THE OFFICIAL®
1999 PRICE GUIDE TO
BASEBALL CARDS

BY
DR. JAMES BECKETT

EIGHTEENTH EDITION

HOUSE OF COLLECTIBLES
The Ballantine Publishing Group • New York

© 1998 by James Beckett III

All rights reserved under International
and Pan-American Copyright Conventions.

 This is a registered trademark of Random House, Inc.

Published by:
House of Collectibles
The Ballantine Publishing Group
201 East 50th Street
New York, New York 10022

Distributed by The Ballantine Publishing Group, a division of Random House, Inc.,
New York, and simultaneously in Canada by
Random House of Canada Limited, Toronto.

Cover design by Min Choi

Cover photo by Doug Pensinger/Allsport

Manufactured in the United States of America

ISSN: 1062-7138

ISBN: 0-676-60138-3

Eighteenth Edition: April 1998

10 9 8 7 6 5 4 3 2 1

Table of Contents

4 / Contents

6 / Contents

About the Author

Jim Beckett, the leading authority on sport card values in the United States, maintains a wide range of activities in the world of sports. He possesses one of the finest collections of sports cards and autographs in the world, has made numerous appearances on radio and television, and has been frequently cited in many national publications. He was awarded the first "Special Achievement Award" for Contributions to the Hobby by the National Sports Collectors Convention in 1980, the "Jock-Jaspersen Award" for Hobby Dedication in 1983, and the "Buck Barker, Spirit of the Hobby" Award in 1991.

Dr. Beckett is the author of *Beckett Baseball Card Price Guide, The Official Price Guide to Baseball Cards, The Sport Americana Price Guide to Baseball Collectibles, The Sport Americana Baseball Memorabilia and Autograph Price Guide, Beckett Football Card Price Guide, The Official Price Guide to Football Cards, Beckett Hockey Card Price Guide, The Official Price Guide to Hockey Cards, Beckett Basketball Card Price Guide, The Official Price Guide to Basketball Cards,* and *The Sport Americana Baseball Card Alphabetical Checklist.* In addition, he is the founder, publisher, and editor of *Beckett Baseball Card Monthly, Beckett Basketball Monthly, Beckett Football Card Monthly, Beckett Hockey Monthly, Beckett Future Stars, Beckett Racing Monthly,* and *Beckett Tribute* magazines.

Jim Beckett received his Ph.D. in Statistics from Southern Methodist University in 1975. Prior to starting Beckett Publications in 1984, Dr. Beckett served as an Associate Professor of Statistics at Bowling Green State University and as a vice president of a consulting firm in Dallas, Texas. He currently resides in Dallas with his wife, Patti, and their daughters, Christina, Rebecca, and Melissa.

How to Use This Book

Isn't it great? Every year this book gets bigger and bigger with all the new sets coming out. But even more exciting is that every year there are more collectors, more shows, more stores, and more interest in the cards we love so much. This edition has been enhanced and expanded from the previous edition. The cards you collect — who appears on them, what they look like, where they are from, and (most important to most of you) what their current values are — are enumerated within. Many of the features contained in the other *Beckett Price Guides* have been incorporated into this volume since condition grading, terminology, and many other aspects of collecting are common to the card hobby in general. We hope you find the book both interesting and useful in your collecting pursuits.

The *Beckett Guide* has been successful where other attempts have failed because it is complete, current, and valid. This Price Guide contains not just one, but three prices by condition for all the baseball cards listed. The prices were added to the card lists just prior to printing and reflect not the author's opinions or desires but the going retail prices for each card, based on the marketplace (sports memorabilia conventions and shows, sports card shops, hobby papers, current mail-order catalogs, local club meetings, auction results, and other firsthand reportings of actually realized prices).

What is the best price guide available on the market today? Of course, card sellers prefer the price guide with the highest prices, while card buyers naturally prefer the one with the lowest prices. Accuracy, however, is the true test. Use the price guide trusted by more collectors and dealers than all the others combined. Look for the *Beckett®* name. I won't put my name on anything I won't stake my reputation on. Not the lowest and not the highest — but the most accurate, with integrity.

To facilitate your use of this book, read the complete introductory section on the following pages before going to the pricing pages. Every collectible field has its own terminology; we've tried to capture most of these terms and definitions in our glossary. Please read carefully the section on grading and the condition of your cards, as you cannot determine which price column is appropriate for a given card without first knowing its condition.

Welcome to the world of baseball cards.

How to Collect

Each collection is personal and reflects the individuality of its owner. There are no set rules on how to collect cards. Since card collecting is a hobby or leisure pastime, what you collect, how much you collect, and how much time and money you spend collecting are entirely up to you. The funds you have available for collecting and your own personal taste should determine how you collect. Information and ideas presented here are intended to help you get the most enjoyment from this hobby.

It is impossible to collect every card ever produced. Therefore, beginners as well as intermediate and advanced collectors usually specialize in some way. One of the reasons this hobby is popular is that individual collectors can define and tailor their collecting methods to match their own tastes. To give you some ideas of the various approaches to collecting, we will list some of the more popular areas of specialization.

Many collectors select complete sets from particular years. For example, they may concentrate on assembling complete sets from all the years since their birth or since they became avid sports fans. They may try to collect a card for every player during that specified period of time.

Many others wish to acquire only certain players. Usually such players are the superstars of the sport, but occasionally collectors will specialize in all the cards of players who attended a particular college or came from a certain town. Some collectors are only interested in the first cards or Rookie Cards of certain players. A handy guide for collectors interested in pursuing the hobby this way is the *Sport Americana Baseball Card Alphabetical Checklist.*

Another fun way to collect cards is by team. Most fans have a favorite team, and it is natural for that loyalty to be translated into a desire for cards of the players on that favorite team. For most of the recent years, team sets (all the cards from a given team for that year) are readily available at a reasonable price. *The Sport Americana Team Baseball Card Checklist* will open up this field to the collector.

Obtaining Cards

Several avenues are open to card collectors. Cards still can be purchased in the traditional way: by the pack at the local candy, grocery, drug or major discount stores.

But there are also thousands of card shops across the country that specialize in selling cards individually or by the pack, box, or set. Another alternative is the thousands of card shows held each month around the country, which feature anywhere from eight to 800 tables of sports cards and memorabilia for sale.

For many years, it has been possible to purchase complete sets of baseball cards through mail-order advertisers found in traditional sports media publications, such as *The Sporting News, Baseball Digest, Street & Smith* year-books, and others. These sets also are advertised in the card collecting periodicals. Many collectors will begin by subscribing to at least one of the hobby periodicals, all with good up-to-date information. In fact, subscription offers can be found in the advertising section of this book.

Most serious card collectors obtain old (and new) cards from one or more of several main sources: (1) trading or buying from other collectors or dealers; (2) responding to sale or auction ads in the hobby publications; (3) buying at a local hobby store; and/or (4) attending sports collectibles shows or conventions.

We advise that you try all four methods since each has its own distinct advantages: (1) trading is a great way to make new friends; (2) hobby periodicals help you keep up with what's going on in the hobby (including when and where the conventions are happening); (3) stores provide the opportunity to enjoy personalized service and consider a great diversity of material in a relaxed sports-oriented atmosphere; and (4) shows allow you to choose from multiple dealers and thousands of cards under one roof in a competitive situation.

Preserving Your Cards

Cards are fragile. They must be handled properly in order to retain their value. Careless handling can easily result in creased or bent cards. It is, however, not recommended that tweezers or tongs be used to pick up your cards since such utensils might mar or indent card surfaces and thus reduce those cards' conditions and values.

In general, your cards should be handled directly as little as possible. This is sometimes easier to say than to do.

Although there are still many who use custom boxes, storage trays, or even shoe boxes, plastic sheets are the preferred method of many collectors for storing cards.

A collection stored in plastic pages in a three-ring album allows you to view your collection at any time without the need to touch the card itself. Cards can also be kept in single holders (of various types and thickness) designed for the enjoyment of each card individually.

For a large collection, some collectors may use a combination of the above methods. When purchasing plastic sheets for your cards, be sure that you find the pocket size that fits the cards snugly. Don't put your 1951 Bowman in a sheet designed to fit 1981 Topps.

Most hobby and collectibles shops and virtually all collectors' conventions will have these plastic pages available in quantity for the various sizes offered, or you can purchase them directly from the advertisers in this book.

Also, remember that pocket size isn't the only factor to consider when looking for plastic sheets. Other factors such as safety, economy, appearance, availability, or personal preference also may indicate which types of sheets a collector may want to buy.

Damp, sunny and/or hot conditions — no, this is not a weather forecast — are three elements to avoid in extremes if you are interested in preserving your collection. Too much (or too little) humidity can cause the gradual deterioration of a card. Direct, bright sun (or fluorescent light) over time will bleach out the color of a card. Extreme heat accelerates the decomposition of the card. On the other hand, many cards have lasted more than 75 years without much scientific intervention. So be cautious, even if the above factors typically present a problem only when present in the extreme. It never hurts to be prudent.

Collecting vs. Investing

Collecting individual players and collecting complete sets are both popular vehicles for investment and speculation.

Most investors and speculators stock up on complete sets or on quantities of players they think have good investment potential.

There is obviously no guarantee in this book, or anywhere else for that matter, that cards will outperform the stock market or other investment alternatives in the future. After all, baseball cards do not pay quarterly dividends and cards cannot be sold at their "current values" as easily as stocks or bonds.

Nevertheless, investors have noticed a favorable long-term trend in the past performance of baseball and other sports collectibles, and certain cards and sets have outperformed just about any other investment in some years.

Many hobbyists maintain that the best investment is and always will be the building of a collection, which traditionally has held up better than outright speculation.

Some of the obvious questions are: Which cards? When to buy? When to sell? The best investment you can make is in your own education.

The more you know about your collection and the hobby, the more informed the decisions you will be able to make. We're not selling investment tips. We're selling information about the current value of baseball cards. It's up to you to use that information to your best advantage.

Terminology

Each hobby has its own language to describe its area of interest. The nomenclature traditionally used for trading cards is derived from the American Card Catalog, published in 1960 by Nostalgia Press. That catalog, written by Jefferson Burdick (who is called the "Father of Card Collecting" for his pioneering work), uses letter and number designations for each separate set of cards. The letter used in the ACC designation refers to the generic type of card. While both sport and non-sport issues are classified in the ACC, we shall confine ourselves to the sport issues. The following list defines the letters and their meanings as used by the American Card Catalog.

(none) or N - 19th Century U.S. Tobacco
B - Blankets
D - Bakery Inserts Including Bread
E - Early Candy and Gum
F - Food Inserts
H - Advertising
M - Periodicals
PC - Postcards
R - Candy and Gum since 1930

Following the letter prefix and an optional hyphen are one-, two-, or three-digit numbers, R(-)999. These typically represent the company or entity issuing the cards. In several cases, the ACC number is extended by an additional hyphen and another one- or two-digit numerical suffix. For example, the 1957 Topps regular-series baseball card issue carries an ACC designation of R414-11. The "R" indicates a Candy or Gum card produced since 1930. The "414" is the ACC designation for Topps Chewing Gum baseball card issues, and the "11" is the ACC designation for the 1957 regular issue (Topps' eleventh baseball set). Like other traditional methods of identification, this system provides order to the process of cataloging cards; however, most serious collectors learn the ACC designation of the popular sets by repetition and familiarity, rather than by attempting to "figure out" what they might or should be. From 1948 forward, collectors and dealers commonly refer to all sets by their year, maker, type of issue, and any other distinguishing characteristic. For example, such a characteristic could be an unusual issue or one of several regular issues put out by a specific maker in a single year. Regional issues are usually referred to by year, maker, and sometimes by title or theme of the set.

Glossary/Legend

Our glossary defines terms used in the card collecting hobby and in this book. Many of these terms are also common to other types of sports memorabilia collecting. Some terms may have several meanings depending on use and context.

ACC - Acronym for American Card Catalog.

ACETATE - A transparent plastic.

ANN- Announcer.

AS - All-Star card. A card portraying an All-Star Player of the previous year that says "All-Star" on its face.

ATG - All-Time Great card.

ATL - All-Time Leaders card.

AU(TO) - Autographed card.

BC - Bonus Card.

BL - Blue letters.

BLANKET - A felt square (normally 5 to 6 inches) portraying a baseball player.

BOX CARD - Card issued on a box (i.e., 1987 Topps Box Bottoms).

BRICK - A group of 50 or more cards having common characteristics that is intended to be bought, sold or traded as a unit.

CABINETS - Popular and highly valuable photographs on thick card stock produced in the 19th and early 20th century.

CHECKLIST - A list of the cards contained in a particular set. The list is always in numerical order if the cards are numbered. Some unnumbered sets are artificially numbered in alphabetical order, by team and alphabetically within the team, or by uniform number for convenience.

CL - Checklist card. A card that lists in order the cards and players in the set or series. Older checklist cards in Mint condition that have not been marked are very desirable and command premiums.

CO - Coach.

COIN - A small disc of metal or plastic portraying a player in its center.

COLLECTOR ISSUE - A set produced for the sake of the card itself with no product or service sponsor. It derives its name from the fact that most of these sets are produced for sale directly to the hobby market.

COM - Card issued by the Post Cereal Company through their mail-in offer.

COMM - Commissioner.

COMMON CARD - The typical card of any set; it has no premium value accruing from subject matter, numerical scarcity, popular demand, or anomaly.

CONVENTION - A gathering of dealers and collectors at a single location for the purpose of buying, selling, and trading sports memorabilia items. Conventions are open to the public and sometimes feature autograph guests, door prizes, contests, seminars, etc. They are frequently referred to simply as "shows."

COOP - Cooperstown.

COR - Corrected card.

COUPON - See Tab.

CY - Cy Young Award.

DEALER - A person who engages in buying, selling, and trading sports collectibles or supplies. A dealer may also be a collector, but as a dealer, his main goal is to earn a profit.

DIE-CUT - A card with part of its stock partially cut, allowing one or more parts to be folded or removed. After removal or appropriate folding, the remaining part of the card can frequently be made to stand up.

DISC - A circular-shaped card.

DISPLAY CARD - A sheet, usually containing three to nine cards, that is printed and used by the manufacturer to advertise and/or display the packages containing his products and cards. The backs of display cards are blank or contain advertisements.

DK - Diamond King.

DL - Division Leaders.

DP - Double Print (a card that was printed in double the quantity compared to the other cards in the same series) or a Draft Pick card.

DUFEX - A method of card manufacturing technology patented by Pinnacle Brands, Inc. It involves a refractive quality to a card with a foil coating.

EMBOSSED - A raised surface; features of a card that are projected from a flat background.

ERA - Earned Run Average.

ERR - Error card. A card with erroneous information, spelling, or depiction on either side of the card. Most errors are not corrected by the producing card company.

ETCHED - Impressions within the surface of a card.

EXHIBIT - The generic name given to thick-stock, postcard-size cards with single color obverse pictures. The name is derived from the Exhibit Supply Co. of Chicago, the principal manufacturer of this type of card. These also are known as Arcade cards since they were found in many arcades.

FDP - First or First Round Draft Pick.

FOIL - Foil embossed stamp on card.

FOLD - Foldout.

FS - Father/son card.

FULL BLEED - A borderless card; a card containing a photo that encompasses the entire card.

FULL SHEET - A complete sheet of cards that has not been cut up into individual cards by the manufacturer. Also called an uncut sheet.

FUN - Fun Cards.

GL - Green letters.

GLOSS - A card with luster; a shiny finish as in a card with UV coating.

HIGH NUMBER - The cards in the last series of numbers in a year in which such higher-numbered cards were printed or distributed in significantly lesser amounts than the lower-numbered cards. The high-number designation refers to a scarcity of the high-numbered cards. Not all years have high numbers in terms of this definition.

HL - Highlight card.

HOF - Hall of Fame, or a card that portrays a Hall of Famer (HOFer).

HOLOGRAM - A three-dimensional photographic image.

HOR - Horizontal pose on card as opposed to the standard vertical orientation found on most cards.

IA - In Action card.

IF - Infielder.

INSERT - A card of a different type or any other sports collectible (typically a poster or sticker) contained and sold in the same package along with a card or cards of a major set. An insert card is either unnumbered or not numbered in the same sequence as the major set. Sometimes the inserts are randomly distributed and are not found in every pack.

INTERACTIVE - A concept that involves collector participation.

ISSUE - Synonymous with set, but usually used in conjunction with a manufacturer, e.g., a Topps issue.

KARAT - A unit of measure for the fineness of gold; i.e. 24K.

LAYERING - The separation or peeling of one or more layers of the card stock, usually at the corner of the card.

LEGITIMATE ISSUE - A set produced to promote or boost sales of a product or service, e.g., bubblegum, cereal, cigarettes, etc. Most collector issues are not legitimate issues in this sense.

LHP - Lefthanded pitcher.

LID - A circular-shaped card (possibly with tab) that forms the top of the container for the product being promoted.

LL - League leaders or large letters on card.

MAJOR SET - A set produced by a national manufacturer of cards containing a large number of cards. Usually 100 or more different cards comprise a major set.

MEM - Memorial card. For example, the 1990 Donruss and Topps Bart Giamatti cards.

METALLIC - A glossy design method that enhances card features.

MG - Manager.

MINI - A small card; for example, a 1975 Topps card of identical design but smaller dimensions than the regular Topps issue of 1975.

ML - Major League.

MULTI-PLAYER CARD - A single card depicting two or more players (but not a team card).

MVP - Most Valuable Player.

NAU - No autograph on card.

NH - No-Hitter.

NNOF - No Name on Front.

NOF - Name on Front.

NON-SPORT CARD - A card from a set whose major theme is a subject other than a sports subject. A card of a sports figure or event that is part of a non-sport set is still a non-sport card, e.g., while the "Look 'N' See" non-sport card set contains a card of Babe Ruth, a sports figure, that card is a non-sport card.

NOTCHING - The grooving of the card, usually caused by fingernails, rubber bands, or bumping card edges against other objects.

OF - Outfield or Outfielder.

OLY - Olympics Card.

ORG - Organist.

P - Pitcher or Pitching pose.

P1 - First Printing.

P2 - Second Printing.

P3 - Third Printing.

PACKS - A means with which cards are issued in terms of pack type (wax, cello, foil, rack, etc.) and channels of distribution (hobby, retail, etc.).

PANEL - An extended card that is composed of two or more individual cards. Often the panel forms the back part of the container for the product being promoted, e.g., a Hostess panel, a Bazooka panel, an Esskay Meat panel.

PARALLEL- A card that is similar in design to its counterpart from a basic set, but offers a distinguishing quality.

PCL - Pacific Coast League.

PF - Profiles.

PLASTIC SHEET - A clear, plastic page that is punched for insertion into a binder (with standard three-ring spacing) containing pockets for displaying cards. Many different styles of sheets exist with pockets of varying sizes to hold the many differing card formats. Also called a display sheet or storage sheet.

PLATINUM - A metallic element used in the process of creating a glossy card.

PR - Printed name on back.

PREMIUM - A card, sometimes on photographic stock, that is purchased or obtained in conjunction with, or redemption for, another card or product. The premium is not packaged in the same unit as the primary item.

PRES - President.

PRISMATIC/PRISM - A glossy or bright design that refracts or disperses light.

PUZZLE CARD - A card whose back contains a part of a picture which, when joined correctly with other puzzle cards, forms the completed picture.

PUZZLE PIECE - A die-cut piece designed to interlock with similar pieces (e.g., early 1980's Donruss).

PVC - Polyvinyl Chloride, a substance used to make many of the popular card display protective sheets. Non-PVC sheets are considered preferable for long-term storage of cards by many.

RARE - A card or series of cards of very limited availability. Unfortunately, "rare" is a subjective term frequently used indiscriminately to hype value. "Rare" cards are harder to obtain than "scarce" cards.

RB - Record Breaker.

REDEMPTION- A program established by multiple card manufacturers that allows collectors to mail in a special card (usually a random insert) in return for special cards, sets or other prizes not available through conventional channels.

REFRACTORS - A card that features a design element which enhances (distorts) its color/appearance through deflecting light.

REGIONAL - A card or set of cards issued and distributed only in a limited geographical area of the country.

REPLICA - An identical copy or reproduction.

REV NEG - Reversed or flopped photo side of the card. This is a major type of error card, but only some are corrected.

RHP - Righthanded pitcher.

ROY - Rookie of the Year.

RP - Relief pitcher.

SA - Super Action card.

SASE - Self-Addressed, Stamped Envelope.

SB - Stolen Bases.

SCARCE - A card or series of cards of limited availability. This subjective term is sometimes used indiscriminately to hype value. "Scarce" cards are not as difficult to obtain as "rare" cards.

SCR - Script name on back.

SD - San Diego Padres.

SEMI-HIGH - A card from the next to last series of a sequentially issued set. It has more value than an average card and generally less value than a high number. A card is not called a semi-high unless the next to last series in which it exists has an additional premium attached to it.

SERIES - The entire set of cards issued by a particular producer in a particular year; e.g., the 1971 Topps series. Also, within a particular set, series can refer to a group of (consecutively numbered) cards printed at the same time; e.g., the first series of the 1957 Topps issue (#1 through #88).

SET - One each of the entire run of cards of the same type produced by a particular manufacturer during a single year. In other words, if you have a complete set of 1976 Topps then you have every card from #1 up to and including #660, i.e., all the different cards that were produced.

SF - Starflics.

SHEEN - Brightness or luster emitted by a card.

SKIP-NUMBERED - A set that has many unissued card numbers between the lowest number in the set and the highest number in the set; e.g., the 1948 Leaf baseball set contains 98 cards skip-numbered from #1 to #168. A major set in which a few numbers were not printed is not considered to be skip-numbered.

SP - Single or Short Print (a card which was printed in lesser quantity compared to the other cards in the same series; see also DP and TP).

SPECIAL CARD - A card that portrays something other than a single player or team; for example, a card that portrays the previous year's statistical leaders or the results from the previous year's World Series.

SS - Shortstop.

STAMP - Adhesive-backed papers depicting a player. The stamp may be individual or in a sheet of many stamps. Moisture must be applied to the adhesive in order for the stamp to be attached to another surface.

STANDARD SIZE - Most modern sports cards measure 2-1/2 by 3-1/2 inches. Exceptions are noted in card descriptions throughout this book.

STAR CARD - A card that portrays a player of some repute, usually determined by his ability, however, sometimes referring to sheer popularity.

STICKER - A card with a removable layer that can be affixed to (stuck onto) another surface.

STOCK - The cardboard or paper on which the card is printed.

STRIP CARDS - A sheet or strip of cards, particularly popular in the 1920s and 1930s, with the individual cards usually separated by broken or dotted lines.

SUPERIMPOSED - To be affixed on top of something, i.e., a player photo over a solid background.

SUPERSTAR CARD - A card that portrays a superstar; e.g., a Hall of Famer or player with strong Hall of Fame potential.

TAB - A card portion set off from the rest of the card, usually with perforations, that may be removed without damaging the central character or event depicted by the card.

TC - Team Checklist.

TEAM CARD - A card that depicts an entire team.

TEST SET - A set, usually containing a small number of cards, issued by a national card producer and distributed in a limited section or sections of the country. Presumably, the purpose of a test set is to test market appeal for a particular type of card.

THREE-DIMENSIONAL (3D) - A visual image that provides an illusion of depth and perspective.

TOPICAL - a subset or group of cards that have a common theme (e.g., MVP award winners).

TP - Triple Print (a card that was printed in triple the quantity compared to the other cards in the same series).

TRANSPARENT - Clear, see through.

TR - Trade reference on card.

TRIMMED - A card cut down from its original size. Trimmed cards are undesirable to most collectors.

UDCA - Upper Deck Classic Alumni.

UER - Uncorrected Error.

UMP - Umpire.

USA - Team USA.

UV - Ultraviolet, a glossy coating used in producing cards.

VAR - Variation card. One of two or more cards from the same series with the same number (or player with identical pose if the series is unnumbered) differing from one another by some aspect, the different feature stemming from the printing or stock of the card. This can be caused when the manufacturer of the cards notices an error in one or more of the cards, makes the changes, and then resumes the print run. In this case there will be two versions or variations of the same card. Sometimes one of the variations is relatively scarce.

VERT - Vertical pose on card.

WAS - Washington National League (1974 Topps).

WC - What's the Call?

WL - White letter on front.

WS - World Series card.

YL - Yellow letters on front.

YT - Yellow team name on front.

* - to denote multi-sport sets.

Understanding Card Values

Determining Value

Why are some cards more valuable than others? Obviously, the economic laws of supply and demand are applicable to card collecting just as they are to any other field where a commodity is bought, sold or traded in a free, unregulated market.

Supply (the number of cards available on the market) is less than the total number of cards originally produced since attrition diminishes that original quantity. Each year a percentage of cards is typically thrown away, destroyed or otherwise lost to collectors. This percentage is much, much smaller today than it was in the past because more and more people have become increasingly aware of the value of their cards.

For those who collect only Mint condition cards, the supply of older cards can be quite small indeed. Until recently, collectors were not so conscious of the need to preserve the condition of their cards. For this reason, it is difficult to know exactly how many 1953 Topps are currently available, Mint or otherwise. It is generally accepted that there are fewer 1953 Topps available than 1963, 1973 or 1983 Topps cards. If demand were equal for each of these sets, the law of supply and demand would increase the price for the least available sets. Demand, however, is never equal for all sets, so price correlations can be complicated. The demand for a card is influenced by many factors. These include: (1) the age of the card; (2) the number of cards printed; (3) the player(s) portrayed on the card; (4) the attractiveness and popularity of the set; and (5) the physical condition of the card.

In general, (1) the older the card, (2) the fewer the number of the cards printed, (3) the more famous, popular and talented the player, (4) the more attractive and popular the set, and (5) the better the condition of the card, the higher the value of the card will be. There are exceptions to all but one of these factors: the condition of the card. Given two cards similar in all respects except condition, the one in the best condition will always be valued higher.

While those guidelines help to establish the value of a card, the countless exceptions and peculiarities make any simple, direct mathematical formula to determine card values impossible.

Regional Variation

Since the market varies from region to region, card prices of local players may be higher. This is known as a regional premium. How significant the premium is — and if there is any premium at all — depends on the local popularity of the team and the player.

The largest regional premiums usually do not apply to superstars, who often are so well-known nationwide that the prices of their key cards are too high for local dealers to realize a premium.

Lesser stars often command the strongest premiums. Their popularity is concentrated in their home region, creating local demand that greatly exceeds overall demand.

Regional premiums can apply to popular retired players and sometimes can be found in the areas where the players grew up or starred in college.

A regional discount is the converse of a regional premium. Regional discounts occur when a player has been so popular in his region for so long that local collectors and dealers have accumulated quantities of his key cards. The abundant supply may make the cards available in that area at the lowest prices anywhere.

Set Prices

A somewhat paradoxical situation exists in the price of a complete set vs. the combined cost of the individual cards in the set. In nearly every case, the sum of the prices for the individual cards is higher than the cost for the complete set. This is prevalent especially in the cards of the last few years. The reasons for this apparent anomaly stem from the habits of collectors and from the carrying costs to dealers. Today, each card in a set normally is produced in the same quantity as all other cards in its set.

Many collectors pick up only stars, superstars and particular teams. As a result, the dealer is left with a shortage of certain player cards and an abundance of others. He therefore incurs an expense in simply "carrying" these less desirable cards in stock. On the other hand, if he sells a complete set, he gets rid of large numbers of cards at one time. For this reason, he generally is willing to receive less money for a complete set. By doing this, he recovers all of his costs and also makes a profit.

The disparity between the price of the complete set and the sum of the individual cards also has been influenced by the fact that some of the major manufacturers now are pre-collating card sets. Since "pulling" individual cards from the sets involves a specific type of labor (and cost), the singles or star card market is not affected significantly by pre-collation.

Set prices also do not include rare card varieties, unless specifically stated. Of course, the prices for sets do include one example of each type for the given set, but this is the least expensive variety.

Scarce Series

Scarce series occur because cards issued before 1974 were made available to the public each year in several series of finite numbers of cards, rather than all cards of the set being available for purchase at one time. At some point during the year, usually toward the end of the baseball season, interest in current year baseball cards waned. Consequently, the manufacturers produced smaller numbers of these later-series cards.

Nearly all nationwide issues from post-World War II manufacturers (1948 to 1973) exhibit these series variations. In the past, Topps, for example, may have issued series consisting of many different numbers of cards, including 55, 66, 80, 88 and others. Recently, Topps has settled on what is now its standard sheet size of 132 cards, six of which comprise its 792-card set.

While the number of cards within a given series is usually the same as the number of cards on one printed sheet, this is not always the case. For example, Bowman used 36 cards on its standard printed sheets, but in 1948 substituted 12 cards during later print runs of that year's baseball cards. Twelve of the cards from the initial sheet of 36 cards were removed and replaced by 12 different cards giving, in effect, a first series of 36 cards and a second series of 12 new cards. This replacement produced a scarcity of 24 cards — the 12 cards removed from the original sheet and the 12 new cards added to the sheet. A full sheet of 1948 Bowman cards (second printing) shows that card numbers 37 through 48 have replaced 12 of the cards on the first printing sheet.

The Topps Company also has created scarcities and/or excesses of certain cards in many of its sets. Topps, however, has most frequently gone the other direction by double printing some of the cards. Double printing causes an abundance of cards of the players who are on the same sheet more than one time. During the years from 1978 to 1981, Topps double printed 66 cards out of their large 726-card set. The Topps practice of double printing cards in earlier years is the most logical explanation for the known scarcities of particular cards in some of these Topps sets.

From 1988 through 1990, Donruss short printed and double printed certain cards in its major sets. Ostensibly this was because of its addition of bonus team MVP cards in its regular-issue wax packs.

We are always looking for information or photographs of printing sheets of cards for research. Each year, we try to update the hobby's knowledge of distribution anomalies. Please let us know at the address in this book if you have first-hand knowledge that would be helpful in this pursuit.

Grading Your Cards

Each hobby has its own grading terminology — stamps, coins, comic books, record collecting, etc. Collectors of sports cards are no exception. The one invariable criterion for determining the value of a card is its condition: The better the condition of the card, the more valuable it is. Condition grading, however, is subjective. Individual card dealers and collectors differ in the strictness of their grading, but the stated condition of a card should be determined without regard to whether it is being bought or sold.

No allowance is made for age. A 1952 card is judged by the same standards as a 1992 card. But there are specific sets and cards that are condition sensitive (marked with "!" in the Price Guide) because of their border color, consistently poor centering, etc. Such cards and sets sometimes command premiums above the listed percentages in Mint condition.

Centering

Current centering terminology uses numbers representing the percentage of border on either side of the main design. Obviously, centering is diminished in importance for borderless cards such as Stadium Club.

Slightly Off-Center (60/40): A slightly off-center card is one that, upon close inspection, is found to have one border bigger than the opposite border. This degree once was offensive to only purists, but now some hobbyists try to avoid cards that are anything other than perfectly centered.

Off-Center (70/30): An off-center card has one border that is noticeably more than twice as wide as the opposite border.

Badly Off-Center (80/20 or worse): A badly off-center card has virtually no border on one side of the card.

Miscut: A miscut card actually shows part of the adjacent card in its larger border and consequently a corresponding amount of its card is cut off.

Corner Wear

Corner wear is the most scrutinized grading criteria in the hobby. These are the major categories of corner wear:

Corner with a slight touch of wear: The corner still is sharp, but there is a slight touch of wear showing. On a dark-bordered card, this shows as a dot of white.

Fuzzy corner: The corner still comes to a point, but the point has just begun to fray. A slightly "dinged" corner is considered the same as a fuzzy corner.

Slightly rounded corner: The fraying of the corner has increased to where there is only a hint of a point. Mild layering may be evident. A "dinged" corner is considered the same as a slightly rounded corner.

Rounded corner: The point is completely gone. Some layering is noticeable.

Badly rounded corner: The corner is completely round and rough. Severe layering is evident.

Creases

A third common defect is the crease. The degree of creasing in a card is difficult to show in a drawing or picture. On giving the specific condition of an expensive card for sale, the seller should note any creases additionally. Creases can be categorized as to severity according to the following scale:

Light Crease: A light crease is a crease that is barely noticeable upon close inspection. In fact, when cards are in plastic sheets or holders, a light crease may not be seen (until the card is taken out of the holder). A light crease on the front is much more serious than a light crease on the card back only.

Medium Crease: A medium crease is noticeable when held and studied at arm's length by the naked eye, but does not overly detract from the appearance of the card. It is an obvious crease, but not one that breaks the picture surface of the card.

Heavy Crease: A heavy crease is one that has torn or broken through the card's picture surface, e.g., puts a tear in the photo surface.

Alterations

Deceptive Trimming: This occurs when someone alters the card in order (1) to shave off edge wear, (2) to improve the sharpness of the corners, or (3) to improve centering — obviously their objective is to falsely increase the perceived value of the card to an unsuspecting buyer. The shrinkage usually is evident only if the trimmed card is compared to an adjacent full-sized card or if the trimmed card is itself measured.

Obvious Trimming: Obvious trimming is noticeable and unfortunate. It is usually performed by non-collectors who give no thought to the present or future value of their cards.

Deceptively Retouched Borders: This occurs when the borders (especially on those cards with dark borders) are touched up on the edges and corners with magic marker or crayons of appropriate color in order to make the card appear Mint.

Categorization of Defects—Miscellaneous Flaws

The following are common minor flaws that, depending on severity, lower a card's condition by one to four grades and often render it no better than Excellent-Mint: bubbles (lumps in surface), gum and wax stains, diamond cutting (slanted borders), notching, off-centered backs, paper wrinkles, scratched-off cartoons or puzzles on back, rubber band marks, scratches, surface impressions and warping.

The following are common serious flaws that, depending on severity, lower a card's condition at least four grades and often render it no better than Good: chemical or sun fading, erasure marks, mildew, miscutting (severe off-centering), holes, bleached or re-touched borders, tape marks, tears, trimming, water or coffee stains and writing.

Condition Guide

Grades

Mint (Mt) - A card with no flaws or wear. The card has four perfect corners, 60/40 or better centering from top to bottom and from left to right, original gloss, smooth edges and original color borders. A Mint card does not have print spots, color or focus imperfections.

Near Mint-Mint (NrMt-Mt) - A card with one minor flaw. Any one of the following would lower a Mint card to Near Mint-Mint: one corner with a slight touch of wear, barely noticeable print spots, color or focus imperfections. The card must have 60/40 or better centering in both directions, original gloss, smooth edges and original color borders.

Near Mint (NrMt) - A card with one minor flaw. Any one of the following would lower a Mint card to Near Mint: one fuzzy corner or two to four corners with slight touches of wear, 70/30 to 60/40 centering, slightly rough edges, minor print spots, color or focus imperfections. The card must have original gloss and original color borders.

Excellent-Mint (ExMt) - A card with two or three fuzzy, but not rounded, corners and centering no worse than 80/20. The card may have no more than two of the following: slightly rough edges, very slightly discolored borders, minor print spots, color or focus imperfections. The card must have original gloss.

Excellent (Ex) - A card with four fuzzy but definitely not rounded corners and centering no worse than 80/20. The card may have a small amount of original gloss lost, rough edges, slightly discolored borders and minor print spots, color or focus imperfections.

Very Good (Vg) - A card that has been handled but not abused: slightly rounded corners with slight layering, slight notching on edges, a significant amount of gloss lost from the surface but no scuffing and moderate discoloration of borders. The card may have a few light creases.

Good (G), Fair (F), Poor (P) - A well-worn, mishandled or abused card: badly rounded and layered corners, scuffing, most or all original gloss missing,

Centering

Well-centered

Slightly Off-centered

Off-centered

Badly Off-centered

Miscut

Corner Wear

The partial cards here have been photographed at 300%. This was done in order to magnify each card's corner wear to such a degree that differences could be shown on a printed page.

The 1962 Topps Mickey Mantle card definitely has a rounded corner. Some may say that this card is badly rounded, but that is a judgement call.

The 1962 Topps Hank Aaron card has a slightly rounded corner. Note that there is definite corner wear evident by the fraying and that there is no longer a sharp point to which the corner converges.

The 1962 Topps Gil Hodges card has corner wear; it is slightly better than the Aaron card above. Nevertheless, some collectors might classify this Hodges corner as slightly rounded.

The 1962 Topps Manager's Dream card showing Mantle and Mays has slight corner wear. This is not a fuzzy corner as very slight wear is noticeable on the card's photo surface.

The 1962 Topps Don Mossi card has very slight corner wear such that it might be called a fuzzy corner. A close look at the original card shows that the corner is not perfect, but almost. However, note that coner wear is somewhat academic on this card. As you can plainly see, the heavy crease going across his name breaks through the photo surface.

seriously discolored borders, moderate or heavy creases, and one or more serious flaws. The grade of Good, Fair or Poor depends on the severity of wear and flaws. Good, Fair and Poor cards generally are used only as fillers.

The most widely used grades are defined above. Obviously, many cards will not perfectly fit one of the definitions.

Therefore, categories between the major grades known as in-between grades are used, such as Good to Very Good (G-Vg), Very Good to Excellent (VgEx), and Excellent-Mint to Near Mint (ExMt-NrMt). Such grades indicate a card with all qualities of the lower category but with at least a few qualities of the higher category.

The Official Price Guide to Baseball Cards lists each card and set in three grades, with the middle grade valued at about 40-45% of the top grade, and the bottom grade valued at about 10-15% of the top grade.

The value of cards that fall between the listed columns can also be calculated using a percentage of the top grade. For example, a card that falls between the top and middle grades (Ex, ExMt or NrMt in most cases) will generally be valued at anywhere from 50% to 90% of the top grade.

Similarly, a card that falls between the middle and bottom grades (G-Vg, Vg or VgEx in most cases) will generally be valued at anywhere from 20% to 40% of the top grade.

There are also cases where cards are in better condition than the top grade or worse than the bottom grade. Cards that grade worse than the lowest grade are generally valued at 5-10% of the top grade.

When a card exceeds the top grade by one — such as NrMt-Mt when the top grade is NrMt, or Mint when the top grade is NrMt-Mt — a premium of up to 50% is possible, with 10-20% the usual norm.

When a card exceeds the top grade by two — such as Mint when the top grade is NrMt, or NrMt-Mt when the top grade is ExMt — a premium of 25-50% is the usual norm. But certain condition sensitive cards or sets, particularly those from the pre-war era, can bring condition premiums of up to 100% or even more.

Unopened packs, boxes and factory-collated sets are considered Mint in their unknown (and presumed perfect) state. Once opened, however, each card can be graded (and valued) in its own right by taking into account any defects that may be present in spite of the fact that the card has never been handled.

Selling Your Cards

Just about every collector sells cards or will sell cards eventually. Someday you may be interested in selling your duplicates or maybe even your whole collection. You may sell to other collectors, friends or dealers. You may even sell cards you purchased from a certain dealer back to that same dealer. In any event, it helps to know some of the mechanics of the typical transaction between buyer and seller.

Dealers will buy cards in order to resell them to other collectors who are interested in the cards. Dealers will always pay a higher percentage for items that (in their opinion) can be resold quickly, and a much lower percentage for those items that are perceived as having low demand and hence are slow moving. In either case, dealers must buy at a price that allows for the expense of doing business and a margin for profit.

If you have cards for sale, the best advice we can give is that you get several offers for your cards — either from card shops or at a card show — and take the best offer, all things considered. Note, the "best" offer may not be the one for the highest amount. And remember, if a dealer really wants your cards, he won't let you get away without making his best competitive offer. Another alternative is to place your cards in an auction as one or several lots.

Many people think nothing of going into a department store and paying $15 for an item of clothing for which the store paid $5. But if you were selling your $15 card to a dealer and he offered you $5 for it, you might consider his mark-up unreasonable. To complete the analogy: Most department stores (and card dealers) that consistently pay $10 for $15 items eventually go out of business. An exception is when the dealer has lined up a willing buyer for the item(s) you are attempting to sell, or if the cards are so Hot that it's likely he'll likely have to hold the cards for just a short period of time.

In those cases, an offer of up to 75 percent of book value still will allow the dealer to make a reasonable profit considering the short time he will need to hold the merchandise. In general, however, most cards and collections will bring offers in the range of 25 to 50 percent of retail price. Also consider that most material from the last five to 10 years is plentiful. If that's what you're selling, don't be surprised if your best offer is well below that range.

Interesting Notes

The first card numerically of an issue is the single card most likely to obtain excessive wear.

Consequently, you typically will find the price on the #1 card (in NrMt or Mint condition) somewhat higher than might otherwise be the case.

Similarly, but to a lesser extent (because normally the less important, reverse side of the card is the one exposed), the last card numerically in an issue also is prone to abnormal wear. This extra wear and tear occurs because the first and last cards are exposed to the elements (human element included) more than any of the other cards. They are generally end cards in any brick formations, rubber bandings, stackings on wet surfaces and like activities.

Sports cards have no intrinsic value. The value of a card, like the value of other collectibles, can be determined only by you and your enjoyment in viewing and possessing these cardboard treasures.

Remember, the buyer ultimately determines the price of each baseball card. You are the determining price factor because you have the ability to say "No" to the price of any card by not exchanging your hard-earned money for a given issue. When the cost of a trading card exceeds the enjoyment you will receive from it, your answer should be "No." We assess and report the prices. You set them!

We are always interested in receiving the price input of collectors and dealers. We happily credit major contributors.

We welcome your opinions, since your contributions assist us in ensuring a better guide each year.

If you would like to join our survey list for the next editions of this book and others authored by Dr. Beckett, please send your name and address to Dr. James Beckett, 15850 Dallas Parkway, Dallas, TX 75248.

History of Baseball Cards

Today's version of the baseball card, with its colorful and oft times high-tech fronts and backs, is a far cry from its earliest predecessors. The issue remains cloudy as to which was the very first baseball card ever produced, but the institution of baseball cards dates from the latter half of the 19th century, more than 100 years ago. Early issues, generally printed on heavy cardboard, were of poor quality, with photographs, drawings, and printing far short of today's standards.

Goodwin & Co., of New York, makers of Gypsy Queen, Old Judge, and other cigarette brands, is considered by many to be the first issuer of baseball and other sports cards. Its issues, predominantly sized 1-1/2 by 2-1/2 inches, generally consisted of photographs of baseball players, boxers, wrestlers, and other subjects mounted on stiff cardboard. More than 2,000 different photos of baseball players alone have been identified. These "Old Judges," a collective name commonly used for the Goodwin & Co. cards, were issued from 1886 to 1890 and are treasured parts of many collections today.

Among the other cigarette companies that issued baseball cards still attracting attention today are Allen & Ginter, D. Buchner & Co. (Gold Coin Chewing Tobacco), and P.H. Mayo & Brother. Cards from the first two companies bear colored line drawings, while the Mayos are sepia photographs on black cardboard. In addition to the small-size cards from this era, several tobacco companies issued cabinet-size baseball cards. These "cabinets" were considerably larger than the small cards, usually about 4-1/4 by 6-1/2 inches, and were printed on heavy stock. Goodwin & Co.'s Old Judge cabinets and the National Tobacco Works' "Newsboy" baseball photos are two that remain popular today.

By 1895, the American Tobacco Company began to dominate its competition. They discontinued baseball card inserts in their cigarette packages (actually slide boxes in those days). The lack of competition in the cigarette market had made these inserts unnecessary. This marked the end of the first era of baseball cards. At the dawn of the 20th century, few baseball cards were being issued. But once again, it was the cigarette companies — particularly, the American Tobacco Company — followed to a lesser extent by the candy and gum makers that revived the practice of including baseball cards with their products. The bulk of these cards, identified in the American Card Catalog (designated hereafter as ACC) as T or E cards for 20th century "Tobacco" or "Early Candy and Gum" issues, respectively, were released from 1909 to 1915.

This romantic and popular era of baseball card collecting produced many desirable items. The most outstanding is the fabled T-206 Honus Wagner card. Other perennial favorites among collectors are the T-206 Eddie Plank card, and the T-206 Magee error card. The former was once the second most valuable card and only recently relinquished that position to a more distinctive and aesthetically pleasing Napoleon Lajoie card from the 1933-34 Goudey Gum series. The latter misspells the player's name as "Magie," the most famous and most valuable blooper card.

The ingenuity and distinctiveness of this era has yet to be surpassed. Highlights include:

• the T-202 Hassan triple-folders, one of the best looking and the most distinctive cards ever issued;

• the durable T-201 Mecca double-folders, one of the first sets with players' records on the reverse;

• the T-3 Turkey Reds, the hobby's most popular cabinet card;

• the E-145 Cracker Jacks, the only major set containing Federal League player cards;

• the T-204 Ramlys, with their distinctive black-and-white oval photos and ornate gold borders.

These are but a few of the varieties issued during this period.

Increasing Popularity

While the American Tobacco Company dominated the field, several other tobacco companies, as well as clothing manufacturers, newspapers and periodicals, game makers, and companies whose identities remain anonymous, also issued cards during this period. In fact, the Collins-McCarthy Candy Company, makers of Zeenuts Pacific Coast League baseball cards, issued cards yearly from 1911 to 1938. Its record for continuous annual card production has been exceeded only by the Topps Chewing Gum Company. The era of the tobacco card issues closed with the onset of World War I, with the exception of the Red Man chewing tobacco sets produced from 1952 to 1955.

The next flurry of card issues broke out in the roaring and prosperous 1920s, the era of the E card. The caramel companies (National Caramel, American Caramel, York Caramel) were the leading distributors of these E cards. In addition, the strip card, a continous strip with several cards divided by dotted lines or other sectioning features, flourished during this time. While the E cards and the strip cards generally are considered less imaginative than the T cards or the recent candy and gum issues, they still are pursued by many advanced collectors.

Another significant event of the 1920s was the introduction of the arcade card. Taking its designation from its issuer, the Exhibit Supply Company of Chicago, it is usually known as the "Exhibit" card. Once a trademark of the penny arcades, amusement parks and county fairs across the country, Exhibit machines dispensed nearly postcard-size photos on thick stock for one penny. These picture cards bore likenesses of a favorite cowboy, actor, actress or baseball player. Exhibit Supply and its associated companies produced baseball cards during a longer time span, although discontinuous, than any other manufacturer. Its first cards appeared in 1921, while its last issue was in 1966. In 1979, the Exhibit Supply Company was bought and somewhat revived by a collector/dealer who has since reprinted Exhibit photos of the past.

If the T card period, from 1909 to 1915, can be designated the "Golden Age" of baseball card collecting, then perhaps the "Silver Age" commenced with the introduction of the Big League Gum series of 239 cards in 1933 (a 240th card was added in 1934). These are the forerunners of today's baseball gum cards, and the Goudey Gum Company of Boston is responsible for their success. This era spanned the period from the Depression days of 1933 to America's formal involvement in World War II in 1941.

Goudey's attractive designs, with full-color line drawings on thick card stock, greatly influenced other cards being issued at that time. As a result, the most attractive and popular vintage cards in history were produced in this "Silver Age." The 1933 Goudey Big League Gum series also owes its popularity to the more than 40 Hall of Fame players in the set. These include four cards of Babe Ruth and two of Lou Gehrig. Goudey's reign continued in 1934, when it issued a 96-card set in color, together with the single remaining card from the 1933 series, #106, the Napoleon Lajoie card.

In addition to Goudey, several other bubblegum manufacturers issued baseball cards during this era. DeLong Gum Company issued an extremely attractive set in 1933. National Chicle Company's 192-card "Batter-Up" series of 1934-1936 became the largest die-cut set in card history. In addition, that company offered the popular "Diamond Stars" series during the same period. Other popular sets included the "Tattoo Orbit" set of 60 color cards issued in 1933 and Gum Products' 75-card "Double Play" set, featuring sepia depictions of two players per card.

In 1939, Gum Inc., which later became Bowman Gum, replaced Goudey Gum as the leading baseball card producer. In 1939 and the following year, it issued two important sets of black-and-white cards. In 1939, its "Play Ball America" set consisted of 162 cards. The larger, 240-card "Play Ball" set of 1940 still is considered by many to be the most attractive black-and-white cards ever produced. That firm introduced its only color set in 1941, consisting of 72 cards titled "Play Ball Sports Hall of Fame." Many of these were colored repeats of poses from the black-and-white 1940 series.

In addition to regular gum cards, many manufacturers distributed premium issues during the 1930s. These premiums were printed on paper or photographic stock, rather than card stock. They were much larger than the regular cards and were sold for a penny across the counter with gum (which was packaged separately from the premium). They often were redeemed at the store or through the mail in exchange for the wrappers of previously purchased gum cards, like proof-of-purchase box-top premiums today. The gum premiums are scarcer than the card issues of the 1930s and in most cases no manufacturer's name is present.

World War II brought an end to this popular era of card collecting when paper and rubber shortages curtailed the production of bubblegum baseball cards. They were resurrected again in 1948 by the Bowman Gum Company (the direct descendent of Gum, Inc.). This marked the beginning of the modern era of card collecting.

In 1948, Bowman Gum issued a 48-card set in black and white consisting of one card and one slab of gum in every 1 cent pack. That same year, the Leaf Gum Company also issued a set of cards. Although rather poor in quality, these cards were issued in color. A squabble over the rights to use players' pictures developed between Bowman and Leaf. Eventually Leaf dropped out of the card market, but not before it had left a lasting heritage to the hobby by issuing some of the rarest cards now in existence. Leaf's baseball card series of 1948-49 contained 98 cards, skip numbered to #168 (not all numbers were printed). Of these 98 cards, 49 are relatively plentiful; the other 49, however, are rare and quite valuable.

Bowman continued its production of cards in 1949 with a color series of 240 cards. Because there are many scarce "high numbers," this series remains the most difficult Bowman regular issue to complete. Although the set was printed in color and commands great interest due to its scarcity, it is considered aesthetically inferior to the Goudey and National Chicle issues of the 1930s. In addition to the regular issue of 1949, Bowman also produced a set of 36 Pacific Coast League players. While this was not a regular issue, it still is prized by collectors. In fact, it has become the most valuable Bowman series.

In 1950 (representing Bowman's one-year monopoly of the baseball card market), the company began a string of top quality cards that continued until its demise in 1955. The 1950 series was itself something of an oddity because the low numbers, rather than the traditional high numbers, were the more difficult cards to obtain.

The year 1951 marked the beginning of the most competitive and perhaps the highest quality period of baseball card production. In that year, Topps Chewing Gum Company of Brooklyn entered the market. Topps' 1951 series consisted of two sets of 52 cards each, one set with red backs and the other with blue backs. In addition, Topps also issued 31 insert cards, three of which remain the rarest Topps cards ("Current All-Stars" Konstanty, Roberts and Stanky). The 1951 Topps cards were unattractive and paled in comparison to the 1951 Bowman issues. They were successful, however, and Topps has continued to produce cards ever since.

Intensified Competition

Topps issued a larger and more attractive card set in 1952. This larger size became standard for the next five years. (Bowman followed with larger-size baseball cards in 1953.) This 1952 Topps set has become, like the 1933

Goudey series and the T-206 white border series, the classic set of its era. The 407-card set is a collector's dream of scarcities, rarities, errors and variations. It also contains the first Topps issues of Mickey Mantle and Willie Mays.

As with Bowman and Leaf in the late 1940s, competition over player rights arose. Ensuing court battles occurred between Topps and Bowman. The market split due to stiff competition, and in January 1956, Topps bought out Bowman. (Topps, using the Bowman name, resurrected Bowman as a later label in 1989.) Topps remained essentially unchallenged as the primary producer of baseball cards through 1980. So, the story of major baseball card sets from 1956 through 1980 is by and large the story of Topps' issues. Notable exceptions include the small sets produced by Fleer Gum in 1959, 1960, 1961 and 1963, and the Kellogg's Cereal and Hostess Cakes baseball cards issued to promote their products.

A court decision in 1980 paved the way for two other large gum companies to enter (or reenter, in Fleer's case) the baseball card arena. Fleer, which had last made photo cards in 1963, and the Donruss Company (then a division of General Mills) secured rights to produce baseball cards of current players, thus breaking Topps' monopoly. Each company issued major card sets in 1981 with bubblegum products.

Then a higher court decision in that year overturned the lower court ruling against Topps. It appeared that Topps had regained its sole position as a producer of baseball cards. Undaunted by the revocation ruling, Fleer and Donruss continued to issue cards in 1982 but without bubblegum or any other edible product. Fleer issued its current player baseball cards with "team logo stickers," while Donruss issued its cards with a piece of a baseball jigsaw puzzle.

Sharing the Pie

Since 1981, these three major baseball card producers all have thrived, sharing relatively equal recognition. Each has steadily increased its involvement in terms of numbers of issues per year. To the delight of collectors, their competition has generated novel, and in some cases exceptional, issues of current Major League Baseball players. Collectors also eagerly accepted the debut efforts of Score (1988) and Upper Deck (1989), the newest companies to enter the baseball card producing derby.

Upper Deck's successful entry into the market turned out to be very important. The company's card stock, photography, packaging and marketing gave baseball cards a new standard for quality, and began the "premium card" trend that continues today. The second premium baseball card set to be issued was the 1990 Leaf set, named for and issued by the parent company of Donruss. To gauge the significance of the premium card trend, one need only note that two of the most valuable post-1986 regular-issue cards in the hobby are the 1989 Upper Deck Ken Griffey Jr. and 1990 Leaf Frank Thomas Rookie Cards.

The impressive debut of Leaf in 1990 was followed by Studio, Ultra, and Stadium Club in 1991. Of those, Stadium Club made the biggest impact. In 1992, Bowman, and Pinnacle joined the premium fray. In 1992, Donruss and Fleer abandoned the traditional 50-cent pack market and instead produced premium sets comparable to (and presumably designed to compete against) Upper Deck's set. Those moves, combined with the almost instantaneous spread of premium cards to the other major team sports cards, serve as strong indicators that premium cards were here to stay. Bowman had been a lower-level product from 1989 to '91.

In 1993, Fleer, Topps and Upper Deck produced the first "super premium" cards with Flair, Finest and SP, respectively. The success of all three products was an indication the baseball card market was headed toward even higher price levels, and that turned out to be the case in 1994 with the introduction of Topps' Bowman's Best (a hybrid of prospect-oriented Bowman and the superpremium Finest) and Leaf Limited. Other 1994 debuts included Upper Deck's entry-level Collector's Choice and Pinnacle's hobby-only Select.

Overall, inserts continued to dominate the hobby scene. Specifically, the parallel chase cards first introduced in 1992 with Topps Gold became the latest major hobby trend. Topps Gold was followed by 1993 Finest Refractors (at the time the scarcest insert ever produced and still a landmark set), and the one-per-box Stadium Club First Day Issue.

Of course, the biggest on-field news of 1994 was the owner-provoked players strike that halted the season prematurely. While the baseball card hobby suffered noticeably from the strike, there was no catastrophic market crash as some had feared. However, the strike pulled the plug on a market that was both strong and growing, and contributed to a serious hobby contraction that continues to this day.

By 1995, parallel insert sets were commonplace and had taken on a new complexion: the most popular ones were those that had announced (or at least suspected) print runs of 500 or less, such as Finest Refractors and Select Artist's Proofs.

This trend continued in 1996, with several parallel inserts that were printed in quantities of 250 or less such as Finest Gold Refractors, Fleer Circa Rave, Studio Silver Press Proofs and three of the six Select Certified parallels. It could be argued that the high price tags on these extremely limited parallel cards (many exceeded the $1000 plateau) were driving many single-player collectors to frustration, and even completely out of the hobby. At the same time, average pack prices soared while average number of cards per pack dropped, making the baseball card hobby increasingly more expensive.

On the positive side, two trends from 1996 clearly brought in new collectors: Topps' Mickey Mantle retrospective inserts in both series of Topps and Stadium Club; and Leaf's Signature Series, which included one certified autograph per pack. While the Mantle craze following his passing seemed to be a short-term phenomenon, the inclusion of autographs in packs seemed to have more long-term significance.

Unfortunately, such positives were clearly overshadowed by the industry's overriding problem: too many products costing too much money, with fewer and fewer buyers willing to ante up. The result? Many dealers going out of business, and a buyer's market in which new products usually were available cheaper to the consumer than original dealer cost from the factory. The hobby still faces this very complex problem with no easy solutions in sight.

In 1997 the print runs in selected sets got even lower. Both Fleer/SkyBox and Pinnacle brands issued cards of which only one exists.

The grouth in popularity of autographs also continued. Many products had autographed cards in their packs. A very positive trend was a return to basics. Many collectors bought Rockie Cards as they understood that concept and worked on finishing sets.

There was also an increase in international players collecting. Hideo Nomo was incredibly popular in Japan while Chan Ho Park was in demand in Korea. This bodes wall for an international growth in the hobby.

Unfortunately, such positives were clearly overshadowed by the industry's overriding problem: too many products costing too much money, with fewer and fewer buyers willing to ante up. The result? Many dealers going out of business, and a buyer's market in which new products usually were available cheaper to the consumer than original dealer cost from the factory. The hobby still faces this very complex problem with no easy solutions in sight.

Finding Out More

The above has been a thumbnail sketch of card collecting from its inception in the 1880s to the present. It is difficult to tell the whole story in just a few pages — there are several other good sources of information. Serious collectors should subscribe to at least one of the excellent hobby periodicals. We also suggest that collectors visit their local card shop(s) and also attend a sports collectibles show in their area. Card collecting is still a young and informal hobby. You can learn more about it in either place. After all, smart dealers realize that spending a few minutes teaching beginners about the hobby often pays off in the long run.

Additional Reading

Each year Beckett Publications produces comprehensive annual price guides for each of the four major sports: *Beckett Baseball Card Price Guide*, *Beckett Football Card Price Guide*, *Beckett Basketball Card Price Guide*, and *Beckett Hockey Card Price Guide*. The aim of these annual guides is to provide information and accurate pricing on a wide array of sports cards, ranging from main issues by the major card manufacturers to various regional, promotional, and food issues. Also alphabetical checklists, such as *Sport Americana Baseball Card Alphabetical Checklist #7*, are published to assist the collector in identifying all the cards of any particular player. The seasoned collector will find these tools valuable sources of information that will enable him to pursue his hobby interests.

In addition, abridged editions of the Beckett Price Guides have been published for each of the four major sports as part of the House of Collectibles series: *The Official Price Guide to Baseball Cards, The Official Price Guide to Football Cards* and *The Official Price Guide to Basketball Cards*. Published in a convenient mass-market paperback format, these price guides provide information and accurate pricing on all the main issues by the major card manufacturers.

Prices in this Guide

Prices found in this guide reflect current retail rates just prior to the printing of this book. They do not reflect the FOR SALE prices of the author, the publisher, the distributors, the advertisers, or any card dealers associated with this guide. No one is obligated in any way to buy, sell or trade his or her cards based on these prices. The price listings were compiled by the author from actual buy/sell transactions at sports conventions, sports card shops, buy/sell advertisements in the hobby papers, for sale prices from dealer catalogs and price lists, and discussions with leading hobbyists in the U.S. and Canada. All prices are in U.S. dollars.

Acknowledgments

A great deal of diligence, hard work, and dedicated effort went into this year's volume. The high standards to which we hold ourselves, however, could not have been met without the expert input and generous amount of time contributed by many people. Our sincere thanks are extended to each and every one of you.

A complete list of these invaluable contributors appears after the Price Guide section.

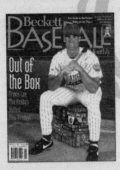

1948 Bowman

The 48-card Bowman set of 1948 was the first major set of the post-war period. Each 2 1/16" by 2 1/2" card had a black and white photo of a current player, with his biographical information printed in black ink on a gray back. Due to the printing process and the 36-card sheet size upon which Bowman was then printing, the 12 cards marked with an SP in the checklist are scarcer numerically, as they were removed from the printing sheet in order to make room for the 12 high numbers (37-48). Cards were issued in one-card penny packs. Many cards are found with overprinted, transposed, or blank backs. The set features the Rookie Cards of Hall of Famers Yogi Berra, Ralph Kiner, Stan Musial, Red Schoendienst, and Warren Spahn. Half of the cards in the set feature New York players (Yankees or Giants).

	NRMT	VG-E
COMPLETE SET (48)	3400.00	1500.00
COMMON CARD (1-36)	20.00	9.00
MINOR STARS 1-36	25.00	11.00
SEMISTARS 1-36	40.00	18.00
UNLISTED STARS 1-36	50.00	22.00
COMMON CARD (37-48)	30.00	13.50
MINOR STARS 37-48	40.00	18.00
SEMISTARS 37-48	60.00	27.00
UNLISTED STARS 37-48	80.00	36.00

*UNLISTED DODGER/YANKEE: 1.25X VALUE
CARDS PRICED IN NM CONDITION !

☐ 1 Bob Elliott	80.00	12.00
☐ 2 Ewell Blackwell	40.00	18.00
☐ 3 Ralph Kiner	150.00	70.00
☐ 4 Johnny Mize	100.00	45.00
☐ 5 Bob Feller	225.00	100.00
☐ 6 Yogi Berra	450.00	200.00
☐ 7 Pete Reiser SP	120.00	55.00
☐ 8 Phil Rizzuto SP	300.00	135.00
☐ 9 Walker Cooper	20.00	9.00
☐ 10 Buddy Rosar	20.00	9.00
☐ 11 Johnny Lindell	25.00	11.00
☐ 12 Johnny Sain	50.00	22.00
☐ 13 Willard Marshall SP	40.00	18.00
☐ 14 Allie Reynolds	50.00	22.00
☐ 15 Eddie Joost	20.00	9.00
☐ 16 Jack Lohrke SP	40.00	18.00
☐ 17 Enos Slaughter	100.00	45.00
☐ 18 Warren Spahn	350.00	160.00
☐ 19 Tommy Henrich	50.00	22.00
☐ 20 Buddy Kerr SP	40.00	18.00
☐ 21 Ferris Fain	40.00	18.00
☐ 22 Floyd Bevens SP	50.00	22.00
☐ 23 Larry Jansen	25.00	11.00
☐ 24 Dutch Leonard SP	40.00	18.00
☐ 25 Barney McCosky	20.00	9.00

☐ 26 Frank Shea SP	50.00	22.00
☐ 27 Sid Gordon	22.50	10.00
☐ 28 Emil Verban SP	40.00	18.00
☐ 29 Joe Page SP	75.00	34.00
☐ 30 Whitey Lockman SP	50.00	22.00
☐ 31 Bill McCahan	20.00	9.00
☐ 32 Bill Rigney	20.00	9.00
☐ 33 Bill Johnson	25.00	11.00
☐ 34 Sheldon Jones SP	40.00	18.00
☐ 35 Snuffy Stirnweiss	40.00	18.00
☐ 36 Stan Musial	825.00	375.00
☐ 37 Clint Hartung	30.00	13.50
☐ 38 Red Schoendienst	150.00	70.00
☐ 39 Augie Galan	30.00	13.50
☐ 40 Marty Marion	75.00	34.00
☐ 41 Rex Barney	60.00	27.00
☐ 42 Ray Poat	30.00	13.50
☐ 43 Bruce Edwards	30.00	13.50
☐ 44 Johnny Wyrostek	30.00	13.50
☐ 45 Hank Sauer	60.00	27.00
☐ 46 Herman Wehmeier	30.00	13.50
☐ 47 Bobby Thomson	100.00	45.00
☐ 48 Dave Koslo	80.00	19.50

1949 Bowman

JOHNNY VANDER MEER

The cards in this 240-card set measure approximately 2 1/16" by 2 1/2". In 1949 Bowman took an intermediate step between black and white and full color with this set of tinted photos on colored backgrounds. Collectors should note the series price variations, which reflect some inconsistencies in the printing process. There are four major varieties in name printing, which are noted in the checklist below: NOF: name on front; NNOF: no name on front; PR: printed name on back; and SCR: script name on back. Cards were issued in five card nickel packs. These variations resulted when Bowman used twelve of the lower numbers to fill out the last press sheet of 36 cards, adding to numbers 217-240. Cards 1-3 and 5-73 can be found with either gray or white backs. The set features the Rookie Cards of Hall of Famers Roy Campanella, Bob Lemon, Robin Roberts, Duke Snider, and Early Wynn as well as Rookie Cards of Richie Ashburn and Gil Hodges.

	NRMT	VG-E
COMPLETE SET (240)	13,000.00	5800.00
COMMON CARD (1-144)	15.00	6.75
MINOR STARS 1-144	25.00	11.00
SEMISTARS 1-144	40.00	18.00
UNLISTED STARS 1-144	60.00	27.00
COMMON CARD (145-240)	50.00	22.00
MINOR STARS 145-240	80.00	36.00

*UNLISTED DODGER/YANKEE: 1.25X VALUE
CARDS PRICED IN NM CONDITION

☐ 1 Vern Bickford	80.00	16.00
☐ 2 Whitey Lockman	40.00	18.00
☐ 3 Bob Porterfield	15.00	6.75
☐ 4A Jerry Priddy NNOF	15.00	6.75
☐ 4B Jerry Priddy NOF	40.00	18.00
☐ 5 Hank Sauer	40.00	18.00
☐ 6 Phil Cavarretta	40.00	18.00
☐ 7 Joe Dobson	15.00	6.75
☐ 8 Murry Dickson	15.00	6.75
☐ 9 Ferris Fain	40.00	18.00
☐ 10 Ted Gray	15.00	6.75
☐ 11 Lou Boudreau	60.00	27.00
☐ 12 Cass Michaels	15.00	6.75
☐ 13 Bob Chesnes	15.00	6.75
☐ 14 Curt Simmons	35.00	16.00
☐ 15 Ned Garver	15.00	6.75
☐ 16 Al Kozar	15.00	6.75
☐ 17 Earl Torgeson	15.00	6.75
☐ 18 Bobby Thomson	35.00	16.00
☐ 19 Bobby Brown	35.00	16.00
☐ 20 Gene Hermanski	15.00	6.75
☐ 21 Frank Baumholtz	40.00	18.00
☐ 22 Peanuts Lowrey	15.00	6.75
☐ 23 Bobby Doerr	60.00	27.00
☐ 24 Stan Musial	500.00	220.00
☐ 25 Carl Scheib	15.00	6.75
☐ 26 George Kell	60.00	27.00
☐ 27 Bob Feller	175.00	80.00
☐ 28 Don Kolloway	15.00	6.75
☐ 29 Ralph Kiner	125.00	55.00
☐ 30 Andy Seminick	40.00	18.00
☐ 31 Dick Kokos	15.00	6.75
☐ 32 Eddie Yost	60.00	27.00
☐ 33 Warren Spahn	175.00	80.00
☐ 34 Dave Koslo	15.00	6.75
☐ 35 Vic Raschi	55.00	25.00
☐ 36 Pee Wee Reese	175.00	80.00
☐ 37 Johnny Wyrostek	15.00	6.75
☐ 38 Emil Verban	15.00	6.75
☐ 39 Billy Goodman	15.00	6.75
☐ 40 Red Munger	15.00	6.75
☐ 41 Lou Brissie	15.00	6.75
☐ 42 Hoot Evers	15.00	6.75
☐ 43 Dale Mitchell	40.00	18.00
☐ 44 Dave Philley	15.00	6.75
☐ 45 Wally Westlake	15.00	6.75
☐ 46 Robin Roberts	200.00	90.00
☐ 47 Johnny Sain	25.00	11.00
☐ 48 Willard Marshall	15.00	6.75
☐ 49 Frank Shea	25.00	11.00
☐ 50 Jackie Robinson	1000.00	450.00
☐ 51 Herman Wehmeier	15.00	6.75
☐ 52 Johnny Schmitz	15.00	6.75
☐ 53 Jack Kramer	15.00	6.75
☐ 54 Marty Marion	60.00	27.00
☐ 55 Eddie Joost	15.00	6.75
☐ 56 Pat Mullin	15.00	6.75
☐ 57 Gene Bearden	40.00	18.00
☐ 58 Bob Elliott	40.00	18.00
☐ 59 Jack Lohrke	15.00	6.75
☐ 60 Yogi Berra	275.00	125.00
☐ 61 Rex Barney	40.00	18.00
☐ 62 Grady Hatton	15.00	6.75
☐ 63 Andy Pafko	40.00	18.00
☐ 64 Dom DiMaggio	35.00	16.00
☐ 65 Enos Slaughter	70.00	32.00
☐ 66 Elmer Valo	15.00	6.75
☐ 67 Alvin Dark	35.00	16.00
☐ 68 Sheldon Jones	15.00	6.75
☐ 69 Tommy Henrich	35.00	16.00
☐ 70 Carl Furillo	100.00	45.00
☐ 71 Vern Stephens	15.00	6.75
☐ 72 Tommy Holmes	40.00	18.00
☐ 73 Billy Cox	35.00	16.00
☐ 74 Tom McBride	15.00	6.75
☐ 75 Eddie Mayo	15.00	6.75
☐ 76 Bill Nicholson	25.00	11.00
☐ 77 Ernie Bonham	15.00	6.75
☐ 78A Sam Zoldak NNOF	15.00	6.75
☐ 78B Sam Zoldak NOF	40.00	18.00
☐ 79 Ron Northey	15.00	6.75
☐ 80 Bill McCahan	15.00	6.75

□ 81 Virgil Stallcup	15.00	6.75
□ 82 Joe Page	60.00	27.00
□ 83A Bob Scheffing NNOF	15.00	6.75
□ 83B Bob Scheffing NOF	40.00	18.00
□ 84 Roy Campanella	725.00	325.00
□ 85A Johnny Mize NNOF	80.00	36.00
□ 85B Johnny Mize NOF	150.00	70.00
□ 86 Johnny Pesky	60.00	27.00
□ 87 Randy Gumpert	15.00	6.75
□ 88A Bill Salkeld NNOF	15.00	6.75
□ 88B Bill Salkeld NOF	40.00	18.00
□ 89 Mizell Platt	15.00	6.75
□ 90 Gil Coan	15.00	6.75
□ 91 Dick Wakefield	15.00	6.75
□ 92 Willie Jones	40.00	18.00
□ 93 Ed Stevens	15.00	6.75
□ 94 Mickey Vernon	35.00	16.00
□ 95 Howie Pollet	15.00	6.75
□ 96 Taft Wright	15.00	6.75
□ 97 Danny Litwhiler	15.00	6.75
□ 98A Phil Rizzuto NNOF	125.00	55.00
□ 98B Phil Rizzuto NOF	200.00	90.00
□ 99 Frank Gustine	15.00	6.75
□ 100 Gil Hodges	250.00	110.00
□ 101 Sid Gordon	15.00	6.75
□ 102 Stan Spence	15.00	6.75
□ 103 Joe Tipton	15.00	6.75
□ 104 Eddie Stanky	35.00	16.00
□ 105 Bill Kennedy	15.00	6.75
□ 106 Jake Early	15.00	6.75
□ 107 Eddie Lake	15.00	6.75
□ 108 Ken Heintzelman	15.00	6.75
□ 109A Ed Fitzgerald SCR	50.00	6.75
□ 109B Ed Fitzgerald PR	40.00	18.00
□ 110 Early Wynn	125.00	55.00
□ 111 Red Schoendienst	70.00	32.00
□ 112 Sam Chapman	60.00	27.00
□ 113 Ray LaManno	15.00	6.75
□ 114 Allie Reynolds	40.00	18.00
□ 115 Dutch Leonard	15.00	6.75
□ 116 Joe Hatton	15.00	6.75
□ 117 Walker Cooper	15.00	6.75
□ 118 Sam Mele	15.00	6.75
□ 119 Floyd Baker	15.00	6.75
□ 120 Cliff Fannin	15.00	6.75
□ 121 Mark Christman	15.00	6.75
□ 122 George Vico	15.00	6.75
□ 123 Johnny Blatnick	15.00	6.75
□ 124A Danny Murtaugh SCR	60.00	27.00
□ 124B Danny Murtaugh PR	45.00	20.00
□ 125 Ken Keltner	40.00	18.00
□ 126A Al Brazle SCR	15.00	6.75
□ 126B Al Brazle PR	40.00	18.00
□ 127A Hank Majeski SCR	15.00	6.75
□ 127B Hank Majeski PR	40.00	18.00
□ 128 Johnny VanderMeer	60.00	27.00
□ 129 Bill Johnson	40.00	18.00
□ 130 Harry Walker	15.00	6.75
□ 131 Paul Lehner	15.00	6.75
□ 132A Al Evans SCR	15.00	6.75
□ 132B Al Evans PR	40.00	18.00
□ 133 Aaron Robinson	15.00	6.75
□ 134 Hank Borowy	15.00	6.75
□ 135 Stan Rojek	15.00	6.75
□ 136 Hank Edwards	15.00	6.75
□ 137 Ted Wilks	15.00	6.75
□ 138 Buddy Rosar	15.00	6.75
□ 139 Hank Arft	15.00	6.75
□ 140 Ray Scarborough	15.00	6.75
□ 141 Tony Lupien	15.00	6.75
□ 142 Eddie Waitkus	40.00	18.00
□ 143A Bob Dillinger SCR	25.00	11.00
□ 143B Bob Dillinger PR	75.00	34.00
□ 144 Mickey Haefner	15.00	6.75
□ 145 Sylvester Donnelly	50.00	22.00
□ 146 Mike McCormick	80.00	36.00
□ 147 Bert Singleton	50.00	22.00
□ 148 Bob Swift	50.00	22.00
□ 149 Roy Partee	50.00	22.00
□ 150 Allie Clark	50.00	22.00
□ 151 Mickey Harris	50.00	22.00
□ 152 Clarence Maddern	50.00	22.00
□ 153 Phil Masi	50.00	22.00
□ 154 Clint Hartung	75.00	34.00
□ 155 Mickey Guerra	50.00	22.00
□ 156 Al Zarilla	50.00	22.00

□ 157 Walt Masterson	50.00	22.00
□ 158 Harry Brecheen	75.00	34.00
□ 159 Glen Moulder	50.00	22.00
□ 160 Jim Blackburn	50.00	22.00
□ 161 Jocko Thompson	50.00	22.00
□ 162 Preacher Roe	125.00	55.00
□ 163 Clyde McCullough	50.00	22.00
□ 164 Vic Wertz	75.00	34.00
□ 165 Snuffy Stirnweiss	75.00	34.00
□ 166 Mike Tresh	50.00	22.00
□ 167 Babe Martin	50.00	22.00
□ 168 Doyle Lade	50.00	22.00
□ 169 Jeff Heath	80.00	36.00
□ 170 Bill Rigney	80.00	36.00
□ 171 Dick Fowler	50.00	22.00
□ 172 Eddie Pellagrini	50.00	22.00
□ 173 Eddie Stewart	50.00	22.00
□ 174 Terry Moore	100.00	45.00
□ 175 Luke Appling	125.00	55.00
□ 176 Ken Raffensberger	50.00	22.00
□ 177 Stan Lopata	80.00	36.00
□ 178 Tom Brown	80.00	36.00
□ 179 Hugh Casey	75.00	34.00
□ 180 Connie Berry	50.00	22.00
□ 181 Gus Niarhos	50.00	22.00
□ 182 Hal Peck	50.00	22.00
□ 183 Lou Stringer	50.00	22.00
□ 184 Bob Chipman	50.00	22.00
□ 185 Pete Reiser	100.00	45.00
□ 186 Buddy Kerr	50.00	22.00
□ 187 Phil Marchildon	50.00	22.00
□ 188 Karl Drews	50.00	22.00
□ 189 Earl Wooten	50.00	22.00
□ 190 Jim Hearn	50.00	22.00
□ 191 Joe Haynes	50.00	22.00
□ 192 Harry Gumbert	50.00	22.00
□ 193 Ken Trinkle	50.00	22.00
□ 194 Ralph Branca	100.00	45.00
□ 195 Eddie Bockman	50.00	22.00
□ 196 Fred Hutchinson	75.00	34.00
□ 197 Johnny Lindell	75.00	34.00
□ 198 Steve Gromek	50.00	22.00
□ 199 Tex Hughson	50.00	22.00
□ 200 Jess Dobernic	50.00	22.00
□ 201 Sibby Sisti	50.00	22.00
□ 202 Larry Jansen	75.00	34.00
□ 203 Barney McCosky	50.00	22.00
□ 204 Bob Savage	50.00	22.00
□ 205 Dick Sisler	80.00	36.00
□ 206 Bruce Edwards	50.00	22.00
□ 207 Johnny Hopp	50.00	22.00
□ 208 Dizzy Trout	75.00	34.00
□ 209 Charlie Keller	100.00	45.00
□ 210 Joe Gordon	100.00	45.00
□ 211 Boo Ferriss	50.00	22.00
□ 212 Ralph Hamner	50.00	22.00
□ 213 Red Barrett	50.00	22.00
□ 214 Richie Ashburn	550.00	250.00
□ 215 Kirby Higbe	50.00	22.00
□ 216 Schoolboy Rowe	75.00	34.00
□ 217 Marino Pieretti	50.00	22.00
□ 218 Dick Kryhoski	50.00	22.00
□ 219 Virgil Fire Trucks	80.00	36.00
□ 220 Johnny McCarthy	50.00	22.00
□ 221 Bob Muncrief	50.00	22.00
□ 222 Alex Kellner	50.00	22.00
□ 223 Bobby Hofman	50.00	22.00
□ 224 Satchell Paige	1000.00	450.00
□ 225 Jerry Coleman	100.00	45.00
□ 226 Duke Snider	900.00	400.00
□ 227 Fritz Ostermueller	50.00	22.00
□ 228 Jackie Mayo	50.00	22.00
□ 229 Ed Lopat	125.00	55.00
□ 230 Augie Galan	80.00	22.00
□ 231 Earl Johnson	50.00	22.00
□ 232 George McQuinn	80.00	22.00
□ 233 Larry Doby	150.00	70.00
□ 234 Rip Sewell	50.00	22.00
□ 235 Jim Russell	50.00	22.00
□ 236 Fred Sanford	50.00	22.00
□ 237 Monte Kennedy	50.00	22.00
□ 238 Bob Lemon	200.00	90.00
□ 239 Frank McCormick	50.00	22.00
□ 240 Babe Young UER	100.00	25.00
	(Photo called	
	Bobby Young)	

1950 Bowman

The cards in this 252-card set measure approximately 2 1/16" by 2 1/2". This set, marketed in 1950 by Bowman, represented a major improvement in terms of quality over their previous efforts. Each card was a beautifully colored line drawing developed from a simple photograph. The first 72 cards are the scarcest in the set, while the final 72 cards may be found with or without the copyright line. This was the only Bowman sports set to carry the famous "5-Star" logo. Cards were issued in five-card nickel packs. Key rookies in this set are Hank Bauer, Don Newcombe, and Al Rosen.

	NRMT	VG-E
COMPLETE SET (252)	8500.00	3800.00
COMMON CARD (1-72)	50.00	22.00
MINOR STARS 1-72	60.00	27.00
SEMISTARS 1-72	80.00	36.00
COMMON CARD (73-252)	15.00	6.75
MINOR STARS 73-252	25.00	11.00
SEMISTARS 73-252	60.00	18.00
UNLISTED STARS 73-252	60.00	27.00

*UNLISTED DODGER/YANKEE: 1.25X VALUE
CARDS PRICED IN NM CONDITION

□ 1 Mel Parnell	150.00	30.00
□ 2 Vern Stephens	65.00	29.00
□ 3 Dom DiMaggio	70.00	32.00
□ 4 Gus Zernial	65.00	29.00
□ 5 Bob Kuzava	50.00	22.00
□ 6 Bob Feller	225.00	100.00
□ 7 Jim Hegan	60.00	27.00
□ 8 George Kell	75.00	34.00
□ 9 Vic Wertz	65.00	29.00
□ 10 Tommy Henrich	80.00	36.00
□ 11 Phil Rizzuto	225.00	100.00
□ 12 Joe Page	75.00	34.00
□ 13 Ferris Fain	65.00	29.00
□ 14 Alex Kellner	50.00	22.00
□ 15 Al Kozar	50.00	22.00
□ 16 Roy Sievers	80.00	36.00
□ 17 Sid Hudson	50.00	22.00
□ 18 Eddie Robinson	50.00	22.00
□ 19 Warren Spahn	225.00	100.00
□ 20 Bob Elliott	65.00	29.00
□ 21 Pee Wee Reese	225.00	100.00
□ 22 Jackie Robinson	750.00	350.00
□ 23 Don Newcombe	150.00	70.00
□ 24 Johnny Schmitz	50.00	22.00
□ 25 Hank Sauer	65.00	29.00
□ 26 Grady Hatton	50.00	22.00
□ 27 Herman Wehmeier	50.00	22.00
□ 28 Bobby Thomson	70.00	32.00
□ 29 Eddie Stanky	65.00	29.00
□ 30 Eddie Waitkus	65.00	29.00
□ 31 Del Ennis	80.00	36.00
□ 32 Robin Roberts	150.00	70.00
□ 33 Ralph Kiner	100.00	45.00
□ 34 Murry Dickson	50.00	22.00

☐ 35	Enos Slaughter	100.00	45.00	☐ 121	Andy Seminick	25.00	11.00	☐ 207	Max Lanier	15.00	6.75
☐ 36	Eddie Kazak	55.00	25.00	☐ 122	Johnny Hopp	25.00	11.00	☐ 208	Jim Hearn	15.00	6.75
☐ 37	Luke Appling	75.00	34.00	☐ 123	Dino Restelli	15.00	6.75	☐ 209	Johnny Lindell	15.00	6.75
☐ 38	Bill Wight	50.00	22.00	☐ 124	Clyde McCullough	15.00	6.75	☐ 210	Ted Gray	15.00	6.75
☐ 39	Larry Doby	75.00	34.00	☐ 125	Del Rice	15.00	6.75	☐ 211	Charlie Keller	25.00	11.00
☐ 40	Bob Lemon	75.00	34.00	☐ 126	Al Brazle	15.00	6.75	☐ 212	Jerry Priddy	15.00	6.75
☐ 41	Hoot Evers	50.00	22.00	☐ 127	Dave Philley	15.00	6.75	☐ 213	Carl Scheib	15.00	6.75
☐ 42	Art Houtteman	50.00	22.00	☐ 128	Phil Masi	15.00	6.75	☐ 214	Dick Fowler	15.00	6.75
☐ 43	Bobby Doerr	75.00	34.00	☐ 129	Joe Gordon	25.00	11.00	☐ 215	Ed Lopat	60.00	27.00
☐ 44	Joe Dobson	50.00	22.00	☐ 130	Dale Mitchell	25.00	11.00	☐ 216	Bob Porterfield	25.00	11.00
☐ 45	Al Zarilla	50.00	22.00	☐ 131	Steve Gromek	15.00	6.75	☐ 217	Casey Stengel MG	125.00	55.00
☐ 46	Yogi Berra	325.00	145.00	☐ 132	Mickey Vernon	25.00	11.00	☐ 218	Cliff Mapes	25.00	11.00
☐ 47	Jerry Coleman	75.00	34.00	☐ 133	Don Kolloway	15.00	6.75	☐ 219	Hank Bauer	75.00	34.00
☐ 48	Lou Brissie	50.00	22.00	☐ 134	Paul Trout	15.00	6.75	☐ 220	Leo Durocher MG	60.00	27.00
☐ 49	Elmer Valo	50.00	22.00	☐ 135	Pat Mullin	15.00	6.75	☐ 221	Don Mueller	40.00	18.00
☐ 50	Dick Kokos	50.00	22.00	☐ 136	Warren Rosar	15.00	6.75	☐ 222	Bobby Morgan	15.00	6.75
☐ 51	Ned Garver	65.00	29.00	☐ 137	Johnny Pesky	25.00	11.00	☐ 223	Jim Russell	15.00	6.75
☐ 52	Sam Mele	50.00	22.00	☐ 138	Allie Reynolds	60.00	27.00	☐ 224	Jack Banta	15.00	6.75
☐ 53	Clyde Vollmer	50.00	22.00	☐ 139	Johnny Mize	75.00	34.00	☐ 225	Eddie Sawyer MG	25.00	11.00
☐ 54	Gil Coan	50.00	22.00	☐ 140	Pete Suder	15.00	6.75	☐ 226	Jim Konstanty	60.00	27.00
☐ 55	Buddy Kerr	50.00	22.00	☐ 141	Joe Coleman	25.00	11.00	☐ 227	Bob Miller	15.00	6.75
☐ 56	Del Crandall	65.00	29.00	☐ 142	Sherman Lollar	40.00	18.00	☐ 228	Bill Nicholson	25.00	11.00
☐ 57	Vern Bickford	50.00	22.00	☐ 143	Eddie Stewart	15.00	6.75	☐ 229	Frank Frisch MG	60.00	27.00
☐ 58	Carl Furillo	80.00	36.00	☐ 144	Al Evans	15.00	6.75	☐ 230	Bill Serena	15.00	6.75
☐ 59	Ralph Branca	75.00	34.00	☐ 145	Jack Graham	15.00	6.75	☐ 231	Preston Ward	15.00	6.75
☐ 60	Andy Pafko	65.00	29.00	☐ 146	Floyd Baker	15.00	6.75	☐ 232	Al Rosen	60.00	27.00
☐ 61	Bob Rush	50.00	22.00	☐ 147	Mike Garcia	40.00	18.00	☐ 233	Allie Clark	15.00	6.75
☐ 62	Ted Kluszewski	100.00	45.00	☐ 148	Early Wynn	75.00	34.00	☐ 234	Bobby Shantz	60.00	27.00
☐ 63	Ewell Blackwell	65.00	29.00	☐ 149	Bob Swift	15.00	6.75	☐ 235	Harold Gilbert	15.00	6.75
☐ 64	Alvin Dark	65.00	29.00	☐ 150	George Vico	15.00	6.75	☐ 236	Bob Cain	15.00	6.75
☐ 65	Dave Koslo	50.00	22.00	☐ 151	Fred Hutchinson	25.00	11.00	☐ 237	Bill Salkeld	15.00	6.75
☐ 66	Larry Jansen	65.00	29.00	☐ 152	Ellis Kinder	15.00	6.75	☐ 238	Nippy Jones	15.00	6.75
☐ 67	Willie Jones	60.00	27.00	☐ 153	Walt Masterson	15.00	6.75	☐ 239	Bill Howerton	15.00	6.75
☐ 68	Curt Simmons	65.00	29.00	☐ 154	Gus Niarhos	15.00	6.75	☐ 240	Eddie Lake	15.00	6.75
☐ 69	Wally Westlake	50.00	22.00	☐ 155	Frank Shea	25.00	11.00	☐ 241	Neil Berry	15.00	6.75
☐ 70	Bob Chesnes	50.00	22.00	☐ 156	Fred Sanford	25.00	11.00	☐ 242	Dick Kryhoski	15.00	6.75
☐ 71	Red Schoendienst	75.00	34.00	☐ 157	Mike Guerra	15.00	6.75	☐ 243	Johnny Groth	15.00	6.75
☐ 72	Howie Pollet	50.00	22.00	☐ 158	Paul Lehner	15.00	6.75	☐ 244	Dale Coogan	15.00	6.75
☐ 73	Willard Marshall	15.00	6.75	☐ 159	Joe Tipton	15.00	6.75	☐ 245	Al Papai	15.00	6.75
☐ 74	Johnny Antonelli	60.00	27.00	☐ 160	Mickey Harris	15.00	6.75	☐ 246	Walt Dropo	40.00	18.00
☐ 75	Roy Campanella	275.00	125.00	☐ 161	Sherry Robertson	15.00	6.75	☐ 247	Irv Noren	25.00	11.00
☐ 76	Rex Barney	40.00	18.00	☐ 162	Eddie Yost	25.00	11.00	☐ 248	Sam Jethroe	60.00	27.00
☐ 77	Duke Snider	275.00	125.00	☐ 163	Earl Torgeson	15.00	6.75	☐ 249	Snuffy Stirnweiss	25.00	11.00
☐ 78	Mickey Owen	25.00	11.00	☐ 164	Sibby Sisti	15.00	6.75	☐ 250	Ray Coleman	15.00	6.75
☐ 79	Johnny VanderMeer	40.00	18.00	☐ 165	Bruce Edwards	15.00	6.75	☐ 251	Les Moss	15.00	6.75
☐ 80	Howard Fox	15.00	6.75	☐ 166	Joe Hatton	15.00	6.75	☐ 252	Billy DeMars	60.00	16.50
☐ 81	Ron Northey	15.00	6.75	☐ 167	Preacher Roe	60.00	27.00			
☐ 82	Whitey Lockman	25.00	11.00	☐ 168	Bob Scheffing	15.00	6.75			
☐ 83	Sheldon Jones	15.00	6.75	☐ 169	Hank Edwards	15.00	6.75			
☐ 84	Richie Ashburn	100.00	45.00	☐ 170	Dutch Leonard	15.00	6.75			
☐ 85	Ken Heintzelman	15.00	6.75	☐ 171	Harry Gumbert	15.00	6.75			
☐ 86	Stan Rojek	15.00	6.75	☐ 172	Peanuts Lowrey	15.00	6.75			
☐ 87	Bill Werle	15.00	6.75	☐ 173	Lloyd Merriman	15.00	6.75			
☐ 88	Marty Marion	40.00	18.00	☐ 174	Hank Thompson	40.00	18.00			
☐ 89	Red Munger	15.00	6.75	☐ 175	Monte Kennedy	15.00	6.75			
☐ 90	Harry Brecheen	40.00	18.00	☐ 176	Sylvester Donnelly	15.00	6.75			
☐ 91	Cass Michaels	15.00	6.75	☐ 177	Hank Borowy	15.00	6.75			
☐ 92	Hank Majeski	15.00	6.75	☐ 178	Ed Fitzgerald	15.00	6.75			
☐ 93	Gene Bearden	40.00	18.00	☐ 179	Chuck Diering	15.00	6.75			
☐ 94	Lou Boudreau	60.00	27.00	☐ 180	Harry Walker	15.00	6.75			
☐ 95	Aaron Robinson	15.00	6.75	☐ 181	Marino Pieretti	15.00	6.75			
☐ 96	Virgil Trucks	25.00	11.00	☐ 182	Sam Zoldak	15.00	6.75			
☐ 97	Maurice McDermott	15.00	6.75	☐ 183	Mickey Haefner	15.00	6.75			
☐ 98	Ted Williams	850.00	375.00	☐ 184	Randy Gumpert	15.00	6.75			
☐ 99	Billy Goodman	25.00	11.00	☐ 185	Howie Judson	15.00	6.75			
☐ 100	Vic Raschi	60.00	27.00	☐ 186	Ken Keltner	25.00	11.00			
☐ 101	Bobby Brown	60.00	27.00	☐ 187	Lou Stringer	15.00	6.75			
☐ 102	Billy Johnson	25.00	11.00	☐ 188	Earl Johnson	15.00	6.75			
☐ 103	Eddie Joost	15.00	6.75	☐ 189	Owen Friend	15.00	6.75			
☐ 104	Sam Chapman	15.00	6.75	☐ 190	Ken Wood	15.00	6.75			
☐ 105	Bob Dillinger	15.00	6.75	☐ 191	Dick Starr	15.00	6.75			
☐ 106	Cliff Fannin	15.00	6.75	☐ 192	Bob Chipman	15.00	6.75			
☐ 107	Sam Dente	15.00	6.75	☐ 193	Pete Reiser	40.00	18.00			
☐ 108	Ray Scarborough	15.00	6.75	☐ 194	Billy Cox	60.00	27.00			
☐ 109	Sid Gordon	15.00	6.75	☐ 195	Phil Cavarretta	40.00	18.00			
☐ 110	Tommy Holmes	25.00	11.00	☐ 196	Doyle Lade	15.00	6.75			
☐ 111	Walker Cooper	15.00	6.75	☐ 197	Johnny Wyrostek	15.00	6.75			
☐ 112	Gil Hodges	100.00	45.00	☐ 198	Danny Litwhiler	15.00	6.75			
☐ 113	Gene Hermanski	15.00	6.75	☐ 199	Jack Kramer	15.00	6.75			
☐ 114	Wayne Terwilliger	15.00	6.75	☐ 200	Kirby Higbe	25.00	11.00			
☐ 115	Roy Smalley	15.00	6.75	☐ 201	Pete Castiglione	15.00	6.75			
☐ 116	Virgil Stallcup	15.00	6.75	☐ 202	Cliff Chambers	15.00	6.75			
☐ 117	Bill Rigney	15.00	6.75	☐ 203	Danny Murtaugh	25.00	11.00			
☐ 118	Clint Hartung	15.00	6.75	☐ 204	Granny Hamner	40.00	18.00			
☐ 119	Dick Sisler	25.00	11.00	☐ 205	Mike Goliat	15.00	6.75			
☐ 120	John Thompson	15.00	6.75	☐ 206	Stan Lopata	25.00	11.00			

1951 Bowman

PHIL RIZZUTO

The cards in this 324-card set measure approximately 2 1/16" by 3 1/8". Many of the obverses of the cards appearing in the 1951 Bowman set are enlargements of those appearing in the previous year. The high number series (253-324) is highly valued and contains the true "Rookie" cards of Mickey Mantle and Willie Mays. Card number 195 depicts Paul Richards in caricature. George Kell's card (number 46) incorrectly lists him as being in the "1941" Bowman series. Cards were issued either in one card penny packs or in five card nickel packs.

Player names are found printed in a panel on the front of the card. These cards were supposedly also sold in sheets in variety stores in the Philadelphia area.

	NRMT	VG-E
COMPLETE SET (324) ..	16000.00	7200.00
COMMON CARD (1-252) ..	18.00	8.00
MINOR STARS 1-252	25.00	11.00
SEMISTARS 1-252	40.00	18.00
UNLISTED STARS 1-252	60.00	27.00
COMMON CARD (253-324) ..	50.00	22.00
MINOR STARS 253-324	60.00	27.00
SEMISTARS 253-324	80.00	36.00

*UNLISTED DODGER/YANKEE: 1.25X VALUE
CARDS PRICED IN NM CONDITION

#	Player	NRMT	VG-E
1	Whitey Ford	800.00	200.00
2	Yogi Berra	275.00	125.00
3	Robin Roberts	75.00	34.00
4	Del Ennis	25.00	11.00
5	Dale Mitchell	25.00	11.00
6	Don Newcombe	50.00	22.00
7	Gil Hodges	90.00	40.00
8	Paul Lehner	18.00	8.00
9	Sam Chapman	18.00	8.00
10	Red Schoendienst	55.00	25.00
11	Red Munger	18.00	8.00
12	Hank Majeski	18.00	8.00
13	Eddie Stanky	25.00	11.00
14	Alvin Dark	40.00	18.00
15	Johnny Pesky	25.00	11.00
16	Maurice McDermott	18.00	8.00
17	Pete Castiglione	18.00	8.00
18	Gil Coan	18.00	8.00
19	Sid Gordon	18.00	8.00
20	Del Crandall UER	25.00	11.00
	(Misspelled Crandell on card)		
21	Snuffy Stirnweiss	25.00	11.00
22	Hank Sauer	25.00	11.00
23	Hoot Evers	18.00	8.00
24	Ewell Blackwell	40.00	18.00
25	Vic Raschi	60.00	27.00
26	Phil Rizzuto	125.00	55.00
27	Jim Konstanty	25.00	11.00
28	Eddie Waitkus	18.00	8.00
29	Allie Clark	18.00	8.00
30	Bob Feller	125.00	55.00
31	Roy Campanella	225.00	100.00
32	Duke Snider	225.00	100.00
33	Bob Hooper	18.00	8.00
34	Marty Marion	40.00	18.00
35	Al Zarilla	18.00	8.00
36	Joe Dobson	18.00	8.00
37	Whitey Lockman	40.00	18.00
38	Al Evans	18.00	8.00
39	Ray Scarborough	18.00	8.00
40	Gus Bell	60.00	27.00
41	Eddie Yost	25.00	11.00
42	Vern Bickford	18.00	8.00
43	Billy DeMars	18.00	8.00
44	Roy Smalley	18.00	8.00
45	Art Houtteman	18.00	8.00
46	George Kell 1941 UER	55.00	25.00
47	Grady Hatton	18.00	8.00
48	Ken Raffensberger	18.00	8.00
49	Jerry Coleman	30.00	13.50
50	Johnny Mize	55.00	25.00
51	Andy Seminick	18.00	8.00
52	Dick Sisler	18.00	8.00
53	Bob Lemon	55.00	25.00
54	Ray Boone	35.00	16.00
55	Gene Hermanski	18.00	8.00
56	Ralph Branca	60.00	27.00
57	Alex Kellner	18.00	8.00
58	Enos Slaughter	55.00	25.00
59	Randy Gumpert	18.00	8.00
60	Chico Carrasquel	18.00	8.00
61	Jim Hearn	22.00	10.00
62	Lou Boudreau	55.00	25.00
63	Bob Dillinger	18.00	8.00
64	Bill Werle	18.00	8.00
65	Mickey Vernon	40.00	18.00
66	Bob Elliott	25.00	11.00
67	Roy Sievers	25.00	11.00
68	Dick Kokos	18.00	8.00
69	Johnny Schmitz	18.00	8.00
70	Ron Northey	18.00	8.00
71	Jerry Priddy	18.00	8.00
72	Lloyd Merriman	18.00	8.00
73	Tommy Byrne	18.00	8.00
74	Billy Johnson	25.00	11.00
75	Russ Meyer	18.00	8.00
76	Stan Lopata	25.00	11.00
77	Mike Goliat	18.00	8.00
78	Early Wynn	55.00	25.00
79	Jim Hegan	25.00	11.00
80	Pee Wee Reese	125.00	55.00
81	Carl Furillo	50.00	22.00
82	Joe Tipton	18.00	8.00
83	Carl Scheib	18.00	8.00
84	Barney McCosky	18.00	8.00
85	Eddie Kazak	18.00	8.00
86	Harry Brecheen	25.00	11.00
87	Floyd Baker	18.00	8.00
88	Eddie Robinson	18.00	8.00
89	Hank Thompson	25.00	11.00
90	Dave Koslo	18.00	8.00
91	Clyde Vollmer	18.00	8.00
92	Vern Stephens	25.00	11.00
93	Danny O'Connell	18.00	8.00
94	Clyde McCullough	18.00	8.00
95	Sherry Robertson	18.00	8.00
96	Sandy Consuegra	18.00	8.00
97	Bob Kuzava	18.00	8.00
98	Willard Marshall	18.00	8.00
99	Earl Torgeson	18.00	8.00
100	Sherm Lollar	25.00	11.00
101	Owen Friend	18.00	8.00
102	Dutch Leonard	18.00	8.00
103	Andy Pafko	40.00	18.00
104	Virgil Trucks	25.00	11.00
105	Don Kolloway	18.00	8.00
106	Pat Mullin	18.00	8.00
107	Johnny Wyrostek	18.00	8.00
108	Virgil Stallcup	18.00	8.00
109	Allie Reynolds	60.00	27.00
110	Bobby Brown	18.00	
111	Curt Simmons	18.00	8.00
112	Willie Jones	18.00	8.00
113	Bill Nicholson	25.00	11.00
114	Sam Zoldak	18.00	8.00
115	Steve Gromek	18.00	8.00
116	Bruce Edwards	18.00	8.00
117	Eddie Miksis	18.00	8.00
118	Preacher Roe	60.00	27.00
119	Eddie Joost	18.00	8.00
120	Joe Coleman	25.00	11.00
121	Jerry Staley	18.00	8.00
122	Joe Garagiola	75.00	34.00
123	Howie Judson	18.00	8.00
124	Gus Niarhos	18.00	8.00
125	Bill Rigney	25.00	11.00
126	Bobby Thomson	60.00	27.00
127	Sal Maglie	55.00	25.00
128	Ellis Kinder	18.00	8.00
129	Matt Batts	18.00	8.00
130	Tom Saffell	18.00	8.00
131	Cliff Chambers	18.00	8.00
132	Cass Michaels	18.00	8.00
133	Sam Dente	18.00	8.00
134	Warren Spahn	125.00	55.00
135	Walker Cooper	18.00	8.00
136	Ray Coleman	18.00	8.00
137	Dick Starr	18.00	8.00
138	Phil Cavarretta	25.00	11.00
139	Doyle Lade	18.00	8.00
140	Eddie Lake	18.00	8.00
141	Fred Hutchinson	25.00	11.00
142	Aaron Robinson	18.00	8.00
143	Ted Kluszewski	60.00	27.00
144	Herman Wehmeier	18.00	8.00
145	Fred Sanford	25.00	11.00
146	Johnny Hopp	25.00	11.00
147	Ken Heintzelman	18.00	8.00
148	Granny Hamner	18.00	8.00
149	Bubba Church	18.00	8.00
150	Mike Garcia	25.00	11.00
151	Larry Doby	60.00	27.00
152	Cal Abrams	18.00	8.00
153	Rex Barney	25.00	11.00
154	Pete Suder	18.00	8.00
155	Lou Brissie	18.00	8.00
156	Del Rice	18.00	8.00
157	Al Brazle	18.00	8.00
158	Chuck Diering	18.00	8.00
159	Eddie Stewart	18.00	8.00
160	Phil Masi	18.00	8.00
161	Wes Westrum	25.00	11.00
162	Larry Jansen	25.00	11.00
163	Monte Kennedy	18.00	8.00
164	Bill Wight	18.00	8.00
165	Ted Williams	700.00	325.00
166	Stan Rojek	18.00	8.00
167	Murry Dickson	18.00	8.00
168	Sam Mele	18.00	8.00
169	Sid Hudson	18.00	8.00
170	Sibby Sisti	18.00	8.00
171	Buddy Kerr	18.00	8.00
172	Ned Garver	18.00	8.00
173	Hank Arft	18.00	8.00
174	Mickey Owen	25.00	11.00
175	Wayne Terwilliger	18.00	8.00
176	Vic Wertz	40.00	18.00
177	Charlie Keller	25.00	11.00
178	Ted Gray	18.00	8.00
179	Danny Litwhiler	25.00	11.00
180	Howie Fox	18.00	8.00
181	Casey Stengel MG	75.00	34.00
182	Tom Ferrick	18.00	8.00
183	Hank Bauer	60.00	27.00
184	Eddie Sawyer MG	40.00	18.00
185	Jimmy Bloodworth	18.00	8.00
186	Richie Ashburn	90.00	40.00
187	Al Rosen	40.00	18.00
188	Bobby Avila	25.00	11.00
189	Erv Palica	18.00	8.00
190	Joe Hatten	18.00	8.00
191	Billy Hitchcock	18.00	8.00
192	Hank Wyse	18.00	8.00
193	Ted Wilks	18.00	8.00
194	Peanuts Lowrey	18.00	8.00
195	Paul Richards MG	25.00	11.00
	(Caricature)		
196	Billy Pierce	60.00	27.00
197	Bob Cain	18.00	8.00
198	Monte Irvin	100.00	45.00
199	Sheldon Jones	18.00	8.00
200	Jack Kramer	18.00	8.00
201	Steve O'Neill MG	18.00	8.00
202	Mike Guerra	18.00	8.00
203	Vernon Law	60.00	27.00
204	Vic Lombardi	18.00	8.00
205	Mickey Grasso	18.00	8.00
206	Conrado Marrero	18.00	8.00
207	Billy Southworth MG	18.00	8.00
208	Blix Donnelly	18.00	8.00
209	Ken Wood	18.00	8.00
210	Les Moss	18.00	8.00
211	Hal Jeffcoat	18.00	8.00
212	Bob Rush	18.00	8.00
213	Neil Berry	18.00	8.00
214	Bob Swift	18.00	8.00
215	Ken Peterson	18.00	8.00
216	Connie Ryan	18.00	8.00
217	Joe Page	25.00	11.00
218	Ed Lopat	60.00	27.00
219	Gene Woodling	60.00	27.00
220	Bob Miller	18.00	8.00
221	Dick Whitman	18.00	8.00
222	Thurman Tucker	18.00	8.00
223	Johnny VanderMeer	40.00	18.00
224	Billy Cox	30.00	13.50
225	Dan Bankhead	40.00	18.00
226	Jimmy Dykes MG	25.00	11.00
227	Bobby Schantz UER	25.00	11.00
	(Sic, Shantz)		
228	Cloyd Boyer	25.00	11.00
229	Bill Howerton	18.00	8.00
230	Max Lanier	18.00	8.00
231	Luis Aloma	18.00	8.00
232	Nelson Fox	225.00	100.00
233	Leo Durocher MG	60.00	27.00
234	Clint Hartung	18.00	8.00
235	Jack Lohrke	18.00	8.00

#	Player	NRMT	VG-E
236	Warren Rosar	18.00	8.00
237	Billy Goodman	25.00	11.00
238	Pete Reiser	40.00	18.00
239	Bill MacDonald	18.00	8.00
240	Joe Haynes	18.00	8.00
241	Irv Noren	25.00	11.00
242	Sam Jethroe	25.00	11.00
243	Johnny Antonelli	25.00	11.00
244	Cliff Fannin	18.00	8.00
245	John Berardino	60.00	27.00
246	Bill Serena	18.00	8.00
247	Bob Ramazzotti	18.00	8.00
248	Johnny Klippstein	18.00	8.00
249	Johnny Groth	18.00	8.00
250	Hank Borowy	18.00	8.00
251	Willard Ramsdell	18.00	8.00
252	Dixie Howell	18.00	8.00
253	Mickey Mantle	8000.00	3600.00
254	Jackie Jensen	100.00	45.00
255	Milo Candini	50.00	22.00
256	Ken Sylvestri	50.00	22.00
257	Birdie Tebbetts	65.00	29.00
258	Luke Easter	65.00	29.00
259	Chuck Dressen MG	75.00	34.00
260	Carl Erskine	100.00	45.00
261	Wally Moses	60.00	27.00
262	Gus Zernial	60.00	27.00
263	Howie Pollet	50.00	22.00
264	Don Richmond	50.00	22.00
265	Steve Bilko	50.00	22.00
266	Harry Dorish	50.00	22.00
267	Ken Holcombe	50.00	22.00
268	Don Mueller	60.00	27.00
269	Ray Noble	50.00	22.00
270	Willard Nixon	50.00	22.00
271	Tommy Wright	50.00	22.00
272	Billy Meyer MG	50.00	22.00
273	Danny Murtaugh	65.00	29.00
274	George Metkovich	50.00	22.00
275	Bucky Harris MG	65.00	29.00
276	Frank Quinn	50.00	22.00
277	Roy Hartsfield	50.00	22.00
278	Norman Roy	50.00	22.00
279	Jim Delsing	50.00	22.00
280	Frank Overmire	50.00	22.00
281	Al Widmar	50.00	22.00
282	Frank Frisch MG	90.00	40.00
283	Walt Dubiel	50.00	22.00
284	Gene Bearden	60.00	27.00
285	Johnny Lipon	50.00	22.00
286	Bob Usher	50.00	22.00
287	Jim Blackburn	50.00	22.00
288	Bobby Adams	50.00	22.00
289	Cliff Mapes	50.00	22.00
290	Bill Dickey CO	100.00	45.00
291	Tommy Henrich CO	90.00	40.00
292	Eddie Pellegrini	50.00	22.00
293	Ken Johnson	50.00	22.00
294	Jocko Thompson	50.00	22.00
295	Al Lopez MG	120.00	55.00
296	Bob Kennedy	50.00	27.00
297	Dave Philley	50.00	22.00
298	Joe Astroth	50.00	22.00
299	Clyde King	50.00	22.00
300	Hal Rice	50.00	22.00
301	Tommy Glaviano	50.00	22.00
302	Jim Busby	50.00	22.00
303	Marv Rotblatt	50.00	22.00
304	Al Gettell	50.00	22.00
305	Willie Mays	3200.00	1450.00
306	Jim Piersall	100.00	45.00
307	Walt Masterson	50.00	22.00
308	Ted Beard	50.00	22.00
309	Mel Queen	50.00	22.00
310	Erv Dusak	50.00	22.00
311	Mickey Harris	50.00	22.00
312	Gene Mauch	65.00	29.00
313	Ray Mueller	50.00	22.00
314	Johnny Sain	65.00	29.00
315	Zack Taylor MG	50.00	22.00
316	Duane Pillette	50.00	22.00
317	Smoky Burgess	75.00	34.00
318	Warren Hacker	50.00	22.00
319	Red Rolfe MG	65.00	29.00
320	Hal White	50.00	22.00
321	Earl Johnson	50.00	22.00
322	Luke Sewell MG	65.00	29.00
323	Joe Adcock	75.00	34.00
324	Johnny Pramesa	80.00	24.00

1952 Bowman

The cards in this 252-card set measure approximately 2 1/16" by 3 1/8". While the Bowman set of 1952 retained the card size introduced in 1951, it employed a modification of color tones from the two preceding years. The cards also appeared with a facsimile autograph on the front and, for the first time since 1949, premium advertising on the back. The 1952 set was apparently sold in sheets as well as in gum packs. Artwork for 15 cards that were never issued was discovered in the early 1980s. Cards were issued in one card penny packs or five card nickel packs. Notable Rookie Cards in this set are Lew Burdette, Gil McDougald, and Minnie Minoso.

	NRMT	VG-E
COMPLETE SET (252)	7500.00	3400.00
COMMON CARD (1-216)	15.00	6.75
MINOR STARS 1-216	25.00	11.00
SEMISTARS 1-216	40.00	18.00
UNLISTED STARS 1-216	60.00	27.00
COMMON CARD (217-252)	50.00	22.00
MINOR STARS 217-252	60.00	27.00
SEMISTARS 217-252	80.00	36.00

*UNLISTED DODGER/YANKEE: 1.25X VALUE
CARDS PRICED IN NM CONDITION

#	Player	NRMT	VG-E
1	Yogi Berra	400.00	125.00
2	Bobby Thomson	40.00	18.00
3	Fred Hutchinson	25.00	11.00
4	Robin Roberts	60.00	27.00
5	Minnie Minoso	125.00	55.00
6	Virgil Stallcup	15.00	6.75
7	Mike Garcia	25.00	11.00
8	Pee Wee Reese	125.00	55.00
9	Vern Stephens	25.00	11.00
10	Bob Hooper	15.00	6.75
11	Ralph Kiner	50.00	22.00
12	Max Surkont	15.00	6.75
13	Cliff Mapes	15.00	6.75
14	Cliff Chambers	15.00	6.75
15	Sam Mele	15.00	6.75
16	Turk Lown	15.00	6.75
17	Ed Lopat	40.00	18.00
18	Don Mueller	25.00	11.00
19	Bob Cain	15.00	6.75
20	Willie Jones	15.00	6.75
21	Nellie Fox	90.00	40.00
22	Willard Ramsdell	15.00	6.75
23	Bob Lemon	50.00	22.00
24	Carl Furillo	40.00	18.00
25	Mickey McDermott	15.00	6.75
26	Eddie Joost	15.00	6.75
27	Joe Garagiola	50.00	22.00
28	Roy Hartsfield	15.00	6.75
29	Ned Garver	15.00	6.75
30	Red Schoendienst	50.00	22.00
31	Eddie Yost	25.00	11.00
32	Eddie Miksis	15.00	6.75
33	Gil McDougald	80.00	36.00
34	Alvin Dark	25.00	11.00
35	Granny Hamner	15.00	6.75
36	Cass Michaels	15.00	6.75
37	Vic Raschi	25.00	11.00
38	Whitey Lockman	25.00	11.00
39	Vic Wertz	25.00	11.00
40	Bubba Church	15.00	6.75
41	Chico Carrasquel	25.00	11.00
42	Johnny Wyrostek	15.00	6.75
43	Bob Feller	125.00	55.00
44	Roy Campanella	250.00	110.00
45	Johnny Pesky	25.00	11.00
46	Carl Scheib	15.00	6.75
47	Pete Castiglione	15.00	6.75
48	Vern Bickford	15.00	6.75
49	Jim Hearn	15.00	6.75
50	Jerry Staley	15.00	6.75
51	Gil Coan	15.00	6.75
52	Phil Rizzuto	125.00	55.00
53	Richie Ashburn	90.00	40.00
54	Billy Pierce	25.00	11.00
55	Ken Raffensberger	15.00	6.75
56	Clyde King	25.00	11.00
57	Clyde Vollmer	15.00	6.75
58	Hank Majeski	15.00	6.75
59	Murry Dickson	15.00	6.75
60	Sid Gordon	20.00	9.00
61	Tommy Byrne	15.00	6.75
62	Joe Presko	15.00	6.75
63	Irv Noren	20.00	9.00
64	Roy Smalley	15.00	6.75
65	Hank Bauer	25.00	11.00
66	Sal Maglie	25.00	11.00
67	Johnny Groth	15.00	6.75
68	Jim Busby	15.00	6.75
69	Joe Adcock	25.00	11.00
70	Carl Erskine	35.00	16.00
71	Vernon Law	25.00	11.00
72	Earl Torgeson	15.00	6.75
73	Jerry Coleman	25.00	11.00
74	Wes Westrum	22.00	10.00
75	George Kell	50.00	22.00
76	Del Ennis	25.00	11.00
77	Eddie Robinson	15.00	6.75
78	Lloyd Merriman	15.00	6.75
79	Lou Brissie	15.00	6.75
80	Gil Hodges	90.00	40.00
81	Billy Goodman	20.00	9.00
82	Gus Zernial	20.00	9.00
83	Howie Pollet	15.00	6.75
84	Sam Jethroe	25.00	11.00
85	Marty Marion CO	25.00	11.00
86	Cal Abrams	20.00	9.00
87	Mickey Vernon	25.00	11.00
88	Bruce Edwards	15.00	6.75
89	Billy Hitchcock	15.00	6.75
90	Larry Jansen	25.00	11.00
91	Don Kolloway	15.00	6.75
92	Eddie Waitkus	20.00	9.00
93	Paul Richards MG	20.00	9.00
94	Luke Sewell MG	15.00	6.75
95	Luke Easter	25.00	11.00
96	Ralph Branca	25.00	11.00
97	Willard Marshall	15.00	6.75
98	Jimmy Dykes MG	25.00	11.00
99	Clyde McCullough	15.00	6.75
100	Sibby Sisti	15.00	6.75
101	Mickey Mantle	2500.00	1100.00
102	Peanuts Lowrey	15.00	6.75
103	Joe Haynes	15.00	6.75
104	Hal Jeffcoat	15.00	6.75
105	Bobby Brown	25.00	11.00
106	Randy Gumpert	15.00	6.75
107	Del Rice	15.00	6.75
108	George Metkovich	20.00	9.00
109	Tom Morgan	20.00	9.00
110	Max Lanier	15.00	6.75
111	Hoot Evers	15.00	6.75
112	Smoky Burgess	25.00	11.00

☐ 113 Al Zarilla	15.00	6.75
☐ 114 Frank Hiller	15.00	6.75
☐ 115 Larry Doby	40.00	18.00
☐ 116 Duke Snider	200.00	90.00
☐ 117 Bill Wight	15.00	6.75
☐ 118 Ray Murray	15.00	6.75
☐ 119 Bill Howerton	15.00	6.75
☐ 120 Chet Nichols	15.00	6.75
☐ 121 Al Corwin	15.00	6.75
☐ 122 Billy Johnson	15.00	6.75
☐ 123 Sid Hudson	15.00	6.75
☐ 124 Birdie Tebbetts	25.00	11.00
☐ 125 Howie Fox	15.00	6.75
☐ 126 Phil Cavarretta	25.00	11.00
☐ 127 Dick Sisler	15.00	6.75
☐ 128 Don Newcombe	35.00	16.00
☐ 129 Gus Niarhos	15.00	6.75
☐ 130 Allie Clark	15.00	6.75
☐ 131 Bob Swift	15.00	6.75
☐ 132 Dave Cole	15.00	6.75
☐ 133 Dick Kryhoski	15.00	6.75
☐ 134 Al Brazle	15.00	6.75
☐ 135 Mickey Harris	15.00	6.75
☐ 136 Gene Hermanski	15.00	6.75
☐ 137 Stan Rojek	15.00	6.75
☐ 138 Ted Wilks	15.00	6.75
☐ 139 Jerry Priddy	15.00	6.75
☐ 140 Ray Scarborough	15.00	6.75
☐ 141 Hank Edwards	15.00	6.75
☐ 142 Early Wynn	50.00	22.00
☐ 143 Sandy Consuegra	15.00	6.75
☐ 144 Joe Hatton	15.00	6.75
☐ 145 Johnny Mize	50.00	22.00
☐ 146 Leo Durocher MG	50.00	22.00
☐ 147 Marlin Stuart	15.00	6.75
☐ 148 Ken Heintzelman	15.00	6.75
☐ 149 Howie Judson	15.00	6.75
☐ 150 Herman Wehmeier	15.00	6.75
☐ 151 Al Rosen	25.00	11.00
☐ 152 Billy Cox	15.00	6.75
☐ 153 Fred Hatfield	15.00	6.75
☐ 154 Ferris Fain	20.00	9.00
☐ 155 Billy Meyer MG	15.00	6.75
☐ 156 Warren Spahn	125.00	55.00
☐ 157 Jim Delsing	15.00	6.75
☐ 158 Bucky Harris MG	25.00	11.00
☐ 159 Dutch Leonard	15.00	6.75
☐ 160 Eddie Stanky	25.00	11.00
☐ 161 Jackie Jensen	35.00	16.00
☐ 162 Monte Irvin	50.00	22.00
☐ 163 Johnny Lipon	15.00	6.75
☐ 164 Connie Ryan	15.00	6.75
☐ 165 Saul Rogovin	15.00	6.75
☐ 166 Bobby Adams	15.00	6.75
☐ 167 Bobby Avila	25.00	11.00
☐ 168 Preacher Roe	25.00	11.00
☐ 169 Walt Dropo	20.00	9.00
☐ 170 Joe Astroth	15.00	6.75
☐ 171 Mel Queen	15.00	6.75
☐ 172 Ebba St.Claire	15.00	6.75
☐ 173 Gene Bearden	15.00	6.75
☐ 174 Mickey Grasso	15.00	6.75
☐ 175 Randy Jackson	15.00	6.75
☐ 176 Harry Brecheen	20.00	9.00
☐ 177 Gene Woodling	25.00	11.00
☐ 178 Dave Williams	20.00	9.00
☐ 179 Pete Suder	15.00	6.75
☐ 180 Ed Fitzgerald	15.00	6.75
☐ 181 Joe Collins	25.00	11.00
☐ 182 Dave Koslo	15.00	6.75
☐ 183 Pat Mullin	15.00	6.75
☐ 184 Curt Simmons	25.00	11.00
☐ 185 Eddie Stewart	15.00	6.75
☐ 186 Frank Smith	15.00	6.75
☐ 187 Jim Hegan	20.00	9.00
☐ 188 Chuck Dressen MG	25.00	11.00
☐ 189 Jimmy Piersall	25.00	11.00
☐ 190 Dick Fowler	15.00	6.75
☐ 191 Bob Friend	40.00	18.00
☐ 192 John Cusick	15.00	6.75
☐ 193 Bobby Young	15.00	6.75
☐ 194 Bob Porterfield	15.00	6.75
☐ 195 Frank Baumholtz	15.00	6.75
☐ 196 Stan Musial	600.00	275.00
☐ 197 Charlie Silvera	15.00	6.75
☐ 198 Chuck Diering	15.00	6.75

☐ 199 Ted Gray	15.00	6.75
☐ 200 Ken Silvestri	15.00	6.75
☐ 201 Ray Coleman	15.00	6.75
☐ 202 Harry Perkowski	15.00	6.75
☐ 203 Steve Gromek	15.00	6.75
☐ 204 Andy Pafko	25.00	11.00
☐ 205 Walt Masterson	15.00	6.75
☐ 206 Elmer Valo	15.00	6.75
☐ 207 George Strickland	15.00	6.75
☐ 208 Walker Cooper	15.00	6.75
☐ 209 Dick Littlefield	15.00	6.75
☐ 210 Archie Wilson	15.00	6.75
☐ 211 Paul Minner	15.00	6.75
☐ 212 Solly Hemus	15.00	6.75
☐ 213 Monte Kennedy	15.00	6.75
☐ 214 Ray Boone	25.00	11.00
☐ 215 Sheldon Jones	15.00	6.75
☐ 216 Matt Batts	15.00	6.75
☐ 217 Casey Stengel MG	150.00	70.00
☐ 218 Willie Mays	1200.00	550.00
☐ 219 Neil Berry	50.00	22.00
☐ 220 Russ Meyer	50.00	22.00
☐ 221 Lou Kretlow	50.00	22.00
☐ 222 Dixie Howell	50.00	22.00
☐ 223 Harry Simpson	50.00	22.00
☐ 224 Johnny Schmitz	50.00	22.00
☐ 225 Del Wilber	50.00	22.00
☐ 226 Alex Kellner	50.00	22.00
☐ 227 Clyde Sukeforth CO	50.00	22.00
☐ 228 Bob Chipman	50.00	22.00
☐ 229 Hank Arft	50.00	22.00
☐ 230 Frank Shea	50.00	22.00
☐ 231 Dee Fondy	50.00	22.00
☐ 232 Enos Slaughter	90.00	40.00
☐ 233 Bob Kuzava	50.00	22.00
☐ 234 Fred Fitzsimmons CO	50.00	22.00
☐ 235 Steve Souchock	50.00	22.00
☐ 236 Tommy Brown	50.00	22.00
☐ 237 Sherm Lollar	50.00	22.00
☐ 238 Roy McMillan	50.00	22.00
☐ 239 Dale Mitchell	50.00	22.00
☐ 240 Billy Loes	50.00	22.00
☐ 241 Mel Parnell	50.00	22.00
☐ 242 Everett Kell	50.00	22.00
☐ 243 Red Munger	50.00	22.00
☐ 244 Lew Burdette	50.00	22.00
☐ 245 George Schmees	50.00	22.00
☐ 246 Jerry Snyder	50.00	22.00
☐ 247 Johnny Pramesa	50.00	22.00
☐ 248 Bill Werle	50.00	22.00
☐ 249 Hank Thompson	50.00	22.00
☐ 250 Ike Delock	50.00	22.00
☐ 251 Jack Lohrke	50.00	22.00
☐ 252 Frank Crosetti CO	100.00	25.00

1953 Bowman B/W

The cards in this 64-card set measure approximately 2 1/2" by 3 3/4". Some collectors believe that the high cost of producing the 1953 color series forced Bowman to issue this set in black and white, since the two sets are identical in design except for the element of color. This set was also produced in fewer numbers than its color

counterpart, and is popular among collectors for the challenge involved in completing it. Cards were issued in five-card nickel packs. There are no key Rookie Cards in this set.

	NRMT	VG-E
COMPLETE SET (64)	2400.00	1100.00
COMMON CARD (1-64)	40.00	18.00
MINOR STARS	70.00	32.00
*UNLISTED DODGER/YANKEE: 1.25X VALUE
CARDS PRICED IN NM CONDITION !

☐ 1 Gus Bell	120.00	24.00
☐ 2 Willard Nixon	40.00	18.00
☐ 3 Bill Rigney	40.00	18.00
☐ 4 Pat Mullin	40.00	18.00
☐ 5 Dee Fondy	40.00	18.00
☐ 6 Ray Murray	40.00	18.00
☐ 7 Andy Seminick	40.00	18.00
☐ 8 Pete Suder	40.00	18.00
☐ 9 Walt Masterson	40.00	18.00
☐ 10 Dick Sisler	70.00	32.00
☐ 11 Dick Gernert	40.00	18.00
☐ 12 Randy Jackson	40.00	18.00
☐ 13 Joe Tipton	40.00	18.00
☐ 14 Bill Nicholson	70.00	32.00
☐ 15 Johnny Mize	125.00	55.00
☐ 16 Stu Miller	70.00	32.00
☐ 17 Virgil Trucks	70.00	32.00
☐ 18 Billy Hoeft	40.00	18.00
☐ 19 Paul LaPalme	40.00	18.00
☐ 20 Eddie Robinson	40.00	18.00
☐ 21 Clarence Podbielan	40.00	18.00
☐ 22 Matt Batts	40.00	18.00
☐ 23 Wilmer Mizell	70.00	32.00
☐ 24 Del Wilber	40.00	18.00
☐ 25 Johnny Sain	60.00	27.00
☐ 26 Preacher Roe	60.00	27.00
☐ 27 Bob Lemon	125.00	55.00
☐ 28 Hoyt Wilhelm	125.00	55.00
☐ 29 Sid Hudson	40.00	18.00
☐ 30 Walker Cooper	40.00	18.00
☐ 31 Gene Woodling	60.00	27.00
☐ 32 Rocky Bridges	40.00	18.00
☐ 33 Bob Kuzava	40.00	18.00
☐ 34 Ebba St.Claire	40.00	18.00
☐ 35 Johnny Wyrostek	40.00	18.00
☐ 36 Jimmy Piersall	60.00	27.00
☐ 37 Hal Jeffcoat	40.00	18.00
☐ 38 Dave Cole	40.00	18.00
☐ 39 Casey Stengel MG	325.00	145.00
☐ 40 Larry Jansen	70.00	32.00
☐ 41 Bob Ramazzotti	40.00	18.00
☐ 42 Howie Judson	40.00	18.00
☐ 43 Hal Bevan	40.00	18.00
☐ 44 Jim Delsing	40.00	18.00
☐ 45 Irv Noren	70.00	32.00
☐ 46 Bucky Harris MG	60.00	27.00
☐ 47 Jack Lohrke	40.00	18.00
☐ 48 Steve Ridzik	40.00	18.00
☐ 49 Floyd Baker	40.00	18.00
☐ 50 Dutch Leonard	40.00	18.00
☐ 51 Lou Burdette	60.00	27.00
☐ 52 Ralph Branca	60.00	27.00
☐ 53 Morrie Martin	40.00	18.00
☐ 54 Bill Miller	40.00	18.00
☐ 55 Don Johnson	40.00	18.00
☐ 56 Roy Smalley	40.00	18.00
☐ 57 Andy Pafko	70.00	32.00
☐ 58 Jim Konstanty	70.00	32.00
☐ 59 Duane Pillette	40.00	18.00
☐ 60 Billy Cox	60.00	27.00
☐ 61 Tom Gorman	40.00	18.00
☐ 62 Keith Thomas	40.00	18.00
☐ 63 Steve Gromek	40.00	18.00
☐ 64 Andy Hansen	60.00	19.00

1953 Bowman Color

The cards in this 160-card set measure approximately 2 1/2"

by 3 3/4". The 1953 Bowman Color set, considered by many to be the best looking set of the modern era, contains Kodachrome photographs with no names or facsimile autographs on the face. Cards were issued in five-card nickel packs. Numbers 113 to 160 are somewhat more difficult to obtain, with numbers 113 to 128 being the most difficult. There are two cards of Al Corwin (126 and 149). There are no key Rookie Cards in this set.

	NRMT	VG-E
COMPLETE SET (160) !	12000.00	5000.00
COMMON CARD (1-112)	40.00	18.00
MINOR STARS 1-112	50.00	22.00
SEMISTARS 1-112	60.00	27.00
UNLISTED STARS 1-112	80.00	36.00
COMMON CARD (113-128)	80.00	36.00
MINOR STARS 113-128	100.00	45.00
SEMISTARS 113-128	120.00	55.00
COMMON CARD (129-160)	60.00	27.00
MINOR STARS 129-160	80.00	36.00
SEMISTARS 129-160	100.00	45.00

*UNLISTED DODGER/YANKEE: 1.25X VALUE
CARDS PRICED IN NM CONDITION !

#	Player	NRMT	VG-E
1	Dave Williams	100.00	20.00
2	Vic Wertz	50.00	22.00
3	Sam Jethroe	50.00	22.00
4	Art Houtteman	40.00	18.00
5	Sid Gordon	40.00	18.00
6	Joe Ginsberg	40.00	18.00
7	Harry Chiti	40.00	18.00
8	Al Rosen	50.00	22.00
9	Phil Rizzuto	175.00	80.00
10	Richie Ashburn	140.00	65.00
11	Bobby Shantz	45.00	20.00
12	Carl Erskine	50.00	22.00
13	Gus Zernial	50.00	22.00
14	Billy Loes	50.00	22.00
15	Jim Busby	40.00	18.00
16	Bob Friend	45.00	20.00
17	Gerry Staley	40.00	18.00
18	Nellie Fox	140.00	65.00
19	Alvin Dark	45.00	20.00
20	Don Lenhardt	40.00	18.00
21	Joe Garagiola	60.00	27.00
22	Bob Porterfield	40.00	18.00
23	Herman Wehmeier	40.00	18.00
24	Jackie Jensen	50.00	22.00
25	Hoot Evers	40.00	18.00
26	Roy McMillan	50.00	22.00
27	Vic Raschi	50.00	22.00
28	Smoky Burgess	45.00	20.00
29	Bobby Avila	45.00	20.00
30	Phil Cavarretta	45.00	20.00
31	Jimmy Dykes MG	45.00	20.00
32	Stan Musial	700.00	325.00
33	Pee Wee Reese	900.00	400.00
34	Gil Coan	40.00	18.00
35	Maurice McDermott	40.00	18.00
36	Minnie Minoso	60.00	27.00
37	Jim Wilson	40.00	18.00
38	Harry Byrd	40.00	18.00
39	Paul Richards MG	45.00	20.00
40	Larry Doby	60.00	27.00
41	Sammy White	40.00	18.00
42	Tommy Brown	40.00	18.00
43	Mike Garcia	50.00	22.00
44	Yogi Berra / Hank Bauer / Mickey Mantle	675.00	300.00
45	Walt Dropo	50.00	22.00
46	Roy Campanella	275.00	125.00
47	Ned Garver	40.00	18.00
48	Hank Sauer	45.00	20.00
49	Eddie Stanky MG	45.00	20.00
50	Lou Kretlow	40.00	18.00
51	Monte Irvin	60.00	27.00
52	Marty Marion MG	50.00	22.00
53	Del Rice	40.00	18.00
54	Chico Carrasquel	45.00	20.00
55	Leo Durocher MG	70.00	32.00
56	Bob Cain	40.00	18.00
57	Lou Boudreau MG	60.00	27.00
58	Willard Marshall	40.00	18.00
59	Mickey Mantle	3000.00	1350.00
60	Granny Hamner	40.00	18.00
61	George Kell	70.00	32.00
62	Ted Kluszewski	60.00	27.00
63	Gil McDougald	60.00	27.00
64	Curt Simmons	45.00	20.00
65	Robin Roberts	100.00	45.00
66	Mel Parnell	50.00	22.00
67	Mel Clark	40.00	18.00
68	Allie Reynolds	50.00	22.00
69	Charlie Grimm MG	45.00	20.00
70	Clint Courtney	40.00	18.00
71	Paul Minner	40.00	18.00
72	Ted Gray	40.00	18.00
73	Billy Pierce	45.00	20.00
74	Don Mueller	50.00	22.00
75	Saul Rogovin	40.00	18.00
76	Jim Hearn	40.00	18.00
77	Mickey Grasso	40.00	18.00
78	Carl Furillo	55.00	22.00
79	Ray Boone	45.00	20.00
80	Ralph Kiner	70.00	32.00
81	Enos Slaughter	60.00	27.00
82	Joe Astroth	40.00	18.00
83	Jack Daniels	40.00	18.00
84	Hank Bauer	50.00	22.00
85	Solly Hemus	40.00	18.00
86	Harry Simpson	40.00	18.00
87	Harry Perkowski	40.00	18.00
88	Joe Dobson	40.00	18.00
89	Sandy Consuegra	40.00	18.00
90	Joe Nuxhall	45.00	20.00
91	Steve Souchock	40.00	18.00
92	Gil Hodges	175.00	80.00
93	Phil Rizzuto and Billy Martin	250.00	110.00
94	Bob Addis	40.00	18.00
95	Wally Moses CO	50.00	22.00
96	Sal Maglie	50.00	22.00
97	Eddie Mathews	300.00	135.00
98	Hector Rodriguez	40.00	18.00
99	Warren Spahn	250.00	110.00
100	Bill Wight	40.00	18.00
101	Red Schoendienst	60.00	27.00
102	Jim Hegan	50.00	22.00
103	Del Ennis	45.00	20.00
104	Luke Easter	50.00	22.00
105	Eddie Joost	40.00	18.00
106	Ken Raffensberger	40.00	18.00
107	Alex Kellner	40.00	18.00
108	Bobby Adams	40.00	18.00
109	Ken Wood	40.00	18.00
110	Bob Rush	40.00	18.00
111	Jim Dyck	40.00	18.00
112	Toby Atwell	40.00	18.00
113	Karl Drews	80.00	36.00
114	Bob Feller	300.00	135.00
115	Cloyd Boyer	80.00	36.00
116	Eddie Yost	100.00	45.00
117	Duke Snider	550.00	250.00
118	Billy Martin	300.00	135.00
119	Dale Mitchell	75.00	34.00
120	Marlin Stuart	80.00	36.00
121	Yogi Berra	575.00	250.00
122	Bill Serena	80.00	36.00
123	Johnny Lipon	80.00	36.00
124	Charlie Dressen MG	90.00	40.00
125	Fred Hatfield	80.00	36.00
126	Al Corwin	80.00	36.00
127	Dick Kryhoski	80.00	36.00
128	Whitey Lockman	100.00	45.00
129	Russ Meyer	60.00	27.00
130	Cass Michaels	60.00	27.00
131	Connie Ryan	60.00	27.00
132	Fred Hutchinson	80.00	36.00
133	Willie Jones	60.00	27.00
134	Johnny Pesky	75.00	34.00
135	Bobby Morgan	60.00	27.00
136	Jim Brideweser	60.00	27.00
137	Sam Dente	60.00	27.00
138	Bubba Church	60.00	27.00
139	Pete Runnels	75.00	34.00
140	Al Brazle	60.00	27.00
141	Frank Shea	60.00	27.00
142	Larry Miggins	60.00	27.00
143	Al Lopez MG	75.00	34.00
144	Warren Hacker	60.00	27.00
145	George Shuba	80.00	36.00
146	Early Wynn	125.00	55.00
147	Clem Koshorek	60.00	27.00
148	Billy Goodman	80.00	36.00
149	Al Corwin	60.00	27.00
150	Carl Scheib	60.00	27.00
151	Joe Adcock	75.00	34.00
152	Clyde Vollmer	60.00	27.00
153	Whitey Ford	500.00	220.00
154	Turk Lown	60.00	27.00
155	Allie Clark	60.00	27.00
156	Max Surkont	60.00	27.00
157	Sherm Lollar	80.00	36.00
158	Howard Fox	60.00	27.00
159	Mickey Vernon UER (Photo actually Floyd Baker)	75.00	34.00
160	Cal Abrams	100.00	34.00

1954 Bowman

The cards in this 224-card set measure approximately 2 1/2" by 3 3/4". The set was distributed in two separate series: 1-128 in first series and 129-224 in second series. A contractual problem apparently resulted in the deletion of the number 66 Ted Williams card from this Bowman set, thereby creating a scarcity that is highly valued among collectors. The set price below does NOT include number 66 Williams but does include number 66 Jim Piersall, the apparent replacement for Williams in spite of the fact that Piersall was already number 210 to appear later in the set. Many errors in players' statistics exist (and some were corrected) while a few players' names *were printed on the front, instead of appearing as a facsimile autograph. Most of these differences are so minor that there is no price differential for either card. The cards which changes were made on are #'s 12, 22, 25, 26, 35, 38, 41, 43, 47, 53, 61, 67, 80, 81, 82, 85, 93, 94, 99, 103, 105, 124, 138, 139, 140, 145, 153, 156, 174, 179, 185, 212, 216 and 217. The set was issued in seven-card nickel packs. The notable Rookie Cards in this set are Harvey Kuenn and Don Larsen.*

	NRMT	VG-E
COMPLETE SET (224)	4000.00	1800.00
COMMON CARD (1-224)		5.50
MINOR STARS	20.00	9.00
SEMISTARS	30.00	13.50
UNLISTED STARS	50.00	22.00

*UNLISTED DODGER/YANKEE: 1.25X VALUE
CARDS PRICED IN NM CONDITION !

☐ 1 Phil Rizzuto	150.00	45.00
☐ 2 Jackie Jensen	20.00	9.00
☐ 3 Marion Fricano	12.00	5.50
☐ 4 Bob Hooper	12.00	5.50
☐ 5 Billy Hunter	12.00	5.50
☐ 6 Nellie Fox	75.00	34.00
☐ 7 Walt Dropo	20.00	9.00
☐ 8 Jim Busby	12.00	5.50
☐ 9 Dave Williams	12.00	5.50
☐ 10 Carl Erskine	20.00	9.00
☐ 11 Sid Gordon	12.00	5.50
☐ 12 Roy McMillan	20.00	9.00
☐ 13 Paul Minner	12.00	5.50
☐ 14 Jerry Staley	12.00	5.50
☐ 15 Richie Ashburn	75.00	34.00
☐ 16 Jim Wilson	12.00	5.50
☐ 17 Tom Gorman	12.00	5.50
☐ 18 Hoot Evers	12.00	5.50
☐ 19 Bobby Shantz	20.00	9.00
☐ 20 Art Houtteman	12.00	5.50
☐ 21 Vic Wertz	20.00	9.00
☐ 22 Sam Mele	12.00	5.50
☐ 23 Harvey Kuenn	35.00	16.00
☐ 24 Bob Porterfield	12.00	5.50
☐ 25 Wes Westrum	20.00	9.00
☐ 26 Billy Cox	20.00	9.00
☐ 27 Dick Cole	12.00	5.50
☐ 28 Jim Greengrass	12.00	5.50
☐ 29 Johnny Klippstein	12.00	5.50
☐ 30 Del Rice	12.00	5.50
☐ 31 Smoky Burgess	20.00	9.00
☐ 32 Del Crandall	20.00	9.00
☐ 33A Vic Raschi		
(No mention of trade on back)		
☐ 33B Vic Raschi	35.00	16.00
(Traded to St.Louis)		
☐ 34 Sammy White	12.00	5.50
☐ 35 Eddie Joost	12.00	5.50
☐ 36 George Strickland	12.00	5.50
☐ 37 Dick Kokos	12.00	5.50
☐ 38 Minnie Minoso	25.00	11.00
☐ 39 Ned Garver	12.00	5.50
☐ 40 Gil Coan	12.00	5.50
☐ 41 Alvin Dark	20.00	9.00
☐ 42 Billy Loes	20.00	9.00
☐ 43 Bob Friend	20.00	9.00
☐ 44 Harry Perkowski	12.00	5.50
☐ 45 Ralph Kiner	40.00	18.00
☐ 46 Rip Repulski	12.00	5.50
☐ 47 Granny Hamner	12.00	5.50
☐ 48 Jack Dittmer	12.00	5.50
☐ 49 Harry Byrd	12.00	5.50
☐ 50 George Kell	40.00	18.00
☐ 51 Alex Kellner	12.00	5.50
☐ 52 Joe Ginsberg	12.00	5.50
☐ 53 Don Lenhardt	12.00	5.50
☐ 54 Chico Carrasquel	12.00	5.50
☐ 55 Jim Delsing	12.00	5.50
☐ 56 Maurice McDermott	12.00	5.50
☐ 57 Hoyt Wilhelm	35.00	16.00
☐ 58 Pee Wee Reese	75.00	34.00
☐ 59 Bob Schultz	12.00	5.50
☐ 60 Fred Baczewski	12.00	5.50
☐ 61 Eddie Miksis	12.00	5.50
☐ 62 Enos Slaughter	40.00	18.00
☐ 63 Earl Torgeson	12.00	5.50
☐ 64 Eddie Mathews	60.00	27.00
☐ 65 Mickey Mantle	1400.00	650.00
☐ 66A Ted Williams	4600.00	2100.00
☐ 66B Jimmy Piersall	75.00	34.00
☐ 67 Carl Scheib	12.00	5.50
☐ 68 Bobby Avila	20.00	9.00
☐ 69 Clint Courtney	12.00	5.50
☐ 70 Willard Marshall	12.00	5.50
☐ 71 Ted Gray	12.00	5.50
☐ 72 Eddie Yost	20.00	9.00
☐ 73 Don Mueller	20.00	9.00
☐ 74 Jim Gilliam	30.00	13.50
☐ 75 Max Surkont	12.00	5.50
☐ 76 Joe Nuxhall	20.00	9.00
☐ 77 Bob Rush	12.00	5.50
☐ 78 Sal Yvars	12.00	5.50
☐ 79 Curt Simmons	20.00	9.00
☐ 80 Johnny Logan	20.00	9.00
☐ 81 Jerry Coleman	20.00	9.00
☐ 82 Billy Goodman	20.00	9.00
☐ 83 Ray Murray	12.00	5.50
☐ 84 Larry Doby	25.00	11.00
☐ 85 Jim Dyck	12.00	5.50
☐ 86 Harry Dorish	12.00	5.50
☐ 87 Don Lund	12.00	5.50
☐ 88 Tom Umphlett	12.00	5.50
☐ 89 Willie Mays	400.00	180.00
☐ 90 Roy Campanella	175.00	80.00
☐ 91 Cal Abrams	12.00	5.50
☐ 92 Ken Raffensberger	12.00	5.50
☐ 93 Bill Serena	12.00	5.50
☐ 94 Solly Hemus	12.00	5.50
☐ 95 Robin Roberts	50.00	22.00
☐ 96 Joe Adcock	20.00	9.00
☐ 97 Gil McDougald	20.00	9.00
☐ 98 Ellis Kinder	12.00	5.50
☐ 99 Pete Suder	12.00	5.50
☐ 100 Mike Garcia	20.00	9.00
☐ 101 Don Larsen	60.00	27.00
☐ 102 Billy Pierce	20.00	9.00
☐ 103 Steve Souchock	12.00	5.50
☐ 104 Frank Shea	12.00	5.50
☐ 105 Sal Maglie	20.00	9.00
☐ 106 Clem Labine	20.00	9.00
☐ 107 Paul LaPalme	12.00	5.50
☐ 108 Bobby Adams	12.00	5.50
☐ 109 Roy Smalley	12.00	5.50
☐ 110 Red Schoendienst	35.00	16.00
☐ 111 Murry Dickson	12.00	5.50
☐ 112 Andy Pafko	20.00	9.00
☐ 113 Allie Reynolds	20.00	9.00
☐ 114 Willard Nixon	12.00	5.50
☐ 115 Don Bollweg	12.00	5.50
☐ 116 Luke Easter	20.00	9.00
☐ 117 Dick Kryhoski	12.00	5.50
☐ 118 Bob Boyd	12.00	5.50
☐ 119 Fred Hatfield	12.00	5.50
☐ 120 Mel Hoderlein	12.00	5.50
☐ 121 Ray Katt	12.00	5.50
☐ 122 Carl Furillo	25.00	11.00
☐ 123 Toby Atwell	12.00	5.50
☐ 124 Gus Bell	20.00	9.00
☐ 125 Warren Hacker	12.00	5.50
☐ 126 Cliff Chambers	12.00	5.50
☐ 127 Del Ennis	20.00	9.00
☐ 128 Ebba St.Claire	12.00	5.50
☐ 129 Hank Bauer	20.00	9.00
☐ 130 Milt Bolling	12.00	5.50
☐ 131 Joe Astroth	12.00	5.50
☐ 132 Bob Feller	75.00	34.00
☐ 133 Duane Pillette	12.00	5.50
☐ 134 Luis Aloma	12.00	5.50
☐ 135 Johnny Pesky	20.00	9.00
☐ 136 Clyde Vollmer	12.00	5.50
☐ 137 Al Corwin	12.00	5.50
☐ 138 Gil Hodges	75.00	34.00
☐ 139 Preston Ward	12.00	5.50
☐ 140 Saul Rogovin	12.00	5.50
☐ 141 Joe Garagiola	30.00	13.50
☐ 142 Al Brazle	12.00	5.50
☐ 143 Willie Jones	12.00	5.50
☐ 144 Ernie Johnson	25.00	11.00
☐ 145 Billy Martin	75.00	34.00
☐ 146 Dick Gernert	12.00	5.50
☐ 147 Joe DeMaestri	12.00	5.50
☐ 148 Dale Mitchell	20.00	9.00
☐ 149 Bob Young	12.00	5.50
☐ 150 Cass Michaels	12.00	5.50
☐ 151 Pat Mullin	12.00	5.50
☐ 152 Mickey Vernon	20.00	9.00
☐ 153 Whitey Lockman	20.00	9.00
☐ 154 Don Newcombe	30.00	13.50
☐ 155 Frank Thomas	20.00	9.00
☐ 156 Rocky Bridges	12.00	5.50
☐ 157 Turk Lown	12.00	5.50
☐ 158 Stu Miller	20.00	9.00
☐ 159 Johnny Lindell	12.00	5.50
☐ 160 Danny O'Connell	12.00	5.50
☐ 161 Yogi Berra	175.00	80.00
☐ 162 Ted Lepcio	12.00	5.50
☐ 163A Dave Philley	20.00	9.00
(No mention of trade on back)		
☐ 163B Dave Philley	36.00	16.00
(Traded to Cleveland)		
☐ 164 Early Wynn	50.00	22.00
☐ 165 Johnny Groth	12.00	5.50
☐ 166 Sandy Consuegra	12.00	5.50
☐ 167 Billy Hoeft	12.00	5.50
☐ 168 Ed Fitzgerald	12.00	5.50
☐ 169 Larry Jansen	20.00	9.00
☐ 170 Duke Snider	125.00	55.00
☐ 171 Carlos Bernier	12.00	5.50
☐ 172 Andy Seminick	12.00	5.50
☐ 173 Dee Fondy	12.00	5.50
☐ 174 Pete Castiglione	12.00	5.50
☐ 175 Mel Clark	12.00	5.50
☐ 176 Vern Bickford	12.00	5.50
☐ 177 Whitey Ford	100.00	45.00
☐ 178 Del Wilber	12.00	5.50
☐ 179 Morrie Martin	12.00	5.50
☐ 180 Joe Tipton	12.00	5.50
☐ 181 Les Moss	12.00	5.50
☐ 182 Sherm Lollar	20.00	9.00
☐ 183 Matt Batts	12.00	5.50
☐ 184 Mickey Grasso	12.00	5.50
☐ 185 Daryl Spencer	12.00	5.50
☐ 186 Russ Meyer	12.00	5.50
☐ 187 Vern Law	20.00	9.00
☐ 188 Frank Smith	12.00	5.50
☐ 189 Randy Jackson	12.00	5.50
☐ 190 Joe Presko	12.00	5.50
☐ 191 Karl Drews	12.00	5.50
☐ 192 Lou Burdette	20.00	9.00
☐ 193 Eddie Robinson	12.00	5.50
☐ 194 Sid Hudson	12.00	5.50
☐ 195 Bob Cain	12.00	5.50
☐ 196 Bob Lemon	40.00	18.00
☐ 197 Lou Kretlow	12.00	5.50
☐ 198 Virgil Trucks	12.00	5.50
☐ 199 Steve Gromek	12.00	5.50
☐ 200 Conrado Marrero	12.00	5.50
☐ 201 Bobby Thomson	25.00	11.00
☐ 202 George Shuba	20.00	9.00
☐ 203 Vic Janowicz	20.00	9.00
☐ 204 Jack Collum	12.00	5.50
☐ 205 Hal Jeffcoat	12.00	5.50
☐ 206 Steve Bilko	12.00	5.50
☐ 207 Stan Lopata	12.00	5.50
☐ 208 Johnny Antonelli	20.00	9.00
☐ 209 Gene Woodling	12.00	5.50
☐ 210 Jimmy Piersall	20.00	9.00
☐ 211 Al Robertson	12.00	5.50
☐ 212 Owen Friend	12.00	5.50
☐ 213 Dick Littlefield	12.00	5.50
☐ 214 Ferris Fain	20.00	9.00
☐ 215 Johnny Bucha	12.00	5.50
☐ 216 Jerry Snyder	12.00	5.50
☐ 217 Hank Thompson	20.00	9.00
☐ 218 Preacher Roe	25.00	11.00
☐ 219 Hal Rice	12.00	5.50
☐ 220 Hobie Landrith	12.00	5.50
☐ 221 Frank Baumholtz	12.00	5.50
☐ 222 Memo Luna	12.00	5.50

☐ 223 Steve Ridzik	12.00	5.50
☐ 224 Bill Bruton	40.00	10.00

1955 Bowman

The cards in this 320-card set measure approximately 2 1/2" by 3 3/4". The Bowman set of 1955 is known as the "TV set" because each player photograph is cleverly shown within a television set design. The set contains umpire cards, some transposed pictures (e.g., Johnsons and Bollings), an incorrect spelling for Harvey Kuenn, and a traded line for Palica (all of which are noted in the checklist below). Some three-card advertising strips exist, the backs of these panels contain advertising for Bowman products. Advertising panels seen include Nellie Fox/Carl Furillo/Carl Erskine, Hank Aaron/Johnny Logan/Eddie Miksis, and a panel including Early Wynn and Pee Wee Reese. Cards were issued either in 9-card nickel packs or one card penny packs. The notable Rookie Cards in this set are Elston Howard and Don Zimmer. Hall of Fame umpires pictured in the set are Al Barlick, Jocko Conlon and Cal Hubbard.

	NRMT	VG-E
COMPLETE SET (320)	4600.00	2100.00
COMMON CARD (1-96)	12.00	5.50
COMMON CARD (97-224)	10.00	4.50
MINOR STARS 1-224	15.00	6.75
SEMISTARS 1-224	20.00	9.00
UNLISTED STARS 1-224	30.00	13.50
COMMON CARD (225-320)	15.00	6.75
MINOR STARS 225-320	20.00	9.00
SEMISTARS 225-320	30.00	13.50
UNLISTED STARS 225-320	40.00	18.00

*UNLISTED DODGER/YANKEE: 1.25X VALUE
CARDS PRICED IN NM CONDITION !

☐ 1 Hoyt Wilhelm	100.00	22.00
☐ 2 Alvin Dark	15.00	6.75
☐ 3 Joe Coleman	15.00	6.75
☐ 4 Eddie Waitkus	12.00	5.50
☐ 5 Jim Robertson	12.00	5.50
☐ 6 Pete Suder	12.00	5.50
☐ 7 Gene Baker	12.00	5.50
☐ 8 Warren Hacker	12.00	5.50
☐ 9 Gil McDougald	20.00	9.00
☐ 10 Phil Rizzuto	65.00	29.00
☐ 11 Bill Bruton	15.00	6.75
☐ 12 Andy Pafko	15.00	6.75
☐ 13 Clyde Vollmer	12.00	5.50
☐ 14 Gus Keriazakos	12.00	5.50
☐ 15 Frank Sullivan	12.00	5.50

☐ 16 Jimmy Piersall	15.00	6.75
☐ 17 Del Ennis	15.00	6.75
☐ 18 Stan Lopata	12.00	5.50
☐ 19 Bobby Avila	15.00	6.75
☐ 20 Al Smith	15.00	6.75
☐ 21 Don Hoak	12.00	5.50
☐ 22 Roy Campanella	125.00	55.00
☐ 23 Al Kaline	150.00	70.00
☐ 24 Al Aber	12.00	5.50
☐ 25 Minnie Minoso	25.00	11.00
☐ 26 Virgil Trucks	15.00	6.75
☐ 27 Preston Ward	12.00	5.50
☐ 28 Dick Cole	12.00	5.50
☐ 29 Red Schoendienst	30.00	13.50
☐ 30 Bill Sarni	12.00	5.50
☐ 31 Johnny Temple	15.00	6.75
☐ 32 Wally Post	15.00	6.75
☐ 33 Nellie Fox	45.00	20.00
☐ 34 Clint Courtney	12.00	5.50
☐ 35 Bill Tuttle	12.00	5.50
☐ 36 Wayne Belardi	12.00	5.50
☐ 37 Pee Wee Reese	65.00	29.00
☐ 38 Early Wynn	30.00	13.50
☐ 39 Bob Darnell	15.00	6.75
☐ 40 Vic Wertz	15.00	6.75
☐ 41 Mel Clark	12.00	5.50
☐ 42 Bob Greenwood	12.00	5.50
☐ 43 Bob Buhl	15.00	6.75
☐ 44 Danny O'Connell	12.00	5.50
☐ 45 Tom Umphlett	12.00	5.50
☐ 46 Mickey Vernon	15.00	6.75
☐ 47 Sammy White	12.00	5.50
☐ 48A Milt Bolling ERR	30.00	13.50
(Name on back is Frank Bolling)		
☐ 48B Milt Bolling COR	15.00	6.75
☐ 49 Jim Greengrass	12.00	5.50
☐ 50 Hobie Landrith	12.00	5.50
☐ 51 Elvin Tappe	12.00	5.50
☐ 52 Hal Rice	12.00	5.50
☐ 53 Alex Kellner	12.00	5.50
☐ 54 Don Bollweg	12.00	5.50
☐ 55 Cal Abrams	15.00	6.75
☐ 56 Billy Cox	15.00	6.75
☐ 57 Bob Friend	15.00	6.75
☐ 58 Frank Thomas	15.00	6.75
☐ 59 Whitey Ford	75.00	34.00
☐ 60 Enos Slaughter	30.00	13.50
☐ 61 Paul LaPalme	12.00	5.50
☐ 62 Royce Lint	12.00	5.50
☐ 63 Irv Noren	15.00	6.75
☐ 64 Curt Simmons	15.00	6.75
☐ 65 Don Zimmer	25.00	11.00
☐ 66 George Shuba	20.00	9.00
☐ 67 Don Larsen	20.00	9.00
☐ 68 Elston Howard	75.00	34.00
☐ 69 Billy Hunter	12.00	5.50
☐ 70 Lou Burdette	15.00	6.75
☐ 71 Dave Jolly	12.00	5.50
☐ 72 Chet Nichols	12.00	5.50
☐ 73 Eddie Yost	15.00	6.75
☐ 74 Jerry Snyder	12.00	5.50
☐ 75 Brooks Lawrence	12.00	5.50
☐ 76 Tom Poholsky	12.00	5.50
☐ 77 Jim McDonald	12.00	5.50
☐ 78 Gil Coan	12.00	5.50
☐ 79 Willie Miranda	12.00	5.50
☐ 80 Lou Limmer	12.00	5.50
☐ 81 Bobby Morgan	12.00	5.50
☐ 82 Lee Walls	12.00	5.50
☐ 83 Max Surkont	12.00	5.50
☐ 84 George Freese	12.00	5.50
☐ 85 Cass Michaels	12.00	5.50
☐ 86 Ted Gray	12.00	5.50
☐ 87 Randy Jackson	12.00	5.50
☐ 88 Steve Bilko	12.00	5.50
☐ 89 Lou Boudreau MG	30.00	13.50
☐ 90 Art Ditmar	15.00	6.75
☐ 91 Dick Marlowe	12.00	5.50
☐ 92 George Zuverink	12.00	5.50
☐ 93 Andy Seminick	12.00	5.50
☐ 94 Hank Thompson	15.00	6.75
☐ 95 Sal Maglie	20.00	9.00
☐ 96 Ray Narleski	12.00	5.50
☐ 97 Johnny Podres	25.00	11.00
☐ 98 Jim Gilliam	25.00	11.00

☐ 99 Jerry Coleman	18.00	8.00
☐ 100 Tom Morgan	10.00	4.50
☐ 101A Don Johnson ERR	15.00	6.75
(Photo actually Ernie Johnson)		
☐ 101B Don Johnson COR	30.00	13.50
☐ 102 Bobby Thomson	15.00	6.75
☐ 103 Eddie Mathews	50.00	22.00
☐ 104 Bob Porterfield	10.00	4.50
☐ 105 Johnny Schmitz	10.00	4.50
☐ 106 Del Rice	10.00	4.50
☐ 107 Solly Hemus	10.00	4.50
☐ 108 Lou Kretlow	10.00	4.50
☐ 109 Vern Stephens	15.00	6.75
☐ 110 Bob Miller	10.00	4.50
☐ 111 Steve Ridzik	10.00	4.50
☐ 112 Granny Hamner	10.00	4.50
☐ 113 Bob Hall	10.00	4.50
☐ 114 Vic Janowicz	15.00	6.75
☐ 115 Roger Bowman	10.00	4.50
☐ 116 Sandy Consuegra	10.00	4.50
☐ 117 Johnny Groth	10.00	4.50
☐ 118 Bobby Adams	10.00	4.50
☐ 119 Joe Astroth	10.00	4.50
☐ 120 Ed Burtschy	10.00	4.50
☐ 121 Rufus Crawford	10.00	4.50
☐ 122 Al Corwin	10.00	4.50
☐ 123 Marv Grissom	10.00	4.50
☐ 124 Johnny Antonelli	15.00	6.75
☐ 125 Paul Giel	15.00	6.75
☐ 126 Billy Goodman	15.00	6.75
☐ 127 Hank Majeski	10.00	4.50
☐ 128 Mike Garcia	15.00	6.75
☐ 129 Hal Naragon	10.00	4.50
☐ 130 Richie Ashburn	45.00	20.00
☐ 131 Willard Marshall	10.00	4.50
☐ 132A Harvey Kueen ERR	20.00	9.00
(Sic, Kuenn)		
☐ 132B Harvey Kuenn COR	30.00	13.50
☐ 133 Charles King	10.00	4.50
☐ 134 Bob Feller	70.00	32.00
☐ 135 Lloyd Merriman	10.00	4.50
☐ 136 Rocky Bridges	10.00	4.50
☐ 137 Bob Talbot	10.00	4.50
☐ 138 Davey Williams	20.00	9.00
☐ 139 Shantz Brothers	15.00	6.75
Wilmer Shantz		
Bobby Shantz		
☐ 140 Bobby Shantz	20.00	9.00
☐ 141 Wes Westrum	20.00	9.00
☐ 142 Rudy Regalado	10.00	4.50
☐ 143 Don Newcombe	25.00	11.00
☐ 144 Art Houtteman	10.00	4.50
☐ 145 Bob Nieman	10.00	4.50
☐ 146 Don Liddle	10.00	4.50
☐ 147 Sam Mele	10.00	4.50
☐ 148 Bob Chakales	10.00	4.50
☐ 149 Cloyd Boyer	10.00	4.50
☐ 150 Billy Klaus	10.00	4.50
☐ 151 Jim Brideweser	10.00	4.50
☐ 152 Johnny Klippstein	10.00	4.50
☐ 153 Eddie Robinson	10.00	4.50
☐ 154 Frank Lary	15.00	6.75
☐ 155 Gerry Staley	10.00	4.50
☐ 156 Jim Hughes	10.00	4.50
☐ 157A Ernie Johnson ERR	20.00	9.00
(Photo actually Don Johnson)		
☐ 157B Ernie Johnson COR	30.00	13.50
☐ 158 Gil Hodges	45.00	20.00
☐ 159 Harry Byrd	10.00	4.50
☐ 160 Bill Skowron	25.00	11.00
☐ 161 Matt Batts	10.00	4.50
☐ 162 Charlie Maxwell	10.00	4.50
☐ 163 Sid Gordon	15.00	6.75
☐ 164 Toby Atwell	10.00	4.50
☐ 165 Maurice McDermott	10.00	4.50
☐ 166 Jim Busby	10.00	4.50
☐ 167 Bob Grim	25.00	11.00
☐ 168 Yogi Berra	90.00	40.00
☐ 169 Carl Furillo	25.00	11.00
☐ 170 Carl Erskine	25.00	11.00
☐ 171 Robin Roberts	35.00	16.00
☐ 172 Willie Jones	10.00	4.50
☐ 173 Chico Carrasquel	10.00	4.50
☐ 174 Sherm Lollar	15.00	6.75

175 Wilmer Shantz	10.00	4.50
176 Joe DeMaestri	10.00	4.50
177 Willard Nixon	10.00	4.50
178 Tom Brewer	10.00	4.50
179 Hank Aaron	200.00	90.00
180 Johnny Logan	15.00	6.75
181 Eddie Miksis	10.00	4.50
182 Bob Rush	10.00	4.50
183 Ray Katt	10.00	4.50
184 Willie Mays	225.00	100.00
185 Vic Raschi	10.00	4.50
186 Alex Grammas	10.00	4.50
187 Fred Hatfield	10.00	4.50
188 Ned Garver	10.00	4.50
189 Jack Collum	10.00	4.50
190 Fred Baczewski	10.00	4.50
191 Bob Lemon	30.00	13.50
192 George Strickland	10.00	4.50
193 Howie Judson	10.00	4.50
194 Joe Nuxhall	15.00	6.75
195A Erv Palica (Without trade)	15.00	6.75
195B Erv Palica (With trade)	30.00	13.50
196 Russ Meyer	15.00	6.75
197 Ralph Kiner	30.00	13.50
198 Dave Pope	10.00	4.50
199 Vern Law	15.00	6.75
200 Dick Littlefield	10.00	4.50
201 Allie Reynolds	18.00	8.00
202 Mickey Mantle UER	900.00	400.00
Birthdate listed as 10/30/31 Should be 10/20/31		
203 Steve Gromek	10.00	4.50
204A Frank Bolling ERR (Name on back is Milt Bolling)	20.00	9.00
204B Frank Bolling COR	20.00	9.00
205 Rip Repulski	10.00	4.50
206 Ralph Beard	10.00	4.50
207 Frank Shea	10.00	4.50
208 Ed Fitzgerald	10.00	4.50
209 Smoky Burgess	15.00	6.75
210 Earl Torgeson	10.00	4.50
211 Sonny Dixon	10.00	4.50
212 Jack Dittmer	10.00	4.50
213 George Kell	30.00	13.50
214 Billy Pierce	15.00	6.75
215 Bob Kuzava	10.00	4.50
216 Preacher Roe	15.00	6.75
217 Del Crandall	15.00	6.75
218 Joe Adcock	15.00	6.75
219 Whitey Lockman	10.00	4.50
220 Jim Hearn	10.00	4.50
221 Hector Brown	10.00	4.50
222 Russ Kemmerer	10.00	4.50
223 Hal Jeffcoat	10.00	4.50
224 Dee Fondy	10.00	4.50
225 Paul Richards MG	15.00	6.75
226 Bill McKinley UMP	30.00	13.50
227 Frank Baumholtz	15.00	6.75
228 John Phillips	15.00	6.75
229 Jim Brosnan	20.00	9.00
230 Al Brazle	15.00	6.75
231 Jim Konstanty	20.00	9.00
232 Birdie Tebbetts MG	22.00	10.00
233 Bill Serena	15.00	6.75
234 Dick Bartell CO	20.00	9.00
235 Joe Paparella UMP	30.00	13.50
236 Murry Dickson	15.00	6.75
237 Johnny Wyrostek	15.00	6.75
238 Eddie Stanky MG	20.00	9.00
239 Edwin Rommel UMP	40.00	18.00
240 Billy Loes	20.00	9.00
241 Johnny Pesky CO	20.00	9.00
242 Ernie Banks	350.00	160.00
243 Gus Bell	15.00	6.75
244 Duane Pillette	15.00	6.75
245 Bill Miller	15.00	6.75
246 Hank Bauer	25.00	11.00
247 Dutch Leonard CO	15.00	6.75
248 Harry Dorish	15.00	6.75
249 Billy Gardner	20.00	9.00
250 Larry Napp UMP	30.00	13.50
251 Stan Jok	15.00	6.75
252 Roy Smalley	15.00	6.75
253 Jim Wilson	15.00	6.75
254 Bennett Flowers	15.00	6.75
255 Pete Runnels	20.00	9.00
256 Owen Friend	15.00	6.75
257 Tom Alston	15.00	6.75
258 John Stevens UMP	30.00	13.50
259 Don Mossi	25.00	11.00
260 Edwin Hurley UMP	30.00	13.50
261 Walt Moryn	20.00	9.00
262 Jim Lemon	15.00	6.75
263 Eddie Joost	15.00	6.75
264 Bill Henry	15.00	6.75
265 Albert Barlick UMP	75.00	34.00
266 Mike Fornieles	15.00	6.75
267 Jim Honochick UMP	75.00	34.00
268 Roy Lee Hawes	15.00	6.75
269 Joe Amalfitano	22.00	10.00
270 Chico Fernandez	20.00	9.00
271 Bob Hooper	15.00	6.75
272 John Flaherty UMP	30.00	13.50
273 Bubba Church	15.00	6.75
274 Jim Delsing	15.00	6.75
275 William Grieve UMP	30.00	13.50
276 Ike Delock	15.00	6.75
277 Ed Runge UMP	30.00	13.50
278 Charlie Neal	35.00	16.00
279 Hank Soar UMP	40.00	18.00
280 Clyde McCullough	15.00	6.75
281 Charles Berry UMP	40.00	18.00
282 Phil Cavarretta	22.00	10.00
283 Nestor Chylak UMP	30.00	13.50
284 Bill Jackowski UMP	30.00	13.50
285 Walt Dropo	20.00	9.00
286 Frank Secory UMP	30.00	13.50
287 Ron Mrozinski	15.00	6.75
288 Dick Smith	15.00	6.75
289 Arthur Gore UMP	30.00	13.50
290 Hershell Freeman	15.00	6.75
291 Frank Dascoli UMP	30.00	13.50
292 Marv Blaylock	15.00	6.75
293 Thomas Gorman UMP	40.00	18.00
294 Wally Moses CO	15.00	6.75
295 Lee Ballanfant UMP	30.00	13.50
296 Bill Virdon	35.00	16.00
297 Dusty Boggess UMP	30.00	13.50
298 Charlie Grimm MG	22.00	10.00
299 Lon Warneke UMP	30.00	13.50
300 Tommy Byrne	20.00	9.00
301 William Engeln UMP	30.00	13.50
302 Frank Malzone	30.00	13.50
303 Jocko Conlan UMP	75.00	34.00
304 Harry Chiti	15.00	6.75
305 Frank Umont UMP	30.00	13.50
306 Bob Cerv	22.00	10.00
307 Babe Pinelli UMP	40.00	18.00
308 Al Lopez MG	50.00	22.00
309 Hal Dixon UMP	30.00	13.50
310 Ken Lehman	15.00	6.75
311 Lawrence Goetz UMP	30.00	13.50
312 Bill Wight	15.00	6.75
313 Augie Donatelli UMP	50.00	22.00
314 Dale Mitchell	22.00	10.00
315 Cal Hubbard UMP	75.00	34.00
316 Marion Fricano	15.00	6.75
317 William Summers UMP	20.00	9.00
318 Sid Hudson	15.00	6.75
319 Al Schroll	15.00	6.75
320 George Susce Jr	45.00	20.00

ing to teams in the AL and NL. Cards 258-261 form a father/son subset. Rookie Cards in this set include Andy Benes, Ken Griffey Jr., Tino Martinez, Charles Nagy, Gary Sheffield, John Smoltz and Robin Ventura.

	MINT	NRMT
COMPLETE SET (484)	12.00	5.50
COMMON CARD (1-484)	.05	.02
MINOR STARS	.10	.05
UNLISTED STARS	.20	.09
COMPLETE REPRINT SET (11)	2.00	.90
REPRINTS: RANDOM INSERTS IN PACKS		

1 Oswald Peraza	.05	.02
2 Brian Holton	.05	.02
3 Jose Bautista	.05	.02
4 Pete Harnisch	.10	.05
5 Dave Schmidt	.05	.02
6 Gregg Olson	.10	.05
7 Jeff Ballard	.05	.02
8 Bob Melvin	.05	.02
9 Cal Ripken	.75	.35
10 Randy Milligan	.05	.02
11 Juan Bell	.05	.02
12 Billy Ripken	.05	.02
13 Jim Traber	.05	.02
14 Pete Stanicek	.05	.02
15 Steve Finley	.25	.11
16 Larry Sheets	.05	.02
17 Phil Bradley	.05	.02
18 Brady Anderson	.50	.23
19 Lee Smith	.10	.05
20 Tom Fischer	.05	.02
21 Mike Boddicker	.05	.02
22 Rob Murphy	.05	.02
23 Wes Gardner	.05	.02
24 John Dopson	.05	.02
25 Bob Stanley	.05	.02
26 Roger Clemens	.40	.18
27 Rich Gedman	.05	.02
28 Marty Barrett	.05	.02
29 Luis Rivera	.05	.02
30 Jody Reed	.05	.02
31 Nick Esasky	.05	.02
32 Wade Boggs	.20	.09
33 Jim Rice	.10	.05
34 Mike Greenwell	.05	.02
35 Dwight Evans	.10	.05
36 Ellis Burks	.10	.05
37 Chuck Finley	.10	.05
38 Kirk McCaskill	.05	.02
39 Jim Abbott	.20	.09
40 Bryan Harvey	.05	.02
41 Bert Blyleven	.10	.05
42 Mike Witt	.05	.02
43 Bob McClure	.05	.02
44 Bill Schroeder	.05	.02
45 Lance Parrish	.05	.02
46 Dick Schofield	.05	.02
47 Wally Joyner	.10	.05
48 Jack Howell	.05	.02
49 Johnny Ray	.05	.02
50 Chili Davis	.10	.05
51 Tony Armas	.05	.02
52 Claudell Washington	.05	.02

1989 Bowman

The 1989 Bowman set, produced by Topps, contains 484 slightly oversized cards (measuring 2 1/2" by 3 3/4"). The cards were produced in midseason 1989 in wax, rack, cello and factory set formats. The fronts have white-bordered color photos with facsimile autographs and small Bowman logos. The backs feature charts detailing 1988 player performances vs. each team. The cards are ordered alphabetically accord-

#	Player	Price	Price
☐ 53	Brian Downing	.05	.02
☐ 54	Devon White	.05	.02
☐ 55	Bobby Thigpen	.05	.02
☐ 56	Bill Long	.05	.02
☐ 57	Jerry Reuss	.05	.02
☐ 58	Shawn Hillegas	.05	.02
☐ 59	Melido Perez	.05	.02
☐ 60	Jeff Bittiger	.05	.02
☐ 61	Jack McDowell	.15	.05
☐ 62	Carlton Fisk	.20	.09
☐ 63	Steve Lyons	.05	.02
☐ 64	Ozzie Guillen	.05	.02
☐ 65	Robin Ventura	.40	.18
☐ 66	Fred Manrique	.05	.02
☐ 67	Dan Pasqua	.05	.02
☐ 68	Ivan Calderon	.05	.02
☐ 69	Ron Kittle	.05	.02
☐ 70	Daryl Boston	.05	.02
☐ 71	Dave Gallagher	.05	.02
☐ 72	Harold Baines	.10	.05
☐ 73	Charles Nagy	.25	.11
☐ 74	John Farrell	.05	.02
☐ 75	Kevin Wickander	.05	.02
☐ 76	Greg Swindell	.05	.02
☐ 77	Mike Walker	.05	.02
☐ 78	Doug Jones	.05	.02
☐ 79	Rich Yett	.05	.02
☐ 80	Tom Candiotti	.05	.02
☐ 81	Jesse Orosco	.05	.02
☐ 82	Bud Black	.05	.02
☐ 83	Andy Allanson	.05	.02
☐ 84	Pete O'Brien	.05	.02
☐ 85	Jerry Browne	.05	.02
☐ 86	Brook Jacoby	.05	.02
☐ 87	Mark Lewis	.20	.09
☐ 88	Luis Aguayo	.05	.02
☐ 89	Cory Snyder	.05	.02
☐ 90	Oddibe McDowell	.05	.02
☐ 91	Joe Carter	.20	.09
☐ 92	Frank Tanana	.05	.02
☐ 93	Jack Morris	.10	.05
☐ 94	Doyle Alexander	.05	.02
☐ 95	Steve Searcy	.05	.02
☐ 96	Randy Bockus	.05	.02
☐ 97	Jeff M. Robinson	.05	.02
☐ 98	Mike Henneman	.05	.02
☐ 99	Paul Gibson	.05	.02
☐ 100	Frank Williams	.05	.02
☐ 101	Matt Nokes	.05	.02
☐ 102	Rico Brogna UER (Misspelled Ricco on card back)	.20	.09
☐ 103	Lou Whitaker	.10	.05
☐ 104	Al Pedrique	.05	.02
☐ 105	Alan Trammell	.10	.05
☐ 106	Chris Brown	.05	.02
☐ 107	Pat Sheridan	.05	.02
☐ 108	Chet Lemon	.05	.02
☐ 109	Keith Moreland	.05	.02
☐ 110	Mel Stottlemyre Jr.	.05	.02
☐ 111	Bret Saberhagen	.05	.02
☐ 112	Floyd Bannister	.05	.02
☐ 113	Jeff Montgomery	.10	.05
☐ 114	Steve Farr	.05	.02
☐ 115	Tom Gordon UER (Front shows autograph of Don Gordon)	.20	.09
☐ 116	Charlie Leibrandt	.05	.02
☐ 117	Mark Gubicza	.05	.02
☐ 118	Mike Macfarlane	.10	.05
☐ 119	Bob Boone	.10	.05
☐ 120	Kurt Stillwell	.05	.02
☐ 121	George Brett	.40	.18
☐ 122	Frank White	.10	.05
☐ 123	Kevin Seitzer	.05	.02
☐ 124	Willie Wilson	.05	.02
☐ 125	Pat Tabler	.05	.02
☐ 126	Bo Jackson	.20	.09
☐ 127	Hugh Walker	.05	.02
☐ 128	Danny Tartabull	.05	.02
☐ 129	Teddy Higuera	.05	.02
☐ 130	Don August	.05	.02
☐ 131	Juan Nieves	.05	.02
☐ 132	Mike Birkbeck	.05	.02
☐ 133	Dan Plesac	.05	.02
☐ 134	Chris Bosio	.05	.02
☐ 135	Bill Wegman	.05	.02
☐ 136	Chuck Crim	.05	.02
☐ 137	B.J. Surhoff	.10	.05
☐ 138	Joey Meyer	.05	.02
☐ 139	Dale Sveum	.05	.02
☐ 140	Paul Molitor	.20	.09
☐ 141	Jim Gantner	.05	.02
☐ 142	Gary Sheffield	.75	.35
☐ 143	Greg Brock	.05	.02
☐ 144	Robin Yount	.20	.09
☐ 145	Glenn Braggs	.05	.02
☐ 146	Rob Deer	.05	.02
☐ 147	Fred Toliver	.05	.02
☐ 148	Jeff Reardon	.10	.05
☐ 149	Allan Anderson	.05	.02
☐ 150	Frank Viola	.05	.02
☐ 151	Shane Rawley	.05	.02
☐ 152	Juan Berenguer	.05	.02
☐ 153	Johnny Ard	.05	.02
☐ 154	Tim Laudner	.05	.02
☐ 155	Brian Harper	.05	.02
☐ 156	Al Newman	.05	.02
☐ 157	Kent Hrbek	.10	.05
☐ 158	Gary Gaetti	.05	.02
☐ 159	Wally Backman	.05	.02
☐ 160	Gene Larkin	.05	.02
☐ 161	Greg Gagne	.05	.02
☐ 162	Kirby Puckett	.40	.18
☐ 163	Dan Gladden	.05	.02
☐ 164	Randy Bush	.05	.02
☐ 165	Dave LaPoint	.05	.02
☐ 166	Andy Hawkins	.05	.02
☐ 167	Dave Righetti	.05	.02
☐ 168	Lance McCullers	.05	.02
☐ 169	Jimmy Jones	.05	.02
☐ 170	Al Leiter	.20	.09
☐ 171	John Candelaria	.05	.02
☐ 172	Don Slaught	.05	.02
☐ 173	Jamie Quirk	.05	.02
☐ 174	Rafael Santana	.05	.02
☐ 175	Mike Pagliarulo	.05	.02
☐ 176	Don Mattingly	.30	.14
☐ 177	Ken Phelps	.05	.02
☐ 178	Steve Sax	.05	.02
☐ 179	Dave Winfield	.20	.09
☐ 180	Stan Jefferson	.05	.02
☐ 181	Rickey Henderson	.20	.09
☐ 182	Bob Brower	.05	.02
☐ 183	Roberto Kelly	.10	.05
☐ 184	Curt Young	.05	.02
☐ 185	Gene Nelson	.05	.02
☐ 186	Bob Welch	.05	.02
☐ 187	Rick Honeycutt	.05	.02
☐ 188	Dave Stewart	.10	.05
☐ 189	Mike Moore	.05	.02
☐ 190	Dennis Eckersley	.10	.05
☐ 191	Eric Plunk	.05	.02
☐ 192	Storm Davis	.05	.02
☐ 193	Terry Steinbach	.10	.05
☐ 194	Ron Hassey	.05	.02
☐ 195	Stan Royer	.05	.02
☐ 196	Walt Weiss	.05	.02
☐ 197	Mark McGwire	.40	.18
☐ 198	Carney Lansford	.10	.05
☐ 199	Glenn Hubbard	.05	.02
☐ 200	Dave Henderson	.05	.02
☐ 201	Jose Canseco	.20	.09
☐ 202	Dave Parker	.10	.05
☐ 203	Scott Bankhead	.05	.02
☐ 204	Tom Niedenfuer	.05	.02
☐ 205	Mark Langston	.05	.02
☐ 206	Erik Hanson	.10	.05
☐ 207	Mike Jackson	.05	.02
☐ 208	Dave Valle	.05	.02
☐ 209	Scott Bradley	.05	.02
☐ 210	Harold Reynolds	.05	.02
☐ 211	Tino Martinez	1.00	.45
☐ 212	Rich Renteria	.05	.02
☐ 213	Rey Quinones	.05	.02
☐ 214	Jim Presley	.05	.02
☐ 215	Alvin Davis	.05	.02
☐ 216	Edgar Martinez	.20	.09
☐ 217	Darnell Coles	.05	.02
☐ 218	Jeffrey Leonard	.05	.02
☐ 219	Jay Buhner	.20	.09
☐ 220	Ken Griffey Jr.	6.00	2.70
☐ 221	Drew Hall	.05	.02
☐ 222	Bobby Witt	.05	.02
☐ 223	Jamie Moyer	.05	.02
☐ 224	Charlie Hough	.10	.05
☐ 225	Nolan Ryan	.75	.35
☐ 226	Jeff Russell	.05	.02
☐ 227	Jim Sundberg	.05	.02
☐ 228	Julio Franco	.05	.02
☐ 229	Buddy Bell	.10	.05
☐ 230	Scott Fletcher	.05	.02
☐ 231	Jeff Kunkel	.05	.02
☐ 232	Steve Buechele	.05	.02
☐ 233	Monty Fariss	.05	.02
☐ 234	Rick Leach	.05	.02
☐ 235	Ruben Sierra	.05	.02
☐ 236	Cecil Espy	.05	.02
☐ 237	Rafael Palmeiro	.20	.09
☐ 238	Pete Incaviglia	.10	.05
☐ 239	Dave Stieb	.05	.02
☐ 240	Jeff Musselman	.05	.02
☐ 241	Mike Flanagan	.05	.02
☐ 242	Todd Stottlemyre	.10	.05
☐ 243	Jimmy Key	.05	.02
☐ 244	Tony Castillo	.05	.02
☐ 245	Alex Sanchez	.05	.02
☐ 246	Tom Henke	.05	.02
☐ 247	John Cerutti	.05	.02
☐ 248	Ernie Whitt	.05	.02
☐ 249	Bob Brenly	.05	.02
☐ 250	Rance Mulliniks	.05	.02
☐ 251	Kelly Gruber	.05	.02
☐ 252	Ed Sprague	.25	.11
☐ 253	Fred McGriff	.20	.09
☐ 254	Tony Fernandez	.05	.02
☐ 255	Tom Lawless	.05	.02
☐ 256	George Bell	.05	.02
☐ 257	Jesse Barfield	.05	.02
☐ 258	Roberto Alomar	.20	.09
☐ 259	Sandy Alomar Jr. / Sandy Alomar	1.00	.45
☐ 260	Cal Ripken Jr. / Ken Griffey Jr.	.30	.14
☐ 261	Mel Stottlemyre Jr. / Cal Ripken Sr.	.05	.02
	Mel Stottlemyre Sr.		
☐ 262	Zane Smith	.05	.02
☐ 263	Charlie Puleo	.05	.02
☐ 264	Derek Lilliquist	.05	.02
☐ 265	Paul Assenmacher	.05	.02
☐ 266	John Smoltz	.50	.23
☐ 267	Tom Glavine	.20	.09
☐ 268	Steve Avery	.05	.05
☐ 269	Pete Smith	.05	.02
☐ 270	Jody Davis	.05	.02
☐ 271	Bruce Benedict	.05	.02
☐ 272	Andres Thomas	.05	.02
☐ 273	Gerald Perry	.05	.02
☐ 274	Ron Gant	.10	.05
☐ 275	Darrell Evans	.10	.05
☐ 276	Dale Murphy	.20	.09
☐ 277	Dion James	.05	.02
☐ 278	Lonnie Smith	.05	.02
☐ 279	Geronimo Berroa	.10	.05
☐ 280	Steve Wilson	.05	.02
☐ 281	Rick Sutcliffe	.05	.02
☐ 282	Kevin Coffman	.05	.02
☐ 283	Mitch Williams	.05	.02
☐ 284	Greg Maddux	.75	.35
☐ 285	Paul Kilgus	.05	.02
☐ 286	Mike Harkey	.05	.02
☐ 287	Lloyd McClendon	.05	.02
☐ 288	Damon Berryhill	.05	.02
☐ 289	Ty Griffin	.05	.02
☐ 290	Ryne Sandberg	.25	.11
☐ 291	Mark Grace	.20	.09
☐ 292	Curt Wilkerson	.05	.02
☐ 293	Vance Law	.05	.02
☐ 294	Shawon Dunston	.05	.02
☐ 295	Jerome Walton	.20	.09
☐ 296	Mitch Webster	.05	.02
☐ 297	Dwight Smith	.10	.05
☐ 298	Andre Dawson	.20	.09
☐ 299	Jeff Sellers	.05	.02
☐ 300	Jose Rijo	.05	.02
☐ 301	John Franco	.05	.02
☐ 302	Rick Mahler	.05	.02

303 Ron Robinson	.05	.02
304 Danny Jackson	.05	.02
305 Rob Dibble	.10	.02
306 Tom Browning	.05	.02
307 Bo Diaz	.05	.02
308 Manny Trillo	.05	.02
309 Chris Sabo	.05	.02
310 Ron Oester	.05	.02
311 Barry Larkin	.20	.09
312 Todd Benzinger	.05	.02
313 Paul O'Neill	.10	.05
314 Kal Daniels	.05	.02
315 Joel Youngblood	.05	.02
316 Eric Davis	.10	.05
317 Dave Smith	.05	.02
318 Mark Portugal	.05	.02
319 Brian Meyer	.05	.02
320 Jim Deshaies	.05	.02
321 Juan Agosto	.05	.02
322 Mike Scott	.05	.02
323 Rick Rhoden	.05	.02
324 Jim Clancy	.05	.02
325 Larry Andersen	.05	.02
326 Alex Trevino	.05	.02
327 Alan Ashby	.05	.02
328 Craig Reynolds	.05	.02
329 Bill Doran	.05	.02
330 Rafael Ramirez	.05	.02
331 Glenn Davis	.05	.02
332 Willie Ansley	.05	.02
333 Gerald Young	.05	.02
334 Cameron Drew	.05	.02
335 Jay Howell	.05	.02
336 Tim Belcher	.05	.02
337 Fernando Valenzuela	.10	.05
338 Ricky Horton	.05	.02
339 Tim Leary	.05	.02
340 Bill Bene	.05	.02
341 Orel Hershiser	.10	.05
342 Mike Scioscia	.05	.02
343 Rick Dempsey	.05	.02
344 Willie Randolph	.10	.05
345 Alfredo Griffin	.05	.02
346 Eddie Murray	.20	.09
347 Mickey Hatcher	.05	.02
348 Mike Sharperson	.05	.02
349 John Shelby	.05	.02
350 Mike Marshall	.05	.02
351 Kirk Gibson	.10	.05
352 Mike Davis	.05	.02
353 Bryn Smith	.05	.02
354 Pascual Perez	.05	.02
355 Kevin Gross	.05	.02
356 Andy McGaffigan	.05	.02
357 Brian Holman	.05	.02
358 Dave Wainhouse	.05	.02
359 Dennis Martinez	.10	.05
360 Tim Burke	.05	.02
361 Nelson Santovenia	.05	.02
362 Tim Wallach	.05	.02
363 Spike Owen	.05	.02
364 Rex Hudler	.05	.02
365 Andres Galarraga	.20	.09
366 Otis Nixon	.05	.02
367 Hubie Brooks	.05	.02
368 Mike Aldrete	.05	.02
369 Tim Raines	.10	.05
370 Dave Martinez	.05	.02
371 Bob Ojeda	.05	.02
372 Ron Darling	.05	.02
373 Wally Whitehurst	.05	.02
374 Randy Myers	.10	.05
375 David Cone	.20	.09
376 Dwight Gooden	.10	.05
377 Sid Fernandez	.05	.02
378 Dave Proctor	.05	.02
379 Gary Carter	.20	.09
380 Keith Miller	.05	.02
381 Gregg Jefferies	.10	.05
382 Tim Teufel	.05	.02
383 Kevin Elster	.05	.02
384 Dave Magadan	.05	.02
385 Keith Hernandez	.10	.05
386 Mookie Wilson	.05	.02
387 Darryl Strawberry	.10	.05
388 Kevin McReynolds	.05	.02
389 Mark Carreon	.05	.02
390 Jeff Parrett	.05	.02
391 Mike Maddux	.05	.02
392 Don Carman	.05	.02
393 Bruce Ruffin	.05	.02
394 Ken Howell	.05	.02
395 Steve Bedrosian	.05	.02
396 Floyd Youmans	.05	.02
397 Larry McWilliams	.05	.02
398 Pat Combs	.05	.02
399 Steve Lake	.05	.02
400 Dickie Thon	.05	.02
401 Ricky Jordan	.05	.02
402 Mike Schmidt	.25	.11
403 Tom Herr	.05	.02
404 Chris James	.05	.02
405 Juan Samuel	.05	.02
406 Von Hayes	.05	.02
407 Ron Jones	.05	.02
408 Curt Ford	.05	.02
409 Bob Walk	.05	.02
410 Jeff D. Robinson	.05	.02
411 Jim Gott	.05	.02
412 Scott Medvin	.05	.02
413 John Smiley	.05	.02
414 Bob Kipper	.05	.02
415 Brian Fisher	.05	.02
416 Doug Drabek	.05	.02
417 Mike LaValliere	.05	.02
418 Ken Oberkfell	.05	.02
419 Sid Bream	.05	.02
420 Austin Manahan	.05	.02
421 Jose Lind	.05	.02
422 Bobby Bonilla	.10	.05
423 Glenn Wilson	.05	.02
424 Andy Van Slyke	.10	.05
425 Gary Redus	.05	.02
426 Barry Bonds	.40	.18
427 Don Heinkel	.05	.02
428 Ken Dayley	.05	.02
429 Todd Worrell	.05	.02
430 Brad DuVall	.05	.02
431 Jose DeLeon	.05	.02
432 Joe Magrane	.05	.02
433 John Ericks	.05	.02
434 Frank DiPino	.05	.02
435 Tony Pena	.05	.02
436 Ozzie Smith	.25	.11
437 Terry Pendleton	.10	.05
438 Jose Oquendo	.05	.02
439 Tim Jones	.05	.02
440 Pedro Guerrero	.10	.05
441 Milt Thompson	.05	.02
442 Willie McGee	.10	.05
443 Vince Coleman	.05	.02
444 Tom Brunansky	.05	.02
445 Walt Terrell	.05	.02
446 Eric Show	.05	.02
447 Mark Davis	.05	.02
448 Andy Benes	.20	.09
449 Ed Whitson	.05	.02
450 Dennis Rasmussen	.05	.02
451 Bruce Hurst	.05	.02
452 Pat Clements	.05	.02
453 Benito Santiago	.05	.02
454 Sandy Alomar Jr	.50	.23
455 Garry Templeton	.05	.02
456 Jack Clark	.10	.05
457 Tim Flannery	.05	.02
458 Roberto Alomar	.30	.14
459 Carmelo Martinez	.05	.02
460 John Kruk	.10	.05
461 Tony Gwynn	.50	.23
462 Jerald Clark	.05	.02
463 Don Robinson	.05	.02
464 Craig Lefferts	.05	.02
465 Kelly Downs	.05	.02
466 Rick Reuschel	.05	.02
467 Scott Garrelts	.05	.02
468 Wil Tejada	.05	.02
469 Kirt Manwaring	.05	.02
470 Terry Kennedy	.05	.02
471 Jose Uribe	.05	.02
472 Royce Clayton	.20	.09
473 Robby Thompson	.05	.02
474 Kevin Mitchell	.10	.05
475 Ernie Riles	.05	.02
476 Will Clark	.20	.09
477 Donell Nixon	.05	.02
478 Candy Maldonado	.05	.02
479 Tracy Jones	.05	.02
480 Brett Butler	.10	.05
481 Checklist 1-121	.05	.02
482 Checklist 122-242	.05	.02
483 Checklist 243-363	.05	.02
484 Checklist 364-484	.05	.02

1990 Bowman

The 1990 Bowman set (produced by Topps) consists of 528 standard-size cards. The cards were issued in wax packs and factory sets. Each wax pack contained one of 11 different 1950's retro art cards. Unlike most sets, player selection focused primarily on rookies instead of proven major leaguers. The cards feature a white border with the player's photo inside and the Bowman logo on top. The card numbering is in team order with the teams themselves being ordered alphabetically within each league. Notable Rookie Cards include Moises Alou, Carlos Baerga, Travis Fryman, Juan Gonzalez, Marquis Grissom, Chuck Knoblauch, Ray Lankford, Ben McDonald, Sammy Sosa, Frank Thomas, Mo Vaughn, Larry Walker, and Bernie Williams.

	MINT	NRMT
COMPLETE SET (528)	10.00	4.50
COMMON CARD (1-528)	.05	.02
MINOR STARS	.10	.05
UNLISTED STARS	.20	.09
COMP.ART SET (11)	2.00	.90
ART CARDS: RANDOM INSERTS IN PACKS		

1 Tommy Greene	.05	.02
2 Tom Glavine	.20	.09
3 Andy Nezelek	.05	.02
4 Mike Stanton	.05	.02
5 Rick Luecken	.05	.02
6 Kent Mercker	.10	.05
7 Derek Lilliquist	.05	.02
8 Charlie Leibrandt	.05	.02
9 Steve Avery	.20	.09
10 John Smoltz	.20	.09
11 Mark Lemke	.05	.02
12 Lonnie Smith	.05	.02
13 Oddibe McDowell	.05	.02
14 Tyler Houston	.20	.09
15 Jeff Blauser	.10	.05
16 Ernie Whitt	.05	.02
17 Alexis Infante	.05	.02
18 Jim Presley	.05	.02
19 Dale Murphy	.20	.09

20	Nick Esasky	.05	.02
21	Rick Sutcliffe	.05	.02
22	Mike Bielecki	.05	.02
23	Steve Wilson	.05	.02
24	Kevin Blankenship	.05	.02
25	Mitch Williams	.05	.02
26	Dean Wilkins	.05	.02
27	Greg Maddux	.60	.25
28	Mike Harkey	.05	.02
29	Mark Grace	.20	.09
30	Ryne Sandberg	.25	.11
31	Greg Smith	.05	.02
32	Dwight Smith	.05	.02
33	Damon Berryhill	.05	.02
34	Earl Cunningham UER (Errant * by the word "in")	.05	.02
35	Jerome Walton	.05	.02
36	Lloyd McClendon	.05	.02
37	Ty Griffin	.05	.02
38	Shawon Dunston	.05	.02
39	Andre Dawson	.20	.09
40	Luis Salazar	.05	.02
41	Tim Layana	.05	.02
42	Rob Dibble	.05	.02
43	Tom Browning	.05	.02
44	Danny Jackson	.05	.02
45	Jose Rijo	.05	.02
46	Scott Scudder	.05	.02
47	Randy Myers UER (Career ERA .274, should be 2.74)	.10	.05
48	Brian Lane	.05	.02
49	Paul O'Neill	.10	.05
50	Barry Larkin	.20	.09
51	Reggie Jefferson	.20	.09
52	Jeff Branson	.05	.02
53	Chris Sabo	.05	.02
54	Joe Oliver	.05	.02
55	Todd Benzinger	.05	.02
56	Rolando Roomes	.05	.02
57	Hal Morris	.05	.02
58	Eric Davis	.10	.05
59	Scott Bryant	.05	.02
60	Ken Griffey Sr.	.05	.02
61	Darryl Kile	.40	.18
62	Dave Smith	.05	.02
63	Mark Portugal	.05	.02
64	Jeff Juden	.05	.02
65	Bill Gullickson	.05	.02
66	Danny Darwin	.05	.02
67	Larry Andersen	.05	.02
68	Jose Cano	.05	.02
69	Dan Schatzeder	.05	.02
70	Jim Deshaies	.05	.02
71	Mike Scott	.05	.02
72	Gerald Young	.05	.02
73	Ken Caminiti	.20	.09
74	Ken Oberkfell	.05	.02
75	Dave Rohde	.05	.02
76	Bill Doran	.05	.02
77	Andujar Cedeno	.05	.02
78	Craig Biggio	.20	.09
79	Karl Rhodes	.05	.02
80	Glenn Davis	.05	.02
81	Eric Anthony	.10	.05
82	John Wetteland	.20	.09
83	Jay Howell	.05	.02
84	Orel Hershiser	.10	.05
85	Tim Belcher	.05	.02
86	Kiki Jones	.05	.02
87	Mike Hartley	.05	.02
88	Ramon Martinez	.15	.07
89	Mike Scioscia	.05	.02
90	Willie Randolph	.10	.05
91	Juan Samuel	.05	.02
92	Jose Offerman	.20	.09
93	Dave Hansen	.05	.02
94	Jeff Hamilton	.05	.02
95	Alfredo Griffin	.05	.02
96	Tom Goodwin	.20	.09
97	Kirk Gibson	.10	.05
98	Jose Vizcaino	.05	.02
99	Kal Daniels	.05	.02
100	Hubie Brooks	.05	.02
101	Eddie Murray	.20	.09
102	Dennis Boyd	.05	.02
103	Tim Burke	.05	.02
104	Bill Sampen	.05	.02
105	Brett Gideon	.05	.02
106	Mark Gardner	.05	.02
107	Howard Farmer	.05	.02
108	Mel Rojas	.20	.09
109	Kevin Gross	.05	.02
110	Dave Schmidt	.05	.02
111	Denny Martinez	.10	.05
112	Jerry Goff	.05	.02
113	Andres Galarraga	.20	.09
114	Tim Wallach	.05	.02
115	Marquis Grissom	.40	.18
116	Spike Owen	.05	.02
117	Larry Walker	1.00	.45
118	Tim Raines	.10	.05
119	Delino DeShields	.20	.09
120	Tom Foley	.05	.02
121	Dave Martinez	.05	.02
122	Frank Viola UER (Career ERA .384 should be 3.84)	.05	.02
123	Julio Valera	.05	.02
124	Alejandro Pena	.05	.02
125	David Cone	.20	.09
126	Dwight Gooden	.10	.05
127	Kevin D. Brown	.05	.02
128	John Franco	.10	.05
129	Terry Bross	.05	.02
130	Blaine Beatty	.05	.02
131	Sid Fernandez	.05	.02
132	Mike Marshall	.05	.02
133	Howard Johnson	.05	.02
134	Jaime Roseboro	.05	.02
135	Alan Zinter	.05	.02
136	Keith Miller	.05	.02
137	Kevin Elster	.05	.02
138	Kevin McReynolds	.05	.02
139	Barry Lyons	.05	.02
140	Gregg Jefferies	.10	.05
141	Darryl Strawberry	.40	.18
142	Todd Hundley	.05	.02
143	Scott Service	.05	.02
144	Chuck Malone	.05	.02
145	Steve Ontiveros	.05	.02
146	Roger McDowell	.05	.02
147	Ken Howell	.05	.02
148	Pat Combs	.05	.02
149	Jeff Parrett	.05	.02
150	Chuck McElroy	.05	.02
151	Jason Grimsley	.05	.02
152	Len Dykstra	.10	.05
153	Mickey Morandini	.20	.09
154	John Kruk	.05	.02
155	Dickie Thon	.05	.02
156	Ricky Jordan	.05	.02
157	Jeff Jackson	.05	.02
158	Darren Daulton	.10	.05
159	Tom Herr	.05	.02
160	Von Hayes	.05	.02
161	Dave Hollins	.20	.09
162	Carmelo Martinez	.05	.02
163	Bob Walk	.05	.02
164	Doug Drabek	.05	.02
165	Walt Terrell	.05	.02
166	Bill Landrum	.05	.02
167	Scott Ruskin	.05	.02
168	Bob Patterson	.05	.02
169	Bobby Bonilla	.10	.05
170	Jose Lind	.05	.02
171	Andy Van Slyke	.10	.05
172	Mike LaValliere	.05	.02
173	Willie Greene	.15	.07
174	Jay Bell	.05	.02
175	Sid Bream	.05	.02
176	Tom Prince	.05	.02
177	Wally Backman	.05	.02
178	Moises Alou	.50	.23
179	Steve Carter	.05	.02
180	Gary Redus	.05	.02
181	Barry Bonds	.25	.11
182	Don Slaught UER (Card back shows headings for a pitcher)	.05	.02
183	Joe Magrane	.05	.02
184	Bryn Smith	.05	.02
185	Todd Worrell	.05	.02
186	Jose DeLeon	.05	.02
187	Frank DiPino	.05	.02
188	John Tudor	.05	.02
189	Howard Hilton	.05	.02
190	John Ericks	.05	.02
191	Ken Dayley	.05	.02
192	Ray Lankford	.50	.23
193	Todd Zeile	.10	.05
194	Willie McGee	.10	.05
195	Ozzie Smith	.25	.11
196	Milt Thompson	.05	.02
197	Terry Pendleton	.10	.05
198	Vince Coleman	.05	.02
199	Paul Coleman	.05	.02
200	Jose Oquendo	.05	.02
201	Pedro Guerrero	.05	.02
202	Tom Brunansky	.05	.02
203	Roger Smithberg	.05	.02
204	Eddie Whitson	.05	.02
205	Dennis Rasmussen	.05	.02
206	Craig Lefferts	.05	.02
207	Andy Benes	.20	.09
208	Bruce Hurst	.05	.02
209	Eric Show	.05	.02
210	Rafael Valdez	.05	.02
211	Joey Cora	.20	.09
212	Thomas Howard	.05	.02
213	Rob Nelson	.05	.02
214	Jack Clark	.10	.05
215	Garry Templeton	.05	.02
216	Fred Lynn	.05	.02
217	Tony Gwynn	.50	.23
218	Benito Santiago	.05	.02
219	Mike Pagliarulo	.05	.02
220	Joe Carter	.10	.05
221	Roberto Alomar	.25	.11
222	Bip Roberts	.05	.02
223	Rick Reuschel	.05	.02
224	Russ Swan	.05	.02
225	Eric Gunderson	.05	.02
226	Steve Bedrosian	.05	.02
227	Mike Remlinger	.05	.02
228	Scott Garrelts	.05	.02
229	Ernie Camacho	.05	.02
230	Andres Santana	.05	.02
231	Will Clark	.05	.02
232	Kevin Mitchell	.10	.05
233	Robby Thompson	.05	.02
234	Bill Bathe	.05	.02
235	Tony Perezchica	.05	.02
236	Gary Carter	.20	.09
237	Brett Butler	.10	.05
238	Matt Williams	.10	.05
239	Earnie Riles	.05	.02
240	Kevin Bass	.05	.02
241	Terry Kennedy	.05	.02
242	Steve Hosey	.05	.02
243	Ben McDonald	.15	.07
244	Jeff Ballard	.05	.02
245	Joe Price	.05	.02
246	Curt Schilling	.20	.09
247	Pete Harnisch	.05	.02
248	Mark Williamson	.05	.02
249	Gregg Olson	.05	.02
250	Chris Myers	.05	.02
251A	David Segui ERR (Missing vital stats at top of card back under name)	.20	.09
251B	David Segui COR	.20	.09
252	Joe Orsulak	.05	.02
253	Craig Worthington	.05	.02
254	Mickey Tettleton	.10	.05
255	Cal Ripken	.75	.35
256	Billy Ripken	.05	.02
257	Randy Milligan	.05	.02
258	Brady Anderson	.20	.09
259	Chris Hoiles UER (Baltimore is spelled Baltimore)	.20	.09
260	Mike Devereaux	.05	.02
261	Phil Bradley	.05	.02
262	Leo Gomez	.05	.02
263	Lee Smith	.10	.05
264	Mike Rochford	.05	.02

☐ 265	Jeff Reardon	.10	.05
☐ 266	Wes Gardner	.05	.02
☐ 267	Mike Boddicker	.05	.02
☐ 268	Roger Clemens	.40	.18
☐ 269	Rob Murphy	.05	.02
☐ 270	Mickey Pina	.05	.02
☐ 271	Tony Pena	.05	.02
☐ 272	Jody Reed	.05	.02
☐ 273	Kevin Romine	.05	.02
☐ 274	Mike Greenwell	.05	.02
☐ 275	Maurice Vaughn	1.25	.55
☐ 276	Danny Heep	.05	.02
☐ 277	Scott Cooper	.05	.02
☐ 278	Greg Blosser	.05	.02
☐ 279	Dwight Evans UER	.10	.05
	(* by "1990 Team Breakdown")		
☐ 280	Ellis Burks	.15	.07
☐ 281	Wade Boggs	.20	.09
☐ 282	Marty Barrett	.05	.02
☐ 283	Kirk McCaskill	.05	.02
☐ 284	Mark Langston	.05	.02
☐ 285	Bert Blyleven	.10	.05
☐ 286	Mike Fetters	.05	.02
☐ 287	Kyle Abbott	.05	.02
☐ 288	Jim Abbott	.10	.05
☐ 289	Chuck Finley	.10	.05
☐ 290	Gary DiSarcina	.05	.02
☐ 291	Dick Schofield	.05	.02
☐ 292	Devon White	.05	.02
☐ 293	Bobby Rose	.05	.02
☐ 294	Brian Downing	.05	.02
☐ 295	Lance Parrish	.05	.02
☐ 296	Jack Howell	.05	.02
☐ 297	Claudell Washington	.05	.02
☐ 298	John Orton	.05	.02
☐ 299	Wally Joyner	.10	.05
☐ 300	Lee Stevens	.05	.02
☐ 301	Chili Davis	.10	.05
☐ 302	Johnny Ray	.05	.02
☐ 303	Greg Hibbard	.05	.02
☐ 304	Eric King	.05	.02
☐ 305	Jack McDowell	.05	.02
☐ 306	Bobby Thigpen	.05	.02
☐ 307	Adam Peterson	.05	.02
☐ 308	Scott Radinsky	.05	.02
☐ 309	Wayne Edwards	.05	.02
☐ 310	Melido Perez	.05	.02
☐ 311	Robin Ventura	.20	.09
☐ 312	Sammy Sosa	.75	.35
☐ 313	Dan Pasqua	.05	.02
☐ 314	Carlton Fisk	.20	.09
☐ 315	Ozzie Guillen	.05	.02
☐ 316	Ivan Calderon	.05	.02
☐ 317	Daryl Boston	.05	.02
☐ 318	Craig Grebeck	.05	.02
☐ 319	Scott Fletcher	.05	.02
☐ 320	Frank Thomas	4.00	1.80
☐ 321	Steve Lyons	.05	.02
☐ 322	Carlos Martinez	.05	.02
☐ 323	Joe Skalski	.05	.02
☐ 324	Tom Candiotti	.05	.02
☐ 325	Greg Swindell	.05	.02
☐ 326	Steve Olin	.10	.05
☐ 327	Kevin Wickander	.05	.02
☐ 328	Doug Jones	.05	.02
☐ 329	Jeff Shaw	.05	.02
☐ 330	Kevin Bearse	.05	.02
☐ 331	Dion James	.05	.02
☐ 332	Jerry Browne	.05	.02
☐ 333	Joey Belle	.50	.23
☐ 334	Felix Fermin	.05	.02
☐ 335	Candy Maldonado	.05	.02
☐ 336	Cory Snyder	.05	.02
☐ 337	Sandy Alomar Jr.	.20	.09
☐ 338	Mark Lewis	.05	.02
☐ 339	Carlos Baerga	.25	.11
☐ 340	Chris James	.05	.02
☐ 341	Brook Jacoby	.05	.02
☐ 342	Keith Hernandez	.10	.05
☐ 343	Frank Tanana	.05	.02
☐ 344	Scott Aldred	.05	.02
☐ 345	Mike Henneman	.05	.02
☐ 346	Steve Wapnick	.05	.02
☐ 347	Greg Gohr	.05	.02
☐ 348	Eric Stone	.05	.02
☐ 349	Brian DuBois	.05	.02
☐ 350	Kevin Ritz	.05	.02
☐ 351	Rico Brogna	.20	.09
☐ 352	Mike Heath	.05	.02
☐ 353	Alan Trammell	.15	.07
☐ 354	Chet Lemon	.05	.02
☐ 355	Dave Bergman	.05	.02
☐ 356	Lou Whitaker	.10	.05
☐ 357	Cecil Fielder UER	.10	.05
	(* by "1990 Team Breakdown")		
☐ 358	Milt Cuyler	.05	.02
☐ 359	Tony Phillips	.05	.02
☐ 360	Travis Fryman	.40	.18
☐ 361	Ed Romero	.05	.02
☐ 362	Lloyd Moseby	.05	.02
☐ 363	Mark Gubicza	.05	.02
☐ 364	Bret Saberhagen	.05	.02
☐ 365	Tom Gordon	.05	.02
☐ 366	Steve Farr	.05	.02
☐ 367	Kevin Appier	.20	.09
☐ 368	Storm Davis	.05	.02
☐ 369	Mark Davis	.05	.02
☐ 370	Jeff Montgomery	.10	.05
☐ 371	Frank White	.10	.05
☐ 372	Brent Mayne	.05	.02
☐ 373	Bob Boone	.10	.05
☐ 374	Jim Eisenreich	.05	.02
☐ 375	Danny Tartabull	.05	.02
☐ 376	Kurt Stillwell	.05	.02
☐ 377	Bill Pecota	.05	.02
☐ 378	Bo Jackson	.20	.09
☐ 379	Bob Hamelin	.20	.09
☐ 380	Kevin Seitzer	.05	.02
☐ 381	Rey Palacios	.05	.02
☐ 382	George Brett	.40	.18
☐ 383	Gerald Perry	.05	.02
☐ 384	Teddy Higuera	.05	.02
☐ 385	Tom Filer	.05	.02
☐ 386	Dan Plesac	.05	.02
☐ 387	Cal Eldred	.20	.09
☐ 388	Jaime Navarro	.05	.02
☐ 389	Chris Bosio	.05	.02
☐ 390	Randy Veres	.05	.02
☐ 391	Gary Sheffield	.25	.11
☐ 392	George Canale	.05	.02
☐ 393	B.J. Surhoff	.10	.05
☐ 394	Tim McIntosh	.05	.02
☐ 395	Greg Brock	.05	.02
☐ 396	Greg Vaughn	.10	.05
☐ 397	Darryl Hamilton	.05	.02
☐ 398	Dave Parker	.10	.05
☐ 399	Paul Molitor	.20	.09
☐ 400	Jim Gantner	.05	.02
☐ 401	Rob Deer	.05	.02
☐ 402	Billy Spiers	.05	.02
☐ 403	Glenn Braggs	.05	.02
☐ 404	Robin Yount	.20	.09
☐ 405	Rick Aguilera	.10	.05
☐ 406	Johnny Ard	.05	.02
☐ 407	Kevin Tapani	.10	.05
☐ 408	Park Pittman	.05	.02
☐ 409	Allan Anderson	.05	.02
☐ 410	Juan Berenguer	.05	.02
☐ 411	Willie Banks	.05	.02
☐ 412	Rich Yett	.05	.02
☐ 413	Dave West	.05	.02
☐ 414	Greg Gagne	.05	.02
☐ 415	Chuck Knoblauch	.75	.35
☐ 416	Randy Bush	.05	.02
☐ 417	Gary Gaetti	.05	.02
☐ 418	Kent Hrbek	.10	.05
☐ 419	Al Newman	.05	.02
☐ 420	Danny Gladden	.05	.02
☐ 421	Paul Sorrento	.20	.09
☐ 422	Derek Parks	.05	.02
☐ 423	Scott Leius	.05	.02
☐ 424	Kirby Puckett	.40	.18
☐ 425	Willie Smith	.05	.02
☐ 426	Dave Righetti	.05	.02
☐ 427	Jeff D. Robinson	.05	.02
☐ 428	Alan Mills	.05	.02
☐ 429	Tim Leary	.05	.02
☐ 430	Pascual Perez	.05	.02
☐ 431	Alvaro Espinoza	.05	.02
☐ 432	Dave Winfield	.20	.09
☐ 433	Jesse Barfield	.05	.02
☐ 434	Randy Velarde	.05	.02
☐ 435	Rick Cerone	.05	.02
☐ 436	Steve Balboni	.05	.02
☐ 437	Mel Hall	.05	.02
☐ 438	Bob Geren	.05	.02
☐ 439	Bernie Williams	.75	.35
☐ 440	Kevin Maas	.10	.05
☐ 441	Mike Blowers	.20	.09
☐ 442	Steve Sax	.05	.02
☐ 443	Don Mattingly	.30	.14
☐ 444	Roberto Kelly	.05	.02
☐ 445	Mike Moore	.05	.02
☐ 446	Reggie Harris	.05	.02
☐ 447	Scott Sanderson	.05	.02
☐ 448	Dave Otto	.05	.02
☐ 449	Dave Stewart	.10	.05
☐ 450	Rick Honeycutt	.05	.02
☐ 451	Dennis Eckersley	.10	.05
☐ 452	Carney Lansford	.05	.02
☐ 453	Scott Hemond	.05	.02
☐ 454	Mark McGwire	.40	.18
☐ 455	Felix Jose	.05	.02
☐ 456	Terry Steinbach	.10	.05
☐ 457	Rickey Henderson	.20	.09
☐ 458	Dave Henderson	.05	.02
☐ 459	Mike Gallego	.05	.02
☐ 460	Jose Canseco	.20	.09
☐ 461	Walt Weiss	.05	.02
☐ 462	Ken Phelps	.05	.02
☐ 463	Darren Lewis	.05	.02
☐ 464	Ron Hassey	.05	.02
☐ 465	Roger Salkeld	.05	.02
☐ 466	Scott Bankhead	.05	.02
☐ 467	Keith Comstock	.05	.02
☐ 468	Randy Johnson	.30	.14
☐ 469	Erik Hanson	.05	.02
☐ 470	Mike Schooler	.05	.02
☐ 471	Gary Eave	.05	.02
☐ 472	Jeffrey Leonard	.05	.02
☐ 473	Dave Valle	.05	.02
☐ 474	Omar Vizquel	.20	.09
☐ 475	Pete O'Brien	.05	.02
☐ 476	Henry Cotto	.05	.02
☐ 477	Jay Buhner	.20	.09
☐ 478	Harold Reynolds	.05	.02
☐ 479	Alvin Davis	.05	.02
☐ 480	Darnell Coles	.05	.02
☐ 481	Ken Griffey Jr.	1.50	.70
☐ 482	Greg Briley	.05	.02
☐ 483	Scott Bradley	.05	.02
☐ 484	Tino Martinez	.20	.09
☐ 485	Jeff Russell	.05	.02
☐ 486	Nolan Ryan	.75	.35
☐ 487	Robb Nen	.20	.09
☐ 488	Kevin Brown	.20	.09
☐ 489	Brian Bohanon	.05	.02
☐ 490	Ruben Sierra	.20	.09
☐ 491	Pete Incaviglia	.05	.02
☐ 492	Juan Gonzalez	2.00	.90
☐ 493	Steve Buechele	.05	.02
☐ 494	Scott Coolbaugh	.05	.02
☐ 495	Geno Petralli	.05	.02
☐ 496	Rafael Palmeiro	.20	.09
☐ 497	Julio Franco	.05	.02
☐ 498	Gary Pettis	.05	.02
☐ 499	Donald Harris	.05	.02
☐ 500	Monty Fariss	.05	.02
☐ 501	Harold Baines	.10	.05
☐ 502	Cecil Espy	.05	.02
☐ 503	Jack Daugherty	.05	.02
☐ 504	Willie Blair	.05	.02
☐ 505	Dave Stieb	.05	.02
☐ 506	Tom Henke	.05	.02
☐ 507	John Cerutti	.05	.02
☐ 508	Paul Kilgus	.05	.02
☐ 509	Jimmy Key	.10	.05
☐ 510	John Olerud	.30	.14
☐ 511	Ed Sprague	.10	.05
☐ 512	Manuel Lee	.05	.02
☐ 513	Fred McGriff	.20	.09
☐ 514	Glenallen Hill	.05	.02
☐ 515	George Bell	.05	.02
☐ 516	Mookie Wilson	.05	.02
☐ 517	Luis Sojo	.05	.02
☐ 518	Nelson Liriano	.05	.02

□ 519 Kelly Gruber .... .05 .02
□ 520 Greg Myers .... .05 .02
□ 521 Pat Borders .... .05 .02
□ 522 Junior Felix .... .05 .02
□ 523 Eddie Zosky .... .05 .02
□ 524 Tony Fernandez .... .05 .02
□ 525 Checklist 1-132 UER .. .05 .02
   (No copyright mark
   on the back)
□ 526 Checklist 133-264 ..... .05 .02
□ 527 Checklist 265-396 ..... .05 .02
□ 528 Checklist 397-528 ..... .05 .02

1991 Bowman

This single-series 704-card standard-size set marked the third straight year that Topps issued a set weighted towards prospects using the Bowman name. Cards were issued in wax packs and factory sets. The cards share a design very similar to the 1990 Bowman set with white borders enframing a color photo. The player name, however, is more prominent than in the previous year set. The cards are arranged in team order by division as follows: AL East, AL West, NL East, and NL West. Subsets include Rod Carew Tribute (1-5), Minor League MVP's (180-185/693-698), AL Silver Sluggers (367-375), NL Silver Sluggers (376-384) and checklists (699-704). Rookie Cards in this set include Jeff Bagwell, Jeff Conine, Carlos Garcia, Pat Hentgen, Chipper Jones, Eric Karros, Ryan Klesko, Kenny Lofton, Javier Lopez, Brian McRae, Raul Mondesi, Mike Mussina, Ivan "Pudge" Rodriguez, Tim Salmon, Reggie Sanders, Jim Thome, Rondell White and Mark Wohlers. There are two instances of misnumbering in the set; Ken Griffey (should be 255) and Ken Griffey Jr. are both numbered 246 and Donovan Osborne (should be 406) and Thomson/Branca share number 410.

	MINT	NRMT
COMPLETE SET (704)	30.00	13.50
COMMON CARD (1-704)	.05	.02
MINOR STARS	.10	.05
UNLISTED STARS	.20	.09

□ 1 Rod Carew I .... .20 .09
□ 2 Rod Carew II .... .20 .09
□ 3 Rod Carew III .... .20 .09
□ 4 Rod Carew IV .... .20 .09
□ 5 Rod Carew V .... .20 .09

□ 6 Willie Fraser .... .05 .02
□ 7 John Olerud .... .10 .05
□ 8 William Suero .... .05 .02
□ 9 Roberto Alomar .... .20 .09
□ 10 Todd Stottlemyre .... .05 .02
□ 11 Joe Carter .... .05 .02
□ 12 Steve Karsay .... .10 .05
□ 13 Mark Whiten .... .05 .02
□ 14 Pat Borders .... .05 .02
□ 15 Mike Timlin .... .05 .02
□ 16 Tom Henke .... .05 .02
□ 17 Eddie Zosky .... .05 .02
□ 18 Kelly Gruber .... .05 .02
□ 19 Jimmy Key .... .10 .05
□ 20 Jerry Schunk .... .05 .02
□ 21 Manuel Lee .... .05 .02
□ 22 Dave Stieb .... .05 .02
□ 23 Pat Hentgen .... .50 .23
□ 24 Glenallen Hill .... .05 .02
□ 25 Rene Gonzales .... .05 .02
□ 26 Ed Sprague .... .05 .02
□ 27 Ken Dayley .... .05 .02
□ 28 Pat Tabler .... .05 .02
□ 29 Denis Boucher .... .05 .02
□ 30 Devon White .... .05 .02
□ 31 Dante Bichette .... .20 .09
□ 32 Paul Molitor .... .20 .09
□ 33 Greg Vaughn .... .05 .02
□ 34 Dan Plesac .... .05 .02
□ 35 Chris George .... .05 .02
□ 36 Tim McIntosh .... .05 .02
□ 37 Franklin Stubbs .... .05 .02
□ 38 Bo Dodson .... .05 .02
□ 39 Ron Robinson .... .05 .02
□ 40 Ed Nunez .... .05 .02
□ 41 Greg Brock .... .05 .02
□ 42 Jaime Navarro .... .05 .02
□ 43 Chris Bosio .... .05 .02
□ 44 B.J. Surhoff .... .10 .05
□ 45 Chris Johnson .... .05 .02
□ 46 Willie Randolph .... .10 .05
□ 47 Narciso Elvira .... .05 .02
□ 48 Jim Gantner .... .05 .02
□ 49 Kevin Brown .... .10 .05
□ 50 Julio Machado .... .05 .02
□ 51 Chuck Crim .... .05 .02
□ 52 Gary Sheffield .... .20 .09
□ 53 Angel Miranda .... .05 .02
□ 54 Teddy Higuera .... .05 .02
□ 55 Robin Yount .... .20 .09
□ 56 Cal Eldred .... .10 .05
□ 57 Sandy Alomar Jr. .... .15 .07
□ 58 Greg Swindell .... .05 .02
□ 59 Brook Jacoby .... .05 .02
□ 60 Efrain Valdez .... .05 .02
□ 61 Ever Magallanes .... .05 .02
□ 62 Tom Candiotti .... .05 .02
□ 63 Eric King .... .05 .02
□ 64 Alex Cole .... .05 .02
□ 65 Charles Nagy .... .20 .09
□ 66 Mitch Webster .... .05 .02
□ 67 Chris James .... .05 .02
□ 68 Jim Thome .... 1.50 .70
□ 69 Carlos Baerga .... .10 .05
□ 70 Mark Lewis .... .05 .02
□ 71 Jerry Browne .... .05 .02
□ 72 Jesse Orosco .... .05 .02
□ 73 Mike Huff .... .05 .02
□ 74 Jose Escobar .... .05 .02
□ 75 Jeff Manto .... .05 .02
□ 76 Turner Ward .... .05 .02
□ 77 Doug Jones .... .05 .02
□ 78 Bruce Egloff .... .05 .02
□ 79 Tim Costo .... .20 .09
□ 80 Beau Allred .... .05 .02
□ 81 Albert Belle .... .30 .14
□ 82 John Farrell .... .05 .02
□ 83 Glenn Davis .... .05 .02
□ 84 Joe Orsulak .... .05 .02
□ 85 Mark Williamson .... .05 .02
□ 86 Ben McDonald .... .05 .02
□ 87 Billy Ripken .... .05 .02
□ 88 Leo Gomez UER .... .05 .02
   Baltimore is spelled Balitmore
□ 89 Bob Melvin .... .05 .02
□ 90 Jeff M. Robinson .... .05 .02

□ 91 Jose Mesa .... .05 .02
□ 92 Gregg Olson .... .05 .02
□ 93 Mike Devereaux .... .05 .02
□ 94 Luis Mercedes .... .05 .02
□ 95 Arthur Rhodes .... .10 .05
□ 96 Juan Bell .... .05 .02
□ 97 Mike Mussina .... 1.25 .55
□ 98 Jeff Ballard .... .05 .02
□ 99 Chris Hoiles .... .05 .02
□ 100 Brady Anderson .... .20 .09
□ 101 Bob Milacki .... .05 .02
□ 102 David Segui .... .05 .02
□ 103 Dwight Evans .... .10 .05
□ 104 Cal Ripken .... .75 .35
□ 105 Mike Linskey .... .05 .02
□ 106 Jeff Tackett .... .05 .02
□ 107 Jeff Reardon .... .10 .05
□ 108 Dana Kiecker .... .05 .02
□ 109 Ellis Burks .... .05 .02
□ 110 Dave Owen .... .05 .02
□ 111 Danny Darwin .... .05 .02
□ 112 Mo Vaughn .... .40 .18
□ 113 Jeff McNeely .... .05 .02
□ 114 Tom Bolton .... .05 .02
□ 115 Greg Blosser .... .05 .02
□ 116 Mike Greenwell .... .05 .02
□ 117 Phil Plantier .... .10 .05
□ 118 Roger Clemens .... .40 .18
□ 119 John Marzano .... .05 .02
□ 120 Jody Reed .... .05 .02
□ 121 Scott Taylor .... .05 .02
□ 122 Jack Clark .... .10 .05
□ 123 Derek Livernois .... .05 .02
□ 124 Tony Pena .... .05 .02
□ 125 Tom Brunansky .... .05 .02
□ 126 Carlos Quintana .... .05 .02
□ 127 Tim Naehring .... .10 .05
□ 128 Matt Young .... .05 .02
□ 129 Wade Boggs .... .20 .09
□ 130 Kevin Morton .... .05 .02
□ 131 Pete Incaviglia .... .05 .02
□ 132 Rob Deer .... .05 .02
□ 133 Bill Gullickson .... .05 .02
□ 134 Rico Brogna .... .15 .07
□ 135 Lloyd Moseby .... .05 .02
□ 136 Cecil Fielder .... .10 .05
□ 137 Tony Phillips .... .05 .02
□ 138 Mark Leiter .... .05 .02
□ 139 John Cerutti .... .05 .02
□ 140 Mickey Tettleton .... .05 .02
□ 141 Milt Cuyler .... .05 .02
□ 142 Greg Gohr .... .05 .02
□ 143 Tony Bernazard .... .05 .02
□ 144 Dan Gakeler .... .05 .02
□ 145 Travis Fryman .... .20 .09
□ 146 Dan Petry .... .05 .02
□ 147 Scott Aldred .... .05 .02
□ 148 John DeSilva .... .05 .02
□ 149 Rusty Meacham .... .05 .02
□ 150 Lou Whitaker .... .10 .05
□ 151 Dave Haas .... .05 .02
□ 152 Luis de los Santos ..... .05 .02
□ 153 Ivan Cruz .... .05 .02
□ 154 Alan Trammell .... .15 .07
□ 155 Pat Kelly .... .05 .02
□ 156 Carl Everett .... .15 .07
□ 157 Greg Cadaret .... .05 .02
□ 158 Kevin Maas .... .05 .02
□ 159 Jeff Johnson .... .05 .02
□ 160 Willie Smith .... .05 .02
□ 161 Gerald Williams .... .05 .02
□ 162 Mike Humphreys .... .05 .02
□ 163 Alvaro Espinoza .... .05 .02
□ 164 Matt Nokes .... .05 .02
□ 165 Wade Taylor .... .05 .02
□ 166 Roberto Kelly .... .20 .09
□ 167 John Habyan .... .05 .02
□ 168 Steve Farr .... .05 .02
□ 169 Jesse Barfield .... .05 .02
□ 170 Steve Sax .... .10 .05
□ 171 Jim Leyritz .... .10 .05
□ 172 Robert Eenhoorn .... .05 .02
□ 173 Bernie Williams .... .25 .11
□ 174 Scott Lusader .... .05 .02
□ 175 Torey Lovullo .... .05 .02
□ 176 Chuck Cary .... .05 .02

177	Scott Sanderson	.05	.02
178	Don Mattingly	.30	.14
179	Mel Hall	.05	.02
180	Juan Gonzalez	.75	.35
181	Hensley Meulens	.05	.02
182	Jose Offerman	.05	.02
183	Jeff Bagwell	2.50	1.10
184	Jeff Conine	.25	.11
185	Henry Rodriguez	.40	.18
186	Jimmie Reese CO	.10	.05
187	Kyle Abbott	.05	.02
188	Lance Parrish	.05	.02
189	Rafael Montalvo	.05	.02
190	Floyd Bannister	.05	.02
191	Dick Schofield	.05	.02
192	Scott Lewis	.05	.02
193	Jeff D. Robinson	.05	.02
194	Kent Anderson	.05	.02
195	Wally Joyner	.10	.05
196	Chuck Finley	.10	.05
197	Luis Sojo	.05	.02
198	Jeff Richardson	.05	.02
199	Dave Parker	.10	.05
200	Jim Abbott	.05	.02
201	Junior Felix	.05	.02
202	Mark Langston	.10	.05
203	Tim Salmon	1.25	.55
204	Cliff Young	.05	.02
205	Scott Bailes	.05	.02
206	Bobby Rose	.05	.02
207	Gary Gaetti	.05	.02
208	Ruben Amaro	.05	.02
209	Luis Polonia	.05	.02
210	Dave Winfield	.20	.09
211	Bryan Harvey	.05	.02
212	Mike Moore	.05	.02
213	Rickey Henderson	.20	.09
214	Steve Chitren	.05	.02
215	Bob Welch	.05	.02
216	Terry Steinbach	.10	.05
217	Earnest Riles	.05	.02
218	Todd Van Poppel	.05	.02
219	Mike Gallego	.05	.02
220	Curt Young	.05	.02
221	Todd Burns	.05	.02
222	Vance Law	.05	.02
223	Eric Show	.05	.02
224	Don Peters	.05	.02
225	Dave Stewart	.10	.05
226	Dave Henderson	.05	.02
227	Jose Canseco	.15	.07
228	Walt Weiss	.05	.02
229	Dann Howitt	.05	.02
230	Willie Wilson	.05	.02
231	Harold Baines	.10	.05
232	Scott Hemond	.05	.02
233	Joe Slusarski	.05	.02
234	Mark McGwire	.40	.18
235	Kirk Dressendorfer	.05	.02
236	Craig Paquette	.05	.02
237	Dennis Eckersley	.10	.05
238	Dana Allison	.05	.02
239	Scott Bradley	.05	.02
240	Brian Holman	.05	.02
241	Mike Schooler	.05	.02
242	Rich DeLucia	.05	.02
243	Edgar Martinez	.20	.09
244	Henry Cotto	.05	.02
245	Omar Vizquel	.20	.09
246	Ken Griffey Jr.	1.50	.70
	(See also 255)		
247	Jay Buhner	.20	.09
248	Bill Krueger	.05	.02
249	Dave Fleming	.05	.02
250	Patrick Lennon	.05	.02
251	Dave Valle	.05	.02
252	Harold Reynolds	.05	.02
253	Randy Johnson	.25	.11
254	Scott Bankhead	.05	.02
255	Ken Griffey Sr. UER	.05	.02
	(Card number is 246)		
256	Greg Briley	.05	.02
257	Tino Martinez	.20	.09
258	Alvin Davis	.05	.02
259	Pete O'Brien	.05	.02
260	Erik Hanson	.05	.02
261	Bret Boone	.10	.05
262	Roger Salkeld	.05	.02
263	Dave Burba	.05	.02
264	Kerry Woodson	.05	.02
265	Julio Franco	.05	.02
266	Dan Peltier	.05	.02
267	Jeff Russell	.05	.02
268	Steve Buechele	.05	.02
269	Donald Harris	.05	.02
270	Rob Nen	.20	.09
271	Rich Gossage	.10	.05
272	Ivan Rodriguez	1.50	.70
273	Jeff Huson	.05	.02
274	Kevin Brown	.10	.05
275	Dan Smith	.05	.02
276	Gary Pettis	.05	.02
277	Jack Daugherty	.05	.02
278	Mike Jeffcoat	.05	.02
279	Brad Arnsberg	.05	.02
280	Nolan Ryan	.75	.35
281	Eric McCray	.05	.02
282	Scott Chiamparino	.05	.02
283	Ruben Sierra	.20	.09
284	Geno Petralli	.05	.02
285	Monty Fariss	.05	.02
286	Rafael Palmeiro	.20	.09
287	Bobby Witt	.05	.02
288	Dean Palmer UER	.10	.05
	Photo is Dan Peltier		
289	Tony Scruggs	.05	.02
290	Kenny Rogers	.05	.02
291	Bret Saberhagen	.05	.02
292	Brian McRae	.20	.09
293	Storm Davis	.05	.02
294	Danny Tartabull	.05	.02
295	David Howard	.05	.02
296	Mike Boddicker	.05	.02
297	Joel Johnston	.05	.02
298	Tim Spehr	.05	.02
299	Hector Wagner	.05	.02
300	George Brett	.40	.18
301	Mike Macfarlane	.05	.02
302	Kirk Gibson	.10	.05
303	Harvey Pulliam	.05	.02
304	Jim Eisenreich	.05	.02
305	Kevin Seitzer	.05	.02
306	Mark Davis	.05	.02
307	Kurt Stillwell	.05	.02
308	Jeff Montgomery	.10	.05
309	Kevin Appier	.20	.09
310	Bob Hamelin	.05	.02
311	Tom Gordon	.05	.02
312	Kerwin Moore	.05	.02
313	Hugh Walker	.05	.02
314	Terry Shumpert	.05	.02
315	Warren Cromartie	.05	.02
316	Gary Thurman	.05	.02
317	Steve Bedrosian	.05	.02
318	Danny Gladden	.05	.02
319	Jack Morris	.10	.05
320	Kirby Puckett	.40	.18
321	Kent Hrbek	.10	.05
322	Kevin Tapani	.05	.02
323	Denny Neagle	.60	.25
324	Rich Garces	.05	.02
325	Larry Casian	.05	.02
326	Shane Mack	.05	.02
327	Allan Anderson	.05	.02
328	Junior Ortiz	.05	.02
329	Paul Abbott	.05	.02
330	Chuck Knoblauch	.25	.11
331	Chili Davis	.10	.05
332	Todd Ritchie	.05	.02
333	Brian Harper	.05	.02
334	Rick Aguilera	.10	.05
335	Scott Erickson	.10	.05
336	Pedro Munoz	.05	.02
337	Scott Leius	.05	.02
338	Greg Gagne	.05	.02
339	Mike Pagliarulo	.05	.02
340	Terry Leach	.05	.02
341	Willie Banks	.05	.02
342	Bobby Thigpen	.05	.02
343	Roberto Hernandez	.20	.09
344	Melido Perez	.05	.02
345	Carlton Fisk	.20	.09
346	Norberto Martin	.05	.02
347	Johnny Ruffin	.05	.02
348	Jeff Carter	.05	.02
349	Lance Johnson	.05	.02
350	Sammy Sosa	.25	.11
351	Alex Fernandez	.10	.05
352	Jack McDowell	.05	.02
353	Bob Wickman	.05	.02
354	Wilson Alvarez	.20	.09
355	Charlie Hough	.05	.02
356	Ozzie Guillen	.05	.02
357	Cory Snyder	.05	.02
358	Robin Ventura	.20	.09
359	Scott Fletcher	.05	.02
360	Cesar Bernhardt	.05	.02
361	Dan Pasqua	.05	.02
362	Tim Raines	.10	.05
363	Brian Drahman	.05	.02
364	Wayne Edwards	.05	.02
365	Scott Radinsky	.05	.02
366	Frank Thomas	1.50	.70
367	Cecil Fielder SLUG	.20	.09
368	Julio Franco SLUG	.05	.02
369	Kelly Gruber SLUG	.05	.02
370	Alan Trammell SLUG	.05	.02
371	Rickey Henderson SLUG	.10	.05
372	Jose Canseco SLUG	.10	.05
373	Ellis Burks SLUG	.05	.02
374	Lance Parrish SLUG	.05	.02
375	Dave Parker SLUG	.05	.02
376	Eddie Murray SLUG	.10	.05
377	Ryne Sandberg SLUG	.20	.09
378	Matt Williams SLUG	.10	.05
379	Barry Larkin SLUG	.10	.05
380	Barry Bonds SLUG	.20	.09
381	Bobby Bonilla SLUG	.05	.02
382	Darryl Strawberry SLUG	.10	.05
383	Benny Santiago SLUG	.05	.02
384	Don Robinson SLUG	.05	.02
385	Paul Coleman	.05	.02
386	Milt Thompson	.05	.02
387	Lee Smith	.10	.05
388	Ray Lankford	.20	.09
389	Tom Pagnozzi	.05	.02
390	Ken Hill	.10	.05
391	Jamie Moyer	.05	.02
392	Greg Carmona	.05	.02
393	John Ericks	.05	.02
394	Bob Tewksbury	.05	.02
395	Jose Oquendo	.05	.02
396	Rheal Cormier	.05	.02
397	Mike Milchin	.05	.02
398	Ozzie Smith	.25	.11
399	Aaron Holbert	.05	.02
400	Jose DeLeon	.05	.02
401	Felix Jose	.05	.02
402	Juan Agosto	.05	.02
403	Pedro Guerrero	.05	.02
404	Todd Zeile	.10	.05
405	Gerald Perry	.05	.02
406	Donovan Osborne UER	.20	.09
	Card number is 410		
407	Bryn Smith	.05	.02
408	Bernard Gilkey	.10	.05
409	Rex Hudler	.05	.02
410	Thomson/Branca Shot	.20	.09
	Bobby Thomson		
	Ralph Branca		
	(See also 406)		
411	Lance Dickson	.05	.02
412	Danny Jackson	.05	.02
413	Jerome Walton	.05	.02
414	Sean Cheetham	.05	.02
415	Joe Girardi	.10	.05
416	Ryne Sandberg	.25	.11
417	Mike Harkey	.05	.02
418	George Bell	.10	.05
419	Rick Wilkins	.05	.02
420	Earl Cunningham	.05	.02
421	Heathcliff Slocumb	.20	.09
422	Mike Bielecki	.05	.02
423	Jessie Hollins	.05	.02
424	Shawon Dunston	.10	.05
425	Doug Dascenzo	.05	.02
426	Greg Maddux	.60	.25
427	Jose Vizcaino	.05	.02

□ 428	Luis Salazar	.05	.02
□ 429	Andre Dawson	.20	.09
□ 430	Rick Sutcliffe	.05	.02
□ 431	Paul Assenmacher	.05	.02
□ 432	Erik Pappas	.05	.02
□ 433	Mark Grace	.20	.09
□ 434	Dennis Martinez	.10	.05
□ 435	Marquis Grissom	.20	.09
□ 436	Wil Cordero	.05	.02
□ 437	Tim Wallach	.05	.02
□ 438	Brian Barnes	.05	.02
□ 439	Barry Jones	.05	.02
□ 440	Ivan Calderon	.05	.02
□ 441	Stan Spencer	.05	.02
□ 442	Larry Walker	.30	.14
□ 443	Chris Haney	.05	.02
□ 444	Hector Rivera	.05	.02
□ 445	Delino DeShields	.05	.02
□ 446	Andres Galarraga	.20	.09
□ 447	Gilberto Reyes	.05	.02
□ 448	Willie Greene	.10	.05
□ 449	Greg Colbrunn	.05	.02
□ 450	Rondell White	.40	.18
□ 451	Steve Frey	.05	.02
□ 452	Shane Andrews	.05	.02
□ 453	Mike Fitzgerald	.05	.02
□ 454	Spike Owen	.05	.02
□ 455	Dave Martinez	.05	.02
□ 456	Dennis Boyd	.05	.02
□ 457	Eric Bullock	.05	.02
□ 458	Reid Cornelius	.05	.02
□ 459	Chris Nabholz	.05	.02
□ 460	David Cone	.10	.05
□ 461	Hubie Brooks	.05	.02
□ 462	Sid Fernandez	.05	.02
□ 463	Doug Simons	.05	.02
□ 464	Howard Johnson	.05	.02
□ 465	Chris Donnels	.05	.02
□ 466	Anthony Young	.05	.02
□ 467	Todd Hundley	.20	.09
□ 468	Rick Cerone	.05	.02
□ 469	Kevin Elster	.05	.02
□ 470	Wally Whitehurst	.05	.02
□ 471	Vince Coleman	.05	.02
□ 472	Dwight Gooden	.10	.05
□ 473	Charlie O'Brien	.05	.02
□ 474	Jeromy Burnitz	.15	.07
□ 475	John Franco	.10	.05
□ 476	Daryl Boston	.05	.02
□ 477	Frank Viola	.05	.02
□ 478	D.J. Dozier	.05	.02
□ 479	Kevin McReynolds	.05	.02
□ 480	Tom Herr	.05	.02
□ 481	Gregg Jefferies	.05	.02
□ 482	Pete Schourek	.10	.05
□ 483	Ron Darling	.05	.02
□ 484	Dave Magadan	.05	.02
□ 485	Andy Ashby	.20	.09
□ 486	Dale Murphy	.20	.09
□ 487	Von Hayes	.05	.02
□ 488	Kim Batiste	.05	.02
□ 489	Tony Longmire	.05	.02
□ 490	Wally Backman	.05	.02
□ 491	Jeff Jackson	.05	.02
□ 492	Mickey Morandini	.05	.02
□ 493	Darrel Akerfelds	.05	.02
□ 494	Ricky Jordan	.05	.02
□ 495	Randy Ready	.05	.02
□ 496	Darrin Fletcher	.05	.02
□ 497	Chuck Malone	.05	.02
□ 498	Pat Combs	.05	.02
□ 499	Dickie Thon	.05	.02
□ 500	Roger McDowell	.05	.02
□ 501	Len Dykstra	.10	.05
□ 502	Joe Boever	.05	.02
□ 503	John Kruk	.10	.05
□ 504	Terry Mulholland	.05	.02
□ 505	Wes Chamberlain	.05	.02
□ 506	Mike Lieberthal	.15	.07
□ 507	Darren Daulton	.10	.05
□ 508	Charlie Hayes	.05	.02
□ 509	John Smiley	.05	.02
□ 510	Gary Varsho	.05	.02
□ 511	Curt Wilkerson	.05	.02
□ 512	Orlando Merced	.10	.05
□ 513	Barry Bonds	.25	.11
□ 514	Mike LaValliere	.05	.02
□ 515	Doug Drabek	.05	.02
□ 516	Gary Redus	.05	.02
□ 517	William Pennyfeather	.05	.02
□ 518	Randy Tomlin	.05	.02
□ 519	Mike Zimmerman	.05	.02
□ 520	Jeff King	.05	.02
□ 521	Kurt Miller	.05	.02
□ 522	Jay Bell	.05	.02
□ 523	Bill Landrum	.05	.02
□ 524	Zane Smith	.05	.02
□ 525	Bobby Bonilla	.10	.05
□ 526	Bob Walk	.05	.02
□ 527	Austin Manahan	.05	.02
□ 528	Joe Ausanio	.05	.02
□ 529	Andy Van Slyke	.10	.05
□ 530	Jose Lind	.05	.02
□ 531	Carlos Garcia	.05	.02
□ 532	Don Slaught	.05	.02
□ 533	Gen. John Powell	.75	.35
□ 534	Frank Bolick	.05	.02
□ 535	Gary Scott	.05	.02
□ 536	Nikco Riesgo	.05	.02
□ 537	Reggie Sanders	.25	.11
□ 538	Tim Howard	.05	.02
□ 539	Ryan Bowen	.05	.02
□ 540	Eric Anthony	.05	.02
□ 541	Jim Deshaies	.05	.02
□ 542	Tom Nevers	.05	.02
□ 543	Ken Caminiti	.20	.09
□ 544	Karl Rhodes	.05	.02
□ 545	Xavier Hernandez	.05	.02
□ 546	Mike Scott	.05	.02
□ 547	Jeff Juden	.05	.02
□ 548	Darryl Kile	.20	.09
□ 549	Willie Ansley	.05	.02
□ 550	Luis Gonzalez	.20	.09
□ 551	Mike Simms	.05	.02
□ 552	Mark Portugal	.05	.02
□ 553	Jimmy Jones	.05	.02
□ 554	Jim Clancy	.05	.02
□ 555	Pete Harnisch	.05	.02
□ 556	Craig Biggio	.20	.09
□ 557	Eric Yelding	.05	.02
□ 558	Dave Rohde	.05	.02
□ 559	Casey Candaele	.05	.02
□ 560	Curt Schilling	.20	.09
□ 561	Steve Finley	.20	.09
□ 562	Javier Ortiz	.05	.02
□ 563	Andujar Cedeno	.05	.02
□ 564	Rafael Ramirez	.05	.02
□ 565	Kenny Lofton	1.50	.70
□ 566	Steve Avery	.05	.02
□ 567	Lonnie Smith	.05	.02
□ 568	Kent Mercker	.05	.02
□ 569	Chipper Jones	4.00	1.80
□ 570	Terry Pendleton	.10	.05
□ 571	Otis Nixon	.05	.02
□ 572	Juan Berenguer	.05	.02
□ 573	Charlie Leibrandt	.05	.02
□ 574	David Justice	.25	.11
□ 575	Keith Mitchell	.05	.02
□ 576	Tom Glavine	.20	.09
□ 577	Greg Olson	.05	.02
□ 578	Rafael Belliard	.05	.02
□ 579	Ben Rivera	.05	.02
□ 580	John Smoltz	.20	.09
□ 581	Tyler Houston	.05	.02
□ 582	Mark Wohlers	.15	.07
□ 583	Ron Gant	.05	.02
□ 584	Ramon Caraballo	.05	.02
□ 585	Sid Bream	.05	.02
□ 586	Jeff Treadway	.05	.02
□ 587	Javier Lopez	.75	.35
□ 588	Deion Sanders	.10	.05
□ 589	Mike Heath	.05	.02
□ 590	Ryan Klesko	1.00	.45
□ 591	Bob Ojeda	.05	.02
□ 592	Alfredo Griffin	.05	.02
□ 593	Raul Mondesi	1.00	.45
□ 594	Greg Smith	.05	.02
□ 595	Orel Hershiser	.10	.05
□ 596	Juan Samuel	.05	.02
□ 597	Brett Butler	.10	.05
□ 598	Gary Carter	.20	.09
□ 599	Stan Javier	.05	.02
□ 600	Kal Daniels	.05	.02
□ 601	Jamie McAndrew	.05	.02
□ 602	Mike Sharperson	.05	.02
□ 603	Jay Howell	.05	.02
□ 604	Eric Karros	.50	.23
□ 605	Tim Belcher	.05	.02
□ 606	Dan Opperman	.05	.02
□ 607	Lenny Harris	.05	.02
□ 608	Tom Goodwin	.10	.05
□ 609	Darryl Strawberry	.10	.05
□ 610	Ramon Martinez	.10	.05
□ 611	Kevin Gross	.05	.02
□ 612	Zakary Shinall	.05	.02
□ 613	Mike Scioscia	.05	.02
□ 614	Eddie Murray	.20	.09
□ 615	Ronnie Walden	.05	.02
□ 616	Will Clark	.20	.09
□ 617	Adam Hyzdu	.05	.02
□ 618	Matt Williams	.20	.09
□ 619	Don Robinson	.05	.02
□ 620	Jeff Brantley	.05	.02
□ 621	Greg Litton	.05	.02
□ 622	Steve Decker	.05	.02
□ 623	Robby Thompson	.05	.02
□ 624	Mark Leonard	.05	.02
□ 625	Kevin Bass	.05	.02
□ 626	Scott Garrelts	.05	.02
□ 627	Jose Uribe	.05	.02
□ 628	Eric Gunderson	.05	.02
□ 629	Steve Hosey	.05	.02
□ 630	Trevor Wilson	.05	.02
□ 631	Terry Kennedy	.05	.02
□ 632	Dave Righetti	.05	.02
□ 633	Kelly Downs	.05	.02
□ 634	Johnny Ard	.05	.02
□ 635	Eric Christopherson	.05	.02
□ 636	Kevin Mitchell	.10	.05
□ 637	John Burkett	.05	.02
□ 638	Kevin Rogers	.05	.02
□ 639	Bud Black	.05	.02
□ 640	Willie McGee	.05	.02
□ 641	Royce Clayton	.10	.05
□ 642	Tony Fernandez	.05	.02
□ 643	Ricky Bones	.05	.02
□ 644	Thomas Howard	.05	.02
□ 645	Dave Staton	.05	.02
□ 646	Jim Presley	.05	.02
□ 647	Tony Gwynn	.50	.23
□ 648	Marty Barrett	.05	.02
□ 649	Scott Coolbaugh	.05	.02
□ 650	Craig Lefferts	.05	.02
□ 651	Eddie Whitson	.05	.02
□ 652	Oscar Azocar	.05	.02
□ 653	Wes Gardner	.05	.02
□ 654	Bip Roberts	.05	.02
□ 655	Robbie Beckett	.05	.02
□ 656	Benito Santiago	.05	.02
□ 657	Greg W.Harris	.05	.02
□ 658	Jerald Clark	.05	.02
□ 659	Fred McGriff	.20	.09
□ 660	Larry Andersen	.05	.02
□ 661	Bruce Hurst	.05	.02
□ 662	Steve Martin UER	.05	.02
	Card said he pitched at Waterloo		
	He's an outfielder		
□ 663	Rafael Valdez	.05	.02
□ 664	Paul Faries	.05	.02
□ 665	Andy Benes	.10	.05
□ 666	Randy Myers	.05	.02
□ 667	Rob Dibble	.05	.02
□ 668	Glenn Sutko	.05	.02
□ 669	Glenn Braggs	.05	.02
□ 670	Billy Hatcher	.05	.02
□ 671	Joe Oliver	.05	.02
□ 672	Freddy Benavides	.05	.02
□ 673	Barry Larkin	.15	.07
□ 674	Chris Sabo	.05	.02
□ 675	Mariano Duncan	.05	.02
□ 676	Chris Jones	.05	.02
□ 677	Gino Minutelli	.05	.02
□ 678	Reggie Jefferson	.15	.07
□ 679	Jack Armstrong	.05	.02
□ 680	Chris Hammond	.05	.02
□ 681	Jose Rijo	.05	.02
□ 682	Bill Doran	.05	.02
□ 683	Terry Lee	.05	.02

		MINT	NRMT
☐ 684	Tom Browning	.05	.02
☐ 685	Paul O'Neill	.10	.05
☐ 686	Eric Davis	.10	.05
☐ 687	Dan Wilson	.25	.11
☐ 688	Ted Power	.05	.02
☐ 689	Tim Layana	.05	.02
☐ 690	Norm Charlton	.05	.02
☐ 691	Hal Morris	.05	.02
☐ 692	Rickey Henderson	.20	.09
☐ 693	Sam Militello	.05	.02
☐ 694	Matt Mieske	.20	.09
☐ 695	Paul Russo	.25	.11
☐ 696	Domingo Mota	.05	.02
☐ 697	Todd Guggiana	.05	.02
☐ 698	Marc Newfield	.15	.07
☐ 699	Checklist 1-122	.05	.02
☐ 700	Checklist 123-244	.05	.02
☐ 701	Checklist 245-366	.05	.02
☐ 702	Checklist 367-471	.05	.02
☐ 703	Checklist 472-593	.05	.02
☐ 704	Checklist 594-704	.05	.02

1992 Bowman

This 705-card standard-size set was issued in one comprehensive series. Unlike the previous Bowman issues, the 1992 set was radically upgraded to slick stock with gold foil subset cards in an attempt to reposition the brand as a premium level product. It initially stumbled out of the gate, but it's superior selection of prospects enabled it to eventually gain acceptance in the hobby and now stands as one of the more important issues of the 1990's. Cards were distributed in plastic wrap packs, retail jumbo packs and special 80-card retail carton packs. Card fronts feature posed and action color player photos on a UV-coated white card face. A gradated orange bar accented with black diagonal stripes carries the player's name at the bottom right corner. Interspersed throughout the set are 45 special cards with an identical front design except for a textured gold-foil border. The foil cards were inserted one per wax pack and two per jumbo (23 regular cards) pack. These foil cards feature past and present Team USA players and minor league POY Award winners. Each foil card has an extremely slight variation in that the photos are cropped differently. There is no additional value to either version. Some of the regular and special cards picture players in civilian clothing who are still in the farm system. Rookie Cards in this set include Garret Anderson, Carlos Delgado, Alex Gonzalez, Butch Huskey, Brian Jordan, Mike Piazza, Manny Ramirez, Mariano Rivera and Michael Tucker.

		MINT	NRMT
	COMPLETE SET (705)	300.00	135.00
	COMMON CARD (1-705)	.25	.11
	MINOR STARS	.50	.23
	SEMISTARS	1.00	.45
	UNLISTED STARS	1.50	.70
☐ 1	Ivan Rodriguez	3.00	1.35
☐ 2	Kirk McCaskill	.25	.11
☐ 3	Scott Livingstone	.25	.11
☐ 4	Salomon Torres	.25	.11
☐ 5	Carlos Hernandez	.25	.11
☐ 6	Dave Hollins	.25	.11
☐ 7	Scott Fletcher	.25	.11
☐ 8	Jorge Fabregas	.25	.11
☐ 9	Andujar Cedeno	.25	.11
☐ 10	Howard Johnson	.25	.11
☐ 11	Trevor Hoffman	1.00	.45
☐ 12	Roberto Kelly	.25	.11
☐ 13	Gregg Jefferies	.25	.11
☐ 14	Marquis Grissom	.50	.23
☐ 15	Mike Ignasiak	.25	.11
☐ 16	Jack Morris	.50	.11
☐ 17	William Pennyfeather	.25	.11
☐ 18	Todd Stottlemyre	.25	.11
☐ 19	Chito Martinez	.25	.11
☐ 20	Roberto Alomar	1.50	.70
☐ 21	Sam Militello	.25	.11
☐ 22	Hector Fajardo	.25	.11
☐ 23	Paul Quantrill	.25	.11
☐ 24	Chuck Knoblauch	1.50	.70
☐ 25	Reggie Jefferson	.25	.23
☐ 26	Jeremy McGarity	.25	.11
☐ 27	Jerome Walton	.25	.11
☐ 28	Chipper Jones	40.00	18.00
☐ 29	Brian Barber	.50	.23
☐ 30	Ron Darling	.25	.11
☐ 31	Roberto Petagine	.25	.11
☐ 32	Chuck Finley	.25	.11
☐ 33	Edgar Martinez	1.00	.45
☐ 34	Napoleon Robinson	.25	.11
☐ 35	Andy Van Slyke	.50	.23
☐ 36	Bobby Thigpen	.25	.11
☐ 37	Travis Fryman	.50	.23
☐ 38	Eric Christopherson	.25	.11
☐ 39	Terry Mulholland	.25	.11
☐ 40	Darryl Strawberry	.50	.23
☐ 41	Manny Alexander	.50	.23
☐ 42	Tracy Sanders	.25	.11
☐ 43	Pete Incaviglia	.25	.11
☐ 44	Kim Batiste	.25	.11
☐ 45	Frank Rodriguez	.50	.23
☐ 46	Greg Swindell	.25	.11
☐ 47	Delino DeShields	.25	.11
☐ 48	John Ericks	.25	.11
☐ 49	Franklin Stubbs	.25	.11
☐ 50	Tony Gwynn	4.00	1.80
☐ 51	Clifton Garrett	.25	.11
☐ 52	Mike Gardella	.25	.11
☐ 53	Scott Erickson	.50	.23
☐ 54	Gary Caraballo	.25	.11
☐ 55	Jose Oliva	.25	.11
☐ 56	Brook Fordyce	.25	.11
☐ 57	Mark Wohlers	.25	.11
☐ 58	Joe Slusarski	.25	.11
☐ 59	J.R. Phillips	.25	.11
☐ 60	Barry Bonds	2.00	.90
☐ 61	Bob Milacki	.25	.11
☐ 62	Keith Mitchell	.25	.11
☐ 63	Angel Miranda	.25	.11
☐ 64	Raul Mondesi	10.00	4.50
☐ 65	Brian Koelling	.25	.11
☐ 66	Brian McRae	.25	.11
☐ 67	John Patterson	.25	.11
☐ 68	John Wetteland	.25	.11
☐ 69	Wilson Alvarez	.50	.23
☐ 70	Wade Boggs	1.50	.70
☐ 71	Darryl Ratliff	.25	.11
☐ 72	Jeff Jackson	.25	.11
☐ 73	Jeremy Hernandez	.25	.11
☐ 74	Darryl Hamilton	.25	.11
☐ 75	Rafael Belliard	.25	.11
☐ 76	Rick Trlicek	.25	.11
☐ 77	Felipe Crespo	.50	.23
☐ 78	Carney Lansford	.50	.23
☐ 79	Ryan Long	.25	.11
☐ 80	Kirby Puckett	3.00	1.35
☐ 81	Earl Cunningham	.25	.11
☐ 82	Pedro Martinez	8.00	3.60
☐ 83	Scott Hatteberg	.25	.11
☐ 84	Juan Gonzalez UER	5.00	2.20
	(65 doubles vs. Tigers)		
☐ 85	Robert Nutting	.25	.11
☐ 86	Calvin Reese	1.00	.45
☐ 87	Dave Silvestri	.25	.11
☐ 88	Scott Ruffcorn	.25	.11
☐ 89	Rick Aguilera	.25	.11
☐ 90	Cecil Fielder	.50	.23
☐ 91	Kirk Dressendorfer	.25	.11
☐ 92	Jerry DiPoto	.25	.11
☐ 93	Mike Felder	.25	.11
☐ 94	Craig Paquette	.25	.11
☐ 95	Elvin Paulino	.25	.11
☐ 96	Donovan Osborne	.25	.11
☐ 97	Hubie Brooks	.25	.11
☐ 98	Derek Lowe	.50	.23
☐ 99	David Zancanaro	.25	.11
☐ 100	Ken Griffey Jr.	10.00	4.50
☐ 101	Todd Hundley	1.00	.45
☐ 102	Mike Trombley	.25	.11
☐ 103	Ricky Gutierrez	.25	.11
☐ 104	Braulio Castillo	.25	.11
☐ 105	Craig Lefferts	.25	.11
☐ 106	Rick Sutcliffe	.25	.11
☐ 107	Dean Palmer	.50	.23
☐ 108	Henry Rodriguez	1.50	.70
☐ 109	Mark Clark	.25	.11
☐ 110	Kenny Lofton	10.00	4.50
☐ 111	Mark Carreon	.25	.11
☐ 112	J.T. Bruett	.25	.11
☐ 113	Gerald Williams	.25	.11
☐ 114	Frank Thomas	8.00	3.60
☐ 115	Kevin Reimer	.25	.11
☐ 116	Sammy Sosa	1.50	.70
☐ 117	Mickey Tettleton	.25	.11
☐ 118	Reggie Sanders	.50	.23
☐ 119	Trevor Wilson	.25	.11
☐ 120	Cliff Brantley	.25	.11
☐ 121	Spike Owen	.25	.11
☐ 122	Jeff Montgomery	.50	.23
☐ 123	Alex Sutherland	.25	.11
☐ 124	Brien Taylor	.25	.11
☐ 125	Brian Williams	.25	.11
☐ 126	Kevin Seitzer	.25	.11
☐ 127	Carlos Delgado	10.00	4.50
☐ 128	Gary Scott	.25	.11
☐ 129	Scott Cooper	.25	.11
☐ 130	Domingo Jean	.25	.11
☐ 131	Pat Mahomes	.25	.11
☐ 132	Mike Boddicker	.25	.11
☐ 133	Roberto Hernandez	1.50	.70
☐ 134	Dave Valle	.25	.11
☐ 135	Kurt Stillwell	.25	.11
☐ 136	Brad Pennington	.25	.11
☐ 137	Jermaine Swinton	.25	.11
☐ 138	Ryan Hawblitzel	.25	.11
☐ 139	Tito Navarro	.25	.11
☐ 140	Sandy Alomar	.50	.23
☐ 141	Todd Benzinger	.25	.11
☐ 142	Danny Jackson	.25	.11
☐ 143	Melvin Nieves	1.50	.70
☐ 144	Jim Campanis	.25	.11
☐ 145	Luis Gonzalez	.25	.11
☐ 146	Dave Doorneweerd	.25	.11
☐ 147	Charlie Hayes	.25	.11
☐ 148	Greg Maddux	5.00	2.20
☐ 149	Brian Harper	.25	.11
☐ 150	Brent Miller	.25	.11
☐ 151	Shawn Estes	5.00	2.20
☐ 152	Mike Williams	.25	.11
☐ 153	Charlie Hough	.25	.11
☐ 154	Randy Myers	.50	.23
☐ 155	Kevin Young	.25	.11
☐ 156	Rick Wilkins	.25	.11

157	Terry Shumpert	.25	.11
158	Steve Karsay	.50	.23
159	Gary DiSarcina	.25	.11
160	Deion Sanders	.50	.23
161	Tom Browning	.25	.11
162	Dickie Thon	.25	.11
163	Luis Mercedes	.25	.11
164	Riccardo Ingram	.25	.11
165	Tavo Alvarez	.25	.11
166	Rickey Henderson	1.00	.45
167	Jaime Navarro	.25	.11
168	Billy Ashley	.50	.23
169	Phil Dauphin	.25	.11
170	Ivan Cruz	.25	.11
171	Harold Baines	.50	.23
172	Bryan Harvey	.25	.11
173	Alex Cole	.25	.11
174	Curtis Shaw	.25	.11
175	Matt Williams	1.00	.45
176	Felix Jose	.25	.11
177	Sam Horn	.25	.11
178	Randy Johnson	1.50	.70
179	Ivan Calderon	.25	.11
180	Steve Avery	.25	.11
181	William Suero	.25	.11
182	Bill Swift	.25	.11
183	Howard Battle	.25	.11
184	Ruben Amaro	.25	.11
185	Jim Abbott	.25	.11
186	Mike Fitzgerald	.25	.11
187	Bruce Hurst	.25	.11
188	Jeff Juden	.25	.11
189	Jeromy Burnitz	.50	.23
190	Dave Burba	.25	.11
191	Kevin Brown	.50	.23
192	Patrick Lennon	.25	.11
193	Jeff McNeely	.25	.11
194	Wil Cordero	.25	.11
195	Chili Davis	.50	.23
196	Milt Cuyler	.25	.11
197	Von Hayes	.25	.11
198	Todd Revenig	.25	.11
199	Joel Johnston	.25	.11
200	Jeff Bagwell	5.00	2.20
201	Alex Fernandez	.50	.23
202	Todd Jones	1.00	.45
203	Charles Nagy	.50	.23
204	Tim Raines	.50	.23
205	Kevin Maas	.25	.11
206	Julio Franco	.25	.11
207	Randy Velarde	.25	.11
208	Lance Johnson	.25	.11
209	Scott Leius	.25	.11
210	Derek Lee	.25	.11
211	Joe Sondrini	.25	.11
212	Royce Clayton	.25	.11
213	Chris George	.25	.11
214	Gary Sheffield	1.50	.70
215	Mark Gubicza	.25	.11
216	Mike Moore	.25	.11
217	Rick Huisman	.25	.11
218	Jeff Russell	.25	.11
219	D.J. Dozier	.25	.11
220	Dave Martinez	.25	.11
221	Alan Newman	.25	.11
222	Nolan Ryan	6.00	2.70
223	Teddy Higuera	.25	.11
224	Damon Buford	.25	.11
225	Ruben Sierra	.50	.23
226	Tom Nevers	.25	.11
227	Tommy Greene	.25	.11
228	Nigel Wilson	.25	.11
229	John DeSilva	.25	.11
230	Bobby Witt	.25	.11
231	Greg Cadaret	.25	.11
232	John Vander Wal	.25	.11
233	Jack Clark	.50	.23
234	Bill Doran	.25	.11
235	Bobby Bonilla	.50	.23
236	Steve Olin	.25	.11
237	Derek Bell	.50	.23
238	David Cone	.50	.23
239	Victor Cole	.25	.11
240	Rod Bolton	.25	.11
241	Tom Pagnozzi	.25	.11
242	Rob Dibble	.25	.11
243	Michael Carter	.25	.11
244	Don Peters	.25	.11
245	Mike LaValliere	.25	.11
246	Joe Perona	.25	.11
247	Mitch Williams	.25	.11
248	Jay Buhner	1.00	.45
249	Andy Benes	.50	.23
250	Alex Ochoa	1.50	.70
251	Greg Blosser	.25	.11
252	Jack Armstrong	.25	.11
253	Juan Samuel	.25	.11
254	Terry Pendleton	.50	.23
255	Ramon Martinez	.25	.11
256	Rico Brogna	.50	.23
257	John Smiley	.25	.11
258	Carl Everett	.50	.23
259	Tim Salmon	6.00	2.70
260	Will Clark	1.00	.45
261	Ugueth Urbina	1.00	.45
262	Jason Wood	.25	.11
263	Dave Magadan	.25	.11
264	Dante Bichette	1.00	.45
265	Jose DeLeon	.25	.11
266	Mike Neill	.25	.11
267	Paul O'Neil	.50	.23
268	Anthony Young	.25	.11
269	Greg W. Harris	.25	.11
270	Todd Van Poppel	.25	.11
271	Pedro Castellano	.25	.11
272	Tony Phillips	.25	.11
273	Mike Gallego	.25	.11
274	Steve Cooke	.25	.11
275	Robin Ventura	.50	.23
276	Kevin Mitchell	.50	.23
277	Doug Linton	.25	.11
278	Robert Eenhoorn	.25	.11
279	Gabe White	.25	.11
280	Dave Stewart	.25	.11
281	Mo Sanford	.25	.11
282	Greg Perschke	.25	.11
283	Kevin Flora	.25	.11
284	Jeff Williams	.25	.11
285	Keith Miller	.25	.11
286	Andy Ashby	.25	.11
287	Doug Dascenzo	.25	.11
288	Eric Karros	2.00	.90
289	Glenn Murray	.25	.11
290	Troy Percival	1.00	.45
291	Orlando Merced	.25	.11
292	Peter Hoy	.25	.11
293	Tony Fernandez	.25	.11
294	Juan Guzman	.50	.23
295	Jesse Barfield	.25	.11
296	Sid Fernandez	.25	.11
297	Scott Cepicky	.25	.11
298	Garret Anderson	4.00	1.80
299	Cal Eldred	.25	.11
300	Ryne Sandberg	2.00	.90
301	Jim Gantner	.25	.11
302	Mariano Rivera	5.00	2.20
303	Ron Lockett	.25	.11
304	Jose Offerman	.25	.11
305	Denny Martinez	.50	.23
306	Luis Ortiz	.25	.11
307	David Howard	.25	.11
308	Russ Springer	.25	.11
309	Chris Howard	.25	.11
310	Kyle Abbott	.25	.11
311	Aaron Sele	1.00	.45
312	David Justice	1.50	.70
313	Pete O'Brien	.25	.11
314	Greg Hansell	.25	.11
315	Dave Winfield	1.50	.70
316	Lance Dickson	.25	.11
317	Eric King	.25	.11
318	Vaughn Eshelman	.25	.11
319	Tim Belcher	.25	.11
320	Andres Galarraga	1.50	.70
321	Scott Bullett	.25	.11
322	Doug Strange	.25	.11
323	Jerald Clark	.25	.11
324	Dave Hansen	.25	.11
325	Greg Hibbard	.25	.11
326	Eric Hillman	.25	.11
327	Shane Reynolds	2.00	.90
328	Chris Hammond	.25	.11
329	Albert Belle	2.00	.90
330	Rich Becker	1.00	.45
331	Eddie Williams	.25	.11
332	Donald Harris	.25	.11
333	Dave Smith	.25	.11
334	Steve Fireovid	.25	.11
335	Steve Buechele	.25	.11
336	Mike Schooler	.25	.11
337	Kevin McReynolds	.25	.11
338	Hensley Meulens	.25	.11
339	Benji Gil	1.00	.45
340	Don Mattingly	2.50	1.10
341	Alvin Davis	.25	.11
342	Alan Mills	.25	.11
343	Kelly Downs	.25	.11
344	Leo Gomez	.25	.11
345	Tarrik Brock	.25	.11
346	Ryan Turner	.25	.11
347	John Smoltz	1.00	.45
348	Bill Sampen	.25	.11
349	Paul Byrd	.25	.11
350	Mike Bordick	.25	.11
351	Jose Lind	.25	.11
352	David Wells	.25	.11
353	Barry Larkin	1.00	.45
354	Bruce Ruffin	.25	.11
355	Luis Rivera	.25	.11
356	Sid Bream	.25	.11
357	Julian Vasquez	.25	.11
358	Jason Bere	.50	.23
359	Ben McDonald	.25	.11
360	Scott Stahoviak	.25	.23
361	Kirt Manwaring	.25	.11
362	Jeff Johnson	.25	.11
363	Rob Deer	.25	.11
364	Tony Pena	.25	.11
365	Melido Perez	.25	.11
366	Clay Parker	.25	.11
367	Dale Sveum	.25	.11
368	Mike Scioscia	.25	.11
369	Roger Salkeld	.25	.11
370	Mike Stanley	.25	.11
371	Jack McDowell	.25	.11
372	Tim Wallach	.25	.11
373	Billy Ripken	.25	.11
374	Mike Christopher	.25	.11
375	Paul Molitor	1.50	.70
376	Dave Stieb	.25	.11
377	Pedro Guerrero	.25	.11
378	Russ Swan	.25	.11
379	Bob Ojeda	.25	.11
380	Donn Pall	.25	.11
381	Eddie Zosky	.25	.11
382	Darnell Coles	.25	.11
383	Tom Smith	.25	.11
384	Mark McGwire	3.00	1.35
385	Gary Carter	1.50	.70
386	Rich Amaral	.25	.11
387	Alan Embree	.25	.11
388	Jonathan Hurst	.25	.11
389	Bobby Jones	2.50	1.10
390	Rico Rossy	.25	.11
391	Dan Smith	.25	.11
392	Terry Steinbach	.50	.23
393	Jon Farrell	.25	.11
394	Dave Anderson	.25	.11
395	Benny Santiago	.25	.11
396	Mark Wohlers	1.00	.45
397	Mo Vaughn	2.50	1.10
398	Randy Kramer	.25	.11
399	John Jaha	1.00	.45
400	Cal Ripken	6.00	2.70
401	Ryan Bowen	.25	.11
402	Tim McIntosh	.25	.11
403	Bernard Gilkey	.50	.23
404	Junior Felix	.25	.11
405	Cris Colon	.25	.11
406	Marc Newfield	1.00	.45
407	Bernie Williams	1.50	.70
408	Jay Howell	.25	.11
409	Zane Smith	.25	.11
410	Jeff Shaw	.25	.11
411	Kerry Woodson	.25	.11
412	Wes Chamberlain	.25	.11
413	Dave Mlicki	.25	.11
414	Benny Distefano	.25	.11

□	#	Name	Price	Price2
□	415	Kevin Rogers	.25	.11
□	416	Tim Naehring	.50	.23
□	417	Clemente Nunez	.50	.23
□	418	Luis Sojo	.25	.11
□	419	Kevin Ritz	.25	.11
□	420	Omar Olivares	.25	.11
□	421	Manuel Lee	.25	.11
□	422	Julio Valera	.25	.11
□	423	Omar Vizquel	.50	.23
□	424	Darren Burton	.25	.11
□	425	Mel Hall	.25	.11
□	426	Dennis Powell	.25	.11
□	427	Lee Stevens	.25	.11
□	428	Glenn Davis	.25	.11
□	429	Willie Greene	.25	.11
□	430	Kevin Wickander	.25	.11
□	431	Dennis Eckersley	.50	.23
□	432	Joe Orsulak	.25	.11
□	433	Eddie Murray	1.50	.70
□	434	Matt Stairs	.25	.11
□	435	Wally Joyner	.50	.23
□	436	Rondell White	4.00	1.80
□	437	Rob Maurer	.25	.11
□	438	Joe Redfield	.25	.11
□	439	Mark Lewis	.25	.11
□	440	Darren Daulton	.50	.23
□	441	Mike Henneman	.25	.11
□	442	John Cangelosi	.25	.11
□	443	Vince Moore	.25	.11
□	444	John Wehner	.25	.11
□	445	Kent Hrbek	.50	.23
□	446	Mark McLemore	.25	.11
□	447	Bill Wegman	.25	.11
□	448	Robby Thompson	.25	.11
□	449	Mark Anthony	.25	.11
□	450	Archi Cianfrocco	.25	.11
□	451	Johnny Ruffin	.25	.11
□	452	Javier Lopez	8.00	3.60
□	453	Greg Gohr	.25	.11
□	454	Tim Scott	.25	.11
□	455	Stan Belinda	.25	.11
□	456	Darrin Jackson	.25	.11
□	457	Chris Gardner	.25	.11
□	458	Esteban Beltre	.25	.11
□	459	Phil Plantier	.25	.11
□	460	Jim Thome	15.00	6.75
□	461	Mike Piazza	60.00	27.00
□	462	Matt Sinatro	.25	.11
□	463	Scott Servais	.25	.11
□	464	Brian Jordan	4.00	1.80
□	465	Doug Drabek	.25	.11
□	466	Carl Willis	.25	.11
□	467	Bret Barberie	.25	.11
□	468	Hal Morris	.25	.11
□	469	Steve Sax	.25	.11
□	470	Jerry Willard	.25	.11
□	471	Dan Wilson	.50	.23
□	472	Chris Hoiles	.25	.11
□	473	Rheal Cormier	.25	.11
□	474	John Morris	.25	.11
□	475	Jeff Reardon	.50	.23
□	476	Mark Leiter	.25	.11
□	477	Tom Gordon	.25	.11
□	478	Kent Bottenfield	.25	.11
□	479	Gene Larkin	.25	.11
□	480	Dwight Gooden	.50	.23
□	481	B.J. Surhoff	.50	.23
□	482	Andy Stankiewicz	.25	.11
□	483	Tino Martinez	1.50	.70
□	484	Craig Biggio	1.00	.45
□	485	Denny Neagle	3.00	1.35
□	486	Rusty Meacham	.25	.11
□	487	Kal Daniels	.25	.11
□	488	Dave Henderson	.25	.11
□	489	Tim Costo	.25	.11
□	490	Doug Davis	.25	.11
□	491	Frank Viola	.25	.11
□	492	Cory Snyder	.25	.11
□	493	Chris Martin	.25	.11
□	494	Dion James	.25	.11
□	495	Randy Tomlin	.25	.11
□	496	Greg Vaughn	.25	.11
□	497	Dennis Cook	.25	.11
□	498	Rosario Rodriguez	.25	.11
□	499	Dave Staton	.25	.11
□	500	George Brett	3.00	1.35

□	#	Name	Price	Price2
□	501	Brian Barnes	.25	.11
□	502	Butch Henry	.25	.11
□	503	Harold Reynolds	.25	.11
□	504	David Nied	.25	.11
□	505	Lee Smith	.50	.23
□	506	Steve Chitren	.25	.11
□	507	Ken Hill	.25	.11
□	508	Robbie Beckett	.25	.11
□	509	Troy Afenir	.25	.11
□	510	Kelly Gruber	.25	.11
□	511	Bret Boone	.50	.23
□	512	Jeff Branson	.25	.11
□	513	Mike Jackson	.25	.11
□	514	Pete Harnisch	.25	.11
□	515	Chad Kreuter	.25	.11
□	516	Joe Vitko	.25	.11
□	517	Orel Hershiser	.50	.23
□	518	John Doherty	.25	.11
□	519	Jay Bell	.50	.23
□	520	Mark Langston	.25	.11
□	521	Dann Howitt	.25	.11
□	522	Bobby Reed	.25	.11
□	523	Roberto Munoz	.25	.11
□	524	Todd Ritchie	.25	.11
□	525	Bip Roberts	.25	.11
□	526	Pat Listach	.25	.11
□	527	Scott Brosius	.25	.11
□	528	John Roper	.25	.11
□	529	Phil Hiatt	.25	.11
□	530	Denny Walling	.25	.11
□	531	Carlos Baerga	.25	.11
□	532	Manny Ramirez	20.00	9.00
□	533	Pat Clements UER	.25	.11
		(Mistakenly numbered 553)		
□	534	Ron Gant	.50	.23
□	535	Pat Kelly	.25	.11
□	536	Billy Spiers	.25	.11
□	537	Darren Reed	.25	.11
□	538	Ken Caminiti	1.00	.45
□	539	Butch Huskey	3.00	1.35
□	540	Matt Nokes	.25	.11
□	541	John Kruk	.50	.23
□	542	John Jaha FOIL	.50	.23
□	543	Justin Thompson	5.00	2.20
□	544	Steve Hosey	.25	.11
□	545	Joe Kmak	.25	.11
□	546	John Franco	.50	.23
□	547	Devon White	.25	.11
□	548	Elston Hansen FOIL	.25	.11
□	549	Ryan Klesko	10.00	4.50
□	550	Danny Tartabull	.25	.11
□	551	Frank Thomas FOIL	10.00	4.50
□	552	Kevin Tapani	.25	.11
□	553	Willie Banks	.25	.11
		(See also 533)		
□	554	B.J. Wallace FOIL	.50	.23
□	555	Orlando Miller	.25	.11
□	556	Mark Smith	.25	.11
□	557	Tim Wallach FOIL	.25	.11
□	558	Bill Gullickson	.25	.11
□	559	Derek Bell FOIL	.50	.23
□	560	Joe Randa FOIL	.50	.23
□	561	Frank Seminara	.25	.11
□	562	Mark Gardner	.25	.11
□	563	Rick Greene FOIL	.25	.11
□	564	Gary Gaetti	.25	.11
□	565	Ozzie Guillen	.25	.11
□	566	Charles Nagy FOIL	.50	.23
□	567	Mike Milchin	.25	.11
□	568	Ben Shelton	.25	.11
□	569	Chris Roberts FOIL	.50	.23
□	570	Ellis Burks	.50	.23
□	571	Scott Scudder	.25	.11
□	572	Jim Abbott FOIL	.25	.11
□	573	Joe Carter	.50	.23
□	574	Steve Finley	.50	.23
□	575	Jim Olander FOIL	.25	.11
□	576	Carlos Garcia	.25	.11
□	577	Gregg Olson	.25	.11
□	578	Greg Swindell FOIL	.25	.11
□	579	Matt Williams FOIL	1.00	.45
□	580	Mark Grace	1.00	.45
□	581	Howard House FOIL	.25	.11
□	582	Luis Polonia	.25	.11
□	583	Erik Hanson	.25	.11
□	584	Salomon Torres FOIL	.25	.11

□	#	Name	Price	Price2
□	585	Carlton Fisk	1.50	.70
□	586	Bret Saberhagen	.25	.11
□	587	Chad McConnell FOIL	.25	.11
□	588	Jimmy Key	.50	.23
□	589	Mike Macfarlane	.25	.11
□	590	Barry Bonds FOIL	2.00	.90
□	591	Jamie McAndrew	.25	.11
□	592	Shane Mack	.25	.11
□	593	Kerwin Moore	.25	.11
□	594	Joe Oliver	.25	.11
□	595	Chris Sabo	.25	.11
□	596	Alex Gonzalez	1.50	.70
□	597	Brett Butler	.25	.11
□	598	Mark Hutton	.25	.11
□	599	Andy Benes FOIL	.50	.23
□	600	Jose Canseco	1.00	.45
□	601	Darryl Kile	.25	.11
□	602	Matt Stairs FOIL	.25	.11
□	603	Robert Butler FOIL	.25	.11
□	604	Willie McGee	.25	.11
□	605	Jack McDowell FOIL	.25	.11
□	606	Tom Candiotti	.25	.11
□	607	Ed Martel	.25	.11
□	608	Matt Mieske FOIL	.50	.23
□	609	Darrin Fletcher	.25	.11
□	610	Rafael Palmeiro	1.00	.45
□	611	Bill Swift FOIL	.25	.11
□	612	Mike Mussina	2.50	1.10
□	613	Vince Coleman	.25	.11
□	614	Scott Cepicky FOIL UER	.25	.11
		(Bats: LEFT)		
□	615	Mike Greenwell	.25	.11
□	616	Kevin McGehee	.25	.11
□	617	Jeffrey Hammonds FOIL	1.50	.70
□	618	Scott Taylor	.25	.11
□	619	Dave Otto	.25	.11
□	620	Mark McGwire FOIL	3.00	1.35
□	621	Kevin Tatar	.25	.11
□	622	Steve Farr	.25	.11
□	623	Ryan Klesko FOIL	2.00	.90
□	624	Dave Fleming	.25	.11
□	625	Andre Dawson	1.00	.45
□	626	Tino Martinez FOIL	1.50	.70
□	627	Chad Curtis	1.50	.70
□	628	Mickey Morandini	.25	.11
□	629	Gregg Olson FOIL	.25	.11
□	630	Lou Whitaker	.50	.23
□	631	Arthur Rhodes	.25	.11
□	632	Brandon Wilson	.25	.11
□	633	Lance Jennings	.25	.11
□	634	Allen Watson	.25	.11
□	635	Len Dykstra	.50	.23
□	636	Joe Girardi	.25	.11
□	637	Kiki Hernandez FOIL	.25	.11
□	638	Mike Hampton	2.00	.90
□	639	Al Osuna	.25	.11
□	640	Kevin Appier	.50	.23
□	641	Rick Helling FOIL	.25	.11
□	642	Jody Reed	.25	.11
□	643	Ray Lankford	1.50	.70
□	644	John Olerud	.50	.23
□	645	Paul Molitor FOIL	1.50	.70
□	646	Pat Borders	.25	.11
□	647	Mike Morgan	.25	.11
□	648	Larry Walker	1.50	.70
□	649	Pedro Castellano FOIL	.25	.11
□	650	Fred McGriff	1.00	.45
□	651	Walt Weiss	.25	.11
□	652	Calvin Murray FOIL	.25	.11
□	653	Dave Nilsson	.50	.23
□	654	Greg Pirkl	.25	.11
□	655	Robin Ventura FOIL	.50	.23
□	656	Mark Portugal	.25	.11
□	657	Roger McDowell	.25	.11
□	658	Rick Hirtensteiner FOIL	.25	.11
□	659	Glenallen Hill	.25	.11
□	660	Greg Gagne	.25	.11
□	661	Charles Johnson FOIL	8.00	3.60
□	662	Brian Hunter	.25	.11
□	663	Mark Lemke	.25	.11
□	664	Tim Belcher FOIL	.25	.11
□	665	Rich DeLucia	.25	.11
□	666	Bob Walk	.25	.11
□	667	Joe Carter FOIL	.50	.23
□	668	Jose Guzman	.25	.11

	MINT	NRMT
669 Otis Nixon	.50	.23
670 Phil Nevin FOIL	.50	.23
671 Eric Davis	.50	.23
672 Damion Easley	1.00	.45
673 Will Clark FOIL	1.00	.45
674 Mark Kiefer	.25	.11
675 Ozzie Smith	2.00	.90
676 Manny Ramirez FOIL	4.00	1.80
677 Gregg Olson	.25	.11
678 Cliff Floyd	2.00	.90
679 Duane Singleton	.25	.11
680 Jose Rijo	.25	.11
681 Willie Randolph	.50	.23
682 Michael Tucker FOIL	4.00	1.80
683 Darren Lewis	.25	.11
684 Dale Murphy	1.50	.70
685 Mike Pagliarulo	.25	.11
686 Paul Miller	.25	.11
687 Mike Robertson	.25	.11
688 Mike Devereaux	.25	.11
689 Pedro Astacio	.50	.23
690 Alan Trammell	1.00	.45
691 Roger Clemens	3.00	1.35
692 Bud Black	.25	.11
693 Turk Wendell	.50	.23
694 Barry Larkin FOIL	1.00	.45
695 Todd Zeile	.25	.11
696 Pat Hentgen	3.00	1.35
697 Eddie Taubensee	.25	.11
698 Guillermo Velasquez	.25	.11
699 Tom Giavine	1.00	.45
700 Robin Yount	1.00	.45
701 Checklist 1-141	.25	.11
702 Checklist 142-282	.25	.11
703 Checklist 283-423	.25	.11
704 Checklist 424-564	.25	.11
705 Checklist 565-705	.25	.11

1993 Bowman

This 708-card standard-size set was issued in one series and features one of the more comprehensive selection of prospects and rookies available that year. Cards were distributed in 14-card plastic wrapped packs and jumbo packs. Each 14-card pack contained one silver foil bordered subset card. The basic issue card fronts feature white-bordered color action player photos. The player's name appears in white lettering at the bottom right, with his last name printed on an ocher rectangle. The 48 foil subset cards (339-374 and 693-704) feature sixteen 1992 MVPs of the Minor Leagues, top prospects and a few father/son combinations. Rookie Cards in this set include James Baldwin, Roger Cedeno, Marty Cordova, Brian L. Hunter, Derek Jeter, Jason Kendall, Andy Pettite and Preston Wilson.

	MINT	NRMT
COMPLETE SET (708)	70.00	32.00
COMMON CARD (1-708)	.15	.07
MINOR STARS	.30	.14
UNLISTED STARS	.60	.25
1 Glenn Davis	.15	.07
2 Hector Roa	.15	.07
3 Ken Ryan	.15	.07
4 Derek Wallace	.15	.07
5 Jorge Fabregas	.15	.07
6 Joe Oliver	.15	.07
7 Brandon Wilson	.15	.07
8 Mark Thompson	.30	.14
9 Tracy Sanders	.15	.07
10 Rich Renteria	.15	.07
11 Lou Whitaker	.30	.14
12 Brian Hunter	2.00	.90
13 Joe Vitiello	.15	.07
14 Eric Karros	.30	.14
15 Joe Kmak	.15	.07
16 Tavo Alvarez	.15	.07
17 Steve Dunn	.15	.07
18 Tony Fernandez	.15	.07
19 Melido Perez	.15	.07
20 Mike Lieberthal	.15	.07
21 Terry Steinbach	.15	.07
22 Stan Belinda	.15	.07
23 Jay Buhner	.40	.18
24 Allen Watson	.15	.07
25 Daryl Henderson	.15	.07
26 Ray McDavid	.15	.07
27 Shawn Green	.75	.35
28 Bud Black	.15	.07
29 Sherman Obando	.15	.07
30 Mike Hostetler	.15	.07
31 Nate Minchey	.15	.07
32 Randy Myers	.30	.14
33 Brian Grebeck	.15	.07
34 John Roper	.15	.07
35 Larry Thomas	.15	.07
36 Alex Cole	.15	.07
37 Tom Kramer	.15	.07
38 Matt Whisenant	.15	.07
39 Chris Gomez	.40	.18
40 Luis Gonzalez	.15	.07
41 Kevin Appier	.30	.14
42 Omar Daal	.15	.07
43 Duane Singleton	.15	.07
44 Bill Risley	.15	.07
45 Pat Meares	.30	.14
46 Butch Huskey	.60	.25
47 Bobby Munoz	.15	.07
48 Juan Bell	.15	.07
49 Scott Lydy	.15	.07
50 Dennis Moeller	.15	.07
51 Marc Newfield	.30	.14
52 Tripp Cromer	.15	.07
53 Kurt Miller	.15	.07
54 Jim Pena	.15	.07
55 Juan Guzman	.30	.14
56 Matt Williams	.40	.18
57 Harold Reynolds	.15	.07
58 Donnie Elliott	.15	.07
59 Jon Shave	.15	.07
60 Kevin Roberson	.15	.07
61 Hilly Hathaway	.15	.07
62 Jose Rijo	.15	.07
63 Kerry Taylor	.15	.07
64 Ryan Hawblitzel	.15	.07
65 Glenallen Hill	.15	.07
66 Ramon Martinez	.30	.14
67 Travis Fryman	.30	.14
68 Tom Nevers	.15	.07
69 Phil Hiatt	.15	.07
70 Tim Wallach	.15	.07
71 B.J. Surhoff	.30	.14
72 Rondell White	.40	.18
73 Denny Hocking	.30	.14
74 Mike Oquist	.15	.07
75 Paul O'Neill	.30	.14
76 Willie Banks	.15	.07
77 Bob Welch	.15	.07
78 Jose Sandoval	.15	.07
79 Bill Haselman	.15	.07
80 Rheal Cormier	.15	.07
81 Dean Palmer	.15	.07
82 Pat Gomez	.15	.07
83 Steve Karsay	.30	.14
84 Carl Hanselman	.15	.07
85 T.R. Lewis	.15	.07
86 Chipper Jones	3.00	1.35
87 Scott Hatteberg	.15	.07
88 Greg Hibbard	.15	.07
89 Lance Painter	.15	.07
90 Chad Mottola	.15	.07
91 Jason Bere	.30	.14
92 Dante Bichette	.40	.18
93 Sandy Alomar Jr	.30	.14
94 Carl Everett	.30	.14
95 Danny Bautista	.30	.14
96 Steve Finley	.30	.14
97 David Cone	.30	.14
98 Todd Hollandsworth	.75	.35
99 Matt Mieske	.30	.14
100 Larry Walker	.60	.25
101 Shane Mack	.15	.07
102 Aaron Ledesma	.15	.07
103 Andy Pettite	5.00	2.20
104 Kevin Stocker	.15	.07
105 Mike Mohler	.15	.07
106 Tony Menendez	.15	.07
107 Derek Lowe	.30	.14
108 Basil Shabazz	.15	.07
109 Dan Smith	.15	.07
110 Scott Sanders	.15	.07
111 Todd Stottlemyre	.15	.07
112 Benji Simonton	.15	.07
113 Rick Sutcliffe	.15	.07
114 Lee Heath	.15	.07
115 Jeff Russell	.15	.07
116 Dave Stevens	.15	.07
117 Mark Holzemer	.15	.07
118 Tim Belcher	.15	.07
119 Bobby Thigpen	.15	.07
120 Roger Bailey	.15	.07
121 Tony Mitchell	.15	.07
122 Junior Felix	.15	.07
123 Rich Robertson	.15	.07
124 Andy Cook	.15	.07
125 Brian Bevil	.30	.14
126 Darryl Strawberry	.30	.14
127 Cal Eldred	.15	.07
128 Cliff Floyd	.30	.14
129 Alan Newman	.15	.07
130 Howard Johnson	.15	.07
131 Jim Abbott	.15	.07
132 Chad McConnell	.15	.07
133 Miguel Jimenez	.30	.14
134 Brett Backlund	.15	.07
135 John Cummings	.15	.07
136 Brian Barber	.15	.07
137 Rafael Palmeiro	.40	.18
138 Tim Worrell	.15	.07
139 Jose Pett	.50	.23
140 Barry Bonds	.60	.25
141 Damon Buford	.15	.07
142 Jeff Blauser	.15	.07
143 Frankie Rodriguez	.15	.07
144 Mike Morgan	.15	.07
145 Gary DiSarcina	.15	.07
146 Calvin Reese	.30	.14
147 Johnny Ruffin	.15	.07
148 David Nied	.15	.07
149 Charles Nagy	.30	.14
150 Mike Myers	.15	.07
151 Kenny Carlyle	.15	.07
152 Eric Anthony	.15	.07
153 Jose Lind	.15	.07
154 Pedro Martinez	.60	.25
155 Mark Kiefer	.15	.07
156 Tim Laker	.15	.07
157 Pat Mahomes	.15	.07
158 Bobby Bonilla	.30	.14
159 Domingo Jean	.15	.07
160 Darren Daulton	.30	.14
161 Mark McGwire	1.25	.55
162 Jason Kendall	2.00	.90
163 Desi Relaford	.30	.14
164 Ozzie Canseco	.15	.07
165 Rick Helling	.15	.07
166 Steve Pegues	.15	.07

#	Player	Val1	Val2
☐ 167	Paul Molitor	.60	.25
☐ 168	Larry Carter	.15	.07
☐ 169	Arthur Rhodes	.15	.07
☐ 170	Damon Hollins	.50	.23
☐ 171	Frank Viola	.15	.07
☐ 172	Steve Trachsel	.30	.14
☐ 173	J.T. Snow	1.50	.70
☐ 174	Keith Gordon	.15	.07
☐ 175	Carlton Fisk	.60	.25
☐ 176	Jason Bates	.30	.14
☐ 177	Mike Crosby	.15	.07
☐ 178	Benny Santiago	.15	.07
☐ 179	Mike Moore	.15	.07
☐ 180	Jeff Juden	.15	.07
☐ 181	Darren Burton	.15	.07
☐ 182	Todd Williams	.15	.07
☐ 183	John Jaha	.30	.14
☐ 184	Mike Lansing	.30	.14
☐ 185	Pedro Grifol	.15	.07
☐ 186	Vince Coleman	.15	.07
☐ 187	Pat Kelly	.15	.07
☐ 188	Clemente Alvarez	.15	.07
☐ 189	Ron Darling	.15	.07
☐ 190	Orlando Merced	.15	.07
☐ 191	Chris Bosio	.15	.07
☐ 192	Steve Dixon	.15	.07
☐ 193	Doug Dascenzo	.15	.07
☐ 194	Ray Holbert	.15	.07
☐ 195	Howard Battle	.15	.07
☐ 196	Willie McGee	.15	.07
☐ 197	John O'Donoghue	.15	.07
☐ 198	Steve Avery	.15	.07
☐ 199	Greg Blosser	.15	.07
☐ 200	Ryne Sandberg	.75	.35
☐ 201	Joe Grahe	.15	.07
☐ 202	Dan Wilson	.30	.14
☐ 203	Domingo Martinez	.15	.07
☐ 204	Andres Galarraga	.60	.25
☐ 205	Jamie Taylor	.15	.07
☐ 206	Darrell Whitmore	.15	.07
☐ 207	Ben Blomdahl	.15	.07
☐ 208	Doug Drabek	.15	.07
☐ 209	Keith Miller	.15	.07
☐ 210	Billy Ashley	.15	.07
☐ 211	Mike Farrell	.15	.07
☐ 212	John Wetteland	.30	.14
☐ 213	Randy Tomlin	.15	.07
☐ 214	Sid Fernandez	.15	.07
☐ 215	Quilvio Veras	.75	.35
☐ 216	Dave Hollins	.30	.14
☐ 217	Mike Neill	.15	.07
☐ 218	Andy Van Slyke	.30	.14
☐ 219	Bret Boone	.15	.07
☐ 220	Tom Pagnozzi	.15	.07
☐ 221	Mike Welch	.15	.07
☐ 222	Frank Seminara	.15	.07
☐ 223	Ron Villone	.15	.07
☐ 224	D.J. Thielen	.15	.07
☐ 225	Cal Ripken	2.50	1.10
☐ 226	Pedro Borbon Jr.	.15	.07
☐ 227	Carlos Quintana	.15	.07
☐ 228	Tommy Shields	.15	.07
☐ 229	Tim Salmon	.75	.35
☐ 230	John Smiley	.15	.07
☐ 231	Ellis Burks	.30	.14
☐ 232	Pedro Castellano	.15	.07
☐ 233	Paul Byrd	.15	.07
☐ 234	Bryan Harvey	.15	.07
☐ 235	Scott Livingstone	.15	.07
☐ 236	James Mouton	.30	.14
☐ 237	Joe Randa	.15	.07
☐ 238	Pedro Astacio	.15	.07
☐ 239	Darryl Hamilton	.15	.07
☐ 240	Joey Eischen	.30	.14
☐ 241	Edgar Herrera	.15	.07
☐ 242	Dwight Gooden	.30	.14
☐ 243	Sam Militello	.15	.07
☐ 244	Ron Blazier	.15	.07
☐ 245	Ruben Sierra	.15	.07
☐ 246	Al Martin	.30	.14
☐ 247	Mike Felder	.15	.07
☐ 248	Bob Tewksbury	.15	.07
☐ 249	Craig Lefferts	.15	.07
☐ 250	Luis Lopez	.15	.07
☐ 251	Devon White	.15	.07
☐ 252	Will Clark	.40	.18
☐ 253	Mark Smith	.15	.07
☐ 254	Terry Pendleton	.30	.14
☐ 255	Aaron Sele	.30	.14
☐ 256	Jose Viera	.15	.07
☐ 257	Damion Easley	.15	.07
☐ 258	Rod Lofton	.15	.07
☐ 259	Chris Snopek	.50	.23
☐ 260	Quinton McCracken	.30	.14
☐ 261	Mike Matthews	.15	.07
☐ 262	Hector Carrasco	.15	.07
☐ 263	Rick Greene	.15	.07
☐ 264	Chris Holt	.15	.07
☐ 265	George Brett	1.25	.55
☐ 266	Rick Gorecki	.15	.07
☐ 267	Francisco Gamez	.15	.07
☐ 268	Marquis Grissom	.30	.14
☐ 269	Kevin Tapani UER	.15	.07
	(Misspelled Tapan on card front)		
☐ 270	Ryan Thompson	.15	.07
☐ 271	Gerald Williams	.15	.07
☐ 272	Paul Fletcher	.15	.07
☐ 273	Lance Blankenship	.15	.07
☐ 274	Marty Neff	.15	.07
☐ 275	Shawn Estes	.75	.35
☐ 276	Rene Arocha	.15	.07
☐ 277	Scott Eyre	.15	.07
☐ 278	Phil Plantier	.15	.07
☐ 279	Paul Spoljaric	.15	.07
☐ 280	Chris Gambs	.15	.07
☐ 281	Harold Baines	.30	.14
☐ 282	Jose Oliva	.15	.07
☐ 283	Matt Whiteside	.15	.07
☐ 284	Brant Brown	.50	.23
☐ 285	Russ Springer	.15	.07
☐ 286	Chris Sabo	.15	.07
☐ 287	Ozzie Guillen	.15	.07
☐ 288	Marcus Moore	.15	.07
☐ 289	Chad Ogea	.30	.14
☐ 290	Walt Weiss	.15	.07
☐ 291	Brian Edmondson	.15	.07
☐ 292	Jimmy Gonzalez	.15	.07
☐ 293	Danny Miceli	.30	.14
☐ 294	Jose Offerman	.15	.07
☐ 295	Greg Vaughn	.15	.07
☐ 296	Frank Bolick	.15	.07
☐ 297	Mike Maksudian	.15	.07
☐ 298	John Franco	.30	.14
☐ 299	Danny Tartabull	.15	.07
☐ 300	Len Dykstra	.30	.14
☐ 301	Bobby Witt	.15	.07
☐ 302	Trey Beamon	.50	.23
☐ 303	Tino Martinez	.60	.25
☐ 304	Aaron Holbert	.15	.07
☐ 305	Juan Gonzalez	1.50	.70
☐ 306	Billy Hall	.15	.07
☐ 307	Duane Ward	.15	.07
☐ 308	Rod Beck	.30	.14
☐ 309	Jose Mercedes	.15	.07
☐ 310	Otis Nixon	.15	.07
☐ 311	Quinton Gittens	.15	.07
☐ 312	Candy Maldonado	.15	.07
☐ 313	Chad Curtis	.30	.14
☐ 314	Tim Costo	.15	.07
☐ 315	Mike Robertson	.15	.07
☐ 316	Nigel Wilson	.15	.07
☐ 317	Greg McMichael	.15	.07
☐ 318	Scott Pose	.15	.07
☐ 319	Ivan Cruz	.15	.07
☐ 320	Greg Swindell	.15	.07
☐ 321	Kevin McReynolds	.15	.07
☐ 322	Tom Candiotti	.15	.07
☐ 323	Rob Wishnevski	.15	.07
☐ 324	Ken Hill	.15	.07
☐ 325	Kirby Puckett	1.25	.55
☐ 326	Tim Bogar	.15	.07
☐ 327	Mariano Rivera	.75	.35
☐ 328	Mitch Williams	.15	.07
☐ 329	Craig Paquette	.15	.07
☐ 330	Jay Bell	.30	.14
☐ 331	Jose Martinez	.15	.07
☐ 332	Rob Deer	.15	.07
☐ 333	Brook Fordyce	.15	.07
☐ 334	Matt Nokes	.15	.07
☐ 335	Derek Lee	.15	.07
☐ 336	Paul Ellis	.15	.07
☐ 337	Desi Wilson	.15	.07
☐ 338	Roberto Alomar	.60	.25
☐ 339	Jim Tatum FOIL	.15	.07
☐ 340	J.T. Snow FOIL	.60	.25
☐ 341	Tim Salmon FOIL	.75	.35
☐ 342	Russ Davis FOIL	1.00	.45
☐ 343	Javier Lopez FOIL	.60	.25
☐ 344	Troy O'Leary FOIL	.30	.14
☐ 345	Marty Cordova FOIL	1.50	.70
☐ 346	Bubba Smith FOIL	.15	.07
☐ 347	Chipper Jones FOIL	3.00	1.35
☐ 348	Jessie Hollins FOIL	.15	.07
☐ 349	Willie Greene FOIL	.30	.14
☐ 350	Mark Thompson FOIL	.30	.14
☐ 351	Nigel Wilson FOIL	.15	.07
☐ 352	Todd Jones FOIL	.30	.14
☐ 353	Raul Mondesi FOIL	.75	.35
☐ 354	Cliff Floyd FOIL	.30	.14
☐ 355	Bobby Jones FOIL	.30	.14
☐ 356	Kevin Stocker FOIL	.15	.07
☐ 357	Midre Cummings FOIL	.30	.14
☐ 358	Allen Watson FOIL	.15	.07
☐ 359	Ray McDavid FOIL	.15	.07
☐ 360	Steve Hosey FOIL	.15	.07
☐ 361	Brad Pennington FOIL	.15	.07
☐ 362	Frankie Rodriguez FOIL	1.15	.07
☐ 363	Troy Percival FOIL	.30	.14
☐ 364	Jason Bere FOIL	.30	.14
☐ 365	Manny Ramirez FOIL	1.25	.55
☐ 366	Justin Thompson FOIL	.75	.35
☐ 367	Joe Vitiello FOIL	.15	.07
☐ 368	Tyrone Hill FOIL	.15	.07
☐ 369	David McCarty FOIL	.15	.07
☐ 370	Brien Taylor FOIL	.15	.07
☐ 371	Todd Van Poppel FOIL	.15	.07
☐ 372	Marc Newfield FOIL	.30	.14
☐ 373	Terrell Lowery FOIL	.15	.07
☐ 374	Alex Gonzalez FOIL	.40	.18
☐ 375	Ken Griffey Jr.	3.00	1.35
☐ 376	Donovan Osborne	.15	.07
☐ 377	Ritchie Moody	.15	.07
☐ 378	Shane Andrews	.15	.07
☐ 379	Carlos Delgado	.60	.25
☐ 380	Bill Swift	.15	.07
☐ 381	Leo Gomez	.15	.07
☐ 382	Ron Gant	.30	.14
☐ 383	Scott Fletcher	.15	.07
☐ 384	Matt Walbeck	.15	.07
☐ 385	Chuck Finley	.15	.07
☐ 386	Kevin Mitchell	.30	.14
☐ 387	Wilson Alvarez UER	.30	.14
	(Misspelled Alverez on card front)		
☐ 388	John Burke	.15	.07
☐ 389	Alan Embree	.15	.07
☐ 390	Trevor Hoffman	.40	.18
☐ 391	Alan Trammell	.40	.18
☐ 392	Todd Jones	.30	.14
☐ 393	Felix Jose	.15	.07
☐ 394	Orel Hershiser	.15	.07
☐ 395	Pat Listach	.15	.07
☐ 396	Gabe White	.15	.07
☐ 397	Dan Serafini	.50	.23
☐ 398	Todd Hundley	.40	.18
☐ 399	Wade Boggs	.60	.25
☐ 400	Tyler Green	.15	.07
☐ 401	Mike Bordick	.15	.07
☐ 402	Scott Bullett	.15	.07
☐ 403	LaGrande Russell	.15	.07
☐ 404	Ray Lankford	.15	.07
☐ 405	Nolan Ryan	2.50	1.10
☐ 406	Robbie Beckett	.15	.07
☐ 407	Brent Bowers	.30	.14
☐ 408	Adell Davenport	.15	.07
☐ 409	Brady Anderson	.40	.18
☐ 410	Tom Glavine	.40	.18
☐ 411	Doug Hecker	.15	.07
☐ 412	Jose Guzman	.15	.07
☐ 413	Luis Polonia	.15	.07
☐ 414	Brian Williams	.15	.07
☐ 415	Bo Jackson	.30	.14
☐ 416	Eric Young	.60	.25
☐ 417	Kenny Lofton	1.25	.55
☐ 418	Orestes Destrade	.15	.07
☐ 419	Tony Phillips	.15	.07
☐ 420	Jeff Bagwell	1.25	.55

421	Mark Gardner	.15	.07
422	Brett Butler	.30	.14
423	Graeme Lloyd	.15	.07
424	Delino DeShields	.15	.07
425	Scott Erickson	.15	.07
426	Jeff Kent	.30	.14
427	Jimmy Key	.30	.14
428	Mickey Morandini	.15	.07
429	Marcos Armas	.15	.07
430	Don Slaught	.15	.07
431	Randy Johnson	.60	.25
432	Omar Olivares	.15	.07
433	Charlie Leibrandt	.15	.07
434	Kurt Stillwell	.15	.07
435	Scott Brow	.15	.07
436	Robby Thompson	.15	.07
437	Ben McDonald	.15	.07
438	Deion Sanders	.30	.14
439	Tony Pena	.15	.07
440	Mark Grace	.40	.18
441	Eduardo Perez	.15	.07
442	Tim Pugh	.15	.07
443	Scott Ruffcorn	.15	.07
444	Jay Gainer	.15	.07
445	Albert Belle	.75	.35
446	Bret Barberie	.15	.07
447	Justin Mashore	.15	.07
448	Pete Harnisch	.15	.07
449	Greg Gagne	.15	.07
450	Eric Davis	.15	.07
451	Dave Mlicki	.15	.07
452	Moises Alou	.30	.14
453	Rick Aguilera	.15	.07
454	Eddie Murray	.60	.25
455	Bob Wickman	.15	.07
456	Wes Chamberlain	.15	.07
457	Brent Gates	.15	.07
458	Paul Wagner	.15	.07
459	Mike Hampton	.40	.18
460	Ozzie Smith	.75	.35
461	Tom Henke	.15	.07
462	Ricky Gutierrez	.15	.07
463	Jack Morris	.30	.14
464	Joel Chimelis	.15	.07
465	Gregg Olson	.15	.07
466	Javier Lopez	.60	.25
467	Scott Cooper	.15	.07
468	Willie Wilson	.15	.07
469	Mark Langston	.15	.07
470	Barry Larkin	.40	.18
471	Rod Bolton	.15	.07
472	Freddie Benavides	.15	.07
473	Ken Ramos	.15	.07
474	Chuck Carr	.15	.07
475	Cecil Fielder	.30	.14
476	Eddie Taubensee	.15	.07
477	Chris Eddy	.15	.07
478	Greg Hansell	.15	.07
479	Kevin Reimer	.15	.07
480	Denny Martinez	.30	.14
481	Chuck Knoblauch	.60	.25
482	Mike Draper	.15	.07
483	Spike Owen	.15	.07
484	Terry Mulholland	.15	.07
485	Dennis Eckersley	.30	.14
486	Blas Minor	.15	.07
487	Dave Fleming	.15	.07
488	Dan Cholowsky	.15	.07
489	Ivan Rodriguez	.75	.35
490	Gary Sheffield	.60	.25
491	Ed Sprague	.15	.07
492	Steve Hosey	.15	.07
493	Jimmy Haynes	.60	.25
494	John Smoltz	.30	.14
495	Andre Dawson	.40	.18
496	Rey Sanchez	.15	.07
497	Ty Van Burkleo	.15	.07
498	Bobby Ayala	.15	.07
499	Tim Raines	.30	.14
500	Charlie Hayes	.15	.07
501	Paul Sorrento	.15	.07
502	Richie Lewis	.15	.07
503	Jason Pfaff	.15	.07
504	Ken Caminiti	.40	.18
505	Mike Macfarlane	.15	.07
506	Jody Reed	.15	.07
507	Bobby Hughes	.15	.07
508	Wil Cordero	.15	.07
509	George Tsamis	.15	.07
510	Bret Saberhagen	.15	.07
511	Derek Jeter	8.00	3.60
512	Gene Schall	.15	.07
513	Curtis Shaw	.15	.07
514	Steve Cooke	.15	.07
515	Edgar Martinez	.40	.18
516	Mike Milchin	.15	.07
517	Billy Ripken	.15	.07
518	Andy Benes	.30	.14
519	Juan de la Rosa	.15	.07
520	John Burkett	.15	.07
521	Alex Ochoa	.15	.07
522	Tony Tarasco	.15	.07
523	Luis Ortiz	.15	.07
524	Rick Wilkins	.15	.07
525	Chris Turner	.15	.07
526	Rob Dibble	.15	.07
527	Jack McDowell	.15	.07
528	Daryl Boston	.15	.07
529	Bill Wertz	.15	.07
530	Charlie Hough	.15	.07
531	Sean Bergman	.15	.07
532	Doug Jones	.15	.07
533	Jeff Montgomery	.30	.14
534	Roger Cedeno	.75	.35
535	Robin Yount	.40	.18
536	Mo Vaughn	.75	.35
537	Brian Harper	.15	.07
538	Juan Castillo	.15	.07
539	Steve Farr	.15	.07
540	John Kruk	.30	.14
541	Troy Neel	.15	.07
542	Danny Clyburn	1.00	.45
543	Jim Converse	.15	.07
544	Gregg Jefferies	.30	.14
545	Jose Canseco	.40	.18
546	Julio Bruno	.15	.07
547	Rob Butler	.15	.07
548	Royce Clayton	.15	.07
549	Chris Hoiles	.15	.07
550	Greg Maddux	2.00	.90
551	Joe Ciccarella	.15	.07
552	Ozzie Timmons	.30	.14
553	Chili Davis	.30	.14
554	Brian Koelling	.15	.07
555	Frank Thomas	2.50	1.10
556	Vinny Castilla	.60	.25
557	Reggie Jefferson	.15	.07
558	Rob Natal	.15	.07
559	Mike Henneman	.15	.07
560	Craig Biggio	.40	.18
561	Billy Brewer	.15	.07
562	Dan Melendez	.15	.07
563	Kenny Felder	.15	.07
564	Miguel Batista	.15	.07
565	Dave Winfield	.40	.18
566	Al Shirley	.30	.14
567	Robert Eenhoorn	.15	.07
568	Mike Williams	.15	.07
569	Tanyon Sturtze	.30	.14
570	Tim Wakefield	.30	.14
571	Greg Pirkl	.15	.07
572	Sean Lowe	.15	.07
573	Terry Burrows	.15	.07
574	Kevin Higgins	.15	.07
575	Joe Carter	.30	.14
576	Kevin Rogers	.15	.07
577	Manny Alexander	.15	.07
578	David Justice	.60	.25
579	Brian Conroy	.15	.07
580	Jesse Hollins	.15	.07
581	Ron Watson	.15	.07
582	Bip Roberts	.15	.07
583	Tom Urbani	.15	.07
584	Jason Hutchins	.15	.07
585	Carlos Baerga	.15	.07
586	Jeff Mutis	.15	.07
587	Justin Thompson	.75	.35
588	Orlando Miller	.30	.14
589	Brian McRae	.15	.07
590	Ramon Martinez	.30	.14
591	Dave Nilsson	.30	.14
592	Jose Vidro	.50	.23
593	Rich Becker	.30	.14
594	Preston Wilson	1.50	.70
595	Don Mattingly	1.00	.45
596	Tony Longmire	.15	.07
597	Kevin Seitzer	.15	.07
598	Midre Cummings	.30	.14
599	Omar Vizquel	.30	.14
600	Lee Smith	.30	.14
601	David Hulse	.15	.07
602	Darrell Sherman	.15	.07
603	Alex Gonzalez	.40	.18
604	Geronimo Pena	.15	.07
605	Mike Devereaux	.15	.07
606	Sterling Hitchcock	.30	.14
607	Mike Greenwell	.15	.07
608	Steve Buechele	.15	.07
609	Troy Percival	.15	.07
610	Roberto Kelly	.15	.07
611	James Baldwin	1.00	.45
612	Jerald Clark	.15	.07
613	Albie Lopez	.30	.14
614	Dave Magadan	.15	.07
615	Mickey Tettleton	.15	.07
616	Sean Runyan	.15	.07
617	Bob Hamelin	.15	.07
618	Raul Mondesi	.75	.35
619	Tyrone Hill	.15	.07
620	Darrin Fletcher	.15	.07
621	Mike Trombley	.15	.07
622	Jeromy Burnitz	.15	.07
623	Bernie Williams	.60	.25
624	Mike Farmer	.15	.07
625	Rickey Henderson	.40	.18
626	Carlos Garcia	.15	.07
627	Jeff Darwin	.15	.07
628	Todd Zeile	.15	.07
629	Benji Gil	.15	.07
630	Tony Gwynn	1.50	.70
631	Aaron Small	.15	.07
632	Joe Rosselli	.15	.07
633	Mike Mussina	.60	.25
634	Ryan Klesko	.75	.35
635	Roger Clemens	1.25	.55
636	Sammy Sosa	.60	.25
637	Orlando Palmeiro	.15	.07
638	Willie Greene	.30	.14
639	George Bell	.15	.07
640	Garvin Alston	.15	.07
641	Pete Janicki	.15	.07
642	Chris Sheff	.15	.07
643	Felipe Lira	.30	.14
644	Roberto Petagine	.15	.07
645	Wally Joyner	.30	.14
646	Mike Piazza	3.00	1.35
647	Jaime Navarro	.15	.07
648	Jeff Hartsock	.15	.07
649	David McCarty	.15	.07
650	Bobby Jones	.30	.14
651	Mark Hutton	.15	.07
652	Kyle Abbott	.15	.07
653	Steve Cox	.50	.23
654	Jeff King	.30	.14
655	Norm Charlton	.15	.07
656	Mike Gulan	.15	.07
657	Julio Franco	.15	.07
658	Cameron Cairncross	.15	.07
659	John Olerud	.30	.14
660	Salomon Torres	.15	.07
661	Brad Pennington	.15	.07
662	Melvin Nieves	.40	.18
663	Ivan Calderon	.15	.07
664	Turk Wendell	.15	.07
665	Chris Pritchett	.15	.07
666	Reggie Sanders	.30	.14
667	Robin Ventura	.30	.14
668	Joe Girardi	.15	.07
669	Manny Ramirez	1.25	.55
670	Jeff Conine	.30	.14
671	Greg Gohr	.15	.07
672	Andujar Cedeno	.15	.07
673	Les Norman	.15	.07
674	Mike James	.15	.07
675	Marshall Boze	.15	.07
676	B.J. Wallace	.15	.07
677	Kent Hrbek	.30	.14
678	Jack Voigt	.15	.07

		MINT	NRMT
□ 679	Brien Taylor	.15	.07
□ 680	Curt Schilling	.15	.07
□ 681	Todd Van Poppel	.15	.07
□ 682	Kevin Young	.15	.07
□ 683	Tommy Adams	.15	.07
□ 684	Bernard Gilkey	.30	.14
□ 685	Kevin Brown	.30	.14
□ 686	Fred McGriff	.40	.18
□ 687	Pat Borders	.15	.07
□ 688	Kirt Manwaring	.15	.07
□ 689	Sid Bream	.15	.07
□ 690	John Valentin	.30	.14
□ 691	Steve Olsen	.15	.07
□ 692	Roberto Mejia	.15	.07
□ 693	Carlos Delgado FOIL	.60	.25
□ 694	Steve Gibralter FOIL	.30	.14
□ 695	Gary Mota FOIL	.15	.07
□ 696	Jose Malave FOIL	.15	.07
□ 697	Larry Sutton FOIL	.15	.07
□ 698	Dan Frye FOIL	.15	.07
□ 699	Tim Clark FOIL	.15	.07
□ 700	Brian Rupp FOIL Moises Alou	.15	.07
□ 701	Felipe Alou FOIL	.30	.14
□ 702	Barry Bonds FOIL Bobby Bonds	.60	.25
□ 703	Ken Griffey Sr. FOIL Ken Griffey Jr.	1.00	.45
□ 704	Brian McRae FOIL Hal McRae	.15	.07
□ 705	Checklist 1	.15	.07
□ 706	Checklist 2	.15	.07
□ 707	Checklist 3	.15	.07
□ 708	Checklist 4	.15	.07

1994 Bowman Previews

This 10-card standard-size set served as a preview to the 1994 Bowman set. The cards were randomly inserted one in every 24 1994 Stadium Club second series packs. The cards were similar to the full-bleed basic issue. The differences are a multi-colored foil stripe up the left-hand border with a red stripe at bottom. Red foil also surrounds the Bowman logo. In the upper right-hand corner is a blue 1994 Bowman Preview logo. The backs are identical to the basic issue with a horizontal layout containing a player photo, text and statistics.

	MINT	NRMT
COMPLETE SET (10)	40.00	18.00
COMMON CARD (1-10)	1.00	.45
SEMISTARS	2.50	1.10
UNLISTED STARS	4.00	1.80
STATED ODDS 1:24 SER.2 STADIUM CLUB		

□ 1	Frank Thomas	15.00	6.75
□ 2	Mike Piazza	12.00	5.50

□ 3	Albert Belle	5.00	2.20
□ 4	Javier Lopez	2.50	1.10
□ 5	Cliff Floyd	.90	.90
□ 6	Alex Gonzalez	2.00	.90
□ 7	Ricky Bottalico	4.00	1.80
□ 8	Tony Clark	10.00	4.50
□ 9	Mac Suzuki	2.00	.90
□ 10	James Mouton Foil	1.00	.45

1994 Bowman

The 1994 Bowman set consists of 682 standard-size, full-bleed cards primarily distributed in plastic wrap packs and jumbo packs. In addition to a color photo on the front, there is a line of gold foil that runs up the far left side and across the bottom of the card. The player's name is also in gold foil at bottom and the Bowman logo at bottom left is enclosed in gold foil. Horizontal backs contain a player photo on the left and statistics and highlights on the right. There are 51 Foil cards (337-388) that include a number of top young stars and prospects. These foil cards were issued one per foil pack and two per jumbo. Rookie Cards of note include Alan Benes, Tony Clark, Brad Fullmer, Derrek Lee, Chan Ho Park, Edgar Renteria and Ruben Rivera.

	MINT	NRMT
COMPLETE SET (682)	125.00	55.00
COMMON CARD (1-682)	.20	.09
MINOR STARS	.40	.18
UNLISTED STARS	.75	.35

□ 1	Joe Carter	.40	.18
□ 2	Marcus Moore	.20	.09
□ 3	Doug Creek	.20	.09
□ 4	Pedro Martinez	.75	.35
□ 5	Ken Griffey Jr.	4.00	1.80
□ 6	Greg Swindell	.20	.09
□ 7	J.J. Johnson	.20	.09
□ 8	Homer Bush	.40	.18
□ 9	Arquimedez Pozo	.60	.25
□ 10	Bryan Harvey	.20	.09
□ 11	J.T. Snow	.75	.35
□ 12	Alan Benes	4.00	1.80
□ 13	Chad Kreuter	.20	.09
□ 14	Eric Karros	.40	.18
□ 15	Frank Thomas	3.00	1.35
□ 16	Bret Saberhagen	.40	.18
□ 17	Terrell Lowery	.20	.09
□ 18	Rod Bolton	.20	.09
□ 19	Harold Baines	.40	.18
□ 20	Matt Walbeck	.20	.09
□ 21	Tom Glavine	.40	.18
□ 22	Todd Jones	.20	.09
□ 23	Alberto Castillo	.40	.18
□ 24	Ruben Sierra	.40	.09

□ 25	Don Mattingly	1.25	.55
□ 26	Mike Morgan	.20	.09
□ 27	Jim Musselwhite	.40	.18
□ 28	Matt Brunson	.20	.09
□ 29	Adam Meinershagen	.20	.09
□ 30	Joe Girardi	.20	.09
□ 31	Shane Halter	.20	.09
□ 32	Jose Paniagua	.40	.18
□ 33	Paul Perkins	.20	.09
□ 34	John Hudek	.20	.09
□ 35	Frank Viola	.20	.09
□ 36	David Lamb	.20	.09
□ 37	Marshall Boze	.20	.09
□ 38	Jorge Posada	.40	.18
□ 39	Brian Anderson	1.00	.45
□ 40	Mark Whiten	.20	.09
□ 41	Sean Bergman	.40	.09
□ 42	Jose Parra	.40	.18
□ 43	Mike Robertson	.20	.09
□ 44	Pete Walker	.20	.09
□ 45	Juan Gonzalez	2.00	.90
□ 46	Cleveland Ladell	.20	.18
□ 47	Mark Smith	.20	.09
□ 48	Kevin Jarvis UER (team listed as Yankees on back)	.20	.09
□ 49	Amaury Telemaco	1.00	.45
□ 50	Andy Van Slyke	.40	.18
□ 51	Rikkert Faneyte	.20	.09
□ 52	Curtis Shaw	.20	.09
□ 53	Matt Drews	.50	.23
□ 54	Wilson Alvarez	.20	.09
□ 55	Manny Ramirez	1.00	.45
□ 56	Bobby Munoz	.20	.09
□ 57	Ed Sprague	.20	.09
□ 58	Jamey Wright	1.50	.70
□ 59	Jeff Montgomery	.20	.09
□ 60	Kirk Rueter	.20	.09
□ 61	Edgar Martinez	.60	.25
□ 62	Luis Gonzalez	.20	.09
□ 63	Tim Vanegmond	.20	.09
□ 64	Bip Roberts	.20	.09
□ 65	John Jaha	.20	.09
□ 66	Chuck Carr	.20	.09
□ 67	Chuck Finley	.20	.09
□ 68	Aaron Holbert	.20	.09
□ 69	Cecil Fielder	.40	.18
□ 70	Tom Engle	.20	.09
□ 71	Ron Karkovice	.20	.09
□ 72	Joe Orsulak	.20	.09
□ 73	Duff Brumley	.20	.09
□ 74	Craig Clayton	.20	.09
□ 75	Cal Ripken	3.00	1.35
□ 76	Brad Fullmer	5.00	2.20
□ 77	Tony Tarasco	.20	.09
□ 78	Terry Farrar	.20	.09
□ 79	Matt Williams	.60	.25
□ 80	Rickey Henderson	.60	.25
□ 81	Terry Mulholland	.20	.09
□ 82	Sammy Sosa	.75	.35
□ 83	Paul Sorrento	.20	.09
□ 84	Pete Incaviglia	.20	.09
□ 85	Darren Hall	.20	.09
□ 86	Scott Klingenbeck	.20	.09
□ 87	Dario Perez	.20	.09
□ 88	Ugueth Urbina	.40	.18
□ 89	Dave Vanhof	.20	.09
□ 90	Domingo Jean	.20	.09
□ 91	Otis Nixon	.20	.09
□ 92	Andres Berumen	.20	.09
□ 93	Jose Valentin	.20	.09
□ 94	Edgar Renteria	4.00	1.80
□ 95	Chris Turner	.20	.09
□ 96	Ray Lankford	.40	.18
□ 97	Danny Bautista	.20	.09
□ 98	Chan Ho Park	6.00	2.70
□ 99	Glenn DiSarcina	.40	.09
□ 100	Butch Huskey	.40	.18
□ 101	Ivan Rodriguez	1.00	.45
□ 102	Johnny Ruffin	.20	.09
□ 103	Alex Ochoa	.20	.09
□ 104	Torii Hunter	.75	.35
□ 105	Ryan Klesko	.75	.35
□ 106	Jay Bell	.40	.18
□ 107	Kurt Peltzer	.20	.09
□ 108	Miguel Jimenez	.20	.09
□ 109	Russ Davis	.40	.18

☐ 110	Derek Wallace	.20	.09
☐ 111	Keith Lockhart	.20	.09
☐ 112	Mike Lieberthal	.20	.09
☐ 113	Dave Stewart	.40	.18
☐ 114	Tom Schmidt	.20	.09
☐ 115	Brian McRae	.20	.09
☐ 116	Moises Alou	.40	.18
☐ 117	Dave Fleming	.20	.09
☐ 118	Jeff Bagwell	1.50	.70
☐ 119	Luis Ortiz	.20	.09
☐ 120	Tony Gwynn	2.00	.90
☐ 121	Jaime Navarro	.20	.09
☐ 122	Benny Santiago	.20	.09
☐ 123	Darrell Whitmore	.20	.09
☐ 124	John Mabry	.75	.35
☐ 125	Mickey Tettleton	.20	.09
☐ 126	Tom Candiotti	.20	.09
☐ 127	Tim Raines	.40	.18
☐ 128	Bobby Bonilla	.40	.18
☐ 129	John Dettmer	.20	.09
☐ 130	Hector Carrasco	.20	.09
☐ 131	Chris Hoiles	.20	.09
☐ 132	Rick Aguilera	.20	.09
☐ 133	David Justice	.75	.35
☐ 134	Esteban Loaiza	1.00	.45
☐ 135	Barry Bonds	1.00	.45
☐ 136	Bob Welch	.20	.09
☐ 137	Mike Stanley	.20	.09
☐ 138	Roberto Hernandez	.20	.09
☐ 139	Sandy Alomar	.40	.18
☐ 140	Darren Daulton	.40	.18
☐ 141	Angel Martinez	.40	.18
☐ 142	Howard Johnson	.20	.09
☐ 143	Bob Hamelin UER	.20	.09

(name and card number colors don't match)

☐ 144	J.J. Thobe	.20	.09
☐ 145	Roger Salkeld	.20	.09
☐ 146	Orlando Miller	.20	.09
☐ 147	Dmitri Young	.60	.25
☐ 148	Tim Hyers	.20	.09
☐ 149	Mark Loretta	.20	.09
☐ 150	Chris Hammond	.20	.09
☐ 151	Joel Moore	.20	.09
☐ 152	Todd Zelle	.20	.09
☐ 153	Wil Cordero	.20	.09
☐ 154	Chris Smith	.20	.09
☐ 155	James Baldwin	.40	.18
☐ 156	Edgardo Alfonzo	3.00	1.35
☐ 157	Kym Ashworth	.40	.18
☐ 158	Paul Bako	.20	.09
☐ 159	Rick Krivda	.20	.09
☐ 160	Pat Mahomes	.20	.09
☐ 161	Damon Hollins	.40	.18
☐ 162	Felix Martinez	.50	.23
☐ 163	Jason Myers	.40	.18
☐ 164	Izzy Molina	.20	.09
☐ 165	Brien Taylor	.20	.09
☐ 166	Kevin Orie	3.00	1.35
☐ 167	Casey Whitten	.40	.18
☐ 168	Tony Longmire	.20	.09
☐ 169	John Olerud	.40	.18
☐ 170	Mark Thompson	.20	.09
☐ 171	Jorge Fabregas	.20	.09
☐ 172	John Wetteland	.20	.09
☐ 173	Dan Wilson	.40	.18
☐ 174	Doug Drabek	.20	.09
☐ 175	Jeffrey McNeely	.20	.09
☐ 176	Melvin Nieves	.20	.09
☐ 177	Doug Glanville	.40	.18
☐ 178	Javier De La Hoya	.20	.09
☐ 179	Chad Curtis	.20	.09
☐ 180	Brian Barber	.20	.09
☐ 181	Mike Henneman	.20	.09
☐ 182	Jose Offerman	.20	.09
☐ 183	Robert Ellis	.20	.09
☐ 184	John Franco	.40	.18
☐ 185	Benji Gil	.20	.09
☐ 186	Hal Morris	.20	.09
☐ 187	Chris Sabo	.20	.09
☐ 188	Blaise Ilsley	.20	.09
☐ 189	Steve Avery	.20	.09
☐ 190	Rick White	.20	.09
☐ 191	Rod Beck	.20	.09
☐ 192	Mark McGwire UER	1.50	.70

(No card number on back)

☐ 193	Jim Abbott	.20	.09
☐ 194	Randy Myers	.20	.09
☐ 195	Kenny Lofton	1.00	.45
☐ 196	Mariano Duncan	.20	.09
☐ 197	Lee Daniels	.20	.09
☐ 198	Armando Reynoso	.20	.09
☐ 199	Joe Randa	.40	.18
☐ 200	Cliff Floyd	.40	.18
☐ 201	Tim Harkrider	.20	.09
☐ 202	Kevin Gallaher	.20	.09
☐ 203	Scott Cooper	.20	.09
☐ 204	Phil Stidham	.20	.09
☐ 205	Jeff D'Amico	1.50	.70
☐ 206	Matt Whisenant	.20	.09
☐ 207	De Shawn Warren	.40	.18
☐ 208	Rene Arocha	.20	.09
☐ 209	Tony Clark	15.00	6.75
☐ 210	Jason Jacome	.20	.09
☐ 211	Scott Christman	.40	.18
☐ 212	Bill Pulsipher	.40	.18
☐ 213	Dean Palmer	.20	.09
☐ 214	Chad Mottola	.20	.09
☐ 215	Manny Alexander	.20	.09
☐ 216	Rich Becker	.20	.09
☐ 217	Andre King	.20	.09
☐ 218	Carlos Garcia	.20	.09
☐ 219	Ron Pezzoni	.20	.09
☐ 220	Steve Karsay	.20	.09
☐ 221	Jose Musset	.20	.09
☐ 222	Karl Rhodes	.20	.09
☐ 223	Frank Cimorelli	.20	.09
☐ 224	Kevin Jordan	.20	.09
☐ 225	Duane Ward	.20	.09
☐ 226	John Burke	.20	.09
☐ 227	Mike Macfarlane	.20	.09
☐ 228	Mike Lansing	.40	.18
☐ 229	Chuck Knoblauch	.75	.35
☐ 230	Ken Caminiti	.60	.25
☐ 231	Gar Finnvold	.20	.09
☐ 232	Derrek Lee	10.00	4.50
☐ 233	Brady Anderson	.60	.25
☐ 234	Vic Darensbourg	.20	.09
☐ 235	Mark Langston	.20	.09
☐ 236	T.J. Mathews	.40	.18
☐ 237	Lou Whitaker	.40	.18
☐ 238	Roger Cedeno	.60	.25
☐ 239	Alex Fernandez	.20	.09
☐ 240	Ryan Thompson	.20	.09
☐ 241	Kerry Lacy	.20	.09
☐ 242	Reggie Sanders	.20	.09
☐ 243	Brad Pennington	.20	.09
☐ 244	Bryan Eversgerd	.20	.09
☐ 245	Greg Maddux	2.50	1.10
☐ 246	Jason Kendall	.75	.35
☐ 247	J.R. Phillips	.20	.09
☐ 248	Bobby Witt	.20	.09
☐ 249	Paul O'Neill	.40	.18
☐ 250	Ryne Sandberg	1.00	.45
☐ 251	Charles Nagy	.40	.18
☐ 252	Kevin Stocker	.20	.09
☐ 253	Shawn Green	.40	.18
☐ 254	Charlie Hayes	.20	.09
☐ 255	Donnie Elliott	.20	.09
☐ 256	Rob Fitzpatrick	.20	.09
☐ 257	Tim Davis	.20	.09
☐ 258	James Mouton	.20	.09
☐ 259	Mike Greenwell	.20	.09
☐ 260	Ray McDavid	.20	.09
☐ 261	Mike Kelly	.20	.09
☐ 262	Andy Larkin	.40	.18
☐ 263	Marquis Riley UER	.20	.09

(No card number on back)

☐ 264	Bob Tewksbury	.20	.09
☐ 265	Brian Edmondson	.20	.09
☐ 266	Eduardo Lantigua	.40	.18
☐ 267	Brandon Wilson	.20	.09
☐ 268	Mike Welch	.20	.09
☐ 269	Tom Henke	.20	.09
☐ 270	Calvin Reese	.40	.18
☐ 271	Greg Zaun	.20	.09
☐ 272	Todd Ritchie	.20	.09
☐ 273	Javier Lopez	.60	.25
☐ 274	Kevin Young	.20	.09
☐ 275	Kirt Manwaring	.20	.09
☐ 276	Bill Taylor	.20	.09
☐ 277	Robert Eenhoorn	.20	.09

☐ 278	Jessie Hollins	.20	.09
☐ 279	Julian Tavarez	.40	.18
☐ 280	Gene Schall	.20	.09
☐ 281	Paul Molitor	.75	.35
☐ 282	Neifi Perez	3.00	1.35
☐ 283	Greg Gagne	.20	.09
☐ 284	Marquis Grissom	.40	.18
☐ 285	Randy Johnson	.75	.35
☐ 286	Pete Harnisch	.20	.09
☐ 287	Joel Bennett	.20	.09
☐ 288	Derek Bell	.20	.09
☐ 289	Darryl Hamilton	.20	.09
☐ 290	Gary Sheffield	.75	.35
☐ 291	Eduardo Perez	.20	.09
☐ 292	Basil Shabazz	.20	.09
☐ 293	Eric Davis	.40	.18
☐ 294	Pedro Astacio	.20	.09
☐ 295	Robin Ventura	.40	.18
☐ 296	Jeff Kent	.20	.09
☐ 297	Rick Helling	.20	.09
☐ 298	Joe Oliver	.20	.09
☐ 299	Lee Smith	.40	.18
☐ 300	Dave Winfield	.60	.25
☐ 301	Deion Sanders	.40	.18
☐ 302	Ravelo Manzanillo	.20	.09
☐ 303	Mark Portugal	.20	.09
☐ 304	Brent Gates	.20	.09
☐ 305	Wade Boggs	.75	.35
☐ 306	Rick Wilkins	.20	.09
☐ 307	Carlos Baerga	.20	.09
☐ 308	Curt Schilling	.40	.18
☐ 309	Shannon Stewart	1.00	.45
☐ 310	Darren Holmes	.20	.09
☐ 311	Robert Toth	.20	.09
☐ 312	Gabe White	.20	.09
☐ 313	Mac Suzuki	.40	.18
☐ 314	Alvin Morman	.20	.09
☐ 315	Mo Vaughn	1.00	.45
☐ 316	Bryce Florie	.20	.09
☐ 317	Gabby Martinez	.50	.23
☐ 318	Carl Everett	.20	.09
☐ 319	Kerwin Moore	.20	.09
☐ 320	Tom Pagnozzi	.20	.09
☐ 321	Chris Gomez	.20	.09
☐ 322	Todd Williams	.20	.09
☐ 323	Pat Hentgen	.40	.18
☐ 324	Kirk Presley	.40	.18
☐ 325	Kevin Brown	.40	.18
☐ 326	Jason Isringhausen	1.50	.70
☐ 327	Rick Forney	.20	.09
☐ 328	Carlos Pulido	.20	.09
☐ 329	Terrell Wade	.40	.18
☐ 330	Al Martin	.20	.09
☐ 331	Dan Carlson	.20	.09
☐ 332	Mark Acre	.20	.09
☐ 333	Sterling Hitchcock	.20	.09
☐ 334	Jon Ratliff	.40	.18
☐ 335	Alex Ramirez	1.50	.70
☐ 336	Phil Geisler	.20	.09
☐ 337	Eddie Zambrano FOIL	.20	.09
☐ 338	Jim Thome FOIL	1.00	.45
☐ 339	James Mouton FOIL	.20	.09
☐ 340	Cliff Floyd FOIL	.40	.18
☐ 341	Carlos Delgado FOIL	.60	.25
☐ 342	Roberto Petagine FOIL	.20	.09
☐ 343	Tim Clark FOIL	.20	.09
☐ 344	Bubba Smith FOIL	.20	.09
☐ 345	Randy Curtis FOIL	.20	.09
☐ 346	Joe Biasucci FOIL	.20	.09
☐ 347	D.J. Boston FOIL	.20	.09
☐ 348	Ruben Rivera FOIL	6.00	2.70
☐ 349	Bryan Link FOIL	.20	.09
☐ 350	Mike Bell FOIL	.75	.35
☐ 351	Marty Watson FOIL	.20	.09
☐ 352	Jason Myers FOIL	.40	.18
☐ 353	Chipper Jones FOIL	2.50	1.10
☐ 354	Brooks Kieschnick FOIL	1.00	.45
☐ 355	Calvin Reese FOIL	.40	.18
☐ 356	John Burke FOIL	.20	.09
☐ 357	Kurt Miller FOIL	.20	.09
☐ 358	Orlando Miller FOIL	.20	.09
☐ 359	Todd Hollandsworth FOIL	.60	.25
☐ 360	Rondell White FOIL	.60	.25
☐ 361	Bill Pulsipher FOIL	.20	.09
☐ 362	Tyler Green FOIL	.20	.09
☐ 363	Midre Cummings FOIL	.20	.09

364	Brian Barber FOIL	.20	.09
365	Melvin Nieves FOIL	.20	.09
366	Salomon Torres FOIL	.20	.09
367	Alex Ochoa FOIL	.20	.09
368	Frankie Rodriguez FOIL	.20	.09
369	Brian Anderson FOIL	1.00	.45
370	James Baldwin FOIL	.40	.18
371	Manny Ramirez FOIL	1.00	.45
372	Justin Thompson FOIL	1.00	.45
373	Johnny Damon FOIL	.75	.35
374	Jeff D'Amico FOIL	1.50	.70
375	Rich Becker FOIL	.20	.09
376	Derek Jeter FOIL	3.00	1.35
377	Steve Karsay FOIL	.40	.18
378	Mac Suzuki FOIL	.40	.18
379	Benji Gil FOIL	.20	.09
380	Alex Gonzalez FOIL	.40	.18
381	Jason Bere FOIL	.20	.09
382	Brett Butler FOIL	.40	.18
383	Jeff Conine FOIL	.40	.18
384	Darren Daulton FOIL	.40	.18
385	Jeff Kent FOIL	.20	.09
386	Don Mattingly FOIL	1.25	.55
387	Mike Piazza FOIL	2.50	1.10
388	Ryne Sandberg FOIL	1.00	.45
389	Rich Amaral	.20	.09
390	Craig Biggio	.60	.25
391	Jeff Suppan	2.00	.90
392	Andy Benes	.40	.18
393	Cal Eldred	.20	.09
394	Jeff Conine	.40	.18
395	Tim Salmon	.75	.35
396	Ray Suplee	.20	.09
397	Tony Phillips	.20	.09
398	Ramon Martinez	.40	.18
399	Julio Franco	.20	.09
400	Dwight Gooden	.40	.18
401	Kevin Lomon	.20	.09
402	Jose Rijo	.20	.09
403	Mike Devereaux	.20	.09
404	Mike Zolecki	.20	.09
405	Fred McGriff	.60	.25
406	Danny Clyburn	.40	.18
407	Robby Thompson	.20	.09
408	Terry Steinbach	.20	.09
409	Luis Polonia	.20	.09
410	Mark Grace	.60	.25
411	Albert Belle	1.00	.45
412	John Kruk	.40	.18
413	Scott Spiezio	2.50	1.10
414	Ellis Burks UER	.40	.18
	(Name spelled Elkis on front)		
415	Joe Vitiello	.20	.09
416	Tim Costo	.20	.09
417	Marc Newfield	.40	.18
418	Oscar Henriquez	.50	.23
419	Matt Perisho	1.00	.45
420	Julio Bruno	.20	.09
421	Kenny Felder	.20	.09
422	Tyler Green	.20	.09
423	Jim Edmonds	.75	.35
424	Ozzie Smith	1.00	.45
425	Rick Greene	.20	.09
426	Todd Hollandsworth	.60	.25
427	Eddie Pearson	.40	.18
428	Quilvio Veras	.40	.18
429	Kenny Rogers	.20	.09
430	Willie Greene	.20	.09
431	Vaughn Eshelman	.20	.09
432	Pat Meares	.20	.09
433	Jermaine Dye	2.00	.90
434	Steve Cooke	.20	.09
435	Bill Swift	.20	.09
436	Fausto Cruz	.20	.09
437	Mark Hutton	.20	.09
438	Brooks Kieschnick	1.00	.45
439	Yorkis Perez	.20	.09
440	Len Dykstra	.40	.18
441	Pat Borders	.20	.09
442	Doug Walls	.40	.18
443	Wally Joyner	.40	.18
444	Ken Hill	.20	.09
445	Eric Anthony	.20	.09
446	Mitch Williams	.20	.09
447	Cory Bailey	.20	.09
448	Dave Staton	.20	.09
449	Greg Vaughn	.20	.09
450	Dave Magadan	.20	.09
451	Chili Davis	.40	.18
452	Gerald Santos	.20	.09
453	Joe Perona	.20	.09
454	Delino DeShields	.20	.09
455	Jack McDowell	.40	.18
456	Todd Hundley	.40	.18
457	Ritchie Moody	.20	.09
458	Bret Boone	.20	.09
459	Ben McDonald	.40	.18
460	Kirby Puckett	1.50	.70
461	Gregg Olson	.20	.09
462	Rich Aude	.20	.09
463	John Burkett	.20	.09
464	Troy Neel	.20	.09
465	Jimmy Key	.40	.18
466	Ozzie Timmons	.20	.09
467	Eddie Murray	.75	.35
468	Mark Tranberg	.20	.09
469	Alex Gonzalez	.40	.18
470	David Nied	.20	.09
471	Barry Larkin	.60	.25
472	Brian Looney	.20	.09
473	Shawn Estes	1.00	.45
474	A.J. Sager	.20	.09
475	Roger Clemens	1.50	.70
476	Vince Moore	.20	.09
477	Scott Karl	.40	.18
478	Kurt Miller	.20	.09
479	Garret Anderson	.75	.35
480	Allen Watson	.20	.09
481	Jose Lima	.40	.18
482	Rick Gorecki	.20	.09
483	Jimmy Hurst	.20	.09
484	Preston Wilson	.75	.35
485	Will Clark	.60	.25
486	Mike Ferry	.20	.09
487	Curtis Goodwin	.40	.18
488	Mike Myers	.20	.09
489	Chipper Jones	2.50	1.10
490	Jeff King	.20	.09
491	William VanLandingham	.40	.18
492	Carlos Reyes	.20	.09
493	Andy Pettitte	1.50	.70
494	Brant Brown	.20	.09
495	Daron Kirkreit	.20	.09
496	Ricky Bottalico	1.00	.45
497	Devon White	.20	.09
498	Jason Johnson	.20	.09
499	Vince Coleman	.20	.09
500	Larry Walker	.75	.35
501	Bobby Ayala	.20	.09
502	Steve Finley	.40	.18
503	Scott Fletcher	.20	.09
504	Brad Ausmus	.20	.09
505	Scott Talanca	.20	.09
506	Orestes Destrade	.20	.09
507	Gary DiSarcina	.20	.09
508	Willie Smith	.20	.09
509	Alan Trammell	.60	.25
510	Mike Piazza	2.50	1.10
511	Ozzie Guillen	.20	.09
512	Jeromy Burnitz	.20	.09
513	Darren Oliver	1.00	.45
514	Kevin Mitchell	.20	.09
515	Rafael Palmeiro	.60	.25
516	David McCarty	.20	.09
517	Jeff Blauser	.20	.09
518	Trey Beamon	.40	.18
519	Royce Clayton	.20	.09
520	Dennis Eckersley	.40	.18
521	Bernie Williams	.75	.35
522	Steve Buechele	.20	.09
523	Denny Martinez	.40	.18
524	Dave Hollins	.20	.09
525	Joey Hamilton	.75	.35
526	Andres Galarraga	.75	.35
527	Jeff Granger	.20	.09
528	Joey Eischen	.20	.09
529	Desi Relaford	.40	.18
530	Roberto Petagine	.20	.09
531	Andre Dawson	.60	.25
532	Ray Holbert	.20	.09
533	Duane Singleton	.20	.09
534	Kurt Abbott	.20	.09
535	Bo Jackson	.40	.18
536	Gregg Jefferies	.20	.09
537	David Mysel	.20	.09
538	Raul Mondesi	.75	.35
539	Chris Snopek	.20	.09
540	Brook Fordyce	.20	.09
541	Ron Frazier	.20	.09
542	Brian Koelling	.20	.09
543	Jimmy Haynes	.40	.18
544	Marty Cordova	.75	.35
545	Jason Green	.40	.18
546	Orlando Merced	.20	.09
547	Lou Pote	.20	.09
548	Todd Van Poppel	.20	.09
549	Pat Kelly	.20	.09
550	Turk Wendell	.20	.09
551	Herbert Perry	.20	.09
552	Ryan Karp	.20	.09
553	Juan Guzman	.40	.18
554	Bryan Rekar	.40	.18
555	Kevin Appier	.40	.18
556	Chris Schwab	.20	.09
557	Jay Buhner	.60	.25
558	Andujar Cedeno	.20	.09
559	Ryan McGuire	.40	.18
560	Ricky Gutierrez	.20	.09
561	Keith Kimsey	.20	.09
562	Tim Clark	.20	.09
563	Damion Easley	.20	.09
564	Clint Davis	.20	.09
565	Mike Moore	.20	.09
566	Orel Hershiser	.40	.18
567	Jason Bere	.20	.09
568	Kevin McReynolds	.20	.09
569	Leland Macon	.20	.09
570	John Courtright	.20	.09
571	Sid Fernandez	.20	.09
572	Chad Roper	.20	.09
573	Terry Pendleton	.20	.09
574	Danny Miceli	.20	.09
575	Joe Rosselli	.20	.09
576	Mike Bordick	.20	.09
577	Danny Tartabull	.20	.09
578	Jose Guzman	.20	.09
579	Omar Vizquel	.40	.18
580	Tommy Greene	.20	.09
581	Paul Spoljaric	.20	.09
582	Walt Weiss	.20	.09
583	Oscar Jimenez	.20	.09
584	Rod Henderson	.20	.09
585	Derek Lowe	.20	.09
586	Richard Hidalgo	6.00	2.70
587	Shayne Bennett	.20	.09
588	Tim Belk	.20	.09
589	Matt Mieske	.20	.09
590	Nigel Wilson	.20	.09
591	Jeff Knox	.20	.09
592	Bernard Gilkey	.20	.09
593	David Cone	.40	.18
594	Paul LoDuca	.40	.18
595	Scott Ruffcorn	.20	.09
596	Chris Roberts	.20	.09
597	Oscar Munoz	.20	.09
598	Scott Sullivan	.20	.09
599	Matt Jarvis	.20	.09
600	Jose Canseco	.60	.25
601	Tony Graffanino	.20	.09
602	Don Slaught	.20	.09
603	Brett King	.40	.18
604	Jose Herrera	.20	.09
605	Melido Perez	.20	.09
606	Mike Hubbard	.20	.09
607	Chad Ogea	.40	.18
608	Wayne Gomes	.20	.09
609	Roberto Alomar	.75	.35
610	Angel Echevarria	.50	.23
611	Jose Lind	.20	.09
612	Darrin Fletcher	.20	.09
613	Chris Bosio	.20	.09
614	Darryl Kile	.40	.18
615	Frankie Rodriguez	.20	.09
616	Phil Plantier	.20	.09
617	Pat Listach	.20	.09
618	Charlie Hough	.20	.09
619	Ryan Hancock	.20	.09
620	Darrel Deak	.20	.09

☐ 621	Travis Fryman	.40	.18
☐ 622	Brett Butler	.40	.18
☐ 623	Lance Johnson	.20	.09
☐ 624	Pete Smith	.20	.09
☐ 625	James Hurst	.20	.09
☐ 626	Roberto Kelly	.20	.09
☐ 627	Mike Mussina	.75	.35
☐ 628	Kevin Tapani	.20	.09
☐ 629	John Smoltz	.40	.18
☐ 630	Midre Cummings	.20	.09
☐ 631	Salomon Torres	.20	.09
☐ 632	Willie Adams	.20	.09
☐ 633	Derek Jeter	3.00	1.35
☐ 634	Steve Trachsel	.40	.18
☐ 635	Albie Lopez	.20	.09
☐ 636	Jason Moler	.20	.09
☐ 637	Carlos Delgado	.60	.25
☐ 638	Roberto Mejia	.20	.09
☐ 639	Darren Burton	.20	.09
☐ 640	B.J. Wallace	.20	.09
☐ 641	Brad Clontz	.20	.09
☐ 642	Billy Wagner	3.00	1.35
☐ 643	Aaron Sele	.20	.09
☐ 644	Cameron Cairncross	.20	.09
☐ 645	Brian Harper	.20	.09
☐ 646	Marc Valdes UER	.20	.09
	(No card number on back)		
☐ 647	Mark Ratekin	.20	.09
☐ 648	Terry Bradshaw	.20	.09
☐ 649	Justin Thompson	1.00	.45
☐ 650	Mike Busch	.40	.18
☐ 651	Joe Hall	.20	.09
☐ 652	Bobby Jones	.40	.18
☐ 653	Kelly Stinnett	.20	.09
☐ 654	Rod Steph	.20	.09
☐ 655	Jay Powell	.40	.18
☐ 656	Keith Garagozzo UER	.20	.09
	(No card number on back)		
☐ 657	Todd Dunn	.40	.18
☐ 658	Charles Peterson	.50	.23
☐ 659	Darren Lewis	.20	.09
☐ 660	John Wasdin	.40	.18
☐ 661	Tate Seefried	.20	.09
☐ 662	Hector Trinidad	.40	.18
☐ 663	John Carter	.20	.09
☐ 664	Larry Mitchell	.20	.09
☐ 665	David Catlett	.20	.09
☐ 666	Dante Bichette	.40	.18
☐ 667	Felix Jose	.20	.09
☐ 668	Rondell White	.60	.25
☐ 669	Tino Martinez	.75	.35
☐ 670	Brian L. Hunter	.75	.35
☐ 671	Jose Malave	.20	.09
☐ 672	Archi Cianfrocco	.20	.09
☐ 673	Mike Matheny	.20	.09
☐ 674	Bret Barberie	.20	.09
☐ 675	Andrew Lorraine	.20	.09
☐ 676	Brian Jordan	.40	.18
☐ 677	Tim Belcher	.20	.09
☐ 678	Antonio Osuna	.75	.35
☐ 679	Checklist	.20	.09
☐ 680	Checklist	.20	.09
☐ 681	Checklist	.20	.09
☐ 682	Checklist	.20	.09

1995 Bowman

Cards from this 439-card standard-size prospect-oriented set were primarily issued in plastic wrapped packs and jumbo packs. Card fronts feature white broders enframing full color photos. The left border is a reversed negative of the photo. The set includes 54 silver foil subset cards (221-274). The foil subset, largely comprising of minor league stars, have embossed borders and are found one per pack and two per jumbo pack. Rookie Cards of note include Bartolo Colon, Karim Garcia, Derrick Gibson, Vladmir Guerrero, Andruw

Jones, Eli Marrero, Hideo Nomo and Scott Rolen.

	MINT	NRMT
COMPLETE SET (439)	240.00	110.00
COMMON CARD (1-439)	.40	.18
COMMON FOIL (221-274)	.40	.18
MINOR STARS	.50	.23
UNLISTED STARS	1.00	.45

☐ 1	Billy Wagner	.75	.35
☐ 2	Chris Widger	.25	.11
☐ 3	Brent Bowers	.25	.11
☐ 4	Bob Abreu	3.00	1.35
☐ 5	Lou Collier	1.00	.45
☐ 6	Juan Acevedo	.25	.11
☐ 7	Jason Kelley	.25	.11
☐ 8	Brian Sackinsky	.25	.11
☐ 9	Scott Christman	.25	.11
☐ 10	Damon Hollins	.50	.23
☐ 11	Willis Otanez	.50	.23
☐ 12	Jason Ryan	.25	.11
☐ 13	Jason Giambi	1.00	.45
☐ 14	Andy Taulbee	.25	.11
☐ 15	Mark Thompson	.25	.11
☐ 16	Hugo Pivaral	.50	.23
☐ 17	Brien Taylor	.50	.23
☐ 18	Antonio Osuna	.25	.11
☐ 19	Edgardo Alfonzo	1.00	.45
☐ 20	Carl Everett	.25	.11
☐ 21	Matt Drews	.25	.11
☐ 22	Bartolo Colon	3.00	1.35
☐ 23	Andruw Jones	30.00	13.50
☐ 24	Robert Person	.25	.11
☐ 25	Derrek Lee	2.00	.90
☐ 26	John Ambrose	.25	.11
☐ 27	Eric Knowles	.50	.23
☐ 28	Chris Roberts	.25	.11
☐ 29	Don Wengert	.25	.11
☐ 30	Marcus Jensen	.50	.23
☐ 31	Brian Barber	.25	.11
☐ 32	Kevin Brown C.	.50	.23
☐ 33	Benji Gil	.25	.11
☐ 34	Mike Hubbard	.25	.11
☐ 35	Bart Evans	.25	.11
☐ 36	Enrique Wilson	2.00	.90
☐ 37	Brian Buchanan	1.50	.70
☐ 38	Ken Ray	.25	.11
☐ 39	Mich Franklin	.25	.11
☐ 40	Ricky Otero	.25	.11
☐ 41	Jason Kendall	1.00	.45
☐ 42	Jimmy Hurst	.25	.11
☐ 43	Jerry Wolak	.25	.11
☐ 44	Jayson Peterson	.50	.23
☐ 45	Allen Battle	.25	.11
☐ 46	Scott Stahoviak	.25	.11
☐ 47	Steve Schrenk	.25	.11
☐ 48	Travis Miller	.25	.11
☐ 49	Eddie Ribs	.25	.11
☐ 50	Mike Hampton	.25	.11
☐ 51	Chad Fontera	.25	.11
☐ 52	Tom Evans	1.00	.45
☐ 53	C.J. Nitkowski	.25	.11
☐ 54	Clay Caruthers	.25	.11
☐ 55	Shannon Stewart	.50	.23
☐ 56	Jorge Posada	.50	.23
☐ 57	Aaron Holbert	.25	.11
☐ 58	Harry Berrios	.25	.11

☐ 59	Steve Rodriguez	.25	.11
☐ 60	Shane Andrews	.25	.11
☐ 61	Will Cunnane	.50	.23
☐ 62	Richard Hidalgo	2.00	.90
☐ 63	Bill Selby	.25	.11
☐ 64	Jay Cranford	.25	.11
☐ 65	Jeff Suppan	.75	.35
☐ 66	Curtis Goodwin	.25	.11
☐ 67	John Thomson	1.50	.70
☐ 68	Justin Thompson	1.00	.45
☐ 69	Troy Percival	.25	.11
☐ 70	Matt Wagner	.50	.23
☐ 71	Terry Bradshaw	.25	.11
☐ 72	Greg Hansell	.25	.11
☐ 73	John Burke	.25	.11
☐ 74	Jeff D'Amico	.50	.23
☐ 75	Ernie Young	.25	.11
☐ 76	Jason Bates	.25	.11
☐ 77	Chris Stynes	.25	.11
☐ 78	Cade Gaspar	.50	.23
☐ 79	Melvin Nieves	.25	.11
☐ 80	Rick Gorecki	.25	.11
☐ 81	Felix Rodriguez	.25	.11
☐ 82	Ryan Hancock	.25	.11
☐ 83	Chris Carpenter	2.00	.90
☐ 84	Ray McDavid	.25	.11
☐ 85	Chris Wimmer	.25	.11
☐ 86	Doug Glanville	.25	.11
☐ 87	DeShawn Warren	.25	.11
☐ 88	Damian Moss	1.00	.45
☐ 89	Rafael Orellano	.50	.23
☐ 90	Vladimir Guerrero	25.00	11.00
☐ 91	Raul Casanova	2.00	.90
☐ 92	Karim Garcia	8.00	3.60
☐ 93	Bryce Florie	.25	.11
☐ 94	Kevin Orie	1.00	.45
☐ 95	Ryan Nye	.50	.23
☐ 96	Matt Sachse	.50	.23
☐ 97	Ivan Arteaga	.25	.11
☐ 98	Glenn Murray	.25	.11
☐ 99	Stacy Hollins	.25	.11
☐ 100	Jim Pittsley	.50	.23
☐ 101	Craig Mattson	.25	.11
☐ 102	Neifi Perez	.50	.23
☐ 103	Keith Williams	.25	.11
☐ 104	Roger Cedeno	.50	.23
☐ 105	Tony Terry	.25	.11
☐ 106	Jose Malave	.25	.11
☐ 107	Joe Rosselli	.25	.11
☐ 108	Kevin Jordan	.25	.11
☐ 109	Sid Roberson	.25	.11
☐ 110	Alan Embree	.25	.11
☐ 111	Terrell Wade	.25	.11
☐ 112	Bob Wolcott	.25	.11
☐ 113	Carlos Perez	.50	.23
☐ 114	Mike Bovee	.50	.23
☐ 115	Tommy Davis	.50	.23
☐ 116	Jeremey Kendall	.25	.11
☐ 117	Rich Aude	.25	.11
☐ 118	Rick Huisman	.25	.11
☐ 119	Tim Belk	.25	.11
☐ 120	Edgar Renteria	1.00	.45
☐ 121	Calvin Maduro	.50	.23
☐ 122	Jerry Martin	.25	.11
☐ 123	Ramon Fermin	.25	.11
☐ 124	Kimera Bartee	.50	.23
☐ 125	Mark Farris	.25	.11
☐ 126	Frank Rodriguez	.25	.11
☐ 127	Bobby Higginson	4.00	1.80
☐ 128	Bret Wagner	.25	.11
☐ 129	Edwin Diaz	1.00	.45
☐ 130	Jimmy Haynes	.50	.23
☐ 131	Chris Weinke	.25	.11
☐ 132	Damian Jackson	1.00	.45
☐ 133	Felix Martinez	.50	.23
☐ 134	Edwin Hurtado	.25	.11
☐ 135	Matt Raleigh	.25	.11
☐ 136	Paul Wilson	.50	.23
☐ 137	Ron Villone	.25	.11
☐ 138	Eric Stuckenschneider	.25	.11
☐ 139	Tate Seefried	.25	.11
☐ 140	Rey Ordonez	2.50	1.10
☐ 141	Eddie Pearson	.25	.11
☐ 142	Kevin Gallaher	.25	.11
☐ 143	Torii Hunter	.50	.23
☐ 144	Daron Kirkreit	.25	.11

145	Craig Wilson	.25	.11
146	Ugueth Urbina	.25	.11
147	Chris Snopek	.25	.11
148	Kym Ashworth	.50	.23
149	Wayne Gomes	.25	.11
150	Mark Loretta	.25	.11
151	Ramon Morel	.50	.23
152	Trot Nixon	.50	.23
153	Desi Relaford	.50	.23
154	Scott Sullivan	.25	.11
155	Marc Barcelo	.25	.11
156	Willie Adams	.25	.11
157	Derrick Gibson	10.00	4.50
158	Brian Meadows	.25	.11
159	Julian Tavarez	.25	.11
160	Bryan Rekar	.25	.11
161	Steve Gibralter	.25	.11
162	Esteban Loaiza	.25	.11
163	John Wasdin	.25	.11
164	Kirk Presley	.25	.11
165	Mariano Rivera	1.00	.45
166	Andy Larkin	.25	.11
167	Sean Whiteside	.25	.11
168	Matt Apana	.25	.11
169	Shawn Senior	.25	.11
170	Scott Gentile	.25	.11
171	Quilvio Veras	.25	.11
172	Eli Marrero	5.00	2.20
173	Mendy Lopez	.50	.23
174	Homer Bush	.25	.11
175	Brian Stephenson	.25	.11
176	Jon Nunnally	.25	.11
177	Jose Herrera	.25	.11
178	Corey Avrard	.50	.23
179	David Bell	.25	.11
180	Jason Isringhausen	.50	.23
181	Jamey Wright	.50	.23
182	Loneli Roberts	.25	.11
183	Marty Cordova	.50	.23
184	Amaury Telemaco	.50	.23
185	John Mabry	.50	.23
186	Andrew Vessel	.50	.23
187	Jim Cole	.25	.11
188	Marquis Riley	.25	.11
189	Todd Dunn	.50	.23
190	John Carter	.25	.11
191	Donnie Sadler	2.00	.90
192	Mike Bell	.50	.23
193	Chris Cumberland	.50	.23
194	Jason Schmidt	.50	.23
195	Matt Brunson	.25	.11
196	James Baldwin	.25	.11
197	Bill Simas	.25	.11
198	Gus Gandarillas	.25	.11
199	Mac Suzuki	.25	.11
200	Rick Holifield	.25	.11
201	Fernando Lunar	.25	.11
202	Kevin Jarvis	.25	.11
203	Everett Stull	.25	.11
204	Steve Wojciechowski	.25	.11
205	Shawn Estes	1.00	.45
206	Jermaine Dye	.75	.35
207	Marc Kroon	.25	.11
208	Peter Munro	.50	.23
209	Pat Watkins	.50	.23
210	Matt Smith	.25	.11
211	Joe Vitiello	.25	.11
212	Gerald Witasick Jr.	.25	.11
213	Freddy Garcia	1.00	.45
214	Glenn Dishman	.50	.23
215	Jay Canizaro	.25	.11
216	Angel Martinez	.25	.11
217	Yamil Benitez	1.00	.45
218	Fausto Macey	.50	.23
219	Eric Owens	.25	.11
220	Checklist	.25	.11
221	Dwayne Hosey FOIL	.40	.18
222	Brad Woodall FOIL	.40	.18
223	Billy Ashley FOIL	.40	.18
224	Mark Grudzielanek FOIL	2.00	.90
225	Mark Johnson FOIL	.40	.18
226	Tim Unroe FOIL	.40	.18
227	Todd Greene FOIL	4.00	1.80
228	Larry Sutton FOIL	.40	.18
229	Derek Jeter FOIL	4.00	1.80
230	Sal Fasano FOIL	.40	.18
231	Ruben Rivera FOIL	2.00	.90
232	Chris Truby FOIL	.40	.18
233	John Donati FOIL	.40	.18
234	Decomba Conner FOIL	.50	.23
235	Sergio Nunez FOIL	.75	.35
236	Ray Brown FOIL	.40	.18
237	Juan Melo FOIL	2.00	.90
238	Hideo Nomo FOIL	12.00	5.50
239	Jamie Bluma FOIL	.40	.18
240	Jay Payton FOIL	1.00	.45
241	Paul Konerko FOIL	20.00	9.00
242	Scott Elarton FOIL	3.00	1.35
243	Jeff Abbott FOIL	1.50	.70
244	Jim Brower FOIL	.40	.18
245	Geoff Blum FOIL	.50	.23
246	Aaron Boone FOIL	1.50	.70
247	J.R. Phillips FOIL	.40	.18
248	Alex Ochoa FOIL	.40	.18
249	Nomar Garciaparra FOIL	25.00	11.00
250	Garret Anderson FOIL	.75	.35
251	Ray Durham FOIL	.50	.23
252	Paul Shuey FOIL	.40	.18
253	Tony Clark FOIL	2.50	1.10
254	Johnny Damon FOIL	.50	.23
255	Duane Singleton FOIL	.40	.18
256	LaTroy Hawkins FOIL	.40	.18
257	Andy Pettitte FOIL	1.50	.70
258	Ben Grieve FOIL	25.00	11.00
259	Marc Newfield FOIL	.40	.18
260	Terrell Lowery FOIL	.40	.18
261	Shawn Green FOIL	.50	.23
262	Chipper Jones FOIL	3.00	1.35
263	Brooks Kieschnick FOIL	.50	.23
264	Calvin Reese FOIL	.40	.18
265	Doug Million FOIL	.40	.18
266	Marc Valdes FOIL	.40	.18
267	Brian L.Hunter FOIL	.50	.23
268	Todd Hollandsworth FOIL	.50	.23
269	Rod Henderson FOIL	.40	.18
270	Bill Pulsipher FOIL	.40	.18
271	Scott Rolen FOIL	25.00	11.00
272	Trey Beamon FOIL	.40	.18
273	Alan Benes FOIL	.75	.35
274	Dustin Hermanson FOIL	.50	.23
275	Ricky Bottalico FOIL	.50	.23
276	Albert Belle	1.25	.55
277	Deion Sanders	.50	.23
278	Matt Williams	.75	.35
279	Jeff Bagwell	2.00	.90
280	Kirby Puckett	2.00	.90
281	Dave Hollins	.25	.11
282	Don Mattingly	1.50	.70
283	Joey Hamilton	.50	.23
284	Bobby Bonilla	.50	.23
285	Moises Alou	.50	.23
286	Tom Glavine	.50	.23
287	Brett Butler	.50	.23
288	Chris Hoiles	.25	.11
289	Kenny Rogers	.25	.11
290	Larry Walker	1.00	.45
291	Tim Raines	.50	.23
292	Kevin Appier	.50	.23
293	Roger Clemens	2.00	.90
294	Chuck Carr	.25	.11
295	Randy Myers	.25	.11
296	Dave Nilsson	.25	.11
297	Joe Carter	.50	.23
298	Chuck Finley	.25	.11
299	Ray Lankford	.50	.23
300	Roberto Kelly	.25	.11
301	Jon Lieber	.25	.11
302	Travis Fryman	.50	.23
303	Mark McGwire	2.00	.90
304	Tony Gwynn	2.50	1.10
305	John Kruk	1.25	.55
306	Mark Whiten	.25	.11
307	Doug Drabek	.25	.11
308	Terry Steinbach	.25	.11
309	Ryan Klesko	.75	.35
310	Mike Piazza	3.00	1.35
311	Ben McDonald	.25	.11
312	Reggie Sanders	.25	.11
313	Alex Fernandez	.25	.11
314	Aaron Sele	.25	.11
315	Gregg Jefferies	.25	.11
316	Rickey Henderson	.75	.35
317	Brian Anderson	.50	.23
318	Jose Valentin	.25	.11
319	Rod Beck	.25	.11
320	Marquis Grissom	.50	.23
321	Ken Griffey Jr.	5.00	2.20
322	Bret Saberhagen	.25	.11
323	Juan Gonzalez	2.50	1.10
324	Paul Molitor	1.00	.45
325	Gary Sheffield	1.00	.45
326	Darren Daulton	.50	.23
327	Bill Swift	.25	.11
328	Brian McRae	.25	.11
329	Robin Ventura	.50	.23
330	Lee Smith	.50	.23
331	Fred McGriff	.75	.35
332	Delino DeShields	.25	.11
333	Edgar Martinez	.75	.35
334	Mike Mussina	1.00	.45
335	Orlando Merced	.25	.11
336	Carlos Baerga	.25	.11
337	Wil Cordero	.25	.11
338	Tom Pagnozzi	.25	.11
339	Pat Hentgen	.75	.35
340	Chad Curtis	.25	.11
341	Darren Lewis	.25	.11
342	Jeff Kent	.25	.11
343	Bip Roberts	.25	.11
344	Ivan Rodriguez	1.25	.55
345	Jeff Montgomery	.25	.11
346	Hal Morris	.25	.11
347	Danny Tartabull	.25	.11
348	Raul Mondesi	.75	.35
349	Ken Hill	.25	.11
350	Pedro Martinez	1.00	.45
351	Frank Thomas	4.00	1.80
352	Manny Ramirez	1.00	.45
353	Tim Salmon	.75	.35
354	W. VanLandingham	.25	.11
355	Andres Galarraga	1.00	.45
356	Paul O'Neill	.50	.23
357	Brady Anderson	.75	.35
358	Ramon Martinez	.50	.23
359	John Olerud	.50	.23
360	Ruben Sierra	.25	.11
361	Cal Eldred	.25	.11
362	Jay Buhner	.75	.35
363	Jay Bell	.50	.23
364	Wally Joyner	.50	.23
365	Chuck Knoblauch	1.00	.45
366	Len Dykstra	.50	.23
367	John Wetteland	.25	.11
368	Roberto Alomar	1.00	.45
369	Craig Biggio	.75	.35
370	Ozzie Smith	1.25	.55
371	Terry Pendleton	.25	.11
372	Sammy Sosa	1.00	.45
373	Carlos Garcia	.25	.11
374	Jose Rijo	.25	.11
375	Chris Gomez	.25	.11
376	Barry Bonds	1.25	.55
377	Steve Avery	.25	.11
378	Rick Wilkins	.25	.11
379	Pete Harnisch	.25	.11
380	Dean Palmer	.25	.11
381	Bob Hamelin	.25	.11
382	Jason Bere	.25	.11
383	Jimmy Key	.50	.23
384	Dante Bichette	.50	.23
385	Rafael Palmeiro	.75	.35
386	David Justice	1.00	.45
387	Chili Davis	.50	.23
388	Mike Greenwell	.25	.11
389	Todd Zeile	.25	.11
390	Jeff Conine	.50	.23
391	Rick Aguilera	.25	.11
392	Eddie Murray	1.00	.45
393	Mike Stanley	.25	.11
394	Cliff Floyd UER (numbered 294)	.25	.11
395	Randy Johnson	1.00	.45
396	David Nied	.25	.11
397	Devon White	.25	.11
398	Royce Clayton	.25	.11
399	Andy Benes	.50	.23
400	John Hudek	.25	.11
401	Bobby Jones	.25	.11

□	402	Eric Karros	.50	.23
□	403	Will Clark	.75	.35
□	404	Mark Langston	.25	.11
□	405	Kevin Brown	.50	.23
□	406	Greg Maddux	3.00	1.35
□	407	David Cone	.50	.23
□	408	Wade Boggs	1.00	.45
□	409	Steve Trachsel	.25	.11
□	410	Greg Vaughn	.25	.11
□	411	Mo Vaughn	1.25	.55
□	412	Wilson Alvarez	.25	.11
□	413	Cal Ripken	4.00	1.80
□	414	Rico Brogna	.25	.11
□	415	Barry Larkin	.75	.35
□	416	Cecil Fielder	.50	.23
□	417	Jose Canseco	.75	.35
□	418	Jack McDowell	.25	.11
□	419	Mike Lieberthal	.25	.11
□	420	Andrew Lorraine	.25	.11
□	421	Rich Becker	.25	.11
□	422	Tony Phillips	.25	.11
□	423	Scott Ruffcorn	.25	.11
□	424	Jeff Granger	.25	.11
□	425	Greg Pirkl	.25	.11
□	426	Dennis Eckersley	.50	.23
□	427	Jose Lima	.25	.11
□	428	Russ Davis	.25	.11
□	429	Armando Benitez	.25	.11
□	430	Alex Gonzalez	.25	.11
□	431	Carlos Delgado	.50	.23
□	432	Chan Ho Park	1.00	.45
□	433	Mickey Tettleton	.25	.11
□	434	Dave Winfield	.75	.35
□	435	John Burkett	.25	.11
□	436	Orlando Miller	.25	.11
□	437	Rondell White	.50	.23
□	438	Jose Oliva	.25	.11
□	439	Checklist	.25	.11

1996 Bowman

The 1996 Bowman set was issued in one series totalling 385 cards. The 11-card packs retail for $2.50 each. The fronts feature color action player photos in a tan-checkered frame with the player's name printed in silver foil at the bottom. The backs carry another color player photo with player information, 1995 and career player statistics. Each pack contained 10 regular issue cards plus either one foil parallel or an insert card. In a special promotional program, Topps offered collectors a $100 guarantee on complete sets. To get the guarantee, collectors had to mail in a Guaranteed Value Certificate request form, found in packs, along with a $5 processing and registration fee before the December 31st, 1996 deadline. Collectors would then receive a $100 Guaranteed Value Certificate, of which they could mail back to Topps between August 31st, 1999 and December 31st, 1999, along with their complete set, to receive $100. A reprint version of the 1952 Bowman Mickey Mantle card was randomly inserted into packs. Rookie Cards in this set include Russell Branyan, Mike Cameron, Jose Guillen, Livan Hernandez, Carl Pavano, Brian Rose and Ron Wright

1995 Bowman Gold Foil

Numbered 221-274, this 54-card standard-size set is the gold insert parallel version of the silver foil subset found in the basic issue. The odds of finding a gold foil version are one in six packs.

	MINT	NRMT
COMPLETE SET (54)	180.00	80.00
COMMON CARD (221-274)	2.00	.90
SEMISTARS	4.00	1.80
UNLISTED STARS	6.00	2.70
STATED ODDS 1:6		

□	229	Derek Jeter	12.00	5.50
□	238	Hideo Nomo	15.00	6.75
□	241	Paul Konerko	25.00	11.00
□	249	Nomar Garciaparra	30.00	13.50
□	253	Tony Clark	8.00	3.60
□	257	Andy Pettitte	8.00	3.60
□	258	Ben Grieve	30.00	13.50
□	262	Chipper Jones	12.00	5.50
□	271	Scott Rolen	30.00	13.50

	MINT	NRMT
COMPLETE SET (385)	125.00	55.00
COMMON CARD (1-385)	.25	.11
MINOR STARS	.40	.18
UNLISTED STARS	.75	.35
COMP.FOIL SET (385)	300.00	135.00
COMMON FOIL (1-385)	.50	.23

*FOIL STARS: 1.25X TO 2.5X HI COLUMN
*FOIL ROOKIES: .75X TO 1.5X HI
ONE FOIL OR INSERT PER PACK
TWO FOILS PER RETAIL PACK
MANTLE STATED ODDS 1:48

□	1	Cal Ripken	3.00	1.35
□	2	Ray Durham	.20	.09
□	3	Ivan Rodriguez	1.00	.45
□	4	Fred McGriff	.60	.25
□	5	Hideo Nomo	2.00	.90
□	6	Troy Percival	.20	.09
□	7	Moises Alou	.40	.18
□	8	Mike Stanley	.20	.09
□	9	Jay Buhner	.60	.25
□	10	Shawn Green	.60	.25
□	11	Ryan Klesko	.60	.25
□	12	Andres Galarraga	.60	.25

□	13	Dean Palmer	.20	.09
□	14	Jeff Conine	.40	.18
□	15	Brian L.Hunter	.40	.18
□	16	J.T. Snow	.40	.18
□	17	Larry Walker	.75	.35
□	18	Barry Larkin	.60	.25
□	19	Alex Gonzalez	.20	.09
□	20	Edgar Martinez	.60	.25
□	21	Mo Vaughn	1.00	.45
□	22	Mark McGwire	1.50	.70
□	23	Jose Canseco	.60	.25
□	24	Jack McDowell	.20	.09
□	25	Dante Bichette	.40	.18
□	26	Wade Boggs	.75	.35
□	27	Mike Piazza	2.50	1.10
□	28	Ray Lankford	.40	.18
□	29	Craig Biggio	.60	.25
□	30	Rafael Palmeiro	.60	.25
□	31	Ron Gant	.40	.18
□	32	Javy Lopez	.40	.18
□	33	Brian Jordan	.40	.18
□	34	Paul O'Neill	.40	.18
□	35	Mark Grace	.60	.25
□	36	Matt Williams	.60	.25
□	37	Pedro Martinez	.75	.35
□	38	Rickey Henderson	.60	.25
□	39	Bobby Bonilla	.40	.18
□	40	Todd Hollandsworth	.20	.09
□	41	Jim Thome	.75	.35
□	42	Gary Sheffield	.75	.35
□	43	Tim Salmon	.75	.35
□	44	Gregg Jefferies	.20	.09
□	45	Roberto Alomar	.75	.35
□	46	Carlos Baerga	.20	.09
□	47	Mark Grudzielanek	.40	.18
□	48	Randy Johnson	.75	.35
□	49	Tino Martinez	.75	.35
□	50	Robin Ventura	.40	.18
□	51	Ryne Sandberg	1.00	.45
□	52	Jay Bell	.40	.18
□	53	Jason Schmidt	.40	.18
□	54	Frank Thomas	3.00	1.35
□	55	Kenny Lofton	1.00	.45
□	56	Ariel Prieto	.20	.09
□	57	David Cone	.40	.18
□	58	Reggie Sanders	.20	.09
□	59	Michael Tucker	.40	.18
□	60	Vinny Castilla	.40	.18
□	61	Len Dykstra	.40	.18
□	62	Todd Hundley	.40	.18
□	63	Brian McRae	.20	.09
□	64	Dennis Eckersley	.40	.18
□	65	Rondell White	.40	.18
□	66	Eric Karros	.40	.18
□	67	Greg Maddux	2.50	1.10
□	68	Kevin Appier	.40	.18
□	69	Eddie Murray	.75	.35
□	70	John Olerud	.40	.18
□	71	Tony Gwynn	2.00	.90
□	72	David Justice	.75	.35
□	73	Ken Caminiti	.60	.25
□	74	Terry Steinbach	.20	.09
□	75	Alan Benes	.40	.18
□	76	Chipper Jones	2.50	1.10
□	77	Jeff Bagwell	1.50	.70
□	78	Barry Bonds	1.00	.45
□	79	Ken Griffey Jr.	4.00	1.80
□	80	Roger Cedeno	.20	.09
□	81	Joe Carter	.40	.18
□	82	Henry Rodriguez	.20	.09
□	83	Jason Isringhausen	.20	.09
□	84	Chuck Knoblauch	.75	.35
□	85	Manny Ramirez	.75	.35
□	86	Tom Glavine	.40	.18
□	87	Jeffrey Hammonds	.20	.09
□	88	Paul Molitor	.75	.35
□	89	Roger Clemens	1.50	.70
□	90	Greg Vaughn	.20	.09
□	91	Marty Cordova	.40	.18
□	92	Albert Belle	1.00	.45
□	93	Mike Mussina	.75	.35
□	94	Garret Anderson	.40	.18
□	95	Juan Gonzalez	2.00	.90
□	96	John Valentin	.20	.09
□	97	Jason Giambi	.40	.18
□	98	Kirby Puckett	1.50	.70

99	Jim Edmonds	.60	.25
100	Cecil Fielder	.40	.18
101	Mike Aldrete	.20	.09
102	Marquis Grissom	.40	.18
103	Derek Bell	.20	.09
104	Raul Mondesi	.60	.25
105	Sammy Sosa	.75	.35
106	Travis Fryman	.40	.18
107	Rico Brogna	.20	.09
108	Will Clark	.60	.25
109	Bernie Williams	.75	.35
110	Brady Anderson	.60	.25
111	Torii Hunter	.40	.18
112	Derek Jeter	2.50	1.10
113	Mike Kusiewicz	.50	.23
114	Scott Rolen	4.00	1.80
115	Ramon Castro	.40	.18
116	Jose Guillen	10.00	4.50
117	Wade Walker	.20	.09
118	Shawn Senior	.20	.09
119	Onan Masaoka	1.00	.45
120	Marlon Anderson	.75	.35
121	Katsuhiro Maeda	2.00	.90
122	Garrett Stephenson	.40	.18
123	Butch Huskey	.40	.18
124	D'Angelo Jimenez	2.50	1.10
125	Tony Mounce	.50	.23
126	Jay Canizaro	.20	.09
127	Juan Melo	.40	.18
128	Steve Gibralter	.20	.09
129	Freddy Garcia	.20	.09
130	Julio Santana UER	.40	.18
	Card has him born in 1993		
131	Richard Hidalgo	.75	.35
132	Jermaine Dye	.40	.18
133	Willie Adams	.20	.09
134	Everett Stull	.20	.09
135	Ramon Morel	.20	.09
136	Chan Ho Park	.75	.35
137	Jamey Wright	.20	.09
138	Luis Garcia	.20	.09
139	Dan Serafini	.20	.09
140	Ryan Dempster	1.00	.45
141	Tate Seefried	.20	.09
142	Jimmy Hurst	.20	.09
143	Travis Miller	.20	.09
144	Curtis Goodwin	.20	.09
145	Rocky Coppinger	.75	.35
146	Enrique Wilson	.20	.09
147	Jaime Bluma	.20	.09
148	Andrew Vessel	.20	.09
149	Damian Moss	.40	.18
150	Shawn Gallagher	1.00	.45
151	Pat Watkins	.40	.18
152	Jose Paniagua	.20	.09
153	Danny Graves	.40	.18
154	Bryon Gainey	.75	.35
155	Steve Soderstrom	.40	.18
156	Cliff Brumbaugh	.20	.09
157	Eugene Kingsale	1.00	.45
158	Lou Collier	.40	.18
159	Todd Walker	3.00	1.35
160	Kris Detmers	.20	.09
161	Josh Booty	2.00	.90
162	Greg Whiteman	.20	.09
163	Damian Jackson	.40	.18
164	Tony Clark	.75	.35
165	Jeff D'Amico	.20	.09
166	Johnny Damon	.40	.18
167	Rafael Orellano	.20	.09
168	Ruben Rivera	.40	.18
169	Alex Ochoa	.20	.09
170	Jay Powell	.20	.09
171	Tom Evans	.20	.09
172	Ron Villone	.20	.09
173	Shawn Estes	.60	.25
174	John Wasdin	.20	.09
175	Bill Simas	.20	.09
176	Kevin Brown	.40	.18
177	Shannon Stewart	.40	.18
178	Todd Greene	.60	.25
179	Bob Wolcott	.20	.09
180	Chris Snopek	.20	.09
181	Nomar Garciaparra	4.00	1.80
182	Cameron Smith	.20	.09
183	Matt Drews	.20	.09
184	Jimmy Haynes	.20	.09
185	Chris Carpenter	.60	.25
186	Desi Relaford	.20	.09
187	Ben Grieve	3.00	1.35
188	Mike Bell	.60	.25
189	Luis Castillo	1.00	.45
190	Ugueth Urbina	.20	.09
191	Paul Wilson	.20	.09
192	Andruw Jones	4.00	1.80
193	Wayne Gomes	.20	.09
194	Craig Counsell	1.00	.45
195	Jim Cole	.20	.09
196	Brooks Kieschnick	.40	.18
197	Trey Beamon	.20	.09
198	Marino Santana	.20	.09
199	Bob Abreu	.60	.25
200	Calvin Reese	.20	.09
201	Dante Powell	2.00	.90
202	George Arias	.20	.09
203	Jorge Velandia	.20	.09
204	George Lombard	3.00	1.35
205	Byron Browne	.20	.09
206	John Frascatore	.20	.09
207	Terry Adams	.20	.09
208	Wilson Delgado	.20	.09
209	Billy McMillon	.20	.09
210	Jeff Abbott	.40	.18
211	Trot Nixon	.40	.18
212	Amaury Telemaco	.40	.18
213	Scott Sullivan	.20	.09
214	Justin Thompson	.60	.25
215	Decomba Conner	.40	.18
216	Ryan McGuire	.20	.09
217	Matt Luke	.20	.09
218	Doug Million	.20	.09
219	Jason Dickson	4.00	1.80
220	Ramon Hernandez	.40	.18
221	Mark Bellhorn	2.50	1.10
222	Eric Ludwick	.20	.09
223	Luke Wilcox	.20	.09
224	Marty Malloy	.50	.23
225	Gary Coffee	.50	.23
226	Wendell Magee	.50	.23
227	Brett Tomko	2.00	.90
228	Derek Lowe	.20	.09
229	Jose Rosado	2.50	1.10
230	Steve Bourgeois	.20	.09
231	Neil Weber	.40	.18
232	Jeff Ware	.20	.09
233	Edwin Diaz	.40	.18
234	Greg Norton	.40	.18
235	Aaron Boone	.40	.18
236	Jeff Suppan	.40	.18
237	Bret Wagner	.20	.09
238	Elieser Marrero	.75	.35
239	Will Cunnane	.40	.18
240	Brian Barkley	.20	.09
241	Jay Payton	.40	.18
242	Marcus Jensen	.20	.09
243	Ryan Nye	.20	.09
244	Chad Mottola	.20	.09
245	Scott McClain	.20	.09
246	Jessie Ibarra	.40	.18
247	Mike Darr	1.50	.70
248	Bobby Estalella	3.00	1.35
249	Michael Barrett	.40	.18
250	Jamie Lopiccolo	.50	.23
251	Shane Dennis	.20	.09
252	Ben Petrick	1.50	.70
253	Jason Bell	.40	.18
254	Arnold Gooch	.50	.23
255	T.J. Mathews	.20	.09
256	Jason Ryan	.20	.09
257	Pat Cline	1.00	.45
258	Rafael Carmona	.20	.09
259	Carl Pavano	6.00	2.70
260	Ben Davis	.75	.35
261	Matt Lawton	.40	.18
262	Kevin Sefcik	.20	.09
263	Chris Fussell	.75	.35
264	Mike Cameron	6.00	2.70
265	Marty Janzen	.20	.09
266	Livan Hernandez	8.00	3.60
267	Raul Ibanez	1.00	.45
268	Juan Encarnacion	1.50	.70
269	David Yocum	.50	.23
270	Jonathan Johnson	.50	.23
271	Reggie Taylor	.60	.25
272	Danny Buxbaum	.75	.35
273	Jacob Cruz	.40	.18
274	Bobby Morris	.20	.09
275	Andy Fox	.20	.09
276	Greg Keagle	.20	.09
277	Charles Peterson	.20	.09
278	Derrek Lee	.75	.35
279	Bryant Nelson	.50	.23
280	Antone Williamson	.40	.18
281	Scott Elarton	.40	.18
282	Shad Williams	.20	.09
283	Rich Hunter	.20	.09
284	Chris Sheff	.20	.09
285	Derrick Gibson	1.50	.70
286	Felix Rodriguez	.20	.09
287	Brian Banks	.20	.09
288	Jason McDonald	.20	.09
289	Glendon Rusch	1.00	.45
290	Gary Rath	.20	.09
291	Peter Munro	.40	.18
292	Tom Fordham	.40	.18
293	Jason Kendall	.60	.25
294	Russ Johnson	.20	.09
295	Joe Long	.20	.09
296	Robert Smith	1.00	.45
297	Jarrod Washburn	1.00	.45
298	Dave Coggin	.50	.23
299	Jeff Yoder	.50	.23
300	Jed Hansen	.40	.18
301	Matt Morris	3.00	1.35
302	Josh Bishop	.50	.23
303	Dustin Hermanson	.20	.09
304	Mike Gulan	.20	.09
305	Felipe Crespo	.20	.09
306	Quinton McCracken	.20	.09
307	Jim Bonnici	.20	.09
308	Sal Fasano	.20	.09
309	Gabe Alvarez	1.25	.55
310	Heath Murray	.50	.23
311	Jose Valentin	1.50	.70
312	Bartolo Colon	.75	.35
313	Olmedo Saenz	.20	.09
314	Norm Hutchins	2.00	.90
315	Chris Holt	.20	.09
316	David Doster	.20	.09
317	Robert Person	.20	.09
318	Donne Wall	.20	.09
319	Adam Riggs	.40	.18
320	Homer Bush	.20	.09
321	Brad Rigby	.20	.09
322	Lou Merloni	.20	.09
323	Neifi Perez	.20	.09
324	Alvie Shepherd	.50	.23
325	Jarrod Patterson	.20	.09
326	Ray Ricken	.40	.18
327	Danny Klassen	1.00	.45
328	David Miller	.50	.23
329	Chad Alexander	.75	.35
330	Matt Beaumont	.40	.18
331	Damon Hollins	.20	.09
332	Todd Dunn	.20	.09
333	Mike Sweeney	2.00	.90
334	Richie Sexson	.50	.25
335	Billy Wagner	.60	.25
336	Ron Wright	5.00	2.20
337	Paul Konerko	2.50	1.10
338	Tommy Phelps	.50	.23
339	Karim Garcia	.60	.25
342	Russell Branyan	8.00	3.60
343	Marty Winn		.45
344	A.J. Pierzynski	1.00	.45
345	Mike Busby	.20	.09
346	Matt Beech	.50	.23
347	Jose Cepeda	.50	.23
348	Brian Stephenson	.20	.09
349	Rey Ordonez	.40	.18
350	Rich Aurilla	.20	.09
351	Edgard Velazquez	2.00	.90
352	Raul Casanova	.20	.09
353	Carlos Guillen	.75	.35
354	Bruce Aven	.20	.09
355	Ryan Jones	1.00	.45

		MINT	NRMT
☐ 356	Derek Aucoin	.20	.09
☐ 357	Brian Rose	6.00	2.70
☐ 358	Richard Almanzar	.50	.23
☐ 359	Fletcher Bates	.75	.35
☐ 360	Russ Ortiz	.20	.09
☐ 361	Wilton Guerrero	2.00	.90
☐ 362	Geoff Jenkins	2.00	.90
☐ 363	Pete Janicki	.20	.09
☐ 364	Yamil Benitez	.40	.18
☐ 365	Aaron Holbert	.20	.09
☐ 366	Tim Belk	.20	.09
☐ 367	Terrell Wade	.20	.09
☐ 368	Terrence Long	.40	.18
☐ 369	Brad Fullmer	.75	.35
☐ 370	Matt Wagner	.20	.09
☐ 371	Craig Wilson	.20	.09
☐ 372	Mark Loretta	.20	.09
☐ 373	Eric Owens	.20	.09
☐ 374	Vladimir Guerrero	3.00	1.35
☐ 375	Tommy Davis	.20	.09
☐ 376	Donnie Sadler	.40	.18
☐ 377	Edgar Renteria	.60	.25
☐ 378	Todd Helton	8.00	3.60
☐ 379	Ralph Milliard	.20	.09
☐ 380	Darin Blood	1.50	.70
☐ 381	Shayne Bennett	.20	.09
☐ 382	Mark Redman	.40	.18
☐ 383	Felix Martinez	.20	.09
☐ 384	Sean Watkins	.75	.35
☐ 385	Oscar Henriquez	.40	.18
☐ M20	1952 B.Mantle Reprint	10.00	4.50
☐ NNO	Unnumbered Checklists	.20	.09

1996 Bowman Minor League POY

Randomly inserted in packs at a rate of one in 12, this 15-card set features top minor league prospects for Player of the Year Candidates. The fronts carry a color player photo with red-and-silver foil printing. The backs display player information including his career bests.

		MINT	NRMT
COMPLETE SET (15)		40.00	18.00
COMMON CARD (1-15)		1.50	.70
SEMISTARS		2.00	.90
STATED ODDS 1:12			
☐ 1	Andruw Jones	12.00	5.50
☐ 2	Derrick Gibson	4.00	1.80
☐ 3	Bob Abreu	2.00	.90
☐ 4	Todd Walker	4.00	1.80
☐ 5	Jamey Wright	1.50	.70
☐ 6	Wes Helms	6.00	2.70
☐ 7	Karim Garcia	2.00	.90
☐ 8	Bartolo Colon	2.50	1.10
☐ 9	Alex Ochoa	1.50	.70
☐ 10	Mike Sweeney	2.50	1.10
☐ 11	Ruben Rivera	1.75	.80
☐ 12	Gabe Alvarez	1.50	.70
☐ 13	Billy Wagner	1.75	.80
☐ 14	Vladimir Guerrero	10.00	4.50
☐ 15	Edgard Velazquez	3.00	1.35

1997 Bowman

The 1997 Bowman set was issued in two series (series one #'s 1-221, series two #'s 222-441) and was distributed in 10 card packs with a suggested retail price of $2.50. The 441-card set features color photos of 300 top prospects with silver and blue foil stamping and 140 veteran stars designated by silver and red foil stamping. An unannounced Hideki Irabu red bordered card (#441) was also included in series 2 packs. Players that were featured for the first time on a Bowman card also carried a blue foil "1st Bowman Card" logo on the card front. Topps offered collectors a $125 guarantee on complete sets. To get the guarantee, collectors had to mail in the Guaranteed Certificate Request Form which was found in every three packs of both series 1 and series 2 along with a $5 registration and processing fee. To redeem the guarantee, collectors had to send a complete set of Bowman regular cards (440 cards in both series) along with the certificate to Topps between August 31 and December 31 in the year 2000. Notable Rookie Cards in this set include Adrian Beltre, Jose Cruz Jr, Hideki Irabu, Travis Lee, Aramis Ramirez, Miguel Tejada and Jaret Wright. Please note that cards 155 and 158 don't exist. Calvin "Pokey" Reese and George Arias are both numbered 156 (Reese is an uncorrected error - should be numbered 155). Chris Carpenter and Eric Milton are both numbered 159 (Carpenter is an uncorrected error - should be numbered 158).

	MINT	NRMT
COMPLETE SET (441)	150.00	150.00
COMPLETE SERIES 1 (220)	90.00	40.00
COMPLETE SERIES 2 (220)	60.00	27.00
COMMON CARD (1-441)	.20	.09
MINOR STARS	.40	.18
UNLISTED STARS	.75	.35
COMP.INT'L SET (440)	300.00	135.00
COMP.INT'L SER.1 (221)	180.00	80.00
COMP.INT'L SER.2 (219)	120.00	55.00
COMMON INT'L (1-440)	.50	.23
*INT'L STARS: 1.25X TO 2.5X HI COLUMN		

*INT'L ROOKIES: .75X TO 1.5X HI
ONE INT'L OR INSERT PER PACK
CARDS 155 AND 158 DON'T EXIST
REESE AND ARIAS BOTH NUMBERED 156
CARPENTER 'N MILTON BOTH NUMBER 159

		MINT	NRMT
☐ 1	Derek Jeter	2.50	1.10
☐ 2	Edgar Renteria	.40	.18
☐ 3	Chipper Jones	2.50	1.10
☐ 4	Hideo Nomo	2.00	.90
☐ 5	Tim Salmon	.75	.35
☐ 6	Jason Giambi	.40	.18
☐ 7	Robin Ventura	.40	.18
☐ 8	Tony Clark	.75	.35
☐ 9	Barry Larkin	.50	.23
☐ 10	Paul Molitor	.75	.35
☐ 11	Bernard Gilkey	.20	.09
☐ 12	Jack McDowell	.20	.09
☐ 13	Andy Benes	.40	.18
☐ 14	Ryan Klesko	.50	.23
☐ 15	Mark McGwire	1.50	.70
☐ 16	Ken Griffey Jr.	4.00	1.80
☐ 17	Robb Nen	.20	.09
☐ 18	Cal Ripken	3.00	1.35
☐ 19	John Valentin	.20	.09
☐ 20	Ricky Bottalico	.20	.09
☐ 21	Mike Lansing	.20	.09
☐ 22	Ryne Sandberg	1.00	.45
☐ 23	Carlos Delgado	.40	.18
☐ 24	Craig Biggio	.50	.23
☐ 25	Eric Karros	.40	.18
☐ 26	Kevin Appier	.40	.18
☐ 27	Mariano Rivera	.40	.18
☐ 28	Vinny Castilla	.40	.18
☐ 29	Juan Gonzalez	2.00	.90
☐ 30	Al Martin	.20	.09
☐ 31	Jeff Cirillo	.40	.18
☐ 32	Eddie Murray	.75	.35
☐ 33	Ray Lankford	.40	.18
☐ 34	Manny Ramirez	.75	.35
☐ 35	Roberto Alomar	.75	.35
☐ 36	Will Clark	.50	.23
☐ 37	Chuck Knoblauch	.75	.35
☐ 38	Harold Baines	.40	.18
☐ 39	Trevor Hoffman	.20	.09
☐ 40	Edgar Martinez	.50	.23
☐ 41	Geronimo Berroa	.20	.09
☐ 42	Rey Ordonez	.20	.09
☐ 43	Mike Stanley	.20	.09
☐ 44	Mike Mussina	.75	.35
☐ 45	Kevin Brown	.40	.18
☐ 46	Dennis Eckersley	.40	.18
☐ 47	Henry Rodriguez	.20	.09
☐ 48	Tino Martinez	.75	.35
☐ 49	Eric Young	.20	.09
☐ 50	Bret Boone	.20	.09
☐ 51	Raul Mondesi	.50	.23
☐ 52	Sammy Sosa	.75	.35
☐ 53	John Smoltz	.40	.18
☐ 54	Billy Wagner	.20	.09
☐ 55	Jeff D'Amico	.20	.09
☐ 56	Ken Caminiti	.50	.23
☐ 57	Jason Kendall	.40	.18
☐ 58	Wade Boggs	.75	.35
☐ 59	Andres Galarraga	.75	.35
☐ 60	Jeff Brantley	.20	.09
☐ 61	Mel Nieves	.20	.09
☐ 62	Brian L. Hunter	.40	.18
☐ 63	Bobby Bonilla	.40	.18
☐ 64	Roger Clemens	1.50	.70
☐ 65	Jeff Kent	.20	.09
☐ 66	Matt Williams	.50	.23
☐ 67	Albert Belle	1.00	.45
☐ 68	Jeff King	.20	.09
☐ 69	John Wetteland	.20	.09
☐ 70	Deion Sanders	.40	.18
☐ 71	Bubba Trammell	1.50	.70
☐ 72	Felix Heredia	1.00	.45
☐ 73	Billy Koch	.50	.23
☐ 74	Sidney Ponson	.60	.25
☐ 75	Ricky Ledee	3.00	1.35
☐ 76	Brett Tomko	.40	.18
☐ 77	Braden Looper	.50	.23
☐ 78	Damian Jackson	.20	.09
☐ 79	Jason Dickson	.40	.18
☐ 80	Chad Green	1.00	.45

81	R.A. Dickey	.50	.23
82	Jeff Liefer	.20	.09
83	Matt Wagner	.20	.09
84	Richard Hidalgo	.40	.18
85	Adam Riggs	.20	.09
86	Robert Smith	.20	.09
87	Chad Hermansen	6.00	2.70
88	Felix Martinez	.20	.09
89	J.J. Johnson	.20	.09
90	Todd Dunwoody	1.00	.45
91	Katsuhiro Maeda	.40	.18
92	Darin Erstad	1.25	.55
93	Elieser Marrero	.40	.18
94	Bartolo Colon	.40	.18
95	Chris Fussell	.20	.09
96	Ugueth Urbina	.20	.09
97	Josh Paul	1.00	.45
98	Jaime Bluma	.20	.09
99	Seth Greisinger	.75	.35
100	Jose Cruz Jr.	15.00	6.75
101	Todd Dunn	.20	.09
102	Joe Young	.50	.23
103	Jonathan Johnson	.20	.09
104	Justin Towle	1.50	.70
105	Brian Rose	1.00	.45
106	Jose Guillen	1.00	.45
107	Andruw Jones	2.00	.90
108	Mark Kotsay	4.00	1.80
109	Wilton Guerrero	.20	.09
110	Jacob Cruz	.40	.18
111	Mike Sweeney	.20	.09
112	Julio Mosquera	.20	.09
113	Matt Morris	.40	.18
114	Wendell Magee	.40	.18
115	John Thomson	.20	.09
116	Javier (Jose) Valentin	.40	.18
117	Tom Fordham	.40	.18
118	Ruben Rivera	.40	.18
119	Mike Drumright	1.00	.45
120	Chris Holt	.20	.09
121	Sean Maloney	.20	.09
122	Michael Barrett	.40	.18
123	Tony Saunders	1.25	.55
124	Kevin Brown C.	.20	.09
125	Richard Almanzar	.20	.09
126	Mark Redman	.20	.09
127	Anthony Sanders	1.50	.70
128	Jeff Abbott	.20	.09
129	Eugene Kingsale	.20	.09
130	Paul Konerko	1.25	.55
131	Randall Simon	3.00	1.35
132	Andy Larkin	.20	.09
133	Rafael Medina	.40	.18
134	Mendy Lopez	.20	.09
135	Freddy Garcia	.40	.18
136	Karim Garcia	.40	.18
137	Larry Rodriguez	.50	.23
138	Carlos Guillen	.20	.09
139	Aaron Boone	.20	.09
140	Donnie Sadler	.20	.09
141	Brooks Kieschnick	.20	.09
142	Scott Spiezio	.40	.18
143	Everett Stull	.20	.09
144	Enrique Wilson	.40	.18
145	Milton Bradley	2.00	.90
146	Kevin Orie	.40	.18
147	Derek Wallace	.20	.09
148	Russ Johnson	.20	.09
149	Joe Lagarde	.50	.23
150	Luis Castillo	.40	.18
151	Jay Payton	.20	.09
152	Joe Long	.40	.18
153	Livan Hernandez	.50	.23
154	Vladimir Nunez	1.00	.45
155	Calvin Reese UER	.20	.09
	Card actually numbered 156		
156	George Arias	.20	.09
157	Homer Bush	.20	.09
158	Chris Carpenter UER	.40	.18
	Card numbered 159		
159	Eric Milton	2.00	.90
160	Richie Sexson	.40	.18
161	Carl Pavano	1.00	.45
162	Chris Gissell	.50	.23
163	Mac Suzuki	.20	.09
164	Pat Cline	.20	.09
165	Ron Wright	.50	.23
166	Dante Powell	.20	.09
167	Mark Bellhorn	.40	.18
168	George Lombard	.40	.18
169	Pee Wee Lopez	1.00	.45
170	Paul Wilder	2.00	.90
171	Brad Fullmer	.20	.09
172	Willie Martinez	1.25	.55
173	Dario Veras	.50	.23
174	Dave Coggin	.20	.09
175	Kris Benson	3.00	1.35
176	Torii Hunter	.20	.09
177	D.T. Cromer	.20	.09
178	Nelson Figueroa	.50	.23
179	Hiram Bocachica	1.25	.55
180	Shane Monahan	.40	.18
181	Jimmy Anderson	.75	.35
182	Juan Melo	.40	.18
183	Pablo Ortega	.75	.35
184	Calvin Pickering	4.00	1.80
185	Reggie Taylor	.40	.18
186	Jeff Farnsworth	.50	.23
187	Terrence Long	.20	.09
188	Geoff Jenkins	.40	.18
189	Steve Rain	.50	.23
190	Nerio Rodriguez	.75	.35
191	Derrick Gibson	.50	.23
192	Darin Blood	.40	.18
193	Ben Davis	.40	.18
194	Adrian Beltre	10.00	4.50
195	Damian Sapp UER	2.00	.90
196	Kerry Wood	5.00	2.20
197	Nate Rolison	1.50	.70
198	Fernando Tatis	4.00	1.80
199	Brad Penny	.75	.35
200	Jake Westbrook	1.25	.55
201	Edwin Diaz	.20	.09
202	Joe Fontenot	.75	.35
203	Matt Halloran	.75	.35
204	Blake Stein	.50	.23
205	Donan Masaoka	.40	.18
206	Ben Petrick	.40	.18
207	Matt Clement	1.50	.70
208	Todd Greene	.40	.18
209	Ray Ricken	.20	.09
210	Eric Chavez	5.00	2.20
211	Edgard Velazquez	.40	.18
212	Bruce Chen	2.00	.90
213	Danny Patterson	.20	.09
214	Jeff Yoder	.20	.09
215	Luis Ordaz	.50	.23
216	Chris Widger	.20	.09
217	Jason Brester	.20	.09
218	Carlton Loewer	.20	.09
219	Chris Reitsma	.50	.23
220	Neifi Perez	.40	.18
221	Hideki Irabu	1.50	.70
222	Ellis Burks	.40	.18
223	Pedro Santana	.75	.35
224	Kenny Lofton	1.00	.45
225	Randy Johnson	.75	.35
226	Terry Steinbach	.20	.09
227	Bernie Williams	.75	.35
228	Dean Palmer	.20	.09
229	Alan Benes	.40	.18
230	Marquis Grissom	.40	.18
231	Gary Sheffield	.75	.35
232	Curt Schilling	.40	.18
233	Reggie Sanders	.20	.09
234	Bobby Higginson	.40	.18
235	Moises Alou	.40	.18
236	Tom Glavine	.50	.23
237	Mark Grace	.50	.23
238	Ramon Martinez	.20	.09
239	Rafael Palmeiro	.50	.23
240	John Olerud	.40	.18
241	Dante Bichette	.40	.18
242	Greg Vaughn	.20	.09
243	Jeff Bagwell	1.50	.70
244	Barry Bonds	1.00	.45
245	Pat Hentgen	.20	.09
246	Jim Thome	.75	.35
247	Jermaine Allensworth	.20	.09
248	Andy Pettitte	.75	.35
249	Jay Bell	.20	.09
250	John Jaha	.20	.09
251	Jim Edmonds	.50	.23
252	Ron Gant	.40	.18
253	David Cone	.50	.23
254	Jose Canseco	.50	.23
255	Jay Buhner	.50	.23
256	Greg Maddux	2.50	1.10
257	Brian McRae	.20	.09
258	Lance Johnson	.20	.09
259	Travis Fryman	.40	.18
260	Paul O'Neill	.40	.18
261	Ivan Rodriguez	1.00	.45
262	Gregg Jefferies	.20	.09
263	Fred McGriff	.50	.23
264	Derek Bell	.20	.09
265	Jeff Conine	.40	.18
266	Mike Piazza	2.50	1.10
267	Mark Grudzielanek	.20	.09
268	Brady Anderson	.50	.23
269	Marty Cordova	.40	.18
270	Ray Durham	.20	.09
271	Joe Carter	.40	.18
272	Brian Jordan	.40	.18
273	David Justice	.75	.35
274	Tony Gwynn	2.00	.90
275	Larry Walker	.75	.35
276	Cecil Fielder	.40	.18
277	Mo Vaughn	1.00	.45
278	Alex Fernandez	.40	.18
279	Michael Tucker	.40	.18
280	Jose Valentin	.20	.09
281	Sandy Alomar	.40	.18
282	Todd Hollandsworth	.20	.09
283	Rico Brogna	.20	.09
284	Rusty Greer	.20	.09
285	Roberto Hernandez	.20	.09
286	Hal Morris	.20	.09
287	Johnny Damon	.20	.09
288	Todd Hundley	.20	.09
289	Rondell White	.40	.18
290	Frank Thomas	3.00	1.35
291	Don Demeter	.20	.09
292	Derek Lee	.50	.23
293	Todd Walker	.40	.18
294	Scott Rolen	2.50	1.10
295	Wes Helms	.40	.18
296	Bob Abreu	.40	.18
297	John Patterson	1.50	.70
298	Alex Gonzalez	1.50	.70
299	Grant Roberts	1.50	.70
300	Jeff Suppan	.40	.18
301	Luke Wilcox	.20	.09
302	Marlon Anderson	.40	.18
303	Ray Brown	.20	.09
304	Mike Caruso	1.50	.70
305	Sam Marsonek	.50	.23
306	Brady Raggio	.20	.09
307	Kevin McGlinchy	1.00	.45
308	Roy Halladay	1.25	.55
309	Jeremi Gonzalez	1.25	.55
310	Aramis Ramirez	8.00	3.60
311	Dermal Brown	4.00	1.80
312	Justin Thompson	.40	.18
313	Jay Tessmer	.20	.09
314	Mike Johnson	.50	.23
315	Danny Clyburn	.20	.09
316	Dean Palmer	.40	.18
317	Keith Foulke	.20	.09
318	Jimmy Osting	.50	.23
319	Valerio De Los Santos	.75	.35
320	Shannon Stewart	.40	.18
321	Willie Adams	.20	.09
322	Larry Barnes	.40	.18
323	Mark Johnson	.50	.23
324	Chris Stowers	.50	.23
325	Brandon Reed	.50	.23
326	Randy Winn	.20	.09
327	Steve Chavez	.75	.35
328	Nomar Garciaparra	2.50	1.10
329	Jacque Jones	2.00	.90
330	Chris Clemons	.20	.09
331	Todd Helton	1.25	.55
332	Ryan Brannan	.50	.23
333	Alex Sanchez	1.25	.55
334	Arnold Gooch	.20	.09
335	Russell Branyan	1.25	.55
336	Daryle Ward	1.50	.70

		MINT	NRMT
☐ 337	John LeRoy	.50	.23
☐ 338	Steve Cox	.20	.09
☐ 339	Kevin Witt	2.50	1.10
☐ 340	Norm Hutchins	.20	.09
☐ 341	Gabby Martinez	.20	.09
☐ 342	Kris Detmers	.20	.09
☐ 343	Mike Villano	.20	.09
☐ 344	Preston Wilson	.40	.18
☐ 345	James Manias	.50	.23
☐ 346	Deivi Cruz	1.25	.55
☐ 347	Donzell McDonald	.50	.23
☐ 348	Rod Myers	.75	.35
☐ 349	Shawn Chacon	1.00	.45
☐ 350	Elvin Hernandez	.50	.23
☐ 351	Orlando Cabrera	.75	.35
☐ 352	Brian Banks	.20	.09
☐ 353	Robbie Bell	.75	.35
☐ 354	Brad Rigby	.20	.09
☐ 355	Scott Elarton	.40	.18
☐ 356	Kevin Sweeney	.50	.23
☐ 357	Steve Soderstrom	.20	.09
☐ 358	Rya Nye	.40	.18
☐ 359	Marlon Allen	.50	.23
☐ 360	Donny Leon	.50	.23
☐ 361	Garrett Neubart	.75	.35
☐ 362	Abraham Nunez	1.25	.55
☐ 363	Adam Eaton	.50	.23
☐ 364	Octavio Dotel	.50	.23
☐ 365	Dean Crow	.20	.09
☐ 366	Jason Baker	.50	.23
☐ 367	Sean Casey	3.00	1.35
☐ 368	Joe Lawrence	.50	.23
☐ 369	Adam Johnson	1.25	.55
☐ 370	Scott Schoeneweis	.75	.35
☐ 371	Gerald Witasick Jr.	.20	.09
☐ 372	Ronnie Belliard	.50	.23
☐ 373	Russ Ortiz	.20	.09
☐ 374	Robert Stratton	.75	.35
☐ 375	Bobby Estalella	.40	.18
☐ 376	Corey Lee	.75	.35
☐ 377	Carlos Beltran	1.00	.45
☐ 378	Mike Cameron	.50	.23
☐ 379	Scott Randall	.50	.23
☐ 380	Corey Erickson	.75	.35
☐ 381	Jay Canizaro	.20	.09
☐ 382	Kerry Robinson	.50	.23
☐ 383	Todd Noel	1.00	.45
☐ 384	A.J. Zapp	3.00	1.35
☐ 385	Jarrod Washburn	.40	.18
☐ 386	Ben Grieve	1.50	.70
☐ 387	Javier Vazquez	1.00	.45
☐ 388	Tony Graffanino	.20	.09
☐ 389	Travis Lee	15.00	6.75
☐ 390	DaRond Stovall	.20	.09
☐ 391	Dennis Reyes	1.25	.55
☐ 392	Danny Buxbaum	.20	.09
☐ 393	Marc Lewis	1.00	.45
☐ 394	Kelvim Escobar	.50	.23
☐ 395	Danny Klassen	.40	.18
☐ 396	Ken Cloude	2.00	.90
☐ 397	Gabe Alvarez	.50	.23
☐ 398	Jaret Wright	10.00	4.50
☐ 399	Raul Casanova	.20	.09
☐ 400	Clayton Bruner	1.00	.45
☐ 401	Jason Marquis	1.25	.55
☐ 402	Marc Kroon	.20	.09
☐ 403	Jamey Wright	.20	.09
☐ 404	Matt Snyder	.50	.23
☐ 405	Josh Garrett	.75	.35
☐ 406	Juan Encarnacion	.75	.35
☐ 407	Heath Murray	.20	.09
☐ 408	Brett Herbison	.50	.23
☐ 409	Brent Butler	3.00	1.35
☐ 410	Danny Peoples	1.50	.70
☐ 411	Miguel Tejada	5.00	2.20
☐ 412	Damian Moss	.20	.09
☐ 413	Jim Pittsley	.20	.09
☐ 414	Dmitri Young	.20	.09
☐ 415	Glendon Rusch	.20	.09
☐ 416	Vladimir Guerrero	1.50	.70
☐ 417	Cole Liniak	2.50	1.10
☐ 418	Ramon Hernandez UER	.40	.18

Card back says 1st Bowman card is 1997
He had a 1996 Bowman

☐ 419	Cliff Politte	.75	.35
☐ 420	Mel Rosario	.50	.23

☐ 421	Jorge Carrion	.50	.23
☐ 422	John Barnes	1.00	.45
☐ 423	Chris Stowe	.50	.23
☐ 424	Vernon Wells	4.00	1.80
☐ 425	Brett Caradonna	2.00	.90
☐ 426	Scott Hodges	1.00	.45
☐ 427	Jon Garland	2.00	.90
☐ 428	Nathan Haynes	1.00	.45
☐ 429	Geoff Goetz	.75	.35
☐ 430	Adam Kennedy	1.00	.45
☐ 431	T.J. Tucker	.50	.23
☐ 432	Aaron Akin	.75	.35
☐ 433	Jayson Werth	3.00	1.35
☐ 434	Glenn Davis	1.25	.55
☐ 435	Mark Mangum	.50	.23
☐ 436	Troy Cameron	2.50	1.10
☐ 437	J.J. Davis	3.00	1.35
☐ 438	Lance Berkman	6.00	2.70
☐ 439	Jason Standridge	1.00	.45
☐ 440	Jason Dellaero	1.25	.55
☐ 441	Hideki Irabu	1.00	.45

1997 Bowman 1998 ROY Favorites

Randomly inserted in 1997 Bowman Series two packs at the rate of one in 12, this 15-card set features color photos of prospective 1998 Rookie of the Year candidates.

		MINT	NRMT
COMPLETE SET (15)		40.00	18.00
COMMON CARD (1-15)		1.00	.45
SER.2 STATED ODDS 1:12			

☐ ROY1	Jeff Abbott	1.00	.45
☐ ROY2	Karim Garcia	1.50	.70
☐ ROY3	Todd Helton	3.00	1.35
☐ ROY4	Richard Hidalgo	1.50	.70
☐ ROY5	Geoff Jenkins	1.50	.70
☐ ROY6	Russ Johnson	1.00	.45
☐ ROY7	Paul Konerko	3.00	1.35
☐ ROY8	Mark Kotsay	4.00	1.80
☐ ROY9	Ricky Ledee	3.00	1.35
☐ ROY10	Travis Lee	15.00	6.75
☐ ROY11	Derrek Lee	2.00	.90
☐ ROY12	Elieser Marrero	1.50	.70
☐ ROY13	Juan Melo	1.50	.70
☐ ROY14	Brian Rose	2.50	1.10
☐ ROY15	Fernando Tatis	4.00	1.80

1997 Bowman Certified Blue Ink Autographs

Randomly inserted in first and second series packs at a rate of one in 96, this 90-card set features color player photos of top prospects with blue ink auto-

graphs and printed on sturdy 16 pt. card stock with the Topps Certified Autograph Issue Stamp. The Derek Jeter blue ink and green ink versions are seeded in every 1,928 packs.

	MINT	NRMT
COMPLETE SET (90)	2200.00	1000.00
COMMON BLUE INK (1-90)	12.00	5.50
BLUE INK MINOR STARS	15.00	6.75
STATED ODDS 1:96, ANCO 1:115		
*BLACK INK: 1X TO 2X HI COLUMN		
BLACK STATED ODDS 1:503, ANCO 1:600		
*GOLD INK: 2.5X TO 5X HI COLUMN		
GOLD: STATED ODDS 1:1509, ANCO 1:1795		
D.JETER BLUE SER.1 ODDS 1:1928		
D.JETER GREEN SER.2 ODDS 1:1928		

☐ CA1	Jeff Abbott	12.00	5.50
☐ CA2	Bob Abreu	20.00	9.00
☐ CA3	Willie Adams	12.00	5.50
☐ CA4	Brian Banks	12.00	5.50
☐ CA5	Kris Benson	40.00	18.00
☐ CA6	Darin Blood	15.00	6.75
☐ CA7	Jaime Bluma	12.00	5.50
☐ CA8	Kevin Brown	15.00	6.75
☐ CA9	Ray Brown	12.00	5.50
☐ CA10	Homer Bush	12.00	5.50
☐ CA11	Mike Cameron	30.00	13.50
☐ CA12	Jay Canizaro	12.00	5.50
☐ CA13	Luis Castillo	15.00	6.75
☐ CA14	Dave Coggin	12.00	5.50
☐ CA15	Bartolo Colon	15.00	6.75
☐ CA16	Rocky Coppinger	12.00	5.50
☐ CA17	Jacob Cruz	25.00	11.00
☐ CA18	Jose Cruz Jr.	150.00	70.00
☐ CA19	Jeff D'Amico	12.00	5.50
☐ CA20	Ben Davis	25.00	11.00
☐ CA21	Mike Drumright	15.00	6.75
☐ CA22	Scott Elarton	15.00	6.75
☐ CA23	Darin Erstad	50.00	22.00
☐ CA24	Bobby Estalella	20.00	9.00
☐ CA25	Joe Fontenot	15.00	6.75
☐ CA26	Tom Fordham	15.00	6.75
☐ CA27	Brad Fullmer	25.00	11.00
☐ CA28	Chris Fussell	12.00	5.50
☐ CA29	Karim Garcia	25.00	11.00
☐ CA30	Kris Detmers	12.00	5.50
☐ CA31	Todd Greene	25.00	11.00
☐ CA32	Ben Grieve	60.00	27.00
☐ CA33	Vladimir Guerrero	60.00	27.00
☐ CA34	Jose Guillen	40.00	18.00
☐ CA35	Roy Halladay	20.00	9.00
☐ CA36	Wes Helms	30.00	13.50
☐ CA37	Chad.Hermansen	60.00	27.00
☐ CA38	Richard Hidalgo	25.00	11.00
☐ CA39	Todd Hollandsworth	12.00	5.50
☐ CA40	Damian Jackson	12.00	5.50
☐ CA41	Derek Jeter Blue DP	100.00	45.00
☐ CA41B	Derek Jeter Green	100.00	45.00
☐ CA42	Andruw Jones	80.00	36.00
☐ CA43	Brooks Kieschnick	12.00	5.50
☐ CA44	Eugene Kingsale	12.00	5.50
☐ CA45	Paul Konerko	50.00	22.00
☐ CA46	Marc Kroon	12.00	5.50
☐ CA47	Derrek Lee	40.00	18.00
☐ CA48	Travis Lee	120.00	55.00

		MINT	NRMT
☐ CA49	Terrence Long......	12.00	5.50
☐ CA50	Curt Lyons	12.00	5.50
☐ CA51	Eli Marrero	25.00	11.00
☐ CA52	Rafael Medina	15.00	6.75
☐ CA53	Juan Melo	15.00	6.75
☐ CA54	Shane Monahan ...	15.00	6.75
☐ CA55	Julio Mosquera	12.00	5.50
☐ CA56	Heath Murray	12.00	5.50
☐ CA57	Ryan Nye	15.00	6.75
☐ CA58	Kevin Orie	30.00	13.50
☐ CA59	Russ Ortiz	12.00	5.50
☐ CA60	Carl Pavano	40.00	18.00
☐ CA61	Jay Payton	12.00	5.50
☐ CA62	Nefi Perez	20.00	9.00
☐ CA63	Sidney Ponson	15.00	6.75
☐ CA64	Calvin Reese	12.00	5.50
☐ CA65	Ray Ricken	12.00	5.50
☐ CA66	Brad Rigby	12.00	5.50
☐ CA67	Adam Riggs	12.00	5.50
☐ CA68	Ruben Rivera	25.00	11.00
☐ CA69	J.J. Johnson	12.00	5.50
☐ CA70	Scott Rolen	80.00	36.00
☐ CA71	Tony Saunders	20.00	9.00
☐ CA72	Donnie Sadler	12.00	5.50
☐ CA73	Richie Sexson	25.00	11.00
☐ CA74	Scott Spiezio	15.00	6.75
☐ CA75	Everett Stull	12.00	5.50
☐ CA76	Mike Sweeney	15.00	6.75
☐ CA77	Fernando Tatis	50.00	22.00
☐ CA78	Miguel Tejada	60.00	27.00
☐ CA79	Justin Thompson ..	30.00	13.50
☐ CA80	Justin Towle	20.00	9.00
☐ CA81	Billy Wagner	20.00	9.00
☐ CA82	Todd Walker	20.00	9.00
☐ CA83	Luke Wilcox	12.00	5.50
☐ CA84	Paul Wilder	25.00	11.00
☐ CA85	Enrique Wilson	15.00	6.75
☐ CA86	Kerry Wood	50.00	22.00
☐ CA87	Jamey Wright	12.00	5.50
☐ CA88	Ron Wright	30.00	13.50
☐ CA89	Dmitri Young	12.00	5.50
☐ CA90	Nelson Figueroa ...	15.00	6.75

1997 Bowman International Best

Randomly inserted in series two packs at the rate of one in 12, this 20-card set features color photos of both prospects and veterans from far and wide who have made an impact on the game.

	MINT	NRMT
COMPLETE SET (20)	100.00	45.00
COMMON CARD (1-20)	1.50	.70
UNLISTED STARS	3.00	1.35
SER.2 STATED ODDS 1:12......		
COMP.ATOMIC SET (20) ..	400.00	180.00
COMMON ATOMIC (1-20) ..	6.00	2.70
*ATOMIC: 2X TO 4X HI COLUMN		
ATOMIC SER.2 STATED ODDS 1:96		
COMP.REF.SET (20)	200.00	90.00
COMMON REF. (1-20)	3.00	1.35

*REFRACTORS: 1X TO 2X HI COLUMN
REFRACTOR SER.2 STATED ODDS 1:48

		MINT	NRMT
☐ BBI1	Frank Thomas	12.00	5.50
☐ BBI2	Ken Griffey Jr.	15.00	6.75
☐ BBI3	Juan Gonzalez	8.00	3.60
☐ BBI4	Bernie Williams	3.00	1.35
☐ BBI5	Hideo Nomo	8.00	3.60
☐ BBI6	Sammy Sosa	3.00	1.35
☐ BBI7	Larry Walker	3.00	1.35
☐ BBI8	Vinny Castilla	1.50	.70
☐ BBI9	Mariano Rivera	1.50	.70
☐ BBI10	Rafael Palmeiro	2.00	.90
☐ BBI11	Nomar Garciaparra	10.00	4.50
☐ BBI12	Todd Walker	1.50	.70
☐ BBI13	Andruw Jones	8.00	3.60
☐ BBI14	Vladimir Guerrero .	6.00	2.70
☐ BBI15	Ruben Rivera	1.50	.70
☐ BBI16	Bob Abreu	1.50	.70
☐ BBI17	Karim Garcia	1.50	.70
☐ BBI18	Katsuhiro Maeda ...	1.50	.70
☐ BBI19	Jose Cruz Jr.	20.00	9.00
☐ BBI20	Damian Moss	1.50	.70

1997 Bowman Scout's Honor Roll

Randomly inserted in first series packs at a rate of one in 12, this 15-card set features color photos of top prospects and rookies printed on double-etched foil cards.

	MINT	NRMT
COMPLETE SET (15)	50.00	22.00
COMMON CARD (1-15)	1.25	.55
UNLISTED STARS	1.50	.70
SER.1 STATED ODDS 1:12......		

		MINT	NRMT
☐ 1	Dmitri Young	1.25	.55
☐ 2	Bob Abreu	1.25	.55
☐ 3	Vladimir Guerrero .	4.00	1.80
☐ 4	Paul Konerko	3.00	1.35
☐ 5	Kevin Orie	1.25	.55
☐ 6	Todd Walker	1.25	.55
☐ 7	Ben Grieve	4.00	1.80
☐ 8	Darin Erstad	3.00	1.35
☐ 9	Derek Lee	1.50	.70
☐ 10	Jose Cruz Jr.	15.00	6.75
☐ 11	Scott Rolen	5.00	2.20
☐ 12	Travis Lee	15.00	6.75
☐ 13	Andruw Jones	5.00	2.20
☐ 14	Wilton Guerrero	1.25	.55
☐ 15	Nomar Garciaparra	6.00	2.70

1997 Bowman Chrome

The 1997 Bowman Chrome set was issued in 300 cards and was distributed in four-card packs with a suggested retail price of $3.00. The product was released in the winter, after the end of the 1997 season. The fronts feature color action player photos printed on dazzling chromium cards. The backs carry player information. Key Rookie Cards in this set include Adrian Beltre, Jose Cruz Jr., Travis Lee, Aramis Ramirez and Miguel Tejada.

	MINT	NRMT
COMPLETE SET (300)	350.00	160.00
COMMON RED (1-100)	.40	.18
MINOR STARS	.75	.35
UNLISTED STARS	1.50	.70
COMMON BLUE (101-300) ..	1.00	.45
BLUE MINOR STARS	1.00	
BLUE SEMISTARS	1.50	
BLUE UNLISTED STARS	2.00	
COMP.INT'L SET (300) ..	1000.00	450.00
COMMON INT'L RED (1-100)	1.00	.45
COMMON INT'L BLUE (101-300)	2.00	.90
*INT'L STARS: 1.5X TO 3X HI COLUMN		
*INT'L ROOKIES: 1X TO 2X HI...		
INT'L STATED ODDS 1:4		

		MINT	NRMT
☐ 1	Derek Jeter	5.00	2.20
☐ 2	Chipper Jones	5.00	2.20
☐ 3	Hideo Nomo	4.00	1.80
☐ 4	Tim Salmon	1.50	.70
☐ 5	Robin Ventura	.75	.35
☐ 6	Tony Clark	1.50	.70
☐ 7	Barry Larkin	1.00	.45
☐ 8	Paul Molitor	1.50	.70
☐ 9	Andy Benes	.75	.35
☐ 10	Ryan Klesko	1.00	.45
☐ 11	Mark McGwire	3.00	1.35
☐ 12	Ken Griffey Jr.	8.00	3.60
☐ 13	Robb Nen	.40	.18
☐ 14	Cal Ripken	6.00	2.70
☐ 15	John Valentin	.40	.18
☐ 16	Ricky Bottalico	.40	.18
☐ 17	Mike Lansing	.40	.18
☐ 18	Ryne Sandberg	2.00	.90
☐ 19	Carlos Delgado	.75	.35
☐ 20	Craig Biggio	1.00	.45
☐ 21	Eric Karros	.75	.35
☐ 22	Kevin Appier	.75	.35
☐ 23	Mariano Rivera	.75	.35
☐ 24	Vinny Castilla	.75	.35
☐ 25	Juan Gonzalez	4.00	1.80
☐ 26	Al Martin	.40	.18
☐ 27	Jeff Cirillo	.75	.35
☐ 28	Ray Lankford	.75	.35
☐ 29	Manny Ramirez	1.50	.70
☐ 30	Roberto Alomar	1.00	.45
☐ 31	Will Clark	1.00	.45
☐ 32	Chuck Knoblauch ..	1.50	.70
☐ 33	Harold Baines	.75	.35
☐ 34	Edgar Martinez	1.00	.45
☐ 35	Mike Mussina	1.50	.70
☐ 36	Kevin Brown	.75	.35
☐ 37	Dennis Eckersley ..	.75	.35
☐ 38	Tino Martinez	1.00	.45
☐ 39	Raul Mondesi	1.00	.45
☐ 40	Sammy Sosa	1.50	.70

41	John Smoltz	.75	.35
42	Billy Wagner	.75	.35
43	Ken Caminiti	1.00	.45
44	Wade Boggs	1.50	.70
45	Andres Galarraga	1.50	.70
46	Roger Clemens	3.00	1.35
47	Matt Williams	1.00	.45
48	Albert Belle	2.00	.90
49	Jeff King	.40	.18
50	John Wetteland	.40	.18
51	Deion Sanders	.75	.35
52	Ellis Burks	.75	.35
53	Pedro Martinez	1.50	.70
54	Kenny Lofton	2.00	.90
55	Randy Johnson	1.50	.70
56	Bernie Williams	1.50	.70
57	Marquis Grissom	.75	.35
58	Gary Sheffield	1.50	.70
59	Curt Schilling	.75	.35
60	Reggie Sanders	.40	.18
61	Bobby Higginson	.75	.35
62	Moises Alou	.75	.35
63	Tom Glavine	.75	.35
64	Mark Grace	1.00	.45
65	Rafael Palmeiro	1.00	.45
66	John Olerud	.75	.35
67	Dante Bichette	.75	.35
68	Jeff Bagwell	3.00	1.35
69	Barry Bonds	2.00	.90
70	Pat Hentgen	.75	.35
71	Jim Thome	1.50	.70
72	Andy Pettitte	1.50	.70
73	Jay Bell	.75	.35
74	Jim Edmonds	1.00	.45
75	Ron Gant	.75	.35
76	David Cone	1.00	.45
77	Jose Canseco	1.00	.45
78	Jay Buhner	1.00	.45
79	Greg Maddux	5.00	2.20
80	Lance Johnson	.40	.18
81	Travis Fryman	.75	.35
82	Paul O'Neill	.75	.35
83	Ivan Rodriguez	2.00	.90
84	Fred McGriff	1.00	.45
85	Mike Piazza	5.00	2.20
86	Brady Anderson	1.00	.45
87	Marty Cordova	.75	.35
88	Joe Carter	.75	.35
89	Brian Jordan	.75	.35
90	David Justice	1.50	.70
91	Tony Gwynn	2.50	1.10
92	Larry Walker	1.50	.70
93	Mo Vaughn	2.00	.90
94	Sandy Alomar	.75	.35
95	Rusty Greer	.75	.35
96	Roberto Hernandez	.40	.18
97	Hal Morris	.40	.18
98	Todd Hundley	.75	.35
99	Rondell White	.75	.35
100	Frank Thomas	6.00	2.70
101	Bubba Trammell	4.00	1.80
102	Sidney Ponson	1.50	.70
103	Ricky Ledee	8.00	3.60
104	Brett Tomko	1.00	.45
105	Braden Looper	1.50	.70
106	Jason Dickson	1.00	.45
107	Chad Green	2.50	1.10
108	R.A. Dickey	.75	.35
109	Jeff Liefer	1.00	.45
110	Richard Hidalgo	1.00	.45
111	Chad Hermansen	15.00	6.75
112	Felix Martinez	1.00	.45
113	J.J. Johnson	1.00	.45
114	Todd Dunwoody	1.50	.70
115	Katsuhiro Maeda	1.00	.45
116	Darin Erstad	2.50	1.10
117	Elieser Marrero	1.00	.45
118	Bartolo Colon	1.00	.45
119	Ugueth Urbina	1.00	.45
120	Jaime Bluma	1.00	.45
121	Seth Greisinger	2.00	.90
122	Jose Cruz Jr.	35.00	16.00
123	Todd Dunn	1.00	.45
124	Justin Towle	4.00	1.80
125	Brian Rose	2.00	.90
126	Jose Guillen	2.00	.90
127	Andruw Jones	4.00	1.80
128	Mark Kotsay	10.00	4.50
129	Wilton Guerrero	1.00	.45
130	Jacob Cruz	1.00	.45
131	Mike Sweeney	1.00	.45
132	Matt Morris	1.00	.45
133	John Thomson	1.00	.45
134	Javier Valentin	1.00	.45
135	Mike Drumright	2.50	1.10
136	Michael Barrett	1.00	.45
137	Tony Saunders	3.00	1.35
138	Kevin Brown	1.00	.45
139	Anthony Sanders	4.00	1.80
140	Jeff Abbott	1.00	.45
141	Eugene Kingsale	1.00	.45
142	Paul Konerko	2.50	1.10
143	Randall Simon	8.00	3.60
144	Freddy Garcia	1.00	.45
145	Karim Garcia	1.00	.45
146	Carlos Guillen	1.00	.45
147	Aaron Boone	1.00	.45
148	Donnie Sadler	1.00	.45
149	Brooks Kieschnick	1.00	.45
150	Scott Spiezio	1.00	.45
151	Kevin Orie	1.00	.45
152	Russ Johnson	1.00	.45
153	Livan Hernandez	1.50	.70
154	Vladimir Nunez	2.50	1.10
155	Calvin Reese	1.00	.45
156	Chris Carpenter	1.00	.45
157	Eric Milton	5.00	2.20
158	Richie Sexson	1.00	.45
159	Carl Pavano	2.00	.90
160	Pat Cline	1.00	.45
161	Ron Wright	1.50	.70
162	Dante Powell	1.00	.45
163	Mark Bellhorn	1.00	.45
164	George Lombard	1.00	.45
165	Paul Wilder	5.00	2.20
166	Brad Fullmer	1.00	.45
167	Kris Benson	8.00	3.60
168	Torii Hunter	1.00	.45
169	D.T. Cromer	1.00	.45
170	Nelson Figueroa	1.50	.70
171	Hiram Bocachica	3.00	1.35
172	Shane Monahan	1.00	.45
173	Juan Melo	1.00	.45
174	Calvin Pickering	10.00	4.50
175	Reggie Taylor	1.00	.45
176	Geoff Jenkins	1.00	.45
177	Steve Rain	1.50	.70
178	Nerio Rodriguez	2.00	.90
179	Derrick Gibson	1.50	.70
180	Darin Blood	1.00	.45
181	Ben Davis	1.00	.45
182	Adrian Beltre	30.00	13.50
183	Kerry Wood	12.00	5.50
184	Nate Rolison	4.00	1.80
185	Fernando Tatis	10.00	4.50
186	Jake Westbrook	3.00	1.35
187	Edwin Diaz	1.00	.45
188	Joe Fontenot	2.00	.90
189	Matt Halloran	2.00	.90
190	Matt Clement	3.00	1.35
191	Todd Greene	1.00	.45
192	Eric Chavez	12.00	5.50
193	Edgard Velazquez	1.00	.45
194	Bruce Chen	5.00	2.20
195	Jason Brester	1.00	.45
196	Chris Reitsma	1.50	.70
197	Neifi Perez	1.00	.45
198	Hideki Irabu	4.00	1.80
199	Don Denbow	1.00	.45
200	Derrek Lee	1.50	.70
201	Todd Walker	1.00	.45
202	Scott Rolen	4.00	1.80
203	Wes Helms	1.00	.45
204	Bob Abreu	1.00	.45
205	John Patterson	4.00	1.80
206	Alex Gonzalez	1.00	.45
207	Grant Roberts	4.00	1.80
208	Jeff Suppan	1.00	.45
209	Luke Wilcox	1.00	.45
210	Marlon Anderson	1.00	.45
211	Mike Caruso	4.00	1.80
212	Roy Halladay	3.00	1.35
213	Jeremi Gonzalez	3.00	1.35
214	Aramis Ramirez	25.00	11.00
215	Dermal Brown	10.00	4.50
216	Justin Thompson	1.00	.45
217	Danny Clyburn	1.00	.45
218	Bruce Aven	1.00	.45
219	Keith Foulke	1.00	.45
220	Shannon Stewart	1.00	.45
221	Larry Barnes	1.00	.45
222	Mark Johnson	1.50	.70
223	Randy Winn	1.00	.45
224	Nomar Garciaparra	5.00	2.20
225	Jacque Jones	5.00	2.20
226	Chris Clemons	1.00	.45
227	Todd Helton	2.50	1.10
228	Ryan Brannan	1.50	.70
229	Alex Sanchez	3.00	1.35
230	Russell Branyan	2.50	1.10
231	Daryle Ward	4.00	1.80
232	Kevin Witt	6.00	2.70
233	Gabby Martinez	1.00	.45
234	Preston Wilson	1.00	.45
235	Donzell McDonald	1.50	.70
236	Orlando Cabrera	2.00	.90
237	Brian Banks	1.00	.45
238	Robbie Bell	2.00	.90
239	Brad Rigby	1.00	.45
240	Scott Elarton	1.00	.45
241	Donny Leon	1.00	.45
242	Abraham Nunez	3.00	1.35
243	Adam Eaton	1.50	.70
244	Octavio Dotel	1.50	.70
245	Sean Casey	8.00	3.60
246	Joe Lawrence	1.50	.70
247	Adam Johnson	3.00	1.35
248	Ronnie Belliard	1.00	.45
249	Bobby Estalella	1.00	.45
250	Corey Lee	2.00	.90
251	Mike Cameron	1.50	.70
252	Kerry Robinson	1.50	.70
253	A.J. Zapp	8.00	3.60
254	Jarrod Washburn	1.00	.45
255	Ben Grieve	8.00	3.60
256	Javier Vazquez	2.50	1.10
257	Travis Lee	35.00	16.00
258	Dennis Reyes	3.00	1.35
259	Danny Buxbaum	1.00	.45
260	Kelvim Escobar	1.50	.70
261	Danny Klassen	1.00	.45
262	Ken Cloude	5.00	2.20
263	Gabe Alvarez	1.00	.45
264	Clayton Bruner	2.50	1.10
265	Jason Marquis	1.00	.45
266	Jamey Wright	1.00	.45
267	Matt Snyder	1.50	.70
268	Josh Garrett	2.00	.90
269	Juan Encarnacion	2.00	.90
270	Heath Murray	1.00	.45
271	Brent Butler	8.00	3.60
272	Danny Peoples	4.00	1.80
273	Miguel Tejada	12.00	5.50
274	Jim Pittsley	1.00	.45
275	Dmitri Young	1.00	.45
276	Vladimir Guerrero	3.00	1.35
277	Cole Liniak	6.00	2.70
278	Ramon Hernandez	2.00	.90
279	Cliff Politte	2.00	.90
280	Mel Rosario	1.50	.70
281	Jorge Carrion	1.50	.70
282	John Barnes	2.50	1.10
283	Chris Stowe	1.00	.45
284	Vernon Wells	10.00	4.50
285	Brett Caradonna	5.00	2.20
286	Scott Hodges	2.50	1.10
287	Jon Garland	5.00	2.20
288	Nathan Haynes	2.50	1.10
289	Geoff Goetz	2.00	.90
290	Adam Kennedy	2.50	1.10
291	T.J. Tucker	1.50	.70
292	Aaron Akin	2.00	.90
293	Jayson Werth	8.00	3.60
294	Glenn Davis	3.00	1.35
295	Mark Mangum	1.50	.70
296	Troy Cameron	6.00	2.70
297	J.J. Davis	8.00	3.60
298	Lance Berkman	15.00	6.75

	MINT	NRMT
□ 299 Jason Standridge	2.50	1.10
□ 300 Jason Dellaero	3.00	1.35

1997 Bowman Chrome Refractors

Randomly inserted in packs at the rate of one in 12, this 300-card set is parallel to the base set and is similar in design. The difference can be found in the refractive quality of the cards.

	MINT	NRMT
COMPLETE SET (300)	3500.00	1600.00
COMMON CARD (1-300)	5.00	2.20
MINOR STARS	8.00	3.60
SEMISTARS	12.00	5.50
UNLISTED STARS	20.00	9.00
*STARS: 6X TO 12X BASIC CARDS		
*YOUNG STARS: 5X TO 10X BASIC CARDS		
*ROOKIES: 2.5X TO 5X BASIC CARDS		
STATED ODDS 1:12		
COMP.INT'L REF.SET (300)	5000.00	2200.00
COMMON INT'L REF. (1-300)	8.00	3.60
*INT'L REF.STARS: .75X TO 1.5X REF.		
*INT'L REF.ROOKIES: .75X TO 1.5X REF.		
INT'L REF.STATED ODDS 1:24		

		MINT	NRMT
□ 1	Derek Jeter	50.00	22.00
□ 2	Chipper Jones	60.00	27.00
□ 3	Hideo Nomo	60.00	27.00
□ 11	Mark McGwire	100.00	45.00
□ 12	Ken Griffey Jr.	100.00	45.00
□ 14	Cal Ripken	80.00	36.00
□ 18	Ryne Sandberg	25.00	11.00
□ 46	Roger Clemens	40.00	18.00
□ 48	Albert Belle	25.00	11.00
□ 54	Kenny Lofton	25.00	11.00
□ 68	Jeff Bagwell	25.00	11.00
□ 69	Barry Bonds	25.00	11.00
□ 79	Greg Maddux	60.00	27.00
□ 83	Ivan Rodriguez	25.00	11.00
□ 85	Mike Piazza	60.00	27.00
□ 91	Tony Gwynn	50.00	22.00
□ 93	Mo Vaughn	25.00	11.00
□ 100	Frank Thomas	80.00	36.00
□ 103	Ricky Ledee	40.00	18.00
□ 111	Chad Hermansen	60.00	27.00
□ 122	Jose Cruz Jr.	175.00	80.00
□ 127	Andruw Jones	30.00	13.50
□ 128	Mark Kotsay	50.00	22.00
□ 142	Paul Konerko	25.00	11.00
□ 143	Randall Simon	40.00	18.00
□ 157	Eric Milton	25.00	11.00
□ 165	Paul Wilder	25.00	11.00
□ 167	Kris Benson	40.00	18.00
□ 174	Calvin Pickering	40.00	18.00
□ 182	Adrian Beltre	120.00	55.00
□ 183	Kerry Wood	50.00	22.00
□ 185	Fernando Tatis	50.00	22.00
□ 192	Eric Chavez	60.00	27.00
□ 202	Scott Rolen	40.00	18.00
□ 214	Aramis Ramirez	80.00	36.00
□ 215	Dermal Brown	25.00	11.00
□ 224	Nomar Garciaparra	50.00	22.00
□ 225	Jacque Jones	25.00	11.00
□ 227	Todd Helton	25.00	11.00
□ 231	Daryle Ward	20.00	9.00
□ 232	Kevin Witt	30.00	13.50
□ 245	Sean Casey	30.00	13.50
□ 253	A.J. Zapp	40.00	18.00
□ 255	Ben Grieve	30.00	13.50
□ 257	Travis Lee	150.00	70.00
□ 262	Ken Cloude	25.00	11.00
□ 271	Brent Butler	40.00	18.00
□ 273	Miguel Tejada	60.00	27.00
□ 276	Vladimir Guerrero	25.00	11.00
□ 277	Cole Liniak	30.00	13.50
□ 284	Vernon Wells	40.00	18.00
□ 293	Jayson Werth	40.00	18.00

		MINT	NRMT
□ 296	Troy Cameron	30.00	13.50
□ 297	J.J. Davis	40.00	18.00
□ 298	Lance Berkman	60.00	27.00

1997 Bowman Chrome 1998 ROY Favorites

Randomly inserted in packs at the rate of one in 24, cards from this 15-card set features color action photos of 1998 Rookie of the Year prospective candidates printed on chromium cards. The backs carry player information.

	MINT	NRMT
COMPLETE SET (15)	60.00	27.00
COMMON CARD (1-15)	1.50	.70
STATED ODDS 1:24		
COMP.REF.SET (15)	120.00	55.00
*REFRACTORS: 1X TO 2X HI COLUMN		
REFRACTOR STATED ODDS 1:72		

		MINT	NRMT
□ ROY1	Jeff Abbott	1.50	.70
□ ROY2	Karim Garcia	2.00	.90
□ ROY3	Todd Helton	5.00	2.20
□ ROY4	Richard Hidalgo	2.00	.90
□ ROY5	Geoff Jenkins	2.00	.90
□ ROY6	Russ Johnson	1.50	.70
□ ROY7	Paul Konerko	5.00	2.20
□ ROY8	Mark Kotsay	6.00	2.70
□ ROY9	Ricky Ledee	5.00	2.20
□ ROY10	Travis Lee	25.00	11.00
□ ROY11	Derrek Lee	3.00	1.35
□ ROY12	Elieser Marrero	2.00	.90
□ ROY13	Juan Melo	2.00	.90
□ ROY14	Brian Rose	4.00	1.80
□ ROY15	Fernando Tatis	6.00	2.70

1997 Bowman Chrome Scout's Honor Roll

Randomly inserted in packs at a rate of one in 12, this 15-card set features color photos of top prospects and rookies printed on chromium cards. The backs carry player information.

	MINT	NRMT
COMPLETE SET (15)	60.00	27.00
COMMON CARD (1-15)	1.50	.70
STATED ODDS 1:12		

	MINT	NRMT
COMP.REF.SET (15)	120.00	55.00
*REFRACTORS: 1X TO 2X HI COLUMN		
REFRACTOR STATED ODDS 1:36		

		MINT	NRMT
□ SHR1	Dmitri Young	1.50	.70
□ SHR2	Bob Abreu	1.50	.70
□ SHR3	Vladimir Guerrero	5.00	2.20
□ SHR4	Paul Konerko	4.00	1.80
□ SHR5	Kevin Orie	1.50	.70
□ SHR6	Todd Walker	1.50	.70
□ SHR7	Ben Grieve	5.00	2.20
□ SHR8	Darin Erstad	4.00	1.80
□ SHR9	Derrek Lee	2.00	.90
□ SHR10	Jose Cruz Jr.	20.00	9.00
□ SHR11	Scott Rolen	6.00	2.70
□ SHR12	Travis Lee	20.00	9.00
□ SHR13	Andruw Jones	6.00	2.70
□ SHR14	Wilton Guerrero	1.50	.70
□ SHR15	Nomar Garciaparra	8.00	3.60

1994 Bowman's Best

This 200-card standard-size set consists of 90 veteran stars, 90 rookies and prospects and 20 Mirror Image cards. The veteran cards have red backs and are designated 1R-90R. The rookies and prospects cards have blue backs and are designated 1B-90B. The Mirror Image cards feature a veteran star and a prospect matched by position. These cards are numbered 91-110. Subsets featured are Super Vet (1R-6R), Super Rookie (82R-90R), and Blue Chip (1B-11B). Rookie Cards include Alan Benes, Tony Clark, Brad Fullmer, Chan Ho Park, Edgar Renteria and Ruben Rivera.

	MINT	NRMT
COMPLETE SET (200)	80.00	36.00
COMMON CARD (B1-X110)	.30	.14
MINOR STARS	.60	.25
UNLISTED STARS	1.25	.55

		MINT	NRMT
□ B1	Chipper Jones	4.00	1.80
□ B2	Derek Jeter	5.00	2.20
□ B3	Bill Pulsipher	.60	.25
□ B4	James Baldwin	.60	.25
□ B5	Brooks Kieschnick	1.00	.45
□ B6	Justin Thompson	2.00	.90
□ B7	Midre Cummings	.30	.14
□ B8	Joey Hamilton	1.25	.55
□ B9	Calvin Reese	.60	.25
□ B10	Brian Barber	.30	.14
□ B11	John Burke	.30	.14
□ B12	DeShawn Warren	.60	.25

☐ B13 Edgardo Alfonzo	3.00	1.35
☐ B14 Eddie Pearson	.60	.25
☐ B15 Jimmy Haynes	.60	.25
☐ B16 Danny Bautista	.30	.14
☐ B17 Roger Cedeno	.75	.35
☐ B18 Jon Lieber	.30	.14
☐ B19 Billy Wagner	3.00	1.35
☐ B20 Tate Seefried	.30	.14
☐ B21 Chad Mottola	.30	.14
☐ B22 Jose Malave	.30	.14
☐ B23 Terrell Wade	.60	.25
☐ B24 Shane Andrews	.30	.14
☐ B25 Chan Ho Park	6.00	2.70
☐ B26 Kirk Presley	.60	.25
☐ B27 Robbie Beckett	.30	.14
☐ B28 Orlando Miller	.30	.14
☐ B29 Jorge Posada	.60	.25
☐ B30 Frankie Rodriguez	.30	.14
☐ B31 Brian L.Hunter	1.25	.55
☐ B32 Billy Ashley	.30	.14
☐ B33 Rondell White	.75	.35
☐ B34 John Roper	.30	.14
☐ B35 Marc Valdes	.30	.14
☐ B36 Scott Ruffcorn	.60	.25
☐ B37 Rod Henderson	.30	.14
☐ B38 Curtis Goodwin	.60	.25
☐ B39 Russ Davis	.60	.25
☐ B40 Rick Gorecki	.30	.14
☐ B41 Johnny Damon	1.25	.55
☐ B42 Roberto Petagine	.30	.14
☐ B43 Chris Snopek	.30	.14
☐ B44 Mark Acre	.30	.14
☐ B45 Todd Hollandsworth	.75	.35
☐ B46 Shawn Green	.60	.25
☐ B47 John Carter	.30	.14
☐ B48 Jim Pittsley	1.25	.55
☐ B49 John Wasdin	.60	.25
☐ B50 D.J.Boston	.30	.14
☐ B51 Tim Clark	.30	.14
☐ B52 Alex Ochoa	.30	.14
☐ B53 Chad Roper	.30	.14
☐ B54 Mike Kelly	.30	.14
☐ B55 Brad Fullmer	4.00	1.80
☐ B56 Carl Everett	.30	.14
☐ B57 Tim Belk	.30	.14
☐ B58 Jimmy Hurst	.60	.25
☐ B59 Mac Suzuki	.30	.14
☐ B60 Michael Moore	.30	.14
☐ B61 Alan Benes	4.00	1.80
☐ B62 Tony Clark	12.00	5.50
☐ B63 Edgar Renteria	4.00	1.80
☐ B64 Trey Beamon	.60	.25
☐ B65 LaTroy Hawkins	.30	.14
☐ B66 Wayne Gomes	.30	.14
☐ B67 Ray McDavid	.30	.14
☐ B68 John Dettmer	.30	.14
☐ B69 Willie Greene	.30	.14
☐ B70 Dave Stevens	.30	.14
☐ B71 Kevin Orie	3.00	1.35
☐ B72 Chad Ogea	.60	.25
☐ B73 Ben Van Ryn	.30	.14
☐ B74 Kym Ashworth	.60	.25
☐ B75 Dmitri Young	.75	.35
☐ B76 Herbert Perry	.30	.14
☐ B77 Joey Eischen	.30	.14
☐ B78 Arquimedez Pozo	.75	.35
☐ B79 Ugueth Urbina	.60	.25
☐ B80 Keith Williams	.30	.14
☐ B81 John Frascatore	.30	.14
☐ B82 Garey Ingram	.30	.14
☐ B83 Aaron Small	.30	.14
☐ B84 Olmedo Saenz	.30	.14
☐ B85 Jesus Tavarez	.30	.14
☐ B86 Jose Silva	.30	.25
☐ B87 Jay Witasick	.30	.14
☐ B88 Jay Maldonado	.30	.14
☐ B89 Keith Heberling	.30	.14
☐ B90 Rusty Greer	6.00	2.70
☐ R1 Paul Molitor	1.25	.55
☐ R2 Eddie Murray	1.25	.55
☐ R3 Ozzie Smith	1.50	.70
☐ R4 Rickey Henderson	.75	.35
☐ R5 Lee Smith	.30	.14
☐ R6 Dave Winfield	.75	.35
☐ R7 Roberto Alomar	1.25	.55
☐ R8 Matt Williams	.75	.35

☐ R9 Mark Grace	.75	.35
☐ R10 Lance Johnson	.30	.14
☐ R11 Darren Daulton	.60	.25
☐ R12 Tom Glavine	.60	.25
☐ R13 Gary Sheffield	1.25	.55
☐ R14 Rod Beck	.30	.14
☐ R15 Fred McGriff	.75	.35
☐ R16 Joe Carter	.60	.25
☐ R17 Dante Bichette	.60	.25
☐ R18 Danny Tartabull	.30	.14
☐ R19 Juan Gonzalez	3.00	1.35
☐ R20 Steve Avery	.30	.14
☐ R21 John Wetteland	.30	.14
☐ R22 Ben McDonald	.30	.14
☐ R23 Jack McDowell	.30	.14
☐ R24 Jose Canseco	.75	.35
☐ R25 Tim Salmon	1.25	.55
☐ R26 Wilson Alvarez	.30	.14
☐ R27 Gregg Jefferies	.30	.14
☐ R28 John Burkett	.30	.14
☐ R29 Greg Vaughn	.30	.14
☐ R30 Robin Ventura	.60	.25
☐ R31 Paul O'Neill	.60	.25
☐ R32 Cecil Fielder	.60	.25
☐ R33 Kevin Mitchell	.30	.14
☐ R34 Jeff Conine	.60	.25
☐ R35 Carlos Baerga	.30	.14
☐ R36 Greg Maddux	4.00	1.80
☐ R37 Roger Clemens	2.50	1.10
☐ R38 Deion Sanders	.60	.25
☐ R39 Delino DeShields	.30	.14
☐ R40 Ken Griffey Jr	6.00	2.70
☐ R41 Albert Belle	1.50	.70
☐ R42 Wade Boggs	1.25	.55
☐ R43 Andres Galarraga	1.25	.55
☐ R44 Aaron Sele	.30	.14
☐ R45 Don Mattingly	2.00	.90
☐ R46 David Cone	.60	.25
☐ R47 Len Dykstra	.30	.14
☐ R48 Brett Butler	.60	.25
☐ R49 Bill Swift	.30	.14
☐ R50 Bobby Bonilla	.60	.25
☐ R51 Rafael Palmeiro	.75	.35
☐ R52 Moises Alou	.60	.25
☐ R53 Jeff Bagwell	2.50	1.10
☐ R54 Mike Mussina	1.25	.55
☐ R55 Frank Thomas	5.00	2.20
☐ R56 Jose Rijo	.30	.14
☐ R57 Ruben Sierra	.30	.14
☐ R58 Randy Myers	.30	.14
☐ R59 Barry Bonds	1.50	.70
☐ R60 Jimmy Key	.60	.25
☐ R61 Travis Fryman	.60	.25
☐ R62 John Olerud	.60	.25
☐ R63 David Justice	1.25	.55
☐ R64 Ray Lankford	.60	.25
☐ R65 Bob Tewksbury	.30	.14
☐ R66 Chuck Carr	.30	.14
☐ R67 Jay Buhner	.75	.35
☐ R68 Kenny Lofton	1.50	.70
☐ R69 Marquis Grissom	.60	.25
☐ R70 Sammy Sosa	1.25	.55
☐ R71 Cal Ripken	5.00	2.20
☐ R72 Ellis Burks	.60	.25
☐ R73 Jeff Montgomery	.30	.14
☐ R74 Julio Franco	.30	.14
☐ R75 Kirby Puckett	2.50	1.10
☐ R76 Larry Walker	1.25	.55
☐ R77 Andy Van Slyke	.60	.25
☐ R78 Tony Gwynn	1.25	.55
☐ R79 Will Clark	.75	.35
☐ R80 Mo Vaughn	1.50	.70
☐ R81 Mike Piazza	4.00	1.80
☐ R82 James Mouton	.30	.14
☐ R83 Carlos Delgado	.75	.35
☐ R84 Ryan Klesko	1.25	.55
☐ R85 Javier Lopez	.75	.35
☐ R86 Raul Mondesi	1.25	.55
☐ R87 Cliff Floyd	.60	.25
☐ R88 Manny Ramirez	1.50	.70
☐ R89 Hector Carrasco	.30	.14
☐ R90 Jeff Granger	.30	.14
☐ X91 Frank Thomas Dmitri Young	2.50	1.10
☐ X92 Fred McGriff Brooks Kieschnick	1.25	.55

☐ X93 Matt Williams Shane Andrews	.30	.14
☐ X94 Cal Ripken Kevin Orie	2.50	1.10
☐ X95 Barry Larkin Derek Jeter	2.50	1.10
☐ X96 Ken Griffey Jr. Johnny Damon	3.00	1.35
☐ X97 Barry Bonds Rondell White	1.25	.55
☐ X98 Albert Belle Jimmy Hurst	1.25	.55
☐ X99 Raul Mondesi Ruben Rivera	5.00	2.20
☐ X100 Roger Clemens Scott Ruffcorn	.75	.35
☐ X101 Greg Maddux John Wasdin	2.00	.90
☐ X102 Tim Salmon Chad Mottola	.75	.35
☐ X103 Carlos Baerga Arquimedez Pozo	.60	.25
☐ X104 Mike Piazza Bobby Hughes	2.00	.90
☐ X105 Carlos Delgado Melvin Nieves	.60	.25
☐ X106 Javier Lopez Jorge Posada	.60	.25
☐ X107 Manny Ramirez Jose Malave	1.25	.55
☐ X108 Travis Fryman Chipper Jones	.60	.25
☐ X109 Steve Avery Bill Pulsipher	.30	.14
☐ X110 John Olerud Shawn Green	.60	.25

1994 Bowman's Best Refractors

This is a 200-card standard-size set is a parallel to the basic Bowman's Best issue. The cards were randomly inserted in packs at a rate of one in nine Bowman's Best packs. The only difference is the refractive coating that allows for a brighter, shinier appearance.

	MINT	NRMT
COMPLETE SET (200)	1300.00	575.00
COMMON CARD	3.00	1.35
SEMISTARS	6.00	2.70
UNLISTED STARS	12.00	5.50
*RED STARS: 5X TO 10X HI COLUMN		
RANDOM INSERTS IN PACKS ..		
☐ B1 Chipper Jones	60.00	27.00
☐ B2 Derek Jeter	60.00	27.00
☐ B6 Justin Thompson	25.00	11.00
☐ B13 Edgardo Alfonzo	20.00	9.00
☐ B19 Billy Wagner	20.00	9.00

	MINT	NRMT
☐ B25 Chan Ho Park	35.00	16.00
☐ B55 Brad Fullmer	25.00	11.00
☐ B61 Alan Benes	25.00	11.00
☐ B62 Tony Clark	60.00	27.00
☐ B63 Edgar Renteria	25.00	11.00
☐ B71 Kevin Orie	20.00	9.00
☐ B90 Rusty Greer	30.00	13.50
☐ X91 Frank Thomas	15.00	6.75
Dmitri Young		
☐ X94 Cal Ripken	15.00	6.75
Kevin Orie		
☐ X96 Ken Griffey Jr.	20.00	9.00
Johnny Damon		
☐ X99 Ruben Rivera	30.00	13.50
Raul Mondesi		

1995 Bowman's Best

This 195 card standard-size set consists of 90 veteran stars, 90 rookies and prospects and 15 Mirror Image cards. The packs contain seven cards, and the suggested retail price was $5. The veteran cards have red backs and are designated R1-R90. Cards of rookies and prospects have blue backs and are designated B1-B90. The Mirror Image cards feature a veteran star and a prospect matched by position. These cards are numbered X1-X15. The fronts have an action photo with the background in silver-foil with the team names at the top and red or blue at the bottom corresponding to the back. The backs have a head shot along with player statistics and information. Rookie Cards include Bartolo Colon, Juan Encarnacion, Karim Garcia, Vladimir Guerrero, Andruw Jones, Hideo Nomo, Jay Payton and Scott Rolen.

	MINT	NRMT
COMPLETE SET (195)	240.00	110.00
COMMON CARD (B1-R90)	.40	.18
COMMON MIR.IM.(X1-X15)	.50	.23
MINOR STARS	.75	.35
UNLISTED STARS	1.50	.70
☐ B1 Derek Jeter	5.00	2.20
☐ B2 Vladimir Guerrero	30.00	13.50
☐ B3 Bob Abreu	4.00	1.80
☐ B4 Chan Ho Park	1.50	.70
☐ B5 Paul Wilson	.40	.18
☐ B6 Chad Ogea	.40	.18
☐ B7 Andruw Jones	35.00	16.00
☐ B8 Brian Barber	.40	.18
☐ B9 Andy Larkin	.40	.18
☐ B10 Richie Sexson	4.00	1.80
☐ B11 Everett Stull	.40	.18
☐ B12 Brooks Kieschnick	.75	.35
☐ B13 Matt Murray	.40	.18
☐ B14 John Wasdin	.40	.18
☐ B15 Shannon Stewart	.75	.35
☐ B16 Luis Ortiz	.40	.18
☐ B17 Marc Kroon	.40	.18
☐ B18 Todd Greene	5.00	2.20
☐ B19 Juan Acevedo	.40	.18
☐ B20 Tony Clark	3.00	1.35
☐ B21 Jermaine Dye	1.00	.45
☐ B22 Derrek Lee	2.50	1.10
☐ B23 Pat Watkins	.75	.35
☐ B24 Calvin Reese	.40	.18
☐ B25 Ben Grieve	30.00	13.50
☐ B26 Julio Santana	.40	.18
☐ B27 Felix Rodriguez	.40	.18
☐ B28 Paul Konerko	25.00	11.00
☐ B29 Nomar Garciaparra	30.00	13.50
☐ B30 Pat Ahearne	.40	.18
☐ B31 Jason Schmidt	.75	.35
☐ B32 Billy Wagner	1.00	.45
☐ B33 Rey Ordonez	3.00	1.35
☐ B34 Curtis Goodwin	.40	.18
☐ B35 Sergio Nunez	.40	.18
☐ B36 Tim Belk	.40	.18
☐ B37 Scott Elarton	1.80	.80
☐ B38 Jason Isringhausen	.75	.35
☐ B39 Trot Nixon	.40	.18
☐ B40 Sid Roberson	.40	.18
☐ B41 Ron Villone	.40	.18
☐ B42 Ruben Rivera	2.50	1.10
☐ B43 Rick Huisman	.40	.18
☐ B44 Todd Hollandsworth	.75	.35
☐ B45 Johnny Damon	.75	.35
☐ B46 Garret Anderson	1.00	.45
☐ B47 Jeff D'Amico	.75	.35
☐ B48 Dustin Hermanson	.75	.35
☐ B49 Juan Encarnacion	12.00	5.50
☐ B50 Andy Pettitte	2.50	1.10
☐ B51 Chris Stynes	.40	.18
☐ B52 Troy Percival	.40	.18
☐ B53 LaTroy Hawkins	.40	.18
☐ B54 Roger Cedeno	.75	.35
☐ B55 Alan Benes	1.00	.45
☐ B56 Karim Garcia	10.00	4.50
☐ B57 Andrew Lorraine	.40	.18
☐ B58 Gary Rath	.40	.18
☐ B59 Bret Wagner	.40	.18
☐ B60 Jeff Suppan	1.00	.45
☐ B61 Bill Pulsipher	.40	.18
☐ B62 Jay Payton	1.25	.55
☐ B63 Alex Ochoa	.40	.18
☐ B64 Ugueth Urbina	.40	.18
☐ B65 Armando Benitez	.40	.18
☐ B66 George Arias	.75	.35
☐ B67 Raul Casanova	2.50	1.10
☐ B68 Matt Drews	.40	.18
☐ B69 Jimmy Haynes	.75	.35
☐ B70 Jimmy Hurst	.40	.18
☐ B71 C.J. Nitkowski	.40	.18
☐ B72 Tommy Davis	.75	.35
☐ B73 Bartolo Colon	1.80	.80
☐ B74 Chris Carpenter	2.50	1.10
☐ B75 Trey Beamon	.40	.18
☐ B76 Bryan Rekar	.40	.18
☐ B77 James Baldwin	.40	.18
☐ B78 Marc Valdes	.40	.18
☐ B79 Tom Fordham	.75	.35
☐ B80 Marc Newfield	.40	.18
☐ B81 Angel Martinez	.40	.18
☐ B82 Brian L. Hunter	1.00	.45
☐ B83 Jose Herrera	.40	.18
☐ B84 Glenn Dishman	.75	.35
☐ B85 Jacob Cruz	5.00	2.20
☐ B86 Paul Shuey	.40	.18
☐ B87 Scott Rolen	30.00	13.50
☐ B88 Doug Million	.40	.18
☐ B89 Desi Relaford	.75	.35
☐ B90 Michael Tucker	.75	.35
☐ R1 Randy Johnson	1.50	.70
☐ R2 Joe Carter	.75	.35
☐ R3 Chili Davis	.75	.35
☐ R4 Moises Alou	.75	.35
☐ R5 Gary Sheffield	1.50	.70
☐ R6 Kevin Appier	.75	.35
☐ R7 Denny Neagle	.75	.35
☐ R8 Ruben Sierra	.40	.18
☐ R9 Darren Daulton	.75	.35
☐ R10 Cal Ripken	6.00	2.70
☐ R11 Bobby Bonilla	.75	.35
☐ R12 Manny Ramirez	1.50	.70
☐ R13 Barry Bonds	2.00	.90
☐ R14 Eric Karros	.75	.35
☐ R15 Greg Maddux	5.00	2.20
☐ R16 Jeff Bagwell	3.00	1.35
☐ R17 Paul Molitor	1.50	.70
☐ R18 Ray Lankford	.75	.35
☐ R19 Mark Grace	1.00	.45
☐ R20 Kenny Lofton	2.00	.90
☐ R21 Tony Gwynn	4.00	1.80
☐ R22 Will Clark	1.00	.45
☐ R23 Roger Clemens	3.00	1.35
☐ R24 Dante Bichette	.75	.35
☐ R25 Barry Larkin	1.00	.45
☐ R26 Wade Boggs	1.50	.70
☐ R27 Kirby Puckett	3.00	1.35
☐ R28 Cecil Fielder	.75	.35
☐ R29 Jose Canseco	1.00	.45
☐ R30 Juan Gonzalez	4.00	1.80
☐ R31 David Cone	.75	.35
☐ R32 Craig Biggio	1.00	.45
☐ R33 Tim Salmon	1.50	.70
☐ R34 David Justice	1.50	.70
☐ R35 Sammy Sosa	1.50	.70
☐ R36 Mike Piazza	5.00	2.20
☐ R37 Carlos Baerga	.40	.18
☐ R38 Jeff Conine	.75	.35
☐ R39 Rafael Palmeiro	1.00	.45
☐ R40 Bret Saberhagen	.40	.18
☐ R41 Len Dykstra	.75	.35
☐ R42 Mo Vaughn	2.00	.90
☐ R43 Wally Joyner	.75	.35
☐ R44 Chuck Knoblauch	1.50	.70
☐ R45 Robin Ventura	.40	.18
☐ R46 Don Mattingly	2.50	1.10
☐ R47 Dave Hollins	.40	.18
☐ R48 Andy Benes	.75	.35
☐ R49 Ken Griffey Jr.	8.00	3.60
☐ R50 Albert Belle	2.00	.90
☐ R51 Matt Williams	1.00	.45
☐ R52 Rondell White	.75	.35
☐ R53 Raul Mondesi	1.00	.45
☐ R54 Brian Jordan	.75	.35
☐ R55 Greg Vaughn	.40	.18
☐ R56 Fred McGriff	1.00	.45
☐ R57 Roberto Alomar	1.50	.70
☐ R58 Dennis Eckersley	.75	.35
☐ R59 Lee Smith	.75	.35
☐ R60 Eddie Murray	1.50	.70
☐ R61 Kenny Rogers	.40	.18
☐ R62 Ron Gant	.75	.35
☐ R63 Larry Walker	1.50	.70
☐ R64 Chad Curtis	.40	.18
☐ R65 Frank Thomas	6.00	2.70
☐ R66 Paul O'Neill	.75	.35
☐ R67 Kevin Seitzer	.40	.18
☐ R68 Marquis Grissom	.75	.35
☐ R69 Mark McGwire	3.00	1.35
☐ R70 Travis Fryman	.75	.35
☐ R71 Andres Galarraga	1.50	.70
☐ R72 Carlos Perez	.75	.35
☐ R73 Tyler Green	.40	.18
☐ R74 Marty Cordova	.75	.35
☐ R75 Shawn Green	.75	.35
☐ R76 Vaughn Eshelman	.40	.18
☐ R77 John Mabry	.75	.35
☐ R78 Jason Bates	.40	.18
☐ R79 Jon Nunnally	.40	.18
☐ R80 Ray Durham	.75	.35
☐ R81 Edgardo Alfonzo	1.50	.70
☐ R82 Esteban Loaiza	.75	.35
☐ R83 Hideo Nomo	15.00	6.75
☐ R84 Orlando Miller	.40	.18
☐ R85 Alex Gonzalez	.40	.18
☐ R86 Mark Grudzielanek	2.50	1.10
☐ R87 Julian Tavarez	.40	.18
☐ R88 Benji Gil	.40	.18
☐ R89 Quilvio Veras	.40	.18
☐ R90 Ricky Bottalico	.75	.35
☐ X1 Ben Davis	4.00	1.80
Ivan Rodriguez		
☐ X2 Mark Redman	1.00	.45

	Manny Ramirez	1.25	.55
☐ X3	Reggie Taylor	1.25	.55
	Deion Sanders		
☐ X4	Ryan Jaroncyk	1.25	.55
	Shawn Green		
☐ X5	Juan LeBron	2.50	1.10
	Juan Gonzalez		
☐ X6	Toby McKnight	1.25	.55
	Craig Biggio		
☐ X7	Michael Barrett	1.25	.55
	Travis Fryman		
☐ X8	Corey Jenkins	2.50	1.10
	Mo Vaughn		
☐ X9	Ruben Rivera	3.00	1.35
	Frank Thomas		
☐ X10	Curtis Goodwin	.50	.23
	Kenny Lofton		
☐ X11	Brian L. Hunter	2.00	.90
	Tony Gwynn		
☐ X12	Todd Greene	4.00	1.80
	Ken Griffey Jr.		
☐ X13	Karim Garcia	2.00	.90
	Matt Williams		
☐ X14	Billy Wagner	.50	.23
	Randy Johnson		
☐ X15	Pat Watkins	1.50	.70
	Jeff Bagwell		

1995 Bowman's Best Refractors

Randomly inserted at a rate of one in six packs, this set is a parallel to the basic Bowman's Best issue. As far as the refractive qualities, the final 15 Mirror Image cards (X1-X15) are considered diffractors which reflects light in a different manner than the typical refractor. The veteran refractor cards have been seen with or without the word refractor on the back. These cards without the refractor markings are currently valued at the same price as the regular refractors.

	MINT	NRMT
COMPLETE SET (195)	2500.00	1100.00
COMMON BLUE (B1-B90)	5.00	2.20
COMMON RED (R1-R90)	4.00	1.80
COMMON MIR. IMAGE (X1-X15)	5.00	2.20
MINOR STARS	6.00	2.70
SEMISTARS	10.00	4.50
UNLISTED STARS	15.00	6.75
*STARS: 5X TO 10X HI COLUMN		
RED/BLUE REF. STATED ODDS 1:6		
MIRROR IMAGE REF. STATED ODDS 1:12		

☐ B1	Derek Jeter	50.00	22.00
☐ B2	Vladimir Guerrero	120.00	55.00
☐ B3	Bob Abreu	25.00	11.00
☐ B7	Andruw Jones	175.00	80.00
☐ B10	Richie Sexson	25.00	11.00
☐ B18	Todd Greene	25.00	11.00
☐ B20	Tony Clark	40.00	18.00
☐ B22	Derrek Lee	40.00	18.00
☐ B25	Ben Grieve	120.00	55.00
☐ B28	Paul Konerko	100.00	45.00
☐ B29	Nomar Garciaparra	120.00	55.00
☐ B33	Rey Ordonez	20.00	9.00
☐ B37	Scott Elarton	25.00	11.00
☐ B42	Ruben Rivera	25.00	11.00
☐ B49	Juan Encarnacion	60.00	27.00
☐ B50	Andy Pettitte	25.00	11.00
☐ B56	Karim Garcia	50.00	22.00
☐ B73	Bartolo Colon	25.00	11.00
☐ B85	Jacob Cruz	30.00	13.50
☐ B87	Scott Rolen	120.00	55.00
☐ R83	Hideo Nomo	100.00	45.00
☐ X1	Ben Davis	25.00	11.00
	Ivan Rodriguez		

1996 Bowman's Best Previews

Printed with Finest technology, this 30-card set features the hottest 15 top prospects and 15 veterans and was randomly inserted in 1996 Bowman packs at the rate of one in 12. The fronts display a color action player photo. The backs carry player information.

	MINT	NRMT
COMPLETE SET (30)	120.00	55.00
COMMON CARD (BBP1-BBP30)	.75	.35
UNLISTED STARS	3.00	1.35
STATED ODDS 1:12	2.50	1.10
*REFRACTORS: .75X TO 1.5X HI COLUMN		
REFRACTOR STATED ODDS 1:24		
*ATOMIC REF: 1.5X TO 3X HI COLUMN		
ATOMIC STATED ODDS 1:48		

☐ BBP1	Chipper Jones	10.00	4.50
☐ BBP2	Alan Benes	1.50	.70
☐ BBP3	Brooks Kieschnick	1.50	.70
☐ BBP4	Barry Bonds	4.00	1.80
☐ BBP5	Rey Ordonez	1.50	.70
☐ BBP6	Tim Salmon	3.00	1.35
☐ BBP7	Mike Piazza	10.00	4.50
☐ BBP8	Billy Wagner	1.50	.70
☐ BBP9	Andruw Jones	10.00	4.50
☐ BBP10	Tony Gwynn	8.00	3.60
☐ BBP11	Paul Wilson	.75	.35
☐ BBP12	Calvin Reese	.75	.35
☐ BBP13	Frank Thomas	12.00	5.50
☐ BBP14	Greg Maddux	10.00	4.50
☐ BBP15	Derek Jeter	8.00	3.60
☐ BBP16	Jeff Bagwell	6.00	2.70
☐ BBP17	Barry Larkin	2.00	.90
☐ BBP18	Todd Greene	2.00	.90
☐ BBP19	Ruben Rivera	1.50	.70
☐ BBP20	Richard Hidalgo	3.00	1.35
☐ BBP21	Larry Walker	3.00	1.35
☐ BBP22	Carlos Baerga	.75	.35
☐ BBP23	Derrick Gibson	3.00	1.35
☐ BBP24	Richie Sexson	2.00	.90
☐ BBP25	Mo Vaughn	4.00	1.80
☐ BBP26	Hideo Nomo	8.00	3.60
☐ BBP27	Nomar Garciaparra	10.00	4.50
☐ BBP28	Cal Ripken	12.00	5.50
☐ BBP29	Karim Garcia	2.00	.90
☐ BBP30	Ken Griffey Jr.	15.00	6.75

1996 Bowman's Best

This 180-card set was issued in packs of six cards at the cost of $4.99 per pack. The fronts feature a color action player cutout of 90 outstanding veteran players on a chromium classic gold background design and 90 up and coming prospects and rook-

ies on a silver design. The backs carry a color player portrait, player information and statistics. Card number 33 was never actually issued. Instead, both Roger Clemens and Rafael Palmeiro are erroneously numbered 32. A chrome reprint of the 1952 Bowman Mickey Mantle was inserted at the rate of one in 24 packs. A Refractor version of the Mantle was seeded at 1:96 packs and an Atomic Refractor version was seeded at 1:192. Notable Rookie Cards include Todd Dunwoody, Jose Guillen and Wes Helms.

	MINT	NRMT
COMPLETE SET (180)	100.00	45.00
COMMON GOLD (1-90)	.25	.11
COMMON SILVER (91-180)	.25	.11
MINOR STARS	.60	.25
UNLISTED STARS	1.25	.55
NUMBER 33 NEVER ISSUED		
CLEMENS AND PALMEIRO NUMBERED 32		
MANTLE CHROME ODDS 1:24 HOB, 1:20 RET		
MANTLE REF. ODDS 1:96 HOB, 1:160 RET		
MANTLE ATOMIC ODDS 1:192 HOB, 1:320 RET		

☐ 1	Hideo Nomo	3.00	1.35
☐ 2	Edgar Martinez	.75	.35
☐ 3	Cal Ripken	5.00	2.20
☐ 4	Wade Boggs	1.25	.55
☐ 5	Cecil Fielder	.60	.25
☐ 6	Albert Belle	1.50	.70
☐ 7	Chipper Jones	4.00	1.80
☐ 8	Ryne Sandberg	1.50	.70
☐ 9	Tim Salmon	1.25	.55
☐ 10	Barry Bonds	1.50	.70
☐ 11	Ken Caminiti	.75	.35
☐ 12	Ron Gant	.60	.25
☐ 13	Frank Thomas	5.00	2.20
☐ 14	Dante Bichette	.60	.25
☐ 15	Jason Kendall	.75	.35
☐ 16	Mo Vaughn	1.50	.70
☐ 17	Rey Ordonez	.60	.25
☐ 18	Henry Rodriguez	.25	.11
☐ 19	Ryan Klesko	.75	.35
☐ 20	Jeff Bagwell	2.50	1.10
☐ 21	Randy Johnson	1.25	.55
☐ 22	Jim Edmonds	.75	.35
☐ 23	Kenny Lofton	1.50	.70
☐ 24	Andy Pettitte	1.50	.70
☐ 25	Brady Anderson	.75	.35
☐ 26	Mike Piazza	4.00	1.80
☐ 27	Greg Vaughn	.25	.11
☐ 28	Joe Carter	.60	.25
☐ 29	Jason Giambi	.60	.25
☐ 30	Ivan Rodriguez	1.50	.70
☐ 31	Jeff Conine	.60	.25
☐ 32	Rafael Palmeiro	.75	.35
☐ 32	Roger Clemens	2.50	1.10
☐ 34	Chuck Knoblauch	1.25	.55
☐ 35	Reggie Sanders	.25	.11
☐ 36	Andres Galarraga	1.25	.55
☐ 37	Paul O'Neill	.60	.25

No	Player	HI	LO
38	Tony Gwynn	3.00	1.35
39	Paul Wilson	.25	.11
40	Garret Anderson	.25	.11
41	David Justice	1.25	.55
42	Eddie Murray	1.25	.55
43	Mike Grace	.25	.11
44	Marty Cordova	.60	.25
45	Kevin Appier	.25	.11
46	Raul Mondesi	.75	.35
47	Jim Thome	1.25	.55
48	Sammy Sosa	1.25	.55
49	Craig Biggio	.75	.35
50	Marquis Grissom	.60	.25
51	Alan Benes	.60	.25
52	Manny Ramirez	1.25	.55
53	Gary Sheffield	1.25	.55
54	Mike Mussina	.60	.25
55	Robin Ventura	.60	.25
56	Johnny Damon	.25	.11
57	Jose Canseco	.75	.35
58	Juan Gonzalez	3.00	1.35
59	Tino Martinez	1.25	.55
60	Brian Hunter	.25	.11
61	Fred McGriff	.75	.35
62	Jay Buhner	.25	.11
63	Carlos Delgado	.60	.25
64	Moises Alou	.60	.25
65	Roberto Alomar	1.25	.55
66	Barry Larkin	.75	.35
67	Vinny Castilla	.60	.25
68	Ray Durham	.25	.11
69	Travis Fryman	.60	.25
70	Jason Isringhausen	.25	.11
71	Ken Griffey Jr.	6.00	2.70
72	John Smoltz	.60	.25
73	Matt Williams	.75	.35
74	Chan Ho Park	1.25	.55
75	Mark McGwire	2.50	1.10
76	Jeffrey Hammonds	.25	.11
77	Will Clark	.75	.35
78	Kirby Puckett	2.50	1.10
79	Derek Jeter	4.00	1.80
80	Derek Bell	.25	.11
81	Eric Karros	.60	.25
82	Len Dykstra	.60	.25
83	Larry Walker	.60	.25
84	Mark Grudzielanek	.25	.11
85	Greg Maddux	4.00	1.80
86	Carlos Baerga	.25	.11
87	Paul Molitor	1.25	.55
88	John Valentin	.25	.11
89	Mark Grace	.75	.35
90	Ray Lankford	.60	.25
91	Andruw Jones	5.00	2.20
92	Nomar Garciaparra	5.00	2.20
93	Alex Ochoa	.25	.11
94	Derrick Gibson	2.00	.90
95	Jeff D'Amico	.25	.11
96	Ruben Rivera	.25	.11
97	Vladimir Guerrero	4.00	1.80
98	Calvin Reese	.25	.11
99	Richard Hidalgo	1.25	.55
100	Bartolo Colon	.25	.11
101	Karim Garcia	.75	.35
102	Ben Davis	.25	.11
103	Jay Powell	.25	.11
104	Chris Snopek	.25	.11
105	Glendon Rusch	1.25	.55
106	Enrique Wilson	.25	.11
107	Antonio Alfonseca	.25	.11
108	Wilton Guerrero	2.50	.11
109	Jose Guillen	12.00	5.50
110	Miguel Mejia	.25	.11
111	Jay Payton	.60	.25
112	Scott Eaton	.60	.25
113	Brooks Kieschnick	.60	.25
114	Dustin Hermanson	.25	.11
115	Roger Cedeno	.25	.11
116	Matt Wagner	.25	.11
117	Lee Daniels	.25	.11
118	Ben Grieve	4.00	1.80
119	Ugueth Urbina	.25	.11
120	Danny Graves	.60	.25
121	Dan Donato	.25	.11
122	Matt Ruebel	.25	.11
123	Mark Sievert	.25	.11
124	Chris Stynes	.25	.11
125	Jeff Abbott	.60	.25
126	Rocky Coppinger	1.00	.45
127	Jermaine Dye	.60	.25
128	Todd Greene	.75	.35
129	Chris Carpenter	.75	.35
130	Edgar Renteria	.75	.35
131	Matt Drews	.25	.11
132	Edgard Velazquez	2.50	1.10
133	Casey Whitten	.25	.11
134	Ryan Jones	1.25	.55
135	Todd Walker	4.00	1.80
136	Geoff Jenkins	2.50	1.10
137	Matt Morris	4.00	1.80
138	Richie Sexson	.75	.35
139	Todd Dunwoody	6.00	2.70
140	Gabe Alvarez	1.50	.70
141	J.J. Johnson	.25	.11
142	Shannon Stewart	.60	.25
143	Brad Fullmer	1.25	.55
144	Julio Santana	.25	.11
145	Scott Rolen	5.00	2.20
146	Amaury Telemaco	.60	.25
147	Trey Beamon	.25	.11
148	Billy Wagner	.25	.11
149	Todd Hollandsworth	.25	.11
150	Doug Million	.25	.11
151	Jose Valentin	2.00	.90
152	Wes Helms	5.00	2.20
153	Jeff Suppan	.60	.25
154	Luis Castillo	1.25	.55
155	Bob Abreu	.75	.35
156	Paul Konerko	3.00	1.35
157	Jamey Wright	.25	.11
158	Eddie Pearson	.25	.11
159	Jimmy Haynes	.25	.11
160	Derrek Lee	1.25	.55
161	Damian Moss	.60	.25
162	Carlos Guillen	1.00	.45
163	Chris Fussell	1.00	.45
164	Mike Sweeney	2.50	1.10
165	Donnie Sadler	.25	.11
166	Desi Relaford	.25	.11
167	Steve Gibralter	.25	.11
168	Neifi Perez	.25	.11
169	Antone Williamson	.60	.25
170	Marty Janzen	.25	.11
171	Todd Helton	10.00	4.50
172	Raul Ibanez	1.25	.55
173	Bill Selby	.25	.11
174	Shane Monahan	1.50	.70
175	Robin Jennings	.25	.11
176	Bobby Chouinard	.25	.11
177	Einar Diaz	.25	.11
178	Jason Thompson	.25	.11
179	Rafael Medina	1.50	.70
180	Kevin Orie	.75	.35
NNO	1952 Mantle Refractor	15.00	6.75
NNO	1952 Mantle Chrome	8.00	3.60
NNO	1952 Mantle At.Ref.	30.00	13.50

1996 Bowman's Best Atomic Refractors

Inserted one in every 48 packs, this 180-card set is parallel to the 1996 Bowman's Best set. It is similar in design to the regular set but was printed with the newest sparkling refractor technology.

	MINT	NRMT
COMMON GOLD (1-90)	10.00	4.50
COMMON SILVER (91-180)	15.00	6.75
MINOR STARS	20.00	9.00
SEMISTARS	30.00	13.50
UNLISTED STARS	50.00	22.00

*STARS: 20X TO 40X HI COLUMN
*YOUNG STARS: 18X TO 30X HI
*ROOKIES: 9X TO 15X HI
STATED ODDS 1:48 HOB, 1:80 RET

1996 Bowman's Best Refractors

This 180-card set is parallel to the regular 1996 Bowman's Best set and is similar in design. The difference is in the refractive quality of the cards. The cards were inserted at the rate of one in every 12 packs.

	MINT	NRMT
COMPLETE SET (180)	1500.00	700.00
COMMON CARD (1-180)	2.50	1.10

*STARS: 5X TO 10X HI COLUMN
*YOUNG STARS: 4X TO 8X HI
*ROOKIES: 2.5X TO 5X HI
STATED ODDS 1:12 HOB, 1:20 RET

No	Player	MINT	NRMT
1	Hideo Nomo	150.00	70.00
3	Cal Ripken	200.00	90.00
6	Albert Belle	60.00	27.00
7	Chipper Jones	120.00	55.00
8	Ryne Sandberg	60.00	27.00
9	Barry Bonds	60.00	27.00
13	Frank Thomas	200.00	90.00
16	Mo Vaughn	60.00	27.00
20	Jeff Bagwell	100.00	45.00
23	Kenny Lofton	60.00	27.00
24	Andy Pettitte	60.00	27.00
26	Mike Piazza	150.00	70.00
29	Ivan Rodriguez	60.00	27.00
33	Roger Clemens	100.00	45.00
38	Tony Gwynn	120.00	55.00
58	Juan Gonzalez	120.00	55.00
71	Ken Griffey Jr.	250.00	110.00
75	Mark McGwire	100.00	45.00
78	Kirby Puckett	100.00	45.00
79	Derek Jeter	150.00	70.00
85	Greg Maddux	150.00	70.00
91	Andruw Jones	150.00	70.00
92	Nomar Garciaparra	150.00	70.00
94	Derrick Gibson	80.00	36.00
96	Ruben Rivera	40.00	18.00
97	Vladimir Guerrero	125.00	55.00
99	Richard Hidalgo	50.00	22.00
101	Karim Garcia	40.00	18.00
102	Ben Davis	40.00	18.00
108	Wilton Guerrero	40.00	18.00
109	Jose Guillen	125.00	55.00
118	Ben Grieve	125.00	55.00
132	Edgard Velazquez	40.00	18.00
135	Todd Walker	60.00	27.00
136	Geoff Jenkins	40.00	18.00
137	Matt Morris	60.00	27.00
139	Todd Dunwoody	100.00	45.00
145	Scott Rolen	150.00	70.00
152	Wes Helms	80.00	36.00
156	Paul Konerko	125.00	55.00
160	Derrek Lee	40.00	18.00
164	Mike Sweeney	40.00	18.00
171	Todd Helton	160.00	70.00

		MINT	NRMT
☐	145 Scott Rolen	50.00	22.00
☐	156 Paul Konerko	30.00	13.50
☐	171 Todd Helton	60.00	27.00

1996 Bowman's Best Cuts

Randomly inserted in packs at a rate of one in 24, this chromium card die-cut set features 15 top hobby stars. The fronts display color action player cutouts over the team name and a background of swinging bars. The backs carry player information.

	MINT	NRMT
COMPLETE SET (15)	200.00	90.00
COMMON CARD (1-15)	1.50	.70
SEMISTARS	3.00	1.35
UNLISTED STARS	6.00	2.70
STATED ODDS 1:24 HOB, 1:40 RET		
*REFRACTORS: .75X TO 1.5X HI COLUMN		
REF.STATED ODDS 1:48 HOB, 1:80 RET		
*ATOMIC REF: 1.5X TO 3X HI COLUMN		
ATOMIC STATED ODDS 1:96 HOB, 1:160 RET		

		MINT	NRMT
☐	1 Ken Griffey Jr.	30.00	13.50
☐	2 Jason Isringhausen	1.50	.70
☐	3 Derek Jeter	15.00	6.75
☐	4 Andruw Jones	20.00	9.00
☐	5 Chipper Jones	20.00	9.00
☐	6 Ryan Klesko	3.00	1.35
☐	7 Raul Mondesi	3.00	1.35
☐	8 Hideo Nomo	15.00	6.75
☐	9 Mike Piazza	20.00	9.00
☐	10 Manny Ramirez	6.00	2.70
☐	11 Cal Ripken	25.00	11.00
☐	12 Ruben Rivera	2.00	.90
☐	13 Tim Salmon	6.00	2.70
☐	14 Frank Thomas	25.00	11.00
☐	15 Jim Thome	6.00	2.70

1996 Bowman's Best Mirror Image

Randomly inserted in packs at a rate of one in 48, this 10-card set features four top players on a single card at one of ten different positions. The fronts display a color photo of an AL veteran with a semicircle containing a color portrait of a prospect who plays the same position. The backs carry a color photo of a NL veteran with a semicircle color portrait of a prospect.

	MINT	NRMT
COMPLETE SET (10)	150.00	70.00
COMMON CARD (1-10)	8.00	3.60
STATED ODDS 1:48 HOB, 1:80 RET		
*REFRACTORS: .75X TO 1.5X HI COLUMN		
REF.STATED ODDS 1:96 HOB, 1:160 RET		

*ATOMIC REFRACTORS: 1.5X TO 3X HI
ATOMIC STATED ODDS 1:192 HOB, 1:320 RET

		MINT	NRMT
☐	1 Jeff Bagwell	25.00	11.00
	Todd Helton		
	Frank Thomas		
	Richie Sexson		
☐	2 Craig Biggio	8.00	3.60
	Luis Castillo		
	Roberto Alomar		
	Desi Relaford		
☐	3 Chipper Jones	25.00	11.00
	Scott Rolen		
	Wade Boggs		
	George Arias		
☐	4 Barry Larkin	20.00	9.00
	Neifi Perez		
	Cal Ripken		
	Mark Bellhorn		
☐	5 Larry Walker	10.00	4.50
	Karim Garcia		
	Albert Belle		
	Ruben Rivera		
☐	6 Barry Bonds	20.00	9.00
	Andruw Jones		
	Kenny Lofton		
	Donnie Sadler		
☐	7 Tony Gwynn	30.00	13.50
	Vladimir Guerrero		
	Ken Griffey		
	Ben Grieve		
☐	8 Mike Piazza	15.00	6.75
	Ben Davis		
	Ivan Rodriguez		
	Jose Valentin		
☐	9 Greg Maddux	15.00	6.75
	Jamey Wright		
	Mike Mussina		
	Bartolo Colon		
☐	10 Tom Glavine	8.00	3.60
	Billy Wagner		
	Randy Johnson		
	Jarrod Washburn		

1997 Bowman's Best Previews

Randomly inserted in packs at a rate of one in 12, this 20-card

set features color photos of 10 rookies and 10 veterans that would be appearing in the 1997 Bowman's Best set.

	MINT	NRMT
COMPLETE SET (20)	100.00	45.00
COMMON CARD (1-20)	1.50	.70
UNLISTED STARS	2.50	1.10
STATED ODDS 1:12		
*REFRACTORS: 1X TO 2X HI COLUMN		
REFRACTOR STATED ODDS 1:48		
*ATOMIC REFRACTORS: 2X TO 4X HI		
ATOMIC STATED ODDS 1:96		

		MINT	NRMT
☐	1 Frank Thomas	12.00	5.50
☐	2 Ken Griffey Jr.	15.00	6.75
☐	3 Barry Bonds	4.00	1.80
☐	4 Derek Jeter	8.00	3.60
☐	5 Chipper Jones	10.00	4.50
☐	6 Mark McGwire	5.00	2.20
☐	7 Cal Ripken	12.00	5.50
☐	8 Kenny Lofton	4.00	1.80
☐	9 Gary Sheffield	2.50	1.10
☐	10 Jeff Bagwell	6.00	2.70
☐	11 Wilton Guerrero	1.50	.70
☐	12 Scott Rolen	6.00	2.70
☐	13 Todd Walker	1.50	.70
☐	14 Ruben Rivera	1.50	.70
☐	15 Andruw Jones	6.00	2.70
☐	16 Nomar Garciaparra	8.00	3.60
☐	17 Vladimir Guerrero	5.00	2.20
☐	18 Miguel Tejada	6.00	2.70
☐	19 Bartolo Colon	1.50	.70
☐	20 Katsuhiro Maeda	1.50	.70

1997 Bowman's Best

The 1997 Bowman's Best set was issued in one series totalling 200 cards and was distributed in six-card packs (SRP $4.99). The fronts feature borderless color player photos printed on chromium card stock. The cards of the 100 current superstars display a classic gold design while the cards of the 100 top prospects carry a sleek silver design. Key Rookie Cards include Adrian Beltre, Jose Cruz Jr., Travis Lee and Miguel Tejada.

	MINT	NRMT
COMPLETE SET (200)	110.00	50.00
COMMON CARD (1-200)	.25	.11
MINOR STARS	.50	.23
UNLISTED STARS	1.00	.45

		MINT	NRMT
☐	1 Ken Griffey Jr.	5.00	2.20
☐	2 Cecil Fielder	.50	.23
☐	3 Albert Belle	1.25	.55
☐	4 Todd Hundley	.50	.23
☐	5 Mike Piazza	3.00	1.35

□	#	Player	Value1	Value2
□	6	Matt Williams	.75	.35
□	7	Mo Vaughn	1.25	.55
□	8	Ryne Sandberg	1.25	.55
□	9	Chipper Jones	3.00	1.35
□	10	Edgar Martinez	.75	.35
□	11	Kenny Lofton	1.25	.55
□	12	Ron Gant	.50	.23
□	13	Moises Alou	.50	.23
□	14	Pat Hentgen	.50	.23
□	15	Steve Finley	.50	.23
□	16	Mark Grace	.75	.35
□	17	Jay Buhner	.75	.35
□	18	Jeff Conine	.50	.23
□	19	Jim Edmonds	.75	.35
□	20	Todd Hollandsworth	.25	.11
□	21	Andy Pettitte	1.00	.45
□	22	Jim Thome	1.00	.45
□	23	Eric Young	.25	.11
□	24	Ray Lankford	.50	.23
□	25	Marquis Grissom	.50	.23
□	26	Tony Clark	1.00	.45
□	27	Jermaine Allensworth	.25	.11
□	28	Ellis Burks	.50	.23
□	29	Tony Gwynn	2.50	1.10
□	30	Barry Larkin	.75	.35
□	31	John Olerud	.50	.23
□	32	Mariano Rivera	.50	.23
□	33	Paul Molitor	1.00	.45
□	34	Ken Caminiti	.75	.35
□	35	Gary Sheffield	1.00	.45
□	36	Al Martin	.25	.11
□	37	John Valentin	.25	.11
□	38	Frank Thomas	4.00	1.80
□	39	John Jaha	.25	.11
□	40	Greg Maddux	3.00	1.35
□	41	Alex Fernandez	.50	.23
□	42	Dean Palmer	.25	.11
□	43	Bernie Williams	1.00	.45
□	44	Deion Sanders	.50	.23
□	45	Mark McGwire	2.00	.90
□	46	Brian Jordan	.50	.23
□	47	Bernard Gilkey	.25	.11
□	48	Will Clark	.75	.35
□	49	Kevin Appier	.50	.23
□	50	Tom Glavine	.50	.23
□	51	Chuck Knoblauch	1.00	.45
□	52	Rondell White	.50	.23
□	53	Greg Vaughn	.25	.11
□	54	Mike Mussina	1.00	.45
□	55	Brian McRae	.25	.11
□	56	Chili Davis	.50	.23
□	57	Wade Boggs	.50	.23
□	58	Jeff Bagwell	2.00	.90
□	59	Roberto Alomar	1.00	.45
□	60	Dennis Eckersley	.50	.23
□	61	Ryan Klesko	.75	.35
□	62	Manny Ramirez	1.00	.45
□	63	John Wetteland	.25	.11
□	64	Cal Ripken	4.00	1.80
□	65	Edgar Renteria	.50	.23
□	66	Tino Martinez	1.00	.45
□	67	Larry Walker	1.00	.45
□	68	Gregg Jefferies	.25	.11
□	69	Lance Johnson	.25	.11
□	70	Carlos Delgado	.50	.23
□	71	Craig Biggio	.75	.35
□	72	Jose Canseco	.75	.35
□	73	Barry Bonds	1.25	.55
□	74	Juan Gonzalez	2.50	1.10
□	75	Eric Karros	.50	.23
□	76	Reggie Sanders	.25	.11
□	77	Robin Ventura	.50	.23
□	78	Hideo Nomo	2.50	1.10
□	79	David Justice	.75	.35
□	80	Vinny Castilla	.50	.23
□	81	Travis Fryman	.50	.23
□	82	Derek Jeter	3.00	1.35
□	83	Sammy Sosa	1.00	.45
□	84	Ivan Rodriguez	1.25	.55
□	85	Rafael Palmeiro	.75	.35
□	86	Roger Clemens	2.00	.90
□	87	Jason Giambi	.50	.23
□	88	Andres Galarraga	1.00	.45
□	89	Jermaine Dye	.25	.11
□	90	Joe Carter	.50	.23
□	91	Brady Anderson	.75	.35

□	#	Player	Value1	Value2
□	92	Derek Bell	.25	.11
□	93	Randy Johnson	1.00	.45
□	94	Fred McGriff	.75	.35
□	95	John Smoltz	.50	.23
□	96	Harold Baines	.50	.23
□	97	Raul Mondesi	.75	.35
□	98	Tim Salmon	1.00	.45
□	99	Carlos Baerga	.25	.11
□	100	Dante Bichette	.50	.23
□	101	Vladimir Guerrero	2.00	.90
□	102	Richard Hidalgo	.50	.23
□	103	Paul Konerko	1.50	.70
□	104	Alex Gonzalez	2.00	.90
□	105	Jason Dickson	.50	.23
□	106	Jose Rosado	.50	.23
□	107	Todd Walker	.50	.23
□	108	Seth Greisinger	1.00	.45
□	109	Todd Helton	1.50	.70
□	110	Ben Davis	.50	.23
□	111	Bartolo Colon	.50	.23
□	112	Elieser Marrero	.50	.23
□	113	Jeff D'Amico	.25	.11
□	114	Miguel Tejada	6.00	2.70
□	115	Darin Erstad	1.50	.70
□	116	Kris Benson	4.00	1.80
□	117	Adrian Beltre	12.00	5.50
□	118	Neifi Perez	.50	.23
□	119	Calvin Reese	.25	.11
□	120	Carl Pavano	1.25	.55
□	121	Juan Melo	.50	.23
□	122	Kevin McGlinchy	1.25	.55
□	123	Pat Cline	.25	.11
□	124	Felix Heredia	1.25	.55
□	125	Aaron Boone	.25	.11
□	126	Glendon Rusch	.25	.11
□	127	Mike Cameron	.75	.35
□	128	Justin Thompson	.50	.23
□	129	Chad Hermansen	8.00	3.60
□	130	Sidney Ponson	.50	.23
□	131	Willie Martinez	1.50	.70
□	132	Paul Wilder	2.50	1.10
□	133	Geoff Jenkins	.50	.23
□	134	Roy Halladay	1.50	.70
□	135	Carlos Guillen	.50	.23
□	136	Tony Batista	.25	.11
□	137	Todd Greene	.50	.23
□	138	Luis Castillo	.50	.23
□	139	Jimmy Anderson	1.00	.45
□	140	Edgard Velazquez	.50	.23
□	141	Chris Snopek	.25	.11
□	142	Ruben Rivera	.50	.23
□	143	Javier Valentin	.50	.23
□	144	Brian Rose	1.25	.55
□	145	Fernando Tatis	5.00	2.20
□	146	Dean Crow	.25	.11
□	147	Karim Garcia	.50	.23
□	148	Dante Powell	.25	.11
□	149	Hideki Irabu	2.00	.90
□	150	Matt Morris	1.00	.45
□	151	Wes Helms	.50	.23
□	152	Russ Johnson	.25	.11
□	153	Jarrod Washburn	.50	.23
□	154	Kerry Wood	6.00	2.70
□	155	Joe Fontenot	1.00	.45
□	156	Eugene Kingsale	.25	.11
□	157	Terrence Long	.50	.23
□	158	Calvin Maduro	.25	.11
□	159	Jeff Suppan	.50	.23
□	160	DaRond Stovall	.25	.11
□	161	Mark Redman	.25	.11
□	162	Ken Cloude	2.50	1.10
□	163	Bobby Estalella	.50	.23
□	164	Abraham Nunez	.75	.35
□	165	Derrick Gibson	.75	.35
□	166	Mike Drumright	1.25	.55
□	167	Katsuhiro Maeda	.50	.23
□	168	Jeff Liefer	.25	.11
□	169	Ben Grieve	2.00	.90
□	170	Bob Abreu	.50	.23
□	171	Shannon Stewart	.50	.23
□	172	Braden Looper	.25	.11
□	173	Brant Brown	.25	.11
□	174	Marlon Anderson	.50	.23
□	175	Brad Fullmer	.50	.23
□	176	Carlos Beltran	1.25	.55
□	177	Nomar Garciaparra	3.00	1.35

□	#	Player	Value1	Value2
□	178	Derrek Lee	.75	.35
□	179	Valerio De Los Santos	1.00	.45
□	180	Dmitri Young	.25	.11
□	181	Jamey Wright	.25	.11
□	182	Hiram Bocachica	1.50	.70
□	183	Wilton Guerrero	.25	.11
□	184	Chris Carpenter	.50	.23
□	185	Scott Spiezio	.50	.23
□	186	Andruw Jones	2.50	1.10
□	187	Travis Lee	20.00	9.00
□	188	Jose Cruz Jr.	20.00	9.00
□	189	Jose Guillen	1.25	.55
□	190	Jeff Abbott	.25	.11
□	191	Ricky Ledee	4.00	1.80
□	192	Mike Sweeney	.50	.23
□	193	Donnie Sadler	.25	.11
□	194	Scott Rolen	2.50	1.10
□	195	Kevin Orie	.50	.23
□	196	Jason Conti	1.50	.70
□	197	Mark Kotsay	5.00	2.20
□	198	Eric Milton	2.50	1.10
□	199	Russell Branyan	1.50	.70
□	200	Alex Sanchez	1.50	.70

1997 Bowman's Best Atomic Refractors

Randomly inserted in packs at a rate of one in 24, cards from this 200 card set parallel the regular Bowman's Best set and were printed with the sparkling cross-weave refractor technology.

	MINT	NRMT
COMPLETE SET (200)	3000.00	1350.00
COMMON CARD (1-200)	6.00	2.70
*STARS: 12.5X TO 25X HI COLUMN		
*YOUNG STARS: 10X TO 20X HI		
*ROOKIES: 5X TO 10X HI		
STATED ODDS 1:24		
COMP.REF.SET (200)	1500.00	700.00
COMMON REF. (1-200)	3.00	1.35
*REFRACTORS: 1/2 VALUE OF ATOMIC		
REFRACTOR STATED ODDS 1:12		

□	#	Player	MINT	NRMT
□	1	Ken Griffey Jr.	120.00	55.00
□	3	Albert Belle	30.00	13.50
□	5	Mike Piazza	80.00	36.00
□	7	Mo Vaughn	30.00	13.50
□	8	Ryne Sandberg	30.00	13.50
□	9	Chipper Jones	80.00	36.00
□	11	Kenny Lofton	30.00	13.50
□	29	Tony Gwynn	60.00	27.00
□	38	Frank Thomas	100.00	45.00
□	40	Greg Maddux	80.00	36.00
□	45	Mark McGwire	50.00	22.00
□	58	Jeff Bagwell	50.00	22.00
□	64	Cal Ripken	100.00	45.00
□	73	Barry Bonds	30.00	13.50
□	74	Juan Gonzalez	80.00	36.00
□	78	Hideo Nomo	80.00	36.00
□	82	Derek Jeter	60.00	27.00
□	84	Ivan Rodriguez	30.00	13.50
□	86	Roger Clemens	50.00	22.00
□	101	Vladimir Guerrero	40.00	18.00
□	103	Paul Konerko	30.00	13.50
□	109	Todd Helton	30.00	13.50
□	114	Miguel Tejada	60.00	27.00
□	116	Kris Benson	40.00	18.00
□	117	Adrian Beltre	120.00	55.00
□	129	Chad Hermansen	60.00	27.00
□	145	Fernando Tatis	50.00	22.00
□	154	Kerry Wood	50.00	22.00
□	169	Ben Grieve	40.00	18.00
□	177	Nomar Garciaparra	60.00	27.00
□	186	Andruw Jones	50.00	22.00
□	187	Travis Lee	150.00	70.00
□	188	Jose Cruz Jr.	200.00	90.00
□	191	Ricky Ledee	40.00	18.00

		MINT	NRMT
☐ 194	Scott Rolen	50.00	22.00
☐ 197	Mark Kotsay	50.00	22.00

1997 Bowman's Best Autographs

Randomly inserted in packs at a rate of 1:170, this 10-card set features five silver rookie cards and five gold veteran cards with authentic autographs and a "Certified Autograph Issue" stamp.

	MINT	NRMT
COMPLETE SET (10)	600.00	275.00
COMMON CARD	12.00	5.50
STATED ODDS 1:170		
*REF.STARS: 1.25X TO 2.5X HI COLUMN		
*REF.YOUNG STARS: 1X TO 2X HI		
REFRACTOR STATED ODDS 1:2036		
*ATOMIC STARS: 3X TO 6X HI COLUMN		
*ATOMIC YOUNG STARS: 2.5X TO 5X HI		
ATOMIC STATED ODDS 1:6107		
SKIP-NUMBERED SET		

		MINT	NRMT
☐ 29	Tony Gwynn	120.00	55.00
☐ 33	Paul Molitor	50.00	22.00
☐ 82	Derek Jeter	120.00	55.00
☐ 91	Brady Anderson	30.00	13.50
☐ 98	Tim Salmon	40.00	18.00
☐ 107	Todd Walker	20.00	9.00
☐ 183	Wilton Guerrero	12.00	5.50
☐ 185	Scott Spiezio	15.00	6.75
☐ 188	Jose Cruz Jr.	120.00	55.00
☐ 194	Scott Rolen	80.00	36.00

1997 Bowman's Best Best Cuts

Randomly inserted in packs at a rate of one in 24, this 20-card set features color player photos printed on intricate, Laser Cut Chromium card stock.

	MINT	NRMT
COMPLETE SET (20)	200.00	90.00
COMMON CARD (BC1-BC20)	3.00	1.35
UNLISTED STARS	5.00	2.20
STATED ODDS 1:24		
*REFRACTORS: .75X TO 1.5X HI COLUMN		
REFRACTOR STATED ODDS 1:48		
*ATOMIC REFRACTORS: 1.5X TO 3X HI		
ATOMIC STATED ODDS 1:96		

		MINT	NRMT
☐ BC1	Derek Jeter	12.00	5.50
☐ BC2	Chipper Jones	15.00	6.75
☐ BC3	Frank Thomas	20.00	9.00
☐ BC4	Cal Ripken	20.00	9.00
☐ BC5	Mark McGwire	10.00	4.50
☐ BC6	Ken Griffey Jr.	25.00	11.00
☐ BC7	Jeff Bagwell	10.00	4.50
☐ BC8	Mike Piazza	15.00	6.75
☐ BC9	Ken Caminiti	3.00	1.35
☐ BC10	Albert Belle	6.00	2.70
☐ BC11	Jose Cruz Jr.	25.00	11.00
☐ BC12	Wilton Guerrero	3.00	1.35
☐ BC13	Darin Erstad	8.00	3.60
☐ BC14	Andruw Jones	12.00	5.50
☐ BC15	Scott Rolen	12.00	5.50
☐ BC16	Jose Guillen	6.00	2.70
☐ BC17	Bob Abreu	3.00	1.35
☐ BC18	Vladimir Guerrero	10.00	4.50
☐ BC19	Todd Walker	3.00	1.35
☐ BC20	Nomar Garciaparra	15.00	6.75

1997 Bowman's Best Mirror Image

Randomly inserted in packs at a rate of one in 48, this 10-card set features color photos of four of the best players in the same position printed on double-sided chromium card stock. Two veterans and two rookies appear on each card. The veteran players are displayed in the larger photos with the rookies appearing in smaller corner photos.

	MINT	NRMT
COMPLETE SET (10)	150.00	70.00
COMMON CARD (MI1-MI10)	5.00	2.20
STATED ODDS 1:48		
*REFRACTORS: .75X TO 1.5X HI COLUMN		
REFRACTOR STATED ODDS 1:96		
*ATOMIC REFRACTORS: 1.5X TO 3X HI		
ATOMIC STATED ODDS 1:192		
*INVERTED: 2X VALUE OF NON-INVERTED		
INVERTED: RANDOM INSERTS IN PACKS		
INVERTED HAVE LARGER ROOKIE PHOTOS		

		MINT	NRMT
☐ MI1	Nomar Garciaparra	20.00	9.00
	Derek Jeter		
	Hiram Bocachica		
	Barry Larkin		
☐ MI2	Travis Lee	30.00	13.50
	Frank Thomas		
	Derrick Lee		
	Jeff Bagwell		
☐ MI3	Kerry Wood	15.00	6.75
	Greg Maddux		
	Kris Benson		
	John Smoltz		
☐ MI4	Kevin Brown	12.00	5.50
	Ivan Rodriguez		
	Eli Marrero		
	Mike Piazza		
☐ MI5	Jose Cruz Jr.	40.00	18.00
	Ken Griffey Jr.		
	Andruw Jones		
	Barry Bonds		
☐ MI6	Jose Guillen	10.00	4.50
	Juan Gonzalez		
	Richard Hidalgo		
	Gary Sheffield		
☐ MI7	Paul Konerko	15.00	6.75
	Mark McGwire		
	Todd Helton		
	Rafael Palmeiro		
☐ MI8	Wilton Guerrero	5.00	2.20
	Craig Biggio		
	Donnie Sadler		
	Chuck Knoblauch		
☐ MI9	Russell Branyan	20.00	9.00
	Matt Williams		
	Adrian Beltre		
	Chipper Jones		
☐ MI10	Bob Abreu	10.00	4.50
	Kenny Lofton		
	Vladimir Guerrero		
	Albert Belle		

1996 Circa

The 1996 Circa set was issued in one series totalling 200 cards. The eight-card packs retail for $1.99 each. The cards feature color action player photos on one of 28 different background designs and colors indicating the player's major league team. The backs carry player information and statistics. The only notable Rookie Card is Darin Erstad.

	MINT	NRMT
COMPLETE SET (200)	25.00	11.00
COMMON CARD (1-200)	.15	.07
MINOR STARS	.30	.14
UNLISTED STARS	.60	.25
SUBSET CARDS HALF VALUE OF BASE CARDS		

		MINT	NRMT
☐ 1	Roberto Alomar	.60	.25
☐ 2	Brady Anderson	.40	.18
☐ 3	Rocky Coppinger	.60	.25
☐ 4	Eddie Murray	.60	.25
☐ 5	Mike Mussina	.60	.25
☐ 6	Randy Myers	.15	.07
☐ 7	Rafael Palmeiro	.40	.18
☐ 8	Cal Ripken	2.50	1.10
☐ 9	Jose Canseco	.40	.18
☐ 10	Roger Clemens	1.25	.55
☐ 11	Mike Greenwell	.15	.07
☐ 12	Tim Naehring	.15	.07

13	John Valentin	.15	.07
14	Mo Vaughn	.75	.35
15	Tim Wakefield	.15	.07
16	Jim Abbott	.15	.07
17	Garret Anderson	.30	.14
18	Jim Edmonds	.15	.07
19	Darin Erstad	3.00	1.35
20	Chuck Finley	.15	.07
21	Troy Percival	.15	.07
22	Tim Salmon	.60	.25
23	J.T. Snow	.30	.14
24	Wilson Alvarez	.15	.07
25	Harold Baines	.30	.14
26	Ray Durham	.15	.07
27	Alex Fernandez	.15	.07
28	Tony Phillips	.15	.07
29	Frank Thomas	2.50	1.10
30	Robin Ventura	.30	.14
31	Sandy Alomar Jr.	.30	.14
32	Albert Belle	.75	.35
33	Kenny Lofton	.75	.35
34	Dennis Martinez	.30	.14
35	Jose Mesa	.15	.07
36	Charles Nagy	.30	.14
37	Manny Ramirez	.60	.25
38	Jim Thome	.60	.25
39	Travis Fryman	.30	.14
40	Bob Higginson	.40	.18
41	Melvin Nieves	.15	.07
42	Alan Trammell	.40	.18
43	Kevin Appier	.30	.14
44	Johnny Damon	.30	.14
45	Keith Lockhart	.15	.07
46	Jeff Montgomery	.15	.07
47	Joe Randa	.15	.07
48	Bip Roberts	.15	.07
49	Ricky Bones	.15	.07
50	Jeff Cirillo	.30	.14
51	Marc Newfield	.15	.07
52	Dave Nilsson	.15	.07
53	Kevin Seitzer	.15	.07
54	Ron Coomer	.15	.07
55	Marty Cordova	.30	.14
56	Roberto Kelly	.15	.07
57	Chuck Knoblauch	.25	.14
58	Paul Molitor	.25	.14
59	Kirby Puckett	1.25	.55
60	Scott Stahoviak	.15	.07
61	Wade Boggs	.60	.25
62	David Cone	.30	.14
63	Cecil Fielder	.30	.14
64	Dwight Gooden	.30	.14
65	Derek Jeter	2.00	.90
66	Tino Martinez	.60	.25
67	Paul O'Neill	.30	.14
68	Andy Pettitte	.75	.35
69	Ruben Rivera	.15	.07
70	Bernie Williams	.60	.25
71	Geronimo Berroa	.15	.07
72	Jason Giambi	.30	.14
73	Mark McGwire	1.25	.55
74	Terry Steinbach	.15	.07
75	Todd Van Poppel	.15	.07
76	Jay Buhner	.40	.18
77	Norm Charlton	.15	.07
78	Ken Griffey Jr.	3.00	1.35
79	Randy Johnson	.25	.18
80	Edgar Martinez	.25	.18
81	Alex Rodriguez	2.00	.90
82	Paul Sorrento	.15	.07
83	Dan Wilson	.15	.07
84	Will Clark	.40	.18
85	Kevin Elster	.15	.07
86	Juan Gonzalez	1.50	.70
87	Rusty Greer	.30	.14
88	Ken Hill	.15	.07
89	Mark McLemore	.15	.07
90	Dean Palmer	.15	.07
91	Roger Pavlik	.15	.07
92	Ivan Rodriguez	.75	.35
93	Joe Carter	.30	.14
94	Carlos Delgado	.30	.14
95	Juan Guzman	.15	.07
96	John Olerud	.30	.14
97	Ed Sprague	.15	.07
98	Jermaine Dye	.30	.14
99	Tom Glavine	.30	.14
100	Marquis Grissom	.30	.14
101	Andruw Jones	2.50	1.10
102	Chipper Jones	2.00	.90
103	David Justice	.60	.25
104	Ryan Klesko	.40	.18
105	Greg Maddux	2.00	.90
106	Fred McGriff	.40	.18
107	John Smoltz	.30	.14
108	Brant Brown	.15	.07
109	Mark Grace	.40	.18
110	Brian McRae	.15	.07
111	Ryne Sandberg	.75	.35
112	Sammy Sosa	.60	.25
113	Steve Trachsel	.15	.07
114	Bret Boone	.15	.07
115	Eric Davis	.30	.14
116	Steve Gibralter	.15	.07
117	Barry Larkin	.40	.18
118	Reggie Sanders	.15	.07
119	John Smiley	.15	.07
120	Dante Bichette	.30	.14
121	Ellis Burks	.30	.14
122	Vinny Castilla	.30	.14
123	Andres Galarraga	.60	.25
124	Larry Walker	.60	.25
125	Eric Young	.15	.07
126	Kevin Brown	.30	.14
127	Greg Colbrunn	.15	.07
128	Jeff Conine	.30	.14
129	Charles Johnson	.30	.14
130	Al Leiter	.15	.07
131	Gary Sheffield	.60	.25
132	Devon White	.15	.07
133	Jeff Bagwell	1.25	.55
134	Derek Bell	.15	.07
135	Craig Biggio	.40	.18
136	Doug Drabek	.15	.07
137	Brian L. Hunter	.30	.14
138	Darryl Kile	.15	.07
139	Shane Reynolds	.15	.07
140	Brett Butler	.15	.07
141	Eric Karros	.30	.14
142	Ramon Martinez	.30	.14
143	Raul Mondesi	.40	.18
144	Hideo Nomo	1.50	.70
145	Chan Ho Park	.60	.25
146	Mike Piazza	2.00	.90
147	Moises Alou	.30	.14
148	Yamil Benitez	.30	.14
149	Mark Grudzielanek	.30	.14
150	Pedro Martinez	.60	.25
151	Henry Rodriguez	.15	.07
152	David Segui	.15	.07
153	Rondell White	.15	.07
154	Carlos Baerga	.15	.07
155	John Franco	.15	.07
156	Bernard Gilkey	.15	.07
157	Todd Hundley	.30	.14
158	Jason Isringhausen	.15	.07
159	Lance Johnson	.30	.14
160	Alex Ochoa	.15	.07
161	Rey Ordonez	.30	.14
162	Paul Wilson	.15	.07
163	Ron Blazier	.15	.07
164	Ricky Bottalico	.15	.07
165	Jim Eisenreich	.15	.07
166	Pete Incaviglia	.15	.07
167	Mickey Morandini	.15	.07
168	Ricky Otero	.15	.07
169	Curt Schilling	.30	.14
170	Jay Bell	.30	.14
171	Charlie Hayes	.15	.07
172	Jason Kendall	.40	.18
173	Jeff King	.15	.07
174	Al Martin	.15	.07
175	Alan Benes	.30	.14
176	Royce Clayton	.15	.07
177	Brian Jordan	.30	.14
178	Ray Lankford	.30	.14
179	John Mabry	.15	.07
180	Willie McGee	.15	.07
181	Ozzie Smith	.75	.35
182	Todd Stottlemyre	.15	.07
183	Andy Ashby	.15	.07
184	Ken Caminiti	.40	.18
185	Steve Finley	.30	.14
186	Tony Gwynn	1.50	.70
187	Rickey Henderson	.40	.18
188	Wally Joyner	.30	.14
189	Fernando Valenzuela	.30	.14
190	Greg Vaughn	.15	.07
191	Rod Beck	.15	.07
192	Barry Bonds	.75	.35
193	Shawon Dunston	.15	.07
194	Chris Singleton	.15	.07
195	Robby Thompson	.15	.07
196	Matt Williams	.40	.18
197	Barry Bonds CL	.40	.18
198	Ken Griffey Jr. CL	1.50	.70
199	Cal Ripken CL	1.25	.55
200	Frank Thomas CL	1.25	.55

1996 Circa Rave

Randomly inserted in packs at a rate of one in 60, this 200-card set is parallel and similar in design to the regular set except for sparkling foil lettering on front. Each card is individually numbered on back with 150 of each card produced.

		MINT	NRMT
COMPLETE SET (200)		8000.00	3600.00
COMMON CARD (1-200)		15.00	6.75
MINOR STARS		25.00	11.00
SEMISTARS		40.00	18.00
UNLISTED STARS		60.00	27.00
STATED ODDS 1:60			
STATED PRINT RUN 150 SERIAL #'d SETS			

#	Player	MINT	NRMT
8	Cal Ripken	250.00	110.00
10	Roger Clemens	150.00	70.00
14	Mo Vaughn	80.00	36.00
19	Darin Erstad	150.00	70.00
29	Frank Thomas	250.00	110.00
32	Albert Belle	80.00	36.00
33	Kenny Lofton	80.00	36.00
59	Kirby Puckett	120.00	55.00
65	Derek Jeter	150.00	70.00
73	Mark McGwire	150.00	70.00
78	Ken Griffey Jr.	300.00	135.00
81	Alex Rodriguez	200.00	90.00
86	Juan Gonzalez	150.00	70.00
92	Ivan Rodriguez	80.00	36.00
101	Andruw Jones	150.00	70.00
102	Chipper Jones	150.00	70.00
105	Greg Maddux	200.00	90.00
111	Ryne Sandberg	100.00	45.00
133	Jeff Bagwell	120.00	55.00
144	Hideo Nomo	200.00	90.00
146	Mike Piazza	200.00	90.00
181	Ozzie Smith	100.00	45.00
186	Tony Gwynn	150.00	70.00
192	Barry Bonds	80.00	36.00
198	Ken Griffey Jr. CL	150.00	70.00
199	Cal Ripken CL	120.00	55.00
200	Frank Thomas CL	120.00	55.00

1996 Circa Access

Randomly inserted in packs at a rate of one in 12, this 30-card limited edition set features a fold-out, three-panel card showcasing some of the hottest superstars of the game. The panels display color player photos, player statistics and personal information on team-colored backgrounds. A promotional card featuring Matt Williams was issued to dealers. The card is similar to the basic Access Williams except for the words "Promotional Sample" written across the card front.

	MINT	NRMT
COMPLETE SET (30)	120.00	55.00
COMMON CARD (1-30)	1.00	.45
STATED ODDS 1:12		

		MINT	NRMT
☐ 1	Cal Ripken	15.00	6.75
☐ 2	Mo Vaughn	5.00	2.20
☐ 3	Tim Salmon	4.00	1.80
☐ 4	Frank Thomas	15.00	6.75
☐ 5	Albert Belle	5.00	2.20
☐ 6	Kenny Lofton	5.00	2.20
☐ 7	Manny Ramirez	4.00	1.80
☐ 8	Paul Molitor	4.00	1.80
☐ 9	Kirby Puckett	8.00	3.60
☐ 10	Paul O'Neill	2.00	.90
☐ 11	Mark McGwire	8.00	3.60
☐ 12	Ken Griffey Jr.	20.00	9.00
☐ 13	Randy Johnson	4.00	1.80
☐ 14	Greg Maddux	12.00	5.50
☐ 15	John Smoltz	2.00	.90
☐ 16	Sammy Sosa	4.00	1.80
☐ 17	Barry Larkin	2.50	1.10
☐ 18	Gary Sheffield	4.00	1.80
☐ 19	Jeff Bagwell	8.00	3.60
☐ 20	Hideo Nomo	10.00	4.50
☐ 21	Mike Piazza	12.00	5.50
☐ 22	Moises Alou	2.00	.90
☐ 23	Henry Rodriguez	1.00	.45
☐ 24	Rey Ordonez	2.00	.90
☐ 25	Jay Bell	2.00	.90
☐ 26	Ozzie Smith	5.00	2.20
☐ 27	Tony Gwynn	10.00	4.50
☐ 28	Rickey Henderson	2.50	1.10
☐ 29	Barry Bonds	5.00	2.20
☐ 30	Matt Williams	1.00	.45
☐ P30	Matt Williams	1.00	.45
	Promo		

1996 Circa Boss

Randomly inserted in packs at a rate of one in six, this 50-card set features a sculpted embossed player image on a team-colored background containing the team logo. The backs carry information about the player's career. A promotional card featuring Cal Ripken was issued to dealers. The card is similar to the basic Boss Ripken except for the words "Promotional Sample" written across the card front.

	MINT	NRMT
COMPLETE SET (50)	100.00	45.00
COMMON CARD (1-50)	1.00	.45
STATED ODDS 1:6		

		MINT	NRMT
☐ 1	Roberto Alomar	3.00	1.35
☐ 2	Cal Ripken	12.00	5.50
☐ 3	Jose Canseco	2.00	.90
☐ 4	Mo Vaughn	4.00	1.80
☐ 5	Tim Salmon	3.00	1.35
☐ 6	Frank Thomas	12.00	5.50
☐ 7	Robin Ventura	1.50	.70
☐ 8	Albert Belle	4.00	1.80
☐ 9	Kenny Lofton	4.00	1.80
☐ 10	Manny Ramirez	3.00	1.35
☐ 11	Dave Nilsson	1.00	.45
☐ 12	Chuck Knoblauch	3.00	1.35
☐ 13	Paul Molitor	3.00	1.35
☐ 14	Kirby Puckett	6.00	2.70
☐ 15	Wade Boggs	3.00	1.35
☐ 16	Dwight Gooden	1.50	.70
☐ 17	Paul O'Neill	1.50	.70
☐ 18	Mark McGwire	6.00	2.70
☐ 19	Jay Buhner	2.00	.90
☐ 20	Ken Griffey Jr.	15.00	6.75
☐ 21	Randy Johnson	3.00	1.35
☐ 22	Will Clark	2.00	.90
☐ 23	Juan Gonzalez	8.00	3.60
☐ 24	Joe Carter	1.50	.70
☐ 25	Tom Glavine	1.50	.70
☐ 26	Ryan Klesko	2.00	.90
☐ 27	Greg Maddux	10.00	4.50
☐ 28	John Smoltz	1.50	.70
☐ 29	Ryne Sandberg	4.00	1.80
☐ 30	Sammy Sosa	3.00	1.35
☐ 31	Barry Larkin	2.00	.90
☐ 32	Reggie Sanders	1.00	.45
☐ 33	Dante Bichette	1.50	.70
☐ 34	Andres Galarraga	3.00	1.35
☐ 35	Charles Johnson	1.50	.70
☐ 36	Gary Sheffield	3.00	1.35
☐ 37	Jeff Bagwell	6.00	2.70
☐ 38	Hideo Nomo	8.00	3.60
☐ 39	Mike Piazza	10.00	4.50
☐ 40	Moises Alou	1.50	.70
☐ 41	Henry Rodriguez	1.00	.45
☐ 42	Rey Ordonez	1.50	.70
☐ 43	Ricky Otero	1.00	.45
☐ 44	Royce Clayton	1.00	.45
☐ 45	Ozzie Smith	4.00	1.80
☐ 46	Tony Gwynn	8.00	3.60
☐ 47	Rickey Henderson	2.00	.90
☐ 48	Barry Bonds	4.00	1.80
☐ 49	Matt Williams	2.00	.90
☐ P2	Cal Ripken	2.00	.90
	Promo		

1997 Circa

The 1997 Circa set was issued in one series totalling 400 cards and was distributed in eight-card foil packs with a suggested retail price of $1.49. The set contains 393 player cards and seven checklist cards. The fronts feature color player photos with new in-your-face graphics that lift the player off the card. The backs carry in-depth player statistics and "Did you know" information. An Alex Rodriguez promo card (P100)

was distributed to dealers with their ordering papers.

	MINT	NRMT
COMPLETE SET (400)	40.00	18.00
COMMON CARD (1-400)	.15	.07
MINOR STARS	.30	.14
UNLISTED STARS	.60	.25
SUBSET CARDS HALF VALUE OF BASE CARDS		

		MINT	NRMT
☐ 1	Kenny Lofton	.75	.35
☐ 2	Ray Durham	.15	.07
☐ 3	Mariano Rivera	.30	.14
☐ 4	Jon Lieber	.15	.07
☐ 5	Tim Salmon	.60	.25
☐ 6	Mark Grudzielanek	.15	.07
☐ 7	Neifi Perez	.30	.14
☐ 8	Cal Ripken	2.50	1.10
☐ 9	John Olerud	.30	.14
☐ 10	Edgar Renteria	.30	.14
☐ 11	Jose Rosado	.30	.14
☐ 12	Mickey Morandini	.15	.07
☐ 13	Orlando Miller	.15	.07
☐ 14	Ben McDonald	.15	.07
☐ 15	Hideo Nomo	1.50	.70
☐ 16	Fred McGriff	.40	.18
☐ 17	Sean Berry	.15	.07
☐ 18	Roger Pavlik	.15	.07
☐ 19	Aaron Sele	.15	.07
☐ 20	Joey Hamilton	.30	.14
☐ 21	Roger Clemens	1.25	.55
☐ 22	Jose Herrera	.15	.07
☐ 23	Ryne Sandberg	.75	.35
☐ 24	Ken Griffey Jr.	3.00	1.35
☐ 25	Barry Bonds	.75	.35
☐ 26	Dan Naulty	.15	.07
☐ 27	Wade Boggs	.60	.25
☐ 28	Ray Lankford	.30	.14
☐ 29	Rico Brogna	.15	.07
☐ 30	Wally Joyner	.15	.07
☐ 31	F.P. Santangelo	.15	.07
☐ 32	Vinny Castilla	.30	.14
☐ 33	Eddie Murray	.60	.25
☐ 34	Kevin Elster	.15	.07
☐ 35	Mike Macfarlane	.15	.07
☐ 36	Jeff Kent	.15	.07
☐ 37	Orlando Merced	.15	.07
☐ 38	Jason Isringhausen	.15	.07
☐ 39	Chad Ogea	.15	.07
☐ 40	Greg Gagne	.15	.07
☐ 41	Curt Lyons	.15	.07
☐ 42	Mo Vaughn	.75	.35
☐ 43	Rusty Greer	.30	.14
☐ 44	Shane Reynolds	.15	.07
☐ 45	Frank Thomas	2.50	1.10
☐ 46	Chris Hoiles	.15	.07
☐ 47	Scott Sanders	.15	.07
☐ 48	Mark Lemke	.15	.07
☐ 49	Fernando Vina	.15	.07
☐ 50	Mark McGwire	1.25	.55
☐ 51	Bernie Williams	.60	.25
☐ 52	Bobby Higginson	.30	.14
☐ 53	Kevin Tapani	.15	.07
☐ 54	Rich Becker	.15	.07
☐ 55	Felix Heredia	.40	.18
☐ 56	Delino DeShields	.15	.07
☐ 57	Rick Wilkins	.15	.07

58	Edgardo Alfonzo	.30	.14
59	Brett Butler	.30	.14
60	Ed Sprague	.15	.07
61	Joe Randa	.15	.07
62	Ugueth Urbina	.15	.07
63	Todd Greene	.30	.14
64	Devon White	.15	.07
65	Bruce Ruffin	.15	.07
66	Mark Gardner	.15	.07
67	Omar Vizquel	.30	.14
68	Luis Gonzalez	.15	.07
69	Tom Glavine	.30	.14
70	Cal Eldred	.15	.07
71	Wm. VanLandingham	.15	.07
72	Jay Buhner	.40	.18
73	James Baldwin	.15	.07
74	Robin Jennings	.15	.07
75	Terry Steinbach	.15	.07
76	Billy Taylor	.15	.07
77	Armando Benitez	.15	.07
78	Joe Girardi	.15	.07
79	Jay Bell	.15	.07
80	Damon Buford	.15	.07
81	Deion Sanders	.30	.14
82	Bill Haselman	.15	.07
83	John Flaherty	.15	.07
84	Todd Stottlemyre	.15	.07
85	J.T. Snow	.30	.14
86	Felipe Lira	.15	.07
87	Steve Avery	.15	.07
88	Trey Beamon	.15	.07
89	Alex Gonzalez	.15	.07
90	Mark Clark	.15	.07
91	Shane Andrews	.15	.07
92	Randy Myers	.15	.07
93	Gary Gaetti	.15	.07
94	Jeff Blauser	.30	.14
95	Tony Batista	.15	.07
96	Todd Worrell	.15	.07
97	Jim Edmonds	.40	.18
98	Eric Young	.15	.07
99	Roberto Kelly	.15	.07
100	Alex Rodriguez	2.00	.90
101	Julio Franco	.15	.07
102	Jeff Bagwell	1.25	.55
103	Bobby Witt	.15	.07
104	Tino Martinez	.60	.25
105	Shannon Stewart	.30	.14
106	Brian Banks	.15	.07
107	Eddie Taubensee	.15	.07
108	Terry Mulholland	.15	.07
109	Lyle Mouton	.15	.07
110	Jeff Conine	.30	.14
111	Johnny Damon	.15	.07
112	Quilvio Veras	.15	.07
113	Wilton Guerrero	.15	.07
114	Dmitri Young	.15	.07
115	Garret Anderson	.30	.14
116	Bill Pulsipher	.15	.07
117	Jacob Brumfield	.15	.07
118	Mike Lansing	.15	.07
119	Jose Canseco	.40	.18
120	Mike Bordick	.15	.07
121	Kevin Stocker	.15	.07
122	Frankie Rodriguez	.15	.07
123	Mike Cameron	.40	.18
124	Tony Womack	.50	.23
125	Bret Boone	.15	.07
126	Moises Alou	.30	.14
127	Tim Naehring	.15	.07
128	Brant Brown	.15	.07
129	Todd Zeile	.15	.07
130	Dave Nilsson	.15	.07
131	Donne Wall	.15	.07
132	Jose Mesa	.15	.07
133	Mark McLemore	.15	.07
134	Mike Stanton	.15	.07
135	Dan Wilson	.15	.07
136	Jose Offerman	.15	.07
137	David Justice	.60	.25
138	Kirt Manwaring	.15	.07
139	Raul Casanova	.15	.07
140	Ron Coomer	.15	.07
141	Dave Hollins	.15	.07
142	Shawn Estes	.30	.14
143	Darren Daulton	.30	.14
144	Turk Wendell	.15	.07
145	Darrin Fletcher	.15	.07
146	Marquis Grissom	.30	.14
147	Andy Benes	.30	.14
148	Nomar Garciaparra	2.00	.90
149	Andy Pettitte	.60	.25
150	Tony Gwynn	1.50	.70
151	Robb Nen	.15	.07
152	Kevin Seitzer	.15	.07
153	Ariel Prieto	.15	.07
154	Scott Karl	.15	.07
155	Carlos Baerga	.15	.07
156	Wilson Alvarez	.15	.07
157	Thomas Howard	.15	.07
158	Kevin Appier	.30	.14
159	Russ Davis	.15	.07
160	Justin Thompson	.30	.14
161	Pete Schourek	.15	.07
162	John Burkett	.15	.07
163	Roberto Alomar	.60	.25
164	Darren Holmes	.15	.07
165	Travis Miller	.15	.07
166	Mark Langston	.15	.07
167	Juan Guzman	.15	.07
168	Pedro Astacio	.15	.07
169	Mark Johnson	.15	.07
170	Mark Leiter	.15	.07
171	Heathcliff Slocumb	.15	.07
172	Dante Bichette	.30	.14
173	Brian Giles	.15	.07
174	Paul Wilson	.15	.07
175	Eric Davis	.30	.14
176	Charles Johnson	.30	.14
177	Willie Greene	.15	.07
178	Geronimo Berroa	.15	.07
179	Mariano Duncan	.15	.07
180	Robert Person	.15	.07
181	David Segui	.15	.07
182	Ozzie Guillen	.15	.07
183	Osvaldo Fernandez	.15	.07
184	Dean Palmer	.15	.07
185	Bob Wickman	.15	.07
186	Eric Karros	.30	.14
187	Travis Fryman	.30	.14
188	Andy Ashby	.15	.07
189	Scott Stahoviak	.15	.07
190	Norm Charlton	.15	.07
191	Craig Paquette	.15	.07
192	John Smoltz UER	.30	.14
	Name spelled "Smotlz" on back		
193	Orel Hershiser	.30	.14
194	Glenallen Hill	.15	.07
195	George Arias	.15	.07
196	Brian Jordan	.30	.14
197	Greg Vaughn	.15	.07
198	Rafael Palmeiro	.40	.18
199	Darryl Kile	.30	.14
200	Derek Jeter	2.00	.90
201	Jose Vizcaino	.15	.07
202	Rick Aguilera	.15	.07
203	Jason Schmidt	.15	.07
204	Trot Nixon	.15	.07
205	Tom Pagnozzi	.15	.07
206	Mark Wohlers	.15	.07
207	Lance Johnson	.15	.07
208	Carlos Delgado	.30	.14
209	Cliff Floyd	.15	.07
210	Kent Mercker	.15	.07
211	Matt Mieske	.15	.07
212	Ismael Valdes	.30	.14
213	Shawon Dunston	.15	.07
214	Melvin Nieves	.15	.07
215	Tony Phillips	.15	.07
216	Scott Spiezio	.30	.14
217	Michael Tucker	.30	.14
218	Matt Williams	.40	.18
219	Ricky Otero	.15	.07
220	Kevin Ritz	.15	.07
221	Darryl Strawberry	.30	.14
222	Troy Percival	.15	.07
223	Eugene Kingsale	.15	.07
224	Julian Tavarez	.15	.07
225	Jermaine Dye	.15	.07
226	Jason Kendall	.30	.14
227	Sterling Hitchcock	.15	.07
228	Jeff Cirillo	.30	.14
229	Roberto Hernandez	.15	.07
230	Ricky Bottalico	.15	.07
231	Bobby Bonilla	.30	.14
232	Edgar Martinez	.40	.18
233	John Valentin	.15	.07
234	Ellis Burks	.30	.14
235	Benito Santiago	.15	.07
236	Terrell Wade	.15	.07
237	Armando Reynoso	.15	.07
238	Danny Graves	.15	.07
239	Ken Hill	.15	.07
240	Dennis Eckersley	.30	.14
241	Darin Erstad	1.00	.45
242	Lee Smith UER	.30	.14
	Position 2b		
243	Cecil Fielder	.30	.14
244	Tony Clark	.60	.25
245	Scott Erickson	.15	.07
246	Bob Abreu	.30	.14
247	Ruben Sierra	.15	.07
248	Chili Davis	.30	.14
249	Darryl Hamilton	.15	.07
250	Albert Belle	.75	.35
251	Todd Hollandsworth	.15	.07
252	Terry Adams	.15	.07
253	Rey Ordonez	.15	.07
254	Steve Finley	.30	.14
255	Jose Valentin	.15	.07
256	Royce Clayton	.15	.07
257	Sandy Alomar	.30	.14
258	Mike Lieberthal	.15	.07
259	Ivan Rodriguez	.75	.35
260	Rod Beck	.15	.07
261	Ron Karkovice	.15	.07
262	Mark Gubicza	.15	.07
263	Chris Holt	.15	.07
264	Jaime Bluma UER	.15	.07
	Name spelled "Jamie" on front and back		
265	Francisco Cordova	.15	.07
266	Javy Lopez	.30	.14
267	Reggie Jefferson	.15	.07
268	Kevin Brown	.30	.14
269	Scott Brosius	.15	.07
270	Dwight Gooden	.30	.14
271	Marty Cordova	.15	.07
272	Jeff Brantley	.15	.07
273	Joe Carter	.30	.14
274	Todd Jones	.15	.07
275	Sammy Sosa	.60	.25
276	Randy Johnson	.60	.25
277	B.J. Surhoff	.15	.07
278	Chan Ho Park	.60	.25
279	Jamey Wright	.15	.07
280	Manny Ramirez	.60	.25
281	John Franco	.30	.14
282	Tim Worrell	.15	.07
283	Scott Rolen	1.50	.70
284	Reggie Sanders	.15	.07
285	Mike Fetters	.15	.07
286	Tim Wakefield	.15	.07
287	Trevor Hoffman	.15	.07
288	Donovan Osborne	.15	.07
289	Phil Nevin	.15	.07
290	Jermaine Allensworth	.15	.07
291	Rocky Coppinger	.15	.07
292	Tim Raines	.30	.14
293	Henry Rodriguez	.15	.07
294	Paul Sorrento	.15	.07
295	Tom Goodwin	.15	.07
296	Raul Mondesi	.40	.18
297	Allen Watson	.15	.07
298	Derek Bell	.15	.07
299	Gary Sheffield	.60	.25
300	Paul Molitor	.60	.25
301	Shawn Green	.15	.07
302	Darren Oliver	.15	.07
303	Jack McDowell	.15	.07
304	Denny Neagle	.30	.14
305	Doug Drabek	.15	.07
306	Mel Rojas	.15	.07
307	Andres Galarraga	.60	.25
308	Alex Ochoa	.15	.07
309	Gary DiSarcina	.15	.07
310	Ron Gant	.30	.14
311	Gregg Jefferies	.15	.07
312	Ruben Rivera	.30	.14

☐ 313	Vladimir Guerrero	1.25	.55
☐ 314	Willie Adams	.15	.07
☐ 315	Bip Roberts	.15	.07
☐ 316	Mark Grace	.40	.18
☐ 317	Bernard Gilkey	.15	.07
☐ 318	Marc Newfield	.15	.07
☐ 319	Al Leiter	.15	.07
☐ 320	Otis Nixon	.15	.07
☐ 321	Tom Candiotti	.15	.07
☐ 322	Mike Stanley	.15	.07
☐ 323	Jeff Fassero	.15	.07
☐ 324	Billy Wagner	.30	.14
☐ 325	Todd Walker	.30	.14
☐ 326	Chad Curtis	.15	.07
☐ 327	Quinton McCracken	.15	.07
☐ 328	Will Clark	.40	.18
☐ 329	Andruw Jones	1.50	.70
☐ 330	Robin Ventura	.30	.14
☐ 331	Curtis Pride	.15	.07
☐ 332	Barry Larkin	.40	.18
☐ 333	Jimmy Key	.30	.14
☐ 334	David Wells	.15	.07
☐ 335	Mike Holtz	.15	.07
☐ 336	Paul Wagner	.15	.07
☐ 337	Greg Maddux	2.00	.90
☐ 338	Curt Schilling	.30	.14
☐ 339	Steve Trachsel	.15	.07
☐ 340	John Wetteland	.15	.07
☐ 341	Rickey Henderson	.40	.18
☐ 342	Ernie Young	.15	.07
☐ 343	Harold Baines	.15	.07
☐ 344	Bobby Jones	.15	.07
☐ 345	Jeff D'Amico	.15	.07
☐ 346	John Mabry	.15	.07
☐ 347	Pedro Martinez	.60	.25
☐ 348	Mark Lewis	.15	.07
☐ 349	Dan Miceli	.15	.07
☐ 350	Chuck Knoblauch	.60	.25
☐ 351	John Smiley	.15	.07
☐ 352	Brady Anderson	.40	.18
☐ 353	Jim Leyritz	.15	.07
☐ 354	Al Martin	.15	.07
☐ 355	Pat Hentgen	.30	.14
☐ 356	Mike Piazza	2.00	.90
☐ 357	Charles Nagy	.30	.14
☐ 358	Luis Castillo	.30	.14
☐ 359	Paul O'Neill	.30	.14
☐ 360	Steve Reed	.15	.07
☐ 361	Tom Gordon	.15	.07
☐ 362	Craig Biggio	.40	.18
☐ 363	Jeff Montgomery	.15	.07
☐ 364	Jamie Moyer	.15	.07
☐ 365	Ryan Klesko	.40	.18
☐ 366	Todd Hundley	.30	.14
☐ 367	Bobby Estalella	.15	.07
☐ 368	Jason Giambi	.30	.14
☐ 369	Brian Hunter	.30	.14
☐ 370	Ramon Martinez	.30	.14
☐ 371	Carlos Garcia	.15	.07
☐ 372	Hal Morris	.15	.07
☐ 373	Juan Gonzalez	1.50	.70
☐ 374	Brian McRae	.15	.07
☐ 375	Mike Mussina	.60	.25
☐ 376	John Ericks	.15	.07
☐ 377	Larry Walker	.60	.25
☐ 378	Chris Gomez	.15	.07
☐ 379	John Jaha	.15	.07
☐ 380	Rondell White	.30	.14
☐ 381	Chipper Jones	2.00	.90
☐ 382	David Cone	.30	.14
☐ 383	Alan Benes	.15	.07
☐ 384	Troy O'Leary	.15	.07
☐ 385	Ken Caminiti	.40	.18
☐ 386	Jeff King	.15	.07
☐ 387	Mike Hampton	.15	.07
☐ 388	Jaime Navarro	.15	.07
☐ 389	Brad Radke	.30	.14
☐ 390	Joey Cora	.15	.07
☐ 391	Jim Thome	.60	.25
☐ 392	Alex Fernandez	.30	.14
☐ 393	Chuck Finley	.15	.07
☐ 394	Andruw Jones CL	.75	.35
☐ 395	Ken Griffey Jr. CL	1.50	.70
☐ 396	Frank Thomas CL	1.25	.55
☐ 397	Alex Rodriguez CL	1.00	.45
☐ 398	Cal Ripken CL	1.25	.55
☐ 399	Mike Piazza CL	1.00	.45
☐ 400	Greg Maddux CL	1.00	.45
☐ P100	Alex Rodriguez Promo	3.00	1.35

1997 Circa Rave

Randomly inserted in packs at a rate of one in 30, this hobby exclusive set is a parallel version of the regular set and is similar in design. One hundred fifty of this limited edition set were produced and are sequentially numbered.

	MINT	NRMT
COMMON CARD (1-400)	10.00	4.50
MINOR STARS	15.00	6.75
SEMISTARS	25.00	11.00
UNLISTED STARS	40.00	18.00
STATED ODDS 1:30 HOBBY		
STATED PRINT RUN 150 SERIAL #'d SETS		

☐ 1	Kenny Lofton	50.00	22.00
☐ 8	Cal Ripken	150.00	70.00
☐ 15	Hideo Nomo	120.00	55.00
☐ 21	Roger Clemens	80.00	36.00
☐ 23	Ryne Sandberg	50.00	22.00
☐ 24	Ken Griffey Jr.	200.00	90.00
☐ 25	Barry Bonds	50.00	22.00
☐ 42	Mo Vaughn	50.00	22.00
☐ 45	Frank Thomas	150.00	70.00
☐ 50	Mark McGwire	80.00	36.00
☐ 100	Alex Rodriguez	120.00	55.00
☐ 102	Jeff Bagwell	80.00	36.00
☐ 148	Nomar Garciaparra	100.00	45.00
☐ 150	Tony Gwynn	100.00	45.00
☐ 200	Derek Jeter	100.00	45.00
☐ 241	Darin Erstad	50.00	22.00
☐ 250	Albert Belle	50.00	22.00
☐ 259	Ivan Rodriguez	50.00	22.00
☐ 283	Scott Rolen	80.00	36.00
☐ 313	Vladimir Guerrero	60.00	27.00
☐ 329	Andruw Jones	80.00	36.00
☐ 337	Greg Maddux	120.00	55.00
☐ 356	Mike Piazza	120.00	55.00
☐ 373	Juan Gonzalez	100.00	45.00
☐ 381	Chipper Jones	100.00	45.00
☐ 395	Ken Griffey Jr. CL	100.00	45.00
☐ 396	Frank Thomas CL	80.00	36.00
☐ 397	Alex Rodriguez CL	60.00	27.00
☐ 398	Cal Ripken CL	60.00	27.00
☐ 399	Mike Piazza CL	50.00	22.00
☐ 400	Greg Maddux CL	50.00	22.00

1997 Circa Boss

Randomly inserted in packs at a rate of one in six, this 20-card set features color player photos of Baseball's leading men on the field and at bat and are printed on sculpted, embossed cards. The backs carry player information.

	MINT	NRMT
COMPLETE SET (20)	40.00	18.00
COMMON CARD (1-20)	.50	.23
STATED ODDS 1:6		
COMP.SUPER BOSS SET (20)	150.00	70.00
*SUPER BOSS: 1.5X TO 4X BASE CARD HI		
SUPER BOSS STATED ODDS 1:36		

☐ 1	Jeff Bagwell	2.50	1.10
☐ 2	Albert Belle	1.50	.70
☐ 3	Barry Bonds	1.50	.70
☐ 4	Ken Caminiti	.75	.35
☐ 5	Juan Gonzalez	3.00	1.35
☐ 6	Ken Griffey Jr.	6.00	2.70
☐ 7	Tony Gwynn	3.00	1.35
☐ 8	Derek Jeter	3.00	1.35
☐ 9	Andruw Jones	3.00	1.35
☐ 10	Chipper Jones	4.00	1.80
☐ 11	Greg Maddux	4.00	1.80
☐ 12	Mark McGwire	2.50	1.10
☐ 13	Mike Piazza	4.00	1.80
☐ 14	Manny Ramirez	1.25	.55
☐ 15	Cal Ripken	5.00	2.20
☐ 16	Alex Rodriguez	4.00	1.80
☐ 17	John Smoltz	.50	.23
☐ 18	Frank Thomas	5.00	2.20
☐ 19	Mo Vaughn	1.50	.70
☐ 20	Bernie Williams	1.25	.55

1997 Circa Emerald Autographs

These autographed cards were made available only to those collectors lucky enough to pull one of the scarce Circa Emerald Autograph Redemption cards (randomly seeded into 1:1000 1997 Circa packs). These cards are identical to the regular issue Circa cards except, of course, for the player's autograph on the card front and an embossed Fleer seal for authenticity. The deadline to redeem these cards was May 1, 1998. In addition, an Emerald Autograph Redemption program entitled "Collect and Win" was featured in 1997 Fleer 2 packs. One in every 4 packs contained one of ten different redemption cards. The object was for collectors to piece together all ten cards and then mail them in to receive a complete set of the Circa Emerald Autographs. The catch was that card #7 was extremely shortprinted (official numbers were not released but speculation is that only a handful of #7 cards made their way into packs). The exchange deadline on this "col-

lect and win" promotion was August 1st, 1998.

	MINT	NRMT
COMPLETE SET (6)	300.00	135.00
COMMON CARD	12.00	5.50

ONE CARD VIA MAIL PER AU RDMP.CARD
EXCHANGE DEADLINE: 5/1/98..

		MINT	NRMT
☐ 100	Alex Rodriguez AU	150.00	70.00
☐ 241	Darin Erstad AU	50.00	22.00
☐ 251	Todd Hollandsworth AU	15.00	6.75
☐ 283	Scott Rolen AU	80.00	36.00
☐ 308	Alex Ochoa AU	12.00	5.50
☐ 325	Todd Walker AU	20.00	9.00

1997 Circa Fast Track

Randomly inserted in packs at a rate of one in 24, this 10-card set features color player photos of young stars and rookies who will carry baseball into the 21st century. The fronts display the player's image on a flocked background design which shows grass as raised fabric.

		MINT	NRMT
COMPLETE SET (10)		50.00	22.00
COMMON CARD		.75	.35
STATED ODDS 1:24			

		MINT	NRMT
☐ 1	Vladimir Guerrero	6.00	2.70
☐ 2	Todd Hollandsworth	.75	.35
☐ 3	Derek Jeter	10.00	4.50
☐ 4	Andruw Jones	8.00	3.60
☐ 5	Chipper Jones	10.00	4.50
☐ 6	Andy Pettitte	3.00	1.35
☐ 7	Mariano Rivera	1.25	.55
☐ 8	Alex Rodriguez	10.00	4.50
☐ 9	Scott Rolen	8.00	3.60
☐ 10	Todd Walker	1.25	.55

1997 Circa Icons

Randomly inserted in packs at a rate of one in 36, this 12-card set features color player images of twelve legendary players printed on 100% holofoil with the word "icon" running across the background. The backs carry player information.

		MINT	NRMT
COMPLETE SET (12)		100.00	45.00
COMMON CARD (1-12)		2.50	1.10
STATED ODDS 1:36			

		MINT	NRMT
☐ 1	Juan Gonzalez	10.00	4.50
☐ 2	Ken Griffey Jr.	20.00	9.00
☐ 3	Tony Gwynn	10.00	4.50
☐ 4	Derek Jeter	10.00	4.50

		MINT	NRMT
☐ 5	Chipper Jones	12.00	5.50
☐ 6	Greg Maddux	12.00	5.50
☐ 7	Mark McGwire	8.00	3.60
☐ 8	Mike Piazza	12.00	5.50
☐ 9	Cal Ripken	15.00	6.75
☐ 10	Alex Rodriguez	12.00	5.50
☐ 11	Frank Thomas	15.00	6.75
☐ 12	Matt Williams	2.50	1.10

1997 Circa Limited Access

Randomly inserted in retail packs only at a rate of one in 18, this 15-card set features color player photos on die-cut, bi-fold cards which track the players from their youth to the present with in-depth statistical analysis.

		MINT	NRMT
COMPLETE SET (15)		180.00	80.00
COMMON CARD (1-15)		6.00	2.70
STATED ODDS 1:18 RETAIL			

		MINT	NRMT
☐ 1	Jeff Bagwell	10.00	4.50
☐ 2	Albert Belle	6.00	2.70
☐ 3	Barry Bonds	6.00	2.70
☐ 4	Juan Gonzalez	12.00	5.50
☐ 5	Ken Griffey Jr.	25.00	11.00
☐ 6	Tony Gwynn	12.00	5.50
☐ 7	Derek Jeter	12.00	5.50
☐ 8	Chipper Jones	15.00	6.75
☐ 9	Greg Maddux	15.00	6.75
☐ 10	Mark McGwire	10.00	4.50
☐ 11	Mike Piazza	15.00	6.75
☐ 12	Cal Ripken	20.00	9.00
☐ 13	Alex Rodriguez	15.00	6.75
☐ 14	Frank Thomas	20.00	9.00
☐ 15	Mo Vaughn	6.00	2.70

1997 Circa Rave Reviews

Randomly inserted in packs at a rate of one in 288, this 12-card

set features color photos of twelve players who generate incredible numbers off the bat and are printed on 100% holofoil. The backs carry player information.

		MINT	NRMT
COMPLETE SET (12)		500.00	220.00
COMMON CARD (1-12)		15.00	6.75
STATED ODDS 1:288			

		MINT	NRMT
☐ 1	Albert Belle	20.00	9.00
☐ 2	Barry Bonds	20.00	9.00
☐ 3	Juan Gonzalez	40.00	18.00
☐ 4	Ken Griffey Jr.	80.00	36.00
☐ 5	Tony Gwynn	40.00	18.00
☐ 6	Greg Maddux	50.00	22.00
☐ 7	Mark McGwire	30.00	13.50
☐ 8	Eddie Murray	15.00	6.75
☐ 9	Mike Piazza	50.00	22.00
☐ 10	Cal Ripken	60.00	27.00
☐ 11	Alex Rodriguez	60.00	27.00
☐ 12	Frank Thomas	60.00	27.00

1994 Collector's Choice

Issued by Upper Deck, this 670 standard-size card set was issued in two series of 320 and 350. Cards were issued in foil-wrapped 12-card packs and factory sets (of which contained five Gold Signature cards for a total of 675 cards). Basic card fronts feature color player action photos with white borders that are highlighted by vertical gray pinstripes. Subsets include Rookie Class (1-20), First Draft Picks (21-30), Top Performers (306-315), Up Close (631-640) and Future Foundation (641-650). Notable Rookie Cards include Michael Jordan, Derrek Lee and Alex Rodriguez.

	MINT	NRMT
COMPLETE SET (670)	25.00	11.00
COMP.FACT.SET (675)	30.00	13.50
COMPLETE SERIES 1 (320)	10.00	4.50
COMPLETE SERIES 2 (350)	15.00	6.75
COMMON CARD (1-670)	.10	.05
MINOR STARS	.20	.09
UNLISTED STARS	.40	.18
SUBSET CARDS HALF VALUE OF BASE CARDS		
COMP.GOLD SIG SET (670)	2400.00	1100.00
COMP.GOLD SIG.SER.1 (320)	1200.00	550.00
COMP.GOLD SIG.SER.2 (350)	1200.00	550.00
COMMON GOLD SIG (1-670)	2.00	.90
*GOLD STARS: 20X TO 40X HI COLUMN		
*GOLD YOUNG STARS: 15X TO 30X HI		
*GOLD ROOKIES: 10X TO 20X HI		
GOLD STATED ODDS 1:36H/R, 1:20J		
FIVE GOLD SIGNATURES PER FACTORY SET		
COMP.SILV.SIG.SET (670)	200.00	90.00
COMP.SILV.SIG.SER.1 (320)	90.00	40.00
COMP.SILV.SIG.SER.2 (350)	110.00	50.00
COMMON SILV SIG (1-670)	.25	.11
*SILV.SIG.STARS: 1.5X TO 4X HI COLUMN		
*SILV.SIG.YOUNG STARS: 1.25X TO 3X HI		
ONE SILVER PER PACK		
COMP.TEAM VS. SET (15)	5.00	2.20
ONE TEAM VS.TEAM CARD PER SER.2 PACK		

#	Player	MINT	NRMT
1	Rich Becker	.10	.05
2	Greg Blosser	.10	.05
3	Midre Cummings	.10	.05
4	Carlos Delgado	.30	.14
5	Steve Dreyer	.10	.05
6	Carl Everett	.10	.05
7	Cliff Floyd	.20	.09
8	Alex Gonzalez	.20	.09
9	Shawn Green	.20	.09
10	Butch Huskey	.20	.09
11	Mark Hutton	.10	.05
12	Miguel Jimenez	.10	.05
13	Steve Karsay	.10	.05
14	Marc Newfield	.20	.09
15	Luis Ortiz	.10	.05
16	Manny Ramirez	.50	.23
17	Johnny Ruffin	.10	.05
18	Scott Stahoviak	.10	.05
19	Salomon Torres	.10	.05
20	Gabe White	.10	.05
21	Brian Anderson	.40	.18
22	Wayne Gomes	.10	.05
23	Jeff Granger	.10	.05
24	Steve Soderstrom	.10	.05
25	Trot Nixon	.20	.09
26	Kirk Presley	.20	.09
27	Matt Brunson	.10	.05
28	Brooks Kieschnick	.40	.18
29	Billy Wagner	.75	.35
30	Matt Drews	.20	.09
31	Kurt Abbott	.10	.05
32	Luis Alicea	.10	.05
33	Roberto Alomar	.40	.18
34	Sandy Alomar Jr.	.20	.09
35	Moises Alou	.20	.09
36	Wilson Alvarez	.10	.05
37	Rich Amaral	.10	.05
38	Eric Anthony	.10	.05
39	Luis Aquino	.10	.05
40	Jack Armstrong	.10	.05
41	Rene Arocha	.10	.05
42	Rich Aude	.10	.05
43	Brad Ausmus	.10	.05
44	Steve Avery	.10	.05
45	Bob Ayrault	.10	.05
46	Willie Banks	.10	.05
47	Bret Barberie	.10	.05
48	Kim Batiste	.10	.05
49	Rod Beck	.10	.05
50	Jason Bere	.10	.05
51	Sean Berry	.10	.05
52	Dante Bichette	.20	.09
53	Jeff Blauser	.20	.09
54	Mike Blowers	.10	.05
55	Tim Bogar	.10	.05
56	Tom Bolton	.10	.05
57	Ricky Bones	.10	.05
58	Bobby Bonilla	.20	.09
59	Bret Boone	.10	.05
60	Pat Borders	.10	.05
61	Mike Bordick	.10	.05
62	Daryl Boston	.10	.05
63	Ryan Bowen	.10	.05
64	Jeff Branson	.10	.05
65	George Brett	.75	.35
66	Steve Buechele	.10	.05
67	Dave Burba	.10	.05
68	John Burkett	.10	.05
69	Jeromy Burnitz	.10	.05
70	Brett Butler	.20	.09
71	Rob Butler	.10	.05
72	Ken Caminiti	.30	.14
73	Cris Carpenter	.10	.05
74	Vinny Castilla	.20	.09
75	Andujar Cedeno	.10	.05
76	Wes Chamberlain	.10	.05
77	Archi Cianfrocco	.10	.05
78	Dave Clark	.10	.05
79	Jerald Clark	.10	.05
80	Royce Clayton	.10	.05
81	David Cone	.20	.09
82	Jeff Conine	.20	.09
83	Steve Cooke	.10	.05
84	Scott Cooper	.10	.05
85	Joey Cora	.20	.09
86	Tim Costo	.10	.05
87	Chad Curtis	.10	.05
88	Ron Darling	.10	.05
89	Danny Darwin	.10	.05
90	Rob Deer	.10	.05
91	Jim Deshaies	.10	.05
92	Delino DeShields	.10	.05
93	Rob Dibble	.10	.05
94	Gary DiSarcina	.10	.05
95	Doug Drabek	.10	.05
96	Scott Erickson	.10	.05
97	Rikkert Faneyte	.10	.05
98	Jeff Fassero	.10	.05
99	Alex Fernandez	.10	.05
100	Cecil Fielder	.20	.09
101	Dave Fleming	.10	.05
102	Darrin Fletcher	.10	.05
103	Scott Fletcher	.10	.05
104	Mike Gallego	.10	.05
105	Carlos Garcia	.10	.05
106	Jeff Gardner	.10	.05
107	Brent Gates	.10	.05
108	Benji Gil	.10	.05
109	Bernard Gilkey	.10	.05
110	Chris Gomez	.10	.05
111	Luis Gonzalez	.10	.05
112	Tom Gordon	.10	.05
113	Jim Gott	.10	.05
114	Mark Grace	.30	.14
115	Tommy Greene	.10	.05
116	Willie Greene	.10	.05
117	Ken Griffey Jr.	2.00	.90
118	Bill Gullickson	.10	.05
119	Ricky Gutierrez	.10	.05
120	Juan Guzman	.20	.09
121	Chris Gwynn	.10	.05
122	Tony Gwynn	1.00	.45
123	Jeffrey Hammonds	.20	.09
124	Erik Hanson	.10	.05
125	Gene Harris	.10	.05
126	Greg W. Harris	.10	.05
127	Bryan Harvey	.10	.05
128	Billy Hatcher	.10	.05
129	Hilly Hathaway	.10	.05
130	Charlie Hayes	.10	.05
131	Rickey Henderson	.30	.14
132	Mike Henneman	.10	.05
133	Pat Hentgen	.20	.09
134	Roberto Hernandez	.10	.05
135	Orel Hershiser	.20	.09
136	Phil Hiatt	.10	.05
137	Glenallen Hill	.10	.05
138	Ken Hill	.10	.05
139	Eric Hillman	.10	.05
140	Chris Hoiles	.10	.05
141	Dave Hollins	.10	.05
142	David Hulse	.10	.05
143	Todd Hundley	.10	.05
144	Pete Incaviglia	.10	.05
145	Danny Jackson	.10	.05
146	John Jaha	.10	.05
147	Domingo Jean	.10	.05
148	Gregg Jefferies	.10	.05
149	Reggie Jefferson	.10	.05
150	Lance Johnson	.10	.05
151	Bobby Jones	.20	.09
152	Chipper Jones	1.25	.55
153	Todd Jones	.10	.05
154	Brian Jordan	.20	.09
155	Wally Joyner	.20	.09
156	David Justice	.40	.18
157	Ron Karkovice	.10	.05
158	Eric Karros	.20	.09
159	Jeff Kent	.10	.05
160	Jimmy Key	.20	.09
161	Mark Kiefer	.10	.05
162	Darryl Kile	.20	.09
163	Jeff King	.10	.05
164	Wayne Kirby	.10	.05
165	Ryan Klesko	.40	.18
166	Chuck Knoblauch	.40	.18
167	Chad Kreuter	.10	.05
168	John Kruk	.20	.09
169	Mark Langston	.10	.05
170	Mike Lansing	.20	.09
171	Barry Larkin	.30	.14
172	Manuel Lee	.10	.05
173	Phil Leftwich	.10	.05
174	Darren Lewis	.10	.05
175	Derek Lilliquist	.10	.05
176	Jose Lind	.10	.05
177	Albie Lopez	.10	.05
178	Javier Lopez	.30	.14
179	Torey Lovullo	.10	.05
180	Scott Lydy	.10	.05
181	Mike Macfarlane	.10	.05
182	Shane Mack	.10	.05
183	Greg Maddux	1.25	.55
184	Dave Magadan	.10	.05
185	Joe Magrane	.10	.05
186	Kirk Manwaring	.10	.05
187	Al Martin	.10	.05
188	Pedro A. Martinez	.10	.05
189	Pedro J. Martinez	.40	.18
190	Ramon Martinez	.20	.09
191	Tino Martinez	.40	.18
192	Don Mattingly	.60	.25
193	Derrick May	.10	.05
194	David McCarty	.10	.05
195	Ben McDonald	.10	.05
196	Roger McDowell	.10	.05
197	Fred McGriff UER	.30	.14
	(Stats on back have 73 stolen bases for 1989; should be 7)		
198	Mark McLemore	.10	.05
199	Greg McMichael	.10	.05
200	Jeff McNeely	.10	.05
201	Brian McRae	.10	.05
202	Pat Meares	.10	.05
203	Roberto Mejia	.10	.05
204	Orlando Merced	.10	.05
205	Jose Mesa	.10	.05
206	Blas Minor	.10	.05
207	Angel Miranda	.10	.05
208	Paul Molitor	.40	.18
209	Raul Mondesi	.40	.18
210	Jeff Montgomery	.10	.05
211	Mickey Morandini	.10	.05
212	Mike Morgan	.10	.05
213	Jamie Moyer	.10	.05
214	Bobby Munoz	.10	.05
215	Troy Neel	.10	.05
216	Dave Nilsson	.10	.05
217	John O'Donoghue	.10	.05
218	Paul O'Neill	.20	.09
219	Jose Offerman	.10	.05
220	Joe Oliver	.10	.05
221	Greg Olson	.10	.05
222	Donovan Osborne	.10	.05
223	J. Owens	.10	.05
224	Mike Pagliarulo	.10	.05
225	Craig Paquette	.10	.05
226	Roger Pavlik	.10	.05
227	Brad Pennington	.10	.05

228	Eduardo Perez	.10	.05
229	Mike Perez	.10	.05
230	Tony Phillips	.10	.05
231	Hipolito Pichardo	.10	.05
232	Phil Plantier	.10	.05
233	Curtis Pride	.10	.05
234	Tim Pugh	.10	.05
235	Scott Radinsky	.10	.05
236	Pat Rapp	.10	.05
237	Kevin Reimer	.10	.05
238	Armando Reynoso	.10	.05
239	Jose Rijo	.10	.05
240	Cal Ripken	1.50	.70
241	Kevin Roberson	.10	.05
242	Kenny Rogers	.10	.05
243	Kevin Rogers	.10	.05
244	Mel Rojas	.10	.05
245	John Roper	.10	.05
246	Kirk Rueter	.10	.05
247	Scott Ruffcorn	.10	.05
248	Ken Ryan	.10	.05
249	Nolan Ryan	1.50	.70
250	Bret Saberhagen	.10	.05
251	Tim Salmon	.35	.18
252	Reggie Sanders	.10	.05
253	Curt Schilling	.20	.09
254	David Segui	.10	.05
255	Aaron Sele	.10	.05
256	Scott Servais	.10	.05
257	Gary Sheffield	.40	.18
258	Reuben Sierra	.10	.05
259	Don Slaught	.10	.05
260	Lee Smith	.20	.09
261	Cory Snyder	.10	.05
262	Paul Sorrento	.10	.05
263	Sammy Sosa	.40	.18
264	Bill Spiers	.10	.05
265	Mike Stanley	.10	.05
266	Dave Staton	.10	.05
267	Terry Steinbach	.10	.05
268	Kevin Stocker	.10	.05
269	Todd Stottlemyre	.10	.05
270	Doug Strange	.10	.05
271	Bill Swift	.10	.05
272	Kevin Tapani	.10	.05
273	Tony Tarasco	.10	.05
274	Julian Tavarez	.20	.09
275	Mickey Tettleton	.10	.05
276	Ryan Thompson	.10	.05
277	Chris Turner	.10	.05
278	John Valentin	.20	.09
279	Todd Van Poppel	.10	.05
280	Andy Van Slyke	.20	.09
281	Mo Vaughn	.50	.23
282	Robin Ventura	.20	.09
283	Frank Viola	.10	.05
284	Jose Vizcaino	.10	.05
285	Omar Vizquel	.20	.09
286	Larry Walker	.40	.18
287	Duane Ward	.10	.05
288	Allen Watson	.10	.05
289	Bill Wegman	.10	.05
290	Turk Wendell	.10	.05
291	Lou Whitaker	.20	.09
292	Devon White	.10	.05
293	Rondell White	.30	.14
294	Mark Whiten	.10	.05
295	Darrel Whitmore	.10	.05
296	Bob Wickman	.10	.05
297	Rick Wilkins	.10	.05
298	Bernie Williams	.30	.14
299	Matt Williams	.30	.14
300	Woody Williams	.10	.05
301	Nigel Wilson	.10	.05
302	Dave Winfield	.30	.14
303	Anthony Young	.10	.05
304	Eric Young	.10	.05
305	Todd Zeile	.10	.05
306	Jack McDowell TP, John Burkett, Tom Glavine	.10	.05
307	Randy Johnson TP	.20	.09
308	Randy Myers TP	.10	.05
309	Jack McDowell TP	.10	.05
310	Mike Piazza TP	.60	.25
311	Barry Bonds TP	.30	.14
312	Andres Galarraga TP	.20	.09
313	Juan Gonzalez TP, Barry Bonds •	.40	.18
314	Albert Belle TP	.30	.14
315	Kenny Lofton TP	.20	.09
316	Barry Bonds CL	.30	.14
317	Ken Griffey Jr. CL	1.00	.45
318	Mike Piazza CL	.50	.25
319	Kirby Puckett CL	.40	.18
320	Nolan Ryan CL	.75	.35
321	Roberto Alomar CL	.20	.09
322	Roger Clemens CL	.40	.18
323	Juan Gonzalez CL	.50	.23
324	Ken Griffey Jr.	.60	.25
325	David Justice CL	.40	.18
326	John Kruk CL	.10	.05
327	Frank Thomas CL	.50	.23
328	Tim Salmon TC	.40	.18
329	Jeff Bagwell TC	.40	.18
330	Mark McGwire TC	.40	.18
331	Roberto Alomar TC	.20	.09
332	David Justice TC	.20	.09
333	Pat Listach TC	.10	.05
334	Ozzie Smith TC	.40	.18
335	Ryne Sandberg TC	.30	.14
336	Mike Piazza TC	.60	.25
337	Cliff Floyd TC	.10	.05
338	Barry Bonds TC	.30	.14
339	Albert Belle TC	.30	.14
340	Ken Griffey Jr. TC	1.00	.45
341	Gary Sheffield TC	.20	.09
342	Dwight Gooden TC	.10	.05
343	Cal Ripken TC	.75	.35
344	Tony Gwynn TC	.40	.18
345	Lenny Dykstra TC	.10	.05
346	Andy Van Slyke TC	.10	.05
347	Juan Gonzalez TC	.50	.23
348	Roger Clemens TC	.40	.18
349	Barry Larkin TC	.20	.09
350	Andres Galarraga TC	.20	.09
351	Kevin Appier TC	.10	.05
352	Cecil Fielder TC	.10	.05
353	Kirby Puckett TC	.40	.18
354	Frank Thomas TC	.75	.35
355	Don Mattingly TC	.30	.14
356	Bo Jackson	.20	.09
357	Randy Johnson	.40	.18
358	Darren Daulton	.10	.05
359	Charlie Hough	.10	.05
360	Andres Galarraga	.40	.18
361	Mike Felder	.10	.05
362	Chris Hammond	.10	.05
363	Shawon Dunston	.10	.05
364	Junior Felix	.10	.05
365	Ray Lankford	.20	.09
366	Darryl Strawberry	.20	.09
367	Dave Magadan	.10	.05
368	Gregg Olson	.10	.05
369	Lenny Dykstra	.20	.09
370	Darrin Jackson	.10	.05
371	Dave Stewart	.20	.09
372	Terry Pendleton	.20	.09
373	Arthur Rhodes	.10	.05
374	Benito Santiago	.20	.09
375	Travis Fryman	.20	.09
376	Scott Brosius	.10	.05
377	Stan Belinda	.10	.05
378	Derek Parks	.10	.05
379	Kevin Seitzer	.10	.05
380	Wade Boggs	.40	.18
381	Wally Whitehurst	.10	.05
382	Scott Leius	.10	.05
383	Danny Tartabull	.20	.09
384	Harold Reynolds	.10	.05
385	Tim Raines	.20	.09
386	Darryl Hamilton	.10	.05
387	Felix Fermin	.10	.05
388	Jim Eisenreich	.10	.05
389	Kurt Abbott	.20	.09
390	Kevin Appier	.20	.09
391	Chris Bosio	.10	.05
392	Randy Tomlin	.10	.05
393	Bob Hamelin	.20	.09
394	Kevin Gross	.10	.05
395	Wil Cordero	.10	.05
396	Joe Girardi	.10	.05
397	Orestes Destrade	.10	.05
398	Chris Haney	.10	.05
399	Xavier Hernandez	.10	.05
400	Mike Piazza	1.25	.55
401	Alex Arias	.10	.05
402	Tom Candiotti	.10	.05
403	Kirk Gibson	.20	.09
404	Chuck Carr	.10	.05
405	Brady Anderson	.30	.14
406	Greg Gagne	.10	.05
407	Bruce Ruffin	.10	.05
408	Scott Hemond	.10	.05
409	Keith Miller	.10	.05
410	John Wetteland	.20	.09
411	Eric Anthony	.10	.05
412	Andre Dawson	.30	.14
413	Doug Henry	.10	.05
414	John Franco	.20	.09
415	Julio Franco	.20	.09
416	Dave Hansen	.10	.05
417	Mike Harkey	.10	.05
418	Jack Armstrong	.10	.05
419	Joe Orsulak	.10	.05
420	John Smoltz	.20	.09
421	Scott Livingstone	.10	.05
422	Darren Holmes	.10	.05
423	Ed Sprague	.10	.05
424	Jay Buhner	.30	.14
425	Kirby Puckett	.75	.35
426	Phil Clark	.10	.05
427	Anthony Young	.10	.05
428	Reggie Jefferson	.10	.05
429	Mariano Duncan	.10	.05
430	Tom Glavine	.20	.09
431	Dave Henderson	.10	.05
432	Melido Perez	.10	.05
433	Paul Wagner	.10	.05
434	Tim Worrell	.10	.05
435	Ozzie Guillen	.10	.05
436	Mike Butcher	.10	.05
437	Jim Deshaies	.10	.05
438	Kevin Young	.10	.05
439	Tom Browning	.10	.05
440	Mike Greenwell	.20	.09
441	Mike Stanton	.10	.05
442	John Doherty	.10	.05
443	John Dopson	.10	.05
444	Carlos Baerga	.30	.14
445	Jack McDowell	.10	.05
446	Kent Mercker	.10	.05
447	Ricky Jordan	.10	.05
448	Jerry Browne	.10	.05
449	Fernando Vina	.10	.05
450	Jim Abbott	.20	.09
451	Teddy Higuera	.10	.05
452	Tim Naehring	.10	.05
453	Jim Leyritz	.10	.05
454	Frank Castillo	.10	.05
455	Joe Carter	.30	.14
456	Craig Biggio	.20	.09
457	Geronimo Pena	.10	.05
458	Alejandro Pena	.10	.05
459	Mike Moore	.10	.05
460	Randy Myers	.10	.05
461	Greg Myers	.10	.05
462	Greg Hibbard	.10	.05
463	Jose Guzman	.10	.05
464	Tom Pagnozzi	.10	.05
465	Marquis Grissom	.20	.09
466	Tim Wallach	.10	.05
467	Joe Grahe	.10	.05
468	Bob Tewksbury	.10	.05
469	B.J. Surhoff	.10	.05
470	Kevin Mitchell	.20	.09
471	Bobby Witt	.10	.05
472	Milt Thompson	.10	.05
473	John Smiley	.10	.05
474	Alan Trammell	.30	.14
475	Mike Mussina	.40	.18
476	Rick Aguilera	.10	.05
477	Jose Valentin	.10	.05
478	Harold Baines	.20	.09
479	Bip Roberts	.10	.05
480	Edgar Martinez	.30	.14
481	Rheal Cormier	.10	.05
482	Hal Morris	.10	.05

☐ 483	Pat Kelly	.10	.05
☐ 484	Roberto Kelly	.10	.05
☐ 485	Chris Sabo	.10	.05
☐ 486	Kent Hrbek	.20	.09
☐ 487	Scott Kamieniecki	.10	.05
☐ 488	Walt Weiss	.10	.05
☐ 489	Karl Rhodes	.10	.05
☐ 490	Derek Bell	.10	.05
☐ 491	Chili Davis	.20	.09
☐ 492	Brian Harper	.10	.05
☐ 493	Felix Jose	.10	.05
☐ 494	Trevor Hoffman	.10	.05
☐ 495	Dennis Eckersley	.20	.09
☐ 496	Pedro Astacio	.10	.05
☐ 497	Jay Bell	.20	.09
☐ 498	Randy Velarde	.10	.05
☐ 499	David Wells	.10	.05
☐ 500	Frank Thomas	1.50	.70
☐ 501	Mark Lemke	.10	.05
☐ 502	Mike Devereaux	.10	.05
☐ 503	Chuck McElroy	.10	.05
☐ 504	Luis Polonia	.10	.05
☐ 505	Damion Easley	.10	.05
☐ 506	Greg A. Harris	.10	.05
☐ 507	Chris James	.10	.05
☐ 508	Terry Mulholland	.10	.05
☐ 509	Pete Smith	.10	.05
☐ 510	Rickey Henderson	.30	.14
☐ 511	Sid Fernandez	.10	.05
☐ 512	Al Leiter	.10	.05
☐ 513	Doug Jones	.10	.05
☐ 514	Steve Farr	.10	.05
☐ 515	Chuck Finley	.10	.05
☐ 516	Bobby Thigpen	.10	.05
☐ 517	Jim Edmonds	.40	.18
☐ 518	Graeme Lloyd	.10	.05
☐ 519	Dwight Gooden	.20	.09
☐ 520	Pat Listach	.10	.05
☐ 521	Kevin Bass	.10	.05
☐ 522	Willie Banks	.10	.05
☐ 523	Steve Finley	.20	.09
☐ 524	Delino DeShields	.10	.05
☐ 525	Mark McGwire	.75	.35
☐ 526	Greg Swindell	.10	.05
☐ 527	Chris Nabholz	.10	.05
☐ 528	Scott Sanders	.10	.05
☐ 529	David Segui	.10	.05
☐ 530	Howard Johnson	.10	.05
☐ 531	Jaime Navarro	.10	.05
☐ 532	Jose Vizcaino	.10	.05
☐ 533	Mark Lewis	.10	.05
☐ 534	Pete Harnisch	.10	.05
☐ 535	Robby Thompson	.10	.05
☐ 536	Marcus Moore	.10	.05
☐ 537	Kevin Brown	.20	.09
☐ 538	Mark Clark	.10	.05
☐ 539	Sterling Hitchcock	.10	.05
☐ 540	Will Clark	.30	.14
☐ 541	Denis Boucher	.10	.05
☐ 542	Jack Morris	.20	.09
☐ 543	Pedro Munoz	.10	.05
☐ 544	Bret Boone	.10	.05
☐ 545	Ozzie Smith	.50	.23
☐ 546	Dennis Martinez	.20	.09
☐ 547	Dan Wilson	.20	.09
☐ 548	Rick Sutcliffe	.10	.05
☐ 549	Kevin McReynolds	.10	.05
☐ 550	Roger Clemens	.75	.35
☐ 551	Todd Benzinger	.10	.05
☐ 552	Bill Haselman	.10	.05
☐ 553	Bobby Munoz	.10	.05
☐ 554	Ellis Burks	.20	.09
☐ 555	Ryne Sandberg	.50	.23
☐ 556	Lee Smith	.20	.09
☐ 557	Danny Bautista	.10	.05
☐ 558	Rey Sanchez	.10	.05
☐ 559	Norm Charlton	.10	.05
☐ 560	Jose Canseco	.30	.14
☐ 561	Tim Belcher	.10	.05
☐ 562	Denny Neagle	.20	.09
☐ 563	Eric Davis	.20	.09
☐ 564	Jody Reed	.10	.05
☐ 565	Kenny Lofton	.50	.23
☐ 566	Gary Gaetti	.10	.05
☐ 567	Todd Worrell	.10	.05
☐ 568	Mark Portugal	.10	.05

☐ 569	Dick Schofield	.10	.05
☐ 570	Andy Benes	.20	.09
☐ 571	Zane Smith	.10	.05
☐ 572	Bobby Ayala	.10	.05
☐ 573	Chip Hale	.10	.05
☐ 574	Bob Welch	.10	.05
☐ 575	Deion Sanders	.20	.09
☐ 576	Dave Nied	.10	.05
☐ 577	Pat Mahomes	.10	.05
☐ 578	Charles Nagy	.20	.09
☐ 579	Otis Nixon	.10	.05
☐ 580	Dean Palmer	.10	.05
☐ 581	Roberto Petagine	.10	.05
☐ 582	Dwight Smith	.10	.05
☐ 583	Jeff Russell	.10	.05
☐ 584	Mark Dewey	.10	.05
☐ 585	Greg Vaughn	.10	.05
☐ 586	Brian Hunter	.10	.05
☐ 587	Willie McGee	.10	.05
☐ 588	Pedro J. Martinez	.40	.18
☐ 589	Roger Salkeld	.10	.05
☐ 590	Jeff Bagwell	.75	.35
☐ 591	Spike Owen	.10	.05
☐ 592	Jeff Reardon	.20	.09
☐ 593	Erik Pappas	.10	.05
☐ 594	Brian Williams	.10	.05
☐ 595	Eddie Murray	.40	.18
☐ 596	Henry Rodriguez	.10	.05
☐ 597	Erik Hanson	.10	.05
☐ 598	Stan Javier	.10	.05
☐ 599	Mitch Williams	.10	.05
☐ 600	John Olerud	.20	.09
☐ 601	Vince Coleman	.10	.05
☐ 602	Damon Berryhill	.10	.05
☐ 603	Tom Brunansky	.10	.05
☐ 604	Robb Nen	.10	.05
☐ 605	Rafael Palmeiro	.30	.14
☐ 606	Cal Eldred	.10	.05
☐ 607	Jeff Brantley	.10	.05
☐ 608	Alan Mills	.10	.05
☐ 609	Jeff Nelson	.10	.05
☐ 610	Barry Bonds	.50	.23
☐ 611	Carlos Pulido	.10	.05
☐ 612	Tim Hyers	.10	.05
☐ 613	Steve Howe	.10	.05
☐ 614	Brian Turang	.10	.05
☐ 615	Leo Gomez	.10	.05
☐ 616	Jesse Orosco	.10	.05
☐ 617	Dan Pasqua	.10	.05
☐ 618	Marvin Freeman	.10	.05
☐ 619	Tony Fernandez	.10	.05
☐ 620	Albert Belle	.50	.23
☐ 621	Eddie Taubensee	.10	.05
☐ 622	Mike Jackson	.10	.05
☐ 623	Jose Bautista	.10	.05
☐ 624	Jim Thome	.50	.23
☐ 625	Ivan Rodriguez	.50	.23
☐ 626	Ben Rivera	.10	.05
☐ 627	Dave Valle	.10	.05
☐ 628	Tom Henke	.10	.05
☐ 629	Omar Vizquel	.20	.09
☐ 630	Juan Gonzalez	1.00	.45
☐ 631	Roberto Alomar UP	.20	.09
☐ 632	Barry Bonds UP	.30	.14
☐ 633	Juan Gonzalez UP	.50	.23
☐ 634	Ken Griffey Jr. UP	1.00	.45
☐ 635	Michael Jordan UP	2.50	1.10
☐ 636	David Justice UP	.20	.09
☐ 637	Mike Piazza UP	.60	.25
☐ 638	Kirby Puckett UP	.40	.18
☐ 639	Tim Salmon UP	.20	.09
☐ 640	Frank Thomas UP	.75	.35
☐ 641	Alan Benes FF	1.00	.45
☐ 642	Johnny Damon FF	.40	.18
☐ 643	Brad Fullmer FF	1.00	.45
☐ 644	Derek Jeter FF	1.50	.70
☐ 645	Derrek Lee FF	1.25	.55
☐ 646	Alex Ochoa FF	.10	.05
☐ 647	Alex Rodriguez FF	5.00	2.20
☐ 648	Jose Silva FF	.20	.09
☐ 649	Terrell Wade FF	.20	.09
☐ 650	Preston Wilson FF	.40	.18
☐ 651	Shane Andrews	.10	.05
☐ 652	James Baldwin	.20	.09
☐ 653	Ricky Bottalico	.40	.18
☐ 654	Tavo Alvarez	.10	.05

☐ 655	Donnie Elliott	.10	.05
☐ 656	Joey Eischen	.10	.05
☐ 657	Jason Giambi	.40	.18
☐ 658	Todd Hollandsworth	.30	.14
☐ 659	Brian L. Hunter	.40	.18
☐ 660	Charles Johnson	.30	.14
☐ 661	Michael Jordan	6.00	2.70
☐ 662	Jeff Juden	.10	.05
☐ 663	Mike Kelly	.10	.05
☐ 664	James Mouton	.10	.05
☐ 665	Ray Holbert	.10	.05
☐ 666	Pokey Reese	.20	.09
☐ 667	Ruben Santana	.10	.05
☐ 668	Paul Spoljaric	.10	.05
☐ 669	Luis Lopez	.10	.05
☐ 670	Matt Walbeck	.10	.05
☐ P50	Ken Griffey Jr. Promo	1.00	.45

1994 Collector's Choice Home Run All-Stars

This 15-card standard-size set served as the eighth place prize in the Crash the Game contest, which was a promotion in both series of Collector's Choice. The series 1 expiration was May 18, 1994; series 2 was Oct. 31, 1994. Horizontal fronts feature holographic images of the player that breaks through a brick wall. A small color photo of the player appears at left or right. The backs, outlined with bricks, features a small photo and text that appears over a stadium background. The cards are numbered with an "HA" prefix.

	MINT	NRMT
COMPLETE SET (8)	4.00	1.80
COMMON CARD (HA1-HA8)	.30	.14
ONE SET VIA MAIL PER 8TH PRIZE CARD		

☐ HA1	Juan Gonzalez	1.50	.70
☐ HA2	Ken Griffey Jr.	3.00	1.35
☐ HA3	Barry Bonds	.75	.35
☐ HA4	Bobby Bonilla	.30	.14
☐ HA5	Cecil Fielder UER	.30	.14
	(Card number is HA4)		
☐ HA6	Albert Belle	.75	.35
☐ HA7	David Justice	.60	.25
☐ HA8	Mike Piazza	2.00	.90

1995 Collector's Choice

This set contains 530 standard-size cards issued in 12-card foil hobby and retail packs for a suggested price of 99 cents. The fronts have a color photo

with a white border and the player's last name at the bottom in his team's color. The backs have an action photo at the top with statistics and information at the bottom with a silver Upper Deck hologram below that. Subsets featured are Rookie Class (1-27), Future Foundation (28-45), Best of the '90s (51-65) and What's the Call? (86-90). Key Rookie Cards that set include Karim Garcia and Hideo Nomo. The 55-card Trade set represents the cards a collector received when the five randomly inserted trade cards were redeemed. They are numbered in continuation of the regular Collector's Choice cards but have a "T" suffix. The cards numbered 542-552 were also issued as a bonus to dealers who ordered collector's choice factory sets. The trade offer expired on February 1, 1996.

	MINT	NRMT
COMPLETE SET (530)	20.00	9.00
COMP.FACT.SET (545)	25.00	11.00
COMMON CARD (1-530)	.10	.05
MINOR STARS	.20	.09
UNLISTED STARS	.40	.18
SUBSET CARDS HALF VALUE OF BASE CARDS		
COMP.TRADE SET (55)	10.00	4.50
COMMON TRADE (531-585)	.15	.07
TEN TRADE VIA MAIL PER TRD.EXCH.CARD		
ONE 542-552 RUN PER DLR.FACT.SET ORDER		
COMP.TRADE EXCH.SET (5)	4.00	1.80
TRD.EXCH.CARDS: RANDOM INS.IN PACKS		
COMP.GOLD SIG SET (530)	1000.00	450.00
COMMON GOLD SIG (1-530)	1.00	.45
*GOLD STARS: 10X TO 20X HI COLUMN		
*GOLD YOUNG STARS: 7.5 TO 15X HI		
GOLD STATED ODDS 1:35		
12 GOLD CARDS PER SUPER PACK		
15 GOLD CARDS PER FACTORY SET		
COMP.SILVER SIG.SET (530)	80.00	36.00
COMMON SILVER (1-530)	.15	.07
*SILV.SIG.STARS: 2X TO 4X HI COLUMN		
*SILV.SIG.YOUNG STARS: 1.5X TO 3X HI		
ONE SILVER PER PACK		

□ 1 Charles Johnson	.20		.09
□ 2 Scott Ruffcorn	.10		.05
□ 3 Ray Durham	.20		.09
□ 4 Armando Benitez	.10		.05
□ 5 Alex Rodriguez	1.50		.70
□ 6 Julian Tavarez	.10		.05
□ 7 Chad Ogea	.10		.05
□ 8 Quilvio Veras	.10		.05
□ 9 Phil Nevin	.10		.05
□ 10 Michael Tucker	.20		.09
□ 11 Mark Thompson	.10		.05
□ 12 Rod Henderson	.10		.05
□ 13 Andrew Lorraine	.10		.05
□ 14 Joe Randa	.10		.05
□ 15 Derek Jeter	1.25		.55
□ 16 Tony Clark	.50		.23
□ 17 Juan Castillo	.10		.05
□ 18 Mark Acre	.10		.05
□ 19 Orlando Miller	.10		.05
□ 20 Paul Wilson	.20		.09
□ 21 John Mabry	.20		.09
□ 22 Garey Ingram	.10		.05
□ 23 Garret Anderson	.30		.14
□ 24 Dave Stevens	.10		.05
□ 25 Dustin Hermanson	.20		.09
□ 26 Paul Shuey	.10		.05
□ 27 J.R. Phillips	.10		.05
□ 28 Ruben Rivera FF	.40		.18
□ 29 Nomar Garciaparra FF	2.50		1.10
□ 30 John Wasdin FF	.10		.05
□ 31 Jim Pittsley FF	.20		.09
□ 32 Scott Elarton FF	.50		.23
□ 33 Raul Casanova FF	.30		.14
□ 34 Todd Greene FF	.40		.18
□ 35 Bill Pulsipher FF	.10		.05
□ 36 Trey Beamon FF	.10		.05
□ 37 Curtis Goodwin FF	.10		.05
□ 38 Doug Million FF	.10		.05
□ 39 Karim Garcia FF	1.00		.45
□ 40 Ben Grieve FF	2.50		1.10
□ 41 Mark Farris FF	.20		.09
□ 42 Juan Acevedo FF	.10		.05
□ 43 C.J. Nitkowski FF	.10		.05
□ 44 Travis Miller FF	.10		.05
□ 45 Reid Ryan FF	.20		.09
□ 46 Nolan Ryan	1.50		.70
□ 47 Robin Yount	.30		.14
□ 48 Ryne Sandberg	.50		.23
□ 49 George Brett	.75		.35
□ 50 Mike Schmidt	.50		.23
□ 51 Cecil Fielder B90	.20		.09
□ 52 Nolan Ryan B90	.75		.35
□ 53 Rickey Henderson B90	.20		.09
□ 54 George Brett B90	.40		.18
Robin Yount			
Dave Winfield			
□ 55 Sid Bream B90	.10		.05
□ 56 Carlos Baerga B90	.10		.05
□ 57 Lee Smith B90	.10		.05
□ 58 Mark Whiten B90	.10		.05
□ 59 Joe Carter B90	.20		.09
□ 60 Barry Bonds B90	.30		.14
□ 61 Tony Gwynn B90	.50		.18
□ 62 Ken Griffey Jr. B90	1.00		.45
□ 63 Greg Maddux B90	.60		.25
□ 64 Frank Thomas B90	.75		.35
□ 65 Dennis Martinez B90	.10		.05
Kenny Rogers			
□ 66 David Cone	.20		.09
□ 67 Greg Maddux	1.25		.55
□ 68 Jimmy Key	.10		.05
□ 69 Fred McGriff	.30		.14
□ 70 Ken Griffey Jr.	2.00		.90
□ 71 Matt Williams	.30		.14
□ 72 Paul O'Neill	.20		.09
□ 73 Tony Gwynn	1.00		.45
□ 74 Randy Johnson	.40		.18
□ 75 Frank Thomas	1.50		.70
□ 76 Jeff Bagwell	.75		.35
□ 77 Kirby Puckett	.75		.35
□ 78 Bob Hamelin	.10		.05
□ 79 Raul Mondesi	.30		.14
□ 80 Mike Piazza	1.25		.55
□ 81 Kenny Lofton	.50		.23
□ 82 Barry Bonds	.50		.23
□ 83 Albert Belle	.50		.23
□ 84 Juan Gonzalez	1.00		.45
□ 85 Cal Ripken Jr.	1.50		.70
□ 86 Barry Bonds WC	.30		.14
□ 87 Mike Piazza WC	.60		.25
□ 88 Ken Griffey Jr. WC	1.00		.45
□ 89 Frank Thomas WC	.75		.35
□ 90 Juan Gonzalez WC	.50		.23
□ 91 Jorge Fabregas	.10		.05
□ 92 J.T. Snow	.20		.09
□ 93 Spike Owen	.10		.05
□ 94 Eduardo Perez	.10		.05
□ 95 Bo Jackson	.20		.09
□ 96 Damion Easley	.10		.05
□ 97 Gary DiSarcina	.10		.05
□ 98 Jim Edmonds	.30		.14
□ 99 Chad Curtis	.10		.05
□ 100 Tim Salmon	.40		.18
□ 101 Chili Davis	.20		.09
□ 102 Chuck Finley	.10		.05
□ 103 Mark Langston	.10		.05
□ 104 Brian Anderson	.20		.09
□ 105 Lee Smith	.20		.09
□ 106 Phil Leftwich	.10		.05
□ 107 Chris Donnels	.10		.05
□ 108 John Hudek	.10		.05
□ 109 Craig Biggio	.30		.14
□ 110 Luis Gonzalez	.20		.09
□ 111 Brian L. Hunter	.30		.14
□ 112 James Mouton	.10		.05
□ 113 Scott Servais	.10		.05
□ 114 Tony Eusebio	.10		.05
□ 115 Derek Bell	.10		.05
□ 116 Doug Drabek	.10		.05
□ 117 Shane Reynolds	.10		.05
□ 118 Darryl Kile	.20		.09
□ 119 Greg Swindell	.10		.05
□ 120 Phil Plantier	.10		.05
□ 121 Todd Jones	.10		.05
□ 122 Steve Ontiveros	.10		.05
□ 123 Bobby Witt	.10		.05
□ 124 Brent Gates	.10		.05
□ 125 Rickey Henderson	.30		.14
□ 126 Scott Brosius	.10		.05
□ 127 Mike Bordick	.10		.05
□ 128 Fausto Cruz	.10		.05
□ 129 Stan Javier	.10		.05
□ 130 Mark McGwire	.75		.35
□ 131 Geronimo Berroa	.10		.05
□ 132 Terry Steinbach	.10		.05
□ 133 Steve Karsay	.10		.05
□ 134 Dennis Eckersley	.20		.09
□ 135 Ruben Sierra	.10		.05
□ 136 Ron Darling	.10		.05
□ 137 Todd Van Poppel	.10		.05
□ 138 Alex Gonzalez	.10		.05
□ 139 John Olerud	.20		.09
□ 140 Roberto Alomar	.40		.18
□ 141 Darren Hall	.10		.05
□ 142 Ed Sprague	.10		.05
□ 143 Devon White	.10		.05
□ 144 Shawn Green	.20		.09
□ 145 Paul Molitor	.40		.18
□ 146 Pat Borders	.10		.05
□ 147 Carlos Delgado	.20		.09
□ 148 Juan Guzman	.10		.05
□ 149 Pat Hentgen	.10		.05
□ 150 Joe Carter	.20		.09
□ 151 Dave Stewart	.20		.09
□ 152 Todd Stottlemyre	.10		.05
□ 153 Dick Schofield	.10		.05
□ 154 Chipper Jones	1.25		.55
□ 155 Ryan Klesko	.30		.14
□ 156 David Justice	.40		.18
□ 157 Mike Kelly	.10		.05
□ 158 Roberto Kelly	.10		.05
□ 159 Tony Tarasco	.10		.05
□ 160 Javier Lopez	.20		.09
□ 161 Steve Avery	.10		.05
□ 162 Greg McMichael	.10		.05
□ 163 Kent Mercker	.10		.05
□ 164 Mark Lemke	.10		.05
□ 165 Tom Glavine	.20		.09
□ 166 Jose Oliva	.10		.05
□ 167 John Smoltz	.20		.09
□ 168 Jeff Blauser	.10		.05
□ 169 Troy O'Leary	.10		.05
□ 170 Greg Vaughn	.10		.05
□ 171 Jody Reed	.10		.05
□ 172 Kevin Seitzer	.10		.05
□ 173 Jeff Cirillo	.20		.09
□ 174 B.J. Surhoff	.10		.05
□ 175 Cal Eldred	.10		.05
□ 176 Jose Valentin	.10		.05
□ 177 Turner Ward	.10		.05
□ 178 Darryl Hamilton	.10		.05
□ 179 Pat Listach	.10		.05
□ 180 Matt Mieske	.10		.05
□ 181 Brian Harper	.10		.05
□ 182 Dave Nilsson	.10		.05

#	Player			#	Player			#	Player		
183	Mike Fetters	.10	.05	269	Omar Vizquel	.20	.09	355	Trevor Hoffman	.10	.05
184	John Jaha	.10	.05	270	Carlos Baerga	.10	.05	356	Mel Nieves	.10	.05
185	Ricky Bones	.10	.05	271	Jeff Russell	.10	.05	357	Brad Ausmus	.10	.05
186	Geronimo Pena	.10	.05	272	Herbert Perry	.10	.05	358	Andy Ashby	.10	.05
187	Bob Tewksbury	.10	.05	273	Sandy Alomar Jr.	.20	.09	359	Scott Sanders	.10	.05
188	Todd Zeile	.10	.05	274	Dennis Martinez	.20	.09	360	Gregg Jefferies	.10	.05
189	Danny Jackson	.10	.05	275	Manny Ramirez	.40	.18	361	Mariano Duncan	.10	.05
190	Ray Lankford	.20	.09	276	Wayne Kirby	.10	.05	362	Dave Hollins	.10	.05
191	Bernard Gilkey	.10	.05	277	Charles Nagy	.20	.09	363	Kevin Stocker	.10	.05
192	Brian Jordan	.20	.09	278	Albie Lopez	.10	.05	364	Fernando Valenzuela	.20	.09
193	Tom Pagnozzi	.10	.05	279	Jeromy Burnitz	.10	.05	365	Lenny Dykstra	.20	.09
194	Rick Sutcliffe	.10	.05	280	Dave Winfield	.30	.14	366	Jim Eisenreich	.10	.05
195	Mark Whiten	.10	.05	281	Tim Davis	.10	.05	367	Ricky Bottalico	.20	.09
196	Tom Henke	.10	.05	282	Marc Newfield	.10	.05	368	Doug Jones	.10	.05
197	Rene Arocha	.10	.05	283	Tino Martinez	.40	.18	369	Ricky Jordan	.10	.05
198	Allen Watson	.10	.05	284	Mike Blowers	.10	.05	370	Darren Daulton	.20	.09
199	Mike Perez	.10	.05	285	Goose Gossage	.20	.09	371	Mike Lieberthal	.10	.05
200	Ozzie Smith	.50	.23	286	Luis Sojo	.10	.05	372	Bobby Munoz	.10	.05
201	Anthony Young	.10	.05	287	Edgar Martinez	.30	.14	373	John Kruk	.20	.09
202	Rey Sanchez	.10	.05	288	Rich Amaral	.10	.05	374	Curt Schilling	.20	.09
203	Steve Buechele	.10	.05	289	Felix Fermin	.10	.05	375	Orlando Merced	.10	.05
204	Shawon Dunston	.10	.05	290	Jay Buhner	.30	.14	376	Carlos Garcia	.10	.05
205	Mark Grace	.30	.14	291	Dan Wilson	.10	.05	377	Lance Parrish	.10	.05
206	Glenallen Hill	.10	.05	292	Bobby Ayala	.10	.05	378	Steve Cooke	.10	.05
207	Eddie Zambrano	.10	.05	293	Dave Fleming	.10	.05	379	Jeff King	.10	.05
208	Rick Wilkins	.10	.05	294	Greg Pirkl	.10	.05	380	Jay Bell	.20	.09
209	Derrick May	.10	.05	295	Reggie Jefferson	.10	.05	381	Al Martin	.10	.05
210	Sammy Sosa	.40	.18	296	Greg Hibbard	.10	.05	382	Paul Wagner	.10	.05
211	Kevin Roberson	.10	.05	297	Yorkis Perez	.10	.05	383	Rick White	.10	.05
212	Steve Trachsel	.10	.05	298	Kurt Miller	.10	.05	384	Midre Cummings	.10	.05
213	Willie Banks	.10	.05	299	Chuck Carr	.05	.05	385	Jon Lieber	.10	.05
214	Kevin Foster	.10	.05	300	Gary Sheffield	.40	.18	386	Dave Clark	.10	.05
215	Randy Myers	.10	.05	301	Jerry Browne	.10	.05	387	Don Slaught	.10	.05
216	Mike Morgan	.10	.05	302	Dave Magadan	.10	.05	388	Denny Neagle	.20	.09
217	Rafael Bournigal	.10	.05	303	Kurt Abbott	.10	.05	389	Zane Smith	.10	.05
218	Delino DeShields	.10	.05	304	Pat Rapp	.10	.05	390	Andy Van Slyke	.20	.09
219	Tim Wallach	.10	.05	305	Jeff Conine	.20	.09	391	Ivan Rodriguez	.50	.23
220	Eric Karros	.20	.09	306	Benito Santiago	.10	.05	392	David Hulse	.10	.05
221	Jose Offerman	.10	.05	307	Dave Weathers	.10	.05	393	John Burkett	.10	.05
222	Tom Candiotti	.10	.05	308	Robb Nen	.10	.05	394	Kevin Brown	.20	.09
223	Ismael Valdes	.30	.14	309	Chris Hammond	.10	.05	395	Dean Palmer	.10	.05
224	Henry Rodriguez	.10	.05	310	Bryan Harvey	.10	.05	396	Otis Nixon	.10	.05
225	Billy Ashley	.10	.05	311	Charlie Hough	.10	.05	397	Rick Helling	.10	.05
226	Darren Dreifort	.10	.05	312	Greg Colbrunn	.10	.05	398	Kenny Rogers	.10	.05
227	Ramon Martinez	.20	.09	313	David Segui	.10	.05	399	Darren Oliver	.20	.09
228	Pedro Astacio	.10	.05	314	Rico Brogna	.10	.05	400	Will Clark	.30	.14
229	Orel Hershiser	.20	.09	315	Jeff Kent	.10	.05	401	Jeff Frye	.10	.05
230	Brett Butler	.10	.05	316	Jose Vizcaino	.10	.05	402	Kevin Gross	.10	.05
231	Todd Hollandsworth	.20	.09	317	Jim Lindeman	.10	.05	403	John Dettmer	.10	.05
232	Chan Ho Park	.40	.18	318	Carl Everett	.10	.05	404	Manny Lee	.10	.05
233	Mike Lansing	.10	.05	319	Ryan Thompson	.10	.05	405	Rusty Greer	.40	.18
234	Sean Berry	.10	.05	320	Bobby Bonilla	.20	.09	406	Aaron Sele	.20	.09
235	Rondell White	.20	.09	321	Joe Orsulak	.10	.05	407	Carlos Rodriguez	.10	.05
236	Ken Hill	.10	.05	322	Pete Harnisch	.10	.05	408	Scott Cooper	.10	.05
237	Marquis Grissom	.20	.09	323	Doug Linton	.10	.05	409	John Valentin	.10	.05
238	Larry Walker	.40	.18	324	Todd Hundley	.20	.09	410	Roger Clemens	.75	.35
239	John Wetteland	.10	.05	325	Bret Saberhagen	.10	.05	411	Mike Greenwell	.10	.05
240	Cliff Floyd	.10	.05	326	Kelly Stinnett	.10	.05	412	Tim Vanegmond	.10	.05
241	Joey Eischen	.10	.05	327	Jason Jacome	.10	.05	413	Tom Brunansky	.10	.05
242	Lou Frazier	.10	.05	328	Bobby Jones	.10	.05	414	Steve Farr	.10	.05
243	Darrin Fletcher	.10	.05	329	John Franco	.20	.09	415	Jose Canseco	.30	.14
244	Pedro J. Martinez	.40	.18	330	Rafael Palmeiro	.30	.14	416	Joe Hesketh	.10	.05
245	Wil Cordero	.10	.05	331	Chris Hoiles	.10	.05	417	Ken Ryan	.10	.05
246	Jeff Fassero	.10	.05	332	Leo Gomez	.10	.05	418	Tim Naehring	.10	.05
247	Butch Henry	.10	.05	333	Chris Sabo	.10	.05	419	Frank Viola	.10	.05
248	Mel Rojas	.10	.05	334	Brady Anderson	.30	.14	420	Andre Dawson	.30	.14
249	Kirk Rueter	.10	.05	335	Jeffrey Hammonds	.20	.09	421	Mo Vaughn	.50	.23
250	Moises Alou	.20	.09	336	Dwight Smith	.10	.05	422	Jeff Brantley	.10	.05
251	Rod Beck	.10	.05	337	Jack Voigt	.10	.05	423	Pete Schourek	.10	.05
252	John Patterson	.10	.05	338	Harold Baines	.20	.09	424	Hal Morris	.10	.05
253	Robby Thompson	.10	.05	339	Ben McDonald	.10	.05	425	Deion Sanders	.20	.09
254	Royce Clayton	.10	.05	340	Mike Mussina	.40	.18	426	Brian R. Hunter	.10	.05
255	Wm. VanLandingham	.10	.05	341	Bret Barberie	.10	.05	427	Bret Boone	.10	.05
256	Darren Lewis	.10	.05	342	Jamie Moyer	.10	.05	428	Willie Greene	.10	.05
257	Kirt Manwaring	.10	.05	343	Mike Oquist	.10	.05	429	Ron Gant	.20	.09
258	Mark Portugal	.10	.05	344	Sid Fernandez	.10	.05	430	Barry Larkin	.30	.14
259	Bill Swift	.10	.05	345	Eddie Williams	.10	.05	431	Reggie Sanders	.10	.05
260	Rikkert Faneyte	.10	.05	346	Joey Hamilton	.20	.09	432	Eddie Taubensee	.10	.05
261	Mike Jackson	.10	.05	347	Brian Williams	.10	.05	433	Jack Morris	.20	.09
262	Todd Benzinger	.10	.05	348	Luis Lopez	.10	.05	434	Jose Rijo	.10	.05
263	Bud Black	.10	.05	349	Steve Finley	.20	.09	435	Johnny Ruffin	.10	.05
264	Salomon Torres	.10	.05	350	Andy Benes	.20	.09	436	John Smiley	.10	.05
265	Eddie Murray	.40	.18	351	Andujar Cedeno	.10	.05	437	John Roper	.10	.05
266	Mark Clark	.10	.05	352	Bip Roberts	.10	.05	438	Dave Nied	.10	.05
267	Paul Sorrento	.10	.05	353	Ray McDavid	.10	.05	439	Roberto Mejia	.10	.05
268	Jim Thome	.40	.18	354	Ken Caminiti	.30	.14	440	Andres Galarraga	.40	.18

☐ 441	Mike Kingery	.10	.05
☐ 442	Curt Leskanic	.10	.05
☐ 443	Walt Weiss	.10	.05
☐ 444	Marvin Freeman	.10	.05
☐ 445	Charlie Hayes	.10	.05
☐ 446	Eric Young	.10	.05
☐ 447	Ellis Burks	.20	.09
☐ 448	Joe Girardi	.10	.05
☐ 449	Lance Painter	.10	.05
☐ 450	Dante Bichette	.20	.09
☐ 451	Bruce Ruffin	.10	.05
☐ 452	Jeff Granger	.10	.05
☐ 453	Wally Joyner	.20	.09
☐ 454	Jose Lind	.10	.05
☐ 455	Jeff Montgomery	.10	.05
☐ 456	Gary Gaetti	.10	.05
☐ 457	Greg Gagne	.10	.05
☐ 458	Vince Coleman	.10	.05
☐ 459	Mike Macfarlane	.10	.05
☐ 460	Brian McRae	.10	.05
☐ 461	Tom Gordon	.10	.05
☐ 462	Kevin Appier	.20	.09
☐ 463	Billy Brewer	.10	.05
☐ 464	Mark Gubicza	.10	.05
☐ 465	Travis Fryman	.20	.09
☐ 466	Danny Bautista	.10	.05
☐ 467	Sean Bergman	.10	.05
☐ 468	Mike Henneman	.10	.05
☐ 469	Mike Moore	.10	.05
☐ 470	Cecil Fielder	.20	.09
☐ 471	Alan Trammell	.30	.14
☐ 472	Kirk Gibson	.20	.09
☐ 473	Tony Phillips	.10	.05
☐ 474	Mickey Tettleton	.10	.05
☐ 475	Lou Whitaker	.20	.09
☐ 476	Chris Gomez	.10	.05
☐ 477	John Doherty	.10	.05
☐ 478	Greg Gohr	.10	.05
☐ 479	Bill Gullickson	.10	.05
☐ 480	Rick Aguilera	.10	.05
☐ 481	Matt Walbeck	.10	.05
☐ 482	Kevin Tapani	.10	.05
☐ 483	Scott Erickson	.10	.05
☐ 484	Steve Dunn	.10	.05
☐ 485	David McCarty	.10	.05
☐ 486	Scott Leius	.10	.05
☐ 487	Pat Meares	.10	.05
☐ 488	Jeff Reboulet	.10	.05
☐ 489	Pedro Munoz	.10	.05
☐ 490	Chuck Knoblauch	.40	.18
☐ 491	Rich Becker	.10	.05
☐ 492	Alex Cole	.10	.05
☐ 493	Pat Mahomes	.10	.05
☐ 494	Ozzie Guillen	.10	.05
☐ 495	Tim Raines	.20	.09
☐ 496	Kirk McCaskill	.10	.05
☐ 497	Olmedo Saenz	.10	.05
☐ 498	Scott Sanderson	.10	.05
☐ 499	Lance Johnson	.10	.05
☐ 500	Michael Jordan	2.50	1.10
☐ 501	Warren Newson	.10	.05
☐ 502	Ron Karkovice	.10	.05
☐ 503	Wilson Alvarez	.10	.05
☐ 504	Jason Bere	.10	.05
☐ 505	Robin Ventura	.20	.09
☐ 506	Alex Fernandez	.10	.05
☐ 507	Roberto Hernandez	.10	.05
☐ 508	Norberto Martin	.10	.05
☐ 509	Bob Wickman	.10	.05
☐ 510	Don Mattingly	.60	.25
☐ 511	Melido Perez	.10	.05
☐ 512	Pat Kelly	.10	.05
☐ 513	Randy Velarde	.10	.05
☐ 514	Tony Fernandez	.10	.05
☐ 515	Jack McDowell	.10	.05
☐ 516	Luis Polonia	.10	.05
☐ 517	Bernie Williams	.40	.18
☐ 518	Danny Tartabull	.10	.05
☐ 519	Mike Stanley	.10	.05
☐ 520	Wade Boggs	.40	.18
☐ 521	Jim Leyritz	.10	.05
☐ 522	Steve Howe	.10	.05
☐ 523	Scott Kamieniecki	.10	.05
☐ 524	Russ Davis	.10	.05
☐ 525	Jim Abbott	.20	.09
☐ 526	Eddie Murray CL	.20	.09

☐ 527	Alex Rodriguez CL	.75	.35
☐ 528	Jeff Bagwell CL	.40	.18
☐ 529	Joe Carter CL	.10	.05
☐ 530	Fred McGriff CL	.20	.09
☐ 531T	Tony Phillips TRADE	.15	.07
☐ 532T	Dave Magadan TRADE	.15	.07
☐ 533T	Mike Gallego TRADE	.15	.07
☐ 534T	Dave Stewart TRADE	.20	.09
☐ 535T	Todd Stottlemyre TRADE	.10	.05
☐ 536T	David Cone TRADE	.20	.09
☐ 537T	Marquis Grissom TRADE	.20	.09
☐ 538T	Derrick May TRADE	.15	.07
☐ 539T	Joe Oliver TRADE	.15	.07
☐ 540T	Scott Cooper TRADE	.15	.07
☐ 541T	Ken Hill TRADE	.15	.07
☐ 542T	Howard Johnson TRADE DP	.15	.07
☐ 543T	Brian McRae TRADE DP	.15	.07
☐ 544T	Jaime Navarro TRADE DP	.15	.07
☐ 545T	Ozzie Timmons TRADE DP	.15	.07
☐ 546T	Roberto Kelly TRADE DP	.15	.07
☐ 547T	Hideo Nomo TRADE DP	5.00	2.20
☐ 548T	Shane Andrews TRADE DP	.15	.07
☐ 549T	M.Grudzielanek TRADE DP	.75	.35
☐ 550T	Carlos Perez TRADE DP		
☐ 551T	Henry Rodriguez TRADE DP		.07
☐ 552T	Tony Tarasco TRADE DP	.15	.07
☐ 553T	Glenallen Hill TRADE	.15	.07
☐ 554T	Terry Mulholland TRADE	.15	.07
☐ 555T	Orel Hershiser TRADE	.20	.09
☐ 556T	Darren Bragg TRADE	.15	.07
☐ 557T	John Burkett TRADE	.15	.07
☐ 558T	Bobby Witt TRADE	.15	.07
☐ 559T	Terry Pendleton TRADE	.15	.07
☐ 560T	Andre Dawson TRADE	.30	.14
☐ 561T	Brett Butler TRADE	.20	.09
☐ 562T	Kevin Brown TRADE		
☐ 563T	Doug Jones TRADE	.15	.07
☐ 564T	Andy Van Slyke TRADE	.20	.09
☐ 565T	Jody Reed TRADE	.15	.07
☐ 566T	Fernando Valenzuela TRADE	.15	.07
☐ 567T	Charlie Hayes TRADE	.15	.07
☐ 568T	Benji Gil TRADE	.15	.07
☐ 569T	Mark McLemore TRADE	.15	.07
☐ 570T	Mickey Tettleton TRADE	.15	.07
☐ 571T	Bob Tewksbury TRADE	.15	.07
☐ 572T	Rheal Cormier TRADE	.15	.07
☐ 573T	Vaughn Eshelman TRADE	.15	.07
☐ 574T	Mike Macfarlane TRADE	.15	.07
☐ 575T	Bill Swift TRADE	.15	.07
☐ 576T	Mark Whiten TRADE	.15	.07
☐ 577T	Benito Santiago TRADE	.15	.07
☐ 578T	Jason Bates TRADE	.15	.07
☐ 579T	Larry Walker TRADE	.75	.35
☐ 580T	Chad Curtis TRADE	.15	.07
☐ 581T	Bobby Higginson TRADE	1.50	.70
☐ 582T	Marty Cordova TRADE	.20	.09
☐ 583T	Mike Devereaux TRADE	.15	.07
☐ 584T	John Kruk TRADE	.20	.09
☐ 585T	John Wetteland TRADE	.20	.09
☐ TC1	Larry Walker	2.00	.90
☐ TC2	David Cone		
☐ TC3	Marquis Grissom		
☐ TC4	Terry Pendleton	1.00	.45
☐ TC5	Fernando Valenzuela		

1995 Collector's Choice Crash the Game

Cards from this 60-card standard-size set were randomly inserted in packs at a rate of one in five. The set is an interactive set in which all 20 players have three cards with a date on it. If the player hit a home run on that date, the collector could redeem the card for a complete enhanced set of all 20 players. The fronts have a color-action photo with the game background in yellow and a large date stamped in silver foil. The

expiration date for redeeming these cards was February 1, 1996. Winning cards eligible for redemption at the time have been highlighted with a "W" in our listings below.

	MINT	NRMT
COMPLETE SET (60)	50.00	22.00
COMMON CARD	.10	.05
COMP.GOLD SET (60)	250.00	110.00
*GOLD CARDS: 2.5X TO 5X BASE CARD HI		
THREE DATES PER PLAYER		
RANDOM INSERTS IN PACKS		
COMP.EXCH.SET (20)	10.00	4.50
*EXCH.CARDS: .25X TO .5X BASE CARD HI		
COMP.GOLD EXCH.SET (20)	50.00	22.00
*GOLD EXCH.CARDS:2X TO 4X BASE CARD HI		
ONE EXCH.SET PER MAIL PER WINNER		

☐ CG1	Jeff Bagwell 7/30	.75	.35
☐ CG1B	Jeff Bagwell 8/13	.75	.35
☐ CG1C	Jeff Bagwell 9/28	.75	.35
☐ CG2	Albert Belle 6/18	.50	.23
☐ CG2B	Albert Belle 8/26	.50	.23
☐ CG2C	Albert Belle 9/20	.50	.23
☐ CG3	Barry Bonds 6/28	.50	.23
☐ CG3B	Barry Bonds 7/9	.50	.23
☐ CG3C	Barry Bonds 9/6	.50	.23
☐ CG4	Jose Canseco 7/9 W	.30	.14
☐ CG4B	Jose Canseco 7/30 W	.30	.14
☐ CG4C	Jose Canseco 9/3	.30	.14
☐ CG5	Joe Carter 7/14	.20	.09
☐ CG5B	Joe Carter 8/8	.20	.09
☐ CG5C	Joe Carter 9/23	.20	.09
☐ CG6	Cecil Fielder 7/4	.20	.09
☐ CG6B	Cecil Fielder 8/2	.20	.09
☐ CG6C	Cecil Fielder 10/1	.20	.09
☐ CG7	Juan Gonzalez 6/29	1.00	.45
☐ CG7B	Juan Gonzalez 8/13	1.00	.45
☐ CG7C	Juan Gonzalez 9/3 W	1.00	.45
☐ CG8	Ken Griffey Jr. 7/2	2.00	.90
☐ CG8B	Ken Griffey Jr. 8/24 W	2.00	.90
☐ CG8C	Ken Griffey Jr. 9/15	2.00	.90
☐ CG9	Bob Hamelin 7/23	.10	.05
☐ CG9B	Bob Hamelin 8/1	.10	.05
☐ CG9C	Bob Hamelin 8/29	.10	.05
☐ CG10	David Justice 6/24	.50	.23
☐ CG10B	David Justice 7/25	.50	.23
☐ CG10C	David Justice 9/17	.50	.23
☐ CG11	Ryan Klesko 7/13	.30	.14
☐ CG11B	Ryan Klesko 8/20	.30	.14
☐ CG11C	Ryan Klesko 9/10	.30	.14
☐ CG12	Fred McGriff 8/25	.30	.14
☐ CG12B	Fred McGriff 9/8	.30	.14
☐ CG12C	Fred McGriff 9/24	.30	.14
☐ CG13	Mark McGwire 7/23	.75	.35
☐ CG13B	Mark McGwire 8/20	.75	.35
☐ CG13C	Mark McGwire 9/27	.75	.35
☐ CG14	Raul Mondesi 7/27 W	.30	.14
☐ CG14B	Raul Mondesi 8/13	.30	.14
☐ CG14C	Raul Mondesi 9/15 W	.30	.14
☐ CG15	Mike Piazza 7/3 W	1.25	.55
☐ CG15B	Mike Piazza 8/27	1.25	.55
☐ CG15C	Mike Piazza 9/19	1.25	.55
☐ CG16	Manny Ramirez 6/21	.40	.18
☐ CG16B	Manny Ramirez 8/13	.40	.18
☐ CG16C	Manny Ramirez 9/26.40		.18

☐ CG17 Alex Rodriguez 9/10	1.50	.70
☐ CG17B Alex Rodriguez 9/18	1.50	.70
☐ CG17C Alex Rodriguez 9/24	1.50	.70
☐ CG18 Gary Sheffield	.25	.11
☐ CG18B Gary Sheffield 8/13	.25	.11
☐ CG18C Gary Sheffield 9/4 W	.25	.11
☐ CG19 Frank Thomas 7/26	1.50	.70
☐ CG19B Frank Thomas 8/17	1.50	.70
☐ CG19C Frank Thomas 9/23	1.50	.70
☐ CG20 Matt Williams 7/29	.30	.14
☐ CG20B Matt Williams 8/12	.30	.14
☐ CG20C Matt Williams 9/19	.30	.14

1996 Collector's Choice

This 790-card standard-size set was issued in 12-card packs with 36 packs per box and 20 boxes per case. Suggested retail price on these packs was 99 cents. The fronts of the regular set feature a player photo, his name and team logo. The backs feature another photo, vital stats and a baseball quiz. The set includes the following subsets: 1995 Stat Leaders (2-9), Rookie Class (10-39), Traditional Threads (100-108), Fantasy Team (268-279), International Flavor (325-342), Series 1 Checklists (358-365), Team Checklists (396-365), First HOF Class (500-504), Award Winners (704-711) and Series 2 Checklists (753-760). Postseason Trade cards were inserted one every 11 packs. These cards had an ordering deadline of May 13 and were each redeemable for 10 cards depicting highlights from the playoffs and World Series, resulting in a 30-card redemption set. Finally, a 30-card Update set was included in each factory set and was also available through a Series 2 wrapper offer.

	MINT	NRMT
COMPLETE SET (730)	24.00	11.00
COMP.FACT.SET (730)	30.00	13.50
COMPLETE SERIES 1 (365)	12.00	5.50
COMPLETE SERIES 2 (365)	12.00	5.50
COMMON (1-365/396-760)	.10	.05
MINOR STARS	.20	.09
UNLISTED STARS	.40	.18
SUBSET CARDS HALF VALUE OF BASE CARDS		
COMP.TRADE SET (30)	15.00	6.75
COMMON TRADE (366T-395T)	.15	.07
TRADE SEMISTARS	.50	.23
TEN TRADE CARDS PER TRADE EXCH.CARD		
SER.1 TRADE EXCH.STATED ODDS 1:11		
COMP.UPDATE SET (30)	4.00	1.80

COMMON UPDATE (761-790)	.25	.11
UPDATE SEMISTARS	.50	.23
ONE UPDATE SET PER FACTORY SET		
ONE UPDATE SET VIA SER.2 WRAP.OFFER		
COMP.GOLD SER. (730)	1500.00	700.00
COMP.GOLD SER.1 (365)	800.00	350.00
COMP.GOLD SER.2 (365)	700.00	325.00
COM.GOLD (1-365/396-760)	1.00	.45
*GOLD STARS: 1.5X TO 2.5X HI COLUMN		
*GOLD YOUNG STARS: 10X TO 20X HI		
GOLD STATED ODDS 1:35		
COMP.SILV.SIG.SET (730)	110.00	50.00
COMP.SILV.SIG.SER.1 (365)	60.00	27.00
COMP.SILV.SIG.SER.2 (365)	50.00	22.00
COM.SILVER (1-365/396-760)	.10	.05
*SILV.SIG.STARS: 1.5X TO 3X HI COLUMN		
*SILV.SIG.YOUNG STARS: 1.25X TO 2.5X HI		
ONE SILVER SIGNATURE PER PACK		
COMP.GRIFFEY ACA SET (10)	8.00	3.60
COMMON GRIFF.(CA1-CA10)	1.00	.45
GRIFFEY ACA: ONE PER SPEC.RETAIL PACK		
COMP.NOMO SET (5)	5.00	2.20
COMMON NOMO (1-5)	1.50	.70
NOMO SER.2 STATED ODDS 1:12		

☐ 1 Cal Ripken	1.50	.70
☐ 2 Edgar Martinez SL Tony Gwynn	.40	.18
☐ 3 Albert Belle SL Dante Bichette	.20	.09
☐ 4 Albert Belle SL Mo Vaughn Dante Bichette	.20	.09
☐ 5 Kenny Lofton SL Quilvio Veras	.20	.09
☐ 6 Mike Mussina SL Greg Maddux	.50	.23
☐ 7 Randy Johnson SL Hideo Nomo	.40	.18
☐ 8 Randy Johnson SL Greg Maddux	.50	.23
☐ 9 Jose Mesa SL Randy Myers	.10	.05
☐ 10 Johnny Damon	.20	.09
☐ 11 Rick Krivda	.10	.05
☐ 12 Roger Cedeno	.10	.05
☐ 13 Angel Martinez	.10	.05
☐ 14 Ariel Prieto	.10	.05
☐ 15 John Wasdin	.10	.05
☐ 16 Edwin Hurtado	.10	.05
☐ 17 Lyle Mouton	.10	.05
☐ 18 Chris Snopek	.10	.05
☐ 19 Mariano Rivera	.30	.14
☐ 20 Ruben Rivera	.20	.09
☐ 21 Juan Castro	.40	.18
☐ 22 Jimmy Haynes	.10	.05
☐ 23 Bob Wolcott	.10	.05
☐ 24 Brian Barber	.10	.05
☐ 25 Frank Rodriguez	.20	.09
☐ 26 Jesus Tavarez	.10	.05
☐ 27 Glenn Dishman	.10	.05
☐ 28 Jose Herrera	.10	.05
☐ 29 Chan Ho Park	.40	.18
☐ 30 Jason Isringhausen	.10	.05
☐ 31 Doug Johns	.10	.05
☐ 32 Gene Schall	.10	.05
☐ 33 Kevin Jordan	.10	.05
☐ 34 Matt Lawton	.30	.14
☐ 35 Karim Garcia	.20	.09
☐ 36 George Williams	.10	.05
☐ 37 Orlando Palmeiro	.10	.05
☐ 38 Jamie Brewington	.10	.05
☐ 39 Robert Person	.10	.05
☐ 40 Greg Maddux	1.25	.55
☐ 41 Marquis Grissom	.20	.09
☐ 42 Chipper Jones	1.25	.55
☐ 43 David Justice	.40	.18
☐ 44 Mark Lemke	.10	.05
☐ 45 Fred McGriff	.30	.14
☐ 46 Javier Lopez	.10	.05
☐ 47 Mark Wohlers	.10	.05
☐ 48 Jason Schmidt	.20	.09
☐ 49 John Smoltz	.20	.09
☐ 50 Curtis Goodwin	.10	.05
☐ 51 Greg Zaun	.10	.05
☐ 52 Armando Benitez	.10	.05

☐ 53 Manny Alexander	.10	.05
☐ 54 Chris Hoiles	.10	.05
☐ 55 Harold Baines	.20	.09
☐ 56 Ben McDonald	.10	.05
☐ 57 Scott Erickson	.10	.05
☐ 58 Jeff Manto	.10	.05
☐ 59 Luis Alicea	.10	.05
☐ 60 Roger Clemens	.75	.35
☐ 61 Rheal Cormier	.10	.05
☐ 62 Vaughn Eshelman	.10	.05
☐ 63 Zane Smith	.10	.05
☐ 64 Mike Macfarlane	.10	.05
☐ 65 Erik Hanson	.10	.05
☐ 66 Tim Naehring	.10	.05
☐ 67 Lee Tinsley	.10	.05
☐ 68 Troy O'Leary	.10	.05
☐ 69 Garret Anderson	.20	.09
☐ 70 Chili Davis	.20	.09
☐ 71 Jim Edmonds	.30	.14
☐ 72 Troy Percival	.10	.05
☐ 73 Mark Langston	.10	.05
☐ 74 Spike Owen	.10	.05
☐ 75 Tim Salmon	.40	.18
☐ 76 Brian Anderson	.10	.05
☐ 77 Lee Smith	.20	.09
☐ 78 Jim Abbott	.10	.05
☐ 79 Jim Bullinger	.10	.05
☐ 80 Mark Grace	.30	.14
☐ 81 Todd Zeile	.10	.05
☐ 82 Kevin Foster	.10	.05
☐ 83 Howard Johnson	.10	.05
☐ 84 Brian McRae	.10	.05
☐ 85 Randy Myers	.10	.05
☐ 86 Jaime Navarro	.10	.05
☐ 87 Luis Gonzalez	.10	.05
☐ 88 Ozzie Timmons	.10	.05
☐ 89 Wilson Alvarez	.10	.05
☐ 90 Frank Thomas	1.50	.70
☐ 91 James Baldwin	.10	.05
☐ 92 Ray Durham	.10	.05
☐ 93 Alex Fernandez	.10	.05
☐ 94 Ozzie Guillen	.10	.05
☐ 95 Tim Raines	.20	.09
☐ 96 Roberto Hernandez	.10	.05
☐ 97 Lance Johnson	.10	.05
☐ 98 John Kruk	.10	.05
☐ 99 Mark Portugal	.10	.05
☐ 100 Don Mattingly TT	.30	.14
☐ 101 Roger Clemens TT	.40	.18
☐ 102 Raul Mondesi TT	.10	.05
☐ 103 Cecil Fielder TT	.10	.05
☐ 104 Ozzie Smith TT	.10	.05
☐ 105 Frank Thomas TT	.75	.35
☐ 106 Sammy Sosa TT	.20	.09
☐ 107 Fred McGriff TT	.10	.05
☐ 108 Barry Bonds TT	.30	.14
☐ 109 Thomas Howard	.10	.05
☐ 110 Ron Gant	.20	.09
☐ 111 Eddie Taubensee	.10	.05
☐ 112 Hal Morris	.10	.05
☐ 113 Jose Rijo	.10	.05
☐ 114 Pete Schourek	.10	.05
☐ 115 Reggie Sanders	.10	.05
☐ 116 Benito Santiago	.10	.05
☐ 117 Jeff Brantley	.10	.05
☐ 118 Julian Tavarez	.10	.05
☐ 119 Carlos Baerga	.10	.05
☐ 120 Jim Thome	.40	.18
☐ 121 Jose Mesa	.10	.05
☐ 122 Dennis Martinez	.20	.09
☐ 123 Dave Winfield	.30	.14
☐ 124 Eddie Murray	.40	.18
☐ 125 Manny Ramirez	.40	.18
☐ 126 Paul Sorrento	.10	.05
☐ 127 Kenny Lofton	.50	.23
☐ 128 Eric Young	.10	.05
☐ 129 Jason Bates	.10	.05
☐ 130 Bret Saberhagen	.10	.05
☐ 131 Andres Galarraga	.40	.18
☐ 132 Joe Girardi	.10	.05
☐ 133 John VanderWal	.10	.05
☐ 134 David Nied	.10	.05
☐ 135 Dante Bichette	.20	.09
☐ 136 Vinny Castilla	.20	.09
☐ 137 Kevin Ritz	.10	.05
☐ 138 Felipe Lira	.10	.05

139	Joe Boever	.10	.05
140	Cecil Fielder	.20	.09
141	John Flaherty	.10	.05
142	Kirk Gibson	.20	.09
143	Brian Maxcy	.10	.05
144	Lou Whitaker	.20	.09
145	Alan Trammell	.30	.14
146	Bobby Higginson	.20	.09
147	Chad Curtis	.10	.05
148	Quilvio Veras	.10	.05
149	Jerry Browne	.10	.05
150	Andre Dawson	.30	.14
151	Robb Nen	.10	.05
152	Greg Colbrunn	.10	.05
153	Chris Hammond	.10	.05
154	Kurt Abbott	.10	.05
155	Charles Johnson	.20	.09
156	Terry Pendleton	.10	.05
157	Dave Weathers	.10	.05
158	Mike Hampton	.10	.05
159	Craig Biggio	.30	.14
160	Jeff Bagwell	.75	.35
161	Brian L.Hunter	.20	.09
162	Mike Henneman	.10	.05
163	Dave Magadan	.10	.05
164	Shane Reynolds	.10	.05
165	Derek Bell	.10	.05
166	Orlando Miller	.10	.05
167	James Mouton	.10	.05
168	Melvin Bunch	.10	.05
169	Tom Gordon	.10	.05
170	Kevin Appier	.20	.09
171	Tom Goodwin	.10	.05
172	Greg Gagne	.10	.05
173	Gary Gaetti	.10	.05
174	Jeff Montgomery	.10	.05
175	Jon Nunnally	.10	.05
176	Michael Tucker	.20	.09
177	Joe Vitiello	.10	.05
178	Billy Ashley	.10	.05
179	Tom Candiotti	.10	.05
180	Hideo Nomo	1.00	.45
181	Chad Fonville	.10	.05
182	Todd Hollandsworth	.10	.05
183	Eric Karros	.20	.09
184	Roberto Kelly	.10	.05
185	Mike Piazza	1.25	.55
186	Ramon Martinez	.20	.09
187	Tim Wallach	.10	.05
188	Jeff Cirillo	.10	.05
189	Sid Roberson	.10	.05
190	Kevin Seitzer	.10	.05
191	Mike Fetters	.10	.05
192	Steve Sparks	.10	.05
193	Matt Mieske	.10	.05
194	Joe Oliver	.10	.05
195	B.J. Surhoff	.10	.05
196	Alberto Reyes	.10	.05
197	Fernando Vina	.10	.05
198	LaTroy Hawkins	.10	.05
199	Marty Cordova	.20	.09
200	Kirby Puckett	.75	.35
201	Brad Radke	.20	.09
202	Pedro Munoz	.10	.05
203	Scott Klingenbeck	.10	.05
204	Pat Meares	.10	.05
205	Chuck Knoblauch	.40	.18
206	Scott Stahoviak	.10	.05
207	Dave Stevens	.10	.05
208	Shane Andrews	.10	.05
209	Moises Alou	.20	.09
210	David Segui	.10	.05
211	Cliff Floyd	.10	.05
212	Carlos Perez	.10	.05
213	Mark Grudzielanek	.20	.09
214	Butch Henry	.10	.05
215	Rondell White	.20	.09
216	Mel Rojas	.10	.05
217	Ugueth Urbina	.20	.09
218	Edgardo Alfonzo	.30	.14
219	Carl Everett	.10	.05
220	John Franco	.20	.09
221	Todd Hundley	.20	.09
222	Bobby Jones	.10	.05
223	Bill Pulsipher	.10	.05
224	Rico Brogna	.10	.05
225	Jeff Kent	.10	.05
226	Chris Jones	.10	.05
227	Butch Huskey	.20	.09
228	Robert Eenhoorn	.10	.05
229	Sterling Hitchcock	.10	.05
230	Wade Boggs	.40	.18
231	Derek Jeter	1.25	.55
232	Tony Fernandez	.10	.05
233	Jack McDowell	.20	.09
234	Andy Pettitte	.50	.23
235	David Cone	.20	.09
236	Mike Stanley	.10	.05
237	Don Mattingly	.60	.25
238	Geronimo Berroa	.10	.05
239	Scott Brosius	.10	.05
240	Rickey Henderson	.30	.14
241	Terry Steinbach	.10	.05
242	Mike Gallego	.10	.05
243	Jason Giambi	.20	.09
244	Steve Ontiveros	.10	.05
245	Dennis Eckersley	.20	.09
246	Dave Stewart	.20	.09
247	Don Wengert	.10	.05
248	Paul Quantrill	.10	.05
249	Ricky Bottalico	.10	.05
250	Kevin Stocker	.10	.05
251	Lenny Dykstra	.20	.09
252	Tony Longmire	.10	.05
253	Tyler Green	.10	.05
254	Mike Mimbs	.10	.05
255	Charlie Hayes	.10	.05
256	Mickey Morandini	.10	.05
257	Heathcliff Slocumb	.10	.05
258	Jeff King	.10	.05
259	Midre Cummings	.10	.05
260	Mark Johnson	.10	.05
261	Freddy Garcia	.10	.05
262	Jon Lieber	.10	.05
263	Esteban Loaiza	.10	.05
264	Dan Miceli	.10	.05
265	Orlando Merced	.10	.05
266	Denny Neagle	.20	.09
267	Steve Parris	.10	.05
268	Greg Maddux	.60	.25
269	Randy Johnson FT	.20	.09
270	Hideo Nomo FT	.50	.23
271	Jose Mesa FT	.10	.05
272	Mike Piazza FT	.60	.25
273	Mo Vaughn FT	.30	.14
274	Craig Biggio FT	.20	.09
275	Edgar Martinez FT	.20	.09
276	Barry Larkin FT	.20	.09
277	Sammy Sosa FT	.20	.09
278	Dante Bichette FT	.20	.09
279	Albert Belle FT	.30	.14
280	Ozzie Smith	.50	.23
281	Mark Sweeney	.10	.05
282	Terry Bradshaw	.10	.05
283	Allen Battle	.10	.05
284	Danny Jackson	.10	.05
285	Tom Henke	.10	.05
286	Scott Cooper	.10	.05
287	Tripp Cromer	.10	.05
288	Bernard Gilkey	.10	.05
289	Brian Jordan	.20	.09
290	Tony Gwynn	1.00	.45
291	Brad Ausmus	.10	.05
292	Bryce Florie	.10	.05
293	Andres Berumen	.10	.05
294	Ken Caminiti	.30	.14
295	Bip Roberts	.10	.05
296	Trevor Hoffman	.10	.05
297	Roberto Petagine	.10	.05
298	Jody Reed	.10	.05
299	Fernando Valenzuela	.20	.09
300	Barry Bonds	.50	.23
301	Mark Leiter	.10	.05
302	Mark Carreon	.10	.05
303	Royce Clayton	.10	.05
304	Kirt Manwaring	.10	.05
305	Glenallen Hill	.10	.05
306	Deion Sanders	.20	.09
307	Joe Roslli	.10	.05
308	Robby Thompson	.10	.05
309	W. VanLandingham	.10	.05
310	Ken Griffey Jr.	2.00	.90
311	Bobby Ayala	.10	.05
312	Joey Cora	.20	.09
313	Mike Blowers	.10	.05
314	Darren Bragg	.10	.05
315	Randy Johnson	.40	.18
316	Alex Rodriguez	1.25	.55
317	Andy Benes	.20	.09
318	Tino Martinez	.40	.18
319	Dan Wilson	.10	.05
320	Will Clark	.30	.14
321	Jeff Frye	.10	.05
322	Benji Gil	.10	.05
323	Rick Helling	.10	.05
324	Mark McLemore	.10	.05
325	Dave Nilsson IF	.20	.09
326	Larry Walker IF	.20	.09
327	Jose Canseco IF	.20	.09
328	Raul Mondesi IF	.20	.09
329	Manny Ramirez IF	.20	.09
330	Robert Eenhoorn IF	.10	.05
331	Chili Davis IF	.10	.05
332	Hideo Nomo IF	.50	.23
333	Benji Gil IF	.10	.05
334	Fernando Valenzuela IF	.10	.05
335	Dennis Martinez IF	.10	.05
336	Roberto Kelly IF	.10	.05
337	Carlos Baerga IF	.20	.09
338	Juan Gonzalez IF	.50	.23
339	Roberto Alomar IF	.20	.09
340	Chan Ho Park IF	.20	.09
341	Andres Galarraga IF	.10	.05
342	Midre Cummings IF	.10	.05
343	Otis Nixon	.10	.05
344	Jeff Russell	.10	.05
345	Ivan Rodriguez	.50	.23
346	Mickey Tettleton	.10	.05
347	Bob Tewksbury	.10	.05
348	Domingo Cedeno	.10	.05
349	Lance Parrish	.10	.05
350	Joe Carter	.20	.09
351	Devon White	.10	.05
352	Carlos Delgado	.20	.09
353	Alex Gonzalez	.10	.05
354	Darren Hall	.10	.05
355	Paul Molitor	.40	.18
356	Al Leiter	.10	.05
357	Randy Knorr	.10	.05
358	Ken Caminiti CL	.20	.09
	Steve Finley		
	Brian Williams		
	Roberto Petagine		
	Andujar Cedeno		
	Phil Plantier		
	Derek Bell		
	Pedro A. Martinez		
	Doug Brocail		
	Craig Shipley		
	Ricky Gutierrez		
359	Hideo Nomo CL	.50	.23
360	Ramon A.Martinez CL	.20	.09
	Ramon J.Martinez		
361	Robin Ventura CL	.10	.05
362	Cal Ripken CL	.75	.35
363	Ken Caminiti CL	.20	.09
364	Albert Belle CL	.30	.14
	Eddie Murray		
365	Randy Johnson CL	.20	.09
366T	Tony Pena TRADE	.15	.07
367T	Jim Thome TRADE	.75	.35
368T	Don Mattingly TRADE	1.25	.55
369T	Jim Leyritz TRADE	.15	.07
370T	Ken Griffey Jr. TRADE	4.00	1.80
371T	Edgar Martinez TRADE	.50	.23
372T	Pete Schourek TRADE	.15	.07
373T	Mark Lewis TRADE	.15	.07
374T	Chipper Jones TRADE	2.50	1.10
375T	Fred McGriff TRADE	.50	.23
376T	Javy Lopez TRADE	.30	.14
377T	Fred McGriff TRADE	.50	.23
378T	Charlie O'Brien TRADE	.15	.07
379T	Mike Devereaux TRADE	.15	.07
380T	Mark Wohlers TRADE	.15	.07
381T	Bob Wolcott TRADE	.15	.07
382T	Manny Ramirez TRADE	.75	.35
383T	Jay Buhner TRADE	.50	.23
384T	Orel Hershiser TRADE	.30	.14

☐ 385T	Kenny Lofton TRADE	1.00	.45
☐ 386T	Greg Maddux TRADE	2.50	1.10
☐ 387T	Javier Lopez TRADE	.30	.14
☐ 388T	Kenny Lofton TRADE	1.00	.45
☐ 389T	Eddie Murray TRADE	.75	.35
☐ 390T	Luis Polonia TRADE	.15	.07
☐ 391T	Pedro Borbon TRADE	.15	.07
☐ 392T	Jim Thome TRADE	.75	.35
☐ 393T	Orel Hershiser TRADE	.30	.14
☐ 394T	David Justice TRADE	.30	.14
☐ 395T	Tom Glavine TRADE	.30	.14
☐ 396	Greg Maddux TC	.60	.25
☐ 397	Darren Daulton TC	.10	.05
☐ 398	Rico Brogna TC	.10	.05
☐ 399	Gary Sheffield TC	.20	.09
☐ 400	Moises Alou TC	.10	.05
☐ 401	Barry Larkin TC	.20	.09
☐ 402	Jeff Bagwell TC	.40	.18
☐ 403	Sammy Sosa TC	.20	.09
☐ 404	Ozzie Smith TC	.30	.14
☐ 405	Jay Bell TC	.10	.05
☐ 406	Mike Piazza TC	.60	.25
☐ 407	Dante Bichette TC	.10	.05
☐ 408	Tony Gwynn TC	.50	.23
☐ 409	Barry Bonds TC	.30	.14
☐ 410	Kenny Lofton TC	.30	.14
☐ 411	Johnny Damon TC	.10	.05
☐ 412	Frank Thomas TC	.75	.35
☐ 413	Greg Vaughn TC	.10	.05
☐ 414	Paul Molitor TC	.20	.09
☐ 415	Ken Griffey Jr. TC	1.00	.45
☐ 416	Tim Salmon TC	.20	.09
☐ 417	Juan Gonzalez TC	.50	.23
☐ 418	Mark McGwire TC	.40	.18
☐ 419	Roger Clemens TC	.40	.18
☐ 420	Wade Boggs TC	.20	.09
☐ 421	Cal Ripken TC	.75	.35
☐ 422	Cecil Fielder TC	.10	.05
☐ 423	Joe Carter TC	.10	.05
☐ 424	Osvaldo Fernandez	.20	.09
☐ 425	Billy Wagner	.20	.09
☐ 426	George Arias	.10	.05
☐ 427	Mendy Lopez	.10	.05
☐ 428	Jeff Suppan	.20	.09
☐ 429	Rey Ordonez	.20	.09
☐ 430	Brooks Kieschnick	.20	.09
☐ 431	Raul Ibanez	.30	.14
☐ 432	Livan Hernandez	1.25	.55
☐ 433	Shannon Stewart	.20	.09
☐ 434	Steve Cox	.10	.05
☐ 435	Trey Beamon	.10	.05
☐ 436	Sergio Nunez	.20	.09
☐ 437	Jermaine Dye	.20	.09
☐ 438	Mike Sweeney	.40	.18
☐ 439	Richard Hidalgo	.40	.18
☐ 440	Todd Greene	.30	.14
☐ 441	Robert Smith	.40	.18
☐ 442	Rafael Orellano	.10	.05
☐ 443	Wilton Guerrero	.40	.18
☐ 444	David Doster	.10	.05
☐ 445	Jason Kendall	.30	.14
☐ 446	Edgar Renteria	.30	.14
☐ 447	Scott Spiezio	.30	.14
☐ 448	Jay Canizaro	.10	.05
☐ 449	Enrique Wilson	.20	.09
☐ 450	Bob Abreu	.50	.23
☐ 451	Dwight Smith	.10	.05
☐ 452	Jeff Blauser	.10	.05
☐ 453	Steve Avery	.10	.05
☐ 454	Brad Clontz	.10	.05
☐ 455	Tom Glavine	.20	.09
☐ 456	Mike Mordecai	.10	.05
☐ 457	Rafael Belliard	.10	.05
☐ 458	Greg McMichael	.10	.05
☐ 459	Pedro Borbon	.10	.05
☐ 460	Ryan Klesko	.30	.14
☐ 461	Terrell Wade	.10	.05
☐ 462	Brady Anderson	.30	.14
☐ 463	Roberto Alomar	.40	.18
☐ 464	Bobby Bonilla	.20	.09
☐ 465	Mike Mussina	.40	.18
☐ 466	Cesar Devarez	.10	.05
☐ 467	Jeffrey Hammonds	.10	.05
☐ 468	Mike Devereaux	.10	.05
☐ 469	B.J. Surhoff	.10	.05
☐ 470	Rafael Palmeiro	.30	.14
☐ 471	John Valentin	.10	.05
☐ 472	Mike Greenwell	.10	.05
☐ 473	Dwayne Hosey	.10	.05
☐ 474	Tim Wakefield	.10	.05
☐ 475	Jose Canseco	.30	.14
☐ 476	Aaron Sele	.10	.05
☐ 477	Stan Belinda	.10	.05
☐ 478	Mike Stanley	.10	.05
☐ 479	Jamie Moyer	.10	.05
☐ 480	Mo Vaughn	.50	.23
☐ 481	Randy Velarde	.10	.05
☐ 482	Gary DiSarcina	.10	.05
☐ 483	Jorge Fabregas	.10	.05
☐ 484	Rex Hudler	.10	.05
☐ 485	Chuck Finley	.10	.05
☐ 486	Tim Wallach	.10	.05
☐ 487	Eduardo Perez	.10	.05
☐ 488	Scott Sanderson	.10	.05
☐ 489	J.T. Snow	.20	.09
☐ 490	Sammy Sosa	.40	.18
☐ 491	Terry Adams	.10	.05
☐ 492	Matt Franco	.10	.05
☐ 493	Scott Servais	.10	.05
☐ 494	Frank Castillo	.10	.05
☐ 495	Ryne Sandberg	.50	.23
☐ 496	Rey Sanchez	.10	.05
☐ 497	Steve Trachsel	.10	.05
☐ 498	Jose Hernandez	.10	.05
☐ 499	Dave Martinez	.10	.05
☐ 500	Babe Ruth FC	.50	.23
☐ 501	Ty Cobb FC	.40	.18
☐ 502	Walter Johnson FC	.30	.14
☐ 503	Christy Mathewson FC	.30	.14
☐ 504	Honus Wagner FC	.30	.14
☐ 505	Robin Ventura	.20	.09
☐ 506	Jason Bere	.10	.05
☐ 507	Mike Cameron	1.00	.45
☐ 508	Ron Karkovice	.10	.05
☐ 509	Matt Karchner	.10	.05
☐ 510	Harold Baines	.20	.09
☐ 511	Kirk McCaskill	.10	.05
☐ 512	Larry Thomas	.10	.05
☐ 513	Danny Tartabull	.10	.05
☐ 514	Steve Gilbralter	.10	.05
☐ 515	Bret Boone	.10	.05
☐ 516	Jeff Branson	.10	.05
☐ 517	Kevin Jarvis	.10	.05
☐ 518	Xavier Hernandez	.10	.05
☐ 519	Eric Owens	.10	.05
☐ 520	Barry Larkin	.30	.14
☐ 521	Dave Burba	.10	.05
☐ 522	John Smiley	.10	.05
☐ 523	Paul Assenmacher	.10	.05
☐ 524	Chad Ogea	.10	.05
☐ 525	Orel Hershiser	.20	.09
☐ 526	Alan Embree	.10	.05
☐ 527	Tony Pena	.10	.05
☐ 528	Omar Vizquel	.20	.09
☐ 529	Mark Clark	.10	.05
☐ 530	Albert Belle	.50	.23
☐ 531	Charles Nagy	.20	.09
☐ 532	Herbert Perry	.10	.05
☐ 533	Darren Holmes	.10	.05
☐ 534	Ellis Burks	.20	.09
☐ 535	Billy Swift	.10	.05
☐ 536	Armando Reynoso	.10	.05
☐ 537	Curtis Leskanic	.10	.05
☐ 538	Quinton McCracken	.10	.05
☐ 539	Steve Reed	.10	.05
☐ 540	Larry Walker	.40	.18
☐ 541	Walt Weiss	.10	.05
☐ 542	Bryan Rekar	.10	.05
☐ 543	Tony Clark	.40	.18
☐ 544	Steve Rodriguez	.10	.05
☐ 545	C.J. Nitkowski	.10	.05
☐ 546	Todd Steverson	.10	.05
☐ 547	Jose Lima	.10	.05
☐ 548	Phil Nevin	.20	.09
☐ 549	Chris Gomez	.10	.05
☐ 550	Travis Fryman	.20	.09
☐ 551	Mark Lewis	.10	.05
☐ 552	Alex Arias	.10	.05
☐ 553	Mark Valdes	.10	.05
☐ 554	Kevin Brown	.20	.09
☐ 555	Jeff Conine	.20	.09
☐ 556	John Burkett	.10	.05
☐ 557	Devon White	.10	.05
☐ 558	Pat Rapp	.10	.05
☐ 559	Jay Powell	.10	.05
☐ 560	Gary Sheffield	.40	.18
☐ 561	Jim Dougherty	.10	.05
☐ 562	Todd Jones	.10	.05
☐ 563	Tony Eusebio	.10	.05
☐ 564	Darryl Kile	.20	.09
☐ 565	Doug Drabek	.10	.05
☐ 566	Mike Simms	.10	.05
☐ 567	Derrick May	.10	.05
☐ 568	Donne Wall	.10	.05
☐ 569	Greg Swindell	.10	.05
☐ 570	Jim Pittsley	.20	.09
☐ 571	Bob Hamelin	.10	.05
☐ 572	Mark Gubicza	.10	.05
☐ 573	Chris Haney	.10	.05
☐ 574	Keith Lockhart	.10	.05
☐ 575	Mike Macfarlane	.10	.05
☐ 576	Les Norman	.10	.05
☐ 577	Joe Randa	.10	.05
☐ 578	Chris Stynes	.10	.05
☐ 579	Greg Gagne	.10	.05
☐ 580	Raul Mondesi	.30	.14
☐ 581	Delino DeShields	.10	.05
☐ 582	Pedro Astacio	.10	.05
☐ 583	Antonio Osuna	.10	.05
☐ 584	Brett Butler	.20	.09
☐ 585	Todd Worrell	.10	.05
☐ 586	Mike Blowers	.10	.05
☐ 587	Felix Rodriguez	.10	.05
☐ 588	Ismael Valdes	.20	.09
☐ 589	Ricky Bones	.10	.05
☐ 590	Greg Vaughn	.10	.05
☐ 591	Mark Loretta	.10	.05
☐ 592	Cal Eldred	.10	.05
☐ 593	Chuck Carr	.10	.05
☐ 594	Dave Nilsson	.10	.05
☐ 595	John Jaha	.10	.05
☐ 596	Scott Karl	.10	.05
☐ 597	Pat Listach	.10	.05
☐ 598	Jose Valentin	.10	.05
☐ 599	Mike Trombley	.10	.05
☐ 600	Paul Molitor	.40	.18
☐ 601	Dave Hollins	.10	.05
☐ 602	Ron Coomer	.10	.05
☐ 603	Matt Walbeck	.10	.05
☐ 604	Roberto Kelly	.10	.05
☐ 605	Rick Aguilera	.10	.05
☐ 606	Pat Mahomes	.10	.05
☐ 607	Jeff Reboulet	.10	.05
☐ 608	Rich Becker	.10	.05
☐ 609	Tim Scott	.10	.05
☐ 610	Pedro J. Martinez	.40	.18
☐ 611	Kirk Rueter	.10	.05
☐ 612	Tavo Alvarez	.10	.05
☐ 613	Yamil Benitez	.20	.09
☐ 614	Darrin Fletcher	.10	.05
☐ 615	Mike Lansing	.10	.05
☐ 616	Henry Rodriguez	.20	.09
☐ 617	Tony Tarasco	.10	.05
☐ 618	Alex Ochoa	.10	.05
☐ 619	Tim Bogar	.10	.05
☐ 620	Bernard Gilkey	.10	.05
☐ 621	Dave Mlicki	.10	.05
☐ 622	Brent Mayne	.10	.05
☐ 623	Ryan Thompson	.10	.05
☐ 624	Pete Harnisch	.10	.05
☐ 625	Lance Johnson	.10	.05
☐ 626	Jose Vizcaino	.10	.05
☐ 627	Doug Henry	.10	.05
☐ 628	Scott Kamieniecki	.10	.05
☐ 629	Jim Leyritz	.10	.05
☐ 630	Ruben Sierra	.20	.09
☐ 631	Pat Kelly	.10	.05
☐ 632	Joe Girardi	.10	.05
☐ 633	John Wetteland	.20	.09
☐ 634	Melido Perez	.10	.05
☐ 635	Paul O'Neill	.20	.09
☐ 636	Jorge Posada	.10	.05
☐ 637	Bernie Williams	.40	.18
☐ 638	Mark Acre	.10	.05
☐ 639	Mike Bordick	.10	.05
☐ 640	Mark McGwire	.75	.35
☐ 641	Fausto Cruz	.10	.05
☐ 642	Ernie Young	.10	.05

☐ 643 Todd Van Poppel	.10	.05
☐ 644 Craig Paquette	.10	.05
☐ 645 Brent Gates	.10	.05
☐ 646 Pedro Munoz	.10	.05
☐ 647 Andrew Lorraine	.10	.05
☐ 648 Sid Fernandez	.10	.05
☐ 649 Jim Eisenreich	.10	.05
☐ 650 Johnny Damon	.20	.09
☐ 651 Dustin Hermanson	.10	.05
☐ 652 Joe Randa	.10	.05
☐ 653 Michael Tucker	.20	.09
☐ 654 Alan Benes	.20	.09
☐ 655 Chad Fonville	.10	.05
☐ 656 David Bell	.10	.05
☐ 657 Jon Nunnally	.10	.05
☐ 658 Chan Ho Park	.40	.18
☐ 659 LaTroy Hawkins	.10	.05
☐ 660 Jamie Brewington	.10	.05
☐ 661 Quinton McCracken	.10	.05
☐ 662 Tim Unroe	.10	.05
☐ 663 Jeff Ware	.10	.05
☐ 664 Todd Greene	.30	.14
☐ 665 Andrew Lorraine	.10	.05
☐ 666 Ernie Young	.10	.05
☐ 667 Toby Borland	.10	.05
☐ 668 Lenny Webster	.10	.05
☐ 669 Benito Santiago	.10	.05
☐ 670 Gregg Jefferies	.10	.05
☐ 671 Darren Daulton	.20	.09
☐ 672 Curt Schilling	.20	.09
☐ 673 Mark Whiten	.10	.05
☐ 674 Todd Zeile	.10	.05
☐ 675 Jay Bell	.20	.09
☐ 676 Paul Wagner	.10	.05
☐ 677 Dave Clark	.10	.05
☐ 678 Nelson Liriano	.10	.05
☐ 679 Ramon Morel	.10	.05
☐ 680 Charlie Hayes	.10	.05
☐ 681 Angelo Encarnacion	.10	.05
☐ 682 Al Martin	.10	.05
☐ 683 Jacob Brumfield	.10	.05
☐ 684 Mike Kingery	.10	.05
☐ 685 Carlos Garcia	.10	.05
☐ 686 Tom Pagnozzi	.10	.05
☐ 687 David Bell	.10	.05
☐ 688 Todd Stottlemyre	.10	.05
☐ 689 Jose Oliva	.10	.05
☐ 690 Ray Lankford	.20	.09
☐ 691 Mike Morgan	.10	.05
☐ 692 John Frascatore	.10	.05
☐ 693 John Mabry	.10	.05
☐ 694 Mark Petkovsek	.10	.05
☐ 695 Alan Benes	.20	.09
☐ 696 Steve Finley	.20	.09
☐ 697 Marc Newfield	.10	.05
☐ 698 Andy Ashby	.10	.05
☐ 699 Mark Kroon	.10	.05
☐ 700 Wally Joyner	.20	.09
☐ 701 Joey Hamilton	.20	.09
☐ 702 Dustin Hermanson	.10	.05
☐ 703 Scott Sanders	.10	.05
☐ 704 Marty Cordova ROY	.10	.05
☐ 705 Hideo Nomo ROY	.50	.23
☐ 706 Mo Vaughn MVP	.30	.14
☐ 707 Barry Larkin MVP	.20	.09
☐ 708 Randy Johnson CY	.20	.09
☐ 709 Greg Maddux CY	.60	.25
☐ 710 Mark McGwire CB	.40	.18
☐ 711 Ron Gant CB	.20	.09
☐ 712 Andujar Cedeno	.10	.05
☐ 713 Brian Johnson	.10	.05
☐ 714 J.R. Phillips	.10	.05
☐ 715 Rod Beck	.10	.05
☐ 716 Sergio Valdez	.10	.05
☐ 717 Marvin Benard	.10	.05
☐ 718 Steve Scarsone	.10	.05
☐ 719 Rich Aurilia	.10	.05
☐ 720 Matt Williams	.30	.14
☐ 721 John Patterson	.10	.05
☐ 722 Shawn Estes	.30	.14
☐ 723 Russ Davis	.10	.05
☐ 724 Rich Amaral	.10	.05
☐ 725 Edgar Martinez	.30	.14
☐ 726 Norm Charlton	.10	.05
☐ 727 Paul Sorrento	.10	.05
☐ 728 Luis Sojo	.10	.05

☐ 729 Arquimedez Pozo	.10	.05
☐ 730 Jay Buhner	.30	.14
☐ 731 Chris Bosio	.10	.05
☐ 732 Chris Widger	.10	.05
☐ 733 Kevin Gross	.10	.05
☐ 734 Darren Oliver	.10	.05
☐ 735 Dean Palmer	.10	.05
☐ 736 Matt Whiteside	.10	.05
☐ 737 Luis Ortiz	.10	.05
☐ 738 Roger Pavlik	.10	.05
☐ 739 Damon Buford	.10	.05
☐ 740 Juan Gonzalez	1.00	.45
☐ 741 Rusty Greer	.20	.09
☐ 742 Lou Frazier	.10	.05
☐ 743 Pat Hentgen	.20	.09
☐ 744 Tomas Perez	.10	.05
☐ 745 Juan Guzman	.10	.05
☐ 746 Otis Nixon	.10	.05
☐ 747 Robert Perez	.10	.05
☐ 748 Ed Sprague	.10	.05
☐ 749 Tony Castillo	.10	.05
☐ 750 John Olerud	.20	.09
☐ 751 Shawn Green	.10	.05
☐ 752 Jeff Ware	.10	.05
☐ 753 Dante Bichette CL	.20	.09
Vinny Castilla		
Andres Galarraga		
Larry Walker		
☐ 754 Greg Maddux CL	.60	.25
☐ 755 Marty Cordova CL	.10	.05
☐ 756 Ozzie Smith CL	.30	.14
☐ 757 John Vanderwal CL	.10	.05
☐ 758 Andres Galarraga CL	.20	.09
☐ 759 Frank Thomas CL	.75	.35
☐ 760 Tony Gwynn CL	.50	.23
☐ 761 Randy Myers UPD	.25	.11
☐ 762 Kent Mercker UPD	.25	.11
☐ 763 David Wells UPD	.25	.11
☐ 764 Tom Gordon UPD	.25	.11
☐ 765 Wil Cordero UPD	.25	.11
☐ 766 Dave Magadan UPD	.25	.11
☐ 767 Doug Jones UPD	.25	.11
☐ 768 Kevin Tapani UPD	.25	.11
☐ 769 Curtis Goodwin UPD	.25	.11
☐ 770 Julio Franco UPD	.25	.11
☐ 771 Jack McDowell UPD	.25	.11
☐ 772 Al Leter UPD	.25	.11
☐ 773 Sean Berry UPD	.25	.11
☐ 774 Big Roberts UPD	.25	.11
☐ 775 Jose Offerman UPD	.25	.11
☐ 776 Ben McDonald UPD	.25	.11
☐ 777 Dan Serafini UPD	.25	.11
☐ 778 Ryan McGuire UPD	.25	.11
☐ 779 Tim Raines UPD	.40	.18
☐ 780 Tino Martinez UPD	.75	.35
☐ 781 Kenny Rogers UPD	.25	.11
☐ 782 Bob Tewksbury UPD	.25	.11
☐ 783 Rickey Henderson UPD	.50	.23
☐ 784 Ron Gant UPD	.40	.18
☐ 785 Gary Gaetti UPD	.25	.11
☐ 786 Andy Benes UPD	.25	.11
☐ 787 Royce Clayton UPD	.25	.11
☐ 788 Darryl Hamilton UPD	.25	.11
☐ 789 Ken Hill UPD	.25	.11
☐ 790 Erik Hanson UPD	.25	.11
☐ P100 Ken Griffey Jr. Promo	3.00	1.35

1996 Collector's Choice Crash the Game

Randomly inserted into one in every five Series 2 packs, silver Crash the Game interactive cards feature a selection of thirty of baseball's top stars. If the featured player hit a home run during the series specified on the card, it was then eligible to be redeemed for a super premium Cell Card of the same player. Winning cards have been highlighted with a "W" in the list-

ings below. The postmark expiration date for exchanging winning cards was November 18th, 1996.

	MINT	NRMT
COMPLETE SET (90)	50.00	22.00
*SINGLES: .6X to 1.5X BASE CARD HI		
SER.2 STATED ODDS 1:5		
COMP.GOLD SET (90)	250.00	110.00
*GOLD: 2.5X to 4X BASE CARD HI		
GOLD SER.2 STATED ODDS 1:48		
THREE DATES PER PLAYER		
COMP.EXCH.SET (27)	100.00	45.00
*EXCH: 2.5X to 5X BASE CARD HI		
COMP.GOLD EXCH.SET (27)	300.00	135.00
*GOLD EXCH: 7.5X to 15X BASE CARD HI		
ONE EXCH.CARD VIA MAIL PER WINNER		

☐ CG1 Chipper Jones 7/11 W	2.00	.90
☐ CG1B Chipper Jones 8/27 W	2.00	.90
☐ CG1C Chipper Jones 9/19	2.00	.90
☐ CG2 Fred McGriff 7/7	.40	.18
☐ CG2B Fred McGriff 8/30	.40	.18
☐ CG2C Fred McGriff 9/10 W	.40	.18
☐ CG3 Rafael Palmeiro 7/4 W	.40	.18
☐ CG3B Rafael Palmeiro 8/29	.40	.18
☐ CG3C Rafael Palmeiro 9/26	.40	.18
☐ CG4 Cal Ripken 6/27	2.50	1.10
☐ CG4B Cal Ripken 7/25 W	2.50	1.10
☐ CG4C Cal Ripken 9/2	2.50	1.10
☐ CG5 Jose Canseco 6/27	.40	.18
☐ CG5B Jose Canseco 7/11 W	.40	.18
☐ CG5C Jose Canseco 8/23	.40	.18
☐ CG6 Mo Vaughn 6/21 W	.75	.35
☐ CG6B Mo Vaughn 7/18 W	.75	.35
☐ CG6C Mo Vaughn 9/20	.75	.35
☐ CG7 Jim Edmonds 7/18 W	.40	.18
☐ CG7B Jim Edmonds 8/16 W	.40	.18
☐ CG7C Jim Edmonds 9/20	.40	.18
☐ CG8 Tim Salmon 6/27	.60	.25
☐ CG8B Tim Salmon 7/30	.60	.25
☐ CG8C Tim Salmon 9/13 W	.60	.25
☐ CG9 Sammy Sosa 7/4 W	.60	.25
☐ CG9B Sammy Sosa 8/1 W	.60	.25
☐ CG9C Sammy Sosa 8/21	.60	.25
☐ CG10 Frank Thomas 6/27	2.50	1.10
☐ CG10B Frank Thomas 7/4	2.50	1.10
☐ CG10C Frank Thomas 9/24	2.50	1.10
☐ CG11 Albert Belle 6/25	.75	.35
☐ CG11B Albert Belle 7/11 W	.75	.35
☐ CG11C Albert Belle 9/6	.75	.35
☐ CG12 Manny Ramirez 7/18	.60	.25
☐ CG12B Manny Ramirez 8/26	.60	.25
☐ CG12C Manny Ramirez 9/6	.60	.25
☐ CG13 Jim Thome 6/27	.60	.25
☐ CG13B Jim Thome 7/4 W	.60	.25
☐ CG13C Jim Thome 9/23	.60	.25
☐ CG14 Dante Bichette 7/11 W	.25	.11
☐ CG14B Dante Bichette 8/9	.25	.11
☐ CG14C Dante Bichette 9/5	.25	.11
☐ CG15 Vinny Castilla 7/1	.25	.11
☐ CG15B Vinny Castilla 8/23 W	.25	.11
☐ CG15C Vinny Castilla 9/13 W	.25	.11
☐ CG16 Larry Walker 6/24	.60	.25
☐ CG16B Larry Walker 7/18	.60	.25
☐ CG16C Larry Walker 9/27	.60	.25
☐ CG17 Cecil Fielder 6/27	.25	.11

☐ CG17B Cecil Fielder 7/30 W .25 .11
☐ CG17C Cecil Fielder 9/17 W .25 .11
☐ CG18 Gary Sheffield 7/4.... .60 .25
☐ CG18B Gary Sheffield 8/2.. .60 .25
☐ CG18C Gary Sheffield 9/5 W .60 .25
☐ CG19 Jeff Bagwell 7/4 W 1.25 .55
☐ CG19B Jeff Bagwell 8/16 1.25 .55
☐ CG19C Jeff Bagwell 9/26 W 1.25 .55
☐ CG20 Eric Karros 7/4 W .25 .11
☐ CG20B Eric Karros 8/13 W .25 .11
☐ CG20C Eric Karros 9/16 .... .25 .11
☐ CG21 Mike Piazza 6/27 W 2.00 .90
☐ CG21B Mike Piazza 7/26 2.00 .90
☐ CG21C Mike Piazza 9/12 W 2.00 .90
☐ CG22 Ken Caminiti 7/11 W .40 .18
☐ CG22B Ken Caminiti 8/16 W .40 .18
☐ CG22C Ken Caminiti 9/19 W .40 .18
☐ CG23 Barry Bonds 6/27 W .75 .35
☐ CG23B Barry Bonds 7/22 .. .75 .35
☐ CG23C Barry Bonds 9/24 .. .75 .35
☐ CG24 Matt Williams 7/11 W .40 .18
☐ CG24B Matt Williams 8/19 .40 .18
☐ CG24C Matt Williams 9/27 .40 .18
☐ CG25 Jay Buhner 6/20 .... .40 .18
☐ CG25B Jay Buhner 7/25.... .40 .18
☐ CG25C Jay Buhner 8/29 W .40 .18
☐ CG26 Ken Griffey Jr. 7/18 W 3.00 1.35
☐ CG26B Ken Griffey Jr. 8/16 W 3.00 1.35
☐ CG26C Ken Griffey Jr. 9/20 W 3.00 1.35
☐ CG27 Ron Gant 6/24 W .25 .11
☐ CG27B Ron Gant 7/11 W .. .25 .11
☐ CG27C Ron Gant 9/27 W .. .25 .11
☐ CG28 Juan Gonzalez 6/28 W 1.50 .70
☐ CG28B Juan Gonzalez 7/15 W 1.50 .70
☐ CG28C Juan Gonzalez 8/6 1.50 .70
☐ CG29 Mickey Tettleton 7/4 W .25 .11
☐ CG29B Mickey Tettleton 8/6 .25 .11
☐ CG29C Mickey Tettleton 9/6 W .25 .11
☐ CG30 Joe Carter 6/25...... .25 .11
☐ CG30B Joe Carter 8/5........ .25 .11
☐ CG30C Joe Carter 9/23...... .25 .11

1996 Collector's Choice You Make the Play

Cards from this 90-card set were inserted one per first series pack. Forty-five players are featured and each player is given two cards. The cards measure just about the standard-size but have rounded corners. In addition to being inserted into packs, dealers also were offered extra You Make the Play cards depending on how many cases ordered. A dealer who ordered one case received two 12-card packs of these cards for a total of 24 cards. Meanwhile, a dealer who ordered two cases received six 12-card packs for a total of 72 packs. Customers could also receive 12 of these cards by sending 10 wrappers and $2 for a mail-in order. This offer expired on May 15, 1996.

	MINT	NRMT
COMPLETE SET (90)	12.00	5.50
COMMON CARD	.10	.05
ONE BASIC CARD PER SER.1 PACK		
COMP GOLD SET (90)	200.00	90.00
*GOLD: 7.5X TO 15X BASE CARD HI		
GOLD SER.1 STATED ODDS 1:35		
TWO MAKE THE PLAY CARDS PER PLAYER		

☐ 1 Kevin Appier .... .20 .09
☐ 1A Kevin Appier .... .20 .09
☐ 2 Carlos Baerga .... .10 .05
☐ 2A Carlos Baerga .... .10 .05
☐ 3 Jeff Bagwell .... .75 .35
☐ 3A Jeff Bagwell .... .75 .35
☐ 4 Jay Bell .... .20 .09
☐ 4A Jay Bell .... .20 .09
☐ 5 Albert Belle .... .50 .23
☐ 5A Albert Belle .... .50 .23
☐ 6 Craig Biggio .... .30 .14
☐ 6A Craig Biggio .... .30 .14
☐ 7 Wade Boggs .... .40 .18
☐ 7A Wade Boggs .... .40 .18
☐ 8 Barry Bonds .... .50 .23
☐ 8A Barry Bonds .... .50 .23
☐ 9 Bobby Bonilla .... .20 .09
☐ 9A Bobby Bonilla .... .20 .09
☐ 10 Jose Canseco .... .30 .14
☐ 10A Jose Canseco .... .30 .14
☐ 11 Joe Carter .... .20 .09
☐ 11A Joe Carter .... .20 .09
☐ 12 Darren Daulton .... .20 .09
☐ 12A Darren Daulton .... .20 .09
☐ 13 Cecil Fielder .... .20 .09
☐ 13A Cecil Fielder .... .20 .09
☐ 14 Ron Gant .... .20 .09
☐ 14A Ron Gant .... .20 .09
☐ 15 Juan Gonzalez .... 1.00 .45
☐ 15A Juan Gonzalez .... 1.00 .45
☐ 16 Ken Griffey Jr. .... 2.00 .90
☐ 16A Ken Griffey Jr. .... 2.00 .90
☐ 17 Tony Gwynn .... 1.00 .45
☐ 17A Tony Gwynn .... 1.00 .45
☐ 18 Randy Johnson .... .50 .23
☐ 18A Randy Johnson .... .50 .23
☐ 19 Chipper Jones .... 1.25 .55
☐ 19A Chipper Jones .... 1.25 .55
☐ 20 Barry Larkin .... .30 .14
☐ 20A Barry Larkin .... .30 .14
☐ 21 Kenny Lofton .... .50 .23
☐ 21A Kenny Lofton .... .50 .23
☐ 22 Greg Maddux .... 1.25 .55
☐ 22A Greg Maddux .... 1.25 .55
☐ 23 Don Mattingly .... .60 .25
☐ 23A Don Mattingly .... .60 .25
☐ 24 Fred McGriff .... .30 .14
☐ 24A Fred McGriff .... .30 .14
☐ 25 Mark McGwire .... .75 .35
☐ 25A Mark McGwire .... .75 .35
☐ 26 Paul Molitor .... .40 .18
☐ 26A Paul Molitor .... .40 .18
☐ 27 Raul Mondesi .... .30 .14
☐ 27A Raul Mondesi .... .30 .14
☐ 28 Eddie Murray .... .40 .18
☐ 28A Eddie Murray .... .40 .18
☐ 29 Hideo Nomo .... 1.00 .45
☐ 29A Hideo Nomo .... 1.00 .45
☐ 30 Jon Nunnally .... .10 .05
☐ 30A Jon Nunnally .... .10 .05
☐ 31 Mike Piazza .... 1.25 .55
☐ 31A Mike Piazza .... 1.25 .55
☐ 32 Kirby Puckett .... .75 .35
☐ 32A Kirby Puckett .... .75 .35
☐ 33 Cal Ripken .... 1.50 .70
☐ 33A Cal Ripken .... 1.50 .70
☐ 34 Alex Rodriguez .... 1.25 .55
☐ 34A Alex Rodriguez .... 1.25 .55
☐ 35 Tim Salmon .... .40 .18
☐ 35A Tim Salmon .... .40 .18
☐ 36 Gary Sheffield .... .40 .18
☐ 36A Gary Sheffield .... .40 .18

☐ 37 Lee Smith .... .20 .09
☐ 37A Lee Smith .... .20 .09
☐ 38 Ozzie Smith .... .50 .23
☐ 38A Ozzie Smith .... .50 .23
☐ 39 Sammy Sosa .... .40 .18
☐ 39A Sammy Sosa .... .40 .18
☐ 40 Frank Thomas .... 1.50 .70
☐ 40A Frank Thomas .... 1.50 .70
☐ 41 Greg Vaughn .... .10 .05
☐ 41A Greg Vaughn .... .10 .05
☐ 42 Mo Vaughn .... .50 .23
☐ 42A Mo Vaughn .... .50 .23
☐ 43 Larry Walker .... .40 .18
☐ 43A Larry Walker .... .40 .18
☐ 44 Rondell White .... .20 .09
☐ 44A Rondell White .... .20 .09
☐ 45 Matt Williams .... .30 .14
☐ 45A Matt Williams .... .30 .14

1997 Collector's Choice

This 506-card set was distributed in 12-card packs with a suggested retail price of $.99. The fronts feature color action player photos while the backs carry player statistics. The set contains the following subsets: Rookie Class (1-27), League Leaders (56-63), Postseason (218-224) which recaps action from the 1996 playoffs and World Series Games and Ken Griffey Jr. Checklist (244-249) which also carry collecting tips. The 260-card second series set was distributed in 14-card packs with a suggested retail price of $1.29 and features color player photos in white borders. The backs carry player statistics. The set contains the following: 199 regular player cards, 10 Ken Griffey Jr.'s Hot List (325-334), 18 Rookie Class, 3 Collecting 101 Set checklists, and 30 full-bleed All-Star cards.

	MINT	NRMT
COMPLETE SET (506)	36.00	16.00
COMP.FACT.SET (516)......	40.00	18.00
COMPLETE SERIES 1 (246)	18.00	8.00
COMPLETE SERIES 2 (260)	18.00	8.00
COMMON CARD (1-506)	.10	.05
COMMON GRIFFEY CL (244-249)	.25	.11
MINOR STARS	.20	.09
UNLISTED STARS	.40	.18
SUBSET CARDS HALF VALUE OF BASE CARDS		
B.WILLIAMS AND D.GOODEN NUMBERED 175		
D.GOODEN 176 AVAIL.ONLY IN FACT.SETS		
TEN JUMBO PREMIER POWER PER FACT.SET		
COMP.GRIFFEY CD SET (5)	80.00	36.00
COMMON GRIFFEY CD (1-5)	20.00	9.00
GRIFFEY CD SER.1 STATED ODDS 1:144		

1	Andruw Jones	1.00	.45
2	Rocky Coppinger	.10	.05
3	Jeff D'Amico	.10	.05
4	Dmitri Young	.10	.05
5	Darin Erstad	.60	.25
6	Jermaine Allensworth	.10	.05
7	Damian Jackson	.10	.05
8	Bill Mueller	.10	.05
9	Jacob Cruz	.20	.09
10	Vladimir Guerrero	.75	.35
11	Marty Janzen	.10	.05
12	Kevin L. Brown	.10	.05
13	Willie Adams	.10	.05
14	Wendell Magee	.10	.05
15	Scott Rolen	1.00	.45
16	Matt Beech	.10	.05
17	Neifi Perez	.20	.09
18	Jamey Wright	.10	.05
19	Jose Paniagua	.10	.05
20	Todd Walker	.20	.09
21	Justin Thompson	.20	.09
22	Robin Jennings	.10	.05
23	Dario Veras	.25	.11
24	Brian Lesher	.10	.05
25	Nomar Garciaparra	1.25	.55
26	Luis Castillo	.20	.09
27	Brian Giles	.20	.09
28	Jermaine Dye	.20	.09
29	Terrell Wade	.10	.05
30	Fred McGriff	.30	.14
31	Marquis Grissom	.20	.09
32	Ryan Klesko	.30	.14
33	Javier Lopez	.20	.09
34	Mark Wohlers	.10	.05
35	Tom Glavine	.20	.09
36	Denny Neagle	.20	.09
37	Scott Erickson	.10	.05
38	Chris Hoiles	.10	.05
39	Roberto Alomar	.40	.18
40	Eddie Murray	.40	.18
41	Cal Ripken	1.50	.70
42	Randy Myers	.10	.05
43	B.J. Surhoff	.10	.05
44	Rick Krivda	.10	.05
45	Jose Canseco	.30	.14
46	Heathcliff Slocumb	.10	.05
47	Jeff Suppan	.20	.09
48	Tom Gordon	.10	.05
49	Aaron Sele	.10	.05
50	Mo Vaughn	.50	.23
51	Darren Bragg	.10	.05
52	Wil Cordero	.10	.05
53	Scott Bullett	.10	.05
54	Terry Adams	.10	.05
55	Jackie Robinson	1.00	.45
56	Tony Gwynn LL Alex Rodriguez	.50	.23
57	Andres Galarraga LL Mark McGwire	.25	.11
58	Andres Galarraga LL Albert Belle	.20	.09
59	Eric Young LL Kenny Lofton	.20	.09
60	John Smoltz LL Andy Pettitte	.10	.05
61	John Smoltz LL Roger Clemens	.25	.11
62	Kevin Brown LL Juan Guzman	.10	.05
63	John Wetteland LL Todd Worrell Jeff Brantley	.10	.05
64	Scott Servais	.10	.05
65	Sammy Sosa	.40	.18
66	Ryne Sandberg	.50	.23
67	Frank Castillo	.10	.05
68	Rey Sanchez	.10	.05
69	Steve Trachsel	.10	.05
70	Robin Ventura	.20	.09
71	Wilson Alvarez	.10	.05
72	Tony Phillips	.10	.05
73	Lyle Mouton	.10	.05
74	Mike Cameron	.30	.14
75	Harold Baines	.20	.09
76	Albert Belle	.50	.23
77	Chris Snopek	.10	.05
78	Reggie Sanders	.10	.05
79	Jeff Brantley	.10	.05
80	Barry Larkin	.30	.14
81	Kevin Jarvis	.10	.05
82	John Smiley	.10	.05
83	Pete Schourek	.10	.05
84	Thomas Howard	.10	.05
85	Lee Smith	.20	.09
86	Omar Vizquel	.20	.09
87	Julio Franco	.20	.09
88	Orel Hershiser	.20	.09
89	Charles Nagy	.20	.09
90	Matt Williams	.30	.14
91	Dennis Martinez	.20	.09
92	Jose Mesa	.10	.05
93	Sandy Alomar Jr.	.20	.09
94	Jim Thome	.40	.18
95	Vinny Castilla	.20	.09
96	Armando Reynoso	.10	.05
97	Kevin Ritz	.10	.05
98	Larry Walker	.40	.18
99	Eric Young	.20	.09
100	Dante Bichette	.20	.09
101	Quinton McCracken	.10	.05
102	John Vander Wal	.10	.05
103	Phil Nevin	.10	.05
104	Tony Clark	.40	.18
105	Alan Trammell	.20	.09
106	Felipe Lira	.10	.05
107	Curtis Pride	.10	.05
108	Bobby Higginson	.20	.09
109	Mark Lewis	.10	.05
110	Travis Fryman	.20	.09
111	Al Leiter	.10	.05
112	Devon White	.10	.05
113	Jeff Conine	.20	.09
114	Charles Johnson	.20	.09
115	Andre Dawson	.30	.14
116	Edgar Renteria	.20	.09
117	Robb Nen	.10	.05
118	Kevin Brown	.20	.09
119	Derek Bell	.10	.05
120	Bob Abreu	.20	.09
121	Mike Hampton	.10	.05
122	Todd Jones	.10	.05
123	Billy Wagner	.20	.09
124	Shane Reynolds	.10	.05
125	Jeff Bagwell	.75	.35
126	Brian L. Hunter	.20	.09
127	Jeff Montgomery	.10	.05
128	Rod Myers	.20	.09
129	Tim Belcher	.10	.05
130	Kevin Appier	.20	.09
131	Mike Sweeney	.20	.09
132	Craig Paquette	.10	.05
133	Joe Randa	.10	.05
134	Michael Tucker	.20	.09
135	Raul Mondesi	.30	.14
136	Tim Wallach	.20	.09
137	Brett Butler	.20	.09
138	Karim Garcia	.20	.09
139	Todd Hollandsworth	.20	.09
140	Eric Karros	.20	.09
141	Hideo Nomo	1.00	.45
142	Ismael Valdes	.20	.09
143	Cal Eldred	.10	.05
144	Scott Karl	.10	.05
145	Matt Mieske	.10	.05
146	Mike Fetters	.10	.05
147	Mark Loretta	.20	.09
148	Fernando Vina	.10	.05
149	Jeff Cirillo	.20	.09
150	Dave Nilsson	.10	.05
151	Kirby Puckett	.75	.35
152	Rich Becker	.10	.05
153	Chuck Knoblauch	.40	.18
154	Marty Cordova	.20	.09
155	Paul Molitor	.40	.18
156	Rick Aguilera	.10	.05
157	Pat Meares	.10	.05
158	Frank Rodriguez	.10	.05
159	David Segui	.10	.05
160	Henry Rodriguez	.20	.09
161	Shane Andrews	.10	.05
162	Pedro Martinez	.40	.18
163	Mark Grudzielanek	.10	.05
164	Mike Lansing	.10	.05
165	Rondell White	.20	.09
166	Ugueth Urbina	.10	.05
167	Rey Ordonez	.20	.09
168	Robert Person	.10	.05
169	Carlos Baerga	.10	.05
170	Bernard Gilkey	.10	.05
171	John Franco	.20	.09
172	Pete Harnisch	.10	.05
173	Butch Huskey	.20	.09
174	Paul Wilson	.20	.09
175	Dwight Gooden ERR incorrectly numbered 175	.20	.09
176	Bernie Williams	.40	.18
177	Wade Boggs	.40	.18
178	Ruben Rivera	.20	.09
179	Jim Leyritz	.10	.05
180	Derek Jeter	1.25	.55
181	Tino Martinez	.40	.18
182	Tim Raines	.20	.09
183	Scott Brosius	.10	.05
184	Jason Giambi	.20	.09
185	Geronimo Berroa	.10	.05
186	Ariel Prieto	.10	.05
187	Scott Spiezio	.20	.09
188	John Wasdin	.10	.05
189	Ernie Young	.10	.05
190	Mark McGwire	.75	.35
191	Jim Eisenreich	.10	.05
192	Ricky Bottalico	.10	.05
193	Darren Daulton	.20	.09
194	David Doster	.10	.05
195	Gregg Jefferies	.10	.05
196	Lenny Dykstra	.20	.09
197	Curt Schilling	.20	.09
198	Todd Stottlemyre	.10	.05
199	Willie McGee	.10	.05
200	Ozzie Smith	.50	.23
201	Dennis Eckersley	.20	.09
202	Ray Lankford	.20	.09
203	John Mabry	.10	.05
204	Alan Benes	.20	.09
205	Ron Gant	.20	.09
206	Archi Cianfrocco	.10	.05
207	Fernando Valenzuela	.20	.09
208	Greg Vaughn	.10	.05
209	Steve Finley	.20	.09
210	Tony Gwynn	1.00	.45
211	Rickey Henderson	.30	.14
212	Trevor Hoffman	.10	.05
213	Jason Thompson	.10	.05
214	Osvaldo Fernandez	.10	.05
215	Glenallen Hill	.10	.05
216	William VanLandingham	.10	.05
217	Marvin Benard	.10	.05
218	Juan Gonzalez POST	.50	.23
219	Roberto Alomar POST	.20	.09
220	Brian Jordan POST	.10	.05
221	John Smoltz POST	.10	.05
222	Javy Lopez POST	.10	.05
223	Bernie Williams POST	.20	.09
224	Jim Leyritz POST John Wetteland	.10	.05
225	Barry Bonds	.50	.23
226	Rich Aurilia	.10	.05
227	Jay Canizaro	.10	.05
228	Dan Wilson	.10	.05
229	Bob Wolcott	.10	.05
230	Ken Griffey Jr.	2.00	.90
231	Sterling Hitchcock	.10	.05
232	Edgar Martinez	.30	.14
233	Joey Cora	.10	.05
234	Norm Charlton	.10	.05
235	Alex Rodriguez	1.25	.55
236	Bobby Witt	.10	.05
237	Darren Oliver	.10	.05
238	Kevin Elster	.10	.05
239	Rusty Greer	.20	.09
240	Juan Gonzalez	1.00	.45
241	Will Clark	.30	.14
242	Dean Palmer	.10	.05
243	Ivan Rodriguez	.50	.23
244	Ken Griffey Jr. CL	.25	.11
245	Ken Griffey Jr. CL	.25	.11
246	Ken Griffey Jr. CL	.25	.11
247	Ken Griffey Jr. CL	.25	.11

248	Ken Griffey Jr. CL	.25	.11
249	Ken Griffey Jr. CL	.25	.11
250	Eddie Murray	.40	.18
251	Troy Percival	.10	.05
252	Garret Anderson	.20	.09
253	Allen Watson	.10	.05
254	Jason Dickson	.20	.09
255	Jim Edmonds	.30	.14
256	Chuck Finley	.10	.05
257	Randy Velarde	.10	.05
258	Shigetoshi Hasegawa	.25	.11
259	Todd Greene	.20	.09
260	Tim Salmon	.40	.18
261	Mark Langston	.10	.05
262	Dave Hollins	.10	.05
263	Gary DiSarcina	.10	.05
264	Kenny Lofton	.50	.23
265	John Smoltz	.20	.09
266	Greg Maddux	1.25	.55
267	Jeff Blauser	.20	.09
268	Alan Embree	.10	.05
269	Mark Lemke	.10	.05
270	Chipper Jones	1.25	.55
271	Mike Mussina	.40	.18
272	Rafael Palmeiro	.30	.14
273	Jimmy Key	.20	.09
274	Mike Bordick	.10	.05
275	Brady Anderson	.30	.14
276	Eric Davis	.20	.09
277	Jeffrey Hammonds	.10	.05
278	Reggie Jefferson	.10	.05
279	Tim Naehring	.10	.05
280	John Valentin	.10	.05
281	Troy O'Leary	.10	.05
282	Shane Mack	.10	.05
283	Mike Stanley	.10	.05
284	Tim Wakefield	.10	.05
285	Brian McRae	.10	.05
286	Brooks Kieschnick	.10	.05
287	Shawon Dunston	.10	.05
288	Kevin Foster	.10	.05
289	Mel Rojas	.10	.05
290	Mark Grace	.30	.14
291	Brant Brown	.10	.05
292	Amaury Telemaco	.10	.05
293	Dave Martinez	.10	.05
294	Jaime Navarro	.10	.05
295	Ray Durham	.10	.05
296	Ozzie Guillen	.10	.05
297	Roberto Hernandez	.10	.05
298	Ron Karkovice	.10	.05
299	James Baldwin	.10	.05
300	Frank Thomas	1.50	.70
301	Eddie Taubensee	.10	.05
302	Bret Boone	.10	.05
303	Willie Greene	.10	.05
304	Dave Burba	.10	.05
305	Deion Sanders	.20	.09
306	Reggie Sanders	.10	.05
307	Hal Morris	.10	.05
308	Pokey Reese	.10	.05
309	Tony Fernandez	.10	.05
310	Manny Ramirez	.40	.18
311	Chad Ogea	.10	.05
312	Jack McDowell	.10	.05
313	Kevin Mitchell	.10	.05
314	Chad Curtis	.10	.05
315	Steve Kline	.10	.05
316	Kevin Seitzer	.10	.05
317	Kirt Manwaring	.10	.05
318	Billy Swift	.10	.05
319	Ellis Burks	.20	.09
320	Andres Galarraga	.40	.18
321	Bruce Ruffin	.10	.05
322	Mark Thompson	.10	.05
323	Walt Weiss	.10	.05
324	Todd Jones	.10	.05
325	Andruw Jones GHL	.50	.23
326	Chipper Jones GHL	.60	.25
327	Mo Vaughn GHL	.25	.11
328	Frank Thomas GHL	.75	.35
329	Albert Belle GHL	.25	.11
330	Mark McGwire GHL	.40	.18
331	Derek Jeter GHL	.25	.11
332	Alex Rodriguez GHL	.60	.25
333	Jay Buhner GHL	.20	.09

	with Ken Griffey Jr.		
334	Ken Griffey Jr. GHL	1.00	.45
335	Brian L. Hunter	.20	.09
336	Brian Johnson	.10	.05
337	Omar Olivares	.10	.05
338	Deivi Cruz	.30	.14
339	Damion Easley	.10	.05
340	Melvin Nieves	.10	.05
341	Moises Alou	.20	.09
342	Jim Eisenreich	.10	.05
343	Mark Hutton	.10	.05
344	Alex Fernandez	.20	.09
345	Gary Sheffield	.40	.18
346	Pat Rapp	.10	.05
347	Brad Ausmus	.10	.05
348	Sean Berry	.10	.05
349	Darryl Kile	.20	.09
350	Craig Biggio	.30	.14
351	Chris Holt	.10	.05
352	Luis Gonzalez	.10	.05
353	Pat Listach	.10	.05
354	Jose Rosado	.10	.05
355	Mike Macfarlane	.10	.05
356	Tom Goodwin	.10	.05
357	Chris Haney	.10	.05
358	Chili Davis	.20	.09
359	Jose Offerman	.10	.05
360	Johnny Damon	.10	.05
361	Bip Roberts	.10	.05
362	Ramon Martinez	.20	.09
363	Pedro Astacio	.10	.05
364	Todd Zeile	.10	.05
365	Mike Piazza	1.25	.55
366	Gregg Gagne	.10	.05
367	Chan Ho Park	.40	.18
368	Wilton Guerrero	.10	.05
369	Todd Worrell	.10	.05
370	John Jaha	.10	.05
371	Steve Sparks	.10	.05
372	Mike Matheny	.10	.05
373	Marc Newfield	.10	.05
374	Jeromy Burnitz	.10	.05
375	Jose Valentin	.10	.05
376	Ben McDonald	.10	.05
377	Roberto Kelly	.10	.05
378	Bob Tewksbury	.10	.05
379	Ron Coomer	.10	.05
380	Brad Radke	.20	.09
381	Matt Lawton	.10	.05
382	Dan Naulty	.10	.05
383	Scott Stahoviak	.10	.05
384	Matt Wagner	.10	.05
385	Jim Bullinger	.10	.05
386	Carlos Perez	.10	.05
387	Darrin Fletcher	.10	.05
388	Chris Widger	.10	.05
389	F.P. Santangelo	.10	.05
390	Lee Smith	.20	.09
391	Bobby Jones	.10	.05
392	John Olerud	.20	.09
393	Mark Clark	.10	.05
394	Jason Isringhausen	.10	.05
395	Todd Hundley	.20	.09
396	Lance Johnson	.10	.05
397	Edgardo Alfonzo	.20	.09
398	Alex Ochoa	.10	.05
399	Darryl Strawberry	.20	.09
400	David Cone	.20	.09
401	Paul O'Neill	.20	.09
402	Joe Girardi	.10	.05
403	Charlie Hayes	.10	.05
404	Andy Pettitte	.40	.18
405	Mariano Rivera	.20	.09
406	Mariano Duncan	.10	.05
407	Kenny Rogers	.10	.05
408	Cecil Fielder	.20	.09
409	George Williams	.10	.05
410	Jose Canseco	.30	.14
411	Tony Batista	.10	.05
412	Steve Karsay	.10	.05
413	Dave Telgheder	.10	.05
414	Billy Taylor	.10	.05
415	Mickey Morandini	.10	.05
416	Calvin Maduro	.10	.05
417	Mark Leiter	.10	.05
418	Kevin Stocker	.10	.05

419	Mike Liebenthal	.10	.05
420	Rico Brogna	.10	.05
421	Mark Portugal	.10	.05
422	Rex Hudler	.10	.05
423	Mark Johnson	.10	.05
424	Esteban Loaiza	.10	.05
425	Lou Collier	.10	.05
426	Kevin Elster	.10	.05
427	Francisco Cordova	.10	.05
428	Marc Wilkins	.10	.05
429	Joe Randa	.10	.05
430	Jason Kendall	.20	.09
431	Jon Lieber	.10	.05
432	Steve Cooke	.10	.05
433	Emil Brown	.20	.09
434	Tony Womack	.30	.14
435	Al Martin	.10	.05
436	Jason Schmidt	.10	.05
437	Andy Benes	.20	.09
438	Delino DeShields	.10	.05
439	Royce Clayton	.10	.05
440	Brian Jordan	.20	.09
441	Donovan Osborne	.10	.05
442	Gary Gaetti	.10	.05
443	Tom Pagnozzi	.10	.05
444	Joey Hamilton	.20	.09
445	Wally Joyner	.10	.05
446	John Flaherty	.10	.05
447	Chris Gomez	.10	.05
448	Sterling Hitchcock	.10	.05
449	Andy Ashby	.10	.05
450	Ken Caminiti	.30	.14
451	Tim Worrell	.10	.05
452	Jose Vizcaino	.10	.05
453	Rod Beck	.10	.05
454	Wilson Delgado	.20	.09
455	Darryl Hamilton	.10	.05
456	Mark Lewis	.10	.05
457	Mark Gardner	.10	.05
458	Rick Wilkins	.10	.05
459	Scott Sanders	.10	.05
460	Kevin Orie	.20	.09
461	Glendon Rusch	.10	.05
462	Juan Melo	.20	.09
463	Richie Sexson	.20	.09
464	Bartolo Colon	.20	.09
465	Jose Guillen	.50	.23
466	Heath Murray	.10	.05
467	Aaron Boone	.10	.05
468	Bubba Trammell	.40	.18
469	Jeff Abbott	.10	.05
470	Derrick Gibson	.30	.14
471	Matt Morris	.20	.09
472	Ryan Jones	.10	.05
473	Pat Cline	.10	.05
474	Adam Riggs	.10	.05
475	Jay Payton	.10	.05
476	Derrek Lee	.30	.14
477	Eli Marrero	.10	.05
478	Lee Tinsley	.10	.05
479	Jamie Moyer	.10	.05
480	Jay Buhner	.30	.14
481	Bob Wells	.10	.05
482	Jeff Fassero	.10	.05
483	Paul Sorrento	.10	.05
484	Russ Davis	.10	.05
485	Randy Johnson	.40	.18
486	Roger Pavlik	.10	.05
487	Damon Buford	.10	.05
488	Julio Santana	.10	.05
489	Mark McLemore	.10	.05
490	Mickey Tettleton	.10	.05
491	Ken Hill	.10	.05
492	Benji Gil	.10	.05
493	Ed Sprague	.10	.05
494	Mike Timlin	.10	.05
495	Pat Hentgen	.20	.09
496	Orlando Merced	.10	.05
497	Carlos Garcia	.10	.05
498	Carlos Delgado	.20	.09
499	Juan Guzman	.10	.05
500	Roger Clemens	.75	.35
501	Erik Hanson	.10	.05
502	Otis Nixon	.10	.05
503	Shawn Green	.10	.05
504	Charlie O'Brien	.10	.05

☐ 505	Joe Carter	.20	.09	☐ 44	Javy Lopez	.20	.09
☐ 506	Alex Gonzalez	.10	.05	☐ 45	Hideo Nomo	1.00	.45

1997 Collector's Choice All-Star Connection

Inserted one in every series two packs, this 45-card set celebrates the unique history of Baseball's All Star Game and highlights the League's top All-Star caliber players. The fronts feature color player cut-outs on a big star background.

		MINT	NRMT
COMPLETE SET (45)		12.00	5.50
COMMON CARD		.10	.05
SER.2 ODDS 1:1 HOBBY, 2:1 RETAIL			

		MINT	NRMT
☐ 1	Mark McGwire	.75	.35
☐ 2	Chuck Knoblauch	.40	.18
☐ 3	Jim Thome	.40	.18
☐ 4	Alex Rodriguez	1.25	.55
☐ 5	Ken Griffey Jr.	2.00	.90
☐ 6	Brady Anderson	.30	.14
☐ 7	Albert Belle	.50	.23
☐ 8	Ivan Rodriguez	.50	.23
☐ 9	Pat Hentgen	.20	.09
☐ 10	Frank Thomas	1.50	.70
☐ 11	Roberto Alomar	.40	.18
☐ 12	Robin Ventura	.20	.09
☐ 13	Cal Ripken	1.50	.70
☐ 14	Juan Gonzalez	1.00	.45
☐ 15	Manny Ramirez	.40	.18
☐ 16	Bernie Williams	.40	.18
☐ 17	Terry Steinbach	.10	.05
☐ 18	Andy Pettitte	.40	.18
☐ 19	Jeff Bagwell	.75	.35
☐ 20	Craig Biggio	.30	.14
☐ 21	Ken Caminiti	.30	.14
☐ 22	Barry Larkin	.30	.14
☐ 23	Tony Gwynn	1.00	.45
☐ 24	Barry Bonds	.50	.23
☐ 25	Kenny Lofton	.50	.23
☐ 26	Mike Piazza	1.25	.55
☐ 27	John Smoltz	.20	.09
☐ 28	Andres Galarraga	.40	.18
☐ 29	Ryne Sandberg	.50	.23
☐ 30	Chipper Jones	1.25	.55
☐ 31	Mark Grudzielanek	.10	.05
☐ 32	Sammy Sosa	.40	.18
☐ 33	Steve Finley	.20	.09
☐ 34	Gary Sheffield	.40	.18
☐ 35	Todd Hundley	.20	.09
☐ 36	Greg Maddux	1.25	.55
☐ 37	Mo Vaughn	.40	.18
☐ 38	Eric Young	.10	.05
☐ 39	Vinny Castilla	.20	.09
☐ 40	Derek Jeter	1.25	.55
☐ 41	Lance Johnson	.10	.05
☐ 42	Ellis Burks	.20	.09
☐ 43	Dante Bichette	.20	.09

1997 Collector's Choice Big Shots

Randomly inserted in series two packs at the rate of one in 12, this 19-card set features unique and exciting photos depicting some of the game's most recognized players.

		MINT	NRMT
COMPLETE SET (19)		60.00	27.00
COMMON CARD		1.00	.45
SER.2 STATED ODDS 1:12			
COMP.GOLD SET (20)		250.00	110.00
*GOLD CARDS: 2X TO 4X BASE CARD HI			
SER.2 GOLD STATED ODDS 1:144			

		MINT	NRMT
☐ 1	Ken Griffey Jr.	10.00	4.50
☐ 2	Nomar Garciaparra	6.00	2.70
☐ 3	Brian Jordan	1.00	.45
☐ 4	Scott Rolen	5.00	2.20
☐ 5	Alex Rodriguez	8.00	3.60
☐ 6	Larry Walker	2.00	.90
☐ 7	Mariano Rivera	1.00	.45
☐ 8	Cal Ripken	8.00	3.60
☐ 9	Deion Sanders	1.00	.45
☐ 10	Frank Thomas	8.00	3.60
☐ 11	Dean Palmer	1.00	.45
☐ 12	Ken Caminiti	1.50	.70
☐ 13	Derek Jeter	6.00	2.70
☐ 14	Barry Bonds	2.50	1.10
☐ 15	Chipper Jones	6.00	2.70
☐ 16	Mo Vaughn	2.50	1.10
☐ 17	Jay Buhner	1.50	.70
☐ 18	Mike Piazza	6.00	2.70
☐ 19	Tony Gwynn	5.00	2.20

1997 Collector's Choice The Big Show

Inserted one in every first series pack, cards from this 45-card set feature color photos of some of the hottest players in baseball. The backs carry comments about the pictured player by ESPN SportsCenter television sportscasters, Keith Olbermann and Dan Patrick.

		MINT	NRMT
COMPLETE SET (45)		10.00	4.50
COMMON CARD (1-45)		.20	.09
SER.1 STATED ODDS 1:1			
COMP.WORLD HQ SET (45)		250.00	110.00
*WHQ STARS: 20X TO 40X BASE CARD HI			
WHQ SER.1 STATED ODDS 1:35			

		MINT	NRMT
☐ 1	Greg Maddux	1.25	.55
☐ 2	Chipper Jones	1.25	.55
☐ 3	Andruw Jones	1.00	.45
☐ 4	John Smoltz	.20	.09
☐ 5	Cal Ripken	1.50	.70
☐ 6	Roberto Alomar	.40	.18
☐ 7	Rafael Palmeiro	.30	.14
☐ 8	Eddie Murray	.40	.18
☐ 9	Jose Canseco	.30	.14
☐ 10	Roger Clemens	.75	.35
☐ 11	Mo Vaughn	.50	.23
☐ 12	Jim Edmonds	.30	.14
☐ 13	Tim Salmon	.40	.18
☐ 14	Sammy Sosa	.40	.18
☐ 15	Albert Belle	.50	.23
☐ 16	Frank Thomas	1.50	.70
☐ 17	Barry Larkin	.30	.14
☐ 18	Kenny Lofton	.50	.23
☐ 19	Manny Ramirez	.40	.18
☐ 20	Matt Williams	.30	.14
☐ 21	Dante Bichette	.20	.09
☐ 22	Gary Sheffield	.40	.18
☐ 23	Craig Biggio	.30	.14
☐ 24	Jeff Bagwell	.75	.35
☐ 25	Todd Hollandsworth	.10	.05
☐ 26	Raul Mondesi	.30	.14
☐ 27	Hideo Nomo	1.00	.45
☐ 28	Mike Piazza	1.25	.55
☐ 29	Paul Molitor	.40	.18
☐ 30	Kirby Puckett	.75	.35
☐ 31	Rondell White	.20	.09
☐ 32	Rey Ordonez	.10	.05
☐ 33	Paul Wilson	.10	.05
☐ 34	Derek Jeter	1.25	.55
☐ 35	Andy Pettitte	.40	.18
☐ 36	Mark McGwire	.75	.35
☐ 37	Jason Kendall	.20	.09
☐ 38	Ozzie Smith	.50	.23
☐ 39	Tony Gwynn	1.00	.45
☐ 40	Barry Bonds	.50	.23
☐ 41	Alex Rodriguez	1.25	.55
☐ 42	Jay Buhner	.30	.14
☐ 43	Ken Griffey Jr.	2.00	.90
☐ 44	Randy Johnson	.40	.18
☐ 45	Juan Gonzalez	1.00	.45

1997 Collector's Choice Crash the Game

Inserted in series two packs at the rate of one in five, cards from this interactive game set features three separate cards each of 30 top home run hitters. If the featured player hit a home run during the series specified on the card, the card could than have been redeemed for a special card of the same player. The postmark expiration date for exchanging winning cards was December 1, 1997.

	MINT	NRMT
COMPLETE SET (90)	60.00	27.00
COMMON CARD	.25	.11
SER.2 STATED ODDS 1:5		

*INSTANT WIN: 10X TO 20X BASE CARD HI
INSTANT WIN SER.2 STATED ODDS 1:721

		MINT	NRMT
☐ 1A	R.Klesko July 28-30 L .50		.23
☐ 1B	R.Klesko Aug 8-11 L .50		.23
☐ 1C	R.Klesko Sept 19-21 L .50		.23
☐ 2A	C.Jones Aug 15-17 L 2.50		1.10
☐ 2B	C.Jones Aug 29-31 L 2.50		1.10
☐ 2C	C.Jones Sept 12-14 L 2.50		1.10
☐ 3A	Andruw Jones Aug 22-24 W 2.00		.90
☐ 3B	Andruw Jones Sept 1-3 2.00		.90
☐ 3C	A.Jones Sept 19-22 L 2.00		.90
☐ 4A	B.Anderson July 31-Aug 3 W .50		.23
☐ 4B	B.Anderson Sept 4-7 L .50		.23
☐ 4C	B.Anderson Sept 19-22 L .50		.23
☐ 5A	R.Palmeiro July 29-30 L .50		.23
☐ 5B	R.Palmeiro Aug 29-31 L .50		.23
☐ 5C	R.Palmeiro Sept 26-28 L .50		.23
☐ 6A	Cal Ripken Aug 8-10 3.00		1.35
☐ 6B	C.Ripken Sept 1-3 L 3.00		1.35
☐ 6C	C.Ripken Sept 11-14 L 3.00		1.35
☐ 7A	M.Vaughn Aug 14-17 L 1.00		.45
☐ 7B	M.Vaughn Aug 29-31 W 1.00		.45
☐ 7C	M.Vaughn Sept 23-25 W 1.00		.45
☐ 8A	S.Sosa Aug 1-3 W .75		.35
☐ 8B	S.Sosa Aug 29-31 L .75		.35
☐ 8C	S.Sosa Sept 19-21 W .75		.35
☐ 9A	A.Belle Aug 7-10 L 1.00		.45
☐ 9B	A.Belle Sept 11-14 L 1.00		.45
☐ 9C	A.Belle Sept 19-21 W 1.00		.45
☐ 10A	F.Thomas Aug 29-31 3.00		1.35
☐ 10B	F.Thomas Sept 1-3 L 3.00		1.35
☐ 10C	F.Thomas Sept 23-25 W 3.00		1.35
☐ 11A	M.Ramirez Aug 12-14 W .75		.35
☐ 11B	M.Ramirez Aug 29-31 L .75		.35
☐ 11C	M.Ramirez Sept 11-14 W .75		.35
☐ 12A	J.Thome July 28-30 L .75		.35
☐ 12B	J.Thome Sept 15-18 W .75		.35
☐ 12C	J.Thome Sept 19-22 L .75		.35
☐ 13A	M.Williams Aug 4-5 L .50		.23
☐ 13B	M.Williams Sept 1-3 W .50		.23
☐ 13C	M.Williams Sept 23-25 L .50		.23
☐ 14A	D.Bichette July 24-27 W .25		.11
☐ 14B	D.Bichette Aug 28-29 L .25		.11
☐ 14C	D.Bichette Sept 26-28 W .25		.11
☐ 15A	V.Castilla Aug 12-13 L .25		.11
☐ 15B	V.Castilla Sept 4-7 W .25		.11
☐ 15C	V.Castilla Sept 19-21 L .25		.11
☐ 16A	A.Galarraga Aug 8-10 W .75		.35
☐ 16B	A.Galarraga Aug 30-31 L .75		.35
☐ 16C	A.Galarraga Sept 12-14 L .75		.35
☐ 17A	G.Sheffield Aug 1-3 W .75		.35
☐ 17B	G.Sheffield Sept 1-3 W .75		.35
☐ 17C	G.Sheffield Sept 12-14 W .75		.35
☐ 18A	J.Bagwell Sept 9-10 L 1.50		.70
☐ 18B	J.Bagwell Sept 19-22 W 1.50		.70
☐ 18C	J.Bagwell Sept 23-25 W 1.50		.70
☐ 19A	E.Karros Aug 1-3 L .25		.11
☐ 19B	E.Karros Sept 15-17 L .25		.11
☐ 19C	E.Karros Sept 25-28 W .25		.11
☐ 20A	M.Piazza Aug 11-12 L 2.50		1.10
☐ 20B	M.Piazza Sept 5-8 W 2.50		1.10
☐ 20C	M.Piazza Sept 19-21 W 2.50		1.10
☐ 21A	V.Guerrero Aug 22-24 L 1.50		.70
☐ 21B	V.Guerrero Aug 29-31 L 1.50		.70
☐ 21C	V.Guerrero Sept 19-22 L 1.50		.70
☐ 22A	C.Fielder Aug 29-31 L .25		.11
☐ 22B	C.Fielder Sept 1-3 L .25		.11
☐ 22C	C.Fielder Sept 26-28 L .25		.11
☐ 23A	J.Canseco Sept 12-14 L .50		.23
☐ 23B	J.Canseco Sept 22-24 L .50		.23
☐ 23C	J.Canseco Sept 26-28 L .50		.23
☐ 24A	M.McGwire July 31-Aug 3 L 1.50		.70
☐ 24B	M.McGwire Aug 30-31 L 1.50		.70
☐ 24C	M.McGwire Sept 19-22 W 1.50		.70
☐ 25A	K.Caminiti Aug 8-10 L .50		.23
☐ 25B	K.Caminiti Sept 4-7 W .50		.23
☐ 25C	K.Caminiti Sept 17-18 W .50		.23
☐ 26A	B.Bonds Aug 5-7 L 1.00		.45
☐ 26B	B.Bonds Sept 4-7 L 1.00		.45
☐ 26C	B.Bonds Sept 23-24 W 1.00		.45
☐ 27A	J.Buhner Aug 7-10 L .50		.23
☐ 27B	J.Buhner Aug 28-29 L .50		.23
☐ 27C	J.Buhner Sept 1-3 L .50		.23
☐ 28A	K.Griffey Jr. Aug 22-24 W 4.00		1.80
☐ 28B	K.Griffey Aug 28-29 L 4.00		1.80
☐ 28C	K.Griffey Sept 19-22 W 4.00		1.80
☐ 29A	A.Rodriguez July 29-31 L 2.50		1.10
☐ 29B	A.Rodriguez Aug 30-31 L 2.50		1.10
☐ 29C	A.Rodriguez Sept 12-15 L 2.50		1.10
☐ 30A	J.Gonzalez Aug 11-13 W 2.00		.90
☐ 30B	J.Gonzalez Aug 30-31 L 2.00		.90
☐ 30C	J.Gonzalez Sept 19-21 W 2.00		.90

1997 Collector's Choice Crash the Game Exchange

This 30-card set was redeemable two ways through the Crash the Game contest. Each player hitting a home run during the dates specified on the card was exchangeable for an upgraded version of that same player. However, only 22 of the players were winners. The remaining eight short-printed cards were only available with a Crash the Game Instant Win card (inserted 1:721 packs), which was redeemable for a complete 30-card upgraded set.

	MINT	NRMT
COMPLETE SET (30)	120.00	55.00
COMMON CARD (CG1-CG30)	1.00	.45

*EXCH.WINNERS: 3X TO 6X BASE CARD HI
ONE CARD VIA MAIL PER CRASH WINNER
ONE SET VIA MAIL PER INSTANT WIN CARD
SP's AVAIL.ONLY W/INSTANT WIN EXCH.

☐ CG1	Ryan Klesko Jr.	6.00	2.70
☐ CG2	Chipper Jones SP	30.00	13.50
☐ CG3	Andruw Jones	5.00	2.20
☐ CG4	Brady Anderson	1.50	.70
☐ CG5	Rafael Palmeiro SP	6.00	2.70
☐ CG6	Cal Ripken Jr.	10.00	4.50
☐ CG7	Mo Vaughn	3.00	1.35
☐ CG8	Sammy Sosa	2.00	.90
☐ CG9	Albert Belle	3.00	1.35
☐ CG10	Frank Thomas	10.00	4.50
☐ CG11	Manny Ramirez	2.50	1.10
☐ CG12	Jim Thome	2.50	1.10
☐ CG13	Matt Williams	1.50	.70
☐ CG14	Dante Bichette	1.00	.45
☐ CG15	Vinny Castilla	1.00	.45
☐ CG16	Andres Galarraga	2.00	.90
☐ CG17	Gary Sheffield	2.00	.90
☐ CG18	Jeff Bagwell	5.00	2.20
☐ CG19	Eric Karros	1.00	.45
☐ CG20	Mike Piazza	8.00	3.60
☐ CG21	Vladimir Guerrero SP	15.00	6.75
☐ CG22	Cecil Fielder SP	4.00	1.80
☐ CG23	Jose Canseco SP	6.00	2.70
☐ CG24	Mark McGwire	5.00	2.20
☐ CG25	Ken Caminiti	1.50	.70
☐ CG26	Barry Bonds	3.00	1.35
☐ CG27	Jay Buhner SP	6.00	2.70
☐ CG28	Ken Griffey Jr.	12.00	5.50
☐ CG29	Alex Rodriguez SP	30.00	13.50
☐ CG30	Juan Gonzalez	6.00	2.70

1997 Collector's Choice New Frontier

Randomly inserted one in every 69 series two packs, this 40-card set showcases the most anticipated InterLeague match-ups. Each card features a color player cut-out of a great player from either the American or National League on half of a baseball diamond background and is designed to fit with another card displaying a great player match-up from the opposite league to complete the diamond.

	MINT	NRMT
COMPLETE SET (40)	450.00	200.00
COMMON CARD (NF1-NF40)	4.00	1.80
UNLISTED STARS	8.00	3.60
SER.2 STATED ODDS 1:69		

☐ NF1	Alex Rodriguez	25.00	11.00
☐ NF2	Tony Gwynn	20.00	9.00
☐ NF3	Jose Canseco	5.00	2.20
☐ NF4	Hideo Nomo	15.00	6.75
☐ NF5	Mark McGwire	15.00	6.75
☐ NF6	Barry Bonds	10.00	4.50
☐ NF7	Juan Gonzalez	20.00	9.00
☐ NF8	Ken Caminiti	5.00	2.20
☐ NF9	Tim Salmon	8.00	3.60
☐ NF10	Mike Piazza	25.00	11.00
☐ NF11	Ken Griffey Jr.	40.00	18.00
☐ NF12	Andres Galarraga	8.00	3.60
☐ NF13	Jay Buhner	5.00	2.20
☐ NF14	Dante Bichette	4.00	1.80
☐ NF15	Frank Thomas	30.00	13.50
☐ NF16	Ryne Sandberg	10.00	4.50

		MINT	NRMT
☐	NF17 Roger Clemens	15.00	6.75
☐	NF18 Andruw Jones	20.00	9.00
☐	NF19 Jim Thome	8.00	3.60
☐	NF20 Sammy Sosa	8.00	3.60
☐	NF21 Dave Justice	4.00	1.80
☐	NF22 Deion Sanders	4.00	1.80
☐	NF23 Todd Walker	4.00	1.80
☐	NF24 Kevin Orie	4.00	1.80
☐	NF25 Albert Belle	10.00	4.50
☐	NF26 Jeff Bagwell	15.00	6.75
☐	NF27 Manny Ramirez	8.00	3.60
☐	NF28 Brian Jordan	4.00	1.80
☐	NF29 Derek Jeter	20.00	9.00
☐	NF30 Chipper Jones	25.00	11.00
☐	NF31 Mo Vaughn	10.00	4.50
☐	NF32 Gary Sheffield	8.00	3.60
☐	NF33 Carlos Delgado	4.00	1.80
☐	NF34 Vladimir Guerrero	30.00	13.50
☐	NF35 Cal Ripken	30.00	13.50
☐	NF36 Greg Maddux	25.00	11.00
☐	NF37 Cecil Fielder	4.00	1.80
☐	NF38 Todd Hundley	4.00	1.80
☐	NF39 Mike Mussina	8.00	3.60
☐	NF40 Scott Rolen	20.00	9.00

1997 Collector's Choice Premier Power

Randomly inserted in first series packs at a rate of one in 15, this silver version 20-card set features borderless color action player photos and information about the 20 top Major League Home Run hitters.

	MINT	NRMT
COMPLETE SET (20)	40.00	18.00
COMMON CARD (PP1-PP20)	1.00	.45
SER.1 STATED ODDS 1:15		
COMP.GOLD SET (20)	150.00	70.00
*GOLD STARS: 7.5X TO 15X BASE CARD HI		
GOLD SER.1 STATED ODDS 1:69		

☐	PP1 Mark McGwire	4.00	1.80
☐	PP2 Brady Anderson	1.50	.70
☐	PP3 Ken Griffey Jr.	10.00	4.50
☐	PP4 Albert Belle	2.50	1.10
☐	PP5 Juan Gonzalez	5.00	2.20
☐	PP6 Andres Galarraga	2.00	.90
☐	PP7 Jay Buhner	1.50	.70
☐	PP8 Mo Vaughn	2.00	.90
☐	PP9 Barry Bonds	2.50	1.10
☐	PP10 Gary Sheffield	2.00	.90
☐	PP11 Todd Hundley	1.00	.45
☐	PP12 Frank Thomas	8.00	3.60
☐	PP13 Sammy Sosa	2.00	.90
☐	PP14 Ken Caminiti	1.50	.70
☐	PP15 Vinny Castilla	1.00	.45
☐	PP16 Ellis Burks	1.00	.45
☐	PP17 Rafael Palmeiro	1.50	.70
☐	PP18 Alex Rodriguez	6.00	2.70
☐	PP19 Mike Piazza	6.00	2.70
☐	PP20 Eddie Murray	2.00	.90

1997 Collector's Choice Stick'Ums

Randomly inserted in first series packs at a rate of one in three, cards from this 30-card set features color sticker images of star players. These interactive reusable stickers could be used to create mini baseball scenes.

	MINT	NRMT
COMPLETE SET (30)	15.00	6.75
COMMON CARD (1-30)	.40	.18
SER.1 STATED ODDS 1:3		

☐	1 Ozzie Smith	.75	.35
☐	2 Andruw Jones	1.50	.70
☐	3 Alex Rodriguez	2.00	.90
☐	4 Paul Molitor	.60	.25
☐	5 Jeff Bagwell	1.25	.55
☐	6 Manny Ramirez	.60	.25
☐	7 Kenny Lofton	.75	.35
☐	8 Albert Belle	.75	.35
☐	9 Jay Buhner	.40	.18
☐	10 Chipper Jones	2.00	.90
☐	11 Barry Larkin	.40	.18
☐	12 Dante Bichette	.25	.11
☐	13 Mike Piazza	2.00	.90
☐	14 Andres Galarraga	.60	.25
☐	15 Barry Bonds	.75	.35
☐	16 Brady Anderson	.40	.18
☐	17 Gary Sheffield	.60	.25
☐	18 Jim Thome	.75	.35
☐	19 Tony Gwynn	1.25	.55
☐	20 Cal Ripken	2.50	1.10
☐	21 Sammy Sosa	.60	.25
☐	22 Juan Gonzalez	1.50	.70
☐	23 Greg Maddux	2.00	.90
☐	24 Ken Griffey Jr.	3.00	1.35
☐	25 Mark McGwire	1.25	.55
☐	26 Kirby Puckett	1.25	.55
☐	27 Mo Vaughn	.75	.35
☐	28 Vladimir Guerrero	1.25	.55
☐	29 Ken Caminiti	.40	.18
☐	30 Frank Thomas	2.50	1.10

1997 Collector's Choice Toast of the Town

Randomly inserted in series two packs at the rate of one in 35, this 30-card set features color photos of some of the best Major League players printed on premium, foil enhanced card stock.

	MINT	NRMT
COMPLETE SET (30)	250.00	110.00
COMMON CARD (T1-T30)	2.50	1.10
UNLISTED STARS	5.00	2.20
SER.2 STATED ODDS 1:35		

☐	T1 Andruw Jones	12.00	5.50
☐	T2 Chipper Jones	15.00	6.75
☐	T3 Greg Maddux	15.00	6.75
☐	T4 John Smoltz	2.50	1.10
☐	T5 Kenny Lofton	6.00	2.70
☐	T6 Brady Anderson	4.00	1.80
☐	T7 Cal Ripken	20.00	9.00
☐	T8 Mo Vaughn	6.00	2.70
☐	T9 Sammy Sosa	5.00	2.20
☐	T10 Albert Belle	6.00	2.70
☐	T11 Frank Thomas	20.00	9.00
☐	T12 Barry Larkin	4.00	1.80
☐	T13 Manny Ramirez	5.00	2.20
☐	T14 Jeff Bagwell	10.00	4.50
☐	T15 Mike Piazza	15.00	6.75
☐	T16 Paul Molitor	5.00	2.20
☐	T17 Vladimir Guerrero	10.00	4.50
☐	T18 Todd Hundley	2.50	1.10
☐	T19 Derek Jeter	12.00	5.50
☐	T20 Andy Pettitte	5.00	2.20
☐	T21 Bernie Williams	5.00	2.20
☐	T22 Mark McGwire	10.00	4.50
☐	T23 Scott Rolen	12.00	5.50
☐	T24 Ken Caminiti	4.00	1.80
☐	T25 Tony Gwynn	12.00	5.50
☐	T26 Barry Bonds	6.00	2.70
☐	T27 Ken Griffey Jr.	25.00	11.00
☐	T28 Alex Rodriguez	15.00	6.75
☐	T29 Juan Gonzalez	12.00	5.50
☐	T30 Roger Clemens	10.00	4.50

1997 Collector's Choice Update

This 30-card Update set was made available to collectors who mailed in 10 series two wrappers (plus a check or money order for $3 to cover postage and handling) prior to the December 1st, 1997 deadline. The cards share the same design as the basic issue 1997 Collector's Choice set and content focuses on traded veterans pictured in their new uniforms and a handful of prospects called up during the season

(including Jose Cruz Jr. and Hideki Irabu).

	MINT	NRMT
COMPLETE SET (30)	6.00	2.70
COMMON CARD (U1-U30)	.10	.05
MINOR STARS	.20	.09
UNLISTED STARS	.40	.18

ONE SET VIA MAIL PER 10 SER.2 WRAPPERS
EXCH.DEADLINE: 12/1/97

		MINT	NRMT
☐ U1	Jim Leyritz	.10	.05
☐ U2	Matt Perisho	.10	.05
☐ U3	Michael Tucker	.20	.09
☐ U4	Mike Johnson	.20	.09
☐ U5	Jaime Navarro	.20	.09
☐ U6	Doug Drabek	.10	.05
☐ U7	Terry Mulholland	.10	.05
☐ U8	Brett Tomko	.20	.09
☐ U9	Marquis Grissom	.20	.09
☐ U10	David Justice	.40	.18
☐ U11	Brian Moehler	.20	.09
☐ U12	Bobby Bonilla	.20	.09
☐ U13	Todd Dunwoody	.30	.14
☐ U14	Tony Saunders	.30	.14
☐ U15	Jay Bell	.20	.09
☐ U16	Jeff King	.10	.05
☐ U17	Terry Steinbach	.10	.05
☐ U18	Steve Bieser	.10	.05
☐ U19	Takashi Kashiwada	.25	.11
☐ U20	Hideki Irabu	.50	.23
☐ U21	Damon Mashore	.10	.05
☐ U22	Quilvio Veras	.20	.09
☐ U23	Will Cunnane	.10	.05
☐ U24	Jeff Kent	.10	.05
☐ U25	J.T. Snow	.20	.09
☐ U26	Dante Powell	.10	.05
☐ U27	Jose Cruz Jr.	4.00	1.80
☐ U28	John Burkett	.10	.05
☐ U29	John Wetteland	.10	.05
☐ U30	Benito Santiago	.10	.05

1998 Collector's Choice

The 1998 Collector's Choice first series was issued with a total of 265 cards and was distributed in 14-card packs with a suggested retail price of $1.29. The fronts feature color action player photos. The backs carry player information. The set contains the topical subsets: Cover Glory (1-18), Rookie Class (100-126), Masked Marauders (181-189), and Top of the Charts (253-261).

	MINT	NRMT
COMPLETE SERIES 1 (265)	18.00	8.00
COMMON CARD (1-265)	.10	.05
MINOR STARS	.20	.09
UNLISTED STARS	.40	.18

☐ 1	Nomar Garciaparra CG	.60	.25
☐ 2	Roger Clemens CG	.40	.18
☐ 3	Larry Walker CG	.20	.09
☐ 4	Mike Piazza CG	.60	.25
☐ 5	Mark McGwire CG	.50	.23
☐ 6	Tony Gwynn CG	.50	.23
☐ 7	Jose Cruz Jr. CG	.75	.35
☐ 8	Frank Thomas CG	.75	.35
☐ 9	Tino Martinez CG	.20	.09
☐ 10	Ken Griffey Jr. CG	1.00	.45
☐ 11	Barry Bonds CG	.30	.14
☐ 12	Scott Rolen CG	.50	.23
☐ 13	Randy Johnson CG	.20	.09
☐ 14	Ryne Sandberg CG	.30	.14
☐ 15	Eddie Murray CG	.20	.09
☐ 16	Kevin Brown CG	.10	.05
☐ 17	Mike Mussina CG	.20	.09
☐ 18	Sandy Alomar Jr. CG	.10	.05
☐ 19	Ken Griffey Jr. CL	.20	.09
	Adam Riggs		
☐ 20	Nomar Garciaparra CL	.20	.09
	Charlie O'Brien		
☐ 21	Ben Grieve CL	.20	.09
	Frank Thomas		
	Tony Gwynn		
☐ 22	Mark McGwire CL	.20	.09
	Cal Ripken		
☐ 23	Tino Martinez CL	.10	.05
☐ 24	Jason Dickson	.20	.09
☐ 25	Darin Erstad	.50	.23
☐ 26	Todd Greene	.20	.09
☐ 27	Chuck Finley	.10	.05
☐ 28	Garret Anderson	.20	.09
☐ 29	Dave Hollins	.10	.05
☐ 30	Rickey Henderson	.30	.14
☐ 31	John Smoltz	.20	.09
☐ 32	Michael Tucker	.20	.09
☐ 33	Jeff Blauser	.20	.09
☐ 34	Javier Lopez	.20	.09
☐ 35	Andruw Jones	.75	.35
☐ 36	Denny Neagle	.20	.09
☐ 37	Randall Simon	.10	.05
☐ 38	Mark Wohlers	.10	.05
☐ 39	Harold Baines	.20	.09
☐ 40	Cal Ripken	1.50	.70
☐ 41	Mike Bordick	.10	.05
☐ 42	Jimmy Key	.10	.05
☐ 43	Armando Benitez	.10	.05
☐ 44	Scott Erickson	.10	.05
☐ 45	Eric Davis	.20	.09
☐ 46	Bret Saberhagen	.10	.05
☐ 47	Darren Bragg	.10	.05
☐ 48	Steve Avery	.10	.05
☐ 49	Jeff Frye	.10	.05
☐ 50	Aaron Sele	.10	.05
☐ 51	Scott Hatteberg	.10	.05
☐ 52	Tom Gordon	.10	.05
☐ 53	Kevin Orie	.20	.09
☐ 54	Kevin Foster	.10	.05
☐ 55	Ryne Sandberg	.50	.23
☐ 56	Doug Glanville	.10	.05
☐ 57	Tyler Houston	.10	.05
☐ 58	Steve Trachsel	.10	.05
☐ 59	Mark Grace	.30	.14
☐ 60	Frank Thomas	1.50	.70
☐ 61	Scott Eyre	.10	.05
☐ 62	Jeff Abbott	.10	.05
☐ 63	Chris Clemons	.10	.05
☐ 64	Jorge Fabregas	.10	.05
☐ 65	Robin Ventura	.20	.09
☐ 66	Matt Karchner	.10	.05
☐ 67	Jon Nunnally	.10	.05
☐ 68	Aaron Boone	.10	.05
☐ 69	Pokey Reese	.10	.05
☐ 70	Deion Sanders	.20	.09
☐ 71	Jeff Shaw	.10	.05
☐ 72	Eduardo Perez	.10	.05
☐ 73	Brett Tomko	.20	.09
☐ 74	Bartolo Colon	.20	.09
☐ 75	Manny Ramirez	.40	.18
☐ 76	Jose Mesa	.10	.05
☐ 77	Brian Giles	.20	.09
☐ 78	Richie Sexson	.20	.09
☐ 79	Orel Hershiser	.10	.05
☐ 80	Matt Williams	.30	.14
☐ 81	Walt Weiss	.10	.05

☐ 82	Jerry DiPoto	.10	.05
☐ 83	Quinton McCracken	.10	.05
☐ 84	Neifi Perez	.20	.09
☐ 85	Vinny Castilla	.20	.09
☐ 86	Ellis Burks	.20	.09
☐ 87	John Thomson	.10	.05
☐ 88	Willie Blair	.10	.05
☐ 89	Bob Hamelin	.10	.05
☐ 90	Tony Clark	.40	.18
☐ 91	Todd Jones	.10	.05
☐ 92	Deivi Cruz	.10	.05
☐ 93	Frank Catalanotto	.25	.11
☐ 94	Justin Thompson	.20	.09
☐ 95	Gary Sheffield	.40	.18
☐ 96	Kevin Brown	.20	.09
☐ 97	Charles Johnson	.20	.09
☐ 98	Bobby Bonilla	.20	.09
☐ 99	Livan Hernandez	.30	.14
☐ 100	Paul Konerko	.60	.25
☐ 101	Craig Counsell	.10	.05
☐ 102	Magglio Ordonez	.50	.23
☐ 103	Garrett Stephenson	.10	.05
☐ 104	Ken Cloude	.20	.09
☐ 105	Miguel Tejada	.50	.23
☐ 106	Juan Encarnacion	.40	.18
☐ 107	Dennis Reyes	.20	.09
☐ 108	Orlando Cabrera	.20	.09
☐ 109	Kelvim Escobar	.10	.05
☐ 110	Ben Grieve	.75	.35
☐ 111	Brian Rose	.30	.14
☐ 112	Fernando Tatis	.40	.18
☐ 113	Tom Evans	.20	.09
☐ 114	Tom Fordham	.10	.05
☐ 115	Mark Kotsay	.40	.18
☐ 116	Mario Valdez	.20	.09
☐ 117	Jeremi Gonzalez	.20	.09
☐ 118	Todd Dunwoody	.20	.09
☐ 119	Javier Valentin	.20	.09
☐ 120	Todd Helton	.50	.23
☐ 121	Jason Varitek	.20	.09
☐ 122	Chris Carpenter	.10	.05
☐ 123	Kevin Millwood	.40	.18
☐ 124	Brad Fullmer	.20	.09
☐ 125	Jaret Wright	1.00	.45
☐ 126	Brad Rigby	.10	.05
☐ 127	Edgar Renteria	.20	.09
☐ 128	Robb Nen	.10	.05
☐ 129	Tony Pena	.10	.05
☐ 130	Craig Biggio	.30	.14
☐ 131	Brad Ausmus	.10	.05
☐ 132	Shane Reynolds	.10	.05
☐ 133	Mike Hampton	.20	.09
☐ 134	Billy Wagner	.20	.09
☐ 135	Richard Hidalgo	.20	.09
☐ 136	Jose Rosado	.10	.05
☐ 137	Yamil Benitez	.10	.05
☐ 138	Felix Martinez	.10	.05
☐ 139	Jeff King	.10	.05
☐ 140	Jose Offerman	.10	.05
☐ 141	Joe Vitiello	.10	.05
☐ 142	Tim Belcher	.10	.05
☐ 143	Brett Butler	.20	.09
☐ 144	Greg Gagne	.10	.05
☐ 145	Mike Piazza	1.25	.55
☐ 146	Ramon Martinez	.20	.09
☐ 147	Raul Mondesi	.30	.14
☐ 148	Adam Riggs	.10	.05
☐ 149	Eddie Murray	.40	.18
☐ 150	Jeff Cirillo	.20	.09
☐ 151	Scott Karl	.10	.05
☐ 152	Mike Fetters	.10	.05
☐ 153	Dave Nilsson	.20	.09
☐ 154	Antone Williamson	.10	.05
☐ 155	Jeff D'Amico	.20	.09
☐ 156	Jose Valentin	.20	.09
☐ 157	Brad Radke	.20	.09
☐ 158	Torii Hunter	.20	.09
☐ 159	Chuck Knoblauch	.40	.18
☐ 160	Paul Molitor	.40	.18
☐ 161	Travis Miller	.10	.05
☐ 162	Rich Robertson	.10	.05
☐ 163	Ron Coomer	.10	.05
☐ 164	Mark Grudzielanek	.10	.05
☐ 165	Lee Smith	.20	.09
☐ 166	Vladimir Guerrero	.60	.25
☐ 167	Dustin Hermanson	.10	.05

☐ 168	Ugueth Urbina	.10	.05
☐ 169	F.P. Santangelo	.10	.05
☐ 170	Rondell White	.20	.09
☐ 171	Bobby Jones	.10	.05
☐ 172	Edgardo Alfonzo	.20	.09
☐ 173	John Franco	.20	.09
☐ 174	Carlos Baerga	.10	.05
☐ 175	Butch Huskey	.10	.05
☐ 176	Rey Ordonez	.10	.05
☐ 177	Matt Franco	.10	.05
☐ 178	Dwight Gooden	.20	.09
☐ 179	Chad Curtis	.10	.05
☐ 180	Tino Martinez	.40	.18
☐ 181	Charlie O'Brien MM	.10	.05
☐ 182	Sandy Alomar Jr. MM	.10	.05
☐ 183	Raul Casanova MM	.10	.05
☐ 184	Javier Lopez MM	.10	.05
☐ 185	Mike Piazza MM	.60	.25
☐ 186	Ivan Rodriguez MM	.30	.14
☐ 187	Charles Johnson MM	.10	.05
☐ 188	Brad Ausmus MM	.10	.05
☐ 189	Brian Johnson MM	.10	.05
☐ 190	Wade Boggs	.40	.18
☐ 191	David Wells	.10	.05
☐ 192	Tim Raines	.20	.09
☐ 193	Ramiro Mendoza	.20	.09
☐ 194	Willie Adams	.10	.05
☐ 195	Matt Stairs	.10	.05
☐ 196	Jason McDonald	.10	.05
☐ 197	Dave Magadan	.10	.05
☐ 198	Mark Bellhorn	.20	.09
☐ 199	Ariel Prieto	.10	.05
☐ 200	Jose Canseco	.30	.14
☐ 201	Bobby Estalella	.20	.09
☐ 202	Tony Barron	.10	.05
☐ 203	Midre Cummings	.10	.05
☐ 204	Ricky Bottalico	.10	.05
☐ 205	Mike Grace	.10	.05
☐ 206	Rico Brogna	.10	.05
☐ 207	Mickey Morandini	.10	.05
☐ 208	Lou Collier	.10	.05
☐ 209	Kevin Polcovich	.10	.05
☐ 210	Kevin Young	.10	.05
☐ 211	Jose Guillen	.40	.18
☐ 212	Esteban Loaiza	.10	.05
☐ 213	Marc Wilkins	.10	.05
☐ 214	Jason Schmidt	.10	.05
☐ 215	Gary Gaetti	.10	.05
☐ 216	Fernando Valenzuela	.20	.09
☐ 217	Willie McGee	.10	.05
☐ 218	Alan Benes	.20	.09
☐ 219	Eli Marrero	.20	.09
☐ 220	Mark McGwire	1.00	.45
☐ 221	Matt Morris	.20	.09
☐ 222	Trevor Hoffman	.10	.05
☐ 223	Will Cunnane	.10	.05
☐ 224	Joey Hamilton	.10	.05
☐ 225	Ken Caminiti	.30	.14
☐ 226	Derrek Lee	.30	.14
☐ 227	Mark Sweeney	.10	.05
☐ 228	Carlos Hernandez	.10	.05
☐ 229	Brian Johnson	.10	.05
☐ 230	Jeff Kent	.20	.09
☐ 231	Kirk Rueter	.10	.05
☐ 232	Bill Mueller	.10	.05
☐ 233	Dante Powell	.10	.05
☐ 234	J.T. Snow	.20	.09
☐ 235	Shawn Estes	.20	.09
☐ 236	Dennis Martinez	.20	.09
☐ 237	Jamie Moyer	.10	.05
☐ 238	Dan Wilson	.10	.05
☐ 239	Joey Cora	.10	.05
☐ 240	Ken Griffey Jr.	2.00	.90
☐ 241	Paul Sorrento	.10	.05
☐ 242	Jay Buhner	.30	.14
☐ 243	Hanley Frias	.25	.11
☐ 244	John Burkett	.10	.05
☐ 245	Juan Gonzalez	1.00	.45
☐ 246	Rick Helling	.10	.05
☐ 247	Darren Oliver	.10	.05
☐ 248	Mickey Tettleton	.10	.05
☐ 249	Ivan Rodriguez	.50	.23
☐ 250	Joe Carter	.20	.09
☐ 251	Pat Hentgen	.20	.09
☐ 252	Marty Janzen	.10	.05
☐ 253	Frank Thomas TOP	.40	.18

☐ 254	Mark McGwire TOP	.50	.23
	Tony Gwynn		
	Ken Griffey Jr.		
	Larry Walker		
☐ 255	Ken Griffey Jr. TOP	.50	.23
	Andres Galarraga		
	Tony Womack		
☐ 256	Brian L.Hunter TOP	.10	.05
	Denny Neagle		
☐ 257	Roger Clemens TOP	.20	.09
	Curt Schilling		
☐ 258	Roger Clemens TOP	.20	.09
	Pedro Martinez		
☐ 259	Roger Clemens TOP	.20	.09
	Jeff Shaw		
☐ 260	Randy Myers TOP	.10	.05
	Scott Rolen		
☐ 261	Nomar Garciaparra TOP	.30	.14
☐ 262	Charlie O'Brien	.10	.05
☐ 263	Shannon Stewart	.20	.09
☐ 264	Robert Person	.10	.05
☐ 265	Carlos Delgado	.20	.09

1998 Collector's Choice Evolution Revolution

Randomly inserted in series one packs at the rate of one in 13, this 28-card set features a color photo of one player from each of the League's 30 teams printed on a baseball jersey shaped card which folded out to display the players accomplishments.

		MINT	NRMT
COMPLETE SET (28)		60.00	27.00
COMMON CARD (ER1-ER28)		.75	.35
SER.1 STATED ODDS 1:13			
☐ ER1	Tim Salmon	1.50	.70
☐ ER2	Greg Maddux	6.00	2.70
☐ ER3	Cal Ripken	8.00	3.60
☐ ER4	Mo Vaughn	2.50	1.10
☐ ER5	Sammy Sosa	1.50	.70
☐ ER6	Frank Thomas	8.00	3.60
☐ ER7	Barry Larkin	1.25	.55
☐ ER8	Jim Thome	2.00	.90
☐ ER9	Larry Walker	2.00	.90
☐ ER10	Travis Fryman	.75	.35
☐ ER11	Gary Sheffield	1.50	.70
☐ ER12	Jeff Bagwell	4.00	1.80
☐ ER13	Johnny Damon	.75	.35
☐ ER14	Mike Piazza	6.00	2.70
☐ ER15	Jeff Cirillo	.75	.35
☐ ER16	Paul Molitor	2.00	.90
☐ ER17	Vladimir Guerrero	3.00	1.35
☐ ER18	Todd Hundley	.75	.35
☐ ER19	Tino Martinez	1.50	.70
☐ ER20	Jose Canseco	1.25	.55
☐ ER21	Scott Rolen	5.00	2.20
☐ ER22	Al Martin	.75	.35
☐ ER23	Mark McGwire	5.00	2.20
☐ ER24	Tony Gwynn	5.00	2.20

☐ ER25	Barry Bonds	2.50	1.10
☐ ER26	Ken Griffey Jr.	10.00	4.50
☐ ER27	Juan Gonzalez	5.00	2.20
☐ ER28	Roger Clemens	4.00	1.80

1998 Collector's Choice StarQuest

The 1998 Series one Collector's Choice 90-card tiered insert set, StarQuest, features color action player photos with a different number of stars printed below the player's name. The more stars on the card, the more collectible the card. The set contains the following subsets: Special Delivery (SQ1-SQ45), inserted one per pack; Students of the Game (SQ46-SQ65), randomly seeded at a rate of 1:21 packs; Super Powers (SQ66-SQ80), randomly seeded at a rate of 1:71 packs; and Superstar Domain (SQ81-SQ90), randomly seeded at a rate of 1:145 packs.

	MINT	NRMT
COMP.DELIV.SET (45)	20.00	9.00
COMM.DELIVERY (1-45)	.15	.07
DELIVERY MINOR STARS	.25	.11
DELIVERY UNLISTED STARS	.50	.23
ONE DELIVERY PER SER.1 PACK		
COMP.STUDENT SET (20)	60.00	27.00
COMM.STUDENTS (46-65)	1.50	.70
STUDENTS SER.1 STATED ODDS 1:21		
COMP.POWERS SET (15)	100.00	45.00
COMMON POWERS (66-80)	4.00	1.80
POWERS SER.1 STATED ODDS 1:71		
COMP.SUPERSTAR SET (10)	300.00	135.00
COMMON SUPERSTAR (81-90)	10.00	4.50
SUPERSTAR SER.1 STATED ODDS 1:145		

☐ SQ1	Nomar Garciaparra SD	1.50	.70
☐ SQ2	Scott Rolen SD	1.25	.55
☐ SQ3	Jason Dickson SD	.25	.11
☐ SQ4	Jaret Wright SD	1.25	.55
☐ SQ5	Kevin Orie SD	.25	.11
☐ SQ6	Jose Guillen SD	.50	.23
☐ SQ7	Matt Morris SD	.25	.11
☐ SQ8	Mike Cameron SD	.25	.11
☐ SQ9	Kevin Polcovich SD	.15	.07
☐ SQ10	Jose Cruz Jr. SD	2.00	.90
☐ SQ11	Miguel Tejada SD	.60	.25
☐ SQ12	Fernando Tatis SD	.50	.23
☐ SQ13	Todd Helton SD	.60	.25
☐ SQ14	Ken Cloude SD	.25	.11
☐ SQ15	Ben Grieve SD	1.00	.45
☐ SQ16	Dante Powell SD	.15	.07
☐ SQ17	Bubba Trammell SD	.25	.11
☐ SQ18	Juan Encarnacion SD	.50	.23
☐ SQ19	Derrek Lee SD	.30	.14
☐ SQ20	Paul Konerko SD	.75	.35
☐ SQ21	Richard Hidalgo SD	.25	.11
☐ SQ22	Denny Neagle SD	.25	.11

☐ SQ23 David Justice SD	.50	.23
☐ SQ24 Pedro Martinez SD	.50	.23
☐ SQ25 Greg Maddux SD	1.50	.70
☐ SQ26 Edgar Martinez SD	.30	.14
☐ SQ27 Cal Ripken SD	2.00	.90
☐ SQ28 Tim Salmon SD	.50	.23
☐ SQ29 Shawn Estes SD	.25	.11
☐ SQ30 Ken Griffey Jr. SD	2.50	1.10
☐ SQ31 Brad Radke SD	.25	.11
☐ SQ32 Andy Pettitte SD	.50	.23
☐ SQ33 Curt Schilling SD	.25	.11
☐ SQ34 Raul Mondesi SD	.30	.14
☐ SQ35 Alex Rodriguez SD	1.50	.70
☐ SQ36 Jeff Kent SD	.15	.07
☐ SQ37 Jeff Bagwell SD	1.00	.45
☐ SQ38 Juan Gonzalez SD	1.25	.55
☐ SQ39 Barry Bonds SD	.60	.25
☐ SQ40 Mark McGwire SD	1.25	.55
☐ SQ41 Frank Thomas SD	2.00	.90
☐ SQ42 Ray Lankford SD	.25	.11
☐ SQ43 Tony Gwynn SD	1.25	.55
☐ SQ44 Mike Piazza SD	1.50	.70
☐ SQ45 Tino Martinez SD	.50	.23
☐ SQ46 Nomar Garciaparra SG	10.00	4.50
☐ SQ47 Raul Mondesi SG	3.00	1.35
☐ SQ48 Chuck Knoblauch SG	2.50	1.10
☐ SQ49 Rusty Greer SG	1.50	.70
☐ SQ50 Cal Ripken SG	12.00	5.50
☐ SQ51 Roberto Alomar SG	3.00	1.35
☐ SQ52 Scott Rolen SG	8.00	3.60
☐ SQ53 Derek Jeter SG	8.00	3.60
☐ SQ54 Mark Grace SG	2.00	.90
☐ SQ55 Randy Johnson SG	3.00	1.35
☐ SQ56 Craig Biggio SG	2.00	.90
☐ SQ57 Kenny Lofton SG	4.00	1.80
☐ SQ58 Eddie Murray SG	3.00	1.35
☐ SQ59 Ryne Sandberg SG	4.00	1.80
☐ SQ60 Rickey Henderson SG	2.00	.90
☐ SQ61 Darin Erstad SG	4.00	1.80
☐ SQ62 Jim Edmonds SG	2.00	.90
☐ SQ63 Ken Caminiti SG	2.00	.90
☐ SQ64 Ivan Rodriguez SG	4.00	1.80
☐ SQ65 Tony Gwynn SG	8.00	3.60
☐ SQ66 Tony Clark SG	6.00	2.70
☐ SQ67 Andres Galarraga SP	6.00	2.70
☐ SQ68 Rafael Palmeiro SP	5.00	2.20
☐ SQ69 Manny Ramirez SP	8.00	3.60
☐ SQ70 Albert Belle SP	5.00	4.50
☐ SQ71 Jay Buhner SP	5.00	2.20
☐ SQ72 Mo Vaughn SP	10.00	4.50
☐ SQ73 Barry Bonds SP	10.00	4.50
☐ SQ74 Chipper Jones SP	25.00	11.00
☐ SQ75 Jeff Bagwell SP	15.00	6.75
☐ SQ76 Jim Thome SP	8.00	3.60
☐ SQ77 Sammy Sosa SP	6.00	2.70
☐ SQ78 Todd Hundley SP	4.00	1.80
☐ SQ79 Matt Williams SP	5.00	2.20
☐ SQ80 Vinny Castilla SP	4.00	1.80
☐ SQ81 Jose Cruz Jr. SS	40.00	18.00
☐ SQ82 Frank Thomas SS	50.00	22.00
☐ SQ83 Juan Gonzalez SS	30.00	13.50
☐ SQ84 Mike Piazza SS	40.00	18.00
☐ SQ85 Alex Rodriguez SS	40.00	18.00
☐ SQ86 Larry Walker SS	12.00	5.50
☐ SQ87 Tino Martinez SS	10.00	4.50
☐ SQ88 Greg Maddux SS	40.00	18.00
☐ SQ89 Mark McGwire SS	25.00	11.00
☐ SQ90 Ken Griffey Jr. SS	60.00	27.00

1998 Collector's Choice Stick 'Ums

Randomly inserted at the rate of one in three first series packs, this 30-card set features color player photos printed on stickers that can be peeled off and restuck anywhere.

	MINT	NRMT
COMPLETE SET (30)	20.00	9.00
COMMON CARD (1-30)	.25	.11
SER.1 STATED ODDS 1:3		

	MINT	NRMT
COMPLETE SET (265)	20.00	9.00
COMMON CARD (1-265)	.15	.07
MINOR STARS	.30	.14
UNLISTED STARS	.60	.25
SUBSET CARDS HALF VALUE OF BASE CARDS		
COMP.GOLD SIG.SET (265)	1500.00	700.00
COMMON GOLD SIG (1-265)	2.50	1.10
*GOLD STARS: 12.5X TO 30X HI COLUMN		
*GOLD YOUNG STARS: 10X TO 25X HI		
GOLD STATED ODDS 1:35		
12 GOLD PER GOLD SUPER PACK		
COMP.SILV.SIG.SET (265)	60.00	27.00
COMMON SILV.SIG. (1-265)	.25	.11
*SILV.SIG.STARS: 1.5X TO 4X HI COLUMN		
*SILV.SIG.YOUNG STARS: 1.25X TO 3X HI		
ONE SILVER SIGNATURE PER PACK		
12 SILVER SIGNATURES PER SUPER PACK		

☐ 1 Andruw Jones	1.25	.55
☐ 2 Chipper Jones	2.00	.90
☐ 3 Cal Ripken	2.50	1.10
☐ 4 Nomar Garciaparra	2.00	.90
☐ 5 Mo Vaughn	.75	.35
☐ 6 Ryne Sandberg	.75	.35
☐ 7 Sammy Sosa	.50	.23
☐ 8 Frank Thomas	1.25	.55
☐ 9 Albert Belle	.75	.35
☐ 10 Jim Thome	.60	.25
☐ 11 Manny Ramirez	.60	.25
☐ 12 Larry Walker	.60	.25
☐ 13 Gary Sheffield	.50	.23
☐ 14 Jeff Bagwell	1.25	.55
☐ 15 Mike Piazza	2.00	.90
☐ 16 Paul Molitor	.50	.23
☐ 17 Pedro Martinez	.50	.23
☐ 18 Todd Hundley	.25	.11
☐ 19 Derek Jeter	1.50	.70
☐ 20 Tino Martinez	.40	.18
☐ 21 Curt Schilling	.25	.11
☐ 22 Mark McGwire	1.50	.70
☐ 23 Tony Gwynn	1.50	.70
☐ 24 Barry Bonds	.75	.35
☐ 25 Ken Griffey Jr.	3.00	1.35
☐ 26 Alex Rodriguez	2.00	.90
☐ 27 Juan Gonzalez	1.50	.70
☐ 28 Ivan Rodriguez	.75	.35
☐ 29 Roger Clemens	1.25	.55
☐ 30 Jose Cruz Jr.	2.50	1.10

1995 Collector's Choice SE

The 1995 Collector's Choice SE set consists of 265 standard-size cards issued in foil packs. The fronts feature color action player photos with blue borders. The player's name, position and the team name are printed on the bottom of the photo. The SE logo in blue-foil appears in a top corner. On a white background, the backs carry another color player photo with a short player biography, career stats and 1994 highlights. Subsets featured include Rookie Class (1-

☐ 1 Alex Rodriguez	2.50	1.10
☐ 2 Derek Jeter	2.00	.90
☐ 3 Dustin Hermanson	.30	.14
☐ 4 Bill Pulsipher	.15	.07
☐ 5 Terrell Wade	.15	.07
☐ 6 Darren Dreifort	.15	.07
☐ 7 LaTroy Hawkins	.15	.07
☐ 8 Alex Ochoa	.15	.07
☐ 9 Paul Wilson	.30	.14
☐ 10 Rod Henderson	.15	.07
☐ 11 Alan Benes	.40	.18
☐ 12 Garret Anderson	.40	.18
☐ 13 Armando Benitez	.15	.07
☐ 14 Mark Thompson	.30	.14
☐ 15 Herbert Perry	.15	.07
☐ 16 Jose Silva	.15	.07
☐ 17 Orlando Miller	.15	.07
☐ 18 Russ Davis	.15	.07
☐ 19 Jason Isringhausen	.30	.14
☐ 20 Ray McDavid	.15	.07
☐ 21 Tim VanEgmond	.15	.07
☐ 22 Paul Shuey	.15	.07
☐ 23 Steve Dunn	.15	.07
☐ 24 Mike Lieberthal	.15	.07
☐ 25 Chan Ho Park	.60	.25
☐ 26 Ken Griffey Jr. RP	1.50	.70
☐ 27 Tony Gwynn RP	.60	.25
☐ 28 Chuck Knoblauch RP	.60	.25
☐ 29 Frank Thomas RP	1.25	.55
☐ 30 Matt Williams RP	.30	.14
☐ 31 Chili Davis	.30	.14
☐ 32 Chad Curtis	.15	.07
☐ 33 Brian Anderson	.15	.07
☐ 34 Chuck Finley	.15	.07
☐ 35 Tim Salmon	.60	.25
☐ 36 Bo Jackson	.30	.14
☐ 37 Doug Drabek	.15	.07
☐ 38 Craig Biggio	.40	.18
☐ 39 Ken Caminiti	.30	.14
☐ 40 Jeff Bagwell	1.25	.55
☐ 41 Darryl Kile	.30	.14
☐ 42 John Hudek	.15	.07
☐ 43 Brian L. Hunter	.40	.18
☐ 44 Dennis Eckersley	.30	.14
☐ 45 Mark McGwire	1.25	.55
☐ 46 Brent Gates	.15	.07
☐ 47 Steve Karsay	.15	.07
☐ 48 Rickey Henderson	.40	.18
☐ 49 Terry Steinbach	.15	.07
☐ 50 Ruben Sierra	.15	.07
☐ 51 Roberto Alomar	.60	.25
☐ 52 Carlos Delgado	.30	.14
☐ 53 Alex Gonzalez	.15	.07
☐ 54 Joe Carter	.30	.14
☐ 55 Paul Molitor	.60	.25
☐ 56 Juan Guzman	.15	.07
☐ 57 John Olerud	.30	.14
☐ 58 Shawn Green	.30	.14
☐ 59 Tom Glavine	.30	.14
☐ 60 Greg Maddux	2.00	.90
☐ 61 Roberto Kelly	.15	.07
☐ 62 Ryan Klesko	.40	.18

Right after the intro text, the listing continues. The intro paragraph notes: "25), Record Pace (26-30), Stat Leaders (137-144), Fantasy Team (249-260). There are no Rookie Cards in this set."

☐ 63 Javier Lopez	.30	.14
☐ 64 Jose Oliva	.15	.07
☐ 65 Fred McGriff	.40	.18
☐ 66 Steve Avery	.15	.07
☐ 67 David Justice	.60	.25
☐ 68 Ricky Bones	.15	.07
☐ 69 Cal Eldred	.15	.07
☐ 70 Greg Vaughn	.15	.07
☐ 71 Dave Nilsson	.15	.07
☐ 72 Jose Valentin	.15	.07
☐ 73 Matt Mieske	.15	.07
☐ 74 Todd Zeile	.15	.07
☐ 75 Ozzie Smith	.75	.35
☐ 76 Bernard Gilkey	.15	.07
☐ 77 Ray Lankford	.30	.14
☐ 78 Bob Tewksbury	.15	.07
☐ 79 Mark Whiten	.15	.07
☐ 80 Gregg Jefferies	.15	.07
☐ 81 Randy Myers	.15	.07
☐ 82 Shawon Dunston	.15	.07
☐ 83 Mark Grace	.40	.18
☐ 84 Derrick May	.15	.07
☐ 85 Sammy Sosa	.60	.25
☐ 86 Steve Trachsel	.15	.07
☐ 87 Brett Butler	.15	.07
☐ 88 Delino DeShields	.15	.07
☐ 89 Orel Hershiser	.15	.07
☐ 90 Mike Piazza	2.00	.90
☐ 91 Todd Hollandsworth	.30	.14
☐ 92 Eric Karros	.30	.14
☐ 93 Ramon Martinez	.30	.14
☐ 94 Tim Wallach	.15	.07
☐ 95 Raul Mondesi	.40	.18
☐ 96 Larry Walker	.60	.25
☐ 97 Wil Cordero	.15	.07
☐ 98 Marquis Grissom	.30	.14
☐ 99 Ken Hill	.15	.07
☐ 100 Cliff Floyd	.15	.07
☐ 101 Pedro J. Martinez	.60	.25
☐ 102 John Wetteland	.15	.07
☐ 103 Rondell White	.30	.14
☐ 104 Moises Alou	.30	.14
☐ 105 Barry Bonds	.75	.35
☐ 106 Darren Lewis	.15	.07
☐ 107 Mark Portugal	.15	.07
☐ 108 Matt Williams	.40	.18
☐ 109 William VanLandingham	.15	.07
☐ 110 Bill Swift	.15	.07
☐ 111 Robby Thompson	.15	.07
☐ 112 Rod Beck	.15	.07
☐ 113 Darryl Strawberry	.30	.14
☐ 114 Jim Thome	.50	.25
☐ 115 Dave Winfield	.40	.18
☐ 116 Eddie Murray	.60	.25
☐ 117 Manny Ramirez	.60	.25
☐ 118 Carlos Baerga	.30	.14
☐ 119 Kenny Lofton	.75	.35
☐ 120 Albert Belle	.75	.35
☐ 121 Mark Clark	.15	.07
☐ 122 Dennis Martinez	.30	.14
☐ 123 Randy Johnson	.60	.25
☐ 124 Jay Buhner	.40	.18
☐ 125 Ken Griffey Jr.	3.00	1.35
☐ 126 Goose Gossage	.30	.14
☐ 127 Tino Martinez	.60	.25
☐ 128 Reggie Jefferson	.15	.07
☐ 129 Edgar Martinez	.40	.18
☐ 130 Gary Sheffield	.60	.25
☐ 131 Pat Rapp	.15	.07
☐ 132 Bret Barberie	.15	.07
☐ 133 Chuck Carr	.15	.07
☐ 134 Jeff Conine	.30	.14
☐ 135 Charles Johnson	.30	.14
☐ 136 Benito Santiago	.15	.07
☐ 137 Matt Williams STL	.30	.14
☐ 138 Jeff Bagwell STL	.60	.25
☐ 139 Kenny Lofton STL	.40	.18
☐ 140 Tony Gwynn STL	.60	.25
☐ 141 Jimmy Key STL	.15	.07
☐ 142 Greg Maddux STL	1.25	.55
☐ 143 Randy Johnson STL	.30	.14
☐ 144 Lee Smith STL	.15	.07
☐ 145 Bobby Bonilla	.15	.07
☐ 146 Jason Jacome	.15	.07
☐ 147 Jeff Kent	.15	.07
☐ 148 Ryan Thompson	.15	.07

☐ 149 Bobby Jones	.15	.07
☐ 150 Bret Saberhagen	.15	.07
☐ 151 John Franco	.30	.14
☐ 152 Lee Smith	.30	.14
☐ 153 Rafael Palmeiro	.40	.18
☐ 154 Brady Anderson	.40	.18
☐ 155 Cal Ripken Jr.	2.50	1.10
☐ 156 Jeffrey Hammonds	.30	.14
☐ 157 Mike Mussina	.60	.25
☐ 158 Chris Hoiles	.15	.07
☐ 159 Ben McDonald	.15	.07
☐ 160 Tony Gwynn	1.50	.70
☐ 161 Joey Hamilton	.30	.14
☐ 162 Andy Benes	.30	.14
☐ 163 Trevor Hoffman	.15	.07
☐ 164 Phil Plantier	.15	.07
☐ 165 Derek Bell	.15	.07
☐ 166 Bip Roberts	.15	.07
☐ 167 Eddie Williams	.15	.07
☐ 168 Fernando Valenzuela	.30	.14
☐ 169 Mariano Duncan	.15	.07
☐ 170 Lenny Dykstra	.30	.14
☐ 171 Darren Daulton	.30	.14
☐ 172 Danny Jackson	.15	.07
☐ 173 Bobby Munoz	.15	.07
☐ 174 Doug Jones	.15	.07
☐ 175 Jay Bell	.30	.14
☐ 176 Zane Smith	.15	.07
☐ 177 Jon Lieber	.15	.07
☐ 178 Carlos Garcia	.15	.07
☐ 179 Orlando Merced	.15	.07
☐ 180 Andy Van Slyke	.30	.14
☐ 181 Rick Helling	.15	.07
☐ 182 Rusty Greer	.60	.25
☐ 183 Kenny Rogers UER	.15	.07
(shows 110 wins in 1990)		
☐ 184 Will Clark	.40	.18
☐ 185 Jose Canseco	.40	.18
☐ 186 Juan Gonzalez	1.50	.70
☐ 187 Dean Palmer	.15	.07
☐ 188 Ivan Rodriguez	.75	.35
☐ 189 John Valentin	.15	.07
☐ 190 Roger Clemens	1.25	.55
☐ 191 Aaron Sele	.15	.07
☐ 192 Scott Cooper	.15	.07
☐ 193 Mike Greenwell	.15	.07
☐ 194 Mo Vaughn	.75	.35
☐ 195 Andre Dawson	.40	.18
☐ 196 Ron Gant	.30	.14
☐ 197 Jose Rijo	.15	.07
☐ 198 Bret Boone	.15	.07
☐ 199 Deion Sanders	.30	.14
☐ 200 Barry Larkin	.40	.18
☐ 201 Hal Morris	.15	.07
☐ 202 Reggie Sanders	.15	.07
☐ 203 Kevin Mitchell	.15	.07
☐ 204 Marvin Freeman	.15	.07
☐ 205 Andres Galarraga	.60	.25
☐ 206 Walt Weiss	.15	.07
☐ 207 Charlie Hayes	.15	.07
☐ 208 Dave Nied	.15	.07
☐ 209 Dante Bichette	.30	.14
☐ 210 David Cone	.30	.14
☐ 211 Jeff Montgomery	.15	.07
☐ 212 Felix Jose	.15	.07
☐ 213 Mike Macfarlane	.15	.07
☐ 214 Wally Joyner	.30	.14
☐ 215 Bob Hamelin	.15	.07
☐ 216 Brian McRae	.15	.07
☐ 217 Kirk Gibson	.30	.14
☐ 218 Lou Whitaker	.30	.14
☐ 219 Chris Gomez	.15	.07
☐ 220 Cecil Fielder	.30	.14
☐ 221 Mickey Tettleton	.15	.07
☐ 222 Travis Fryman	.30	.14
☐ 223 Tony Phillips	.15	.07
☐ 224 Rick Aguilera	.15	.07
☐ 225 Scott Erickson	.15	.07
☐ 226 Chuck Knoblauch	.60	.25
☐ 227 Kent Hrbek	.30	.14
☐ 228 Shane Mack	.15	.07
☐ 229 Kevin Tapani	.15	.07
☐ 230 Kirby Puckett	1.25	.55
☐ 231 Julio Franco	.15	.07
☐ 232 Jack McDowell	.15	.07
☐ 233 Jason Bere	.15	.07

☐ 234 Alex Fernandez	.15	.07
☐ 235 Frank Thomas	2.50	1.10
☐ 236 Ozzie Guillen	.30	.14
☐ 237 Robin Ventura	.30	.14
☐ 238 Michael Jordan	4.00	1.80
☐ 239 Wilson Alvarez	.15	.07
☐ 240 Don Mattingly	1.00	.45
☐ 241 Jim Abbott	.15	.07
☐ 242 Jim Leyritz	.15	.07
☐ 243 Paul O'Neill	.30	.14
☐ 244 Melido Perez	.15	.07
☐ 245 Wade Boggs	.60	.25
☐ 246 Mike Stanley	.15	.07
☐ 247 Danny Tartabull	.15	.07
☐ 248 Jimmy Key	.30	.14
☐ 249 Greg Maddux FT	1.25	.55
☐ 250 Randy Johnson FT	.30	.14
☐ 251 Bret Saberhagen FT	.15	.07
☐ 252 John Wetteland FT	.15	.07
☐ 253 Mike Piazza FT	1.25	.55
☐ 254 Jeff Bagwell FT	.60	.25
☐ 255 Craig Biggio FT	.30	.14
☐ 256 Matt Williams FT	.30	.14
☐ 257 Wil Cordero FT	.15	.07
☐ 258 Kenny Lofton FT	.40	.18
☐ 259 Barry Bonds FT	.40	.18
☐ 260 Dante Bichette FT	.15	.07
☐ 261 Ken Griffey Jr. CL	1.50	.70
☐ 262 Goose Gossage CL	.15	.07
☐ 263 Cal Ripken CL	1.25	.55
☐ 264 Kenny Rogers CL	.15	.07
☐ 265 John Valentin CL	.15	.07
☐ P125 Ken Griffey Jr. Promo	3.00	1.35

1981 Donruss

In 1981 Donruss launched itself into the baseball card market with a 600-card set. Wax packs contained 15 cards as well as a piece of gum. This would be the only year that Donruss was allowed to have any confectionary product in their packs. The standard-size cards are printed on thin stock and more than one pose exists for several popular players. Numerous errors of the first print run were later corrected by the company. These are marked P1 and P2 in the checklist below. The key Rookie Cards in this set are Danny Ainge, Tim Raines, and Jeff Reardon.

	NRMT	VG-E
COMPLETE SET (605)	30.00	13.50
COMMON CARD (1-605)	.10	.05
MINOR STARS	.25	.11
SEMISTARS	.50	.23
UNLISTED STARS	1.00	.45

☐ 1 Ozzie Smith	4.00	1.80
☐ 2 Rollie Fingers	.50	.23
☐ 3 Rick Wise	.10	.05
☐ 4 Gene Richards	.10	.05

#	Card	Price 1	Price 2
☐ 5	Alan Trammell	1.25	.55
☐ 6	Tom Brookens	.10	.05
☐ 7A	Duffy Dyer P1	.25	.11
	1980 batting average has decimal point		
☐ 7B	Duffy Dyer P2	.10	.05
	1980 batting average has no decimal point		
☐ 8	Mark Fidrych	1.00	.45
☐ 9	Dave Rozema	.10	.05
☐ 10	Ricky Peters	.10	.05
☐ 11	Mike Schmidt	1.25	.55
☐ 12	Willie Stargell	1.00	.45
☐ 13	Tim Foli	.10	.05
☐ 14	Manny Sanguillen	.25	.11
☐ 15	Grant Jackson	.10	.05
☐ 16	Eddie Solomon	.10	.05
☐ 17	Omar Moreno	.10	.05
☐ 18	Joe Morgan	1.00	.45
☐ 19	Rafael Landestoy	.10	.05
☐ 20	Bruce Bochy	.10	.05
☐ 21	Joe Sambito	.10	.05
☐ 22	Manny Trillo	.10	.05
☐ 23A	Dave Smith P1	.25	.11
	Line box around stats is not complete		
☐ 23B	Dave Smith P2	.25	.11
	Box totally encloses stats at top		
☐ 24	Terry Puhl	.10	.05
☐ 25	Bump Wills	.10	.05
☐ 26A	John Ellis P1 ERR	.50	.23
	Danny Walton photo on front		
☐ 26B	John Ellis P2 COR	.25	.11
☐ 27	Jim Kern	.10	.05
☐ 28	Richie Zisk	.10	.05
☐ 29	John Mayberry	.10	.05
☐ 30	Bob Davis	.10	.05
☐ 31	Jackson Todd	.10	.05
☐ 32	Alvis Woods	.10	.05
☐ 33	Steve Carlton	1.00	.45
☐ 34	Lee Mazzilli	.10	.05
☐ 35	John Stearns	.10	.05
☐ 36	Roy Lee Jackson	.10	.05
☐ 37	Mike Scott	.25	.11
☐ 38	Lamar Johnson	.10	.05
☐ 39	Kevin Bell	.10	.05
☐ 40	Ed Farmer	.10	.05
☐ 41	Ross Baumgarten	.10	.05
☐ 42	Leo Sutherland	.10	.05
☐ 43	Dan Meyer	.10	.05
☐ 44	Ron Reed	.10	.05
☐ 45	Mario Mendoza	.10	.05
☐ 46	Rick Honeycutt	.10	.05
☐ 47	Glenn Abbott	.10	.05
☐ 48	Leon Roberts	.10	.05
☐ 49	Rod Carew	.75	.35
☐ 50	Bert Campaneris	.25	.11
☐ 51A	Tom Donahue P1 ERR	.25	.11
	Name on front misspelled Donahue		
☐ 51B	Tom Donohue P2 COR	.10	.05
☐ 52	Dave Frost	.10	.05
☐ 53	Ed Halicki	.10	.05
☐ 54	Dan Ford	.10	.05
☐ 55	Garry Maddox	.10	.05
☐ 56A	Steve Garvey P1	1.00	.45
	Surpassed 25 HR		
☐ 56B	Steve Garvey P2	1.00	.45
	Surpassed 21 HR		
☐ 57	Bill Russell	.25	.11
☐ 58	Don Sutton	1.00	.45
☐ 59	Reggie Smith	.25	.11
☐ 60	Rick Monday	.25	.11
☐ 61	Ray Knight	.25	.11
☐ 62	Johnny Bench	1.25	.55
☐ 63	Mario Soto	.10	.05
☐ 64	Doug Bair	.10	.05
☐ 65	George Foster	.25	.11
☐ 66	Jeff Burroughs	.10	.05
☐ 67	Keith Hernandez	.25	.11
☐ 68	Tom Herr	.25	.11
☐ 69	Bob Forsch	.10	.05
☐ 70	John Fulgham	.10	.05
☐ 71A	Bobby Bonds P1 ERR	1.00	.45
	986 lifetime HR		
☐ 71B	Bobby Bonds P2 COR	.50	.23
	326 lifetime HR		
☐ 72A	Rennie Stennett P1	.25	.11
	Breaking broke leg		
☐ 72B	Rennie Stennett P2	.10	.05
	Word "broke" deleted		
☐ 73	Joe Strain	.10	.05
☐ 74	Ed Whitson	.10	.05
☐ 75	Tom Griffin	.10	.05
☐ 76	Billy North	.10	.05
☐ 77	Gene Garber	.10	.05
☐ 78	Mike Hargrove	.25	.11
☐ 79	Dave Rosello	.10	.05
☐ 80	Ron Hassey	.10	.05
☐ 81	Sid Monge	.10	.05
☐ 82A	Joe Charboneau P1...	1.00	.45
	'78 highlights For some reason		
☐ 82B	Joe Charboneau P2...	1.00	.45
	Phrase 'For some reason' deleted		
☐ 83	Cecil Cooper	.25	.11
☐ 84	Sal Bando	.25	.11
☐ 85	Moose Haas	.10	.05
☐ 86	Mike Caldwell	.10	.05
☐ 87A	Larry Hisle P1	.25	.11
	'77 highlights line ends with "28 RBI"		
☐ 87B	Larry Hisle P2	.25	.11
	Correct line '28 HR'		
☐ 88	Luis Gomez	.10	.05
☐ 89	Larry Parrish	.10	.05
☐ 90	Gary Carter	1.00	.45
☐ 91	Bill Gullickson	.50	.23
☐ 92	Fred Norman	.10	.05
☐ 93	Tommy Hutton	.10	.05
☐ 94	Carl Yastrzemski	1.00	.45
☐ 95	Glenn Hoffman	.10	.05
☐ 96	Dennis Eckersley	1.00	.45
☐ 97A	Tom Burgmeier P1	.25	.11
	ERR Throws: Right		
☐ 97B	Tom Burgmeier P2	.10	.05
	COR Throws: Left		
☐ 98	Win Remmerswaal	.10	.05
☐ 99	Bob Horner	.25	.11
☐ 100	George Brett	2.50	1.10
☐ 101	Dave Chalk	.10	.05
☐ 102	Dennis Leonard	.10	.05
☐ 103	Renie Martin	.10	.05
☐ 104	Amos Otis	.25	.11
☐ 105	Graig Nettles	.25	.11
☐ 106	Eric Soderholm	.10	.05
☐ 107	Tommy John	.50	.23
☐ 108	Tom Underwood	.10	.05
☐ 109	Lou Piniella	.25	.11
☐ 110	Mickey Klutts	.10	.05
☐ 111	Bobby Murcer	.25	.11
☐ 112	Eddie Murray	2.00	.90
☐ 113	Rick Dempsey	.25	.11
☐ 114	Scott McGregor	.10	.05
☐ 115	Ken Singleton	.25	.11
☐ 116	Gary Roenicke	.10	.05
☐ 117	Dave Revering	.10	.05
☐ 118	Mike Norris	.10	.05
☐ 119	Rickey Henderson	2.50	1.10
☐ 120	Mike Heath	.10	.05
☐ 121	Dave Cash	.10	.05
☐ 122	Randy Jones	.10	.05
☐ 123	Eric Rasmussen	.10	.05
☐ 124	Jerry Mumphrey	.10	.05
☐ 125	Richie Hebner	.10	.05
☐ 126	Mark Wagner	.10	.05
☐ 127	Jack Morris	1.00	.45
☐ 128	Dan Petry	.25	.11
☐ 129	Bruce Robbins	.10	.05
☐ 130	Champ Summers	.10	.05
☐ 131	Pete Rose P1	1.25	.55
	Last line ends with see card 251		
☐ 131B	Pete Rose P2	1.50	.70
	Last line corrected see card 371		
☐ 132	Willie Stargell	1.00	.45
☐ 133	Ed Ott	.10	.05
☐ 134	Jim Bibby	.10	.05
☐ 135	Bert Blyleven	.50	.23
☐ 136	Dave Parker	.25	.11
☐ 137	Bill Robinson	.25	.11
☐ 138	Enos Cabell	.10	.05
☐ 139	Dave Bergman	.10	.05
☐ 140	J.R. Richard	.25	.11
☐ 141	Ken Forsch	.10	.05
☐ 142	Larry Bowa UER	.25	.11
	Shortshop on front		
☐ 143	Frank LaCorte UER	.10	.05
	Photo actually Randy Niemann		
☐ 144	Denny Walling	.10	.05
☐ 145	Buddy Bell	.25	.11
☐ 146	Ferguson Jenkins	1.00	.45
☐ 147	Danny Darwin	.25	.11
☐ 148	John Grubb	.10	.05
☐ 149	Alfredo Griffin	.10	.05
☐ 150	Jerry Garvin	.10	.05
☐ 151	Paul Mirabella	.10	.05
☐ 152	Rick Bosetti	.10	.05
☐ 153	Dick Ruthven	.10	.05
☐ 154	Frank Taveras	.10	.05
☐ 155	Craig Swan	.10	.05
☐ 156	Jeff Reardon	1.00	.45
☐ 157	Steve Henderson	.10	.05
☐ 158	Jim Morrison	.10	.05
☐ 159	Glenn Borgmann	.10	.05
☐ 160	LaMarr Hoyt	.25	.11
☐ 161	Rich Wortham	.10	.05
☐ 162	Thad Bosley	.10	.05
☐ 163	Julio Cruz	.10	.05
☐ 164A	Del Unser P1	.25	.11
	No '3B' heading		
☐ 164B	Del Unser P2	.10	.05
	Batting record on back corrected '3B'		
☐ 165	Jim Anderson	.10	.05
☐ 166	Jim Beattie	.10	.05
☐ 167	Shane Rawley	.10	.05
☐ 168	Joe Simpson	.10	.05
☐ 169	Rod Carew	.75	.35
☐ 170	Fred Patek	.10	.05
☐ 171	Frank Tanana	.25	.11
☐ 172	Alfredo Martinez	.10	.05
☐ 173	Chris Knapp	.10	.05
☐ 174	Joe Rudi	.25	.11
☐ 175	Greg Luzinski	.25	.11
☐ 176	Steve Garvey	.50	.23
☐ 177	Joe Ferguson	.10	.05
☐ 178	Bob Welch	.25	.11
☐ 179	Dusty Baker	.50	.23
☐ 180	Rudy Law	.10	.05
☐ 181	Dave Concepcion	.25	.11
☐ 182	Johnny Bench	1.25	.55
☐ 183	Mike LaCoss	.10	.05
☐ 184	Ken Griffey	.50	.23
☐ 185	Dave Collins	.10	.05
☐ 186	Brian Asselstine	.10	.05
☐ 187	Garry Templeton	.25	.11
☐ 188	Mike Phillips	.10	.05
☐ 189	Pete Vuckovich	.25	.11
☐ 190	John Urrea	.10	.05
☐ 191	Tony Scott	.10	.05
☐ 192	Darrell Evans	.25	.11
☐ 193	Milt May	.10	.05
☐ 194	Bob Knepper	.25	.11
☐ 195	Randy Moffitt	.10	.05
☐ 196	Larry Herndon	.10	.05
☐ 197	Rick Camp	.10	.05
☐ 198	Andre Thornton	.25	.11
☐ 199	Tom Veryzer	.10	.05
☐ 200	Gary Alexander	.10	.05
☐ 201	Rick Waits	.10	.05
☐ 202	Rick Manning	.10	.05
☐ 203	Paul Molitor	2.00	.90
☐ 204	Jim Gantner	.25	.11
☐ 205	Paul Mitchell	.10	.05
☐ 206	Reggie Cleveland	.10	.05
☐ 207	Sixto Lezcano	.10	.05
☐ 208	Bruce Benedict	.10	.05
☐ 209	Rodney Scott	.10	.05
☐ 210	John Tamargo	.10	.05
☐ 211	Bill Lee	.25	.11
☐ 212	Andre Dawson UER	1.25	.55
	Middle name Fernando should be Nolan		
☐ 213	Rowland Office	.10	.05

#	Player	Price	Price
214	Carl Yastrzemski	1.00	.45
215	Jerry Remy	.10	.05
216	Mike Torrez	.10	.05
217	Skip Lockwood	.10	.05
218	Fred Lynn	.25	.11
219	Chris Chambliss	.25	.11
220	Willie Aikens	.10	.05
221	John Wathan	.10	.05
222	Dan Quisenberry	.25	.11
223	Willie Wilson	.25	.11
224	Clint Hurdle	.10	.05
225	Bob Watson	.25	.11
226	Jim Spencer	.10	.05
227	Ron Guidry	.25	.11
228	Reggie Jackson	1.25	.55
229	Oscar Gamble	.10	.05
230	Jeff Cox	.10	.05
231	Luis Tiant	.25	.11
232	Rich Dauer	.10	.05
233	Dan Graham	.10	.05
234	Mike Flanagan	.25	.11
235	John Lowenstein	.10	.05
236	Benny Ayala	.10	.05
237	Wayne Gross	.10	.05
238	Rick Langford	.10	.05
239	Tony Armas	.25	.11
240A	Bob Lacey P1 ERR	.50	.23
	Name misspelled Lacy		
240B	Bob Lacey P2 COR	.10	.05
241	Gene Tenace	.25	.11
242	Bob Shirley	.10	.05
243	Gary Lucas	.10	.05
244	Jerry Turner	.10	.05
245	John Wockenfuss	.10	.05
246	Stan Papi	.10	.05
247	Milt Wilcox	.10	.05
248	Dan Schatzeder	.10	.05
249	Steve Kemp	.10	.05
250	Jim Lentine	.10	.05
251	Pete Rose	1.25	.55
252	Bill Madlock	.25	.11
253	Dale Berra	.10	.05
254	Kent Tekulve	.25	.11
255	Enrique Romo	.10	.05
256	Mike Easler	.10	.05
257	Chuck Tanner MG	.25	.11
258	Art Howe	.10	.05
259	Alan Ashby	.10	.05
260	Nolan Ryan	5.00	2.20
261A	Vern Ruhle P1 ERR	.50	.23
	Ken Forsch photo on front		
261B	Vern Ruhle P2 COR	.10	.05
262	Bob Boone	.25	.11
263	Cesar Cedeno	.25	.11
264	Jeff Leonard	.25	.11
265	Pat Putnam	.10	.05
266	Jon Matlack	.10	.05
267	Dave Rajsich	.10	.05
268	Billy Sample	.10	.05
269	Damaso Garcia	.10	.05
270	Tom Buskey	.10	.05
271	Joey McLaughlin	.10	.05
272	Barry Bonnell	.10	.05
273	Tug McGraw	.25	.11
274	Mike Jorgensen	.10	.05
275	Pat Zachry	.10	.05
276	Neil Allen	.10	.05
277	Joel Youngblood	.10	.05
278	Greg Pryor	.10	.05
279	Britt Burns	.10	.05
280	Rich Dotson	.10	.05
281	Chet Lemon	.10	.05
282	Rusty Kuntz	.10	.05
283	Ted Cox	.10	.05
284	Sparky Lyle	.25	.11
285	Larry Cox	.10	.05
286	Floyd Bannister	.10	.05
287	Byron McLaughlin	.10	.05
288	Rodney Craig	.10	.05
289	Bobby Grich	.25	.11
290	Dickie Thon	.10	.05
291	Mark Clear	.10	.05
292	Dave Lemanczyk	.10	.05
293	Jason Thompson	.10	.05
294	Rick Miller	.10	.05
295	Lonnie Smith	.25	.11
296	Ron Cey	.25	.11
297	Steve Yeager	.10	.05
298	Bobby Castillo	.10	.05
299	Manny Mota	.25	.11
300	Jay Johnstone	.25	.11
301	Dan Driessen	.10	.05
302	Joe Nolan	.10	.05
303	Paul Householder	.10	.05
304	Harry Spilman	.10	.05
305	Cesar Geronimo	.10	.05
306A	Gary Mathews P1 ERR	.50	.23
	Name misspelled		
306B	Gary Matthews P2	.25	.11
	COR		
307	Ken Reitz	.10	.05
308	Ted Simmons	.25	.11
309	John Littlefield	.10	.05
310	George Frazier	.10	.05
311	Dane Iorg	.10	.05
312	Mike Ivie	.10	.05
313	Dennis Littlejohn	.10	.05
314	Gary Lavelle	.10	.05
315	Jack Clark	.25	.11
316	Jim Wohlford	.10	.05
317	Rick Matula	.10	.05
318	Toby Harrah	.25	.11
319A	Dwane Kuiper P1 ERR	.25	.11
	Name misspelled		
319B	Duane Kuiper P2 COR	.10	.05
320	Len Barker	.10	.05
321	Victor Cruz	.10	.05
322	Dell Alston	.10	.05
323	Robin Yount	1.25	.55
324	Charlie Moore	.10	.05
325	Lary Sorensen	.10	.05
326A	Gorman Thomas P1	.50	.23
	2nd line on back:		
	'30 HR mark 4th'		
326B	Gorman Thomas P2	.25	.11
	30 HR mark 3rd		
327	Bob Rodgers MG	.10	.05
328	Phil Niekro	1.00	.45
329	Chris Speier	.10	.05
330A	Steve Rodgers P1	.25	.11
	ERR name misspelled		
330B	Steve Rogers P2 COR	.10	.05
331	Woodie Fryman	.10	.05
332	Warren Cromartie	.10	.05
333	Jerry White	.10	.05
334	Tony Perez	1.00	.45
335	Carlton Fisk	1.25	.55
336	Dick Drago	.10	.05
337	Steve Renko	.10	.05
338	Jim Rice	.25	.11
339	Jerry Royster	.10	.05
340	Frank White	.25	.11
341	Jamie Quirk	.10	.05
342A	Paul Spittorff P1 ERR	.25	.11
	Name misspelled		
342B	Paul Splittorff	.10	.05
	P2 COR		
343	Marty Pattin	.10	.05
344	Pete LaCock	.10	.05
345	Willie Randolph	.25	.11
346	Rick Cerone	.10	.05
347	Rich Gossage	.25	.11
348	Reggie Jackson	1.25	.55
349	Ruppert Jones	.10	.05
350	Dave McKay	.10	.05
351	Yogi Berra CO	1.00	.45
352	Doug DeCinces	.25	.11
353	Jim Palmer	.60	.25
354	Tippy Martinez	.10	.05
355	Al Bumbry	.10	.05
356	Earl Weaver MG	1.00	.45
357A	Bob Picciolo P1 ERR	.25	.11
	Name misspelled		
357B	Rob Picciolo P2 COR	.10	.05
358	Matt Keough	.10	.05
359	Dwayne Murphy	.10	.05
360	Brian Kingman	.10	.05
361	Bill Fahey	.10	.05
362	Steve Mura	.10	.05
363	Dennis Kinney	.10	.05
364	Dave Winfield	1.50	.70
365	Lou Whitaker	1.00	.45
366	Lance Parrish	.25	.11
367	Tim Corcoran	.10	.05
368	Pat Underwood	.10	.05
369	Al Cowens	.10	.05
370	Sparky Anderson MG	1.25	.55
371	Pete Rose	1.25	.55
372	Phil Garner	.25	.11
373	Steve Nicosia	.10	.05
374	John Candelaria	.25	.11
375	Don Robinson	.10	.05
376	Lee Lacy	.10	.05
377	John Milner	.10	.05
378	Craig Reynolds	.10	.05
379A	Luis Pujols P1 ERR	.25	.11
	Name misspelled Pujois		
379B	Luis Pujols P2 COR	.10	.05
380	Joe Niekro	.25	.11
381	Joaquin Andujar	.25	.11
382	Keith Moreland	.25	.11
383	Jose Cruz	.25	.11
384	Bill Virdon MG	.10	.05
385	Jim Sundberg	.25	.11
386	Doc Medich	.10	.05
387	Al Oliver	.25	.11
388	Jim Norris	.10	.05
389	Bob Bailor	.10	.05
390	Ernie Whitt	.10	.05
391	Otto Velez	.10	.05
392	Roy Howell	.10	.05
393	Bob Walk	.25	.11
394	Doug Flynn	.10	.05
395	Pete Falcone	.10	.05
396	Tom Hausman	.10	.05
397	Elliott Maddox	.10	.05
398	Mike Squires	.10	.05
399	Marvis Foley	.10	.05
400	Steve Trout	.10	.05
401	Wayne Nordhagen	.10	.05
402	Tony LaRussa MG	.25	.11
403	Bruce Bochte	.10	.05
404	Bake McBride	.10	.05
405	Jerry Narron	.10	.05
406	Rob Dressler	.10	.05
407	Dave Heaverlo	.10	.05
408	Tom Paciorek	.10	.05
409	Carney Lansford	.25	.11
410	Brian Downing	.10	.05
411	Don Aase	.10	.05
412	Jim Barr	.10	.05
413	Don Baylor	.50	.23
414	Jim Fregosi MG	.25	.11
415	Dallas Green MG	.10	.05
416	Dave Lopes	.25	.11
417	Jerry Reuss	.25	.11
418	Rick Sutcliffe	.25	.11
419	Derrel Thomas	.10	.05
420	Tom Lasorda MG	1.00	.45
421	Charlie Leibrandt	.50	.23
422	Tom Seaver	1.25	.55
423	Ron Oester	.10	.05
424	Junior Kennedy	.10	.05
425	Tom Seaver	1.25	.55
426	Bobby Cox MG	.25	.11
427	Leon Durham	.25	.11
428	Terry Kennedy	.25	.11
429	Silvio Martinez	.10	.05
430	George Hendrick	.10	.05
431	Red Schoendienst MG	1.00	.45
432	Johnnie LeMaster	.10	.05
433	Vida Blue	.25	.11
434	John Montefusco	.10	.05
435	Terry Whitfield	.10	.05
436	Dave Bristol MG	.10	.05
437	Dale Murphy	1.00	.45
438	Jerry Dybzinski	.10	.05
439	Jorge Orta	.10	.05
440	Wayne Garland	.10	.05
441	Miguel Dilone	.10	.05
442	Dave Garcia MG	.10	.05
443	Don Money	.10	.05
444A	Buck Martinez P1 ERR	.25	.11
	Reverse negative		
444B	Buck Martinez	.10	.05
	P2 COR		
445	Jerry Augustine	.10	.05
446	Ben Oglivie	.25	.11

☐ 447	Jim Slaton	.10	.05
☐ 448	Doyle Alexander	.10	.05
☐ 449	Tony Bernazard	.10	.05
☐ 450	Scott Sanderson	.10	.05
☐ 451	David Palmer	.10	.05
☐ 452	Stan Bahnsen	.10	.05
☐ 453	Dick Williams MG	.10	.05
☐ 454	Rick Burleson	.10	.05
☐ 455	Gary Allenson	.10	.05
☐ 456	Bob Stanley	.10	.05
☐ 457A	John Tudor P1 ERR Lifetime W-L 9.7	.25	.11
☐ 457B	John Tudor P2 COR Lifetime W-L 9-7	.25	.11
☐ 458	Dwight Evans	.50	.23
☐ 459	Glenn Hubbard	.10	.05
☐ 460	U.L. Washington	.10	.05
☐ 461	Larry Gura	.10	.05
☐ 462	Rich Gale	.10	.05
☐ 463	Hal McRae	.50	.23
☐ 464	Jim Frey MG	.10	.05
☐ 465	Bucky Dent	.25	.11
☐ 466	Dennis Werth	.10	.05
☐ 467	Ron Davis	.10	.05
☐ 468	Reggie Jackson UER 32 HR in 1970 should be 23	1.25	.55
☐ 469	Bobby Brown	.10	.05
☐ 470	Mike Davis	.10	.05
☐ 471	Gaylord Perry	1.00	.45
☐ 472	Mark Belanger	.25	.11
☐ 473	Jim Palmer	.60	.25
☐ 474	Sammy Stewart	.10	.05
☐ 475	Tim Stoddard	.10	.05
☐ 476	Steve Stone	.25	.11
☐ 477	Jeff Newman	.10	.05
☐ 478	Steve McCatty	.10	.05
☐ 479	Billy Martin MG	.50	.23
☐ 480	Mitchell Page	.10	.05
☐ 481	Steve Carlton CY	1.00	.45
☐ 482	Bill Buckner	.25	.11
☐ 483A	Ivan DeJesus P1 ERR Lifetime hits 702	.25	.11
☐ 483B	Ivan DeJesus P2 COR Lifetime hits 642	.10	.05
☐ 484	Cliff Johnson	.10	.05
☐ 485	Lenny Randle	.10	.05
☐ 486	Larry Milbourne	.10	.05
☐ 487	Roy Smalley	.10	.05
☐ 488	John Castino	.10	.05
☐ 489	Ron Jackson	.10	.05
☐ 490A	Dave Roberts P1 Career Highlights Showed pop in	.25	.11
☐ 490B	Dave Roberts P2 Declared himself		.05
☐ 491	George Brett MVP	1.25	.55
☐ 492	Mike Cubbage	.10	.05
☐ 493	Rob Wilfong	.10	.05
☐ 494	Danny Goodwin	.10	.05
☐ 495	Jose Morales	.10	.05
☐ 496	Mickey Rivers	.25	.11
☐ 497	Mike Edwards	.10	.05
☐ 498	Mike Sadek	.10	.05
☐ 499	Lenn Sakata	.10	.05
☐ 500	Gene Michael MG	.10	.05
☐ 501	Dave Roberts	.10	.05
☐ 502	Steve Dillard	.10	.05
☐ 503	Jim Essian	.10	.05
☐ 504	Rance Mulliniks	.10	.05
☐ 505	Darrell Porter	.10	.05
☐ 506	Joe Torre MG	.25	.11
☐ 507	Terry Crowley	.10	.05
☐ 508	Bill Travers	.10	.05
☐ 509	Nelson Norman	.10	.05
☐ 510	Bob McClure	.10	.05
☐ 511	Steve Howe	.25	.11
☐ 512	Dave Rader	.10	.05
☐ 513	Mick Kelleher	.10	.05
☐ 514	Kiko Garcia	.10	.05
☐ 515	Larry Biittner	.10	.05
☐ 516A	Willie Norwood P1 Career Highlights Spent most of	.25	.11
☐ 516B	Willie Norwood P2 Traded to Seattle	.10	.05

☐ 517	Bo Diaz	.10	.05
☐ 518	Juan Beniquez	.10	.05
☐ 519	Scot Thompson	.10	.05
☐ 520	Jim Tracy	.10	.05
☐ 521	Carlos Lezcano	.10	.05
☐ 522	Joe Amalfitano MG	.10	.05
☐ 523	Preston Hanna	.10	.05
☐ 524A	Ray Burris P1 Career Highlights Went on 0	.25	.11
☐ 524B	Ray Burris P2 Drafted by 0	.10	.05
☐ 525	Broderick Perkins	.10	.05
☐ 526	Mickey Hatcher	.25	.11
☐ 527	John Goryl MG	.10	.05
☐ 528	Dick Davis	.10	.05
☐ 529	Butch Wynegar	.10	.05
☐ 530	Sal Butera	.10	.05
☐ 531	Jerry Koosman	.25	.11
☐ 532A	Geoff Zahn P1 (Career Highlights Was 2nd in	.25	.11
☐ 532B	Geoff Zahn P2 Signed a 3 year		.05
☐ 533	Dennis Martinez	.50	.23
☐ 534	Gary Thomasson	.10	.05
☐ 535	Steve Macko	.10	.05
☐ 536	Jim Kaat	.50	.23
☐ 537	Best Hitters George Brett Rod Carew	1.50	.70
☐ 538	Tim Raines	2.00	.90
☐ 539	Keith Smith	.10	.05
☐ 540	Ken Macha	.10	.05
☐ 541	Burt Hooton	.10	.05
☐ 542	Butch Hobson	.10	.05
☐ 543	Bill Stein	.10	.05
☐ 544	Dave Stapleton	.10	.05
☐ 545	Bob Pate	.10	.05
☐ 546	Doug Corbett	.10	.05
☐ 547	Darrell Jackson	.10	.05
☐ 548	Pete Redfern	.10	.05
☐ 549	Roger Erickson	.10	.05
☐ 550	Al Hrabosky	.25	.11
☐ 551	Dick Tidrow	.10	.05
☐ 552	Dave Ford	.10	.05
☐ 553	Dave Kingman	.50	.23
☐ 554A	Mike Vail P1 Career Highlights After two	.25	.11
☐ 554B	Mike Vail P2	.10	.05
☐ 555A	Jerry Martin P1 Career Highlights Overcame a	.25	.11
☐ 555B	Jerry Martin P2 Traded to	.10	.05
☐ 556A	Jesus Figueroa P1 Career Highlights Had an	.25	.11
☐ 556B	Jesus Figueroa P2 Traded to	.10	.05
☐ 557	Don Stanhouse	.10	.05
☐ 558	Barry Foote	.10	.05
☐ 559	Tim Blackwell	.10	.05
☐ 560	Bruce Sutter	.25	.11
☐ 561	Rick Reuschel	.25	.11
☐ 562	Lynn McGlothen	.10	.05
☐ 563A	Bob Owchinko P1 Career Highlights Traded to	.25	.11
☐ 563B	Bob Owchinko P2 Involved in a	.10	.05
☐ 564	John Verhoeven	.10	.05
☐ 565	Ken Landreaux	.10	.05
☐ 566A	Glen Adams P1 ERR Name misspelled	.25	.11
☐ 566B	Glenn Adams P2 COR	.10	.05
☐ 567	Hosken Powell	.10	.05
☐ 568	Dick Noles	.10	.05
☐ 569	Danny Ainge	2.00	.90
☐ 570	Bobby Mattick MG	.10	.05
☐ 571	Joe Lefebvre	.10	.05
☐ 572	Bobby Clark	.10	.05
☐ 573	Dennis Lamp	.10	.05
☐ 574	Randy Lerch	.10	.05

☐ 575	Mookie Wilson	.50	.23
☐ 576	Ron LeFlore	.25	.11
☐ 577	Jim Dwyer	.10	.05
☐ 578	Bill Castro	.10	.05
☐ 579	Greg Minton	.10	.05
☐ 580	Mark Littell	.10	.05
☐ 581	Andy Hassler	.10	.05
☐ 582	Dave Stieb	.25	.11
☐ 583	Ken Oberkfell	.10	.05
☐ 584	Larry Bradford	.10	.05
☐ 585	Fred Stanley	.10	.05
☐ 586	Bill Caudill	.10	.05
☐ 587	Doug Capilla	.10	.05
☐ 588	George Riley	.10	.05
☐ 589	Willie Hernandez	.25	.11
☐ 590	Mike Schmidt MVP	1.25	.55
☐ 591	Steve Stone CY	.10	.05
☐ 592	Rick Sofield	.10	.05
☐ 593	Bombo Rivera	.10	.05
☐ 594	Gary Ward	.10	.05
☐ 595A	Dave Edwards P1 Career Highlights Sidelined the	.25	.11
☐ 595B	Dave Edwards P2 Traded to	.10	.05
☐ 596	Mike Proly	.10	.05
☐ 597	Tommy Boggs	.10	.05
☐ 598	Greg Gross	.10	.05
☐ 599	Elias Sosa	.10	.05
☐ 600	Pat Kelly	.10	.05
☐ 601A	Checklist 1-120 P1 ERR Unnumbered 51 Donahue	.25	.11
☐ 601B	Checklist 1-120 P2 COR Unnumbered 51 Donohue	.50	.23
☐ 602	Checklist 121-240 Unnumbered	.25	.11
☐ 603A	Checklist 241-360 P1 ERR Unnumbered 306 Mathews	.25	.11
☐ 603B	Checklist 241-360 P2 COR Unnumbered 306 Mathews	.25	.11
☐ 604A	Checklist 361-480 P1 ERR Unnumbered 379 Pujois	.25	.11
☐ 604B	Checklist 361-480 P2 COR Unnumbered 379 Pujois	.25	.11
☐ 605A	Checklist 481-600 P1 ERR Unnumbered 566 Glen Adams	.25	.11
☐ 605B	Checklist 481-600 P2 COR Unnumbered 566 Glenn Adams	.25	.11

1982 Donruss

The 1982 Donruss set contains 653 numbered standard-size cards and seven unnumbered checklists. The first 26 cards of this set are entitled Diamond Kings (DK) and feature the art-work of Dick Perez of Perez-Steele Galleries. The set was marketed with puzzle pieces in 15-card packs rather than with bubble gum. There are 63 pieces to the puzzle, which, when put together, make a collage of Babe Ruth entitled "Hall of Fame Diamond King." The card stock in this year's Donruss cards is considerably thicker than the 1981 cards. The seven unnumbered checklist cards are arbitrarily assigned numbers 654 through 660 and are listed at the end of the list below. Notable Rookie Cards in this set include Brett Butler, Cal Ripken Jr., Lee Smith and Dave Stewart.

	NRMT	VG-E
COMPLETE SET (660)	65.00	29.00
COMP.FACT.SET (660)	65.00	29.00
COMMON CARD (1-660)	.10	.05
MINOR STARS	.20	.09
SEMISTARS	.40	.18
UNLISTED STARS	.75	.35

☐ 1 Pete Rose DK	2.00	.90
☐ 2 Gary Carter DK	.20	.09
☐ 3 Steve Garvey DK	.40	.18
☐ 4 Vida Blue DK	.20	.09
☐ 5 Alan Trammell DK	.40	.18
COR		
☐ 5A Alan Trammell DK ERR	.75	.35
(Name misspelled)		
☐ 6 Len Barker DK	.20	.09
☐ 7 Dwight Evans DK	.40	.18
☐ 8 Rod Carew DK	.75	.35
☐ 9 George Hendrick DK	.20	.09
☐ 10 Phil Niekro DK	.40	.18
☐ 11 Richie Zisk DK	.20	.09
☐ 12 Dave Parker DK	.20	.09
☐ 13 Nolan Ryan DK	4.00	1.80
☐ 14 Ivan DeJesus DK	.20	.09
☐ 15 George Brett DK	2.00	.90
☐ 16 Tom Seaver DK	1.00	.45
☐ 17 Dave Kingman DK	.40	.18
☐ 18 Dave Winfield DK	1.50	.70
☐ 19 Mike Norris DK	.20	.09
☐ 20 Carlton Fisk DK	.40	.18
☐ 21 Ozzie Smith DK	1.25	.55
☐ 22 Roy Smalley DK	.20	.09
☐ 23 Buddy Bell DK	.20	.09
☐ 24 Ken Singleton DK	.20	.09
☐ 25 John Mayberry DK	.20	.09
☐ 26 Gorman Thomas DK	.20	.09
☐ 27 Earl Weaver MG	.40	.18
☐ 28 Rollie Fingers	.75	.35
☐ 29 Sparky Anderson MG	.20	.09
☐ 30 Dennis Eckersley	.75	.35
☐ 31 Dave Winfield	1.50	.70
☐ 32 Burt Hooton	.10	.05
☐ 33 Rick Waits	.10	.05
☐ 34 George Brett	1.50	.70
☐ 35 Steve McCatty	.10	.05
☐ 36 Steve Rogers	.10	.05
☐ 37 Bill Stein	.10	.05
☐ 38 Steve Renko	.10	.05
☐ 39 Mike Squires	.10	.05
☐ 40 George Hendrick	.10	.05
☐ 41 Bob Knepper	.10	.05
☐ 42 Steve Carlton	.75	.35
☐ 43 Larry Bittner	.10	.05
☐ 44 Chris Welsh	.10	.05
☐ 45 Steve Nicosia	.10	.05
☐ 46 Jack Clark	.20	.09
☐ 47 Chris Chambliss	.20	.09
☐ 48 Ivan DeJesus	.10	.05
☐ 49 Lee Mazzilli	.10	.05
☐ 50 Julio Cruz	.10	.05
☐ 51 Pete Redfern	.10	.05
☐ 52 Dave Stieb	.20	.09
☐ 53 Doug Corbett	.10	.05
☐ 54 Jorge Bell	.75	.35
☐ 55 Joe Simpson	.10	.05
☐ 56 Rusty Staub	.20	.09
☐ 57 Hector Cruz	.10	.05
☐ 58 Claudell Washington	.10	.05
☐ 59 Enrique Romo	.10	.05
☐ 60 Gary Lavelle	.10	.05
☐ 61 Tim Flannery	.10	.05
☐ 62 Joe Nolan	.10	.05
☐ 63 Larry Bowa	.20	.09
☐ 64 Sixto Lezcano	.10	.05
☐ 65 Joe Sambito	.10	.05
☐ 66 Bruce Kison	.10	.05
☐ 67 Wayne Nordhagen	.10	.05
☐ 68 Woodie Fryman	.10	.05
☐ 69 Billy Sample	.10	.05
☐ 70 Amos Otis	.20	.09
☐ 71 Matt Keough	.10	.05
☐ 72 Toby Harrah	.20	.09
☐ 73 Dave Righetti	.75	.35
☐ 74 Carl Yastrzemski	.75	.35
☐ 75 Bob Welch	.20	.09
☐ 76 Alan Trammell COR	.40	.18
☐ 76A Alan Trammell ERR	1.00	.45
(Name misspelled)		
☐ 77 Rick Dempsey	.20	.09
☐ 78 Paul Molitor	1.25	.55
☐ 79 Dennis Martinez	.40	.18
☐ 80 Jim Slaton	.10	.05
☐ 81 Champ Summers	.10	.05
☐ 82 Carney Lansford	.20	.09
☐ 83 Barry Foote	.10	.05
☐ 84 Steve Garvey	.40	.18
☐ 85 Rick Manning	.10	.05
☐ 86 John Wathan	.10	.05
☐ 87 Brian Kingman	.10	.05
☐ 88 Andre Dawson UER	.75	.35
(Middle name Fernando		
should be Nolan)		
☐ 89 Jim Kern	.10	.05
☐ 90 Bobby Grich	.20	.09
☐ 91 Bob Forsch	.10	.05
☐ 92 Art Howe	.10	.05
☐ 93 Marty Bystrom	.10	.05
☐ 94 Ozzie Smith	2.00	.90
☐ 95 Dave Parker	.20	.09
☐ 96 Doyle Alexander	.10	.05
☐ 97 Al Hrabosky	.10	.05
☐ 98 Frank Taveras	.10	.05
☐ 99 Tim Blackwell	.10	.05
☐ 100 Floyd Bannister	.10	.05
☐ 101 Alfredo Griffin	.10	.05
☐ 102 Dave Engle	.10	.05
☐ 103 Mario Soto	.10	.05
☐ 104 Ross Baumgarten	.10	.05
☐ 105 Ken Singleton	.20	.09
☐ 106 Ted Simmons	.20	.09
☐ 107 Jack Morris	.75	.35
☐ 108 Bob Watson	.20	.09
☐ 109 Dwight Evans	.40	.18
☐ 110 Tom Lasorda MG	.40	.18
☐ 111 Bert Blyleven	.40	.18
☐ 112 Dan Quisenberry	.20	.09
☐ 113 Rickey Henderson	1.50	.70
☐ 114 Gary Carter	.75	.35
☐ 115 Brian Downing	.20	.09
☐ 116 Al Oliver	.20	.09
☐ 117 LaMarr Hoyt	.10	.05
☐ 118 Cesar Cedeno	.20	.09
☐ 119 Keith Moreland	.10	.05
☐ 120 Bob Shirley	.10	.05
☐ 121 Terry Kennedy	.10	.05
☐ 122 Frank Pastore	.10	.05
☐ 123 Gene Garber	.10	.05
☐ 124 Tony Pena	.20	.09
☐ 125 Allen Ripley	.10	.05
☐ 126 Randy Martz	.10	.05
☐ 127 Richie Zisk	.10	.05
☐ 128 Mike Scott	.20	.09
☐ 129 Lloyd Moseby	.20	.09
☐ 130 Rob Wilfong	.10	.05
☐ 131 Tim Stoddard	.10	.05
☐ 132 Gorman Thomas	.20	.09
☐ 133 Dan Petry	.10	.05
☐ 134 Bob Stanley	.10	.05
☐ 135 Lou Piniella	.20	.09
☐ 136 Pedro Guerrero	.20	.09
☐ 137 Len Barker	.10	.05
☐ 138 Rich Gale	.10	.05
☐ 139 Wayne Gross	.10	.05
☐ 140 Tim Wallach	.40	.18
☐ 141 Gene Mauch MG	.10	.05
☐ 142 Doc Medich	.10	.05
☐ 143 Tony Bernazard	.10	.05
☐ 144 Bill Virdon MG	.10	.05
☐ 145 John Littlefield	.10	.05
☐ 146 Dave Bergman	.10	.05
☐ 147 Dick Davis	.10	.05
☐ 148 Tom Seaver	1.00	.45
☐ 149 Matt Sinatro	.10	.05
☐ 150 Chuck Tanner MG	.10	.05
☐ 151 Leon Durham	.20	.09
☐ 152 Gene Tenace	.20	.09
☐ 153 Al Bumbry	.10	.05
☐ 154 Mark Brouhard	.10	.05
☐ 155 Rick Peters	.10	.05
☐ 156 Jerry Remy	.10	.05
☐ 157 Rick Reuschel	.20	.09
☐ 158 Steve Howe	.10	.05
☐ 159 Alan Bannister	.10	.05
☐ 160 U.L. Washington	.10	.05
☐ 161 Rick Langford	.10	.05
☐ 162 Bill Gullickson	.20	.09
☐ 163 Mark Wagner	.10	.05
☐ 164 Geoff Zahn	.10	.05
☐ 165 Ron LeFlore	.20	.09
☐ 166 Dane Iorg	.10	.05
☐ 167 Joe Niekro	.20	.09
☐ 168 Pete Rose	1.00	.45
☐ 169 Dave Collins	.10	.05
☐ 170 Rick Wise	.10	.05
☐ 171 Jim Bibby	.10	.05
☐ 172 Larry Herndon	.10	.05
☐ 173 Bob Horner	.20	.09
☐ 174 Steve Dillard	.10	.05
☐ 175 Mookie Wilson	.20	.09
☐ 176 Dan Meyer	.10	.05
☐ 177 Fernando Arroyo	.10	.05
☐ 178 Jackson Todd	.10	.05
☐ 179 Darrell Jackson	.10	.05
☐ 180 Alvis Woods	.10	.05
☐ 181 Jim Anderson	.10	.05
☐ 182 Dave Kingman	.40	.18
☐ 183 Steve Henderson	.10	.05
☐ 184 Brian Asselstine	.10	.05
☐ 185 Rod Scurry	.10	.05
☐ 186 Fred Breining	.10	.05
☐ 187 Danny Boone	.10	.05
☐ 188 Junior Kennedy	.10	.05
☐ 189 Sparky Lyle	.20	.09
☐ 190 Whitey Herzog MG	.20	.09
☐ 191 Dave Smith	.10	.05
☐ 192 Ed Ott	.10	.05
☐ 193 Greg Luzinski	.20	.09
☐ 194 Bill Lee	.10	.05
☐ 195 Don Zimmer MG	.10	.05
☐ 196 Hal McRae	.20	.09
☐ 197 Mike Norris	.10	.05
☐ 198 Duane Kuiper	.10	.05
☐ 199 Rick Cerone	.10	.05
☐ 200 Jim Rice	.40	.18
☐ 201 Steve Yeager	.10	.05
☐ 202 Tom Brookens	.10	.05
☐ 203 Jose Morales	.10	.05
☐ 204 Roy Howell	.10	.05
☐ 205 Tippy Martinez	.10	.05
☐ 206 Moose Haas	.10	.05
☐ 207 Al Cowens	.10	.05
☐ 208 Dave Stapleton	.10	.05
☐ 209 Bucky Dent	.20	.09
☐ 210 Ron Cey	.20	.09
☐ 211 Jorge Orta	.10	.05
☐ 212 Jamie Quirk	.10	.05
☐ 213 Jeff Jones	.10	.05
☐ 214 Tim Raines	.75	.35
☐ 215 Jon Matlack	.10	.05
☐ 216 Rod Carew	.75	.35
☐ 217 Jim Kaat	.20	.09
☐ 218 Joe Pittman	.10	.05
☐ 219 Larry Christenson	.10	.05
☐ 220 Juan Bonilla	.10	.05
☐ 221 Mike Easler	.10	.05
☐ 222 Vida Blue	.20	.09
☐ 223 Rick Camp	.10	.05
☐ 224 Mike Jorgensen	.10	.05

☐ 225 Jody Davis	.10	.05
☐ 226 Mike Parrott	.10	.05
☐ 227 Jim Clancy	.10	.05
☐ 228 Hosken Powell	.10	.05
☐ 229 Tom Hume	.10	.05
☐ 230 Britt Burns	.10	.05
☐ 231 Jim Palmer	.75	.35
☐ 232 Bob Rodgers MG	.10	.05
☐ 233 Milt Wilcox	.10	.05
☐ 234 Dave Revering	.10	.05
☐ 235 Mike Torrez	.10	.05
☐ 236 Robert Castillo	.10	.05
☐ 237 Von Hayes	.20	.09
☐ 238 Renie Martin	.10	.05
☐ 239 Dwayne Murphy	.10	.05
☐ 240 Rodney Scott	.10	.05
☐ 241 Fred Patek	.10	.05
☐ 242 Mickey Rivers	.10	.05
☐ 243 Steve Trout	.10	.05
☐ 244 Jose Cruz	.20	.09
☐ 245 Manny Trillo	.10	.05
☐ 246 Lary Sorensen	.10	.05
☐ 247 Dave Edwards	.10	.05
☐ 248 Dan Driessen	.10	.05
☐ 249 Tommy Boggs	.10	.05
☐ 250 Dale Berra	.10	.05
☐ 251 Ed Whitson	.10	.05
☐ 252 Lee Smith	2.50	1.10
☐ 253 Tom Paciorek	.10	.05
☐ 254 Pat Zachry	.10	.05
☐ 255 Luis Leal	.10	.05
☐ 256 John Castino	.10	.05
☐ 257 Rich Dauer	.10	.05
☐ 258 Cecil Cooper	.20	.09
☐ 259 Dave Rozema	.10	.05
☐ 260 John Tudor	.10	.05
☐ 261 Jerry Mumphrey	.10	.05
☐ 262 Jay Johnstone	.20	.09
☐ 263 Bo Diaz	.10	.05
☐ 264 Dennis Leonard	.10	.05
☐ 265 Jim Spencer	.10	.05
☐ 266 John Milner	.10	.05
☐ 267 Don Aase	.10	.05
☐ 268 Jim Sundberg	.20	.09
☐ 269 Lamar Johnson	.10	.05
☐ 270 Frank LaCorte	.10	.05
☐ 271 Barry Evans	.10	.05
☐ 272 Enos Cabell	.10	.05
☐ 273 Del Unser	.10	.05
☐ 274 George Foster	.20	.09
☐ 275 Brett Butler	1.25	.55
☐ 276 Lee Lacy	.10	.05
☐ 277 Ken Reitz	.10	.05
☐ 278 Keith Hernandez	.20	.09
☐ 279 Doug DeCinces	.20	.09
☐ 280 Charlie Moore	.10	.05
☐ 281 Lance Parrish	.40	.18
☐ 282 Ralph Houk MG	.10	.05
☐ 283 Rich Gossage	.40	.18
☐ 284 Jerry Reuss	.20	.09
☐ 285 Mike Stanton	.10	.05
☐ 286 Frank White	.20	.09
☐ 287 Bob Owchinko	.10	.05
☐ 288 Scott Sanderson	.10	.05
☐ 289 Bump Wills	.10	.05
☐ 290 Dave Frost	.10	.05
☐ 291 Chet Lemon	.10	.05
☐ 292 Tito Landrum	.10	.05
☐ 293 Vern Ruhle	.10	.05
☐ 294 Mike Schmidt	1.00	.45
☐ 295 Sam Mejias	.10	.05
☐ 296 Gary Lucas	.10	.05
☐ 297 John Candelaria	.10	.05
☐ 298 Jerry Martin	.10	.05
☐ 299 Dale Murphy	.75	.35
☐ 300 Mike Lum	.10	.05
☐ 301 Tom Hausman	.10	.05
☐ 302 Glenn Abbott	.10	.05
☐ 303 Roger Erickson	.10	.05
☐ 304 Otto Velez	.10	.05
☐ 305 Danny Goodwin	.10	.05
☐ 306 John Mayberry	.10	.05
☐ 307 Lenny Randle	.10	.05
☐ 308 Bob Bailor	.10	.05
☐ 309 Jerry Morales	.10	.05
☐ 310 Rufino Linares	.10	.05

☐ 311 Kent Tekulve	.20	.09
☐ 312 Joe Morgan	.75	.35
☐ 313 John Urrea	.10	.05
☐ 314 Paul Householder	.10	.05
☐ 315 Garry Maddox	.10	.05
☐ 316 Mike Ramsey	.10	.05
☐ 317 Alan Ashby	.10	.05
☐ 318 Bob Clark	.10	.05
☐ 319 Tony LaRussa MG	.20	.09
☐ 320 Charlie Lea	.10	.05
☐ 321 Danny Darwin	.10	.05
☐ 322 Cesar Geronimo	.10	.05
☐ 323 Tom Underwood	.10	.05
☐ 324 Andre Thornton	.10	.05
☐ 325 Rudy May	.10	.05
☐ 326 Frank Tanana	.20	.09
☐ 327 Dave Lopes	.20	.09
☐ 328 Richie Hebner	.20	.09
☐ 329 Mike Flanagan	.20	.09
☐ 330 Mike Caldwell	.10	.05
☐ 331 Scott McGregor	.10	.05
☐ 332 Jerry Augustine	.10	.05
☐ 333 Stan Papi	.10	.05
☐ 334 Rick Miller	.10	.05
☐ 335 Graig Nettles	.20	.09
☐ 336 Dusty Baker	.40	.18
☐ 337 Dave Garcia MG	.10	.05
☐ 338 Larry Gura	.10	.05
☐ 339 Cliff Johnson	.10	.05
☐ 340 Warren Cromartie	.10	.05
☐ 341 Steve Comer	.10	.05
☐ 342 Rick Burleson	.10	.05
☐ 343 John Martin	.10	.05
☐ 344 Craig Reynolds	.10	.05
☐ 345 Mike Proly	.10	.05
☐ 346 Ruppert Jones	.10	.05
☐ 347 Omar Moreno	.10	.05
☐ 348 Greg Minton	.10	.05
☐ 349 Rick Mahler	.10	.05
☐ 350 Alex Trevino	.10	.05
☐ 351 Mike Krukow	.10	.05
☐ 352A Shane Rawley ERR	.40	.18
(Photo actually		
Jim Anderson)		
☐ 352B Shane Rawley COR	.10	.05
☐ 353 Garth Iorg	.10	.05
☐ 354 Pete Mackanin	.10	.05
☐ 355 Paul Moskau	.10	.05
☐ 356 Richard Dotson	.10	.05
☐ 357 Steve Stone	.20	.09
☐ 358 Larry Hisle	.10	.05
☐ 359 Aurelio Lopez	.10	.05
☐ 360 Oscar Gamble	.10	.05
☐ 361 Tom Burgmeier	.10	.05
☐ 362 Terry Forster	.10	.05
☐ 363 Joe Charboneau	.20	.09
☐ 364 Ken Brett	.10	.05
☐ 365 Tony Armas	.20	.09
☐ 366 Chris Speier	.10	.05
☐ 367 Fred Lynn	.20	.09
☐ 368 Buddy Bell	.20	.09
☐ 369 Jim Essian	.10	.05
☐ 370 Terry Puhl	.10	.05
☐ 371 Greg Gross	.10	.05
☐ 372 Bruce Sutter	.20	.09
☐ 373 Joe Lefebvre	.10	.05
☐ 374 Ray Knight	.10	.05
☐ 375 Bruce Benedict	.10	.05
☐ 376 Tim Foli	.10	.05
☐ 377 Al Holland	.10	.05
☐ 378 Ken Kravec	.10	.05
☐ 379 Jeff Burroughs	.10	.05
☐ 380 Pete Falcone	.10	.05
☐ 381 Ernie Whitt	.10	.05
☐ 382 Brad Havens	.10	.05
☐ 383 Terry Crowley	.10	.05
☐ 384 Don Money	.10	.05
☐ 385 Dan Schatzeder	.10	.05
☐ 386 Gary Allenson	.10	.05
☐ 387 Yogi Berra CO	.75	.35
☐ 388 Ken Landreaux	.10	.05
☐ 389 Mike Hargrove	.20	.09
☐ 390 Darryl Motley	.10	.05
☐ 391 Dave McKay	.10	.05
☐ 392 Stan Bahnsen	.10	.05
☐ 393 Ken Forsch	.10	.05

☐ 394 Mario Mendoza	.10	.05
☐ 395 Jim Morrison	.10	.05
☐ 396 Mike Ivie	.10	.05
☐ 397 Broderick Perkins	.10	.05
☐ 398 Darrell Evans	.20	.09
☐ 399 Ron Reed	.10	.05
☐ 400 Johnny Bench	1.00	.45
☐ 401 Steve Bedrosian	.20	.09
☐ 402 Bill Robinson	.10	.05
☐ 403 Bill Buckner	.20	.09
☐ 404 Ken Oberkfell	.10	.05
☐ 405 Cal Ripken	40.00	18.00
☐ 406 Jim Gantner	.10	.05
☐ 407 Kirk Gibson	.75	.35
☐ 408 Tony Perez	.75	.35
☐ 409 Tommy John UER	.40	.18
(Text says 52-56 as		
Yankee, should be		
52-26)		
☐ 410 Dave Stewart	1.00	.45
☐ 411 Dan Spillner	.10	.05
☐ 412 Willie Aikens	.10	.05
☐ 413 Mike Heath	.10	.05
☐ 414 Ray Burris	.10	.05
☐ 415 Leon Roberts	.10	.05
☐ 416 Mike Witt	.20	.09
☐ 417 Bob Molinaro	.10	.05
☐ 418 Steve Braun	.10	.05
☐ 419 Nolan Ryan UER	5.00	2.20
(Nisnumbering of		
Nolan's no-hitters		
on card back)		
☐ 420 Tug McGraw	.20	.09
☐ 421 Dave Concepcion	.20	.09
☐ 422A Juan Eichelberger	.40	.18
ERR (Photo actually		
Gary Lucas)		
☐ 422B Juan Eichelberger	.10	.05
COR		
☐ 423 Rick Rhoden	.10	.05
☐ 424 Frank Robinson MG	.40	.18
☐ 425 Eddie Miller	.10	.05
☐ 426 Bill Caudill	.10	.05
☐ 427 Doug Flynn	.10	.05
☐ 428 Larry Andersen UER	.10	.05
(Misspelled Anderson		
on card front)		
☐ 429 Al Williams	.10	.05
☐ 430 Jerry Garvin	.10	.05
☐ 431 Glenn Adams	.10	.05
☐ 432 Barry Bonnell	.10	.05
☐ 433 Jerry Narron	.10	.05
☐ 434 John Stearns	.10	.05
☐ 435 Mike Tyson	.10	.05
☐ 436 Glenn Hubbard	.10	.05
☐ 437 Eddie Solomon	.10	.05
☐ 438 Jeff Leonard	.10	.05
☐ 439 Randy Bass	.10	.05
☐ 440 Mike LaCoss	.10	.05
☐ 441 Gary Matthews	.20	.09
☐ 442 Mark Littell	.10	.05
☐ 443 Don Sutton	.75	.35
☐ 444 John Harris	.10	.05
☐ 445 Vada Pinson CO	.20	.09
☐ 446 Elias Sosa	.10	.05
☐ 447 Charlie Hough	.20	.09
☐ 448 Willie Wilson	.20	.09
☐ 449 Fred Stanley	.10	.05
☐ 450 Tom Veryzer	.10	.05
☐ 451 Ron Davis	.10	.05
☐ 452 Mark Clear	.10	.05
☐ 453 Bill Russell	.20	.09
☐ 454 Lou Whitaker	.75	.35
☐ 455 Dan Graham	.10	.05
☐ 456 Reggie Cleveland	.10	.05
☐ 457 Sammy Stewart	.10	.05
☐ 458 Pete Vuckovich	.10	.05
☐ 459 John Wockenfuss	.10	.05
☐ 460 Glenn Hoffman	.10	.05
☐ 461 Willie Randolph	.20	.09
☐ 462 Fernando Valenzuela	.75	.35
☐ 463 Ron Hassey	.10	.05
☐ 464 Paul Splittorff	.10	.05
☐ 465 Rob Picciolo	.10	.05
☐ 466 Larry Parrish	.10	.05
☐ 467 Johnny Grubb	.10	.05

☐ 468 Dan Ford	.10	.05
☐ 469 Silvio Martinez	.10	.05
☐ 470 Kiko Garcia	.10	.05
☐ 471 Bob Boone	.20	.09
☐ 472 Luis Salazar	.10	.05
☐ 473 Randy Niemann	.10	.05
☐ 474 Tom Griffin	.10	.05
☐ 475 Phil Niekro	.75	.35
☐ 476 Hubie Brooks	.20	.09
☐ 477 Dick Tidrow	.10	.05
☐ 478 Jim Beattie	.10	.05
☐ 479 Damaso Garcia	.10	.05
☐ 480 Mickey Hatcher	.10	.05
☐ 481 Joe Price	.10	.05
☐ 482 Ed Farmer	.10	.05
☐ 483 Eddie Murray	1.25	.55
☐ 484 Ben Oglivie	.20	.09
☐ 485 Kevin Saucier	.10	.05
☐ 486 Bobby Murcer	.20	.09
☐ 487 Bill Campbell	.10	.05
☐ 488 Reggie Smith	.20	.09
☐ 489 Wayne Garland	.10	.05
☐ 490 Jim Wright	.10	.05
☐ 491 Billy Martin MG	.20	.09
☐ 492 Jim Fanning MG	.10	.05
☐ 493 Don Baylor	.40	.18
☐ 494 Rick Honeycutt	.10	.05
☐ 495 Carlton Fisk	.75	.35
☐ 496 Denny Walling	.10	.05
☐ 497 Bake McBride	.10	.05
☐ 498 Darrell Porter	.20	.09
☐ 499 Gene Richards	.10	.05
☐ 500 Ron Oester	.10	.05
☐ 501 Ken Dayley	.10	.05
☐ 502 Jason Thompson	.10	.05
☐ 503 Milt May	.10	.05
☐ 504 Doug Bird	.10	.05
☐ 505 Bruce Bochte	.10	.05
☐ 506 Neil Allen	.10	.05
☐ 507 Joey McLaughlin	.10	.05
☐ 508 Butch Wynegar	.10	.05
☐ 509 Gary Roenicke	.10	.05
☐ 510 Robin Yount	1.50	.70
☐ 511 Dave Tobik	.10	.05
☐ 512 Rich Gedman	.20	.09
☐ 513 Gene Nelson	.10	.05
☐ 514 Rick Monday	.10	.05
☐ 515 Miguel Dilone	.10	.05
☐ 516 Clint Hurdle	.10	.05
☐ 517 Jeff Newman	.10	.05
☐ 518 Grant Jackson	.10	.05
☐ 519 Andy Hassler	.10	.05
☐ 520 Pat Putnam	.10	.05
☐ 521 Greg Pryor	.10	.05
☐ 522 Tony Scott	.10	.05
☐ 523 Steve Mura	.10	.05
☐ 524 Johnnie LeMaster	.10	.05
☐ 525 Dick Ruthven	.10	.05
☐ 526 John McNamara MG	.10	.05
☐ 527 Larry McWilliams	.10	.05
☐ 528 Johnny Ray	.20	.09
☐ 529 Pat Tabler	.20	.09
☐ 530 Tom Herr	.20	.09
☐ 531A San Diego Chicken	.75	.35
ERR (Without TM)		
☐ 531B San Diego Chicken	.75	.35
COR (With TM)		
☐ 532 Sal Butera	.10	.05
☐ 533 Mike Griffin	.10	.05
☐ 534 Kelvin Moore	.10	.05
☐ 535 Reggie Jackson	1.00	.45
☐ 536 Ed Romero	.10	.05
☐ 537 Derrel Thomas	.10	.05
☐ 538 Mike O'Berry	.10	.05
☐ 539 Jack O'Connor	.10	.05
☐ 540 Bob Ojeda	.40	.18
☐ 541 Roy Lee Jackson	.10	.05
☐ 542 Lynn Jones	.10	.05
☐ 543 Gaylord Perry	.75	.35
☐ 544A Phil Garner ERR	.40	.18
(Reverse negative)		
☐ 544B Phil Garner COR	.20	.09
☐ 545 Garry Templeton	.10	.05
☐ 546 Rafael Ramirez	.10	.05
☐ 547 Jeff Reardon	.40	.18
☐ 548 Ron Guidry	.20	.09

☐ 549 Tim Laudner	.10	.05
☐ 550 John Henry Johnson	.10	.05
☐ 551 Chris Bando	.10	.05
☐ 552 Bobby Brown	.10	.05
☐ 553 Larry Bradford	.10	.05
☐ 554 Scott Fletcher	.20	.09
☐ 555 Jerry Royster	.10	.05
☐ 556 Shooty Babitt UER	.10	.05
(Spelled Babbitt		
on front)		
☐ 557 Kent Hrbek	1.00	.45
☐ 558 Yankee Winners	.20	.09
Ron Guidry		
Tommy John		
☐ 559 Mark Bomback	.10	.05
☐ 560 Julio Valdez	.10	.05
☐ 561 Buck Martinez	.10	.05
☐ 562 Mike A. Marshall	.20	.09
☐ 563 Rennie Stennett	.10	.05
☐ 564 Steve Crawford	.10	.05
☐ 565 Bob Babcock	.10	.05
☐ 566 Johnny Podres CO	.20	.09
☐ 567 Paul Serna	.10	.05
☐ 568 Harold Baines	.40	.18
☐ 569 Dave LaRoche	.10	.05
☐ 570 Lee May	.20	.09
☐ 571 Gary Ward	.10	.05
☐ 572 John Denny	.10	.05
☐ 573 Roy Smalley	.10	.05
☐ 574 Bob Brenly	.10	.05
☐ 575 Bronx Bombers	1.50	.70
Reggie Jackson		
Dave Winfield		
☐ 576 Luis Pujols	.10	.05
☐ 577 Butch Hobson	.10	.05
☐ 578 Harvey Kuenn MG	.20	.09
☐ 579 Cal Ripken Sr. CO	.20	.09
☐ 580 Juan Berenguer	.10	.05
☐ 581 Benny Ayala	.10	.05
☐ 582 Vance Law	.10	.05
☐ 583 Rick Leach	.10	.05
☐ 584 George Frazier	.10	.05
☐ 585 Phillies Finest	1.00	.45
Pete Rose		
Mike Schmidt		
☐ 586 Joe Rudi	.10	.05
☐ 587 Juan Beniquez	.10	.05
☐ 588 Luis DeLeon	.10	.05
☐ 589 Craig Swan	.10	.05
☐ 590 Dave Chalk	.10	.05
☐ 591 Billy Gardner MG	.10	.05
☐ 592 Sal Bando	.20	.09
☐ 593 Bert Campaneris	.20	.09
☐ 594 Steve Kemp	.10	.05
☐ 595A Randy Lerch ERR	.40	.18
(Braves)		
☐ 595B Randy Lerch COR		.05
(Brewers)		
☐ 596 Bryan Clark	.10	.05
☐ 597 Dave Ford	.10	.05
☐ 598 Mike Scioscia	.20	.09
☐ 599 John Lowenstein	.10	.05
☐ 600 Rene Lachemann MG	.10	.05
☐ 601 Mick Kelleher	.10	.05
☐ 602 Ron Jackson	.10	.05
☐ 603 Jerry Koosman	.20	.09
☐ 604 Dave Goltz	.10	.05
☐ 605 Ellis Valentine	.10	.05
☐ 606 Lonnie Smith	.20	.09
☐ 607 Joaquin Andujar	.20	.09
☐ 608 Garry Hancock	.10	.05
☐ 609 Jerry Turner	.10	.05
☐ 610 Bob Bonner	.10	.05
☐ 611 Jim Dwyer	.10	.05
☐ 612 Terry Bulling	.10	.05
☐ 613 Joel Youngblood	.10	.05
☐ 614 Larry Milbourne	.10	.05
☐ 615 Gene Roof UER	.10	.05
(Name on front		
is Phil Roof)		
☐ 616 Keith Drumwright	.10	.05
☐ 617 Dave Rosello	.10	.05
☐ 618 Rickey Keeton	.10	.05
☐ 619 Dennis Lamp	.10	.05
☐ 620 Sid Monge	.10	.05
☐ 621 Jerry White	.10	.05

☐ 622 Luis Aguayo	.10	.05
☐ 623 Jamie Easterly	.10	.05
☐ 624 Steve Sax	.75	.35
☐ 625 Dave Roberts	.10	.05
☐ 626 Rick Bosetti	.10	.05
☐ 627 Terry Francona	.10	.05
☐ 628 Pride of Reds	1.00	.45
Tom Seaver		
Johnny Bench		
☐ 629 Paul Mirabella	.10	.05
☐ 630 Rance Mulliniks	.10	.05
☐ 631 Kevin Hickey	.10	.05
☐ 632 Reid Nichols	.10	.05
☐ 633 Dave Geisel	.10	.05
☐ 634 Ken Griffey	.20	.09
☐ 635 Bob Lemon MG	.75	.35
☐ 636 Orlando Sanchez	.10	.05
☐ 637 Bill Almon	.10	.05
☐ 638 Danny Ainge	1.00	.45
☐ 639 Willie Stargell	.75	.35
☐ 640 Bob Sykes	.10	.05
☐ 641 Ed Lynch	.10	.05
☐ 642 John Ellis	.10	.05
☐ 643 Ferguson Jenkins	.75	.35
☐ 644 Lenn Sakata	.10	.05
☐ 645 Julio Gonzalez	.10	.05
☐ 646 Jesse Orosco	.20	.09
☐ 647 Jerry Dybzinski	.10	.05
☐ 648 Tommy Davis CO	.20	.09
☐ 649 Ron Gardenhire	.10	.05
☐ 650 Felipe Alou CO	.20	.09
☐ 651 Harvey Haddix CO	.20	.09
☐ 652 Willie Upshaw	.10	.05
☐ 653 Bill Madlock	.20	.09
☐ 654A DK Checklist 1-26	.75	.35
ERR (Unnumbered)		
(With Trammel)		
☐ 654B DK Checklist 1-26	.20	.09
COR (Unnumbered)		
(With Trammell)		
☐ 655 Checklist 27-130	.20	.09
(Unnumbered)		
☐ 656 Checklist 131-234	.20	.09
(Unnumbered)		
☐ 657 Checklist 235-338	.20	.09
(Unnumbered)		
☐ 658 Checklist 339-442	.20	.09
(Unnumbered)		
☐ 659 Checklist 443-544	.75	.35
(Unnumbered)		
☐ 660 Checklist 545-653	.20	.09
(Unnumbered)		

1983 Donruss

The 1983 Donruss baseball set leads off with a 26-card Diamond Kings (DK) series. Of the remaining 634 standard-size cards, two are combination cards, one portrays the San Diego Chicken, one shows the completed Ty Cobb puzzle, and seven are unnumbered checklist cards. The seven unnumbered checklist cards are arbitrarily assigned numbers 654 *through 660 and are listed at the end of the list below. All cards measure the standard size. Card fronts feature full color photos around a framed white broder. Several printing variations are available but the complete set price below includes only the more common of each variation. Cards were issued in 15-card packs which included a three-piece Ty Cobb puzzle panel (21 different panels were needed to complete the puzzle). Notable Rookie Cards include Wade Boggs, Tony Gwynn and Ryne Sandberg.*

	NRMT	VG-E
COMPLETE SET (660)	80.00	36.00
COMMON CARD (1-660)	.10	.05
MINOR STARS	.20	.09
SEMISTARS	.40	.18
UNLISTED STARS	.75	.35

☐ 1 Fernando Valenzuela DK	.75	.35
☐ 2 Rollie Fingers DK	.75	.35
☐ 3 Reggie Jackson DK	.75	.35
☐ 4 Jim Palmer DK	.75	.35
☐ 5 Jack Morris DK	.20	.09
☐ 6 George Foster DK	.20	.09
☐ 7 Jim Sundberg DK	.20	.09
☐ 8 Willie Stargell DK	.40	.18
☐ 9 Dave Stieb DK	.20	.09
☐ 10 Joe Niekro DK	.20	.09
☐ 11 Rickey Henderson DK	1.25	.55
☐ 12 Dale Murphy DK	.75	.35
☐ 13 Toby Harrah DK	.20	.09
☐ 14 Bill Buckner DK	.20	.09
☐ 15 Willie Wilson DK	.20	.09
☐ 16 Steve Carlton DK	.40	.18
☐ 17 Ron Guidry DK	.20	.09
☐ 18 Steve Rogers DK	.20	.09
☐ 19 Kent Hrbek DK	.20	.09
☐ 20 Keith Hernandez DK	.20	.09
☐ 21 Floyd Bannister DK	.20	.09
☐ 22 Johnny Bench DK	.40	.18
☐ 23 Britt Burns DK	.20	.09
☐ 24 Joe Morgan DK	.40	.18
☐ 25 Carl Yastrzemski DK	.40	.18
☐ 26 Terry Kennedy DK	.20	.09
☐ 27 Gary Roenicke	.10	.05
☐ 28 Dwight Bernard	.10	.05
☐ 29 Pat Underwood	.10	.05
☐ 30 Gary Allenson	.10	.05
☐ 31 Ron Guidry	.20	.09
☐ 32 Burt Hooton	.10	.05
☐ 33 Chris Bando	.10	.05
☐ 34 Vida Blue	.20	.09
☐ 35 Rickey Henderson	1.00	.45
☐ 36 Ray Burris	.10	.05
☐ 37 John Butcher	.10	.05
☐ 38 Don Aase	.10	.05
☐ 39 Jerry Koosman	.20	.09
☐ 40 Bruce Sutter	.20	.09
☐ 41 Jose Cruz	.20	.09
☐ 42 Pete Rose	1.00	.45
☐ 43 Cesar Cedeno	.20	.09
☐ 44 Floyd Chiffer	.10	.05
☐ 45 Larry McWilliams	.10	.05
☐ 46 Alan Fowlkes	.10	.05
☐ 47 Dale Murphy	.75	.35
☐ 48 Doug Bird	.10	.05
☐ 49 Hubie Brooks	.20	.09
☐ 50 Floyd Bannister	.10	.05
☐ 51 Jack O'Connor	.10	.05
☐ 52 Steve Senteney	.10	.05
☐ 53 Gary Gaetti	.75	.35
☐ 54 Damaso Garcia	.10	.05
☐ 55 Gene Nelson	.10	.05
☐ 56 Mookie Wilson	.20	.09
☐ 57 Allen Ripley	.10	.05
☐ 58 Bob Horner	.20	.09
☐ 59 Tony Pena	.20	.09
☐ 60 Gary Lavelle	.10	.05

☐ 61 Tim Lollar	.10	.05
☐ 62 Frank Pastore	.10	.05
☐ 63 Garry Maddox	.10	.05
☐ 64 Bob Forsch	.10	.05
☐ 65 Harry Spilman	.10	.05
☐ 66 Geoff Zahn	.10	.05
☐ 67 Salome Barojas	.10	.05
☐ 68 David Palmer	.10	.05
☐ 69 Charlie Hough	.20	.09
☐ 70 Dan Quisenberry	.20	.09
☐ 71 Tony Armas	.20	.09
☐ 72 Rick Sutcliffe	.20	.09
☐ 73 Steve Balboni	.10	.05
☐ 74 Jerry Remy	.10	.05
☐ 75 Mike Scioscia	.10	.05
☐ 76 John Wockenfuss	.10	.05
☐ 77 Jim Palmer	.75	.35
☐ 78 Rollie Fingers	.75	.35
☐ 79 Joe Nolan	.10	.05
☐ 80 Pete Vuckovich	.10	.05
☐ 81 Rick Leach	.10	.05
☐ 82 Rick Miller	.10	.05
☐ 83 Graig Nettles	.20	.09
☐ 84 Ron Cey	.20	.09
☐ 85 Miguel Dilone	.10	.05
☐ 86 John Wathan	.10	.05
☐ 87 Kelvin Moore	.10	.05
☐ 88A Byrn Smith ERR	.20	.09
(Sic, Bryn)		
☐ 88B Bryn Smith COR	.40	.18
☐ 89 Dave Hostetler	.10	.05
☐ 90 Rod Carew	.60	.25
☐ 91 Lonnie Smith	.10	.05
☐ 92 Bob Knepper	.10	.05
☐ 93 Marty Bystrom	.10	.05
☐ 94 Chris Welsh	.10	.05
☐ 95 Jason Thompson	.10	.05
☐ 96 Tom O'Malley	.10	.05
☐ 97 Phil Niekro	.75	.35
☐ 98 Neil Allen	.10	.05
☐ 99 Bill Buckner	.20	.09
☐ 100 Ed VandeBerg	.10	.05
☐ 101 Jim Clancy	.10	.05
☐ 102 Robert Castillo	.10	.05
☐ 103 Bruce Berenyi	.10	.05
☐ 104 Carlton Fisk	.75	.35
☐ 105 Mike Flanagan	.20	.09
☐ 106 Cecil Cooper	.20	.09
☐ 107 Jack Morris	.20	.09
☐ 108 Mike Morgan	.10	.05
☐ 109 Luis Aponte	.10	.05
☐ 110 Pedro Guerrero	.20	.09
☐ 111 Len Barker	.10	.05
☐ 112 Willie Wilson	.20	.09
☐ 113 Dave Beard	.10	.05
☐ 114 Mike Gates	.10	.05
☐ 115 Reggie Jackson	1.00	.45
☐ 116 George Wright	.10	.05
☐ 117 Vance Law	.10	.05
☐ 118 Nolan Ryan	4.00	1.80
☐ 119 Mike Krukow	.10	.05
☐ 120 Ozzie Smith	1.50	.70
☐ 121 Broderick Perkins	.10	.05
☐ 122 Tom Seaver	1.00	.45
☐ 123 Chris Chambliss	.20	.09
☐ 124 Chuck Tanner MG	.10	.05
☐ 125 Johnnie LeMaster	.10	.05
☐ 126 Mel Hall	.20	.09
☐ 127 Bruce Bochte	.10	.05
☐ 128 Charlie Puleo	.10	.05
☐ 129 Luis Leal	.10	.05
☐ 130 John Pacella	.10	.05
☐ 131 Glenn Gulliver	.10	.05
☐ 132 Don Money	.10	.05
☐ 133 Dave Rozema	.10	.05
☐ 134 Bruce Hurst	.20	.09
☐ 135 Rudy May	.10	.05
☐ 136 Tom Lasorda MG	.40	.18
☐ 137 Dan Spillner UER	.10	.05
(Photo actually		
Ed Whitson)		
☐ 138 Jerry Martin	.10	.05
☐ 139 Mike Norris	.10	.05
☐ 140 Al Oliver	.20	.09
☐ 141 Daryl Sconiers	.10	.05
☐ 142 Lamar Johnson	.10	.05

☐ 143 Harold Baines	.40	.18
☐ 144 Alan Ashby	.10	.05
☐ 145 Garry Templeton	.10	.05
☐ 146 Al Holland	.10	.05
☐ 147 Bo Diaz	.10	.05
☐ 148 Dave Concepcion	.20	.09
☐ 149 Rick Camp	.10	.05
☐ 150 Jim Morrison	.10	.05
☐ 151 Randy Martz	.10	.05
☐ 152 Keith Hernandez	.20	.09
☐ 153 John Lowenstein	.10	.05
☐ 154 Mike Caldwell	.10	.05
☐ 155 Milt Wilcox	.10	.05
☐ 156 Rich Gedman	.10	.05
☐ 157 Rich Gossage	.40	.18
☐ 158 Jerry Reuss	.20	.09
☐ 159 Ron Hassey	.10	.05
☐ 160 Larry Gura	.10	.05
☐ 161 Dwayne Murphy	.10	.05
☐ 162 Woodie Fryman	.10	.05
☐ 163 Steve Comer	.10	.05
☐ 164 Ken Forsch	.10	.05
☐ 165 Dennis Lamp	.10	.05
☐ 166 David Green	.10	.05
☐ 167 Terry Puhl	.10	.05
☐ 168 Mike Schmidt	1.00	.45
(Wearing 37		
rather than 20)		
☐ 169 Eddie Milner	.10	.05
☐ 170 John Curtis	.10	.05
☐ 171 Don Robinson	.10	.05
☐ 172 Rich Gale	.10	.05
☐ 173 Steve Bedrosian	.20	.09
☐ 174 Willie Hernandez	.20	.09
☐ 175 Ron Gardenhire	.10	.05
☐ 176 Jim Beattie	.10	.05
☐ 177 Tim Laudner	.10	.05
☐ 178 Buck Martinez	.10	.05
☐ 179 Kent Hrbek	.20	.09
☐ 180 Alfredo Griffin	.10	.05
☐ 181 Larry Andersen	.10	.05
☐ 182 Pete Falcone	.10	.05
☐ 183 Jody Davis	.10	.05
☐ 184 Glenn Hubbard	.10	.05
☐ 185 Dale Berra	.10	.05
☐ 186 Greg Minton	.10	.05
☐ 187 Gary Lucas	.10	.05
☐ 188 Dave Van Gorder	.10	.05
☐ 189 Bob Dernier	.10	.05
☐ 190 Willie McGee	.75	.35
☐ 191 Dickie Thon	.10	.05
☐ 192 Bob Boone	.20	.09
☐ 193 Britt Burns	.10	.05
☐ 194 Jeff Reardon	.20	.09
☐ 195 Jon Matlack	.10	.05
☐ 196 Don Slaught	.40	.18
☐ 197 Fred Stanley	.10	.05
☐ 198 Rick Manning	.10	.05
☐ 199 Dave Righetti	.20	.09
☐ 200 Dave Stapleton	.10	.05
☐ 201 Steve Yeager	.10	.05
☐ 202 Enos Cabell	.10	.05
☐ 203 Sammy Stewart	.10	.05
☐ 204 Moose Haas	.10	.05
☐ 205 Lenn Sakata	.10	.05
☐ 206 Charlie Moore	.10	.05
☐ 207 Alan Trammell	.75	.35
☐ 208 Jim Rice	.40	.18
☐ 209 Roy Smalley	.10	.05
☐ 210 Bill Russell	.20	.09
☐ 211 Andre Thornton	.10	.05
☐ 212 Willie Aikens	.10	.05
☐ 213 Dave McKay	.10	.05
☐ 214 Tim Blackwell	.10	.05
☐ 215 Buddy Bell	.20	.09
☐ 216 Doug DeCinces	.20	.09
☐ 217 Tom Herr	.20	.09
☐ 218 Frank LaCorte	.10	.05
☐ 219 Steve Carlton	.75	.35
☐ 220 Terry Kennedy	.10	.05
☐ 221 Mike Easler	.10	.05
☐ 222 Jack Clark	.20	.09
☐ 223 Gene Garber	.10	.05
☐ 224 Scott Holman	.10	.05
☐ 225 Mike Proly	.10	.05
☐ 226 Terry Bulling	.10	.05

☐ 227	Jerry Garvin	.10	.05
☐ 228	Ron Davis	.10	.05
☐ 229	Tom Hume	.10	.05
☐ 230	Marc Hill	.10	.05
☐ 231	Dennis Martinez	.20	.09
☐ 232	Jim Gantner	.20	.09
☐ 233	Larry Pashnick	.10	.05
☐ 234	Dave Collins	.10	.05
☐ 235	Tom Burgmeier	.10	.05
☐ 236	Ken Landreaux	.10	.05
☐ 237	John Denny	.10	.05
☐ 238	Hal McRae	.20	.09
☐ 239	Matt Keough	.10	.05
☐ 240	Doug Flynn	.10	.05
☐ 241	Fred Lynn	.20	.09
☐ 242	Billy Sample	.10	.05
☐ 243	Tom Paciorek	.20	.09
☐ 244	Joe Sambito	.10	.05
☐ 245	Sid Monge	.10	.05
☐ 246	Ken Oberkfell	.10	.05
☐ 247	Joe Pittman UER	.10	.05
	(Photo actually Mario Soto Juan Eichelberger)		
☐ 248	Mario Soto	.10	.05
☐ 249	Claudell Washington	.10	.05
☐ 250	Rick Rhoden	.10	.05
☐ 251	Darrell Evans	.20	.09
☐ 252	Steve Henderson	.10	.05
☐ 253	Manny Castillo	.10	.05
☐ 254	Craig Swan	.10	.05
☐ 255	Joey McLaughlin	.10	.05
☐ 256	Pete Redfern	.10	.05
☐ 257	Ken Singleton	.10	.05
☐ 258	Robin Yount	1.25	.55
☐ 259	Elias Sosa	.10	.05
☐ 260	Bob Ojeda	.10	.05
☐ 261	Bobby Murcer	.20	.09
☐ 262	Candy Maldonado	.20	.09
☐ 263	Rick Waits	.10	.05
☐ 264	Greg Pryor	.10	.05
☐ 265	Bob Owchinko	.10	.05
☐ 266	Chris Speier	.10	.05
☐ 267	Bruce Kison	.10	.05
☐ 268	Mark Wagner	.10	.05
☐ 269	Steve Kemp	.10	.05
☐ 270	Phil Garner	.20	.09
☐ 271	Gene Richards	.10	.05
☐ 272	Renie Martin	.10	.05
☐ 273	Dave Roberts	.10	.05
☐ 274	Dan Driessen	.10	.05
☐ 275	Rufino Linares	.10	.05
☐ 276	Lee Lacy	.10	.05
☐ 277	Ryne Sandberg	12.00	5.50
☐ 278	Darrell Porter	.10	.05
☐ 279	Cal Ripken	10.00	4.50
☐ 280	Jamie Easterly	.10	.05
☐ 281	Bill Fahey	.10	.05
☐ 282	Glenn Hoffman	.10	.05
☐ 283	Willie Randolph	.20	.09
☐ 284	Fernando Valenzuela	.40	.18
☐ 285	Alan Bannister	.10	.05
☐ 286	Paul Splittorff	.10	.05
☐ 287	Joe Rudi	.10	.05
☐ 288	Bill Gullickson	.20	.09
☐ 289	Danny Darwin	.10	.05
☐ 290	Andy Hassler	.10	.05
☐ 291	Ernesto Escarrega	.10	.05
☐ 292	Steve Mura	.10	.05
☐ 293	Tony Scott	.10	.05
☐ 294	Manny Trillo	.10	.05
☐ 295	Greg Harris	.10	.05
☐ 296	Luis DeLeon	.10	.05
☐ 297	Kent Tekulve	.20	.09
☐ 298	Atlee Hammaker	.10	.05
☐ 299	Bruce Benedict	.10	.05
☐ 300	Fergie Jenkins	.75	.35
☐ 301	Dave Kingman	.40	.18
☐ 302	Bill Caudill	.10	.05
☐ 303	John Castino	.10	.05
☐ 304	Ernie Whitt	.10	.05
☐ 305	Randy Johnson	.10	.05
☐ 306	Garth Iorg	.10	.05
☐ 307	Gaylord Perry	.75	.35
☐ 308	Ed Lynch	.10	.05
☐ 309	Keith Moreland	.10	.05
☐ 310	Rafael Ramirez	.10	.05
☐ 311	Bill Madlock	.20	.09
☐ 312	Milt May	.10	.05
☐ 313	John Montefusco	.10	.05
☐ 314	Wayne Krenchicki	.10	.05
☐ 315	George Vukovich	.10	.05
☐ 316	Joaquin Andujar	.10	.05
☐ 317	Craig Reynolds	.10	.05
☐ 318	Rick Burleson	.10	.05
☐ 319	Richard Dotson	.10	.05
☐ 320	Steve Rogers	.10	.05
☐ 321	Dave Schmidt	.10	.05
☐ 322	Bud Black	.20	.09
☐ 323	Jeff Burroughs	.10	.05
☐ 324	Von Hayes	.20	.09
☐ 325	Butch Wynegar	.10	.05
☐ 326	Carl Yastrzemski	.75	.35
☐ 327	Ron Roenicke	.10	.05
☐ 328	Howard Johnson	.75	.35
☐ 329	Rick Dempsey UER	.20	.09
	(Posing as a left-handed batter)		
☐ 330A	Jim Slaton	.10	.05
	(Bio printed black on white)		
☐ 330B	Jim Slaton	.20	.09
	(Bio printed black on yellow)		
☐ 331	Benny Ayala	.10	.05
☐ 332	Ted Simmons	.20	.09
☐ 333	Lou Whitaker	.20	.09
☐ 334	Chuck Rainey	.10	.05
☐ 335	Lou Piniella	.20	.09
☐ 336	Steve Sax	.20	.09
☐ 337	Toby Harrah	.10	.05
☐ 338	George Brett	1.50	.70
☐ 339	Dave Lopes	.20	.09
☐ 340	Gary Carter	.75	.35
☐ 341	John Grubb	.10	.05
☐ 342	Tim Foli	.10	.05
☐ 343	Jim Kaat	.20	.09
☐ 344	Mike LaCoss	.10	.05
☐ 345	Larry Christenson	.10	.05
☐ 346	Juan Bonilla	.10	.05
☐ 347	Omar Moreno	.10	.05
☐ 348	Chili Davis	.20	.09
☐ 349	Tommy Boggs	.10	.05
☐ 350	Rusty Staub	.20	.09
☐ 351	Bump Wills	.10	.05
☐ 352	Rick Sweet	.10	.05
☐ 353	Jim Gott	.10	.05
☐ 354	Terry Felton	.10	.05
☐ 355	Jim Kern	.10	.05
☐ 356	Bill Almon UER	.10	.05
	(Expos/Mets in 1983, not Padres/Mets)		
☐ 357	Tippy Martinez	.10	.05
☐ 358	Roy Howell	.10	.05
☐ 359	Dan Petry	.10	.05
☐ 360	Jerry Mumphrey	.10	.05
☐ 361	Mark Clear	.10	.05
☐ 362	Mike Marshall	.10	.05
☐ 363	Lary Sorensen	.10	.05
☐ 364	Amos Otis	.20	.09
☐ 365	Rick Langford	.10	.05
☐ 366	Brad Mills	.10	.05
☐ 367	Brian Downing	.10	.05
☐ 368	Mike Richardt	.10	.05
☐ 369	Aurelio Rodriguez	.10	.05
☐ 370	Dave Bergman	.10	.05
☐ 371	Tug McGraw	.20	.09
☐ 372	Doug Bair	.10	.05
☐ 373	Ruppert Jones	.10	.05
☐ 374	Alex Trevino	.10	.05
☐ 375	Ken Dayley	.10	.05
☐ 376	Rod Scurry	.10	.05
☐ 377	Bob Brenly	.10	.05
☐ 378	Scot Thompson	.10	.05
☐ 379	Julio Cruz	.10	.05
☐ 380	John Stearns	.10	.05
☐ 381	Dale Murray	.10	.05
☐ 382	Frank Viola	.75	.35
☐ 383	Al Bumbry	.10	.05
☐ 384	Ben Oglivie	.10	.05
☐ 385	Dave Tobik	.10	.05
☐ 386	Bob Stanley	.10	.05
☐ 387	Andre Robertson	.10	.05
☐ 388	Jorge Orta	.10	.05
☐ 389	Ed Whitson	.10	.05
☐ 390	Don Hood	.10	.05
☐ 391	Tom Underwood	.10	.05
☐ 392	Tim Wallach	.20	.09
☐ 393	Steve Renko	.10	.05
☐ 394	Mickey Rivers	.10	.05
☐ 395	Greg Luzinski	.20	.09
☐ 396	Art Howe	.10	.05
☐ 397	Alan Wiggins	.10	.05
☐ 398	Jim Barr	.10	.05
☐ 399	Ivan DeJesus	.10	.05
☐ 400	Tom Lawless	.10	.05
☐ 401	Bob Walk	.10	.05
☐ 402	Jimmy Smith	.10	.05
☐ 403	Lee Smith	2.00	.90
☐ 404	George Hendrick	.10	.05
☐ 405	Eddie Murray	1.00	.45
☐ 406	Marshall Edwards	.10	.05
☐ 407	Lance Parrish	.20	.09
☐ 408	Carney Lansford	.20	.09
☐ 409	Dave Winfield	1.25	.55
☐ 410	Bob Welch	.20	.09
☐ 411	Larry Milbourne	.10	.05
☐ 412	Dennis Leonard	.10	.05
☐ 413	Dan Meyer	.10	.05
☐ 414	Charlie Lea	.10	.05
☐ 415	Rick Honeycutt	.10	.05
☐ 416	Mike Witt	.10	.05
☐ 417	Steve Trout	.10	.05
☐ 418	Glenn Brummer	.10	.05
☐ 419	Denny Walling	.10	.05
☐ 420	Gary Matthews	.20	.09
☐ 421	Charlie Leibrandt UER	.10	.05
	(Liebrandt on front of card)		
☐ 422	Juan Eichelberger UER	.10	.05
	(Photo actually Joe Pittman)		
☐ 423	Cecilio Guante UER	.10	.05
	(Listed as Matt on card)		
☐ 424	Bill Laskey	.10	.05
☐ 425	Jerry Royster	.10	.05
☐ 426	Dickie Noles	.10	.05
☐ 427	George Foster	.20	.09
☐ 428	Mike Moore	.75	.35
☐ 429	Gary Ward	.10	.05
☐ 430	Barry Bonnell	.10	.05
☐ 431	Ron Washington	.10	.05
☐ 432	Rance Mulliniks	.10	.05
☐ 433	Mike Stanton	.10	.05
☐ 434	Jesse Orosco	.20	.09
☐ 435	Larry Bowa	.20	.09
☐ 436	Biff Pocoroba	.10	.05
☐ 437	Johnny Ray	.10	.05
☐ 438	Joe Morgan	.75	.35
☐ 439	Eric Show	.10	.05
☐ 440	Larry Biittner	.10	.05
☐ 441	Greg Gross	.10	.05
☐ 442	Gene Tenace	.20	.09
☐ 443	Danny Heep	.10	.05
☐ 444	Bobby Clark	.10	.05
☐ 445	Kevin Hickey	.10	.05
☐ 446	Scott Sanderson	.10	.05
☐ 447	Frank Tanana	.20	.09
☐ 448	Cesar Geronimo	.10	.05
☐ 449	Jimmy Sexton	.10	.05
☐ 450	Mike Hargrove	.20	.09
☐ 451	Doyle Alexander	.10	.05
☐ 452	Dwight Evans	.20	.09
☐ 453	Terry Forster	.10	.05
☐ 454	Tom Brookens	.10	.05
☐ 455	Rich Dauer	.10	.05
☐ 456	Rob Picciolo	.10	.05
☐ 457	Terry Crowley	.10	.05
☐ 458	Ned Yost	.10	.05
☐ 459	Kirk Gibson	.75	.35
☐ 460	Reid Nichols	.10	.05
☐ 461	Oscar Gamble	.10	.05
☐ 462	Dusty Baker	.20	.09
☐ 463	Jack Perconte	.10	.05
☐ 464	Frank White	.20	.09
☐ 465	Mickey Klutts	.10	.05
☐ 466	Warren Cromartie	.10	.05
☐ 467	Larry Parrish	.10	.05

☐ 468	Bobby Grich	.20	.09
☐ 469	Dane Iorg	.10	.05
☐ 470	Joe Niekro	.20	.09
☐ 471	Ed Farmer	.10	.05
☐ 472	Tim Flannery	.10	.05
☐ 473	Dave Parker	.20	.09
☐ 474	Jeff Leonard	.10	.05
☐ 475	Al Hrabosky	.10	.05
☐ 476	Ron Hodges	.10	.05
☐ 477	Leon Durham	.10	.05
☐ 478	Jim Essian	.10	.05
☐ 479	Roy Lee Jackson	.10	.05
☐ 480	Brad Havens	.10	.05
☐ 481	Joe Price	.10	.05
☐ 482	Tony Bernazard	.10	.05
☐ 483	Scott McGregor	.10	.05
☐ 484	Paul Molitor	1.00	.45
☐ 485	Mike Ivie	.10	.05
☐ 486	Ken Griffey	.20	.09
☐ 487	Dennis Eckersley	.75	.35
☐ 488	Steve Garvey	.40	.18
☐ 489	Mike Fischlin	.10	.05
☐ 490	U.L. Washington	.10	.05
☐ 491	Steve McCatty	.10	.05
☐ 492	Roy Johnson	.10	.05
☐ 493	Don Baylor	.40	.18
☐ 494	Bobby Johnson	.10	.05
☐ 495	Mike Squires	.10	.05
☐ 496	Bert Roberge	.10	.05
☐ 497	Dick Ruthven	.10	.05
☐ 498	Tito Landrum	.10	.05
☐ 499	Sixto Lezcano	.10	.05
☐ 500	Johnny Bench	1.00	.45
☐ 501	Larry Whisenton	.10	.05
☐ 502	Manny Sarmiento	.10	.05
☐ 503	Fred Breining	.10	.05
☐ 504	Bill Campbell	.10	.05
☐ 505	Todd Cruz	.10	.05
☐ 506	Bob Bailor	.10	.05
☐ 507	Dave Stieb	.20	.09
☐ 508	Al Williams	.10	.05
☐ 509	Dan Ford	.10	.05
☐ 510	Gorman Thomas	.10	.05
☐ 511	Chet Lemon	.10	.05
☐ 512	Mike Torrez	.10	.05
☐ 513	Shane Rawley	.10	.05
☐ 514	Mark Belanger	.10	.05
☐ 515	Rodney Craig	.10	.05
☐ 516	Onix Concepcion	.10	.05
☐ 517	Mike Heath	.10	.05
☐ 518	Andre Dawson UER	.75	.35
	(Middle name Fernando, should be Nolan)		
☐ 519	Luis Sanchez	.10	.05
☐ 520	Terry Bogener	.10	.05
☐ 521	Rudy Law	.10	.05
☐ 522	Ray Knight	.20	.09
☐ 523	Joe Lefebvre	.10	.05
☐ 524	Jim Wohlford	.10	.05
☐ 525	Julio Franco	1.00	.45
☐ 526	Ron Oester	.10	.05
☐ 527	Rick Mahler	.10	.05
☐ 528	Steve Nicosia	.10	.05
☐ 529	Junior Kennedy	.10	.05
☐ 530A	Whitey Herzog MG	.20	.09
	(Bio printed black on white)		
☐ 530B	Whitey Herzog MG	.20	.09
	(Bio printed black on yellow)		
☐ 531A	Don Sutton	.75	.35
	(Blue border on photo)		
☐ 531B	Don Sutton	.75	.35
	(Green border on photo)		
☐ 532	Mark Brouhard	.10	.05
☐ 533A	Sparky Anderson MG	.20	.09
	(Bio printed black on white)		
☐ 533B	Sparky Anderson MG	.20	.09
	(Bio printed black on yellow)		
☐ 534	Roger LaFrancois	.10	.05
☐ 535	George Frazier	.10	.05
☐ 536	Tom Niedenfuer	.10	.05

☐ 537	Ed Glynn	.10	.05
☐ 538	Lee May	.20	.09
☐ 539	Bob Kearney	.10	.05
☐ 540	Tim Raines	.75	.35
☐ 541	Paul Mirabella	.10	.05
☐ 542	Luis Tiant	.20	.09
☐ 543	Ron LeFlore	.10	.05
☐ 544	Dave LaPoint	.10	.05
☐ 545	Randy Moffitt	.10	.05
☐ 546	Luis Aguayo	.10	.05
☐ 547	Brad Lesley	.20	.09
☐ 548	Luis Salazar	.10	.05
☐ 549	John Candelaria	.10	.05
☐ 550	Dave Bergman	.10	.05
☐ 551	Bob Watson	.20	.09
☐ 552	Pat Tabler	.10	.05
☐ 553	Brent Gaff	.10	.05
☐ 554	Al Cowens	.10	.05
☐ 555	Tom Brunansky	.20	.09
☐ 556	Lloyd Moseby	.10	.05
☐ 557A	Pascual Perez ERR	2.00	.90
	(Twins in glove)		
☐ 557B	Pascual Perez COR	.20	.09
	(Braves in glove)		
☐ 558	Willie Upshaw	.10	.05
☐ 559	Richie Zisk	.10	.05
☐ 560	Pat Zachry	.10	.05
☐ 561	Jay Johnstone	.20	.09
☐ 562	Carlos Diaz	.10	.05
☐ 563	John Tudor	.10	.05
☐ 564	Frank Robinson MG	.40	.18
☐ 565	Dave Edwards	.10	.05
☐ 566	Paul Householder	.10	.05
☐ 567	Ron Reed	.10	.05
☐ 568	Mike Ramsey	.10	.05
☐ 569	Kiko Garcia	.10	.05
☐ 570	Tommy John	.40	.18
☐ 571	Tony LaRussa MG	.20	.09
☐ 572	Joel Youngblood	.10	.05
☐ 573	Wayne Tolleson	.10	.05
☐ 574	Keith Creel	.10	.05
☐ 575	Billy Martin MG	.20	.09
☐ 576	Jerry Dybzinski	.10	.05
☐ 577	Rick Cerone	.10	.05
☐ 578	Tony Perez	.75	.35
☐ 579	Greg Brock	.10	.05
☐ 580	Glenn Wilson	.10	.05
☐ 581	Tim Stoddard	.10	.05
☐ 582	Bob McClure	.10	.05
☐ 583	Jim Dwyer	.10	.05
☐ 584	Ed Romero	.10	.05
☐ 585	Larry Herndon	.10	.05
☐ 586	Wade Boggs	8.00	3.60
☐ 587	Jay Howell	.10	.05
☐ 588	Dave Stewart	.20	.09
☐ 589	Bert Blyleven	.40	.18
☐ 590	Dick Howser MG	.10	.05
☐ 591	Wayne Gross	.10	.05
☐ 592	Terry Francona	.10	.05
☐ 593	Don Werner	.10	.05
☐ 594	Bill Stein	.10	.05
☐ 595	Jesse Barfield	.20	.09
☐ 596	Bob Molinaro	.10	.05
☐ 597	Mike Vail	.10	.05
☐ 598	Tony Gwynn	25.00	11.00
☐ 599	Gary Rajsich	.10	.05
☐ 600	Jerry Ujdur	.10	.05
☐ 601	Cliff Johnson	.10	.05
☐ 602	Jerry White	.10	.05
☐ 603	Bryan Clark	.10	.05
☐ 604	Joe Ferguson	.10	.05
☐ 605	Guy Sularz	.10	.05
☐ 606A	Ozzie Virgil	.20	.09
	(Green border on photo)		
☐ 606B	Ozzie Virgil	.20	.09
	(Orange border on photo)		
☐ 607	Terry Harper	.10	.05
☐ 608	Harvey Kuenn MG	.20	.09
☐ 609	Jim Sundberg	.20	.09
☐ 610	Willie Stargell	.75	.35
☐ 611	Reggie Smith	.20	.09
☐ 612	Rob Wilfong	.10	.05
☐ 613	The Niekro Brothers	.40	.18
	Joe Niekro		

	Phil Niekro		
☐ 614	Lee Elia MG	.10	.05
☐ 615	Mickey Hatcher	.10	.05
☐ 616	Jerry Hairston	.10	.05
☐ 617	John Martin	.10	.05
☐ 618	Wally Backman	.10	.05
☐ 619	Storm Davis	.10	.05
☐ 620	Alan Knicely	.10	.05
☐ 621	John Stuper	.10	.05
☐ 622	Matt Sinatro	.10	.05
☐ 623	Geno Petralli	.40	.18
☐ 624	Duane Walker	.10	.05
☐ 625	Dick Williams MG	.10	.05
☐ 626	Pat Corrales MG	.10	.05
☐ 627	Vern Ruhle	.10	.05
☐ 628	Joe Torre MG	.40	.18
☐ 629	Anthony Johnson	.10	.05
☐ 630	Steve Howe	.10	.05
☐ 631	Gary Woods	.10	.05
☐ 632	LaMarr Hoyt	.20	.09
☐ 633	Steve Swisher	.10	.05
☐ 634	Terry Leach	.10	.05
☐ 635	Jeff Newman	.10	.05
☐ 636	Brett Butler	.40	.18
☐ 637	Gary Gray	.10	.05
☐ 638	Lee Mazzilli	.10	.05
☐ 639A	Ron Jackson ERR	5.00	2.20
	(A's in glove)		
☐ 639B	Ron Jackson COR	.10	.05
	(Angels in glove, red border on photo)		
☐ 639C	Ron Jackson COR	.20	.35
	(Angels in glove, green border on photo)		
☐ 640	Juan Beniquez	.10	.05
☐ 641	Dave Rucker	.10	.05
☐ 642	Luis Pujols	.10	.05
☐ 643	Rick Monday	.10	.05
☐ 644	Hosken Powell	.10	.05
☐ 645	The Chicken	.75	.35
☐ 646	Dave Engle	.10	.05
☐ 647	Dick Davis	.10	.05
☐ 648	Frank Robinson	.20	.09
	Vida Blue		
	Joe Morgan		
☐ 649	Al Chambers	.10	.05
☐ 650	Jesus Vega	.10	.05
☐ 651	Jeff Jones	.10	.05
☐ 652	Marvis Foley	.10	.05
☐ 653	Ty Cobb Puzzle Card	.75	.35
☐ 654A	Dick Perez/Diamond King Checklist 1-26 (Unnumbered) ERR (Word "checklist" omitted from back)	.75	.35
☐ 654B	Dick Perez/Diamond King Checklist 1-26 (Unnumbered) COR (Word "checklist" is on back)		.35
☐ 655	Checklist 27-130 (Unnumbered)	.10	.05
☐ 656	Checklist 131-234 (Unnumbered)	.10	.05
☐ 657	Checklist 235-338 (Unnumbered)	.10	.05
☐ 658	Checklist 339-442 (Unnumbered)	.10	.05
☐ 659	Checklist 443-544 (Unnumbered)	.10	.05
☐ 660	Checklist 545-653 (Unnumbered)	.10	.05

1984 Donruss

The 1984 Donruss set contains a total of 660 standard-size cards; however, only 658 are numbered. The first 26 cards in the set are again Diamond Kings (DK). A new feature, Rated Rookies (RR), was introduced with this set with Bill

KEITH HERNANDEZ 1b

Madden's 20 selections comprising numbers 27 through 46. Two "Living Legend" cards designated A (featuring Gaylord Perry and Rollie Fingers) and B (featuring Johnny Bench and Carl Yastrzemski) were issued as bonus cards in wax packs, but were not issued in the factory sets sold to hobby dealers. The seven unnumbered checklist cards are arbitrarily assigned numbers 652 through 658 and are listed at the end of the list below. The attractive card front designs changed considerably from the previous two years. The backs contain statistics and are printed in green and black ink. The cards were distributed with a 3-piece puzzle panel of Duke Snider. There are no extra variation cards included in the complete set price below. The variation cards apparently resulted from a different printing for the factory sets as the Darling and Stenhouse no number variations as well as the Perez-Steele errors were corrected in the factory sets which were released later in the year. The Diamond King cards found in packs spelled Perez-Steele as Perez-Steel. Notable Rookie Cards in this set include Joe Carter, Don Mattingly, Tony Phillips, Darryl Strawberry, and Andy Van Slyke. The Joe Carter card is almost never found well centered.

	NRMT	VG-E
COMPLETE SET (660)	200.00	90.00
COMP.FACT.SET (658)	200.00	90.00
COMMON CARD (1-658)	.25	.11
MINOR STARS	.75	.35
SEMISTARS	1.50	.70
UNLISTED STARS	3.00	1.35

DIAMOND KING ERR: 80% VALUE OF COR
BEWARE OF COUNTERFEITS

☐ 1 Robin Yount DK COR	5.00	2.20
☐ 1A Robin Yount DK ERR	1.50	.70
☐ 2 Dave Concepcion DK	1.50	.70
COR		
☐ 2A Dave Concepcion DK	.75	.35
ERR		
☐ 3 Dwayne Murphy DK	.75	.35
COR		
☐ 3A Dwayne Murphy DK	.25	.11
ERR		
☐ 4 John Castino DK COR	.75	.35
☐ 4A John Castino DK ERR	.25	.11
☐ 5 Leon Durham DK COR	.75	.35
☐ 5A Leon Durham DK ERR	.25	.11

☐ 6 Rusty Staub DK COR	.75	.35
☐ 6A Rusty Staub DK ERR	.75	.35
☐ 7 Jack Clark DK COR	.75	.35
☐ 7A Jack Clark DK ERR	.75	.35
☐ 8 Dave Dravecky DK	.75	.35
COR		
☐ 8A Dave Dravecky DK	.75	.35
ERR		
☐ 9 Al Oliver DK COR	.75	.35
☐ 9A Al Oliver DK ERR	.75	.35
☐ 10 Dave Righetti DK	.75	.35
COR		
☐ 10A Dave Righetti DK	.75	.35
ERR		
☐ 11 Hal McRae DK COR	.75	.35
☐ 11A Hal McRae DK ERR	.75	.35
☐ 12 Ray Knight DK COR	.75	.35
☐ 12A Ray Knight DK ERR	.75	.35
☐ 13 Bruce Sutter DK COR	.75	.35
☐ 13A Bruce Sutter DK ERR	.75	.35
☐ 14 Bob Horner DK COR	.75	.35
☐ 14A Bob Horner DK ERR	.75	.35
☐ 15 Lance Parrish DK	.75	.35
COR		
☐ 15A Lance Parrish DK	.75	.35
ERR		
☐ 16 Matt Young DK COR	.75	.35
☐ 16A Matt Young DK ERR	.25	.11
☐ 17 Fred Lynn DK COR	.75	.35
☐ 17A Fred Lynn DK ERR	.25	.11
☐ 18 Ron Kittle DK COR	.75	.35
☐ 18A Ron Kittle DK ERR	.25	.11
☐ 19 Jim Clancy DK COR	.75	.35
☐ 19A Jim Clancy DK ERR	.25	.11
☐ 20 Bill Madlock DK COR	.75	.35
☐ 20A Bill Madlock DK ERR	.75	.35
☐ 21 Larry Parrish DK	.75	.35
COR		
☐ 21A Larry Parrish DK	.25	.11
ERR		
☐ 22 Eddie Murray DK COR	3.00	1.35
☐ 22A Eddie Murray DK ERR	1.50	.70
☐ 23 Mike Schmidt DK COR	5.00	2.20
☐ 23A Mike Schmidt DK ERR	3.00	1.35
☐ 24 Pedro Guerrero DK	.75	.35
COR		
☐ 24A Pedro Guerrero DK	.75	.35
ERR		
☐ 25 Andre Thornton DK	.75	.35
COR		
☐ 25A Andre Thornton DK	.75	.35
ERR		
☐ 26 Wade Boggs DK COR	3.50	1.55
☐ 26A Wade Boggs DK ERR	2.50	1.10
☐ 27 Joel Skinner RR	.25	.11
☐ 28 Tommy Dunbar RR	.25	.11
☐ 29 Mike Stenhouse RR	.75	.35
ERR No number on back		
☐ 29B Mike Stenhouse RR	3.00	1.35
COR Numbered on back		
☐ 30A Ron Darling RR ERR	.75	.35
(No number on back)		
☐ 30B Ron Darling RR COR	3.00	1.35
(Numbered on back)		
☐ 31 Dion James RR	.75	.35
☐ 32 Tony Fernandez RR	1.50	.70
☐ 33 Angel Salazar RR	.25	.11
☐ 34 Kevin McReynolds RR	1.50	.70
☐ 35 Dick Schofield RR	.75	.35
☐ 36 Brad Komminsk RR	.25	.11
☐ 37 Tim Teufel RR	.25	.11
☐ 38 Doug Frobel RR	.25	.11
☐ 39 Greg Gagne RR	.75	.35
☐ 40 Mike Fuentes RR	.25	.11
☐ 41 Joe Carter RR	20.00	9.00
☐ 42 Mike Brown RR	.25	.11
(Angels OF)		
☐ 43 Mike Jeffcoat RR	.25	.11
☐ 44 Sid Fernandez RR	1.50	.70
☐ 45 Brian Dayett RR	.25	.11
☐ 46 Chris Smith RR	.25	.11
☐ 47 Eddie Murray	4.00	1.80
☐ 48 Robin Yount	4.00	1.80
☐ 49 Lance Parrish	.75	.35
☐ 50 Jim Rice	.75	.35
☐ 51 Dave Winfield	5.00	2.20

☐ 52 Fernando Valenzuela	.75	.35
☐ 53 George Brett	8.00	3.60
☐ 54 Rickey Henderson	4.00	1.80
☐ 55 Gary Carter	3.00	1.35
☐ 56 Buddy Bell	.75	.35
☐ 57 Reggie Jackson	5.00	2.20
☐ 58 Harold Baines	1.50	.70
☐ 59 Ozzie Smith	6.00	2.70
☐ 60 Nolan Ryan UER	20.00	9.00
(Text on back refers to 1972 as the year he struck out 383; the year was 1973)		
☐ 61 Pete Rose	5.00	2.20
☐ 62 Ron Oester	.25	.11
☐ 63 Steve Garvey	1.50	.70
☐ 64 Jason Thompson	.25	.11
☐ 65 Jack Clark	.75	.35
☐ 66 Dale Murphy	3.00	1.35
☐ 67 Leon Durham	.25	.11
☐ 68 Darryl Strawberry	10.00	4.50
☐ 69 Richie Zisk	.25	.11
☐ 70 Kent Hrbek	.75	.35
☐ 71 Dave Stieb	.25	.11
☐ 72 Ken Schrom	.25	.11
☐ 73 George Bell	.75	.35
☐ 74 John Moses	.25	.11
☐ 75 Ed Lynch	.25	.11
☐ 76 Chuck Rainey	.25	.11
☐ 77 Biff Pocoroba	.25	.11
☐ 78 Cecilio Guante	.25	.11
☐ 79 Jim Barr	.25	.11
☐ 80 Kurt Bevacqua	.25	.11
☐ 81 Tom Foley	.25	.11
☐ 82 Joe Lefebvre	.25	.11
☐ 83 Andy Van Slyke	2.50	1.10
☐ 84 Bob Lillis MG	.25	.11
☐ 85 Ricky Adams	.25	.11
☐ 86 Jerry Hairston	.25	.11
☐ 87 Bob James	.25	.11
☐ 88 Joe Altobelli MG	.25	.11
☐ 89 Ed Romero	.25	.11
☐ 90 John Grubb	.25	.11
☐ 91 John Henry Johnson	.25	.11
☐ 92 Juan Espino	.25	.11
☐ 93 Candy Maldonado	.25	.11
☐ 94 Andre Thornton	.25	.11
☐ 95 Onix Concepcion	.25	.11
☐ 96 Donnie Hill UER	.25	.11
(Listed as P, should be 2B)		
☐ 97 Andre Dawson UER	3.00	1.35
(Wrong middle name, should be Nolan)		
☐ 98 Frank Tanana	.75	.35
☐ 99 Curt Wilkerson	.25	.11
☐ 100 Larry Gura	.25	.11
☐ 101 Dwayne Murphy	.25	.11
☐ 102 Tom Brennan	.25	.11
☐ 103 Dave Righetti	.75	.35
☐ 104 Steve Sax	.75	.35
☐ 105 Dan Petry	.75	.35
☐ 106 Cal Ripken	30.00	13.50
☐ 107 Paul Molitor UER	4.00	1.80
('83 stats should say .270 BA, 608 AB, and 164 hits)		
☐ 108 Fred Lynn	.75	.35
☐ 109 Neil Allen	.25	.11
☐ 110 Joe Niekro	.75	.35
☐ 111 Steve Carlton	4.00	1.80
☐ 112 Terry Kennedy	.25	.11
☐ 113 Bill Madlock	.75	.35
☐ 114 Chili Davis	1.50	.70
☐ 115 Jim Gantner	.75	.35
☐ 116 Tom Seaver	5.00	2.20
☐ 117 Bill Buckner	.75	.35
☐ 118 Bill Caudill	.25	.11
☐ 119 Jim Clancy	.25	.11
☐ 120 John Castino	.25	.11
☐ 121 Dave Concepcion	.75	.35
☐ 122 Greg Luzinski	.75	.35
☐ 123 Mike Boddicker	.25	.11
☐ 124 Pete Ladd	.25	.11
☐ 125 Juan Berenguer	.25	.11
☐ 126 John Montefusco	.25	.11
☐ 127 Ed Jurak	.25	.11

128	Tom Niedenfuer	.25	.11
129	Bert Blyleven	.75	.35
130	Bud Black	.25	.11
131	Gorman Heimueller	.25	.11
132	Dan Schatzeder	.25	.11
133	Ron Jackson	.25	.11
134	Tom Henke	1.50	.70
135	Kevin Hickey	.25	.11
136	Mike Scott	.75	.35
137	Bo Diaz	.25	.11
138	Glenn Brummer	.25	.11
139	Sid Monge	.25	.11
140	Rich Gale	.25	.11
141	Brett Butler	1.50	.70
142	Brian Harper	.75	.35
143	John Rabb	.25	.11
144	Gary Woods	.25	.11
145	Pat Putnam	.25	.11
146	Jim Acker	.25	.11
147	Mickey Hatcher	.25	.11
148	Todd Cruz	.25	.11
149	Tom Tellmann	.25	.11
150	John Wockenfuss	.25	.11
151	Wade Boggs UER ..	8.00	3.60
	1983 runs 10; should be 100		
152	Don Baylor	1.50	.70
153	Bob Welch	.25	.11
154	Alan Bannister	.25	.11
155	Willie Aikens	.25	.11
156	Jeff Burroughs	.25	.11
157	Bryan Little	.25	.11
158	Bob Boone	.75	.35
159	Dave Hostetler	.25	.11
160	Jerry Dybzinski	.25	.11
161	Mike Madden	.25	.11
162	Luis DeLeon	.25	.11
163	Willie Hernandez	.75	.35
164	Frank Pastore	.25	.11
165	Rick Camp	.25	.11
166	Lee Mazzilli	.25	.11
167	Scot Thompson	.25	.11
168	Bob Forsch	.25	.11
169	Mike Flanagan	.25	.11
170	Rick Manning	.25	.11
171	Chet Lemon	.75	.35
172	Jerry Remy	.25	.11
173	Ron Guidry	.75	.35
174	Pedro Guerrero	.75	.35
175	Willie Wilson	.75	.35
176	Carney Lansford	.75	.35
177	Al Oliver	.75	.35
178	Jim Sundberg	.75	.35
179	Bobby Grich	.75	.35
180	Rich Dotson	.25	.11
181	Joaquin Andujar	.25	.11
182	Jose Cruz	.75	.35
183	Mike Schmidt	5.00	2.20
184	Gary Redus	.25	.11
185	Garry Templeton	.25	.11
186	Tony Pena	.25	.11
187	Greg Minton	.25	.11
188	Phil Niekro	3.00	1.35
189	Ferguson Jenkins	3.00	1.35
190	Mookie Wilson	.75	.35
191	Jim Beattie	.25	.11
192	Gary Ward	.25	.11
193	Jesse Barfield	.75	.35
194	Pete Filson	.25	.11
195	Roy Lee Jackson	.25	.11
196	Rick Sweet	.25	.11
197	Jesse Orosco	.25	.11
198	Steve Lake	.25	.11
199	Ken Dayley	.25	.11
200	Manny Sarmiento	.25	.11
201	Mark Davis	.25	.11
202	Tim Flannery	.25	.11
203	Bill Scherrer	.25	.11
204	Al Holland	.25	.11
205	Dave Von Ohlen	.25	.11
206	Mike LaCoss	.25	.11
207	Juan Beniquez	.25	.11
208	Juan Agosto	.25	.11
209	Bobby Ramos	.25	.11
210	Al Bumbry	.75	.35
211	Mark Brouhard	.25	.11
212	Howard Bailey	.25	.11
213	Bruce Hurst	.25	.11
214	Bob Shirley	.25	.11
215	Pat Zachry	.25	.11
216	Julio Franco	1.50	.70
217	Mike Armstrong	.25	.11
218	Dave Beard	.25	.11
219	Steve Rogers	.25	.11
220	John Butcher	.25	.11
221	Mike Smithson	.25	.11
222	Frank White	.75	.35
223	Mike Heath	.25	.11
224	Chris Bando	.25	.11
225	Roy Smalley	.25	.11
226	Dusty Baker	1.50	.70
227	Lou Whitaker	3.00	1.35
228	John Lowenstein	.25	.11
229	Ben Oglivie	.25	.11
230	Doug DeCinces	.25	.11
231	Lonnie Smith	.25	.11
232	Ray Knight	.75	.35
233	Gary Matthews	.75	.35
234	Juan Bonilla	.25	.11
235	Rod Scurry	.25	.11
236	Atlee Hammaker	.25	.11
237	Mike Caldwell	.25	.11
238	Keith Hernandez	.75	.35
239	Larry Bowa	.75	.35
240	Tony Bernazard	.25	.11
241	Damaso Garcia	.25	.11
242	Tom Brunansky	.75	.35
243	Dan Driessen	.25	.11
244	Ron Kittle	.25	.11
245	Tim Stoddard	.25	.11
246	Bob L. Gibson	.25	.11
	(Brewers Pitcher)		
247	Marty Castillo	.25	.11
248	Don Mattingly UER	40.00	18.00
	('Traiing' on back)		
249	Jeff Newman	.25	.11
250	Alejandro Pena	.75	.35
251	Toby Harrah	.75	.35
252	Cesar Geronimo	.25	.11
253	Tom Underwood	.25	.11
254	Doug Flynn	.25	.11
255	Andy Hassler	.25	.11
256	Odell Jones	.25	.11
257	Rudy Law	.25	.11
258	Harry Spilman	.25	.11
259	Marty Bystrom	.25	.11
260	Dave Rucker	.25	.11
261	Ruppert Jones	.25	.11
262	Jeff R. Jones	.25	.11
	(Reds OF)		
263	Gerald Perry	.75	.35
264	Gene Tenace	.25	.11
265	Brad Wellman	.25	.11
266	Dickie Noles	.25	.11
267	Jamie Allen	.25	.11
268	Jim Gott	.25	.11
269	Ron Davis	.25	.11
270	Benny Ayala	.25	.11
271	Ned Yost	.25	.11
272	Dave Rozema	.25	.11
273	Dave Stapleton	.25	.11
274	Lou Piniella	.75	.35
275	Jose Morales	.25	.11
276	Broderick Perkins	.25	.11
277	Butch Davis	.25	.11
278	Tony Phillips	4.00	1.80
279	Jeff Reardon	.75	.35
280	Ken Forsch	.25	.11
281	Pete O'Brien	.75	.35
282	Tom Paciorek	.25	.11
283	Frank LaCorte	.25	.11
284	Tim Lollar	.25	.11
285	Greg Gross	.25	.11
286	Alex Trevino	.25	.11
287	Gene Garber	.25	.11
288	Dave Parker	.75	.35
289	Lee Smith	3.00	1.35
290	Dave LaPoint	.25	.11
291	John Shelby	.25	.11
292	Charlie Moore	.25	.11
293	Alan Trammell	3.00	1.35
294	Tony Armas	.25	.11
295	Shane Rawley	.25	.11
296	Greg Brock	.25	.11
297	Hal McRae	.75	.35
298	Mike Davis	.25	.11
299	Tim Raines	1.50	.70
300	Bucky Dent	.75	.35
301	Tommy John	1.50	.70
302	Carlton Fisk	3.00	1.35
303	Darrell Porter	.25	.11
304	Dickie Thon	.25	.11
305	Garry Maddox	.25	.11
306	Cesar Cedeno	.75	.35
307	Gary Lucas	.25	.11
308	Johnny Ray	.25	.11
309	Andy McGaffigan	.25	.11
310	Claudell Washington	.25	.11
311	Ryne Sandberg	12.00	5.50
312	George Foster	.75	.35
313	Spike Owen	.75	.35
314	Gary Gaetti	1.50	.70
315	Willie Upshaw	.25	.11
316	Al Williams	.25	.11
317	Jorge Orta	.25	.11
318	Orlando Mercado	.25	.11
319	Junior Ortiz	.25	.11
320	Mike Proly	.25	.11
321	Randy Johnson UER ..	.25	.11
	('72-'82 stats are from Twins' Randy Johnson, '83 stats are from Braves' Randy Johnson)		
322	Jim Morrison	.25	.11
323	Max Venable	.25	.11
324	Tony Gwynn	25.00	11.00
325	Duane Walker	.25	.11
326	Ozzie Virgil	.25	.11
327	Jeff Lahti	.25	.11
328	Bill Dawley	.25	.11
329	Rob Wilfong	.25	.11
330	Marc Hill	.25	.11
331	Ray Burris	.25	.11
332	Allan Ramirez	.25	.11
333	Chuck Porter	.25	.11
334	Wayne Krenchicki	.25	.11
335	Gary Allenson	.25	.11
336	Bobby Meacham	.25	.11
337	Joe Beckwith	.25	.11
338	Rick Sutcliffe	.75	.35
339	Mark Huismann	.25	.11
340	Tim Conroy	.25	.11
341	Scott Sanderson	.25	.11
342	Larry Biittner	.25	.11
343	Dave Stewart	.75	.35
344	Darryl Motley	.25	.11
345	Chris Codiroli	.25	.11
346	Rich Behenna	.25	.11
347	Andre Robertson	.25	.11
348	Mike Marshall	.75	.35
349	Larry Herndon	.25	.11
350	Rich Dauer	.25	.11
351	Cecil Cooper	.75	.35
352	Rod Carew	4.00	1.80
353	Willie McGee	1.50	.70
354	Phil Garner	.75	.35
355	Joe Morgan	3.00	1.35
356	Luis Salazar	.25	.11
357	John Candelaria	.25	.11
358	Bill Laskey	.25	.11
359	Bob McClure	.25	.11
360	Dave Kingman	.75	.35
361	Ron Cey	.75	.35
362	Matt Young	.25	.11
363	Lloyd Moseby	.25	.11
364	Frank Viola	1.50	.70
365	Eddie Milner	.25	.11
366	Floyd Bannister	.25	.11
367	Dan Ford	.25	.11
368	Moose Haas	.25	.11
369	Doug Bair	.25	.11
370	Ray Fontenot	.25	.11
371	Luis Aponte	.25	.11
372	Jack Fimple	.25	.11
373	Neal Heaton	.25	.11
374	Greg Pryor	.25	.11
375	Wayne Gross	.25	.11
376	Charlie Lea	.25	.11
377	Steve Lubratich	.25	.11

No. Name		
378 Jon Matlack	.25	.11
379 Julio Cruz	.25	.11
380 John Mizerock	.25	.11
381 Kevin Gross	.75	.35
382 Mike Ramsey	.25	.11
383 Doug Gwosdz	.25	.11
384 Kelly Paris	.25	.11
385 Pete Falcone	.25	.11
386 Milt May	.25	.11
387 Fred Breining	.25	.11
388 Craig Lefferts	.25	.11
389 Steve Henderson	.25	.11
390 Randy Moffitt	.25	.11
391 Ron Washington	.25	.11
392 Gary Roenicke	.25	.11
393 Tom Candiotti	3.00	1.35
394 Larry Pashnick	.25	.11
395 Dwight Evans	.75	.35
396 Goose Gossage	1.50	.70
397 Derrel Thomas	.25	.11
398 Juan Eichelberger	.25	.11
399 Leon Roberts	.25	.11
400 Dave Lopes	.75	.35
401 Bill Gullickson	.25	.11
402 Geoff Zahn	.25	.11
403 Billy Sample	.25	.11
404 Mike Squires	.25	.11
405 Craig Reynolds	.25	.11
406 Eric Show	.25	.11
407 John Denny	.25	.11
408 Dann Bilardello	.25	.11
409 Bruce Benedict	.25	.11
410 Kent Tekulve	.75	.35
411 Mel Hall	.75	.35
412 John Stuper	.25	.11
413 Rick Dempsey	.25	.11
414 Don Sutton	3.00	1.35
415 Jack Morris	3.00	1.35
416 John Tudor	.25	.11
417 Willie Randolph	.75	.35
418 Jerry Reuss	.25	.11
419 Don Slaught	.75	.35
420 Steve McCatty	.25	.11
421 Tim Wallach	.75	.35
422 Larry Parrish	.25	.11
423 Brian Downing	.25	.11
424 Britt Burns	.25	.11
425 David Green	.25	.11
426 Jerry Mumphrey	.25	.11
427 Ivan DeJesus	.25	.11
428 Mario Soto	.25	.11
429 Gene Richards	.25	.11
430 Dale Berra	.25	.11
431 Darrell Evans	.75	.35
432 Glenn Hubbard	.25	.11
433 Jody Davis	.25	.11
434 Danny Heep	.25	.11
435 Ed Nunez	.25	.11
436 Bobby Castillo	.25	.11
437 Ernie Whitt	.25	.11
438 Scott Ullger	.25	.11
439 Doyle Alexander	.25	.11
440 Domingo Ramos	.25	.11
441 Craig Swan	.25	.11
442 Warren Brusstar	.25	.11
443 Len Barker	.25	.11
444 Mike Easler	.25	.11
445 Renie Martin	.25	.11
446 Dennis Rasmussen	.25	.11
447 Ted Power	.25	.11
448 Charles Hudson	.25	.11
449 Danny Cox	.25	.11
450 Kevin Bass	.25	.11
451 Daryl Sconiers	.25	.11
452 Scott Fletcher	.25	.11
453 Bryn Smith	.25	.11
454 Jim Dwyer	.25	.11
455 Rob Picciolo	.25	.11
456 Enos Cabell	.25	.11
457 Dennis Boyd	.75	.35
458 Butch Wynegar	.25	.11
459 Burt Hooton	.25	.11
460 Ron Hassey	.25	.11
461 Danny Jackson	1.50	.70
462 Bob Kearney	.25	.11
463 Terry Francona	.25	.11
464 Wayne Tolleson	.25	.11
465 Mickey Rivers	.25	.11
466 John Wathan	.25	.11
467 Bill Almon	.25	.11
468 George Vukovich	.25	.11
469 Steve Kemp	.25	.11
470 Ken Landreaux	.25	.11
471 Milt Wilcox	.25	.11
472 Tippy Martinez	.25	.11
473 Ted Simmons	.75	.35
474 Tim Foli	.25	.11
475 George Hendrick	.25	.11
476 Terry Puhl	.25	.11
477 Von Hayes	.25	.11
478 Bobby Brown	.25	.11
479 Lee Lacy	.25	.11
480 Joel Youngblood	.25	.11
481 Jim Slaton	.25	.11
482 Mike Fitzgerald	.25	.11
483 Keith Moreland	.25	.11
484 Ron Roenicke	.25	.11
485 Luis Leal	.25	.11
486 Bryan Oelkers	.25	.11
487 Bruce Berenyi	.25	.11
488 LaMarr Hoyt	.25	.11
489 Joe Nolan	.25	.11
490 Marshall Edwards	.25	.11
491 Mike Laga	.75	.35
492 Rick Cerone	.25	.11
493 Rick Miller UER	.25	.11
(Listed as Mike on card front)		
494 Rick Honeycutt	.25	.11
495 Mike Hargrove	.75	.35
496 Joe Simpson	.25	.11
497 Keith Atherton	.25	.11
498 Chris Welsh	.25	.11
499 Bruce Kison	.25	.11
500 Bobby Johnson	.25	.11
501 Jerry Koosman	.75	.35
502 Frank DiPino	.25	.11
503 Tony Perez	3.00	1.35
504 Ken Oberkfell	.25	.11
505 Mark Thurmond	.25	.11
506 Joe Price	.25	.11
507 Pascual Perez	.25	.11
508 Marvell Wynne	.25	.11
509 Mike Krukow	.25	.11
510 Dick Ruthven	.25	.11
511 Al Cowens	.25	.11
512 Cliff Johnson	.25	.11
513 Randy Bush	.25	.11
514 Sammy Stewart	.25	.11
515 Bill Schroeder	.25	.11
516 Aurelio Lopez	.75	.35
517 Mike G. Brown	.25	.11
518 Graig Nettles	.75	.35
519 Dave Sax	.25	.11
520 Jerry Willard	.25	.11
521 Paul Splittorff	.25	.11
522 Tom Burgmeier	.25	.11
523 Chris Speier	.25	.11
524 Bobby Clark	.25	.11
525 George Wright	.25	.11
526 Dennis Lamp	.25	.11
527 Tony Scott	.25	.11
528 Ed Whitson	.25	.11
529 Ron Reed	.25	.11
530 Charlie Puleo	.25	.11
531 Jerry Royster	.25	.11
532 Don Robinson	.25	.11
533 Steve Trout	.25	.11
534 Bruce Sutter	.75	.35
535 Bob Horner	.25	.11
536 Pat Tabler	.25	.11
537 Chris Chambliss	.25	.11
538 Bob Ojeda	.25	.11
539 Alan Ashby	.25	.11
540 Jay Johnstone	.75	.35
541 Bob Dernier	.25	.11
542 Brook Jacoby	.75	.35
543 U.L. Washington	.25	.11
544 Danny Darwin	.75	.35
545 Kiko Garcia	.25	.11
546 Vance Law UER	.25	.11
(Listed as P on card front)		
547 Tug McGraw	.75	.35
548 Dave Smith	.25	.11
549 Len Matuszek	.25	.11
550 Tom Hume	.25	.11
551 Dave Dravecky	.75	.35
552 Rick Rhoden	.25	.11
553 Duane Kuiper	.25	.11
554 Rusty Staub	.75	.35
555 Bill Campbell	.25	.11
556 Mike Torrez	.25	.11
557 Dave Henderson	.75	.35
558 Len Whitehouse	.25	.11
559 Barry Bonnell	.25	.11
560 Rick Lysander	.25	.11
561 Garth Iorg	.25	.11
562 Bryan Clark	.25	.11
563 Brian Giles	.25	.11
564 Vern Ruhle	.25	.11
565 Steve Bedrosian	.25	.11
566 Larry McWilliams	.25	.11
567 Jeff Leonard UER	.25	.11
(Listed as P on card front)		
568 Alan Wiggins	.25	.11
569 Jeff Russell	.75	.35
570 Salome Barojas	.25	.11
571 Dane Iorg	.25	.11
572 Bob Knepper	.25	.11
573 Gary Lavelle	.25	.11
574 Gorman Thomas	.25	.11
575 Manny Trillo	.25	.11
576 Jim Palmer	4.00	1.80
577 Dale Murray	.25	.11
578 Tom Brookens	.75	.35
579 Rich Gedman	.25	.11
580 Bill Doran	.75	.35
581 Steve Yeager	.25	.11
582 Dan Spillner	.25	.11
583 Dan Quisenberry	.25	.11
584 Rance Mulliniks	.25	.11
585 Storm Davis	.25	.11
586 Dave Schmidt	.25	.11
587 Bill Russell	.75	.35
588 Pat Sheridan	.25	.11
589 Rafael Ramirez	.25	.11
UER (A's on front)		
590 Bud Anderson	.25	.11
591 George Frazier	.25	.11
592 Lee Tunnell	.25	.11
593 Kirk Gibson	3.00	1.35
594 Scott McGregor	.25	.11
595 Bob Bailor	.25	.11
596 Tommy Herr	.75	.35
597 Luis Sanchez	.25	.11
598 Dave Engle	.25	.11
599 Craig McMurtry	.25	.11
600 Carlos Diaz	.25	.11
601 Tom O'Malley	.25	.11
602 Nick Esasky	.25	.11
603 Ron Hodges	.25	.11
604 Ed Vandeberg	.25	.11
605 Alfredo Griffin	.25	.11
606 Glenn Hoffman	.25	.11
607 Hubie Brooks	.25	.11
608 Richard Barnes UER	.25	.11
(Photo actually Neal Heaton)		
609 Greg Walker	.75	.35
610 Ken Singleton	.75	.35
611 Mark Clear	.25	.11
612 Buck Martinez	.25	.11
613 Ken Griffey	.75	.35
614 Reid Nichols	.25	.11
615 Doug Sisk	.25	.11
616 Bob Brenly	.25	.11
617 Joey McLaughlin	.25	.11
618 Glenn Wilson	.75	.35
619 Bob Stoddard	.25	.11
620 Lenn Sakata UER	.25	.11
(Listed as Len on card front)		
621 Mike Young	.25	.11
622 John Stefero	.25	.11
623 Carmelo Martinez	.25	.11
624 Dave Bergman	.25	.11

☐ 625	Runnin' Reds UER....	3.00	1.35				
	(Sic, Redbirds)						
	David Green						
	Willie McGee						
	Lonnie Smith						
	Ozzie Smith						
☐ 626	Rudy May	.25	.11				
☐ 627	Matt Keough	.25	.11				
☐ 628	Jose DeLeon	.25	.11				
☐ 629	Jim Essian	.25	.11				
☐ 630	Darnell Coles	.25	.11				
☐ 631	Mike Warren	.25	.11				
☐ 632	Del Crandall MG	.25	.11				
☐ 633	Dennis Martinez	.75	.35				
☐ 634	Mike Moore	.75	.35				
☐ 635	Lary Sorensen	.25	.11				
☐ 636	Ricky Nelson	.25	.11				
☐ 637	Omar Moreno	.25	.11				
☐ 638	Charlie Hough	.75	.35				
☐ 639	Dennis Eckersley	3.00	1.35				
☐ 640	Walt Terrell	.25	.11				
☐ 641	Denny Walling	.25	.11				
☐ 642	Dave Anderson	.25	.11				
☐ 643	Jose Oquendo	.75	.35				
☐ 644	Bob Stanley	.25	.11				
☐ 645	Dave Geisel	.25	.11				
☐ 646	Scott Garrelts	.25	.11				
☐ 647	Gary Pettis	.25	.11				
☐ 648	Duke Snider	1.50	.70				
	Puzzle Card						
☐ 649	Johnnie LeMaster	.25	.11				
☐ 650	Dave Collins	.25	.11				
☐ 651	The Chicken	1.50	.70				
☐ 652	DK Checklist 1-26	.75	.35				
	(Unnumbered)						
☐ 653	Checklist 27-130	.25	.11				
	(Unnumbered)						
☐ 654	Checklist 131-234	.25	.11				
	(Unnumbered)						
☐ 655	Checklist 235-338	.25	.11				
	(Unnumbered)						
☐ 656	Checklist 339-442	.25	.11				
	(Unnumbered)						
☐ 657	Checklist 443-546	.25	.11				
	(Unnumbered)						
☐ 658	Checklist 547-651	.25	.11				
	(Unnumbered)						
☐ A	Living Legends A	2.50	1.10				
	Gaylord Perry						
	Rollie Fingers						
☐ B	Living Legends B	5.00	2.20				
	Carl Yastrzemski						
	Johnny Bench						

1985 Donruss

The 1985 Donruss set consists of 660 standard-size cards. Wax packs contained 15 cards and a Lou Gehrig puzzle panel. The fronts feature full color photos framed by jet black borders (making the cards condition sensitive). The first 26 cards of the set feature Diamond Kings (DK), for the fourth year in a row; the artwork on the

Diamond Kings was again produced by the Perez-Steele Galleries. Cards 27-46 feature Rated Rookies (RR). The unnumbered checklist cards are arbitrarily numbered below as numbers 654 through 660. Rookie Cards in this set include Roger Clemens, Eric Davis, Shawon Dunston, Dwight Gooden, Orel Hershiser, Jimmy Key, Mark Langston, Terry Pendleton, Kirby Puckett, Jose Rijo, Bret Saberhagen, and Danny Tartabull.

		NRMT	VG-E
COMPLETE SET (660)		100.00	45.00
COMP.FACT.SET (660).		120.00	55.00
COMMON CARD (1-660)		.15	.07
MINOR STARS		.40	.11
SEMISTARS		.75	.35
UNLISTED STARS		1.50	.70
CONDITION SENSITIVE SET		....	

☐ 1	Ryne Sandberg DK	2.00	.90
☐ 2	Doug DeCinces DK	.15	.07
☐ 3	Richard Dotson DK	.15	.07
☐ 4	Bert Blyleven DK	.15	.07
☐ 5	Lou Whitaker DK	.40	.18
☐ 6	Dan Quisenberry DK	.15	.07
☐ 7	Don Mattingly DK	2.50	1.10
☐ 8	Carney Lansford DK	.15	.07
☐ 9	Frank Tanana DK	.15	.07
☐ 10	Willie Upshaw DK	.15	.07
☐ 11	Claudell Washington DK	.15	.07
☐ 12	Mike Marshall DK	.15	.07
☐ 13	Joaquin Andujar DK	.15	.07
☐ 14	Cal Ripken DK	4.00	1.80
☐ 15	Jim Rice DK	.40	.18
☐ 16	Don Sutton DK	.40	.18
☐ 17	Frank Viola DK	.15	.07
☐ 18	Alvin Davis DK	.15	.07
☐ 19	Mario Soto DK	.15	.07
☐ 20	Jose Cruz DK	.15	.07
☐ 21	Charlie Lea DK	.15	.07
☐ 22	Jesse Orosco DK	.15	.07
☐ 23	Juan Samuel DK	.15	.07
☐ 24	Tony Pena DK	.15	.07
☐ 25	Tony Gwynn DK	3.00	1.35
☐ 26	Bob Brenly DK	.15	.07
☐ 27	Mike Tartabull RR	1.50	.70
☐ 28	Mike Bielecki RR	.15	.07
☐ 29	Steve Lyons RR	.40	.18
☐ 30	Jeff Reed RR	.15	.07
☐ 31	Tony Brewer RR	.15	.07
☐ 32	John Morris RR	.15	.07
☐ 33	Daryl Boston RR	.15	.07
☐ 34	Al Pulido RR	.15	.07
☐ 35	Steve Kiefer RR	.15	.07
☐ 36	Larry Sheets RR	.15	.07
☐ 37	Scott Bradley RR	.15	.07
☐ 38	Calvin Schiraldi RR	.15	.07
☐ 39	Shawon Dunston RR	1.50	.70
☐ 40	Charlie Mitchell RR	.15	.07
☐ 41	Billy Hatcher RR	.75	.35
☐ 42	Russ Stephans RR	.15	.07
☐ 43	Alejandro Sanchez RR	.15	.07
☐ 44	Steve Jeltz RR	.15	.07
☐ 45	Jim Traber RR	.15	.07
☐ 46	Doug Loman RR	.15	.07
☐ 47	Eddie Murray	1.50	.70
☐ 48	Robin Yount	1.50	.70
☐ 49	Lance Parrish	.40	.18
☐ 50	Jim Rice	.40	.18
☐ 51	Dave Winfield	1.50	.70
☐ 52	Fernando Valenzuela	.40	.18
☐ 53	George Brett	3.00	1.35
☐ 54	Dave Kingman	.40	.18
☐ 55	Gary Carter	1.50	.70
☐ 56	Buddy Bell	.40	.18
☐ 57	Reggie Jackson	2.00	.90
☐ 58	Harold Baines	.40	.18
☐ 59	Ozzie Smith	2.00	.90
☐ 60	Nolan Ryan UER	8.00	3.60
	(Set strikeout record		

	in 1973, not 1972)		
☐ 61	Mike Schmidt	2.00	.90
☐ 62	Dave Parker	.40	.18
☐ 63	Tony Gwynn	6.00	2.70
☐ 64	Tony Pena	.15	.07
☐ 65	Jack Clark	.40	.18
☐ 66	Dale Murphy	1.50	.70
☐ 67	Ryne Sandberg	3.00	1.35
☐ 68	Keith Hernandez	.40	.18
☐ 69	Alvin Davis	.40	.18
☐ 70	Kent Hrbek	.40	.18
☐ 71	Willie Upshaw	.15	.07
☐ 72	Dave Engle	.15	.07
☐ 73	Alfredo Griffin	.15	.07
☐ 74A	Jack Perconte	.15	.07
	(Career Highlights		
	takes four lines)		
☐ 74B	Jack Perconte	.15	.07
	(Career Highlights		
	takes three lines)		
☐ 75	Jesse Orosco	.15	.07
☐ 76	Jody Davis	.15	.07
☐ 77	Bob Horner	.15	.07
☐ 78	Larry McWilliams	.15	.07
☐ 79	Joel Youngblood	.15	.07
☐ 80	Alan Wiggins	.15	.07
☐ 81	Ron Oester	.15	.07
☐ 82	Ozzie Virgil	.15	.07
☐ 83	Ricky Horton	.15	.07
☐ 84	Bill Doran	.15	.07
☐ 85	Rod Carew	1.50	.70
☐ 86	LaMarr Hoyt	.15	.07
☐ 87	Tim Wallach	.40	.18
☐ 88	Mike Flanagan	.15	.07
☐ 89	Jim Sundberg	.15	.07
☐ 90	Chet Lemon	.15	.07
☐ 91	Bob Stanley	.15	.07
☐ 92	Willie Randolph	.40	.18
☐ 93	Bill Russell	.15	.07
☐ 94	Julio Franco	.75	.35
☐ 95	Dan Quisenberry	.40	.18
☐ 96	Bill Caudill	.15	.07
☐ 97	Bill Gullickson	.15	.07
☐ 98	Danny Darwin	.15	.07
☐ 99	Curtis Wilkerson	.15	.07
☐ 100	Bud Black	.15	.07
☐ 101	Tony Phillips	.15	.07
☐ 102	Tony Bernazard	.15	.07
☐ 103	Jay Howell	.15	.07
☐ 104	Burt Hooton	.15	.07
☐ 105	Milt Wilcox	.15	.07
☐ 106	Rich Dauer	.15	.07
☐ 107	Don Sutton	1.50	.70
☐ 108	Mike Witt	.15	.07
☐ 109	Bruce Sutter	.40	.18
☐ 110	Enos Cabell	.15	.07
☐ 111	John Denny	.15	.07
☐ 112	Dave Dravecky	.40	.18
☐ 113	Marvell Wynne	.15	.07
☐ 114	Johnnie LeMaster	.15	.07
☐ 115	Chuck Porter	.15	.07
☐ 116	John Gibbons	.15	.07
☐ 117	Keith Moreland	.15	.07
☐ 118	Darnell Coles	.15	.07
☐ 119	Dennis Lamp	.15	.07
☐ 120	Ron Davis	.15	.07
☐ 121	Nick Esasky	.15	.07
☐ 122	Vance Law	.15	.07
☐ 123	Gary Roenicke	.15	.07
☐ 124	Bill Schroeder	.15	.07
☐ 125	Dave Rozema	.15	.07
☐ 126	Bobby Meacham	.15	.07
☐ 127	Marty Barrett	.15	.07
☐ 128	R.J. Reynolds	.15	.07
☐ 129	Ernie Camacho UER	.15	.07
	(Photo actually		
	Rich Thompson)		
☐ 130	Jorge Orta	.15	.07
☐ 131	Lary Sorensen	.15	.07
☐ 132	Terry Francona	.15	.07
☐ 133	Fred Lynn	.40	.18
☐ 134	Bob Jones	.15	.07
☐ 135	Jerry Hairston	.15	.07
☐ 136	Kevin Bass	.15	.07
☐ 137	Garry Maddox	.15	.07
☐ 138	Dave LaPoint	.15	.07

No.	Name		
139	Kevin McReynolds	.40	.18
140	Wayne Krenchicki	.15	.07
141	Rafael Ramirez	.15	.07
142	Rod Scurry	.15	.07
143	Greg Minton	.15	.07
144	Tim Stoddard	.15	.07
145	Steve Henderson	.15	.07
146	George Bell	.40	.18
147	Dave Meier	.15	.07
148	Sammy Stewart	.15	.07
149	Mark Brouhard	.15	.07
150	Larry Herndon	.15	.07
151	Oil Can Boyd	.15	.07
152	Brian Dayett	.15	.07
153	Tom Niedenfuer	.15	.07
154	Brook Jacoby	.15	.07
155	Onix Concepcion	.15	.07
156	Tim Conroy	.15	.07
157	Joe Hesketh	.15	.07
158	Brian Downing	.15	.07
159	Tommy Dunbar	.15	.07
160	Marc Hill	.15	.07
161	Phil Garner	.15	.07
162	Jerry Davis	.15	.07
163	Bill Campbell	.15	.07
164	John Franco	1.50	.70
165	Len Barker	.15	.07
166	Benny Distefano	.15	.07
167	George Frazier	.15	.07
168	Tito Landrum	.15	.07
169	Cal Ripken	8.00	3.60
170	Cecil Cooper	.40	.18
171	Alan Trammell	.75	.35
172	Wade Boggs	2.00	.90
173	Don Baylor	.40	.18
174	Pedro Guerrero	.40	.18
175	Frank White	.40	.18
176	Rickey Henderson	1.50	.70
177	Charlie Lea	.15	.07
178	Pete O'Brien	.15	.07
179	Doug DeCinces	.15	.07
180	Ron Kittle	.15	.07
181	George Hendrick	.15	.07
182	Joe Niekro	.15	.07
183	Juan Samuel	.15	.07
184	Mario Soto	.15	.07
185	Goose Gossage	.40	.18
186	Johnny Ray	.15	.07
187	Bob Brenly	.15	.07
188	Craig McMurtry	.15	.07
189	Leon Durham	.15	.07
190	Dwight Gooden	4.00	1.80
191	Barry Bonnell	.15	.07
192	Tim Teufel	.15	.07
193	Dave Stieb	.40	.18
194	Mickey Hatcher	.15	.07
195	Jesse Barfield	.15	.07
196	Al Cowens	.15	.07
197	Hubie Brooks	.15	.07
198	Steve Trout	.15	.07
199	Glenn Hubbard	.15	.07
200	Bill Madlock	.40	.18
201	Jeff D. Robinson	.15	.07
202	Eric Show	.15	.07
203	Dave Concepcion	.15	.07
204	Ivan DeJesus	.15	.07
205	Neil Allen	.15	.07
206	Jerry Mumphrey	.15	.07
207	Mike C. Brown	.15	.07
208	Carlton Fisk	1.50	.70
209	Bryn Smith	.15	.07
210	Tippy Martinez	.15	.07
211	Dion James	.15	.07
212	Willie Hernandez	.15	.07
213	Mike Easler	.15	.07
214	Ron Guidry	.40	.18
215	Rick Honeycutt	.15	.07
216	Brett Butler	.40	.18
217	Larry Gura	.15	.07
218	Ray Burris	.15	.07
219	Steve Rogers	.15	.07
220	Frank Tanana UER	.15	.07
	(Bats Left listed twice on card back)		
221	Ned Yost	.15	.07
222	Bret Saberhagen UER	1.50	.70
	(18 career IP on back)		
223	Mike Davis	.15	.07
224	Bert Blyleven	.40	.18
225	Steve Kemp	.15	.07
226	Jerry Reuss	.15	.07
227	Darrell Evans UER	.40	.18
	(80 homers in 1980)		
228	Wayne Gross	.15	.07
229	Jim Gantner	.15	.07
230	Bob Boone	.40	.18
231	Lonnie Smith	.15	.07
232	Frank DiPino	.15	.07
233	Jerry Koosman	.15	.07
234	Graig Nettles	.40	.18
235	John Tudor	.15	.07
236	John Rabb	.15	.07
237	Rick Manning	.15	.07
238	Mike Fitzgerald	.15	.07
239	Gary Matthews	.15	.07
240	Jim Presley	.40	.18
241	Dave Collins	.15	.07
242	Gary Gaetti	.40	.18
243	Dann Bilardello	.15	.07
244	Rudy Law	.15	.07
245	John Lowenstein	.15	.07
246	Tom Tellmann	.15	.07
247	Howard Johnson	.40	.18
248	Ray Fontenot	.15	.07
249	Tony Armas	.15	.07
250	Candy Maldonado	.15	.07
251	Mike Jeffcoat	.15	.07
252	Dane Iorg	.15	.07
253	Bruce Bochte	.15	.07
254	Pete Rose	2.00	.90
255	Don Aase	.15	.07
256	George Wright	.15	.07
257	Britt Burns	.15	.07
258	Mike Scott	.15	.07
259	Len Matuszek	.15	.07
260	Dave Rucker	.15	.07
261	Craig Lefferts	.15	.07
262	Jay Tibbs	.15	.07
263	Bruce Benedict	.15	.07
264	Don Robinson	.15	.07
265	Gary Lavelle	.15	.07
266	Scott Sanderson	.15	.07
267	Matt Young	.15	.07
268	Ernie Whitt	.15	.07
269	Houston Jimenez	.15	.07
270	Ken Dixon	.15	.07
271	Pete Ladd	.15	.07
272	Juan Berenguer	.15	.07
273	Roger Clemens	30.00	13.50
274	Rick Cerone	.15	.07
275	Dave Anderson	.15	.07
276	George Vukovich	.15	.07
277	Greg Pryor	.15	.07
278	Mike Warren	.15	.07
279	Bob James	.15	.07
280	Bobby Grich	.40	.18
281	Mike Mason	.15	.07
282	Ron Reed	.15	.07
283	Alan Ashby	.15	.07
284	Mark Thurmond	.15	.07
285	Joe Lefebvre	.15	.07
286	Ted Power	.15	.07
287	Chris Chambliss	.15	.07
288	Lee Tunnell	.15	.07
289	Rich Bordi	.15	.07
290	Glenn Brummer	.15	.07
291	Mike Boddicker	.15	.07
292	Rollie Fingers	1.50	.70
293	Lou Whitaker	.75	.35
294	Dwight Evans	.40	.18
295	Don Mattingly	5.00	2.20
296	Mike Marshall	.15	.07
297	Willie Wilson	.15	.07
298	Mike Heath	.15	.07
299	Tim Raines	.40	.18
300	Larry Parrish	.15	.07
301	Geoff Zahn	.15	.07
302	Rich Dotson	.15	.07
303	David Green	.15	.07
304	Jose Cruz	.40	.18
305	Steve Carlton	1.50	.70
306	Gary Redus	.15	.07
307	Steve Garvey	.75	.35
308	Jose DeLeon	.15	.07
309	Randy Lerch	.15	.07
310	Claudell Washington	.15	.07
311	Lee Smith	.75	.35
312	Darryl Strawberry	1.50	.70
313	Jim Beattie	.15	.07
314	John Butcher	.15	.07
315	Damaso Garcia	.15	.07
316	Mike Smithson	.15	.07
317	Luis Leal	.15	.07
318	Ken Phelps	.15	.07
319	Wally Backman	.15	.07
320	Ron Cey	.40	.18
321	Brad Komminsk	.15	.07
322	Jason Thompson	.15	.07
323	Frank Williams	.15	.07
324	Tim Lollar	.15	.07
325	Eric Davis	2.00	.90
326	Von Hayes	.15	.07
327	Andy Van Slyke	.75	.35
328	Craig Reynolds	.15	.07
329	Dick Schofield	.15	.07
330	Scott Fletcher	.15	.07
331	Jeff Reardon	.40	.18
332	Rick Dempsey	.15	.07
333	Ben Oglivie	.15	.07
334	Dan Petry	.15	.07
335	Jackie Gutierrez	.15	.07
336	Dave Righetti	.40	.18
337	Alejandro Pena	.15	.07
338	Mel Hall	.15	.07
339	Pat Sheridan	.15	.07
340	Keith Atherton	.15	.07
341	David Palmer	.15	.07
342	Gary Ward	.15	.07
343	Dave Stewart	.40	.18
344	Mark Gubicza	.40	.18
345	Carney Lansford	.40	.18
346	Jerry Willard	.15	.07
347	Ken Griffey	.40	.18
348	Franklin Stubbs	.15	.07
349	Aurelio Lopez	.15	.07
350	Al Bumbry	.15	.07
351	Charlie Moore	.15	.07
352	Luis Sanchez	.15	.07
353	Darrell Porter	.15	.07
354	Bill Dawley	.15	.07
355	Charles Hudson	.15	.07
356	Garry Templeton	.15	.07
357	Cecilio Guante	.15	.07
358	Jeff Leonard	.15	.07
359	Paul Molitor	1.50	.70
360	Ron Gardenhire	.15	.07
361	Larry Bowa	.40	.18
362	Bob Kearney	.15	.07
363	Garth Iorg	.15	.07
364	Tom Brunansky	.40	.18
365	Brad Gulden	.15	.07
366	Greg Walker	.15	.07
367	Mike Young	.15	.07
368	Rick Waits	.15	.07
369	Doug Bair	.15	.07
370	Bob Shirley	.15	.07
371	Bob Ojeda	.15	.07
372	Bob Welch	.40	.18
373	Neal Heaton	.15	.07
374	Danny Jackson UER	.15	.07
	(Photo actually Frank Wills)		
375	Donnie Hill	.15	.07
376	Mike Stenhouse	.15	.07
377	Bruce Kison	.15	.07
378	Wayne Tolleson	.15	.07
379	Floyd Bannister	.15	.07
380	Vern Ruhle	.15	.07
381	Tim Corcoran	.15	.07
382	Kurt Kepshire	.15	.07
383	Bobby Brown	.15	.07
384	Dave Van Gorder	.15	.07
385	Rick Mahler	.15	.07
386	Lee Mazzilli	.15	.07
387	Bill Laskey	.15	.07
388	Thad Bosley	.15	.07
389	Al Chambers	.15	.07
390	Tony Fernandez	.40	.18

No.	Name		
391	Ron Washington	.15	.07
392	Bill Swaggerty	.15	.07
393	Bob L. Gibson	.15	.07
394	Marty Castillo	.15	.07
395	Steve Crawford	.15	.07
396	Clay Christiansen	.15	.07
397	Bob Bailor	.15	.07
398	Mike Hargrove	.40	.18
399	Charlie Leibrandt	.15	.07
400	Tom Burgmeier	.15	.07
401	Razor Shines	.15	.07
402	Rob Wifong	.15	.07
403	Tom Henke	.40	.18
404	Al Jones	.15	.07
405	Mike LaCoss	.15	.07
406	Luis DeLeon	.15	.07
407	Greg Gross	.15	.07
408	Tom Hume	.15	.07
409	Rick Camp	.15	.07
410	Milt May	.15	.07
411	Henry Cotto	.15	.07
412	David Von Ohlen	.15	.07
413	Scott McGregor	.15	.07
414	Ted Simmons	.40	.18
415	Jack Morris	.40	.18
416	Bill Buckner	.40	.18
417	Butch Wynegar	.15	.07
418	Steve Sax	.15	.07
419	Steve Balboni	.15	.07
420	Dwayne Murphy	.15	.07
421	Andre Dawson	1.50	.70
422	Charlie Hough	.40	.18
423	Tommy John	.75	.35
424A	Tom Seaver ERR	2.00	.90
	(Photo actually Floyd Bannister)		
424B	Tom Seaver COR	25.00	11.00
425	Tommy Herr	.15	.07
426	Terry Puhl	.15	.07
427	Al Holland	.15	.07
428	Eddie Milner	.15	.07
429	Terry Kennedy	.15	.07
430	John Candelaria	.15	.07
431	Manny Trillo	.15	.07
432	Ken Oberkfell	.15	.07
433	Rick Sutcliffe	.15	.07
434	Ron Darling	.40	.18
435	Spike Owen	.15	.07
436	Frank Viola	.40	.18
437	Lloyd Moseby	.15	.07
438	Kirby Puckett	25.00	11.00
439	Jim Clancy	.15	.07
440	Mike Moore	.15	.07
441	Doug Sisk	.15	.07
442	Dennis Eckersley	1.50	.70
443	Gerald Perry	.15	.07
444	Dale Berra	.15	.07
445	Dusty Baker	.40	.18
446	Ed Whitson	.15	.07
447	Cesar Cedeno	.40	.18
448	Rick Schu	.15	.07
449	Joaquin Andujar	.15	.07
450	Mark Bailey	.15	.07
451	Ron Romanick	.15	.07
452	Julio Cruz	.15	.07
453	Miguel Dilone	.15	.07
454	Storm Davis	.15	.07
455	Jaime Cocanower	.15	.07
456	Barbaro Garbey	.15	.07
457	Rich Gedman	.15	.07
458	Phil Niekro	1.50	.70
459	Mike Scioscia	.15	.07
460	Pat Tabler	.15	.07
461	Darryl Motley	.15	.07
462	Chris Codiroli	.15	.07
463	Doug Flynn	.15	.07
464	Billy Sample	.15	.07
465	Mickey Rivers	.15	.07
466	John Wathan	.15	.07
467	Bill Krueger	.15	.07
468	Andre Thornton	.15	.07
469	Rex Hudler	.15	.07
470	Sid Bream	.40	.18
471	Kirk Gibson	.40	.18
472	John Shelby	.15	.07
473	Moose Haas	.15	.07
474	Doug Corbett	.15	.07
475	Willie McGee	.40	.18
476	Bob Knepper	.15	.07
477	Kevin Gross	.15	.07
478	Carmelo Martinez	.15	.07
479	Kent Tekulve	.15	.07
480	Chili Davis	.40	.18
481	Bobby Clark	.15	.07
482	Mookie Wilson	.40	.18
483	Dave Owen	.15	.07
484	Ed Nunez	.15	.07
485	Rance Mulliniks	.15	.07
486	Ken Schrom	.15	.07
487	Jeff Russell	.15	.07
488	Tom Paciorek	.15	.07
489	Dan Ford	.15	.07
490	Mike Caldwell	.15	.07
491	Scottie Earl	.15	.07
492	Jose Rijo	.75	.35
493	Bruce Hurst	.15	.07
494	Ken Landreaux	.15	.07
495	Mike Fischlin	.15	.07
496	Don Slaught	.15	.07
497	Steve McCatty	.15	.07
498	Gary Lucas	.15	.07
499	Gary Pettis	.15	.07
500	Marvis Foley	.15	.07
501	Mike Squires	.15	.07
502	Jim Pankovits	.15	.07
503	Luis Aguayo	.15	.07
504	Ralph Citarella	.15	.07
505	Bruce Bochy	.15	.07
506	Bob Owchinko	.15	.07
507	Pascual Perez	.15	.07
508	Lee Lacy	.15	.07
509	Atlee Hammaker	.15	.07
510	Bob Dernier	.15	.07
511	Ed VandeBerg	.15	.07
512	Cliff Johnson	.15	.07
513	Len Whitehouse	.15	.07
514	Dennis Martinez	.40	.18
515	Ed Romero	.15	.07
516	Rusty Kuntz	.15	.07
517	Rick Miller	.15	.07
518	Dennis Rasmussen	.15	.07
519	Steve Yeager	.15	.07
520	Chris Bando	.15	.07
521	U.L. Washington	.15	.07
522	Curt Young	.15	.07
523	Angel Salazar	.15	.07
524	Curt Kaufman	.15	.07
525	Odell Jones	.15	.07
526	Juan Agosto	.15	.07
527	Denny Walling	.15	.07
528	Andy Hawkins	.15	.07
529	Sixto Lezcano	.15	.07
530	Skeeter Barnes	.15	.07
531	Randy Johnson	.15	.07
532	Jim Morrison	.15	.07
533	Warren Brusstar	.15	.07
534A	Jeff Pendleton ERR	1.50	.70
	(Wrong first name)		
534B	Terry Pendleton COR	5.00	2.20
535	Vic Rodriguez	.15	.07
536	Bob McClure	.15	.07
537	Dave Bergman	.15	.07
538	Mark Clear	.15	.07
539	Mike Pagliarulo	.15	.07
540	Terry Whitfield	.15	.07
541	Joe Beckwith	.15	.07
542	Jeff Burroughs	.15	.07
543	Dan Schatzeder	.15	.07
544	Donnie Scott	.15	.07
545	Jim Slaton	.15	.07
546	Greg Luzinski	.40	.18
547	Mark Salas	.15	.07
548	Dave Smith	.15	.07
549	John Wockenfuss	.15	.07
550	Frank Pastore	.15	.07
551	Tim Flannery	.15	.07
552	Rick Rhoden	.15	.07
553	Mark Davis	.15	.07
554	Jeff Dedmon	.15	.07
555	Gary Woods	.15	.07
556	Danny Heep	.15	.07
557	Mark Langston	.75	.35
558	Darrell Brown	.15	.07
559	Jimmy Key	2.00	.90
560	Rick Lysander	.15	.07
561	Doyle Alexander	.15	.07
562	Mike Stanton	.15	.07
563	Sid Fernandez	.40	.18
564	Richie Hebner	.15	.07
565	Alex Trevino	.15	.07
566	Brian Harper	.15	.07
567	Dan Gladden	.40	.18
568	Luis Salazar	.15	.07
569	Tom Foley	.15	.07
570	Larry Andersen	.15	.07
571	Danny Cox	.15	.07
572	Joe Sambito	.15	.07
573	Juan Beniquez	.15	.07
574	Joel Skinner	.15	.07
575	Randy St.Claire	.15	.07
576	Floyd Rayford	.15	.07
577	Roy Howell	.15	.07
578	John Grubb	.15	.07
579	Ed Jurak	.15	.07
580	John Montefusco	.15	.07
581	Orel Hershiser	2.00	.90
582	Tom Waddell	.15	.07
583	Mark Huismann	.15	.07
584	Joe Morgan	1.50	.70
585	Jim Wohlford	.15	.07
586	Dave Schmidt	.15	.07
587	Jeff Kunkel	.15	.07
588	Hal McRae	.40	.18
589	Bill Almon	.15	.07
590	Carmen Castillo	.15	.07
591	Omar Moreno	.15	.07
592	Ken Howell	.15	.07
593	Tom Brookens	.15	.07
594	Joe Nolan	.15	.07
595	Willie Lozado	.15	.07
596	Tom Nieto	.15	.07
597	Walt Terrell	.15	.07
598	Al Oliver	.40	.18
599	Shane Rawley	.15	.07
600	Denny Gonzalez	.15	.07
601	Mark Grant	.15	.07
602	Mike Armstrong	.15	.07
603	George Foster	.40	.18
604	Dave Lopes	.40	.18
605	Salome Barojas	.15	.07
606	Roy Lee Jackson	.15	.07
607	Pete Filson	.15	.07
608	Duane Walker	.15	.07
609	Glenn Wilson	.15	.07
610	Rafael Santana	.15	.07
611	Roy Smith	.15	.07
612	Ruppert Jones	.15	.07
613	Joe Cowley	.15	.07
614	Al Nipper UER	.15	.07
	(Photo actually Mike Brown)		
615	Gene Nelson	.15	.07
616	Joe Carter	1.50	.70
617	Ray Knight	.15	.07
618	Chuck Rainey	.15	.07
619	Dan Driessen	.15	.07
620	Daryl Sconiers	.15	.07
621	Bill Stein	.15	.07
622	Roy Smalley	.15	.07
623	Ed Lynch	.15	.07
624	Jeff Stone	.15	.07
625	Bruce Berenyi	.15	.07
626	Kelvin Chapman	.15	.07
627	Joe Price	.15	.07
628	Steve Bedrosian	.15	.07
629	Vic Mata	.15	.07
630	Mike Krukow	.15	.07
631	Phil Bradley	.40	.18
632	Jim Gott	.15	.07
633	Randy Bush	.15	.07
634	Tom Browning	.40	.18
635	Lou Gehrig Puzzle Card	1.50	.70
636	Reid Nichols	.15	.07
637	Dan Pasqua	.40	.18
638	German Rivera	.15	.07
639	Don Schulze	.15	.07
640A	Mike Jones	.15	.07

		MINT	NRMT
	(Career Highlights, takes five lines)		
☐ 640B	Mike Jones .15		.07
	(Career Highlights, takes four lines)		
☐ 641	Pete Rose	2.00	.90
☐ 642	Wade Rowdon .15		.07
☐ 643	Jerry Narron .15		.07
☐ 644	Darrell Miller .15		.07
☐ 645	Tim Hulett .15		.07
☐ 646	Andy McGaffigan .15		.07
☐ 647	Kurt Bevacqua .15		.07
☐ 648	John Russell .15		.07
☐ 649	Ron Robinson .15		.07
☐ 650	Donnie Moore .15		.07
☐ 651A	Two for the Title	2.00	.90
	Dave Winfield		
	Don Mattingly		
	(Yellow letters)		
☐ 651B	Two for the Title	5.00	2.20
	Dave Winfield		
	Don Mattingly		
	(White letters)		
☐ 652	Tim Laudner .15		.07
☐ 653	Steve Farr .40		.18
☐ 654	DK Checklist 1-26 .15		.07
	(Unnumbered)		
☐ 655	Checklist 27-130 .15		.07
	(Unnumbered)		
☐ 656	Checklist 131-234 .15		.07
	(Unnumbered)		
☐ 657	Checklist 235-338 .15		.07
	(Unnumbered)		
☐ 658	Checklist 339-442 .15		.07
	(Unnumbered)		
☐ 659	Checklist 443-546 .15		.07
	(Unnumbered)		
☐ 660	Checklist 547-653 .15		.07
	(Unnumbered)		

1986 Donruss

The 1986 Donruss set consists of 660 standard-size cards. Wax packs contained 15 cards plus a Hank Aaron puzzle panel. The card fronts feature blue borders, the standard team logo, player's name, position, and Donruss logo. The first 26 cards of the set are Diamond Kings (DK), for the fifth year in a row; the artwork on the Diamond Kings was again produced by the Perez-Steele Galleries. Cards 27-46 again feature Rated Rookies (RR). The unnumbered checklist cards are arbitrarily numbered below as numbers 654 through 660. Rookie Cards in this set include Jose Canseco, Darren Daulton, Len Dykstra, Cecil Fielder, Andres Galarraga, Fred McGriff, Paul O'Neill, and Mickey Tettleton.

		MINT	NRMT
	COMPLETE SET (660)	40.00	18.00
	COMP.FACT.SET (660)	50.00	22.00
	COMMON CARD (1-660)	.10	.05
	MINOR STARS		.11
	SEMISTARS	.50	.23
	UNLISTED STARS	1.00	.45
	BEWARE CANSECO COUNTERFEITS		
	1986-PRESENT PRICED IN MINT CONDITION		
☐ 1	Kirk Gibson DK	.10	.05
☐ 2	Goose Gossage DK	.10	.05
☐ 3	Willie McGee DK	.10	.05
☐ 4	George Bell DK	.10	.05
☐ 5	Tony Armas DK	.10	.05
☐ 6	Chili Davis DK	.50	.23
☐ 7	Cecil Cooper DK	.10	.05
☐ 8	Mike Boddicker DK	.10	.05
☐ 9	Dave Lopes DK	.10	.05
☐ 10	Bill Doran DK	.10	.05
☐ 11	Bret Saberhagen DK	.25	.11
☐ 12	Brett Butler DK	.25	.11
☐ 13	Harold Baines DK	.50	.23
☐ 14	Mike Davis DK	.10	.05
☐ 15	Tony Perez DK	.25	.11
☐ 16	Willie Randolph DK	.10	.05
☐ 17	Bob Boone DK	.10	.05
☐ 18	Orel Hershiser DK	.25	.11
☐ 19	Johnny Ray DK	.10	.05
☐ 20	Gary Ward DK	.10	.05
☐ 21	Rick Mahler DK	.10	.05
☐ 22	Phil Bradley DK	.10	.05
☐ 23	Jerry Koosman DK	.25	.11
☐ 24	Tom Brunansky DK	.25	.11
☐ 25	Andre Dawson DK	.25	.11
☐ 26	Dwight Gooden DK	.25	.11
☐ 27	Kal Daniels RR	.25	.11
☐ 28	Fred McGriff RR	6.00	2.70
☐ 29	Cory Snyder RR	.10	.05
☐ 30	Jose Guzman RR	.10	.05
☐ 31	Ty Gainey RR	.10	.05
☐ 32	Johnny Abrego RR	.10	.05
☐ 33	Andres Galarraga RR	6.00	2.70
	(No accent)		
☐ 33B	Andre's Galarraga RR	6.00	2.70
	(Accent over e)		
☐ 34	Dave Shipanoff RR	.10	.05
☐ 35	Mark McLemore RR	.50	.23
☐ 36	Marty Clary RR	.10	.05
☐ 37	Paul O'Neill RR	2.00	.90
☐ 38	Danny Tartabull RR	.25	.11
☐ 39	Jose Canseco RR	8.00	3.60
☐ 40	Juan Nieves RR	.10	.05
☐ 41	Lance McCullers RR	.10	.05
☐ 42	Rick Surhoff RR	.10	.05
☐ 43	Todd Worrell RR	1.00	.45
☐ 44	Bob Kipper RR	.10	.05
☐ 45	John Habyan RR	.10	.05
☐ 46	Mike Woodard RR	.10	.05
☐ 47	Mike Boddicker	.10	.05
☐ 48	Robin Yount	1.00	.45
☐ 49	Lou Whitaker	.25	.11
☐ 50	Oil Can Boyd	.10	.05
☐ 51	Rickey Henderson	1.00	.45
☐ 52	Mike Marshall	.10	.05
☐ 53	George Brett	2.00	.90
☐ 54	Dave Kingman	.25	.11
☐ 55	Hubie Brooks	.10	.05
☐ 56	Oddibe McDowell	.10	.05
☐ 57	Doug DeCinces	.10	.05
☐ 58	Britt Burns	.10	.05
☐ 59	Ozzie Smith	1.25	.55
☐ 60	Jose Cruz	.25	.11
☐ 61	Mike Schmidt	1.25	.55
☐ 62	Pete Rose	1.25	.55
☐ 63	Steve Garvey	.50	.23
☐ 64	Tony Pena	.10	.05
☐ 65	Chili Davis	.50	.23
☐ 66	Dale Murphy	1.00	.45
☐ 67	Ryne Sandberg	1.25	.55
☐ 68	Gary Carter	1.00	.45
☐ 69	Alvin Davis	.10	.05
☐ 70	Kent Hrbek	.25	.11
☐ 71	George Bell	.25	.11
☐ 72	Kirby Puckett	4.00	1.80
☐ 73	Lloyd Moseby	.10	.05
☐ 74	Bob Kearney	.10	.05
☐ 75	Dwight Gooden	1.00	.45
☐ 76	Gary Matthews	.10	.05
☐ 77	Rick Mahler	.10	.05
☐ 78	Benny Distefano	.10	.05
☐ 79	Jeff Leonard	.10	.05
☐ 80	Kevin McReynolds	.25	.11
☐ 81	Ron Oester	.10	.05
☐ 82	John Russell	.10	.05
☐ 83	Tommy Herr	.10	.05
☐ 84	Jerry Mumphrey	.10	.05
☐ 85	Ron Romanick	.10	.05
☐ 86	Daryl Boston	.10	.05
☐ 87	Andre Dawson	1.00	.45
☐ 88	Eddie Murray	1.00	.45
☐ 89	Dion James	.10	.05
☐ 90	Chet Lemon	.10	.05
☐ 91	Bob Stanley	.10	.05
☐ 92	Willie Randolph	.25	.11
☐ 93	Mike Scioscia	.10	.05
☐ 94	Tom Waddell	.10	.05
☐ 95	Danny Jackson	.10	.05
☐ 96	Mike Davis	.10	.05
☐ 97	Mike Fitzgerald	.10	.05
☐ 98	Gary Ward	.10	.05
☐ 99	Pete O'Brien	.10	.05
☐ 100	Bret Saberhagen	.25	.11
☐ 101	Alfredo Griffin	.10	.05
☐ 102	Brett Butler	.25	.11
☐ 103	Ron Guidry	.25	.11
☐ 104	Jerry Reuss	.10	.05
☐ 105	Jack Morris	.25	.11
☐ 106	Rick Dempsey	.10	.05
☐ 107	Ray Burris	.10	.05
☐ 108	Brian Downing	.10	.05
☐ 109	Willie McGee	.25	.11
☐ 110	Bill Doran	.10	.05
☐ 111	Kent Tekulve	.10	.05
☐ 112	Tony Gwynn	2.50	1.10
☐ 113	Marvell Wynne	.10	.05
☐ 114	David Green	.10	.05
☐ 115	Jim Gantner	.10	.05
☐ 116	George Foster	.25	.11
☐ 117	Steve Trout	.10	.05
☐ 118	Mark Langston	.25	.11
☐ 119	Tony Fernandez	.25	.11
☐ 120	John Butcher	.10	.05
☐ 121	Ron Robinson	.10	.05
☐ 122	Dan Spillner	.10	.05
☐ 123	Mike Young	.10	.05
☐ 124	Paul Molitor	1.00	.45
☐ 125	Kirk Gibson	.25	.11
☐ 126	Ken Griffey	.25	.11
☐ 127	Tony Armas	.10	.05
☐ 128	Mariano Duncan	1.00	.45
☐ 129	Pat Tabler	.10	.05
☐ 130	Frank White	.25	.11
☐ 131	Carney Lansford	.25	.11
☐ 132	Vance Law	.10	.05
☐ 133	Dick Schofield	.10	.05
☐ 134	Wayne Tolleson	.10	.05
☐ 135	Greg Walker	.10	.05
☐ 136	Denny Walling	.10	.05
☐ 137	Ozzie Virgil	.10	.05
☐ 138	Ricky Horton	.10	.05
☐ 139	LaMarr Hoyt	.10	.05
☐ 140	Wayne Krenchicki	.10	.05
☐ 141	Glenn Hubbard	.10	.05
☐ 142	Cecilio Guante	.10	.05
☐ 143	Mike Krukow	.10	.05
☐ 144	Lee Smith	.50	.23
☐ 145	Edwin Nunez	.10	.05
☐ 146	Dave Stieb	.10	.05
☐ 147	Mike Smithson	.10	.05
☐ 148	Ken Dixon	.10	.05
☐ 149	Danny Darwin	.10	.05
☐ 150	Chris Pittaro	.10	.05
☐ 151	Bill Buckner	.25	.11
☐ 152	Mike Pagliarulo	.10	.05
☐ 153	Bill Russell	.10	.05
☐ 154	Brook Jacoby	.10	.05
☐ 155	Pat Sheridan	.10	.05
☐ 156	Mike Gallego	.25	.11
☐ 157	Jim Wohlford	.10	.05
☐ 158	Gary Pettis	.10	.05
☐ 159	Toby Harrah	.10	.05

□			
160	Richard Dotson	.10	.05
161	Bob Knepper	.10	.05
162	Dave Dravecky	.25	.11
163	Greg Gross	.10	.05
164	Eric Davis	.50	.23
165	Gerald Perry	.10	.05
166	Rick Rhoden	.10	.05
167	Keith Moreland	.10	.05
168	Jack Clark	.25	.11
169	Storm Davis	.10	.05
170	Cecil Cooper	.25	.11
171	Alan Trammell	.50	.23
172	Roger Clemens	4.00	1.80
173	Don Mattingly	1.50	.70
174	Pedro Guerrero	.25	.11
175	Willie Wilson	.10	.05
176	Dwayne Murphy	.10	.05
177	Tim Raines	.25	.11
178	Larry Parrish	.10	.05
179	Mike Witt	.10	.05
180	Harold Baines	.50	.23
181	Vince Coleman UER	1.00	.45
	(BA 2.67 on back)		
182	Jeff Heathcock	.10	.05
183	Steve Carlton	1.00	.45
184	Mario Soto	.10	.05
185	Goose Gossage	.25	.11
186	Johnny Ray	.10	.05
187	Dan Gladden	.10	.05
188	Bob Horner	.10	.05
189	Rick Sutcliffe	.10	.05
190	Keith Hernandez	.25	.11
191	Phil Bradley	.10	.05
192	Tom Brunansky	.10	.05
193	Jesse Barfield	.10	.05
194	Frank Viola	.10	.05
195	Willie Upshaw	.10	.05
196	Jim Beattie	.10	.05
197	Darryl Strawberry	1.00	.45
198	Ron Cey	.25	.11
199	Steve Bedrosian	.10	.05
200	Steve Kemp	.10	.05
201	Manny Trillo	.10	.05
202	Garry Templeton	.10	.05
203	Dave Parker	.25	.11
204	John Denny	.10	.05
205	Terry Pendleton	.50	.23
206	Terry Puhl	.10	.05
207	Bobby Grich	.25	.11
208	Ozzie Guillen	.50	.23
209	Jeff Reardon	.25	.11
210	Cal Ripken	4.00	1.80
211	Bill Schroeder	.10	.05
212	Dan Petry	.10	.05
213	Jim Rice	.25	.11
214	Dave Righetti	.10	.05
215	Fernando Valenzuela	.25	.11
216	Julio Franco	.25	.11
217	Darryl Motley	.10	.05
218	Dave Collins	.10	.05
219	Tim Wallach	.10	.05
220	George Wright	.10	.05
221	Tommy Dunbar	.10	.05
222	Steve Balboni	.10	.05
223	Jay Howell	.10	.05
224	Joe Carter	1.00	.45
225	Ed Whitson	.10	.05
226	Orel Hershiser	.50	.23
227	Willie Hernandez	.10	.05
228	Lee Lacy	.10	.05
229	Rollie Fingers	1.00	.45
230	Bob Boone	.25	.11
231	Joaquin Andujar	.10	.05
232	Craig Reynolds	.10	.05
233	Shane Rawley	.10	.05
234	Eric Show	.10	.05
235	Jose DeLeon	.10	.05
236	Jose Uribe	.10	.05
237	Moose Haas	.10	.05
238	Wally Backman	.10	.05
239	Dennis Eckersley	1.00	.45
240	Mike Moore	.25	.11
241	Damaso Garcia	.10	.05
242	Tim Teufel	.10	.05
243	Dave Concepcion	.25	.11
244	Floyd Bannister	.10	.05
245	Fred Lynn	.25	.11
246	Charlie Moore	.10	.05
247	Walt Terrell	.10	.05
248	Dave Winfield	1.00	.45
249	Dwight Evans	.25	.11
250	Dennis Powell	.10	.05
251	Andre Thornton	.10	.05
252	Onix Concepcion	.10	.05
253	Mike Heath	.10	.05
254A	David Palmer ERR	.10	.05
	(Position 2B)		
254B	David Palmer COR	1.00	.45
	(Position P)		
255	Donnie Moore	.10	.05
256	Curtis Wilkerson	.10	.05
257	Julio Cruz	.10	.05
258	Nolan Ryan	4.00	1.80
259	Jeff Stone	.10	.05
260	John Tudor	.10	.05
261	Mark Thurmond	.10	.05
262	Jay Tibbs	.10	.05
263	Rafael Ramirez	.10	.05
264	Larry McWilliams	.10	.05
265	Mark Davis	.10	.05
266	Bob Dernier	.10	.05
267	Matt Young	.10	.05
268	Jim Clancy	.10	.05
269	Mickey Hatcher	.10	.05
270	Sammy Stewart	.10	.05
271	Bob L. Gibson	.10	.05
272	Nelson Simmons	.10	.05
273	Rich Gedman	.10	.05
274	Butch Wynegar	.10	.05
275	Ken Howell	.10	.05
276	Mel Hall	.10	.05
277	Jim Sundberg	.10	.05
278	Chris Codiroli	.10	.05
279	Herm Winningham	.10	.05
280	Rod Carew	1.00	.45
281	Don Slaught	.10	.05
282	Scott Fletcher	.10	.05
283	Bill Dawley	.10	.05
284	Andy Hawkins	.10	.05
285	Glenn Wilson	.10	.05
286	Nick Esasky	.10	.05
287	Claudell Washington	.10	.05
288	Lee Mazzilli	.10	.05
289	Jody Davis	.10	.05
290	Darrell Porter	.10	.05
291	Scott McGregor	.10	.05
292	Ted Simmons	.25	.11
293	Aurelio Lopez	.10	.05
294	Marty Barrett	.10	.05
295	Dale Berra	.10	.05
296	Greg Brock	.10	.05
297	Charlie Leibrandt	.10	.05
298	Bill Krueger	.10	.05
299	Bryn Smith	.10	.05
300	Burt Hooton	.10	.05
301	Stu Cliburn	.10	.05
302	Luis Salazar	.10	.05
303	Ken Dayley	.10	.05
304	Frank DiPino	.10	.05
305	Von Hayes	.10	.05
306	Gary Redus	.10	.05
307	Craig Lefferts	.10	.05
308	Sammy Khalifa	.10	.05
309	Scott Garrelts	.10	.05
310	Rick Cerone	.10	.05
311	Shawon Dunston	.25	.11
312	Howard Johnson	.25	.11
313	Jim Presley	.10	.05
314	Gary Gaetti	.25	.11
315	Luis Leal	.10	.05
316	Mark Salas	.10	.05
317	Bill Caudill	.10	.05
318	Dave Henderson	.10	.05
319	Rafael Santana	.10	.05
320	Leon Durham	.10	.05
321	Bruce Sutter	.25	.11
322	Jason Thompson	.10	.05
323	Bob Brenly	.10	.05
324	Carmelo Martinez	.10	.05
325	Eddie Milner	.10	.05
326	Juan Samuel	.10	.05
327	Tom Nieto	.10	.05
328	Dave Smith	.10	.05
329	Urbano Lugo	.10	.05
330	Joel Skinner	.10	.05
331	Bill Gullickson	.10	.05
332	Floyd Rayford	.10	.05
333	Ben Oglivie	.10	.05
334	Lance Parrish	.25	.11
335	Jackie Gutierrez	.10	.05
336	Dennis Rasmussen	.10	.05
337	Terry Whitfield	.10	.05
338	Neal Heaton	.10	.05
339	Jorge Orta	.10	.05
340	Donnie Hill	.10	.05
341	Joe Hesketh	.10	.05
342	Charlie Hough	.25	.11
343	Dave Rozema	.10	.05
344	Greg Pryor	.10	.05
345	Mickey Tettleton	1.00	.45
346	George Vukovich	.10	.05
347	Don Baylor	.50	.23
348	Carlos Diaz	.10	.05
349	Barbaro Garbey	.10	.05
350	Larry Sheets	.10	.05
351	Ted Higuera	.25	.11
352	Juan Beniquez	.10	.05
353	Bob Forsch	.10	.05
354	Mark Bailey	.10	.05
355	Larry Andersen	.10	.05
356	Terry Kennedy	.10	.05
357	Don Robinson	.10	.05
358	Jim Gott	.10	.05
359	Earnie Riles	.10	.05
360	John Christensen	.10	.05
361	Ray Fontenot	.10	.05
362	Spike Owen	.10	.05
363	Jim Acker	.10	.05
364	Ron Davis	.10	.05
365	Tom Hume	.10	.05
366	Carlton Fisk	1.00	.45
367	Nate Snell	.10	.05
368	Rick Manning	.10	.05
369	Darrell Evans	.25	.11
370	Ron Hassey	.10	.05
371	Wade Boggs	1.00	.45
372	Rick Honeycutt	.10	.05
373	Chris Bando	.10	.05
374	Bud Black	.10	.05
375	Steve Henderson	.10	.05
376	Charlie Lea	.10	.05
377	Reggie Jackson	1.25	.55
378	Dave Schmidt	.10	.05
379	Bob James	.10	.05
380	Glenn Davis	.25	.11
381	Tim Corcoran	.10	.05
382	Danny Cox	.10	.05
383	Tim Flannery	.10	.05
384	Tom Browning	.10	.05
385	Rick Camp	.10	.05
386	Jim Morrison	.10	.05
387	Dave LaPoint	.10	.05
388	Dave Lopes	.25	.11
389	Al Cowens	.10	.05
390	Doyle Alexander	.10	.05
391	Tim Laudner	.10	.05
392	Don Aase	.10	.05
393	Jaime Cocanower	.10	.05
394	Randy O'Neal	.10	.05
395	Mike Easier	.10	.05
396	Scott Bradley	.10	.05
397	Tom Niedenfuer	.10	.05
398	Jerry Willard	.10	.05
399	Lonnie Smith	.10	.05
400	Bruce Bochte	.10	.05
401	Terry Francona	.10	.05
402	Jim Slaton	.10	.05
403	Bill Stein	.10	.05
404	Tim Hulett	.10	.05
405	Alan Ashby	.10	.05
406	Tim Stoddard	.10	.05
407	Garry Maddox	.10	.05
408	Ted Power	.10	.05
409	Len Barker	.10	.05
410	Denny Gonzalez	.10	.05
411	George Frazier	.10	.05
412	Andy Van Slyke	.25	.11
413	Jim Dwyer	.10	.05

414	Paul Householder	.10	.05
415	Alejandro Sanchez	.10	.05
416	Steve Crawford	.10	.05
417	Dan Pasqua	.10	.05
418	Enos Cabell	.10	.05
419	Mike Jones	.10	.05
420	Steve Kiefer	.10	.05
421	Tim Burke	.10	.05
422	Mike Mason	.10	.05
423	Ruppert Jones	.10	.05
424	Jerry Hairston	.10	.05
425	Tito Landrum	.10	.05
426	Jeff Calhoun	.10	.05
427	Don Carman	.10	.05
428	Tony Perez	1.00	.45
429	Jerry Davis	.10	.05
430	Bob Walk	.10	.05
431	Brad Wellman	.10	.05
432	Terry Forster	.10	.05
433	Billy Hatcher	.10	.05
434	Clint Hurdle	.10	.05
435	Ivan Calderon	.11	.05
436	Pete Filson	.10	.05
437	Tom Henke	.25	.11
438	Dave Engle	.10	.05
439	Tom Filer	.10	.05
440	Gorman Thomas	.10	.05
441	Rick Aguilera	1.00	.45
442	Scott Sanderson	.10	.05
443	Jeff Dedmon	.10	.05
444	Joe Orsulak	.10	.05
445	Atlee Hammaker	.10	.05
446	Jerry Royster	.10	.05
447	Buddy Bell	.25	.11
448	Dave Rucker	.10	.05
449	Ivan DeJesus	.10	.05
450	Jim Pankovits	.10	.05
451	Jerry Narron	.10	.05
452	Bryan Little	.10	.05
453	Gary Lucas	.10	.05
454	Dennis Martinez	.25	.11
455	Ed Romero	.10	.05
456	Bob Melvin	.10	.05
457	Glenn Hoffman	.10	.05
458	Bob Shirley	.10	.05
459	Bob Welch	.10	.05
460	Carmen Castillo	.10	.05
461	Dave Leeper	.10	.05
462	Tim Birtsas	.10	.05
463	Randy St.Claire	.10	.05
464	Chris Welsh	.10	.05
465	Greg Harris	.10	.05
466	Lynn Jones	.10	.05
467	Dusty Baker	.25	.11
468	Roy Smith	.10	.05
469	Andre Robertson	.10	.05
470	Ken Landreaux	.10	.05
471	Dave Bergman	.10	.05
472	Gary Roenicke	.10	.05
473	Pete Vuckovich	.10	.05
474	Kirk McCaskill	.25	.11
475	Jeff Lahti	.10	.05
476	Mike Scott	.10	.05
477	Darren Daulton	2.00	.90
478	Graig Nettles	.25	.11
479	Bill Almon	.10	.05
480	Greg Minton	.10	.05
481	Randy Ready	.10	.05
482	Len Dykstra	2.00	.90
483	Thad Bosley	.10	.05
484	Harold Reynolds	1.00	.45
485	Al Oliver	.25	.11
486	Roy Smalley	.10	.05
487	John Franco	1.00	.45
488	Juan Agosto	.10	.05
489	Al Pardo	.10	.05
490	Bill Wegman	.10	.05
491	Frank Tanana	.10	.05
492	Brian Fisher	.10	.05
493	Mark Clear	.10	.05
494	Len Matuszek	.10	.05
495	Ramon Romero	.10	.05
496	John Wathan	.10	.05
497	Rob Picciolo	.10	.05
498	U.L. Washington	.10	.05
499	John Candelaria	.10	.05
500	Duane Walker	.10	.05
501	Gene Nelson	.10	.05
502	John Mizerock	.10	.05
503	Luis Aguayo	.10	.05
504	Kurt Kepshire	.10	.05
505	Ed Wojna	.10	.05
506	Joe Price	.10	.05
507	Milt Thompson	.25	.11
508	Junior Ortiz	.10	.05
509	Vida Blue	.25	.11
510	Steve Engel	.10	.05
511	Karl Best	.10	.05
512	Cecil Fielder	3.00	1.35
513	Frank Eufemia	.10	.05
514	Tippy Martinez	.10	.05
515	Billy Joe Robidoux	.10	.05
516	Bill Scherrer	.10	.05
517	Bruce Hurst	.10	.05
518	Rich Bordi	.10	.05
519	Steve Yeager	.10	.05
520	Tony Bernazard	.10	.05
521	Hal McRae	.25	.11
522	Jose Rijo	.10	.05
523	Mitch Webster	.10	.05
524	Jack Howell	.10	.05
525	Alan Bannister	.10	.05
526	Ron Kittle	.10	.05
527	Phil Garner	.10	.05
528	Kurt Bevacqua	.10	.05
529	Kevin Gross	.10	.05
530	Bo Diaz	.10	.05
531	Ken Oberkfell	.10	.05
532	Rick Reuschel	.10	.05
533	Ron Meridith	.10	.05
534	Steve Braun	.10	.05
535	Wayne Gross	.10	.05
536	Ray Searage	.10	.05
537	Tom Brookens	.10	.05
538	Al Nipper	.10	.05
539	Billy Sample	.10	.05
540	Steve Sax	.10	.05
541	Dan Quisenberry	.10	.05
542	Tony Phillips	.10	.05
543	Floyd Youmans	.10	.05
544	Steve Buechele	.25	.11
545	Craig Gerber	.10	.05
546	Joe DeSa	.10	.05
547	Brian Harper	.10	.05
548	Kevin Bass	.10	.05
549	Tom Foley	.10	.05
550	Dave Van Gorder	.10	.05
551	Bruce Bochy	.10	.05
552	R.J. Reynolds	.10	.05
553	Chris Brown	.10	.05
554	Bruce Benedict	.10	.05
555	Warren Brusstar	.10	.05
556	Danny Heep	.10	.05
557	Darnell Coles	.10	.05
558	Greg Gagne	.10	.05
559	Ernie Whitt	.10	.05
560	Ron Washington	.10	.05
561	Billy Key	1.00	.45
562	Billy Swift	.10	.05
563	Ron Darling	.10	.05
564	Dick Ruthven	.10	.05
565	Zane Smith	.10	.05
566	Sid Bream	.10	.05
567A	Joel Youngblood ERR (Position P)	.10	.05
567B	Joel Youngblood COR (Position IF)	1.00	.45
568	Mario Ramirez	.10	.05
569	Tom Runnells	.10	.05
570	Rick Schu	.10	.05
571	Bill Campbell	.10	.05
572	Dickie Thon	.10	.05
573	Al Holland	.10	.05
574	Reid Nichols	.10	.05
575	Bert Roberge	.10	.05
576	Mike Flanagan	.10	.05
577	Tim Leary	.10	.05
578	Mike Laga	.10	.05
579	Steve Lyons	.10	.05
580	Phil Niekro	1.00	.45
581	Gilberto Reyes	.10	.05
582	Jamie Easterly	.10	.05
583	Mark Gubicza	.10	.05
584	Stan Javier	.25	.11
585	Bill Laskey	.10	.05
586	Jeff Russell	.10	.05
587	Dickie Noles	.10	.05
588	Steve Farr	.10	.05
589	Steve Ontiveros	.25	.11
590	Mike Hargrove	.25	.11
591	Marty Bystrom	.10	.05
592	Franklin Stubbs	.10	.05
593	Larry Herndon	.10	.05
594	Bill Swaggerty	.10	.05
595	Carlos Ponce	.10	.05
596	Pat Perry	.10	.05
597	Ray Knight	.25	.11
598	Steve Lombardozzi	.10	.05
599	Brad Havens	.10	.05
600	Pat Clements	.10	.05
601	Joe Niekro	.10	.05
602	Hank Aaron Puzzle Card	1.00	.45
603	Dwayne Henry	.10	.05
604	Mookie Wilson	.25	.11
605	Buddy Biancalana	.10	.05
606	Rance Mulliniks	.10	.05
607	Alan Wiggins	.10	.05
608	Joe Cowley	.10	.05
609	Tom Seaver (Green borders on name)	1.25	.55
609B	Tom Seaver (Yellow borders on name)	2.00	.90
610	Neil Allen	.10	.05
611	Don Sutton	1.00	.45
612	Fred Toliver	.10	.05
613	Jay Baller	.10	.05
614	Marc Sullivan	.10	.05
615	John Grubb	.10	.05
616	Bruce Kison	.10	.05
617	Bill Madlock	.10	.05
618	Chris Chambliss	.25	.11
619	Dave Stewart	.25	.11
620	Tim Lollar	.10	.05
621	Gary Lavelle	.10	.05
622	Charles Hudson	.10	.05
623	Joel Davis	.10	.05
624	Joe Johnson	.10	.05
625	Sid Fernandez	.25	.11
626	Dennis Lamp	.10	.05
627	Terry Harper	.10	.05
628	Jack Lazorko	.10	.05
629	Roger McDowell	.25	.11
630	Mark Funderburk	.10	.05
631	Ed Lynch	.10	.05
632	Rudy Law	.10	.05
633	Roger Mason	.10	.05
634	Mike Felder	.10	.05
635	Ken Schrom	.10	.05
636	Bob Ojeda	.10	.05
637	Ed VandeBerg	.10	.05
638	Bobby Meacham	.10	.05
639	Cliff Johnson	.10	.05
640	Garth Iorg	.10	.05
641	Dan Driessen	.10	.05
642	Mike Brown P	.10	.05
643	John Shelby	.10	.05
644	Pete Rose (Ty-Breaking)	.60	.25
645	The Knuckle Brothers Phil Niekro Joe Niekro	.25	.11
646	Jesse Orosco	.10	.05
647	Billy Beane	.10	.05
648	Cesar Cedeno	.25	.11
649	Bert Blyleven	.25	.11
650	Max Venable	.10	.05
651	Fleet Feet Vince Coleman Willie McGee	.10	.05
652	Calvin Schiraldi	.10	.05
653	King of Kings (Pete Rose)	1.00	.45
654	Diamond Kings CL 1-26 (Unnumbered)	.10	.05
655A	CL 1: 27-130	.10	.05

(Unnumbered)		
(45 Beane ERR)		
☐ 655B CL 1: 27-130	.10	.05
(Unnumbered)		
(45 Habyan COR)		
☐ 656 CL 2: 131-234	.10	.05
(Unnumbered)		
☐ 657 CL 3: 235-338	.10	.05
(Unnumbered)		
☐ 658 CL 4: 339-442	.10	.05
(Unnumbered)		
☐ 659 CL 5: 443-546	.10	.05
(Unnumbered)		
☐ 660 CL 6: 547-653	.10	.05
(Unnumbered)		

1986 Donruss Rookies

KELLY GRUBER

The 1986 Donruss "The Rookies" set features 56 full-color standard-size cards plus a 15-piece puzzle of Hank Aaron. The set was distributed through hobby dealers in a small green, cellophane wrapped factory box. Although the set was wrapped in cellophane, the top card was number 1 Joyner, resulting in a percentage of the Joyner cards arriving in less than perfect condition. Donruss fixed the problem after it was called to their attention and even went so far as to include a customer service phone number in their second printing. Card fronts are similar in design to the 1986 Donruss regular issue except for the presence of "The Rookies" logo in the lower left corner and a bluish green border instead of a blue border. The key extended Rookie Cards in this set are Barry Bonds, Bobby Bonilla, Will Clark, Bo Jackson, Wally Joyner, John Kruk, Kevin Mitchell, and Ruben Sierra.

	MINT	NRMT
COMP.FACT.SET (56)	25.00	11.00
COMMON CARD (1-56)	.10	.05
MINOR STARS	.25	.11
SEMISTARS	.50	.23
UNLISTED STARS	1.00	.45
☐ 1 Wally Joyner	1.00	.45
☐ 2 Tracy Jones	.10	.05
☐ 3 Allan Anderson	.10	.05
☐ 4 Ed Correa	.10	.05
☐ 5 Reggie Williams	.10	.05
☐ 6 Charlie Kerfeld	.10	.05
☐ 7 Andres Galarraga	3.00	1.35
☐ 8 Bob Tewksbury	.25	.11
☐ 9 Al Newman	.25	.11

☐ 10 Andres Thomas	.10	.05
☐ 11 Barry Bonds	8.00	3.60
☐ 12 Juan Nieves	.10	.05
☐ 13 Mark Eichhorn	.10	.05
☐ 14 Dan Plesac	.10	.05
☐ 15 Cory Snyder	.10	.05
☐ 16 Kelly Gruber	.10	.05
☐ 17 Kevin Mitchell	1.00	.45
☐ 18 Steve Lombardozzi	.10	.05
☐ 19 Mitch Williams	.25	.11
☐ 20 John Cerutti	.10	.05
☐ 21 Todd Worrell	1.00	.45
☐ 22 Jose Canseco	3.00	1.35
☐ 23 Pete Incaviglia	1.00	.45
☐ 24 Jose Guzman	.10	.05
☐ 25 Scott Bailes	.10	.05
☐ 26 Greg Mathews	.10	.05
☐ 27 Eric King	.10	.05
☐ 28 Paul Assenmacher	.10	.05
☐ 29 Jeff Sellers	.10	.05
☐ 30 Bobby Bonilla	2.00	.90
☐ 31 Doug Drabek	1.00	.45
☐ 32 Will Clark UER	3.00	1.35
(Listed as throwing right, should be left)		
☐ 33 Bip Roberts	1.00	.45
☐ 34 Jim Deshaies	.10	.05
☐ 35 Mike LaValliere	.10	.05
☐ 36 Scott Bankhead	.10	.05
☐ 37 Dale Sveum	.10	.05
☐ 38 Bo Jackson	2.00	.90
☐ 39 Robby Thompson	.25	.11
☐ 40 Eric Plunk	.10	.05
☐ 41 Bill Bathe	.10	.05
☐ 42 John Kruk	1.00	.45
☐ 43 Andy Allanson	.10	.05
☐ 44 Mark Portugal	.25	.11
☐ 45 Danny Tartabull	.25	.11
☐ 46 Bob Kipper	.10	.05
☐ 47 Gene Walter	.10	.05
☐ 48 Rey Quinones UER	.10	.05
(Misspelled Quinonez)		
☐ 49 Bobby Witt	.50	.23
☐ 50 Bill Mooneyham	.10	.05
☐ 51 John Cangelosi	.10	.05
☐ 52 Ruben Sierra	1.00	.45
☐ 53 Rob Woodward	.10	.05
☐ 54 Ed Hearn	.10	.05
☐ 55 Joel McKeon	.10	.05
☐ 56 Checklist 1-56	.10	.05

1987 Donruss

ANDY VAN SLYKE OF

This set consists of 660 standard-size cards. Cards were primarily distributed in 15-card wax packs, rack packs and a factory set. All packs included a Roberto Clemente puzzle panel and the factory sets contained a complete puzzle. The regular-issue cards feature a black and gold border on the front. The backs of the cards in the factory sets are oriented differently than cards taken from wax packs, giving the appearance that one

version or the other is upside down when sorting from the card backs. There are no premiums or discounts for either version. The popular Diamond King subset returns for the sixth consecutive year. Some of the Diamond King (1-26) selections are repeats from prior years; Perez-Steele Galleries had indicated in 1987 that a five-year rotation would be maintained in order to avoid depleting the pool of available worthy "Kings" on some of the teams. Rookie Cards in this set include Barry Bonds, Bobby Bonilla, Kevin Brown, Will Clark, David Cone, Chuck Finley, Bo Jackson, Wally Joyner, Barry Larkin, Greg Maddux and Rafael Palmeiro. The Greg Maddux card has been noted to have a premium for perfectly centered copies.

	MINT	NRMT
COMPLETE SET (660)	30.00	13.50
COMMON CARD (1-660)	.10	.05
MINOR STARS	.20	.09
UNLISTED STARS	.40	.18
☐ 1 Wally Joyner DK	.10	.05
☐ 2 Roger Clemens DK	.40	.18
☐ 3 Dale Murphy DK	.20	.09
☐ 4 Darryl Strawberry DK	.10	.05
☐ 5 Ozzie Smith DK	.40	.18
☐ 6 Jose Canseco DK	.40	.18
☐ 7 Charlie Hough DK	.10	.05
☐ 8 Brook Jacoby DK	.10	.05
☐ 9 Fred Lynn DK	.20	.09
☐ 10 Rick Rhoden DK	.10	.05
☐ 11 Chris Brown DK	.10	.05
☐ 12 Von Hayes DK	.10	.05
☐ 13 Jack Morris DK	.20	.09
☐ 14A Kevin McReynolds DK	.40	.18
ERR (Yellow strip missing on back)		
☐ 14B Kevin McReynolds DK	.10	.05
COR		
☐ 15 George Brett DK	.40	.18
☐ 16 Ted Higuera DK	.10	.05
☐ 17 Hubie Brooks DK	.10	.05
☐ 18 Mike Scott DK	.10	.05
☐ 19 Kirby Puckett DK	.50	.23
☐ 20 Dave Winfield DK	.20	.09
☐ 21 Lloyd Moseby DK	.10	.05
☐ 22A Eric Davis DK ERR	.40	.18
(Yellow strip missing on back)		
☐ 22B Eric Davis DK COR		.09
☐ 23 Jim Presley DK	.10	.05
☐ 24 Keith Moreland DK	.10	.05
☐ 25A Greg Walker DK ERR	.40	.18
(Yellow strip missing on back)		
☐ 25B Greg Walker DK COR		.05
☐ 26 Steve Sax DK	.10	.05
☐ 27 DK Checklist 1-26	.10	.05
☐ 28 B.J. Surhoff RR	.40	.18
☐ 29 Randy Myers RR	.40	.18
☐ 30 Ken Gerhart RR	.10	.05
☐ 31 Benito Santiago RR	.20	.09
☐ 32 Greg Swindell RR	.40	.18
☐ 33 Mike Birkbeck RR	.10	.05
☐ 34 Terry Steinbach RR	.40	.18
☐ 35 Bo Jackson RR	1.00	.45
☐ 36 Greg Maddux UER	20.00	9.00
(middle name misspelled "Allen")		
☐ 37 Jim Lindeman RR	.10	.05
☐ 38 Devon White RR	.40	.18
☐ 39 Eric Bell RR	.10	.05
☐ 40 Willie Fraser RR	.10	.05
☐ 41 Jerry Browne RR	.10	.05
☐ 42 Chris James RR	.10	.05
☐ 43 Rafael Palmeiro RR	2.00	.90

44	Pat Dodson RR	.10	.05
45	Duane Ward RR	.20	.09
46	Mark McGwire RR	4.00	1.80
47	Bruce Fields RR UER (Photo actually Darnell Coles)	.10	.05
48	Eddie Murray	.40	.18
49	Ted Higuera	.10	.05
50	Kirk Gibson	.20	.09
51	Oil Can Boyd	.10	.05
52	Don Mattingly	.60	.25
53	Pedro Guerrero	.20	.09
54	George Brett	.75	.35
55	Jose Rijo	.10	.05
56	Tim Raines	.20	.09
57	Ed Correa	.10	.05
58	Mike Witt	.10	.05
59	Greg Walker	.10	.05
60	Ozzie Smith	.50	.23
61	Glenn Davis	.10	.05
62	Glenn Wilson	.10	.05
63	Tom Browning	.10	.05
64	Tony Gwynn	1.00	.45
65	R.J. Reynolds	.10	.05
66	Will Clark	1.50	.70
67	Ozzie Virgil	.10	.05
68	Rick Sutcliffe	.10	.05
69	Gary Carter	.20	.09
70	Mike Moore	.10	.05
71	Bert Blyleven	.20	.09
72	Tony Fernandez	.20	.09
73	Kent Hrbek	.20	.09
74	Lloyd Moseby	.10	.05
75	Alvin Davis	.10	.05
76	Keith Hernandez	.20	.09
77	Ryne Sandberg	.50	.23
78	Dale Murphy	.40	.18
79	Sid Bream	.10	.05
80	Chris Brown	.10	.05
81	Steve Garvey	.40	.18
82	Mario Soto	.10	.05
83	Shane Rawley	.10	.05
84	Willie McGee	.20	.09
85	Jose Cruz	.20	.09
86	Brian Downing	.10	.05
87	Ozzie Guillen	.20	.09
88	Hubie Brooks	.10	.05
89	Cal Ripken	1.50	.70
90	Juan Nieves	.10	.05
91	Lance Parrish	.20	.09
92	Jim Rice	.20	.09
93	Ron Guidry	.20	.09
94	Fernando Valenzuela	.20	.09
95	Andy Allanson	.10	.05
96	Willie Wilson	.10	.05
97	Jose Canseco	.50	.23
98	Jeff Reardon	.20	.09
99	Bobby Witt	.20	.09
100	Checklist 28-133	.10	.05
101	Jose Guzman	.10	.05
102	Steve Balboni	.10	.05
103	Tony Phillips	.10	.05
104	Brook Jacoby	.10	.05
105	Dave Winfield	.40	.18
106	Orel Hershiser	.20	.09
107	Lou Whitaker	.20	.09
108	Fred Lynn	.20	.09
109	Bill Wegman	.10	.05
110	Donnie Moore	.10	.05
111	Jack Clark	.20	.09
112	Bob Knepper	.10	.05
113	Von Hayes	.20	.09
114	Bip Roberts	.40	.18
115	Tony Pena	.10	.05
116	Scott Garrelts	.10	.05
117	Paul Molitor	.40	.18
118	Darryl Strawberry	.20	.09
119	Shawon Dunston	.10	.05
120	Jim Presley	.10	.05
121	Jesse Barfield	.10	.05
122	Gary Gaetti	.10	*.05
123	Kurt Stillwell	.10	.05
124	Joel Davis	.10	.05
125	Mike Boddicker	.10	.05
126	Robin Yount	.40	.18
127	Alan Trammell	.10	.05
128	Dave Righetti	.10	.05
129	Dwight Evans	.20	.09
130	Mike Scioscia	.10	.05
131	Julio Franco	.10	.05
132	Bret Saberhagen	.10	.05
133	Mike Davis	.10	.05
134	Joe Hesketh	.10	.05
135	Wally Joyner	.40	.18
136	Don Slaught	.10	.05
137	Daryl Boston	.10	.05
138	Nolan Ryan	1.50	.70
139	Mike Schmidt	.50	.23
140	Tommy Herr	.10	.05
141	Garry Templeton	.10	.05
142	Kal Daniels	.10	.05
143	Billy Sample	.10	.05
144	Johnny Ray	.10	.05
145	Rob Thompson	.20	.09
146	Bob Dernier	.10	.05
147	Danny Tartabull	.10	.05
148	Ernie Whitt	.10	.05
149	Kirby Puckett	1.00	.45
150	Mike Young	.10	.05
151	Ernest Riles	.10	.05
152	Frank Tanana	.10	.05
153	Rich Gedman	.10	.05
154	Willie Randolph	.10	.05
155	Bill Madlock	.20	.09
156	Joe Carter	.40	.18
157	Danny Jackson	.10	.05
158	Carney Lansford	.20	.09
159	Bryn Smith	.10	.05
160	Gary Pettis	.10	.05
161	Oddibe McDowell	.10	.05
162	John Cangelosi	.10	.05
163	Mike Scott	.10	.05
164	Eric Show	.10	.05
165	Juan Samuel	.10	.05
166	Nick Esasky	.10	.05
167	Zane Smith	.10	.05
168	Mike C. Brown OF	.10	.05
169	Keith Moreland	.10	.05
170	John Tudor	.10	.05
171	Ken Dixon	.10	.05
172	Jim Gantner	.10	.05
173	Jack Morris	.20	.09
174	Bruce Hurst	.10	.05
175	Dennis Rasmussen	.10	.05
176	Mike Marshall	.10	.05
177	Dan Quisenberry	.10	.05
178	Eric Plunk	.10	.05
179	Tim Wallach	.10	.05
180	Steve Buechele	.10	.05
181	Don Sutton	.40	.18
182	Dave Schmidt	.10	.05
183	Terry Pendleton	.20	.09
184	Jim Deshaies	.10	.05
185	Steve Bedrosian	.10	.05
186	Pete Rose	.50	.23
187	Dave Dravecky	.20	.09
188	Rick Reuschel	.10	.05
189	Dan Gladden	.10	.05
190	Rick Mahler	.10	.05
191	Thad Bosley	.10	.05
192	Ron Darling	.10	.05
193	Matt Young	.10	.05
194	Tom Brunansky	.10	.05
195	Dave Stieb	.10	.05
196	Frank Viola	.10	.05
197	Tom Henke	.10	.05
198	Karl Best	.10	.05
199	Dwight Gooden	.10	.05
200	Checklist 134-239	.10	.05
201	Steve Trout	.10	.05
202	Rafael Ramirez	.10	.05
203	Bob Walk	.10	.05
204	Roger Mason	.10	.05
205	Terry Kennedy	.10	.05
206	Ron Oester	.10	.05
207	John Russell	.10	.05
208	Greg Mathews	.10	.05
209	Charlie Kerfeld	.10	.05
210	Reggie Jackson	.50	.23
211	Floyd Bannister	.10	.05
212	Vance Law	.10	.05
213	Rich Bordi	.10	.05
214	Dan Plesac	.10	.05
215	Dave Collins	.10	.05
216	Bob Stanley	.10	.05
217	Joe Niekro	.10	.05
218	Tom Niedenfuer	.10	.05
219	Brett Butler	.20	.09
220	Charlie Leibrandt	.10	.05
221	Steve Ontiveros	.10	.05
222	Tim Burke	.10	.05
223	Curtis Wilkerson	.10	.05
224	Pete Incaviglia	.20	.09
225	Lonnie Smith	.10	.05
226	Chris Codiroli	.10	.05
227	Scott Bailes	.10	.05
228	Rickey Henderson	.40	.18
229	Ken Howell	.10	.05
230	Darnell Coles	.10	.05
231	Don Aase	.10	.05
232	Tim Leary	.10	.05
233	Bob Boone	.20	.09
234	Ricky Horton	.10	.05
235	Mark Bailey	.10	.05
236	Kevin Gross	.10	.05
237	Lance McCullers	.10	.05
238	Cecilio Guante	.10	.05
239	Bob Melvin	.10	.05
240	Billy Joe Robidoux	.10	.05
241	Roger McDowell	.10	.05
242	Leon Durham	.10	.05
243	Ed Nunez	.10	.05
244	Jimmy Key	.10	.05
245	Mike Smithson	.10	.05
246	Bo Diaz	.10	.05
247	Carlton Fisk	.40	.18
248	Larry Sheets	.10	.05
249	Juan Castillo	.10	.05
250	Eric King	.10	.05
251	Doug Drabek	.40	.18
252	Wade Boggs	.40	.18
253	Mariano Duncan	.10	.05
254	Pat Tabler	.10	.05
255	Frank White	.20	.09
256	Alfredo Griffin	.10	.05
257	Floyd Youmans	.10	.05
258	Rob Wilfong	.10	.05
259	Pete O'Brien	.10	.05
260	Tim Hulett	.10	.05
261	Dickie Thon	.10	.05
262	Darren Daulton	.10	.05
263	Vince Coleman	.20	.09
264	Andy Hawkins	.10	.05
265	Eric Davis	.10	.05
266	Andres Thomas	.10	.05
267	Mike Diaz	.10	.05
268	Chili Davis	.10	.05
269	Jody Davis	.10	.05
270	Phil Bradley	.10	.05
271	George Bell	.10	.05
272	Keith Atherton	.10	.05
273	Storm Davis	.10	.05
274	Rob Deer	.10	.05
275	Walt Terrell	.10	.05
276	Roger Clemens	1.00	.45
277	Mike Easler	.10	.05
278	Steve Sax	.10	.05
279	Andre Thornton	.10	.05
280	Jim Sundberg	.10	.05
281	Bill Bathe	.10	.05
282	Jay Tibbs	.10	.05
283	Dick Schofield	.10	.05
284	Mike Mason	.10	.05
285	Jerry Hairston	.10	.05
286	Bill Doran	.10	.05
287	Tim Flannery	.10	.05
288	Gary Redus	.10	.05
289	John Franco	.20	.09
290	Paul Assenmacher	.10	.05
291	Joe Orsulak	.10	.05
292	Lee Smith	.20	.09
293	Mike Laga	.10	.05
294	Rick Dempsey	.20	.09
295	Mike Felder	.10	.05
296	Tom Brookens	.10	.05
297	Al Nipper	.10	.05
298	Mike Pagliarulo	.10	.05
299	Franklin Stubbs	.10	.05

☐ 300	Checklist 240-345	.10	.05
☐ 301	Steve Farr	.10	.05
☐ 302	Bill Mooneyham	.10	.05
☐ 303	Andres Galarraga	.50	.23
☐ 304	Scott Fletcher	.10	.05
☐ 305	Jack Howell	.10	.05
☐ 306	Russ Morman	.10	.05
☐ 307	Todd Worrell	.20	.09
☐ 308	Dave Smith	.10	.05
☐ 309	Jeff Stone	.10	.05
☐ 310	Ron Robinson	.10	.05
☐ 311	Bruce Bochy	.10	.05
☐ 312	Jim Winn	.10	.05
☐ 313	Mark Davis	.10	.05
☐ 314	Jeff Dedmon	.10	.05
☐ 315	Jamie Moyer	.10	.05
☐ 316	Wally Backman	.10	.05
☐ 317	Ken Phelps	.10	.05
☐ 318	Steve Lombardozzi	.10	.05
☐ 319	Rance Mulliniks	.10	.05
☐ 320	Tim Laudner	.10	.05
☐ 321	Mark Eichhorn	.10	.05
☐ 322	Lee Guetterman	.10	.05
☐ 323	Sid Fernandez	.10	.05
☐ 324	Jerry Mumphrey	.10	.05
☐ 325	David Palmer	.10	.05
☐ 326	Bill Almon	.10	.05
☐ 327	Candy Maldonado	.10	.05
☐ 328	John Kruk	.40	.18
☐ 329	John Denny	.10	.05
☐ 330	Milt Thompson	.10	.05
☐ 331	Mike LaValliere	.10	.05
☐ 332	Alan Ashby	.10	.05
☐ 333	Doug Corbett	.10	.05
☐ 334	Ron Karkovice	.20	.09
☐ 335	Mitch Webster	.10	.05
☐ 336	Lee Lacy	.10	.05
☐ 337	Glenn Braggs	.10	.05
☐ 338	Dwight Lowry	.10	.05
☐ 339	Don Baylor	.20	.09
☐ 340	Brian Fisher	.10	.05
☐ 341	Reggie Williams	.10	.05
☐ 342	Tom Candiotti	.10	.05
☐ 343	Rudy Law	.10	.05
☐ 344	Curt Young	.10	.05
☐ 345	Mike Fitzgerald	.10	.05
☐ 346	Ruben Sierra	.40	.18
☐ 347	Mitch Williams	.20	.09
☐ 348	Jorge Orta	.10	.05
☐ 349	Mickey Tettleton	.20	.09
☐ 350	Ernie Camacho	.10	.05
☐ 351	Ron Kittle	.10	.05
☐ 352	Ken Landreaux	.10	.05
☐ 353	Chet Lemon	.10	.05
☐ 354	John Shelby	.10	.05
☐ 355	Mark Clear	.10	.05
☐ 356	Doug DeCinces	.10	.05
☐ 357	Ken Dayley	.10	.05
☐ 358	Phil Garner	.10	.05
☐ 359	Steve Jeltz	.10	.05
☐ 360	Ed Whitson	.10	.05
☐ 361	Barry Bonds	4.00	1.80
☐ 362	Vida Blue	.20	.09
☐ 363	Cecil Cooper	.20	.09
☐ 364	Bob Ojeda	.10	.05
☐ 365	Dennis Eckersley	.40	.18
☐ 366	Mike Morgan	.10	.05
☐ 367	Willie Upshaw	.10	.05
☐ 368	Allan Anderson	.10	.05
☐ 369	Bill Gullickson	.10	.05
☐ 370	Bobby Thigpen	.20	.09
☐ 371	Juan Beniquez	.10	.05
☐ 372	Charlie Moore	.10	.05
☐ 373	Dan Petry	.10	.05
☐ 374	Rod Scurry	.10	.05
☐ 375	Tom Seaver	.40	.18
☐ 376	Ed VandeBerg	.10	.05
☐ 377	Tony Bernazard	.10	.05
☐ 378	Greg Pryor	.10	.05
☐ 379	Dwayne Murphy	.10	.05
☐ 380	Andy McGaffigan	.10	.05
☐ 381	Kirk McCaskill	.10	.05
☐ 382	Greg Harris	.10	.05
☐ 383	Rich Dotson	.10	.05
☐ 384	Craig Reynolds	.10	.05
☐ 385	Greg Gross	.10	.05
☐ 386	Tito Landrum	.10	.05
☐ 387	Craig Lefferts	.10	.05
☐ 388	Dave Parker	.20	.09
☐ 389	Bob Horner	.10	.05
☐ 390	Pat Clements	.10	.05
☐ 391	Jeff Leonard	.10	.05
☐ 392	Chris Speier	.10	.05
☐ 393	John Moses	.10	.05
☐ 394	Garth Iorg	.10	.05
☐ 395	Greg Gagne	.10	.05
☐ 396	Nate Snell	.10	.05
☐ 397	Bryan Clutterbuck	.10	.05
☐ 398	Darrell Evans	.20	.09
☐ 399	Steve Crawford	.10	.05
☐ 400	Checklist 346-451	.10	.05
☐ 401	Phil Lombardi	.10	.05
☐ 402	Rick Honeycutt	.10	.05
☐ 403	Ken Schrom	.10	.05
☐ 404	Bud Black	.10	.05
☐ 405	Donnie Hill	.10	.05
☐ 406	Wayne Krenchicki	.10	.05
☐ 407	Chuck Finley	.40	.18
☐ 408	Toby Harrah	.10	.05
☐ 409	Steve Lyons	.10	.05
☐ 410	Kevin Bass	.10	.05
☐ 411	Marvell Wynne	.10	.05
☐ 412	Ron Roenicke	.10	.05
☐ 413	Tracy Jones	.10	.05
☐ 414	Gene Garber	.10	.05
☐ 415	Mike Bielecki	.10	.05
☐ 416	Frank DiPino	.10	.05
☐ 417	Andy Van Slyke	.20	.09
☐ 418	Jim Dwyer	.10	.05
☐ 419	Ben Oglivie	.10	.05
☐ 420	Dave Bergman	.10	.05
☐ 421	Joe Sambito	.10	.05
☐ 422	Bob Tewksbury	.20	.09
☐ 423	Len Matuszek	.10	.05
☐ 424	Mike Kingery	.10	.05
☐ 425	Dave Kingman	.20	.09
☐ 426	Al Newman	.10	.05
☐ 427	Gary Ward	.10	.05
☐ 428	Ruppert Jones	.10	.05
☐ 429	Harold Baines	.20	.09
☐ 430	Pat Perry	.10	.05
☐ 431	Terry Puhl	.10	.05
☐ 432	Don Carman	.10	.05
☐ 433	Eddie Milner	.10	.05
☐ 434	LaMarr Hoyt	.10	.05
☐ 435	Rick Rhoden	.10	.05
☐ 436	Jose Uribe	.10	.05
☐ 437	Ken Oberkfell	.10	.05
☐ 438	Ron Davis	.10	.05
☐ 439	Jesse Orosco	.10	.05
☐ 440	Scott Bradley	.10	.05
☐ 441	Randy Bush	.10	.05
☐ 442	John Cerutti	.10	.05
☐ 443	Roy Smalley	.10	.05
☐ 444	Kelly Gruber	.10	.05
☐ 445	Bob Kearney	.10	.05
☐ 446	Ed Hearn	.10	.05
☐ 447	Scott Sanderson	.10	.05
☐ 448	Bruce Benedict	.10	.05
☐ 449	Junior Ortiz	.10	.05
☐ 450	Mike Aldrete	.20	.09
☐ 451	Kevin McReynolds	.10	.05
☐ 452	Rob Murphy	.10	.05
☐ 453	Kent Tekulve	.10	.05
☐ 454	Curt Ford	.10	.05
☐ 455	Dave Lopes	.20	.09
☐ 456	Bob Grich	.20	.09
☐ 457	Jose DeLeon	.10	.05
☐ 458	Andre Dawson	.40	.18
☐ 459	Mike Flanagan	.10	.05
☐ 460	Joey Meyer	.10	.05
☐ 461	Chuck Cary	.10	.05
☐ 462	Bill Buckner	.20	.09
☐ 463	Bob Shirley	.10	.05
☐ 464	Jeff Hamilton	.10	.05
☐ 465	Phil Niekro	.40	.18
☐ 466	Mark Gubicza	.10	.05
☐ 467	Jerry Willard	.10	.05
☐ 468	Bob Sebra	.10	.05
☐ 469	Larry Parrish	.10	.05
☐ 470	Charlie Hough	.10	.05
☐ 471	Hal McRae	.20	.09
☐ 472	Dave Leiper	.10	.05
☐ 473	Mel Hall	.10	.05
☐ 474	Dan Pasqua	.10	.05
☐ 475	Bob Welch	.10	.05
☐ 476	Johnny Grubb	.10	.05
☐ 477	Jim Traber	.10	.05
☐ 478	Chris Bosio	.20	.09
☐ 479	Mark McLemore	.10	.05
☐ 480	John Morris	.10	.05
☐ 481	Billy Hatcher	.10	.05
☐ 482	Dan Schatzeder	.10	.05
☐ 483	Rich Gossage	.20	.09
☐ 484	Jim Morrison	.10	.05
☐ 485	Bob Brenly	.10	.05
☐ 486	Bill Schroeder	.10	.05
☐ 487	Mookie Wilson	.20	.09
☐ 488	Dave Martinez	.10	.05
☐ 489	Harold Reynolds	.10	.05
☐ 490	Jeff Hearron	.10	.05
☐ 491	Mickey Hatcher	.10	.05
☐ 492	Barry Larkin	2.00	.90
☐ 493	Bob James	.10	.05
☐ 494	John Habyan	.10	.05
☐ 495	Jim Adduci	.10	.05
☐ 496	Mike Heath	.10	.05
☐ 497	Tim Stoddard	.10	.05
☐ 498	Tony Armas	.10	.05
☐ 499	Dennis Powell	.10	.05
☐ 500	Checklist 452-557	.10	.05
☐ 501	Chris Bando	.10	.05
☐ 502	David Cone	1.50	.70
☐ 503	Jay Howell	.10	.05
☐ 504	Tom Foley	.10	.05
☐ 505	Ray Chadwick	.10	.05
☐ 506	Mike Loynd	.10	.05
☐ 507	Neil Allen	.10	.05
☐ 508	Danny Darwin	.10	.05
☐ 509	Rick Schu	.10	.05
☐ 510	Jose Oquendo	.10	.05
☐ 511	Gene Walter	.10	.05
☐ 512	Terry McGriff	.10	.05
☐ 513	Ken Griffey	.20	.09
☐ 514	Benny Distefano	.10	.05
☐ 515	Terry Mulholland	.20	.09
☐ 516	Ed Lynch	.10	.05
☐ 517	Bill Swift	.10	.05
☐ 518	Manny Lee	.10	.05
☐ 519	Andre David	.10	.05
☐ 520	Scott McGregor	.10	.05
☐ 521	Rick Manning	.10	.05
☐ 522	Willie Hernandez	.10	.05
☐ 523	Marty Barrett	.10	.05
☐ 524	Wayne Tolleson	.10	.05
☐ 525	Jose Gonzalez	.10	.05
☐ 526	Cory Snyder	.20	.09
☐ 527	Buddy Biancalana	.10	.05
☐ 528	Moose Haas	.10	.05
☐ 529	Wilfredo Tejada	.10	.05
☐ 530	Stu Cliburn	.10	.05
☐ 531	Dale Mohorcic	.10	.05
☐ 532	Ron Hassey	.10	.05
☐ 533	Ty Gainey	.10	.05
☐ 534	Jerry Royster	.10	.05
☐ 535	Mike Maddux	.10	.05
☐ 536	Ted Power	.10	.05
☐ 537	Ted Simmons	.20	.09
☐ 538	Rafael Belliard	.10	.05
☐ 539	Chico Walker	.10	.05
☐ 540	Bob Forsch	.10	.05
☐ 541	John Stefero	.10	.05
☐ 542	Dale Sveum	.10	.05
☐ 543	Mark Thurmond	.10	.05
☐ 544	Jeff Sellers	.10	.05
☐ 545	Joel Skinner	.10	.05
☐ 546	Alex Trevino	.10	.05
☐ 547	Randy Kutcher	.10	.05
☐ 548	Joaquin Andujar	.10	.05
☐ 549	Casey Candaele	.10	.05
☐ 550	Jeff Russell	.10	.05
☐ 551	John Candelaria	.10	.05
☐ 552	Joe Cowley	.10	.05
☐ 553	Danny Cox	.10	.05
☐ 554	Denny Walling	.10	.05
☐ 555	Bruce Ruffin	.10	.05
☐ 556	Buddy Bell	.20	.09
☐ 557	Jimmy Jones	.10	.05

558 Bobby Bonilla	1.00	.45
559 Jeff D. Robinson	.10	.05
560 Ed Olwine	.10	.05
561 Glenallen Hill	.40	.18
562 Lee Mazzilli	.10	.05
563 Mike G. Brown P	.10	.05
564 George Frazier	.10	.05
565 Mike Sharperson	.10	.05
566 Mark Portugal	.20	.09
567 Rick Leach	.10	.05
568 Mark Langston	.10	.05
569 Rafael Santana	.10	.05
570 Manny Trillo	.10	.05
571 Cliff Speck	.10	.05
572 Bob Kipper	.10	.05
573 Kelly Downs	.10	.05
574 Randy Asadoor	.10	.05
575 Dave Magadan	.10	.05
576 Marvin Freeman	.10	.05
577 Jeff Lahti	.10	.05
578 Jeff Calhoun	.10	.05
579 Gus Polidor	.10	.05
580 Gene Nelson	.10	.05
581 Tim Teufel	.10	.05
582 Odell Jones	.10	.05
583 Mark Ryal	.10	.05
584 Randy O'Neal	.10	.05
585 Mike Greenwell	.40	.18
586 Ray Knight	.10	.05
587 Ralph Bryant	.10	.05
588 Carmen Castillo	.10	.05
589 Ed Wojna	.10	.05
590 Stan Javier	.10	.05
591 Jeff Musselman	.10	.05
592 Mike Stanley	.40	.18
593 Darrell Porter	.10	.05
594 Drew Hall	.10	.05
595 Rob Nelson	.10	.05
596 Bryan Oelkers	.10	.05
597 Scott Nielsen	.10	.05
598 Brian Holton	.10	.05
599 Kevin Mitchell	.10	.05
600 Checklist 558-660	.10	.05
601 Jackie Gutierrez	.10	.05
602 Barry Jones	.10	.05
603 Jerry Narron	.10	.05
604 Steve Lake	.10	.05
605 Jim Pankovits	.10	.05
606 Ed Romero	.10	.05
607 Dave LaPoint	.10	.05
608 Don Robinson	.10	.05
609 Mike Krukow	.10	.05
610 Dave Valle	.10	.05
611 Len Dykstra	.40	.18
612 Roberto Clemente PUZ	.50	.23
613 Mike Trujillo	.10	.05
614 Damaso Garcia	.10	.05
615 Neal Heaton	.10	.05
616 Juan Berenguer	.10	.05
617 Steve Carlton	.40	.18
618 Gary Lucas	.10	.05
619 Geno Petralli	.10	.05
620 Rick Aguilera	.20	.09
621 Fred McGriff	.50	.23
622 Dave Henderson	.10	.05
623 Dave Clark	.20	.09
624 Angel Salazar	.10	.05
625 Randy Hunt	.10	.05
626 John Gibbons	.10	.05
627 Kevin Brown	1.50	.70
628 Bill Dawley	.10	.05
629 Aurelio Lopez	.10	.05
630 Charles Hudson	.10	.05
631 Ray Soff	.10	.05
632 Ray Hayward	.10	.05
633 Spike Owen	.10	.05
634 Glenn Hubbard	.10	.05
635 Kevin Elster	.40	.18
636 Mike LaCoss	.10	.05
637 Dwayne Henry	.10	.05
638 Rey Quinones	.10	.05
639 Jim Clancy	.10	.05
640 Larry Andersen	.10	.05
641 Calvin Schiraldi	.10	.05
642 Stan Jefferson	.10	.05
643 Marc Sullivan	.10	.05
644 Mark Grant	.10	.05
645 Cliff Johnson	.10	.05
646 Howard Johnson	.10	.05
647 Dave Sax	.10	.05
648 Dave Stewart	.20	.09
649 Danny Heep	.10	.05
650 Joe Johnson	.10	.05
651 Bob Brower	.10	.05
652 Rob Woodward	.10	.05
653 John Mizerock	.10	.05
654 Tim Pyznarski	.10	.05
655 Luis Aquino	.10	.05
656 Mickey Brantley	.10	.05
657 Doyle Alexander	.10	.23
658 Sammy Stewart	.10	.05
659 Jim Acker	.10	.05
660 Pete Ladd	.10	.05

1987 Donruss Rookies

The 1987 Donruss "The Rookies" set features 56 full-color standard-size cards plus a 15-piece puzzle of Roberto Clemente. The set was distributed in factory set form packaged in a small green and black box through hobby dealers. Card fronts are similar in design to the 1987 Donruss regular issue except for the presence of "The Rookies" logo in the lower left corner and a green border instead of a black border. The key extended Rookie Cards in this set are Ellis Burks and Matt Williams. The second Donruss-issued cards of Greg Maddux and Rafael Palmeiro are also in this set.

	MINT	NRMT
COMP.FACT.SET (56)	20.00	9.00
COMMON CARD (1-56)	.10	.05
MINOR STARS	.25	.11
SEMISTARS	.50	.23
UNLISTED STARS	.75	.35
1 Mark McGwire	3.00	1.35
2 Eric Bell	.10	.05
3 Mark Williamson	.10	.05
4 Mike Greenwell	.75	.35
5 Ellis Burks	1.50	.70
6 DeWayne Buice	.10	.05
7 Mark McLemore	.10	.05
8 Devon White	.75	.35
9 Willie Fraser	.10	.05
10 Les Lancaster	.10	.05
11 Ken Williams	.10	.05
12 Matt Nokes	.25	.11
13 Jeff M. Robinson	.10	.05
14 Bo Jackson	1.00	.45
15 Kevin Seitzer	.75	.35
16 Billy Ripken	.10	.05
17 B.J. Surhoff	.10	.35
18 Chuck Crim	.10	.05
19 Mike Birkbeck	.10	.05
20 Chris Bosio	.25	.11
21 Les Straker	.10	.05
22 Mark Davidson	.10	.05
23 Gene Larkin	.10	.05
24 Ken Gerhart	.10	.05
25 Luis Polonia	.25	.11
26 Terry Steinbach	.75	.35
27 Mickey Brantley	.10	.05
28 Mike Stanley	.75	.35
29 Jerry Browne	.10	.05
30 Todd Benzinger	.10	.05
31 Fred McGriff	1.00	.45
32 Mike Henneman	.75	.35
33 Casey Candaele	.10	.05
34 Dave Magadan	.25	.11
35 David Cone	1.50	.70
36 Mike Jackson	.75	.35
37 John Mitchell	.10	.05
38 Mike Dunne	.10	.05
39 John Smiley	.25	.11
40 Joe Magrane	.10	.05
41 Jim Lindeman	.10	.05
42 Shane Mack	.25	.11
43 Stan Jefferson	.10	.05
44 Benito Santiago	.25	.11
45 Matt Williams	5.00	2.20
46 Dave Meads	.10	.05
47 Rafael Palmeiro	2.00	.90
48 Bill Long	.10	.05
49 Bob Brower	.10	.05
50 James Steels	.10	.05
51 Paul Noce	.10	.05
52 Greg Maddux	15.00	6.75
53 Jeff Musselman	.10	.05
54 Brian Holton	.10	.05
55 Chuck Jackson	.10	.05
56 Checklist 1-56	.10	.05

1988 Donruss

This set consists of 660 standard-size cards. For the seventh straight year, wax packs consisted of 15 cards plus a puzzle panel (featuring Stan Musial this time around). Cards were also distributed in rack packs and retail and hobby factory sets. Card fronts feature a distinctive black and blue border on the front. The card front border design pattern of the factory set card fronts is oriented differently from that of the regular wax pack cards. No premium or discount exists for either version. Subsets include Diamond Kings (1-27) and Rated Rookies (28-47). Cards marked as SP (short printed) from 648-660 are more difficult to find than the other 13 SP's in the lower 600s. These 26 cards listed as SP were apparently pulled from the printing sheet to make room for the 26 Bonus MVP cards. Numbered with the prefix "BC" for bonus card, this 26-card set featuring the most valuable player from each of the 26 teams was randomly inserted in the wax and rack packs. The cards are distinguished by the MVP logo in the upper left corner of the obverse, and cards BC14-BC26 are considered to be more difficult to find than cards BC1-BC13. Six of the checklist cards were done two different ways to reflect the inclusion or exclusion of the Bonus MVP cards. In the checklist below, the A variations (for the checklist cards) are from the wax packs and the B variations are from the factory-collated sets. The key Rookie Cards in this set are Roberto Alomar, Jay Bell, Jay Buhner, Ellis Burks, Ken Caminiti, Tom Glavine, Mark Grace, Gregg Jefferies and Matt Williams. There was also a Kirby Puckett card issued as the package back of Donruss blister packs; it uses a different photo from both of Kirby's regular and Bonus MVP cards and is unnumbered on the back.

	MINT	NRMT
COMPLETE SET (660)	8.00	3.60
COMMON CARD (1-660)	.05	.02
MINOR STARS	.10	.05
UNLISTED STARS	.20	.09
COMPLETE MVP SET (26)	3.00	1.35
MVP'S: RANDOM INSERTS IN PACKS		

☐ 1	Mark McGwire DK	.30	.14
☐ 2	Tim Raines DK	.07	.03
☐ 3	Benito Santiago DK	.05	.02
☐ 4	Alan Trammell DK	.10	.05
☐ 5	Danny Tartabull DK	.05	.02
☐ 6	Ron Darling DK	.05	.02
☐ 7	Paul Molitor DK	.20	.09
☐ 8	Devon White DK	.05	.02
☐ 9	Andre Dawson DK	.20	.09
☐ 10	Julio Franco DK	.05	.02
☐ 11	Scott Fletcher DK	.05	.02
☐ 12	Tony Fernandez DK	.05	.02
☐ 13	Shane Rawley DK	.05	.02
☐ 14	Kal Daniels DK	.05	.02
☐ 15	Jack Clark DK	.05	.02
☐ 16	Dwight Evans DK	.05	.02
☐ 17	Tommy John DK	.05	.02
☐ 18	Andy Van Slyke DK	.05	.02
☐ 19	Gary Gaetti DK	.05	.02
☐ 20	Mark Langston DK	.05	.02
☐ 21	Will Clark DK	.20	.09
☐ 22	Glenn Hubbard DK	.05	.02
☐ 23	Billy Hatcher DK	.05	.02
☐ 24	Bob Welch DK	.05	.02
☐ 25	Ivan Calderon DK	.05	.02
☐ 26	Cal Ripken DK	.40	.18
☐ 27	DK Checklist 1-26	.05	.02
☐ 28	Mackey Sasser RR	.05	.02
☐ 29	Jeff Treadway RR	.05	.02
☐ 30	Mike Campbell RR	.05	.02
☐ 31	Lance Johnson RR	.15	.07
☐ 32	Nelson Liriano RR	.05	.02
☐ 33	Shawn Abner RR	.05	.02
☐ 34	Roberto Alomar RR	1.00	.45
☐ 35	Shawn Hillegas RR	.05	.02
☐ 36	Joey Meyer RR	.05	.02
☐ 37	Kevin Elster RR	.10	.05
☐ 38	Jose Lind RR	.05	.02
☐ 39	Kirt Manwaring RR	.10	.05
☐ 40	Mark Grace RR	.60	.25
☐ 41	Jody Reed RR	.10	.05
☐ 42	John Farrell RR	.05	.02
☐ 43	Al Leiter RR	.20	.09
☐ 44	Gary Thurman RR	.05	.02
☐ 45	Vicente Palacios RR	.05	.02
☐ 46	Eddie Williams RR	.05	.02
☐ 47	Jack McDowell RR	.20	.09
☐ 48	Ken Dixon	.05	.02
☐ 49	Mike Birkbeck	.05	.02
☐ 50	Eric King	.05	.02
☐ 51	Roger Clemens	.40	.18
☐ 52	Pat Clements	.05	.02
☐ 53	Fernando Valenzuela	.10	.05
☐ 54	Mark Gubicza	.05	.02
☐ 55	Jay Howell	.05	.02
☐ 56	Floyd Youmans	.05	.02
☐ 57	Ed Correa	.05	.02
☐ 58	DeWayne Buice	.05	.02
☐ 59	Jose DeLeon	.05	.02
☐ 60	Danny Cox	.05	.02
☐ 61	Nolan Ryan	.75	.35
☐ 62	Steve Bedrosian	.05	.02
☐ 63	Tom Browning	.05	.02
☐ 64	Mark Davis	.05	.02
☐ 65	R.J. Reynolds	.05	.02
☐ 66	Kevin Mitchell	.10	.05
☐ 67	Ken Oberkfell	.05	.02
☐ 68	Rick Sutcliffe	.05	.02
☐ 69	Dwight Gooden	.10	.05
☐ 70	Scott Bankhead	.05	.02
☐ 71	Bert Blyleven	.10	.05
☐ 72	Jimmy Key	.10	.05
☐ 73	Les Straker	.05	.02
☐ 74	Jim Clancy	.05	.02
☐ 75	Mike Moore	.05	.02
☐ 76	Ron Darling	.05	.02
☐ 77	Ed Lynch	.05	.02
☐ 78	Dale Murphy	.20	.09
☐ 79	Doug Drabek	.05	.02
☐ 80	Scott Garrelts	.05	.02
☐ 81	Ed Whitson	.05	.02
☐ 82	Rob Murphy	.05	.02
☐ 83	Shane Rawley	.05	.02
☐ 84	Greg Mathews	.05	.02
☐ 85	Jim Deshaies	.05	.02
☐ 86	Mike Witt	.05	.02
☐ 87	Donnie Hill	.05	.02
☐ 88	Jeff Reed	.05	.02
☐ 89	Mike Boddicker	.05	.02
☐ 90	Ted Higuera	.05	.02
☐ 91	Walt Terrell	.05	.02
☐ 92	Bob Stanley	.05	.02
☐ 93	Dave Righetti	.05	.02
☐ 94	Orel Hershiser	.10	.05
☐ 95	Chris Bando	.05	.02
☐ 96	Bret Saberhagen	.05	.02
☐ 97	Curt Young	.05	.02
☐ 98	Tim Burke	.05	.02
☐ 99	Charlie Hough	.10	.05
☐ 100A	Checklist 28-137	.05	.02
☐ 100B	Checklist 28-133	.05	.02
☐ 101	Bobby Witt	.05	.02
☐ 102	George Brett	.40	.18
☐ 103	Mickey Tettleton	.10	.05
☐ 104	Scott Bailes	.05	.02
☐ 105	Mike Pagliarulo	.05	.02
☐ 106	Mike Scioscia	.05	.02
☐ 107	Tom Brookens	.05	.02
☐ 108	Ray Knight	.05	.02
☐ 109	Dan Plesac	.05	.02
☐ 110	Wally Joyner	.20	.09
☐ 111	Bob Forsch	.05	.02
☐ 112	Mike Scott	.05	.02
☐ 113	Kevin Gross	.05	.02
☐ 114	Benito Santiago	.05	.02
☐ 115	Bob Kipper	.05	.02
☐ 116	Mike Krukow	.05	.02
☐ 117	Chris Bosio	.05	.02
☐ 118	Sid Fernandez	.05	.02
☐ 119	Jody Davis	.05	.02
☐ 120	Mike Morgan	.05	.02
☐ 121	Mark Eichhorn	.05	.02
☐ 122	Jeff Reardon	.05	.02
☐ 123	John Franco	.10	.05
☐ 124	Richard Dotson	.05	.02
☐ 125	Eric Bell	.05	.02
☐ 126	Juan Nieves	.05	.02
☐ 127	Jack Morris	.15	.07
☐ 128	Rick Rhoden	.05	.02
☐ 129	Rich Gedman	.05	.02
☐ 130	Ken Howell	.05	.02
☐ 131	Brook Jacoby	.05	.02
☐ 132	Danny Jackson	.05	.02
☐ 133	Gene Nelson	.05	.02
☐ 134	Neal Heaton	.05	.02
☐ 135	Willie Fraser	.05	.02
☐ 136	Jose Guzman	.05	.02
☐ 137	Ozzie Guillen	.05	.02
☐ 138	Bob Knepper	.05	.02
☐ 139	Mike Jackson	.10	.05
☐ 140	Joe Magrane	.05	.02
☐ 141	Jimmy Jones	.05	.02
☐ 142	Ted Power	.05	.02
☐ 143	Ozzie Virgil	.05	.02
☐ 144	Felix Fermin	.05	.02
☐ 145	Kelly Downs	.05	.02
☐ 146	Shawon Dunston	.05	.02
☐ 147	Scott Bradley	.05	.02
☐ 148	Dave Stieb	.05	.02
☐ 149	Frank Viola	.05	.02
☐ 150	Terry Kennedy	.05	.02
☐ 151	Bill Wegman	.05	.02
☐ 152	Matt Nokes	.05	.02
☐ 153	Wade Boggs	.20	.09
☐ 154	Wayne Tolleson	.05	.02
☐ 155	Mariano Duncan	.05	.02
☐ 156	Julio Franco	.05	.02
☐ 157	Charlie Leibrandt	.05	.02
☐ 158	Terry Steinbach	.15	.07
☐ 159	Mike Fitzgerald	.05	.02
☐ 160	Jack Lazorko	.05	.02
☐ 161	Mitch Williams	.05	.02
☐ 162	Greg Walker	.05	.02
☐ 163	Alan Ashby	.05	.02
☐ 164	Tony Gwynn	.50	.23
☐ 165	Bruce Ruffin	.05	.02
☐ 166	Ron Robinson	.05	.02
☐ 167	Zane Smith	.05	.02
☐ 168	Junior Ortiz	.05	.02
☐ 169	Jamie Moyer	.05	.02
☐ 170	Tony Pena	.05	.02
☐ 171	Cal Ripken	.75	.35
☐ 172	B.J. Surhoff	.10	.05
☐ 173	Lou Whitaker	.10	.05
☐ 174	Ellis Burks	.30	.14
☐ 175	Ron Guidry	.05	.02
☐ 176	Steve Sax	.05	.02
☐ 177	Danny Tartabull	.05	.02
☐ 178	Carney Lansford	.10	.05
☐ 179	Casey Candaele	.05	.02
☐ 180	Scott Fletcher	.05	.02
☐ 181	Mark McLemore	.05	.02
☐ 182	Ivan Calderon	.05	.02
☐ 183	Jack Clark	.10	.05
☐ 184	Glenn Davis	.05	.02
☐ 185	Luis Aguayo	.05	.02
☐ 186	Bo Diaz	.05	.02
☐ 187	Stan Jefferson	.05	.02
☐ 188	Sid Bream	.05	.02
☐ 189	Bob Brenly	.05	.02
☐ 190	Dion James	.05	.02
☐ 191	Leon Durham	.05	.02
☐ 192	Jesse Orosco	.05	.02
☐ 193	Alvin Davis	.05	.02
☐ 194	Gary Gaetti	.05	.02
☐ 195	Fred McGriff	.20	.09
☐ 196	Steve Lombardozzi	.05	.02
☐ 197	Rance Mulliniks	.05	.02
☐ 198	Rey Quinones	.05	.02
☐ 199	Gary Carter	.15	.07
☐ 200A	Checklist 138-247	.05	.02
☐ 200B	Checklist 134-239	.05	.02
☐ 201	Keith Moreland	.05	.02
☐ 202	Ken Griffey	.05	.02
☐ 203	Tommy Gregg	.05	.02
☐ 204	Will Clark	.25	.11
☐ 205	John Kruk	.10	.05
☐ 206	Buddy Bell	.10	.05
☐ 207	Von Hayes	.05	.02
☐ 208	Tommy Herr	.05	.02
☐ 209	Craig Reynolds	.05	.02
☐ 210	Gary Pettis	.05	.02
☐ 211	Harold Baines	.15	.07
☐ 212	Vance Law	.05	.02
☐ 213	Ken Gerhart	.05	.02

□	No.	Player		
□	214	Jim Gantner	.05	.02
□	215	Chet Lemon	.05	.02
□	216	Dwight Evans	.10	.05
□	217	Don Mattingly	.30	.14
□	218	Franklin Stubbs	.05	.02
□	219	Pat Tabler	.05	.02
□	220	Bo Jackson	.20	.09
□	221	Tony Phillips	.05	.02
□	222	Tim Wallach	.05	.02
□	223	Ruben Sierra	.05	.02
□	224	Steve Buechele	.05	.02
□	225	Frank White	.10	.05
□	226	Alfredo Griffin	.05	.02
□	227	Greg Swindell	.05	.02
□	228	Willie Randolph	.10	.05
□	229	Mike Marshall	.05	.02
□	230	Alan Trammell	.15	.07
□	231	Eddie Murray	.20	.09
□	232	Dale Sveum	.05	.02
□	233	Dick Schofield	.05	.02
□	234	Jose Oquendo	.05	.02
□	235	Bill Doran	.05	.02
□	236	Milt Thompson	.05	.02
□	237	Marvell Wynne	.05	.02
□	238	Bobby Bonilla	.15	.07
□	239	Chris Speier	.05	.02
□	240	Glenn Braggs	.05	.02
□	241	Wally Backman	.05	.02
□	242	Ryne Sandberg	.25	.11
□	243	Phil Bradley	.05	.02
□	244	Kelly Gruber	.05	.02
□	245	Tom Brunansky	.05	.02
□	246	Ron Oester	.05	.02
□	247	Bobby Thigpen	.05	.02
□	248	Fred Lynn	.05	.02
□	249	Paul Molitor	.20	.09
□	250	Darrell Evans	.10	.05
□	251	Gary Ward	.05	.02
□	252	Bruce Hurst	.05	.02
□	253	Bob Welch	.05	.02
□	254	Joe Carter	.20	.09
□	255	Willie Wilson	.05	.02
□	256	Mark McGwire	.60	.25
□	257	Mitch Webster	.05	.02
□	258	Brian Downing	.05	.02
□	259	Mike Stanley	.10	.05
□	260	Carlton Fisk	.20	.09
□	261	Billy Hatcher	.05	.02
□	262	Glenn Wilson	.05	.02
□	263	Ozzie Smith	.25	.11
□	264	Randy Ready	.05	.02
□	265	Kurt Stillwell	.05	.02
□	266	David Palmer	.05	.02
□	267	Mike Diaz	.05	.02
□	268	Robby Thompson	.05	.02
□	269	Andre Dawson	.20	.09
□	270	Lee Guetterman	.05	.02
□	271	Willie Upshaw	.05	.02
□	272	Randy Bush	.05	.02
□	273	Larry Sheets	.05	.02
□	274	Rob Deer	.05	.02
□	275	Kirk Gibson	.10	.05
□	276	Marty Barrett	.05	.02
□	277	Rickey Henderson	.20	.09
□	278	Pedro Guerrero	.10	.05
□	279	Brett Butler	.10	.05
□	280	Kevin Seitzer	.10	.05
□	281	Mike Davis	.05	.02
□	282	Andres Galarraga	.20	.09
□	283	Devon White	.10	.05
□	284	Pete O'Brien	.05	.02
□	285	Jerry Hairston	.05	.02
□	286	Kevin Bass	.05	.02
□	287	Carmelo Martinez	.05	.02
□	288	Juan Samuel	.05	.02
□	289	Kal Daniels	.05	.02
□	290	Albert Hall	.05	.02
□	291	Andy Van Slyke	.10	.05
□	292	Lee Smith	.10	.05
□	293	Vince Coleman	.05	.02
□	294	Tom Niedenfuer	.05	.02
□	295	Robin Yount	.20	.09
□	296	Jeff M. Robinson	.05	.02
□	297	Todd Benzinger	.05	.02
□	298	Dave Winfield	.20	.09
□	299	Mickey Hatcher	.05	.02
□	300A	Checklist 248-357	.05	.02
□	300B	Checklist 240-345	.05	.02
□	301	Bud Black	.05	.02
□	302	Jose Canseco	.20	.09
□	303	Tom Foley	.05	.02
□	304	Pete Incaviglia	.05	.02
□	305	Bob Boone	.10	.05
□	306	Bill Long	.05	.02
□	307	Willie McGee	.05	.02
□	308	Ken Caminiti	.75	.35
□	309	Darren Daulton	.10	.05
□	310	Tracy Jones	.05	.02
□	311	Greg Booker	.05	.02
□	312	Mike LaValliere	.05	.02
□	313	Chili Davis	.15	.07
□	314	Glenn Hubbard	.05	.02
□	315	Paul Noce	.05	.02
□	316	Keith Hernandez	.05	.02
□	317	Mark Langston	.05	.02
□	318	Keith Atherton	.05	.02
□	319	Tony Fernandez	.05	.02
□	320	Kent Hrbek	.10	.05
□	321	John Cerutti	.05	.02
□	322	Mike Kingery	.05	.02
□	323	Dave Magadan	.05	.02
□	324	Rafael Palmeiro	.20	.09
□	325	Jeff Dedmon	.05	.02
□	326	Barry Bonds	.50	.23
□	327	Jeffrey Leonard	.05	.02
□	328	Tim Flannery	.05	.02
□	329	Dave Concepcion	.05	.02
□	330	Mike Schmidt	.25	.11
□	331	Bill Dawley	.05	.02
□	332	Larry Andersen	.05	.02
□	333	Jack Howell	.05	.02
□	334	Ken Williams	.05	.02
□	335	Bryn Smith	.05	.02
□	336	Billy Ripken	.10	.05
□	337	Greg Brock	.05	.02
□	338	Mike Heath	.05	.02
□	339	Mike Greenwell	.05	.02
□	340	Claudell Washington	.05	.02
□	341	Jose Gonzalez	.05	.02
□	342	Mel Hall	.05	.02
□	343	Jim Eisenreich	.20	.09
□	344	Tony Bernazard	.05	.02
□	345	Tim Raines	.10	.05
□	346	Bob Brower	.05	.02
□	347	Larry Parrish	.05	.02
□	348	Thad Bosley	.05	.02
□	349	Dennis Eckersley	.10	.05
□	350	Cory Snyder	.05	.02
□	351	Rick Cerone	.05	.02
□	352	John Shelby	.05	.02
□	353	Larry Herndon	.05	.02
□	354	John Habyan	.05	.02
□	355	Chuck Crim	.05	.02
□	356	Gus Polidor	.05	.02
□	357	Ken Dayley	.05	.02
□	358	Danny Darwin	.05	.02
□	359	Lance Parrish	.05	.02
□	360	James Steels	.05	.02
□	361	Al Pedrique	.05	.02
□	362	Mike Aldrete	.05	.02
□	363	Juan Castillo	.05	.02
□	364	Len Dykstra	.10	.05
□	365	Luis Quinones	.05	.02
□	366	Jim Presley	.05	.02
□	367	Lloyd Moseby	.05	.02
□	368	Kirby Puckett	.40	.18
□	369	Eric Davis	.10	.05
□	370	Gary Redus	.05	.02
□	371	Dave Schmidt	.05	.02
□	372	Mark Clear	.05	.02
□	373	Dave Bergman	.05	.02
□	374	Charles Hudson	.05	.02
□	375	Calvin Schiraldi	.05	.02
□	376	Alex Trevino	.05	.02
□	377	Tom Candiotti	.05	.02
□	378	Steve Farr	.05	.02
□	379	Mike Gallego	.05	.02
□	380	Andy McGaffigan	.05	.02
□	381	Kirk McCaskill	.05	.02
□	382	Oddibe McDowell	.05	.02
□	383	Floyd Bannister	.05	.02
□	384	Denny Walling	.05	.02
□	385	Don Carman	.05	.02
□	386	Todd Worrell	.10	.05
□	387	Eric Show	.05	.02
□	388	Dave Parker	.10	.05
□	389	Rick Mahler	.05	.02
□	390	Mike Dunne	.05	.02
□	391	Candy Maldonado	.05	.02
□	392	Bob Dernier	.05	.02
□	393	Dave Valle	.05	.02
□	394	Ernie Whitt	.05	.02
□	395	Juan Berenguer	.05	.02
□	396	Mike Young	.05	.02
□	397	Mike Felder	.05	.02
□	398	Willie Hernandez	.05	.02
□	399	Jim Rice	.10	.05
□	400A	Checklist 358-467	.05	.02
□	400B	Checklist 346-451	.05	.02
□	401	Tommy John	.05	.02
□	402	Brian Holton	.05	.02
□	403	Carmen Castillo	.05	.02
□	404	Jamie Quirk	.05	.02
□	405	Dwayne Murphy	.05	.02
□	406	Jeff Parrett	.05	.02
□	407	Don Sutton	.20	.09
□	408	Jerry Browne	.05	.02
□	409	Jim Winn	.05	.02
□	410	Dave Smith	.05	.02
□	411	Shane Mack	.05	.02
□	412	Greg Gross	.05	.02
□	413	Nick Esasky	.05	.02
□	414	Damaso Garcia	.05	.02
□	415	Brian Fisher	.05	.02
□	416	Brian Dayett	.05	.02
□	417	Curt Ford	.05	.02
□	418	Mark Williamson	.05	.02
□	419	Bill Schroeder	.05	.02
□	420	Mike Henneman	.10	.05
□	421	John Marzano	.05	.02
□	422	Ron Kittle	.05	.02
□	423	Matt Young	.05	.02
□	424	Steve Balboni	.05	.02
□	425	Luis Polonia	.10	.05
□	426	Randy St.Claire	.05	.02
□	427	Greg Harris	.05	.02
□	428	Johnny Ray	.05	.02
□	429	Ray Searage	.05	.02
□	430	Ricky Horton	.05	.02
□	431	Gerald Young	.05	.02
□	432	Rick Schu	.05	.02
□	433	Paul O'Neill	.15	.07
□	434	Rich Gossage	.10	.05
□	435	John Cangelosi	.05	.02
□	436	Mike LaCoss	.05	.02
□	437	Gerald Perry	.05	.02
□	438	Dave Martinez	.05	.02
□	439	Darryl Strawberry	.10	.05
□	440	John Moses	.05	.02
□	441	Greg Gagne	.05	.02
□	442	Jesse Barfield	.05	.02
□	443	George Frazier	.05	.02
□	444	Garth Iorg	.05	.02
□	445	Ed Nunez	.05	.02
□	446	Rick Aguilera	.05	.02
□	447	Jerry Mumphrey	.05	.02
□	448	Rafael Ramirez	.05	.02
□	449	John Smiley	.05	.02
□	450	Atlee Hammaker	.05	.02
□	451	Lance McCullers	.05	.02
□	452	Guy Hoffman	.05	.02
□	453	Chris James	.05	.02
□	454	Terry Pendleton	.05	.02
□	455	Dave Meads	.05	.02
□	456	Bill Buckner	.05	.02
□	457	John Pawlowski	.05	.02
□	458	Bob Sebra	.05	.02
□	459	Jim Dwyer	.05	.02
□	460	Jay Aldrich	.05	.02
□	461	Frank Tanana	.05	.02
□	462	Oil Can Boyd	.05	.02
□	463	Dan Pasqua	.05	.02
□	464	Tim Crews	.05	.02
□	465	Andy Allanson	.05	.02
□	466	Bill Pecota	.05	.02
□	467	Steve Ontiveros	.05	.02
□	468	Hubie Brooks	.05	.02
□	469	Paul Kilgus	.05	.02

☐ 470 Dale Mohorcic	.05	.02
☐ 471 Dan Quisenberry	.05	.02
☐ 472 Dave Stewart	.10	.05
☐ 473 Dave Clark	.05	.02
☐ 474 Joel Skinner	.05	.02
☐ 475 Dave Anderson	.05	.02
☐ 476 Dan Petry	.05	.02
☐ 477 Carl Nichols	.05	.02
☐ 478 Ernest Riles	.05	.02
☐ 479 George Hendrick	.05	.02
☐ 480 John Morris	.05	.02
☐ 481 Manny Hernandez	.05	.02
☐ 482 Jeff Stone	.05	.02
☐ 483 Chris Brown	.05	.02
☐ 484 Mike Bielecki	.05	.02
☐ 485 Dave Dravecky	.10	.05
☐ 486 Rick Manning	.05	.02
☐ 487 Bill Almon	.05	.02
☐ 488 Jim Sundberg	.05	.02
☐ 489 Ken Phelps	.05	.02
☐ 490 Tom Henke	.05	.02
☐ 491 Dan Gladden	.05	.02
☐ 492 Barry Larkin	.20	.09
☐ 493 Fred Manrique	.05	.02
☐ 494 Mike Griffin	.05	.02
☐ 495 Mark Knudson	.05	.02
☐ 496 Bill Madlock	.10	.05
☐ 497 Tim Stoddard	.05	.02
☐ 498 Sam Horn	.05	.02
☐ 499 Tracy Woodson	.05	.02
☐ 500A Checklist 468-577	.05	.02
☐ 500B Checklist 452-557	.05	.02
☐ 501 Ken Schrom	.05	.02
☐ 502 Angel Salazar	.05	.02
☐ 503 Eric Plunk	.05	.02
☐ 504 Joe Hesketh	.05	.02
☐ 505 Greg Minton	.05	.02
☐ 506 Geno Petralli	.05	.02
☐ 507 Bob James	.05	.02
☐ 508 Robbie Wine	.05	.02
☐ 509 Jeff Calhoun	.05	.02
☐ 510 Steve Lake	.05	.02
☐ 511 Mark Grant	.05	.02
☐ 512 Frank Williams	.05	.02
☐ 513 Jeff Blauser	.25	.11
☐ 514 Bob Walk	.05	.02
☐ 515 Craig Lefferts	.05	.02
☐ 516 Manny Trillo	.05	.02
☐ 517 Jerry Reed	.05	.02
☐ 518 Rick Leach	.05	.02
☐ 519 Mark Davidson	.05	.02
☐ 520 Jeff Ballard	.05	.02
☐ 521 Dave Stapleton	.05	.02
☐ 522 Pat Sheridan	.05	.02
☐ 523 Al Nipper	.05	.02
☐ 524 Steve Trout	.05	.02
☐ 525 Jeff Hamilton	.05	.02
☐ 526 Tommy Hinzo	.05	.02
☐ 527 Lonnie Smith	.05	.02
☐ 528 Greg Cadaret	.05	.02
☐ 529 Bob McClure UER	.05	.02
(Rob on front)		
☐ 530 Chuck Finley	.10	.05
☐ 531 Jeff Russell	.05	.02
☐ 532 Steve Lyons	.05	.02
☐ 533 Terry Puhl	.05	.02
☐ 534 Eric Nolte	.05	.02
☐ 535 Kent Tekulve	.05	.02
☐ 536 Pat Pacillo	.05	.02
☐ 537 Charlie Puleo	.05	.02
☐ 538 Tom Prince	.05	.02
☐ 539 Greg Maddux	1.25	.55
☐ 540 Jim Lindeman	.05	.02
☐ 541 Pete Stanicek	.05	.02
☐ 542 Steve Kiefer	.05	.02
☐ 543A Jim Morrison ERR	.20	.09
(No decimal before lifetime average)		
☐ 543B Jim Morrison COR	.05	.02
☐ 544 Spike Owen	.05	.02
☐ 545 Jay Buhner	.60	.25
☐ 546 Mike Devereaux	.15	.07
☐ 547 Jerry Don Gleaton	.05	.02
☐ 548 Jose Rijo	.05	.02
☐ 549 Dennis Martinez	.10	.05
☐ 550 Mike Loynd	.05	.02

☐ 551 Darrell Miller	.05	.02
☐ 552 Dave LaPoint	.05	.02
☐ 553 John Tudor	.05	.02
☐ 554 Rocky Childress	.05	.02
☐ 555 Wally Ritchie	.05	.02
☐ 556 Terry McGriff	.05	.02
☐ 557 Dave Leiper	.05	.02
☐ 558 Jeff D. Robinson	.05	.02
☐ 559 Jose Uribe	.05	.02
☐ 560 Ted Simmons	.10	.05
☐ 561 Les Lancaster	.05	.02
☐ 562 Keith A. Miller	.05	.02
☐ 563 Harold Reynolds	.05	.02
☐ 564 Gene Larkin	.05	.02
☐ 565 Cecil Fielder	.15	.07
☐ 566 Roy Smalley	.05	.02
☐ 567 Duane Ward	.05	.02
☐ 568 Bill Wilkinson	.05	.02
☐ 569 Howard Johnson	.05	.02
☐ 570 Frank DiPino	.05	.02
☐ 571 Pete Smith	.05	.02
☐ 572 Darnell Coles	.05	.02
☐ 573 Don Robinson	.05	.02
☐ 574 Rob Nelson UER	.05	.02
(Career 0 RBI, but 1 RBI in '87)		
☐ 575 Dennis Rasmussen	.05	.02
☐ 576 Steve Jeltz UER	.05	.02
(Photo actually Juan Samuel; Samuel noted for one batting glove and black bat)		
☐ 577 Tom Pagnozzi	.10	.05
☐ 578 Ty Gainey	.05	.02
☐ 579 Gary Lucas	.05	.02
☐ 580 Ron Hassey	.05	.02
☐ 581 Herm Winningham	.05	.02
☐ 582 Rene Gonzales	.05	.02
☐ 583 Brad Komminsk	.05	.02
☐ 584 Doyle Alexander	.05	.02
☐ 585 Jeff Sellers	.05	.02
☐ 586 Bill Gullickson	.05	.02
☐ 587 Tim Belcher	.10	.05
☐ 588 Doug Jones	.20	.09
☐ 589 Melido Perez	.10	.05
☐ 590 Rick Honeycutt	.05	.02
☐ 591 Pascual Perez	.05	.02
☐ 592 Curt Wilkerson	.05	.02
☐ 593 Steve Howe	.05	.02
☐ 594 John Davis	.05	.02
☐ 595 Storm Davis	.05	.02
☐ 596 Sammy Stewart	.05	.02
☐ 597 Neil Allen	.05	.02
☐ 598 Alejandro Pena	.05	.02
☐ 599 Mark Thurmond	.05	.02
☐ 600A Checklist 578-660/BC1-BC26	.05	.02
☐ 600B Checklist 558-660	.05	.02
☐ 601 Jose Mesa	.20	.09
☐ 602 Don August	.05	.02
☐ 603 Terry Leach SP	.07	.03
☐ 604 Tom Newell		.03
☐ 605 Randall Byers SP	.07	.03
☐ 606 Jim Gott	.05	.02
☐ 607 Harry Spilman	.05	.02
☐ 608 John Candelaria	.05	.02
☐ 609 Mike Brumley	.05	.02
☐ 610 Mickey Brantley	.05	.02
☐ 611 Jose Nunez SP	.07	.03
☐ 612 Tom Nieto	.05	.02
☐ 613 Rick Reuschel	.05	.02
☐ 614 Lee Mazzilli SP	.07	.03
☐ 615 Scott Lusader	.05	.02
☐ 616 Bobby Meacham	.05	.02
☐ 617 Ken McReynolds SP	.07	.03
☐ 618 Gene Garber	.05	.02
☐ 619 Barry Lyons SP	.07	.03
☐ 620 Randy Myers	.15	.07
☐ 621 Donnie Moore	.05	.02
☐ 622 Domingo Ramos	.05	.02
☐ 623 Ed Romero	.05	.02
☐ 624 Greg Myers	.05	.02
☐ 625 Ripken Family	.40	.18
Cal Ripken Sr.		
Cal Ripken Jr.		
Billy Ripken		

☐ 626 Pat Perry	.05	.02
☐ 627 Andres Thomas SP	.07	.03
☐ 628 Matt Williams SP	.75	.35
☐ 629 Dave Hengel	.05	.02
☐ 630 Jeff Musselman SP	.07	.03
☐ 631 Tim Laudner	.05	.02
☐ 632 Bob Ojeda SP	.07	.03
☐ 633 Rafael Santana	.05	.02
☐ 634 Wes Gardner	.05	.02
☐ 635 Roberto Kelly SP	.20	.09
☐ 636 Mike Flanagan SP	.07	.03
☐ 637 Jay Bell	.25	.11
☐ 638 Bob Melvin	.05	.02
☐ 639 Damon Berryhill UER	.05	.02
(Bats: Switchl)		
☐ 640 David Wells SP	.07	.03
☐ 641 Stan Musial PUZ	.20	.09
☐ 642 Doug Sisk	.05	.02
☐ 643 Keith Hughes	.05	.02
☐ 644 Tom Glavine	.50	.23
☐ 645 Al Newman	.05	.02
☐ 646 Scott Sanderson	.05	.02
☐ 647 Scott Terry	.05	.02
☐ 648 Tim Teufel SP	.07	.03
☐ 649 Garry Templeton SP	.07	.03
☐ 650 Manny Lee SP	.07	.03
☐ 651 Roger McDowell SP	.07	.03
☐ 652 Mookie Wilson SP	.20	.09
☐ 653 David Cone SP	.20	.09
☐ 654 Ron Gant SP	.15	.07
☐ 655 Joe Price SP	.07	.03
☐ 656 George Bell SP	.10	.05
☐ 657 Gregg Jefferies SP	.25	.11
☐ 658 Todd Stottlemyre SP	.20	.09
☐ 659 Geronimo Berroa SP	.25	.11
☐ 660 Jerry Royster SP	.07	.03

1988 Donruss Rookies

The 1988 Donruss "The Rookies" set features 56 standard-size full-color cards plus a 15-piece puzzle of Stan Musial. This set was distributed exclusively in factory set form in a small, cellophane-wrapped, green and black through hobby dealers. Card fronts are similar in design to the 1988 Donruss regular issue except for the presence of "The Rookies" logo in the lower right corner and a green and black border instead of a blue and black border on the fronts. Extended Rookie Cards in this set include Brady Anderson, Edgar Martinez, and Walt Weiss. Notable second cards were issued of Roberto Alomar and Jay Buhner.

	MINT	NRMT
COMP.FACT.SET (56)	12.00	5.50
COMMON CARD (1-56)	.15	.07

	MINT	NRMT
MINOR STARS	.30	.14
UNLISTED STARS	.60	.25
□ 1 Mark Grace	2.00	.90
□ 2 Mike Campbell	.15	.07
□ 3 Todd Frohwirth	.15	.07
□ 4 Dave Stapleton	.15	.07
□ 5 Shawn Abner	.15	.07
□ 6 Jose Cecena	.15	.07
□ 7 Dave Gallagher	.15	.07
□ 8 Mark Parent	.15	.07
□ 9 Cecil Espy	.15	.07
□ 10 Pete Smith	.15	.07
□ 11 Jay Buhner	2.50	1.10
□ 12 Pat Borders	.30	.14
□ 13 Doug Jennings	.15	.07
□ 14 Brady Anderson	2.50	1.10
□ 15 Pete Stanicek	.15	.07
□ 16 Roberto Kelly	.60	.25
□ 17 Jeff Treadway	.15	.07
□ 18 Walt Weiss	.15	.07
□ 19 Paul Gibson	.15	.07
□ 20 Tim Crews	.15	.07
□ 21 Melido Perez	.15	.07
□ 22 Steve Peters	.15	.07
□ 23 Craig Worthington	.15	.07
□ 24 John Trautwein	.15	.07
□ 25 DeWayne Vaughn	.15	.07
□ 26 David Wells	.30	.14
□ 27 Al Leiter	.60	.25
□ 28 Tim Belcher	.30	.14
□ 29 Johnny Paredes	.15	.07
□ 30 Chris Sabo	.30	.14
□ 31 Damon Berryhill	.15	.07
□ 32 Randy Milligan	.15	.07
□ 33 Gary Thurman	.15	.07
□ 34 Kevin Elster	.15	.07
□ 35 Roberto Alomar	5.00	2.20
□ 36 Edgar Martinez UER	2.50	1.10
(Photo actually name Nunez)		
□ 37 Todd Stottlemyre	.60	.25
□ 38 Joey Meyer	.15	.07
□ 39 Carl Nichols	.15	.07
□ 40 Jack McDowell	.65	.25
□ 41 Jose Bautista	.15	.07
□ 42 Sil Campusano	.15	.07
□ 43 John Dopson	.15	.07
□ 44 Jody Reed	.30	.14
□ 45 Darrin Jackson	.15	.07
□ 46 Mike Capel	.15	.07
□ 47 Ron Gant	.60	.25
□ 48 John Davis	.15	.07
□ 49 Kevin Coffman	.15	.07
□ 50 Cris Carpenter	.15	.07
□ 51 Mackey Sasser	.15	.07
□ 52 Luis Alicea	.30	.14
□ 53 Bryan Harvey	.30	.14
□ 54 Steve Ellsworth	.15	.07
□ 55 Mike Macfarlane	.30	.14
□ 56 Checklist 1-56	.15	.07

1989 Donruss

This set consists of 660 standard-size cards. The cards were primarily issued 15-card wax packs, rack packs and hobby and retail factory sets. Each wax pack also contained a puzzle panel (featuring Warren Spahn this year). The cards feature a distinctive black side border with an alternating coating. Subsets include Diamond Kings (1-27) and Rated Rookies (28-47). There are two variations that occur throughout most of the set. On the card backs "Denotes Led League" can be found with one asterisk to the left or with an asterisk on each side. On the card fronts the horizontal lines on the left and right borders can be glossy or non-glossy. Since both of these variation types and seem equally common, there is no premium value for either type. Rather than short-printing 26 cards in order to make room for printing the Bonus MVP's this year, Donruss apparently chose to double print 106 cards. These double prints are listed below by DP. Numbered with the prefix "BC" for bonus card, the 26-card set featuring the most valuable player from each of the 26 teams was randomly inserted in the wax and rack packs. These cards are distinguished by the bold MVP logo in the upper background of the obverse. Rookie Cards in this set are Sandy Alomar Jr., Brady Anderson, Dante Bichette, Craig Biggio, Ken Griffey Jr., Ken Hill, Randy Johnson, Ramon Martinez, Hal Morris, Gary Sheffield, and John Smoltz.

	MINT	NRMT
COMPLETE SET (660)	10.00	4.50
COMP.FACT.SET (672)	12.00	5.50
COMMON CARD (1-660)	.05	.02
MINOR STARS		.25
UNLISTED STARS	.20	.09
COMP.GRANDSLAMMERS (12)	2.00	.90
ONE G'SLAMMERS SET PER FACT.SET		
COMP.MVP SET (26)	1.50	.70
MVP'S: RANDOM INSERTS IN PACKS		
□ 1 Mike Greenwell DK	.05	.02
□ 2 Bobby Bonilla DK DP	.10	.05
□ 3 Pete Incaviglia DK	.05	.02
□ 4 Chris Sabo DK DP	.05	.02
□ 5 Robin Yount DK	.10	.05
□ 6 Tony Gwynn DK DP	.20	.09
□ 7 Carlton Fisk DK UER	.10	.05
(OF on back)		
□ 8 Cory Snyder DK	.05	.02
□ 9 David Cone DK UER	.10	.05
("hurdiers")		
□ 10 Kevin Seitzer DK	.05	.02
□ 11 Rick Reuschel DK	.05	.02
□ 12 Johnny Ray DK	.05	.02
□ 13 Dave Schmidt DK	.05	.02
□ 14 Andres Galarraga DK	.10	.05
□ 15 Kirk Gibson DK	.05	.02
□ 16 Fred McGriff DK	.10	.05
□ 17 Mark Grace DK	.10	.05
□ 18 Jeff M. Robinson DK	.05	.02
□ 19 Vince Coleman DK DP	.05	.02
□ 20 Dave Henderson DK	.05	.02
□ 21 Harold Reynolds DK	.05	.02
□ 22 Gerald Perry DK	.05	.02
□ 23 Frank Viola DK	.05	.02
□ 24 Steve Bedrosian DK	.05	.02
□ 25 Glenn Davis DK	.05	.02
□ 26 Don Mattingly DK UER	.10	.05
(Doesn't mention Don's previous DK in 1985)		
□ 27 DK Checklist 1-26 DP	.05	.02
□ 28 Sandy Alomar Jr. RR	.50	.23
□ 29 Steve Searcy RR	.05	.02
□ 30 Cameron Drew RR	.05	.02
□ 31 Gary Sheffield RR	.75	.35
□ 32 Erik Hanson RR	.10	.05
□ 33 Ken Griffey Jr. RR	6.00	2.70
□ 34 Greg W. Harris RR	.05	.02
□ 35 Gregg Jefferies RR	.10	.05
□ 36 Luis Medina RR	.05	.02
□ 37 Carlos Quintana RR	.05	.02
□ 38 Felix Jose RR	.05	.02
□ 39 Cris Carpenter RR	.05	.02
□ 40 Ron Jones RR	.05	.02
□ 41 Dave West RR	.05	.02
□ 42 Randy Johnson RR UER	1.00	.45
Card says born in 1964 he was born in 1963		
□ 43 Mike Harkey RR	.05	.02
□ 44 Pete Harnisch RR	.10	.05
□ 45 Tom Gordon RR DP	.20	.09
□ 46 Gregg Olson RR DP	.10	.05
□ 47 Alex Sanchez RR DP	.05	.02
□ 48 Ruben Sierra RR	.20	.09
□ 49 Rafael Palmeiro RR	.20	.09
□ 50 Ron Gant	.10	.05
□ 51 Cal Ripken	.75	.35
□ 52 Wally Joyner	.10	.05
□ 53 Gary Carter	.20	.09
□ 54 Andy Van Slyke	.10	.05
□ 55 Robin Yount	.20	.09
□ 56 Pete Incaviglia	.10	.05
□ 57 Greg Brock	.05	.02
□ 58 Melido Perez	.05	.02
□ 59 Craig Lefferts	.05	.02
□ 60 Gary Pettis	.05	.02
□ 61 Danny Tartabull	.05	.02
□ 62 Guillermo Hernandez	.05	.02
□ 63 Ozzie Smith	.25	.11
□ 64 Gary Gaetti	.05	.02
□ 65 Mark Davis	.05	.02
□ 66 Lee Smith	.10	.05
□ 67 Dennis Eckersley	.20	.09
□ 68 Wade Boggs	.20	.09
□ 69 Mike Scott	.05	.02
□ 70 Fred McGriff	.20	.09
□ 71 Tom Browning	.05	.02
□ 72 Claudell Washington	.05	.02
□ 73 Mel Hall	.05	.02
□ 74 Don Mattingly	.30	.14
□ 75 Steve Bedrosian	.05	.02
□ 76 Juan Samuel	.05	.02
□ 77 Mike Scioscia	.05	.02
□ 78 Dave Righetti	.05	.02
□ 79 Alfredo Griffin	.05	.02
□ 80 Eric Davis UER	.10	.05
(165 games in 1988, should be 135)		
□ 81 Juan Berenguer	.05	.02
□ 82 Todd Worrell	.05	.02
□ 83 Joe Carter	.20	.09
□ 84 Steve Sax	.05	.02
□ 85 Frank White	.05	.02
□ 86 John Kruk	.10	.05
□ 87 Rance Mulliniks	.05	.02
□ 88 Alan Ashby	.05	.02
□ 89 Charlie Leibrandt	.05	.02
□ 90 Frank Tanana	.05	.02
□ 91 Jose Canseco	.20	.09
□ 92 Barry Bonds	.40	.18
□ 93 Harold Reynolds	.05	.02
□ 94 Mark McLemore	.05	.02
□ 95 Mark McGwire	.40	.18
□ 96 Eddie Murray	.20	.09
□ 97 Tim Raines	.10	.05
□ 98 Robby Thompson	.05	.02
□ 99 Kevin McReynolds	.05	.02
□ 100 Checklist 28-137	.05	.02
□ 101 Carlton Fisk	.20	.09
□ 102 Dave Martinez	.05	.02
□ 103 Glenn Braggs	.05	.02
□ 104 Dale Murphy	.20	.09
□ 105 Ryne Sandberg	.25	.11
□ 106 Dennis Martinez	.05	.02

107	Pete O'Brien	.05	.02
108	Dick Schofield	.05	.02
109	Henry Cotto	.05	.02
110	Mike Marshall	.05	.02
111	Keith Moreland	.05	.02
112	Tom Brunansky	.05	.02
113	Kelly Gruber UER (Wrong birthdate)	.05	.02
114	Brook Jacoby	.05	.02
115	Keith Brown	.05	.02
116	Matt Nokes	.05	.02
117	Keith Hernandez	.10	.05
118	Bob Boone	.05	.02
119	Bert Blyleven UER (... 3000 strikeouts in 1987, should be 1986)	.10	.05
120	Willie Wilson	.05	.02
121	Tommy Gregg	.05	.02
122	Jim Rice	.10	.05
123	Bob Knepper	.05	.02
124	Danny Jackson	.05	.02
125	Eric Plunk	.05	.02
126	Brian Fisher	.05	.02
127	Mike Pagliarulo	.05	.02
128	Tony Gwynn	.50	.23
129	Lance McCullers	.05	.02
130	Andres Galarraga	.20	.09
131	Jose Uribe	.05	.02
132	Kirk Gibson UER (Wrong birthdate)	.10	.05
133	David Palmer	.05	.02
134	R.J. Reynolds	.05	.02
135	Greg Walker	.05	.02
136	Kirk McCaskill UER (Wrong birthdate)	.05	.02
137	Shawon Dunston	.05	.02
138	Andy Allanson	.05	.02
139	Rob Murphy	.05	.02
140	Mike Aldrete	.05	.02
141	Terry Kennedy	.05	.02
142	Scott Fletcher	.05	.02
143	Steve Balboni	.05	.02
144	Bret Saberhagen	.05	.02
145	Ozzie Virgil	.05	.02
146	Dale Sveum	.05	.02
147	Darryl Strawberry	.10	.05
148	Harold Baines	.05	.02
149	George Bell	.05	.02
150	Dave Parker	.05	.02
151	Bobby Bonilla	.10	.05
152	Mookie Wilson	.05	.02
153	Ted Power	.05	.02
154	Nolan Ryan	.75	.35
155	Jeff Reardon	.10	.05
156	Tim Wallach	.05	.02
157	Jamie Moyer	.05	.02
158	Rich Gossage	.10	.05
159	Dave Winfield	.20	.09
160	Von Hayes	.05	.02
161	Willie McGee	.10	.05
162	Rich Gedman	.05	.02
163	Tony Pena	.05	.02
164	Mike Morgan	.05	.02
165	Charlie Hough	.05	.02
166	Mike Stanley	.05	.02
167	Andre Dawson	.20	.09
168	Joe Boever	.05	.02
169	Pete Stanicek	.05	.02
170	Bob Boone	.10	.05
171	Ron Darling	.05	.02
172	Bob Walk	.05	.02
173	Rob Deer	.05	.02
174	Steve Buechele	.05	.02
175	Ted Higuera	.05	.02
176	Ozzie Guillen	.05	.02
177	Candy Maldonado	.05	.02
178	Doyle Alexander	.05	.02
179	Mark Gubicza	.05	.02
180	Alan Trammell	.10	.05
181	Vince Coleman	.05	.02
182	Kirby Puckett	.40	.18
183	Chris Brown	.05	.02
184	Marty Barrett	.05	.02
185	Stan Javier	.05	.02
186	Mike Greenwell	.05	.02
187	Billy Hatcher	.05	.02
188	Jimmy Key	.10	.05
189	Nick Esasky	.05	.02
190	Don Slaught	.05	.02
191	Cory Snyder	.05	.02
192	John Candelaria	.05	.02
193	Mike Schmidt	.25	.11
194	Kevin Gross	.05	.02
195	John Tudor	.05	.02
196	Neil Allen	.05	.02
197	Orel Hershiser	.10	.05
198	Kal Daniels	.05	.02
199	Kent Hrbek	.05	.02
200	Checklist 136-247	.05	.02
201	Joe Magrane	.05	.02
202	Scott Bailes	.05	.02
203	Tim Belcher	.05	.02
204	George Brett	.40	.18
205	Benito Santiago	.05	.02
206	Tony Fernandez	.05	.02
207	Gerald Young	.05	.02
208	Bo Jackson	.20	.09
209	Chet Lemon	.05	.02
210	Storm Davis	.05	.02
211	Doug Drabek	.05	.02
212	Mickey Brantley UER (Photo actually Nelson Simmons)	.05	.02
213	Devon White	.05	.02
214	Dave Stewart	.10	.05
215	Dave Schmidt	.05	.02
216	Bryn Smith	.05	.02
217	Brett Butler	.10	.05
218	Bob Ojeda	.05	.02
219	Steve Rosenberg	.05	.02
220	Hubie Brooks	.05	.02
221	B.J. Surhoff	.10	.05
222	Rick Mahler	.05	.02
223	Rick Sutcliffe	.05	.02
224	Neal Heaton	.05	.02
225	Mitch Williams	.05	.02
226	Chuck Finley	.05	.02
227	Mark Langston	.05	.02
228	Jesse Orosco	.05	.02
229	Ed Whitson	.05	.02
230	Terry Pendleton	.10	.05
231	Lloyd Moseby	.05	.02
232	Greg Swindell	.05	.02
233	John Franco	.10	.05
234	Jack Morris	.10	.05
235	Howard Johnson	.05	.02
236	Glenn Davis	.05	.02
237	Frank Viola	.05	.02
238	Kevin Seitzer	.05	.02
239	Gerald Perry	.05	.02
240	Dwight Evans	.10	.05
241	Jim Deshaies	.05	.02
242	Bo Diaz	.05	.02
243	Carney Lansford	.10	.05
244	Mike LaValliere	.05	.02
245	Rickey Henderson	.20	.09
246	Roberto Alomar	.30	.14
247	Jimmy Jones	.05	.02
248	Pascual Perez	.05	.02
249	Will Clark	.20	.09
250	Fernando Valenzuela	.10	.05
251	Shane Rawley	.05	.02
252	Sid Bream	.05	.02
253	Steve Lyons	.05	.02
254	Brian Downing	.05	.02
255	Mark Grace	.20	.09
256	Tom Candiotti	.05	.02
257	Barry Larkin	.20	.09
258	Mike Krukow	.05	.02
259	Billy Ripken	.05	.02
260	Cecilio Guante	.05	.02
261	Scott Bradley	.05	.02
262	Floyd Bannister	.05	.02
263	Pete Smith	.05	.02
264	Jim Gantner UER (Wrong birthdate)	.05	.02
265	Roger McDowell	.05	.02
266	Bobby Thigpen	.05	.02
267	Jim Clancy	.05	.02
268	Terry Steinbach	.10	.05
269	Mike Dunne	.05	.02
270	Dwight Gooden	.10	.05
271	Mike Heath	.05	.02
272	Dave Smith	.05	.02
273	Keith Atherton	.05	.02
274	Tim Burke	.05	.02
275	Damon Berryhill	.05	.02
276	Vance Law	.05	.02
277	Rich Dotson	.05	.02
278	Lance Parrish	.05	.02
279	Denny Walling	.05	.02
280	Roger Clemens	.40	.18
281	Greg Mathews	.05	.02
282	Tom Niedenfuer	.05	.02
283	Paul Kilgus	.05	.02
284	Jose Guzman	.05	.02
285	Calvin Schiraldi	.05	.02
286	Charlie Puleo UER (Career ERA 4.24, should be 4.23)	.05	.02
287	Joe Orsulak	.05	.02
288	Jack Howell	.05	.02
289	Kevin Elster	.05	.02
290	Jose Lind	.05	.02
291	Paul Molitor	.20	.09
292	Cecil Espy	.05	.02
293	Bill Wegman	.05	.02
294	Dan Pasqua	.05	.02
295	Scott Garrelts UER (Wrong birthdate)	.05	.02
296	Walt Terrell	.05	.02
297	Ed Hearn	.05	.02
298	Lou Whitaker	.10	.05
299	Ken Dayley	.05	.02
300	Checklist 248-357	.05	.02
301	Tommy Herr	.05	.02
302	Mike Brumley	.05	.02
303	Ellis Burks	.10	.05
304	Curt Young UER (Wrong birthdate)	.05	.02
305	Jody Reed	.05	.02
306	Bill Doran	.05	.02
307	David Wells	.05	.02
308	Don Robinson	.05	.02
309	Rafael Santana	.05	.02
310	Julio Franco	.05	.02
311	Jack Clark	.10	.05
312	Chris James	.05	.02
313	Milt Thompson	.05	.02
314	John Shelby	.05	.02
315	Al Leiter	.20	.09
316	Mike Davis	.05	.02
317	Chris Sabo	.05	.02
318	Greg Gagne	.05	.02
319	Jose Oquendo	.05	.02
320	John Farrell	.05	.02
321	Franklin Stubbs	.05	.02
322	Kurt Stillwell	.05	.02
323	Shawn Abner	.05	.02
324	Mike Flanagan	.05	.02
325	Kevin Bass	.05	.02
326	Pat Tabler	.05	.02
327	Mike Henneman	.05	.02
328	Rick Honeycutt	.05	.02
329	John Smiley	.05	.02
330	Rey Quinones	.05	.02
331	Johnny Ray	.05	.02
332	Bob Welch	.05	.02
333	Larry Sheets	.05	.02
334	Jeff Parrett	.05	.02
335	Rick Reuschel UER (For Don Robinson, should be Jeff)	.05	.02
336	Randy Myers	.10	.05
337	Ken Williams	.05	.05
338	Andy McGaffigan	.05	.05
339	Joey Meyer	.05	.05
340	Dion James	.05	.05
341	Les Lancaster	.05	.05
342	Tom Foley	.05	.05
343	Geno Petralli	.05	.05
344	Dan Petry	.05	.05
345	Alvin Davis	.05	.05
346	Mickey Hatcher	.05	.05
347	Marvell Wynne	.05	.05
348	Danny Cox	.05	.05
349	Dave Stieb	.05	.02
350	Jay Bell	.10	.05

☐ 351	Jeff Treadway	.05	.02
☐ 352	Luis Salazar	.05	.02
☐ 353	Len Dykstra	.10	.05
☐ 354	Juan Agosto	.05	.02
☐ 355	Gene Larkin	.05	.02
☐ 356	Steve Farr	.05	.02
☐ 357	Paul Assenmacher	.05	.02
☐ 358	Todd Benzinger	.05	.02
☐ 359	Larry Andersen	.05	.02
☐ 360	Paul O'Neill	.10	.05
☐ 361	Ron Hassey	.05	.02
☐ 362	Jim Gott	.05	.02
☐ 363	Ken Phelps	.05	.02
☐ 364	Tim Flannery	.05	.02
☐ 365	Randy Ready	.05	.02
☐ 366	Nelson Santovenia	.05	.02
☐ 367	Kelly Downs	.05	.02
☐ 368	Danny Heep	.05	.02
☐ 369	Phil Bradley	.05	.02
☐ 370	Jeff D. Robinson	.05	.02
☐ 371	Ivan Calderon	.05	.02
☐ 372	Mike Witt	.05	.02
☐ 373	Greg Maddux	.75	.35
☐ 374	Carmen Castillo	.05	.02
☐ 375	Jose Rijo	.05	.02
☐ 376	Joe Price	.05	.02
☐ 377	Rene Gonzales	.05	.02
☐ 378	Oddibe McDowell	.05	.02
☐ 379	Jim Presley	.05	.02
☐ 380	Brad Wellman	.05	.02
☐ 381	Tom Glavine	.20	.09
☐ 382	Dan Plesac	.05	.02
☐ 383	Wally Backman	.05	.02
☐ 384	Dave Gallagher	.05	.02
☐ 385	Tom Henke	.05	.02
☐ 386	Luis Polonia	.05	.02
☐ 387	Junior Ortiz	.05	.02
☐ 388	David Cone	.20	.09
☐ 389	Dave Bergman	.05	.02
☐ 390	Danny Darwin	.05	.02
☐ 391	Dan Gladden	.05	.02
☐ 392	John Dopson	.05	.02
☐ 393	Frank DiPino	.05	.02
☐ 394	Al Nipper	.05	.02
☐ 395	Willie Randolph	.10	.05
☐ 396	Don Carman	.05	.02
☐ 397	Scott Terry	.05	.02
☐ 398	Rick Cerone	.05	.02
☐ 399	Tom Pagnozzi	.05	.02
☐ 400	Checklist 358-467	.05	.02
☐ 401	Mickey Tettleton	.10	.05
☐ 402	Curtis Wilkerson	.05	.02
☐ 403	Jeff Russell	.05	.02
☐ 404	Pat Perry	.05	.02
☐ 405	Jose Alvarez	.05	.02
☐ 406	Rick Schu	.05	.02
☐ 407	Sherman Corbett	.05	.02
☐ 408	Dave Magadan	.05	.02
☐ 409	Bob Kipper	.05	.02
☐ 410	Don August	.05	.02
☐ 411	Bob Brower	.05	.02
☐ 412	Chris Bosio	.05	.02
☐ 413	Jerry Reuss	.05	.02
☐ 414	Atlee Hammaker	.05	.02
☐ 415	Jim Walewander	.05	.02
☐ 416	Mike Macfarlane	.10	.05
☐ 417	Pat Sheridan	.05	.02
☐ 418	Pedro Guerrero	.10	.05
☐ 419	Allan Anderson	.05	.02
☐ 420	Mark Parent	.05	.02
☐ 421	Bob Stanley	.05	.02
☐ 422	Mike Gallego	.05	.02
☐ 423	Bruce Hurst	.05	.02
☐ 424	Dave Meads	.05	.02
☐ 425	Jesse Barfield	.05	.02
☐ 426	Rob Dibble	.10	.05
☐ 427	Joel Skinner	.05	.02
☐ 428	Ron Kittle	.05	.02
☐ 429	Rick Rhoden	.05	.02
☐ 430	Bob Dernier	.05	.02
☐ 431	Steve Jeltz	.05	.02
☐ 432	Rick Dempsey	.05	.02
☐ 433	Roberto Kelly	.10	.05
☐ 434	Dave Anderson	.05	.02
☐ 435	Herm Winningham	.05	.02
☐ 436	Al Newman	.05	.02
☐ 437	Jose DeLeon	.05	.02
☐ 438	Doug Jones	.05	.02
☐ 439	Brian Holton	.05	.02
☐ 440	Jeff Montgomery	.10	.05
☐ 441	Dickie Thon	.05	.02
☐ 442	Cecil Fielder	.10	.05
☐ 443	John Fishel	.05	.02
☐ 444	Jerry Don Gleaton	.05	.02
☐ 445	Paul Gibson	.05	.02
☐ 446	Walt Weiss	.05	.02
☐ 447	Glenn Wilson	.05	.02
☐ 448	Mike Moore	.05	.02
☐ 449	Chili Davis	.05	.02
☐ 450	Dave Henderson	.05	.02
☐ 451	Jose Bautista	.05	.02
☐ 452	Rex Hudler	.05	.02
☐ 453	Bob Brenly	.05	.02
☐ 454	Mackey Sasser	.05	.02
☐ 455	Daryl Boston	.05	.02
☐ 456	Mike R. Fitzgerald	.05	.02
☐ 457	Jeffrey Leonard	.05	.02
☐ 458	Bruce Sutter	.05	.02
☐ 459	Mitch Webster	.05	.02
☐ 460	Joe Hesketh	.05	.02
☐ 461	Bobby Witt	.05	.02
☐ 462	Stew Cliburn	.05	.02
☐ 463	Scott Bankhead	.05	.02
☐ 464	Ramon Martinez	.25	.11
☐ 465	Dave Leiper	.05	.02
☐ 466	Luis Alicea	.05	.02
☐ 467	John Cerutti	.05	.02
☐ 468	Ron Washington	.05	.02
☐ 469	Jeff Reed	.05	.02
☐ 470	Jeff M. Robinson	.05	.02
☐ 471	Sid Fernandez	.05	.02
☐ 472	Terry Puhl	.05	.02
☐ 473	Charlie Lea	.05	.02
☐ 474	Israel Sanchez	.05	.02
☐ 475	Bruce Benedict	.05	.02
☐ 476	Oil Can Boyd	.05	.02
☐ 477	Craig Reynolds	.05	.02
☐ 478	Frank Williams	.05	.02
☐ 479	Greg Cadaret	.05	.02
☐ 480	Randy Kramer	.05	.02
☐ 481	Dave Eiland	.05	.02
☐ 482	Eric Show	.05	.02
☐ 483	Garry Templeton	.05	.02
☐ 484	Wallace Johnson	.05	.02
☐ 485	Kevin Mitchell	.10	.05
☐ 486	Tim Crews	.05	.02
☐ 487	Mike Maddux	.05	.02
☐ 488	Dave LaPoint	.05	.02
☐ 489	Fred Manrique	.05	.02
☐ 490	Greg Minton	.05	.02
☐ 491	Doug Dascenzo UER	.05	.02
	(Photo actually Damon Berryhill)		
☐ 492	Willie Upshaw	.05	.02
☐ 493	Jack Armstrong	.05	.02
☐ 494	Kirt Manwaring	.05	.02
☐ 495	Jeff Ballard	.05	.02
☐ 496	Jeff Kunkel	.05	.02
☐ 497	Mike Campbell	.05	.02
☐ 498	Gary Thurman	.05	.02
☐ 499	Zane Smith	.05	.02
☐ 500	Checklist 468-577 DP	.05	.02
☐ 501	Mike Birkbeck	.05	.02
☐ 502	Terry Leach	.05	.02
☐ 503	Shawn Hillegas	.05	.02
☐ 504	Manny Lee	.05	.02
☐ 505	Doug Jennings	.05	.02
☐ 506	Ken Oberkfell	.05	.02
☐ 507	Tim Teufel	.05	.02
☐ 508	Tom Brookens	.05	.02
☐ 509	Rafael Ramirez	.05	.02
☐ 510	Fred Toliver	.05	.02
☐ 511	Brian Holman	.05	.02
☐ 512	Mike Bielecki	.05	.02
☐ 513	Jeff Pico	.05	.02
☐ 514	Charles Hudson	.05	.02
☐ 515	Bruce Ruffin	.05	.02
☐ 516	Larry McWilliams UER	.05	.02
	(New Richland, should be North Richland)		
☐ 517	Jeff Sellers	.05	.02
☐ 518	John Costello	.05	.02
☐ 519	Brady Anderson	.50	.23
☐ 520	Craig McMurtry	.05	.02
☐ 521	Ray Hayward DP	.05	.02
☐ 522	Drew Hall DP	.05	.02
☐ 523	Mark Lemke DP	.10	.05
☐ 524	Oswald Peraza DP	.05	.02
☐ 525	Bryan Harvey DP	.05	.02
☐ 526	Rick Aguilera DP	.10	.05
☐ 527	Tom Prince DP	.05	.02
☐ 528	Mark Clear DP	.05	.02
☐ 529	Jerry Browne DP	.05	.02
☐ 530	Juan Castillo DP	.05	.02
☐ 531	Jack McDowell DP	.10	.05
☐ 532	Chris Speier DP	.05	.02
☐ 533	Darrell Evans DP	.10	.05
☐ 534	Luis Aquino DP	.05	.02
☐ 535	Eric King DP	.05	.02
☐ 536	Ken Hill DP	.20	.09
☐ 537	Randy Bush DP	.05	.02
☐ 538	Shane Mack DP	.05	.02
☐ 539	Tom Bolton DP	.05	.02
☐ 540	Gene Nelson DP	.05	.02
☐ 541	Wes Gardner DP	.05	.02
☐ 542	Ken Caminiti DP	.20	.09
☐ 543	Duane Ward DP	.05	.02
☐ 544	Norm Charlton DP	.10	.05
☐ 545	Hal Morris DP	.10	.05
☐ 546	Rich Yett DP	.05	.02
☐ 547	Hensley Meulens DP	.05	.02
☐ 548	Greg A. Harris DP	.05	.02
☐ 549	Darren Daulton DP	.10	.05
	(Posing as right-handed hitter)		
☐ 550	Jeff Hamilton DP	.05	.02
☐ 551	Luis Aguayo DP	.05	.02
☐ 552	Tim Leary DP	.05	.02
	(Resembles M.Marshall)		
☐ 553	Ron Oester DP	.05	.02
☐ 554	Steve Lombardozzi DP	.05	.02
☐ 555	Tim Jones DP	.05	.02
☐ 556	Bud Black DP	.05	.02
☐ 557	Alejandro Pena DP	.05	.02
☐ 558	Jose DeJesus DP	.05	.02
☐ 559	Dennis Rasmussen DP	.05	.02
☐ 560	Pat Borders DP	.10	.05
☐ 561	Craig Biggio DP	.50	.23
☐ 562	Luis DeLosSantos DP	.05	.02
☐ 563	Fred Lynn DP	.05	.02
☐ 564	Todd Burns DP	.05	.02
☐ 565	Felix Fermin DP	.05	.02
☐ 566	Darnell Coles DP	.05	.02
☐ 567	Willie Fraser DP	.05	.02
☐ 568	Glenn Hubbard DP	.05	.02
☐ 569	Craig Worthington DP	.05	.02
☐ 570	Johnny Paredes DP	.05	.02
☐ 571	Don Robinson DP	.05	.02
☐ 572	Barry Lyons DP	.05	.02
☐ 573	Bill Long DP	.05	.02
☐ 574	Tracy Jones DP	.05	.02
☐ 575	Juan Nieves DP	.05	.02
☐ 576	Andres Thomas DP	.05	.02
☐ 577	Rolando Roomes DP	.05	.02
☐ 578	Luis Rivera UER DP	.05	.02
	(Wrong birthdate)		
☐ 579	Chad Kreuter DP	.05	.02
☐ 580	Tony Armas DP	.05	.02
☐ 581	Jay Buhner	.20	.09
☐ 582	Ricky Horton DP	.05	.02
☐ 583	Andy Hawkins DP	.05	.02
☐ 584	Sil Campusano	.05	.02
☐ 585	Dave Clark	.05	.02
☐ 586	Van Snider DP	.05	.02
☐ 587	Todd Frohwirth DP	.05	.02
☐ 588	Warren Spahn DP PUZ	.20	.09
☐ 589	William Brennan	.05	.02
☐ 590	German Gonzalez	.05	.02
☐ 591	Ernie Whitt DP	.05	.02
☐ 592	Jeff Blauser	.10	.05
☐ 593	Spike Owen DP	.05	.02
☐ 594	Matt Williams	.20	.09
☐ 595	Floyd McClendon DP	.05	.02
☐ 596	Steve Ontiveros	.05	.02
☐ 597	Scott Medvin	.05	.02
☐ 598	Hipolito Pena DP	.05	.02
☐ 599	Jerald Clark DP	.05	.02
☐ 600A	Checklist 578-660 DP	.05	.02

	(635 Kurt Schilling)		
☐ 600B	Checklist 578-660 DP	.05	.02
	(635 Curt Schilling;		
	MVP's not listed		
	on checklist back)		
☐ 600C	Checklist 578-660 DP	.05	.02
	(635 Curt Schilling;		
	MVP's listed		
	following 660)		
☐ 601	Carmelo Martinez DP	.05	.02
☐ 602	Mike LaCoss	.05	.02
☐ 603	Mike Devereaux	.05	.02
☐ 604	Alex Madrid DP	.05	.02
☐ 605	Gary Redus DP	.05	.02
☐ 606	Lance Johnson	.10	.05
☐ 607	Terry Clark DP	.05	.02
☐ 608	Manny Trillo DP	.05	.02
☐ 609	Scott Jordan	.10	.05
☐ 610	Jay Howell DP	.05	.02
☐ 611	Francisco Melendez	.05	.02
☐ 612	Mike Boddicker	.05	.02
☐ 613	Kevin Brown DP	.20	.09
☐ 614	Dave Valle	.05	.02
☐ 615	Tim Laudner DP	.05	.02
☐ 616	Andy Nezelek UER	.05	.02
	(Wrong birthdate)		
☐ 617	Chuck Crim	.05	.02
☐ 618	Jack Savage DP	.05	.02
☐ 619	Adam Peterson	.05	.02
☐ 620	Todd Stottlemyre	.10	.05
☐ 621	Lance Blankenship	.05	.02
☐ 622	Miguel Garcia DP	.05	.02
☐ 623	Keith A. Miller DP	.05	.02
☐ 624	Ricky Jordan DP	.10	.05
☐ 625	Ernest Riles DP	.05	.02
☐ 626	John Moses DP	.05	.02
☐ 627	Nelson Liriano DP	.05	.02
☐ 628	Mike Smithson DP	.05	.02
☐ 629	Scott Sanderson	.05	.02
☐ 630	Dale Mohorcic	.05	.02
☐ 631	Marvin Freeman DP	.05	.02
☐ 632	Mike Young DP	.05	.02
☐ 633	Dennis Lamp	.05	.02
☐ 634	Danny Darwin DP	.40	.18
☐ 635	Curt Schilling DP	.50	.23
☐ 636	Scott May DP	.05	.02
☐ 637	Mike Schooler	.05	.02
☐ 638	Rick Leach	.05	.02
☐ 639	Tom Lampkin UER	.05	.02
	(Throws Left, should		
	be Throws Right)		
☐ 640	Brian Meyer	.05	.02
☐ 641	Brian Harper	.05	.02
☐ 642	John Smoltz	.50	.23
☐ 643	Jose Canseco	.10	.05
	(40/40 Club)		
☐ 644	Bill Schroeder	.05	.02
☐ 645	Edgar Martinez	.20	.09
☐ 646	Dennis Cook	.05	.02
☐ 647	Barry Jones	.05	.02
☐ 648	Orel Hershiser	.10	.05
	(59 and Counting)		
☐ 649	Rod Nichols	.05	.02
☐ 650	Jody Davis	.05	.02
☐ 651	Bob Milacki	.05	.02
☐ 652	Mike Jackson	.05	.02
☐ 653	Derek Lilliquist	.05	.02
☐ 654	Paul Mirabella	.05	.02
☐ 655	Mike Diaz	.05	.02
☐ 656	Jeff Musselman	.05	.02
☐ 657	Jerry Reed	.05	.02
☐ 658	Kevin Blankenship	.05	.02
☐ 659	Wayne Tolleson	.05	.02
☐ 660	Eric Hetzel	.05	.02

1989 Donruss Rookies

The 1989 Donruss Rookies set contains 56 standard-size cards. The cards were distributed exclusively in factory set form in small, emerald green, cellophane-wrapped boxes through

hobby dealers. The cards are almost identical in design to geular 1989 Donruss except for the green borders. Rookie Cards in this set include Jim Abbott, Steve Finley, Kenny Rogers and Deion Sanders. Ken Griffey Jr. is also featured on a card within the set.

		MINT	NRMT
COMP.FACT.SET (56)		10.00	4.50
COMMON CARD (1-56)		.05	.02
MINOR STARS		.10	.05
UNLISTED STARS		.20	.09
☐ 1	Gary Sheffield	.75	.35
☐ 2	Gregg Jefferies	.15	.07
☐ 3	Ken Griffey Jr.	6.00	2.70
☐ 4	Tom Gordon	.20	.09
☐ 5	Billy Spiers	.05	.02
☐ 6	Deion Sanders	.75	.35
☐ 7	Donn Pall	.05	.02
☐ 8	Steve Carter	.05	.02
☐ 9	Francisco Oliveras	.05	.02
☐ 10	Steve Wilson	.05	.02
☐ 11	Bob Geren	.05	.02
☐ 12	Tony Castillo	.05	.02
☐ 13	Kenny Rogers	.10	.05
☐ 14	Carlos Martinez	.05	.02
☐ 15	Edgar Martinez	.20	.09
☐ 16	Jim Abbott	.20	.09
☐ 17	Torey Lovullo	.05	.02
☐ 18	Mark Carreon	.05	.02
☐ 19	Geronimo Berroa	.10	.05
☐ 20	Luis Medina	.05	.02
☐ 21	Sandy Alomar Jr.	.50	.23
☐ 22	Bob Milacki	.05	.02
☐ 23	Joe Girardi	.05	.02
☐ 24	German Gonzalez	.05	.02
☐ 25	Craig Worthington	.05	.02
☐ 26	Jerome Walton	.05	.02
☐ 27	Gary Wayne	.05	.02
☐ 28	Tim Jones	.05	.02
☐ 29	Dante Bichette	.40	.18
☐ 30	Alexis Infante	.05	.02
☐ 31	Ken Hill	.20	.09
☐ 32	Dwight Smith	.10	.05
☐ 33	Luis de los Santos	.05	.02
☐ 34	Eric Yelding	.05	.02
☐ 35	Gregg Olson	.10	.05
☐ 36	Phil Stephenson	.05	.02
☐ 37	Ken Patterson	.05	.02
☐ 38	Rick Wrona	.05	.02
☐ 39	Mike Brumley	.05	.02
☐ 40	Cris Carpenter	.05	.02
☐ 41	Jeff Brantley	.20	.09
☐ 42	Ron Jones	.05	.02
☐ 43	Randy Johnson	1.00	.45
☐ 44	Kevin Brown	.20	.09
☐ 45	Ramon Martinez	.20	.09
☐ 46	Greg W.Harris	.05	.02
☐ 47	Steve Finley	.25	.11
☐ 48	Randy Kramer	.05	.02
☐ 49	Erik Hanson	.10	.05
☐ 50	Matt Merullo	.05	.02
☐ 51	Mike Devereaux	.05	.02
☐ 52	Clay Parker	.05	.02
☐ 53	Omar Vizquel	.40	.18
☐ 54	Derek Lilliquist	.05	.02
☐ 55	Junior Felix	.05	.02
☐ 56	Checklist 1-56	.05	.02

1990 Donruss

The 1990 Donruss set contains 716 standard-size cards. Cards were issued in wax packs and hobby and retail factory sets. The card fronts feature bright red borders. Subsets include Diamond Kings (1-27) and Rated Rookies (28-47). The set was the largest ever produced by Donruss, unfortunately it also had a large number of errors which were corrected after the cards were released. Most of these feature minor printing flaws and insignificant variations that collectors have found unworthy of price differentials. There are several double-printed cards within the set indicated in the checklists below with a "DP" coding. Rookie Cards of note include Juan Gonzalez, Marquis Grissom, Dave Justice, Ben McDonald, Dean Palmer, Sammy Sosa, Larry Walker and Bernie Williams. Numbered with the prefix "BC", Special Bonus Cards from a set featuring one most valuable player from each of the 26 teams were randomly inserted in all 1990 Donruss unopened pack formats. The factory sets were distributed without the Bonus Cards.

		MINT	NRMT
COMPLETE SET (716)		8.00	3.60
COMP.FACT.SET (728)		8.00	3.60
COMMON CARD (1-716)		.05	.02
MINOR STARS		.10	.05
UNLISTED STARS		.20	.09
SUBSET CARDS HALF VALUE OF BASE CARDS			
COMP.BONUS MVP SET (26)		1.50	.70
MVP'S: RANDOM INSERTS IN PACKS			
COMP.G'SLAMMERS SET (12)		1.50	.70
ONE G.SLAM SET PER FACT.SET			
☐ 1	Bo Jackson DK	.10	.05
☐ 2	Steve Sax DK	.05	.02
☐ 3A	Ruben Sierra DK ERR	.05	.02
	(No small line on top		
	border on card back)		
☐ 3B	Ruben Sierra DK COR	.05	.02
☐ 4	Ken Griffey Jr. DK	.75	.35
☐ 5	Mickey Tettleton DK	.05	.02
☐ 6	Dave Stewart DK	.05	.02
☐ 7	Jim Deshaies DK DP	.05	.02
☐ 8	John Smoltz DK	.20	.09
☐ 9	Mike Bielecki DK	.05	.02
☐ 10A	Brian Downing DK	.20	.09

ERR (Reverse negative on card front)

□ 10B Brian Downing DK	.05	.02

COR

□ 11 Kevin Mitchell DK	.05	.02
□ 12 Kelly Gruber DK	.05	.02
□ 13 Joe Magrane DK	.05	.02
□ 14 John Franco DK	.05	.02
□ 15 Ozzie Guillen DK	.05	.02
□ 16 Lou Whitaker DK	.05	.02
□ 17 John Smiley DK	.05	.02
□ 18 Howard Johnson DK	.05	.02
□ 19 Willie Randolph DK	.10	.05
□ 20 Chris Bosio DK	.05	.02
□ 21 Tommy Herr DK DP	.05	.02
□ 22 Dan Gladden DK	.05	.02
□ 23 Ellis Burks DK	.10	.05
□ 24 Pete O'Brien DK	.05	.02
□ 25 Bryn Smith DK	.05	.02
□ 26 Ed Whitson DK DP	.05	.02
□ 27 DK Checklist 1-27 DP	.05	.02

(Comments on Perez-Steele on back)

□ 28 Robin Ventura RR	.20	.09
□ 29 Todd Zeile RR	.10	.05
□ 30 Sandy Alomar Jr. RR	.20	.09
□ 31 Kent Mercker RR	.10	.05
□ 32 Ben McDonald RR UER	.15	.07

(Middle name Benard, not Benjamin)

□ 33A Juan Gonzalez RR ERR	5.00	2.20

(Reverse negative)

□ 33B Juan Gonzalez RR COR	2.00	.90
□ 34 Eric Anthony RR	.10	.05
□ 35 Mike Fetters RR	.05	.02
□ 36 Marquis Grissom RR	.40	.18
□ 37 Greg Vaughn RR	.10	.05
□ 38 Brian DuBois RR	.05	.02
□ 39 Steve Avery RR UER	.05	.02

(Born in MI, not NJ)

□ 40 Mark Gardner RR	.05	.02
□ 41 Andy Benes RR	.20	.09
□ 42 Delino DeShields RR	.10	.05
□ 43 Scott Coolbaugh RR	.05	.02
□ 44 Pat Combs RR DP	.05	.02
□ 45 Alex Sanchez RR DP	.05	.02
□ 46 Kelly Mann RR DP	.05	.02
□ 47 Julio Machado RR DP	.05	.02
□ 48 Pete Incaviglia	.05	.02
□ 49 Shawon Dunston	.05	.02
□ 50 Jeff Treadway	.05	.02
□ 51 Jeff Ballard	.05	.02
□ 52 Claudell Washington	.05	.02
□ 53 Juan Samuel	.05	.02
□ 54 John Smiley	.05	.02
□ 55 Rob Deer	.05	.02
□ 56 Geno Petralli	.05	.02
□ 57 Chris Bosio	.05	.02
□ 58 Carlton Fisk	.20	.09
□ 59 Kirt Manwaring	.05	.02
□ 60 Chet Lemon	.05	.02
□ 61 Bo Jackson	.20	.09
□ 62 Doyle Alexander	.05	.02
□ 63 Pedro Guerrero	.05	.02
□ 64 Allan Anderson	.05	.02
□ 65 Greg W. Harris	.05	.02
□ 66 Mike Greenwell	.05	.02
□ 67 Walt Weiss	.05	.02
□ 68 Wade Boggs	.20	.09
□ 69 Jim Clancy	.05	.02
□ 70 Junior Felix	.05	.02
□ 71 Barry Larkin	.20	.09
□ 72 Dave LaPoint	.05	.02
□ 73 Joel Skinner	.05	.02
□ 74 Jesse Barfield	.05	.02
□ 75 Tommy Herr	.05	.02
□ 76 Ricky Jordan	.05	.02
□ 77 Eddie Murray	.20	.09
□ 78 Steve Sax	.05	.02
□ 79 Tim Belcher	.05	.02
□ 80 Danny Jackson	.05	.02
□ 81 Kent Hrbek	.10	.05
□ 82 Milt Thompson	.05	.02
□ 83 Brook Jacoby	.05	.02
□ 84 Mike Marshall	.05	.02
□ 85 Kevin Seitzer	.05	.02
□ 86 Tony Gwynn	.50	.23
□ 87 Dave Stieb	.05	.02
□ 88 Dave Smith	.05	.02
□ 89 Bret Saberhagen	.05	.02
□ 90 Alan Trammell	.15	.07
□ 91 Tony Phillips	.05	.02
□ 92 Doug Drabek	.05	.02
□ 93 Jeffrey Leonard	.05	.02
□ 94 Wally Joyner	.10	.05
□ 95 Carney Lansford	.10	.05
□ 96 Cal Ripken	.75	.35
□ 97 Andres Galarraga	.20	.09
□ 98 Kevin Mitchell	.10	.05
□ 99 Howard Johnson	.05	.02
□ 100A Checklist 28-129	.05	.02
□ 100B Checklist 28-125	.05	.02
□ 101 Melido Perez	.05	.02
□ 102 Spike Owen	.05	.02
□ 103 Paul Molitor	.20	.09
□ 104 Geronimo Berroa	.10	.05
□ 105 Ryne Sandberg	.25	.11
□ 106 Bryn Smith	.05	.02
□ 107 Steve Buechele	.05	.02
□ 108 Jim Abbott	.10	.05
□ 109 Alvin Davis	.05	.02
□ 110 Lee Smith	.10	.05
□ 111 Roberto Alomar	.25	.11
□ 112 Rick Reuschel	.05	.02
□ 113A Kelly Gruber ERR	.05	.02
□ 113B Kelly Gruber COR	.05	.02

(Born 2/26; corrected in factory sets)

□ 114 Joe Carter	.10	.05
□ 115 Jose Rijo	.05	.02
□ 116 Greg Minton	.05	.02
□ 117 Bob Ojeda	.05	.02
□ 118 Glenn Davis	.05	.02
□ 119 Jeff Reardon	.10	.05
□ 120 Kurt Stillwell	.05	.02
□ 121 John Smoltz	.20	.09
□ 122 Dwight Evans	.10	.05
□ 123 Eric Yelding	.05	.02
□ 124 John Franco	.05	.02
□ 125 Jose Canseco	.20	.09
□ 126 Barry Bonds	.25	.11
□ 127 Lee Guetterman	.05	.02
□ 128 Jack Clark	.05	.02
□ 129 Dave Valle	.05	.02
□ 130 Hubie Brooks	.05	.02
□ 131 Ernest Riles	.05	.02
□ 132 Mike Morgan	.05	.02
□ 133 Steve Jeltz	.05	.02
□ 134 Jeff D. Robinson	.05	.02
□ 135 Ozzie Guillen	.05	.02
□ 136 Chili Davis	.10	.05
□ 137 Mitch Webster	.05	.02
□ 138 Jerry Browne	.05	.02
□ 139 Bo Diaz	.05	.02
□ 140 Robby Thompson	.05	.02
□ 141 Craig Worthington	.05	.02
□ 142 Julio Franco	.05	.02
□ 143 Brian Holman	.05	.02
□ 144 George Brett	.40	.18
□ 145 Tom Glavine	.20	.09
□ 146 Robin Yount	.20	.09
□ 147 Gary Carter	.20	.09
□ 148 Ron Kittle	.05	.02
□ 149 Tony Fernandez	.05	.02
□ 150 Dave Stewart	.10	.05
□ 151 Gary Gaetti	.05	.02
□ 152 Kevin Elster	.05	.02
□ 153 Gerald Perry	.05	.02
□ 154 Jesse Orosco	.05	.02
□ 155 Wally Backman	.05	.02
□ 156 Dennis Martinez	.10	.05
□ 157 Rick Sutcliffe	.05	.02
□ 158 Greg Maddux	.60	.25
□ 159 Andy Hawkins	.05	.02
□ 160 John Kruk	.10	.05
□ 161 Jose Oquendo	.05	.02
□ 162 John Dopson	.05	.02
□ 163 Joe Magrane	.05	.02
□ 164 Bill Ripken	.05	.02
□ 165 Fred Manrique	.05	.02
□ 166 Nolan Ryan UER	.75	.35

(Did not lead NL in K's in '89 as he was in AL in '89)

□ 167 Damon Berryhill	.05	.02
□ 168 Dale Murphy	.20	.09
□ 169 Mickey Tettleton	.10	.05
□ 170A Kirk McCaskill ERR	.05	.02

(Born 4/19)

□ 170B Kirk McCaskill COR	.05	.02

(Born 4/9; corrected in factory sets)

□ 171 Dwight Gooden	.10	.05
□ 172 Jose Lind	.05	.02
□ 173 B.J. Surhoff	.10	.05
□ 174 Ruben Sierra	.05	.02
□ 175 Dan Plesac	.05	.02
□ 176 Dan Pasqua	.05	.02
□ 177 Kelly Downs	.05	.02
□ 178 Matt Nokes	.05	.02
□ 179 Luis Aquino	.05	.02
□ 180 Frank Tanana	.05	.02
□ 181 Tony Pena	.05	.02
□ 182 Dan Gladden	.05	.02
□ 183 Bruce Hurst	.05	.02
□ 184 Roger Clemens	.40	.18
□ 185 Mark McGwire	.40	.18
□ 186 Rob Murphy	.05	.02
□ 187 Jim Deshaies	.05	.02
□ 188 Fred McGriff	.20	.09
□ 189 Rob Dibble	.05	.02
□ 190 Don Mattingly	.30	.14
□ 191 Felix Fermin	.05	.02
□ 192 Roberto Kelly	.05	.02
□ 193 Dennis Cook	.05	.02
□ 194 Darren Daulton	.10	.05
□ 195 Alfredo Griffin	.05	.02
□ 196 Eric Plunk	.05	.02
□ 197 Orel Hershiser	.10	.05
□ 198 Paul O'Neill	.10	.05
□ 199 Randy Bush	.05	.02
□ 200A Checklist 130-231	.05	.02
□ 200B Checklist 126-223	.05	.02
□ 201 Ozzie Smith	.25	.11
□ 202 Pete O'Brien	.05	.02
□ 203 Jay Howell	.05	.02
□ 204 Mark Gubicza	.05	.02
□ 205 Ed Whitson	.05	.02
□ 206 George Bell	.05	.02
□ 207 Mike Scott	.05	.02
□ 208 Charlie Leibrandt	.05	.02
□ 209 Mike Heath	.05	.02
□ 210 Dennis Eckersley	.10	.05
□ 211 Mike LaValliere	.05	.02
□ 212 Darnell Coles	.05	.02
□ 213 Lance Parrish	.05	.02
□ 214 Mike Moore	.05	.02
□ 215 Steve Finley	.05	.02
□ 216 Tim Raines	.10	.05
□ 217A Scott Garrelts ERR	.05	.02

(Born 10/30)

□ 217B Scott Garrelts COR	.05	.02

(Born 10/30; corrected in factory sets)

□ 218 Kevin McReynolds	.05	.02
□ 219 Dave Gallagher	.05	.02
□ 220 Tim Wallach	.05	.02
□ 221 Chuck Crim	.05	.02
□ 222 Lonnie Smith	.05	.02
□ 223 Andre Dawson	.20	.09
□ 224 Nelson Santovenia	.05	.02
□ 225 Rafael Palmeiro	.20	.09
□ 226 Devon White	.05	.02
□ 227 Harold Reynolds	.05	.02
□ 228 Ellis Burks	.15	.07
□ 229 Mark Parent	.05	.02
□ 230 Will Clark	.20	.09
□ 231 Jimmy Key	.10	.05
□ 232 John Farrell	.05	.02
□ 233 Eric Davis	.10	.05
□ 234 Johnny Ray	.05	.02
□ 235 Darryl Strawberry	.10	.05
□ 236 Bill Doran	.05	.02
□ 237 Greg Gagne	.05	.02
□ 238 Jim Eisenreich	.05	.02
□ 239 Tommy Gregg	.05	.02
□ 240 Marty Barrett	.05	.02

241	Rafael Ramirez	.05	.02
242	Chris Sabo	.05	.02
243	Dave Henderson	.05	.02
244	Andy Van Slyke	.10	.05
245	Alvaro Espinoza	.05	.02
246	Garry Templeton	.05	.02
247	Gene Harris	.05	.02
248	Kevin Gross	.05	.02
249	Brett Butler	.10	.05
250	Willie Randolph	.10	.05
251	Roger McDowell	.05	.02
252	Rafael Belliard	.05	.02
253	Steve Rosenberg	.05	.02
254	Jack Howell	.05	.02
255	Marvell Wynne	.05	.02
256	Tom Candiotti	.05	.02
257	Todd Benzinger	.05	.02
258	Don Robinson	.05	.02
259	Phil Bradley	.05	.02
260	Cecil Espy	.05	.02
261	Scott Bankhead	.05	.02
262	Frank White	.10	.05
263	Andres Thomas	.05	.02
264	Glenn Braggs	.05	.02
265	David Cone	.20	.09
266	Bobby Thigpen	.05	.02
267	Nelson Liriano	.05	.02
268	Terry Steinbach	.10	.05
269	Kirby Puckett UER	.40	.18
	(Back doesn't consider Joe Torre's .363 in '71)		
270	Gregg Jefferies	.10	.05
271	Jeff Blauser	.10	.05
272	Cory Snyder	.05	.02
273	Roy Smith	.05	.02
274	Tom Foley	.05	.02
275	Mitch Williams	.05	.02
276	Paul Kilgus	.05	.02
277	Don Slaught	.05	.02
278	Von Hayes	.05	.02
279	Vince Coleman	.05	.02
280	Mike Boddicker	.05	.02
281	Ken Dayley	.05	.02
282	Mike Devereaux	.05	.02
283	Kenny Rogers	.05	.02
284	Jeff Russell	.05	.02
285	Jerome Walton	.05	.02
286	Derek Lilliquist	.05	.02
287	Joe Orsulak	.05	.02
288	Dick Schofield	.05	.02
289	Ron Darling	.05	.02
290	Bobby Bonilla	.10	.05
291	Jim Gantner	.05	.02
292	Bobby Witt	.05	.02
293	Greg Brock	.05	.02
294	Ivan Calderon	.05	.02
295	Steve Bedrosian	.05	.02
296	Mike Henneman	.05	.02
297	Tom Gordon	.05	.02
298	Lou Whitaker	.10	.05
299	Terry Pendleton	.10	.05
300A	Checklist 232-333	.05	
300B	Checklist 224-321	.05	
301	Juan Berenguer	.05	.02
302	Mark Davis	.05	.02
303	Nick Esasky	.05	.02
304	Rickey Henderson	.20	.09
305	Rick Cerone	.05	.02
306	Craig Biggio	.20	.09
307	Duane Ward	.05	.02
308	Tom Browning	.05	.02
309	Walt Terrell	.05	.02
310	Greg Swindell	.05	.02
311	Dave Righetti	.05	.02
312	Mike Maddux	.05	.02
313	Len Dykstra	.05	.02
314	Jose Gonzalez	.05	.02
315	Steve Balboni	.05	.02
316	Mike Scioscia	.05	.02
317	Ron Oester	.05	.02
318	Gary Wayne	.05	.02
319	Todd Worrell	.05	.02
320	Doug Jones	.05	.02
321	Jeff Hamilton	.05	.02
322	Danny Tartabull	.10	.05
323	Chris James	.05	.02
324	Mike Flanagan	.05	.02
325	Gerald Young	.05	.02
326	Bob Boone	.10	.05
327	Frank Williams	.05	.02
328	Dave Parker	.10	.05
329	Sid Bream	.05	.02
330	Mike Schooler	.05	.02
331	Bert Blyleven	.05	.02
332	Bob Welch	.05	.02
333	Bob Milacki	.05	.02
334	Tim Burke	.05	.02
335	Jose Uribe	.05	.02
336	Randy Myers	.10	.05
337	Eric King	.05	.02
338	Mark Langston	.05	.02
339	Teddy Higuera	.05	.02
340	Oddibe McDowell	.05	.02
341	Lloyd McClendon	.05	.02
342	Pascual Perez	.05	.02
343	Kevin Brown UER	.20	.09
	(Signed is misspelled as signed on back)		
344	Chuck Finley	.10	.05
345	Erik Hanson	.05	.02
346	Rich Gedman	.05	.02
347	Bip Roberts	.05	.02
348	Matt Williams	.20	.09
349	Tom Henke	.05	.02
350	Brad Komminsk	.05	.02
351	Jeff Reed	.05	.02
352	Brian Downing	.05	.02
353	Frank Viola	.05	.02
354	Terry Puhl	.05	.02
355	Brian Harper	.05	.02
356	Steve Farr	.05	.02
357	Joe Boever	.05	.02
358	Danny Heep	.05	.02
359	Larry Andersen	.05	.02
360	Rolando Roomes	.05	.02
361	Mike Gallego	.05	.02
362	Bob Kipper	.05	.02
363	Clay Parker	.05	.02
364	Mike Pagliarulo	.05	.02
365	Ken Griffey Jr. UER	1.50	.70
	(Signed through 1990, should be 1991)		
366	Rex Hudler	.05	.02
367	Pat Sheridan	.05	.02
368	Kirk Gibson	.10	.05
369	Jeff Parrett	.05	.02
370	Bob Walk	.05	.02
371	Ken Patterson	.05	.02
372	Bryan Harvey	.05	.02
373	Mike Bielecki	.05	.02
374	Tom Magrann	.05	.02
375	Rick Mahler	.05	.02
376	Craig Lefferts	.05	.02
377	Gregg Olson	.05	.02
378	Jamie Moyer	.05	.02
379	Randy Johnson	.30	.14
380	Jeff Montgomery	.10	.05
381	Marty Clary	.05	.02
382	Bill Spiers	.05	.02
383	Dave Magadan	.05	.02
384	Greg Hibbard	.05	.02
385	Ernie Whitt	.05	.02
386	Rick Honeycutt	.05	.02
387	Dave West	.05	.02
388	Keith Hernandez	.10	.05
389	Jose Alvarez	.05	.02
390	Joey Belle	.50	.23
391	Rick Aguilera	.10	.05
392	Mike Fitzgerald	.05	.02
393	Dwight Smith	.05	.02
394	Steve Wilson	.05	.02
395	Bob Geren	.05	.02
396	Randy Ready	.05	.02
397	Ken Hill	.15	.07
398	Jody Reed	.05	.02
399	Tom Brunansky	.05	.02
400A	Checklist 334-435	.05	.02
400B	Checklist 322-419	.05	.02
401	Rene Gonzales	.05	.02
402	Harold Baines	.10	.05
403	Cecilio Guante	.05	.02
404	Joe Girardi	.10	.05
405A	Sergio Valdez ERR	.05	.02
	(Card front shows black line crossing S in Sergio)		
405B	Sergio Valdez COR	.05	.02
406	Mark Williamson	.05	.02
407	Glenn Hoffman	.05	.02
408	Jeff Innis	.05	.02
409	Randy Kramer	.05	.02
410	Charlie O'Brien	.05	.02
411	Charlie Hough	.05	.02
412	Gus Polidor	.05	.02
413	Ron Karkovice	.05	.02
414	Trevor Wilson	.05	.02
415	Kevin Ritz	.05	.02
416	Gary Thurman	.05	.02
417	Jeff M. Robinson	.05	.02
418	Scott Terry	.05	.02
419	Tim Laudner	.05	.02
420	Dennis Rasmussen	.05	.02
421	Luis Rivera	.05	.02
422	Jim Corsi	.05	.02
423	Dennis Lamp	.05	.02
424	Ken Caminiti	.20	.09
425	David Wells	.05	.02
426	Norm Charlton	.05	.02
427	Deion Sanders	.20	.09
428	Dion James	.05	.02
429	Chuck Cary	.05	.02
430	Ken Howell	.05	.02
431	Steve Lake	.05	.02
432	Kal Daniels	.05	.02
433	Lance McCullers	.05	.02
434	Lenny Harris	.05	.02
435	Scott Scudder	.05	.02
436	Gene Larkin	.05	.02
437	Dan Quisenberry	.05	.02
438	Steve Olin	.10	.05
439	Mickey Hatcher	.05	.02
440	Willie Wilson	.05	.02
441	Mark Grant	.05	.02
442	Mookie Wilson	.05	.02
443	Alex Trevino	.05	.02
444	Pat Tabler	.05	.02
445	Dave Bergman	.05	.02
446	Todd Burns	.05	.02
447	R.J. Reynolds	.05	.02
448	Jay Buhner	.20	.09
449	Lee Stevens	.05	.02
450	Ron Hassey	.05	.02
451	Bob Melvin	.05	.02
452	Dave Martinez	.05	.02
453	Greg Litton	.05	.02
454	Mark Carreon	.05	.02
455	Scott Fletcher	.05	.02
456	Otis Nixon	.10	.05
457	Tony Fossas	.05	.02
458	John Russell	.05	.02
459	Paul Assenmacher	.05	.02
460	Zane Smith	.05	.02
461	Jack Daugherty	.05	.02
462	Rich Monteleone	.05	.02
463	Greg Briley	.05	.02
464	Mike Smithson	.05	.02
465	Benito Santiago	.05	.02
466	Jeff Brantley	.05	.02
467	Jose Nunez	.05	.02
468	Scott Bailes	.05	.02
469	Ken Griffey Sr.	.05	.02
470	Bob McClure	.05	.02
471	Mackey Sasser	.05	.02
472	Glenn Wilson	.05	.02
473	Kevin Tapani	.10	.05
474	Bill Buckner	.10	.05
475	Ron Gant	.10	.05
476	Kevin Romine	.05	.02
477	Juan Agosto	.05	.02
478	Herm Winningham	.05	.02
479	Storm Davis	.05	.02
480	Jeff King	.10	.05
481	Kevin Mmahat	.05	.02
482	Carmelo Martinez	.05	.02
483	Omar Vizquel	.20	.09
484	Jim Dwyer	.05	.02
485	Bob Knepper	.05	.02
486	Dave Anderson	.05	.02

☐ 487	Ron Jones	.05	.02
☐ 488	Jay Bell	.10	.05
☐ 489	Sammy Sosa	.75	.35
☐ 490	Kent Anderson	.05	.02
☐ 491	Domingo Ramos	.05	.02
☐ 492	Dave Clark	.05	.02
☐ 493	Tim Birtsas	.05	.02
☐ 494	Ken Oberkfell	.05	.02
☐ 495	Larry Sheets	.05	.02
☐ 496	Jeff Kunkel	.05	.02
☐ 497	Jim Presley	.05	.02
☐ 498	Mike Macfarlane	.05	.02
☐ 499	Pete Smith	.05	.02
☐ 500A	Checklist 436-537 DP	.05	
☐ 500B	Checklist 420-517	.05	.02
☐ 501	Gary Sheffield	.25	.11
☐ 502	Terry Bross	.05	.02
☐ 503	Jerry Kutzler	.05	.02
☐ 504	Lloyd Moseby	.05	.02
☐ 505	Curt Young	.05	.02
☐ 506	Al Newman	.05	.02
☐ 507	Keith Miller	.05	.02
☐ 508	Mike Stanton	.05	.02
☐ 509	Rich Yett	.05	.02
☐ 510	Tim Drummond	.05	.02
☐ 511	Joe Hesketh	.05	.02
☐ 512	Rick Wrona	.05	.02
☐ 513	Luis Salazar	.05	.02
☐ 514	Hal Morris	.05	.02
☐ 515	Terry Mulholland	.05	.02
☐ 516	John Morris	.05	.02
☐ 517	Carlos Quintana	.05	.02
☐ 518	Frank DiPino	.05	.02
☐ 519	Randy Milligan	.05	.02
☐ 520	Chad Kreuter	.05	.02
☐ 521	Mike Jeffcoat	.05	.02
☐ 522	Mike Harkey	.05	.02
☐ 523A	Andy Nezelek ERR (Wrong birth year)	.05	.02
☐ 523B	Andy Nezelek COR (Finally corrected in factory sets)	.20	.09
☐ 524	Dave Schmidt	.05	.02
☐ 525	Tony Armas	.05	.02
☐ 526	Barry Lyons	.05	.02
☐ 527	Rick Reed	.05	.02
☐ 528	Jerry Reuss	.05	.02
☐ 529	Dean Palmer	.25	.11
☐ 530	Jeff Peterek	.05	.02
☐ 531	Carlos Martinez	.05	.02
☐ 532	Atlee Hammaker	.05	.02
☐ 533	Mike Brumley	.05	.02
☐ 534	Terry Leach	.05	.02
☐ 535	Doug Strange	.05	.02
☐ 536	Jose DeLeon	.05	.02
☐ 537	Shane Rawley	.05	.02
☐ 538	Joey Cora	.20	.09
☐ 539	Eric Hetzel	.05	.02
☐ 540	Gene Nelson	.05	.02
☐ 541	Wes Gardner	.05	.02
☐ 542	Mark Portugal	.05	.02
☐ 543	Al Leiter	.20	.09
☐ 544	Jack Armstrong	.05	.02
☐ 545	Greg Cadaret	.05	.02
☐ 546	Rod Nichols	.05	.02
☐ 547	Luis Polonia	.05	.02
☐ 548	Charlie Hayes	.05	.02
☐ 549	Dickie Thon	.05	.02
☐ 550	Tim Crews	.05	.02
☐ 551	Dave Winfield	.20	.09
☐ 552	Mike Davis	.05	.02
☐ 553	Ron Robinson	.05	.02
☐ 554	Carmen Castillo	.05	.02
☐ 555	John Costello	.05	.02
☐ 556	Bud Black	.05	.02
☐ 557	Rick Dempsey	.05	.02
☐ 558	Jim Acker	.05	.02
☐ 559	Eric Show	.05	.02
☐ 560	Pat Borders	.05	.02
☐ 561	Danny Darwin	.05	.02
☐ 562	Rick Luecken	.05	.02
☐ 563	Edwin Nunez	.05	.02
☐ 564	Felix Jose	.05	.02
☐ 565	John Cangelosi	.05	.02
☐ 566	Bill Swift	.05	.02
☐ 567	Bill Schroeder	.05	.02
☐ 568	Stan Javier	.05	.02
☐ 569	Jim Traber	.05	.02
☐ 570	Wallace Johnson	.05	.02
☐ 571	Donell Nixon	.05	.02
☐ 572	Sid Fernandez	.05	.02
☐ 573	Lance Johnson	.05	.02
☐ 574	Andy McGaffigan	.05	.02
☐ 575	Mark Knudson	.05	.02
☐ 576	Tommy Greene	.05	.02
☐ 577	Mark Grace	.20	.09
☐ 578	Larry Walker	1.00	.45
☐ 579	Mike Stanley	.05	.02
☐ 580	Mike Witt DP	.05	.02
☐ 581	Scott Bradley	.05	.02
☐ 582	Greg A. Harris	.05	.02
☐ 583A	Kevin Hickey ERR	.20	.09
☐ 583B	Kevin Hickey COR	.05	.02
☐ 584	Lee Mazzilli	.05	.02
☐ 585	Jeff Pico	.05	.02
☐ 586	Joe Oliver	.05	.02
☐ 587	Willie Fraser DP	.05	.02
☐ 588	Carl Yastrzemski Puzzle Card DP	.20	.09
☐ 589	Kevin Bass DP	.05	.02
☐ 590	John Moses DP	.05	.02
☐ 591	Tom Pagnozzi DP	.05	.02
☐ 592	Tony Castillo DP	.05	.02
☐ 593	Jerald Clark DP	.05	.02
☐ 594	Dan Schatzeder	.05	.02
☐ 595	Luis Quinones DP	.05	.02
☐ 596	Pete Harnisch DP	.05	.02
☐ 597	Gary Redus	.05	.02
☐ 598	Mel Hall	.05	.02
☐ 599	Rick Schu	.05	.02
☐ 600A	Checklist 538-639	.05	.02
☐ 600B	Checklist 518-617	.05	.02
☐ 601	Mike Kingery DP	.05	.02
☐ 602	Terry Kennedy DP	.05	.02
☐ 603	Mike Sharperson DP	.05	.02
☐ 604	Don Carman DP	.05	.02
☐ 605	Jim Gott	.05	.02
☐ 606	Donn Pall DP	.05	.02
☐ 607	Rance Mulliniks	.05	.02
☐ 608	Curt Wilkerson DP	.05	.02
☐ 609	Mike Felder DP	.05	.02
☐ 610	Guillermo Hernandez DP	.05	.02
☐ 611	Candy Maldonado DP	.05	.02
☐ 612	Mark Thurmond DP	.05	.02
☐ 613	Rick Leach DP	.05	.02
☐ 614	Jerry Reed DP	.05	.02
☐ 615	Franklin Stubbs	.05	.02
☐ 616	Billy Hatcher DP	.05	.02
☐ 617	Don August DP	.05	.02
☐ 618	Tim Teufel	.05	.02
☐ 619	Shawn Hillegas DP	.05	.02
☐ 620	Manny Lee	.05	.02
☐ 621	Gary Ward DP	.05	.02
☐ 622	Mark Guthrie DP	.05	.02
☐ 623	Jeff Musselman DP	.05	.02
☐ 624	Mark Lemke DP	.05	.02
☐ 625	Fernando Valenzuela	.10	.05
☐ 626	Paul Sorrento DP	.20	.09
☐ 627	Glenallen Hill DP	.05	.02
☐ 628	Les Lancaster DP	.05	.02
☐ 629	Vance Law DP	.05	.02
☐ 630	Randy Velarde DP	.05	.02
☐ 631	Todd Frohwirth DP	.05	.02
☐ 632	Willie McGee	.10	.05
☐ 633	Dennis Boyd DP	.05	.02
☐ 634	Cris Carpenter DP	.05	.02
☐ 635	Brian Holton	.05	.02
☐ 636	Tracy Jones DP	.05	.02
☐ 637A	Terry Steinbach AS (Recent Major League Performance)	.05	.02
☐ 637B	Terry Steinbach AS (All-Star Game Performance)	.05	.02
☐ 638	Brady Anderson	.20	.09
☐ 639A	Jack Morris ERR (Card front shows black line crossing J in Jack)	.05	.02
☐ 639B	Jack Morris COR	.05	.02
☐ 640	Jaime Navarro	.05	.02
☐ 641	Darrin Jackson	.05	.02
☐ 642	Mike Dyer	.05	.02
☐ 643	Mike Schmidt	.25	.11
☐ 644	Henry Cotto	.05	.02
☐ 645	John Cerutti	.05	.02
☐ 646	Francisco Cabrera	.05	.02
☐ 647	Scott Sanderson	.05	.02
☐ 648	Brian Meyer	.05	.02
☐ 649	Ray Searage	.05	.02
☐ 650A	Bo Jackson AS (Recent Major League Performance)	.10	.05
☐ 650B	Bo Jackson AS (All-Star Game Performance)	.10	.05
☐ 651	Steve Lyons	.05	.02
☐ 652	Mike LaCoss	.05	.02
☐ 653	Ted Power	.05	.02
☐ 654A	Howard Johnson AS (Recent Major League Performance)	.05	.02
☐ 654B	Howard Johnson AS (All-Star Game Performance)	.05	.02
☐ 655	Mauro Gozzo	.05	.02
☐ 656	Mike Blowers	.05	.09
☐ 657	Paul Gibson	.05	.02
☐ 658	Neal Heaton	.05	.02
☐ 659	Nolan Ryan 5000K COR (Still an error as Ryan did not lead AL in K's in '75)	.40	.18
☐ 659A	Nolan Ryan 5000K (665 King of Kings back) ERR	1.50	.70
☐ 660A	Harold Baines AS (Black line through star on front; Recent Major League Performance)	.75	.35
☐ 660B	Harold Baines AS (Black line through star on front; All-Star Game Performance)	1.00	.45
☐ 660C	Harold Baines AS (Black line behind star on front; Recent Major League Performance)	.20	.09
☐ 660D	Harold Baines AS (Black line behind star on front; All-Star Game Performance)	.05	.02
☐ 661	Gary Pettis	.05	.02
☐ 662	Clint Zavaras	.05	.02
☐ 663A	Rick Reuschel AS (Recent Major League Performance)	.05	.02
☐ 663B	Rick Reuschel AS (All-Star Game Performance)	.05	.02
☐ 664	Alejandro Pena	.05	.02
☐ 665	Nolan Ryan KING COR	.40	.18
☐ 665A	Nolan Ryan KING (659 5000 K back) ERR	1.50	.70
☐ 665C	Nolan Ryan KING ERR (No number on back; in factory sets)	.75	.35
☐ 666	Ricky Horton	.05	.02
☐ 667	Curt Schilling	.20	.09
☐ 668	Bill Landrum	.05	.02
☐ 669	Todd Stottlemyre	.10	.05
☐ 670	Tim Leary	.05	.02
☐ 671	John Wetteland	.20	.09
☐ 672	Calvin Schiraldi	.05	.02
☐ 673A	Ruben Sierra AS (Recent Major League Performance)	.05	.02
☐ 673B	Ruben Sierra AS (All-Star Game Performance)	.05	.02
☐ 674A	Pedro Guerrero AS (Recent Major League Performance)	.05	.02

674B Pedro Guerrero AS .05 .02
(All-Star Game Performance)
675 Ken Phelps .05 .02
676 Cal Ripken AS .40 .18
676A Cal Ripken AS .75 .35
(Recent Major League Performance)
677 Denny Walling .05 .02
678 Goose Gossage .10 .05
679 Gary Mielke .05 .02
680 Bill Bathe .05 .02
681 Tom Lawless .05 .02
682 Xavier Hernandez .05 .02
683A Kirby Puckett AS .20 .09
(Recent Major League Performance)
683B Kirby Puckett AS .20 .09
(All-Star Game Performance)
684 Mariano Duncan .05 .02
685 Ramon Martinez .15 .07
686 Tim Jones .05 .02
687 Tom Filer .05 .02
688 Steve Lombardozzi .05 .02
689 Bernie Williams .75 .35
690 Chip Hale .05 .02
691 Beau Allred .05 .02
692A Ryne Sandberg AS .. .20
(Recent Major League Performance)
692B Ryne Sandberg AS .. .09
(All-Star Game Performance)
693 Jeff Huson .05 .02
694 Curt Ford .05 .02
695A Eric Davis AS .05 .02
(Recent Major League Performance)
695B Eric Davis AS .05 .02
(All-Star Game Performance)
696 Scott Lusader .05 .02
697A Mark McGwire AS .20 .09
(Recent Major League Performance)
697B Mark McGwire AS .10 .05
(All-Star Game Performance)
698 Steve Cummings .05 .02
699 George Canale .05 .02
700A Checklist 640-715 .20 .09
and BC1-BC26
700B Checklist 640-716 .10 .05
and BC1-BC26
700C Checklist 618-716 .05 .02
701A Julio Franco AS .05 .02
(Recent Major League Performance)
701B Julio Franco AS .05 .02
(All-Star Game Performance)
702 Dave Johnson (P) .05 .02
703A Dave Stewart AS .05 .02
(Recent Major League Performance)
703B Dave Stewart AS .05 .02
(All-Star Game Performance)
704 Dave Justice .75 .35
705 Tony Gwynn AS .25 .11
(All-Star Game Performance)
705A Tony Gwynn AS .20 .09
(Recent Major League Performance)
706 Greg Myers .05 .02
707A Will Clark AS .20 .09
(Recent Major League Performance)
707B Will Clark AS .20 .09
(All-Star Game Performance)
708A Benito Santiago AS .. .05
(Recent Major League Performance)
708B Benito Santiago AS .. .05 .02
(All-Star Game Performance)
709 Larry McWilliams .05 .02
710A Ozzie Smith AS .20 .09
(Recent Major League Performance)
710B Ozzie Smith AS .10 .05
(All-Star Game Performance)
711 John Olerud .20 .09
712A Wade Boggs AS .10 .05
(Recent Major League Performance)
712B Wade Boggs AS .10 .05
(All-Star Game Performance)
713 Gary Eave .05 .02
714 Bob Tewksbury .05 .02
715A Kevin Mitchell AS .05 .02
(Recent Major League Performance)
715B Kevin Mitchell AS .05 .02
(All-Star Game Performance)
716 Bart Giamatti COMM .20 .09
(In Memoriam)

1990 Donruss Rookies

The 1990 Donruss Rookies set marked the fifth consecutive year that Donruss issued a boxed set honoring the best rookies of the season. This set, which used the 1990 Donruss design but featured a green border, was issued exclusively through the Donruss dealer network to hobby stores. This 56-card, standard size set came in its own box and the words "The Rookies" are featured prominently on the front of the cards. The only notable Rookie Card in this set is Carlos Baerga.

	MINT	NRMT
COMPLETE SET (56)	2.00	.90
COMMON CARD (1-56)	.05	.02
MINOR STARS	.10	.05
UNLISTED STARS	.20	.09

1 Sandy Alomar Jr. UER .20 .09
(No stitches on baseball on Donruss logo on card front)
2 John Olerud .20 .09
3 Pat Combs .05 .02
4 Brian DuBois .05 .02
5 Felix Jose .05 .02
6 Delino DeShields .10 .05
7 Mike Stanton .05 .02
8 Mike Munoz .05 .02
9 Craig Grebeck .05 .02
10 Joe Kraemer .05 .02
11 Jeff Huson .05 .02
12 Bill Sampen .05 .02
13 Brian Bohanon .05 .02
14 Dave Justice .75 .35
15 Robin Ventura .20 .09
16 Greg Vaughn .10 .05
17 Wayne Edwards .05 .02
18 Shawn Boskie .05 .02
19 Carlos Baerga .25 .11
20 Mark Gardner .05 .02
21 Kevin Appier .20 .09
22 Mike Harkey .05 .02
23 Tim Layana .05 .02
24 Glenallen Hill .05 .02
25 Jerry Kutzler .05 .02
26 Mike Blowers .20 .09
27 Scott Ruskin .05 .02
28 Dana Kiecker .05 .02
29 Willie Blair .05 .02
30 Ben McDonald .15 .07
31 Todd Zeile .10 .05
32 Scott Coolbaugh .05 .02
33 Xavier Hernandez .05 .02
34 Mike Hartley .05 .02
35 Kevin Tapani .10 .05
36 Kevin Wickander .05 .02
37 Carlos Hernandez .05 .02
38 Brian Traxler .05 .02
39 Marty Brown .05 .02
40 Scott Radinsky .05 .02
41 Julio Machado .05 .02
42 Steve Avery .05 .02
43 Mark Lemke .05 .02
44 Alan Mills .05 .02
45 Marquis Grissom .40 .18
46 Greg Olson .05 .02
47 Dave Hollins .20 .09
48 Jerald Clark .05 .02
49 Eric Anthony .10 .05
50 Tim Drummond .05 .02
51 John Burkett .10 .05
52 Brent Knackert .05 .02
53 Jeff Shaw .05 .02
54 John Orton .05 .02
55 Terry Shumpert .05 .02
56 Checklist 1-56 .05 .02

1991 Donruss

The 1991 Donruss set was issued in two series of 386 and 384 for a total of 770 standard-size cards. This set marked the first time Donruss issued cards in multiple series. The second series was issued approximately three months after the first series was issued. Cards were issued in wax packs and factory sets. As a separate promotion, wax packs were also given away with six and 12-packs of Coke and Diet Coke. First series cards feature blue bor-

ders and second series green borders with some stripes and the players name in white against a red background. Subsets include Diamond Kings (1-27), Rated Rookies (28-47/413-432), AL All-Stars (48-56), MVP's (387-412) and NL All-Stars (433-441). There were also special cards to honor the award winners and the heroes of the World Series. Rookie Cards in the set include Jeff Conine and Brian McRae. On cards 60, 70, 127, 182, 239, 294, 355, 368, and 377, the border stripes are red and yellow.

	MINT	NRMT
COMPLETE SET (770)	8.00	3.60
COMP.FACT.w/LEAF PREV.	10.00	4.50
COMP.FACT.w/STUDIO PREV	10.00	4.50
COMMON CARD (1-770)	.05	.02
MINOR STARS	.10	.05
UNLISTED STARS	.20	.09
SUBSET CARDS HALF VALUE OF BASE CARDS		
COMP.BONUS CARD SET (22)	1.50	.70
BONUS CARDS: RANDOM INSERTS IN PACKS		
COMP.'G'SLAMMERS (14)	2.00	.90
ONE G'SLAMMER SET PER FACT.SET		

□ 1 Dave Stieb DK ... .05 .02
□ 2 Craig Biggio DK ... .10 .05
□ 3 Cecil Fielder DK ... .05 .02
□ 4 Barry Bonds DK ... .20 .09
□ 5 Barry Larkin DK ... .10 .05
□ 6 Dave Parker DK ... .05 .02
□ 7 Len Dykstra DK ... .05 .02
□ 8 Bobby Thigpen DK ... .05 .02
□ 9 Roger Clemens DK ... .20 .09
□ 10 Ron Gant DK UER ... .10 .05
(No trademark on team logo on back)
□ 11 Delino DeShields DK ... .05 .02
□ 12 Roberto Alomar DK UER .10 .05
(No trademark on team logo on back)
□ 13 Sandy Alomar Jr. DK ... .10 .05
□ 14 Ryne Sandberg DK UER .20 .09
(Was DK in '85, not '83 as shown)
□ 15 Ramon Martinez DK ... .05 .02
□ 16 Edgar Martinez DK ... .10 .05
□ 17 Dave Magadan DK ... .05 .02
□ 18 Matt Williams DK ... .10 .05
□ 19 Rafael Palmeiro DK ... .05 .02
UER (No trademark on team logo on back)
□ 20 Bob Welch DK ... .05 .02
□ 21 Dave Righetti DK ... .05 .02
□ 22 Brian Harper DK ... .05 .02
□ 23 Gregg Olson DK ... .05 .02
□ 24 Kurt Stillwell DK ... .05 .02
□ 25 Pedro Guerrero DK UER .05 .02
(No trademark on team logo on back)
□ 26 Chuck Finley DK UER .. .05 .02
(No trademark on team logo on back)
□ 27 DK Checklist 1-27 ... .05 .02
□ 28 Tino Martinez RR ... .20 .09
□ 29 Mark Lewis RR ... .05 .02
□ 30 Bernard Gilkey RR ... .10 .05
□ 31 Hensley Meulens RR ... .05 .02
□ 32 Derek Bell RR ... .20 .09
□ 33 Jose Offerman RR ... .05 .02
□ 34 Terry Bross RR ... .05 .02
□ 35 Leo Gomez RR ... .05 .02
□ 36 Derrick May RR ... .05 .02
□ 37 Kevin Morton RR ... .05 .02
□ 38 Moises Alou RR ... .20 .09
□ 39 Julio Valera RR ... .05 .02
□ 40 Milt Cuyler RR ... .05 .02
□ 41 Phil Plantier RR ... .10 .05
□ 42 Scott Chiamparino RR.. .05 .02
□ 43 Ray Lankford RR ... .20 .09

□ 44 Mickey Morandini RR .. .05 .02
□ 45 Dave Hansen RR ... .05 .02
□ 46 Kevin Belcher RR ... .05 .02
□ 47 Darrin Fletcher RR ... .05 .02
□ 48 Steve Sax AS ... .05 .02
□ 49 Ken Griffey AS ... .75 .35
□ 50A Jose Canseco AS ERR .10 .05
(Team in stat box should be AL, not A's)
□ 50B Jose Canseco AS COR .75 .35
□ 51 Sandy Alomar Jr. AS ... .10 .05
□ 52 Cal Ripken AS ... .40 .18
□ 53 Rickey Henderson AS ... .05 .02
□ 54 Bob Welch AS ... .05 .02
□ 55 Wade Boggs AS ... .10 .05
□ 56 Mark McGwire AS ... .20 .09
□ 57A Jack McDowell ERR .. .20 .09
(Career stats do not include 1990)
□ 57B Jack McDowell COR .. .25 .11
(Career stats do not include 1990)
□ 58 Jose Lind ... .05 .02
□ 59 Alex Fernandez ... .10 .05
□ 60 Pat Combs ... .05 .02
□ 61 Mike Walker ... .05 .02
□ 62 Juan Samuel ... .05 .02
□ 63 Mike Blowers UER ... .05 .02
(Last line has aseball, not baseball)
□ 64 Mark Guthrie ... .05 .02
□ 65 Mark Salas ... .05 .02
□ 66 Tim Jones ... .05 .02
□ 67 Tim Leary ... .05 .02
□ 68 Andres Galarraga ... .05 .02
□ 69 Bob Milacki ... .05 .02
□ 70 Tim Belcher ... .05 .02
□ 71 Todd Zeile ... .10 .05
□ 72 Jerome Walton ... .05 .02
□ 73 Kevin Seitzer ... .05 .02
□ 74 Jerald Clark ... .05 .02
□ 75 John Smoltz UER ... .20 .09
(Born in Detroit, not Warren)
□ 76 Mike Henneman ... .05 .02
□ 77 Ken Griffey Jr. ... 1.50 .70
□ 78 Jim Abbott ... .10 .05
□ 79 Gregg Jefferies ... .05 .02
□ 80 Kevin Reimer ... .05 .02
□ 81 Roger Clemens ... .40 .18
□ 82 Mike Fitzgerald ... .05 .02
□ 83 Bruce Hurst UER ... .05 .02
(Middle name is Lee, not Vee)
□ 84 Eric Davis ... .10 .05
□ 85 Paul Molitor ... .20 .09
□ 86 Will Clark ... .20 .09
□ 87 Mike Bielecki ... .05 .02
□ 88 Bret Saberhagen ... .05 .02
□ 89 Nolan Ryan ... .75 .35
□ 90 Bobby Thigpen ... .05 .02
□ 91 Dickie Thon ... .05 .02
□ 92 Duane Ward ... .05 .02
□ 93 Luis Polonia ... .05 .02
□ 94 Terry Kennedy ... .05 .02
□ 95 Kent Hrbek ... .10 .05
□ 96 Danny Jackson ... .05 .02
□ 97 Sid Fernandez ... .05 .02
□ 98 Jimmy Key ... .10 .05
□ 99 Franklin Stubbs ... .05 .02
□ 100 Checklist 28-103 ... .05 .02
□ 101 R.J. Reynolds ... .05 .02
□ 102 Dave Stewart ... .10 .05
□ 103 Dan Pasqua ... .05 .02
□ 104 Dan Plesac ... .05 .02
□ 105 Mark McGwire ... .40 .18
□ 106 John Farrell ... .05 .02
□ 107 Don Mattingly ... .30 .14
□ 108 Carlton Fisk ... .20 .09
□ 109 Ken Oberkfell ... .05 .02
□ 110 Darrel Akerfelds ... .05 .02
□ 111 Gregg Olson ... .05 .02
□ 112 Mike Scioscia ... .05 .02
□ 113 Bryn Smith ... .05 .02
□ 114 Bob Geren ... .05 .02
□ 115 Tom Candiotti ... .05 .02

□ 116 Kevin Tapani ... .05 .02
□ 117 Jeff Treadway ... .05 .02
□ 118 Alan Trammell ... .15 .07
□ 119 Pete O'Brien ... .05 .02
(Blue shading goes through stats)
□ 120 Joel Skinner ... .05 .02
□ 121 Mike LaValliere ... .05 .02
□ 122 Dwight Evans ... .10 .05
□ 123 Jody Reed ... .05 .02
□ 124 Lee Guetterman ... .05 .02
□ 125 Tim Burke ... .05 .02
□ 126 Dave Johnson ... .05 .02
□ 127 Fernando Valenzuela .. .10 .05
(Lower large stripe in yellow instead of blue)
□ 128 Jose DeLeon ... .05 .02
□ 129 Andre Dawson ... .20 .09
□ 130 Gerald Perry ... .05 .02
□ 131 Greg W. Harris ... .05 .02
□ 132 Tom Glavine ... .20 .09
□ 133 Lance McCullers ... .05 .02
□ 134 Randy Johnson ... .25 .11
□ 135 Lance Parrish UER ... .05 .02
(Born in McKeesport, not Clairton)
□ 136 Mackey Sasser ... .05 .02
□ 137 Geno Petralli ... .05 .02
□ 138 Dennis Lamp ... .05 .02
□ 139 Dennis Martinez ... .10 .05
□ 140 Mike Pagliarulo ... .05 .02
□ 141 Hal Morris ... .05 .02
□ 142 Dave Parker ... .10 .05
□ 143 Brett Butler ... .05 .02
□ 144 Paul Assenmacher ... .05 .02
□ 145 Mark Gubicza ... .05 .02
□ 146 Charlie Hough ... .05 .02
□ 147 Sammy Sosa ... .25 .11
□ 148 Randy Ready ... .05 .02
□ 149 Kelly Gruber ... .05 .02
□ 150 Devon White ... .05 .02
□ 151 Gary Carter ... .20 .09
□ 152 Gene Larkin ... .05 .02
□ 153 Chris Sabo ... .05 .02
□ 154 David Cone ... .10 .05
□ 155 Todd Stottlemyre ... .05 .02
□ 156 Glenn Wilson ... .05 .02
□ 157 Bob Walk ... .05 .02
□ 158 Mike Gallego ... .05 .02
□ 159 Greg Hibbard ... .05 .02
□ 160 Chris Bosio ... .05 .02
□ 161 Mike Moore ... .05 .02
□ 162 Jerry Browne UER ... .05 .02
(Born Christiansted, should be St. Croix)
□ 163 Steve Sax UER ... .05 .02
(No asterisk next to his 1989 At Bats)
□ 164 Melido Perez ... .05 .02
□ 165 Danny Darwin ... .05 .02
□ 166 Roger McDowell ... .05 .02
□ 167 Bill Ripken ... .05 .02
□ 168 Mike Sharperson ... .05 .02
□ 169 Lee Smith ... .10 .05
□ 170 Matt Nokes ... .05 .02
□ 171 Jesse Orosco ... .05 .02
□ 172 Rick Aguilera ... .10 .05
□ 173 Jim Presley ... .05 .02
□ 174 Lou Whitaker ... .10 .05
□ 175 Harold Reynolds ... .05 .02
□ 176 Brook Jacoby ... .05 .02
□ 177 Wally Backman ... .05 .02
□ 178 Wade Boggs ... .20 .09
□ 179 Chuck Cary ... .05 .02
(Comma after DOB, not on other cards)
□ 180 Tom Foley ... .05 .02
□ 181 Pete Harnisch ... .05 .02
□ 182 Mike Morgan ... .05 .02
□ 183 Bob Tewksbury ... .05 .02
□ 184 Joe Girardi ... .10 .05
□ 185 Storm Davis ... .05 .02
□ 186 Ed Whitson ... .05 .02
□ 187 Steve Avery UER ... .05 .02
(Born in New Jersey,

should be Michigan)
□ 188 Lloyd Moseby	.05	.02
□ 189 Scott Bankhead	.05	.02
□ 190 Mark Langston	.05	.02
□ 191 Kevin McReynolds	.05	.02
□ 192 Julio Franco	.05	.02
□ 193 John Dopson	.05	.02
□ 194 Dennis Boyd	.05	.02
□ 195 Bip Roberts	.05	.02
□ 196 Billy Hatcher	.05	.02
□ 197 Edgar Diaz	.05	.02
□ 198 Greg Litton	.05	.02
□ 199 Mark Grace	.20	.09
□ 200 Checklist 104-179	.05	.02
□ 201 George Brett	.40	.18
□ 202 Jeff Russell	.05	.02
□ 203 Ivan Calderon	.05	.02
□ 204 Ken Howell	.05	.02
□ 205 Tom Henke	.05	.02
□ 206 Bryan Harvey	.05	.02
□ 207 Steve Bedrosian	.05	.02
□ 208 Al Newman	.05	.02
□ 209 Randy Myers	.05	.02
□ 210 Daryl Boston	.05	.02
□ 211 Manny Lee	.05	.02
□ 212 Dave Smith	.05	.02
□ 213 Don Slaught	.05	.02
□ 214 Walt Weiss	.05	.02
□ 215 Donn Pall	.05	.02
□ 216 Jaime Navarro	.05	.02
□ 217 Willie Randolph	.10	.05
□ 218 Rudy Seanez	.05	.02
□ 219 Jim Leyritz	.10	.05
□ 220 Ron Karkovice	.05	.02
□ 221 Ken Caminiti	.20	.09
□ 222 Von Hayes	.05	.02
□ 223 Cal Ripken	.75	.35
□ 224 Lenny Harris	.05	.02
□ 225 Milt Thompson	.05	.02
□ 226 Alvaro Espinoza	.05	.02
□ 227 Chris James	.05	.02
□ 228 Dan Gladden	.05	.02
□ 229 Jeff Blauser	.05	.02
□ 230 Mike Heath	.05	.02
□ 231 Omar Vizquel	.20	.09
□ 232 Doug Jones	.05	.02
□ 233 Jeff King	.10	.05
□ 234 Luis Rivera	.05	.02
□ 235 Ellis Burks	.10	.05
□ 236 Greg Cadaret	.05	.02
□ 237 Dave Martinez	.05	.02
□ 238 Mark Williamson	.05	.02
□ 239 Stan Javier	.05	.02
□ 240 Ozzie Smith	.25	.11
□ 241 Shawn Boskie	.05	.02
□ 242 Tom Gordon	.05	.02
□ 243 Tony Gwynn	.50	.23
□ 244 Tommy Gregg	.05	.02
□ 245 Jeff M. Robinson	.05	.02
□ 246 Keith Comstock	.05	.02
□ 247 Jack Howell	.05	.02
□ 248 Keith Miller	.05	.02
□ 249 Bobby Witt	.05	.02
□ 250 Rob Murphy UER	.05	.02

(Shown as on Reds in '89 in stats, should be Red Sox)

□ 251 Spike Owen	.05	.02
□ 252 Garry Templeton	.05	.02
□ 253 Glenn Braggs	.05	.02
□ 254 Ron Robinson	.05	.02
□ 255 Kevin Mitchell	.10	.05
□ 256 Les Lancaster	.05	.02
□ 257 Mel Stottlemyre Jr.	.05	.02
□ 258 Kenny Rogers UER	.05	.02

(IP listed as 171, should be 172)

□ 259 Lance Johnson	.05	.02
□ 260 John Kruk	.10	.05
□ 261 Fred McGriff	.20	.09
□ 262 Dick Schofield	.05	.02
□ 263 Trevor Wilson	.05	.02
□ 264 David West	.05	.02
□ 265 Scott Scudder	.05	.02
□ 266 Dwight Gooden	.10	.05
□ 267 Willie Blair	.05	.02

□ 268 Mark Portugal	.05	.02
□ 269 Doug Drabek	.05	.02
□ 270 Dennis Eckersley	.10	.05
□ 271 Eric King	.05	.02
□ 272 Robin Yount	.20	.09
□ 273 Carney Lansford	.05	.02
□ 274 Carlos Baerga	.10	.05
□ 275 Dave Righetti	.05	.02
□ 276 Scott Fletcher	.05	.02
□ 277 Eric Yelding	.05	.02
□ 278 Charlie Hayes	.05	.02
□ 279 Jeff Ballard	.05	.02
□ 280 Orel Hershiser	.10	.05
□ 281 Jose Oquendo	.05	.02
□ 282 Mike Witt	.05	.02
□ 283 Mitch Webster	.05	.02
□ 284 Greg Gagne	.05	.02
□ 285 Greg Olson	.05	.02
□ 286 Tony Phillips UER	.05	.02

(Born 4/15, should be 4/25)

□ 287 Scott Bradley	.05	.02
□ 288 Cory Snyder UER	.05	.02

(In text, led is repeated and Inglewood is misspelled as Englewood)

□ 289 Jay Bell UER	.10	.05

(Born in Pensacola, not Eglin AFB)

□ 290 Kevin Romine	.05	.02
□ 291 Jeff D. Robinson	.05	.02
□ 292 Steve Frey UER	.05	.02

(Bats left, should be right)

□ 293 Craig Worthington	.05	.02
□ 294 Tim Crews	.05	.02
□ 295 Joe Magrane	.05	.02
□ 296 Hector Villanueva	.05	.02
□ 297 Terry Shumpert	.05	.02
□ 298 Joe Carter	.10	.05
□ 299 Kent Mercker UER	.05	.02

(IP listed as 53, should be 52)

□ 300 Checklist 180-255	.05	.02
□ 301 Chet Lemon	.05	.02
□ 302 Mike Schooler	.05	.02
□ 303 Dante Bichette	.20	.09
□ 304 Kevin Elster	.05	.02
□ 305 Jeff Huson	.05	.02
□ 306 Greg A. Harris	.05	.02
□ 307 Marquis Grissom UER	.20	.09

(Middle name Deon, should be Dean)

□ 308 Calvin Schiraldi	.05	.02
□ 309 Mariano Duncan	.05	.02
□ 310 Bill Spiers	.05	.02
□ 311 Scott Garrelts	.05	.02
□ 312 Mitch Williams	.05	.02
□ 313 Mike Macfarlane	.05	.02
□ 314 Kevin Brown	.10	.05
□ 315 Robin Ventura	.20	.09
□ 316 Darren Daulton	.10	.05
□ 317 Pat Borders	.05	.02
□ 318 Mark Knudson	.05	.02
□ 319 Jeff Brantley	.05	.02
□ 320 Shane Mack	.05	.02
□ 321 Rob Dibble	.05	.02
□ 322 John Franco	.10	.05
□ 323 Junior Felix	.05	.02
□ 324 Casey Candaele	.05	.02
□ 325 Bobby Bonilla	.10	.05
□ 326 Dave Henderson	.05	.02
□ 327 Wayne Edwards	.05	.02
□ 328 Mark Knudson	.05	.02
□ 329 Terry Steinbach	.05	.02
□ 330 Colby Ward UER	.05	.02

(No comma between city and state)

□ 331 Oscar Azocar	.05	.02
□ 332 Scott Radinsky	.05	.02
□ 333 Eric Anthony	.05	.02
□ 334 Steve Lake	.05	.02
□ 335 Bob Melvin	.05	.02
□ 336 Kal Daniels	.05	.02
□ 337 Tom Pagnozzi	.05	.02
□ 338 Alan Mills	.05	.02

□ 339 Steve Olin	.05	.02
□ 340 Juan Berenguer	.05	.02
□ 341 Francisco Cabrera	.05	.02
□ 342 Dave Bergman	.05	.02
□ 343 Henry Cotto	.05	.02
□ 344 Sergio Valdez	.05	.02
□ 345 Bob Patterson	.05	.02
□ 346 John Marzano	.05	.02
□ 347 Dana Kiecker	.05	.02
□ 348 Dion James	.05	.02
□ 349 Hubie Brooks	.05	.02
□ 350 Bill Landrum	.05	.02
□ 351 Bill Sampen	.05	.02
□ 352 Greg Briley	.05	.02
□ 353 Paul Gibson	.05	.02
□ 354 Dave Eiland	.05	.02
□ 355 Steve Finley	.20	.09
□ 356 Bob Boone	.10	.05
□ 357 Steve Buechele	.05	.02
□ 358 Chris Hoiles	.05	.02
□ 359 Larry Walker	.30	.14
□ 360 Frank DiPino	.05	.02
□ 361 Mark Grant	.05	.02
□ 362 Dave Magadan	.05	.02
□ 363 Robby Thompson	.05	.02
□ 364 Lonnie Smith	.05	.02
□ 365 Steve Farr	.05	.02
□ 366 Dave Valle	.05	.02
□ 367 Tim Naehring	.10	.05
□ 368 Jim Acker	.05	.02
□ 369 Jeff Reardon UER	.10	.05

(Born in Pittsfield, not Dalton)

□ 370 Tim Teufel	.05	.02
□ 371 Juan Gonzalez	.75	.35
□ 372 Luis Salazar	.05	.02
□ 373 Rick Honeycutt	.05	.02
□ 374 Greg Maddux	.60	.25
□ 375 Jose Uribe UER	.05	.02

(Middle name Elta, should be Alta)

□ 376 Donnie Hill	.05	.02
□ 377 Don Carman	.05	.02
□ 378 Craig Grebeck	.05	.02
□ 379 Willie Fraser	.05	.02
□ 380 Glenallen Hill	.05	.02
□ 381 Joe Oliver	.05	.02
□ 382 Randy Bush	.05	.02
□ 383 Alex Cole	.05	.02
□ 384 Norm Charlton	.05	.02
□ 385 Gene Nelson	.05	.02
□ 386 Checklist 256-331	.05	.05
□ 387 Rickey Henderson MVP	.10	.05
□ 388 Lance Parrish MVP	.05	.02
□ 389 Fred McGriff MVP	.10	.05
□ 390 Dave Parker MVP	.05	.02
□ 391 Candy Maldonado MVP	.05	.02
□ 392 Ken Griffey Jr. MVP	.75	.35
□ 393 Gregg Olson MVP	.05	.02
□ 394 Rafael Palmeiro MVP	.05	.02
□ 395 Roger Clemens MVP	.20	.09
□ 396 George Brett MVP	.20	.09
□ 397 Cecil Fielder MVP	.10	.05
□ 398 Brian Harper MVP	.05	.02

UER (Major League Performance, should be Career)

□ 399 Bobby Thigpen MVP	.05	.02
□ 400 Roberto Kelly MVP	.05	.02

UER (Second Base on front and OF on back)

□ 401 Danny Darwin MVP	.05	.02
□ 402 Dave Justice MVP	.10	.05
□ 403 Lee Smith MVP	.05	.02
□ 404 Ryne Sandberg MVP	.20	.09
□ 405 Eddie Murray MVP	.10	.05
□ 406 Tim Wallach MVP	.05	.02
□ 407 Kevin Mitchell MVP	.05	.02
□ 408 Darryl Strawberry MVP	.05	.02
□ 409 Joe Carter MVP	.05	.02
□ 410 Len Dykstra MVP	.05	.02
□ 411 Doug Drabek MVP	.05	.02
□ 412 Chris Sabo MVP	.05	.02
□ 413 Paul Marak RR	.05	.02
□ 414 Tim McIntosh RR	.05	.02
□ 415 Brian Barnes RR	.05	.02

416	Eric Gunderson RR	.05	.02
417	Mike Gardiner RR	.05	.02
418	Steve Carter RR	.05	.02
419	Gerald Alexander RR	.05	.02
420	Rich Garces RR	.05	.02
421	Chuck Knoblauch RR	.25	.11
422	Scott Aldred RR	.05	.02
423	Wes Chamberlain RR	.05	.02
424	Larice Dickson RR	.05	.02
425	Greg Colbrunn RR	.05	.02
426	Rich DeLucia RR UER	.05	.02
	(Misspelled Delucia on card)		
427	Jeff Conine RR	.25	.11
428	Steve Decker RR	.05	.02
429	Turner Ward RR	.05	.02
430	Mo Vaughn RR	.40	.18
431	Steve Chitren RR	.05	.02
432	Mike Benjamin RR	.05	.02
433	Ryne Sandberg AS	.20	.09
434	Len Dykstra AS	.05	.02
435	Andre Dawson AS	.10	.05
436A	Mike Scioscia AS	.05	.02
	(White star by name)		
436B	Mike Scioscia AS	.05	.02
	(Yellow star by name)		
437	Ozzie Smith AS	.20	.09
438	Kevin Mitchell AS	.05	.02
439	Jack Armstrong AS	.05	.02
440	Chris Sabo AS	.05	.02
441	Will Clark AS	.05	.02
442	Mel Hall	.05	.02
443	Mark Gardner	.05	.02
444	Mike Devereaux	.05	.02
445	Kirk Gibson	.10	.05
446	Terry Pendleton	.10	.05
447	Mike Harkey	.05	.02
448	Jim Eisenreich	.05	.02
449	Benito Santiago	.05	.02
450	Oddibe McDowell	.05	.02
451	Cecil Fielder	.10	.05
452	Ken Griffey Sr.	.05	.02
453	Bert Blyleven	.10	.05
454	Howard Johnson	.05	.02
455	Monty Fariss UER	.05	.02
	(Misspelled Farris on card)		
456	Tony Pena	.05	.02
457	Tim Raines	.10	.05
458	Dennis Rasmussen	.05	.02
459	Luis Quinones	.05	.02
460	B.J. Surhoff	.10	.05
461	Ernest Riles	.05	.02
462	Rick Sutcliffe	.05	.02
463	Danny Tartabull	.05	.02
464	Pete Incaviglia	.05	.02
465	Carlos Martinez	.05	.02
466	Ricky Jordan	.05	.02
467	John Cerutti	.05	.02
468	Dave Winfield	.20	.09
469	Francisco Oliveras	.05	.02
470	Roy Smith	.05	.02
471	Barry Larkin	.15	.07
472	Ron Darling	.05	.02
473	David Wells	.05	.02
474	Glenn Davis	.05	.02
475	Neal Heaton	.05	.02
476	Ron Hassey	.05	.02
477	Frank Thomas	1.50	.70
478	Greg Vaughn	.05	.02
479	Todd Burns	.05	.02
480	Candy Maldonado	.05	.02
481	Dave LaPoint	.05	.02
482	Alvin Davis	.05	.02
483	Mike Scott	.05	.02
484	Dale Murphy	.20	.09
485	Ben McDonald	.05	.02
486	Jay Howell	.05	.02
487	Vince Coleman	.05	.02
488	Alfredo Griffin	.05	.02
489	Sandy Alomar Jr.	.05	.02
490	Kirby Puckett	.40	.18
491	Andres Thomas	.05	.02
492	Jack Morris	.10	.05
493	Matt Young	.05	.02
494	Greg Myers	.05	.02
495	Barry Bonds	.25	.11
496	Scott Cooper UER	.05	.02
	(No BA for 1990 and career)		
497	Dan Schatzeder	.05	.02
498	Jesse Barfield	.05	.02
499	Jerry Goff	.05	.02
500	Checklist 332-408	.05	.02
501	Anthony Telford	.05	.02
502	Eddie Murray	.20	.09
503	Omar Olivares	.05	.02
504	Ryne Sandberg	.25	.11
505	Jeff Montgomery	.10	.05
506	Mark Parent	.05	.02
507	Ron Gant	.10	.05
508	Frank Tanana	.05	.02
509	Jay Buhner	.20	.09
510	Max Venable	.05	.02
511	Wally Whitehurst	.05	.02
512	Gary Pettis	.05	.02
513	Tom Brunansky	.05	.02
514	Tim Wallach	.05	.02
515	Craig Lefferts	.05	.02
516	Tim Layana	.05	.02
517	Darryl Hamilton	.05	.02
518	Rick Reuschel	.05	.02
519	Steve Wilson	.05	.02
520	Kurt Stillwell	.05	.02
521	Rafael Palmeiro	.20	.09
522	Ken Patterson	.05	.02
523	Len Dykstra	.10	.05
524	Tony Fernandez	.05	.02
525	Kent Anderson	.05	.02
526	Mark Leonard	.05	.02
527	Allan Anderson	.05	.02
528	Tom Browning	.05	.02
529	Frank Viola	.05	.02
530	John Olerud	.10	.05
531	Juan Agosto	.05	.02
532	Zane Smith	.05	.02
533	Scott Sanderson	.05	.02
534	Barry Jones	.05	.02
535	Mike Felder	.05	.02
536	Jose Canseco	.15	.07
537	Felix Fermin	.05	.02
538	Roberto Kelly	.05	.02
539	Brian Holman	.05	.02
540	Mark Davidson	.05	.02
541	Terry Mulholland	.05	.02
542	Randy Milligan	.05	.02
543	Jose Gonzalez	.05	.02
544	Craig Wilson	.05	.02
545	Mike Hartley	.05	.02
546	Greg Swindell	.05	.02
547	Gary Gaetti	.05	.02
548	Dave Justice	.25	.11
549	Steve Searcy	.05	.02
550	Erik Hanson	.05	.02
551	Dave Stieb	.05	.02
552	Andy Van Slyke	.10	.05
553	Mike Greenwell	.05	.02
554	Kevin Maas	.05	.02
555	Delino DeShields	.05	.02
556	Curt Schilling	.20	.09
557	Ramon Martinez	.05	.02
558	Pedro Guerrero	.05	.02
559	Dwight Smith	.05	.02
560	Mark Davis	.05	.02
561	Shawn Abner	.05	.02
562	Charlie Leibrandt	.05	.02
563	John Shelby	.05	.02
564	Bill Swift	.05	.02
565	Mike Fetters	.05	.02
566	Alejandro Pena	.05	.02
567	Ruben Sierra	.25	.11
568	Carlos Quintana	.05	.02
569	Kevin Gross	.05	.02
570	Derek Lilliquist	.05	.02
571	Jack Armstrong	.05	.02
572	Greg Brock	.05	.02
573	Mike Kingery	.05	.02
574	Greg Smith	.05	.02
575	Brian McRae	.20	.09
576	Jack Daugherty	.05	.02
577	Ozzie Guillen	.05	.02
578	Joe Boever	.05	.02
579	Luis Sojo UER	.05	.02
580	Chili Davis	.10	.05
581	Don Robinson	.05	.02
582	Brian Harper	.05	.02
583	Paul O'Neill	.10	.05
584	Bob Ojeda	.05	.02
585	Mookie Wilson	.10	.05
586	Rafael Ramirez	.05	.02
587	Gary Redus	.05	.02
588	Jamie Quirk	.05	.02
589	Shawn Hillegas	.05	.02
590	Tom Edens	.05	.02
591	Joe Klink	.05	.02
592	Charles Nagy	.20	.09
593	Eric Plunk	.05	.02
594	Tracy Jones	.05	.02
595	Craig Biggio	.20	.09
596	Jose DeJesus	.05	.02
597	Mickey Tettleton	.10	.05
598	Chris Gwynn	.05	.02
599	Rex Hudler	.05	.02
600	Checklist 409-506	.05	.02
601	Jim Gott	.05	.02
602	Jeff Manto	.05	.02
603	Nelson Liriano	.05	.02
604	Mark Lemke	.05	.02
605	Clay Parker	.05	.02
606	Edgar Martinez	.20	.09
607	Mark Whiten	.05	.02
608	Ted Power	.05	.02
609	Tom Bolton	.05	.02
610	Tom Herr	.05	.02
611	Andy Hawkins UER	.05	.02
	(Pitched No-Hitter on 7/1, not 7/2)		
612	Scott Ruskin	.05	.02
613	Ron Kittle	.05	.02
614	John Wetteland	.20	.09
615	Mike Perez	.05	.02
616	Dave Clark	.05	.02
617	Brent Mayne	.05	.02
618	Jack Clark	.10	.05
619	Marvin Freeman	.05	.02
620	Edwin Nunez	.05	.02
621	Russ Swan	.05	.02
622	Johnny Ray	.05	.02
623	Charlie O'Brien	.05	.02
624	Joe Bitker	.05	.02
625	Mike Marshall	.05	.02
626	Otis Nixon	.05	.02
627	Andy Benes	.10	.05
628	Ron Oester	.05	.02
629	Ted Higuera	.05	.02
630	Kevin Bass	.05	.02
631	Damon Berryhill	.05	.02
632	Bo Jackson	.15	.07
633	Brad Arnsberg	.05	.02
634	Jerry Willard	.05	.02
635	Tommy Greene	.05	.02
636	Bob MacDonald	.05	.02
637	Kirk McCaskill	.05	.02
638	John Burkett	.05	.02
639	Paul Abbott	.05	.02
640	Todd Benzinger	.05	.02
641	Todd Hundley	.20	.09
642	George Bell	.10	.05
643	Javier Ortiz	.05	.02
644	Sid Bream	.05	.02
645	Bob Welch	.05	.02
646	Phil Bradley	.05	.02
647	Bill Krueger	.05	.02
648	Rickey Henderson	.20	.09
649	Kevin Wickander	.05	.02
650	Steve Balboni	.05	.02
651	Gene Harris	.05	.02
652	Jim Deshaies	.05	.02
653	Jason Grimsley	.05	.02
654	Joe Orsulak	.05	.02
655	Jim Poole	.05	.02
656	Felix Jose	.05	.02
657	Denis Cook	.05	.02
658	Tom Brookens	.05	.02
659	Junior Ortiz	.05	.02
660	Jeff Parrett	.05	.02
661	Jerry Don Gleaton	.05	.02
662	Brent Knackert	.05	.02

☐ 663 Rance Mulliniks	.05	.02
☐ 664 John Smiley	.05	.02
☐ 665 Larry Andersen	.05	.02
☐ 666 Willie McGee	.05	.02
☐ 667 Chris Nabholz	.05	.02
☐ 668 Brady Anderson	.20	.09
☐ 669 Darren Holmes UER	.05	.02
(19 CG's, should be 0)		
☐ 670 Ken Hill	.10	.05
☐ 671 Gary Varsho	.05	.02
☐ 672 Bill Pecota	.05	.02
☐ 673 Fred Lynn	.05	.02
☐ 674 Kevin D. Brown	.05	.02
☐ 675 Dan Petry	.05	.02
☐ 676 Mike Jackson	.05	.02
☐ 677 Wally Joyner	.10	.05
☐ 678 Danny Jackson	.05	.02
☐ 679 Bill Haselman	.05	.02
☐ 680 Mike Boddicker	.05	.02
☐ 681 Mel Rojas	.20	
☐ 682 Roberto Alomar	.20	.09
☐ 683 Dave Justice ROY	.10	.05
☐ 684 Chuck Crim	.05	.02
☐ 685 Matt Williams	.20	.09
☐ 686 Shawon Dunston	.05	.02
☐ 687 Jeff Schulz	.05	.02
☐ 688 John Barfield	.05	.02
☐ 689 Gerald Young	.05	.02
☐ 690 Luis Gonzalez	.20	.09
☐ 691 Frank Wills	.05	.02
☐ 692 Chuck Finley	.05	.02
☐ 693 Sandy Alomar Jr. ROY	.10	.05
☐ 694 Tim Drummond	.05	.02
☐ 695 Herm Winningham	.05	.02
☐ 696 Darryl Strawberry	.10	.05
☐ 697 Al Leiter	.05	.02
☐ 698 Karl Rhodes	.05	.02
☐ 699 Stan Belinda	.05	.02
☐ 700 Checklist 507-604	.05	.02
☐ 701 Lance Blankenship	.05	.02
☐ 702 Willie Stargell PUZ	.20	.09
☐ 703 Jim Gantner	.05	.02
☐ 704 Reggie Harris	.05	.02
☐ 705 Rob Ducey	.05	.02
☐ 706 Tim Hulett	.05	.02
☐ 707 Atlee Hammaker	.05	.02
☐ 708 Xavier Hernandez	.05	.02
☐ 709 Chuck McElroy	.05	.02
☐ 710 John Mitchell	.05	.02
☐ 711 Carlos Hernandez	.05	.02
☐ 712 Geronimo Pena	.05	.02
☐ 713 Jim Neidlinger	.05	.02
☐ 714 John Orton	.05	.02
☐ 715 Terry Leach	.05	.02
☐ 716 Mike Stanton	.05	.02
☐ 717 Walt Terrell	.05	.02
☐ 718 Luis Aquino	.05	.02
☐ 719 Bud Black	.05	.02
(Blue Jays uniform, but Giants logo)		
☐ 720 Bob Kipper	.05	.02
☐ 721 Jeff Gray	.05	.02
☐ 722 Jose Rijo	.05	.02
☐ 723 Curt Young	.05	.02
☐ 724 Jose Vizcaino	.05	.02
☐ 725 Randy Tomlin	.05	.02
☐ 726 Junior Noboa	.05	.02
☐ 727 Bob Welch CY	.05	.02
☐ 728 Gary Ward	.05	.02
☐ 729 Rob Deer	.05	.02
(Brewers uniform, but Tigers logo)		
☐ 730 David Segui	.10	.05
☐ 731 Mark Carreon	.05	.02
☐ 732 Vicente Palacios	.05	.02
☐ 733 Sam Horn	.05	.02
☐ 734 Howard Farmer	.05	.02
☐ 735 Ken Dayley	.05	.02
(Cardinals uniform, but Blue Jays logo)		
☐ 736 Kelly Mann	.05	.02
☐ 737 Joe Grahe	.05	.02
☐ 738 Kelly Downs	.05	.02
☐ 739 Jimmy Kremers	.05	.02
☐ 740 Kevin Appier	.20	.09
☐ 741 Jeff Reed	.05	.02

☐ 742 Jose Rijo WS	.05	.02
☐ 743 Dave Rohde	.05	.02
☐ 744 Dr.Dirt/Mr.Clean	.10	.05
Len Dykstra		
Dale Murphy		
UER (No '91 Donruss logo on card front)		
☐ 745 Paul Sorrento	.05	.02
☐ 746 Thomas Howard	.05	.02
☐ 747 Matt Stark	.05	.02
☐ 748 Harold Baines	.10	.05
☐ 749 Doug Dascenzo	.05	.02
☐ 750 Doug Drabek CY	.05	.02
☐ 751 Gary Sheffield	.20	.09
☐ 752 Terry Lee	.05	.02
☐ 753 Jim Vatcher	.05	.02
☐ 754 Lee Stevens	.05	.02
☐ 755 Randy Veres	.05	.02
☐ 756 Bill Doran	.05	.02
☐ 757 Gary Wayne	.05	.02
☐ 758 Pedro Munoz	.05	.02
☐ 759 Chris Hammond	.05	.02
☐ 760 Checklist 605-702	.05	.02
☐ 761 Rickey Henderson MVP	.10	.05
☐ 762 Barry Bonds MVP	.20	.09
☐ 763 Billy Hatcher WS	.05	.02
UER (Line 13, on should be one)		
☐ 764 Julio Machado	.05	.02
☐ 765 Jose Mesa	.05	.02
☐ 766 Willie Randolph WS	.05	.02
☐ 767 Scott Erickson	.10	.05
☐ 768 Travis Fryman	.20	.09
☐ 769 Rich Rodriguez	.05	.02
☐ 770 Checklist 703-770	.05	.02
and BC1-BC22		

1991 Donruss Elite

These special cards were inserted in the 1991 Donruss first and second series wax packs. Production was limited to a maximum of 10,000 cards for each card in the Elite series, and lesser production for the Sandberg Signature (5,000) and Ryan Legend (7,500) cards. This was the first time that mainstream insert cards were ever numbered allowing for verifiable proof of print runs. The regular Elite cards are photos enclosed in a bronze marble borders which surround an evenly squared photo of the players. The Sandberg Signature card has a green marble border and is signed in a blue sharpie. The Nolan Ryan Legend card is a Dick Perez drawing with silver borders. The cards are all numbered on the back, 1 out of 10,000, etc.

	MINT	NRMT
COMPLETE SET (10)	1000.00	450.00
COMMON CARD (1-8)	20.00	9.00
MINOR STARS	30.00	13.50
SEMISTARS	40.00	18.00
RANDOM INSERTS IN PACKS		
STATED PRINT RUN 10,000 SERIAL #'d SETS		
☐ 1 Barry Bonds	80.00	36.00
☐ 2 George Brett	120.00	55.00
☐ 3 Jose Canseco	60.00	27.00
☐ 4 Andre Dawson	40.00	18.00
☐ 5 Doug Drabek	20.00	9.00
☐ 6 Cecil Fielder	30.00	13.50
☐ 7 Rickey Henderson	40.00	18.00
☐ 8 Matt Williams	60.00	27.00
☐ L1 Nolan Ryan (Legend)	200.00	90.00
☐ S1 Ryne Sandberg	300.00	135.00
(Signature Series)		

1991 Donruss Rookies

The 1991 Donruss Rookies set was issued exclusively in factory set form through hobby dealers. The cards measure the standard size and a mini puzzle featuring Hall of Famer Willie Stargell was included with the set. The fronts feature color action player photos, with white and red borders. Rookie Cards include Jeff Bagwell and Ivan Rodriguez.

	MINT	NRMT
COMPLETE SET (56)	4.00	1.80
COMMON CARD (1-56)	.05	.02
MINOR STARS	.10	.05
UNLISTED STARS	.20	.09
☐ 1 Pat Kelly	.05	.02
☐ 2 Rich DeLucia	.05	.02
☐ 3 Wes Chamberlain	.05	.02
☐ 4 Scott Leius	.05	.02
☐ 5 Darryl Kile	.20	.09
☐ 6 Milt Cuyler	.05	.02
☐ 7 Todd Van Poppel	.20	.09
☐ 8 Ray Lankford	.20	.09
☐ 9 Brian R. Hunter	.05	.02
☐ 10 Tony Perezchica	.05	.02
☐ 11 Ced Landrum	.05	.02
☐ 12 Dave Burba	.05	.02
☐ 13 Ramon Garcia	.05	.02
☐ 14 Ed Sprague	.05	.02
☐ 15 Warren Newson	.05	.02
☐ 16 Paul Faries	.05	.02
☐ 17 Luis Gonzalez	.10	.05
☐ 18 Charles Nagy	.20	.09
☐ 19 Chris Hammond	.05	.02
☐ 20 Frank Castillo	.10	.05
☐ 21 Pedro Munoz	.05	.02
☐ 22 Orlando Merced	.10	.05
☐ 23 Jose Melendez	.05	.02
☐ 24 Kirk Dressendorfer	.05	.02

☐ 25 Heathcliff Slocumb ...... .20 .09
☐ 26 Doug Simons .... .05 .02
☐ 27 Mike Timlin .... .05 .02
☐ 28 Jeff Fassero .... .25 .11
☐ 29 Mark Leiter .... .05 .02
☐ 30 Jeff Bagwell 2.50 1.10
☐ 31 Brian McRae .... .20 .09
☐ 32 Mark Whiten .... .05 .02
☐ 33 Ivan Rodriguez .... 1.50 .70
☐ 34 Wade Taylor .... .05 .02
☐ 35 Darren Lewis .... .05 .02
☐ 36 Mo Vaughn .... .40 .18
☐ 37 Mike Remlinger .... .05 .02
☐ 38 Rick Wilkins .... .05 .02
☐ 39 Chuck Knoblauch .... .25 .11
☐ 40 Kevin Morton .... .05 .02
☐ 41 Carlos Rodriguez .... .05 .02
☐ 42 Mark Lewis .... .05 .02
☐ 43 Brent Mayne .... .05 .02
☐ 44 Chris Haney .... .05 .02
☐ 45 Denis Boucher .... .05 .02
☐ 46 Mike Gardiner .... .05 .02
☐ 47 Jeff Johnson .... .05 .02
☐ 48 Dean Palmer .... .10 .05
☐ 49 Chuck McElroy .... .05 .02
☐ 50 Chris Jones .... .05 .02
☐ 51 Scott Kamieniecki .... .05 .02
☐ 52 Al Osuna .... .05 .02
☐ 53 Rusty Meacham .... .05 .02
☐ 54 Chito Martinez .... .05 .02
☐ 55 Reggie Jefferson .... .15 .07
☐ 56 Checklist 1-56 .... .05 .02

1992 Donruss

JUAN GONZALEZ

The 1992 Donruss set contains 784 standard-size cards issued in two separate series of 396. Cards were issued in first and second series foil wrapped packs in addition to hobby and retail factory sets. One of 21 different puzzle panels featuring Hall of Famer Rod Carew was inserted into each pack. The basic card design features glossy color player photos with white borders. Two-toned blue stripes overlay the top and bottom of the picture. Subsets include Rated Rookies (1-20, 397-421), All-Stars (21-30/422, 431) and Highlights (33, 34, 154, 215, 276, 434, 495, 555, 616, 677). The only notable Rookie Card in the set features John Jaha.

	MINT	NRMT
COMPLETE SET (784)	8.00	3.60
COMP.HOBBY SET (788)	15.00	6.75
COMP.RETAIL SET (788)	8.00	3.60
COMPLETE SERIES 1 (396)	4.00	1.80
COMPLETE SERIES 2 (388)	4.00	1.80
COMMON CARD (1-784)	.05	.02
MINOR STARS	.10	.05
UNLISTED STARS	.20	.09

SUBSET CARDS HALF VALUE OF BASE CARDS
COMP.BONUS CARD SET (8) 2.00 .90
BONUS CARDS: RANDOM INSERTS IN PACKS

☐ 1 Mark Wohlers RR .... .15 .07
☐ 2 Wil Cordero RR .... .05 .02
☐ 3 Kyle Abbott RR .... .05 .02
☐ 4 Dave Nilsson RR .... .10 .05
☐ 5 Kenny Lofton RR .... .75 .35
☐ 6 Luis Mercedes RR .... .05 .02
☐ 7 Roger Salkeld RR .... .05 .02
☐ 8 Eddie Zosky RR .... .05 .02
☐ 9 Todd Van Poppel RR ..... .05 .02
☐ 10 Frank Seminara RR ...... .05 .02
☐ 11 Andy Ashby RR .... .05 .02
☐ 12 Reggie Jefferson RR ..... .10 .05
☐ 13 Ryan Klesko RR .... .40 .18
☐ 14 Carlos Garcia RR .... .05 .02
☐ 15 John Ramos RR .... .05 .02
☐ 16 Eric Karros RR .... .15 .07
☐ 17 Patrick Lennon RR .... .05 .02
☐ 18 Eddie Taubensee RR ..... .05 .02
☐ 19 Roberto Hernandez RR .. .20 .09
☐ 20 D.J. Dozier RR .... .05 .02
☐ 21 Dave Henderson AS ...... .05 .02
☐ 22 Cal Ripken AS .... .20 .09
☐ 23 Wade Boggs AS .... .20 .09
☐ 24 Ken Griffey Jr. AS .... .60 .25
☐ 25 Jack Morris AS .... .05 .02
☐ 26 Danny Tartabull AS ...... .05 .02
☐ 27 Cecil Fielder AS .... .10 .05
☐ 28 Roberto Alomar AS .... .10 .05
☐ 29 Sandy Alomar Jr. AS ..... .05 .02
☐ 30 Rickey Henderson AS .... .10 .05
☐ 31 Ken Hill .... .05 .02
☐ 32 John Habyan .... .05 .02
☐ 33 Otis Nixon HL .... .05 .02
☐ 34 Tim Wallach .... .05 .02
☐ 35 Cal Ripken .... .75 .35
☐ 36 Gary Carter .... .20 .09
☐ 37 Juan Agosto .... .05 .02
☐ 38 Doug Dascenzo .... .05 .02
☐ 39 Kirk Gibson .... .10 .05
☐ 40 Benito Santiago .... .10 .05
☐ 41 Otis Nixon .... .10 .05
☐ 42 Andy Allanson .... .05 .02
☐ 43 Brian Holman .... .05 .02
☐ 44 Dick Schofield .... .05 .02
☐ 45 Dave Magadan .... .05 .02
☐ 46 Rafael Palmeiro .... .15 .07
☐ 47 Jody Reed .... .05 .02
☐ 48 Ivan Calderon .... .05 .02
☐ 49 Greg W. Harris .... .05 .02
☐ 50 Chris Sabo .... .05 .02
☐ 51 Paul Molitor .... .20 .09
☐ 52 Robby Thompson .... .05 .02
☐ 53 Dave Smith .... .05 .02
☐ 54 Mark Davis .... .05 .02
☐ 55 Kevin Brown .... .10 .05
☐ 56 Donn Pall .... .05 .02
☐ 57 Len Dykstra .... .10 .05
☐ 58 Roberto Alomar .... .20 .09
☐ 59 Jeff D. Robinson .... .05 .02
☐ 60 Willie McGee .... .05 .02
☐ 61 Jay Buhner .... .15 .07
☐ 62 Mike Pagliarulo .... .05 .02
☐ 63 Paul O'Neill .... .10 .05
☐ 64 Hubie Brooks .... .05 .02
☐ 65 Kelly Gruber .... .05 .02
☐ 66 Ken Caminiti .... .15 .07
☐ 67 Gary Redus .... .05 .02
☐ 68 Harold Baines .... .10 .05
☐ 69 Charlie Hough .... .05 .02
☐ 70 B.J. Surhoff .... .10 .05
☐ 71 Walt Weiss .... .05 .02
☐ 72 Shawn Hillegas .... .05 .02
☐ 73 Roberto Kelly .... .05 .02
☐ 74 Jeff Ballard .... .05 .02
☐ 75 Craig Biggio .... .15 .07
☐ 76 Pat Combs .... .05 .02
☐ 77 Jeff M. Robinson .... .05 .02
☐ 78 Tim Belcher .... .05 .02
☐ 79 Cris Carpenter .... .05 .02
☐ 80 Checklist 1-79 .... .05 .02
☐ 81 Steve Avery .... .05 .02
☐ 82 Chris James .... .05 .02

☐ 83 Brian Harper .... .05 .02
☐ 84 Charlie Leibrandt .... .05 .02
☐ 85 Mickey Tettleton .... .05 .02
☐ 86 Pete O'Brien .... .05 .02
☐ 87 Danny Darwin .... .05 .02
☐ 88 Bob Walk .... .05 .02
☐ 89 Jeff Reardon .... .10 .05
☐ 90 Bobby Rose .... .05 .02
☐ 91 Danny Jackson .... .05 .02
☐ 92 John Morris .... .05 .02
☐ 93 Bud Black .... .05 .02
☐ 94 Tommy Greene HL .... .05 .02
☐ 95 Rick Aguilera .... .05 .02
☐ 96 Gary Gaetti .... .05 .02
☐ 97 David Cone .... .10 .05
☐ 98 John Olerud .... .10 .05
☐ 99 Joel Skinner .... .05 .02
☐ 100 Jay Bell .... .10 .05
☐ 101 Bob Milacki .... .05 .02
☐ 102 Norm Charlton .... .05 .02
☐ 103 Chuck Crim .... .05 .02
☐ 104 Terry Steinbach .... .10 .05
☐ 105 Juan Samuel .... .05 .02
☐ 106 Steve Howe .... .05 .02
☐ 107 Rafael Belliard .... .05 .02
☐ 108 Joey Cora .... .10 .05
☐ 109 Tommy Greene .... .05 .02
☐ 110 Gregg Olson .... .05 .02
☐ 111 Frank Tanana .... .05 .02
☐ 112 Lee Smith .... .10 .05
☐ 113 Greg A. Harris .... .05 .02
☐ 114 Dwayne Henry .... .05 .02
☐ 115 Chili Davis .... .10 .05
☐ 116 Kent Mercker .... .05 .02
☐ 117 Brian Barnes .... .05 .02
☐ 118 Rich DeLucia .... .05 .02
☐ 119 Andre Dawson .... .15 .07
☐ 120 Carlos Baerga .... .05 .02
☐ 121 Mike LaValliere .... .05 .02
☐ 122 Jeff Gray .... .05 .02
☐ 123 Bruce Hurst .... .05 .02
☐ 124 Alvin Davis .... .05 .02
☐ 125 John Candelaria .... .05 .02
☐ 126 Matt Nokes .... .05 .02
☐ 127 George Bell .... .05 .02
☐ 128 Bret Saberhagen .... .05 .02
☐ 129 Jeff Russell .... .05 .02
☐ 130 Jim Abbott .... .10 .05
☐ 131 Bill Gullickson .... .05 .02
☐ 132 Todd Zeile .... .05 .02
☐ 133 Dave Winfield .... .20 .09
☐ 134 Wally Whitehurst .... .05 .02
☐ 135 Matt Williams .... .15 .07
☐ 136 Tom Browning .... .05 .02
☐ 137 Marquis Grissom .... .10 .05
☐ 138 Erik Hanson .... .05 .02
☐ 139 Rob Dibble .... .05 .02
☐ 140 Don August .... .05 .02
☐ 141 Tom Henke .... .05 .02
☐ 142 Dan Pasqua .... .05 .02
☐ 143 George Brett .... .40 .18
☐ 144 Jerald Clark .... .05 .02
☐ 145 Robin Ventura .... .10 .05
☐ 146 Dale Murphy .... .20 .09
☐ 147 Dennis Eckersley .... .10 .05
☐ 148 Eric Yelding .... .05 .02
☐ 149 Mario Diaz .... .05 .02
☐ 150 Casey Candaele .... .05 .02
☐ 151 Steve Olin .... .05 .02
☐ 152 Luis Salazar .... .05 .02
☐ 153 Kevin Maas .... .05 .02
☐ 154 Nolan Ryan HL .... .40 .18
☐ 155 Barry Jones .... .05 .02
☐ 156 Chris Hoiles .... .05 .02
☐ 157 Bobby Ojeda .... .05 .02
☐ 158 Pedro Guerrero .... .05 .02
☐ 159 Paul Assenmacher .... .05 .02
☐ 160 Checklist 80-157 .... .05 .02
☐ 161 Mike Macfarlane .... .05 .02
☐ 162 Craig Lefferts .... .05 .02
☐ 163 Brian Hunter .... .05 .02
☐ 164 Alan Trammell .... .15 .07
☐ 165 Ken Griffey Jr. .... 1.25 .55
☐ 166 Lance Parrish .... .05 .02
☐ 167 Brian Downing .... .05 .02
☐ 168 John Barfield .... .05 .02

427	Bobby Bonilla AS	.05	.02
428	Will Clark AS	.10	.02
429	Ryne Sandberg AS	.20	.09
430	Benito Santiago AS	.05	.02
431	Ivan Calderon AS	.05	.02
432	Ozzie Smith	.25	.11
433	Tim Leary	.05	.02
434	Bret Saberhagen HL	.05	.02
435	Mel Rojas	.10	.05
436	Ben McDonald	.05	.02
437	Tim Crews	.05	.02
438	Rex Hudler	.05	.02
439	Chico Walker	.05	.02
440	Kurt Stillwell	.05	.02
441	Tony Gwynn	.50	.23
442	John Smoltz	.15	.07
443	Lloyd Moseby	.05	.02
444	Mike Schooler	.05	.02
445	Joe Grahe	.05	.02
446	Dwight Gooden	.10	.05
447	Oil Can Boyd	.05	.02
448	John Marzano	.05	.02
449	Bret Barberie	.05	.02
450	Mike Maddux	.05	.02
451	Jeff Reed	.05	.02
452	Dale Sveum	.05	.02
453	Jose Uribe	.05	.02
454	Bob Scanlan	.05	.02
455	Kevin Appier	.10	.05
456	Jeff Huson	.05	.02
457	Ken Patterson	.05	.02
458	Ricky Jordan	.05	.02
459	Tom Candiotti	.05	.02
460	Lee Stevens	.05	.02
461	Rod Beck	.20	.09
462	Dave Valle	.05	.02
463	Scott Erickson	.10	.05
464	Chris Jones	.05	.02
465	Mark Carreon	.05	.02
466	Rob Ducey	.05	.02
467	Jim Corsi	.05	.02
468	Jeff King	.10	.05
469	Curt Young	.05	.02
470	Bo Jackson	.10	.05
471	Chris Bosio	.05	.02
472	Jamie Quirk	.05	.02
473	Jesse Orosco	.05	.02
474	Alvaro Espinoza	.05	.02
475	Joe Orsulak	.05	.02
476	Checklist 397-477	.05	.02
477	Gerald Young	.05	.02
478	Wally Backman	.05	.02
479	Juan Bell	.05	.02
480	Mike Scioscia	.05	.02
481	Omar Olivares	.05	.02
482	Francisco Cabrera	.05	.02
483	Greg Swindell UER	.05	.02
	(Shown on Indians, but listed on Reds)		
484	Terry Leach	.05	.02
485	Tommy Gregg	.05	.02
486	Scott Aldred	.05	.02
487	Greg Briley	.05	.02
488	Phil Plantier	.05	.02
489	Curtis Wilkerson	.05	.02
490	Tom Brunansky	.05	.02
491	Mike Fetters	.05	.02
492	Frank Castillo	.05	.02
493	Joe Boever	.05	.02
494	Kirt Manwaring	.05	.02
495	Wilson Alvarez HL	.05	.02
496	Gene Larkin	.05	.02
497	Gary DiSarcina	.05	.02
498	Frank Viola	.05	.02
499	Manuel Lee	.05	.02
500	Albert Belle	.25	.11
501	Stan Belinda	.05	.02
502	Dwight Evans	.05	.02
503	Eric Davis	.10	.05
504	Darren Holmes	.05	.02
505	Mike Bordick	.05	.02
506	Dave Hansen	.05	.02
507	Lee Guetterman	.05	.02
508	Keith Mitchell	.05	.02
509	Melido Perez	.05	.02
510	Dickie Thon	.05	.02
511	Mark Williamson	.05	.02
512	Mark Salas	.05	.02
513	Milt Thompson	.05	.02
514	Mo Vaughn	.30	.14
515	Jim Deshaies	.05	.02
516	Rich Garces	.05	.02
517	Lonnie Smith	.05	.02
518	Spike Owen	.05	.02
519	Tracy Jones	.05	.02
520	Greg Maddux	.60	.25
521	Carlos Martinez	.05	.02
522	Neal Heaton	.05	.02
523	Mike Greenwell	.05	.02
524	Andy Benes	.10	.05
525	Jeff Schaefer UER	.05	.02
	(Photo actually Tino Martinez)		
526	Mike Sharperson	.05	.02
527	Wade Taylor	.05	.02
528	Jerome Walton	.05	.02
529	Storm Davis	.05	.02
530	Jose Hernandez	.05	.02
531	Mark Langston	.05	.02
532	Rob Deer	.05	.02
533	Geronimo Pena	.05	.02
534	Juan Guzman	.05	.02
535	Pete Schourek	.05	.02
536	Todd Benzinger	.05	.02
537	Billy Hatcher	.05	.02
538	Tom Foley	.05	.02
539	Dave Cochrane	.05	.02
540	Mariano Duncan	.05	.02
541	Edwin Nunez	.05	.02
542	Rance Mulliniks	.05	.02
543	Carlton Fisk	.20	.09
544	Luis Aquino	.05	.02
545	Ricky Bones	.05	.02
546	Craig Grebeck	.05	.02
547	Charlie Hayes	.05	.02
548	Jose Canseco	.15	.07
549	Andujar Cedeno	.05	.02
550	Geno Petralli	.05	.02
551	Javier Ortiz	.05	.02
552	Rudy Seanez	.05	.02
553	Rich Gedman	.05	.02
554	Eric Plunk	.05	.02
555	Nolan Ryan HL	.25	.11
	(With Rich Gossage)		
556	Checklist 478-555	.05	.02
557	Greg Colbrunn	.05	.02
558	Chito Martinez	.05	.02
559	Darryl Strawberry	.10	.05
560	Luis Alicea	.05	.02
561	Dwight Smith	.05	.02
562	Terry Shumpert	.05	.02
563	Jim Vatcher	.05	.02
564	Deion Sanders	.10	.05
565	Walt Terrell	.05	.02
566	Dave Burba	.05	.02
567	Dave Howard	.05	.02
568	Todd Hundley	.15	.07
569	Jack Daugherty	.05	.02
570	Scott Cooper	.05	.02
571	Bill Sampen	.05	.02
572	Jose Melendez	.05	.02
573	Freddie Benavides	.05	.02
574	Jim Gantner	.05	.02
575	Trevor Wilson	.05	.02
576	Ryne Sandberg	.25	.11
577	Kevin Seitzer	.05	.02
578	Gerald Alexander	.05	.02
579	Mike Huff	.05	.02
580	Von Hayes	.05	.02
581	Derek Bell	.10	.05
582	Mike Stanley	.05	.02
583	Kevin Mitchell	.05	.02
584	Mike Jackson	.05	.02
585	Dan Gladden	.05	.02
586	Ted Power UER	.05	.02
	(Wrong year given for signing with Reds)		
587	Jeff Innis	.05	.02
588	Bob MacDonald	.05	.02
589	Jose Tolentino	.05	.02
590	Bob Patterson	.05	.02
591	Scott Brosius	.05	.02
592	Frank Thomas	1.00	.45
593	Darryl Hamilton	.05	.02
594	Kirk Dressendorfer	.05	.02
595	Jeff Shaw	.05	.02
596	Don Mattingly	.30	.14
597	Glenn Davis	.05	.02
598	Andy Mota	.05	.02
599	Jason Grimsley	.05	.02
600	Jimmy Poole	.05	.02
601	Jim Gott	.05	.02
602	Stan Royer	.05	.02
603	Marvin Freeman	.05	.02
604	Denis Boucher	.05	.02
605	Denny Neagle	.15	.07
606	Mark Lemke	.05	.02
607	Jerry Don Gleaton	.05	.02
608	Brent Knackert	.05	.02
609	Carlos Quintana	.05	.02
610	Bobby Bonilla	.10	.05
611	Joe Hesketh	.05	.02
612	Daryl Boston	.05	.02
613	Shawon Dunston	.05	.02
614	Danny Cox	.05	.02
615	Darren Lewis	.05	.02
616	Braves No-Hitter UER	.05	.02
	Kent Mercker (Misspelled Merker on card front) Alejandro Pena Mark Wohlers		
617	Kirby Puckett	.40	.18
618	Franklin Stubbs	.05	.02
619	Chris Donnels	.05	.02
620	David Wells UER	.05	.02
	(Career Highlights in black not red)		
621	Mike Aldrete	.05	.02
622	Bob Kipper	.05	.02
623	Anthony Telford	.05	.02
624	Randy Myers	.10	.05
625	Willie Randolph	.10	.05
626	Joe Slusarski	.05	.02
627	John Wetteland	.10	.05
628	Greg Cadaret	.05	.02
629	Tom Glavine	.15	.07
630	Wilson Alvarez	.10	.05
631	Wally Ritchie	.05	.02
632	Mike Mussina	.30	.14
633	Mark Leiter	.05	.02
634	Gerald Perry	.05	.02
635	Matt Young	.05	.02
636	Checklist 556-635	.05	.02
637	Scott Hemond	.05	.02
638	David West	.05	.02
639	Jim Clancy	.05	.02
640	Doug Piatt UER	.05	.02
	(Not born in 1955 as on card; incorrect info on How Acquired)		
641	Omar Vizquel	.10	.05
642	Rick Sutcliffe	.05	.02
643	Glenallen Hill	.05	.02
644	Gary Varsho	.05	.02
645	Tony Fossas	.05	.02
646	Jack Howell	.05	.02
647	Jim Campanis	.05	.02
648	Chris Gwynn	.05	.02
649	Jim Leyritz	.05	.02
650	Chuck McElroy	.05	.02
651	Sean Berry	.05	.02
652	Donald Harris	.05	.02
653	Don Slaught	.05	.02
654	Rusty Meacham	.05	.02
655	Scott Terry	.05	.02
656	Ramon Martinez	.10	.05
657	Keith Miller	.05	.02
658	Ramon Garcia	.05	.02
659	Milt Hill	.05	.02
660	Steve Frey	.05	.02
661	Bob McClure	.05	.02
662	Ced Landrum	.05	.02
663	Doug Henry	.05	.02
664	Candy Maldonado	.05	.02
665	Carl Willis	.05	.02
666	Jeff Montgomery	.10	.05
667	Craig Shipley	.05	.02

		MINT	NRMT
☐ 668	Warren Newson	.05	.02
☐ 669	Mickey Morandini	.05	.02
☐ 670	Brook Jacoby	.05	.02
☐ 671	Ryan Bowen	.05	.02
☐ 672	Bill Krueger	.05	.02
☐ 673	Rob Mallicoat	.05	.02
☐ 674	Doug Jones	.05	.02
☐ 675	Scott Livingstone	.05	.02
☐ 676	Danny Tartabull	.05	.02
☐ 677	Joe Carter HL	.10	.05
☐ 678	Cecil Espy	.05	.02
☐ 679	Randy Velarde	.05	.02
☐ 680	Bruce Ruffin	.05	.02
☐ 681	Ted Wood	.05	.02
☐ 682	Dan Plesac	.05	.02
☐ 683	Eric Bullock	.05	.02
☐ 684	Junior Ortiz	.05	.02
☐ 685	Dave Hollins	.05	.02
☐ 686	Dennis Martinez	.10	.05
☐ 687	Larry Andersen	.05	.02
☐ 688	Doug Simons	.05	.02
☐ 689	Tim Spehr	.05	.02
☐ 690	Calvin Jones	.05	.02
☐ 691	Mark Guthrie	.05	.02
☐ 692	Alfredo Griffin	.05	.02
☐ 693	Joe Carter	.10	.05
☐ 694	Terry Mathews	.05	.02
☐ 695	Pascual Perez	.05	.02
☐ 696	Gene Nelson	.05	.02
☐ 697	Gerald Williams	.05	.02
☐ 698	Chris Cron	.05	.02
☐ 699	Steve Buechele	.05	.02
☐ 700	Paul McClellan	.05	.02
☐ 701	Jim Lindeman	.05	.02
☐ 702	Francisco Oliveras	.05	.02
☐ 703	Rob Maurer	.05	.02
☐ 704	Pat Hentgen	.20	.09
☐ 705	Jaime Navarro	.05	.02
☐ 706	Mike Magnante	.05	.02
☐ 707	Nolan Ryan	.75	.35
☐ 708	Bobby Thigpen	.05	.02
☐ 709	John Cerutti	.05	.02
☐ 710	Steve Wilson	.05	.02
☐ 711	Hensley Meulens	.05	.02
☐ 712	Rheal Cormier	.05	.02
☐ 713	Scott Bradley	.05	.02
☐ 714	Mitch Webster	.05	.02
☐ 715	Roger Mason	.05	.02
☐ 716	Checklist 636-716	.05	.02
☐ 717	Jeff Fassero	.05	.02
☐ 718	Cal Eldred	.05	.02
☐ 719	Sid Fernandez	.05	.02
☐ 720	Bob Zupcic	.05	.02
☐ 721	Jose Offerman	.05	.02
☐ 722	Cliff Brantley	.05	.02
☐ 723	Ron Darling	.05	.02
☐ 724	Dave Stieb	.05	.02
☐ 725	Hector Villanueva	.05	.02
☐ 726	Mike Hartley	.05	.02
☐ 727	Arthur Rhodes	.05	.02
☐ 728	Randy Bush	.05	.02
☐ 729	Steve Sax	.05	.02
☐ 730	Dave Otto	.05	.02
☐ 731	John Wehner	.05	.02
☐ 732	Dave Martinez	.05	.02
☐ 733	Ruben Amaro	.05	.02
☐ 734	Billy Ripken	.05	.02
☐ 735	Steve Farr	.05	.02
☐ 736	Shawn Abner	.05	.02
☐ 737	Gil Heredia	.05	.02
☐ 738	Ron Jones	.05	.02
☐ 739	Tony Castillo	.05	.02
☐ 740	Sammy Sosa	.20	.09
☐ 741	Julio Franco	.10	.05
☐ 742	Tim Naehring	.10	.05
☐ 743	Steve Wapnick	.05	.02
☐ 744	Craig Wilson	.05	.02
☐ 745	Darrin Chapin	.05	.02
☐ 746	Chris George	.05	.02
☐ 747	Mike Simms	.05	.02
☐ 748	Rosario Rodriguez	.05	.02
☐ 749	Skeeter Barnes	.05	.02
☐ 750	Roger McDowell	.05	.02
☐ 751	Dann Howitt	.05	.02
☐ 752	Paul Sorrento	.05	.02
☐ 753	Braulio Castillo	.05	.02

		MINT	NRMT
☐ 754	Yorkis Perez	.05	.02
☐ 755	Willie Fraser	.05	.02
☐ 756	Jeremy Hernandez	.05	.02
☐ 757	Curt Schilling	.05	.02
☐ 758	Steve Lyons	.05	.02
☐ 759	Dave Anderson	.05	.02
☐ 760	Willie Banks	.05	.02
☐ 761	Mark Leonard	.05	.02
☐ 762	Jack Armstrong	.05	.02
	(Listed on Indians,		
	but shown on Reds)		
☐ 763	Scott Servais	.05	.02
☐ 764	Ray Stephens	.05	.02
☐ 765	Junior Noboa	.05	.02
☐ 766	Jim Olander	.05	.02
☐ 767	Joe Magrane	.05	.02
☐ 768	Lance Blankenship	.05	.02
☐ 769	Mike Humphreys	.05	.02
☐ 770	Jarvis Brown	.05	.02
☐ 771	Damon Berryhill	.05	.02
☐ 772	Alejandro Pena	.05	.02
☐ 773	Jose Mesa	.05	.02
☐ 774	Gary Cooper	.05	.02
☐ 775	Carney Lansford	.10	.05
☐ 776	Mike Bielecki	.05	.02
	(Shown on Cubs,		
	but listed on Braves)		
☐ 777	Charlie O'Brien	.05	.02
☐ 778	Carlos Hernandez	.05	.02
☐ 779	Howard Farmer	.05	.02
☐ 780	Mike Stanton	.05	.02
☐ 781	Reggie Harris	.05	.02
☐ 782	Xavier Hernandez	.05	.02
☐ 783	Bryan Hickerson	.05	.02
☐ 784	Checklist 717-784	.05	.02
	and BC1-BC8		

1992 Donruss Diamond Kings

These standard-size cards were randomly inserted in 1992 Donruss I foil packs (cards 1-13 and the checklist only) and in 1992 Donruss II foil packs (cards 14-26). The fronts feature player portraits by noted sports artist Dick Perez. The words "Donruss Diamond Kings" are superimposed in a gold-trimmed blue and black banner, with the player's name in a similarly designed black stripe at the card bottom. A very limited amount of 5" by 7" cards were produced. These issues were never formally released but these cards were intended to be premiums in retail products. We are not valuing them currently since trading in these cards is very thin.

	MINT	NRMT
COMPLETE SET (27)	20.00	9.00
COMPLETE SERIES 1 (14)	16.00	7.25

	MINT	NRMT
COMPLETE SERIES 2 (13)	4.00	1.80
COMMON CARD (DK1-DK27)	.50	.23
RANDOM INSERTS IN PACKS		
☐ DK1 Paul Molitor	1.50	.70
☐ DK2 Will Clark	1.00	.45
☐ DK3 Joe Carter	.75	.35
☐ DK4 Julio Franco	.50	.23
☐ DK5 Cal Ripken	6.00	2.70
☐ DK6 Dave Justice	1.50	.70
☐ DK7 George Bell	.50	.23
☐ DK8 Frank Thomas	6.00	2.70
☐ DK9 Wade Boggs	1.50	.70
☐ DK10 Scott Sanderson	.50	.23
☐ DK11 Jeff Bagwell	4.00	1.80
☐ DK12 John Kruk	.75	.35
☐ DK13 Felix Jose	.50	.23
☐ DK14 Harold Baines	.75	.35
☐ DK15 Dwight Gooden	.75	.35
☐ DK16 Brian McRae	.50	.23
☐ DK17 Jay Bell	.75	.35
☐ DK18 Brett Butler	1.00	.45
☐ DK19 Hal Morris	.50	.23
☐ DK20 Mark Langston	.50	.23
☐ DK21 Scott Erickson	.75	.35
☐ DK22 Randy Johnson	1.50	.70
☐ DK23 Greg Swindell	.50	.23
☐ DK24 Dennis Martinez	.75	.35
☐ DK25 Tony Phillips	.50	.23
☐ DK26 Fred McGriff	1.00	.45
☐ DK27 Checklist 1-26 DP	.50	.23
(Dick Perez)		

1992 Donruss Elite

These cards were random inserts in 1992 Donruss first and second series foil packs. Like the previous year, the cards were individually numbered of 10,000. Card fronts feature dramatic prismatic borders encasing a full color action or posed shot of the player. The numbering of the set is essentially a continuation of the series started the year before. Only 5,000 Ripken Signature Series cards were printed and only 7,500 Henderson Legends cards were printed.

	MINT	NRMT
COMPLETE SET (12)	800.00	350.00
COMMON CARD (9-18)	15.00	6.75
SEMISTARS	25.00	11.00
RANDOM INSERTS IN PACKS		
STATED PRINT RUN 10,000 SERIAL #'d SETS		
☐ 9 Wade Boggs	25.00	11.00
☐ 10 Joe Carter	20.00	9.00
☐ 11 Will Clark	25.00	11.00
☐ 12 Dwight Gooden	20.00	9.00
☐ 13 Ken Griffey Jr.	150.00	70.00
☐ 14 Tony Gwynn	60.00	27.00
☐ 15 Howard Johnson	15.00	6.75
☐ 16 Terry Pendleton	15.00	6.75

		MINT	NRMT
☐ 17	Kirby Puckett	50.00	22.00
☐ 18	Frank Thomas	120.00	55.00
☐ L2	Rickey Henderson	30.00	13.50
	(Legend Series)		
☐ S2	Cal Ripken	400.00	180.00
	(Signature Series)		

1992 Donruss Update

GEORGE BELL

STEVE HOSEY

set, Donruss expanded it to a 132-card standard-size set and distributed the cards exclusively in hobby and retail foil packs. The card design is the same as the 1992 Donruss regular issue except that the two-tone blue color bars have been replaced by green, as in the previous six Donruss Rookies sets. The cards are arranged in alphabetical order and numbered on the back. Rookie Cards in this set include Manny Ramirez, Shane Reynolds and Eric Young.

Four cards from this 22-card standard-size set were included in each retail factory set. Card design is identical to regular issue 1992 Donruss cards except for the U-prefixed numbering on back. Card numbers U1-U6 are Rated Rookie cards, while card numbers U7-U9 are Highlights cards. A tough early Kenny Lofton card, his first as a member of the Cleveland Indians, highlights the set.

		MINT	NRMT
COMPLETE SET (22)		60.00	27.00
COMMON CARD (U1-U22)		1.00	.45
MINOR STARS		2.00	.90
SEMISTARS		4.00	1.80
UNLISTED STARS		6.00	2.70
FOUR PER RETAIL FACTORY SET			

☐ U1	Pat Listach RR	1.00	.45
☐ U2	Andy Stankiewicz RR	1.00	.45
☐ U3	Brian Jordan RR	6.00	2.70
☐ U4	Dan Walters RR	2.00	.90
☐ U5	Chad Curtis RR	6.00	2.70
☐ U6	Kenny Lofton RR	30.00	13.50
☐ U7	Mark McGwire HL	12.00	5.50
☐ U8	Eddie Murray HL	6.00	2.70
☐ U9	Jeff Reardon HL	2.00	.90
☐ U10	Frank Viola	1.00	.45
☐ U11	Gary Sheffield	6.00	2.70
☐ U12	George Bell	1.00	.45
☐ U13	Rick Sutcliffe	1.00	.45
☐ U14	Wally Joyner	2.00	.90
☐ U15	Kevin Seitzer	1.00	.45
☐ U16	Bill Krueger	1.00	.45
☐ U17	Danny Tartabull	1.00	.45
☐ U18	Dave Winfield	6.00	2.70
☐ U19	Gary Carter	6.00	2.70
☐ U20	Bobby Bonilla	2.00	.90
☐ U21	Cory Snyder	1.00	.45
☐ U22	Bill Swift	1.00	.45

1992 Donruss Rookies

After six years of issuing "The Rookies" as a 56-card boxed

		MINT	NRMT
COMPLETE SET (132)		5.00	2.20
COMMON CARD (1-132)		.05	.02
MINOR STARS		.10	.05
UNLISTED STARS		.20	.09

☐ 1	Kyle Abbott	.05	.02
☐ 2	Troy Afenir	.05	.02
☐ 3	Rich Amaral	.05	.02
☐ 4	Ruben Amaro	.05	.02
☐ 5	Billy Ashley	.05	.02
☐ 6	Pedro Astacio	.10	.05
☐ 7	Jim Austin	.05	.02
☐ 8	Robert Ayrault	.05	.02
☐ 9	Kevin Baez	.05	.02
☐ 10	Esteban Beltre	.05	.02
☐ 11	Brian Bohanon	.05	.02
☐ 12	Kent Bottenfield	.05	.02
☐ 13	Jeff Branson	.05	.02
☐ 14	Brad Brink	.05	.02
☐ 15	John Briscoe	.05	.02
☐ 16	Doug Brocail	.05	.02
☐ 17	Rico Brogna	.10	.05
☐ 18	J.T. Bruett	.05	.02
☐ 19	Jacob Brumfield	.05	.02
☐ 20	Jim Bullinger	.05	.02
☐ 21	Kevin Campbell	.05	.02
☐ 22	Pedro Castellano	.05	.02
☐ 23	Mike Christopher	.05	.02
☐ 24	Archi Cianfrocco	.05	.02
☐ 25	Mark Clark	.05	.02
☐ 26	Craig Colbert	.05	.02
☐ 27	Victor Cole	.05	.02
☐ 28	Steve Cooke	.05	.02
☐ 29	Tim Costo	.05	.02
☐ 30	Chad Curtis	.20	.09
☐ 31	Doug Davis	.05	.02
☐ 32	Gary DiSarcina	.05	.02
☐ 33	John Doherty	.05	.02
☐ 34	Mike Draper	.05	.02
☐ 35	Monty Fariss	.05	.02
☐ 36	Bien Figueroa	.05	.02
☐ 37	John Flaherty	.05	.02
☐ 38	Tim Fortugno	.05	.02
☐ 39	Eric Fox	.05	.02
☐ 40	Jeff Frye	.05	.02
☐ 41	Ramon Garcia	.05	.02
☐ 42	Brent Gates	.05	.02
☐ 43	Tom Goodwin	.10	.05
☐ 44	Buddy Groom	.05	.02
☐ 45	Jeff Grotewold	.05	.02
☐ 46	Juan Guerrero	.05	.02

☐ 47	Johnny Guzman	.05	.02
☐ 48	Shawn Hare	.05	.02
☐ 49	Ryan Hawblitzel	.05	.02
☐ 50	Bert Heffernan	.05	.02
☐ 51	Butch Henry	.05	.02
☐ 52	Cesar Hernandez	.05	.02
☐ 53	Vince Horsman	.05	.02
☐ 54	Steve Hosey	.05	.02
☐ 55	Pat Howell	.05	.02
☐ 56	Peter Hoy	.05	.02
☐ 57	Jonathan Hurst	.05	.02
☐ 58	Mark Hutton	.05	.02
☐ 59	Shawn Jeter	.05	.02
☐ 60	Joel Johnston	.05	.02
☐ 61	Jeff Kent	.20	.09
☐ 62	Kurt Knudsen	.05	.02
☐ 63	Kevin Koslofski	.05	.02
☐ 64	Danny Leon	.05	.02
☐ 65	Jesse Levis	.05	.02
☐ 66	Tom Marsh	.05	.02
☐ 67	Ed Martin	.05	.02
☐ 68	Al Martin	.20	.09
☐ 69	Pedro Martinez	.40	.18
☐ 70	Derrick May	.05	.02
☐ 71	Matt Maysey	.05	.02
☐ 72	Russ McGinnis	.05	.02
☐ 73	Tim McIntosh	.05	.02
☐ 74	Jim McNamara	.05	.02
☐ 75	Jeff McNeely	.05	.02
☐ 76	Rusty Meacham	.05	.02
☐ 77	Tony Menendez	.05	.02
☐ 78	Henry Mercedes	.05	.02
☐ 79	Paul Miller	.05	.02
☐ 80	Joe Millette	.05	.02
☐ 81	Blas Minor	.05	.02
☐ 82	Dennis Moeller	.05	.02
☐ 83	Raul Mondesi	.40	.18
☐ 84	Rob Natal	.05	.02
☐ 85	Troy Neel	.05	.02
☐ 86	David Nied	.05	.02
☐ 87	Jerry Nielson	.05	.02
☐ 88	Donovan Osborne	.05	.02
☐ 89	John Patterson	.05	.02
☐ 90	Roger Pavlik	.10	.05
☐ 91	Dan Peltier	.05	.02
☐ 92	Jim Pena	.05	.02
☐ 93	William Pennyfeather	.05	.02
☐ 94	Mike Perez	.05	.02
☐ 95	Hipolito Pichardo	.05	.02
☐ 96	Greg Pirkl	.05	.02
☐ 97	Harvey Pulliam	.05	.02
☐ 98	Manny Ramirez	1.25	.55
☐ 99	Pat Rapp	.05	.02
☐ 100	Jeff Reboulet	.05	.02
☐ 101	Darren Reed	.05	.02
☐ 102	Shane Reynolds	.20	.09
☐ 103	Bill Risley	.05	.02
☐ 104	Ben Rivera	.05	.02
☐ 105	Henry Rodriguez	.20	.09
☐ 106	Rico Rossy	.05	.02
☐ 107	Johnny Ruffin	.05	.02
☐ 108	Steve Scarsone	.05	.02
☐ 109	Tim Scott	.05	.02
☐ 110	Steve Shifflett	.05	.02
☐ 111	Dave Silvestri	.05	.02
☐ 112	Matt Stairs	.05	.02
☐ 113	William Suero	.05	.02
☐ 114	Jeff Tackett	.05	.02
☐ 115	Eddie Taubensee	.05	.02
☐ 116	Rick Trlicek	.05	.02
☐ 117	Scooter Tucker	.05	.02
☐ 118	Shane Turner	.05	.02
☐ 119	Julio Valera	.05	.02
☐ 120	Paul Wagner	.05	.02
☐ 121	Tim Wakefield	.20	.09
☐ 122	Mike Walker	.05	.02
☐ 123	Bruce Walton	.05	.02
☐ 124	Lenny Webster	.05	.02
☐ 125	Bob Wickman	.05	.02
☐ 126	Mike Williams	.05	.02
☐ 127	Kerry Woodson	.05	.02
☐ 128	Eric Young	.20	.09
☐ 129	Kevin Young	.05	.02
☐ 130	Pete Young	.05	.02
☐ 131	Checklist 1-66	.05	.02
☐ 132	Checklist 67-132	.05	.02

1992 Donruss Rookies Phenoms

This 20-card standard size set features a selection young prospects. The first twelve cards were randomly inserted into 1992 Donruss The Rookies 12-card foil packs. The last eight were inserted one per 1992 Donruss Rookies 30-card jumbo pack. Each glossy card front features a black border surrounding a full color photo and gold foil type.

young prospects. There are no key Rookie Cards in this set.

	MINT	NRMT
COMPLETE FOIL SET (12)	25.00	11.00
COMMON FOIL (BC1-BC12)	.50	.23
FOIL MINOR STARS	1.00	.45
FOIL UNLISTED STARS	1.50	.70
FOIL: RANDOM INSERTS IN PACKS		
COMPLETE JUMBO SET (8)	10.00	4.50
COMMON JUMBO (BC13-BC20)	.50	.23
JUMBO MINOR STARS	1.00	.45
JUMBO UNLISTED STARS	1.50	.70
JUMBOS: ONE PER JUMBO PACK		

		MINT	NRMT
☐ BC1	Moises Alou	1.25	.55
☐ BC2	Bret Boone	.50	.23
☐ BC3	Jeff Conine	1.25	.55
☐ BC4	Dave Fleming	.50	.23
☐ BC5	Tyler Green	.50	.23
☐ BC6	Eric Karros	1.25	.55
☐ BC7	Pat Listach	.50	.23
☐ BC8	Kenny Lofton	8.00	3.60
☐ BC9	Mike Piazza	20.00	9.00
☐ BC10	Tim Salmon	5.00	2.20
☐ BC11	Andy Stankiewicz	.50	.23
☐ BC12	Dan Walters	.50	.23
☐ BC13	Ramon Caraballo	.50	.23
☐ BC14	Brian Jordan	1.50	.70
☐ BC15	Ryan Klesko	3.00	1.35
☐ BC16	Sam Militello	.50	.23
☐ BC17	Frank Seminara	.50	.23
☐ BC18	Salomon Torres	.50	.23
☐ BC19	John Valentin	1.50	.70
☐ BC20	Wil Cordero	.50	.23

1993 Donruss

The 792-card 1993 Donruss set was issued in two series, each with 396 standard-size cards. Cards were distributed in foil packs. The basic card fronts feature glossy color action photos with white borders. At the bottom of the picture, the team logo appears in a team color-coded diamond with the player's name in a color-coded bar extending to the right. A Rated Rookies (RR) subset , sprinkled throughout the set, spotlights 20 young prospects. There are no key Rookie Cards in this set.

	MINT	NRMT
COMPLETE SET (792)	30.00	13.50
COMPLETE SERIES 1 (396)	15.00	6.75
COMPLETE SERIES 2 (396)	15.00	6.75
COMMON CARD (1-792)	.10	.05
MINOR STARS	.20	.09
UNLISTED STARS	.40	.18

		MINT	NRMT
☐ 1	Craig Lefferts	.10	.05
☐ 2	Kent Mercker	.10	.05
☐ 3	Phil Plantier	.10	.05
☐ 4	Alex Arias	.10	.05
☐ 5	Julio Valera	.10	.05
☐ 6	Dan Wilson	.20	.09
☐ 7	Frank Thomas	1.50	.70
☐ 8	Eric Anthony	.10	.05
☐ 9	Derek Lilliquist	.10	.05
☐ 10	Rafael Bournigal	.10	.05
☐ 11	Manny Alexander RR	.10	.05
☐ 12	Bret Barberie	.10	.05
☐ 13	Mickey Tettleton	.10	.05
☐ 14	Anthony Young	.10	.05
☐ 15	Tim Spehr	.10	.05
☐ 16	Bob Ayrault	.10	.05
☐ 17	Bill Wegman	.10	.05
☐ 18	Jay Bell	.20	.09
☐ 19	Rick Aguilera	.10	.05
☐ 20	Todd Zeile	.10	.05
☐ 21	Steve Farr	.10	.05
☐ 22	Andy Benes	.20	.09
☐ 23	Lance Blankenship	.10	.05
☐ 24	Ted Wood	.10	.05
☐ 25	Omar Vizquel	.20	.09
☐ 26	Steve Avery	.10	.05
☐ 27	Brian Bohanon	.10	.05
☐ 28	Rick Wilkins	.10	.05
☐ 29	Devon White	.10	.05
☐ 30	Bobby Ayala	.10	.05
☐ 31	Leo Gomez	.10	.05
☐ 32	Mike Simms	.10	.05
☐ 33	Ellis Burks	.20	.09
☐ 34	Steve Wilson	.10	.05
☐ 35	Jim Abbott	.10	.05
☐ 36	Tim Wallach	.10	.05
☐ 37	Wilson Alvarez	.20	.09
☐ 38	Daryl Boston	.10	.05
☐ 39	Sandy Alomar Jr	.20	.09
☐ 40	Mitch Williams	.10	.05
☐ 41	Rico Brogna	.20	.09
☐ 42	Gary Varsho	.10	.05
☐ 43	Kevin Appier	.20	.09
☐ 44	Eric Wedge RR	.10	.05
☐ 45	Dante Bichette	.30	.14
☐ 46	Jose Oquendo	.10	.05
☐ 47	Mike Trombley	.10	.05
☐ 48	Dan Walters	.10	.05
☐ 49	Gerald Williams	.10	.05
☐ 50	Bud Black	.10	.05
☐ 51	Bobby Witt	.10	.05
☐ 52	Mark Davis	.10	.05
☐ 53	Shawn Barton	.10	.05
☐ 54	Paul Assenmacher	.10	.05
☐ 55	Kevin Reimer	.10	.05
☐ 56	Billy Ashley RR	.10	.05
☐ 57	Eddie Zosky	.10	.05
☐ 58	Chris Sabo	.10	.05
☐ 59	Billy Ripken	.10	.05
☐ 60	Scooter Tucker	.10	.05
☐ 61	Tim Wakefield RR	.20	.09
☐ 62	Mitch Webster	.10	.05
☐ 63	Jack Clark	.10	.05
☐ 64	Mark Gardner	.10	.05
☐ 65	Lee Stevens	.10	.05
☐ 66	Todd Hundley	.30	.14
☐ 67	Bobby Thigpen	.10	.05
☐ 68	Dave Hollins	.10	.05
☐ 69	Jack Armstrong	.10	.05
☐ 70	Alex Cole	.10	.05
☐ 71	Mark Carreon	.10	.05
☐ 72	Todd Worrell	.10	.05
☐ 73	Steve Shifflett	.10	.05
☐ 74	Jerald Clark	.10	.05
☐ 75	Paul Molitor	.40	.18
☐ 76	Larry Carter	.10	.05
☐ 77	Rich Rowland RR	.10	.05
☐ 78	Damon Berryhill	.10	.05
☐ 79	Willie Banks	.10	.05
☐ 80	Hector Villanueva	.10	.05
☐ 81	Mike Gallego	.10	.05
☐ 82	Tim Belcher	.10	.05
☐ 83	Mike Bordick	.10	.05
☐ 84	Craig Biggio	.30	.14
☐ 85	Lance Parrish	.10	.05
☐ 86	Brett Butler	.20	.09
☐ 87	Mike Timlin	.10	.05
☐ 88	Brian Barnes	.10	.05
☐ 89	Brady Anderson	.30	.14
☐ 90	D.J. Dozier	.10	.05
☐ 91	Frank Viola	.10	.05
☐ 92	Darren Daulton	.20	.09
☐ 93	Chad Curtis	.20	.09
☐ 94	Zane Smith	.10	.05
☐ 95	George Bell	.10	.05
☐ 96	Rex Hudler	.10	.05
☐ 97	Mark Whiten	.10	.05
☐ 98	Tim Teufel	.10	.05
☐ 99	Kevin Ritz	.10	.05
☐ 100	Jeff Brantley	.10	.05
☐ 101	Jeff Conine	.20	.09
☐ 102	Vinny Castilla	.40	.18
☐ 103	Greg Vaughn	.10	.05
☐ 104	Steve Buechele	.10	.05
☐ 105	Darren Reed	.10	.05
☐ 106	Bip Roberts	.10	.05
☐ 107	John Habyan	.10	.05
☐ 108	Scott Servais	.10	.05
☐ 109	Walt Weiss	.10	.05
☐ 110	J.T. Snow RR	.50	.23
☐ 111	Jay Buhner	.30	.14
☐ 112	Darryl Strawberry	.20	.09
☐ 113	Roger Pavlik	.10	.05
☐ 114	Chris Nabholz	.10	.05
☐ 115	Pat Borders	.10	.05
☐ 116	Pat Howell	.10	.05
☐ 117	Gregg Olson	.10	.05
☐ 118	Curt Schilling	.20	.09
☐ 119	Roger Clemens	.75	.35
☐ 120	Victor Cole	.10	.05
☐ 121	Gary DiSarcina	.10	.05
☐ 122	Checklist 1-80	.20	.09
	Gary Carter and		
	Kirt Manwaring		
☐ 123	Steve Sax	.10	.05
☐ 124	Chuck Carr	.10	.05
☐ 125	Mark Lewis	.10	.05
☐ 126	Tony Gwynn	1.00	.45
☐ 127	Travis Fryman	.20	.09
☐ 128	Dave Burba	.10	.05
☐ 129	Wally Joyner	.20	.09
☐ 130	John Smoltz	.20	.09
☐ 131	Cal Eldred	.10	.05
☐ 132	Checklist 81-159	.20	.09
	Roberto Alomar and		
	Devon White		
☐ 133	Arthur Rhodes	.10	.05
☐ 134	Jeff Blauser	.10	.05
☐ 135	Scott Cooper	.10	.05
☐ 136	Doug Strange	.10	.05
☐ 137	Luis Sojo	.10	.05
☐ 138	Jeff Branson	.10	.05
☐ 139	Alex Fernandez	.20	.09

140	Ken Caminiti	.30	.14
141	Charles Nagy	.20	.09
142	Tom Candiotti	.10	.05
143	Willie Greene RR	.20	.09
144	John Vander Wal	.10	.05
145	Kurt Knudsen	.10	.05
146	John Franco	.20	.09
147	Eddie Pierce	.10	.05
148	Kim Batiste	.10	.05
149	Darren Holmes	.10	.05
150	Steve Cooke	.10	.05
151	Terry Jorgensen	.10	.05
152	Mark Clark	.10	.05
153	Randy Velarde	.10	.05
154	Greg W. Harris	.10	.05
155	Kevin Campbell	.10	.05
156	John Burkett	.10	.05
157	Kevin Mitchell	.20	.09
158	Deion Sanders	.20	.09
159	Jose Canseco	.30	.14
160	Jeff Hartsock	.10	.05
161	Tom Quinlan	.10	.05
162	Tim Pugh	.10	.05
163	Glenn Davis	.10	.05
164	Shane Reynolds	.20	.09
165	Jody Reed	.10	.05
166	Mike Sharperson	.10	.05
167	Scott Lewis	.10	.05
168	Dennis Martinez	.20	.09
169	Scott Radinsky	.10	.05
170	Dave Gallagher	.10	.05
171	Jim Thome	.75	.35
172	Terry Mulholland	.10	.05
173	Milt Cuyler	.10	.05
174	Bob Patterson	.10	.05
175	Jeff Montgomery	.20	.09
176	Tim Salmon RR	.50	.23
177	Franklin Stubbs	.10	.05
178	Donovan Osborne	.10	.05
179	Jeff Reboulet	.10	.05
180	Jeremy Hernandez	.10	.05
181	Charlie Hayes	.10	.05
182	Matt Williams	.30	.14
183	Mike Raczka	.10	.05
184	Francisco Cabrera	.10	.05
185	Rich DeLucia	.10	.05
186	Sammy Sosa	.40	.18
187	Ivan Rodriguez	.50	.23
188	Bret Boone RR	.10	.05
189	Juan Guzman	.10	.05
190	Tom Browning	.10	.05
191	Randy Milligan	.10	.05
192	Steve Finley	.20	.09
193	John Patterson RR	.10	.05
194	Kip Gross	.10	.05
195	Tony Fossas	.10	.05
196	Ivan Calderon	.10	.05
197	Junior Felix	.10	.05
198	Pete Schourek	.10	.05
199	Craig Grebeck	.10	.05
200	Juan Bell	.10	.05
201	Glenallen Hill	.10	.05
202	Danny Jackson	.10	.05
203	John Kiely	.10	.05
204	Bob Tewksbury	.10	.05
205	Kevin Koslofski	.10	.05
206	Craig Shipley	.10	.05
207	John Jaha	.20	.09
208	Royce Clayton	.10	.05
209	Mike Piazza RR	2.00	.90
210	Ron Gant	.20	.09
211	Scott Erickson	.10	.05
212	Doug Dascenzo	.10	.05
213	Andy Stankiewicz	.10	.05
214	Geronimo Berroa	.20	.09
215	Dennis Eckersley	.20	.09
216	Al Osuna	.10	.05
217	Tino Martinez	.40	.18
218	Henry Rodriguez	.20	.09
219	Ed Sprague	.10	.05
220	Ken Hill	.10	.05
221	Chito Martinez	.10	.05
222	Bret Saberhagen	.10	.05
223	Mike Greenwell	.10	.05
224	Mickey Morandini	.10	.05
225	Chuck Finley	.10	.05
226	Denny Neagle	.20	.09
227	Kirk McCaskill	.10	.05
228	Rheal Cormier	.10	.05
229	Paul Sorrento	.10	.05
230	Darrin Jackson	.10	.05
231	Rob Deer	.20	.09
232	Bill Swift	.10	.05
233	Kevin McReynolds	.10	.05
234	Terry Pendleton	.20	.09
235	Dave Nilsson	.20	.09
236	Chuck McElroy	.10	.05
237	Derek Parks	.10	.05
238	Norm Charlton	.10	.05
239	Matt Nokes	.10	.05
240	Juan Guerrero	.10	.05
241	Jeff Parrett	.10	.05
242	Ryan Thompson RR	.10	.05
243	Dave Fleming	.20	.09
244	Dave Hansen	.10	.05
245	Monty Fariss	.10	.05
246	Archi Cianfrocco	.10	.05
247	Pat Hentgen	.30	.14
248	Bill Pecota	.10	.05
249	Ben McDonald	.10	.05
250	Cliff Brantley	.10	.05
251	John Valentin	.20	.09
252	Jeff King	.20	.09
253	Reggie Williams	.10	.05
254	Checklist 160-238	.10	.05
	(Damon Berryhill and Alex Arias)		
255	Ozzie Guillen	.10	.05
256	Mike Perez	.10	.05
257	Thomas Howard	.10	.05
258	Kurt Stillwell	.10	.05
259	Mike Henneman	.10	.05
260	Steve Decker	.10	.05
261	Brent Mayne	.10	.05
262	Otis Nixon	.10	.05
263	Mark Kiefer	.10	.05
264	Checklist 239-317	.30	.14
	(Don Mattingly and Mike Bordick)		
265	Richie Lewis	.10	.05
266	Pat Gomez	.10	.05
267	Scott Taylor	.10	.05
268	Shawon Dunston	.10	.05
269	Greg Myers	.10	.05
270	Tim Costo	.10	.05
271	Greg Hibbard	.10	.05
272	Pete Harnisch	.10	.05
273	Dave Mlicki	.10	.05
274	Orel Hershiser	.20	.09
275	Sean Berry RR	.10	.05
276	Doug Simons	.10	.05
277	John Doherty	.10	.05
278	Eddie Murray	.40	.18
279	Chris Haney	.10	.05
280	Stan Javier	.10	.05
281	Jaime Navarro	.10	.05
282	Orlando Merced	.10	.05
283	Kent Hrbek	.20	.09
284	Bernard Gilkey	.20	.09
285	Russ Springer	.10	.05
286	Mike Maddux	.10	.05
287	Eric Fox	.10	.05
288	Mark Leonard	.10	.05
289	Tim Leary	.10	.05
290	Brian Hunter	.10	.05
291	Donald Harris	.10	.05
292	Bob Scanlan	.10	.05
293	Turner Ward	.10	.05
294	Hal Morris	.10	.05
295	Jimmy Poole	.10	.05
296	Doug Jones	.10	.05
297	Tony Pena	.10	.05
298	Ramon Martinez	.20	.09
299	Tim Fortugno	.10	.05
300	Marquis Grissom	.20	.09
301	Lance Johnson	.10	.05
302	Jeff Kent	.20	.09
303	Reggie Jefferson	.10	.05
304	Wes Chamberlain	.10	.05
305	Shawn Hare	.10	.05
306	Mike LaValliere	.10	.05
307	Gregg Jefferies	.10	.05
308	Troy Neel RR	.10	.05
309	Pat Listach	.20	.09
310	Geronimo Pena	.10	.05
311	Pedro Munoz	.10	.05
312	Guillermo Velasquez	.10	.05
313	Roberto Kelly	.10	.05
314	Mike Jackson	.10	.05
315	Rickey Henderson	.30	.14
316	Mark Lemke	.10	.05
317	Erik Hanson	.10	.05
318	Derrick May	.10	.05
319	Geno Petralli	.10	.05
320	Melvin Nieves RR	.20	.09
321	Doug Linton	.10	.05
322	Rob Dibble	.10	.05
323	Chris Hoiles	.10	.05
324	Jimmy Jones	.10	.05
325	Dave Staton RR	.10	.05
326	Pedro Martinez	.40	.18
327	Paul Quantrill	.10	.05
328	Greg Colbrunn	.10	.05
329	Hilly Hathaway	.10	.05
330	Jeff Innis	.10	.05
331	Ron Karkovice	.10	.05
332	Keith Shepherd	.10	.05
333	Alan Embree	.10	.05
334	Paul Wagner	.10	.05
335	Dave Haas	.10	.05
336	Ozzie Canseco	.10	.05
337	Bill Sampen	.10	.05
338	Rich Rodriguez	.10	.05
339	Dean Palmer	.10	.05
340	Greg Litton	.10	.05
341	Jim Tatum RR	.10	.05
342	Todd Haney	.10	.05
343	Larry Casian	.10	.05
344	Ryne Sandberg	.50	.23
345	Sterling Hitchcock	.20	.09
346	Chris Hammond	.10	.05
347	Vince Horsman	.10	.05
348	Butch Henry	.10	.05
349	Dann Howitt	.10	.05
350	Roger McDowell	.10	.05
351	Jack Morris	.20	.09
352	Bill Krueger	.10	.05
353	Cris Colon	.10	.05
354	Joe Vitko	.10	.05
355	Willie McGee	.10	.05
356	Jay Baller	.10	.05
357	Pat Mahomes	.10	.05
358	Roger Mason	.10	.05
359	Jerry Nielsen	.10	.05
360	Tom Pagnozzi	.10	.05
361	Kevin Baez	.10	.05
362	Tim Scott	.10	.05
363	Domingo Martinez	.10	.05
364	Kirt Manwaring	.10	.05
365	Rafael Palmeiro	.30	.14
366	Ray Lankford	.30	.14
367	Tim McIntosh	.10	.05
368	Jessie Hollins	.10	.05
369	Scott Leius	.10	.05
370	Bill Doran	.10	.05
371	Sam Militello	.10	.05
372	Ryan Bowen	.10	.05
373	Dave Henderson	.10	.05
374	Dan Smith RR	.10	.05
375	Steve Reed RR	.10	.05
376	Jose Offerman	.10	.05
377	Kevin Brown	.20	.09
378	Darrin Fletcher	.10	.05
379	Duane Ward	.10	.05
380	Wayne Kirby RR	.10	.05
381	Steve Scarsone	.10	.05
382	Mariano Duncan	.10	.05
383	Ken Ryan	.10	.05
384	Lloyd McClendon	.10	.05
385	Brian Holman	.10	.05
386	Braulio Castillo	.10	.05
387	Danny Leon	.10	.05
388	Omar Olivares	.10	.05
389	Kevin Wickander	.10	.05
390	Fred McGriff	.30	.14
391	Phil Clark	.10	.05
392	Darren Lewis	.10	.05
393	Phil Hiatt	.10	.05

394	Mike Morgan	.10	.05
395	Shane Mack	.10	.05
396	Checklist 318-396	.20	.09
	(Dennis Eckersley and Art Kusnyer CO)		
397	David Segui	.10	.05
398	Rafael Belliard	.10	.05
399	Tim Naehring	.10	.05
400	Frank Castillo	.10	.05
401	Joe Grahe	.10	.05
402	Reggie Sanders	.20	.09
403	Roberto Hernandez	.20	.09
404	Luis Gonzalez	.10	.05
405	Carlos Baerga	.10	.05
406	Carlos Hernandez	.10	.05
407	Pedro Astacio RR	.10	.05
408	Mel Rojas	.20	.09
409	Scott Livingstone	.10	.05
410	Chico Walker	.10	.05
411	Brian McRae	.10	.05
412	Ben Rivera	.10	.05
413	Ricky Bones	.10	.05
414	Andy Van Slyke	.20	.09
415	Chuck Knoblauch	.18	.08
416	Luis Alicea	.10	.05
417	Bob Wickman	.10	.05
418	Doug Brocail	.10	.05
419	Scott Brosius	.10	.05
420	Rod Beck	.10	.05
421	Edgar Martinez	.30	.14
422	Ryan Klesko	.50	.23
423	Nolan Ryan	1.50	.70
424	Rey Sanchez	.10	.05
425	Roberto Alomar	.40	.18
426	Barry Larkin	.30	.14
427	Mike Mussina	.18	.08
428	Jeff Bagwell	.75	.35
429	Mo Vaughn	.50	.23
430	Eric Karros	.20	.09
431	John Orton	.10	.05
432	Wil Cordero	.10	.05
433	Jack McDowell	.10	.05
434	Howard Johnson	.10	.05
435	Albert Belle	.50	.23
436	John Kruk	.20	.09
437	Skeeter Barnes	.10	.05
438	Don Slaught	.10	.05
439	Rusty Meacham	.10	.05
440	Tim Laker RR	.10	.05
441	Robin Yount	.30	.14
442	Brian Jordan	.20	.09
443	Kevin Tapani	.10	.05
444	Gary Sheffield	.40	.18
445	Rich Monteleone	.10	.05
446	Wil Clark	.30	.14
447	Jerry Browne	.10	.05
448	Jeff Treadway	.10	.05
449	Mike Schooler	.10	.05
450	Mike Harkey	.10	.05
451	Julio Franco	.10	.05
452	Kevin Young RR	.10	.05
453	Kelly Gruber	.10	.05
454	Jose Rijo	.10	.05
455	Mike Devereaux	.10	.05
456	Andujar Cedeno	.10	.05
457	Damion Easley RR	.10	.05
458	Kevin Gross	.10	.05
459	Matt Young	.10	.05
460	Matt Stairs	.10	.05
461	Luis Polonia	.10	.05
462	Dwight Gooden	.20	.09
463	Warren Newson	.10	.05
464	Jose DeLeon	.10	.05
465	Jose Mesa	.10	.05
466	Danny Cox	.10	.05
467	Dan Gladden	.10	.05
468	Gerald Perry	.10	.05
469	Mike Boddicker	.10	.05
470	Jeff Gardner	.10	.05
471	Doug Henry	.10	.05
472	Mike Benjamin	.10	.05
473	Dan Peltier RR	.10	.05
474	Mike Stanton	.10	.05
475	John Smiley	.10	.05
476	Dwight Smith	.10	.05
477	Jim Leyritz	.10	.05
478	Dwayne Henry	.10	.05
479	Mark McGwire	.75	.35
480	Pete Incaviglia	.10	.05
481	Dave Cochrane	.10	.05
482	Eric Davis	.20	.09
483	John Olerud	.10	.05
484	Kent Bottenfield	.10	.05
485	Mark McLemore	.10	.05
486	Dave Magadan	.10	.05
487	John Marzano	.10	.05
488	Ruben Amaro	.10	.05
489	Rob Ducey	.10	.05
490	Stan Belinda	.10	.05
491	Dan Pasqua	.10	.05
492	Joe Magrane	.10	.05
493	Brook Jacoby	.10	.05
494	Gene Harris	.10	.05
495	Mark Leiter	.10	.05
496	Bryan Hickerson	.10	.05
497	Tom Gordon	.10	.05
498	Pete Smith	.10	.05
499	Chris Bosio	.10	.05
500	Shawn Boskie	.10	.05
501	Dave West	.10	.05
502	Milt Hill	.10	.05
503	Pat Kelly	.10	.05
504	Joe Boever	.10	.05
505	Terry Steinbach	.10	.05
506	Butch Huskey RR	.40	.18
507	David Valle	.10	.05
508	Mike Scioscia	.10	.05
509	Kenny Rogers	.10	.05
510	Moises Alou	.20	.09
511	David Wells	.10	.05
512	Mackey Sasser	.10	.05
513	Todd Frohwirth	.10	.05
514	Ricky Jordan	.10	.05
515	Mike Gardiner	.10	.05
516	Gary Redus	.10	.05
517	Gary Gaetti	.10	.05
518	Checklist	.10	.05
519	Carlton Fisk	.40	.18
520	Ozzie Smith	.50	.23
521	Rod Nichols	.10	.05
522	Benito Santiago	.10	.05
523	Bill Gullickson	.10	.05
524	Robby Thompson	.10	.05
525	Mike Macfarlane	.10	.05
526	Sid Bream	.10	.05
527	Darryl Hamilton	.10	.05
528	Checklist	.10	.05
529	Jeff Tackett	.10	.05
530	Greg Olson	.10	.05
531	Bob Zupcic	.10	.05
532	Mark Grace	.30	.14
533	Steve Frey	.10	.05
534	Dave Martinez	.10	.05
535	Robin Ventura	.20	.09
536	Casey Candaele	.10	.05
537	Kenny Lofton	.75	.35
538	Jay Howell	.10	.05
539	Fernando Ramsey RR	.10	.05
540	Larry Walker	.40	.18
541	Cecil Fielder	.20	.09
542	Lee Guetterman	.10	.05
543	Keith Miller	.10	.05
544	Len Dykstra	.10	.05
545	B.J. Surhoff	.20	.09
546	Bob Walk	.10	.05
547	Brian Harper	.10	.05
548	Lee Smith	.20	.09
549	Danny Tartabull	.20	.09
550	Frank Seminara	.10	.05
551	Henry Mercedes	.10	.05
552	Dave Righetti	.10	.05
553	Ken Griffey Jr.	2.00	.90
554	Tom Glavine	.30	.14
555	Juan Gonzalez	1.00	.45
556	Jim Bullinger	.10	.05
557	Derek Bell	.20	.09
558	Cesar Hernandez	.10	.05
559	Cal Ripken	1.50	.70
560	Eddie Taubensee	.10	.05
561	John Flaherty	.10	.05
562	Todd Benzinger	.10	.05
563	Hubie Brooks	.10	.05
564	Delino DeShields	.10	.05
565	Tim Raines	.20	.09
566	Sid Fernandez	.10	.05
567	Steve Olin	.10	.05
568	Tommy Greene	.10	.05
569	Buddy Groom	.10	.05
570	Randy Tomlin	.10	.05
571	Hipolito Pichardo	.10	.05
572	Rene Arocha RR	.10	.05
573	Mike Fetters	.10	.05
574	Felix Jose	.10	.05
575	Gene Larkin	.10	.05
576	Bruce Hurst	.10	.05
577	Bernie Williams	.40	.18
578	Trevor Wilson	.10	.05
579	Bob Welch	.10	.05
580	David Justice	.40	.18
581	Randy Johnson	.40	.18
582	Jose Vizcaino	.10	.05
583	Jeff Huson	.10	.05
584	Rob Maurer RR	.10	.05
585	Todd Stottlemyre	.10	.05
586	Joe Oliver	.10	.05
587	Bob Milacki	.10	.05
588	Rob Murphy	.10	.05
589	Greg Pirkl RR	.10	.05
590	Lenny Harris	.10	.05
591	Luis Rivera	.10	.05
592	John Wetteland	.20	.09
593	Mark Langston	.20	.09
594	Bobby Bonilla	.20	.09
595	Esteban Beltre	.10	.05
596	Mike Hartley	.10	.05
597	Felix Fermin	.10	.05
598	Carlos Garcia	.10	.05
599	Frank Tanana	.10	.05
600	Pedro Guerrero	.10	.05
601	Terry Shumpert	.10	.05
602	Wally Whitehurst	.10	.05
603	Kevin Seitzer	.10	.05
604	Chris James	.10	.05
605	Greg Gohr RR	.10	.05
606	Mark Wohlers	.20	.09
607	Kirby Puckett	.75	.35
608	Greg Maddux	1.25	.55
609	Don Mattingly	.60	.25
610	Greg Cadaret	.10	.05
611	Dave Stewart	.20	.09
612	Mark Portugal	.10	.05
613	Pete O'Brien	.10	.05
614	Bobby Ojeda	.10	.05
615	Joe Carter	.20	.09
616	Pete Young	.10	.05
617	Sam Horn	.10	.05
618	Vince Coleman	.10	.05
619	Wade Boggs	.40	.18
620	Todd Pratt	.10	.05
621	Ron Tingley	.10	.05
622	Doug Drabek	.10	.05
623	Scott Hemond	.10	.05
624	Tim Jones	.10	.05
625	Dennis Cook	.10	.05
626	Jose Melendez	.10	.05
627	Mike Munoz	.10	.05
628	Jim Pena	.10	.05
629	Gary Thurman	.10	.05
630	Charlie Leibrandt	.10	.05
631	Scott Fletcher	.10	.05
632	Andre Dawson	.30	.14
633	Greg Gagne	.10	.05
634	Greg Swindell	.10	.05
635	Kevin Maas	.10	.05
636	Xavier Hernandez	.10	.05
637	Ruben Sierra	.40	.18
638	Dmitri Young RR	.40	.18
639	Harold Reynolds	.10	.05
640	Tom Goodwin	.10	.05
641	Todd Burns	.10	.05
642	Jeff Fassero	.10	.05
643	Dave Winfield	.30	.14
644	Willie Randolph	.20	.09
645	Luis Mercedes	.10	.05
646	Dale Murphy	.30	.14
647	Danny Darwin	.10	.05
648	Dennis Moeller	.10	.05
649	Chuck Crim	.10	.05

□			MINT	NRMT
□	650 Checklist	.10		.05
□	651 Shawn Abner	.10		.05
□	652 Tracy Woodson	.10		.05
□	653 Scott Scudder	.10		.05
□	654 Tom Lampkin	.10		.05
□	655 Alan Trammell	.30		.14
□	656 Cory Snyder	.10		.05
□	657 Chris Gwynn	.10		.05
□	658 Lonnie Smith	.10		.05
□	659 Jim Austin	.10		.05
□	660 Checklist	.10		.05
□	661 Tim Hulett	.10		.05
□	662 Marvin Freeman	.10		.05
□	663 Greg A. Harris	.10		.05
□	664 Heathcliff Slocumb	.10		.05
□	665 Mike Butcher	.10		.05
□	666 Steve Foster	.10		.05
□	667 Donn Pall	.10		.05
□	668 Darryl Kile	.20		.09
□	669 Jesse Levis	.10		.05
□	670 Jim Gott	.10		.05
□	671 Mark Hutton RR	.10		.05
□	672 Brian Drahman	.10		.05
□	673 Chad Kreuter	.10		.05
□	674 Tony Fernandez	.10		.05
□	675 Jose Lind	.10		.05
□	676 Kyle Abbott	.10		.05
□	677 Dan Plesac	.10		.05
□	678 Barry Bonds	.50		.23
□	679 Chili Davis	.20		.09
□	680 Stan Royer	.10		.05
□	681 Scott Kamieniecki	.10		.05
□	682 Carlos Martinez	.10		.05
□	683 Mike Moore	.10		.05
□	684 Candy Maldonado	.10		.05
□	685 Jeff Nelson	.10		.05
□	686 Lou Whitaker	.20		.09
□	687 Jose Guzman	.10		.05
□	688 Manuel Lee	.10		.05
□	689 Bob MacDonald	.10		.05
□	690 Scott Bankhead	.10		.05
□	691 Alan Mills	.10		.05
□	692 Brian Williams	.10		.05
□	693 Tom Brunansky	.10		.05
□	694 Lenny Webster	.10		.05
□	695 Greg Briley	.10		.05
□	696 Paul O'Neill	.20		.09
□	697 Joey Cora	.10		.05
□	698 Charlie O'Brien	.10		.05
□	699 Junior Ortiz	.10		.05
□	700 Ron Darling	.10		.05
□	701 Tony Phillips	.10		.05
□	702 William Pennyfeather	.10		.05
□	703 Mark Gubicza	.10		.05
□	704 Steve Hosey RR	.10		.05
□	705 Henry Cotto	.10		.05
□	706 David Hulse	.10		.05
□	707 Mike Pagliarulo	.10		.05
□	708 Dave Stieb	.10		.05
□	709 Melido Perez	.10		.05
□	710 Jimmy Key	.20		.09
□	711 Jeff Russell	.10		.05
□	712 David Cone	.20		.09
□	713 Russ Swan	.10		.05
□	714 Mark Guthrie	.10		.05
□	715 Checklist	.10		.05
□	716 Al Martin RR	.20		.09
□	717 Randy Knorr	.10		.05
□	718 Mike Stanley	.10		.05
□	719 Rick Sutcliffe	.10		.05
□	720 Terry Leach	.10		.05
□	721 Chipper Jones RR	2.00		.90
□	722 Jim Eisenreich	.10		.05
□	723 Tom Henke	.10		.05
□	724 Jeff Frye	.10		.05
□	725 Harold Baines	.10		.05
□	726 Scott Sanderson	.10		.05
□	727 Tom Foley	.10		.05
□	728 Bryan Harvey	.10		.05
□	729 Tom Edens	.10		.05
□	730 Eric Young	.40		.18
□	731 Dave Weathers	.10		.05
□	732 Spike Owen	.10		.05
□	733 Scott Aldred	.10		.05
□	734 Cris Carpenter	.10		.05
□	735 Dion James	.10		.05
□	736 Joe Girardi	.10		.05
□	737 Nigel Wilson RR	.10		.05
□	738 Scott Chiamparino	.10		.05
□	739 Jeff Reardon	.20		.09
□	740 Willie Blair	.10		.05
□	741 Jim Corsi	.10		.05
□	742 Ken Patterson	.10		.05
□	743 Andy Ashby	.10		.05
□	744 Rob Natal	.10		.05
□	745 Kevin Bass	.10		.05
□	746 Freddie Benavides	.10		.05
□	747 Chris Donnels	.10		.05
□	748 Kerry Woodson	.10		.05
□	749 Calvin Jones	.10		.05
□	750 Gary Scott	.10		.05
□	751 Joe Orsulak	.10		.05
□	752 Armando Reynoso	.10		.05
□	753 Monty Fariss	.10		.05
□	754 Billy Hatcher	.10		.05
□	755 Denis Boucher	.10		.05
□	756 Walt Weiss	.10		.05
□	757 Mike Fitzgerald	.10		.05
□	758 Rudy Seanez	.10		.05
□	759 Bret Barberie	.10		.05
□	760 Mo Sanford	.10		.05
□	761 Pedro Castellano	.10		.05
□	762 Chuck Carr	.10		.05
□	763 Steve Howe	.10		.05
□	764 Andres Galarraga	.40		.18
□	765 Jeff Conine	.20		.09
□	766 Ted Power	.10		.05
□	767 Butch Henry	.10		.05
□	768 Steve Decker	.10		.05
□	769 Storm Davis	.10		.05
□	770 Vinny Castilla	.40		.18
□	771 Junior Felix	.10		.05
□	772 Walt Terrell	.10		.05
□	773 Brad Ausmus	.10		.05
□	774 Jamie McAndrew	.10		.05
□	775 Milt Thompson	.10		.05
□	776 Charlie Hayes	.10		.05
□	777 Jack Armstrong	.10		.05
□	778 Dennis Rasmussen	.10		.05
□	779 Darren Holmes	.10		.05
□	780 Alex Arias	.10		.05
□	781 Randy Bush	.10		.05
□	782 Javier Lopez RR	.10		.05
□	783 Dante Bichette	.30		.14
□	784 John Johnstone	.10		.05
□	785 Rene Gonzales	.10		.05
□	786 Alex Cole	.10		.05
□	787 Jeromy Burnitz RR	.10		.05
□	788 Michael Huff	.10		.05
□	789 Anthony Telford	.10		.05
□	790 Jerald Clark	.10		.05
□	791 Joel Johnston	.10		.05
□	792 David Nied RR	.10		.05

first 15 cards were available in the first series of the 1993 Donruss and cards 16-31 were inserted with the second series. The cards are gold-foil stamped and feature player portraits by noted sports artist Dick Perez. Card numbers 27-28 honor the first draft picks of the new Florida Marlins and Colorado Rockies franchises. Collectors 16 years of age and younger could enter Donruss' Diamond King contest by writing an essay of 75 words or less explaining who their favorite Diamond King player was and why. Winners were awarded one of 30 framed watercolors at the National Convention, held in Chicago, July 22-25, 1993.

		MINT	NRMT
COMPLETE SET (31)		30.00	13.50
COMPLETE SERIES 1 (15)		20.00	9.00
COMPLETE SERIES 2 (16)		10.00	4.50
COMMON CARD (DK1-DK31)		.75	.35
RANDOM INSERTS IN FOIL PACKS			
□ DK1 Ken Griffey Jr.		12.00	5.50
□ DK2 Ryne Sandberg		3.00	1.35
□ DK3 Roger Clemens		5.00	2.20
□ DK4 Kirby Puckett		4.00	1.80
□ DK5 Bill Swift		.75	.35
□ DK6 Larry Walker		2.50	1.10
□ DK7 Juan Gonzalez		6.00	2.70
□ DK8 Wally Joyner		.75	.35
□ DK9 Andy Van Slyke		.75	.35
□ DK10 Robin Ventura		1.25	.55
□ DK11 Bip Roberts		.75	.35
□ DK12 Roberto Kelly		.75	.35
□ DK13 Carlos Baerga		.75	.35
□ DK14 Orel Hershiser		1.25	.55
□ DK15 Cecil Fielder		1.25	.55
□ DK16 Robin Yount		2.00	.90
□ DK17 Darren Daulton		.75	.35
□ DK18 Mark McGwire		4.00	1.80
□ DK19 Tom Glavine		2.00	.90
□ DK20 Roberto Alomar		2.50	1.10
□ DK21 Gary Sheffield		2.50	1.10
□ DK22 Bob Tewksbury		.75	.35
□ DK23 Brady Anderson		2.00	.90
□ DK24 Craig Biggio		2.00	.90
□ DK25 Eddie Murray		2.50	1.10
□ DK26 Luis Polonia		.75	.35
□ DK27 Nigel Wilson		.75	.35
□ DK28 David Nied		.75	.35
□ DK29 Pat Listach ROY		.75	.35
□ DK30 Eric Karros ROY		1.25	.55
□ DK31 Checklist 1-31		.75	.35

1993 Donruss Diamond Kings

These standard-size cards, commemorating Donruss' annual selection of the games top players, were randomly inserted in 1993 Donruss packs. The

1993 Donruss Elite

Cards 19-27 were random inserts in 1993 Donruss series I foil packs while cards 28-36 were inserted in series II packs.

The numbering on the 1993 Elite cards follows consecutively after that of the 1992 Elite series cards, and each of the 10,000 Elite cards is serially numbered. The backs of the Elite cards also carry the serial number ("X" of 10,000) as well as the card number. The Signature Series Will Clark card was randomly inserted in 1993 Donruss foil packs: he personally autographed 5,000 cards. Featuring a Dick Perez portrait, the ten thousand Legends Series cards honor Robin Yount for his 3,000th hit achievement. The front design of the Elite cards features a cutout color player photo superimposed on a neon-colored panel framed by a gray inner border and a variegated silver metallic outer border.

	MINT	NRMT
COMPLETE SET (20)	400.00	180.00
COMMON CARD (19-36)	10.00	4.50
SEMISTARS	15.00	6.75
RANDOM INSERTS IN PACKS ..		

		MINT	NRMT
☐ 19	Fred McGriff	15.00	6.75
☐ 20	Ryne Sandberg	30.00	13.50
☐ 21	Eddie Murray	25.00	11.00
☐ 22	Paul Molitor	25.00	11.00
☐ 23	Barry Larkin	15.00	6.75
☐ 24	Don Mattingly	40.00	18.00
☐ 25	Dennis Eckersley	12.00	5.50
☐ 26	Roberto Alomar	25.00	11.00
☐ 27	Edgar Martinez	15.00	6.75
☐ 28	Gary Sheffield	20.00	9.00
☐ 29	Darren Daulton	12.00	5.50
☐ 30	Larry Walker	25.00	11.00
☐ 31	Barry Bonds	30.00	13.50
☐ 32	Andy Van Slyke	10.00	4.50
☐ 33	Mark McGwire	50.00	22.00
☐ 34	Cecil Fielder	12.00	5.50
☐ 35	Dave Winfield	15.00	6.75
☐ 36	Juan Gonzalez	60.00	27.00
☐ L3	Robin Yount	15.00	6.75
	(Legend Series)		
☐ S3	Will Clark AU	150.00	70.00
	(Signature Series)		

1993 Donruss Long Ball Leaders

Randomly inserted in 26-card magazine distributor packs (1-9 in series I and 10-18 in series II), these standard-size cards feature some of MLB's outstanding sluggers. The fronts feature full-bleed color action player photos with a red and bright yellow stripe design

across the bottom that carries the player's name and team. The Donruss Long Ball Leaders icon rests on the stripe at the lower left. The player's longest home run is printed in gold foil at the upper left.

		MINT	NRMT
COMPLETE SET (18)		60.00	27.00
COMPLETE SERIES 1 (9)		30.00	13.50
COMPLETE SERIES 2 (9)		30.00	13.50
COMMON CARD (LL1-LL18)		1.00	.45
RANDOM INSERTS IN 26-CARD JUMBOS			

		MINT	NRMT
☐ LL1	Rob Deer	1.00	.45
☐ LL2	Fred McGriff	2.50	1.10
☐ LL3	Albert Belle	5.00	2.20
☐ LL4	Mark McGwire	8.00	3.60
☐ LL5	David Justice	4.00	1.80
☐ LL6	Jose Canseco	2.50	1.10
☐ LL7	Kent Hrbek	1.00	.45
☐ LL8	Roberto Alomar	4.00	1.80
☐ LL9	Ken Griffey Jr.	20.00	9.00
☐ LL10	Frank Thomas	15.00	6.75
☐ LL11	Darryl Strawberry	2.00	.90
☐ LL12	Felix Jose	1.00	.45
☐ LL13	Cecil Fielder	2.00	.90
☐ LL14	Juan Gonzalez	10.00	4.50
☐ LL15	Ryne Sandberg	5.00	2.20
☐ LL16	Gary Sheffield	4.00	1.80
☐ LL17	Jeff Bagwell	8.00	3.60
☐ LL18	Larry Walker	4.00	1.80

1993 Donruss MVPs

These twenty-six standard-size MVP cards were issued 13 cards in each series, and they were inserted one per 23-card jumbo packs. The fronts feature full-bleed color action player photos with a red, white, and blue ribbon design across the bottom that contains the player's name and team. The Donruss MVP icon is gold-foil stamped over the ribbon.

	MINT	NRMT
COMPLETE SET (26)	30.00	13.50
COMPLETE SERIES 1 (13)	10.00	4.50
COMPLETE SERIES 2 (13)	20.00	9.00
COMMON CARD (1-26)	.50	.23
ONE PER 23-CARD JUMBO PACK		

		MINT	NRMT
☐ 1	Luis Polonia	.50	.23
☐ 2	Frank Thomas	6.00	2.70
☐ 3	George Brett	3.00	1.35
☐ 4	Paul Molitor	1.00	.45
☐ 5	Don Mattingly	3.00	1.35
☐ 6	Roberto Alomar	1.00	.45
☐ 7	Terry Pendleton	.50	.23
☐ 8	Eric Karros	.60	.25
☐ 9	Larry Walker	1.00	.45

		MINT	NRMT
☐ 10	Eddie Murray	1.00	.45
☐ 11	Darren Daulton	.60	.25
☐ 12	Ray Lankford	.75	.35
☐ 13	Will Clark	.75	.35
☐ 14	Cal Ripken	6.00	2.70
☐ 15	Roger Clemens	3.00	1.35
☐ 16	Carlos Baerga	.50	.23
☐ 17	Cecil Fielder	.60	.25
☐ 18	Kirby Puckett	3.00	1.35
☐ 19	Mark McGwire	3.00	1.35
☐ 20	Ken Griffey Jr.	8.00	3.60
☐ 21	Juan Gonzalez	4.00	1.80
☐ 22	Ryne Sandberg	2.00	.90
☐ 23	Bip Roberts	.50	.23
☐ 24	Jeff Bagwell	3.00	1.35
☐ 25	Barry Bonds	2.00	.90
☐ 26	Gary Sheffield	1.00	.45

1993 Donruss Spirit of the Game

These 20 standard-size cards were randomly inserted in 1993 Donruss packs and packed approximately two per box. Cards 1-10 were first-series inserts, and cards 11-20 were second-series inserts. The fronts feature borderless glossy color action player photos. The set title, "Spirit of the Game," is stamped in gold foil script across the top or bottom of the picture.

	MINT	NRMT
COMPLETE SET (20)	20.00	9.00
COMPLETE SERIES 1 (10)	8.00	3.60
COMPLETE SERIES 2 (10)	12.00	5.50
COMMON CARD (SG1-SG20)	.50	.23
RANDOM INSERTS IN FOIL/JUMBO PACKS		

		MINT	NRMT
☐ SG1	Mike Bordick Turning Two	.50	.23
☐ SG2	Dave Justice Play at the Plate	1.50	.70
☐ SG3	Roberto Alomar In There	1.50	.70
☐ SG4	Dennis Eckersley Pumped	.75	.35
☐ SG5	Juan Gonzalez and Jose Canseco Dynamic Duo	4.00	1.80
☐ SG6	George Bell and Frank Thomas - Gone	1.50	.70
☐ SG7	Wade Boggs and Luis Polonia Safe or Out	1.50	.70
☐ SG8	Will Clark The Thrill	1.50	.70
☐ SG9	Bip Roberts Safe at Home	.50	.23
☐ SG10	Cecil Fielder Rob Deer Mickey Tettleton	.75	.35

Thirty 3
		MINT	NRMT
SG11	Kenny Lofton	4.00	1.80
	Bag Bandit		
SG12	Gary Sheffield	1.50	.70
	Fred McGriff		
	Back to Back		
SG13	Greg Gagne	.75	.35
	Barry Larkin		
SG14	Ryne Sandberg	2.50	1.10
	The Ball Stops Here		
SG15	Carlos Baerga	.75	.35
	Gary Gaetti		
	Over the Top		
SG16	Danny Tartabull	.50	.23
	At the Wall		
SG17	Brady Anderson	1.00	.45
	Head First		
SG18	Frank Thomas	10.00	4.50
	Big Hurt		
SG19	Kevin Gross	.50	.23
	No Hitter		
SG20	Robin Yount	1.50	.70
	3,000 Hits		

1994 Donruss

The 1994 Donruss set was issued in two separate series of 330 standard-size cards for a total of 660. The fronts feature borderless color player action photos on front. The player's name and position appear in gold foil within a team color-coded stripe near the bottom. The team logo appears within a black rectangle framed by a team color near the bottom. The set name and year, stamped in gold foil, also appear in this rectangle. Most of the backs are horizontal, and feature another borderless color player action photo. A black rectangle framed by a team color appears on one side and carries the player's name, team, uniform number, and biography. The player's stats appear within ghosted stripes near the bottom. Rookie Cards include Curtis Pride and Julian Tavarez.

	MINT	NRMT
COMPLETE SET (660)	40.00	18.00
COMPLETE SERIES 1 (330)	20.00	9.00
COMPLETE SERIES 2 (330)	20.00	9.00
COMMON CARD (1-660)	.15	.07
MINOR STARS	.30	.14
UNLISTED STARS	.60	.25
COMP.SPEC.ED.SET (100)	20.00	9.00
COMP.SPEC.ED.SER.1 (50)	10.00	4.50
COMP.SPEC.ED.SER.2 (50)	10.00	4.50
COMMON SPEC.ED (1-100)	.25	.11

*SPEC.EDITION: 1X TO 2X HI COLUMN
ONE SPECIAL EDITION PER PACK
SE #51-100 CORRESPOND w/ #331-380

#	Player	MINT	NRMT
1	Nolan Ryan	3.00	1.35
2	Mike Piazza	2.00	.90
3	Moises Alou	.30	.14
4	Ken Griffey Jr.	3.00	1.35
5	Gary Sheffield	.60	.25
6	Roberto Alomar	.60	.25
7	John Kruk	.30	.14
8	Gregg Olson	.15	.07
9	Gregg Jefferies	.15	.07
10	Tony Gwynn	1.50	.70
11	Chad Curtis	.15	.07
12	Craig Biggio	.40	.18
13	John Burkett	.15	.07
14	Carlos Baerga	.15	.07
15	Robin Yount	.40	.18
16	Dennis Eckersley	.30	.14
17	Dwight Gooden	.30	.14
18	Ryne Sandberg	.75	.35
19	Rickey Henderson	.40	.18
20	Jack McDowell	.15	.07
21	Jay Bell	.30	.14
22	Kevin Brown	.30	.14
23	Robin Ventura	.30	.14
24	Paul Molitor	.60	.25
25	David Justice	.60	.25
26	Rafael Palmeiro	.40	.18
27	Cecil Fielder	.30	.14
28	Chuck Knoblauch	.60	.25
29	Dave Hollins	.15	.07
30	Jimmy Key	.30	.14
31	Mark Langston	.15	.07
32	Darryl Kile	.30	.14
33	Ruben Sierra	.15	.07
34	Ron Gant	.30	.14
35	Ozzie Smith	.75	.35
36	Wade Boggs	.60	.25
37	Marquis Grissom	.30	.14
38	Will Clark	.40	.18
39	Kenny Lofton	.75	.35
40	Cal Ripken	2.50	1.10
41	Steve Avery	.15	.07
42	Mo Vaughn	.75	.35
43	Brian McRae	.15	.07
44	Mickey Tettleton	.15	.07
45	Barry Larkin	.40	.18
46	Charlie Hayes	.15	.07
47	Kevin Appier	.30	.14
48	Robby Thompson	.15	.07
49	Juan Gonzalez	1.50	.70
50	Paul O'Neill	.30	.14
51	Marcos Armas	.15	.07
52	Mike Butcher	.15	.07
53	Ken Caminiti	.40	.18
54	Pat Borders	.15	.07
55	Pedro Munoz	.15	.07
56	Tim Belcher	.15	.07
57	Paul Assenmacher	.15	.07
58	Damon Berryhill	.15	.07
59	Ricky Bones	.15	.07
60	Rene Arocha	.15	.07
61	Shawn Boskie	.15	.07
62	Pedro Astacio	.15	.07
63	Frank Bolick	.15	.07
64	Bud Black	.15	.07
65	Sandy Alomar Jr.	.30	.14
66	Rich Amaral	.15	.07
67	Luis Aquino	.15	.07
68	Kevin Baez	.15	.07
69	Mike Devereaux	.15	.07
70	Andy Ashby	.15	.07
71	Larry Andersen	.15	.07
72	Steve Cooke	.15	.07
73	Mario Diaz	.15	.07
74	Rob Deer	.15	.07
75	Bobby Ayala	.15	.07
76	Freddie Benavides	.15	.07
77	Stan Belinda	.15	.07
78	John Doherty	.15	.07
79	Willie Banks	.15	.07
80	Spike Owen	.15	.07
81	Mike Bordick	.15	.07
82	Chili Davis	.30	.14
83	Luis Gonzalez	.15	.07
84	Ed Sprague	.15	.07
85	Jeff Reboulet	.15	.07
86	Jason Bere	.15	.07
87	Mark Hutton	.15	.07
88	Jeff Blauser	.30	.14
89	Cal Eldred	.15	.07
90	Bernard Gilkey	.15	.07
91	Frank Castillo	.15	.07
92	Jim Gott	.15	.07
93	Greg Colbrunn	.15	.07
94	Jeff Brantley	.15	.07
95	Jeremy Hernandez	.15	.07
96	Norm Charlton	.15	.07
97	Alex Arias	.15	.07
98	John Franco	.30	.14
99	Chris Hoiles	.15	.07
100	Brad Ausmus	.15	.07
101	Wes Chamberlain	.15	.07
102	Mark Dewey	.15	.07
103	Benji Gil	.15	.07
104	John Dopson	.15	.07
105	John Smiley	.15	.07
106	David Nied	.15	.07
107	George Brett	1.25	.55
108	Kirk Gibson	.30	.14
109	Larry Casian	.15	.07
110	Ryne Sandberg CL	.40	.18
111	Brent Gates	.15	.07
112	Damion Easley	.15	.07
113	Pete Harnisch	.15	.07
114	Danny Cox	.15	.07
115	Kevin Tapani	.15	.07
116	Roberto Hernandez	.15	.07
117	Domingo Jean	.15	.07
118	Sid Bream	.15	.07
119	Doug Henry	.15	.07
120	Omar Olivares	.15	.07
121	Mike Harkey	.15	.07
122	Carlos Hernandez	.15	.07
123	Jeff Fassero	.15	.07
124	Dave Burba	.15	.07
125	Wayne Kirby	.15	.07
126	John Cummings	.15	.07
127	Bret Barberie	.15	.07
128	Todd Hundley	.30	.14
129	Tim Hulett	.15	.07
130	Phil Clark	.15	.07
131	Danny Jackson	.15	.07
132	Tom Foley	.15	.07
133	Donald Harris	.15	.07
134	Scott Fletcher	.15	.07
135	Johnny Ruffin	.15	.07
136	Jerald Clark	.15	.07
137	Billy Brewer	.15	.07
138	Dan Gladden	.15	.07
139	Eddie Guardado	.15	.07
140	Cal Ripken CL	.75	.35
141	Scott Hemond	.15	.07
142	Steve Frey	.15	.07
143	Xavier Hernandez	.15	.07
144	Mark Eichhorn	.15	.07
145	Elis Burks	.30	.14
146	Jim Leyritz	.15	.07
147	Mark Lemke	.15	.07
148	Pat Listach	.15	.07
149	Donovan Osborne	.15	.07
150	Glenallen Hill	.15	.07
151	Orel Hershiser	.30	.14
152	Darrin Fletcher	.15	.07
153	Royce Clayton	.15	.07
154	Derek Lilliquist	.15	.07
155	Mike Felder	.15	.07
156	Jeff Conine	.30	.14
157	Ryan Thompson	.15	.07
158	Ben McDonald	.15	.07
159	Ricky Gutierrez	.15	.07
160	Terry Mulholland	.15	.07
161	Carlos Garcia	.15	.07
162	Tom Henke	.15	.07
163	Mike Greenwell	.15	.07
164	Thomas Howard	.15	.07
165	Joe Girardi	.15	.07
166	Hubie Brooks	.15	.07
167	Greg Gohr	.15	.07
168	Chip Hale	.15	.07
169	Rick Honeycutt	.15	.07
170	Hilly Hathaway	.15	.07
171	Todd Jones	.15	.07
172	Tony Fernandez	.15	.07

173	Bo Jackson	.30	.14
174	Bobby Munoz	.15	.07
175	Greg McMichael	.15	.07
176	Graeme Lloyd	.15	.07
177	Tom Pagnozzi	.15	.07
178	Derrick May	.15	.07
179	Pedro Martinez	.60	.25
180	Ken Hill	.15	.07
181	Bryan Hickerson	.15	.07
182	Jose Mesa	.15	.07
183	Dave Fleming	.15	.07
184	Henry Cotto	.15	.07
185	Jeff Kent	.15	.07
186	Mark McLemore	.15	.07
187	Trevor Hoffman	.15	.07
188	Todd Pratt	.15	.07
189	Blas Minor	.15	.07
190	Charlie Leibrandt	.15	.07
191	Tony Pena	.15	.07
192	Larry Luebbers	.15	.07
193	Greg W. Harris	.15	.07
194	David Cone	.30	.14
195	Bill Gullickson	.15	.07
196	Brian Harper	.15	.07
197	Steve Karsay	.15	.07
198	Greg Myers	.15	.07
199	Mark Portugal	.15	.07
200	Pat Hentgen	.30	.14
201	Mike LaValliere	.15	.07
202	Mike Stanley	.15	.07
203	Kent Mercker	.15	.07
204	Dave Nilsson	.15	.07
205	Erik Pappas	.15	.07
206	Mike Morgan	.15	.07
207	Roger McDowell	.15	.07
208	Mike Lansing	.30	.14
209	Kirt Manwaring	.15	.07
210	Randy Milligan	.15	.07
211	Erik Hanson	.15	.07
212	Orestes Destrade	.15	.07
213	Mike Maddux	.15	.07
214	Alan Mills	.15	.07
215	Tim Mauser	.15	.07
216	Ben Rivera	.15	.07
217	Don Slaught	.15	.07
218	Bob Patterson	.15	.07
219	Carlos Quintana	.15	.07
220	Tim Raines CL	.15	.07
221	Hal Morris	.15	.07
222	Darren Holmes	.15	.07
223	Chris Gwynn	.15	.07
224	Chad Kreuter	.15	.07
225	Mike Hartley	.15	.07
226	Scott Lydy	.15	.07
227	Eduardo Perez	.15	.07
228	Greg Swindell	.15	.07
229	Al Leiter	.15	.07
230	Scott Radinsky	.15	.07
231	Bob Wickman	.15	.07
232	Otis Nixon	.15	.07
233	Kevin Reimer	.15	.07
234	Geronimo Pena	.15	.07
235	Kevin Roberson	.15	.07
236	Jody Reed	.15	.07
237	Kirk Rueter	.15	.07
238	Willie McGee	.15	.07
239	Charles Nagy	.30	.14
240	Tim Leary	.15	.07
241	Carl Everett	.15	.07
242	Charlie O'Brien	.15	.07
243	Mike Pagliarulo	.15	.07
244	Kerry Taylor	.15	.07
245	Kevin Stocker	.15	.07
246	Joel Johnston	.15	.07
247	Geno Petralli	.15	.07
248	Jeff Russell	.15	.07
249	Joe Oliver	.15	.07
250	Roberto Mejia	.15	.07
251	Chris Haney	.15	.07
252	Bill Krueger	.15	.07
253	Shane Mack	.15	.07
254	Terry Steinbach	.15	.07
255	Luis Polonia	.15	.07
256	Eddie Taubensee	.15	.07
257	Dave Stewart	.30	.14
258	Tim Raines	.30	.14
259	Bernie Williams	.60	.25
260	John Smoltz	.30	.14
261	Kevin Seitzer	.15	.07
262	Bob Tewksbury	.15	.07
263	Bob Scanlan	.15	.07
264	Henry Rodriguez	.15	.07
265	Tim Scott	.15	.07
266	Scott Sanderson	.15	.07
267	Eric Plunk	.15	.07
268	Edgar Martinez	.40	.18
269	Charlie Hough	.15	.07
270	Joe Orsulak	.15	.07
271	Harold Reynolds	.15	.07
272	Tim Teufel	.15	.07
273	Bobby Thigpen	.15	.07
274	Randy Tomlin	.15	.07
275	Gary Redus	.15	.07
276	Ken Ryan	.15	.07
277	Tim Pugh	.15	.07
278	J. Owens	.15	.07
279	Phil Hiatt	.15	.07
280	Mark Langston	.40	.18
281	Dave McCarty	.15	.07
282	Bob Welch	.15	.07
283	J.T. Snow	.60	.25
284	Brian Williams	.15	.07
285	Devon White	.15	.07
286	Steve Sax	.15	.07
287	Tony Tarasco	.15	.07
288	Bill Spiers	.15	.07
289	Allen Watson	.15	.07
290	Rickey Henderson CL	.30	.14
291	Jose Vizcaino	.15	.07
292	Darryl Strawberry	.30	.14
293	John Wetteland	.15	.07
294	Bill Swift	.15	.07
295	Jeff Treadway	.15	.07
296	Tino Martinez	.60	.25
297	Richie Lewis	.15	.07
298	Bret Saberhagen	.15	.07
299	Arthur Rhodes	.15	.07
300	Guillermo Velasquez	.15	.07
301	Milt Thompson	.15	.07
302	Doug Strange	.15	.07
303	Aaron Sele	.15	.07
304	Bip Roberts	.15	.07
305	Bruce Ruffin	.15	.07
306	Jose Lind	.15	.07
307	David Wells	.15	.07
308	Bobby Witt	.15	.07
309	Mark Wohlers	.15	.07
310	B.J. Surhoff	.15	.07
311	Mark Whiten	.15	.07
312	Turk Wendell	.15	.07
313	Raul Mondesi	.60	.25
314	Brian Turang	.15	.07
315	Chris Hammond	.15	.07
316	Tim Bogar	.15	.07
317	Brad Pennington	.15	.07
318	Tim Worrell	.15	.07
319	Mitch Williams	.15	.07
320	Rondell White	.40	.18
321	Frank Viola	.15	.07
322	Manny Ramirez	.75	.35
323	Gary Wayne	.15	.07
324	Mike Macfarlane	.15	.07
325	Russ Springer	.15	.07
326	Tim Wallach	.15	.07
327	Salomon Torres	.15	.07
328	Omar Vizquel	.30	.14
329	Andy Tomberlin	.15	.07
330	Chris Sabo	.15	.07
331	Mike Mussina	.60	.25
332	Andy Benes	.30	.14
333	Darren Daulton	.30	.14
334	Orlando Merced	.15	.07
335	Mark McGwire	1.25	.55
336	Dave Winfield	.40	.18
337	Sammy Sosa	.60	.25
338	Eric Karros	.30	.14
339	Greg Vaughn	.15	.07
340	Don Mattingly	1.00	.45
341	Frank Thomas	2.50	1.10
342	Fred McGriff	.40	.18
343	Kirby Puckett	1.25	.55
344	Roberto Kelly	.15	.07
345	Wally Joyner	.30	.14
346	Andres Galarraga	.60	.25
347	Bobby Bonilla	.30	.14
348	Benito Santiago	.15	.07
349	Barry Bonds	.75	.35
350	Delino DeShields	.15	.07
351	Albert Belle	.75	.35
352	Randy Johnson	.60	.25
353	Tim Salmon	.60	.25
354	John Olerud	.30	.14
355	Dean Palmer	.15	.07
356	Roger Clemens	1.25	.55
357	Jim Abbott	.15	.07
358	Mark Grace	.40	.18
359	Ozzie Guillen	.15	.07
360	Lou Whitaker	.30	.14
361	Jose Rijo	.15	.07
362	Jeff Montgomery	.15	.07
363	Chuck Finley	.15	.07
364	Tom Glavine	.30	.14
365	Jeff Bagwell	1.25	.55
366	Joe Carter	.30	.14
367	Ray Lankford	.30	.14
368	Ramon Martinez	.30	.14
369	Jay Buhner	.40	.18
370	Matt Williams	.40	.18
371	Larry Walker	.60	.25
372	Jose Canseco	.40	.18
373	Lenny Dykstra	.15	.07
374	Bryan Harvey	.15	.07
375	Andy Van Slyke	.30	.14
376	Ivan Rodriguez	.75	.35
377	Kevin Mitchell	.15	.07
378	Travis Fryman	.30	.14
379	Duane Ward	.15	.07
380	Greg Maddux	2.00	.90
381	Scott Servais	.15	.07
382	Greg Olson	.15	.07
383	Rey Sanchez	.15	.07
384	Tom Kramer	.15	.07
385	David Valle	.15	.07
386	Eddie Murray	.60	.25
387	Kevin Higgins	.15	.07
388	Dan Wilson	.30	.14
389	Todd Frohwirth	.15	.07
390	Gerald Williams	.15	.07
391	Hipolito Pichardo	.15	.07
392	Pat Meares	.15	.07
393	Luis Lopez	.15	.07
394	Ricky Jordan	.15	.07
395	Bob Walk	.15	.07
396	Sid Fernandez	.15	.07
397	Todd Worrell	.15	.07
398	Darryl Hamilton	.15	.07
399	Randy Myers	.15	.07
400	Rod Brewer	.15	.07
401	Lance Blankenship	.15	.07
402	Steve Finley	.30	.14
403	Phil Leftwich	.15	.07
404	Juan Guzman	.15	.07
405	Anthony Young	.15	.07
406	Jeff Gardner	.15	.07
407	Ryan Bowen	.15	.07
408	Fernando Valenzuela	.30	.14
409	David West	.15	.07
410	Kenny Rogers	.15	.07
411	Bob Zupcic	.15	.07
412	Eric Young	.15	.07
413	Bret Boone	.15	.07
414	Danny Tartabull	.15	.07
415	Bob MacDonald	.15	.07
416	Ron Karkovice	.15	.07
417	Scott Cooper	.15	.07
418	Dante Bichette	.30	.14
419	Tripp Cromer	.15	.07
420	Billy Ashley	.15	.07
421	Roger Smithberg	.15	.07
422	Dennis Martinez	.30	.14
423	Mike Blowers	.15	.07
424	Darren Lewis	.15	.07
425	Junior Ortiz	.15	.07
426	Butch Huskey	.30	.14
427	Jimmy Poole	.15	.07
428	Walt Weiss	.15	.07
429	Scott Bankhead	.15	.07
430	Deion Sanders	.30	.14

☐ 431	Scott Bullett	.15	.07
☐ 432	Jeff Huson	.15	.07
☐ 433	Tyler Green	.15	.07
☐ 434	Billy Hatcher	.15	.07
☐ 435	Bob Hamelin	.15	.07
☐ 436	Reggie Sanders	.15	.07
☐ 437	Scott Erickson	.15	.07
☐ 438	Steve Reed	.15	.07
☐ 439	Randy Velarde	.15	.07
☐ 440	Tony Gwynn CL	.15	.25
☐ 441	Terry Leach	.15	.07
☐ 442	Danny Bautista	.15	.07
☐ 443	Kent Hrbek	.30	.14
☐ 444	Rick Wilkins	.15	.07
☐ 445	Tony Phillips	.15	.07
☐ 446	Dion James	.15	.07
☐ 447	Joey Cora	.30	.14
☐ 448	Andre Dawson	.40	.18
☐ 449	Pedro Castellano	.15	.07
☐ 450	Tom Gordon	.15	.07
☐ 451	Rob Dibble	.15	.07
☐ 452	Ron Darling	.15	.07
☐ 453	Chipper Jones	2.00	.90
☐ 454	Joe Grahe	.15	.07
☐ 455	Domingo Cedeno	.15	.07
☐ 456	Tom Edens	.15	.07
☐ 457	Mitch Webster	.15	.07
☐ 458	Jose Bautista	.15	.07
☐ 459	Troy O'Leary	.15	.07
☐ 460	Todd Zeile	.15	.07
☐ 461	Sean Berry	.15	.07
☐ 462	Brad Holman	.15	.07
☐ 463	Dave Martinez	.15	.07
☐ 464	Mark Lewis	.15	.07
☐ 465	Paul Carey	.15	.07
☐ 466	Jack Armstrong	.15	.07
☐ 467	David Telgheder	.15	.07
☐ 468	Gene Harris	.15	.07
☐ 469	Danny Darwin	.15	.07
☐ 470	Kim Batiste	.15	.07
☐ 471	Tim Wakefield	.15	.07
☐ 472	Craig Lefferts	.15	.07
☐ 473	Jacob Brumfield	.15	.07
☐ 474	Lance Painter	.15	.07
☐ 475	Milt Cuyler	.15	.07
☐ 476	Melido Perez	.15	.07
☐ 477	Derek Parks	.15	.07
☐ 478	Gary DiSarcina	.15	.07
☐ 479	Steve Bedrosian	.15	.07
☐ 480	Eric Anthony	.15	.07
☐ 481	Julio Franco	.15	.07
☐ 482	Tommy Greene	.15	.07
☐ 483	Pat Kelly	.15	.07
☐ 484	Nate Minchey	.15	.07
☐ 485	William Pennyfeather	.15	.07
☐ 486	Harold Baines	.30	.14
☐ 487	Howard Johnson	.15	.07
☐ 488	Angel Miranda	.15	.07
☐ 489	Scott Sanders	.15	.07
☐ 490	Shawon Dunston	.15	.07
☐ 491	Mel Rojas	.15	.07
☐ 492	Jeff Nelson	.15	.07
☐ 493	Arch Cianfrocco	.15	.07
☐ 494	Al Martin	.15	.07
☐ 495	Mike Gallego	.15	.07
☐ 496	Mike Henneman	.15	.07
☐ 497	Armando Reynoso	.15	.07
☐ 498	Mickey Morandini	.15	.07
☐ 499	Rick Renteria	.15	.07
☐ 500	Rick Sutcliffe	.15	.07
☐ 501	Bobby Jones	.30	.14
☐ 502	Gary Gaetti	.15	.07
☐ 503	Rick Aguilera	.15	.07
☐ 504	Todd Stottlemyre	.15	.07
☐ 505	Mike Mohler	.15	.07
☐ 506	Mike Stanton	.15	.07
☐ 507	Jose Guzman	.15	.07
☐ 508	Kevin Rogers	.15	.07
☐ 509	Chuck Carr	.15	.07
☐ 510	Chris Jones	.15	.07
☐ 511	Brent Mayne	.15	.07
☐ 512	Greg Harris	.15	.07
☐ 513	Dave Henderson	.15	.07
☐ 514	Eric Hillman	.15	.07
☐ 515	Dan Peltier	.15	.07
☐ 516	Craig Shipley	.15	.07
☐ 517	John Valentin	.30	.14
☐ 518	Wilson Alvarez	.15	.07
☐ 519	Andujar Cedeno	.15	.07
☐ 520	Troy Neel	.15	.07
☐ 521	Tom Candiotti	.15	.07
☐ 522	Matt Mieske	.15	.07
☐ 523	Jim Thome	.75	.35
☐ 524	Lou Frazier	.15	.07
☐ 525	Mike Jackson	.15	.07
☐ 526	Pedro Martinez	.60	.25
☐ 527	Roger Pavlik	.15	.07
☐ 528	Kent Bottenfield	.15	.07
☐ 529	Felix Jose	.15	.07
☐ 530	Mark Guthrie	.15	.07
☐ 531	Steve Farr	.15	.07
☐ 532	Craig Paquette	.15	.07
☐ 533	Doug Jones	.15	.07
☐ 534	Luis Alicea	.15	.07
☐ 535	Cory Snyder	.15	.07
☐ 536	Paul Sorrento	.15	.07
☐ 537	Nigel Wilson	.15	.07
☐ 538	Jeff King	.15	.07
☐ 539	Willie Greene	.15	.07
☐ 540	Kirk McCaskill	.15	.07
☐ 541	Al Osuna	.15	.07
☐ 542	Greg Hibbard	.15	.07
☐ 543	Brett Butler	.30	.14
☐ 544	Jose Valentin	.15	.07
☐ 545	Wil Cordero	.15	.07
☐ 546	Chris Bosio	.15	.07
☐ 547	Jamie Moyer	.15	.07
☐ 548	Jim Eisenreich	.15	.07
☐ 549	Vinny Castilla	.30	.14
☐ 550	Dave Winfield CL	.30	.14
☐ 551	John Roper	.15	.07
☐ 552	Lance Johnson	.15	.07
☐ 553	Scott Kamieniecki	.15	.07
☐ 554	Mike Moore	.15	.07
☐ 555	Steve Buechele	.15	.07
☐ 556	Terry Pendleton	.15	.07
☐ 557	Todd Van Poppel	.15	.07
☐ 558	Rob Butler	.15	.07
☐ 559	Zane Smith	.15	.07
☐ 560	David Hulse	.15	.07
☐ 561	Tim Costo	.15	.07
☐ 562	John Habyan	.15	.07
☐ 563	Terry Jorgensen	.15	.07
☐ 564	Matt Nokes	.15	.07
☐ 565	Kevin McReynolds	.15	.07
☐ 566	Phil Plantier	.15	.07
☐ 567	Chris Turner	.15	.07
☐ 568	Carlos Delgado	.40	.18
☐ 569	John Jaha	.15	.07
☐ 570	Dwight Smith	.15	.07
☐ 571	John Vander Wal	.15	.07
☐ 572	Trevor Wilson	.15	.07
☐ 573	Felix Fermin	.15	.07
☐ 574	Marc Newfield	.30	.14
☐ 575	Jeromy Burnitz	.15	.07
☐ 576	Leo Gomez	.15	.07
☐ 577	Curt Schilling	.30	.14
☐ 578	Kevin Young	.15	.07
☐ 579	Jerry Spradlin	.15	.07
☐ 580	Curt Leskanic	.15	.07
☐ 581	Carl Willis	.15	.07
☐ 582	Alex Fernandez	.15	.07
☐ 583	Mark Holzemer	.15	.07
☐ 584	Domingo Martinez	.15	.07
☐ 585	Pete Smith	.15	.07
☐ 586	Brian Jordan	.30	.14
☐ 587	Kevin Gross	.15	.07
☐ 588	J.R. Phillips	.15	.07
☐ 589	Chris Nabholz	.15	.07
☐ 590	Bill Wertz	.15	.07
☐ 591	Derek Bell	.15	.07
☐ 592	Brady Anderson	.40	.18
☐ 593	Matt Turner	.15	.07
☐ 594	Pete Incaviglia	.15	.07
☐ 595	Greg Gagne	.15	.07
☐ 596	John Flaherty	.15	.07
☐ 597	Scott Livingstone	.15	.07
☐ 598	Rod Bolton	.15	.07
☐ 599	Mike Perez	.15	.07
☐ 600	Roger Clemens CL	.60	.25
☐ 601	Tony Castillo	.15	.07
☐ 602	Henry Mercedes	.15	.07
☐ 603	Mike Fetters	.15	.07
☐ 604	Rod Beck	.15	.07
☐ 605	Damon Buford	.15	.07
☐ 606	Matt Whiteside	.15	.07
☐ 607	Shawn Green	.30	.14
☐ 608	Midre Cummings	.15	.07
☐ 609	Jeff McNeely	.15	.07
☐ 610	Danny Sheaffer	.15	.07
☐ 611	Paul Wagner	.15	.07
☐ 612	Torey Lovullo	.15	.07
☐ 613	Javier Lopez	.40	.18
☐ 614	Mariano Duncan	.15	.07
☐ 615	Doug Brocail	.15	.07
☐ 616	Dave Hansen	.15	.07
☐ 617	Ryan Klesko	.60	.25
☐ 618	Eric Davis	.30	.14
☐ 619	Scott Ruffcorn	.15	.07
☐ 620	Mike Trombley	.15	.07
☐ 621	Jaime Navarro	.15	.07
☐ 622	Rheal Cormier	.15	.07
☐ 623	Jose Offerman	.15	.07
☐ 624	David Segui	.15	.07
☐ 625	Robb Nen	.15	.07
☐ 626	Dave Gallagher	.15	.07
☐ 627	Julian Tavarez	.30	.14
☐ 628	Chris Gomez	.15	.07
☐ 629	Jeffrey Hammonds	.30	.14
☐ 630	Scott Brosius	.15	.07
☐ 631	Willie Blair	.15	.07
☐ 632	Doug Drabek	.15	.07
☐ 633	Bill Wegman	.15	.07
☐ 634	Jeff McKnight	.15	.07
☐ 635	Rich Rodriguez	.15	.07
☐ 636	Steve Trachsel	.30	.14
☐ 637	Buddy Groom	.15	.07
☐ 638	Sterling Hitchcock	.15	.07
☐ 639	Chuck McElroy	.15	.07
☐ 640	Rene Gonzales	.15	.07
☐ 641	Dan Plesac	.15	.07
☐ 642	Jeff Branson	.15	.07
☐ 643	Darrell Whitmore	.15	.07
☐ 644	Paul Quantrill	.15	.07
☐ 645	Rich Rowland	.15	.07
☐ 646	Curtis Pride	.15	.07
☐ 647	Erik Plantenberg	.15	.07
☐ 648	Albie Lopez	.15	.07
☐ 649	Rich Batchelor	.15	.07
☐ 650	Lee Smith	.30	.14
☐ 651	Cliff Floyd	.30	.14
☐ 652	Pete Schourek	.15	.07
☐ 653	Reggie Jefferson	.15	.07
☐ 654	Bill Haselman	.15	.07
☐ 655	Steve Hosey	.15	.07
☐ 656	Mark Clark	.15	.07
☐ 657	Mark Davis	.15	.07
☐ 658	Dave Magadan	.15	.07
☐ 659	Candy Maldonado	.15	.07
☐ 660	Mark Langston CL	.15	.07

1994 Donruss Anniversary '84

Randomly inserted in hobby foil packs at a rate of one in 12, this ten-card standard-size set reproduces selected cards from the 1984 Donruss baseball set. The cards feature white bordered color player photos on their fronts. The player's name appears in yellow lettering within a colored stripe at the bottom. The player's gold-foil team name is shown within wavy gold-foil lines near the bottom of the photo. The horizontal and white-bordered back carries the player's name and biography within a green-colored stripe across the top. A white area below contains the player's stats and, within a green panel further below, his career highlights. The cards are numbered on the back at the bottom right as "X of 10," and also carry the numbers from the original 1984 set at the upper left.

	MINT	NRMT
COMPLETE SET (10)	50.00	22.00
COMMON CARD (1-10)	2.00	.90

RANDOM INSERTS IN SER.1 HOBBY PACKS

☐ 1 Joe Carter	2.00	.90
☐ 2 Robin Yount	2.50	1.10
☐ 3 George Brett	5.00	2.20
☐ 4 Rickey Henderson	2.50	1.10
☐ 5 Nolan Ryan	15.00	6.75
☐ 6 Cal Ripken	15.00	6.75
☐ 7 Wade Boggs UER	4.00	1.80
1983 runs 10, should be 100		
☐ 8 Don Mattingly	6.00	2.70
☐ 9 Ryne Sandberg	5.00	2.20
☐ 10 Tony Gwynn	10.00	4.50

1994 Donruss Award Winner Jumbos

This 10-card set was issued one per jumbo foil and Canadian foil boxes and spotlights players that won various awards in 1993. Cards 1-5 were included in first series boxes and 6-10 with the second series. The cards measure approximately 3 1/2" by 5". Ten-thousand of each card were produced. Card fronts are full-bleed with a color player photo and the Award Winner logo at the top. The backs are individually numbered out of 10,000.

	MINT	NRMT
COMPLETE SET (10)	90.00	40.00
COMPLETE SERIES 1 (5)	50.00	22.00
COMPLETE SERIES 2 (5)	40.00	18.00

COMMON CARD (1-10) .... 2.00 .90
ONE PER JUMBO BOX OR CDN FOIL BOX

☐ 1 Barry Bonds MVP	8.00	3.60
☐ 2 Greg Maddux CY	20.00	9.00
☐ 3 Mike Piazza ROY	20.00	9.00
☐ 4 Barry Bonds HR King	8.00	3.60
☐ 5 Kirby Puckett AS MVP	12.00	5.50
☐ 6 Frank Thomas MVP	25.00	11.00
☐ 7 Jack McDowell CY	2.00	.90
☐ 8 Tim Salmon ROY	6.00	2.70
☐ 9 Juan Gonzalez HR King	15.00	6.75
☐ 10 Paul Molitor WS MVP	6.00	2.70

1994 Donruss Diamond Kings

This 30-card standard-size set was split in two series. Cards 1-14 and 29 were randomly inserted in first series packs, while cards 15-28 and 30 were inserted in second series packs. With each series, the insertion rate was one in nine. The fronts feature full-bleed player portraits by noted sports artist Dick Perez. The cards are numbered on the back with the prefix DK. Jumbo versions of these cards were inserted one per retail box.

	MINT	NRMT
COMPLETE SET (30)	50.00	22.00
COMPLETE SERIES 1 (15)	25.00	11.00
COMPLETE SERIES 2 (15)	25.00	11.00
COMMON CARD (DK1-DK30)	.50	.23

STATED ODDS 1:9
*JUMBO DK's: 1X TO 12X BASE CARD HI
ONE JUMBO DK PER RETAIL BOX

☐ DK1 Barry Bonds	2.50	1.10
☐ DK2 Mo Vaughn	2.00	.90
☐ DK3 Steve Avery	.50	.23
☐ DK4 Tim Salmon	2.00	.90
☐ DK5 Rick Wilkins	.50	.23
☐ DK6 Brian Harper	.50	.23
☐ DK7 Andres Galarraga	2.00	.90
☐ DK8 Albert Belle	2.00	.90
☐ DK9 John Kruk	1.00	.45
☐ DK10 Ivan Rodriguez	2.50	1.10
☐ DK11 Tony Gwynn	5.00	2.20
☐ DK12 Brian McRae	.50	.23
☐ DK13 Bobby Bonilla	1.00	.45
☐ DK14 Ken Griffey Jr.	10.00	4.50
☐ DK15 Mike Piazza	6.00	2.70
☐ DK16 Don Mattingly	3.00	1.35
☐ DK17 Barry Larkin	1.25	.55
☐ DK18 Ruben Sierra	.50	.23
☐ DK19 Orlando Merced	.50	.23
☐ DK20 Greg Vaughn	.50	.23
☐ DK21 Gregg Jefferies	.50	.23
☐ DK22 Cecil Fielder	1.00	.45
☐ DK23 Moises Alou	1.00	.45
☐ DK24 John Olerud	1.00	.45
☐ DK25 Gary Sheffield	2.00	.90

☐ DK26 Mike Mussina	2.00	.90
☐ DK27 Jeff Bagwell	4.00	1.80
☐ DK28 Frank Thomas	8.00	3.60
☐ DK29 Dave Winfield	1.25	.55
☐ DK30 Checklist	.50	.23

1994 Donruss Dominators

This 20-card, standard-size set was randomly inserted in all packs at a rate of one in 12. The 10 series 1 cards feature the top home run hitters of the '90s, while the 10 series 2 cards depict the decade's batting average leaders. The fronts displayed full-bleed color action shots with the set title printed along the bottom in gold and black lettering. Jumbo Dominators (3 1/2" by 5") were issued one per hobby box.

	MINT	NRMT
COMPLETE SET (20)	50.00	22.00
COMPLETE SERIES 1 (10)	20.00	9.00
COMPLETE SERIES 2 (10)	30.00	13.50
COMMON CARD (A1-B10)	.50	.23

RANDOM INSERTS IN PACKS
*JUMBOS: 3X TO 6X BASE CARD HI
ONE JUMBO DOMINATOR PER HOBBY BOX

☐ A1 Cecil Fielder	1.00	.45
☐ A2 Barry Bonds	2.50	1.10
☐ A3 Fred McGriff	1.25	.55
☐ A4 Matt Williams	1.25	.55
☐ A5 Joe Carter	1.00	.45
☐ A6 Juan Gonzalez	5.00	2.20
☐ A7 Jose Canseco	1.25	.55
☐ A8 Ron Gant	1.00	.45
☐ A9 Ken Griffey Jr.	10.00	4.50
☐ A10 Mark McGwire	4.00	1.80
☐ B1 Tony Gwynn	5.00	2.20
☐ B2 Frank Thomas	8.00	3.60
☐ B3 Paul Molitor	2.00	.90
☐ B4 Edgar Martinez	1.25	.55
☐ B5 Kirby Puckett	4.00	1.80
☐ B6 Ken Griffey Jr.	10.00	4.50
☐ B7 Barry Bonds	2.50	1.10
☐ B8 Willie McGee	.50	.23
☐ B9 Lenny Dykstra	1.00	.45
☐ B10 John Kruk	1.00	.45

1994 Donruss Elite

This 12-card set was issued in two series of six. Using a continued numbering system from previous years, cards 37-42 were randomly inserted in first series foil packs with cards 43-48 a second series offering. The cards measure the standard size. Only 10,000 of each card were produced. The color play-

er photo inside a diamond design on the front rests on a marbleized panel framed by a red-and-white inner border and a silver foil outer border. Silver foil stripes radiate away from the edges of the picture. The player's name appears across the bottom of the front. The back design is similar, but with a color head shot in a small diamond and a player profile, both resting on a marbleized panel. The bottom carries the card number, the serial number, and the production run figure.

	MINT	NRMT
COMPLETE SET (12)	200.00	90.00
COMPLETE SERIES 1 (6)	110.00	50.00
COMPLETE SERIES 2 (6)	90.00	40.00
COMMON CARD (37-48)	8.00	3.60
UNLISTED STARS	10.00	4.50
RANDOM INSERTS IN HOBBY/RETAIL PACKS		

		MINT	NRMT
☐ 37	Frank Thomas	40.00	18.00
☐ 38	Tony Gwynn	25.00	11.00
☐ 39	Tim Salmon	10.00	4.50
☐ 40	Albert Belle	12.00	5.50
☐ 41	John Kruk	10.00	4.50
☐ 42	Juan Gonzalez	25.00	11.00
☐ 43	John Olerud	10.00	4.50
☐ 44	Barry Bonds	12.00	5.50
☐ 45	Ken Griffey Jr.	50.00	22.00
☐ 46	Mike Piazza	30.00	13.50
☐ 47	Jack McDowell	8.00	3.60
☐ 48	Andres Galarraga	10.00	4.50

1994 Donruss Long Ball Leaders

Inserted in second series hobby foil packs at a rate of one in 12, this 10-card standard-size set features some of top home run hitters and the distance of their longest home run of 1993. The card fronts have a color photo with a black right-hand border.

Within the border is the Long Ball Leaders logo in silver foil. Also in silver foil at bottom, is the player's last name and the distance of the clout. Card backs contain a photo of the park with which the home run occurred as well as information such as the date, the pitcher and other particulars.

	MINT	NRMT
COMPLETE SET (10)	40.00	18.00
COMMON CARD (1-10)	1.00	.45
RANDOM INSERTS IN SER.2 HOBBY PACKS		

		MINT	NRMT
☐ 1	Cecil Fielder	1.50	.70
☐ 2	Dean Palmer	1.00	.45
☐ 3	Andres Galarraga	3.00	1.35
☐ 4	Bo Jackson	1.50	.70
☐ 5	Ken Griffey Jr.	15.00	6.75
☐ 6	David Justice	3.00	1.35
☐ 7	Mike Piazza	10.00	4.50
☐ 8	Frank Thomas	12.00	5.50
☐ 9	Barry Bonds	4.00	1.80
☐ 10	Juan Gonzalez	8.00	3.60

1994 Donruss MVPs

Inserted at a rate of one per first and second series jumbo pack, this 28-card standard-size set was split into two series of 14; one player for each team. The first 14 are of National League players with the latter group being American Leaguers. Full-bleed card fronts feature an action photo of the player with "MVP" in large red (American League) or blue (National) letters at the bottom. The player's name and, for Amercian League player cards only, team name are beneath the "MVP." A number of white stars stretches up the left border. The backs, which are horizontal, contain a photo, 1993 statistics, a short write-up and white stars within blue foil along the left border.

	MINT	NRMT
COMPLETE SET (28)	75.00	34.00
COMPLETE SERIES 1 (14)	15.00	6.75
COMPLETE SERIES 2 (14)	60.00	27.00
COMMON CARD (1-10)	1.00	.45
ONE PER JUMBO PACK		

		MINT	NRMT
☐ 1	David Justice	2.50	1.10
☐ 2	Mark Grace	1.50	.70
☐ 3	Jose Rijo	.75	.35
☐ 4	Andres Galarraga	2.50	1.10
☐ 5	Bryan Harvey	.75	.35
☐ 6	Jeff Bagwell	6.00	2.70
☐ 7	Mike Piazza	10.00	4.50
☐ 8	Moises Alou	1.00	.45
☐ 9	Bobby Bonilla	1.00	.45
☐ 10	Len Dykstra	1.00	.45
☐ 11	Jeff King	.75	.35
☐ 12	Gregg Jefferies	.75	.35
☐ 13	Tony Gwynn	8.00	3.60
☐ 14	Barry Bonds	4.00	1.80
☐ 15	Cal Ripken Jr.	12.00	5.50
☐ 16	Mo Vaughn	4.00	1.80
☐ 17	Tim Salmon	2.50	1.10
☐ 18	Frank Thomas	12.00	5.50
☐ 19	Albert Belle	4.00	1.80
☐ 20	Cecil Fielder	1.00	.45
☐ 21	Wally Joyner	1.00	.45
☐ 22	Greg Vaughn	.75	.35
☐ 23	Kirby Puckett	6.00	2.70
☐ 24	Don Mattingly	5.00	2.20
☐ 25	Ruben Sierra	.75	.35
☐ 26	Ken Griffey Jr.	15.00	6.75
☐ 27	Juan Gonzalez	8.00	3.60
☐ 28	John Olerud	1.00	.45

1994 Donruss Spirit of the Game

This ten card set features a selection of the games top stars. Cards 1-5 were randomly inserted in first-series magazine jumbo packs and cards 6-10 in second series magazine jumbo packs. Card fronts feature borderless, horizontal designs that have color action player photos superposed over triple exposure sepia-toned action shots. Jumbo sized Spirit of the Game cards, individually numbered out of 10,000, were issued one per magazine jumbo box.

	MINT	NRMT
COMPLETE SET (10)	60.00	27.00
COMPLETE SERIES 1 (5)	30.00	13.50
COMPLETE SERIES 2 (5)	30.00	13.50
COMMON CARD (1-10)	1.50	.70
RANDOM INSERTS IN MAG.JUMBO PACKS		
*JUMBOS: 1X TO 12X BASE CARD HI		
ONE JUMBO SPIRIT PER MAG.JUMBO BOX		

		MINT	NRMT
☐ 1	John Olerud	1.50	.70
☐ 2	Barry Bonds	5.00	2.20
☐ 3	Ken Griffey Jr.	20.00	9.00
☐ 4	Mike Piazza	12.00	5.50
☐ 5	Juan Gonzalez	10.00	4.50
☐ 6	Frank Thomas	15.00	6.75
☐ 7	Tim Salmon	4.00	1.80
☐ 8	David Justice	4.00	1.80
☐ 9	Don Mattingly	6.00	2.70
☐ 10	Lenny Dykstra	1.50	.70

1995 Donruss

The 1995 Donruss set consists of 550 standard-size cards. The

first series had 330 cards while 220 cards comprised the second series. The fronts feature borderless color action player photos. A second, smaller color player photo in a homeplate shape with team color-coded borders appears in the lower left corner. The player's position in silver-foil is above this smaller photo, while his name is printed in a silver-foil bar under the photo. The borderless backs carry a color action player cutout superimposed over the team logo, along with player biography and stats for the last five years. There are no key Rookie Cards in this set.

	MINT	NRMT
COMPLETE SET (550)	40.00	18.00
COMPLETE SERIES 1 (330)	25.00	11.00
COMPLETE SERIES 2 (220)	15.00	6.75
COMMON CARD (1-550)	.15	.07
MINOR STARS	.30	.14
UNLISTED STARS	.60	.25
COMP.PP SET (550)	1500.00	700.00
COMP.PP SER.1 (330)	900.00	400.00
COMP.PP SER.2 (220)	600.00	275.00
COMMON PP (1-550)	2.50	1.10

*PP STARS: 12.5X TO 25X HI COLUMN
*PP YOUNG STARS: 10X TO 20X HI
PP SER.1 STAT.ODDS 1:20H/R, 1:18J, 1:24M
PP SER.2 STAT.ODDS 1:24H/R, 1:18J, 1:24M
PP STATED PRINT RUN 2000 SETS

1	David Justice	.60	.25
2	Rene Arocha	.15	.07
3	Sandy Alomar Jr.	.30	.14
4	Luis Lopez	.15	.07
5	Mike Piazza	2.00	.90
6	Bobby Jones	.15	.07
7	Damion Easley	.15	.07
8	Barry Bonds	.75	.35
9	Mike Mussina	.60	.25
10	Kevin Seitzer	.15	.07
11	John Smiley	.15	.07
12	Wm.VanLandingham	.15	.07
13	Ron Darling	.15	.07
14	Walt Weiss	.15	.07
15	Mike Lansing	.15	.07
16	Allen Watson	.15	.07
17	Aaron Sele	.15	.07
18	Randy Johnson	.40	.18
19	Dean Palmer	.15	.07
20	Jeff Bagwell	1.25	.55
21	Curt Schilling	.30	.14
22	Darrell Whitmore	.15	.07
23	Steve Trachsel	.15	.07
24	Dan Wilson	.15	.07
25	Steve Finley	.30	.14
26	Bret Boone	.15	.07
27	Charles Johnson	.30	.14
28	Mike Stanton	.15	.07
29	Ismael Valdes	.40	.18
30	Salomon Torres	.15	.07
31	Eric Anthony	.15	.07
32	Spike Owen	.15	.07
33	Joey Cora	.30	.14
34	Robert Eenhoorn	.15	.07
35	Rick White	.15	.07
36	Omar Vizquel	.30	.14
37	Carlos Delgado	.30	.14
38	Eddie Williams	.15	.07
39	Shawon Dunston	.15	.07
40	Darrin Fletcher	.15	.07
41	Leo Gomez	.15	.07
42	Juan Gonzalez	1.50	.70
43	Luis Alicea	.15	.07
44	Ken Ryan	.15	.07
45	Lou Whitaker	.30	.14
46	Mike Blowers	.15	.07
47	Willie Blair	.15	.07
48	Todd Van Poppel	.15	.07
49	Roberto Alomar	.60	.25
50	Ozzie Smith	.75	.35
51	Sterling Hitchcock	.15	.07
52	Mo Vaughn	.75	.35
53	Rick Aguilera	.15	.07
54	Kent Mercker	.15	.07
55	Don Mattingly	1.00	.45
56	Bob Scanlan	.15	.07
57	Wilson Alvarez	.15	.07
58	Jose Mesa	.15	.07
59	Scott Kamieniecki	.15	.07
60	Todd Jones	.15	.07
61	John Kruk	.30	.14
62	Mike Stanley	.15	.07
63	Tino Martinez	.60	.25
64	Eddie Zambrano	.15	.07
65	Todd Hundley	.30	.14
66	Jamie Moyer	.15	.07
67	Rich Amaral	.15	.07
68	Jose Valentin	.15	.07
69	Alex Gonzalez	.15	.07
70	Kurt Abbott	.15	.07
71	Delino DeShields	.15	.07
72	Brian Anderson	.30	.14
73	John Vander Wal	.15	.07
74	Turner Ward	.15	.07
75	Tim Raines	.30	.14
76	Mark Acre	.15	.07
77	Jose Offerman	.15	.07
78	Jimmy Key	.30	.14
79	Mark Whiten	.15	.07
80	Mark Gubicza	.15	.07
81	Darren Hall	.15	.07
82	Travis Fryman	.30	.14
83	Cal Ripken	2.50	1.10
84	Geronimo Berroa	.15	.07
85	Bret Barberie	.15	.07
86	Andy Ashby	.15	.07
87	Steve Avery	.15	.07
88	Rich Becker	.15	.07
89	John Valentin	.15	.07
90	Glenallen Hill	.15	.07
91	Carlos Garcia	.15	.07
92	Dennis Martinez	.30	.14
93	Pat Kelly	.15	.07
94	Orlando Miller	.15	.07
95	Felix Jose	.15	.07
96	Mike Kingery	.15	.07
97	Jeff Kent	.15	.07
98	Pete Incaviglia	.15	.07
99	Chad Curtis	.15	.07
100	Thomas Howard	.15	.07
101	Hector Carrasco	.15	.07
102	Tom Pagnozzi	.15	.07
103	Danny Tartabull	.15	.07
104	Donnie Elliott	.15	.07
105	Danny Jackson	.15	.07
106	Steve Dunn	.15	.07
107	Roger Salkeld	.15	.07
108	Jeff King	.15	.07
109	Cecil Fielder	.30	.14
110	Paul Molitor CL	.30	.14
111	Denny Neagle	.30	.14
112	Troy Neel	.15	.07
113	Rod Beck	.15	.07
114	Alex Rodriguez	2.50	1.10
115	Joey Eischen	.15	.07
116	Tom Candiotti	.15	.07
117	Ray McDavid	.15	.07
118	Vince Coleman	.15	.07
119	Pete Harnisch	.15	.07
120	David Nied	.15	.07
121	Pat Rapp	.15	.07
122	Sammy Sosa	.60	.25
123	Steve Reed	.15	.07
124	Jose Oliva	.15	.07
125	Ricky Bottalico	.30	.14
126	Jose DeLeon	.15	.07
127	Pat Hentgen	.30	.14
128	Will Clark	.40	.18
129	Mark Dewey	.15	.07
130	Greg Vaughn	.15	.07
131	Darren Dreifort	.15	.07
132	Ed Sprague	.15	.07
133	Lee Smith	.30	.14
134	Charles Nagy	.15	.07
135	Phil Plantier	.15	.07
136	Jason Jacome	.15	.07
137	Jose Lima	.15	.07
138	J.R. Phillips	.15	.07
139	J.T. Snow	.30	.14
140	Michael Huff	.15	.07
141	Billy Brewer	.15	.07
142	Jeromy Burnitz	.15	.07
143	Ricky Bones	.15	.07
144	Carlos Rodriguez	.15	.07
145	Luis Gonzalez	.15	.07
146	Mark Lemke	.15	.07
147	Al Martin	.15	.07
148	Mike Bordick	.15	.07
149	Robb Nen	.15	.07
150	Wil Cordero	.15	.07
151	Edgar Martinez	.40	.18
152	Gerald Williams	.15	.07
153	Esteban Beltre	.15	.07
154	Mike Moore	.15	.07
155	Mark Langston	.15	.07
156	Mark Clark	.15	.07
157	Bobby Ayala	.15	.07
158	Rick Wilkins	.15	.07
159	Bobby Munoz	.15	.07
160	Brett Butler CL	.30	.14
161	Scott Erickson	.15	.07
162	Paul Molitor	.60	.25
163	Jon Lieber	.15	.07
164	Jason Grimsley	.15	.07
165	Norberto Martin	.15	.07
166	Javier Lopez	.30	.14
167	Brian McRae	.15	.07
168	Gary Sheffield	.60	.25
169	Marcus Moore	.15	.07
170	John Hudek	.15	.07
171	Kelly Stinnett	.15	.07
172	Chris Gomez	.15	.07
173	Rey Sanchez	.15	.07
174	Juan Guzman	.15	.07
175	Chan Ho Park	.60	.25
176	Terry Shumpert	.15	.07
177	Steve Ontiveros	.15	.07
178	Brad Ausmus	.15	.07
179	Tim Davis	.15	.07
180	Billy Ashley	.15	.07
181	Vinny Castilla	.30	.14
182	Bill Spiers	.15	.07
183	Randy Knorr	.15	.07
184	Brian Hunter	.40	.18
185	Pat Meares	.15	.07
186	Steve Buechele	.15	.07
187	Kirt Manwaring	.15	.07
188	Tim Naehring	.15	.07
189	Matt Mieske	.15	.07
190	Josias Manzanillo	.15	.07
191	Greg McMichael	.15	.07
192	Chuck Carr	.15	.07
193	Midre Cummings	.15	.07
194	Darryl Strawberry	.30	.14
195	Greg Gagne	.15	.07
196	Steve Cooke	.15	.07
197	Woody Williams	.15	.07
198	Ron Karkovice	.15	.07
199	Phil Leftwich	.15	.07
200	Jim Thome	.60	.25
201	Brady Anderson	.40	.18
202	Pedro Martinez	.60	.25
203	Steve Karsay	.15	.07

204	Reggie Sanders	.15	.07
205	Bill Risley	.15	.07
206	Jay Bell	.30	.14
207	Kevin Brown	.30	.14
208	Tim Scott	.15	.07
209	Lenny Dykstra	.30	.14
210	Willie Greene	.15	.07
211	Jim Eisenreich	.15	.07
212	Cliff Floyd	.15	.07
213	Otis Nixon	.15	.07
214	Eduardo Perez	.15	.07
215	Manuel Lee	.15	.07
216	Armando Benitez	.15	.07
217	Dave McCarty	.15	.07
218	Scott Livingstone	.15	.07
219	Chad Kreuter	.15	.07
220	Don Mattingly CL	.60	.25
221	Brian Jordan	.30	.14
222	Matt Whiteside	.15	.07
223	Jim Edmonds	.40	.18
224	Tony Gwynn	1.50	.70
225	Jose Lind	.15	.07
226	Marvin Freeman	.15	.07
227	Ken Hill	.15	.07
228	David Hulse	.15	.07
229	Joe Hesketh	.15	.07
230	Roberto Petagine	.15	.07
231	Jeffrey Hammonds	.30	.14
232	John Jaha	.15	.07
233	John Burkett	.15	.07
234	Hal Morris	.15	.07
235	Tony Castillo	.15	.07
236	Ryan Bowen	.15	.07
237	Wayne Kirby	.15	.07
238	Brent Mayne	.15	.07
239	Jim Bullinger	.15	.07
240	Mike Lieberthal	.15	.07
241	Barry Larkin	.40	.18
242	David Segui	.15	.07
243	Jose Bautista	.15	.07
244	Hector Fajardo	.15	.07
245	Orel Hershiser	.30	.14
246	James Mouton	.15	.07
247	Scott Leius	.15	.07
248	Tom Glavine	.30	.14
249	Danny Bautista	.15	.07
250	Jose Mercedes	.15	.07
251	Marquis Grissom	.30	.14
252	Charlie Hayes	.15	.07
253	Ryan Klesko	.40	.18
254	Vicente Palacios	.15	.07
255	Matias Carrillo	.15	.07
256	Gary DiSarcina	.15	.07
257	Kirk Gibson	.30	.14
258	Garey Ingram	.15	.07
259	Alex Fernandez	.15	.07
260	John Mabry	.30	.14
261	Chris Howard	.15	.07
262	Miguel Jimenez	.15	.07
263	Heath Slocumb	.15	.07
264	Albert Belle	.75	.35
265	Dave Clark	.15	.07
266	Joe Orsulak	.15	.07
267	Joey Hamilton	.30	.14
268	Mark Portugal	.15	.07
269	Kevin Tapani	.15	.07
270	Sid Fernandez	.15	.07
271	Steve Dreyer	.15	.07
272	Denny Hocking	.15	.07
273	Troy O'Leary	.15	.07
274	Milt Cuyler	.15	.07
275	Frank Thomas	2.50	1.10
276	Jorge Fabregas	.15	.07
277	Mike Gallego	.15	.07
278	Mickey Morandini	.15	.07
279	Roberto Hernandez	.15	.07
280	Henry Rodriguez	.15	.07
281	Garret Anderson	.40	.18
282	Bob Wickman	.15	.07
283	Gar Finnvold	.15	.07
284	Paul O'Neill	.30	.14
285	Royce Clayton	.15	.07
286	Chuck Knoblauch	.60	.25
287	Johnny Ruffin	.15	.07
288	Dave Nilsson	.15	.07
289	David Cone	.30	.14
290	Chuck McElroy	.15	.07
291	Kevin Stocker	.15	.07
292	Jose Rijo	.15	.07
293	Sean Berry	.15	.07
294	Ozzie Guillen	.15	.07
295	Chris Hoiles	.15	.07
296	Kevin Foster	.15	.07
297	Jeff Frye	.15	.07
298	Lance Johnson	.15	.07
299	Mike Kelly	.15	.07
300	Ellis Burks	.30	.14
301	Roberto Kelly	.15	.07
302	Dante Bichette	.30	.14
303	Alvaro Espinoza	.15	.07
304	Alex Cole	.15	.07
305	Rickey Henderson	.40	.18
306	Dave Weathers	.15	.07
307	Shane Reynolds	.15	.07
308	Bobby Bonilla	.30	.14
309	Junior Felix	.15	.07
310	Jeff Fassero	.15	.07
311	Darren Lewis	.15	.07
312	John Doherty	.15	.07
313	Scott Servais	.15	.07
314	Rick Helling	.15	.07
315	Pedro Martinez	.60	.25
316	Wes Chamberlain	.15	.07
317	Bryan Eversgerd	.15	.07
318	Trevor Hoffman	.15	.07
319	John Patterson	.15	.07
320	Matt Walbeck	.15	.07
321	Jeff Montgomery	.15	.07
322	Mel Rojas	.15	.07
323	Eddie Taubensee	.15	.07
324	Ray Lankford	.30	.14
325	Jose Vizcaino	.15	.07
326	Carlos Baerga	.15	.07
327	Jack Voigt	.15	.07
328	Julio Franco	.15	.07
329	Brent Gates	.15	.07
330	Kirby Puckett CL	.60	.25
331	Greg Maddux	2.00	.90
332	Jason Bere	.15	.07
333	Bill Wegman	.15	.07
334	Tuffy Rhodes	.15	.07
335	Kevin Young	.15	.07
336	Andy Benes	.30	.14
337	Pedro Astacio	.15	.07
338	Reggie Jefferson	.15	.07
339	Tim Belcher	.15	.07
340	Ken Griffey Jr.	3.00	1.35
341	Mariano Duncan	.15	.07
342	Andres Galarraga	.60	.25
343	Rondell White	.30	.14
344	Cory Bailey	.15	.07
345	Bryan Harvey	.15	.07
346	John Franco	.15	.07
347	Greg Swindell	.15	.07
348	David West	.15	.07
349	Fred McGriff	.40	.18
350	Jose Canseco	.40	.18
351	Orlando Merced	.15	.07
352	Rheal Cormier	.15	.07
353	Carlos Pulido	.15	.07
354	Terry Steinbach	.15	.07
355	Wade Boggs	.60	.25
356	B.J. Surhoff	.15	.07
357	Rafael Palmeiro	.40	.18
358	Anthony Young	.15	.07
359	Tom Brunansky	.15	.07
360	Todd Stottlemyre	.15	.07
361	Chris Turner	.15	.07
362	Joe Boever	.15	.07
363	Jeff Blauser	.30	.14
364	Derek Bell	.15	.07
365	Matt Williams	.40	.18
366	Jeremy Hernandez	.15	.07
367	Joe Girardi	.15	.07
368	Mike Devereaux	.15	.07
369	Jim Abbott	.15	.07
370	Manny Ramirez	.60	.25
371	Kenny Lofton	.75	.35
372	Mark Smith	.15	.07
373	Dave Fleming	.15	.07
374	Dave Stewart	.30	.14
375	Roger Pavlik	.15	.07
376	Hipolito Pichardo	.15	.07
377	Bill Taylor	.15	.07
378	Robin Ventura	.30	.14
379	Bernard Gilkey	.15	.07
380	Kirby Puckett	1.25	.55
381	Steve Howe	.15	.07
382	Devon White	.15	.07
383	Roberto Mejia	.15	.07
384	Darrin Jackson	.15	.07
385	Mike Morgan	.15	.07
386	Rusty Meacham	.15	.07
387	Bill Swift	.15	.07
388	Lou Frazier	.15	.07
389	Andy Van Slyke	.30	.14
390	Brett Butler	.30	.14
391	Bobby Witt	.15	.07
392	Jeff Conine	.30	.14
393	Tim Hyers	.15	.07
394	Terry Pendleton	.15	.07
395	Ricky Jordan	.15	.07
396	Eric Plunk	.15	.07
397	Melido Perez	.15	.07
398	Darryl Kile	.30	.14
399	Mark McLemore	.15	.07
400	Greg W.Harris	.15	.07
401	Jim Leyritz	.15	.07
402	Doug Strange	.15	.07
403	Tim Salmon	.60	.25
404	Terry Mulholland	.15	.07
405	Robby Thompson	.15	.07
406	Ruben Sierra	.15	.07
407	Tony Phillips	.15	.07
408	Moises Alou	.30	.14
409	Felix Fermin	.15	.07
410	Pat Listach	.15	.07
411	Kevin Bass	.15	.07
412	Ben McDonald	.15	.07
413	Scott Cooper	.15	.07
414	Jody Reed	.15	.07
415	Deion Sanders	.30	.14
416	Ricky Gutierrez	.15	.07
417	Gregg Jefferies	.15	.07
418	Jack McDowell	.15	.07
419	Al Leiter	.15	.07
420	Tony Longmire	.15	.07
421	Paul Wagner	.15	.07
422	Geronimo Pena	.15	.07
423	Ivan Rodriguez	.75	.35
424	Kevin Gross	.15	.07
425	Kirk McCaskill	.15	.07
426	Greg Myers	.15	.07
427	Roger Clemens	1.25	.55
428	Chris Hammond	.15	.07
429	Randy Myers	.15	.07
430	Roger Mason	.15	.07
431	Bret Saberhagen	.15	.07
432	Jeff Reboulet	.15	.07
433	John Olerud	.30	.14
434	Bill Gullickson	.15	.07
435	Eddie Murray	.60	.25
436	Pedro Munoz	.15	.07
437	Charlie O'Brien	.15	.07
438	Jeff Nelson	.15	.07
439	Mike Macfarlane	.15	.07
440	Don Mattingly CL	.60	.25
441	Derrick May	.15	.07
442	John Roper	.15	.07
443	Darryl Hamilton	.15	.07
444	Dan Miceli	.15	.07
445	Tony Eusebio	.15	.07
446	Jerry Browne	.15	.07
447	Wally Joyner	.30	.14
448	Brian Harper	.15	.07
449	Scott Fletcher	.15	.07
450	Bip Roberts	.15	.07
451	Pete Smith	.15	.07
452	Chili Davis	.30	.14
453	Dave Hollins	.15	.07
454	Tony Pena	.15	.07
455	Butch Henry	.15	.07
456	Craig Biggio	.40	.18
457	Zane Smith	.15	.07
458	Ryan Thompson	.15	.07
459	Mike Jackson	.15	.07
460	Mark McGwire	1.25	.55
461	John Smoltz	.30	.14

☐ 462	Steve Scarsone	.15 .07
☐ 463	Greg Colbrunn	.15 .07
☐ 464	Shawn Green	.30 .14
☐ 465	David Wells	.15 .07
☐ 466	Jose Hernandez	.15 .07
☐ 467	Chip Hale	.15 .07
☐ 468	Tony Tarasco	.15 .07
☐ 469	Kevin Mitchell	.15 .07
☐ 470	Billy Hatcher	.15 .07
☐ 471	Jay Buhner	.40 .18
☐ 472	Ken Caminiti	.40 .18
☐ 473	Tom Henke	.15 .07
☐ 474	Todd Worrell	.15 .07
☐ 475	Mark Eichhorn	.15 .07
☐ 476	Bruce Ruffin	.15 .07
☐ 477	Chuck Finley	.15 .07
☐ 478	Marc Newfield	.15 .07
☐ 479	Paul Shuey	.15 .07
☐ 480	Bob Tewksbury	.15 .07
☐ 481	Ramon J.Martinez	.30 .14
☐ 482	Melvin Nieves	.15 .07
☐ 483	Todd Zeile	.15 .07
☐ 484	Benito Santiago	.15 .07
☐ 485	Stan Javier	.15 .07
☐ 486	Kirk Rueter	.15 .07
☐ 487	Andre Dawson	.40 .18
☐ 488	Eric Karros	.30 .14
☐ 489	Dave Magadan	.15 .07
☐ 490	Joe Carter CL	.15 .07
☐ 491	Randy Velarde	.15 .07
☐ 492	Larry Walker	.60 .25
☐ 493	Cris Carpenter	.15 .07
☐ 494	Tom Gordon	.15 .07
☐ 495	Dave Burba	.15 .07
☐ 496	Darren Bragg	.30 .14
☐ 497	Darren Daulton	.30 .14
☐ 498	Don Slaught	.15 .07
☐ 499	Pat Borders	.15 .07
☐ 500	Lenny Harris	.15 .07
☐ 501	Joe Ausanio	.15 .07
☐ 502	Alan Trammell	.40 .18
☐ 503	Mike Fetters	.15 .07
☐ 504	Scott Ruffcorn	.15 .07
☐ 505	Rich Rowland	.15 .07
☐ 506	Juan Samuel	.15 .07
☐ 507	Bo Jackson	.30 .14
☐ 508	Jeff Branson	.30 .14
☐ 509	Bernie Williams	.60 .25
☐ 510	Paul Sorrento	.15 .07
☐ 511	Dennis Eckersley	.30 .14
☐ 512	Pat Mahomes	.15 .07
☐ 513	Rusty Greer	.60 .25
☐ 514	Luis Polonia	.15 .07
☐ 515	Willie Banks	.15 .07
☐ 516	John Wetteland	.15 .07
☐ 517	Mike LaValliere	.15 .07
☐ 518	Tommy Greene	.15 .07
☐ 519	Mark Grace	.40 .18
☐ 520	Bob Hamelin	.15 .07
☐ 521	Scott Sanderson	.15 .07
☐ 522	Joe Carter	.30 .14
☐ 523	Jeff Brantley	.15 .07
☐ 524	Andrew Lorraine	.15 .07
☐ 525	Rico Brogna	.15 .07
☐ 526	Shane Mack	.15 .07
☐ 527	Mark Wohlers	.15 .07
☐ 528	Scott Sanders	.15 .07
☐ 529	Chris Bosio	.15 .07
☐ 530	Andujar Cedeno	.15 .07
☐ 531	Kenny Rogers	.15 .07
☐ 532	Doug Drabek	.15 .07
☐ 533	Curt Leskanic	.15 .07
☐ 534	Craig Shipley	.15 .07
☐ 535	Craig Grebeck	.15 .07
☐ 536	Cal Eldred	.15 .07
☐ 537	Mickey Tettleton	.15 .07
☐ 538	Harold Baines	.30 .14
☐ 539	Tim Wallach	.15 .07
☐ 540	Damon Buford	.15 .07
☐ 541	Lenny Webster	.15 .07
☐ 542	Kevin Appier	.30 .14
☐ 543	Raul Mondesi	.40 .18
☐ 544	Eric Young	.15 .07
☐ 545	Russ Davis	.15 .07
☐ 546	Mike Benjamin	.15 .07
☐ 547	Mike Greenwell	.15 .07

☐ 548	Scott Brosius	.15 .07
☐ 549	Brian Dorsett	.15 .07
☐ 550	Chili Davis CL	.15 .07

1995 Donruss All-Stars

This 18-card standard-size set was randomly inserted into retail packs. The first series has the nine 1994 American League starters while the second series honored the National League starters. The fronts feature the player's photo against a background of his league's all-star logo. The player and his team are identified on the bottom. His team is noted in the upper left corner. All of this is on a borderless card with a gray background. The horizontal backs have a player photo, a quick blurb about his starting role in the game and his performance in the 1994 All-Star game. The cards are numbered in the upper right with either an "AL-X" or an "NL-X".

	MINT	NRMT
COMPLETE SET (18)	150.00	70.00
COMPLETE SERIES AL (9)	100.00	45.00
COMPLETE SERIES NL (9)	50.00	22.00
COMMON CARD (AL1-NL9)	2.00	.90
STATED ODDS 1:8 JUMBO		

		MINT	NRMT
☐ AL1	Jimmy Key	3.00	1.35
☐ AL2	Ivan Rodriguez	7.50	3.40
☐ AL3	Frank Thomas	25.00	11.00
☐ AL4	Roberto Alomar	6.00	2.70
☐ AL5	Wade Boggs	6.00	2.70
☐ AL6	Cal Ripken	25.00	11.00
☐ AL7	Joe Carter	3.00	1.35
☐ AL8	Ken Griffey Jr.	30.00	13.50
☐ AL9	Kirby Puckett	12.50	5.50
☐ NL1	Greg Maddux	20.00	9.00
☐ NL2	Mike Piazza	20.00	9.00
☐ NL3	Gregg Jefferies	2.00	.90
☐ NL4	Mariano Duncan	2.00	.90
☐ NL5	Matt Williams	4.00	1.80
☐ NL6	Ozzie Smith	7.50	3.40
☐ NL7	Barry Bonds	7.50	3.40
☐ NL8	Tony Gwynn	15.00	6.75
☐ NL9	David Justice	6.00	2.70

1995 Donruss Bomb Squad

Randomly inserted one in every 24 retail packs and one in every 16 magazine packs, this set features the top six home run hitters in the National and American League. These cards

were only included in first series packs. Each of the six cards shows a different slugger on the either side of the card. Both the fronts and backs are horizontal and feature the player photo with a bomber as background. There are foil bombs to the left indicating how many homers the player hit in 1994. A dog tag indicates the player's position and rank among home run leaders in his league.

	MINT	NRMT
COMPLETE SET (6)	25.00	11.00
COMMON CARD (1-6)	1.50	.70
SER.1 STATED ODDS 1:24 RET, 1:16 MAG		

		MINT	NRMT
☐ 1	Ken Griffey	8.00	3.60
	Matt Williams		
☐ 2	Frank Thomas	8.00	3.60
	Jeff Bagwell		
☐ 3	Albert Belle	2.50	1.10
	Barry Bonds		
☐ 4	Jose Canseco	2.50	1.10
	Fred McGriff		
☐ 5	Cecil Fielder	1.50	.70
	Andres Galarraga		
☐ 6	Joe Carter	2.00	.90
	Kevin Mitchell		

1995 Donruss Diamond Kings

The 1995 Donruss Diamond King set consists of 29 standard-size cards that were randomly inserted in packs. The fronts feature water color player portraits by noted sports artist Dick Perez. The player's name and "Diamond Kings" are in gold foil. The backs have a dark blue border with a player photo and text. The cards are numbered on back with a DK prefix.

	MINT	NRMT
COMPLETE SET (29)	50.00	22.00
COMPLETE SERIES 1 (14) ..	20.00	9.00
COMPLETE SERIES 1 (15) ..	30.00	13.50
COMMON CARD (DK1-DK29)	1.00	.45
STATED ODDS 1:10 H/R, 1:9 JUM, 1:10 MAG		

		MINT	NRMT
☐ DK1	Frank Thomas	10.00	4.50
☐ DK2	Jeff Bagwell	5.00	2.20
☐ DK3	Chili Davis	1.50	.70
☐ DK4	Dante Bichette	1.50	.70
☐ DK5	Ruben Sierra	1.00	.45
☐ DK6	Jeff Conine	1.50	.70
☐ DK7	Paul O'Neill	1.50	.70
☐ DK8	Bobby Bonilla	1.50	.70
☐ DK9	Joe Carter	1.50	.70
☐ DK10	Moises Alou	1.50	.70
☐ DK11	Kenny Lofton	3.00	1.35
☐ DK12	Matt Williams	2.00	.90
☐ DK13	Kevin Seitzer	1.00	.45
☐ DK14	Sammy Sosa	2.50	1.10
☐ DK15	Scott Cooper	1.00	.45
☐ DK16	Raul Mondesi	2.00	.90
☐ DK17	Will Clark	2.00	.90
☐ DK18	Lenny Dykstra	1.50	.70
☐ DK19	Kirby Puckett	5.00	2.20
☐ DK20	Hal Morris	1.00	.45
☐ DK21	Travis Fryman	1.50	.70
☐ DK22	Greg Maddux	8.00	3.60
☐ DK23	Rafael Palmeiro	2.00	.90
☐ DK24	Tony Gwynn	6.00	2.70
☐ DK25	David Cone	1.50	.70
☐ DK26	Al Martin	1.00	.45
☐ DK27	Ken Griffey Jr.	12.00	5.50
☐ DK28	Gregg Jefferies	1.00	.45
☐ DK29	Checklist	1.00	.45

1995 Donruss Dominators

This nine-card standard-size set was randomly inserted in second series hobby packs. Each of these cards features three of the leading players at each position. The horizontal fronts have photos of all three players and identify only their last name. The words "remove protective film" cover a significant portion of the fronts as well. The backs have small action photos of the three players along with their 1994 stats. The cards are numbered in the upper right corner as "X" of 9.

	MINT	NRMT
COMPLETE SET (9)	25.00	11.00
COMMON CARD (1-9)	1.00	.45
SER.2 STATED ODDS 1:24 HOBBY		

		MINT	NRMT
☐ 1	David Cone	5.00	2.20
	Mike Mussina		

		MINT	NRMT
	Greg Maddux		
☐ 2	Ivan Rodriguez	5.00	2.20
	Mike Piazza		
	Darren Daulton		
☐ 3	Fred McGriff	8.00	3.60
	Frank Thomas		
	Jeff Bagwell		
☐ 4	Roberto Alomar	1.00	.45
	Carlos Baerga		
	Craig Biggio		
☐ 5	Robin Ventura	1.00	.45
	Travis Fryman		
	Matt Williams		
☐ 6	Cal Ripken	6.00	2.70
	Barry Larkin		
	Wil Cordero		
☐ 7	Albert Belle	1.50	.70
	Barry Bonds		
	Moises Alou		
☐ 8	Ken Griffey	8.00	3.60
	Kenny Lofton		
	Marquis Grissom		
☐ 9	Kirby Puckett	3.00	1.35
	Paul O'Neill		
	Tony Gwynn		

1995 Donruss Elite

Randomly inserted one in every 210 Series 1 and 2 packs, this set consists of 12 standard-size cards that are numbered (49-60) based on where the previous year's set left off. The fronts contain an action photo surrounded by a marble border. Silver holographic foil borders the card on all four sides. Limited to 10,000, the backs are individually numbered, contain a small photo and write-up.

	MINT	NRMT
COMPLETE SET (12)	275.00	125.00
COMPLETE SERIES 1 (6)	150.00	70.00
COMPLETE SERIES 2 (6)	125.00	55.00
COMMON CARD (49-60)	6.00	2.70
SEMISTARS	8.00	3.60
SER.1 STAT.ODDS 1:210H/R, 1:120J, 1:210M		
SER.2 STAT.ODDS 1:180H/R, 1:120J, 1:180M		

		MINT	NRMT
☐ 49	Jeff Bagwell	25.00	11.00
☐ 50	Paul O'Neill	6.00	2.70
☐ 51	Greg Maddux	40.00	18.00
☐ 52	Mike Piazza	40.00	18.00
☐ 53	Matt Williams	8.00	3.60
☐ 54	Ken Griffey	60.00	27.00
☐ 55	Frank Thomas	50.00	22.00
☐ 56	Barry Bonds	15.00	6.75
☐ 57	Kirby Puckett	25.00	11.00
☐ 58	Fred McGriff	8.00	3.60
☐ 59	Jose Canseco	8.00	3.60
☐ 60	Albert Belle	15.00	6.75

1995 Donruss Long Ball Leaders

Inserted one in every 24 series one hobby packs, this set features eight top home run hitters. Metallic fronts have much ornamentation including a player photo, the length of the player's home run, the stadium and the date. Horizontal backs have a player photo and photo of the stadium with which the home run occurred. The back also includes all the particulars concerning the home run.

	MINT	NRMT
COMPLETE SET (8)	20.00	9.00
COMMON CARD (1-8)	1.25	.55
SER.1 STATED ODDS 1:24 HOBBY		

		MINT	NRMT
☐ 1	Frank Thomas	8.00	3.60
☐ 2	Fred McGriff	1.25	.55
☐ 3	Ken Griffey	8.00	3.60
☐ 4	Matt Williams	1.25	.55
☐ 5	Mike Piazza	6.00	2.70
☐ 6	Jose Canseco	1.25	.55
☐ 7	Barry Bonds	2.00	.90
☐ 8	Jeff Bagwell	4.00	1.80

1995 Donruss Mound Marvels

This eight-card standard-size set was randomly inserted into second series magazine jumbo and retail packs at a rate of one every 16 packs. This set features eight of the leading major league starters. The horizontal fronts feature the player's photo on the left with the words "Donruss Mound Marvels" and the player's name on the right. The back features the player's

photo within a circular inset
along with all his 1994 stats.

	MINT	NRMT
COMPLETE SET (8)	20.00	9.00
COMMON CARD (1-8)	1.00	.65
SER.2 STATED ODDS 1:16 RET/MAG		

☐ 1	Greg Maddux	10.00	4.50
☐ 2	David Cone	1.50	.70
☐ 3	Mike Mussina	3.00	1.35
☐ 4	Bret Saberhagen	1.00	.45
☐ 5	Jimmy Key	1.50	.70
☐ 6	Doug Drabek	1.00	.45
☐ 7	Randy Johnson	3.00	1.35
☐ 8	Jason Bere	1.00	.45

1996 Donruss

The 1996 Donruss set was issued in two series of 330 and 220 cards respectively, for a total of 550. The 12-card packs had a suggested retail price of $1.79. The full-bleed fronts feature full-color action photos. The player's name is in white ink in the upper right. The Donruss logo, team name and team logo as well as uniform number and position are located in the bottom middle set against a silver foil background. The horizontal backs feature season and career stats, text, vital stats and another photo. There are no notable Rookie Cards in this set.

	MINT	NRMT
COMPLETE SET (550)	40.00	18.00
COMPLETE SERIES 1 (330)	25.00	11.00
COMPLETE SERIES 2 (220)	15.00	6.75
COMMON CARD (1-550)	.15	.07
MINOR STARS	.30	.14
UNLISTED STARS	.60	.25
SUBSET CARDS HALF VALUE OF BASE CARDS		
COMP.PP SET (550)	1500.00	700.00
COMP.PP SER.1 (330)	900.00	400.00
COMP.PP SER.2 (220)	600.00	275.00
COMMON PP (1-550)	2.00	.90

*PP STARS: 10X TO 20X HI COLUMN
*PP YOUNG STARS: 7.5X TO 15X HI
PP SER.1 STATED ODDS 1:12
PP SER.2 STATED ODDS 1:10
PP STATED PRINT RUN 2000 SETS

☐ 1	Frank Thomas	2.50	1.10
☐ 2	Jason Bates	.15	.07
☐ 3	Steve Sparks	.15	.07
☐ 4	Scott Servais	.15	.07
☐ 5	Angelo Encarnacion	.15	.07
☐ 6	Scott Sanders	.15	.07
☐ 7	Billy Ashley	.15	.07
☐ 8	Alex Rodriguez	2.00	.90
☐ 9	Sean Bergman	.15	.07
☐ 10	Brad Radke	.15	.07
☐ 11	Andy Van Slyke	.30	.14
☐ 12	Joe Girardi	.15	.07
☐ 13	Mark Grudzielanek	.30	.14
☐ 14	Rick Aguilera	.15	.07
☐ 15	Randy Veres	.15	.07
☐ 16	Tim Bogar	.15	.07
☐ 17	Dave Veres	.15	.07
☐ 18	Kevin Stocker	.15	.07
☐ 19	Marquis Grissom	.30	.14
☐ 20	Will Clark	.40	.18
☐ 21	Jay Bell	.15	.07
☐ 22	Allen Battle	.15	.07
☐ 23	Frank Rodriguez	.15	.07
☐ 24	Terry Steinbach	.15	.07
☐ 25	Gerald Williams	.15	.07
☐ 26	Sid Roberson	.15	.07
☐ 27	Greg Zaun	.15	.07
☐ 28	Ozzie Timmons	.15	.07
☐ 29	Vaughn Eshelman	.15	.07
☐ 30	Ed Sprague	.15	.07
☐ 31	Gary DiSarcina	.15	.07
☐ 32	Joe Boever	.15	.07
☐ 33	Steve Avery	.15	.07
☐ 34	Brad Ausmus	.15	.07
☐ 35	Kirt Manwaring	.15	.07
☐ 36	Gary Sheffield	.60	.25
☐ 37	Jason Bere	.15	.07
☐ 38	Jeff Manto	.15	.07
☐ 39	David Cone	.15	.07
☐ 40	Manny Ramirez	.60	.25
☐ 41	Sandy Alomar Jr.	.15	.07
☐ 42	Curtis Goodwin	.15	.07
☐ 43	Tino Martinez	.60	.25
☐ 44	Woody Williams	.15	.07
☐ 45	Dean Palmer	.15	.07
☐ 46	Hipolito Pichardo	.15	.07
☐ 47	Jason Giambi	.30	.14
☐ 48	Lance Johnson	.15	.07
☐ 49	Bernard Gilkey	.15	.07
☐ 50	Kirby Puckett	1.25	.55
☐ 51	Tony Fernandez	.15	.07
☐ 52	Alex Gonzalez	.15	.07
☐ 53	Bret Saberhagen	.15	.07
☐ 54	Lyle Mouton	.15	.07
☐ 55	Brian McRae	.15	.07
☐ 56	Mark Gubicza	.15	.07
☐ 57	Sergio Valdez	.15	.07
☐ 58	Darrin Fletcher	.15	.07
☐ 59	Steve Parris	.15	.07
☐ 60	Johnny Damon	.30	.14
☐ 61	Rickey Henderson	.40	.18
☐ 62	Darrell Whitmore	.15	.07
☐ 63	Roberto Petagine	.15	.07
☐ 64	Trenidad Hubbard	.15	.07
☐ 65	Heathcliff Slocumb	.15	.07
☐ 66	Steve Finley	.30	.14
☐ 67	Mariano Rivera	.40	.18
☐ 68	Brian L.Hunter	.30	.14
☐ 69	Jamie Moyer	.15	.07
☐ 70	Ellis Burks	.30	.14
☐ 71	Pat Kelly	.15	.07
☐ 72	Mickey Tettleton	.15	.07
☐ 73	Garret Anderson	.30	.14
☐ 74	Andy Pettitte	.75	.35
☐ 75	Glenallen Hill	.15	.07
☐ 76	Brent Gates	.15	.07
☐ 77	Lou Whitaker	.30	.14
☐ 78	David Segui	.15	.07
☐ 79	Dan Wilson	.15	.07
☐ 80	Pat Listach	.15	.07
☐ 81	Jeff Bagwell	1.25	.55
☐ 82	Ben McDonald	.15	.07
☐ 83	John Valentin	.15	.07
☐ 84	John Jaha	.15	.07
☐ 85	Pete Schourek	.15	.07
☐ 86	Bryce Florie	.15	.07
☐ 87	Brian Jordan	.30	.14
☐ 88	Ron Karkovice	.15	.07
☐ 89	Al Leiter	.15	.07
☐ 90	Tony Longmire	.15	.07
☐ 91	Nelson Liriano	.15	.07
☐ 92	David Bell	.15	.07
☐ 93	Kevin Gross	.15	.07
☐ 94	Tom Candiotti	.15	.07
☐ 95	Dave Martinez	.15	.07
☐ 96	Greg Myers	.15	.07
☐ 97	Rheal Cormier	.15	.07
☐ 98	Chris Hammond	.15	.07
☐ 99	Randy Myers	.15	.07
☐ 100	Bill Pulsipher	.15	.07
☐ 101	Jason Isringhausen	.15	.07
☐ 102	Dave Stevens	.15	.07
☐ 103	Roberto Alomar	.60	.25
☐ 104	Bob Higginson	.40	.18
☐ 105	Eddie Murray	.60	.25
☐ 106	Matt Walbeck	.15	.07
☐ 107	Mark Wohlers	.15	.07
☐ 108	Jeff Nelson	.15	.07
☐ 109	Tom Goodwin	.15	.07
☐ 110	Cal Ripken CL	1.25	.55
☐ 111	Rey Sanchez	.15	.07
☐ 112	Hector Carrasco	.15	.07
☐ 113	B.J. Surhoff	.15	.07
☐ 114	Dan Miceli	.15	.07
☐ 115	Dean Hartgraves	.15	.07
☐ 116	John Burkett	.15	.07
☐ 117	Gary Gaetti	.15	.07
☐ 118	Ricky Bones	.15	.07
☐ 119	Mike Macfarlane	.15	.07
☐ 120	Bip Roberts	.15	.07
☐ 121	Dave Mlicki	.15	.07
☐ 122	Chili Davis	.30	.14
☐ 123	Mark Whiten	.15	.07
☐ 124	Herbert Perry	.15	.07
☐ 125	Butch Henry	.15	.07
☐ 126	Derek Bell	.15	.07
☐ 127	Al Martin	.15	.07
☐ 128	John Franco	.30	.14
☐ 129	W. VanLandingham	.15	.07
☐ 130	Mike Bordick	.15	.07
☐ 131	Mike Mordecai	.15	.07
☐ 132	Robby Thompson	.15	.07
☐ 133	Greg Colbrunn	.15	.07
☐ 134	Domingo Cedeno	.15	.07
☐ 135	Chad Curtis	.15	.07
☐ 136	Jose Hernandez	.15	.07
☐ 137	Scott Klingenbeck	.15	.07
☐ 138	Ryan Klesko	.40	.18
☐ 139	John Smiley	.15	.07
☐ 140	Charlie Hayes	.15	.07
☐ 141	Jay Buhner	.40	.18
☐ 142	Doug Drabek	.15	.07
☐ 143	Roger Pavlik	.15	.07
☐ 144	Todd Worrell	.15	.07
☐ 145	Cal Ripken	2.50	1.10
☐ 146	Steve Reed	.15	.07
☐ 147	Chuck Finley	.15	.07
☐ 148	Mike Blowers	.15	.07
☐ 149	Orel Hershiser	.30	.14
☐ 150	Allen Watson	.15	.07
☐ 151	Ramon Martinez	.30	.14
☐ 152	Melvin Nieves	.15	.07
☐ 153	Tripp Cromer	.15	.07
☐ 154	Yorkis Perez	.15	.07
☐ 155	Stan Javier	.15	.07
☐ 156	Mel Rojas	.15	.07
☐ 157	Aaron Sele	.15	.07
☐ *158	Eric Karros	.30	.14
☐ 159	Robb Nen	.15	.07
☐ 160	Raul Mondesi	.40	.18
☐ 161	John Wetteland	.15	.07
☐ 162	Tim Scott	.15	.07
☐ 163	Kenny Rogers	.15	.07
☐ 164	Melvin Bunch	.15	.07
☐ 165	Rod Beck	.15	.07
☐ 166	Andy Benes	.30	.14
☐ 167	Lenny Dykstra	.30	.14
☐ 168	Orlando Merced	.15	.07
☐ 169	Tomas Perez	.15	.07
☐ 170	Xavier Hernandez	.15	.07
☐ 171	Ruben Sierra	.15	.07
☐ 172	Alan Trammell	.40	.18
☐ 173	Mike Fetters	.15	.07
☐ 174	Wilson Alvarez	.15	.07
☐ 175	Erik Hanson	.15	.07
☐ 176	Travis Fryman	.30	.14
☐ 177	Jim Abbott	.15	.07
☐ 178	Bret Boone	.15	.07
☐ 179	Sterling Hitchcock	.15	.07
☐ 180	Pat Mahomes	.15	.07
☐ 181	Mark Acre	.15	.07
☐ 182	Charles Nagy	.30	.14
☐ 183	Rusty Greer	.30	.14

184	Mike Stanley	.15	.07
185	Jim Bullinger	.15	.07
186	Shane Andrews	.15	.07
187	Brian Keyser	.15	.07
188	Tyler Green	.15	.07
189	Mark Grace	.40	.18
190	Bob Hamelin	.15	.07
191	Luis Ortiz	.15	.07
192	Joe Carter	.30	.14
193	Eddie Taubensee	.15	.07
194	Brian Anderson	.15	.07
195	Edgardo Alfonzo	.40	.18
196	Pedro Munoz	.15	.07
197	David Justice	.60	.25
198	Trevor Hoffman	.15	.07
199	Bobby Ayala	.15	.07
200	Tony Eusebio	.15	.07
201	Jeff Russell	.15	.07
202	Mike Hampton	.15	.07
203	Walt Weiss	.15	.07
204	Joey Hamilton	.30	.14
205	Roberto Hernandez	.15	.07
206	Greg Vaughn	.15	.07
207	Felipe Lira	.15	.07
208	Harold Baines	.30	.14
209	Tim Wallach	.15	.07
210	Manny Alexander	.15	.07
211	Tim Laker	.15	.07
212	Chris Haney	.15	.07
213	Brian Maxcy	.15	.07
214	Eric Young	.15	.07
215	Darryl Strawberry	.75	.35
216	Barry Bonds	.75	.35
217	Tim Naehring	.15	.07
218	Scott Brosius	.15	.07
219	Reggie Sanders	.30	.14
220	Eddie Murray CL	.30	.14
221	Luis Alicea	.15	.07
222	Albert Belle	.75	.35
223	Benji Gil	.15	.07
224	Dante Bichette	.30	.14
225	Bobby Bonilla	.30	.14
226	Todd Stottlemyre	.15	.07
227	Jim Edmonds	.40	.18
228	Todd Jones	.15	.07
229	Shawn Green	.15	.07
230	Javier Lopez	.30	.14
231	Ariel Prieto	.15	.07
232	Tony Phillips	.15	.07
233	James Mouton	.15	.07
234	Jose Oquendo	.15	.07
235	Royce Clayton	.15	.07
236	Chuck Carr	.15	.07
237	Doug Jones	.15	.07
238	Mark McLemore	.15	.07
239	Bill Swift	.15	.07
240	Scott Leius	.15	.07
241	Russ Davis	.15	.07
242	Ray Durham	.15	.07
243	Matt Mieske	.15	.07
244	Brent Mayne	.15	.07
245	Thomas Howard	.15	.07
246	Troy O'Leary	.15	.07
247	Jacob Brumfield	.15	.07
248	Mickey Morandini	.15	.07
249	Todd Hundley	.30	.14
250	Chris Bosio	.15	.07
251	Omar Vizquel	.30	.14
252	Mike Lansing	.15	.07
253	John Mabry	.15	.07
254	Mike Perez	.15	.07
255	Delino DeShields	.15	.07
256	Wil Cordero	.15	.07
257	Mike James	.15	.07
258	Todd Van Poppel	.15	.07
259	Joey Cora	.30	.14
260	Andre Dawson	.40	.18
261	Jerry DiPoto	.15	.07
262	Rick Krivda	.15	.07
263	Glenn Dishman	.15	.07
264	Mike Mimbs	.15	.07
265	John Ericks	.15	.07
266	Jose Canseco	.40	.18
267	Jeff Branson	.15	.07
268	Curt Leskanic	.15	.07
269	Jon Nunnally	.15	.07
270	Scott Stahoviak	.15	.07
271	Jeff Montgomery	.15	.07
272	Hal Morris	.15	.07
273	Esteban Loaiza	.15	.07
274	Rico Brogna	.15	.07
275	Dave Winfield	.40	.18
276	J.R. Phillips	.15	.07
277	Todd Zeile	.15	.07
278	Tom Pagnozzi	.15	.07
279	Mark Lemke	.15	.07
280	Dave Magadan	.15	.07
281	Greg McMichael	.15	.07
282	Mike Morgan	.15	.07
283	Moises Alou	.30	.14
284	Dennis Martinez	.30	.14
285	Jeff Kent	.15	.07
286	Mark Johnson	.15	.07
287	Darren Lewis	.15	.07
288	Brad Clontz	.15	.07
289	Chad Fonville	.15	.07
290	Paul Sorrento	.15	.07
291	Lee Smith	.30	.14
292	Tom Glavine	.30	.14
293	Antonio Osuna	.15	.07
294	Kevin Foster	.15	.07
295	Sandy Martinez	.15	.07
296	Mark Leiter	.15	.07
297	Julian Tavarez	.15	.07
298	Mike Kelly	.15	.07
299	Joe Oliver	.15	.07
300	John Flaherty	.15	.07
301	Don Mattingly	1.00	.45
302	Pat Meares	.15	.07
303	John Doherty	.15	.07
304	Joe Vitiello	.15	.07
305	Vinny Castilla	.30	.14
306	Jeff Brantley	.15	.07
307	Mike Greenwell	.15	.07
308	Midre Cummings	.15	.07
309	Curt Schilling	.30	.14
310	Ken Caminiti	.40	.18
311	Scott Erickson	.15	.07
312	Carl Everett	.15	.07
313	Charles Johnson	.30	.14
314	Alex Diaz	.15	.07
315	Jose Mesa	.15	.07
316	Mark Carreon	.15	.07
317	Carlos Perez	.15	.07
318	Ismael Valdes	.30	.14
319	Frank Castillo	.15	.07
320	Tom Henke	.15	.07
321	Spike Owen	.15	.07
322	Joe Orsulak	.15	.07
323	Paul Menhart	.15	.07
324	Pedro Borbon	.15	.07
325	Paul Molitor CL	.30	.14
326	Jeff Cirillo	.30	.14
327	Edwin Hurtado	.15	.07
328	Orlando Miller	.15	.07
329	Steve Ontiveros	.15	.07
330	Kirby Puckett CL	.60	.25
331	Scott Bullett	.15	.07
332	Andres Galarraga	.60	.25
333	Cal Eldred	.15	.07
334	Sammy Sosa	.60	.25
335	Don Slaught	.15	.07
336	Jody Reed	.15	.07
337	Roger Cedeno	.15	.07
338	Ken Griffey Jr.	3.00	1.35
339	Todd Hollandsworth	.15	.07
340	Mike Trombley	.15	.07
341	Gregg Jefferies	.15	.07
342	Larry Walker	.60	.25
343	Pedro Martinez	.60	.25
344	Dwayne Hosey	.15	.07
345	Terry Pendleton	.15	.07
346	Pete Harnisch	.15	.07
347	Tony Castillo	.15	.07
348	Paul Quantrill	.15	.07
349	Fred McGriff	.40	.18
350	Ivan Rodriguez	.75	.35
351	Butch Huskey	.30	.14
352	Ozzie Smith	.75	.35
353	Marty Cordova	.30	.14
354	John Wasdin	.15	.07
355	Wade Boggs	.60	.25
356	Dave Nilsson	.15	.07
357	Rafael Palmeiro	.40	.18
358	Luis Gonzalez	.15	.07
359	Reggie Jefferson	.15	.07
360	Carlos Delgado	.30	.14
361	Orlando Palmeiro	.15	.07
362	Chris Gomez	.15	.07
363	John Smoltz	.30	.14
364	Marc Newfield	.15	.07
365	Matt Williams	.40	.18
366	Jesus Tavarez	.15	.07
367	Bruce Ruffin	.15	.07
368	Sean Berry	.15	.07
369	Randy Velarde	.15	.07
370	Tony Pena	.15	.07
371	Jim Thome	.60	.25
372	Jeffrey Hammonds	.15	.07
373	Bob Wolcott	.15	.07
374	Juan Guzman	.15	.07
375	Juan Gonzalez	1.50	.70
376	Michael Tucker	.30	.14
377	Doug Johns	.15	.07
378	Mike Cameron	1.50	.70
379	Ray Lankford	.30	.14
380	Jose Herrera	.15	.07
381	Jimmy Key	.30	.14
382	John Olerud	.30	.14
383	Kevin Ritz	.15	.07
384	Tim Raines	.30	.14
385	Rich Amaral	.15	.07
386	Keith Lockhart	.15	.07
387	Steve Scarsone	.15	.07
388	Cliff Floyd	.15	.07
389	Rich Aude	.15	.07
390	Hideo Nomo	1.50	.70
391	Geronimo Berroa	.15	.07
392	Pat Rapp	.15	.07
393	Dustin Hermanson	.15	.07
394	Greg Maddux	2.00	.90
395	Darren Daulton	.30	.14
396	Kenny Lofton	.75	.35
397	Ruben Rivera	.30	.14
398	Billy Wagner	.30	.14
399	Kevin Brown	.30	.14
400	Mike Kingery	.15	.07
401	Bernie Williams	.60	.25
402	Otis Nixon	.15	.07
403	Damion Easley	.15	.07
404	Paul O'Neill	.30	.14
405	Deion Sanders	.30	.14
406	Dennis Eckersley	.30	.14
407	Tony Clark	.60	.25
408	Rondell White	.30	.14
409	Luis Sojo	.15	.07
410	David Hulse	.15	.07
411	Shane Reynolds	.15	.07
412	Chris Hoiles	.15	.07
413	Lee Tinsley	.15	.07
414	Scott Karl	.15	.07
415	Ron Gant	.30	.14
416	Brian Johnson	.15	.07
417	Jose Oliva	.15	.07
418	Jack McDowell	.15	.07
419	Paul Molitor	.60	.25
420	Ricky Bottalico	.15	.07
421	Paul Wagner	.15	.07
422	Terry Bradshaw	.15	.07
423	Bob Tewksbury	.15	.07
424	Mike Piazza	2.00	.90
425	Luis Andujar	.30	.14
426	Mark Langston	.15	.07
427	Stan Belinda	.15	.07
428	Kurt Abbott	.15	.07
429	Shawon Dunston	.15	.07
430	Bobby Jones	.15	.07
431	Jose Vizcaino	.15	.07
432	Matt Lawton	.40	.18
433	Pat Hentgen	.30	.14
434	Cecil Fielder	.30	.14
435	Carlos Baerga	.15	.07
436	Rich Becker	.15	.07
437	Chipper Jones	2.00	.90
438	Bill Risley	.15	.07
439	Kevin Appier	.30	.14
440	Wade Boggs CL	.30	.14
441	Jaime Navarro	.15	.07

		MINT	NRMT
442	Barry Larkin	.40	.18
443	Jose Valentin	.15	.07
444	Bryan Rekar	.15	.07
445	Rick Wilkins	.15	.07
446	Quilvio Veras	.15	.07
447	Greg Gagne	.15	.07
448	Mark Kiefer	.15	.07
449	Bobby Witt	.15	.07
450	Andy Ashby	.15	.07
451	Alex Ochoa	.15	.07
452	Jorge Fabregas	.15	.07
453	Gene Schall	.15	.07
454	Ken Hill	.15	.07
455	Tony Tarasco	.15	.07
456	Donnie Wall	.15	.07
457	Carlos Garcia	.15	.07
458	Ryan Thompson	.15	.07
459	Marvin Benard	.15	.07
460	Jose Herrera	.15	.07
461	Jeff Blauser	.30	.14
462	Chris Hook	.15	.07
463	Jeff Conine	.30	.14
464	Devon White	.15	.07
465	Danny Bautista	.15	.07
466	Steve Trachsel	.15	.07
467	C.J. Nitkowski	.15	.07
468	Mike Devereaux	.15	.07
469	David Wells	.15	.07
470	Jim Eisenreich	.15	.07
471	Edgar Martinez	.40	.18
472	Craig Biggio	.40	.18
473	Jeff Frye	.15	.07
474	Karim Garcia	.40	.18
475	Jimmy Haynes	.15	.07
476	Darren Holmes	.15	.07
477	Tim Salmon	.60	.25
478	Randy Johnson	.60	.25
479	Eric Plunk	.15	.07
480	Scott Cooper	.15	.07
481	Chan Ho Park	.60	.25
482	Ray McDavid	.15	.07
483	Mark Petkovsek	.15	.07
484	Greg Swindell	.15	.07
485	George Williams	.15	.07
486	Yamil Benitez	.30	.14
487	Tim Wakefield	.30	.14
488	Kevin Tapani	.15	.07
489	Derrick May	.15	.07
490	Ken Griffey Jr. CL	1.50	.70
491	Derek Jeter	2.00	.90
492	Jeff Fassero	.15	.07
493	Benito Santiago	.15	.07
494	Tom Gordon	.15	.07
495	Jamie Brewington	.15	.07
496	Vince Coleman	.15	.07
497	Kevin Jordan	.15	.07
498	Jeff King	.15	.07
499	Mike Simms	.15	.07
500	Jose Rijo	.15	.07
501	Denny Neagle	.30	.14
502	Jose Lima	.15	.07
503	Kevin Seitzer	.15	.07
504	Alex Fernandez	.15	.07
505	Mo Vaughn	.75	.35
506	Phil Nevin	.15	.07
507	J.T. Snow	.30	.14
508	Andujar Cedeno	.15	.07
509	Ozzie Guillen	.15	.07
510	Mark Clark	.15	.07
511	Mark McGwire	1.25	.55
512	Jeff Reboulet	.15	.07
513	Armando Benitez	.15	.07
514	LaTroy Hawkins	.15	.07
515	Brett Butler	.30	.14
516	Tavo Alvarez	.15	.07
517	Chris Snopek	.15	.07
518	Mike Mussina	.60	.25
519	Darryl Kile	.30	.14
520	Wally Joyner	.30	.14
521	Willie McGee	.15	.07
522	Kent Mercker	.15	.07
523	Mike Jackson	.15	.07
524	Troy Percival	.15	.07
525	Tony Gwynn	1.50	.70
526	Ron Coomer	.15	.07
527	Darryl Hamilton	.15	.07
528	Phil Plantier	.15	.07
529	Norm Charlton	.15	.07
530	Craig Paquette	.15	.07
531	Dave Burba	.15	.07
532	Mike Henneman	.15	.07
533	Terrell Wade	.15	.07
534	Eddie Williams	.15	.07
535	Robin Ventura	.30	.14
536	Chuck Knoblauch	.60	.25
537	Les Norman	.15	.07
538	Brady Anderson	.40	.18
539	Roger Clemens	1.25	.55
540	Mark Portugal	.15	.07
541	Mike Matheny	.15	.07
542	Jeff Parrett	.15	.07
543	Roberto Kelly	.15	.07
544	Damon Buford	.15	.07
545	Chad Ogea	.15	.07
546	Jose Offerman	.15	.07
547	Brian Barber	.15	.07
548	Danny Tartabull	.15	.07
549	Duane Singleton	.15	.07
550	Tony Gwynn CL	.75	.35

1996 Donruss Diamond Kings

These 31 standard-size cards were randomly inserted into packs and inserted in two series of 14 and 17 cards. They were inserted in first series packs at a ratio of approximately one every 60 packs. Second series cards were inserted one every 30 packs. The cards are sequentially numbered in the back lower right as "X" of 10,000. The fronts feature player portraits by noted sports artist Dick Perez. These cards are gold-foil stamped and the portraits are surrounded by gold-foil borders. The backs feature text about the player as well as a player photo. The cards are numbered on back with a "DK" prefix.

		MINT	NRMT
COMPLETE SET (31)		300.00	135.00
COMPLETE SERIES 1 (14)		150.00	70.00
COMPLETE SERIES 2 (17)		150.00	70.00
COMMON CARD (1-31)		4.00	1.80
SEMISTARS		6.00	2.70
UNLISTED STARS		10.00	4.50
SER.1 STATED ODDS 1:60			
SER.2 STATED ODDS 1:30			
STATED PRINT RUN 10,000 SERIAL #'d SETS			

1	Frank Thomas	40.00	18.00
2	Mo Vaughn	12.00	5.50
3	Manny Ramirez	10.00	4.50
4	Mark McGwire	20.00	9.00
5	Juan Gonzalez	25.00	11.00

1996 Donruss Elite

Randomly inserted approximately one in Donruss packs, this 12-card standard-size set is continuously numbered (61-72) from the previous year. First series cards were inserted one every 40 packs. Second series cards were inserted one every 75 packs. The fronts contain an action photo surrounded by a silver border. Limited to 10,000 and sequentially numbered, the backs contain a small photo and write up.

		MINT	NRMT
COMPLETE SET (12)		270.00	120.00
COMPLETE SERIES 1 (6)		150.00	70.00
COMPLETE SERIES 2 (6)		120.00	55.00
COMMON CARD (61-72)		5.00	2.20
UNLISTED STARS		8.00	3.60
SER.1 STATED ODDS 1:140			
SER.2 STATED ODDS 1:75			
STATED PRINT RUN 10,000 SERIAL #'d SETS			

6	Roberto Alomar	10.00	4.50
7	Tim Salmon	10.00	4.50
8	Barry Bonds	12.00	5.50
9	Tony Gwynn	25.00	11.00
10	Reggie Sanders	4.00	1.80
11	Larry Walker	10.00	4.50
12	Pedro Martinez	10.00	4.50
13	Jeff King	4.00	1.80
14	Mark Grace	6.00	2.70
15	Greg Maddux	25.00	11.00
16	Don Mattingly	12.00	5.50
17	Gregg Jefferies	4.00	1.80
18	Chad Curtis	4.00	1.80
19	Jason Isringhausen	4.00	1.80
20	B.J. Surhoff	4.00	1.80
21	Jeff Conine	5.00	2.20
22	Kirby Puckett	15.00	6.75
23	Derek Bell	4.00	1.80
24	Wally Joyner	5.00	2.20
25	Brian Jordan	5.00	2.20
26	Edgar Martinez	6.00	2.70
27	Hideo Nomo	20.00	9.00
28	Mike Mussina	10.00	4.50
29	Eddie Murray	10.00	4.50
30	Cal Ripken	30.00	13.50
31	Checklist	4.00	1.80
61	Cal Ripken	50.00	22.00
62	Hideo Nomo	40.00	18.00
63	Reggie Sanders	5.00	2.20
64	Mo Vaughn	15.00	6.75
65	Tim Salmon	8.00	3.60
66	Chipper Jones	40.00	18.00
67	Manny Ramirez	8.00	3.60
68	Greg Maddux	25.00	11.00
69	Frank Thomas	30.00	13.50
70	Ken Griffey Jr.	40.00	18.00
71	Dante Bichette	6.00	2.70
72	Tony Gwynn	20.00	9.00

1996 Donruss Freeze Frame

Randomly inserted in second series packs at a rate of one in 60, this 8-card standard-size set features the top hitters and pitchers in baseball. Just 5,000 of each card were produced and sequentially numbered. In a horizontal format with round corners, the fronts display a crosshatched color player photo that is bordered on the left and bottom by thick black borders. A second color player cutout is superposed on the photo. The backs have three small color photos, '95 season highlights, and a brief note.

	MINT	NRMT
COMPLETE SET (8)	180.00	80.00
COMMON CARD (1-8)	10.00	4.50
SER.2 STATED ODDS 1:60		
STATED PRINT RUN 5000 SERIAL #'d SETS		

		MINT	NRMT
☐ 1	Frank Thomas	30.00	13.50
☐ 2	Ken Griffey Jr.	40.00	18.00
☐ 3	Cal Ripken	30.00	13.50
☐ 4	Hideo Nomo	20.00	9.00
☐ 5	Greg Maddux	25.00	11.00
☐ 6	Albert Belle	10.00	4.50
☐ 7	Chipper Jones	25.00	11.00
☐ 8	Mike Piazza	25.00	11.00

1996 Donruss Hit List

This 16-card standard-size set was randomly inserted in 97 Donruss and salutes the most consistent hitters in the game. The first series cards were inserted one every 105 packs while the second series cards were inserted one every 60

packs. The cards are sequentially numbered out of 10,000. The fronts feature full-color shots set against a silver-foil background that is complemented by a team color duotone and features a gold foil team logo and "Hit List" logo. The backs have a color action photo as well as having year-by-year and career hit and batting average stats.

	MINT	NRMT
COMPLETE SET (16)	100.00	45.00
COMPLETE SERIES 1 (8)	60.00	27.00
COMPLETE SERIES 2 (8)	40.00	18.00
COMMON CARD (1-16)	2.50	1.10
SEMISTARS	3.00	1.35
UNLISTED STARS	5.00	2.20
SER.1 STATED ODDS 1:105		
SER.2 STATED ODDS 1:60		
STATED PRINT RUN 10,000 SERIAL #'d SETS		

		MINT	NRMT
☐ 1	Tony Gwynn	15.00	6.75
☐ 2	Ken Griffey Jr.	30.00	13.50
☐ 3	Will Clark	3.00	1.35
☐ 4	Mike Piazza	20.00	9.00
☐ 5	Carlos Baerga	2.50	1.10
☐ 6	Mo Vaughn	8.00	3.60
☐ 7	Mark Grace	3.00	1.35
☐ 8	Kirby Puckett	12.00	5.50
☐ 9	Frank Thomas	20.00	9.00
☐ 10	Barry Bonds	6.00	2.70
☐ 11	Jeff Bagwell	10.00	4.50
☐ 12	Edgar Martinez	3.00	1.35
☐ 13	Tim Salmon	5.00	2.20
☐ 14	Wade Boggs	5.00	2.20
☐ 15	Don Mattingly	8.00	3.60
☐ 16	Eddie Murray	5.00	2.20

1996 Donruss Long Ball Leaders

This eight-card standard-size set was randomly inserted into series one retail packs. They were inserted at a rate of approximately one in every 96 packs. The cards are sequentially numbered out of 5,000. The set highlights eight top sluggers and their farthest home run distance of 1995. The fronts feature a player photo set against a silver-foil background. The words "Long Ball Leaders" are on the top of the card while the stadium, date and distance of the blast are in the middle. The player's name is at the bottom. The back has a player photo and information about the game in which the mighty clout occurred.

	MINT	NRMT
COMPLETE SET (8)	200.00	90.00
COMMON CARD (1-8)	8.00	3.60
SER.1 STATED ODDS 1:96 RETAIL		
STATED PRINT RUN 5000 SERIAL #'d SETS		

		MINT	NRMT
☐ 1	Barry Bonds	20.00	9.00
☐ 2	Ryan Klesko	12.00	5.50
☐ 3	Mark McGwire	30.00	13.50
☐ 4	Raul Mondesi	12.00	5.50
☐ 5	Cecil Fielder	10.00	4.50
☐ 6	Ken Griffey Jr.	80.00	36.00
☐ 7	Larry Walker	15.00	6.75
☐ 8	Frank Thomas	60.00	27.00

1996 Donruss Power Alley

This ten-card standard-size set was randomly inserted into series one hobby packs. They were inserted at a rate of approximately one in every 92 packs. These cards are all sequentially numbered out of 5,000. These cards feature a player photo set against a diamond design and team holographic background. The horizontal backs feature a player photo, some text and the player's 1995 power statistics.

	MINT	NRMT
COMPLETE SET (10)	150.00	70.00
COMMON CARD (1-10)	4.00	1.80
SEMISTARS	6.00	2.70
UNLISTED STARS	10.00	4.50
SER.1 STATED ODDS 1:92 HOBBY		
STATED PRINT RUN 4500 SERIAL #'d SETS		
COMP.DIE CUT SET (10) ..	800.00	350.00
*DIE CUTS: 2X TO 4X HI COLUMN		
SER.1 DC STATED ODDS 1:920 HOBBY		
DC STATED PRINT RUN 500 SERIAL #'d SETS		

		MINT	NRMT
☐ 1	Frank Thomas	40.00	18.00
☐ 2	Barry Bonds	12.00	5.50
☐ 3	Reggie Sanders	4.00	1.80
☐ 4	Albert Belle	12.00	5.50
☐ 5	Tim Salmon	10.00	4.50
☐ 6	Dante Bichette	5.00	2.20
☐ 7	Mo Vaughn	12.00	5.50
☐ 8	Jim Edmonds	6.00	2.70
☐ 9	Manny Ramirez	10.00	4.50
☐ 10	Ken Griffey Jr.	50.00	22.00

1996 Donruss Pure Power

Randomly inserted in retail and magazine packs only at a rate of one in eight, this eight-card set features color action player photos of eight of the most pow-

erful players in Major League baseball.

	MINT	NRMT
COMPLETE SET (8)	175.00	80.00
COMMON CARD (1-8)	10.00	4.50
UNLISTED STARS	12.00	5.50
RANDOM INSERTS IN SER.2 RETAIL PACKS		
STATED PRINT RUN 5000 SETS		

		MINT	NRMT
☐ 1	Raul Mondesi		4.50
☐ 2	Barry Bonds	15.00	6.75
☐ 3	Albert Belle	15.00	6.75
☐ 4	Frank Thomas	40.00	18.00
☐ 5	Mike Piazza	40.00	18.00
☐ 6	Dante Bichette	10.00	4.50
☐ 7	Manny Ramirez	12.00	5.50
☐ 8	Mo Vaughn	15.00	6.75

1996 Donruss
Round Trippers

Randomly inserted in second series hobby packs at a rate of one in 55, this 10-card standard-size set honors ten of Baseball's top homerun hitters. Just 5,000 of each card were produced and consecutively numbered. On a sepia-tone background with a home plate icon carrying the 1995 season home run total, the fronts superpose a color player cutout. The player's name and "Round Trippers" are bronze foil stamped at the bottom. The backs have a similar design and present 1995 and career home run statistics by a bar graph.

	MINT	NRMT
COMPLETE SET (10)	150.00	70.00
COMMON CARD (1-10)	5.00	2.20
SER.2 STATED ODDS 1:55 HOBBY		
STATED PRINT RUN 5000 SERIAL #'d SETS		

		MINT	NRMT
☐ 1	Albert Belle	10.00	4.50
☐ 2	Barry Bonds	10.00	4.50

		MINT	NRMT
☐ 3	Jeff Bagwell	15.00	6.75
☐ 4	Tim Salmon	8.00	3.60
☐ 5	Mo Vaughn	10.00	4.50
☐ 6	Ken Griffey Jr.	40.00	18.00
☐ 7	Mike Piazza	25.00	11.00
☐ 8	Cal Ripken	30.00	13.50
☐ 9	Frank Thomas	30.00	13.50
☐ 10	Dante Bichette	5.00	2.20

1996 Donruss
Showdown

This eight-card standard-size set was randomly inserted in series one packs at a rate of one every 105 packs. These cards feature one top hitter and one top pitcher from each league. The cards are sequentially numbered out of 10,000. The horizontal fronts feature gold foil stamping and have the words "Show Down" in the middle. The backs feature color player photos as well as some text about their accomplishments.

	MINT	NRMT
COMPLETE SET (8)	120.00	55.00
COMMON CARD (1-8)	4.00	1.80
SER.1 STATED ODDS 1:105		
STATED PRINT RUN 10,000 SERIAL #'d SETS		

		MINT	NRMT
☐ 1	Frank Thomas	30.00	13.50
	Hideo Nomo		
☐ 2	Barry Bonds	10.00	4.50
	Randy Johnson		
☐ 3	Greg Maddux	40.00	18.00
	Ken Griffey Jr.		
☐ 4	Roger Clemens	20.00	9.00
	Tony Gwynn		
☐ 5	Mike Piazza	20.00	9.00
	Mike Mussina		
☐ 6	Cal Ripken	25.00	11.00
	Pedro J.Martinez		
☐ 7	Tim Wakefield	4.00	1.80
	Matt Williams		
☐ 8	Manny Ramirez	8.00	3.60
	Carlos Perez		

1997 Donruss

The 1997 Donruss set was issued in two separate series of 270 and 180 cards respectively. Both first series and Update cards were distributed in 10-card packs carrying a suggested retail price of $1.99 each. Card fronts feature color action player photos while the backs carry another color player photo with player information and career statistics. The following subsets are included within the

set: Checklists (267-270/448-450), Rookies (353-397), Hit List (398-422), King of the Hill (423-437) and Interleague Showdown (438-447). The only key RCs in this set are Jose Cruz Jr. and Hideki Irabu.

	MINT	NRMT
COMPLETE SET (450)	45.00	20.00
COMPLETE SERIES 1 (270)	25.00	11.00
COMPLETE UPDATE (180)	20.00	9.00
COMMON CARD (1-450)	.15	.07
MINOR STARS	.30	.14
UNLISTED STARS	.60	.25
SUBSET CARDS HALF VALUE OF BASE CARDS		
COMP.SILV.PP SET (450)	1200.00	550.00
COMP.SILV.PP SER.1 (270)	700.00	325.00
COMP.SILV.PP UPD. (180)	500.00	220.00
COMMON SILVER PP (1-450)	2.00	.90
*SILV.PP STARS: 6X TO 12X HI COLUMN		
*SILV.PP YOUNG STARS: 5X TO 10X HI		
*SILV.PP ROOKIES: 3X TO 6X HI		
SILVER PP SER.1 STATED ODDS 1:8		
SILVER PP PRINT RUN 2000 SETS		
COMP.GOLD PP SET (450)	3200.00	1450.00
COMP.GOLD PP SER.1 (270)	2000.00	900.00
COMP.GOLD PP UPD. (180)	1200.00	550.00
COMMON GOLD PP (1-450)	6.00	2.70
*GOLD PP STARS: 15X TO 40X HI COL.		
*GOLD PP YOUNG STARS: 12.5X TO 30X HI		
*GOLD PP ROOKIES: 8X TO 20X HI		
GOLD PP SER.1 STATED ODDS 1:32		
GOLD PRESS PROOF PRINT RUN 500 SETS		
COMP.RIPKEN SET (9)	100.00	45.00
COMMON RIPKEN (1-9)	12.00	5.50
RIPKEN: RANDOM INS.IN UPDATE PACKS		
RIPKEN PRINT RUN 5000 SERIAL #'d SETS		
RIPKEN #10 DIST.ONLY W/HIS BOOK		

		MINT	NRMT
☐ 1	Juan Gonzalez	1.50	.70
☐ 2	Jim Edmonds	.40	.18
☐ 3	Tony Gwynn	1.50	.70
☐ 4	Andres Galarraga	.60	.25
☐ 5	Joe Carter	.30	.14
☐ 6	Raul Mondesi	.40	.18
☐ 7	Greg Maddux	2.00	.90
☐ 8	Travis Fryman	.30	.14
☐ 9	Brian Jordan	.30	.14
☐ 10	Henry Rodriguez	.15	.07
☐ 11	Manny Ramirez	.60	.25
☐ 12	Mark McGwire	1.25	.55
☐ 13	Marc Newfield	.15	.07
☐ 14	Craig Biggio	.40	.18
☐ 15	Sammy Sosa	.60	.25
☐ 16	Brady Anderson	.30	.18
☐ 17	Wade Boggs	.60	.25
☐ 18	Charles Johnson	.30	.14
☐ 19	Matt Williams	.40	.18
☐ 20	Denny Neagle	.30	.14
☐ 21	Ken Griffey Jr.	3.00	1.35
☐ 22	Robin Ventura	.30	.14
☐ 23	Barry Larkin	.40	.18
☐ 24	Todd Zeile	.15	.07
☐ 25	Chuck Knoblauch	.60	.25
☐ 26	Todd Hundley	.30	.14
☐ 27	Roger Clemens	1.25	.55
☐ 28	Michael Tucker	.30	.14

29	Rondell White	.30	.14
30	Osvaldo Fernandez	.15	.07
31	Ivan Rodriguez	.30	.14
32	Alex Fernandez	.15	.07
33	Jason Isringhausen	.15	.07
34	Chipper Jones	2.00	.90
35	Paul O'Neill	.30	.14
36	Hideo Nomo	1.50	.70
37	Roberto Alomar	.60	.25
38	Derek Bell	.15	.07
39	Paul Molitor	.60	.25
40	Andy Benes	.30	.14
41	Steve Trachsel	.15	.07
42	J.T. Snow	.30	.14
43	Jason Kendall	.30	.14
44	Alex Rodriguez	2.00	.90
45	Joey Hamilton	.30	.14
46	Carlos Delgado	.30	.14
47	Jason Giambi	.30	.14
48	Larry Walker	.60	.25
49	Derek Jeter	2.00	.90
50	Kenny Lofton	.75	.35
51	Devon White	.15	.07
52	Matt Mieske	.15	.07
53	Melvin Nieves	.15	.07
54	Jose Canseco	.40	.18
55	Tino Martinez	.40	.18
56	Rafael Palmeiro	.40	.18
57	Edgardo Alfonzo	.30	.14
58	Jay Buhner	.40	.18
59	Shane Reynolds	.15	.07
60	Steve Finley	.30	.14
61	Bobby Higginson	.30	.14
62	Dean Palmer	.15	.07
63	Terry Pendleton	.15	.07
64	Marquis Grissom	.30	.14
65	Mike Stanley	.15	.07
66	Moises Alou	.30	.14
67	Ray Lankford	.30	.14
68	Marty Cordova	.30	.14
69	John Olerud	.30	.14
70	David Cone	.30	.14
71	Benito Santiago	.15	.07
72	Ryne Sandberg	.75	.35
73	Rickey Henderson	.40	.18
74	Roger Cedeno	.15	.07
75	Wilson Alvarez	.15	.07
76	Tim Salmon	.60	.25
77	Orlando Merced	.15	.07
78	Vinny Castilla	.30	.14
79	Ismael Valdes	.30	.14
80	Dante Bichette	.30	.14
81	Kevin Brown	.30	.14
82	Andy Pettitte	.60	.25
83	Scott Stahoviak	.15	.07
84	Mickey Tettleton	.15	.07
85	Jack McDowell	.15	.07
86	Tom Glavine	.30	.14
87	Gregg Jefferies	.15	.07
88	Chili Davis	.15	.07
89	Randy Johnson	.60	.25
90	John Mabry	.15	.07
91	Billy Wagner	.30	.14
92	Jeff Cirillo	.15	.07
93	Trevor Hoffman	.15	.07
94	Juan Guzman	.15	.07
95	Geronimo Berroa	.15	.07
96	Bernard Gilkey	.15	.07
97	Danny Tartabull	.15	.07
98	Johnny Damon	.15	.07
99	Charlie Hayes	.15	.07
100	Reggie Sanders	.15	.07
101	Robby Thompson	.15	.07
102	Bobby Bonilla	.30	.14
103	Reggie Jefferson	.15	.07
104	John Smoltz	.30	.14
105	Jim Thome	.60	.25
106	Ruben Rivera	.30	.14
107	Darren Oliver	.15	.07
108	Mo Vaughn	.75	.35
109	Roger Pavlik	.15	.07
110	Terry Steinbach	.15	.07
111	Jermaine Dye	.30	.14
112	Mark Grudzielanek	.15	.07
113	Rick Aguilera	.15	.07
114	Jamey Wright	.15	.07
115	Eddie Murray	.60	.25
116	Brian L. Hunter	.30	.14
117	Hal Morris	.15	.07
118	Tom Pagnozzi	.15	.07
119	Mike Mussina	.60	.25
120	Mark Grace	.40	.18
121	Cal Ripken	2.50	1.10
122	Tom Goodwin	.15	.07
123	Paul Sorrento	.15	.07
124	Jay Bell	.30	.14
125	Todd Hollandsworth	.15	.07
126	Edgar Martinez	.40	.18
127	George Arias	.15	.07
128	Greg Vaughn	.15	.07
129	Roberto Hernandez	.15	.07
130	Delino DeShields	.15	.07
131	Bill Pulsipher	.15	.07
132	Joey Cora	.30	.14
133	Mariano Rivera	.30	.14
134	Mike Piazza	2.00	.90
135	Carlos Baerga	.15	.07
136	Jose Mesa	.15	.07
137	Will Clark	.40	.18
138	Frank Thomas	2.50	1.10
139	John Wetteland	.15	.07
140	Shawn Estes	.30	.14
141	Garret Anderson	.30	.14
142	Andre Dawson	.40	.18
143	Eddie Taubensee	.15	.07
144	Ryan Klesko	.40	.18
145	Rocky Coppinger	.15	.07
146	Jeff Bagwell	1.25	.55
147	Donovan Osborne	.15	.07
148	Greg Myers	.15	.07
149	Brant Brown	.15	.07
150	Kevin Elster	.15	.07
151	Bob Wells	.15	.07
152	Wally Joyner	.30	.14
153	Rico Brogna	.15	.07
154	Dwight Gooden	.30	.14
155	Jermaine Allensworth	.15	.07
156	Ray Durham	.30	.14
157	Cecil Fielder	.30	.14
158	John Burkett	.15	.07
159	Gary Sheffield	.60	.25
160	Albert Belle	.75	.35
161	Tomas Perez	.15	.07
162	David Doster	.15	.07
163	John Valentin	.15	.07
164	Danny Graves	.15	.07
165	Jose Paniagua	.15	.07
166	Brian Giles	.15	.07
167	Barry Bonds	.75	.35
168	Sterling Hitchcock	.15	.07
169	Bernie Williams	.60	.25
170	Fred McGriff	.40	.18
171	George Williams	.15	.07
172	Amaury Telemaco	.15	.07
173	Ken Caminiti	.40	.18
174	Ron Gant	.30	.14
175	Dave Justice	.30	.14
176	James Baldwin	.15	.07
177	Pat Hentgen	.30	.14
178	Ben McDonald	.15	.07
179	Tim Naehring	.15	.07
180	Jim Eisenreich	.15	.07
181	Ken Hill	.15	.07
182	Paul Wilson	.15	.07
183	Marvin Benard	.15	.07
184	Alan Benes	.30	.14
185	Ellis Burks	.30	.14
186	Scott Servais	.15	.07
187	David Segui	.15	.07
188	Scott Brosius	.15	.07
189	Jose Offerman	.15	.07
190	Eric Davis	.30	.14
191	Brett Butler	.30	.14
192	Curtis Pride	.15	.07
193	Yamil Benitez	.15	.07
194	Chan Ho Park	.60	.25
195	Bret Boone	.15	.07
196	Omar Vizquel	.30	.14
197	Orlando Miller	.15	.07
198	Ramon Martinez	.30	.14
199	Harold Baines	.30	.14
200	Eric Young	.15	.07
201	Fernando Vina	.15	.07
202	Alex Gonzalez	.15	.07
203	Fernando Valenzuela	.30	.14
204	Steve Avery	.15	.07
205	Ernie Young	.15	.07
206	Kevin Appier	.30	.14
207	Randy Myers	.15	.07
208	Jeff Suppan	.30	.14
209	James Mouton	.15	.07
210	Russ Davis	.15	.07
211	Al Martin	.15	.07
212	Troy Percival	.15	.07
213	Al Leiter	.15	.07
214	Dennis Eckersley	.30	.14
215	Mark Johnson	.15	.07
216	Eric Karros	.30	.14
217	Royce Clayton	.15	.07
218	Tony Phillips	.15	.07
219	Tim Wakefield	.30	.14
220	Alan Trammell	.30	.14
221	Eduardo Perez	.15	.07
222	Butch Huskey	.30	.14
223	Tim Belcher	.15	.07
224	Jamie Moyer	.15	.07
225	F.P. Santangelo	.15	.07
226	Rusty Greer	.30	.14
227	Jeff Brantley	.15	.07
228	Mark Langston	.15	.07
229	Ray Montgomery	.15	.07
230	Rich Becker	.15	.07
231	Ozzie Smith	.75	.35
232	Rey Ordonez	.15	.07
233	Ricky Otero	.15	.07
234	Mike Cameron	.40	.18
235	Mike Sweeney	.30	.14
236	Mark Lewis	.15	.07
237	Luis Gonzalez	.15	.07
238	Marcus Jensen	.15	.07
239	Ed Sprague	.15	.07
240	Jose Valentin	.15	.07
241	Jeff Frye	.15	.07
242	Charles Nagy	.30	.14
243	Carlos Garcia	.15	.07
244	Mike Hampton	.15	.07
245	B.J. Surhoff	.15	.07
246	Wilton Guerrero	.15	.07
247	Frank Rodriguez	.15	.07
248	Gary Gaetti	.15	.07
249	Lance Johnson	.15	.07
250	Darren Bragg	.15	.07
251	Darryl Hamilton	.15	.07
252	John Jaha	.15	.07
253	Craig Paquette	.15	.07
254	Jaime Navarro	.15	.07
255	Shawon Dunston	.15	.07
256	Mark Loretta	.15	.07
257	Tim Belk	.15	.07
258	Jeff Darwin	.15	.07
259	Ruben Sierra	.15	.07
260	Chuck Finley	.15	.07
261	Darryl Strawberry	.30	.14
262	Shannon Stewart	.30	.14
263	Pedro Martinez	.60	.25
264	Neifi Perez	.30	.14
265	Jeff Conine	.30	.14
266	Orel Hershiser	.30	.14
267	Eddie Murray CL	.30	.14
268	Paul Molitor CL	.30	.14
269	Barry Bonds CL	.40	.18
270	Mark McGwire CL	.60	.25
271	Matt Williams	.30	.14
272	Todd Zeile	.15	.07
273	Roger Clemens	1.25	.55
274	Michael Tucker	.30	.14
275	J.T. Snow	.30	.14
276	Kenny Lofton	.75	.35
277	Jose Canseco	.40	.18
278	Marquis Grissom	.30	.14
279	Moises Alou	.30	.14
280	Benito Santiago	.15	.07
281	Willie McGee	.15	.07
282	Chili Davis	.30	.14
283	Ron Coomer	.15	.07
284	Orlando Merced	.15	.07
285	Delino DeShields	.15	.07
286	John Wetteland	.15	.07

☐ 287	Darren Daulton	.30	.14
☐ 288	Lee Stevens	.15	.07
☐ 289	Albert Belle	.75	.35
☐ 290	Sterling Hitchcock	.15	.07
☐ 291	David Justice	.60	.25
☐ 292	Eric Davis	.60	.14
☐ 293	Brian Hunter	.30	.14
☐ 294	Darryl Hamilton	.15	.07
☐ 295	Steve Avery	.15	.07
☐ 296	Joe Vitiello	.15	.07
☐ 297	Jaime Navarro	.15	.07
☐ 298	Eddie Murray	.60	.25
☐ 299	Randy Myers	.15	.07
☐ 300	Francisco Cordova	.15	.07
☐ 301	Javier Lopez	.30	.14
☐ 302	Geronimo Berroa	.15	.07
☐ 303	Jeffrey Hammonds	.15	.07
☐ 304	Deion Sanders	.30	.14
☐ 305	Jeff Fassero	.15	.07
☐ 306	Curt Schilling	.30	.14
☐ 307	Robb Nen	.15	.07
☐ 308	Mark McLemore	.15	.07
☐ 309	Jimmy Key	.30	.14
☐ 310	Quilvio Veras	.15	.07
☐ 311	Bip Roberts	.15	.07
☐ 312	Esteban Loaiza	.15	.07
☐ 313	Andy Ashby	.15	.07
☐ 314	Sandy Alomar Jr	.30	.14
☐ 315	Shawn Green	.15	.07
☐ 316	Luis Castillo	.30	.14
☐ 317	Benji Gil	.15	.07
☐ 318	Otis Nixon	.15	.07
☐ 319	Aaron Sele	.15	.07
☐ 320	Brad Ausmus	.15	.07
☐ 321	Troy O'Leary	.15	.07
☐ 322	Terrell Wade	.15	.07
☐ 323	Jeff King	.15	.07
☐ 324	Kevin Seitzer	.15	.07
☐ 325	Mark Wohlers	.15	.07
☐ 326	Edgar Renteria	.30	.14
☐ 327	Dan Wilson	.15	.07
☐ 328	Brian McRae	.15	.07
☐ 329	Rod Beck	.15	.07
☐ 330	Julio Franco	.30	.14
☐ 331	Dave Nilsson	.15	.07
☐ 332	Glenallen Hill	.15	.07
☐ 333	Kevin Elster	.15	.07
☐ 334	Joe Girardi	.15	.07
☐ 335	David Wells	.15	.07
☐ 336	Jeff Blauser	.30	.14
☐ 337	Darryl Kile	.30	.14
☐ 338	Jeff Kent	.15	.07
☐ 339	Jim Leyritz	.15	.07
☐ 340	Todd Stottlemyre	.15	.07
☐ 341	Tony Clark	.60	.25
☐ 342	Chris Hoiles	.15	.07
☐ 343	Mike Lieberthal	.15	.07
☐ 344	Matt Lawton	.15	.07
☐ 345	Alex Ochoa	.15	.07
☐ 346	Chris Snopek	.15	.07
☐ 347	Rudy Pemberton	.15	.07
☐ 348	Eric Owens	.15	.07
☐ 349	Joe Randa	.15	.07
☐ 350	John Olerud	.30	.14
☐ 351	Steve Karsay	.15	.07
☐ 352	Mark Whiten	.15	.07
☐ 353	Bob Abreu	.30	.14
☐ 354	Bartolo Colon	.30	.14
☐ 355	Vladimir Guerrero	1.25	.55
☐ 356	Darin Erstad	1.00	.45
☐ 357	Scott Rolen	1.50	.70
☐ 358	Andruw Jones	1.50	.70
☐ 359	Scott Spiezio	.30	.14
☐ 360	Karim Garcia	.30	.14
☐ 361	Hideki Irabu	.60	.25
☐ 362	Nomar Garciaparra	2.00	.90
☐ 363	Dmitri Young	.15	.07
☐ 364	Bubba Trammell	.60	.25
☐ 365	Kevin Orie	.30	.14
☐ 366	Jose Rosado	.30	.14
☐ 367	Jose Guillen	.75	.35
☐ 368	Brooks Kieschnick	.15	.07
☐ 369	Pokey Reese	.15	.07
☐ 370	Glendon Rusch	.15	.07
☐ 371	Jason Dickson	.30	.14
☐ 372	Todd Walker	.30	.14

☐ 373	Justin Thompson	.30	.14
☐ 374	Todd Greene	.30	.14
☐ 375	Jeff Suppan	.30	.14
☐ 376	Trey Beamon	.15	.07
☐ 377	Damon Mashore	.15	.07
☐ 378	Wendell Magee	.15	.07
☐ 379	Shigetoshi Hasegawa	.40	.18
☐ 380	Bill Mueller	.15	.07
☐ 381	Chris Widger	.15	.07
☐ 382	Tony Graffanino	.15	.07
☐ 383	Derrek Lee	.40	.18
☐ 384	Brian Moehler	.15	.07
☐ 385	Quinton McCracken	.15	.07
☐ 386	Matt Morris	.30	.14
☐ 387	Marvin Benard	.15	.07
☐ 388	Deivi Cruz	.50	.23
☐ 389	Javier Valentin	.30	.14
☐ 390	Todd Dunwoody	.40	.18
☐ 391	Derrick Gibson	.40	.18
☐ 392	Raul Casanova	.15	.07
☐ 393	George Arias	.15	.07
☐ 394	Tony Womack	.50	.23
☐ 395	Antone Williamson	.15	.07
☐ 396	Jose Cruz Jr.	5.00	2.20
☐ 397	Desi Relaford	.15	.07
☐ 398	Frank Thomas HIT	1.25	.55
☐ 399	Ken Griffey Jr. HIT	1.50	.70
☐ 400	Cal Ripken HIT	1.25	.55
☐ 401	Chipper Jones HIT	1.00	.45
☐ 402	Mike Piazza HIT	1.00	.45
☐ 403	Gary Sheffield HIT	.30	.14
☐ 404	Alex Rodriguez HIT	1.00	.45
☐ 405	Wade Boggs HIT	.30	.14
☐ 406	Juan Gonzalez HIT	.75	.35
☐ 407	Tony Gwynn HIT	.75	.35
☐ 408	Edgar Martinez HIT	.30	.14
☐ 409	Jeff Bagwell HIT	.60	.25
☐ 410	Larry Walker HIT	.15	.07
☐ 411	Kenny Lofton HIT	.40	.18
☐ 412	Manny Ramirez HIT	.50	.23
☐ 413	Mark McGwire HIT	.60	.25
☐ 414	Roberto Alomar HIT	.30	.14
☐ 415	Derek Jeter HIT	1.00	.45
☐ 416	Brady Anderson HIT	.30	.14
☐ 417	Paul Molitor HIT	.30	.14
☐ 418	Dante Bichette HIT	.15	.07
☐ 419	Jim Edmonds HIT	.30	.14
☐ 420	Mo Vaughn HIT	.40	.18
☐ 421	Barry Bonds HIT	.40	.18
☐ 422	Rusty Greer HIT	.15	.07
☐ 423	Greg Maddux KING	1.00	.45
☐ 424	Andy Pettitte KING	.30	.14
☐ 425	John Smoltz KING	.15	.07
☐ 426	Randy Johnson KING	.30	.14
☐ 427	Hideo Nomo KING	.75	.35
☐ 428	Roger Clemens KING	.60	.25
☐ 429	Tom Glavine KING	.15	.07
☐ 430	Pat Hentgen KING	.15	.07
☐ 431	Kevin Brown KING	.15	.07
☐ 432	Mike Mussina KING	.30	.14
☐ 433	Alex Fernandez KING	.15	.07
☐ 434	Kevin Appier KING	.15	.07
☐ 435	David Cone KING	.15	.07
☐ 436	Jeff Fassero KING	.15	.07
☐ 437	John Wetteland KING	.15	.07
☐ 438	Ivan Rodriguez	.55	.25
☐ 439	Ken Griffey Jr. IS	1.00	.45
☐ 440	Fred McGriff IS	.15	.07
☐ 441	Barry Larkin IS	.15	.07
☐ 442	Sammy Sosa IS	.25	.11
☐ 443	Bernie Williams IS	.15	.07
☐ 444	Chuck Knoblauch IS	.15	.07
☐ 445	Mo Vaughn IS	.25	.11
☐ 446	Ken Caminiti IS	.15	.07
☐ 447	Raul Mondesi IS	.15	.07
☐ 448	Cal Ripken CL	1.25	.55

☐ 449	Greg Maddux CL	1.00	.45
☐ 450	Ken Griffey Jr. CL	1.50	.70

1997 Donruss Armed and Dangerous

Randomly inserted in hobby packs at a rate of one in 58 packs, this 15-card set features the League's hottest arms in the game. The fronts carry color action player photos with foil printing. The backs display player information and a color player head portrait at the end of a ribbon representing a medal. Only 5,000 of this set were produced and are sequentially numbered.

	MINT	NRMT
COMPLETE SET (15)	150.00	70.00
COMMON CARD (1-15)	4.00	1.80
UNLISTED STARS	6.00	2.70
SER.1 STATED ODDS 1:58 HOBBY		
STATED PRINT RUN 5000 SERIAL #'d SETS		

☐ 1	Ken Griffey Jr.	30.00	13.50
☐ 2	Raul Mondesi	4.00	1.80
☐ 3	Chipper Jones	20.00	9.00
☐ 4	Ivan Rodriguez	8.00	3.60
☐ 5	Randy Johnson	6.00	2.70
☐ 6	Alex Rodriguez	20.00	9.00
☐ 7	Larry Walker	6.00	2.70
☐ 8	Cal Ripken	25.00	11.00
☐ 9	Kenny Lofton	8.00	3.60
☐ 10	Barry Bonds	8.00	3.60
☐ 11	Derek Jeter	15.00	6.75
☐ 12	Charles Johnson	4.00	1.80
☐ 13	Greg Maddux	20.00	9.00
☐ 14	Roberto Alomar	6.00	2.70
☐ 15	Barry Larkin	4.00	1.80

1997 Donruss Diamond Kings

Randomly inserted in all first series packs at a rate of one in 45, this 10-card set commemorates the 15th anniversary of the annual art cards in Donruss baseball sets. Only 10,000 sets were produced each of which is sequentially numbered. Ten cards were printed with the number 1,982 representing the year the insert began and could be redeemed for an original piece of artwork by Diamond Kings artist Dan Gardiner. This was the first year Gardiner painted the Diamond King series.

	MINT	NRMT
□ 11 Roger Clemens	6.00	2.70
□ 12 John Smoltz	1.50	.70
□ 13 Mike Piazza	10.00	4.50
□ 14 Sammy Sosa	3.00	1.35
□ 15 Matt Williams	2.00	.90
□ 16 Kenny Lofton	4.00	1.80
□ 17 Barry Larkin	2.00	.90
□ 18 Rafael Palmeiro	2.00	.90
□ 19 Ken Caminiti	2.00	.90
□ 20 Gary Sheffield	3.00	1.35

1997 Donruss Elite Inserts

	MINT	NRMT
COMPLETE SET (10)	180.00	80.00
COMMON CARD (1-10)	4.00	1.80
UNLISTED STARS	6.00	2.70

SER.1 STATED ODDS 1:45......
STATED PRINT RUN 9500 SERIAL #'d SETS
COMP.CANVAS SET (10) .. 750.00 350.00
*CANVAS: 2X TO 4X HI COLUMN
CANVAS: RANDOM INS.IN SER.1 PACKS
CANVAS PRINT RUN 500 SERIAL #'d SETS
EACH CARD #1982 WINS ORIGINAL ART

□ 1 Ken Griffey Jr.	40.00	18.00
□ 2 Cal Ripken	30.00	13.50
□ 3 Mo Vaughn	10.00	4.50
□ 4 Chuck Knoblauch	6.00	2.70
□ 5 Jeff Bagwell	15.00	6.75
□ 6 Henry Rodriguez	4.00	1.80
□ 7 Mike Piazza	25.00	11.00
□ 8 Ivan Rodriguez	10.00	4.50
□ 9 Frank Thomas	30.00	13.50
□ 10 Chipper Jones	25.00	11.00

1997 Donruss Dominators

Randomly inserted in Update packs, cards from this 20-card set feature top stars with either incredible speed, awesome power, or unbelievable pitching ability. Card fronts feature red borders and silver foil stamping.

	MINT	NRMT
COMPLETE SET (20)	90.00	40.00
COMMON CARD (1-20)	1.50	.70

RANDOM INSERTS IN UPDATE PACKS

□ 1 Frank Thomas	12.00	5.50
□ 2 Ken Griffey Jr.	15.00	6.75
□ 3 Greg Maddux	10.00	4.50
□ 4 Cal Ripken	12.00	5.50
□ 5 Alex Rodriguez	10.00	4.50
□ 6 Albert Belle	4.00	1.80
□ 7 Mark McGwire	6.00	2.70
□ 8 Juan Gonzalez	8.00	3.60
□ 9 Chipper Jones	10.00	4.50
□ 10 Hideo Nomo	8.00	3.60

Randomly inserted in all first series packs, this 12-card set honors perennial all-star players of the League. The fronts feature Micro-etched color action player photos, while the backs carry player information. Only 2,500 of this set were produced and are sequentially numbered.

	MINT	NRMT
COMPLETE SET (12)	500.00	220.00
COMMON CARD (1-12)	12.00	5.50

SER.1 STATED ODDS 1:144......
STATED PRINT RUN 2500 SERIAL #'d SETS

□ 1 Frank Thomas	60.00	27.00
□ 2 Paul Molitor	15.00	6.75
□ 3 Sammy Sosa	12.00	5.50
□ 4 Barry Bonds	20.00	9.00
□ 5 Chipper Jones	50.00	22.00
□ 6 Alex Rodriguez	50.00	22.00
□ 7 Ken Griffey Jr.	80.00	36.00
□ 8 Jeff Bagwell	30.00	13.50
□ 9 Cal Ripken	60.00	27.00
□ 10 Mo Vaughn	20.00	9.00
□ 11 Mike Piazza	50.00	22.00
□ 12 Juan Gonzalez UER	40.00	18.00

name mispelled as Gonzales

1997 Donruss Franchise Features

Randomly inserted in Update hobby packs only at an approximate rate of 1:48, cards from this 15-card set feature color player photos on a unique "movie-poster" style, double-front card design. Each card highlights a superstar veteran on one side displaying a "Now Playing" banner, while the other side features a rookie prospect with a "Coming Attraction" banner. Each card is printed on an all foil stock and serial numbered to 3,000.

	MINT	NRMT
COMPLETE SET (15)	250.00	110.00
COMMON CARD (1-15)	6.00	2.70
UNLISTED STARS	8.00	3.60

RANDOM INSERTS IN UPDATE PACKS
STATED PRINT RUN 3000 SERIAL #'d SETS

□ 1 Ken Griffey Jr.	40.00	18.00
Andruw Jones		
□ 2 Frank Thomas	30.00	13.50
Darin Erstad		
□ 3 Alex Rodriguez	30.00	13.50
Nomar Garciaparra		
□ 4 Chuck Knoblauch	8.00	3.60
Wilton Guerrero		
□ 5 Juan Gonzalez	20.00	9.00
BubbaTrammell		
□ 6 Chipper Jones	25.00	11.00
Todd Walker		
□ 7 Barry Bonds	12.00	5.50
Vladimir Guerrero		
□ 8 Mark McGwire	15.00	6.75
Dmitri Young		
□ 9 Mike Piazza	25.00	11.00
Mike Sweeney		
□ 10 Mo Vaughn	10.00	4.50
Tony Clark		
□ 11 Gary Sheffield	8.00	3.60
Jose Guillen		
□ 12 Kenny Lofton	10.00	4.50
Shannon Stewart		
□ 13 Cal Ripken	30.00	13.50
Scott Rolen		
□ 14 Derek Jeter	20.00	9.00
Pokey Reese		
□ 15 Tony Gwynn	20.00	9.00
Bob Abreu		

1997 Donruss Longball Leaders

Randomly inserted in first series retail packs only, this 15-card set honors the league's most fearsome long-ball hitters. The fronts feature color action player photos and foil stamping. The backs carry player information.

	MINT	NRMT
COMPLETE SET (15)	120.00	55.00
COMMON CARD (1-15)	2.50	1.10
UNLISTED STARS	5.00	2.20
RANDOM INSERTS IN SER.1 RETAIL PACKS		
STATED PRINT RUN 5000 SERIAL #'d SETS		

		MINT	NRMT
☐ 1	Frank Thomas	25.00	11.00
☐ 2	Albert Belle	8.00	3.60
☐ 3	Mo Vaughn	8.00	3.60
☐ 4	Brady Anderson	4.00	1.80
☐ 5	Greg Vaughn	2.50	1.10
☐ 6	Ken Griffey Jr.	30.00	13.50
☐ 7	Jay Buhner	4.00	1.80
☐ 8	Juan Gonzalez	15.00	6.75
☐ 9	Mike Piazza	20.00	9.00
☐ 10	Jeff Bagwell	12.00	5.50
☐ 11	Sammy Sosa	5.00	2.20
☐ 12	Mark McGwire	12.00	5.50
☐ 13	Cecil Fielder	2.50	1.10
☐ 14	Ryan Klesko	4.00	1.80
☐ 15	Jose Canseco	4.00	1.80

1997 Donruss Power Alley

This 24-card set features color images of some of the league's top hitters printed on a micro-etched, all-foil card stock with holographic foil stamping. Using a "fractured" printing structure, 12 players utilize a green finish and are numbered to 4,000. Eight players are printed on all blue finish and number to 2,000, with the last four players utilizing a gold finish and are numbered to 1,000.

		MINT	NRMT
COMPLETE SET (24)		600.00	275.00
COMMON CARD (1-24)		5.00	2.20
UNLISTED STARS		8.00	3.60
RANDOM INSERTS IN UPDATE PACKS			
GREEN PRINT RUN 3750 SERIAL #'d SETS			
BLUE PRINT RUN 1750 SERIAL #'d SETS			
GOLD PRINT RUN 750 SERIAL #'d SETS			
*GREEN DIE CUT: 2.5X TO 6X BASIC GREEN			
*BLUE DIE CUT: 1.5X TO 4X BASIC BLUE			
*GOLD DIE CUT: 1X TO 2.5X BASIC GOLD			
DIE CUTS: RANDOM INS.IN UPDATE PACKS			
DIE CUTS PRINT RUN 250 SERIAL #'d SETS			

		MINT	NRMT
☐ 1	Frank Thomas G	80.00	36.00
☐ 2	Ken Griffey Jr. G	100.00	45.00
☐ 3	Cal Ripken B	80.00	36.00
☐ 4	Jeff Bagwell B	25.00	11.00
☐ 5	Mike Piazza B	40.00	18.00
☐ 6	Andruw Jones GR	15.00	6.75
☐ 7	Alex Rodriguez G	60.00	27.00
☐ 8	Albert Belle GR	10.00	4.50
☐ 9	Mo Vaughn GR	10.00	4.50
☐ 10	Chipper Jones B	40.00	18.00
☐ 11	Juan Gonzalez B	30.00	13.50

		MINT	NRMT
☐ 12	Ken Caminiti GR	5.00	2.20
☐ 13	Manny Ramirez GR	8.00	3.60
☐ 14	Mark McGwire GR	15.00	6.75
☐ 15	Kenny Lofton B	15.00	6.75
☐ 16	Barry Bonds GR	10.00	4.50
☐ 17	Gary Sheffield GR	8.00	3.60
☐ 18	Tony Gwynn G	20.00	9.00
☐ 19	Vladimir Guerrero B	20.00	9.00
☐ 20	Ivan Rodriguez GR	15.00	6.75
☐ 21	Paul Molitor B	12.00	5.50
☐ 22	Sammy Sosa GR	8.00	3.60
☐ 23	Matt Williams GR	5.00	2.20
☐ 24	Derek Jeter GR	20.00	9.00

1997 Donruss Rated Rookies

Randomly inserted in all first series packs, this 30-card set honors the top rookie prospects as chosen by Donruss to be the most likely to succeed. The fronts feature color action player photos and silver foil printing. The backs carry a player portrait and player information.

		MINT	NRMT
COMPLETE SET (30)		50.00	22.00
COMMON CARD (1-30)		1.00	.45
SEMISTARS		2.00	.90
UNLISTED STARS		4.00	1.80
RANDOM INSERTS IN SER.1 PACKS			

		MINT	NRMT
☐ 1	Jason Thompson	1.00	.45
☐ 2	LaTroy Hawkins	1.00	.45
☐ 3	Scott Rolen	10.00	4.50
☐ 4	Trey Beamon	1.00	.45
☐ 5	Kimera Bartee	1.00	.45
☐ 6	Nerio Rodriguez	1.50	.70
☐ 7	Jeff D'Amico	1.00	.45
☐ 8	Quinton McCracken	1.00	.45
☐ 9	John Wasdin	1.00	.45
☐ 10	Robin Jennings	1.00	.45
☐ 11	Steve Gibralter	1.00	.45
☐ 12	Tyler Houston	1.00	.45
☐ 13	Tony Clark	4.00	1.80
☐ 14	Ugueth Urbina	1.00	.45
☐ 15	Karim Garcia	1.50	.70
☐ 16	Raul Casanova	1.00	.45
☐ 17	Brooks Kieschnick	1.00	.45
☐ 18	Luis Castillo	1.50	.70
☐ 19	Edgar Renteria	1.50	.70
☐ 20	Andruw Jones	10.00	4.50
☐ 21	Chad Mottola	1.00	.45
☐ 22	Mac Suzuki	1.00	.45
☐ 23	Justin Thompson	1.50	.70
☐ 24	Darin Erstad	6.00	2.70
☐ 25	Todd Walker	1.50	.70
☐ 26	Todd Greene	1.50	.70
☐ 27	Vladimir Guerrero	8.00	3.60
☐ 28	Darren Dreifort	1.00	.45
☐ 29	John Burke	1.00	.45
☐ 30	Damon Mashore	1.00	.45

1997 Donruss Rocket Launchers

Randomly inserted in first series magazine packs only, this 15-card set honers baseball's top power hitters. The fronts feature color player photos, while the backs carry player information. Only 5,000 of this set were produced and are sequentially numbered.

		MINT	NRMT
COMPLETE SET (15)		120.00	55.00
COMMON CARD (1-15)		3.00	1.35
UNLISTED STARS		6.00	2.70
RANDOM INSERTS IN SER.1 MAG.PACKS			
STATED PRINT RUN 5000 SERIAL #'d SETS			

		MINT	NRMT
☐ 1	Frank Thomas	25.00	11.00
☐ 2	Albert Belle	8.00	3.60
☐ 3	Chipper Jones	20.00	9.00
☐ 4	Mike Piazza	20.00	9.00
☐ 5	Mo Vaughn	8.00	3.60
☐ 6	Juan Gonzalez	15.00	6.75
☐ 7	Fred McGriff	4.00	1.80
☐ 8	Jeff Bagwell	12.00	5.50
☐ 9	Matt Williams	4.00	1.80
☐ 10	Gary Sheffield	6.00	2.70
☐ 11	Barry Bonds	8.00	3.60
☐ 12	Manny Ramirez	6.00	2.70
☐ 13	Henry Rodriguez	3.00	1.35
☐ 14	Jason Giambi	3.00	1.35
☐ 15	Cal Ripken	25.00	11.00

1997 Donruss Rookie Diamond Kings

Randomly inserted in Update packs at an approximate rate of 1:24, cards from this 10-card set feature color portraits of some of the season's hottest rookie prospects in gold borders. Only 9,500 of each card were printed and are sequentially numbered. Please note that the numbering of each card runs to 10,000, but the first 500 of each card were Canvas parallels.

	MINT	NRMT
COMPLETE SET (10)	110.00	50.00
COMMON CARD (1-10)	4.00	1.80
UNLISTED STARS	6.00	2.70

STATED PRINT RUN 9500 SERIAL #'d SETS
*CANVAS: 2X TO 4X HI COLUMN
CANVAS PRINT RUN 500 SERIAL #'d SETS
RANDOM INSERTS IN UPDATE PACKS

☐ 1	Andruw Jones	20.00	9.00
☐ 2	Vladimir Guerrero	15.00	6.75
☐ 3	Scott Rolen	20.00	9.00
☐ 4	Todd Walker	4.00	1.80
☐ 5	Bartolo Colon	4.00	1.80
☐ 6	Jose Guillen	10.00	4.50
☐ 7	Nomar Garciaparra	25.00	11.00
☐ 8	Darin Erstad	12.00	5.50
☐ 9	Dmitri Young	4.00	1.80
☐ 10	Wilton Guerrero	4.00	1.80

1998 Donruss

The 1998 Donruss set was issued in one series totalling 170 cards and was distributed in 10-card packs with a suggested retail price of $1.99. The fronts feature color player photos with player information on the backs. The set contains the topical subset: Fan Club (156-165). Each Fan Club card carried instructions on how the fan could vote for their favorite players to be included in the 1998 Donruss Update set.

	MINT	NRMT
COMPLETE SET (170)	20.00	9.00
COMMON CARD (1-170)	.10	.05
MINOR STARS	.25	.11
UNLISTED STARS	.50	.23
COMP.GOLD PP SET (170)	2000.00	900.00
COMMON GOLD PP (1-170)	5.00	2.20

*GOLD PP STARS: 20X TO 40X HI COLUMN
*GOLD PP YOUNG STARS: 15X TO 30X HI
GOLD PP: RANDOM INSERTS IN PACKS
GOLD PP STATED PRINT RUN 500 SETS

COMP.SILVER PP SET (170)	800.00	350.00
COMMON SILVER PP (1-170)	2.00	.90

*SILVER PP STARS: 6X TO 15X HI COLUMN
*SILVER PP YOUNG STARS: 5X TO 12X HI
SILVER PP: RANDOM INSERTS IN PACKS
SILVER PP STATED PRINT RUN 1500 SETS
SILVER PP'S CONDITION SENSITIVE

☐ 1	Paul Molitor	.50	.23
☐ 2	Juan Gonzalez	1.25	.55
☐ 3	Darryl Kile	.25	.11
☐ 4	Randy Johnson	.50	.23
☐ 5	Tom Glavine	.25	.11
☐ 6	Pat Hentgen	.25	.11
☐ 7	David Justice	.50	.23
☐ 8	Kevin Brown	.25	.11
☐ 9	Mike Mussina	.50	.23
☐ 10	Ken Caminiti	.30	.14
☐ 11	Todd Hundley	.25	.11
☐ 12	Frank Thomas	2.00	.90
☐ 13	Ray Lankford	.25	.11
☐ 14	Justin Thompson	.25	.11
☐ 15	Jason Dickson	.25	.11
☐ 16	Kenny Lofton	.60	.25
☐ 17	Ivan Rodriguez	.60	.25
☐ 18	Pedro Martinez	.50	.23
☐ 19	Brady Anderson	.30	.14
☐ 20	Barry Larkin	.30	.14
☐ 21	Chipper Jones	1.50	.70
☐ 22	Tony Gwynn	1.25	.55
☐ 23	Roger Clemens	1.00	.45
☐ 24	Sandy Alomar Jr.	.25	.11
☐ 25	Tino Martinez	.50	.23
☐ 26	Jeff Bagwell	1.00	.45
☐ 27	Shawn Estes	.25	.11
☐ 28	Ken Griffey Jr.	2.50	1.10
☐ 29	Javier Lopez	.25	.11
☐ 30	Denny Neagle	.25	.11
☐ 31	Mike Piazza	1.50	.70
☐ 32	Andres Galarraga	.50	.23
☐ 33	Larry Walker	.25	.11
☐ 34	Alex Rodriguez	1.50	.70
☐ 35	Greg Maddux	1.50	.70
☐ 36	Albert Belle	.50	.25
☐ 37	Barry Bonds	.60	.25
☐ 38	Mo Vaughn	.60	.25
☐ 39	Kevin Appier	.25	.11
☐ 40	Wade Boggs	.50	.23
☐ 41	Garret Anderson	.25	.11
☐ 42	Jeffrey Hammonds	.10	.05
☐ 43	Marquis Grissom	.25	.11
☐ 44	Jim Edmonds	.30	.14
☐ 45	Brian Jordan	.25	.11
☐ 46	Raul Mondesi	.30	.14
☐ 47	John Valentin	.10	.05
☐ 48	Brad Radke	.25	.11
☐ 49	Ismael Valdes	.25	.11
☐ 50	Matt Stairs	.10	.05
☐ 51	Matt Williams	.30	.14
☐ 52	Reggie Jefferson	.10	.05
☐ 53	Alan Benes	.25	.11
☐ 54	Charles Johnson	.25	.11
☐ 55	Chuck Knoblauch	.50	.23
☐ 56	Edgar Martinez	.30	.14
☐ 57	Nomar Garciaparra	1.50	.70
☐ 58	Craig Biggio	.50	.23
☐ 59	Bernie Williams	.50	.23
☐ 60	David Cone	.25	.11
☐ 61	Cal Ripken	2.00	.90
☐ 62	Mark McGwire	1.25	.55
☐ 63	Roberto Alomar	.50	.23
☐ 64	Fred McGriff	.30	.14
☐ 65	Eric Karros	.25	.11
☐ 66	Robin Ventura	.25	.11
☐ 67	Darin Erstad	.60	.25
☐ 68	Michael Tucker	.25	.11
☐ 69	Jim Thome	.50	.23
☐ 70	Mark Grace	.30	.14
☐ 71	Lou Collier	.10	.05
☐ 72	Karim Garcia	.25	.11
☐ 73	Alex Fernandez	.10	.05
☐ 74	J.T. Snow	.25	.11
☐ 75	Reggie Sanders	.10	.05
☐ 76	John Smoltz	.25	.11
☐ 77	Tim Salmon	.50	.23
☐ 78	Paul O'Neill	.25	.11
☐ 79	Vinny Castilla	.25	.11
☐ 80	Rafael Palmeiro	.30	.14
☐ 81	Jaret Wright	1.25	.55
☐ 82	Jay Buhner	.30	.14
☐ 83	Brett Butler	.25	.11
☐ 84	Todd Greene	.25	.11
☐ 85	Scott Rolen	1.25	.55
☐ 86	Sammy Sosa	.50	.23
☐ 87	Jason Giambi	.25	.11
☐ 88	Carlos Delgado	.25	.11
☐ 89	Deion Sanders	.25	.11
☐ 90	Wilton Guerrero	.10	.05
☐ 91	Andy Pettitte	.50	.23
☐ 92	Brian Giles	.10	.05
☐ 93	Dmitri Young	.10	.05
☐ 94	Ron Coomer	.10	.05
☐ 95	Mike Cameron	.25	.11
☐ 96	Edgardo Alfonzo	.25	.11
☐ 97	Jimmy Key	.25	.11
☐ 98	Ryan Klesko	.30	.14
☐ 99	Andy Benes	.25	.11
☐ 100	Derek Jeter	1.25	.55
☐ 101	Jeff Fassero	.10	.05
☐ 102	Neifi Perez	.25	.11
☐ 103	Hideo Nomo	1.25	.55
☐ 104	Andruw Jones	1.00	.45
☐ 105	Todd Helton	.60	.25
☐ 106	Livan Hernandez	.30	.14
☐ 107	Brett Tomko	.25	.11
☐ 108	Shannon Stewart	.25	.11
☐ 109	Bartolo Colon	.25	.11
☐ 110	Matt Morris	.25	.11
☐ 111	Miguel Tejada	.60	.25
☐ 112	Pokey Reese	.10	.05
☐ 113	Fernando Tatis	.50	.23
☐ 114	Todd Dunwoody	.25	.11
☐ 115	Jose Cruz Jr.	2.00	.90
☐ 116	Chan Ho Park	.50	.23
☐ 117	Kevin Young	.10	.05
☐ 118	Rickey Henderson	.30	.14
☐ 119	Hideki Irabu	.25	.11
☐ 120	Francisco Cordova	.10	.05
☐ 121	Al Martin	.10	.05
☐ 122	Tony Clark	.50	.23
☐ 123	Curt Schilling	.25	.11
☐ 124	Rusty Greer	.25	.11
☐ 125	Jose Canseco	.30	.14
☐ 126	Edgar Renteria	.25	.11
☐ 127	Todd Walker	.25	.11
☐ 128	Wally Joyner	.25	.11
☐ 129	Bill Mueller	.10	.05
☐ 130	Jose Guillen	.50	.23
☐ 131	Manny Ramirez	.50	.23
☐ 132	Bobby Higginson	.25	.11
☐ 133	Kevin Orie	.25	.11
☐ 134	Will Clark	.30	.14
☐ 135	Dave Nilsson	.10	.05
☐ 136	Jason Kendall	.25	.11
☐ 137	Ivan Cruz	.10	.05
☐ 138	Gary Sheffield	.25	.11
☐ 139	Bubba Trammell	.25	.11
☐ 140	Vladimir Guerrero	.75	.35
☐ 141	Dennis Reyes	.25	.11
☐ 142	Bobby Bonilla	.25	.11
☐ 143	Ruben Rivera	.25	.11
☐ 144	Ben Grieve	1.00	.45
☐ 145	Moises Alou	.25	.11
☐ 146	Tony Womack	.10	.05
☐ 147	Eric Young	.10	.05
☐ 148	Paul Konerko	.75	.35
☐ 149	Dante Bichette	.25	.11
☐ 150	Joe Carter	.25	.11
☐ 151	Rondell White	.25	.11
☐ 152	Chris Holt	.10	.05
☐ 153	Shawn Green	.10	.05
☐ 154	Mark Grudzielanek	.10	.05
	UER back rudzielanek		
☐ 155	Andujar Dye	.10	.05
☐ 156	Ken Griffey Jr. FC	1.25	.55
☐ 157	Frank Thomas FC	1.00	.45
☐ 158	Chipper Jones FC	.75	.35
☐ 159	Mike Piazza FC	.75	.35
☐ 160	Cal Ripken FC	1.00	.45
☐ 161	Greg Maddux FC	.75	.35
☐ 162	Juan Gonzalez FC	.60	.25
☐ 163	Alex Rodriguez FC	.75	.35
☐ 164	Mark McGwire FC	.60	.25
☐ 165	Derek Jeter FC	.60	.25
☐ 166	Larry Walker CL	.25	.11
☐ 167	Tony Gwynn CL	.60	.25
☐ 168	Tino Martinez CL	.25	.11
☐ 169	Scott Rolen CL	.60	.25
☐ 170	Nomar Garciaparra CL	.75	.35

1998 Donruss Crusade Green

This 40-card set is skip numbered and was combined with cards from two other sets to make a complete set consisting of a total of 100 cards. The spread over the three programs were as follows: 40 players from 1998 Donruss, 30 from 1998 Leaf, and 30 from 1998 Donruss Update. The fronts feature color player photos printed with Limited 'refractive' technology. The backs carry player information. Only 250 of each of these Green cards were produced and sequentially numbered.

	MINT	NRMT
COMMON CARD	12.00	5.50
MINOR STARS	20.00	9.00
*PURPLE STARS: .75X TO 1.5X GREEN HI		
*RED STARS: 3X TO 6X GREEN HI		
GREEN PRINT RUN 250 SERIAL #'d SETS		
PURPLE PRINT RUN 100 SERIAL #'d SETS		
RED PRINT RUN 25 SERIAL #'d SETS		
RANDOM INSERTS IN PACKS		
SKIP-NUMBERED SET		

			MINT	NRMT
☐ 5	Jason Dickson	20.00	9.00
☐ 6	Todd Greene	20.00	9.00
☐ 7	Roberto Alomar CTA	50.00	22.00
☐ 8	Cal Ripken	200.00	90.00
☐ 12	Mo Vaughn CTA	60.00	27.00
☐ 13	Nomar Garciaparra	120.00	55.00
☐ 16	Mike Cameron	25.00	11.00
☐ 20	Sandy Alomar Jr.	25.00	11.00
☐ 21	David Justice	40.00	18.00
☐ 25	Justin Thompson	25.00	11.00
☐ 27	Kevin Appier	20.00	9.00
☐ 33	Tino Martinez	40.00	18.00
☐ 36	Hideki Irabu	25.00	11.00
☐ 37	Jose Canseco	30.00	13.50
☐ 39	Ken Griffey Jr.	250.00	110.00
☐ 42	Edgar Martinez	30.00	13.50
☐ 45	Will Clark	30.00	13.50
☐ 47	Rusty Greer	20.00	9.00
☐ 50	Shawn Green	12.00	5.50
☐ 51	Jose Cruz Jr.	150.00	70.00
☐ 52	Kenny Lofton	60.00	27.00
☐ 53	Chipper Jones	120.00	55.00
☐ 62	Kevin Orie	20.00	9.00
☐ 65	Deion Sanders	25.00	11.00
☐ 67	Larry Walker	50.00	22.00
☐ 68	Dante Bichette CTA	25.00	11.00
☐ 71	Todd Helton	50.00	22.00
☐ 74	Bobby Bonilla	20.00	9.00
☐ 75	Kevin Brown	20.00	9.00
☐ 78	Craig Biggio	30.00	13.50
☐ 82	Wilton Guerrero	12.00	5.50
☐ 85	Pedro Martinez	40.00	18.00
☐ 86	Edgardo Alfonzo	20.00	9.00
☐ 88	Scott Rolen	100.00	45.00
☐ 89	Francisco Cordova	12.00	5.50
☐ 90	Jose Guillen	40.00	18.00
☐ 92	Ray Lankford	20.00	9.00
☐ 93	M.McGwire CTA NNO	100.00	45.00
☐ 94	Matt Morris	20.00	9.00
☐ 100	Shawn Estes	20.00	9.00

1998 Donruss Diamond Kings

Randomly inserted in packs, this 20-card set features color player portraits of some of the greatest names in Baseball. Only 9,500 sets were produced and are sequentially numbered. The first 500 of each card were printed on actual canvas card stock. In addition, a Frank Thomas sample card was created as a promo for the 1998 Donruss 1 product. The card was sent to all wholesale accounts along with the order forms for the product. The large "SAMPLE" stamp across the back of the card makes it easy to differentiate from Thomas' standard 1998 Diamond King insert card.

	MINT	NRMT
COMPLETE SET (20)	250.00	110.00
COMMON CARD (1-20)	5.00	2.20
UNLISTED STARS	8.00	3.60
RANDOM INSERTS IN PACKS		
STATED PRINT RUN 9500 SERIAL #'d SETS		
COMP.CANVAS SET (20)	1200.00	550.00
*CANVAS: 2X TO 4X HI COLUMN		
CANVAS: RANDOM INSERTS IN PACKS		
CANVAS PRINT RUN 500 SERIAL #'d SETS		

			MINT	NRMT
☐ 1	Cal Ripken	30.00	13.50
☐ 2	Greg Maddux	25.00	11.00
☐ 3	Ivan Rodriguez	10.00	4.50
☐ 4	Tony Gwynn	20.00	9.00
☐ 5	Paul Molitor	8.00	3.60
☐ 6	Kenny Lofton	10.00	4.50
☐ 7	Andy Pettitte	8.00	3.60
☐ 8	Darin Erstad	8.00	3.60
☐ 9	Randy Johnson	8.00	3.60
☐ 10	Derek Jeter	20.00	9.00
☐ 11	Hideo Nomo	8.00	3.60
☐ 12	David Justice	8.00	3.60
☐ 13	Bernie Williams	8.00	3.60
☐ 14	Roger Clemens	15.00	6.75
☐ 15	Barry Larkin	5.00	2.20
☐ 16	Andruw Jones	12.00	5.50
☐ 17	Mike Piazza	25.00	11.00
☐ 18	Frank Thomas	30.00	13.50
☐ 19	Alex Rodriguez	25.00	11.00
☐ 20	Ken Griffey Jr.	40.00	18.00
☐ S20	Frank Thomas Sample	3.00	1.35

1998 Donruss Longball Leaders

Randomly inserted in packs, this 24-card set features color photos of the top sluggers in baseball printed on micro-etched cards. Only 5000 of each card were produced and are sequentially numbered.

	MINT	NRMT
COMPLETE SET (24)	200.00	90.00
COMMON CARD (1-24)	4.00	1.80
UNLISTED STARS	6.00	2.70
RANDOM INSERTS IN PACKS		
STATED PRINT RUN 5000 SERIAL #'d SETS		

			MINT	NRMT
☐ 1	Ken Griffey Jr.	30.00	13.50
☐ 2	Mark McGwire	12.00	5.50
☐ 3	Tino Martinez	6.00	2.70
☐ 4	Barry Bonds	8.00	3.60
☐ 5	Frank Thomas	25.00	11.00
☐ 6	Albert Belle	8.00	3.60
☐ 7	Mike Piazza	20.00	9.00
☐ 8	Chipper Jones	15.00	6.75
☐ 9	Vladimir Guerrero	8.00	3.60
☐ 10	Matt Williams	4.00	1.80
☐ 11	Sammy Sosa	6.00	2.70
☐ 12	Tim Salmon	6.00	2.70
☐ 13	Raul Mondesi	4.00	1.80
☐ 14	Jeff Bagwell	12.00	5.50
☐ 15	Mo Vaughn	8.00	3.60
☐ 16	Manny Ramirez	6.00	2.70
☐ 17	Jim Thome	6.00	2.70
☐ 18	Jim Edmonds	4.00	1.80
☐ 19	Tony Clark	6.00	2.70
☐ 20	Nomar Garciaparra	15.00	6.75
☐ 21	Juan Gonzalez	15.00	6.75
☐ 22	Scott Rolen	12.00	5.50
☐ 23	Larry Walker	6.00	2.70
☐ 24	Andres Galarraga	6.00	2.70

1998 Donruss Production Line On-Base

Randomly inserted in pre-priced packs only, this 20-card set features color player images printed on holographic board with green highlights. Each card is sequentially numbered according to the player's on-base percentage.

	MINT	NRMT
COMPLETE SET (20)	800.00	350.00
COMMON CARD (1-20)	15.00	6.75

RANDOM INSERTS IN PRE-PRICED PACKS
PRINT RUN BASED ON PLAYER STATS

			MINT	NRMT
☐	1	Frank Thomas/456	120.00	55.00
☐	2	Edgar Martinez/456	20.00	9.00
☐	3	Roberto Alomar/390	30.00	13.50
☐	4	Chuck Knoblauch/390	25.00	11.00
☐	5	Mike Piazza/443	100.00	45.00
☐	6	Barry Larkin/440	20.00	9.00
☐	7	Kenny Lofton/400	40.00	18.00
☐	8	Jeff Bagwell/425	60.00	27.00
☐	9	Barry Bonds/446	40.00	18.00
☐	10	Rusty Greer/405	15.00	6.75
☐	11	Gary Sheffield/424	25.00	11.00
☐	12	Mark McGwire/393	80.00	36.00
☐	13	Chipper Jones/371	100.00	45.00
☐	14	Tony Gwynn/409	80.00	36.00
☐	15	Craig Biggio/415	20.00	9.00
☐	16	Mo Vaughn/420	40.00	18.00
☐	17	Bernie Williams/408	25.00	11.00
☐	18	Ken Griffey Jr./382	150.00	70.00
☐	19	Brady Anderson/393	20.00	9.00
☐	20	Derek Jeter/370	80.00	36.00

1998 Donruss Production Line Power Index

Randomly inserted in hobby packs only, this 20-card set features color player images printed on holographic board with blue highlights. Each card is sequentially numbered according to the player's power index.

		MINT	NRMT
COMPLETE SET (1-20)		600.00	275.00
COMMON CARD (1-20)		12.00	5.50
UNLISTED STARS			9.00

RANDOM INSERTS IN HOBBY PACKS
PRINT RUN BASED ON PLAYER STATS

			MINT	NRMT
☐	1	Frank Thomas/1067	80.00	36.00
☐	2	Mark McGwire/1039	50.00	22.00
☐	3	Barry Bonds/1031	25.00	11.00
☐	4	Jeff Bagwell/1017	40.00	18.00
☐	5	Ken Griffey Jr./1008	100.00	45.00
☐	6	Alex Rodriguez/846	60.00	27.00
☐	7	Chipper Jones/850	50.00	22.00
☐	8	Mike Piazza/1070	60.00	27.00
☐	9	Mo Vaughn/980	25.00	11.00
☐	10	Brady Anderson/863	12.00	5.50
☐	11	Manny Ramirez/953	20.00	9.00
☐	12	Albert Belle/823	25.00	11.00
☐	13	Jim Thome/1001	20.00	9.00
☐	14	Bernie Williams/952	20.00	9.00
☐	15	Scott Rolen/846	40.00	18.00
☐	16	Vladimir Guerrero/833	25.00	11.00
☐	17	Larry Walker/1013	20.00	9.00
☐	18	David Justice/1011	20.00	9.00
☐	19	Tino Martinez/948	20.00	9.00
☐	20	Tony Gwynn/957	50.00	22.00

1998 Donruss Production Line Slugging

Randomly inserted in retail packs only, this 20-card set features color player images printed on holographic board with red highlights. Each card is sequentially numbered according to the player's slugging percentage.

		MINT	NRMT
COMPLETE SET (20)		800.00	350.00
COMMON CARD (1-20)		15.00	6.75

RANDOM INSERTS IN RETAIL PACKS
PRINT RUN BASED ON PLAYER STATS

			MINT	NRMT
☐	1	Mark McGwire/646	60.00	27.00
☐	2	Ken Griffey Jr./646	120.00	55.00
☐	3	Andres Galarraga/585	20.00	9.00
☐	4	Barry Bonds/585	30.00	13.50
☐	5	Juan Gonzalez/589	60.00	27.00
☐	6	Mike Piazza/638	80.00	36.00
☐	7	Jeff Bagwell/592	50.00	22.00
☐	8	Manny Ramirez/538	25.00	11.00
☐	9	Jim Thome/579	25.00	11.00
☐	10	Mo Vaughn/560	30.00	13.50
☐	11	Larry Walker/720	25.00	11.00
☐	12	Tino Martinez/577	20.00	9.00
☐	13	Frank Thomas/611	100.00	45.00
☐	14	Tim Salmon/517	20.00	9.00
☐	15	Raul Mondesi/541	15.00	6.75
☐	16	Alex Rodriguez/496	80.00	36.00
☐	17	Nomar Garciaparra/534	60.00	27.00
☐	18	Jose Cruz Jr./499	80.00	36.00
☐	19	Tony Clark/500	20.00	9.00
☐	20	Cal Ripken/402	100.00	45.00

1998 Donruss Rated Rookies

Randomly inserted in packs, this 30-card set features color action photos of some of the top rookie prospects as chosen by Donruss to be the most likely to succeed. The backs carry player information.

		MINT	NRMT
COMPLETE SET (30)		60.00	27.00
COMMON CARD (1-30)		1.00	.45
MINOR STARS		1.50	.70
SEMISTARS		2.50	1.10
COMP. MEDALIST SET (30)		800.00	350.00
*MEDALISTS: 5X TO 10X HI COLUMN			
MEDALIST PRINT RUN 250 SETS			

RANDOM INSERTS IN PACKS

			MINT	NRMT
☐	1	Mark Kotsay	4.00	1.80
☐	2	Neifi Perez	1.50	.70
☐	3	Paul Konerko	6.00	2.70

			MINT	NRMT
☐	4	Jose Cruz Jr.	15.00	6.75
☐	5	Hideki Irabu	1.50	.70
☐	6	Mike Cameron	1.50	.70
☐	7	Jeff Suppan	1.00	.45
☐	8	Kevin Orie	1.50	.70
☐	9	Pokey Reese	1.00	.45
☐	10	Todd Dunwoody	1.50	.70
☐	11	Miguel Tejada	5.00	2.20
☐	12	Jose Guillen	4.00	1.80
☐	13	Bartolo Colon	1.50	.70
☐	14	Derrek Lee	2.50	1.10
☐	15	Antone Williamson	1.00	.45
☐	16	Wilton Guerrero	1.00	.45
☐	17	Jaret Wright	10.00	4.50
☐	18	Todd Helton	5.00	2.20
☐	19	Shannon Stewart	1.50	.70
☐	20	Nomar Garciaparra	12.00	5.50
☐	21	Brett Tomko	1.50	.70
☐	22	Fernando Tatis	4.00	1.80
☐	23	Raul Ibanez	1.00	.45
☐	24	Dennis Reyes	1.50	.70
☐	25	Bobby Estalella	1.50	.70
☐	26	Lou Collier	1.00	.45
☐	27	Bubba Trammell	1.50	.70
☐	28	Ben Grieve	8.00	3.60
☐	29	Ivan Cruz	1.00	.45
☐	30	Karim Garcia	1.50	.70

1997 Donruss Elite

The 1997 Donruss Elite set was issued in one series totalling 150 cards. The product was distributed exclusively to hobby dealers. Each foil-wrapped pack contained eight cards and carried a suggested retail price of $3.49. Player selection was limited to the top stars (plus three player checklist cards) and card design is very similar to the Donruss Elite hockey set that was released one year earlier. Basic card fronts feature a color player photo encased by a thick silver and marble border. Backs contain another color photo and player information. Strangely enough, the backs only provide career statistics neglecting statistics from the previous season. The cards were released around February 1997.

	MINT	NRMT
COMPLETE SET (150)	40.00	18.00
COMMON CARD (1-150)	.20	.09
MINOR STARS	.40	.18
UNLISTED STARS	.75	.35
COMP.GOLD SET (150)	1000.00	450.00
COMMON GOLD (1-150)	2.00	.90
*GOLD STARS: 6X TO 15X HI COLUMN		
*GOLD YOUNG STARS: 5X TO 12X HI		
GOLD: RANDOM INSERTS IN PACKS		

			MINT	NRMT
☐	1	Juan Gonzalez	2.00	.90
☐	2	Alex Rodriguez	2.50	1.10

□ 3 Frank Thomas	3.00	1.35
□ 4 Greg Maddux	2.50	1.10
□ 5 Ken Griffey Jr.	4.00	1.80
□ 6 Cal Ripken	3.00	1.35
□ 7 Mike Piazza	2.50	1.10
□ 8 Chipper Jones	2.50	1.10
□ 9 Albert Belle	1.00	.45
□ 10 Andruw Jones	2.00	.90
□ 11 Vladimir Guerrero	1.50	.70
□ 12 Mo Vaughn	1.00	.45
UER front Gonzales		
□ 13 Ivan Rodriguez	1.00	.45
□ 14 Andy Pettitte	.75	.35
□ 15 Tony Gwynn	2.00	.90
□ 16 Barry Bonds	1.00	.45
□ 17 Jeff Bagwell	1.50	.70
□ 18 Manny Ramirez	.75	.35
□ 19 Kenny Lofton	1.00	.45
□ 20 Roberto Alomar	.75	.35
□ 21 Mark McGwire	1.50	.70
□ 22 Ryan Klesko	.50	.23
□ 23 Tim Salmon	.75	.35
□ 24 Derek Jeter	2.50	1.10
□ 25 Eddie Murray	.75	.35
□ 26 Jermaine Dye	.20	.09
□ 27 Ruben Rivera	.40	.18
□ 28 Jim Edmonds	.20	.09
□ 29 Mike Mussina	.75	.35
□ 30 Randy Johnson	.75	.35
□ 31 Sammy Sosa	.75	.35
□ 32 Hideo Nomo	2.00	.90
□ 33 Chuck Knoblauch	.50	.23
□ 34 Paul Molitor	.75	.35
□ 35 Rafael Palmeiro	.50	.23
□ 36 Brady Anderson	.50	.23
□ 37 Will Clark	.50	.23
□ 38 Craig Biggio	.50	.23
□ 39 Jason Giambi	.40	.18
□ 40 Roger Clemens	1.50	.70
□ 41 Jay Buhner	.50	.23
□ 42 Edgar Martinez	.50	.23
□ 43 Gary Sheffield	.75	.35
□ 44 Fred McGriff	.50	.23
□ 45 Bobby Bonilla	.40	.18
□ 46 Tom Glavine	.40	.18
□ 47 Wade Boggs	.75	.35
□ 48 Jeff Conine	.40	.18
□ 49 John Smoltz	.40	.18
□ 50 Jim Thome	.75	.35
□ 51 Billy Wagner	.40	.18
□ 52 Jose Canseco	.50	.23
□ 53 Javy Lopez	.40	.18
□ 54 Cecil Fielder	.40	.18
□ 55 Garret Anderson	.40	.18
□ 56 Alex Ochoa	.20	.09
□ 57 Scott Rolen	2.00	.90
□ 58 Darin Erstad	1.25	.55
□ 59 Rey Ordonez	.20	.09
□ 60 Dante Bichette	.40	.18
□ 61 Joe Carter	.40	.18
□ 62 Moises Alou	.40	.18
□ 63 Jason Isringhausen	.20	.09
□ 64 Karim Garcia	.40	.18
□ 65 Brian Jordan	.40	.18
□ 66 Ruben Sierra	.20	.09
□ 67 Todd Hollandsworth	.20	.09
□ 68 Paul Wilson	.20	.09
□ 69 Ernie Young	.20	.09
□ 70 Ryne Sandberg	1.00	.45
□ 71 Raul Mondesi	.50	.23
□ 72 George Arias	.20	.09
□ 73 Ray Durham	.20	.09
□ 74 Dean Palmer	.20	.09
□ 75 Shawn Green	.20	.09
□ 76 Eric Young	.20	.09
□ 77 Jason Kendall	.40	.18
□ 78 Greg Vaughn	.20	.09
□ 79 Terrell Wade	.20	.09
□ 80 Bill Pulsipher	.20	.09
□ 81 Bobby Higginson	.40	.18
□ 82 Mark Grudzielanek	.20	.09
□ 83 Ken Caminiti	.50	.23
□ 84 Todd Greene	.40	.18
□ 85 Carlos Delgado	.40	.18
□ 86 Mark Grace	.50	.23
□ 87 Rondell White	.40	.18

□ 88 Barry Larkin	.50	.23
□ 89 J.T. Snow	.40	.18
□ 90 Alex Gonzalez	.20	.09
□ 91 Raul Casanova	.20	.09
□ 92 Marc Newfield	.20	.09
□ 93 Jermaine Allensworth	.20	.09
□ 94 John Mabry	.20	.09
□ 95 Kirby Puckett	1.50	.70
□ 96 Travis Fryman	.40	.18
□ 97 Kevin Brown	.40	.18
□ 98 Andres Galarraga	.75	.35
□ 99 Marty Cordova	.40	.18
□ 100 Henry Rodriguez	.20	.09
□ 101 Sterling Hitchcock	.20	.09
□ 102 Trey Beamon	.20	.09
□ 103 Brett Butler	.40	.18
□ 104 Rickey Henderson	.50	.23
□ 105 Tino Martinez	.75	.35
□ 106 Kevin Appier	.40	.18
□ 107 Brian Hunter	.40	.18
□ 108 Eric Karros	.40	.18
□ 109 Andre Dawson	.50	.23
□ 110 Darryl Strawberry	.40	.18
□ 111 James Baldwin	.20	.09
□ 112 Chad Mottola	.20	.09
□ 113 Dave Nilsson	.20	.09
□ 114 Carlos Baerga	.20	.09
□ 115 Chan Ho Park	.75	.35
□ 116 John Jaha	.20	.09
□ 117 Alan Benes	.40	.18
□ 118 Mariano Rivera	.40	.18
□ 119 Ellis Burks	.40	.18
□ 120 Tony Clark	.75	.35
□ 121 Todd Walker	.40	.18
□ 122 Dwight Gooden	.40	.18
□ 123 Ugueth Urbina	.20	.09
□ 124 David Cone	.40	.18
□ 125 Ozzie Smith	1.00	.45
□ 126 Kimera Bartee	.20	.09
□ 127 Rusty Greer	.40	.18
□ 128 Pat Hentgen	.40	.18
□ 129 Charles Johnson	.40	.18
□ 130 Quinton McCracken	.20	.09
□ 131 Troy Percival	.20	.09
□ 132 Shane Reynolds	.20	.09
□ 133 Charles Nagy	.40	.18
□ 134 Tom Goodwin	.20	.09
□ 135 Ron Gant	.40	.18
□ 136 Dan Wilson	.20	.09
□ 137 Matt Williams	.50	.23
□ 138 LaTroy Hawkins	.20	.09
□ 139 Kevin Seitzer	.20	.09
□ 140 Michael Tucker	.40	.18
□ 141 Todd Hundley	.40	.18
□ 142 Alex Fernandez	.40	.18
□ 143 Marquis Grissom	.40	.18
□ 144 Steve Finley	.40	.18
□ 145 Curtis Pride	.20	.09
□ 146 Derek Bell	.40	.18
□ 147 Butch Huskey	.40	.18
□ 148 Dwight Gooden CL	.40	.18
□ 149 Al Leiter CL	.20	.09
□ 150 Hideo Nomo CL	1.00	.45

	MINT	NRMT
COMPLETE SET (10)	1000.00	450.00
COMMON CARD (1-10)	30.00	13.50
RANDOM INSERTS IN PACKS		
STATED PRINT RUN 500 SERIAL #'d SETS		

□ 1 Ken Griffey Jr.	200.00	90.00
□ 2 Alex Rodriguez	120.00	55.00
□ 3 Frank Thomas	150.00	70.00
□ 4 Chipper Jones	100.00	45.00
□ 5 Ivan Rodriguez	50.00	22.00
□ 6 Cal Ripken	150.00	70.00
□ 7 Barry Bonds	50.00	22.00
□ 8 Chuck Knoblauch	30.00	13.50
□ 9 Manny Ramirez	40.00	18.00
□ 10 Mark McGwire	80.00	36.00

1997 Donruss Elite Passing the Torch

This 12-card insert set features eight players on four double-sided cards. A color portrait of a superstar veteran is displayed on one side with a gold foil background, and a portrait of a rising young star is printed on the flipside. Each of the eight players also has his own card to round out the 12-card set. Only 1500 of this set were produced and are sequentially numbered. However, only 1,350 of each card are available without autographs.

	MINT	NRMT
COMPLETE SET (12)	500.00	220.00
COMMON CARD (1-12)	8.00	3.60
RANDOM INSERTS IN PACKS		
STATED PRINT RUN 1350 SERIAL #'d SETS		

□ 1 Cal Ripken	60.00	27.00
□ 2 Alex Rodriguez	50.00	22.00
□ 3 Cal Ripken	100.00	45.00
Alex Rodriguez		
□ 4 Kirby Puckett	30.00	13.50
□ 5 Andruw Jones	30.00	13.50
□ 6 Kirby Puckett	30.00	13.50

1997 Donruss Elite Leather and Lumber

This ten-card insert set features color action veteran player photos printed on two unique materials. The fronts display a player image on real wood stock with the end of a baseball bat as background. The backs carry another player photo printed on genuine leather card stock with a baseball and glove as background. Only 500 of each card was produced and are sequentially numbered.

Andruw Jones

		MINT	NRMT
☐ 7	Cecil Fielder	8.00	3.60
☐ 8	Frank Thomas	60.00	27.00
☐ 9	Cecil Fielder	60.00	27.00

Frank Thomas

☐ 10	Ozzie Smith	20.00	9.00
☐ 11	Derek Jeter	40.00	18.00
☐ 12	Ozzie Smith	40.00	18.00

Derek Jeter

1997 Donruss Elite Passing the Torch Autographs

This 12-card set consists of the first 150 sets of the regular "Passing the Torch" set with each card displaying an authentic player autograph. The set features a double front design which captures eight of the league's top superstars, alternating one of four different megastars on the flipside. An individual card for each of the eight players rounds out the set. Each set is sequentially numbered to 150.

		MINT	NRMT
	COMPLETE SET (12)	5000.00	2200.00
	COMMON CARD (1-12)	100.00	45.00
	RANDOM INSERTS IN PACKS ..		
	STATED PRINT RUN 150 SERIAL #'d SETS		

☐ 1	Cal Ripken	600.00	275.00
☐ 2	Alex Rodriguez	500.00	220.00
☐ 3	Cal Ripken	1200.00	550.00

Alex Rodriguez

☐ 4	Kirby Puckett	400.00	180.00
☐ 5	Andruw Jones	250.00	110.00
☐ 6	Kirby Puckett	500.00	220.00

Andruw Jones

☐ 7	Cecil Fielder	100.00	45.00
☐ 8	Frank Thomas	500.00	220.00
☐ 9	Cecil Fielder	500.00	220.00

Frank Thomas

☐ 10	Ozzie Smith	300.00	135.00
☐ 11	Derek Jeter	300.00	135.00
☐ 12	Ozzie Smith	500.00	220.00

Derek Jeter

1997 Donruss Elite Turn of the Century

This 20-card set showcases the stars of the next millennium and features a color player image on a silver-and-black background. The backs display another player photo with a short paragraph about the player. Only 3,500 of this set were produced and are sequentially numbered.

		MINT	NRMT
	COMPLETE SET (20)	150.00	70.00
	COMMON CARD (1-20)	4.00	1.80
	UNLISTED STARS	8.00	3.60
	STATED PRINT RUN 3000 SERIAL #'d SETS		
	COMP.DIE CUT SET (20)	400.00	180.00
	*DIE CUTS: 1.25X TO 3X HI COLUMN		
	DC STATED PRINT RUN 500 SERIAL #'d SETS		
	RANDOM INSERTS IN PACKS ..		

☐ 1	Alex Rodriguez	25.00	11.00
☐ 2	Andruw Jones	20.00	9.00
☐ 3	Chipper Jones	25.00	11.00
☐ 4	Todd Walker	4.00	1.80
☐ 5	Scott Rolen	20.00	9.00
☐ 6	Trey Beamon	4.00	1.80
☐ 7	Derek Jeter	25.00	11.00
☐ 8	Darin Erstad	12.00	5.50
☐ 9	Tony Clark	8.00	3.60
☐ 10	Todd Greene	4.00	1.80
☐ 11	Jason Giambi	4.00	1.80
☐ 12	Justin Thompson	4.00	1.80
☐ 13	Ernie Young	4.00	1.80
☐ 14	Jason Kendall	4.00	1.80
☐ 15	Alex Ochoa	4.00	1.80
☐ 16	Brooks Kieschnick	4.00	1.80
☐ 17	Bobby Higginson	4.00	1.80
☐ 18	Ruben Rivera	4.00	1.80
☐ 19	Chan Ho Park	8.00	3.60
☐ 20	Chad Mottola	4.00	1.80
☐ P5	Scott Rolen Promo	5.00	2.20
☐ P7	Derek Jeter Promo	5.00	2.20

1998 Donruss Elite

The 1998 Donruss Elite set was issued in one series totalling 150 cards and distributed in five-card packs with a suggested retail price of $3.99. The fronts feature color player action photos. The backs carry player information. The set contains the topical subset: Generations (118-147).

		MINT	NRMT
	COMPLETE SET (150)	40.00	18.00
	COMMON CARD (1-150)	.20	.09
	MINOR STARS		.18

	UNLISTED STARS	.75	.35
	COMP.ASPIR.SET (150)	1500.00	700.00
	COMMON ASPIR. (1-150)	3.00	1.35
	*ASPIR.STARS: 7.5X TO 15X HI COL.		
	*ASPIR.YOUNG STARS: 6X TO 12X HI		
	ASPIRATIONS: RANDOM INS.IN PACKS		
	ASPIRATION PRINT RUN 750 SETS		

☐ 1	Ken Griffey Jr.	4.00	1.80
☐ 2	Frank Thomas	3.00	1.35
☐ 3	Alex Rodriguez	2.50	1.10
☐ 4	Mike Piazza	2.50	1.10
☐ 5	Greg Maddux	2.50	1.10
☐ 6	Cal Ripken	3.00	1.35
☐ 7	Chipper Jones	2.00	.90
☐ 8	Derek Jeter	2.00	.90
☐ 9	Tony Gwynn	2.00	.90
☐ 10	Andruw Jones	1.50	.70
☐ 11	Juan Gonzalez	2.00	.90
☐ 12	Jeff Bagwell	1.50	.70
☐ 13	Mark McGwire	2.00	.90
☐ 14	Roger Clemens	1.50	.70
☐ 15	Albert Belle	1.00	.45
☐ 16	Barry Bonds	1.00	.45
☐ 17	Kenny Lofton	1.00	.45
☐ 18	Ivan Rodriguez	1.00	.45
☐ 19	Manny Ramirez	.75	.35
☐ 20	Jim Thome	.75	.35
☐ 21	Chuck Knoblauch	.75	.35
☐ 22	Paul Molitor	.75	.35
☐ 23	Barry Larkin	.50	.23
☐ 24	Andy Pettitte	.75	.35
☐ 25	John Smoltz	.40	.18
☐ 26	Randy Johnson	.75	.35
☐ 27	Bernie Williams	.75	.35
☐ 28	Larry Walker	.75	.35
☐ 29	Mo Vaughn	1.00	.45
☐ 30	Bobby Higginson	.40	.18
☐ 31	Edgardo Alfonzo	.40	.18
☐ 32	Justin Thompson	.40	.18
☐ 33	Jeff Suppan	.20	.09
☐ 34	Roberto Alomar	.75	.35
☐ 35	Hideo Nomo	2.00	.90
☐ 36	Rusty Greer	.40	.18
☐ 37	Tim Salmon	.75	.35
☐ 38	Jim Edmonds	.50	.23
☐ 39	Gary Sheffield	.75	.35
☐ 40	Ken Caminiti	.50	.23
☐ 41	Sammy Sosa	.75	.35
☐ 42	Tony Womack	.20	.09
☐ 43	Matt Williams	.50	.23
☐ 44	Andres Galarraga	.75	.35
☐ 45	Garret Anderson	.40	.18
☐ 46	Rafael Palmeiro	.50	.23
☐ 47	Mike Mussina	.75	.35
☐ 48	Craig Biggio	.75	.35
☐ 49	Wade Boggs	.75	.35
☐ 50	Tom Glavine	.40	.18
☐ 51	Jason Giambi	.40	.18
☐ 52	Will Clark	.50	.23
☐ 53	David Justice	.75	.35
☐ 54	Sandy Alomar Jr.	.40	.18
☐ 55	Edgar Martinez	.50	.23
☐ 56	Brady Anderson	.50	.23
☐ 57	Eric Young	.20	.09
☐ 58	Ray Lankford	.40	.18
☐ 59	Kevin Brown	.40	.18
☐ 60	Raul Mondesi	.50	.23
☐ 61	Bobby Bonilla	.40	.18
☐ 62	Javier Lopez	.40	.18
☐ 63	Fred McGriff	.50	.23
☐ 64	Rondell White	.40	.18
☐ 65	Todd Hundley	.40	.18
☐ 66	Mark Grace	.50	.23
☐ 67	Alan Benes	.20	.09
☐ 68	Jeff Abbott	.20	.09
☐ 69	Bob Abreu	.40	.18
☐ 70	Deion Sanders	.40	.18
☐ 71	Tino Martinez	.75	.35
☐ 72	Shannon Stewart	.40	.18
☐ 73	Homer Bush	.20	.09
☐ 74	Carlos Delgado	.40	.18
☐ 75	Raul Ibanez	.20	.09
☐ 76	Hideki Irabu	.40	.18
☐ 77	Jose Cruz Jr.	2.50	1.10
☐ 78	Tony Clark	.75	.35

☐ 79	Wilton Guerrero	.20	.09
☐ 80	Vladimir Guerrero	1.25	.55
☐ 81	Scott Rolen	2.00	.90
☐ 82	Nomar Garciaparra	2.50	1.10
☐ 83	Darin Erstad	1.00	.45
☐ 84	Chan Ho Park	.75	.35
☐ 85	Mike Cameron	.40	.18
☐ 86	Todd Walker	.40	.18
☐ 87	Todd Dunwoody	.40	.18
☐ 88	Neifi Perez	.40	.18
☐ 89	Brett Tomko	.40	.18
☐ 90	Jose Guillen	.75	.35
☐ 91	Matt Morris	.40	.18
☐ 92	Bartolo Colon	.40	.18
☐ 93	Jaret Wright	2.50	1.10
☐ 94	Shawn Estes	.40	.18
☐ 95	Livan Hernandez	.50	.23
☐ 96	Bobby Estalella	.40	.18
☐ 97	Ben Grieve	1.50	.70
☐ 98	Paul Konerko	1.25	.55
☐ 99	David Ortiz	.40	.18
☐ 100	Todd Helton	1.00	.45
☐ 101	Juan Encarnacion	.75	.35
☐ 102	Bubba Trammell	.40	.18
☐ 103	Miguel Tejada	1.00	.45
☐ 104	Jacob Cruz	.40	.18
☐ 105	Todd Greene	.40	.18
☐ 106	Kevin Orie	.40	.18
☐ 107	Mark Kotsay	.75	.35
☐ 108	Fernando Tatis	.75	.35
☐ 109	Jay Payton	.20	.09
☐ 110	Pokey Reese	.20	.09
☐ 111	Derrek Lee	.50	.23
☐ 112	Richard Hidalgo	.40	.18
☐ 113	Ricky Ledee	.40	.18
	UER front Rickey		
☐ 114	Lou Collier	.20	.09
☐ 115	Ruben Rivera	.40	.18
☐ 116	Shawn Green	.20	.09
☐ 117	Moises Alou	.40	.18
☐ 118	Ken Griffey Jr. GEN	2.00	.90
☐ 119	Frank Thomas GEN	1.50	.70
☐ 120	Alex Rodriguez GEN	1.25	.55
☐ 121	Mike Piazza GEN	1.25	.55
☐ 122	Greg Maddux GEN	1.25	.55
☐ 123	Cal Ripken GEN	1.50	.70
☐ 124	Chipper Jones GEN	1.00	.45
☐ 125	Derek Jeter GEN	1.00	.45
☐ 126	Tony Gwynn GEN	1.00	.45
☐ 127	Andruw Jones GEN	.75	.35
☐ 128	Juan Gonzalez GEN	1.00	.45
☐ 129	Jeff Bagwell GEN	.75	.35
☐ 130	Mark McGwire GEN	1.00	.45
☐ 131	Roger Clemens GEN	.75	.35
☐ 132	Albert Belle GEN	.50	.23
☐ 133	Barry Bonds GEN	.50	.23
☐ 134	Kenny Lofton GEN	.50	.23
☐ 135	Ivan Rodriguez GEN	.50	.23
☐ 136	Manny Ramirez GEN	.40	.18
☐ 137	Jim Thome GEN	.40	.18
☐ 138	Chuck Knoblauch GEN	.40	.18
☐ 139	Paul Molitor GEN	.40	.18
☐ 140	Barry Larkin GEN	.40	.18
☐ 141	Mo Vaughn GEN	.50	.23
☐ 142	Hideki Irabu GEN	.20	.09
☐ 143	Jose Cruz Jr. GEN	1.25	.55
☐ 144	Tony Clark GEN	.40	.18
☐ 145	Vladimir Guerrero GEN	.50	.23
☐ 146	Scott Rolen GEN	1.00	.45
☐ 147	Nomar Garciaparra GEN	1.25	.55
☐ 148	Nomar Garciaparra CL	1.25	.55
☐ 149	Larry Walker CL	.40	.18
☐ 150	Tino Martinez CL	.40	.18

1998 Donruss Elite Status

Randomly inserted in packs, this 150-card set is parallel to the base set. Only 100 of this set were produced and are serially numbered.

	MINT	NRMT
COMPLETE SET (150) ..	10000.00	4500.00
COMPLETE SET (1-150)	20.00	9.00
MINOR STARS	30.00	13.50
SEMISTARS	50.00	22.00
UNLISTED STARS	80.00	36.00
*STARS: 40X TO 100X HI COLUMN		
*YOUNG STARS: 30X TO 80X HI		
RANDOM INSERTS IN PACKS		
STATED PRINT RUN 100 SERIAL #'d SETS		

		MINT	NRMT
☐ 1	Ken Griffey Jr.	400.00	180.00
☐ 2	Frank Thomas	300.00	135.00
☐ 3	Alex Rodriguez	250.00	110.00
☐ 4	Mike Piazza	250.00	110.00
☐ 5	Greg Maddux	250.00	110.00
☐ 6	Cal Ripken	300.00	135.00
☐ 7	Chipper Jones	200.00	90.00
☐ 8	Derek Jeter	200.00	90.00
☐ 9	Tony Gwynn	200.00	90.00
☐ 11	Juan Gonzalez	200.00	90.00
☐ 12	Jeff Bagwell	150.00	70.00
☐ 13	Mark McGwire	200.00	90.00
☐ 14	Roger Clemens	150.00	70.00
☐ 35	Hideo Nomo	250.00	110.00
☐ 77	Jose Cruz Jr.	250.00	110.00
☐ 81	Scott Rolen	200.00	90.00
☐ 82	Nomar Garciaparra	200.00	90.00
☐ 93	Jaret Wright	200.00	90.00
☐ 118	Ken Griffey Jr. GEN	200.00	90.00
☐ 119	Frank Thomas GEN	150.00	70.00
☐ 123	Cal Ripken GEN	150.00	70.00

1998 Donruss Elite Back to the Future

Randomly inserted in packs, this eight-card set is double-sided and features color images of top veteran and new players on a tile background. Only 1,500 of each card were produced and sequentially numbered. The first 100 of each card were autographed by both players pictured on the card. There is no autographed card number six.

	MINT	NRMT
COMPLETE SET (8)	400.00	180.00
COMMON CARD (1-8)	40.00	18.00
RANDOM INSERTS IN PACKS ..		
STATED PRINT RUN 1400 SERIAL #'d SETS		
COMP.SET INCLUDES CARD 6B		

		MINT	NRMT
☐ 1	Cal Ripken	80.00	36.00
	Paul Konerko		
☐ 2	Jeff Bagwell	40.00	18.00
	Todd Helton		
☐ 3	Eddie Matthews	50.00	22.00
	Chipper Jones		
☐ 4	Juan Gonzalez	50.00	22.00
	Ben Grieve		
☐ 5	Hank Aaron	60.00	27.00
	Jose Cruz Jr.		

		MINT	NRMT
☐ 6A	F.Thomas/D.Ortiz 1-100	500.00	
	220.00		
☐ 6B	Frank Thomas	60.00	27.00
	David Ortiz		
☐ 7	Nolan Ryan	80.00	36.00
	Greg Maddux		
☐ 8	Alex Rodriguez	60.00	27.00
	Nomar Garciaparra		

1998 Donruss Elite Back to the Future Autographs

Randomly inserted in packs, this seven-card set is a parallel version of the regular 1998 Donruss Elite Back to the Future insert and contains the first 100 cards of the regular set signed by both pictured players. Card number six does not exist. Cal Ripken did not sign the card along with Paul Konerko. Special redemption cards were issed for the Ripken card.

	MINT	NRMT
COMPLETE SET (7)	3500.00	1600.00
COMMON CARD (1-5/7-8)	350.00	160.00
RANDOM INSERTS IN PACKS ..		
STATED PRINT RUN 100 SERIAL #'d SETS		
CARD NUM.1 SIGNED BY KONERKO ONLY		
AU CARD NUMBER 6 DOES NOT EXIST		
COMP.SET EXCLUDES NNO RIPKEN EXCH		

		MINT	NRMT
☐ 1	Cal Ripken	600.00	275.00
	Paul Konerko		
☐ 2	Jeff Bagwell	350.00	160.00
	Todd Helton		
☐ 3	Eddie Mathews	400.00	180.00
	Chipper Jones		
☐ 4	Juan Gonzalez	400.00	180.00
	Ben Grieve		
☐ 5	Hank Aaron	600.00	275.00
	Jose Cruz Jr.		
☐ 7	Nolan Ryan	1200.00	550.00
	Greg Maddux		
☐ 8	Alex Rodriguez	600.00	275.00
	Nomar Garciaparra		
NNO	Cal Ripken EXCH/100	500.00	220.00

1998 Donruss Elite Craftsmen

Randomly inserted in packs, this 30-card set features color photos of players who are the best at what they do. Only 3,500 of this set were produced and are sequentially numbered.

	MINT	NRMT
COMPLETE SET (30)	250.00	110.00
COMMON CARD (1-30)	4.00	
RANDOM INSERTS IN PACKS ..		
STATED PRINT RUN 3500 SERIAL #'d SETS		

		MINT	NRMT
☐ 1	Ken Griffey Jr.	30.00	13.50
☐ 2	Frank Thomas	25.00	11.00
☐ 3	Alex Rodriguez	20.00	9.00
☐ 4	Cal Ripken	25.00	11.00
☐ 5	Greg Maddux	20.00	9.00
☐ 6	Mike Piazza	20.00	9.00
☐ 7	Chipper Jones	15.00	6.75
☐ 8	Derek Jeter	15.00	6.75
☐ 9	Tony Gwynn	15.00	6.75
☐ 10	Nomar Garciaparra	15.00	6.75
☐ 11	Scott Rolen	12.00	5.50
☐ 12	Jose Cruz Jr.	20.00	9.00
☐ 13	Tony Clark	5.00	2.20
☐ 14	Vladimir Guerrero	8.00	3.60
☐ 15	Todd Helton	6.00	2.70
☐ 16	Ben Grieve	10.00	4.50
☐ 17	Andruw Jones	10.00	4.50
☐ 18	Jeff Bagwell	12.00	5.50
☐ 19	Mark McGwire	15.00	6.75
☐ 20	Juan Gonzalez	15.00	6.75
☐ 21	Roger Clemens	12.00	5.50
☐ 22	Albert Belle	8.00	3.60
☐ 23	Barry Bonds	8.00	3.60
☐ 24	Kenny Lofton	8.00	3.60
☐ 25	Ivan Rodriguez	8.00	3.60
☐ 26	Paul Molitor	6.00	2.70
☐ 27	Barry Larkin	5.00	2.20
☐ 28	Mo Vaughn	8.00	3.60
☐ 29	Larry Walker	6.00	2.70
☐ 30	Tino Martinez	5.00	2.20

1998 Donruss Elite Master Craftsmen

Randomly inserted in packs, this 30-card set is parallel to the 1998 Donruss Elite Craftsmen insert set. Only 100 of this set were produced and are sequentially numbered.

	MINT	NRMT
COMPLETE SET (30)	4000.00	1800.00
COMMON CARD (1-30)	60.00	27.00
RANDOM INSERTS IN PACKS ..		
STATED PRINT RUN 100 SERIAL #'d SETS		

		MINT	NRMT
☐ 1	Ken Griffey Jr.	400.00	180.00
☐ 2	Frank Thomas	300.00	135.00
☐ 3	Alex Rodriguez	250.00	110.00
☐ 4	Cal Ripken	300.00	135.00
☐ 5	Greg Maddux	250.00	110.00
☐ 6	Mike Piazza	250.00	110.00
☐ 7	Chipper Jones	200.00	90.00
☐ 8	Derek Jeter	200.00	90.00
☐ 9	Tony Gwynn	200.00	90.00
☐ 10	Nomar Garciaparra	200.00	90.00
☐ 11	Scott Rolen	150.00	70.00
☐ 12	Jose Cruz Jr.	250.00	110.00
☐ 13	Tony Clark	60.00	27.00
☐ 14	Vladimir Guerrero	100.00	45.00
☐ 15	Todd Helton	80.00	36.00
☐ 16	Ben Grieve	120.00	55.00
☐ 17	Andruw Jones	120.00	55.00
☐ 18	Jeff Bagwell	150.00	70.00
☐ 19	Mark McGwire	200.00	90.00
☐ 20	Juan Gonzalez	200.00	90.00
☐ 21	Roger Clemens	150.00	70.00
☐ 22	Albert Belle	100.00	45.00
☐ 23	Barry Bonds	100.00	45.00
☐ 24	Kenny Lofton	100.00	45.00
☐ 25	Ivan Rodriguez	100.00	45.00
☐ 26	Paul Molitor	80.00	36.00
☐ 27	Barry Larkin	60.00	27.00
☐ 28	Mo Vaughn	100.00	45.00
☐ 29	Larry Walker	80.00	36.00
☐ 30	Tino Martinez	60.00	27.00

1998 Donruss Elite Prime Numbers

Randomly inserted in packs, this 36-card set features three cards each of 12 top players in the league printed with three different numerical backgrounds (which form a statistical benchmark when placed together). The total number of each card produced depended on the player's particular statistic. Print runs are included below in parentheses at the end of each card description.

	MINT	NRMT
COMPLETE SET (36)	5000.00	2200.00
COMMON CARD (1-36)	40.00	18.00
RANDOM INSERTS IN PACKS ..		
PRINT RUNS IN PARENTHESIS BELOW		

		MINT	NRMT
☐ 1A	Ken Griffey Jr. 2 (94)	400.00	180.00
☐ 1B	Ken Griffey Jr. 9 (204)	200.00	90.00
☐ 1C	Ken Griffey Jr. 4 (290)	150.00	70.00
☐ 2A	Frank Thomas 4 (56)	400.00	180.00
☐ 2B	Frank Thomas 5 (406)	100.00	45.00
☐ 2C	Frank Thomas 6 (456)	100.00	45.00
☐ 3A	Mark McGwire 3 (87)	200.00	90.00
☐ 3B	Mark McGwire 8 (307)	80.00	36.00
☐ 3C	Mark McGwire 7 (380)	80.00	36.00
☐ 4A	Cal Ripken 1 (71)	1200.00	550.00
☐ 4B	Cal Ripken 7 (507)	100.00	45.00
☐ 4C	Cal Ripken 7 (510)	100.00	45.00
☐ 5A	Mike Piazza 5 (76)	250.00	110.00
☐ 5B	Mike Piazza 7 (506)	80.00	36.00
☐ 5C	Mike Piazza 6 (570)	80.00	36.00
☐ 6A	Chipper Jones 4 (89)	200.00	90.00
☐ 6B	Chipper Jones 8 (409)	60.00	27.00
☐ 6C	Chipper Jones 9 (480)	60.00	27.00
☐ 7A	Tony Gwynn 3 (72)	200.00	90.00
☐ 7B	Tony Gwynn 7 (302)	80.00	36.00
☐ 7C	Tony Gwynn 2 (370)	80.00	36.00
☐ 8A	Barry Bonds 3 (74)	100.00	45.00
☐ 8B	Barry Bonds 7 (304)	40.00	18.00
☐ 8C	Barry Bonds 4 (370)	40.00	18.00
☐ 9A	Jeff Bagwell 4 (25)	400.00	180.00
☐ 9B	Jeff Bagwell 2 (405)	50.00	22.00
☐ 9C	Jeff Bagwell 5 (420)	50.00	22.00
☐ 10A	Juan Gonzalez 5 (89)	200.00	90.00
☐ 10B	Juan Gonzalez 8 (509)	60.00	27.00
☐ 10C	Juan Gonzalez 9 (580)	60.00	27.00
☐ 11A	Alex Rodriguez 5 (34)	400.00	180.00
☐ 11B	Alex Rodriguez 3 (504)	80.00	36.00
☐ 11C	Alex Rodriguez 4 (530)	80.00	36.00
☐ 12A	Kenny Lofton 3 (54)	120.00	55.00
☐ 12B	Kenny Lofton 5 (304)	40.00	18.00
☐ 12C	Kenny Lofton 4 (350)	40.00	18.00

1998 Donruss Elite Prime Numbers Die Cuts

Randomly inserted in packs, this 36-card set is a die-cut parallel version to the regular Donruss Elite Prime Numbers set. Print runs are included below in parentheses at the end of each card description. Cards printed in quantites of 10 or less are identified in the checklist but not priced below.

	MINT	NRMT
COMMON CARD (1-36)	40.00	18.00
RANDOM INSERTS IN PACKS ..		
PRINT RUNS IN PARENTHESES BELOW		

		MINT	NRMT
☐ 1A	Ken Griffey Jr. 2 (200)	200.00	90.00
☐ 1B	Ken Griffey Jr. 9 (90)	400.00	180.00
☐ 1C	Ken Griffey Jr. 4 (4)		
☐ 2A	Frank Thomas 4 (400)	100.00	45.00
☐ 2B	Frank Thomas 5 (400)	400.00	180.00
☐ 2C	Frank Thomas 6 (6)		
☐ 3A	Mark McGwire 3 (400)	80.00	36.00
☐ 3B	Mark McGwire 8 (80)	200.00	90.00
☐ 3C	Mark McGwire 7 (7)		
☐ 4A	Cal Ripken 5 (500)	100.00	45.00
☐ 4B	Cal Ripken 1 (10)		
☐ 4C	Cal Ripken 7 (7)		
☐ 5A	Mike Piazza 5 (50)	80.00	36.00
☐ 5B	Mike Piazza 7 (70)	250.00	110.00
☐ 5C	Mike Piazza 6 (6)		
☐ 6A	Chipper Jones 4 (400)	60.00	27.00
☐ 6B	Chipper Jones 8 (80)	200.00	90.00
☐ 6C	Chipper Jones 9 (9)	40.00	18.00
☐ 7A	Tony Gwynn 3 (300)	80.00	36.00
☐ 7B	Tony Gwynn 7 (70)	200.00	90.00
☐ 7C	Tony Gwynn 2 (2)		
☐ 8A	Barry Bonds 3 (300)	40.00	18.00
☐ 8B	Barry Bonds 7 (70)	100.00	45.00
☐ 8C	Barry Bonds 4 (4)		
☐ 9A	Jeff Bagwell 4 (400)	50.00	22.00
☐ 9B	Jeff Bagwell 2 (20)	500.00	220.00
☐ 9C	Jeff Bagwell 5 (5)		
☐ 10A	Juan Gonzalez 5 (500)	60.00	27.00
☐ 10B	Juan Gonzalez 8 (80)	200.00	90.00
☐ 10C	Juan Gonzalez 9 (9)		
☐ 11A	Alex Rodriguez 5 (500)	80.00	36.00
☐ 11B	Alex Rodriguez 3 (30)	500.00	220.00
☐ 11C	Alex Rodriguez 4 (4)		
☐ 12A	Kenny Lofton 3 (300)	40.00	18.00
☐ 12B	Kenny Lofton 5 (50)	120.00	55.00
☐ 12C	Kenny Lofton 4 (4)		

1997 Donruss Limited

The 1997 Donruss Limited set was issued in one series totalling 200 cards and distributed in five-card packs with a suggested retail price of $4.99.

The set is divided into four unique subsets: Counterparts, Double Team, Star Factor and Unlimited Potential/Talent. The Counterparts subset features 100 double-sided cards with full-bleed photos of two star players who play the same position. The Double Team subset displays color action photos of two star teammates back-to-back on 40 double-sided cards. The Star Factor subset highlights 40 superstars with a different photo of the same player on each side of the card plus unique player statistics. The Unlimited Potential/Talent subset features double-front cards with color photo matchups of a veteran and a rookie. Less than 1100 of each Unlimited Potential/Talent card was produced. Judging from case breakdowns provided to us from dealers in the field, the odds appear to be as follows: Double Team 1:6, Star Factor 1:24 and Unlimited Potential/Talent 1:36.

	MINT	NRMT
COMPLETE SET (200)	1900.00	850.00
COMP.COUNTER SET (100)	40.00	18.00
COMMON COUNTERPART	.25	.11
COUNTERPART MINORS	.50	.23
COUNTERPART UNLISTED	1.00	.45
COMP.DOUBLE SET (40)	120.00	55.00
COMMON DOUBLE TEAM	1.50	.70
DOUBLE TEAM MINORS	3.00	1.35
DOUBLE TEAM UNLISTED	6.00	2.70
COMP.STAR FACT.SET (40)	1000.00	450.00
COMMON STAR FACTOR	5.00	2.20
STAR FACTOR MINORS	10.00	4.50
STAR FACTOR UNLISTED	20.00	9.00
COMP.UNLIMITED SET (20)	800.00	350.00
COMMON UNLIMITED	4.00	1.80
UNLIMITED MINORS	8.00	3.60
UNLIMITED UNLISTED	15.00	6.75
LESS THAN 1100 OF EACH STAR FACT.MADE		

□ 1 Ken Griffey Jr. C	5.00	2.20
Rondell White		
□ 2 Greg Maddux S	3.00	1.35
David Cone		
□ 3 Gary Sheffield D	6.00	2.70
Moises Alou		
□ 4 Frank Thomas S	80.00	36.00
Kevin Orie		
□ 5 Cal Ripken D	4.00	1.80
Barry Bonds		
□ 6 Vladimir Guerrero U	25.00	11.00
Reggie Jefferson		
□ 7 Eddie Murray C	1.00	.45
Marquis Grissom		
□ 8 Manny Ramirez S	6.00	2.70
Derek Jeter		
□ 9 Mike Piazza S	60.00	27.00
Barry Larkin		
□ 10 Barry Larkin C	.75	.35
Rey Ordonez		

□ 11 Jeff Bagwell C	2.00	.90
Eric Karros		
□ 12 Chuck Knoblauch C	1.00	.45
Ray Durham		
□ 13 Alex Rodriguez C	4.00	1.80
Edgar Renteria		
□ 14 Matt Williams C	.75	.35
Vinny Castilla		
□ 15 Todd Hollandsworth C	.50	.23
Bob Abreu		
□ 16 John Smoltz C	1.00	.45
Pedro Martinez		
□ 17 Jose Canseco C	.75	.35
Chili Davis		
□ 18 Jose Cruz Jr. U	120.00	55.00
Ken Griffey Jr.		
□ 19 Ken Griffey Jr. S	100.00	45.00
□ 20 Paul Molitor C	1.00	.45
John Olerud		
□ 21 Roberto Alomar C	1.00	.45
Luis Castillo		
□ 22 Derek Jeter C	3.00	1.35
Lou Collier		
□ 23 Chipper Jones C	3.00	1.35
Robin Ventura		
□ 24 Gary Sheffield C	1.00	.45
Ron Gant		
□ 25 Ramon Martinez C	.50	.23
Bobby Jones		
□ 26 Mike Piazza D	20.00	9.00
Raul Mondesi		
□ 27 Darin Erstad U	40.00	18.00
Jeff Bagwell		
□ 28 Ivan Rodriguez S	25.00	11.00
□ 29 J.T.Snow C	.50	.23
Kevin Young		
□ 30 Ryne Sandberg C	1.25	.55
Julio Franco		
□ 31 Travis Fryman C	.50	.23
Chris Snopek		
□ 32 Wade Boggs C	1.00	.45
Russ Davis		
□ 33 Brooks Kieschnick C	.50	.23
Marty Cordova		
□ 34 Andy Pettitte C	1.00	.45
Denny Neagle		
□ 35 Paul Molitor D	6.00	2.70
Matt Lawton		
□ 36 Scott Rolen U	80.00	36.00
Cal Ripken		
□ 37 Cal Ripken S	80.00	36.00
□ 38 Jim Thome C	1.00	.45
Dave Nilsson		
□ 39 Tony Womack C	1.25	.55
Carlos Baerga		
□ 40 Nomar Garciaparra C	3.00	1.35
Mark Grudzielanek		
□ 41 Todd Greene C	.50	.23
Chris Widger		
□ 42 Deion Sanders C	.50	.23
Bernard Gilkey		
□ 43 Hideo Nomo C	2.50	1.10
Charles Nagy		
□ 44 Ivan Rodriguez D	8.00	3.60
Rusty Greer		
□ 45 Todd Walker U	50.00	22.00
Chipper Jones		
□ 46 Greg Maddux S	60.00	27.00
□ 47 Mo Vaughn C	1.25	.55
Cecil Fielder		
□ 48 Craig Biggio C	.75	.35
Scott Spiezio		
□ 49 Pokey Reese C	.50	.23
Jeff Blauser		
□ 50 Ken Caminiti C	.75	.35
Joe Randa		
□ 51 Albert Belle C	1.25	.55
Shawn Green		
□ 52 Randy Johnson C	1.00	.45
Jason Dickson		
□ 53 Hideo Nomo S	15.00	6.75
Chan Ho Park		
□ 54 Scott Spiezio U	15.00	6.75
Chuck Knoblauch		
□ 55 Chipper Jones S	60.00	27.00
□ 56 Tino Martinez C	1.00	.45

Ryan McGuire		
□ 57 Eric Young C	.25	.11
Wilton Guerrero		
□ 58 Ron Coomer C	.25	.11
Dave Hollins		
□ 59 Sammy Sosa C	1.00	.45
Angel Echevarria		
□ 60 Dennis Reyes C	1.00	.45
Jimmy Key		
□ 61 Barry Larkin D	4.00	1.80
Deion Sanders		
□ 62 Wilton Guerrero U	15.00	6.75
Roberto Alomar		
□ 63 Albert Belle S	25.00	11.00
□ 64 Mark McGwire C	2.00	.90
Andre Galarraga		
□ 65 Edgar Martinez C	.75	.35
Todd Walker		
□ 66 Steve Finley C	.50	.23
Rich Becker		
□ 67 Tom Glavine C	.50	.23
Andy Ashby		
□ 68 Sammy Sosa S	8.00	3.60
Ryne Sandberg		
□ 69 Nomar Garciaparra U	80.00	36.00
Alex Rodriguez		
□ 70 Jeff Bagwell S	40.00	18.00
□ 71 Darin Erstad C	1.50	.70
Mark Grace		
□ 72 Scott Rolen C	2.50	1.10
Edgardo Alfonzo		
□ 73 Kenny Lofton C	1.25	.55
Lance Johnson		
□ 74 Joey Hamilton C	.50	.23
Brett Tomko		
□ 75 Eddie Murray D	6.00	2.70
Tim Salmon		
□ 76 Dmitri Young U	20.00	9.00
Mo Vaughn		
□ 77 Juan Gonzalez S	50.00	22.00
□ 78 Frank Thomas C	5.00	2.20
Tony Clark		
□ 79 Shannon Stewart C	.50	.23
Bip Roberts		
□ 80 Shawn Estes C	.50	.23
Alex Fernandez		
□ 81 John Smoltz D	3.00	1.35
Javier Lopez		
□ 82 Todd Greene U	50.00	22.00
Mike Piazza		
□ 83 Derek Jeter S	50.00	22.00
□ 84 Dmitri Young C	.25	.11
Antone Williamson		
□ 85 Rickey Henderson C	.75	.35
Darryl Hamilton		
□ 86 Billy Wagner C	.50	.23
Dennis Eckersley		
□ 87 Larry Walker U	6.00	2.70
Eric Young		
□ 88 Mark Kotsay U	50.00	22.00
Juan Gonzalez		
□ 89 Barry Bonds S	25.00	11.00
□ 90 Will Clark C	.75	.35
Jeff Conine		
□ 91 Tony Gwynn C	2.50	1.10
Brett Butler		
□ 92 John Wetteland C	.25	.11
Rod Beck		
□ 93 Bernie Williams D	6.00	2.70
Tony Martinez		
□ 94 Andruw Jones U	30.00	13.50
Kenny Lofton		
□ 95 Mo Vaughn S	25.00	11.00
□ 96 Joe Carter C	.75	.35
Derrek Lee		
□ 97 John Mabry C	.25	.11
F.P. Santangelo		
□ 98 Esteban Loaiza C	.25	.11
Wilson Alvarez		
□ 99 Matt Williams D	6.00	2.70
David Justice		
□ 100 Derrek Lee U	60.00	27.00
Frank Thomas		
□ 101 Mark McGwire S	40.00	18.00
□ 102 Fred McGriff C	.75	.35
Paul Sorrento		

		MINT	NRMT
103	Jermaine Allensworth C 1.00		.45
	Bernie Williams		
104	Ismael Valdes C .50		.23
	Chris Holt		
105	Fred McGriff D 4.00		1.80
	Ryan Klesko		
106	Tony Clark U 30.00		13.50
	Mark McGwire		
107	Tony Gwynn S 50.00		22.00
	Ellis Burks		
108	Jeffrey Hammonds C .50		.23
	Andy Benes		
109	Shane Reynolds C .50		.23
	Carlos Delgado		
110	Roger Clemens D .. 12.00		5.50
111	Karim Garcia U 25.00		11.00
	Albert Belle		
112	Paul Molitor S 20.00		9.00
113	Trey Beamon C .25		.11
	Eric Owens		
114	Curt Schilling C .50		.23
	Darryl Kile		
115	Tom Glavine D 3.00		1.35
	Michael Tucker		
116	Pokey Reese U 40.00		18.00
	Derek Jeter		
117	Manny Ramirez S 20.00		9.00
118	Juan Gonzalez C 2.50		1.10
	Brant Brown		
119	Juan Guzman C .25		.11
	Francisco Cordova		
120	Randy Johnson D 6.00		2.70
	Edgar Martinez		
121	Hideki Irabu U 50.00		22.00
	Greg Maddux		
122	Alex Rodriguez S 60.00		27.00
123	Barry Bonds C 1.25		.55
	Quinton McCracken		
124	Roger Clemens C 2.00		.90
	Andy Benes		
125	Wade Boggs D 6.00		2.70
	Paul O'Neill		
126	Mike Cameron U 15.00		6.75
	Larry Walker		
127	Gary Sheffield S 15.00		6.75
128	Andruw Jones C 2.50		1.10
	Raul Mondesi		
129	Brady Anderson C .75		.35
	Terrell Wade		
130	Brady Anderson D 4.00		1.80
	Rafael Palmeiro		
131	Neifi Perez U 10.00		4.50
	Barry Larkin		
132	Ken Caminiti S 12.00		5.50
133	Larry Walker C 1.00		.45
	Rusty Greer		
134	Mariano Rivera C .50		.23
	Mark Wohlers		
135	Hideki Irabu D 5.00		2.20
	Andy Pettitte		
136	Jose Guillen U 40.00		18.00
	Tony Gwynn		
137	Hideo Nomo S 50.00		22.00
138	Vladimir Guerrero C 2.00		.90
	Jim Edmonds		
139	Justin Thompson C .50		.23
	Dwight Gooden		
140	Andres Galarraga D .. 6.00		2.70
	Dante Bichette		
141	Kenny Lofton S 25.00		11.00
142	Tim Salmon C 1.00		.45
	Manny Ramirez		
143	Kevin Brown C .50		.23
	Matt Morris		
144	Craig Biggio C 4.00		1.80
	Bob Abreu		
145	Roberto Alomar S 20.00		9.00
146	Jose Guillen C 1.25		.55
	Brian Jordan		
147	Bartolo Colon C .50		.23
	Kevin Appier		
148	Ray Lankford S 3.00		1.35
	Brian Jordan		
149	Chuck Knoblauch S 15.00		6.75
150	Henry Rodriguez C .50		.23
	Ray Lankford		
151	Jaret Wright C 6.00		2.70
	Ben McDonald		
152	Bobby Bonilla D 3.00		1.35
	Kevin Brown		
153	Barry Larkin S 12.00		5.50
154	David Justice C 1.00		.45
	Reggie Sanders		
155	Mike Mussina C 1.00		.45
	Ken Hill		
156	Mark Grace D 4.00		1.80
	Brooks Kieschnick		
157	Jim Thome S 20.00		9.00
158	Michael Tucker C .50		.23
	Curtis Goodwin		
159	Jeff Suppan C .50		.23
	Jeff Fassero		
160	Mike Mussina D 6.00		2.70
	Jeffrey Hammonds		
161	John Smoltz S 10.00		4.50
162	Moises Alou C .50		.23
	Eric Davis		
163	Sandy Alomar Jr. C .50		.23
	Dan Wilson		
164	Rondell White D 3.00		1.35
	Henry Rodriguez		
165	Roger Clemens S 40.00		18.00
166	Brady Anderson C .75		.35
	Charles Johnson		
167	Jason Kendall C .50		.23
	Jose Canseco		
168	Jason Giambi D 4.00		1.80
	Jose Rosado		
169	Larry Walker S 20.00		9.00
170	Jay Buhner C .75		.35
	Geronimo Berroa		
171	Ivan Rodriguez C 1.25		.55
	Mike Sweeney		
172	Kevin Appier D 1.00		.45
	Jose Rosado		
173	Bernie Williams S 15.00		6.75
174	Todd Dunwoody C .75		.35
	Brian Giles		
175	Javier Lopez C .50		.23
	Scott Hatteberg		
176	John Jaha D 1.00		.45
	Jeff Cirillo		
177	Andy Pettitte S 20.00		9.00
	Butch Huskey		
178	Dante Bichette C .50		.23
	Butch Huskey		
179	Raul Casanova D .50		.23
	Todd Hundley		
180	Jim Edmonds D 4.00		1.80
	Garrett Anderson		
181	Deion Sanders S 10.00		4.50
182	Ryan Klesko C .75		.35
	Paul O'Neill		
183	Joe Carter D 3.00		1.35
	Pat Hentgen		
184	Brady Anderson S 12.00		5.50
185	Carlos Delgado C .50		.23
	Wally Joyner		
186	Jermaine Dye D 1.50		.70
	Johnny Damon		
187	Randy Johnson S 20.00		9.00
188	Todd Hundley D 3.00		1.35
	Carlos Baerga		
189	Tom Glavine S 10.00		4.50
190	Damon Mashore D 1.50		.70
	Jason McDonald		
191	Wade Boggs S 20.00		9.00
192	Al Martin D 3.00		1.35
	Jason Kendall		
193	Matt Williams S 15.00		6.75
194	Will Clark D 4.00		1.80
	Dean Palmer		
195	Sammy Sosa S 15.00		6.75
196	Jose Cruz Jr. D 30.00		13.50
	Jay Buhner		
197	Eddie Murray S 20.00		9.00
198	Darin Erstad D 10.00		4.50
	Jason Dickson		
199	Fred McGriff S 10.00		4.50
200	Bubba Trammell D .. 5.00		2.20
	Bobby Higginson		

1997 Donruss Limited Exposure

Randomly inserted in packs, this 200-card set is parallel to the base set and was printed using Holographic Poly-Chromium technology on both sides. The set is designated by an exclusive "Limited Exposure" stamp. Less than 40 of the "Star Factor" subsets exist.

	MINT	NRMT
COMPLETE SET (200)	15000.00	6800.00
COMP.COUNTER SET (100)	1000.00	450.00
COMMON COUNTERPART	4.00	1.80
COUNTERPART MINORS	6.00	2.70
COUNTER.SEMIS	10.00	4.50
COUNTERPART UNLISTED	15.00	6.75
COMP.DOUBLE SET (40)	1000.00	450.00
COMMON DOUBLE TEAM ..	12.00	5.50
DOUBLE TEAM MINORS	20.00	9.00
DOUBLE SEMIS	30.00	13.50
DOUBLE TEAM UNLISTED ..	50.00	22.00
COMP.STAR FACT.SET (40)	8000.00	3600.00
COMMON STAR FACTOR	40.00	18.00
STAR FACTOR MINORS	60.00	27.00
STAR FACTOR SEMIS	100.00	45.00
STAR FACTOR UNLISTED ..	150.00	70.00
COMP.UNLIMITED SET (20)	5000.00	2200.00
COMMON UNLIMITED	25.00	11.00
UNLIMITED MINORS	40.00	18.00
UNLIMITED SEMIS	60.00	27.00
UNLIMITED UNLISTED	100.00	45.00
RANDOM INSERTS IN PACKS ..		
LESS THAN 40 OF EACH STAR FACTOR EXIST		
COMP.NON-GLOSS SET (100)	250.00	110.00
COMMON NON-GLOSS	1.00	.45
*NON-GLOSS: .1X TO .25X HI COLUMN		
NON-GLOSS: RANDOM ERRORS IN PACKS		
NO EXCHANGE AVAIL.ON NON-GLOSS CARDS		
1 Ken Griffey Jr. C	80.00	36.00
Rondell White		
2 Greg Maddux C	50.00	22.00
David Cone		
4 Frank Thomas S	800.00	350.00
5 Cal Ripken C	60.00	27.00
Kevin Orie		
6 Vladimir Guerrero U	150.00	70.00
Barry Bonds		
9 Mike Piazza S	500.00	220.00
11 Jeff Bagwell C	30.00	13.50
Eric Karros		
13 Alex Rodriguez C	60.00	27.00
Edgar Renteria		
18 Jose Cruz Jr. U	800.00	350.00
Ken Griffey Jr.		
19 Ken Griffey Jr. S ..	1000.00	450.00
22 Derek Jeter C	40.00	18.00
Lou Collier		
23 Chipper Jones C	50.00	22.00
Robin Ventura		
26 Mike Piazza D	150.00	70.00
Raul Mondesi		
27 Darin Erstad U	250.00	110.00
Jeff Bagwell		
28 Ivan Rodriguez S	200.00	90.00
30 Ryne Sandberg C	20.00	9.00
Julio Franco		
36 Scott Rolen U	500.00	220.00
Cal Ripken		
37 Cal Ripken S	600.00	275.00
40 Nomar Garciaparra C	50.00	22.00
Mark Grudzielanek		
43 Hideo Nomo C	40.00	18.00
Charles Nagy		
44 Ivan Rodriguez U	60.00	27.00
Rusty Greer		
45 Todd Walker U	250.00	110.00
Chipper Jones		
46 Greg Maddux S	500.00	220.00
47 Mo Vaughn C	20.00	9.00

Cecil Fielder
☐ 51 Albert Belle C .... 20.00 — 9.00
Shawn Green
☐ 53 Hideo Nomo U ...... 120.00 — 55.00
Chan Ho Park
☐ 55 Chipper Jones S ...... 400.00 — 180.00
☐ 63 Albert Belle S .... 200.00 — 90.00
☐ 64 Mark McGwire S ...... 30.00 — 13.50
Andre Galarraga
☐ 68 Sammy Sosa D .... 60.00 — 27.00
Ryne Sandberg
☐ 69 Nomar Garciaparra U 500.00 — 220.00
Alex Rodriguez
☐ 70 Jeff Bagwell S .... 300.00 — 135.00
☐ 71 Darin Erstad C .... 25.00 — 11.00
Mark Grace
☐ 72 Scott Rolen C .... 40.00 — 18.00
Edgardo Alfonzo
☐ 73 Kenny Lofton C .... 20.00 — 9.00
Lance Johnson
☐ 76 Dmitri Young U ...... 120.00 — 55.00
☐ 77 Juan Gonzalez S ...... 400.00 — 180.00
☐ 78 Frank Thomas C ...... 60.00 — 27.00
Tony Clark
☐ 82 Todd Greene U ...... 300.00 — 135.00
Mike Piazza
☐ 83 Derek Jeter S .... 400.00 — 180.00
☐ 88 Mark Kotsay S .... 300.00 — 135.00
Juan Gonzalez
☐ 89 Barry Bonds S .... 200.00 — 90.00
☐ 91 Tony Gwynn C .... 40.00 — 18.00
Brett Butler
☐ 94 Andruw Jones U ...... 200.00 — 90.00
Kenny Lofton
☐ 95 Mo Vaughn S .... 200.00 — 90.00
☐ 100 Derrek Lee U .... 500.00 — 220.00
Frank Thomas
☐ 101 Mark McGwire S ... 300.00 — 135.00
☐ 106 Tony Clark U .... 200.00 — 90.00
Mark McGwire
☐ 107 Tony Gwynn S .... 400.00 — 180.00
☐ 110 Roger Clemens D ... 100.00 — 45.00
Carlos Delgado
☐ 111 Karim Garcia U ...... 150.00 — 70.00
Albert Belle
☐ 116 Pokey Reese U .... 250.00 — 110.00
Derek Jeter
☐ 118 Juan Gonzalez C ...... 40.00 — 18.00
Brant Brown
☐ 121 Hideki Irabu U .... 300.00 — 135.00
Greg Maddux
☐ 122 Alex Rodriguez S ... 500.00 — 220.00
☐ 123 Barry Bonds C .... 20.00 — 9.00
Quinton McCracken
☐ 124 Roger Clemens C ...... 30.00 — 13.50
Andy Benes
☐ 128 Andruw Jones C ...... 40.00 — 18.00
Raul Mondesi
☐ 135 Hideki Irabu D .... 30.00 — 13.50
Andy Pettitte
☐ 136 Jose Guillen U .... 250.00 — 110.00
Tony Gwynn
☐ 137 Hideo Nomo S ...... 600.00 — 275.00
Jim Edmonds
☐ 138 Vladimir Guerrero C 30.00 — 13.50
Jim Edmonds
☐ 141 Kenny Lofton S ...... 200.00 — 90.00
☐ 151 Jaret Wright C .... 30.00 — 13.50
Ben McDonald
☐ 165 Roger Clemens S ...... 300.00 — 135.00
☐ 171 Ivan Rodriguez C ...... 20.00 — 9.00
Mike Sweeney
☐ 196 Jose Cruz Jr. D ...... 150.00 — 70.00
Jay Buhner
☐ 198 Darin Erstad U .... 60.00 — 27.00
Jason Dickson

1997 Donruss Limited Fabric of the Game

Randomly inserted in packs at a rate of 1:20, cards from this 69-

card multi-fractured chase set highlights color player photos using three different technologies, each of which represents a different statistical category: Canvas (Stolen Bases), Leather (Doubles), and Wood (Homeruns). Five more levels cross the sections and are sequentially numbered: Legendary Material (numbered to 100), Hall of Fame Material (numbered to 250), Superstar Material (numbered to 500), Star Material (numbered to 750), and Major League Material (numbered to 1000)

	MINT	NRMT
COMPLETE SET (69)	2000.00	900.00
COMMON MAJOR LG MAT. ..	3.00	1.35
MAJOR LG.MINORS	5.00	2.20
MAJOR LG.SEMIS	8.00	3.60
MAJOR LG.UNLISTED	12.00	5.50
1000 OF EACH MAJOR LG.MATERIAL		
COMMON STAR MAT. ..	5.00	2.20
STAR MAT.MINORS	8.00	3.60
STAR MAT.SEMIS	12.00	5.50
STAR MAT.UNLISTED	20.00	9.00
750 OF EACH STAR MATERIAL		
COMMON SUPERSTAR MAT.	12.00	5.50
SUPERSTAR SEMIS	15.00	6.75
SUPERSTAR UNLISTED	25.00	11.00
500 OF EACH SUPERSTAR MATERIAL		
COMMON HOF MAT. ..	20.00	9.00
250 OF EACH HOF MATERIAL ..		
COMMON LEGEND ..	50.00	22.00
100 OF EACH LEGENDARY MATERIAL		
RANDOM INSERTS IN PACKS ..		

☐ 1 Cal Ripken HF .... 150.00 — 70.00
☐ 2 Tony Gwynn SS .... 60.00 — 27.00
☐ 3 Ivan Rodriguez S ...... 25.00 — 11.00
☐ 4 Rickey Henderson L .... 6.00 — 2.70
☐ 5 Ken Griffey Jr. SS ...... 120.00 — 55.00
☐ 6 Chipper Jones ML ...... 40.00 — 18.00
☐ 7 Sammy Sosa S .... 20.00 — 9.00
☐ 8 Wade Boggs HF .... 30.00 — 13.50
☐ 9 Manny Ramirez ML ... 12.00 — 5.50
☐ 10 Barry Bonds HF .... 50.00 — 22.00
☐ 11 Mike Piazza S .... 60.00 — 27.00
☐ 12 Rondell White ML ...... 5.00 — 2.20
☐ 13 Albert Belle S .... 25.00 — 11.00
☐ 14 Tony Clark ML .... 12.00 — 5.50
☐ 15 Edgar Martinez SS ...... 15.00 — 6.75
☐ 16 Deion Sanders ML ...... 8.00 — 3.60
☐ 17 Juan Gonzalez SS ...... 60.00 — 27.00
☐ 18 Nomar Garciaparra ML 40.00 — 18.00
☐ 19 Rafael Palmeiro SS ...... 15.00 — 6.75
☐ 20 Dave Justice ML .... 20.00 — 9.00
☐ 21 Bob Abreu ML .... 5.00 — 2.20
☐ 22 Paul Molitor S .... 80.00 — 36.00
☐ 23 Vladimir Guerrero ML ... 25.00 — 11.00
☐ 24 Chuck Knoblauch SS ... 25.00 — 11.00
☐ 25 Tony Gwynn HF ...... 100.00 — 45.00
☐ 26 Darin Erstad ML .... 20.00 — 9.00
☐ 27 Mark McGwire HF ...... 80.00 — 36.00
☐ 28 Larry Walker S .... 20.00 — 9.00

☐ 29 Gary Sheffield S .... 20.00 — 9.00
☐ 30 Jose Cruz Jr. ML .... 60.00 — 27.00
☐ 31 Kenny Lofton HF ...... 50.00 — 22.00
☐ 32 Andres Galarraga SS ... 25.00 — 11.00
☐ 33 Raul Mondesi ML .... 8.00 — 3.60
☐ 34 Eddie Murray L .... 80.00 — 36.00
☐ 35 Tino Martinez ML ...... 12.00 — 5.50
☐ 36 Todd Walker ML .... 5.00 — 2.20
☐ 37 Frank Thomas SS ...... 100.00 — 45.00
☐ 38 Ken Caminiti S .... 12.00 — 5.50
☐ 39 Pokey Reese ML .... 3.00 — 1.35
☐ 40 Barry Bonds HF .... 50.00 — 22.00
☐ 41 Barry Larkin SS .... 15.00 — 6.75
☐ 42 Bernie Williams S ...... 20.00 — 9.00
☐ 43 Cal Ripken HF ...... 150.00 — 70.00
☐ 44 Bobby Bonilla SS ...... 15.00 — 6.75
☐ 45 Ken Griffey Jr. S ...... 100.00 — 45.00
☐ 46 Tim Salmon S .... 20.00 — 9.00
☐ 47 Ryne Sandberg HF ...... 50.00 — 22.00
☐ 48 Rusty Greer ML .... 5.00 — 2.20
☐ 49 Matt Williams SS ...... 15.00 — 6.75
☐ 50 Eric Young S .... 5.00 — 2.20
☐ 51 Andruw Jones ML ...... 30.00 — 13.50
☐ 52 Jeff Bagwell S .... 40.00 — 18.00
☐ 53 Wilton Guerrero ML .... 3.00 — 1.35
☐ 54 Fred McGriff HF ...... 25.00 — 11.00
☐ 55 Jose Guillen ML .... 12.00 — 5.50
☐ 56 Brady Anderson SS ... 15.00 — 6.75
☐ 57 Mo Vaughn S .... 25.00 — 11.00
☐ 58 Craig Biggio SS .... 15.00 — 6.75
☐ 59 Dmitri Young ML .... 3.00 — 1.35
☐ 60 Frank Thomas S .... 80.00 — 36.00
☐ 61 Derek Jeter ML .... 40.00 — 18.00
☐ 62 Albert Belle SS .... 30.00 — 13.50
☐ 63 Scott Rolen ML .... 30.00 — 13.50
☐ 64 Roberto Alomar HF ...... 40.00 — 18.00
☐ 65 Jeff Bagwell S .... 40.00 — 18.00
☐ 66 Mark Grace SS .... 15.00 — 6.75
☐ 67 Gary Sheffield S .... 20.00 — 9.00
☐ 68 Joe Carter HF .... 20.00 — 9.00
☐ 69 Jim Thome ML .... 12.00 — 5.50

1997 Donruss Preferred

The 1997 Donruss Preferred set was issued in one series totalling 200 cards and distributed in five-card packs with a suggested retail of $4.99. The set features color player photos on an all-foil, micro-etched card stock. The set is divided into 100 bronze (5:1 insert odds), 60 silver (1:3), 30 gold (1:12), and 10 platinum (1:48) cards.

	MINT	NRMT
COMPLETE SET (200)	950.00	425.00
COMP.BRONZE SET (100) ..	30.00	13.50
COMMON BRONZE ...	.25	.11
BRONZE SEMISTARS ...	.50	.23
BRONZE UNLISTED STARS ..	.75	.35
COMP.SILVER SET (60) ...	150.00	70.00
COMMON SILVER	2.00	.90
SILVER SEMISTARS	3.00	1.35

#	Card	MINT	NRMT
	SILVER UNLISTED STARS	5.00	2.20
	SILVER STATED ODDS 1:3		
	COMP.GOLD SET (30)	300.00	135.00
	COMMON GOLD	6.00	2.70
	GOLD UNLISTED STARS	10.00	4.50
	GOLD STATED ODDS 1:12		
	COMP.PLAT.SET (10)	500.00	220.00
	COMMON PLATINUM	40.00	18.00
	PLATINUM STATED ODDS 1:48		
1	Frank Thomas P	60.00	27.00
2	Ken Griffey Jr. P	80.00	36.00
3	Cecil Fielder B	.40	.18
4	Chuck Knoblauch B	10.00	4.50
5	Garret Anderson B	.40	.18
6	Greg Maddux P	50.00	22.00
7	Matt Williams S	3.00	1.35
8	Marquis Grissom S	2.50	1.10
9	Jason Isringhausen B	.25	.11
10	Larry Walker S	6.00	2.70
11	Charles Nagy B	.40	.18
12	Dan Wilson B	.25	.11
13	Albert Belle G	15.00	6.75
14	Javier Lopez B	.40	.18
15	David Cone B	.40	.18
16	Bernard Gilkey B	.25	.11
17	Andres Galarraga S	5.00	2.20
18	Bill Pulsipher B	.25	.11
19	Alex Fernandez B	.40	.18
20	Andy Pettitte S	6.00	2.70
21	Mark Grudzielanek B	.25	.11
22	Juan Gonzalez P	40.00	18.00
23	Reggie Sanders B	.25	.11
24	Kenny Lofton S	15.00	6.75
25	Andy Ashby B	.25	.11
26	John Wetteland B	.25	.11
27	Bobby Bonilla B	.40	.18
28	Hideo Nomo S	30.00	13.50
29	Joe Carter B	.40	.18
30	Jose Canseco S	.50	.23
31	Ellis Burks B	.40	.18
32	Edgar Martinez S	3.00	1.35
33	Chan Ho Park S	.75	.35
34	Dave Justice B	.75	.35
35	Carlos Delgado B	.40	.18
36	Jeff Cirillo S	2.50	1.10
37	Charles Johnson B	.40	.18
38	Manny Ramirez G	12.00	5.50
39	Greg Vaughn B	.25	.11
40	Henry Rodriguez B	.25	.11
41	Darryl Strawberry B	.40	.18
42	Jim Thome G	12.00	5.50
43	Ryan Klesko S	3.00	1.35
44	Ruben Sierra B	.25	.11
45	Brian Jordan G	6.00	2.70
46	Tony Gwynn P	40.00	18.00
47	Rafael Palmeiro S	8.00	3.60
48	Dante Bichette S	2.50	1.10
49	Ivan Rodriguez G	15.00	6.75
50	Mark McGwire G	25.00	11.00
51	Tim Salmon S	5.00	2.20
52	Roger Clemens B	1.50	.70
53	Matt Lawton B	.25	.11
54	Wade Boggs S	5.00	2.20
55	Travis Fryman B	.40	.18
56	Bobby Higginson S	2.50	1.10
57	John Jaha S	2.00	.90
58	Rondell White S	2.50	1.10
59	Tom Glavine S	2.50	1.10
60	Eddie Murray S	6.00	2.70
61	Vinny Castilla B	.40	.18
62	Todd Hundley B	.40	.18
63	Jay Buhner S	3.00	1.35
64	Paul O'Neill B	.40	.18
65	Steve Finley B	.40	.18
66	Kevin Appier B	.40	.18
67	Ray Durham B	.25	.11
68	Dave Nilsson B	.25	.11
69	Jeff Bagwell G	25.00	11.00
70	Al Martin S	2.00	.90
71	Paul Molitor G	12.00	5.50
72	Kevin Brown S	2.50	1.10
73	Ron Gant B	.40	.18
74	Dwight Gooden B	.40	.18
75	Quinton McCracken B	.25	.11
76	Rusty Greer S	2.50	1.10
77	Juan Guzman B	.25	.11
78	Fred McGriff S	3.00	1.35
79	Tino Martinez B	.75	.35
80	Ray Lankford B	.40	.18
81	Ken Caminiti G	8.00	3.60
82	James Baldwin B	.25	.11
83	Jermaine Dye G	6.00	2.70
84	Mark Grace S	3.00	1.35
85	Pat Hentgen S	2.50	1.10
86	Jason Giambi S	2.50	1.10
87	Brian Hunter B	.40	.18
88	Andy Benes B	.40	.18
89	Jose Rosado B	.40	.18
90	Shawn Green B	.25	.11
91	Jason Kendall B	.40	.18
92	Alex Rodriguez P	50.00	22.00
93	Chipper Jones P	50.00	22.00
94	Barry Bonds S	15.00	6.75
95	Brady Anderson S	8.00	3.60
96	Ryne Sandberg S	8.00	3.60
97	Lance Johnson B	.25	.11
98	Cal Ripken P	60.00	27.00
99	Craig Biggio S	8.00	3.60
100	Dean Palmer B	.25	.11
101	Gary Sheffield G	10.00	4.50
102	Johnny Damon B	.25	.11
103	Mo Vaughn S	15.00	6.75
104	Randy Johnson S	6.00	2.70
105	Raul Mondesi S	3.00	1.35
106	Roberto Alomar G	12.00	5.50
107	Mike Piazza P	50.00	22.00
108	Rey Ordonez B	.25	.11
109	Barry Larkin G	8.00	3.60
110	Tony Clark S	5.00	2.20
111	Bernie Williams S	5.00	2.20
112	John Smoltz G	6.00	2.70
113	Moises Alou B	.40	.18
114	Will Clark B	.50	.23
115	Sammy Sosa G	10.00	4.50
116	Jim Edmonds S	3.00	1.35
117	Jeff Conine B	.40	.18
118	Joey Hamilton B	.40	.18
119	Todd Hollandsworth B	.25	.11
120	Troy Percival B	.25	.11
121	Paul Wilson B	.25	.11
122	Ken Hill B	.25	.11
123	Mariano Rivera S	2.50	1.10
124	Eric Karros B	.40	.18
125	Derek Jeter S	30.00	13.50
126	Eric Young S	.25	.11
127	John Mabry B	.25	.11
128	Gregg Jefferies B	.25	.11
129	Ismael Valdes S	2.50	1.10
130	Marty Cordova B	.40	.18
131	Omar Vizquel B	.40	.18
132	Mike Mussina S	6.00	2.70
133	Darin Erstad B	1.25	.55
134	Edgar Renteria S	2.50	1.10
135	Billy Wagner B	.40	.18
136	Alex Ochoa B	.25	.11
137	Luis Castillo B	.25	.11
138	Rocky Coppinger B	.25	.11
139	Mike Sweeney B	.40	.18
140	Michael Tucker B	.25	.11
141	Chris Snopek B	.25	.11
142	Dmitri Young S	2.00	.90
143	Andruw Jones P	30.00	13.50
144	Mike Cameron S	3.00	1.35
145	Brant Brown B	.25	.11
146	Todd Walker G	6.00	2.70
147	Nomar Garciaparra G	30.00	13.50
148	Glendon Rusch B	.25	.11
149	Karim Garcia S	2.50	1.10
150	Bubba Trammell S	5.00	2.20
151	Todd Greene B	.40	.18
152	Wilton Guerrero G	6.00	2.70
153	Scott Spiezio B	.40	.18
154	Brooks Kieschnick B	.25	.11
155	Vladimir Guerrero G	20.00	9.00
156	Brian Giles S	2.00	.90
157	Pokey Reese B	.25	.11
158	Jason Dickson G	6.00	2.70
159	Kevin Orie S	2.50	1.10
160	Scott Rolen G	25.00	11.00
161	Bartolo Colon S	2.50	1.10
162	Shannon Stewart G	6.00	2.70
163	Wendell Magee B	.25	.11
164	Jose Guillen S	6.00	2.70
165	Bob Abreu S	2.50	1.10
166	Deivi Cruz B	1.00	.45
167	Alex Rodriguez NT B	2.50	1.10
168	Frank Thomas NT B	3.00	1.35
169	Cal Ripken NT B	3.00	1.35
170	Chipper Jones NT B	2.50	1.10
171	Mike Piazza NT S	2.50	1.10
172	Tony Gwynn NT S	15.00	6.75
173	Juan Gonzalez NT B	2.00	.90
174	Kenny Lofton NT S	8.00	3.60
175	Ken Griffey Jr. NT B	4.00	1.80
176	Mark McGwire NT B	1.50	.70
177	Jeff Bagwell NT B	1.50	.70
178	Paul Molitor NT S	6.00	2.70
179	Andruw Jones NT B	2.00	.90
180	Manny Ramirez NT S	6.00	2.70
181	Ken Caminiti NT S	3.00	1.35
182	Barry Bonds NT B	1.00	.45
183	Mo Vaughn NT B	1.00	.45
184	Derek Jeter NT B	2.50	1.10
185	Barry Larkin NT S	3.00	1.35
186	Ivan Rodriguez NT B	1.00	.45
187	Albert Belle NT S	8.00	3.60
188	John Smoltz NT S	2.50	1.10
189	Chuck Knoblauch NT S	5.00	2.20
190	Brian Jordan NT S	2.50	1.10
191	Gary Sheffield NT S	5.00	2.20
192	Jim Thome NT S	6.00	2.70
193	Brady Anderson NT S	3.00	1.35
194	Hideo Nomo NT S	15.00	6.75
195	Sammy Sosa NT S	5.00	2.20
196	Greg Maddux NT B	2.50	1.10
197	Vladimir Guerrero CL B	1.25	.55
198	Scott Rolen CL B	1.50	.70
199	Todd Walker CL B	.25	.11
200	Nomar Garciaparra CL B	2.00	.90

1997 Donruss Preferred Precious Metals

Randomly inserted in packs, this 25-card set is a partial parallel version of the regular set printed on actual silver, gold, or platinum. No more than 100 of each card was produced.

#	Card	MINT	NRMT
	COMPLETE SET (25)	6000.00	2700.00
	COMMON CARD (1-25)	80.00	36.00
	RANDOM INSERTS IN PACKS		
	STATED PRINT RUN 100 SETS		
	ONE GRAM OF PRECIOUS METAL PER CARD		
1	Frank Thomas P	500.00	220.00
2	Ken Griffey Jr. P	600.00	275.00
3	Greg Maddux P	400.00	180.00
4	Albert Belle G	150.00	70.00
5	Juan Gonzalez P	300.00	135.00
6	Kenny Lofton G	150.00	70.00
7	Tony Gwynn P	300.00	135.00
8	Ivan Rodriguez G	150.00	70.00

		MINT	NRMT
☐ 9	Mark McGwire G	250.00	110.00
☐ 10	Matt Williams S	80.00	36.00
☐ 11	Wade Boggs S	100.00	45.00
☐ 12	Eddie Murray S	120.00	55.00
☐ 13	Jeff Bagwell G	250.00	110.00
☐ 14	Ken Caminiti G	80.00	36.00
☐ 15	Alex Rodriguez G	400.00	180.00
☐ 16	Chipper Jones P	300.00	135.00
☐ 17	Barry Bonds S	150.00	70.00
☐ 18	Cal Ripken P	500.00	220.00
☐ 19	Mo Vaughn G	150.00	70.00
☐ 20	Mike Piazza P	400.00	180.00
☐ 21	Derek Jeter S	300.00	135.00
☐ 22	Bernie Williams S	100.00	45.00
☐ 23	Andruw Jones P	250.00	110.00
☐ 24	Vladimir Guerrero G	200.00	90.00
☐ 25	Jose Guillen S	100.00	45.00

1997 Donruss Preferred Staremasters

Randomly inserted in packs, this 20-card set features up-close face photos of superstar players printed on all-foil card stock and accented with holographic foil stamping. Each card is sequentially numbered out of 1,500.

		MINT	NRMT
COMPLETE SET (20)		600.00	275.00
COMMON CARD (1-20)		12.00	5.50
RANDOM INSERTS IN PACKS			
STATED PRINT RUN 1500 SERIAL #'d SETS			

☐ 1	Alex Rodriguez	50.00	22.00
☐ 2	Frank Thomas	60.00	27.00
☐ 3	Chipper Jones	50.00	22.00
☐ 4	Cal Ripken	60.00	27.00
☐ 5	Mike Piazza	50.00	22.00
☐ 6	Juan Gonzalez	40.00	18.00
☐ 7	Derek Jeter	40.00	18.00
☐ 8	Jeff Bagwell	30.00	13.50
☐ 9	Ken Griffey Jr.	80.00	36.00
☐ 10	Tony Gwynn	40.00	18.00
☐ 11	Barry Bonds	20.00	9.00
☐ 12	Albert Belle	20.00	9.00
☐ 13	Greg Maddux	50.00	22.00
☐ 14	Mark McGwire	30.00	13.50
☐ 15	Ken Caminiti	12.00	5.50
☐ 16	Hideo Nomo	40.00	18.00
☐ 17	Gary Sheffield	15.00	6.75
☐ 18	Andruw Jones	30.00	13.50
☐ 19	Mo Vaughn	20.00	9.00
☐ 20	Ivan Rodriguez	20.00	9.00

1997 Donruss Preferred Tin Packs

Each pack of Donruss Preferred Baseball cards comes in one of 25 different player tins. These 25 tins come packed in hobby only, sequentially numbered display tins. Less than 1,200 of each Hobby-Only Display Master Tins were produced with each featuring one of 25 star players. The tins are unnumbered and checklisted below alphabetically.

	MINT	NRMT
COMPLETE SET (25)	20.00	
COMMON PACK (1-25)	.25	.11
UNLISTED STARS	.50	.23
COMMON SEALED PACK	5.00	2.20

*SEALED: 1.5X TO 3X HI ON 2.00+ PACKS
COMP.GOLD PACK SET (25) 250.00 110.00
*GOLD PACKS: 4X TO 10X HI COLUMN
*GOLD SEALED PACKS: 7.5X TO 15X HI
ONE GOLD PACK PER BOX
GOLD PACKS: 1200 SERIAL #'d SETS
COMP.BLUE BOX SET (25) 150.00 70.00
*BLUE BOXES: 3X TO 8X HI COLUMN
BLUE BOXES: 1200 SERIAL #'d SETS
*GOLD BOXES: 8X TO 20X HI COLUMN
GOLD BOXES: 299 SERIAL #'d SETS
PRICES BELOW REFER TO OPENED PACKS*

☐ 1	Jeff Bagwell	1.00	.45
☐ 2	Albert Belle	.60	.25
☐ 3	Barry Bonds	.60	.25
☐ 4	Roger Clemens	1.00	.45
☐ 5	Juan Gonzalez	1.25	.55
☐ 6	Ken Griffey Jr.	2.50	1.10
☐ 7	Tony Gwynn	1.25	.55
☐ 8	Derek Jeter	1.50	.70
☐ 9	Andruw Jones	1.25	.55
☐ 10	Chipper Jones	1.50	.70
☐ 11	Kenny Lofton	.60	.25
☐ 12	Greg Maddux	1.50	.70
☐ 13	Mark McGwire	1.00	.45
☐ 14	Hideo Nomo	1.25	.55
☐ 15	Mike Piazza	1.50	.70
☐ 16	Manny Ramirez	.50	.23
☐ 17	Cal Ripken	2.00	.90
☐ 18	Alex Rodriguez	1.50	.70
☐ 19	Ivan Rodriguez	.60	.25
☐ 20	Ryne Sandberg	.60	.25
☐ 21	Gary Sheffield	.50	.23
☐ 22	John Smoltz	.50	.23
☐ 23	Sammy Sosa	.50	.23
☐ 24	Frank Thomas	2.00	.90
☐ 25	Mo Vaughn	.60	.25

1997 Donruss Preferred X-Ponential Power

Randomly inserted in packs, this 20-card set features color player action photos from 10 of the best hitters from 10 of the

hottest teams in the league printed on die-cut thick plastic card stock with gold holographic foil treatment. When the cards of both superstar teammates are placed side-by-side, their cards form a complete "X." Only 3,000 of each card was produced and sequentially numbered.

	MINT	NRMT
COMPLETE SET (10)	300.00	135.00
COMMON CARD (1A-10B)	5.00	2.20
UNLISTED STARS	10.00	4.50
RANDOM INSERTS IN PACKS		
STATED PRINT RUN 3000 SERIAL #'d SETS		

☐ 1A	Manny Ramirez	10.00	4.50
☐ 1B	Jim Thome	10.00	4.50
☐ 2A	Paul Molitor	10.00	4.50
☐ 2B	Chuck Knoblauch	10.00	4.50
☐ 3A	Ivan Rodriguez	12.00	5.50
☐ 3B	Juan Gonzalez	25.00	11.00
☐ 4A	Albert Belle	12.00	5.50
☐ 4B	Frank Thomas	40.00	18.00
☐ 5A	Roberto Alomar	10.00	4.50
☐ 5B	Cal Ripken	40.00	18.00
☐ 6A	Tim Salmon	10.00	4.50
☐ 6B	Jim Edmonds	6.00	2.70
☐ 7A	Ken Griffey Jr.	50.00	22.00
☐ 7B	Alex Rodriguez	30.00	13.50
☐ 8A	Chipper Jones	30.00	13.50
☐ 8B	Andruw Jones	20.00	9.00
☐ 9A	Mike Piazza	30.00	13.50
☐ 9B	Raul Mondesi	6.00	2.70
☐ 10A	Tony Gwynn	25.00	11.00
☐ 10B	Ken Caminiti	6.00	2.70

1997 Donruss Signature

Distributed in five-card packs with one authentic autographed card per pack, this 100-card set was issued in two series. However, these regular cards were issued with both series and one could make sets from either series. The fronts feature color player photos with player information on the backs. These packs carried a suggested retail price of $14.99. The only Rookie Cards of note in this set are Jose Cruz Jr. and Mark Kotsay.

	MINT	NRMT
COMPLETE SET (100)	50.00	22.00
COMMON CARD (1-100)	.25	.11
MINOR STARS	.50	.23
UNLISTED STARS	1.00	.45
COMP.PLAT.PP SET (100)	3000.00	1350.00
COMMON PLAT.PP (1-100)	10.00	4.50
*PLAT.PP STARS: 20X TO 40X HI COLUMN		

*PLAT.PP YOUNG STARS: 15X TO 30X HI
*PLAT.PP ROOKIES: 7.5X TO 15X HI
PLATINUM PP: RANDOM INSERTS IN PACKS
PLAT.PP STATED PRINT RUN 150 SETS

#	Player	MINT	NRMT
1	Mark McGwire	2.50	1.10
2	Kenny Lofton	1.25	.55
3	Tony Gwynn	2.50	1.10
4	Tony Clark	1.00	.45
5	Tim Salmon	1.00	.45
6	Ken Griffey Jr.	5.00	2.20
7	Mike Piazza	3.00	1.35
8	Greg Maddux	3.00	1.35
9	Roberto Alomar	1.00	.45
10	Andres Galarraga	1.00	.45
11	Roger Clemens	2.00	.90
12	Bernie Williams	1.00	.45
13	Rondell White	.50	.23
14	Kevin Appier	.50	.23
15	Ray Lankford	.50	.23
16	Frank Thomas	4.00	1.80
17	Will Clark	.75	.35
18	Chipper Jones	3.00	1.35
19	Jeff Bagwell	2.00	.90
20	Manny Ramirez	1.00	.45
21	Ryne Sandberg	1.25	.55
22	Paul Molitor	1.00	.45
23	Gary Sheffield	1.00	.45
24	Jim Edmonds	.75	.35
25	Barry Larkin	.75	.35
26	Rafael Palmeiro	.75	.35
27	Alan Benes	.50	.23
28	Dave Justice	1.00	.45
29	Randy Johnson	1.00	.45
30	Barry Bonds	1.25	.55
31	Mo Vaughn	1.25	.55
32	Michael Tucker	.50	.23
33	Larry Walker	1.00	.45
34	Tino Martinez	1.00	.45
35	Jose Guillen	.50	.23
36	Carlos Delgado	.50	.23
37	Jason Dickson	.50	.23
38	Tom Glavine	.50	.23
39	Raul Mondesi	.75	.35
40	Jose Cruz Jr.	8.00	3.60
41	Johnny Damon	.25	.11
42	Mark Grace	.75	.35
43	Juan Gonzalez	2.50	1.10
44	Vladimir Guerrero	2.00	.90
45	Kevin Brown	.50	.23
46	Justin Thompson	.50	.23
47	Eric Young	.25	.11
48	Ron Coomer	.25	.11
49	Mark Kotsay	2.00	.90
50	Scott Rolen	2.50	1.10
51	Derek Jeter	3.00	1.35
52	Jim Thome	1.00	.45
53	Fred McGriff	.75	.35
54	Albert Belle	1.25	.55
55	Garret Anderson	.50	.23
56	Wilton Guerrero	.25	.11
57	Jose Canseco	.75	.35
58	Cal Ripken	4.00	1.80
59	Sammy Sosa	1.00	.45
60	Dmitri Young	.25	.11
61	Alex Rodriguez	3.00	1.35
62	Javier Lopez	.50	.23
63	Sandy Alomar Jr.	.50	.23
64	Joe Carter	.50	.23
65	Dante Bichette	.50	.23
66	Al Martin	.25	.11
67	Darin Erstad	1.50	.70
68	Pokey Reese	.25	.11
69	Brady Anderson	.75	.35
70	Andruw Jones	2.50	1.10
71	Ivan Rodriguez	1.25	.55
72	Nomar Garciaparra	3.00	1.35
73	Moises Alou	1.00	.45
74	Andy Pettitte	1.00	.45
75	Jay Buhner	.75	.35
76	Craig Biggio	.75	.35
77	Wade Boggs	1.00	.45
78	Shawn Estes	.50	.23
79	Neifi Perez	.25	.11
80	Rusty Greer	.50	.23
81	Pedro Martinez	1.00	.45
82	Mike Mussina	1.00	.45
83	Jason Giambi	.50	.23
84	Hideo Nomo	2.50	1.10
85	Todd Hundley	.50	.23
86	Deion Sanders	.50	.23
87	Mike Cameron	.75	.35
88	Bobby Bonilla	.50	.23
89	Todd Greene	.50	.23
90	Kevin Orie	.50	.23
91	Ken Caminiti	.75	.35
92	Chuck Knoblauch	1.00	.45
93	Matt Morris	.50	.23
94	Matt Williams	.75	.35
95	Pat Hentgen	.50	.23
96	John Smoltz	.50	.23
97	Edgar Martinez	.75	.35
98	Jason Kendall	.50	.23
99	Ken Griffey Jr. CL	2.50	1.10
100	Frank Thomas CL	2.00	.90

1997 Donruss Signature Autographs

Inserted one per pack, this 117-card set features color player autographed photos. The first 100 cards each player signed were blue, sequentially numbered to 100, and designated as "Century Marks." The next 100 cards signed were green, sequentially numbered 101-1,100, and designated "Millenium Marks." Player autographs surpassing 1100 were red and were not numbered. Some autographed signature cards were not available at first and were designated by blank-backed redemption cards which could be redeemed by mail for the player's autograph card. The cards are checklisted below in alphabetical order. Asterisk cards were found in both Series A and B. Print runs for how many cards each player signed is noted below next to the players' name.

	MINT	NRMT
COMPLETE SET (117)	2000.00	900.00
COMMON CARD	6.00	2.70
MINOR STARS	8.00	3.60
ONE AUTOGRAPH PER PACK		
ASTERISK CARDS ARE IN SERIES A AND B		
NNO CARDS LISTED IN ALPH.ORDER		

#	Player	MINT	NRMT
1	Jeff Abbott/3900	6.00	2.70
2	Bob Abreu/3900	8.00	3.60
3	Edgardo Alfonzo/3900	10.00	4.50
4	Roberto Alomar/150 *	100.00	45.00
5	Sandy Alomar Jr./1400	20.00	9.00
6	Moises Alou/900	20.00	9.00
7	Garret Anderson/3900	10.00	4.50
8	Andy Ashby/3900	6.00	2.70
9	Trey Beamon/3900	6.00	2.70
10	Alan Benes/3900	10.00	4.50
11	Geronimo Berroa/3900	6.00	2.70
12	Wade Boggs/150 *	100.00	45.00
13	Kevin Brown C/3900	6.00	2.70
14	Brett Butler/1400	20.00	9.00
15	Mike Cameron/3900	15.00	6.75
16	Giovanni Carrara/2900	6.00	2.70
17	Luis Castillo/3900	8.00	3.60
18	Tony Clark/3900	15.00	6.75
19	Will Clark/1400	30.00	13.50
20	Lou Collier/3900	6.00	2.70
21	Bartolo Colon/3900	8.00	3.60
22	Ron Coomer/3900	8.00	3.60
23	Marty Cordova/3900	8.00	3.60
24	Jacob Cruz/3900 *	10.00	4.50
25	Jose Cruz Jr./900 *	120.00	55.00
26	Russ Davis/3900	10.00	4.50
27	Jason Dickson/3900	10.00	4.50
28	Todd Dunwoody/3900	15.00	6.75
29	Jermaine Dye/3900	10.00	4.50
30	Jim Edmonds/3900	15.00	6.75
31	Darin Erstad/900 *	50.00	22.00
32	Bobby Estalella/3900	10.00	4.50
33	Shawn Estes/3900	6.00	2.70
34	Jeff Fassero/3900	6.00	2.70
35	Andres Galarraga/900	40.00	18.00
36	Karim Garcia/3900	12.00	5.50
37	Derrick Gibson/3900	15.00	6.75
38	Brian Giles/3900	6.00	2.70
39	Tom Glavine/150	50.00	22.00
40	Rick Gorecki/3900	6.00	2.70
41	Shawn Green/1900	12.00	5.50
42	Todd Greene/3900	12.00	5.50
43	Rusty Greer/3900	10.00	4.50
44	Ben Grieve/3900	30.00	13.50
45	Mark Grudzielanek/3900	6.00	2.70
46	Vlad.Guerrero/1900 *	40.00	18.00
47	Wilton Guerrero/2150	10.00	4.50
48	Jose Guillen/2900	20.00	9.00
49	Jeffrey Hammonds/2150	10.00	4.50
50	Todd Helton/1400	30.00	13.50
51	Todd Hollandsworth/2900	10.00	4.50
52	Trenidad Hubbard/900	10.00	4.50
53	Todd Hundley/1400	15.00	6.75
54	Bobby Jones/3900	6.00	2.70
55	Brian Jordan/1400	12.00	5.50
56	David Justice/900	40.00	18.00
57	Eric Karros/650	25.00	11.00
58	Jason Kendall/3900	10.00	4.50
59	Jimmy Key/3900	10.00	4.50
60	Brooks Kieschnick/3900	6.00	2.70
61	Ryan Klesko/225	50.00	22.00
62	Paul Konerko/3900	25.00	11.00
63	Mark Kotsay/2400	30.00	13.50
64	Ray Lankford/3900	6.00	2.70
65	Barry Larkin/150 *	60.00	27.00
66	Derrek Lee/3900	15.00	6.75
67	Esteban Loaiza/3900	6.00	2.70
68	Javier Lopez/1400	20.00	9.00
69	Edgar Martinez/150 *	60.00	27.00
70	Pedro Martinez/3900	40.00	18.00
71	Rafael Medina/3900	8.00	3.60
72	Raul Mondesi EXCH/650	40.00	18.00
73	Matt Morris/3900	8.00	3.60
74	Paul O'Neill/900	25.00	11.00
75	Kevin Orie/3900	12.00	5.50
76	David Ortiz/3900	12.00	5.50
77	Rafael Palmeiro/3900	25.00	11.00
78	Jay Payton/3900	6.00	2.70
79	Neifi Perez/3900	8.00	3.60
80	Manny Ramirez/900	40.00	18.00
81	Joe Randa/3900	6.00	2.70
82	Calvin Reese/3900	6.00	2.70
83	Ed.Renteria EXCH/3900	10.00	4.50
84	Dennis Reyes/3900	8.00	3.60
85	Henry Rodriguez/3900	6.00	2.70
86	Scott Rolen/1900 *	50.00	22.00
87	Kirk Rueter/2900	8.00	3.60
88	Ryne Sandberg/420	120.00	55.00
89	Dwight Smith/3900	6.00	2.70
90	J.T. Snow/900	15.00	6.75
91	Scott Spiezio/3900	8.00	3.60
92	Shannon Stewart/2900	10.00	4.50

☐ 93 Jeff Suppan/1900	12.00	5.50
☐ 94 Mike Sweeney/3900 ..	8.00	3.60
☐ 95 Miguel Tejada/3900..	25.00	11.00
☐ 96 Justin Thompson/2400	15.00	6.75
☐ 97 Brett Tomko/3900	10.00	4.50
☐ 98 Bubba Trammell/3900	12.00	5.50
☐ 99 Michael Tucker/3900..	8.00	3.60
☐ 100 Javier Valentin/3900	10.00	4.50
☐ 101 Mo Vaughn/150 *	100.00	45.00
☐ 102 Robin Ventura/1400	20.00	9.00
☐ 103 Terrell Wade/3900.....	6.00	2.70
☐ 104 Billy Wagner/3900..	10.00	4.50
☐ 105 Larry Walker/900.....	50.00	22.00
☐ 106 Todd Walker/2400..	15.00	6.75
☐ 107 Rondell White/3900..	8.00	3.60
☐ 108 Kevin Wickander/900	10.00	4.50
☐ 109 Chris Widger/3900 ..	6.00	2.70
☐ 110 Matt Williams/150 *	60.00	27.00
☐ 111 Ant.Williamson/3900	6.00	2.70
☐ 112 Dan Wilson/3900......	6.00	2.70
☐ 113 Tony Womack/3900..	8.00	3.60
☐ 114 Jaret Wright/3900..	40.00	18.00
☐ 115 Dmitri Young/3900 ..	6.00	2.70
☐ 116 Eric Young/3900......	6.00	2.70
☐ 117 Kevin Young/3900....	6.00	2.70

1997 Donruss Signature Autographs Century

Randomly inserted in packs, this set, designated as blue, features the first 100 cards signed by each player. The cards are sequentially numbered. Raul Mondesi, Eddie Murray, Edgar Renteria and Jim Thome are exchange cards. The cards are checklisted below in alphabetical order. It's believed a number of Nomar Garciaparra Century marks were lost or destroyed during packaging and as few as 62 of these cards may have been inserted into packs.

	MINT	NRMT
COMMON CARD..................	40.00	18.00
MINOR STARS.....................	80.00	36.00

RANDOM INSERTS IN PACKS ..
STATED PRINT RUN 100 SERIAL #'d SETS
ASTERISK CARDS ARE IN SERIES A AND B
NNO CARDS LISTED IN ALPH.ORDER

☐ 4 Roberto Alomar *	150.00	70.00
☐ 9 Jeff Bagwell...............	250.00	110.00
☐ 11 Albert Belle	200.00	90.00
☐ 14 Wade Boggs *..........	150.00	70.00
☐ 15 Barry Bonds	200.00	90.00
☐ 19 Jay Buhner	100.00	45.00
☐ 24 Tony Clark	100.00	45.00
☐ 25 Will Clark	100.00	45.00

☐ 26 Roger Clemens *	350.00	160.00
☐ 32 Jose Cruz Jr. *	300.00	135.00
☐ 37 Jim Edmonds	100.00	45.00
☐ 38 Darin Erstad *	120.00	55.00
☐ 42 Andres Galarraga....	120.00	55.00
☐ 44 N.Garciaparra SP62 *	300.00	135.00
☐ 48 Juan Gonzalez	400.00	180.00
☐ 53 Ben Grieve	150.00	70.00
☐ 55 Vladimir Guerrero *	150.00	70.00
☐ 57 Jose Guillen.............	100.00	45.00
☐ 58 Tony Gwynn *	400.00	180.00
☐ 60 Todd Helton.............	120.00	55.00
☐ 64 Derek Jeter *	300.00	135.00
☐ 65 Andruw Jones *	200.00	90.00
☐ 67 Chipper Jones *	400.00	180.00
☐ 69 David Justice...........	120.00	55.00
☐ 74 Ryan Klesko	100.00	45.00
☐ 75 Chuck Knoblauch *	100.00	45.00
☐ 76 Paul Konerko	120.00	55.00
☐ 77 Mark Kotsay	100.00	45.00
☐ 79 Barry Larkin *	100.00	45.00
☐ 83 Greg Maddux *	500.00	220.00
☐ 84 Edgar Martinez *	100.00	45.00
☐ 85 Pedro Martinez	120.00	55.00
☐ 86 Tino Martinez *	100.00	45.00
☐ 88 Raul Mondesi EXCH.	100.00	45.00
☐ 90 Eddie Murray EXCH*	150.00	70.00
☐ 91 Mike Mussina	150.00	70.00
☐ 98 Andy Pettitte	150.00	70.00
☐ 99 Manny Ramirez	120.00	55.00
☐ 104 Cal Ripken	600.00	275.00
☐ 105 Alex Rodriguez	500.00	220.00
☐ 107 Ivan Rodriguez	200.00	90.00
☐ 108 Scott Rolen *	200.00	90.00
☐ 110 Ryne Sandberg	250.00	110.00
☐ 111 Gary Sheffield *	120.00	55.00
☐ 118 Miguel Tejada	120.00	55.00
☐ 119 Frank Thomas	500.00	220.00
☐ 120 Jim Thome EXCH	150.00	70.00
☐ 126 Mo Vaughn *	150.00	70.00
☐ 130 Larry Walker	150.00	70.00
☐ 135 Bernie Williams *	120.00	55.00
☐ 136 Matt Williams *	100.00	45.00
☐ 140 Jaret Wright	200.00	90.00

1997 Donruss Signature Autographs Millenium

Randomly inserted in packs, this set, designated as green, features the second 100 cards signed by each player. The cards are sequentially numbered 101-1,100 and are checklisted below in alphabetical order. It has been noted that there are some cards in existence not serially numbered.

	MINT	NRMT
COMMON CARD..................	15.00	6.75
MINOR STARS.....................	30.00	13.50

RANDOM INSERTS IN PACKS ..
1000 OF EACH CARD UNLESS NOTED BELOW
ASTERISK CARDS ARE IN SERIES A AND B
NNO CARDS LISTED IN ALPH.ORDER

☐ 1 Jeff Abbott.................	15.00	6.75
☐ 2 Bob Abreu.................	20.00	9.00
☐ 3 Edgardo Alfonzo	20.00	9.00
☐ 4 Roberto Alomar *	60.00	27.00
☐ 5 Sandy Alomar Jr.......	30.00	13.50
☐ 6 Moises Alou	30.00	13.50
☐ 7 Garret Anderson	30.00	13.50
☐ 8 Andy Ashby	15.00	6.75
☐ 9 Jeff Bagwell/400	150.00	70.00
☐ 10 Trey Beamon	15.00	6.75
☐ 11 Albert Belle/400.......	120.00	55.00
☐ 12 Alan Benes	30.00	13.50
☐ 13 Geronimo Berroa......	15.00	6.75
☐ 14 Wade Boggs *	60.00	27.00
☐ 15 Barry Bonds/400	150.00	70.00
☐ 16 Bobby Bonilla/900 *	40.00	18.00
☐ 17 Kevin Brown/900......	40.00	18.00
☐ 18 Kevin Brown C	15.00	6.75
☐ 19 Jay Buhner/900	50.00	22.00
☐ 20 Brett Butler	30.00	13.50
☐ 21 Mike Cameron	40.00	18.00
☐ 22 Giovanni Carrara	15.00	6.75
☐ 23 Luis Castillo	20.00	9.00
☐ 24 Tony Clark	30.00	13.50
☐ 25 Will Clark.................	40.00	18.00
☐ 26 Roger Clemens/400 *	200.00	90.00
☐ 27 Lou Collier	15.00	6.75
☐ 28 Bartolo Colon	20.00	9.00
☐ 29 Ron Coomer	15.00	6.75
☐ 30 Marty Cordova.........	30.00	13.50
☐ 31 Jacob Cruz	20.00	9.00
☐ 32 Jose Cruz Jr. *	120.00	55.00
☐ 33 Russ Davis	15.00	6.75
☐ 34 Jason Dickson	20.00	9.00
☐ 35 Todd Dunwoody	30.00	13.50
☐ 36 Jermaine Dye	15.00	6.75
☐ 37 Jim Edmonds	40.00	18.00
☐ 38 Darin Erstad *	50.00	22.00
☐ 39 Bobby Estalella	20.00	9.00
☐ 40 Shawn Estes	30.00	13.50
☐ 41 Jeff Fassero.............	15.00	6.75
☐ 42 Andres Galarraga.....	50.00	22.00
☐ 43 Karim Garcia	20.00	9.00
☐ 44 Nomar Garciaparra/650 *	200.00	90.00
☐ 45 Derrick Gibson	30.00	13.50
☐ 46 Brian Giles	15.00	6.75
☐ 47 Tom Glavine	30.00	13.50
☐ 48 Juan Gonzalez/900	150.00	70.00
☐ 49 Rick Gorecki	15.00	6.75
☐ 50 Shawn Green	15.00	6.75
☐ 51 Todd Greene	20.00	9.00
☐ 52 Rusty Greer	30.00	13.50
☐ 53 Ben Grieve..............	60.00	27.00
☐ 54 Mark Grudzielanek...	15.00	6.75
☐ 55 Vladimir Guerrero *	80.00	36.00
☐ 56 Wilton Guerrero	15.00	6.75
☐ 57 Jose Guillen.............	40.00	18.00
☐ 58 Tony Gwynn/900 *	150.00	70.00
☐ 59 Jeffrey Hammonds ..	15.00	6.75
☐ 60 Todd Helton.............	40.00	18.00
☐ 61 Todd Hundley	30.00	13.50
☐ 62 Todd Hollandsworth	15.00	6.75
☐ 63 Trenidad Hubbard ...	15.00	6.75
☐ 64 Derek Jeter/400 * ...	200.00	90.00
☐ 65 Andruw Jones/900 *	100.00	45.00
☐ 66 Bobby Jones............	15.00	6.75
☐ 67 Chipper Jones/900 *	150.00	70.00
☐ 68 Brian Jordan	30.00	13.50
☐ 69 David Justice............	50.00	22.00
☐ 70 Eric Karros	30.00	13.50
☐ 71 Jason Kendall	30.00	13.50
☐ 72 Jimmy Key	30.00	13.50
☐ 73 Brooks Kieschnick ..	15.00	6.75
☐ 74 Ryan Klesko	30.00	13.50
☐ 75 Chuck Knoblauch/900 *	50.00	22.00
☐ 76 Paul Konerko...........	50.00	22.00
☐ 77 Mark Kotsay	40.00	18.00
☐ 78 Ray Lankford...........	30.00	13.50
☐ 79 Barry Larkin *	40.00	18.00
☐ 80 Derrek Lee	30.00	13.50
☐ 81 Esteban Loaiza	15.00	6.75

		MINT	NRMT
☐ 82	Javier Lopez	30.00	13.50
☐ 83	Greg Maddux/400 *	350.00	160.00
☐ 84	Edgar Martinez *	40.00	18.00
☐ 85	Pedro Martinez	50.00	22.00
☐ 86	Tino Martinez/900	50.00	22.00
☐ 87	Rafael Medina	20.00	9.00
☐ 88	Raul Mondesi EXCH	40.00	18.00
☐ 89	Matt Morris	20.00	9.00
☐ 90	Eddie Murray/900 *	60.00	27.00
☐ 91	Mike Mussina/900	60.00	27.00
☐ 92	Paul O'Neill	30.00	13.50
☐ 93	Kevin Orie	20.00	9.00
☐ 94	David Ortiz	20.00	9.00
☐ 95	Rafael Palmeiro	40.00	18.00
☐ 96	Jay Payton	15.00	6.75
☐ 97	Neifi Perez	20.00	9.00
☐ 98	Andy Pettitte/900 *	60.00	27.00
☐ 99	Manny Ramirez	50.00	22.00
☐ 100	Joe Randa	15.00	6.75
☐ 101	Calvin Reese	15.00	6.75
☐ 102	Edgar Renteria	30.00	13.50
☐ 103	Dennis Reyes	20.00	9.00
☐ 104	Cal Ripken/400	400.00	180.00
☐ 105	Alex Rodriguez/400	300.00	135.00
☐ 106	Henry Rodriguez	15.00	6.75
☐ 107	Ivan Rodriguez/900	80.00	36.00
☐ 108	Scott Rolen *	100.00	45.00
☐ 109	Kirk Rueter	15.00	6.75
☐ 110	Ryne Sandberg	100.00	45.00
☐ 111	Gary Sheffield/400 *	80.00	36.00
☐ 112	Dwight Smith	15.00	6.75
☐ 113	J.T. Snow	30.00	13.50
☐ 114	Scott Spiezio	20.00	9.00
☐ 115	Shannon Stewart	20.00	9.00
☐ 116	Jeff Suppan	20.00	9.00
☐ 117	Mike Sweeney	20.00	9.00
☐ 118	Miguel Tejada	50.00	22.00
☐ 119	Frank Thomas/400	300.00	135.00
☐ 120	Jim Thome EXCH/900	60.00	27.00
☐ 121	Justin Thompson	30.00	13.50
☐ 122	Brett Tomko	20.00	9.00
☐ 123	Bubba Trammell	30.00	13.50
☐ 124	Michael Tucker	20.00	9.00
☐ 125	Javier Valentin	20.00	9.00
☐ 126	Mo Vaughn *	60.00	27.00
☐ 127	Robin Ventura	30.00	13.50
☐ 128	Terrell Wade	15.00	6.75
☐ 129	Billy Wagner	30.00	13.50
☐ 130	Larry Walker	60.00	27.00
☐ 131	Todd Walker	20.00	9.00
☐ 132	Rondell White	30.00	13.50
☐ 133	Kevin Wickander	15.00	6.75
☐ 134	Chris Widger	15.00	6.75
☐ 135	Bernie Williams/400	80.00	36.00
☐ 136	Matt Williams *	40.00	18.00
☐ 137	Antone Williamson	15.00	6.75
☐ 138	Dan Wilson	15.00	6.75
☐ 139	Tony Womack	20.00	9.00
☐ 140	Jaret Wright	80.00	36.00
☐ 141	Dmitri Young	15.00	6.75
☐ 142	Eric Young	15.00	6.75
☐ 143	Kevin Young	15.00	6.75

1997 Donruss Signature Notable Nicknames

Randomly inserted in packs, this 10-card set features photos of players with notable nicknames. Only 200 of this serial numbered set were produced. The cards are unnumbered and checklisted below in alphabetical order.

	MINT	NRMT
COMPLETE SET (10)	1800.00	800.00
COMMON CARD	60.00	27.00
RANDOM INSERTS IN PACKS		
STATED PRINT RUN 200 SERIAL #'d SETS		
NNO CARDS LISTED IN ALPH.ORDER		

		MINT	NRMT
☐ 1	Ernie Banks Mr. Cub	225.00	100.00
☐ 2	Tony Clark The Tiger	120.00	55.00
☐ 3	Roger Clemens The Rocket	300.00	135.00
☐ 4	Reggie Jackson Mr. October	250.00	110.00
☐ 5	Randy Johnson The Big Unit	150.00	70.00
☐ 6	Stan Musial The Man	300.00	135.00
☐ 7	Ivan Rodriguez Pudge	150.00	70.00
☐ 8	Frank Thomas The Big Hurt	400.00	180.00
☐ 9	Mo Vaughn The Hit Dog	120.00	55.00
☐ 10	Billy Wagner The Kid	60.00	27.00

1997 Donruss Signature Significant Signatures

Randomly inserted in packs, this 22-card set features photos with autographs of legendary Hall of Fame players. Only 2000 of each card was produced and serially numbered. The cards are checklisted below in alphabetical order.

	MINT	NRMT
COMPLETE SET (22)	1000.00	450.00
COMMON CARD	30.00	13.50
RANDOM INSERTS IN PACKS		
STATED PRINT RUN 2000 SERIAL #'d SETS		
NNO CARDS LISTED IN ALPH.ORDER		

		MINT	NRMT
☐ 1	Ernie Banks	50.00	22.00
☐ 2	Johnny Bench	60.00	27.00
☐ 3	Yogi Berra	60.00	27.00
☐ 4	George Brett	60.00	27.00
☐ 5	Lou Brock	40.00	18.00

		MINT	NRMT
☐ 6	Rod Carew	40.00	18.00
☐ 7	Steve Carlton	40.00	18.00
☐ 8	Larry Doby	30.00	13.50
☐ 9	Carlton Fisk	40.00	18.00
☐ 10	Bob Gibson	40.00	18.00
☐ 11	Reggie Jackson	60.00	27.00
☐ 12	Al Kaline	50.00	22.00
☐ 13	Harmon Killebrew	40.00	18.00
☐ 14	Don Mattingly	100.00	45.00
☐ 15	Stan Musial	80.00	36.00
☐ 16	Jim Palmer	40.00	18.00
☐ 17	Brooks Robinson	40.00	18.00
☐ 18	Frank Robinson	50.00	22.00
☐ 19	Mike Schmidt	80.00	36.00
☐ 20	Tom Seaver	60.00	27.00
☐ 21	Duke Snider	60.00	27.00
☐ 22	Carl Yastrzemski	60.00	27.00

1995 Emotion

This 200-card standard-size set was produced by Fleer/SkyBox. The first-year brand has double-thick card stock with borderless fronts. Card fronts and backs are either horizontal or vertical. On the front of each player card is a theme such as Class (Cal Ripken) and Confident (Barry Bonds). The backs have two player photos, '94 stats and career numbers. The checklist is arranged alphabetically by team with AL preceding NL.

	MINT	NRMT
COMPLETE SET (200)	40.00	18.00
COMMON CARD (1-200)	.25	.11
MINOR STARS	.50	.23
UNLISTED STARS	1.00	.45
COMP.RIPKEN SET (10)	50.00	22.00
COMMON RIPKEN (1-10)	6.00	2.70
STATED ODDS 1:12		
COMMON MAIL-IN (11-15)	6.00	2.70
MAIL-IN CARDS AVAIL.VIA WRAPPER EXCH.		

		MINT	NRMT
☐ 1	Brady Anderson	.75	.35
☐ 2	Kevin Brown	.50	.23
☐ 3	Curtis Goodwin	.25	.11
☐ 4	Jeffrey Hammonds	.50	.23
☐ 5	Ben McDonald	.25	.11
☐ 6	Mike Mussina	1.00	.45
☐ 7	Rafael Palmeiro	.75	.35
☐ 8	Cal Ripken Jr.	4.00	1.80
☐ 9	Jose Canseco	.75	.35
☐ 10	Roger Clemens	2.00	.90
☐ 11	Vaughn Eshelman	.25	.11
☐ 12	Mike Greenwell	.25	.11
☐ 13	Erik Hanson	.25	.11
☐ 14	Tim Naehring	.25	.11
☐ 15	Aaron Sele	.25	.11
☐ 16	John Valentin	.25	.11
☐ 17	Mo Vaughn	1.25	.55
☐ 18	Chili Davis	.50	.23
☐ 19	Gary DiSarcina	.25	.11
☐ 20	Chuck Finley	.25	.11
☐ 21	Tim Salmon	1.00	.45

□ 22 Lee Smith	.50	.23
□ 23 J.T. Snow	.50	.23
□ 24 Jim Abbott	.25	.11
□ 25 Jason Bere	.25	.11
□ 26 Ray Durham	.50	.23
□ 27 Ozzie Guillen	.25	.11
□ 28 Tim Raines	.50	.23
□ 29 Frank Thomas	4.00	1.80
□ 30 Robin Ventura	.50	.23
□ 31 Carlos Baerga	.25	.11
□ 32 Albert Belle	1.25	.55
□ 33 Orel Hershiser	.50	.23
□ 34 Kenny Lofton	1.25	.55
□ 35 Dennis Martinez	.50	.23
□ 36 Eddie Murray	1.00	.45
□ 37 Manny Ramirez	1.00	.45
□ 38 Julian Tavarez	.25	.11
□ 39 Jim Thome	1.00	.45
□ 40 Dave Winfield	.75	.35
□ 41 Chad Curtis	.25	.11
□ 42 Cecil Fielder	.50	.23
□ 43 Travis Fryman	.50	.23
□ 44 Kirk Gibson	.50	.23
□ 45 Bob Higginson	1.50	.70
□ 46 Alan Trammell	.75	.35
□ 47 Lou Whitaker	.50	.23
□ 48 Kevin Appier	.50	.23
□ 49 Gary Gaetti	.25	.11
□ 50 Jeff Montgomery	.25	.11
□ 51 Jon Nunnally	.25	.11
□ 52 Ricky Bones	.25	.11
□ 53 Cal Eldred	.25	.11
□ 54 Joe Oliver	.25	.11
□ 55 Kevin Seitzer	.25	.11
□ 56 Marty Cordova	.50	.23
□ 57 Chuck Knoblauch	1.00	.45
□ 58 Kirby Puckett	2.00	.90
□ 59 Wade Boggs	1.00	.45
□ 60 Derek Jeter	3.00	1.35
□ 61 Jimmy Key	.25	.11
□ 62 Don Mattingly	1.50	.70
□ 63 Jack McDowell	.50	.23
□ 64 Paul O'Neill	.50	.23
□ 65 Andy Pettitte	1.50	.70
□ 66 Ruben Rivera	1.00	.45
□ 67 Mike Stanley	.25	.11
□ 68 John Wetteland	.25	.11
□ 69 Geronimo Berroa	.25	.11
□ 70 Dennis Eckersley	.50	.23
□ 71 Rickey Henderson	.75	.35
□ 72 Mark McGwire	2.00	.90
□ 73 Steve Ontiveros	.25	.11
□ 74 Ruben Sierra	.25	.11
□ 75 Terry Steinbach	.25	.11
□ 76 Jay Buhner	.75	.35
□ 77 Ken Griffey Jr.	5.00	2.20
□ 78 Randy Johnson	1.00	.45
□ 79 Edgar Martinez	.75	.35
□ 80 Tino Martinez	1.00	.45
□ 81 Marc Newfield	.25	.11
□ 82 Alex Rodriguez	4.00	1.80
□ 83 Will Clark	.75	.35
□ 84 Benji Gil	.25	.11
□ 85 Juan Gonzalez	2.50	1.10
□ 86 Rusty Greer	1.00	.45
□ 87 Dean Palmer	.25	.11
□ 88 Ivan Rodriguez	1.25	.55
□ 89 Kenny Rogers	.25	.11
□ 90 Roberto Alomar	1.00	.45
□ 91 Joe Carter	.50	.23
□ 92 David Cone	.50	.23
□ 93 Alex Gonzalez	.25	.11
□ 94 Shawn Green	.50	.23
□ 95 Pat Hentgen	.25	.11
□ 96 Paul Molitor	1.00	.45
□ 97 John Olerud	.50	.23
□ 98 Devon White	.25	.11
□ 99 Steve Avery	.25	.11
□ 100 Tom Glavine	.50	.23
□ 101 Marquis Grissom	.50	.23
□ 102 Chipper Jones	3.00	1.35
□ 103 David Justice	1.00	.45
□ 104 Ryan Klesko	.75	.35
□ 105 Javier Lopez	.50	.23
□ 106 Greg Maddux	3.00	1.35
□ 107 Fred McGriff	.75	.35

□ 108 John Smoltz	.50	.23
□ 109 Shawon Dunston	.25	.11
□ 110 Mark Grace	.75	.35
□ 111 Brian McRae	.25	.11
□ 112 Randy Myers	.25	.11
□ 113 Sammy Sosa	1.00	.45
□ 114 Steve Trachsel	.25	.11
□ 115 Bret Boone	.25	.11
□ 116 Ron Gant	.50	.23
□ 117 Barry Larkin	.75	.35
□ 118 Deion Sanders	.50	.23
□ 119 Reggie Sanders	.25	.11
□ 120 Pete Schourek	.25	.11
□ 121 John Smiley	.25	.11
□ 122 Jason Bates	.25	.11
□ 123 Dante Bichette	.50	.23
□ 124 Vinny Castilla	.50	.23
□ 125 Andres Galarraga	1.00	.45
□ 126 Larry Walker	1.00	.45
□ 127 Greg Colbrunn	.25	.11
□ 128 Jeff Conine	.50	.23
□ 129 Andre Dawson	.75	.35
□ 130 Chris Hammond	.25	.11
□ 131 Charles Johnson	.50	.23
□ 132 Gary Sheffield	1.00	.45
□ 133 Quilvio Veras	.25	.11
□ 134 Jeff Bagwell	2.00	.90
□ 135 Derek Bell	.25	.11
□ 136 Craig Biggio	.75	.35
□ 137 Jim Dougherty	.25	.11
□ 138 John Hudek	.25	.11
□ 139 Orlando Miller	.25	.11
□ 140 Phil Plantier	.25	.11
□ 141 Eric Karros	.50	.23
□ 142 Ramon Martinez	.50	.23
□ 143 Raul Mondesi	.75	.35
□ 144 Hideo Nomo	5.00	2.20
□ 145 Mike Piazza	3.00	1.35
□ 146 Ismael Valdes	.75	.35
□ 147 Todd Worrell	.25	.11
□ 148 Moises Alou	.50	.23
□ 149 Yamil Benitez	.75	.35
□ 150 Wil Cordero	.25	.11
□ 151 Jeff Fassero	.25	.11
□ 152 Cliff Floyd	.25	.11
□ 153 Pedro Martinez	1.00	.45
□ 154 Carlos Perez	.25	.11
□ 155 Tony Tarasco	.25	.11
□ 156 Rondell White	.50	.23
□ 157 Edgardo Alfonzo	1.00	.45
□ 158 Bobby Bonilla	.50	.23
□ 159 Rico Brogna	.25	.11
□ 160 Bobby Jones	.25	.11
□ 161 Bill Pulsipher	.25	.11
□ 162 Bret Saberhagen	.25	.11
□ 163 Ricky Bottalico	.25	.11
□ 164 Darren Daulton	.50	.23
□ 165 Lenny Dykstra	.50	.23
□ 166 Charlie Hayes	.25	.11
□ 167 Dave Hollins	.25	.11
□ 168 Gregg Jefferies	.25	.11
□ 169 Michael Mimbs	.25	.11
□ 170 Curt Schilling	.25	.11
□ 171 Heathcliff Slocumb	.25	.11
□ 172 Jay Bell	.50	.23
□ 173 Micah Franklin	.25	.11
□ 174 Mark Johnson	.25	.11
□ 175 Jeff King	.25	.11
□ 176 Al Martin	.25	.11
□ 177 Dan Miceli	.25	.11
□ 178 Denny Neagle	.25	.11
□ 179 Bernard Gilkey	.25	.11
□ 180 Ken Hill	.25	.11
□ 181 Brian Jordan	.50	.23
□ 182 Ray Lankford	.50	.23
□ 183 Ozzie Smith	1.25	.55
□ 184 Andy Benes	.50	.23
□ 185 Ken Caminiti	.75	.35
□ 186 Steve Finley	.50	.23
□ 187 Tony Gwynn	2.50	1.10
□ 188 Joey Hamilton	.50	.23
□ 189 Melvin Nieves	.25	.11
□ 190 Scott Sanders	.25	.11
□ 191 Rod Beck	.25	.11
□ 192 Barry Bonds	1.25	.55
□ 193 Royce Clayton	.25	.11

□ 194 Glenallen Hill	.25	.11
□ 195 Darren Lewis	.25	.11
□ 196 Mark Portugal	.25	.11
□ 197 Matt Williams	.75	.35
□ 198 Checklist 1-82	.25	.11
□ 199 Checklist 83-162	.25	.11
□ 200 Checklist 163-200/Inserts	.25	.11
□ P8 Cal Ripken Promo	7.50	3.40

1995 Emotion Masters

The theme of this 10-card standard-size set is the showcasing of players that come through in the clutch. Randomly inserted at a rate of one in eight packs, a player photo is superimposed over a larger photo that is ghosted in a color emblematic of that team. The player's name and the Emotion logo are at the bottom. The backs have a photo to the left and text to the right. Both sides of the card are shaded in the color scheme of the player's team.

	MINT	NRMT
COMPLETE SET (10)	60.00	27.00
COMMON CARD (1-10)	2.00	.90
STATED ODDS 1:8		

□ 1 Barry Bonds	4.00	1.80
□ 2 Juan Gonzalez	7.50	3.40
□ 3 Ken Griffey Jr.	15.00	6.75
□ 4 Tony Gwynn	8.00	3.60
□ 5 Kenny Lofton	4.00	1.80
□ 6 Greg Maddux	10.00	4.50
□ 7 Raul Mondesi	2.00	.90
□ 8 Cal Ripken	12.00	5.50
□ 9 Frank Thomas	12.00	5.50
□ 10 Matt Williams	2.00	.90

1995 Emotion N-Tense

Randomly inserted at a rate of one in 37 packs, this 12-card standard-size set features fronts that have a player photo surrounded by a swirling color scheme and a large holographic "N" in the background. The backs feature a like color scheme with text and player photo.

	MINT	NRMT
COMPLETE SET (12)	150.00	70.00
COMMON CARD (1-12)	4.00	1.80
UNLISTED STARS	8.00	3.60
STATED ODDS 1:37		

	MINT	NRMT
☐ 1 Jeff Bagwell	15.00	6.75
☐ 2 Albert Belle	10.00	4.50
☐ 3 Barry Bonds	10.00	4.50
☐ 4 Cecil Fielder	4.00	1.80
☐ 5 Ron Gant	4.00	1.80
☐ 6 Ken Griffey Jr.	40.00	18.00
☐ 7 Mark McGwire	15.00	6.75
☐ 8 Mike Piazza	25.00	11.00
☐ 9 Manny Ramirez	8.00	3.60
☐ 10 Frank Thomas	30.00	13.50
☐ 11 Mo Vaughn	10.00	4.50
☐ 12 Matt Williams	5.00	2.20

1995 Emotion Rookies

This 10-card standard-size set was inserted at a rate of one in five packs. Card fronts feature an action photo superimposed over background that is in a color consistent with that of the team's. The backs feature a player photo and a write-up.

	MINT	NRMT
COMPLETE SET (10)	25.00	11.00
COMMON CARD (1-10)	1.00	.45
STATED ODDS 1:5		

☐ 1 Edgardo Alfonzo	4.00	1.80
☐ 2 Jason Bates	1.00	.45
☐ 3 Marty Cordova	2.00	.90
☐ 4 Ray Durham	2.00	.90
☐ 5 Alex Gonzalez	1.00	.45
☐ 6 Shawn Green	2.00	.90
☐ 7 Charles Johnson	2.00	.90
☐ 8 Chipper Jones	8.00	3.60
☐ 9 Hideo Nomo	8.00	3.60
☐ 10 Alex Rodriguez	10.00	4.50

1996 Emotion-XL

The 1996 Emotion-XL set was issued in one series totalling

300 standard-size cards. The 7-card packs retail for $4.99 each. The fronts feature a color action player photo with either a blue, green or maroon frame and the player's name and team printed in a foil-stamped medallion. A descriptive term describing the player completes the front. The backs carry player information and statistics. The cards are grouped alphabetically by team with AL preceding NL.

	MINT	NRMT
COMPLETE SET (300)	80.00	36.00
COMMON CARD (1-300)	.40	.18
MINOR STARS	.75	.35
UNLISTED STARS	1.50	.70
PRODUCED BY FLEER		

☐ 1 Roberto Alomar	1.50	.70
☐ 2 Brady Anderson	1.00	.45
☐ 3 Bobby Bonilla	.75	.35
☐ 4 Jeffrey Hammonds	.40	.18
☐ 5 Chris Hoiles	.40	.18
☐ 6 Mike Mussina	1.50	.70
☐ 7 Randy Myers	.40	.18
☐ 8 Rafael Palmeiro	1.00	.45
☐ 9 Cal Ripken	6.00	2.70
☐ 10 B.J. Surhoff	.40	.18
☐ 11 Jose Canseco	1.00	.45
☐ 12 Roger Clemens	3.00	1.35
☐ 13 Wil Cordero	.40	.18
☐ 14 Mike Greenwell	.40	.18
☐ 15 Dwayne Hosey	.40	.18
☐ 16 Tim Naehring	.40	.18
☐ 17 Troy O'Leary	.40	.18
☐ 18 Mike Stanley	.40	.18
☐ 19 John Valentin	.40	.18
☐ 20 Mo Vaughn	2.00	.90
☐ 21 Jim Abbott	.40	.18
☐ 22 Garret Anderson	.75	.35
☐ 23 George Arias	.40	.18
☐ 24 Chili Davis	.40	.18
☐ 25 Jim Edmonds	1.00	.45
☐ 26 Chuck Finley	.40	.18
☐ 27 Todd Greene	1.00	.45
☐ 28 Mark Langston	.40	.18
☐ 29 Troy Percival	.40	.18
☐ 30 Tim Salmon	1.50	.70
☐ 31 Lee Smith	.75	.35
☐ 32 J.T. Snow	.75	.35
☐ 33 Harold Baines	.40	.18
☐ 34 Jason Bere	.40	.18
☐ 35 Ray Durham	.40	.18
☐ 36 Alex Fernandez	.40	.18
☐ 37 Ozzie Guillen	.40	.18
☐ 38 Darren Lewis	.40	.18
☐ 39 Lyle Mouton	.40	.18
☐ 40 Tony Phillips	.40	.18
☐ 41 Danny Tartabull	.40	.18
☐ 42 Frank Thomas	6.00	2.70
☐ 43 Robin Ventura	.75	.35
☐ 44 Sandy Alomar Jr.	.75	.35
☐ 45 Carlos Baerga	.40	.18
☐ 46 Albert Belle	2.00	.90

☐ 47 Julio Franco	.40	.18
☐ 48 Orel Hershiser	.75	.35
☐ 49 Kenny Lofton	2.00	.90
☐ 50 Dennis Martinez	.75	.35
☐ 51 Jack McDowell	.40	.18
☐ 52 Jose Mesa	.40	.18
☐ 53 Eddie Murray	1.50	.70
☐ 54 Charles Nagy	.75	.35
☐ 55 Manny Ramirez	1.50	.70
☐ 56 Jim Thome	1.50	.70
☐ 57 Omar Vizquel	.75	.35
☐ 58 Chad Curtis	.40	.18
☐ 59 Cecil Fielder	.75	.35
☐ 60 Travis Fryman	.75	.35
☐ 61 Chris Gomez	.40	.18
☐ 62 Felipe Lira	.40	.18
☐ 63 Atan Trammell	1.00	.45
☐ 64 Kevin Appier	.75	.35
☐ 65 Johnny Damon	.75	.35
☐ 66 Tom Goodwin	.40	.18
☐ 67 Mark Gubicza	.40	.18
☐ 68 Jeff Montgomery	.40	.18
☐ 69 Jon Nunnally	.40	.18
☐ 70 Bip Roberts	.40	.18
☐ 71 Ricky Bones	.40	.18
☐ 72 Chuck Carr	.40	.18
☐ 73 John Jaha	.40	.18
☐ 74 Ben McDonald	.40	.18
☐ 75 Matt Mieske	.40	.18
☐ 76 Dave Nilsson	.40	.18
☐ 77 Kevin Seitzer	.40	.18
☐ 78 Greg Vaughn	.40	.18
☐ 79 Rick Aguilera	.40	.18
☐ 80 Marty Cordova	.75	.35
☐ 81 Roberto Kelly	.40	.18
☐ 82 Chuck Knoblauch	1.50	.70
☐ 83 Pat Meares	.40	.18
☐ 84 Paul Molitor	1.50	.70
☐ 85 Kirby Puckett	3.00	1.35
☐ 86 Brad Radke	.75	.35
☐ 87 Wade Boggs	1.50	.70
☐ 88 David Cone	.75	.35
☐ 89 Dwight Gooden	.75	.35
☐ 90 Derek Jeter	5.00	2.20
☐ 91 Tino Martinez	1.50	.70
☐ 92 Paul O'Neill	.75	.35
☐ 93 Andy Pettitte	2.00	.90
☐ 94 Tim Raines	.75	.35
☐ 95 Ruben Rivera	.75	.35
☐ 96 Kenny Rogers	.40	.18
☐ 97 Ruben Sierra	.40	.18
☐ 98 John Wetteland	.40	.18
☐ 99 Bernie Williams	1.50	.70
☐ 100 Allen Battle	.40	.18
☐ 101 Geronimo Berroa	.40	.18
☐ 102 Brent Gates	.40	.18
☐ 103 Doug Johns	.40	.18
☐ 104 Mark McGwire	3.00	1.35
☐ 105 Pedro Munoz	.40	.18
☐ 106 Ariel Prieto	.40	.18
☐ 107 Terry Steinbach	.40	.18
☐ 108 Todd Van Poppel	.40	.18
☐ 109 Chris Bosio	.40	.18
☐ 110 Jay Buhner	1.00	.45
☐ 111 Joey Cora	.75	.35
☐ 112 Russ Davis	.40	.18
☐ 113 Ken Griffey Jr.	8.00	3.60
☐ 114 Sterling Hitchcock	.40	.18
☐ 115 Randy Johnson	1.50	.70
☐ 116 Edgar Martinez	1.00	.45
☐ 117 Alex Rodriguez	5.00	2.20
☐ 118 Paul Sorrento	.40	.18
☐ 119 Dan Wilson	.40	.18
☐ 120 Will Clark	1.00	.45
☐ 121 Juan Gonzalez	4.00	1.80
☐ 122 Rusty Greer	.75	.35
☐ 123 Kevin Gross	.40	.18
☐ 124 Ken Hill	.40	.18
☐ 125 Dean Palmer	.40	.18
☐ 126 Roger Pavlik	.40	.18
☐ 127 Ivan Rodriguez	2.00	.90
☐ 128 Mickey Tettleton	.40	.18
☐ 129 Joe Carter	.75	.35
☐ 130 Carlos Delgado	.75	.35
☐ 131 Alex Gonzalez	.40	.18
☐ 132 Shawn Green	.40	.18

		MINT	NRMT
☐ 133 Erik Hanson		.40	.18
☐ 134 Pat Hentgen		.75	.35
☐ 135 Otis Nixon		.40	.18
☐ 136 John Olerud		.75	.35
☐ 137 Ed Sprague		.40	.18
☐ 138 Steve Avery		.40	.18
☐ 139 Jermaine Dye		.75	.35
☐ 140 Tom Glavine		.75	.35
☐ 141 Marquis Grissom		.75	.35
☐ 142 Chipper Jones		5.00	2.20
☐ 143 David Justice		1.50	.70
☐ 144 Ryan Klesko		1.00	.45
☐ 145 Javier Lopez		.75	.35
☐ 146 Greg Maddux		5.00	2.20
☐ 147 Fred McGriff		1.00	.45
☐ 148 Jason Schmidt		.75	.35
☐ 149 John Smoltz		.75	.35
☐ 150 Mark Wohlers		.40	.18
☐ 151 Jim Bullinger		.40	.18
☐ 152 Frank Castillo		.40	.18
☐ 153 Kevin Foster		.40	.18
☐ 154 Luis Gonzalez		.40	.18
☐ 155 Mark Grace		1.00	.45
☐ 156 Brian McRae		.40	.18
☐ 157 Jaime Navarro		.40	.18
☐ 158 Rey Sanchez		.40	.18
☐ 159 Ryne Sandberg		2.00	.90
☐ 160 Sammy Sosa		1.50	.70
☐ 161 Bret Boone		.40	.18
☐ 162 Jeff Brantley		.40	.18
☐ 163 Vince Coleman		.40	.18
☐ 164 Steve Gibralter		.40	.18
☐ 165 Barry Larkin		1.00	.45
☐ 166 Hal Morris		.40	.18
☐ 167 Mark Portugal		.40	.18
☐ 168 Reggie Sanders		.40	.18
☐ 169 Pete Schourek		.40	.18
☐ 170 John Smiley		.40	.18
☐ 171 Jason Bates		.40	.18
☐ 172 Dante Bichette		.75	.35
☐ 173 Ellis Burks		.75	.35
☐ 174 Vinny Castilla		.75	.35
☐ 175 Andres Galarraga		1.50	.70
☐ 176 Kevin Ritz		.40	.18
☐ 177 Bill Swift		.40	.18
☐ 178 Larry Walker		1.50	.70
☐ 179 Walt Weiss		.40	.18
☐ 180 Eric Young		.40	.18
☐ 181 Kurt Abbott		.40	.18
☐ 182 Kevin Brown		.75	.35
☐ 183 John Burkett		.40	.18
☐ 184 Greg Colbrunn		.40	.18
☐ 185 Jeff Conine		.75	.35
☐ 186 Chris Hammond		.40	.18
☐ 187 Charles Johnson		.75	.35
☐ 188 Terry Pendleton		.40	.18
☐ 189 Pat Rapp		.40	.18
☐ 190 Gary Sheffield		1.50	.70
☐ 191 Quilvio Veras		.40	.18
☐ 192 Devon White		.40	.18
☐ 193 Jeff Bagwell		3.00	1.35
☐ 194 Derek Bell		.40	.18
☐ 195 Sean Berry		.40	.18
☐ 196 Craig Biggio		1.00	.45
☐ 197 Doug Drabek		.40	.18
☐ 198 Tony Eusebio		.40	.18
☐ 199 Mike Hampton		.40	.18
☐ 200 Brian L.Hunter		.75	.35
☐ 201 Derrick May		.40	.18
☐ 202 Orlando Miller		.40	.18
☐ 203 Shane Reynolds		.40	.18
☐ 204 Mike Blowers		.40	.18
☐ 205 Tom Candiotti		.40	.18
☐ 206 Delino DeShields		.40	.18
☐ 207 Greg Gagne		.40	.18
☐ 208 Karim Garcia		1.00	.45
☐ 209 Todd Hollandsworth		.40	.18
☐ 210 Eric Karros		.75	.35
☐ 211 Ramon Martinez		.75	.35
☐ 212 Raul Mondesi		1.00	.45
☐ 213 Hideo Nomo		4.00	1.80
☐ 214 Chan Ho Park		1.50	.70
☐ 215 Mike Piazza		5.00	2.20
☐ 216 Ismael Valdes		.75	.35
☐ 217 Todd Worrell		.40	.18
☐ 218 Moises Alou		.75	.35
☐ 219 Yamil Benitez		.75	.35
☐ 220 Jeff Fassero		.40	.18
☐ 221 Darrin Fletcher		.40	.18
☐ 222 Cliff Floyd		.40	.18
☐ 223 Pedro Martinez		1.50	.70
☐ 224 Carlos Perez		.40	.18
☐ 225 Mel Rojas		.40	.18
☐ 226 David Segui		.40	.18
☐ 227 Rondell White		.75	.35
☐ 228 Rico Brogna		.40	.18
☐ 229 Carl Everett		.40	.18
☐ 230 John Franco		.40	.18
☐ 231 Bernard Gilkey		.40	.18
☐ 232 Todd Hundley		.75	.35
☐ 233 Jason Isringhausen		.40	.18
☐ 234 Lance Johnson		.40	.18
☐ 235 Bobby Jones		.40	.18
☐ 236 Jeff Kent		.40	.18
☐ 237 Rey Ordonez		.75	.35
☐ 238 Bill Pulsipher		.40	.18
☐ 239 Jose Vizcaino		.40	.18
☐ 240 Paul Wilson		.40	.18
☐ 241 Ricky Bottalico		.40	.18
☐ 242 Darren Daulton		.75	.35
☐ 243 Lenny Dykstra		.75	.35
☐ 244 Jim Eisenreich		.40	.18
☐ 245 Sid Fernandez		.40	.18
☐ 246 Gregg Jefferies		.40	.18
☐ 247 Mickey Morandini		.40	.18
☐ 248 Benito Santiago		.40	.18
☐ 249 Curt Schilling		.75	.35
☐ 250 Mark Whiten		.40	.18
☐ 251 Todd Zeile		.40	.18
☐ 252 Jay Bell		.75	.35
☐ 253 Carlos Garcia		.40	.18
☐ 254 Charlie Hayes		.40	.18
☐ 255 Jason Kendall		1.00	.45
☐ 256 Jeff King		.40	.18
☐ 257 Al Martin		.40	.18
☐ 258 Orlando Merced		.40	.18
☐ 259 Dan Miceli		.40	.18
☐ 260 Denny Neagle		.75	.35
☐ 261 Alan Benes		.75	.35
☐ 262 Andy Benes		.40	.18
☐ 263 Royce Clayton		.40	.18
☐ 264 Dennis Eckersley		.75	.35
☐ 265 Gary Gaetti		.40	.18
☐ 266 Ron Gant		.75	.35
☐ 267 Brian Jordan		.75	.35
☐ 268 Ray Lankford		.75	.35
☐ 269 John Mabry		.40	.18
☐ 270 Tom Pagnozzi		.40	.18
☐ 271 Ozzie Smith		2.00	.90
☐ 272 Todd Stottlemyre		.40	.18
☐ 273 Andy Ashby		.40	.18
☐ 274 Brad Ausmus		.40	.18
☐ 275 Ken Caminiti		1.00	.45
☐ 276 Steve Finley		.75	.35
☐ 277 Tony Gwynn		4.00	1.80
☐ 278 Joey Hamilton		.75	.35
☐ 279 Rickey Henderson		1.00	.45
☐ 280 Trevor Hoffman		.40	.18
☐ 281 Wally Joyner		.75	.35
☐ 282 Jody Reed		.40	.18
☐ 283 Bob Tewksbury		.40	.18
☐ 284 Fernando Valenzuela		.75	.35
☐ 285 Rod Beck		.40	.18
☐ 286 Barry Bonds		2.00	.90
☐ 287 Mark Carreon		.40	.18
☐ 288 Shawon Dunston		.40	.18
☐ 289 Osvaldo Fernandez		.75	.35
☐ 290 Glenallen Hill		.40	.18
☐ 291 Stan Javier		.40	.18
☐ 292 Mark Leiter		.40	.18
☐ 293 Kirt Manwaring		.40	.18
☐ 294 Robby Thompson		.40	.18
☐ 295 William VanLandingham		.40	.18
☐ 296 Allen Watson		.40	.18
☐ 297 Matt Williams		1.00	.45
☐ 298 Checklist		.40	.18
☐ 299 Checklist		.40	.18
☐ 300 Checklist		.40	.18
☐ P55 Manny Ramirez Promo		2.00	.90

1996 Emotion-XL D-Fense

Randomly inserted in packs at a rate of one in four, this 10-card set showcases outstanding defensive players. The fronts feature a color action player cut-out on a sepia portrait background with silver foil print and border. The backs carry information about the player on another sepia portrait background.

	MINT	NRMT
COMPLETE SET (10)	25.00	11.00
COMMON CARD (1-10)	1.00	.45
STATED ODDS 1:4		

		MINT	NRMT
☐ 1 Roberto Alomar		1.50	.70
☐ 2 Barry Bonds		2.50	1.10
☐ 3 Mark Grace		1.00	.45
☐ 4 Ken Griffey Jr.		10.00	4.50
☐ 5 Kenny Lofton		2.50	1.10
☐ 6 Greg Maddux		6.00	2.70
☐ 7 Raul Mondesi		1.00	.45
☐ 8 Cal Ripken		8.00	3.60
☐ 9 Ivan Rodriguez		2.50	1.10
☐ 10 Matt Williams		1.00	.45

1996 Emotion-XL Legion of Boom

Randomly inserted in packs at a rate of one in 36, this 12-card set features the game's big hitters on cards with translucent card backs. The fronts carry a color action player cut-out with silver foil print.

	MINT	NRMT
COMPLETE SET (12)	200.00	90.00
COMMON CARD (1-12)	6.00	2.70
UNLISTED STARS	10.00	4.50
STATED ODDS 1:36 HOBBY		

		MINT	NRMT
☐ 1	Albert Belle	12.00	5.50
☐ 2	Barry Bonds	12.00	5.50
☐ 3	Juan Gonzalez	25.00	11.00
☐ 4	Ken Griffey Jr	50.00	22.00
☐ 5	Mark McGwire	20.00	9.00
☐ 6	Mike Piazza	30.00	13.50
☐ 7	Manny Ramirez	10.00	4.50
☐ 8	Tim Salmon	10.00	4.50
☐ 9	Sammy Sosa	10.00	4.50
☐ 10	Frank Thomas	40.00	18.00
☐ 11	Mo Vaughn	12.00	5.50
☐ 12	Matt Williams	6.00	2.70

1996 Emotion-XL N-Tense

Randomly inserted in packs at a rate of one in 12, this 10-card set highlights top-clutch performers on special, front N-shaped die-cut cards. The backs carry information about the player on a player portrait background.

		MINT	NRMT
COMPLETE SET (10)		100.00	45.00
COMMON CARD (1-10)		4.00	1.80
STATED ODDS 1:12			

		MINT	NRMT
☐ 1	Albert Belle	6.00	2.70
☐ 2	Barry Bonds	6.00	2.70
☐ 3	Jose Canseco	4.00	1.80
☐ 4	Ken Griffey Jr.	25.00	11.00
☐ 5	Tony Gwynn	12.00	5.50
☐ 6	Randy Johnson	5.00	2.20
☐ 7	Greg Maddux	15.00	6.75
☐ 8	Cal Ripken	20.00	9.00
☐ 9	Frank Thomas	20.00	9.00
☐ 10	Matt Williams	4.00	1.80

1996 Emotion-XL Rare Breed

Randomly inserted in packs at a rate of one in 100, this 10-card set showcases young stars on lenticular cards. The fronts feature color action player cut-outs on a baseball graphics background. The backs carry player information over a color player portrait.

		MINT	NRMT
COMPLETE SET (10)		200.00	90.00
COMMON CARD (1-10)		6.00	2.70
SEMISTARS		12.00	5.50
STATED ODDS 1:100			

		MINT	NRMT
☐ 1	Garret Anderson	8.00	3.60
☐ 2	Marty Cordova	8.00	3.60
☐ 3	Brian L.Hunter	8.00	3.60
☐ 4	Jason Isringhausen	6.00	2.70
☐ 5	Charles Johnson	8.00	3.60
☐ 6	Chipper Jones	80.00	36.00
☐ 7	Raul Mondesi	12.00	5.50
☐ 8	Hideo Nomo	60.00	27.00
☐ 9	Manny Ramirez	25.00	11.00
☐ 10	Rondell White	8.00	3.60

1993 Finest

This 199-card standard-size single series set is widely recognized as one of the most important issues of the 1990's. The Finest brand was Topps first attempt at the super-premium card market. Production was announced at 4,000 cases and cards were distributed exclusively through hobby dealers in the fall of 1993. This was the first time in the history of the hobby that a major manufacturer publicly released production figures. Cards were issued in 7-card foil fin-wrapped packs that carried a suggested retail price of $3.99. The product was a smashing success upon release with pack prices immediately soaring well above suggested retail prices. The popularity of the product has continued to grow throughout the years as it's place in hobby lore is now well solidified. The cards have silver-blue metallic finishes on their fronts and feature color player action photos. The set's title appears at the top, and the player's name is shown at the bottom. J.T. Snow is the only key Rookie Card in this set.

	MINT	NRMT
COMPLETE SET (199)	250.00	110.00
COMMON CARD (1-199)	1.00	.45
MINOR STARS	1.50	.70
SEMISTARS	3.00	1.35
UNLISTED STARS	5.00	2.20

		MINT	NRMT
☐ 1	David Justice	5.00	2.20
☐ 2	Lou Whitaker	1.50	.70
☐ 3	Bryan Harvey	1.00	.45
☐ 4	Carlos Garcia	1.00	.45
☐ 5	Sid Fernandez	1.00	.45
☐ 6	Brett Butler	1.50	.70
☐ 7	Scott Cooper	1.00	.45
☐ 8	B.J. Surhoff	1.50	.70
☐ 9	Steve Finley	1.50	.70
☐ 10	Curt Schilling	1.50	.70
☐ 11	Jeff Bagwell	10.00	4.50
☐ 12	Alex Cole	1.00	.45
☐ 13	John Olerud	1.00	.45
☐ 14	John Smiley	1.00	.45
☐ 15	Bip Roberts	1.00	.45
☐ 16	Albert Belle	6.00	2.70
☐ 17	Duane Ward	1.00	.45
☐ 18	Alan Trammell	3.00	1.35
☐ 19	Andy Benes	1.50	.70
☐ 20	Reggie Sanders	1.50	.70
☐ 21	Todd Zeile	1.00	.45
☐ 22	Rick Aguilera	1.00	.45
☐ 23	Dave Hollins	1.00	.45
☐ 24	Jose Rijo	1.00	.45
☐ 25	Matt Williams	3.00	1.35
☐ 26	Sandy Alomar	1.50	.70
☐ 27	Alex Fernandez	1.50	.70
☐ 28	Ozzie Smith	6.00	2.70
☐ 29	Ramon Martinez	1.00	.70
☐ 30	Bernie Williams	5.00	2.20
☐ 31	Gary Sheffield	5.00	2.20
☐ 32	Eric Karros	1.50	.70
☐ 33	Frank Viola	1.00	.45
☐ 34	Kevin Young	1.00	.45
☐ 35	Ken Hill	1.00	.45
☐ 36	Tony Fernandez	1.00	.45
☐ 37	Tim Wakefield	1.50	.70
☐ 38	John Kruk	1.50	.70
☐ 39	Chris Sabo	1.00	.45
☐ 40	Marquis Grissom	1.50	.70
☐ 41	Glenn Davis	1.00	.45
☐ 42	Jeff Montgomery	1.50	.70
☐ 43	Kenny Lofton	10.00	4.50
☐ 44	John Burkett	1.00	.45
☐ 45	Darryl Hamilton	1.00	.45
☐ 46	Jim Abbott	1.50	.70
☐ 47	Ivan Rodriguez	6.00	2.70
☐ 48	Eric Young	5.00	2.20
☐ 49	Mitch Williams	1.00	.45
☐ 50	Harold Reynolds	1.00	.45
☐ 51	Brian Harper	1.00	.45
☐ 52	Rafael Palmeiro	3.00	1.35
☐ 53	Bret Saberhagen	1.00	.45
☐ 54	Jeff Conine	1.50	.70
☐ 55	Ivan Calderon	1.00	.45
☐ 56	Juan Guzman	1.00	.45
☐ 57	Carlos Baerga	1.50	.70
☐ 58	Charles Nagy	1.50	.70
☐ 59	Wally Joyner	1.50	.70
☐ 60	Charlie Hayes	1.00	.45
☐ 61	Shane Mack	1.00	.45
☐ 62	Pete Harnisch	1.00	.45
☐ 63	George Brett	10.00	4.50
☐ 64	Lance Johnson	1.00	.45
☐ 65	Ben McDonald	1.00	.45
☐ 66	Bobby Bonilla	1.50	.70
☐ 67	Terry Steinbach	1.00	.45
☐ 68	Ron Gant	1.50	.70
☐ 69	Doug Jones	1.00	.45
☐ 70	Paul Molitor	5.00	2.20
☐ 71	Brady Anderson	3.00	1.35
☐ 72	Chuck Finley	1.00	.45
☐ 73	Mark Grace	3.00	1.35
☐ 74	Mike Devereaux	1.00	.45
☐ 75	Tony Phillips	1.00	.45
☐ 76	Chuck Knoblauch	5.00	2.20
☐ 77	Tony Gwynn	12.00	5.50
☐ 78	Kevin Appier	1.50	.70
☐ 79	Sammy Sosa	5.00	2.20
☐ 80	Mickey Tettleton	1.00	.45
☐ 81	Felix Jose	1.00	.45
☐ 82	Mark Langston	1.00	.45
☐ 83	Gregg Jefferies	1.00	.45
☐ 84	Andre Dawson AS	3.00	1.35
☐ 85	Greg Maddux AS	15.00	6.75
☐ 86	Rickey Henderson AS	3.00	1.35

87	Tom Glavine AS	3.00	1.35
88	Roberto Alomar AS	5.00	2.20
89	Darryl Strawberry AS	1.50	.70
90	Wade Boggs AS	5.00	2.20
91	Bo Jackson AS	1.50	.70
92	Mark McGwire AS	10.00	4.50
93	Robin Ventura AS	1.50	.70
94	Joe Carter AS	1.50	.70
95	Lee Smith AS	1.50	.70
96	Cal Ripken AS	20.00	9.00
97	Larry Walker AS	5.00	2.20
98	Don Mattingly AS	8.00	3.60
99	Jose Canseco AS	3.00	1.35
100	Dennis Eckersley AS	1.00	.45
101	Terry Pendleton AS	1.50	.70
102	Frank Thomas AS	20.00	9.00
103	Barry Bonds AS	6.00	2.70
104	Roger Clemens AS	10.00	4.50
105	Ryne Sandberg AS	6.00	2.70
106	Fred McGriff AS	3.00	1.35
107	Nolan Ryan AS	20.00	9.00
108	Will Clark AS	3.00	1.35
109	Pat Listach AS	1.00	.45
110	Ken Griffey Jr. AS	25.00	11.00
111	Cecil Fielder AS	1.50	.70
112	Kirby Puckett AS	10.00	4.50
113	Dwight Gooden AS	1.50	.70
114	Barry Larkin AS	3.00	1.35
115	David Cone AS	1.50	.70
116	Juan Gonzalez AS	12.00	5.50
117	Kent Hrbek	1.50	.70
118	Tim Wallach	1.00	.45
119	Craig Biggio	3.00	1.35
120	Roberto Kelly	1.00	.45
121	Gregg Olson	1.00	.45
122	Eddie Murray UER	5.00	2.20
	122 career strikeouts should be 1224		
123	Wil Cordero	1.00	.45
124	Jay Buhner	3.00	1.35
125	Carlton Fisk	5.00	2.20
126	Eric Davis	1.50	.70
127	Doug Drabek	1.00	.45
128	Ozzie Guillen	1.00	.45
129	John Wetteland	1.50	.70
130	Andres Galarraga	5.00	2.20
131	Ken Caminiti	3.00	1.35
132	Tom Candiotti	1.00	.45
133	Pat Borders	1.00	.45
134	Kevin Brown	1.50	.70
135	Travis Fryman	1.50	.70
136	Kevin Mitchell	1.50	.70
137	Greg Swindell	1.00	.45
138	Benito Santiago	1.00	.45
139	Reggie Jefferson	1.00	.45
140	Chris Bosio	1.00	.45
141	Deion Sanders	1.50	.70
142	Scott Erickson	1.00	.45
143	Howard Johnson	1.00	.45
144	Orestes Destrade	1.00	.45
145	Jose Guzman	1.00	.45
146	Chad Curtis	1.50	.70
147	Cal Eldred	1.00	.45
148	Willie Greene	1.50	.70
149	Tommy Greene	1.00	.45
150	Erik Hanson	1.00	.45
151	Bob Welch	1.00	.45
152	John Jaha	1.50	.70
153	Harold Baines	1.50	.70
154	Randy Johnson	5.00	2.20
155	Al Martin	1.50	.70
156	J.T. Snow	6.00	2.70
157	Mike Mussina	6.00	2.70
158	Ruben Sierra	1.00	.45
159	Dean Palmer	1.50	.70
160	Steve Avery	1.50	.70
161	Julio Franco	1.00	.45
162	Dave Winfield	3.00	1.35
163	Tim Salmon	6.00	2.70
164	Tom Henke	1.00	.45
165	Mo Vaughn	6.00	2.70
166	John Smoltz	1.50	.70
167	Danny Tartabull	1.00	.45
168	Delino DeShields	1.00	.45
169	Charlie Hough	1.00	.45
170	Paul O'Neill	1.50	.70
171	Darren Daulton	1.50	.70
172	Jack McDowell	1.00	.45
173	Junior Felix	1.00	.45
174	Jimmy Key	1.50	.70
175	George Bell	1.00	.45
176	Mike Stanton	1.00	.45
177	Len Dykstra	1.50	.70
178	Norm Charlton	1.00	.45
179	Eric Anthony	1.00	.45
180	Rob Dibble	1.00	.45
181	Otis Nixon	1.00	.45
182	Randy Myers	1.50	.70
183	Tim Raines	1.50	.70
184	Orel Hershiser	1.50	.70
185	Andy Van Slyke	1.50	.70
186	Mike Lansing	1.50	.70
187	Ray Lankford	3.00	1.35
188	Mike Morgan	1.00	.45
189	Moises Alou	1.50	.70
190	Edgar Martinez	3.00	1.35
191	John Franco	1.50	.70
192	Robin Yount	3.00	1.35
193	Bob Tewksbury	1.00	.45
194	Jay Bell	1.50	.70
195	Luis Gonzalez	1.00	.45
196	Dave Fleming	1.50	.70
197	Mike Greenwell	1.00	.45
198	David Nied	1.00	.45
199	Mike Piazza	25.00	11.00

1993 Finest Refractors

Randomly inserted in packs at a rate of one in 18, these 199 standard-size cards are identical to the regular-issue 1993 Topps Finest except that their fronts have been laminated with a plastic diffraction grating that gives the card a colorful 3-D appearance. Because of the known production numbers, these cards are believed to have a print run of 241 of each card. Several cards are believed to be in short supply and are notated with an asterisk. Topps, however, has never publicly released any verification of the shortprinted singles, but some of the singles are accepted as being tough to find due to poor regional distribution and hoarding. Due to their high value, these cards are extremely condition sensitive, with much attention paid to centering and minor scratches on the card fronts.

	MINT	NRMT
COMPLETE SET (199)	35000.00	15800.00
COMMON CARD (1-199)	50.00	22.00
MINOR STARS	100.00	45.00
STATED ODDS 1:18		
ASTERISK CARDS: PERCEIVED SCARCITY		

#	Player	MINT	NRMT
1	David Justice	250.00	110.00
3	Bryan Harvey*	200.00	90.00
10	Curt Schilling*	250.00	110.00
11	Jeff Bagwell	1000.00	450.00
12	Alex Cole	250.00	110.00
16	Albert Belle	600.00	275.00
25	Matt Williams	500.00	220.00
26	Sandy Alomar	150.00	70.00
27	Alex Fernandez	150.00	70.00
28	Ozzie Smith	300.00	135.00
30	Bernie Williams	400.00	180.00
31	Gary Sheffield	350.00	160.00
32	Eric Karros	150.00	70.00
38	John Kruk*	200.00	90.00
39	Chris Sabo*	200.00	90.00
40	Marquis Grissom*	350.00	160.00
41	Glenn Davis*	250.00	110.00
43	Kenny Lofton	400.00	180.00
47	Ivan Rodriguez*	800.00	350.00
52	Rafael Palmeiro	200.00	90.00
63	George Brett	700.00	325.00
70	Paul Molitor	500.00	220.00
71	Brady Anderson	250.00	110.00
73	Mark Grace	250.00	110.00
76	Chuck Knoblauch	350.00	160.00
77	Tony Gwynn	700.00	325.00
79	Sammy Sosa*	500.00	220.00
84	Andre Dawson AS*	200.00	90.00
85	Greg Maddux AS	1200.00	550.00
86	Rickey Henderson	250.00	110.00
87	Tom Glavine AS !	150.00	70.00
88	Roberto Alomar AS	500.00	220.00
90	Wade Boggs AS	250.00	110.00
92	Mark McGwire AS	700.00	325.00
96	Cal Ripken AS	2000.00	900.00
97	Larry Walker AS	350.00	160.00
98	Don Mattingly AS	400.00	180.00
99	Jose Canseco AS !	250.00	110.00
102	Frank Thomas AS	1200.00	550.00
103	Barry Bonds AS	700.00	325.00
104	Roger Clemens AS	600.00	275.00
105	Ryne Sandberg AS	300.00	135.00
106	Fred McGriff AS	200.00	90.00
107	Nolan Ryan AS	1500.00	700.00
108	Will Clark AS	250.00	110.00
110	Ken Griffey Jr. AS !	2000.00	900.00
112	Kirby Puckett AS	400.00	180.00
114	Barry Larkin AS	250.00	110.00
116	Juan Gonzalez AS	1500.00	700.00
119	Craig Biggio	150.00	70.00
122	Eddie Murray UER	400.00	180.00
	122 career strikeouts should be 1224		
124	Jay Buhner	250.00	110.00
125	Carlton Fisk	175.00	80.00
130	Andres Galarraga	250.00	110.00
131	Ken Caminiti	250.00	110.00
134	Kevin Brown*	200.00	90.00
135	Travis Fryman	150.00	70.00
141	Deion Sanders	200.00	90.00
154	Randy Johnson	500.00	220.00
156	J.T. Snow	150.00	70.00
157	Mike Mussina	400.00	180.00
159	Dean Palmer	150.00	70.00
162	Dave Winfield	150.00	70.00
163	Tim Salmon	400.00	180.00
165	Mo Vaughn	400.00	180.00
166	John Smoltz	200.00	90.00
187	Ray Lankford	150.00	70.00
189	Moises Alou*	200.00	90.00
190	Edgar Martinez	250.00	110.00
192	Robin Yount	200.00	90.00
193	Bob Tewksbury*	150.00	70.00
199	Mike Piazza	1200.00	550.00

1993 Finest Jumbos

These oversized (approximately 4" by 6") cards were inserted one per sealed box of 1993 Topps Finest packs and feature reproductions of 33 players from that set's All-Star subset (84-116). Some hobby dealers believe because of the known production numbers that slightly less than 1,500 of each of these cards were produced.

	MINT	NRMT
COMPLETE SET (33)	500.00	220.00
COMMON CARD (84-116)	5.00	2.20
SEMISTARS	8.00	3.60
SIMILAR STARS	12.00	5.50
ONE CARD PER SEALED BOX		

#	Player	MINT	NRMT
84	Andre Dawson	8.00	3.60
85	Greg Maddux	40.00	18.00
86	Rickey Henderson	8.00	3.60

□ 87 Tom Glavine	8.00	3.60
□ 88 Roberto Alomar	12.00	5.50
□ 89 Darryl Strawberry	6.00	2.70
□ 90 Wade Boggs	12.00	5.50
□ 91 Bo Jackson	6.00	2.70
□ 92 Mark McGwire	25.00	11.00
□ 93 Robin Ventura	6.00	2.70
□ 94 Joe Carter	6.00	2.70
□ 95 Lee Smith	6.00	2.70
□ 96 Cal Ripken	50.00	22.00
□ 97 Larry Walker	12.00	5.50
□ 98 Don Mattingly	20.00	9.00
□ 99 Jose Canseco	8.00	3.60
□ 100 Dennis Eckersley	6.00	2.70
□ 101 Terry Pendleton	6.00	2.70
□ 102 Frank Thomas	50.00	22.00
□ 103 Barry Bonds	15.00	6.75
□ 104 Roger Clemens	25.00	11.00
□ 105 Ryne Sandberg	15.00	6.75
□ 106 Fred McGriff	8.00	3.60
□ 107 Nolan Ryan	50.00	22.00
□ 108 Will Clark	8.00	3.60
□ 109 Pat Listach	5.00	2.20
□ 110 Ken Griffey Jr.	60.00	27.00
□ 111 Cecil Fielder	6.00	2.70
□ 112 Kirby Puckett	25.00	11.00
□ 113 Dwight Gooden	6.00	2.70
□ 114 Barry Larkin	8.00	3.60
□ 115 David Cone	6.00	2.70
□ 116 Juan Gonzalez	30.00	13.50

□ 59P Dante Bichette	6.00	2.70
□ 61P Orlando Merced	3.00	1.35
□ 62P Brian McRae	3.00	1.35
□ 66P Mike Mussina	20.00	9.00
□ 76P Mike Stanley	3.00	1.35
□ 78P Mark McGwire	40.00	18.00
□ 79P Pat Listach	3.00	1.35
□ 82P Dwight Gooden	6.00	2.70
□ 84P Phil Plantier	3.00	1.35
□ 90P Jeff Russell	3.00	1.35
□ 92P Gregg Jefferies	3.00	1.35
□ 93P Jose Guzman	3.00	1.35
□ 100P John Smoltz	6.00	2.70
□ 102P Jim Thome	25.00	11.00
□ 121P Moises Alou	6.00	2.70
□ 125P Devon White	3.00	1.35
□ 126P Ivan Rodriguez	25.00	11.00
□ 130P Dave Magadan	3.00	1.35
□ 136P Ozzie Smith	25.00	11.00
□ 141P Chris Hoiles	3.00	1.35
□ 149P Jim Abbott	3.00	1.35
□ 151P Bill Swift	3.00	1.35
□ 154P Edgar Martinez	12.00	5.50
□ 157P J.T. Snow	15.00	6.75
□ 159P Alan Trammell	12.00	5.50
□ 163P Roberto Kelly	3.00	1.35
□ 166P Scott Erickson	3.00	1.35
□ 168P Scott Cooper	3.00	1.35
□ 169P Paul Molitor	6.00	2.70
□ 177P Dean Palmer	3.00	1.35
□ 182P Todd Van Poppel	3.00	1.35
□ 185P Paul Sorrento	3.00	1.35

*REF.STARS: 5X TO 10X HI COLUMN		
*REF.ROOKIES: 2.5X TO 5X HI		
REFRACTOR STATED ODDS 1:9		
COMP JUMBO SET (80)	350.00	160.00
COMP JUMBO SER.1 (40)	200.00	90.00
COMP JUMBO SER.2 (40)	150.00	70.00
COMMON 1 (1-20/201-220)..	1.00	.45
COMMON 2 (221-240/421-440)	1.00	.45
*JUMBO STARS: 1.5X TO 3X HI COLUMN		
ONE JUMBO PER BOX		

1994 Finest Pre-Production

This 40-card preview standard-size set is identical in design to the basic Finest set. Cards were randomly inserted at a rate of one in 36 in second series Topps packs and three cards were issued with each Topps factory set. The card numbers on back correspond to those of the regular issue. The only way to distinguish between the preview and basic cards is "Pre-Production" in small red letters on back.

	MINT	NRMT
COMPLETE SET (40)	175.00	80.00
COMMON CARD	3.00	1.35
MINOR STARS	6.00	2.70
SEMISTARS	12.00	5.50

NUMBERS CORRESPOND TO BASIC SET
TOPPS SER.2 ODDS 1:36H/R, 1:15J, 1:28 CEL
THREE PER REGULAR TOPPS FACTORY SET

□ 22P Deion Sanders	6.00	2.70
□ 23P Jose Offerman	3.00	1.35
□ 26P Alex Fernandez	3.00	1.35
□ 31P Steve Finley	6.00	2.70
□ 35P Andres Galarraga	15.00	6.75
□ 43P Reggie Sanders	3.00	1.35
□ 47P Dave Hollins	3.00	1.35
□ 52P David Cone	6.00	2.70

1994 Finest

The 1994 Topps Finest baseball set consists of two series of 220 cards each, for a total of 440 standard-size cards. Each series includes 40 special design Finest cards: 20 top 1993 rookies (1-20), 20 top 1994 rookies (421-440) and 40 top veterans (201-240). These glossy and metallic cards have a color photo on front with green and gold borders. A color photo on back is accompanied by statistics and a "Finest Moment" note. Some series 2 packs contained either one or two series 1 cards. The only notable Rookie Card is Chan Ho Park.

	MINT	NRMT
COMPLETE SET (440)	180.00	80.00
COMPLETE SERIES 1 (220)	90.00	40.00
COMPLETE SERIES 2 (220)	90.00	40.00
COMMON CARD (1-440)	.50	.23
MINOR STARS	1.00	.45
SEMISTARS	1.50	.70
UNLISTED STARS	2.50	1.10
COMP.REF.SET (440)	2800.00	1250.00
COMP.REF.SER.1 (220)	1400.00	650.00
COMP.REF.SER.2 (220)	1400.00	650.00
COMMON REF. (1-440)	4.00	1.80

□ 1 Mike Piazza FIN	8.00	3.60
□ 2 Kevin Stocker FIN	.50	.23
□ 3 Greg McMichael FIN	.50	.23
□ 4 Jeff Conine FIN	1.00	.45
□ 5 Rene Arocha FIN	.50	.23
□ 6 Aaron Sele FIN	.50	.23
□ 7 Brent Gates FIN	.50	.23
□ 8 Chuck Carr FIN	.50	.23
□ 9 Kirk Rueter FIN	.50	.23
□ 10 Mike Lansing FIN	1.00	.45
□ 11 Al Martin FIN	.50	.23
□ 12 Jason Bere FIN	.50	.23
□ 13 Troy Neel FIN	.50	.23
□ 14 Armando Reynoso FIN	.50	.23
□ 15 Jeromy Burnitz FIN	.50	.23
□ 16 Rich Amaral FIN	.50	.23
□ 17 David McCarty FIN	.50	.23
□ 18 Tim Salmon FIN	2.50	1.10
□ 19 Steve Cooke FIN	.50	.23
□ 20 Wil Cordero FIN	.50	.23
□ 21 Kevin Tapani FIN	.50	.23
□ 22 Deion Sanders FIN	1.00	.45
□ 23 Jose Offerman FIN	.50	.23
□ 24 Mark Langston FIN	.50	.23
□ 25 Ken Hill FIN	.50	.23
□ 26 Alex Fernandez FIN	.50	.23
□ 27 Jeff Blauser FIN	1.00	.45
□ 28 Royce Clayton FIN	.50	.23
□ 29 Brad Ausmus FIN	.50	.23
□ 30 Ryan Bowen FIN	.50	.23
□ 31 Steve Finley FIN	1.00	.45
□ 32 Charlie Hayes FIN	.50	.23
□ 33 Jeff Kent FIN	.50	.23
□ 34 Mike Henneman FIN	.50	.23
□ 35 Andres Galarraga FIN	2.50	1.10
□ 36 Wayne Kirby FIN	.50	.23
□ 37 Joe Oliver FIN	.50	.23
□ 38 Terry Steinbach FIN	.50	.23
□ 39 Ryan Thompson FIN	.50	.23
□ 40 Luis Alicea FIN	.50	.23
□ 41 Randy Velarde FIN	.50	.23
□ 42 Bob Tewksbury FIN	.50	.23
□ 43 Reggie Sanders FIN	.50	.23
□ 44 Brian Williams FIN	.50	.23
□ 45 Joe Orsulak FIN	.50	.23
□ 46 Jose Lind FIN	.50	.23
□ 47 Dave Hollins FIN	.50	.23
□ 48 Graeme Lloyd FIN	.50	.23
□ 49 Jim Gott FIN	.50	.23
□ 50 Andre Dawson FIN	1.50	.70
□ 51 Steve Buechele FIN	.50	.23
□ 52 David Cone FIN	1.00	.45
□ 53 Ricky Gutierrez FIN	.50	.23
□ 54 Lance Johnson FIN	.50	.23
□ 55 Tino Martinez FIN	2.50	1.10
□ 56 Phil Hiatt FIN	.50	.23
□ 57 Carlos Garcia FIN	.50	.23
□ 58 Danny Darwin FIN	.50	.23
□ 59 Dante Bichette FIN	1.00	.45
□ 60 Scott Kamieniecki FIN	.50	.23
□ 61 Orlando Merced FIN	.50	.23
□ 62 Brian McRae FIN	.50	.23
□ 63 Pat Kelly FIN	.50	.23
□ 64 Tom Henke FIN	.50	.23
□ 65 Jeff King FIN	.50	.23
□ 66 Mike Mussina FIN	2.50	1.10
□ 67 Tim Pugh FIN	.50	.23
□ 68 Robby Thompson FIN	.50	.23
□ 69 Paul O'Neill FIN	1.00	.45
□ 70 Hal Morris FIN	.50	.23
□ 71 Ron Karkovice FIN	.50	.23
□ 72 Joe Girardi FIN	.50	.23
□ 73 Eduardo Perez FIN	.50	.23
□ 74 Raul Mondesi FIN	2.50	1.10
□ 75 Mike Gallego FIN	.50	.23

□ 76	Mike Stanley	.50	.23
□ 77	Kevin Roberson	.50	.23
□ 78	Mark McGwire	5.00	2.20
□ 79	Pat Listach	.50	.23
□ 80	Eric Davis	1.00	.45
□ 81	Mike Bordick	.50	.23
□ 82	Doc Gooden	1.00	.45
□ 83	Mike Moore	.50	.23
□ 84	Phil Plantier	.50	.23
□ 85	Darren Lewis	.50	.23
□ 86	Rick Wilkins	.50	.23
□ 87	Darryl Strawberry	1.00	.45
□ 88	Rob Dibble	.50	.23
□ 89	Greg Vaughn	.50	.23
□ 90	Jeff Russell	.50	.23
□ 91	Mark Lewis	.50	.23
□ 92	Gregg Jefferies	.50	.23
□ 93	Jose Guzman	.50	.23
□ 94	Kenny Rogers	.50	.23
□ 95	Mark Lemke	.50	.23
□ 96	Mike Morgan	.50	.23
□ 97	Andujar Cedeno	.50	.23
□ 98	Orel Hershiser	1.00	.45
□ 99	Greg Swindell	.50	.23
□ 100	John Smoltz	1.00	.45
□ 101	Pedro Martinez	2.50	1.10
□ 102	Jim Thome	3.00	1.35
□ 103	David Segui	.50	.23
□ 104	Charles Nagy	1.00	.45
□ 105	Shane Mack	.50	.23
□ 106	John Jaha	.50	.23
□ 107	Tom Candiotti	.50	.23
□ 108	David Wells	.50	.23
□ 109	Bobby Jones	1.00	.45
□ 110	Bob Hamelin	.50	.23
□ 111	Bernard Gilkey	.50	.23
□ 112	Chili Davis	1.00	.45
□ 113	Todd Stottlemyre	.50	.23
□ 114	Derek Bell	.50	.23
□ 115	Mark McLemore	.50	.23
□ 116	Mark Whiten	.50	.23
□ 117	Mike Devereaux	.50	.23
□ 118	Terry Pendleton	.50	.23
□ 119	Pat Meares	.50	.23
□ 120	Pete Harnisch	.50	.23
□ 121	Moises Alou	1.00	.45
□ 122	Jay Buhner	1.50	.70
□ 123	Wes Chamberlain	.50	.23
□ 124	Mike Perez	.50	.23
□ 125	Devon White	.50	.23
□ 126	Ivan Rodriguez	3.00	1.35
□ 127	Don Slaught	.50	.23
□ 128	John Valentin	1.00	.45
□ 129	Jaime Navarro	.50	.23
□ 130	Dave Magadan	.50	.23
□ 131	Brady Anderson	1.50	.70
□ 132	Juan Guzman	.50	.23
□ 133	John Wetteland	.50	.23
□ 134	Dave Stewart	1.00	.45
□ 135	Scott Servais	.50	.23
□ 136	Ozzie Smith	3.00	1.35
□ 137	Darrin Fletcher	.50	.23
□ 138	Jose Mesa	.50	.23
□ 139	Wilson Alvarez	.50	.23
□ 140	Pete Incaviglia	.50	.23
□ 141	Chris Hoiles	.50	.23
□ 142	Darryl Hamilton	.50	.23
□ 143	Chuck Finley	.50	.23
□ 144	Archi Cianfrocco	.50	.23
□ 145	Bill Wegman	.50	.23
□ 146	Joey Cora	1.00	.45
□ 147	Darrell Whitmore	.50	.23
□ 148	David Hulse	.50	.23
□ 149	Jim Abbott	1.00	.45
□ 150	Curt Schilling	1.00	.45
□ 151	Bill Swift	.50	.23
□ 152	Tommy Greene	.50	.23
□ 153	Roberto Mejia	.50	.23
□ 154	Edgar Martinez	1.50	.70
□ 155	Roger Pavlik	.50	.23
□ 156	Randy Tomlin	.50	.23
□ 157	J.T. Snow	2.50	1.10
□ 158	Bob Welch	.50	.23
□ 159	Alan Trammell	1.50	.70
□ 160	Ed Sprague	.50	.23
□ 161	Ben McDonald	.50	.23
□ 162	Derrick May	.50	.23
□ 163	Roberto Kelly	.50	.23
□ 164	Bryan Harvey	.50	.23
□ 165	Ron Gant	1.00	.45
□ 166	Scott Erickson	.50	.23
□ 167	Anthony Young	.50	.23
□ 168	Scott Cooper	.50	.23
□ 169	Rod Beck	.50	.23
□ 170	John Franco	1.00	.45
□ 171	Gary DiSarcina	.50	.23
□ 172	Dave Fleming	.50	.23
□ 173	Wade Boggs	2.50	1.10
□ 174	Kevin Appier	1.00	.45
□ 175	Jose Bautista	.50	.23
□ 176	Wally Joyner	1.00	.45
□ 177	Dean Palmer	.50	.23
□ 178	Tony Phillips	.50	.23
□ 179	John Smiley	.50	.23
□ 180	Charlie Hough	.50	.23
□ 181	Scott Fletcher	.50	.23
□ 182	Todd Van Poppel	.50	.23
□ 183	Mike Blowers	.50	.23
□ 184	Willie McGee	.50	.23
□ 185	Paul Sorrento	.50	.23
□ 186	Eric Young	.50	.23
□ 187	Bret Barberie	.50	.23
□ 188	Manuel Lee	.50	.23
□ 189	Jeff Branson	.50	.23
□ 190	Jim Deshaies	.50	.23
□ 191	Ken Caminiti	1.50	.70
□ 192	Tim Raines	1.00	.45
□ 193	Joe Grahe	.50	.23
□ 194	Hipolito Pichardo	.50	.23
□ 195	Denny Neagle	1.00	.45
□ 196	Jeff Gardner	.50	.23
□ 197	Mike Benjamin	.50	.23
□ 198	Milt Thompson	.50	.23
□ 199	Bruce Ruffin	.50	.23
□ 200	Chris Hammond UER	.50	.23
	(Back of card has Mariners; should be Marlins)		
□ 201	Tony Gwynn FIN	6.00	2.70
□ 202	Robin Ventura FIN	1.00	.45
□ 203	Frank Thomas FIN	10.00	4.50
□ 204	Kirby Puckett FIN	5.00	2.20
□ 205	Roberto Alomar FIN	2.50	1.10
□ 206	Dennis Eckersley FIN	1.00	.45
□ 207	Joe Carter FIN	1.00	.45
□ 208	Albert Belle FIN	3.00	1.35
□ 209	Greg Maddux FIN	8.00	3.60
□ 210	Ryne Sandberg FIN	3.00	1.35
□ 211	Juan Gonzalez FIN	6.00	2.70
□ 212	Jeff Bagwell FIN	5.00	2.20
□ 213	Randy Johnson FIN	2.50	1.10
□ 214	Matt Williams FIN	1.50	.70
□ 215	Dave Winfield FIN	1.50	.70
□ 216	Larry Walker FIN	2.50	1.10
□ 217	Roger Clemens FIN	5.00	2.20
□ 218	Kenny Lofton FIN	3.00	1.35
□ 219	Cecil Fielder FIN	1.00	.45
□ 220	Darren Daulton FIN	1.00	.45
□ 221	John Olerud FIN	1.00	.45
□ 222	Jose Canseco FIN	1.50	.70
□ 223	Rickey Henderson FIN	1.50	.70
□ 224	Fred McGriff FIN	1.50	.70
□ 225	Gary Sheffield FIN	2.50	1.10
□ 226	Jack McDowell FIN	.50	.23
□ 227	Rafael Palmeiro FIN	1.50	.70
□ 228	Travis Fryman FIN	1.00	.45
□ 229	Marquis Grissom FIN	1.00	.45
□ 230	Barry Bonds FIN	3.00	1.35
□ 231	Carlos Baerga FIN	.50	.23
□ 232	Ken Griffey Jr. FIN	12.00	5.50
□ 233	David Justice FIN	2.50	1.10
□ 234	Bobby Bonilla FIN	1.00	.45
□ 235	Cal Ripken FIN	10.00	4.50
□ 236	Sammy Sosa FIN	2.50	1.10
□ 237	Len Dykstra FIN	1.00	.45
□ 238	Will Clark FIN	1.50	.70
□ 239	Paul Molitor FIN	2.50	1.10
□ 240	Barry Larkin FIN	1.50	.70
□ 241	Bo Jackson FIN	1.00	.45
□ 242	Mitch Williams	.50	.23
□ 243	Ron Darling	.50	.23
□ 244	Darryl Kile	1.00	.45
□ 245	Geronimo Berroa	.50	.23
□ 246	Gregg Olson	.50	.23
□ 247	Brian Harper	.50	.23
□ 248	Rheal Cormier	.50	.23
□ 249	Rey Sanchez	.50	.23
□ 250	Jeff Fassero	.50	.23
□ 251	Sandy Alomar	1.00	.45
□ 252	Chris Bosio	.50	.23
□ 253	Andy Stankiewicz	.50	.23
□ 254	Harold Baines	1.00	.45
□ 255	Andy Ashby	.50	.23
□ 256	Tyler Green	.50	.23
□ 257	Kevin Brown	1.00	.45
□ 258	Mo Vaughn	3.00	1.35
□ 259	Mike Harkey	.50	.23
□ 260	Dave Henderson	.50	.23
□ 261	Kent Hrbek	1.00	.45
□ 262	Darrin Jackson	.50	.23
□ 263	Bob Wickman	.50	.23
□ 264	Spike Owen	.50	.23
□ 265	Todd Jones	.50	.23
□ 266	Pat Borders	.50	.23
□ 267	Tom Glavine	1.00	.45
□ 268	Dave Nilsson	.50	.23
□ 269	Rich Batchelor	.50	.23
□ 270	Delino DeShields	.50	.23
□ 271	Felix Fermin	.50	.23
□ 272	Orestes Destrade	.50	.23
□ 273	Mickey Morandini	.50	.23
□ 274	Otis Nixon	.50	.23
□ 275	Ellis Burks	1.00	.45
□ 276	Greg Gagne	.50	.23
□ 277	John Doherty	.50	.23
□ 278	Julio Franco	.50	.23
□ 279	Bernie Williams	2.50	1.10
□ 280	Rick Aguilera	.50	.23
□ 281	Mickey Tettleton	.50	.23
□ 282	David Nied	.50	.23
□ 283	Johnny Ruffin	.50	.23
□ 284	Dan Wilson	1.00	.45
□ 285	Omar Vizquel	1.00	.45
□ 286	Willie Banks	.50	.23
□ 287	Erik Pappas	.50	.23
□ 288	Cal Eldred	.50	.23
□ 289	Bobby Witt	.50	.23
□ 290	Luis Gonzalez	.50	.23
□ 291	Greg Perki	.50	.23
□ 292	Alex Cole	.50	.23
□ 293	Ricky Bones	.50	.23
□ 294	Denis Boucher	.50	.23
□ 295	John Burkett	.50	.23
□ 296	Steve Trachsel	1.00	.45
□ 297	Ricky Jordan	.50	.23
□ 298	Mark Dewey	.50	.23
□ 299	Jimmy Key	1.00	.45
□ 300	Mike Macfarlane	.50	.23
□ 301	Tim Belcher	.50	.23
□ 302	Carlos Reyes	.50	.23
□ 303	Greg A. Harris	.50	.23
□ 304	Brian Anderson	2.50	1.10
□ 305	Terry Mulholland	.50	.23
□ 306	Felix Jose	.50	.23
□ 307	Darren Holmes	.50	.23
□ 308	Jose Rijo	.50	.23
□ 309	Paul Wagner	.50	.23
□ 310	Bob Scanlan	.50	.23
□ 311	Mike Jackson	.50	.23
□ 312	Jose Vizcaino	.50	.23
□ 313	Rob Butler	.50	.23
□ 314	Kevin Seitzer	.50	.23
□ 315	Geronimo Pena	.50	.23
□ 316	Hector Carrasco	.50	.23
□ 317	Eddie Murray	2.50	1.10
□ 318	Roger Salkeld	.50	.23
□ 319	Todd Hundley	1.00	.45
□ 320	Danny Jackson	.50	.23
□ 321	Kevin Young	.50	.23
□ 322	Mike Greenwell	.50	.23
□ 323	Kevin Mitchell	.50	.23
□ 324	Chuck Knoblauch	2.50	1.10
□ 325	Danny Tartabull	.50	.23
□ 326	Vince Coleman	.50	.23
□ 327	Marvin Freeman	.50	.23
□ 328	Andy Benes	1.00	.45
□ 329	Mike Kelly	.50	.23
□ 330	Karl Rhodes	.50	.23
□ 331	Allen Watson	.50	.23

332 Damion Easley	.50	.23	418 Chris Sabo	.50	.23	6 William VanLandingham	.40	.18
333 Reggie Jefferson	.50	.23	419 Bret Saberhagen	.50	.23	7 Jon Lieber	.40	.18
334 Kevin McReynolds	.50	.23	420 Chris Nabholz	.50	.23	8 Ryan Klesko	1.25	.55
335 Arthur Rhodes	.50	.23	421 James Mouton FIN	.50	.23	9 John Hudek	.40	.18
336 Brian R. Hunter	.50	.23	422 Tony Tarasco FIN	.50	.23	10 Joey Hamilton	.75	.35
337 Tom Browning	.50	.23	423 Carlos Delgado FIN	1.50	.70	11 Bob Hamelin	.40	.18
338 Pedro Munoz	.50	.23	424 Rondell White FIN	1.00	.45	12 Brian Anderson	.75	.35
339 Billy Ripken	.50	.23	425 Javier Lopez FIN	1.50	.70	13 Mike Lieberthal	.40	.18
340 Gene Harris	.50	.23	426 Chan Ho Park FIN	10.00	4.50	14 Rico Brogna	.40	.18
341 Fernando Vina	.50	.23	427 Cliff Floyd FIN	1.00	.45	15 Rusty Greer	2.00	.90
342 Sean Berry	.50	.23	428 Dave Staton FIN	.50	.23	16 Carlos Delgado	.75	.35
343 Pedro Astacio	.50	.23	429 J.R. Phillips FIN	.50	.23	17 Jim Edmonds	1.25	.55
344 B.J. Surhoff	.50	.23	430 Manny Ramirez FIN	3.00	1.35	18 Steve Trachsel	.40	.18
345 Doug Drabek	.50	.23	431 Kurt Abbott FIN	.50	.23	19 Matt Walbeck	.40	.18
346 Jody Reed	.50	.23	432 Melvin Nieves FIN	.50	.23	20 Armando Benitez	.40	.18
347 Ray Lankford	1.00	.45	433 Alex Gonzalez FIN	1.00	.45	21 Steve Karsay	.40	.18
348 Steve Farr	.50	.23	434 Rick Helling FIN	.50	.23	22 Jose Oliva	.40	.18
349 Eric Anthony	.50	.23	435 Danny Bautista FIN	.50	.23	23 Cliff Floyd	.40	.18
350 Pete Smith	.50	.23	436 Matt Walbeck FIN	.50	.23	24 Kevin Foster	.40	.18
351 Lee Smith	1.00	.45	437 Ryan Klesko FIN	2.50	1.10	25 Javier Lopez	.75	.35
352 Mariano Duncan	.50	.23	438 Steve Karsay FIN	.50	.23	26 Jose Valentin	.40	.18
353 Doug Strange	.50	.23	439 Salomon Torres FIN	.50	.23	27 James Mouton	.40	.18
354 Tim Bogar	.50	.23	440 Scott Ruffcorn FIN	.50	.23	28 Hector Carrasco	.40	.18
355 Dave Weathers	.50	.23				29 Orlando Miller	.40	.18
356 Eric Karros	1.00	.45				30 Garret Anderson	1.25	.55
357 Randy Myers	.50	.23				31 Marvin Freeman	.40	.18
358 Chad Curtis	.50	.23				32 Brett Butler	.75	.35
359 Steve Avery	.50	.23				33 Roberto Kelly	.40	.18
360 Brian Jordan	1.00	.45				34 Rod Beck	.40	.18
361 Tim Wallach	.50	.23				35 Jose Rijo	.40	.18
362 Pedro Martinez	2.50	1.10				36 Edgar Martinez	1.25	.55
363 Bip Roberts	.50	.23				37 Jim Thome	2.00	.90
364 Lou Whitaker	1.00	.45				38 Rick Wilkins	.40	.18
365 Luis Polonia	.50	.23				39 Wally Joyner	.75	.35
366 Benny Santiago	.50	.23				40 Wil Cordero	.40	.18
367 Brett Butler	1.00	.45				41 Tommy Greene	.40	.18
368 Shawon Dunston	.50	.23				42 Travis Fryman	.75	.35
369 Kelly Stinnett	.50	.23				43 Don Slaught	.40	.18
370 Chris Turner	.50	.23				44 Brady Anderson	1.25	.55
371 Ruben Sierra	.50	.23				45 Matt Williams	1.25	.55
372 Greg A. Harris	.50	.23				46 Rene Arocha	.40	.18
373 Xavier Hernandez	.50	.23				47 Rickey Henderson	1.25	.55
374 Howard Johnson	.50	.23				48 Mike Mussina	2.00	.90
375 Duane Ward	.50	.23				49 Greg McMichael	.40	.18
376 Roberto Hernandez	.50	.23				50 Jody Reed	.40	.18
377 Scott Leius	.50	.23				51 Tino Martinez	2.00	.90
378 Dave Valle	.50	.23				52 Dave Clark	.40	.18
379 Sid Fernandez	.50	.23				53 John Valentin	.40	.18
380 Doug Jones	.50	.23				54 Bret Boone	.40	.18
381 Zane Smith	.50	.23				55 Walt Weiss	.40	.18
382 Craig Biggio	1.50	.70				56 Kenny Lofton	2.50	1.10
383 Rick White	.50	.23				57 Scott Leius	.40	.18
384 Tom Pagnozzi	.50	.23				58 Eric Karros	.75	.35
385 Chris James	.50	.23				59 John Olerud	.75	.35
386 Bret Boone	.50	.23				60 Chris Hoiles	.40	.18
387 Jeff Montgomery	.50	.23				61 Sandy Alomar Jr	.75	.35
388 Chad Kreuter	.50	.23				62 Tim Wallach	.40	.18
389 Greg Hibbard	.50	.23				63 Cal Eldred	.40	.18
390 Mark Grace	1.50	.70				64 Tom Glavine	.75	.35
391 Phil Leftwich	.50	.23				65 Mark Grace	1.25	.55
392 Don Mattingly	4.00	1.80				66 Rey Sanchez	.40	.18
393 Ozzie Guillen	.50	.23				67 Bobby Ayala	.40	.18
394 Gary Gaetti	.50	.23				68 Dante Bichette	.75	.35
395 Erik Hanson	.50	.23				69 Andres Galarraga	2.00	.90
396 Scott Brosius	.50	.23				70 Chuck Carr	.40	.18
397 Tom Gordon	.50	.23				71 Bobby Witt	.40	.18
398 Bill Gullickson	.50	.23				72 Steve Avery	.40	.18
399 Matt Mieske	.50	.23				73 Bobby Jones	.40	.18
400 Pat Hentgen	1.00	.45				74 Delino DeShields	.40	.18
401 Walt Weiss	.50	.23				75 Kevin Tapani	.40	.18
402 Greg Blosser	.50	.23				76 Randy Johnson	2.00	.90
403 Stan Javier	.50	.23				77 David Nied	.40	.18
404 Doug Henry	.50	.23				78 Pat Hentgen	.75	.35
405 Ramon Martinez	1.00	.45				79 Tim Salmon	2.00	.90
406 Frank Viola	.50	.23				80 Todd Zeile	.40	.18
407 Mike Hampton	1.00	.45				81 John Wetteland	.40	.18
408 Andy Van Slyke	1.00	.45				82 Albert Belle	2.50	1.10
409 Bobby Ayala	.50	.23				83 Ben McDonald	.40	.18
410 Todd Zeile	.50	.23				84 Bobby Munoz	.40	.18
411 Jay Bell	1.00	.45				85 Bip Roberts	.40	.18
412 Denny Martinez	1.00	.45				86 Mo Vaughn	2.50	1.10
413 Mark Portugal	.50	.23				87 Chuck Finley	.40	.18
414 Bobby Munoz	.50	.23				88 Chuck Knoblauch	2.00	.90
415 Kirt Manwaring	.50	.23				89 Frank Thomas	8.00	3.60
416 John Kruk	1.00	.45				90 Danny Tartabull	.40	.18
417 Trevor Hoffman	.50	.23				91 Dean Palmer	.40	.18

1995 Finest

Consisting of 330 standard-size cards, this set was issued in series of 220 and 110. A protective film, designed to keep the card from scratching and to maintain original gloss, covers the front. With the Finest logo at the top, a silver baseball diamond design surrounded by green (field) form the background to an action photo. Horizontally designed backs have a photo to the right with statistical information to the left. A Finest Moment, or career highlight, is also included. Rookie Cards in this set include Bobby Higginson and Hideo Nomo.

	MINT	NRMT
COMPLETE SET (330)	120.00	55.00
COMPLETE SERIES 1 (220)	80.00	36.00
COMPLETE SERIES 2 (110)	40.00	18.00
COMMON CARD (1-330)	.40	.18
MINOR STARS	.75	.35
SEMISTARS	1.25	.55
UNLISTED STARS	2.00	.90
COMP.REF.SET (330)	4500.00	2000.00
COMP.REF.SER.1 (220)	3500.00	1600.00
COMP.REF.SER.2 (110)	1000.00	450.00
COMMON REF. (1-330)	10.00	4.50

*REF.STARS: 10X TO 25X HI COLUMN
*REF.ROOKIES: 5X TO 12X HI.
REFRACTOR STATED ODDS 1:12

1 Raul Mondesi	1.25	.55
2 Kurt Abbott	.40	.18
3 Chris Gomez	.40	.18
4 Manny Ramirez	2.00	.90
5 Rondell White	.75	.35

92	Len Dykstra	.75	.35
93	J.R. Phillips	.40	.18
94	Tom Candiotti	.40	.18
95	Marquis Grissom	.75	.35
96	Barry Larkin	1.25	.55
97	Bryan Harvey	.40	.18
98	David Justice	2.00	.90
99	David Cone	.75	.35
100	Wade Boggs	2.00	.90
101	Jason Bere	.40	.18
102	Hal Morris	.40	.18
103	Fred McGriff	1.25	.55
104	Bobby Bonilla	.75	.35
105	Jay Buhner	1.25	.55
106	Allen Watson	.40	.18
107	Mickey Tettleton	.40	.18
108	Kevin Appier	.75	.35
109	Ivan Rodriguez	2.50	1.10
110	Carlos Garcia	.40	.18
111	Andy Benes	.75	.35
112	Eddie Murray	2.00	.90
113	Mike Piazza	6.00	2.70
114	Greg Vaughn	.40	.18
115	Paul Molitor	2.00	.90
116	Terry Steinbach	.40	.18
117	Jeff Bagwell	4.00	1.80
118	Ken Griffey Jr.	10.00	4.50
119	Gary Sheffield	2.00	.90
120	Cal Ripken	8.00	3.60
121	Jeff Kent	.40	.18
122	Jay Bell	.75	.35
123	Will Clark	1.25	.55
124	Cecil Fielder	.75	.35
125	Alex Fernandez	.40	.18
126	Don Mattingly	3.00	1.35
127	Reggie Sanders	.40	.18
128	Moises Alou	.75	.35
129	Craig Biggio	1.25	.55
130	Eddie Williams	.40	.18
131	John Franco	.75	.35
132	John Kruk	.75	.35
133	Jeff King	.40	.18
134	Royce Clayton	.40	.18
135	Doug Drabek	.40	.18
136	Ray Lankford	.75	.35
137	Roberto Alomar	2.00	.90
138	Todd Hundley	.75	.35
139	Alex Cole	.40	.18
140	Shawon Dunston	.40	.18
141	John Roper	.40	.18
142	Mark Langston	.40	.18
143	Tom Pagnozzi	.40	.18
144	Wilson Alvarez	.40	.18
145	Scott Cooper	.40	.18
146	Kevin Mitchell	.40	.18
147	Mark Whiten	.40	.18
148	Jeff Conine	.75	.35
149	Chili Davis	.75	.35
150	Luis Gonzalez	.40	.18
151	Juan Guzman	.40	.18
152	Mike Greenwell	.40	.18
153	Mike Henneman	.40	.18
154	Rick Aguilera	.40	.18
155	Dennis Eckersley	.75	.35
156	Darrin Fletcher	.40	.18
157	Darren Lewis	.40	.18
158	Juan Gonzalez	5.00	2.20
159	Dave Hollins	.40	.18
160	Jimmy Key	.75	.35
161	Roberto Hernandez	.40	.18
162	Randy Myers	.40	.18
163	Joe Carter	.75	.35
164	Darren Daulton	.40	.18
165	Mike Macfarlane	.40	.18
166	Bret Saberhagen	.40	.18
167	Kirby Puckett	4.00	1.80
168	Lance Johnson	.40	.18
169	Mark McGwire	4.00	1.80
170	Jose Canseco	1.25	.55
171	Mike Stanley	.40	.18
172	Lee Smith	.75	.35
173	Robin Ventura	.75	.35
174	Greg Gagne	.40	.18
175	Brian McRae	.40	.18
176	Mike Bordick	.40	.18
177	Rafael Palmeiro	1.25	.55
178	Kenny Rogers	.40	.18
179	Chad Curtis	.40	.18
180	Devon White	.40	.18
181	Paul O'Neill	.75	.35
182	Ken Caminiti	1.25	.55
183	Dave Nilsson	.40	.18
184	Tim Naehring	.40	.18
185	Roger Clemens	4.00	1.80
186	Otis Nixon	.40	.18
187	Tim Raines	.75	.35
188	Denny Martinez	.75	.35
189	Pedro Martinez	2.00	.90
190	Jim Abbott	.40	.18
191	Ryan Thompson	.40	.18
192	Barry Bonds	2.50	1.10
193	Joe Girardi	.40	.18
194	Steve Finley	.75	.35
195	John Jaha	.40	.18
196	Tony Gwynn	5.00	2.20
197	Sammy Sosa	2.00	.90
198	John Burkett	.40	.18
199	Carlos Baerga	.75	.35
200	Ramon Martinez	.75	.35
201	Aaron Sele	.40	.18
202	Eduardo Perez	.40	.18
203	Alan Trammell	1.25	.55
204	Orlando Merced	.40	.18
205	Deion Sanders	.75	.35
206	Robb Nen	.40	.18
207	Jack McDowell	.40	.18
208	Ruben Sierra	.40	.18
209	Bernie Williams	2.00	.90
210	Kevin Seitzer	.40	.18
211	Charles Nagy	.75	.35
212	Tony Phillips	.40	.18
213	Greg Maddux	6.00	2.70
214	Jeff Montgomery	.40	.18
215	Larry Walker	2.00	.90
216	Andy Van Slyke	.75	.35
217	Ozzie Smith	2.50	1.10
218	Geronimo Pena	.40	.18
219	Gregg Jefferies	.40	.18
220	Lou Whitaker	.75	.35
221	Chipper Jones	6.00	2.70
222	Benji Gil	.40	.18
223	Tony Phillips	.40	.18
224	Trevor Wilson	.40	.18
225	Tony Tarasco	.40	.18
226	Roberto Petagine	.40	.18
227	Mike Macfarlane	.40	.18
228	Hideo Nomo UER	15.00	6.75
	(In 3rd line agianst)		
229	Mark McLemore	.40	.18
230	Ron Gant	.75	.35
231	Andujar Cedeno	.40	.18
232	Mike Kingery	.40	.18
233	Jim Abbott	.40	.18
234	Ricky Bones	.40	.18
235	Marty Cordova	.75	.35
236	Mark Johnson	.40	.18
237	Marquis Grissom	.75	.35
238	Tom Henke	.40	.18
239	Terry Pendleton	.40	.18
240	John Wetteland	.40	.18
241	Lee Smith	.75	.35
242	Jaime Navarro	.40	.18
243	Luis Alicea	.40	.18
244	Scott Cooper	.40	.18
245	Gary Gaetti	.40	.18
246	Edgardo Alfonzo UER	2.00	.90
	(Incomplete career BA)		
247	Brad Clontz	.40	.18
248	Dave Mlicki	.40	.18
249	Dave Winfield	1.25	.55
250	Mark Grudzielanek	2.50	1.10
251	Alex Gonzalez	.40	.18
252	Kevin Brown	.75	.35
253	Esteban Loaiza	.40	.18
254	Vaughn Eshelman	.40	.18
255	Bill Swift	.40	.18
256	Brian McRae	.40	.18
257	Bobby Higginson	5.00	2.20
258	Jack McDowell	.40	.18
259	Scott Stahoviak	.40	.18
260	Jon Nunnally	.40	.18
261	Charlie Hayes	.40	.18
262	Jacob Brumfield	.40	.18
263	Chad Curtis	.40	.18
264	Heathcliff Slocumb	.40	.18
265	Mark Whiten	.40	.18
266	Mickey Tettleton	.40	.18
267	Jose Mesa	.40	.18
268	Doug Jones	.40	.18
269	Trevor Hoffman	.40	.18
270	Paul Sorrento	.40	.18
271	Shane Andrews	.40	.18
272	Brett Butler	.75	.35
273	Curtis Goodwin	.40	.18
274	Larry Walker	2.00	.90
275	Phil Plantier	.40	.18
276	Ken Hill	.40	.18
277	Vinny Castilla UER	.75	.35
	Rockies spelled Rockie		
278	Billy Ashley	.40	.18
279	Derek Jeter	6.00	2.70
280	Bob Tewksbury	.40	.18
281	Jose Offerman	.40	.18
282	Glenallen Hill	.40	.18
283	Tony Fernandez	.40	.18
284	Mike Devereaux	.40	.18
285	John Burkett	.40	.18
286	Geronimo Berroa	.40	.18
287	Quilvio Veras	.40	.18
288	Jason Bates	.40	.18
289	Lee Tinsley	.40	.18
290	Derek Bell	.40	.18
291	Jeff Fassero	.40	.18
292	Ray Durham	.75	.35
293	Chad Ogea	.40	.18
294	Bill Pulsipher	.40	.18
295	Phil Nevin	.40	.18
296	Carlos Perez	.75	.35
297	Roberto Kelly	.40	.18
298	Tim Wakefield	.40	.18
299	Jeff Manto	.40	.18
300	Brian Hunter	1.25	.55
301	C.J. Nitkowski	.40	.18
302	Dustin Hermanson	.75	.35
303	John Mabry	.75	.35
304	Orel Hershiser	.75	.35
305	Ron Villone	.40	.18
306	Sean Bergman	.40	.18
307	Tom Goodwin	.40	.18
308	Al Reyes	.40	.18
309	Todd Stottlemyre	.40	.18
310	Rich Becker	.40	.18
311	Joey Cora	.75	.35
312	Ed Sprague	.40	.18
313	John Smoltz UER	.75	.35
	(3rd line; then spelled as form)		
314	Frank Castillo	.40	.18
315	Chris Hammond	.40	.18
316	Ismael Valdes	1.25	.55
317	Pete Harnisch	.40	.18
318	Bernard Gilkey	.40	.18
319	John Kruk	.75	.35
320	Marc Newfield	.40	.18
321	Brian Johnson	.40	.18
322	Mark Portugal	.40	.18
323	David Hulse	.40	.18
324	Luis Ortiz UER	.40	.18
	(Below spelled beloe)		
325	Mike Benjamin	.40	.18
326	Brian Jordan	.75	.35
327	Shawn Green	.75	.35
328	Joe Oliver	.40	.18
329	Felipe Lira	.40	.18
330	Andre Dawson	1.25	.55

1995 Finest Flame Throwers

Randomly inserted in first series packs at a rate of 1:48, this nine-card set showcases strike-out leaders who bring on the heat. With a protective coating, a player photo is superimposed over a fiery orange background. The backs have a player photo

with skills ratings such as velocity.

	MINT	NRMT
COMPLETE SET (9)	40.00	18.00
COMMON CARD (FT1-FT9)	3.00	1.35
SER.1 STATED ODDS 1:48		

		MINT	NRMT
☐ FT1	Jason Bere	3.00	1.35
☐ FT2	Roger Clemens	25.00	11.00
☐ FT3	Juan Guzman	3.00	1.35
☐ FT4	John Hudek	3.00	1.35
☐ FT5	Randy Johnson	12.00	5.50
☐ FT6	Pedro Martinez	8.00	3.60
☐ FT7	Jose Rijo	3.00	1.35
☐ FT8	Bret Saberhagen	3.00	1.35
☐ FT9	John Wetteland	3.00	1.35

1995 Finest Power Kings

Randomly inserted in series one packs at a rate of one in 24, Power Kings is an 18-card set highlighting top sluggers. With a protective coating, the fronts feature chromium technology that allows the player photo to be further enhanced as if to jump out from a blue lightning bolt background. The horizontal backs contain two small photos and power production figures.

	MINT	NRMT
COMPLETE SET (18)	200.00	90.00
COMMON CARD (PK1-PK18)	4.00	1.80
SEMISTARS	6.00	2.70
SER.1 STATED ODDS 1:24		

		MINT	NRMT
☐ PK1	Bob Hamelin	4.00	1.80
☐ PK2	Raul Mondesi	6.00	2.70
☐ PK3	Ryan Klesko	6.00	2.70
☐ PK4	Carlos Delgado	5.00	2.20
☐ PK5	Manny Ramirez	10.00	4.50
☐ PK6	Mike Piazza	30.00	13.50
☐ PK7	Jeff Bagwell	20.00	9.00
☐ PK8	Mo Vaughn	12.00	5.50
☐ PK9	Frank Thomas	40.00	18.00
☐ PK10	Ken Griffey Jr.	50.00	22.00
☐ PK11	Albert Belle	12.00	5.50
☐ PK12	Sammy Sosa	10.00	4.50
☐ PK13	Dante Bichette	5.00	2.20
☐ PK14	Gary Sheffield	10.00	4.50
☐ PK15	Matt Williams	6.00	2.70
☐ PK16	Fred McGriff	6.00	2.70
☐ PK17	Barry Bonds	12.00	5.50
☐ PK18	Cecil Fielder	5.00	2.20

1996 Finest

The 1996 Finest set was issued in two series of 191 cards and 168 cards respectively, for a total of 359 cards. The six-card foil packs originally retailed for $5.00 each. A protective film, designed to keep the card from scratching and to maintain original gloss, covers the front. This product provides collectors with the opportunity to complete a number of sets within sets, each with a different degree of insertion. Each card is numbered twice to indicate the set count and the theme count. Series 1 set covers four distinct themes: Finest Phenoms, Finest Intimidators, Finest Gamers and Finest Sterling. Within the first three themes, some players will be common (bronze trim), some uncommon (silver) and some rare (gold). Finest Sterling consists of star players included within one of the other three themes, but featured with a new design and different photography. The breakdown for the player selection of common, uncommon and rare cards is completely random. There are 110 common, 55 uncommon (1:4 packs) and 25 rare cards (1:24 packs). Series 2 covers four distict themes also with common, uncommon and rare cards seeded at the same ratio. The four themes are: Finest Franchises which features 36 team leaders and bonafide superstars, Finest Additions which features 47 players who have switched teams in '96, Finest Prodigies which features 45 best up-and-coming players, and Finest Sterling with 39 top stars. In addition to the cards' special borders, each card will also have either "common," "uncommon," or "rare" written within the numbering box on the card backs to let collectors know what type of card they hold.

	MINT	NRMT
COMPLETE SET (359)	1150.00	525.00
COMPLETE SERIES 1 (191)	750.00	350.00
COMPLETE SERIES 2 (168)	400.00	180.00
COMP.BRONZE SET (220)	50.00	22.00
COMP.BRONZE SER.1 (110)	25.00	11.00
COMP.BRONZE SER.2 (110)	30.00	13.50
COMMON BRONZE	.25	.11
BRONZE MINOR STARS	.50	.23
BRONZE UNLISTED STARS	1.00	.45
COMP.GOLD SET (48)	900.00	400.00
COMP.GOLD SER.1 (26)	600.00	275.00
COMP.GOLD SER.2 (22)	300.00	135.00
COMMON GOLD	8.00	3.60
GOLD SEMISTARS	10.00	4.50
GOLD UNLISTED STARS	15.00	6.75
GOLD STATED ODDS 1:24		
COMP.SILVER SET (91)	230.00	105.00
COMP.SILVER SER.1 (55)	150.00	70.00
COMP.SILVER SER.2 (36)	80.00	36.00
COMMON SILVER	1.50	.70
SILVER MINOR STARS	2.50	1.10
SILVER UNLISTED STARS	5.00	2.20
SILVER STATED ODDS 1:4		
SETS SKIP-NUMBERED BY COLOR		

		MINT	NRMT
☐ B5	Roberto Hernandez B	.25	.11
☐ B8	Terry Pendleton B	.25	.11
☐ B12	Ken Caminiti B	.75	.35
☐ B15	Dan Miceli B	.25	.11
☐ B16	Chipper Jones C	3.00	1.35
☐ B17	John Wetteland B	.25	.11
☐ B19	Tim Naehring B	.25	.11
☐ B21	Eddie Murray B	1.00	.45
☐ B23	Kevin Appier B	.50	.23
☐ B24	Ken Griffey Jr. B	5.00	2.20
☐ B26	Brian McRae B	.25	.11
☐ B27	Pedro Martinez B	1.00	.45
☐ B28	Brian Jordan B	.50	.23
☐ B29	Mike Fetters B	.25	.11
☐ B30	Carlos Delgado B	.50	.23
☐ B31	Shane Reynolds B	.25	.11
☐ B32	Terry Steinbach B	.25	.11
☐ B34	Mark Leiter B	.25	.11
☐ B36	David Segui B	.25	.11
☐ B40	Fred McGriff B	.75	.35
☐ B44	Glenallen Hill B	.25	.11
☐ B45	Brady Anderson B	.75	.35
☐ B47	Jim Thome B	1.00	.45
☐ B48	Frank Thomas B	4.00	1.80
☐ B49	Chuck Knoblauch B	1.00	.45
☐ B50	Len Dykstra B	.50	.23
☐ B53	Tom Pagnozzi B	.25	.11
☐ B55	Ricky Bones B	.25	.11
☐ B56	David Justice B	1.00	.45
☐ B57	Steve Avery B	.25	.11
☐ B58	Robby Thompson B	.25	.11
☐ B61	Tony Gwynn B	2.50	1.10
☐ B63	Denny Neagle B	.25	.23
☐ B67	Robin Ventura B	.50	.23
☐ B70	Kevin Seitzer B	.25	.11
☐ B71	Ramon Martinez B	.50	.23
☐ B75	Brian L.Hunter B	.50	.23
☐ B76	Alan Benes B	.50	.23
☐ B80	Ozzie Guillen B	.25	.11
☐ B82	Benji Gil B	.25	.11
☐ B85	Todd Hundley B	.50	.23
☐ B87	Pat Hentgen B	.50	.23
☐ B89	Chuck Finley B	.25	.11
☐ B92	Derek Jeter B	3.00	1.35
☐ B93	Paul O'Neill B	.50	.23
☐ B94	Darrin Fletcher B	.25	.11
☐ B96	Delino DeShields B	.25	.11
☐ B97	Tim Salmon B	1.00	.45
☐ B98	John Olerud B	.50	.23
☐ B101	Tim Wakefield B	.25	.11
☐ B103	Dave Stevens B	.25	.11
☐ B104	Orlando Merced B	.25	.11
☐ B106	Jay Bell B	.50	.23
☐ B107	John Burkett B	.25	.11
☐ B108	Chris Hoiles B	.25	.11
☐ B110	Dave Nilsson B	.25	.11
☐ B111	Rod Beck B	.25	.11
☐ B113	Mike Piazza B	3.00	1.35
☐ B114	Mark Langston B	.25	.11
☐ B116	Rico Brogna B	.25	.11

Card	Player	Price	
B118	Tom Goodwin B	.25	.11
B119	Bryan Rekar B	.25	.11
B120	David Cone B	.50	.23
B122	Andy Pettitte B	1.25	.55
B123	Chili Davis B	.50	.23
B124	John Smoltz B	.50	.23
B125	Heathcliff Slocumb B	.25	.11
B126	Dante Bichette B	.50	.23
B128	Alex Gonzalez B	.25	.11
B129	Jeff Montgomery B	.25	.11
B131	Denny Martinez B	.50	.23
B132	Mel Rojas B	.25	.11
B133	Derek Bell B	.50	.23
B134	Trevor Hoffman B	.25	.11
B136	Darren Daulton B	.50	.23
B137	Pete Schourek B	.25	.11
B138	Phil Nevin B	.25	.11
B139	Andres Galarraga B	.75	.35
B140	Chad Fonville B	.25	.11
B144	J.T. Snow B	.50	.23
B146	Barry Bonds B	1.25	.55
B147	Orel Hershiser B	.50	.23
B148	Quilvio Veras B	.25	.11
B149	Will Clark B	.75	.35
B150	Jose Rijo B	.25	.11
B152	Travis Fryman B	.50	.23
B154	Alex Fernandez B	.25	.11
B155	Wade Boggs B	1.00	.45
B156	Troy Percival B	.25	.11
B157	Moises Alou B	.50	.23
B158	Javy Lopez B	.50	.23
B160	Jason Giambi B	.50	.23
B162	Mark McGwire B	2.00	.90
B163	Eric Karros B	.50	.23
B166	Mickey Tettleton B	.25	.11
B167	Barry Larkin B	.75	.35
B169	Ruben Sierra B	.25	.11
B170	Bill Swift B	.25	.11
B172	Chad Curtis B	.25	.11
B173	Dean Palmer B	.50	.23
B175	Bobby Bonilla B	.50	.23
B176	Greg Colbrunn B	.25	.11
B177	Jose Mesa B	.25	.11
B178	Mike Greenwell B	.25	.11
B181	Doug Drabek B	.25	.11
B183	Wilson Alvarez B	.25	.11
B184	Marty Cordova B	.50	.23
B185	Hal Morris B	.25	.11
B187	Carlos Garcia B	.25	.11
B190	Marquis Grissom B	.50	.23
B193	Will Clark B	.75	.35
B194	Paul Molitor B	1.00	.45
B195	Kenny Rogers B	.25	.11
B196	Reggie Sanders B	.25	.11
B199	Raul Mondesi B	.75	.35
B200	Lance Johnson B	.25	.11
B201	Alvin Morman B	.25	.11
B203	Jack McDowell B	.25	.11
B204	Randy Myers B	.25	.11
B205	Harold Baines B	.50	.23
B206	Marty Cordova B	.50	.23
B207	Rich Hunter B	.25	.11
B208	Al Leiter B	.25	.11
B209	Greg Gagne B	.25	.11
B210	Ben McDonald B	.25	.11
B212	Terry Adams B	.25	.11
B213	Paul Sorrento B	.25	.11
B214	Albert Belle B	1.25	.55
B215	Mike Blowers B	.25	.11
B216	Jim Edmonds B	.75	.35
B217	Felipe Crespo B	.25	.11
B219	Shawon Dunston B	.25	.11
B220	Jimmy Haynes B	.25	.11
B221	Jose Canseco B	.75	.35
B222	Eric Davis B	.50	.23
B224	Tim Raines B	.50	.23
B225	Tony Phillips B	.25	.11
B226	Charlie Hayes B	.25	.11
B227	Eric Owens B	.25	.11
B228	Roberto Alomar B	1.00	.45
B233	Kenny Lofton B	1.25	.55
B236	Mark McGwire B	2.00	.90
B237	Jay Buhner B	.75	.35
B238	Craig Biggio B	.75	.35
B240	Barry Bonds B	1.25	.55
B244	Ron Gant B	.50	.23
B245	Paul Wilson B	.25	.11
B246	Todd Hollandsworth B	.25	.11
B247	Todd Zeile B	.25	.11
B248	David Justice B	1.00	.45
B250	Moises Alou B	.50	.23
B251	Bob Wolcott B	.25	.11
B252	David Wells B	.25	.11
B253	Juan Gonzalez B	2.50	1.10
B254	Andres Galarraga B	.75	.35
B255	Dave Hollins B	.25	.11
B256	Sammy Sosa B	1.00	.45
B258	Ivan Rodriguez B	1.00	.45
B259	Bip Roberts B	.25	.11
B260	Tino Martinez B	1.00	.45
B262	Mike Stanley B	.25	.11
B264	Butch Huskey B	.50	.23
B265	Jeff Conine B	.50	.23
B267	Mark Grace B	.75	.35
B268	Jason Schmidt B	.25	.23
B269	Otis Nixon B	.25	.23
B271	Kirby Puckett B	2.00	.90
B273	Andy Benes B	.50	.23
B275	Mike Piazza B	3.00	1.35
B278	Rey Ordonez B	.50	.23
B278	Gary Gaetti B	.25	.11
B280	Robin Ventura B	.50	.23
B281	Cal Ripken B	4.00	1.80
B282	Carlos Baerga B	.25	.11
B283	Roger Cedeno B	.25	.11
B285	Terrell Wade B	.25	.11
B286	Kevin Brown B	.25	.11
B287	Rafael Palmeiro B	.75	.35
B288	Mo Vaughn B	1.25	.55
B292	Bob Tewksbury B	.25	.11
B298	Manny Ramirez B	1.00	.45
B297	Jeff Bagwell B	2.00	.90
B301	Wade Boggs B	1.00	.45
B303	Steve Gibralter B	.25	.11
B304	B.J. Surhoff B	.25	.11
B306	Royce Clayton B	.25	.11
B307	Sal Fasano B	.25	.11
B309	Gary Sheffield B	1.00	.45
B310	Ken Hill B	.25	.11
B311	Joe Girardi B	.25	.11
B312	Matt Lawton B	.25	.35
B314	Julio Franco B	.25	.11
B315	Joe Carter B	.50	.23
B316	Brooks Kieschnick B	.50	.23
B318	Heathcliff Slocumb B	.25	.11
B319	Barry Larkin B	.75	.35
B320	Tony Gwynn B	2.50	1.10
B322	Frank Thomas B	4.00	1.80
B323	Edgar Martinez B	.75	.35
B325	Henry Rodriguez B	.25	.11
B326	Marvin Benard B	.25	.11
B329	Ugueth Urbina B	.25	.11
B331	Roger Salkeld B	.25	.11
B332	Edgar Renteria B	.75	.35
B334	Ryan Klesko B	.75	.35
B334	Ray Lankford B	.50	.23
B336	Justin Thompson B	.75	.35
B339	Mark Clark B	.25	.11
B340	Ruben Rivera B	.50	.23
B342	Matt Williams B	.75	.35
B343	Francisco Cordova B	.25	.11
B344	Cecil Fielder B	.50	.23
B348	Mark Grudzielanek B	.50	.23
B349	Ron Coomer B	.25	.11
B351	Rich Aurilia B	.25	.11
B352	Jose Herrera B	.25	.11
B356	Tony Clark B	1.00	.45
B358	Dan Naulty B	.25	.11
B359	Checklist B	.25	.11
G4	Marty Cordova G	8.00	3.60
G6	Tony Gwynn G	40.00	18.00
G9	Albert Belle G	20.00	9.00
G18	Kirby Puckett G	30.00	13.50
G20	Karim Garcia G	10.00	4.50
G25	Cal Ripken G	60.00	27.00
G33	Hideo Nomo G	40.00	18.00
G39	Ryne Sandberg G	20.00	9.00
G42	Jeff Bagwell G	30.00	13.50
G51	Jason Isringhausen G	8.00	3.60
G64	Mo Vaughn G	20.00	9.00
G66	Dante Bichette G	8.00	3.60
G74	Mark McGwire G	30.00	13.50
G81	Kenny Lofton G	20.00	9.00
G83	Jim Edmonds G	10.00	4.50
G90	Mike Mussina G	15.00	6.75
G100	Jeff Conine G	8.00	3.60
G105	Barry Bonds G	20.00	9.00
G117	Jose Canseco G	10.00	4.50
G135	Ken Griffey Jr. G	80.00	36.00
G141	Chipper Jones G	50.00	22.00
G145	Greg Maddux G	50.00	22.00
G164	Jay Buhner G	10.00	4.50
G186	Frank Thomas G	60.00	27.00
G191	Checklist G	8.00	3.60
G192	Chipper Jones G	50.00	22.00
G197	Roberto Alomar G	15.00	6.75
G198	Dennis Eckersley G	8.00	3.60
G202	George Arias G	8.00	3.60
G232	Hideo Nomo G	40.00	18.00
G243	Chris Snopek G	8.00	3.60
G249	Tim Salmon G	15.00	6.75
G266	Matt Williams G	10.00	4.50
G270	Randy Johnson G	15.00	6.75
G279	Paul Molitor G	15.00	6.75
G290	Cecil Fielder G	8.00	3.60
G294	Livan Hernandez G	30.00	13.50
G300	Marty Janzen G	8.00	3.60
G308	Ron Gant G	8.00	3.60
G321	Ryan Klesko G	10.00	4.50
G324	Jermaine Dye G	8.00	3.60
G330	Jason Giambi G	8.00	3.60
G338	Edgar Martinez G	10.00	4.50
G338	Rey Ordonez G	8.00	3.60
G347	Sammy Sosa G	15.00	6.75
G354	Juan Gonzalez G	40.00	18.00
G355	Craig Biggio G	10.00	4.50
S1	Greg Maddux S UER	15.00	6.75
	95 stats listed as Mariners		
S2	Bernie Williams S	5.00	2.20
S3	Ivan Rodriguez S	6.00	2.70
S7	Barry Larkin S	3.00	1.35
S10	Ray Lankford S	2.50	1.10
S11	Mike Piazza S	15.00	6.75
S13	Larry Walker S	5.00	2.20
S14	Matt Williams S	3.00	1.35
S22	Tim Salmon S	5.00	2.20
S35	Edgar Martinez S	3.00	1.35
S37	Gregg Jefferies S	1.50	.70
S38	Bill Pulsipher S	1.50	.70
S41	Shawn Green S	1.50	.70
S43	Jim Abbott S	1.50	.70
S46	Roger Clemens S	10.00	4.50
S52	Rondell White S	2.50	1.10
S54	Dennis Eckersley S	2.50	1.10
S59	Hideo Nomo S	12.00	5.50
S60	Gary Sheffield S	5.00	2.20
S62	Will Clark S	3.00	1.35
S65	Bret Boone S	1.50	.70
S68	Rafael Palmeiro S	3.00	1.35
S69	Carlos Baerga S	1.50	.70
S72	Tom Glavine S	2.50	1.10
S73	Garret Anderson S	2.50	1.10
S77	Randy Johnson S	5.00	2.20
S78	Jeff King S	1.50	.70
S79	Kirby Puckett S	10.00	4.50
S82	Cecil Fielder S	2.50	1.10
S86	Reggie Sanders S	1.50	.70
S88	Ryan Klesko S	3.00	1.35
S91	John Valentin S	1.50	.70
S99	Manny Ramirez S	5.00	2.20
S109	Carlos Perez S	1.50	.70
S112	Craig Biggio S	3.00	1.35
S115	Juan Gonzalez S	12.00	5.50
S121	Ray Durham S	1.50	.70
S124	C.J. Nitkowski S	1.50	.70
S130	Raul Mondesi S	3.00	1.35
S142	Lee Smith S	2.50	1.10
S143	Joe Carter S	2.50	1.10
S151	Mo Vaughn S	6.00	2.70
S153	Frank Rodriguez S	1.50	.70
S160	Steve Finley S	2.50	1.10
S165	Jeff Bagwell S	10.00	4.50
S165	Cal Ripken S	20.00	9.00
S168	Lyle Mouton S	1.50	.70
S171	Sammy Sosa S	5.00	2.20

☐ S174	John Franco S	2.50	1.10
☐ S179	Greg Vaughn S	1.50	.70
☐ S180	Mark Wohlers S	1.50	.70
☐ S182	Paul O'Neill S	2.50	1.10
☐ S188	Albert Belle S	6.00	2.70
☐ S189	Mark Grace S	3.00	1.35
☐ S211	Ernie Young S	1.50	.70
☐ S218	Fred McGriff S	3.00	1.35
☐ S223	Kimera Bartee S	1.50	.70
☐ S229	Rickey Henderson S	3.00	1.35
☐ S230	Sterling Hitchcock S	1.50	.70
☐ S231	Bernard Gilkey S	1.50	.70
☐ S234	Ryne Sandberg S	6.00	2.70
☐ S235	Greg Maddux S	15.00	6.75
☐ S239	Todd Stottlemyre S	1.50	.70
☐ S241	Jason Kendall S	3.00	1.35
☐ S242	Paul O'Neill S	2.50	1.10
☐ S256	Devon White S	1.50	.70
☐ S261	Chuck Knoblauch S	5.00	2.20
☐ S263	Wally Joyner S	2.50	1.10
☐ S272	Andy Fox S	1.50	.70
☐ S274	Sean Berry S	1.50	.70
☐ S277	Benito Santiago S	1.50	.70
☐ S284	Chad Mottola S	1.50	.70
☐ S289	Dante Bichette S	2.50	1.10
☐ S291	Deo Gooden S	2.50	1.10
☐ S293	Kevin Mitchell S	1.50	.70
☐ S295	Russ Davis S	1.50	.70
☐ S296	Chan Ho Park S	5.00	2.20
☐ S302	Larry Walker S	5.00	2.20
☐ S305	Ken Griffey Jr. S	25.00	11.00
☐ S313	Billy Wagner S	2.50	1.10
☐ S317	Mike Grace S	1.50	.70
☐ S327	Kenny Lofton S	6.00	2.70
☐ S328	Derek Bell S	1.50	.70
☐ S337	Gary Sheffield S	3.00	1.35
☐ S341	Mark Grace S	3.00	1.35
☐ S345	Andres Galarraga S	5.00	2.20
☐ S346	Brady Anderson S	3.00	1.35
☐ S350	Derek Jeter S	12.00	5.50
☐ S353	Jay Buhner S	3.00	1.35
☐ S357	Tino Martinez S	5.00	2.20

1996 Finest Refractors

This 359-card set is parallel to the basic 1996 Finest set. The first 191 cards are parallel to the regular Series 1 with the second 168 cards parallel to regular Series 2. The word "refractor" is printed above the numbers on the card backs. The rate of insertion is one in 12 for a Bronze refractor (common), one in 48 for a Silver refractor (uncommon), and one in 288 for a Gold refractor (rare).

	MINT	NRMT
COMPLETE SET (359)	6000.00	2700.00
COMP.SERIES 1 (191)	3800.00	1700.00
COMP.SERIES 2 (168)	2200.00	1000.00
COMP.BRONZE SET (220)	1100.00	500.00
COMP.BRONZE SER.1 (110)	500.00	220.00
COMP.BRONZE SER.2 (110)	600.00	275.00
COMMON BRONZE	3.00	1.35
*BRONZE STARS: 5X TO 12X HI COLUMN
BRONZE STATED ODDS 1:12
COMP.GOLD SET (48)	3500.00	1600.00
COMP.GOLD SER.1 (26)	2500.00	1100.00
COMP.GOLD SER.2 (22)	1000.00	450.00
COMMON GOLD	25.00	11.00
*GOLD STARS: 2X TO 4X HI
GOLD STATED ODDS 1:288
COMP.SILVER SET (91)	1400.00	650.00
COMP.SILVER SER.1 (55)	800.00	350.00
COMP.SILVER SER.2 (36)	600.00	275.00
COMMON SILVER	6.00	2.70
*SILVER STARS: 2.5X TO 5X HI
SILVER STATED ODDS 1:48

1997 Finest

The 1997 Finest set was issued in two series of 175 cards each and was distributed in six-card packs with a suggested retail price of $5.00. The fronts feature a borderless action player photo while the backs carry another player photo. Series 1 is divided into five distinct themes: Finest Hurlers (top pitchers), Finest Blue Chips (up-and-coming future stars), Finest Power (long-ball hitters), Finest Warriors (superstar players), and Finest Masters (hottest player photo). Series 2 is also divided into five distinct themes: Finest Power (power hitters, pitchers), Finest Masters (top players), Finest Blue Chips (top new players), Finest Competitors (hottest players), and Finest Acquisitions (latest trades and new signings). All five themes of each series have common cards (1-100, 176-275) designated with bronze trim, uncommon (101-150, 276-325) with silver trim and an insertion rate of one in four for both series, and rare (151-175, 326-350) with gold trim and an insertion rate of one in 24 for both series. The cards are numbered on the backs within the whole set and within the theme set.

	MINT	NRMT
COMPLETE SET (350)	1250.00	550.00
COMPLETE SERIES 1 (175)	650.00	300.00
COMPLETE SERIES 2 (175)	600.00	275.00
COMP.BRONZE SET (200)	60.00	27.00
COMP.BRONZE SER.1 (100)	30.00	13.50
COMP.BRONZE SER.2 (100)	30.00	13.50
COM.BRON.(1-100/176-275)	.25	.11
BRONZE MINOR STARS	.50	.23
BRONZE UNLISTED STARS	1.00	.45
COMP.SILVER SET (100)	350.00	160.00
COMP.SILVER SER.1 (50)	150.00	70.00
COMP.SILVER SER.2 (50)	200.00	90.00
COM.SILV.(101-150/276-325)	1.50	.70
SILVER MINOR STARS	2.50	1.10
SILVER UNLISTED STARS	4.00	1.80
SILVER STATED ODDS 1:4
COMP.GOLD SET (50)	900.00	400.00
COMP.GOLD SER.1 (25)	500.00	220.00
COMP.GOLD SER.2 (25)	400.00	180.00
GOLD.(151-175/326-350)	8.00	3.60
GOLD UNLISTED STARS	12.00	5.50
GOLD STATED ODDS 1:24
BICHETTE/MCGWIRE BOTH NUMBERED 155
BICHETTE UER SHOULD BE NUMBER 5

☐ 1	Barry Bonds B	1.25	.55
☐ 2	Ryne Sandberg B	1.25	.55
☐ 3	Brian Jordan B	.50	.23
☐ 4	Rocky Coppinger B	.25	.11
☐ 5	Dante Bichette B UER	.25	.23
	Card is erroneously numbered 155
☐ 6	Al Martin B	.25	.11
☐ 7	Charles Nagy B	.50	.23
☐ 8	Otis Nixon B	.25	.11
☐ 9	Mark Johnson B	.25	.11
☐ 10	Jeff Bagwell B	2.00	.90
☐ 11	Ken Hill B	.25	.11
☐ 12	Willie Adams B	.25	.11
☐ 13	Raul Mondesi B	.75	.35
☐ 14	Reggie Sanders B	.25	.11
☐ 15	Derek Jeter B	3.00	1.35
☐ 16	Jermaine Dye B	.25	.11
☐ 17	Edgar Renteria B	.50	.23
☐ 18	Travis Fryman B	.50	.23
☐ 19	Roberto Hernandez B	.25	.11
☐ 20	Sammy Sosa B	1.00	.45
☐ 21	Garret Anderson B	.50	.23
☐ 22	Rey Ordonez B	.25	.11
☐ 23	Glenallen Hill B	.25	.11
☐ 24	Dave Nilsson B	.25	.11
☐ 25	Kevin Brown B	.50	.23
☐ 26	Brian McRae B	.25	.11
☐ 27	Joey Hamilton B	.25	.11
☐ 28	Jamey Wright B	.25	.11
☐ 29	Frank Thomas B	4.00	1.80
☐ 30	Mark McGwire B	2.00	.90
☐ 31	Ramon Martinez B	.50	.23
☐ 32	Jaime Bluma B	.25	.11
☐ 33	Frank Rodriguez B	.25	.11
☐ 34	Andy Benes B	.50	.23
☐ 35	Jay Buhner B	.75	.35
☐ 36	Justin Thompson B	.50	.23
☐ 37	Darin Erstad B	1.50	.70
☐ 38	Gregg Jefferies B	.25	.11
☐ 39	Jeff D'Amico B	.25	.11
☐ 40	Pedro Martinez B	1.00	.45
☐ 41	Nomar Garciaparra B	3.00	1.35
☐ 42	Jose Valentin B	.25	.11
☐ 43	Pat Hentgen B	.50	.23
☐ 44	Will Clark B	.75	.35
☐ 45	Bernie Williams B	1.00	.45
☐ 46	Luis Castillo B	.50	.23
☐ 47	B.J. Surhoff B	.25	.11
☐ 48	Greg Gagne B	.25	.11
☐ 49	Pete Schourek B	.25	.11
☐ 50	Mike Piazza B	3.00	1.35
☐ 51	Dwight Gooden B	.50	.23
☐ 52	Javy Lopez B	.50	.23
☐ 53	Chuck Finley B	.25	.11
☐ 54	James Baldwin B	.25	.11
☐ 55	Jack McDowell B	.25	.11
☐ 56	Royce Clayton B	.25	.11
☐ 57	Carlos Delgado B	.50	.23
☐ 58	Neifi Perez B	.50	.23
☐ 59	Eddie Taubensee B	.25	.11
☐ 60	Rafael Palmeiro B	.75	.35
☐ 61	Marty Cordova B	.50	.23
☐ 62	Wade Boggs B	1.00	.45
☐ 63	Rickey Henderson B	.75	.35
☐ 64	Mike Hampton B	.25	.11
☐ 65	Troy Percival B	.25	.11
☐ 66	Barry Larkin B	.75	.35
☐ 67	Jermaine Allensworth B	.25	.11
☐ 68	Mark Clark B	.25	.11
☐ 69	Mike Lansing B	.25	.11
☐ 70	Mark Grudzielanek B	.25	.11
☐ 71	Todd Stottlemyre B	.25	.11
☐ 72	Juan Guzman B	.25	.11
☐ 73	John Burkett B	.25	.11
☐ 74	Wilson Alvarez B	.25	.11
☐ 75	Ellis Burks B	.50	.23
☐ 76	Bobby Higginson B	.50	.23
☐ 77	Ricky Bottalico B	.25	.11
☐ 78	Omar Vizquel B	.50	.23
☐ 79	Paul Sorrento B	.25	.11
☐ 80	Denny Neagle B	.25	.11
☐ 81	Roger Pavlik B	.25	.11
☐ 82	Mike Lieberthal B	.25	.11
☐ 83	Devon White B	.25	.11
☐ 84	John Olerud B	.50	.23
☐ 85	Kevin Appier B	.50	.23

□ 86	Joe Girardi B	.25	.11		□ 172	Jay Buhner G UER#'d 164	10.00	4.50		□ 258	Shane Reynolds B	.25	.11
□ 87	Paul O'Neill B	.50	.23		□ 173	Paul Molitor G	15.00	6.75		□ 259	Jaime Navarro B	.25	.11
□ 88	Mike Sweeney B	.50	.23		□ 174	Kenny Lofton G	20.00	9.00		□ 260	Eric Davis B	.50	.23
□ 89	John Smiley B	.25	.11		□ 175	Barry Bonds G	20.00	9.00		□ 261	Orel Hershiser B	.50	.23
□ 90	Ivan Rodriguez B	1.25	.55		□ 176	Gary Sheffield B	1.00	.45		□ 262	Mark Grace B	.75	.35
□ 91	Randy Myers B	.25	.11		□ 177	Dmitri Young B	.25	.11		□ 263	Rod Beck B	.25	.11
□ 92	Bip Roberts B	.25	.11		□ 178	Jay Bell B	.50	.23		□ 264	Ismael Valdes B	.50	.23
□ 93	Jose Mesa B	.25	.11		□ 179	David Wells B	.25	.11		□ 265	Manny Ramirez B	1.00	.45
□ 94	Paul Wilson B	.25	.11		□ 180	Walt Weiss B	.25	.11		□ 266	Ken Caminiti B	.75	.35
□ 95	Mike Mussina B	1.00	.45		□ 181	Paul Molitor B	1.00	.45		□ 267	Tim Naehring B	.25	.11
□ 96	Ben McDonald B	.25	.11		□ 182	Jose Guillen B	1.25	.55		□ 268	Jose Rosado B	.50	.23
□ 97	John Mabry B	.25	.11		□ 183	Al Leiter B	.25	.11		□ 269	Greg Colbrunn B	.25	.11
□ 98	Tom Goodwin B	.25	.11		□ 184	Mike Fetters B	.25	.11		□ 270	Dean Palmer B	.25	.11
□ 99	Edgar Martinez B	.75	.35		□ 185	Mark Langston B	.25	.11		□ 271	David Justice B	1.00	.45
□ 100	Andruw Jones B	2.50	1.10		□ 186	Fred McGriff B	.75	.35		□ 272	Scott Spiezio B	.50	.23
□ 101	Jose Canseco S	3.00	1.35		□ 187	Darrin Fletcher B	.25	.11		□ 273	Chipper Jones B	3.00	1.35
□ 102	Billy Wagner S	2.50	1.10		□ 188	Brant Brown B	.25	.11		□ 274	Mel Rojas B	.25	.11
□ 103	Dante Bichette S	2.50	1.10		□ 189	Geronimo Berroa B	.25	.11		□ 275	Bartolo Colon B	.50	.23
□ 104	Curt Schilling S	2.50	1.10		□ 190	Jim Thome B	1.00	.45		□ 276	Darin Erstad S	8.00	3.60
□ 105	Dean Palmer S	1.50	.70		□ 191	Jose Vizcaino B	.25	.11		□ 277	Sammy Sosa S	4.00	1.80
□ 106	Larry Walker S	5.00	2.20		□ 192	Andy Ashby B	.25	.11		□ 278	Rafael Palmeiro S	3.00	1.35
□ 107	Bernie Williams S	4.00	1.80		□ 193	Rusty Greer B	.50	.23		□ 279	Frank Thomas S	20.00	9.00
□ 108	Chipper Jones S	15.00	6.75		□ 194	Brian Hunter B	.50	.23		□ 280	Ruben Rivera S	2.50	1.10
□ 109	Gary Sheffield S	4.00	1.80		□ 195	Chris Hoiles B	.25	.11		□ 281	Hal Morris S	1.50	.70
□ 110	Randy Johnson S	5.00	2.20		□ 196	Orlando Merced B	.25	.11		□ 282	Jay Buhner S	3.00	1.35
□ 111	Roberto Alomar S	5.00	2.20		□ 197	Brett Butler B	.50	.23		□ 283	Kenny Lofton S	6.00	2.70
□ 112	Todd Walker S	2.50	1.10		□ 198	Derek Bell B	.25	.11		□ 284	Jose Canseco S	3.00	1.35
□ 113	Sandy Alomar Jr. S	2.50	1.10		□ 199	Bobby Bonilla B	.50	.23		□ 285	Alex Fernandez S	2.50	1.10
□ 114	John Jaha S	1.50	.70		□ 200	Alex Ochoa B	.25	.11		□ 286	Todd Helton S	8.00	3.60
□ 115	Ken Caminiti S UER#'d 135	3.00	1.35		□ 201	Wally Joyner B	.50	.23		□ 287	Andy Pettitte S	5.00	2.20
□ 116	Ryan Klesko S	2.50	1.10		□ 202	Mo Vaughn B	1.25	.55		□ 288	John Franco S	2.50	1.10
□ 117	Mariano Rivera S	2.50	1.10		□ 203	Doug Drabek B	.25	.11		□ 289	Ivan Rodriguez S	6.00	2.70
□ 118	Jason Giambi S	2.50	1.10		□ 204	Tino Martinez B	1.00	.45		□ 290	Ellis Burks S	2.50	1.10
□ 119	Lance Johnson S	1.50	.70		□ 205	Roberto Alomar B	1.00	.45		□ 291	Julio Franco S	2.50	1.10
□ 120	Robin Ventura S	2.50	1.10		□ 206	Brian Giles B	.25	.11		□ 292	Mike Piazza S	15.00	6.75
□ 121	Todd Hollandsworth S	1.50	.70		□ 207	Todd Worrell B	.25	.11		□ 293	Brian Jordan S	2.50	1.10
□ 122	Johnny Damon S	1.50	.70		□ 208	Alan Benes B	.25	.11		□ 294	Greg Maddux S	15.00	6.75
□ 123	William VanLandingham S	1.50	.70		□ 209	Jim Leyritz B	.25	.11		□ 295	Bob Abreu S	2.50	1.10
□ 124	Jason Kendall S	2.50	1.10		□ 210	Darryl Hamilton B	.25	.11		□ 296	Ronde? White S	2.50	1.10
□ 125	Vinny Castilla S	2.50	1.10		□ 211	Jimmy Key B	.50	.23		□ 297	Moises Alou S	2.50	1.10
□ 126	Harold Baines S	2.50	1.10		□ 212	Juan Gonzalez B	2.50	1.10		□ 298	Tony Gwynn S	12.00	5.50
□ 127	Joe Carter S	2.50	1.10		□ 213	Vinny Castilla B	.50	.23		□ 299	Deion Sanders S	2.50	1.10
□ 128	Craig Biggio S	3.00	1.35		□ 214	Chuck Knoblauch B	1.00	.45		□ 300	Jeff Montgomery S	1.50	.70
□ 129	Tony Clark S	4.00	1.80		□ 215	Tony Phillips B	.25	.11		□ 301	Ray Durham S	1.50	.70
□ 130	Ron Gant S	2.50	1.10		□ 216	Jeff Cirillo B	.50	.23		□ 302	John Wasdin S	1.50	.70
□ 131	David Segui S	1.50	.70		□ 217	Carlos Garcia B	.25	.11		□ 303	Ryne Sandberg S	6.00	2.70
□ 132	Steve Trachsel S	1.50	.70		□ 218	Brooks Kieschnick B	.25	.11		□ 304	Delino DeShields S	1.50	.70
□ 133	Scott Rolen S	12.00	5.50		□ 219	Marquis Grissom B	.50	.23		□ 305	Mark McGwire S	10.00	4.50
□ 134	Mike Stanley S	1.50	.70		□ 220	Dan Wilson B	.25	.11		□ 306	Andruw Jones S	12.00	5.50
□ 135	Cal Ripken S	20.00	9.00		□ 221	Greg Vaughn B	.25	.11		□ 307	Kevin Orie S	2.50	1.10
□ 136	John Smoltz S	2.50	1.10		□ 222	John Wetteland B	.25	.11		□ 308	Matt Williams S	3.00	1.35
□ 137	Bobby Jones S	1.50	.70		□ 223	Andres Galarraga B	1.00	.45		□ 309	Karim Garcia S	2.50	1.10
□ 138	Manny Ramirez S	5.00	2.20		□ 224	Ozzie Guillen B	.25	.11		□ 310	Derek Jeter S	15.00	6.75
□ 139	Ken Griffey Jr. S	25.00	11.00		□ 225	Kevin Elster B	.25	.11		□ 311	Mo Vaughn S	6.00	2.70
□ 140	Chuck Knoblauch S	4.00	1.80		□ 226	Bernard Gilkey B	.25	.11		□ 312	Brady Anderson S	3.00	1.35
□ 141	Mark Grace S	3.00	1.35		□ 227	Mike Macfarlane B	.25	.11		□ 313	Barry Bonds S	6.00	2.70
□ 142	Chris Snopek S	1.50	.70		□ 228	Heathcliff Slocumb B	.25	.11		□ 314	Steve Finley S	2.50	1.10
□ 143	Hideo Nomo S	12.00	5.50		□ 229	Wendell Magee Jr. B	.25	.11		□ 315	Vladimir Guerrero S	10.00	4.50
□ 144	Tim Salmon S	4.00	1.80		□ 230	Carlos Baerga B	.25	.11		□ 316	Matt Morris S	2.50	1.10
□ 145	David Cone S	2.50	1.10		□ 231	Kevin Seitzer B	.25	.11		□ 317	Tom Glavine S	2.50	1.10
□ 146	Eric Young S	1.50	.70		□ 232	Henry Rodriguez B	.25	.11		□ 318	Jeff Bagwell S	10.00	4.50
□ 147	Jeff Brantley S	1.50	.70		□ 233	Roger Clemens B	2.00	.90		□ 319	Albert Belle S	6.00	2.70
□ 148	Jim Thome S	5.00	2.20		□ 234	Mark Wohlers B	.25	.11		□ 320	Hideki Irabu S	5.00	2.20
□ 149	Trevor Hoffman S	1.50	.70		□ 235	Eddie Murray B	1.00	.45		□ 321	Andres Galarraga S	4.00	1.80
□ 150	Juan Gonzalez S	12.00	5.50		□ 236	Todd Zeile B	.25	.11		□ 322	Cecil Fielder S	2.50	1.10
□ 151	Mike Piazza S	50.00	22.00		□ 237	J.T. Snow B	.25	.23		□ 323	Barry Larkin S	3.00	1.35
□ 152	Ivan Rodriguez S	20.00	9.00		□ 238	Ken Griffey Jr. B	5.00	2.20		□ 324	Todd Hundley S	2.50	1.10
□ 153	Mo Vaughn S	20.00	9.00		□ 239	Sterling Hitchcock B	.25	.11		□ 325	Fred McGriff S	3.00	1.35
□ 154	Brady Anderson S	10.00	4.50		□ 240	Albert Belle B	1.25	.55		□ 326	Gary Sheffield S	12.00	5.50
□ 155	Mark McGwire S	30.00	13.50		□ 241	Terry Steinbach B	.25	.11		□ 327	Craig Biggio S	10.00	4.50
□ 156	Rafael Palmeiro S	10.00	4.50		□ 242	Robb Nen B	.25	.11		□ 328	Raul Mondesi S	10.00	4.50
□ 157	Barry Larkin S	10.00	4.50		□ 243	Mark McLemore B	.25	.11		□ 329	Edgar Martinez S	10.00	4.50
□ 158	Greg Maddux S	50.00	22.00		□ 244	Jeff King B	.25	.11		□ 330	Chipper Jones S	50.00	22.00
□ 159	Jeff Bagwell S	30.00	13.50		□ 245	Tony Clark B	1.00	.45		□ 331	Bernie Williams S	12.00	5.50
□ 160	Frank Thomas S	60.00	27.00		□ 246	Tim Salmon B	1.00	.45		□ 332	Juan Gonzalez S	40.00	18.00
□ 161	Ken Caminiti S	10.00	4.50		□ 247	Benito Santiago B	.25	.11		□ 333	Ron Gant S	8.00	3.60
□ 162	Andruw Jones S	40.00	18.00		□ 248	Robin Ventura B	.50	.23		□ 334	Cal Ripken S	60.00	27.00
□ 163	Dennis Eckersley S	8.00	3.60		□ 249	Bubba Trammell B	.50	.45		□ 335	Larry Walker S	15.00	6.75
□ 164	Jeff Conine S	8.00	3.60		□ 250	Chili Davis B	.25	.23		□ 336	Matt Williams S	10.00	4.50
□ 165	Jim Edmonds S	10.00	4.50		□ 251	John Valentin B	.25	.11		□ 337	Jose Cruz Jr. S	80.00	36.00
□ 166	Derek Jeter S	50.00	22.00		□ 252	Cal Ripken B	4.00	1.80		□ 338	Joe Carter S	8.00	3.60
□ 167	Vladimir Guerrero S	30.00	13.50		□ 253	Matt Williams B	.75	.35		□ 339	Wilton Guerrero S	8.00	3.60
□ 168	Sammy Sosa S	12.00	5.50		□ 254	Jeff Kent B	.25	.11		□ 340	Cecil Fielder S	8.00	3.60
□ 169	Tony Gwynn S	40.00	18.00		□ 255	Eric Karros B	.25	.23		□ 341	Todd Walker S	8.00	3.60
□ 170	Andres Galarraga S	12.00	5.50		□ 256	Ray Lankford B	.50	.23		□ 342	Ken Griffey Jr. S	80.00	36.00
□ 171	Todd Hundley S	8.00	3.60		□ 257	Ed Sprague B	.25	.11		□ 343	Ryan Klesko S	10.00	4.50

□ 344 Roger Clemens G 30.00 13.50
□ 345 Hideo Nomo G...... 40.00 18.00
□ 346 Dante Bichette G ... 10.00 4.50
□ 347 Albert Belle G 20.00 9.00
□ 348 Randy Johnson G .. 15.00 6.75
□ 349 Manny Ramirez G .. 15.00 6.75
□ 350 John Smoltz G....... 8.00 3.60

1997 Finest Embossed

This 150-card set is parallel to regular set numbers 101-175 of Finest Series 1 and 276-350 of Finest Series 2. There is an embossed version of cards 101-150 and 276-325 with an insertion rate of one in 16 for each series. There is an embossed die-cut version of cards 151-175 and 326-350 with an insertion rate of one in 96 packs for each series.

	MINT	NRMT
COMPLETE SET (150)	2800.00	1250.00
COMPLETE SERIES 1 (75)	1400.00	650.00
COMPLETE SERIES 2 (75)	1400.00	650.00
COMP.SILVER SER.1 (50)	400.00	180.00
COMP.SILVER SER.2 (50)	600.00	275.00
COM.SILV.(101-150/276-325)	4.00	1.80

*SILV.STARS: 1X TO 2.5X BASE CARD HI
*SILVER YOUNG STARS: .75X TO 2X BASE HI
SILVER STATED ODDS 1:16 ....
ALL SILVER CARDS ARE NON DIE CUT

COMP.GOLD SER.1 (25)	1000.00	450.00
COMP.GOLD SER.2 (25) ..	800.00	350.00
COM.GOLD (151-175/326-350)	15.00	6.75

*GOLD STARS: .75X TO 2X BASE CARD HI
*GOLD YOUNG STARS: .6X TO 1.5X BASE HI
GOLD STATED ODDS 1:96 ....
ALL GOLD CARDS ARE DIE CUT

1997 Finest Embossed Refractors

This 150-card set is a parallel version of the regular Finest Embossed set and is similar in design. The difference is found in the refractive quality of the cards.

	MINT	NRMT
COM.SILV.(101-150/276-325)	30.00	13.50
SILVER MINOR STARS	40.00	18.00
SILVER UNLISTED STARS ...	60.00	27.00

SILVER STATED ODDS 1:192 ....
ALL SILVER CARDS ARE NON DIE CUT

COM.GOLD (151-175/326-350)	120.00	55.00
GOLD MINOR STARS	150.00	70.00
GOLD UNLISTED STARS ..	200.00	90.00

GOLD STATED ODDS 1:1152 ....
ALL GOLD CARDS ARE DIE CUT

□ 106 Larry Walker S 80.00 36.00
□ 108 Chipper Jones S .. 200.00 90.00
□ 110 Randy Johnson S .. 80.00 36.00
□ 111 Roberto Alomar S .. 80.00 36.00
□ 133 Scott Rolen S 150.00 70.00
□ 135 Cal Ripken S 300.00 135.00
□ 138 Manny Ramirez S .. 80.00 36.00
□ 139 Ken Griffey Jr. S .. 500.00 220.00
□ 143 Hideo Nomo S...... 250.00 110.00
□ 148 Jim Thome S........ 80.00 36.00
□ 150 Juan Gonzalez S .. 200.00 90.00
□ 151 Mike Piazza G 800.00 350.00
□ 152 Ivan Rodriguez G.. 300.00 135.00
□ 153 Mo Vaughn G 300.00 135.00
□ 155 Mark McGwire G .. 500.00 220.00
□ 158 Greg Maddux G 800.00 350.00
□ 159 Jeff Bagwell G...... 500.00 220.00
□ 160 Frank Thomas G .. 1200.00 550.00
□ 162 Andruw Jones G .. 500.00 220.00
□ 166 Derek Jeter G 600.00 275.00
□ 167 Vladimir Guerrero G 400.00 180.00
□ 169 Tony Gwynn G 600.00 275.00
□ 173 Paul Molitor G 250.00 110.00
□ 174 Kenny Lofton G 300.00 135.00
□ 175 Barry Bonds G...... 300.00 135.00
□ 276 Darin Erstad S 100.00 45.00
□ 279 Frank Thomas S ... 400.00 180.00
□ 283 Kenny Lofton S 100.00 45.00
□ 286 Todd Helton S 100.00 45.00
□ 287 Andy Pettitte S 80.00 36.00
□ 292 Mike Piazza S 250.00 110.00
□ 294 Greg Maddux S 250.00 110.00
□ 298 Tony Gwynn S 200.00 90.00
□ 303 Ryne Sandberg S .. 100.00 45.00
□ 305 Mark McGwire S .. 150.00 70.00
□ 306 Andruw Jones S .. 150.00 70.00
□ 310 Derek Jeter S 200.00 90.00
□ 311 Mo Vaughn S 100.00 45.00
□ 313 Barry Bonds S...... 100.00 45.00
□ 315 Vladimir Guerrero S 120.00 55.00
□ 318 Jeff Bagwell S 150.00 70.00
□ 319 Albert Belle S........ 100.00 45.00
□ 320 Hideki Irabu S 50.00 22.00
□ 330 Chipper Jones G .. 600.00 275.00
□ 332 Juan Gonzalez G .. 600.00 275.00
□ 334 Cal Ripken G 1000.00 450.00
□ 335 Larry Walker S 250.00 110.00
□ 337 Jose Cruz Jr. G 600.00 275.00
□ 342 Ken Griffey G 1200.00 550.00
□ 344 Roger Clemens G .. 500.00 220.00
□ 345 Hideo Nomo G...... 800.00 350.00
□ 347 Albert Belle G 300.00 135.00
□ 348 Randy Johnson G .. 250.00 110.00
□ 349 Manny Ramirez G .. 250.00 110.00

1997 Finest Refractors

This 350-card set is parallel and similar in design to the regular Finest set. The distinction is in the refractive quality of the card.

Cards 1-100 and 176-275 have an insertion rate of one in 12 in each series packs. Cards 101-150 and 276-325 have an insertion rate of one in 48 in each series packs. Cards 151-175 and 326-350 have an insertion rate of one in 288.

	MINT	NRMT
COMPLETE SET (350)	6200.00	2800.00
COMPLETE SERIES 1 (175)	3200.00	1450.00
COMPLETE SERIES 2 (175)	3000.00	1350.00
COMP.BRONZE SER.1 (100)	500.00	220.00
COMP.BRONZE SER.2 (100)	400.00	180.00
COM.BRON.(1-100/176-275)	3.00	1.35

*BRONZE STARS: 5X TO 12X BASE CARD HI
*BRONZE YOUNG STARS: 4X TO 10X BASE HI
BRONZE STATED ODDS 1:12...

COMP.SILVER SER.1 (50)	800.00	350.00
COMP.SILVER SER.2 (50)	1200.00	550.00
COM.SILV.(101-150/276-325)	30.00	3.60

*SILVER STARS: 2X TO 5X BASE CARD HI
*SILVER YOUNG STARS: 1.5X TO 4X BASE HI
SILVER STATED ODDS 1:48 ....

COMP.GOLD SER.1 (25)	2000.00	900.00
COMP.GOLD SER.2 (25)	1500.00	700.00
COM.GOLD (151-175/326-350)	30.00	13.50

*GOLD STARS: 2X TO 5X BASE CARD HI
*GOLD YOUNG STARS: 1.5X TO 4X BASE HI
GOLD STATED ODDS 1:288...

1993 Flair

This 300-card standard-size set represents Fleer's entrance into the super-premium category of trading cards. Cards were distributed exclusively in specially encased "hardpacks." The cards are made from heavy 24 point board card stock, with an additional three points of high-gloss laminate on each side, and feature full-bleed color fronts that sport two photos of each player, one superposed upon the other. The Flair logo appears at the top and the player's name rests at the bottom, both stamped in gold foil. The cards are numbered alphabetically within teams with National League preceding American league. There are no key Rookie Cards in this set.

	MINT	NRMT
COMPLETE SET (300)	60.00	27.00
COMMON CARD (1-300)	.40	.18
MINOR STARS	.60	.25
SEMISTARS	1.00	.45
UNLISTED STARS	1.50	.70

□ 1 Steve Avery .... .40 .18
□ 2 Jeff Blauser .... .40 .18

3	Ron Gant	.60	.25
4	Tom Glavine	1.00	.45
5	David Justice	1.50	.70
6	Mark Lemke	.40	.18
7	Greg Maddux	5.00	2.20
8	Fred McGriff	1.00	.45
9	Terry Pendleton	.60	.25
10	Deion Sanders	.60	.25
11	John Smoltz	.60	.25
12	Mike Stanton	.40	.18
13	Steve Buechele	.40	.18
14	Mark Grace	1.00	.45
15	Greg Hibbard	.40	.18
16	Derrick May	.40	.18
17	Chuck McElroy	.40	.18
18	Mike Morgan	.40	.18
19	Randy Myers	.60	.25
20	Ryne Sandberg	2.00	.90
21	Dwight Smith	.40	.18
22	Sammy Sosa	1.50	.70
23	Jose Vizcaino	.40	.18
24	Tim Belcher	.40	.18
25	Rob Dibble	.40	.18
26	Roberto Kelly	.40	.18
27	Barry Larkin	1.00	.45
28	Kevin Mitchell	.60	.25
29	Hal Morris	.40	.18
30	Joe Oliver	.40	.18
31	Jose Rijo	.40	.18
32	Bip Roberts	.40	.18
33	Chris Sabo	.40	.18
34	Reggie Sanders	.60	.25
35	Dante Bichette	1.00	.45
36	Willie Blair	.40	.18
37	Jerald Clark	.40	.18
38	Alex Cole	.40	.18
39	Andres Galarraga	1.50	.70
40	Joe Girardi	.40	.18
41	Charlie Hayes	.40	.18
42	Chris Jones	.40	.18
43	David Nied	1.50	.70
44	Eric Young	1.50	.70
45	Alex Arias	.40	.18
46	Jack Armstrong	.40	.18
47	Bret Barberie	.40	.18
48	Chuck Carr	.40	.18
49	Jeff Conine	.60	.25
50	Orestes Destrade	.40	.18
51	Chris Hammond	.40	.18
52	Bryan Harvey	.40	.18
53	Benito Santiago	.40	.18
54	Gary Sheffield	1.50	.70
55	Walt Weiss	.40	.18
56	Eric Anthony	.40	.18
57	Jeff Bagwell	3.00	1.35
58	Craig Biggio	1.00	.45
59	Ken Caminiti	.40	.18
60	Andujar Cedeno	.40	.18
61	Doug Drabek	.40	.18
62	Steve Finley	.60	.25
63	Luis Gonzalez	.40	.18
64	Pete Harnisch	.40	.18
65	Doug Jones	.40	.18
66	Darryl Kile	.60	.25
67	Greg Swindell	.40	.18
68	Brett Butler	.60	.25
69	Jim Gott	.40	.18
70	Orel Hershiser	.60	.25
71	Eric Karros	.60	.25
72	Pedro Martinez	1.50	.70
73	Ramon Martinez	.40	.25
74	Roger McDowell	.40	
75	Mike Piazza	8.00	3.60
76	Jody Reed	.40	.18
77	Tim Wallach	.40	.18
78	Moises Alou	.60	.25
79	Greg Colbrunn	.40	.18
80	Wil Cordero	.40	.18
81	Delino DeShields	.60	.25
82	Jeff Fassero	.40	.18
83	Marquis Grissom	.60	.25
84	Ken Hill	.40	.18
85	Mike Lansing	.60	.25
86	Dennis Martinez	.60	.25
87	Larry Walker	1.50	.70
88	John Wetteland	.60	.25
89	Bobby Bonilla	.60	.25
90	Vince Coleman	.40	.18
91	Dwight Gooden	.60	.25
92	Todd Hundley	1.00	.45
93	Howard Johnson	.40	.18
94	Eddie Murray	1.50	.70
95	Joe Orsulak	.40	.18
96	Bret Saberhagen	.40	.18
97	Darren Daulton	.60	.25
98	Mariano Duncan	.40	.18
99	Len Dykstra	.60	.25
100	Jim Eisenreich	.40	.18
101	Tommy Greene	.40	.18
102	Dave Hollins	.40	.18
103	Pete Incaviglia	.40	.18
104	Danny Jackson	.40	.18
105	John Kruk	.60	.25
106	Terry Mulholland	.40	.18
107	Curt Schilling	.60	.25
108	Mitch Williams	.40	.18
109	Stan Belinda	.40	.18
110	Jay Bell	.60	.25
111	Steve Cooke	.40	.18
112	Carlos Garcia	.40	.18
113	Jeff King	.60	.25
114	Al Martin	.40	.18
115	Orlando Merced	.40	.18
116	Don Slaught	.40	.18
117	Andy Van Slyke	.60	.25
118	Tim Wakefield	.60	.25
119	Rene Arocha	.60	.25
120	Bernard Gilkey	.60	.25
121	Gregg Jefferies	.40	.18
122	Ray Lankford	1.00	.45
123	Donovan Osborne	.40	.18
124	Tom Pagnozzi	.40	.18
125	Erik Pappas	.40	.18
126	Geronimo Pena	.40	.18
127	Lee Smith	.60	.25
128	Ozzie Smith	2.00	.90
129	Bob Tewksbury	.40	.18
130	Mark Whiten	.40	.18
131	Derek Bell	.60	.25
132	Andy Benes	.60	.25
133	Tony Gwynn	4.00	1.80
134	Gene Harris	.40	.18
135	Trevor Hoffman	1.00	.45
136	Phil Plantier	.40	.18
137	Rod Beck	.60	.25
138	Barry Bonds	2.00	.90
139	John Burkett	.40	.18
140	Will Clark	1.00	.45
141	Royce Clayton	.40	.18
142	Mike Jackson	.40	.18
143	Darren Lewis	.40	.18
144	Kirt Manwaring	.40	.18
145	Willie McGee	.40	.18
146	Bill Swift	.40	.18
147	Robby Thompson	.40	.18
148	Matt Williams	1.00	.45
149	Brady Anderson	1.00	.45
150	Mike Devereaux	.40	.18
151	Chris Hoiles	.40	.18
152	Ben McDonald	.40	.18
153	Mark McLemore	.40	.18
154	Mike Mussina	1.50	.70
155	Gregg Olson	.40	.18
156	Harold Reynolds	.40	.18
157	Cal Ripken UER	6.00	2.70
	(Back refers to his games streak going into 1992; should be 1993) Also streak is spelled steak		
158	Rick Sutcliffe	.40	.18
159	Fernando Valenzuela	.40	.25
160	Roger Clemens	3.00	1.35
161	Scott Cooper	.40	.18
162	Andre Dawson	1.00	.45
163	Scott Fletcher	.40	.18
164	Mike Greenwell	.40	.18
165	Greg A. Harris	.40	.18
166	Billy Hatcher	.40	.18
167	Jeff Russell	.40	.18
168	Mo Vaughn	2.00	.90
169	Frank Viola	.40	.18
170	Chad Curtis	.60	.25
171	Chili Davis	.60	.25
172	Gary DiSarcina	.40	.18
173	Damion Easley	.40	.18
174	Chuck Finley	.40	.18
175	Mark Langston	.40	.18
176	Luis Polonia	.40	.18
177	Tim Salmon	2.00	.90
178	Scott Sanderson	.40	.18
179	J.T.Snow	2.00	.90
180	Wilson Alvarez	.60	.25
181	Ellis Burks	.60	.25
182	Joey Cora	.40	.18
183	Alex Fernandez	.40	.18
184	Ozzie Guillen	.40	.18
185	Roberto Hernandez	.60	.25
186	Bo Jackson	.60	.25
187	Lance Johnson	.40	.18
188	Jack McDowell	.40	.18
189	Frank Thomas	6.00	2.70
190	Robin Ventura	.60	.25
191	Carlos Baerga	.40	.18
192	Albert Belle	2.00	.90
193	Wayne Kirby	.40	.18
194	Derek Lilliquist	.40	.18
195	Kenny Lofton	3.00	1.35
196	Carlos Martinez	.40	.18
197	Jose Mesa	.40	.18
198	Eric Plunk	.40	.18
199	Paul Sorrento	.40	.18
200	John Doherty	.40	.18
201	Cecil Fielder	.60	.25
202	Travis Fryman	.60	.25
203	Kirk Gibson	.60	.25
204	Mike Henneman	.40	.18
205	Chad Kreuter	.40	.18
206	Scott Livingstone	.40	.18
207	Tony Phillips	.40	.18
208	Mickey Tettleton	.40	.18
209	Alan Trammell	1.00	.45
210	David Wells	.40	.18
211	Lou Whitaker	.60	.25
212	Kevin Appier	.60	.25
213	George Brett	3.00	1.35
214	David Cone	.60	.25
215	Tom Gordon	.40	.18
216	Phil Hiatt	.40	.18
217	Felix Jose	.40	.18
218	Wally Joyner	.60	.25
219	Jose Lind	.40	.18
220	Mike Macfarlane	.40	.18
221	Brian McRae	.40	.18
222	Jeff Montgomery	.60	.25
223	Cal Eldred	.40	.18
224	Darryl Hamilton	.40	.18
225	John Jaha	.60	.25
226	Pat Listach	.40	.18
227	Graeme Lloyd	.40	.18
228	Kevin Reimer	.40	.18
229	Bill Spiers	.40	.18
230	B.J.Surhoff	.60	.25
231	Greg Vaughn	.40	.18
232	Robin Yount	1.00	.45
233	Rick Aguilera	.40	.18
234	Jim Deshaies	.40	.18
235	Brian Harper	.40	.18
236	Kent Hrbek	.60	.25
237	Chuck Knoblauch	1.50	.70
238	Shane Mack	.40	.18
239	David McCarty	.40	.18
240	Pedro Munoz	.40	.18
241	Mike Pagliarulo	.40	.18
242	Kirby Puckett	3.00	1.35
243	Dave Winfield	1.00	.45
244	Jim Abbott	.40	.18
245	Wade Boggs	1.50	.70
246	Pat Kelly	.40	.18
247	Jimmy Key	.60	.25
248	Jim Leyritz	.40	.18
249	Don Mattingly	2.50	1.10
250	Matt Nokes	.40	.18
251	Paul O'Neill	.60	.25
252	Mike Stanley	.40	.18
253	Danny Tartabull	.40	.18
254	Bob Wickman	.40	.18
255	Bernie Williams	1.50	.70
256	Mike Bordick	.40	.18
257	Dennis Eckersley	.60	.25

☐ 258 Brent Gates	.40	.18
☐ 259 Goose Gossage	.60	.25
☐ 260 Rickey Henderson	1.00	.45
☐ 261 Mark McGwire	3.00	1.35
☐ 262 Ruben Sierra	.40	.18
☐ 263 Terry Steinbach	.40	.18
☐ 264 Bob Welch	.40	.18
☐ 265 Bobby Witt	.40	.18
☐ 266 Rich Amaral	.40	.18
☐ 267 Chris Bosio	.40	.18
☐ 268 Jay Buhner	1.00	.45
☐ 269 Norm Charlton	.40	.18
☐ 270 Ken Griffey Jr.	8.00	3.60
☐ 271 Erik Hanson	.40	.18
☐ 272 Randy Johnson	1.50	.70
☐ 273 Edgar Martinez	1.00	.45
☐ 274 Tino Martinez	1.50	.70
☐ 275 Dave Valle	.40	.18
☐ 276 Omar Vizquel	.60	.25
☐ 277 Kevin Brown	.60	.25
☐ 278 Jose Canseco	1.00	.45
☐ 279 Julio Franco	.40	.18
☐ 280 Juan Gonzalez	4.00	1.80
☐ 281 Tom Henke	.40	.18
☐ 282 David Hulse	.40	.18
☐ 283 Rafael Palmeiro	1.00	.45
☐ 284 Dean Palmer	.40	.18
☐ 285 Ivan Rodriguez	2.00	.90
☐ 286 Nolan Ryan	6.00	2.70
☐ 287 Roberto Alomar	1.50	.70
☐ 288 Pat Borders	.40	.18
☐ 289 Joe Carter	.60	.25
☐ 290 Juan Guzman	.40	.18
☐ 291 Pat Hentgen	1.00	.45
☐ 292 Paul Molitor	1.50	.70
☐ 293 John Olerud	.40	.18
☐ 294 Ed Sprague	.40	.18
☐ 295 Dave Stewart	.60	.25
☐ 296 Duane Ward	.40	.18
☐ 297 Devon White	.40	.18
☐ 298 Checklist 1-100	.40	.18
☐ 299 Checklist 101-200	.40	.18
☐ 300 Checklist 201-300	.40	.18

1993 Flair Wave of the Future

This 20-card standard-size limited edition insert set features a selection of top prospects. Cards were randomly seeded into 1993 Flair packs. Each card is made of the same thick card stock as the regular-issue set and features full-bleed color player action photos on the fronts, with the Flair logo, player's name, and the "Wave of the Future" name and logo in gold foil, all superimposed upon an ocean breaker.

	MINT	NRMT
COMPLETE SET (20)	40.00	18.00
COMMON CARD (1-20)	1.00	.45

SEMISTARS	2.00	.90
STATED ODDS 1:4		

☐ 1 Jason Bere	1.00	.45
☐ 2 Jeromy Burnitz	1.00	.45
☐ 3 Russ Davis	1.50	.70
☐ 4 Jim Edmonds	10.00	4.50
☐ 5 Cliff Floyd	1.00	.45
☐ 6 Jeffrey Hammonds	2.00	.90
☐ 7 Trevor Hoffman	2.00	.90
☐ 8 Domingo Jean	1.00	.45
☐ 9 David McCarty	1.00	.45
☐ 10 Bobby Munoz	1.00	.45
☐ 11 Brad Pennington	1.00	.45
☐ 12 Mike Piazza	15.00	6.75
☐ 13 Manny Ramirez	8.00	3.60
☐ 14 John Roper	1.00	.45
☐ 15 Tim Salmon	5.00	2.20
☐ 16 Aaron Sele	1.00	.45
☐ 17 Allen Watson	1.00	.45
☐ 18 Rondell White	2.00	.90
☐ 19 Darrell Whitmore UER	1.00	.45
(Nigel Wilson back)		
☐ 20 Nigel Wilson UER	1.00	.45
(Darrell Whitmore back)		

1994 Flair

For the second consecutive year Fleer issued a Flair brand. The set consists of 450 full bleed cards in two series of 250 and 200. The card stock is thicker than the traditional standard card. Card fronts feature two photos with the player's name and team name at the bottom in gold foil. The first letter of the player's last name appears within a gold shield to add style to this premium brand product. The backs are horizontal with a player photo and statistics. The team logo and player's name are done in gold foil. The cards are grouped alphabetically by team within each league with AL preceding NL. Notable Rookie Cards include Chan Ho Park and Alex Rodriguez.

	MINT	NRMT
COMPLETE SET (450)	60.00	27.00
COMPLETE SERIES 1 (250)	25.00	11.00
COMPLETE SERIES 2 (200)	35.00	16.00
COMMON CARD (1-450)	.25	.11
MINOR STARS	.50	.23
UNLISTED STARS	1.00	.45

☐ 1 Harold Baines	.50	.23
☐ 2 Jeffrey Hammonds	.50	.23
☐ 3 Chris Hoiles	.25	.11
☐ 4 Ben McDonald	.25	.11
☐ 5 Mark McLemore	.25	.11
☐ 6 Jamie Moyer	.25	.11
☐ 7 Jim Poole	.25	.11
☐ 8 Cal Ripken Jr.	4.00	1.80
☐ 9 Chris Sabo	.25	.11
☐ 10 Scott Bankhead	.25	.11
☐ 11 Scott Cooper	.25	.11
☐ 12 Danny Darwin	.25	.11
☐ 13 Andre Dawson	.75	.35
☐ 14 Billy Hatcher	.25	.11
☐ 15 Aaron Sele	.25	.11
☐ 16 John Valentin	.50	.23
☐ 17 Dave Valle	.25	.11
☐ 18 Mo Vaughn	1.25	.55
☐ 19 Brian Anderson	1.00	.45
☐ 20 Gary DiSarcina	.25	.11
☐ 21 Jim Edmonds	1.00	.45
☐ 22 Chuck Finley	.25	.11
☐ 23 Bo Jackson	.50	.23
☐ 24 Mark Leiter	.25	.11
☐ 25 Greg Myers	.25	.11
☐ 26 Eduardo Perez	.25	.11
☐ 27 Tim Salmon	1.00	.45
☐ 28 Wilson Alvarez	.25	.11
☐ 29 Jason Bere	.25	.11
☐ 30 Alex Fernandez	.25	.11
☐ 31 Ozzie Guillen	.25	.11
☐ 32 Joe Hall	.25	.11
☐ 33 Darrin Jackson	.25	.11
☐ 34 Kirk McCaskill	.25	.11
☐ 35 Tim Raines	.25	.11
☐ 36 Frank Thomas	4.00	1.80
☐ 37 Carlos Baerga	.25	.11
☐ 38 Albert Belle	1.25	.55
☐ 39 Mark Clark	.25	.11
☐ 40 Wayne Kirby	.25	.11
☐ 41 Dennis Martinez	.50	.23
☐ 42 Charles Nagy	.50	.23
☐ 43 Manny Ramirez	1.25	.55
☐ 44 Paul Sorrento	.25	.11
☐ 45 Jim Thome	1.25	.55
☐ 46 Eric Davis	.50	.23
☐ 47 John Doherty	.25	.11
☐ 48 Junior Felix	.25	.11
☐ 49 Cecil Fielder	.50	.23
☐ 50 Kirk Gibson	.50	.23
☐ 51 Mike Moore	.25	.11
☐ 52 Tony Phillips	.25	.11
☐ 53 Alan Trammell	.75	.35
☐ 54 Kevin Appier	.50	.23
☐ 55 Stan Belinda	.25	.11
☐ 56 Vince Coleman	.25	.11
☐ 57 Greg Gagne	.25	.11
☐ 58 Bob Hamelin	.25	.11
☐ 59 Dave Henderson	.25	.11
☐ 60 Wally Joyner	.50	.23
☐ 61 Mike Macfarlane	.25	.11
☐ 62 Jeff Montgomery	.25	.11
☐ 63 Ricky Bones	.25	.11
☐ 64 Jeff Bronkey	.25	.11
☐ 65 Alex Diaz	.25	.11
☐ 66 Cal Eldred	.25	.11
☐ 67 Darryl Hamilton	.25	.11
☐ 68 John Jaha	.25	.11
☐ 69 Mark Kiefer	.25	.11
☐ 70 Kevin Seitzer	.25	.11
☐ 71 Turner Ward	.25	.11
☐ 72 Rich Becker	.25	.11
☐ 73 Scott Erickson	.25	.11
☐ 74 Keith Garagozzo	.25	.11
☐ 75 Kent Hrbek	.50	.23
☐ 76 Scott Leius	.25	.11
☐ 77 Kirby Puckett	2.00	.90
☐ 78 Matt Walbeck	.25	.11
☐ 79 Dave Winfield	.75	.35
☐ 80 Mike Gallego	.25	.11
☐ 81 Xavier Hernandez	.25	.11
☐ 82 Jimmy Key	.50	.23
☐ 83 Jim Leyritz	.25	.11
☐ 84 Don Mattingly	1.50	.70
☐ 85 Matt Nokes	.25	.11
☐ 86 Paul O'Neill	.50	.23
☐ 87 Melido Perez	.25	.11
☐ 88 Danny Tartabull	.25	.11
☐ 89 Mike Bordick	.25	.11
☐ 90 Ron Darling	.25	.11
☐ 91 Dennis Eckersley	.50	.23
☐ 92 Stan Javier	.25	.11
☐ 93 Steve Karsay	.25	.11

#	Player	Price	Price
94	Mark McGwire	2.00	.90
95	Troy Neel	.25	.11
96	Terry Steinbach	.25	.11
97	Bill Taylor	.25	.11
98	Eric Anthony	.25	.11
99	Chris Bosio	.25	.11
100	Tim Davis	.25	.11
101	Felix Fermin	.25	.11
102	Dave Fleming	.25	.11
103	Ken Griffey Jr.	5.00	2.20
104	Greg Hibbard	.25	.11
105	Reggie Jefferson	.25	.11
106	Tino Martinez	1.00	.45
107	Jack Armstrong	.25	.11
108	Will Clark	.75	.35
109	Juan Gonzalez	2.50	1.10
110	Rick Helling	.25	.11
111	Tom Henke	.25	.11
112	David Hulse	.25	.11
113	Manuel Lee	.25	.11
114	Doug Strange	.25	.11
115	Roberto Alomar	1.00	.45
116	Joe Carter	.50	.23
117	Carlos Delgado	.75	.35
118	Pat Hentgen	.25	.23
119	Paul Molitor	1.00	.45
120	John Olerud	.25	.23
121	Dave Stewart	.50	.23
122	Todd Stottlemyre	.25	.11
123	Mike Timlin	.25	.11
124	Jeff Blauser	.50	.23
125	Tom Glavine	.50	.23
126	David Justice	1.00	.45
127	Mike Kelly	.25	.11
128	Ryan Klesko	1.00	.45
129	Javier Lopez	.75	.35
130	Greg Maddux	3.00	1.35
131	Fred McGriff	.75	.35
132	Kent Mercker	.25	.11
133	Mark Wohlers	.25	.11
134	Willie Banks	.25	.11
135	Steve Buechele	.25	.11
136	Shawon Dunston	.25	.11
137	Jose Guzman	.25	.11
138	Glenallen Hill	.25	.11
139	Randy Myers	.25	.11
140	Karl Rhodes	.25	.11
141	Ryne Sandberg	1.25	.55
142	Steve Trachsel	.50	.23
143	Bret Boone	.25	.11
144	Tom Browning	.25	.11
145	Hector Carrasco	.25	.11
146	Barry Larkin	.75	.35
147	Hal Morris	.25	.11
148	Jose Rijo	.25	.11
149	Reggie Sanders	.25	.11
150	John Smiley	.25	.11
151	Dante Bichette	.50	.23
152	Ellis Burks	.50	.23
153	Joe Girardi	.25	.11
154	Mike Harkey	.25	.11
155	Roberto Mejia	.25	.11
156	Marcus Moore	.25	.11
157	Armando Reynoso	.25	.11
158	Bruce Ruffin	.25	.11
159	Eric Young	.25	.11
160	Kurt Abbott	.25	.11
161	Jeff Conine	.50	.23
162	Orestes Destrade	.25	.11
163	Chris Hammond	.25	.11
164	Bryan Harvey	.25	.11
165	Dave Magadan	.25	.11
166	Gary Sheffield	1.00	.45
167	David Weathers	.25	.11
168	Andujar Cedeno	.25	.11
169	Tom Edens	.25	.11
170	Luis Gonzalez	.25	.11
171	Pete Harnisch	.25	.11
172	Todd Jones	.25	.11
173	Darryl Kile	.25	.23
174	James Mouton	.25	.11
175	Scott Servais	.25	.11
176	Mitch Williams	.25	.11
177	Pedro Astacio	.25	.11
178	Orel Hershiser	.50	.23
179	Raul Mondesi	1.00	.45
180	Jose Offerman	.25	.11
181	Chan Ho Park	4.00	1.80
182	Mike Piazza	3.00	1.35
183	Cory Snyder	.25	.11
184	Tim Wallach	.25	.11
185	Todd Worrell	.25	.11
186	Sean Berry	.25	.11
187	Wil Cordero	.25	.11
188	Darrin Fletcher	.25	.11
189	Cliff Floyd	.50	.23
190	Marquis Grissom	.50	.23
191	Rod Henderson	.25	.11
192	Ken Hill	.25	.11
193	Pedro Martinez	1.00	.45
194	Kirk Rueter	.25	.11
195	Jeromy Burnitz	.25	.11
196	John Franco	.50	.23
197	Dwight Gooden	.50	.23
198	Todd Hundley	.25	.23
199	Bobby Jones	.50	.23
200	Jeff Kent	.25	.11
201	Mike Maddux	.25	.11
202	Ryan Thompson	.25	.11
203	Jose Vizcaino	.25	.11
204	Darren Daulton	.50	.23
205	Lenny Dykstra	.50	.23
206	Jim Eisenreich	.25	.11
207	Dave Hollins	.25	.11
208	Danny Jackson	.25	.11
209	Doug Jones	.25	.11
210	Jeff Juden	.25	.11
211	Ben Rivera	.25	.11
212	Kevin Stocker	.25	.11
213	Milt Thompson	.25	.11
214	Jay Bell	.50	.23
215	Steve Cooke	.25	.11
216	Mark Dewey	.25	.11
217	Al Martin	.25	.11
218	Orlando Merced	.25	.11
219	Don Slaught	.25	.11
220	Zane Smith	.25	.11
221	Rick White	.25	.11
222	Kevin Young	.25	.11
223	Rene Arocha	.25	.11
224	Rheal Cormier	.25	.11
225	Brian Jordan	.50	.23
226	Ray Lankford	.50	.23
227	Mike Perez	.25	.11
228	Ozzie Smith	1.25	.55
229	Mark Whiten	.25	.11
230	Todd Zeile	.25	.11
231	Derek Bell	.25	.11
232	Archi Cianfrocco	.25	.11
233	Ricky Gutierrez	.25	.11
234	Trevor Hoffman	.25	.11
235	Phil Plantier	.25	.11
236	Dave Staton	.25	.11
237	Wally Whitehurst	.25	.11
238	Todd Benzinger	.25	.11
239	Barry Bonds	1.25	.55
240	John Burkett	.25	.11
241	Royce Clayton	.25	.11
242	Bryan Hickerson	.25	.11
243	Mike Jackson	.25	.11
244	Darren Lewis	.25	.11
245	Kirt Manwaring	.25	.11
246	Mark Portugal	.25	.11
247	Salomon Torres	.25	.11
248	Checklist	.25	.11
249	Checklist	.25	.11
250	Checklist	.25	.11
251	Brady Anderson	.35	.11
252	Mike Devereaux	.25	.11
253	Sid Fernandez	.25	.11
254	Leo Gomez	.25	.11
255	Mike Mussina	1.00	.45
256	Mike Oquist	.25	.11
257	Rafael Palmeiro	.75	.35
258	Lee Smith	.50	.23
259	Damon Berryhill	.25	.11
260	Wes Chamberlain	.25	.11
261	Roger Clemens	2.00	.90
262	Gar Finnvold	.25	.11
263	Mike Greenwell	.25	.23
264	Tim Naehring	.25	.11
265	Otis Nixon	.25	.11
266	Ken Ryan	.25	.11
267	Chad Curtis	.25	.11
268	Chili Davis	.50	.23
269	Damion Easley	.25	.11
270	Jorge Fabregas	.25	.11
271	Mark Langston	.25	.11
272	Phil Leftwich	.25	.11
273	Harold Reynolds	.25	.11
274	J.T. Snow	1.00	.45
275	Joey Cora	.50	.23
276	Julio Franco	.25	.11
277	Roberto Hernandez	.25	.11
278	Lance Johnson	.25	.11
279	Ron Karkovice	.25	.11
280	Jack McDowell	.25	.11
281	Robin Ventura	.50	.23
282	Sandy Alomar Jr.	.50	.23
283	Kenny Lofton	1.25	.55
284	Jose Mesa	.25	.11
285	Jack Morris	.50	.23
286	Eddie Murray	1.00	.45
287	Chad Ogea	.50	.23
288	Eric Plunk	.25	.11
289	Paul Shuey	.25	.11
290	Omar Vizquel	.50	.23
291	Danny Bautista	.25	.11
292	Travis Fryman	.50	.23
293	Greg Gohr	.25	.11
294	Chris Gomez	.25	.11
295	Mickey Tettleton	.25	.11
296	Lou Whitaker	.50	.23
297	David Cone	.50	.23
298	Gary Gaetti	.25	.11
299	Tom Gordon	.25	.11
300	Felix Jose	.25	.11
301	Jose Lind	.25	.11
302	Brian McRae	.25	.11
303	Mike Fetters	.25	.11
304	Brian Harper	.25	.11
305	Pat Listach	.25	.11
306	Matt Mieske	.25	.11
307	Dave Nilsson	.25	.11
308	Jody Reed	.25	.11
309	Greg Vaughn	.25	.11
310	Bill Wegman	.25	.11
311	Rick Aguilera	.25	.11
312	Alex Cole	.25	.11
313	Denny Hocking	.25	.11
314	Chuck Knoblauch	1.00	.45
315	Shane Mack	.25	.11
316	Pat Meares	.25	.11
317	Kevin Tapani	.25	.11
318	Jim Abbott	.25	.11
319	Wade Boggs	1.00	.45
320	Sterling Hitchcock	.25	.11
321	Pat Kelly	.25	.11
322	Terry Mulholland	.25	.11
323	Luis Polonia	.25	.11
324	Mike Stanley	.25	.11
325	Bob Wickman	.25	.11
326	Bernie Williams	1.00	.45
327	Mark Acre	.25	.11
328	Geronimo Berroa	.25	.11
329	Scott Brosius	.25	.11
330	Brent Gates	.25	.11
331	Rickey Henderson	.75	.35
332	Carlos Reyes	.25	.11
333	Ruben Sierra	.25	.11
334	Bobby Witt	.25	.11
335	Bobby Ayala	.25	.11
336	Jay Buhner	.75	.35
337	Randy Johnson	1.00	.45
338	Edgar Martinez	.75	.35
339	Bill Risley	.25	.11
340	Alex Rodriguez	20.00	9.00
341	Roger Salkeld	.25	.11
342	Dan Wilson	.50	.23
343	Kevin Brown	.50	.23
344	Jose Canseco	.75	.35
345	Dean Palmer	.25	.11
346	Ivan Rodriguez	1.25	.55
347	Kenny Rogers	.25	.11
348	Pat Borders	.25	.11
349	Juan Guzman	.25	.11
350	Ed Sprague	.25	.11
351	Devon White	.25	.11

☐ 352 Steve Avery	.25	.11
☐ 353 Roberto Kelly	.25	.11
☐ 354 Mark Lemke	.25	.11
☐ 355 Greg McMichael	.25	.11
☐ 356 Terry Pendleton	.25	.11
☐ 357 John Smoltz	.50	.23
☐ 358 Mike Stanton	.25	.11
☐ 359 Tony Tarasco	.25	.11
☐ 360 Mark Grace	.75	.35
☐ 361 Derrick May	.25	.11
☐ 362 Rey Sanchez	.25	.11
☐ 363 Sammy Sosa	1.00	.45
☐ 364 Rick Wilkins	.25	.11
☐ 365 Jeff Brantley	.25	.11
☐ 366 Tony Fernandez	.25	.11
☐ 367 Chuck McElroy	.25	.11
☐ 368 Kevin Mitchell	.25	.11
☐ 369 John Roper	.25	.11
☐ 370 Johnny Ruffin	.25	.11
☐ 371 Deion Sanders	.50	.23
☐ 372 Marvin Freeman	.25	.11
☐ 373 Andres Galarraga	1.00	.45
☐ 374 Charlie Hayes	.25	.11
☐ 375 Nelson Liriano	.25	.11
☐ 376 David Nied	.25	.11
☐ 377 Walt Weiss	.25	.11
☐ 378 Bret Barberie	.25	.11
☐ 379 Jerry Browne	.25	.11
☐ 380 Chuck Carr	.25	.11
☐ 381 Greg Colbrunn	.25	.11
☐ 382 Charlie Hough	.25	.11
☐ 383 Kurt Miller	.25	.11
☐ 384 Benito Santiago	.25	.11
☐ 385 Jeff Bagwell	2.00	.90
☐ 386 Craig Biggio	.75	.35
☐ 387 Ken Caminiti	.75	.35
☐ 388 Doug Drabek	.25	.11
☐ 389 Steve Finley	.50	.23
☐ 390 John Hudek	.25	.11
☐ 391 Orlando Miller	.25	.11
☐ 392 Shane Reynolds	.25	.11
☐ 393 Brett Butler	.50	.23
☐ 394 Tom Candiotti	.25	.11
☐ 395 Delino DeShields	.25	.11
☐ 396 Kevin Gross	.25	.11
☐ 397 Eric Karros	.50	.23
☐ 398 Ramon Martinez	.50	.23
☐ 399 Henry Rodriguez	.25	.11
☐ 400 Moises Alou	.50	.23
☐ 401 Jeff Fassero	.25	.11
☐ 402 Mike Lansing	.50	.23
☐ 403 Mel Rojas	.25	.11
☐ 404 Larry Walker	1.00	.45
☐ 405 John Wetteland	.25	.11
☐ 406 Gabe White	.25	.11
☐ 407 Bobby Bonilla	.50	.23
☐ 408 Josias Manzanillo	.25	.11
☐ 409 Bret Saberhagen	.25	.11
☐ 410 David Segui	.25	.11
☐ 411 Mariano Duncan	.25	.11
☐ 412 Tommy Greene	.25	.11
☐ 413 Billy Hatcher	.25	.11
☐ 414 Ricky Jordan	.25	.11
☐ 415 John Kruk	.50	.23
☐ 416 Bobby Munoz	.25	.11
☐ 417 Curt Schilling	.50	.23
☐ 418 Fernando Valenzuela	.50	.23
☐ 419 David West	.25	.11
☐ 420 Carlos Garcia	.25	.11
☐ 421 Brian Hunter	.25	.11
☐ 422 Jeff King	.25	.11
☐ 423 Jon Lieber	.25	.11
☐ 424 Ravelo Manzanillo	.25	.11
☐ 425 Denny Neagle	.50	.23
☐ 426 Andy Van Slyke	.50	.23
☐ 427 Bryan Eversgerd	.25	.11
☐ 428 Bernard Gilkey	.25	.11
☐ 429 Gregg Jefferies	.50	.23
☐ 430 Tom Pagnozzi	.25	.11
☐ 431 Bob Tewksbury	.25	.11
☐ 432 Allen Watson	.25	.11
☐ 433 Andy Ashby	.25	.11
☐ 434 Andy Benes	.50	.23
☐ 435 Donnie Elliott	.25	.11
☐ 436 Tony Gwynn	2.50	1.10
☐ 437 Joey Hamilton	1.00	.45

☐ 438 Tim Hyers	.25	.11
☐ 439 Luis Lopez	.25	.11
☐ 440 Bip Roberts	.25	.11
☐ 441 Scott Sanders	.25	.11
☐ 442 Rod Beck	.25	.11
☐ 443 Dave Burba	.25	.11
☐ 444 Darryl Strawberry	.50	.23
☐ 445 Bill Swift	.25	.11
☐ 446 Robby Thompson	.25	.11
☐ 447 Bill VanLandingham	.50	.23
☐ 448 Matt Williams	.75	.35
☐ 449 Checklist	.25	.11
☐ 450 Checklist	.25	.11
☐ P15 Aaron Sele Promo	1.50	.70

1994 Flair Hot Gloves

Randomly inserted in second series packs at a rate of one in 24, this set highlights 10 of the game's top players that also have outstanding defensive ability. The cards feature a special die-cut "glove" design with the player appearing within the glove. The back has a short write-up and a photo.

	MINT	NRMT
COMPLETE SET (10)	180.00	80.00
COMMON CARD (1-10)	8.00	3.60
UNLISTED STARS	10.00	4.50
RANDOM INSERTS IN SER.2 PACKS		

☐ 1 Barry Bonds	15.00	6.75
☐ 2 Will Clark	10.00	4.50
☐ 3 Ken Griffey Jr.	60.00	27.00
☐ 4 Kenny Lofton	15.00	6.75
☐ 5 Greg Maddux	40.00	18.00
☐ 6 Don Mattingly	20.00	9.00
☐ 7 Kirby Puckett	25.00	11.00
☐ 8 Cal Ripken Jr.	50.00	22.00
☐ 9 Tim Salmon	10.00	4.50
☐ 10 Matt Williams	10.00	4.50

1994 Flair Hot Numbers

This 10-card set was randomly inserted in first series packs at a rate of one in 24. Metallic fronts feature a player photo with various numbers or statistics serving as background. The player's uniform number is part of the Hot Numbers logo at bottom left or right. The player's name is also at the bottom. The backs have a small photo centered in the middle surrounded by text highlighting achievements.

	MINT	NRMT
COMPLETE SET (10)	90.00	40.00
COMMON CARD (1-10)	1.50	.70
RANDOM INSERTS IN SER.1 PACKS		

☐ 1 Roberto Alomar	6.00	2.70
☐ 2 Carlos Baerga	1.50	.70
☐ 3 Will Clark	4.00	1.80
☐ 4 Fred McGriff	4.00	1.80
☐ 5 Paul Molitor	6.00	2.70
☐ 6 John Olerud	3.00	1.35
☐ 7 Mike Piazza	20.00	9.00
☐ 8 Cal Ripken Jr.	25.00	11.00
☐ 9 Ryne Sandberg	7.50	3.40
☐ 10 Frank Thomas	25.00	11.00

1994 Flair Infield Power

Randomly inserted in second series packs at a rate of one in five, this 10-card standard-size set spotlights major league infielders who are power hitters. Card fronts feature a horizontal format with two photos of the player. The backs contain a short write-up with emphasis on power numbers. The back also has a small photo.

	MINT	NRMT
COMPLETE SET (10)	18.00	8.00
COMMON CARD (1-10)	.75	.35
RANDOM INSERTS IN SER.2 PACKS		

☐ 1 Jeff Bagwell	3.00	1.35
☐ 2 Will Clark	1.00	.45
☐ 3 Darren Daulton	.75	.35
☐ 4 Don Mattingly	2.00	.90
☐ 5 Fred McGriff	1.00	.45
☐ 6 Rafael Palmeiro	1.00	.45
☐ 7 Mike Piazza	5.00	2.20
☐ 8 Cal Ripken Jr.	6.00	2.70
☐ 9 Frank Thomas	6.00	2.70
☐ 10 Matt Williams	1.00	.45

1994 Flair Outfield Power

	MINT	NRMT
COMPLETE SET (20)	55.00	25.00
COMPLETE SERIES 1 (10)	15.00	6.75
COMPLETE SERIES 2 (10)	40.00	18.00
COMMON CARD (A1-B10)	1.00	.45
MINOR STARS	1.50	.70
RANDOM INSERTS IN BOTH SERIES PACKS		

		MINT	NRMT
☐ A1	Kurt Abbott	1.00	.45
☐ A2	Carlos Delgado	2.50	1.10
☐ A3	Steve Karsay	1.00	.45
☐ A4	Ryan Klesko	3.00	1.35
☐ A5	Javier Lopez	2.50	1.10
☐ A6	Raul Mondesi	3.00	1.35
☐ A7	James Mouton	1.00	.45
☐ A8	Chan Ho Park	8.00	3.60
☐ A9	Dave Staton	1.00	.45
☐ A10	Rick White	1.00	.45
☐ B1	Mark Acre	1.00	.45
☐ B2	Chris Gomez	1.00	.45
☐ B3	Joey Hamilton	2.50	1.10
☐ B4	John Hudek	1.00	.45
☐ B5	Jon Lieber	1.00	.45
☐ B6	Matt Mieske	1.00	.45
☐ B7	Orlando Miller	1.00	.45
☐ B8	Alex Rodriguez	30.00	13.50
☐ B9	Tony Tarasco	1.00	.45
☐ B10	William VanLandingham	1.50	.70

This 10-card standard-size set was randomly inserted in both first and second series packs at a rate of one in five. Two photos on the front feature the player fielding and hitting. The player's name and Outfield Power serve as a dividing point between the photos. The back contains a small photo and text.

	MINT	NRMT
COMPLETE SET (10)	25.00	11.00
COMMON CARD (1-10)	.50	.23
RANDOM INSERTS IN SER.1 PACKS		

		MINT	NRMT
☐ 1	Albert Belle	2.50	1.10
☐ 2	Barry Bonds	2.50	1.10
☐ 3	Joe Carter	1.00	.45
☐ 4	Lenny Dykstra	.50	.23
☐ 5	Juan Gonzalez	5.00	2.20
☐ 6	Ken Griffey Jr.	10.00	4.50
☐ 7	David Justice	2.00	.90
☐ 8	Kirby Puckett	4.00	1.80
☐ 9	Tim Salmon	2.00	.90
☐ 10	Dave Winfield	1.50	.70

1994 Flair Wave of the Future

This 20-card standard-size set takes a look at potential big league stars. The cards were randomly inserted in packs at a rate of one in five -- the first 10 in series 1, the second 10 in series 2. The fronts and backs have the player superimposed over a wavy colored background. The front has the Wave of the Future logo and a paragraph or two about the player along with a photo on the back.

1995 Flair

This set was issued in two series of 216 cards for a total of 432 standard-size cards. Horizontally designed fronts have a 100 percent etched foil surface containing two player photos. The backs feature a full-bleed photo with yearly statistics superimposed. The checklist is arranged alphabetically by league with AL preceding NL.

	MINT	NRMT
COMPLETE SET (432)	80.00	36.00
COMPLETE SERIES 1 (216)	50.00	22.00
COMPLETE SERIES 2 (216)	30.00	13.50
COMMON CARD (1-432)	.25	.11
MINOR STARS	.50	.23
UNLISTED STARS	1.00	.45
COMP.RIPKEN SET (10)	80.00	36.00
COMMON RIPKEN (1-10)	10.00	4.50
RIPKEN SER.2 STATED ODDS 1:12		
COMMON MAIL-IN (11-15)	.25	.11
MAIL-IN AVAIL.VIA WRAPPER EXCH.		2.70

		MINT	NRMT
☐ 1	Brady Anderson	.75	.35
☐ 2	Harold Baines	.50	.23
☐ 3	Leo Gomez	.25	.11
☐ 4	Alan Mills	.25	.11
☐ 5	Jamie Moyer	.25	.11
☐ 6	Mike Mussina	1.00	.45
☐ 7	Mike Oquist	.25	.11
☐ 8	Arthur Rhodes	.25	.11
☐ 9	Cal Ripken Jr.	4.00	1.80
☐ 10	Roger Clemens	2.00	.90
☐ 11	Scott Cooper	.25	.11
☐ 12	Mike Greenwell	.25	.11
☐ 13	Aaron Sele	.25	.11
☐ 14	John Valentin	.25	.11
☐ 15	Mo Vaughn	1.25	.55
☐ 16	Chad Curtis	.25	.11
☐ 17	Gary DiSarcina	.25	.11
☐ 18	Chuck Finley	.25	.11
☐ 19	Andrew Lorraine	.25	.11
☐ 20	Spike Owen	.25	.11
☐ 21	Tim Salmon	1.00	.45
☐ 22	J.T. Snow	.50	.23
☐ 23	Wilson Alvarez	.25	.11
☐ 24	Jason Bere	.25	.11
☐ 25	Ozzie Guillen	.25	.11
☐ 26	Mike LaValliere	.25	.11
☐ 27	Frank Thomas	4.00	1.80
☐ 28	Robin Ventura	.50	.23
☐ 29	Carlos Baerga	.25	.11
☐ 30	Albert Belle	1.25	.55
☐ 31	Jason Grimsley	.25	.11
☐ 32	Dennis Martinez	.50	.23
☐ 33	Eddie Murray	1.00	.45
☐ 34	Charles Nagy	.50	.23
☐ 35	Manny Ramirez	1.00	.45
☐ 36	Paul Sorrento	.25	.11
☐ 37	John Doherty	.25	.11
☐ 38	Cecil Fielder	.50	.23
☐ 39	Travis Fryman	.50	.23
☐ 40	Chris Gomez	.25	.11
☐ 41	Tony Phillips	.25	.11
☐ 42	Lou Whitaker	.50	.23
☐ 43	David Cone	.50	.23
☐ 44	Gary Gaetti	.25	.11
☐ 45	Mark Gubicza	.25	.11
☐ 46	Bob Hamelin	.25	.11
☐ 47	Wally Joyner	.50	.23
☐ 48	Rusty Meacham	.25	.11
☐ 49	Jeff Montgomery	.25	.11
☐ 50	Ricky Bones	.25	.11
☐ 51	Cal Eldred	.25	.11
☐ 52	Pat Listach	.25	.11
☐ 53	Matt Mieske	.25	.11
☐ 54	Dave Nilsson	.25	.11
☐ 55	Greg Vaughn	.25	.11
☐ 56	Bill Wegman	.25	.11
☐ 57	Chuck Knoblauch	1.00	.45
☐ 58	Scott Leius	.25	.11
☐ 59	Pat Mahomes	.25	.11
☐ 60	Pat Meares	.25	.11
☐ 61	Pedro Munoz	.25	.11
☐ 62	Kirby Puckett	2.00	.90
☐ 63	Wade Boggs	1.00	.45
☐ 64	Jimmy Key	.50	.23
☐ 65	Jim Leyritz	.25	.11
☐ 66	Don Mattingly	1.50	.70
☐ 67	Paul O'Neill	.50	.23
☐ 68	Melido Perez	.25	.11
☐ 69	Danny Tartabull	.25	.11
☐ 70	John Briscoe	.25	.11
☐ 71	Scott Brosius	.25	.11
☐ 72	Ron Darling	.25	.11
☐ 73	Brent Gates	.25	.11
☐ 74	Rickey Henderson	.75	.35
☐ 75	Stan Javier	.25	.11
☐ 76	Mark McGwire	2.00	.90
☐ 77	Todd Van Poppel	.25	.11
☐ 78	Bobby Ayala	.25	.11
☐ 79	Mike Blowers	.25	.11
☐ 80	Jay Buhner	.75	.35
☐ 81	Ken Griffey Jr.	5.00	2.20
☐ 82	Randy Johnson	1.00	.45
☐ 83	Tino Martinez	1.00	.45
☐ 84	Jeff Nelson	.25	.11
☐ 85	Alex Rodriguez	4.00	1.80
☐ 86	Will Clark	.75	.35
☐ 87	Jeff Frye	.25	.11
☐ 88	Juan Gonzalez	2.50	1.10
☐ 89	Rusty Greer	1.00	.45
☐ 90	Darren Oliver	.50	.23
☐ 91	Dean Palmer	.25	.11
☐ 92	Ivan Rodriguez	1.25	.55
☐ 93	Matt Whiteside	.25	.11
☐ 94	Roberto Alomar	1.00	.45
☐ 95	Joe Carter	.50	.23
☐ 96	Tony Castillo	.25	.11
☐ 97	Juan Guzman	.25	.11

#	Player			#	Player			#	Player		
98	Pat Hentgen	.50	.23	184	Jay Bell	.50	.23	270	Darryl Hamilton	.25	.11
99	Mike Huff	.25	.11	185	Steve Cooke	.25	.11	271	David Hulse	.25	.11
100	John Olerud	.50	.23	186	Ravelo Manzanillo	.25	.11	272	Mark Kiefer	.25	.11
101	Woody Williams	.25	.11	187	Al Martin	.25	.11	273	Graeme Lloyd	.25	.11
102	Roberto Kelly	.25	.11	188	Denny Neagle	.50	.23	274	Joe Oliver	.25	.11
103	Ryan Klesko	.75	.35	189	Don Slaught	.25	.11	275	Al Reyes	.25	.11
104	Javier Lopez	.50	.23	190	Paul Wagner	.25	.11	276	Kevin Seitzer	.25	.11
105	Greg Maddux	3.00	1.35	191	Rene Arocha	.25	.11	277	Rick Aguilera	.25	.11
106	Fred McGriff	.75	.35	192	Bernard Gilkey	.25	.11	278	Marty Cordova	.50	.23
107	Jose Oliva	.25	.11	193	Jose Oquendo	.25	.11	279	Scott Erickson	.25	.11
108	John Smoltz	.50	.23	194	Tom Pagnozzi	.25	.11	280	LaTroy Hawkins	.25	.11
109	Tony Tarasco	.25	.11	195	Ozzie Smith	1.25	.55	281	Brad Radke	1.25	.55
110	Mark Wohlers	.25	.11	196	Allen Watson	.25	.11	282	Kevin Tapani	.25	.11
111	Jim Bullinger	.25	.11	197	Mark Whiten	.25	.11	283	Tony Fernandez	.25	.11
112	Shawon Dunston	.25	.11	198	Andy Ashby	.25	.11	284	Sterling Hitchcock	.25	.11
113	Derrick May	.25	.11	199	Donnie Elliott	.25	.11	285	Pat Kelly	.25	.11
114	Randy Myers	.25	.11	200	Bryce Florie	.25	.11	286	Jack McDowell	.25	.11
115	Karl Rhodes	.25	.11	201	Tony Gwynn	2.50	1.10	287	Andy Pettitte	1.50	.70
116	Rey Sanchez	.25	.11	202	Trevor Hoffman	.25	.11	288	Mike Stanley	.25	.11
117	Steve Trachsel	.25	.11	203	Brian Johnson	.25	.11	289	John Wetteland	.25	.11
118	Eddie Zambrano	.25	.11	204	Tim Mauser	.25	.11	290	Bernie Williams	1.00	.45
119	Bret Boone	.25	.11	205	Bip Roberts	.25	.11	291	Mark Acre	.25	.11
120	Brian Dorsett	.25	.11	206	Rod Beck	.25	.11	292	Geronimo Berroa	.25	.11
121	Hal Morris	.25	.11	207	Barry Bonds	1.25	.55	293	Dennis Eckersley	.50	.23
122	Jose Rijo	.25	.11	208	Royce Clayton	.25	.11	294	Steve Ontiveros	.25	.11
123	John Roper	.25	.11	209	Darren Lewis	.25	.11	295	Ruben Sierra	.25	.11
124	Reggie Sanders	.25	.11	210	Mark Portugal	.25	.11	296	Terry Steinbach	.25	.11
125	Pete Schourek	.25	.11	211	Kevin Rogers	.25	.11	297	Dave Stewart	.50	.23
126	John Smiley	.25	.11	212	Wm. VanLandingham	.25	.11	298	Todd Stottlemyre	.25	.11
127	Ellis Burks	.50	.23	213	Matt Williams	.75	.35	299	Darren Bragg	.25	.11
128	Vinny Castilla	.50	.23	214	Checklist	.25	.11	300	Joey Cora	.50	.23
129	Marvin Freeman	.25	.11	215	Checklist	.25	.11	301	Edgar Martinez	.75	.35
130	Andres Galarraga	1.00	.45	216	Checklist	.25	.11	302	Bill Risley	.25	.11
131	Mike Munoz	.25	.11	217	Bret Barberie	.25	.11	303	Ron Villone	.25	.11
132	David Nied	.25	.11	218	Armando Benitez	.25	.11	304	Dan Wilson	.25	.11
133	Bruce Ruffin	.25	.11	219	Kevin Brown	.50	.23	305	Benji Gil	.25	.11
134	Walt Weiss	.25	.11	220	Sid Fernandez	.25	.11	306	Wilson Heredia	.25	.11
135	Eric Young	.25	.11	221	Chris Hoiles	.25	.11	307	Mark McLemore	.25	.11
136	Greg Colbrunn	.25	.11	222	Doug Jones	.25	.11	308	Otis Nixon	.25	.11
137	Jeff Conine	.50	.23	223	Ben McDonald	.25	.11	309	Kenny Rogers	.25	.11
138	Jeremy Hernandez	.25	.11	224	Rafael Palmeiro	.75	.35	310	Jeff Russell	.25	.11
139	Charles Johnson	.50	.23	225	Andy Van Slyke	.50	.23	311	Mickey Tettleton	.25	.11
140	Robb Nen	.25	.11	226	Jose Canseco	.75	.35	312	Bob Tewksbury	.25	.11
141	Gary Sheffield	1.00	.45	227	Vaughn Eshelman	.25	.11	313	David Cone	.50	.23
142	Dave Weathers	.25	.11	228	Mike Macfarlane	.25	.11	314	Carlos Delgado	.50	.23
143	Jeff Bagwell	2.00	.90	229	Tim Naehring	.25	.11	315	Alex Gonzalez	.25	.11
144	Craig Biggio	.75	.35	230	Frank Rodriguez	.25	.11	316	Shawn Green	.50	.23
145	Tony Eusebio	.25	.11	231	Lee Tinsley	.25	.11	317	Paul Molitor	1.00	.45
146	Luis Gonzalez	.25	.11	232	Mark Whiten	.25	.11	318	Ed Sprague	.25	.11
147	John Hudek	.25	.11	233	Garret Anderson	.75	.35	319	Devon White	.25	.11
148	Darryl Kile	.50	.23	234	Chili Davis	.50	.23	320	Steve Avery	.25	.11
149	Dave Veres	.25	.11	235	Jim Edmonds	.75	.35	321	Jeff Blauser	.50	.23
150	Billy Ashley	.25	.11	236	Mark Langston	.25	.11	322	Brad Clontz	.25	.11
151	Pedro Astacio	.25	.11	237	Troy Percival	.25	.11	323	Tom Glavine	.50	.23
152	Rafael Bournigal	.25	.11	238	Tony Phillips	.25	.11	324	Marquis Grissom	.50	.23
153	Delino DeShields	.25	.11	239	Lee Smith	.50	.23	325	Chipper Jones	3.00	1.35
154	Raul Mondesi	.75	.35	240	Jim Abbott	.25	.11	326	David Justice	1.00	.45
155	Mike Piazza	3.00	1.35	241	James Baldwin	.25	.11	327	Mark Lemke	.25	.11
156	Rudy Seanez	.25	.11	242	Mike Devereaux	.25	.11	328	Kent Mercker	.25	.11
157	Ismael Valdes	.75	.35	243	Ray Durham	.50	.23	329	Jason Schmidt	.50	.23
158	Tim Wallach	.25	.11	244	Alex Fernandez	.25	.11	330	Steve Buechele	.25	.11
159	Todd Worrell	.25	.11	245	Roberto Hernandez	.25	.11	331	Kevin Foster	.25	.11
160	Moises Alou	.50	.23	246	Lance Johnson	.25	.11	332	Mark Grace	.75	.35
161	Cliff Floyd	.25	.11	247	Ron Karkovice	.25	.11	333	Brian McRae	.25	.11
162	Gil Heredia	.25	.11	248	Tim Raines	.50	.23	334	Sammy Sosa	1.00	.45
163	Mike Lansing	.25	.11	249	Sandy Alomar Jr	.50	.23	335	Ozzie Timmons	.25	.11
164	Pedro Martinez	1.00	.45	250	Orel Hershiser	.50	.23	336	Rick Wilkins	.25	.11
165	Kirk Rueter	.25	.11	251	Julian Tavarez	.25	.11	337	Hector Carrasco	.25	.11
166	Tim Scott	.25	.11	252	Jim Thome	1.00	.45	338	Ron Gant	.50	.23
167	Jeff Shaw	.25	.11	253	Omar Vizquel	.50	.23	339	Barry Larkin	.75	.35
168	Rondell White	.50	.23	254	Dave Winfield	.75	.35	340	Deion Sanders	.50	.23
169	Bobby Bonilla	.50	.23	255	Chad Curtis	.25	.11	341	Benito Santiago	.25	.11
170	Rico Brogna	.25	.11	256	Kirk Gibson	.50	.23	342	Roger Bailey	.25	.11
171	Todd Hundley	.25	.11	257	Mike Henneman	.25	.11	343	Jason Bates	.25	.11
172	Jeff Kent	.25	.11	258	Bob Higginson	1.50	.70	344	Dante Bichette	.50	.23
173	Jim Lindeman	.25	.11	259	Felipe Lira	.25	.11	345	Joe Girardi	.25	.11
174	Joe Orsulak	.25	.11	260	Rudy Pemberton	.25	.11	346	Bill Swift	.25	.11
175	Bret Saberhagen	.25	.11	261	Alan Trammell	.75	.35	347	Mark Thompson	.50	.23
176	Toby Borland	.25	.11	262	Kevin Appier	.50	.23	348	Larry Walker	1.00	.45
177	Darren Daulton	.50	.23	263	Pat Borders	.25	.11	349	Kurt Abbott	.25	.11
178	Lenny Dykstra	.50	.23	264	Tom Gordon	.25	.11	350	John Burkett	.25	.11
179	Jim Eisenreich	.25	.11	265	Jose Lind	.25	.11	351	Chuck Carr	.25	.11
180	Tommy Greene	.25	.11	266	Jon Nunnally	.25	.11	352	Andre Dawson	.75	.35
181	Tony Longmire	.25	.11	267	Dilson Torres	.25	.11	353	Chris Hammond	.25	.11
182	Bobby Munoz	.25	.11	268	Michael Tucker	.50	.23	354	Charles Johnson	.50	.23
183	Kevin Stocker	.25	.11	269	Jeff Cirillo	.50	.23	355	Terry Pendleton	.25	.11

			MINT	NRMT
☐	356	Quilvio Veras	.25	.11
☐	357	Derek Bell	.25	.11
☐	358	Jim Dougherty	.25	.11
☐	359	Doug Drabek	.25	.11
☐	360	Todd Jones	.25	.11
☐	361	Orlando Miller	.25	.11
☐	362	James Mouton	.25	.11
☐	363	Phil Plantier	.25	.11
☐	364	Shane Reynolds	.25	.11
☐	365	Todd Hollandsworth	.50	.23
☐	366	Eric Karros	.50	.23
☐	367	Ramon Martinez	.50	.23
☐	368	Hideo Nomo	5.00	2.20
☐	369	Jose Offerman	.25	.11
☐	370	Antonio Osuna	.25	.11
☐	371	Todd Williams	.25	.11
☐	372	Shane Andrews	.25	.11
☐	373	Wil Cordero	.25	.11
☐	374	Jeff Fassero	.25	.11
☐	375	Darren Fletcher	.25	.11
☐	376	Mark Grudzielanek	.75	.35
☐	377	Carlos Perez	.50	.23
☐	378	Mel Rojas	.25	.11
☐	379	Tony Tarasco	.25	.11
☐	380	Edgardo Alfonzo	1.00	.45
☐	381	Brett Butler	.50	.23
☐	382	Carl Everett	.50	.23
☐	383	John Franco	.50	.23
☐	384	Pete Harnisch	.25	.11
☐	385	Bobby Jones	.25	.11
☐	386	Dave Mlicki	.25	.11
☐	387	Jose Vizcaino	.25	.11
☐	388	Ricky Bottalico	.50	.23
☐	389	Tyler Green	.25	.11
☐	390	Charlie Hayes	.25	.11
☐	391	Dave Hollins	.25	.11
☐	392	Gregg Jefferies	.25	.11
☐	393	Michael Mimbs	.25	.11
☐	394	Mickey Morandini	.25	.11
☐	395	Curt Schilling	.50	.23
☐	396	Heathcliff Slocumb	.25	.11
☐	397	Jason Christiansen	.25	.11
☐	398	Midre Cummings	.25	.11
☐	399	Carlos Garcia	.25	.11
☐	400	Mark Johnson	.25	.11
☐	401	Jeff King	.25	.11
☐	402	Jon Lieber	.25	.11
☐	403	Esteban Loaiza	.50	.23
☐	404	Orlando Merced	.25	.11
☐	405	Gary Wilson	.25	.11
☐	406	Scott Cooper	.25	.11
☐	407	Tom Henke	.25	.11
☐	408	Ken Hill	.25	.11
☐	409	Danny Jackson	.25	.11
☐	410	Brian Jordan	.50	.23
☐	411	Ray Lankford	.50	.23
☐	412	John Mabry	.50	.23
☐	413	Todd Zeile	.25	.11
☐	414	Andy Benes	.50	.23
☐	415	Andres Berumen	.25	.11
☐	416	Ken Caminiti	.75	.35
☐	417	Andujar Cedeno	.25	.11
☐	418	Steve Finley	.50	.23
☐	419	Joey Hamilton	.50	.23
☐	420	Dustin Hermanson	.25	.11
☐	421	Melvin Nieves	.25	.11
☐	422	Roberto Petagine	.25	.11
☐	423	Eddie Williams	.25	.11
☐	424	Glenallen Hill	.25	.11
☐	425	Kirt Manwaring	.25	.11
☐	426	Terry Mulholland	.25	.11
☐	427	J.R. Phillips	.25	.11
☐	428	Joe Rosselli	.25	.11
☐	429	Robby Thompson	.25	.11
☐	430	Checklist	.25	.11
☐	431	Checklist	.25	.11
☐	432	Checklist	.25	.11

1995 Flair Hot Gloves

This 12-card standard-size set features players that are known for their defensive prowess.

Randomly inserted in series two packs at a rate of one in 25, a player photo is superimposed over an embossed design of a bronze glove. The backs have a photo and write-up with a glove as background.

	MINT	NRMT
COMPLETE SET (12)	175.00	80.00
COMMON CARD (1-12)	5.00	2.20
SEMISTARS	8.00	3.60
UNLISTED STARS	12.00	5.50
SER.2 STATED ODDS 1:25		

			MINT	NRMT
☐	1	Roberto Alomar	12.00	5.50
☐	2	Barry Bonds	15.00	6.75
☐	3	Ken Griffey Jr.	60.00	27.00
☐	4	Marquis Grissom	6.00	2.70
☐	5	Barry Larkin	8.00	3.60
☐	6	Darren Lewis	5.00	2.20
☐	7	Kenny Lofton	15.00	6.75
☐	8	Don Mattingly	20.00	9.00
☐	9	Cal Ripken	50.00	22.00
☐	10	Ivan Rodriguez	15.00	6.75
☐	11	Devon White	5.00	2.20
☐	12	Matt Williams	8.00	3.60

1995 Flair Hot Numbers

Randomly inserted in series 1 packs at a rate of 1 in nine, this 10-card standard-size set showcases top players. A player photo on front is superimposed over a gold background that contains player stats from 1994. Horizontal backs have a ghosted player photo to the right with highlights on the left.

	MINT	NRMT
COMPLETE SET (10)	60.00	27.00
COMMON CARD (1-10)	2.00	.90
SER.1 STATED ODDS 1:9		

			MINT	NRMT
☐	1	Jeff Bagwell	6.00	2.70
☐	2	Albert Belle	4.00	1.80
☐	3	Barry Bonds	4.00	1.80
☐	4	Ken Griffey Jr.	15.00	6.75
☐	5	Kenny Lofton	4.00	1.80
☐	6	Greg Maddux	10.00	4.50
☐	7	Mike Piazza	10.00	4.50
☐	8	Cal Ripken	8.00	3.60
☐	9	Frank Thomas	12.00	5.50
☐	10	Matt Williams	2.00	.90

1995 Flair Infield Power

Randomly inserted in second series packs at a rate of one in six, this 10-card standard-size set features sluggers that man the infield. A player photo on front is surrounded by multiple color schemes with a horizontal back offering a player photo and highlights.

	MINT	NRMT
COMPLETE SET (10)	15.00	6.75
COMMON CARD (1-10)	.75	.35
SER.2 STATED ODDS 1:6		

			MINT	NRMT
☐	1	Jeff Bagwell	3.00	1.35
☐	2	Darren Daulton	.75	.35
☐	3	Cecil Fielder	.75	.35
☐	4	Andres Galarraga	1.50	.70
☐	5	Fred McGriff	1.00	.45
☐	6	Rafael Palmeiro	1.00	.45
☐	7	Mike Piazza	5.00	2.20
☐	8	Frank Thomas	5.00	2.20
☐	9	Mo Vaughn	2.00	.90
☐	10	Matt Williams	1.00	.45

1995 Flair Outfield Power

Randomly inserted in first series packs at a rate of one in six, this 10-card standard-size set features sluggers that patrol the outfield. A player photo on front is surrounded by multiple color

schemes with a horizontal back offering a player photo and highlights.

	MINT	NRMT
COMPLETE SET (10)	15.00	6.75
COMMON CARD (1-10)	.50	.23
SER.1 STATED ODDS 1:6		

		MINT	NRMT
☐ 1	Albert Belle	2.00	.90
☐ 2	Dante Bichette	.75	.35
☐ 3	Barry Bonds	2.00	.90
☐ 4	Jose Canseco	1.00	.45
☐ 5	Joe Carter	.75	.35
☐ 6	Juan Gonzalez	4.00	1.80
☐ 7	Ken Griffey Jr.	8.00	3.60
☐ 8	Kirby Puckett	3.00	1.35
☐ 9	Gary Sheffield	1.50	.70
☐ 10	Ruben Sierra	.50	.23

1995 Flair Today's Spotlight

This 12-card die-cut set was randomly inserted in first series packs at a rate of one in 25. The upper portion of the player photo on front has the spotlight effect as the remainder of the photo is darkened. Horizontal backs have a circular player photo to the right with text off to the left.

	MINT	NRMT
COMPLETE SET (12)	120.00	55.00
COMMON CARD (1-12)	4.00	1.80
SEMISTARS	6.00	2.70
UNLISTED STARS	10.00	4.50
SER.1 STATED ODDS 1:25		

		MINT	NRMT
☐ 1	Jeff Bagwell	20.00	9.00
☐ 2	Jason Bere	4.00	1.80
☐ 3	Cliff Floyd	4.00	1.80
☐ 4	Chuck Knoblauch	10.00	4.50
☐ 5	Kenny Lofton	12.00	5.50
☐ 6	Javier Lopez	5.00	2.20
☐ 7	Raul Mondesi	6.00	2.70
☐ 8	Mike Mussina	10.00	4.50
☐ 9	Mike Piazza	30.00	13.50
☐ 10	Manny Ramirez	10.00	4.50
☐ 11	Tim Salmon	10.00	4.50
☐ 12	Frank Thomas	40.00	18.00

1995 Flair Wave of the Future

Spotlighting 10 of the game's hottest young stars, cards were randomly inserted in second series packs at a rate of one in nine. An action photo is super-imposed over primarily a solid background save for the player's name, team and same

name which appear several times. The backs are horizontal with a photo and write-up.

	MINT	NRMT
COMPLETE SET (10)	25.00	11.00
COMMON CARD (1-10)	1.00	.45
SER.2 STATED ODDS 1:9		

		MINT	NRMT
☐ 1	Jason Bates	1.00	.45
☐ 2	Armando Benitez	1.00	.45
☐ 3	Marty Cordova	2.00	.90
☐ 4	Ray Durham	2.00	.90
☐ 5	Vaughn Eshelman	1.00	.45
☐ 6	Carl Everett	1.00	.45
☐ 7	Shawn Green	2.00	.90
☐ 8	Dustin Hermanson	2.00	.90
☐ 9	Chipper Jones	10.00	4.50
☐ 10	Hideo Nomo	10.00	4.50

1996 Flair

Released in July 1996, this 400-card set was issued in one series and sold in seven-card packs at a suggested retail price of $4.99. Gold and Silver etched foil front variations exist for all cards. These color variations were printed in similar quantities and are valued equally. The fronts and backs each carry a color action player cut-out on a player portrait background with player statistics on the backs. The cards are grouped alphabetically within teams and checklisted below alphabetically according to teams for each league."

	MINT	NRMT
COMPLETE SET (400)	200.00	90.00
COMMON CARD (1-400)	.50	.23
MINOR STARS	.75	.35
SEMISTARS	1.25	.55
UNLISTED STARS	2.00	.90
GOLD AND SILVER EQUAL VALUE		

		MINT	NRMT
☐ 1	Roberto Alomar	2.00	.90
☐ 2	Brady Anderson	1.25	.55
☐ 3	Bobby Bonilla	.75	.35
☐ 4	Scott Erickson	.50	.23
☐ 5	Jeffrey Hammonds	.50	.23
☐ 6	Jimmy Haynes	.50	.23
☐ 7	Chris Hoiles	.50	.23
☐ 8	Kent Mercker	.50	.23
☐ 9	Mike Mussina	2.00	.90
☐ 10	Randy Myers	.50	.23
☐ 11	Rafael Palmeiro	1.25	.55
☐ 12	Cal Ripken	8.00	3.60
☐ 13	B.J. Surhoff	.50	.23
☐ 14	David Wells	.50	.23
☐ 15	Jose Canseco	1.25	.55
☐ 16	Roger Clemens	4.00	1.80
☐ 17	Wil Cordero	.50	.23
☐ 18	Tom Gordon	.50	.23
☐ 19	Mike Greenwell	.50	.23
☐ 20	Dwayne Hosey	.50	.23
☐ 21	Jose Malave	.50	.23
☐ 22	Tim Naehring	.50	.23
☐ 23	Troy O'Leary	.50	.23
☐ 24	Aaron Sele	.50	.23
☐ 25	Heathcliff Slocumb	.50	.23
☐ 26	Mike Stanley	.50	.23
☐ 27	Jeff Suppan	.75	.35
☐ 28	John Valentin	.50	.23
☐ 29	Mo Vaughn	2.50	1.10
☐ 30	Tim Wakefield	.50	.23
☐ 31	Jim Abbott	.50	.23
☐ 32	Garret Anderson	.75	.35
☐ 33	George Arias	.50	.23
☐ 34	Chili Davis	.75	.35
☐ 35	Gary DiSarcina	.50	.23
☐ 36	Jim Edmonds	1.25	.55
☐ 37	Chuck Finley	.50	.23
☐ 38	Todd Greene	1.25	.55
☐ 39	Mark Langston	.50	.23
☐ 40	Troy Percival	.50	.23
☐ 41	Tim Salmon	2.00	.90
☐ 42	Lee Smith	.75	.35
☐ 43	J.T. Snow	.75	.35
☐ 44	Randy Velarde	.50	.23
☐ 45	Tim Wallach	.50	.23
☐ 46	Wilson Alvarez	.50	.23
☐ 47	Harold Baines	.75	.35
☐ 48	Jason Bere	.50	.23
☐ 49	Ray Durham	.50	.23
☐ 50	Alex Fernandez	.50	.23
☐ 51	Ozzie Guillen	.50	.23
☐ 52	Roberto Hernandez	.50	.23
☐ 53	Ron Karkovice	.50	.23
☐ 54	Darren Lewis	.50	.23
☐ 55	Lyle Mouton	.50	.23
☐ 56	Tony Phillips	.50	.23
☐ 57	Chris Snopek	.50	.23
☐ 58	Kevin Tapani	.50	.23
☐ 59	Danny Tartabull	.50	.23
☐ 60	Frank Thomas	8.00	3.60
☐ 61	Robin Ventura	.75	.35
☐ 62	Sandy Alomar Jr.	.50	.35
☐ 63	Carlos Baerga	.50	.23
☐ 64	Albert Belle	2.50	1.10
☐ 65	Julio Franco	.50	.23
☐ 66	Orel Hershiser	.75	.35
☐ 67	Kenny Lofton	2.50	1.10
☐ 68	Dennis Martinez	.75	.35
☐ 69	Jack McDowell	.50	.23
☐ 70	Jose Mesa	.50	.23
☐ 71	Eddie Murray	2.00	.90
☐ 72	Charles Nagy	.75	.35
☐ 73	Tony Pena	.50	.23
☐ 74	Manny Ramirez	2.00	.90
☐ 75	Julian Tavarez	.50	.23
☐ 76	Jim Thome	2.00	.90
☐ 77	Omar Vizquel	.75	.35
☐ 78	Chad Curtis	.50	.23
☐ 79	Cecil Fielder	.75	.35
☐ 80	Travis Fryman	.75	.35
☐ 81	Chris Gomez	.50	.23
☐ 82	Bob Higginson	1.25	.55
☐ 83	Mark Lewis	.50	.23
☐ 84	Felipe Lira	.50	.23
☐ 85	Alan Trammell	1.25	.55
☐ 86	Kevin Appier	.75	.35

87	Johnny Damon	.75	.35
88	Tom Goodwin	.50	.23
89	Mark Gubicza	.50	.23
90	Bob Hamelin	.50	.23
91	Keith Lockhart	.50	.23
92	Jeff Montgomery	.50	.23
93	Jon Nunnally	.50	.23
94	Bip Roberts	.50	.23
95	Michael Tucker	.75	.35
96	Joe Vitiello	.50	.23
97	Ricky Bones	.50	.23
98	Chuck Carr	.50	.23
99	Jeff Cirillo	.75	.35
100	Mike Fetters	.50	.23
101	John Jaha	.50	.23
102	Mike Matheny	.50	.23
103	Ben McDonald	.50	.23
104	Matt Mieske	.50	.23
105	Dave Nilsson	.50	.23
106	Kevin Seitzer	.50	.23
107	Steve Sparks	.50	.23
108	Jose Valentin	.50	.23
109	Greg Vaughn	.50	.23
110	Rick Aguilera	.50	.23
111	Rich Becker	.50	.23
112	Marty Cordova	.75	.35
113	LaTroy Hawkins	.50	.23
114	Dave Hollins	.50	.23
115	Roberto Kelly	.50	.23
116	Chuck Knoblauch	2.00	.90
117	Matt Lawton	1.25	.55
118	Pat Meares	.50	.23
119	Paul Molitor	2.00	.90
120	Kirby Puckett	4.00	1.80
121	Brad Radke	.75	.35
122	Frank Rodriguez	.50	.23
123	Scott Stahoviak	.50	.23
124	Matt Walbeck	.50	.23
125	Wade Boggs	2.00	.90
126	David Cone	.75	.35
127	Joe Girardi	.50	.23
128	Dwight Gooden	.75	.35
129	Derek Jeter	6.00	2.70
130	Jimmy Key	.75	.35
131	Jim Leyritz	.50	.23
132	Tino Martinez	2.00	.90
133	Paul O'Neill	.75	.35
134	Andy Pettitte	2.50	1.10
135	Tim Raines	.75	.35
136	Ruben Rivera	.75	.35
137	Kenny Rogers	.50	.23
138	Ruben Sierra	.50	.23
139	John Wetteland	.50	.23
140	Bernie Williams	2.00	.90
141	Tony Batista	.75	.35
142	Allen Battle	.50	.23
143	Geronimo Berroa	.50	.23
144	Mike Bordick	.50	.23
145	Scott Brosius	.50	.23
146	Steve Cox	.50	.23
147	Brent Gates	.50	.23
148	Jason Giambi	.75	.35
149	Doug Johns	.50	.23
150	Mark McGwire	4.00	1.80
151	Pedro Munoz	.50	.23
152	Ariel Prieto	.50	.23
153	Terry Steinbach	.50	.23
154	Todd Van Poppel	.50	.23
155	Bobby Ayala	.50	.23
156	Chris Bosio	.50	.23
157	Jay Buhner	1.25	.55
158	Joey Cora	.75	.35
159	Russ Davis	.50	.23
160	Ken Griffey Jr.	10.00	4.50
161	Sterling Hitchcock	.50	.23
162	Randy Johnson	2.00	.90
163	Edgar Martinez	1.25	.55
164	Alex Rodriguez	6.00	2.70
165	Paul Sorrento	.50	.23
166	Dan Wilson	.50	.23
167	Will Clark	1.25	.55
168	Benji Gil	.50	.23
169	Juan Gonzalez	5.00	2.20
170	Rusty Greer	.75	.35
171	Kevin Gross	.50	.23
172	Darryl Hamilton	.50	.23
173	Mike Henneman	.50	.23
174	Ken Hill	.50	.23
175	Mark McLemore	.50	.23
176	Dean Palmer	.50	.23
177	Roger Pavlik	.50	.23
178	Ivan Rodriguez	2.50	1.10
179	Mickey Tettleton	.50	.23
180	Bobby Witt	.50	.23
181	Joe Carter	.75	.35
182	Felipe Crespo	.50	.23
183	Alex Gonzalez	.50	.23
184	Shawn Green	.50	.23
185	Juan Guzman	.50	.23
186	Erik Hanson	.50	.23
187	Pat Hentgen	.75	.35
188	Sandy Martinez	.50	.23
189	Otis Nixon	.50	.23
190	John Olerud	.75	.35
191	Paul Quantrill	.50	.23
192	Bill Risley	.50	.23
193	Ed Sprague	.50	.23
194	Steve Avery	.50	.23
195	Jeff Blauser	.75	.35
196	Brad Clontz	.50	.23
197	Jermaine Dye	.75	.35
198	Tom Glavine	.75	.35
199	Marquis Grissom	.75	.35
200	Chipper Jones	6.00	2.70
201	David Justice	2.00	.90
202	Ryan Klesko	1.25	.55
203	Mark Lemke	.50	.23
204	Javier Lopez	.75	.35
205	Greg Maddux	6.00	2.70
206	Fred McGriff	1.25	.55
207	Greg McMichael	.50	.23
208	Wonderful Monds	.50	.23
209	Jason Schmidt	.50	.23
210	John Smoltz	.75	.35
211	Mark Wohlers	.50	.23
212	Jim Bullinger	.50	.23
213	Frank Castillo	.50	.23
214	Kevin Foster	.50	.23
215	Luis Gonzalez	.50	.23
216	Mark Grace	1.25	.55
217	Robin Jennings	.50	.23
218	Doug Jones	.50	.23
219	Dave Magadan	.50	.23
220	Brian McRae	.50	.23
221	Jaime Navarro	.50	.23
222	Rey Sanchez	.50	.23
223	Ryne Sandberg	2.50	1.10
224	Scott Servais	.50	.23
225	Sammy Sosa	2.00	.90
226	Ozzie Timmons	.50	.23
227	Bret Boone	.50	.23
228	Jeff Branson	.50	.23
229	Jeff Brantley	.50	.23
230	Dave Burba	.50	.23
231	Vince Coleman	.50	.23
232	Steve Gibralter	.50	.23
233	Mike Kelly	.50	.23
234	Barry Larkin	1.25	.55
235	Hal Morris	.50	.23
236	Mark Portugal	.50	.23
237	Jose Rijo	.50	.23
238	Reggie Sanders	.50	.23
239	Pete Schourek	.50	.23
240	John Smiley	.50	.23
241	Eddie Taubensee	.50	.23
242	Jason Bates	.50	.23
243	Dante Bichette	.75	.35
244	Ellis Burks	.75	.35
245	Vinny Castilla	.75	.35
246	Andres Galarraga	2.00	.90
247	Darren Holmes	.50	.23
248	Curt Leskanic	.50	.23
249	Steve Reed	.50	.23
250	Kevin Ritz	.50	.23
251	Bret Saberhagen	.50	.23
252	Bill Swift	.50	.23
253	Larry Walker	2.00	.90
254	Walt Weiss	.50	.23
255	Eric Young	.50	.23
256	Kurt Abbott	.50	.23
257	Kevin Brown	.75	.35
258	John Burkett	.50	.23
259	Greg Colbrunn	.50	.23
260	Jeff Conine	.75	.35
261	Andre Dawson	1.25	.55
262	Chris Hammond	.50	.23
263	Charles Johnson	.75	.35
264	Al Leiter	.50	.23
265	Robb Nen	.50	.23
266	Terry Pendleton	.50	.23
267	Pat Rapp	.50	.23
268	Gary Sheffield	2.00	.90
269	Quilvio Veras	.50	.23
270	Devon White	.50	.23
271	Bob Abreu	1.25	.55
272	Jeff Bagwell	4.00	1.80
273	Derek Bell	.50	.23
274	Sean Berry	.50	.23
275	Craig Biggio	1.25	.55
276	Doug Drabek	.50	.23
277	Tony Eusebio	.50	.23
278	Richard Hidalgo	2.00	.90
279	Brian L. Hunter	.75	.35
280	Todd Jones	.50	.23
281	Derrick May	.50	.23
282	Orlando Miller	.50	.23
283	James Mouton	.50	.23
284	Shane Reynolds	.50	.23
285	Greg Swindell	.50	.23
286	Mike Blowers	.50	.23
287	Brett Butler	.75	.35
288	Tom Candiotti	.50	.23
289	Roger Cedeno	.50	.23
290	Delino DeShields	.50	.23
291	Greg Gagne	.50	.23
292	Karim Garcia	1.25	.55
293	Todd Hollandsworth	.50	.23
294	Eric Karros	.75	.35
295	Ramon Martinez	.75	.35
296	Raul Mondesi	1.25	.55
297	Hideo Nomo	5.00	2.20
298	Mike Piazza	6.00	2.70
299	Ismael Valdes	.75	.35
300	Todd Worrell	.50	.23
301	Moises Alou	.75	.35
302	Shane Andrews	.50	.23
303	Yamil Benitez	.75	.35
304	Jeff Fassero	.50	.23
305	Darrin Fletcher	.50	.23
306	Cliff Floyd	.50	.23
307	Mark Grudzielanek	.75	.35
308	Mike Lansing	.50	.23
309	Pedro Martinez	2.00	.90
310	Ryan McGuire	.50	.23
311	Carlos Perez	.50	.23
312	Mel Rojas	.50	.23
313	David Segui	.50	.23
314	Rondell White	.75	.35
315	Edgardo Alfonzo	1.25	.55
316	Rico Brogna	.50	.23
317	Carl Everett	.50	.23
318	John Franco	.75	.35
319	Bernard Gilkey	.50	.23
320	Todd Hundley	.75	.35
321	Jason Isringhausen	.50	.23
322	Lance Johnson	.50	.23
323	Bobby Jones	.50	.23
324	Jeff Kent	.50	.23
325	Rey Ordonez	.75	.35
326	Bill Pulsipher	.50	.23
327	Jose Vizcaino	.50	.23
328	Paul Wilson	.50	.23
329	Ricky Bottalico	.50	.23
330	Darren Daulton	.75	.35
331	David Doster	.50	.23
332	Lenny Dykstra	.75	.35
333	Jim Eisenreich	.50	.23
334	Sid Fernandez	.50	.23
335	Gregg Jefferies	.50	.23
336	Mickey Morandini	.50	.23
337	Benito Santiago	.50	.23
338	Curt Schilling	.75	.35
339	Kevin Stocker	.50	.23
340	David West	.50	.23
341	Mark Whiten	.50	.23
342	Todd Zeile	.50	.23
343	Jay Bell	.75	.35
344	John Ericks	.50	.23

☐ 345 Carlos Garcia	.50	.23
☐ 346 Charlie Hayes	.50	.23
☐ 347 Jason Kendall	1.25	.55
☐ 348 Jeff King	.50	.23
☐ 349 Mike Kingery	.50	.23
☐ 350 Al Martin	.50	.23
☐ 351 Orlando Merced	.50	.23
☐ 352 Dan Miceli	.50	.23
☐ 353 Denny Neagle	.75	.35
☐ 354 Alan Benes	.75	.35
☐ 355 Andy Benes	.75	.35
☐ 356 Royce Clayton	.50	.23
☐ 357 Dennis Eckersley	.75	.35
☐ 358 Gary Gaetti	.50	.23
☐ 359 Ron Gant	.75	.35
☐ 360 Brian Jordan	.75	.35
☐ 361 Ray Lankford	.75	.35
☐ 362 John Mabry	.50	.23
☐ 363 T.J. Mathews	.50	.23
☐ 364 Mike Morgan	.50	.23
☐ 365 Donovan Osborne	.50	.23
☐ 366 Tom Pagnozzi	.50	.23
☐ 367 Ozzie Smith	2.50	1.10
☐ 368 Todd Stottlemyre	.50	.23
☐ 369 Andy Ashby	.50	.23
☐ 370 Brad Ausmus	.50	.23
☐ 371 Ken Caminiti	1.25	.55
☐ 372 Andujar Cedeno	.50	.23
☐ 373 Steve Finley	.75	.35
☐ 374 Tony Gwynn	5.00	2.20
☐ 375 Joey Hamilton	.75	.35
☐ 376 Rickey Henderson	1.25	.55
☐ 377 Trevor Hoffman	.50	.23
☐ 378 Wally Joyner	.75	.35
☐ 379 Marc Newfield	.50	.23
☐ 380 Jody Reed	.50	.23
☐ 381 Bob Tewksbury	.50	.23
☐ 382 Fernando Valenzuela	.75	.35
☐ 383 Rod Beck	.50	.23
☐ 384 Barry Bonds	2.50	1.10
☐ 385 Mark Carreon	.50	.23
☐ 386 Shawon Dunston	.50	.23
☐ 387 Osvaldo Fernandez	.75	.35
☐ 388 Glenallen Hill	.50	.23
☐ 389 Stan Javier	.50	.23
☐ 390 Mark Leiter	.50	.23
☐ 391 Kirt Manwaring	.50	.23
☐ 392 Robby Thompson	.50	.23
☐ 393 William VanLandingham	.50	.23
☐ 394 Allen Watson	.50	.23
☐ 395 Matt Williams	1.25	.55
☐ 396 Checklist (1-92)	.50	.23
☐ 397 Checklist (93-180)	.50	.23
☐ 398 Checklist (181-272)	.50	.23
☐ 399 Checklist (273-365)	.50	.23
☐ 400 Checklist (366-400/Inserts)	.50	.23

1996 Flair Diamond Cuts

Randomly inserted in packs at a rate of one in 20, this 12-card set showcases the game's greatest stars with rainbow holofoil and glitter coating on the card.

	MINT	NRMT
COMPLETE SET (12)	150.00	70.00
COMMON CARD (1-12)	4.00	1.80
UNLISTED STARS	6.00	2.70
STATED ODDS 1:20		

☐ 1 Jeff Bagwell	12.00	5.50
☐ 2 Albert Belle	8.00	3.60
☐ 3 Barry Bonds	8.00	3.60
☐ 4 Juan Gonzalez	15.00	6.75
☐ 5 Ken Griffey Jr.	30.00	13.50
☐ 6 Greg Maddux	20.00	9.00
☐ 7 Eddie Murray	6.00	2.70
☐ 8 Mike Piazza	20.00	9.00
☐ 9 Cal Ripken	25.00	11.00
☐ 10 Frank Thomas	25.00	11.00
☐ 11 Mo Vaughn	8.00	3.60
☐ 12 Matt Williams	4.00	1.80

1996 Flair Hot Gloves

Randomly inserted in hobby packs only at a rate of one in 90, this 10-card set is printed on special, thermo-embossed die-cut cards and spotlights the best defensive players.

	MINT	NRMT
COMPLETE SET (10)	500.00	220.00
COMMON CARD (1-10)	20.00	9.00
STATED ODDS 1:90 HOBBY		

☐ 1 Roberto Alomar	30.00	13.50
☐ 2 Barry Bonds	40.00	18.00
☐ 3 Will Clark	20.00	9.00
☐ 4 Ken Griffey Jr.	150.00	70.00
☐ 5 Kenny Lofton	40.00	18.00
☐ 6 Greg Maddux	100.00	45.00
☐ 7 Mike Piazza	100.00	45.00
☐ 8 Cal Ripken	120.00	55.00
☐ 9 Ivan Rodriguez	40.00	18.00
☐ 10 Matt Williams	20.00	9.00

1996 Flair Powerline

Randomly inserted in packs at a rate of one in 6, this 10-card set features baseball's leading power hitters. The fronts display a color action close-up player photo with a green overlay indicating his power. The backs carry a player portrait and a statement about the player's hitting power.

	MINT	NRMT
COMPLETE SET (10)	30.00	13.50
COMMON CARD (1-10)	1.50	.70
STATED ODDS 1:6		

☐ 1 Albert Belle	2.50	1.10
☐ 2 Barry Bonds	2.50	1.10
☐ 3 Juan Gonzalez	5.00	2.20
☐ 4 Ken Griffey Jr.	10.00	4.50
☐ 5 Mark McGwire	4.00	1.80
☐ 6 Mike Piazza	6.00	2.70
☐ 7 Manny Ramirez	2.00	.90
☐ 8 Sammy Sosa	2.00	.90
☐ 9 Frank Thomas	8.00	3.60
☐ 10 Matt Williams	1.50	.70

1996 Flair Wave of the Future

Randomly inserted in packs at a rate of one in 72, this 20-card set highlights the top 1996 rookies and prospects on lenticular cards.

	MINT	NRMT
COMPLETE SET (20)	250.00	110.00
COMMON CARD (1-20)	10.00	4.50
STATED ODDS 1:72		

☐ 1 Bob Abreu	15.00	6.75
☐ 2 George Arias	10.00	4.50
☐ 3 Tony Batista	20.00	9.00
☐ 4 Alan Benes	25.00	11.00
☐ 5 Yamil Benitez	20.00	9.00
☐ 6 Steve Cox	10.00	4.50
☐ 7 David Doster	10.00	4.50
☐ 8 Jermaine Dye	20.00	9.00
☐ 9 Osvaldo Fernandez	20.00	9.00
☐ 10 Karim Garcia	25.00	11.00
☐ 11 Steve Gibralter	10.00	4.50
☐ 12 Todd Greene	20.00	9.00
☐ 13 Richard Hidalgo	25.00	11.00
☐ 14 Robin Jennings	10.00	4.50
☐ 15 Jason Kendall	20.00	9.00
☐ 16 Jose Malave	10.00	4.50
☐ 17 Wonderful Monds	10.00	4.50
☐ 18 Rey Ordonez	15.00	6.75
☐ 19 Ruben Rivera	25.00	11.00
☐ 20 Paul Wilson	10.00	4.50

1997 Flair Showcase Row 2

The 1997 Flair Showcase set was issued in one series totalling 540 cards and was distributed in five-card packs with a suggested retail price of $4.99. This hobby exclusive set is divided into three 180-card sets (Row2/Style, Row1/Grace, and Row0/Showcase) and features holographic foil fronts with an action photo of the player silhouetted over a larger black-and-white head-shot image in the background. The thick card stock is laminated with a shiny glossy coating for a super-premium "feel." Also inserted one in every pack was a Million Dollar Moments card: Finally, 25 serial-numbered Alex Rodriguez Emerald Exchange cards were randomly seeded into packs. The card fronts were very similar in design to the regular Row 2 Rodriguez, except for green foil accents. The card back, however, consisted entirely of text explaining prize guidelines. The deadline to exchange the card was 8/1/98.

	MINT	NRMT
COMPLETE SET (180)	100.00	45.00
COMMON CARD (1-60)	.25	.11
MINOR STARS 1-60	.40	.18
SEMISTARS 1-60	.60	.25
UNLISTED STARS 1-60	1.00	.45
ROW 2 1-60 ODDS 1.5:1		
COMMON CARD (61-120)	.40	.18
MINOR STARS 61-120	.60	.25
SEMISTARS 61-120	1.00	.45
ROW 2 61-120 ODDS 1:1.5		
COMMON CARD (121-180)	.30	.14
MINOR STARS 121-180	.50	.23
SEMISTARS 121-180	.75	.35
ROW 2 121-180 STATED ODDS 1:1		
A.ROD GLOVE EXCH.DEADLINE: 8/1/98		

☐ 1 Andruw Jones .... 2.50 ...... 1.10
☐ 2 Derek Jeter .... 3.00 ...... 1.35
☐ 3 Alex Rodriguez .... 3.00 ...... 1.35
☐ 4 Paul Molitor .... 1.00 ...... .45
☐ 5 Jeff Bagwell .... 2.00 ...... .90
☐ 6 Scott Rolen .... 2.50 ...... 1.10
☐ 7 Kenny Lofton .... 1.25 ...... .55
☐ 8 Cal Ripken .... 4.00 ...... 1.80
☐ 9 Brady Anderson .... .60 ...... .25
☐ 10 Chipper Jones .... 3.00 ...... 1.35
☐ 11 Todd Greene .... .40 ...... .18
☐ 12 Todd Walker .... .40 ...... .18
☐ 13 Billy Wagner .... .40 ...... .18
☐ 14 Craig Biggio .... .60 ...... .25
☐ 15 Kevin Orie .... .40 ...... .18
☐ 16 Hideo Nomo .... 2.50 ...... 1.10
☐ 17 Kevin Appier .... .40 ...... .18
☐ 18 Bubba Trammell STY 1.00 ...... .45
☐ 19 Juan Gonzalez .... 2.50 ...... 1.10
☐ 20 Randy Johnson .... 1.00 ...... .45
☐ 21 Roger Clemens .... 2.00 ...... .90
☐ 22 Johnny Damon .... .25 ...... .11
☐ 23 Ryne Sandberg .... 1.25 ...... .55
☐ 24 Ken Griffey Jr. .... 5.00 ...... 2.20
☐ 25 Barry Bonds .... 1.25 ...... .55
☐ 26 Nomar Garciaparra ... 3.00 ...... 1.35
☐ 27 Vladimir Guerrero ..... 2.00 ...... .90
☐ 28 Ron Gant .... .40 ...... .18
☐ 29 Joe Carter .... .40 ...... .18
☐ 30 Tim Salmon .... 1.00 ...... .45
☐ 31 Mike Piazza .... 3.00 ...... 1.35
☐ 32 Barry Larkin .... .60 ...... .25
☐ 33 Manny Ramirez .... 1.00 ...... .45
☐ 34 Sammy Sosa .... 1.00 ...... .45
☐ 35 Frank Thomas .... 4.00 ...... 1.80
☐ 36 Melvin Nieves .... .25 ...... .11
☐ 37 Tony Gwynn .... 2.50 ...... 1.10
☐ 38 Gary Sheffield .... 1.00 ...... .45
☐ 39 Darin Erstad .... 1.50 ...... .70
☐ 40 Ken Caminiti .... .60 ...... .25
☐ 41 Jermaine Dye .... .25 ...... .11
☐ 42 Mo Vaughn .... 1.25 ...... .55
☐ 43 Raul Mondesi .... .60 ...... .25
☐ 44 Greg Maddux .... 3.00 ...... 1.35
☐ 45 Chuck Knoblauch ..... 1.00 ...... .45
☐ 46 Andy Pettitte .... 1.00 ...... .45
☐ 47 Deion Sanders .... .40 ...... .18
☐ 48 Albert Belle .... 1.25 ...... .55
☐ 49 Jamey Wright .... .25 ...... .11
☐ 50 Rey Ordonez .... .25 ...... .11
☐ 51 Bernie Williams .... 1.00 ...... .45
☐ 52 Mark McGwire .... 2.00 ...... .90
☐ 53 Mike Mussina .... 1.00 ...... .45
☐ 54 Bob Abreu .... .40 ...... .18
☐ 55 Reggie Sanders .... .25 ...... .11
☐ 56 Brian Jordan .... .40 ...... .18
☐ 57 Ivan Rodriguez .... 1.25 ...... .55
☐ 58 Roberto Alomar .... 1.00 ...... .45
☐ 59 Tim Naehring .... .25 ...... .11
☐ 60 Edgar Renteria .... .40 ...... .18
☐ 61 Dean Palmer .... .40 ...... .18
☐ 62 Benito Santiago .... .40 ...... .18
☐ 63 David Cone .... .25 ...... .11
☐ 64 Carlos Delgado .... .60 ...... .25
☐ 65 Brian Giles .... .40 ...... .18
☐ 66 Alex Ochoa .... .40 ...... .18
☐ 67 Rondell White .... .40 ...... .18
☐ 68 Robin Ventura .... .60 ...... .25
☐ 69 Eric Karros .... .40 ...... .18
☐ 70 Jose Valentin .... .40 ...... .18
☐ 71 Rafael Palmeiro .... 1.00 ...... .45
☐ 72 Chris Snopek .... .40 ...... .18
☐ 73 David Justice .... 1.25 ...... .55
☐ 74 Tom Glavine .... .60 ...... .25
☐ 75 Rudy Pemberton .... .40 ...... .18
☐ 76 Larry Walker .... 1.50 ...... .70
☐ 77 Jim Thome .... 1.50 ...... .70
☐ 78 Charles Johnson .... .60 ...... .25
☐ 79 Dante Powell .... .40 ...... .18
☐ 80 Derrek Lee .... 1.25 ...... .55
☐ 81 Jason Kendall .... .60 ...... .25
☐ 82 Todd Hollandsworth ... .40 ...... .18
☐ 83 Bernard Gilkey .... .40 ...... .18
☐ 84 Mel Rojas .... .40 ...... .18
☐ 85 Dmitri Young .... .40 ...... .18
☐ 86 Bret Boone .... .40 ...... .18
☐ 87 Pat Hentgen .... .60 ...... .25
☐ 88 Bobby Bonilla .... .60 ...... .25
☐ 89 John Wetteland .... .40 ...... .18
☐ 90 Todd Hundley .... .40 ...... .18
☐ 91 Wilton Guerrero .... .40 ...... .18
☐ 92 Geronimo Berroa .... .40 ...... .18
☐ 93 Al Martin .... .40 ...... .18
☐ 94 Danny Tartabull .... .40 ...... .18
☐ 95 Mel McRae .... .40 ...... .18
☐ 96 Steve Finley .... .60 ...... .25
☐ 97 John Stottlemyre .... .40 ...... .18
☐ 98 John Smoltz .... .60 ...... .25
☐ 99 Matt Williams .... 1.00 ...... .45
☐ 100 Eddie Murray .... 1.50 ...... .70
☐ 101 Henry Rodriguez .... .40 ...... .18
☐ 102 Marty Cordova .... .60 ...... .25
☐ 103 Juan Guzman .... .40 ...... .18
☐ 104 Chili Davis .... .60 ...... .25
☐ 105 Eric Young .... .40 ...... .18
☐ 106 Jeff Abbott .... .40 ...... .18
☐ 107 Shannon Stewart .... .60 ...... .25
☐ 108 Rocky Coppinger .... .40 ...... .18
☐ 109 Jose Canseco .... 1.00 ...... .45
☐ 110 Dante Bichette .... .60 ...... .25
☐ 111 Dwight Gooden .... .60 ...... .25
☐ 112 Scott Brosius .... .40 ...... .18
☐ 113 Steve Avery .... .40 ...... .18
☐ 114 Andres Galarraga ...... 1.25 ...... .55
☐ 115 Sandy Alomar Jr .... .60 ...... .25
☐ 116 Ray Lankford .... .60 ...... .25
☐ 117 Jorge Posada .... .40 ...... .18
☐ 118 Ryan Klesko .... 1.00 ...... .45
☐ 119 Jay Buhner .... 1.00 ...... .45
☐ 120 Jose Guillen .... 2.00 ...... .90
☐ 121 Paul O'Neill .... .50 ...... .23
☐ 122 Jimmy Key .... .50 ...... .23
☐ 123 Hal Morris .... .30 ...... .14
☐ 124 Travis Fryman .... .50 ...... .23
☐ 125 Jim Edmonds .... .75 ...... .35
☐ 126 Jeff Cirillo .... .50 ...... .23
☐ 127 Fred McGriff .... .75 ...... .35
☐ 128 Alan Benes .... .50 ...... .23
☐ 129 Derek Bell .... .30 ...... .14
☐ 130 Tony Graffanino .... .30 ...... .14
☐ 131 Shawn Green .... .50 ...... .23
☐ 132 Denny Neagle .... .50 ...... .23
☐ 133 Alex Fernandez .... .50 ...... .23
☐ 134 Mickey Morandini .... .30 ...... .14
☐ 135 Royce Clayton .... .50 ...... .23
☐ 136 Jose Mesa .... .30 ...... .14
☐ 137 Edgar Martinez .... .75 ...... .35
☐ 138 Curt Schilling .... .50 ...... .23
☐ 139 Lance Johnson .... .30 ...... .14
☐ 140 Andy Benes .... .50 ...... .23
☐ 141 Charles Nagy .... .50 ...... .23
☐ 142 Mariano Rivera .... .50 ...... .23
☐ 143 Mark Wohlers .... .30 ...... .14
☐ 144 Ken Hill .... .30 ...... .14
☐ 145 Jay Bell .... .50 ...... .23
☐ 146 Bob Higginson .... .50 ...... .23
☐ 147 Mark Grudzielanek ..... .30 ...... .14
☐ 148 Ray Durham .... .50 ...... .23
☐ 149 John Olerud .... .50 ...... .23
☐ 150 Joey Hamilton .... .50 ...... .23
☐ 151 Trevor Hoffman .... .50 ...... .23
☐ 152 Dan Wilson .... .30 ...... .14
☐ 153 J.T. Snow .... .50 ...... .23
☐ 154 Marquis Grissom .... .50 ...... .23
☐ 155 Yamil Benitez .... .30 ...... .14
☐ 156 Rusty Greer .... .50 ...... .23
☐ 157 Darryl Kile .... .50 ...... .23
☐ 158 Ismael Valdes .... .50 ...... .23
☐ 159 Jeff Conine .... .50 ...... .23
☐ 160 Darren Daulton .... .50 ...... .23
☐ 161 Chan Ho Park .... 1.00 ...... .45
☐ 162 Troy Percival .... .50 ...... .23
☐ 163 Wade Boggs .... 1.00 ...... .45
☐ 164 Dave Nilsson .... .30 ...... .14
☐ 165 Vinny Castilla .... .50 ...... .23
☐ 166 Kevin Brown .... .50 ...... .23
☐ 167 Dennis Eckersley .... .50 ...... .23
☐ 168 Wendell Magee Jr .... .30 ...... .14
☐ 169 John Jaha .... .30 ...... .14
☐ 170 Garret Anderson .... .50 ...... .23
☐ 171 Jason Giambi .... .50 ...... .23
☐ 172 Mark Grace .... .75 ...... .35
☐ 173 Tony Clark .... 1.00 ...... .45
☐ 174 Moises Alou .... .50 ...... .23
☐ 175 Brett Butler .... .50 ...... .23
☐ 176 Cecil Fielder .... .50 ...... .23
☐ 177 Chris Widger .... .30 ...... .14
☐ 178 Doug Drabek .... .30 ...... .14
☐ 179 Ellis Burks .... .50 ...... .23
☐ 180 Shigetoshi Hasegawa STY .75 ...... .35
☐ NNO Alex Rodr.Glove EXCH 1000.00 450.00

1997 Flair Showcase Row 1

Randomly inserted in packs at the rate of one in 25, this 180-

card Grace set is parallel to the base Flair Showcase Row 2 (Style) set and features holographic foil fronts with an action photo of the player silhouetted over a larger color head-shot image in the background.

	MINT	NRMT
COMPLETE SET (180)	200.00	90.00
COMMON CARD (1-60)	.60	.25
MINOR STARS 1-60	1.00	.45
SEMISTARS 1-60	1.50	.70
UNLISTED STARS 1-60	2.50	1.10
*STARS 1-60: 1.25X TO 2.5X ROW 2		
ROW 1 1-60 ODDS 1:2.5		
COMMON CARD (61-120)	.50	.23
MINOR STARS 61-120	.75	.35
SEMISTARS 61-120	1.25	.55
UNLISTED STARS 61-120	2.00	.90
*STARS 61-120: .6X TO 1.2X ROW 2		
ROW 1 61-120 ODDS 1:2		
COMMON CARD (121-180)	1.00	.45
MINOR STARS 121-180	1.50	.70
SEMISTARS 121-180	2.50	1.10
UNLISTED STARS 121-180	4.00	1.80
*STARS 121-180: 1.5X TO 3X ROW 2		
ROW 1 121-180 ODDS 1:3		

1997 Flair Showcase Row 0

Randomly inserted in packs at the rate of one in 24, this 180-card Showcase set is parallel to the base Flair Showcase Row 2 (Style) set and features holographic foil fronts with a head-shot image of the player silhouetted over a larger player action-shot in the background.

	MINT	NRMT
COMPLETE SET (180)	2000.00	900.00
COMMON CARD (1-60)	8.00	3.60
MINOR STARS 1-60	10.00	4.50
SEMISTARS 1-60	15.00	6.75
UNLISTED STARS 1-60	20.00	9.00
*STARS 1-60: 12.5X TO 25X ROW 2		
*YOUNG STARS 1-60: 10X TO 20X ROW 2		
ROW 0 1-60 ODDS 1:24		
COMMON CARD (61-120)	3.00	1.35
MINOR STARS 61-120	5.00	2.20
SEMISTARS 61-120	8.00	3.60
*STARS 61-120: 4X TO 8X ROW 2		
*YOUNG STARS 61-120: 3X TO 6X ROW 2		
ROW 0 61-120 ODDS 1:12		
COMMON CARD (121-180)	1.25	.55
MINOR STARS 121-180	2.00	.90
SEMISTARS 121-180	3.00	1.35
*STARS 121-180: 2.5X TO 5X ROW 2		
*YOUNG STARS 121-180: 2X TO 4X ROW 2		
ROW 0 121-180 ODDS 1:5		

☐ 1	Andruw Jones	50.00	22.00
☐ 2	Derek Jeter	60.00	27.00
☐ 3	Alex Rodriguez	80.00	36.00
☐ 4	Paul Molitor	25.00	11.00
☐ 5	Jeff Bagwell	50.00	22.00
☐ 6	Scott Rolen	50.00	22.00
☐ 7	Kenny Lofton	30.00	13.50
☐ 8	Cal Ripken	100.00	45.00
☐ 10	Chipper Jones	80.00	36.00
☐ 16	Hideo Nomo	60.00	27.00
☐ 18	Bubba Trammell STY	20.00	9.00
☐ 19	Juan Gonzalez	60.00	27.00
☐ 20	Randy Johnson	25.00	11.00
☐ 21	Roger Clemens	50.00	22.00
☐ 23	Ryne Sandberg	30.00	13.50
☐ 24	Ken Griffey Jr.	120.00	55.00
☐ 25	Barry Bonds	30.00	13.50
☐ 26	Nomar Garciaparra	60.00	27.00
☐ 27	Vladimir Guerrero	40.00	18.00
☐ 31	Mike Piazza	80.00	36.00

☐ 33	Manny Ramirez	25.00	11.00
☐ 35	Frank Thomas	100.00	45.00
☐ 37	Tony Gwynn	60.00	27.00
☐ 39	Darin Erstad	30.00	13.50
☐ 42	Mo Vaughn	30.00	13.50
☐ 44	Greg Maddux	80.00	36.00
☐ 46	Andy Pettitte	25.00	11.00
☐ 48	Albert Belle	30.00	13.50
☐ 52	Mark McGwire	50.00	22.00
☐ 53	Mike Mussina	25.00	11.00
☐ 57	Ivan Rodriguez	30.00	13.50
☐ 58	Roberto Alomar	25.00	11.00
☐ 76	Larry Walker	12.00	5.50
☐ 77	Jim Thome	12.00	5.50
☐ 100	Eddie Murray	12.00	5.50
☐ 120	Jose Guillen	12.00	5.50
☐ 161	Chan Ho Park	4.00	1.80
☐ 163	Wade Boggs	4.00	1.80
☐ 173	Tony Clark	4.00	1.80

1997 Flair Showcase Legacy Collection

Randomly inserted in packs at a rate of one in 30, this 180-card set is parallel to the regular set. Only 100 sequentially numbered sets were produced, each featuring an "alternate" player photo printed on a matte finish/foil stamped card. Similar to the regular Showcase set, each player has three different cards. We are treating the pricing of the cards the same irregardless of the row. One of one Masterpiece cards were also made. Since there are so few produced, we are not providing pricing for them. Please refer to future issues of Beckett Baseball Card Monthly for occassional updates on key players.

	MINT	NRMT
COMMON CARD (1-180)	25.00	11.00
MINOR STARS	40.00	18.00
SEMISTARS	60.00	27.00
UNLISTED STARS	100.00	45.00
STATED ODDS 1:30		
STATED PRINT RUN 100 SERIAL #'d SETS		
THREE CARDS PER PLAYER		

☐ 1	Andruw Jones	200.00	90.00
☐ 2	Derek Jeter	250.00	110.00
☐ 3	Alex Rodriguez	300.00	135.00
☐ 5	Jeff Bagwell	200.00	90.00
☐ 6	Scott Rolen	200.00	90.00
☐ 7	Kenny Lofton	120.00	55.00
☐ 8	Cal Ripken	400.00	180.00
☐ 10	Chipper Jones	250.00	110.00
☐ 16	Hideo Nomo	350.00	160.00
☐ 19	Juan Gonzalez	250.00	110.00
☐ 21	Roger Clemens	200.00	90.00
☐ 23	Ryne Sandberg	120.00	55.00
☐ 24	Ken Griffey Jr.	500.00	220.00
☐ 25	Barry Bonds	120.00	55.00
☐ 26	Nomar Garciaparra	250.00	110.00
☐ 27	Vladimir Guerrero	150.00	70.00
☐ 31	Mike Piazza	300.00	135.00
☐ 35	Frank Thomas	400.00	180.00
☐ 37	Tony Gwynn	250.00	110.00
☐ 39	Darin Erstad	120.00	55.00
☐ 42	Mo Vaughn	120.00	55.00
☐ 44	Greg Maddux	300.00	135.00
☐ 48	Albert Belle	120.00	55.00
☐ 52	Mark McGwire	200.00	90.00
☐ 57	Ivan Rodriguez	120.00	55.00

1997 Flair Showcase Diamond Cuts

Randomly inserted in packs at a rate of one in 20, this 20-card set features color images of baseball's brightest stars silhouetted on a holofoil-stamped die-cut diamond-design background.

	MINT	NRMT
COMPLETE SET (20)	300.00	135.00
COMMON CARD (1-20)	5.00	2.20
UNLISTED STARS	8.00	3.60
STATED ODDS 1:20		

☐ 1	Jeff Bagwell	15.00	6.75
☐ 2	Albert Belle	10.00	4.50
☐ 3	Ken Caminiti	6.00	2.70
☐ 4	Juan Gonzalez	20.00	9.00
☐ 5	Ken Griffey Jr.	40.00	18.00
☐ 6	Tony Gwynn	20.00	9.00
☐ 7	Todd Hundley	5.00	2.20
☐ 8	Andruw Jones	15.00	6.75
☐ 9	Chipper Jones	25.00	11.00
☐ 10	Greg Maddux	25.00	11.00
☐ 11	Mark McGwire	15.00	6.75
☐ 12	Mike Piazza	25.00	11.00
☐ 13	Derek Jeter	20.00	9.00
☐ 14	Manny Ramirez	8.00	3.60
☐ 15	Cal Ripken	30.00	13.50
☐ 16	Alex Rodriguez	25.00	11.00
☐ 17	Frank Thomas	30.00	13.50
☐ 18	Mo Vaughn	10.00	4.50
☐ 19	Bernie Williams	8.00	3.60
☐ 20	Matt Williams	6.00	2.70

1997 Flair Showcase Hot Gloves

Randomly inserted in packs at a rate of one in 90, this 15-card set features color images of baseball's top glovemen silhouetted against a die-cut flame and glove background with temperature-sensitive inks.

	MINT	NRMT
COMPLETE SET (15)	700.00	325.00
COMMON CARD (1-15)	10.00	4.50
SEMISTARS	12.00	5.50
STATED ODDS 1:90		

☐ 1	Roberto Alomar	20.00	9.00
☐ 2	Barry Bonds	25.00	11.00
☐ 3	Juan Gonzalez	50.00	22.00
☐ 4	Ken Griffey Jr.	100.00	45.00
☐ 5	Marquis Grissom	10.00	4.50
☐ 6	Derek Jeter	50.00	22.00

		MINT	NRMT
☐ 7	Chipper Jones	60.00	27.00
☐ 8	Barry Larkin	12.00	5.50
☐ 9	Kenny Lofton	25.00	11.00
☐ 10	Greg Maddux	60.00	27.00
☐ 11	Mike Piazza	60.00	27.00
☐ 12	Cal Ripken	80.00	36.00
☐ 13	Alex Rodriguez	60.00	27.00
☐ 14	Ivan Rodriguez	25.00	11.00
☐ 15	Frank Thomas	80.00	36.00

1997 Flair Showcase Wave of the Future

Randomly inserted in packs at a rate of one in four, this 27-card set features color images of top rookies silhouetted against a background of an embossed wave design with simulated sand.

		MINT	NRMT
COMPLETE SET (27)		70.00	32.00
COMMON (1-25/WF1-WF2)		1.00	.45
UNLISTED STARS		2.00	.90
STATED ODDS 1:4			

		MINT	NRMT
☐ 1	Todd Greene	1.50	.70
☐ 2	Andruw Jones	6.00	2.70
☐ 3	Randall Simon	5.00	2.20
☐ 4	Wady Almonte	1.50	.70
☐ 5	Pat Cline	1.00	.45
☐ 6	Jeff Abbott	1.00	.45
☐ 7	Justin Towle	2.00	.90
☐ 8	Richie Sexson	1.50	.70
☐ 9	Bubba Trammell	2.50	1.10
☐ 10	Bob Abreu	1.50	.70
☐ 11	David Arias-Ortiz	4.00	1.80
☐ 12	Todd Walker	1.50	.70
☐ 13	Orlando Cabrera	1.50	.70
☐ 14	Vladimir Guerrero	5.00	2.20
☐ 15	Ricky Ledee	5.00	2.20
☐ 16	Jorge Posada	1.00	.45
☐ 17	Ruben Rivera	1.50	.70
☐ 18	Scott Spiezio	1.50	.70
☐ 19	Scott Rolen	6.00	2.70
☐ 20	Emil Brown	1.50	.70
☐ 21	Jose Guillen	3.00	1.35
☐ 22	T.J. Staton	1.50	.70
☐ 23	Eli Marrero	1.50	.70
☐ 24	Fernando Tatis	6.00	2.70
☐ 25	Ryan Jones	1.00	.45
☐ WF1	Hideki Irabu	5.00	2.20
☐ WF2	Jose Cruz Jr.	30.00	13.50

1963 Fleer

The Fleer set of current baseball players was marketed in 1963 in a gum card-style waxed wrapper package which contained a cherry cookie instead of gum. The cards were printed in sheets of 66 with the scarce

card of Joe Adcock (#46) replaced by the unnumbered checklist card for the final press run. The complete set price includes the checklist card. The catalog designation for this set is R418-4. The key Rookie Card in this set is Maury Wills. The set is basically arranged numerically in alphabetical order by teams which are also in alphabetical order.

		NRMT	VG-E
COMPLETE SET (67)		2000.00	900.00
COMMON CARD (1-66)		15.00	6.75
MINOR STARS		20.00	9.00
SEMISTARS		25.00	11.00
UNLISTED STARS		30.00	13.50

CARDS PRICED IN NM CONDITION !

		NRMT	VG-E
☐ 1	Steve Barber	30.00	9.00
☐ 2	Ron Hansen	15.00	6.75
☐ 3	Milt Pappas	20.00	9.00
☐ 4	Brooks Robinson	100.00	45.00
☐ 5	Willie Mays	200.00	90.00
☐ 6	Lou Clinton	15.00	6.75
☐ 7	Bill Monbouquette	15.00	6.75
☐ 8	Carl Yastrzemski	120.00	55.00
☐ 9	Ray Herbert	15.00	6.75
☐ 10	Jim Landis	15.00	6.75
☐ 11	Dick Donovan	15.00	6.75
☐ 12	Tito Francona	15.00	6.75
☐ 13	Jerry Kindall	15.00	6.75
☐ 14	Frank Lary	20.00	9.00
☐ 15	Dick Howser	20.00	9.00
☐ 16	Jerry Lumpe	15.00	6.75
☐ 17	Norm Siebern	15.00	6.75
☐ 18	Don Lee	15.00	6.75
☐ 19	Albie Pearson	20.00	9.00
☐ 20	Bob Rodgers	20.00	9.00
☐ 21	Leon Wagner	15.00	6.75
☐ 22	Jim Kaat	25.00	11.00
☐ 23	Vic Power	20.00	9.00
☐ 24	Rich Rollins	20.00	9.00
☐ 25	Bobby Richardson	30.00	13.50
☐ 26	Ralph Terry	20.00	9.00
☐ 27	Tom Cheney	15.00	6.75
☐ 28	Chuck Cottier	15.00	6.75
☐ 29	Jimmy Piersall	20.00	9.00
☐ 30	Dave Stenhouse	15.00	6.75
☐ 31	Glen Hobbie	15.00	6.75
☐ 32	Ron Santo	25.00	11.00
☐ 33	Gene Freese	15.00	6.75
☐ 34	Vada Pinson	20.00	9.00
☐ 35	Bob Purkey	15.00	6.75
☐ 36	Joe Amalfitano	15.00	6.75
☐ 37	Bob Aspromonte	15.00	6.75
☐ 38	Dick Farrell	15.00	6.75
☐ 39	Al Spangler	15.00	6.75
☐ 40	Tommy Davis	20.00	9.00
☐ 41	Don Drysdale	60.00	27.00
☐ 42	Sandy Koufax	200.00	90.00
☐ 43	Maury Wills	100.00	45.00
☐ 44	Frank Bolling	15.00	6.75
☐ 45	Warren Spahn	70.00	32.00
☐ 46	Joe Adcock SP	200.00	90.00
☐ 47	Roger Craig	20.00	9.00

		NRMT	VG-E
☐ 48	Al Jackson	20.00	9.00
☐ 49	Rod Kanehl	20.00	9.00
☐ 50	Ruben Amaro	15.00	6.75
☐ 51	Johnny Callison	20.00	9.00
☐ 52	Clay Dalrymple	15.00	6.75
☐ 53	Don Demeter	15.00	6.75
☐ 54	Art Mahaffey	15.00	6.75
☐ 55	Smoky Burgess	20.00	9.00
☐ 56	Roberto Clemente	250.00	110.00
☐ 57	Roy Face	20.00	9.00
☐ 58	Vern Law	20.00	9.00
☐ 59	Bill Mazeroski	30.00	13.50
☐ 60	Ken Boyer	25.00	11.00
☐ 61	Bob Gibson	70.00	32.00
☐ 62	Gene Oliver	15.00	6.75
☐ 63	Bill White	25.00	11.00
☐ 64	Orlando Cepeda	30.00	13.50
☐ 65	Jim Davenport	15.00	6.75
☐ 66	Billy O'Dell	30.00	9.00
☐ NNO	Checklist card	700.00	230.00

1981 Fleer

This issue of cards marks Fleer's first entry into the current player baseball card market since 1963. Cards are grouped in team order and teams are ordered based upon their standings from the 1980 season with the World Series champion Philadelphia Phillies starting off the set. Cards 638-660 feature specials and checklists. The cards of pitchers in this set erroneously show a heading (on the card backs) of 'Batting Record' over their career pitching statistics. There are three distinct printings: the two following the primary run were designed to correct numerous errors. The variations caused by these multiple printings are noted in the checklist below (P1, P2, or P3). The Craig Nettles variation was corrected before the end of the first printing and thus is not included in the complete set consideration due to scarcity. Unopened packs contained 17 cards as well as a piece of gum. Unopened boxes contained 38 packs. The key Rookie Cards in this set are Danny Ainge, Harold Baines, Kirk Gibson, Jeff Reardon, and Fernando Valenzuela, whose first name was erroneously spelled Fernand on the card front.

		NRMT	VG-E
COMPLETE SET (660)		30.00	13.50
COMMON CARD (1-660)		.10	.05
MINOR STARS		.25	.11
SEMISTARS		.50	.23
UNLISTED STARS		1.00	.45

□ 1	Pete Rose UER (270 hits in '63, should be 170)	1.25	.55
□ 2	Larry Bowa	.25	.11
□ 3	Manny Trillo	.10	.05
□ 4	Bob Boone	.25	.11
□ 5	Mike Schmidt (See also 640A)	1.25	.55
□ 6	Steve Carlton P1 Golden Arm (Back "1066 Cardinals"; Number on back 6)	1.50	.70
□ 6B	Steve Carlton P2 Pitcher of Year (Back "1066 Cardinals")	1.50	.70
□ 6C	Steve Carlton P3 (1966 Cardinals)	2.00	.90
□ 7	Tug McGraw (See 657A)	.25	.11
□ 8	Larry Christenson	.10	.05
□ 9	Bake McBride	.10	.05
□ 10	Greg Luzinski	.25	.11
□ 11	Ron Reed	.10	.05
□ 12	Dickie Noles	.10	.05
□ 13	Keith Moreland	.25	.11
□ 14	Bob Walk	.25	.11
□ 15	Lonnie Smith	.25	.11
□ 16	Dick Ruthven	.10	.05
□ 17	Sparky Lyle	.25	.11
□ 18	Greg Gross	.10	.05
□ 19	Garry Maddox	.10	.05
□ 20	Nino Espinosa	.10	.05
□ 21	George Vukovich	.10	.05
□ 22	John Vukovich	.10	.05
□ 23	Ramon Aviles	.10	.05
□ 24A	Kevin Saucier P1 (Name on back "Ken")	.10	
□ 24B	Kevin Saucier P2 (Name on back "Ken")	.10	.05
□ 24C	Kevin Saucier P3 (Name on back "Kevin")	1.00	.45
□ 25	Randy Lerch	.10	.05
□ 26	Del Unser	.10	.05
□ 27	Tim McCarver	.50	.23
□ 28	George Brett (See also 655A)	2.50	1.10
□ 29	Willie Wilson (See also 653A)	.10	.05
□ 30	Paul Splittorff	.10	.05
□ 31	Dan Quisenberry	.25	.11
□ 32A	Amos Otis P1 (Batting Pose; "Outfield"; 32 on back)	.25	.11
□ 32B	Amos Otis P2 Series Starter 483 on back	.25	.11
□ 33	Steve Busby	.10	.05
□ 34	U.L. Washington	.10	.05
□ 35	Dave Chalk	.10	.05
□ 36	Darrell Porter	.10	.05
□ 37	Marty Pattin	.10	.05
□ 38	Larry Gura	.10	.05
□ 39	Renie Martin	.10	.05
□ 40	Rich Gale	.10	.05
□ 41A	Hal McRae P1 ("Royals" on front in black letters)	.50	.23
□ 41B	Hal McRae P2 ("Royals" on front in blue letters)	.25	.11
□ 42	Dennis Leonard	.10	.05
□ 43	Willie Aikens	.10	.05
□ 44	Frank White	.25	.11
□ 45	Clint Hurdle	.10	.05
□ 46	John Wathan	.10	.05
□ 47	Pete LaCock	.10	.05
□ 48	Rance Mulliniks	.10	.05
□ 49	Jeff Twitty	.10	.05
□ 50	Jamie Quirk	.10	.05
□ 51	Art Howe	.10	.05
□ 52	Ken Forsch	.10	.05
□ 53	Vern Ruhle	.10	.05
□ 54	Joe Niekro	.25	.11
□ 55	Frank LaCorte	.10	.05
□ 56	J.R. Richard	.25	.11
□ 57	Nolan Ryan	5.00	2.20
□ 58	Enos Cabell	.10	.05
□ 59	Cesar Cedeno	.25	.11
□ 60	Jose Cruz	.50	.23
□ 61	Bill Virdon MG	.10	.05
□ 62	Terry Puhl	.10	.05
□ 63	Joaquin Andujar	.25	.11
□ 64	Alan Ashby	.10	.05
□ 65	Joe Sambito	.10	.05
□ 66	Denny Walling	.10	.05
□ 67	Jeff Leonard	.25	.11
□ 68	Luis Pujols	.10	.05
□ 69	Bruce Bochy	.10	.05
□ 70	Rafael Landestoy	.10	.05
□ 71	Dave Smith	.25	.11
□ 72	Danny Heep	.10	.05
□ 73	Julio Gonzalez	.10	.05
□ 74	Craig Reynolds	.10	.05
□ 75	Gary Woods	.10	.05
□ 76	Dave Bergman	.10	.05
□ 77	Randy Niemann	.10	.05
□ 78	Joe Morgan	1.00	.45
□ 79	Reggie Jackson (See also 650A)	1.25	.55
□ 80	Bucky Dent	.25	.11
□ 81	Tommy John	.50	.23
□ 82	Luis Tiant	.25	.11
□ 83	Rick Cerone	.10	.05
□ 84	Dick Howser MG	.25	.11
□ 85	Lou Piniella	.25	.11
□ 86	Ron Davis	.10	.05
□ 87A	Graig Nettles P1 ERR (Name on back misspelled "Craig")	8.00	3.60
□ 87B	Graig Nettles P2 COR ("Graig")	.25	.11
□ 88	Ron Guidry	.25	.11
□ 89	Rich Gossage	.50	.23
□ 90	Rudy May	.10	.05
□ 91	Gaylord Perry	1.00	.45
□ 92	Eric Soderholm	.10	.05
□ 93	Bob Watson	.10	.05
□ 94	Bobby Murcer	.25	.11
□ 95	Bobby Brown	.10	.05
□ 96	Jim Spencer	.10	.05
□ 97	Tom Underwood	.10	.05
□ 98	Oscar Gamble	.10	.05
□ 99	Johnny Oates	.25	.11
□ 100	Fred Stanley	.10	.05
□ 101	Ruppert Jones	.10	.05
□ 102	Dennis Werth	.10	.05
□ 103	Joe Lefebvre	.10	.05
□ 104	Brian Doyle	.10	.05
□ 105	Aurelio Rodriguez	.10	.05
□ 106	Doug Bird	.10	.05
□ 107	Mike Griffin	.10	.05
□ 108	Tim Lollar	.10	.05
□ 109	Willie Randolph	.25	.11
□ 110	Steve Garvey	.50	.23
□ 111	Reggie Smith	.25	.11
□ 112	Don Sutton	1.00	.45
□ 113	Burt Hooton	.10	.05
□ 114A	Dave Lopes P1 (Small hand on back)	.50	.23
□ 114B	Dave Lopes P2 (No hand)	.25	.11
□ 115	Dusty Baker	.50	.23
□ 116	Tom Lasorda MG	.25	.11
□ 117	Bill Russell	.25	.11
□ 118	Jerry Reuss UER ("Home:" omitted)	.25	.11
□ 119	Terry Forster	.25	.11
□ 120A	Bob Welch P1 (Name on back is "Bob")	.25	.11
□ 120B	Bob Welch P2 (Name on back is "Robert")	.50	.23
□ 121	Don Stanhouse	.10	.05
□ 122	Rick Monday	.25	.11
□ 123	Derrel Thomas	.10	.05
□ 124	Joe Ferguson	.10	.05
□ 125	Rick Sutcliffe	.25	.11
□ 126A	Ron Cey P1 (Small hand on back)	.50	.23
□ 126B	Ron Cey P2	.25	.11
	(No hand)		
□ 127	Dave Goltz	.10	.05
□ 128	Jay Johnstone	.25	.11
□ 129	Steve Yeager	.10	.05
□ 130	Gary Weiss	.10	.05
□ 131	Mike Scioscia	1.00	.45
□ 132	Vic Davalillo	.10	.05
□ 133	Doug Rau	.10	.05
□ 134	Pepe Frias	.10	.05
□ 135	Mickey Hatcher	.25	.11
□ 136	Steve Howe	.25	.11
□ 137	Robert Castillo	.10	.05
□ 138	Gary Thomasson	.10	.05
□ 139	Rudy Law	.10	.05
□ 140	Fernando Valenzuela UER (Misspelled Fernand on card)	2.00	.90
□ 141	Manny Mota	.25	.11
□ 142	Gary Carter	1.00	.45
□ 143	Steve Rogers	.10	.05
□ 144	Warren Cromartie	.10	.05
□ 145	Andre Dawson	1.50	.70
□ 146	Larry Parrish	.10	.05
□ 147	Rowland Office	.10	.05
□ 148	Ellis Valentine	.10	.05
□ 149	Dick Williams MG	.10	.05
□ 150	Bill Gullickson	.50	.23
□ 151	Elias Sosa	.10	.05
□ 152	John Tamargo	.10	.05
□ 153	Chris Speier	.10	.05
□ 154	Ron LeFlore	.25	.11
□ 155	Rodney Scott	.10	.05
□ 156	Stan Bahnsen	.10	.05
□ 157	Bill Lee	.25	.11
□ 158	Fred Norman	.10	.05
□ 159	Woodie Fryman	.10	.05
□ 160	David Palmer	.10	.05
□ 161	Jerry White	.10	.05
□ 162	Roberto Ramos	.10	.05
□ 163	John D'Acquisto	.10	.05
□ 164	Tommy Hutton	.10	.05
□ 165	Charlie Lea	.10	.05
□ 166	Scott Sanderson	.10	.05
□ 167	Ken Macha	.10	.05
□ 168	Tony Bernazard	.10	.05
□ 169	Jim Palmer	.75	.35
□ 170	Steve Stone	.25	.11
□ 171	Mike Flanagan	.25	.11
□ 172	Al Bumbry	.10	.05
□ 173	Doug DeCinces	.25	.11
□ 174	Scott McGregor	.10	.05
□ 175	Mark Belanger	.25	.11
□ 176	Tim Stoddard	.10	.05
□ 177A	Rick Dempsey P1 (Small hand on front)	.50	.23
□ 177B	Rick Dempsey P2 (No hand)	.25	.11
□ 178	Earl Weaver MG	1.00	.45
□ 179	Tippy Martinez	.10	.05
□ 180	Dennis Martinez	.50	.23
□ 181	Sammy Stewart	.10	.05
□ 182	Rich Dauer	.10	.05
□ 183	Lee May	.25	.11
□ 184	Eddie Murray	2.00	.90
□ 185	Benny Ayala	.10	.05
□ 186	John Lowenstein	.10	.05
□ 187	Gary Roenicke	.10	.05
□ 188	Ken Singleton	.25	.11
□ 189	Dan Graham	.10	.05
□ 190	Terry Crowley	.10	.05
□ 191	Kiko Garcia	.10	.05
□ 192	Dave Ford	.10	.05
□ 193	Mark Corey	.10	.05
□ 194	Lenn Sakata	.10	.05
□ 195	Doug DeCinces	.25	.11
□ 196	Johnny Bench	1.25	.55
□ 197	Dave Concepcion	.25	.11
□ 198	Ray Knight	.25	.11
□ 199	Ken Griffey	.50	.23
□ 200	Tom Seaver	1.25	.55
□ 201	Dave Collins	.10	.05
□ 202A	George Foster P1 Slugger (Number on back 216)	.50	.23
□ 202B	George Foster P2 Slugger	.50	.23

(Number on back 202)

☐ 203 Junior Kennedy .10	.05	
☐ 204 Frank Pastore .10	.05	
☐ 205 Dan Driessen .10	.05	
☐ 206 Hector Cruz .10	.05	
☐ 207 Paul Moskau .10	.05	
☐ 208 Charlie Leibrandt .50	.23	
☐ 209 Harry Spilman .10	.05	
☐ 210 Joe Price .10	.05	
☐ 211 Tom Hume .10	.05	
☐ 212 Joe Nolan .10	.05	
☐ 213 Doug Bair .10	.05	
☐ 214 Mario Soto .10	.05	
☐ 215A Bill Bonham P1 .50	.23	
(Small hand on back)		
☐ 215B Bill Bonham P2 .10	.05	
(No hand)		
☐ 216 George Foster .25	.11	
(See 202)		
☐ 217 Paul Householder .10	.05	
☐ 218 Ron Oester .10	.05	
☐ 219 Sam Mejias .10	.05	
☐ 220 Sheldon Burnside .10	.05	
☐ 221 Carl Yastrzemski 1.00	.45	
☐ 222 Jim Rice .25	.11	
☐ 223 Fred Lynn .25	.11	
☐ 224 Carlton Fisk 1.25	.55	
☐ 225 Rick Burleson .10	.05	
☐ 226 Dennis Eckersley 1.00	.45	
☐ 227 Butch Hobson .10	.05	
☐ 228 Tom Burgmeier .10	.05	
☐ 229 Garry Hancock .10	.05	
☐ 230 Don Zimmer MG .10	.05	
☐ 231 Steve Renko .10	.05	
☐ 232 Dwight Evans .50	.23	
☐ 233 Mike Torrez .10	.05	
☐ 234 Bob Stanley .10	.05	
☐ 235 Jim Dwyer .10	.05	
☐ 236 Dave Stapleton .10	.05	
☐ 237 Glenn Hoffman .10	.05	
☐ 238 Jerry Remy .10	.05	
☐ 239 Dick Drago .10	.05	
☐ 240 Bill Campbell .10	.05	
☐ 241 Tony Perez 1.00	.45	
☐ 242 Phil Niekro 1.00	.45	
☐ 243 Dale Murphy 1.00	.45	
☐ 244 Bob Horner .25	.11	
☐ 245 Jeff Burroughs .10	.05	
☐ 246 Rick Camp .10	.05	
☐ 247 Bobby Cox MG .25	.11	
☐ 248 Bruce Benedict .10	.05	
☐ 249 Gene Garber .10	.05	
☐ 250 Jerry Royster .10	.05	
☐ 251A Gary Matthews P1 .50	.23	
(Small hand on back)		
☐ 251B Gary Matthews P2 .25	.11	
(No hand)		
☐ 252 Chris Chambliss .25	.11	
☐ 253 Luis Gomez .10	.05	
☐ 254 Bill Nahorodny .10	.05	
☐ 255 Doyle Alexander .10	.05	
☐ 256 Brian Asselstine .10	.05	
☐ 257 Biff Pocoroba .10	.05	
☐ 258 Mike Lum .10	.05	
☐ 259 Charlie Spikes .10	.05	
☐ 260 Glenn Hubbard .10	.05	
☐ 261 Tommy Boggs .10	.05	
☐ 262 Al Hrabosky .10	.05	
☐ 263 Rick Matula .10	.05	
☐ 264 Preston Hanna .10	.05	
☐ 265 Larry Bradford .10	.05	
☐ 266 Rafael Ramirez .25	.11	
☐ 267 Larry McWilliams .10	.05	
☐ 268 Rod Carew .75	.35	
☐ 269 Bobby Grich .25	.11	
☐ 270 Carney Lansford .25	.11	
☐ 271 Don Baylor .50	.23	
☐ 272 Joe Rudi .25	.11	
☐ 273 Dan Ford .10	.05	
☐ 274 Jim Fregosi MG .10	.05	
☐ 275 Dave Frost .10	.05	
☐ 276 Frank Tanana .25	.11	
☐ 277 Dickie Thon .10	.05	
☐ 278 Jason Thompson .10	.05	
☐ 279 Rick Miller .10	.05	
☐ 280 Bert Campaneris .25	.11	

☐ 281 Tom Donohue .10	.05	
☐ 282 Brian Downing .25	.11	
☐ 283 Fred Patek .10	.05	
☐ 284 Bruce Kison .10	.05	
☐ 285 Dave LaRoche .10	.05	
☐ 286 Don Aase .10	.05	
☐ 287 Jim Barr .10	.05	
☐ 288 Alfredo Martinez .10	.05	
☐ 289 Larry Harlow .10	.05	
☐ 290 Andy Hassler .10	.05	
☐ 291 Dave Kingman .50	.23	
☐ 292 Bill Buckner .25	.11	
☐ 293 Rick Reuschel .25	.11	
☐ 294 Bruce Sutter .25	.11	
☐ 295 Jerry Martin .10	.05	
☐ 296 Scot Thompson .10	.05	
☐ 297 Ivan DeJesus .10	.05	
☐ 298 Steve Dillard .10	.05	
☐ 299 Dick Tidrow .10	.05	
☐ 300 Randy Martz .10	.05	
☐ 301 Lenny Randle .10	.05	
☐ 302 Lynn McGlothen .10	.05	
☐ 303 Cliff Johnson .10	.05	
☐ 304 Tim Blackwell .10	.05	
☐ 305 Dennis Lamp .10	.05	
☐ 306 Bill Caudill .10	.05	
☐ 307 Carlos Lezcano .10	.05	
☐ 308 Jim Tracy .10	.05	
☐ 309 Doug Capilla UER .10	.05	
(Cubs on front but		
Braves on back)		
☐ 310 Willie Hernandez .25	.11	
☐ 311 Mike Vail .10	.05	
☐ 312 Mike Krukow .10	.05	
☐ 313 Barry Foote .10	.05	
☐ 314 Larry Biittner .10	.05	
☐ 315 Mike Tyson .10	.05	
☐ 316 Lee Mazzilli .10	.05	
☐ 317 John Stearns .10	.05	
☐ 318 Alex Trevino .10	.05	
☐ 319 Craig Swan .10	.05	
☐ 320 Frank Taveras .10	.05	
☐ 321 Steve Henderson .10	.05	
☐ 322 Neil Allen .10	.05	
☐ 323 Mark Bomback .10	.05	
☐ 324 Mike Jorgensen .10	.05	
☐ 325 Joe Torre MG .25	.11	
☐ 326 Elliott Maddox .10	.05	
☐ 327 Pete Falcone .10	.05	
☐ 328 Ray Burris .10	.05	
☐ 329 Claudell Washington .10	.05	
☐ 330 Doug Flynn .10	.05	
☐ 331 Joel Youngblood .10	.05	
☐ 332 Bill Almon .10	.05	
☐ 333 Tom Hausman .10	.05	
☐ 334 Pat Zachry .10	.05	
☐ 335 Jeff Reardon 1.00	.45	
☐ 336 Wally Backman .25	.11	
☐ 337 Dan Norman .10	.05	
☐ 338 Jerry Morales .10	.05	
☐ 339 Ed Farmer .10	.05	
☐ 340 Bob Molinaro .10	.05	
☐ 341 Todd Cruz .10	.05	
☐ 342A Britt Burns P1 .50	.23	
(Small hand on front)		
☐ 342B Britt Burns P2 .25	.11	
(No hand)		
☐ 343 Kevin Bell .10	.05	
☐ 344 Tony LaRussa MG .25	.11	
☐ 345 Steve Trout .10	.05	
☐ 346 Harold Baines 1.50	.70	
☐ 347 Richard Wortham .10	.05	
☐ 348 Wayne Nordhagen .10	.05	
☐ 349 Mike Squires .10	.05	
☐ 350 Lamar Johnson .10	.05	
☐ 351 Rickey Henderson 2.00	.90	
(Most Stolen Bases AL)		
☐ 352 Francisco Barrios .10	.05	
☐ 353 Thad Bosley .10	.05	
☐ 354 Chet Lemon .25	.11	
☐ 355 Bruce Kimm .10	.05	
☐ 356 Richard Dotson .25	.11	
☐ 357 Jim Morrison .10	.05	
☐ 358 Mike Proly .10	.05	
☐ 359 Greg Pryor .10	.05	
☐ 360 Dave Parker .50	.23	

☐ 361 Omar Moreno .10	.05	
☐ 362A Kent Tekulve P1 .25	.11	
(Back "1071 Waterbury"		
and "1078 Pirates")		
☐ 362B Kent Tekulve P2 .10	.05	
("1971 Waterbury" and		
"1978 Pirates")		
☐ 363 Willie Stargell .75	.35	
☐ 364 Phil Garner .25	.11	
☐ 365 Ed Ott .10	.05	
☐ 366 Don Robinson .10	.05	
☐ 367 Chuck Tanner MG .25	.11	
☐ 368 Jim Rooker .10	.05	
☐ 369 Dale Berra .10	.05	
☐ 370 Jim Bibby .10	.05	
☐ 371 Steve Nicosia .10	.05	
☐ 372 Mike Easler .10	.05	
☐ 373 Bill Robinson .25	.11	
☐ 374 Lee Lacy .10	.05	
☐ 375 John Candelaria .25	.11	
☐ 376 Manny Sanguillen .25	.11	
☐ 377 Rick Rhoden .10	.05	
☐ 378 Grant Jackson .10	.05	
☐ 379 Tim Foli .10	.05	
☐ 380 Rod Scurry .10	.05	
☐ 381 Bill Madlock .50	.23	
☐ 382A Kurt Bevacqua .25	.11	
P1 ERR		
(P on cap backwards)		
☐ 382B Kurt Bevacqua P2 .10	.05	
COR		
☐ 383 Bert Blyleven .50	.23	
☐ 384 Eddie Solomon .10	.05	
☐ 385 Enrique Romo .10	.05	
☐ 386 John Milner .10	.05	
☐ 387 Mike Hargrove .25	.11	
☐ 388 Jorge Orta .10	.05	
☐ 389 Toby Harrah .25	.11	
☐ 390 Tom Veryzer .10	.05	
☐ 391 Miguel Dilone .10	.05	
☐ 392 Dan Spillner .10	.05	
☐ 393 Jack Brohamer .10	.05	
☐ 394 Wayne Garland .10	.05	
☐ 395 Sid Monge .10	.05	
☐ 396 Rick Waits .10	.05	
☐ 397 Joe Charboneau 1.00	.45	
☐ 398 Gary Alexander .10	.05	
☐ 399 Jerry Dybzinski .10	.05	
☐ 400 Mike Stanton .10	.05	
☐ 401 Mike Paxton .10	.05	
☐ 402 Gary Gray .10	.05	
☐ 403 Rick Manning .10	.05	
☐ 404 Bo Diaz .10	.05	
☐ 405 Ron Hassey .10	.05	
☐ 406 Ross Grimsley .10	.05	
☐ 407 Victor Cruz .10	.05	
☐ 408 Len Barker .10	.05	
☐ 409 Bob Bailor .10	.05	
☐ 410 Otto Velez .10	.05	
☐ 411 Ernie Whitt .10	.05	
☐ 412 Jim Clancy .10	.05	
☐ 413 Barry Bonnell .10	.05	
☐ 414 Dave Stieb .25	.11	
☐ 415 Damaso Garcia .10	.05	
☐ 416 John Mayberry .10	.05	
☐ 417 Roy Howell .10	.05	
☐ 418 Danny Ainge 2.00	.90	
☐ 419A Jesse Jefferson P1 .10	.05	
(Back says Pirates)		
☐ 419B Jesse Jefferson P2 .10	.05	
(Back says Pirates)		
☐ 419C Jesse Jefferson P3 1.00	.45	
(Back says Blue Jays)		
☐ 420 Joey McLaughlin .10	.05	
☐ 421 Lloyd Moseby .25	.11	
☐ 422 Alvis Woods .10	.05	
☐ 423 Garth Iorg .10	.05	
☐ 424 Doug Ault .10	.05	
☐ 425 Ken Schrom .10	.05	
☐ 426 Mike Willis .10	.05	
☐ 427 Steve Braun .10	.05	
☐ 428 Bob Davis .10	.05	
☐ 429 Jerry Garvin .10	.05	
☐ 430 Alfredo Griffin .10	.05	
☐ 431 Bob Mattick MG .10	.05	
☐ 432 Vida Blue .25	.11	

☐ 433	Jack Clark	.25	.11
☐ 434	Willie McCovey	.75	.35
☐ 435	Mike Ivie	.05	
☐ 436A	Darrel Evans P1 ERR	.50	.23
	(Name on front "Darrel")		
☐ 436B	Darrell Evans P2 COR	.50	.23
	(Name on front "Darrell")		
☐ 437	Terry Whitfield	.10	.05
☐ 438	Rennie Stennett	.10	.05
☐ 439	John Montefusco	.10	.05
☐ 440	Jim Wohlford	.10	.05
☐ 441	Bill North	.10	.05
☐ 442	Milt May	.10	.05
☐ 443	Max Venable	.10	.05
☐ 444	Ed Whitson	.10	.05
☐ 445	Al Holland	.10	.05
☐ 446	Randy Moffitt	.10	.05
☐ 447	Bob Knepper	.10	.05
☐ 448	Gary Lavelle	.10	.05
☐ 449	Greg Minton	.10	.05
☐ 450	Johnnie LeMaster	.10	.05
☐ 451	Larry Herndon	.10	.05
☐ 452	Rich Murray	.10	.05
☐ 453	Joe Pettini	.10	.05
☐ 454	Allen Ripley	.10	.05
☐ 455	Dennis Littlejohn	.10	.05
☐ 456	Tom Griffin	.10	.05
☐ 457	Alan Hargesheimer	.10	.05
☐ 458	Joe Strain	.10	.05
☐ 459	Steve Kemp	.10	.05
☐ 460	Sparky Anderson MG	.10	.05
☐ 461	Alan Trammell	1.25	.55
☐ 462	Mark Fidrych	1.00	.45
☐ 463	Lou Whitaker	1.00	.45
☐ 464	Dave Rozema	.10	.05
☐ 465	Milt Wilcox	.10	.05
☐ 466	Champ Summers	.10	.05
☐ 467	Lance Parrish	.25	.11
☐ 468	Dan Petry	.10	.05
☐ 469	Pat Underwood	.10	.05
☐ 470	Rick Peters	.10	.05
☐ 471	Al Cowens	.10	.05
☐ 472	John Wockenfuss	.10	.05
☐ 473	Tom Brookens	.10	.05
☐ 474	Richie Hebner	.10	.05
☐ 475	Jack Morris	1.00	.45
☐ 476	Jim Lentine	.10	.05
☐ 477	Bruce Robbins	.10	.05
☐ 478	Mark Wagner	.10	.05
☐ 479	Tim Corcoran	.10	.05
☐ 480A	Stan Papi P1	.25	.11
	(Front as Pitcher)		
☐ 480B	Stan Papi P2	.10	.05
	(Front as Shortstop)		
☐ 481	Kirk Gibson	2.00	.90
☐ 482	Dan Schatzeder	.10	.05
☐ 483A	Amos Otis P1	.25	.11
	(See card 32)		
☐ 483B	Amos Otis P2	.25	.11
	(See card 32)		
☐ 484	Dave Winfield	1.50	.70
☐ 485	Rollie Fingers	1.00	.45
☐ 486	Gene Richards	.10	.05
☐ 487	Randy Jones	.10	.05
☐ 488	Ozzie Smith	4.00	1.80
☐ 489	Gene Tenace	.25	.11
☐ 490	Bill Fahey	.10	.05
☐ 491	John Curtis	.10	.05
☐ 492	Dave Cash	.10	.05
☐ 493A	Tim Flannery P1	.25	.11
	(Batting right)		
☐ 493B	Tim Flannery P2	.10	.05
	(Batting left)		
☐ 494	Jerry Mumphrey	.10	.05
☐ 495	Bob Shirley	.10	.05
☐ 496	Steve Mura	.10	.05
☐ 497	Eric Rasmussen	.10	.05
☐ 498	Broderick Perkins	.10	.05
☐ 499	Barry Evans	.10	.05
☐ 500	Chuck Baker	.10	.05
☐ 501	Luis Salazar	.10	.05
☐ 502	Gary Lucas	.10	.05
☐ 503	Mike Armstrong	.10	.05
☐ 504	Jerry Turner	.10	.05
☐ 505	Dennis Kinney	.10	.05
☐ 506	Willie Montanez UER	.10	.05
	(Misspelled Willy on card front)		
☐ 507	Gorman Thomas	.25	.11
☐ 508	Ben Oglivie	.25	.11
☐ 509	Larry Hisle	.10	.05
☐ 510	Sal Bando	.25	.11
☐ 511	Robin Yount	1.25	.55
☐ 512	Mike Caldwell	.10	.05
☐ 513	Sixto Lezcano	.10	.05
☐ 514A	Bill Travers P1 ERR	.25	.11
	("Jerry Augustine" with Augustine back)		
☐ 514B	Bill Travers P2 COR	.10	.05
☐ 515	Paul Molitor	2.00	.90
☐ 516	Moose Haas	.10	.05
☐ 517	Bill Castro	.10	.05
☐ 518	Jim Slaton	.10	.05
☐ 519	Lary Sorensen	.10	.05
☐ 520	Bob McClure	.10	.05
☐ 521	Charlie Moore	.10	.05
☐ 522	Jim Gantner	.25	.11
☐ 523	Reggie Cleveland	.10	.05
☐ 524	Don Money	.10	.05
☐ 525	Bill Travers	.10	.05
☐ 526	Buck Martinez	.10	.05
☐ 527	Dick Davis	.10	.05
☐ 528	Ted Simmons	.25	.11
☐ 529	Garry Templeton	.10	.05
☐ 530	Ken Reitz	.10	.05
☐ 531	Tony Scott	.10	.05
☐ 532	Ken Oberkfell	.10	.05
☐ 533	Bob Sykes	.10	.05
☐ 534	Keith Smith	.10	.05
☐ 535	John Littlefield	.10	.05
☐ 536	Jim Kaat	.25	.11
☐ 537	Bob Forsch	.10	.05
☐ 538	Mike Phillips	.10	.05
☐ 539	Terry Landrum	.10	.05
☐ 540	Leon Durham	.25	.11
☐ 541	Terry Kennedy	.10	.05
☐ 542	George Hendrick	.10	.05
☐ 543	Dane Iorg	.10	.05
☐ 544	Mark Littell	.10	.05
☐ 545	Keith Hernandez	.25	.11
☐ 546	Silvio Martinez	.10	.05
☐ 547A	Don Hood P1 ERR	.25	.11
	("Pete Vuckovich" with Vuckovich back)		
☐ 547B	Don Hood P2 COR	.10	.05
☐ 548	Bobby Bonds	.25	.11
☐ 549	Mike Ramsey	.10	.05
☐ 550	Tom Herr	.25	.11
☐ 551	Roy Smalley	.10	.05
☐ 552	Jerry Koosman	.25	.11
☐ 553	Ken Landreaux	.10	.05
☐ 554	John Castino	.10	.05
☐ 555	Doug Corbett	.10	.05
☐ 556	Bombo Rivera	.10	.05
☐ 557	Ron Jackson	.10	.05
☐ 558	Butch Wynegar	.10	.05
☐ 559	Hosken Powell	.10	.05
☐ 560	Pete Redfern	.10	.05
☐ 561	Roger Erickson	.10	.05
☐ 562	Glenn Adams	.10	.05
☐ 563	Rick Sofield	.10	.05
☐ 564	Geoff Zahn	.10	.05
☐ 565	Pete Mackanin	.10	.05
☐ 566	Mike Cubbage	.10	.05
☐ 567	Darrell Jackson	.10	.05
☐ 568	Dave Edwards	.10	.05
☐ 569	Rob Wilfong	.10	.05
☐ 570	Sal Butera	.10	.05
☐ 571	Jose Morales	.10	.05
☐ 572	Rick Langford	.10	.05
☐ 573	Mike Norris	.10	.05
☐ 574	Rickey Henderson	2.50	1.10
☐ 575	Tony Armas	.25	.11
☐ 576	Dave Revering	.10	.05
☐ 577	Jeff Newman	.10	.05
☐ 578	Bob Lacey	.10	.05
☐ 579	Brian Kingman	.10	.05
☐ 580	Mitchell Page	.10	.05
☐ 581	Billy Martin MG	.50	.23
☐ 582	Rob Picciolo	.10	.05
☐ 583	Mike Heath	.10	.05
☐ 584	Mickey Klutts	.10	.05
☐ 585	Orlando Gonzalez	.10	.05
☐ 586	Mike Davis	.10	.05
☐ 587	Wayne Gross	.10	.05
☐ 588	Matt Keough	.10	.05
☐ 589	Steve McCatty	.10	.05
☐ 590	Dwayne Murphy	.10	.05
☐ 591	Mario Guerrero	.10	.05
☐ 592	Dave McKay	.10	.05
☐ 593	Jim Essian	.10	.05
☐ 594	Dave Heaverlo	.10	.05
☐ 595	Maury Wills MG	.25	.11
☐ 596	Juan Beniquez	.10	.05
☐ 597	Rodney Craig	.10	.05
☐ 598	Jim Anderson	.10	.05
☐ 599	Floyd Bannister	.10	.05
☐ 600	Bruce Bochte	.10	.05
☐ 601	Julio Cruz	.10	.05
☐ 602	Ted Cox	.10	.05
☐ 603	Dan Meyer	.10	.05
☐ 604	Larry Cox	.10	.05
☐ 605	Bill Stein	.10	.05
☐ 606	Steve Garvey	.50	.23
	(Most Hits NL)		
☐ 607	Dave Roberts	.10	.05
☐ 608	Leon Roberts	.10	.05
☐ 609	Reggie Walton	.10	.05
☐ 610	Dave Edler	.10	.05
☐ 611	Larry Milbourne	.10	.05
☐ 612	Kim Allen	.10	.05
☐ 613	Mario Mendoza	.10	.05
☐ 614	Tom Paciorek	.10	.05
☐ 615	Glenn Abbott	.10	.05
☐ 616	Joe Simpson	.10	.05
☐ 617	Mickey Rivers	.25	.11
☐ 618	Jim Kern	.10	.05
☐ 619	Jim Sundberg	.25	.11
☐ 620	Richie Zisk	.10	.05
☐ 621	Jon Matlack	.10	.05
☐ 622	Ferguson Jenkins	1.00	.45
☐ 623	Pat Corrales MG	.10	.05
☐ 624	Ed Figueroa	.10	.05
☐ 625	Buddy Bell	.25	.11
☐ 626	Al Oliver	.25	.11
☐ 627	Doc Medich	.10	.05
☐ 628	Bump Wills	.10	.05
☐ 629	Rusty Staub	.25	.11
☐ 630	Pat Putnam	.10	.05
☐ 631	John Grubb	.10	.05
☐ 632	Danny Darwin	.25	.11
☐ 633	Ken Clay	.10	.05
☐ 634	Jim Norris	.10	.05
☐ 635	John Butcher	.10	.05
☐ 636	Dave Roberts	.10	.05
☐ 637	Billy Sample	.10	.05
☐ 638	Carl Yastrzemski	1.00	.45
☐ 639	Cecil Cooper	.25	.11
☐ 640	Mike Schmidt P1	1.25	.55
	(Portrait; "Third Base"; number on back 5)		
☐ 640B	Mike Schmidt P2	2.00	.90
	("1980 Home Run King"; 640 on back)		
☐ 641A	CL: Phils/Royals P1..	.25	.11
	41 is Hal McRae		
☐ 641B	CL: Phils/Royals P2..	.25	.11
	(41 is Hal McRae, Double Threat)		
☐ 642	CL: Astros/Yankees	.10	.05
☐ 643	CL: Expos/Dodgers	.10	.05
☐ 644A	CL: Reds/Orioles P1	.25	.11
	(202 is George Foster; Joe Nolan pitcher, should be catcher)		
☐ 644B	CL: Reds/Orioles P2	.25	.11
	(202 is Foster Slugger; Joe Nolan pitcher, should be catcher)		
☐ 645	Pete Rose	1.25	.55
	Larry Bowa		
	Mike Schmidt		
	Triple Threat P1		
	(No number on back)		
☐ 645B	Pete Rose	2.50	1.10

Larry Bowa
Mike Schmidt
Triple Threat P2
(Back numbered 645)

- □ 646 CL: Braves/Red Sox.... .10 .05
- □ 647 CL: Cubs/Angels .... .10 .05
- □ 648 CL: Mets/White Sox..... .10 .05
- □ 649 CL: Indians/Pirates ..... .10 .05
- □ 650 Reggie Jackson ...... 1.25 .55
  Mr. Baseball P1
  (Number on back 79)
- □ 650B Reggie Jackson...... 1.25 .55
  Mr. Baseball P2
  (Number on back 650)
- □ 651 CL: Giants/Blue Jays .. .10 .05
- □ 652A CL: Tigers/Padres P1 .25 .11
  (483 is listed)
- □ 652B CL: Tigers/Padres P2 .25 .11
  (483 is deleted)
- □ 653A Willie Wilson P1 ...... .25 .11
  Most Hits Most Runs
  (Number on back 29)
- □ 653B Willie Wilson P2 ...... .25 .11
  Most Hits Most Runs
  (Number on back 653)
- □ 654A CL:Brewers/Cards P1 .25 .11
  (514 Jerry Augustine;
  547 Pete Vuckovich)
- □ 654B CL:Brewers/Cards P2 .25 .11
  (514 Billy Travers;
  547 Don Hood)
- □ 655 George Brett P1...... 2.50 1.10
  .390 Average
  (Number on back 28)
- □ 655B George Brett P2 ...... 4.00 1.80
  .390 Average
  (Number on back 655)
- □ 656 CL: Twins/Oakland A's .25
- □ 657A Tug McGraw P1 ...... .25 .11
  Game Saver
  (Number on back 7)
- □ 657B Tug McGraw P2 ...... .25 .11
  Game Saver
  (Number on back 657)
- □ 658 CL: Rangers/Mariners .10 .05
- □ 659A Checklist P1 ...... .10 .05
  of Special Cards
  (Last lines on front,
  Wilson Most Hits)
- □ 659B Checklist P2 ...... .10 .05
  of Special Cards
  (Last lines on front,
  Otis Series Starter)
- □ 660 Steve Carlton P1 ...... 1.50 .70
  Golden Arm
  (Number on back 660;
  Back "1066 Cardinals")
- □ 660B Steve Carlton P2 ...... 1.50 .70
  Golden Arm
  ("1966 Cardinals")

1982 Fleer

Tim Raines
EXPOS • OUTFIELDER

*The 1982 Fleer set contains
660-card standard-size cards,
of which are grouped in team
order based upon standings*

from the previous season.
Cards numbered 628 through
646 are special cards highlighting some of the stars and leaders of the 1981 season. The last
14 cards in the set (647-660)
are checklist cards. The backs
feature player statistics and a
full-color team logo in the upper
right-hand corner of each card.
The complete set price below
does not include any of the
more valuable variation cards
listed. Fleer was not allowed to
insert bubble gum or other confectionary products into these
packs; therefore logo stickers
were included in these 15-card
packs. Notable Rookie Cards in
this set include Cal Ripken Jr.,
Lee Smith, and Dave Stewart.

	NRMT	VG-E
COMPLETE SET (660)	65.00	29.00
COMMON CARD (1-660)	.10	.05
MINOR STARS	.20	.09
SEMISTARS	.40	.18
UNLISTED STARS	.75	.35

- □ 1 Dusty Baker ...... .40 .18
- □ 2 Robert Castillo ...... .10 .05
- □ 3 Ron Cey ...... .20 .09
- □ 4 Terry Forster ...... .10 .05
- □ 5 Steve Garvey ...... .40 .18
- □ 6 Dave Goltz ...... .10 .05
- □ 7 Pedro Guerrero ...... .20 .09
- □ 8 Burt Hooton ...... .10 .05
- □ 9 Steve Howe ...... .10 .05
- □ 10 Jay Johnstone ...... .20 .09
- □ 11 Ken Landreaux ...... .10 .05
- □ 12 Dave Lopes ...... .20 .09
- □ 13 Mike A. Marshall ...... .20 .09
- □ 14 Bobby Mitchell ...... .10 .05
- □ 15 Rick Monday ...... .10 .05
- □ 16 Tom Niedenfuer ...... .10 .05
- □ 17 Ted Power ...... .10 .05
- □ 18 Jerry Reuss UER ...... .20 .09
  ("Home:" omitted)
- □ 19 Ron Roenicke ...... .10 .05
- □ 20 Bill Russell ...... .20 .09
- □ 21 Steve Sax ...... .75 .35
- □ 22 Mike Scioscia ...... .20 .09
- □ 23 Reggie Smith ...... .20 .09
- □ 24 Dave Stewart ...... 1.00 .45
- □ 25 Rick Sutcliffe ...... .20 .09
- □ 26 Derrel Thomas ...... .10 .05
- □ 27 Fernando Valenzuela ...... .40 .18
- □ 28 Bob Welch ...... .20 .09
- □ 29 Steve Yeager ...... .10 .05
- □ 30 Bobby Brown ...... .10 .05
- □ 31 Rick Cerone ...... .10 .05
- □ 32 Ron Davis ...... .10 .05
- □ 33 Bucky Dent ...... .20 .09
- □ 34 Barry Foote ...... .10 .05
- □ 35 George Frazier ...... .10 .05
- □ 36 Oscar Gamble ...... .10 .05
- □ 37 Rich Gossage ...... .40 .18
- □ 38 Ron Guidry ...... .20 .09
- □ 39 Reggie Jackson ...... 1.00 .45
- □ 40 Tommy John ...... .40 .18
- □ 41 Rudy May ...... .10 .05
- □ 42 Larry Milbourne ...... .10 .05
- □ 43 Jerry Mumphrey ...... .10 .05
- □ 44 Bobby Murcer ...... .20 .09
- □ 45 Gene Nelson ...... .10 .05
- □ 46 Graig Nettles ...... .20 .09
- □ 47 Johnny Oates ...... .20 .09
- □ 48 Lou Piniella ...... .20 .09
- □ 49 Willie Randolph ...... .20 .09
- □ 50 Rick Reuschel ...... .20 .09
- □ 51 Dave Revering ...... .10 .05
- □ 52 Dave Righetti ...... .75 .35
- □ 53 Aurelio Rodriguez ...... .10 .05
- □ 54 Bob Watson ...... .20 .09
- □ 55 Dennis Werth ...... .10 .05
- □ 56 Dave Winfield ...... 1.50 .70

- □ 57 Johnny Bench ...... 1.00 .45
- □ 58 Bruce Berenyi ...... .10 .05
- □ 59 Larry Biittner ...... .10 .05
- □ 60 Scott Brown ...... .10 .05
- □ 61 Dave Collins ...... .10 .05
- □ 62 Geoff Combe ...... .10 .05
- □ 63 Dave Concepcion ...... .20 .09
- □ 64 Dan Driessen ...... .10 .05
- □ 65 Joe Edelen ...... .10 .05
- □ 66 George Foster ...... .20 .09
- □ 67 Ken Griffey ...... .20 .09
- □ 68 Paul Householder ...... .10 .05
- □ 69 Tom Hume ...... .10 .05
- □ 70 Junior Kennedy ...... .10 .05
- □ 71 Ray Knight ...... .20 .09
- □ 72 Mike LaCoss ...... .10 .05
- □ 73 Rafael Landestoy ...... .10 .05
- □ 74 Charlie Leibrandt ...... .10 .05
- □ 75 Sam Mejias ...... .10 .05
- □ 76 Paul Moskau ...... .10 .05
- □ 77 Joe Nolan ...... .10 .05
- □ 78 Mike O'Berry ...... .10 .05
- □ 79 Ron Oester ...... .10 .05
- □ 80 Frank Pastore ...... .10 .05
- □ 81 Joe Price ...... .10 .05
- □ 82 Tom Seaver ...... 1.00 .45
- □ 83 Mario Soto ...... .10 .05
- □ 84 Mike Vail ...... .10 .05
- □ 85 Tony Armas ...... .10 .05
- □ 86 Shooty Babitt ...... .10 .05
- □ 87 Dave Beard ...... .10 .05
- □ 88 Rick Bosetti ...... .10 .05
- □ 89 Keith Drumwright ...... .10 .05
- □ 90 Wayne Gross ...... .10 .05
- □ 91 Mike Heath ...... .10 .05
- □ 92 Rickey Henderson ...... 1.50 .70
- □ 93 Cliff Johnson ...... .10 .05
- □ 94 Jeff Jones ...... .10 .05
- □ 95 Matt Keough ...... .10 .05
- □ 96 Brian Kingman ...... .10 .05
- □ 97 Mickey Klutts ...... .10 .05
- □ 98 Rick Langford ...... .10 .05
- □ 99 Steve McCatty ...... .10 .05
- □ 100 Dave McKay ...... .10 .05
- □ 101 Dwayne Murphy ...... .10 .05
- □ 102 Jeff Newman ...... .10 .05
- □ 103 Mike Norris ...... .10 .05
- □ 104 Bob Owchinko ...... .10 .05
- □ 105 Mitchell Page ...... .10 .05
- □ 106 Rob Piccioli ...... .10 .05
- □ 107 Jim Spencer ...... .10 .05
- □ 108 Fred Stanley ...... .10 .05
- □ 109 Tom Underwood ...... .10 .05
- □ 110 Joaquin Andujar ...... .20 .09
- □ 111 Steve Braun ...... .10 .05
- □ 112 Bob Forsch ...... .10 .05
- □ 113 George Hendrick ...... .20 .09
- □ 114 Keith Hernandez ...... .20 .09
- □ 115 Tom Herr ...... .20 .09
- □ 116 Dane Iorg ...... .10 .05
- □ 117 Jim Kaat ...... .40 .18
- □ 118 Tito Landrum ...... .10 .05
- □ 119 Sixto Lezcano ...... .10 .05
- □ 120 Mark Littell ...... .10 .05
- □ 121 John Martin ...... .10 .05
- □ 122 Silvio Martinez ...... .10 .05
- □ 123 Ken Oberkfell ...... .10 .05
- □ 124 Darrell Porter ...... .20 .09
- □ 125 Mike Ramsey ...... .10 .05
- □ 126 Orlando Sanchez ...... .10 .05
- □ 127 Bob Shirley ...... .10 .05
- □ 128 Lary Sorensen ...... .10 .05
- □ 129 Bruce Sutter ...... .20 .09
- □ 130 Bob Sykes ...... .10 .05
- □ 131 Garry Templeton ...... .10 .05
- □ 132 Gene Tenace ...... .20 .09
- □ 133 Jerry Augustine ...... .10 .05
- □ 134 Sal Bando ...... .20 .09
- □ 135 Mark Brouhard ...... .10 .05
- □ 136 Mike Caldwell ...... .10 .05
- □ 137 Reggie Cleveland ...... .10 .05
- □ 138 Cecil Cooper ...... .20 .09
- □ 139 Jamie Easterly ...... .10 .05
- □ 140 Marshall Edwards ...... .10 .05
- □ 141 Rollie Fingers ...... .75 .35
- □ 142 Jim Gantner ...... .20 .09

143	Moose Haas	.10	.05
144	Larry Hisle	.10	.05
145	Roy Howell	.10	.05
146	Rickey Keeton	.10	.05
147	Randy Lerch	.10	.05
148	Paul Molitor	1.25	.55
149	Don Money	.10	.05
150	Charlie Moore	.10	.05
151	Ben Oglivie	.20	.09
152	Ted Simmons	.20	.09
153	Jim Slaton	.10	.05
154	Gorman Thomas	.20	.09
155	Robin Yount	1.50	.70
156	Pete Vuckovich	.10	.05
	(Should precede Yount in the team order)		
157	Benny Ayala	.10	.05
158	Mark Belanger	.20	.09
159	Al Bumbry	.20	.09
160	Terry Crowley	.10	.05
161	Rich Dauer	.10	.05
162	Doug DeCinces	.20	.09
163	Rick Dempsey	.20	.09
164	Jim Dwyer	.10	.05
165	Mike Flanagan	.20	.09
166	Dave Ford	.10	.05
167	Dan Graham	.10	.05
168	Wayne Krenchicki	.10	.05
169	John Lowenstein	.10	.05
170	Dennis Martinez	.20	.09
171	Tippy Martinez	.10	.05
172	Scott McGregor	.10	.05
173	Jose Morales	.10	.05
174	Eddie Murray	1.25	.55
175	Jim Palmer	.75	.35
176	Cal Ripken	40.00	18.00
	(Fleer Ripken cards from 1982 through 1993 erroneously have 22 games played in 1981; not 23.)		
177	Gary Roenicke	.10	.05
178	Lenn Sakata	.10	.05
179	Ken Singleton	.20	.09
180	Sammy Stewart	.10	.05
181	Tim Stoddard	.10	.05
182	Steve Stone	.20	.09
183	Stan Bahnsen	.10	.05
184	Ray Burris	.10	.05
185	Gary Carter	.75	.35
186	Warren Cromartie	.10	.05
187	Andre Dawson	.75	.35
188	Terry Francona	.10	.05
189	Woodie Fryman	.10	.05
190	Bill Gullickson	.10	.05
191	Grant Jackson	.10	.05
192	Wallace Johnson	.10	.05
193	Charlie Lea	.10	.05
194	Bill Lee	.20	.09
195	Jerry Manuel	.10	.05
196	Brad Mills	.10	.05
197	John Milner	.10	.05
198	Rowland Office	.10	.05
199	David Palmer	.10	.05
200	Larry Parrish	.10	.05
201	Mike Phillips	.10	.05
202	Tim Raines	.75	.35
203	Bobby Ramos	.10	.05
204	Jeff Reardon	.20	.09
205	Steve Rogers	.10	.05
206	Scott Sanderson	.10	.05
207	Rodney Scott UER	.40	.18
	(Photo actually Tim Raines)		
208	Elias Sosa	.10	.05
209	Chris Speier	.10	.05
210	Tim Wallach	.75	.35
211	Jerry White	.10	.05
212	Alan Ashby	.10	.05
213	Cesar Cedeno	.20	.09
214	Jose Cruz	.20	.09
215	Kiko Garcia	.10	.05
216	Phil Garner	.20	.09
217	Danny Heep	.10	.05
218	Art Howe	.10	.05
219	Bob Knepper	.10	.05
220	Frank LaCorte	.10	.05
221	Joe Niekro	.20	.09
222	Joe Pittman	.10	.05
223	Terry Puhl	.10	.05
224	Luis Pujols	.10	.05
225	Craig Reynolds	.10	.05
226	J.R. Richard	.20	.09
227	Dave Roberts	.10	.05
228	Vern Ruhle	.10	.05
229	Nolan Ryan	5.00	2.20
230	Joe Sambito	.10	.05
231	Tony Scott	.10	.05
232	Dave Smith	.10	.05
233	Harry Spilman	.10	.05
234	Don Sutton	.75	.35
235	Dickie Thon	.10	.05
236	Denny Walling	.10	.05
237	Gary Woods	.10	.05
238	Luis Aguayo	.10	.05
239	Ramon Aviles	.10	.05
240	Bob Boone	.20	.09
241	Larry Bowa	.20	.09
242	Warren Brusstar	.10	.05
243	Steve Carlton	.75	.35
244	Larry Christenson	.10	.05
245	Dick Davis	.10	.05
246	Greg Gross	.10	.05
247	Sparky Lyle	.20	.09
248	Garry Maddox	.10	.05
249	Garry Matthews	.20	.09
250	Bake McBride	.10	.05
251	Tug McGraw	.20	.09
252	Keith Moreland	.10	.05
253	Dickie Noles	.10	.05
254	Mike Proly	.10	.05
255	Ron Reed	.10	.05
256	Pete Rose	1.00	.45
257	Dick Ruthven	.10	.05
258	Mike Schmidt	1.00	.45
259	Lonnie Smith	.20	.09
260	Manny Trillo	.10	.05
261	Del Unser	.10	.05
262	George Vukovich	.10	.05
263	Tom Brookens	.10	.05
264	George Cappuzzello	.10	.05
265	Marty Castillo	.10	.05
266	Al Cowens	.10	.05
267	Kirk Gibson	.75	.35
268	Richie Hebner	.20	.09
269	Ron Jackson	.10	.05
270	Lynn Jones	.10	.05
271	Steve Kemp	.10	.05
272	Rick Leach	.10	.05
273	Aurelio Lopez	.10	.05
274	Jack Morris	.75	.35
275	Kevin Saucier	.10	.05
276	Lance Parrish	.40	.18
277	Rick Peters	.10	.05
278	Dan Petry	.10	.05
279	Dave Rozema	.10	.05
280	Stan Papi	.10	.05
281	Dan Schatzeder	.10	.05
282	Champ Summers	.10	.05
283	Alan Trammell	.75	.35
284	Lou Whitaker	.40	.18
285	Milt Wilcox	.10	.05
286	John Wockenfuss	.10	.05
287	Gary Allenson	.10	.05
288	Tom Burgmeier	.10	.05
289	Bill Campbell	.10	.05
290	Mark Clear	.10	.05
291	Steve Crawford	.10	.05
292	Dennis Eckersley	.75	.35
293	Dwight Evans	.40	.18
294	Rich Gedman	.10	.05
295	Garry Hancock	.10	.05
296	Glenn Hoffman	.10	.05
297	Bruce Hurst	.20	.09
298	Carney Lansford	.20	.09
299	Rick Miller	.10	.05
300	Reid Nichols	.10	.05
301	Bob Ojeda	.40	.18
302	Tony Perez	.75	.35
303	Chuck Rainey	.10	.05
304	Jerry Remy	.10	.05
305	Jim Rice	.20	.09
306	Joe Rudi	.10	.05
307	Bob Stanley	.10	.05
308	Dave Stapleton	.10	.05
309	Frank Tanana	.20	.09
310	Mike Torrez	.10	.05
311	John Tudor	.20	.09
312	Carl Yastrzemski	.75	.35
313	Buddy Bell	.20	.09
314	Steve Comer	.10	.05
315	Danny Darwin	.10	.05
316	John Ellis	.10	.05
317	John Grubb	.10	.05
318	Rick Honeycutt	.10	.05
319	Charlie Hough	.20	.09
320	Ferguson Jenkins	.75	.35
321	John Henry Johnson	.10	.05
322	Jim Kern	.10	.05
323	Jon Matlack	.10	.05
324	Doc Medich	.10	.05
325	Mario Mendoza	.10	.05
326	Al Oliver	.20	.09
327	Pat Putnam	.10	.05
328	Mickey Rivers	.10	.05
329	Leon Roberts	.10	.05
330	Billy Sample	.10	.05
331	Bill Stein	.10	.05
332	Jim Sundberg	.20	.09
333	Mark Wagner	.10	.05
334	Bump Wills	.10	.05
335	Bill Almon	.10	.05
336	Harold Baines	.75	.35
337	Ross Baumgarten	.10	.05
338	Tony Bernazard	.10	.05
339	Britt Burns	.10	.05
340	Richard Dotson	.10	.05
341	Jim Essian	.10	.05
342	Ed Farmer	.10	.05
343	Carlton Fisk	.75	.35
344	Kevin Hickey	.10	.05
345	LaMarr Hoyt	.10	.05
346	Lamar Johnson	.10	.05
347	Jerry Koosman	.20	.09
348	Rusty Kuntz	.10	.05
349	Dennis Lamp	.10	.05
350	Ron LeFlore	.20	.09
351	Chet Lemon	.20	.09
352	Greg Luzinski	.20	.09
353	Bob Molinaro	.10	.05
354	Jim Morrison	.10	.05
355	Wayne Nordhagen	.10	.05
356	Greg Pryor	.10	.05
357	Mike Squires	.10	.05
358	Steve Trout	.10	.05
359	Alan Bannister	.10	.05
360	Len Barker	.20	.09
361	Bert Blyleven	.75	.35
362	Joe Charboneau	.10	.05
363	John Denny	.10	.05
364	Bo Diaz	.10	.05
365	Miguel Dilone	.10	.05
366	Jerry Dybzinski	.10	.05
367	Wayne Garland	.10	.05
368	Mike Hargrove	.20	.09
369	Toby Harrah	.20	.09
370	Ron Hassey	.10	.05
371	Von Hayes	.20	.09
372	Pat Kelly	.10	.05
373	Duane Kuiper	.10	.05
374	Rick Manning	.10	.05
375	Sid Monge	.10	.05
376	Jorge Orta	.10	.05
377	Dave Rosello	.10	.05
378	Dan Spillner	.10	.05
379	Mike Stanton	.10	.05
380	Andre Thornton	.20	.09
381	Tom Veryzer	.10	.05
382	Rick Waits	.10	.05
383	Doyle Alexander	.10	.05
384	Vida Blue	.20	.09
385	Fred Breining	.10	.05
386	Enos Cabell	.10	.05
387	Jack Clark	.20	.09
388	Darrell Evans	.20	.09
389	Tom Griffin	.10	.05
390	Larry Herndon	.10	.05
391	Al Holland	.10	.05
392	Gary Lavelle	.10	.05
393	Johnnie LeMaster	.10	.05

☐ 394	Jerry Martin	.10	.05
☐ 395	Milt May	.10	.05
☐ 396	Greg Minton	.10	.05
☐ 397	Joe Morgan	.75	.35
☐ 398	Joe Pettini	.10	.05
☐ 399	Allen Ripley	.10	.05
☐ 400	Billy Smith	.10	.05
☐ 401	Rennie Stennett	.10	.05
☐ 402	Ed Whitson	.10	.05
☐ 403	Jim Wohlford	.10	.05
☐ 404	Willie Aikens	.10	.05
☐ 405	George Brett	1.50	.70
☐ 406	Ken Brett	.10	.05
☐ 407	Dave Chalk	.10	.05
☐ 408	Rich Gale	.10	.05
☐ 409	Cesar Geronimo	.10	.05
☐ 410	Larry Gura	.10	.05
☐ 411	Clint Hurdle	.10	.05
☐ 412	Mike Jones	.10	.05
☐ 413	Dennis Leonard	.10	.05
☐ 414	Renie Martin	.10	.05
☐ 415	Lee May	.20	.09
☐ 416	Hal McRae	.10	.05
☐ 417	Darryl Motley	.10	.05
☐ 418	Rance Mulliniks	.10	.05
☐ 419	Amos Otis	.20	.09
☐ 420	Ken Phelps	.10	.05
☐ 421	Jamie Quirk	.10	.05
☐ 422	Dan Quisenberry	.20	.09
☐ 423	Paul Splittorff	.10	.05
☐ 424	U.L. Washington	.10	.05
☐ 425	John Wathan	.10	.05
☐ 426	Frank White	.20	.09
☐ 427	Willie Wilson	.20	.09
☐ 428	Brian Asselstine	.10	.05
☐ 429	Bruce Benedict	.10	.05
☐ 430	Tommy Boggs	.10	.05
☐ 431	Larry Bradford	.10	.05
☐ 432	Rick Camp	.10	.05
☐ 433	Chris Chambliss	.10	.05
☐ 434	Gene Garber	.10	.05
☐ 435	Preston Hanna	.10	.05
☐ 436	Bob Horner	.20	.09
☐ 437	Glenn Hubbard	.10	.05
☐ 438A	Al Hrabosky ERR (Height 5'1" All on reverse)	15.00	6.75
☐ 438B	Al Hrabosky ERR (Height 5'1")	.40	.18
☐ 438C	Al Hrabosky (Height 5'10")	.20	.09
☐ 439	Rufino Linares	.10	.05
☐ 440	Rick Mahler	.10	.05
☐ 441	Ed Miller	.10	.05
☐ 442	John Montefusco	.10	.05
☐ 443	Dale Murphy	.75	.35
☐ 444	Phil Niekro	.75	.35
☐ 445	Gaylord Perry	.75	.35
☐ 446	Biff Pocoroba	.10	.05
☐ 447	Rafael Ramirez	.10	.05
☐ 448	Jerry Royster	.10	.05
☐ 449	Claudell Washington	.10	.05
☐ 450	Don Aase	.40	.18
☐ 451	Don Baylor	.40	.18
☐ 452	Juan Beniquez	.10	.05
☐ 453	Rick Burleson	.10	.05
☐ 454	Bert Campaneris	.20	.09
☐ 455	Rod Carew	.75	.35
☐ 456	Bob Clark	.10	.05
☐ 457	Brian Downing	.10	.05
☐ 458	Dan Ford	.10	.05
☐ 459	Ken Forsch	.10	.05
☐ 460A	Dave Frost (5 mm space before ERA)	.10	.05
☐ 460B	Dave Frost (1 mm space)	.10	.05
☐ 461	Bobby Grich	.20	.09
☐ 462	Larry Harlow	.10	.05
☐ 463	John Harris	.10	.05
☐ 464	Andy Hassler	.10	.05
☐ 465	Butch Hobson	.10	.05
☐ 466	Jesse Jefferson	.10	.05
☐ 467	Bruce Kison	.10	.05
☐ 468	Fred Lynn	.20	.09
☐ 469	Angel Moreno	.10	.05
☐ 470	Ed Ott	.10	.05
☐ 471	Fred Patek	.10	.05
☐ 472	Steve Renko	.10	.05
☐ 473	Mike Witt	.20	.09
☐ 474	Geoff Zahn	.10	.05
☐ 475	Gary Alexander	.10	.05
☐ 476	Dale Berra	.10	.05
☐ 477	Kurt Bevacqua	.10	.05
☐ 478	Jim Bibby	.10	.05
☐ 479	John Candelaria	.10	.05
☐ 480	Victor Cruz	.10	.05
☐ 481	Mike Easler	.10	.05
☐ 482	Tim Foli	.10	.05
☐ 483	Lee Lacy	.10	.05
☐ 484	Vance Law	.10	.05
☐ 485	Bill Madlock	.20	.09
☐ 486	Willie Montanez	.10	.05
☐ 487	Omar Moreno	.10	.05
☐ 488	Steve Nicosia	.10	.05
☐ 489	Dave Parker	.20	.09
☐ 490	Tony Pena	.10	.05
☐ 491	Pascual Perez	.10	.05
☐ 492	Johnny Ray	.20	.09
☐ 493	Rick Rhoden	.10	.05
☐ 494	Bill Robinson	.10	.05
☐ 495	Don Robinson	.10	.05
☐ 496	Enrique Romo	.10	.05
☐ 497	Rod Scurry	.10	.05
☐ 498	Eddie Solomon	.10	.05
☐ 499	Willie Stargell	.75	.35
☐ 500	Kent Tekulve	.20	.09
☐ 501	Jason Thompson	.10	.05
☐ 502	Glenn Abbott	.10	.05
☐ 503	Jim Anderson	.10	.05
☐ 504	Floyd Bannister	.10	.05
☐ 505	Bruce Bochte	.10	.05
☐ 506	Jeff Burroughs	.10	.05
☐ 507	Bryan Clark	.10	.05
☐ 508	Ken Clay	.10	.05
☐ 509	Julio Cruz	.10	.05
☐ 510	Dick Drago	.10	.05
☐ 511	Gary Gray	.10	.05
☐ 512	Dan Meyer	.10	.05
☐ 513	Jerry Narron	.10	.05
☐ 514	Tom Paciorek	.20	.09
☐ 515	Casey Parsons	.10	.05
☐ 516	Lenny Randle	.10	.05
☐ 517	Shane Rawley	.10	.05
☐ 518	Joe Simpson	.10	.05
☐ 519	Richie Zisk	.10	.05
☐ 520	Neil Allen	.10	.05
☐ 521	Bob Bailor	.10	.05
☐ 522	Hubie Brooks	.20	.09
☐ 523	Mike Cubbage	.10	.05
☐ 524	Pete Falcone	.10	.05
☐ 525	Doug Flynn	.10	.05
☐ 526	Tom Hausman	.10	.05
☐ 527	Ron Hodges	.10	.05
☐ 528	Randy Jones	.10	.05
☐ 529	Mike Jorgensen	.10	.05
☐ 530	Dave Kingman	.20	.09
☐ 531	Ed Lynch	.10	.05
☐ 532	Mike G. Marshall	.10	.05
☐ 533	Lee Mazzilli	.10	.05
☐ 534	Dyar Miller	.10	.05
☐ 535	Mike Scott	.20	.09
☐ 536	Rusty Staub	.20	.09
☐ 537	John Stearns	.10	.05
☐ 538	Craig Swan	.10	.05
☐ 539	Frank Taveras	.10	.05
☐ 540	Alex Trevino	.10	.05
☐ 541	Ellis Valentine	.10	.05
☐ 542	Mookie Wilson	.20	.09
☐ 543	Joel Youngblood	.10	.05
☐ 544	Pat Zachry	.10	.05
☐ 545	Glenn Adams	.10	.05
☐ 546	Fernando Arroyo	.10	.05
☐ 547	John Verhoeven	.10	.05
☐ 548	Sal Butera	.10	.05
☐ 549	John Castino	.10	.05
☐ 550	Don Cooper	.10	.05
☐ 551	Doug Corbett	.10	.05
☐ 552	Dave Engle	.10	.05
☐ 553	Roger Erickson	.10	.05
☐ 554	Danny Goodwin	.10	.05
☐ 555A	Darrell Jackson (Black cap)	.40	.18
☐ 555B	Darrell Jackson (Red cap with T)	.20	.09
☐ 555C	Darrell Jackson (Red cap, no emblem)	3.00	1.35
☐ 556	Pete Mackanin	.10	.05
☐ 557	Jack O'Connor	.10	.05
☐ 558	Hosken Powell	.10	.05
☐ 559	Pete Redfern	.10	.05
☐ 560	Roy Smalley	.10	.05
☐ 561	Chuck Baker UER (Shortstop on front)	.10	.05
☐ 562	Gary Ward	.10	.05
☐ 563	Rob Wilfong	.10	.05
☐ 564	Al Williams	.10	.05
☐ 565	Butch Wynegar	.10	.05
☐ 566	Randy Bass	.10	.05
☐ 567	Juan Bonilla	.10	.05
☐ 568	Danny Boone	.10	.05
☐ 569	John Curtis	.10	.05
☐ 570	Juan Eichelberger	.10	.05
☐ 571	Barry Evans	.10	.05
☐ 572	Tim Flannery	.10	.05
☐ 573	Ruppert Jones	.10	.05
☐ 574	Terry Kennedy	.10	.05
☐ 575	Joe Lefebvre	.10	.05
☐ 576A	John Littlefield ERR (Left handed; reverse negative)	200.00	90.00
☐ 576B	John Littlefield COR (Right handed)	.20	.09
☐ 577	Gary Lucas	.10	.05
☐ 578	Steve Mura	.10	.05
☐ 579	Broderick Perkins	.10	.05
☐ 580	Gene Richards	.10	.05
☐ 581	Luis Salazar	.10	.05
☐ 582	Ozzie Smith	2.00	.90
☐ 583	John Urrea	.10	.05
☐ 584	Chris Welsh	.10	.05
☐ 585	Rick Wise	.10	.05
☐ 586	Doug Bird	.10	.05
☐ 587	Tim Blackwell	.10	.05
☐ 588	Bobby Bonds	.20	.09
☐ 589	Bill Buckner	.20	.09
☐ 590	Bill Caudill	.10	.05
☐ 591	Hector Cruz	.10	.05
☐ 592	Jody Davis	.10	.05
☐ 593	Ivan DeJesus	.10	.05
☐ 594	Steve Dillard	.10	.05
☐ 595	Leon Durham	.10	.05
☐ 596	Rawly Eastwick	.10	.05
☐ 597	Steve Henderson	.10	.05
☐ 598	Mike Krukow	.10	.05
☐ 599	Mike Lum	.10	.05
☐ 600	Randy Martz	.10	.05
☐ 601	Jerry Morales	.10	.05
☐ 602	Ken Reitz	.10	.05
☐ 603	Lee Smith ERR (Cubs logo reversed)	2.50	1.10
☐ 603B	Lee Smith COR	2.50	1.10
☐ 604	Dick Tidrow	.10	.05
☐ 605	Jim Tracy	.10	.05
☐ 606	Mike Tyson	.10	.05
☐ 607	Ty Waller	.10	.05
☐ 608	Danny Ainge	1.00	.45
☐ 609	Jorge Bell	.75	.35
☐ 610	Mark Bomback	.10	.05
☐ 611	Barry Bonnell	.10	.05
☐ 612	Jim Clancy	.10	.05
☐ 613	Damaso Garcia	.10	.05
☐ 614	Jerry Garvin	.10	.05
☐ 615	Alfredo Griffin	.10	.05
☐ 616	Garth Iorg	.10	.05
☐ 617	Luis Leal	.10	.05
☐ 618	Ken Macha	.10	.05
☐ 619	John Mayberry	.10	.05
☐ 620	Joey McLaughlin	.10	.05
☐ 621	Lloyd Moseby	.20	.09
☐ 622	Dave Stieb	.20	.09
☐ 623	Jackson Todd	.10	.05
☐ 624	Willie Upshaw	.10	.05
☐ 625	Otto Velez	.10	.05
☐ 626	Ernie Whitt	.10	.05
☐ 627	Alvis Woods	.10	.05
☐ 628	All Star Game Cleveland, Ohio	.20	.09
☐ 629	All Star Infielders	.20	.09

Frank White and
Bucky Dent
☐ 630 Big Red Machine .... .20 .09
Dan Driessen
Dave Concepcion
George Foster
☐ 631 Bruce Sutter .... .20 .09
Top NL Relief Pitcher
☐ 632 Steve and Carlton ...... .40 .18
Steve Carlton
Carlton Fisk
☐ 633 Carl Yastrzemski .... .75 .35
3000th Game
☐ 634 Dynamic Duo .... 1.00 .45
Johnny Bench and
Tom Seaver
☐ 635 West Meets East .... .20 .09
Fernando Valenzuela
and Gary Carter
☐ 636A Fernando Valenzuela: .75 .35
NL SO King ('he' NL)
☐ 636B Fernando Valenzuela: .75 .35
NL SO King ('the' NL)
☐ 637 Mike Schmidt .... 1.00 .45
Home Run King
☐ 638 NL All Stars .... .20 .09
Gary Carter and
Dave Parker
☐ 639 Perfect Game UER ..... .20 .09
Len Barker and
Bo Diaz
(Catcher actually
Ron Hassey)
☐ 640 Pete and Re-Pete .... 1.00 .45
Pete Rose and Son
☐ 641 Phillies Finest .... .75 .35
Lonnie Smith
Mike Schmidt
Steve Carlton
☐ 642 Red Sox Reunion ...... .20 .09
Fred Lynn and
Dwight Evans
☐ 643 Rickey Henderson .... 1.00 .45
Most Hits and Runs
☐ 644 Rollie Fingers .... .20 .09
Most Saves AL
☐ 645 Tom Seaver .... .75 .35
Most 1981 Wins
☐ 646 Yankee Powerhouse 2.00 .90
Reggie Jackson and
Dave Winfield
(Comma on back
after outfielder)
☐ 646B Yankee Powerhouse 2.00 .90
Reggie Jackson and
Dave Winfield
(No comma)
☐ 647 CL: Yankees/Dodgers .10 .05
☐ 648 CL: A's/Reds .... .10 .05
☐ 649 CL: Cards/Brewers .... .10 .05
☐ 650 CL: Expos/Orioles ..... .10 .05
☐ 651 CL: Astros/Phillies .... .10 .05
☐ 652 CL: Tigers/Red Sox ... .10 .05
☐ 653 CL: Rangers/White Sox .10 .05
☐ 654 CL: Giants/Indians .... .10 .05
☐ 655 CL: Royals/Braves ..... .10 .05
☐ 656 CL: Angels/Pirates .... .10 .05
☐ 657 CL: Mariners/Mets .... .10 .05
☐ 658 CL: Padres/Twins ...... .10 .05
☐ 659 CL: Blue Jays/Cubs ... .10 .05
☐ 660 Specials Checklist .... .10 .05

1983 Fleer

In 1983, for the third straight year, Fleer produced a baseball series of 660 standard-size cards. Of these, 1-628 are player cards, 629-646 are special cards, and 647-660 are checklist cards. The player cards are again ordered alphabetically within team and teams seeded in descending order based upon the previous season's stand-

Rod Carew
FIRST BASE

ings. The front of each card has a colorful team logo at bottom left and the player's name and position at lower right. The reverses are done in shades of brown on white. Wax packs consisted of 15 cards plus logo stickers in a 38-pack box. Notable Rookie Cards include Wade Boggs, Tony Gwynn and Ryne Sandberg.

	NRMT	VG-E
COMPLETE SET (660)	80.00	36.00
COMMON CARD (1-660)	.10	.05
MINOR STARS	.20	.09
SEMISTARS	.40	.18
UNLISTED STARS	.75	.35

☐ 1 Joaquin Andujar .... .10 .05
☐ 2 Doug Bair .... .10 .05
☐ 3 Steve Braun .... .10 .05
☐ 4 Glenn Brummer .... .10 .05
☐ 5 Bob Forsch .... .10 .05
☐ 6 David Green .... .10 .05
☐ 7 George Hendrick .... .10 .05
☐ 8 Keith Hernandez .... .20 .09
☐ 9 Tom Herr .... .10 .05
☐ 10 Dane Iorg .... .10 .05
☐ 11 Jim Kaat .... .20 .09
☐ 12 Jeff Lahti .... .10 .05
☐ 13 Tito Landrum .... .10 .05
☐ 14 Dave LaPoint .... .10 .05
☐ 15 Willie McGee .... .75 .35
☐ 16 Steve Mura .... .10 .05
☐ 17 Ken Oberkfell .... .10 .05
☐ 18 Darrell Porter .... .10 .05
☐ 19 Mike Ramsey .... .10 .05
☐ 20 Gene Roof .... .10 .05
☐ 21 Lonnie Smith .... .10 .05
☐ 22 Ozzie Smith .... 1.50 .70
☐ 23 John Stuper .... .10 .05
☐ 24 Bruce Sutter .... .20 .09
☐ 25 Gene Tenace .... .10 .05
☐ 26 Jerry Augustine .... .10 .05
☐ 27 Dwight Bernard .... .10 .05
☐ 28 Mark Brouhard .... .10 .05
☐ 29 Mike Caldwell .... .10 .05
☐ 30 Cecil Cooper .... .20 .09
☐ 31 Jamie Easterly .... .10 .05
☐ 32 Marshall Edwards ..... .10 .05
☐ 33 Rollie Fingers .... .75 .35
☐ 34 Jim Gantner .... .10 .05
☐ 35 Moose Haas .... .10 .05
☐ 36 Roy Howell .... .10 .05
☐ 37 Pete Ladd .... .10 .05
☐ 38 Bob McClure .... .10 .05
☐ 39 Doc Medich .... .10 .05
☐ 40 Paul Molitor .... 1.00 .45
☐ 41 Don Money .... .10 .05
☐ 42 Charlie Moore .... .10 .05
☐ 43 Ben Oglivie .... .10 .05
☐ 44 Ed Romero .... .10 .05
☐ 45 Ted Simmons .... .20 .09
☐ 46 Jim Slaton .... .10 .05
☐ 47 Don Sutton .... .40 .18
☐ 48 Gorman Thomas .... .10 .05
☐ 49 Pete Vuckovich .... .10 .05

☐ 50 Ned Yost .... .10 .05
☐ 51 Robin Yount .... 1.25 .55
☐ 52 Benny Ayala .... .10 .05
☐ 53 Bob Bonner .... .10 .05
☐ 54 Al Bumbry .... .20 .09
☐ 55 Terry Crowley .... .10 .05
☐ 56 Storm Davis .... .10 .05
☐ 57 Rich Dauer .... .10 .05
☐ 58 Rick Dempsey UER .... .20 .09
(Posing batting lefty)
☐ 59 Jim Dwyer .... .10 .05
☐ 60 Mike Flanagan .... .20 .09
☐ 61 Dan Ford .... .10 .05
☐ 62 Glenn Gulliver .... .10 .05
☐ 63 John Lowenstein .... .10 .05
☐ 64 Dennis Martinez .... .20 .09
☐ 65 Tippy Martinez .... .10 .05
☐ 66 Scott McGregor .... .10 .05
☐ 67 Eddie Murray .... 1.00 .45
☐ 68 Joe Nolan .... .10 .05
☐ 69 Jim Palmer .... .75 .35
☐ 70 Cal Ripken 10.00 4.50
☐ 71 Gary Roenicke .... .10 .05
☐ 72 Lenn Sakata .... .10 .05
☐ 73 Ken Singleton .... .20 .09
☐ 74 Sammy Stewart .... .10 .05
☐ 75 Tim Stoddard .... .10 .05
☐ 76 Don Aase .... .10 .05
☐ 77 Don Baylor .... .40 .18
☐ 78 Juan Beniquez .... .10 .05
☐ 79 Bob Boone .... .20 .09
☐ 80 Rick Burleson .... .10 .05
☐ 81 Rod Carew .... .60 .25
☐ 82 Bobby Clark .... .10 .05
☐ 83 Doug Corbett .... .10 .05
☐ 84 John Curtis .... .10 .05
☐ 85 Doug DeCinces .... .20 .09
☐ 86 Brian Downing .... .10 .05
☐ 87 Joe Ferguson .... .10 .05
☐ 88 Tim Foli .... .10 .05
☐ 89 Ken Forsch .... .10 .05
☐ 90 Dave Goltz .... .10 .05
☐ 91 Bobby Grich .... .20 .09
☐ 92 Andy Hassler .... .10 .05
☐ 93 Reggie Jackson ...... 1.00 .45
☐ 94 Ron Jackson .... .10 .05
☐ 95 Tommy John .... .40 .18
☐ 96 Bruce Kison .... .10 .05
☐ 97 Fred Lynn .... .20 .09
☐ 98 Ed Ott .... .10 .05
☐ 99 Steve Renko .... .10 .05
☐ 100 Luis Sanchez .... .10 .05
☐ 101 Rob Wilfong .... .10 .05
☐ 102 Mike Witt .... .10 .05
☐ 103 Geoff Zahn .... .10 .05
☐ 104 Willie Aikens .... .10 .05
☐ 105 Mike Armstrong ...... .10 .05
☐ 106 Vida Blue .... .20 .09
☐ 107 Bud Black .... .10 .05
☐ 108 George Brett .... 1.50 .70
☐ 109 Bill Castro .... .10 .05
☐ 110 Onix Concepcion ..... .10 .05
☐ 111 Dave Frost .... .10 .05
☐ 112 Cesar Geronimo ...... .10 .05
☐ 113 Larry Gura .... .10 .05
☐ 114 Steve Hammond ..... .10 .05
☐ 115 Don Hood .... .10 .05
☐ 116 Dennis Leonard ...... .10 .05
☐ 117 Jerry Martin .... .10 .05
☐ 118 Lee May .... .20 .09
☐ 119 Hal McRae .... .20 .09
☐ 120 Amos Otis .... .20 .09
☐ 121 Greg Pryor .... .10 .05
☐ 122 Dan Quisenberry ..... .20 .09
☐ 123 Don Slaught .... .40 .18
☐ 124 Paul Splittorff .... .10 .05
☐ 125 U.L. Washington ..... .10 .05
☐ 126 John Wathan .... .10 .05
☐ 127 Frank White .... .20 .09
☐ 128 Willie Wilson .... .20 .09
☐ 129 Steve Bedrosian UER .20 .09
(Height 6'33')
☐ 130 Bruce Benedict ...... .10 .05
☐ 131 Tommy Boggs .... .10 .05
☐ 132 Brett Butler .... .75 .35
☐ 133 Rick Camp .... .10 .05

#	Player	Price 1	Price 2
134	Chris Chambliss	.20	.09
135	Ken Dayley	.10	.05
136	Gene Garber	.10	.05
137	Terry Harper	.10	.05
138	Bob Horner	.10	.05
139	Glenn Hubbard	.10	.05
140	Rufino Linares	.10	.05
141	Rick Mahler	.10	.05
142	Dale Murphy	.75	.35
143	Phil Niekro	.75	.35
144	Pascual Perez	.10	.05
145	Biff Pocoroba	.10	.05
146	Rafael Ramirez	.10	.05
147	Jerry Royster	.10	.05
148	Ken Smith	.10	.05
149	Bob Walk	.10	.05
150	Claudell Washington	.10	.05
151	Bob Watson	.20	.09
152	Larry Whisenton	.10	.05
153	Porfirio Altamirano	.10	.05
154	Marty Bystrom	.10	.05
155	Steve Carlton	.75	.35
156	Larry Christenson	.10	.05
157	Ivan DeJesus	.10	.05
158	John Denny	.10	.05
159	Bob Dernier	.10	.05
160	Bo Diaz	.10	.05
161	Ed Farmer	.10	.05
162	Greg Gross	.10	.05
163	Mike Krukow	.10	.05
164	Garry Maddox	.10	.05
165	Gary Matthews	.20	.09
166	Tug McGraw	.20	.09
167	Bob Molinaro	.10	.05
168	Sid Monge	.10	.05
169	Ron Reed	.10	.05
170	Bill Robinson	.10	.05
171	Pete Rose	1.00	.45
172	Dick Ruthven	.10	.05
173	Mike Schmidt	1.00	.45
174	Manny Trillo	.10	.05
175	Ozzie Virgil	.10	.05
176	George Vukovich	.10	.05
177	Gary Allenson	.10	.05
178	Luis Aponte	.10	.05
179	Wade Boggs	8.00	3.60
180	Tom Burgmeier	.10	.05
181	Mark Clear	.10	.05
182	Dennis Eckersley	.75	.35
183	Dwight Evans	.20	.09
184	Rich Gedman	.10	.05
185	Glenn Hoffman	.10	.05
186	Bruce Hurst	.10	.05
187	Carney Lansford	.20	.09
188	Rick Miller	.10	.05
189	Reid Nichols	.10	.05
190	Bob Ojeda	.10	.05
191	Tony Perez	.75	.35
192	Chuck Rainey	.10	.05
193	Jerry Remy	.10	.05
194	Jim Rice	.20	.09
195	Bob Stanley	.10	.05
196	Dave Stapleton	.10	.05
197	Mike Torrez	.10	.05
198	John Tudor	.10	.05
199	Julio Valdez	.10	.05
200	Carl Yastrzemski	.75	.35
201	Dusty Baker	.20	.09
202	Joe Beckwith	.10	.05
203	Greg Brock	.10	.05
204	Ron Cey	.20	.09
205	Terry Forster	.10	.05
206	Steve Garvey	.40	.18
207	Pedro Guerrero	.20	.09
208	Burt Hooton	.10	.05
209	Steve Howe	.10	.05
210	Ken Landreaux	.10	.05
211	Mike Marshall	.10	.05
212	Candy Maldonado	.20	.09
213	Rick Monday	.10	.05
214	Tom Niedenfuer	.10	.05
215	Jorge Orta	.10	.05
216	Jerry Reuss UER ("Home." omitted)	.20	.09
217	Ron Roenicke	.10	.05
218	Vicente Romo	.10	.05
219	Bill Russell	.20	.09
220	Steve Sax	.20	.09
221	Mike Scioscia	.20	.09
222	Dave Stewart	.20	.09
223	Derrel Thomas	.10	.05
224	Fernando Valenzuela	.40	.18
225	Bob Welch	.20	.09
226	Ricky Wright	.10	.05
227	Steve Yeager	.10	.05
228	Bill Almon	.10	.05
229	Harold Baines	.40	.18
230	Salome Barojas	.10	.05
231	Tony Bernazard	.10	.05
232	Britt Burns	.10	.05
233	Richard Dotson	.10	.05
234	Ernesto Escarrega	.10	.05
235	Carlton Fisk	.75	.35
236	Jerry Hairston	.10	.05
237	Kevin Hickey	.10	.05
238	LaMarr Hoyt	.20	.09
239	Steve Kemp	.10	.05
240	Jim Kern	.10	.05
241	Ron Kittle	.40	.18
242	Jerry Koosman	.20	.09
243	Dennis Lamp	.10	.05
244	Rudy Law	.10	.05
245	Vance Law	.10	.05
246	Ron LeFlore	.10	.05
247	Greg Luzinski	.20	.09
248	Tom Paciorek	.10	.05
249	Aurelio Rodriguez	.10	.05
250	Mike Squires	.10	.05
251	Steve Trout	.10	.05
252	Jim Barr	.10	.05
253	Dave Bergman	.10	.05
254	Fred Breining	.10	.05
255	Bob Brenly	.10	.05
256	Jack Clark	.20	.09
257	Chili Davis	.75	.35
258	Darrell Evans	.20	.09
259	Alan Fowlkes	.10	.05
260	Rich Gale	.10	.05
261	Atlee Hammaker	.10	.05
262	Al Holland	.10	.05
263	Duane Kuiper	.10	.05
264	Bill Laskey	.10	.05
265	Gary Lavelle	.10	.05
266	Johnnie LeMaster	.10	.05
267	Renie Martin	.10	.05
268	Milt May	.10	.05
269	Greg Minton	.10	.05
270	Joe Morgan	.75	.35
271	Tom O'Malley	.10	.05
272	Reggie Smith	.20	.09
273	Guy Sularz	.10	.05
274	Champ Summers	.10	.05
275	Max Venable	.10	.05
276	Jim Wohlford	.10	.05
277	Ray Burris	.10	.05
278	Gary Carter	.75	.35
279	Warren Cromartie	.10	.05
280	Andre Dawson	.75	.35
281	Terry Francona	.10	.05
282	Doug Flynn	.10	.05
283	Woodie Fryman	.10	.05
284	Bill Gullickson	.20	.09
285	Wallace Johnson	.10	.05
286	Charlie Lea	.10	.05
287	Randy Lerch	.10	.05
288	Brad Mills	.10	.05
289	Dan Norman	.10	.05
290	Al Oliver	.20	.09
291	David Palmer	.10	.05
292	Tim Raines	.75	.35
293	Jeff Reardon	.20	.09
294	Steve Rogers	.10	.05
295	Scott Sanderson	.10	.05
296	Dan Schatzeder	.10	.05
297	Bryn Smith	.10	.05
298	Chris Speier	.10	.05
299	Tim Wallach	.20	.09
300	Jerry White	.10	.05
301	Joel Youngblood	.10	.05
302	Ross Baumgarten	.10	.05
303	Dale Berra	.10	.05
304	John Candelaria	.10	.05
305	Dick Davis	.10	.05
306	Mike Easler	.10	.05
307	Richie Hebner	.20	.09
308	Lee Lacy	.10	.05
309	Bill Madlock	.20	.09
310	Larry McWilliams	.10	.05
311	John Milner	.10	.05
312	Omar Moreno	.10	.05
313	Jim Morrison	.10	.05
314	Steve Nicosia	.10	.05
315	Dave Parker	.20	.09
316	Tony Pena	.10	.05
317	Johnny Ray	.10	.05
318	Rick Rhoden	.10	.05
319	Don Robinson	.10	.05
320	Enrique Romo	.10	.05
321	Manny Sarmiento	.10	.05
322	Rod Scurry	.10	.05
323	Jimmy Smith	.10	.05
324	Willie Stargell	.75	.35
325	Jason Thompson	.10	.05
326	Kent Tekulve	.20	.09
327A	Tom Brookens (Short .375" brown box shaded in on card back)	.10	.05
327B	Tom Brookens (Longer 1.25" brown box shaded in on card back)		.05
328	Enos Cabell	.10	.05
329	Kirk Gibson	.75	.35
330	Larry Herndon	.10	.05
331	Mike Ivie	.10	.05
332	Howard Johnson	.75	.35
333	Lynn Jones	.10	.05
334	Rick Leach	.10	.05
335	Chet Lemon	.10	.05
336	Jack Morris	.40	.18
337	Lance Parrish	.20	.09
338	Larry Pashnick	.10	.05
339	Dan Petry	.10	.05
340	Dave Rozema	.10	.05
341	Dave Rucker	.10	.05
342	Elias Sosa	.10	.05
343	Dave Tobik	.10	.05
344	Alan Trammell	.75	.35
345	Jerry Turner	.10	.05
346	Jerry Ujdur	.10	.05
347	Pat Underwood	.10	.05
348	Lou Whitaker	.40	.18
349	Milt Wilcox	.10	.05
350	Glenn Wilson	.20	.09
351	John Wockenfuss	.10	.05
352	Kurt Bevacqua	.10	.05
353	Juan Bonilla	.10	.05
354	Floyd Chiffer	.10	.05
355	Luis DeLeon	.10	.05
356	Dave Dravecky	.75	.35
357	Dave Edwards	.10	.05
358	Juan Eichelberger	.10	.05
359	Tim Flannery	.10	.05
360	Tony Gwynn	25.00	11.00
361	Ruppert Jones	.10	.05
362	Terry Kennedy	.10	.05
363	Joe Lefebvre	.10	.05
364	Sixto Lezcano	.10	.05
365	Tim Lollar	.10	.05
366	Gary Lucas	.10	.05
367	John Montefusco	.10	.05
368	Broderick Perkins	.10	.05
369	Joe Pittman	.10	.05
370	Gene Richards	.10	.05
371	Luis Salazar	.10	.05
372	Eric Show	.10	.05
373	Garry Templeton	.10	.05
374	Chris Welsh	.10	.05
375	Alan Wiggins	.10	.05
376	Rick Cerone	.10	.05
377	Dave Collins	.10	.05
378	Roger Erickson	.10	.05
379	George Frazier	.10	.05
380	Oscar Gamble	.10	.05
381	Rich Gossage	.20	.18
382	Ken Griffey	.20	.09
383	Ron Guidry	.20	.09
384	Dave LaRoche	.10	.05
385	Rudy May	.10	.05

☐ 386 John Mayberry	.10	.05	☐ 470 Larry Andersen	.10	.05	☐ 552 Charlie Puleo	.10	.05
☐ 387 Lee Mazzilli	.10	.05	☐ 471 Floyd Bannister	.10	.05	☐ 553 Gary Rajsich	.10	.05
☐ 388 Mike Morgan	.10	.05	☐ 472 Jim Beattie	.10	.05	☐ 554 Mike Scott	.20	.09
☐ 389 Jerry Mumphrey	.10	.05	☐ 473 Bruce Bochte	.10	.05	☐ 555 Rusty Staub	.20	.09
☐ 390 Bobby Murcer	.20	.09	☐ 474 Manny Castillo	.10	.05	☐ 556 John Stearns	.10	.05
☐ 391 Graig Nettles	.20	.09	☐ 475 Bill Caudill	.10	.05	☐ 557 Craig Swan	.10	.05
☐ 392 Lou Piniella	.20	.09	☐ 476 Bryan Clark	.10	.05	☐ 558 Ellis Valentine	.10	.05
☐ 393 Willie Randolph	.20	.09	☐ 477 Al Cowens	.10	.05	☐ 559 Tom Veryzer	.10	.05
☐ 394 Shane Rawley	.10	.05	☐ 478 Julio Cruz	.10	.05	☐ 560 Mookie Wilson	.20	.09
☐ 395 Dave Righetti	.20	.09	☐ 479 Todd Cruz	.10	.05	☐ 561 Pat Zachry	.10	.05
☐ 396 Andre Robertson	.10	.05	☐ 480 Gary Gray	.10	.05	☐ 562 Buddy Bell	.20	.09
☐ 397 Roy Smalley	.10	.05	☐ 481 Dave Henderson	.10	.05	☐ 563 John Butcher	.10	.05
☐ 398 Dave Winfield	1.25	.55	☐ 482 Mike Moore	.20	.09	☐ 564 Steve Comer	.10	.05
☐ 399 Butch Wynegar	.10	.05	☐ 483 Gaylord Perry	.75	.35	☐ 565 Danny Darwin	.10	.05
☐ 400 Chris Bando	.10	.05	☐ 484 Dave Revering	.10	.05	☐ 566 Bucky Dent	.20	.09
☐ 401 Alan Bannister	.10	.05	☐ 485 Joe Simpson	.10	.05	☐ 567 John Grubb	.10	.05
☐ 402 Len Barker	.10	.05	☐ 486 Mike Stanton	.10	.05	☐ 568 Rick Honeycutt	.10	.05
☐ 403 Tom Brennan	.10	.05	☐ 487 Rick Sweet	.10	.05	☐ 569 Dave Hostetler	.10	.05
☐ 404 Carmelo Castillo	.10	.05	☐ 488 Ed VandeBerg	.10	.05	☐ 570 Charlie Hough	.20	.09
☐ 405 Miguel Dilone	.10	.05	☐ 489 Richie Zisk	.10	.05	☐ 571 Lamar Johnson	.10	.05
☐ 406 Jerry Dybzinski	.10	.05	☐ 490 Doug Bird	.10	.05	☐ 572 Jon Matlack	.10	.05
☐ 407 Mike Fischlin	.10	.05	☐ 491 Larry Bowa	.20	.09	☐ 573 Paul Mirabella	.10	.05
☐ 408 Ed Glynn UER	.10	.05	☐ 492 Bill Buckner	.20	.09	☐ 574 Larry Parrish	.10	.05
(Photo actually Bud Anderson)			☐ 493 Bill Campbell	.10	.05	☐ 575 Mike Richardt	.10	.05
			☐ 494 Jody Davis	.10	.05	☐ 576 Mickey Rivers	.10	.05
☐ 409 Mike Hargrove	.20	.09	☐ 495 Leon Durham	.10	.05	☐ 577 Billy Sample	.10	.05
☐ 410 Toby Harrah	.10	.05	☐ 496 Steve Henderson	.10	.05	☐ 578 Dave Schmidt	.10	.05
☐ 411 Ron Hassey	.10	.05	☐ 497 Willie Hernandez	.20	.09	☐ 579 Bill Stein	.10	.05
☐ 412 Von Hayes	.20	.09	☐ 498 Ferguson Jenkins	.75	.35	☐ 580 Jim Sundberg	.20	.09
☐ 413 Rick Manning	.10	.05	☐ 499 Jay Johnstone	.20	.09	☐ 581 Frank Tanana	.20	.09
☐ 414 Bake McBride	.10	.05	☐ 500 Junior Kennedy	.10	.05	☐ 582 Mark Wagner	.10	.05
☐ 415 Larry Milbourne	.10	.05	☐ 501 Randy Martz	.10	.05	☐ 583 George Wright	.10	.05
☐ 416 Bill Nahorodny	.10	.05	☐ 502 Jerry Morales	.10	.05	☐ 584 Johnny Bench	1.00	.45
☐ 417 Jack Perconte	.10	.05	☐ 503 Keith Moreland	.10	.05	☐ 585 Bruce Berenyi	.10	.05
☐ 418 Lary Sorensen	.10	.05	☐ 504 Dickie Noles	.10	.05	☐ 586 Larry Biittner	.10	.05
☐ 419 Dan Spillner	.10	.05	☐ 505 Mike Proly	.10	.05	☐ 587 Cesar Cedeno	.20	.09
☐ 420 Rick Sutcliffe	.10	.05	☐ 506 Allen Ripley	.10	.05	☐ 588 Dave Concepcion	.20	.09
☐ 421 Andre Thornton	.10	.05	☐ 507 Ryne Sandberg UER	12.00	5.50	☐ 589 Dan Driessen	.10	.05
☐ 422 Rick Waits	.10	.05	(Should say High School in Spokane, Washington)			☐ 590 Greg Harris	.10	.05
☐ 423 Eddie Whitson	.10	.05				☐ 591 Ben Hayes	.10	.05
☐ 424 Jesse Barfield	.20	.09	☐ 508 Lee Smith	2.00	.90	☐ 592 Paul Householder	.10	.05
☐ 425 Barry Bonnell	.10	.05	☐ 509 Pat Tabler	.10	.05	☐ 593 Tom Hume	.10	.05
☐ 426 Jim Clancy	.10	.05	☐ 510 Dick Tidrow	.10	.05	☐ 594 Wayne Krenchicki	.10	.05
☐ 427 Damaso Garcia	.10	.05	☐ 511 Bump Wills	.10	.05	☐ 595 Rafael Landestoy	.10	.05
☐ 428 Jerry Garvin	.10	.05	☐ 512 Gary Woods	.10	.05	☐ 596 Charlie Leibrandt	.10	.05
☐ 429 Alfredo Griffin	.10	.05	☐ 513 Tony Armas	.20	.09	☐ 597 Eddie Milner	.10	.05
☐ 430 Garth Iorg	.10	.05	☐ 514 Dave Beard	.10	.05	☐ 598 Ron Oester	.10	.05
☐ 431 Roy Lee Jackson	.10	.05	☐ 515 Jeff Burroughs	.10	.05	☐ 599 Frank Pastore	.10	.05
☐ 432 Luis Leal	.10	.05	☐ 516 John D'Acquisto	.10	.05	☐ 600 Joe Price	.10	.05
☐ 433 Buck Martinez	.10	.05	☐ 517 Wayne Gross	.10	.05	☐ 601 Tom Seaver	1.00	.45
☐ 434 Joey McLaughlin	.10	.05	☐ 518 Mike Heath	.10	.05	☐ 602 Bob Shirley	.10	.05
☐ 435 Lloyd Moseby	.10	.05	☐ 519 Rickey Henderson UER	1.00	.45	☐ 603 Mario Soto	.10	.05
☐ 436 Rance Mulliniks	.10	.05	(Brock record listed as 120 steals)			☐ 604 Alex Trevino	.10	.05
☐ 437 Dale Murray	.10	.05				☐ 605 Mike Vail	.10	.05
☐ 438 Wayne Nordhagen	.10	.05	☐ 520 Cliff Johnson	.10	.05	☐ 606 Duane Walker	.10	.05
☐ 439 Geno Petralli	.20	.09	☐ 521 Matt Keough	.10	.05	☐ 607 Tom Brunansky	.20	.09
☐ 440 Hosken Powell	.10	.05	☐ 522 Brian Kingman	.10	.05	☐ 608 Bobby Castillo	.10	.05
☐ 441 Dave Stieb	.20	.09	☐ 523 Rick Langford	.10	.05	☐ 609 John Castino	.10	.05
☐ 442 Willie Upshaw	.10	.05	☐ 524 Dave Lopes	.20	.09	☐ 610 Ron Davis	.10	.05
☐ 443 Ernie Whitt	.10	.05	☐ 525 Steve McCatty	.10	.05	☐ 611 Lenny Faedo	.10	.05
☐ 444 Alvis Woods	.10	.05	☐ 526 Dave McKay	.10	.05	☐ 612 Terry Felton	.10	.05
☐ 445 Alan Ashby	.10	.05	☐ 527 Dan Meyer	.10	.05	☐ 613 Gary Gaetti	.75	.35
☐ 446 Jose Cruz	.20	.09	☐ 528 Dwayne Murphy	.10	.05	☐ 614 Mickey Hatcher	.10	.05
☐ 447 Kiko Garcia	.10	.05	☐ 529 Jeff Newman	.10	.05	☐ 615 Brad Havens	.10	.05
☐ 448 Phil Garner	.20	.09	☐ 530 Mike Norris	.10	.05	☐ 616 Kent Hrbek	.20	.09
☐ 449 Danny Heep	.10	.05	☐ 531 Bob Owchinko	.10	.05	☐ 617 Randy Johnson	.10	.05
☐ 450 Art Howe	.10	.05	☐ 532 Joe Rudi	.10	.05	☐ 618 Tim Laudner	.10	.05
☐ 451 Bob Knepper	.10	.05	☐ 533 Jimmy Sexton	.10	.05	☐ 619 Jeff Little	.10	.05
☐ 452 Alan Knicely	.10	.05	☐ 534 Fred Stanley	.10	.05	☐ 620 Bobby Mitchell	.10	.05
☐ 453 Ray Knight	.20	.09	☐ 535 Tom Underwood	.10	.05	☐ 621 Jack O'Connor	.10	.05
☐ 454 Frank LaCorte	.10	.05	☐ 536 Neil Allen	.10	.05	☐ 622 John Pacella	.10	.05
☐ 455 Mike LaCoss	.10	.05	☐ 537 Wally Backman	.10	.05	☐ 623 Pete Redfern	.10	.05
☐ 456 Randy Moffitt	.10	.05	☐ 538 Bob Bailor	.10	.05	☐ 624 Jesus Vega	.10	.05
☐ 457 Joe Niekro	.20	.09	☐ 539 Hubie Brooks	.10	.05	☐ 625 Frank Viola	.75	.35
☐ 458 Terry Puhl	.10	.05	☐ 540 Carlos Diaz	.10	.05	☐ 626 Ron Washington	.10	.05
☐ 459 Luis Pujols	.10	.05	☐ 541 Pete Falcone	.10	.05	☐ 627 Gary Ward	.10	.05
☐ 460 Craig Reynolds	.10	.05	☐ 542 George Foster	.20	.09	☐ 628 Al Williams	.10	.05
☐ 461 Bert Roberge	.10	.05	☐ 543 Ron Gardenhire	.10	.05	☐ 629 Red Sox All-Stars	.75	.35
☐ 462 Vern Ruhle	.10	.05	☐ 544 Brian Giles	.10	.05	Carl Yastrzemski		
☐ 463 Nolan Ryan	4.00	1.80	☐ 545 Ron Hodges	.10	.05	Dennis Eckersley		
☐ 464 Joe Sambito	.10	.05	☐ 546 Randy Jones	.10	.05	Mark Clear		
☐ 465 Tony Scott	.10	.05	☐ 547 Mike Jorgensen	.10	.05	☐ 630 300 Career Wins	.20	.09
☐ 466 Dave Smith	.10	.05	☐ 548 Dave Kingman	.40	.18	Gaylord Perry		
☐ 467 Harry Spilman	.10	.05	☐ 549 Ed Lynch	.10	.05	Terry Bulling 5/6/82		
☐ 468 Dickie Thon	.10	.05	☐ 550 Jesse Orosco	.10	.05	☐ 631 Pride of Venezuela	.20	.09
☐ 469 Denny Walling	.10	.05	☐ 551 Rick Ownbey	.10	.05	Dave Concepcion and		

☐ 632	All-Star Infielders .... Robin Yount and Buddy Bell	.75	.35
☐ 633	Mr.Vet and Mr.Rookie Dave Winfield and Kent Hrbek	.75	.35
☐ 634	Fountain of Youth .... Willie Stargell and Pete Rose	.75	.35
☐ 635	Big Chiefs .... Toby Harrah and Andre Thornton	.20	.09
☐ 636	Smith Brothers .... Ozzie Smith Lonnie Smith	.75	.35
☐ 637	Base Stealers' Threat.. Bo Diaz and Gary Carter	.20	.09
☐ 638	All-Star Catchers .... Carlton Fisk and Gary Carter	.75	.35
☐ 639	The Silver Shoe .... Rickey Henderson	1.00	.45
☐ 640	Home Run Threats .... Ben Oglivie and Reggie Jackson	.75	.35
☐ 641	Two Teams Same Day Joel Youngblood August 4, 1982	.10	.05
☐ 642	Last Perfect Game ..... Ron Hassey and Len Barker	.20	.09
☐ 643	Black and Blue........... Vida Blue	.20	.09
☐ 644	Black and Blue........... Bud Black	.10	.05
☐ 645	Speed and Power .... Reggie Jackson	.75	.35
☐ 646	Speed and Power .... Rickey Henderson	1.00	.45
☐ 647	CL: Cards/Brewers	.10	
☐ 648	CL: Orioles/Angels	.10	.05
☐ 649	CL: Royals/Braves	.10	.05
☐ 650	CL: Phillies/Red Sox ..	.10	
☐ 651	CL: Dodgers/White Sox	.10	
☐ 652	CL: Giants/Expos	.10	.05
☐ 653	CL: Pirates/Tigers	.10	.05
☐ 654	CL: Padres/Yankees ..	.10	.05
☐ 655	CL: Indians/Blue Jays	.10	.05
☐ 656	CL: Astros/Mariners ..	.10	.05
☐ 657	CL: Cubs/A's	.10	.05
☐ 658	CL: Mets/Rangers	.10	.05
☐ 659	CL: Reds/Twins	.10	.05
☐ 660	CL: Specials/Teams ...	.10	.05

1984 Fleer

The 1984 Fleer card 660-card standard-size set featured fronts with full-color team logos along with the player's name and position and the Fleer identification. The set features several imaginative photos, several multi-player cards, and many more action shots than the 1983

card set. The backs are quite similar to the 1983 backs except that blue rather than brown ink is used. The player cards are alphabetized within team and the teams are ordered by their 1983 season finish and won-lost record. Specials (626-646) and checklist cards (647-660) make up the end of the set. Wax packs again consisted of 15 cards plus logo stickers. The key Rookie Cards in this set are Don Mattingly, Tony Phillips, Darryl Strawberry, and Andy Van Slyke.

	NRMT	VG-E
COMPLETE SET (660)	80.00	36.00
COMMON CARD (1-660)	.15	.07
MINOR STARS	.40	.18
SEMISTARS	.75	.35
UNLISTED STARS	1.50	.70

☐ 1	Mike Boddicker	.40	.18
☐ 2	Al Bumbry	.40	.18
☐ 3	Todd Cruz	.15	.07
☐ 4	Rich Dauer	.15	.07
☐ 5	Storm Davis	.15	.07
☐ 6	Rick Dempsey	.15	.07
☐ 7	Jim Dwyer	.15	.07
☐ 8	Mike Flanagan	.15	.07
☐ 9	Dan Ford	.15	.07
☐ 10	John Lowenstein	.15	.07
☐ 11	Dennis Martinez	.40	.18
☐ 12	Tippy Martinez	.15	.07
☐ 13	Scott McGregor	.15	.07
☐ 14	Eddie Murray	4.00	1.80
☐ 15	Joe Nolan	.15	.07
☐ 16	Jim Palmer	1.25	.55
☐ 17	Cal Ripken	12.00	5.50
☐ 18	Gary Roenicke	.15	.07
☐ 19	Lenn Sakata	.15	.07
☐ 20	John Shelby	.15	.07
☐ 21	Ken Singleton	.15	.07
☐ 22	Sammy Stewart	.15	.07
☐ 23	Tim Stoddard	.15	.07
☐ 24	Marty Bystrom	.15	.07
☐ 25	Steve Carlton	2.00	.90
☐ 26	Ivan DeJesus............	.15	.07
☐ 27	John Denny	.15	.07
☐ 28	Bob Dernier	.15	.07
☐ 29	Bo Diaz	.15	.07
☐ 30	Kiko Garcia	.15	.07
☐ 31	Greg Gross	.15	.07
☐ 32	Kevin Gross	.40	.18
☐ 33	Von Hayes	.15	.07
☐ 34	Willie Hernandez	.40	.18
☐ 35	Al Holland	.15	.07
☐ 36	Charles Hudson	.15	.07
☐ 37	Joe Lefebvre	.15	.07
☐ 38	Sixto Lezcano	.15	.07
☐ 39	Garry Maddox	.15	.07
☐ 40	Gary Matthews	.15	.07
☐ 41	Len Matuszek	.15	.07
☐ 42	Tug McGraw	.40	.18
☐ 43	Joe Morgan	1.50	.70
☐ 44	Tony Perez	1.50	.70
☐ 45	Ron Reed	.15	.07
☐ 46	Pete Rose	2.00	.90
☐ 47	Juan Samuel	.75	.35
☐ 48	Mike Schmidt	2.00	.90
☐ 49	Ozzie Virgil	.15	.07
☐ 50	Juan Agosto	.15	.07
☐ 51	Harold Baines	.75	.35
☐ 52	Floyd Bannister	.15	.07
☐ 53	Salome Barojas	.15	.07
☐ 54	Britt Burns	.15	.07
☐ 55	Julio Cruz	.15	.07
☐ 56	Richard Dotson	.15	.07
☐ 57	Jerry Dybzinski	.15	.07
☐ 58	Carlton Fisk	2.00	.90
☐ 59	Scott Fletcher	.15	.07
☐ 60	Jerry Hairston	.15	.07
☐ 61	Kevin Hickey	.15	.07
☐ 62	Marc Hill	.15	.07
☐ 63	LaMarr Hoyt	.15	.07
☐ 64	Ron Kittle	.15	.07
☐ 65	Jerry Koosman	.40	.18
☐ 66	Dennis Lamp	.15	.07
☐ 67	Rudy Law	.15	.07
☐ 68	Vance Law	.15	.07
☐ 69	Greg Luzinski	.40	.18
☐ 70	Tom Paciorek	.15	.07
☐ 71	Mike Squires	.15	.07
☐ 72	Dick Tidrow	.15	.07
☐ 73	Greg Walker	.40	.18
☐ 74	Glenn Abbott	.15	.07
☐ 75	Howard Bailey	.15	.07
☐ 76	Doug Bair	.15	.07
☐ 77	Juan Berenguer	.15	.07
☐ 78	Tom Brookens	.40	.18
☐ 79	Enos Cabell	.15	.07
☐ 80	Kirk Gibson	1.50	.70
☐ 81	John Grubb	.15	.07
☐ 82	Larry Herndon	.40	.18
☐ 83	Wayne Krenchicki	.15	.07
☐ 84	Rick Leach	.15	.07
☐ 85	Chet Lemon	.40	.18
☐ 86	Aurelio Lopez	.40	.18
☐ 87	Jack Morris	1.50	.70
☐ 88	Lance Parrish	.75	.35
☐ 89	Dan Petry	.40	.18
☐ 90	Dave Rozema	.15	.07
☐ 91	Alan Trammell	1.50	.70
☐ 92	Lou Whitaker	1.50	.70
☐ 93	Milt Wilcox	.15	.07
☐ 94	Glenn Wilson	.40	.18
☐ 95	John Wockenfuss	.15	.07
☐ 96	Dusty Baker	.75	.35
☐ 97	Joe Beckwith	.15	.07
☐ 98	Greg Brock	.15	.07
☐ 99	Jack Fimple	.15	.07
☐ 100	Pedro Guerrero	.40	.18
☐ 101	Rick Honeycutt	.15	.07
☐ 102	Burt Hooton	.15	.07
☐ 103	Steve Howe	.15	.07
☐ 104	Ken Landreaux	.15	.07
☐ 105	Mike Marshall	.15	.07
☐ 106	Rick Monday	.15	.07
☐ 107	Jose Morales	.15	.07
☐ 108	Tom Niedenfuer	.15	.07
☐ 109	Alejandro Pena	.40	.18
☐ 110	Jerry Reuss UER	.15	.07
	("Home:" omitted)		
☐ 111	Bill Russell	.40	.18
☐ 112	Steve Sax	.40	.18
☐ 113	Mike Scioscia	.15	.07
☐ 114	Derrel Thomas	.15	.07
☐ 115	Fernando Valenzuela ..	.40	.18
☐ 116	Bob Welch	.40	.18
☐ 117	Steve Yeager	.15	.07
☐ 118	Pat Zachry	.15	.07
☐ 119	Don Baylor	.75	.35
☐ 120	Bert Campaneris	.40	.18
☐ 121	Rick Cerone	.15	.07
☐ 122	Ray Fontenot	.15	.07
☐ 123	George Frazier	.15	.07
☐ 124	Oscar Gamble	.15	.07
☐ 125	Rich Gossage	.75	.35
☐ 126	Ken Griffey	.40	.18
☐ 127	Ron Guidry	.40	.18
☐ 128	Jay Howell	.40	.18
☐ 129	Steve Kemp	.15	.07
☐ 130	Matt Keough	.15	.07
☐ 131	Don Mattingly	20.00	9.00
☐ 132	John Montefusco	.15	.07
☐ 133	Omar Moreno	.15	.07
☐ 134	Dale Murray	.15	.07
☐ 135	Graig Nettles	.40	.18
☐ 136	Lou Piniella	.40	.18
☐ 137	Willie Randolph	.40	.18
☐ 138	Shane Rawley	.15	.07
☐ 139	Dave Righetti	.40	.18
☐ 140	Andre Robertson	.15	.07
☐ 141	Bob Shirley	.15	.07
☐ 142	Roy Smalley	.15	.07
☐ 143	Dave Winfield	3.00	1.35
☐ 144	Butch Wynegar	.15	.07
☐ 145	Jim Acker	.15	.07
☐ 146	Doyle Alexander	.15	.07
☐ 147	Jesse Barfield	.40	.18

148	Jorge Bell	.40	.18
149	Barry Bonnell	.15	.07
150	Jim Clancy	.15	.07
151	Dave Collins	.15	.07
152	Tony Fernandez	1.50	.70
153	Damaso Garcia	.15	.07
154	Dave Geisel	.15	.07
155	Jim Gott	.15	.07
156	Alfredo Griffin	.15	.07
157	Garth Iorg	.15	.07
158	Roy Lee Jackson	.15	.07
159	Cliff Johnson	.15	.07
160	Luis Leal	.15	.07
161	Buck Martinez	.15	.07
162	Joey McLaughlin	.15	.07
163	Randy Moffitt	.15	.07
164	Lloyd Moseby	.15	.07
165	Rance Mulliniks	.15	.07
166	Jorge Orta	.15	.07
167	Dave Stieb	.15	.07
168	Willie Upshaw	.15	.07
169	Ernie Whitt	.15	.07
170	Len Barker	.15	.07
171	Steve Bedrosian	.15	.07
172	Bruce Benedict	.15	.07
173	Brett Butler	.75	.35
174	Rick Camp	.15	.07
175	Chris Chambliss	.15	.07
176	Ken Dayley	.15	.07
177	Pete Falcone	.15	.07
178	Terry Forster	.15	.07
179	Gene Garber	.15	.07
180	Terry Harper	.15	.07
181	Bob Horner	.15	.07
182	Glenn Hubbard	.15	.07
183	Randy Johnson	.15	.07
184	Craig McMurtry	.15	.07
185	Donnie Moore	.15	.07
186	Dale Murphy	1.50	.70
187	Phil Niekro	1.50	.70
188	Pascual Perez	.15	.07
189	Biff Pocoroba	.15	.07
190	Rafael Ramirez	.15	.07
191	Jerry Royster	.15	.07
192	Claudell Washington	.15	.07
193	Bob Watson	.40	.18
194	Jerry Augustine	.15	.07
195	Mark Brouhard	.15	.07
196	Mike Caldwell	.15	.07
197	Tom Candiotti	1.50	.70
198	Cecil Cooper	.40	.18
199	Rollie Fingers	1.50	.70
200	Jim Gantner	.40	.18
201	Bob L. Gibson	.15	.07
202	Moose Haas	.15	.07
203	Roy Howell	.15	.07
204	Pete Ladd	.15	.07
205	Rick Manning	.15	.07
206	Bob McClure	.15	.07
207	Paul Molitor UER ('83 stats should say .270 BA and 608 AB)	3.00	1.35
208	Don Money	.15	.07
209	Charlie Moore	.15	.07
210	Ben Oglivie	.15	.07
211	Chuck Porter	.15	.07
212	Ed Romero	.15	.07
213	Ted Simmons	.40	.18
214	Jim Slaton	.15	.07
215	Don Sutton	1.50	.70
216	Tom Tellmann	.15	.07
217	Pete Vuckovich	.15	.07
218	Ned Yost	.15	.07
219	Robin Yount	3.00	1.35
220	Alan Ashby	.15	.07
221	Kevin Bass	.15	.07
222	Jose Cruz	.40	.18
223	Bill Dawley	.15	.07
224	Frank DiPino	.15	.07
225	Bill Doran	.40	.18
226	Phil Garner	.40	.18
227	Art Howe	.15	.07
228	Bob Knepper	.15	.07
229	Ray Knight	.40	.18
230	Frank LaCorte	.15	.07
231	Mike LaCoss	.15	.07
232	Mike Madden	.15	.07
233	Jerry Mumphrey	.15	.07
234	Joe Niekro	.40	.18
235	Terry Puhl	.15	.07
236	Luis Pujols	.15	.07
237	Craig Reynolds	.15	.07
238	Vern Ruhle	.15	.07
239	Nolan Ryan	10.00	4.50
240	Mike Scott	.40	.18
241	Tony Scott	.15	.07
242	Dave Smith	.15	.07
243	Dickie Thon	.15	.07
244	Denny Walling	.15	.07
245	Dale Berra	.15	.07
246	Jim Bibby	.15	.07
247	John Candelaria	.15	.07
248	Jose DeLeon	.15	.07
249	Mike Easler	.15	.07
250	Cecilio Guante	.15	.07
251	Richie Hebner	.15	.07
252	Lee Lacy	.15	.07
253	Bill Madlock	.40	.18
254	Milt May	.15	.07
255	Lee Mazzilli	.15	.07
256	Larry McWilliams	.15	.07
257	Jim Morrison	.15	.07
258	Dave Parker	.40	.18
259	Tony Pena	.15	.07
260	Johnny Ray	.15	.07
261	Rick Rhoden	.15	.07
262	Don Robinson	.15	.07
263	Manny Sarmiento	.15	.07
264	Rod Scurry	.15	.07
265	Kent Tekulve	.40	.18
266	Gene Tenace	.40	.18
267	Jason Thompson	.15	.07
268	Lee Tunnell	.15	.07
269	Marvell Wynne	.15	.07
270	Ray Burris	.15	.07
271	Gary Carter	1.50	.70
272	Warren Cromartie	.15	.07
273	Andre Dawson	1.50	.70
274	Doug Flynn	.15	.07
275	Terry Francona	.15	.07
276	Bill Gullickson	.15	.07
277	Bob James	.15	.07
278	Charlie Lea	.15	.07
279	Bryan Little	.15	.07
280	Al Oliver	.40	.18
281	Tim Raines	.75	.35
282	Bobby Ramos	.15	.07
283	Jeff Reardon	.40	.18
284	Steve Rogers	.15	.07
285	Scott Sanderson	.15	.07
286	Dan Schatzeder	.15	.07
287	Bryn Smith	.15	.07
288	Chris Speier	.15	.07
289	Manny Trillo	.15	.07
290	Mike Vail	.15	.07
291	Tim Wallach	.40	.18
292	Chris Welsh	.15	.07
293	Jim Wohlford	.15	.07
294	Kurt Bevacqua	.15	.07
295	Juan Bonilla	.15	.07
296	Bobby Brown	.15	.07
297	Luis DeLeon	.15	.07
298	Dave Dravecky	.40	.18
299	Tim Flannery	.15	.07
300	Steve Garvey	.75	.35
301	Tony Gwynn	10.00	4.50
302	Andy Hawkins	.15	.07
303	Ruppert Jones	.15	.07
304	Terry Kennedy	.15	.07
305	Tim Lollar	.15	.07
306	Gary Lucas	.15	.07
307	Kevin McReynolds	.75	.35
308	Sid Monge	.15	.07
309	Mario Ramirez	.15	.07
310	Gene Richards	.15	.07
311	Luis Salazar	.15	.07
312	Eric Show	.15	.07
313	Elias Sosa	.15	.07
314	Garry Templeton	.15	.07
315	Mark Thurmond	.15	.07
316	Ed Whitson	.15	.07
317	Alan Wiggins	.15	.07
318	Neil Allen	.15	.07
319	Joaquin Andujar	.15	.07
320	Steve Braun	.15	.07
321	Glenn Brummer	.15	.07
322	Bob Forsch	.15	.07
323	David Green	.15	.07
324	George Hendrick	.15	.07
325	Tom Herr	.40	.18
326	Dane Iorg	.15	.07
327	Jeff Lahti	.15	.07
328	Dave LaPoint	.15	.07
329	Willie McGee	.75	.35
330	Ken Oberkfell	.15	.07
331	Darrell Porter	.15	.07
332	Jamie Quirk	.15	.07
333	Mike Ramsey	.15	.07
334	Floyd Rayford	.15	.07
335	Lonnie Smith	.15	.07
336	Ozzie Smith	2.50	1.10
337	John Stuper	.15	.07
338	Bruce Sutter	.40	.18
339	Andy Van Slyke UER (Batting and throwing both wrong on card back)	1.50	.70
340	Dave Von Ohlen	.15	.07
341	Willie Aikens	.15	.07
342	Mike Armstrong	.15	.07
343	Bud Black	.15	.07
344	George Brett	3.00	1.35
345	Onix Concepcion	.15	.07
346	Keith Creel	.15	.07
347	Larry Gura	.15	.07
348	Don Hood	.15	.07
349	Dennis Leonard	.15	.07
350	Hal McRae	.40	.18
351	Amos Otis	.40	.18
352	Gaylord Perry	1.50	.70
353	Greg Pryor	.15	.07
354	Dan Quisenberry	.15	.07
355	Steve Renko	.15	.07
356	Leon Roberts	.15	.07
357	Pat Sheridan	.15	.07
358	Joe Simpson	.15	.07
359	Don Slaught	.40	.18
360	Paul Splittorff	.15	.07
361	U.L. Washington	.15	.07
362	John Wathan	.15	.07
363	Frank White	.40	.18
364	Willie Wilson	.40	.18
365	Jim Barr	.15	.07
366	Dave Bergman	.15	.07
367	Fred Breining	.15	.07
368	Bob Brenly	.15	.07
369	Jack Clark	.40	.18
370	Chili Davis	.75	.35
371	Mark Davis	.15	.07
372	Darrell Evans	.40	.18
373	Atlee Hammaker	.15	.07
374	Mike Krukow	.15	.07
375	Duane Kuiper	.15	.07
376	Bill Laskey	.15	.07
377	Gary Lavelle	.15	.07
378	Johnnie LeMaster	.15	.07
379	Jeff Leonard	.15	.07
380	Randy Lerch	.15	.07
381	Renie Martin	.15	.07
382	Andy McGaffigan	.15	.07
383	Greg Minton	.15	.07
384	Tom O'Malley	.15	.07
385	Max Venable	.15	.07
386	Brad Wellman	.15	.07
387	Joel Youngblood	.15	.07
388	Gary Allenson	.15	.07
389	Luis Aponte	.15	.07
390	Tony Armas	.15	.07
391	Doug Bird	.15	.07
392	Wade Boggs	3.00	1.35
393	Dennis Boyd	.40	.18
394	Mike Brown UER P (shown with record of 31-104)	.15	.07
395	Mark Clear	.15	.07
396	Dennis Eckersley	1.50	.70
397	Dwight Evans	.40	.18
398	Rich Gedman	.15	.07
399	Glenn Hoffman	.15	.07

400	Bruce Hurst	.15	.07
401	John Henry Johnson	.15	.07
402	Ed Jurak	.15	.07
403	Rick Miller	.15	.07
404	Jeff Newman	.15	.07
405	Reid Nichols	.15	.07
406	Bob Ojeda	.15	.07
407	Jerry Remy	.15	.07
408	Jim Rice	.40	.18
409	Bob Stanley	.15	.07
410	Dave Stapleton	.15	.07
411	John Tudor	.15	.07
412	Carl Yastrzemski	1.50	.70
413	Buddy Bell	.40	.18
414	Larry Biittner	.15	.07
415	John Butcher	.15	.07
416	Danny Darwin	.15	.07
417	Bucky Dent	.40	.18
418	Dave Hostetler	.15	.07
419	Charlie Hough	.40	.18
420	Bobby Johnson	.15	.07
421	Odell Jones	.15	.07
422	Jon Matlack	.15	.07
423	Pete O'Brien	.40	.18
424	Larry Parrish	.15	.07
425	Mickey Rivers	.15	.07
426	Billy Sample	.15	.07
427	Dave Schmidt	.15	.07
428	Mike Smithson	.15	.07
429	Bill Stein	.15	.07
430	Dave Stewart	.40	.18
431	Jim Sundberg	.40	.18
432	Frank Tanana	.40	.18
433	Dave Tobik	.15	.07
434	Wayne Tolleson	.15	.07
435	George Wright	.15	.07
436	Bill Almon	.15	.07
437	Keith Atherton	.15	.07
438	Dave Beard	.15	.07
439	Tom Burgmeier	.15	.07
440	Jeff Burroughs	.15	.07
441	Chris Codiroli	.15	.07
442	Tim Conroy	.15	.07
443	Mike Davis	.15	.07
444	Wayne Gross	.15	.07
445	Garry Hancock	.15	.07
446	Mike Heath	.15	.07
447	Rickey Henderson	3.00	1.35
448	Donnie Hill	.15	.07
449	Bob Kearney	.15	.07
450	Bill Krueger	.15	.07
451	Rick Langford	.15	.07
452	Carney Lansford	.40	.18
453	Dave Lopes	.40	.18
454	Steve McCatty	.15	.07
455	Dan Meyer	.15	.07
456	Dwayne Murphy	.15	.07
457	Mike Norris	.15	.07
458	Ricky Peters	.15	.07
459	Tony Phillips	2.00	.90
460	Tom Underwood	.15	.07
461	Mike Warren	.15	.07
462	Johnny Bench	2.00	.90
463	Bruce Berenyi	.15	.07
464	Dann Bilardello	.15	.07
465	Cesar Cedeno	.40	.18
466	Dave Concepcion	.40	.18
467	Dan Driessen	.15	.07
468	Nick Esasky	.15	.07
469	Rich Gale	.15	.07
470	Ben Hayes	.15	.07
471	Paul Householder	.15	.07
472	Tom Hume	.15	.07
473	Alan Knicely	.15	.07
474	Eddie Milner	.15	.07
475	Ron Oester	.15	.07
476	Kelly Paris	.15	.07
477	Frank Pastore	.15	.07
478	Ted Power	.15	.07
479	Joe Price	.15	.07
480	Charlie Puleo	.15	.07
481	Gary Redus	.15	.07
482	Bill Scherrer	.15	.07
483	Mario Soto	.15	.07
484	Alex Trevino	.15	.07
485	Duane Walker	.15	.07
486	Larry Bowa	.40	.18
487	Warren Brusstar	.15	.07
488	Bill Buckner	.40	.18
489	Bill Campbell	.15	.07
490	Ron Cey	.40	.18
491	Jody Davis	.15	.07
492	Leon Durham	.15	.07
493	Mel Hall	.40	.18
494	Ferguson Jenkins	1.50	.70
495	Jay Johnstone	.40	.18
496	Craig Lefferts	.15	.07
497	Carmelo Martinez	.15	.07
498	Jerry Morales	.15	.07
499	Keith Moreland	.15	.07
500	Dickie Noles	.15	.07
501	Mike Proly	.15	.07
502	Chuck Rainey	.15	.07
503	Dick Ruthven	.15	.07
504	Ryne Sandberg	5.00	2.20
505	Lee Smith	1.50	.70
506	Steve Trout	.15	.07
507	Gary Woods	.15	.07
508	Juan Beniquez	.15	.07
509	Bob Boone	.40	.18
510	Rick Burleson	.15	.07
511	Rod Carew	1.25	.55
512	Bobby Clark	.15	.07
513	John Curtis	.15	.07
514	Doug DeCinces	.15	.07
515	Brian Downing	.15	.07
516	Tim Foli	.15	.07
517	Ken Forsch	.15	.07
518	Bobby Grich	.40	.18
519	Andy Hassler	.15	.07
520	Reggie Jackson	2.00	.90
521	Ron Jackson	.15	.07
522	Tommy John	.75	.35
523	Bruce Kison	.15	.07
524	Steve Lubratich	.15	.07
525	Fred Lynn	.40	.18
526	Gary Pettis	.15	.07
527	Luis Sanchez	.15	.07
528	Daryl Sconiers	.15	.07
529	Ellis Valentine	.15	.07
530	Rob Wilfong	.15	.07
531	Mike Witt	.15	.07
532	Geoff Zahn	.15	.07
533	Bud Anderson	.15	.07
534	Chris Bando	.15	.07
535	Alan Bannister	.15	.07
536	Bert Blyleven	.40	.18
537	Tom Brennan	.15	.07
538	Jamie Easterly	.15	.07
539	Juan Eichelberger	.15	.07
540	Jim Essian	.15	.07
541	Mike Fischlin	.15	.07
542	Julio Franco	.75	.35
543	Mike Hargrove	.40	.18
544	Toby Harrah	.40	.18
545	Ron Hassey	.15	.07
546	Neal Heaton	.15	.07
547	Bake McBride	.15	.07
548	Broderick Perkins	.15	.07
549	Lary Sorensen	.15	.07
550	Dan Spillner	.15	.07
551	Rick Sutcliffe	.40	.18
552	Pat Tabler	.15	.07
553	Gorman Thomas	.15	.07
554	Andre Thornton	.15	.07
555	George Vukovich	.15	.07
556	Darrell Brown	.15	.07
557	Tom Brunansky	.40	.18
558	Randy Bush	.15	.07
559	Bobby Castillo	.15	.07
560	John Castino	.15	.07
561	Ron Davis	.15	.07
562	Dave Engle	.15	.07
563	Lenny Faedo	.15	.07
564	Pete Filson	.15	.07
565	Gary Gaetti	.75	.35
566	Mickey Hatcher	.15	.07
567	Kent Hrbek	.40	.18
568	Rusty Kuntz	.15	.07
569	Tim Laudner	.15	.07
570	Rick Lysander	.15	.07
571	Bobby Mitchell	.15	.07
572	Ken Schrom	.15	.07
573	Ray Smith	.15	.07
574	Tim Teufel	.15	.07
575	Frank Viola	.75	.35
576	Gary Ward	.15	.07
577	Ron Washington	.15	.07
578	Len Whitehouse	.15	.07
579	Al Williams	.15	.07
580	Bob Bailor	.15	.07
581	Mark Bradley	.15	.07
582	Hubie Brooks	.15	.07
583	Carlos Diaz	.15	.07
584	George Foster	.40	.18
585	Brian Giles	.15	.07
586	Danny Heep	.15	.07
587	Keith Hernandez	.40	.18
588	Ron Hodges	.15	.07
589	Scott Holman	.15	.07
590	Dave Kingman	.75	.35
591	Ed Lynch	.15	.07
592	Jose Oquendo	.40	.18
593	Jesse Orosco	.15	.07
594	Junior Ortiz	.15	.07
595	Tom Seaver	2.00	.90
596	Doug Sisk	.15	.07
597	Rusty Staub	.40	.18
598	John Stearns	.15	.07
599	Darryl Strawberry	5.00	2.20
600	Craig Swan	.15	.07
601	Walt Terrell	.15	.07
602	Mike Torrez	.15	.07
603	Mookie Wilson	.40	.18
604	Jamie Allen	.15	.07
605	Jim Beattie	.15	.07
606	Tony Bernazard	.15	.07
607	Manny Castillo	.15	.07
608	Bill Caudill	.15	.07
609	Bryan Clark	.15	.07
610	Al Cowens	.15	.07
611	Dave Henderson	.40	.18
612	Steve Henderson	.15	.07
613	Orlando Mercado	.15	.07
614	Mike Moore	.15	.07
615	Ricky Nelson UER (Jamie Nelson's stats on back)	.15	.07
616	Spike Owen	.40	.18
617	Pat Putnam	.15	.07
618	Ron Roenicke	.15	.07
619	Mike Stanton	.15	.07
620	Bob Stoddard	.15	.07
621	Rick Sweet	.15	.07
622	Roy Thomas	.15	.07
623	Ed VandeBerg	.15	.07
624	Matt Young	.15	.07
625	Richie Zisk	.15	.07
626	Fred Lynn 1982 AS Game RB	.40	.18
627	Manny Trillo 1983 AS Game RB	.15	.07
628	Steve Garvey NL Iron Man	.75	.35
629	Rod Carew AL Batting Runner-up	1.50	.70
630	Wade Boggs AL Batting Champion	1.50	.70
631	Tim Raines: Letting Go of the Raines	.40	.18
632	Al Oliver Double Trouble	.40	.18
633	Steve Sax AS Second Base	.15	.07
634	Dickie Thon AS Shortstop	.15	.07
635	Ace Firemen Dan Quisenberry and Tippy Martinez	.15	.07
636	Reds Reunited Joe Morgan Pete Rose Tony Perez	1.50	.70
637	Backstop Stars Lance Parrish Bob Boone	.75	.35
638	George Brett and Gaylord Perry	2.00	.90

Pine Tar 7/24/83
☐ 639 1983 No Hitters .... .75   .35
  Dave Righetti
  Mike Warren
  Bob Forsch
☐ 640 Johnny Bench and.... 2.00   .90
  Carl Yastrzemski
  Retiring Superstars
☐ 641 Gaylord Perry 1.50   .70
  300 Club and
  Going Out in Style
☐ 642 Steve Carlton 1.50   .70
  300 Club and
  Strikeout Record
☐ 643 Joe Altobelli and .... .15   .07
  Paul Owens
  World Series Managers
☐ 644 Rick Dempsey ...... .40   .18
  WS Rookie MVP
☐ 645 Mike Boddicker .15   .07
  WS Rookie Winner
☐ 646 Scott McGregor .15   .07
  WS Clincher
☐ 647 CL: Orioles/Royals. .15   .07
  Joe Altobelli MG
☐ 648 CL: Phillies/Giants. .15   .07
  Paul Owens MG
☐ 649 CL: White Sox/Red Sox .75   .35
  Tony LaRussa MG
☐ 650 CL: Tigers/Rangers ... .75   .35
  Sparky Anderson MG
☐ 651 CL: Dodgers/A's ...... .75   .35
  Tommy Lasorda MG
☐ 652 CL: Yankees/Reds ...... .75   .35
  Billy Martin MG
☐ 653 CL: Blue Jays/Cubs .... .40   .18
  Bobby Cox MG
☐ 654 CL: Braves/Angels ... .75   .35
  Joe Torre MG
☐ 655 CL: Brewers/Indians .. .15   .07
  Rene Lachemann MG
☐ 656 CL: Astros/Twins ...... .15   .07
  Bob Lillis MG
☐ 657 CL: Pirates/Mets .... .15   .07
  Chuck Tanner MG
☐ 658 CL: Expos/Mariners .... .15   .07
  Bill Virdon MG
☐ 659 CL: Padres/Specials .. .40   .18
  Dick Williams MG
☐ 660 CL: Cardinals/Teams .. .75   .35
  Whitey Herzog MG

1984 Fleer Update

This set was Fleer's first update set and portrayed players with their proper team for the current year and to rookies who were not in their regular issue. Like the Topps Traded sets of the time, the Fleer Update sets were distributed in factory set form through hobby dealers only. The set was quite popular with collectors, and, apparently, the print run was relatively short, as the set was quickly in short supply and exhibited a rapid

and dramatic price increase. The cards are numbered on the back with a U prefix and placed in alphabetical order by player name. The key (extended) Rookie Cards in this set are Roger Clemens, John Franco, Dwight Gooden, Jimmy Key, Mark Langston, Kirby Puckett, Jose Rijo, and Bret Saberhagen. Collectors are urged to be careful if purchasing single cards of Clemens, Darling, Gooden, Puckett, Rose, or Saberhagen as these specific cards have been illegally reprinted. These fakes are blurry when compared to the real cards.

	NRMT	VG-E
COMP.FACT.SET (132)	400.00	180.00
COMMON CARD (1-132)	1.00	.45
MINOR STARS	4.00	1.80
BEWARE OF COUNTERFEITS		

☐ 1 Willie Aikens .... 1.00 .45
☐ 2 Luis Aponte .... 1.00 .45
☐ 3 Mark Bailey .... 1.00 .45
☐ 4 Bob Bailor .... 1.00 .45
☐ 5 Dusty Baker 4.00 1.80
☐ 6 Steve Balboni .... 1.00 .45
☐ 7 Alan Bannister .... 1.00 .45
☐ 8 Marty Barrett 4.00 1.80
☐ 9 Dave Beard .... 1.00 .45
☐ 10 Joe Beckwith .... 1.00 .45
☐ 11 Dave Bergman .... 1.00 .45
☐ 12 Tony Bernazard .... 1.00 .45
☐ 13 Bruce Bochte .... 1.00 .45
☐ 14 Barry Bonnell .... 1.00 .45
☐ 15 Phil Bradley 4.00 1.80
☐ 16 Fred Breining .... 1.00 .45
☐ 17 Mike C. Brown .... 1.00 .45
☐ 18 Bill Buckner 4.00 1.80
☐ 19 Ray Burris .... 1.00 .45
☐ 20 John Butcher .... 1.00 .45
☐ 21 Brett Butler 5.00 2.20
☐ 22 Enos Cabell .... 1.00 .45
☐ 23 Bill Campbell .... 1.00 .45
☐ 24 Bill Caudill .... 1.00 .45
☐ 25 Bobby Clark .... 1.00 .45
☐ 26 Bryan Clark .... 1.00 .45
☐ 27 Roger Clemens 200.00 90.00
☐ 28 Jaime Cocanower .... 1.00 .45
☐ 29 Ron Darling 5.00 2.20
☐ 30 Alvin Davis 4.00 1.80
☐ 31 Bob Dernier .... 1.00 .45
☐ 32 Carlos Diaz .... 1.00 .45
☐ 33 Mike Easler .... 1.00 .45
☐ 34 Dennis Eckersley 6.00 2.70
☐ 35 Jim Essian .... 1.00 .45
☐ 36 Darrell Evans 4.00 1.80
☐ 37 Mike Fitzgerald .... 1.00 .45
☐ 38 Tim Foli .... 1.00 .45
☐ 39 John Franco 8.00 3.60
☐ 40 George Frazier .... 1.00 .45
☐ 41 Rich Gale .... 1.00 .45
☐ 42 Barbaro Garbey .... 1.00 .45
☐ 43 Dwight Gooden 40.00 18.00
☐ 44 Rich Gossage 5.00 2.20
☐ 45 Wayne Gross .... 1.00 .45
☐ 46 Mark Gubicza 4.00 1.80
☐ 47 Jackie Gutierrez .... 1.00 .45
☐ 48 Toby Harrah .... 1.00 .45
☐ 49 Ron Hassey .... 1.00 .45
☐ 50 Richie Hebner .... 1.00 .45
☐ 51 Willie Hernandez 4.00 1.80
☐ 52 Ed Hodge .... 1.00 .45
☐ 53 Ricky Horton .... 1.00 .45
☐ 54 Art Howe .... 1.00 .45
☐ 55 Dane Iorg .... 1.00 .45
☐ 56 Brook Jacoby 4.00 1.80
☐ 57 Dion James 4.00 1.80
☐ 58 Mike Jeffcoat .... 1.00 .45
☐ 59 Ruppert Jones .... 1.00 .45
☐ 60 Bob Kearney .... 1.00 .45

☐ 61 Jimmy Key 15.00 6.75
☐ 62 Dave Kingman 5.00 2.20
☐ 63 Brad Komminsk .... 1.00 .45
☐ 64 Jerry Koosman 4.00 1.80
☐ 65 Wayne Krenchicki .... 1.00 .45
☐ 66 Rusty Kuntz .... 1.00 .45
☐ 67 Frank LaCorte .... 1.00 .45
☐ 68 Dennis Lamp .... 1.00 .45
☐ 69 Tito Landrum .... 1.00 .45
☐ 70 Mark Langston 8.00 3.60
☐ 71 Rick Leach .... 1.00 .45
☐ 72 Craig Lefferts 4.00 1.80
☐ 73 Gary Lucas .... 1.00 .45
☐ 74 Jerry Martin .... 1.00 .45
☐ 75 Carmelo Martinez .... 1.00 .45
☐ 76 Mike Mason .... 1.00 .45
☐ 77 Gary Matthews .... 1.00 .45
☐ 78 Andy McGaffigan .... 1.00 .45
☐ 79 Joey McLaughlin .... 1.00 .45
☐ 80 Joe Morgan 8.00 3.60
☐ 81 Darryl Motley .... 1.00 .45
☐ 82 Graig Nettles 4.00 1.80
☐ 83 Phil Niekro 5.00 2.20
☐ 84 Ken Oberkfell .... 1.00 .45
☐ 85 Al Oliver 4.00 1.80
☐ 86 Jorge Orta .... 1.00 .45
☐ 87 Amos Otis 4.00 1.80
☐ 88 Bob Owchinko .... 1.00 .45
☐ 89 Dave Parker 4.00 1.80
☐ 90 Jack Perconte .... 1.00 .45
☐ 91 Tony Perez 6.00 2.70
☐ 92 Gerald Perry 4.00 1.80
☐ 93 Kirby Puckett 180.00 80.00
☐ 94 Shane Rawley .... 1.00 .45
☐ 95 Floyd Rayford .... 1.00 .45
☐ 96 Ron Reed .... 1.00 .45
☐ 97 R.J. Reynolds .... 1.00 .45
☐ 98 Gene Richards .... 1.00 .45
☐ 99 Jose Rijo 5.00 2.20
☐ 100 Jeff D. Robinson .... 1.00 .45
☐ 101 Ron Romanick .... 1.00 .45
☐ 102 Pete Rose 15.00 6.75
☐ 103 Bret Saberhagen 8.00 3.60
☐ 104 Scott Sanderson .... 1.00 .45
☐ 105 Dick Schofield 4.00 1.80
☐ 106 Tom Seaver 15.00 6.75
☐ 107 Jim Slaton .... 1.00 .45
☐ 108 Mike Smithson .... 1.00 .45
☐ 109 Lary Sorensen .... 1.00 .45
☐ 110 Tim Stoddard .... 1.00 .45
☐ 111 Jeff Stone .... 1.00 .45
☐ 112 Champ Summers .... 1.00 .45
☐ 113 Jim Sundberg 4.00 1.80
☐ 114 Rick Sutcliffe 4.00 1.80
☐ 115 Craig Swan .... 1.00 .45
☐ 116 Derrel Thomas .... 1.00 .45
☐ 117 Gorman Thomas 4.00 1.80
☐ 118 Alex Trevino .... 1.00 .45
☐ 119 Manny Trillo .... 1.00 .45
☐ 120 John Tudor .... 1.00 .45
☐ 121 Tom Underwood .... 1.00 .45
☐ 122 Mike Vail .... 1.00 .45
☐ 123 Tom Waddell .... 1.00 .45
☐ 124 Gary Ward .... 1.00 .45
☐ 125 Terry Whitfield .... 1.00 .45
☐ 126 Curtis Wilkerson .... 1.00 .45
☐ 127 Frank Williams .... 1.00 .45
☐ 128 Glenn Wilson .... 1.00 .45
☐ 129 John Wockenfuss .... 1.00 .45
☐ 130 Ned Yost .... 1.00 .45
☐ 131 Mike Young .... 1.00 .45
☐ 132 Checklist 1-132 .... 1.00 .45

1985 Fleer

The 1985 Fleer set consists of 660 standard-size cards. Wax packs contained 15 cards plus logo stickers. Card fronts feature a full color photo, team logo along with the player's name and position. The borders enclosing the photo are color-coded to correspond to the player's team. The cards are

ordered alphabetically within team. The teams are ordered based on their respective performance during the prior year. Subsets include Specials (626-643) and Major League Prospects (644-653). The black and white photo on the reverse is included for the third straight year. Notable Rookie Cards include Roger Clemens, Eric Davis, Shawon Dunston, John Franco, Dwight Gooden, Orel Hershiser, Jimmy Key, Mark Langston, Terry Pendleton, Kirby Puckett, Jose Rijo, Bret Saberhagen, and Danny Tartabull.

	NRMT	VG-E
COMPLETE SET (660)	100.00	45.00
COMMON CARD (1-660)	.15	.07
MINOR STARS	.40	.18
SEMISTARS	.75	.35
UNLISTED STARS	1.50	.70
CONDITION SENSITIVE SET		

#	Player	NRMT	VG-E
1	Doug Bair	.15	.07
2	Juan Berenguer	.15	.07
3	Dave Bergman	.15	.07
4	Tom Brookens	.15	.07
5	Marty Castillo	.15	.07
6	Darrell Evans	.40	.18
7	Barbaro Garbey	.15	.07
8	Kirk Gibson	.40	.18
9	John Grubb	.15	.07
10	Willie Hernandez	.15	.07
11	Larry Herndon	.15	.07
12	Howard Johnson	.40	.18
13	Ruppert Jones	.15	.07
14	Rusty Kuntz	.15	.07
15	Chet Lemon	.15	.07
16	Aurelio Lopez	.15	.07
17	Sid Monge	.15	.07
18	Jack Morris	.40	.18
19	Lance Parrish	.40	.18
20	Dan Petry	.15	.07
21	Dave Rozema	.15	.07
22	Bill Scherrer	.15	.07
23	Alan Trammell	.75	.35
24	Lou Whitaker	.75	.35
25	Milt Wilcox	.15	.07
26	Kurt Bevacqua	.15	.07
27	Greg Booker	.15	.07
28	Bobby Brown	.15	.07
29	Luis DeLeon	.15	.07
30	Dave Dravecky	.40	.18
31	Tim Flannery	.15	.07
32	Steve Garvey	.75	.35
33	Rich Gossage	.40	.18
34	Tony Gwynn	6.00	2.70
35	Greg Harris	.15	.07
36	Andy Hawkins	.15	.07
37	Terry Kennedy	.15	.07
38	Craig Lefferts	.15	.07
39	Tim Lollar	.15	.07
40	Carmelo Martinez	.15	.07
41	Kevin McReynolds	.40	.18
42	Graig Nettles	.40	.18
43	Luis Salazar	.15	.07
44	Eric Show	.15	.07
45	Garry Templeton	.15	.07
46	Mark Thurmond	.15	.07
47	Ed Whitson	.15	.07
48	Alan Wiggins	.15	.07
49	Rich Bordi	.15	.07
50	Larry Bowa	.40	.18
51	Warren Brusstar	.15	.07
52	Ron Cey	.40	.18
53	Henry Cotto	.15	.07
54	Jody Davis	.15	.07
55	Bob Dernier	.15	.07
56	Leon Durham	.15	.07
57	Dennis Eckersley	1.50	.70
58	George Frazier	.15	.07
59	Richie Hebner	.15	.07
60	Dave Lopes	.40	.18
61	Gary Matthews	.15	.07
62	Keith Moreland	.15	.07
63	Rick Reuschel	.15	.07
64	Dick Ruthven	.15	.07
65	Ryne Sandberg	3.00	1.35
66	Scott Sanderson	.15	.07
67	Lee Smith	.75	.35
68	Tim Stoddard	.15	.07
69	Rick Sutcliffe	.15	.07
70	Steve Trout	.15	.07
71	Gary Woods	.15	.07
72	Wally Backman	.15	.07
73	Bruce Berenyi	.15	.07
74	Hubie Brooks UER	.15	.07
	(Kelvin Chapman's stats on card back)		
75	Kelvin Chapman	.15	.07
76	Ron Darling	.40	.18
77	Sid Fernandez	.40	.18
78	Mike Fitzgerald	.15	.07
79	George Foster	.40	.18
80	Brent Gaff	.15	.07
81	Ron Gardenhire	.15	.07
82	Dwight Gooden	4.00	1.80
83	Tom Gorman	.15	.07
84	Danny Heep	.15	.07
85	Keith Hernandez	.40	.18
86	Ray Knight	.15	.07
87	Ed Lynch	.15	.07
88	Jose Oquendo	.15	.07
89	Jesse Orosco	.15	.07
90	Rafael Santana	.15	.07
91	Doug Sisk	.15	.07
92	Rusty Staub	.40	.18
93	Darryl Strawberry	1.50	.70
94	Walt Terrell	.15	.07
95	Mookie Wilson	.40	.18
96	Jim Acker	.15	.07
97	Willie Aikens	.15	.07
98	Doyle Alexander	.15	.07
99	Jesse Barfield	.15	.07
100	George Bell	.40	.18
101	Jim Clancy	.15	.07
102	Dave Collins	.15	.07
103	Tony Fernandez	.40	.18
104	Damaso Garcia	.15	.07
105	Jim Gott	.15	.07
106	Alfredo Griffin	.15	.07
107	Garth Iorg	.15	.07
108	Roy Lee Jackson	.15	.07
109	Cliff Johnson	.15	.07
110	Jimmy Key	2.00	.90
111	Dennis Lamp	.15	.07
112	Rick Leach	.15	.07
113	Luis Leal	.15	.07
114	Buck Martinez	.15	.07
115	Lloyd Moseby	.15	.07
116	Rance Mulliniks	.15	.07
117	Dave Stieb	.40	.18
118	Willie Upshaw	.15	.07
119	Ernie Whitt	.15	.07
120	Mike Armstrong	.15	.07
121	Don Baylor	.40	.18
122	Marty Bystrom	.15	.07
123	Rick Cerone	.15	.07
124	Joe Cowley	.15	.07
125	Brian Dayett	.15	.07
126	Tim Foli	.15	.07
127	Ray Fontenot	.15	.07
128	Ken Griffey	.40	.18
129	Ron Guidry	.40	.18
130	Toby Harrah	.15	.07
131	Jay Howell	.15	.07
132	Steve Kemp	.15	.07
133	Don Mattingly	5.00	2.20
134	Bobby Meacham	.15	.07
135	John Montefusco	.15	.07
136	Omar Moreno	.15	.07
137	Dale Murray	.15	.07
138	Phil Niekro	1.50	.70
139	Mike Pagliarulo	.15	.07
140	Willie Randolph	.40	.18
141	Dennis Rasmussen	.15	.07
142	Dave Righetti	.40	.18
143	Jose Rijo	.75	.35
144	Andre Robertson	.15	.07
145	Bob Shirley	.15	.07
146	Dave Winfield	1.50	.70
147	Butch Wynegar	.15	.07
148	Gary Allenson	.15	.07
149	Tony Armas	.15	.07
150	Marty Barrett	.15	.07
151	Wade Boggs	2.00	.90
152	Dennis Boyd	.15	.07
153	Bill Buckner	.40	.18
154	Mark Clear	.15	.07
155	Roger Clemens	30.00	13.50
156	Steve Crawford	.15	.07
157	Mike Easler	.15	.07
158	Dwight Evans	.40	.18
159	Rich Gedman	.15	.07
160	Jackie Gutierrez	.40	.18
	(Wade Boggs shown on deck)		
161	Bruce Hurst	.15	.07
162	John Henry Johnson	.15	.07
163	Rick Miller	.15	.07
164	Reid Nichols	.15	.07
165	Al Nipper	.15	.07
166	Bob Ojeda	.15	.07
167	Jerry Remy	.15	.07
168	Jim Rice	.40	.18
169	Bob Stanley	.15	.07
170	Mike Boddicker	.15	.07
171	Al Bumbry	.15	.07
172	Todd Cruz	.15	.07
173	Rich Dauer	.15	.07
174	Storm Davis	.15	.07
175	Rick Dempsey	.15	.07
176	Jim Dwyer	.15	.07
177	Mike Flanagan	.15	.07
178	Dan Ford	.15	.07
179	Wayne Gross	.15	.07
180	John Lowenstein	.15	.07
181	Dennis Martinez	.40	.18
182	Tippy Martinez	.15	.07
183	Scott McGregor	.15	.07
184	Eddie Murray	1.50	.70
185	Joe Nolan	.15	.07
186	Floyd Rayford	.15	.07
187	Cal Ripken	8.00	3.60
188	Gary Roenicke	.15	.07
189	Lenn Sakata	.15	.07
190	John Shelby	.15	.07
191	Ken Singleton	.15	.07
192	Sammy Stewart	.15	.07
193	Bill Swaggerty	.15	.07
194	Tom Underwood	.15	.07
195	Mike Young	.15	.07
196	Steve Balboni	.15	.07
197	Joe Beckwith	.15	.07
198	Bud Black	.15	.07
199	George Brett	3.00	1.35
200	Onix Concepcion	.15	.07
201	Mark Gubicza	.40	.18
202	Larry Gura	.15	.07
203	Mark Huismann	.15	.07
204	Dane Iorg	.15	.07
205	Danny Jackson	.15	.07
206	Charlie Leibrandt	.15	.07
207	Hal McRae	.40	.18
208	Darryl Motley	.15	.07
209	Jorge Orta	.15	.07

☐ 210	Greg Pryor	.15	.07
☐ 211	Dan Quisenberry	.40	.18
☐ 212	Bret Saberhagen	1.50	.70
☐ 213	Pat Sheridan	.15	.07
☐ 214	Don Slaught	.15	.07
☐ 215	U.L. Washington	.15	.07
☐ 216	John Wathan	.15	.07
☐ 217	Frank White	.40	.18
☐ 218	Willie Wilson	.15	.07
☐ 219	Neil Allen	.15	.07
☐ 220	Joaquin Andujar	.15	.07
☐ 221	Steve Braun	.15	.07
☐ 222	Danny Cox	.15	.07
☐ 223	Bob Forsch	.15	.07
☐ 224	David Green	.15	.07
☐ 225	George Hendrick	.15	.07
☐ 226	Tom Herr	.15	.07
☐ 227	Ricky Horton	.15	.07
☐ 228	Art Howe	.15	.07
☐ 229	Mike Jorgensen	.15	.07
☐ 230	Kurt Kepshire	.15	.07
☐ 231	Jeff Lahti	.15	.07
☐ 232	Tito Landrum	.15	.07
☐ 233	Dave LaPoint	.15	.07
☐ 234	Willie McGee	.40	.18
☐ 235	Tom Nieto	.15	.07
☐ 236	Terry Pendleton	1.50	.70
☐ 237	Darrell Porter	.15	.07
☐ 238	Dave Rucker	.15	.07
☐ 239	Lonnie Smith	.15	.07
☐ 240	Ozzie Smith	2.00	.90
☐ 241	Bruce Sutter	.40	.18
☐ 242	Andy Van Slyke UER	.75	.35
	(Bats Right,		
	Throws Left)		
☐ 243	Dave Von Ohlen	.15	.07
☐ 244	Larry Andersen	.15	.07
☐ 245	Bill Campbell	.15	.07
☐ 246	Steve Carlton	1.50	.70
☐ 247	Tim Corcoran	.15	.07
☐ 248	Ivan DeJesus	.15	.07
☐ 249	John Denny	.15	.07
☐ 250	Bo Diaz	.15	.07
☐ 251	Greg Gross	.15	.07
☐ 252	Kevin Gross	.15	.07
☐ 253	Von Hayes	.15	.07
☐ 254	Al Holland	.15	.07
☐ 255	Charles Hudson	.15	.07
☐ 256	Jerry Koosman	.15	.07
☐ 257	Joe Lefebvre	.15	.07
☐ 258	Sixto Lezcano	.15	.07
☐ 259	Garry Maddox	.15	.07
☐ 260	Len Matuszek	.15	.07
☐ 261	Tug McGraw	.40	.18
☐ 262	Al Oliver	.40	.18
☐ 263	Shane Rawley	.15	.07
☐ 264	Juan Samuel	.15	.07
☐ 265	Mike Schmidt	2.00	.90
☐ 266	Jeff Stone	.15	.07
☐ 267	Ozzie Virgil	.15	.07
☐ 268	Glenn Wilson	.15	.07
☐ 269	John Wockenfuss	.15	.07
☐ 270	Darrell Brown	.15	.07
☐ 271	Tom Brunansky	.40	.18
☐ 272	Randy Bush	.15	.07
☐ 273	John Butcher	.15	.07
☐ 274	Bobby Castillo	.15	.07
☐ 275	Ron Davis	.15	.07
☐ 276	Dave Engle	.15	.07
☐ 277	Pete Filson	.15	.07
☐ 278	Gary Gaetti	.40	.18
☐ 279	Mickey Hatcher	.15	.07
☐ 280	Ed Hodge	.15	.07
☐ 281	Kent Hrbek	.40	.18
☐ 282	Houston Jimenez	.15	.07
☐ 283	Tim Laudner	.15	.07
☐ 284	Rick Lysander	.15	.07
☐ 285	Dave Meier	.15	.07
☐ 286	Kirby Puckett	25.00	11.00
☐ 287	Pat Putnam	.15	.07
☐ 288	Ken Schrom	.15	.07
☐ 289	Mike Smithson	.15	.07
☐ 290	Tim Teufel	.15	.07
☐ 291	Frank Viola	.40	.18
☐ 292	Ron Washington	.15	.07
☐ 293	Don Aase	.15	.07
☐ 294	Juan Beniquez	.15	.07
☐ 295	Bob Boone	.40	.18
☐ 296	Mike C. Brown	.15	.07
☐ 297	Rod Carew	1.50	.70
☐ 298	Doug Corbett	.15	.07
☐ 299	Doug DeCinces	.15	.07
☐ 300	Brian Downing	.15	.07
☐ 301	Ken Forsch	.15	.07
☐ 302	Bobby Grich	.40	.18
☐ 303	Reggie Jackson	2.00	.90
☐ 304	Tommy John	.75	.35
☐ 305	Curt Kaufman	.15	.07
☐ 306	Bruce Kison	.15	.07
☐ 307	Fred Lynn	.40	.18
☐ 308	Gary Pettis	.15	.07
☐ 309	Ron Romanick	.15	.07
☐ 310	Luis Sanchez	.15	.07
☐ 311	Dick Schofield	.15	.07
☐ 312	Daryl Sconiers	.15	.07
☐ 313	Jim Slaton	.15	.07
☐ 314	Derrel Thomas	.15	.07
☐ 315	Rob Wilfong	.15	.07
☐ 316	Mike Witt	.15	.07
☐ 317	Geoff Zahn	.15	.07
☐ 318	Len Barker	.15	.07
☐ 319	Steve Bedrosian	.15	.07
☐ 320	Bruce Benedict	.15	.07
☐ 321	Rick Camp	.15	.07
☐ 322	Chris Chambliss	.15	.07
☐ 323	Jeff Dedmon	.15	.07
☐ 324	Terry Forster	.15	.07
☐ 325	Gene Garber	.15	.07
☐ 326	Albert Hall	.15	.07
☐ 327	Terry Harper	.15	.07
☐ 328	Bob Horner	.15	.07
☐ 329	Glenn Hubbard	.15	.07
☐ 330	Randy Johnson	.15	.07
☐ 331	Brad Komminsk	.15	.07
☐ 332	Rick Mahler	.15	.07
☐ 333	Craig McMurtry	.15	.07
☐ 334	Donnie Moore	.15	.07
☐ 335	Dale Murphy	1.50	.70
☐ 336	Ken Oberkfell	.15	.07
☐ 337	Pascual Perez	.15	.07
☐ 338	Gerald Perry	.15	.07
☐ 339	Rafael Ramirez	.15	.07
☐ 340	Jerry Royster	.15	.07
☐ 341	Alex Trevino	.15	.07
☐ 342	Claudell Washington	.15	.07
☐ 343	Alan Ashby	.15	.07
☐ 344	Mark Bailey	.15	.07
☐ 345	Kevin Bass	.15	.07
☐ 346	Enos Cabell	.15	.07
☐ 347	Jose Cruz	.40	.18
☐ 348	Bill Dawley	.15	.07
☐ 349	Frank DiPino	.15	.07
☐ 350	Bill Doran	.15	.07
☐ 351	Phil Garner	.15	.07
☐ 352	Bob Knepper	.15	.07
☐ 353	Mike LaCoss	.15	.07
☐ 354	Jerry Mumphrey	.15	.07
☐ 355	Joe Niekro	.15	.07
☐ 356	Terry Puhl	.15	.07
☐ 357	Craig Reynolds	.15	.07
☐ 358	Vern Ruhle	.15	.07
☐ 359	Nolan Ryan	8.00	3.60
☐ 360	Joe Sambito	.15	.07
☐ 361	Mike Scott	.15	.07
☐ 362	Dave Smith	.15	.07
☐ 363	Julio Solano	.15	.07
☐ 364	Dickie Thon	.15	.07
☐ 365	Denny Walling	.15	.07
☐ 366	Dave Anderson	.15	.07
☐ 367	Bob Bailor	.15	.07
☐ 368	Greg Brock	.15	.07
☐ 369	Carlos Diaz	.15	.07
☐ 370	Pedro Guerrero	.40	.18
☐ 371	Orel Hershiser	2.00	.90
☐ 372	Rick Honeycutt	.15	.07
☐ 373	Burt Hooton	.15	.07
☐ 374	Ken Howell	.15	.07
☐ 375	Ken Landreaux	.15	.07
☐ 376	Candy Maldonado	.15	.07
☐ 377	Mike Marshall	.15	.07
☐ 378	Tom Niedenfuer	.15	.07
☐ 379	Alejandro Pena	.15	.07
☐ 380	Jerry Reuss UER	.15	.07
	("Home:" omitted)		
☐ 381	R.J. Reynolds	.15	.07
☐ 382	German Rivera	.15	.07
☐ 383	Bill Russell	.15	.07
☐ 384	Steve Sax	.15	.07
☐ 385	Mike Scioscia	.15	.07
☐ 386	Franklin Stubbs	.15	.07
☐ 387	Fernando Valenzuela	.40	.18
☐ 388	Bob Welch	.15	.07
☐ 389	Terry Whitfield	.15	.07
☐ 390	Steve Yeager	.15	.07
☐ 391	Pat Zachry	.15	.07
☐ 392	Fred Breining	.15	.07
☐ 393	Gary Carter	1.50	.70
☐ 394	Andre Dawson	1.50	.70
☐ 395	Miguel Dilone	.15	.07
☐ 396	Dan Driessen	.15	.07
☐ 397	Doug Flynn	.15	.07
☐ 398	Terry Francona	.15	.07
☐ 399	Bill Gullickson	.15	.07
☐ 400	Bob James	.15	.07
☐ 401	Charlie Lea	.15	.07
☐ 402	Bryan Little	.15	.07
☐ 403	Gary Lucas	.15	.07
☐ 404	David Palmer	.15	.07
☐ 405	Tim Raines	.40	.18
☐ 406	Mike Ramsey	.15	.07
☐ 407	Jeff Reardon	.40	.18
☐ 408	Steve Rogers	.15	.07
☐ 409	Dan Schatzeder	.15	.07
☐ 410	Bryn Smith	.15	.07
☐ 411	Mike Stenhouse	.15	.07
☐ 412	Tim Wallach	.40	.18
☐ 413	Jim Wohlford	.15	.07
☐ 414	Bill Almon	.15	.07
☐ 415	Keith Atherton	.15	.07
☐ 416	Bruce Bochte	.15	.07
☐ 417	Tom Burgmeier	.15	.07
☐ 418	Ray Burris	.15	.07
☐ 419	Bill Caudill	.15	.07
☐ 420	Chris Codiroli	.15	.07
☐ 421	Tim Conroy	.15	.07
☐ 422	Mike Davis	.15	.07
☐ 423	Jim Essian	.15	.07
☐ 424	Mike Heath	.15	.07
☐ 425	Rickey Henderson	1.50	.70
☐ 426	Donnie Hill	.15	.07
☐ 427	Dave Kingman	.40	.18
☐ 428	Bill Krueger	.15	.07
☐ 429	Carney Lansford	.40	.18
☐ 430	Steve McCatty	.15	.07
☐ 431	Joe Morgan	1.50	.70
☐ 432	Dwayne Murphy	.15	.07
☐ 433	Tony Phillips	.15	.07
☐ 434	Lary Sorensen	.15	.07
☐ 435	Mike Warren	.15	.07
☐ 436	Curt Young	.15	.07
☐ 437	Luis Aponte	.15	.07
☐ 438	Chris Bando	.15	.07
☐ 439	Tony Bernazard	.15	.07
☐ 440	Bert Blyleven	.40	.18
☐ 441	Brett Butler	.40	.18
☐ 442	Ernie Camacho	.15	.07
☐ 443	Joe Carter	1.50	.70
☐ 444	Carmelo Castillo	.15	.07
☐ 445	Jamie Easterly	.15	.07
☐ 446	Steve Farr	.40	.18
☐ 447	Mike Fischlin	.15	.07
☐ 448	Julio Franco	.75	.35
☐ 449	Mel Hall	.15	.07
☐ 450	Mike Hargrove	.40	.18
☐ 451	Neal Heaton	.15	.07
☐ 452	Brook Jacoby	.15	.07
☐ 453	Mike Jeffcoat	.15	.07
☐ 454	Don Schulze	.15	.07
☐ 455	Roy Smith	.15	.07
☐ 456	Pat Tabler	.15	.07
☐ 457	Andre Thornton	.15	.07
☐ 458	George Vukovich	.15	.07
☐ 459	Tom Waddell	.15	.07
☐ 460	Jerry Willard	.15	.07
☐ 461	Dale Berra	.15	.07
☐ 462	John Candelaria	.15	.07
☐ 463	Jose DeLeon	.15	.07
☐ 464	Doug Frobel	.15	.07

☐ 465	Cecilio Guante	.15	.07
☐ 466	Brian Harper	.15	.07
☐ 467	Lee Lacy	.15	.07
☐ 468	Bill Madlock	.40	.18
☐ 469	Lee Mazzilli	.15	.07
☐ 470	Larry McWilliams	.15	.07
☐ 471	Jim Morrison	.15	.07
☐ 472	Tony Pena	.15	.07
☐ 473	Johnny Ray	.15	.07
☐ 474	Rick Rhoden	.15	.07
☐ 475	Don Robinson	.15	.07
☐ 476	Rod Scurry	.15	.07
☐ 477	Kent Tekulve	.15	.07
☐ 478	Jason Thompson	.15	.07
☐ 479	John Tudor	.15	.07
☐ 480	Lee Tunnell	.15	.07
☐ 481	Marvell Wynne	.15	.07
☐ 482	Salome Barojas	.15	.07
☐ 483	Dave Beard	.15	.07
☐ 484	Jim Beattie	.15	.07
☐ 485	Barry Bonnell	.15	.07
☐ 486	Phil Bradley	.40	.18
☐ 487	Al Cowens	.15	.07
☐ 488	Alvin Davis	.40	.18
☐ 489	Dave Henderson	.15	.07
☐ 490	Steve Henderson	.15	.07
☐ 491	Bob Kearney	.15	.07
☐ 492	Mark Langston	.75	.35
☐ 493	Larry Milbourne	.15	.07
☐ 494	Paul Mirabella	.15	.07
☐ 495	Mike Moore	.15	.07
☐ 496	Edwin Nunez	.15	.07
☐ 497	Spike Owen	.15	.07
☐ 498	Jack Perconte	.15	.07
☐ 499	Ken Phelps	.15	.07
☐ 500	Jim Presley	.40	.18
☐ 501	Mike Stanton	.15	.07
☐ 502	Bob Stoddard	.15	.07
☐ 503	Gorman Thomas	.15	.07
☐ 504	Ed VandeBerg	.15	.07
☐ 505	Matt Young	.15	.07
☐ 506	Juan Agosto	.15	.07
☐ 507	Harold Baines	.40	.18
☐ 508	Floyd Bannister	.15	.07
☐ 509	Britt Burns	.15	.07
☐ 510	Julio Cruz	.15	.07
☐ 511	Richard Dotson	.15	.07
☐ 512	Jerry Dybzinski	.15	.07
☐ 513	Carlton Fisk	1.50	.70
☐ 514	Scott Fletcher	.15	.07
☐ 515	Jerry Hairston	.15	.07
☐ 516	Marc Hill	.15	.07
☐ 517	LaMarr Hoyt	.15	.07
☐ 518	Ron Kittle	.15	.07
☐ 519	Rudy Law	.15	.07
☐ 520	Vance Law	.15	.07
☐ 521	Greg Luzinski	.40	.18
☐ 522	Gene Nelson	.15	.07
☐ 523	Tom Paciorek	.40	.18
☐ 524	Ron Reed	.15	.07
☐ 525	Bert Roberge	.15	.07
☐ 526	Tom Seaver	2.00	.90
☐ 527	Roy Smalley	.15	.07
☐ 528	Dan Spillner	.15	.07
☐ 529	Mike Squires	.15	.07
☐ 530	Greg Walker	.15	.07
☐ 531	Cesar Cedeno	.40	.18
☐ 532	Dave Concepcion	.40	.18
☐ 533	Eric Davis	2.00	.90
☐ 534	Nick Esasky	.15	.07
☐ 535	Tom Foley	.15	.07
☐ 536	John Franco UER	1.50	.70
	(Koufax misspelled as Kofax on back)		
☐ 537	Brad Gulden	.15	.07
☐ 538	Tom Hume	.15	.07
☐ 539	Wayne Krenchicki	.15	.07
☐ 540	Andy McGaffigan	.15	.07
☐ 541	Eddie Milner	.15	.07
☐ 542	Ron Oester	.15	.07
☐ 543	Bob Owchinko	.15	.07
☐ 544	Dave Parker	.40	.18
☐ 545	Frank Pastore	.15	.07
☐ 546	Tony Perez	1.50	.70
☐ 547	Ted Power	.15	.07
☐ 548	Joe Price	.15	.07
☐ 549	Gary Redus	.15	.07
☐ 550	Pete Rose	2.00	.90
☐ 551	Jeff Russell	.15	.07
☐ 552	Mario Soto	.15	.07
☐ 553	Jay Tibbs	.15	.07
☐ 554	Duane Walker	.15	.07
☐ 555	Alan Bannister	.15	.07
☐ 556	Buddy Bell	.40	.18
☐ 557	Danny Darwin	.15	.07
☐ 558	Charlie Hough	.40	.18
☐ 559	Bobby Jones	.15	.07
☐ 560	Odell Jones	.15	.07
☐ 561	Jeff Kunkel	.15	.07
☐ 562	Mike Mason	.15	.07
☐ 563	Pete O'Brien	.15	.07
☐ 564	Larry Parrish	.15	.07
☐ 565	Mickey Rivers	.15	.07
☐ 566	Billy Sample	.15	.07
☐ 567	Dave Schmidt	.15	.07
☐ 568	Donnie Scott	.15	.07
☐ 569	Dave Stewart	.40	.18
☐ 570	Frank Tanana	.15	.07
☐ 571	Wayne Tolleson	.15	.07
☐ 572	Gary Ward	.15	.07
☐ 573	Curtis Wilkerson	.15	.07
☐ 574	George Wright	.15	.07
☐ 575	Ned Yost	.15	.07
☐ 576	Mark Brouhard	.15	.07
☐ 577	Mike Caldwell	.15	.07
☐ 578	Bobby Clark	.15	.07
☐ 579	Jaime Cocanower	.15	.07
☐ 580	Cecil Cooper	.40	.18
☐ 581	Rollie Fingers	1.50	.70
☐ 582	Jim Gantner	.15	.07
☐ 583	Moose Haas	.15	.07
☐ 584	Dion James	.15	.07
☐ 585	Pete Ladd	.15	.07
☐ 586	Rick Manning	.15	.07
☐ 587	Bob McClure	.15	.07
☐ 588	Paul Molitor	1.50	.70
☐ 589	Charlie Moore	.15	.07
☐ 590	Ben Oglivie	.15	.07
☐ 591	Chuck Porter	.15	.07
☐ 592	Randy Ready	.15	.07
☐ 593	Ed Romero	.15	.07
☐ 594	Bill Schroeder	.15	.07
☐ 595	Ray Searage	.15	.07
☐ 596	Ted Simmons	.40	.18
☐ 597	Jim Sundberg	.15	.07
☐ 598	Don Sutton	1.50	.70
☐ 599	Tom Tellmann	.15	.07
☐ 600	Rick Waits	.15	.07
☐ 601	Robin Yount	1.50	.70
☐ 602	Dusty Baker	.40	.18
☐ 603	Bob Brenly	.15	.07
☐ 604	Jack Clark	.40	.18
☐ 605	Chili Davis	.40	.18
☐ 606	Mark Davis	.15	.07
☐ 607	Dan Gladden	.40	.18
☐ 608	Atlee Hammaker	.15	.07
☐ 609	Mike Krukow	.15	.07
☐ 610	Duane Kuiper	.15	.07
☐ 611	Bob Lacey	.15	.07
☐ 612	Bill Laskey	.15	.07
☐ 613	Gary Lavelle	.15	.07
☐ 614	Johnnie LeMaster	.15	.07
☐ 615	Jeff Leonard	.15	.07
☐ 616	Randy Lerch	.15	.07
☐ 617	Greg Minton	.15	.07
☐ 618	Steve Nicosia	.15	.07
☐ 619	Gene Richards	.15	.07
☐ 620	Jeff D. Robinson	.15	.07
☐ 621	Scot Thompson	.15	.07
☐ 622	Manny Trillo	.15	.07
☐ 623	Brad Wellman	.15	.07
☐ 624	Frank Williams	.15	.07
☐ 625	Joel Youngblood	.15	.07
☐ 626	Cal Ripken IA	4.00	1.80
☐ 627	Mike Schmidt IA	1.00	.45
☐ 628	Giving The Signs, Sparky Anderson	.40	.18
☐ 629	AL Pitcher's Nightmare, Dave Winfield, Rickey Henderson	1.50	.70
☐ 630	NL Pitcher's Nightmare, Mike Schmidt, Ryne Sandberg	1.50	.70
☐ 631	NL All-Stars, Darryl Strawberry, Gary Carter, Steve Garvey, Ozzie Smith	.75	.35
☐ 632	A-S Winning Battery, Gary Carter, Charlie Lea	.75	.35
☐ 633	NL Pennant Clinchers, Steve Garvey, Rich Gossage	.75	.35
☐ 634	NL Rookie Phenoms, Dwight Gooden, Juan Samuel	1.50	.70
☐ 635	Toronto's Big Guns, Willie Upshaw	.15	.07
☐ 636	Toronto's Big Guns, Lloyd Moseby	.15	.07
☐ 637	HOLLAND: Al Holland	.15	.07
☐ 638	TUNNELL: Lee Tunnell	.15	.07
☐ 639	500th Homer, Reggie Jackson	1.00	.45
☐ 640	4000th Hit, Pete Rose	1.00	.45
☐ 641	Father and Son, Cal Ripken Jr., Cal Ripken Sr.	4.00	1.80
☐ 642	Cubs: Division Champs	.40	.18
☐ 643	Two Perfect Games and One No-Hitter: Mike Witt, David Palmer, Jack Morris	.40	.18
☐ 644	Willie Lozado and Vic Mata	.15	.07
☐ 645	Kelly Gruber and Randy O'Neal	.40	.18
☐ 646	Jose Roman and Joel Skinner	.15	.07
☐ 647	Steve Kiefer and Danny Tartabull	1.50	.70
☐ 648	Rob Deer and Alejandro Sanchez	.40	.18
☐ 649	Billy Hatcher and Shawon Dunston	1.50	.70
☐ 650	Ron Robinson and Mike Bielecki	.15	.07
☐ 651	Zane Smith and Paul Zuvella	.40	.18
☐ 652	Joe Hesketh and Glenn Davis	.40	.18
☐ 653	John Russell and Steve Jeltz	.15	.07
☐ 654	CL: Tigers/Padres and Cubs/Mets	.15	.07
☐ 655	CL: Blue Jays/Yankees and Red Sox/Orioles	.15	.07
☐ 656	CL: Royals/Cardinals and Phillies/Twins	.15	.07
☐ 657	CL: Angels/Braves and Astros/Dodgers	.15	.07
☐ 658	CL: Expos/A's and Indians/Pirates	.15	.07
☐ 659	CL: Mariners/White Sox and Reds/Rangers	.15	.07
☐ 660	CL: Brewers/Giants and Special Cards	.15	.07

1985 Fleer Update

This 132-card standard-size update set was issued in factory set form exclusively through hobby dealers. Design is identical to the regular-issue 1985 Fleer cards except for the U prefixed card numbers on back. Cards are ordered alphabetically by the player's name. This set features the extended Rookie Cards of Vince Coleman, Darren Daulton, Mariano Duncan, Ozzie Guillen and Mickey Tettleton.

	NRMT	VG-E
COMP.FACT.SET (132)	12.00	5.50
COMMON CARD (1-132)	.15	.07
MINOR STARS	.40	.18
SEMISTARS	.75	.35

		NRMT	VG-E
☐ 1	Don Aase	.15	.07
☐ 2	Bill Almon	.15	.07
☐ 3	Dusty Baker	.40	.18
☐ 4	Dale Berra	.15	.07
☐ 5	Karl Best	.15	.07
☐ 6	Tim Birtsas	.15	.07
☐ 7	Vida Blue	.40	.18
☐ 8	Rich Bordi	.15	.07
☐ 9	Daryl Boston	.15	.07
☐ 10	Hubie Brooks	.15	.07
☐ 11	Chris Brown	.15	.07
☐ 12	Tom Browning	.40	.18
☐ 13	Al Bumbry	.15	.07
☐ 14	Tim Burke	.15	.07
☐ 15	Ray Burris	.15	.07
☐ 16	Jeff Burroughs	.15	.07
☐ 17	Ivan Calderon	.15	.07
☐ 18	Jeff Calhoun	.15	.07
☐ 19	Bill Campbell	.15	.07
☐ 20	Don Carman	.15	.07
☐ 21	Gary Carter	.75	.35
☐ 22	Bobby Castillo	.15	.07
☐ 23	Bill Caudill	.15	.07
☐ 24	Rick Cerone	.15	.07
☐ 25	Jack Clark	.40	.18
☐ 26	Pat Clements	.15	.07
☐ 27	Stewart Cliburn	.15	.07
☐ 28	Vince Coleman	.75	.35
☐ 29	Dave Collins	.15	.07
☐ 30	Fritz Connally	.15	.07
☐ 31	Henry Cotto	.15	.07
☐ 32	Danny Darwin	.15	.07
☐ 33	Darren Daulton	8.00	3.60
☐ 34	Jerry Davis	.15	.07
☐ 35	Brian Dayett	.15	.07
☐ 36	Ken Dixon	.15	.07
☐ 37	Tommy Dunbar	.15	.07
☐ 38	Mariano Duncan	.75	.35
☐ 39	Bob Fallon	.15	.07
☐ 40	Brian Fisher	.15	.07
☐ 41	Mike Fitzgerald	.15	.07
☐ 42	Ray Fontenot	.15	.07
☐ 43	Greg Gagne	.40	.18
☐ 44	Oscar Gamble	.15	.07
☐ 45	Jim Gott	.15	.07
☐ 46	David Green	.15	.07
☐ 47	Alfredo Griffin	.15	.07
☐ 48	Ozzie Guillen	1.50	.70
☐ 49	Toby Harrah	.15	.07
☐ 50	Ron Hassey	.15	.07
☐ 51	Rickey Henderson	1.00	.45
☐ 52	Steve Henderson	.15	.07
☐ 53	George Hendrick	.15	.07
☐ 54	Teddy Higuera	.40	.18
☐ 55	Al Holland	.15	.07
☐ 56	Burt Hooton	.15	.07
☐ 57	Jay Howell	.15	.07
☐ 58	LaMarr Hoyt	.15	.07
☐ 59	Tim Hulett	.15	.07
☐ 60	Bob James	.15	.07
☐ 61	Cliff Johnson	.15	.07
☐ 62	Howard Johnson	.40	.18

☐ 63	Ruppert Jones	.15	.07
☐ 64	Steve Kemp	.15	.07
☐ 65	Bruce Kison	.15	.07
☐ 66	Mike LaCoss	.15	.07
☐ 67	Lee Lacy	.15	.07
☐ 68	Dave LaPoint	.15	.07
☐ 69	Gary Lavelle	.15	.07
☐ 70	Vance Law	.15	.07
☐ 71	Manny Lee	.15	.07
☐ 72	Sixto Lezcano	.15	.07
☐ 73	Tim Lollar	.15	.07
☐ 74	Urbano Lugo	.15	.07
☐ 75	Fred Lynn	.40	.18
☐ 76	Steve Lyons	.40	.18
☐ 77	Mickey Mahler	.15	.07
☐ 78	Ron Mathis	.15	.07
☐ 79	Len Matuszek	.15	.07
☐ 80	Oddibe McDowell UER	.40	.18
	(Part of bio		
	actually Roger's)		
☐ 81	Roger McDowell UER	.40	.18
	(Part of bio		
	actually Oddibe's)		
☐ 82	Donnie Moore	.15	.07
☐ 83	Ron Musselman	.15	.07
☐ 84	Al Oliver	.15	.07
☐ 85	Joe Orsulak	.40	.18
☐ 86	Dan Pasqua	.40	.18
☐ 87	Chris Pittaro	.15	.07
☐ 88	Rick Reuschel	.15	.07
☐ 89	Earnie Riles	.15	.07
☐ 90	Jerry Royster	.15	.07
☐ 91	Dave Rozema	.15	.07
☐ 92	Dave Rucker	.15	.07
☐ 93	Vern Ruhle	.15	.07
☐ 94	Mark Salas	.15	.07
☐ 95	Luis Salazar	.15	.07
☐ 96	Joe Sambito	.15	.07
☐ 97	Billy Sample	.15	.07
☐ 98	Alejandro Sanchez	.15	.07
☐ 99	Calvin Schiraldi	.15	.07
☐ 100	Rick Schu	.15	.07
☐ 101	Larry Sheets	.15	.07
☐ 102	Ron Shephard	.15	.07
☐ 103	Nelson Simmons	.15	.07
☐ 104	Don Slaught	.15	.07
☐ 105	Roy Smalley	.15	.07
☐ 106	Lonnie Smith	.15	.07
☐ 107	Nate Snell	.15	.07
☐ 108	Lary Sorensen	.15	.07
☐ 109	Chris Speier	.15	.07
☐ 110	Mike Stenhouse	.15	.07
☐ 111	Tim Stoddard	.15	.07
☐ 112	John Stuper	.15	.07
☐ 113	Jim Sundberg	.15	.07
☐ 114	Bruce Sutter	.40	.18
☐ 115	Don Sutton	.75	.35
☐ 116	Bruce Tanner	.15	.07
☐ 117	Kent Tekulve	.15	.07
☐ 118	Walt Terrell	.15	.07
☐ 119	Mickey Tettleton	1.50	.70
☐ 120	Rich Thompson	.15	.07
☐ 121	Louis Thornton	.15	.07
☐ 122	Alex Trevino	.15	.07
☐ 123	John Tudor	.15	.07
☐ 124	Jose Uribe	.15	.07
☐ 125	Dave Valle	.15	.07
☐ 126	Dave Von Ohlen	.15	.07
☐ 127	Curt Wardle	.15	.07
☐ 128	U.L. Washington	.15	.07
☐ 129	Ed Whitson	.15	.07
☐ 130	Herm Winningham	.15	.07
☐ 131	Rich Yett	.15	.07
☐ 132	Checklist U1-U132	.15	.07

1986 Fleer

The 1986 Fleer set consists of 660-card standard-size cards. Wax packs included 15 cards plus logo stickers. Card fronts feature dark blue borders, a team logo along with the player's name and position. The player cards are alphabetized within team and the teams are ordered by their 1985 season finish and won-lost record. Subsets include Specials (626-643) and Major League Prospects (644-653). The Dennis and Tippy Martinez cards were apparently switched in the set numbering, as their adjacent numbers (279 and 280) were reversed on the Orioles checklist card. The set includes the Rookie Cards of Rick Aguilera, Jose Canseco, Darren Daulton, Len Dykstra, Cecil Fielder, Andres Galarraga, Paul O'Neill, and Mickey Tettleton.

	MINT	NRMT
COMPLETE SET (660)	40.00	18.00
COMMON CARD (1-660)	.10	.05
MINOR STARS	.25	.11
SEMISTARS	.50	.23
UNLISTED STARS	1.00	.45

		MINT	NRMT
☐ 1	Steve Balboni	.10	.05
☐ 2	Joe Beckwith	.10	.05
☐ 3	Buddy Biancalana	.10	.05
☐ 4	Bud Black	.10	.05
☐ 5	George Brett	2.00	.90
☐ 6	Onix Concepcion	.10	.05
☐ 7	Steve Farr	.10	.05
☐ 8	Mark Gubicza	.10	.05
☐ 9	Dane Iorg	.10	.05
☐ 10	Danny Jackson	.10	.05
☐ 11	Lynn Jones	.10	.05
☐ 12	Mike Jones	.10	.05
☐ 13	Charlie Leibrandt	.10	.05
☐ 14	Hal McRae	.25	.11
☐ 15	Omar Moreno	.10	.05
☐ 16	Darryl Motley	.10	.05
☐ 17	Jorge Orta	.10	.05
☐ 18	Dan Quisenberry	.10	.05
☐ 19	Bret Saberhagen	.25	.11
☐ 20	Pat Sheridan	.10	.05
☐ 21	Lonnie Smith	.10	.05
☐ 22	Jim Sundberg	.10	.05
☐ 23	John Wathan	.10	.05
☐ 24	Frank White	.25	.11
☐ 25	Willie Wilson	.10	.05
☐ 26	Joaquin Andujar	.10	.05
☐ 27	Steve Braun	.10	.05
☐ 28	Bill Campbell	.10	.05
☐ 29	Cesar Cedeno	.25	.11
☐ 30	Jack Clark	.25	.11
☐ 31	Vince Coleman	1.00	.45
☐ 32	Danny Cox	.10	.05
☐ 33	Ken Dayley	.10	.05
☐ 34	Ivan DeJesus	.10	.05
☐ 35	Bob Forsch	.10	.05
☐ 36	Brian Harper	.10	.05
☐ 37	Tom Herr	.10	.05
☐ 38	Ricky Horton	.10	.05
☐ 39	Kurt Kepshire	.10	.05
☐ 40	Jeff Lahti	.10	.05
☐ 41	Tito Landrum	.10	.05
☐ 42	Willie McGee	.25	.11

43	Tom Nieto	.10	.05
44	Terry Pendleton	.50	.23
45	Darrell Porter	.25	.11
46	Ozzie Smith	1.25	.55
47	John Tudor	.10	.05
48	Andy Van Slyke	.25	.11
49	Todd Worrell	1.00	.45
50	Jim Acker	.10	.05
51	Doyle Alexander	.10	.05
52	Jesse Barfield	.10	.05
53	George Bell	.25	.11
54	Jeff Burroughs	.10	.05
55	Bill Caudill	.10	.05
56	Jim Clancy	.10	.05
57	Tony Fernandez	.25	.11
58	Tom Filer	.10	.05
59	Damaso Garcia	.10	.05
60	Tom Henke	.25	.11
61	Garth Iorg	.10	.05
62	Cliff Johnson	.10	.05
63	Jimmy Key	1.00	.45
64	Dennis Lamp	.10	.05
65	Gary Lavelle	.10	.05
66	Buck Martinez	.10	.05
67	Lloyd Moseby	.10	.05
68	Rance Mulliniks	.10	.05
69	Al Oliver	.25	.11
70	Dave Stieb	.10	.05
71	Louis Thornton	.10	.05
72	Willie Upshaw	.10	.05
73	Ernie Whitt	.10	.05
74	Rick Aguilera	1.00	.45
75	Wally Backman	.10	.05
76	Gary Carter	1.00	.45
77	Ron Darling	.10	.05
78	Len Dykstra	2.00	.90
79	Sid Fernandez	.25	.11
80	George Foster	.25	.11
81	Dwight Gooden	1.00	.45
82	Tom Gorman	.10	.05
83	Danny Heep	.10	.05
84	Keith Hernandez	.25	.11
85	Howard Johnson	.25	.11
86	Ray Knight	.25	.11
87	Terry Leach	.10	.05
88	Ed Lynch	.10	.05
89	Roger McDowell	.25	.11
90	Jesse Orosco	.10	.05
91	Tom Paciorek	.25	.11
92	Ronn Reynolds	.10	.05
93	Rafael Santana	.10	.05
94	Doug Sisk	.10	.05
95	Rusty Staub	.25	.11
96	Darryl Strawberry	1.00	.45
97	Mookie Wilson	.25	.11
98	Neil Allen	.10	.05
99	Don Baylor	.50	.23
100	Dale Berra	.10	.05
101	Rich Bordi	.10	.05
102	Marty Bystrom	.10	.05
103	Joe Cowley	.10	.05
104	Brian Fisher	.10	.05
105	Ken Griffey	.25	.11
106	Ron Guidry	.25	.11
107	Ron Hassey	.10	.05
108	Rickey Henderson UER (SB Record of 120, sic)	1.00	.45
109	Don Mattingly	1.50	.70
110	Bobby Meacham	.10	.05
111	John Montefusco	.10	.05
112	Phil Niekro	1.00	.45
113	Mike Pagliarulo	.10	.05
114	Dan Pasqua	.10	.05
115	Willie Randolph	.25	.11
116	Dave Righetti	.10	.05
117	Andre Robertson	.10	.05
118	Billy Sample	.10	.05
119	Bob Shirley	.10	.05
120	Ed Whitson	.10	.05
121	Dave Winfield	1.00	.45
122	Butch Wynegar	.10	.05
123	Dave Anderson	.10	.05
124	Bob Bailor	.10	.05
125	Greg Brock	.10	.05
126	Enos Cabell	.10	.05
127	Bobby Castillo	.10	
128	Carlos Diaz	.10	.05
129	Mariano Duncan	1.00	.45
130	Pedro Guerrero	.25	.11
131	Orel Hershiser	.50	.23
132	Rick Honeycutt	.10	.05
133	Ken Howell	.10	.05
134	Ken Landreaux	.10	.05
135	Bill Madlock	.10	.05
136	Candy Maldonado	.10	.05
137	Mike Marshall	.10	.05
138	Len Matuszek	.10	.05
139	Tom Niedenfuer	.10	.05
140	Alejandro Pena	.10	.05
141	Jerry Reuss	.10	.05
142	Bill Russell	.25	.11
143	Steve Sax	.10	.05
144	Mike Scioscia	.10	.05
145	Fernando Valenzuela	.25	.11
146	Bob Welch	.10	.05
147	Terry Whitfield	.10	.05
148	Juan Beniquez	.10	.05
149	Bob Boone	.25	.11
150	John Candelaria	.10	.05
151	Rod Carew	1.00	.45
152	Stewart Cliburn	.10	.05
153	Doug DeCinces	.10	.05
154	Brian Downing	.10	.05
155	Ken Forsch	.10	.05
156	Craig Gerber	.10	.05
157	Bobby Grich	.25	.11
158	George Hendrick	.10	.05
159	Al Holland	.10	.05
160	Reggie Jackson	1.25	.55
161	Ruppert Jones	.10	.05
162	Urbano Lugo	.10	.05
163	Kirk McCaskill	.25	.11
164	Donnie Moore	.10	.05
165	Gary Pettis	.10	.05
166	Ron Romanick	.10	.05
167	Dick Schofield	.10	.05
168	Daryl Sconiers	.10	.05
169	Jim Slaton	.10	.05
170	Don Sutton	1.00	.45
171	Mike Witt	.10	.05
172	Buddy Bell	.25	.11
173	Tom Browning	.10	.05
174	Dave Concepcion	.25	.11
175	Eric Davis	.50	.23
176	Bo Diaz	.10	.05
177	Nick Esasky	.10	.05
178	John Franco	1.00	.45
179	Tom Hume	.10	.05
180	Wayne Krenchicki	.10	.05
181	Andy McGaffigan	.10	.05
182	Eddie Milner	.10	.05
183	Ron Oester	.10	.05
184	Dave Parker	.25	.11
185	Frank Pastore	.10	.05
186	Tony Perez	1.00	.45
187	Ted Power	.10	.05
188	Joe Price	.10	.05
189	Gary Redus	.10	.05
190	Ron Robinson	.10	.05
191	Pete Rose	1.25	.55
192	Mario Soto	.10	.05
193	John Stuper	.10	.05
194	Jay Tibbs	.10	.05
195	Dave Van Gorder	.10	.05
196	Max Venable	.10	.05
197	Juan Agosto	.10	.05
198	Harold Baines	.50	.23
199	Floyd Bannister	.10	.05
200	Britt Burns	.10	.05
201	Julio Cruz	.10	.05
202	Joel Davis	.10	.05
203	Richard Dotson	.10	.05
204	Carlton Fisk	1.00	.45
205	Scott Fletcher	.10	.05
206	Ozzie Guillen	.50	.23
207	Jerry Hairston	.10	.05
208	Tim Hulett	.10	.05
209	Bob James	.10	.05
210	Ron Kittle	.10	.05
211	Rudy Law	.10	.05
212	Bryan Little	.10	.05
213	Gene Nelson	.10	.05
214	Reid Nichols	.10	.05
215	Luis Salazar	.10	.05
216	Tom Seaver	1.25	.55
217	Dan Spillner	.10	.05
218	Bruce Tanner	.10	.05
219	Greg Walker	.10	.05
220	Dave Wehrmeister	.10	.05
221	Juan Berenguer	.10	.05
222	Dave Bergman	.10	.05
223	Tom Brookens	.10	.05
224	Darrell Evans	.25	.11
225	Barbaro Garbey	.10	.05
226	Kirk Gibson	.25	.11
227	John Grubb	.10	.05
228	Willie Hernandez	.10	.05
229	Larry Herndon	.10	.05
230	Chet Lemon	.10	.05
231	Aurelio Lopez	.10	.05
232	Jack Morris	.25	.11
233	Randy O'Neal	.10	.05
234	Lance Parrish	.25	.11
235	Dan Petry	.10	.05
236	Alejandro Sanchez	.10	.05
237	Bill Scherrer	.10	.05
238	Nelson Simmons	.10	.05
239	Frank Tanana	.10	.05
240	Walt Terrell	.10	.05
241	Alan Trammell	.50	.23
242	Lou Whitaker	.25	.11
243	Milt Wilcox	.10	.05
244	Hubie Brooks	.10	.05
245	Tim Burke	.10	.05
246	Andre Dawson	1.00	.45
247	Mike Fitzgerald	.10	.05
248	Terry Francona	.10	.05
249	Bill Gullickson	.10	.05
250	Joe Hesketh	.10	.05
251	Bill Laskey	.10	.05
252	Vance Law	.10	.05
253	Charlie Lea	.10	.05
254	Gary Lucas	.10	.05
255	David Palmer	.10	.05
256	Tim Raines	.25	.11
257	Jeff Reardon	.25	.11
258	Bert Roberge	.10	.05
259	Dan Schatzeder	.10	.05
260	Bryn Smith	.10	.05
261	Randy St.Claire	.10	.05
262	Scot Thompson	.10	.05
263	Tim Wallach	.10	.05
264	U.L. Washington	.10	.05
265	Mitch Webster	.10	.05
266	Herm Winningham	.10	.05
267	Floyd Youmans	.10	.05
268	Don Aase	.10	.05
269	Mike Boddicker	.10	.05
270	Rich Dauer	.10	.05
271	Storm Davis	.10	.05
272	Rick Dempsey	.10	.05
273	Ken Dixon	.10	.05
274	Jim Dwyer	.10	.05
275	Mike Flanagan	.10	.05
276	Wayne Gross	.10	.05
277	Lee Lacy	.10	.05
278	Fred Lynn	.25	.11
279	Tippy Martinez	.10	.05
280	Dennis Martinez	.25	.11
281	Scott McGregor	.10	.05
282	Eddie Murray	1.00	.45
283	Floyd Rayford	.10	.05
284	Cal Ripken	4.00	1.80
285	Gary Roenicke	.10	.05
286	Larry Sheets	.10	.05
287	John Shelby	.10	.05
288	Nate Snell	.10	.05
289	Sammy Stewart	.10	.05
290	Alan Wiggins	.10	.05
291	Mike Young	.10	.05
292	Alan Ashby	.10	.05
293	Mark Bailey	.10	.05
294	Kevin Bass	.10	.05
295	Jeff Calhoun	.10	.05
296	Jose Cruz	.25	.11
297	Glenn Davis	.25	.11
298	Bill Dawley	.10	.05
299	Frank DiPino	.10	.05

☐ 556 Alan Bannister	.10	.05
☐ 557 Glenn Brummer	.10	.05
☐ 558 Steve Buechele	.25	.11
☐ 559 Jose Guzman	.10	.05
☐ 560 Toby Harrah	.10	.05
☐ 561 Greg Harris	.10	.05
☐ 562 Dwayne Henry	.10	.05
☐ 563 Burt Hooton	.10	.05
☐ 564 Charlie Hough	.25	.11
☐ 565 Mike Mason	.10	.05
☐ 566 Oddibe McDowell	.10	.05
☐ 567 Dickie Noies	.10	.05
☐ 568 Pete O'Brien	.10	.05
☐ 569 Larry Parrish	.10	.05
☐ 570 Dave Rozema	.10	.05
☐ 571 Dave Schmidt	.10	.05
☐ 572 Don Slaught	.10	.05
☐ 573 Wayne Tolleson	.10	.05
☐ 574 Duane Walker	.10	.05
☐ 575 Gary Ward	.10	.05
☐ 576 Chris Welsh	.10	.05
☐ 577 Curtis Wilkerson	.10	.05
☐ 578 George Wright	.10	.05
☐ 579 Chris Bando	.10	.05
☐ 580 Tony Bernazard	.10	.05
☐ 581 Brett Butler	.25	.11
☐ 582 Ernie Camacho	.10	.05
☐ 583 Joe Carter	1.00	.45
☐ 584 Carmen Castillo	.10	.05
☐ 585 Jamie Easterly	.10	.05
☐ 586 Julio Franco	.25	.11
☐ 587 Mel Hall	.10	.05
☐ 588 Mike Hargrove	.25	.11
☐ 589 Neal Heaton	.10	.05
☐ 590 Brook Jacoby	.10	.05
☐ 591 Otis Nixon	1.00	.45
☐ 592 Jerry Reed	.10	.05
☐ 593 Vern Ruhle	.10	.05
☐ 594 Pat Tabler	.10	.05
☐ 595 Rich Thompson	.10	.05
☐ 596 Andre Thornton	.10	.05
☐ 597 Dave Von Ohlen	.10	.05
☐ 598 George Vukovich	.10	.05
☐ 599 Tom Waddell	.10	.05
☐ 600 Curt Wardle	.10	.05
☐ 601 Jerry Willard	.10	.05
☐ 602 Bill Almon	.10	.05
☐ 603 Mike Bielecki	.10	.05
☐ 604 Sid Bream	.10	.05
☐ 605 Mike C. Brown	.10	.05
☐ 606 Pat Clements	.10	.05
☐ 607 Jose DeLeon	.10	.05
☐ 608 Denny Gonzalez	.10	.05
☐ 609 Cecilio Guante	.10	.05
☐ 610 Steve Kemp	.10	.05
☐ 611 Sammy Khalifa	.10	.05
☐ 612 Lee Mazzilli	.10	.05
☐ 613 Larry McWilliams	.10	.05
☐ 614 Jim Morrison	.10	.05
☐ 615 Joe Orsulak	.10	.05
☐ 616 Tony Pena	.10	.05
☐ 617 Johnny Ray	.10	.05
☐ 618 Rick Reuschel	.10	.05
☐ 619 R.J. Reynolds	.10	.05
☐ 620 Rick Rhoden	.10	.05
☐ 621 Don Robinson	.10	.05
☐ 622 Jason Thompson	.10	.05
☐ 623 Lee Tunnell	.10	.05
☐ 624 Jim Winn	.10	.05
☐ 625 Marvell Wynne	.10	.05
☐ 626 Dwight Gooden IA	.25	.11
☐ 627 Don Mattingly IA	1.25	.55
☐ 628 4192 (Pete Rose)	.60	.25
☐ 629 3000 Career Hits	1.00	.45
Rod Carew		
☐ 630 300 Career Wins	1.00	.45
Tom Seaver		
Phil Niekro		
☐ 631 Ouch (Don Baylor)	.25	.11
☐ 632 Instant Offense	.50	.23
Darryl Strawberry		
Tim Raines		
☐ 633 Shortstops Supreme	2.00	.90
Cal Ripken		
Alan Trammell		
☐ 634 Boggs and "Hero"	1.00	.45

Wade Boggs		
George Brett		
☐ 635 Braves Dynamic Duo	.25	.11
Bob Horner		
Dale Murphy		
☐ 636 Cardinal Ignitors	.25	.11
Willie McGee		
Vince Coleman		
☐ 637 Terror on Basepaths	.25	.11
Vince Coleman		
☐ 638 Charlie Hustle / Dr.K	1.00	.45
Pete Rose		
Dwight Gooden		
☐ 639 1984 and 1985 AL	1.00	.45
Batting Champs		
Wade Boggs		
Don Mattingly		
☐ 640 NL West Sluggers	.25	.11
Dale Murphy		
Steve Garvey		
Dave Parker		
☐ 641 Staff Aces	.25	.11
Fernando Valenzuela		
Dwight Gooden		
☐ 642 Blue Jay Stoppers	.25	.11
Jimmy Key		
Dave Stieb		
☐ 643 AL All-Star Backstops	.25	.11
Carlton Fisk		
Rich Gedman		
☐ 644 Gene Walter and	1.00	.45
Benito Santiago		
☐ 645 Mike Woodard and	.10	.05
Colin Ward		
☐ 646 Kal Daniels and	2.00	.90
Paul O'Neill		
☐ 647 Andres Galarraga and	6.00	2.70
Fred Toliver		
☐ 648 Bob Kipper and	.10	.05
Curt Ford		
☐ 649 Jose Canseco and	8.00	3.60
Eric Plunk		
☐ 650 Mark McLemore and	1.00	.45
Gus Polidor		
☐ 651 Rob Woodward and	.10	.05
Mickey Brantley		
☐ 652 Billy Joe Robidoux and	.10	.05
Mark Funderburk		
☐ 653 Cecil Fielder and	3.00	1.35
Cory Snyder		
☐ 654 CL: Royals/Cardinals	.10	.05
Blue Jays/Mets		
☐ 655 CL: Yankees/Dodgers	.10	.05
Angels/Reds UER		
(168 Darly Sconiers)		
☐ 656 CL: White Sox/Tigers	.10	.05
Expos/Orioles		
(279 Dennis,		
280 Tippy)		
☐ 657 CL: Astros/Padres	.10	.05
Red Sox/Cubs		
☐ 658 CL: Twins/A's	.10	.05
Phillies/Mariners		
☐ 659 CL: Brewers/Braves	.10	.45
Giants/Rangers		
☐ 660 CL: Indians/Pirates	.10	.05
Special Cards		

1986 Fleer All-Stars

Randomly inserted in wax and cello packs, this 12-card standard-size set features top stars. The cards feature red backgrounds (American Leaguers) and blue backgrounds (National Leaguers). The 12 selections cover each position, left and right-handed starting pitchers, a reliever, and a designated hitter.

Cal Ripken, Jr.
ORIOLES · SHORTSTOP

	MINT	NRMT
COMPLETE SET (12)	30.00	13.50
COMMON CARD (1-12)	.25	.11
RANDOM INSERTS IN PACKS		

☐ 1 Don Mattingly	6.00	2.70
☐ 2 Tom Herr	.25	.11
☐ 3 George Brett	6.00	2.70
☐ 4 Gary Carter	.75	.35
☐ 5 Cal Ripken	15.00	6.75
☐ 6 Dave Parker	.35	.16
☐ 7 Rickey Henderson UER	2.50	1.10
(Misspelled Ricky		
on card back)		
☐ 8 Pedro Guerrero	.35	.16
☐ 9 Dan Quisenberry	.25	.11
☐ 10 Dwight Gooden	.75	.35
☐ 11 Gorman Thomas	.25	.11
☐ 12 John Tudor	.25	.11

1986 Fleer Future Hall of Famers

Tom Seaver
WHITE SOX · PITCHER

These six standard-size cards were issued one per Fleer three-packs. This set features players that Fleer predicts will be "Future Hall of Famers." The card backs describe career highlights, records, and honors won by the player.

	MINT	NRMT
COMPLETE SET (6)	15.00	6.75
COMMON CARD (1-6)	2.00	.90
ONE PER RACK PACK		

☐ 1 Pete Rose	3.00	1.35
☐ 2 Steve Carlton	2.00	.90
☐ 3 Tom Seaver	2.00	.90
☐ 4 Rod Carew	2.00	.90
☐ 5 Nolan Ryan	10.00	4.50
☐ 6 Reggie Jackson	2.50	1.10

1986 Fleer Update

This 132-card standard-size set was distributed in factory set form through hobby dealers. In addition to the complete set of 132 cards, the box also contains 25 Team Logo Stickers. The card fronts look very similar to the 1986 Fleer regular issue. The cards are numbered (with a U prefix) alphabetically according to player's last name. The extended Rookie Cards in this set include Barry Bonds, Bobby Bonilla, Will Clark, Wally Joyner, John Kruk, Kevin Mitchell, and Ruben Sierra.

	MINT	NRMT
COMP.FACT.SET (132)	12.00	5.50
COMMON CARD (1-132)	.10	.05
MINOR STARS	.20	.09
SEMISTARS	.40	.18
UNLISTED STARS	.75	.35

		MINT	NRMT
☐ 1	Mike Aldrete	.10	.05
☐ 2	Andy Allanson	.10	.05
☐ 3	Neil Allen	.10	.05
☐ 4	Joaquin Andujar	.10	.05
☐ 5	Paul Assenmacher	.10	.05
☐ 6	Scott Bailes	.10	.05
☐ 7	Jay Baller	.10	.05
☐ 8	Scott Bankhead	.10	.05
☐ 9	Bill Bathe	.10	.05
☐ 10	Don Baylor	.40	.18
☐ 11	Billy Beane	.10	.05
☐ 12	Steve Bedrosian	.10	.05
☐ 13	Juan Beniquez	.10	.05
☐ 14	Barry Bonds	6.00	2.70
☐ 15	Bobby Bonilla UER	1.50	.70
	(Wrong birthday)		
☐ 16	Rich Bordi	.10	.05
☐ 17	Bill Campbell	.10	.05
☐ 18	Tom Candiotti	.10	.05
☐ 19	John Cangelosi	.10	.05
☐ 20	Jose Canseco UER	2.50	1.10
	(Headings on back		
	for a pitcher)		
☐ 21	Chuck Cary	.10	.05
☐ 22	Juan Castillo	.10	.05
☐ 23	Rick Cerone	.10	.05
☐ 24	John Cerutti	.10	.05
☐ 25	Will Clark	2.50	1.10
☐ 26	Mark Clear	.10	.05
☐ 27	Darnell Coles	.10	.05
☐ 28	Dave Collins	.10	.05
☐ 29	Tim Conroy	.10	.05
☐ 30	Ed Correa	.10	.05
☐ 31	Joe Cowley	.10	.05
☐ 32	Bill Dawley	.10	.05
☐ 33	Rob Deer	.20	.09
☐ 34	John Denny	.10	.05
☐ 35	Jim Deshaies	.10	.05
☐ 36	Doug Drabek	.75	.35
☐ 37	Mike Easler	.10	.05
☐ 38	Mark Eichhorn	.10	.05
☐ 39	Dave Engle	.10	.05
☐ 40	Mike Fischlin	.10	.05
☐ 41	Scott Fletcher	.10	.05
☐ 42	Terry Forster	.10	.05
☐ 43	Terry Francona	.10	.05
☐ 44	Andres Galarraga	2.50	1.10
☐ 45	Lee Guetterman	.10	.05
☐ 46	Bill Gullickson	.10	.05
☐ 47	Jackie Gutierrez	.10	.05
☐ 48	Moose Haas	.10	.05
☐ 49	Billy Hatcher	.10	.05
☐ 50	Mike Heath	.10	.05
☐ 51	Guy Hoffman	.10	.05
☐ 52	Tom Hume	.10	.05
☐ 53	Pete Incaviglia	.75	.35
☐ 54	Dane Iorg	.10	.05
☐ 55	Chris James	.10	.05
☐ 56	Stan Javier	.20	.09
☐ 57	Tommy John	.75	.35
☐ 58	Tracy Jones	.10	.05
☐ 59	Wally Joyner	.75	.35
☐ 60	Wayne Krenchicki	.10	.05
☐ 61	John Kruk	.75	.35
☐ 62	Mike LaCoss	.10	.05
☐ 63	Pete Ladd	.10	.05
☐ 64	Dave LaPoint	.10	.05
☐ 65	Mike LaValliere	.10	.05
☐ 66	Rudy Law	.10	.05
☐ 67	Dennis Leonard	.10	.05
☐ 68	Steve Lombardozzi	.10	.05
☐ 69	Aurelio Lopez	.10	.05
☐ 70	Mickey Mahler	.10	.05
☐ 71	Candy Maldonado	.10	.05
☐ 72	Roger Mason	.10	.05
☐ 73	Greg Mathews	.10	.05
☐ 74	Andy McGaffigan	.10	.05
☐ 75	Joel McKeon	.10	.05
☐ 76	Kevin Mitchell	.75	.35
☐ 77	Bill Mooneyham	.10	.05
☐ 78	Omar Moreno	.10	.05
☐ 79	Jerry Mumphrey	.10	.05
☐ 80	Al Newman	.20	.09
☐ 81	Phil Niekro	.75	.35
☐ 82	Randy Niemann	.10	.05
☐ 83	Juan Nieves	.10	.05
☐ 84	Bob Ojeda	.10	.05
☐ 85	Rick Ownbey	.10	.05
☐ 86	Tom Paciorek	.20	.09
☐ 87	David Palmer	.10	.05
☐ 88	Jeff Parrett	.10	.05
☐ 89	Pat Perry	.10	.05
☐ 90	Dan Plesac	.10	.05
☐ 91	Darrell Porter	.10	.05
☐ 92	Luis Quinones	.10	.05
☐ 93	Rey Quinones UER	.10	.05
	(Misspelled Quinonez)		
☐ 94	Gary Redus	.10	.05
☐ 95	Jeff Reed	.10	.05
☐ 96	Bip Roberts	.75	.35
☐ 97	Billy Joe Robidoux	.10	.05
☐ 98	Gary Roenicke	.10	.05
☐ 99	Ron Roenicke	.10	.05
☐ 100	Angel Salazar	.10	.05
☐ 101	Joe Sambito	.10	.05
☐ 102	Billy Sample	.10	.05
☐ 103	Dave Schmidt	.10	.05
☐ 104	Ken Schrom	.10	.05
☐ 105	Ruben Sierra	.75	.35
☐ 106	Ted Simmons	.20	.09
☐ 107	Sammy Stewart	.10	.05
☐ 108	Kurt Stillwell	.10	.05
☐ 109	Dale Sveum	.10	.05
☐ 110	Tim Teufel	.10	.05
☐ 111	Bob Tewksbury	.20	.09
☐ 112	Andres Thomas	.10	.05
☐ 113	Jason Thompson	.10	.05
☐ 114	Milt Thompson	.20	.09
☐ 115	Robby Thompson	.20	.09
☐ 116	Jay Tibbs	.10	.05
☐ 117	Fred Toliver	.10	.05
☐ 118	Wayne Tolleson	.10	.05
☐ 119	Alex Trevino	.10	.05
☐ 120	Manny Trillo	.10	.05
☐ 121	Ed VandeBerg	.10	.05
☐ 122	Ozzie Virgil	.10	.05
☐ 123	Tony Walker	.10	.05
☐ 124	Gene Walter	.10	.05
☐ 125	Duane Ward	.20	.09
☐ 126	Jerry Willard	.10	.05
☐ 127	Mitch Williams	.20	.09
☐ 128	Reggie Williams	.10	.05
☐ 129	Bobby Witt	.40	.18
☐ 130	Marvell Wynne	.10	.05
☐ 131	Steve Yeager	.10	.05
☐ 132	Checklist 1-132	.10	.05

1987 Fleer

This set consists of 660 standard-size cards. Cards were primarily issued in 17-card wax packs, rack packs and hobby and retail factory sets. Card fronts feature a distinctive light blue and white blended border encasing a color photo. Cards are again organized numerically by teams with team ordering based on the previous seasons record. The last 36 cards in the set consist of Specials (625-643), Rookie Pairs (644-653), and checklists (654-660). The key Rookie Cards in this set are Barry Bonds, Bobby Bonilla, Will Clark, Chuck Finley, Bo Jackson, Wally Joyner, John Kruk, Barry Larkin, Kevin Mitchell, Kevin Seitzer, Ruben Sierra and Devon White.

	MINT	NRMT
COMPLETE SET (660)	40.00	18.00
COMP.FACT.SET (672)	40.00	18.00
COMMON CARD (1-660)	.20	.09
MINOR STARS	.40	.18
UNLISTED STARS	.75	.35
COMP.WORLD SERIES SET (12)	2.00	.90
ONE WORLD SERIES SET PER FACT.SET		

		MINT	NRMT
☐ 1	Rick Aguilera	.40	.18
☐ 2	Richard Anderson	.20	.09
☐ 3	Wally Backman	.20	.09
☐ 4	Gary Carter	.10	.05
☐ 5	Ron Darling	.20	.09
☐ 6	Len Dykstra	.75	.35
☐ 7	Kevin Elster	.75	.35
☐ 8	Sid Fernandez	.20	.09
☐ 9	Dwight Gooden	.10	.05
☐ 10	Ed Hearn	.20	.09
☐ 11	Danny Heep	.20	.09
☐ 12	Keith Hernandez	.40	.18
☐ 13	Howard Johnson	.20	.09
☐ 14	Ray Knight	.20	.09
☐ 15	Lee Mazzilli	.20	.09
☐ 16	Roger McDowell	.20	.09
☐ 17	Kevin Mitchell	.10	.05
☐ 18	Randy Niemann	.20	.09
☐ 19	Bob Ojeda	.20	.09
☐ 20	Jesse Orosco	.20	.09
☐ 21	Rafael Santana	.20	.09
☐ 22	Doug Sisk	.20	.09
☐ 23	Darryl Strawberry	.40	.18
☐ 24	Tim Teufel	.20	.09

☐ 25	Mookie Wilson	.40	.18
☐ 26	Tony Armas	.20	.09
☐ 27	Marty Barrett	.20	.09
☐ 28	Don Baylor	.40	.18
☐ 29	Wade Boggs	.75	.35
☐ 30	Oil Can Boyd	.20	.09
☐ 31	Bill Buckner	.40	.18
☐ 32	Roger Clemens	2.00	.90
☐ 33	Steve Crawford	.20	.09
☐ 34	Dwight Evans	.40	.18
☐ 35	Rich Gedman	.20	.09
☐ 36	Dave Henderson	.20	.09
☐ 37	Bruce Hurst	.20	.09
☐ 38	Tim Lollar	.20	.09
☐ 39	Al Nipper	.20	.09
☐ 40	Spike Owen	.20	.09
☐ 41	Jim Rice	.40	.18
☐ 42	Ed Romero	.20	.09
☐ 43	Joe Sambito	.20	.09
☐ 44	Calvin Schiraldi	.20	.09
☐ 45	Tom Seaver UER	.75	.35
	(Lifetime saves total 0, should be 1)		
☐ 46	Jeff Sellers	.20	.09
☐ 47	Bob Stanley	.20	.09
☐ 48	Sammy Stewart	.20	.09
☐ 49	Larry Andersen	.20	.09
☐ 50	Alan Ashby	.20	.09
☐ 51	Kevin Bass	.20	.09
☐ 52	Jeff Calhoun	.20	.09
☐ 53	Jose Cruz	.40	.18
☐ 54	Danny Darwin	.20	.09
☐ 55	Glenn Davis	.20	.09
☐ 56	Jim Deshaies	.20	.09
☐ 57	Bill Doran	.20	.09
☐ 58	Phil Garner	.20	.09
☐ 59	Billy Hatcher	.20	.09
☐ 60	Charlie Kerfeld	.20	.09
☐ 61	Bob Knepper	.20	.09
☐ 62	Dave Lopes	.40	.18
☐ 63	Aurelio Lopez	.20	.09
☐ 64	Jim Pankovits	.20	.09
☐ 65	Terry Puhl	.20	.09
☐ 66	Craig Reynolds	.20	.09
☐ 67	Nolan Ryan	3.00	1.35
☐ 68	Mike Scott	.20	.09
☐ 69	Dave Smith	.20	.09
☐ 70	Dickie Thon	.20	.09
☐ 71	Tony Walker	.20	.09
☐ 72	Denny Walling	.20	.09
☐ 73	Bob Boone	.40	.18
☐ 74	Rick Burleson	.20	.09
☐ 75	John Candelaria	.20	.09
☐ 76	Doug Corbett	.20	.09
☐ 77	Doug DeCinces	.20	.09
☐ 78	Brian Downing	.20	.09
☐ 79	Chuck Finley	.75	.35
☐ 80	Terry Forster	.20	.09
☐ 81	Bob Grich	.40	.18
☐ 82	George Hendrick	.20	.09
☐ 83	Jack Howell	.20	.09
☐ 84	Reggie Jackson	1.00	.45
☐ 85	Ruppert Jones	.20	.09
☐ 86	Wally Joyner	1.00	.45
☐ 87	Gary Lucas	.20	.09
☐ 88	Kirk McCaskill	.20	.09
☐ 89	Donnie Moore	.20	.09
☐ 90	Gary Pettis	.20	.09
☐ 91	Vern Ruhle	.20	.09
☐ 92	Dick Schofield	.20	.09
☐ 93	Don Sutton	.75	.35
☐ 94	Rob Wilfong	.20	.09
☐ 95	Mike Witt	.20	.09
☐ 96	Doug Drabek	.75	.35
☐ 97	Mike Easler	.20	.09
☐ 98	Mike Fischlin	.20	.09
☐ 99	Brian Fisher	.20	.09
☐ 100	Ron Guidry	.40	.18
☐ 101	Rickey Henderson	.75	.35
☐ 102	Tommy John	.40	.18
☐ 103	Ron Kittle	.20	.09
☐ 104	Don Mattingly	1.25	.55
☐ 105	Bobby Meacham	.20	.09
☐ 106	Joe Niekro	.20	.09
☐ 107	Mike Pagliarulo	.20	.09
☐ 108	Dan Pasqua	.20	.09
☐ 109	Willie Randolph	.40	.18
☐ 110	Dennis Rasmussen	.20	.09
☐ 111	Dave Righetti	.20	.09
☐ 112	Gary Roenicke	.20	.09
☐ 113	Rod Scurry	.20	.09
☐ 114	Bob Shirley	.20	.09
☐ 115	Joel Skinner	.20	.09
☐ 116	Tim Stoddard	.20	.09
☐ 117	Bob Tewksbury	.40	.18
☐ 118	Wayne Tolleson	.20	.09
☐ 119	Claudell Washington	.20	.09
☐ 120	Dave Winfield	.75	.35
☐ 121	Steve Buechele	.20	.09
☐ 122	Ed Correa	.20	.09
☐ 123	Scott Fletcher	.20	.09
☐ 124	Jose Guzman	.20	.09
☐ 125	Toby Harrah	.20	.09
☐ 126	Greg Harris	.20	.09
☐ 127	Charlie Hough	.20	.09
☐ 128	Pete Incaviglia	.40	.18
☐ 129	Mike Mason	.20	.09
☐ 130	Oddibe McDowell	.20	.09
☐ 131	Dale Mohorcic	.20	.09
☐ 132	Pete O'Brien	.20	.09
☐ 133	Tom Paciorek	.20	.09
☐ 134	Larry Parrish	.20	.09
☐ 135	Geno Petralli	.20	.09
☐ 136	Darrell Porter	.20	.09
☐ 137	Jeff Russell	.20	.09
☐ 138	Ruben Sierra	1.00	.45
☐ 139	Don Slaught	.20	.09
☐ 140	Gary Ward	.20	.09
☐ 141	Curtis Wilkerson	.20	.09
☐ 142	Mitch Williams	.40	.18
☐ 143	Bobby Witt UER	.40	.18
	(Tulsa misspelled as Tusla; ERA should be 6.43, not .643)		
☐ 144	Dave Bergman	.20	.09
☐ 145	Tom Brookens	.20	.09
☐ 146	Bill Campbell	.20	.09
☐ 147	Chuck Cary	.20	.09
☐ 148	Darnell Coles	.20	.09
☐ 149	Dave Collins	.20	.09
☐ 150	Darrell Evans	.40	.18
☐ 151	Kirk Gibson	.40	.18
☐ 152	John Grubb	.20	.09
☐ 153	Willie Hernandez	.20	.09
☐ 154	Larry Herndon	.20	.09
☐ 155	Eric King	.20	.09
☐ 156	Chet Lemon	.20	.09
☐ 157	Dwight Lowry	.20	.09
☐ 158	Jack Morris	.40	.18
☐ 159	Randy O'Neal	.20	.09
☐ 160	Lance Parrish	.40	.18
☐ 161	Dan Petry	.20	.09
☐ 162	Pat Sheridan	.20	.09
☐ 163	Jim Slaton	.20	.09
☐ 164	Frank Tanana	.20	.09
☐ 165	Walt Terrell	.20	.09
☐ 166	Mark Thurmond	.20	.09
☐ 167	Alan Trammell	.10	.05
☐ 168	Lou Whitaker	.40	.18
☐ 169	Luis Aguayo	.20	.09
☐ 170	Steve Bedrosian	.20	.09
☐ 171	Don Carman	.20	.09
☐ 172	Darren Daulton	.10	.05
☐ 173	Greg Gross	.20	.09
☐ 174	Kevin Gross	.20	.09
☐ 175	Von Hayes	.20	.09
☐ 176	Charles Hudson	.20	.09
☐ 177	Tom Hume	.20	.09
☐ 178	Steve Jeltz	.20	.09
☐ 179	Mike Maddux	.20	.09
☐ 180	Shane Rawley	.20	.09
☐ 181	Gary Redus	.20	.09
☐ 182	Ron Roenicke	.20	.09
☐ 183	Bruce Ruffin	.20	.09
☐ 184	John Russell	.20	.09
☐ 185	Juan Samuel	.20	.09
☐ 186	Dan Schatzeder	.20	.09
☐ 187	Mike Schmidt	1.00	.45
☐ 188	Rick Schu	.20	.09
☐ 189	Jeff Stone	.20	.09
☐ 190	Kent Tekulve	.20	.09
☐ 191	Milt Thompson	.20	.09
☐ 192	Glenn Wilson	.20	.09
☐ 193	Buddy Bell	.40	.18
☐ 194	Tom Browning	.20	.09
☐ 195	Sal Butera	.20	.09
☐ 196	Dave Concepcion	.40	.18
☐ 197	Kal Daniels	.20	.09
☐ 198	Eric Davis	.10	.05
☐ 199	John Denny	.20	.09
☐ 200	Bo Diaz	.20	.09
☐ 201	Nick Esasky	.20	.09
☐ 202	John Franco	.40	.18
☐ 203	Bill Gullickson	.20	.09
☐ 204	Barry Larkin	5.00	2.20
☐ 205	Eddie Milner	.20	.09
☐ 206	Rob Murphy	.20	.09
☐ 207	Ron Oester	.20	.09
☐ 208	Dave Parker	.40	.18
☐ 209	Tony Perez	.75	.35
☐ 210	Ted Power	.20	.09
☐ 211	Joe Price	.20	.09
☐ 212	Ron Robinson	.20	.09
☐ 213	Pete Rose	1.00	.45
☐ 214	Mario Soto	.20	.09
☐ 215	Kurt Stillwell	.20	.09
☐ 216	Max Venable	.20	.09
☐ 217	Chris Welsh	.20	.09
☐ 218	Carl Willis	.20	.09
☐ 219	Jesse Barfield	.20	.09
☐ 220	George Bell	.20	.09
☐ 221	Bill Caudill	.20	.09
☐ 222	John Cerutti	.20	.09
☐ 223	Jim Clancy	.20	.09
☐ 224	Mark Eichhorn	.20	.09
☐ 225	Tony Fernandez	.20	.09
☐ 226	Damaso Garcia	.20	.09
☐ 227	Kelly Gruber ERR	.20	.09
	(Wrong birth year)		
☐ 228	Tom Henke	.20	.09
☐ 229	Garth Iorg	.20	.09
☐ 230	Joe Johnson	.20	.09
☐ 231	Cliff Johnson	.20	.09
☐ 232	Jimmy Key	.10	.05
☐ 233	Dennis Lamp	.20	.09
☐ 234	Rick Leach	.20	.09
☐ 235	Buck Martinez	.20	.09
☐ 236	Lloyd Moseby	.20	.09
☐ 237	Rance Mulliniks	.20	.09
☐ 238	Dave Stieb	.20	.09
☐ 239	Willie Upshaw	.20	.09
☐ 240	Ernie Whitt	.20	.09
☐ 241	Andy Allanson	.20	.09
☐ 242	Scott Bailes	.20	.09
☐ 243	Chris Bando	.20	.09
☐ 244	Tony Bernazard	.20	.09
☐ 245	John Butcher	.20	.09
☐ 246	Brett Butler	.40	.18
☐ 247	Ernie Camacho	.20	.09
☐ 248	Tom Candiotti	.20	.09
☐ 249	Joe Carter	.75	.35
☐ 250	Carmen Castillo	.20	.09
☐ 251	Julio Franco	.20	.09
☐ 252	Mel Hall	.20	.09
☐ 253	Brook Jacoby	.20	.09
☐ 254	Phil Niekro	.75	.35
☐ 255	Otis Nixon	.10	.05
☐ 256	Dickie Noles	.20	.09
☐ 257	Bryan Oelkers	.20	.09
☐ 258	Ken Schrom	.20	.09
☐ 259	Don Schulze	.20	.09
☐ 260	Cory Snyder	.20	.09
☐ 261	Pat Tabler	.20	.09
☐ 262	Andre Thornton	.20	.09
☐ 263	Rich Yett	.20	.09
☐ 264	Mike Aldrete	.40	.18
☐ 265	Juan Berenguer	.20	.09
☐ 266	Vida Blue	.40	.18
☐ 267	Bob Brenly	.20	.09
☐ 268	Chris Brown	.20	.09
☐ 269	Will Clark	5.00	2.20
☐ 270	Chili Davis	.10	.05
☐ 271	Mark Davis	.20	.09
☐ 272	Kelly Downs	.20	.09
☐ 273	Scott Garrelts	.20	.09
☐ 274	Dan Gladden	.20	.09
☐ 275	Mike Krukow	.20	.09
☐ 276	Randy Kutcher	.20	.09
☐ 277	Mike LaCoss	.20	.09

☐ 278	Jeff Leonard	.20	.09
☐ 279	Candy Maldonado	.20	.09
☐ 280	Roger Mason	.20	.09
☐ 281	Bob Melvin	.20	.09
☐ 282	Greg Minton	.20	.09
☐ 283	Jeff D. Robinson	.20	.09
☐ 284	Harry Spilman	.20	.09
☐ 285	Robby Thompson	.40	.18
☐ 286	Jose Uribe	.20	.09
☐ 287	Frank Williams	.20	.09
☐ 288	Joel Youngblood	.20	.09
☐ 289	Jack Clark	.40	.18
☐ 290	Vince Coleman	.20	.09
☐ 291	Tim Conroy	.20	.09
☐ 292	Danny Cox	.20	.09
☐ 293	Ken Dayley	.20	.09
☐ 294	Curt Ford	.20	.09
☐ 295	Bob Forsch	.20	.09
☐ 296	Tom Herr	.20	.09
☐ 297	Ricky Horton	.20	.09
☐ 298	Clint Hurdle	.20	.09
☐ 299	Jeff Lahti	.20	.09
☐ 300	Steve Lake	.20	.09
☐ 301	Tito Landrum	.20	.09
☐ 302	Mike LaValliere	.20	.09
☐ 303	Greg Mathews	.20	.09
☐ 304	Willie McGee	.20	.09
☐ 305	Jose Oquendo	.20	.09
☐ 306	Terry Pendleton	.40	.18
☐ 307	Pat Perry	.20	.09
☐ 308	Ozzie Smith	1.00	.45
☐ 309	Ray Soff	.20	.09
☐ 310	John Tudor	.20	.09
☐ 311	Andy Van Slyke UER (Bats R, Throws L)	.40	.18
☐ 312	Todd Worrell	.40	.18
☐ 313	Dann Bilardello	.20	.09
☐ 314	Hubie Brooks	.20	.09
☐ 315	Tim Burke	.20	.09
☐ 316	Andre Dawson	.75	.35
☐ 317	Mike Fitzgerald	.20	.09
☐ 318	Tom Foley	.20	.09
☐ 319	Andres Galarraga	1.00	.45
☐ 320	Joe Hesketh	.20	.09
☐ 321	Wallace Johnson	.20	.09
☐ 322	Wayne Krenchicki	.20	.09
☐ 323	Vance Law	.20	.09
☐ 324	Dennis Martinez	.40	.18
☐ 325	Bob McClure	.20	.09
☐ 326	Andy McGaffigan	.20	.09
☐ 327	Al Newman	.20	.09
☐ 328	Tim Raines	.40	.18
☐ 329	Jeff Reardon	.40	.18
☐ 330	Luis Rivera	.20	.09
☐ 331	Bob Sebra	.20	.09
☐ 332	Bryn Smith	.20	.09
☐ 333	Jay Tibbs	.20	.09
☐ 334	Tim Wallach	.20	.09
☐ 335	Mitch Webster	.20	.09
☐ 336	Jim Wohlford	.20	.09
☐ 337	Floyd Youmans	.20	.09
☐ 338	Chris Bosio	.40	.18
☐ 339	Glenn Braggs	.20	.09
☐ 340	Rick Cerone	.20	.09
☐ 341	Mark Clear	.20	.09
☐ 342	Bryan Clutterbuck	.20	.09
☐ 343	Cecil Cooper	.40	.18
☐ 344	Rob Deer	.20	.09
☐ 345	Jim Gantner	.20	.09
☐ 346	Ted Higuera	.20	.09
☐ 347	John Henry Johnson	.20	.09
☐ 348	Tim Leary	.20	.09
☐ 349	Rick Manning	.20	.09
☐ 350	Paul Molitor	.75	.35
☐ 351	Charlie Moore	.20	.09
☐ 352	Juan Nieves	.20	.09
☐ 353	Ben Oglivie	.20	.09
☐ 354	Dan Plesac	.20	.09
☐ 355	Ernest Riles	.20	.09
☐ 356	Billy Joe Robidoux	.20	.09
☐ 357	Bill Schroeder	.20	.09
☐ 358	Dale Sveum	.20	.09
☐ 359	Gorman Thomas	.20	.09
☐ 360	Bill Wegman	.20	.09
☐ 361	Robin Yount	.75	.35
☐ 362	Steve Balboni	.20	.09
☐ 363	Scott Bankhead	.20	.09
☐ 364	Buddy Biancalana	.20	.09
☐ 365	Bud Black	.20	.09
☐ 366	George Brett	1.50	.70
☐ 367	Steve Farr	.20	.09
☐ 368	Mark Gubicza	.20	.09
☐ 369	Bo Jackson	2.50	1.10
☐ 370	Danny Jackson	.20	.09
☐ 371	Mike Kingery	.40	.18
☐ 372	Rudy Law	.20	.09
☐ 373	Charlie Leibrandt	.20	.09
☐ 374	Dennis Leonard	.20	.09
☐ 375	Hal McRae	.40	.18
☐ 376	Jorge Orta	.20	.09
☐ 377	Jamie Quirk	.20	.09
☐ 378	Dan Quisenberry	.20	.09
☐ 379	Bret Saberhagen	.20	.09
☐ 380	Angel Salazar	.20	.09
☐ 381	Lonnie Smith	.20	.09
☐ 382	Jim Sundberg	.20	.09
☐ 383	Frank White	.40	.18
☐ 384	Willie Wilson	.20	.09
☐ 385	Joaquin Andujar	.20	.09
☐ 386	Doug Bair	.20	.09
☐ 387	Dusty Baker	.40	.18
☐ 388	Bruce Bochte	.20	.09
☐ 389	Jose Canseco	1.50	.70
☐ 390	Chris Codiroli	.20	.09
☐ 391	Mike Davis	.20	.09
☐ 392	Alfredo Griffin	.20	.09
☐ 393	Moose Haas	.20	.09
☐ 394	Donnie Hill	.20	.09
☐ 395	Jay Howell	.20	.09
☐ 396	Dave Kingman	.40	.18
☐ 397	Carney Lansford	.40	.18
☐ 398	Dave Leiper	.20	.09
☐ 399	Bill Mooneyham	.20	.09
☐ 400	Dwayne Murphy	.20	.09
☐ 401	Steve Ontiveros	.20	.09
☐ 402	Tony Phillips	.20	.09
☐ 403	Eric Plunk	.20	.09
☐ 404	Jose Rijo	.20	.09
☐ 405	Terry Steinbach	1.00	.45
☐ 406	Dave Stewart	.40	.18
☐ 407	Mickey Tettleton	.40	.18
☐ 408	Dave Von Ohlen	.20	.09
☐ 409	Jerry Willard	.20	.09
☐ 410	Curt Young	.20	.09
☐ 411	Bruce Bochy	.20	.09
☐ 412	Dave Dravecky	.40	.18
☐ 413	Tim Flannery	.20	.09
☐ 414	Steve Garvey	.75	.35
☐ 415	Rich Gossage	.40	.18
☐ 416	Tony Gwynn	2.00	.90
☐ 417	Andy Hawkins	.20	.09
☐ 418	LaMarr Hoyt	.20	.09
☐ 419	Terry Kennedy	.20	.09
☐ 420	John Kruk	1.00	.45
☐ 421	Dave LaPoint	.20	.09
☐ 422	Craig Lefferts	.20	.09
☐ 423	Carmelo Martinez	.20	.09
☐ 424	Lance McCullers	.20	.09
☐ 425	Kevin McReynolds	.20	.09
☐ 426	Graig Nettles	.40	.18
☐ 427	Bip Roberts	1.00	.45
☐ 428	Jerry Royster	.20	.09
☐ 429	Benito Santiago	.40	.18
☐ 430	Eric Show	.20	.09
☐ 431	Bob Stoddard	.20	.09
☐ 432	Garry Templeton	.20	.09
☐ 433	Gene Walter	.20	.09
☐ 434	Ed Whitson	.20	.09
☐ 435	Marvell Wynne	.20	.09
☐ 436	Dave Anderson	.20	.09
☐ 437	Greg Brock	.20	.09
☐ 438	Enos Cabell	.20	.09
☐ 439	Mariano Duncan	.20	.09
☐ 440	Pedro Guerrero	.40	.18
☐ 441	Orel Hershiser	.40	.18
☐ 442	Rick Honeycutt	.20	.09
☐ 443	Ken Howell	.20	.09
☐ 444	Ken Landreaux	.20	.09
☐ 445	Bill Madlock	.40	.18
☐ 446	Mike Marshall	.20	.09
☐ 447	Len Matuszek	.20	.09
☐ 448	Tom Niedenfuer	.20	.09
☐ 449	Alejandro Pena	.20	.09
☐ 450	Dennis Powell	.20	.09
☐ 451	Jerry Reuss	.20	.09
☐ 452	Bill Russell	.20	.09
☐ 453	Steve Sax	.20	.09
☐ 454	Mike Scioscia	.20	.09
☐ 455	Franklin Stubbs	.20	.09
☐ 456	Alex Trevino	.20	.09
☐ 457	Fernando Valenzuela	.40	.18
☐ 458	Ed VandeBerg	.20	.09
☐ 459	Bob Welch	.20	.09
☐ 460	Reggie Williams	.20	.09
☐ 461	Don Aase	.20	.09
☐ 462	Juan Beniquez	.20	.09
☐ 463	Mike Boddicker	.20	.09
☐ 464	Juan Bonilla	.20	.09
☐ 465	Rich Bordi	.20	.09
☐ 466	Storm Davis	.20	.09
☐ 467	Rick Dempsey	.40	.18
☐ 468	Ken Dixon	.20	.09
☐ 469	Jim Dwyer	.20	.09
☐ 470	Mike Flanagan	.20	.09
☐ 471	Jackie Gutierrez	.20	.09
☐ 472	Brad Havens	.20	.09
☐ 473	Lee Lacy	.20	.09
☐ 474	Fred Lynn	.40	.18
☐ 475	Scott McGregor	.20	.09
☐ 476	Eddie Murray	.75	.35
☐ 477	Tom O'Malley	.20	.09
☐ 478	Cal Ripken Jr.	3.00	1.35
☐ 479	Larry Sheets	.20	.09
☐ 480	John Shelby	.20	.09
☐ 481	Nate Snell	.20	.09
☐ 482	Jim Traber	.20	.09
☐ 483	Mike Young	.20	.09
☐ 484	Neil Allen	.20	.09
☐ 485	Harold Baines	.40	.18
☐ 486	Floyd Bannister	.20	.09
☐ 487	Daryl Boston	.20	.09
☐ 488	Ivan Calderon	.20	.09
☐ 489	John Cangelosi	.20	.09
☐ 490	Steve Carlton	.75	.35
☐ 491	Joe Cowley	.20	.09
☐ 492	Julio Cruz	.20	.09
☐ 493	Bill Dawley	.20	.09
☐ 494	Jose DeLeon	.20	.09
☐ 495	Richard Dotson	.20	.09
☐ 496	Carlton Fisk	.75	.35
☐ 497	Ozzie Guillen	.40	.18
☐ 498	Jerry Hairston	.20	.09
☐ 499	Ron Hassey	.20	.09
☐ 500	Tim Hulett	.20	.09
☐ 501	Bob James	.20	.09
☐ 502	Steve Lyons	.20	.09
☐ 503	Joel McKeon	.20	.09
☐ 504	Gene Nelson	.20	.09
☐ 505	Dave Schmidt	.20	.09
☐ 506	Ray Searage	.20	.09
☐ 507	Bobby Thigpen	.40	.18
☐ 508	Greg Walker	.20	.09
☐ 509	Jim Acker	.20	.09
☐ 510	Doyle Alexander	.20	.09
☐ 511	Paul Assenmacher	.20	.09
☐ 512	Bruce Benedict	.20	.09
☐ 513	Chris Chambliss	.20	.09
☐ 514	Jeff Dedmon	.20	.09
☐ 515	Gene Garber	.20	.09
☐ 516	Ken Griffey	.40	.18
☐ 517	Terry Harper	.20	.09
☐ 518	Bob Horner	.20	.09
☐ 519	Glenn Hubbard	.20	.09
☐ 520	Rick Mahler	.20	.09
☐ 521	Omar Moreno	.20	.09
☐ 522	Dale Murphy	.75	.35
☐ 523	Ken Oberkfell	.20	.09
☐ 524	Ed Olwine	.20	.09
☐ 525	David Palmer	.20	.09
☐ 526	Rafael Ramirez	.20	.09
☐ 527	Billy Sample	.20	.09
☐ 528	Ted Simmons	.40	.18
☐ 529	Zane Smith	.20	.09
☐ 530	Bruce Sutter	.20	.09
☐ 531	Andres Thomas	.20	.09
☐ 532	Ozzie Virgil	.20	.09
☐ 533	Allan Anderson	.20	.09
☐ 534	Keith Atherton	.20	.09

☐ 535	Billy Beane	.20		.09
☐ 536	Bert Blyleven	.40		.18
☐ 537	Tom Brunansky	.20		.09
☐ 538	Randy Bush	.20		.09
☐ 539	George Frazier	.20		.09
☐ 540	Gary Gaetti	.20		.09
☐ 541	Greg Gagne	.20		.09
☐ 542	Mickey Hatcher	.20		.09
☐ 543	Neal Heaton	.20		.09
☐ 544	Kent Hrbek	.40		.18
☐ 545	Roy Lee Jackson	.20		.09
☐ 546	Tim Laudner	.20		.09
☐ 547	Steve Lombardozzi	.20		.09
☐ 548	Mark Portugal	.40		.18
☐ 549	Kirby Puckett	2.00		.90
☐ 550	Jeff Reed	.20		.09
☐ 551	Mark Salas	.20		.09
☐ 552	Roy Smalley	.20		.09
☐ 553	Mike Smithson	.20		.09
☐ 554	Frank Viola	.20		.09
☐ 555	Thad Bosley	.20		.09
☐ 556	Ron Cey	.40		.18
☐ 557	Jody Davis	.20		.09
☐ 558	Ron Davis	.20		.09
☐ 559	Bob Dernier	.20		.09
☐ 560	Frank DiPino	.20		.09
☐ 561	Shawon Dunston UER	.20		
	(Wrong birth year listed on card back)			
☐ 562	Leon Durham	.20		.09
☐ 563	Dennis Eckersley	.75		.35
☐ 564	Terry Francona	.20		.09
☐ 565	Dave Gumpert	.20		.09
☐ 566	Guy Hoffman	.20		.09
☐ 567	Ed Lynch	.20		.09
☐ 568	Gary Matthews	.20		.09
☐ 569	Keith Moreland	.20		.09
☐ 570	Jamie Moyer	.10		.05
☐ 571	Jerry Mumphrey	.20		.09
☐ 572	Ryne Sandberg	1.00		.45
☐ 573	Scott Sanderson	.20		.09
☐ 574	Lee Smith	.10		.05
☐ 575	Chris Speier	.20		.09
☐ 576	Rick Sutcliffe	.20		.09
☐ 577	Manny Trillo	.20		.09
☐ 578	Steve Trout	.20		.09
☐ 579	Karl Best	.20		.09
☐ 580	Scott Bradley	.20		.09
☐ 581	Phil Bradley	.20		.09
☐ 582	Mickey Brantley	.20		.09
☐ 583	Mike G. Brown P	.20		.09
☐ 584	Alvin Davis	.20		.09
☐ 585	Lee Guetterman	.20		.09
☐ 586	Mark Huismann	.20		.09
☐ 587	Bob Kearney	.20		.09
☐ 588	Pete Ladd	.20		.09
☐ 589	Mark Langston	.20		.09
☐ 590	Mike Moore	.20		.09
☐ 591	Mike Morgan	.20		.09
☐ 592	John Moses	.20		.09
☐ 593	Ken Phelps	.20		.09
☐ 594	Jim Presley	.20		.09
☐ 595	Rey Quinones UER	.20		
	(Quinonez on front)			
☐ 596	Harold Reynolds	.20		.09
☐ 597	Billy Swift	.20		.09
☐ 598	Danny Tartabull	.40		.18
☐ 599	Steve Yeager	.20		.09
☐ 600	Matt Young	.20		.09
☐ 601	Bill Almon	.20		.09
☐ 602	Rafael Belliard	.20		.09
☐ 603	Mike Bielecki	.20		.09
☐ 604	Barry Bonds	20.00		9.00
☐ 605	Bobby Bonilla	2.50		1.10
☐ 606	Sid Bream	.20		.09
☐ 607	Mike C. Brown	.20		.09
☐ 608	Pat Clements	.20		.09
☐ 609	Mike Diaz	.20		.09
☐ 610	Cecilio Guante	.20		.09
☐ 611	Barry Jones	.20		.09
☐ 612	Bob Kipper	.20		.09
☐ 613	Larry McWilliams	.20		.09
☐ 614	Jim Morrison	.20		.09
☐ 615	Joe Orsulak	.20		.09
☐ 616	Junior Ortiz	.20		.09
☐ 617	Tony Pena	.20		.09
☐ 618	Johnny Ray	.20		.09
☐ 619	Rick Reuschel	.20		.09
☐ 620	R.J. Reynolds	.20		.09
☐ 621	Rick Rhoden	.20		.09
☐ 622	Don Robinson	.20		.09
☐ 623	Bob Walk	.20		.09
☐ 624	Jim Winn	.20		.09
☐ 625	Youthful Power	.75		.35
	Pete Incaviglia			
	Jose Canseco			
☐ 626	300 Game Winners	.10		.05
	Don Sutton			
	Phil Niekro			
☐ 627	AL Firemen	.20		.09
	Dave Righetti			
	Don Aase			
☐ 628	Rookie All-Stars	.75		.35
	Wally Joyner			
	Jose Canseco			
☐ 629	Magic Mets	.10		.05
	Gary Carter			
	Sid Fernandez			
	Dwight Gooden			
	Keith Hernandez			
	Darryl Strawberry			
	Mike Scott			
☐ 630	NL Best Righties	.20		.09
	Mike Krukow			
☐ 631	Sensational Southpaws	.20		.09
	Fernando Valenzuela			
	John Franco			
☐ 632	Count'Em	.20		.09
	Bob Horner			
☐ 633	AL Pitcher's Nightmare	1.00		.45
	Jose Canseco			
	Jim Rice			
	Kirby Puckett			
☐ 634	All-Star Battery	.40		.18
	Gary Carter			
	Roger Clemens			
☐ 635	4000 Strikeouts	.40		.18
	Steve Carlton			
☐ 636	Big Bats at First	.75		.35
	Glenn Davis			
	Eddie Murray			
☐ 637	On Base	.40		.18
	Wade Boggs			
	Keith Hernandez			
☐ 638	Sluggers Left Side	.75		.35
	Don Mattingly			
	Darryl Strawberry			
☐ 639	Former MVP's	.40		.18
	Dave Parker			
	Ryne Sandberg			
☐ 640	Dr. K and Super K	.10		.05
	Dwight Gooden			
	Roger Clemens			
☐ 641	AL West Stoppers	.20		.09
	Mike Witt			
	Charlie Hough			
☐ 642	Doubles and Triples	.40		.18
	Juan Samuel			
	Tim Raines			
☐ 643	Outfielders with Punch	.40		.18
	Harold Baines			
	Jesse Barfield			
☐ 644	Dave Clark and	.75		.35
	Greg Swindell			
☐ 645	Ron Karkovice and	.40		.18
	Russ Morman			
☐ 646	Devon White and	1.00		.45
	Willie Fraser			
☐ 647	Mike Stanley and	.75		.35
	Jerry Browne			
☐ 648	Dave Magadan and	.10		.05
	Phil Lombardi			
☐ 649	Jose Gonzalez and	.20		.09
	Ralph Bryant			
☐ 650	Jimmy Jones and	.20		
	Randy Asadoor			
☐ 651	Tracy Jones and	.20		
	Marvin Freeman			
☐ 652	John Stefero and	.75		.35
	Kevin Seitzer			
☐ 653	Rob Nelson and	.20		.09
	Steve Fireovid			

☐ 654	CL: Mets/Red Sox	.20		.09
	Astros/Angels			
☐ 655	CL: Yankees/Rangers	.20		.09
	Tigers/Phillies			
☐ 656	CL: Reds/Blue Jays	.20		.09
	Indians/Giants			
	ERR (230/231 wrong)			
☐ 657	CL: Cardinals/Expos	.20		.09
	Brewers/Royals			
☐ 658	CL: A's/Padres	.20		.09
	Dodgers/Orioles			
☐ 659	CL: White Sox/Braves	.20		.09
	Twins/Cubs			
☐ 660	CL: Mariners/Pirates	.20		.09
	Special Cards			
	ER (580/581 wrong)			

1987 Fleer All-Stars

Steve Sax
2ND BASE • SECOND BASE

This 12-card standard-size set was distributed as an insert in packs of the Fleer regular issue. The cards are designed with a color player photo superimposed on a gray or black background with yellow stars. The player's name, team, and position are printed in orange on black or gray at the bottom of the obverse. The card backs are done predominantly in gray, red, and black and are numbered on the back in the upper right hand corner.

		MINT	NRMT
COMPLETE SET (12)		20.00	9.00
COMMON CARD (1-12)		.30	.10
RANDOM INSERTS IN PACKS ..			
☐ 1	Don Mattingly	6.00	2.70
☐ 2	Gary Carter	1.50	.70
☐ 3	Tony Fernandez	.30	.14
☐ 4	Steve Sax	.30	.14
☐ 5	Kirby Puckett	10.00	4.50
☐ 6	Mike Schmidt	2.50	1.10
☐ 7	Mike Easler	.30	.14
☐ 8	Todd Worrell	.30	.14
☐ 9	George Bell	.30	.14
☐ 10	Fernando Valenzuela	.75	.35
☐ 11	Roger Clemens	5.00	2.20
☐ 12	Tim Raines	.75	.35

1987 Fleer Headliners

This six-card standard-size set was distributed one per rack pack as well as with three-pack wax pack rack packs. The obverse features the player photo against a beige background with irregular red stripes. The checklist below also lists

each player's team affiliation. The set is sequenced in alphabetical order.

	MINT	NRMT
COMPLETE SET (6)	6.00	2.70
COMMON CARD (1-6)	.50	.23
ONE PER RACK PACK		
☐ 1 Wade Boggs	1.50	.70
☐ 2 Jose Canseco	3.00	1.35
☐ 3 Dwight Gooden	.75	.35
☐ 4 Rickey Henderson	1.50	.70
☐ 5 Keith Hernandez	.50	.23
☐ 6 Jim Rice	.50	.23

1987 Fleer Update

This 132-card standard-size set was distributed exclusively in factory set form by hobby dealers. In addition to the complete set of 132 cards, the box also contained 25 Team Logo stickers. The cards look very similar to the 1987 Fleer regular issue except for the U-prefixed numbering on back. Cards are ordered alphabetically according to player's last name. The key extended Rookie Cards in this set are Ellis Burks, Mike Greenwell, Greg Maddux, Fred McGriff, Mark McGwire, and Matt Williams.

	MINT	NRMT
COMP.FACT.SET (132)	12.00	5.50
COMMON CARD (1-132)	.10	.05
MINOR STARS	.25	.11
UNLISTED STARS	.50	.23
☐ 1 Scott Bankhead	.10	.05
☐ 2 Eric Bell	.10	.05
☐ 3 Juan Beniquez	.10	.05
☐ 4 Juan Berenguer	.10	.05
☐ 5 Mike Birkbeck	.10	.05

☐ 6 Randy Bockus	.10	.05
☐ 7 Rod Booker	.10	.05
☐ 8 Thad Bosley	.10	.05
☐ 9 Greg Brock	.10	.05
☐ 10 Bob Brower	.10	.05
☐ 11 Chris Brown	.10	.05
☐ 12 Jerry Browne	.10	.05
☐ 13 Ralph Bryant	.10	.05
☐ 14 DeWayne Buice	.10	.05
☐ 15 Ellis Burks	1.00	.45
☐ 16 Casey Candaele	.10	.05
☐ 17 Steve Carlton	.50	.23
☐ 18 Juan Castillo	.10	.05
☐ 19 Chuck Crim	.10	.05
☐ 20 Mark Davidson	.10	.05
☐ 21 Mark Davis	.10	.05
☐ 22 Storm Davis	.10	.05
☐ 23 Bill Dawley	.10	.05
☐ 24 Andre Dawson	.50	.23
☐ 25 Brian Dayett	.10	.05
☐ 26 Rick Dempsey	.25	.11
☐ 27 Ken Dowell	.10	.05
☐ 28 Dave Dravecky	.25	.11
☐ 29 Mike Dunne	.10	.05
☐ 30 Dennis Eckersley	.50	.23
☐ 31 Cecil Fielder	.10	.05
☐ 32 Brian Fisher	.10	.05
☐ 33 Willie Fraser	.10	.05
☐ 34 Ken Gerhart	.10	.05
☐ 35 Jim Gott	.10	.05
☐ 36 Dan Gladden	.10	.05
☐ 37 Mike Greenwell	.50	.23
☐ 38 Cecilio Guante	.10	.05
☐ 39 Albert Hall	.10	.05
☐ 40 Atlee Hammaker	.10	.05
☐ 41 Mickey Hatcher	.10	.05
☐ 42 Mike Heath	.10	.05
☐ 43 Neal Heaton	.10	.05
☐ 44 Mike Henneman	.50	.23
☐ 45 Guy Hoffman	.10	.05
☐ 46 Charles Hudson	.10	.05
☐ 47 Chuck Jackson	.10	.05
☐ 48 Mike Jackson	.50	.23
☐ 49 Reggie Jackson	.60	.25
☐ 50 Chris James	.10	.05
☐ 51 Dion James	.10	.05
☐ 52 Stan Javier	.10	.05
☐ 53 Stan Jefferson	.10	.05
☐ 54 Jimmy Jones	.10	.05
☐ 55 Tracy Jones	.10	.05
☐ 56 Terry Kennedy	.10	.05
☐ 57 Mike Kingery	.25	.11
☐ 58 Ray Knight	.10	.05
☐ 59 Gene Larkin	.10	.05
☐ 60 Mike LaValliere	.10	.05
☐ 61 Jack Lazorko	.10	.05
☐ 62 Terry Leach	.10	.05
☐ 63 Rick Leach	.10	.05
☐ 64 Craig Lefferts	.10	.05
☐ 65 Jim Lindeman	.10	.05
☐ 66 Bill Long	.10	.05
☐ 67 Mike Loynd	.10	.05
☐ 68 Greg Maddux	8.00	3.60
☐ 69 Bill Madlock	.25	.11
☐ 70 Dave Magadan	.25	.11
☐ 71 Joe Magrane	.10	.05
☐ 72 Fred Manrique	.10	.05
☐ 73 Mike Mason	.10	.05
☐ 74 Lloyd McClendon	.10	.05
☐ 75 Fred McGriff	.60	.25
☐ 76 Mark McGwire	2.50	1.10
☐ 77 Mark McLemore	.10	.05
☐ 78 Kevin McReynolds	.10	.05
☐ 79 Dave Meads	.10	.05
☐ 80 Greg Minton	.10	.05
☐ 81 John Mitchell	.10	.05
☐ 82 Kevin Mitchell	.10	.05
☐ 83 John Morris	.10	.05
☐ 84 Jeff Musselman	.10	.05
☐ 85 Randy Myers	.50	.23
☐ 86 Gene Nelson	.10	.05
☐ 87 Joe Niekro	.10	.05
☐ 88 Tom Nieto	.10	.05
☐ 89 Reid Nichols	.10	.05
☐ 90 Matt Nokes	.25	.11
☐ 91 Dickie Noles	.10	.05

☐ 92 Edwin Nunez	.10	.05
☐ 93 Jose Nunez	.10	.05
☐ 94 Paul O'Neill	.25	.11
☐ 95 Jim Paciorek	.10	.05
☐ 96 Lance Parrish	.25	.11
☐ 97 Bill Pecota	.10	.05
☐ 98 Tony Pena	.10	.05
☐ 99 Luis Polonia	.25	.11
☐ 100 Randy Ready	.10	.05
☐ 101 Jeff Reardon	.25	.11
☐ 102 Gary Redus	.10	.05
☐ 103 Rick Rhoden	.10	.05
☐ 104 Wally Ritchie	.10	.05
☐ 105 Jeff M. Robinson UER	.10	.05
(Wrong Jeff's stats on back)		
☐ 106 Mark Salas	.10	.05
☐ 107 Dave Schmidt	.10	.05
☐ 108 Kevin Seitzer UER	.25	.11
(Wrong birth year)		
☐ 109 John Shelby	.10	.05
☐ 110 John Smiley	.25	.11
☐ 111 Lary Sorensen	.10	.05
☐ 112 Chris Speier	.10	.05
☐ 113 Randy St.Claire	.10	.05
☐ 114 Jim Sundberg	.10	.05
☐ 115 B.J. Surhoff	.50	.23
☐ 116 Greg Swindell	.50	.23
☐ 117 Danny Tartabull	.25	.11
☐ 118 Dorn Taylor	.10	.05
☐ 119 Lee Tunnell	.10	.05
☐ 120 Ed VandeBerg	.10	.05
☐ 121 Andy Van Slyke	.25	.11
☐ 122 Gary Ward	.10	.05
☐ 123 Devon White	.50	.23
☐ 124 Alan Wiggins	.10	.05
☐ 125 Bill Wilkinson	.10	.05
☐ 126 Jim Winn	.10	.05
☐ 127 Frank Williams	.10	.05
☐ 128 Ken Williams	.10	.05
☐ 129 Matt Williams	3.00	1.35
☐ 130 Herm Winningham	.10	.05
☐ 131 Matt Young	.10	.05
☐ 132 Checklist 1-132	.10	.05

1988 Fleer

This set consists of 660 standard-size cards. Cards were primarily issued in 15-card wax packs and hobby and retail factory sets. Each wax pack contained one of 26 different "Stadium Card" stickers. Card fronts feature a distinctive white background with red and blue diagonal stripes across the card. Cards are again organized numerically by teams and team order is based upon the previous season's record. Subsets include Specials (622-640), Rookie Pairs (641-653), and checklists (654-660). Rookie Cards in this set include Jay

Bell, John Burkett, Ellis Burks, Ken Caminiti, Ron Gant, Tom Glavine, Mark Grace, Gregg Jefferies, Edgar Martinez, Jack McDowell, Jeff Montgomery, and Matt Williams.

	MINT	NRMT
COMPLETE SET (660)	20.00	9.00
COMPLETE RETAIL SET (660)	20.00	9.00
COMPLETE HOBBY SET (672)	25.00	11.00
COMMON CARD (1-660)	.10	.05
MINOR STARS	.20	.09
UNLISTED STARS	.40	.18
COMP.WORLD SERIES SET (12)	2.00	.90
ONE WORLD SERIES SET PER FACT.SET		

No.	Player	MINT	NRMT
1	Keith Atherton	.10	.05
2	Don Baylor	.20	.09
3	Juan Berenguer	.10	.05
4	Bert Blyleven	.20	.09
5	Tom Brunansky	.10	.05
6	Randy Bush	.10	.05
7	Steve Carlton	.40	.18
8	Mark Davidson	.10	.05
9	George Frazier	.10	.05
10	Gary Gaetti	.10	.05
11	Greg Gagne	.10	.05
12	Dan Gladden	.10	.05
13	Kent Hrbek	.20	.09
14	Gene Larkin	.10	.05
15	Tim Laudner	.10	.05
16	Steve Lombardozzi	.10	.05
17	Al Newman	.10	.05
18	Joe Niekro	.10	.05
19	Kirby Puckett	.75	.35
20	Jeff Reardon	.20	.09
21A	Dan Schatzeder ERR (Misspelled Schatzader on card front)	.20	
21B	Dan Schatzeder COR	.10	.05
22	Roy Smalley	.10	.05
23	Mike Smithson	.10	.05
24	Les Straker	.10	.05
25	Frank Viola	.10	.05
26	Jack Clark	.20	.09
27	Vince Coleman	.10	.05
28	Danny Cox	.10	.05
29	Bill Dawley	.10	.05
30	Ken Dayley	.10	.05
31	Doug DeCinces	.10	.05
32	Curt Ford	.10	.05
33	Bob Forsch	.10	.05
34	David Green	.10	.05
35	Tom Herr	.10	.05
36	Ricky Horton	.10	.05
37	Lance Johnson	.50	.23
38	Steve Lake	.10	.05
39	Jim Lindeman	.10	.05
40	Joe Magrane	.10	.05
41	Greg Mathews	.10	.05
42	Willie McGee	.10	.05
43	John Morris	.10	.05
44	Jose Oquendo	.10	.05
45	Tony Pena	.10	.05
46	Terry Pendleton	.20	.09
47	Ozzie Smith	.50	.23
48	John Tudor	.10	.05
49	Lee Tunnell	.10	.05
50	Todd Worrell	.20	.09
51	Doyle Alexander	.10	.05
52	Dave Bergman	.10	.05
53	Tom Brookens	.10	.05
54	Darrell Evans	.20	.09
55	Kirk Gibson	.20	.09
56	Mike Heath	.10	.05
57	Mike Henneman	.20	.09
58	Willie Hernandez	.10	.05
59	Larry Herndon	.10	.05
60	Eric King	.10	.05
61	Chet Lemon	.10	.05
62	Scott Lusader	.10	.05
63	Bill Madlock	.20	.09
64	Jack Morris	.10	.05
65	Jim Morrison	.10	.05
66	Matt Nokes	.10	.05
67	Dan Petry	.10	.05
68A	Jeff M. Robinson ERR (Stats for Jeff D. Robinson on card back, Born 12-13-60)	.40	.18
68B	Jeff M. Robinson COR (Born 12-14-61)	.10	.05
69	Pat Sheridan	.10	.05
70	Nate Snell	.10	.05
71	Frank Tanana	.10	.05
72	Walt Terrell	.10	.05
73	Mark Thurmond	.10	.05
74	Alan Trammell	.10	.05
75	Lou Whitaker	.20	.09
76	Mike Aldrete	.10	.05
77	Bob Brenly	.10	.05
78	Will Clark	.50	.23
79	Chili Davis	.10	.05
80	Kelly Downs	.10	.05
81	Dave Dravecky	.20	.09
82	Scott Garrelts	.10	.05
83	Atlee Hammaker	.10	.05
84	Dave Henderson	.10	.05
85	Mike Krukow	.10	.05
86	Mike LaCoss	.10	.05
87	Craig Lefferts	.10	.05
88	Jeff Leonard	.10	.05
89	Candy Maldonado	.10	.05
90	Eddie Milner	.10	.05
91	Bob Melvin	.10	.05
92	Kevin Mitchell	.20	.09
93	Jon Perlman	.10	.05
94	Rick Reuschel	.10	.05
95	Don Robinson	.10	.05
96	Chris Speier	.10	.05
97	Harry Spilman	.10	.05
98	Robby Thompson	.10	.05
99	Jose Uribe	.10	.05
100	Mark Wasinger	.10	.05
101	Matt Williams	2.00	.90
102	Jesse Barfield	.10	.05
103	George Bell	.20	.09
104	Juan Beniquez	.10	.05
105	John Cerutti	.10	.05
106	Jim Clancy	.10	.05
107	Rob Ducey	.10	.05
108	Mark Eichhorn	.10	.05
109	Tony Fernandez	.10	.05
110	Cecil Fielder	.40	.18
111	Kelly Gruber	.10	.05
112	Tom Henke	.10	.05
113A	Garth Iorg ERR (Misspelled Iorq on card front)	.40	.18
113B	Garth Iorg COR	.10	.05
114	Jimmy Key	.20	.09
115	Rick Leach	.10	.05
116	Manny Lee	.10	.05
117	Nelson Liriano	.10	.05
118	Fred McGriff	.40	.18
119	Lloyd Moseby	.10	.05
120	Rance Mulliniks	.10	.05
121	Jeff Musselman	.10	.05
122	Jose Nunez	.10	.05
123	Dave Stieb	.20	.09
124	Willie Upshaw	.10	.05
125	Duane Ward	.10	.05
126	Ernie Whitt	.10	.05
127	Rick Aguilera	.20	.09
128	Wally Backman	.10	.05
129	Mark Carreon	.20	.09
130	Gary Carter	.10	.05
131	David Cone	.18	.07
132	Ron Darling	.10	.05
133	Len Dykstra	.20	.09
134	Sid Fernandez	.10	.05
135	Dwight Gooden	.20	.09
136	Keith Hernandez	.20	.09
137	Gregg Jefferies	.50	.23
138	Howard Johnson	.10	.05
139	Terry Leach	.10	.05
140	Barry Lyons	.10	.05
141	Dave Magadan	.10	.05
142	Roger McDowell	.10	.05
143	Kevin McReynolds	.10	.05
144	Keith A. Miller	.10	.05
145	John Mitchell	.10	.05
146	Randy Myers	.10	.05
147	Bob Ojeda	.10	.05
148	Jesse Orosco	.10	.05
149	Rafael Santana	.10	.05
150	Doug Sisk	.10	.05
151	Darryl Strawberry	.20	.09
152	Tim Teufel	.10	.05
153	Gene Walter	.10	.05
154	Mookie Wilson	.20	.09
155	Jay Aldrich	.10	.05
156	Chris Bosio	.10	.05
157	Glenn Braggs	.10	.05
158	Greg Brock	.10	.05
159	Juan Castillo	.10	.05
160	Mark Clear	.10	.05
161	Cecil Cooper	.20	.09
162	Chuck Crim	.10	.05
163	Rob Deer	.10	.05
164	Mike Felder	.10	.05
165	Jim Gantner	.10	.05
166	Ted Higuera	.10	.05
167	Steve Kiefer	.10	.05
168	Rick Manning	.10	.05
169	Paul Molitor	.40	.18
170	Juan Nieves	.10	.05
171	Dan Plesac	.10	.05
172	Earnest Riles	.10	.05
173	Bill Schroeder	.10	.05
174	Steve Stanicek	.10	.05
175	B.J. Surhoff	.20	.09
176	Dale Sveum	.10	.05
177	Bill Wegman	.10	.05
178	Robin Yount	.40	.18
179	Hubie Brooks	.10	.05
180	Tim Burke	.10	.05
181	Casey Candaele	.10	.05
182	Mike Fitzgerald	.10	.05
183	Tom Foley	.10	.05
184	Andres Galarraga	.40	.18
185	Neal Heaton	.10	.05
186	Wallace Johnson	.10	.05
187	Vance Law	.10	.05
188	Dennis Martinez	.20	.09
189	Bob McClure	.10	.05
190	Andy McGaffigan	.10	.05
191	Reid Nichols	.10	.05
192	Pascual Perez	.10	.05
193	Tim Raines	.20	.09
194	Jeff Reed	.10	.05
195	Bob Sebra	.10	.05
196	Bryn Smith	.10	.05
197	Randy St.Claire	.10	.05
198	Tim Wallach	.20	.09
199	Mitch Webster	.10	.05
200	Herm Winningham	.10	.05
201	Floyd Youmans	.10	.05
202	Brad Arnsberg	.10	.05
203	Rick Cerone	.10	.05
204	Pat Clements	.10	.05
205	Henry Cotto	.10	.05
206	Mike Easler	.10	.05
207	Ron Guidry	.20	.09
208	Bill Gullickson	.10	.05
209	Rickey Henderson	.40	.18
210	Charles Hudson	.10	.05
211	Tommy John	.20	.09
212	Roberto Kelly	.40	.18
213	Ron Kittle	.10	.05
214	Don Mattingly	.60	.25
215	Bobby Meacham	.10	.05
216	Mike Pagliarulo	.10	.05
217	Dan Pasqua	.10	.05
218	Willie Randolph	.20	.09
219	Rick Rhoden	.10	.05
220	Dave Righetti	.20	.09
221	Jerry Royster	.10	.05
222	Tim Stoddard	.10	.05
223	Wayne Tolleson	.10	.05
224	Gary Ward	.10	.05
225	Claudell Washington	.10	.05
226	Dave Winfield	.40	.18
227	Buddy Bell	.20	.09
228	Tom Browning	.10	.05
229	Dave Concepcion	.20	.09
230	Kal Daniels	.10	.05

231	Eric Davis	.20	.09
232	Bo Diaz	.10	.05
233	Nick Esasky	.10	.05
	(Has a dollar sign before '87 SB totals)		
234	John Franco	.20	.09
235	Guy Hoffman	.10	.05
236	Tom Hume	.10	.05
237	Tracy Jones	.10	.05
238	Bill Landrum	.10	.05
239	Barry Larkin	.40	.18
240	Terry McGriff	.10	.05
241	Rob Murphy	.10	.05
242	Ron Oester	.10	.05
243	Dave Parker	.20	.09
244	Pat Perry	.10	.05
245	Ted Power	.10	.05
246	Dennis Rasmussen	.10	.05
247	Ron Robinson	.10	.05
248	Kurt Stillwell	.10	.05
249	Jeff Treadway	.10	.05
250	Frank Williams	.10	.05
251	Steve Balboni	.10	.05
252	Bud Black	.10	.05
253	Thad Bosley	.10	.05
254	George Brett	.75	.35
255	John Davis	.10	.05
256	Steve Farr	.10	.05
257	Gene Garber	.10	.05
258	Jerry Don Gleaton	.10	.05
259	Mark Gubicza	.10	.05
260	Bo Jackson	.40	.18
261	Danny Jackson	.10	.05
262	Ross Jones	.10	.05
263	Charlie Leibrandt	.10	.05
264	Bill Pecota	.10	.05
265	Melido Perez	.20	.09
266	Jamie Quirk	.10	.05
267	Dan Quisenberry	.10	.05
268	Bret Saberhagen	.10	.05
269	Angel Salazar	.10	.05
270	Kevin Seitzer UER	.20	.09
	(Wrong birth year)		
271	Danny Tartabull	.10	.05
272	Gary Thurman	.10	.05
273	Frank White	.20	.09
274	Willie Wilson	.10	.05
275	Tony Bernazard	.10	.05
276	Jose Canseco	.40	.18
277	Mike Davis	.10	.05
278	Storm Davis	.10	.05
279	Dennis Eckersley	.20	.09
280	Alfredo Griffin	.10	.05
281	Rick Honeycutt	.10	.05
282	Jay Howell	.10	.05
283	Reggie Jackson	.50	.23
284	Dennis Lamp	.10	.05
285	Carney Lansford	.20	.09
286	Mark McGwire	1.50	.70
287	Dwayne Murphy	.10	.05
288	Gene Nelson	.10	.05
289	Steve Ontiveros	.10	.05
290	Tony Phillips	.10	.05
291	Eric Plunk	.10	.05
292	Luis Polonia	.20	.09
293	Rick Rodriguez	.10	.05
294	Terry Steinbach	.10	.05
295	Dave Stewart	.20	.09
296	Curt Young	.10	.05
297	Luis Aguayo	.10	.05
298	Steve Bedrosian	.10	.05
299	Jeff Calhoun	.10	.05
300	Don Carman	.10	.05
301	Todd Frohwirth	.10	.05
302	Greg Gross	.10	.05
303	Kevin Gross	.10	.05
304	Von Hayes	.10	.05
305	Keith Hughes	.10	.05
306	Mike Jackson	.20	.09
307	Chris James	.10	.05
308	Steve Jeltz	.10	.05
309	Mike Maddux	.10	.05
310	Lance Parrish	.10	.05
311	Shane Rawley	.10	.05
312	Wally Ritchie	.10	.05
313	Bruce Ruffin	.10	.05
314	Juan Samuel	.10	.05
315	Mike Schmidt	.50	.23
316	Rick Schu	.10	.05
317	Jeff Stone	.10	.05
318	Kent Tekulve	.10	.05
319	Milt Thompson	.10	.05
320	Glenn Wilson	.10	.05
321	Rafael Belliard	.10	.05
322	Barry Bonds	1.00	.45
323	Bobby Bonilla UER	.10	.05
	(Wrong birth year)		
324	Sid Bream	.10	.05
325	John Cangelosi	.10	.05
326	Mike Diaz	.10	.05
327	Doug Drabek	.10	.05
328	Mike Dunne	.10	.05
329	Brian Fisher	.10	.05
330	Brett Gideon	.10	.05
331	Terry Harper	.10	.05
332	Bob Kipper	.10	.05
333	Mike LaValliere	.10	.05
334	Jose Lind	.10	.05
335	Junior Ortiz	.10	.05
336	Vicente Palacios	.10	.05
337	Bob Patterson	.10	.05
338	Al Pedrique	.10	.05
339	R.J. Reynolds	.10	.05
340	John Smiley	.20	.09
341	Andy Van Slyke UER	.20	.09
	(Wrong batting and throwing listed)		
342	Bob Walk	.10	.05
343	Marty Barrett	.10	.05
344	Todd Benzinger	.10	.05
345	Wade Boggs	.40	.18
346	Tom Bolton	.10	.05
347	Oil Can Boyd	.10	.05
348	Ellis Burks	1.00	.45
349	Roger Clemens	.75	.35
350	Steve Crawford	.10	.05
351	Dwight Evans	.10	.05
352	Wes Gardner	.10	.05
353	Rich Gedman	.10	.05
354	Mike Greenwell	.20	.09
355	Sam Horn	.10	.05
356	Bruce Hurst	.10	.05
357	John Marzano	.10	.05
358	Al Nipper	.10	.05
359	Spike Owen	.10	.05
360	Jody Reed	.10	.05
361	Jim Rice	.20	.09
362	Ed Romero	.10	.05
363	Kevin Romine	.10	.05
364	Joe Sambito	.10	.05
365	Calvin Schiraldi	.10	.05
366	Jeff Sellers	.10	.05
367	Bob Stanley	.10	.05
368	Scott Bankhead	.10	.05
369	Phil Bradley	.10	.05
370	Scott Bradley	.10	.05
371	Mickey Brantley	.10	.05
372	Mike Campbell	.10	.05
373	Alvin Davis	.10	.05
374	Lee Guetterman	.10	.05
375	Dave Hengel	.10	.05
376	Mike Kingery	.10	.05
377	Mark Langston	.10	.05
378	Edgar Martinez	2.00	.90
379	Mike Moore	.10	.05
380	Mike Morgan	.10	.05
381	John Moses	.10	.05
382	Donell Nixon	.10	.05
383	Edwin Nunez	.10	.05
384	Ken Phelps	.10	.05
385	Jim Presley	.10	.05
386	Rey Quinones	.10	.05
387	Jerry Reed	.10	.05
388	Harold Reynolds	.10	.05
389	Dave Valle	.10	.05
390	Bill Wilkinson	.10	.05
391	Harold Baines	.20	.09
392	Floyd Bannister	.10	.05
393	Daryl Boston	.10	.05
394	Ivan Calderon	.10	.05
395	Jose DeLeon	.10	.05
396	Richard Dotson	.10	.05
397	Carlton Fisk	.40	.18
398	Ozzie Guillen	.10	.05
399	Ron Hassey	.10	.05
400	Donnie Hill	.10	.05
401	Bob James	.10	.05
402	Dave LaPoint	.10	.05
403	Bill Lindsey	.10	.05
404	Bill Long	.10	.05
405	Steve Lyons	.10	.05
406	Fred Manrique	.10	.05
407	Jack McDowell	.40	.18
408	Gary Redus	.10	.05
409	Ray Searage	.10	.05
410	Bobby Thigpen	.10	.05
411	Greg Walker	.10	.05
412	Ken Williams	.10	.05
413	Jim Winn	.10	.05
414	Jody Davis	.10	.05
415	Andre Dawson	.40	.18
416	Brian Dayett	.10	.05
417	Bob Dernier	.10	.05
418	Frank DiPino	.10	.05
419	Shawon Dunston	.10	.05
420	Leon Durham	.10	.05
421	Les Lancaster	.10	.05
422	Ed Lynch	.10	.05
423	Greg Maddux	2.50	1.10
424	Dave Martinez	.10	.05
425A	Keith Moreland ERR	1.50	.70
	(Photo actually Jody Davis)		
425B	Keith Moreland COR	.20	.09
	(Bat on shoulder)		
426	Jamie Moyer	.10	.05
427	Jerry Mumphrey	.10	.05
428	Paul Noce	.10	.05
429	Rafael Palmeiro	.40	.18
430	Wade Rowdon	.10	.05
431	Ryne Sandberg	.50	.23
432	Scott Sanderson	.10	.05
433	Lee Smith	.20	.09
434	Jim Sundberg	.10	.05
435	Rick Sutcliffe	.10	.05
436	Manny Trillo	.10	.05
437	Juan Agosto	.10	.05
438	Larry Andersen	.10	.05
439	Alan Ashby	.10	.05
440	Kevin Bass	.10	.05
441	Ken Caminiti	2.00	.90
442	Rocky Childress	.10	.05
443	Jose Cruz	.10	.05
444	Danny Darwin	.10	.05
445	Glenn Davis	.10	.05
446	Jim Deshaies	.10	.05
447	Bill Doran	.10	.05
448	Ty Gainey	.10	.05
449	Billy Hatcher	.10	.05
450	Jeff Heathcock	.10	.05
451	Bob Knepper	.10	.05
452	Rob Mallicoat	.10	.05
453	Dave Meads	.10	.05
454	Craig Reynolds	.10	.05
455	Nolan Ryan	1.50	.70
456	Mike Scott	.10	.05
457	Dave Smith	.10	.05
458	Denny Walling	.10	.05
459	Robbie Wine	.10	.05
460	Gerald Young	.10	.05
461	Bob Brower	.10	.05
462A	Jerry Browne ERR..	1.50	.70
	(Photo actually Bob Brower, white player)		
462B	Jerry Browne COR ..	.20	.09
	(Black player)		
463	Steve Buechele	.10	.05
464	Edwin Correa	.10	.05
465	Cecil Espy	.10	.05
466	Scott Fletcher	.10	.05
467	Jose Guzman	.10	.05
468	Greg Harris	.10	.05
469	Charlie Hough	.10	.09
470	Pete Incaviglia	.10	.05
471	Paul Kilgus	.10	.05
472	Mike Loynd	.10	.05
473	Oddibe McDowell	.10	.05

☐ 474 Dale Mohorcic .... .05
☐ 475 Pete O'Brien .... .10 .05
☐ 476 Larry Parrish ...... .05 .05
☐ 477 Geno Petralli ...... .05 .05
☐ 478 Jeff Russell .... .05 .05
☐ 479 Ruben Sierra ...... .20
☐ 480 Mike Stanley ...... .20 .09
☐ 481 Curtis Wilkerson .. .10
☐ 482 Mitch Williams .... .20 .09
☐ 483 Bobby Witt .... .10
☐ 484 Tony Armas .... .10 .05
☐ 485 Bob Boone .... .20 .09
☐ 486 Bill Buckner .... .20 .09
☐ 487 DeWayne Buice .... .10
☐ 488 Brian Downing ...... .10 .05
☐ 489 Chuck Finley .... .20 .09
☐ 490 Willie Fraser UER .. .05
    (Wrong bio stats,
    for George Hendrick)
☐ 491 Jack Howell .... .10 .05
☐ 492 Ruppert Jones ...... .10 .05
☐ 493 Wally Joyner .... .40 .18
☐ 494 Jack Lazorko ...... .10 .05
☐ 495 Gary Lucas .... .10 .05
☐ 496 Kirk McCaskill ...... .10 .05
☐ 497 Mark McLemore .... .10 .05
☐ 498 Darrell Miller ...... .10 .05
☐ 499 Greg Minton .... .10 .05
☐ 500 Donnie Moore ...... .10 .05
☐ 501 Gus Polidor .... .10 .05
☐ 502 Johnny Ray .... .10 .05
☐ 503 Mark Ryal .... .10 .05
☐ 504 Dick Schofield ...... .10 .05
☐ 505 Don Sutton .... .40 .18
☐ 506 Devon White .... .20 .09
☐ 507 Mike Witt .... .10 .05
☐ 508 Dave Anderson .... .10 .05
☐ 509 Tim Belcher .... .20 .09
☐ 510 Ralph Bryant ...... .10 .05
☐ 511 Tim Crews .... .10 .05
☐ 512 Mike Devereaux .... .10 .05
☐ 513 Mariano Duncan .... .10 .05
☐ 514 Pedro Guerrero .... .20 .09
☐ 515 Jeff Hamilton ...... .10 .05
☐ 516 Mickey Hatcher .... .10 .05
☐ 517 Brad Havens .... .10 .05
☐ 518 Orel Hershiser .... .20 .09
☐ 519 Shawn Hillegas .... .10 .05
☐ 520 Ken Howell .... .10 .05
☐ 521 Tim Leary .... .10 .05
☐ 522 Mike Marshall ...... .10 .05
☐ 523 Steve Sax .... .10 .05
☐ 524 Mike Scioscia ...... .10 .05
☐ 525 Mike Sharperson .. .10 .05
☐ 526 John Shelby .... .10 .05
☐ 527 Franklin Stubbs .... .10 .05
☐ 528 Fernando Valenzuela .20 .09
☐ 529 Bob Welch .... .10 .05
☐ 530 Matt Young .... .10 .05
☐ 531 Jim Acker .... .10 .05
☐ 532 Paul Assenmacher .10 .05
☐ 533 Jeff Blauser .... .75 .35
☐ 534 Joe Boever .... .10 .05
☐ 535 Martin Clary .... .10 .05
☐ 536 Kevin Coffman ...... .10 .05
☐ 537 Jeff Dedmon .... .10 .05
☐ 538 Ron Gant .... .50 .23
☐ 539 Tom Glavine .... 1.50 .70
☐ 540 Ken Griffey .... .10 .05
☐ 541 Albert Hall .... .10 .05
☐ 542 Glenn Hubbard .... .10 .05
☐ 543 Dion James .... .10 .05
☐ 544 Dale Murphy ...... .40 .18
☐ 545 Ken Oberkfell ...... .10 .05
☐ 546 David Palmer ...... .10 .05
☐ 547 Gerald Perry .... .10 .05
☐ 548 Charlie Puleo ...... .10 .05
☐ 549 Ted Simmons ...... .20 .09
☐ 550 Zane Smith .... .10 .05
☐ 551 Andres Thomas .... .10 .05
☐ 552 Ozzie Virgil .... .10 .05
☐ 553 Don Aase .... .10 .05
☐ 554 Jeff Ballard .... .10 .05
☐ 555 Eric Bell .... .10 .05
☐ 556 Mike Boddicker .... .10 .05
☐ 557 Ken Dixon .... .10 .05

☐ 558 Jim Dwyer .... .10 .05
☐ 559 Ken Gerhart .... .10 .05
☐ 560 Rene Gonzales .... .10 .05
☐ 561 Mike Griffin .... .10 .05
☐ 562 John Habyan UER .. .10 .05
    (Misspelled Hayban on
    both sides of card)
☐ 563 Terry Kennedy ...... .10 .05
☐ 564 Ray Knight .... .10 .05
☐ 565 Lee Lacy .... .10 .05
☐ 566 Fred Lynn .... .10 .05
☐ 567 Eddie Murray ...... .40 .18
☐ 568 Tom Niedenfuer .... .10 .05
☐ 569 Bill Ripken .... .20 .09
☐ 570 Cal Ripken .... 1.50 .70
☐ 571 Dave Schmidt ...... .10 .05
☐ 572 Larry Sheets ...... .10 .05
☐ 573 Pete Stanicek ...... .10 .05
☐ 574 Mark Williamson .. .10 .05
☐ 575 Mike Young .... .10 .05
☐ 576 Shawn Abner ...... .10 .05
☐ 577 Greg Booker .... .10 .05
☐ 578 Chris Brown .... .10 .05
☐ 579 Keith Comstock .... .10 .05
☐ 580 Joey Cora .... .75 .35
☐ 581 Mark Davis .... .10 .05
☐ 582 Tim Flannery .... .40 .18
    (With surfboard)
☐ 583 Goose Gossage .... .10 .05
☐ 584 Mark Grant .... .10 .05
☐ 585 Tony Gwynn .... 1.00 .45
☐ 586 Andy Hawkins ...... .10 .05
☐ 587 Stan Jefferson ...... .10 .05
☐ 588 Jimmy Jones .... .10 .05
☐ 589 John Kruk .... .20 .09
☐ 590 Shane Mack .... .10 .05
☐ 591 Carmelo Martinez .. .10 .05
☐ 592 Lance McCullers UER .10 .05
    (6'11" tall)
☐ 593 Eric Nolte .... .10 .05
☐ 594 Randy Ready .... .10 .05
☐ 595 Luis Salazar .... .10 .05
☐ 596 Benito Santiago .... .20 .09
☐ 597 Eric Show .... .10 .05
☐ 598 Garry Templeton .... .10 .05
☐ 599 Ed Whitson .... .10 .05
☐ 600 Scott Bailes .... .10 .05
☐ 601 Chris Bando .... .10 .05
☐ 602 Jay Bell .... .75 .35
☐ 603 Brett Butler .... .20 .09
☐ 604 Tom Candiotti ...... .10 .05
☐ 605 Joe Carter .... .40 .18
☐ 606 Carmen Castillo .... .10 .05
☐ 607 Brian Dorsett ...... .10 .05
☐ 608 John Farrell .... .10 .05
☐ 609 Julio Franco .... .20 .09
☐ 610 Mel Hall .... .10 .05
☐ 611 Tommy Hinzo ...... .10 .05
☐ 612 Brook Jacoby ...... .10 .05
☐ 613 Doug Jones .... .40 .18
☐ 614 Ken Schrom .... .10 .05
☐ 615 Cory Snyder .... .20 .09
☐ 616 Sammy Stewart .... .10 .05
☐ 617 Greg Swindell ...... .20 .09
☐ 618 Pat Tabler .... .10 .05
☐ 619 Ed Vande Berg .... .10 .05
☐ 620 Eddie Williams .... .20 .09
☐ 621 Rich Yett .... .10 .05
☐ 622 Slugging Sophomores .20 .09
    Wally Joyner,
    Cory Snyder
☐ 623 Dominican Dynamite .10 .05
    George Bell
    Pedro Guerrero
☐ 624 Oakland's Power Team .75 .35
    Mark McGwire
    Jose Canseco
☐ 625 Classic Relief ...... .10 .05
    Dave Righetti
    Dan Plesac
☐ 626 All Star Righties .... .20 .09
    Bret Saberhagen
    Mike Witt
    Jack Morris
☐ 627 Game Closers ...... .10 .05
    John Franco

    Steve Bedrosian
☐ 628 Masters/Double Play .50 .23
    Ozzie Smith
    Ryne Sandberg
☐ 629 Rookie Record Setter .75 .35
    Mark McGwire
☐ 630 Changing the Guard .40 .18
    Mike Greenwell
    Ellis Burks
    Todd Benzinger
☐ 631 NL Batting Champs .40 .18
    Tony Gwynn
    Tim Raines
☐ 632 Pitching Magic ...... .20 .09
    Mike Scott
    Orel Hershiser
☐ 633 Big Bats at First .... .50 .23
    Pat Tabler
    Mark McGwire
☐ 634 Hitting King/Thief .... .40 .18
    Tony Gwynn
    Vince Coleman
☐ 635 Slugging Shortstops .50 .23
    Tony Fernandez
    Cal Ripken
☐ 636 Tried/True Sluggers .10 .05
    Mike Schmidt
    Gary Carter
☐ 637 Crunch Time .... .20 .09
    Darryl Strawberry
    Eric Davis
☐ 638 AL All-Stars .... .10 .05
    Matt Nokes
    Kirby Puckett
☐ 639 NL All-Stars .... .20 .09
    Keith Hernandez
    Dale Murphy
☐ 640 The O's Brothers .... .75 .35
    Billy Ripken
    Cal Ripken
☐ 641 Mark Grace and .... 2.00 .90
    Darrin Jackson
☐ 642 Damon Berryhill and .40 .18
    Jeff Montgomery
☐ 643 Felix Fermin and .... .10 .05
    Jesse Reid
☐ 644 Greg Myers and .... .10 .05
    Greg Tabor
☐ 645 Joey Meyer and .... .10 .05
    Jim Eppard
☐ 646 Adam Peterson and .20 .09
    Randy Velarde
☐ 647 Pete Smith and .... .20 .09
    Chris Gwynn
☐ 648 Tom Newell and .... .10 .05
    Greg Jelks
☐ 649 Mario Diaz and ...... .10 .05
    Clay Parker
☐ 650 Jack Savage and .... .10 .05
    Todd Simmons
☐ 651 John Burkett and .... .40 .18
    Kirt Manwaring
☐ 652 Dave Otto and ...... .10 .05
    Walt Weiss
☐ 653 Jeff King and .... .50 .23
    Randell Byers
☐ 654 CL: Twins/Cards .... .10 .05
    Tigers/Giants UER
    (90 Bob Melvin,
    91 Eddie Milner)
☐ 655 CL: Blue Jays/Mets .10 .05
    Brewers/Expos UER
    (Mets listed before
    Blue Jays on card)
☐ 656 CL: Yankees/Reds .. .10 .05
    Royals/A's
☐ 657 CL: Phillies/Pirates .. .10 .05
    Red Sox/Mariners
☐ 658 CL: White Sox/Cubs .10 .05
    Astros/Rangers
☐ 659 CL: Angels/Dodgers .10 .05
    Braves/Orioles
☐ 660 CL: Padres/Indians .10 .05
    Rookies/Specials

1988 Fleer All-Stars

These 12 standard-size cards were inserted randomly in wax and cello packs of the 1988 Fleer set. The cards show the player silhouetted against a light green background with dark green stripes. The player's name, team, and position are printed in yellow at the bottom of the obverse. The card backs are done predominantly in green, white, and black. The players are the "best" at each position, three pitchers, eight position players, and a designated hitter.

	MINT	NRMT
COMPLETE SET (12)	6.00	2.70
COMMON CARD (1-12)	.30	.14
RANDOM INSERTS IN PACKS ..		
☐ 1 Matt Nokes	.30	.14
☐ 2 Tom Henke	.30	.14
☐ 3 Ted Higuera	.30	.14
☐ 4 Roger Clemens	3.00	1.35
☐ 5 George Bell	.30	.14
☐ 6 Andre Dawson	1.00	.45
☐ 7 Eric Davis	.75	.35
☐ 8 Wade Boggs	1.00	.45
☐ 9 Alan Trammell	.40	.18
☐ 10 Juan Samuel	.30	.14
☐ 11 Jack Clark	.30	.14
☐ 12 Paul Molitor	1.50	.70

1988 Fleer Headliners

This six-card standard-size set was distributed one per rack pack. The obverse features the player photo superimposed on a gray newspaper background. The cards are printed in red, black,

and white on the back describing why that particular player made headlines the previous season. The set is sequenced in alphabetical order.

	MINT	NRMT
COMPLETE SET (6)	5.00	2.20
COMMON CARD (1-6)	.75	.35
ONE PER RACK PACK		
☐ 1 Don Mattingly	1.00	.45
☐ 2 Mark McGwire	2.50	1.10
☐ 3 Jack Morris	1.25	.55
☐ 4 Darryl Strawberry	1.00	.45
☐ 5 Dwight Gooden	1.00	.45
☐ 6 Tim Raines	.75	.35

1988 Fleer Update

This 132-card standard-size set was distributed exclusively in factory set form in a red, white and blue, cellophane-wrapped box through hobby dealers. In addition to the complete set of 132 cards, the box also contained 25 Team Logo stickers. The cards look very similar to the 1988 Fleer regular issue except for the U-prefixed numbering on back. Cards are ordered alphabetically by player's last name. This was the first Fleer Update set to adopt the Fleer "alphabetical within team" numbering system. The key extended Rookie Cards in this set are Roberto Alomar, Craig Biggio and John Smoltz.

	MINT	NRMT
COMP.FACT.SET (132)	8.00	3.60
COMMON CARD (1-132)	.10	.05
MINOR STARS	.20	.09
SEMISTARS	.40	.18
UNLISTED STARS	.75	.35
☐ 1 Jose Bautista	.10	.05
☐ 2 Joe Orsulak	.10	.05
☐ 3 Doug Sisk	.10	.05
☐ 4 Craig Worthington	.10	.05
☐ 5 Mike Boddicker	.10	.05
☐ 6 Rick Cerone	.10	.05
☐ 7 Larry Parrish	.10	.05
☐ 8 Lee Smith	.20	.09
☐ 9 Mike Smithson	.10	.05
☐ 10 John Trautwein	.10	.05
☐ 11 Sherman Corbett	.10	.05
☐ 12 Chili Davis	.40	.18
☐ 13 Jim Eppard	.10	.05
☐ 14 Bryan Harvey	.20	.09
☐ 15 John Davis	.10	.05
☐ 16 Dave Gallagher	.10	.05
☐ 17 Ricky Horton	.10	.05
☐ 18 Dan Pasqua	.10	.05
☐ 19 Melido Perez	.20	.09

☐ 20 Jose Segura	.10	.05
☐ 21 Andy Allanson	.10	.05
☐ 22 Jon Perlman	.10	.05
☐ 23 Domingo Ramos	.10	.05
☐ 24 Rick Rodriguez	.10	.05
☐ 25 Willie Upshaw	.10	.05
☐ 26 Paul Gibson	.10	.05
☐ 27 Don Heinkel	.10	.05
☐ 28 Ray Knight	.10	.05
☐ 29 Gary Pettis	.10	.05
☐ 30 Luis Salazar	.10	.05
☐ 31 Mike Macfarlane	.20	.09
☐ 32 Jeff Montgomery	.75	.35
☐ 33 Ted Power	.10	.05
☐ 34 Israel Sanchez	.10	.05
☐ 35 Kurt Stillwell	.10	.05
☐ 36 Pat Tabler	.10	.05
☐ 37 Don August	.10	.05
☐ 38 Darryl Hamilton	.20	.09
☐ 39 Jeff Leonard	.10	.05
☐ 40 Joey Meyer	.10	.05
☐ 41 Allan Anderson	.10	.05
☐ 42 Brian Harper	.10	.05
☐ 43 Tom Herr	.10	.05
☐ 44 Charlie Lea	.10	.05
☐ 45 John Moses	.10	.05
(Listed as Hohn on checklist card)		
☐ 46 John Candelaria	.10	.05
☐ 47 Jack Clark	.20	.09
☐ 48 Richard Dotson	.10	.05
☐ 49 Al Leiter	.75	.35
☐ 50 Rafael Santana	.10	.05
☐ 51 Don Slaught	.10	.05
☐ 52 Todd Burns	.10	.05
☐ 53 Dave Henderson	.10	.05
☐ 54 Doug Jennings	.10	.05
☐ 55 Dave Parker	.20	.09
☐ 56 Walt Weiss	.40	.18
☐ 57 Bob Welch	.10	.05
☐ 58 Henry Cotto	.10	.05
☐ 59 Mario Diaz UER	.10	.05
(Listed as Marion on card front)		
☐ 60 Mike Jackson	.10	.05
☐ 61 Bill Swift	.10	.05
☐ 62 Jose Cecena	.10	.05
☐ 63 Ray Hayward	.10	.05
☐ 64 Jim Steels UER	.10	.05
(Listed as Jim Steele on card back)		
☐ 65 Pat Borders	.20	.09
☐ 66 Sil Campusano	.10	.05
☐ 67 Mike Flanagan	.10	.05
☐ 68 Todd Stottlemyre	.75	.35
☐ 69 David Wells	.75	.35
☐ 70 Jose Alvarez	.10	.05
☐ 71 Paul Runge	.10	.05
☐ 72 Cesar Jimenez	.10	.05
(Card was intended for German Jiminez, it's his photo)		
☐ 73 Pete Smith	.10	.05
☐ 74 John Smoltz	2.00	.90
☐ 75 Damon Berryhill	.10	.05
☐ 76 Goose Gossage	.40	.18
☐ 77 Mark Grace	1.50	.70
☐ 78 Darrin Jackson	.10	.05
☐ 79 Vance Law	.10	.05
☐ 80 Jeff Pico	.10	.05
☐ 81 Gary Varsho	.10	.05
☐ 82 Tim Birtsas	.10	.05
☐ 83 Rob Dibble	.20	.09
☐ 84 Danny Jackson	.10	.05
☐ 85 Paul O'Neill	.40	.18
☐ 86 Jose Rijo	.10	.05
☐ 87 Chris Sabo	.20	.09
☐ 88 John Fishel	.10	.05
☐ 89 Craig Biggio	2.50	1.10
☐ 90 Terry Puhl	.10	.05
☐ 91 Rafael Ramirez	.10	.05
☐ 92 Louie Meadows	.10	.05
☐ 93 Kirk Gibson	.75	.35
☐ 94 Alfredo Griffin	.10	.05
☐ 95 Jay Howell	.10	.05
☐ 96 Jesse Orosco	.10	.05

□ 97 Alejandro Pena ....10 .05
□ 98 Tracy Woodson ....10 .05
□ 99 John Dopson.................10 .05
□ 100 Brian Holman ....10 .05
□ 101 Rex Hudler ....10 .05
□ 102 Jeff Parrett ....10 .05
□ 103 Nelson Santovenia ....10 .05
□ 104 Kevin Elster ....20 .09
□ 105 Jeff Innis ....10 .05
□ 106 Mackey Sasser ....10 .05
□ 107 Phil Bradley ....10 .05
□ 108 Danny Clay ....10 .05
□ 109 Greg A.Harris ....10 .05
□ 110 Ricky Jordan ....20 .09
□ 111 David Palmer ....10 .05
□ 112 Jim Gott ....10 .05
□ 113 Tommy Gregg UER ....10 .05
  (Photo actually Randy Milligan)
□ 114 Barry Jones ....10 .05
□ 115 Randy Milligan ....10 .05
□ 116 Luis Alicea ....20 .09
□ 117 Tom Brunansky ....10 .05
□ 118 John Costello ....10 .05
□ 119 Jose DeLeon ....10 .05
□ 120 Bob Horner ....10 .05
□ 121 Scott Terry ....10 .05
□ 122 Roberto Alomar 4.00 1.80
□ 123 Dave Leiper ....10 .05
□ 124 Keith Moreland ....10 .05
□ 125 Mark Parent ....10 .05
□ 126 Dennis Rasmussen ....10 .05
□ 127 Randy Bockus ....10 .05
□ 128 Brett Butler ....20 .09
□ 129 Donell Nixon ....10 .05
□ 130 Earnest Riles ....10 .05
□ 131 Roger Samuels ....10 .05
□ 132 Checklist U1-U132 ....10 .05

1989 Fleer

This set consists of 660 standard-size cards. Cards were primarily issued in 15-card wax packs, rack packs and hobby and retail factory sets. Card fronts feature a distinctive gray border background with white and yellow trim. Cards are again organized alphabetically within teams and teams ordered by previous season record. The last 33 cards in the set consist of Specials (628-639), Rookie Pairs (640-653), and checklists (654-660). Approximately half of the California Angels players have white rather than yellow halos. Certain Oakland A's player cards have red instead of green lines for front photo borders. Checklist cards are available either with or without positions listed for each player. Rookie Cards in this set include Sandy Alomar Jr., Brady Anderson, Dante Bichette,

Craig Biggio, Ken Griffey Jr., Charlie Hayes, Ken Hill, Randy Johnson, Ramon Martinez, Hal Morris, Gary Sheffield, and John Smoltz.

	MINT	NRMT
COMPLETE SET (660)	10.00	4.50
COMP.HOBBY SET (672)	12.00	5.50
COMMON CARD (1-660)	.05	
MINOR STARS	.10	
UNLISTED STARS	.20	.09
COMP.WORLD SERIES SET (12)	2.00	.90
ONE W.SERIES SET PER HOBBY SET		

□ 1 Don Baylor ....10 .05
□ 2 Lance Blankenship ......05 .02
□ 3 Todd Burns UER ....05 .02
  (Wrong birthdate; before/after All-Star stats missing)
□ 4 Greg Cadaret UER ......05 .02
  (All-Star Break stats show 3 losses, should be 2)
□ 5 Jose Canseco ....20 .09
□ 6 Storm Davis ....05 .02
□ 7 Dennis Eckersley ....10 .05
□ 8 Mike Gallego ....05 .02
□ 9 Ron Hassey ....05 .02
□ 10 Dave Henderson ....05 .02
□ 11 Rick Honeycutt ....05 .02
□ 12 Glenn Hubbard ....05 .02
□ 13 Stan Javier ....05 .02
□ 14 Doug Jennings ....05 .02
□ 15 Felix Jose ....05 .02
□ 16 Carney Lansford ....10 .05
□ 17 Mark McGwire ....40 .18
□ 18 Gene Nelson ....05 .02
□ 19 Dave Parker ....10 .05
□ 20 Eric Plunk ....05 .02
□ 21 Luis Polonia ....05 .02
□ 22 Terry Steinbach ....10 .05
□ 23 Dave Stewart ....10 .05
□ 24 Walt Weiss ....05 .02
□ 25 Bob Welch ....05 .02
□ 26 Curt Young ....05 .02
□ 27 Rick Aguilera ....10 .05
□ 28 Wally Backman ....05 .02
□ 29 Mark Carreon UER ......05 .02
  (After All-Star batting 7.14)
□ 30 Gary Carter ....20 .09
□ 31 David Cone ....20 .09
□ 32 Ron Darling ....05 .02
□ 33 Len Dykstra ....10 .05
□ 34 Kevin Elster ....05 .02
□ 35 Sid Fernandez ....05 .02
□ 36 Dwight Gooden ....10 .05
□ 37 Keith Hernandez ....10 .05
□ 38 Gregg Jefferies ....10 .05
□ 39 Howard Johnson ....10 .05
□ 40 Terry Leach ....05 .02
□ 41 Dave Magadan UER .....05 .02
  (Bio says 15 doubles, should be 13)
□ 42 Bob McClure ....05 .02
□ 43 Roger McDowell UER ...05 .02
  (Led Mets with 58, should be 62)
□ 44 Kevin McReynolds ......05 .02
□ 45 Keith A. Miller ....05 .02
□ 46 Randy Myers ....10 .05
□ 47 Bob Ojeda ....05 .02
□ 48 Mackey Sasser ....05 .02
□ 49 Darryl Strawberry ....10 .05
□ 50 Tim Teufel ....05 .02
□ 51 Dave West ....05 .02
□ 52 Mookie Wilson ....10 .05
□ 53 Dave Anderson ....05 .02
□ 54 Tim Belcher ....05 .02
□ 55 Mike Davis ....05 .02
□ 56 Mike Devereaux ....05 .02
□ 57 Kirk Gibson ....10 .05
□ 58 Alfredo Griffin ....05 .02
□ 59 Chris Gwynn ....05 .02

□ 60 Jeff Hamilton..............05 .02
□ 61A Danny Heep...............20 .09
  (Home: Lake Hills)
□ 61B Danny Heep..............05 .02
  (Home: San Antonio)
□ 62 Orel Hershiser ....10 .05
□ 63 Brian Holton ....05 .02
□ 64 Jay Howell ....05 .02
□ 65 Tim Leary ....05 .02
□ 66 Mike Marshall ....05 .02
□ 67 Ramon Martinez ....25 .11
□ 68 Jesse Orosco ....05 .02
□ 69 Alejandro Pena ....05 .02
□ 70 Steve Sax ....10 .05
□ 71 Mike Scioscia ....05 .02
□ 72 Mike Sharperson ....05 .02
□ 73 John Shelby ....05 .02
□ 74 Franklin Stubbs ....05 .02
□ 75 John Tudor ....05 .02
□ 76 Fernando Valenzuela ...10 .05
□ 77 Tracy Woodson ....05 .02
□ 78 Marty Barrett ....05 .02
□ 79 Todd Benzinger ....05 .02
□ 80 Mike Boddicker UER ....05 .02
  (Rochester in '76, should be '78)
□ 81 Wade Boggs ....20 .09
□ 82 Oil Can Boyd ....05 .02
□ 83 Ellis Burks ....10 .05
□ 84 Rick Cerone ....05 .02
□ 85 Roger Clemens ....40 .18
□ 86 Steve Curry ....05 .02
□ 87 Dwight Evans ....05 .02
□ 88 Wes Gardner ....05 .02
□ 89 Rich Gedman ....05 .02
□ 90 Mike Greenwell ....05 .02
□ 91 Bruce Hurst ....05 .02
□ 92 Dennis Lamp ....05 .02
□ 93 Spike Owen ....05 .02
□ 94 Larry Parrish UER ....05 .02
  (Before All-Star Break batting 1.90)
□ 95 Carlos Quintana ....05 .02
□ 96 Jody Reed ....05 .02
□ 97 Jim Rice ....10 .05
□ 98A Kevin Romine ERR .....20 .09
  (Photo actually Randy Kutcher batting)
□ 98B Kevin Romine COR .....05 .02
  (Arms folded)
□ 99 Lee Smith ....10 .05
□ 100 Mike Smithson ....05 .02
□ 101 Bob Stanley ....05 .02
□ 102 Allan Anderson ....05 .02
□ 103 Keith Atherton ....05 .02
□ 104 Juan Berenguer ....05 .02
□ 105 Bert Blyleven ....10 .05
□ 106 Eric Bullock UER ....05 .02
  (Bats/Throws Right, should be Left)
□ 107 Randy Bush ....05 .02
□ 108 John Christensen ....05 .02
□ 109 Mark Davidson ....05 .02
□ 110 Gary Gaetti ....05 .02
□ 111 Greg Gagne ....05 .02
□ 112 Dan Gladden ....05 .02
□ 113 German Gonzalez ....05 .02
□ 114 Brian Harper ....05 .02
□ 115 Tom Herr ....05 .02
□ 116 Kent Hrbek ....10 .05
□ 117 Gene Larkin ....05 .02
□ 118 Tim Laudner ....05 .02
□ 119 Charlie Lea ....05 .02
□ 120 Steve Lombardozzi .....05 .02
□ 121A John Moses ....20 .09
  (Home: Tempe)
□ 121B John Moses ....05 .02
  (Home: Phoenix)
□ 122 Al Newman ....05 .02
□ 123 Mark Portugal ....05 .02
□ 124 Kirby Puckett ....40 .18
□ 125 Jeff Reardon ....10 .05
□ 126 Fred Toliver ....05 .02
□ 127 Frank Viola ....05 .02
□ 128 Doyle Alexander ....05 .02
□ 129 Dave Bergman ....05 .02

☐ 130A	Tom Brookens ERR (Mike Heath back)	.75	.35
☐ 130B	Tom Brookens COR	.05	.02
☐ 131	Paul Gibson	.05	.02
☐ 132A	Mike Heath ERR (Tom Brookens back)	.75	.35
☐ 132B	Mike Heath COR	.05	.02
☐ 133	Don Heinkel	.05	.02
☐ 134	Mike Henneman	.05	.02
☐ 135	Guillermo Hernandez	.05	.02
☐ 136	Eric King	.05	.02
☐ 137	Chet Lemon	.05	.02
☐ 138	Fred Lynn UER ('74, '75 stats missing)	.05	.02
☐ 139	Jack Morris	.10	.05
☐ 140	Matt Nokes	.05	.02
☐ 141	Gary Pettis	.05	.02
☐ 142	Ted Power	.05	.02
☐ 143	Jeff M. Robinson	.05	.02
☐ 144	Luis Salazar	.05	.02
☐ 145	Steve Searcy	.05	.02
☐ 146	Pat Sheridan	.05	.02
☐ 147	Frank Tanana	.05	.02
☐ 148	Alan Trammell	.05	.02
☐ 149	Walt Terrell	.05	.02
☐ 150	Jim Walewander	.05	.02
☐ 151	Lou Whitaker	.10	.05
☐ 152	Tim Birtsas	.05	.02
☐ 153	Tom Browning	.05	.02
☐ 154	Keith Brown	.05	.02
☐ 155	Norm Charlton	.10	.05
☐ 156	Dave Concepcion	.05	.02
☐ 157	Kal Daniels	.05	.02
☐ 158	Eric Davis	.05	.02
☐ 159	Bo Diaz	.05	.02
☐ 160	Rob Dibble	.10	.05
☐ 161	Nick Esasky	.05	.02
☐ 162	John Franco	.10	.05
☐ 163	Danny Jackson	.05	.02
☐ 164	Barry Larkin	.20	.09
☐ 165	Rob Murphy	.05	.02
☐ 166	Paul O'Neill	.10	.05
☐ 167	Jeff Reed	.05	.02
☐ 168	Jose Rijo	.05	.02
☐ 169	Ron Robinson	.05	.02
☐ 170	Chris Sabo	.05	.02
☐ 171	Candy Sierra	.05	.02
☐ 172	Van Snider	.05	.02
☐ 173A	Jeff Treadway (Target registration mark above head on front in light blue)	5.00	2.20
☐ 173B	Jeff Treadway (No target on front)	.05	.02
☐ 174	Frank Williams (After All-Star Break stats are jumbled)	.05	.02
☐ 175	Herm Winningham	.05	.02
☐ 176	Jim Adduci	.05	.02
☐ 177	Don August	.05	.02
☐ 178	Mike Birkbeck	.05	.02
☐ 179	Chris Bosio	.05	.02
☐ 180	Glenn Braggs	.05	.02
☐ 181	Greg Brock	.05	.02
☐ 182	Mark Clear	.05	.02
☐ 183	Chuck Crim	.05	.02
☐ 184	Rob Deer	.05	.02
☐ 185	Tom Filer	.05	.02
☐ 186	Jim Gantner	.05	.02
☐ 187	Darryl Hamilton	.10	.05
☐ 188	Ted Higuera	.05	.02
☐ 189	Odell Jones	.05	.02
☐ 190	Jeffrey Leonard	.05	.02
☐ 191	Joey Meyer	.05	.02
☐ 192	Paul Mirabella	.05	.02
☐ 193	Paul Molitor	.20	.09
☐ 194	Charlie O'Brien	.05	.02
☐ 195	Dan Plesac	.05	.02
☐ 196	Gary Sheffield	.75	.35
☐ 197	B.J. Surhoff	.10	.05
☐ 198	Dale Sveum	.05	.02
☐ 199	Bill Wegman	.05	.02
☐ 200	Robin Yount	.20	.09
☐ 201	Rafael Belliard	.05	.02
☐ 202	Barry Bonds	.40	.18
☐ 203	Bobby Bonilla	.05	.02
☐ 204	Sid Bream	.05	.02
☐ 205	Benny Distefano	.05	.02
☐ 206	Doug Drabek	.05	.02
☐ 207	Mike Dunne	.05	.02
☐ 208	Felix Fermin	.05	.02
☐ 209	Brian Fisher	.05	.02
☐ 210	Jim Gott	.05	.02
☐ 211	Bob Kipper	.05	.02
☐ 212	Dave LaPoint	.05	.02
☐ 213	Mike LaValliere	.05	.02
☐ 214	Jose Lind	.05	.02
☐ 215	Junior Ortiz	.05	.02
☐ 216	Vicente Palacios	.05	.02
☐ 217	Tom Prince	.05	.02
☐ 218	Gary Redus	.05	.02
☐ 219	R.J. Reynolds	.05	.02
☐ 220	Jeff D. Robinson	.05	.02
☐ 221	John Smiley	.05	.02
☐ 222	Andy Van Slyke	.10	.05
☐ 223	Bob Walk	.05	.02
☐ 224	Glenn Wilson	.05	.02
☐ 225	Jesse Barfield	.05	.02
☐ 226	George Bell	.10	.05
☐ 227	Pat Borders	.10	.05
☐ 228	John Cerutti	.05	.02
☐ 229	Jim Clancy	.05	.02
☐ 230	Mark Eichhorn	.05	.02
☐ 231	Tony Fernandez	.05	.02
☐ 232	Cecil Fielder	.05	.02
☐ 233	Mike Flanagan	.05	.02
☐ 234	Kelly Gruber	.05	.02
☐ 235	Tom Henke	.05	.02
☐ 236	Jimmy Key	.10	.05
☐ 237	Rick Leach	.05	.02
☐ 238	Manny Lee UER (Bio says regular shortstop, sic, Tony Fernandez)	.05	.02
☐ 239	Nelson Liriano	.05	.02
☐ 240	Fred McGriff	.20	.09
☐ 241	Lloyd Moseby	.05	.02
☐ 242	Rance Mulliniks	.05	.02
☐ 243	Jeff Musselman	.05	.02
☐ 244	Dave Stieb	.05	.02
☐ 245	Todd Stottlemyre	.10	.05
☐ 246	Duane Ward	.05	.02
☐ 247	David Wells	.05	.02
☐ 248	Ernie Whitt UER (HR total 21, should be 121)	.05	.02
☐ 249	Luis Aguayo	.05	.02
☐ 250A	Neil Allen (Home: Sarasota, FL)	.75	.35
☐ 250B	Neil Allen (Home: Syosset, NY)	.05	.02
☐ 251	John Candelaria	.05	.02
☐ 252	Jack Clark	.10	.05
☐ 253	Richard Dotson	.05	.02
☐ 254	Rickey Henderson	.20	.09
☐ 255	Tommy John	.10	.05
☐ 256	Roberto Kelly	.10	.05
☐ 257	Al Leiter	.20	.09
☐ 258	Don Mattingly	.30	.14
☐ 259	Dale Mohorcic	.05	.02
☐ 260	Hal Morris	.20	.09
☐ 261	Scott Nielsen	.05	.02
☐ 262	Mike Pagliarulo UER (Wrong birthdate)	.05	.02
☐ 263	Hipolito Pena	.05	.02
☐ 264	Ken Phelps	.05	.02
☐ 265	Willie Randolph	.10	.05
☐ 266	Rick Rhoden	.05	.02
☐ 267	Dave Righetti	.05	.02
☐ 268	Rafael Santana	.05	.02
☐ 269	Steve Shields	.05	.02
☐ 270	Joel Skinner	.05	.02
☐ 271	Don Slaught	.05	.02
☐ 272	Claudell Washington	.05	.02
☐ 273	Gary Ward	.05	.02
☐ 274	Dave Winfield	.20	.09
☐ 275	Luis Aquino	.05	.02
☐ 276	Floyd Bannister	.05	.02
☐ 277	George Brett	.40	.18
☐ 278	Bill Buckner	.10	.05
☐ 279	Nick Capra	.05	.02
☐ 280	Jose DeJesus	.05	.02
☐ 281	Steve Farr	.05	.02
☐ 282	Jerry Don Gleaton	.05	.02
☐ 283	Mark Gubicza	.05	.02
☐ 284	Tom Gordon UER (16.2 innings in '88, should be 15.2)	.20	.09
☐ 285	Bo Jackson	.20	.09
☐ 286	Charlie Leibrandt	.05	.02
☐ 287	Mike Macfarlane	.05	.02
☐ 288	Jeff Montgomery	.10	.05
☐ 289	Bill Pecota UER (Photo actually Brad Wellman)	.05	.02
☐ 290	Jamie Quirk	.05	.02
☐ 291	Bret Saberhagen	.05	.02
☐ 292	Kevin Seitzer	.05	.02
☐ 293	Kurt Stillwell	.05	.02
☐ 294	Pat Tabler	.05	.02
☐ 295	Danny Tartabull	.05	.02
☐ 296	Gary Thurman	.05	.02
☐ 297	Frank White	.10	.05
☐ 298	Willie Wilson	.05	.02
☐ 299	Roberto Alomar	.30	.14
☐ 300	Sandy Alomar Jr. UER (Wrong birthdate, says 6/16/66, should say 6/18/66)	.50	.23
☐ 301	Chris Brown	.05	.02
☐ 302	Mike Brumley UER (133 hits in '88, should be 134)	.05	.02
☐ 303	Mark Davis	.05	.02
☐ 304	Mark Grant	.05	.02
☐ 305	Tony Gwynn	.50	.23
☐ 306	Greg W. Harris	.05	.02
☐ 307	Andy Hawkins	.05	.02
☐ 308	Jimmy Jones	.05	.02
☐ 309	John Kruk	.10	.05
☐ 310	Dave Leiper	.05	.02
☐ 311	Carmelo Martinez	.05	.02
☐ 312	Lance McCullers	.05	.02
☐ 313	Keith Moreland	.05	.02
☐ 314	Dennis Rasmussen	.05	.02
☐ 315	Randy Ready UER (1214 games in '88, should be 114)	.05	.02
☐ 316	Benito Santiago	.05	.02
☐ 317	Eric Show	.05	.02
☐ 318	Todd Simmons	.05	.02
☐ 319	Garry Templeton	.05	.02
☐ 320	Dickie Thon	.05	.02
☐ 321	Ed Whitson	.05	.02
☐ 322	Marvell Wynne	.05	.02
☐ 323	Mike Aldrete	.05	.02
☐ 324	Brett Butler	.10	.05
☐ 325	Will Clark UER (Three consecutive 100 RBI seasons)	.20	.09
☐ 326	Kelly Downs UER ('88 stats missing)	.05	.02
☐ 327	Dave Dravecky	.10	.05
☐ 328	Scott Garrelts	.05	.02
☐ 329	Atlee Hammaker	.05	.02
☐ 330	Charlie Hayes	.20	.09
☐ 331	Mike Krukow	.05	.02
☐ 332	Craig Lefferts	.05	.02
☐ 333	Candy Maldonado	.05	.02
☐ 334	Kirt Manwaring UER (Bats Rights)	.05	.02
☐ 335	Bob Melvin	.05	.02
☐ 336	Kevin Mitchell	.05	.02
☐ 337	Donell Nixon	.05	.02
☐ 338	Tony Perezchica	.05	.02
☐ 339	Joe Price	.05	.02
☐ 340	Rick Reuschel	.05	.02
☐ 341	Earnest Riles	.05	.02
☐ 342	Don Robinson	.05	.02
☐ 343	Chris Speier	.05	.02
☐ 344	Robby Thompson UER (West Plam Beach)	.05	.02
☐ 345	Jose Uribe	.05	.02
☐ 346	Matt Williams	.20	.09
☐ 347	Trevor Wilson	.05	.02
☐ 348	Juan Agosto	.05	.02

☐ 349 Larry Andersen	.05	.02
☐ 350A Alan Ashby ERR	2.00	.90
(Throws Rig)		
☐ 350B Alan Ashby COR	.05	.02
☐ 351 Kevin Bass	.05	.02
☐ 352 Buddy Bell	.10	.05
☐ 353 Craig Biggio	.50	.23
☐ 354 Danny Darwin	.05	.02
☐ 355 Glenn Davis	.05	.02
☐ 356 Jim Deshaies	.05	.02
☐ 357 Bill Doran	.05	.02
☐ 358 John Fishel	.05	.02
☐ 359 Billy Hatcher	.05	.02
☐ 360 Bob Knepper	.05	.02
☐ 361 Louie Meadows UER	.05	.02
(Bio says 10 EBH's		
and 6 SB's in '88,		
should be 3 and 4)		
☐ 362 Dave Meads	.05	.02
☐ 363 Jim Pankovits	.05	.02
☐ 364 Terry Puhl	.05	.02
☐ 365 Rafael Ramirez	.05	.02
☐ 366 Craig Reynolds	.05	.02
☐ 367 Mike Scott	.05	.02
(Card number listed		
as 368 on Astros CL)		
☐ 368 Nolan Ryan	.75	.35
(Card number listed		
as 367 on Astros CL)		
☐ 369 Dave Smith	.05	.02
☐ 370 Gerald Young	.05	.02
☐ 371 Hubie Brooks	.05	.02
☐ 372 Tim Burke	.05	.02
☐ 373 John Dopson	.05	.02
☐ 374 Mike R. Fitzgerald	.05	.02
☐ 375 Tom Foley	.05	.02
☐ 376 Andres Galarraga UER	.20	.09
(Home: Caracus)		
☐ 377 Neal Heaton	.05	.02
☐ 378 Joe Hesketh	.05	.02
☐ 379 Brian Holman	.05	.02
☐ 380 Rex Hudler	.05	.02
☐ 381 Randy Johnson UER	1.00	.45
(Innings for '85 and		
'86 shown as 27 and		
120, should be 27.1		
and 119.2)		
☐ 382 Wallace Johnson	.05	.02
☐ 383 Tracy Jones	.05	.02
☐ 384 Dave Martinez	.05	.02
☐ 385 Dennis Martinez	.10	.05
☐ 386 Andy McGaffigan	.05	.02
☐ 387 Otis Nixon	.10	.05
☐ 388 Johnny Paredes	.05	.02
☐ 389 Jeff Parrett	.05	.02
☐ 390 Pascual Perez	.05	.02
☐ 391 Tim Raines	.10	.05
☐ 392 Luis Rivera	.05	.02
☐ 393 Nelson Santovenia	.05	.02
☐ 394 Bryn Smith	.05	.02
☐ 395 Tim Wallach	.05	.02
☐ 396 Andy Allanson UER	.05	.02
(1214 hits in '88,		
should be 114)		
☐ 397 Rod Allen	.05	.02
☐ 398 Scott Bailes	.05	.02
☐ 399 Tom Candiotti	.05	.02
☐ 400 Joe Carter	.20	.09
☐ 401 Carmen Castillo UER	.05	.02
(After All-Star Break		
batting 2.50)		
☐ 402 Dave Clark UER	.05	.02
(Card front shows		
position as Rookie;		
after All-Star Break		
batting 3.14)		
☐ 403 John Farrell UER	.05	.02
(Typo in runs		
allowed in '88)		
☐ 404 Julio Franco	.05	.02
☐ 405 Don Gordon	.05	.02
☐ 406 Mel Hall	.05	.02
☐ 407 Brad Havens	.05	.02
☐ 408 Brook Jacoby	.05	.02
☐ 409 Doug Jones	.05	.02
☐ 410 Jeff Kaiser	.05	.02

☐ 411 Luis Medina	.05	.02
☐ 412 Cory Snyder	.05	.02
☐ 413 Greg Swindell	.05	.02
☐ 414 Ron Tingley UER	.05	.02
(Hit HR in first ML		
at-bat, should be		
first AL at-bat)		
☐ 415 Willie Upshaw	.05	.02
☐ 416 Ron Washington	.05	.02
☐ 417 Rich Yett	.05	.02
☐ 418 Damon Berryhill	.05	.02
☐ 419 Mike Bielecki	.05	.02
☐ 420 Doug Dascenzo	.05	.02
☐ 421 Jody Davis UER	.05	.02
(Braves stats for		
'88 missing)		
☐ 422 Andre Dawson	.20	.09
☐ 423 Frank DiPino	.05	.02
☐ 424 Shawon Dunston	.05	.02
☐ 425 Rich Gossage	.10	.05
☐ 426 Mark Grace UER	.20	.09
(Minor League stats		
for '88 missing)		
☐ 427 Mike Harkey	.05	.02
☐ 428 Darrin Jackson	.05	.02
☐ 429 Les Lancaster	.05	.02
☐ 430 Vance Law	.05	.02
☐ 431 Greg Maddux	.75	.35
☐ 432 Jamie Moyer	.05	.02
☐ 433 Al Nipper	.05	.02
☐ 434 Rafael Palmeiro UER	.20	.09
(170 hits in '88,		
should be 178)		
☐ 435 Pat Perry	.05	.02
☐ 436 Jeff Pico	.05	.02
☐ 437 Ryne Sandberg	.25	.11
☐ 438 Calvin Schiraldi	.05	.02
☐ 439 Rick Sutcliffe	.05	.02
☐ 440A Manny Trillo ERR	2.00	.90
(Throws Rig)		
☐ 440B Manny Trillo COR	.05	.02
☐ 441 Gary Varsho UER	.05	.02
(Wrong birthdate;		
.303 should be .302;		
11/28 should be 9/19)		
☐ 442 Mitch Webster	.05	.02
☐ 443 Luis Alicea	.05	.02
☐ 444 Tom Brunansky	.05	.02
☐ 445 Vince Coleman UER	.05	.02
(Third straight with		
83, should be fourth		
straight with 81)		
☐ 446 John Costello UER	.05	.02
(Home California,		
should be New York)		
☐ 447 Danny Cox	.05	.02
☐ 448 Ken Dayley	.05	.02
☐ 449 Jose DeLeon	.05	.02
☐ 450 Curt Ford	.05	.02
☐ 451 Pedro Guerrero	.10	.05
☐ 452 Bob Horner	.05	.02
☐ 453 Tim Jones	.05	.02
☐ 454 Steve Lake	.05	.02
☐ 455 Joe Magrane UER	.05	.02
(Des Moines, IO)		
☐ 456 Greg Mathews	.05	.02
☐ 457 Willie McGee	.10	.05
☐ 458 Larry McWilliams	.05	.02
☐ 459 Jose Oquendo	.05	.02
☐ 460 Tony Pena	.05	.02
☐ 461 Terry Pendleton	.10	.05
☐ 462 Steve Peters UER	.05	.02
(Lives in Harrah,		
not Harah)		
☐ 463 Ozzie Smith	.25	.11
☐ 464 Scott Terry	.05	.02
☐ 465 Denny Walling	.05	.02
☐ 466 Todd Worrell	.05	.02
☐ 467 Tony Armas UER	.05	.02
(Before All-Star Break		
batting 2.39)		
☐ 468 Dante Bichette	.18	.08
☐ 469 Bob Boone	.10	.05
☐ 470 Terry Clark	.05	.02
☐ 471 Stew Cliburn	.05	.02
☐ 472 Mike Cook UER	.05	.02

(TM near Angels logo		
missing from front)		
☐ 473 Sherman Corbett	.05	.02
☐ 474 Chili Davis	.10	.05
☐ 475 Brian Downing	.05	.02
☐ 476 Jim Eppard	.05	.02
☐ 477 Chuck Finley	.10	.05
☐ 478 Willie Fraser	.05	.02
☐ 479 Bryan Harvey UER	.10	.05
(ML record shows 0-0,		
should be 7-5)		
☐ 480 Jack Howell	.05	.02
☐ 481 Wally Joyner UER	.10	.05
(Yorba Linda, GA)		
☐ 482 Jack Lazorko	.05	.02
☐ 483 Kirk McCaskill	.05	.02
☐ 484 Mark McLemore	.05	.02
☐ 485 Greg Minton	.05	.02
☐ 486 Dan Petry	.05	.02
☐ 487 Johnny Ray	.05	.02
☐ 488 Dick Schofield	.05	.02
☐ 489 Devon White	.05	.02
☐ 490 Mike Witt	.05	.02
☐ 491 Harold Baines	.10	.05
☐ 492 Daryl Boston	.05	.02
☐ 493 Ivan Calderon UER	.05	.02
('80 stats shifted)		
☐ 494 Mike Diaz	.05	.02
☐ 495 Carlton Fisk	.20	.09
☐ 496 Dave Gallagher	.05	.02
☐ 497 Ozzie Guillen	.05	.02
☐ 498 Shawn Hillegas	.05	.02
☐ 499 Lance Johnson	.10	.05
☐ 500 Barry Jones	.05	.02
☐ 501 Bill Long	.05	.02
☐ 502 Steve Lyons	.05	.02
☐ 503 Fred Manrique	.05	.02
☐ 504 Jack McDowell	.10	.05
☐ 505 Donn Pall	.05	.02
☐ 506 Kelly Paris	.05	.02
☐ 507 Dan Pasqua	.05	.02
☐ 508 Ken Patterson	.05	.02
☐ 509 Melido Perez	.05	.02
☐ 510 Jerry Reuss	.05	.02
☐ 511 Mark Salas	.05	.02
☐ 512 Bobby Thigpen UER	.05	.02
('86 ERA 4.69,		
should be 4.68)		
☐ 513 Mike Woodard	.05	.02
☐ 514 Bob Brower	.05	.02
☐ 515 Steve Buechele	.05	.02
☐ 516 Jose Cecena	.05	.02
☐ 517 Cecil Espy	.05	.02
☐ 518 Scott Fletcher	.05	.02
☐ 519 Cecilio Guante	.05	.02
('87 Yankee stats		
are off-centered)		
☐ 520 Jose Guzman	.05	.02
☐ 521 Ray Hayward	.05	.02
☐ 522 Charlie Hough	.10	.05
☐ 523 Pete Incaviglia	.10	.05
☐ 524 Mike Jeffcoat	.05	.02
☐ 525 Paul Kilgus	.05	.02
☐ 526 Chad Kreuter	.05	.02
☐ 527 Jeff Kunkel	.05	.02
☐ 528 Oddibe McDowell	.05	.02
☐ 529 Pete O'Brien	.05	.02
☐ 530 Geno Petralli	.05	.02
☐ 531 Jeff Russell	.05	.02
☐ 532 Ruben Sierra	.20	.09
☐ 533 Mike Stanley	.05	.02
☐ 534A Ed VandeBerg ERR	2.00	.90
(Throws Lef)		
☐ 534B Ed VandeBerg COR	.05	.02
☐ 535 Curtis Wilkerson ERR	.05	.02
(Pitcher headings		
at bottom)		
☐ 536 Mitch Williams	.05	.02
☐ 537 Bobby Witt UER	.05	.02
('85 ERA .643,		
should be 6.43)		
☐ 538 Steve Balboni	.05	.02
☐ 539 Scott Bankhead	.05	.02
☐ 540 Scott Bradley	.05	.02
☐ 541 Mickey Brantley	.05	.02
☐ 542 Jay Buhner	.20	.09

☐ 543 Mike Campbell............ .05	.02
☐ 544 Darnell Coles .... .05	.02
☐ 545 Henry Cotto .... .05	.02
☐ 546 Alvin Davis .... .05	.02
☐ 547 Mario Diaz .... .05	.02
☐ 548 Ken Griffey Jr. 6.00	2.70
☐ 549 Erik Hanson .... .10	.05
☐ 550 Mike Jackson UER .... .05	.02
(Lifetime ERA 3.345,	
should be 3.45)	
☐ 551 Mark Langston .... .05	.02
☐ 552 Edgar Martinez .... .20	.09
☐ 553 Bill McGuire............. .05	.02
☐ 554 Mike Moore .... .05	.02
☐ 555 Jim Presley .... .05	.02
☐ 556 Rey Quinones .... .05	.02
☐ 557 Jerry Reed .... .05	.02
☐ 558 Harold Reynolds .... .05	.02
☐ 559 Mike Schooler .... .05	.02
☐ 560 Bill Swift .... .05	.02
☐ 561 Dave Valle .... .05	.02
☐ 562 Steve Bedrosian .... .05	.02
☐ 563 Phil Bradley .... .05	.02
☐ 564 Don Carman .... .05	.02
☐ 565 Bob Dernier .... .05	.02
☐ 566 Marvin Freeman .... .05	.02
☐ 567 Todd Frohwirth .... .05	.02
☐ 568 Greg Gross .... .05	.02
☐ 569 Kevin Gross .... .05	.02
☐ 570 Greg A. Harris .... .05	.02
☐ 571 Von Hayes .... .05	.02
☐ 572 Chris James .... .05	.02
☐ 573 Steve Jeltz .... .05	.02
☐ 574 Ron Jones UER .... .05	.02
(Led IL in '88 with	
85, should be 75)	
☐ 575 Ricky Jordan .... .10	.05
☐ 576 Mike Maddux .... .05	.02
☐ 577 David Palmer .... .05	.02
☐ 578 Lance Parrish .... .05	.02
☐ 579 Shane Rawley .... .05	.02
☐ 580 Bruce Ruffin .... .05	.02
☐ 581 Juan Samuel .... .05	.02
☐ 582 Mike Schmidt .... .25	.11
☐ 583 Kent Tekulve .... .05	.02
☐ 584 Milt Thompson UER .. .05	.02
(19 hits in '88,	
should be 109)	
☐ 585 Jose Alvarez .... .05	.02
☐ 586 Paul Assenmacher ..... .05	.02
☐ 587 Bruce Benedict .... .05	.02
☐ 588 Jeff Blauser .... .10	.05
☐ 589 Terry Blocker .... .05	.02
☐ 590 Ron Gant .... .10	.05
☐ 591 Tom Glavine .... .20	.09
☐ 592 Tommy Gregg .... .05	.02
☐ 593 Albert Hall .... .05	.02
☐ 594 Dion James .... .05	.02
☐ 595 Rick Mahler .... .05	.02
☐ 596 Dale Murphy .... .20	.09
☐ 597 Gerald Perry .... .05	.02
☐ 598 Charlie Puleo .... .05	.02
☐ 599 Ted Simmons .... .10	.05
☐ 600 Pete Smith .... .05	.02
☐ 601 Zane Smith .... .05	.02
☐ 602 John Smoltz .... .50	.23
☐ 603 Bruce Sutter .... .05	.02
☐ 604 Andres Thomas .... .05	.02
☐ 605 Ozzie Virgil .... .05	.02
☐ 606 Brady Anderson .... .50	.23
☐ 607 Jeff Ballard .... .05	.02
☐ 608 Jose Bautista .... .05	.02
☐ 609 Ken Gerhart .... .05	.02
☐ 610 Terry Kennedy .... .05	.02
☐ 611 Eddie Murray .... .20	.09
☐ 612 Carl Nichols UER ...... .05	.02
(Before All-Star Break	
batting 1.88)	
☐ 613 Tom Niedenfuer........ .05	.02
☐ 614 Joe Orsulak .... .05	.02
☐ 615 Oswald Peraza UER ... .05	.02
(Shown as Oswaldo)	
☐ 616A Bill Ripken ERR 5.00	2.20
(Rick Face written	
on knob of bat)	
☐ 616B Bill Ripken 30.00	13.50

(Bat knob	
whited out)	
☐ 616C Bill Ripken............ 5.00	2.20
(Words on bat knob	
scribbled out)	
☐ 616D Bill Ripken DP .... .10	.05
(Black box covering	
bat knob)	
☐ 617 Cal Ripken .... .75	.35
☐ 618 Dave Schmidt .... .05	.02
☐ 619 Rick Schu .... .05	.02
☐ 620 Larry Sheets .... .05	.02
☐ 621 Doug Sisk .... .05	.02
☐ 622 Pete Stanicek........... .05	.02
☐ 623 Mickey Tettleton ...... .10	.05
☐ 624 Jay Tibbs .... .05	.02
☐ 625 Jim Traber .... .05	.02
☐ 626 Mark Williamson ...... .05	.02
☐ 627 Craig Worthington...... .05	.02
☐ 628 Speed/Power............ .05	.02
Jose Canseco	
☐ 629 Pitcher Perfect.......... .05	.02
Tom Browning	
☐ 630 Like Father/Like Sons .20	.09
Roberto Alomar	
Sandy Alomar Jr.	
(Names on card listed	
in wrong order) UER	
☐ 631 NL All Stars UER .... .20	.09
Will Clark	
Rafael Palmeiro	
(Gallaraga, sic;	
Clark 3 consecutive	
100 RBI seasons;	
third with 102 RBI's)	
☐ 632 Homeruns - Coast ..... .10	.05
to Coast UER	
Darryl Strawberry	
Will Clark (Homeruns	
should be two words)	
☐ 633 Hot Corners - Hot ...... .10	.05
Hitters UER	
Wade Boggs	
Carney Lansford	
(Boggs hit .366 in	
'86, should be '88)	
☐ 634 Triple A's................. .10	.05
Jose Canseco	
Terry Steinbach	
Mark McGwire	
☐ 635 Dual Heat................. .10	.05
Mark Davis	
Dwight Gooden	
☐ 636 NL Pitching Power UER.10	.05
Danny Jackson	
David Cone	
(Hersheiser, sic)	
☐ 637 Cannon Arms UER ..... .10	.05
Chris Sabo	
Bobby Bonilla	
(Bobby Bonds, sic)	
☐ 638 Double Trouble UER .. .10	.05
Andres Galarraga	
(Misspelled Galarraga	
on card back)	
Gerald Perry	
☐ 639 Power Center............ .20	.09
Kirby Puckett	
Eric Davis	
☐ 640 Steve Wilson and ...... .05	.02
Cameron Drew	
☐ 641 Kevin Brown and .... .20	.09
Kevin Reimer	
☐ 642 Brad Pounders and ..... .05	.02
Jerald Clark	
☐ 643 Mike Capel and .... .05	.02
Drew Hall	
☐ 644 Joe Girardi and .... .20	.09
Rolando Roomes	
☐ 645 Lenny Harris and ...... .10	.05
Marty Brown	
☐ 646 Luis DeLosSantos ...... .05	.02
and Jim Campbell	
☐ 647 Randy Kramer and ..... .05	.02
Miguel Garcia	
☐ 648 Torey Lovullo and ..... .05	.02

Robert Palacios	
☐ 649 Jim Corsi and .... .05	.02
Bob Milacki	
☐ 650 Grady Hall and.......... .05	.02
Mike Rochford	
☐ 651 Terry Taylor and .... .05	.02
Vance Lovelace	
☐ 652 Ken Hill and .... .20	.09
Dennis Cook	
☐ 653 Scott Service and ...... .05	.02
Shane Turner	
☐ 654 CL: Oakland/Mets ...... .05	.02
Dodgers/Red Sox	
(10 Hendersor;	
68 Jess Orosco)	
☐ 655A CL: Twins/Tigers ERR .05	.02
Reds/Brewers	
(179 Boslo and	
Twins/Tigers positions	
listed)	
☐ 655B CL: Twins/Tigers COR .05	.02
Reds/Brewers	
(179 Boslo but	
Twins/Tigers positions	
not listed)	
☐ 656 CL: Pirates/Blue Jays.. .05	.02
Yankees/Royals	
(225 Jess Barfield)	
☐ 657 CL: Padres/Giants ..... .05	.02
Astros/Expos	
(367/368 wrong)	
☐ 658 CL: Indians/Cubs .... .05	.02
Cardinals/Angels	
(449 Deleon)	
☐ 659 CL: White Sox/Rangers .05	.02
Mariners/Phillies	
☐ 660 CL: Braves/Orioles..... .05	.02
Specials/Checklists	
(632 hyphenated diff-	
erently and 650 Hall;	
595 Rich Mahler;	
619 Rich Schu)	

1989 Fleer All-Stars

89FLEERALLSTAR team

WILL CLARK
FIRST BASE-GIANTS

This twelve-card standard-size subset was randomly inserted in Fleer wax and cello packs. The players selected are the 1989 Fleer Major League All-Star team. One player has been selected for each position along with a DH and three pitchers. The cards feature a distinctive green background on the card fronts. The set is sequenced in alphabetical order.

	MINT	NRMT
COMPLETE SET (12) 5.00	2.20
COMMON CARD (1-50) .... .25	.11
RANDOM INSERTS IN PACKS	
☐ 1 Bobby Bonilla .... .40	.18
☐ 2 Jose Canseco .... .50	.23

		MINT	NRMT
□ 3	Will Clark	.50	.23
□ 4	Dennis Eckersley	.35	.16
□ 5	Julio Franco	.25	.11
□ 6	Mike Greenwell	.25	.11
□ 7	Orel Hershiser	.40	.18
□ 8	Paul Molitor	.50	.23
□ 9	Mike Scioscia	.25	.11
□ 10	Darryl Strawberry	.35	.16
□ 11	Alan Trammell	.40	.18
□ 12	Frank Viola	.25	.11

1989 Fleer For The Record

Roger Clemens RED SOX PITCHER

This six-card standard-size insert set was distributed one per rack pack. The set is subtitled "For The Record" and commemorates record-breaking events for those players from the previous season. The card backs are printed in red, black, and gray on white card stock. The set is sequenced in alphabetical order.

		MINT	NRMT
COMPLETE SET (6)		8.00	3.60
COMMON CARD (1-6)		.75	.35
ONE PER RACK PACK			
□ 1	Wade Boggs	.75	.35
□ 2	Roger Clemens	2.50	1.10
□ 3	Andres Galarraga	.75	.35
□ 4	Kirk Gibson	.30	.14
□ 5	Greg Maddux	5.00	2.20
□ 6	Don Mattingly UER	2.00	.90
	(Won batting title '83, should say '84)		

1989 Fleer Update

MARK LANGSTON PITCHER

The 1989 Fleer Update set contains 132 standard-size cards. The cards were distributed exclusively in factory set form in grey and white, cellophane wrapped boxes through hobby

dealers. The cards are identical in design to regular issue 1989 Fleer cards except for the U-prefixed numbering on back. The set numbering is in team order with players within teams ordered alphabetically. The set includes special cards for Nolan Ryan's 5,000th strikeout and Mike Schmidt's retirement. Rookie Cards include Kevin Appier, Joey (Albert) Belle, Deion Sanders, Greg Vaughn, Robin Ventura and Todd Zeile.

		MINT	NRMT
COMP.FACT.SET (132)		5.00	2.20
COMMON CARD (1-132)		.05	.02
MINOR STARS		.10	.05
UNLISTED STARS		.20	.09
□ 1	Phil Bradley	.05	.02
□ 2	Mike Devereaux	.05	.02
□ 3	Steve Finley	.25	.11
□ 4	Kevin Hickey	.05	.02
□ 5	Brian Holton	.05	.02
□ 6	Bob Milacki	.05	.02
□ 7	Randy Milligan	.05	.02
□ 8	John Dopson	.05	.02
□ 9	Nick Esasky	.05	.02
□ 10	Rob Murphy	.05	.02
□ 11	Jim Abbott	.20	.09
□ 12	Bert Blyleven	.10	.05
□ 13	Jeff Manto	.05	.02
□ 14	Bob McClure	.05	.02
□ 15	Lance Parrish	.05	.02
□ 16	Lee Stevens	.05	.02
□ 17	Claudell Washington	.05	.02
□ 18	Mark Davis	.05	.02
□ 19	Eric King	.05	.02
□ 20	Ron Kittle	.05	.02
□ 21	Matt Merullo	.05	.02
□ 22	Steve Rosenberg	.05	.02
□ 23	Robin Ventura	.40	.18
□ 24	Keith Atherton	.05	.02
□ 25	Joey Belle	2.00	.90
□ 26	Jerry Browne	.05	.02
□ 27	Felix Fermin	.05	.02
□ 28	Brad Komminsk	.05	.02
□ 29	Pete O'Brien	.05	.02
□ 30	Mike Brumley	.05	.02
□ 31	Tracy Jones	.05	.02
□ 32	Mike Schwabe	.05	.02
□ 33	Gary Ward	.05	.02
□ 34	Frank Williams	.05	.02
□ 35	Kevin Appier	.25	.11
□ 36	Bob Boone	.10	.05
□ 37	Luis DeLosSantos	.05	.02
□ 38	Jim Eisenreich	.05	.02
□ 39	Jaime Navarro	.05	.02
□ 40	Bill Spiers	.05	.02
□ 41	Greg Vaughn	.50	.23
□ 42	Randy Veres	.05	.02
□ 43	Wally Backman	.05	.02
□ 44	Shane Rawley	.05	.02
□ 45	Steve Balboni	.05	.02
□ 46	Jesse Barfield	.05	.02
□ 47	Alvaro Espinoza	.05	.02
□ 48	Bob Geren	.05	.02
□ 49	Mel Hall	.05	.02
□ 50	Andy Hawkins	.05	.02
□ 51	Hensley Meulens	.05	.02
□ 52	Steve Sax	.05	.02
□ 53	Deion Sanders	.75	.35
□ 54	Rickey Henderson	.20	.09
□ 55	Mike Moore	.05	.02
□ 56	Tony Phillips	.05	.02
□ 57	Greg Briley	.05	.02
□ 58	Gene Harris	.05	.02
□ 59	Randy Johnson	1.00	.45
□ 60	Jeffrey Leonard	.05	.02
□ 61	Dennis Powell	.05	.02
□ 62	Omar Vizquel	.40	.18
□ 63	Kevin Brown	.20	.09
□ 64	Julio Franco	.05	.02
□ 65	Jamie Moyer	.05	.02

		MINT	NRMT
□ 66	Rafael Palmeiro	.20	.09
□ 67	Nolan Ryan	1.50	.70
□ 68	Francisco Cabrera	.10	.05
□ 69	Junior Felix	.05	.02
□ 70	Al Leiter	.20	.09
□ 71	Alex Sanchez	.05	.02
□ 72	Geronimo Berroa	.10	.05
□ 73	Derek Lilliquist	.05	.02
□ 74	Lonnie Smith	.05	.02
□ 75	Jeff Treadway	.05	.02
□ 76	Paul Kilgus	.05	.02
□ 77	Lloyd McClendon	.05	.02
□ 78	Scott Sanderson	.05	.02
□ 79	Dwight Smith	.10	.05
□ 80	Jerome Walton	.20	.09
□ 81	Mitch Williams	.05	.02
□ 82	Steve Wilson	.05	.02
□ 83	Todd Benzinger	.05	.02
□ 84	Ken Griffey Sr.	.05	.02
□ 85	Rick Mahler	.05	.02
□ 86	Rolando Roomes	.05	.02
□ 87	Scott Scudder	.05	.02
□ 88	Jim Clancy	.05	.02
□ 89	Rick Rhoden	.05	.02
□ 90	Dan Schatzeder	.05	.02
□ 91	Mike Morgan	.05	.02
□ 92	Eddie Murray	.20	.09
□ 93	Willie Randolph	.10	.05
□ 94	Ray Searage	.05	.02
□ 95	Mike Aldrete	.05	.02
□ 96	Kevin Gross	.05	.02
□ 97	Mark Langston	.05	.02
□ 98	Spike Owen	.05	.02
□ 99	Zane Smith	.05	.02
□ 100	Don Aase	.05	.02
□ 101	Barry Lyons	.05	.02
□ 102	Juan Samuel	.05	.02
□ 103	Wally Whitehurst	.05	.02
□ 104	Dennis Cook	.05	.02
□ 105	Len Dykstra	.10	.05
□ 106	Charlie Hayes	.20	.09
□ 107	Tommy Herr	.05	.02
□ 108	Ken Howell	.05	.02
□ 109	John Kruk	.10	.05
□ 110	Roger McDowell	.05	.02
□ 111	Terry Mulholland	.05	.02
□ 112	Jeff Parrett	.05	.02
□ 113	Neal Heaton	.05	.02
□ 114	Jeff King	.10	.05
□ 115	Randy Kramer	.05	.02
□ 116	Bill Landrum	.05	.02
□ 117	Cris Carpenter	.05	.02
□ 118	Frank DiPino	.05	.02
□ 119	Ken Hill	.20	.09
□ 120	Dan Quisenberry	.05	.02
□ 121	Milt Thompson	.05	.02
□ 122	Todd Zeile	.20	.09
□ 123	Jack Clark	.10	.05
□ 124	Bruce Hurst	.05	.02
□ 125	Mark Parent	.05	.02
□ 126	Bip Roberts	.10	.05
□ 127	Jeff Brantley UER	.10	.05
	(Photo actually Joe Kmak)		
□ 128	Terry Kennedy	.05	.02
□ 129	Mike LaCoss	.05	.02
□ 130	Greg Litton	.05	.02
□ 131	Mike Schmidt	.50	.23
□ 132	Checklist 1-132	.05	.02

1990 Fleer

The 1990 Fleer set contains 660 standard-size cards. Cards were primarily issued in wax packs, rack packs and hobby and retail factory sets. Card fronts feature white outer borders with ribbon-like, colored inner borders. The set is again ordered numerically by teams based upon the previous season's record. Subsets include Decade Greats (621-630), Superstar Combinations (631-

639), Rookie Prospects (640-653) and checklists (654-660). Rookie Cards of note include Moises Alou, Juan Gonzalez, Marquis Grissom, Dave Justice, Ben McDonald, Sammy Sosa, and Larry Walker.

	MINT	NRMT
COMPLETE SET (660)	8.00	3.60
COMP.HOBBY SET (672)	10.00	4.50
COMMON CARD (1-660)	.05	.02
MINOR STARS	.10	.05
UNLISTED STARS	.20	.09
COMP.WORLD SERIES SET (12)	2.00	.90
ONE WORLD SERIES SET PER FACT.SET		

☐ 1	Lance Blankenship	.05	.02
☐ 2	Todd Burns	.05	.02
☐ 3	Jose Canseco	.20	.09
☐ 4	Jim Corsi	.05	.02
☐ 5	Storm Davis	.05	.02
☐ 6	Dennis Eckersley	.10	.05
☐ 7	Mike Gallego	.05	.02
☐ 8	Ron Hassey	.05	.02
☐ 9	Dave Henderson	.05	.02
☐ 10	Rickey Henderson	.20	.09
☐ 11	Rick Honeycutt	.05	.02
☐ 12	Stan Javier	.05	.02
☐ 13	Felix Jose	.05	.02
☐ 14	Carney Lansford	.10	.05
☐ 15	Mark McGwire UER	.40	.18
	(1989 runs listed as 4, should be 74)		
☐ 16	Mike Moore		.02
☐ 17	Gene Nelson	.05	.02
☐ 18	Dave Parker	.10	.05
☐ 19	Tony Phillips	.05	.02
☐ 20	Terry Steinbach	.10	.05
☐ 21	Dave Stewart	.05	.02
☐ 22	Walt Weiss	.05	.02
☐ 23	Bob Welch	.05	.02
☐ 24	Curt Young	.05	.02
☐ 25	Paul Assenmacher	.05	.02
☐ 26	Damon Berryhill	.05	.02
☐ 27	Mike Bielecki	.05	.02
☐ 28	Kevin Blankenship	.05	.02
☐ 29	Andre Dawson	.20	.09
☐ 30	Shawon Dunston	.05	.02
☐ 31	Joe Girardi	.10	.05
☐ 32	Mark Grace	.20	.09
☐ 33	Mike Harkey	.05	.02
☐ 34	Paul Kilgus	.05	.02
☐ 35	Les Lancaster	.05	.02
☐ 36	Vance Law	.05	.02
☐ 37	Greg Maddux	.60	.25
☐ 38	Lloyd McClendon	.05	.02
☐ 39	Jeff Pico	.05	.02
☐ 40	Ryne Sandberg	.25	.11
☐ 41	Scott Sanderson	.05	.02
☐ 42	Dwight Smith	.05	.02
☐ 43	Rick Sutcliffe	.05	.02
☐ 44	Jerome Walton	.05	.02
☐ 45	Mitch Webster	.05	.02
☐ 46	Curt Wilkerson	.05	.02
☐ 47	Dean Wilkins	.05	.02
☐ 48	Mitch Williams	.05	.02
☐ 49	Steve Wilson	.05	.02
☐ 50	Steve Bedrosian	.05	
☐ 51	Mike Benjamin	.05	.02
☐ 52	Jeff Brantley	.05	.02
☐ 53	Brett Butler	.10	.05
☐ 54	Will Clark UER	.20	.09
	(Did You Know says first in runs, should say tied for first)		
☐ 55	Kelly Downs	.05	.02
☐ 56	Scott Garrelts	.05	.02
☐ 57	Atlee Hammaker	.05	.02
☐ 58	Terry Kennedy	.05	.02
☐ 59	Mike LaCoss	.05	.02
☐ 60	Craig Lefferts	.05	.02
☐ 61	Greg Litton	.05	.02
☐ 62	Candy Maldonado	.05	.02
☐ 63	Kirt Manwaring UER	.05	.02
	(No '88 Phoenix stats as noted in box)		
☐ 64	Randy McCament	.05	.02
☐ 65	Kevin Mitchell	.10	.05
☐ 66	Donell Nixon	.05	.02
☐ 67	Ken Oberkfell	.05	.02
☐ 68	Rick Reuschel	.05	.02
☐ 69	Ernest Riles	.05	.02
☐ 70	Don Robinson	.05	.02
☐ 71	Pat Sheridan	.05	.02
☐ 72	Chris Speier	.05	.02
☐ 73	Robby Thompson	.05	.02
☐ 74	Jose Uribe	.05	.02
☐ 75	Matt Williams	.20	.09
☐ 76	George Bell	.05	.02
☐ 77	Pat Borders	.05	.02
☐ 78	John Cerutti	.05	.02
☐ 79	Junior Felix	.05	.02
☐ 80	Tony Fernandez	.05	.02
☐ 81	Mike Flanagan	.05	.02
☐ 82	Mauro Gozzo	.05	.02
☐ 83	Kelly Gruber	.05	.02
☐ 84	Tom Henke	.05	.02
☐ 85	Jimmy Key	.10	.05
☐ 86	Manny Lee	.05	.02
☐ 87	Nelson Liriano UER	.05	.02
	(Should say 'led the IL' instead of 'led the TL')		
☐ 88	Lee Mazzilli	.05	.02
☐ 89	Fred McGriff	.20	.09
☐ 90	Lloyd Moseby	.05	.02
☐ 91	Rance Mulliniks	.05	.02
☐ 92	Alex Sanchez	.05	.02
☐ 93	Dave Stieb	.05	.02
☐ 94	Todd Stottlemyre	.10	.05
☐ 95	Duane Ward UER	.05	.02
	(Double line of '87 Syracuse stats)		
☐ 96	David Wells	.05	.02
☐ 97	Ernie Whitt	.05	.02
☐ 98	Frank Wills	.05	.02
☐ 99	Mookie Wilson	.05	.02
☐ 100	Kevin Appier	.20	.09
☐ 101	Luis Aquino	.05	.02
☐ 102	Bob Boone	.10	.05
☐ 103	George Brett	.40	.18
☐ 104	Jose DeJesus	.05	.02
☐ 105	Luis De Los Santos	.05	.02
☐ 106	Jim Eisenreich	.05	.02
☐ 107	Steve Farr	.05	.02
☐ 108	Tom Gordon	.05	.02
☐ 109	Mark Gubicza	.05	.02
☐ 110	Bo Jackson	.20	.09
☐ 111	Terry Leach	.05	.02
☐ 112	Charlie Leibrandt	.05	.02
☐ 113	Rick Luecken	.05	.02
☐ 114	Mike Macfarlane	.05	.02
☐ 115	Jeff Montgomery	.10	.05
☐ 116	Bret Saberhagen	.10	.05
☐ 117	Kevin Seitzer	.05	.02
☐ 118	Kurt Stillwell	.05	.02
☐ 119	Pat Tabler	.05	.02
☐ 120	Danny Tartabull	.05	.02
☐ 121	Gary Thurman	.05	.02
☐ 122	Frank White	.10	.05
☐ 123	Willie Wilson	.05	.02
☐ 124	Matt Winters	.05	.02
☐ 125	Jim Abbott	.10	.05
☐ 126	Tony Armas	.05	.02
☐ 127	Dante Bichette	.20	.09
☐ 128	Bert Blyleven	.10	.05
☐ 129	Chili Davis	.05	.02
☐ 130	Brian Downing	.05	.02
☐ 131	Mike Fetters	.05	.02
☐ 132	Chuck Finley	.10	.05
☐ 133	Willie Fraser	.05	.02
☐ 134	Bryan Harvey	.05	.02
☐ 135	Jack Howell	.05	.02
☐ 136	Wally Joyner	.10	.05
☐ 137	Jeff Manto	.05	.02
☐ 138	Kirk McCaskill	.05	.02
☐ 139	Bob McClure	.05	.02
☐ 140	Greg Minton	.05	.02
☐ 141	Lance Parrish	.05	.02
☐ 142	Dan Petry	.05	.02
☐ 143	Johnny Ray	.05	.02
☐ 144	Dick Schofield	.05	.02
☐ 145	Lee Stevens	.05	.02
☐ 146	Claudell Washington	.05	.02
☐ 147	Devon White	.05	.02
☐ 148	Mike Witt	.05	.02
☐ 149	Roberto Alomar	.25	.11
☐ 150	Sandy Alomar Jr.	.20	.09
☐ 151	Andy Benes	.20	.09
☐ 152	Jack Clark	.10	.05
☐ 153	Pat Clements	.05	.02
☐ 154	Joey Cora	.20	.09
☐ 155	Mark Davis	.05	.02
☐ 156	Mark Grant	.05	.02
☐ 157	Tony Gwynn	.50	.23
☐ 158	Greg W. Harris	.05	.02
☐ 159	Bruce Hurst	.05	.02
☐ 160	Darrin Jackson	.05	.02
☐ 161	Chris James	.05	.02
☐ 162	Carmelo Martinez	.05	.02
☐ 163	Mike Pagliarulo	.05	.02
☐ 164	Mark Parent	.05	.02
☐ 165	Dennis Rasmussen	.05	.02
☐ 166	Bip Roberts	.05	.02
☐ 167	Benito Santiago	.05	.02
☐ 168	Calvin Schiraldi	.05	.02
☐ 169	Eric Show	.05	.02
☐ 170	Garry Templeton	.05	.02
☐ 171	Ed Whitson	.05	.02
☐ 172	Brady Anderson	.20	.09
☐ 173	Jeff Ballard	.05	.02
☐ 174	Phil Bradley	.05	.02
☐ 175	Mike Devereaux	.05	.02
☐ 176	Steve Finley	.20	.09
☐ 177	Pete Harnisch	.05	.02
☐ 178	Kevin Hickey	.05	.02
☐ 179	Brian Holton	.05	.02
☐ 180	Ben McDonald	.15	.07
☐ 181	Bob Melvin	.05	.02
☐ 182	Bob Milacki	.05	.02
☐ 183	Randy Milligan UER	.05	.02
	(Double line of '87 stats)		
☐ 184	Gregg Olson	.05	.02
☐ 185	Joe Orsulak	.05	.02
☐ 186	Bill Ripken	.05	.02
☐ 187	Cal Ripken	.75	.35
☐ 188	Dave Schmidt	.05	.02
☐ 189	Larry Sheets	.05	.02
☐ 190	Mickey Tettleton	.10	.05
☐ 191	Mark Thurmond	.05	.02
☐ 192	Jay Tibbs	.05	.02
☐ 193	Jim Traber	.05	.02
☐ 194	Mark Williamson	.05	.02
☐ 195	Craig Worthington	.05	.02
☐ 196	Don Aase	.05	.02
☐ 197	Blaine Beatty	.05	.02
☐ 198	Mark Carreon	.05	.02
☐ 199	Gary Carter	.20	.09
☐ 200	David Cone	.20	.09
☐ 201	Ron Darling	.05	.02
☐ 202	Kevin Elster	.05	.02
☐ 203	Sid Fernandez	.05	.02
☐ 204	Dwight Gooden	.10	.05
☐ 205	Keith Hernandez	.10	.05
☐ 206	Jeff Innis	.05	.02
☐ 207	Gregg Jefferies	.10	.05
☐●208	Howard Johnson	.05	.02
☐ 209	Barry Lyons UER	.05	.02

(Double line of '87 stats)

210	Dave Magadan	.05	.02
211	Kevin McReynolds	.05	.02
212	Jeff Musselman	.05	.02
213	Randy Myers	.10	.05
214	Bob Ojeda	.05	.02
215	Juan Samuel	.05	.02
216	Mackey Sasser	.05	.02
217	Darryl Strawberry	.10	.05
218	Tim Teufel	.05	.02
219	Frank Viola	.05	.02
220	Juan Agosto	.05	.02
221	Larry Andersen	.05	.02
222	Eric Anthony	.10	.05
223	Kevin Bass	.05	.02
224	Craig Biggio	.20	.09
225	Ken Caminiti	.20	.09
226	Jim Clancy	.05	.02
227	Danny Darwin	.05	.02
228	Glenn Davis	.05	.02
229	Jim Deshaies	.05	.02
230	Bill Doran	.05	.02
231	Bob Forsch	.05	.02
232	Brian Meyer	.05	.02
233	Terry Puhl	.05	.02
234	Rafael Ramirez	.05	.02
235	Rick Rhoden	.05	.02
236	Dan Schatzeder	.05	.02
237	Mike Scott	.05	.02
238	Dave Smith	.05	.02
239	Alex Trevino	.05	.02
240	Glenn Wilson	.05	.02
241	Gerald Young	.05	.02
242	Tom Brunansky	.05	.02
243	Cris Carpenter	.05	.02
244	Alex Cole	.05	.02
245	Vince Coleman	.05	.02
246	John Costello	.05	.02
247	Ken Dayley	.05	.02
248	Jose DeLeon	.05	.02
249	Frank DiPino	.05	.02
250	Pedro Guerrero	.05	.02
251	Ken Hill	.15	.07
252	Joe Magrane	.05	.02
253	Willie McGee UER	.05	.02

(No decimal point before 353)

254	John Morris	.05	.02
255	Jose Oquendo	.05	.02
256	Tony Pena	.05	.02
257	Terry Pendleton	.10	.05
258	Ted Power	.05	.02
259	Dan Quisenberry	.05	.02
260	Ozzie Smith	.25	.11
261	Scott Terry	.05	.02
262	Milt Thompson	.05	.02
263	Denny Walling	.05	.02
264	Todd Worrell	.05	.02
265	Todd Zeile	.10	.05
266	Marty Barrett	.05	.02
267	Mike Boddicker	.05	.02
268	Wade Boggs	.20	.09
269	Ellis Burks	.15	.07
270	Rick Cerone	.05	.02
271	Roger Clemens	.40	.18
272	John Dopson	.05	.02
273	Nick Esasky	.05	.02
274	Dwight Evans	.10	.05
275	Wes Gardner	.05	.02
276	Rich Gedman	.05	.02
277	Mike Greenwell	.05	.02
278	Danny Heep	.05	.02
279	Eric Hetzel	.05	.02
280	Dennis Lamp	.05	.02
281	Rob Murphy UER	.05	.02

('89 stats say Reds, should say Red Sox)

282	Joe Price	.05	.02
283	Carlos Quintana	.05	.02
284	Jody Reed	.05	.02
285	Luis Rivera	.05	.02
286	Kevin Romine	.05	.02
287	Lee Smith	.05	.02
288	Mike Smithson	.05	.02
289	Bob Stanley	.05	.02
290	Harold Baines	.10	.05
291	Kevin Brown	.20	.09
292	Steve Buechele	.05	.02
293	Scott Coolbaugh	.05	.02
294	Jack Daugherty	.05	.02
295	Cecil Espy	.05	.02
296	Julio Franco	.05	.02
297	Juan Gonzalez	2.00	.90
298	Cecilio Guante	.05	.02
299	Drew Hall	.05	.02
300	Charlie Hough	.05	.02
301	Pete Incaviglia	.05	.02
302	Mike Jeffcoat	.05	.02
303	Chad Kreuter	.05	.02
304	Jeff Kunkel	.05	.02
305	Rick Leach	.05	.02
306	Fred Manrique	.05	.02
307	Jamie Moyer	.05	.02
308	Rafael Palmeiro	.20	.09
309	Geno Petralli	.05	.02
310	Kevin Reimer	.05	.02
311	Kenny Rogers	.05	.02
312	Jeff Russell	.05	.02
313	Nolan Ryan	.75	.35
314	Ruben Sierra	.05	.02
315	Bobby Witt	.05	.02
316	Chris Bosio	.05	.02
317	Glenn Braggs UER	.05	.02

(Stats say 111 K's, but bio says 117 K's)

318	Greg Brock	.05	.02
319	Chuck Crim	.05	.02
320	Rob Deer	.05	.02
321	Mike Felder	.05	.02
322	Tom Filer	.05	.02
323	Tony Fossas	.05	.02
324	Jim Gantner	.05	.02
325	Darryl Hamilton	.05	.02
326	Teddy Higuera	.05	.02
327	Mark Knudson	.05	.02
328	Bill Krueger UER	.05	.02

('86 stats missing)

329	Tim McIntosh	.05	.02
330	Paul Molitor	.20	.09
331	Jaime Navarro	.05	.02
332	Charlie O'Brien	.05	.02
333	Jeff Peterek	.05	.02
334	Dan Plesac	.05	.02
335	Jerry Reuss	.05	.02
336	Gary Sheffield UER	.25	.11

(Bio says played for 3 teams in '87, but stats say in '88)

337	Bill Spiers	.05	.02
338	B.J. Surhoff	.05	.02
339	Greg Vaughn	.10	.05
340	Robin Yount	.20	.09
341	Hubie Brooks	.05	.02
342	Tim Burke	.05	.02
343	Mike Fitzgerald	.05	.02
344	Tom Foley	.05	.02
345	Andres Galarraga	.20	.09
346	Damaso Garcia	.05	.02
347	Marquis Grissom	.40	.18
348	Kevin Gross	.05	.02
349	Joe Hesketh	.05	.02
350	Jeff Huson	.05	.02
351	Wallace Johnson	.05	.02
352	Mark Langston	.05	.02
353A	Dave Martinez	2.00	.90

(Yellow on front)

353B	Dave Martinez	.05	.02

(Red on front)

354	Dennis Martinez UER	.05	.02

('87 ERA is 616, should be 6.16)

355	Andy McGaffigan	.05	.02
356	Otis Nixon	.05	.02
357	Spike Owen	.05	.02
358	Pascual Perez	.05	.02
359	Tim Raines	.10	.05
360	Nelson Santovenia	.05	.02
361	Bryn Smith	.05	.02
362	Zane Smith	.05	.02
363	Larry Walker	1.00	.45
364	Tim Wallach	.05	.02
365	Rick Aguilera	.10	.05
366	Allan Anderson	.05	.02
367	Wally Backman	.05	.02
368	Doug Baker	.05	.02
369	Juan Berenguer	.05	.02
370	Randy Bush	.05	.02
371	Carmen Castillo	.05	.02
372	Mike Dyer	.05	.02
373	Gary Gaetti	.05	.02
374	Greg Gagne	.05	.02
375	Dan Gladden	.05	.02
376	German Gonzalez UER	.05	.02

(Bio says 31 saves in '88, but stats say 30)

377	Brian Harper	.05	.02
378	Kent Hrbek	.10	.05
379	Gene Larkin	.05	.02
380	Tim Laudner UER	.05	.02

(No decimal point before '85 BA of 238)

381	John Moses	.05	.02
382	Al Newman	.05	.02
383	Kirby Puckett	.40	.18
384	Shane Rawley	.05	.02
385	Jeff Reardon	.10	.05
386	Roy Smith	.05	.02
387	Gary Wayne	.05	.02
388	Dave West	.05	.02
389	Tim Belcher	.05	.02
390	Tim Crews UER	.05	.02

(Stats say 163 IP for '83, but bio says 136)

391	Mike Davis	.05	.02
392	Rick Dempsey	.05	.02
393	Kirk Gibson	.10	.05
394	Jose Gonzalez	.05	.02
395	Alfredo Griffin	.05	.02
396	Jeff Hamilton	.05	.02
397	Lenny Harris	.05	.02
398	Mickey Hatcher	.05	.02
399	Orel Hershiser	.10	.05
400	Jay Howell	.05	.02
401	Mike Marshall	.05	.02
402	Ramon Martinez	.15	.07
403	Mike Morgan	.05	.02
404	Eddie Murray	.20	.09
405	Alejandro Pena	.05	.02
406	Willie Randolph	.10	.05
407	Mike Scioscia	.05	.02
408	Ray Searage	.05	.02
409	Fernando Valenzuela	.10	.05
410	Jose Vizcaino	.20	.09
411	John Wetteland	.20	.09
412	Jack Armstrong	.05	.02
413	Todd Benzinger UER	.05	.02

(Bio says .323 at Pawtucket, but stats say .321)

414	Tim Birtsas	.05	.02
415	Tom Browning	.05	.02
416	Norm Charlton	.05	.02
417	Eric Davis	.10	.05
418	Rob Dibble	.05	.02
419	John Franco	.10	.05
420	Ken Griffey Sr.	.05	.02
421	Chris Hammond	.05	.02

(No 1989 used for 'Did Not Play' stat, actually did play for Nashville in 1989)

422	Danny Jackson	.05	.02
423	Barry Larkin	.20	.09
424	Tim Leary	.05	.02
425	Rick Mahler	.05	.02
426	Joe Oliver	.05	.02
427	Paul O'Neill	.10	.05
428	Luis Quinones UER	.05	.02

('86-'88 stats are omitted from card but included in totals)

429	Jeff Reed	.05	.02
430	Jose Rijo	.05	.02
431	Ron Robinson	.05	.02
432	Rolando Roomes	.05	.02
433	Chris Sabo	.05	.02
434	Scott Scudder	.05	.02

□	#	Player		
□	435	Herm Winningham	.05	.02
□	436	Steve Balboni	.05	.02
□	437	Jesse Barfield	.05	.02
□	438	Mike Blowers	.20	.09
□	439	Tom Brookens	.05	.02
□	440	Greg Cadaret	.05	.02
□	441	Alvaro Espinoza UER	.05	.02

(Career games say
218, should be 219)

□	442	Bob Geren	.05	.02
□	443	Lee Guetterman	.05	.02
□	444	Mel Hall	.05	.02
□	445	Andy Hawkins	.05	.02
□	446	Roberto Kelly	.05	.02
□	447	Don Mattingly	.30	.14
□	448	Lance McCullers	.05	.02
□	449	Hensley Meulens	.05	.02
□	450	Dale Mohorcic	.05	.02
□	451	Clay Parker	.05	.02
□	452	Eric Plunk	.05	.02
□	453	Dave Righetti	.05	.02
□	454	Deion Sanders	.20	.09
□	455	Steve Sax	.05	.02
□	456	Don Slaught	.05	.02
□	457	Walt Terrell	.05	.02
□	458	Dave Winfield	.20	.09
□	459	Jay Bell	.10	.05
□	460	Rafael Belliard	.05	.02
□	461	Barry Bonds	.25	.11
□	462	Bobby Bonilla	.05	.02
□	463	Sid Bream	.05	.02
□	464	Benny Distefano	.05	.02
□	465	Doug Drabek	.05	.02
□	466	Jim Gott	.05	.02
□	467	Billy Hatcher UER	.05	.02

(.1 hits for Cubs
in 1984)

□	468	Neal Heaton	.05	.02
□	469	Jeff King	.10	.05
□	470	Bob Kipper	.05	.02
□	471	Randy Kramer	.05	.02
□	472	Bill Landrum	.05	.02
□	473	Mike LaValliere	.05	.02
□	474	Jose Lind	.05	.02
□	475	Junior Ortiz	.05	.02
□	476	Gary Redus	.05	.02
□	477	Rick Reed	.05	.02
□	478	R.J. Reynolds	.05	.02
□	479	Jeff D. Robinson	.05	.02
□	480	John Smiley	.05	.02
□	481	Andy Van Slyke	.10	.05
□	482	Bob Walk	.05	.02
□	483	Andy Allanson	.05	.02
□	484	Scott Bailes	.05	.02
□	485	Joey Belle UER	.50	.23

(Has Jay Bell
'Did You Know')

□	486	Bud Black	.05	.02
□	487	Jerry Browne	.05	.02
□	488	Tom Candiotti	.05	.02
□	489	Joe Carter	.10	.05
□	490	Dave Clark	.05	.02

(No '84 stats)

□	491	John Farrell	.05	.02
□	492	Felix Fermin	.05	.02
□	493	Brook Jacoby	.05	.02
□	494	Dion James	.05	.02
□	495	Doug Jones	.05	.02
□	496	Brad Komminsk	.05	.02
□	497	Rod Nichols	.05	.02
□	498	Pete O'Brien	.05	.02
□	499	Steve Olin	.10	.05
□	500	Jesse Orosco	.05	.02
□	501	Joel Skinner	.05	.02
□	502	Cory Snyder	.05	.02
□	503	Greg Swindell	.05	.02
□	504	Rich Yett	.05	.02
□	505	Scott Bankhead	.05	.02
□	506	Scott Bradley	.05	.02
□	507	Greg Briley UER	.05	.02

(28 SB's in bio,
but 27 in stats)

□	508	Jay Buhner	.20	.09
□	509	Darnell Coles	.05	.02
□	510	Keith Comstock	.05	.02
□	511	Henry Cotto	.05	.02

□	512	Alvin Davis	.05	.02
□	513	Ken Griffey Jr.	1.50	.70
□	514	Erik Hanson	.05	.02
□	515	Gene Harris	.05	.02
□	516	Brian Holman	.05	.02
□	517	Mike Jackson	.05	.02
□	518	Randy Johnson	.30	.14
□	519	Jeffrey Leonard	.05	.02
□	520	Edgar Martinez	.20	.09
□	521	Dennis Powell	.05	.02
□	522	Jim Presley	.05	.02
□	523	Jerry Reed	.05	.02
□	524	Harold Reynolds	.05	.02
□	525	Mike Schooler	.05	.02
□	526	Bill Swift	.05	.02
□	527	Dave Valle	.05	.02
□	528	Omar Vizquel	.20	.09
□	529	Ivan Calderon	.05	.02
□	530	Carlton Fisk UER	.20	.09

(Bellows Falls, should
be Bellows Falls)

□	531	Scott Fletcher	.05	.02
□	532	Dave Gallagher	.05	.02
□	533	Ozzie Guillen	.05	.02
□	534	Greg Hibbard	.05	.02
□	535	Shawn Hillegas	.05	.02
□	536	Lance Johnson	.05	.02
□	537	Eric King	.05	.02
□	538	Ron Kittle	.05	.02
□	539	Steve Lyons	.05	.02
□	540	Carlos Martinez	.05	.02
□	541	Tom McCarthy	.05	.02
□	542	Matt Merullo	.05	.02

(Had 5 ML runs scored
entering '90, not 6)

| □ | 543 | Donn Pall UER | .05 | .02 |

(Stats say pro career
began in '85,
bio says '88)

□	544	Dan Pasqua	.05	.02
□	545	Ken Patterson	.05	.02
□	546	Melido Perez	.05	.02
□	547	Steve Rosenberg	.05	.02
□	548	Sammy Sosa	.75	.35
□	549	Bobby Thigpen	.05	.02
□	550	Robin Ventura	.20	.09
□	551	Greg Walker	.05	.02
□	552	Don Carman	.05	.02
□	553	Pat Combs	.05	.02

(6 walks for Phillies
in '89 in stats,
brief bio says 4)

□	554	Dennis Cook	.05	.02
□	555	Darren Daulton	.10	.05
□	556	Len Dykstra	.10	.05
□	557	Curt Ford	.05	.02
□	558	Charlie Hayes	.05	.02
□	559	Von Hayes	.05	.02
□	560	Tommy Herr	.05	.02
□	561	Ken Howell	.05	.02
□	562	Steve Jeltz	.05	.02
□	563	Ron Jones	.05	.02
□	564	Ricky Jordan UER	.05	.02

(Duplicate line of
statistics on back)

□	565	John Kruk	.10	.05
□	566	Steve Lake	.05	.02
□	567	Roger McDowell	.05	.02
□	568	Terry Mulholland UER	.05	.02

(Did You Know refers
to Dave Magadan)

□	569	Dwayne Murphy	.05	.02
□	570	Jeff Parrett	.05	.02
□	571	Randy Ready	.05	.02
□	572	Bruce Ruffin	.05	.02
□	573	Dickie Thon	.05	.02
□	574	Jose Alvarez UER	.05	.02

('78 and '79 stats
are reversed)

□	575	Geronimo Berroa	.10	.05
□	576	Jeff Blauser	.05	.02
□	577	Joe Boever	.05	.02
□	578	Marty Clary UER	.05	.02

(No comma between
city and state)

| □ | 579 | Jody Davis | .05 | .02 |

□	580	Mark Eichhorn	.05	.02
□	581	Darrell Evans	.10	.05
□	582	Ron Gant	.10	.05
□	583	Tom Glavine	.20	.09
□	584	Tommy Greene	.05	.02
□	585	Tommy Gregg	.05	.02
□	586	Dave Justice UER	.75	.35

(Actually had 16 2B
in Sumter in '86)

□	587	Mark Lemke	.05	.02
□	588	Derek Lilliquist	.05	.02
□	589	Oddibe McDowell	.05	.02
□	590	Kent Mercker ERA	.10	.05

(Bio says 2.75 ERA,
stats say 2.68 ERA)

□	591	Dale Murphy	.20	.09
□	592	Gerald Perry	.05	.02
□	593	Lonnie Smith	.05	.02
□	594	Pete Smith	.05	.02
□	595	John Smoltz	.20	.09
□	596	Mike Stanton UER	.05	.02

(No comma between
city and state)

□	597	Andres Thomas	.05	.02
□	598	Jeff Treadway	.05	.02
□	599	Doyle Alexander	.05	.02
□	600	Dave Bergman	.05	.02
□	601	Brian DuBois	.05	.02
□	602	Paul Gibson	.05	.02
□	603	Mike Heath	.05	.02
□	604	Mike Henneman	.05	.02
□	605	Guillermo Hernandez	.05	.02
□	606	Shawn Holman	.05	.02
□	607	Tracy Jones	.05	.02
□	608	Chet Lemon	.05	.02
□	609	Fred Lynn	.05	.02
□	610	Jack Morris	.10	.05
□	611	Matt Nokes	.05	.02
□	612	Gary Pettis	.05	.02
□	613	Kevin Ritz	.05	.02
□	614	Jeff M. Robinson	.05	.02

('88 stats are
not in line)

□	615	Steve Searcy	.05	.02
□	616	Frank Tanana	.05	.02
□	617	Alan Trammell	.15	.07
□	618	Gary Ward	.05	.02
□	619	Lou Whitaker	.10	.05
□	620	Frank Williams	.05	.02
□	621A	George Brett '80	1.50	.70

ERR (Had 10 .390
hitting seasons)

| □ | 621B | George Brett '80 | .20 | .09 |

COR

□	622	Fern.Valenzuela '81	.05	.02
□	623	Dale Murphy '82	.10	.05
□	624A	Cal Ripken '83 ERR	5.00	2.20

(Misspelled Ripklin
on card back)

□	624B	Cal Ripken '83 COR	.40	.18
□	625	Ryne Sandberg '84	.20	.09
□	626	Don Mattingly '85	.20	.09
□	627	Roger Clemens '86	.20	.09
□	628	George Bell '87	.05	.02
□	629	Jose Canseco '88 UER	.10	.05

(Reggie won MVP in
'83, should say '73)

| □ | 630A | Will Clark '89 ERR. | 1.00 | .45 |

(32 total bases
on card back)

| □ | 630B | Will Clark '89 COR | .20 | .09 |

(321 total bases;
technically still
an error, listing
only 24 runs)

| □ | 631 | Game Savers | .05 | .02 |

Mark Davis
Mitch Williams

| □ | 632 | Boston Igniters | .20 | .09 |

Wade Boggs
Mike Greenwell

| □ | 633 | Starter and Stopper | .05 | .02 |

Mark Gubicza
Jeff Russell

| □ | 634 | League's Best | .25 | .11 |

Shortstops

	Tony Fernandez		
	Cal Ripken		
☐ 635	Human Dynamos........	.20	.09
	Kirby Puckett		
	Bo Jackson		
☐ 636	300 Strikeout Club	.25	.11
	Nolan Ryan		
	Mike Scott		
☐ 637	The Dynamic Duo	.10	.05
	Will Clark		
	Kevin Mitchell		
☐ 638	AL All-Stars	.25	.11
	Don Mattingly		
	Mark McGwire		
☐ 639	NL East Rivals	.20	.09
	Howard Johnson		
	Ryne Sandberg		
☐ 640	Rudy Seanez	.05	.02
	Colin Charland		
☐ 641	George Canale..........	.20	.09
	Kevin Maas UER		
	(Canale listed as INF		
	on front, 1B on back)		
☐ 642	Kelly Mann	.05	.02
	and Dave Hansen		
☐ 643	Greg Smith	.05	.02
	and Stu Tate		
☐ 644	Tom Drees................	.05	.02
	and Dann Howitt		
☐ 645	Mike Roesler	.20	.09
	and Derrick May		
☐ 646	Scott Hemond	.05	.02
	and Mark Gardner		
☐ 647	John Orton	.05	.02
	and Scott Leius		
☐ 648	Rich Monteleone	.05	.02
	and Dana Williams		
☐ 649	Mike Huff.................	.05	.02
	and Steve Frey		
☐ 650	Chuck McElroy	.50	.23
	and Moises Alou		
☐ 651	Bobby Rose	.05	.02
	and Mike Hartley		
☐ 652	Matt Kinzer	.05	.02
	and Wayne Edwards		
☐ 653	Delino DeShields	.10	.05
	and Jason Grimsley		
☐ 654	CL: A's/Cubs	.05	.02
	Giants/Blue Jays		
☐ 655	CL: Royals/Angels	.05	.02
	Padres/Orioles		
☐ 656	CL: Mets/Astros	.05	.02
	Cards/Red Sox		
☐ 657	CL: Rangers/Brewers	.05	.02
	Expos/Twins		
☐ 658	CL: Dodgers/Reds	.05	.02
	Yankees/Pirates		
☐ 659	CL: Indians/Mariners..	.05	.02
	White Sox/Phillies		
☐ 660A	CL: Braves/Tigers	.05	.02
	Specials/Checklists		
	(Checklist-660 in small-		
	er print on card front)		
☐ 660B	CL: Braves/Tigers	.05	.02
	Specials/Checklists		
	(Checklist-660 in nor-		
	mal print on card front)		

1990 Fleer All-Stars

The 1990 Fleer All-Star insert set includes 12 standard-size cards. The set was randomly inserted in 33-card cellos and wax packs. The set is sequenced in alphabetical order. The fronts are white with a light gray screen and bright red stripes. The player selection for the set is Fleer's opinion of the best Major Leaguer at each position.

	MINT	NRMT
COMPLETE SET (12)	3.00	1.35
COMMON CARD (1-12)	.15	.07
RANDOM INSERTS IN PACKS ..		
☐ 1 Harold Baines	.35	.16
☐ 2 Will Clark..................	.50	.23
☐ 3 Mark Davis	.15	.07
☐ 4 Howard Johnson UER ..	.15	.07
(In middle of 5th		
line, the is		
misspelled th)		
☐ 5 Joe Magrane	.15	.07
☐ 6 Kevin Mitchell	.15	.07
☐ 7 Kirby Puckett.............	1.00	.45
☐ 8 Cal Ripken	2.00	.90
☐ 9 Ryne Sandberg	.75	.35
☐ 10 Mike Scott UER	.15	.07
Astros spelled Asatros on back		
☐ 11 Ruben Sierra	.15	.07
☐ 12 Mickey Tettleton	.15	.07

1990 Fleer League Standouts

This six-card standard-size insert set was distributed one per 45-card rack pack. The set is subtitled "Standouts" and commemorates outstanding events for those players from the previous season.

	MINT	NRMT
COMPLETE SET (6)	6.00	2.70
COMMON CARD (1-6)	.50	.23
ONE PER RACK PACK		
☐ 1 Barry Larkin	1.00	.45
☐ 2 Don Mattingly	2.50	1.10
☐ 3 Darryl Strawberry	.50	.23
☐ 4 Jose Canseco	1.00	.45
☐ 5 Wade Boggs	.75	.35
☐ 6 Mark Sabo UER	.75	.35
(Chris Sabo misspelled		
as Cris)		

1990 Fleer Soaring Stars

The 1990 Fleer Soaring Stars set was issued exclusively in jumbo cello packs. This 12-card, standard-size set features some of the most popular young players entering the 1990 season. The set gives the visual impression of rockets exploding in the air to honor these young players.

	MINT	NRMT
COMPLETE SET (12)	25.00	11.00
COMMON CARD (1-12)	.50	.23
MINOR STARS	1.00	.45
SEMISTARS	1.50	.70
RANDOM INSERTS IN JUMBO PACKS		
☐ 1 Todd Zeile	1.00	.45
☐ 2 Mike Stanton	.50	.23
☐ 3 Larry Walker	6.00	2.70
☐ 4 Robin Ventura	2.00	.90
☐ 5 Scott Coolbaugh	.50	.23
☐ 6 Ken Griffey Jr.	15.00	6.75
☐ 7 Tom Gordon	.50	.23
☐ 8 Jerome Walton	.50	.23
☐ 9 Junior Felix	.50	.23
☐ 10 Jim Abbott.............	1.00	.45
☐ 11 Ricky Jordan	.50	.23
☐ 12 Dwight Smith	.50	.23

1990 Fleer Update

The 1990 Fleer Update set contains 132 standard-size cards. This set marked the seventh consecutive year Fleer issued an end of season Update set. The set was issued exclusively as a boxed set through hobby dealers. The set is checklisted alphabetically by team for each league and then alphabetically within each team. The fronts are styled the same as the 1990

Fleer regular issue set. The backs are numbered with the prefix "U" for Update. Rookie Cards in this set include Carlos Baerga, Alex Fernandez, Travis Fryman, Todd Hundley and Frank Thomas.

	MINT	NRMT
COMPLETE SET (132)	5.00	2.20
COMMON CARD (1-132)	.05	.02
MINOR STARS	.10	.05
UNLISTED STARS	.20	.09

☐ 1 Steve Avery	.05	.02
☐ 2 Francisco Cabrera	.05	.02
☐ 3 Nick Esasky	.05	.02
☐ 4 Jim Kremers	.05	.02
☐ 5 Greg Olson	.05	.02
☐ 6 Jim Presley	.05	.02
☐ 7 Shawn Boskie	.05	.02
☐ 8 Joe Kraemer	.05	.02
☐ 9 Luis Salazar	.05	.02
☐ 10 Hector Villanueva	.05	.02
☐ 11 Glenn Braggs	.05	.02
☐ 12 Mariano Duncan	.05	.02
☐ 13 Billy Hatcher	.05	.02
☐ 14 Tim Layana	.05	.02
☐ 15 Hal Morris	.05	.02
☐ 16 Javier Ortiz	.05	.02
☐ 17 Dave Rohde	.05	.02
☐ 18 Eric Yelding	.05	.02
☐ 19 Hubie Brooks	.05	.02
☐ 20 Kal Daniels	.05	.02
☐ 21 Dave Hansen	.05	.02
☐ 22 Mike Hartley	.05	.02
☐ 23 Stan Javier	.05	.02
☐ 24 Jose Offerman	.20	.09
☐ 25 Juan Samuel	.05	.02
☐ 26 Dennis Boyd	.05	.02
☐ 27 Delino DeShields	.10	.05
☐ 28 Steve Frey	.05	.02
☐ 29 Mark Gardner	.05	.02
☐ 30 Chris Nabholz	.05	.02
☐ 31 Bill Sampen	.05	.02
☐ 32 Dave Schmidt	.05	.02
☐ 33 Daryl Boston	.05	.02
☐ 34 Chuck Carr	.20	.09
☐ 35 John Franco	.10	.05
☐ 36 Todd Hundley	.40	.18
☐ 37 Julio Machado	.05	.02
☐ 38 Alejandro Pena	.05	.02
☐ 39 Darren Reed	.05	.02
☐ 40 Kelvin Torve	.05	.02
☐ 41 Darrel Akerfelds	.05	.02
☐ 42 Jose DeJesus	.05	.02
☐ 43 Dave Hollins UER	.20	.09
(Misspelled Dane on card back)		
☐ 44 Carmelo Martinez	.05	.02
☐ 45 Brad Moore	.05	.02
☐ 46 Dale Murphy	.20	.09
☐ 47 Wally Backman	.05	.02
☐ 48 Stan Belinda	.05	.02
☐ 49 Bob Patterson	.05	.02
☐ 50 Ted Power	.05	.02
☐ 51 Don Slaught	.05	.02
☐ 52 Geronimo Pena	.05	.02
☐ 53 Lee Smith	.10	.05
☐ 54 John Tudor	.05	.02
☐ 55 Joe Carter	.10	.05
☐ 56 Thomas Howard	.05	.02
☐ 57 Craig Lefferts	.05	.02
☐ 58 Rafael Valdez	.05	.02
☐ 59 Dave Anderson	.05	.02
☐ 60 Kevin Bass	.05	.02
☐ 61 John Burkett	.10	.05
☐ 62 Gary Carter	.20	.09
☐ 63 Rick Parker	.05	.02
☐ 64 Trevor Wilson	.05	.02
☐ 65 Chris Hoiles	.20	.09
☐ 66 Tim Hulett	.05	.02
☐ 67 Dave Johnson	.05	.02
☐ 68 Curt Schilling	.20	.09
☐ 69 David Segui	.20	.09
☐ 70 Tom Brunansky	.05	.02

☐ 71 Greg A. Harris	.05	.02
☐ 72 Dana Kiecker	.05	.02
☐ 73 Tim Naehring	.20	.09
☐ 74 Tony Pena	.05	.02
☐ 75 Jeff Reardon	.10	.05
☐ 76 Jerry Reed	.05	.02
☐ 77 Mark Eichhorn	.05	.02
☐ 78 Mark Langston	.05	.02
☐ 79 John Orton	.05	.02
☐ 80 Luis Polonia	.05	.02
☐ 81 Dave Winfield	.20	.09
☐ 82 Cliff Young	.05	.02
☐ 83 Wayne Edwards	.05	.02
☐ 84 Alex Fernandez	.50	.23
☐ 85 Craig Grebeck	.05	.02
☐ 86 Scott Radinsky	.05	.02
☐ 87 Frank Thomas	4.00	1.80
☐ 88 Beau Allred	.05	.02
☐ 89 Sandy Alomar Jr.	.20	.09
☐ 90 Carlos Baerga	.25	.11
☐ 91 Kevin Bearse	.05	.02
☐ 92 Chris James	.05	.02
☐ 93 Candy Maldonado	.05	.02
☐ 94 Jeff Manto	.05	.02
☐ 95 Cecil Fielder	.10	.05
☐ 96 Travis Fryman	.40	.18
☐ 97 Lloyd Moseby	.05	.02
☐ 98 Edwin Nunez	.05	.02
☐ 99 Tony Phillips	.05	.02
☐ 100 Larry Sheets	.05	.02
☐ 101 Mark Davis	.05	.02
☐ 102 Storm Davis	.05	.02
☐ 103 Gerald Perry	.05	.02
☐ 104 Terry Shumpert	.05	.02
☐ 105 Edgar Diaz	.05	.02
☐ 106 Dave Parker	.10	.05
☐ 107 Tim Drummond	.05	.02
☐ 108 Junior Ortiz	.05	.02
☐ 109 Park Pittman	.05	.02
☐ 110 Kevin Tapani	.10	.05
☐ 111 Oscar Azocar	.05	.02
☐ 112 Jim Leyritz	.20	.09
☐ 113 Kevin Maas	.10	.05
☐ 114 Alan Mills	.05	.02
☐ 115 Matt Nokes	.05	.02
☐ 116 Pascual Perez	.05	.02
☐ 117 Ozzie Canseco	.05	.02
☐ 118 Scott Sanderson	.05	.02
☐ 119 Tino Martinez	.40	.18
☐ 120 Jeff Schaefer	.05	.02
☐ 121 Matt Young	.05	.02
☐ 122 Brian Bohanon	.05	.02
☐ 123 Jeff Huson	.05	.02
☐ 124 Ramon Manon	.05	.02
☐ 125 Gary Mielke UER	.05	.02
(Shown as Blue Jay on front)		
☐ 126 Willie Blair	.05	.02
☐ 127 Glenallen Hill	.05	.02
☐ 128 John Olerud UER	.20	.09
(Listed as throwing right, should be left)		
☐ 129 Luis Sojo	.05	.02
☐ 130 Mark Whiten	.10	.05
☐ 131 Nolan Ryan	.75	.35
☐ 132 Checklist U1-U132	.05	.02

1991 Fleer

The 1991 Fleer set consists of 720 standard-size cards. Cards were primarily issued in wax packs, cello packs and factory sets. This set does not have what has been a Fleer tradition in recent years, the two-player rookie cards and there are less two-player special cards than in prior years. The design features solid yellow borders with the information in black indicating name, position, and team. The set is again ordered numerically by teams, followed by combination cards, rookie prospect

pairs, and checklists. Rookie Cards in this set include Jeff Conine and Brian McRae. A number of the cards in the set can be found with photos cropped (very slightly) differently as Fleer used two separate printers in their attempt to maximize production.

	MINT	NRMT
COMPLETE SET (720)	8.00	3.60
COMP.RETAIL SET (732)	10.00	4.50
COMP.HOBBY SET (732)	10.00	4.50
COMMON CARD (1-720)	.05	.02
MINOR STARS	.10	.05
UNLISTED STARS	.20	.09
COMP.WORLD SERIES SET (8)	2.00	.90
ONE WORLD SERIES SET PER FACT.SET		

☐ 1 Troy Afenir	.05	.02
☐ 2 Harold Baines	.10	.05
☐ 3 Lance Blankenship	.05	.02
☐ 4 Todd Burns	.05	.02
☐ 5 Jose Canseco	.15	.07
☐ 6 Dennis Eckersley	.10	.05
☐ 7 Mike Gallego	.05	.02
☐ 8 Ron Hassey	.05	.02
☐ 9 Dave Henderson	.05	.02
☐ 10 Rickey Henderson	.20	.09
☐ 11 Rick Honeycutt	.05	.02
☐ 12 Doug Jennings	.05	.02
☐ 13 Joe Klink	.05	.02
☐ 14 Carney Lansford	.10	.05
☐ 15 Darren Lewis	.05	.02
☐ 16 Willie McGee UER	.05	.02
(Height 6'11")		
☐ 17 Mark McGwire UER	.40	.18
(183 extra base hits in 1987)		
☐ 18 Mike Moore	.05	.02
☐ 19 Gene Nelson	.05	.02
☐ 20 Dave Otto	.05	.02
☐ 21 Jamie Quirk	.05	.02
☐ 22 Willie Randolph	.10	.05
☐ 23 Scott Sanderson	.05	.02
☐ 24 Terry Steinbach	.05	.02
☐ 25 Dave Stewart	.10	.05
☐ 26 Walt Weiss	.05	.02
☐ 27 Bob Welch	.05	.02
☐ 28 Curt Young	.05	.02
☐ 29 Wally Backman	.05	.02
☐ 30 Stan Belinda UER	.05	.02
(Born in Huntington, should be State College)		
☐ 31 Jay Bell	.10	.05
☐ 32 Rafael Belliard	.05	.02
☐ 33 Barry Bonds	.25	.11
☐ 34 Bobby Bonilla	.10	.05
☐ 35 Sid Bream	.05	.02
☐ 36 Doug Drabek	.05	.02
☐ 37 Carlos Garcia	.05	.02
☐ 38 Neal Heaton	.05	.02
☐ 39 Jeff King	.10	.05
☐ 40 Bob Kipper	.05	.02
☐ 41 Bill Landrum	.05	.02
☐ 42 Mike LaValliere	.05	.02
☐ 43 Jose Lind	.05	.02

□ 44 Carmelo Martinez .05 .02
□ 45 Bob Patterson .05 .02
□ 46 Ted Power .05 .02
□ 47 Gary Redus .05 .02
□ 48 R.J. Reynolds .05 .02
□ 49 Don Slaught .05 .02
□ 50 John Smiley .05 .02
□ 51 Zane Smith .05 .02
□ 52 Randy Tomlin .05 .02
□ 53 Andy Van Slyke .10 .05
□ 54 Bob Walk .05 .02
□ 55 Jack Armstrong .05 .02
□ 56 Todd Benzinger .05 .02
□ 57 Glenn Braggs .05 .02
□ 58 Keith Brown .05 .02
□ 59 Tom Browning .05 .02
□ 60 Norm Charlton .05 .02
□ 61 Eric Davis .10 .05
□ 62 Rob Dibble .05 .02
□ 63 Bill Doran .05 .02
□ 64 Mariano Duncan .05 .02
□ 65 Chris Hammond .05 .02
□ 66 Billy Hatcher .05 .02
□ 67 Danny Jackson .05 .02
□ 68 Barry Larkin .15 .07
□ 69 Tim Layana .05 .02
(Black line over made in first text line)
□ 70 Terry Lee .05 .02
□ 71 Rick Mahler .05 .02
□ 72 Hal Morris .05 .02
□ 73 Randy Myers .05 .02
□ 74 Ron Oester .05 .02
□ 75 Joe Oliver .05 .02
□ 76 Paul O'Neill .10 .05
□ 77 Luis Quinones .05 .02
□ 78 Jeff Reed .05 .02
□ 79 Jose Rijo .05 .02
□ 80 Chris Sabo .05 .02
□ 81 Scott Scudder .05 .02
□ 82 Herm Winningham .05 .02
□ 83 Larry Andersen .05 .02
□ 84 Marty Barrett .05 .02
□ 85 Mike Boddicker .05 .02
□ 86 Wade Boggs .20 .09
□ 87 Tom Bolton .05 .02
□ 88 Tom Brunansky .05 .02
□ 89 Ellis Burks .10 .05
□ 90 Roger Clemens .40 .18
□ 91 Scott Cooper .05 .02
□ 92 John Dopson .05 .02
□ 93 Dwight Evans .10 .05
□ 94 Wes Gardner .05 .02
□ 95 Jeff Gray .05 .02
□ 96 Mike Greenwell .05 .02
□ 97 Greg A. Harris .05 .02
□ 98 Daryl Irvine .05 .02
□ 99 Dana Kiecker .05 .02
□ 100 Randy Kutcher .05 .02
□ 101 Dennis Lamp .05 .02
□ 102 Mike Marshall .05 .02
□ 103 John Marzano .05 .02
□ 104 Rob Murphy .05 .02
□ 105 Tim Naehring .10 .05
□ 106 Tony Pena .05 .02
□ 107 Phil Plantier .10 .05
□ 108 Carlos Quintana .05 .02
□ 109 Jeff Reardon .10 .05
□ 110 Jerry Reed .05 .02
□ 111 Jody Reed .05 .02
□ 112 Luis Rivera UER .05 .02
(Born 1/3/84)
□ 113 Kevin Romine .05 .02
□ 114 Phil Bradley .05 .02
□ 115 Ivan Calderon .05 .02
□ 116 Wayne Edwards .05 .02
□ 117 Alex Fernandez .10 .05
□ 118 Carlton Fisk .20 .09
□ 119 Scott Fletcher .05 .02
□ 120 Craig Grebeck .05 .02
□ 121 Ozzie Guillen .05 .02
□ 122 Greg Hibbard .05 .02
□ 123 Lance Johnson UER .05 .02
(Born Cincinnati, should be Lincoln Heights)
□ 124 Barry Jones .05 .02

□ 125 Ron Karkovice .05 .02
□ 126 Eric King .05 .02
□ 127 Steve Lyons .05 .02
□ 128 Carlos Martinez .05 .02
□ 129 Jack McDowell UER .05 .02
(Stanford misspelled as Standford on back)
□ 130 Donn Pall .05 .02
(No dots over any i's in text)
□ 131 Dan Pasqua .05 .02
□ 132 Ken Patterson .05 .02
□ 133 Melido Perez .05 .02
□ 134 Adam Peterson .05 .02
□ 135 Scott Radinsky .05 .02
□ 136 Sammy Sosa .25 .11
□ 137 Bobby Thigpen .05 .02
□ 138 Frank Thomas 1.50 .70
□ 139 Robin Ventura .20 .09
□ 140 Daryl Boston .05 .02
□ 141 Chuck Carr .05 .02
□ 142 Mark Carreon .05 .02
□ 143 David Cone .10 .05
□ 144 Ron Darling .05 .02
□ 145 Kevin Elster .05 .02
□ 146 Sid Fernandez .05 .02
□ 147 John Franco .10
□ 148 Dwight Gooden .10 .05
□ 149 Tom Herr .05 .02
□ 150 Todd Hundley .20 .09
□ 151 Gregg Jefferies .05 .02
□ 152 Howard Johnson .05 .02
□ 153 Dave Magadan .05 .02
□ 154 Kevin McReynolds .05 .02
□ 155 Keith Miller UER .05 .02
(Text says Rochester in '87, stats say Tidewater, mixed up with other Keith Miller)
□ 156 Bob Ojeda .05 .02
□ 157 Tom O'Malley .05 .02
□ 158 Alejandro Pena .05 .02
□ 159 Darren Reed .05 .02
□ 160 Mackey Sasser .05 .02
□ 161 Darryl Strawberry .10 .05
□ 162 Tim Teufel .05 .02
□ 163 Kelvin Torve .05 .02
□ 164 Julio Valera .05 .02
□ 165 Frank Viola .05 .02
□ 166 Wally Whitehurst .05 .02
□ 167 Jim Acker .05 .02
□ 168 Derek Bell .20 .09
□ 169 George Bell .05 .02
□ 170 Willie Blair .05 .02
□ 171 Pat Borders .05 .02
□ 172 John Cerutti .05 .02
□ 173 Junior Felix .05 .02
□ 174 Tony Fernandez .05 .02
□ 175 Kelly Gruber UER .05 .02
(Born in Houston, should be Bellaire)
□ 176 Tom Henke .05 .02
□ 177 Glenallen Hill .05 .02
□ 178 Jimmy Key .10 .05
□ 179 Manny Lee .05 .02
□ 180 Fred McGriff .20 .09
□ 181 Rance Mulliniks .05 .02
□ 182 Greg Myers .05 .02
□ 183 John Olerud UER .10 .05
(Listed as throwing right, should be left)
□ 184 Luis Sojo .05 .02
□ 185 Dave Stieb .05 .02
□ 186 Todd Stottlemyre .05 .02
□ 187 Duane Ward .05 .02
□ 188 David Wells .05 .02
□ 189 Mark Whiten .05 .02
□ 190 Ken Williams .05 .02
□ 191 Frank Wills .05 .02
□ 192 Mookie Wilson .10 .05
□ 193 Don Aase .05 .02
□ 194 Tim Belcher UER .05 .02
(Born Sparta, Ohio, should say Mt. Gilead)
□ 195 Hubie Brooks .05 .02
□ 196 Dennis Cook .05 .02

□ 197 Tim Crews .05 .02
□ 198 Kal Daniels .05 .02
□ 199 Kirk Gibson .10 .05
□ 200 Jim Gott .05 .02
□ 201 Alfredo Griffin .05 .02
□ 202 Chris Gwynn .05 .02
□ 203 Dave Hansen .05 .02
□ 204 Lenny Harris .05 .02
□ 205 Mike Hartley .05 .02
□ 206 Mickey Hatcher .05 .02
□ 207 Carlos Hernandez .05 .02
□ 208 Orel Hershiser .10 .05
□ 209 Jay Howell UER .05 .02
(No 1982 Yankee stats)
□ 210 Mike Huff .05 .02
□ 211 Stan Javier .05 .02
□ 212 Ramon Martinez .10 .05
□ 213 Mike Morgan .05 .02
□ 214 Eddie Murray .20 .09
□ 215 Jim Neidlinger .05 .02
□ 216 Jose Offerman .05 .02
□ 217 Jim Poole .05 .02
□ 218 Juan Samuel .05 .02
□ 219 Mike Scioscia .05 .02
□ 220 Ray Searage .05 .02
□ 221 Mike Sharperson .05 .02
□ 222 Fernando Valenzuela .10 .05
□ 223 Jose Vizcaino .05 .02
□ 224 Mike Aldrete .05 .02
□ 225 Scott Anderson .05 .02
□ 226 Dennis Boyd .05 .02
□ 227 Tim Burke .05 .02
□ 228 Delino DeShields .05 .02
□ 229 Mike Fitzgerald .05 .02
□ 230 Tom Foley .05 .02
□ 231 Steve Frey .05 .02
□ 232 Andres Galarraga .20 .09
□ 233 Mark Gardner .05 .02
□ 234 Marquis Grissom .20 .09
□ 235 Kevin Gross .05 .02
(No date given for first Expos win)
□ 236 Drew Hall .05 .02
□ 237 Dave Martinez .05 .02
□ 238 Dennis Martinez .10 .05
□ 239 Dale Mohorcic .05 .02
□ 240 Chris Nabholz .05 .02
□ 241 Otis Nixon .05 .02
□ 242 Junior Noboa .05 .02
□ 243 Spike Owen .05 .02
□ 244 Tim Raines .10 .05
□ 245 Mel Rojas UER .20 .09
(Stats show 3.60 ERA, bio says 3.19 ERA)
□ 246 Scott Ruskin .05 .02
□ 247 Bill Sampen .05 .02
□ 248 Nelson Santovenia .05 .02
□ 249 Dave Schmidt .05 .02
□ 250 Larry Walker .30 .14
□ 251 Tim Wallach .05 .02
□ 252 Dave Anderson .05 .02
□ 253 Kevin Bass .05 .02
□ 254 Steve Bedrosian .05 .02
□ 255 Jeff Brantley .05 .02
□ 256 John Burkett .05 .02
□ 257 Brett Butler .10 .05
□ 258 Gary Carter .20 .09
□ 259 Will Clark .30 .14
□ 260 Steve Decker .05 .02
□ 261 Kelly Downs .05 .02
□ 262 Scott Garrelts .05 .02
□ 263 Terry Kennedy .05 .02
□ 264 Mike LaCoss .05 .02
□ 265 Mark Leonard .05 .02
□ 266 Greg Litton .05 .02
□ 267 Kevin Mitchell .10 .05
□ 268 Randy O'Neal .05 .02
□ 269 Rick Parker .05 .02
□ 270 Rick Reuschel .05 .02
□ 271 Ernest Riles .05 .02
□ 272 Don Robinson .05 .02
□ 273 Robby Thompson .05 .02
□ 274 Mark Thurmond .05 .02
□ 275 Jose Uribe .05 .02
□ 276 Matt Williams .20 .09
□ 277 Trevor Wilson .05 .02

☐ 278 Gerald Alexander	.05	.02
☐ 279 Brad Arnsberg	.05	.02
☐ 280 Kevin Belcher	.05	.02
☐ 281 Joe Bitker	.05	.02
☐ 282 Kevin Brown	.10	.05
☐ 283 Steve Buechele	.05	.02
☐ 284 Jack Daugherty	.05	.02
☐ 285 Julio Franco	.05	.02
☐ 286 Juan Gonzalez	.75	.35
☐ 287 Bill Haselman	.05	.02
☐ 288 Charlie Hough	.05	.02
☐ 289 Jeff Huson	.05	.02
☐ 290 Pete Incaviglia	.05	.02
☐ 291 Mike Jeffcoat	.05	.02
☐ 292 Jeff Kunkel	.05	.02
☐ 293 Gary Mielke	.05	.02
☐ 294 Jamie Moyer	.05	.02
☐ 295 Rafael Palmeiro	.20	.09
☐ 296 Geno Petralli	.05	.02
☐ 297 Gary Pettis	.05	.02
☐ 298 Kevin Reimer	.05	.02
☐ 299 Kenny Rogers	.05	.02
☐ 300 Jeff Russell	.05	.02
☐ 301 John Russell	.05	.02
☐ 302 Nolan Ryan	.75	.35
☐ 303 Ruben Sierra	.20	.09
☐ 304 Bobby Witt	.05	.02
☐ 305 Jim Abbott UER	.05	.02
(Text on back states he won Sullivan Award (outstanding amateur athlete) in 1989;should be '88)		
☐ 306 Kent Anderson	.05	.02
☐ 307 Dante Bichette	.20	.09
☐ 308 Bert Blyleven	.10	.05
☐ 309 Chili Davis	.10	.05
☐ 310 Brian Downing	.05	.02
☐ 311 Mark Eichhorn	.05	.02
☐ 312 Mike Fetters	.05	.02
☐ 313 Chuck Finley	.10	.05
☐ 314 Willie Fraser	.05	.02
☐ 315 Bryan Harvey	.05	.02
☐ 316 Donnie Hill	.05	.02
☐ 317 Wally Joyner	.10	.05
☐ 318 Mark Langston	.05	.02
☐ 319 Kirk McCaskill	.05	.02
☐ 320 John Orton	.05	.02
☐ 321 Lance Parrish	.05	.02
☐ 322 Luis Polonia UER	.05	.02
(1984 Madfison, should be Madison)		
☐ 323 Johnny Ray	.05	.02
☐ 324 Bobby Rose	.05	.02
☐ 325 Dick Schofield	.05	.02
☐ 326 Rick Schu	.05	.02
☐ 327 Lee Stevens	.05	.02
☐ 328 Devon White	.05	.02
☐ 329 Dave Winfield	.20	.09
☐ 330 Cliff Young	.05	.02
☐ 331 Dave Bergman	.05	.02
☐ 332 Phil Clark	.05	.02
☐ 333 Darnell Coles	.05	.02
☐ 334 Milt Cuyler	.10	.05
☐ 335 Cecil Fielder	.10	.05
☐ 336 Travis Fryman	.20	.09
☐ 337 Paul Gibson	.05	.02
☐ 338 Jerry Don Gleaton	.05	.02
☐ 339 Mike Heath	.05	.02
☐ 340 Mike Henneman	.05	.02
☐ 341 Chet Lemon	.05	.02
☐ 342 Lance McCullers	.05	.02
☐ 343 Jack Morris	.10	.05
☐ 344 Lloyd Moseby	.05	.02
☐ 345 Edwin Nunez	.05	.02
☐ 346 Clay Parker	.05	.02
☐ 347 Dan Petry	.05	.02
☐ 348 Tony Phillips	.05	.02
☐ 349 Jeff M. Robinson	.05	.02
☐ 350 Mark Salas	.05	.02
☐ 351 Mike Schwabe	.05	.02
☐ 352 Larry Sheets	.05	.02
☐ 353 John Shelby	.05	.02
☐ 354 Frank Tanana	.05	.02
☐ 355 Alan Trammell	.15	.07
☐ 356 Gary Ward	.05	.02
☐ 357 Lou Whitaker	.10	.05
☐ 358 Beau Allred	.05	.02
☐ 359 Sandy Alomar Jr.	.15	.07
☐ 360 Carlos Baerga	.10	.05
☐ 361 Kevin Bearse	.05	.02
☐ 362 Tom Brookens	.05	.02
☐ 363 Jerry Browne UER	.05	.02
(No dot over i in first text line)		
☐ 364 Tom Candiotti	.05	.02
☐ 365 Alex Cole	.05	.02
☐ 366 John Farrell UER	.05	.02
(Born in Neptune, should be Monmouth)		
☐ 367 Felix Fermin	.05	.02
☐ 368 Keith Hernandez	.10	.05
☐ 369 Brook Jacoby	.05	.02
☐ 370 Chris James	.05	.02
☐ 371 Dion James	.05	.02
☐ 372 Doug Jones	.05	.02
☐ 373 Candy Maldonado	.05	.02
☐ 374 Steve Olin	.05	.02
☐ 375 Jesse Orosco	.05	.02
☐ 376 Rudy Seanez	.05	.02
☐ 377 Joel Skinner	.05	.02
☐ 378 Cory Snyder	.05	.02
☐ 379 Greg Swindell	.05	.02
☐ 380 Sergio Valdez	.05	.02
☐ 381 Mike Walker	.05	.02
☐ 382 Colby Ward	.05	.02
☐ 383 Turner Ward	.05	.02
☐ 384 Mitch Webster	.05	.02
☐ 385 Kevin Wickander	.05	.02
☐ 386 Darrel Akerfelds	.05	.02
☐ 387 Joe Boever	.05	.02
☐ 388 Rod Booker	.05	.02
☐ 389 Sil Campusano	.05	.02
☐ 390 Don Carman	.05	.02
☐ 391 Wes Chamberlain	.05	.02
☐ 392 Pat Combs	.05	.02
☐ 393 Darren Daulton	.10	.05
☐ 394 Jose DeJesus	.05	.02
☐ 395A Lenny Dykstra	.05	.02
(Name spelled Lenny on back)		
☐ 395B Len Dykstra	.10	.05
(Name spelled Len on back)		
☐ 396 Jason Grimsley	.05	.02
☐ 397 Charlie Hayes	.05	.02
☐ 398 Von Hayes	.05	.02
☐ 399 David Hollins UER	.05	.02
(Ati-bats, should say at-bats)		
☐ 400 Ken Howell	.05	.02
☐ 401 Ricky Jordan	.05	.02
☐ 402 John Kruk	.10	.05
☐ 403 Steve Lake	.05	.02
☐ 404 Chuck Malone	.05	.02
☐ 405 Roger McDowell UER	.05	.02
(Says Phillies is saves, should say in)		
☐ 406 Chuck McElroy	.05	.02
☐ 407 Mickey Morandini	.05	.02
☐ 408 Terry Mulholland	.05	.02
☐ 409 Dale Murphy	.10	.05
☐ 410A Randy Ready ERR	.05	.02
(No Brewers stats listed for 1983)		
☐ 410B Randy Ready COR	.05	.02
☐ 411 Bruce Ruffin	.05	.02
☐ 412 Dickie Thon	.05	.02
☐ 413 Paul Assenmacher	.05	.02
☐ 414 Damon Berryhill	.05	.02
☐ 415 Mike Bielecki	.05	.02
☐ 416 Shawn Boskie	.05	.02
☐ 417 Dave Clark	.05	.02
☐ 418 Doug Dascenzo	.05	.02
☐ 419A Andre Dawson ERR	.20	.09
(No stats for 1976)		
☐ 419B Andre Dawson COR	.20	.09
☐ 420 Shawon Dunston	.05	.02
☐ 421 Joe Girardi	.10	.05
☐ 422 Mark Grace	.20	.09
☐ 423 Mike Harkey	.05	.02
☐ 424 Les Lancaster	.05	.02
☐ 425 Bill Long	.05	.02
☐ 426 Greg Maddux	.60	.25
☐ 427 Derrick May	.05	.02
☐ 428 Jeff Pico	.05	.02
☐ 429 Domingo Ramos	.05	.02
☐ 430 Luis Salazar	.05	.02
☐ 431 Ryne Sandberg	.25	.11
☐ 432 Dwight Smith	.05	.02
☐ 433 Greg Smith	.05	.02
☐ 434 Rick Sutcliffe	.05	.02
☐ 435 Gary Varsho	.05	.02
☐ 436 Hector Villanueva	.05	.02
☐ 437 Jerome Walton	.05	.02
☐ 438 Curtis Wilkerson	.05	.02
☐ 439 Mitch Williams	.05	.02
☐ 440 Steve Wilson	.05	.02
☐ 441 Marvell Wynne	.05	.02
☐ 442 Scott Bankhead	.05	.02
☐ 443 Scott Bradley	.05	.02
☐ 444 Greg Briley	.05	.02
☐ 445 Mike Brumley UER	.05	.02
(Text 40 SB's in 1988, stats say 41)		
☐ 446 Jay Buhner	.20	.09
☐ 447 Dave Burba	.05	.02
☐ 448 Henry Cotto	.05	.02
☐ 449 Alvin Davis	.05	.02
☐ 450 Ken Griffey Jr.	1.50	.70
(Bat around .300)		
☐ 450A Ken Griffey Jr.	1.50	.70
(Bat .300)		
☐ 451 Erik Hanson	.05	.02
☐ 452 Gene Harris UER	.05	.02
(63 career runs, should be 73)		
☐ 453 Brian Holman	.05	.02
☐ 454 Mike Jackson	.05	.02
☐ 455 Randy Johnson	.25	.11
☐ 456 Jeffrey Leonard	.05	.02
☐ 457 Edgar Martinez	.20	.09
☐ 458 Tino Martinez	.20	.09
☐ 459 Pete O'Brien UER	.05	.02
(1987 BA .266, should be .286)		
☐ 460 Harold Reynolds	.05	.02
☐ 461 Mike Schooler	.05	.02
☐ 462 Bill Swift	.05	.02
☐ 463 David Valle	.05	.02
☐ 464 Omar Vizquel	.20	.09
☐ 465 Matt Young	.05	.02
☐ 466 Brady Anderson	.05	.02
☐ 467 Jeff Ballard UER	.05	.02
(Missing top of right parenthesis after Saberhagen in last text line)		
☐ 468 Juan Bell	.05	.02
☐ 469A Mike Devereaux	.10	.05
(First line of text ends with six)		
☐ 469B Mike Devereaux	.10	.05
(First line of text ends with runs)		
☐ 470 Steve Finley	.20	.09
☐ 471 Dave Gallagher	.05	.02
☐ 472 Leo Gomez	.20	.09
☐ 473 Rene Gonzales	.05	.02
☐ 474 Pete Harnisch	.05	.02
☐ 475 Kevin Hickey	.05	.02
☐ 476 Chris Holles	.05	.02
☐ 477 Sam Horn	.05	.02
☐ 478 Tim Hulett	.05	.02
(Photo shows National Leaguer sliding into second base)		
☐ 479 Dave Johnson	.05	.02
☐ 480 Ron Kittle UER	.05	.02
(Edmonton misspelled as Edmundton)		
☐ 481 Ben McDonald	.05	.02
☐ 482 Bob Melvin	.05	.02
☐ 483 Bob Milacki	.05	.02
☐ 484 Randy Milligan	.05	.02
☐ 485 John Mitchell	.05	.02
☐ 486 Gregg Olson	.05	.02
☐ 487 Joe Orsulak	.05	.02
☐ 488 Joe Price	.05	.02
☐ 489 Bill Ripken	.05	.02
☐ 490 Cal Ripken	.75	.35
☐ 491 Curt Schilling	.20	.09

#	Player		
492	David Segui	.10	.05
493	Anthony Telford	.05	.02
494	Mickey Tettleton	.10	.05
495	Mark Williamson	.05	.02
496	Craig Worthington	.05	.02
497	Juan Agosto	.05	.02
498	Eric Anthony	.05	.02
499	Craig Biggio	.05	.09
500	Ken Caminiti UER (Born 4/4, should be 4/21)	.20	.09
501	Casey Candaele	.05	.02
502	Andujar Cedeno	.05	.02
503	Danny Darwin	.05	.02
504	Mark Davidson	.05	.02
505	Glenn Davis	.05	.02
506	Jim Deshaies	.05	.02
507	Luis Gonzalez	.20	.09
508	Bill Gullickson	.05	.02
509	Xavier Hernandez	.05	.02
510	Brian Meyer	.05	.02
511	Ken Oberkfell	.05	.02
512	Mark Portugal	.05	.02
513	Rafael Ramirez	.05	.02
514	Karl Rhodes	.05	.02
515	Mike Scott	.05	.02
516	Mike Simms	.05	.02
517	Dave Smith	.05	.02
518	Franklin Stubbs	.05	.02
519	Glenn Wilson	.05	.02
520	Eric Yelding UER (Text has 63 steals, stats have 64, which is correct)	.05	.02
521	Gerald Young	.05	.02
522	Shawn Abner	.05	.02
523	Roberto Alomar	.20	.09
524	Andy Benes	.10	.05
525	Joe Carter	.10	.05
526	Jack Clark	.10	.05
527	Joey Cora	.15	.07
528	Paul Faries	.05	.02
529	Tony Gwynn	.50	.23
530	Atlee Hammaker	.05	.02
531	Greg W. Harris	.05	.02
532	Thomas Howard	.05	.02
533	Bruce Hurst	.05	.02
534	Craig Lefferts	.05	.02
535	Derek Lilliquist	.05	.02
536	Fred Lynn	.05	.02
537	Mike Pagliarulo	.05	.02
538	Mark Parent	.05	.02
539	Dennis Rasmussen	.05	.02
540	Bip Roberts	.05	.02
541	Richard Rodriguez	.05	.02
542	Benito Santiago	.05	.02
543	Calvin Schiraldi	.05	.02
544	Eric Show	.05	.02
545	Phil Stephenson	.05	.02
546	Garry Templeton UER (Born 3/24/57, should be 3/24/56)	.05	.02
547	Ed Whitson	.05	.02
548	Eddie Williams	.05	.02
549	Kevin Appier	.20	.09
550	Luis Aquino	.05	.02
551	Bob Boone	.10	.05
552	George Brett	.40	.18
553	Jeff Conine	.25	.11
554	Steve Crawford	.05	.02
555	Mark Davis	.05	.02
556	Storm Davis	.05	.02
557	Jim Eisenreich	.05	.02
558	Steve Farr	.05	.02
559	Tom Gordon	.05	.02
560	Mark Gubicza	.05	.02
561	Bo Jackson	.15	.07
562	Mike Macfarlane	.05	.02
563	Brian McRae	.20	.09
564	Jeff Montgomery	.10	.05
565	Bill Pecota	.05	.02
566	Gerald Perry	.05	.02
567	Bret Saberhagen	.05	.02
568	Jeff Schulz	.05	.02
569	Kevin Seitzer	.05	.02
570	Terry Shumpert	.05	.02
571	Kurt Stillwell	.05	.02
572	Danny Tartabull	.05	.02
573	Gary Thurman	.05	.02
574	Frank White	.10	.05
575	Willie Wilson	.05	.02
576	Chris Bosio	.05	.02
577	Greg Brock	.05	.02
578	George Canale	.05	.02
579	Chuck Crim	.05	.02
580	Rob Deer	.05	.02
581	Edgar Diaz	.05	.02
582	Tom Edens	.05	.02
583	Mike Felder	.05	.02
584	Jim Gantner	.05	.02
585	Darryl Hamilton	.05	.02
586	Ted Higuera	.05	.02
587	Mark Knudson	.05	.02
588	Bill Krueger	.05	.02
589	Tim McIntosh	.05	.02
590	Paul Mirabella	.05	.02
591	Paul Molitor	.20	.09
592	Jaime Navarro	.05	.02
593	Dave Parker	.10	.05
594	Dan Plesac	.05	.02
595	Ron Robinson	.05	.02
596	Gary Sheffield	.20	.09
597	Bill Spiers	.05	.02
598	B.J. Surhoff	.05	.02
599	Greg Vaughn	.20	.09
600	Randy Veres	.05	.02
601	Robin Yount	.20	.09
602	Rick Aguilera	.10	.05
603	Allan Anderson	.05	.02
604	Juan Berenguer	.05	.02
605	Randy Bush	.05	.02
606	Carmen Castillo	.05	.02
607	Tim Drummond	.05	.02
608	Scott Erickson	.10	.05
609	Gary Gaetti	.05	.02
610	Greg Gagne	.05	.02
611	Dan Gladden	.05	.02
612	Mark Guthrie	.05	.02
613	Brian Harper	.05	.02
614	Kent Hrbek	.10	.05
615	Gene Larkin	.05	.02
616	Terry Leach	.05	.02
617	Nelson Liriano	.05	.02
618	Shane Mack	.05	.02
619	John Moses	.05	.02
620	Pedro Munoz	.05	.02
621	Al Newman	.05	.02
622	Junior Ortiz	.05	.02
623	Kirby Puckett	.40	.18
624	Roy Smith	.05	.02
625	Kevin Tapani	.05	.02
626	Gary Wayne	.05	.02
627	David West	.05	.02
628	Cris Carpenter	.05	.02
629	Vince Coleman	.05	.02
630	Ken Dayley	.05	.02
631A	Jose DeLeon ERR (missing '79 Bradenton stats)	.05	
631B	Jose DeLeon COR (with '79 Bradenton stats)	.05	.02
632	Frank DiPino	.05	.02
633	Bernard Gilkey	.05	.02
634A	Pedro Guerrero ERR (career SB shown as "$91")	.15	.07
634B	Pedro Guerrero COR	.10	.05
635	Ken Hill	.10	.05
636	Felix Jose	.05	.02
637	Ray Lankford	.20	.09
638	Joe Magrane	.05	.02
639	Tom Niedenfuer	.05	.02
640	Jose Oquendo	.05	.02
641	Tom Pagnozzi	.05	.02
642	Terry Pendleton	.10	.05
643	Mike Perez	.05	.02
644	Bryn Smith	.05	.02
645	Lee Smith	.10	.05
646	Ozzie Smith	.25	.11
647	Scott Terry	.05	.02
648	Bob Tewksbury	.05	.02
649	Milt Thompson	.05	.02
650	John Tudor	.05	.02
651	Denny Walling	.05	.02
652	Craig Wilson	.05	.02
653	Todd Worrell	.05	.02
654	Todd Zeile	.10	.05
655	Oscar Azocar	.05	.02
656	Steve Balboni UER (Born 1/5/57, should be 1/16)	.05	.02
657	Jesse Barfield	.05	.02
658	Greg Cadaret	.05	.02
659	Chuck Cary	.05	.02
660	Rick Cerone	.05	.02
661	Dave Eiland	.05	.02
662	Alvaro Espinoza	.05	.02
663	Bob Geren	.05	.02
664	Lee Guetterman	.05	.02
665	Mel Hall	.05	.02
666	Andy Hawkins	.05	.02
667	Jimmy Jones	.05	.02
668	Roberto Kelly	.05	.02
669	Dave LaPoint UER (No '81 Brewers stats, totals also are wrong)	.05	.02
670	Tim Leary	.05	.02
671	Jim Leyritz	.10	.05
672	Kevin Maas	.30	.14
673	Don Mattingly	.30	.14
674	Matt Nokes	.05	.02
675	Pascual Perez	.05	.02
676	Eric Plunk	.05	.02
677	Dave Righetti	.05	.02
678	Jeff D. Robinson	.05	.02
679	Steve Sax	.05	.02
680	Mike Witt	.05	.02
681	Steve Avery UER (Born in New Jersey, should say Michigan)	.05	.02
682	Mike Bell	.05	.02
683	Jeff Blauser	.05	.02
684	Francisco Cabrera UER (Born 10/16, should say 10/10)	.05	.02
685	Tony Castillo	.05	.02
686	Marty Clary UER (Shown pitching righty, but bio has left)	.05	.02
687	Nick Esasky	.05	.02
688	Ron Gant	.10	.05
689	Tom Glavine	.20	.09
690	Mark Grant	.05	.02
691	Tommy Gregg	.05	.02
692	Dwayne Henry	.05	.02
693	Dave Justice	.25	.11
694	Jimmy Kremers	.05	.02
695	Charlie Leibrandt	.05	.02
696	Mark Lemke	.05	.02
697	Oddibe McDowell	.05	.02
698	Greg Olson	.05	.02
699	Jeff Parrett	.05	.02
700	Jim Presley	.05	.02
701	Victor Rosario	.05	.02
702	Lonnie Smith	.05	.02
703	Pete Smith	.05	.02
704	John Smoltz	.20	.09
705	Mike Stanton	.05	.02
706	Andres Thomas	.05	.02
707	Jeff Treadway	.05	.02
708	Jim Vatcher	.05	.02
709	Ryne Sandberg / Cecil Fielder — Home Run Kings	.20	.09
710	Barry Bonds / Ken Griffey Jr. — 2nd Generation Stars	.50	.23
711	Bobby Bonilla / Barry Larkin — NLCS Team Leaders	.20	.09
712	Bobby Thigpen / John Franco — Top Game Savers	.05	.02
713	Chicago's 100 Club / Andre Dawson / Ryne Sandberg UER (Ryno misspelled Rhino)	.10	.05
714	CL:A's/Pirates / Reds/Red Sox	.05	.02
715	CL:White Sox/Mets	.05	.02

	MINT	NRMT
Blue Jays/Dodgers		
☐ 716 CL:Expos/Giants .05		.02
Rangers/Angels		
☐ 717 CL:Tigers/Indians .05		.02
Phillies/Cubs		
☐ 718 CL:Mariners/Orioles .. .05		.02
Astros/Padres		
☐ 719 CL:Royals/Brewers .05		.02
Twins/Cardinals		
☐ 720 CL:Yankees/Braves .05		.02
Superstars/Specials		

1991 Fleer All-Stars

For the sixth consecutive year Fleer issued an All-Star insert set. This year the cards were only available as random inserts in Fleer cello packs. This ten-card standard-size set is reminiscent of the 1971 Topps Greatest Moments set with two pictures on the (black-bordered) front as well as a photo on the back.

	MINT	NRMT
COMPLETE SET (10)	15.00	6.75
COMMON CARD (1-10)	.50	.23
RANDOM INSERTS IN CELLO PACKS		

		MINT	NRMT
☐ 1	Ryne Sandberg	2.00	.90
☐ 2	Barry Larkin	1.50	.70
☐ 3	Matt Williams	2.50	1.10
☐ 4	Cecil Fielder	1.00	.45
☐ 5	Barry Bonds	2.00	.90
☐ 6	Rickey Henderson	2.50	1.10
☐ 7	Ken Griffey Jr.	12.00	5.50
☐ 8	Jose Canseco	1.50	.70
☐ 9	Benito Santiago	.50	.23
☐ 10	Roger Clemens	3.00	1.35

1991 Fleer Pro-Visions

This 12-card standard-size insert set features paintings by artist Terry Smith framed by distinctive black borders on each card front. The cards were randomly inserted in wax and rack packs. An additional four-card set was issued only in 1991 Fleer factory sets. Those cards are numbered F1-F4. Unlike the 12 cards inserted in packs, these factory set cards feature white borders on front.

	MINT	NRMT
COMP.WAX SET (12)	4.00	1.80
COMP.FACT.SET (4)	2.00	.90
COMMON CARD	.20	.09

1-12: RANDOM INSERTS IN PACKS
F1-F4: ONE SET PER FACT.SET

		MINT	NRMT
☐ 1	Kirby Puckett UER	1.25	.55
	(.326 average, should be .328)		
☐ 2	Will Clark UER	.50	.23
	(On tenth line, pennant misspelled pennent)		
☐ 3	Ruben Sierra UER	.20	.09
	(No apostrophe in hasn't)		
☐ 4	Mark McGwire UER	1.25	.55
	(Fisk won ROY in '72, not '82)		
☐ 5	Bo Jackson	.30	.14
	(Bio says 6', others have him at 6'1")		
☐ 6	Jose Canseco UER	.40	.18
	(Bio 6'3", 230, text has 6'4", 240)		
☐ 7	Dwight Gooden UER	.30	.14
	(2.80 ERA in Lynchburg, should be 2.50)		
☐ 8	Mike Greenwell UER	.20	.09
	(.328 BA and 87 RBI, should be .325 and 95)		
☐ 9	Roger Clemens	1.25	.55
☐ 10	Eric Davis	.30	.14
☐ 11	Don Mattingly	1.00	.45
☐ 12	Darryl Strawberry	.30	.14
☐ F1	Barry Bonds	.75	.35
☐ F2	Rickey Henderson	.50	.23
☐ F3	Ryne Sandberg	.75	.35
☐ F4	Dave Stewart	.25	.11

1991 Fleer Update

The 1991 Fleer Update set contains 132 standard-size cards. The cards were distributed exclusively in factory set form through hobby dealers. Card design is identical to regular issue 1991 Fleer cards except for the U-prefixed numbering on back. The cards are ordered alphabetically by team. The key Rookie Cards in this set are Jeff Bagwell and Ivan Rodriguez.

	MINT	NRMT
COMPLETE SET (132)	4.00	1.80
COMMON CARD (1-132)	.05	.02
MINOR STARS	.10	.05
UNLISTED STARS	.20	.09

		MINT	NRMT
☐ 1	Glenn Davis	.05	.02
☐ 2	Dwight Evans	.10	.05
☐ 3	Jose Mesa	.05	.02
☐ 4	Jack Clark	.10	.05
☐ 5	Danny Darwin	.05	.02
☐ 6	Steve Lyons	.05	.02
☐ 7	Mo Vaughn	.40	.18
☐ 8	Floyd Bannister	.05	.02
☐ 9	Gary Gaetti	.05	.02
☐ 10	Dave Parker	.10	.05
☐ 11	Joey Cora	.15	.07
☐ 12	Charlie Hough	.05	.02
☐ 13	Matt Merullo	.05	.02
☐ 14	Warren Newson	.05	.02
☐ 15	Tim Raines	.10	.05
☐ 16	Albert Belle	.30	.14
☐ 17	Glenallen Hill	.05	.02
☐ 18	Shawn Hillegas	.05	.02
☐ 19	Mark Lewis	.05	.02
☐ 20	Charles Nagy	.20	.09
☐ 21	Mark Whiten	.05	.02
☐ 22	John Cerutti	.05	.02
☐ 23	Rob Deer	.05	.02
☐ 24	Mickey Tettleton	.10	.05
☐ 25	Warren Cromartie	.05	.02
☐ 26	Kirk Gibson	.10	.05
☐ 27	David Howard	.05	.02
☐ 28	Brent Mayne	.05	.02
☐ 29	Dante Bichette	.20	.09
☐ 30	Mark Lee	.05	.02
☐ 31	Julio Machado	.05	.02
☐ 32	Edwin Nunez	.05	.02
☐ 33	Willie Randolph	.10	.05
☐ 34	Franklin Stubbs	.05	.02
☐ 35	Bill Wegman	.05	.02
☐ 36	Chili Davis	.10	.05
☐ 37	Chuck Knoblauch	.25	.11
☐ 38	Scott Leius	.05	.02
☐ 39	Jack Morris	.10	.05
☐ 40	Mike Pagliarulo	.05	.02
☐ 41	Lenny Webster	.05	.02
☐ 42	John Habyan	.05	.02
☐ 43	Steve Howe	.05	.02
☐ 44	Jeff Johnson	.05	.02
☐ 45	Scott Kamieniecki	.05	.02
☐ 46	Pat Kelly	.10	.05
☐ 47	Hensley Meulens	.05	.02
☐ 48	Wade Taylor	.05	.02
☐ 49	Bernie Williams	.25	.11
☐ 50	Kirk Dressendorfer	.05	.02
☐ 51	Ernest Riles	.05	.02
☐ 52	Rich DeLucia	.05	.02
☐ 53	Tracy Jones	.05	.02
☐ 54	Bill Krueger	.05	.02
☐ 55	Alonzo Powell	.05	.02
☐ 56	Jeff Schaefer	.05	.02
☐ 57	Russ Swan	.05	.02
☐ 58	John Barfield	.05	.02
☐ 59	Rich Gossage	.10	.05
☐ 60	Jose Guzman	.05	.02
☐ 61	Dean Palmer	.25	.11
☐ 62	Ivan Rodriguez	1.50	.70
☐ 63	Roberto Alomar	.20	.09
☐ 64	Tom Candiotti	.05	.02
☐ 65	Joe Carter	.10	.05
☐ 66	Ed Sprague	.05	.02
☐ 67	Pat Tabler	.05	.02
☐ 68	Mike Timlin	.05	.02
☐ 69	Devon White	.05	.02
☐ 70	Rafael Belliard	.05	.02
☐ 71	Juan Berenguer	.05	.02
☐ 72	Sid Bream	.05	.02
☐ 73	Marvin Freeman	.05	.02
☐ 74	Kent Mercker	.05	.02
☐ 75	Otis Nixon	.05	.02
☐ 76	Terry Pendleton	.10	.05
☐ 77	George Bell	.05	.02
☐ 78	Danny Jackson	.05	.02
☐ 79	Chuck McElroy	.05	.02
☐ 80	Gary Scott	.05	.02

				MINT	NRMT
☐ 81	Heathcliff Slocumb	.20	.09		
☐ 82	Dave Smith	.05	.02		
☐ 83	Rick Wilkins	.05	.02		
☐ 84	Freddie Benavides	.05	.02		
☐ 85	Ted Power	.05	.02		
☐ 86	Mo Sanford	.05	.02		
☐ 87	Jeff Bagwell	2.50	1.10		
☐ 88	Steve Finley	.20	.09		
☐ 89	Pete Harnisch	.05	.02		
☐ 90	Darryl Kile	.20	.09		
☐ 91	Brett Butler	.10	.05		
☐ 92	John Candelaria	.05	.02		
☐ 93	Gary Carter	.20	.09		
☐ 94	Kevin Gross	.05	.02		
☐ 95	Bob Ojeda	.05	.02		
☐ 96	Darryl Strawberry	.10	.05		
☐ 97	Ivan Calderon	.05	.02		
☐ 98	Ron Hassey	.05	.02		
☐ 99	Gilberto Reyes	.05	.02		
☐ 100	Hubie Brooks	.05	.02		
☐ 101	Rick Cerone	.05	.02		
☐ 102	Vince Coleman	.05	.02		
☐ 103	Jeff Innis	.05	.02		
☐ 104	Pete Schourek	.10	.05		
☐ 105	Andy Ashby	.20	.09		
☐ 106	Wally Backman	.05	.02		
☐ 107	Darrin Fletcher	.05	.02		
☐ 108	Tommy Greene	.05	.02		
☐ 109	John Morris	.05	.02		
☐ 110	Mitch Williams	.05	.02		
☐ 111	Lloyd McClendon	.05	.02		
☐ 112	Orlando Merced	.10	.05		
☐ 113	Vicente Palacios	.05	.02		
☐ 114	Gary Varsho	.05	.02		
☐ 115	John Wehner	.05	.02		
☐ 116	Rex Hudler	.05	.02		
☐ 117	Tim Jones	.05	.02		
☐ 118	Geronimo Pena	.05	.02		
☐ 119	Gerald Perry	.05	.02		
☐ 120	Larry Andersen	.05	.02		
☐ 121	Jerald Clark	.05	.02		
☐ 122	Scott Coolbaugh	.05	.02		
☐ 123	Tony Fernandez	.05	.02		
☐ 124	Darrin Jackson	.05	.02		
☐ 125	Fred McGriff	.20	.09		
☐ 126	Jose Mota	.05	.02		
☐ 127	Tim Teufel	.05	.02		
☐ 128	Bud Black	.05	.02		
☐ 129	Mike Felder	.05	.02		
☐ 130	Willie McGee	.05	.02		
☐ 131	Dave Righetti	.05	.02		
☐ 132	Checklist U1-U132	.05	.02		

1992 Fleer

The 1992 Fleer set contains 720 standard-size cards issued in one comprehensive series. The cards were distributed in plastic wrapped packs, 35-card cello packs, 42-card rack packs and factory sets. The card fronts shade from metallic pale green to white as one moves down the face. The team logo and player's name appear to the right of the picture, running the length of the card. The cards are ordered alphabetically within and according to teams for each league with AL preceding NL. Topical subsets feature Major League Prospects (652-680), Record Setters (681-687), League Leaders (688-697), Super Star Specials (698-707) and Pro Visions (708-713). The only notable Rookie Card features Vinny Castilla.

	MINT	NRMT
COMPLETE SET (720)	10.00	4.50
COMP.HOBBY SET (732)	20.00	9.00
COMP.RETAIL SET (732)	20.00	9.00
COMMON CARD (1-720)	.05	.02
MINOR STARS	.10	.05
UNLISTED STARS	.20	.09
SUBSET CARDS HALF VALUE OF BASE CARDS		
COMP.CLEMENS SET (12)	10.00	4.50
COMMON CLEMENS (1-12)	1.00	.45
CLEMENS: RANDOM INSERTS IN PACKS		
CLEMENS MAIL-IN (13-15)	1.00	.45
MAIL-IN CLEMENS: VIA WRAPPER EXCH.		

☐ 1	Brady Anderson	.15	.07
☐ 2	Jose Bautista	.05	.02
☐ 3	Juan Bell	.05	.02
☐ 4	Glenn Davis	.05	.02
☐ 5	Mike Devereaux	.05	.02
☐ 6	Dwight Evans	.10	.05
☐ 7	Mike Flanagan	.05	.02
☐ 8	Leo Gomez	.05	.02
☐ 9	Chris Hoiles	.05	.02
☐ 10	Sam Horn	.05	.02
☐ 11	Tim Hulett	.05	.02
☐ 12	Dave Johnson	.05	.02
☐ 13	Chito Martinez	.05	.02
☐ 14	Ben McDonald	.05	.02
☐ 15	Bob Melvin	.05	.02
☐ 16	Luis Mercedes	.05	.02
☐ 17	Jose Mesa	.05	.02
☐ 18	Bob Milacki	.05	.02
☐ 19	Randy Milligan	.05	.02
☐ 20	Mike Mussina UER	.30	.14
	(Card refers to him as Jeff)		
☐ 21	Gregg Olson	.05	.02
☐ 22	Joe Orsulak	.05	.02
☐ 23	Jim Poole	.05	.02
☐ 24	Arthur Rhodes	.05	.02
☐ 25	Billy Ripken	.05	.02
☐ 26	Cal Ripken	.75	.35
☐ 27	David Segui	.05	.02
☐ 28	Roy Smith	.05	.02
☐ 29	Anthony Telford	.05	.02
☐ 30	Mark Williamson	.05	.02
☐ 31	Craig Worthington	.05	.02
☐ 32	Wade Boggs	.20	.09
☐ 33	Tom Bolton	.05	.02
☐ 34	Tom Brunansky	.05	.02
☐ 35	Ellis Burks	.10	.05
☐ 36	Jack Clark	.10	.05
☐ 37	Roger Clemens	.40	.18
☐ 38	Danny Darwin	.05	.02
☐ 39	Mike Greenwell	.05	.02
☐ 40	Joe Hesketh	.05	.02
☐ 41	Daryl Irvine	.05	.02
☐ 42	Dennis Lamp	.05	.02
☐ 43	Tony Pena	.05	.02
☐ 44	Phil Plantier	.05	.02
☐ 45	Carlos Quintana	.05	.02
☐ 46	Jeff Reardon	.10	.05
☐ 47	Jody Reed	.05	.02
☐ 48	Luis Rivera	.05	.02
☐ 49	Mo Vaughn	.30	.14
☐ 50	Jim Abbott	.05	.02
☐ 51	Kyle Abbott	.05	.02
☐ 52	Ruben Amaro Jr.	.05	.02
☐ 53	Scott Bailes	.05	.02
☐ 54	Chris Beasley	.05	.02
☐ 55	Mark Eichhorn	.05	.02
☐ 56	Mike Fetters	.05	.02
☐ 57	Chuck Finley	.05	.02
☐ 58	Gary Gaetti	.05	.02
☐ 59	Dave Gallagher	.05	.02
☐ 60	Donnie Hill	.05	.02
☐ 61	Bryan Harvey UER	.05	.02
	(Lee Smith led the Majors with 47 saves)		
☐ 62	Wally Joyner	.10	.05
☐ 63	Mark Langston	.05	.02
☐ 64	Kirk McCaskill	.05	.02
☐ 65	John Orton	.05	.02
☐ 66	Lance Parrish	.05	.02
☐ 67	Luis Polonia	.05	.02
☐ 68	Bobby Rose	.05	.02
☐ 69	Dick Schofield	.05	.02
☐ 70	Luis Sojo	.05	.02
☐ 71	Lee Stevens	.05	.02
☐ 72	Dave Winfield	.20	.09
☐ 73	Cliff Young	.05	.02
☐ 74	Wilson Alvarez	.10	.05
☐ 75	Esteban Beltre	.05	.02
☐ 76	Joey Cora	.10	.05
☐ 77	Brian Drahman	.05	.02
☐ 78	Alex Fernandez	.10	.05
☐ 79	Carlton Fisk	.20	.09
☐ 80	Scott Fletcher	.05	.02
☐ 81	Craig Grebeck	.05	.02
☐ 82	Ozzie Guillen	.05	.02
☐ 83	Greg Hibbard	.05	.02
☐ 84	Charlie Hough	.05	.02
☐ 85	Mike Huff	.05	.02
☐ 86	Bo Jackson	.10	.05
☐ 87	Lance Johnson	.05	.02
☐ 88	Ron Karkovice	.05	.02
☐ 89	Jack McDowell	.05	.02
☐ 90	Matt Merullo	.05	.02
☐ 91	Warren Newson	.05	.02
☐ 92	Donn Pall UER	.05	.02
	(Called Dunn on card back)		
☐ 93	Dan Pasqua	.05	.02
☐ 94	Ken Patterson	.05	.02
☐ 95	Melido Perez	.05	.02
☐ 96	Scott Radinsky	.05	.02
☐ 97	Tim Raines	.10	.05
☐ 98	Sammy Sosa	.20	.09
☐ 99	Bobby Thigpen	.05	.02
☐ 100	Frank Thomas	1.00	.45
☐ 101	Robin Ventura	.10	.05
☐ 102	Mike Aldrete	.05	.02
☐ 103	Sandy Alomar Jr.	.10	.05
☐ 104	Carlos Baerga	.05	.02
☐ 105	Albert Belle	.25	.11
☐ 106	Willie Blair	.05	.02
☐ 107	Jerry Browne	.05	.02
☐ 108	Alex Cole	.05	.02
☐ 109	Felix Fermin	.05	.02
☐ 110	Glenallen Hill	.05	.02
☐ 111	Shawn Hillegas	.05	.02
☐ 112	Chris James	.05	.02
☐ 113	Reggie Jefferson	.10	.05
☐ 114	Doug Jones	.05	.02
☐ 115	Eric King	.05	.02
☐ 116	Mark Lewis	.05	.02
☐ 117	Carlos Martinez	.05	.02
☐ 118	Charles Nagy UER	.10	.05
	(Throws right, but card says left)		
☐ 119	Rod Nichols	.05	.02
☐ 120	Steve Olin	.05	.02
☐ 121	Jesse Orosco	.05	.02
☐ 122	Rudy Seanez	.05	.02
☐ 123	Joel Skinner	.05	.02
☐ 124	Greg Swindell	.05	.02
☐ 125	Jim Thome	.60	.25
☐ 126	Mark Whiten	.05	.02
☐ 127	Scott Aldred	.05	.02
☐ 128	Andy Allanson	.05	.02
☐ 129	John Cerutti	.05	.02
☐ 130	Milt Cuyler	.05	.02
☐ 131	Mike Dalton	.05	.02
☐ 132	Rob Deer	.05	.02
☐ 133	Cecil Fielder	.10	.05
☐ 134	Travis Fryman	.05	.02
☐ 135	Dan Gakeler	.05	.02
☐ 136	Paul Gibson	.05	.02
☐ 137	Bill Gullickson	.05	.02

138	Mike Henneman	.05	.02
139	Pete Incaviglia	.05	.02
140	Mark Leiter	.05	.02
141	Scott Livingstone	.05	.02
142	Lloyd Moseby	.05	.02
143	Tony Phillips	.05	.02
144	Mark Salas	.05	.02
145	Frank Tanana	.05	.02
146	Walt Terrell	.05	.02
147	Mickey Tettleton	.05	.02
148	Alan Trammell	.15	.07
149	Lou Whitaker	.10	.05
150	Kevin Appier	.10	.05
151	Luis Aquino	.05	.02
152	Todd Benzinger	.05	.02
153	Mike Boddicker	.05	.02
154	George Brett	.40	.18
155	Storm Davis	.05	.02
156	Jim Eisenreich	.05	.02
157	Kirk Gibson	.10	.05
158	Tom Gordon	.05	.02
159	Mark Gubicza	.05	.02
160	David Howard	.05	.02
161	Mike Macfarlane	.05	.02
162	Brent Mayne	.05	.02
163	Brian McRae	.05	.02
164	Jeff Montgomery	.10	.05
165	Bill Pecota	.05	.02
166	Harvey Pulliam	.05	.02
167	Bret Saberhagen	.05	.02
168	Kevin Seitzer	.05	.02
169	Terry Shumpert	.05	.02
170	Kurt Stillwell	.05	.02
171	Danny Tartabull	.05	.02
172	Gary Thurman	.05	.02
173	Dante Bichette	.15	.07
174	Kevin D. Brown	.05	.02
175	Chuck Crim	.05	.02
176	Jim Gantner	.05	.02
177	Darryl Hamilton	.05	.02
178	Ted Higuera	.05	.02
179	Darren Holmes	.05	.02
180	Mark Lee	.05	.02
181	Julio Machado	.05	.02
182	Paul Molitor	.20	.09
183	Jaime Navarro	.05	.02
184	Edwin Nunez	.05	.02
185	Dan Plesac	.05	.02
186	Willie Randolph	.10	.05
187	Ron Robinson	.05	.02
188	Gary Sheffield	.20	.09
189	Bill Spiers	.05	.02
190	B.J. Surhoff	.10	.05
191	Dale Sveum	.05	.02
192	Greg Vaughn	.10	.05
193	Bill Wegman	.05	.02
194	Robin Yount	.15	.07
195	Rick Aguilera	.05	.02
196	Allan Anderson	.05	.02
197	Steve Bedrosian	.05	.02
198	Randy Bush	.05	.02
199	Larry Casian	.05	.02
200	Chili Davis	.10	.05
201	Scott Erickson	.15	.07
202	Greg Gagne	.05	.02
203	Dan Gladden	.05	.02
204	Brian Harper	.05	.02
205	Kent Hrbek	.10	.05
206	Chuck Knoblauch UER (Career hit total of 59 is wrong)	.20	.09
207	Gene Larkin	.05	.02
208	Terry Leach	.05	.02
209	Scott Leius	.05	.02
210	Shane Mack	.05	.02
211	Jack Morris	.10	.05
212	Pedro Munoz	.05	.02
213	Denny Neagle	.15	.07
214	Al Newman	.05	.02
215	Junior Ortiz	.05	.02
216	Mike Pagliarulo	.05	.02
217	Kirby Puckett	.40	.18
218	Paul Sorrento	.05	.02
219	Kevin Tapani	.05	.02
220	Lenny Webster	.05	.02
221	Jesse Barfield	.05	.02
222	Greg Cadaret	.05	.02
223	Dave Eiland	.05	.02
224	Alvaro Espinoza	.05	.02
225	Steve Farr	.05	.02
226	Bob Geren	.05	.02
227	Lee Guetterman	.05	.02
228	John Habyan	.05	.02
229	Mel Hall	.05	.02
230	Steve Howe	.05	.02
231	Mike Humphreys	.05	.02
232	Scott Kamieniecki	.05	.02
233	Pat Kelly	.05	.02
234	Roberto Kelly	.05	.02
235	Tim Leary	.05	.02
236	Kevin Maas	.05	.02
237	Don Mattingly	.30	.14
238	Hensley Meulens	.05	.02
239	Matt Nokes	.05	.02
240	Pascual Perez	.05	.02
241	Eric Plunk	.05	.02
242	John Ramos	.05	.02
243	Scott Sanderson	.05	.02
244	Steve Sax	.05	.02
245	Wade Taylor	.05	.02
246	Randy Velarde	.05	.02
247	Bernie Williams	.20	.09
248	Troy Afenir	.05	.02
249	Harold Baines	.10	.05
250	Lance Blankenship	.05	.02
251	Mike Bordick	.05	.02
252	Jose Canseco	.15	.07
253	Steve Chitren	.05	.02
254	Ron Darling	.05	.02
255	Dennis Eckersley	.10	.05
256	Mike Gallego	.05	.02
257	Dave Henderson	.05	.02
258	Rickey Henderson UER (Wearing 24 on front and 22 on back)	.15	.07
259	Rick Honeycutt	.05	.02
260	Brook Jacoby	.05	.02
261	Carney Lansford	.05	.02
262	Mark McGwire	.40	.18
263	Mike Moore	.05	.02
264	Gene Nelson	.05	.02
265	Jamie Quirk	.05	.02
266	Joe Slusarski	.05	.02
267	Terry Steinbach	.05	.02
268	Dave Stewart	.10	.05
269	Todd Van Poppel	.05	.02
270	Walt Weiss	.05	.02
271	Bob Welch	.05	.02
272	Curt Young	.05	.02
273	Scott Bradley	.05	.02
274	Greg Briley	.05	.02
275	Jay Buhner	.15	.07
276	Henry Cotto	.05	.02
277	Alvin Davis	.05	.02
278	Rich DeLucia	.05	.02
279	Ken Griffey Jr.	1.25	.55
280	Erik Hanson	.05	.02
281	Brian Holman	.05	.02
282	Mike Jackson	.05	.02
283	Randy Johnson	.20	.09
284	Tracy Jones	.05	.02
285	Bill Krueger	.05	.02
286	Edgar Martinez	.15	.07
287	Tino Martinez	.20	.09
288	Rob Murphy	.05	.02
289	Pete O'Brien	.05	.02
290	Alonzo Powell	.05	.02
291	Harold Reynolds	.05	.02
292	Mike Schooler	.05	.02
293	Russ Swan	.05	.02
294	Bill Swift	.05	.02
295	Dave Valle	.05	.02
296	Omar Vizquel	.10	.05
297	Gerald Alexander	.05	.02
298	Brad Arnsberg	.05	.02
299	Kevin Brown	.10	.05
300	Jack Daugherty	.05	.02
301	Mario Diaz	.05	.02
302	Brian Downing	.05	.02
303	Julio Franco	.05	.02
304	Juan Gonzalez	.60	.25
305	Rich Gossage	.10	.05
306	Jose Guzman	.05	.02
307	Jose Hernandez	.05	.02
308	Jeff Huson	.05	.02
309	Mike Jeffcoat	.05	.02
310	Terry Mathews	.05	.02
311	Rafael Palmeiro	.15	.07
312	Dean Palmer	.10	.05
313	Geno Petralli	.05	.02
314	Gary Pettis	.05	.02
315	Kevin Reimer	.05	.02
316	Ivan Rodriguez	.40	.18
317	Kenny Rogers	.05	.02
318	Wayne Rosenthal	.05	.02
319	Jeff Russell	.05	.02
320	Nolan Ryan	.75	.35
321	Ruben Sierra	.25	.11
322	Jim Acker	.05	.02
323	Roberto Alomar	.20	.09
324	Derek Bell	.10	.05
325	Pat Borders	.05	.02
326	Tom Candiotti	.05	.02
327	Joe Carter	.10	.05
328	Rob Ducey	.05	.02
329	Kelly Gruber	.05	.02
330	Juan Guzman	.05	.02
331	Tom Henke	.05	.02
332	Jimmy Key	.10	.05
333	Manny Lee	.05	.02
334	Al Leiter	.10	.05
335	Bob MacDonald	.05	.02
336	Candy Maldonado	.05	.02
337	Rance Mulliniks	.05	.02
338	Greg Myers	.05	.02
339	John Olerud UER (1991 BA has .256, but text says .258)	.10	.05
340	Ed Sprague	.05	.02
341	Dave Stieb	.05	.02
342	Todd Stottlemyre	.05	.02
343	Mike Timlin	.05	.02
344	Duane Ward	.05	.02
345	David Wells	.05	.02
346	Devon White	.05	.02
347	Mookie Wilson	.05	.02
348	Eddie Zosky	.05	.02
349	Steve Avery	.20	.09
350	Mike Bell	.05	.02
351	Rafael Belliard	.05	.02
352	Juan Berenguer	.05	.02
353	Jeff Blauser	.05	.02
354	Sid Bream	.05	.02
355	Francisco Cabrera	.05	.02
356	Marvin Freeman	.05	.02
357	Ron Gant	.10	.05
358	Tom Glavine	.15	.07
359	Brian Hunter	.05	.02
360	Dave Justice	.20	.09
361	Charlie Leibrandt	.05	.02
362	Mark Lemke	.05	.02
363	Kent Mercker	.05	.02
364	Keith Mitchell	.05	.02
365	Greg Olson	.05	.02
366	Terry Pendleton	.10	.05
367	Armando Reynoso	.05	.02
368	Deion Sanders	.10	.05
369	Lonnie Smith	.05	.02
370	Pete Smith	.05	.02
371	John Smoltz	.15	.07
372	Mike Stanton	.05	.02
373	Jeff Treadway	.05	.02
374	Mark Wohlers	.15	.07
375	Paul Assenmacher	.05	.02
376	George Bell	.05	.02
377	Shawn Boskie	.05	.02
378	Frank Castillo	.05	.02
379	Andre Dawson	.15	.07
380	Shawon Dunston	.05	.02
381	Mark Grace	.15	.07
382	Mike Harkey	.05	.02
383	Danny Jackson	.05	.02
384	Les Lancaster	.05	.02
385	Ced Landrum	.05	.02
386	Greg Maddux	.60	.25
387	Derrick May	.05	.02
388	Chuck McElroy	.05	.02
389	Ryne Sandberg	.25	.11

390	Heathcliff Slocumb	.05	
391	Dave Smith	.05	.02
392	Dwight Smith	.05	.02
393	Rick Sutcliffe	.05	.02
394	Hector Villanueva	.05	.02
395	Chico Walker	.05	.02
396	Jerome Walton	.05	.02
397	Rick Wilkins	.05	.02
398	Jack Armstrong	.05	.02
399	Freddie Benavides	.05	.02
400	Glenn Braggs	.05	.02
401	Tom Browning	.05	.02
402	Norm Charlton	.05	.02
403	Eric Davis	.10	.05
404	Rob Dibble	.05	.02
405	Bill Doran	.05	.02
406	Mariano Duncan	.05	.02
407	Kip Gross	.05	.02
408	Chris Hammond	.05	.02
409	Billy Hatcher	.05	.02
410	Chris Jones	.05	.02
411	Barry Larkin	.15	.07
412	Hal Morris	.10	.05
413	Randy Myers	.10	.05
414	Joe Oliver	.05	.02
415	Paul O'Neill	.10	.05
416	Ted Power	.05	.02
417	Luis Quinones	.05	.02
418	Jeff Reed	.05	.02
419	Jose Rijo	.05	.02
420	Chris Sabo	.05	.02
421	Reggie Sanders	.10	.05
422	Scott Scudder	.05	.02
423	Glenn Sutko	.05	.02
424	Eric Anthony	.05	.02
425	Jeff Bagwell	.60	.25
426	Craig Biggio	.15	.07
427	Ken Caminiti	.15	.07
428	Casey Candaele	.05	.02
429	Mike Capel	.05	.02
430	Andujar Cedeno	.05	.02
431	Jim Corsi	.05	.02
432	Mark Davidson	.05	.02
433	Steve Finley	.10	.05
434	Luis Gonzalez	.05	.02
435	Pete Harnisch	.05	.02
436	Dwayne Henry	.05	.02
437	Xavier Hernandez	.05	.02
438	Jimmy Jones	.05	.02
439	Darryl Kile	.10	.05
440	Rob Mallicoat	.05	.02
441	Andy Mota	.05	.02
442	Al Osuna	.05	.02
443	Mark Portugal	.05	.02
444	Scott Servais	.05	.02
445	Mike Simms	.05	.02
446	Gerald Young	.05	.02
447	Tim Belcher	.05	.02
448	Brett Butler	.10	.05
449	John Candelaria	.05	.02
450	Gary Carter	.20	.09
451	Dennis Cook	.05	.02
452	Tim Crews	.05	.02
453	Kal Daniels	.05	.02
454	Jim Gott	.05	.02
455	Alfredo Griffin	.05	.02
456	Kevin Gross	.05	.02
457	Chris Gwynn	.05	.02
458	Lenny Harris	.05	.02
459	Orel Hershiser	.10	.05
460	Jay Howell	.05	.02
461	Stan Javier	.05	.02
462	Eric Karros	.15	.07
463	Ramon Martinez UER	.10	
	(Card says bats right, should be left)		
464	Roger McDowell UER	.05	.02
	(Wins add up to 54, totals have 51)		
465	Mike Morgan	.05	.02
466	Eddie Murray	.20	.09
467	Jose Offerman	.05	.02
468	Bob Ojeda	.05	.02
469	Juan Samuel	.05	.02
470	Mike Scioscia	.05	.02
471	Darryl Strawberry	.10	.05
472	Bret Barberie	.05	.02
473	Brian Barnes	.05	.02
474	Eric Bullock	.05	.02
475	Ivan Calderon	.05	.02
476	Delino DeShields	.05	.02
477	Jeff Fassero	.05	.02
478	Mike Fitzgerald	.05	.02
479	Steve Frey	.05	.02
480	Andres Galarraga	.20	.09
481	Mark Gardner	.05	.02
482	Marquis Grissom	.10	.05
483	Chris Haney	.05	.02
484	Barry Jones	.05	.02
485	Dave Martinez	.05	.02
486	Dennis Martinez	.10	.05
487	Chris Nabholz	.05	.02
488	Spike Owen	.05	.02
489	Gilberto Reyes	.05	.02
490	Mel Rojas	.10	.05
491	Scott Ruskin	.05	.02
492	Bill Sampen	.05	.02
493	Larry Walker	.20	.09
494	Tim Wallach	.05	.02
495	Daryl Boston	.05	.02
496	Hubie Brooks	.05	.02
497	Tim Burke	.05	.02
498	Mark Carreon	.05	.02
499	Tony Castillo	.05	.02
500	Vince Coleman	.05	.02
501	David Cone	.10	.05
502	Kevin Elster	.05	.02
503	Sid Fernandez	.05	.02
504	John Franco	.10	.05
505	Dwight Gooden	.10	.05
506	Todd Hundley	.15	.07
507	Jeff Innis	.05	.02
508	Gregg Jefferies	.05	.02
509	Howard Johnson	.05	.02
510	Dave Magadan	.05	.02
511	Terry McDaniel	.05	.02
512	Kevin McReynolds	.05	.02
513	Keith Miller	.05	.02
514	Charlie O'Brien	.05	.02
515	Mackey Sasser	.05	.02
516	Pete Schourek	.05	.02
517	Julio Valera	.05	.02
518	Frank Viola	.05	.02
519	Wally Whitehurst	.05	.02
520	Anthony Young	.05	.02
521	Andy Ashby	.05	.02
522	Kim Batiste	.05	.02
523	Joe Boever	.05	.02
524	Wes Chamberlain	.05	.02
525	Pat Combs	.05	.02
526	Danny Cox	.05	.02
527	Darren Daulton	.10	.05
528	Jose DeJesus	.05	.02
529	Len Dykstra	.10	.05
530	Darrin Fletcher	.05	.02
531	Tommy Greene	.05	.02
532	Jason Grimsley	.05	.02
533	Charlie Hayes	.05	.02
534	Von Hayes	.05	.02
535	Dave Hollins	.05	.02
536	Ricky Jordan	.05	.02
537	John Kruk	.10	.05
538	Jim Lindeman	.05	.02
539	Mickey Morandini	.05	.02
540	Terry Mulholland	.05	.02
541	Dale Murphy	.20	.09
542	Randy Ready	.05	.02
543	Wally Ritchie UER	.05	
	(Letters in data are cut off on card)		
544	Bruce Ruffin	.05	.02
545	Steve Searcy	.05	.02
546	Dickie Thon	.05	.02
547	Mitch Williams	.05	.02
548	Stan Belinda	.05	
549	Jay Bell	.10	.05
550	Barry Bonds	.25	.11
551	Bobby Bonilla	.10	.05
552	Steve Buechele	.05*	.02
553	Doug Drabek	.10	.05
554	Neal Heaton	.05	.02
555	Jeff King	.10	.05
556	Bob Kipper	.05	.02
557	Bill Landrum	.05	.02
558	Mike LaValliere	.05	.02
559	Jose Lind	.05	.02
560	Lloyd McClendon	.05	.02
561	Orlando Merced	.05	.02
562	Bob Patterson	.05	.02
563	Joe Redfield	.05	.02
564	Gary Redus	.05	.02
565	Rosario Rodriguez	.05	.02
566	Don Slaught	.05	.02
567	John Smiley	.05	.02
568	Zane Smith	.05	.02
569	Randy Tomlin	.05	.02
570	Andy Van Slyke	.10	.05
571	Gary Varsho	.05	.02
572	Bob Walk	.05	.02
573	John Wehner UER	.05	.02
	(Actually played for Carolina in 1991, not Cards)		
574	Juan Agosto	.05	.02
575	Cris Carpenter	.05	.02
576	Jose DeLeon	.05	.02
577	Rich Gedman	.05	.02
578	Bernard Gilkey	.10	.05
579	Pedro Guerrero	.05	.02
580	Ken Hill	.05	.02
581	Rex Hudler	.05	.02
582	Felix Jose	.05	.02
583	Ray Lankford	.20	.09
584	Omar Olivares	.05	.02
585	Jose Oquendo	.05	.02
586	Tom Pagnozzi	.05	.02
587	Geronimo Pena	.05	.02
588	Mike Perez	.05	.02
589	Gerald Perry	.05	.02
590	Bryn Smith	.05	.02
591	Lee Smith	.10	.05
592	Ozzie Smith	.25	.11
593	Scott Terry	.05	.02
594	Bob Tewksbury	.05	.02
595	Milt Thompson	.05	.02
596	Todd Zeile	.05	.02
597	Larry Andersen	.05	.02
598	Oscar Azocar	.05	.02
599	Andy Benes	.10	.05
600	Ricky Bones	.05	.02
601	Jerald Clark	.05	.02
602	Pat Clements	.05	.02
603	Paul Faries	.05	.02
604	Tony Fernandez	.05	.02
605	Tony Gwynn	.50	.23
606	Greg W. Harris	.05	.02
607	Thomas Howard	.05	.02
608	Bruce Hurst	.05	.02
609	Darrin Jackson	.05	.02
610	Tom Lampkin	.05	.02
611	Craig Lefferts	.05	.02
612	Jim Lewis	.05	.02
613	Mike Maddux	.05	.02
614	Fred McGriff	.15	.07
615	Jose Melendez	.05	.02
616	Jose Mota	.05	.02
617	Dennis Rasmussen	.05	.02
618	Bip Roberts	.05	.02
619	Rich Rodriguez	.05	.02
620	Benito Santiago	.05	.02
621	Craig Shipley	.05	.02
622	Tim Teufel	.05	.02
623	Kevin Ward	.05	.02
624	Ed Whitson	.05	.02
625	Dave Anderson	.05	.02
626	Kevin Bass	.05	.02
627	Rod Beck	.20	.09
628	Bud Black	.05	.02
629	Jeff Brantley	.05	.02
630	John Burkett	.05	.02
631	Will Clark	.15	.07
632	Royce Clayton	.05	.02
633	Steve Decker	.05	.02
634	Kelly Downs	.05	.02
635	Mike Felder	.05	.02
636	Scott Garrelts	.05	.02
637	Eric Gunderson	.05	.02
638	Bryan Hickerson	.05	.02

		MINT	NRMT
☐ 639	Darren Lewis	.05	.02
☐ 640	Greg Litton	.05	.02
☐ 641	Kirt Manwaring	.05	.02
☐ 642	Paul McClellan	.05	.02
☐ 643	Willie McGee	.05	.02
☐ 644	Kevin Mitchell	.10	.05
☐ 645	Francisco Oliveras	.05	.02
☐ 646	Mike Remlinger	.05	.02
☐ 647	Dave Righetti	.05	.02
☐ 648	Robby Thompson	.05	.02
☐ 649	Jose Uribe	.05	.02
☐ 650	Matt Williams	.15	.07
☐ 651	Trevor Wilson	.05	.02
☐ 652	Tom Goodwin MLP UER	.10	.05
	(Timed in 3.5, should be be timed)		
☐ 653	Terry Bross MLP	.05	.02
☐ 654	Mike Christopher MLP	.05	.02
☐ 655	Kenny Lofton MLP	.75	.35
☐ 656	Chris Cron MLP	.05	.02
☐ 657	Willie Banks MLP	.05	.02
☐ 658	Pat Rice MLP	.05	.02
☐ 659A	Rob Maurer MLP ERR	.75	.35
	(Name misspelled as Mauer on card front)		
☐ 659B	Rob Maurer MLP COR	.10	.05
☐ 660	Don Harris MLP	.05	.02
☐ 661	Henry Rodriguez MLP	.20	.09
☐ 662	Cliff Brantley MLP	.05	.02
☐ 663	Mike Linskey MLP UER	.05	.02
	(220 pounds in 205, 200 in text)		
☐ 664	Gary DiSarcina MLP	.05	.02
☐ 665	Gil Heredia MLP	.05	.02
☐ 666	Vinny Castilla MLP	.50	.23
☐ 667	Paul Abbott MLP	.05	.02
☐ 668	Monty Fariss MLP UER	.05	.02
	(Called Paul on back)		
☐ 669	Jarvis Brown MLP	.05	.02
☐ 670	Wayne Kirby MLP	.05	.02
☐ 671	Scott Brosius MLP	.05	.02
☐ 672	Bob Hamelin MLP	.05	.02
☐ 673	Joel Johnston MLP	.05	.02
☐ 674	Tim Spehr MLP	.05	.02
☐ 675A	Jeff Gardner MLP ERR	.75	.35
	(P on front, should be SS)		
☐ 675B	Jeff Gardner MLP COR	.25	.11
☐ 676	Rico Rossy MLP	.05	.02
☐ 677	Roberto Hernandez MLP	.20	.09
☐ 678	Ted Wood MLP	.05	.02
☐ 679	Cal Eldred MLP	.05	.02
☐ 680	Sean Berry MLP	.05	.02
☐ 681	Rickey Henderson RS	.10	.05
☐ 682	Nolan Ryan RS	.40	.18
☐ 683	Dennis Martinez RS	.05	.02
☐ 684	Wilson Alvarez RS	.05	.02
☐ 685	Joe Carter RS	.05	.02
☐ 686	Dave Winfield RS	.10	.05
☐ 687	David Cone RS	.05	.02
☐ 688	Jose Canseco LL UER	.10	.05
	(Text on back has 42 stolen bases in '88; should be 40)		
☐ 689	Howard Johnson LL	.05	.02
☐ 690	Julio Franco LL	.05	.02
☐ 691	Terry Pendleton LL	.05	.02
☐ 692	Cecil Fielder LL	.05	.02
☐ 693	Scott Erickson LL	.05	.02
☐ 694	Tom Glavine LL	.10	.05
☐ 695	Dennis Martinez LL	.05	.02
☐ 696	Bryan Harvey LL	.05	.02
☐ 697	Lee Smith LL	.05	.02
☐ 698	Super Siblings	.10	.05
	Roberto Alomar Sandy Alomar Jr.		
☐ 699	The Indispensables	.10	.05
	Bobby Bonilla Will Clark		
☐ 700	Teamwork	.05	.02
	Mark Wohlers Kent Mercker Alejandro Pena		
☐ 701	Tiger Tandems	.50	.23
	Stacy Jones Bo Jackson Gregg Olson		

		MINT	NRMT
	Frank Thomas		
☐ 702	The Ignitors	.20	.09
	Paul Molitor Brett Butler		
☐ 703	Indispensables II	.40	.18
	Cal Ripken Joe Carter		
☐ 704	Power Packs	.20	.09
	Barry Larkin Kirby Puckett		
☐ 705	Today and Tomorrow	.20	.09
	Mo Vaughn Cecil Fielder		
☐ 706	Teenage Sensations	.10	.05
	Ramon Martinez Ozzie Guillen		
☐ 707	Designated Hitters	.15	.07
	Harold Baines Wade Boggs		
☐ 708	Robin Yount PV	.10	.05
☐ 709	Ken Griffey Jr. PV UER	.60	.25
	(Missing quotations on back; BA has .322, but was actually .327)		
☐ 710	Nolan Ryan PV	.40	.18
☐ 711	Cal Ripken PV	.20	.09
☐ 712	Frank Thomas PV	.60	.25
☐ 713	Dave Justice PV	.10	.05
☐ 714	Checklist 1-101	.05	.02
☐ 715	Checklist 102-194	.05	.02
☐ 716	Checklist 195-296	.05	.02
☐ 717	Checklist 297-397	.05	.02
☐ 718	Checklist 398-494	.05	.02
☐ 719	Checklist 495-596	.05	.02
☐ 720A	Checklist 597-720 ERR	.05	.02
	(659 Rob Mauer)		
☐ 720B	Checklist 597-720 COR	.05	.02
	(659 Rob Mauer)		

1992 Fleer All-Stars

Cards from this 24-card standard-size set were randomly inserted in plastic wrap packs. Selected members of the American and National League 1991 All-Star squads comprise this set. The glossy color photos on the fronts are bordered in black and accented above and below with gold stripes and lettering. A diamond with a color head shot of the player is superimposed at the lower right corner of the picture.

	MINT	NRMT
COMPLETE SET (24)	35.00	16.00
COMMON CARD (1-24)	.50	.23
RANDOM INSERTS IN WAX PACKS		

		MINT	NRMT
☐ 1	Felix Jose	.50	.23
☐ 2	Tony Gwynn	4.00	1.80
☐ 3	Barry Bonds	2.00	.90
☐ 4	Bobby Bonilla	1.00	.45

		MINT	NRMT
☐ 5	Mike LaValliere	.50	.23
☐ 6	Tom Glavine	1.50	.70
☐ 7	Ramon Martinez	1.00	.45
☐ 8	Lee Smith	1.00	.45
☐ 9	Mickey Tettleton	.50	.23
☐ 10	Scott Erickson	1.00	.45
☐ 11	Frank Thomas	8.00	3.60
☐ 12	Danny Tartabull	.50	.23
☐ 13	Will Clark	1.50	.70
☐ 14	Ryne Sandberg	1.50	.70
☐ 15	Terry Pendleton	.50	.23
☐ 16	Barry Larkin	1.50	.70
☐ 17	Rafael Palmeiro	1.50	.70
☐ 18	Julio Franco	.50	.23
☐ 19	Robin Ventura	1.00	.45
☐ 20	Cal Ripken UER	6.00	2.70
	(Candide; total bases misspelled as based)		
☐ 21	Joe Carter	1.00	.45
☐ 22	Kirby Puckett	3.00	1.35
☐ 23	Ken Griffey Jr.	10.00	4.50
☐ 24	Jose Canseco	1.50	.70

1992 Fleer Lumber Company

The 1992 Fleer Lumber Company standard-size set features nine outstanding hitters in Major League Baseball. This set was only available as a bonus in Fleer hobby factory sets. Inside a black glossy frame, the fronts display color action player photos, with the player's name printed in black in a gold foil bar beneath the picture. The wider right border contains the catch phrase "The Lumber Co." in the shape of a baseball bat, complete with woodgrain streaks.

	MINT	NRMT
COMPLETE SET (9)	10.00	4.50
COMMON CARD (L1-L9)	.50	.23
ONE SET PER HOBBY FACTORY SET		

		MINT	NRMT
☐ L1	Cecil Fielder	.75	.35
☐ L2	Mickey Tettleton	.50	.23
☐ L3	Darryl Strawberry	.75	.35
☐ L4	Ryne Sandberg	1.50	.70
☐ L5	Jose Canseco	1.00	.45
☐ L6	Matt Williams UER	1.00	.45
	In 17th line, cycle is spelled cyle		
☐ L7	Cal Ripken	6.00	2.70
☐ L8	Barry Bonds	1.50	.70
☐ L9	Ron Gant	.75	.35

1992 Fleer Rookie Sensations

Cards from the 20-card Fleer Rookie Sensations set were randomly inserted in 1992 Fleer 35-card cello packs. The cards

were extremely popular upon release resulting in packs selling for levels far above suggested retail levels. The glossy color photos on the fronts have a white border on a royal blue card face. The words "Rookie Sensations" appear above the picture in gold foil lettering, while the player's name appears on a gold foil plaque beneath the picture. Through a mail-in offer for ten Fleer baseball card wrappers and 1.00 for postage and handling, Fleer offered an uncut 8 1/2" by 11" numbered promo sheet picturing ten of the 20-card set on each side in a reduced-size front-only format. The offer indicated an expiration date of July 31, 1992, or whenever the production quantity of 250,000 sheets was exhausted.

	MINT	NRMT
COMPLETE SET (20)	50.00	22.00
COMMON CARD (1-20)	1.00	.45
MINOR STARS	2.00	.90
SEMISTARS	3.00	1.35
RANDOM INSERTS IN CELLO PACKS		
☐ 1 Frank Thomas	25.00	11.00
☐ 2 Todd Van Poppel	1.00	.45
☐ 3 Orlando Merced	1.00	.45
☐ 4 Jeff Bagwell	12.00	5.50
☐ 5 Jeff Fassero	1.00	.45
☐ 6 Darren Lewis	1.00	.45
☐ 7 Milt Cuyler	1.00	.45
☐ 8 Mike Timlin	1.00	.45
☐ 9 Brian McRae	1.00	.45
☐ 10 Chuck Knoblauch	4.00	1.80
☐ 11 Rich DeLucia	1.00	.45
☐ 12 Ivan Rodriguez	8.00	3.60
☐ 13 Juan Guzman	1.00	.45
☐ 14 Steve Chitren	1.00	.45
☐ 15 Mark Wohlers	3.00	1.35
☐ 16 Wes Chamberlain	1.00	.45
☐ 17 Ray Lankford	4.00	1.80
☐ 18 Chito Martinez	1.00	.45
☐ 19 Phil Plantier	1.00	.45
☐ 20 Scott Leius UER	1.00	.45
(Misspelled Lieus on card front)		

1992 Fleer Smoke 'n Heat

This 12-card standard-size set features outstanding major league pitchers, especially the premier fastball pitchers in both leagues. These cards were only available in Fleer's 1992 Christmas factory set. The front design features color action player photos bordered in black.

The player's name appears in a gold foil bar beneath the picture, and the words "Smoke 'n Heat" are printed vertically in the wider right border.

	MINT	NRMT
COMPLETE SET (12)	10.00	4.50
COMMON CARD (S1-S12)	.50	.23
ONE SET PER RETAIL FACTORY SET		
☐ S1 Lee Smith	.75	.35
☐ S2 Jack McDowell	.50	.23
☐ S3 David Cone	.75	.35
☐ S4 Roger Clemens	3.00	1.35
☐ S5 Nolan Ryan	6.00	2.70
☐ S6 Scott Erickson	.50	.23
☐ S7 Tom Glavine	1.00	.45
☐ S8 Dwight Gooden	.75	.35
☐ S9 Andy Benes	.75	.35
☐ S10 Steve Avery	.50	.23
☐ S11 Randy Johnson	1.50	.70
☐ S12 Jim Abbott	.50	.23

1992 Fleer Team Leaders

Cards from the 20-card Fleer Team Leaders set were randomly inserted in 1992 Fleer 42-card rack packs. The glossy color photos on the fronts are bordered in white and green. Two gold foil stripes below the picture intersect a diamond-shaped "Team Leaders" emblem.

	MINT	NRMT
COMPLETE SET (20)	45.00	20.00
COMMON CARD (1-20)	1.00	.45
ONE TL OR CLEMENS PER RACK PACK		
☐ 1 Don Mattingly	5.00	2.20
☐ 2 Howard Johnson	1.00	.45
☐ 3 Chris Sabo UER	1.00	.45
(Where he it, should be Where he hit)		
☐ 4 Carlton Fisk	4.00	1.80

☐ 5 Kirby Puckett	6.00	2.70
☐ 6 Cecil Fielder	2.00	.90
☐ 7 Tony Gwynn	8.00	3.60
☐ 8 Will Clark	2.50	1.10
☐ 9 Bobby Bonilla	2.00	.90
☐ 10 Len Dykstra	2.00	.90
☐ 11 Tom Glavine	2.50	1.10
☐ 12 Rafael Palmeiro	2.50	1.10
☐ 13 Wade Boggs	4.00	1.80
☐ 14 Joe Carter	2.00	.90
☐ 15 Ken Griffey Jr.	20.00	9.00
☐ 16 Darryl Strawberry	2.00	.90
☐ 17 Cal Ripken	12.00	5.50
☐ 18 Danny Tartabull	1.00	.45
☐ 19 Jose Canseco	2.50	1.10
☐ 20 Andre Dawson	2.50	1.10

1992 Fleer Update

The 1992 Fleer Update set contains 132 standard-size cards. Cards were distributed exclusively in factory sets through hobby dealers. Factory sets included a four-card, black-bordered "92 Headliners" insert set for a total of 136 cards. Due to lackluster retail response for previous Fleer Update sets, wholesale orders for this product were low, resulting in a short print run. As word got out that the cards were in short supply, the secondary market prices soared not soon after release. The basic card design is identical to the regular issue 1992 Fleer Update except the U-prefixed numbering on back. The cards are checklisted alphabetically within and according to teams for each league with AL preceding NL. Rookie Cards in this set include John Jaha, Mike Piazza, John Valentin and Eric Young. The Piazza card is widely recognized as one of the more desirable singles issued in the 1990s.

	MINT	NRMT
COMP.FACT.SET (136)	160.00	70.00
COMPLETE SET (132)	150.00	70.00
COMMON CARD (U1-U132)	.25	.11
MINOR STARS	.75	.35
SEMISTARS	1.50	.70
☐ 1 Todd Frohwirth	.25	.11
☐ 2 Alan Mills	.25	.11
☐ 3 Rick Sutcliffe	.25	.11
☐ 4 John Valentin	2.00	.90
☐ 5 Frank Viola	.25	.11
☐ 6 Bob Zupcic	.25	.11
☐ 7 Mike Butcher	.25	.11
☐ 8 Chad Curtis	2.00	.90
☐ 9 Damion Easley	1.50	.70

□		MINT	NRMT
10	Tim Salmon	18.00	8.00
11	Julio Valera	.25	.11
12	George Bell	.25	.11
13	Roberto Hernandez	2.00	.90
14	Shawn Jeter	.25	.11
15	Thomas Howard	.25	.11
16	Jesse Levis	.25	.11
17	Kenny Lofton	30.00	13.50
18	Paul Sorrento	.25	.11
19	Rico Brogna	.75	.35
20	John Doherty	.25	.11
21	Dan Gladden	.25	.11
22	Buddy Groom	.25	.11
23	Shawn Hare	.25	.11
24	John Kiely	.25	.11
25	Kurt Knudsen	.25	.11
26	Gregg Jefferies	.25	.11
27	Wally Joyner	.75	.35
28	Kevin Koslofski	.25	.11
29	Kevin McReynolds	.25	.11
30	Rusty Meacham	.25	.11
31	Keith Miller	.25	.11
32	Hipolito Pichardo	.25	.11
33	James Austin	.25	.11
34	Scott Fletcher	.25	.11
35	John Jaha	2.00	.90
36	Pat Listach	.25	.11
37	Dave Nilsson	2.00	.90
38	Kevin Seitzer	.25	.11
39	Tom Edens	.25	.11
40	Pat Mahomes	.25	.11
41	John Smiley	.25	.11
42	Charlie Hayes	.25	.11
43	Sam Militello	.25	.11
44	Andy Stankiewicz	.25	.11
45	Danny Tartabull	.25	.11
46	Bob Wickman	.25	.11
47	Jerry Browne	.25	.11
48	Kevin Campbell	.25	.11
49	Vince Horsman	.25	.11
50	Troy Neel	.25	.11
51	Ruben Sierra	.25	.11
52	Bruce Walton	.25	.11
53	Willie Wilson	.25	.11
54	Bret Boone	.75	.35
55	Dave Fleming	.75	.11
56	Kevin Mitchell	.75	.35
57	Jeff Nelson	.25	.11
58	Shane Turner	.25	.11
59	Jose Canseco	1.50	.70
60	Jeff Frye	.25	.11
61	Danny Leon	.25	.11
62	Roger Pavlik	.75	.35
63	David Cone	.75	.35
64	Pat Hentgen	6.00	2.70
65	Randy Knorr	.25	.11
66	Jack Morris	.75	.35
67	Dave Winfield	2.00	.90
68	David Nied	.25	.11
69	Otis Nixon	.75	.35
70	Alejandro Pena	.25	.11
71	Jeff Reardon	.75	.35
72	Alex Arias	.25	.11
73	Jim Bullinger	.25	.11
74	Mike Morgan	.25	.11
75	Rey Sanchez	.25	.11
76	Bob Scanlan	.25	.11
77	Sammy Sosa	2.00	.90
78	Scott Bankhead	.25	.11
79	Tim Belcher	.25	.11
80	Steve Foster	.25	.11
81	Willie Greene	.25	.11
82	Bip Roberts	.25	.11
83	Scott Ruskin	.25	.11
84	Greg Swindell	.25	.11
85	Juan Guerrero	.25	.11
86	Butch Henry	.25	.11
87	Doug Jones	.25	.11
88	Brian Williams	.25	.11
89	Tom Candiotti	.25	.11
90	Eric Davis	.75	.35
91	Carlos Hernandez	.25	.11
92	Mike Piazza	100.00	45.00
93	Mike Sharperson	.25	.11
94	Eric Young	2.00	.90
95	Moises Alou	3.00	1.35

□			
96	Greg Colbrunn	.25	.11
97	Wil Cordero	.25	.11
98	Ken Hill	.75	.35
99	John Vander Wal	.25	.11
100	John Wetteland	.75	.35
101	Bobby Bonilla	.75	.35
102	Eric Hillman	.25	.11
103	Pat Howell	.25	.11
104	Jeff Kent	2.00	.90
105	Dick Schofield	.25	.11
106	Ryan Thompson	.25	.11
107	Chico Walker	.25	.11
108	Juan Bell	.25	.11
109	Mariano Duncan	.25	.11
110	Jeff Grotewold	.25	.11
111	Ben Rivera	.25	.11
112	Curt Schilling	3.00	1.35
113	Victor Cole	.25	.11
114	Al Martin	2.00	.90
115	Roger Mason	.25	.11
116	Blas Minor	.25	.11
117	Tim Wakefield	2.00	.90
118	Mark Clark	.25	.11
119	Rheal Cormier	.25	.11
120	Donovan Osborne	.25	.11
121	Todd Worrell	.25	.11
122	Jeremy Hernandez	.25	.11
123	Randy Myers	.75	.35
124	Frank Seminara	.25	.11
125	Gary Sheffield	2.00	.90
126	Dan Walters	.25	.11
127	Steve Hosey	.25	.11
128	Mike Jackson	.25	.11
129	Jim Pena	.25	.11
130	Cory Snyder	.25	.11
131	Bill Swift	.25	.11
132	Checklist U1-U132	.25	.11

1992 Fleer Update Headliners

Each 1992 Fleer Update factory set included a four-card set of Headliner inserts. The cards are numbered separately and have a completely different design to the base cards. Each Headliner features UV coating and black borders. The set features a selection of stars that made headlines in the 1991 season. Cards are numbered on back X of 4.

		MINT	NRMT
COMPLETE SET (4)		15.00	6.75
COMMON CARD (1-4)		.50	.23
ONE SET PER FACTORY SET			

□			
1	Ken Griffey Jr.	12.00	5.50
2	Robin Yount	1.50	.70
3	Jeff Reardon	.50	.23
4	Cecil Fielder	1.00	.45

1993 Fleer

The 720-card 1993 Fleer baseball set contains two series of 360 standard-size cards. Cards were distributed in plastic wrapped packs, cello packs, jumbo packs and rack packs. For the first time in years, Fleer did not issue a factory set. In fact, Fleer discontinued issuing factory sets from 1993-on. The card fronts show glossy color action player photos bordered in silver. A team color-coded stripe edges the left side of the picture and carries the player's name and team name. The cards are checklisted below alphabetically within and according to teams for each league with NL preceding AL. Topical subsets include League Leaders (344-348/704-708), Round Trippers (349-353/709-713), and Super Star Specials (354-357/714-717). Each series concludes with checklists (358-360/718-720). There are no key Rookie Cards in this set.

		MINT	NRMT
COMPLETE SET (720)		40.00	18.00
COMPLETE SERIES 1 (360)		20.00	9.00
COMPLETE SERIES 2 (360)		20.00	9.00
COMMON CARD (1-720)		.10	.05
MINOR STARS		.20	.09
UNLISTED STARS		.40	.18
COMP.GLAVINE SET (12)		4.00	1.80
COMMON GLAVINE (1-12)		.50	.23
CERTIFIED GLAVINE AUTO		80.00	36.00
GLAVINE: RANDOM INSERTS IN ALL PACKS			
COMMON GLAV.MAIL (13-15)		2.00	.90
GLAVINE MAIL-IN DIST.VIA WRAPPER EXCH.			

□			
1	Steve Avery	.10	.05
2	Sid Bream	.10	.05
3	Ron Gant	.20	.09
4	Tom Glavine	.30	.14
5	Brian Hunter	.25	.11
6	Ryan Klesko	.50	.23
7	Charlie Leibrandt	.10	.05
8	Kent Mercker	.10	.05
9	David Nied	.10	.05
10	Otis Nixon	.10	.05
11	Greg Olson	.10	.05
12	Terry Pendleton	.20	.09
13	Deion Sanders	.20	.09
14	John Smoltz	.20	.09
15	Mike Stanton	.10	.05
16	Mark Wohlers	.20	.09
17	Paul Assenmacher	.10	.05
18	Steve Buechele	.10	.05
19	Shawon Dunston	.10	.05
20	Mark Grace	.30	.14
21	Derrick May	.10	.05
22	Chuck McElroy	.10	.05
23	Mike Morgan	.10	.05

24	Rey Sanchez	.10	.05
25	Ryne Sandberg	.50	.23
26	Bob Scanlan	.10	.05
27	Sammy Sosa	.40	.18
28	Rick Wilkins	.10	.05
29	Bobby Ayala	.10	.05
30	Tim Belcher	.10	.05
31	Jeff Branson	.10	.05
32	Norm Charlton	.10	.05
33	Steve Foster	.10	.05
34	Willie Greene	.20	.09
35	Chris Hammond	.10	.05
36	Milt Hill	.10	.05
37	Hal Morris	.10	.05
38	Joe Oliver	.10	.05
39	Paul O'Neill	.20	.09
40	Tim Pugh	.10	.05
41	Jose Rijo	.10	.05
42	Bip Roberts	.10	.05
43	Chris Sabo	.10	.05
44	Reggie Sanders	.20	.09
45	Eric Anthony	.10	.05
46	Jeff Bagwell	.75	.35
47	Craig Biggio	.30	.14
48	Joe Boever	.10	.05
49	Casey Candaele	.10	.05
50	Steve Finley	.20	.09
51	Luis Gonzalez	.10	.05
52	Pete Harnisch	.10	.05
53	Xavier Hernandez	.10	.05
54	Doug Jones	.10	.05
55	Eddie Taubensee	.10	.05
56	Brian Williams	.10	.05
57	Pedro Astacio	.10	.05
58	Todd Benzinger	.10	.05
59	Brett Butler	.20	.09
60	Tom Candiotti	.10	.05
61	Lenny Harris	.10	.05
62	Carlos Hernandez	.10	.05
63	Orel Hershiser	.20	.09
64	Eric Karros	.20	.09
65	Ramon Martinez	.20	.09
66	Jose Offerman	.10	.05
67	Mike Scioscia	.10	.05
68	Mike Sharperson	.10	.05
69	Eric Young	.40	.18
70	Moises Alou	.20	.09
71	Ivan Calderon	.10	.05
72	Archi Cianfrocco	.10	.05
73	Wil Cordero	.10	.05
74	Delino DeShields	.10	.05
75	Mark Gardner	.10	.05
76	Ken Hill	.10	.05
77	Tim Laker	.10	.05
78	Chris Nabholz	.10	.05
79	Mel Rojas	.20	.09
80	John Vander Wal UER (Misspelled Vander Wall in letters on back)	.10	.05
81	Larry Walker	.40	.18
82	Tim Wallach	.20	.09
83	John Wetteland	.20	.09
84	Bobby Bonilla	.20	.09
85	Daryl Boston	.10	.05
86	Sid Fernandez	.10	.05
87	Eric Hillman	.10	.05
88	Todd Hundley	.30	.14
89	Howard Johnson	.10	.05
90	Jeff Kent	.40	.18
91	Eddie Murray	.40	.18
92	Bill Pecota	.10	.05
93	Bret Saberhagen	.10	.05
94	Dick Schofield	.10	.05
95	Pete Schourek	.10	.05
96	Anthony Young	.10	.05
97	Ruben Amaro Jr.	.10	.05
98	Juan Bell	.10	.05
99	Wes Chamberlain	.10	.05
100	Darren Daulton	.20	.09
101	Mariano Duncan	.10	.05
102	Mike Hartley	.10	.05
103	Ricky Jordan	.10	.05
104	John Kruk	.20	.09
105	Mickey Morandini	.10	.05
106	Terry Mulholland	.10	.05
107	Ben Rivera	.10	.05
108	Curt Schilling	.20	.09
109	Keith Shepherd	.10	.05
110	Stan Belinda	.10	.05
111	Jay Bell	.20	.09
112	Barry Bonds	.50	.23
113	Jeff King	.20	.09
114	Mike LaValliere	.10	.05
115	Jose Lind	.10	.05
116	Roger Mason	.10	.05
117	Orlando Merced	.10	.05
118	Bob Patterson	.10	.05
119	Don Slaught	.10	.05
120	Zane Smith	.10	.05
121	Randy Tomlin	.10	.05
122	Andy Van Slyke	.20	.09
123	Tim Wakefield	.20	.09
124	Rheal Cormier	.10	.05
125	Bernard Gilkey	.20	.09
126	Felix Jose	.10	.05
127	Ray Lankford	.30	.14
128	Bob McClure	.10	.05
129	Donovan Osborne	.10	.05
130	Tom Pagnozzi	.10	.05
131	Geronimo Pena	.10	.05
132	Mike Perez	.10	.05
133	Lee Smith	.20	.09
134	Bob Tewksbury	.10	.05
135	Todd Worrell	.10	.05
136	Todd Zeile	.10	.05
137	Jerald Clark	.10	.05
138	Tony Gwynn	1.00	.45
139	Greg W. Harris	.10	.05
140	Jeremy Hernandez	.10	.05
141	Darrin Jackson	.10	.05
142	Mike Maddux	.10	.05
143	Fred McGriff	.30	.14
144	Jose Melendez	.10	.05
145	Rich Rodriguez	.10	.05
146	Frank Seminara	.10	.05
147	Gary Sheffield	.40	.18
148	Kurt Stillwell	.10	.05
149	Dan Walters	.10	.05
150	Rod Beck	.20	.09
151	Bud Black	.10	.05
152	Jeff Brantley	.10	.05
153	John Burkett	.10	.05
154	Will Clark	.30	.14
155	Royce Clayton	.10	.05
156	Mike Jackson	.10	.05
157	Darren Lewis	.10	.05
158	Kirt Manwaring	.10	.05
159	Willie McGee	.10	.05
160	Cory Snyder	.10	.05
161	Bill Swift	.10	.05
162	Trevor Wilson	.10	.05
163	Brady Anderson	.30	.14
164	Glenn Davis	.10	.05
165	Mike Devereaux	.10	.05
166	Todd Frohwirth	.10	.05
167	Leo Gomez	.10	.05
168	Chris Hoiles	.10	.05
169	Ben McDonald	.10	.05
170	Randy Milligan	.10	.05
171	Alan Mills	.10	.05
172	Mike Mussina	.40	.18
173	Gregg Olson	.10	.05
174	Arthur Rhodes	.10	.05
175	David Segui	.10	.05
176	Ellis Burks	.10	.05
177	Roger Clemens	.75	.35
178	Scott Cooper	.10	.05
179	Danny Darwin	.10	.05
180	Tony Fossas	.10	.05
181	Paul Quantrill	.10	.05
182	Jody Reed	.10	.05
183	John Valentin	.20	.09
184	Mo Vaughn	.50	.23
185	Frank Viola	.20	.09
186	Bob Zupcic	.10	.05
187	Jim Abbott	.20	.09
188	Gary DiSarcina	.10	.05
189	Damion Easley	.10	.05
190	Junior Felix	.10	.05
191	Chuck Finley	.10	.05
192	Joe Grahe	.10	.05
193	Bryan Harvey	.10	.05
194	Mark Langston	.10	.05
195	John Orton	.10	.05
196	Luis Polonia	.10	.05
197	Tim Salmon	.50	.23
198	Luis Sojo	.10	.05
199	Wilson Alvarez	.20	.09
200	George Bell	.20	.09
201	Alex Fernandez	.20	.09
202	Craig Grebeck	.10	.05
203	Ozzie Guillen	.10	.05
204	Lance Johnson	.10	.05
205	Ron Karkovice	.10	.05
206	Kirk McCaskill	.10	.05
207	Jack McDowell	.20	.09
208	Scott Radinsky	.10	.05
209	Tim Raines	.20	.09
210	Frank Thomas	1.50	.70
211	Robin Ventura	.20	.09
212	Sandy Alomar Jr.	.20	.09
213	Carlos Baerga	.20	.09
214	Dennis Cook	.10	.05
215	Thomas Howard	.10	.05
216	Mark Lewis	.10	.05
217	Derek Lilliquist	.10	.05
218	Kenny Lofton	.75	.35
219	Charles Nagy	.20	.09
220	Steve Olin	.10	.05
221	Paul Sorrento	.10	.05
222	Jim Thome	.75	.35
223	Mark Whiten	.10	.05
224	Milt Cuyler	.10	.05
225	Rob Deer	.10	.05
226	John Doherty	.10	.05
227	Cecil Fielder	.20	.09
228	Travis Fryman	.40	.18
229	Mike Henneman	.10	.05
230	John Kiely UER (Card has batting stats of Pat Kelly)	.10	.05
231	Kurt Knudsen	.10	.05
232	Scott Livingstone	.10	.05
233	Tony Phillips	.10	.05
234	Mickey Tettleton	.10	.05
235	Kevin Appier	.20	.09
236	George Brett	.75	.35
237	Tom Gordon	.10	.05
238	Gregg Jefferies	.20	.09
239	Wally Joyner	.20	.09
240	Kevin Koslofski	.10	.05
241	Mike Macfarlane	.10	.05
242	Brian McRae	.10	.05
243	Rusty Meacham	.10	.05
244	Keith Miller	.10	.05
245	Jeff Montgomery	.20	.09
246	Hipolito Pichardo	.10	.05
247	Ricky Bones	.10	.05
248	Cal Eldred	.20	.09
249	Mike Fetters	.10	.05
250	Darryl Hamilton	.10	.05
251	Doug Henry	.10	.05
252	John Jaha	.20	.09
253	Pat Listach	.40	.18
254	Paul Molitor	.40	.18
255	Jaime Navarro	.10	.05
256	Kevin Seitzer	.10	.05
257	B.J. Surhoff	.20	.09
258	Greg Vaughn	.10	.05
259	Bill Wegman	.10	.05
260	Robin Yount	.30	.14
261	Rick Aguilera	.10	.05
262	Chili Davis	.20	.09
263	Scott Erickson	.20	.09
264	Greg Gagne	.10	.05
265	Mark Guthrie	.10	.05
266	Brian Harper	.10	.05
267	Kent Hrbek	.20	.09
268	Terry Jorgensen	.10	.05
269	Gene Larkin	.10	.05
270	Scott Leius	.10	.05
271	Pat Mahomes	.20	.09
272	Pedro Munoz	.10	.05
273	Kirby Puckett	.75	.35
274	Kevin Tapani	.10	.05
275	Carl Willis	.10	.05
276	Steve Farr	.10	.05
277	John Habyan	.10	.05

278	Mel Hall	.10	.05
279	Charlie Hayes	.10	.05
280	Pat Kelly	.10	.05
281	Don Mattingly	.60	.25
282	Sam Militello	.10	.05
283	Matt Nokes	.10	.05
284	Melido Perez	.10	.05
285	Andy Stankiewicz	.10	.05
286	Danny Tartabull	.10	.05
287	Randy Velarde	.10	.05
288	Bob Wickman	.10	.05
289	Bernie Williams	.40	.18
290	Lance Blankenship	.10	.05
291	Mike Bordick	.10	.05
292	Jerry Browne	.10	.05
293	Dennis Eckersley	.20	.09
294	Rickey Henderson	.30	.14
295	Vince Horsman	.10	.05
296	Mark McGwire	.75	.35
297	Jeff Parrett	.10	.05
298	Ruben Sierra	.10	.05
299	Terry Steinbach	.10	.05
300	Walt Weiss	.10	.05
301	Bob Welch	.10	.05
302	Willie Wilson	.10	.05
303	Bobby Witt	.10	.05
304	Bret Boone	.10	.05
305	Jay Buhner	.30	.14
306	Dave Fleming	.10	.05
307	Ken Griffey Jr.	2.00	.90
308	Erik Hanson	.10	.05
309	Edgar Martinez	.30	.14
310	Tino Martinez	.40	.18
311	Jeff Nelson	.10	.05
312	Dennis Powell	.10	.05
313	Mike Schooler	.10	.05
314	Russ Swan	.10	.05
315	Dave Valle	.10	.05
316	Omar Vizquel	.20	.09
317	Kevin Brown	.20	.09
318	Todd Burns	.10	.05
319	Jose Canseco	.30	.14
320	Julio Franco	.10	.05
321	Jeff Frye	.10	.05
322	Juan Gonzalez	1.00	.45
323	Jose Guzman	.10	.05
324	Jeff Huson	.10	.05
325	Dean Palmer	.10	.05
326	Kevin Reimer	.10	.05
327	Ivan Rodriguez	.50	.23
328	Kenny Rogers	.10	.05
329	Dan Smith	.10	.05
330	Roberto Alomar	.40	.18
331	Derek Bell	.20	.09
332	Pat Borders	.10	.05
333	Joe Carter	.20	.09
334	Kelly Gruber	.10	.05
335	Tom Henke	.10	.05
336	Jimmy Key	.20	.09
337	Manuel Lee	.10	.05
338	Candy Maldonado	.10	.05
339	John Olerud	.10	.05
340	Todd Stottlemyre	.10	.05
341	Duane Ward	.10	.05
342	Devon White	.10	.05
343	Dave Winfield	.30	.14
344	Edgar Martinez LL	.20	.09
345	Cecil Fielder LL	.10	.05
346	Kenny Lofton LL	.40	.18
347	Jack Morris LL	.10	.05
348	Roger Clemens LL	.40	.18
349	Fred McGriff RT	.20	.09
350	Barry Bonds RT	.30	.14
351	Gary Sheffield RT	.20	.09
352	Darren Daulton RT	.10	.05
353	Dave Hollins RT	.10	.05
354	Brothers in Blue	.10	.05
	Pedro Martinez		
	Ramon Martinez		
355	Power Packs	.50	.23
	Ivan Rodriguez		
	Kirby Puckett		
356	Triple Threats	.40	.18
	Ryne Sandberg		
	Gary Sheffield		
357	Infield Trifecta	.40	.18
	Roberto Alomar		
	Chuck Knoblauch		
	Carlos Baerga		
358	Checklist 1-120	.10	.05
359	Checklist 121-240	.10	.05
360	Checklist 241-360	.10	.05
361	Rafael Belliard	.10	.05
362	Damon Berryhill	.10	.05
363	Mike Bielecki	.10	.05
364	Jeff Blauser	.10	.05
365	Francisco Cabrera	.10	.05
366	Marvin Freeman	.10	.05
367	David Justice	.40	.18
368	Mark Lemke	.10	.05
369	Alejandro Pena	.10	.05
370	Jeff Reardon	.20	.09
371	Lonnie Smith	.10	.05
372	Pete Smith	.10	.05
373	Shawn Boskie	.10	.05
374	Jim Bullinger	.10	.05
375	Frank Castillo	.10	.05
376	Doug Dascenzo	.10	.05
377	Andre Dawson	.30	.14
378	Mike Harkey	.10	.05
379	Greg Hibbard	.10	.05
380	Greg Maddux	1.25	.55
381	Ken Patterson	.10	.05
382	Jeff D. Robinson	.10	.05
383	Luis Salazar	.10	.05
384	Dwight Smith	.10	.05
385	Jose Vizcaino	.10	.05
386	Scott Bankhead	.10	.05
387	Tom Browning	.10	.05
388	Darnell Coles	.10	.05
389	Rob Dibble	.10	.05
390	Bill Doran	.10	.05
391	Dwayne Henry	.10	.05
392	Cesar Hernandez	.10	.05
393	Roberto Kelly	.10	.05
394	Barry Larkin	.30	.14
395	Dave Martinez	.10	.05
396	Kevin Mitchell	.20	.09
397	Jeff Reed	.10	.05
398	Scott Ruskin	.10	.05
399	Greg Swindell	.10	.05
400	Dan Wilson	.20	.09
401	Andy Ashby	.10	.05
402	Freddie Benavides	.10	.05
403	Dante Bichette	.30	.14
404	Willie Blair	.10	.05
405	Denis Boucher	.10	.05
406	Vinny Castilla	.10	.05
407	Braulio Castillo	.10	.05
408	Alex Cole	.10	.05
409	Andres Galarraga	.40	.18
410	Joe Girardi	.10	.05
411	Butch Henry	.10	.05
412	Darren Holmes	.10	.05
413	Calvin Jones	.10	.05
414	Steve Reed	.10	.05
415	Kevin Ritz	.10	.05
416	Jim Tatum	.10	.05
417	Jack Armstrong	.10	.05
418	Bret Barberie	.10	.05
419	Ryan Bowen	.10	.05
420	Cris Carpenter	.10	.05
421	Chuck Carr	.10	.05
422	Scott Chiamparino	.10	.05
423	Jeff Conine	.20	.09
424	Jim Corsi	.10	.05
425	Chris Donnels	.10	.05
426	Monty Fariss	.10	.05
427	Bob Natal	.10	.05
428	Pat Rapp	.10	.05
429	Dave Weathers	.10	.05
430	Nigel Wilson	.10	.05
431	Ken Caminiti	.30	.14
432	Andujar Cedeno	.10	.05
433	Tom Edens	.10	.05
434	Juan Guerrero	.10	.05
435	Pete Incaviglia	.10	.05
436	Jimmy Jones	.10	.05
437	Darryl Kile	.20	.09
438	Rob Murphy	.10	.05
439	Al Osuna	.10	.05
440			
441	Mark Portugal	.10	.05
442	Scott Servais	.10	.05
443	John Candelaria	.10	.05
444	Tim Crews	.10	.05
445	Eric Davis	.20	.09
446	Tom Goodwin	.10	.05
447	Jim Gott	.10	.05
448	Kevin Gross	.10	.05
449	Dave Hansen	.10	.05
450	Jay Howell	.10	.05
451	Roger McDowell	.10	.05
452	Bob Ojeda	.10	.05
453	Henry Rodriguez	.20	.09
454	Darryl Strawberry	.20	.09
455	Mitch Webster	.10	.05
456	Steve Wilson	.10	.05
457	Brian Barnes	.10	.05
458	Sean Berry	.10	.05
459	Jeff Fassero	.10	.05
460	Darrin Fletcher	.10	.05
461	Marquis Grissom	.20	.09
462	Dennis Martinez	.20	.09
463	Spike Owen	.10	.05
464	Matt Stairs	.10	.05
465	Sergio Valdez	.10	.05
466	Kevin Bass	.10	.05
467	Vince Coleman	.10	.05
468	Mark Dewey	.10	.05
469	Kevin Elster	.10	.05
470	Tony Fernandez	.10	.05
471	John Franco	.20	.09
472	Dave Gallagher	.10	.05
473	Paul Gibson	.10	.05
474	Dwight Gooden	.20	.09
475	Lee Guetterman	.10	.05
476	Jeff Innis	.10	.05
477	Dave Magadan	.10	.05
478	Charlie O'Brien	.10	.05
479	Willie Randolph	.20	.09
480	Mackey Sasser	.10	.05
481	Ryan Thompson	.10	.05
482	Chico Walker	.10	.05
483	Kyle Abbott	.10	.05
484	Bob Ayrault	.10	.05
485	Kim Batiste	.10	.05
486	Cliff Brantley	.10	.05
487	Jose DeLeon	.10	.05
488	Len Dykstra	.20	.09
489	Tommy Greene	.10	.05
490	Jeff Grotewold	.10	.05
491	Dave Hollins	.10	.05
492	Danny Jackson	.10	.05
493	Stan Javier	.10	.05
494	Tom Marsh	.10	.05
495	Greg Mathews	.10	.05
496	Dale Murphy	.30	.14
497	Todd Pratt	.10	.05
498	Mitch Williams	.10	.05
499	Danny Cox	.10	.05
500	Doug Drabek	.10	.05
501	Carlos Garcia	.10	.05
502	Lloyd McClendon	.10	.05
503	Denny Neagle	.20	.09
504	Gary Redus	.10	.05
505	Bob Walk	.10	.05
506	John Wehner	.10	.05
507	Luis Alicea	.10	.05
508	Mark Clark	.10	.05
509	Pedro Guerrero	.10	.05
510	Rex Hudler	.10	.05
511	Brian Jordan	.20	.09
512	Omar Olivares	.10	.05
513	Jose Oquendo	.10	.05
514	Gerald Perry	.10	.05
515	Bryn Smith	.10	.05
516	Craig Wilson	.10	.05
517	Tracy Woodson	.10	.05
518	Larry Andersen	.10	.05
519	Andy Benes	.20	.09
520	Jim Deshaies	.10	.05
521	Bruce Hurst	.10	.05
522	Randy Myers	.20	.09
523	Benito Santiago	.20	.09
524	Tim Scott	.10	.05
525	Tim Teufel	.10	.05
526	Mike Benjamin	.10	.05

☐ 527 Dave Burba	.10	.05		
☐ 528 Craig Colbert	.10	.05		
☐ 529 Mike Felder	.10	.05		
☐ 530 Bryan Hickerson	.10	.05		
☐ 531 Chris James	.10	.05		
☐ 532 Mark Leonard	.10	.05		
☐ 533 Greg Litton	.10	.05		
☐ 534 Francisco Oliveras	.10	.05		
☐ 535 John Patterson	.10	.05		
☐ 536 Jim Pena	.10	.05		
☐ 537 Dave Righetti	.10	.05		
☐ 538 Robby Thompson	.10	.05		
☐ 539 Jose Uribe	.10	.05		
☐ 540 Matt Williams	.30	.14		
☐ 541 Storm Davis	.10	.05		
☐ 542 Sam Horn	.10	.05		
☐ 543 Tim Hulett	.10	.05		
☐ 544 Craig Lefferts	.10	.05		
☐ 545 Chito Martinez	.10	.05		
☐ 546 Mark McLemore	.10	.05		
☐ 547 Luis Mercedes	.10	.05		
☐ 548 Bob Milacki	.10	.05		
☐ 549 Joe Orsulak	.10	.05		
☐ 550 Billy Ripken	.10	.05		
☐ 551 Cal Ripken Jr.	1.50	.70		
☐ 552 Rick Sutcliffe	.10	.05		
☐ 553 Jeff Tackett	.10	.05		
☐ 554 Wade Boggs	.40	.18		
☐ 555 Tom Brunansky	.10	.05		
☐ 556 Jack Clark	.10	.05		
☐ 557 John Dopson	.10	.05		
☐ 558 Mike Gardiner	.10	.05		
☐ 559 Mike Greenwell	.10	.05		
☐ 560 Greg A. Harris	.10	.05		
☐ 561 Billy Hatcher	.10	.05		
☐ 562 Joe Hesketh	.10	.05		
☐ 563 Tony Pena	.10	.05		
☐ 564 Phil Plantier	.10	.05		
☐ 565 Luis Rivera	.10	.05		
☐ 566 Herm Winningham	.10	.05		
☐ 567 Matt Young	.10	.05		
☐ 568 Bert Blyleven	.20	.09		
☐ 569 Mike Butcher	.10	.05		
☐ 570 Chuck Crim	.10	.05		
☐ 571 Chad Curtis	.20	.09		
☐ 572 Tim Fortugno	.10	.05		
☐ 573 Steve Frey	.10	.05		
☐ 574 Gary Gaetti	.10	.05		
☐ 575 Scott Lewis	.10	.05		
☐ 576 Lee Stevens	.10	.05		
☐ 577 Ron Tingley	.10	.05		
☐ 578 Julio Valera	.10	.05		
☐ 579 Shawn Abner	.10	.05		
☐ 580 Joey Cora	.20	.09		
☐ 581 Chris Cron	.10	.05		
☐ 582 Carlton Fisk	.40	.18		
☐ 583 Roberto Hernandez	.20	.09		
☐ 584 Charlie Hough	.10	.05		
☐ 585 Terry Leach	.10	.05		
☐ 586 Donn Pall	.10	.05		
☐ 587 Dan Pasqua	.10	.05		
☐ 588 Steve Sax	.10	.05		
☐ 589 Bobby Thigpen	.10	.05		
☐ 590 Albert Belle	.50	.23		
☐ 591 Felix Fermin	.10	.05		
☐ 592 Glenallen Hill	.10	.05		
☐ 593 Brook Jacoby	.10	.05		
☐ 594 Reggie Jefferson	.10	.05		
☐ 595 Carlos Martinez	.10	.05		
☐ 596 Jose Mesa	.10	.05		
☐ 597 Rod Nichols	.10	.05		
☐ 598 Junior Ortiz	.10	.05		
☐ 599 Eric Plunk	.10	.05		
☐ 600 Ted Power	.10	.05		
☐ 601 Scott Scudder	.10	.05		
☐ 602 Kevin Wickander	.10	.05		
☐ 603 Skeeter Barnes	.10	.05		
☐ 604 Mark Carreon	.10	.05		
☐ 605 Dan Gladden	.10	.05		
☐ 606 Bill Gullickson	.10	.05		
☐ 607 Chad Kreuter	.10	.05		
☐ 608 Mark Leiter	.10	.05		
☐ 609 Mike Munoz	.10	.05		
☐ 610 Rich Rowland	.10	.05		
☐ 611 Frank Tanana	.10	.05		
☐ 612 Walt Terrell	.10	.05		

☐ 613 Alan Trammell	.30	.14		
☐ 614 Lou Whitaker	.20	.09		
☐ 615 Luis Aquino	.10	.05		
☐ 616 Mike Boddicker	.10	.05		
☐ 617 Jim Eisenreich	.10	.05		
☐ 618 Mark Gubicza	.10	.05		
☐ 619 David Howard	.10	.05		
☐ 620 Mike Magnante	.10	.05		
☐ 621 Brent Mayne	.10	.05		
☐ 622 Kevin McReynolds	.10	.05		
☐ 623 Ed Pierce	.10	.05		
☐ 624 Bill Sampen	.10	.05		
☐ 625 Steve Shifflett	.10	.05		
☐ 626 Gary Thurman	.10	.05		
☐ 627 Curtis Wilkerson	.10	.05		
☐ 628 Chris Bosio	.10	.05		
☐ 629 Scott Fletcher	.10	.05		
☐ 630 Jim Gantner	.10	.05		
☐ 631 Dave Nilsson	.20	.09		
☐ 632 Jesse Orosco	.10	.05		
☐ 633 Dan Plesac	.10	.05		
☐ 634 Ron Robinson	.10	.05		
☐ 635 Bill Spiers	.10	.05		
☐ 636 Franklin Stubbs	.10	.05		
☐ 637 Willie Banks	.10	.05		
☐ 638 Randy Bush	.10	.05		
☐ 639 Chuck Knoblauch	.40	.18		
☐ 640 Shane Mack	.10	.05		
☐ 641 Mike Pagliarulo	.10	.05		
☐ 642 Jeff Reboulet	.10	.05		
☐ 643 John Smiley	.10	.05		
☐ 644 Mike Trombley	.10	.05		
☐ 645 Gary Wayne	.10	.05		
☐ 646 Lenny Webster	.10	.05		
☐ 647 Tim Burke	.10	.05		
☐ 648 Mike Gallego	.10	.05		
☐ 649 Dion James	.10	.05		
☐ 650 Jeff Johnson	.10	.05		
☐ 651 Scott Kamieniecki	.10	.05		
☐ 652 Kevin Maas	.10	.05		
☐ 653 Rich Monteleone	.10	.05		
☐ 654 Jerry Nielsen	.10	.05		
☐ 655 Scott Sanderson	.10	.05		
☐ 656 Mike Stanley	.10	.05		
☐ 657 Gerald Williams	.10	.05		
☐ 658 Curt Young	.10	.05		
☐ 659 Harold Baines	.20	.09		
☐ 660 Kevin Campbell	.10	.05		
☐ 661 Ron Darling	.10	.05		
☐ 662 Kelly Downs	.10	.05		
☐ 663 Eric Fox	.10	.05		
☐ 664 Dave Henderson	.10	.05		
☐ 665 Rick Honeycutt	.10	.05		
☐ 666 Mike Moore	.10	.05		
☐ 667 Jamie Quirk	.10	.05		
☐ 668 Jeff Russell	.10	.05		
☐ 669 Dave Stewart	.20	.09		
☐ 670 Greg Briley	.10	.05		
☐ 671 Dave Cochrane	.10	.05		
☐ 672 Henry Cotto	.10	.05		
☐ 673 Rich DeLucia	.10	.05		
☐ 674 Brian Fisher	.10	.05		
☐ 675 Mark Grant	.10	.05		
☐ 676 Randy Johnson	.40	.18		
☐ 677 Tim Leary	.10	.05		
☐ 678 Pete O'Brien	.10	.05		
☐ 679 Lance Parrish	.10	.05		
☐ 680 Harold Reynolds	.10	.05		
☐ 681 Shane Turner	.10	.05		
☐ 682 Jack Daugherty	.10	.05		
☐ 683 David Hulse	.10	.05		
☐ 684 Terry Mathews	.10	.05		
☐ 685 Al Newman	.10	.05		
☐ 686 Edwin Nunez	.10	.05		
☐ 687 Rafael Palmeiro	.30	.14		
☐ 688 Roger Pavlik	.10	.05		
☐ 689 Geno Petralli	.10	.05		
☐ 690 Nolan Ryan	1.50	.70		
☐ 691 David Cone	.20	.09		
☐ 692 Alfredo Griffin	.10	.05		
☐ 693 Juan Guzman	.10	.05		
☐ 694 Pat Hentgen	.30	.14		
☐ 695 Randy Knorr	.10	.05		
☐ 696 Bob MacDonald	.10	.05		
☐ 697 Jack Morris	.20	.09		
☐ 698 Ed Sprague	.10	.05		

☐ 699 Dave Stieb	.10	.05
☐ 700 Pat Tabler	.10	.05
☐ 701 Mike Timlin	.10	.05
☐ 702 David Wells	.10	.05
☐ 703 Eddie Zosky	.10	.05
☐ 704 Gary Sheffield LL	.20	.09
☐ 705 Darren Daulton LL	.10	.05
☐ 706 Marquis Grissom LL	.10	.05
☐ 707 Greg Maddux LL	.60	.25
☐ 708 Bill Swift LL	.10	.05
☐ 709 Juan Gonzalez RT	.50	.23
☐ 710 Mark McGwire RT	.50	.23
☐ 711 Cecil Fielder RT	.10	.05
☐ 712 Albert Belle RT	.20	.09
☐ 713 Joe Carter RT	.10	.05
☐ 714 Cecil Fielder SS	.40	.18
	Frank Thomas	
	Power Brokers	
☐ 715 Larry Walker SS	.40	.18
	Darren Daulton	
	Unsung Heroes	
☐ 716 Edgar Martinez SS	.20	.09
	Robin Ventura	
	Hot Corner Hammers	
☐ 717 Roger Clemens SS	.40	.18
	Dennis Eckersley	
	Start to Finish	
☐ 718 Checklist 361-480	.10	.05
☐ 719 Checklist 481-600	.10	.05
☐ 720 Checklist 601-720	.10	.05

1993 Fleer All-Stars

This 24-card standard-size set featuring members of the American and National league All-Star squads, was randomly inserted in wax packs. 12 American League players were seeded in series 1 packs and 12 National League players in series 2. The horizontal fronts feature a color close-up photo cut out and superposed upon a black-and-white action scene framed by white borders. The player's name and the word "All-Stars" are printed in gold foil lettering across the bottom of the picture.

	MINT	NRMT
COMPLETE SET (24)	40.00	18.00
COMPLETE SERIES 1 (12)	25.00	11.00
COMPLETE SERIES 2 (12)	15.00	6.75
COMMON CARD (AL1-NL12)	.50	.23
AL: RANDOM INSERTS IN SER.1 PACKS		
NL: RANDOM INSERTS IN SER.2 PACKS		

☐ AL1 Frank Thomas	10.00	4.50
☐ AL2 Roberto Alomar	2.50	1.10
☐ AL3 Edgar Martinez	1.50	.70
☐ AL4 Pat Listach	.50	.23
☐ AL5 Cecil Fielder	1.00	.45
☐ AL6 Juan Gonzalez	6.00	2.70

☐ AL7 Ken Griffey Jr.	12.00	5.50
☐ AL8 Joe Carter	1.00	.45
☐ AL9 Kirby Puckett	5.00	2.20
☐ AL10 Brian Harper	.50	.23
☐ AL11 Dave Fleming	.50	.23
☐ AL12 Jack McDowell	.50	.23
☐ NL1 Fred McGriff	1.50	.70
☐ NL2 Delino DeShields	.50	.23
☐ NL3 Gary Sheffield	2.50	1.10
☐ NL4 Barry Larkin	1.50	.70
☐ NL5 Felix Jose	.50	.23
☐ NL6 Larry Walker	2.50	1.10
☐ NL7 Barry Bonds	3.00	1.35
☐ NL8 Andy Van Slyke	1.00	.45
☐ NL9 Darren Daulton	1.00	.45
☐ NL10 Greg Maddux	8.00	3.60
☐ NL11 Tom Glavine	1.50	.70
☐ NL12 Lee Smith	1.00	.45

1993 Fleer Golden Moments

Cards from this six-card standard-size set, featuring memorable moments from the previous season, were randomly inserted in 1993 Fleer wax packs, three in series 1 and 2. The fronts feature glossy color action photos framed by thin aqua and white lines and a black outer border. A gold foil baseball icon appears at each corner of the picture, and the player's name and the set title "Golden Moments" appears in a gold foil bar toward the bottom of the picture. The cards are unnumbered and checklisted below in alphabetical order.

	MINT	NRMT
COMPLETE SET (6)	12.00	5.50
COMPLETE SERIES 1 (3)	4.00	1.80
COMPLETE SERIES 2 (3)	8.00	3.60
COMMON CARD (A1-B3)	.50	.23
RANDOM INSERTS IN WAX PACKS		
☐ A1 George Brett	4.00	1.80
☐ A2 Mickey Morandini	.50	.23
☐ A3 Dave Winfield	2.00	.90
☐ B1 Dennis Eckersley	1.00	.45
☐ B2 Bip Roberts	.50	.23
☐ B3 Frank Thomas	8.00	3.60
and Juan Gonzalez		

1993 Fleer Major League Prospects

Cards from this 36-card standard-size set, featuring a selection of prospects, were randomly inserted in wax packs, 18 each in series 1 and 2. These cards feature black-bordered

---

color player action photos on their fronts. The player's name appears in gold foil at the top, and the set's name and logo appear in gold foil and black at the bottom. The key card in this set is Mike Piazza.

	MINT	NRMT
COMPLETE SET (36)	30.00	13.50
COMPLETE SERIES 1 (18)	20.00	9.00
COMPLETE SERIES 2 (18)	10.00	4.50
COMMON SERIES 1 (A1-A18)	.50	.23
COMMON SERIES 2 (B1-B18)	.50	.23
SEMISTARS	1.00	.45
RANDOM INSERTS IN WAX PACKS		
☐ A1 Melvin Nieves	.75	.35
☐ A2 Sterling Hitchcock	.50	.23
☐ A3 Tim Costo	.50	.23
☐ A4 Manny Alexander	.50	.23
☐ A5 Alan Embree	.50	.23
☐ A6 Kevin Young	.50	.23
☐ A7 J.T. Snow	1.50	.70
☐ A8 Russ Springer	.50	.23
☐ A9 Billy Ashley	.50	.23
☐ A10 Kevin Rogers	.50	.23
☐ A11 Steve Hosey	.50	.23
☐ A12 Eric Wedge	.50	.23
☐ A13 Mike Piazza	15.00	6.75
☐ A14 Jesse Levis	.50	.23
☐ A15 Rico Brogna	.75	.35
☐ A16 Alex Arias	.50	.23
☐ A17 Rod Brewer	.50	.23
☐ A18 Troy Neel	.50	.23
☐ B1 Scooter Tucker	.50	.23
☐ B2 Kerry Woodson	.50	.23
☐ B3 Greg Colbrunn	.50	.23
☐ B4 Pedro Martinez	5.00	2.20
☐ B5 Dave Silvestri	.50	.23
☐ B6 Kent Bottenfield	.50	.23
☐ B7 Rafael Bournigal	.50	.23
☐ B8 J.T. Bruett	.50	.23
☐ B9 Dave Mlicki	.50	.23
☐ B10 Paul Wagner	.50	.23
☐ B11 Mike Williams	.50	.23
☐ B12 Henry Mercedes	.50	.23
☐ B13 Scott Taylor	.50	.23
☐ B14 Dennis Moeller	.50	.23
☐ B15 Javier Lopez	3.00	1.35
☐ B16 Steve Cooke	.50	.23
☐ B17 Pete Young	.50	.23
☐ B18 Ken Ryan	.50	.23

1993 Fleer Pro-Visions

Cards from this six-card standard-size set, featuring a selection of superstars in fantasy paintings, were randomly inserted in poly packs, three in series 1 and 2. These cards feature black-bordered fanciful color artwork of the players in action. The player's name

---

appears in gold foil within the bottom black margin of each.

	MINT	NRMT
COMPLETE SET (6)	5.00	2.20
COMPLETE SERIES 1 (3)	3.00	1.35
COMPLETE SERIES 2 (3)	2.00	.90
COMMON SERIES 1 (A1-B3)	.75	.35
COMMON SERIES 2 (A1-B3)	.75	.35
RANDOM INSERTS IN WAX PACKS		
☐ A1 Roberto Alomar	2.00	.90
☐ A2 Dennis Eckersley	1.00	.45
☐ A3 Gary Sheffield	2.00	.90
☐ A4 Andy Van Slyke	.75	.35
☐ B2 Tom Glavine	1.50	.70
☐ B3 Cecil Fielder	1.00	.45

1993 Fleer Rookie Sensations

Cards from this 20-card standard-size set, featuring a selection of 1993's top rookies, were randomly inserted in cello packs, 10 each in series 1 and 2. The cards feature blue-bordered fronts with cutout color player photos, each superposed upon a silver-colored background. The set's title and the player's name appear in gold foil in an upper corner. The key card in this set is Kenny Lofton.

	MINT	NRMT
COMPLETE SET (20)	30.00	13.50
COMPLETE SERIES 1 (10)	20.00	9.00
COMPLETE SERIES 2 (10)	10.00	4.50
COMMON CARD (RSA1-RSB10)	1.00	.45
RANDOM INSERTS IN CELLO PACKS		
☐ RSA1 Kenny Lofton	15.00	6.75
☐ RSA2 Cal Eldred	1.00	.45
☐ RSA3 Pat Listach	1.00	.45
☐ RSA4 Roberto Hernandez	1.50	.70
☐ RSA5 Dave Fleming	1.00	.45
☐ RSA6 Eric Karros	1.50	.70

		MINT	NRMT
☐ RSA7	Reggie Sanders	1.50	.70
☐ RSA8	Derrick May	1.00	.45
☐ RSA9	Mike Perez	1.00	.45
☐ RSA10	Donovan Osborne	1.00	.45
☐ RSB1	Moises Alou	1.50	.70
☐ RSB2	Pedro Astacio	1.00	.45
☐ RSB3	Jim Austin	1.00	.45
☐ RSB4	Chad Curtis	1.50	.70
☐ RSB5	Gary DiSarcina	1.00	.45
☐ RSB6	Scott Livingstone	1.00	.45
☐ RSB7	Sam Militello	1.00	.45
☐ RSB8	Arthur Rhodes	1.00	.45
☐ RSB9	Tim Wakefield	1.50	.70
☐ RSB10	Bob Zupcic	1.00	.45

1993 Fleer Team Leaders

One Team Leader or Tom Glavine insert was seeded into each Fleer rack pack. Series 1 racks included 10 American League players, while series 2 racks included 10 National League players. Each of the tan-bordered standard-size cards comprising this set feature a posed color player photo on its front with a smaller cutout color action photo superposed in a lower corner. The player's name and the set's title appear vertically in gold foil along the left side within team color-coded bars.

		MINT	NRMT
COMPLETE SET (20)		70.00	32.00
COMPLETE SERIES 1 (10)		50.00	22.00
COMPLETE SERIES 2 (10)		20.00	9.00
*SINGLES: 4X TO 10X BASE CARD HI			
ONE TL OR GLAVINE PER RACK PACK			
AL: RANDOM INSERTS IN SER.1 PACKS			
NL: RANDOM INSERTS IN SER.2 PACKS			

		MINT	NRMT
☐ AL1	Kirby Puckett	8.00	3.60
☐ AL2	Mark McGwire	8.00	3.60
☐ AL3	Pat Listach	1.00	.45
☐ AL4	Roger Clemens	8.00	3.60
☐ AL5	Frank Thomas	15.00	6.75
☐ AL6	Carlos Baerga	1.00	.45
☐ AL7	Brady Anderson	2.50	1.10
☐ AL8	Juan Gonzalez	10.00	4.50
☐ AL9	Roberto Alomar	4.00	1.80
☐ AL10	Ken Griffey Jr.	20.00	9.00
☐ NL1	Will Clark	2.50	1.10
☐ NL2	Terry Pendleton	1.00	.45
☐ NL3	Ray Lankford	2.00	.90
☐ NL4	Eric Karros	2.00	.90
☐ NL5	Gary Sheffield	4.00	1.80
☐ NL6	Ryne Sandberg	5.00	2.20
☐ NL7	Marquis Grissom	2.00	.90
☐ NL8	John Kruk	2.00	.90
☐ NL9	Jeff Bagwell	8.00	3.60
☐ NL10	Andy Van Slyke	2.00	.90

1993 Fleer Final Edition

This 300-card standard-size set was issued exclusively in factory set form (along with ten Diamond Tribute inserts) to update and feature rookies not in the regular 1993 Fleer set. The cards are identical in design to regular issue 1993 Fleer cards except for the F-prefixed numbering. Cards are ordered alphabetically within teams with NL preceding AL. The set closes with checklist cards (298-300). The only key Rookie Card in this set features Jim Edmonds.

	MINT	NRMT
COMP.FACT.SET (310)	10.00	4.50
COMPLETE SET (300)	6.00	2.70
COMMON CARD (F1-F300)	.10	.05
MINOR STARS	.20	.09
SEMISTARS	.30	.14
UNLISTED STARS	.40	.18

☐ 1	Steve Bedrosian	.10	.05
☐ 2	Jay Howell	.10	.05
☐ 3	Greg Maddux	1.25	.55
☐ 4	Greg McMichael	.10	.05
☐ 5	Tony Tarasco	.10	.05
☐ 6	Jose Bautista	.10	.05
☐ 7	Jose Guzman	.10	.05
☐ 8	Greg Hibbard	.10	.05
☐ 9	Candy Maldonado	.10	.05
☐ 10	Randy Myers	.20	.09
☐ 11	Matt Walbeck	.10	.05
☐ 12	Turk Wendell	.10	.05
☐ 13	Willie Wilson	.10	.05
☐ 14	Greg Cadaret	.10	.05
☐ 15	Roberto Kelly	.10	.05
☐ 16	Randy Milligan	.10	.05
☐ 17	Kevin Mitchell	.20	.09
☐ 18	Jeff Reardon	.20	.09
☐ 19	John Roper	.10	.05
☐ 20	John Smiley	.10	.05
☐ 21	Andy Ashby	.10	.05
☐ 22	Dante Bichette	.30	.14
☐ 23	Willie Blair	.10	.05
☐ 24	Pedro Castellano	.10	.05
☐ 25	Vinny Castilla	.40	.18
☐ 26	Jerald Clark	.10	.05
☐ 27	Alex Cole	.10	.05
☐ 28	Scott Fredrickson	.10	.05
☐ 29	Jay Gainer	.10	.05
☐ 30	Andres Galarraga	.40	.18
☐ 31	Joe Girardi	.10	.05
☐ 32	Ryan Hawblitzel	.10	.05
☐ 33	Charlie Hayes	.10	.05
☐ 34	Darren Holmes	.10	.05
☐ 35	Chris Jones	.10	.05
☐ 36	David Nied	.40	.18
☐ 37	J.Owens	.10	.05
☐ 38	Lance Painter	.10	.05
☐ 39	Jeff Parrett	.10	.05
☐ 40	Steve Reed	.10	.05
☐ 41	Armando Reynoso	.10	.05
☐ 42	Bruce Ruffin	.10	.05
☐ 43	Danny Sheaffer	.10	.05
☐ 44	Keith Shepherd	.10	.05
☐ 45	Jim Tatum	.10	.05
☐ 46	Gary Wayne	.10	.05
☐ 47	Eric Young	.40	.18
☐ 48	Luis Aquino	.10	.05
☐ 49	Alex Arias	.10	.05
☐ 50	Jack Armstrong	.10	.05
☐ 51	Bret Barberie	.10	.05
☐ 52	Geronimo Berroa	.20	.09
☐ 53	Ryan Bowen	.10	.05
☐ 54	Greg Briley	.10	.05
☐ 55	Cris Carpenter	.10	.05
☐ 56	Chuck Carr	.10	.05
☐ 57	Jeff Conine	.20	.09
☐ 58	Jim Corsi	.10	.05
☐ 59	Orestes Destrade	.10	.05
☐ 60	Junior Felix	.10	.05
☐ 61	Chris Hammond	.10	.05
☐ 62	Bryan Harvey	.10	.05
☐ 63	Charlie Hough	.10	.05
☐ 64	Joe Klink	.10	.05
☐ 65	Richie Lewis UER	.10	.05
	(Refers to place of birth and residence as Illinois instead of Indiana)		
☐ 66	Mitch Lyden	.10	.05
☐ 67	Bob Natal	.10	.05
☐ 68	Scott Pose	.10	.05
☐ 69	Rich Renteria	.10	.05
☐ 70	Benito Santiago	.10	.05
☐ 71	Gary Sheffield	.40	.18
☐ 72	Matt Turner	.10	.05
☐ 73	Walt Weiss	.10	.05
☐ 74	Darrell Whitmore	.10	.05
☐ 75	Nigel Wilson	.10	.05
☐ 76	Kevin Bass	.10	.05
☐ 77	Doug Drabek	.10	.05
☐ 78	Tom Edens	.10	.05
☐ 79	Chris James	.10	.05
☐ 80	Greg Swindell	.10	.05
☐ 81	Omar Daal	.20	.09
☐ 82	Raul Mondesi	.50	.23
☐ 83	Jody Reed	.10	.05
☐ 84	Cory Snyder	.10	.05
☐ 85	Rick Trlicek	.10	.05
☐ 86	Tim Wallach	.10	.05
☐ 87	Todd Worrell	.10	.05
☐ 88	Tavo Alvarez	.10	.05
☐ 89	Frank Bolick	.10	.05
☐ 90	Kent Bottenfield	.10	.05
☐ 91	Greg Colbrunn	.10	.05
☐ 92	Cliff Floyd	.20	.09
☐ 93	Lou Frazier	.10	.05
☐ 94	Mike Gardiner	.10	.05
☐ 95	Mike Lansing	.20	.09
☐ 96	Bill Risley	.10	.05
☐ 97	Jeff Shaw	.10	.05
☐ 98	Kevin Baez	.10	.05
☐ 99	Tim Bogar	.10	.05
☐ 100	Jeromy Burnitz	.10	.05
☐ 101	Mike Draper	.10	.05
☐ 102	Darrin Jackson	.10	.05
☐ 103	Mike Maddux	.10	.05
☐ 104	Joe Orsulak	.10	.05
☐ 105	Doug Saunders	.10	.05
☐ 106	Frank Tanana	.10	.05
☐ 107	Dave Telgheder	.10	.05
☐ 108	Larry Andersen	.10	.05
☐ 109	Jim Eisenreich	.10	.05
☐ 110	Pete Incaviglia	.10	.05
☐ 111	Danny Jackson	.10	.05
☐ 112	David West	.10	.05
☐ 113	Al Martin	.20	.09
☐ 114	Blas Minor	.10	.05
☐ 115	Dennis Moeller	.10	.05
☐ 116	William Pennyfeather	.10	.05
☐ 117	Rich Robertson	.10	.05
☐ 118	Ben Shelton	.10	.05
☐ 119	Lonnie Smith	.10	.05
☐ 120	Freddie Toliver	.10	.05
☐ 121	Paul Wagner	.10	.05
☐ 122	Kevin Young	.10	.05
☐ 123	Rene Arocha	.10	.05

□ 124	Gregg Jefferies	.10	.05
□ 125	Paul Kilgus	.10	.05
□ 126	Les Lancaster	.10	.05
□ 127	Joe Magrane	.10	.05
□ 128	Rob Murphy	.10	.05
□ 129	Erik Pappas	.10	.05
□ 130	Stan Royer	.10	.05
□ 131	Ozzie Smith	.50	.23
□ 132	Tom Urbani	.10	.05
□ 133	Mark Whiten	.10	.05
□ 134	Derek Bell	.20	.09
□ 135	Doug Brocail	.10	.05
□ 136	Phil Clark	.10	.05
□ 137	Mark Ettles	.10	.05
□ 138	Jeff Gardner	.10	.05
□ 139	Pat Gomez	.10	.05
□ 140	Ricky Gutierrez	.10	.05
□ 141	Gene Harris	.10	.05
□ 142	Kevin Higgins	.10	.05
□ 143	Trevor Hoffman	.30	.14
□ 144	Phil Plantier	.10	.05
□ 145	Kerry Taylor	.10	.05
□ 146	Guillermo Velasquez	.10	.05
□ 147	Wally Whitehurst	.10	.05
□ 148	Tim Worrell	.10	.05
□ 149	Todd Benzinger	.10	.05
□ 150	Barry Bonds	.50	.23
□ 151	Greg Brummett	.10	.05
□ 152	Mark Carreon	.10	.05
□ 153	Dave Martinez	.10	.05
□ 154	Jeff Reed	.10	.05
□ 155	Kevin Rogers	.10	.05
□ 156	Harold Baines	.20	.09
□ 157	Damon Buford	.10	.05
□ 158	Paul Carey	.10	.05
□ 159	Jeffrey Hammonds	.30	.14
□ 160	Jamie Moyer	.10	.05
□ 161	Sherman Obando	.10	.05
□ 162	John O'Donoghue	.10	.05
□ 163	Brad Pennington	.10	.05
□ 164	Jim Poole	.10	.05
□ 165	Harold Reynolds	.10	.05
□ 166	Fernando Valenzuela	.20	.09
□ 167	Jack Voigt	.10	.05
□ 168	Mark Williamson	.10	.05
□ 169	Scott Bankhead	.10	.05
□ 170	Greg Blosser	.10	.05
□ 171	Jim Byrd	.10	.05
□ 172	Ivan Calderon	.10	.05
□ 173	Andre Dawson	.30	.14
□ 174	Scott Fletcher	.10	.05
□ 175	Jose Melendez	.10	.05
□ 176	Carlos Quintana	.10	.05
□ 177	Jeff Russell	.10	.05
□ 178	Aaron Sele	.20	.09
□ 179	Rod Correia	.10	.05
□ 180	Chili Davis	.20	.09
□ 181	Jim Edmonds	1.00	.45
□ 182	Rene Gonzales	.10	.05
□ 183	Hilly Hathaway	.10	.05
□ 184	Torey Lovullo	.10	.05
□ 185	Greg Myers	.10	.05
□ 186	Gene Nelson	.10	.05
□ 187	Troy Percival	.20	.09
□ 188	Scott Sanderson	.10	.05
□ 189	Darryl Scott	.10	.05
□ 190	J.T. Snow	.50	.23
□ 191	Russ Springer	.10	.05
□ 192	Jason Bere	.20	.09
□ 193	Rodney Bolton	.10	.05
□ 194	Ellis Burks	.20	.09
□ 195	Bo Jackson	.20	.09
□ 196	Mike LaValliere	.10	.05
□ 197	Scott Ruffcorn	.10	.05
□ 198	Jeff Schwartz	.10	.05
□ 199	Jerry DiPoto	.10	.05
□ 200	Alvaro Espinoza	.10	.05
□ 201	Wayne Kirby	.10	.05
□ 202	Tom Kramer	.10	.05
□ 203	Jesse Levis	.10	.05
□ 204	Manny Ramirez	.75	.35
□ 205	Jeff Treadway	.10	.05
□ 206	Bill Wertz	.10	.05
□ 207	Cliff Young	.10	.05
□ 208	Matt Young	.10	.05
□ 209	Kirk Gibson	.20	.09

□ 210	Greg Gohr	.10	.05
□ 211	Bill Krueger	.10	.05
□ 212	Bob MacDonald	.10	.05
□ 213	Mike Moore	.10	.05
□ 214	David Wells	.10	.05
□ 215	Billy Brewer	.10	.05
□ 216	David Cone	.20	.09
□ 217	Greg Gagne	.10	.05
□ 218	Mark Gardner	.10	.05
□ 219	Chris Haney	.10	.05
□ 220	Phil Hiatt	.10	.05
□ 221	Jose Lind	.10	.05
□ 222	Juan Bell	.10	.05
□ 223	Tom Brunansky	.10	.05
□ 224	Mike Ignasiak	.10	.05
□ 225	Joe Kmak	.10	.05
□ 226	Tom Lampkin	.10	.05
□ 227	Graeme Lloyd	.10	.05
□ 228	Carlos Maldonado	.10	.05
□ 229	Matt Mieske	.20	.09
□ 230	Angel Miranda	.10	.05
□ 231	Troy O'Leary	.20	.09
□ 232	Kevin Reimer	.10	.05
□ 233	Larry Casian	.10	.05
□ 234	Jim Deshaies	.10	.05
□ 235	Eddie Guardado	.10	.05
□ 236	Chip Hale	.10	.05
□ 237	Mike Maksudian	.10	.05
□ 238	David McCarty	.10	.05
□ 239	Pat Meares	.20	.09
□ 240	George Tsamis	.10	.05
□ 241	Dave Winfield	.30	.14
□ 242	Jim Abbott	.20	.09
□ 243	Wade Boggs	.40	.18
□ 244	Andy Cook	.10	.05
□ 245	Russ Davis	.40	.18
□ 246	Mike Humphreys	.10	.05
□ 247	Jimmy Key	.20	.09
□ 248	Jim Leyritz	.10	.05
□ 249	Bobby Munoz	.10	.05
□ 250	Paul O'Neill	.20	.09
□ 251	Spike Owen	.10	.05
□ 252	Dave Silvestri	.10	.05
□ 253	Marcos Armas	.10	.05
□ 254	Brent Gates	.20	.09
□ 255	Goose Gossage	.20	.09
□ 256	Scott Lydy	.10	.05
□ 257	Henry Mercedes	.10	.05
□ 258	Mike Mohler	.10	.05
□ 259	Troy Neel	.10	.05
□ 260	Edwin Nunez	.10	.05
□ 261	Craig Paquette	.10	.05
□ 262	Kevin Seitzer	.10	.05
□ 263	Rich Amaral	.10	.05
□ 264	Mike Blowers	.10	.05
□ 265	Chris Bosio	.10	.05
□ 266	Norm Charlton	.10	.05
□ 267	Jim Converse	.10	.05
□ 268	John Cummings	.10	.05
□ 269	Mike Felder	.10	.05
□ 270	Mike Hampton	.30	.14
□ 271	Bill Haselman	.10	.05
□ 272	Dwayne Henry	.10	.05
□ 273	Greg Litton	.10	.05
□ 274	Mackey Sasser	.10	.05
□ 275	Lee Tinsley	.20	.09
□ 276	David Wainhouse	.10	.05
□ 277	Jeff Bronkey	.10	.05
□ 278	Benji Gil	.10	.05
□ 279	Tom Henke	.10	.05
□ 280	Charlie Leibrandt	.10	.05
□ 281	Robb Nen	.30	.14
□ 282	Bill Ripken	.10	.05
□ 283	Jon Shave	.10	.05
□ 284	Doug Strange	.10	.05
□ 285	Matt Whiteside	.10	.05
□ 286	Scott Brow	.10	.05
□ 287	Willie Canate	.10	.05
□ 288	Tony Castillo	.10	.05
□ 289	Domingo Cedeno	.10	.05
□ 290	Darnell Coles	.10	.05
□ 291	Danny Cox	.10	.05
□ 292	Mark Eichhorn	.10	.05
□ 293	Tony Fernandez	.10	.05
□ 294	Al Leiter	.20	.09
□ 295	Paul Molitor	.40	.18

□ 296	Dave Stewart	.20	.09
□ 297	Woody Williams	.10	.05
□ 298	Checklist F1-F100	.10	.05
□ 299	Checklist F101-F200	.10	.05
□ 300	Checklist F201-F300	.10	.05

1993 Fleer Final Edition Diamond Tribute

Each Fleer Final Edition factory set contained a complete 10-card set of Diamond Tribute inserts. These cards are numbered separately and feature a totally different design from the base cards. Each horizontally-designed Diamond Tribute card front features UV coating and two player images (one chest up and one full body action shot) set against the background of a blurred crowd. The set highlights a selection of top active veterans. Each card is numbered X of 10 on back.

	MINT	NRMT
COMPLETE SET (10)	4.00	1.80
COMMON CARD (1-10)	.20	.09
ONE SET PER FINAL EDITION FACTORY SET		

□ 1	Wade Boggs	.50	.23
□ 2	George Brett	1.25	.55
□ 3	Andre Dawson	.30	.14
□ 4	Carlton Fisk	.50	.23
□ 5	Paul Molitor	.50	.23
□ 6	Nolan Ryan	2.00	.90
□ 7	Lee Smith	.20	.09
□ 8	Ozzie Smith	.75	.35
□ 9	Dave Winfield	.30	.14
□ 10	Robin Yount	.30	.14

1994 Fleer

The 1994 Fleer baseball set consists of 720 standard-size

cards. The white-bordered fronts feature color player action photos. In one corner, the player's name and position appear in a gold foil lettered arc; his team logo appears within. The backs are also white-bordered and feature a color player photo, some action, others posed. One side of the picture is ghosted and color-screened, and carries the player's name, biography, and career highlights. The bottom of the picture is also color-screened and ghosted, and carries the player's statistics. The cards are numbered on the back, grouped alphabetically within teams, and checklisted below alphabetically according to teams for each league with AL preceding NL. The set closes with a Superstar Specials (706-713) subset. There are no key Rookie Cards in this set.

	MINT	NRMT
COMPLETE SET (720)	50.00	22.00
COMMON CARD (1-720)	.15	.07
MINOR STARS	.30	.14
UNLISTED STARS	.60	.25
COMP.ALL-ROOKIE SET (9)	8.00	3.60
ONE SET PER EXCHANGE CARD VIA MAIL		
COMP.SALMON SET (12)	25.00	11.00
COMMON SALMON (1-12)	2.50	1.10
CERTIFIED SALMON AUTO	80.00	36.00
SALMON: RANDOM INSERTS IN ALL PACKS		
COMMON SALMON.EXCH. (13-15)	2.50	1.10
SALMON EXCH.AVAIL.VIA WRAPPER EXCH.		

□	1	Brady Anderson	.40	.18
□	2	Harold Baines	.30	.14
□	3	Mike Devereaux	.15	.07
□	4	Todd Frohwirth	.15	.07
□	5	Jeffrey Hammonds	.30	.14
□	6	Chris Hoiles	.15	.07
□	7	Tim Hulett	.15	.07
□	8	Ben McDonald	.15	.07
□	9	Mark McLemore	.15	.07
□	10	Alan Mills	.15	.07
□	11	Jamie Moyer	.15	.07
□	12	Mike Mussina	.60	.25
□	13	Gregg Olson	.15	.07
□	14	Mike Pagliarulo	.15	.07
□	15	Brad Pennington	.15	.07
□	16	Jim Poole	.15	.07
□	17	Harold Reynolds	.15	.07
□	18	Arthur Rhodes	.15	.07
□	19	Cal Ripken Jr.	2.50	1.10
□	20	David Segui	.15	.07
□	21	Rick Sutcliffe	.15	.07
□	22	Fernando Valenzuela	.30	.14
□	23	Jack Voigt	.15	.07
□	24	Mark Williamson	.15	.07
□	25	Scott Bankhead	.15	.07
□	26	Roger Clemens	1.25	.55
□	27	Scott Cooper	.15	.07
□	28	Danny Darwin	.15	.07
□	29	Andre Dawson	.40	.18
□	30	Rob Deer	.15	.07
□	31	John Dopson	.15	.07
□	32	Scott Fletcher	.15	.07
□	33	Mike Greenwell	.15	.07
□	34	Greg A. Harris	.15	.07
□	35	Billy Hatcher	.15	.07
□	36	Bob Melvin	.15	.07
□	37	Tony Pena	.15	.07
□	38	Paul Quantrill	.15	.07
□	39	Carlos Quintana	.15	.07
□	40	Ernest Riles	.15	.07
□	41	Jeff Russell	.15	.07
□	42	Ken Ryan	.15	.07
□	43	Aaron Sele	.15	.07
□	44	John Valentin	.30	.14
□	45	Mo Vaughn	.75	.35
□	46	Frank Viola	.15	.07
□	47	Bob Zupcic	.15	.07
□	48	Mike Butcher	.15	.07
□	49	Rod Correia	.15	.07
□	50	Chad Curtis	.15	.07
□	51	Chili Davis	.30	.14
□	52	Gary DiSarcina	.15	.07
□	53	Damion Easley	.15	.07
□	54	Jim Edmonds	.60	.25
□	55	Chuck Finley	.15	.07
□	56	Steve Frey	.15	.07
□	57	Rene Gonzales	.15	.07
□	58	Joe Grahe	.15	.07
□	59	Hilly Hathaway	.15	.07
□	60	Stan Javier	.15	.07
□	61	Mark Langston	.15	.07
□	62	Phil Leftwich	.15	.07
□	63	Torey Lovullo	.15	.07
□	64	Joe Magrane	.15	.07
□	65	Greg Myers	.15	.07
□	66	Ken Patterson	.15	.07
□	67	Eduardo Perez	.15	.07
□	68	Luis Polonia	.15	.07
□	69	Tim Salmon	.60	.25
□	70	J.T. Snow	.60	.25
□	71	Ron Tingley	.15	.07
□	72	Julio Valera	.15	.07
□	73	Wilson Alvarez	.15	.07
□	74	Tim Belcher	.15	.07
□	75	George Bell	.15	.07
□	76	Jason Bere	.15	.07
□	77	Rod Bolton	.15	.07
□	78	Ellis Burks	.30	.14
□	79	Joey Cora	.30	.14
□	80	Alex Fernandez	.15	.07
□	81	Craig Grebeck	.15	.07
□	82	Ozzie Guillen	.15	.07
□	83	Roberto Hernandez	.15	.07
□	84	Bo Jackson	.30	.14
□	85	Lance Johnson	.15	.07
□	86	Ron Karkovice	.15	.07
□	87	Mike LaValliere	.15	.07
□	88	Kirk McCaskill	.15	.07
□	89	Jack McDowell	.15	.07
□	90	Warren Newson	.15	.07
□	91	Dan Pasqua	.15	.07
□	92	Scott Radinsky	.15	.07
□	93	Tim Raines	.30	.14
□	94	Steve Sax	.15	.07
□	95	Jeff Schwarz	.15	.07
□	96	Frank Thomas	2.50	1.10
□	97	Robin Ventura	.30	.14
□	98	Sandy Alomar Jr.	.30	.14
□	99	Carlos Baerga	.15	.07
□	100	Albert Belle	.75	.35
□	101	Mark Clark	.15	.07
□	102	Jerry DiPoto	.15	.07
□	103	Alvaro Espinoza	.15	.07
□	104	Felix Fermin	.15	.07
□	105	Jeremy Hernandez	.15	.07
□	106	Reggie Jefferson	.15	.07
□	107	Wayne Kirby	.15	.07
□	108	Tom Kramer	.15	.07
□	109	Mark Lewis	.15	.07
□	110	Derek Lilliquist	.15	.07
□	111	Kenny Lofton	.75	.35
□	112	Candy Maldonado	.15	.07
□	113	Jose Mesa	.15	.07
□	114	Jeff Mutis	.15	.07
□	115	Charles Nagy	.30	.14
□	116	Bob Ojeda	.15	.07
□	117	Junior Ortiz	.15	.07
□	118	Eric Plunk	.15	.07
□	119	Manny Ramirez	.75	.35
□	120	Paul Sorrento	.15	.07
□	121	Jim Thome	.75	.35
□	122	Jeff Treadway	.15	.07
□	123	Bill Wertz	.15	.07
□	124	Skeeter Barnes	.15	.07
□	125	Milt Cuyler	.15	.07
□	126	Eric Davis	.30	.14
□	127	John Doherty	.15	.07
□	128	Cecil Fielder	.30	.14
□	129	Travis Fryman	.30	.14
□	130	Kirk Gibson	.15	.07
□	131	Dan Gladden	.15	.07
□	132	Greg Gohr	.15	.07
□	133	Chris Gomez	.15	.07
□	134	Bill Gullickson	.15	.07
□	135	Mike Henneman	.15	.07
□	136	Kurt Knudsen	.15	.07
□	137	Chad Kreuter	.15	.07
□	138	Bill Krueger	.15	.07
□	139	Scott Livingstone	.15	.07
□	140	Bob MacDonald	.15	.07
□	141	Mike Moore	.15	.07
□	142	Tony Phillips	.15	.07
□	143	Mickey Tettleton	.15	.07
□	144	Alan Trammell	.40	.18
□	145	David Wells	.15	.07
□	146	Lou Whitaker	.30	.14
□	147	Kevin Appier	.30	.14
□	148	Stan Belinda	.15	.07
□	149	George Brett	1.25	.55
□	150	Billy Brewer	.15	.07
□	151	Hubie Brooks	.15	.07
□	152	David Cone	.30	.14
□	153	Gary Gaetti	.15	.07
□	154	Greg Gagne	.15	.07
□	155	Tom Gordon	.15	.07
□	156	Mark Gubicza	.15	.07
□	157	Chris Gwynn	.15	.07
□	158	John Habyan	.15	.07
□	159	Chris Haney	.15	.07
□	160	Phil Hiatt	.15	.07
□	161	Felix Jose	.15	.07
□	162	Wally Joyner	.30	.14
□	163	Jose Lind	.15	.07
□	164	Mike Macfarlane	.15	.07
□	165	Mike Magnante	.15	.07
□	166	Brent Mayne	.15	.07
□	167	Brian McRae	.15	.07
□	168	Kevin McReynolds	.15	.07
□	169	Keith Miller	.15	.07
□	170	Jeff Montgomery	.15	.07
□	171	Hipolito Pichardo	.15	.07
□	172	Rico Rossy	.15	.07
□	173	Juan Bell	.15	.07
□	174	Ricky Bones	.15	.07
□	175	Cal Eldred	.15	.07
□	176	Mike Fetters	.15	.07
□	177	Darryl Hamilton	.15	.07
□	178	Doug Henry	.15	.07
□	179	Mike Ignasiak	.15	.07
□	180	John Jaha	.15	.07
□	181	Pat Listach	.15	.07
□	182	Graeme Lloyd	.15	.07
□	183	Matt Mieske	.15	.07
□	184	Angel Miranda	.15	.07
□	185	Jaime Navarro	.15	.07
□	186	Dave Nilsson	.15	.07
□	187	Troy O'Leary	.15	.07
□	188	Jesse Orosco	.15	.07
□	189	Kevin Reimer	.15	.07
□	190	Kevin Seitzer	.15	.07
□	191	Bill Spiers	.15	.07
□	192	B.J. Surhoff	.15	.07
□	193	Dickie Thon	.15	.07
□	194	Jose Valentin	.15	.07
□	195	Greg Vaughn	.15	.07
□	196	Bill Wegman	.15	.07
□	197	Robin Yount	.40	.18
□	198	Rick Aguilera	.15	.07
□	199	Willie Banks	.15	.07
□	200	Bernardo Brito	.15	.07
□	201	Larry Casian	.15	.07
□	202	Scott Erickson	.15	.07
□	203	Eddie Guardado	.15	.07
□	204	Mark Guthrie	.15	.07
□	205	Chip Hale	.15	.07
□	206	Brian Harper	.15	.07
□	207	Mike Hartley	.15	.07
□	208	Kent Hrbek	.30	.14
□	209	Terry Jorgensen	.15	.07
□	210	Chuck Knoblauch	.60	.25
□	211	Gene Larkin	.15	.07
□	212	Shane Mack	.15	.07
□	213	David McCarty	.15	.07
□	214	Pat Meares	.15	.07
□	215	Pedro Munoz	.15	.07
□	216	Derek Parks	.15	.07
□	217	Kirby Puckett	1.25	.55
□	218	Jeff Reboulet	.15	.07

219	Kevin Tapani	.15	.07
220	Mike Trombley	.15	.07
221	George Tsamis	.15	.07
222	Carl Willis	.15	.07
223	Dave Winfield	.40	.18
224	Jim Abbott	.15	.07
225	Paul Assenmacher	.15	.07
226	Wade Boggs	.60	.25
227	Russ Davis	.30	.14
228	Steve Farr	.15	.07
229	Mike Gallego	.15	.07
230	Paul Gibson	.15	.07
231	Steve Howe	.15	.07
232	Dion James	.15	.07
233	Domingo Jean	.15	.07
234	Scott Kamieniecki	.15	.07
235	Pat Kelly	.15	.07
236	Jimmy Key	.30	.14
237	Jim Leyritz	.15	.07
238	Kevin Maas	.15	.07
239	Don Mattingly	1.00	.45
240	Rich Monteleone	.15	.07
241	Bobby Munoz	.15	.07
242	Matt Nokes	.15	.07
243	Paul O'Neill	.30	.14
244	Spike Owen	.15	.07
245	Melido Perez	.15	.07
246	Lee Smith	.30	.14
247	Mike Stanley	.15	.07
248	Danny Tartabull	.15	.07
249	Randy Velarde	.15	.07
250	Bob Wickman	.15	.07
251	Bernie Williams	.60	.25
252	Mike Aldrete	.15	.07
253	Marcos Armas	.15	.07
254	Lance Blankenship	.15	.07
255	Mike Bordick	.15	.07
256	Scott Brosius	.15	.07
257	Jerry Browne	.15	.07
258	Ron Darling	.15	.07
259	Kelly Downs	.15	.07
260	Dennis Eckersley	.30	.14
261	Brent Gates	.15	.07
262	Goose Gossage	.30	.14
263	Scott Hemond	.15	.07
264	Dave Henderson	.15	.07
265	Rick Honeycutt	.15	.07
266	Vince Horsman	.15	.07
267	Scott Lydy	.15	.07
268	Mark McGwire	1.25	.55
269	Mike Mohler	.15	.07
270	Troy Neel	.15	.07
271	Edwin Nunez	.15	.07
272	Craig Paquette	.15	.07
273	Ruben Sierra	.15	.07
274	Terry Steinbach	.15	.07
275	Todd Van Poppel	.15	.07
276	Bob Welch	.15	.07
277	Bobby Witt	.15	.07
278	Rich Amaral	.15	.07
279	Mike Blowers	.15	.07
280	Bret Boone UER	.15	.07
	(Name spelled Brett on front)		
281	Chris Bosio	.15	.07
282	Jay Buhner	.40	.18
283	Norm Charlton	.15	.07
284	Mike Felder	.15	.07
285	Dave Fleming	.15	.07
286	Ken Griffey Jr.	3.00	1.35
287	Erik Hanson	.15	.07
288	Bill Haselman	.15	.07
289	Brad Holman	.15	.07
290	Randy Johnson	.60	.25
291	Tim Leary	.15	.07
292	Greg Litton	.15	.07
293	Dave Magadan	.15	.07
294	Edgar Martinez	.40	.18
295	Tino Martinez	.60	.25
296	Jeff Nelson	.15	.07
297	Erik Plantenberg	.15	.07
298	Mackey Sasser	.15	.07
299	Brian Turang	.15	.07
300	Dave Valle	.15	.07
301	Omar Vizquel	.30	.14
302	Brian Bohanon	.15	.07
303	Kevin Brown	.30	.14
304	Jose Canseco UER	.40	.18
	(Back mentions 1991 as his 40/40 MVP season; should be '88)		
305	Mario Diaz	.15	.07
306	Julio Franco	.15	.07
307	Juan Gonzalez	1.50	.70
308	Tom Henke	.15	.07
309	David Hulse	.15	.07
310	Manuel Lee	.15	.07
311	Craig Lefferts	.15	.07
312	Charlie Leibrandt	.15	.07
313	Rafael Palmeiro	.40	.18
314	Dean Palmer	.15	.07
315	Roger Pavlik	.15	.07
316	Dan Peltier	.15	.07
317	Gene Petralli	.15	.07
318	Gary Redus	.15	.07
319	Ivan Rodriguez	.75	.35
320	Kenny Rogers	.15	.07
321	Nolan Ryan	2.50	1.10
322	Doug Strange	.15	.07
323	Matt Whiteside	.15	.07
324	Roberto Alomar	.60	.25
325	Pat Borders	.15	.07
326	Joe Carter	.30	.14
327	Tony Castillo	.15	.07
328	Darnell Coles	.15	.07
329	Danny Cox	.15	.07
330	Mark Eichhorn	.15	.07
331	Tony Fernandez	.15	.07
332	Alfredo Griffin	.15	.07
333	Juan Guzman	.15	.07
334	Rickey Henderson	.40	.18
335	Pat Hentgen	.30	.14
336	Randy Knorr	.15	.07
337	Al Leiter	.15	.07
338	Paul Molitor	.60	.25
339	Jack Morris	.30	.14
340	John Olerud	.30	.14
341	Dick Schofield	.15	.07
342	Ed Sprague	.15	.07
343	Dave Stewart	.30	.14
344	Todd Stottlemyre	.15	.07
345	Mike Timlin	.15	.07
346	Duane Ward	.15	.07
347	Turner Ward	.15	.07
348	Devon White	.15	.07
349	Woody Williams	.15	.07
350	Steve Avery	.30	.14
351	Steve Bedrosian	.15	.07
352	Rafael Belliard	.15	.07
353	Damon Berryhill	.15	.07
354	Jeff Blauser	.30	.14
355	Sid Bream	.15	.07
356	Francisco Cabrera	.15	.07
357	Marvin Freeman	.15	.07
358	Ron Gant	.30	.14
359	Tom Glavine	.30	.14
360	Jay Howell	.15	.07
361	David Justice	.60	.25
362	Ryan Klesko	.60	.25
363	Mark Lemke	.15	.07
364	Javier Lopez	.40	.18
365	Greg Maddux	2.00	.90
366	Fred McGriff	.40	.18
367	Greg McMichael	.15	.07
368	Kent Mercker	.15	.07
369	Otis Nixon	.15	.07
370	Greg Olson	.15	.07
371	Bill Pecota	.15	.07
372	Terry Pendleton	.30	.14
373	Deion Sanders	.30	.14
374	Pete Smith	.15	.07
375	John Smoltz	.30	.14
376	Mike Stanton	.15	.07
377	Tony Tarasco	.15	.07
378	Mark Wohlers	.15	.07
379	Jose Bautista	.15	.07
380	Shawn Boskie	.15	.07
381	Steve Buechele	.15	.07
382	Frank Castillo	.15	.07
383	Mark Grace	.40	.18
384	Jose Guzman	.15	.07
385	Mike Harkey	.15	.07
386	Greg Hibbard	.15	.07
387	Glenallen Hill	.15	.07
388	Steve Lake	.15	.07
389	Derrick May	.15	.07
390	Chuck McElroy	.15	.07
391	Mike Morgan	.15	.07
392	Randy Myers	.15	.07
393	Dan Plesac	.15	.07
394	Kevin Roberson	.15	.07
395	Rey Sanchez	.15	.07
396	Ryne Sandberg	.75	.35
397	Bob Scanlan	.15	.07
398	Dwight Smith	.15	.07
399	Sammy Sosa	.60	.25
400	Jose Vizcaino	.15	.07
401	Rick Wilkins	.15	.07
402	Willie Wilson	.15	.07
403	Eric Yelding	.15	.07
404	Bobby Ayala	.15	.07
405	Jeff Branson	.15	.07
406	Tom Browning	.15	.07
407	Jacob Brumfield	.15	.07
408	Tim Costo	.15	.07
409	Rob Dibble	.15	.07
410	Willie Greene	.15	.07
411	Thomas Howard	.15	.07
412	Roberto Kelly	.15	.07
413	Bill Landrum	.15	.07
414	Barry Larkin	.40	.18
415	Larry Luebbers	.15	.07
416	Kevin Mitchell	.15	.07
417	Hal Morris	.15	.07
418	Joe Oliver	.15	.07
419	Tim Pugh	.15	.07
420	Jeff Reardon	.30	.14
421	Jose Rijo	.15	.07
422	Bip Roberts	.15	.07
423	John Roper	.15	.07
424	Johnny Ruffin	.15	.07
425	Chris Sabo	.15	.07
426	Juan Samuel	.15	.07
427	Reggie Sanders	.15	.07
428	Scott Service	.15	.07
429	John Smiley	.15	.07
430	Jerry Spradlin	.15	.07
431	Kevin Wickander	.15	.07
432	Freddie Benavides	.15	.07
433	Dante Bichette	.30	.14
434	Willie Blair	.15	.07
435	Daryl Boston	.15	.07
436	Kent Bottenfield	.15	.07
437	Vinny Castilla	.30	.14
438	Jerald Clark	.15	.07
439	Alex Cole	.15	.07
440	Andres Galarraga	.60	.25
441	Joe Girardi	.15	.07
442	Greg W. Harris	.15	.07
443	Charlie Hayes	.15	.07
444	Darren Holmes	.15	.07
445	Chris Jones	.15	.07
446	Roberto Mejia	.15	.07
447	David Nied	.15	.07
448	J. Owens	.15	.07
449	Jeff Parrett	.15	.07
450	Steve Reed	.15	.07
451	Armando Reynoso	.15	.07
452	Bruce Ruffin	.15	.07
453	Mo Sanford	.15	.07
454	Danny Sheaffer	.15	.07
455	Jim Tatum	.15	.07
456	Gary Wayne	.15	.07
457	Eric Young	.15	.07
458	Luis Aquino	.15	.07
459	Alex Arias	.15	.07
460	Jack Armstrong	.15	.07
461	Bret Barberie	.15	.07
462	Ryan Bowen	.15	.07
463	Chuck Carr	.15	.07
464	Jeff Conine	.30	.14
465	Henry Cotto	.15	.07
466	Orestes Destrade	.15	.07
467	Chris Hammond	.15	.07
468	Bryan Harvey	.15	.07
469	Charlie Hough	.15	.07
470	Joe Klink	.15	.07
471	Richie Lewis	.15	.07
472	Bob Natal	.15	.07
473	Pat Rapp	.15	.07

☐ 474 Rich Renteria	.15	.07	
☐ 475 Rich Rodriguez	.15	.07	
☐ 476 Benito Santiago	.15	.07	
☐ 477 Gary Sheffield	.60	.25	
☐ 478 Matt Turner	.15	.07	
☐ 479 David Weathers	.15	.07	
☐ 480 Walt Weiss	.15	.07	
☐ 481 Darrell Whitmore	.15	.07	
☐ 482 Eric Anthony	.15	.07	
☐ 483 Jeff Bagwell	1.25	.55	
☐ 484 Kevin Bass	.15	.07	
☐ 485 Craig Biggio	.40	.18	
☐ 486 Ken Caminiti	.40	.18	
☐ 487 Andujar Cedeno	.15	.07	
☐ 488 Chris Donnels	.15	.07	
☐ 489 Doug Drabek	.15	.07	
☐ 490 Steve Finley	.30	.14	
☐ 491 Luis Gonzalez	.15	.07	
☐ 492 Pete Harnisch	.15	.07	
☐ 493 Xavier Hernandez	.15	.07	
☐ 494 Doug Jones	.15	.07	
☐ 495 Todd Jones	.15	.07	
☐ 496 Darryl Kile	.30	.14	
☐ 497 Al Osuna	.15	.07	
☐ 498 Mark Portugal	.15	.07	
☐ 499 Scott Servais	.15	.07	
☐ 500 Greg Swindell	.15	.07	
☐ 501 Eddie Taubensee	.15	.07	
☐ 502 Jose Uribe	.15	.07	
☐ 503 Brian Williams	.15	.07	
☐ 504 Billy Ashley	.15	.07	
☐ 505 Pedro Astacio	.15	.07	
☐ 506 Brett Butler	.30	.14	
☐ 507 Tom Candiotti	.15	.07	
☐ 508 Omar Daal	.15	.07	
☐ 509 Jim Gott	.15	.07	
☐ 510 Kevin Gross	.15	.07	
☐ 511 Dave Hansen	.15	.07	
☐ 512 Carlos Hernandez	.15	.07	
☐ 513 Orel Hershiser	.30	.14	
☐ 514 Eric Karros	.30	.14	
☐ 515 Pedro Martinez	.60	.25	
☐ 516 Ramon Martinez	.30	.14	
☐ 517 Roger McDowell	.15	.07	
☐ 518 Raul Mondesi	.60	.25	
☐ 519 Jose Offerman	.15	.07	
☐ 520 Mike Piazza	2.00	.90	
☐ 521 Jody Reed	.15	.07	
☐ 522 Henry Rodriguez	.15	.07	
☐ 523 Mike Sharperson	.15	.07	
☐ 524 Cory Snyder	.15	.07	
☐ 525 Darryl Strawberry	.30	.14	
☐ 526 Rick Trlicek	.15	.07	
☐ 527 Tim Wallach	.15	.07	
☐ 528 Mitch Webster	.15	.07	
☐ 529 Steve Wilson	.15	.07	
☐ 530 Todd Worrell	.15	.07	
☐ 531 Moises Alou	.30	.14	
☐ 532 Brian Barnes	.15	.07	
☐ 533 Sean Berry	.15	.07	
☐ 534 Greg Colbrunn	.15	.07	
☐ 535 Delino DeShields	.15	.07	
☐ 536 Jeff Fassero	.15	.07	
☐ 537 Darrin Fletcher	.15	.07	
☐ 538 Cliff Floyd	.30	.14	
☐ 539 Lou Frazier	.15	.07	
☐ 540 Marquis Grissom	.30	.14	
☐ 541 Butch Henry	.15	.07	
☐ 542 Ken Hill	.15	.07	
☐ 543 Mike Lansing	.30	.14	
☐ 544 Brian Looney	.15	.07	
☐ 545 Dennis Martinez	.30	.14	
☐ 546 Chris Nabholz	.15	.07	
☐ 547 Randy Ready	.15	.07	
☐ 548 Mel Rojas	.15	.07	
☐ 549 Kirk Rueter	.15	.07	
☐ 550 Tim Scott	.15	.07	
☐ 551 Jeff Shaw	.15	.07	
☐ 552 Tim Spehr	.15	.07	
☐ 553 John VanderWal	.15	.07	
☐ 554 Larry Walker	.60	.25	
☐ 555 John Wetteland	.15	.07	
☐ 556 Rondell White	.40	.18	
☐ 557 Tim Bogar	.15	.07	
☐ 558 Bobby Bonilla	.30	.14	
☐ 559 Jeromy Burnitz	.15	.07	
☐ 560 Sid Fernandez	.15	.07	
☐ 561 John Franco	.30	.14	
☐ 562 Dave Gallagher	.15	.07	
☐ 563 Dwight Gooden	.30	.14	
☐ 564 Eric Hillman	.15	.07	
☐ 565 Todd Hundley	.30	.14	
☐ 566 Jeff Innis	.15	.07	
☐ 567 Darrin Jackson	.15	.07	
☐ 568 Howard Johnson	.15	.07	
☐ 569 Bobby Jones	.30	.14	
☐ 570 Jeff Kent	.15	.07	
☐ 571 Mike Maddux	.15	.07	
☐ 572 Jeff McKnight	.15	.07	
☐ 573 Eddie Murray	.60	.25	
☐ 574 Charlie O'Brien	.15	.07	
☐ 575 Joe Orsulak	.15	.07	
☐ 576 Bret Saberhagen	.15	.07	
☐ 577 Pete Schourek	.15	.07	
☐ 578 Dave Telgheder	.15	.07	
☐ 579 Ryan Thompson	.15	.07	
☐ 580 Anthony Young	.15	.07	
☐ 581 Ruben Amaro	.15	.07	
☐ 582 Larry Andersen	.15	.07	
☐ 583 Kim Batiste	.15	.07	
☐ 584 Wes Chamberlain	.15	.07	
☐ 585 Darren Daulton	.30	.14	
☐ 586 Mariano Duncan	.15	.07	
☐ 587 Lenny Dykstra	.30	.14	
☐ 588 Jim Eisenreich	.15	.07	
☐ 589 Tommy Greene	.15	.07	
☐ 590 Dave Hollins	.15	.07	
☐ 591 Pete Incaviglia	.15	.07	
☐ 592 Danny Jackson	.15	.07	
☐ 593 Ricky Jordan	.15	.07	
☐ 594 John Kruk	.30	.14	
☐ 595 Roger Mason	.15	.07	
☐ 596 Mickey Morandini	.15	.07	
☐ 597 Terry Mulholland	.15	.07	
☐ 598 Todd Pratt	.15	.07	
☐ 599 Ben Rivera	.15	.07	
☐ 600 Curt Schilling	.30	.14	
☐ 601 Kevin Stocker	.15	.07	
☐ 602 Milt Thompson	.15	.07	
☐ 603 David West	.15	.07	
☐ 604 Mitch Williams	.15	.07	
☐ 605 Jay Bell	.30	.14	
☐ 606 Dave Clark	.15	.07	
☐ 607 Steve Cooke	.15	.07	
☐ 608 Tom Foley	.15	.07	
☐ 609 Carlos Garcia	.15	.07	
☐ 610 Joel Johnston	.15	.07	
☐ 611 Jeff King	.15	.07	
☐ 612 Al Martin	.15	.07	
☐ 613 Lloyd McClendon	.15	.07	
☐ 614 Orlando Merced	.15	.07	
☐ 615 Blas Minor	.15	.07	
☐ 616 Denny Neagle	.30	.14	
☐ 617 Mark Petkovsek	.15	.07	
☐ 618 Tom Prince	.15	.07	
☐ 619 Don Slaught	.15	.07	
☐ 620 Zane Smith	.15	.07	
☐ 621 Randy Tomlin	.15	.07	
☐ 622 Andy Van Slyke	.30	.14	
☐ 623 Paul Wagner	.15	.07	
☐ 624 Tim Wakefield	.15	.07	
☐ 625 Bob Walk	.15	.07	
☐ 626 Kevin Young	.15	.07	
☐ 627 Luis Alicea	.15	.07	
☐ 628 Rene Arocha	.15	.07	
☐ 629 Rod Brewer	.15	.07	
☐ 630 Rheal Cormier	.15	.07	
☐ 631 Bernard Gilkey	.15	.07	
☐ 632 Lee Guetterman	.15	.07	
☐ 633 Gregg Jefferies	.15	.07	
☐ 634 Brian Jordan	.30	.14	
☐ 635 Les Lancaster	.15	.07	
☐ 636 Ray Lankford	.30	.14	
☐ 637 Rob Murphy	.15	.07	
☐ 638 Omar Olivares	.15	.07	
☐ 639 Jose Oquendo	.15	.07	
☐ 640 Donovan Osborne	.15	.07	
☐ 641 Tom Pagnozzi	.15	.07	
☐ 642 Erik Pappas	.15	.07	
☐ 643 Geronimo Pena	.15	.07	
☐ 644 Mike Perez	.15	.07	
☐ 645 Gerald Perry	.15	.07	
☐ 646 Ozzie Smith	.75	.35	
☐ 647 Bob Tewksbury	.15	.07	
☐ 648 Allen Watson	.15	.07	
☐ 649 Mark Whiten	.15	.07	
☐ 650 Tracy Woodson	.15	.07	
☐ 651 Todd Zeile	.15	.07	
☐ 652 Andy Ashby	.15	.07	
☐ 653 Brad Ausmus	.15	.07	
☐ 654 Billy Bean	.15	.07	
☐ 655 Derek Bell	.15	.07	
☐ 656 Andy Benes	.30	.14	
☐ 657 Doug Brocail	.15	.07	
☐ 658 Jarvis Brown	.15	.07	
☐ 659 Archi Cianfrocco	.15	.07	
☐ 660 Phil Clark	.15	.07	
☐ 661 Mark Davis	.15	.07	
☐ 662 Jeff Gardner	.15	.07	
☐ 663 Pat Gomez	.15	.07	
☐ 664 Ricky Gutierrez	.15	.07	
☐ 665 Tony Gwynn	1.50	.70	
☐ 666 Gene Harris	.15	.07	
☐ 667 Kevin Higgins	.15	.07	
☐ 668 Trevor Hoffman	.15	.07	
☐ 669 Pedro Martinez	.15	.07	
☐ 670 Tim Mauser	.15	.07	
☐ 671 Melvin Nieves	.15	.07	
☐ 672 Phil Plantier	.15	.07	
☐ 673 Frank Seminara	.15	.07	
☐ 674 Craig Shipley	.15	.07	
☐ 675 Kerry Taylor	.15	.07	
☐ 676 Tim Teufel	.15	.07	
☐ 677 Guillermo Velasquez	.15	.07	
☐ 678 Wally Whitehurst	.15	.07	
☐ 679 Tim Worrell	.15	.07	
☐ 680 Rod Beck	.15	.07	
☐ 681 Mike Benjamin	.15	.07	
☐ 682 Todd Benzinger	.15	.07	
☐ 683 Bud Black	.15	.07	
☐ 684 Barry Bonds	.75	.35	
☐ 685 Jeff Brantley	.15	.07	
☐ 686 Dave Burba	.15	.07	
☐ 687 John Burkett	.15	.07	
☐ 688 Mark Carreon	.15	.07	
☐ 689 Will Clark	.40	.18	
☐ 690 Royce Clayton	.15	.07	
☐ 691 Bryan Hickerson	.15	.07	
☐ 692 Mike Jackson	.15	.07	
☐ 693 Darren Lewis	.15	.07	
☐ 694 Kirt Manwaring	.15	.07	
☐ 695 Dave Martinez	.15	.07	
☐ 696 Willie McGee	.15	.07	
☐ 697 John Patterson	.15	.07	
☐ 698 Jeff Reed	.15	.07	
☐ 699 Kevin Rogers	.15	.07	
☐ 700 Scott Sanderson	.15	.07	
☐ 701 Steve Scarsone	.15	.07	
☐ 702 Billy Swift	.15	.07	
☐ 703 Robby Thompson	.15	.07	
☐ 704 Matt Williams	.40	.18	
☐ 705 Trevor Wilson	.15	.07	
☐ 706 Brave New World	.60	.25	
	Fred McGriff		
	Ron Gant		
	David Justice		
☐ 707 1-2 Punch	.30	.14	
	John Olerud		
	Paul Molitor		
☐ 708 American Heat	.30	.14	
	Mike Mussina		
	Jack McDowell		
☐ 709 Together Again	.40	.18	
	Lou Whitaker		
	Alan Trammell		
☐ 710 Lone Star Lumber	.40	.18	
	Rafael Palmeiro		
	Juan Gonzalez		
☐ 711 Batmen	.40	.18	
	Brett Butler		
	Tony Gwynn		
☐ 712 Twin Peaks	.60	.25	
	Kirby Puckett		
	Chuck Knoblauch		
☐ 713 Back to Back	.75	.35	
	Mike Piazza		
	Eric Karros		
☐ 714 Checklist 1	.15	.07	

☐ 715 Checklist 2	.15	.07
☐ 716 Checklist 3	.15	.07
☐ 717 Checklist 4	.15	.07
☐ 718 Checklist 5	.15	.07
☐ 719 Checklist 6	.15	.07
☐ 720 Checklist 7	.15	.07
☐ P69 Tim Salmon Promo	1.00	.45

1994 Fleer All-Stars

Fleer issued this 50-card standard-size set in 1994, to commemorate the All-Stars of the 1993 season. The cards were exclusively available in the Fleer wax packs at a rate of one in two. The set features 25 American League (1-25) and 25 National League (26-50) All-Stars. The full-bleed fronts feature color action player cut-out photos with an American flag background. The player's name is stamped in gold foil along the bottom edge adjacent to a 1993 All-Stars Game logo. The borderless backs carry a similar flag background with a player head shot near the bottom. The player's name and career highlights round out the back. Each league's all-stars are sequenced in alphabetical order.

	MINT	NRMT
COMPLETE SET (50)	25.00	11.00
COMMON CARD (1-50)	.25	.11
RANDOM INSERTS IN ALL PACKS		

☐ 1 Roberto Alomar	.75	.35
☐ 2 Carlos Baerga	.25	.11
☐ 3 Albert Belle	1.00	.45
☐ 4 Wade Boggs	.75	.35
☐ 5 Joe Carter	.40	.18
☐ 6 Scott Cooper	.25	.11
☐ 7 Cecil Fielder	.40	.18
☐ 8 Travis Fryman	.40	.18
☐ 9 Juan Gonzalez	2.00	.90
☐ 10 Ken Griffey Jr.	4.00	1.80
☐ 11 Pat Hentgen	.40	.18
☐ 12 Randy Johnson	.75	.35
☐ 13 Jimmy Key	.40	.18
☐ 14 Mark Langston	.25	.11
☐ 15 Jack McDowell	.25	.11
☐ 16 Paul Molitor	.75	.35
☐ 17 Jeff Montgomery	.25	.11
☐ 18 Mike Mussina	.75	.35
☐ 19 John Olerud	.40	.18
☐ 20 Kirby Puckett	1.50	.70
☐ 21 Cal Ripken	3.00	1.35
☐ 22 Ivan Rodriguez	1.00	.45
☐ 23 Frank Thomas	3.00	1.35
☐ 24 Greg Vaughn	.25	.11
☐ 25 Duane Ward	.25	.11

☐ 26 Steve Avery	.25	.11
☐ 27 Rod Beck	.25	.11
☐ 28 Jay Bell	.40	.18
☐ 29 Andy Benes	.40	.18
☐ 30 Jeff Blauser	.40	.18
☐ 31 Barry Bonds	1.00	.45
☐ 32 Bobby Bonilla	.40	.18
☐ 33 John Burkett	.25	.11
☐ 34 Darren Daulton	.40	.18
☐ 35 Andres Galarraga	.75	.35
☐ 36 Tom Glavine	.40	.18
☐ 37 Mark Grace	.50	.23
☐ 38 Marquis Grissom	.40	.18
☐ 39 Tony Gwynn	2.00	.90
☐ 40 Bryan Harvey	.25	.11
☐ 41 Dave Hollins	.25	.11
☐ 42 David Justice	.75	.35
☐ 43 Darryl Kile	.40	.18
☐ 44 John Kruk	.40	.18
☐ 45 Barry Larkin	.50	.23
☐ 46 Terry Mulholland	.25	.11
☐ 47 Mike Piazza	2.50	1.10
☐ 48 Ryne Sandberg	1.00	.45
☐ 49 Gary Sheffield	.75	.35
☐ 50 John Smoltz	.40	.18

1994 Fleer Award Winners

Randomly inserted in foil packs at a rate of one in 37, this six-card standard-size set spotlights six outstanding players who received awards. Inside beige borders, the horizontal fronts feature three views of the same color player photo. The words "Fleer Award Winners" and the player's name are printed in gold foil toward the bottom. The backs have a similar design to the fronts, only with one color player cutout and a season summary.

	MINT	NRMT
COMPLETE SET (6)	12.00	5.50
COMMON CARD (1-6)	.25	.11
RANDOM INSERTS IN ALL PACKS		

☐ 1 Frank Thomas	4.00	1.80
☐ 2 Barry Bonds	1.25	.55
☐ 3 Jack McDowell	.25	.11
☐ 4 Greg Maddux	3.00	1.35
☐ 5 Tim Salmon	1.00	.45
☐ 6 Mike Piazza	3.00	1.35

1994 Fleer Golden Moments

These standard-size cards were issued one per blue retail jumbo pack. The fronts feature borderless color player action photos. A shrink-wrapped package con-

taining a jumbo set was issued one per Fleer hobby case. Jumbos were later issued for retail purposes. The production number out of a total of 10,000 appears near the bottom of the jumbos. The standard-size cards are not individually numbered.

	MINT	NRMT
COMPLETE SET (10)	40.00	18.00
COMMON CARD (1-10)	.75	.35
ONE PER BLUE RETAIL JUMBO PACK		
*JUMBOS: 5X TO 1X BASE CARD HI		
ONE JUMBO SET PER HOBBY CASE		

☐ 1 Mark Whiten	.75	.35
☐ 2 Carlos Baerga	.75	.35
☐ 3 Dave Winfield	1.50	.70
☐ 4 Ken Griffey Jr.	12.00	5.50
☐ 5 Bo Jackson	1.00	.45
☐ 6 George Brett	4.00	1.80
☐ 7 Nolan Ryan	10.00	4.50
☐ 8 Fred McGriff	1.50	.70
☐ 9 Frank Thomas	40.00	18.00
☐ 10 Chris Bosio	.75	.35
	Jim Abbott	
	Darryl Kile	

1994 Fleer League Leaders

Randomly inserted in all pack types at a rate of one in 17, this 28-card set features six statistical leaders each for the American (1-6) and the National (7-12) Leagues. Inside a beige border, the fronts feature color action player cutout superimposed on a black-and-white player photo. The player's name and the set title are gold foil stamped in the bottom border, while the player's achievement is printed vertically along the right edge of the picture. The horizontal backs have a color close-up shot on the left portion and a player summary on the right.

	MINT	NRMT
COMPLETE SET (12)	5.00	2.20
COMMON CARD (1-12)	.25	.11
RANDOM INSERTS IN ALL PACKS		
☐ 1 John Olerud	.40	.18
☐ 2 Albert Belle	1.00	.45
☐ 3 Rafael Palmeiro	.60	.25
☐ 4 Kenny Lofton	1.25	.55
☐ 5 Jack McDowell	.25	.11
☐ 6 Kevin Appier	.40	.18
☐ 7 Andres Galarraga	.75	.35
☐ 8 Barry Bonds	1.25	.55
☐ 9 Lenny Dykstra	.40	.18
☐ 10 Chuck Carr	.25	.11
☐ 11 Tom Glavine UER	.40	.18
No number on back of card		
☐ 12 Greg Maddux	3.00	1.35

1994 Fleer Lumber Company

Randomly inserted in jumbo packs at a rate of one in five, this ten-card standard-size set features the best hitters in the game. The full-bleed fronts have a color action player cutout on a wood background. The player's name, team name, and the set title "Lumber Company" appear in an oval-shaped seal burned in the wood, just as one would find on a bat. On a background consisting of wooden bats laying on infield sand, the backs present a color headshot and a player profile on a ghosted panel. The cards are numbered alphabetically.

	MINT	NRMT
COMPLETE SET (10)	12.00	5.50
COMMON CARD (1-10)	.60	.25
RANDOM INSERTS IN JUMBO PACKS		
☐ 1 Albert Belle	1.00	.45
☐ 2 Barry Bonds	1.25	.55
☐ 3 Ron Gant	.60	.25
☐ 4 Juan Gonzalez	2.50	1.10
☐ 5 Ken Griffey Jr.	5.00	2.20
☐ 6 David Justice	1.00	.45
☐ 7 Fred McGriff	.75	.35
☐ 8 Rafael Palmeiro	.75	.35
☐ 9 Frank Thomas	4.00	1.80
☐ 10 Matt Williams	.75	.35

1994 Fleer Major League Prospects

Randomly inserted in all pack types at a rate of one in six, this 35-card standard-size set show-cases some of the outstanding young players in Major League Baseball. Inside beige borders, the fronts display color action photos superimposed over ghosted versions of the team logos. The set title and the player's name are gold foil stamped across the bottom of the card. On a beige background with thin blue pinstripes, the backs show a color player cutout and, on a powder blue panel, a player profile. The cards are numbered on the back "X of 35" and are sequenced in alphabetical order.

	MINT	NRMT
COMPLETE SET (35)	15.00	6.75
COMMON CARD (1-35)	.25	.11
MINOR STARS	.50	.23
SEMISTARS	1.00	.45
RANDOM INSERTS IN ALL PACKS		
☐ 1 Kurt Abbott	.25	.11
☐ 2 Brian Anderson	1.50	.70
☐ 3 Rich Aude	.25	.11
☐ 4 Cory Bailey	.25	.11
☐ 5 Danny Bautista	.25	.11
☐ 6 Marty Cordova	1.50	.70
☐ 7 Tripp Cromer	.25	.11
☐ 8 Midre Cummings	.25	.11
☐ 9 Carlos Delgado	2.00	.90
☐ 10 Steve Dreyer	.25	.11
☐ 11 Steve Dunn	.25	.11
☐ 12 Jeff Granger	.25	.11
☐ 13 Tyrone Hill	.25	.11
☐ 14 Denny Hocking	.25	.11
☐ 15 John Hope	.25	.11
☐ 16 Butch Huskey	.50	.23
☐ 17 Miguel Jimenez	.25	.11
☐ 18 Chipper Jones	6.00	2.70
☐ 19 Steve Karsay	.25	.11
☐ 20 Mike Kelly	.25	.11
☐ 21 Mike Lieberthal	.25	.11
☐ 22 Albie Lopez	.25	.11
☐ 23 Jeff McNeely	.25	.11
☐ 24 Dan Miceli	.25	.11
☐ 25 Nate Minchey	.25	.11
☐ 26 Marc Newfield	.50	.23
☐ 27 Darren Oliver	1.50	.70
☐ 28 Luis Ortiz	.25	.11
☐ 29 Curtis Pride	.25	.11
☐ 30 Roger Salkeld	.25	.11
☐ 31 Scott Sanders	.25	.11
☐ 32 Dave Staton	.25	.11
☐ 33 Salomon Torres	.25	.11
☐ 34 Steve Trachsel	.50	.23
☐ 35 Chris Turner	.25	.11

1994 Fleer Pro-Visions

Randomly inserted in all pack types at a rate of one in 12, this nine-card standard-size set features on its fronts colorful artistic player caricatures with surrealistic backgrounds drawn by illustrator Wayne Still. The player's name is gold foil stamped at the lower right corner. When all nine cards are placed in order in a collector sheet, the backgrounds fit together to form a composite. The backs shade from one bright color to another and present career summaries. The cards are numbered on the back "X of 9."

	MINT	NRMT
COMPLETE SET (9)	4.00	1.80
COMMON CARD (1-9)	.25	.11
RANDOM INSERTS IN ALL PACKS		
☐ 1 Darren Daulton	.40	.18
☐ 2 John Olerud	.40	.18
☐ 3 Matt Williams	.60	.25
☐ 4 Carlos Baerga	.25	.11
☐ 5 Ozzie Smith	1.00	.45
☐ 6 Juan Gonzalez	2.00	.90
☐ 7 Jack McDowell	.25	.11
☐ 8 Mike Piazza	2.50	1.10
☐ 9 Tony Gwynn	2.00	.90

1994 Fleer Rookie Sensations

Randomly inserted in jumbo packs at a rate of one in four, this 20-card standard-size set features outstanding rookies. The fronts are "double exposed," with a player action cutout superimposed over a second photo. The team logo also appears in the team color-coded background. The set title is gold foil stamped toward the top, and the player's name is gold foil stamped on a team color-coded ribbon toward the bottom. On a white background featuring a ghosted version of the team logo, the backs have a player cutout photo and a season summary. The cards are numbered on the back "X of 20" and are sequenced in alphabetical order.

	MINT	NRMT
COMPLETE SET (20)	18.00	8.00
COMMON CARD (1-20)	.75	.35
STATED ODDS 1:4 JUMBO		

☐ 1 Rene Arocha	.75	.35
☐ 2 Jason Bere	.75	.35
☐ 3 Jeromy Burnitz	.75	.35
☐ 4 Chuck Carr	.75	.35
☐ 5 Jeff Conine	1.50	.70
☐ 6 Steve Cooke	.75	.35
☐ 7 Cliff Floyd	1.50	.70
☐ 8 Jeffrey Hammonds	1.50	.70
☐ 9 Wayne Kirby	.75	.35
☐ 10 Mike Lansing	1.50	.70
☐ 11 Al Martin	.75	.35
☐ 12 Greg McMichael	.75	.35
☐ 13 Troy Neel	.75	.35
☐ 14 Mike Piazza	12.00	5.50
☐ 15 Armando Reynoso	.75	.35
☐ 16 Kirk Rueter	.75	.35
☐ 17 Tim Salmon	2.50	1.10
☐ 18 Aaron Sele	.75	.35
☐ 19 J.T. Snow	2.50	1.10
☐ 20 Kevin Stocker	.75	.35

1994 Fleer Smoke 'n Heat

Randomly inserted in wax packs at a rate of one in 36, this 12-card standard-size set showcases the best pitchers in the game. On the fronts, color action player cutouts are superimposed on a red-and-gold fiery background that has a metallic sheen to it. The set title "Smoke 'n Heat" is printed in large block lettering. On a reddish marbleized background, the backs have another player cutout and season summary. The cards are numbered on the back "X of 12." and are sequenced in alphabetical order.

	MINT	NRMT
COMPLETE SET (12)	70.00	32.00
COMMON CARD (1-12)	2.00	.90
RANDOM INSERTS IN ALL PACKS		

☐ 1 Roger Clemens	12.00	5.50
☐ 2 David Cone	3.00	1.35
☐ 3 Juan Guzman	2.00	.90
☐ 4 Pete Harnisch	2.00	.90
☐ 5 Randy Johnson	6.00	2.70
☐ 6 Mark Langston	2.00	.90
☐ 7 Greg Maddux	20.00	9.00
☐ 8 Mike Mussina	6.00	2.70
☐ 9 Jose Rijo	2.00	.90
☐ 10 Nolan Ryan	30.00	13.50
☐ 11 Curt Schilling	3.00	1.35
☐ 12 John Smoltz	3.00	1.35

1994 Fleer Team Leaders

Randomly inserted in all pack types, this 28-card standard-size set features Fleer's selected top player from each of the 28 major league teams. The fronts feature an action player cutout superposed on a team close-up photo with a team color-coded background, all inside beige borders. The set title, player's name, team name, and position are printed in gold foil across the bottom. On a white background with a ghosted version of the team logo, the horizontal backs carry a second color player cutout and a summary of the player's performance. The card numbering is arranged alphabetically by city according to the American (1-14) and the National (15-28) Leagues.

	MINT	NRMT
COMPLETE SET (28)	25.00	11.00
COMMON CARD (1-28)	.25	.11
RANDOM INSERTS IN ALL PACKS		

☐ 1 Cal Ripken	4.00	1.80
☐ 2 Mo Vaughn	1.25	.55
☐ 3 Tim Salmon	1.00	.45
☐ 4 Frank Thomas	4.00	1.80
☐ 5 Carlos Baerga	.25	.11
☐ 6 Cecil Fielder	.50	.23
☐ 7 Brian McRae	.25	.11
☐ 8 Greg Vaughn	.25	.11
☐ 9 Kirby Puckett	2.00	.90
☐ 10 Don Mattingly	1.50	.70
☐ 11 Mark McGwire	2.00	.90
☐ 12 Ken Griffey Jr.	5.00	2.20
☐ 13 Juan Gonzalez	2.50	1.10
☐ 14 Paul Molitor	1.00	.45
☐ 15 David Justice	1.00	.45
☐ 16 Ryne Sandberg	1.25	.55
☐ 17 Barry Larkin	.75	.35
☐ 18 Andres Galarraga	1.00	.45
☐ 19 Gary Sheffield	1.00	.45

☐ 20 Jeff Bagwell	2.00	.90
☐ 21 Mike Piazza	3.00	1.35
☐ 22 Marquis Grissom	.50	.23
☐ 23 Bobby Bonilla	.50	.23
☐ 24 Lenny Dykstra	.50	.23
☐ 25 Jay Bell	.50	.23
☐ 26 Gregg Jefferies	.25	.11
☐ 27 Tony Gwynn	2.50	1.10
☐ 28 Will Clark	.75	.35

1994 Fleer Update

This 200-card standard-size set highlights traded players in their new uniforms and promising young rookies. The Update set was exclusively distributed in factory set form through hobby dealers. A ten card Diamond Tribute set was included in each factory set for a total of 210 cards. The cards are numbered on the back, grouped alphabetically by team by league with AL preceding NL. Key Rookie Cards include Chan Ho Park and Alex Rodriguez.

	MINT	NRMT
COMP.FACT.SET (210)	18.00	8.00
COMPLETE SET (200)	15.00	6.75
COMMON CARD (U1-U200)	.15	.07
MINOR STARS	.25	.11
SEMISTARS	.50	.23
UNLISTED STARS	1.00	.45

☐ 1 Mark Eichhorn	.15	.07
☐ 2 Sid Fernandez	.15	.07
☐ 3 Leo Gomez	.15	.07
☐ 4 Mike Oquist	.15	.07
☐ 5 Rafael Palmeiro	.50	.23
☐ 6 Chris Sabo	.15	.07
☐ 7 Dwight Smith	.15	.07
☐ 8 Lee Smith	.25	.11
☐ 9 Damon Berryhill	.15	.07
☐ 10 Wes Chamberlain	.15	.07
☐ 11 Gar Finnvold	.15	.07
☐ 12 Chris Howard	.15	.07
☐ 13 Tim Naehring	.15	.07
☐ 14 Otis Nixon	.15	.07
☐ 15 Brian Anderson	1.00	.45
☐ 16 Jorge Fabregas	.15	.07
☐ 17 Rex Hudler	.15	.07
☐ 18 Bo Jackson	.25	.11
☐ 19 Mark Leiter	.15	.07
☐ 20 Spike Owen	.15	.07
☐ 21 Harold Reynolds	.15	.07
☐ 22 Chris Turner	.15	.07
☐ 23 Dennis Cook	.15	.07
☐ 24 Jose DeLeon	.15	.07
☐ 25 Julio Franco	.15	.07
☐ 26 Joe Hall	.15	.07
☐ 27 Darrin Jackson	.15	.07
☐ 28 Dane Johnson	.15	.07
☐ 29 Norberto Martin	.15	.07

☐ 30 Scott Sanderson	.15	.07	
☐ 31 Jason Grimsley	.15	.07	
☐ 32 Dennis Martinez	.25	.11	
☐ 33 Jack Morris	.25	.11	
☐ 34 Eddie Murray	1.00	.45	
☐ 35 Chad Ogea	.25	.11	
☐ 36 Tony Pena	.15	.07	
☐ 37 Paul Shuey	.15	.07	
☐ 38 Omar Vizquel	.25	.11	
☐ 39 Danny Bautista	.15	.07	
☐ 40 Tim Belcher	.15	.07	
☐ 41 Joe Boever	.15	.07	
☐ 42 Storm Davis	.15	.07	
☐ 43 Junior Felix	.15	.07	
☐ 44 Mike Gardiner	.15	.07	
☐ 45 Buddy Groom	.15	.07	
☐ 46 Juan Samuel	.15	.07	
☐ 47 Vince Coleman	.15	.07	
☐ 48 Bob Hamelin	.15	.07	
☐ 49 Dave Henderson	.15	.07	
☐ 50 Rusty Meacham	.15	.07	
☐ 51 Terry Shumpert	.15	.07	
☐ 52 Jeff Bronkey	.15	.07	
☐ 53 Alex Diaz	.15	.07	
☐ 54 Brian Harper	.15	.07	
☐ 55 Jose Mercedes	.15	.07	
☐ 56 Jody Reed	.15	.07	
☐ 57 Bob Scanlan	.15	.07	
☐ 58 Turner Ward	.15	.07	
☐ 59 Rich Becker	.15	.07	
☐ 60 Alex Cole	.15	.07	
☐ 61 Denny Hocking	.15	.07	
☐ 62 Scott Leius	.15	.07	
☐ 63 Pat Mahomes	.15	.07	
☐ 64 Carlos Pulido	.15	.07	
☐ 65 Dave Stevens	.15	.07	
☐ 66 Matt Walbeck	.15	.07	
☐ 67 Xavier Hernandez	.15	.07	
☐ 68 Sterling Hitchcock	.15	.07	
☐ 69 Terry Mulholland	.15	.07	
☐ 70 Luis Polonia	.15	.07	
☐ 71 Gerald Williams	.15	.07	
☐ 72 Mark Acre	.15	.07	
☐ 73 Geronimo Berroa	.15	.07	
☐ 74 Rickey Henderson	.50	.23	
☐ 75 Stan Javier	.15	.07	
☐ 76 Steve Karsay	.15	.07	
☐ 77 Carlos Reyes	.15	.07	
☐ 78 Bill Taylor	.15	.07	
☐ 79 Eric Anthony	.15	.07	
☐ 80 Bobby Ayala	.15	.07	
☐ 81 Tim Davis	.15	.07	
☐ 82 Felix Fermin	.15	.07	
☐ 83 Reggie Jefferson	.15	.07	
☐ 84 Keith Mitchell	.15	.07	
☐ 85 Bill Risley	.15	.07	
☐ 86 Alex Rodriguez	10.00	4.50	
☐ 87 Roger Salkeld	.15	.07	
☐ 88 Dan Wilson	.25	.11	
☐ 89 Cris Carpenter	.15	.07	
☐ 90 Will Clark	.50	.23	
☐ 91 Jeff Frye	.15	.07	
☐ 92 Rick Helling	.15	.07	
☐ 93 Chris James	.15	.07	
☐ 94 Oddibe McDowell	.15	.07	
☐ 95 Billy Ripken	.15	.07	
☐ 96 Carlos Delgado	.50	.23	
☐ 97 Alex Gonzalez	.25	.11	
☐ 98 Shawn Green	.25	.11	
☐ 99 Darren Hall	.15	.07	
☐ 100 Mike Huff	.15	.07	
☐ 101 Mike Kelly	.15	.07	
☐ 102 Roberto Kelly	.15	.07	
☐ 103 Charlie O'Brien	.15	.07	
☐ 104 Jose Oliva	.15	.07	
☐ 105 Gregg Olson	.15	.07	
☐ 106 Willie Banks	.15	.07	
☐ 107 Jim Bullinger	.15	.07	
☐ 108 Chuck Crim	.15	.07	
☐ 109 Shawon Dunston	.15	.07	
☐ 110 Karl Rhodes	.15	.07	
☐ 111 Steve Trachsel	.25	.11	
☐ 112 Anthony Young	.15	.07	
☐ 113 Eddie Zambrano	.15	.07	
☐ 114 Bret Boone	.15	.07	
☐ 115 Jeff Brantley	.15	.07	

☐ 116 Hector Carrasco	.15	.07	
☐ 117 Tony Fernandez	.15	.07	
☐ 118 Tim Fortugno	.15	.07	
☐ 119 Erik Hanson	.15	.07	
☐ 120 Chuck McElroy	.15	.07	
☐ 121 Deion Sanders	.25	.11	
☐ 122 Ellis Burks	.25	.11	
☐ 123 Marvin Freeman	.15	.07	
☐ 124 Mike Harkey	.15	.07	
☐ 125 Howard Johnson	.15	.07	
☐ 126 Mike Kingery	.15	.07	
☐ 127 Nelson Liriano	.15	.07	
☐ 128 Marcus Moore	.15	.07	
☐ 129 Mike Munoz	.15	.07	
☐ 130 Kevin Ritz	.15	.07	
☐ 131 Walt Weiss	.15	.07	
☐ 132 Kurt Abbott	.15	.07	
☐ 133 Jerry Browne	.15	.07	
☐ 134 Greg Colbrunn	.15	.07	
☐ 135 Jeremy Hernandez	.15	.07	
☐ 136 Dave Magadan	.15	.07	
☐ 137 Kurt Miller	.15	.07	
☐ 138 Robb Nen	.15	.07	
☐ 139 Jesus Tavarez	.15	.07	
☐ 140 Sid Bream	.15	.07	
☐ 141 Tom Edens	.15	.07	
☐ 142 Tony Eusebio	.15	.07	
☐ 143 John Hudek	.15	.07	
☐ 144 Brian L. Hunter	1.00	.45	
☐ 145 Orlando Miller	.15	.07	
☐ 146 James Mouton	.15	.07	
☐ 147 Shane Reynolds	.15	.07	
☐ 148 Rafael Bournigal	.15	.07	
☐ 149 Delino DeShields	.15	.07	
☐ 150 Garey Ingram	.15	.07	
☐ 151 Chan Ho Park	2.50	1.10	
☐ 152 Wil Cordero	.15	.07	
☐ 153 Pedro Martinez	1.00	.45	
☐ 154 Randy Milligan	.15	.07	
☐ 155 Lenny Webster	.15	.07	
☐ 156 Rico Brogna	.15	.07	
☐ 157 Josias Manzanillo	.15	.07	
☐ 158 Kevin McReynolds	.15	.07	
☐ 159 Mike Remlinger	.15	.07	
☐ 160 David Segui	.15	.07	
☐ 161 Pete Smith	.15	.07	
☐ 162 Kelly Stinnett	.15	.07	
☐ 163 Jose Vizcaino	.15	.07	
☐ 164 Billy Hatcher	.15	.07	
☐ 165 Doug Jones	.15	.07	
☐ 166 Mike Lieberthal	.15	.07	
☐ 167 Tony Longmire	.15	.07	
☐ 168 Bobby Munoz	.15	.07	
☐ 169 Paul Quantrill	.15	.07	
☐ 170 Heathcliff Slocumb	.15	.07	
☐ 171 Fernando Valenzuela	.25	.11	
☐ 172 Mark Dewey	.15	.07	
☐ 173 Brian R. Hunter	.15	.07	
☐ 174 Jon Lieber	.15	.07	
☐ 175 Ravelo Manzanillo	.15	.07	
☐ 176 Dan Miceli	.15	.07	
☐ 177 Rick White	.15	.07	
☐ 178 Bryan Eversgerd	.15	.07	
☐ 179 John Habyan	.15	.07	
☐ 180 Terry McGriff	.15	.07	
☐ 181 Vicente Palacios	.15	.07	
☐ 182 Rich Rodriguez	.15	.07	
☐ 183 Rick Sutcliffe	.15	.07	
☐ 184 Donnie Elliott	.15	.07	
☐ 185 Joey Hamilton	1.00	.45	
☐ 186 Tim Hyers	.15	.07	
☐ 187 Luis Lopez	.15	.07	
☐ 188 Ray McDavid	.15	.07	
☐ 189 Bip Roberts	.15	.07	
☐ 190 Scott Sanders	.15	.07	
☐ 191 Eddie Williams	.15	.07	
☐ 192 Steve Frey	.15	.07	
☐ 193 Pat Gomez	.15	.07	
☐ 194 Rich Monteleone	.15	.07	
☐ 195 Mark Portugal	.15	.07	
☐ 196 Darryl Strawberry	.25	.11	
☐ 197 Salomon Torres	.15	.07	
☐ 198 W.VanLandingham	.25	.11	
☐ 199 Checklist	.15	.07	
☐ 200 Checklist	.15	.07	

1994 Fleer Update Diamond Tribute

Each 1994 Fleer Update factory set contained a complete 10-card set of Diamond Tribute inserts. This was the third and final year that Fleer included an insert set in their factory boxed sets. The 1994 Diamond Tribute inserts feature a player action shot cut out against a backdrop of clouds and baseballs. The selection once again focuses on the game's top veterans. Cards are numbered X of 10 on the back.

	MINT	NRMT
COMPLETE SET (10)	3.00	1.35
COMMON CARD (1-10)	.25	.11
ONE SET PER UPDATE FACTORY SET		

☐ 1 Barry Bonds	.40	.18
☐ 2 Joe Carter	.25	.11
☐ 3 Will Clark	.40	.18
☐ 4 Roger Clemens	.60	.25
☐ 5 Tony Gwynn	.75	.35
☐ 6 Don Mattingly	.50	.23
☐ 7 Fred McGriff	.40	.18
☐ 8 Eddie Murray	.60	.25
☐ 9 Kirby Puckett	.75	.35
☐ 10 Cal Ripken	2.00	.90

1995 Fleer

The 1995 Fleer set consists of 600 standard-size cards issued as one series. Each pack contained at least one insert card with some 'Hot Packs' containing nothing but insert cards. Full-bleed fronts have two player photos and, atypical of baseball cards fronts, biographical information such as height, weight, etc. The backgrounds are multi-colored. The backs are horizontal and contain year-by-

year statistics along with a photo. There was a different design for each of baseball's six divisions. The checklist is arranged alphabetically by teams within each league with AL preceding NL. Eight card promo sets were issued to hobby dealers. These cards are extremely difficult to tell apart from the regular cards and have the same value as the regular cards. The players in this set are Marquis Grissom, David Cone, Ozzie Smith, Roger Clemens, Tim Salmon, Paul O'Neill, Juan Gonzalez and Dante Bichette.

	MINT	NRMT
COMPLETE SET (600)	50.00	22.00
COMMON CARD (1-600)	.15	.07
MINOR STARS	.30	.14
UNLISTED STARS	.60	.25
COMP.ALL-ROOKIE SET (9)	5.00	2.20
ONE ROOKIE SET VIA MAIL PER EXCH.CARD		

#	Name	MINT	NRMT
1	Brady Anderson	.40	.18
2	Harold Baines	.30	.14
3	Damon Buford	.15	.07
4	Mike Devereaux	.15	.07
5	Mark Eichhorn	.15	.07
6	Sid Fernandez	.15	.07
7	Leo Gomez	.15	.07
8	Jeffrey Hammonds	.30	.14
9	Chris Hoiles	.15	.07
10	Rick Krivda	.15	.07
11	Ben McDonald	.15	.07
12	Mark McLemore	.15	.07
13	Alan Mills	.15	.07
14	Jamie Moyer	.15	.07
15	Mike Mussina	.60	.25
16	Mike Oquist	.15	.07
17	Rafael Palmeiro	.40	.18
18	Arthur Rhodes	.15	.07
19	Cal Ripken Jr.	2.50	1.10
20	Chris Sabo	.15	.07
21	Lee Smith	.30	.14
22	Jack Voigt	.15	.07
23	Damon Berryhill	.15	.07
24	Tom Brunansky	.15	.07
25	Wes Chamberlain	.15	.07
26	Roger Clemens	1.25	.55
27	Scott Cooper	.15	.07
28	Andre Dawson	.40	.18
29	Gar Finnvold	.15	.07
30	Tony Fossas	.15	.07
31	Mike Greenwell	.15	.07
32	Joe Hesketh	.15	.07
33	Chris Howard	.15	.07
34	Chris Nabholz	.15	.07
35	Tim Naehring	.15	.07
36	Otis Nixon	.15	.07
37	Carlos Rodriguez	.15	.07
38	Rich Rowland	.15	.07
39	Ken Ryan	.15	.07
40	Aaron Sele	.15	.07
41	John Valentin	.15	.07
42	Mo Vaughn	.75	.35
43	Frank Viola	.15	.07
44	Danny Bautista	.15	.07
45	Joe Boever	.15	.07
46	Milt Cuyler	.15	.07
47	Storm Davis	.15	.07
48	John Doherty	.15	.07
49	Junior Felix	.15	.07
50	Cecil Fielder	.30	.14
51	Travis Fryman	.30	.14
52	Mike Gardiner	.15	.07
53	Kirk Gibson	.30	.14
54	Chris Gomez	.15	.07
55	Buddy Groom	.15	.07
56	Mike Henneman	.15	.07
57	Chad Kreuter	.15	.07
58	Mike Moore	.15	.07
59	Tony Phillips	.15	.07
60	Juan Samuel	.15	.07
61	Mickey Tettleton	.15	.07
62	Alan Trammell	.40	.18
63	David Wells	.15	.07
64	Lou Whitaker	.30	.14
65	Jim Abbott	.15	.07
66	Joe Ausanio	.15	.07
67	Wade Boggs	.60	.25
68	Mike Gallego	.15	.07
69	Xavier Hernandez	.15	.07
70	Sterling Hitchcock	.15	.07
71	Steve Howe	.15	.07
72	Scott Kamieniecki	.15	.07
73	Pat Kelly	.15	.07
74	Jimmy Key	.30	.14
75	Jim Leyritz	.15	.07
76	Don Mattingly UER Photo is a reversed negative	1.00	.45
77	Terry Mulholland	.15	.07
78	Paul O'Neill	.30	.14
79	Melido Perez	.15	.07
80	Luis Polonia	.15	.07
81	Mike Stanley	.15	.07
82	Danny Tartabull	.15	.07
83	Randy Velarde	.15	.07
84	Bob Wickman	.15	.07
85	Bernie Williams	.60	.25
86	Gerald Williams	.15	.07
87	Roberto Alomar	.30	.14
88	Pat Borders	.15	.07
89	Joe Carter	.30	.14
90	Tony Castillo	.15	.07
91	Brad Cornett	.15	.07
92	Carlos Delgado	.30	.14
93	Alex Gonzalez	.15	.07
94	Shawn Green	.30	.14
95	Juan Guzman	.15	.07
96	Darren Hall	.15	.07
97	Pat Hentgen	.30	.14
98	Mike Huff	.15	.07
99	Randy Knorr	.15	.07
100	Al Leiter	.15	.07
101	Paul Molitor	.60	.25
102	John Olerud	.30	.14
103	Dick Schofield	.15	.07
104	Ed Sprague	.15	.07
105	Dave Stewart	.30	.14
106	Todd Stottlemyre	.15	.07
107	Devon White	.15	.07
108	Woody Williams	.15	.07
109	Wilson Alvarez	.15	.07
110	Paul Assenmacher	.15	.07
111	Jason Bere	.15	.07
112	Dennis Cook	.15	.07
113	Joey Cora	.30	.14
114	Jose DeLeon	.15	.07
115	Alex Fernandez	.15	.07
116	Julio Franco	.15	.07
117	Craig Grebeck	.15	.07
118	Ozzie Guillen	.15	.07
119	Roberto Hernandez	.15	.07
120	Darrin Jackson	.15	.07
121	Lance Johnson	.15	.07
122	Ron Karkovice	.15	.07
123	Mike LaValliere	.15	.07
124	Norberto Martin	.15	.07
125	Kirk McCaskill	.15	.07
126	Jack McDowell	.15	.07
127	Tim Raines	.30	.14
128	Frank Thomas	2.50	1.10
129	Robin Ventura	.30	.14
130	Sandy Alomar Jr.	.30	.14
131	Carlos Baerga	.15	.07
132	Albert Belle	.75	.35
133	Mark Clark	.15	.07
134	Alvaro Espinoza	.15	.07
135	Jason Grimsley	.15	.07
136	Wayne Kirby	.15	.07
137	Kenny Lofton	.75	.35
138	Albie Lopez	.15	.07
139	Dennis Martinez	.30	.14
140	Jose Mesa	.15	.07
141	Eddie Murray	.60	.25
142	Charles Nagy	.30	.14
143	Tony Pena	.15	.07
144	Eric Plunk	.15	.07
145	Manny Ramirez	.60	.25
146	Jeff Russell	.15	.07
147	Paul Shuey	.15	.07
148	Paul Sorrento	.15	.07
149	Jim Thome	.60	.25
150	Omar Vizquel	.30	.14
151	Dave Winfield	.40	.18
152	Kevin Appier	.30	.14
153	Billy Brewer	.15	.07
154	Vince Coleman	.15	.07
155	David Cone	.30	.14
156	Gary Gaetti	.15	.07
157	Greg Gagne	.15	.07
158	Tom Gordon	.15	.07
159	Mark Gubicza	.15	.07
160	Bob Hamelin	.15	.07
161	Dave Henderson	.15	.07
162	Felix Jose	.15	.07
163	Wally Joyner	.30	.14
164	Jose Lind	.15	.07
165	Mike Macfarlane	.15	.07
166	Mike Magnante	.15	.07
167	Brent Mayne	.15	.07
168	Brian McRae	.15	.07
169	Rusty Meacham	.15	.07
170	Jeff Montgomery	.15	.07
171	Hipolito Pichardo	.15	.07
172	Terry Shumpert	.15	.07
173	Michael Tucker	.30	.14
174	Ricky Bones	.15	.07
175	Jeff Cirillo	.30	.14
176	Alex Diaz	.15	.07
177	Cal Eldred	.15	.07
178	Mike Fetters	.15	.07
179	Darryl Hamilton	.15	.07
180	Brian Harper	.15	.07
181	John Jaha	.15	.07
182	Pat Listach	.15	.07
183	Graeme Lloyd	.15	.07
184	Jose Mercedes	.15	.07
185	Matt Mieske	.15	.07
186	Dave Nilsson	.15	.07
187	Jody Reed	.15	.07
188	Bob Scanlan	.15	.07
189	Kevin Seitzer	.15	.07
190	Bill Spiers	.15	.07
191	B.J. Surhoff	.15	.07
192	Jose Valentin	.15	.07
193	Greg Vaughn	.15	.07
194	Turner Ward	.15	.07
195	Bill Wegman	.15	.07
196	Rick Aguilera	.15	.07
197	Rich Becker	.15	.07
198	Alex Cole	.15	.07
199	Marty Cordova	.30	.14
200	Steve Dunn	.15	.07
201	Scott Erickson	.15	.07
202	Mark Guthrie	.15	.07
203	Chip Hale	.15	.07
204	LaTroy Hawkins	.15	.07
205	Denny Hocking	.15	.07
206	Chuck Knoblauch	.60	.25
207	Scott Leius	.15	.07
208	Shane Mack	.15	.07
209	Pat Mahomes	.15	.07
210	Pat Meares	.15	.07
211	Pedro Munoz	.15	.07
212	Kirby Puckett	1.25	.55
213	Jeff Reboulet	.15	.07
214	Dave Stevens	.15	.07
215	Kevin Tapani	.15	.07
216	Matt Walbeck	.15	.07
217	Carl Willis	.15	.07
218	Brian Anderson	.30	.14
219	Chad Curtis	.15	.07
220	Chili Davis	.30	.14
221	Gary DiSarcina	.15	.07
222	Damion Easley	.15	.07
223	Jim Edmonds	.40	.18
224	Chuck Finley	.15	.07
225	Joe Grahe	.15	.07
226	Rex Hudler	.15	.07
227	Bo Jackson	.30	.14
228	Mark Langston	.15	.07
229	Phil Leftwich	.15	.07
230	Mark Leiter	.15	.07

□	#	Name	Price 1	Price 2
□	231	Spike Owen	.15	.07
□	232	Bob Patterson	.15	.07
□	233	Troy Percival	.15	.07
□	234	Eduardo Perez	.15	.07
□	235	Tim Salmon	.60	.25
□	236	J.T. Snow	.30	.14
□	237	Chris Turner	.15	.07
□	238	Mark Acre	.15	.07
□	239	Geronimo Berroa	.15	.07
□	240	Mike Bordick	.15	.07
□	241	John Briscoe	.15	.07
□	242	Scott Brosius	.15	.07
□	243	Ron Darling	.15	.07
□	244	Dennis Eckersley	.30	.14
□	245	Brent Gates	.15	.07
□	246	Rickey Henderson	.40	.18
□	247	Stan Javier	.15	.07
□	248	Steve Karsay	.15	.07
□	249	Mark McGwire	1.25	.55
□	250	Troy Neel	.15	.07
□	251	Steve Ontiveros	.15	.07
□	252	Carlos Reyes	.15	.07
□	253	Ruben Sierra	.15	.07
□	254	Terry Steinbach	.15	.07
□	255	Bill Taylor	.15	.07
□	256	Todd Van Poppel	.15	.07
□	257	Bobby Witt	.15	.07
□	258	Rich Amaral	.15	.07
□	259	Eric Anthony	.15	.07
□	260	Bobby Ayala	.15	.07
□	261	Mike Blowers	.15	.07
□	262	Chris Bosio	.15	.07
□	263	Jay Buhner	.40	.18
□	264	John Cummings	.15	.07
□	265	Tim Davis	.15	.07
□	266	Felix Fermin	.15	.07
□	267	Dave Fleming	.15	.07
□	268	Goose Gossage	.30	.14
□	269	Ken Griffey Jr.	3.00	1.35
□	270	Reggie Jefferson	.15	.07
□	271	Randy Johnson	.60	.25
□	272	Edgar Martinez	.40	.18
□	273	Tino Martinez	.60	.25
□	274	Greg Pirkl	.15	.07
□	275	Bill Risley	.15	.07
□	276	Roger Salkeld	.15	.07
□	277	Luis Sojo	.15	.07
□	278	Mac Suzuki	.15	.07
□	279	Dan Wilson	.15	.07
□	280	Kevin Brown	.30	.14
□	281	Jose Canseco	.40	.18
□	282	Cris Carpenter	.15	.07
□	283	Will Clark	.40	.18
□	284	Jeff Frye	.15	.07
□	285	Juan Gonzalez	1.50	.70
□	286	Rick Helling	.15	.07
□	287	Tom Henke	.15	.07
□	288	David Hulse	.15	.07
□	289	Chris James	.15	.07
□	290	Manuel Lee	.15	.07
□	291	Oddibe McDowell	.15	.07
□	292	Dean Palmer	.15	.07
□	293	Roger Pavlik	.15	.07
□	294	Bill Ripken	.15	.07
□	295	Ivan Rodriguez	.75	.35
□	296	Kenny Rogers	.15	.07
□	297	Doug Strange	.15	.07
□	298	Matt Whiteside	.15	.07
□	299	Steve Avery	.15	.07
□	300	Steve Bedrosian	.15	.07
□	301	Rafael Belliard	.15	.07
□	302	Jeff Blauser	.30	.14
□	303	Dave Gallagher	.15	.07
□	304	Tom Glavine	.30	.14
□	305	David Justice	.60	.25
□	306	Mike Kelly	.15	.07
□	307	Roberto Kelly	.15	.07
□	308	Ryan Klesko	.40	.18
□	309	Mark Lemke	.15	.07
□	310	Javier Lopez	.30	.14
□	311	Greg Maddux	2.00	.90
□	312	Fred McGriff	.40	.18
□	313	Greg McMichael	.15	.07
□	314	Kent Mercker	.15	.07
□	315	Charlie O'Brien	.15	.07
□	316	Jose Oliva	.15	.07
□	317	Terry Pendleton	.15	.07
□	318	John Smoltz	.30	.14
□	319	Mike Stanton	.15	.07
□	320	Tony Tarasco	.15	.07
□	321	Terrell Wade	.15	.07
□	322	Mark Wohlers	.15	.07
□	323	Kurt Abbott	.15	.07
□	324	Luis Aquino	.15	.07
□	325	Bret Barberie	.15	.07
□	326	Ryan Bowen	.15	.07
□	327	Jerry Browne	.15	.07
□	328	Chuck Carr	.15	.07
□	329	Matias Carrillo	.15	.07
□	330	Greg Colbrunn	.15	.07
□	331	Jeff Conine	.30	.14
□	332	Mark Gardner	.15	.07
□	333	Chris Hammond	.15	.07
□	334	Bryan Harvey	.15	.07
□	335	Richie Lewis	.15	.07
□	336	Dave Magadan	.15	.07
□	337	Terry Mathews	.15	.07
□	338	Robb Nen	.15	.07
□	339	Yorkis Perez	.15	.07
□	340	Pat Rapp	.15	.07
□	341	Benito Santiago	.15	.07
□	342	Gary Sheffield	.60	.25
□	343	Dave Weathers	.15	.07
□	344	Moises Alou	.30	.14
□	345	Sean Berry	.15	.07
□	346	Wil Cordero	.15	.07
□	347	Joey Eischen	.15	.07
□	348	Jeff Fassero	.15	.07
□	349	Darrin Fletcher	.15	.07
□	350	Cliff Floyd	.15	.07
□	351	Marquis Grissom	.30	.14
□	352	Butch Henry	.15	.07
□	353	Gil Heredia	.15	.07
□	354	Ken Hill	.15	.07
□	355	Mike Lansing	.15	.07
□	356	Pedro Martinez	.60	.25
□	357	Mel Rojas	.15	.07
□	358	Kirk Rueter	.15	.07
□	359	Tim Scott	.15	.07
□	360	Jeff Shaw	.15	.07
□	361	Larry Walker	.60	.25
□	362	Lenny Webster	.15	.07
□	363	John Wetteland	.15	.07
□	364	Rondell White	.30	.14
□	365	Bobby Bonilla	.30	.14
□	366	Rico Brogna	.15	.07
□	367	Jeromy Burnitz	.15	.07
□	368	John Franco	.30	.14
□	369	Dwight Gooden	.30	.14
□	370	Todd Hundley	.30	.14
□	371	Jason Jacome	.15	.07
□	372	Bobby Jones	.15	.07
□	373	Jeff Kent	.15	.07
□	374	Jim Lindeman	.15	.07
□	375	Josias Manzanillo	.15	.07
□	376	Roger Mason	.15	.07
□	377	Kevin McReynolds	.15	.07
□	378	Joe Orsulak	.15	.07
□	379	Bill Pulsipher	.15	.07
□	380	Bret Saberhagen	.15	.07
□	381	David Segui	.15	.07
□	382	Pete Smith	.15	.07
□	383	Kelly Stinnett	.15	.07
□	384	Ryan Thompson	.15	.07
□	385	Jose Vizcaino	.15	.07
□	386	Toby Borland	.15	.07
□	387	Ricky Bottalico	.30	.14
□	388	Darren Daulton	.30	.14
□	389	Mariano Duncan	.15	.07
□	390	Lenny Dykstra	.30	.14
□	391	Jim Eisenreich	.15	.07
□	392	Tommy Greene	.15	.07
□	393	Dave Hollins	.15	.07
□	394	Pete Incaviglia	.15	.07
□	395	Danny Jackson	.15	.07
□	396	Doug Jones	.15	.07
□	397	Ricky Jordan	.15	.07
□	398	John Kruk	.30	.14
□	399	Mike Lieberthal	.15	.07
□	400	Tony Longmire	.15	.07
□	401	Mickey Morandini	.15	.07
□	402	Bobby Munoz	.15	.07
□	403	Curt Schilling	.30	.14
□	404	Heathcliff Slocumb	.15	.07
□	405	Kevin Stocker	.15	.07
□	406	Fernando Valenzuela	.30	.14
□	407	David West	.15	.07
□	408	Willie Banks	.15	.07
□	409	Jose Bautista	.15	.07
□	410	Steve Buechele	.15	.07
□	411	Jim Bullinger	.15	.07
□	412	Chuck Crim	.15	.07
□	413	Shawon Dunston	.15	.07
□	414	Kevin Foster	.15	.07
□	415	Mark Grace	.40	.18
□	416	Jose Hernandez	.15	.07
□	417	Glenallen Hill	.15	.07
□	418	Brooks Kieschnick	.30	.14
□	419	Derrick May	.15	.07
□	420	Randy Myers	.15	.07
□	421	Dan Plesac	.15	.07
□	422	Karl Rhodes	.15	.07
□	423	Rey Sanchez	.15	.07
□	424	Sammy Sosa	.60	.25
□	425	Steve Trachsel	.15	.07
□	426	Rick Wilkins	.15	.07
□	427	Anthony Young	.15	.07
□	428	Eddie Zambrano	.15	.07
□	429	Bret Boone	.15	.07
□	430	Jeff Branson	.30	.14
□	431	Jeff Brantley	.15	.07
□	432	Hector Carrasco	.15	.07
□	433	Brian Dorsett	.15	.07
□	434	Tony Fernandez	.15	.07
□	435	Tim Fortugno	.15	.07
□	436	Erik Hanson	.15	.07
□	437	Thomas Howard	.15	.07
□	438	Kevin Jarvis	.15	.07
□	439	Barry Larkin	.40	.18
□	440	Chuck McElroy	.15	.07
□	441	Kevin Mitchell	.15	.07
□	442	Hal Morris	.15	.07
□	443	Jose Rijo	.15	.07
□	444	John Roper	.15	.07
□	445	Johnny Ruffin	.15	.07
□	446	Deion Sanders	.30	.14
□	447	Reggie Sanders	.15	.07
□	448	Pete Schourek	.15	.07
□	449	John Smiley	.15	.07
□	450	Eddie Taubensee	.15	.07
□	451	Jeff Bagwell	1.25	.55
□	452	Kevin Bass	.15	.07
□	453	Craig Biggio	.40	.18
□	454	Ken Caminiti	.40	.18
□	455	Andujar Cedeno	.15	.07
□	456	Doug Drabek	.15	.07
□	457	Tony Eusebio	.15	.07
□	458	Mike Felder	.15	.07
□	459	Steve Finley	.30	.14
□	460	Luis Gonzalez	.15	.07
□	461	Mike Hampton	.15	.07
□	462	Pete Harnisch	.15	.07
□	463	John Hudek	.15	.07
□	464	Todd Jones	.15	.07
□	465	Darryl Kile	.30	.14
□	466	James Mouton	.15	.07
□	467	Shane Reynolds	.15	.07
□	468	Scott Servais	.15	.07
□	469	Greg Swindell	.15	.07
□	470	Dave Veres	.15	.07
□	471	Brian Williams	.15	.07
□	472	Jay Bell	.30	.14
□	473	Jacob Brumfield	.15	.07
□	474	Dave Clark	.15	.07
□	475	Steve Cooke	.15	.07
□	476	Midre Cummings	.15	.07
□	477	Mark Dewey	.15	.07
□	478	Tom Foley	.15	.07
□	479	Carlos Garcia	.15	.07
□	480	Jeff King	.15	.07
□	481	Jon Lieber	.15	.07
□	482	Ravelo Manzanillo	.15	.07
□	483	Al Martin	.15	.07
□	484	Orlando Merced	.15	.07
□	485	Danny Miceli	.15	.07
□	486	Denny Neagle	.30	.14
□	487	Lance Parrish	.15	.07
□	488	Don Slaught	.15	.07

☐ 489	Zane Smith	.15	.07	☐ 575	Dave Burba	.15	.07
☐ 490	Andy Van Slyke	.30	.14	☐ 576	John Burkett	.15	.07
☐ 491	Paul Wagner	.15	.07	☐ 577	Mark Carreon	.15	.07
☐ 492	Rick White	.15	.07	☐ 578	Royce Clayton	.15	.07
☐ 493	Luis Alicea	.15	.07	☐ 579	Steve Frey	.15	.07
☐ 494	Rene Arocha	.15	.07	☐ 580	Bryan Hickerson	.15	.07
☐ 495	Rheal Cormier	.15	.07	☐ 581	Mike Jackson	.15	.07
☐ 496	Bryan Eversgerd	.15	.07	☐ 582	Darren Lewis	.15	.07
☐ 497	Bernard Gilkey	.15	.07	☐ 583	Kirt Manwaring	.15	.07
☐ 498	John Habyan	.15	.07	☐ 584	Rich Monteleone	.15	.07
☐ 499	Gregg Jefferies	.15	.07	☐ 585	John Patterson	.15	.07
☐ 500	Brian Jordan	.30	.14	☐ 586	J.R. Phillips	.15	.07
☐ 501	Ray Lankford	.30	.14	☐ 587	Mark Portugal	.15	.07
☐ 502	John Mabry	.30	.14	☐ 588	Joe Rosselli	.15	.07
☐ 503	Terry McGriff	.15	.07	☐ 589	Darryl Strawberry	.30	.14
☐ 504	Tom Pagnozzi	.15	.07	☐ 590	Bill Swift	.15	.07
☐ 505	Vicente Palacios	.15	.07	☐ 591	Robby Thompson	.15	.07
☐ 506	Geronimo Pena	.15	.07	☐ 592	William VanLandingham	.15	.07
☐ 507	Gerald Perry	.15	.07	☐ 593	Matt Williams	.40	.18
☐ 508	Rich Rodriguez	.15	.07	☐ 594	Checklist	.15	.07
☐ 509	Ozzie Smith	.75	.35	☐ 595	Checklist	.15	.07
☐ 510	Bob Tewksbury	.15	.07	☐ 596	Checklist	.15	.07
☐ 511	Allen Watson	.15	.07	☐ 597	Checklist	.15	.07
☐ 512	Mark Whiten	.15	.07	☐ 598	Checklist	.15	.07
☐ 513	Todd Zeile	.15	.07	☐ 599	Checklist	.15	.07
☐ 514	Dante Bichette	.30	.14	☐ 600	Checklist	.15	.07
☐ 515	Willie Blair	.15	.07				
☐ 516	Ellis Burks	.30	.14				
☐ 517	Marvin Freeman	.15	.07				
☐ 518	Andres Galarraga	.60	.25				
☐ 519	Joe Girardi	.15	.07				
☐ 520	Greg W. Harris	.15	.07				
☐ 521	Charlie Hayes	.15	.07				
☐ 522	Mike Kingery	.15	.07				
☐ 523	Nelson Liriano	.15	.07				
☐ 524	Mike Munoz	.15	.07				
☐ 525	David Nied	.15	.07				
☐ 526	Steve Reed	.15	.07				
☐ 527	Kevin Ritz	.15	.07				
☐ 528	Bruce Ruffin	.15	.07				
☐ 529	John Vander Wal	.15	.07				
☐ 530	Walt Weiss	.15	.07				
☐ 531	Eric Young	.15	.07				
☐ 532	Billy Ashley	.15	.07				
☐ 533	Pedro Astacio	.15	.07				
☐ 534	Rafael Bournigal	.15	.07				
☐ 535	Brett Butler	.30	.14				
☐ 536	Tom Candiotti	.15	.07				
☐ 537	Omar Daal	.15	.07				
☐ 538	Delino DeShields	.15	.07				
☐ 539	Darren Dreifort	.15	.07				
☐ 540	Kevin Gross	.15	.07				
☐ 541	Orel Hershiser	.30	.14				
☐ 542	Garey Ingram	.15	.07				
☐ 543	Eric Karros	.30	.14				
☐ 544	Ramon Martinez	.30	.14				
☐ 545	Raul Mondesi	.40	.18				
☐ 546	Chan Ho Park	.60	.25				
☐ 547	Mike Piazza	2.00	.90				
☐ 548	Henry Rodriguez	.15	.07				
☐ 549	Rudy Seanez	.15	.07				
☐ 550	Ismael Valdes	.40	.18				
☐ 551	Tim Wallach	.15	.07				
☐ 552	Todd Worrell	.15	.07				
☐ 553	Andy Ashby	.15	.07				
☐ 554	Brad Ausmus	.15	.07				
☐ 555	Derek Bell	.30	.14				
☐ 556	Andy Benes	.30	.14				
☐ 557	Phil Clark	.15	.07				
☐ 558	Donnie Elliott	.15	.07				
☐ 559	Ricky Gutierrez	.15	.07				
☐ 560	Tony Gwynn	1.50	.70				
☐ 561	Joey Hamilton	.30	.14				
☐ 562	Trevor Hoffman	.15	.07				
☐ 563	Luis Lopez	.15	.07				
☐ 564	Pedro A. Martinez	.15	.07				
☐ 565	Tim Mauser	.15	.07				
☐ 566	Phil Plantier	.15	.07				
☐ 567	Bip Roberts	.15	.07				
☐ 568	Scott Sanders	.15	.07				
☐ 569	Craig Shipley	.15	.07				
☐ 570	Jeff Tabaka	.15	.07				
☐ 571	Eddie Williams	.15	.07				
☐ 572	Rod Beck	.15	.07				
☐ 573	Mike Benjamin	.15	.07				
☐ 574	Barry Bonds	.75	.35				

1995 Fleer All-Fleer

This nine-card standard-size set was available through a 1995 Fleer wrapper offer. Nine of the leading players for each position are featured in this set. The wrapper redemption offer expired on September 30, 1995. The fronts feature the player's photo covering most of the card with a small section on the right set off for the words "All Fleer 9" along with the player's name. The backs feature player information as to why they are among the best in the game.

		MINT	NRMT
COMPLETE SET (9)		10.00	4.50
COMMON CARD (1-9)		.50	.23
SETS WERE AVAILABLE VIA WRAPPER OFFER			
☐ 1	Mike Piazza	2.00	.90
☐ 2	Frank Thomas	2.50	1.10
☐ 3	Roberto Alomar	.75	.35
☐ 4	Cal Ripken Jr.	2.50	1.10
☐ 5	Matt Williams	.50	.23
☐ 6	Barry Bonds	.75	.35
☐ 7	Ken Griffey Jr.	3.00	1.35
☐ 8	Tony Gwynn	1.00	.45
☐ 9	Greg Maddux	2.00	.90

1995 Fleer All-Stars

Randomly inserted in all pack types at a rate of one in

three, this 25-card standard-size set showcases those that participated in the 1994 mid-season classic held in Pittsburgh. Horizontally designed, the fronts contain photos of American League stars with the back portraying the National League player from the same position. On each side, the 1994 All-Star Game logo appears in gold foil as does either the A.L. or N.L. logo in silver foil.

		MINT	NRMT
COMPLETE SET (25)		12.00	5.50
COMMON CARD (1-25)		.25	.11
SEMISTARS		.50	.23
RANDOM INSERTS IN PACKS		..	
☐ 1	Ivan Rodriguez / Mike Piazza	2.00	.90
☐ 2	Frank Thomas / Gregg Jefferies	2.50	1.10
☐ 3	Robert Alomar / Mariano Duncan	.60	.25
☐ 4	Wade Boggs / Matt Williams	.60	.25
☐ 5	Cal Ripken Jr. / Ozzie Smith	2.50	1.10
☐ 6	Joe Carter / Barry Bonds	.75	.35
☐ 7	Ken Griffey Jr. / Tony Gwynn	4.00	1.80
☐ 8	Kirby Puckett / David Justice	1.25	.55
☐ 9	Jimmy Key / Greg Maddux	2.00	.90
☐ 10	Chuck Knoblauch / Wil Cordero	.60	.25
☐ 11	Scott Cooper / Ken Caminiti	.25	.11
☐ 12	Will Clark / Carlos Garcia	.50	.23
☐ 13	Paul Molitor / Jeff Bagwell	1.25	.55
☐ 14	Travis Fryman / Craig Biggio	.35	.16
☐ 15	Mickey Tettleton / Fred McGriff	.35	.16
☐ 16	Kenny Lofton / Moises Alou	.35	.16
☐ 17	Albert Belle / Marquis Grissom	.75	.35
☐ 18	Paul O'Neill / Dante Bichette	.35	.16
☐ 19	David Cone / Ken Hill	.35	.16
☐ 20	Mike Mussina / Doug Drabek	.35	.16
☐ 21	Randy Johnson / John Hudek	.35	.16
☐ 22	Pat Hentgen / Danny Jackson	.35	.16
☐ 23	Wilson Alvarez / Rod Beck	.25	.11
☐ 24	Lee Smith / Randy Myers	.35	.16

☐ 25 Jason Bere .... .25 .11
    Doug Jones

1995 Fleer Award Winners

Randomly inserted in all pack types at a rate of one in 24, this six card standard-size set highlights the major award winners of 1994. Card fronts feature action photos that are full-bleed on the right border and have gold border on the left. Within the gold border are the player's name and Fleer Award Winner. The backs contain a photo with text that references 1994 accomplishments.

	MINT	NRMT
COMPLETE SET (6)	8.00	3.60
COMMON CARD (1-6)	.50	.23
STATED ODDS 1:24		
☐ 1 Frank Thomas	4.00	1.80
☐ 2 Jeff Bagwell	2.00	.90
☐ 3 David Cone	.75	.35
☐ 4 Greg Maddux	3.00	1.35
☐ 5 Bob Hamelin	.50	.23
☐ 6 Raul Mondesi	1.00	.45

1995 Fleer League Leaders

Randomly inserted in all pack types at a rate of one in 12, this 10-card standard-size set features 1994 American and National League leaders in various categories. The horizontal cards have player photos on front and back. The back also has a brief write-up concerning the accomplishment.

	MINT	NRMT
COMPLETE SET (10)	8.00	3.60

COMMON CARD (1-10) .... .50 .23
STATED ODDS 1:12 ....

☐ 1 Paul O'Neill	.50	.23
☐ 2 Ken Griffey Jr.	5.00	2.20
☐ 3 Kirby Puckett	2.00	.90
☐ 4 Jimmy Key	.50	.23
☐ 5 Randy Johnson	1.00	.45
☐ 6 Tony Gwynn	2.00	.90
☐ 7 Matt Williams	.75	.35
☐ 8 Jeff Bagwell	2.00	.90
☐ 9 Greg Maddux	1.50	.70
Ken Hill		
☐ 10 Andy Benes	.50	.23

1995 Fleer Lumber Company

Randomly inserted in retail packs at a rate of one in 24, this standard-size set highlights 10 of the game's top sluggers. Full-bleed card fronts feature an action photo with the Lumber Company logo, which includes the player's name, toward the bottom of the photo. Card backs have a player photo and wood-grain background with a write-up that highlights individual achievements. The set is sequenced in alphabetical order.

	MINT	NRMT
COMPLETE SET (10)	40.00	18.00
COMMON CARD (1-10)	1.00	.45
STATED ODDS 1:24 RETAIL		
☐ 1 Jeff Bagwell..............	6.00	2.70
☐ 2 Albert Belle	4.00	1.80
☐ 3 Barry Bonds	4.00	1.80
☐ 4 Jose Canseco	2.00	.90
☐ 5 Joe Carter	1.50	.70
☐ 6 Ken Griffey Jr.	15.00	6.75
☐ 7 Fred McGriff	2.00	.90
☐ 8 Kevin Mitchell	1.00	.45
☐ 9 Frank Thomas	12.00	5.50
☐ 10 Matt Williams	2.00	.90

1995 Fleer Major League Prospects

Randomly inserted in all pack types at a rate of one in six, this 10-card standard-size set spotlights major league hopefuls. Card fronts feature a player photo with the words "Major League Prospects" serving as part of the background. The player's name and team appear in silver foil at the bottom. The backs have a photo and a write-up on his minor league career. The cards are sequenced in alphabetical order.

CHARLES JOHNSON • MARLINS

	MINT	NRMT
COMPLETE SET (10)	10.00	4.50
COMMON CARD (1-10)	.50	.23
SEMISTARS	1.00	.45
STATED ODDS 1:6		
☐ 1 Garret Anderson	1.00	.45
☐ 2 James Baldwin	.50	.23
☐ 3 Alan Benes	1.00	.45
☐ 4 Armando Benitez	.50	.23
☐ 5 Ray Durham	.75	.35
☐ 6 Brian L. Hunter	1.00	.45
☐ 7 Derek Jeter	4.00	1.80
☐ 8 Charles Johnson	.75	.35
☐ 9 Orlando Miller	.50	.23
☐ 10 Alex Rodriguez	5.00	2.20

1995 Fleer Pro-Visions

Randomly inserted in all pack types at a rate of one in nine, this six card standard-size set features top players illustrated by Wayne Anthony Still. The colorful artwork on front features the player in a surrealistic setting. The backs offer write-up on the player's previous season.

	MINT	NRMT
COMPLETE SET (6)	3.00	1.35
COMMON CARD (1-6)	.75	.35
STATED ODDS 1:9		
☐ 1 Mike Mussina	1.00	.45
☐ 2 Raul Mondesi	.75	.35
☐ 3 Jeff Bagwell	1.25	.55
☐ 4 Greg Maddux	2.00	.90
☐ 5 Tim Salmon	1.00	.45
☐ 6 Manny Ramirez	1.00	.45

1995 Fleer Rookie Sensations

Randomly inserted in 18-card packs, this 20-card standard-size set features top rookies

from the 1994 season. The fronts have full-bleed color photos with the team and player's name in gold foil along the right edge. The backs also have full-bleed color photos along with player information. The set is sequenced in alphabetical order.

er's name are gold foil stamped on front and back.

	MINT	NRMT
COMPLETE SET (28)	225.00	100.00
COMMON CARD (1-28)	2.50	1.10
SEMISTARS	5.00	2.20
UNLISTED STARS	8.00	3.60
STATED ODDS 1:24 HOBBY		

		MINT	NRMT
☐ 1	Cal Ripken Jr.	30.00	13.50
	Mike Mussina		
☐ 2	Mo Vaughn	15.00	6.75
	Roger Clemens		
☐ 3	Tim Salmon	2.50	1.10
	Chuck Finley		
☐ 4	Frank Thomas	30.00	13.50
	Jack McDowell		
☐ 5	Albert Belle	10.00	4.50
	Dennis Martinez		
☐ 6	Cecil Fielder	4.00	1.80
	Mike Moore		
☐ 7	Bob Hamelin	2.50	1.10
	David Cone		
☐ 8	Greg Vaughn	2.50	1.10
	Ricky Bones		
☐ 9	Kirby Puckett	15.00	6.75
	Rick Aguilera		
☐ 10	Don Mattingly	12.00	5.50
	Jimmy Key		
☐ 11	Ruben Sierra	2.50	1.10
	Dennis Eckersley		
☐ 12	Ken Griffey Jr.	40.00	18.00
	Randy Johnson		
☐ 13	Jose Canseco	5.00	2.20
	Kenny Rogers		
☐ 14	Joe Carter	4.00	1.80
	Pat Hentgen		
☐ 15	David Justice	25.00	11.00
	Greg Maddux		
☐ 16	Sammy Sosa	8.00	3.60
	Steve Trachsel		
☐ 17	Kevin Mitchell	2.50	1.10
	Jose Rijo		
☐ 18	Dante Bichette	2.50	1.10
	Bruce Ruffin		
☐ 19	Jeff Conine	2.50	1.10
	Robb Nen		
☐ 20	Jeff Bagwell	15.00	6.75
	Doug Drabek		
☐ 21	Mike Piazza	20.00	9.00
	Ramon Martinez		
☐ 22	Moises Alou	4.00	1.80
	Ken Hill		
☐ 23	Bobby Bonilla	2.50	1.10
	Bret Saberhagen		
☐ 24	Darren Daulton	4.00	1.80
	Danny Jackson		
☐ 25	Jay Bell	4.00	1.80
	Zane Smith		
☐ 26	Gregg Jefferies	2.50	1.10
	Bob Tewksbury		
☐ 27	Tony Gwynn	20.00	9.00
	Andy Benes		
☐ 28	Matt Williams	2.50	1.10
	Rod Beck		

	MINT	NRMT
COMPLETE SET (20)	50.00	22.00
COMMON CARD (1-20)	2.00	.90
SEMISTARS	4.00	1.80
RANDOM INSERTS IN JUMBO PACKS		

		MINT	NRMT
☐ 1	Kurt Abbott	2.00	.90
☐ 2	Rico Brogna	2.00	.90
☐ 3	Hector Carrasco	2.00	.90
☐ 4	Kevin Foster	2.00	.90
☐ 5	Chris Gomez	2.00	.90
☐ 6	Darren Hall	2.00	.90
☐ 7	Bob Hamelin	2.00	.90
☐ 8	Joey Hamilton	3.00	1.35
☐ 9	John Hudek	2.00	.90
☐ 10	Ryan Klesko	6.00	2.70
☐ 11	Javier Lopez	3.00	1.35
☐ 12	Matt Mieske	2.00	.90
☐ 13	Raul Mondesi	6.00	2.70
☐ 14	Manny Ramirez	10.00	4.50
☐ 15	Shane Reynolds	2.00	.90
☐ 16	Bill Risley	2.00	.90
☐ 17	Johnny Ruffin	2.00	.90
☐ 18	Steve Trachsel	2.00	.90
☐ 19	William VanLandingham	2.00	.90
☐ 20	Rondell White	3.00	1.35

1995 Fleer Team Leaders

MATT WILLIAMS

Randomly inserted in 12-card hobby packs at a rate of one in 24, this 28-card standard-size set features top players from each team. Each team is represented with card the has the team's leading hitter on one side with the leading pitcher on the other side. The team logo, "Team Leaders" and the play-

1995 Fleer Update

This 200-card standard-size set features many players who were either rookies in 1995 or played for new teams. These cards were issued in either 12-card packs with a suggested retail price of $1.49 or 18-card packs that had a suggested retail price of $2.29. Each Fleer Update pack included one card from several insert sets pro-duced with this product. Hot packs featuring only these insert cards were included one every 72 packs. The full-bleed fronts have two player photos and, atypical of baseball card

fronts, biographical information such as height, weight, etc. The backgrounds are multi-colored. The backs are horizontal, have yearly statistics, a photo, and are numbered with the prefix "U." The checklist is arranged alpha-betically by team within each leagueis divisions. Key Rookie Cards in this set include Bobby Higginson and Hideo Nomo.

	MINT	NRMT
COMPLETE SET (200)	15.00	6.75
COMMON CARD (1-200)	.10	.05
MINOR STARS	.20	.09
UNLISTED STARS	.40	.18

		MINT	NRMT
☐ 1	Manny Alexander	.10	.05
☐ 2	Bret Barberie	.10	.05
☐ 3	Armando Benitez	.10	.05
☐ 4	Kevin Brown	.20	.09
☐ 5	Doug Jones	.10	.05
☐ 6	Sherman Obando	.10	.05
☐ 7	Andy Van Slyke	.20	.09
☐ 8	Stan Belinda	.10	.05
☐ 9	Jose Canseco	.30	.14
☐ 10	Vaughn Eshelman	.10	.05
☐ 11	Mike Macfarlane	.10	.05
☐ 12	Troy O'Leary	.10	.05
☐ 13	Steve Rodriguez	.10	.05
☐ 14	Lee Tinsley	.10	.05
☐ 15	Tim Vanegmond	.10	.05
☐ 16	Mark Whiten	.10	.05
☐ 17	Sean Bergman	.10	.05
☐ 18	Chad Curtis	.10	.05
☐ 19	John Flaherty	.10	.05
☐ 20	Bob Higginson	.60	.25
☐ 21	Felipe Lira	.10	.05
☐ 22	Shannon Penn	.10	.05
☐ 23	Todd Steverson	.10	.05
☐ 24	Sean Whiteside	.10	.05
☐ 25	Tony Fernandez	.10	.05
☐ 26	Jack McDowell	.10	.05
☐ 27	Andy Pettitte	.60	.25
☐ 28	John Wetteland	.10	.05
☐ 29	David Cone	.20	.09
☐ 30	Mike Timlin	.10	.05
☐ 31	Duane Ward	.10	.05
☐ 32	Jim Abbott	.10	.05
☐ 33	James Baldwin	.10	.05
☐ 34	Mike Devereaux	.10	.05
☐ 35	Ray Durham	.20	.09
☐ 36	Tim Fortugno	.10	.05
☐ 37	Scott Ruffcorn	.10	.05
☐ 38	Chris Sabo	.10	.05
☐ 39	Paul Assenmacher	.10	.05
☐ 40	Bud Black	.10	.05
☐ 41	Orel Hershiser	.20	.09
☐ 42	Julian Tavarez	.10	.05
☐ 43	Dave Winfield	.30	.14
☐ 44	Pat Borders	.10	.05
☐ 45	Melvin Bunch	.10	.05
☐ 46	Tom Goodwin	.10	.05
☐ 47	Jon Nunnally	.10	.05
☐ 48	Joe Randa	.10	.05
☐ 49	Dilson Torres	.10	.05
☐ 50	Joe Vitiello	.10	.05

☐ 51	David Hulse	.10	.05	☐ 137	Scott Sullivan	.10	.05
☐ 52	Scott Karl	.10	.05	☐ 138	Derek Bell	.10	.05
☐ 53	Mark Kiefer	.10	.05	☐ 139	Doug Brocail	.10	.05
☐ 54	Derrick May	.10	.05	☐ 140	Ricky Gutierrez	.10	.05
☐ 55	Joe Oliver	.10	.05	☐ 141	Pedro Martinez	.10	.05
☐ 56	Al Reyes	.10	.05	☐ 142	Orlando Miller	.10	.05
☐ 57	Steve Sparks	.10	.05	☐ 143	Phil Plantier	.10	.05
☐ 58	Jerald Clark	.10	.05	☐ 144	Craig Shipley	.10	.05
☐ 59	Eddie Guardado	.10	.05	☐ 145	Rich Aude	.10	.05
☐ 60	Kevin Maas	.10	.05	☐ 146	Jason Christiansen	.10	.05
☐ 61	David McCarty	.10	.05	☐ 147	Freddy Garcia	.30	.14
☐ 62	Brad Radke	.50	.23	☐ 148	Jim Gott	.10	.05
☐ 63	Scott Stahoviak	.05		☐ 149	Mark Johnson	.10	.05
☐ 64	Garret Anderson	.30	.14	☐ 150	Esteban Loaiza	.20	.09
☐ 65	Shawn Boskie	.10	.05	☐ 151	Dan Plesac	.10	.05
☐ 66	Mike James	.10	.05	☐ 152	Gary Wilson	.10	.05
☐ 67	Tony Phillips	.10	.05	☐ 153	Allen Battle	.10	.05
☐ 68	Lee Smith	.20	.05	☐ 154	Terry Bradshaw	.10	.05
☐ 69	Mitch Williams	.10	.05	☐ 155	Scott Cooper	.10	.05
☐ 70	Jim Corsi	.10	.05	☐ 156	Tripp Cromer	.10	.05
☐ 71	Mark Harkey	.10	.05	☐ 157	John Frascatore	.10	.05
☐ 72	Dave Stewart	.20	.09	☐ 158	John Habyan	.10	.05
☐ 73	Todd Stottlemyre	.10	.05	☐ 159	Tom Henke	.10	.05
☐ 74	Joey Cora	.10	.05	☐ 160	Ken Hill	.10	.05
☐ 75	Chad Kreuter	.10	.05	☐ 161	Danny Jackson	.10	.05
☐ 76	Jeff Nelson	.10	.05	☐ 162	Donovan Osborne	.10	.05
☐ 77	Alex Rodriguez	1.50	.70	☐ 163	Tom Urbani	.10	.05
☐ 78	Ron Villone	.10	.05	☐ 164	Roger Bailey	.10	.05
☐ 79	Bob Wells	.10	.05	☐ 165	Jorge Brito	.10	.05
☐ 80	Jose Alberro	.10	.05	☐ 166	Vinny Castilla	.20	.09
☐ 81	Terry Burrows	.10	.05	☐ 167	Darren Holmes	.10	.05
☐ 82	Kevin Gross	.10	.05	☐ 168	Roberto Mejia	.10	.05
☐ 83	Wilson Heredia	.10	.05	☐ 169	Bill Swift	.10	.05
☐ 84	Mark McLemore	.10	.05	☐ 170	Mark Thompson	.10	.05
☐ 85	Otis Nixon	.10	.05	☐ 171	Larry Walker	.40	.18
☐ 86	Jeff Russell	.10	.05	☐ 172	Greg Hansell	.10	.05
☐ 87	Mickey Tettleton	.10	.05	☐ 173	Dave Hansen	.10	.05
☐ 88	Bob Tewksbury	.10	.05	☐ 174	Carlos Hernandez	.10	.05
☐ 89	Pedro Borbon	.10	.05	☐ 175	Hideo Nomo	2.00	.90
☐ 90	Marquis Grissom	.20	.09	☐ 176	Jose Offerman	.10	.05
☐ 91	Chipper Jones	1.25	.55	☐ 177	Antonio Osuna	.10	.05
☐ 92	Mike Mordecai	.10	.05	☐ 178	Reggie Williams	.10	.05
☐ 93	Jason Schmidt	.10	.05	☐ 179	Todd Williams	.10	.05
☐ 94	John Burkett	.10	.05	☐ 180	Andres Berumen	.10	.05
☐ 95	Andre Dawson	.30	.14	☐ 181	Ken Caminiti	.30	.14
☐ 96	Matt Dunbar	.10	.05	☐ 182	Andujar Cedeno	.10	.05
☐ 97	Charles Johnson	.20	.09	☐ 183	Steve Finley	.20	.09
☐ 98	Terry Pendleton	.10	.05	☐ 184	Bryce Florie	.10	.05
☐ 99	Rich Scheid	.10	.05	☐ 185	Dustin Hermanson	.20	.09
☐ 100	Quilvio Veras	.10	.05	☐ 186	Ray Holbert	.10	.05
☐ 101	Bobby Witt	.10	.05	☐ 187	Melvin Nieves	.10	.05
☐ 102	Eddie Zosky	.10	.05	☐ 188	Roberto Petagine	.10	.05
☐ 103	Shane Andrews	.10	.05	☐ 189	Jody Reed	.10	.05
☐ 104	Reid Cornelius	.10	.05	☐ 190	Fernando Valenzuela	.20	.09
☐ 105	Chad Fonville	.10	.05	☐ 191	Brian Williams	.10	.05
☐ 106	Mark Grudzielanek	.30	.14	☐ 192	Mark Dewey	.10	.05
☐ 107	Roberto Kelly	.10	.05	☐ 193	Glenallen Hill	.10	.05
☐ 108	Carlos Perez	.20	.09	☐ 194	Chris Hook	.10	.05
☐ 109	Tony Tarasco	.10	.05	☐ 195	Terry Mulholland	.10	.05
☐ 110	Brett Butler	.20	.09	☐ 196	Steve Scarsone	.10	.05
☐ 111	Carl Everett	.10	.05	☐ 197	Trevor Wilson	.10	.05
☐ 112	Pete Harnisch	.10	.05	☐ 198	Checklist	.10	.05
☐ 113	Doug Henry	.10	.05	☐ 199	Checklist	.10	.05
☐ 114	Kevin Lomon	.10	.05	☐ 200	Checklist	.10	.05
☐ 115	Blas Minor	.10	.05				
☐ 116	Dave Mlicki	.10	.05				
☐ 117	Ricky Otero	.10	.05				
☐ 118	Norm Charlton	.10	.05				
☐ 119	Tyler Green	.10	.05				
☐ 120	Gene Harris	.10	.05				
☐ 121	Charlie Hayes	.10	.05				
☐ 122	Gregg Jefferies	.10	.05				
☐ 123	Michael Mimbs	.10	.05				
☐ 124	Paul Quantrill	.10	.05				
☐ 125	Frank Castillo	.10	.05				
☐ 126	Brian McRae	.10	.05				
☐ 127	Jaime Navarro	.10	.05				
☐ 128	Mike Perez	.10	.05				
☐ 129	Tanyon Sturtze	.10	.05				
☐ 130	Ozzie Timmons	.10	.05				
☐ 131	John Courtright	.10	.05				
☐ 132	Ron Gant	.20	.09				
☐ 133	Xavier Hernandez	.10	.05				
☐ 134	Brian Hunter	.10	.05				
☐ 135	Benito Santiago	.10	.05				
☐ 136	Pete Smith	.10					

	MINT	NRMT
COMPLETE SET (10)	8.00	3.60
COMMON CARD (1-10)	.50	.23
STATED ODDS 1:5 HOB/RET		

			MINT	NRMT
☐ 1	Jeff Bagwell		1.25	.55
☐ 2	Albert Belle		.75	.35
☐ 3	Barry Bonds		.75	.35
☐ 4	David Cone		.30	.14
☐ 5	Dennis Eckersley		.30	.14
☐ 6	Ken Griffey Jr.		3.00	1.35
☐ 7	Rickey Henderson		.50	.23
☐ 8	Greg Maddux		2.00	.90
☐ 9	Frank Thomas		2.50	1.10
☐ 10	Matt Williams		.50	.23

1995 Fleer Update Headliners

Inserted one every three packs, this 20-card standard-size set features various major league stars. The fronts feature the player's photo set against a newspaper headline. The word "Headliner" as well as the player's name is printed on the bottom on the card in gold foil. The backs have some player information as well as another player photo. The cards are numbered in the lower left as "X" of 20. The cards are sequenced in alphabetical order.

	MINT	NRMT
COMPLETE SET (20)	12.00	5.50
COMMON CARD (1-20)	.25	.11
STATED ODDS 1:3		

		MINT	NRMT
☐ 1	Jeff Bagwell	1.25	.55
☐ 2	Albert Belle	.75	.35
☐ 3	Barry Bonds	.75	.35
☐ 4	Jose Canseco	.50	.23
☐ 5	Joe Carter	.25	.11
☐ 6	Will Clark	.50	.23
☐ 7	Roger Clemens	1.25	.55
☐ 8	Lenny Dykstra	.25	.11
☐ 9	Cecil Fielder	.25	.11

1995 Fleer Update Diamond Tribute

This 10-card standard-size set was inserted at a rate of one in five packs. This set features ten top players. The full-bleed fronts feature a player photo, the "Fleer 95" logo in the upper left corner, the words "Diamond Tribute" surrounding the player's team logo and the player's name on the bottom. All the words in front are in gold foil. The back is split between player information and a player photo. The cards are numbered in the lower right with an "X" of 10. The cards are sequenced in alphabetical order.

		MINT	NRMT
☐ 10	Juan Gonzalez	1.50	.70
☐ 11	Ken Griffey Jr.	3.00	1.35
☐ 12	Kenny Lofton	.75	.35
☐ 13	Greg Maddux.	2.00	.90
☐ 14	Fred McGriff	.50	.23
☐ 15	Mike Piazza	2.00	.90
☐ 16	Kirby Puckett	1.25	.55
☐ 17	Tim Salmon	.60	.25
☐ 18	Frank Thomas	2.50	1.10
☐ 19	Mo Vaughn	.75	.35
☐ 20	Matt Williams	.50	.23

1995 Fleer Update Rookie Update

Inserted one in every four packs, this 10-card standard-size set features some of 1995s best rookies. The horizontal fronts feature the words "Rookie Update" in large letters at the top, and the "Fleer 95" logo as well as the player's name at the bottom. The rest of the card has the player's photo. To the left, the back has background information as well as a photo on the right. The cards are numbered as "X of 10." Chipper Jones and Hideo Nomo are among the players included in this set. The set is sequenced in alphabetical order.

		MINT	NRMT
COMPLETE SET (10)		15.00	6.75
COMMON CARD (1-10)		.25	.11
MINOR STARS		.50	.23
UNLISTED STARS		1.00	.45
STATED ODDS 1:4			

		MINT	NRMT
☐ 1	Shane Andrews	.25	.11
☐ 2	Ray Durham	.50	.23
☐ 3	Shawn Green	.50	.23
☐ 4	Charles Johnson	.50	.23
☐ 5	Chipper Jones	4.00	1.80
☐ 6	Esteban Loaiza	.50	.23
☐ 7	Hideo Nomo	4.00	1.80
☐ 8	Jon Nunnally	.25	.11
☐ 9	Alex Rodriguez	5.00	2.20
☐ 10	Julian Tavarez	.25	.11

1995 Fleer Update Smooth Leather

Inserted one every five jumbo packs, this 10-card standard-size set features many leading defensive wizards. The card fronts feature a player photo. Underneath the player photo, is his name along with the words "smooth leather" on the bottom. The right corner features a

glove. All of this information as well as the "Fleer 95" logo is in gold print. All of this is on a card with a special leather-like coating. The back features a photo as well as fielding information. The cards are numbered in the lower left as "X of 10" and are sequenced in alphabetical order.

		MINT	NRMT
COMPLETE SET (10)		25.00	11.00
COMMON CARD (1-10)		.75	.35
STATED ODDS 1:5 JUMBO			

		MINT	NRMT
☐ 1	Roberto Alomar	2.00	.90
☐ 2	Barry Bonds	2.50	1.10
☐ 3	Ken Griffey Jr.	10.00	4.50
☐ 4	Marquis Grissom	.75	.35
☐ 5	Darren Lewis	.75	.35
☐ 6	Kenny Lofton	2.50	1.10
☐ 7	Don Mattingly	3.00	1.35
☐ 8	Cal Ripken	8.00	3.60
☐ 9	Ivan Rodriguez	2.50	1.10
☐ 10	Matt Williams	1.25	.55

1995 Fleer Update Soaring Stars

This nine-card standard-size set was inserted one every 36 packs. The fronts feature the player's photo set against a prismatic background of baseballs. The player's name, the "Soaring Stars" logo as well as a star are all printed in gold foil at the bottom. The back has a player photo, his name as well as some career information. The cards are numbered in the upper right "X of 9" and are sequenced in alphabetical order.

	MINT	NRMT
COMPLETE SET (10)	60.00	27.00
COMMON CARD (1-10)	2.50	1.10

		MINT	NRMT
SEMISTARS		5.00	2.20
UNLISTED STARS		8.00	3.60
STATED ODDS 1:36			

		MINT	NRMT
☐ 1	Moises Alou UER (says .399 BA in 1994)	3.00	1.35
☐ 2	Jason Bere	2.50	1.10
☐ 3	Jeff Conine	3.00	1.35
☐ 4	Cliff Floyd	2.50	1.10
☐ 5	Pat Hentgen	3.00	1.35
☐ 6	Kenny Lofton	12.00	5.50
☐ 7	Raul Mondesi	5.00	2.20
☐ 8	Mike Piazza	30.00	13.50
☐ 9	Tim Salmon,	8.00	3.60

1996 Fleer

The 1996 Fleer baseball set consists of 600 standard-size cards. Cards were issued in 11-card packs with a suggested retail price of $1.49. Borderless fronts are matte-finished and have full-color action shots with the player's name, team and position stamped in gold foil. Backs contain a biography and career stats on the top and a full-color head shot with a 1995 synopsis on the bottom. The matte finish on the cards was designed so collectors could have an easier surface for cards to be autographed. Fleer included in each pack a "Thanks a Million" scratch-off game card redeemable for instant-win prizes and a chance to bat for a million-dollar prize in a Major League park. Rookie Cards in this set include Matt Lawton and Mike Sweeney.

		MINT	NRMT
COMPLETE SET (600)		80.00	36.00
COMMON CARD (1-600)		.15	.07
MINOR STARS		.30	.14
UNLISTED STARS		.60	.25
COMP.TIFFANY SET (600)		200.00	90.00
COMMON TIFFANY (1-600)		.25	.11
*TIFFANY STARS: 2X TO 4X HI COLUMN			
ONE TIFFANY PER PACK			

		MINT	NRMT
☐ 1	Manny Alexander	.15	.07
☐ 2	Brady Anderson	.40	.18
☐ 3	Harold Baines	.30	.14
☐ 4	Armando Benitez	.15	.07
☐ 5	Bobby Bonilla	.30	.14
☐ 6	Kevin Brown	.30	.14
☐ 7	Scott Erickson	.15	.07
☐ 8	Curtis Goodwin	.15	.07
☐ 9	Jeffrey Hammonds	.15	.07
☐ 10	Jimmy Haynes	.15	.07
☐ 11	Chris Hoiles	.15	.07
☐ 12	Doug Jones	.15	.07
☐ 13	Rick Krivda	.15	.07
☐ 14	Jeff Manto	.15	.07

#	Player			#	Player			#	Player		
15	Ben McDonald	.15	.07	101	Julian Tavarez	.15	.07	187	Jim Leyritz	.15	.07
16	Jamie Moyer	.15	.07	102	Jim Thome	.60	.25	188	Tino Martinez	.60	.25
17	Mike Mussina	.60	.25	103	Omar Vizquel	.30	.14	189	Don Mattingly	1.00	.45
18	Jesse Orosco	.15	.07	104	Dave Winfield	.40	.18	190	Jack McDowell	.15	.07
19	Rafael Palmeiro	.40	.18	105	Danny Bautista	.15	.07	191	Jeff Nelson	.15	.07
20	Cal Ripken	2.50	1.10	106	Joe Boever	.15	.07	192	Paul O'Neill	.30	.14
21	Rick Aguilera	.15	.07	107	Chad Curtis	.15	.07	193	Melido Perez	.15	.07
22	Luis Alicea	.15	.07	108	John Doherty	.15	.07	194	Andy Pettitte	.60	.25
23	Stan Belinda	.15	.07	109	Cecil Fielder	.30	.14	195	Mariano Rivera	.40	.18
24	Jose Canseco	.40	.18	110	John Flaherty	.15	.07	196	Ruben Sierra	.15	.07
25	Roger Clemens	1.25	.55	111	Travis Fryman	.30	.14	197	Mike Stanley	.15	.07
26	Vaughn Eshelman	.15	.07	112	Chris Gomez	.15	.07	198	Darryl Strawberry	.30	.14
27	Mike Greenwell	.15	.07	113	Bob Higginson	.40	.18	199	John Wetteland	.15	.07
28	Erik Hanson	.15	.07	114	Mark Lewis	.15	.07	200	Bob Wickman	.15	.07
29	Dwayne Hosey	.15	.07	115	Jose Lima	.15	.07	201	Bernie Williams	.60	.25
30	Mike Macfarlane UER	.15	.07	116	Felipe Lira	.15	.07	202	Mark Acre	.15	.07
31	Tim Naehring	.15	.07	117	Brian Maxcy	.15	.07	203	Geronimo Berroa	.15	.07
32	Troy O'Leary	.15	.07	118	C.J. Nitkowski	.15	.07	204	Mike Bordick	.15	.07
33	Aaron Sele	.15	.07	119	Phil Plantier	.15	.07	205	Scott Brosius	.15	.07
34	Zane Smith	.15	.07	120	Clint Sodowsky	.15	.07	206	Dennis Eckersley	.30	.14
35	Jeff Suppan	.30	.14	121	Alan Trammell	.40	.18	207	Brent Gates	.15	.07
36	Lee Tinsley	.15	.07	122	Lou Whitaker	.30	.14	208	Jason Giambi	.30	.14
37	John Valentin	.15	.07	123	Kevin Appier	.30	.14	209	Rickey Henderson	.40	.18
38	Mo Vaughn	.75	.35	124	Johnny Damon	.30	.14	210	Jose Herrera	.15	.07
39	Tim Wakefield	.15	.07	125	Gary Gaetti	.15	.07	211	Stan Javier	.15	.07
40	Jim Abbott	.15	.07	126	Tom Goodwin	.15	.07	212	Doug Johns	.15	.07
41	Brian Anderson	.15	.07	127	Tom Gordon	.15	.07	213	Mark McGwire	1.25	.55
42	Garret Anderson	.30	.14	128	Mark Gubicza	.15	.07	214	Steve Ontiveros	.15	.07
43	Chili Davis	.15	.07	129	Bob Hamelin	.15	.07	215	Craig Paquette	.15	.07
44	Gary DiSarcina	.15	.07	130	David Howard	.15	.07	216	Ariel Prieto	.15	.07
45	Damion Easley	.15	.07	131	Jason Jacome	.15	.07	217	Carlos Reyes	.15	.07
46	Jim Edmonds	.40	.18	132	Wally Joyner	.30	.14	218	Terry Steinbach	.15	.07
47	Chuck Finley	.15	.07	133	Keith Lockhart	.15	.07	219	Todd Stottlemyre	.15	.07
48	Todd Greene	.40	.18	134	Brent Mayne	.15	.07	220	Danny Tartabull	.15	.07
49	Mike Harkey	.15	.07	135	Jeff Montgomery	.15	.07	221	Todd Van Poppel	.15	.07
50	Mike James	.15	.07	136	Jon Nunnally	.15	.07	222	John Wasdin	.15	.07
51	Mark Langston	.15	.07	137	Juan Samuel	.15	.07	223	George Williams	.15	.07
52	Greg Myers	.15	.07	138	Mike Sweeney	.60	.25	224	Steve Wojciechowski	.15	.07
53	Orlando Palmeiro	.15	.07	139	Michael Tucker	.30	.14	225	Rich Amaral	.15	.07
54	Bob Patterson	.15	.07	140	Joe Vitiello	.15	.07	226	Bobby Ayala	.15	.07
55	Troy Percival	.15	.07	141	Ricky Bones	.15	.07	227	Tim Belcher	.15	.07
56	Tony Phillips	.15	.07	142	Chuck Carr	.15	.07	228	Andy Benes	.30	.14
57	Tim Salmon	.60	.25	143	Jeff Cirillo	.30	.14	229	Chris Bosio	.15	.07
58	Lee Smith	.30	.14	144	Mike Fetters	.15	.07	230	Darren Bragg	.15	.07
59	J.T. Snow	.30	.14	145	Darryl Hamilton	.15	.07	231	Jay Buhner	.40	.18
60	Randy Velarde	.15	.07	146	David Hulse	.15	.07	232	Norm Charlton	.15	.07
61	Wilson Alvarez	.15	.07	147	John Jaha	.15	.07	233	Vince Coleman	.15	.07
62	Luis Andujar	.15	.07	148	Scott Karl	.15	.07	234	Joey Cora	.30	.14
63	Jason Bere	.15	.07	149	Mark Kiefer	.15	.07	235	Russ Davis	.15	.07
64	Ray Durham	.15	.07	150	Pat Listach	.15	.07	236	Alex Diaz	.15	.07
65	Alex Fernandez	.15	.07	151	Mark Loretta	.15	.07	237	Felix Fermin	.15	.07
66	Ozzie Guillen	.15	.07	152	Mike Matheny	.15	.07	238	Ken Griffey Jr.	3.00	1.35
67	Roberto Hernandez	.15	.07	153	Matt Mieske	.15	.07	239	Sterling Hitchcock	.15	.07
68	Lance Johnson	.15	.07	154	Dave Nilsson	.15	.07	240	Randy Johnson	.60	.25
69	Matt Karchner	.15	.07	155	Joe Oliver	.15	.07	241	Edgar Martinez	.40	.18
70	Ron Karkovice	.15	.07	156	Al Reyes	.15	.07	242	Bill Risley	.15	.07
71	Norberto Martin	.15	.07	157	Kevin Seitzer	.15	.07	243	Alex Rodriguez	2.00	.90
72	Dave Martinez	.15	.07	158	Steve Sparks	.15	.07	244	Luis Sojo	.15	.07
73	Kirk McCaskill	.15	.07	159	B.J. Surhoff	.15	.07	245	Dan Wilson	.15	.07
74	Lyle Mouton	.15	.07	160	Jose Valentin	.15	.07	246	Bob Wolcott	.15	.07
75	Tim Raines	.30	.14	161	Greg Vaughn	.30	.14	247	Will Clark	.40	.18
76	Mike Sirotka	.15	.07	162	Fernando Vina	.15	.07	248	Jeff Frye	.15	.07
77	Frank Thomas	2.50	1.10	163	Rich Becker	.15	.07	249	Benji Gil	.15	.07
78	Larry Thomas	.15	.07	164	Ron Coomer	.15	.07	250	Juan Gonzalez	1.50	.70
79	Robin Ventura	.30	.14	165	Marty Cordova	.30	.14	251	Rusty Greer	.30	.14
80	Sandy Alomar Jr.	.30	.14	166	Chuck Knoblauch	.60	.25	252	Kevin Gross	.15	.07
81	Paul Assenmacher	.15	.07	167	Matt Lawton	.40	.18	253	Roger McDowell	.15	.07
82	Carlos Baerga	.15	.07	168	Pat Meares	.15	.07	254	Mark McLemore	.15	.07
83	Albert Belle	.75	.35	169	Paul Molitor	.60	.25	255	Otis Nixon	.15	.07
84	Mark Clark	.15	.07	170	Pedro Munoz	.15	.07	256	Luis Ortiz	.15	.07
85	Alan Embree	.15	.07	171	Jose Parra	.15	.07	257	Mike Pagliarulo	.15	.07
86	Alvaro Espinoza	.15	.07	172	Kirby Puckett	1.25	.55	258	Dean Palmer	.15	.07
87	Orel Hershiser	.15	.07	173	Brad Radke	.30	.14	259	Roger Pavlik	.15	.07
88	Ken Hill	.15	.07	174	Jeff Reboulet	.15	.07	260	Ivan Rodriguez	.75	.35
89	Kenny Lofton	.75	.35	175	Rich Robertson	.15	.07	261	Kenny Rogers	.15	.07
90	Dennis Martinez	.30	.14	176	Frank Rodriguez	.15	.07	262	Jeff Russell	.15	.07
91	Jose Mesa	.15	.07	177	Scott Stahoviak	.15	.07	263	Mickey Tettleton	.15	.07
92	Eddie Murray	.60	.25	178	Dave Stevens	.15	.07	264	Bob Tewksbury	.15	.07
93	Charles Nagy	.30	.14	179	Matt Walbeck	.15	.07	265	Dave Valle	.15	.07
94	Chad Ogea	.15	.07	180	Wade Boggs	.60	.25	266	Matt Whiteside	.15	.07
95	Tony Pena	.15	.07	181	David Cone	.30	.14	267	Roberto Alomar	.60	.25
96	Herb Perry	.15	.07	182	Tony Fernandez	.15	.07	268	Joe Carter	.30	.14
97	Eric Plunk	.15	.07	183	Joe Girardi	.15	.07	269	Tony Castillo	.15	.07
98	Jim Poole	.15	.07	184	Derek Jeter	2.00	.90	270	Domingo Cedeno	.15	.07
99	Manny Ramirez	.60	.25	185	Scott Kamieniecki	.15	.07	271	Tim Crabtree UER	.15	.07
100	Paul Sorrento	.15	.07	186	Pat Kelly	.15	.07	272	Carlos Delgado	.30	.14

	#	Name	Price	Price
☐	273	Alex Gonzalez	.15	.07
☐	274	Shawn Green	.15	.07
☐	275	Juan Guzman	.15	.07
☐	276	Pat Hentgen	.30	.14
☐	277	Al Leiter	.15	.07
☐	278	Sandy Martinez	.15	.07
☐	279	Paul Menhart	.15	.07
☐	280	John Olerud	.30	.14
☐	281	Paul Quantrill	.15	.07
☐	282	Ken Robinson	.15	.07
☐	283	Ed Sprague	.15	.07
☐	284	Mike Timlin	.15	.07
☐	285	Steve Avery	.15	.07
☐	286	Rafael Belliard	.15	.07
☐	287	Jeff Blauser	.30	.14
☐	288	Pedro Borbon	.15	.07
☐	289	Brad Clontz	.15	.07
☐	290	Mike Devereaux	.15	.07
☐	291	Tom Glavine	.30	.14
☐	292	Marquis Grissom	.30	.14
☐	293	Chipper Jones	2.00	.90
☐	294	David Justice	.60	.25
☐	295	Mike Kelly	.15	.07
☐	296	Ryan Klesko	.40	.18
☐	297	Mark Lemke	.15	.07
☐	298	Javier Lopez	.30	.14
☐	299	Greg Maddux	2.00	.90
☐	300	Fred McGriff	.40	.18
☐	301	Greg McMichael	.15	.07
☐	302	Kent Mercker	.15	.07
☐	303	Mike Mordecai	.15	.07
☐	304	Charlie O'Brien	.15	.07
☐	305	Eduardo Perez	.15	.07
☐	306	Luis Polonia	.15	.07
☐	307	Jason Schmidt	.30	.14
☐	308	John Smoltz	.30	.14
☐	309	Terrell Wade	.15	.07
☐	310	Mark Wohlers	.15	.07
☐	311	Scott Bullett	.15	.07
☐	312	Jim Bullinger	.15	.07
☐	313	Larry Casian	.15	.07
☐	314	Frank Castillo	.15	.07
☐	315	Shawon Dunston	.15	.07
☐	316	Kevin Foster	.15	.07
☐	317	Matt Franco	.15	.07
☐	318	Luis Gonzalez	.15	.07
☐	319	Mark Grace	.40	.18
☐	320	Jose Hernandez	.15	.07
☐	321	Mike Hubbard	.15	.07
☐	322	Brian McRae	.15	.07
☐	323	Randy Myers	.15	.07
☐	324	Jaime Navarro	.15	.07
☐	325	Mark Parent	.15	.07
☐	326	Mike Perez	.15	.07
☐	327	Rey Sanchez	.15	.07
☐	328	Ryne Sandberg	.75	.35
☐	329	Scott Servais	.15	.07
☐	330	Sammy Sosa	.60	.25
☐	331	Ozzie Timmons	.15	.07
☐	332	Steve Trachsel	.15	.07
☐	333	Todd Zeile	.15	.07
☐	334	Bret Boone	.15	.07
☐	335	Jeff Branson	.15	.07
☐	336	Jeff Brantley	.15	.07
☐	337	Dave Burba	.15	.07
☐	338	Hector Carrasco	.15	.07
☐	339	Mariano Duncan	.15	.07
☐	340	Ron Gant	.30	.14
☐	341	Lenny Harris	.15	.07
☐	342	Xavier Hernandez	.15	.07
☐	343	Thomas Howard	.15	.07
☐	344	Mike Jackson	.15	.07
☐	345	Barry Larkin	.40	.18
☐	346	Darren Lewis	.15	.07
☐	347	Hal Morris	.15	.07
☐	348	Eric Owens	.15	.07
☐	349	Mark Portugal	.15	.07
☐	350	Jose Rijo	.15	.07
☐	351	Reggie Sanders	.15	.07
☐	352	Benito Santiago	.15	.07
☐	353	Pete Schourek	.15	.07
☐	354	John Smiley	.15	.07
☐	355	Eddie Taubensee	.15	.07
☐	356	Jerome Walton	.15	.07
☐	357	David Wells	.15	.07
☐	358	Roger Bailey	.15	.07
☐	359	Jason Bates	.15	.07
☐	360	Dante Bichette	.30	.14
☐	361	Ellis Burks	.30	.14
☐	362	Vinny Castilla	.30	.14
☐	363	Andres Galarraga	.60	.25
☐	364	Darren Holmes	.15	.07
☐	365	Mike Kingery	.15	.07
☐	366	Curt Leskanic	.15	.07
☐	367	Quinton McCracken	.15	.07
☐	368	Mike Munoz	.15	.07
☐	369	David Nied	.15	.07
☐	370	Steve Reed	.15	.07
☐	371	Bryan Rekar	.15	.07
☐	372	Kevin Ritz	.15	.07
☐	373	Bruce Ruffin	.15	.07
☐	374	Bret Saberhagen	.15	.07
☐	375	Bill Swift	.15	.07
☐	376	John Vander Wal	.15	.07
☐	377	Larry Walker	.60	.25
☐	378	Walt Weiss	.15	.07
☐	379	Eric Young	.15	.07
☐	380	Kurt Abbott	.15	.07
☐	381	Alex Arias	.15	.07
☐	382	Jerry Browne	.15	.07
☐	383	John Burkett	.15	.07
☐	384	Greg Colbrunn	.15	.07
☐	385	Jeff Conine	.30	.14
☐	386	Andre Dawson	.40	.18
☐	387	Chris Hammond	.15	.07
☐	388	Charles Johnson	.30	.14
☐	389	Terry Mathews	.15	.07
☐	390	Robb Nen	.15	.07
☐	391	Joe Orsulak	.15	.07
☐	392	Terry Pendleton	.15	.07
☐	393	Pat Rapp	.15	.07
☐	394	Gary Sheffield	.60	.25
☐	395	Jesus Tavarez	.15	.07
☐	396	Marc Valdes	.15	.07
☐	397	Quilvio Veras	.15	.07
☐	398	Randy Veres	.15	.07
☐	399	Devon White	.15	.07
☐	400	Jeff Bagwell	1.25	.55
☐	401	Derek Bell	.15	.07
☐	402	Craig Biggio	.40	.18
☐	403	John Cangelosi	.15	.07
☐	404	Jim Dougherty	.15	.07
☐	405	Doug Drabek	.15	.07
☐	406	Tony Eusebio	.15	.07
☐	407	Ricky Gutierrez	.15	.07
☐	408	Mike Hampton	.15	.07
☐	409	Dean Hartgraves	.15	.07
☐	410	John Hudek	.15	.07
☐	411	Brian L. Hunter	.30	.14
☐	412	Todd Jones	.15	.07
☐	413	Darryl Kile	.30	.14
☐	414	Dave Magadan	.15	.07
☐	415	Derrick May	.15	.07
☐	416	Orlando Miller	.15	.07
☐	417	James Mouton	.15	.07
☐	418	Shane Reynolds	.15	.07
☐	419	Greg Swindell	.15	.07
☐	420	Jeff Tabaka	.15	.07
☐	421	Dave Veres	.15	.07
☐	422	Billy Wagner	.30	.14
☐	423	Donne Wall	.15	.07
☐	424	Rick Wilkins	.15	.07
☐	425	Billy Ashley	.15	.07
☐	426	Mike Blowers	.15	.07
☐	427	Brett Butler	.30	.14
☐	428	Tom Candiotti	.15	.07
☐	429	Juan Castro	.15	.07
☐	430	John Cummings	.15	.07
☐	431	Delino DeShields	.15	.07
☐	432	Joey Eischen	.15	.07
☐	433	Chad Fonville	.15	.07
☐	434	Greg Gagne	.15	.07
☐	435	Dave Hansen	.15	.07
☐	436	Carlos Hernandez	.15	.07
☐	437	Todd Hollandsworth	.15	.07
☐	438	Eric Karros	.30	.14
☐	439	Roberto Kelly	.15	.07
☐	440	Ramon Martinez	.30	.14
☐	441	Raul Mondesi	.40	.18
☐	442	Hideo Nomo	1.50	.70
☐	443	Antonio Osuna	.15	.07
☐	444	Chan Ho Park	.60	.25
☐	445	Mike Piazza	2.00	.90
☐	446	Felix Rodriguez	.15	.07
☐	447	Kevin Tapani	.15	.07
☐	448	Ismael Valdes	.30	.14
☐	449	Todd Worrell	.15	.07
☐	450	Moises Alou	.30	.14
☐	451	Shane Andrews	.15	.07
☐	452	Yamil Benitez	.30	.14
☐	453	Sean Berry	.15	.07
☐	454	Wil Cordero	.15	.07
☐	455	Jeff Fassero	.15	.07
☐	456	Darrin Fletcher	.15	.07
☐	457	Cliff Floyd	.15	.07
☐	458	Mark Grudzielanek	.30	.14
☐	459	Gil Heredia	.15	.07
☐	460	Tim Laker	.15	.07
☐	461	Mike Lansing	.15	.07
☐	462	Pedro J.Martinez	.60	.25
☐	463	Carlos Perez	.15	.07
☐	464	Curtis Pride	.15	.07
☐	465	Mel Rojas	.15	.07
☐	466	Kirk Rueter	.15	.07
☐	467	F.P. Santangelo	.15	.07
☐	468	Tim Scott	.15	.07
☐	469	David Segui	.15	.07
☐	470	Tony Tarasco	.15	.07
☐	471	Rondell White	.30	.14
☐	472	Edgardo Alfonzo	.40	.18
☐	473	Tim Bogar	.15	.07
☐	474	Rico Brogna	.15	.07
☐	475	Damon Buford	.15	.07
☐	476	Paul Byrd	.15	.07
☐	477	Carl Everett	.15	.07
☐	478	John Franco	.30	.14
☐	479	Todd Hundley	.30	.14
☐	480	Butch Huskey	.30	.14
☐	481	Jason Isringhausen	.15	.07
☐	482	Bobby Jones	.15	.07
☐	483	Chris Jones	.15	.07
☐	484	Jeff Kent	.15	.07
☐	485	Dave Mlicki	.15	.07
☐	486	Robert Person	.15	.07
☐	487	Bill Pulsipher	.15	.07
☐	488	Kelly Stinnett	.15	.07
☐	489	Ryan Thompson	.15	.07
☐	490	Jose Vizcaino	.15	.07
☐	491	Howard Battle	.15	.07
☐	492	Tony Borland	.15	.07
☐	493	Ricky Bottalico	.15	.07
☐	494	Darren Daulton	.30	.14
☐	495	Lenny Dykstra	.30	.14
☐	496	Jim Eisenreich	.15	.07
☐	497	Sid Fernandez	.15	.07
☐	498	Tyler Green	.15	.07
☐	499	Charlie Hayes	.15	.07
☐	500	Gregg Jefferies	.15	.07
☐	501	Kevin Jordan	.15	.07
☐	502	Tony Longmire	.15	.07
☐	503	Tom Marsh	.15	.07
☐	504	Michael Mimbs	.15	.07
☐	505	Mickey Morandini	.15	.07
☐	506	Gene Schall	.15	.07
☐	507	Curt Schilling	.30	.14
☐	508	Heathcliff Slocumb	.15	.07
☐	509	Kevin Stocker	.15	.07
☐	510	Andy Van Slyke	.30	.14
☐	511	Lenny Webster	.15	.07
☐	512	Mark Whiten	.15	.07
☐	513	Mike Williams	.15	.07
☐	514	Jay Bell	.30	.14
☐	515	Jacob Brumfield	.15	.07
☐	516	Jason Christiansen	.15	.07
☐	517	Dave Clark	.15	.07
☐	518	Midre Cummings	.15	.07
☐	519	Angelo Encarnacion	.15	.07
☐	520	John Ericks	.15	.07
☐	521	Carlos Garcia	.15	.07
☐	522	Mark Johnson	.15	.07
☐	523	Jeff King	.15	.07
☐	524	Nelson Liriano	.15	.07
☐	525	Esteban Loaiza	.15	.07
☐	526	Al Martin	.15	.07
☐	527	Orlando Merced	.15	.07
☐	528	Dan Miceli	.15	.07
☐	529	Ramon Morel	.15	.07
☐	530	Denny Neagle	.30	.14

		MINT	NRMT
☐ 531	Steve Parris	.15	.07
☐ 532	Dan Plesac	.15	.07
☐ 533	Don Slaught	.15	.07
☐ 534	Paul Wagner	.15	.07
☐ 535	John Wehner	.15	.07
☐ 536	Kevin Young	.15	.07
☐ 537	Allen Battle	.15	.07
☐ 538	David Bell	.15	.07
☐ 539	Alan Benes	.30	.14
☐ 540	Scott Cooper	.15	.07
☐ 541	Tripp Cromer	.15	.07
☐ 542	Tony Fossas	.15	.07
☐ 543	Bernard Gilkey	.15	.07
☐ 544	Tom Henke	.15	.07
☐ 545	Brian Jordan	.30	.14
☐ 546	Ray Lankford	.30	.14
☐ 547	John Mabry	.15	.07
☐ 548	T.J. Mathews	.15	.07
☐ 549	Mike Morgan	.15	.07
☐ 550	Jose Oliva	.15	.07
☐ 551	Jose Oquendo	.15	.07
☐ 552	Donovan Osborne	.15	.07
☐ 553	Tom Pagnozzi	.15	.07
☐ 554	Mark Petkovsek	.15	.07
☐ 555	Danny Sheaffer	.15	.07
☐ 556	Ozzie Smith	.75	.35
☐ 557	Mark Sweeney	.15	.07
☐ 558	Allen Watson	.15	.07
☐ 559	Andy Ashby	.15	.07
☐ 560	Brad Ausmus	.15	.07
☐ 561	Willie Blair	.15	.07
☐ 562	Ken Caminiti	.40	.18
☐ 563	Andujar Cedeno	.15	.07
☐ 564	Glenn Dishman	.15	.07
☐ 565	Steve Finley	.30	.14
☐ 566	Bryce Florie	.15	.07
☐ 567	Tony Gwynn	1.50	.70
☐ 568	Joey Hamilton	.30	.14
☐ 569	Dustin Hermanson UER	.15	.07
☐ 570	Trevor Hoffman	.15	.07
☐ 571	Brian Johnson	.15	.07
☐ 572	Marc Kroon	.15	.07
☐ 573	Scott Livingstone	.15	.07
☐ 574	Marc Newfield	.15	.07
☐ 575	Melvin Nieves	.15	.07
☐ 576	Jody Reed	.15	.07
☐ 577	Bip Roberts	.15	.07
☐ 578	Scott Sanders	.15	.07
☐ 579	Fernando Valenzuela	.30	.14
☐ 580	Eddie Williams	.15	.07
☐ 581	Rod Beck	.15	.07
☐ 582	Marvin Benard	.15	.07
☐ 583	Barry Bonds	.75	.35
☐ 584	Jamie Brewington	.15	.07
☐ 585	Mark Carreon	.15	.07
☐ 586	Royce Clayton	.15	.07
☐ 587	Shawn Estes	.40	.18
☐ 588	Glenallen Hill	.15	.07
☐ 589	Mark Leiter	.15	.07
☐ 590	Kirt Manwaring	.15	.07
☐ 591	Darryl McCarty	.15	.07
☐ 592	Terry Mulholland	.15	.07
☐ 593	John Patterson	.15	.07
☐ 594	J.R. Phillips	.15	.07
☐ 595	Deion Sanders	.30	.14
☐ 596	Steve Scarsone	.15	.07
☐ 597	Robby Thompson	.15	.07
☐ 598	Sergio Valdez	.15	.07
☐ 599	William Van Landingham	.15	.07
☐ 600	Matt Williams	.40	.18
☐ P20	Cal Ripken	2.00	.90
	Promo		

1996 Fleer Checklists

Checklist cards were seeded one per six regular packs and have glossy, borderless fronts with full-color shots of the Major League's best. "Checklist" and the player's name are stamped in gold foil. Backs list the entire rundown of '96 Fleer cards

printed in black type on a white background.

	MINT	NRMT
COMPLETE SET (10)	4.00	1.80
COMMON CARD (1-10)	.20	.09
STATED ODDS 1:6		

		MINT	NRMT
☐ 1	Barry Bonds	.30	.14
☐ 2	Ken Griffey Jr.	1.50	.70
☐ 3	Chipper Jones	1.00	.45
☐ 4	Greg Maddux	1.00	.45
☐ 5	Mike Piazza	1.00	.45
☐ 6	Manny Ramirez	.30	.14
☐ 7	Cal Ripken	1.25	.55
☐ 8	Frank Thomas	1.25	.55
☐ 9	Mo Vaughn	.30	.14
☐ 10	Matt Williams	.20	.09

1996 Fleer Golden Memories

Randomly inserted at a rate of one in 10 regular packs, this 10-card standard-size set features important highlights of the 1995 season. Fronts have two action shots, one serving as a background, the other a full-color cutout. "Golden Memories" and player's name are printed vertically in white type. Backs contain a biography, player close-up and career statistics.

	MINT	NRMT
COMPLETE SET (10)	8.00	3.60
COMMON CARD (1-10)	.25	.11
STATED ODDS 1:10		

		MINT	NRMT
☐ 1	Albert Belle	1.00	.45
☐ 2	Barry Bonds	1.25	.55
	Sammy Sosa		
☐ 3	Greg Maddux	3.00	1.35
☐ 4	Edgar Martinez	.60	.25
☐ 5	Ramon Martinez	.25	.11
☐ 6	Mark McGwire	1.50	.70
☐ 7	Eddie Murray	1.00	.45
☐ 8	Cal Ripken	4.00	1.80

		MINT	NRMT
☐ 9	Frank Thomas	4.00	1.80
☐ 10	Alan Trammell	.60	.25
	Lou Whitaker		

1996 Fleer Lumber Company

This retail-exclusive 12-card set was inserted one in every nine packs and features RBI and HR power hitters. The fronts display a color action player cut-out on a wood background with embossed printing. The backs carry a player photo and information about the player.

	MINT	NRMT
COMPLETE SET (12)	25.00	11.00
COMMON CARD (1-12)	1.00	.45
STATED ODDS 1:9 RETAIL		

		MINT	NRMT
☐ 1	Albert Belle	2.00	.90
☐ 2	Dante Bichette	1.00	.45
☐ 3	Barry Bonds	2.00	.90
☐ 4	Ken Griffey Jr.	10.00	4.50
☐ 5	Mark McGwire	4.00	1.80
☐ 6	Mike Piazza	6.00	2.70
☐ 7	Manny Ramirez	2.00	.90
☐ 8	Tim Salmon	2.00	.90
☐ 9	Sammy Sosa	2.00	.90
☐ 10	Frank Thomas	8.00	3.60
☐ 11	Mo Vaughn	2.50	1.10
☐ 12	Matt Williams	1.50	.70

1996 Fleer Postseason Glory

Randomly inserted in regular packs at a rate of one in five, this five-card standard-size set highlights great moments of the 1996 Divisional, League Championship and World Series games. Horizontal, white-bordered fronts feature a player in three full-color action cutouts

with black strips on top and bottom. "Post-Season Glory" appears on top and the player's name is printed in silver hologram foil. White-bordered backs are split between a full-color player close-up and a description of his post-season play printed in white type on a black background.

	MINT	NRMT
COMPLETE SET (5)	2.00	.90
COMMON CARD (1-5)	.15	.07
STATED ODDS 1:5		

		MINT	NRMT
☐ 1	Tom Glavine	.15	.07
☐ 2	Ken Griffey Jr.	1.50	.70
☐ 3	Orel Hershiser	.15	.07
☐ 4	Randy Johnson	.25	.11
☐ 5	Jim Thome	.25	.11

1996 Fleer Prospects

Randomly inserted at a rate of one in six regular packs, this ten-card standard-size set focuses on players moving up through the farm system. Borderless fronts have full-color head shots on one-color backgrounds. "Prospect" and the player's name are stamped in silver hologram foil. Backs feature a full-color action shot with a synopsis of talent printed in a green box.

	MINT	NRMT
COMPLETE SET (10)	5.00	2.20
COMMON CARD (1-10)	.25	.11
MINOR STARS	.50	.23
SEMISTARS	1.00	.45
STATED ODDS 1:6		

		MINT	NRMT
☐ 1	Yamil Benitez	.50	.23
☐ 2	Roger Cedeno	.25	.11
☐ 3	Tony Clark	1.50	.70
☐ 4	Micah Franklin	.25	.11
☐ 5	Karim Garcia	1.50	.70
☐ 6	Todd Greene	1.50	.70
☐ 7	Alex Ochoa	.25	.11
☐ 8	Ruben Rivera	1.50	.70
☐ 9	Chris Snopek	.25	.11
☐ 10	Shannon Stewart	.50	.23

1996 Fleer Road Warriors

Randomly inserted in regular packs at a rate of one in 13, this 10-card standard-size set focuses on players who thrive on the road. Fronts feature a full-color

player cutout set against a winding rural highway background. "Road Warriors" is printed in reverse type with a hazy white border and the player's name is printed in white type underneath. Backs include the player's road stats, biography and a close-up image.

	MINT	NRMT
COMPLETE SET (10)	12.00	5.50
COMMON CARD (1-10)	.25	.11
STATED ODDS 1:13		

		MINT	NRMT
☐ 1	Derek Bell	.25	.11
☐ 2	Tony Gwynn	2.00	.90
☐ 3	Greg Maddux	3.00	1.35
☐ 4	Mark McGwire	2.00	.90
☐ 5	Mike Piazza	3.00	1.35
☐ 6	Manny Ramirez	1.00	.45
☐ 7	Tim Salmon	1.00	.45
☐ 8	Frank Thomas	4.00	1.80
☐ 9	Mo Vaughn	1.25	.55
☐ 10	Matt Williams	.75	.35

1996 Fleer Rookie Sensations

Randomly inserted at a rate of one in 11 regular packs, this 15-card standard-size set highlights 1995's best rookies. Borderless, horizontal fronts have a full-color action shot and a silver hologram strip containing the player's name and team logo. Horizontal backs have full-color head shots with a player profile all printed on a white background.

	MINT	NRMT
COMPLETE SET (15)	20.00	9.00
COMMON CARD (1-15)	1.00	.45
STATED ODDS 1:11		

		MINT	NRMT
☐ 1	Garret Anderson	1.50	.70
☐ 2	Marty Cordova	1.50	.70

		MINT	NRMT
☐ 3	Johnny Damon	1.50	.70
☐ 4	Ray Durham	1.00	.45
☐ 5	Carl Everett	1.00	.45
☐ 6	Shawn Green	1.00	.45
☐ 7	Brian L.Hunter	1.50	.70
☐ 8	Jason Isringhausen	1.00	.45
☐ 9	Charles Johnson	1.50	.70
☐ 10	Chipper Jones	10.00	4.50
☐ 11	John Mabry	1.00	.45
☐ 12	Hideo Nomo	8.00	3.60
☐ 13	Troy Percival	1.00	.45
☐ 14	Andy Pettitte	5.00	2.20
☐ 15	Quivlio Veras	1.00	.45

1996 Fleer Smoke 'n Heat

Randomly inserted at a rate of one in nine regular packs, this 10-card standard-size set celebrates the pitchers with rifle arms and a high strikeout count. Fronts feature a full-color player cutout set against a red flame background. "Smoke 'n Heat" and the player's name are printed in gold type. Backs feature the pitcher's 1995 numbers, a biography and career stats along with a full-color close-up.

	MINT	NRMT
COMPLETE SET (10)	6.00	2.70
COMMON CARD (1-10)	.25	.11
STATED ODDS 1:9		

		MINT	NRMT
☐ 1	Kevin Appier	.35	.16
☐ 2	Roger Clemens	2.00	.90
☐ 3	David Cone	.35	.16
☐ 4	Chuck Finley	.25	.11
☐ 5	Randy Johnson	1.00	.45
☐ 6	Greg Maddux	3.00	1.35
☐ 7	Pedro Martinez	1.00	.45
☐ 8	Hideo Nomo	2.50	1.10
☐ 9	John Smoltz	.35	.16
☐ 10	Todd Stottlemyre	.25	.11

1996 Fleer Team Leaders

This hobby-exclusive 28-card set was randomly inserted one in every nine packs and features statistical and inspirational leaders. The fronts display color action player cut-out on a foil background of the team name and logo. The backs carry a player portrait and player information.

	MINT	NRMT
COMPLETE SET (28)	80.00	36.00
COMMON CARD (1-28)	.75	.35
STATED ODDS 1:9 HOBBY		

	MINT	NRMT
COMPLETE SET (10)	10.00	4.50
COMMON CARD (1-10)	1.00	.45
STATED ODDS 1:13		

		MINT	NRMT
☐ 1	Garret Anderson	1.25	.55
☐ 2	Jim Edmonds	1.50	.70
☐ 3	Brian L.Hunter	1.25	.55
☐ 4	Jason Isringhausen	1.00	.45
☐ 5	Charles Johnson	1.25	.55
☐ 6	Chipper Jones	6.00	2.70
☐ 7	Ryan Klesko	1.50	.70
☐ 8	Hideo Nomo	5.00	2.20
☐ 9	Manny Ramirez	2.00	.90
☐ 10	Rondell White	1.25	.55

		MINT	NRMT
☐ 1	Cal Ripken	12.00	5.50
☐ 2	Mo Vaughn	4.00	1.80
☐ 3	Jim Edmonds	2.00	.90
☐ 4	Frank Thomas	12.00	5.50
☐ 5	Kenny Lofton	4.00	1.80
☐ 6	Travis Fryman	1.50	.70
☐ 7	Gary Gaetti	.75	.35
☐ 8	B.J. Surhoff	.75	.35
☐ 9	Kirby Puckett	6.00	2.70
☐ 10	Don Mattingly	5.00	2.20
☐ 11	Mark McGwire	6.00	2.70
☐ 12	Ken Griffey Jr.	15.00	6.75
☐ 13	Juan Gonzalez	8.00	3.60
☐ 14	Joe Carter	1.50	.70
☐ 15	Greg Maddux	10.00	4.50
☐ 16	Sammy Sosa	3.00	1.35
☐ 17	Barry Larkin	2.00	.90
☐ 18	Dante Bichette	1.50	.70
☐ 19	Jeff Conine	1.50	.70
☐ 20	Jeff Bagwell	6.00	2.70
☐ 21	Mike Piazza	10.00	4.50
☐ 22	Rondell White	1.50	.70
☐ 23	Rico Brogna	.75	.35
☐ 24	Darren Daulton	1.50	.70
☐ 25	Jeff King	.75	.35
☐ 26	Ray Lankford	1.50	.70
☐ 27	Tony Gwynn	8.00	3.60
☐ 28	Barry Bonds	4.00	1.80

1996 Fleer Zone

This 12-card set was randomly inserted one in every 90 packs and features "unstoppable" hitters and "unhittable" pitchers. The fronts display a color action player cut-out printed on holographic foil. The backs carry a player portrait with information as to why they were selected for this set.

	MINT	NRMT
COMPLETE SET (12)	200.00	90.00
COMMON CARD (1-12)	5.00	2.20
UNLISTED STARS	8.00	3.60
STATED ODDS 1:90		

		MINT	NRMT
☐ 1	Albert Belle	10.00	4.50
☐ 2	Barry Bonds	10.00	4.50
☐ 3	Ken Griffey Jr.	40.00	18.00
☐ 4	Tony Gwynn	20.00	9.00
☐ 5	Randy Johnson	8.00	3.60
☐ 6	Kenny Lofton	10.00	4.50
☐ 7	Greg Maddux	25.00	11.00
☐ 8	Edgar Martinez	7.00	3.10
☐ 9	Mike Piazza	25.00	11.00
☐ 10	Frank Thomas	30.00	13.50
☐ 11	Mo Vaughn	10.00	4.50
☐ 12	Matt Williams	7.00	3.10

1996 Fleer Tomorrow's Legends

Randomly inserted in regular packs at a rate of one in 13, this 10-card set focuses on young talent with bright futures. Multicolored fronts have four panels of art that serve as a background and a full-color player cutout. "Tomorrow's Legends" and player's name are printed in white type at the bottom. Backs include the player's '95 stats, biography and a full-color close-up shot.

1996 Fleer Update

The 1996 Fleer Update set was issued in one series totalling 250 cards. The 11-card packs retail for $1.49 each. The fronts feature color action player photos. The backs carry complete player stats and a "Did you know?" fact. The cards are grouped alphabetically within teams and checklisted below alphabetically according to teams for each league with AL preceding NL. The set contains the subset: Encore (U211-U245). Notable Rookie Cards include Mike Cameron and Wilton Guerrero.

	MINT	NRMT
COMPLETE SET (250)	30.00	13.50
COMMON CARD (U1-U250)	.15	.07
MINOR STARS	.30	.14
UNLISTED STARS	.60	.25
COMP.TIFFANY SET (250)	120.00	55.00
COMMON TIFFANY (1-250)	.25	.11
*TIFFANY STARS: 2.5X TO 5X HI COLUMN		
*TIFFANY YOUNG STARS: 2X TO 4X HI		
ONE TIFFANY PER PACK		

		MINT	NRMT
☐ U1	Roberto Alomar	.60	.25
☐ U2	Mike Devereaux	.15	.07
☐ U3	Scott McClain	.15	.07
☐ U4	Roger McDowell	.15	.07
☐ U5	Kent Mercker	.15	.07
☐ U6	Jimmy Myers	.15	.07
☐ U7	Randy Myers	.15	.07
☐ U8	B.J. Surhoff	.15	.07
☐ U9	Tony Tarasco	.15	.07
☐ U10	David Wells	.15	.07
☐ U11	Wil Cordero	.15	.07
☐ U12	Tom Gordon	.15	.07
☐ U13	Reggie Jefferson	.15	.07
☐ U14	Jose Malave	.15	.07
☐ U15	Kevin Mitchell	.15	.07
☐ U16	Jamie Moyer	.15	.07
☐ U17	Heathcliff Slocumb	.15	.07
☐ U18	Mike Stanley	.15	.07
☐ U19	George Arias	.15	.07
☐ U20	Jorge Fabregas	.15	.07
☐ U21	Don Slaught	.15	.07
☐ U22	Randy Velarde	.15	.07
☐ U23	Harold Baines	.30	.14
☐ U24	Mike Cameron	1.50	.70
☐ U25	Darren Lewis	.15	.07
☐ U26	Tony Phillips	.15	.07
☐ U27	Bill Simas	.15	.07
☐ U28	Chris Snopek	.15	.07
☐ U29	Kevin Tapani	.15	.07
☐ U30	Danny Tartabull	.15	.07
☐ U31	Julio Franco	.15	.07
☐ U32	Jack McDowell	.15	.07
☐ U33	Kimera Bartee	.15	.07
☐ U34	Mark Lewis	.15	.07
☐ U35	Melvin Nieves	.15	.07
☐ U36	Mark Parent	.15	.07
☐ U37	Eddie Williams	.15	.07
☐ U38	Tim Belcher	.15	.07
☐ U39	Sal Fasano	.15	.07
☐ U40	Chris Haney	.15	.07
☐ U41	Mike Macfarlane	.15	.07
☐ U42	Jose Offerman	.15	.07
☐ U43	Joe Randa	.15	.07
☐ U44	Bip Roberts	.15	.07
☐ U45	Chuck Carr	.15	.07
☐ U46	Bobby Hughes	.15	.07
☐ U47	Graeme Lloyd	.15	.07
☐ U48	Ben McDonald	.15	.07
☐ U49	Kevin Wickander	.15	.07
☐ U50	Rick Aguilera	.15	.07
☐ U51	Mike Durant	.15	.07
☐ U52	Chip Hale	.15	.07
☐ U53	LaTroy Hawkins	.15	.07
☐ U54	Dave Hollins	.15	.07
☐ U55	Roderick Kelly	.15	.07
☐ U56	Paul Molitor	.60	.25
☐ U57	Dan Naulty	.15	.07

U58 Mariano Duncan	.15	.07	U144 Karim Garcia	.40	.18	U230 Barry Larkin ENC	.30	.14
U59 Andy Fox	.15	.07	U145 Wilton Guerrero	.60	.25	U231 Kenny Lofton ENC	.40	.18
U60 Joe Girardi	.15	.07	U146 Israel Alcantara	.15	.07	U232 Greg Maddux ENC	1.00	.45
U61 Dwight Gooden	.30	.14	U147 Omar Daal	.15	.07	U233 Raul Mondesi ENC	.30	.14
U62 Jimmy Key	.30	.14	U148 Ryan McGuire	.15	.07	U234 Hideo Nomo ENC	.75	.35
U63 Matt Luke	.15	.07	U149 Sherman Obando	.15	.07	U235 Mike Piazza ENC	1.00	.45
U64 Tino Martinez	.60	.25	U150 Jose Paniagua	.15	.07	U236 Manny Ramirez ENC	.30	.14
U65 Jeff Nelson	.15	.07	U151 Henry Rodriguez	.15	.07	U237 Cal Ripken ENC	1.25	.55
U66 Tim Raines	.30	.14	U152 Andy Stankiewicz	.15	.07	U238 Tim Salmon ENC	.30	.14
U67 Ruben Rivera	.30	.14	U153 Dave Veres	.15	.07	U239 Ryne Sandberg ENC	.40	.18
U68 Kenny Rogers	.15	.07	U154 Juan Acevedo	.15	.07	U240 Reggie Sanders ENC	.15	.07
U69 Gerald Williams	.15	.07	U155 Mark Clark	.15	.07	U241 Gary Sheffield ENC	.30	.14
U70 Tony Batista	.30	.14	U156 Bernard Gilkey	.15	.07	U242 Sammy Sosa ENC	.30	.14
U71 Allen Battle	.15	.07	U157 Pete Harnisch	.15	.07	U243 Frank Thomas ENC	1.25	.55
U72 Jim Corsi	.15	.07	U158 Lance Johnson	.15	.07	U244 Mo Vaughn ENC	.50	.23
U73 Steve Cox	.15	.07	U159 Brent Mayne	.15	.07	U245 Matt Williams ENC	.30	.14
U74 Pedro Munoz	.15	.07	U160 Rey Ordonez	.30	.14	U246 Barry Bonds CL	.40	.18
U75 Phil Plantier	.15	.07	U161 Kevin Roberson	.15	.07	U247 Ken Griffey Jr. CL	1.50	.70
U76 Scott Spiezio	.40	.18	U162 Paul Wilson	.15	.07	U248 Rey Ordonez CL	.15	.07
U77 Ernie Young	.15	.07	U163 David Doster	.15	.07	U249 Ryne Sandberg CL	.40	.18
U78 Russ Davis	.15	.07	U164 Mike Grace	.15	.07	U250 Frank Thomas CL	1.25	.55
U79 Sterling Hitchcock	.15	.07	U165 Rich Hunter	.15	.07			
U80 Edwin Hurtado	.15	.07	U166 Pete Incaviglia	.15	.07			
U81 Raul Ibanez	.40	.18	U167 Mike Lieberthal	.15	.07			
U82 Mike Jackson	.15	.07	U168 Terry Mulholland	.15	.07			
U83 Ricky Jordan	.15	.07	U169 Ken Ryan	.15	.07			
U84 Paul Sorrento	.15	.07	U170 Benito Santiago	.15	.07			
U85 Doug Strange	.15	.07	U171 Kevin Sefcik	.15	.07			
U86 Mark Brandenburg	.15	.07	U172 Lee Tinsley	.15	.07			
U87 Damon Buford	.15	.07	U173 Todd Zeile	.15	.07			
U88 Kevin Elster	.15	.07	U174 Francisco Cordova	.15	.07			
U89 Darryl Hamilton	.15	.07	U175 Danny Darwin	.15	.07			
U90 Ken Hill	.15	.07	U176 Charlie Hayes	.15	.07			
U91 Ed Vosberg	.15	.07	U177 Jason Kendall	.40	.18			
U92 Craig Worthington	.15	.07	U178 Mike Kingery	.15	.07			
U93 Tilson Brito	.15	.07	U179 Jon Lieber	.15	.07			
U94 Giovanni Carrara	.15	.07	U180 Zane Smith	.15	.07			
U95 Felipe Crespo	.15	.07	U181 Luis Alicea	.15	.07			
U96 Erik Hanson	.15	.07	U182 Cory Bailey	.15	.07			
U97 Marty Janzen	.15	.07	U183 Andy Benes	.30	.14			
U98 Otis Nixon	.15	.07	U184 Pat Borders	.15	.07			
U99 Charlie O'Brien	.15	.07	U185 Mike Busby	.15	.07			
U100 Robert Perez	.15	.07	U186 Royce Clayton	.15	.07			
U101 Paul Quantrill	.15	.07	U187 Dennis Eckersley	.30	.14			
U102 Bill Risley	.15	.07	U188 Gary Gaetti	.15	.07			
U103 Juan Samuel	.15	.07	U189 Ron Gant	.30	.14			
U104 Jermaine Dye	.30	.14	U190 Aaron Holbert	.15	.07			
U105 Wonderful Monds	.15	.07	U191 Willie McGee	.15	.07			
U106 Dwight Smith	.15	.07	U192 Miguel Mejia	.15	.07			
U107 Jerome Walton	.15	.07	U193 Jeff Parrett	.15	.07			
U108 Terry Adams	.15	.07	U194 Todd Stottlemyre	.15	.07			
U109 Leo Gomez	.15	.07	U195 Sean Bergman	.15	.07			
U110 Robin Jennings	.15	.07	U196 Archi Cianfrocco	.15	.07			
U111 Doug Jones	.15	.07	U197 Rickey Henderson	.40	.18			
U112 Brooks Kieschnick	.30	.14	U198 Wally Joyner	.30	.14			
U113 Dave Magadan	.15	.07	U199 Craig Shipley	.15	.07			
U114 Jason Maxwell	.15	.07	U200 Bob Tewksbury	.15	.07			
U115 Rodney Myers	.15	.07	U201 Tim Worrell	.15	.07			
U116 Eric Anthony	.15	.07	U202 Rich Aurilia	.15	.07			
U117 Vince Coleman	.15	.07	U203 Doug Creek	.15	.07			
U118 Eric Davis	.30	.14	U204 Shawon Dunston	.15	.07			
U119 Steve Gibralter	.15	.07	U205 Osvaldo Fernandez	.30	.14			
U120 Curtis Goodwin	.15	.07	U206 Mark Gardner	.15	.07			
U121 Willie Greene	.15	.07	U207 Stan Javier	.15	.07			
U122 Mike Kelly	.15	.07	U208 Marcus Jensen	.15	.07			
U123 Marcus Moore	.15	.07	U209 Chris Singleton	.15	.07			
U124 Chad Mottola	.15	.07	U210 Allen Watson	.15	.07			
U125 Chris Sabo	.15	.07	U211 Jeff Bagwell ENC	.60	.25			
U126 Roger Salkeld	.15	.07	U212 Derek Bell ENC	.15	.07			
U127 Pedro Castellano	.15	.07	U213 Albert Belle ENC	.40	.18			
U128 Trenidad Hubbard	.15	.07	U214 Wade Boggs ENC	.30	.14			
U129 Jayhawk Owens	.15	.07	U215 Barry Bonds ENC	.40	.18			
U130 Jeff Reed	.15	.07	U216 Jose Canseco ENC	.30	.14			
U131 Kevin Brown	.30	.14	U217 Marty Cordova ENC	.15	.07			
U132 Al Leiter	.15	.07	U218 Jim Edmonds ENC	.30	.14			
U133 Matt Mantei	.15	.07	U219 Cecil Fielder ENC	.15	.07			
U134 Dave Weathers	.15	.07	U220 Andres Galarraga ENC	.30	.14			
U135 Devon White	.15	.07	U221 Juan Gonzalez ENC	.75	.35			
U136 Bob Abreu	.40	.18	U222 Mark Grace ENC	.15	.07			
U137 Sean Berry	.15	.07	U223 Ken Griffey Jr. ENC	1.50	.70			
U138 Doug Brocail	.15	.07	U224 Tony Gwynn ENC	.75	.35			
U139 Richard Hidalgo	.60	.25	U225 Jason Isringhausen ENC	.15	.07			
U140 Alvin Morman	.15	.07	U226 Derek Jeter ENC	1.00	.45			
U141 Mike Blowers	.15	.07	U227 Randy Johnson ENC	.30	.14			
U142 Roger Cedeno	.15	.07	U228 Chipper Jones ENC	1.00	.45			
U143 Greg Gagne	.15	.07	U229 Ryan Klesko ENC	.30	.14			

1996 Fleer Update Diamond Tribute

Randomly inserted in packs at a rate of one in 100, this 10-card set spotlights future Hall of Famers with holographic foils in a diamond design.

	MINT	NRMT
COMPLETE SET (10)	150.00	70.00
COMMON CARD (1-10)	5.00	2.20
UNLISTED STARS	8.00	3.60
STATED ODDS 1:100		

		MINT	NRMT
1	Wade Boggs	8.00	3.60
2	Barry Bonds	10.00	4.50
3	Ken Griffey Jr.	40.00	18.00
4	Tony Gwynn	15.00	6.75
5	Rickey Henderson	5.00	2.20
6	Greg Maddux	25.00	11.00
7	Eddie Murray	8.00	3.60
8	Cal Ripken	30.00	13.50
9	Ozzie Smith	10.00	4.50
10	Frank Thomas	30.00	13.50

1996 Fleer Update Headliners

Randomly inserted exclusively in retail packs at a rate of one in 20, cards from this 20-card set feature raised textured printing. The fronts carry color action player photos with the word "headliner" running continuously across the background.

	MINT	NRMT
COMPLETE SET (20)	40.00	18.00
COMMON CARD (1-20)	.75	.35
STATED ODDS 1:5 RETAIL		

		MINT	NRMT
☐ 1	Roberto Alomar	1.50	.70
☐ 2	Jeff Bagwell	3.00	1.35
☐ 3	Albert Belle	2.00	.90
☐ 4	Barry Bonds	2.00	.90
☐ 5	Cecil Fielder	.75	.35
☐ 6	Juan Gonzalez	4.00	1.80
☐ 7	Ken Griffey Jr.	8.00	3.60
☐ 8	Tony Gwynn	4.00	1.80
☐ 9	Randy Johnson	1.50	.70
☐ 10	Chipper Jones	5.00	2.20
☐ 11	Ryan Klesko	1.00	.45
☐ 12	Kenny Lofton	1.00	.45
☐ 13	Greg Maddux	5.00	2.20
☐ 14	Hideo Nomo	4.00	1.80
☐ 15	Mike Piazza	5.00	2.20
☐ 16	Manny Ramirez	1.50	.70
☐ 17	Cal Ripken	6.00	2.70
☐ 18	Tim Salmon	1.50	.70
☐ 19	Frank Thomas	6.00	2.70
☐ 20	Matt Williams	1.00	.45

1996 Fleer Update New Horizons

Randomly inserted in hobby packs only at a rate of one in five, this 20-card set features 1996 rookies and prospects. The fronts carry player action color photos printed on foil cards. The backs display a player portrait and information about the player.

		MINT	NRMT
COMPLETE SET (20)		15.00	6.75
COMMON CARD (1-20)		.25	.11
MINOR STARS		.50	.23
SEMISTARS		1.00	.45
STATED ODDS 1:5 HOBBY			
☐ 1	Bob Abreu	1.00	.45
☐ 2	George Arias	.25	.11
☐ 3	Tony Batista	.50	.23
☐ 4	Steve Cox	.25	.11
☐ 5	Jermaine Dye	.50	.23
☐ 6	Andy Fox	.25	.11
☐ 7	Mike Grace	.25	.11
☐ 8	Todd Greene	1.50	.70

☐ 9	Wilton Guerrero	2.50	1.10
☐ 10	Richard Hidalgo	2.00	.90
☐ 11	Raul Ibanez	1.00	.45
☐ 12	Robin Jennings	.25	.11
☐ 13	Marcus Jensen	.25	.11
☐ 14	Jason Kendall	1.50	.70
☐ 15	Jason Maxwell	.25	.11
☐ 16	Ryan McGuire	.25	.11
☐ 17	Miguel Mejia	.25	.11
☐ 18	Wonderful Monds	.25	.11
☐ 19	Rey Ordonez	.50	.23
☐ 20	Paul Wilson	.25	.11

1996 Fleer Update Smooth Leather

Randomly inserted in packs at a rate of one in 5, this 10-card set features ten defensive stars. The fronts display color player photos and gold foil printing. The backs carry a player portrait and information about why the player was selected for this set.

		MINT	NRMT
COMPLETE SET (10)		10.00	4.50
COMMON CARD (1-10)		.40	.18
STATED ODDS 1:5			
☐ 1	Roberto Alomar	.75	.35
☐ 2	Barry Bonds	1.00	.45
☐ 3	Will Clark	.60	.25
☐ 4	Ken Griffey Jr.	4.00	1.80
☐ 5	Kenny Lofton	1.00	.45
☐ 6	Greg Maddux	2.50	1.10
☐ 7	Raul Mondesi	.60	.25
☐ 8	Rey Ordonez	.40	.18
☐ 9	Cal Ripken	3.00	1.35
☐ 10	Matt Williams	.60	.25

1996 Fleer Update Soaring Stars

Randomly inserted in packs at a rate of one in 11, this 10-card

set features 10 of the hottest young players. The fronts carry color player cut-outs on a background of soaring baseballs in etched foil. The backs display another player photo on the same background with player information.

		MINT	NRMT
COMPLETE SET (10)		25.00	11.00
COMMON CARD (1-10)		1.00	.45
STATED ODDS 1:11			
☐ 1	Jeff Bagwell	3.00	1.35
☐ 2	Barry Bonds	2.00	.90
☐ 3	Juan Gonzalez	4.00	1.80
☐ 4	Ken Griffey Jr.	8.00	3.60
☐ 5	Chipper Jones	5.00	2.20
☐ 6	Greg Maddux	5.00	2.20
☐ 7	Mike Piazza	5.00	2.20
☐ 8	Manny Ramirez	1.50	.70
☐ 9	Frank Thomas	6.00	2.70
☐ 10	Matt Williams	1.00	.45

1997 Fleer

The 1997 Fleer Set was issued in two series totaling 761 cards and distributed in 10-card packs with a suggested retail price of $1.49. The fronts feature color action player photos with a matte finish and gold foil printing. The backs carry another player photo with player information and career statistics. Cards 491-500 are a Checklist subset of Series 1 and feature black-and-white or sepia tone photos of big-name players. Series 2 contains the following subsets: Encore (696-720) which are redesigned cards of the big-name players from Series 1, and Checklists (721-748). Cards 749 and 750 are expansion team logo cards with the insert checklists on the backs. Many dealers believe that cards numbered 751-761 were shortprinted. An Andruw Jones autographed Circa card numbered to 200 was also randomly inserted into packs.

	MINT	NRMT
COMPLETE SET (761)	85.00	38.00
COMPLETE SERIES 1 (500)	50.00	22.00
COMPLETE SERIES 2 (261)	35.00	16.00
COMMON CARD (1-750)	.15	.07
COMMON CARD (751-761)	.25	.11
MINOR STARS	.30	.14
UNLISTED STARS	.60	.25
SUBSET CARDS HALF VALUE OF BASE CARDS		
COMP.TIFFANY SET (761)	5500.00	2500.00
COMP.TIFFANY SER.1 (500)	4000.00	1800.00

COMP.TIFFANY SER.2 (261) 1500.00 700.00
COMMON TIFFANY (1-761) .. 4.00   1.80
*TIFFANY STARS: 15X TO 40X HI COLUMN
*TIFFANY YOUNG STARS: 12.5X TO 30X HI
*TIFFANY ROOKIES: 6X TO 15X HI
*TIFFANY 751-761: 5X TO 12X HI
TIFFANY STATED ODDS 1:20....

☐ 1 Roberto Alomar	.60	.25	
☐ 2 Brady Anderson	.40	.18	
☐ 3 Bobby Bonilla	.30	.14	
☐ 4 Rocky Coppinger	.15	.07	
☐ 5 Cesar Devarez	.15	.07	
☐ 6 Scott Erickson	.15	.07	
☐ 7 Jeffrey Hammonds	.15	.07	
☐ 8 Chris Hoiles	.15	.07	
☐ 9 Eddie Murray	.60	.25	
☐ 10 Mike Mussina	.60	.25	
☐ 11 Randy Myers	.15	.07	
☐ 12 Rafael Palmeiro	.40	.18	
☐ 13 Cal Ripken	2.50	1.10	
☐ 14 B.J. Surhoff	.15	.07	
☐ 15 David Wells	.15	.07	
☐ 16 Todd Zeile	.15	.07	
☐ 17 Darren Bragg	.15	.07	
☐ 18 Jose Canseco	.40	.18	
☐ 19 Roger Clemens	1.25	.55	
☐ 20 Wil Cordero	.15	.07	
☐ 21 Jeff Frye	.15	.07	
☐ 22 Nomar Garciaparra	2.00	.90	
☐ 23 Tom Gordon	.15	.07	
☐ 24 Mike Greenwell	.15	.07	
☐ 25 Reggie Jefferson	.15	.07	
☐ 26 Jose Malave	.15	.07	
☐ 27 Tim Naehring	.15	.07	
☐ 28 Troy O'Leary	.15	.07	
☐ 29 Heathcliff Slocumb	.15	.07	
☐ 30 Mike Stanley	.15	.07	
☐ 31 John Valentin	.15	.07	
☐ 32 Mo Vaughn	.75	.35	
☐ 33 Tim Wakefield	.15	.07	
☐ 34 Garret Anderson	.30	.14	
☐ 35 George Arias	.15	.07	
☐ 36 Shawn Boskie	.15	.07	
☐ 37 Chili Davis	.30	.14	
☐ 38 Jason Dickson	.30	.14	
☐ 39 Gary DiSarcina	.15	.07	
☐ 40 Jim Edmonds	.40	.18	
☐ 41 Darin Erstad	1.00	.45	
☐ 42 Jorge Fabregas	.15	.07	
☐ 43 Chuck Finley	.15	.07	
☐ 44 Todd Greene	.30	.14	
☐ 45 Mike Holtz	.15	.07	
☐ 46 Rex Hudler	.15	.07	
☐ 47 Mike James	.15	.07	
☐ 48 Mark Langston	.15	.07	
☐ 49 Troy Percival	.15	.07	
☐ 50 Tim Salmon	.60	.25	
☐ 51 Jeff Schmidt	.15	.07	
☐ 52 J.T. Snow	.30	.14	
☐ 53 Randy Velarde	.15	.07	
☐ 54 Wilson Alvarez	.15	.07	
☐ 55 Harold Baines	.30	.14	
☐ 56 James Baldwin	.15	.07	
☐ 57 Jason Bere	.15	.07	
☐ 58 Mike Cameron	.40	.18	
☐ 59 Ray Durham	.30	.14	
☐ 60 Alex Fernandez	.30	.14	
☐ 61 Ozzie Guillen	.15	.07	
☐ 62 Roberto Hernandez	.15	.07	
☐ 63 Ron Karkovice	.15	.07	
☐ 64 Darren Lewis	.15	.07	
☐ 65 Dave Martinez	.15	.07	
☐ 66 Lyle Mouton	.15	.07	
☐ 67 Greg Norton	.15	.07	
☐ 68 Tony Phillips	.15	.07	
☐ 69 Chris Snopek	.15	.07	
☐ 70 Kevin Tapani	.15	.07	
☐ 71 Danny Tartabull	.15	.07	
☐ 72 Frank Thomas	2.50	1.10	
☐ 73 Robin Ventura	.30	.14	
☐ 74 Sandy Alomar Jr	.30	.14	
☐ 75 Albert Belle	.75	.35	
☐ 76 Mark Carreon	.15	.07	
☐ 77 Julio Franco	.30	.14	
☐ 78 Brian Giles	.15	.07	
☐ 79 Orel Hershiser	.30	.14	
☐ 80 Kenny Lofton	.75	.35	
☐ 81 Dennis Martinez	.30	.14	
☐ 82 Jack McDowell	.15	.07	
☐ 83 Jose Mesa	.15	.07	
☐ 84 Charles Nagy	.30	.14	
☐ 85 Chad Ogea	.15	.07	
☐ 86 Eric Plunk	.15	.07	
☐ 87 Manny Ramirez	.60	.25	
☐ 88 Kevin Seitzer	.15	.07	
☐ 89 Julian Tavarez	.15	.07	
☐ 90 Jim Thome	.60	.25	
☐ 91 Jose Vizcaino	.15	.07	
☐ 92 Omar Vizquel	.30	.14	
☐ 93 Brad Ausmus	.15	.07	
☐ 94 Kimera Bartee	.15	.07	
☐ 95 Raul Casanova	.15	.07	
☐ 96 Tony Clark	.60	.25	
☐ 97 John Cummings	.15	.07	
☐ 98 Travis Fryman	.30	.14	
☐ 99 Bob Higginson	.30	.14	
☐ 100 Mark Lewis	.15	.07	
☐ 101 Felipe Lira	.15	.07	
☐ 102 Phil Nevin	.15	.07	
☐ 103 Melvin Nieves	.15	.07	
☐ 104 Curtis Pride	.15	.07	
☐ 105 A.J. Sager	.15	.07	
☐ 106 Ruben Sierra	.15	.07	
☐ 107 Justin Thompson	.30	.14	
☐ 108 Alan Trammell	.30	.14	
☐ 109 Kevin Appier	.30	.14	
☐ 110 Tim Belcher	.15	.07	
☐ 111 Jaime Bluma	.15	.07	
☐ 112 Johnny Damon	.15	.07	
☐ 113 Tom Goodwin	.15	.07	
☐ 114 Chris Haney	.15	.07	
☐ 115 Keith Lockhart	.15	.07	
☐ 116 Mike Macfarlane	.15	.07	
☐ 117 Jeff Montgomery	.15	.07	
☐ 118 Jose Offerman	.15	.07	
☐ 119 Craig Paquette	.15	.07	
☐ 120 Joe Randa	.15	.07	
☐ 121 Bip Roberts	.15	.07	
☐ 122 Jose Rosado	.30	.14	
☐ 123 Mike Sweeney	.30	.14	
☐ 124 Michael Tucker	.30	.14	
☐ 125 Jeromy Burnitz	.15	.07	
☐ 126 Jeff Cirillo	.30	.14	
☐ 127 Jeff D'Amico	.15	.07	
☐ 128 Mike Fetters	.15	.07	
☐ 129 John Jaha	.15	.07	
☐ 130 Scott Karl	.15	.07	
☐ 131 Jesse Levis	.15	.07	
☐ 132 Mark Loretta	.15	.07	
☐ 133 Mike Matheny	.15	.07	
☐ 134 Ben McDonald	.15	.07	
☐ 135 Matt Mieske	.15	.07	
☐ 136 Marc Newfield	.15	.07	
☐ 137 Dave Nilsson	.15	.07	
☐ 138 Jose Valentin	.15	.07	
☐ 139 Fernando Vina	.15	.07	
☐ 140 Bob Wickman	.15	.07	
☐ 141 Gerald Williams	.15	.07	
☐ 142 Rick Aguilera	.15	.07	
☐ 143 Rich Becker	.15	.07	
☐ 144 Ron Coomer	.15	.07	
☐ 145 Marty Cordova	.30	.14	
☐ 146 Roberto Kelly	.15	.07	
☐ 147 Chuck Knoblauch	.60	.25	
☐ 148 Matt Lawton	.15	.07	
☐ 149 Pat Meares	.15	.07	
☐ 150 Travis Miller	.15	.07	
☐ 151 Paul Molitor	.60	.25	
☐ 152 Greg Myers	.15	.07	
☐ 153 Dan Naulty	.15	.07	
☐ 154 Kirby Puckett	1.25	.55	
☐ 155 Brad Radke	.30	.14	
☐ 156 Frank Rodriguez	.15	.07	
☐ 157 Scott Stahoviak	.15	.07	
☐ 158 Dave Stevens	.15	.07	
☐ 159 Matt Walbeck	.15	.07	
☐ 160 Todd Walker	.30	.14	
☐ 161 Wade Boggs	.60	.25	
☐ 162 David Cone	.30	.14	
☐ 163 Mariano Duncan	.15	.07	
☐ 164 Cecil Fielder	.30	.14	
☐ 165 Joe Girardi	.15	.07	
☐ 166 Dwight Gooden	.30	.14	
☐ 167 Charlie Hayes	.15	.07	
☐ 168 Derek Jeter	2.00	.90	
☐ 169 Jimmy Key	.30	.14	
☐ 170 Jim Leyritz	.15	.07	
☐ 171 Tino Martinez	.60	.25	
☐ 172 Ramiro Mendoza	.40	.18	
☐ 173 Jeff Nelson	.15	.07	
☐ 174 Paul O'Neill	.30	.14	
☐ 175 Andy Pettitte	.60	.25	
☐ 176 Mariano Rivera	.30	.14	
☐ 177 Ruben Rivera	.30	.14	
☐ 178 Kenny Rogers	.15	.07	
☐ 179 Darryl Strawberry	.30	.14	
☐ 180 John Wetteland	.15	.07	
☐ 181 Bernie Williams	.60	.25	
☐ 182 Willie Adams	.15	.07	
☐ 183 Tony Batista	.15	.07	
☐ 184 Geronimo Berroa	.15	.07	
☐ 185 Mike Bordick	.15	.07	
☐ 186 Scott Brosius	.15	.07	
☐ 187 Bobby Chouinard	.15	.07	
☐ 188 Jim Corsi	.15	.07	
☐ 189 Brent Gates	.15	.07	
☐ 190 Jason Giambi	.30	.14	
☐ 191 Jose Herrera	.15	.07	
☐ 192 Damon Mashore	.15	.07	
☐ 193 Mark McGwire	1.25	.55	
☐ 194 Mike Mohler	.15	.07	
☐ 195 Scott Spiezio	.30	.14	
☐ 196 Terry Steinbach	.15	.07	
☐ 197 Bill Taylor	.15	.07	
☐ 198 John Wasdin	.15	.07	
☐ 199 Steve Wojciechowski	.15	.07	
☐ 200 Ernie Young	.15	.07	
☐ 201 Rich Amaral	.15	.07	
☐ 202 Jay Buhner	.40	.18	
☐ 203 Norm Charlton	.15	.07	
☐ 204 Joey Cora	.30	.14	
☐ 205 Russ Davis	.15	.07	
☐ 206 Ken Griffey Jr.	3.00	1.35	
☐ 207 Sterling Hitchcock	.15	.07	
☐ 208 Brian Hunter	.30	.14	
☐ 209 Raul Ibanez	.15	.07	
☐ 210 Randy Johnson	.60	.25	
☐ 211 Edgar Martinez	.40	.18	
☐ 212 Jamie Moyer	.15	.07	
☐ 213 Alex Rodriguez	2.00	.90	
☐ 214 Paul Sorrento	.15	.07	
☐ 215 Matt Wagner	.15	.07	
☐ 216 Bob Wells	.15	.07	
☐ 217 Dan Wilson	.15	.07	
☐ 218 Damon Buford	.15	.07	
☐ 219 Will Clark	.40	.18	
☐ 220 Kevin Elster	.15	.07	
☐ 221 Juan Gonzalez	1.50	.70	
☐ 222 Rusty Greer	.15	.07	
☐ 223 Kevin Gross	.15	.07	
☐ 224 Darryl Hamilton	.15	.07	
☐ 225 Mike Henneman	.15	.07	
☐ 226 Ken Hill	.15	.07	
☐ 227 Mark McLemore	.15	.07	
☐ 228 Darren Oliver	.15	.07	
☐ 229 Dean Palmer	.15	.07	
☐ 230 Roger Pavlik	.15	.07	
☐ 231 Ivan Rodriguez	.75	.35	
☐ 232 Mickey Tettleton	.15	.07	
☐ 233 Bobby Witt	.15	.07	
☐ 234 Jacob Brumfield	.15	.07	
☐ 235 Joe Carter	.30	.14	
☐ 236 Tim Crabtree	.15	.07	
☐ 237 Carlos Delgado	.30	.14	
☐ 238 Huck Flener	.15	.07	
☐ 239 Alex Gonzalez	.15	.07	
☐ 240 Shawn Green	.15	.07	
☐ 241 Juan Guzman	.15	.07	
☐ 242 Pat Hentgen	.30	.14	
☐ 243 Marty Janzen	.15	.07	
☐ 244 Sandy Martinez	.15	.07	
☐ 245 Otis Nixon	.15	.07	
☐ 246 Charlie O'Brien	.15	.07	
☐ 247 John Olerud	.30	.14	
☐ 248 Robert Perez	.15	.07	
☐ 249 Ed Sprague	.15	.07	
☐ 250 Mike Timlin	.15	.07	

251	Steve Avery	.15	.07
252	Jeff Blauser	.30	.14
253	Brad Clontz	.15	.07
254	Jermaine Dye	.15	.07
255	Tom Glavine	.30	.14
256	Marquis Grissom	.30	.14
257	Andruw Jones	1.50	.70
258	Chipper Jones	2.00	.90
259	David Justice	.60	.25
260	Ryan Klesko	.40	.18
261	Mark Lemke	.15	.07
262	Javier Lopez	.30	.14
263	Greg Maddux	2.00	.90
264	Fred McGriff	.40	.18
265	Greg McMichael	.15	.07
266	Denny Neagle	.30	.14
267	Terry Pendleton	.15	.07
268	Eddie Perez	.15	.07
269	John Smoltz	.30	.14
270	Terrell Wade	.15	.07
271	Mark Wohlers	.15	.07
272	Terry Adams	.15	.07
273	Brant Brown	.15	.07
274	Leo Gomez	.15	.07
275	Luis Gonzalez	.15	.07
276	Mark Grace	.40	.18
277	Tyler Houston	.15	.07
278	Robin Jennings	.15	.07
279	Brooks Kieschnick	.15	.07
280	Brian McRae	.15	.07
281	Jaime Navarro	.15	.07
282	Ryne Sandberg	.75	.35
283	Scott Servais	.15	.07
284	Sammy Sosa	.60	.25
285	Dave Swartzbaugh	.15	.07
286	Amaury Telemaco	.15	.07
287	Steve Trachsel	.15	.07
288	Pedro Valdes	.15	.07
289	Turk Wendell	.15	.07
290	Bret Boone	.15	.07
291	Jeff Branson	.15	.07
292	Jeff Brantley	.15	.07
293	Eric Davis	.30	.14
294	Willie Greene	.15	.07
295	Thomas Howard	.15	.07
296	Barry Larkin	.40	.18
297	Kevin Mitchell	.15	.07
298	Hal Morris	.15	.07
299	Chad Mottola	.15	.07
300	Joe Oliver	.15	.07
301	Mark Portugal	.15	.07
302	Roger Salkeld	.15	.07
303	Reggie Sanders	.15	.07
304	Pete Schourek	.15	.07
305	John Smiley	.15	.07
306	Eddie Taubensee	.15	.07
307	Dante Bichette	.30	.14
308	Ellis Burks	.30	.14
309	Vinny Castilla	.30	.14
310	Andres Galarraga	.60	.25
311	Curt Leskanic	.15	.07
312	Quinton McCracken	.15	.07
313	Neifi Perez	.30	.14
314	Jeff Reed	.15	.07
315	Steve Reed	.15	.07
316	Armando Reynoso	.15	.07
317	Kevin Ritz	.15	.07
318	Bruce Ruffin	.15	.07
319	Larry Walker	.60	.25
320	Walt Weiss	.15	.07
321	Jamey Wright	.15	.07
322	Eric Young	.15	.07
323	Kurt Abbott	.15	.07
324	Alex Arias	.15	.07
325	Kevin Brown	.30	.14
326	Luis Castillo	.30	.14
327	Greg Colbrunn	.15	.07
328	Jeff Conine	.30	.14
329	Andre Dawson	.40	.18
330	Charles Johnson	.30	.14
331	Al Leiter	.15	.07
332	Ralph Milliard	.15	.07
333	Robb Nen	.15	.07
334	Pat Rapp	.15	.07
335	Edgar Renteria	.30	.14
336	Gary Sheffield	.60	.25
337	Devon White	.15	.07
338	Bob Abreu	.30	.14
339	Jeff Bagwell	1.25	.55
340	Derek Bell	.15	.07
341	Sean Berry	.15	.07
342	Craig Biggio	.40	.18
343	Doug Drabek	.15	.07
344	Tony Eusebio	.15	.07
345	Ricky Gutierrez	.15	.07
346	Mike Hampton	.15	.07
347	Brian Hunter	.30	.14
348	Todd Jones	.15	.07
349	Darryl Kile	.30	.14
350	Derrick May	.15	.07
351	Orlando Miller	.15	.07
352	James Mouton	.15	.07
353	Shane Reynolds	.15	.07
354	Billy Wagner	.30	.14
355	Donne Wall	.15	.07
356	Mike Blowers	.15	.07
357	Brett Butler	.30	.14
358	Roger Cedeno	.15	.07
359	Chad Curtis	.15	.07
360	Delino DeShields	.15	.07
361	Greg Gagne	.15	.07
362	Karim Garcia	.30	.14
363	Wilton Guerrero	.15	.07
364	Todd Hollandsworth	.15	.07
365	Eric Karros	.30	.14
366	Ramon Martinez	.30	.14
367	Raul Mondesi	.40	.18
368	Hideo Nomo	1.50	.70
369	Antonio Osuna	.15	.07
370	Chan Ho Park	.60	.25
371	Mike Piazza	2.00	.90
372	Ismael Valdes	.30	.14
373	Todd Worrell	.15	.07
374	Moises Alou	.30	.14
375	Shane Andrews	.15	.07
376	Yamil Benitez	.15	.07
377	Jeff Fassero	.15	.07
378	Darrin Fletcher	.15	.07
379	Cliff Floyd	.15	.07
380	Mark Grudzielanek	.15	.07
381	Mike Lansing	.15	.07
382	Barry Manuel	.15	.07
383	Pedro Martinez	.60	.25
384	Henry Rodriguez	.15	.07
385	Mel Rojas	.15	.07
386	F.P. Santangelo	.15	.07
387	David Segui	.15	.07
388	Ugueth Urbina	.15	.07
389	Rondell White	.30	.14
390	Edgardo Alfonzo	.30	.14
391	Carlos Baerga	.15	.07
392	Mark Clark	.15	.07
393	Alvaro Espinoza	.15	.07
394	John Franco	.30	.14
395	Bernard Gilkey	.15	.07
396	Pete Harnisch	.15	.07
397	Todd Hundley	.30	.14
398	Butch Huskey	.30	.14
399	Jason Isringhausen	.15	.07
400	Lance Johnson	.15	.07
401	Bobby Jones	.15	.07
402	Alex Ochoa	.15	.07
403	Rey Ordonez	.15	.07
404	Robert Person	.15	.07
405	Paul Wilson	.15	.07
406	Matt Beech	.15	.07
407	Ron Blazier	.15	.07
408	Ricky Bottalico	.15	.07
409	Lenny Dykstra	.30	.14
410	Jim Eisenreich	.15	.07
411	Bobby Estalella	.30	.14
412	Mike Grace	.15	.07
413	Gregg Jefferies	.15	.07
414	Mike Lieberthal	.15	.07
415	Wendell Magee	.15	.07
416	Mickey Morandini	.15	.07
417	Ricky Otero	.15	.07
418	Scott Rolen	1.50	.70
419	Ken Ryan	.15	.07
420	Benito Santiago	.15	.07
421	Curt Schilling	.30	.14
422	Kevin Sefcik	.15	.07
423	Jermaine Allensworth	.15	.07
424	Trey Beamon	.15	.07
425	Jay Bell	.30	.14
426	Francisco Cordova	.15	.07
427	Carlos Garcia	.15	.07
428	Mark Johnson	.15	.07
429	Jason Kendall	.30	.14
430	Jeff King	.15	.07
431	Jon Lieber	.15	.07
432	Al Martin	.15	.07
433	Orlando Merced	.15	.07
434	Ramon Morel	.15	.07
435	Matt Ruebel	.15	.07
436	Jason Schmidt	.15	.07
437	Marc Wilkins	.15	.07
438	Alan Benes	.30	.14
439	Andy Benes	.30	.14
440	Royce Clayton	.15	.07
441	Dennis Eckersley	.30	.14
442	Gary Gaetti	.15	.07
443	Ron Gant	.30	.14
444	Aaron Holbert	.15	.07
445	Brian Jordan	.30	.14
446	Ray Lankford	.30	.14
447	John Mabry	.15	.07
448	T.J. Mathews	.15	.07
449	Willie McGee	.15	.07
450	Donovan Osborne	.15	.07
451	Tom Pagnozzi	.15	.07
452	Ozzie Smith	.75	.35
453	Todd Stottlemyre	.15	.07
454	Mark Sweeney	.15	.07
455	Dmitri Young	.15	.07
456	Andy Ashby	.15	.07
457	Ken Caminiti	.40	.18
458	Archi Cianfrocco	.15	.07
459	Steve Finley	.30	.14
460	John Flaherty	.15	.07
461	Chris Gomez	.15	.07
462	Tony Gwynn	1.50	.70
463	Joey Hamilton	.30	.14
464	Rickey Henderson	.40	.18
465	Trevor Hoffman	.15	.07
466	Brian Johnson	.15	.07
467	Wally Joyner	.30	.14
468	Jody Reed	.15	.07
469	Scott Sanders	.15	.07
470	Bob Tewksbury	.15	.07
471	Fernando Valenzuela	.30	.14
472	Greg Vaughn	.15	.07
473	Tim Worrell	.15	.07
474	Rich Aurilia	.15	.07
475	Rod Beck	.15	.07
476	Marvin Benard	.15	.07
477	Barry Bonds	.75	.35
478	Jay Canizaro	.15	.07
479	Shawn Dunston	.15	.07
480	Shawn Estes	.30	.14
481	Mark Gardner	.15	.07
482	Glenallen Hill	.15	.07
483	Stan Javier	.15	.07
484	Marcus Jensen	.15	.07
485	Bill Mueller	.15	.07
486	Wm. VanLandingham	.15	.07
487	Allen Watson	.15	.07
488	Rick Wilkins	.15	.07
489	Matt Williams	.40	.18
490	Desi Wilson	.15	.07
491	Albert Belle CL	.30	.14
492	Ken Griffey Jr. CL	1.50	.70
493	Andruw Jones CL	.75	.35
494	Chipper Jones CL	1.00	.45
495	Mark McGwire CL	.60	.25
496	Paul Molitor CL	.30	.14
497	Mike Piazza CL	1.00	.45
498	Cal Ripken CL	1.25	.55
499	Alex Rodriguez CL	1.00	.45
500	Frank Thomas CL	1.25	.55
501	Kenny Lofton	.75	.35
502	Carlos Perez	.15	.07
503	Tim Raines	.30	.14
504	Danny Patterson	.15	.07
505	Derrick May	.15	.07
506	Dave Hollins	.15	.07
507	Felipe Crespo	.15	.07
508	Brian Banks	.15	.07

509	Jeff Kent	.15	.07
510	Bubba Trammell	.60	.25
511	Robert Person	.15	.07
512	David Arias-Ortiz	1.00	.45
513	Ryan Jones	.15	.07
514	David Justice	.60	.25
515	Will Cunnane	.15	.07
516	Russ Johnson	.15	.07
517	John Burkett	.15	.07
518	Robinson Checo	.15	.07
519	Ricardo Rincon	.15	.07
520	Woody Williams	.15	.07
521	Rick Helling	.15	.07
522	Jorge Posada	.15	.07
523	Kevin Orie	.30	.14
524	Fernando Tatis	1.50	.70
525	Jermaine Dye	.15	.07
526	Brian Hunter	.30	.14
527	Greg McMichael	.15	.07
528	Matt Wagner	.15	.07
529	Richie Sexson	.30	.14
530	Scott Ruffcorn	.15	.07
531	Luis Gonzalez	.15	.07
532	Mike Johnson	.40	.18
533	Mark Petkovsek	.15	.07
534	Doug Drabek	.15	.07
535	Jose Canseco	.40	.18
536	Bobby Bonilla	.30	.14
537	J.T. Snow	.30	.14
538	Shawon Dunston	.15	.07
539	John Ericks	.15	.07
540	Terry Steinbach	.15	.07
541	Jay Bell	.30	.14
542	Joe Borowski	.15	.07
543	David Wells	.15	.07
544	Justin Towle	.60	.25
545	Mike Blowers	.15	.07
546	Shannon Stewart	.30	.14
547	Rudy Pemberton	.15	.07
548	Bill Swift	.15	.07
549	Osvaldo Fernandez	.15	.07
550	Eddie Murray	.60	.25
551	Don Wengert	.15	.07
552	Brad Ausmus	.15	.07
553	Carlos Garcia	.15	.07
554	Jose Guillen	.60	.25
555	Rheal Cormier	.15	.07
556	Doug Brocail	.15	.07
557	Rex Hudler	.15	.07
558	Armando Benitez	.15	.07
559	Eli Marrero	.30	.14
560	Ricky Ledee	1.25	.55
561	Bartolo Colon	.30	.14
562	Quilvio Veras	.15	.07
563	Alex Fernandez	.30	.14
564	Darren Dreifort	.15	.07
565	Benji Gil	.15	.07
566	Kent Mercker	.15	.07
567	Glendon Rusch	.15	.07
568	Ramon Tatis	.15	.07
569	Roger Clemens	1.25	.55
570	Mark Lewis	.15	.07
571	Emil Brown	.40	.18
572	Jaime Navarro	.15	.07
573	Sherman Obando	.15	.07
574	John Wasdin	.15	.07
575	Calvin Maduro	.15	.07
576	Todd Jones	.15	.07
577	Orlando Merced	.15	.07
578	Cal Eldred	.15	.07
579	Mark Gubicza	.15	.07
580	Michael Tucker	.30	.14
581	Tony Saunders	.50	.23
582	Garvin Alston	.15	.07
583	Joe Roa	.15	.07
584	Brady Raggio	.15	.07
585	Jimmy Key	.30	.14
586	Marc Sagmoen	.15	.07
587	Jim Bullinger	.15	.07
588	Yorkis Perez	.15	.07
589	Jose Cruz Jr.	5.00	2.20
590	Mike Stanton	.15	.07
591	Deivi Cruz	.50	.23
592	Steve Karsay	.15	.07
593	Mike Trombley	.15	.07
594	Doug Glanville	.15	.07
595	Scott Sanders	.15	.07
596	Thomas Howard	.15	.07
597	T.J. Staton	.40	.18
598	Garrett Stephenson	.15	.07
599	Rico Brogna	.15	.07
600	Albert Belle	.75	.35
601	Jose Vizcaino	.15	.07
602	Chili Davis	.30	.14
603	Shane Mack	.15	.07
604	Jim Eisenreich	.15	.07
605	Todd Zeile	.15	.07
606	Brian Boehringer	.15	.07
607	Paul Shuey	.15	.07
608	Kevin Tapani	.15	.07
609	John Wetteland	.15	.07
610	Jim Leyritz	.15	.07
611	Ray Montgomery	.15	.07
612	Doug Bochtler	.15	.07
613	Wady Almonte	.40	.18
614	Danny Tartabull	.15	.07
615	Orlando Miller	.15	.07
616	Bobby Ayala	.15	.07
617	Tony Graffanino	.15	.07
618	Marc Valdes	.15	.07
619	Ron Villone	.15	.07
620	Derrek Lee	.40	.18
621	Greg Colbrunn	.15	.07
622	Felix Heredia	.40	.18
623	Carl Everett	.15	.07
624	Mark Thompson	.15	.07
625	Jeff Granger	.15	.07
626	Damian Jackson	.15	.07
627	Mark Leiter	.15	.07
628	Chris Holt	.15	.07
629	Dario Veras	.40	.18
630	Dave Burba	.15	.07
631	Darryl Hamilton	.15	.07
632	Mark Acre	.15	.07
633	Fernando Hernandez	.15	.07
634	Terry Mulholland	.15	.07
635	Dustin Hermanson	.15	.07
636	Delino DeShields	.15	.07
637	Steve Avery	.15	.07
638	Tony Womack	.50	.23
639	Mark Whiten	.15	.07
640	Marquis Grissom	.30	.14
641	Xavier Hernandez	.15	.07
642	Eric Davis	.30	.14
643	Bob Tewksbury	.15	.07
644	Dante Powell	.15	.07
645	Carlos Castillo	.15	.18
646	Chris Widger	.15	.07
647	Moises Alou	.30	.14
648	Pat Listach	.15	.07
649	Edgar Ramos	.40	.18
650	Deion Sanders	.30	.14
651	John Olerud	.30	.14
652	Todd Dunwoody	.40	.18
653	Randall Simon	1.25	.55
654	Dan Carlson	.15	.07
655	Matt Williams	.40	.18
656	Jeff King	.15	.07
657	Luis Alicea	.15	.07
658	Brian Moehler	.15	.07
659	Ariel Prieto	.15	.07
660	Kevin Elster	.15	.07
661	Mark Hutton	.15	.07
662	Aaron Sele	.15	.07
663	Graeme Lloyd	.15	.07
664	John Burke	.15	.07
665	Mel Rojas	.15	.07
666	Sid Fernandez	.15	.07
667	Pedro Astacio	.15	.07
668	Jeff Abbott	.15	.07
669	Darren Daulton	.30	.14
670	Mike Bordick	.15	.07
671	Sterling Hitchcock	.15	.07
672	Damion Easley	.15	.07
673	Armando Reynoso	.15	.07
674	Pat Cline	.15	.07
675	Orlando Cabrera	.30	.14
676	Alan Embree	.15	.07
677	Brian Bevil	.15	.07
678	David Weathers	.15	.07
679	Cliff Floyd	.15	.07
680	Joe Randa	.15	.07
681	Bill Haselman	.15	.07
682	Jeff Fassero	.15	.07
683	Matt Morris	.30	.14
684	Mark Portugal	.15	.07
685	Lee Smith	.30	.14
686	Pokey Reese	.15	.07
687	Benito Santiago	.15	.07
688	Brian Johnson	.15	.07
689	Brent Brede	.30	.14
690	Shigetoshi Hasegawa	.40	.18
691	Julio Santana	.15	.07
692	Steve Kline	.15	.07
693	Julian Tavarez	.15	.07
694	John Hudek	.15	.07
695	Manny Alexander	.15	.07
696	Roberto Alomar ENC	.30	.14
697	Jeff Bagwell ENC	.60	.25
698	Barry Bonds ENC	.40	.18
699	Ken Caminiti ENC	.30	.14
700	Juan Gonzalez ENC	.75	.35
701	Ken Griffey Jr. ENC	1.50	.70
702	Tony Gwynn ENC	.75	.35
703	Derek Jeter ENC	1.00	.45
704	Andruw Jones ENC	.75	.35
705	Chipper Jones ENC	1.00	.45
706	Barry Larkin ENC	.30	.14
707	Greg Maddux ENC	1.00	.45
708	Mark McGwire ENC	.60	.25
709	Paul Molitor ENC	.30	.14
710	Hideo Nomo ENC	.75	.35
711	Andy Pettitte ENC	.30	.14
712	Mike Piazza ENC	1.00	.45
713	Manny Ramirez ENC	.30	.14
714	Cal Ripken ENC	1.25	.55
715	Alex Rodriguez ENC	1.00	.45
716	Ryne Sandberg ENC	.40	.18
717	John Smoltz ENC	.15	.07
718	Frank Thomas ENC	1.25	.55
719	Mo Vaughn ENC	.40	.18
720	Bernie Williams ENC	.30	.14
721	Tim Salmon ENC	.30	.14
722	Greg Maddux CL	1.00	.45
723	Cal Ripken CL	1.25	.55
724	Mo Vaughn CL	.40	.18
725	Ryne Sandberg CL	.40	.18
726	Frank Thomas CL	1.25	.55
727	Barry Larkin CL	.30	.14
728	Manny Ramirez CL	.30	.14
729	Andres Galarraga CL	.30	.14
730	Tony Clark CL	.30	.14
731	Gary Sheffield CL	.30	.14
732	Jeff Bagwell CL	.60	.25
733	Kevin Appier CL	.15	.07
734	Mike Piazza CL	1.00	.45
735	Jeff Cirillo CL	.15	.07
736	Paul Molitor CL	.30	.14
737	Henry Rodriguez CL	.15	.07
738	Todd Hundley CL	.15	.07
739	Derek Jeter CL	1.00	.45
740	Mark McGwire CL	.60	.25
741	Curt Schilling CL	.15	.07
742	Jason Kendall CL	.15	.07
743	Tony Gwynn CL	.75	.35
744	Barry Bonds CL	.40	.18
745	Ken Griffey Jr. CL	1.50	.70
746	Brian Jordan CL	.15	.07
747	Juan Gonzalez CL	.75	.35
748	Joe Carter CL	.15	.07
749	Arizona Diamondbacks CL	.30	.14
750	Tampa Bay Devil Rays CL	.30	.14
751	Hideki Irabu	1.00	.45
752	Jeremi Gonzalez	.75	.35
753	Mario Valdez	.75	.35
754	Aaron Boone	.25	.11
755	Brett Tomko	.25	.11
756	Jaret Wright	6.00	2.70
757	Ryan McGuire	.25	.11
758	Jason McDonald	.25	.11
759	Adrian Brown	.25	.11
760	Keith Foulke	.25	.11
761	Bonus Checklist	.25	.11
P489	Matt Williams Promo	3.00	1.35
NNO	A.Jones Circa AU200	100.00	45.00

1997 Fleer Bleacher Blasters

Randomly inserted in Fleer 2 retail packs only at a rate of one in 36, this 10-card set features color action photos of power hitters who reach the bleachers with great frequency.

	MINT	NRMT
COMPLETE SET (10)	100.00	45.00
COMMON CARD (1-10)	3.00	1.35
SER.2 STATED ODDS 1:36 RETAIL		

		MINT	NRMT
☐ 1	Albert Belle	6.00	2.70
☐ 2	Barry Bonds	6.00	2.70
☐ 3	Juan Gonzalez	12.00	5.50
☐ 4	Ken Griffey Jr.	25.00	11.00
☐ 5	Mark McGwire	10.00	4.50
☐ 6	Mike Piazza	15.00	6.75
☐ 7	Alex Rodriguez	15.00	6.75
☐ 8	Frank Thomas	20.00	9.00
☐ 9	Mo Vaughn	6.00	2.70
☐ 10	Matt Williams	3.00	1.35

1997 Fleer Decade of Excellence

Randomly inserted in Fleer Series 2 hobby packs only at a rate of one in 36, this 12-card set spotlights players who started their major league careers no later than 1987. The set features photos of these players from the 1987 Fleer Baseball card design.

	MINT	NRMT
COMPLETE SET (12)	60.00	27.00
COMMON CARD (1-12)	2.50	1.10
UNLISTED STARS	4.00	1.80
SER.2 STATED ODDS 1:36 HOBBY		
*RARE TRADITION: 2.5X TO 5X HI COLUMN		
RARE TRAD.STATED ODDS 1:360 HOBBY		

		MINT	NRMT
☐ 1	Wade Boggs	4.00	1.80
☐ 2	Barry Bonds	5.00	2.20
☐ 3	Roger Clemens	8.00	3.60
☐ 4	Tony Gwynn	10.00	4.50
☐ 5	Rickey Henderson	2.50	1.10
☐ 6	Greg Maddux	12.00	5.50
☐ 7	Mark McGwire	8.00	3.60
☐ 8	Paul Molitor	4.00	1.80
☐ 9	Eddie Murray	4.00	1.80
☐ 10	Cal Ripken	15.00	6.75
☐ 11	Ryne Sandberg	5.00	2.20
☐ 12	Matt Williams	2.50	1.10

1997 Fleer Diamond Tribute

Randomly inserted in Fleer Series 2 packs at a rate of one in 288, this 12-card set features color action images of Baseball's top players on a dazzling foil background.

	MINT	NRMT
COMPLETE SET (12)	600.00	275.00
COMMON CARD (1-12)	20.00	9.00
SER.2 STATED ODDS 1:288		

		MINT	NRMT
☐ 1	Albert Belle	25.00	11.00
☐ 2	Barry Bonds	25.00	11.00
☐ 3	Juan Gonzalez	50.00	22.00
☐ 4	Ken Griffey Jr.	100.00	45.00
☐ 5	Tony Gwynn	50.00	22.00
☐ 6	Greg Maddux	60.00	27.00
☐ 7	Mark McGwire	40.00	18.00
☐ 8	Eddie Murray	20.00	9.00
☐ 9	Mike Piazza	60.00	27.00
☐ 10	Cal Ripken	80.00	36.00
☐ 11	Alex Rodriguez	60.00	27.00
☐ 12	Frank Thomas	80.00	36.00

1997 Fleer Golden Memories

Randomly inserted in first series packs at a rate of one in 16, this ten-card set commemorates

major achievements by individual players from the 1996 season. The fronts feature color player images on a background of the top portion of the sun and its rays. The backs carry player information.

	MINT	NRMT
COMPLETE SET (10)	10.00	4.50
COMMON CARD (1-10)	.50	.23
SER.1 STATED ODDS 1:16 HOBBY		

		MINT	NRMT
☐ 1	Barry Bonds	1.50	.70
☐ 2	Dwight Gooden	.50	.23
☐ 3	Todd Hundley	.50	.23
☐ 4	Mark McGwire	2.50	1.10
☐ 5	Paul Molitor	1.25	.55
☐ 6	Eddie Murray	1.25	.55
☐ 7	Hideo Nomo	3.00	1.35
☐ 8	Mike Piazza	4.00	1.80
☐ 9	Cal Ripken	5.00	2.20
☐ 10	Ozzie Smith	1.50	.70

1997 Fleer Goudey Greats

FRANK H. FLEER

Randomly inserted in Fleer Series 2 packs at a rate of one in eight, this 15-card set features color player photos of today's stars on cards styled and sized to resemble the 1933 Goudey Baseball card set.

	MINT	NRMT
COMPLETE SET (15)	30.00	13.50
COMMON CARD (1-15)	1.25	.55
SER.2 STATED ODDS 1:8		
*FOIL CARDS: 25X TO 50X BASE CARD HI		
FOIL SER.2 STATED ODDS 1:800		

		MINT	NRMT
☐ 1	Barry Bonds	1.25	.55
☐ 2	Ken Griffey Jr.	5.00	2.20
☐ 3	Tony Gwynn	2.50	1.10
☐ 4	Derek Jeter	3.00	1.35
☐ 5	Chipper Jones	3.00	1.35
☐ 6	Kenny Lofton	1.25	.55
☐ 7	Greg Maddux	3.00	1.35
☐ 8	Mark McGwire	2.00	.90
☐ 9	Eddie Murray	1.00	.45
☐ 10	Mike Piazza	3.00	1.35
☐ 11	Cal Ripken	4.00	1.80
☐ 12	Alex Rodriguez	3.00	1.35
☐ 13	Ryne Sandberg	1.25	.55
☐ 14	Frank Thomas	4.00	1.80
☐ 15	Mo Vaughn	1.25	.55

1997 Fleer Headliners

Randomly inserted in Fleer Series 2 packs at a rate of one in two, this 20-card set features color action photos of top players who make headlines for

their teams. The backs carry player information.

	MINT	NRMT
COMPLETE SET (20)	12.00	5.50
COMMON CARD (1-20)	.30	.14
SER.2 STATED ODDS 1:2		

		MINT	NRMT
☐ 1	Jeff Bagwell	.75	.35
☐ 2	Albert Belle	.50	.23
☐ 3	Barry Bonds	.50	.23
☐ 4	Ken Caminiti	.30	.14
☐ 5	Juan Gonzalez	1.00	.45
☐ 6	Ken Griffey Jr.	2.00	.90
☐ 7	Tony Gwynn	1.00	.45
☐ 8	Derek Jeter	1.25	.55
☐ 9	Andruw Jones	1.00	.45
☐ 10	Chipper Jones	1.25	.55
☐ 11	Greg Maddux	1.25	.55
☐ 12	Mark McGwire	.75	.35
☐ 13	Paul Molitor	.40	.18
☐ 14	Eddie Murray	.40	.18
☐ 15	Mike Piazza	1.25	.55
☐ 16	Cal Ripken	1.50	.70
☐ 17	Alex Rodriguez	1.25	.55
☐ 18	Ryne Sandberg	.50	.23
☐ 19	John Smoltz	.20	.09
☐ 20	Frank Thomas	1.50	.70

1997 Fleer Lumber Company

Randomly inserted exclusively in Fleer Series 1 retail packs, this 18-card set features a selection of the game's top sluggers. The innovative design displays pure die-cut circular borders, simulating the effect of a cut tree.

	MINT	NRMT
COMPLETE SET (18)	180.00	80.00
COMMON CARD (1-18)	3.00	1.35
UNLISTED STARS	5.00	2.20
SER.1 STATED ODDS 1:48 RETAIL		

		MINT	NRMT
☐ 1	Brady Anderson	4.00	1.80
☐ 2	Jeff Bagwell	12.00	5.50

		MINT	NRMT
☐ 3	Albert Belle	8.00	3.60
☐ 4	Barry Bonds	8.00	3.60
☐ 5	Jay Buhner	4.00	1.80
☐ 6	Ellis Burks	3.00	1.35
☐ 7	Andres Galarraga	5.00	2.20
☐ 8	Juan Gonzalez	15.00	6.75
☐ 9	Ken Griffey Jr.	30.00	13.50
☐ 10	Todd Hundley	3.00	1.35
☐ 11	Ryan Klesko	4.00	1.80
☐ 12	Mark McGwire	12.00	5.50
☐ 13	Mike Piazza	20.00	9.00
☐ 14	Alex Rodriguez	20.00	9.00
☐ 15	Gary Sheffield	5.00	2.20
☐ 16	Sammy Sosa	5.00	2.20
☐ 17	Frank Thomas	25.00	11.00
☐ 18	Mo Vaughn	8.00	3.60

1997-98 Fleer Million Dollar Moments

Inserted one per pack into 1997 Fleer 2, 1997 Flair Showcase, 1998 Fleer 1 and 1998 Ultra 1; these 50 cards mix a selection of retired legends with today's stars, highlighting key moments in baseball history. The first 45 cards in the set are common to find. Cards 46-50 are extremely shortprinted with each card being tougher to find than the next as you work your way up to card #50. Prior to the July 31, 1998 deadline, collectors could mail in their 45-card sets (plus $5.99 for postage and handling) and receive a complete 50-card exchange set. The lucky collectors that managed to obtain one or more of the shortprinted cards could receive a shopping spree at card shops nationwide selected by Fleer. Each shortprinted card had to be mailed in along with a complete 45-card set to receive the following shopping allowances: #46/$100, #47/$250, #48/$500, #49/$1000. A grand prize of $1,000,000 cash (payable in increments of $50,000 annually over 20 years) was available for one collector that could obtain and redeem all five shortprint cards (#s 46-50). This set was actually a part of a multi-sport promotion (baseball, basketball and football) for Fleer with each sport offering a separate $1,000,000 grand prize. In addition, 10,000 instant winner cards per sport (good for an assortment of material including

shopping sprees, video games and various Fleer sets) were randomly seeded into packs. We are listing cards #46-50, however no prices are assigned for these cards.

	MINT	NRMT
COMPLETE SET (45)	8.00	3.60
COMMON CARD (1-45)	.10	.05
UNLISTED STARS	.25	.11
#'s 1-45: ONE PER '97 FLEER 2/FLAIR PACK		
#'s 1-45: ONE PER '98 FLEER 1/ULT.1 PACK		
#'s 46-50: RAND.IN '97 FLEER 2/FLAIR PACKS		
#'s 46-50: RAND.IN '98 FLEER 1/ULT.1 PACKS		
1-45 SET REDEEMABLE FOR 1-50 EXCH.SET		
EXCHANGE DEADLINE: 7/31/98		

		MINT	NRMT
☐ 1	Checklist	.10	.05
☐ 2	Derek Jeter	.60	.25
☐ 3	Babe Ruth	1.50	.70
☐ 4	Barry Bonds	.25	.11
☐ 5	Brooks Robinson	.25	.11
☐ 6	Todd Hundley	.10	.05
☐ 7	Johnny Vander Meer	.10	.05
☐ 8	Cal Ripken	.75	.35
☐ 9	Bill Mazeroski	.10	.05
☐ 10	Chipper Jones	.60	.25
☐ 11	Frank Robinson	.25	.11
☐ 12	Roger Clemens	.40	.18
☐ 13	Bob Feller	.10	.05
☐ 14	Mike Piazza	.60	.25
☐ 15	Joe Nuxhall	.10	.05
☐ 16	Hideo Nomo	.50	.23
☐ 17	Jackie Robinson	1.00	.45
☐ 18	Orel Hershiser	.10	.05
☐ 19	Bobby Thomson	.10	.05
☐ 20	Joe Carter	.10	.05
☐ 21	Al Kaline	.25	.11
☐ 22	Bernie Williams	.25	.11
☐ 23	Don Larsen	.10	.05
☐ 24	Rickey Henderson	.15	.07
☐ 25	Maury Wills	.10	.05
☐ 26	Andruw Jones	.50	.23
☐ 27	Bobby Richardson	.10	.05
☐ 28	Alex Rodriguez	.60	.25
☐ 29	Jim Bunning	.10	.05
☐ 30	Ken Caminiti	.15	.07
☐ 31	Bob Gibson	.25	.11
☐ 32	Frank Thomas	.75	.35
☐ 33	Mickey Lolich	.10	.05
☐ 34	John Smoltz	.10	.05
☐ 35	Ron Swoboda	.10	.05
☐ 36	Albert Belle	.25	.11
☐ 37	Chris Chambliss	.10	.05
☐ 38	Juan Gonzalez	.50	.23
☐ 39	Ron Blomberg	.10	.05
☐ 40	John Wetteland	.10	.05
☐ 41	Carlton Fisk	.25	.11
☐ 42	Mo Vaughn	.25	.11
☐ 43	Bucky Dent	.10	.05
☐ 44	Greg Maddux	.60	.25
☐ 45	Willie Stargell	.10	.05
☐ 46	Tony Gwynn SP		
☐ 47	Joel Youngblood SP		
☐ 48	Andy Pettitte SP		
☐ 49	Mookie Wilson SP		
☐ 50	Jeff Bagwell SP		

1997 Fleer New Horizons

Randomly inserted in Fleer Series 2 packs at a rate of one in four, this 15-card set features borderless color action photos of Rookies and prospects. The backs carry player information.

	MINT	NRMT
COMPLETE SET (15)	12.00	5.50
COMMON CARD (1-12)	.25	.11
SER.2 STATED ODDS 1:4		

☐ 1 Bob Abreu	.25	.11
☐ 2 Jose Cruz Jr.	5.00	2.20
☐ 3 Darin Erstad	1.25	.55
☐ 4 Nomar Garciaparra	2.50	1.10
☐ 5 Vladimir Guerrero	1.50	.70
☐ 6 Wilton Guerrero	.25	.11
☐ 7 Jose Guillen	1.00	.45
☐ 8 Hideki Irabu	.75	.35
☐ 9 Andruw Jones	2.00	.90
☐ 10 Kevin Orie	.25	.11
☐ 11 Scott Rolen	2.00	.90
☐ 12 Scott Spiezio	.25	.11
☐ 13 Bubba Trammell	.75	.35
☐ 14 Todd Walker	.25	.11
☐ 15 Dmitri Young	.25	.11

1997 Fleer Night and Day

Randomly inserted in Fleer Series 1 packs at a rate of one in 240, this ten-card set features color action player photos of superstars who excel in day games, night games, or both and are printed on lenticular 3D cards. The backs carry player information.

	MINT	NRMT
COMPLETE SET (10)	350.00	160.00
COMMON CARD (1-10)	15.00	4.50
UNLISTED STARS	15.00	6.75
SER.1 STATED ODDS 1:240		
☐ 1 Barry Bonds	20.00	9.00
☐ 2 Ellis Burks	10.00	4.50
☐ 3 Juan Gonzalez	40.00	18.00
☐ 4 Ken Griffey Jr.	80.00	36.00
☐ 5 Mark McGwire	30.00	13.50
☐ 6 Mike Piazza	50.00	22.00
☐ 7 Manny Ramirez	15.00	6.75
☐ 8 Alex Rodriguez	50.00	22.00
☐ 9 John Smoltz	10.00	4.50
☐ 10 Frank Thomas	60.00	27.00

1997 Fleer Rookie Sensations

Randomly inserted in Fleer Series 1 packs at a rate of one in six, this 20-card set honors the top rookies from the 1996 season and the 1997 season rookies/prospects. The fronts feature color action player images on a multi-color swirling background. The backs carry a paragraph with information about the player.

	MINT	NRMT
COMPLETE SET (20)	25.00	11.00
COMMON CARD (1-20)	.40	.18
SER.1 STATED ODDS 1:6		
☐ 1 Jermaine Allensworth	.40	.18
☐ 2 James Baldwin	.40	.18
☐ 3 Alan Benes	.60	.25
☐ 4 Jermaine Dye	.40	.18
☐ 5 Darin Erstad	2.50	1.10
☐ 6 Todd Hollandsworth	.40	.18
☐ 7 Derek Jeter	5.00	2.20
☐ 8 Jason Kendall	.60	.25
☐ 9 Alex Ochoa	.40	.18
☐ 10 Rey Ordonez	.40	.18
☐ 11 Edgar Renteria	.60	.25
☐ 12 Bob Abreu	.60	.25
☐ 13 Nomar Garciaparra	5.00	2.20
☐ 14 Wilton Guerrero	.40	.18
☐ 15 Andruw Jones	4.00	1.80
☐ 16 Wendell Magee	.40	.18
☐ 17 Neifi Perez	.60	.25
☐ 18 Scott Rolen	4.00	1.80
☐ 19 Scott Spiezio	.60	.25
☐ 20 Todd Walker	.60	.25

1997 Fleer Soaring Stars

Randomly inserted in Fleer Series 2 packs at a rate of one in 12, this 12-card set features

color action photos of players who enjoyed a meteoric rise to stardom and have all the skills to stay there. The player's image is set on a background of twinkling stars.

	MINT	NRMT
COMPLETE SET (12)	40.00	18.00
COMMON CARD (1-12)	1.50	.70
SER.2 STATED ODDS 1:12		
*GLOWING: 5X TO 10X BASE CARD HI		
GLOWING: RANDOM INS.IN SER.2 PACKS		
☐ 1 Albert Belle	1.50	.70
☐ 2 Barry Bonds	1.50	.70
☐ 3 Juan Gonzalez	3.00	1.35
☐ 4 Ken Griffey Jr.	6.00	2.70
☐ 5 Derek Jeter	4.00	1.80
☐ 6 Andruw Jones	3.00	1.35
☐ 7 Chipper Jones	4.00	1.80
☐ 8 Greg Maddux	4.00	1.80
☐ 9 Mark McGwire	2.50	1.10
☐ 10 Mike Piazza	4.00	1.80
☐ 11 Alex Rodriguez	4.00	1.80
☐ 12 Frank Thomas	5.00	2.20

1997 Fleer Team Leaders

Randomly inserted in Fleer Series 1 packs at a rate of one in 20, this 28-card set honors statistical or inspirational leaders from each team on a die-cut card. The fronts feature color action player images with the player's face in the background. The backs carry a paragraph with information about the player.

	MINT	NRMT
COMPLETE SET (28)	110.00	50.00
COMMON CARD (1-28)	1.50	.70
UNLISTED STARS	4.00	1.80
SER.1 STATED ODDS 1:20		
☐ 1 Cal Ripken	15.00	6.75
☐ 2 Mo Vaughn	5.00	2.20
☐ 3 Jim Edmonds	2.50	1.10
☐ 4 Frank Thomas	15.00	6.75
☐ 5 Albert Belle	5.00	2.20
☐ 6 Bob Higginson	2.00	.90
☐ 7 Kevin Appier	2.00	.90
☐ 8 John Jaha	1.50	.70
☐ 9 Paul Molitor	4.00	1.80
☐ 10 Andy Pettitte	4.00	1.80
☐ 11 Mark McGwire	8.00	3.60
☐ 12 Ken Griffey Jr.	20.00	9.00
☐ 13 Juan Gonzalez	10.00	4.50
☐ 14 Pat Hentgen	2.00	.90
☐ 15 Chipper Jones	12.00	5.50
☐ 16 Mark Grace	2.50	1.10
☐ 17 Barry Larkin	2.50	1.10
☐ 18 Ellis Burks	2.00	.90

		MINT	NRMT
☐ 19	Gary Sheffield	4.00	1.80
☐ 20	Jeff Bagwell	8.00	3.60
☐ 21	Mike Piazza	12.00	5.50
☐ 22	Henry Rodriguez	1.50	.70
☐ 23	Todd Hundley	2.00	.90
☐ 24	Curt Schilling	2.00	.90
☐ 25	Jeff King	1.50	.70
☐ 26	Brian Jordan	2.00	.90
☐ 27	Tony Gwynn	10.00	4.50
☐ 28	Barry Bonds	5.00	2.20

1997 Fleer Zone

Randomly inserted in Fleer Series 1 hobby packs only at a rate of one in 80, this 20-card set features color player images of some of the 1996 season's unstoppable hitters and unhittable pitchers on a holographic card. The backs carry another color photo with a paragraph about the player.

		MINT	NRMT
COMPLETE SET (20)		250.00	110.00
COMMON CARD (1-20)		4.00	1.80
UNLISTED STARS		8.00	3.60
SER.1 STATED ODDS 1:80 HOBBY			

		MINT	NRMT
☐ 1	Jeff Bagwell	15.00	6.75
☐ 2	Albert Belle	10.00	4.50
☐ 3	Barry Bonds	10.00	4.50
☐ 4	Ken Caminiti	5.00	2.20
☐ 5	Andres Galarraga	8.00	3.60
☐ 6	Juan Gonzalez	20.00	9.00
☐ 7	Ken Griffey Jr.	40.00	18.00
☐ 8	Tony Gwynn	20.00	9.00
☐ 9	Chipper Jones	25.00	11.00
☐ 10	Greg Maddux	25.00	11.00
☐ 11	Mark McGwire	15.00	6.75
☐ 12	Dean Palmer	4.00	1.80
☐ 13	Andy Pettitte	8.00	3.60
☐ 14	Mike Piazza	25.00	11.00
☐ 15	Alex Rodriguez	25.00	11.00
☐ 16	Gary Sheffield	8.00	3.60
☐ 17	John Smoltz	4.00	1.80
☐ 18	Frank Thomas	30.00	13.50
☐ 19	Jim Thome	8.00	3.60
☐ 20	Matt Williams	5.00	2.20

1998 Fleer

The 1998 Fleer set was issued in two series. Series one consists of 350 cards and features borderless color action player photos with UV-coating and foil stamping. The backs display player information and career statistics. The set contains the following topical subsets: Smoke 'N Heat (301-310), Golden Memories (311-320), and Tale of the Tape (321-340). The Golden Memories (1:6) and Tale of the Tape (1:4) cards are

shortprinted. An Alex Rodriguez Promo card was distributed to dealers along with their 1998 Fleer 1 order forms. The card can be readily distinguished by the "Promotional Sample" text running diagonally across both the front and back of the card. 50 Fleer Flashback Exchange cards were hand-numbered and randomly inserted into packs. Each of these cards could be exchanged for a framed, uncut press sheet from one of Fleer's baseball sets dating anywhere from 1981 to 1993.

	MINT	NRMT
COMPLETE SERIES 1 (350)	80.00	36.00
COMMON CARD (1-350)	.15	.07
MINOR STARS	.30	.14
UNLISTED STARS	.60	.25
COMMON GM (311-320)	.60	.23
GM MINOR STARS	.50	.23
GM SEMISTARS	.75	.35
GM UNLISTED STARS	1.00	.45
GOLDEN MOMENT STATED ODDS 1:6		
COMMON TT (321-340)	.75	.35
TT MINOR STARS	.75	.35
TT SEMISTARS	.75	.35
TT UNLISTED STARS	1.25	.55
TALE OF TAPE STATED ODDS 1:4		

		MINT	NRMT
☐ 1	Ken Griffey Jr.	3.00	1.35
☐ 2	Derek Jeter	1.50	.70
☐ 3	Gerald Williams	.15	.07
☐ 4	Carlos Delgado	.30	.14
☐ 5	Nomar Garciaparra	2.00	.90
☐ 6	Gary Sheffield	.60	.25
☐ 7	Jeff King	.15	.07
☐ 8	Cal Ripken	2.50	1.10
☐ 9	Matt Williams	.40	.18
☐ 10	Chipper Jones	2.00	.90
☐ 11	Chuck Knoblauch	.60	.25
☐ 12	Mark Grudzielanek	.15	.07
☐ 13	Edgardo Alfonzo	.30	.14
☐ 14	Andres Galarraga	.60	.25
☐ 15	Tim Salmon	.60	.25
☐ 16	Reggie Sanders	.15	.07
☐ 17	Tony Clark	.60	.25
☐ 18	Jason Kendall	.30	.14
☐ 19	Juan Gonzalez	1.50	.70
☐ 20	Ben Grieve	1.25	.55
☐ 21	Roger Clemens	1.25	.55
☐ 22	Raul Mondesi	.40	.18
☐ 23	Robin Ventura	.30	.14
☐ 24	Derrek Lee	.40	.18
☐ 25	Mark McGwire	1.50	.70
☐ 26	Luis Gonzalez	.15	.07
☐ 27	Kevin Brown	.30	.14
☐ 28	Kirk Rueter	.15	.07
☐ 29	Bobby Estalella	.15	.07
☐ 30	Shawn Green	.15	.07
☐ 31	Greg Maddux	2.00	.90
☐ 32	Jorge Velandia	.15	.07
☐ 33	Larry Walker	.60	.25
☐ 34	Joey Cora	.30	.14
☐ 35	Frank Thomas	2.50	1.10

		MINT	NRMT
☐ 36	Curtis King	.25	.11
☐ 37	Aaron Boone	.15	.07
☐ 38	Curt Schilling	.30	.14
☐ 39	Bruce Aven	.15	.07
☐ 40	Ben McDonald	.15	.07
☐ 41	Andy Ashby	.15	.07
☐ 42	Jason McDonald	.15	.07
☐ 43	Eric Davis	.30	.14
☐ 44	Mark Grace	.40	.18
☐ 45	Pedro Martinez	.60	.25
☐ 46	Lou Collier	.15	.07
☐ 47	Chan Ho Park	.60	.25
☐ 48	Shane Halter	.15	.07
☐ 49	Brian Hunter	.30	.14
☐ 50	Jeff Bagwell	1.25	.55
☐ 51	Bernie Williams	.60	.25
☐ 52	J.T. Snow	.30	.14
☐ 53	Todd Greene	.30	.14
☐ 54	Shannon Stewart	.30	.14
☐ 55	Darren Bragg	.15	.07
☐ 56	Fernando Tatis	.60	.25
☐ 57	Darryl Kile	.30	.14
☐ 58	Chris Stynes	.15	.07
☐ 59	Javier Valentin	.30	.14
☐ 60	Brian McRae	.15	.07
☐ 61	Tom Evans	.30	.14
☐ 62	Randall Simon	.15	.07
☐ 63	Darrin Fletcher	.15	.07
☐ 64	Jaret Wright	1.50	.70
☐ 65	Luis Ordaz	.15	.07
☐ 66	Jose Canseco	.40	.18
☐ 67	Edgar Renteria	.30	.14
☐ 68	Jay Buhner	.40	.18
☐ 69	Paul Konerko	1.00	.45
☐ 70	Adrian Brown	.15	.07
☐ 71	Chris Carpenter	.15	.07
☐ 72	Mike Lieberthal	.15	.07
☐ 73	Dean Palmer	.15	.07
☐ 74	Jorge Fabregas	.15	.07
☐ 75	Stan Javier	.15	.07
☐ 76	Damion Easley	.15	.07
☐ 77	David Cone	.30	.14
☐ 78	Aaron Sele	.15	.07
☐ 79	Antonio Alfonseca	.15	.07
☐ 80	Bobby Jones	.15	.07
☐ 81	David Justice	.60	.25
☐ 82	Jeffrey Hammonds	.15	.07
☐ 83	Doug Glanville	.15	.07
☐ 84	Jason Dickson	.30	.14
☐ 85	Brad Radke	.30	.14
☐ 86	David Segui	.15	.07
☐ 87	Greg Vaughn	.15	.07
☐ 88	Mike Cather	.25	.11
☐ 89	Alex Fernandez	.15	.07
☐ 90	Billy Taylor	.15	.07
☐ 91	Jason Schmidt	.15	.07
☐ 92	Mike DeJean	.25	.11
☐ 93	Domingo Cedeno	.15	.07
☐ 94	Jeff Cirillo	.30	.14
☐ 95	Manny Aybar	.50	.23
☐ 96	Jaime Navarro	.15	.07
☐ 97	Dennis Reyes	.30	.14
☐ 98	Barry Larkin	.40	.18
☐ 99	Troy O'Leary	.15	.07
☐ 100	Alex Rodriguez	2.00	.90
☐ 101	Pat Hentgen	.30	.14
☐ 102	Bubba Trammell	.30	.14
☐ 103	Gordon Rusch	.15	.07
☐ 104	Kenny Lofton	.75	.35
☐ 105	Craig Biggio	.40	.18
☐ 106	Kelvin Escobar	.15	.07
☐ 107	Mark Kotsay	.60	.25
☐ 108	Rondell White	.30	.14
☐ 109	Darren Oliver	.15	.07
☐ 110	Jim Thome	.60	.25
☐ 111	Rich Becker	.15	.07
☐ 112	Chad Curtis	.15	.07
☐ 113	Dave Hollins	.15	.07
☐ 114	Bill Mueller	.15	.07
☐ 115	Antone Williamson	.15	.07
☐ 116	Tony Womack	.30	.14
☐ 117	Randy Myers	.15	.07
☐ 118	Rico Brogna	.15	.07
☐ 119	Pat Watkins	.15	.07
☐ 120	Eli Marrero	.30	.14
☐ 121	Jay Bell	.30	.14

□ 122	Kevin Tapani	.15	.07
□ 123	Todd Erdos	.25	.11
□ 124	Neifi Perez	.30	.14
□ 125	Todd Hundley	.30	.14
□ 126	Jeff Abbott	.15	.07
□ 127	Todd Zeile	.15	.07
□ 128	Travis Fryman	.30	.14
□ 129	Sandy Alomar	.30	.14
□ 130	Fred McGriff	.40	.18
□ 131	Richard Hidalgo	.30	.14
□ 132	Scott Spiezio	.30	.14
□ 133	John Valentin	.15	.07
□ 134	Quilvio Veras	.15	.07
□ 135	Mike Lansing	.15	.07
□ 136	Paul Molitor	.60	.25
□ 137	Randy Johnson	.60	.25
□ 138	Harold Baines	.15	.07
□ 139	Doug Jones	.15	.07
□ 140	Abraham Nunez	.30	.14
□ 141	Alan Benes	.30	.14
□ 142	Matt Perisho	.15	.07
□ 143	Chris Clemons	.15	.07
□ 144	Andy Pettitte	.60	.25
□ 145	Jason Giambi	.30	.14
□ 146	Moises Alou	.30	.14
□ 147	Chad Fox	.15	.07
□ 148	Felix Martinez	.15	.07
□ 149	Carlos Mendoza	.25	.11
□ 150	Scott Rolen	1.50	.70
□ 151	Jose Cabrera	.25	.11
□ 152	Justin Thompson	.30	.14
□ 153	Ellis Burks	.30	.14
□ 154	Pokey Reese	.15	.07
□ 155	Bartolo Colon	.30	.14
□ 156	Ray Durham	.15	.07
□ 157	Ugueth Urbina	.15	.07
□ 158	Tom Goodwin	.15	.07
□ 159	Dave Dellucci	.25	.11
□ 160	Rod Beck	.15	.07
□ 161	Ramon Martinez	.30	.14
□ 162	Joe Carter	.30	.14
□ 163	Kevin Orie	.30	.14
□ 164	Trevor Hoffman	.15	.07
□ 165	Emil Brown	.15	.07
□ 166	Robb Nen	.15	.07
□ 167	Paul O'Neill	.30	.14
□ 168	Ryan Long	.15	.07
□ 169	Ray Lankford	.30	.14
□ 170	Ivan Rodriguez	.75	.35
□ 171	Rick Aguilera	.15	.07
□ 172	Deivi Cruz	.15	.07
□ 173	Ricky Bottalico	.15	.07
□ 174	Garret Anderson	.30	.14
□ 175	Jose Vizcaino	.15	.07
□ 176	Omar Vizquel	.30	.14
□ 177	Jeff Blauser	.30	.14
□ 178	Orlando Cabrera	.30	.14
□ 179	Russ Johnson	.15	.07
□ 180	Matt Stairs	.15	.07
□ 181	Will Cunnane	.15	.07
□ 182	Adam Riggs	.15	.07
□ 183	Matt Morris	.30	.14
□ 184	Mario Valdez	.30	.14
□ 185	Larry Sutton	.15	.07
□ 186	Marc Pisciotta	.25	.11
□ 187	Dan Wilson	.15	.07
□ 188	John Franco	.30	.14
□ 189	Darren Daulton	.30	.14
□ 190	Todd Helton	.75	.35
□ 191	Brady Anderson	.40	.18
□ 192	Ricardo Rincon	.15	.07
□ 193	Kevin Stocker	.15	.07
□ 194	Jose Valentin	.15	.07
□ 195	Ed Sprague	.15	.07
□ 196	Ryan McGuire	.15	.07
□ 197	Scott Eyre	.15	.07
□ 198	Steve Finley	.30	.14
□ 199	T.J. Mathews	.15	.07
□ 200	Mike Piazza	2.00	.90
□ 201	Mark Wohlers	.15	.07
□ 202	Brian Giles	.15	.07
□ 203	Eduardo Perez	.15	.07
□ 204	Shigetoshi Hasegawa	.30	.14
□ 205	Mariano Rivera	.30	.14
□ 206	Jose Rosado	.15	.07
□ 207	Michael Coleman	.40	.18
□ 208	James Baldwin	.15	.07
□ 209	Russ Davis	.15	.07
□ 210	Billy Wagner	.30	.14
□ 211	Sammy Sosa	.60	.25
□ 212	Frank Catalanotto	.25	.11
□ 213	Delino DeShields	.15	.07
□ 214	John Olerud	.30	.14
□ 215	Heath Murray	.15	.07
□ 216	Jose Vidro	.30	.14
□ 217	Jim Edmonds	.40	.18
□ 218	Shawon Dunston	.15	.07
□ 219	Homer Bush	.15	.07
□ 220	Midre Cummings	.15	.07
□ 221	Tony Saunders	.30	.14
□ 222	Jeromy Burnitz	.15	.07
□ 223	Enrique Wilson	.30	.14
□ 224	Chili Davis	.30	.14
□ 225	Jerry DiPoto	.15	.07
□ 226	Dante Powell	.15	.07
□ 227	Javier Lopez	.30	.14
□ 228	Kevin Polcovich	.15	.07
□ 229	Deion Sanders	.30	.14
□ 230	Jimmy Key	.15	.07
□ 231	Rusty Greer	.30	.14
□ 232	Reggie Jefferson	.15	.07
□ 233	Ron Coomer	.15	.07
□ 234	Bobby Higginson	.30	.14
□ 235	Magglio Ordonez	.75	.35
□ 236	Miguel Tejada	.75	.35
□ 237	Rick Gorecki	.15	.07
□ 238	Charles Johnson	.15	.07
□ 239	Lance Johnson	.15	.07
□ 240	Derek Bell	.15	.07
□ 241	Will Clark	.40	.18
□ 242	Brady Raggio	.15	.07
□ 243	Orel Hershiser	.30	.14
□ 244	Vladimir Guerrero	1.00	.45
□ 245	John LeRoy	.15	.07
□ 246	Shawn Estes	.30	.14
□ 247	Brett Tomko	.30	.14
□ 248	Dave Nilsson	.15	.07
□ 249	Edgar Martinez	.40	.18
□ 250	Tony Gwynn	1.50	.70
□ 251	Mark Bellhorn	.15	.07
□ 252	Jed Hansen	.15	.07
□ 253	Butch Huskey	.30	.14
□ 254	Eric Young	.15	.07
□ 255	Vinny Castilla	.30	.14
□ 256	Hideki Irabu	.30	.14
□ 257	Mike Cameron	.30	.14
□ 258	Juan Encarnacion	.60	.25
□ 259	Brian Rose	.40	.18
□ 260	Brad Ausmus	.15	.07
□ 261	Dan Serafini	.15	.07
□ 262	Willie Greene	.15	.07
□ 263	Troy Percival	.15	.07
□ 264	Jeff Wallace	.15	.07
□ 265	Richie Sexson	.30	.14
□ 266	Rafael Palmeiro	.40	.18
□ 267	Brad Fullmer	.30	.14
□ 268	Jeremi Gonzalez	.30	.14
□ 269	Rob Stanifer	.15	.07
□ 270	Mickey Morandini	.15	.07
□ 271	Andruw Jones	1.25	.55
□ 272	Royce Clayton	.15	.07
□ 273	Takashi Kashiwada	.50	.23
□ 274	Steve Woodard	.30	.14
□ 275	Jose Cruz Jr.	2.50	1.10
□ 276	Keith Foulke	.15	.07
□ 277	Brad Rigby	.15	.07
□ 278	Tino Martinez	.60	.25
□ 279	Todd Jones	.15	.07
□ 280	John Wetteland	.15	.07
□ 281	Alex Gonzalez	.15	.07
□ 282	Ken Cloude	.30	.14
□ 283	Jose Guillen	.60	.25
□ 284	Danny Clyburn	.15	.07
□ 285	David Ortiz	.30	.14
□ 286	John Thomson	.15	.07
□ 287	Kevin Appier	.30	.14
□ 288	Ismael Valdes	.30	.14
□ 289	Gary DiSarcina	.15	.07
□ 290	Todd Dunwoody	.30	.14
□ 291	Wally Joyner	.30	.14
□ 292	Charles Nagy	.30	.14
□ 293	Jeff Shaw	.15	.07
□ 294	Kevin Millwood	.50	.23
□ 295	Rigo Beltran	.25	.11
□ 296	Jeff Frye	.15	.07
□ 297	Oscar Henriquez	.30	.14
□ 298	Mike Thurman	.15	.07
□ 299	Garrett Stephenson	.15	.07
□ 300	Barry Bonds	.75	.35
□ 301	Roger Clemens SH	.60	.25
□ 302	David Cone SH	.15	.07
□ 303	Hideki Irabu SH	.15	.07
□ 304	Randy Johnson SH	.30	.14
□ 305	Greg Maddux SH	1.00	.45
□ 306	Pedro Martinez SH	.30	.14
□ 307	Mike Mussina SH	.30	.14
□ 308	Andy Pettitte SH	.30	.14
□ 309	Curt Schilling SH	.15	.07
□ 310	John Smoltz SH	.15	.07
□ 311	Roger Clemens GM	2.00	.90
□ 312	Jose Cruz JR. GM	4.00	1.80
□ 313	Nomar Garciaparra GM	3.00	1.35
□ 314	Ken Griffey Jr. GM	5.00	2.20
□ 315	Tony Gwynn GM	2.50	1.10
□ 316	Hideki Irabu GM	.50	.23
□ 317	Randy Johnson GM	1.00	.45
□ 318	Mark McGwire GM	2.50	1.10
□ 319	Curt Schilling GM	.50	.23
□ 320	Larry Walker GM	1.00	.45
□ 321	Jeff Bagwell TT	2.50	1.10
□ 322	Albert Belle TT	1.50	.70
□ 323	Barry Bonds TT	1.50	.70
□ 324	Jay Buhner TT	.75	.35
□ 325	Tony Clark TT	1.25	.55
□ 326	Jose Cruz Jr. TT	5.00	2.20
□ 327	Andres Galarraga TT	1.25	.55
□ 328	Juan Gonzalez TT	3.00	1.35
□ 329	Ken Griffey Jr. TT	6.00	2.70
□ 330	Andruw Jones TT	2.50	1.10
□ 331	Tino Martinez TT	1.25	.55
□ 332	Mark McGwire TT	3.00	1.35
□ 333	Rafael Palmeiro TT	.75	.35
□ 334	Mike Piazza TT	4.00	1.80
□ 335	Manny Ramirez TT	1.25	.55
□ 336	Alex Rodriguez TT	4.00	1.80
□ 337	Frank Thomas TT	5.00	2.20
□ 338	Jim Thome TT	1.25	.55
□ 339	Mo Vaughn TT	1.50	.70
□ 340	Larry Walker TT	1.25	.55
□ 341	Jose Cruz Jr. CL	1.25	.55
□ 342	Ken Griffey Jr. CL	1.50	.70
□ 343	Derek Jeter CL	.75	.35
□ 344	Andruw Jones CL	.60	.25
□ 345	Chipper Jones CL	1.00	.45
□ 346	Greg Maddux CL	1.00	.45
□ 347	Mike Piazza CL	1.00	.45
□ 348	Cal Ripken CL	1.25	.55
□ 349	Alex Rodriguez CL	1.00	.45
□ 350	Frank Thomas CL	1.25	.55
□ P100	Alex Rodriguez Promo	3.00	1.35

1998 Fleer Vintage '63

CHIPPER JONES
Atlanta Braves—26

Randomly inserted one in every hobby pack only, this 63-card set commemorates the 35th anniversary of the Fleer set and features color photos of top players printed in the 1963 Fleer Baseball card design.

	MINT	NRMT
COMPLETE SET (64)	25.00	11.00
COMMON CARD (1-63/CL)	.25	.11
MINOR STARS	.40	.18
UNLISTED STARS	.75	.35
STATED ODDS 1:1 HOBBY		
☐ 1 Jason Dickson	.40	.18
☐ 2 Tim Salmon	.75	.35
☐ 3 Andruw Jones	1.50	.70
☐ 4 Chipper Jones	2.50	1.10
☐ 5 Kenny Lofton	1.00	.45
☐ 6 Greg Maddux	2.50	1.10
☐ 7 Rafael Palmeiro	.50	.23
☐ 8 Cal Ripken	3.00	1.35
☐ 9 Nomar Garciaparra	2.50	1.10
☐ 10 Mark Grace	.50	.23
☐ 11 Sammy Sosa	.75	.35
☐ 12 Frank Thomas	3.00	1.35
☐ 13 Deion Sanders	.40	.18
☐ 14 Sandy Alomar	.40	.18
☐ 15 David Justice	.75	.35
☐ 16 Jim Thome	.75	.35
☐ 17 Matt Williams	.50	.23
☐ 18 Jaret Wright	2.00	.90
☐ 19 Vinny Castilla	.40	.18
☐ 20 Andres Galarraga	.75	.35
☐ 21 Todd Helton	1.00	.45
☐ 22 Larry Walker	.75	.35
☐ 23 Tony Clark	.75	.35
☐ 24 Moises Alou	.40	.18
☐ 25 Kevin Brown	.40	.18
☐ 26 Charles Johnson	.40	.18
☐ 27 Edgar Renteria	.40	.18
☐ 28 Gary Sheffield	.75	.35
☐ 29 Jeff Bagwell	1.50	.70
☐ 30 Craig Biggio	.50	.23
☐ 31 Paul Molitor	.50	.23
☐ 32 Mike Piazza	2.50	1.10
☐ 33 Chuck Knoblauch	.75	.35
☐ 34 Paul Molitor	.75	.35
☐ 35 Vladimir Guerrero	1.25	.55
☐ 36 Pedro Martinez	.75	.35
☐ 37 Todd Hundley	.40	.18
☐ 38 Derek Jeter	2.00	.90
☐ 39 Tino Martinez	.75	.35
☐ 40 Paul O'Neill	.75	.35
☐ 41 Andy Pettitte	.75	.35
☐ 42 Mariano Rivera	.40	.18
☐ 43 Bernie Williams	.75	.35
☐ 44 Ben Grieve	1.50	.70
☐ 45 Scott Rolen	2.00	.90
☐ 46 Curt Schilling	.40	.18
☐ 47 Jason Kendall	.40	.18
☐ 48 Tony Womack	.25	.11
☐ 49 Ray Lankford	.40	.18
☐ 50 Mark McGwire	2.00	.90
☐ 51 Matt Morris	.40	.18
☐ 52 Tony Gwynn	2.00	.90
☐ 53 Barry Bonds	1.00	.45
☐ 54 Jay Buhner	.50	.23
☐ 55 Ken Griffey Jr.	4.00	1.80
☐ 56 Randy Johnson	.75	.35
☐ 57 Edgar Martinez	.50	.23
☐ 58 Alex Rodriguez	2.50	1.10
☐ 59 Juan Gonzalez	2.00	.90
☐ 60 Rusty Greer	.40	.18
☐ 61 Ivan Rodriguez	1.00	.45
☐ 62 Roger Clemens	1.50	.70
☐ 63 Jose Cruz Jr.	3.00	1.35
☐ NNO Vintage '63 Checklist	.25	.11

1998 Fleer Vintage '63 Classic

Randomly inserted in hobby packs only, this 63-card set is parallel to the regular Vintage '63. Only 63 of these sets were produced and serially num-bered. All Cards are Numbered with a "C" suffix.

	MINT	NRMT
COMMON CARD (1-63/CL)	30.00	13.50
MINOR STARS	40.00	18.00
SEMISTARS	60.00	27.00
UNLISTED STARS	100.00	45.00
*STARS: 60X TO 120X HI COLUMN		
*YOUNG STARS: 50X TO 100X HI		
RANDOM INSERTS IN HOBBY PACKS		
STATED PRINT RUN 63 SERIAL #'d SETS		
☐ 3 Andruw Jones	150.00	70.00
☐ 4 Chipper Jones	250.00	110.00
☐ 5 Kenny Lofton	120.00	55.00
☐ 6 Greg Maddux	300.00	135.00
☐ 8 Cal Ripken	400.00	180.00
☐ 9 Nomar Garciaparra	250.00	110.00
☐ 12 Frank Thomas	400.00	180.00
☐ 18 Jaret Wright	150.00	70.00
☐ 29 Jeff Bagwell	200.00	90.00
☐ 32 Mike Piazza	300.00	135.00
☐ 35 Vladimir Guerrero	120.00	55.00
☐ 38 Derek Jeter	250.00	110.00
☐ 44 Ben Grieve	150.00	70.00
☐ 45 Scott Rolen	200.00	90.00
☐ 50 Mark McGwire	250.00	110.00
☐ 52 Tony Gwynn	250.00	110.00
☐ 53 Barry Bonds	120.00	55.00
☐ 55 Ken Griffey Jr.	500.00	220.00
☐ 58 Alex Rodriguez	300.00	135.00
☐ 59 Juan Gonzalez	250.00	110.00
☐ 61 Ivan Rodriguez	120.00	55.00
☐ 62 Roger Clemens	200.00	90.00
☐ 63 Jose Cruz Jr.	300.00	135.00

1998 Fleer Decade of Excellence

Randomly inserted in hobby packs only, this 12-card set features 1988 season photos in Fleer's 1988 card design of current players who have been in Baseball for ten years or more.

	MINT	NRMT
COMPLETE SET (12)	120.00	55.00
COMMON CARD (1-12)	4.00	1.80
STATED ODDS 1:72 HOBBY		
*RARE TRADITIONS: 2.5X TO 5X HI COLUMN		
RARE TRAD. STATED ODDS 1:720 HOBBY		
☐ 1 Roberto Alomar	8.00	3.60
☐ 2 Barry Bonds	10.00	4.50
☐ 3 Roger Clemens	15.00	6.75
☐ 4 David Cone	4.00	1.80
☐ 5 Andres Galarraga	6.00	2.70
☐ 6 Mark Grace	5.00	2.20
☐ 7 Tony Gwynn	20.00	9.00
☐ 8 Randy Johnson	8.00	3.60
☐ 9 Greg Maddux	25.00	11.00
☐ 10 Mark McGwire	20.00	9.00

	MINT	NRMT
☐ 11 Paul O'Neill	4.00	1.80
☐ 12 Cal Ripken	30.00	13.50

1998 Fleer Diamond Ink

Randomly inserted one per Series 1 Fleer and Ultra packs, these point cards feature a selection of top stars. Collectors that saved up 500 points of a specific player could redeem the cards for a baseball signed by that player. Point cards came in 1, 5 and 10 point increments. Judging from supplies on the secondary market at the time of the promotion it appears that a few players were in much short-er supply than other - most notably Roger Clemens, Tony Gwynn, Greg Maddux and Alex Rodriguez. Finally, Greg Maddux was a late additon to the promotion, thus his point cards were made available only in Fleer 1 packs (which hap-pened to be released about four to six weeks after Ultra 1).

	MINT	NRMT
J.BUHNER POINT	.10	.05
R.CLEMENS POINT	.30	.14
J.CRUZ JR. POINT	.25	.11
N.GARCIAPARRA POINT	.20	.09
T.GWYNN POINT	.25	.11
R.HERNANDEZ POINT	.05	.02
G.MADDUX POINT	.40	.18
A.RODRIGUEZ POINT	.30	.14
S.ROLEN POINT	.15	.07
T.WOMACK POINT	.05	.02
ONE PER SERIES 1 PACK		
PRICES LISTED ARE PER POINT		
EXCHANGE 500 PTS. FOR SIGNED BALL		

1998 Fleer Diamond Standouts

Randomly inserted in packs at the rate of one in 12, this 20-card set features color photos of great players on a diamond design silver foil background. The backs display detailed play-er information.

	MINT	NRMT
COMPLETE SET (20)	50.00	22.00
COMMON CARD (1-20)	.75	.35
STATED ODDS 1:12		
☐ 1 Jeff Bagwell	3.00	1.35
☐ 2 Barry Bonds	2.00	.90
☐ 3 Roger Clemens	3.00	1.35
☐ 4 Jose Cruz Jr.	6.00	2.70

☐ 5 Andres Galarraga	1.25	.55
☐ 6 Nomar Garciaparra	5.00	2.20
☐ 7 Juan Gonzalez	4.00	1.80
☐ 8 Ken Griffey Jr.	8.00	3.60
☐ 9 Derek Jeter	4.00	1.80
☐ 10 Randy Johnson	1.50	.70
☐ 11 Chipper Jones	5.00	2.20
☐ 12 Kenny Lofton	2.00	.90
☐ 13 Greg Maddux	5.00	2.20
☐ 14 Pedro Martinez	1.25	.55
☐ 15 Mark McGwire	4.00	1.80
☐ 16 Mike Piazza	5.00	2.20
☐ 17 Alex Rodriguez	5.00	2.20
☐ 18 Curt Schilling	.75	.35
☐ 19 Frank Thomas	6.00	2.70
☐ 20 Larry Walker	1.50	.70

1998 Fleer Power Game

Randomly inserted in packs at the rate of one in 36, this 20-card set features color action player photos of great pitchers and hitters highlighted with purple metallic foil and glossy UV coating. The backs display player statistics.

	MINT	NRMT
COMPLETE SET (20)	120.00	55.00
COMMON CARD (1-20)	2.50	1.10
STATED ODDS 1:36		
☐ 1 Jeff Bagwell	10.00	4.50
☐ 2 Albert Belle	6.00	2.70
☐ 3 Barry Bonds	6.00	2.70
☐ 4 Tony Clark	4.00	1.80
☐ 5 Roger Clemens	10.00	4.50
☐ 6 Jose Cruz Jr.	15.00	6.75
☐ 7 Andres Galarraga	4.00	1.80
☐ 8 Nomar Garciaparra	12.00	5.50
☐ 9 Juan Gonzalez	12.00	5.50
☐ 10 Ken Griffey Jr.	25.00	11.00
☐ 11 Randy Johnson	5.00	2.20
☐ 12 Greg Maddux	15.00	6.75
☐ 13 Pedro Martinez	4.00	1.80

☐ 14 Tino Martinez	4.00	1.80
☐ 15 Mark McGwire	12.00	5.50
☐ 16 Mike Piazza	15.00	6.75
☐ 17 Curt Schilling	2.50	1.10
☐ 18 Frank Thomas	20.00	9.00
☐ 19 Jim Thome	5.00	2.20
☐ 20 Larry Walker	5.00	2.20

1998 Fleer Rookie Sensations

Randomly inserted in packs at the rate of one in 18, this 20-card set features gray-bordered action color images of the 1997 most promising players who were eligible for Rookie of the Year honors on multi-colored backgrounds.

	MINT	NRMT
COMPLETE SET (20)	60.00	27.00
COMMON CARD (1-20)	1.00	.45
STATED ODDS 1:18		
☐ 1 Mike Cameron	2.00	.90
☐ 2 Jose Cruz Jr.	12.00	5.50
☐ 3 Jason Dickson	1.00	.45
☐ 4 Kelvim Escobar	1.00	.45
☐ 5 Nomar Garciaparra	10.00	4.50
☐ 6 Ben Grieve	6.00	2.70
☐ 7 Vladimir Guerrero	5.00	2.20
☐ 8 Wilton Guerrero	1.00	.45
☐ 9 Jose Guillen	3.00	1.35
☐ 10 Todd Helton	4.00	1.80
☐ 11 Livan Hernandez	2.50	1.10
☐ 12 Hideki Irabu	2.00	.90
☐ 13 Andruw Jones	6.00	2.70
☐ 14 Matt Morris	1.50	.70
☐ 15 Magglio Ordonez	2.00	.90
☐ 16 Neifi Perez	1.50	.70
☐ 17 Scott Rolen	8.00	3.60
☐ 18 Fernando Tatis	3.00	1.35
☐ 19 Brett Tomko	1.00	.45
☐ 20 Jaret Wright	8.00	3.60

1998 Fleer Zone

Randomly inserted in packs at the rate of one in 288, this 15-card set features color photos of unstoppable players printed on cards with custom pattern rainbow foil and etching.

	MINT	NRMT
COMPLETE SET (15)	600.00	275.00
COMMON CARD (1-15)	20.00	9.00
STATED ODDS 1:288		
☐ 1 Jeff Bagwell	40.00	18.00
☐ 2 Barry Bonds	25.00	11.00
☐ 3 Roger Clemens	40.00	18.00

☐ 4 Jose Cruz Jr.	60.00	27.00
☐ 5 Nomar Garciaparra	50.00	22.00
☐ 6 Juan Gonzalez	50.00	22.00
☐ 7 Ken Griffey Jr.	100.00	45.00
☐ 8 Tony Gwynn	50.00	22.00
☐ 9 Chipper Jones	60.00	27.00
☐ 10 Greg Maddux	60.00	27.00
☐ 11 Mark McGwire	50.00	22.00
☐ 12 Mike Piazza	60.00	27.00
☐ 13 Alex Rodriguez	60.00	27.00
☐ 14 Frank Thomas	80.00	36.00
☐ 15 Larry Walker	20.00	9.00

1949 Leaf

The cards in this 98-card set measure 2 3/8" by 2 7/8". The 1949 Leaf set was the first postwar baseball series issued in color. In hobby circles, it has been speculated that the set was issued in the spring of 1949. This effort was not entirely successful due to a lack of refinement which resulted in many color variations and cards out of register. In addition, the set was skip numbered from 1-168, with 49 of the 98 cards printed in limited quantities (marked with SP in the checklist). Cards 102 and 136 have variations, and cards are sometimes found with overprinted, incorrect or blank backs. The notable Rookie Cards in this set include Stan Musial, Satchel Paige, and Jackie Robinson.

	NRMT	VG-E
COMPLETE SET (98)	25000.00	11200.00
COMMON CARD (1-168)	25.00	11.00
MINOR STARS	40.00	18.00
SEMISTARS	60.00	27.00
UNLISTED STARS	100.00	45.00
COMMON SP's	275.00	125.00
MINOR STAR SP's	375.00	170.00
*UNLISTED DODGER/YANKEE: 1.25X VALUE		
SET IS SKIP NUMBERED		
CARDS PRICED IN NM CONDITION !		
☐ 1 Joe DiMaggio	2100.00	850.00
☐ 3 Babe Ruth	2500.00	1100.00
☐ 4 Stan Musial	850.00	375.00
☐ 5 Virgil Trucks SP	350.00	160.00
☐ 8 Satchel Paige SP	2300.00	1050.00
☐ 10 Dizzy Trout	35.00	16.00
☐ 11 Phil Rizzuto	250.00	110.00
☐ 13 Cass Michaels SP	275.00	125.00
☐ 14 Billy Johnson	40.00	18.00
☐ 17 Frank Overmire	25.00	11.00
☐ 19 Johnny Wyrostek SP	275.00	125.00
☐ 20 Hank Sauer SP	350.00	160.00
☐ 22 Al Evans	25.00	11.00
☐ 26 Sam Chapman	35.00	16.00
☐ 27 Mickey Harris	25.00	11.00

	MINT	NRMT
28 Jim Hegan	35.00	16.00
29 Elmer Valo	35.00	16.00
30 Billy Goodman SP	300.00	135.00
31 Lou Brissie	25.00	11.00
32 Warren Spahn	275.00	125.00
33 Peanuts Lowrey SP	275.00	125.00
36 Al Zarilla SP	275.00	125.00
38 Ted Kluszewski	150.00	70.00
39 Ewell Blackwell	55.00	25.00
42 Kent Peterson	25.00	11.00
43 Ed Stevens SP	275.00	125.00
45 Ken Keltner SP	275.00	125.00
46 Johnny Mize	100.00	45.00
47 George Vico	25.00	11.00
48 Johnny Schmitz SP	275.00	125.00
49 Del Ennis	55.00	25.00
50 Dick Wakefield	25.00	11.00
51 Al Dark SP	450.00	200.00
53 Johnny VanderMeer	100.00	45.00
54 Bobby Adams SP	275.00	125.00
55 Tommy Henrich SP	450.00	200.00
56 Larry Jansen UER	35.00	16.00
(Misspelled Jensen)		
57 Bob McCall	25.00	11.00
59 Luke Appling	100.00	45.00
61 Jake Early	25.00	11.00
62 Eddie Joost SP	275.00	125.00
63 Barney McCosky SP	275.00	125.00
65 Robert Elliott UER	100.00	45.00
(Misspelled Elliot on card front)		
66 Orval Grove SP	275.00	125.00
68 Eddie Miller SP	275.00	125.00
70 Honus Wagner CO	275.00	125.00
72 Hank Edwards	25.00	11.00
73 Pat Seerey	25.00	11.00
75 Dom DiMaggio SP	550.00	250.00
76 Ted Williams	850.00	375.00
77 Roy Smalley	25.00	11.00
78 Hoot Evers SP	275.00	125.00
79 Jackie Robinson	1000.00	450.00
81 Whitey Kurowski SP	275.00	125.00
82 Johnny Lindell	35.00	16.00
83 Bobby Doerr	100.00	45.00
84 Sid Hudson	25.00	11.00
85 Dave Philley SP	300.00	135.00
86 Ralph Weigel	25.00	11.00
88 Frank Gustine SP	275.00	125.00
91 Ralph Kiner	200.00	90.00
93 Bob Feller SP	1300.00	575.00
95 George Stirnweiss	35.00	16.00
97 Marty Marion	55.00	25.00
98 Hal Newhouser SP	550.00	250.00
102A Gene Hermanski ERR	250.00	110.00
102B Gene Hermanski COR	40.00	18.00
104 Eddie Stewart SP	275.00	125.00
106 Lou Boudreau	100.00	45.00
108 Matt Batts SP	275.00	125.00
111 Jerry Priddy	25.00	11.00
113 Dutch Leonard SP	275.00	125.00
117 Joe Gordon	35.00	16.00
120 George Kell SP	550.00	250.00
121 Johnny Pesky SP	350.00	160.00
123 Cliff Fannin SP	275.00	125.00
125 Andy Pafko	25.00	11.00
127 Enos Slaughter SP	650.00	300.00
128 Buddy Rosar	25.00	11.00
129 Kirby Higbe SP	375.00	170.00
131 Sid Gordon SP	375.00	170.00
133 Tommy Holmes SP	450.00	200.00
136A Cliff Aberson	25.00	11.00
(Full sleeve)		
136B Cliff Aberson	250.00	110.00
(Short sleeve)		
137 Harry Walker SP	275.00	125.00
138 Larry Doby SP	550.00	250.00
139 Johnny Hopp	25.00	11.00
142 Danny Murtaugh SP	350.00	160.00
143 Dick Sisler SP	275.00	125.00
144 Bob Dillinger SP	375.00	170.00
146 Pete Reiser SP	450.00	200.00
149 Hank Majeski SP	275.00	125.00
153 Floyd Baker SP	275.00	125.00
158 Harry Brecheen SP	350.00	160.00
159 Mizell Platt	25.00	11.00
160 Bob Scheffing SP	275.00	125.00
161 Vern Stephens SP	350.00	160.00
163 Fred Hutchinson SP	350.00	160.00
165 Dale Mitchell SP	350.00	160.00
168 Phil Cavaretta UER	450.00	180.00
Name spelled Cavaretta		

1990 Leaf

GREG OLSON

The 1990 Leaf set was the first premium set introduced by Donruss. The cards were issued in 15-card foil wrapped packs and were not available in factory sets. Each pack also contained one three-piece puzzle panel of a 63-piece Yogi Berra "Donruss Hall of Fame Diamond King" puzzle. This set, which was produced on high quality paper stock, was issued in two separate series of 264 standard-size cards each. The second series was issued approximately six weeks after the release of the first series. The cards feature full-color photos on the front and back. Rookie Cards in the set include Carlos Baerga, Bernard Gilkey, Marquis Grissom, David Justice, Ben McDonald, Sammy Sosa, Frank Thomas and Larry Walker.

	MINT	NRMT
COMPLETE SET (528)	200.00	90.00
COMPLETE SERIES 1 (264)	80.00	36.00
COMPLETE SERIES 2 (264)	120.00	55.00
COMMON CARD (1-528)	.25	.11
MINOR STARS		.23
SEMISTARS	1.00	.45
UNLISTED STARS	1.50	.70
BEWARE THOMAS COUNTERFEIT		

1 Introductory Card	.25	.11
2 Mike Henneman	.25	.11
3 Steve Bedrosian	.25	.11
4 Mike Scott	.25	.11
5 Allan Anderson	.25	.11
6 Rick Sutcliffe	.25	.11
7 Gregg Olson	.25	.11
8 Kevin Elster	.25	.11
9 Pete O'Brien	.25	.11
10 Carlton Fisk	1.50	.70
11 Joe Magrane	.25	.11
12 Roger Clemens	3.00	1.35
13 Tom Glavine	2.00	.90
14 Tom Gordon	.50	.23
15 Todd Benzinger	.25	.11
16 Hubie Brooks	.25	.11
17 Roberto Kelly	.25	.11
18 Barry Larkin	1.50	.70
19 Mike Boddicker	.25	.11
20 Roger McDowell	.25	.11
21 Nolan Ryan	6.00	2.70
22 John Farrell	.25	.11
23 Bruce Hurst	.25	.11
24 Wally Joyner	.50	.23
25 Greg Maddux	15.00	6.75
26 Chris Bosio	.25	.11
27 John Cerutti	.25	.11
28 Tim Burke	.25	.11
29 Dennis Eckersley	.50	.23
30 Glenn Davis	.25	.11
31 Jim Abbott	.50	.23
32 Mike LaValliere	.25	.11
33 Andres Thomas	.25	.11
34 Lou Whitaker	.50	.23
35 Alvin Davis	.25	.11
36 Melido Perez	.25	.11
37 Craig Biggio	1.50	.70
38 Rick Aguilera	.50	.23
39 Pete Harnisch	.25	.11
40 David Cone	1.50	.70
41 Scott Garrelts	.25	.11
42 Jay Howell	.25	.11
43 Eric King	.25	.11
44 Pedro Guerrero	.25	.11
45 Mike Bielecki	.25	.11
46 Bob Boone	.50	.23
47 Kevin Brown	1.50	.70
48 Jerry Browne	.25	.11
49 Mike Scioscia	.25	.11
50 Chuck Cary	.25	.11
51 Wade Boggs	1.50	.70
52 Von Hayes	.25	.11
53 Tony Fernandez	.25	.11
54 Dennis Martinez	.50	.23
55 Tom Candiotti	.25	.11
56 Andy Benes	1.50	.70
57 Rob Dibble	.25	.11
58 Chuck Crim	.25	.11
59 John Smoltz	2.50	1.10
60 Mike Heath	.25	.11
61 Kevin Gross	.25	.11
62 Mark McGwire	3.00	1.35
63 Bert Blyleven	.50	.23
64 Bob Walk	.25	.11
65 Mickey Tettleton	.50	.23
66 Sid Fernandez	.25	.11
67 Terry Kennedy	.25	.11
68 Fernando Valenzuela	.50	.23
69 Don Mattingly	2.50	1.10
70 Paul O'Neill	.50	.23
71 Robin Yount	1.50	.70
72 Bret Saberhagen	.50	.23
73 Geno Petralli	.25	.11
74 Brook Jacoby	.25	.11
75 Roberto Alomar	2.00	.90
76 Devon White	.25	.11
77 Jose Lind	.25	.11
78 Pat Combs	.25	.11
79 Dave Steib	.25	.11
80 Tim Wallach	.25	.11
81 Dave Stewart	.50	.23
82 Eric Anthony	.50	.23
83 Randy Bush	.25	.11
84 Rickey Henderson CL	.50	.23
85 Jaime Navarro	.25	.11
86 Tommy Gregg	.25	.11
87 Frank Tanana	.25	.11
88 Omar Vizquel	2.00	.90
89 Ivan Calderon	.25	.11
90 Vince Coleman	.25	.11
91 Barry Bonds	2.00	.90
92 Randy Milligan	.25	.11
93 Frank Viola	.25	.11
94 Matt Williams	2.00	.90
95 Alfredo Griffin	.25	.11
96 Steve Sax	.25	.11
97 Gary Gaetti	.25	.11
98 Ryne Sandberg	2.00	.90
99 Danny Tartabull	.25	.11
100 Rafael Palmeiro	1.50	.70
101 Jesse Orosco	.25	.11
102 Garry Templeton	.25	.11
103 Frank DiPino	.25	.11
104 Tony Pena	.25	.11
105 Dickie Thon	.25	.11
106 Kelly Gruber	.25	.11
107 Marquis Grissom	4.00	1.80
108 Jose Canseco	1.50	.70
109 Mike Blowers	1.50	.70
110 Tom Browning	.25	.11

☐ 111	Greg Vaughn	.50	.23
☐ 112	Oddibe McDowell	.25	.11
☐ 113	Gary Ward	.25	.11
☐ 114	Jay Buhner	1.50	.70
☐ 115	Eric Show	.25	.11
☐ 116	Bryan Harvey	.25	.11
☐ 117	Andy Van Slyke	.50	.23
☐ 118	Jeff Ballard	.25	.11
☐ 119	Barry Lyons	.25	.11
☐ 120	Kevin Mitchell	.50	.23
☐ 121	Mike Gallego	.25	.11
☐ 122	Dave Smith	.25	.11
☐ 123	Kirby Puckett	3.00	1.35
☐ 124	Jerome Walton	.25	.11
☐ 125	Bo Jackson	1.50	.70
☐ 126	Harold Baines	.50	.23
☐ 127	Scott Bankhead	.25	.11
☐ 128	Ozzie Guillen	.25	.11
☐ 129	Jose Oquendo UER (League misspelled as Legue)	.25	.11
☐ 130	John Dopson	.25	.11
☐ 131	Charlie Hayes	.25	.11
☐ 132	Fred McGriff	1.50	.70
☐ 133	Chet Lemon	.25	.11
☐ 134	Gary Carter	1.50	.70
☐ 135	Rafael Ramirez	.25	.11
☐ 136	Shane Mack	.25	.11
☐ 137	Mark Grace UER (Card back has OB:L, should be B:L)	1.50	.70
☐ 138	Phil Bradley	.25	.11
☐ 139	Dwight Gooden	.50	.23
☐ 140	Harold Reynolds	.25	.11
☐ 141	Scott Fletcher	.25	.11
☐ 142	Ozzie Smith	2.00	.90
☐ 143	Mike Greenwell	.25	.11
☐ 144	Pete Smith	.25	.11
☐ 145	Mark Gubicza	.25	.11
☐ 146	Chris Sabo	.25	.11
☐ 147	Ramon Martinez	1.00	.45
☐ 148	Tim Leary	.25	.11
☐ 149	Randy Myers	.50	.23
☐ 150	Jody Reed	.25	.11
☐ 151	Bruce Ruffin	.25	.11
☐ 152	Jeff Russell	.25	.11
☐ 153	Doug Jones	.25	.11
☐ 154	Tony Gwynn	4.00	1.80
☐ 155	Mark Langston	.25	.11
☐ 156	Mitch Williams	.25	.11
☐ 157	Gary Sheffield	4.00	1.80
☐ 158	Tom Henke	.25	.11
☐ 159	Oil Can Boyd	.25	.11
☐ 160	Rickey Henderson	1.50	.70
☐ 161	Bill Doran	.25	.11
☐ 162	Chuck Finley	.50	.23
☐ 163	Jeff King	.50	.23
☐ 164	Nick Esasky	.25	.11
☐ 165	Cecil Fielder	1.00	.45
☐ 166	Dave Valle	.25	.11
☐ 167	Robin Ventura	2.00	.90
☐ 168	Jim Deshaies	.25	.11
☐ 169	Juan Berenguer	.25	.11
☐ 170	Craig Worthington	.25	.11
☐ 171	Gregg Jefferies	.50	.23
☐ 172	Will Clark	1.50	.70
☐ 173	Kirk Gibson	.50	.23
☐ 174	Carlton Fisk CL	1.00	.45
☐ 175	Bobby Thigpen	.25	.11
☐ 176	John Tudor	.25	.11
☐ 177	Andre Dawson	1.50	.70
☐ 178	George Brett	3.00	1.35
☐ 179	Steve Buechele	.25	.11
☐ 180	Joey Belle	10.00	4.50
☐ 181	Eddie Murray	1.50	.70
☐ 182	Bob Geren	.25	.11
☐ 183	Rob Murphy	.25	.11
☐ 184	Tom Herr	.25	.11
☐ 185	George Bell	.50	.23
☐ 186	Spike Owen	.25	.11
☐ 187	Cory Snyder	.25	.11
☐ 188	Fred Lynn	.25	.11
☐ 189	Eric Davis	.50	.23
☐ 190	Dave Parker	.50	.23
☐ 191	Jeff Blauser	.50	.23
☐ 192	Matt Nokes	.25	.11
☐ 193	Delino DeShields	1.50	.70
☐ 194	Scott Sanderson	.25	.11
☐ 195	Lance Parrish	.25	.11
☐ 196	Bobby Bonilla	.50	.23
☐ 197	Cal Ripken UER (Reisterstown, should be Reisterstown)	6.00	2.70
☐ 198	Kevin McReynolds	.25	.11
☐ 199	Robby Thompson	.25	.11
☐ 200	Tim Belcher	.25	.11
☐ 201	Jesse Barfield	.25	.11
☐ 202	Mariano Duncan	.25	.11
☐ 203	Bill Spiers	.25	.11
☐ 204	Frank White	.50	.23
☐ 205	Julio Franco	.25	.11
☐ 206	Greg Swindell	.25	.11
☐ 207	Benito Santiago	.25	.11
☐ 208	Johnny Ray	.25	.11
☐ 209	Gary Redus	.25	.11
☐ 210	Jeff Parrett	.25	.11
☐ 211	Jimmy Key	.50	.23
☐ 212	Tim Raines	.50	.23
☐ 213	Carney Lansford	.50	.23
☐ 214	Gerald Young	.25	.11
☐ 215	Gene Larkin	.25	.11
☐ 216	Dan Plesac	.25	.11
☐ 217	Lonnie Smith	.25	.11
☐ 218	Alan Trammell	1.00	.45
☐ 219	Jeffrey Leonard	.25	.11
☐ 220	Sammy Sosa	8.00	3.60
☐ 221	Todd Zeile	.50	.23
☐ 222	Bill Landrum	.25	.11
☐ 223	Mike Devereaux	.25	.11
☐ 224	Mike Marshall	.25	.11
☐ 225	Jose Uribe	.25	.11
☐ 226	Juan Samuel	.25	.11
☐ 227	Mel Hall	.25	.11
☐ 228	Kent Hrbek	.50	.23
☐ 229	Shawon Dunston	.25	.11
☐ 230	Kevin Seitzer	.25	.11
☐ 231	Pete Incaviglia	.25	.11
☐ 232	Sandy Alomar Jr.	2.00	.90
☐ 233	Bip Roberts	.25	.11
☐ 234	Scott Terry	.25	.11
☐ 235	Dwight Evans	.50	.23
☐ 236	Ricky Jordan	.25	.11
☐ 237	John Olerud	2.00	.90
☐ 238	Zane Smith	.25	.11
☐ 239	Walt Weiss	.25	.11
☐ 240	Alvaro Espinoza	.25	.11
☐ 241	Billy Hatcher	.25	.11
☐ 242	Paul Molitor	1.50	.70
☐ 243	Dale Murphy	1.50	.70
☐ 244	Dave Bergman	.25	.11
☐ 245	Ken Griffey Jr.	25.00	11.00
☐ 246	Ed Whitson	.25	.11
☐ 247	Kirk McCaskill	.25	.11
☐ 248	Jay Bell	.50	.23
☐ 249	Ben McDonald	1.00	.45
☐ 250	Darryl Strawberry	.50	.23
☐ 251	Brett Butler	.50	.23
☐ 252	Terry Steinbach	.50	.23
☐ 253	Ken Caminiti	2.50	1.10
☐ 254	Dan Gladden	.25	.11
☐ 255	Dwight Smith	.25	.11
☐ 256	Kurt Stillwell	.25	.11
☐ 257	Ruben Sierra	.50	.23
☐ 258	Mike Schooler	.25	.11
☐ 259	Lance Johnson	.25	.11
☐ 260	Terry Pendleton	.50	.23
☐ 261	Ellis Burks	1.00	.45
☐ 262	Len Dykstra	.50	.23
☐ 263	Mookie Wilson	.25	.11
☐ 264	Nolan Ryan CL UER (No TM after Ranger logo)	1.50	.70
☐ 265	Nolan Ryan (No Hit King)	3.00	1.35
☐ 266	Brian DuBois	.25	.11
☐ 267	Don Robinson	.25	.11
☐ 268	Glenn Wilson	.25	.11
☐ 269	Kevin Tapani	.50	.23
☐ 270	Marvell Wynne	.25	.11
☐ 271	Billy Ripken	.25	.11
☐ 272	Howard Johnson	.25	.11
☐ 273	Brian Holman	.25	.11
☐ 274	Dan Pasqua	.25	.11
☐ 275	Ken Dayley	.25	.11
☐ 276	Jeff Reardon	.50	.23
☐ 277	Jim Presley	.25	.11
☐ 278	Jim Eisenreich	.25	.11
☐ 279	Danny Jackson	.25	.11
☐ 280	Orel Hershiser	.50	.23
☐ 281	Andy Hawkins	.25	.11
☐ 282	Jose Rijo	.25	.11
☐ 283	Luis Rivera	.25	.11
☐ 284	John Kruk	.50	.23
☐ 285	Jeff Huson	.25	.11
☐ 286	Joel Skinner	.25	.11
☐ 287	Jack Clark	.50	.23
☐ 288	Chili Davis	.50	.23
☐ 289	Joe Girardi	.50	.23
☐ 290	B.J. Surhoff	.50	.23
☐ 291	Luis Sojo	.25	.11
☐ 292	Tom Foley	.25	.11
☐ 293	Mike Moore	.25	.11
☐ 294	Ken Oberkfell	.25	.11
☐ 295	Luis Polonia	.25	.11
☐ 296	Doug Drabek	.25	.11
☐ 297	Dave Justice	8.00	3.60
☐ 298	Paul Gibson	.25	.11
☐ 299	Edgar Martinez	2.00	.90
☐ 300	Frank Thomas UER (No B in front of birthdate)	85.00	38.00
☐ 301	Eric Yelding	.25	.11
☐ 302	Greg Gagne	.25	.11
☐ 303	Brad Komminsk	.25	.11
☐ 304	Ron Darling	.25	.11
☐ 305	Kevin Bass	.25	.11
☐ 306	Jeff Hamilton	.25	.11
☐ 307	Ron Karkovice	.25	.11
☐ 308	Milt Thompson UER (Ray Lankford pictured on card back)	1.50	.70
☐ 309	Mike Harkey	.25	.11
☐ 310	Mel Stottlemyre Jr.	.25	.11
☐ 311	Kenny Rogers	.25	.11
☐ 312	Mitch Webster	.25	.11
☐ 313	Kal Daniels	.25	.11
☐ 314	Matt Nokes	.25	.11
☐ 315	Dennis Lamp	.25	.11
☐ 316	Ken Howell	.25	.11
☐ 317	Glenallen Hill	.25	.11
☐ 318	Dave Martinez	.25	.11
☐ 319	Chris James	.25	.11
☐ 320	Mike Pagliarulo	.25	.11
☐ 321	Hal Morris	.25	.11
☐ 322	Rob Deer	.25	.11
☐ 323	Greg Olson	.25	.11
☐ 324	Tony Phillips	.25	.11
☐ 325	Larry Walker	12.00	5.50
☐ 326	Ron Hassey	.25	.11
☐ 327	Jack Howell	.25	.11
☐ 328	John Smiley	.25	.11
☐ 329	Steve Finley	1.50	.70
☐ 330	Dave Magadan	.25	.11
☐ 331	Greg Litton	.25	.11
☐ 332	Mickey Hatcher	.25	.11
☐ 333	Lee Guetterman	.25	.11
☐ 334	Norm Charlton	.25	.11
☐ 335	Edgar Diaz	.25	.11
☐ 336	Willie Wilson	.25	.11
☐ 337	Bobby Witt	.25	.11
☐ 338	Candy Maldonado	.25	.11
☐ 339	Craig Lefferts	.25	.11
☐ 340	Dante Bichette	2.00	.90
☐ 341	Wally Backman	.25	.11
☐ 342	Dennis Cook	.25	.11
☐ 343	Pat Borders	.25	.11
☐ 344	Wallace Johnson	.25	.11
☐ 345	Willie Randolph	.50	.23
☐ 346	Danny Darwin	.25	.11
☐ 347	Al Newman	.25	.11
☐ 348	Mark Knudson	.25	.11
☐ 349	Joe Boever	.25	.11
☐ 350	Larry Sheets	.25	.11
☐ 351	Mike Jackson	.25	.11
☐ 352	Wayne Edwards	.25	.11
☐ 353	Bernard Gilkey	2.50	1.10
☐ 354	Don Slaught	.25	.11
☐ 355	Joe Orsulak	.25	.11
☐ 356	John Franco	.50	.23

☐ 357 Jeff Brantley	.25	.11
☐ 358 Mike Morgan	.25	.11
☐ 359 Deion Sanders	3.00	1.35
☐ 360 Terry Leach	.25	.11
☐ 361 Les Lancaster	.25	.11
☐ 362 Storm Davis	.25	.11
☐ 363 Scott Coolbaugh	.25	.11
☐ 364 Ozzie Smith CL	1.00	.45
☐ 365 Cecilio Guante	.25	.11
☐ 366 Joey Cora	1.50	.70
☐ 367 Willie McGee	.50	.23
☐ 368 Jerry Reed	.25	.11
☐ 369 Darren Daulton	.50	.23
☐ 370 Manny Lee	.25	.11
☐ 371 Mark Gardner	.25	.11
☐ 372 Rick Honeycutt	.25	.11
☐ 373 Steve Balboni	.25	.11
☐ 374 Jack Armstrong	.25	.11
☐ 375 Charlie O'Brien	.25	.11
☐ 376 Ron Gant	1.00	.45
☐ 377 Lloyd Moseby	.25	.11
☐ 378 Gene Harris	.25	.11
☐ 379 Joe Carter	.50	.23
☐ 380 Scott Bailes	.25	.11
☐ 381 R.J. Reynolds	.25	.11
☐ 382 Bob Melvin	.25	.11
☐ 383 Tim Teufel	.25	.11
☐ 384 John Burkett	.50	.23
☐ 385 Felix Jose	.25	.11
☐ 386 Larry Andersen	.25	.11
☐ 387 David West	.25	.11
☐ 388 Luis Salazar	.25	.11
☐ 389 Mike Macfarlane	.25	.11
☐ 390 Charlie Hough	.25	.11
☐ 391 Greg Briley	.25	.11
☐ 392 Donn Pall	.25	.11
☐ 393 Bryn Smith	.25	.11
☐ 394 Carlos Quintana	.25	.11
☐ 395 Steve Lake	.25	.11
☐ 396 Mark Whiten	.50	.23
☐ 397 Edwin Nunez	.25	.11
☐ 398 Rick Parker	.25	.11
☐ 399 Mark Portugal	.25	.11
☐ 400 Roy Smith	.25	.11
☐ 401 Hector Villanueva	.25	.11
☐ 402 Bob Milacki	.25	.11
☐ 403 Alejandro Pena	.25	.11
☐ 404 Scott Bradley	.25	.11
☐ 405 Ron Kittle	.25	.11
☐ 406 Bob Tewksbury	.25	.11
☐ 407 Wes Gardner	.25	.11
☐ 408 Ernie Whitt	.25	.11
☐ 409 Terry Shumpert	.25	.11
☐ 410 Tim Layana	.25	.11
☐ 411 Chris Gwynn	.25	.11
☐ 412 Jeff D. Robinson	.25	.11
☐ 413 Scott Scudder	.25	.11
☐ 414 Kevin Romine	.25	.11
☐ 415 Jose DeJesus	.25	.11
☐ 416 Mike Jeffcoat	.25	.11
☐ 417 Rudy Seanez	.25	.11
☐ 418 Mike Dunne	.25	.11
☐ 419 Dick Schofield	.25	.11
☐ 420 Steve Wilson	.25	.11
☐ 421 Bill Krueger	.25	.11
☐ 422 Junior Felix	.25	.11
☐ 423 Drew Hall	.25	.11
☐ 424 Curt Young	.25	.11
☐ 425 Franklin Stubbs	.25	.11
☐ 426 Dave Winfield	1.50	.70
☐ 427 Rick Reed	.25	.11
☐ 428 Charlie Leibrandt	.25	.11
☐ 429 Jeff M. Robinson	.25	.11
☐ 430 Erik Hanson	.25	.11
☐ 431 Barry Jones	.25	.11
☐ 432 Alex Trevino	.25	.11
☐ 433 John Moses	.25	.11
☐ 434 Dave Johnson	.25	.11
☐ 435 Mackey Sasser	.25	.11
☐ 436 Rick Leach	.25	.11
☐ 437 Lenny Harris	.25	.11
☐ 438 Carlos Martinez	.25	.11
☐ 439 Rex Hudler	.25	.11
☐ 440 Domingo Ramos	.25	.11
☐ 441 Gerald Perry	.25	.11
☐ 442 Jeff Russell	.25	.11

☐ 443 Carlos Baerga	2.50	1.10
☐ 444 Will Clark CL	1.00	.45
☐ 445 Stan Javier	.25	.11
☐ 446 Kevin Maas	.50	.23
☐ 447 Tom Brunansky	.25	.11
☐ 448 Carmelo Martinez	.25	.11
☐ 449 Willie Blair	1.50	.70
☐ 450 Andres Galarraga	1.50	.70
☐ 451 Bud Black	.25	.11
☐ 452 Greg W. Harris	.25	.11
☐ 453 Joe Oliver	.25	.11
☐ 454 Greg Brock	.25	.11
☐ 455 Jeff Treadway	.25	.11
☐ 456 Lance McCullers	.25	.11
☐ 457 Dave Schmidt	.25	.11
☐ 458 Todd Burns	.25	.11
☐ 459 Max Venable	.25	.11
☐ 460 Neal Heaton	.25	.11
☐ 461 Mark Williamson	.25	.11
☐ 462 Keith Miller	.25	.11
☐ 463 Mike LaCoss	.25	.11
☐ 464 Jose Offerman	1.50	.70
☐ 465 Jim Leyritz	1.50	.70
☐ 466 Glenn Braggs	.25	.11
☐ 467 Ron Robinson	.25	.11
☐ 468 Mark Davis	.25	.11
☐ 469 Gary Pettis	.25	.11
☐ 470 Keith Hernandez	.50	.23
☐ 471 Dennis Rasmussen	.25	.11
☐ 472 Mark Eichhorn	.25	.11
☐ 473 Ted Power	.25	.11
☐ 474 Terry Mulholland	.25	.11
☐ 475 Todd Stottlemyre	.50	.23
☐ 476 Jerry Goff	.25	.11
☐ 477 Gene Nelson	.25	.11
☐ 478 Rich Gedman	.25	.11
☐ 479 Brian Harper	.25	.11
☐ 480 Mike Felder	.25	.11
☐ 481 Steve Avery	.50	.23
☐ 482 Jack Morris	.50	.23
☐ 483 Randy Johnson	5.00	2.20
☐ 484 Scott Radinsky	.25	.11
☐ 485 Jose DeLeon	.25	.11
☐ 486 Stan Belinda	.25	.11
☐ 487 Brian Holton	.25	.11
☐ 488 Mark Carreon	.25	.11
☐ 489 Trevor Wilson	.25	.11
☐ 490 Mike Sharperson	.25	.11
☐ 491 Alan Mills	.25	.11
☐ 492 John Candelaria	.25	.11
☐ 493 Paul Assenmacher	.25	.11
☐ 494 Steve Crawford	.25	.11
☐ 495 Brad Arnsberg	.25	.11
☐ 496 Sergio Valdez	.25	.11
☐ 497 Mark Parent	.25	.11
☐ 498 Tom Pagnozzi	.25	.11
☐ 499 Greg A. Harris	.25	.11
☐ 500 Randy Ready	.25	.11
☐ 501 Duane Ward	.25	.11
☐ 502 Nelson Santovenia	.25	.11
☐ 503 Joe Klink	.25	.11
☐ 504 Eric Plunk	.25	.11
☐ 505 Jeff Reed	.25	.11
☐ 506 Ted Higuera	.25	.11
☐ 507 Joe Hesketh	.25	.11
☐ 508 Dan Petry	.25	.11
☐ 509 Matt Young	.25	.11
☐ 510 Jerald Clark	.25	.11
☐ 511 John Orton	.25	.11
☐ 512 Scott Ruskin	.25	.11
☐ 513 Chris Hoiles	1.50	.70
☐ 514 Daryl Boston	.25	.11
☐ 515 Francisco Oliveras	.25	.11
☐ 516 Ozzie Canseco	.25	.11
☐ 517 Xavier Hernandez	.25	.11
☐ 518 Fred Manrique	.25	.11
☐ 519 Shawn Boskie	.25	.11
☐ 520 Jeff Montgomery	.50	.23
☐ 521 Jack Daugherty	.25	.11
☐ 522 Keith Comstock	.25	.11
☐ 523 Greg Hibbard	.25	.11
☐ 524 Lee Smith	.50	.23
☐ 525 Dana Kiecker	.25	.11
☐ 526 Darrel Akerfelds	.25	.11
☐ 527 Greg Myers	.25	.11
☐ 528 Ryne Sandberg CL	1.50	.70

1991 Leaf Previews

The 1991 Leaf Previews set consists of 26 standard-size cards. Cards from this set were issued as inserts (four at a time) inside specially marked 1991 Donruss hobby factory sets. The front design has color action player photos, with white and silver borders.

	MINT	NRMT
COMPLETE SET (26)	35.00	16.00
COMMON CARD (1-26)	1.00	.45
FOUR PER DONRUSS HOBBY FACT.SET		

		MINT	NRMT
☐ 1 Dave Justice		3.00	1.35
☐ 2 Ryne Sandberg		4.00	1.80
☐ 3 Barry Larkin		2.50	1.10
☐ 4 Craig Biggio		3.00	1.35
☐ 5 Ramon Martinez		1.50	.70
☐ 6 Tim Wallach		1.00	.45
☐ 7 Dwight Gooden		1.50	.70
☐ 8 Len Dykstra		1.50	.70
☐ 9 Barry Bonds		4.00	1.80
☐ 10 Ray Lankford		3.00	1.35
☐ 11 Tony Gwynn		8.00	3.60
☐ 12 Will Clark		3.00	1.35
☐ 13 Leo Gomez		1.00	.45
☐ 14 Wade Boggs		3.00	1.35
☐ 15 Chuck Finley UER		1.00	.45
(Position on card back is First Base)			
☐ 16 Carlton Fisk		3.00	1.35
☐ 17 Sandy Alomar Jr.		2.50	1.10
☐ 18 Cecil Fielder		1.50	.70
☐ 19 Bo Jackson		2.50	1.10
☐ 20 Paul Molitor		3.00	1.35
☐ 21 Kirby Puckett		6.00	2.70
☐ 22 Don Mattingly		5.00	2.20
☐ 23 Rickey Henderson		3.00	1.35
☐ 24 Tino Martinez		3.00	1.35
☐ 25 Nolan Ryan		12.00	5.50
☐ 26 Dave Stieb		1.00	.45

1991 Leaf

This 528-card standard size set was issued by Donruss in two separate series of 264 cards. Cards were exclusively issued in foil packs. The front design has color action player photos, with white and silver borders. A thicker stock was used for these (then) premium level cards. Rookie Cards in the set include Brian McRae and Denny Neagle.

	MINT	NRMT
COMPLETE SET (528)	15.00	6.75
COMPLETE SERIES 1 (264)	5.00	2.20
COMPLETE SERIES 2 (264)	10.00	4.50

COMMON CARD (1-528)	.10	.05
MINOR STARS	.20	.09
UNLISTED STARS	.40	.18

☐ 1	The Leaf Card	.10	.05
☐ 2	Kurt Stillwell	.10	.05
☐ 3	Bobby Witt	.10	.05
☐ 4	Tony Phillips	.10	.05
☐ 5	Scott Garrelts	.10	.05
☐ 6	Greg Swindell	.10	.05
☐ 7	Billy Ripken	.10	.05
☐ 8	Dave Martinez	.10	.05
☐ 9	Kelly Gruber	.10	.05
☐ 10	Juan Samuel	.10	.05
☐ 11	Brian Holman	.10	.05
☐ 12	Craig Biggio	.40	.18
☐ 13	Lonnie Smith	.10	.05
☐ 14	Ron Robinson	.10	.05
☐ 15	Mike LaValliere	.10	.05
☐ 16	Mark Davis	.10	.05
☐ 17	Jack Daugherty	.10	.05
☐ 18	Mike Henneman	.10	.05
☐ 19	Mike Greenwell	.10	.05
☐ 20	Dave Magadan	.10	.05
☐ 21	Mark Williamson	.10	.05
☐ 22	Marquis Grissom	.40	.18
☐ 23	Pat Borders	.10	.05
☐ 24	Mike Scioscia	.10	.05
☐ 25	Shawon Dunston	.10	.05
☐ 26	Randy Bush	.10	.05
☐ 27	John Smoltz	.40	.18
☐ 28	Chuck Crim	.10	.05
☐ 29	Don Slaught	.10	.05
☐ 30	Mike Macfarlane	.10	.05
☐ 31	Wally Joyner	.30	.14
☐ 32	Pat Combs	.10	.05
☐ 33	Tony Pena	.10	.05
☐ 34	Howard Johnson	.10	.05
☐ 35	Leo Gomez	.10	.05
☐ 36	Spike Owen	.10	.05
☐ 37	Eric Davis	.30	.14
☐ 38	Roberto Kelly	.10	.05
☐ 39	Jerome Walton	.10	.05
☐ 40	Shane Mack	.10	.05
☐ 41	Kent Mercker	.10	.05
☐ 42	B.J. Surhoff	.30	.14
☐ 43	Jerry Browne	.10	.05
☐ 44	Lee Smith	.20	.09
☐ 45	Chuck Finley	.30	.14
☐ 46	Terry Mulholland	.10	.05
☐ 47	Tom Bolton	.10	.05
☐ 48	Tom Herr	.10	.05
☐ 49	Jim Deshaies	.10	.05
☐ 50	Walt Weiss	.10	.05
☐ 51	Hal Morris	.10	.05
☐ 52	Lee Guetterman	.10	.05
☐ 53	Paul Assenmacher	.10	.05
☐ 54	Brian Harper	.10	.05
☐ 55	Paul Gibson	.10	.05
☐ 56	John Burkett	.10	.05
☐ 57	Doug Jones	.10	.05
☐ 58	Jose Oquendo	.10	.05
☐ 59	Dick Schofield	.10	.05
☐ 60	Dickie Thon	.10	.05
☐ 61	Ramon Martinez	.30	.14
☐ 62	Jay Buhner	.40	.18
☐ 63	Mark Portugal	.10	.05
☐ 64	Bob Welch	.10	.05
☐ 65	Chris Sabo	.10	.05
☐ 66	Chuck Cary	.10	.05
☐ 67	Mark Langston	.10	.05
☐ 68	Joe Boever	.10	.05
☐ 69	Jody Reed	.10	.05
☐ 70	Alejandro Pena	.10	.05
☐ 71	Jeff King	.30	.14
☐ 72	Tom Pagnozzi	.10	.05
☐ 73	Joe Oliver	.10	.05
☐ 74	Mike Witt	.10	.05
☐ 75	Hector Villanueva	.10	.05
☐ 76	Dan Gladden	.10	.05
☐ 77	Dave Justice	.50	.23
☐ 78	Mike Gallego	.10	.05
☐ 79	Tom Candiotti	.10	.05
☐ 80	Ozzie Smith	.50	.23
☐ 81	Luis Polonia	.10	.05
☐ 82	Randy Ready	.10	.05
☐ 83	Greg A. Harris	.10	.05
☐ 84	David Justice CL	.20	.09
☐ 85	Kevin Mitchell	.30	.14
☐ 86	Mark McLemore	.10	.05
☐ 87	Terry Steinbach	.30	.14
☐ 88	Tom Browning	.10	.05
☐ 89	Matt Nokes	.10	.05
☐ 90	Mike Harkey	.10	.05
☐ 91	Omar Vizquel	.40	.18
☐ 92	Dave Bergman	.10	.05
☐ 93	Matt Williams	.40	.18
☐ 94	Steve Olin	.10	.05
☐ 95	Craig Wilson	.10	.05
☐ 96	Dave Stieb	.10	.05
☐ 97	Ruben Sierra	.30	.14
☐ 98	Jay Howell	.10	.05
☐ 99	Scott Bradley	.10	.05
☐ 100	Eric Yelding	.10	.05
☐ 101	Rickey Henderson	.40	.18
☐ 102	Jeff Reed	.10	.05
☐ 103	Jimmy Key	.30	.14
☐ 104	Terry Shumpert	.10	.05
☐ 105	Kenny Rogers	.10	.05
☐ 106	Cecil Fielder	.30	.14
☐ 107	Robby Thompson	.10	.05
☐ 108	Alex Cole	.10	.05
☐ 109	Randy Milligan	.10	.05
☐ 110	Andres Galarraga	.40	.18
☐ 111	Bill Spiers	.10	.05
☐ 112	Kal Daniels	.10	.05
☐ 113	Henry Cotto	.10	.05
☐ 114	Casey Candaele	.10	.05
☐ 115	Jeff Blauser	.10	.05
☐ 116	Robin Yount	.40	.18
☐ 117	Ben McDonald	.10	.05
☐ 118	Bret Saberhagen	.10	.05
☐ 119	Juan Gonzalez	1.50	.70
☐ 120	Lou Whitaker	.30	.14
☐ 121	Ellis Burks	.20	.09
☐ 122	Charlie O'Brien	.10	.05
☐ 123	John Smiley	.10	.05
☐ 124	Tim Burke	.10	.05
☐ 125	John Olerud	.30	.14
☐ 126	Eddie Murray	.40	.18
☐ 127	Greg Maddux	1.25	.55
☐ 128	Kevin Tapani	.10	.05
☐ 129	Ron Gant	.30	.14
☐ 130	Jay Bell	.30	.14
☐ 131	Chris Hoiles	.10	.05
☐ 132	Tom Gordon	.10	.05
☐ 133	Kevin Seitzer	.10	.05
☐ 134	Jeff Huson	.10	.05
☐ 135	Jerry Don Gleaton	.10	.05
☐ 136	Jeff Brantley UER	.10	.05
	(Photo actually Rick Leach on back)		
☐ 137	Felix Fermin	.10	.05
☐ 138	Mike Devereaux	.10	.05
☐ 139	Delino DeShields	.10	.05
☐ 140	David Wells	.10	.05
☐ 141	Tim Crews	.10	.05
☐ 142	Erik Hanson	.10	.05
☐ 143	Mark Davidson	.10	.05
☐ 144	Tommy Gregg	.10	.05
☐ 145	Jim Gantner	.10	.05
☐ 146	Jose Lind	.10	.05
☐ 147	Danny Tartabull	.10	.05
☐ 148	Geno Petralli	.10	.05
☐ 149	Travis Fryman	.40	.18
☐ 150	Tim Naehring	.30	.14
☐ 151	Kevin McReynolds	.10	.05
☐ 152	Joe Orsulak	.10	.05
☐ 153	Steve Frey	.10	.05
☐ 154	Duane Ward	.10	.05
☐ 155	Stan Javier	.10	.05
☐ 156	Damon Berryhill	.10	.05
☐ 157	Gene Larkin	.10	.05
☐ 158	Greg Olson	.10	.05
☐ 159	Mark Knudson	.10	.05
☐ 160	Carmelo Martinez	.10	.05
☐ 161	Storm Davis	.10	.05
☐ 162	Jim Abbott	.10	.05
☐ 163	Len Dykstra	.30	.14
☐ 164	Tom Brunansky	.10	.05
☐ 165	Dwight Gooden	.30	.14
☐ 166	Jose Mesa	.10	.05
☐ 167	Oil Can Boyd	.10	.05
☐ 168	Barry Larkin	.30	.14
☐ 169	Scott Sanderson	.10	.05
☐ 170	Mark Grace	.40	.18
☐ 171	Mark Guthrie	.10	.05
☐ 172	Tom Glavine	.40	.18
☐ 173	Gary Sheffield	.40	.18
☐ 174	Roger Clemens CL	.40	.18
☐ 175	Chris James	.10	.05
☐ 176	Milt Thompson	.10	.05
☐ 177	Donnie Hill	.10	.05
☐ 178	Wes Chamberlain	.10	.05
☐ 179	John Marzano	.10	.05
☐ 180	Frank Viola	.10	.05
☐ 181	Eric Anthony	.10	.05
☐ 182	Jose Canseco	.30	.14
☐ 183	Scott Scudder	.10	.05
☐ 184	Dave Eiland	.10	.05
☐ 185	Luis Salazar	.10	.05
☐ 186	Pedro Munoz	.10	.05
☐ 187	Steve Searcy	.10	.05
☐ 188	Don Robinson	.10	.05
☐ 189	Sandy Alomar Jr.	.30	.14
☐ 190	Jose DeLeon	.10	.05
☐ 191	John Orton	.10	.05
☐ 192	Darren Daulton	.30	.14
☐ 193	Mike Morgan	.10	.05
☐ 194	Greg Briley	.10	.05
☐ 195	Karl Rhodes	.10	.05
☐ 196	Harold Baines	.20	.09
☐ 197	Bill Doran	.10	.05
☐ 198	Alvaro Espinoza	.10	.05
☐ 199	Kirk McCaskill	.10	.05
☐ 200	Jose DeJesus	.10	.05
☐ 201	Jack Clark	.30	.14
☐ 202	Daryl Boston	.10	.05
☐ 203	Randy Tomlin	.10	.05
☐ 204	Pedro Guerrero	.10	.05
☐ 205	Billy Hatcher	.10	.05
☐ 206	Tim Leary	.10	.05
☐ 207	Ryne Sandberg	.50	.23
☐ 208	Kirby Puckett	.75	.35
☐ 209	Charlie Leibrandt	.10	.05
☐ 210	Rick Honeycutt	.10	.05
☐ 211	Joel Skinner	.10	.05
☐ 212	Rex Hudler	.10	.05
☐ 213	Bryan Harvey	.10	.05
☐ 214	Charlie Hayes	.10	.05
☐ 215	Matt Young	.10	.05
☐ 216	Terry Kennedy	.10	.05
☐ 217	Carl Nichols	.10	.05
☐ 218	Mike Moore	.10	.05
☐ 219	Paul O'Neill	.30	.14
☐ 220	Steve Sax	.10	.05
☐ 221	Shawn Boskie	.10	.05
☐ 222	Rich DeLucia	.10	.05
☐ 223	Lloyd Moseby	.10	.05
☐ 224	Mike Kingery	.10	.05
☐ 225	Carlos Baerga	.30	.14
☐ 226	Bryn Smith	.10	.05
☐ 227	Todd Stottlemyre	.10	.05
☐ 228	Julio Franco	.10	.05
☐ 229	Jim Gott	.10	.05
☐ 230	Mike Schooler	.10	.05
☐ 231	Steve Finley	.40	.18
☐ 232	Dave Henderson	.10	.05
☐ 233	Luis Quinones	.10	.05
☐ 234	Mark Whiten	.10	.05

☐ 235	Brian McRae	.40	.18
☐ 236	Rich Gossage	.30	.14
☐ 237	Rob Deer	.10	.05
☐ 238	Will Clark	.40	.18
☐ 239	Albert Belle	.60	.25
☐ 240	Bob Melvin	.10	.05
☐ 241	Larry Walker	.60	.25
☐ 242	Dante Bichette	.40	.18
☐ 243	Orel Hershiser	.30	.14
☐ 244	Pete O'Brien	.10	.05
☐ 245	Pete Harnisch	.10	.05
☐ 246	Jeff Treadway	.10	.05
☐ 247	Julio Machado	.10	.05
☐ 248	Dave Johnson	.10	.05
☐ 249	Kirk Gibson	.30	.14
☐ 250	Kevin Brown	.20	.09
☐ 251	Milt Cuyler	.10	.05
☐ 252	Jeff Reardon	.30	.14
☐ 253	David Cone	.30	.14
☐ 254	Gary Redus	.10	.05
☐ 255	Junior Noboa	.10	.05
☐ 256	Greg Myers	.10	.05
☐ 257	Dennis Cook	.10	.05
☐ 258	Joe Girardi	.30	.14
☐ 259	Allan Anderson	.10	.05
☐ 260	Paul Marak	.10	.05
☐ 261	Barry Bonds	.50	.23
☐ 262	Juan Bell	.10	.05
☐ 263	Russ Morman	.10	.05
☐ 264	George Brett CL	.40	.18
☐ 265	Jerald Clark	.10	.05
☐ 266	Dwight Evans	.30	.14
☐ 267	Roberto Alomar	.40	.18
☐ 268	Danny Jackson	.10	.05
☐ 269	Brian Downing	.10	.05
☐ 270	John Cerutti	.10	.05
☐ 271	Robin Ventura	.40	.18
☐ 272	Gerald Perry	.10	.05
☐ 273	Wade Boggs	.40	.18
☐ 274	Dennis Martinez	.30	.14
☐ 275	Andy Benes	.20	.09
☐ 276	Tony Fossas	.10	.05
☐ 277	Franklin Stubbs	.10	.05
☐ 278	John Kruk	.30	.14
☐ 279	Kevin Gross	.10	.05
☐ 280	Von Hayes	.10	.05
☐ 281	Frank Thomas	3.00	1.35
☐ 282	Rob Dibble	.10	.05
☐ 283	Mel Hall	.10	.05
☐ 284	Rick Mahler	.10	.05
☐ 285	Dennis Eckersley	.20	.09
☐ 286	Bernard Gilkey	.30	.14
☐ 287	Dan Plesac	.10	.05
☐ 288	Jason Grimsley	.10	.05
☐ 289	Mark Lewis	.10	.05
☐ 290	Tony Gwynn	1.00	.45
☐ 291	Jeff Russell	.10	.05
☐ 292	Curt Schilling	.40	.18
☐ 293	Pascual Perez	.10	.05
☐ 294	Jack Morris	.30	.14
☐ 295	Hubie Brooks	.10	.05
☐ 296	Alex Fernandez	.20	.09
☐ 297	Harold Reynolds	.10	.05
☐ 298	Craig Worthington	.10	.05
☐ 299	Willie Wilson	.10	.05
☐ 300	Mike Maddux	.10	.05
☐ 301	Dave Righetti	.10	.05
☐ 302	Paul Molitor	.40	.18
☐ 303	Gary Gaetti	.10	.05
☐ 304	Terry Pendleton	.30	.14
☐ 305	Kevin Elster	.10	.05
☐ 306	Scott Fletcher	.10	.05
☐ 307	Jeff Robinson	.10	.05
☐ 308	Jesse Barfield	.10	.05
☐ 309	Mike LaCoss	.10	.05
☐ 310	Andy Van Slyke	.30	.14
☐ 311	Glenallen Hill	.10	.05
☐ 312	Bud Black	.10	.05
☐ 313	Kent Hrbek	.10	.05
☐ 314	Tim Teufel	.10	.05
☐ 315	Tony Fernandez	.10	.05
☐ 316	Beau Allred	.10	.05
☐ 317	Curtis Wilkerson	.10	.05
☐ 318	Bill Sampen	.10	.05
☐ 319	Randy Johnson	.50	.23
☐ 320	Mike Heath	.10	.05
☐ 321	Sammy Sosa	.50	.23
☐ 322	Mickey Tettleton	.30	.14
☐ 323	Jose Vizcaino	.10	.05
☐ 324	John Candelaria	.10	.05
☐ 325	Dave Howard	.10	.05
☐ 326	Jose Rijo	.10	.05
☐ 327	Todd Zeile	.30	.14
☐ 328	Gene Nelson	.10	.05
☐ 329	Dwayne Henry	.10	.05
☐ 330	Mike Boddicker	.10	.05
☐ 331	Ozzie Guillen	.10	.05
☐ 332	Sam Horn	.10	.05
☐ 333	Wally Whitehurst	.10	.05
☐ 334	Dave Parker	.30	.14
☐ 335	George Brett	.75	.35
☐ 336	Bobby Thigpen	.10	.05
☐ 337	Ed Whitson	.10	.05
☐ 338	Ivan Calderon	.10	.05
☐ 339	Mike Pagliarulo	.10	.05
☐ 340	Jack McDowell	.30	.14
☐ 341	Dana Kiecker	.10	.05
☐ 342	Fred McGriff	.40	.18
☐ 343	Mark Lee	.10	.05
☐ 344	Alfredo Griffin	.10	.05
☐ 345	Scott Bankhead	.10	.05
☐ 346	Darrin Jackson	.10	.05
☐ 347	Rafael Palmeiro	.40	.18
☐ 348	Steve Farr	.10	.05
☐ 349	Hensley Meulens	.10	.05
☐ 350	Danny Cox	.10	.05
☐ 351	Alan Trammell	.20	.09
☐ 352	Edwin Nunez	.10	.05
☐ 353	Joe Carter	.20	.09
☐ 354	Eric Show	.10	.05
☐ 355	Vance Law	.10	.05
☐ 356	Jeff Gray	.10	.05
☐ 357	Bobby Bonilla	.20	.09
☐ 358	Ernest Riles	.10	.05
☐ 359	Ron Hassey	.10	.05
☐ 360	Willie McGee	.10	.05
☐ 361	Mackey Sasser	.10	.05
☐ 362	Glenn Braggs	.10	.05
☐ 363	Mario Diaz	.10	.05
☐ 364	Barry Bonds CL	.40	.18
☐ 365	Jarvis Bass	.10	.05
☐ 366	Pete Incaviglia	.10	.05
☐ 367	Luis Sojo UER	.10	.05
	(1989 stats interspersed with 1990's)		
☐ 368	Lance Parrish	.10	.05
☐ 369	Mark Leonard	.10	.05
☐ 370	Heathcliff Slocumb	.40	.18
☐ 371	Jimmy Jones	.10	.05
☐ 372	Ken Griffey Jr.	3.00	1.35
☐ 373	Chris Hammond	.10	.05
☐ 374	Chili Davis	.30	.14
☐ 375	Joey Cora	.20	.09
☐ 376	Ken Hill	.30	.14
☐ 377	Darryl Strawberry	.30	.14
☐ 378	Ron Darling	.10	.05
☐ 379	Sid Bream	.10	.05
☐ 380	Bill Swift	.10	.05
☐ 381	Shawn Abner	.10	.05
☐ 382	Eric King	.10	.05
☐ 383	Mickey Morandini	.10	.05
☐ 384	Carlton Fisk	.40	.18
☐ 385	Steve Lake	.10	.05
☐ 386	Mike Jeffcoat	.10	.05
☐ 387	Darren Holmes	.10	.05
☐ 388	Tim Wallach	.10	.05
☐ 389	George Bell	.10	.05
☐ 390	Craig Lefferts	.10	.05
☐ 391	Ernie Whitt	.10	.05
☐ 392	Felix Jose	.10	.05
☐ 393	Kevin Maas	.10	.05
☐ 394	Devon White	.10	.05
☐ 395	Otis Nixon	.30	.14
☐ 396	Chuck Knoblauch	.50	.23
☐ 397	Scott Coolbaugh	.10	.05
☐ 398	Glenn Davis	.10	.05
☐ 399	Manny Lee	.10	.05
☐ 400	Andre Dawson	.40	.18
☐ 401	Scott Chiamparino	.10	.05
☐ 402	Bill Gullickson	.10	.05
☐ 403	Lance Johnson	.10	.05
☐ 404	Juan Agosto	.10	.05
☐ 405	Danny Darwin	.10	.05
☐ 406	Barry Jones	.10	.05
☐ 407	Larry Andersen	.10	.05
☐ 408	Luis Rivera	.10	.05
☐ 409	Jaime Navarro	.10	.05
☐ 410	Roger McDowell	.10	.05
☐ 411	Brett Butler	.30	.14
☐ 412	Dale Murphy	.40	.18
☐ 413	Tim Raines UER	.20	.09
	(Listed as hitting .500 in 1980, should be .050)		
☐ 414	Norm Charlton	.10	.05
☐ 415	Greg Cadaret	.10	.05
☐ 416	Chris Nabholz	.10	.05
☐ 417	Dave Stewart	.30	.14
☐ 418	Rich Gedman	.10	.05
☐ 419	Willie Randolph	.30	.14
☐ 420	Mitch Williams	.10	.05
☐ 421	Brook Jacoby	.10	.05
☐ 422	Greg W. Harris	.10	.05
☐ 423	Nolan Ryan	1.50	.70
☐ 424	Dave Rohde	.10	.05
☐ 425	Don Mattingly	.60	.25
☐ 426	Greg Gagne	.10	.05
☐ 427	Vince Coleman	.10	.05
☐ 428	Dan Pasqua	.10	.05
☐ 429	Alvin Davis	.10	.05
☐ 430	Cal Ripken	1.50	.70
☐ 431	Jamie Quirk	.10	.05
☐ 432	Benito Santiago	.10	.05
☐ 433	Jose Uribe	.10	.05
☐ 434	Candy Maldonado	.10	.05
☐ 435	Junior Felix	.10	.05
☐ 436	Deion Sanders	.20	.09
☐ 437	John Franco	.20	.09
☐ 438	Greg Hibbard	.10	.05
☐ 439	Floyd Bannister	.10	.05
☐ 440	Steve Howe	.10	.05
☐ 441	Steve Decker	.10	.05
☐ 442	Vicente Palacios	.10	.05
☐ 443	Pat Tabler	.10	.05
☐ 444	Darryl Strawberry CL	.30	.14
☐ 445	Mike Felder	.10	.05
☐ 446	Al Newman	.10	.05
☐ 447	Chris Donnels	.10	.05
☐ 448	Rich Rodriguez	.10	.05
☐ 449	Turner Ward	.10	.05
☐ 450	Bob Walk	.10	.05
☐ 451	Gilberto Reyes	.10	.05
☐ 452	Mike Jackson	.10	.05
☐ 453	Rafael Belliard	.10	.05
☐ 454	Wayne Edwards	.10	.05
☐ 455	Andy Allanson	.10	.05
☐ 456	Dave Smith	.10	.05
☐ 457	Gary Carter	.40	.18
☐ 458	Warren Cromartie	.10	.05
☐ 459	Jack Armstrong	.10	.05
☐ 460	Bob Tewksbury	.10	.05
☐ 461	Joe Klink	.10	.05
☐ 462	Xavier Hernandez	.10	.05
☐ 463	Scott Radinsky	.10	.05
☐ 464	Jeff Robinson	.10	.05
☐ 465	Gregg Jefferies	.10	.05
☐ 466	Denny Neagle	1.25	.55
☐ 467	Carmelo Martinez	.10	.05
☐ 468	Donn Pall	.10	.05
☐ 469	Bruce Hurst	.10	.05
☐ 470	Eric Bullock	.10	.05
☐ 471	Rick Aguilera	.30	.14
☐ 472	Charlie Hough	.10	.05
☐ 473	Carlos Quintana	.10	.05
☐ 474	Marty Barrett	.10	.05
☐ 475	Kevin D. Brown	.10	.05
☐ 476	Bobby Ojeda	.10	.05
☐ 477	Edgar Martinez	.40	.18
☐ 478	Bip Roberts	.10	.05
☐ 479	Mike Flanagan	.10	.05
☐ 480	John Habyan	.10	.05
☐ 481	Larry Casian	.10	.05
☐ 482	Wally Backman	.10	.05
☐ 483	Doug Dascenzo	.10	.05
☐ 484	Rick Dempsey	.10	.05
☐ 485	Ed Sprague	.10	.05
☐ 486	Steve Ontiveros	.10	.05
☐ 487	Mark McGwire	.75	.35
☐ 488	Roger Clemens	.75	.35

		MINT	NRMT
☐ 489	Orlando Merced	.20	.09
☐ 490	Rene Gonzales	.10	.05
☐ 491	Mike Stanton	.10	.05
☐ 492	Al Osuna	.10	.05
☐ 493	Rick Cerone	.10	.05
☐ 494	Mariano Duncan	.10	.05
☐ 495	Zane Smith	.10	.05
☐ 496	John Morris	.10	.05
☐ 497	Frank Tanana	.10	.05
☐ 498	Junior Ortiz	.10	.05
☐ 499	Dave Winfield	.40	.18
☐ 500	Gary Varsho	.10	.05
☐ 501	Chico Walker	.10	.05
☐ 502	Ken Caminiti	.40	.18
☐ 503	Ken Griffey Sr.	.10	.05
☐ 504	Randy Myers	.10	.05
☐ 505	Steve Bedrosian	.10	.05
☐ 506	Cory Snyder	.10	.05
☐ 507	Cris Carpenter	.10	.05
☐ 508	Tim Belcher	.10	.05
☐ 509	Jeff Hamilton	.10	.05
☐ 510	Steve Avery	.10	.05
☐ 511	Dave Valle	.10	.05
☐ 512	Tom Lampkin	.10	.05
☐ 513	Shawn Hillegas	.10	.05
☐ 514	Reggie Jefferson	.30	.14
☐ 515	Ron Karkovice	.10	.05
☐ 516	Doug Drabek	.10	.05
☐ 517	Tom Henke	.10	.05
☐ 518	Chris Bosio	.10	.05
☐ 519	Gregg Olson	.10	.05
☐ 520	Bob Scanlan	.10	.05
☐ 521	Alonzo Powell	.10	.05
☐ 522	Jeff Ballard	.10	.05
☐ 523	Ray Lankford	.40	.18
☐ 524	Tommy Greene	.10	.05
☐ 525	Mike Timlin	.10	.05
☐ 526	Juan Berenguer	.10	.05
☐ 527	Scott Erickson	.30	.14
☐ 528	Sandy Alomar Jr. CL	.10	.05

1991 Leaf Gold Rookies

KIRK DRESSENDORFER P

This 26-card standard size set was issued by Leaf as an insert to their 1991 Leaf regular issue. The first twelve cards were issued as random inserts in the first series of 1991 Leaf foil packs. The rest were issued as random inserts in with the second series. The set features a selection of rookie prospects. The earliest Leaf Gold Rookie cards issued with the first series can sometimes be found with erroneous regular numbered backs 265 through 276 instead of the correct BC1 through BC12. These numbered variations are very tough to find and are valued at ten times the values listed below.

		MINT	NRMT
COMPLETE SET (26)		20.00	9.00
COMMON CARD (BC1-BC26)		.50	.23
SEMISTARS		1.00	.45
RANDOM INSERTS IN BOTH SERIES			
☐ BC1	Scott Leius	.50	.23
☐ BC2	Luis Gonzalez	.75	.35
☐ BC3	Wil Cordero	.50	.23
☐ BC4	Gary Scott	.50	.23
☐ BC5	Willie Banks	.50	.23
☐ BC6	Arthur Rhodes	.75	.35
☐ BC7	Mo Vaughn	5.00	2.20
☐ BC8	Henry Rodriguez	1.50	.70
☐ BC9	Todd Van Poppel	.50	.23
☐ BC10	Reggie Sanders	1.00	.45
☐ BC11	Rico Brogna	1.00	.45
☐ BC12	Mike Mussina	3.00	1.35
☐ BC13	Kirk Dressendorfer	.50	.23
☐ BC14	Jeff Bagwell	6.00	2.70
☐ BC15	Pete Schourek	.75	.35
☐ BC16	Wade Taylor	.50	.23
☐ BC17	Pat Kelly	.50	.23
☐ BC18	Tim Costo	.50	.23
☐ BC19	Roger Salkeld	.50	.23
☐ BC20	Andujar Cedeno	.50	.23
☐ BC21	Ryan Klesko UER	3.00	1.35
	(1990 Sumter BA .289; should be .368)		
☐ BC22	Mike Huff	.50	.23
☐ BC23	Anthony Young	.50	.23
☐ BC24	Eddie Zosky	.50	.23
☐ BC25	Nolan Ryan DP UER	1.50	.70
	No Hitter 7 (Word other repeated in 7th line)		
☐ BC26	Rickey Henderson DP	.75	.35
	Record Steal		

1992 Leaf Previews

MARK WHITTEN RF

Four Leaf Preview standard-size cards were included in each 1992 Donruss hobby factory set. The cards were intended to show collectors and dealers the style of the 1992 Leaf set. The fronts carry glossy color player photos framed by silver borders.

		MINT	NRMT
COMPLETE SET (26)		50.00	22.00
COMMON CARD (1-26)		.50	.23
FOUR PER DONRUSS HOBBY FACTORY SET			
☐ 1	Steve Avery	.50	.23
☐ 2	Ryne Sandberg	2.50	1.10
☐ 3	Chris Sabo	.50	.23
☐ 4	Jeff Bagwell	6.00	2.70
☐ 5	Darryl Strawberry	1.00	.45
☐ 6	Bret Barberie	.50	.23
☐ 7	Howard Johnson	.50	.23
☐ 8	John Kruk	1.00	.45
☐ 9	Andy Van Slyke	1.00	.45

		MINT	NRMT
☐ 10	Felix Jose	.50	.23
☐ 11	Fred McGriff	1.50	.70
☐ 12	Will Clark	1.50	.70
☐ 13	Cal Ripken	8.00	3.60
☐ 14	Phil Plantier	.50	.23
☐ 15	Lee Stevens	.50	.23
☐ 16	Frank Thomas	10.00	4.50
☐ 17	Mark Whiten	.50	.23
☐ 18	Cecil Fielder	1.00	.45
☐ 19	George Brett	4.00	1.80
☐ 20	Robin Yount	1.50	.70
☐ 21	Scott Erickson	.50	.23
☐ 22	Don Mattingly	3.00	1.35
☐ 23	Jose Canseco	1.50	.70
☐ 24	Ken Griffey Jr.	12.00	5.50
☐ 25	Nolan Ryan	8.00	3.60
☐ 26	Joe Carter	1.00	.45

1992 Leaf

STEVE SAX 2B

The 1992 Leaf set consists of 528 cards, issued in two separate 264-card series. Cards were distributed in first and second series 15-card foil packs. Each pack contained a selection of basic cards and one black gold parallel card. The basic card fronts feature color action player photos on a silver card face. The player's name appears in a black bar edged at the bottom by a thin red stripe. The team logo overlaps the bar at the right corner. There are no significant Rookie Cards in this set.

	MINT	NRMT
COMPLETE SET (528)	15.00	6.75
COMPLETE SERIES 1 (264)	5.00	2.20
COMPLETE SERIES 2 (264)	10.00	4.50
COMMON CARD (1-528)	.05	.02
MINOR STARS	.15	.07
UNLISTED STARS	.30	.14
COMP.B.GOLD SET (528)	80.00	36.00
COMP.B.GOLD SER.1 (264)	30.00	13.50
COMP.B.GOLD SER.2 (264)	50.00	22.00
COMMON BLACK GOLD (1-528)	.15	.07
*B.GOLD STARS: 2.5X TO 5X HI COLUMN		
*BLACK GOLD RCs: 1.5X TO 3X HI		
ONE BLACK GOLD IN EVERY PACK		

		MINT	NRMT
☐ 1	Jim Abbott	.05	.02
☐ 2	Cal Eldred	.05	.02
☐ 3	Bud Black	.05	.02
☐ 4	Dave Howard	.05	.02
☐ 5	Luis Sojo	.05	.02
☐ 6	Gary Scott	.05	.02
☐ 7	Joe Oliver	.05	.02
☐ 8	Chris Gardner	.05	.02
☐ 9	Sandy Alomar Jr.	.15	.07
☐ 10	Greg W. Harris	.05	.02
☐ 11	Doug Drabek	.05	.02
☐ 12	Darryl Hamilton	.05	.02
☐ 13	Mike Mussina	.50	.23
☐ 14	Kevin Tapani	.05	.02
☐ 15	Ron Gant	.15	.07

☐ 16	Mark McGwire	.60	.25
☐ 17	Robin Ventura	.15	.07
☐ 18	Pedro Guerrero	.05	.02
☐ 19	Roger Clemens	.60	.25
☐ 20	Steve Farr	.05	.02
☐ 21	Frank Tanana	.05	.02
☐ 22	Joe Hesketh	.05	.02
☐ 23	Erik Hanson	.05	.02
☐ 24	Greg Cadaret	.05	.02
☐ 25	Rex Hudler	.05	.02
☐ 26	Mark Grace	.20	.09
☐ 27	Kelly Gruber	.05	.02
☐ 28	Jeff Bagwell	1.00	.45
☐ 29	Darryl Strawberry	.15	.07
☐ 30	Dave Smith	.05	.02
☐ 31	Kevin Appier	.15	.07
☐ 32	Steve Chitren	.05	.02
☐ 33	Kevin Gross	.05	.02
☐ 34	Rick Aguilera	.05	.02
☐ 35	Juan Guzman	.05	.02
☐ 36	Joe Orsulak	.05	.02
☐ 37	Tim Raines	.15	.07
☐ 38	Harold Reynolds	.05	.02
☐ 39	Charlie Hough	.05	.02
☐ 40	Tony Phillips	.05	.02
☐ 41	Nolan Ryan	1.25	.55
☐ 42	Vince Coleman	.05	.02
☐ 43	Andy Van Slyke	.15	.07
☐ 44	Tim Burke	.05	.02
☐ 45	Luis Polonia	.05	.02
☐ 46	Tom Browning	.05	.02
☐ 47	Willie McGee	.05	.02
☐ 48	Gary DiSarcina	.05	.02
☐ 49	Mark Lewis	.05	.02
☐ 50	Phil Plantier	.05	.02
☐ 51	Doug Dascenzo	.05	.02
☐ 52	Cal Ripken	1.25	.55
☐ 53	Pedro Munoz	.05	.02
☐ 54	Carlos Hernandez	.05	.02
☐ 55	Jerald Clark	.05	.02
☐ 56	Jeff Brantley	.05	.02
☐ 57	Don Mattingly	.50	.23
☐ 58	Roger McDowell	.05	.02
☐ 59	Steve Avery	.05	.02
☐ 60	John Olerud	.15	.07
☐ 61	Bill Gullickson	.05	.02
☐ 62	Juan Gonzalez	1.00	.45
☐ 63	Felix Jose	.05	.02
☐ 64	Robin Yount	.20	.09
☐ 65	Greg Briley	.05	.02
☐ 66	Steve Finley	.05	.07
☐ 67	Frank Thomas CL	.30	.14
☐ 68	Tom Gordon	.05	.02
☐ 69	Rob Dibble	.05	.02
☐ 70	Glenallen Hill	.05	.02
☐ 71	Calvin Jones	.05	.02
☐ 72	Joe Girardi	.05	.02
☐ 73	Barry Larkin	.20	.09
☐ 74	Andy Benes	.15	.07
☐ 75	Milt Cuyler	.05	.02
☐ 76	Kevin Bass	.05	.02
☐ 77	Pete Harnisch	.05	.02
☐ 78	Wilson Alvarez	.15	.07
☐ 79	Mike Devereaux	.05	.02
☐ 80	Doug Henry	.05	.02
☐ 81	Orel Hershiser	.15	.07
☐ 82	Shane Mack	.05	.02
☐ 83	Mike Macfarlane	.05	.02
☐ 84	Thomas Howard	.05	.02
☐ 85	Alex Fernandez	.15	.07
☐ 86	Reggie Jefferson	.05	.02
☐ 87	Leo Gomez	.05	.02
☐ 88	Mel Hall	.05	.02
☐ 89	Mike Greenwell	.05	.02
☐ 90	Jeff Russell	.05	.02
☐ 91	Steve Buechele	.05	.02
☐ 92	David Cone	.15	.07
☐ 93	Kevin Reimer	.05	.02
☐ 94	Mark Lemke	.05	.02
☐ 95	Bob Tewksbury	.05	.02
☐ 96	Zane Smith	.05	.02
☐ 97	Mark Eichhorn	.05	.02
☐ 98	Kirby Puckett	.60	.25
☐ 99	Paul O'Neill	.15	.07
☐ 100	Dennis Eckersley	.15	.07
☐ 101	Duane Ward	.05	.02
☐ 102	Matt Nokes	.05	.02
☐ 103	Mo Vaughn	.50	.23
☐ 104	Pat Kelly	.05	.02
☐ 105	Ron Karkovice	.05	.02
☐ 106	Bill Spiers	.05	.02
☐ 107	Gary Gaetti	.05	.02
☐ 108	Mackey Sasser	.05	.02
☐ 109	Robby Thompson	.05	.02
☐ 110	Marvin Freeman	.05	.02
☐ 111	Jimmy Key	.15	.07
☐ 112	Dwight Gooden	.15	.07
☐ 113	Charlie Leibrandt	.05	.02
☐ 114	Devon White	.05	.02
☐ 115	Charles Nagy	.15	.07
☐ 116	Rickey Henderson	.20	.09
☐ 117	Paul Assenmacher	.05	.02
☐ 118	Junior Felix	.05	.02
☐ 119	Julio Franco	.05	.02
☐ 120	Norm Charlton	.05	.02
☐ 121	Scott Servais	.05	.02
☐ 122	Gerald Perry	.05	.02
☐ 123	Brian McRae	.05	.02
☐ 124	Don Slaught	.05	.02
☐ 125	Juan Samuel	.05	.02
☐ 126	Harold Baines	.15	.07
☐ 127	Scott Livingstone	.05	.02
☐ 128	Jay Buhner	.20	.09
☐ 129	Darrin Jackson	.05	.02
☐ 130	Luis Mercedes	.05	.02
☐ 131	Brian Harper	.05	.02
☐ 132	Howard Johnson	.05	.02
☐ 133	Nolan Ryan CL	.30	.14
☐ 134	Dante Bichette	.20	.09
☐ 135	Dave Righetti	.05	.02
☐ 136	Jeff Montgomery	.15	.07
☐ 137	Joe Grahe	.05	.02
☐ 138	Delino DeShields	.05	.02
☐ 139	Jose Rijo	.05	.02
☐ 140	Ken Caminiti	.20	.09
☐ 141	Steve Olin	.05	.02
☐ 142	Kurt Stillwell	.05	.02
☐ 143	Jay Bell	.15	.07
☐ 144	Jaime Navarro	.05	.02
☐ 145	Ben McDonald	.05	.02
☐ 146	Greg Gagne	.05	.02
☐ 147	Jeff Blauser	.05	.02
☐ 148	Carney Lansford	.15	.07
☐ 149	Ozzie Guillen	.05	.02
☐ 150	Milt Thompson	.05	.02
☐ 151	Jeff Reardon	.15	.07
☐ 152	Scott Sanderson	.05	.02
☐ 153	Cecil Fielder	.15	.07
☐ 154	Greg A. Harris	.05	.02
☐ 155	Rich DeLucia	.05	.02
☐ 156	Roberto Kelly	.05	.02
☐ 157	Bryn Smith	.05	.02
☐ 158	Chuck McElroy	.05	.02
☐ 159	Tom Henke	.05	.02
☐ 160	Luis Gonzalez	.05	.02
☐ 161	Steve Wilson	.05	.02
☐ 162	Shawn Boskie	.05	.02
☐ 163	Mark Davis	.05	.02
☐ 164	Mike Moore	.05	.02
☐ 165	Mike Scioscia	.05	.02
☐ 166	Scott Erickson	.15	.07
☐ 167	Todd Stottlemyre	.05	.02
☐ 168	Alvin Davis	.05	.02
☐ 169	Greg Hibbard	.05	.02
☐ 170	David Valle	.05	.02
☐ 171	Dave Winfield	.30	.14
☐ 172	Alan Trammell	.20	.09
☐ 173	Kenny Rogers	.05	.02
☐ 174	John Franco	.15	.07
☐ 175	Jose Lind	.05	.02
☐ 176	Pete Schourek	.05	.02
☐ 177	Von Hayes	.05	.02
☐ 178	Chris Hammond	.05	.02
☐ 179	John Burkett	.05	.02
☐ 180	Dickie Thon	.05	.02
☐ 181	Joel Skinner	.05	.02
☐ 182	Scott Cooper	.05	.02
☐ 183	Andre Dawson	.20	.09
☐ 184	Kevin Maas	.25	.11
☐ 185	Kevin Mitchell	.15	.07
☐ 186	Brett Butler	.15	.07
☐ 187	Tony Fernandez	.05	.02
☐ 188	Cory Snyder	.05	.02
☐ 189	John Habyan	.05	.02
☐ 190	Dennis Martinez	.15	.07
☐ 191	John Smoltz	.20	.09
☐ 192	Greg Myers	.05	.02
☐ 193	Rob Deer	.05	.02
☐ 194	Ivan Rodriguez	.60	.25
☐ 195	Ray Lankford	.30	.14
☐ 196	Bill Wegman	.05	.02
☐ 197	Edgar Martinez	.20	.09
☐ 198	Darryl Kile	.15	.07
☐ 199	Cal Ripken CL	.30	.14
☐ 200	Brent Mayne	.05	.02
☐ 201	Larry Walker	.30	.14
☐ 202	Carlos Baerga	.05	.02
☐ 203	Russ Swan	.05	.02
☐ 204	Mike Morgan	.05	.02
☐ 205	Hal Morris	.05	.02
☐ 206	Tony Gwynn	.75	.35
☐ 207	Mark Leiter	.05	.02
☐ 208	Kirt Manwaring	.05	.02
☐ 209	Al Osuna	.05	.02
☐ 210	Bobby Thigpen	.05	.02
☐ 211	Chris Hoiles	.05	.02
☐ 212	B.J. Surhoff	.15	.07
☐ 213	Lenny Harris	.05	.02
☐ 214	Scott Leius	.05	.02
☐ 215	Gregg Jefferies	.05	.02
☐ 216	Bruce Hurst	.05	.02
☐ 217	Steve Sax	.05	.02
☐ 218	Dave Otto	.05	.02
☐ 219	Sam Horn	.05	.02
☐ 220	Charlie Hayes	.05	.02
☐ 221	Frank Viola	.05	.02
☐ 222	Jose Guzman	.05	.02
☐ 223	Gary Redus	.05	.02
☐ 224	Dave Gallagher	.05	.02
☐ 225	Dean Palmer	.15	.07
☐ 226	Greg Olson	.05	.02
☐ 227	Jose DeLeon	.05	.02
☐ 228	Mike LaValliere	.05	.02
☐ 229	Mark Langston	.05	.02
☐ 230	Chuck Knoblauch	.30	.14
☐ 231	Bill Doran	.05	.02
☐ 232	Dave Henderson	.05	.02
☐ 233	Roberto Alomar	.30	.14
☐ 234	Scott Fletcher	.05	.02
☐ 235	Tim Naehring	.15	.07
☐ 236	Mike Gallego	.05	.02
☐ 237	Lance Johnson	.05	.02
☐ 238	Paul Molitor	.30	.14
☐ 239	Dan Gladden	.05	.02
☐ 240	Willie Randolph	.15	.07
☐ 241	Will Clark	.20	.09
☐ 242	Sid Bream	.05	.02
☐ 243	Derek Bell	.15	.07
☐ 244	Bill Pecota	.05	.02
☐ 245	Terry Pendleton	.15	.07
☐ 246	Randy Ready	.05	.02
☐ 247	Jack Armstrong	.05	.02
☐ 248	Todd Van Poppel	.05	.02
☐ 249	Shawon Dunston	.05	.02
☐ 250	Bobby Rose	.05	.02
☐ 251	Jeff Huson	.05	.02
☐ 252	Bip Roberts	.05	.02
☐ 253	Doug Jones	.05	.02
☐ 254	Lee Smith	.15	.07
☐ 255	George Brett	.60	.25
☐ 256	Randy Tomlin	.05	.02
☐ 257	Todd Benzinger	.05	.02
☐ 258	Dave Stewart	.05	.02
☐ 259	Mark Carreon	.05	.02
☐ 260	Pete O'Brien	.05	.02
☐ 261	Tim Teufel	.05	.02
☐ 262	Bob Milacki	.05	.02
☐ 263	Mark Guthrie	.05	.02
☐ 264	Darrin Fletcher	.05	.02
☐ 265	Omar Vizquel	.15	.07
☐ 266	Chris Bosio	.05	.02
☐ 267	Jose Canseco	.20	.09
☐ 268	Mike Boddicker	.05	.02
☐ 269	Lance Parrish	.05	.02
☐ 270	Jose Vizcaino	.05	.02
☐ 271	Chris Sabo	.05	.02
☐ 272	Royce Clayton	.05	.02
☐ 273	Marquis Grissom	.15	.07

274	Fred McGriff	.20	.09
275	Barry Bonds	.40	.18
276	Greg Vaughn	.05	.02
277	Gregg Olson	.05	.02
278	Dave Hollins	.05	.02
279	Tom Glavine	.20	.09
280	Bryan Hickerson UER	.05	.02
	Name spelled Brian on front		
281	Scott Radinsky	.05	.02
282	Omar Olivares	.05	.02
283	Ivan Calderon	.05	.02
284	Kevin Maas	.05	.02
285	Mickey Tettleton	.05	.02
286	Wade Boggs	.30	.14
287	Stan Belinda	.05	.02
288	Bret Barberie	.05	.02
289	Jose Oquendo	.05	.02
290	Frank Castillo	.05	.02
291	Dave Stieb	.05	.02
292	Tommy Greene	.05	.02
293	Eric Karros	.20	.09
294	Greg Maddux	1.00	.45
295	Jim Eisenreich	.05	.02
296	Rafael Palmeiro	.20	.09
297	Ramon Martinez	.15	.07
298	Tim Wallach	.05	.02
299	Jim Thome	1.00	.45
300	Chito Martinez	.05	.02
301	Mitch Williams	.05	.02
302	Randy Johnson	.30	.14
303	Carlton Fisk	.30	.14
304	Travis Fryman	.15	.07
305	Bobby Witt	.05	.02
306	Dave Magadan	.05	.02
307	Alex Cole	.05	.02
308	Bobby Bonilla	.15	.07
309	Bryan Harvey	.05	.02
310	Rafael Belliard	.05	.02
311	Mariano Duncan	.05	.02
312	Chuck Crim	.05	.02
313	John Kruk	.05	.02
314	Ellis Burks	.15	.07
315	Craig Biggio	.20	.09
316	Glenn Davis	.05	.02
317	Ryne Sandberg	.40	.18
318	Mike Sharperson	.05	.02
319	Rich Rodriguez	.05	.02
320	Lee Guetterman	.05	.02
321	Benito Santiago	.05	.02
322	Jose Offerman	.05	.02
323	Tony Pena	.05	.02
324	Pat Borders	.05	.02
325	Mike Henneman	.05	.02
326	Kevin Brown	.15	.07
327	Chris Nabholz	.05	.02
328	Franklin Stubbs	.05	.02
329	Tino Martinez	.30	.14
330	Mickey Morandini	.05	.02
331	Ryne Sandberg CL	.30	.14
332	Mark Gubicza	.05	.02
333	Bill Landrum	.05	.02
334	Mark Whiten	.15	.07
335	Darren Daulton	.15	.07
336	Rick Wilkins	.05	.02
337	Brian Jordan	.40	.18
338	Kevin Ward	.05	.02
339	Ruben Amaro	.05	.02
340	Trevor Wilson	.05	.02
341	Andujar Cedeno	.05	.02
342	Michael Huff	.05	.02
343	Brady Anderson	.20	.09
344	Craig Grebeck	.05	.02
345	Bobby Ojeda	.05	.02
346	Mike Pagliarulo	.05	.02
347	Terry Shumpert	.05	.02
348	Dann Bilardello	.05	.02
349	Frank Thomas	1.50	.70
350	Albert Belle	.40	.18
351	Jose Mesa	.05	.02
352	Rich Monteleone	.05	.02
353	Bob Walk	.05	.02
354	Monty Fariss	.05	.02
355	Luis Rivera	.05	.02
356	Anthony Young	.05	.02
357	Geno Petralli	.05	.02
358	Otis Nixon	.15	.07
359	Tom Pagnozzi	.05	.02
360	Reggie Sanders	.15	
361	Lee Stevens	.05	.02
362	Kent Hrbek	.15	.07
363	Orlando Merced	.05	.02
364	Mike Bordick	.05	.02
365	Dion James UER	.05	.02
	(Blue Jays logo on card back)		
366	Jack Clark	.15	.07
367	Mike Stanley	.05	.02
368	Randy Velarde	.05	.02
369	Dan Pasqua	.05	.02
370	Pat Listach	.05	.02
371	Mike Fitzgerald	.05	.02
372	Tom Foley	.05	.02
373	Matt Williams	.20	.09
374	Brian Hunter	.05	.02
375	Joe Carter	.15	.07
376	Bret Saberhagen	.05	.02
377	Mike Stanton	.05	.02
378	Hubie Brooks	.05	.02
379	Eric Bell	.05	.02
380	Walt Weiss	.05	.02
381	Danny Jackson	.05	.02
382	Manuel Lee	.05	.02
383	Ruben Sierra	.05	.02
384	Greg Swindell	.05	.02
385	Ryan Bowen	.05	.02
386	Kevin Ritz	.05	.02
387	Curtis Wilkerson	.05	.02
388	Gary Varsho	.05	.02
389	Dave Hansen	.05	.02
390	Bob Welch	.05	.02
391	Lou Whitaker	.15	.07
392	Ken Griffey Jr.	2.00	.90
393	Mike Maddux	.05	.02
394	Arthur Rhodes	.05	.02
395	Chili Davis	.05	.02
396	Eddie Murray	.30	.14
397	Robin Yount CL	.20	.09
398	Dave Cochrane	.05	.02
399	Kevin Seitzer	.05	.02
400	Ozzie Smith	.40	.18
401	Paul Sorrento	.05	.02
402	Les Lancaster	.05	.02
403	Junior Noboa	.05	.02
404	David Justice	.30	.14
405	Andy Ashby	.05	.02
406	Danny Tartabull	.05	.02
407	Bill Swift	.05	.02
408	Craig Lefferts	.05	.02
409	Tom Candiotti	.05	.02
410	Lance Blankenship	.05	.02
411	Jeff Tackett	.05	.02
412	Sammy Sosa	.30	.14
413	Jody Reed	.05	.02
414	Bruce Ruffin	.05	.02
415	Gene Larkin	.05	.02
416	John Vander Wal	.05	.02
417	Tim Belcher	.05	.02
418	Steve Frey	.05	.02
419	Dick Schofield	.05	.02
420	Jeff King	.15	.07
421	Kim Batiste	.05	.02
422	Jack McDowell	.05	.02
423	Damon Berryhill	.05	.02
424	Gary Wayne	.05	.02
425	Jack Morris	.15	.07
426	Moises Alou	.20	.09
427	Mark McLemore	.05	.02
428	Juan Guerrero	.05	.02
429	Scott Scudder	.05	.02
430	Eric Davis	.15	.07
431	Joe Slusarski	.05	.02
432	Todd Zeile	.05	.02
433	Dwayne Henry	.05	.02
434	Cliff Brantley	.05	.02
435	Butch Henry	.05	.02
436	Todd Worrell	.05	.02
437	Bob Scanlan	.05	.02
438	Wally Joyner	.15	.07
439	John Flaherty	.05	.02
440	Brian Downing	.05	.02
441	Darren Lewis	.05	.02
442	Gary Carter	.30	.14
443	Wally Ritchie	.05	.02
444	Chris Jones	.05	.02
445	Jeff Kent	.30	.14
446	Gary Sheffield	.30	.14
447	Ron Darling	.05	.02
448	Deion Sanders	.15	.07
449	Andres Galarraga	.30	.14
450	Chuck Finley	.05	.02
451	Derek Lilliquist	.05	.02
452	Carl Willis	.05	.02
453	Wes Chamberlain	.05	.02
454	Roger Mason	.05	.02
455	Spike Owen	.05	.02
456	Thomas Howard	.05	.02
457	Dave Martinez	.05	.02
458	Pete Incaviglia	.05	.02
459	Keith A. Miller	.05	.02
460	Mike Fetters	.05	.02
461	Paul Gibson	.05	.02
462	George Bell	.05	.02
463	Bobby Bonilla CL	.15	.07
464	Terry Mulholland	.05	.02
465	Storm Davis	.05	.02
466	Gary Pettis	.05	.02
467	Randy Bush	.05	.02
468	Ken Hill	.05	.02
469	Rheal Cormier	.05	.02
470	Andy Stankiewicz	.05	.02
471	Dave Burba	.05	.02
472	Henry Cotto	.05	.02
473	Dale Sveum	.05	.02
474	Rich Gossage	.15	.07
475	William Suero	.05	.02
476	Doug Strange	.05	.02
477	Bill Krueger	.05	.02
478	John Wetteland	.15	.07
479	Melido Perez	.05	.02
480	Lonnie Smith	.05	.02
481	Mike Jackson	.05	.02
482	Mike Gardiner	.05	.02
483	David Wells	.05	.02
484	Barry Jones	.05	.02
485	Scott Bankhead	.05	.02
486	Terry Leach	.05	.02
487	Vince Horsman	.05	.02
488	Dave Eiland	.05	.02
489	Alejandro Pena	.05	.02
490	Julio Valera	.05	.02
491	Joe Boever	.05	.02
492	Paul Miller	.05	.02
493	Archi Cianfrocco	.05	.02
494	Dave Fleming	.05	.02
495	Kyle Abbott	.05	.02
496	Chad Kreuter	.05	.02
497	Chris James	.05	.02
498	Donnie Hill	.05	.02
499	Jacob Brumfield	.05	.02
500	Ricky Bones	.05	.02
501	Terry Steinbach	.15	.07
502	Bernard Gilkey	.15	.07
503	Dennis Cook	.05	.02
504	Len Dykstra	.15	.07
505	Mike Bielecki	.05	.02
506	Bob Kipper	.05	.02
507	Jose Melendez	.05	.02
508	Rick Sutcliffe	.05	.02
509	Ken Patterson	.05	.02
510	Andy Allanson	.05	.02
511	Al Newman	.05	.02
512	Mark Gardner	.05	.02
513	Jeff Schaefer	.05	.02
514	Jim McNamara	.05	.02
515	Peter Hoy	.05	.02
516	Curt Schilling	.20	.09
517	Kirk McCaskill	.05	.02
518	Chris Gwynn	.05	.02
519	Sid Fernandez	.05	.02
520	Jeff Parrett	.05	.02
521	Scott Ruskin	.05	.02
522	Kevin McReynolds	.05	.02
523	Rick Cerone	.05	.02
524	Jesse Orosco	.05	.02
525	Troy Afenir	.05	.02
526	John Smiley	.05	.02
527	Dale Murphy	.30	.14
528	Leaf Set Card	.05	.02

1992 Leaf Gold Rookies

This 24-card standard-size set honors 1992's most promising newcomers. The first 12 cards were randomly inserted in Leaf series I foil packs, while the second 12 cards were featured only in series II packs. The fronts display full-bleed color action photos highlighted by gold foil border stripes. A gold foil diamond appears at the corners of the picture frame, and the player's name appears in a black bar that extends between the bottom two diamonds. The key cards in this set are Kenny Lofton and Raul Mondesi.

color action photos that are full-bleed except at the bottom where a diagonal black stripe (gold-foil stamped with the player's name) separates the picture from a team color-coded slate triangle. The Leaf seal embossed with gold foil is superimposed at the lower right corner. J.T. Snow is the only key Rookie Card in this set.

	MINT	NRMT
COMPLETE SET (550)	35.00	16.00
COMPLETE SERIES 1 (220)	15.00	6.75
COMPLETE SERIES 2 (220)	15.00	6.75
COMPLETE UPDATE (110)	5.00	2.20
COMMON CARD (1-550)	.15	.07
MINOR STARS	.30	.14
UNLISTED STARS	.60	.25
COMP.F.THOMAS SET (10)	40.00	18.00
COMMON F.THOMAS (1-10)	5.00	2.20
THOMAS: RANDOM INS.IN BOTH SER.PACKS		
COMP.JUM.THOM.SET (10)	60.00	27.00
COMMON JUM.THOM. (1-10)	6.00	2.70
ONE JUMBO THOMAS PER UPDATE BOX		

	MINT	NRMT
COMPLETE SET (24)	16.00	7.25
COMPLETE SERIES 1 (12)	6.00	2.70
COMPLETE SERIES 2 (12)	10.00	4.50
COMMON CARD (BC1-BC24)	.50	.23
MINOR STARS	1.00	.45
RANDOM INSERTS IN BOTH SERIES		

☐ BC1	Chad Curtis	1.50	.70
☐ BC2	Brent Gates	.50	.23
☐ BC3	Pedro Martinez	4.00	1.80
☐ BC4	Kenny Lofton	6.00	2.70
☐ BC5	Turk Wendell	.50	.23
☐ BC6	Mark Hutton	.50	.23
☐ BC7	Todd Hundley	1.25	.55
☐ BC8	Matt Stairs	.50	.23
☐ BC9	Eddie Taubensee	.50	.23
☐ BC10	David Nied	.50	.23
☐ BC11	Salomon Torres	.50	.23
☐ BC12	Bret Boone	1.00	.45
☐ BC13	Johnny Ruffin	.50	.23
☐ BC14	Ed Martel	.50	.23
☐ BC15	Rick Trlicek	.50	.23
☐ BC16	Raul Mondesi	4.00	1.80
☐ BC17	Pat Mahomes	.50	.23
☐ BC18	Dan Wilson	1.00	.45
☐ BC19	Donovan Osborne	.50	.23
☐ BC20	Dave Silvestri	.50	.23
☐ BC21	Gary DiSarcina	.50	.23
☐ BC22	Denny Neagle	1.25	.55
☐ BC23	Steve Hosey	.50	.23
☐ BC24	John Doherty	.50	.23

1993 Leaf

The 1993 Leaf baseball set consists of three series of 220, 220, and 110 standard-size cards, respectively. Cards were distributed in 14-card foil packs, jumbo packs and magazine packs. The card fronts feature

☐ 1	Ben McDonald	.15	.07
☐ 2	Sid Fernandez	.15	.07
☐ 3	Juan Guzman	.15	.07
☐ 4	Curt Schilling	.30	.14
☐ 5	Ivan Rodriguez	.75	.35
☐ 6	Don Slaught	.15	.07
☐ 7	Terry Steinbach	.15	.07
☐ 8	Todd Zeile	.15	.07
☐ 9	Andy Stankiewicz	.15	.07
☐ 10	Tim Teufel	.15	.07
☐ 11	Marvin Freeman	.15	.07
☐ 12	Jim Austin	.15	.07
☐ 13	Bob Scanlan	.15	.07
☐ 14	Rusty Meacham	.15	.07
☐ 15	Casey Candaele	.15	.07
☐ 16	Travis Fryman	.30	.14
☐ 17	Jose Offerman	.15	.07
☐ 18	Albert Belle	.75	.35
☐ 19	John Vander Wal	.15	.07
☐ 20	Dan Pasqua	.15	.07
☐ 21	Frank Viola	.15	.07
☐ 22	Terry Mulholland	.15	.07
☐ 23	Gregg Olson	.15	.07
☐ 24	Randy Tomlin	.15	.07
☐ 25	Todd Stottlemyre	.15	.07
☐ 26	Jose Oquendo	.15	.07
☐ 27	Julio Franco	.15	.07
☐ 28	Tony Gwynn	1.50	.70
☐ 29	Ruben Sierra	.15	.07
☐ 30	Robby Thompson	.15	.07
☐ 31	Jim Bullinger	.15	.07
☐ 32	Rick Aguilera	.15	.07
☐ 33	Scott Servais	.15	.07
☐ 34	Cal Eldred	.15	.07
☐ 35	Mike Piazza	3.00	1.35
☐ 36	Brent Mayne	.15	.07
☐ 37	Wil Cordero	.15	.07
☐ 38	Milt Cuyler	.15	.07
☐ 39	Howard Johnson	.15	.07
☐ 40	Kenny Lofton	1.25	.55
☐ 41	Alex Fernandez	.30	.14

☐ 42	Denny Neagle	.30	.14
☐ 43	Tony Pena	.15	.07
☐ 44	Bob Tewksbury	.15	.07
☐ 45	Glenn Davis	.15	.07
☐ 46	Fred McGriff	.40	.18
☐ 47	John Olerud	.15	.07
☐ 48	Steve Hosey	.15	.07
☐ 49	Rafael Palmeiro	.40	.18
☐ 50	David Justice	.60	.25
☐ 51	Pete Harnisch	.15	.07
☐ 52	Sam Militello	.15	.07
☐ 53	Orel Hershiser	.30	.14
☐ 54	Pat Mahomes	.15	.07
☐ 55	Greg Colbrunn	.15	.07
☐ 56	Greg Vaughn	.15	.07
☐ 57	Vince Coleman	.15	.07
☐ 58	Brian McRae	.15	.07
☐ 59	Len Dykstra	.30	.14
☐ 60	Dan Gladden	.15	.07
☐ 61	Ted Power	.15	.07
☐ 62	Donovan Osborne	.15	.07
☐ 63	Ron Karkovice	.15	.07
☐ 64	Frank Seminara	.15	.07
☐ 65	Bob Zupcic	.15	.07
☐ 66	Kirt Manwaring	.15	.07
☐ 67	Mike Devereaux	.15	.07
☐ 68	Mark Lemke	.15	.07
☐ 69	Devon White	.15	.07
☐ 70	Sammy Sosa	.60	.25
☐ 71	Pedro Astacio	.15	.07
☐ 72	Dennis Eckersley	.30	.14
☐ 73	Chris Nabholz	.15	.07
☐ 74	Melido Perez	.15	.07
☐ 75	Todd Hundley	.40	.18
☐ 76	Kent Hrbek	.30	.14
☐ 77	Mickey Morandini	.15	.07
☐ 78	Tim McIntosh	.15	.07
☐ 79	Andy Van Slyke	.30	.14
☐ 80	Kevin McReynolds	.15	.07
☐ 81	Mike Henneman	.15	.07
☐ 82	Greg W. Harris	.15	.07
☐ 83	Sandy Alomar Jr.	.30	.14
☐ 84	Mike Jackson	.15	.07
☐ 85	Ozzie Guillen	.15	.07
☐ 86	Jeff Blauser	.15	.07
☐ 87	John Valentin	.30	.14
☐ 88	Rey Sanchez	.15	.07
☐ 89	Rick Sutcliffe	.15	.07
☐ 90	Luis Gonzalez	.15	.07
☐ 91	Jeff Fassero	.15	.07
☐ 92	Kenny Rogers	.15	.07
☐ 93	Bret Saberhagen	.15	.07
☐ 94	Bob Welch	.15	.07
☐ 95	Darren Daulton	.30	.14
☐ 96	Mike Gallego	.15	.07
☐ 97	Orlando Merced	.15	.07
☐ 98	Chuck Knoblauch	.60	.25
☐ 99	Bernard Gilkey	.15	.07
☐ 100	Billy Ashley	.30	.14
☐ 101	Kevin Appier	.15	.07
☐ 102	Jeff Brantley	.15	.07
☐ 103	Bill Gullickson	.15	.07
☐ 104	John Smoltz	.30	.14
☐ 105	Paul Sorrento	.15	.07
☐ 106	Steve Buechele	.15	.07
☐ 107	Steve Sax	.15	.07
☐ 108	Andujar Cedeno	.15	.07
☐ 109	Billy Hatcher	.15	.07
☐ 110	Checklist	.15	.07
☐ 111	John Franco	.30	.14
☐ 112	Alan Mills	.15	.07
☐ 113	Jack Morris	.30	.14
☐ 114	Mitch Williams	.15	.07
☐ 115	Nolan Ryan	2.50	1.10
☐ 116	Jay Bell	.30	.14
☐ 117	Mike Bordick	.15	.07
☐ 118	Geronimo Pena	.15	.07
☐ 119	Danny Tartabull	.15	.07
☐ 120	Checklist	.15	.07
☐ 121	Steve Avery	.15	.07
☐ 122	Ricky Bones	.15	.07
☐ 123	Mike Morgan	.15	.07
☐ 124	Jeff Montgomery	.30	.14
☐ 125	Jeff Bagwell	1.25	.55
☐ 126	Tony Phillips	.15	.07
☐ 127	Lenny Harris	.15	.07

#	Name				#	Name				#	Name		
128	Glenallen Hill	.15	.07		212	Bud Black	.15	.07		298	Greg Hibbard	.15	.07
129	Marquis Grissom	.30	.14		213	Mickey Tettleton	.15	.07		299	Jody Reed	.15	.07
130	Gerald Williams UER	.15	.07		214	Pete Smith	.15	.07		300	Dennis Martinez	.30	.14
	(Bernie Williams				215	Felix Fermin	.15	.07		301	Dave Martinez	.15	.07
	picture and stats)				216	Rick Wilkins	.15	.07		302	Reggie Jefferson	.15	.07
131	Greg A. Harris	.15	.07		217	George Bell	.15	.07		303	John Cummings	.15	.07
132	Tommy Greene	.15	.07		218	Eric Anthony	.15	.07		304	Orestes Destrade	.15	.07
133	Chris Hoiles	.15	.07		219	Pedro Munoz	.15	.07		305	Mike Maddux	.15	.07
134	Bob Walk	.15	.07		220	Checklist	.15	.07		306	David Segui	.15	.07
135	Duane Ward	.15	.07		221	Lance Blankenship	.15	.07		307	Gary Sheffield	.60	.25
136	Tom Pagnozzi	.15	.07		222	Deion Sanders	.30	.14		308	Danny Jackson	.15	.07
137	Jeff Huson	.15	.07		223	Craig Biggio	.40	.18		309	Craig Lefferts	.15	.07
138	Kurt Stillwell	.15	.07		224	Ryne Sandberg	.75	.35		310	Andre Dawson	.40	.18
139	Dave Henderson	.15	.07		225	Ron Gant	.30	.14		311	Barry Larkin	.40	.18
140	Darrin Jackson	.15	.07		226	Tom Brunansky	.15	.07		312	Alex Cole	.15	.07
141	Frank Castillo	.15	.07		227	Chad Curtis	.30	.14		313	Mark Gardner	.15	.07
142	Scott Erickson	.15	.07		228	Joe Carter	.30	.14		314	Kirk Gibson	.30	.14
143	Darryl Kile	.30	.14		229	Brian Jordan	.30	.14		315	Shane Mack	.15	.07
144	Bill Wegman	.15	.07		230	Brett Butler	.30	.14		316	Bo Jackson	.30	.14
145	Steve Wilson	.15	.07		231	Frank Bolick	.15	.07		317	Jimmy Key	.30	.14
146	George Brett	1.25	.55		232	Rod Beck	.30	.14		318	Greg Myers	.15	.07
147	Moises Alou	.30	.14		233	Carlos Baerga	.15	.07		319	Ken Griffey Jr.	3.00	1.35
148	Lou Whitaker	.30	.14		234	Eric Karros	.30	.14		320	Monty Fariss	.15	.07
149	Chico Walker	.15	.07		235	Jack Armstrong	.15	.07		321	Kevin Mitchell	.30	.14
150	Jerry Browne	.15	.07		236	Bobby Bonilla	.30	.14		322	Andres Galarraga	.60	.25
151	Kirk McCaskill	.15	.07		237	Don Mattingly	1.00	.45		323	Mark McGwire	1.25	.55
152	Zane Smith	.15	.07		238	Jeff Gardner	.15	.07		324	Mark Langston	.15	.07
153	Matt Young	.15	.07		239	Dave Hollins	.15	.07		325	Steve Finley	.30	.14
154	Lee Smith	.30	.14		240	Steve Cooke	.15	.07		326	Greg Maddux	2.00	.90
155	Leo Gomez	.15	.07		241	Jose Canseco	.40	.18		327	Dave Nilsson	.30	.14
156	Dan Walters	.15	.07		242	Ivan Calderon	.15	.07		328	Ozzie Smith	.75	.35
157	Pat Borders	.15	.07		243	Tim Belcher	.15	.07		329	Candy Maldonado	.15	.07
158	Matt Williams	.40	.18		244	Freddie Benavides	.15	.07		330	Checklist	.15	.07
159	Dean Palmer	.15	.07		245	Roberto Alomar	.60	.25		331	Tim Pugh	.15	.07
160	John Patterson	.15	.07		246	Rob Deer	.15	.07		332	Joe Girardi	.15	.07
161	Doug Jones	.15	.07		247	Will Clark	.40	.18		333	Junior Felix	.15	.07
162	John Habyan	.15	.07		248	Mike Felder	.15	.07		334	Greg Swindell	.15	.07
163	Pedro Martinez	.60	.25		249	Harold Baines	.30	.14		335	Ramon Martinez	.30	.14
164	Carl Willis	.15	.07		250	David Cone	.30	.14		336	Sean Berry	.15	.07
165	Darrin Fletcher	.15	.07		251	Mark Guthrie	.15	.07		337	Joe Orsulak	.15	.07
166	B.J. Surhoff	.30	.14		252	Ellis Burks	.30	.14		338	Wes Chamberlain	.15	.07
167	Eddie Murray	.60	.25		253	Jim Abbott	.30	.14		339	Stan Belinda	.15	.07
168	Keith Miller	.15	.07		254	Chili Davis	.30	.14		340	Checklist UER	.15	.07
169	Ricky Jordan	.15	.07		255	Chris Bosio	.15	.07			(306 Luis Mercedes)		
170	Juan Gonzalez	1.50	.70		256	Bret Barberie	.15	.07		341	Bruce Hurst	.15	.07
171	Charles Nagy	.30	.14		257	Hal Morris	.15	.07		342	John Burkett	.15	.07
172	Mark Clark	.15	.07		258	Dante Bichette	.40	.18		343	Mike Mussina	.60	.25
173	Bobby Thigpen	.15	.07		259	Storm Davis	.15	.07		344	Scott Fletcher	.15	.07
174	Tim Scott	.15	.07		260	Gary DiSarcina	.15	.07		345	Rene Gonzales	.15	.07
175	Scott Cooper	.15	.07		261	Ken Caminiti	.40	.18		346	Roberto Hernandez	.30	.14
176	Royce Clayton	.15	.07		262	Paul Molitor	.60	.25		347	Carlos Martinez	.15	.07
177	Brady Anderson	.40	.18		263	Joe Oliver	.15	.07		348	Bill Krueger	.15	.07
178	Sid Bream	.15	.07		264	Pat Listach	.15	.07		349	Felix Jose	.15	.07
179	Derek Bell	.30	.14		265	Gregg Jefferies	.15	.07		350	John Jaha	.30	.14
180	Otis Nixon	.15	.07		266	Jose Guzman	.15	.07		351	Willie Banks	.15	.07
181	Kevin Gross	.15	.07		267	Eric Davis	.30	.14		352	Matt Nokes	.15	.07
182	Ron Darling	.15	.07		268	Delino DeShields	.15	.07		353	Kevin Seitzer	.15	.07
183	John Wetteland	.30	.14		269	Barry Bonds	.75	.35		354	Erik Hanson	.15	.07
184	Mike Stanley	.15	.07		270	Mike Bielecki	.15	.07		355	David Hulse	.15	.07
185	Jeff Kent	.30	.14		271	Jay Buhner	.40	.18		356	Domingo Martinez	.15	.07
186	Brian Harper	.15	.07		272	Scott Pose	.15	.07		357	Greg Olson	.15	.07
187	Mariano Duncan	.15	.07		273	Tony Fernandez	.15	.07		358	Randy Myers	.30	.14
188	Robin Yount	.40	.18		274	Chito Martinez	.15	.07		359	Tom Browning	.15	.07
189	Al Martin	.30	.14		275	Phil Plantier	.15	.07		360	Charlie Hayes	.15	.07
190	Eddie Zosky	.15	.07		276	Pete Incaviglia	.15	.07		361	Bryan Harvey	.15	.07
191	Mike Munoz	.15	.07		277	Carlos Garcia	.15	.07		362	Eddie Taubensee	.15	.07
192	Andy Benes	.30	.14		278	Tom Henke	.15	.07		363	Tim Wallach	.15	.07
193	Dennis Cook	.15	.07		279	Roger Clemens	1.25	.55		364	Mel Rojas	.30	.14
194	Bill Swift	.15	.07		280	Rob Dibble	.15	.07		365	Frank Tanana	.15	.07
195	Frank Thomas	2.50	1.10		281	Daryl Boston	.15	.07		366	John Kruk	.30	.14
196	Damon Berryhill	.15	.07		282	Greg Gagne	.15	.07		367	Tim Laker	.15	.07
197	Mike Greenwell	.15	.07		283	Cecil Fielder	.30	.14		368	Rich Rodriguez	.15	.07
198	Mark Grace	.40	.18		284	Carlton Fisk	.60	.25		369	Darren Lewis	.15	.07
199	Darryl Hamilton	.15	.07		285	Wade Boggs	.60	.25		370	Harold Reynolds	.15	.07
200	Derrick May	.15	.07		286	Damion Easley	.15	.07		371	Jose Melendez	.15	.07
201	Ken Hill	.15	.07		287	Norm Charlton	.15	.07		372	Joe Grahe	.15	.07
202	Kevin Brown	.30	.14		288	Jeff Conine	.30	.14		373	Lance Johnson	.15	.07
203	Dwight Gooden	.30	.14		289	Roberto Kelly	.15	.07		374	Jose Mesa	.15	.07
204	Bobby Witt	.15	.07		290	Jerald Clark	.15	.07		375	Scott Livingstone	.15	.07
205	Juan Bell	.15	.07		291	Rickey Henderson	.40	.18		376	Wally Joyner	.30	.14
206	Kevin Maas	.15	.07		292	Chuck Finley	.15	.07		377	Kevin Reimer	.15	.07
207	Jeff King	.30	.14		293	Doug Drabek	.15	.07		378	Kirby Puckett	1.25	.55
208	Scott Leius	.15	.07		294	Dave Stewart	.30	.14		379	Paul O'Neill	.30	.14
209	Rheal Cormier	.15	.07		295	Tom Glavine	.40	.18		380	Randy Johnson	.60	.25
210	Darryl Strawberry	.30	.14		296	Jaime Navarro	.15	.07		381	Manuel Lee	.15	.07
211	Tom Gordon	.15	.07		297	Ray Lankford	.40	.18		382	Dick Schofield	.15	.07

☐ 383 Darren Holmes	.15	.07
☐ 384 Charlie Hough	.15	.07
☐ 385 John Orton	.15	.07
☐ 386 Edgar Martinez	.40	.18
☐ 387 Terry Pendleton	.30	.14
☐ 388 Dan Plesac	.15	.07
☐ 389 Jeff Reardon	.30	.14
☐ 390 David Nied	.15	.07
☐ 391 Dave Magadan	.15	.07
☐ 392 Larry Walker	.60	.25
☐ 393 Ben Rivera	.15	.07
☐ 394 Lonnie Smith	.15	.07
☐ 395 Craig Shipley	.15	.07
☐ 396 Willie McGee	.15	.07
☐ 397 Arthur Rhodes	.15	.07
☐ 398 Mike Stanton	.15	.07
☐ 399 Luis Polonia	.15	.07
☐ 400 Jack McDowell	.15	.07
☐ 401 Mike Moore	.15	.07
☐ 402 Jose Lind	.15	.07
☐ 403 Bill Spiers	.15	.07
☐ 404 Kevin Tapani	.15	.07
☐ 405 Spike Owen	.15	.07
☐ 406 Tino Martinez	.60	.25
☐ 407 Charlie Leibrandt	.15	.07
☐ 408 Ed Sprague	.15	.07
☐ 409 Bryn Smith	.15	.07
☐ 410 Benito Santiago	.15	.07
☐ 411 Jose Rijo	.15	.07
☐ 412 Pete O'Brien	.15	.07
☐ 413 Willie Wilson	.15	.07
☐ 414 Bip Roberts	.15	.07
☐ 415 Eric Young	.60	.25
☐ 416 Walt Weiss	.15	.07
☐ 417 Milt Thompson	.15	.07
☐ 418 Chris Sabo	.15	.07
☐ 419 Scott Sanderson	.15	.07
☐ 420 Tim Raines	.30	.14
☐ 421 Alan Trammell	.40	.18
☐ 422 Mike Macfarlane	.15	.07
☐ 423 Dave Winfield	.40	.18
☐ 424 Bob Wickman	.15	.07
☐ 425 David Valle	.15	.07
☐ 426 Gary Redus	.15	.07
☐ 427 Turner Ward	.15	.07
☐ 428 Reggie Sanders	.30	.14
☐ 429 Todd Worrell	.15	.07
☐ 430 Julio Valera	.15	.07
☐ 431 Cal Ripken Jr.	2.50	1.10
☐ 432 Mo Vaughn	.75	.35
☐ 433 John Smiley	.15	.07
☐ 434 Omar Vizquel	.30	.14
☐ 435 Billy Ripken	.15	.07
☐ 436 Cory Snyder	.15	.07
☐ 437 Carlos Quintana	.15	.07
☐ 438 Omar Olivares	.15	.07
☐ 439 Robin Ventura	.30	.14
☐ 440 Checklist	.15	.07
☐ 441 Kevin Higgins	.15	.07
☐ 442 Carlos Hernandez	.15	.07
☐ 443 Dan Peltier	.15	.07
☐ 444 Derek Lilliquist	.15	.07
☐ 445 Tim Salmon	.75	.35
☐ 446 Sherman Obando	.15	.07
☐ 447 Pat Kelly	.15	.07
☐ 448 Todd Van Poppel	.15	.07
☐ 449 Mark Whiten	.15	.07
☐ 450 Checklist	.15	.07
☐ 451 Pat Meares	.30	.14
☐ 452 Tony Tarasco	.15	.07
☐ 453 Chris Gwynn	.15	.07
☐ 454 Armando Reynoso	.15	.07
☐ 455 Danny Darwin	.15	.07
☐ 456 Willie Greene	.30	.14
☐ 457 Mike Blowers	.15	.07
☐ 458 Kevin Roberson	.15	.07
☐ 459 Graeme Lloyd	.15	.07
☐ 460 David West	.15	.07
☐ 461 Joey Cora	.30	.14
☐ 462 Alex Arias	.15	.07
☐ 463 Chad Kreuter	.15	.07
☐ 464 Mike Lansing	.30	.14
☐ 465 Mike Timlin	.15	.07
☐ 466 Paul Wagner	.15	.07
☐ 467 Mark Portugal	.15	.07
☐ 468 Jim Leyritz	.15	.07

☐ 469 Ryan Klesko	.75	.35
☐ 470 Mario Diaz	.15	.07
☐ 471 Guillermo Velasquez	.15	.07
☐ 472 Fernando Valenzuela	.30	.14
☐ 473 Raul Mondesi	.75	.35
☐ 474 Mike Pagliarulo	.15	.07
☐ 475 Chris Hammond	.15	.07
☐ 476 Torey Lovullo	.15	.07
☐ 477 Trevor Wilson	.15	.07
☐ 478 Marcos Armas	.15	.07
☐ 479 Dave Gallagher	.15	.07
☐ 480 Jeff Treadway	.15	.07
☐ 481 Jeff Branson	.15	.07
☐ 482 Dickie Thon	.15	.07
☐ 483 Eduardo Perez	.15	.07
☐ 484 David Wells	.15	.07
☐ 485 Brian Williams	.15	.07
☐ 486 Domingo Cedeno	.15	.07
☐ 487 Tom Candiotti	.15	.07
☐ 488 Steve Frey	.15	.07
☐ 489 Greg McMichael	.15	.07
☐ 490 Marc Newfield	.30	.14
☐ 491 Larry Andersen	.15	.07
☐ 492 Damon Buford	.15	.07
☐ 493 Ricky Gutierrez	.15	.07
☐ 494 Jeff Russell	.15	.07
☐ 495 Vinny Castilla	.60	.25
☐ 496 Wilson Alvarez	.30	.14
☐ 497 Scott Bullett	.15	.07
☐ 498 Larry Casian	.15	.07
☐ 499 Jose Vizcaino	.15	.07
☐ 500 J.T. Snow	.75	.35
☐ 501 Bryan Hickerson	.15	.07
☐ 502 Jeremy Hernandez	.15	.07
☐ 503 Jeromy Burnitz	.15	.07
☐ 504 Steve Farr	.15	.07
☐ 505 S. Owens	.15	.07
☐ 506 Craig Paquette	.15	.07
☐ 507 Jim Eisenreich	.15	.07
☐ 508 Matt Whiteside	.15	.07
☐ 509 Luis Aquino	.15	.07
☐ 510 Mike LaValliere	.15	.07
☐ 511 Jim Gott	.15	.07
☐ 512 Mark McLemore	.15	.07
☐ 513 Randy Milligan	.15	.07
☐ 514 Gary Gaetti	.15	.07
☐ 515 Lou Frazier	.15	.07
☐ 516 Rich Amaral	.15	.07
☐ 517 Gene Harris	.15	.07
☐ 518 Aaron Sele	.30	.14
☐ 519 Mark Wohlers	.30	.14
☐ 520 Scott Kamieniecki	.15	.07
☐ 521 Kent Mercker	.15	.07
☐ 522 Jim Deshaies	.15	.07
☐ 523 Kevin Stocker	.15	.07
☐ 524 Jason Bere	.30	.14
☐ 525 Tim Bogar	.15	.07
☐ 526 Brad Pennington	.15	.07
☐ 527 Curt Leskanic	.15	.07
☐ 528 Wayne Kirby	.15	.07
☐ 529 Tim Costo	.15	.07
☐ 530 Doug Henry	.15	.07
☐ 531 Trevor Hoffman	.40	.18
☐ 532 Kelly Gruber	.15	.07
☐ 533 Mike Harkey	.15	.07
☐ 534 John Doherty	.15	.07
☐ 535 Erik Pappas	.15	.07
☐ 536 Brent Gates	.15	.07
☐ 537 Roger McDowell	.15	.07
☐ 538 Chris Haney	.15	.07
☐ 539 Blas Minor	.15	.07
☐ 540 Pat Hentgen	.40	.18
☐ 541 Chuck Carr	.15	.07
☐ 542 Doug Strange	.15	.07
☐ 543 Xavier Hernandez	.15	.07
☐ 544 Paul Quantrill	.15	.07
☐ 545 Anthony Young	.15	.07
☐ 546 Bret Boone	.15	.07
☐ 547 Dwight Smith	.15	.07
☐ 548 Bobby Munoz	.15	.07
☐ 549 Russ Springer	.15	.07
☐ 550 Roger Pavlik	.15	.07
☐ DW Dave Winfield 3000 Hits	1.00	.45
☐ FT Frank Thomas AU/3500 (Certified autograph)	200.00	90.00

1993 Leaf Fasttrack

These 20 standard-size cards, featuring a selection of talented young stars, were randomly inserted into 1993 Leaf retail packs; the first ten were series I inserts, the second ten were series II inserts. The fronts feature borderless color player action photos, except in the lower right corner, where an oblique white stripe carries the motion-streaked set title.

	MINT	NRMT
COMPLETE SET (20)	100.00	45.00
COMPLETE SERIES 1 (10)	60.00	27.00
COMPLETE SERIES 2 (10)	40.00	18.00
COMMON CARD (1-20)	2.00	.90
RANDOM INSERTS IN RETAIL PACKS		
☐ 1 Frank Thomas	30.00	13.50
☐ 2 Tim Wakefield	2.00	.90
☐ 3 Kenny Lofton	15.00	6.75
☐ 4 Mike Mussina	8.00	3.60
☐ 5 Juan Gonzalez	20.00	9.00
☐ 6 Chuck Knoblauch	6.00	2.70
☐ 7 Eric Karros	3.00	1.35
☐ 8 Ray Lankford	5.00	2.20
☐ 9 Juan Guzman	2.00	.90
☐ 10 Pat Listach	2.00	.90
☐ 11 Carlos Baerga	2.00	.90
☐ 12 Felix Jose	2.00	.90
☐ 13 Steve Avery	2.00	.90
☐ 14 Robin Ventura	3.00	1.35
☐ 15 Ivan Rodriguez	10.00	4.50
☐ 16 Cal Eldred	2.00	.90
☐ 17 Jeff Bagwell	15.00	6.75
☐ 18 David Justice	6.00	2.70
☐ 19 Travis Fryman	3.00	1.35
☐ 20 Marquis Grissom	3.00	1.35

1993 Leaf Gold All-Stars

These 30 standard-size dual-sided cards feature members of the American and National league All-Star squads. The first 20 were inserted one per 1993 Leaf jumbo packs; the first ten were series I inserts, the second ten were series II inserts. The final ten cards were randomly inserted in 1993 Leaf Update packs. The card design features full color action photos with a diagonal stripe at the base.

	MINT	NRMT
COMPLETE REG.SET (20) ..	40.00	18.00
COMPLETE UPDATE SET (10)	12.00	5.50
COMMON CARD (R1-U10)......	.50	.23
SEMISTARS	1.00	.45

R1-R20 ONE PER JUMBO PACK
U1-U10 INSERTS IN UPDATE PACKS

			MINT	NRMT
☐	R1	Ivan Rodriguez	.75	.35
		Darren Daulton		
☐	R2	Don Mattingly	1.50	.70
		Fred McGriff		
☐	R3	Cecil Fielder	2.00	.90
		Jeff Bagwell		
☐	R4	Carlos Baerga	1.50	.70
		Ryne Sandberg		
☐	R5	Chuck Knoblauch	1.00	.45
		Delino DeShields		
☐	R6	Robin Ventura........	.50	.23
		Terry Pendleton		
☐	R7	Ken Griffey Jr.	5.00	2.20
		Andy Van Slyke		
☐	R8	Joe Carter	.75	.35
		Dave Justice		
☐	R9	Jose Canseco	2.50	1.10
		Tony Gwynn		
☐	R10	Dennis Eckersley.....	.50	.23
		Rob Dibble		
☐	R11	Mark McGwire	2.00	.90
		Will Clark		
☐	R12	Frank Thomas.....	4.00	1.80
		Mark Grace		
☐	R13	Roberto Alomar	1.50	.70
		Craig Biggio		
☐	R14	Cal Ripken...........	4.00	1.80
		Barry Larkin		
☐	R15	Edgar Martinez	1.00	.45
		Gary Sheffield		
☐	R16	Juan Gonzalez.........	2.50	1.10
		Barry Bonds		
☐	R17	Kirby Puckett	2.00	.90
		Marquis Grissom		
☐	R18	Jim Abbott	.75	.35
		Tom Glavine		
☐	R19	Nolan Ryan	8.00	3.60
		Greg Maddux		
☐	R20	Roger Clemens	1.00	.45
		Doug Drabek		
☐	U1	Mark Langston	.50	.23
		Terry Mulholland		
☐	U2	Ivan Rodriguez	.75	.35
		Darren Daulton		
☐	U3	John Olerud	.50	.23
		John Kruk		
☐	U4	Roberto Alomar	1.50	.70
		Ryne Sandberg		
☐	U5	Wade Boggs	1.50	.70
		Gary Sheffield		
☐	U6	Cal Ripken............	4.00	1.80
		Barry Larkin		
☐	U7	Kirby Puckett	2.50	1.10
		Barry Bonds		
☐	U8	Ken Griffey Jr.	5.00	2.20
		Marquis Grissom		
☐	U9	Joe Carter	1.00	.45
		David Justice		
☐	U10	Paul Molitor	1.00	.45
		Mark Grace		

1993 Leaf Gold Rookies

These cards of promising new-comers were randomly inserted into 1993 Leaf packs; the first ten in series I, the last ten in series II, and five in the Update product. The front of each standard-size card features a borderless color player action shot. The player's name appears in white cursive lettering within a wide gray lithic stripe near the bottom, which is set off by gold-foil lines and carries the set's title in simulated bas-relief. Leaf produced jumbo (3 1/2 by 5 inch) versions for retail repacks; they are valued at approximately double the prices below.

	MINT	NRMT
COMPLETE REG.SET (20) ..	40.00	18.00
COMPLETE UPDATE SET (5)	20.00	9.00
COMMON CARD (R1-U5)......	1.00	.45
SEMISTARS	1.50	.70

R1-R20 INSERTS IN HOBBY FOIL PACKS
U1-U5 INSERTS IN UPDATE PACKS

			MINT	NRMT
☐	R1	Kevin Young	1.25	.55
☐	R2	Wil Cordero............	1.00	.45
☐	R3	Mark Kiefer	1.00	.45
☐	R4	Gerald Williams.......	1.00	.45
☐	R5	Brandon Wilson	1.00	.45
☐	R6	Greg Gohr.............	1.00	.45
☐	R7	Ryan Thompson	1.00	.45
☐	R8	Tim Wakefield	1.25	.55
☐	R9	Troy Neel	1.00	.45
☐	R10	Tim Salmon	8.00	3.60
☐	R11	Kevin Rogers	1.00	.45
☐	R12	Rod Bolton	1.00	.45
☐	R13	Ken Ryan	1.00	.45
☐	R14	Phil Hiatt	1.00	.45
☐	R15	Rene Arocha	1.00	.45
☐	R16	Nigel Wilson	1.00	.45
☐	R17	J.T. Snow	3.00	1.35
☐	R18	Benji Gil	1.00	.45
☐	R19	Chipper Jones	20.00	9.00
☐	R20	Darrell Sherman	1.00	.45
☐	U1	Allen Watson...........	1.00	.45
☐	U2	Jeffrey Hammonds	1.50	.70
☐	U3	Dave McCarty	1.00	.45
☐	U4	Mike Piazza	15.00	6.75
☐	U5	Roberto Mejia	1.00	.45

1993 Leaf Heading for the Hall

Randomly inserted into 1993 Leaf series 1 and 2 packs, this ten-card standard-size set features potential Hall of Famers. Cards 1-5 were series I inserts and cards 6-10 were series II

inserts. The fronts feature borderless color player action shots, with the player's name appearing within a lithic banner near the bottom, below the set's logo.

	MINT	NRMT
COMPLETE SET (10)	30.00	13.50
COMPLETE SERIES 1 (5)	20.00	9.00
COMPLETE SERIES 2 (5)	10.00	4.50
COMMON CARD (1-10)	2.50	1.10

RANDOM INSERTS IN PACKS ..

			MINT	NRMT
☐	1	Nolan Ryan	10.00	4.50
☐	2	Tony Gwynn	6.00	2.70
☐	3	Robin Yount	2.50	1.10
☐	4	Eddie Murray	3.00	1.35
☐	5	Cal Ripken...........	10.00	4.50
☐	6	Roger Clemens	5.00	2.20
☐	7	George Brett	3.00	1.35
☐	8	Ryne Sandberg	3.00	1.35
☐	9	Kirby Puckett.........	5.00	2.20
☐	10	Ozzie Smith	3.00	1.35

1994 Leaf

The 1994 Leaf baseball set consists of two series of 220 standard-size cards for a total of 440. Certain "Super Packs" contained complete insert sets. The fronts feature color action player photos, with team color-coded designs on the bottom. The player's name and the Leaf logo are foil stamped, the team name appears under the player's name. The backs carry a photo of the player's home stadium in the background with a silhouetted photo of the player in the foreground. Additionally, a headshot appears in a ticket stub-like design with biographical information, while player statistics appear on the bottom. Cards featuring players from the Texas Rangers, Cleveland Indians, Milwaukee Brewers

*and Houston Astros were held
out of the first series in order to
have up-to-date photography in
each team's new uniforms. A
limited number of players from
the San Francisco Giants are
featured in the first series
because of minor modifications
to the team's uniforms.
Randomly inserted in hobby
packs at a rate of one in 36 was
a stamped version of Frank
Thomas' 1990 Leaf rookie card.*

	MINT	NRMT
COMPLETE SET (440)	24.00	11.00
COMPLETE SERIES 1 (220)	12.00	5.50
COMPLETE SERIES 2 (220)	12.00	5.50
COMMON CARD (1-440)	.15	.07
MINOR STARS	.30	.14
UNLISTED STARS	.60	.25
THOMAS ANN. STATED ODDS 1:36		

☐ 1 Cal Ripken Jr.	2.50		1.10
☐ 2 Tony Tarasco	.15		.07
☐ 3 Joe Girardi	.15		.07
☐ 4 Bernie Williams	.60		.25
☐ 5 Chad Kreuter	.15		.07
☐ 6 Troy Neel	.15		.07
☐ 7 Tom Pagnozzi	.15		.07
☐ 8 Kirk Rueter	.15		.07
☐ 9 Chris Bosio	.15		.07
☐ 10 Dwight Gooden	.30		.14
☐ 11 Mariano Duncan	.15		.07
☐ 12 Jay Bell	.30		.14
☐ 13 Lance Johnson	.15		.07
☐ 14 Richie Lewis	.15		.07
☐ 15 Dave Martinez	.15		.07
☐ 16 Orel Hershiser	.30		.14
☐ 17 Rob Butler	.15		.07
☐ 18 Glenallen Hill	.15		.07
☐ 19 Chad Curtis	.15		.07
☐ 20 Mike Stanton	.15		.07
☐ 21 Tim Wallach	.15		.07
☐ 22 Milt Thompson	.15		.07
☐ 23 Kevin Young	.15		.07
☐ 24 John Smiley	.15		.07
☐ 25 Jeff Montgomery	.15		.07
☐ 26 Robin Ventura	.30		.14
☐ 27 Scott Lydy	.15		.07
☐ 28 Todd Stottlemyre	.15		.07
☐ 29 Mark Whiten	.15		.07
☐ 30 Robby Thompson	.15		.07
☐ 31 Bobby Bonilla	.30		.14
☐ 32 Andy Ashby	.15		.07
☐ 33 Greg Myers	.15		.07
☐ 34 Billy Hatcher	.15		.07
☐ 35 Brad Holman	.15		.07
☐ 36 Mark McLemore	.15		.07
☐ 37 Scott Sanders	.15		.07
☐ 38 Jim Abbott	.15		.07
☐ 39 David Wells	.15		.07
☐ 40 Roberto Kelly	.15		.07
☐ 41 Jeff Conine	.30		.14
☐ 42 Sean Berry	.15		.07
☐ 43 Mark Grace	.40		.18
☐ 44 Eric Young	.15		.07
☐ 45 Rick Aguilera	.15		.07
☐ 46 Chipper Jones	2.00		.90
☐ 47 Mel Rojas	.15		.07
☐ 48 Ryan Thompson	.15		.07
☐ 49 Al Martin	.15		.07
☐ 50 Cecil Fielder	.30		.14
☐ 51 Pat Kelly	.15		.07
☐ 52 Kevin Tapani	.15		.07
☐ 53 Tim Costo	.15		.07
☐ 54 Dave Hollins	.15		.07
☐ 55 Kirt Manwaring	.15		.07
☐ 56 Gregg Jefferies	.15		.07
☐ 57 Ron Darling	.15		.07
☐ 58 Bill Haselman	.15		.07
☐ 59 Phil Plantier	.15		.07
☐ 60 Frank Viola	.15		.07
☐ 61 Todd Zeile	.15		.07
☐ 62 Bret Barberie	.15		.07
☐ 63 Roberto Mejia	.15		.07
☐ 64 Chuck Knoblauch	.60		.25
☐ 65 Jose Lind	.15		.07
☐ 66 Brady Anderson	.40		.18
☐ 67 Ruben Sierra	.15		.07
☐ 68 Jose Vizcaino	.15		.07
☐ 69 Joe Grahe	.15		.07
☐ 70 Kevin Appier	.30		.14
☐ 71 Wilson Alvarez	.15		.07
☐ 72 Tom Candiotti	.15		.07
☐ 73 John Burkett	.15		.07
☐ 74 Anthony Young	.15		.07
☐ 75 Scott Cooper	.15		.07
☐ 76 Nigel Wilson	.15		.07
☐ 77 John Valentin	.30		.14
☐ 78 Dave McCarty	.15		.07
☐ 79 Archi Cianfrocco	.15		.07
☐ 80 Lou Whitaker	.30		.14
☐ 81 Dante Bichette	.30		.14
☐ 82 Mark Dewey	.15		.07
☐ 83 Danny Jackson	.15		.07
☐ 84 Harold Baines	.30		.14
☐ 85 Todd Benzinger	.15		.07
☐ 86 Damion Easley	.15		.07
☐ 87 Danny Cox	.15		.07
☐ 88 Jose Bautista	.15		.07
☐ 89 Mike Lansing	.30		.14
☐ 90 Phil Hiatt	.15		.07
☐ 91 Tim Pugh	.15		.07
☐ 92 Tino Martinez	.60		.25
☐ 93 Raul Mondesi	.60		.25
☐ 94 Greg Maddux	2.00		.90
☐ 95 Al Leiter	.15		.07
☐ 96 Benito Santiago	.15		.07
☐ 97 Lenny Dykstra	.30		.14
☐ 98 Sammy Sosa	.60		.25
☐ 99 Tim Bogar	.15		.07
☐ 100 Checklist	.15		.07
☐ 101 Deion Sanders	.30		.14
☐ 102 Bobby Witt	.15		.07
☐ 103 Wil Cordero	.15		.07
☐ 104 Rich Amaral	.15		.07
☐ 105 Mike Mussina	.60		.25
☐ 106 Reggie Sanders	.15		.07
☐ 107 Ozzie Guillen	.15		.07
☐ 108 Paul O'Neill	.30		.14
☐ 109 Tim Salmon	.60		.25
☐ 110 Rheal Cormier	.15		.07
☐ 111 Billy Ashley	.15		.07
☐ 112 Jeff Kent	.15		.07
☐ 113 Derek Bell	.15		.07
☐ 114 Danny Darwin	.15		.07
☐ 115 Chip Hale	.15		.07
☐ 116 Tim Raines	.30		.14
☐ 117 Ed Sprague	.15		.07
☐ 118 Darrin Fletcher	.15		.07
☐ 119 Darren Holmes	.15		.07
☐ 120 Alan Trammell	.40		.18
☐ 121 Don Mattingly	1.00		.45
☐ 122 Greg Gagne	.15		.07
☐ 123 Jose Offerman	.15		.07
☐ 124 Joe Orsulak	.15		.07
☐ 125 Jack McDowell	.15		.07
☐ 126 Barry Larkin	.40		.18
☐ 127 Ben McDonald	.15		.07
☐ 128 Mike Bordick	.15		.07
☐ 129 Devon White	.15		.07
☐ 130 Mike Perez	.15		.07
☐ 131 Jay Buhner	.40		.18
☐ 132 Phil Leftwich	.15		.07
☐ 133 Tommy Greene	.15		.07
☐ 134 Charlie Hayes	.15		.07
☐ 135 Don Slaught	.15		.07
☐ 136 Mike Gallego	.15		.07
☐ 137 Dave Winfield	.40		.18
☐ 138 Steve Avery	.15		.07
☐ 139 Derrick May	.15		.07
☐ 140 Bryan Harvey	.15		.07
☐ 141 Wally Joyner	.30		.14
☐ 142 Andre Dawson	.40		.18
☐ 143 Andy Benes	.30		.14
☐ 144 John Franco	.30		.14
☐ 145 Jeff King	.15		.07
☐ 146 Joe Oliver	.15		.07
☐ 147 Bill Gullickson	.15		.07
☐ 148 Armando Reynoso	.15		.07
☐ 149 Dave Fleming	.15		.07
☐ 150 Checklist	.15		.07
☐ 151 Todd Van Poppel	.15		.07
☐ 152 Bernard Gilkey	.15		.07
☐ 153 Kevin Gross	.15		.07
☐ 154 Mike Devereaux	.15		.07
☐ 155 Tim Wakefield	.15		.07
☐ 156 Andres Galarraga	.60		.25
☐ 157 Pat Meares	.15		.07
☐ 158 Jim Leyritz	.15		.07
☐ 159 Mike Macfarlane	.15		.07
☐ 160 Tony Phillips	.15		.07
☐ 161 Brent Gates	.15		.07
☐ 162 Mark Langston	.15		.07
☐ 163 Allen Watson	.15		.07
☐ 164 Randy Johnson	.60		.25
☐ 165 Doug Brocail	.15		.07
☐ 166 Rob Dibble	.15		.07
☐ 167 Roberto Hernandez	.15		.07
☐ 168 Felix Jose	.15		.07
☐ 169 Steve Cooke	.15		.07
☐ 170 Darren Daulton	.30		.14
☐ 171 Eric Karros	.30		.14
☐ 172 Geronimo Pena	.15		.07
☐ 173 Gary DiSarcina	.15		.07
☐ 174 Marquis Grissom	.30		.14
☐ 175 Joey Cora	.30		.14
☐ 176 Jim Eisenreich	.15		.07
☐ 177 Brad Pennington	.15		.07
☐ 178 Terry Steinbach	.15		.07
☐ 179 Pat Borders	.15		.07
☐ 180 Steve Buechele	.15		.07
☐ 181 Jeff Fassero	.15		.07
☐ 182 Mike Greenwell	.15		.07
☐ 183 Mike Henneman	.15		.07
☐ 184 Ron Karkovice	.15		.07
☐ 185 Pat Hentgen	.30		.14
☐ 186 Jose Guzman	.15		.07
☐ 187 Brett Butler	.30		.14
☐ 188 Charlie Hough	.15		.07
☐ 189 Terry Pendleton	.15		.07
☐ 190 Melido Perez	.15		.07
☐ 191 Orestes Destrade	.15		.07
☐ 192 Mike Morgan	.15		.07
☐ 193 Joe Carter	.30		.14
☐ 194 Jeff Blauser	.30		.14
☐ 195 Chris Hoiles	.15		.07
☐ 196 Ricky Gutierrez	.15		.07
☐ 197 Mike Moore	.15		.07
☐ 198 Carl Willis	.15		.07
☐ 199 Aaron Sele	.15		.07
☐ 200 Checklist	.15		.07
☐ 201 Tim Naehring	.15		.07
☐ 202 Scott Livingstone	.15		.07
☐ 203 Luis Alicea	.15		.07
☐ 204 Torey Lovullo	.15		.07
☐ 205 Jim Gott	.15		.07
☐ 206 Bob Wickman	.15		.07
☐ 207 Greg McMichael	.15		.07
☐ 208 Scott Brosius	.15		.07
☐ 209 Chris Gwynn	.15		.07
☐ 210 Steve Sax	.15		.07
☐ 211 Dick Schofield	.15		.07
☐ 212 Robb Nen	.15		.07
☐ 213 Ben Rivera	.15		.07
☐ 214 Vinny Castilla	.30		.14
☐ 215 Jamie Moyer	.15		.07
☐ 216 Wally Whitehurst	.15		.07
☐ 217 Frank Castillo	.15		.07
☐ 218 Mike Blowers	.15		.07
☐ 219 Tim Scott	.15		.07
☐ 220 Paul Wagner	.15		.07
☐ 221 Jeff Bagwell	1.25		.55
☐ 222 Ricky Bones	.15		.07
☐ 223 Sandy Alomar Jr.	.30		.14
☐ 224 Rod Beck	.15		.07
☐ 225 Roberto Alomar	.60		.25
☐ 226 Jack Armstrong	.15		.07
☐ 227 Scott Erickson	.15		.07
☐ 228 Rene Arocha	.15		.07
☐ 229 Eric Anthony	.15		.07
☐ 230 Jeromy Burnitz	.15		.07
☐ 231 Kevin Brown	.30		.14
☐ 232 Tim Belcher	.15		.07
☐ 233 Bret Boone	.15		.07
☐ 234 Dennis Eckersley	.30		.14
☐ 235 Tom Glavine	.30		.14

☐ 236 Craig Biggio	.40		.18
☐ 237 Pedro Astacio	.15		.07
☐ 238 Ryan Bowen	.15		.07
☐ 239 Brad Ausmus	.15		.07
☐ 240 Vince Coleman	.15		.07
☐ 241 Jason Bere	.15		.07
☐ 242 Ellis Burks	.30		.14
☐ 243 Wes Chamberlain	.15		.07
☐ 244 Ken Caminiti	.40		.18
☐ 245 Willie Banks	.15		.07
☐ 246 Sid Fernandez	.15		.07
☐ 247 Carlos Baerga	.15		.07
☐ 248 Carlos Garcia	.15		.07
☐ 249 Jose Canseco	.40		.18
☐ 250 Alex Diaz	.15		.07
☐ 251 Albert Belle	.75		.35
☐ 252 Moises Alou	.30		.14
☐ 253 Bobby Ayala	.15		.07
☐ 254 Tony Gwynn	1.50		.70
☐ 255 Roger Clemens	1.25		.55
☐ 256 Eric Davis	.30		.14
☐ 257 Wade Boggs	.60		.25
☐ 258 Chili Davis	.15		.14
☐ 259 Rickey Henderson	.40		.18
☐ 260 Andujar Cedeno	.15		.07
☐ 261 Cris Carpenter	.15		.07
☐ 262 Juan Guzman	.15		.07
☐ 263 David Justice	.60		.25
☐ 264 Barry Bonds	.75		.07
☐ 265 Pete Incaviglia	.15		.07
☐ 266 Tony Fernandez	.15		.07
☐ 267 Cal Eldred	.15		.07
☐ 268 Alex Fernandez	.15		.07
☐ 269 Kent Hrbek	.30		.14
☐ 270 Steve Farr	.15		.07
☐ 271 Doug Drabek	.15		.07
☐ 272 Brian Jordan	.30		.14
☐ 273 Xavier Hernandez	.15		.07
☐ 274 David Cone	.30		.14
☐ 275 Brian Hunter	.15		.07
☐ 276 Mike Harkey	.15		.07
☐ 277 Delino DeShields	.15		.07
☐ 278 David Hulse	.15		.07
☐ 279 Mickey Tettleton	.15		.07
☐ 280 Kevin McReynolds	.15		.07
☐ 281 Darryl Hamilton	.15		.07
☐ 282 Ken Hill	.15		.07
☐ 283 Wayne Kirby	.15		.07
☐ 284 Chris Hammond	.15		.07
☐ 285 Mo Vaughn	.75		.35
☐ 286 Ryan Klesko	.60		.25
☐ 287 Rick Wilkins	.15		.07
☐ 288 Bill Swift	.15		.07
☐ 289 Rafael Palmeiro	.40		.18
☐ 290 Brian Harper	.15		.07
☐ 291 Chris Turner	.15		.07
☐ 292 Luis Gonzalez	.15		.07
☐ 293 Kenny Rogers	.15		.07
☐ 294 Kirby Puckett	1.25		.55
☐ 295 Mike Stanley	.15		.07
☐ 296 Carlos Reyes	.15		.07
☐ 297 Charles Nagy	.30		.14
☐ 298 Reggie Jefferson	.15		.07
☐ 299 Bip Roberts	.15		.07
☐ 300 Darrin Jackson	.15		.07
☐ 301 Mike Jackson	.15		.07
☐ 302 Dave Nilsson	.15		.07
☐ 303 Ramon Martinez	.30		.14
☐ 304 Bobby Jones	.30		.14
☐ 305 Johnny Ruffin	.15		.07
☐ 306 Brian McRae	.15		.07
☐ 307 Bo Jackson	.30		.14
☐ 308 Dave Stewart	.30		.14
☐ 309 John Smoltz	.30		.14
☐ 310 Dennis Martinez	.30		.14
☐ 311 Dean Palmer	.15		.07
☐ 312 David Nied	.15		.07
☐ 313 Eddie Murray	.60		.25
☐ 314 Darryl Kile	.30		.14
☐ 315 Rick Sutcliffe	.15		.07
☐ 316 Shawon Dunston	.15		.07
☐ 317 John Jaha	.15		.07
☐ 318 Salomon Torres	.15		.07
☐ 319 Gary Sheffield	.60		.25
☐ 320 Curt Schilling	.30		.14
☐ 321 Greg Vaughn	.15		.07

☐ 322 Jay Howell	.15		.07
☐ 323 Todd Hundley	.15		.14
☐ 324 Chris Sabo	.15		.07
☐ 325 Stan Javier	.15		.07
☐ 326 Willie Greene	.15		.07
☐ 327 Hipolito Pichardo	.15		.07
☐ 328 Doug Strange	.15		.07
☐ 329 Dan Wilson	.30		.14
☐ 330 Checklist	.15		.07
☐ 331 Omar Vizquel	.30		.14
☐ 332 Scott Servais	.15		.07
☐ 333 Bob Tewksbury	.15		.07
☐ 334 Matt Williams	.40		.18
☐ 335 Tom Foley	.15		.07
☐ 336 Jeff Russell	.15		.07
☐ 337 Scott Leius	.15		.07
☐ 338 Ivan Rodriguez	.75		.35
☐ 339 Kevin Seitzer	.15		.07
☐ 340 Jose Rijo	.15		.07
☐ 341 Eduardo Perez	.15		.07
☐ 342 Kirk Gibson	.30		.14
☐ 343 Randy Milligan	.15		.07
☐ 344 Edgar Martinez	.40		.18
☐ 345 Fred McGriff	.40		.18
☐ 346 Kurt Abbott	.15		.07
☐ 347 John Kruk	.30		.14
☐ 348 Mike Felder	.15		.07
☐ 349 Dave Staton	.15		.07
☐ 350 Kenny Lofton	.75		.35
☐ 351 Graeme Lloyd	.15		.07
☐ 352 David Segui	.15		.07
☐ 353 Danny Tartabull	.15		.07
☐ 354 Bob Welch	.15		.07
☐ 355 Duane Ward	.15		.07
☐ 356 Karl Rhodes	.15		.07
☐ 357 Lee Smith	.30		.14
☐ 358 Chris James	.15		.07
☐ 359 Walt Weiss	.15		.07
☐ 360 Pedro Munoz	.15		.07
☐ 361 Paul Sorrento	.15		.07
☐ 362 Todd Worrell	.15		.07
☐ 363 Bob Hamelin	.15		.07
☐ 364 Julio Franco	.15		.07
☐ 365 Roberto Petagine	.15		.07
☐ 366 Willie McGee	.15		.07
☐ 367 Pedro Martinez	.60		.25
☐ 368 Ken Griffey Jr.	3.00		1.35
☐ 369 B.J. Surhoff	.15		.07
☐ 370 Kevin Mitchell	.15		.07
☐ 371 John Doherty	.15		.07
☐ 372 Manuel Lee	.15		.07
☐ 373 Terry Mulholland	.15		.07
☐ 374 Zane Smith	.15		.07
☐ 375 Otis Nixon	.15		.07
☐ 376 Jody Reed	.15		.07
☐ 377 Doug Jones	.15		.07
☐ 378 John Olerud	.30		.14
☐ 379 Greg Swindell	.15		.07
☐ 380 Checklist	.15		.07
☐ 381 Royce Clayton	.15		.07
☐ 382 Jim Thome	.75		.35
☐ 383 Steve Finley	.15		.07
☐ 384 Ray Lankford	.30		.14
☐ 385 Henry Rodriguez	.15		.07
☐ 386 Dave Magadan	.15		.07
☐ 387 Gary Redus	.15		.07
☐ 388 Orlando Merced	.15		.07
☐ 389 Tom Gordon	.15		.07
☐ 390 Luis Polonia	.15		.07
☐ 391 Mark McGwire	1.25		.55
☐ 392 Mark Lemke	.15		.07
☐ 393 Doug Henry	.15		.07
☐ 394 Chuck Finley	.15		.07
☐ 395 Paul Molitor	.60		.25
☐ 396 Randy Myers	.15		.07
☐ 397 Larry Walker	.60		.25
☐ 398 Pete Harnisch	.15		.07
☐ 399 Darren Lewis	.15		.07
☐ 400 Frank Thomas	2.50		1.10
☐ 401 Jack Morris	.30		.14
☐ 402 Greg Hibbard	.15		.07
☐ 403 Jeffrey Hammonds	.30		.14
☐ 404 Will Clark	.40		.18
☐ 405 Travis Fryman	.30		.14
☐ 406 Scott Sanderson	.15		.07
☐ 407 Gene Harris	.15		.07

☐ 408 Chuck Carr	.15		.07
☐ 409 Ozzie Smith	.75		.35
☐ 410 Kent Mercker	.15		.07
☐ 411 Andy Van Slyke	.30		.14
☐ 412 Jimmy Key	.30		.14
☐ 413 Pat Mahomes	.15		.07
☐ 414 John Wetteland	.15		.07
☐ 415 Todd Jones	.15		.07
☐ 416 Greg Harris	.15		.07
☐ 417 Kevin Stocker	.15		.07
☐ 418 Juan Gonzalez	1.50		.70
☐ 419 Pete Smith	.15		.07
☐ 420 Pat Listach	.15		.07
☐ 421 Trevor Hoffman	.15		.07
☐ 422 Scott Fletcher	.15		.07
☐ 423 Mark Lewis	.15		.07
☐ 424 Mickey Morandini	.15		.07
☐ 425 Ryne Sandberg	.75		.35
☐ 426 Erik Hanson	.15		.07
☐ 427 Gary Gaetti	.15		.07
☐ 428 Harold Reynolds	.15		.07
☐ 429 Mark Portugal	.15		.07
☐ 430 David Valle	.15		.07
☐ 431 Mitch Williams	.15		.07
☐ 432 Howard Johnson	.15		.07
☐ 433 Hal Morris	.15		.07
☐ 434 Tom Henke	.15		.07
☐ 435 Shane Mack	.15		.07
☐ 436 Mike Piazza	2.00		.90
☐ 437 Bret Saberhagen	.15		.07
☐ 438 Jose Mesa	.15		.07
☐ 439 Jaime Navarro	.15		.07
☐ 440 Checklist	.15		.07
☐ A300 Frank Thomas	2.50		1.10
Leaf 5th Anniversary			

1994 Leaf Clean-Up Crew

Inserted in magazine jumbo packs at a rate of one in 12, this 12-card set was issued in two series of six. Full-bleed fronts contain an action photo with the Clean-Up Crew logo at bottom right and the player's name in a colored band toward bottom left. The backs contain a photo and 1993 statistics when batting fourth. The home plate area serves as background.

	MINT	NRMT
COMPLETE SET (12)	60.00	27.00
COMPLETE SERIES 1 (6)	10.00	4.50
COMPLETE SERIES 2 (6)	50.00	22.00
COMMON CARD (1-12)	3.00	1.35
SEMISTARS	6.00	2.70
UNLISTED STARS	10.00	4.50
STATED ODDS 1:12 MAG-JUMBOS		

☐ 1 Larry Walker	10.00		4.50
☐ 2 Andres Galarraga	10.00		4.50
☐ 3 Dave Hollins	3.00		1.35
☐ 4 Bobby Bonilla	4.00		1.80
☐ 5 Cecil Fielder	4.00		1.80

☐ 6 Danny Tartabull	3.00	1.35
☐ 7 Juan Gonzalez	25.00	11.00
☐ 8 Joe Carter	4.00	1.80
☐ 9 Fred McGriff	6.00	2.70
☐ 10 Matt Williams	6.00	2.70
☐ 11 Albert Belle	12.00	5.50
☐ 12 Harold Baines	4.00	1.80

1994 Leaf Gamers

A close-up photo of the player highlights this 12-card standard-size set that was issued in two series of six. They were randomly inserted in jumbo packs at a rate of one in eight. The player's name appears at the top of the photo with the Leaf Gamers hologram logo at the bottom. The backs feature a variety of color photos including a frame by frame series resembling a film strip. There is also a small write-up.

	MINT	NRMT
COMPLETE SET (12)	150.00	70.00
COMPLETE SERIES 1 (6)	70.00	32.00
COMPLETE SERIES 2 (6)	80.00	36.00
COMMON CARD (1-12)	2.50	1.10
SEMISTARS	5.00	2.20
UNLISTED STARS	8.00	3.60
STATED ODDS 1:8 JUMBO		

☐ 1 Ken Griffey Jr.	40.00	18.00
☐ 2 Lenny Dykstra	4.00	1.80
☐ 3 Juan Gonzalez	20.00	9.00
☐ 4 Don Mattingly	12.00	5.50
☐ 5 David Justice	8.00	3.60
☐ 6 Mark Grace	5.00	2.20
☐ 7 Frank Thomas	30.00	13.50
☐ 8 Barry Bonds	10.00	4.50
☐ 9 Kirby Puckett	15.00	6.75
☐ 10 Will Clark	5.00	2.20
☐ 11 John Kruk	4.00	1.80
☐ 12 Mike Piazza	25.00	11.00

1994 Leaf Gold Rookies

This set, which was randomly inserted in first series packs at a rate of one in 18 and second series packs at a rate of one in twelve, features 20 of the hottest young stars in the majors. A color player cutout is layed over a dark brownish background that contains "94 Gold Leaf Rookie." The player's name and team appear at the bottom in silver. Horizontal backs include career highlights and two photos.

	MINT	NRMT
COMPLETE SET (20)	16.00	7.25
COMPLETE SERIES 1 (10)	12.00	5.50
COMPLETE SERIES 2 (10)	4.00	1.80
COMMON CARD (1-20)	.50	.23
MINOR STARS	1.00	.45
STAT. ODDS 1:18 SER.1, 1:12 SER.2		

☐ 1 Javier Lopez	1.50	.70
☐ 2 Rondell White	1.50	.70
☐ 3 Butch Huskey	1.00	.45
☐ 4 Midre Cummings	.50	.23
☐ 5 Scott Ruffcorn	.50	.23
☐ 6 Manny Ramirez	4.00	1.80
☐ 7 Danny Bautista	.50	.23
☐ 8 Russ Davis	1.00	.45
☐ 9 Steve Karsay	.50	.23
☐ 10 Carlos Delgado	2.00	.90
☐ 11 Bob Hamelin	.50	.23
☐ 12 Marcus Moore	.50	.23
☐ 13 Miguel Jimenez	.50	.23
☐ 14 Matt Walbeck	.50	.23
☐ 15 James Mouton	.50	.23
☐ 16 Rich Becker	.50	.23
☐ 17 Brian Anderson	2.00	.90
☐ 18 Cliff Floyd	1.00	.45
☐ 19 Steve Trachsel	1.00	.45
☐ 20 Hector Carrasco	.50	.23

1994 Leaf Gold Stars

Randomly inserted in all packs at a rate of one in 90, the 15 standard-size cards in this set are individually numbered and limited to 10,000 per player. The cards were issued in two series with eight cards in Series I and seven in Series II. The fronts are bordered by gold and have a green marble appearance with the player appearing within a diamond (outlined in gold) in the card's upper half. The player's name, gold facsimile autograph and team name appear below the photo. The backs are

similar to the fronts except for 1993 highlights and the individual numbering. They are numbered "X/10,000."

	MINT	NRMT
COMPLETE SET (15)	200.00	90.00
COMPLETE SERIES 1 (8)	120.00	55.00
COMPLETE SERIES 2 (7)	80.00	36.00
COMMON CARD (1-15)	5.00	2.20
UNLISTED STARS	10.00	4.50
SER.1 STAT.ODDS 1:90H/R, 1:288J, 1:240M		
STATED PRINT RUN 10,000 SERIAL #'d SETS		

☐ 1 Roberto Alomar	10.00	4.50
☐ 2 Barry Bonds	12.00	5.50
☐ 3 David Justice	10.00	4.50
☐ 4 Ken Griffey Jr.	50.00	22.00
☐ 5 Lenny Dykstra	6.00	2.70
☐ 6 Don Mattingly	15.00	6.75
☐ 7 Andres Galarraga	10.00	4.50
☐ 8 Greg Maddux	30.00	13.50
☐ 9 Carlos Baerga	5.00	2.20
☐ 10 Paul Molitor	10.00	4.50
☐ 11 Frank Thomas	40.00	18.00
☐ 12 John Olerud	6.00	2.70
☐ 13 Juan Gonzalez	25.00	11.00
☐ 14 Fred McGriff	8.00	3.60
☐ 15 Jack McDowell	5.00	2.20

1994 Leaf MVP Contenders

This 30-card standard-size set contains 15 players from each league who were projected to be 1994 MVP hopefuls. These unnumbered cards were randomly inserted in all second series packs at a rate of one in 36. If the player appearing on the card was named his league's MVP (Frank Thomas American League and Jeff Bagwell National League), the card could be redeemed for a 5" x 7" Frank Thomas card individually numbered out of 20,000. The backs contain all the rules and read "1 of 10,000." The expiration for redeeming Thomas and Bagwell cards was Jan. 19, 1995.

	MINT	NRMT
COMPLETE SET (30)	150.00	70.00
*SINGLES: 4X TO 10X BASE CARD HI		
SER.2 STAT.ODDS 1:36H/R, 1:90MAG		
COMP.GOLD SET (30)	150.00	70.00
*GOLD: 4X TO 10X BASE CARD HI		
ONE GOLD SET PER A13 OR N1 VIA MAIL		
ONE THOMAS J400 PER A13 OR N1 VIA MAIL		

☐ A1 Carlos Baerga	2.00	.90
☐ A2 Albert Belle	8.00	3.60

		MINT	NRMT
☐ A3	Jose Canseco	4.00	1.80
☐ A4	Joe Carter	3.00	1.35
☐ A5	Will Clark	4.00	1.80
☐ A6	Cecil Fielder	3.00	1.35
☐ A7	Juan Gonzalez	15.00	6.75
☐ A8	Ken Griffey Jr.	30.00	13.50
☐ A9	Paul Molitor	6.00	2.70
☐ A10	Rafael Palmeiro	4.00	1.80
☐ A11	Kirby Puckett	12.00	5.50
☐ A12	Cal Ripken Jr.	25.00	11.00
☐ A13	Frank Thomas W	25.00	11.00
☐ A14	Mo Vaughn	8.00	3.60
☐ A15	AL Bonus Card	2.00	.90
☐ N1	Jeff Bagwell W	12.00	5.50
☐ N2	Dante Bichette	3.00	1.35
☐ N3	Barry Bonds	8.00	3.60
☐ N4	Darren Daulton	3.00	1.35
☐ N5	Andres Galarraga	6.00	2.70
☐ N6	Gregg Jefferies	2.00	.90
☐ N7	David Justice	6.00	2.70
☐ N8	Ray Lankford	3.00	1.35
☐ N9	Barry Larkin	4.00	1.80
☐ N10	Fred McGriff	4.00	1.80
☐ N11	Mike Piazza	20.00	9.00
☐ N12	Deion Sanders	3.00	1.35
☐ N13	Gary Sheffield	6.00	2.70
☐ N14	Matt Williams	4.00	1.80
☐ N15	NL Bonus Card	2.00	.90
☐ J400	Frank Thomas Jumbo	12.00	5.50

1994 Leaf Power Brokers

Inserted in second series retail and hobby foil packs at a rate of one in 12, this 10-card standard-size set spotlights top sluggers. Both fronts and backs are horizontal. The fronts have a small player cutout with a black background and "Power Brokers" dominating the card. Fireworks appear within "Power." The backs contain various pie charts that document the player's home run tendencies as far as home vs. away etc. There is also a small photo.

	MINT	NRMT
COMPLETE SET (10)	20.00	9.00
COMMON CARD (1-10)	.75	.35
SER.2 STATED ODDS 1:12 HOB/RET		

		MINT	NRMT
☐ 1	Frank Thomas	6.00	2.70
☐ 2	David Justice	1.50	.70
☐ 3	Barry Bonds	2.00	.90
☐ 4	Juan Gonzalez	4.00	1.80
☐ 5	Ken Griffey Jr.	8.00	3.60
☐ 6	Mike Piazza	5.00	2.20
☐ 7	Cecil Fielder	.75	.35
☐ 8	Fred McGriff	1.00	.45
☐ 9	Joe Carter	.75	.35
☐ 10	Albert Belle	2.00	.90

1994 Leaf Slideshow

Randomly inserted in first and second series packs at a rate of one in 54, these ten standard-size cards simulate mounted photographic slides, but the images of the players are actually printed on acetate. The color transparencies can be seen best when they are held up to the light. The front of each transparency is framed by a simulated white slide holder, which at its bottom bears the player's name and the game from which the photo was shot. The insert set's title is shown in blue and merges with the blue-edged bottom. The remaining edges are black. The back, in addition to the appearance of the slide's reverse image, carries comments about the player from Frank Thomas.

	MINT	NRMT
COMPLETE SET (10)	60.00	27.00
COMPLETE SERIES 1 (5)	30.00	13.50
COMPLETE SERIES 2 (5)	30.00	13.50
COMMON CARD (1-10)	2.00	.90
STATED ODDS 1:54H/R, 1:36J, 1:36M		

		MINT	NRMT
☐ 1	Frank Thomas	15.00	6.75
☐ 2	Mike Piazza	12.00	5.50
☐ 3	Darren Daulton	2.00	.90
☐ 4	Ryne Sandberg	5.00	2.20
☐ 5	Roberto Alomar	4.00	1.80
☐ 6	Barry Bonds	5.00	2.20
☐ 7	Juan Gonzalez	10.00	4.50
☐ 8	Tim Salmon	4.00	1.80
☐ 9	Ken Griffey Jr.	20.00	9.00
☐ 10	David Justice	4.00	1.80

1994 Leaf Statistical Standouts

Inserted in retail and hobby foil packs at a rate of one in 12, this 10-card standard-size set features players that had significant statistical achievements in 1993. For example: Cal Ripken's home run record for a shortstop. Card fronts contain a player photo that stands out from a background that is the colors of that player's team. The back contains a photo and statistical information.

	MINT	NRMT
COMPLETE SET (10)	20.00	9.00
COMMON CARD (1-10)	.50	.23
SER.1 STATED ODDS 1:12 HOB/RET		

		MINT	NRMT
☐ 1	Frank Thomas	4.00	1.80
☐ 2	Barry Bonds	1.25	.55
☐ 3	Juan Gonzalez	2.50	1.10
☐ 4	Mike Piazza	3.00	1.35
☐ 5	Greg Maddux	3.00	1.35
☐ 6	Ken Griffey Jr.	5.00	2.20
☐ 7	Joe Carter	.50	.23
☐ 8	Dave Winfield	.75	.35
☐ 9	Tony Gwynn	2.50	1.10
☐ 10	Cal Ripken	4.00	1.80

1995 Leaf

The 1995 Leaf set was issued in two series of 200 standard-size cards for a total of 400. Full-bleed fronts contain diamond-shaped player hologram in the upper left. The team name is done in silver foil up the left side. Peculiar backs contain two photos, the card number within a stamp or seal like emblem in the upper right and '94 and career stats graph toward bottom left. Hideo Nomo is the only key Rookie Card in this set.

	MINT	NRMT
COMPLETE SET (400)	40.00	18.00
COMPLETE SERIES 1 (200)	15.00	6.75
COMPLETE SERIES 2 (200)	25.00	11.00
COMMON CARD (1-400)	.15	.07
MINOR STARS	.30	.14
UNLISTED STARS	.60	.25
COMP.F.THOMAS SET (6)	25.00	11.00
COMMON F.THOMAS (1-6)	5.00	2.20
SER. 2 THOMAS STATED ODDS 1:18		

		MINT	NRMT
☐ 1	Frank Thomas	2.50	1.10
☐ 2	Carlos Garcia	.15	.07
☐ 3	Todd Hundley	.30	.14
☐ 4	Damion Easley	.15	.07

5	Roberto Mejia	.15	.07
6	John Mabry	.30	.14
7	Aaron Sele	.15	.07
8	Kenny Lofton	.75	.35
9	John Doherty	.15	.07
10	Joe Carter	.30	.14
11	Mike Lansing	.15	.07
12	John Valentin	.15	.07
13	Ismael Valdes	.40	.18
14	Dave McCarty	.15	.07
15	Melvin Nieves	.15	.07
16	Bobby Jones	.15	.07
17	Trevor Hoffman	.15	.07
18	John Smoltz	.30	.14
19	Leo Gomez	.15	.07
20	Roger Pavlik	.15	.07
21	Dean Palmer	.15	.07
22	Rickey Henderson	.40	.18
23	Eddie Taubensee	.15	.07
24	Damon Buford	.15	.07
25	Mark Wohlers	.15	.07
26	Jim Edmonds	.40	.18
27	Wilson Alvarez	.15	.07
28	Matt Williams	.40	.18
29	Jeff Montgomery	.15	.07
30	Shawon Dunston	.15	.07
31	Tom Pagnozzi	.15	.07
32	Jose Lind	.15	.07
33	Royce Clayton	.15	.07
34	Cal Eldred	.15	.07
35	Chris Gomez	.15	.07
36	Henry Rodriguez	.15	.07
37	Dave Fleming	.15	.07
38	Jon Lieber	.15	.07
39	Scott Servais	.15	.07
40	Wade Boggs	.60	.25
41	John Olerud	.30	.14
42	Eddie Williams	.15	.07
43	Paul Sorrento	.15	.07
44	Ron Karkovice	.15	.07
45	Kevin Foster	.15	.07
46	Miguel Jimenez	.15	.07
47	Reggie Sanders	.15	.07
48	Rondell White	.30	.14
49	Scott Leius	.15	.07
50	Jose Valentin	.15	.07
51	Wm. VanLandingham	.15	.07
52	Denny Hocking	.15	.07
53	Jeff Fassero	.15	.07
54	Chris Hoiles	.15	.07
55	Walt Weiss	.15	.07
56	Geronimo Berroa	.15	.07
57	Rich Rowland	.15	.07
58	Dave Weathers	.15	.07
59	Sterling Hitchcock	.15	.07
60	Raul Mondesi	.40	.18
61	Rusty Greer	.60	.25
62	David Justice	.60	.25
63	Cecil Fielder	.30	.14
64	Brian Jordan	.30	.14
65	Mike Lieberthal	.15	.07
66	Rick Aguilera	.15	.07
67	Chuck Finley	.15	.07
68	Andy Ashby	.15	.07
69	Alex Fernandez	.15	.07
70	Ed Sprague	.15	.07
71	Steve Buechele	.15	.07
72	Willie Greene	.15	.07
73	Dave Nilsson	.15	.07
74	Bret Saberhagen	.15	.07
75	Jimmy Key	.30	.14
76	Darren Lewis	.15	.07
77	Steve Cooke	.15	.07
78	Kirk Gibson	.30	.14
79	Ray Lankford	.30	.14
80	Paul O'Neill	.30	.14
81	Mike Bordick	.15	.07
82	Wes Chamberlain	.15	.07
83	Rico Brogna	.15	.07
84	Kevin Appier	.30	.14
85	Juan Guzman	.15	.07
86	Kevin Seitzer	.15	.07
87	Mickey Morandini	.15	.07
88	Pedro Martinez	.60	.25
89	Matt Mieske	.15	.07
90	Tino Martinez	.60	.25
91	Paul Shuey	.15	.07
92	Bip Roberts	.15	.07
93	Chili Davis	.30	.14
94	Deion Sanders	.30	.14
95	Darrell Whitmore	.15	.07
96	Joe Orsulak	.15	.07
97	Bret Boone	.15	.07
98	Kent Mercker	.15	.07
99	Scott Livingstone	.15	.07
100	Brady Anderson	.40	.18
101	James Mouton	.15	.07
102	Jose Rijo	.15	.07
103	Bobby Munoz	.15	.07
104	Ramon Martinez	.30	.14
105	Bernie Williams	.60	.25
106	Troy Neel	.15	.07
107	Ivan Rodriguez	.75	.35
108	Salomon Torres	.15	.07
109	Johnny Ruffin	.15	.07
110	Darryl Kile	.30	.14
111	Bobby Ayala	.15	.07
112	Ron Darling	.15	.07
113	Jose Lima	.15	.07
114	Joey Hamilton	.30	.14
115	Greg Maddux	2.00	.90
116	Greg Colbrunn	.15	.07
117	Ozzie Guillen	.15	.07
118	Brian Anderson	.30	.14
119	Jeff Bagwell	1.25	.55
120	Pat Listach	.15	.07
121	Sandy Alomar Jr.	.30	.14
122	Jose Vizcaino	.15	.07
123	Rick Helling	.15	.07
124	Allen Watson	.15	.07
125	Pedro Munoz	.15	.07
126	Craig Biggio	.40	.18
127	Kevin Stocker	.15	.07
128	Wil Cordero	.15	.07
129	Rafael Palmeiro	.40	.18
130	Gar Finnvold	.15	.07
131	Darren Hall	.15	.07
132	Heath Slocumb	.15	.07
133	Darrin Fletcher	.15	.07
134	Cal Ripken	2.50	1.10
135	Dante Bichette	.30	.14
136	Don Slaught	.15	.07
137	Pedro Astacio	.15	.07
138	Ryan Thompson	.15	.07
139	Greg Gohr	.15	.07
140	Javier Lopez	.30	.14
141	Lenny Dykstra	.30	.14
142	Pat Rapp	.15	.07
143	Mark Kiefer	.15	.07
144	Greg Gagne	.15	.07
145	Eduardo Perez	.15	.07
146	Felix Fermin	.15	.07
147	Jeff Frye	.15	.07
148	Terry Steinbach	.15	.07
149	Jim Eisenreich	.15	.07
150	Brad Ausmus	.15	.07
151	Randy Myers	.15	.07
152	Rick White	.15	.07
153	Mark Portugal	.15	.07
154	Delino DeShields	.15	.07
155	Scott Cooper	.15	.07
156	Pat Hentgen	.30	.14
157	Mark Gubicza	.15	.07
158	Carlos Baerga	.30	.14
159	Joe Girardi	.15	.07
160	Rey Sanchez	.15	.07
161	Todd Jones	.15	.07
162	Luis Polonia	.15	.07
163	Steve Trachsel	.15	.07
164	Roberto Hernandez	.15	.07
165	John Patterson	.15	.07
166	Rene Arocha	.15	.07
167	Will Clark	.40	.18
168	Jim Leyritz	.15	.07
169	Todd Van Poppel	.15	.07
170	Robb Nen	.15	.07
171	Midre Cummings	.15	.07
172	Jay Buhner	.40	.18
173	Kevin Tapani	.15	.07
174	Mark Lemke	.15	.07
175	Marcus Moore	.15	.07
176	Wayne Kirby	.15	.07
177	Rich Amaral	.15	.07
178	Lou Whitaker	.30	.14
179	Jay Bell	.30	.14
180	Rick Wilkins	.15	.07
181	Paul Molitor	.60	.25
182	Gary Sheffield	.60	.25
183	Kirby Puckett	1.25	.55
184	Cliff Floyd	.15	.07
185	Darren Oliver	.30	.14
186	Tim Naehring	.15	.07
187	John Hudek	.15	.07
188	Eric Young	.15	.07
189	Roger Salkeld	.15	.07
190	Kirt Manwaring	.15	.07
191	Kurt Abbott	.15	.07
192	David Nied	.15	.07
193	Todd Zeile	.15	.07
194	Wally Joyner	.30	.14
195	Dennis Martinez	.30	.14
196	Billy Ashley	.15	.07
197	Ben McDonald	.15	.07
198	Bob Hamelin	.15	.07
199	Chris Turner	.15	.07
200	Lance Johnson	.15	.07
201	Willie Banks	.15	.07
202	Juan Gonzalez	1.50	.70
203	Scott Sanders	.15	.07
204	Scott Brosius	.15	.07
205	Curt Schilling	.30	.14
206	Alex Gonzalez	.15	.07
207	Travis Fryman	.30	.14
208	Tim Raines	.30	.14
209	Steve Avery	.15	.07
210	Hal Morris	.15	.07
211	Ken Griffey Jr.	3.00	1.35
212	Ozzie Smith	.75	.35
213	Chuck Carr	.15	.07
214	Ryan Klesko	.40	.18
215	Robin Ventura	.30	.14
216	Luis Gonzalez	.15	.07
217	Ken Ryan	.15	.07
218	Mike Piazza	2.00	.90
219	Matt Walbeck	.15	.07
220	Jeff Kent	.15	.07
221	Orlando Miller	.15	.07
222	Kenny Rogers	.15	.07
223	J.T. Snow	.30	.14
224	Alan Trammell	.40	.18
225	John Franco	.30	.14
226	Gerald Williams	.15	.07
227	Andy Benes	.30	.14
228	Dan Wilson	.15	.07
229	Dave Hollins	.15	.07
230	Vinny Castilla	.30	.14
231	Devon White	.15	.07
232	Fred McGriff	.40	.18
233	Quilvio Veras	.15	.07
234	Tom Candiotti	.15	.07
235	Jason Bere	.15	.07
236	Mark Langston	.15	.07
237	Mel Rojas	.15	.07
238	Chuck Knoblauch	.60	.25
239	Bernard Gilkey	.15	.07
240	Mark McGwire	1.25	.55
241	Kirk Rueter	.15	.07
242	Pat Kelly	.15	.07
243	Ruben Sierra	.30	.14
244	Randy Johnson	.60	.25
245	Shane Reynolds	.15	.07
246	Danny Tartabull	.15	.07
247	Darryl Hamilton	.15	.07
248	Danny Bautista	.15	.07
249	Tom Gordon	.15	.07
250	Tom Glavine	.30	.14
251	Orlando Merced	.15	.07
252	Eric Karros	.30	.14
253	Benji Gil	.15	.07
254	Sean Bergman	.15	.07
255	Roger Clemens	1.25	.55
256	Roberto Alomar	.60	.25
257	Benito Santiago	.15	.07
258	Robby Thompson	.15	.07
259	Marvin Freeman	.15	.07
260	Jose Offerman	.15	.07
261	Greg Vaughn	.15	.07
262	David Segui	.15	.07

□	#	Player		
□	263	Geronimo Pena	.15	.07
□	264	Tim Salmon	.60	.25
□	265	Eddie Murray	.60	.25
□	266	Mariano Duncan	.15	.07
□	267	Hideo Nomo	3.00	1.35
□	268	Derek Bell	.15	.07
□	269	Mo Vaughn	.75	.35
□	270	Jeff King	.15	.07
□	271	Edgar Martinez	.40	.18
□	272	Sammy Sosa	.60	.25
□	273	Scott Ruffcorn	.15	.07
□	274	Darren Daulton	.30	.14
□	275	John Jaha	.15	.07
□	276	Andres Galarraga	.60	.25
□	277	Mark Grace	.40	.18
□	278	Mike Moore	.15	.07
□	279	Barry Bonds	.75	.35
□	280	Manny Ramirez	.60	.25
□	281	Ellis Burks	.30	.14
□	282	Greg Swindell	.15	.07
□	283	Barry Larkin	.40	.18
□	284	Albert Belle	.75	.35
□	285	Shawn Green	.30	.14
□	286	John Roper	.15	.07
□	287	Scott Erickson	.15	.07
□	288	Moises Alou	.30	.14
□	289	Mike Blowers	.15	.07
□	290	Brent Gates	.15	.07
□	291	Sean Berry	.15	.07
□	292	Mike Stanley	.15	.07
□	293	Jeff Conine	.30	.14
□	294	Tim Wallach	.15	.07
□	295	Bobby Bonilla	.30	.14
□	296	Bruce Ruffin	.15	.07
□	297	Chad Curtis	.15	.07
□	298	Mike Greenwell	.15	.07
□	299	Tony Gwynn	1.50	.70
□	300	Russ Davis	.15	.07
□	301	Danny Jackson	.15	.07
□	302	Pete Harnisch	.15	.07
□	303	Don Mattingly	1.00	.45
□	304	Rheal Cormier	.15	.07
□	305	Larry Walker	.60	.25
□	306	Hector Carrasco	.15	.07
□	307	Jason Jacome	.15	.07
□	308	Phil Plantier	.15	.07
□	309	Harold Baines	.30	.14
□	310	Mitch Williams	.15	.07
□	311	Charles Nagy	.30	.14
□	312	Ken Caminiti	.40	.18
□	313	Alex Rodriguez	2.50	1.10
□	314	Chris Sabo	.15	.07
□	315	Gary Gaetti	.15	.07
□	316	Andre Dawson	.40	.18
□	317	Mark Clark	.15	.07
□	318	Vince Coleman	.15	.07
□	319	Brad Clontz	.15	.07
□	320	Steve Finley	.30	.14
□	321	Doug Drabek	.15	.07
□	322	Mark McLemore	.15	.07
□	323	Stan Javier	.15	.07
□	324	Ron Gant	.30	.14
□	325	Charlie Hayes	.15	.07
□	326	Carlos Delgado	.30	.14
□	327	Ricky Bottalico	.30	.14
□	328	Rod Beck	.15	.07
□	329	Mark Acre	.15	.07
□	330	Chris Bosio	.15	.07
□	331	Tony Phillips	.15	.07
□	332	Garret Anderson	.40	.18
□	333	Pat Meares	.15	.07
□	334	Todd Worrell	.15	.07
□	335	Marquis Grissom	.30	.14
□	336	Brent Mayne	.15	.07
□	337	Lee Tinsley	.15	.07
□	338	Terry Pendleton	.15	.07
□	339	David Cone	.30	.14
□	340	Tony Fernandez	.15	.07
□	341	Jim Bullinger	.15	.07
□	342	Armando Benitez	.15	.07
□	343	John Smiley	.15	.07
□	344	Dan Miceli	.15	.07
□	345	Charles Johnson	.30	.14
□	346	Lee Smith	.30	.14
□	347	Brian McRae	.15	.07
□	348	Jim Thome	.60	.25
□	349	Jose Oliva	.15	.07
□	350	Terry Mulholland	.15	.07
□	351	Tom Henke	.15	.07
□	352	Dennis Eckersley	.30	.14
□	353	Sid Fernandez	.15	.07
□	354	Paul Wagner	.15	.07
□	355	John Dettmer	.15	.07
□	356	John Wetteland	.15	.07
□	357	John Burkett	.15	.07
□	358	Marty Cordova	.30	.14
□	359	Norm Charlton	.15	.07
□	360	Mike Devereaux	.15	.07
□	361	Alex Cole	.15	.07
□	362	Brett Butler	.30	.14
□	363	Mickey Tettleton	.15	.07
□	364	Al Martin	.15	.07
□	365	Tony Tarasco	.15	.07
□	366	Pat Mahomes	.15	.07
□	367	Gary DiSarcina	.15	.07
□	368	Bill Swift	.15	.07
□	369	Chipper Jones	2.00	.90
□	370	Orel Hershiser	.30	.14
□	371	Kevin Gross	.15	.07
□	372	Dave Winfield	.40	.18
□	373	Andujar Cedeno	.15	.07
□	374	Jim Abbott	.15	.07
□	375	Glenallen Hill	.15	.07
□	376	Otis Nixon	.15	.07
□	377	Roberto Kelly	.15	.07
□	378	Chris Hammond	.15	.07
□	379	Mike Macfarlane	.15	.07
□	380	J.R. Phillips	.15	.07
□	381	Luis Alicea	.15	.07
□	382	Bret Barberie	.15	.07
□	383	Tom Goodwin	.15	.07
□	384	Mark Whiten	.15	.07
□	385	Jeffrey Hammonds	.30	.14
□	386	Omar Vizquel	.30	.14
□	387	Mike Mussina	.60	.25
□	388	Ricky Bones	.15	.07
□	389	Steve Ontiveros	.15	.07
□	390	Jeff Blauser	.30	.14
□	391	Jose Canseco	.40	.18
□	392	Bob Tewksbury	.15	.07
□	393	Jacob Brumfield	.15	.07
□	394	Doug Jones	.15	.07
□	395	Ken Hill	.15	.07
□	396	Pat Borders	.15	.07
□	397	Carl Everett	.15	.07
□	398	Gregg Jefferies	.15	.07
□	399	Jack McDowell	.15	.07
□	400	Denny Neagle	.30	.14

	MINT	NRMT
COMPLETE SET (8)	8.00	3.60
COMPLETE SERIES 1 (4)	4.00	1.80
COMPLETE SERIES 2 (4)	4.00	1.80
COMMON CARD (1-8)	.50	.23
RANDOM INSERTS IN BOTH SERIES PACKS		
□ 1 Bob Hamelin UER	.50	.23
(Name spelled Hamlin)		
□ 2 David Cone	.75	.35
□ 3 Frank Thomas	2.50	1.10
□ 4 Paul O'Neill	.75	.35
□ 5 Raul Mondesi	1.00	.45
□ 6 Greg Maddux	2.00	.90
□ 7 Tony Gwynn	1.50	.70
□ 8 Jeff Bagwell	1.25	.55

1995 Leaf Cornerstones

Cards from this six-card standard-size set were randomly inserted in first series packs. Horizontally designed, leading first and third basemen from the same team are featured. The fronts have silver foil borders and team names with the team logo serving as background to the photos. The backs have a photo of either player with offensive and defensive stats.

	MINT	NRMT
COMPLETE SET (6)	10.00	4.50
COMMON CARD (1-6)	1.00	.45
SER.1 STATED ODDS 1:18 HOB/RET		
□ 1 Frank Thomas	5.00	2.20
Robin Ventura		
□ 2 Cecil Fielder	1.25	.55
Travis Fryman		
□ 3 Don Mattingly	2.00	.90
Wade Boggs		
□ 4 Jeff Bagwell	2.50	1.10
Ken Caminiti		
□ 5 Will Clark	1.50	.70
Dean Palmer		
□ 6 J.R. Phillips	1.00	.45
Matt Williams		

1995 Leaf Checklists

Four checklist cards were randomly inserted in either series for a total of eight standard-size cards. Checklist fronts feature a player photo from left to center with the start of the checklist to the right which continues on the back.

1995 Leaf Gold Rookies

Inserted in every other first series pack, this 16-card standard-size set showcases those that were expected to have an impact in 1995. Card fronts offer two photos with various gold foil ornamentation. The backs have a large black and white photo with a smaller color photo inset at top left. The backs also contain career minor league stats.

	MINT	NRMT
COMPLETE SET (16)	6.00	2.70
COMMON CARD (1-16)	.25	.11
SER.1 STATED ODDS 1:2 HOB/RET		

		MINT	NRMT
☐ 1	Alex Rodriguez	4.00	1.80
☐ 2	Garret Anderson	1.00	.45
☐ 3	Shawn Green	.50	.23
☐ 4	Armando Benitez	.25	.11
☐ 5	Darren Dreifort	.25	.11
☐ 6	Orlando Miller	.25	.11
☐ 7	Jose Oliva	.25	.11
☐ 8	Ricky Bottalico	.50	.23
☐ 9	Charles Johnson	.50	.23
☐ 10	Brian L.Hunter	1.00	.45
☐ 11	Ray McDavid	.25	.11
☐ 12	Chan Ho Park	1.50	.70
☐ 13	Mike Kelly	.25	.11
☐ 14	Cory Bailey	.25	.11
☐ 15	Alex Gonzalez	.25	.11
☐ 16	Andrew Lorraine	.25	.11

1995 Leaf Gold Stars

Randomly inserted in first and second series packs at a rate of one in 110, this 14-card standard-size set (eight first series, six second series) showcases some of the game's superstars. Individually numbered on back out of 10,000, the cards feature fronts that have a player photo superimposed with metallic, refractive background. A die-cut player star is in the lower left corner. The backs have a small player photo and brief write-up in addition to the numbering.

	MINT	NRMT
COMPLETE SET (14)	300.00	135.00
COMPLETE SERIES 1 (8)	150.00	70.00
COMPLETE SERIES 2 (6)	150.00	70.00
COMMON CARD (1-14)	8.00	3.60
STATED ODDS 1:110 HOB/RET		
STATED PRINT RUN 10,000 SERIAL #'d SETS		

		MINT	NRMT
☐ 1	Jeff Bagwell	20.00	9.00
☐ 2	Albert Belle	12.00	5.50
☐ 3	Tony Gwynn	25.00	11.00
☐ 4	Ken Griffey Jr.	50.00	22.00
☐ 5	Barry Bonds	12.00	5.50
☐ 6	Don Mattingly	15.00	6.75
☐ 7	Raul Mondesi	8.00	3.60
☐ 8	Joe Carter	8.00	3.60
☐ 9	Greg Maddux	30.00	13.50
☐ 10	Frank Thomas	40.00	18.00
☐ 11	Mike Piazza	30.00	13.50
☐ 12	Jose Canseco	8.00	3.60
☐ 13	Kirby Puckett	20.00	9.00
☐ 14	Matt Williams	8.00	3.60

1995 Leaf Great Gloves

This 16-card standard-size set was randomly inserted in series two packs at a rate of one every two packs. The players featured are leading defensive players. Action photos are set against a background that includes part of a glove. The player's name and team are stamped in gold foil. The horizontal backs feature a photo set against a glove, information about the player and their 1994 defensive statistics. The cards are numbered "X" of 16 in the upper right.

	MINT	NRMT
COMPLETE SET (16)	8.00	3.60
COMMON CARD (1-16)	.30	.14
SER.2 STATED ODDS 1:2		

		MINT	NRMT
☐ 1	Jeff Bagwell	1.25	.55
☐ 2	Roberto Alomar	.60	.25
☐ 3	Barry Bonds	.75	.35
☐ 4	Wade Boggs	.60	.25
☐ 5	Andres Galarraga	.60	.25
☐ 6	Ken Griffey Jr.	3.00	1.35
☐ 7	Marquis Grissom	.30	.14
☐ 8	Kenny Lofton	.75	.35
☐ 9	Barry Larkin	.40	.18
☐ 10	Don Mattingly	1.00	.45
☐ 11	Greg Maddux	2.00	.90
☐ 12	Kirby Puckett	1.25	.55
☐ 13	Ozzie Smith	.75	.35
☐ 14	Cal Ripken Jr.	2.50	1.10
☐ 15	Matt Williams	.40	.18
☐ 16	Ivan Rodriguez	.75	.35

1995 Leaf Heading for the Hall

This eight-card standard-size set was randomly inserted into series two packs. The cards are cut in the shape of a Hall of Fame plaque and are designed as if this were the actual information on the player's plaque in Cooperstown. The backs feature a black and white photo along with career statistics. The cards are individually numbered out of 5,000 as well.

	MINT	NRMT
COMPLETE SET (8)	250.00	110.00
COMMON CARD (1-8)	12.00	5.50
SER.2 STATED ODDS 1:75 HOBBY		
STATED PRINT RUN 5000 SERIAL #'d SETS		

		MINT	NRMT
☐ 1	Frank Thomas	50.00	22.00
☐ 2	Ken Griffey Jr.	60.00	27.00
☐ 3	Jeff Bagwell	25.00	11.00
☐ 4	Barry Bonds	15.00	6.75
☐ 5	Kirby Puckett	25.00	11.00
☐ 6	Cal Ripken	50.00	22.00
☐ 7	Tony Gwynn	30.00	13.50
☐ 8	Paul Molitor	12.00	5.50

1995 Leaf Slideshow

This 16-card standard-size set was issued eight per series and randomly inserted at a rate of per box. The eight cards in the first series are numbered 1A-8A and repeated with different photos in the second series as 1B-8B. Both version carry the same value. The left side of the card front is semi-circular featuring three player translucent "slides."

	MINT	NRMT
COMPLETE SET (16)	80.00	36.00
COMPLETE SERIES 1 (8)	40.00	18.00
COMPLETE SERIES 2 (8)	40.00	18.00
COMMON CARD (1A-8B)	1.50	.70
SERIES 1 AND 2 CARDS SAME VALUE		
STATED ODDS 1:30 HOB, 1:36 RET		

		MINT	NRMT
☐ 1A	Raul Mondesi	1.50	.70
☐ 1B	Raul Mondesi	1.50	.70
☐ 2A	Frank Thomas	12.00	5.50

☐ 2B	Frank Thomas	12.00	5.50
☐ 3A	Fred McGriff	1.50	.70
☐ 3B	Fred McGriff	1.50	.70
☐ 4A	Cal Ripken	12.00	5.50
☐ 4B	Cal Ripken	12.00	5.50
☐ 5A	Jeff Bagwell	6.00	2.70
☐ 5B	Jeff Bagwell	6.00	2.70
☐ 6A	Will Clark	1.50	.70
☐ 6B	Will Clark	1.50	.70
☐ 7A	Matt Williams	1.50	.70
☐ 7B	Matt Williams	1.50	.70
☐ 8A	Ken Griffey Jr.	15.00	6.75
☐ 8B	Ken Griffey Jr.	15.00	6.75

1995 Leaf Statistical Standouts

Randomly inserted in first series hobby packs at a rate of one in 70, this set features nine players who stood out from the rest statistically. The fronts contain a player photo between embossed seams or stitches of a baseball. The backs have a small circular player photo with 1994 highlights.

	MINT	NRMT
COMPLETE SET (9)	450.00	200.00
COMMON CARD (1-9)	15.00	6.75
SER.1 STATED ODDS 1:70 HOBBY		

☐ 1	Joe Carter	15.00	6.75
☐ 2	Ken Griffey Jr.	120.00	55.00
☐ 3	Don Mattingly	40.00	18.00
☐ 4	Fred McGriff	20.00	9.00
☐ 5	Paul Molitor	25.00	11.00
☐ 6	Kirby Puckett	50.00	22.00
☐ 7	Cal Ripken	100.00	45.00
☐ 8	Frank Thomas	100.00	45.00
☐ 9	Matt Williams	20.00	9.00

1995 Leaf 300 Club

Randomly inserted in first and second series mini and retail packs at a rate of one every 12 packs, this set depicts all 18 players who had a career average of .300 or better entering the 1995 campaign. A large ghosted 300 serves as background to a player photo. Gold foil is at the bottom in either corner including career average in the right corner. Full-bleed backs list the 18 players and their averages to that point.

	MINT	NRMT
COMPLETE SET (18)	120.00	55.00
COMPLETE SERIES 1 (9)	50.00	22.00
COMPLETE SERIES 2 (9)	70.00	32.00

COMMON CARD (1-18)		1.50	.70
STATED ODDS 1:12 RETAIL/MINI			

☐ 1	Frank Thomas	20.00	9.00
☐ 2	Paul Molitor	5.00	2.20
☐ 3	Mike Piazza	15.00	6.75
☐ 4	Moises Alou	3.00	1.35
☐ 5	Mike Greenwell	1.50	.70
☐ 6	Will Clark	4.00	1.80
☐ 7	Hal Morris	1.50	.70
☐ 8	Edgar Martinez	4.00	1.80
☐ 9	Carlos Baerga	1.50	.70
☐ 10	Ken Griffey Jr.	25.00	11.00
☐ 11	Wade Boggs	5.00	2.20
☐ 12	Jeff Bagwell	10.00	4.50
☐ 13	Tony Gwynn	12.00	5.50
☐ 14	John Kruk	3.00	1.35
☐ 15	Don Mattingly	8.00	3.60
☐ 16	Mark Grace	4.00	1.80
☐ 17	Kirby Puckett	10.00	4.50
☐ 18	Kenny Lofton	6.00	2.70

1996 Leaf

The 1996 Leaf set was issued in one series totalling 220 cards. The fronts feature color action player photos with silver foil printing and lines forming a border on the left and bottom. The backs display another player photo with 1995 season and career statistics. Card number 210 is a checklist for the insert sets and cards number 211-220 feature rookies. The fronts of these 10 cards are different in design from the first 200 with a color action player cut-out over a green-shadow background of the same picture and gold lettering. The horizontal backs carry another player cut-out on a purple-and-black background with 1995 season statistics and personal information.

	MINT	NRMT
COMPLETE SET (220)	20.00	9.00
COMMON CARD (1-220)	.15	.07

MINOR STARS	.30	.14
UNLISTED STARS	.60	.25
COMP.BRZ.PP SET (220)..	600.00	275.00
COMMON BRZ PP (1-220)..	1.00	.45
*BRONZE PP STARS: 5X TO 12X HI COLUMN		
*BRONZE PP YOUNG STARS: 4X TO 10X HI		
BRONZE PP STATED PRINT RUN 2000 SETS		
COMP.GOLD PP SET (220)	2500.00	1100.00
COMMON GOLD PP (1-220)	5.00	2.20
*GOLD PP STARS: 20X TO 50X HI COLUMN		
*GOLD PP YOUNG STARS: 15X TO 40X HI		
GOLD PP STATED PRINT RUN 500 SETS		
COMP.SILV.PP SET (220)	1200.00	550.00
COMMON SILV.PP (1-220) ..	2.00	.90
*SILV.PP STARS: 10X TO 25X HI COLUMN		
*SILV.PP YOUNG STARS: 8X TO 20X HI		
SILVER PP STATED PRINT RUN 1000 SETS		
1:10 PACKS CONTAINS EITHER B, G OR S PP		
COMP.F.THOMAS SET (8)	150.00	70.00
COMMON THOMAS (1-7)..	25.00	11.00
THOMAS EXCHANGE (8) ...	30.00	13.50
THOMAS 1-4: STATED ODDS 1:210 HOBBY		
THOMAS 5-7: STATED ODDS 1:210 RETAIL		
THOMAS: CARD 8 WAS AVAIL.VIA MAIL-IN		
THOMAS STATED PRINT RUN 5000 SETS		

☐ 1	John Smoltz	.30	.14
☐ 2	Dennis Eckersley	.30	.14
☐ 3	Delino DeShields	.15	.07
☐ 4	Cliff Floyd	.15	.07
☐ 5	Chuck Finley	.30	.14
☐ 6	Cecil Fielder	.30	.14
☐ 7	Tim Naehring	.15	.07
☐ 8	Carlos Perez	.15	.07
☐ 9	Brad Ausmus	.15	.07
☐ 10	Matt Lawton	.40	.18
☐ 11	Alan Trammell	.40	.18
☐ 12	Steve Finley	.30	.14
☐ 13	Paul O'Neil	.30	.14
☐ 14	Gary Sheffield	.60	.25
☐ 15	Mark McGwire	1.25	.55
☐ 16	Bernie Williams	.60	.25
☐ 17	Jeff Montgomery	.15	.07
☐ 18	Chan Ho Park	.60	.25
☐ 19	Greg Vaughn	.15	.07
☐ 20	Jeff Kent	.15	.07
☐ 21	Cal Ripken	2.50	1.10
☐ 22	Charles Johnson	.30	.14
☐ 23	Eric Karros	.30	.14
☐ 24	Alex Rodriguez	2.00	.90
☐ 25	Chris Snopek	.15	.07
☐ 26	Jason Isringhausen	.15	.07
☐ 27	Chili Davis	.30	.14
☐ 28	Chipper Jones	2.00	.90
☐ 29	Bret Saberhagen	.15	.07
☐ 30	Tony Clark	.60	.25
☐ 31	Marty Cordova	.30	.14
☐ 32	Dwayne Hosey	.15	.07
☐ 33	Fred McGriff	.40	.18
☐ 34	Deion Sanders	.30	.14
☐ 35	Orlando Merced	.15	.07
☐ 36	Brady Anderson	.40	.18
☐ 37	Ray Lankford	.30	.14
☐ 38	Manny Ramirez	.60	.25
☐ 39	Alex Fernandez	.15	.07
☐ 40	Greg Colbrunn	.15	.07
☐ 41	Ken Griffey Jr.	3.00	1.35
☐ 42	Mickey Morandini	.15	.07
☐ 43	Chuck Knoblauch	.60	.25
☐ 44	Quinton McCracken	.15	.07
☐ 45	Tim Salmon	.60	.25
☐ 46	Jose Mesa	.15	.07
☐ 47	Marquis Grissom	.30	.14
☐ 48	Checklist	.15	.07
☐ 49	Raul Mondesi	.40	.18
☐ 50	Mark Grudzielanek	.30	.14
☐ 51	Ray Durham	.15	.07
☐ 52	Matt Williams	.40	.18
☐ 53	Bob Hamelin	.15	.07
☐ 54	Lenny Dykstra	.30	.14
☐ 55	Jeff King	.15	.07
☐ 56	LaTroy Hawkins	.15	.07
☐ 57	Terry Pendleton	.15	.07
☐ 58	Kevin Stocker	.15	.07
☐ 59	Ozzie Timmons	.15	.07

#	Player		
□ 60	David Justice	.60	.25
□ 61	Ricky Bottalico	.15	.07
□ 62	Andy Ashby	.15	.07
□ 63	Larry Walker	.60	.25
□ 64	Jose Canseco	.40	.18
□ 65	Bret Boone	.15	.07
□ 66	Shawn Green	.15	.07
□ 67	Chad Curtis	.15	.07
□ 68	Travis Fryman	.30	.14
□ 69	Roger Clemens	1.25	.55
□ 70	David Bell	.15	.07
□ 71	Rusty Greer	.30	.14
□ 72	Bob Higginson	.40	.18
□ 73	Joey Hamilton	.30	.14
□ 74	Kevin Seitzer	.15	.07
□ 75	Julian Tavarez	.15	.07
□ 76	Troy Percival	.15	.07
□ 77	Kirby Puckett	1.25	.55
□ 78	Barry Bonds	.75	.35
□ 79	Michael Tucker	.30	.14
□ 80	Paul Molitor	.60	.25
□ 81	Carlos Garcia	.15	.07
□ 82	Johnny Damon	.30	.14
□ 83	Mike Hampton	.15	.07
□ 84	Ariel Prieto	.15	.07
□ 85	Tony Tarasco	.15	.07
□ 86	Pete Schourek	.15	.07
□ 87	Tom Glavine	.30	.14
□ 88	Rondell White	.30	.14
□ 89	Jim Edmonds	.40	.18
□ 90	Robby Thompson	.15	.07
□ 91	Wade Boggs	.60	.25
□ 92	Pedro Martinez	.60	.25
□ 93	Gregg Jefferies	.15	.07
□ 94	Albert Belle	.75	.35
□ 95	Benji Gil	.15	.07
□ 96	Denny Neagle	.30	.14
□ 97	Mark Langston	.15	.07
□ 98	Sandy Alomar Jr.	.30	.14
□ 99	Tony Gwynn	1.50	.70
□ 100	Todd Hundley	.30	.14
□ 101	Dante Bichette	.30	.14
□ 102	Eddie Murray	.60	.25
□ 103	Lyle Mouton	.15	.07
□ 104	John Jaha	.15	.07
□ 105	Checklist	.15	.07
□ 106	Jon Nunnally	.15	.07
□ 107	Juan Gonzalez	1.50	.70
□ 108	Kevin Appier	.30	.14
□ 109	Brian McRae	.15	.07
□ 110	Lee Smith	.30	.14
□ 111	Tim Wakefield	.30	.14
□ 112	Sammy Sosa	.60	.25
□ 113	Jay Buhner	.30	.18
□ 114	Garret Anderson	.30	.14
□ 115	Edgar Martinez	.40	.18
□ 116	Edgardo Alfonzo	.40	.18
□ 117	Billy Ashley	.15	.07
□ 118	Joe Carter	.30	.14
□ 119	Javy Lopez	.30	.14
□ 120	Bobby Bonilla	.30	.14
□ 121	Ken Caminiti	.40	.18
□ 122	Barry Larkin	.40	.18
□ 123	Shannon Stewart	.30	.14
□ 124	Orel Hershiser	.30	.14
□ 125	Jeff Conine	.30	.14
□ 126	Mark Grace	.40	.18
□ 127	Kenny Lofton	.75	.35
□ 128	Luis Gonzalez	.15	.07
□ 129	Rico Brogna	.15	.07
□ 130	Mo Vaughn	.75	.35
□ 131	Brad Radke	.30	.14
□ 132	Jose Herrera	.15	.07
□ 133	Rick Aguilera	.15	.07
□ 134	Gary DiSarcina	.15	.07
□ 135	Andres Galarraga	.60	.25
□ 136	Carl Everett	.15	.07
□ 137	Steve Avery	.15	.07
□ 138	Vinny Castilla	.30	.14
□ 139	Dennis Martinez	.30	.14
□ 140	John Wetteland	.15	.07
□ 141	Alex Gonzalez	.15	.07
□ 142	Brian Jordan	.30	.14
□ 143	Todd Hollandsworth	.30	.14
□ 144	Terrell Wade	.15	.07
□ 145	Wilson Alvarez	.15	.07
□ 146	Reggie Sanders	.15	.07
□ 147	Will Clark	.40	.18
□ 148	Hideo Nomo	1.50	.70
□ 149	J.T.Snow	.30	.14
□ 150	Frank Thomas	2.50	1.10
□ 151	Ivan Rodriguez	.75	.35
□ 152	Jay Bell	.30	.14
□ 153	Checklist	.15	.07
□ 154	David Cone	.30	.14
□ 155	Roberto Alomar	.60	.25
□ 156	Carlos Delgado	.30	.14
□ 157	Carlos Baerga	.15	.07
□ 158	Geronimo Berroa	.15	.07
□ 159	Joe Vitiello	.15	.07
□ 160	Terry Steinbach	.15	.07
□ 161	Doug Drabek	.15	.07
□ 162	David Segui	.15	.07
□ 163	Ozzie Smith	.75	.35
□ 164	Kurt Abbott	.15	.07
□ 165	Randy Johnson	.60	.25
□ 166	John Valentin	.15	.07
□ 167	Mickey Tettleton	.15	.07
□ 168	Ruben Sierra	.15	.07
□ 169	Jim Thome	.60	.25
□ 170	Mike Greenwell	.15	.07
□ 171	Quilvio Veras	.15	.07
□ 172	Robin Ventura	.30	.14
□ 173	Bill Pulsipher	.15	.07
□ 174	Rafael Palmeiro	.40	.18
□ 175	Hal Morris	.15	.07
□ 176	Ryan Klesko	.40	.18
□ 177	Eric Young	.15	.07
□ 178	Shane Andrews	.15	.07
□ 179	Brian L.Hunter	.30	.14
□ 180	Brett Butler	.30	.14
□ 181	John Olerud	.30	.14
□ 182	Moises Alou	.30	.14
□ 183	Glenallen Hill	.15	.07
□ 184	Ismael Valdes	.30	.14
□ 185	Andy Pettitte	.75	.35
□ 186	Vinny Benitez	.30	.14
□ 187	Jason Bere	.15	.07
□ 188	Dean Palmer	.15	.07
□ 189	Jimmy Haynes	.15	.07
□ 190	Trevor Hoffman	.15	.07
□ 191	Mike Mussina	.60	.25
□ 192	Greg Maddux	2.00	.90
□ 193	Ozzie Guillen	.15	.07
□ 194	Pat Listach	.15	.07
□ 195	Derek Bell	.15	.07
□ 196	Darren Daulton	.30	.14
□ 197	John Mabry	.15	.07
□ 198	Ramon Martinez	.30	.14
□ 199	Jeff Bagwell	1.25	.55
□ 200	Mike Piazza	2.00	.90
□ 201	Al Martin	.15	.07
□ 202	Aaron Sele	.15	.07
□ 203	Ed Sprague	.15	.07
□ 204	Rod Beck	.15	.07
□ 205	Checklist	.15	.07
□ 206	Mike Lansing	.15	.07
□ 207	Craig Biggio	.30	.18
□ 208	Jeffrey Hammonds	.15	.07
□ 209	Dave Nilsson	.15	.07
□ 210	Checklist	.15	.07
□ 211	Derek Jeter	2.00	.90
□ 212	Alan Benes	.30	.14
□ 213	Jason Schmidt	.15	.07
□ 214	Alex Ochoa	.15	.07
□ 215	Ruben Rivera	.30	.14
□ 216	Roger Cedeno	.15	.07
□ 217	Jeff Suppan	.30	.14
□ 218	Billy Wagner	.30	.14
□ 219	Mark Loretta	.15	.07
□ 220	Karim Garcia	.40	.18

Philadelphia. The cards were randomly inserted into packs. If the player on the front of the card won the MVP Award (which turned out to be Mike Piazza), the holder could send it in for a special Gold MVP Contenders set of which only 5,000 were produced. The fronts display a color action player photo. The backs carry the instructions on how to redeem the card. The expiration date for the redemption was August 15th, 1996. The Piazza card when returned with the redemption set had a hole in it to indicate the set had been redeemed.

	MINT	NRMT
COMPLETE SET (20)	40.00	18.00
*SINGLES: .75X TO 2X BASE CARD HI		
RANDOM INSERTS IN PACKS ..		
COMP.GOLD SET (20)	40.00	18.00
*GOLD CARDS: .75X TO 2X BASE CARD HI		
ONE GOLD SET PER PIAZZA VIA MAIL		

#	Player	MINT	NRMT
□ 1	Frank Thomas	5.00	2.20
□ 2	Mike Piazza	6.00	2.70
□ 3	Sammy Sosa	1.25	.55
□ 4	Cal Ripken	5.00	2.20
□ 5	Jeff Bagwell	2.50	1.10
□ 6	Reggie Sanders	.50	.23
□ 7	Mo Vaughn	1.50	.70
□ 8	Tony Gwynn	3.00	1.35
□ 9	Dante Bichette	.75	.35
□ 10	Tim Salmon	1.25	.55
□ 11	Chipper Jones	4.00	1.80
□ 12	Kenny Lofton	1.50	.70
□ 13	Manny Ramirez	1.25	.55
□ 14	Barry Bonds	1.50	.70
□ 15	Raul Mondesi	1.00	.45
□ 16	Kirby Puckett	2.50	1.10
□ 17	Albert Belle	1.50	.70
□ 18	Ken Griffey Jr.	6.00	2.70
□ 19	Greg Maddux	4.00	1.80
□ 20	Bonus Card	.50	.23

1996 Leaf Gold Stars

Randomly inserted in hobby and retail packs at a rate of one in 190, this 15-card set honors some of the games great players on 22 karat gold trim cards. Only 2,500 cards of each player were printed and are individually numbered.

	MINT	NRMT
COMPLETE SET (15)	500.00	220.00
COMMON CARD (1-15)	10.00	4.50
UNLISTED STARS	15.00	6.75
STATED ODDS 1:190		
STATED PRINT RUN 2500 SERIAL #'d SETS		

1996 Leaf All-Star Game MVP Contenders

This 20 card set features possible contenders for the MVP at the 1996 All-Star Game held in

		MINT	NRMT
COMPLETE SET (8)		450.00	200.00
COMMON CARD (1-8)		25.00	11.00
STATED ODDS 1:210 HOBBY			
STATED PRINT RUN 2500 SERIAL #'d SETS			

			MINT	NRMT
☐	1	Cal Ripken	80.00	36.00
☐	2	Tony Gwynn	50.00	22.00
☐	3	Frank Thomas	80.00	36.00
☐	4	Ken Griffey Jr.	100.00	45.00
☐	5	Hideo Nomo	50.00	22.00
☐	6	Greg Maddux	60.00	27.00
☐	7	Albert Belle	25.00	11.00
☐	8	Chipper Jones	60.00	27.00

			MINT	NRMT
☐	1	Frank Thomas	60.00	27.00
☐	2	Dante Bichette	12.00	5.50
☐	3	Sammy Sosa	15.00	6.75
☐	4	Ken Griffey Jr.	80.00	36.00
☐	5	Mike Piazza	50.00	22.00
☐	6	Tim Salmon	15.00	6.75
☐	7	Hideo Nomo	40.00	18.00
☐	8	Cal Ripken	60.00	27.00
☐	9	Chipper Jones	50.00	22.00
☐	10	Albert Belle	20.00	9.00
☐	11	Tony Gwynn	40.00	18.00
☐	12	Mo Vaughn	20.00	9.00
☐	13	Barry Larkin	12.00	5.50
☐	14	Manny Ramirez	15.00	6.75
☐	15	Greg Maddux	50.00	22.00

1996 Leaf Total Bases

PAUL MOLITOR

1996 Leaf Hats Off

Randomly inserted in hobby packs only at a rate of one in 72, this 12-card set is printed on canvas and features the top offensive stars. Only 5,000 of each card was printed and are individually numbered. The fronts carry a color action player cut-out over a base background. The backs display another player photo and 1995 stats.

Randomly inserted in retail packs only at a rate of one in 72, this 8-card set was printed and embossed on a wool-like material with the feel of a Major League ball cap. Only 5,000 of each player was produced and is individually numbered.

		MINT	NRMT
COMPLETE SET (12)		150.00	70.00
COMMON CARD (1-12)		3.00	1.35
UNLISTED STARS		6.00	2.70
STATED ODDS 1:72 HOBBY			
STATED PRINT RUN 5000 SERIAL #'d SETS			

		MINT	NRMT
COMPLETE SET (8)		200.00	90.00
COMMON CARD (1-8)		5.00	2.20
STATED ODDS 1:72 RETAIL			
STATED PRINT RUN 5000 SERIAL #'d SETS			

			MINT	NRMT
☐	1	Cal Ripken	30.00	13.50
☐	2	Barry Larkin	5.00	2.20
☐	3	Frank Thomas	30.00	13.50
☐	4	Mo Vaughn	10.00	4.50
☐	5	Ken Griffey Jr.	40.00	18.00
☐	6	Hideo Nomo	20.00	9.00
☐	7	Albert Belle	10.00	4.50
☐	8	Greg Maddux	25.00	11.00

			MINT	NRMT
☐	1	Frank Thomas	25.00	11.00
☐	2	Albert Belle	8.00	3.60
☐	3	Rafael Palmeiro	5.00	2.20
☐	4	Barry Bonds	8.00	3.60
☐	5	Kirby Puckett	12.00	5.50
☐	6	Joe Carter	4.00	1.80
☐	7	Paul Molitor	6.00	2.70
☐	8	Fred McGriff	5.00	2.20
☐	9	Ken Griffey Jr.	30.00	13.50
☐	10	Carlos Baerga	3.00	1.35
☐	11	Juan Gonzalez	15.00	6.75
☐	12	Cal Ripken	25.00	11.00

1996 Leaf Picture Perfect

Randomly inserted in hobby (1-6) and retail (7-12) packs at a rate of one in 140, this 12-card set is printed on real wood with gold foil trim. The fronts feature a color player action framed photo. The backs carry another player photo with player information. Only 5,000 of each card were printed and are individually numbered.

		MINT	NRMT
COMPLETE SET (12)		250.00	110.00
COMMON CARD (1-12)		10.00	4.50
CARDS 1-6 STATED ODDS 1:140 HOBBY			
CARDS 7-12 RANDOM INS.IN RET.PACKS			
STATED PRINT RUN 5000 SERIAL #'d SETS			

			MINT	NRMT
☐	1	Frank Thomas	30.00	13.50
☐	2	Cal Ripken	30.00	13.50
☐	3	Greg Maddux	25.00	11.00
☐	4	Manny Ramirez	10.00	4.50
☐	5	Chipper Jones	25.00	11.00
☐	6	Tony Gwynn	20.00	9.00
☐	7	Ken Griffey Jr.	40.00	18.00
☐	8	Albert Belle	10.00	4.50
☐	9	Jeff Bagwell	15.00	6.75
☐	10	Mike Piazza	25.00	11.00
☐	11	Mo Vaughn	10.00	4.50
☐	12	Barry Bonds	10.00	4.50
☐	P10	Mike Piazza Promo	3.00	1.35

1996 Leaf Statistical Standouts

Randomly inserted in hobby packs only at a rate of one in 210, this 8-card set features eight players who stood out from the rest statistically. The cards were printed on a material with the feel of a baseball. Only 2,500 of each card was printed and is numbered individually.

1997 Leaf

The 400-card Leaf set was issued in two separate 200-card series. 10-card packs carried a suggested retail of $2.99. Each card features color action player photos with foil enhancement. The backs carry another player photo and season and career statistics. The set contains the following subsets: Legacy (188-197/348-367), Checklists (198-200/398-400) and Gamers (368-397). The only key Rookie

Cards in the set are Jose Cruz Jr. and Hideki Irabu. In a tie in with the 50th anniversary of Jackie Robinson's major league debut, Donruss/Leaf also issued some collectible items. They made 42 all-leather jackets (issued to match Robinson's uniform number). There were also 311 leather jackets produced (to match Robinson's career batting average). 1,500 lithographs were also produced of which Rachel Robinson signed 500 of them.

	MINT	NRMT
COMPLETE SET (400)	40.00	18.00
COMPLETE SERIES 1 (200)	20.00	9.00
COMPLETE SERIES 2 (200)	20.00	9.00
COMMON CARD (1-400)	.15	.07
MINOR STARS	.30	.14
UNLISTED STARS	.60	.25
SUBSET CARDS HALF VALUE OF BASE CARDS		

☐ 1 Wade Boggs	.60		.25
☐ 2 Brian McRae	.15		.07
☐ 3 Jeff D'Amico	.15		.07
☐ 4 George Arias	.15		.07
☐ 5 Billy Wagner	.30		.14
☐ 6 Ray Lankford	.30		.14
☐ 7 Will Clark	.40		.18
☐ 8 Edgar Renteria	.30		.14
☐ 9 Alex Ochoa	.15		.07
☐ 10 Roberto Hernandez	.15		.07
☐ 11 Joe Carter	.30		.14
☐ 12 Gregg Jefferies	.15		.07
☐ 13 Mark Grace	.40		.18
☐ 14 Roberto Alomar	.60		.25
☐ 15 Joe Randa	.15		.07
☐ 16 Alex Rodriguez	2.00		.90
☐ 17 Tony Gwynn	1.50		.70
☐ 18 Steve Gibralter	.15		.07
☐ 19 Scott Stahoviak	.15		.07
☐ 20 Matt Williams	.40		.18
☐ 21 Quinton McCracken	.15		.07
☐ 22 Ugueth Urbina	.15		.07
☐ 23 Jermaine Allensworth	.15		.07
☐ 24 Paul Molitor	.60		.25
☐ 25 Carlos Delgado	.30		.14
☐ 26 Bob Abreu	.30		.14
☐ 27 Jon Jaha	.15		.07
☐ 28 Rusty Greer	.30		.14
☐ 29 Kimera Bartee	.15		.07
☐ 30 Ruben Rivera	.30		.14
☐ 31 Jason Kendall	.30		.14
☐ 32 Lance Johnson	.15		.07
☐ 33 Robin Ventura	.30		.14
☐ 34 Kevin Appier	.15		.07
☐ 35 John Mabry	.15		.07
☐ 36 Ricky Otero	.15		.07
☐ 37 Mike Lansing	.15		.07
☐ 38 Mark McGwire	1.25		.55
☐ 39 Tim Naehring	.15		.07
☐ 40 Tom Glavine	.30		.14
☐ 41 Rey Ordonez	.15		.07
☐ 42 Tony Clark	.60		.25
☐ 43 Rafael Palmeiro	.40		.18

☐ 44 Pedro Martinez	.60		.25
☐ 45 Keith Lockhart	.15		.07
☐ 46 Dan Wilson	.15		.07
☐ 47 John Wetteland	.15		.07
☐ 48 Chan Ho Park	.60		.25
☐ 49 Gary Sheffield	.60		.25
☐ 50 Shawn Estes	.30		.14
☐ 51 Royce Clayton	.15		.07
☐ 52 Jaime Navarro	.15		.07
☐ 53 Raul Casanova	.15		.07
☐ 54 Jeff Bagwell	1.25		.55
☐ 55 Barry Larkin	.40		.18
☐ 56 Charles Nagy	.30		.14
☐ 57 Ken Caminiti	.40		.18
☐ 58 Todd Hollandsworth	.15		.07
☐ 59 Pat Hentgen	.30		.14
☐ 60 Jose Valentin	.15		.07
☐ 61 Frank Rodriguez	.15		.07
☐ 62 Mickey Tettleton	.15		.07
☐ 63 Marty Cordova	.30		.14
☐ 64 Cecil Fielder	.30		.14
☐ 65 Barry Bonds	.75		.35
☐ 66 Scott Servais	.15		.07
☐ 67 Ernie Young	.15		.07
☐ 68 Wilson Alvarez	.15		.07
☐ 69 Mike Grace	.15		.07
☐ 70 Shane Reynolds	.15		.07
☐ 71 Henry Rodriguez	.15		.07
☐ 72 Eric Karros	.30		.14
☐ 73 Mark Langston	.15		.07
☐ 74 Scott Karl	.15		.07
☐ 75 Trevor Hoffman	.15		.07
☐ 76 Orel Hershiser	.30		.14
☐ 77 John Smoltz	.30		.14
☐ 78 Raul Mondesi	.40		.18
☐ 79 Jeff Brantley	.15		.07
☐ 80 Donne Wall	.15		.07
☐ 81 Joey Cora	.30		.14
☐ 82 Mel Rojas	.15		.07
☐ 83 Chad Mottola	.15		.07
☐ 84 Omar Vizquel	.30		.14
☐ 85 Greg Maddux	2.00		.90
☐ 86 Jamey Wright	.15		.07
☐ 87 Chuck Finley	.15		.07
☐ 88 Brady Anderson	.40		.18
☐ 89 Alex Gonzalez	.15		.07
☐ 90 Andy Benes	.30		.14
☐ 91 Reggie Jefferson	.15		.07
☐ 92 Paul O'Neill	.30		.14
☐ 93 Javier Lopez	.30		.14
☐ 94 Mark Grudzielanek	.15		.07
☐ 95 Marc Newfield	.15		.07
☐ 96 Kevin Ritz	.15		.07
☐ 97 Fred McGriff	.30		.14
☐ 98 Dwight Gooden	.30		.14
☐ 99 Hideo Nomo	1.50		.70
☐ 100 Steve Finley	.30		.14
☐ 101 Juan Gonzalez	1.50		.70
☐ 102 Jay Buhner	.40		.18
☐ 103 Paul Wilson	.15		.07
☐ 104 Alan Benes	.30		.14
☐ 105 Manny Ramirez	.60		.25
☐ 106 Kevin Elster	.15		.07
☐ 107 Frank Thomas	2.50		1.10
☐ 108 Orlando Miller	.15		.07
☐ 109 Ramon Martinez	.30		.14
☐ 110 Kenny Lofton	.75		.35
☐ 111 Bernie Williams	.60		.25
☐ 112 Robby Thompson	.15		.07
☐ 113 Bernard Gilkey	.15		.07
☐ 114 Ray Durham	.15		.07
☐ 115 Jeff Cirillo	.30		.14
☐ 116 Brian Jordan	.30		.14
☐ 117 Rich Becker	.15		.07
☐ 118 Al Leiter	.15		.07
☐ 119 Mark Johnson	.15		.07
☐ 120 Ellis Burks	.30		.14
☐ 121 Sammy Sosa	.60		.25
☐ 122 Willie Greene	.15		.07
☐ 123 Michael Tucker	.30		.14
☐ 124 Eddie Murray	.60		.25
☐ 125 Joey Hamilton	.30		.14
☐ 126 Antonio Osuna	.15		.07
☐ 127 Bobby Higginson	.30		.14
☐ 128 Tomas Perez	.15		.07
☐ 129 Tim Salmon	.60		.25

☐ 130 Mark Wohlers	.15		.07
☐ 131 Charles Johnson	.30		.14
☐ 132 Randy Johnson	.60		.25
☐ 133 Brooks Kieschnick	.15		.07
☐ 134 Al Martin	.15		.07
☐ 135 Dante Bichette	.30		.14
☐ 136 Andy Pettitte	.60		.25
☐ 137 Jason Giambi	.30		.14
☐ 138 James Baldwin	.15		.07
☐ 139 Ben McDonald	.15		.07
☐ 140 Shawn Green	.15		.07
☐ 141 Geronimo Berroa	.15		.07
☐ 142 Jose Offerman	.15		.07
☐ 143 Curtis Pride	.15		.07
☐ 144 Terrell Wade	.15		.07
☐ 145 Ismael Valdes	.30		.14
☐ 146 Mike Mussina	.60		.25
☐ 147 Mariano Rivera	.30		.14
☐ 148 Ken Hill	.15		.07
☐ 149 Darin Erstad	1.00		.45
☐ 150 Jay Bell	.30		.14
☐ 151 Mo Vaughn	.75		.35
☐ 152 Ozzie Smith	.75		.35
☐ 153 Jose Mesa	.15		.07
☐ 154 Osvaldo Fernandez	.15		.07
☐ 155 Vinny Castilla	.30		.14
☐ 156 Jason Isringhausen	.15		.07
☐ 157 B.J. Surhoff	.15		.07
☐ 158 Robert Perez	.15		.07
☐ 159 Ron Coomer	.15		.07
☐ 160 Darren Oliver	.15		.07
☐ 161 Mike Mohler	.15		.07
☐ 162 Russ Davis	.15		.07
☐ 163 Bret Boone	.15		.07
☐ 164 Ricky Bottalico	.15		.07
☐ 165 Derek Jeter	2.00		.90
☐ 166 Orlando Merced	.15		.07
☐ 167 John Valentin	.15		.07
☐ 168 Andruw Jones	1.50		.70
☐ 169 Angel Echevarria	.15		.07
☐ 170 Todd Walker	.30		.14
☐ 171 Desi Relaford	.15		.07
☐ 172 Trey Beamon	.15		.07
☐ 173 Brian Giles	.15		.07
☐ 174 Scott Rolen	1.50		.70
☐ 175 Shannon Stewart	.30		.14
☐ 176 Dmitri Young	.15		.07
☐ 177 Justin Thompson	.30		.14
☐ 178 Trot Nixon	.15		.07
☐ 179 Josh Booty	.40		.18
☐ 180 Robin Jennings	.15		.07
☐ 181 Marvin Benard	.15		.07
☐ 182 Luis Castillo	.30		.14
☐ 183 Wendell Magee	.15		.07
☐ 184 Vladimir Guerrero	1.25		.55
☐ 185 Nomar Garciaparra	2.00		.90
☐ 186 Ryan Hancock	.15		.07
☐ 187 Mike Cameron	.40		.18
☐ 188 Cal Ripken Jr.	1.25		.55
☐ 189 Chipper Jones LG	1.00		.45
☐ 190 Albert Belle LG	.40		.18
☐ 191 Mike Piazza LG	1.00		.45
☐ 192 Chuck Knoblauch LG.	.30		.14
☐ 193 Ken Griffey Jr. LG	1.50		.70
☐ 194 Ivan Rodriguez LG	.40		.18
☐ 195 Jose Canseco LG	.40		.18
☐ 196 Ryne Sandberg LG	.40		.18
☐ 197 Jim Thome LG	.30		.14
☐ 198 Andy Pettitte CL	.30		.14
☐ 199 Andruw Jones CL	.75		.35
☐ 200 Derek Jeter CL	1.00		.45
☐ 201 Chipper Jones	2.00		.90
☐ 202 Albert Belle	.75		.35
☐ 203 Mike Piazza	2.00		.90
☐ 204 Ken Griffey Jr.	3.00		1.35
☐ 205 Ryne Sandberg	.75		.35
☐ 206 Jose Canseco	.40		.18
☐ 207 Chili Davis	.30		.14
☐ 208 Roger Clemens	1.25		.55
☐ 209 Deion Sanders	.30		.14
☐ 210 Darryl Hamilton	.15		.07
☐ 211 Jermaine Dye	.15		.07
☐ 212 Matt Williams	.40		.18
☐ 213 Kevin Elster	.15		.07
☐ 214 John Wetteland	.15		.07
☐ 215 Garret Anderson	.30		.14

#	Player		
216	Kevin Brown	.30	.14
217	Matt Lawton	.15	.07
218	Cal Ripken	2.50	1.10
219	Moises Alou	.30	.14
220	Chuck Knoblauch	.60	.25
221	Ivan Rodriguez	.75	.35
222	Travis Fryman	.30	.14
223	Jim Thome	.60	.25
224	Eddie Murray	.60	.25
225	Eric Young	.15	.07
226	Ron Gant	.30	.14
227	Tony Phillips	.15	.07
228	Reggie Sanders	.15	.07
229	Johnny Damon	.15	.07
230	Bill Pulsipher	.15	.07
231	Jim Edmonds	.40	.18
232	Melvin Nieves	.15	.07
233	Ryan Klesko	.40	.18
234	David Cone	.30	.14
235	Derek Bell	.15	.07
236	Julio Franco	.30	.14
237	Juan Gonzalez	.15	.07
238	Larry Walker	.60	.25
239	Delino DeShields	.15	.07
240	Troy Percival	.15	.07
241	Andres Galarraga	.60	.25
242	Rondell White	.30	.14
243	John Burkett	.15	.07
244	J.T. Snow	.30	.14
245	Alex Fernandez	.30	.14
246	Edgar Martinez	.40	.18
247	Craig Biggio	.40	.18
248	Todd Hundley	.30	.14
249	Jimmy Key	.30	.14
250	Cliff Floyd	.15	.07
251	Jeff Conine	.30	.14
252	Curt Schilling	.30	.14
253	Jeff King	.15	.07
254	Tino Martinez	.60	.25
255	Carlos Baerga	.15	.07
256	Jeff Fassero	.15	.07
257	Dean Palmer	.15	.07
258	Robb Nen	.15	.07
259	Sandy Alomar Jr.	.30	.14
260	Carlos Perez	.15	.07
261	Rickey Henderson	.30	.14
262	Bobby Bonilla	.30	.14
263	Darren Daulton	.30	.14
264	Jim Leyritz	.15	.07
265	Dennis Martinez	.15	.07
266	Butch Huskey	.30	.14
267	Joe Vitiello	.15	.07
268	Steve Trachsel	.15	.07
269	Glenallen Hill	.15	.07
270	Terry Steinbach	.15	.07
271	Mark McLemore	.15	.07
272	Devon White	.15	.07
273	Jeff Kent	.15	.07
274	Tim Raines	.30	.14
275	Carlos Garcia	.15	.07
276	Hal Morris	.15	.07
277	Gary Gaetti	.15	.07
278	John Olerud	.30	.14
279	Wally Joyner	.30	.14
280	Brian Hunter	.30	.14
281	Steve Karsay	.15	.07
282	Denny Neagle	.30	.14
283	Jose Herrera	.15	.07
284	Todd Stottlemyre	.15	.07
285	Bip Roberts	.15	.07
286	Kevin Seitzer	.15	.07
287	Benji Gil	.15	.07
288	Dennis Eckersley	.30	.14
289	Brad Ausmus	.15	.07
290	Otis Nixon	.15	.07
291	Darryl Strawberry	.30	.14
292	Marquis Grissom	.30	.14
293	Darryl Kile	.30	.14
294	Quilvio Veras	.15	.07
295	Tom Goodwin	.15	.07
296	Benito Santiago	.15	.07
297	Mike Bordick	.15	.07
298	Roberto Kelly	.15	.07
299	David Justice	.60	.25
300	Carl Everett	.15	.07
301	Mark Whiten	.15	.07
302	Aaron Sele	.15	.07
303	Darren Dreifort	.15	.07
304	Bobby Jones	.15	.07
305	Fernando Vina	.15	.07
306	Ed Sprague	.15	.07
307	Andy Ashby	.15	.07
308	Tony Fernandez	.15	.07
309	Roger Pavlik	.15	.07
310	Mark Clark	.15	.07
311	Mariano Duncan	.15	.07
312	Tyler Houston	.15	.07
313	Eric Davis	.30	.14
314	Greg Vaughn	.15	.07
315	David Segui	.15	.07
316	Dave Nilsson	.15	.07
317	F.P. Santangelo	.15	.07
318	Wilton Guerrero	.15	.07
319	Jose Guillen	.75	.35
320	Kevin Orie	.30	.14
321	Derrek Lee	.40	.18
322	Bubba Trammell	.60	.25
323	Pokey Reese	.15	.07
324	Hideki Irabu	.60	.25
325	Scott Spiezio	.30	.14
326	Bartolo Colon	.30	.14
327	Damon Mashore	.15	.07
329	Chris Carpenter	.30	.14
330	Jose Cruz Jr.	5.00	2.20
331	Todd Greene	.30	.14
332	Brian Moehler	.15	.07
333	Mike Sweeney	.30	.14
334	Neifi Perez	.30	.14
335	Matt Morris	.30	.14
336	Marvin Benard	.15	.07
337	Karim Garcia	.30	.14
338	Jason Dickson	.30	.14
339	Brant Brown	.15	.07
340	Jeff Suppan	.30	.14
341	Deivi Cruz	.50	.23
342	Antone Williamson	.15	.07
343	Curtis Goodwin	.15	.07
344	Brooks Kieschnick	.15	.07
345	Tony Womack	.50	.23
346	Rudy Pemberton	.15	.07
347	Todd Dunwoody	.40	.18
348	Frank Thomas LG	1.25	.55
349	Andruw Jones LG	.75	.35
350	Alex Rodriguez LG	1.00	.45
351	Greg Maddux LG	1.00	.45
352	Jeff Bagwell LG	.60	.25
353	Juan Gonzalez LG	.75	.35
354	Barry Bonds LG	.40	.18
355	Mark McGwire LG	.60	.25
356	Tony Gwynn LG	.75	.35
357	Gary Sheffield LG	.30	.14
358	Derek Jeter LG	1.00	.45
359	Manny Ramirez LG	.30	.14
360	Hideo Nomo LG	1.00	.45
361	Sammy Sosa LG	.30	.14
362	Paul Molitor LG	.30	.14
363	Kenny Lofton LG	.40	.18
364	Eddie Murray LG	.30	.14
365	Barry Larkin LG	.30	.14
366	Roger Clemens LG	.60	.25
367	John Smoltz LG	.15	.07
368	Alex Rodriguez GM	1.00	.45
369	Frank Thomas GM	1.25	.55
370	Cal Ripken GM	1.25	.55
371	Ken Griffey Jr. GM	1.50	.70
372	Greg Maddux GM	1.00	.45
373	Mike Piazza GM	1.00	.45
374	Chipper Jones GM	1.00	.45
375	Albert Belle GM	.40	.18
376	Chuck Knoblauch GM	.30	.14
377	Brady Anderson GM	.30	.14
378	David Justice GM	.30	.14
379	Randy Johnson GM	.30	.14
380	Wade Boggs GM	.30	.14
381	Kevin Brown GM	.30	.14
382	Tom Glavine GM	.15	.07
383	Raul Mondesi GM	.30	.14
384	Ivan Rodriguez GM	.40	.18
385	Larry Walker GM	.30	.14
386	Bernie Williams GM	.30	.14
387	Rusty Greer GM	.30	.14
388	Rafael Palmeiro GM	.30	.14
389	Matt Williams GM	.30	.14
390	Eric Young GM	.15	.07
391	Fred McGriff GM	.30	.14
392	Ken Caminiti GM	.30	.14
393	Roberto Alomar GM	.30	.14
394	Brian Jordan GM	.15	.07
395	Mark Grace GM	.30	.14
396	Jim Edmonds GM	.30	.14
397	Deion Sanders GM	.30	.14
398	Vladimir Guerrero CL	.75	.35
399	Darin Erstad CL	.40	.18
400	Nomar Garciaparra CL	1.00	.45
NNO	J.Robinson Reprint	50.00	22.00

1997 Leaf Fractal Matrix

This 400-card set is parallel to the regular Leaf issue and features color player photos with either a bronze, silver or gold finish. Only 200 cards are bronze, 120 cards are silver, and 80 cards are gold. No card is available in more than one of the colors.

	MINT	NRMT
COMMON BRONZE	1.50	.70
BRONZE MINOR STARS .	2.50	1.10
BRONZE SEMISTARS	4.00	1.80
BRONZE UNLISTED STARS ..	6.00	2.70
COMMON SILVER	5.00	2.20
SILVER MINOR STARS	8.00	3.60
SILVER SEMISTARS	12.00	5.50
SILVER UNLISTED STARS .	20.00	9.00
COMMON GOLD	8.00	3.60
GOLD MINOR STARS	12.00	5.50
GOLD SEMISTARS	20.00	9.00
GOLD UNLISTED STARS .	30.00	13.50
RANDOM INSERTS IN PACKS ..		

#	Player		
1	Wade Boggs GY	40.00	18.00
2	Brian McRae BY	1.50	.70
3	Jeff D'Amico BY	1.50	.70
4	George Arias SY	5.00	2.20
5	Billy Wagner SY	8.00	3.60
6	Ray Lankford BZ	2.50	1.10
7	Will Clark SY	12.00	5.50
8	Edgar Renteria SY	8.00	3.60
9	Alex Ochoa SY	5.00	2.20
10	Roberto Hernandez BX	1.50	.70
11	Joe Carter SY	8.00	3.60
12	Gregg Jefferies BY	1.50	.70
13	Mark Grace SY	12.00	5.50
14	Roberto Alomar GY	40.00	18.00
15	Joe Randa BX	1.50	.70
16	Alex Rodriguez GZ.	100.00	45.00
17	Tony Gwynn GZ.	80.00	36.00
18	Steve Gibralter BY	1.50	.70
19	Scott Stahoviak BX	1.50	.70
20	Matt Williams SZ.	12.00	5.50
21	Quinton McCracken BY	1.50	.70
22	Ugueth Urbina BX	1.50	.70
23	Jermaine Allensworth SX	5.00	2.20
24	Paul Molitor GX	60.00	27.00

#	Player		
25	Carlos Delgado SY	8.00	3.60
26	Bob Abreu SY	8.00	3.60
27	John Jaha SY	5.00	2.20
28	Rusty Greer SZ	8.00	3.60
29	Kimera Bartee BX	1.50	.70
30	Ruben Rivera SY	8.00	3.60
31	Jason Kendall SY	8.00	3.60
32	Lance Johnson SX	1.50	.70
33	Robin Ventura BY	2.50	1.10
34	Kevin Appier SX	8.00	3.60
35	John Mabry SY	5.00	2.20
36	Ricky Otero BX	1.50	.70
37	Mike Lansing BX	1.50	.70
38	Mark McGwire GZ	60.00	27.00
39	Tim Naehring BX	1.50	.70
40	Tom Glavine SZ	8.00	3.60
41	Rey Ordonez SY	5.00	2.20
42	Tony Clark SY	20.00	9.00
43	Rafael Palmeiro SY	12.00	5.50
44	Pedro Martinez BX	6.00	2.70
45	Keith Lockhart BX	1.50	.70
46	Dan Wilson BY	1.50	.70
47	John Wetteland BY	1.50	.70
48	Chan Ho Park BX	6.00	2.70
49	Gary Sheffield GZ	30.00	13.50
50	Shawn Estes BX	2.50	1.10
51	Royce Clayton BX	1.50	.70
52	Jaime Navarro BX	1.50	.70
53	Raul Casanova BX	1.50	.70
54	Jeff Bagwell GZ	60.00	27.00
55	Barry Larkin GX	40.00	18.00
56	Charles Nagy BY	2.50	1.10
57	Ken Caminiti GY	20.00	9.00
58	Todd Hollandsworth SZ	5.00	2.20
59	Pat Hentgen SX	8.00	3.60
60	Jose Valentin BX	1.50	.70
61	Frank Rodriguez BX	1.50	.70
62	Mickey Tettleton BX	1.50	.70
63	Marty Cordova GX	12.00	5.50
64	Cecil Fielder SX	8.00	3.60
65	Barry Bonds GZ	40.00	18.00
66	Scott Servais BX	1.50	.70
67	Ernie Young BX	1.50	.70
68	Wilson Alvarez BX	1.50	.70
69	Mike Grace BX	1.50	.70
70	Shane Reynolds SY	5.00	2.20
71	Henry Rodriguez SY	5.00	2.20
72	Eric Karros BX	2.50	1.10
73	Mark Langston BX	1.50	.70
74	Scott Karl BX	1.50	.70
75	Trevor Hoffman BX	1.50	.70
76	Orel Hershiser SX	8.00	3.60
77	John Smoltz GY	12.00	5.50
78	Raul Mondesi GZ	20.00	9.00
79	Jeff Brantley BX	1.50	.70
80	Donne Wall BX	1.50	.70
81	Joey Cora BX	2.50	1.10
82	Mel Rojas BX	1.50	.70
83	Chad Mottola BX	1.50	.70
84	Omar Vizquel BX	1.50	1.10
85	Greg Maddux GZ	100.00	45.00
86	Jamey Wright SY	5.00	2.20
87	Chuck Finley BX	1.50	.70
88	Brady Anderson GY	20.00	9.00
89	Alex Gonzalez SX	5.00	2.20
90	Andy Benes BX	2.50	1.10
91	Reggie Jefferson BX	1.50	.70
92	Paul O'Neill BY	2.50	1.10
93	Javier Lopez SX	8.00	3.60
94	Mark Grudzielanek SX	5.00	2.20
95	Marc Newfield BX	1.50	.70
96	Kevin Ritz BX	1.50	.70
97	Fred McGriff GY	20.00	9.00
98	Dwight Gooden SX	8.00	3.60
99	Hideo Nomo SY	50.00	22.00
100	Steve Finley SY	2.50	1.10
101	Juan Gonzalez GZ	80.00	36.00
102	Jay Buhner SZ	12.00	5.50
103	Paul Wilson SY	5.00	2.20
104	Alan Benes BY	2.50	1.10
105	Manny Ramirez GZ	30.00	13.50
106	Kevin Elster BX	1.50	.70
107	Frank Thomas GZ	120.00	55.00
108	Orlando Miller BX	1.50	.70
109	Ramon Martinez BX	2.50	1.10
110	Kenny Lofton GZ	40.00	18.00
111	Bernie Williams GY	30.00	13.50
112	Robby Thompson BX	1.50	.70
113	Bernard Gilkey BZ	1.50	.70
114	Ray Durham BX	1.50	.70
115	Jeff Cirillo BZ	8.00	3.60
116	Brian Jordan GZ	12.00	5.50
117	Rich Becker SY	5.00	2.20
118	Al Leiter BX	1.50	.70
119	Mark Johnson BX	1.50	.70
120	Ellis Burks BY	2.50	1.10
121	Sammy Sosa GZ	30.00	13.50
122	Willie Greene BX	1.50	.70
123	Michael Tucker BX	2.50	1.10
124	Eddie Murray GY	40.00	18.00
125	Joey Hamilton SY	8.00	3.60
126	Antonio Osuna BX	1.50	.70
127	Bobby Higginson SY	8.00	3.60
128	Tomas Perez BX	1.50	.70
129	Tim Salmon GZ	30.00	13.50
130	Mark Wohlers BX	1.50	.70
131	Charles Johnson SX	8.00	3.60
132	Randy Johnson SY	20.00	9.00
133	Brooks Kieschnick SX	5.00	2.20
134	Al Martin SY	8.00	3.60
135	Dante Bichette BX	2.50	1.10
136	Andy Pettitte GZ	30.00	13.50
137	Jason Giambi GY	12.00	5.50
138	James Baldwin SX	5.00	2.20
139	Ben McDonald BX	1.50	.70
140	Shawn Green SX	5.00	2.20
141	Geronimo Berroa BY	1.50	.70
142	Jose Offerman BX	1.50	.70
143	Curtis Pride BX	1.50	.70
144	Terrell Wade BX	1.50	.70
145	Ismael Valdes SX	8.00	3.60
146	Mike Mussina SY	20.00	9.00
147	Mariano Rivera SX	8.00	3.60
148	Ken Hill BY	1.50	.70
149	Darin Erstad GZ	40.00	18.00
150	Jay Bell BX	2.50	1.10
151	Mo Vaughn GZ	40.00	18.00
152	Ozzie Smith GY	50.00	22.00
153	Jose Mesa BX	1.50	.70
154	Osvaldo Fernandez BX	1.50	.70
155	Vinny Castilla BY	2.50	1.10
156	Jason Isringhausen SY	5.00	2.20
157	B.J. Surhoff BX	1.50	.70
158	Robert Perez BX	1.50	.70
159	Ron Coomer BX	1.50	.70
160	Darren Oliver BX	1.50	.70
161	Mike Mohler BX	1.50	.70
162	Russ Davis BX	1.50	.70
163	Bret Boone BX	1.50	.70
164	Ricky Bottalico BX	1.50	.70
165	Derek Jeter GZ	80.00	36.00
166	Orlando Merced BX	1.50	.70
167	John Valentin BX	1.50	.70
168	Andruw Jones GZ	60.00	27.00
169	Angel Echeverria BX	1.50	.70
170	Todd Walker GZ	12.00	5.50
171	Desi Relaford BY	1.50	.70
172	Trey Beamon SX	5.00	2.20
173	Brian Giles SY	5.00	2.20
174	Scott Rolen GZ	60.00	27.00
175	Shannon Stewart SZ	8.00	3.60
176	Dmitri Young GZ	8.00	3.60
177	Justin Thompson BX	2.50	1.10
178	Trot Nixon SY	5.00	2.20
179	Josh Booty SY	12.00	5.50
180	Robin Jennings BX	1.50	.70
181	Marvin Benard BX	1.50	.70
182	Luis Castillo BY	2.50	1.10
183	Wendell Magee BX	1.50	.70
184	Vladimir Guerrero GX	80.00	36.00
185	Nomar Garciaparra GX	150.00	70.00
186	Ryan Hancock BX	1.50	.70
187	Mike Cameron SX	12.00	5.50
188	Cal Ripken LG BZ	25.00	11.00
189	Chipper Jones LG SZ	50.00	22.00
190	Albert Belle LG GZ	20.00	9.00
191	Mike Piazza LG BZ	20.00	9.00
192	Chuck Knoblauch LG SY	20.00	9.00
193	Ken Griffey Jr. LG BZ	30.00	13.50
194	Ivan Rodriguez LG GZ	40.00	18.00
195	Jose Canseco LG SX	12.00	5.50
196	Ryne Sandberg LG SX	30.00	13.50
197	Jim Thome LG GY	40.00	18.00
198	Andy Pettitte CL BY	6.00	2.70
199	Andruw Jones CL BY	12.00	5.50
200	Derek Jeter CL SY	50.00	22.00
201	Chipper Jones GX	250.00	110.00
202	Albert Belle GY	50.00	22.00
203	Mike Piazza GY	120.00	55.00
204	Ken Griffey Jr. GX	500.00	220.00
205	Ryne Sandberg GZ	40.00	18.00
206	Jose Canseco SY	12.00	5.50
207	Chili Davis BX	2.50	1.10
208	Roger Clemens GZ	60.00	27.00
209	Deion Sanders GZ	12.00	5.50
210	Darryl Hamilton BX	1.50	.70
211	Jermaine Dye SX	5.00	2.20
212	Matt Williams GY	20.00	9.00
213	Kevin Elster BX	1.50	.70
214	John Wetteland SX	5.00	2.20
215	Garret Anderson GZ	12.00	5.50
216	Kevin Brown GY	12.00	5.50
217	Matt Lawton SY	5.00	2.20
218	Cal Ripken GX	400.00	180.00
219	Moises Alou GY	12.00	5.50
220	Chuck Knoblauch GZ	30.00	13.50
221	Ivan Rodriguez GY	50.00	22.00
222	Travis Fryman BY	2.50	1.10
223	Jim Thome GZ	30.00	13.50
224	Eddie Murray SZ	15.00	6.75
225	Eric Young GZ	8.00	3.60
226	Ron Gant SX	8.00	3.60
227	Tony Phillips BX	1.50	.70
228	Reggie Sanders BY	1.50	.70
229	Johnny Damon SZ	5.00	2.20
230	Bill Pulsipher BX	1.50	.70
231	Jim Edmonds GZ	20.00	9.00
232	Melvin Nieves BX	1.50	.70
233	Ryan Klesko GZ	20.00	9.00
234	David Cone SX	8.00	3.60
235	Derek Bell BY	1.50	.70
236	Julio Franco SX	8.00	3.60
237	Juan Guzman BX	1.50	.70
238	Larry Walker GZ	30.00	13.50
239	Delino DeShields BX	1.50	.70
240	Troy Percival BY	1.50	.70
241	Andres Galarraga GZ	30.00	13.50
242	Rondell White GZ	12.00	5.50
243	John Burkett BX	1.50	.70
244	J.T. Snow BY	2.50	1.10
245	Alex Fernandez SY	8.00	3.60
246	Edgar Martinez GZ	20.00	9.00
247	Craig Biggio GZ	20.00	9.00
248	Todd Hundley GY	12.00	5.50
249	Jimmy Key SX	8.00	3.60
250	Cliff Floyd BY	1.50	.70
251	Jeff Conine BY	2.50	1.10
252	Curt Schilling BX	2.50	1.10
253	Jeff King BX	1.50	.70
254	Tino Martinez GZ	30.00	13.50
255	Carlos Baerga SY	5.00	2.20
256	Jeff Fassero BY	1.50	.70
257	Dean Palmer SY	5.00	2.20
258	Robb Nen BX	1.50	.70
259	Sandy Alomar Jr. SY	8.00	3.60
260	Carlos Perez BX	1.50	.70
261	Rickey Henderson SY	12.00	5.50
262	Bobby Bonilla SY	8.00	3.60
263	Darren Daulton BX	2.50	1.10
264	Jim Leyritz BX	1.50	.70
265	Dennis Martinez BX	2.50	1.10
266	Butch Huskey BX	2.50	1.10
267	Joe Vitiello SY	5.00	2.20
268	Steve Trachsel BX	1.50	.70
269	Glenallen Hill BX	1.50	.70
270	Terry Steinbach BX	1.50	.70
271	Mark McLemore BX	1.50	.70
272	Devon White BX	1.50	.70
273	Jeff Kent BX	1.50	.70
274	Tim Raines BX	2.50	1.10
275	Carlos Garcia BX	1.50	.70
276	Hal Morris BX	1.50	.70
277	Gary Gaetti BX	1.50	.70
278	John Olerud SX	8.00	3.60
279	Wally Joyner BX	2.50	1.10
280	Brian Hunter SX	8.00	3.60
281	Steve Karsay BX	1.50	.70
282	Denny Neagle SX	8.00	3.60

☐ 283 Jose Herrera BX	1.50	.70	☐ 369 Frank Thomas GM BX	30.00	13.50
☐ 284 Todd Stottlemyre BX	1.50	.70	☐ 370 Cal Ripken GM SY	80.00	36.00
☐ 285 Bip Roberts SX	5.00	2.20	☐ 371 Ken Griffey Jr. GM SY	100.00	45.00
☐ 286 Kevin Seitzer BX	1.50	.70	☐ 372 Greg Maddux GM BX	25.00	11.00
☐ 287 Benji Gil BX	1.50	.70	☐ 373 Mike Piazza GM SX	80.00	36.00
☐ 288 Dennis Eckersley SX	8.00	3.60	☐ 374 Chipper Jones GM BY	20.00	9.00
☐ 289 Brad Ausmus BX	1.50	.70	☐ 375 Albert Belle GM	10.00	4.50
☐ 290 Otis Nixon BX	1.50	.70	☐ 376 Chuck Knoblauch GM BX	6.00	2.70
☐ 291 Darryl Strawberry BX	2.50	1.10	☐ 377 Brady Anderson GM BZ	2.50	1.10
☐ 292 Marquis Grissom SY	8.00	3.60	☐ 378 David Justice GM SX	20.00	9.00
☐ 293 Darryl Kile BX	2.50	1.10	☐ 379 Randy Johnson GM BZ	6.00	2.70
☐ 294 Quilvio Veras BX	1.50	.70	☐ 380 Wade Boggs GM BX	6.00	2.70
☐ 295 Tom Goodwin BX	1.50	.70	☐ 381 Kevin Brown GM BZ	2.50	1.10
☐ 296 Benito Santiago BX	1.50	.70	☐ 382 Tom Glavine GM SY	12.00	5.50
☐ 297 Mike Bordick BX	1.50	.70	☐ 383 Raul Mondesi GM SX	12.00	5.50
☐ 298 Roberto Kelly BX	1.50	.70	☐ 384 Ivan Rodriguez GM SX	30.00	13.50
☐ 299 David Justice GZ	30.00	13.50	☐ 385 Larry Walker GM BY	6.00	2.70
☐ 300 Carl Everett BX	1.50	.70	☐ 386 Bernie Williams GM BZ	6.00	2.70
☐ 301 Mark Whiten BX	1.50	.70	☐ 387 Rusty Greer GM BY	12.00	5.50
☐ 302 Aaron Sele BX	1.50	.70	☐ 388 Rafael Palmeiro GM GY	12.00	5.50
☐ 303 Darren Dreifort BX	1.50	.70	☐ 389 Matt Williams GM BX	4.00	1.80
☐ 304 Bobby Jones BX	1.50	.70	☐ 390 Eric Young GM BX	1.50	.70
☐ 305 Fernando Vina BX	1.50	.70	☐ 391 Fred McGriff GM BX	4.00	1.80
☐ 306 Ed Sprague BX	1.50	.70	☐ 392 Ken Caminiti GM BX	4.00	1.80
☐ 307 Andy Ashby SX	5.00	2.20	☐ 393 Roberto Alomar GM BZ	6.00	2.70
☐ 308 Tony Fernandez BX	1.50	.70	☐ 394 Brian Jordan BX	2.50	1.10
☐ 309 Roger Pavlik BX	1.50	.70	☐ 395 Mark Grace GM GZ	4.00	1.80
☐ 310 Mark Clark BX	1.50	.70	☐ 396 Jim Edmonds GM BY	4.00	1.80
☐ 311 Mariano Duncan BX	1.50	.70	☐ 397 Deion Sanders GM SY	8.00	3.60
☐ 312 Tyler Houston BX	1.50	.70	☐ 398 Vladimir Guerrero CL SZ	25.00	11.00
☐ 313 Eric Davis SY	8.00	3.60	☐ 399 Darin Erstad CL SX	25.00	11.00
☐ 314 Greg Vaughn BY	1.50	.70	☐ 400 Nomar Garciaparra CL SZ	40.00	18.00
☐ 315 David Segui SY	5.00	2.20			
☐ 316 Dave Nilsson SX	5.00	2.20			
☐ 317 F.P. Santangelo SX	5.00	2.20			
☐ 818 Wilton Guerrero GZ	8.00	3.60			
☐ 319 Jose Guillen GZ	30.00	13.50			
☐ 320 Kevin Orie SY	8.00	3.60			
☐ 321 Derrek Lee GZ	20.00	9.00			
☐ 322 Bubba Trammell SY	20.00	9.00			
☐ 323 Pokey Reese GZ	8.00	3.60			
☐ 324 Hideki Irabu GX	30.00	13.50			
☐ 325 Scott Spiezio SZ	8.00	3.60			
☐ 326 Bartolo Colon GZ	12.00	5.50			
☐ 327 Damon Mashore SY	5.00	2.20			
☐ 328 Ryan McGuire SY	5.00	2.20			
☐ 329 Chris Carpenter BX	2.50	1.10			
☐ 330 Jose Cruz Jr. GX	300.00	135.00			
☐ 331 Todd Greene SZ	8.00	3.60			
☐ 332 Brian Moehler BX	1.50	.70			
☐ 333 Mike Sweeney BX	2.50	1.10			
☐ 334 Neifi Perez GZ	12.00	5.50			
☐ 335 Matt Morris SX	8.00	3.60			
☐ 336 Marvin Benard BY	1.50	.70			
☐ 337 Karim Garcia SZ	8.00	3.60			
☐ 338 Jason Dickson SY	8.00	3.60			
☐ 339 Brant Brown SY	5.00	2.20			
☐ 340 Jeff Suppan SZ	8.00	3.60			
☐ 341 Deivi Cruz BX	6.00	2.70			
☐ 342 Antone Williamson GZ	8.00	3.60			
☐ 343 Curtis Goodwin BX	1.50	.70			
☐ 344 Brooks Kieschnick SY	5.00	2.20			
☐ 345 Tony Womack BX	4.00	1.80			
☐ 346 Rudy Pemberton BX	1.50	.70			
☐ 347 Todd Dunwoody BX	4.00	1.80			
☐ 348 Frank Thomas LG BY	36.00	16.00			
☐ 349 Andruw Jones LG SX	50.00	22.00			
☐ 350 Alex Rodriguez LG BY	20.00	9.00			
☐ 351 Greg Maddux LG SY	60.00	27.00			
☐ 352 Jeff Bagwell LG BY	12.00	5.50			
☐ 353 Juan Gonzalez LG SY	12.00	5.50			
☐ 354 Barry Bonds LG BY	8.00	3.60			
☐ 355 Mark McGwire LG BY	12.00	5.50			
☐ 356 Tony Gwynn LG BY	15.00	6.75			
☐ 357 Gary Sheffield LG BY	6.00	2.70			
☐ 358 Derek Jeter LG SX	60.00	27.00			
☐ 359 Manny Ramirez LG SY	20.00	9.00			
☐ 360 Hideo Nomo LG BZ	80.00	36.00			
☐ 361 Sammy Sosa LG BX	6.00	2.70			
☐ 362 Paul Molitor LG SZ	20.00	9.00			
☐ 363 Kenny Lofton LG BY	8.00	3.60			
☐ 364 Eddie Murray LG BX	8.00	3.60			
☐ 365 Barry Larkin LG BZ	12.00	5.50			
☐ 366 Roger Clemens LG SY	40.00	18.00			
☐ 367 John Smoltz BX	2.50	1.10			
☐ 368 Alex Rodriguez GM SX	80.00	36.00			

1997 Leaf Fractal Matrix Die Cuts

This 200-card series 1 set is parallel to the regular set and features three different die-cut versions in three different finishes. Only 100 of the 200-card set are produced in the X-Axis cut with 75 of those bronze, 20 of those silver, and 5 of those gold. Only 60 of the 200-card set are available in type Y-Axis cut with 20 of those bronze, 30 silver, and 10 gold. Only 40 of the 200-card set are produced in the Z-Axis cut with 5 of those bronze, 10 of those silver and 25 of those gold. No card was available in more than one color nor in more than one die-cut version.

	MINT	NRMT
COMMON X-AXIS	6.00	2.70
X-AXIS MINOR STARS	10.00	4.50
X-AXIS SEMISTARS	15.00	6.75
X-AXIS UNLISTED STARS	25.00	11.00
COMMON Y-AXIS	10.00	4.50
Y-AXIS MINOR STARS	15.00	6.75
Y-AXIS SEMISTARS	25.00	11.00
Y-AXIS UNLISTED STARS	40.00	18.00
COMMON Z-AXIS	15.00	6.75
Z-AXIS MINOR STARS	25.00	11.00

Z-AXIS SEMISTARS	40.00	18.00
Z-AXIS UNLISTED STARS	60.00	27.00
RANDOM INSERTS IN PACKS		

☐ 1 Wade Boggs GY	60.00	27.00
☐ 2 Brian McRae BY	6.00	2.70
☐ 3 Jeff D'Amico BY	6.00	2.70
☐ 4 George Arias SY	10.00	4.50
☐ 5 Billy Wagner SY	15.00	6.75
☐ 6 Ray Lankford BZ	10.00	4.50
☐ 7 Will Clark SY	25.00	11.00
☐ 8 Edgar Renteria SY	15.00	6.75
☐ 9 Alex Ochoa SY	10.00	4.50
☐ 10 Roberto Hernandez BX	6.00	2.70
☐ 11 Joe Carter SY	15.00	6.75
☐ 12 Gregg Jefferies BY	6.00	2.70
☐ 13 Mark Grace SY	25.00	11.00
☐ 14 Roberto Alomar GY	60.00	27.00
☐ 15 Joe Randa BX	6.00	2.70
☐ 16 Alex Rodriguez GZ	200.00	90.00
☐ 17 Tony Gwynn SZ	150.00	70.00
☐ 18 Steve Gibralter BY	6.00	2.70
☐ 19 Scott Stahoviak BX	6.00	2.70
☐ 20 Matt Williams SZ	25.00	11.00
☐ 21 Quinton McCracken BY	6.00	2.70
☐ 22 Ugueth Urbina BY	6.00	2.70
☐ 23 Jermaine Allensworth SX	10.00	4.50
☐ 24 Paul Molitor SX	60.00	27.00
☐ 25 Carlos Delgado SY	15.00	6.75
☐ 26 Bob Abreu SY	15.00	6.75
☐ 27 John Jaha SY	10.00	4.50
☐ 28 Rusty Greer SZ	15.00	6.75
☐ 29 Kimera Bartee BX	6.00	2.70
☐ 30 Ruben Rivera SY	15.00	6.75
☐ 31 Jason Kendall SY	15.00	6.75
☐ 32 Lance Johnson BX	6.00	2.70
☐ 33 Robin Ventura BY	10.00	4.50
☐ 34 Kevin Appier SX	15.00	6.75
☐ 35 John Mabry SY	10.00	4.50
☐ 36 Ricky Otero BY	6.00	2.70
☐ 37 Mike Lansing BX	6.00	2.70
☐ 38 Mark McGwire GZ	120.00	55.00
☐ 39 Tim Naehring BX	6.00	2.70
☐ 40 Tom Glavine SZ	15.00	6.75
☐ 41 Rey Ordonez SY	10.00	4.50
☐ 42 Tony Clark SY	40.00	18.00
☐ 43 Rafael Palmeiro SZ	25.00	11.00
☐ 44 Pedro Martinez BX	25.00	11.00
☐ 45 Keith Lockhart BX	6.00	2.70
☐ 46 Dan Wilson BY	6.00	2.70
☐ 47 John Wetteland BY	6.00	2.70
☐ 48 Chan Ho Park BX	25.00	11.00
☐ 49 Gary Sheffield SY	60.00	27.00
☐ 50 Shawn Estes BX	10.00	4.50
☐ 51 Royce Clayton BX	6.00	2.70
☐ 52 Jaime Navarro BX	6.00	2.70
☐ 53 Raul Casanova BX	6.00	2.70
☐ 54 Barry Larkin GX	120.00	55.00
☐ 55 Barry Larkin SX	40.00	18.00
☐ 56 Charles Nagy BY	10.00	4.50
☐ 57 Ken Caminiti SX	40.00	18.00
☐ 58 Todd Hollandsworth SZ	10.00	4.50
☐ 59 Pat Hentgen SX	15.00	6.75
☐ 60 Jose Valentin BX	6.00	2.70
☐ 61 Frank Rodriguez BX	6.00	2.70
☐ 62 Mickey Tettleton BX	6.00	2.70
☐ 63 Marty Cordova GX	25.00	11.00
☐ 64 Cecil Fielder SX	15.00	6.75
☐ 65 Barry Bonds BZ	80.00	36.00
☐ 66 Scott Servais BX	6.00	2.70
☐ 67 Ernie Young BX	6.00	2.70
☐ 68 Wilson Alvarez BX	6.00	2.70
☐ 69 Mike Grace BX	6.00	2.70
☐ 70 Shane Reynolds SX	10.00	4.50
☐ 71 Henry Rodriguez SY	10.00	4.50
☐ 72 Eric Karros BX	10.00	4.50
☐ 73 Mark Langston BX	6.00	2.70
☐ 74 Scott Karl BX	6.00	2.70
☐ 75 Trevor Hoffman BX	6.00	2.70
☐ 76 Orel Hershiser SX	15.00	6.75
☐ 77 John Smoltz GY	25.00	11.00
☐ 78 Raul Mondesi GZ	40.00	18.00
☐ 79 Jeff Brantley BX	6.00	2.70
☐ 80 Donne Wall BX	6.00	2.70
☐ 81 Joey Cora BX	10.00	4.50
☐ 82 Mel Rojas BX	6.00	2.70

#	Player	Price 1	Price 2
83	Chad Mottola BX	6.00	2.70
84	Omar Vizquel BX	10.00	4.50
85	Greg Maddux GZ	200.00	90.00
86	Jamey Wright SY	10.00	4.50
87	Chuck Finley BX	6.00	2.70
88	Brady Anderson GY	40.00	18.00
89	Alex Gonzalez SX	10.00	4.50
90	Andy Benes BX	10.00	4.50
91	Reggie Jefferson BX	6.00	2.70
92	Paul O'Neill BY	10.00	4.50
93	Javier Lopez BX	15.00	6.75
94	Mark Grudzielanek SX	10.00	4.50
95	Marc Newfield BX	6.00	2.70
96	Kevin Ritz BX	6.00	2.70
97	Fred McGriff GY	40.00	18.00
98	Dwight Gooden SX	15.00	6.75
99	Hideo Nomo SY	100.00	45.00
100	Steve Finley BX	10.00	4.50
101	Juan Gonzalez GZ	150.00	70.00
102	Jay Buhner BX	25.00	11.00
103	Paul Wilson SY	10.00	4.50
104	Alan Benes BY	10.00	4.50
105	Manny Ramirez GZ	60.00	27.00
106	Kevin Elster BX	6.00	2.70
107	Frank Thomas GZ	250.00	110.00
108	Orlando Miller BX	6.00	2.70
109	Ramon Martinez BX	10.00	4.50
110	Kenny Lofton GZ	80.00	36.00
111	Bernie Williams GY	60.00	27.00
112	Robby Thompson BX	6.00	2.70
113	Bernard Gilkey BZ	6.00	2.70
114	Ray Durham BX	6.00	2.70
115	Jeff Cirillo SZ	15.00	6.75
116	Brian Jordan GZ	25.00	11.00
117	Rich Becker SY	10.00	4.50
118	Al Leiter BX	6.00	2.70
119	Mark Johnson BX	6.00	2.70
120	Elis Burks BY	10.00	4.50
121	Sammy Sosa GZ	60.00	27.00
122	Willie Greene BX	6.00	2.70
123	Michael Tucker BX	10.00	4.50
124	Eddie Murray GY	60.00	27.00
125	Joey Hamilton SY	15.00	6.75
126	Antonio Osuna BX	6.00	2.70
127	Bobby Higginson SY	15.00	6.75
128	Tomas Perez BX	6.00	2.70
129	Tim Salmon GZ	60.00	27.00
130	Mark Wohlers BX	6.00	2.70
131	Charles Johnson SX	15.00	6.75
132	Randy Johnson SY	40.00	18.00
133	Brooks Kieschnick SX	10.00	4.50
134	Al Martin SY	15.00	6.75
135	Dante Bichette BX	10.00	4.50
136	Andy Pettitte GZ	60.00	27.00
137	Jason Giambi GZ	25.00	11.00
138	James Baldwin SX	10.00	4.50
139	Ben McDonald BX	6.00	2.70
140	Shawn Green SX	10.00	4.50
141	Geronimo Berroa BY	6.00	2.70
142	Jose Offerman BX	6.00	2.70
143	Curtis Pride BX	6.00	2.70
144	Terrell Wade BX	6.00	2.70
145	Ismael Valdes SX	15.00	6.75
146	Mike Mussina GY	40.00	18.00
147	Mariano Rivera SX	15.00	6.75
148	Ken Hill BY	6.00	2.70
149	Darin Erstad GZ	80.00	36.00
150	Jay Bell BX	10.00	4.50
151	Mo Vaughn GZ	80.00	36.00
152	Ozzie Smith GY	50.00	22.00
153	Jose Mesa BX	6.00	2.70
154	Osvaldo Fernandez BX	6.00	2.70
155	Vinny Castilla BY	10.00	4.50
156	Jason Isringhausen SY	10.00	4.50
157	B.J. Surhoff BX	6.00	2.70
158	Robert Perez BX	6.00	2.70
159	Ron Coomer BX	6.00	2.70
160	Darren Oliver BX	6.00	2.70
161	Mike Mohler BX	6.00	2.70
162	Russ Davis BX	6.00	2.70
163	Bret Boone BX	6.00	2.70
164	Ricky Bottalico BX	6.00	2.70
165	Derek Jeter GZ	150.00	70.00
166	Orlando Merced BX	6.00	2.70
167	John Valentin BX	6.00	2.70
168	Andruw Jones GZ	120.00	55.00
169	Angel Echevarria BX	6.00	2.70
170	Todd Walker GZ	25.00	11.00
171	Desi Relaford BY	6.00	2.70
172	Trey Beamon SX	10.00	4.50
173	Brian Giles SX	10.00	4.50
174	Scott Rolen GZ	120.00	55.00
175	Shannon Stewart SZ	15.00	6.75
176	Dmitri Young GZ	15.00	6.75
177	Justin Thompson BX	10.00	4.50
178	Trot Nixon SY	10.00	4.50
179	Josh Booty SY	25.00	11.00
180	Robin Jennings BX	6.00	2.70
181	Marvin Benard BX	6.00	2.70
182	Luis Castillo BY	10.00	4.50
183	Wendell Magee BX	6.00	2.70
184	Vladimir Guerrero GX	40.00	18.00
185	Nomar Garciaparra GX	60.00	27.00
186	Ryan Hancock BX	6.00	2.70
187	Mike Cameron SX	25.00	11.00
188	Cal Ripken LGD BZ	250.00	110.00
189	Chipper Jones LGD SZ	150.00	70.00
190	Albert Belle LGD SZ	80.00	36.00
191	Mike Piazza LGD BY	200.00	90.00
192	Chuck Knoblauch LGD SY	40.00	18.00
193	Ken Griffey Jr. LGD BZ	300.00	135.00
194	Ivan Rodriguez LGD GZ	80.00	36.00
195	Jose Canseco LGD SX	30.00	13.50
196	Ryne Sandberg LGD SX	30.00	13.50
197	Jim Thome LGD GY	60.00	27.00
198	Andy Pettitte CL BY	25.00	11.00
199	Andruw Jones CL BY	80.00	36.00
200	Derek Jeter CL SY	100.00	45.00
201	Chipper Jones GX	80.00	36.00
202	Albert Belle GY	50.00	22.00
203	Mike Piazza GX	120.00	55.00
204	Ken Griffey Jr. GZ	120.00	55.00
205	Ryne Sandberg GZ	80.00	36.00
206	Jose Canseco SY	25.00	11.00
207	Chili Davis BX	10.00	4.50
208	Roger Clemens GZ	120.00	55.00
209	Deion Sanders GZ	25.00	11.00
210	Darryl Hamilton BX	6.00	2.70
211	Jermaine Dye SX	10.00	4.50
212	Matt Williams GY	40.00	18.00
213	Kevin Elster BX	6.00	2.70
214	John Wetteland SX	10.00	4.50
215	Garret Anderson GZ	25.00	11.00
216	Kevin Brown GY	25.00	11.00
217	Matt Lawton SY	10.00	4.50
218	Cal Ripken GX	100.00	45.00
219	Moises Alou GY	15.00	6.75
220	Chuck Knoblauch GZ	60.00	27.00
221	Ivan Rodriguez GY	50.00	22.00
222	Travis Fryman BY	10.00	4.50
223	Jim Thome GZ	60.00	27.00
224	Eddie Murray SZ	40.00	18.00
225	Eric Young GZ	15.00	6.75
226	Ron Gant SX	15.00	6.75
227	Tony Phillips BX	6.00	2.70
228	Reggie Sanders BY	6.00	2.70
229	Johnny Damon SZ	10.00	4.50
230	Bill Pulsipher BX	6.00	2.70
231	Jim Edmonds GZ	40.00	18.00
232	Melvin Nieves BX	6.00	2.70
233	Ryan Klesko GZ	40.00	18.00
234	David Cone SX	15.00	6.75
235	Derek Bell BY	6.00	2.70
236	Julio Franco SX	15.00	6.75
237	Juan Guzman BX	6.00	2.70
238	Larry Walker GZ	60.00	27.00
239	Delino DeShields BX	6.00	2.70
240	Troy Percival BY	6.00	2.70
241	Andres Galarraga GZ	60.00	27.00
242	Rondell White GZ	25.00	11.00
243	John Burkett BX	6.00	2.70
244	J.T. Snow BY	10.00	4.50
245	Alex Fernandez SY	15.00	6.75
246	Edgar Martinez GZ	40.00	18.00
247	Craig Biggio GZ	40.00	18.00
248	Todd Hundley GY	25.00	11.00
249	Jimmy Key SX	15.00	6.75
250	Cliff Floyd BY	6.00	2.70
251	Jeff Conine BY	10.00	4.50
252	Curt Schilling BX	10.00	4.50
253	Jeff King BX	6.00	2.70
254	Tino Martinez GZ	60.00	27.00
255	Carlos Baerga SY	10.00	4.50
256	Jeff Fassero BY	6.00	2.70
257	Dean Palmer SY	10.00	4.50
258	Robb Nen BX	6.00	2.70
259	Sandy Alomar Jr. SY	15.00	6.75
260	Carlos Perez BX	6.00	2.70
261	Rickey Henderson SY	25.00	11.00
262	Bobby Bonilla BY	15.00	6.75
263	Darren Daulton BX	10.00	4.50
264	Jim Leyritz BX	6.00	2.70
265	Dennis Martinez BX	10.00	4.50
266	Butch Huskey BX	10.00	4.50
267	Joe Vitiello SY	10.00	4.50
268	Steve Trachsel BX	6.00	2.70
269	Glenallen Hill BX	6.00	2.70
270	Terry Steinbach BX	6.00	2.70
271	Mark McLemore BX	6.00	2.70
272	Devon White BX	6.00	2.70
273	Jeff Kent BX	6.00	2.70
274	Tim Raines BX	10.00	4.50
275	Carlos Garcia BX	6.00	2.70
276	Hal Morris BX	6.00	2.70
277	Gary Gaetti BX	6.00	2.70
278	John Olerud SY	15.00	6.75
279	Wally Joyner BX	10.00	4.50
280	Brian Hunter SX	15.00	6.75
281	Steve Karsay BX	6.00	2.70
282	Denny Neagle SX	15.00	6.75
283	Jose Herrera BX	6.00	2.70
284	Todd Stottlemyre BX	6.00	2.70
285	Bip Roberts SX	10.00	4.50
286	Kevin Seitzer BX	6.00	2.70
287	Benji Gil BX	6.00	2.70
288	Dennis Eckersley SX	15.00	6.75
289	Brad Ausmus BX	6.00	2.70
290	Otis Nixon BX	6.00	2.70
291	Darryl Strawberry BX	10.00	4.50
292	Marquis Grissom SY	15.00	6.75
293	Darryl Kile BX	10.00	4.50
294	Quilvio Veras BX	6.00	2.70
295	Tom Goodwin BX	6.00	2.70
296	Benito Santiago BX	6.00	2.70
297	Mike Bordick BX	6.00	2.70
298	Roberto Kelly BX	6.00	2.70
299	David Justice GZ	60.00	27.00
300	Carl Everett BX	6.00	2.70
301	Mark Whiten BX	6.00	2.70
302	Aaron Sele BX	6.00	2.70
303	Darren Dreifort BX	6.00	2.70
304	Bobby Jones BX	6.00	2.70
305	Fernando Vina BX	6.00	2.70
306	Ed Sprague BX	6.00	2.70
307	Andy Ashby SX	10.00	4.50
308	Tony Fernandez BX	6.00	2.70
309	Roger Pavlik BX	6.00	2.70
310	Mark Clark BX	6.00	2.70
311	Mariano Duncan BX	6.00	2.70
312	Tyler Houston BX	6.00	2.70
313	Eric Davis SY	15.00	6.75
314	Greg Vaughn BY	10.00	4.50
315	David Segui SY	10.00	4.50
316	Dave Nilsson SX	10.00	4.50
317	F.P. Santangelo SX	10.00	4.50
318	Wilton Guerrero GZ	15.00	6.75
319	Jose Guillen GZ	60.00	27.00
320	Kevin Orie SY	15.00	6.75
321	Derrek Lee GZ	40.00	18.00
322	Bubba Trammell SY	40.00	18.00
323	Pokey Reese GZ	15.00	6.75
324	Hideki Irabu GX	12.00	5.50
325	Scott Spiezio SZ	15.00	6.75
326	Bartolo Colon GZ	25.00	11.00
327	Damon Mashore SY	10.00	4.50
328	Ryan McGuire SY	10.00	4.50
329	Chris Carpenter BX	10.00	4.50
330	Jose Cruz Jr. GX	100.00	45.00
331	Todd Greene SZ	15.00	6.75
332	Brian Moehler BX	6.00	2.70
333	Mike Sweeney BY	10.00	4.50
334	Neifi Perez GZ	25.00	11.00
335	Matt Morris SY	15.00	6.75
336	Marvin Benard BY	6.00	2.70
337	Karim Garcia SZ	15.00	6.75
338	Jason Dickson SY	15.00	6.75
339	Brant Brown SY	10.00	4.50
340	Jeff Suppan SZ	15.00	6.75

☐ 341 Deivi Cruz BX	25.00	11.00
☐ 342 Antone Williamson GZ	15.00	6.75
☐ 343 Curtis Goodwin BX	6.00	2.70
☐ 344 Brooks Kieschnick SY	10.00	4.50
☐ 345 Tony Womack BX	15.00	6.75
☐ 346 Rudy Pemberton BX	6.00	2.70
☐ 347 Todd Dunwoody BX	15.00	6.75
☐ 348 Frank Thomas LG SY	150.00	70.00
☐ 349 Andruw Jones LG SX	50.00	22.00
☐ 350 Alex Rodriguez LG GM	120.00	55.00
☐ 351 Greg Maddux LG SY	120.00	55.00
☐ 352 Jeff Bagwell LG BY	80.00	36.00
☐ 353 Juan Gonzalez LG SY	100.00	45.00
☐ 354 Barry Bonds LG BY	50.00	22.00
☐ 355 Mark McGwire LG BY	80.00	36.00
☐ 356 Tony Gwynn LG BY	100.00	45.00
☐ 357 Gary Sheffield LG SX	25.00	11.00
☐ 358 Derek Jeter LG SX	60.00	27.00
☐ 359 Manny Ramirez LG SY	40.00	18.00
☐ 360 Hideo Nomo LG GZ	200.00	90.00
☐ 361 Sammy Sosa LG BX	25.00	11.00
☐ 362 Paul Molitor LG SZ	40.00	18.00
☐ 363 Kenny Lofton LG BY	50.00	22.00
☐ 364 Eddie Murray LG BX	25.00	11.00
☐ 365 Barry Larkin LG SZ	25.00	11.00
☐ 366 Roger Clemens LG SY	80.00	36.00
☐ 367 John Smoltz LG BZ	10.00	4.50
☐ 368 Alex Rodriguez GM SX	80.00	36.00
☐ 369 Frank Thomas GM BX	100.00	45.00
☐ 370 Cal Ripken GM SY	150.00	70.00
☐ 371 Ken Griffey Jr. GM SY	200.00	90.00
☐ 372 Greg Maddux GM BX	80.00	36.00
☐ 373 Mike Piazza GM SX	80.00	36.00
☐ 374 Chipper Jones GM BY	100.00	45.00
☐ 375 Albert Belle GM BX	30.00	13.50
☐ 376 Chuck Knoblauch GM BZ	25.00	11.00
☐ 377 Brady Anderson GM BZ	10.00	4.50
☐ 378 David Justice GM SX	40.00	18.00
☐ 379 Randy Johnson GM BZ	25.00	11.00
☐ 380 Wade Boggs GM BX	25.00	11.00
☐ 381 Kevin Brown GM BX	10.00	4.50
☐ 382 Tom Glavine GM GY	25.00	11.00
☐ 383 Raul Mondesi GM SX	25.00	11.00
☐ 384 Ivan Rodriguez GM SX	30.00	13.50
☐ 385 Larry Walker GM BY	25.00	11.00
☐ 386 Bernie Williams GM BZ	25.00	11.00
☐ 387 Rusty Greer GM GY	25.00	11.00
☐ 388 Rafael Palmeiro GM BX	25.00	11.00
☐ 389 Matt Williams GM SY	15.00	6.75
☐ 390 Eric Young GM BX	6.00	2.70
☐ 391 Fred McGriff GM BX	15.00	6.75
☐ 392 Ken Caminiti GM BX	15.00	6.75
☐ 393 Roberto Alomar GM BZ	25.00	11.00
☐ 394 Brian Jordan GM BX	10.00	4.50
☐ 395 Mark Grace GM GZ	15.00	6.75
☐ 396 Jim Edmonds GM BY	15.00	6.75
☐ 397 Deion Sanders GM SY	15.00	6.75
☐ 398 Vladimir Guerrero CL SZ	100.00	45.00
☐ 399 Darin Erstad CL SY	50.00	22.00
☐ 400 Nomar Garciaparra CL SZ	150.00	70.00

1997 Leaf Banner Season

Randomly inserted in series one magazine packs, this 15-card

---

set features color action player photos on die-cut cards and is printed on canvas card stock. Only 2500 of each card was produced and are sequentially numbered.

	MINT	NRMT
COMPLETE SET (15)	250.00	110.00
COMMON CARD (1-15)	4.00	1.80
UNLISTED STARS	8.00	3.60
RANDOM INS.IN SER.1 MAGAZINE PACKS		
STATED PRINT RUN 2500 SERIAL #'d SETS		

☐ 1 Jeff Bagwell	20.00	9.00
☐ 2 Ken Griffey Jr.	60.00	27.00
☐ 3 Juan Gonzalez	25.00	11.00
☐ 4 Frank Thomas	50.00	22.00
☐ 5 Alex Rodriguez	30.00	13.50
☐ 6 Kenny Lofton	12.00	5.50
☐ 7 Chuck Knoblauch	8.00	3.60
☐ 8 Mo Vaughn	12.00	5.50
☐ 9 Chipper Jones	30.00	13.50
☐ 10 Ken Caminiti	6.00	2.70
☐ 11 Craig Biggio	6.00	2.70
☐ 12 John Smoltz	5.00	2.20
☐ 13 Pat Hentgen	5.00	2.20
☐ 14 Derek Jeter	25.00	11.00
☐ 15 Todd Hollandsworth	4.00	1.80

1997 Leaf Dress for Success

Randomly inserted in series one retail only set features color player photos printed on a jersey-simulated, nylon card stock and is accented with flocking on the team logo and gold-foil stamping. Only 3,500 of each card were produced and are sequentially numbered.

	MINT	NRMT
COMPLETE SET (18)	300.00	135.00
COMMON CARD (1-18)	4.00	1.80
UNLISTED STARS	6.00	2.70
RANDOM INS.IN SER.1 RETAIL PACKS		
STATED PRINT RUN 3500 SERIAL #'d SETS		

☐ 1 Greg Maddux	25.00	11.00
☐ 2 Cal Ripken	30.00	13.50
☐ 3 Albert Belle	10.00	4.50
☐ 4 Frank Thomas	30.00	13.50
☐ 5 Dante Bichette	5.00	2.20
☐ 6 Gary Sheffield	6.00	2.70
☐ 7 Jeff Bagwell	15.00	6.75
☐ 8 Mike Piazza	25.00	11.00
☐ 9 Mark McGwire	15.00	6.75
☐ 10 Ken Caminiti	5.00	2.20
☐ 11 Alex Rodriguez	20.00	9.00
☐ 12 Ken Griffey Jr.	40.00	18.00
☐ 13 Juan Gonzalez	20.00	9.00
☐ 14 Brian Jordan	5.00	2.20
☐ 15 Mo Vaughn	10.00	4.50

☐ 16 Ivan Rodriguez	10.00	4.50
☐ 17 Andruw Jones	15.00	6.75
☐ 18 Chipper Jones	25.00	11.00

1997 Leaf Get-A-Grip

Randomly inserted in series one hobby packs, this 16-card double player insert set features color player photos of some of the current top pitchers matched against some of the league's current power hitters. The set is printed on full-silver, ploy-laminated card stock with gold-foil stamping. Only 3,500 of each card was produced and are sequentially numbered.

	MINT	NRMT
COMPLETE SET (16)	250.00	110.00
COMMON CARD (1-16)	6.00	2.70
RANDOM INS.IN SER.1 HOBBY PACKS		
STATED PRINT RUN 3500 SERIAL #'d SETS		

☐ 1 Ken Griffey Jr.	40.00	18.00
Greg Maddux		
☐ 2 John Smoltz	25.00	11.00
Frank Thomas		
☐ 3 Mike Piazza	25.00	11.00
Andy Pettitte		
☐ 4 Randy Johnson	25.00	11.00
Chipper Jones		
☐ 5 Tom Glavine	30.00	13.50
Alex Rodriguez		
☐ 6 Pat Hentgen	12.00	5.50
Jeff Bagwell		
☐ 7 Kevin Brown	15.00	6.75
Juan Gonzalez		
☐ 8 Barry Bonds	10.00	4.50
Mike Mussina		
☐ 9 Hideo Nomo	15.00	6.75
Albert Belle		
☐ 10 Troy Percival	15.00	6.75
Andruw Jones		
☐ 11 Roger Clemens	10.00	4.50
Brian Jordan		
☐ 12 Paul Wilson	8.00	3.60
Ivan Rodriguez		
☐ 13 Alan Benes	8.00	3.60
Mo Vaughn		
☐ 14 Al Leiter	12.00	5.50
Derek Jeter		
☐ 15 Bill Pulsipher	25.00	11.00
Cal Ripken		
☐ 16 Mariano Rivera	6.00	2.70
Ken Caminiti		

1997 Leaf Gold Stars

Randomly inserted in series two packs, this 36-card set features

color action images of some of Baseball's hottest names with actual 24kt. gold foil stamping. Only 2,500 of each card were produced and are sequentially numbered.

	MINT	NRMT
COMPLETE SET (36)	600.00	275.00
COMMON CARD (1-36)	8.00	3.60
UNLISTED STARS	12.00	5.50
RANDOM INSERTS IN SER.2 PACKS		
STATED PRINT RUN 2500 SERIAL #'d SETS		
☐ 1 Frank Thomas	50.00	22.00
☐ 2 Alex Rodriguez	40.00	18.00
☐ 3 Ken Griffey Jr.	60.00	27.00
☐ 4 Andruw Jones	25.00	11.00
☐ 5 Chipper Jones	40.00	18.00
☐ 6 Jeff Bagwell	25.00	11.00
☐ 7 Derek Jeter	30.00	13.50
☐ 8 Deion Sanders	8.00	3.60
☐ 9 Ivan Rodriguez	15.00	6.75
☐ 10 Juan Gonzalez	30.00	13.50
☐ 11 Greg Maddux	40.00	18.00
☐ 12 Andy Pettitte	12.00	5.50
☐ 13 Roger Clemens	25.00	11.00
☐ 14 Hideo Nomo	30.00	13.50
☐ 15 Tony Gwynn	30.00	13.50
☐ 16 Barry Bonds	15.00	6.75
☐ 17 Kenny Lofton	15.00	6.75
☐ 18 Paul Molitor	12.00	5.50
☐ 19 Jim Thome	12.00	5.50
☐ 20 Albert Belle	15.00	6.75
☐ 21 Cal Ripken	50.00	22.00
☐ 22 Mark McGwire	25.00	11.00
☐ 23 Barry Larkin	8.00	3.60
☐ 24 Mike Piazza	40.00	18.00
☐ 25 Darin Erstad	15.00	6.75
☐ 26 Chuck Knoblauch	12.00	5.50
☐ 27 Vladimir Guerrero	20.00	9.00
☐ 28 Tony Clark	12.00	5.50
☐ 29 Scott Rolen	25.00	11.00
☐ 30 Nomar Garciaparra	20.00	9.00
☐ 31 Eric Young	8.00	3.60
☐ 32 Ryne Sandberg	15.00	6.75
☐ 33 Roberto Alomar	12.00	5.50
☐ 34 Eddie Murray	12.00	5.50
☐ 35 Rafael Palmeiro	8.00	3.60
☐ 36 Jose Guillen	12.00	5.50

1997 Leaf Knot-Hole Gang

This 12-card insert set features color action player photos printed on wooden card stock. The die-cut card resembles a wooden fence with the player being seen in action through a knot hole. Only 5,000 of this set was produced and is sequentially numbered. In addition, a promo card featuring Ryan Klesko was distributed to dealers with ordering forms for the product.

	MINT	NRMT
COMPLETE SET (12)	150.00	70.00
COMMON CARD (1-12)	3.00	1.35
UNLISTED STARS	6.00	2.70
RANDOM INSERTS IN SER.1 PACKS		
STATED PRINT RUN 5000 SERIAL #'d SETS		
☐ 1 Chuck Knoblauch	6.00	2.70
☐ 2 Ken Griffey Jr.	30.00	13.50
☐ 3 Frank Thomas	25.00	11.00
☐ 4 Tony Gwynn	15.00	6.75
☐ 5 Mike Piazza	20.00	9.00
☐ 6 Jeff Bagwell	12.00	5.50
☐ 7 Rusty Greer	3.00	1.35
☐ 8 Cal Ripken	25.00	11.00
☐ 9 Chipper Jones	20.00	9.00
☐ 10 Ryan Klesko	4.00	1.80
☐ 11 Barry Larkin	4.00	1.80
☐ 12 Paul Molitor	6.00	2.70
☐ P10 Ryan Klesko Promo	2.00	.90

1997 Leaf Leagues of the Nation

Randomly inserted in series two packs, this 15-card set celebrates the first season of interleague play with double-sided, die-cut cards that highlight some of the best interleague match-ups. Using flocking technology, the cards display color action player photos with the place and date of the game where the match-up between the pictured players took place. Only 2,500 of each card were produced and are sequentially numbered.

	MINT	NRMT
COMPLETE SET (15)	350.00	160.00
COMMON CARD (1-15)	10.00	4.50
RANDOM INSERTS IN SER.2 PACKS		
STATED PRINT RUN 2500 SERIAL #'d SETS		
☐ 1 Juan Gonzalez	25.00	11.00
Barry Bonds		
☐ 2 Cal Ripken	40.00	18.00
Chipper Jones		
☐ 3 Mark McGwire	20.00	9.00
Ken Caminiti		
☐ 4 Derek Jeter	25.00	11.00
Kenny Lofton		
☐ 5 Ivan Rodriguez	30.00	13.50
Mike Piazza		
☐ 6 Ken Griffey Jr.	60.00	27.00
Larry Walker		
☐ 7 Frank Thomas	40.00	18.00
Sammy Sosa		
☐ 8 Paul Molitor	10.00	4.50
Barry Larkin		
☐ 9 Albert Belle	12.00	5.50
Deion Sanders		
☐ 10 Matt Williams	20.00	9.00
Jeff Bagwell		
☐ 11 Mo Vaughn	12.00	5.50
Gary Sheffield		
☐ 12 Alex Rodriguez	40.00	18.00
Tony Gwynn		
☐ 13 Tino Martinez	20.00	9.00
Scott Rolen		
☐ 14 Darin Erstad	12.00	5.50
Wilton Guerrero		
☐ 15 Tony Clark	20.00	9.00
Vladimir Guerrero		

1997 Leaf Statistical Standouts

This 15-card insert set showcases some of the league's statistical leaders and is printed on full-leather, die-cut, foil-stamped card stock. The player's statistics are displayed beside a color player photo. Only 1,000 of this set were produced and are sequentially numbered.

	MINT	NRMT
COMPLETE SET (15)	1000.00	450.00
COMMON CARD (1-15)	15.00	6.75
UNLISTED STARS	25.00	11.00
RANDOM INSERTS IN SER.1 PACKS		
STATED PRINT RUN 1000 SERIAL #'d SETS		
☐ 1 Albert Belle	40.00	18.00
☐ 2 Juan Gonzalez	80.00	36.00
☐ 3 Ken Griffey Jr.	150.00	70.00
☐ 4 Alex Rodriguez	100.00	45.00
☐ 5 Frank Thomas	120.00	55.00
☐ 6 Chipper Jones	80.00	36.00
☐ 7 Greg Maddux	100.00	45.00
☐ 8 Mike Piazza	100.00	45.00
☐ 9 Cal Ripken	120.00	55.00
☐ 10 Mark McGwire	60.00	27.00
☐ 11 Barry Bonds	40.00	18.00
☐ 12 Derek Jeter	80.00	36.00
☐ 13 Ken Caminiti	20.00	9.00
☐ 14 John Smoltz	15.00	6.75
☐ 15 Paul Molitor	30.00	13.50

1997 Leaf Thomas Collection

Randomly inserted in series two packs, this six-card set commemorates the multi-faceted talents of first baseman Frank Thomas with actual pieces of his game-used hats, jerseys (home and away), sweatbands, batting gloves or bats embedded in the cards. Only 100 of each set were produced and are sequentially numbered.

	MINT	NRMT
COMPLETE SET (6)	2500.00	1100.00
COMMON CARD (1-6)	400.00	180.00
RANDOM INSERTS IN SER.2 PACKS		
STATED PRINT RUN 100 SETS		
☐ 1 Frank Thomas	400.00	180.00
Game Hat/Blue Text		
☐ 2 Frank Thomas	500.00	220.00
Home Jersey/Orange Text		
☐ 3 Frank Thomas	400.00	180.00
Batting Glove/Yellow Text		
☐ 4 Frank Thomas	400.00	180.00
Bat/Green Text		
☐ 5 Frank Thomas	400.00	180.00
Sweatband/Purple Text		
☐ 6 Frank Thomas	500.00	220.00
Away Jersey/Red Text		

1997 Leaf Warning Track

Randomly inserted in series two packs, this 18-card set features color action photos of outstanding outfielders printed on embossed canvas card stock. Only 3,500 of each card were produced and are sequentially numbered.

	MINT	NRMT
COMPLETE SET (18)	120.00	55.00
COMMON CARD (1-18)	3.00	1.35
UNLISTED STARS	6.00	2.70
RANDOM INSERTS IN SER.2 PACKS		
STATED PRINT RUN 3500 SERIAL #'d SETS		
☐ 1 Ken Griffey Jr.	30.00	13.50
☐ 2 Albert Belle	8.00	3.60
☐ 3 Barry Bonds	8.00	3.60
☐ 4 Andruw Jones	12.00	5.50
☐ 5 Kenny Lofton	8.00	3.60
☐ 6 Tony Gwynn	15.00	6.75
☐ 7 Manny Ramirez	6.00	2.70
☐ 8 Rusty Greer	3.00	1.35
☐ 9 Bernie Williams	6.00	2.70
☐ 10 Gary Sheffield	6.00	2.70
☐ 11 Juan Gonzalez	15.00	6.75
☐ 12 Raul Mondesi	4.00	1.80
☐ 13 Brady Anderson	4.00	1.80
☐ 14 Rondell White	3.00	1.35
☐ 15 Sammy Sosa	6.00	2.70
☐ 16 Deion Sanders	3.00	1.35
☐ 17 Dave Justice	6.00	2.70
☐ 18 Jim Edmonds	4.00	1.80

1994 Leaf Limited

This 160-card standard-size set was issued exclusively to hobby dealers. The fronts display silver holographic Spectra Tech foiling and a silhouetted player action photo over full silver foil. The backs contain silver holographic Spectra Tech foil, two photos, and a quote about the player by well-known baseball personalities. The set is organized alphabetically within teams with AL preceding NL.

	MINT	NRMT
COMPLETE SET (160)	100.00	45.00
COMMON CARD (1-160)	.50	.23
MINOR STARS	.75	.35
SEMISTARS	1.25	.55
UNLISTED STARS	2.00	.90
☐ 1 Jeffrey Hammonds	.75	.35
☐ 2 Ben McDonald	.50	.23
☐ 3 Mike Mussina	2.00	.90
☐ 4 Rafael Palmeiro	1.25	.55
☐ 5 Cal Ripken Jr.	8.00	3.60
☐ 6 Lee Smith	.75	.35
☐ 7 Roger Clemens	4.00	1.80
☐ 8 Scott Cooper	.50	.23
☐ 9 Andre Dawson	1.25	.55
☐ 10 Mike Greenwell	.50	.23
☐ 11 Aaron Sele	.50	.23
☐ 12 Mo Vaughn	2.50	1.10
☐ 13 Brian Anderson	2.00	.90
☐ 14 Chad Curtis	.50	.23
☐ 15 Chili Davis	.75	.35
☐ 16 Gary DiSarcina	.50	.23
☐ 17 Mark Langston	.50	.23
☐ 18 Tim Salmon	2.00	.90
☐ 19 Wilson Alvarez	.50	.23
☐ 20 Jason Bere	.50	.23
☐ 21 Julio Franco	.50	.23
☐ 22 Jack McDowell	.50	.23
☐ 23 Tim Raines	.75	.35
☐ 24 Frank Thomas	8.00	3.60
☐ 25 Robin Ventura	.75	.35
☐ 26 Carlos Baerga	.50	.23
☐ 27 Albert Belle	2.50	1.10
☐ 28 Kenny Lofton	2.50	1.10
☐ 29 Eddie Murray	2.00	.90
☐ 30 Manny Ramirez	2.50	1.10
☐ 31 Cecil Fielder	.75	.35
☐ 32 Travis Fryman	.75	.35
☐ 33 Mickey Tettleton	.50	.23
☐ 34 Alan Trammell	1.25	.55
☐ 35 Lou Whitaker	.75	.35
☐ 36 David Cone	.75	.35
☐ 37 Gary Gaetti	.50	.23
☐ 38 Greg Gagne	.50	.23
☐ 39 Bob Hamelin	.50	.23
☐ 40 Wally Joyner	.75	.35
☐ 41 Brian McRae	.50	.23
☐ 42 Ricky Bones	.50	.23
☐ 43 Brian Harper	.50	.23
☐ 44 John Jaha	.50	.23
☐ 45 Pat Listach	.50	.23
☐ 46 Dave Nilsson	.50	.23
☐ 47 Greg Vaughn	.50	.23
☐ 48 Kent Hrbek	.75	.35
☐ 49 Chuck Knoblauch	2.00	.90
☐ 50 Shane Mack	.50	.23
☐ 51 Kirby Puckett	4.00	1.80
☐ 52 Dave Winfield	1.25	.55
☐ 53 Jim Abbott	.50	.23
☐ 54 Wade Boggs	2.00	.90
☐ 55 Jimmy Key	.75	.35
☐ 56 Don Mattingly	3.00	1.35
☐ 57 Paul O'Neil	.75	.35
☐ 58 Danny Tartabull	.50	.23
☐ 59 Dennis Eckersley	.75	.35
☐ 60 Rickey Henderson	1.25	.55
☐ 61 Mark McGwire	4.00	1.80
☐ 62 Troy Neel	.50	.23
☐ 63 Ruben Sierra	.50	.23
☐ 64 Eric Anthony	.50	.23
☐ 65 Jay Buhner	1.25	.55
☐ 66 Ken Griffey Jr.	10.00	4.50
☐ 67 Randy Johnson	2.00	.90
☐ 68 Edgar Martinez	1.25	.55
☐ 69 Tino Martinez	2.00	.90
☐ 70 Jose Canseco	1.25	.55
☐ 71 Will Clark	1.25	.55
☐ 72 Juan Gonzalez	5.00	2.20
☐ 73 Dean Palmer	.50	.23
☐ 74 Ivan Rodriguez	2.50	1.10
☐ 75 Roberto Alomar	2.00	.90
☐ 76 Joe Carter	.75	.35
☐ 77 Carlos Delgado	1.25	.55
☐ 78 Paul Molitor	2.00	.90
☐ 79 John Olerud	.75	.35
☐ 80 Devon White	.50	.23
☐ 81 Steve Avery	.50	.23
☐ 82 Tom Glavine	.75	.35
☐ 83 David Justice	2.00	.90
☐ 84 Roberto Kelly	.50	.23
☐ 85 Ryan Klesko	2.00	.90
☐ 86 Javier Lopez	1.25	.55
☐ 87 Greg Maddux	6.00	2.70
☐ 88 Fred McGriff	1.25	.55
☐ 89 Shawon Dunston	.50	.23
☐ 90 Mark Grace	1.25	.55
☐ 91 Derrick May	.50	.23
☐ 92 Sammy Sosa	2.00	.90
☐ 93 Rick Wilkins	.50	.23
☐ 94 Bret Boone	.50	.23
☐ 95 Barry Larkin	1.25	.55
☐ 96 Kevin Mitchell	.50	.23
☐ 97 Hal Morris	.50	.23
☐ 98 Deion Sanders	.75	.35
☐ 99 Reggie Sanders	.50	.23
☐ 100 Dante Bichette	.75	.35
☐ 101 Ellis Burks	.75	.35
☐ 102 Andres Galarraga	2.00	.90
☐ 103 Joe Girardi	.50	.23
☐ 104 Charlie Hayes	.50	.23

☐ 105	Chuck Carr	.50	.23
☐ 106	Jeff Conine	.75	.35
☐ 107	Bryan Harvey	.50	.23
☐ 108	Benito Santiago	.50	.23
☐ 109	Gary Sheffield	2.00	.90
☐ 110	Jeff Bagwell	4.00	1.90
☐ 111	Craig Biggio	1.25	.55
☐ 112	Ken Caminiti	1.25	.55
☐ 113	Andujar Cedeno	.50	.23
☐ 114	Doug Drabek	.50	.23
☐ 115	Luis Gonzalez	.50	.23
☐ 116	Brett Butler	.75	.35
☐ 117	Delino DeShields	.50	.23
☐ 118	Eric Karros	.75	.35
☐ 119	Raul Mondesi	2.00	.90
☐ 120	Mike Piazza	6.00	2.70
☐ 121	Henry Rodriguez	.50	.23
☐ 122	Tim Wallach	.50	.23
☐ 123	Moises Alou	.75	.35
☐ 124	Cliff Floyd	.75	.35
☐ 125	Marquis Grissom	.75	.35
☐ 126	Ken Hill	.50	.23
☐ 127	Larry Walker	2.00	.90
☐ 128	John Wetteland	.50	.23
☐ 129	Bobby Bonilla	.75	.35
☐ 130	John Franco	.50	.23
☐ 131	Jeff Kent	.50	.23
☐ 132	Bret Saberhagen	.50	.23
☐ 133	Ryan Thompson	.50	.23
☐ 134	Darren Daulton	.75	.35
☐ 135	Mariano Duncan	.50	.23
☐ 136	Lenny Dykstra	.75	.35
☐ 137	Danny Jackson	.50	.23
☐ 138	John Kruk	.75	.35
☐ 139	Jay Bell	.75	.35
☐ 140	Jeff King	.50	.23
☐ 141	Al Martin	.50	.23
☐ 142	Orlando Merced	.50	.23
☐ 143	Andy Van Slyke	.75	.35
☐ 144	Bernard Gilkey	.50	.23
☐ 145	Gregg Jefferies	.75	.35
☐ 146	Ray Lankford	.75	.35
☐ 147	Ozzie Smith	2.50	1.10
☐ 148	Mark Whiten	.50	.23
☐ 149	Todd Zeile	.50	.23
☐ 150	Derek Bell	.50	.23
☐ 151	Andy Benes	.75	.35
☐ 152	Tony Gwynn	5.00	2.20
☐ 153	Phil Plantier	.50	.23
☐ 154	Bip Roberts	.50	.23
☐ 155	Rod Beck	.50	.23
☐ 156	Barry Bonds	2.50	1.10
☐ 157	John Burkett	.50	.23
☐ 158	Royce Clayton	.50	.23
☐ 159	Bill Swift	.50	.23
☐ 160	Matt Williams	1.25	.55

1994 Leaf Limited Gold All-Stars

Randomly inserted in packs at a rate of one in seven, this 18-card standard-size set features the starting players at each position in both the National and American leagues for the *1994 All-Star Game. They are identical in design to the basic Limited product except for being gold and individually numbered out of 10,000.*

		MINT	NRMT
COMPLETE SET (18)		175.00	80.00
COMMON CARD (1-18)		2.00	.90
STATED ODDS 1:7			
STAT.PRINT RUN 10,000 SERIAL #'d SETS			

☐ 1	Frank Thomas	30.00	13.50
☐ 2	Gregg Jefferies	2.00	.90
☐ 3	Roberto Alomar	8.00	3.60
☐ 4	Mariano Duncan	2.00	.90
☐ 5	Wade Boggs	8.00	3.60
☐ 6	Matt Williams	6.00	2.70
☐ 7	Cal Ripken Jr.	30.00	13.50
☐ 8	Ozzie Smith	10.00	4.50
☐ 9	Kirby Puckett	15.00	6.75
☐ 10	Barry Bonds	10.00	4.50
☐ 11	Ken Griffey Jr.	40.00	18.00
☐ 12	Tony Gwynn	20.00	9.00
☐ 13	Joe Carter	4.00	1.80
☐ 14	David Justice	8.00	3.60
☐ 15	Ivan Rodriguez	10.00	4.50
☐ 16	Mike Piazza	25.00	11.00
☐ 17	Jimmy Key	4.00	1.80
☐ 18	Greg Maddux	25.00	11.00

1994 Leaf Limited Rookies

This 80-card standard-size set was issued exclusively to hobby dealers. The set showcases top rookies and prospects of 1994. The fronts display silver holographic Spectra Tech foiling and a silhouetted player action photo over full silver foil. The word "Rookies" appears in black letters above the Leaf Limited logo at top. The backs contain silver holographic Spectra Tech foil, two photos, and a quote about the player by well-known baseball personalities. Rookie Cards in this set include Kurt Abbott, Rusty Greer, Chan Ho Park and Ismael Valdes.

		MINT	NRMT
COMPLETE SET (80)		25.00	11.00
COMMON CARD (1-80)		.40	.18
MINOR STARS		.75	.35
UNLISTED STARS		1.50	.70

☐ 1	Charles Johnson	1.00	.45
☐ 2	Rico Brogna	.40	.18
☐ 3	Melvin Nieves	.40	.18
☐ 4	Rich Becker	.40	.18
☐ 5	Russ Davis	.75	.35
☐ 6	Matt Mieske	.40	.18
☐ 7	Paul Shuey	.40	.18
☐ 8	Hector Carrasco	.40	.18
☐ 9	J.R. Phillips	.40	.18
☐ 10	Scott Ruffcorn	.40	.18
☐ 11	Kurt Abbott	.40	.18
☐ 12	Danny Bautista	.40	.18
☐ 13	Rick White	.40	.18
☐ 14	Steve Dunn	.40	.18
☐ 15	Joe Ausanio	.40	.18
☐ 16	Salomon Torres	.40	.45
☐ 17	Ricky Bottalico	1.00	.45
☐ 18	Johnny Ruffin	.40	.18
☐ 19	Kevin Foster	.40	.18
☐ 20	W.VanLandingham	.75	.35
☐ 21	Troy O'Leary	.40	.18
☐ 22	Mark Acre	.40	.18
☐ 23	Norberto Martin	.40	.18
☐ 24	Jason Jacome	.40	.18
☐ 25	Steve Trachsel	.75	.35
☐ 26	Denny Hocking	.40	.18
☐ 27	Mike Lieberthal	.40	.18
☐ 28	Gerald Williams	.40	.18
☐ 29	John Mabry	1.50	.70
☐ 30	Greg Blosser	.40	.18
☐ 31	Carl Everett	.40	.18
☐ 32	Steve Karsay	.40	.18
☐ 33	Jose Valentin	.40	.18
☐ 34	Jon Lieber	.40	.18
☐ 35	Chris Gomez	.40	.18
☐ 36	Jesus Tavarez	.40	.18
☐ 37	Tony Longmire	.40	.18
☐ 38	Luis Lopez	.40	.18
☐ 39	Matt Walbeck	.40	.18
☐ 40	Rikkert Faneyte	.40	.18
☐ 41	Shane Reynolds	.40	.18
☐ 42	Joey Hamilton	1.50	.70
☐ 43	Ismael Valdes	2.00	.90
☐ 44	Danny Micell	.40	.18
☐ 45	Darren Bragg	.75	.35
☐ 46	Alex Gonzalez	.75	.35
☐ 47	Rick Helling	.40	.18
☐ 48	Jose Oliva	.40	.18
☐ 49	Jim Edmonds	1.50	.70
☐ 50	Miguel Jimenez	.40	.18
☐ 51	Tony Eusebio	.40	.18
☐ 52	Shawn Green	.75	.35
☐ 53	Billy Ashley	.40	.18
☐ 54	Rondell White	1.00	.45
☐ 55	Cory Bailey	.40	.18
☐ 56	Tim Davis	.40	.18
☐ 57	John Hudek	.40	.18
☐ 58	Darren Hall	.40	.18
☐ 59	Darren Dreifort	.75	.35
☐ 60	Mike Kelly	.40	.18
☐ 61	Marcus Moore	.40	.18
☐ 62	Garret Anderson	1.50	.70
☐ 63	Brian L.Hunter	1.50	.70
☐ 64	Mark Smith	.40	.18
☐ 65	Garey Ingram	.40	.18
☐ 66	Rusty Greer	6.00	2.70
☐ 67	Marc Newfield	.75	.35
☐ 68	Gar Finnvold	.40	.18
☐ 69	Paul Spoljaric	.40	.18
☐ 70	Ray McDavid	.40	.18
☐ 71	Orlando Miller	.40	.18
☐ 72	Jorge Fabregas	.40	.18
☐ 73	Ray Holbert	.40	.18
☐ 74	Armando Benitez	.40	.18
☐ 75	Ernie Young	.40	.18
☐ 76	James Mouton	.40	.18
☐ 77	Robert Perez	.40	.18
☐ 78	Chan Ho Park	6.00	2.70
☐ 79	Roger Salkeld	.40	.18
☐ 80	Tony Tarasco	.40	.18

1994 Leaf Limited Rookies Phenoms

This 10-card standard-size set was randomly inserted in Leaf Limited Rookies packs at a rate of approximately of one in twelve. Limited to 5,000, the set

showcases top 1994 rookies. The fronts are designed much like the Limited Rookies except the card is comprised of gold foil instead of silver. Gold backs are also virtually identical to the Limited Rookies in terms of content and layout. The cards are individually numbered on back out of 5,000.

	MINT	NRMT
COMPLETE SET (10)	150.00	70.00
COMMON CARD (1-10)	8.00	3.60
MINOR STARS	10.00	4.50
STATED ODDS 1:12		
STATED PRINT RUN 5000 SERIAL #'d SETS		

		MINT	NRMT
☐ 1	Raul Mondesi	15.00	6.75
☐ 2	Bob Hamelin	8.00	3.60
☐ 3	Midre Cummings	8.00	3.60
☐ 4	Carlos Delgado	12.00	5.50
☐ 5	Cliff Floyd	10.00	4.50
☐ 6	Jeffrey Hammonds	10.00	4.50
☐ 7	Ryan Klesko	15.00	6.75
☐ 8	Javier Lopez	12.00	5.50
☐ 9	Manny Ramirez	25.00	11.00
☐ 10	Alex Rodriguez	80.00	36.00

1995 Leaf Limited

This 192 standard-size card set was issued in two series. Each series contained 96 cards. These cards were issued in six-box cases with 20 packs per box and four cards per pack. Forty-five thousand boxes of each series was produced. The fronts feature a player photo shot against a silver holographic foil background. The player is identified on the top with his team name on the right. The "Leaf Limited" logo is on the bottom of the card. The horizontal backs contain two player photos along with career stats broken down on a monthly basis. The cards are numbered in the upper right corner. Rookie Cards in this set include Bob Higginson and Hideo Nomo.

	MINT	NRMT
COMPLETE SET (192)	60.00	27.00
COMPLETE SERIES 1 (96)	30.00	13.50
COMPLETE SERIES 2 (96)	30.00	13.50
COMMON CARD (1-192)	.25	.11
MINOR STARS	.50	.23
SEMISTARS	1.00	.45
UNLISTED STARS	1.50	.70
COMP. GOLD SET (24)	35.00	16.00
*GOLD: .5X TO 1X HI COLUMN		
ONE GOLD PER SERIES 1 PACK		

☐ 1	Frank Thomas	6.00	2.70
☐ 2	Geronimo Berroa	.25	.11
☐ 3	Tony Phillips	.25	.11
☐ 4	Roberto Alomar	1.50	.70
☐ 5	Steve Avery	.25	.11
☐ 6	Darryl Hamilton	.25	.11
☐ 7	Scott Cooper	.25	.11
☐ 8	Mark Grace	1.00	.45
☐ 9	Billy Ashley	.25	.11
☐ 10	Wil Cordero	.25	.11
☐ 11	Barry Bonds	2.00	.90
☐ 12	Kenny Lofton	2.00	.90
☐ 13	Jay Buhner	1.00	.45
☐ 14	Alex Rodriguez	6.00	2.70
☐ 15	Bobby Bonilla	.50	.23
☐ 16	Brady Anderson	1.00	.45
☐ 17	Ken Caminiti	1.00	.45
☐ 18	Charlie Hayes	.25	.11
☐ 19	Jay Bell	.50	.23
☐ 20	Will Clark	1.00	.45
☐ 21	Jose Canseco	1.00	.45
☐ 22	Bret Boone	.25	.11
☐ 23	Dante Bichette	.50	.23
☐ 24	Kevin Appier	.50	.23
☐ 25	Chad Curtis	.25	.11
☐ 26	Marty Cordova	.50	.23
☐ 27	Jason Bere	.25	.11
☐ 28	Jimmy Key	.50	.23
☐ 29	Rickey Henderson	1.00	.45
☐ 30	Tim Salmon	1.50	.70
☐ 31	Joe Carter	.50	.23
☐ 32	Tom Glavine	.50	.23
☐ 33	Pat Listach	.25	.11
☐ 34	Brian Jordan	.50	.23
☐ 35	Brian McRae	.25	.11
☐ 36	Eric Karros	.50	.23
☐ 37	Pedro Martinez	1.50	.70
☐ 38	Royce Clayton	.25	.11
☐ 39	Eddie Murray	1.50	.70
☐ 40	Randy Johnson	1.50	.70
☐ 41	Jeff Conine	.50	.23
☐ 42	Brett Butler	.50	.23
☐ 43	Jeffrey Hammonds	.50	.23
☐ 44	Andujar Cedeno	.25	.11
☐ 45	Dave Hollins	.25	.11
☐ 46	Jeff King	.25	.11
☐ 47	Benji Gil	.25	.11
☐ 48	Roger Clemens	3.00	1.35
☐ 49	Barry Larkin	1.00	.45
☐ 50	Joe Girardi	.25	.11
☐ 51	Bob Hamelin	.25	.11
☐ 52	Travis Fryman	.50	.23
☐ 53	Chuck Knoblauch	1.50	.70
☐ 54	Ray Durham	.50	.23
☐ 55	Don Mattingly	2.50	1.10
☐ 56	Ruben Sierra	.50	.23
☐ 57	J.T. Snow	.50	.23
☐ 58	Derek Bell	.25	.11
☐ 59	David Cone	.50	.23
☐ 60	Marquis Grissom	.50	.23
☐ 61	Kevin Seitzer	.25	.11
☐ 62	Ozzie Smith	2.00	.90
☐ 63	Rick Wilkins	.25	.11
☐ 64	Hideo Nomo	8.00	3.60
☐ 65	Tony Tarasco	.25	.11
☐ 66	Manny Ramirez	1.50	.70
☐ 67	Charles Johnson	.50	.23
☐ 68	Craig Biggio	1.00	.45
☐ 69	Bobby Jones	.25	.11
☐ 70	Mike Mussina	1.50	.70
☐ 71	Alex Gonzalez	.25	.11
☐ 72	Gregg Jefferies	.25	.11
☐ 73	Rusty Greer	1.50	.70
☐ 74	Mike Greenwell	.25	.11
☐ 75	Hal Morris	.25	.11
☐ 76	Paul O'Neill	.50	.23
☐ 77	Luis Gonzalez	.25	.11
☐ 78	Chipper Jones	5.00	2.20
☐ 79	Mike Piazza	5.00	2.20
☐ 80	Rondell White	.50	.23
☐ 81	Glenallen Hill	.25	.11
☐ 82	Shawn Green	.50	.23
☐ 83	Bernie Williams	1.50	.70
☐ 84	Jim Thome	1.50	.70
☐ 85	Terry Pendleton	.25	.11
☐ 86	Rafael Palmeiro	1.00	.45
☐ 87	Tony Gwynn	4.00	1.80
☐ 88	Mickey Tettleton	.25	.11
☐ 89	John Valentin	.25	.11
☐ 90	Deion Sanders	.50	.23
☐ 91	Larry Walker	1.50	.70
☐ 92	Michael Tucker	.50	.23
☐ 93	Alan Trammell	1.00	.45
☐ 94	Tim Raines	.50	.23
☐ 95	David Justice	1.50	.70
☐ 96	Tino Martinez	1.50	.70
☐ 97	Cal Ripken Jr.	6.00	2.70
☐ 98	Deion Sanders	.50	.23
☐ 99	Darren Daulton	.50	.23
☐ 100	Paul Molitor	1.50	.70
☐ 101	Randy Myers	.25	.11
☐ 102	Wally Joyner	.50	.23
☐ 103	Carlos Perez	.50	.23
☐ 104	Brian Hunter	1.00	.45
☐ 105	Wade Boggs	1.50	.70
☐ 106	Bob Higginson	2.50	1.10
☐ 107	Jeff Kent	.25	.11
☐ 108	Jose Offerman	.25	.11
☐ 109	Dennis Eckersley	.50	.23
☐ 110	Dave Nilsson	.50	.23
☐ 111	Chuck Finley	.25	.11
☐ 112	Devon White	.25	.11
☐ 113	Bip Roberts	.25	.11
☐ 114	Ramon Martinez	.50	.23
☐ 115	Greg Maddux	5.00	2.20
☐ 116	Curtis Goodwin	.25	.11
☐ 117	John Jaha	.25	.11
☐ 118	Ken Griffey Jr.	8.00	3.60
☐ 119	Geronimo Pena	.25	.11
☐ 120	Shawon Dunston	.25	.11
☐ 121	Ariel Prieto	.50	.23
☐ 122	Kirby Puckett	3.00	1.35
☐ 123	Carlos Baerga	.25	.11
☐ 124	Todd Hundley	.50	.23
☐ 125	Tim Naehring	.25	.11
☐ 126	Gary Sheffield	1.50	.70
☐ 127	Dean Palmer	.25	.11
☐ 128	Rondell White	.50	.23
☐ 129	Greg Gagne	.25	.11
☐ 130	Jose Rijo	.25	.11
☐ 131	Ivan Rodriguez	2.00	.90
☐ 132	Jeff Bagwell	3.00	1.35
☐ 133	Greg Vaughn	.25	.11
☐ 134	Chili Davis	.50	.23
☐ 135	Al Martin	.25	.11
☐ 136	Kenny Rogers	.25	.11
☐ 137	Aaron Sele	.25	.11
☐ 138	Raul Mondesi	1.00	.45
☐ 139	Cecil Fielder	.50	.23
☐ 140	Tim Wallach	.25	.11
☐ 141	Andres Galarraga	1.50	.70
☐ 142	Lou Whitaker	.25	.11
☐ 143	Jack McDowell	.25	.11
☐ 144	Matt Williams	1.00	.45
☐ 145	Ryan Klesko	1.00	.45
☐ 146	Carlos Garcia	.25	.11
☐ 147	Albert Belle	2.00	.90
☐ 148	Ryan Thompson	.25	.11
☐ 149	Roberto Kelly	.25	.11
☐ 150	Edgar Martinez	1.00	.45
☐ 151	Robby Thompson	.25	.11
☐ 152	Mo Vaughn	2.00	.90
☐ 153	Todd Zeile	.25	.11
☐ 154	Harold Baines	.50	.23
☐ 155	Phil Plantier	.25	.11
☐ 156	Mike Stanley	.25	.11

		MINT	NRMT
☐ 157	Ed Sprague	.25	.11
☐ 158	Moises Alou	.50	.23
☐ 159	Quivilo Veras	.25	.11
☐ 160	Reggie Sanders	.25	.11
☐ 161	Delino DeShields	.25	.11
☐ 162	Rico Brogna	.25	.11
☐ 163	Greg Colbrunn	.25	.11
☐ 164	Steve Finley	.50	.23
☐ 165	Orlando Merced	.25	.11
☐ 166	Mark McGwire	3.00	1.35
☐ 167	Garret Anderson	1.00	.45
☐ 168	Paul Sorrento	.25	.11
☐ 169	Mark Langston	.25	.11
☐ 170	Danny Tartabull	.25	.11
☐ 171	Vinny Castilla	.50	.23
☐ 172	Javier Lopez	.50	.23
☐ 173	Bret Saberhagen	.25	.11
☐ 174	Eddie Williams	.25	.11
☐ 175	Scott Leius	.25	.11
☐ 176	Juan Gonzalez	4.00	1.80
☐ 177	Gary Gaetti	.25	.11
☐ 178	Jim Edmonds	1.00	.45
☐ 179	John Olerud	.50	.23
☐ 180	Lenny Dykstra	.50	.23
☐ 181	Ray Lankford	.50	.23
☐ 182	Ron Gant	.50	.23
☐ 183	Doug Drabek	.25	.11
☐ 184	Fred McGriff	1.00	.45
☐ 185	Andy Benes	.50	.23
☐ 186	Kurt Abbott	.25	.11
☐ 187	Bernard Gilkey	.25	.11
☐ 188	Sammy Sosa	1.50	.70
☐ 189	Lee Smith	.50	.23
☐ 190	Dennis Martinez	.50	.23
☐ 191	Ozzie Guillen	.25	.11
☐ 192	Robin Ventura	.50	.23

☐ 9	Kenny Lofton	2.00	.90
☐ 10	Mike Piazza	5.00	2.20
☐ 11	Will Clark	1.00	.45
☐ 12	Mo Vaughn	2.00	.90
☐ 13	Carlos Baerga	.50	.23
☐ 14	Rafael Palmeiro	1.00	.45
☐ 15	Barry Bonds	2.00	.90
☐ 16	Kirby Puckett	3.00	1.35
☐ 17	Roberto Alomar	1.50	.70
☐ 18	Barry Larkin	1.00	.45
☐ 19	Eddie Murray	1.50	.70
☐ 20	Tim Salmon	1.50	.70
☐ 21	Don Mattingly	2.50	1.10
☐ 22	Fred McGriff	1.00	.45
☐ 23	Albert Belle	5.00	2.20
☐ 24	Dante Bichette	.75	.35

1995 Leaf Limited Lumberjacks

These eight standard-size cards were randomly inserted into second series packs. The cards are individually numbered out of 5,000. The fronts feature a player photo surrounded by his name, the word "Lumberjacks" and "Handcrafted" in a semi-circular pattern. The team logo is in the background. The UV-coated horizontal backs feature a player photo against a forest background on the right along with some information on the left side. The player's career statistics are directly above the individual numbering (out of 5,000) of the card. The cards are numbered in the upper right corner.

	MINT	NRMT
COMPLETE SET (16)	450.00	200.00
COMPLETE SERIES 1 (8)	250.00	110.00
COMPLETE SERIES 2 (8)	200.00	90.00
COMMON CARD (1-16)	8.00	3.60
UNLISTED STARS	15.00	6.75
STATED ODDS 1:23		
STATED PRINT RUN 5000 SERIAL-#'d SETS		

		MINT	NRMT
☐ 1	Albert Belle	20.00	9.00
☐ 2	Barry Bonds	20.00	9.00
☐ 3	Juan Gonzalez	40.00	18.00
☐ 4	Ken Griffey Jr.	80.00	36.00
☐ 5	Fred McGriff	12.00	5.50
☐ 6	Mike Piazza	40.00	18.00
☐ 7	Kirby Puckett	30.00	13.50
☐ 8	Mo Vaughn	20.00	9.00
☐ 9	Frank Thomas	60.00	27.00
☐ 10	Jeff Bagwell	30.00	13.50
☐ 11	Matt Williams	12.00	5.50
☐ 12	Jose Canseco	12.00	5.50
☐ 13	Raul Mondesi	12.00	5.50
☐ 14	Manny Ramirez	15.00	6.75
☐ 15	Cecil Fielder	8.00	3.60
☐ 16	Cal Ripken Jr.	60.00	27.00

1995 Leaf Limited Bat Patrol

These 24 standard-size cards were inserted one per series two pack. The fronts feature a full-bleed player photo with the player being identified on the top and the words "Bat Patrol" covering most of the middle. The horizontal backs feature another player photo as well as a year by year breakdown. The cards are numbered in the upper right corner as "X" of 24.

	MINT	NRMT
COMPLETE SET (24)	25.00	11.00
COMMON CARD (1-24)	.50	.23
ONE PER SERIES 2 PACK		

☐ 1	Frank Thomas	6.00	2.70
☐ 2	Tony Gwynn	4.00	1.80
☐ 3	Wade Boggs	1.50	.70
☐ 4	Larry Walker	1.50	.70
☐ 5	Ken Griffey, Jr.	8.00	3.60
☐ 6	Jeff Bagwell	3.00	1.35
☐ 7	Manny Ramirez	1.50	.70
☐ 8	Mark Grace	1.00	.45

1996 Leaf Limited

The 1996 Leaf Limited set was issued exclusively to hobby outlets with a maximum production run of 45,000 boxes. Each box contained two smaller mini-boxes, enabling the dealer to use his imagination in the marketing of this product. The five-card packs carried a suggested retail price of $3.24. Each Master Box was sequentially-numbered via a box topper. If this number matched the 1996 year-ending stats, the collector and the dealer both had a chance to win prizes such as a Frank Thomas game-used bat, autographed batting glove, or a "Two Biggest Weapons" poster. The collector would return the winning box number to the hobby shop, and the dealer would mail it to Donruss and both receiving the same prize. The card fronts displayed color player photos with another photo and player information on the backs.

	MINT	NRMT
COMPLETE SET (90)	50.00	22.00
COMMON CARD (1-90)	.40	.18
MINOR STARS	.75	.35
UNLISTED STARS	1.50	.70
COMP.GOLD SET (90)	500.00	220.00
COMMON GOLD (1-90)	2.50	1.10
*GOLD: 4X TO 10X HI COLUMN		
GOLD STATED ODDS 1:11		

☐ 1	Ivan Rodriguez	2.00	.90
☐ 2	Roger Clemens	3.00	1.35
☐ 3	Gary Sheffield	1.50	.70
☐ 4	Tino Martinez	1.50	.70
☐ 5	Sammy Sosa	1.50	.70
☐ 6	Reggie Sanders	.40	.18
☐ 7	Ray Lankford	.75	.35
☐ 8	Manny Ramirez	1.50	.70
☐ 9	Jeff Bagwell	3.00	1.35
☐ 10	Greg Maddux	5.00	2.20
☐ 11	Ken Griffey Jr.	8.00	3.60
☐ 12	Rondell White	.75	.35
☐ 13	Mike Piazza	5.00	2.20
☐ 14	Marc Newfield	.40	.18
☐ 15	Cal Ripken	6.00	2.70
☐ 16	Carlos Delgado	.75	.35
☐ 17	Tim Salmon	1.50	.70
☐ 18	Andres Galarraga	1.50	.70
☐ 19	Chuck Knoblauch	1.50	.70
☐ 20	Matt Williams	1.00	.45
☐ 21	Mark McGwire	3.00	1.35
☐ 22	Ben McDonald	.40	.18
☐ 23	Frank Thomas	6.00	2.70
☐ 24	Johnny Damon	.75	.35
☐ 25	Gregg Jefferies	.40	.18
☐ 26	Travis Fryman	.75	.35
☐ 27	Chipper Jones	5.00	2.20

		MINT	NRMT
☐ 28	David Cone	.75	.35
☐ 29	Kenny Lofton	2.00	.90
☐ 30	Mike Mussina	1.50	.70
☐ 31	Alex Rodriguez	5.00	2.20
☐ 32	Carlos Baerga	.40	.18
☐ 33	Brian Hunter	.75	.35
☐ 34	Juan Gonzalez	4.00	1.80
☐ 35	Bernie Williams	1.50	.70
☐ 36	Wally Joyner	.75	.35
☐ 37	Fred McGriff	1.00	.45
☐ 38	Randy Johnson	1.50	.70
☐ 39	Marty Cordova	.75	.35
☐ 40	Garret Anderson	.75	.35
☐ 41	Albert Belle	2.00	.90
☐ 42	Edgar Martinez	1.00	.45
☐ 43	Barry Larkin	1.00	.45
☐ 44	Paul O'Neil	.75	.35
☐ 45	Cecil Fielder	.75	.35
☐ 46	Rusty Greer	.75	.35
☐ 47	Mo Vaughn	2.00	.90
☐ 48	Dante Bichette	.75	.35
☐ 49	Ryan Klesko	1.00	.45
☐ 50	Roberto Alomar	1.50	.70
☐ 51	Raul Mondesi	1.00	.45
☐ 52	Robin Ventura	.75	.35
☐ 53	Tony Gwynn	4.00	1.80
☐ 54	Mark Grace	1.00	.45
☐ 55	Jim Thome	1.50	.70
☐ 56	Jason Giambi	.75	.35
☐ 57	Tom Glavine	.75	.35
☐ 58	Jim Edmonds	1.00	.45
☐ 59	Pedro Martinez	1.50	.70
☐ 60	Charles Johnson	.75	.35
☐ 61	Wade Boggs	1.50	.70
☐ 62	Orlando Merced	.40	.18
☐ 63	Craig Biggio	1.00	.45
☐ 64	Brady Anderson	1.00	.45
☐ 65	Hideo Nomo	4.00	1.80
☐ 66	Ozzie Smith	2.00	.90
☐ 67	Eddie Murray	1.50	.70
☐ 68	Will Clark	1.00	.45
☐ 69	Jay Buhner	1.00	.45
☐ 70	Kirby Puckett	3.00	1.35
☐ 71	Barry Bonds	2.00	.90
☐ 72	Ray Durham	.40	.18
☐ 73	Sterling Hitchcock	.40	.18
☐ 74	John Smoltz	.75	.35
☐ 75	Andre Dawson	1.00	.45
☐ 76	Joe Carter	.75	.35
☐ 77	Ryne Sandberg	2.00	.90
☐ 78	Rickey Henderson	1.00	.45
☐ 79	Brian Jordan	.75	.35
☐ 80	Greg Vaughn	.40	.18
☐ 81	Andy Pettitte	2.00	.90
☐ 82	Dean Palmer	.40	.18
☐ 83	Paul Molitor	1.50	.70
☐ 84	Rafael Palmeiro	1.00	.45
☐ 85	Henry Rodriguez	.40	.18
☐ 86	Larry Walker	1.50	.70
☐ 87	Ismael Valdes	.75	.35
☐ 88	Derek Bell	.40	.18
☐ 89	J.T. Snow	.75	.35
☐ 90	Jack McDowell	.40	.18

1996 Leaf Limited Lumberjacks

Printed with maple stock that puts wood grains on both sides, this 10-card insert set features the league's top sluggers. The fronts carry color player photos with player information and statistics on the backs. Only 5,000 sets were produced and each card was individually numbered.

	MINT	NRMT
COMPLETE SET (10)	200.00	90.00
COMMON CARD (1-10)	6.00	2.70
RANDOM INSERTS IN PACKS ..		
STATED PRINT RUN 4500 SERIAL #'d SETS		
*BLACK: 1.5X TO 4X HI COLUMN		
BLACK PRINT RUN 500 SERIAL #'d SETS		

		MINT	NRMT
☐ 1	Ken Griffey Jr.	40.00	18.00
☐ 2	Sammy Sosa	8.00	3.60
☐ 3	Cal Ripken	30.00	13.50
☐ 4	Frank Thomas	30.00	13.50
☐ 5	Alex Rodriguez	25.00	11.00
☐ 6	Mo Vaughn	10.00	4.50
☐ 7	Chipper Jones	25.00	11.00
☐ 8	Mike Piazza	25.00	11.00
☐ 9	Jeff Bagwell	15.00	6.75
☐ 10	Mark McGwire	15.00	6.75
☐ P8	Mike Piazza Promo	5.00	2.20

1996 Leaf Limited Pennant Craze

This 10-card insert set features 10 superstars who have a thirst for the pennant. A special flocking technique puts the felt feel of a pennant on a die cut card. Only 2,500 sets were produced and are individually numbered.

	MINT	NRMT
COMPLETE SET (10)	500.00	220.00
COMMON CARD (1-10)	15.00	6.75
RANDOM INSERTS IN PACKS ..		
STATED PRINT RUN 2500 SERIAL #'d SETS		

		MINT	NRMT
☐ 1	Juan Gonzalez	40.00	18.00
☐ 2	Cal Ripken	60.00	27.00
☐ 3	Frank Thomas	60.00	27.00
☐ 4	Ken Griffey Jr.	80.00	36.00
☐ 5	Albert Belle	20.00	9.00
☐ 6	Greg Maddux	50.00	22.00
☐ 7	Paul Molitor	15.00	6.75
☐ 8	Alex Rodriguez	50.00	22.00
☐ 9	Barry Bonds	20.00	9.00
☐ 10	Chipper Jones	50.00	22.00

1996 Leaf Limited Rookies

Randomly inserted in packs at a rate of one in seven, this 10-card set printed in silver holo

graphic foil features some of the hottest rookies of the year.

	MINT	NRMT
COMPLETE SET (10)	70.00	32.00
COMMON CARD (1-10)	2.50	1.10
UNLISTED STARS	5.00	2.20
STATED ODDS 1:7		
COMP.GOLD SET (10)	180.00	80.00
*GOLD: 1X TO 2.5X HI COLUMN		
GOLD: RANDOM INSERTS IN PACKS		

		MINT	NRMT
☐ 1	Alex Ochoa	2.50	1.10
☐ 2	Darin Erstad	15.00	6.75
☐ 3	Ruben Rivera	3.00	1.35
☐ 4	Derek Jeter	15.00	6.75
☐ 5	Jermaine Dye	3.00	1.35
☐ 6	Jason Kendall	4.00	1.80
☐ 7	Mike Grace	2.50	1.10
☐ 8	Andruw Jones	15.00	6.75
☐ 9	Rey Ordonez	3.00	1.35
☐ 10	George Arias	2.50	1.10

1996 Leaf Preferred

The 1996 Leaf Preferred set was issued in one series totalling 150 cards. The 6-card packs retail for $3.49 each. Each card was printed on 20-point stock for extra thickness and durability. The fronts feature a color action player photo and silver foil printing. The backs carry another player photo, player information and statistics. One in every ten packs contains an insert card.

	MINT	NRMT
COMPLETE SET (150)	25.00	11.00
COMMON CARD (1-150)	.15	.07
MINOR STARS	.30	.14
UNLISTED STARS	.60	.25
SUBSET CARDS HALF VALUE OF BASE CARDS		
COMP.PP SET (150)	2000.00	900.00
COMMON PP (1-150)	4.00	1.80
*PP STARS: 15X TO 40X HI COLUMN		

*PP YOUNG STARS: 12.5X TO 30X HI
PRESS PROOFS: RANDOM INS.IN PACKS
PP STATED PRINT RUN 500 SETS

□ 1	Ken Griffey Jr.	3.00	1.35
□ 2	Rico Brogna	.15	.07
□ 3	Gregg Jefferies	.15	.07
□ 4	Reggie Sanders	.15	.07
□ 5	Manny Ramirez	.60	.25
□ 6	Shawn Green	.15	.07
□ 7	Tino Martinez	.60	.25
□ 8	Jeff Bagwell	1.25	.55
□ 9	Marc Newfield	.15	.07
□ 10	Ray Lankford	.30	.14
□ 11	Jay Bell	.30	.14
□ 12	Greg Maddux	2.00	.90
□ 13	Frank Thomas	2.50	1.10
□ 14	Travis Fryman	.30	.14
□ 15	Mark McGwire	1.25	.55
□ 16	Chuck Knoblauch	.60	.25
□ 17	Sammy Sosa	.60	.25
□ 18	Matt Williams	.40	.18
□ 19	Roger Clemens	1.25	.55
□ 20	Rondell White	.30	.14
□ 21	Ivan Rodriguez	.75	.35
□ 22	Cal Ripken	2.50	1.10
□ 23	Ben McDonald	.15	.07
□ 24	Kenny Lofton	.75	.35
□ 25	Mike Piazza	2.00	.90
□ 26	David Cone	.30	.14
□ 27	Gary Sheffield	.60	.25
□ 28	Tim Salmon	.60	.25
□ 29	Andres Galarraga	.60	.25
□ 30	Johnny Damon	.30	.14
□ 31	Ozzie Smith	.75	.35
□ 32	Carlos Baerga	.15	.07
□ 33	Raul Mondesi	.40	.18
□ 34	Moises Alou	.30	.14
□ 35	Alex Rodriguez	2.00	.90
□ 36	Mike Mussina	.15	.07
□ 37	Jason Isringhausen	.15	.07
□ 38	Barry Larkin	.40	.18
□ 39	Bernie Williams	.60	.25
□ 40	Chipper Jones	2.00	.90
□ 41	Joey Hamilton	.30	.14
□ 42	Charles Johnson	.30	.14
□ 43	Juan Gonzalez	1.50	.70
□ 44	Greg Vaughn	.15	.07
□ 45	Robin Ventura	.30	.14
□ 46	Albert Belle	.75	.35
□ 47	Rafael Palmeiro	.40	.18
□ 48	Brian L.Hunter	.30	.14
□ 49	Mo Vaughn	.75	.35
□ 50	Paul O'Neill	.30	.14
□ 51	Mark Grace	.40	.18
□ 52	Randy Johnson	.60	.25
□ 53	Pedro Martinez	.60	.25
□ 54	Marty Cordova	.30	.14
□ 55	Garret Anderson	.30	.14
□ 56	Joe Carter	.30	.14
□ 57	Jim Thome	.60	.25
□ 58	Edgardo Alfonzo	.40	.18
□ 59	Dante Bichette	.30	.14
□ 60	Darryl Hamilton	.15	.07
□ 61	Roberto Alomar	.60	.25
□ 62	Fred McGriff	.40	.18
□ 63	Kirby Puckett	1.25	.55
□ 64	Hideo Nomo	1.50	.70
□ 65	Alex Fernandez	.15	.07
□ 66	Ryan Klesko	.40	.18
□ 67	Wade Boggs	.60	.25
□ 68	Eddie Murray	.60	.25
□ 69	Eric Karros	.30	.14
□ 70	Jim Edmonds	.40	.18
□ 71	Edgar Martinez	.40	.18
□ 72	Andy Pettitte	.75	.35
□ 73	Mark Grudzielanek	.30	.14
□ 74	Tom Glavine	.40	.18
□ 75	Ken Caminiti	.40	.18
□ 76	Will Clark	.40	.18
□ 77	Craig Biggio	.40	.18
□ 78	Brady Anderson	.40	.18
□ 79	Tony Gwynn	1.50	.70
□ 80	Larry Walker	.60	.25
□ 81	Brian Jordan	.30	.14
□ 82	Lenny Dykstra	.30	.14
□ 83	Butch Huskey	.30	.14
□ 84	Jack McDowell	.15	.07
□ 85	Cecil Fielder	.30	.14
□ 86	Jose Canseco	.40	.18
□ 87	Jason Giambi	.30	.14
□ 88	Rickey Henderson	.40	.18
□ 89	Kevin Seitzer	.15	.07
□ 90	Carlos Delgado	.30	.14
□ 91	Ryne Sandberg	.75	.35
□ 92	Dwight Gooden	.30	.14
□ 93	Michael Tucker	.15	.07
□ 94	Barry Bonds	.75	.35
□ 95	Eric Young	.15	.07
□ 96	Dean Palmer	.15	.07
□ 97	Henry Rodriguez	.15	.07
□ 98	John Mabry	.15	.07
□ 99	J.T. Snow	.30	.14
□ 100	Andre Dawson	.40	.18
□ 101	Ismael Valdes	.30	.14
□ 102	Charles Nagy	.30	.14
□ 103	Jay Buhner	.40	.18
□ 104	Derek Bell	.15	.07
□ 105	Paul Molitor	.60	.25
□ 106	Hal Morris	.15	.07
□ 107	Ray Durham	.30	.14
□ 108	Bernard Gilkey	.15	.07
□ 109	John Valentin	.15	.07
□ 110	Melvin Nieves	.15	.07
□ 111	John Smoltz	.30	.14
□ 112	Terrell Wade	.15	.07
□ 113	Chad Mottola	.15	.07
□ 114	Tony Clark	.60	.25
□ 115	John Wasdin	.15	.07
□ 116	Derek Jeter	2.00	.90
□ 117	Rey Ordonez	.30	.14
□ 118	Jason Thompson	.15	.07
□ 119	Robin Jennings	.15	.07
□ 120	Rocky Coppinger	.60	.25
□ 121	Billy Wagner	.30	.14
□ 122	Steve Gibralter	.15	.07
□ 123	Jermaine Dye	.40	.18
□ 124	Jason Kendall	.30	.14
□ 125	Mike Grace	.15	.07
□ 126	Jason Schmidt	.30	.14
□ 127	Paul Wilson	.15	.07
□ 128	Alan Benes	.30	.14
□ 129	Justin Thompson	.40	.18
□ 130	Brooks Kieschnick	.30	.14
□ 131	George Arias	.15	.07
□ 132	Osvaldo Fernandez	.30	.14
□ 133	Todd Hollandsworth	.15	.07
□ 134	Eric Owens	.15	.07
□ 135	Chan Ho Park	.60	.25
□ 136	Mark Loretta	.15	.07
□ 137	Ruben Rivera	.30	.14
□ 138	Jeff Suppan	.30	.14
□ 139	Ugueth Urbina	.15	.07
□ 140	LaTroy Hawkins	.15	.07
□ 141	Chris Snopek	.15	.07
□ 142	Edgar Renteria	.40	.18
□ 143	Raul Casanova	.15	.07
□ 144	Jose Herrera	.15	.07
□ 145	Matt Lawton	.40	.18
□ 146	Ralph Milliard	.15	.07
□ 147	Frank Thomas CL	1.25	.55
□ 148	Jeff Bagwell CL	.60	.25
□ 149	Ken Griffey Jr. CL	1.50	.70
□ 150	Mike Piazza CL	1.00	.45

	MINT	NRMT
COMPLETE SET (12)	400.00	180.00
COMMON CARD (1-12)	15.00	6.75
RANDOM INSERTS IN PACKS		
STATED PRINT RUN 2500 SERIAL #'d SETS		

□ 1	Chipper Jones	40.00	18.00
□ 2	Alex Rodriguez	40.00	18.00
□ 3	Derek Jeter	30.00	13.50
□ 4	Tony Gwynn	30.00	13.50
□ 5	Frank Thomas	50.00	22.00
□ 6	Ken Griffey Jr.	60.00	27.00
□ 7	Cal Ripken	50.00	22.00
□ 8	Greg Maddux	40.00	18.00
□ 9	Albert Belle	15.00	6.75
□ 10	Barry Bonds	15.00	6.75
□ 11	Jeff Bagwell	25.00	11.00
□ 12	Mike Piazza	40.00	18.00

1996 Leaf Preferred Steel

Seeded one-per-pack, this all-steel, metalized set features silver framed color action player photos of the leagues most dominant players on a silver tinted background with a scriptive letter "S." The backs carry another player photo with the card logo as background and player statistics.

	MINT	NRMT
COMPLETE SET (77)	120.00	55.00
*STARS: 1.25X TO 3X BASE CARD HI		
*YOUNG STARS: 1X TO 2.5X BASE HI		
ONE SILVER STEEL PER PACK		
COMP.GOLD SET (77)	1200.00	550.00
*GOLD STARS: 12.5X TO 30X BASE CARD HI		
*GOLD YOUNG STARS: 10X TO 25X BASE HI		
GOLD: RANDOM INSERTS IN PACKS		

□ 1	Frank Thomas	8.00	3.60
□ 2	Paul Molitor	2.00	.90
□ 3	Kenny Lofton	2.50	1.10
□ 4	Travis Fryman	1.00	.45
□ 5	Jeff Conine	1.00	.45
□ 6	Barry Bonds	2.50	1.10

1996 Leaf Preferred Staremaster

Randomly inserted at an approximate rate of one in every 144 packs, these twelve cards feature mug shots of the games most intense stares. Each card is printed on silver holographic card stock. Only 2,500 of each card was produced and are individually numbered.

☐ 7	Gregg Jefferies	.50	.23
☐ 8	Alex Rodriguez	6.00	2.70
☐ 9	Wade Boggs	2.00	.90
☐ 10	David Justice	2.00	.90
☐ 11	Hideo Nomo	5.00	2.20
☐ 12	Roberto Alomar	2.00	.90
☐ 13	Todd Hollandsworth	.50	.23
☐ 14	Mark McGwire	4.00	1.80
☐ 15	Rafael Palmeiro	1.50	.70
☐ 16	Will Clark	1.50	.70
☐ 17	Cal Ripken	8.00	3.60
☐ 18	Derek Bell	.50	.23
☐ 19	Gary Sheffield	2.00	.90
☐ 20	Juan Gonzalez	5.00	2.20
☐ 21	Garret Anderson	1.00	.45
☐ 22	Mo Vaughn	2.50	1.10
☐ 23	Robin Ventura	1.00	.45
☐ 24	Carlos Baerga	.50	.23
☐ 25	Tim Salmon	2.00	.90
☐ 26	Matt Williams	1.50	.70
☐ 27	Fred McGriff	1.50	.70
☐ 28	Rondell White	1.00	.45
☐ 29	Ray Lankford	1.00	.45
☐ 30	Lenny Dykstra	1.00	.45
☐ 31	J.T. Snow	1.00	.45
☐ 32	Sammy Sosa	2.00	.90
☐ 33	Chipper Jones	6.00	2.70
☐ 34	Bobby Bonilla	1.00	.45
☐ 35	Paul Wilson	.50	.23
☐ 36	Darren Daulton	1.00	.45
☐ 37	Larry Walker	2.00	.90
☐ 38	Raul Mondesi	1.50	.70
☐ 39	Jeff Bagwell	4.00	1.80
☐ 40	Derek Jeter	6.00	2.70
☐ 41	Kirby Puckett	4.00	1.80
☐ 42	Jason Isringhausen	.50	.23
☐ 43	Vinny Castilla	1.00	.45
☐ 44	Jim Edmonds	1.50	.70
☐ 45	Ron Gant	1.00	.45
☐ 46	Carlos Delgado	1.00	.45
☐ 47	Jose Canseco	1.50	.70
☐ 48	Tony Gwynn	5.00	2.20
☐ 49	Mike Mussina	2.00	.90
☐ 50	Charles Johnson	1.00	.45
☐ 51	Mike Piazza	6.00	2.70
☐ 52	Ken Griffey Jr.	10.00	4.50
☐ 53	Greg Maddux	6.00	2.70
☐ 54	Mark Grace	1.50	.70
☐ 55	Ryan Klesko	1.50	.70
☐ 56	Dennis Eckersley	1.00	.45
☐ 57	Rickey Henderson	1.50	.70
☐ 58	Michael Tucker	1.00	.45
☐ 59	Joe Carter	1.00	.45
☐ 60	Randy Johnson	2.00	.90
☐ 61	Brian Jordan	1.00	.45
☐ 62	Shawn Green	.50	.23
☐ 63	Roger Clemens	4.00	1.80
☐ 64	Andres Galarraga	2.00	.90
☐ 65	Johnny Damon	1.00	.45
☐ 66	Ryne Sandberg	2.50	1.10
☐ 67	Alan Benes	1.00	.45
☐ 68	Albert Belle	2.00	.90
☐ 69	Barry Larkin	1.50	.70
☐ 70	Marty Cordova	1.00	.45
☐ 71	Dante Bichette	1.00	.45
☐ 72	Craig Biggio	1.50	.70
☐ 73	Reggie Sanders	.50	.23
☐ 74	Moises Alou	1.00	.45
☐ 75	Chuck Knoblauch	2.00	.90
☐ 76	Cecil Fielder	1.00	.45
☐ 77	Manny Ramirez	2.00	.90

1996 Leaf Preferred Steel Power

This eight-card set combines a micro-etched foil card with corner interior lightening-symbol diecutting and honors eight of the top power hitters. The fronts carry a color player photo while the backs display a statement

explaining why the player is included in the set along with his 1995 season hitting statistics. Only 5,000 sets were produced, and each card carries a serial number.

	MINT	NRMT
COMPLETE SET (8)	150.00	70.00
COMMON CARD (1-8)	10.00	4.50
RANDOM INSERTS IN PACKS		

☐ 1	Albert Belle	10.00	4.50
☐ 2	Mo Vaughn	10.00	4.50
☐ 3	Ken Griffey Jr.	40.00	18.00
☐ 4	Cal Ripken	30.00	13.50
☐ 5	Mike Piazza	25.00	11.00
☐ 6	Barry Bonds	10.00	4.50
☐ 7	Jeff Bagwell	15.00	6.75
☐ 8	Frank Thomas	30.00	13.50

1996 Leaf Signature

The 1996 Leaf Signature Set was issued in two series totalling 150 cards. The four-card packs have a suggested retail price of $9.99 each. It's interesting to note that the Extended Series was the last of the 1996 releases. In fact, it was released in January 1997 - so late in the year that it's categorization as a 1996 issue is a bit of a stretch. Production for the Extended Series was only 40% that of the regular issue. Extended series packs actually contained a mix of both Series 1 and 2 cards, thus the Extended series cards are somewhat scarcer. Card fronts feature borderless color action player photos with the card name printed in a silver foil emblem. The backs carry player information. The only notable Rookie Card is of Darin Erstad.

	MINT	NRMT
COMPLETE SET (150)	100.00	45.00
COMPLETE SERIES 1 (100)	60.00	27.00
COMMON CARD (1-100)	.25	.11
SERIES 1 MINOR STARS	.50	.23
SERIES 1 UNLISTED STARS	1.00	.45
COMPLETE SERIES 2 (50)	40.00	18.00
COMMON CARD (101-150)	.25	.23
SERIES 2 MINOR STARS	1.00	.45
SERIES 2 UNLISTED STARS	2.00	.90
COMP.GOLD SET (150)	1200.00	550.00
COMP.GOLD SER.1 (100)	800.00	350.00
COMP.GOLD SER.2 (50)	400.00	180.00
COMMON GOLD (1-150)	3.00	1.35

*SER.1 GOLD STARS: 6X TO 15X HI COL.
*SER.1 GOLD Y.STARS: 5X TO 12X HI
*SER.2 GOLD STARS: 3X TO 8X HI
*SER.2 GOLD Y.STARS: 2.5X TO 6X HI
GOLD PRESS PROOFS STATED ODDS 1:12
GOLD PLAT.SET (150) ... 4000.00 1800.00
GOLD PLAT. (1-150) ... 8.00 3.60
*SER.1 PLAT.STARS: 20X TO 40X HI COLUMN
*SER.1 PLAT.YOUNG STARS: 15X TO 30X HI
*SER.2 PLAT.STARS: 10X TO 20X HI
*SER.2 PLAT.YNG.STARS: 7.5X TO 15X HI
PLATINUM SER.2 STATED ODDS 1:24
PLATINUM STATED PRINT RUN 150 SETS

☐ 1	Mike Piazza	3.00	1.35
☐ 2	Juan Gonzalez	2.50	1.10
☐ 3	Greg Maddux	3.00	1.35
☐ 4	Marc Newfield	.25	.11
☐ 5	Wade Boggs	1.00	.45
☐ 6	Ray Lankford	.50	.23
☐ 7	Frank Thomas	4.00	1.80
☐ 8	Rico Brogna	.25	.11
☐ 9	Tim Salmon	1.00	.45
☐ 10	Ken Griffey Jr.	5.00	2.20
☐ 11	Manny Ramirez	1.00	.45
☐ 12	Cecil Fielder	.50	.23
☐ 13	Gregg Jefferies	.25	.11
☐ 14	Rondell White	.50	.23
☐ 15	Cal Ripken	4.00	1.80
☐ 16	Alex Rodriguez	3.00	1.35
☐ 17	Bernie Williams	1.00	.45
☐ 18	Andres Galarraga	1.00	.45
☐ 19	Mike Mussina	1.00	.45
☐ 20	Chuck Knoblauch	1.00	.45
☐ 21	Joe Carter	.50	.23
☐ 22	Jeff Bagwell	2.00	.90
☐ 23	Mark McGwire	2.00	.90
☐ 24	Sammy Sosa	1.00	.45
☐ 25	Reggie Sanders	.25	.11
☐ 26	Chipper Jones	3.00	1.35
☐ 27	Jeff Cirillo	.50	.23
☐ 28	Roger Clemens	2.00	.90
☐ 29	Craig Biggio	.75	.35
☐ 30	Gary Sheffield	1.00	.45
☐ 31	Paul O'Neill	.50	.23
☐ 32	Johnny Damon	.50	.23
☐ 33	Jason Isringhausen	.25	.11
☐ 34	Jay Bell	.50	.23
☐ 35	Henry Rodriguez	.25	.11
☐ 36	Matt Williams	.75	.35
☐ 37	Randy Johnson	1.00	.45
☐ 38	Fred McGriff	.75	.35
☐ 39	Jason Giambi	.50	.23
☐ 40	Ivan Rodriguez	1.25	.55
☐ 41	Raul Mondesi	.75	.35
☐ 42	Barry Larkin	.75	.35
☐ 43	Ryan Klesko	.75	.35
☐ 44	Joey Hamilton	.50	.23
☐ 45	Todd Hundley	.50	.23
☐ 46	Jim Edmonds	.75	.35
☐ 47	Dante Bichette	.50	.23
☐ 48	Roberto Alomar	1.00	.45
☐ 49	Mark Grace	.75	.35
☐ 50	Brady Anderson	.75	.35
☐ 51	Hideo Nomo	2.50	1.10
☐ 52	Ozzie Smith	1.25	.55
☐ 53	Robin Ventura	.50	.23
☐ 54	Andy Pettitte	1.25	.55
☐ 55	Kenny Lofton	1.25	.55
☐ 56	John Mabry	.25	.11
☐ 57	Paul Molitor	1.00	.45
☐ 58	Rey Ordonez	.50	.23

☐ 59 Albert Belle	1.25	.55
☐ 60 Charles Johnson	.50	.23
☐ 61 Edgar Martinez	.75	.35
☐ 62 Derek Bell	.25	.11
☐ 63 Carlos Delgado	.50	.23
☐ 64 Raul Casanova	.25	.11
☐ 65 Ismael Valdes	.50	.23
☐ 66 J.T. Snow	.50	.23
☐ 67 Derek Jeter	3.00	1.50
☐ 68 Jason Kendall	.75	.35
☐ 69 John Smoltz	.50	.23
☐ 70 Chad Mottola	.25	.11
☐ 71 Jim Thome	1.00	.45
☐ 72 Will Clark	.75	.35
☐ 73 Mo Vaughn	1.25	.55
☐ 74 John Wasdin	.25	.11
☐ 75 Rafael Palmeiro	.75	.35
☐ 76 Mark Grudzielanek	.50	.23
☐ 77 Larry Walker	1.00	.45
☐ 78 Alan Benes	.50	.23
☐ 79 Michael Tucker	.50	.23
☐ 80 Billy Wagner	.50	.23
☐ 81 Paul Wilson	.25	.11
☐ 82 Greg Vaughn	.25	.11
☐ 83 Dean Palmer	.25	.11
☐ 84 Ryne Sandberg	1.25	.55
☐ 85 Eric Young	.25	.11
☐ 86 Jay Buhner	.75	.35
☐ 87 Tony Clark	1.00	.45
☐ 88 Jermaine Dye	.50	.23
☐ 89 Barry Bonds	1.25	.55
☐ 90 Ugueth Urbina	.25	.11
☐ 91 Charles Nagy	.50	.23
☐ 92 Ruben Rivera	.50	.23
☐ 93 Todd Hollandsworth	.25	.11
☐ 94 Darin Erstad	5.00	2.20
☐ 95 Brooks Kieschnick	.50	.23
☐ 96 Edgar Renteria	.50	.23
☐ 97 Lenny Dykstra	.50	.23
☐ 98 Tony Gwynn	2.50	1.10
☐ 99 Kirby Puckett	2.00	.90
☐ 100 Checklist	.25	.11
☐ 101 Andruw Jones	5.00	2.20
☐ 102 Alex Ochoa	.50	.23
☐ 103 David Cone	1.00	.45
☐ 104 Rusty Greer	.50	.23
☐ 105 Jose Canseco	1.50	.70
☐ 106 Ken Caminiti	1.50	.70
☐ 107 Mariano Rivera	1.50	.70
☐ 108 Ron Gant	1.00	.45
☐ 109 Darryl Strawberry	1.00	.45
☐ 110 Vladimir Guerrero	4.00	1.80
☐ 111 George Arias	.50	.23
☐ 112 Jeff Conine	1.00	.45
☐ 113 Bobby Higginson	1.00	.45
☐ 114 Eric Karros	1.00	.45
☐ 115 Brian Hunter	1.00	.45
☐ 116 Eddie Murray	2.00	.90
☐ 117 Todd Walker	3.00	1.35
☐ 118 Chan Ho Park	2.00	.90
☐ 119 John Jaha	.50	.23
☐ 120 Dave Justice	2.00	.90
☐ 121 Makoto Suzuki	.50	.23
☐ 122 Scott Rolen	5.00	2.20
☐ 123 Tino Martinez	1.00	.45
☐ 124 Kimera Bartee	.50	.23
☐ 125 Garret Anderson	1.00	.45
☐ 126 Brian Jordan	1.00	.45
☐ 127 Andre Dawson	2.00	.90
☐ 128 Javier Lopez	1.00	.45
☐ 129 Bill Pulsipher	.50	.23
☐ 130 Dwight Gooden	1.00	.45
☐ 131 Al Martin	.50	.23
☐ 132 Terrell Wade	.50	.23
☐ 133 Steve Gibralter	.50	.23
☐ 134 Tom Glavine	1.00	.45
☐ 135 Kevin Appier	1.00	.45
☐ 136 Tim Raines	1.00	.45
☐ 137 Curtis Pride	.50	.23
☐ 138 Todd Greene	1.50	.70
☐ 139 Bobby Bonilla	1.00	.45
☐ 140 Trey Beamon	.50	.23
☐ 141 Marty Cordova	1.00	.45
☐ 142 Rickey Henderson	1.50	.70
☐ 143 Ellis Burks	1.00	.45
☐ 144 Dennis Eckersley	1.00	.45

☐ 145 Kevin Brown	1.00	.45
☐ 146 Carlos Baerga	.50	.23
☐ 147 Brett Butler	1.00	.45
☐ 148 Marquis Grissom	1.00	.45
☐ 149 Karim Garcia	1.50	.70
☐ 150 Frank Thomas CL	4.00	1.80

1996 Leaf Signature Autographs

Inserted into 1996 Leaf Signature Series first series packs, these unnumbered cards were one of the first major autograph issues featured in an MLB-licensed trading card set. First series packs contained at least one autograph, with the chance of getting more. Donruss/Leaf reports that all but 10 players in the Leaf Signature Series signed close to 5,000 total autographs (3,500 bronze, 1,000 silver, 500 gold). The 10 players who signed 1,000 (700 bronze, 200 silver, 100 gold) are: Roberto Alomar, Wade Boggs, Derek Jeter, Kenny Lofton, Paul Molitor, Raul Mondesi, Manny Ramirez, Alex Rodriguez, Frank Thomas and Mo Vaughn. It's also important to note that six additional players did not submit their cards in time to be included in first series packs. Thus, their cards were thrown into Extended series packs. Those six players are as follows: Brian L. Hunter, Carlos Delgado, Phil Plantier, Jim Thome, Terrell Wade and Ernie Young. Thome signed only silver and gold foil cards, thus the Bronze set is considered complete at 251 cards. Prices below refer exclusively to Bronze versions. Blue and black ink variations have been found for Carlos Delgado, Alex Rodriguez and Michael Tucker. No consistent premiums for these variations has been tracked. Finally, an autographed jumbo silver foil version of the Frank Thomas card was distributed to dealers in March 1997. Dealers received either this first series or the Extended Series jumbo Thomas for every Extended Series jumbo case ordered. Each Thomas jumbo is individually serial numbered to 1,500.

	MINT	NRMT
COMP. BRONZE SET (251)	2200.00	1000.00
COMMON BRONZE (1-251)	4.00	1.80
BRONZE MINOR STARS	8.00	3.60
*SILVER: .75X TO 1.5X HI COLUMN		
*GOLD: 1X TO 2X HI		
ONE OR MORE AUTOGRAPHS PER PACK		
NON-SP: 3500 BRONZE/1000 SILV/500 GOLD		
SP: 700 BRONZE/200 SILV/100 GOLD		

☐ 1 Kurt Abbott	4.00	1.80
☐ 2 Juan Acevedo	4.00	1.80
☐ 3 Terry Adams	4.00	1.80
☐ 4 Manny Alexander	4.00	1.80
☐ 5 Roberto Alomar SP	120.00	55.00
☐ 6 Moises Alou	8.00	3.60
☐ 7 Wilson Alvarez	4.00	1.80
☐ 8 Garret Anderson	8.00	3.60
☐ 9 Shane Andrews	4.00	1.80
☐ 10 Andy Ashby	4.00	1.80
☐ 11 Pedro Astacio	4.00	1.80
☐ 12 Brad Ausmus	4.00	1.80
☐ 13 Bobby Ayala	4.00	1.80
☐ 14 Carlos Baerga	4.00	1.80
☐ 15 Harold Baines	8.00	3.60
☐ 16 Jason Bates	4.00	1.80
☐ 17 Allen Battle	4.00	1.80
☐ 18 Rich Becker	4.00	1.80
☐ 19 David Bell	4.00	1.80
☐ 20 Rafael Belliard	4.00	1.80
☐ 21 Andy Benes	8.00	3.60
☐ 22 Armando Benitez	4.00	1.80
☐ 23 Jason Bere	4.00	1.80
☐ 24 Geronimo Berroa	4.00	1.80
☐ 25 Willie Blair	4.00	1.80
☐ 26 Mike Blowers	4.00	1.80
☐ 27 Wade Boggs SP	200.00	90.00
☐ 28 Ricky Bones	4.00	1.80
☐ 29 Mike Bordick	4.00	1.80
☐ 30 Toby Borland	4.00	1.80
☐ 31 Ricky Bottalico	4.00	1.80
☐ 32 Darren Bragg	4.00	1.80
☐ 33 Jeff Branson	4.00	1.80
☐ 34 Tilson Brito	4.00	1.80
☐ 35 Rico Brogna	4.00	1.80
☐ 36 Scott Brosius	4.00	1.80
☐ 37 Damon Buford	4.00	1.80
☐ 38 Mike Busby	4.00	1.80
☐ 39 Tom Candiotti	4.00	1.80
☐ 40 Frank Castillo	4.00	1.80
☐ 41 Andujar Cedeno	4.00	1.80
☐ 42 Domingo Cedeno	4.00	1.80
☐ 43 Roger Cedeno	4.00	1.80
☐ 44 Norm Charlton	4.00	1.80
☐ 45 Jeff Cirillo	8.00	3.60
☐ 46 Will Clark	15.00	6.75
☐ 47 Jeff Conine	8.00	3.60
☐ 48 Steve Cooke	4.00	1.80
☐ 49 Joey Cora	8.00	3.60
☐ 50 Marty Cordova	8.00	3.60
☐ 51 Rheal Cormier	4.00	1.80
☐ 52 Felipe Crespo	4.00	1.80
☐ 53 Chad Curtis	4.00	1.80
☐ 54 Johnny Damon	8.00	3.60
☐ 55 Russ Davis	4.00	1.80
☐ 56 Andre Dawson	12.00	5.50
☐ 57 Carlos Delgado	8.00	3.60
☐ 58 Doug Drabek	4.00	1.80
☐ 59 Darren Dreifort	4.00	1.80
☐ 60 Shawon Dunston	4.00	1.80
☐ 61 Ray Durham	4.00	1.80
☐ 62 Jim Edmonds	15.00	6.75
☐ 63 Joey Eischen	4.00	1.80
☐ 64 Jim Eisenreich	4.00	1.80
☐ 65 Sal Fasano	4.00	1.80
☐ 66 Jeff Fassero	4.00	1.80
☐ 67 Alex Fernandez	4.00	1.80
☐ 68 Darrin Fletcher	4.00	1.80
☐ 69 Chad Fonville	4.00	1.80
☐ 70 Kevin Foster	4.00	1.80
☐ 71 John Franco	8.00	3.60
☐ 72 Julio Franco	4.00	1.80
☐ 73 Marvin Freeman	4.00	1.80
☐ 74 Travis Fryman	8.00	3.60
☐ 75 Gary Gaetti	4.00	1.80
☐ 76 Carlos Garcia	4.00	1.80

□		MINT	NRMT
□ 77	Jason Giambi	8.00	3.60
□ 78	Benji Gil	4.00	1.80
□ 79	Greg Gohr	4.00	1.80
□ 80	Chris Gomez	4.00	1.80
□ 81	Leo Gomez	4.00	1.80
□ 82	Tom Goodwin	4.00	1.80
□ 83	Mike Grace	4.00	1.80
□ 84	Mike Greenwell	4.00	1.80
□ 85	Rusty Greer	12.00	5.50
□ 86	Mark Grudzielanek	8.00	3.60
□ 87	Mark Gubicza	4.00	1.80
□ 88	Juan Guzman	4.00	1.80
□ 89	Darryl Hamilton	4.00	1.80
□ 90	Joey Hamilton	8.00	3.60
□ 91	Chris Hammond	4.00	1.80
□ 92	Mike Hampton	4.00	1.80
□ 93	Chris Haney	4.00	1.80
□ 94	Todd Haney	4.00	1.80
□ 95	Erik Hanson	4.00	1.80
□ 96	Pete Harnisch	4.00	1.80
□ 97	LaTroy Hawkins	4.00	1.80
□ 98	Charlie Hayes	4.00	1.80
□ 99	Jimmy Haynes	4.00	1.80
□ 100	Roberto Hernandez	4.00	1.80
□ 101	Bobby Higginson	8.00	3.60
□ 102	Glenallen Hill	4.00	1.80
□ 103	Ken Hill	4.00	1.80
□ 104	Sterling Hitchcock	4.00	1.80
□ 105	Trevor Hoffman	4.00	1.80
□ 106	Dave Hollins	4.00	1.80
□ 107	Dwayne Hosey	4.00	1.80
□ 108	Thomas Howard	4.00	1.80
□ 109	Steve Howe	4.00	1.80
□ 110	John Hudek	4.00	1.80
□ 111	Rex Hudler	4.00	1.80
□ 112	Brian L. Hunter	8.00	3.60
□ 113	Butch Huskey	8.00	3.60
□ 114	Mark Hutton	4.00	1.80
□ 115	Jason Jacome	4.00	1.80
□ 116	John Jaha	4.00	1.80
□ 117	Reggie Jefferson	4.00	1.80
□ 118	Derek Jeter SP	175.00	80.00
□ 119	Bobby Jones	4.00	1.80
□ 120	Todd Jones	4.00	1.80
□ 121	Brian Jordan	8.00	3.60
□ 122	Kevin Jordan	4.00	1.80
□ 123	Jeff Juden	4.00	1.80
□ 124	Ron Karkovice	4.00	1.80
□ 125	Roberto Kelly	4.00	1.80
□ 126	Mark Kiefer	4.00	1.80
□ 127	Brooks Kieschnick	8.00	3.60
□ 128	Jeff King	4.00	1.80
□ 129	Mike Lansing	4.00	1.80
□ 130	Matt Lawton	12.00	5.50
□ 131	Al Leiter	4.00	1.80
□ 132	Mark Leiter	4.00	1.80
□ 133	Curtis Leskanic	4.00	1.80
□ 134	Darren Lewis	4.00	1.80
□ 135	Mark Lewis	4.00	1.80
□ 136	Felipe Lira	4.00	1.80
□ 137	Pat Listach	4.00	1.80
□ 138	Keith Lockhart	4.00	1.80
□ 139	Kenny Lofton SP	120.00	55.00
□ 140	John Mabry	4.00	1.80
□ 141	Mike Macfarlane	4.00	1.80
□ 142	Kirt Manwaring	4.00	1.80
□ 143	Al Martin	4.00	1.80
□ 144	Norberto Martin	4.00	1.80
□ 145	Dennis Martinez	8.00	3.60
□ 146	Pedro Martinez	18.00	8.00
□ 147	Sandy Martinez	4.00	1.80
□ 148	Mike Matheny	4.00	1.80
□ 149	T.J. Mathews	4.00	1.80
□ 150	David McCarty	4.00	1.80
□ 151	Ben McDonald	4.00	1.80
□ 152	Pat Meares	4.00	1.80
□ 153	Orlando Merced	4.00	1.80
□ 154	Jose Mesa	4.00	1.80
□ 155	Matt Mieske	4.00	1.80
□ 156	Orlando Miller	4.00	1.80
□ 157	Mike Mimbs	4.00	1.80
□ 158	Paul Molitor SP	100.00	45.00
□ 159A	R.Mondesi SP Bronze	80.00	36.00
□ 160	Jeff Montgomery	4.00	1.80
□ 161	Mickey Morandini	4.00	1.80
□ 162	Lyle Mouton	4.00	1.80
□ 163	James Mouton	4.00	1.80
□ 164	Jamie Moyer	4.00	1.80
□ 165	Rodney Myers	4.00	1.80
□ 166	Denny Neagle	12.00	5.50
□ 167	Robb Nen	4.00	1.80
□ 168	Marc Newfield	4.00	1.80
□ 169	Dave Nilsson	4.00	1.80
□ 170	Jon Nunnally	4.00	1.80
□ 171	Chad Ogea	4.00	1.80
□ 172	Troy O'Leary	4.00	1.80
□ 173	Rey Ordonez	8.00	3.60
□ 174	Jayhawk Owens	4.00	1.80
□ 175	Tom Pagnozzi	4.00	1.80
□ 176	Dean Palmer	4.00	1.80
□ 177	Roger Pavlik	4.00	1.80
□ 178	Troy Percival	4.00	1.80
□ 179	Carlos Perez	4.00	1.80
□ 180	Robert Perez	4.00	1.80
□ 181	Andy Pettitte	30.00	13.50
□ 182	Phil Plantier	4.00	1.80
□ 183	Mike Potts	4.00	1.80
□ 184	Curtis Pride	4.00	1.80
□ 185	Ariel Prieto	4.00	1.80
□ 186	Bill Pulsipher	4.00	1.80
□ 187	Brad Radke	8.00	3.60
□ 188	Manny Ramirez SP	40.00	18.00
□ 189	Joe Randa	4.00	1.80
□ 190	Pat Rapp	4.00	1.80
□ 191	Bryan Rekar	4.00	1.80
□ 192	Shane Reynolds	4.00	1.80
□ 193	Arthur Rhodes	4.00	1.80
□ 194	Mariano Rivera	12.00	5.50
□ 195	Alex Rodriguez SP	250.00	110.00
□ 196	Frank Rodriguez	4.00	1.80
□ 197	Mel Rojas	4.00	1.80
□ 198	Ken Ryan	4.00	1.80
□ 199	Bret Saberhagen	4.00	1.80
□ 200	Tim Salmon	20.00	9.00
□ 201	Rey Sanchez	4.00	1.80
□ 202	Scott Sanders	4.00	1.80
□ 203	Steve Scarsone	4.00	1.80
□ 204	Curt Schilling	8.00	3.60
□ 205	Jason Schmidt	8.00	3.60
□ 206	David Segui	4.00	1.80
□ 207	Kevin Seitzer	4.00	1.80
□ 208	Scott Servais	4.00	1.80
□ 209	Don Slaught	4.00	1.80
□ 210	Zane Smith	4.00	1.80
□ 211	Paul Sorrento	4.00	1.80
□ 212	Scott Stahoviak	4.00	1.80
□ 213	Mike Stanley	4.00	1.80
□ 214	Terry Steinbach	4.00	1.80
□ 215	Kevin Stocker	4.00	1.80
□ 216	Jeff Suppan	8.00	3.60
□ 217	Bill Swift	4.00	1.80
□ 218	Greg Swindell	4.00	1.80
□ 219	Kevin Tapani	4.00	1.80
□ 220	Danny Tartabull	4.00	1.80
□ 221	Julian Tavarez	4.00	1.80
□ 222	Frank Thomas SP	250.00	110.00
□ 223	Ozzie Timmons	4.00	1.80
□ 224	Michael Tucker	8.00	3.60
□ 225	Ismael Valdes	8.00	3.60
□ 226	Jose Valentin	4.00	1.80
□ 227	Todd Van Poppel	4.00	1.80
□ 228	Mo Vaughn SP	100.00	45.00
□ 229	Quilvio Veras	4.00	1.80
□ 230	Fernando Vina	4.00	1.80
□ 231	Joe Vitiello	4.00	1.80
□ 232	Jose Vizcaino	4.00	1.80
□ 233	Omar Vizquel	8.00	3.60
□ 234	Terrell Wade	4.00	1.80
□ 235	Paul Wagner	4.00	1.80
□ 236	Matt Walbeck	4.00	1.80
□ 237	Jerome Walton	4.00	1.80
□ 238	Turner Ward	4.00	1.80
□ 239	Allen Watson	4.00	1.80
□ 240	David Weathers	4.00	1.80
□ 241	Walt Weiss	4.00	1.80
□ 242	Turk Wendell	4.00	1.80
□ 243	Rondell White	8.00	3.60
□ 244	Brian Williams	4.00	1.80
□ 245	George Williams	4.00	1.80
□ 246	Paul Wilson	4.00	1.80
□ 247	Bobby Witt	4.00	1.80
□ 248	Bob Wolcott	4.00	1.80
□ 249	Eric Young	4.00	1.80
□ 250	Ernie Young	4.00	1.80
□ 251	Greg Zaun	4.00	1.80
□ NNO	F.Thomas Jumbo AU	80.00	36.00

1996 Leaf Signature Extended Autographs

At least two autographed cards from this 217-card set were inserted in every Extended Series pack. Super Packs with four autographed cards were seeded one in every 12 packs. Most players signed 5000 cards, but short prints (500-2500 of each) do exist. On average, one in every nine packs contains a short print. All short print cards are individually noted below. By mistake, Andruw Jones, Ryan Klesko, Andy Pettitte, Kirby Puckett and Frank Thomas signed a few hundred of each of their cards in blue ink instead of black. No difference in price has been noted. Also, the Juan Gonzalez, Andruw Jones and Alex Rodriguez cards available in packs were not signed. All three cards had information on the back on how to mail them into Donruss/Leaf for an actual signed version. The deadline to exchange these cards was December 31, 1998. In addition, middle relievers Doug Creek and Steve Parris failed to sign all 5000 of their cards. Creek submitted 1,950 cards and Parris submitted 1,800. Finally, an autographed jumbo version of the Extended Series Frank Thomas card was distributed to dealers in March 1997. Dealers received either this card or the first series jumbo Thomas for every Extended Series case ordered. Each Extended Thomas jumbo is individually serial numbered to 1,500.

	MINT	NRMT
COMPLETE SET (217)	3000.00	1350.00
COMMON CARD (1-217)	4.00	1.80
TWO OR MORE AUTOGRAPHS PER PACK		
NON-SP PRINT RUN 5000 OF EACH CARD		
EXCH. DEADLINE: 12/31/98		

☐ 1	Scott Aldred	4.00	1.80
☐ 2	Mike Aldrete	4.00	1.80
☐ 3	Rich Amaral	4.00	1.80
☐ 4	Alex Arias	4.00	1.80
☐ 5	Paul Assenmacher	4.00	1.80
☐ 6	Roger Bailey	4.00	1.80
☐ 7	Erik Bennett	4.00	1.80
☐ 8	Sean Bergman	4.00	1.80
☐ 9	Doug Bochtler	4.00	1.80
☐ 10	Tim Bogar	4.00	1.80
☐ 11	Pat Borders	4.00	1.80
☐ 12	Pedro Borbon	4.00	1.80
☐ 13	Shawn Boskie	4.00	1.80
☐ 14	Rafael Bournigal	4.00	1.80
☐ 15	Mark Brandenburg	4.00	1.80
☐ 16	John Briscoe	4.00	1.80
☐ 17	Jorge Brito	4.00	1.80
☐ 18	Doug Brocail	4.00	1.80
☐ 19	Jay Buhner SP1000	50.00	22.00
☐ 20	Scott Bullett	4.00	1.80
☐ 21	Dave Burba	4.00	1.80
☐ 22	Ken Caminiti SP1000	50.00	22.00
☐ 23	John Cangelosi	4.00	1.80
☐ 24	Cris Carpenter	4.00	1.80
☐ 25	Chuck Carr	4.00	1.80
☐ 26	Larry Casian	4.00	1.80
☐ 27	Tony Castillo	4.00	1.80
☐ 28	Jason Christiansen	4.00	1.80
☐ 29	Archi Cianfrocco	4.00	1.80
☐ 30	Mark Clark	4.00	1.80
☐ 31	Terry Clark	4.00	1.80
☐ 32	Roger Clemens SP1000	150.00	70.00
☐ 33	Jim Converse	4.00	1.80
☐ 34	Dennis Cook	4.00	1.80
☐ 35	Francisco Cordova	4.00	1.80
☐ 36	Jim Corsi	4.00	1.80
☐ 37	Tim Crabtree	4.00	1.80
☐ 38	Doug Creek SP1950	12.00	5.50
☐ 39	John Cummings	4.00	1.80
☐ 40	Omar Daal	4.00	1.80
☐ 41	Rich DeLucia	4.00	1.80
☐ 42	Mark Dewey	4.00	1.80
☐ 43	Alex Diaz	4.00	1.80
☐ 44	Jermaine Dye SP2500	15.00	6.75
☐ 45	Ken Edenfield	4.00	1.80
☐ 46	Mark Eichhorn	4.00	1.80
☐ 47	John Ericks	4.00	1.80
☐ 48	Darin Erstad	40.00	18.00
☐ 49	Alvaro Espinoza	4.00	1.80
☐ 50	Jorge Fabregas	4.00	1.80
☐ 51	Mike Fetters	4.00	1.80
☐ 52	John Flaherty	4.00	1.80
☐ 53	Bryce Florie	4.00	1.80
☐ 54	Tony Fossas	4.00	1.80
☐ 55	Lou Frazier	4.00	1.80
☐ 56	Mike Gallego	4.00	1.80
☐ 57	Karim Garcia SP2500	25.00	11.00
☐ 58	Jason Giambi	6.00	2.70
☐ 59	Ed Giovanola	4.00	1.80
☐ 60	Tom Glavine SP1250	40.00	18.00
☐ 61	Juan Gonzalez SP1000	150.00	70.00
☐ 62	Craig Grebeck	4.00	1.80
☐ 63	Buddy Groom	4.00	1.80
☐ 64	Kevin Gross	4.00	1.80
☐ 65	Eddie Guardado	4.00	1.80
☐ 66	Mark Guthrie	4.00	1.80
☐ 67	Tony Gwynn SP1000	150.00	70.00
☐ 68	Chip Hale	4.00	1.80
☐ 69	Darren Hall	4.00	1.80
☐ 70	Lee Hancock	4.00	1.80
☐ 71	Dave Hansen	4.00	1.80
☐ 72	Bryan Harvey	4.00	1.90
☐ 73	Bill Haselman	4.00	1.80
☐ 74	Mike Henneman	4.00	1.80
☐ 75	Doug Henry	4.00	1.80
☐ 76	Gil Heredia	4.00	1.80
☐ 77	Carlos Hernandez	4.00	1.80
☐ 78	Jose Hernandez	4.00	1.80
☐ 79	Darren Holmes	4.00	1.80
☐ 80	Mark Holzemer	4.00	1.80
☐ 81	Rick Honeycutt	4.00	1.80
☐ 82	Chris Hook	4.00	1.80
☐ 83	Chris Howard	4.00	1.80
☐ 84	Jack Howell	4.00	1.80
☐ 85	David Hulse	4.00	1.80
☐ 86	Edwin Hurtado	4.00	1.80
☐ 87	Jeff Huson	4.00	1.80
☐ 88	Mike James	4.00	1.80
☐ 89	Derek Jeter SP1000	150.00	70.00
☐ 90	Brian Johnson	4.00	1.80
☐ 91	Randy Johnson SP1000	80.00	36.00
☐ 92	Mark Johnson	4.00	1.80
☐ 93	Andruw Jones SP2000	80.00	36.00
☐ 94	Chris Jones	4.00	1.80
☐ 95	Ricky Jordan	4.00	1.80
☐ 96	Matt Karchner	4.00	1.80
☐ 97	Scott Karl	4.00	1.80
☐ 98	Jason Kendall SP2500	20.00	9.00
☐ 99	Brian Keyser	4.00	1.80
☐ 100	Mike Kingery	4.00	1.80
☐ 101	Wayne Kirby	4.00	1.80
☐ 102	Ryan Klesko SP1000	50.00	22.00
☐ 103	Chuck Knoblauch SP1000	60.00	27.00
☐ 104	Chad Kreuter	4.00	1.80
☐ 105	Tom Lampkin	4.00	1.80
☐ 106	Scott Leius	4.00	1.80
☐ 107	Jon Lieber	4.00	1.80
☐ 108	Nelson Liriano	4.00	1.80
☐ 109	Scott Livingstone	4.00	1.80
☐ 110	Graeme Lloyd	4.00	1.80
☐ 111	Kenny Lofton SP1000	80.00	36.00
☐ 112	Luis Lopez	4.00	1.80
☐ 113	Torey Lovullo	4.00	1.80
☐ 114	Greg Maddux SP500	400.00	180.00
☐ 115	Mike Maddux	4.00	1.80
☐ 116	Dave Magadan	4.00	1.80
☐ 117	Mike Magnante	4.00	1.80
☐ 118	Joe Magrane	4.00	1.80
☐ 119	Pat Mahomes	4.00	1.80
☐ 120	Matt Mantei	4.00	1.80
☐ 121	John Marzano	4.00	1.80
☐ 122	Terry Mathews	4.00	1.80
☐ 123	Chuck McElroy	4.00	1.80
☐ 124	Fred McGriff SP1000	40.00	18.00
☐ 125	Mark McLemore	4.00	1.80
☐ 126	Greg McMichael	4.00	1.80
☐ 127	Blas Minor	4.00	1.80
☐ 128	Dave Mlicki	4.00	1.80
☐ 129	Mike Mohler	4.00	1.80
☐ 130	Paul Molitor SP1000	80.00	36.00
☐ 131	Steve Montgomery	4.00	1.80
☐ 132	Mike Mordecai	4.00	1.80
☐ 133	Mike Morgan	4.00	1.80
☐ 134	Mike Munoz	4.00	1.80
☐ 135	Greg Myers	4.00	1.80
☐ 136	Jimmy Myers	4.00	1.80
☐ 137	Mike Myers	4.00	1.80
☐ 138	Bob Natal	4.00	1.80
☐ 139	Dan Naulty	4.00	1.80
☐ 140	Jeff Nelson	4.00	1.80
☐ 141	Warren Newson	4.00	1.80
☐ 142	Chris Nichting	4.00	1.80
☐ 143	Melvin Nieves	4.00	1.80
☐ 144	Charlie O'Brien	4.00	1.80
☐ 145	Alex Ochoa	4.00	1.80
☐ 146	Omar Olivares	4.00	1.80
☐ 147	Joe Oliver	4.00	1.80
☐ 148	Lance Painter	4.00	1.80
☐ 149	Rafael Palmeiro SP2000	25.00	11.00
☐ 150	Mark Parent	4.00	1.80
☐ 151	Steve Parris SP1800	20.00	9.00
☐ 152	Bob Patterson	4.00	1.80
☐ 153	Tony Pena	4.00	1.80
☐ 154	Eddie Perez	4.00	1.80
☐ 155	Yorkis Perez	4.00	1.80
☐ 156	Robert Person	4.00	1.80
☐ 157	Mark Petkovsek	4.00	1.80
☐ 158	Andy Pettitte SP1000	60.00	27.00
☐ 159	J.R. Phillips	4.00	1.80
☐ 160	Hipolito Pichardo	4.00	1.80
☐ 161	Eric Plunk	4.00	1.80
☐ 162	Jimmy Poole	4.00	1.80
☐ 163	Kirby Puckett SP1000	150.00	70.00
☐ 164	Paul Quantrill	4.00	1.80
☐ 165	Tom Quinlan	4.00	1.80
☐ 166	Jeff Reboulet	4.00	1.80
☐ 167	Jeff Reed	4.00	1.80
☐ 168	Steve Reed	4.00	1.80
☐ 169	Carlos Reyes	4.00	1.80
☐ 170	Bill Risley	4.00	1.80
☐ 171	Kevin Ritz	4.00	1.80
☐ 172	Kevin Roberson	4.00	1.80
☐ 173	Rich Robertson	4.00	1.80
☐ 174	Alex Rodriguez SP500	300.00	135.00
☐ 175	Ivan Rodriguez SP1250	80.00	36.00
☐ 176	Bruce Ruffin	4.00	1.80
☐ 177	Juan Samuel	4.00	1.80
☐ 178	Tim Scott	4.00	1.80
☐ 179	Kevin Sefcik	4.00	1.80
☐ 180	Jeff Shaw	4.00	1.80
☐ 181	Danny Sheaffer	4.00	1.80
☐ 182	Craig Shipley	4.00	1.80
☐ 183	Dave Silvestri	4.00	1.80
☐ 184	Aaron Small	4.00	1.80
☐ 185	John Smoltz SP1000	40.00	18.00
☐ 186	Luis Sojo	4.00	1.80
☐ 187	Sammy Sosa SP1000	60.00	27.00
☐ 188	Steve Sparks	4.00	1.80
☐ 189	Tim Spehr	4.00	1.80
☐ 190	Russ Springer	4.00	1.80
☐ 191	Matt Stairs	4.00	1.80
☐ 192	Andy Stankiewicz	4.00	1.80
☐ 193	Mike Stanton	4.00	1.80
☐ 194	Kelly Stinnett	4.00	1.80
☐ 195	Doug Strange	4.00	1.80
☐ 196	Mark Sweeney	4.00	1.80
☐ 197	Jeff Tabaka	4.00	1.80
☐ 198	Jesus Tavarez	4.00	1.80
☐ 199	Frank Thomas SP1000	200.00	90.00
☐ 200	Larry Thomas	4.00	1.80
☐ 201	Mark Thompson	4.00	1.80
☐ 202	Mike Timlin	4.00	1.80
☐ 203	Steve Trachsel	4.00	1.80
☐ 204	Tom Urbani	4.00	1.80
☐ 205	Julio Valera	4.00	1.80
☐ 206	Dave Valle	4.00	1.80
☐ 207	William VanLandingham	4.00	1.80
☐ 208	Mo Vaughn SP1000	80.00	36.00
☐ 209	Dave Veres	4.00	1.80
☐ 210	Ed Vosberg	4.00	1.80
☐ 211	Don Wengert	4.00	1.80
☐ 212	Matt Whiteside	4.00	1.80
☐ 213	Bob Wickman	4.00	1.80
☐ 214	Matt Williams SP1250	50.00	22.00
☐ 215	Mike Williams	4.00	1.80
☐ 216	Woody Williams	4.00	1.80
☐ 217	Craig Worthington	4.00	1.80
☐ NNO	F.Thomas Jumbo AU	80.00	36.00

1996 Leaf Signature Extended Autographs Century Marks

Randomly inserted exclusively into Extended Series packs, cards from this 31-card parallel set feature a selection of star and rising young prospect players taken from the more comprehensive 217-card Extended Autograph set. The cards differ by a special blue holographic foil treatment. Only 100 of each card exists. In addition, Juan Gonzalez, Derek Jeter, Andrew Jones, Rafael Palmeiro and Alex Rodriguez did not sign the cards distributed in packs. All of these players cards had information on the back on how to mail them into Leaf/Donruss to receive a signed version.

	MINT	NRMT
COMPLETE SET (31)	6000.00	2700.00
COMMON CARD (1-31)	50.00	22.00
RANDOM INSERTS IN PACKS		
STATED PRINT RUN 100 SETS		

☐ 1 Jay Buhner	100.00	45.00
☐ 2 Ken Caminiti	100.00	45.00

☐ 3 Roger Clemens	400.00	180.00
☐ 4 Jermaine Dye	50.00	22.00
☐ 5 Darin Erstad	200.00	90.00
☐ 6 Karim Garcia	100.00	45.00
☐ 7 Jason Giambi	80.00	36.00
☐ 8 Tom Glavine	80.00	36.00
☐ 9 Juan Gonzalez	400.00	180.00
☐ 10 Tony Gwynn	400.00	180.00
☐ 11 Derek Jeter	325.00	145.00
☐ 12 Randy Johnson	200.00	90.00
☐ 13 Andruw Jones	300.00	135.00
☐ 14 Jason Kendall	80.00	36.00
☐ 15 Ryan Klesko	100.00	45.00
☐ 16 Chuck Knoblauch	125.00	55.00
☐ 17 Kenny Lofton	200.00	90.00
☐ 18 Greg Maddux	600.00	275.00
☐ 19 Fred McGriff	100.00	45.00
☐ 20 Paul Molitor	150.00	70.00
☐ 21 Alex Ochoa	50.00	22.00
☐ 22 Rafael Palmeiro	100.00	45.00
☐ 23 Andy Pettitte	150.00	70.00
☐ 24 Kirby Puckett	400.00	180.00
☐ 25 Alex Rodriguez	500.00	220.00
☐ 26 Ivan Rodriguez	200.00	90.00
☐ 27 John Smoltz	80.00	36.00
☐ 28 Sammy Sosa	125.00	55.00
☐ 29 Frank Thomas	500.00	220.00
☐ 30 Mo Vaughn	200.00	90.00
☐ 31 Matt Williams	100.00	45.00

1996 Metal Universe

The Fleer Metal Universe set was issued in one series totalling 250 standard-size cards. The cards were issued in foil-wrapped packs. The theme for the set was based on inter-mingling fantasy comic book elements with baseball, thus each card features a player set against a wide variety of bizarre backgrounds. The cards are grouped alphabetically within teams below.

	MINT	NRMT
COMPLETE SET (250)	40.00	18.00
COMMON CARD (1-250)	.15	.07
MINOR STARS	.30	.14
UNLISTED STARS	.60	.25
COMP.PLAT.SET (250)	150.00	70.00
COMMON PLATINUM (1-250)	.25	.11
*PLAT.STARS: 2X TO 4X HI COLUMN		
*PLAT.YOUNG STARS: 1.5X TO 3X HI		
ONE PLATINUM PER PACK		

☐ 1 Roberto Alomar	.60	.25
☐ 2 Brady Anderson	.40	.18
☐ 3 Bobby Bonilla	.30	.14
☐ 4 Chris Hoiles	.15	.07
☐ 5 Ben McDonald	.15	.07
☐ 6 Mike Mussina	.60	.25
☐ 7 Randy Myers	.15	.07
☐ 8 Rafael Palmeiro	.40	.18
☐ 9 Cal Ripken	2.50	1.10
☐ 10 B.J. Surhoff	.15	.07
☐ 11 Luis Alicea	.15	.07
☐ 12 Jose Canseco	.40	.18
☐ 13 Roger Clemens	1.25	.55
☐ 14 Wil Cordero	.15	.07
☐ 15 Tom Gordon	.15	.07
☐ 16 Mike Greenwell	.15	.07
☐ 17 Tim Naehring	.15	.07
☐ 18 Troy O'Leary	.15	.07
☐ 19 Mike Stanley	.15	.07
☐ 20 John Valentin	.15	.07
☐ 21 Mo Vaughn	.75	.35
☐ 22 Tim Wakefield	.15	.07
☐ 23 Garret Anderson	.30	.14
☐ 24 Chili Davis	.30	.14
☐ 25 Gary DiSarcina	.15	.07
☐ 26 Jim Edmonds	.40	.18
☐ 27 Chuck Finley	.15	.07
☐ 28 Todd Greene	.40	.18
☐ 29 Mark Langston	.15	.07
☐ 30 Troy Percival	.15	.07
☐ 31 Tony Phillips	.15	.07
☐ 32 Tim Salmon	.60	.25
☐ 33 Lee Smith	.30	.14
☐ 34 J.T. Snow	.30	.14
☐ 35 Ray Durham	.15	.07
☐ 36 Alex Fernandez	.15	.07
☐ 37 Ozzie Guillen	.15	.07
☐ 38 Roberto Hernandez	.15	.07
☐ 39 Lyle Mouton	.15	.07
☐ 40 Frank Thomas	2.50	1.10
☐ 41 Robin Ventura	.30	.14
☐ 42 Sandy Alomar Jr.	.30	.14
☐ 43 Carlos Baerga	.15	.07
☐ 44 Albert Belle	.75	.35
☐ 45 Orel Hershiser	.30	.14
☐ 46 Kenny Lofton	.75	.35
☐ 47 Dennis Martinez	.30	.14
☐ 48 Jack McDowell	.15	.07
☐ 49 Jose Mesa	.15	.07
☐ 50 Eddie Murray	.60	.25
☐ 51 Charles Nagy	.30	.14
☐ 52 Manny Ramirez	.60	.25
☐ 53 Julian Tavarez	.15	.07
☐ 54 Jim Thome	.60	.25
☐ 55 Omar Vizquel	.30	.14
☐ 56 Chad Curtis	.15	.07
☐ 57 Cecil Fielder	.30	.14
☐ 58 John Flaherty	.15	.07
☐ 59 Travis Fryman	.30	.14
☐ 60 Chris Gomez	.15	.07
☐ 61 Felipe Lira	.15	.07
☐ 62 Kevin Appier	.30	.14
☐ 63 Johnny Damon	.30	.14
☐ 64 Tom Goodwin	.15	.07
☐ 65 Mark Gubicza	.15	.07
☐ 66 Jeff Montgomery	.15	.07
☐ 67 Jon Nunnally	.15	.07
☐ 68 Ricky Bones	.15	.07
☐ 69 Jeff Cirillo	.30	.14
☐ 70 John Jaha	.15	.07
☐ 71 Dave Nilsson	.15	.07
☐ 72 Joe Oliver	.15	.07
☐ 73 Kevin Seitzer	.15	.07
☐ 74 Greg Vaughn	.15	.07
☐ 75 Marty Cordova	.30	.14
☐ 76 Chuck Knoblauch	.60	.25
☐ 77 Pat Meares	.15	.07
☐ 78 Paul Molitor	.60	.25
☐ 79 Pedro Munoz	.15	.07
☐ 80 Kirby Puckett	1.25	.55
☐ 81 Brad Radke	.30	.14
☐ 82 Scott Stahoviak	.15	.07
☐ 83 Matt Walbeck	.15	.07
☐ 84 Wade Boggs	.60	.25
☐ 85 David Cone	.30	.14
☐ 86 Joe Girardi	.15	.07
☐ 87 Derek Jeter	2.00	.90
☐ 88 Jim Leyritz	.15	.07
☐ 89 Tino Martinez	.60	.25
☐ 90 Don Mattingly	1.00	.45
☐ 91 Paul O'Neill	.30	.14
☐ 92 Andy Pettitte	.75	.35
☐ 93 Tim Raines	.30	.14
☐ 94 Kenny Rogers	.15	.07
☐ 95 Ruben Sierra	.15	.07
☐ 96 John Wetteland	.15	.07
☐ 97 Bernie Williams	.60	.25
☐ 98 Geronimo Berroa	.15	.07
☐ 99 Dennis Eckersley	.30	.14
☐ 100 Brent Gates	.15	.07
☐ 101 Mark McGwire	1.25	.55
☐ 102 Steve Ontiveros	.15	.07
☐ 103 Terry Steinbach	.15	.07
☐ 104 Jay Buhner	.40	.18
☐ 105 Vince Coleman	.15	.07
☐ 106 Joey Cora	.30	.14
☐ 107 Ken Griffey, Jr.	3.00	1.35
☐ 108 Randy Johnson	.60	.25
☐ 109 Edgar Martinez	.40	.18
☐ 110 Alex Rodriguez	2.00	.90
☐ 111 Paul Sorrento	.15	.07
☐ 112 Will Clark	.40	.18
☐ 113 Juan Gonzalez	1.50	.70
☐ 114 Rusty Greer	.30	.14
☐ 115 Dean Palmer	.15	.07
☐ 116 Ivan Rodriguez	.75	.35
☐ 117 Mickey Tettleton	.15	.07
☐ 118 Joe Carter	.30	.14
☐ 119 Alex Gonzalez	.15	.07
☐ 120 Shawn Green	.15	.07
☐ 121 Erik Hanson	.15	.07
☐ 122 Pat Hentgen	.30	.14
☐ 123 Sandy Martinez	.15	.07
☐ 124 Otis Nixon	.15	.07
☐ 125 John Olerud	.30	.14
☐ 126 Steve Avery	.15	.07
☐ 127 Tom Glavine	.30	.14
☐ 128 Marquis Grissom	.30	.14
☐ 129 Chipper Jones	2.00	.90
☐ 130 David Justice	.60	.25
☐ 131 Ryan Klesko	.40	.18
☐ 132 Mark Lemke	.15	.07
☐ 133 Javier Lopez	.30	.14
☐ 134 Greg Maddux	2.00	.90
☐ 135 Fred McGriff	.40	.18
☐ 136 John Smoltz	.30	.14
☐ 137 Mark Wohlers	.15	.07
☐ 138 Frank Castillo	.15	.07
☐ 139 Shawon Dunston	.15	.07
☐ 140 Luis Gonzalez	.15	.07
☐ 141 Mark Grace	.40	.18
☐ 142 Briar. ..lcRae	.15	.07
☐ 143 Jaime Navarro	.15	.07
☐ 144 Rey Sanchez	.15	.07
☐ 145 Ryne Sandberg	.75	.35
☐ 146 Sammy Sosa	.60	.25
☐ 147 Bret Boone	.15	.07
☐ 148 Curtis Goodwin	.15	.07
☐ 149 Barry Larkin	.40	.18
☐ 150 Hal Morris	.15	.07
☐ 151 Reggie Sanders	.15	.07
☐ 152 Pete Schourek	.15	.07
☐ 153 John Smiley	.15	.07
☐ 154 Dante Bichette	.30	.14
☐ 155 Vinny Castilla	.30	.14
☐ 156 Andres Galarraga	.60	.25
☐ 157 Bret Saberhagen	.15	.07
☐ 158 Bill Swift	.15	.07
☐ 159 Larry Walker	.60	.25
☐ 160 Walt Weiss	.15	.07
☐ 161 Kurt Abbott	.15	.07
☐ 162 John Burkett	.15	.07
☐ 163 Greg Colbrunn	.15	.07
☐ 164 Jeff Conine	.30	.14
☐ 165 Chris Hammond	.15	.07
☐ 166 Charles Johnson	.30	.14
☐ 167 Al Leiter	.15	.07
☐ 168 Pat Rapp	.15	.07
☐ 169 Gary Sheffield	.60	.25
☐ 170 Quivio Veras	.15	.07
☐ 171 Devon White	.15	.07
☐ 172 Jeff Bagwell	1.25	.55
☐ 173 Derek Bell	.15	.07
☐ 174 Sean Berry	.15	.07
☐ 175 Craig Biggio	.40	.18
☐ 176 Doug Drabek	.15	.07
☐ 177 Tony Eusebio	.15	.07
☐ 178 Brian L.Hunter	.30	.14
☐ 179 Orlando Miller	.15	.07
☐ 180 Shane Reynolds	.15	.07

□ 181 Mike Blowers	.15	.07
□ 182 Roger Cedeno	.15	.07
□ 183 Eric Karros	.30	.14
□ 184 Ramon Martinez	.30	.14
□ 185 Raul Mondesi	.40	.18
□ 186 Hideo Nomo	1.50	.70
□ 187 Mike Piazza	2.00	.90
□ 188 Moises Alou	.30	.14
□ 189 Yamil Benitez	.30	.14
□ 190 Darrin Fletcher	.15	.07
□ 191 Cliff Floyd	.15	.07
□ 192 Pedro Martinez	.60	.25
□ 193 Carlos Perez	.15	.07
□ 194 David Segui	.15	.07
□ 195 Tony Tarasco	.15	.07
□ 196 Rondell White	.30	.14
□ 197 Edgardo Alfonzo	.40	.18
□ 198 Rico Brogna	.15	.07
□ 199 Carl Everett	.15	.07
□ 200 Todd Hundley	.30	.14
□ 201 Jason Isringhausen	.15	.07
□ 202 Lance Johnson	.15	.07
□ 203 Bobby Jones	.15	.07
□ 204 Jeff Kent	.15	.07
□ 205 Bill Pulsipher	.15	.07
□ 206 Jose Vizcaino	.15	.07
□ 207 Ricky Bottalico	.15	.07
□ 208 Darren Daulton	.30	.14
□ 209 Lenny Dykstra	.30	.14
□ 210 Jim Eisenreich	.15	.07
□ 211 Gregg Jefferies	.15	.07
□ 212 Mickey Morandini	.15	.07
□ 213 Heathcliff Slocumb	.15	.07
□ 214 Jay Bell	.30	.14
□ 215 Carlos Garcia	.15	.07
□ 216 Jeff King	.15	.07
□ 217 Al Martin	.15	.07
□ 218 Orlando Merced	.15	.07
□ 219 Dan Miceli	.15	.07
□ 220 Denny Neagle	.30	.14
□ 221 Andy Benes	.30	.14
□ 222 Royce Clayton	.15	.07
□ 223 Gary Gaetti	.15	.07
□ 224 Ron Gant	.30	.14
□ 225 Bernard Gilkey	.15	.07
□ 226 Brian Jordan	.30	.14
□ 227 Ray Lankford	.30	.14
□ 228 John Mabry	.15	.07
□ 229 Ozzie Smith	.75	.35
□ 230 Todd Stottlemyre	.15	.07
□ 231 Andy Ashby	.15	.07
□ 232 Brad Ausmus	.15	.07
□ 233 Ken Caminiti	.40	.18
□ 234 Steve Finley	.30	.14
□ 235 Tony Gwynn	1.50	.70
□ 236 Joey Hamilton	.15	.07
□ 237 Rickey Henderson	.40	.18
□ 238 Trevor Hoffman	.15	.07
□ 239 Wally Joyner	.30	.14
□ 240 Rod Beck	.15	.07
□ 241 Barry Bonds	.75	.35
□ 242 Glenallen Hill	.15	.07
□ 243 Stan Javier	.15	.07
□ 244 Mark Leiter	.15	.07
□ 245 Deion Sanders	.30	.14
□ 246 William Van Landingham	.15	.07
□ 247 Matt Williams	.40	.18
□ 248 Checklist	.15	.07
□ 249 Checklist	.15	.07
□ 250 Checklist	.15	.07

1996 Metal Universe Heavy Metal

Randomly inserted in packs at a rate of one in 8 this 10-card set features the Power Hitters of Baseball. The fronts feature a color action player cut-out over a silver foil background. The

backs carry a player portrait and information about the player.

	MINT	NRMT
COMPLETE SET (10)	25.00	11.00
COMMON CARD (1-10)	2.00	.90
STATED ODDS 1:8		

		MINT	NRMT
□ 1 Albert Belle		2.50	1.10
□ 2 Barry Bonds		2.50	1.10
□ 3 Juan Gonzalez		5.00	2.20
□ 4 Ken Griffey Jr.		10.00	4.50
□ 5 Mark McGwire		4.00	1.80
□ 6 Mike Piazza		6.00	2.70
□ 7 Sammy Sosa		2.50	1.10
□ 8 Frank Thomas		8.00	3.60
□ 9 Mo Vaughn		2.50	1.10
□ 10 Matt Williams		2.00	.90

1996 Metal Universe Mining For Gold

Randomly inserted in retail packs only at a rate of one in 12, this 12-card set highlights major prospects and rookies.

	MINT	NRMT
COMPLETE SET (12)	60.00	27.00
COMMON CARD (1-12)	1.50	.70
MINOR STARS	2.50	1.10
SEMISTARS	4.00	1.80
STATED ODDS 1:12 RETAIL		

		MINT	NRMT
□ 1 Yamil Benitez		2.50	1.10
□ 2 Marty Cordova		2.50	1.10
□ 3 Shawn Green		1.50	.70
□ 4 Todd Greene		4.00	1.80
□ 5 Brian Hunter		2.50	1.10
□ 6 Derek Jeter		15.00	6.75
□ 7 Charles Johnson		2.50	1.10
□ 8 Chipper Jones		20.00	9.00
□ 9 Hideo Nomo		15.00	6.75
□ 10 Alex Ochoa		1.50	.70
□ 11 Andy Pettitte		8.00	3.60
□ 12 Quivio Veras		1.50	.70

1996 Metal Universe Mother Lode

Randomly inserted in hobby packs only at a rate of one in 12, this 12-card set features multi-tool players. The fronts carry a color action player cut-out over a silver-foil, scroll-design background. The backs

display another player photo and information about the player.

	MINT	NRMT
COMPLETE SET (12)	60.00	27.00
COMMON CARD (1-12)	2.00	.90
STATED ODDS 1:12 HOBBY		

		MINT	NRMT
□ 1 Barry Bonds		4.00	1.80
□ 2 Jim Edmonds		2.00	.90
□ 3 Ken Griffey Jr.		15.00	6.75
□ 4 Kenny Lofton		4.00	1.80
□ 5 Raul Mondesi		2.00	.90
□ 6 Rafael Palmeiro		2.00	.90
□ 7 Manny Ramirez		3.00	1.35
□ 8 Cal Ripken		12.00	5.50
□ 9 Tim Salmon		3.00	1.35
□ 10 Ryne Sandberg		4.00	1.80
□ 11 Frank Thomas		12.00	5.50
□ 12 Matt Williams		2.00	.90

1996 Metal Universe Platinum Portraits

Randomly inserted in packs at a rate of one in four, this 10-card set features ten of the hottest young stars. The fronts display a player portrait on a platinum foil background. The backs carry a color action player photo and why the player is hot.

	MINT	NRMT
COMPLETE SET (10)	12.00	5.50
COMMON CARD (1-12)	.50	.23
STATED ODDS 1:4		

		MINT	NRMT
□ 1 Garret Anderson		.75	.35
□ 2 Marty Cordova		.75	.35
□ 3 Jim Edmonds		1.00	.45
□ 4 Jason Isringhausen		.50	.23
□ 5 Chipper Jones		5.00	2.20
□ 6 Ryan Klesko		1.00	.45
□ 7 Hideo Nomo		4.00	1.80
□ 8 Carlos Perez		.50	.23

	Player	MINT	NRMT
☐ 9	Manny Ramirez	1.50	.70
☐ 10	Rondell White	.75	.35

1996 Metal Universe Titanium

Randomly inserted in packs at a rate of one in 24, this 10-card set features ten of the fans' favorite players. The fronts feature an action color player cut-out on a foil baseball background. The backs display a player portrait and why the player is liked by the fans.

		MINT	NRMT
COMPLETE SET (10)		125.00	55.00
COMMON CARD (1-10)		3.00	1.35
STATED ODDS 1:24			

	Player	MINT	NRMT
☐ 1	Albert Belle	6.00	2.70
☐ 2	Barry Bonds	6.00	2.70
☐ 3	Ken Griffey Jr.	25.00	11.00
☐ 4	Tony Gwynn	12.00	5.50
☐ 5	Greg Maddux	15.00	6.75
☐ 6	Mike Piazza	15.00	6.75
☐ 7	Cal Ripken	20.00	9.00
☐ 8	Frank Thomas	20.00	9.00
☐ 9	Mo Vaughn	6.00	2.70
☐ 10	Matt Williams	3.00	1.35

1997 Metal Universe

The 1997 Metal Universe set was issued in one series totalling 250 cards and distributed in eight-card foil packs with a suggested retail price of $2.49. Printed in 100% etched foil with UV-coating, the fronts features color photos of star players on full-bleed backgrounds of comic book art with the player's name, team, position and card logo printed near the bottom of the card. The backs carry another player photo and statistics.

		MINT	NRMT
COMPLETE SET (250)		40.00	18.00
COMMON CARD (1-250)		.15	.07
MINOR STARS		.30	.14
UNLISTED STARS		.60	.25

	Player	MINT	NRMT
☐ 1	Roberto Alomar	.60	.25
☐ 2	Brady Anderson	.40	.18
☐ 3	Rocky Coppinger	.15	.07
☐ 4	Chris Hoiles	.15	.07
☐ 5	Eddie Murray	.60	.25
☐ 6	Mike Mussina	.40	.18
☐ 7	Rafael Palmeiro	.40	.18
☐ 8	Cal Ripken	2.50	1.10
☐ 9	B.J. Surhoff	.15	.07
☐ 10	Brant Brown	.15	.07
☐ 11	Mark Grace	.40	.18
☐ 12	Brian McRae	.15	.07
☐ 13	Jaime Navarro	.15	.07
☐ 14	Ryne Sandberg	.75	.35
☐ 15	Sammy Sosa	.60	.25
☐ 16	Amaury Telemaco	.15	.07
☐ 17	Steve Trachsel	.15	.07
☐ 18	Darren Bragg	.15	.07
☐ 19	Jose Canseco	.40	.18
☐ 20	Roger Clemens	1.25	.55
☐ 21	Nomar Garciaparra	2.00	.90
☐ 22	Tom Gordon	.15	.07
☐ 23	Tim Naehring	.15	.07
☐ 24	Mike Stanley	.15	.07
☐ 25	John Valentin	.15	.07
☐ 26	Mo Vaughn	.75	.35
☐ 27	Jermaine Dye	.15	.07
☐ 28	Tom Glavine	.30	.14
☐ 29	Marquis Grissom	.15	.07
☐ 30	Andruw Jones	1.50	.70
☐ 31	Chipper Jones	2.00	.90
☐ 32	Ryan Klesko	.40	.18
☐ 33	Greg Maddux	2.00	.90
☐ 34	Fred McGriff	.40	.18
☐ 35	John Smoltz	.30	.14
☐ 36	Garret Anderson	.30	.14
☐ 37	George Arias	.15	.07
☐ 38	Gary DiSarcina	.15	.07
☐ 39	Jim Edmonds	.40	.18
☐ 40	Darin Erstad	1.00	.45
☐ 41	Chuck Finley	.15	.07
☐ 42	Troy Percival	.15	.07
☐ 43	Tim Salmon	.60	.25
☐ 44	Bret Boone	.15	.07
☐ 45	Jeff Brantley	.15	.07
☐ 46	Eric Davis	.30	.14
☐ 47	Barry Larkin	.40	.18
☐ 48	Hal Morris	.15	.07
☐ 49	Mark Portugal	.15	.07
☐ 50	Reggie Sanders	.15	.07
☐ 51	John Smiley	.15	.07
☐ 52	Wilson Alvarez	.15	.07
☐ 53	Harold Baines	.30	.14
☐ 54	James Baldwin	.15	.07
☐ 55	Albert Belle	1.00	.45
☐ 56	Mike Cameron	.40	.18
☐ 57	Ray Durham	.15	.07
☐ 58	Alex Fernandez	.30	.14
☐ 59	Roberto Hernandez	.15	.07
☐ 60	Tony Phillips	.15	.07
☐ 61	Frank Thomas	2.50	1.10
☐ 62	Robin Ventura	.30	.14
☐ 63	Jeff Cirillo	.30	.14
☐ 64	Jeff D'Amico	.15	.07
☐ 65	John Jaha	.15	.07
☐ 66	Scott Karl	.15	.07
☐ 67	Ben McDonald	.15	.07
☐ 68	Marc Newfield	.15	.07
☐ 69	Dave Nilsson	.15	.07
☐ 70	Jose Valentin	.15	.07
☐ 71	Dante Bichette	.30	.14
☐ 72	Ellis Burks	.30	.14
☐ 73	Vinny Castilla	.30	.14
☐ 74	Andres Galarraga	.60	.25
☐ 75	Kevin Ritz	.15	.07
☐ 76	Larry Walker	.60	.25
☐ 77	Walt Weiss	.15	.07
☐ 78	Jamey Wright	.15	.07
☐ 79	Eric Young	.15	.07
☐ 80	Julio Franco	.30	.14
☐ 81	Orel Hershiser	.30	.14
☐ 82	Kenny Lofton	.75	.35
☐ 83	Jack McDowell	.15	.07
☐ 84	Jose Mesa	.15	.07
☐ 85	Charles Nagy	.30	.14
☐ 86	Manny Ramirez	.60	.25
☐ 87	Jim Thome	.60	.25
☐ 88	Omar Vizquel	.30	.14
☐ 89	Matt Williams	.40	.18
☐ 90	Kevin Appier	.15	.07
☐ 91	Johnny Damon	.15	.07
☐ 92	Chili Davis	.30	.14
☐ 93	Tom Goodwin	.15	.07
☐ 94	Keith Lockhart	.15	.07
☐ 95	Jeff Montgomery	.15	.07
☐ 96	Craig Paquette	.15	.07
☐ 97	Jose Rosado	.30	.14
☐ 98	Michael Tucker	.30	.14
☐ 99	Wilton Guerrero	.15	.07
☐ 100	Todd Hollandsworth	.15	.07
☐ 101	Eric Karros	.30	.14
☐ 102	Ramon Martinez	.30	.14
☐ 103	Raul Mondesi	.40	.18
☐ 104	Hideo Nomo	1.25	.55
☐ 105	Mike Piazza	2.00	.90
☐ 106	Ismael Valdes	.30	.14
☐ 107	Todd Worrell	.15	.07
☐ 108	Tony Clark	.60	.25
☐ 109	Travis Fryman	.30	.14
☐ 110	Bob Higginson	.30	.14
☐ 111	Mark Lewis	.15	.07
☐ 112	Melvin Nieves	.15	.07
☐ 113	Justin Thompson	.30	.14
☐ 114	Wade Boggs	.60	.25
☐ 115	David Cone	.30	.14
☐ 116	Cecil Fielder	.30	.14
☐ 117	Dwight Gooden	.30	.14
☐ 118	Derek Jeter	2.00	.90
☐ 119	Tino Martinez	.60	.25
☐ 120	Paul O'Neill	.30	.14
☐ 121	Andy Pettitte	.60	.25
☐ 122	Mariano Rivera	.30	.14
☐ 123	Darryl Strawberry	.30	.14
☐ 124	John Wetteland	.15	.07
☐ 125	Bernie Williams	.60	.25
☐ 126	Tony Batista	.15	.07
☐ 127	Geronimo Berroa	.15	.07
☐ 128	Scott Brosius	.15	.07
☐ 129	Jason Giambi	.30	.14
☐ 130	Jose Herrera	.15	.07
☐ 131	Mark McGwire	1.25	.55
☐ 132	John Wasdin	.15	.07
☐ 133	Bob Abreu	.30	.14
☐ 134	Jeff Bagwell	1.25	.55
☐ 135	Derek Bell	.15	.07
☐ 136	Craig Biggio	.40	.18
☐ 137	Brian Hunter	.30	.14
☐ 138	Darryl Kile	.30	.14
☐ 139	Orlando Miller	.15	.07
☐ 140	Shane Reynolds	.15	.07
☐ 141	Billy Wagner	.30	.14
☐ 142	Donne Wall	.15	.07
☐ 143	Jay Buhner	.40	.18
☐ 144	Jeff Fassero	.15	.07
☐ 145	Ken Griffey Jr.	3.00	1.35
☐ 146	Sterling Hitchcock	.15	.07
☐ 147	Randy Johnson	.60	.25
☐ 148	Edgar Martinez	.40	.18
☐ 149	Alex Rodriguez	2.00	.90
☐ 150	Paul Sorrento	.15	.07
☐ 151	Dan Wilson	.15	.07
☐ 152	Moises Alou	.30	.14
☐ 153	Darrin Fletcher	.15	.07
☐ 154	Cliff Floyd	.15	.07
☐ 155	Mark Grudzielanek	.15	.07
☐ 156	Vladimir Guerrero	1.25	.55
☐ 157	Mike Lansing	.15	.07
☐ 158	Pedro Martinez	.60	.25
☐ 159	Henry Rodriguez	.15	.07
☐ 160	Rondell White	.30	.14
☐ 161	Will Clark	.40	.18
☐ 162	Juan Gonzalez	1.50	.70

☐ 163 Rusty Greer	.30	.14
☐ 164 Ken Hill	.15	.07
☐ 165 Mark McLemore	.15	.07
☐ 166 Dean Palmer	.15	.07
☐ 167 Roger Pavlik	.15	.07
☐ 168 Ivan Rodriguez	.75	.35
☐ 169 Mickey Tettleton	.15	.07
☐ 170 Bobby Bonilla	.30	.14
☐ 171 Kevin Brown	.30	.14
☐ 172 Greg Colbrunn	.15	.07
☐ 173 Jeff Conine	.30	.14
☐ 174 Jim Eisenreich	.15	.07
☐ 175 Charles Johnson	.30	.14
☐ 176 Al Leiter	.15	.07
☐ 177 Robb Nen	.15	.07
☐ 178 Edgar Renteria	.30	.14
☐ 179 Gary Sheffield	.60	.25
☐ 180 Devon White	.15	.07
☐ 181 Joe Carter	.30	.14
☐ 182 Carlos Delgado	.15	.07
☐ 183 Alex Gonzalez	.15	.07
☐ 184 Shawn Green	.15	.07
☐ 185 Juan Guzman	.15	.07
☐ 186 Pat Hentgen	.30	.14
☐ 187 Orlando Merced	.15	.07
☐ 188 John Olerud	.30	.14
☐ 189 Robert Perez	.15	.07
☐ 190 Ed Sprague	.15	.07
☐ 191 Mark Clark	.15	.07
☐ 192 John Franco	.30	.14
☐ 193 Bernard Gilkey	.15	.07
☐ 194 Todd Hundley	.30	.14
☐ 195 Lance Johnson	.15	.07
☐ 196 Bobby Jones	.15	.07
☐ 197 Alex Ochoa	.15	.07
☐ 198 Rey Ordonez	.15	.07
☐ 199 Paul Wilson	.15	.07
☐ 200 Ricky Bottalico	.15	.07
☐ 201 Gregg Jefferies	.15	.07
☐ 202 Wendell Magee	.15	.07
☐ 203 Mickey Morandini	.15	.07
☐ 204 Ricky Otero	.15	.07
☐ 205 Scott Rolen	1.50	.70
☐ 206 Benito Santiago	.15	.07
☐ 207 Curt Schilling	.30	.14
☐ 208 Rich Becker	.15	.07
☐ 209 Marty Cordova	.30	.14
☐ 210 Chuck Knoblauch	.60	.25
☐ 211 Pat Meares	.15	.07
☐ 212 Paul Molitor	.60	.25
☐ 213 Frank Rodriguez	.15	.07
☐ 214 Terry Steinbach	.15	.07
☐ 215 Todd Walker	.30	.14
☐ 216 Andy Ashby	.15	.07
☐ 217 Ken Caminiti	.40	.18
☐ 218 Steve Finley	.30	.14
☐ 219 Tony Gwynn	1.50	.70
☐ 220 Joey Hamilton	.30	.14
☐ 221 Rickey Henderson	.40	.18
☐ 222 Trevor Hoffman	.15	.07
☐ 223 Wally Joyner	.30	.14
☐ 224 Scott Sanders	.15	.07
☐ 225 Fernando Valenzuela	.30	.14
☐ 226 Greg Vaughn	.30	.14
☐ 227 Alan Benes	.30	.14
☐ 228 Andy Benes	.30	.14
☐ 229 Dennis Eckersley	.30	.14
☐ 230 Ron Gant	.30	.14
☐ 231 Brian Jordan	.30	.14
☐ 232 Ray Lankford	.30	.14
☐ 233 John Mabry	.15	.07
☐ 234 Tom Pagnozzi	.15	.07
☐ 235 Todd Stottlemyre	.15	.07
☐ 236 Jermaine Allensworth	.15	.07
☐ 237 Francisco Cordova	.15	.07
☐ 238 Jason Kendall	.30	.14
☐ 239 Jeff King	.15	.07
☐ 240 Al Martin	.15	.07
☐ 241 Rod Beck	.15	.07
☐ 242 Barry Bonds	.75	.35
☐ 243 Shawn Estes	.30	.14
☐ 244 Mark Gardner	.15	.07
☐ 245 Glenallen Hill	.15	.07
☐ 246 Bill Mueller	.15	.07
☐ 247 J.T. Snow	.30	.14
☐ 248 Checklist (1-107)	.15	.07

☐ 249 Checklist (108-207)	.15	.07
☐ 250 Checklist (208-250/Inserts)	.15	.07
☐ P149 Alex Rodriguez Promo	2.00	.90

1997 Metal Universe Blast Furnace

Randomly inserted in hobby packs only at a rate of one in 48, this 12-card set features color photos of some of base- ball's biggest sluggers.

	MINT	NRMT
COMPLETE SET (12)	200.00	90.00
COMMON CARD (1-12)	4.00	1.80
SEMISTARS	5.00	2.20
STATED ODDS 1:48 HOBBY		
☐ 1 Jeff Bagwell	15.00	6.75
☐ 2 Albert Belle	10.00	4.50
☐ 3 Barry Bonds	10.00	4.50
☐ 4 Andres Galarraga	6.00	2.70
☐ 5 Juan Gonzalez	20.00	9.00
☐ 6 Ken Griffey Jr.	40.00	18.00
☐ 7 Todd Hundley	4.00	1.80
☐ 8 Mark McGwire	15.00	6.75
☐ 9 Mike Piazza	25.00	11.00
☐ 10 Alex Rodriguez	25.00	11.00
☐ 11 Frank Thomas	30.00	13.50
☐ 12 Mo Vaughn	10.00	4.50

1997 Metal Universe Emerald Autographs

One of six different exchange cards were randomly inserted in hobby boxes as chiptoppers (sealed inside the box, but lay- ing on top of the packs) at a rate of one in 20 hobby boxes The exchange cards parallel the cor- responding basic cards except for emerald foil on front. In addi- tion, the area used for the card number on back of the regular issue card is replaced by a logo stating "certified emerald auto- graph." The exchange cards are unnumbered and have been assigned numbers based upon alphabetical order of each play- er's last name for cataloguing purposes. The deadline to exchange these cards was February 1, 1998.

	MINT	NRMT
COMPLETE SET (6)	300.00	135.00
COMMON CARD	12.00	5.50
ONE CARD VIA MAIL PER EXCH.CARD		

*EXCH.CARDS: .1X TO .2X HI COLUMN
EXCHANGE CARDS: 1:20 BOXES

		MINT	NRMT
☐ AU1 Darin Erstad		50.00	22.00
☐ AU2 Todd Hollandsworth		15.00	6.75
☐ AU3 Alex Ochoa		12.00	5.50
☐ AU4 Alex Rodriguez		150.00	70.00
☐ AU5 Scott Rolen		80.00	36.00
☐ AU6 Todd Walker		20.00	9.00

1997 Metal Universe Magnetic Field

Randomly inserted in packs at a rate of one in 12, this ten-card set honors "Gold Glovers" who appear to have a special attrac- tion to the ball. The fronts fea- ture color player photos on refractive foil backgrounds.

	MINT	NRMT
COMPLETE SET (10)	40.00	18.00
COMMON CARD (1-10)	1.00	.45
STATED ODDS 1:12		
☐ 1 Roberto Alomar	2.50	1.10
☐ 2 Jeff Bagwell	5.00	2.20
☐ 3 Barry Bonds	3.00	1.35
☐ 4 Ken Griffey Jr.	12.00	5.50
☐ 5 Derek Jeter	8.00	3.60
☐ 6 Kenny Lofton	3.00	1.35
☐ 7 Edgar Renteria	1.00	.45
☐ 8 Cal Ripken	10.00	4.50
☐ 9 Alex Rodriguez	8.00	3.60
☐ 10 Matt Williams	1.50	.70

1997 Metal Universe Mining for Gold

Randomly inserted in packs at a rate of one in nine, this 10-card set features some of baseball's brightest young stars on die-cut "ingot" cards with pearlized gold coating.

	MINT	NRMT
COMPLETE SET (10)	20.00	9.00
COMMON CARD (1-10)	.50	.23
STATED ODDS 1:8		
☐ 1 Bob Abreu	1.00	.45
☐ 2 Kevin L.Brown C	.50	.23
☐ 3 Nomar Garciaparra	6.00	2.70
☐ 4 Vladimir Guerrero	4.00	1.80
☐ 5 Wilton Guerrero	.50	.23
☐ 6 Andruw Jones	5.00	2.20
☐ 7 Curt Lyons	.50	.23
☐ 8 Neifi Perez	1.00	.45
☐ 9 Scott Rolen	5.00	2.20
☐ 10 Todd Walker	1.00	.45

1997 Metal Universe Mother Lode

Randomly inserted in packs at a rate of one in 288, this 12-card set features color player photos on die-cut cards in 100% etched foil.

	MINT	NRMT
COMPLETE SET (12)	800.00	350.00
COMMON CARD (1-12)	20.00	9.00
STATED ODDS 1:288		
☐ 1 Roberto Alomar	25.00	11.00
☐ 2 Jeff Bagwell	50.00	22.00
☐ 3 Barry Bonds	30.00	13.50
☐ 4 Ken Griffey Jr.	120.00	55.00
☐ 5 Andruw Jones	50.00	22.00
☐ 6 Chipper Jones	80.00	36.00
☐ 7 Kenny Lofton	30.00	13.50
☐ 8 Mike Piazza	80.00	36.00
☐ 9 Cal Ripken	100.00	45.00
☐ 10 Alex Rodriguez	80.00	36.00
☐ 11 Frank Thomas	100.00	45.00
☐ 12 Matt Williams	20.00	9.00

1997 Metal Universe Platinum Portraits

Randomly inserted in packs at a rate of one in 36, this 10-card set features color photos of some of Baseball's rising stars with backgrounds of platinum-colored etched foil.

	MINT	NRMT
COMPLETE SET (10)	80.00	36.00
COMMON CARD (1-10)	2.50	1.10

UNLISTED STARS	6.00	2.70
STATED ODDS 1:36		
☐ 1 James Baldwin	2.50	1.10
☐ 2 Jermaine Dye	2.50	1.10
☐ 3 Todd Hollandsworth	2.50	1.10
☐ 4 Derek Jeter	15.00	6.75
☐ 5 Chipper Jones	20.00	9.00
☐ 6 Jason Kendall	3.00	1.35
☐ 7 Rey Ordonez	2.50	1.10
☐ 8 Andy Pettitte	6.00	2.70
☐ 9 Edgar Renteria	3.00	1.35
☐ 10 Alex Rodriguez	20.00	9.00

1997 Metal Universe Titanium

Randomly inserted in packs at a rate of one in 24, this 10-card set honors some of baseball's favorite superstars. The fronts feature color player photos printed on die-cut embossed cards and sculpted on 100% etched foil.

	MINT	NRMT
COMPLETE SET (10)	100.00	45.00
COMMON CARD (1-10)	5.00	2.20
STATED ODDS 1:24 RETAIL		
☐ 1 Jeff Bagwell	8.00	3.60
☐ 2 Albert Belle	5.00	2.20
☐ 3 Ken Griffey Jr.	20.00	9.00
☐ 4 Chipper Jones	12.00	5.50
☐ 5 Greg Maddux	12.00	5.50
☐ 6 Mark McGwire	8.00	3.60
☐ 7 Mike Piazza	12.00	5.50
☐ 8 Cal Ripken	15.00	6.75
☐ 9 Alex Rodriguez	12.00	5.50
☐ 10 Frank Thomas	15.00	6.75

1997 New Pinnacle

The 1997 New Pinnacle set was issued in one series totalling 200 cards and distributed in 10-card packs with a suggested

retail price of $2.99. The fronts feature borderless color action player photos with gold printing. The backs carry another smaller player photo and biographical and statistical information.

	MINT	NRMT
COMPLETE SET (200)	25.00	11.00
COMMON CARD (1-200)	.15	.07
MINOR STARS	.30	.14
UNLISTED STARS	.60	.25
SUBSET CARDS HALF VALUE OF BASE CARDS		
COMP.MUSEUM SET (200)	600.00	275.00
COMMON MUSEUM (1-200)	1.50	.70
*MUSEUM STARS: 7.5X TO 15X HI COLUMN		
*MUSEUM YOUNG STARS: 6X TO 12 X HI		
MUSEUM STATED ODDS 1:9		
☐ 1 Ken Griffey Jr.	3.00	1.35
☐ 2 Sammy Sosa	.60	.25
☐ 3 Greg Maddux	2.00	.90
☐ 4 Matt Williams	.40	.18
☐ 5 Jason Isringhausen	.15	.07
☐ 6 Gregg Jefferies	.15	.07
☐ 7 Chili Davis	.30	.14
☐ 8 Paul O'Neill	.30	.14
☐ 9 Larry Walker	.60	.25
☐ 10 Ellis Burks	.30	.14
☐ 11 Cliff Floyd	.15	.07
☐ 12 Albert Belle	.75	.35
☐ 13 Javier Lopez	.30	.14
☐ 14 David Cone	.30	.14
☐ 15 Jose Canseco	.40	.18
☐ 16 Todd Zeile	.15	.07
☐ 17 Bernard Gilkey	.15	.07
☐ 18 Andres Galarraga	.60	.25
☐ 19 Chris Snopek	.15	.07
☐ 20 Tim Salmon	.60	.25
☐ 21 Roger Clemens	1.25	.55
☐ 22 Reggie Sanders	.15	.07
☐ 23 John Jaha	.15	.07
☐ 24 Andy Pettitte	.60	.25
☐ 25 Kenny Lofton	.75	.35
☐ 26 Robb Nen	.15	.07
☐ 27 John Wetteland	.15	.07
☐ 28 Bobby Bonilla	.30	.14
☐ 29 Hideo Nomo	1.50	.70
☐ 30 Cecil Fielder	.30	.14
☐ 31 Garret Anderson	.30	.14
☐ 32 Pat Hentgen	.30	.14
☐ 33 Dave Justice	.60	.25
☐ 34 Billy Wagner	.30	.14
☐ 35 Al Leiter	.15	.07
☐ 36 Mark Wohlers	.15	.07
☐ 37 Rondell White	.30	.14
☐ 38 Charles Johnson	.30	.14
☐ 39 Mark Grace	.40	.18
☐ 40 Pedro Martinez	.60	.25
☐ 41 Tom Goodwin	.15	.07
☐ 42 Manny Ramirez	.60	.25
☐ 43 Greg Vaughn	.15	.07
☐ 44 Brian Jordan	.30	.14
☐ 45 Mike Piazza	2.00	.90
☐ 46 Roberto Hernandez	.15	.07
☐ 47 Wade Boggs	.60	.25
☐ 48 Scott Sanders	.15	.07
☐ 49 Alex Gonzalez	.15	.07

#	Player	MINT	NRMT
50	Kevin Brown	.30	.14
51	Bob Higginson	.30	.14
52	Ken Caminiti	.40	.18
53	Derek Jeter	2.00	.90
54	Carlos Baerga	.15	.07
55	Jay Buhner	.40	.18
56	Tim Naehring	.15	.07
57	Jeff Bagwell	1.25	.55
58	Steve Finley	.30	.14
59	Kevin Appier	.30	.14
60	Jay Bell	.30	.14
61	Ivan Rodriguez	.75	.35
62	Terrell Wade	.15	.07
63	Rusty Greer	.30	.14
64	Juan Guzman	.15	.07
65	Fred McGriff	.40	.18
66	Tino Martinez	.60	.25
67	Ray Lankford	.15	.07
68	Juan Gonzalez	1.50	.70
69	Ron Gant	.30	.14
70	Jack McDowell	.15	.07
71	Tony Gwynn	1.50	.70
72	Joe Carter	.30	.14
73	Wilson Alvarez	.15	.07
74	Jason Giambi	.30	.14
75	Brian Hunter	.30	.14
76	Michael Tucker	.15	.07
77	Andy Benes	.30	.14
78	Brady Anderson	.40	.18
79	Ramon Martinez	.30	.14
80	Troy Percival	.15	.07
81	Alex Rodriguez	2.00	.90
82	Jim Thome	.60	.25
83	Denny Neagle	.30	.14
84	Rafael Palmeiro	.15	.07
85	Jose Valentin	.15	.07
86	Marc Newfield	.15	.07
87	Mariano Rivera	.30	.14
88	Alan Benes	.30	.14
89	Jimmy Key	.15	.07
90	Joe Randa	.15	.07
91	Cal Ripken	2.50	1.10
92	Craig Biggio	.40	.18
93	Dean Palmer	.15	.07
94	Gary Sheffield	.60	.25
95	Ismael Valdes	.30	.14
96	John Valentin	.15	.07
97	Johnny Damon	.15	.07
98	Mo Vaughn	.75	.35
99	Paul Sorrento	.15	.07
100	Randy Johnson	.60	.25
101	Raul Mondesi	.40	.18
102	Roberto Alomar	.60	.25
103	Royce Clayton	.15	.07
104	Mark Grudzielanek	.15	.07
105	Wally Joyner	.30	.14
106	Wil Cordero	.15	.07
107	Will Clark	.40	.18
108	Chuck Knoblauch	.60	.25
109	Derek Bell	.15	.07
110	Henry Rodriguez	.15	.07
111	Edgar Renteria	.30	.14
112	Travis Fryman	.30	.14
113	Eric Young	.15	.07
114	Sandy Alomar Jr.	.30	.14
115	Darin Erstad	1.00	.45
116	Barry Larkin	.40	.18
117	Barry Bonds	.75	.35
118	Frank Thomas	2.50	1.10
119	Carlos Delgado	.30	.14
120	Jason Kendall	.30	.14
121	Todd Hollandsworth	.15	.07
122	Jim Edmonds	.40	.18
123	Chipper Jones	2.00	.90
124	Jeff Fassero	.15	.07
125	Deion Sanders	.30	.14
126	Matt Lawton	.15	.07
127	Ryan Klesko	.40	.18
128	Mike Mussina	.60	.25
129	Paul Molitor	.60	.25
130	Dante Bichette	.30	.14
131	Bill Pulsipher	.15	.07
132	Todd Hundley	.30	.14
133	J.T. Snow	.30	.14
134	Chuck Finley	.15	.07
135	Shawn Green	.15	.07
136	Charles Nagy	.30	.14
137	Willie Greene	.15	.07
138	Marty Cordova	.30	.14
139	Eddie Murray	.60	.25
140	Ryne Sandberg	.75	.35
141	Alex Fernandez	.30	.14
142	Mark McGwire	1.25	.55
143	Eric Davis	.30	.14
144	Jermaine Dye	.15	.07
145	Ruben Sierra	.15	.07
146	Damon Buford	.15	.07
147	John Smoltz	.30	.14
148	Alex Ochoa	.15	.07
149	Moises Alou	.30	.14
150	Rico Brogna	.15	.07
151	Terry Steinbach	.15	.07
152	Jeff King	.15	.07
153	Carlos Garcia	.15	.07
154	Tom Glavine	.30	.14
155	Edgar Martinez	.40	.18
156	Kevin Elster	.15	.07
157	Darryl Hamilton	.15	.07
158	Jason Dickson	.30	.14
159	Kevin Orie	.30	.14
160	Bubba Trammell	.60	.25
161	Jose Guillen	.75	.35
162	Brant Brown	.15	.07
163	Wendell Magee	.15	.07
164	Scott Spiezio	.30	.14
165	Todd Walker	.30	.14
166	Rod Myers	.30	.14
167	Damon Mashore	.15	.07
168	Wilton Guerrero	.15	.07
169	Vladimir Guerrero	1.25	.55
170	Nomar Garciaparra	2.00	.90
171	Shannon Stewart	.30	.14
172	Scott Rolen	1.50	.70
173	Bob Abreu	.30	.14
174	Danny Patterson	.15	.07
175	Andruw Jones	1.50	.70
176	Brian Giles	.15	.07
177	Dmitri Young	.15	.07
178	Cal Ripken EMW	1.25	.55
179	Chuck Knoblauch EMW	.30	.14
180	Alex Rodriguez EMW	1.00	.45
181	Andres Galarraga EMW	.30	.14
182	Pedro Martinez EMW	.30	.14
183	Brady Anderson EMW	.30	.14
184	Barry Bonds EMW	.40	.18
185	Ivan Rodriguez EMW	.40	.18
186	Gary Sheffield EMW	.30	.14
187	Denny Neagle EMW	.15	.07
188	Mark McGwire AURA	.60	.25
189	Ellis Burks AURA	.15	.07
190	Alex Rodriguez AURA	1.00	.45
191	Mike Piazza AURA	1.00	.45
192	Barry Bonds AURA	.40	.18
193	Albert Belle AURA	.40	.18
194	Chipper Jones AURA	1.00	.45
195	Juan Gonzalez AURA	.75	.35
196	Brady Anderson AURA	.30	.14
197	Frank Thomas AURA	1.25	.55
198	Vladimir Guerrero CL	.60	.25
199	Todd Walker CL	.15	.07
200	Scott Rolen CL	.75	.35

1997 New Pinnacle Artist's Proof

Randomly inserted in packs at a rate of one in 39, this 200-card set is a fractured parallel version of the regular set and features exclusive Dufex all-foil print technology in varying levels of scarcity utilizing finishes of Red, Blue and Green foil. The 125 Reds are scarce, 50 Blues are scarcer, and the 25 Greens represent the top stars with the scarcest printing. Each card is stamped with the "Artist's Proof" seal.

	MINT	NRMT
COMPLETE SET (200)	4300.00	1900.00
COMP.RED SET (125)	600.00	275.00
COMMON RED	5.00	2.20
RED MINOR STARS	8.00	3.60
RED UNLISTED STARS	15.00	6.75
COMP.BLUE SET (50)	1200.00	550.00
COMMON BLUE	20.00	9.00
BLUE UNLISTED STARS	40.00	18.00
COMP.GREEN SET (25)	2500.00	1100.00
COMMON GREEN	30.00	13.50
STATED ODDS 1:39		

#	Player	MINT	NRMT
1	Ken Griffey Jr. G	250.00	110.00
2	Sammy Sosa B	40.00	18.00
3	Greg Maddux G	150.00	70.00
4	Matt Williams B	25.00	11.00
5	Jason Isringhausen R	5.00	2.20
6	Gregg Jefferies R	5.00	2.20
7	Chili Davis R	8.00	3.60
8	Paul O'Neill R	8.00	3.60
9	Larry Walker R	15.00	6.75
10	Ellis Burks B	20.00	9.00
11	Cliff Floyd R	5.00	2.20
12	Albert Belle G	60.00	27.00
13	Javier Lopez R	8.00	3.60
14	David Cone R	8.00	3.60
15	Jose Canseco R	25.00	11.00
16	Todd Zeile R	5.00	2.20
17	Bernard Gilkey B	20.00	9.00
18	Andres Galarraga B	40.00	18.00
19	Chris Snopek R	5.00	2.20
20	Tim Salmon B	40.00	18.00
21	Roger Clemens B	80.00	36.00
22	Reggie Sanders R	5.00	2.20
23	John Jaha R	5.00	2.20
24	Andy Pettitte B	40.00	18.00
25	Kenny Lofton G	60.00	27.00
26	Robb Nen R	5.00	2.20
27	John Wetteland B	20.00	9.00
28	Bobby Bonilla R	8.00	3.60
29	Hideo Nomo G	150.00	70.00
30	Cecil Fielder R	8.00	3.60
31	Garret Anderson R	8.00	3.60
32	Pat Hentgen R	8.00	3.60
33	Dave Justice R	15.00	6.75
34	Billy Wagner R	8.00	3.60
35	Al Leiter R	5.00	2.20
36	Mark Wohlers R	5.00	2.20
37	Rondell White R	8.00	3.60
38	Charles Johnson R	8.00	3.60
39	Mark Grace R	10.00	4.50
40	Pedro Martinez R	15.00	6.75
41	Tom Goodwin R	5.00	2.20
42	Manny Ramirez B	40.00	18.00
43	Greg Vaughn R	5.00	2.20
44	Brian Jordan B	20.00	9.00
45	Mike Piazza G	150.00	70.00
46	Roberto Hernandez R	5.00	2.20
47	Wade Boggs B	40.00	18.00
48	Scott Sanders R	5.00	2.20
49	Alex Gonzalez R	5.00	2.20
50	Kevin Brown R	8.00	3.60
51	Bob Higginson B	20.00	9.00
52	Ken Caminiti B	25.00	11.00
53	Derek Jeter G	120.00	55.00
54	Carlos Baerga R	5.00	2.20
55	Jay Buhner B	25.00	11.00
56	Tim Naehring R	5.00	2.20
57	Jeff Bagwell G	100.00	45.00
58	Steve Finley R	8.00	3.60
59	Kevin Appier R	8.00	3.60
60	Jay Bell R	8.00	3.60
61	Ivan Rodriguez B	50.00	22.00
62	Terrell Wade R	5.00	2.20
63	Rusty Greer R	8.00	3.60
64	Juan Guzman R	5.00	2.20
65	Fred McGriff R	10.00	4.50
66	Tino Martinez R	15.00	6.75
67	Ray Lankford R	5.00	2.20
68	Juan Gonzalez G	120.00	55.00
69	Ron Gant R	8.00	3.60
70	Jack McDowell R	5.00	2.20
71	Tony Gwynn B	100.00	45.00
72	Joe Carter B	20.00	9.00
73	Wilson Alvarez R	5.00	2.20

☐ 74 Jason Giambi R	8.00	3.60
☐ 75 Brian Hunter R	8.00	3.60
☐ 76 Michael Tucker R	8.00	3.60
☐ 77 Andy Benes R	8.00	3.60
☐ 78 Brady Anderson B	25.00	11.00
☐ 79 Ramon Martinez R	8.00	3.60
☐ 80 Troy Percival R	9.00	4.00
☐ 81 Alex Rodriguez G	150.00	70.00
☐ 82 Jim Thome B	18.00	9.00
☐ 83 Denny Neagle R	8.00	3.60
☐ 84 Rafael Palmeiro B	25.00	11.00
☐ 85 Jose Valentin R	5.00	2.20
☐ 86 Marc Newfield R	5.00	2.20
☐ 87 Mariano Rivera B	20.00	9.00
☐ 88 Alan Benes R	8.00	3.60
☐ 89 Jimmy Key R	8.00	3.60
☐ 90 Joe Randa R	5.00	2.20
☐ 91 Cal Ripken G	200.00	90.00
☐ 92 Craig Biggio R	10.00	4.50
☐ 93 Dean Palmer R	5.00	2.20
☐ 94 Gary Sheffield B	40.00	18.00
☐ 95 Ismael Valdes R	8.00	3.60
☐ 96 John Valentin R	5.00	2.20
☐ 97 Johnny Damon R	5.00	2.20
☐ 98 Mo Vaughn G	60.00	27.00
☐ 99 Paul Sorrento R	5.00	2.20
☐ 100 Randy Johnson B	40.00	18.00
☐ 101 Raul Mondesi B	25.00	11.00
☐ 102 Roberto Alomar B	40.00	18.00
☐ 103 Royce Clayton R	5.00	2.20
☐ 104 Mark Grudzielanek R	5.00	2.20
☐ 105 Wally Joyner R	8.00	3.60
☐ 106 Wil Cordero R	5.00	2.20
☐ 107 Will Clark B	25.00	11.00
☐ 108 Chuck Knoblauch B	40.00	18.00
☐ 109 Derek Bell R	5.00	2.20
☐ 110 Henry Rodriguez R	5.00	2.20
☐ 111 Edgar Renteria R	8.00	3.60
☐ 112 Travis Fryman R	8.00	3.60
☐ 113 Eric Young R	5.00	2.20
☐ 114 Sandy Alomar Jr. R	8.00	3.60
☐ 115 Darin Erstad B	50.00	22.00
☐ 116 Barry Larkin B	25.00	11.00
☐ 117 Barry Bonds B	50.00	22.00
☐ 118 Frank Thomas G	200.00	90.00
☐ 119 Carlos Delgado R	8.00	3.60
☐ 120 Jason Kendall R	8.00	3.60
☐ 121 Todd Hollandsworth R	5.00	2.20
☐ 122 Jim Edmonds R	10.00	4.50
☐ 123 Chipper Jones G	120.00	55.00
☐ 124 Jeff Fassero R	5.00	2.20
☐ 125 Deion Sanders B	20.00	9.00
☐ 126 Matt Lawton R	5.00	2.20
☐ 127 Ryan Klesko R	10.00	4.50
☐ 128 Mike Mussina R	15.00	6.75
☐ 129 Paul Molitor B	40.00	18.00
☐ 130 Dante Bichette R	8.00	3.60
☐ 131 Bill Pulsipher R	5.00	2.20
☐ 132 Todd Hundley B	20.00	9.00
☐ 133 J.T. Snow R	8.00	3.60
☐ 134 Chuck Finley R	5.00	2.20
☐ 135 Shawn Green R	5.00	2.20
☐ 136 Charles Nagy R	8.00	3.60
☐ 137 Willie Greene R	5.00	2.20
☐ 138 Marty Cordova R	8.00	3.60
☐ 139 Eddie Murray R	15.00	6.75
☐ 140 Ryne Sandberg R	20.00	9.00
☐ 141 Alex Fernandez R	5.00	3.60
☐ 142 Mark McGwire G	100.00	45.00
☐ 143 Eric Davis R	8.00	3.60
☐ 144 Jermaine Dye R	5.00	2.20
☐ 145 Ruben Sierra R	5.00	2.20
☐ 146 Damon Buford R	5.00	2.20
☐ 147 John Smoltz B	20.00	9.00
☐ 148 Alex Ochoa R	5.00	2.20
☐ 149 Moises Alou R	8.00	3.60
☐ 150 Rico Brogna R	5.00	2.20
☐ 151 Terry Steinbach R	5.00	2.20
☐ 152 Jeff King R	5.00	2.20
☐ 153 Carlos Garcia R	5.00	2.20
☐ 154 Tom Glavine R	8.00	3.60
☐ 155 Edgar Martinez B	25.00	11.00
☐ 156 Kevin Elster R	5.00	2.20
☐ 157 Darryl Hamilton R	5.00	2.20
☐ 158 Jason Dickson R	8.00	3.60
☐ 159 Kevin Orie R	8.00	3.60
☐ 160 Bubba Trammell R	15.00	6.75
☐ 161 Jose Guillen B	40.00	18.00
☐ 162 Brant Brown R	5.00	2.20
☐ 163 Wendell Magee R	5.00	2.20
☐ 164 Scott Spiezio R	8.00	3.60
☐ 165 Todd Walker R	20.00	9.00
☐ 166 Rod Myers R	8.00	3.60
☐ 167 Damon Mashore R	5.00	2.20
☐ 168 Wilton Guerrero R	20.00	9.00
☐ 169 Vladimir Guerrero G	80.00	36.00
☐ 170 Nomar Garciaparra R	100.00	45.00
☐ 171 Shannon Stewart R	8.00	3.60
☐ 172 Scott Rolen R	30.00	13.50
☐ 173 Bob Abreu R	8.00	3.60
☐ 174 Danny Patterson R	5.00	2.20
☐ 175 Andruw Jones G	100.00	45.00
☐ 176 Brian Giles R	5.00	2.20
☐ 177 Dmitri Young R	5.00	2.20
☐ 178 Cal Ripken EMW G	100.00	45.00
☐ 179 Chuck Knoblauch EMW D	20.00	9.00
☐ 180 Alex Rodriguez EMW G	80.00	36.00
☐ 181 Andres Galarraga EMW R	8.00	3.60
☐ 182 Pedro Martinez EMW R	8.00	3.60
☐ 183 Brady Anderson EMW R	8.00	3.60
☐ 184 Barry Bonds EMW B	25.00	11.00
☐ 185 Ivan Rodriguez EMW B	25.00	11.00
☐ 186 Gary Sheffield EMW R	20.00	9.00
☐ 187 Denny Neagle EMW B	20.00	9.00
☐ 188 Mark McGwire AURA G	40.00	18.00
☐ 189 Ellis Burks AURA R	8.00	3.60
☐ 190 Alex Rodriguez AURA G	80.00	36.00
☐ 191 Mike Piazza AURA G	80.00	36.00
☐ 192 Barry Bonds AURA B	25.00	11.00
☐ 193 Albert Belle AURA G	30.00	13.50
☐ 194 Chipper Jones AURA G	80.00	36.00
☐ 195 Juan Gonzalez AURA G	60.00	27.00
☐ 196 Brady Anderson AURA B	20.00	9.00
☐ 197 Frank Thomas AURA G	100.00	45.00
☐ 198 Vladimir Guerrero CL R	10.00	4.50
☐ 199 Todd Walker CL R	5.00	2.20
☐ 200 Scott Rolen CL R	15.00	6.75

1997 New Pinnacle Keeping the Pace

Randomly inserted in packs at a rate of one in 89, this 18-card set features dot matrix holograms of the 18 hitters most likely to keep a 61-home run pace.

	MINT	NRMT
COMPLETE SET (18)	600.00	275.00
COMMON CARD (1-18)	6.00	2.70
UNLISTED STARS	15.00	6.75
STATED ODDS 1:89		

☐ 1 Juan Gonzalez	40.00	18.00
☐ 2 Greg Maddux	50.00	22.00
☐ 3 Ivan Rodriguez	20.00	9.00
☐ 4 Ken Griffey Jr.	80.00	36.00
☐ 5 Alex Rodriguez	50.00	22.00
☐ 6 Barry Bonds	20.00	9.00
☐ 7 Frank Thomas	60.00	27.00
☐ 8 Chuck Knoblauch	15.00	6.75
☐ 9 Derek Jeter	40.00	18.00
☐ 10 Roger Clemens	30.00	13.50
☐ 11 Kenny Lofton	20.00	9.00
☐ 12 Tony Gwynn	40.00	18.00
☐ 13 Troy Percival	6.00	2.70
☐ 14 Cal Ripken	60.00	27.00
☐ 15 Andy Pettitte	15.00	6.75
☐ 16 Hideo Nomo	40.00	18.00
☐ 17 Randy Johnson	15.00	6.75
☐ 18 Mike Piazza	50.00	22.00

1997 New Pinnacle Interleague Encounter

Randomly inserted in packs at a rate of one in 240, this 10-card set features a double-front card design printed on mirror blue mylar foil with red foil treatments. A top AL star player is carried on one side with a top NL mega-star on the flipside and the date of the first match-up of the two teams.

	MINT	NRMT
COMPLETE SET (10)	600.00	275.00
COMMON CARD (1-10)	30.00	13.50
STATED ODDS 1:240		

☐ 1 Albert Belle Brian Jordan	30.00	13.50
☐ 2 Andruw Jones Brady Anderson	50.00	22.00
☐ 3 Ken Griffey Jr. Tony Gwynn	120.00	55.00
☐ 4 Cal Ripken Chipper Jones	100.00	45.00
☐ 5 Mike Piazza Ivan Rodriguez	80.00	36.00
☐ 6 Derek Jeter Vladimir Guerrero	80.00	36.00
☐ 7 Greg Maddux Mo Vaughn	80.00	36.00
☐ 8 Alex Rodriguez Hideo Nomo	100.00	45.00
☐ 9 Juan Gonzalez Barry Bonds	60.00	27.00
☐ 10 Frank Thomas Jeff Bagwell	100.00	45.00

1997 New Pinnacle Spellbound

Randomly inserted in both hobby and retail packs at a rate of one in 19, this 50-card set features color action player photos superimposed over one of the letters of the player's name and printed on a full-foil, micro-etched card. The completed set for each star player spells both the player's name and the word "Spellbound."

	MINT	NRMT
COMMON A.BELLE	6.00	2.70
COMMON A.JONES	12.00	5.50
COMMON A.RODRIGUEZ	20.00	9.00
COMMON C.JONES	15.00	6.75
COMMON C.RIPKEN	20.00	9.00
COMMON F.THOMAS	20.00	9.00
COMMON I.RODRIGUEZ	6.00	2.70
COMMON K.GRIFFEY JR.	25.00	11.00
COMMON M.PIAZZA	15.00	6.75
STATED ODDS 1:19		

HOBBY: JUNIOR, ANDRUW, RIPKEN, CHIPPER
RETAIL: FRANK,PIAZZA,
ALEX,PUDGE,BELLE ....

1994 Pacific

The 660 standard-size cards comprising this set feature color player action shots on their fronts that are borderless, except at the bottom, where a team color-coded marbleized border set off by a gold-foil line carries the team color-coded player's name. The set's gold-foil-stamped crown logo rests at the lower left. The back carries another color player action photo that is bordered only at the bottom, where the photo appears "torn away," revealing the gray marbleized area that carries the player's name, biography in both English and Spanish, statistics, and a ghosted team logo. The cards are numbered on the back, grouped alphabetically within teams. The set closes with an Award Winners subset (655-660). There are no key Rookie Cards in this set.

	MINT	NRMT
COMPLETE SET (660)	35.00	16.00
COMMON CARD (1-660)	.10	.05
MINOR STARS	.20	.09
UNLISTED STARS	.40	.18
SUBSET CARDS HALF VALUE OF BASE CARDS		
COMP.CHECKLIST SET (6)	2.00	.90
CL: RANDOM INSERTS IN PACKS		

☐ 1 Steve Avery	.10	.05
☐ 2 Steve Bedrosian	.10	.05
☐ 3 Damon Berryhill	.10	.05
☐ 4 Jeff Blauser	.20	.09
☐ 5 Sid Bream	.10	.05
☐ 6 Francisco Cabrera	.10	.05
☐ 7 Ramon Caraballo	.10	.05
☐ 8 Ron Gant	.20	.09
☐ 9 Tom Glavine	.20	.09
☐ 10 Chipper Jones	1.25	.55
☐ 11 Dave Justice	.40	.18
☐ 12 Ryan Klesko	.40	.18
☐ 13 Mark Lemke	.10	.05
☐ 14 Javier Lopez	.30	.14
☐ 15 Greg Maddux	1.25	.55
☐ 16 Fred McGriff	.30	.14
☐ 17 Greg McMichael	.10	.05
☐ 18 Kent Mercker	.10	.05
☐ 19 Otis Nixon	.10	.05
☐ 20 Terry Pendleton	.10	.05
☐ 21 Deion Sanders	.20	.09
☐ 22 John Smoltz	.20	.09
☐ 23 Tony Tarasco	.10	.05
☐ 24 Manny Alexander	.10	.05
☐ 25 Brady Anderson	.30	.14
☐ 26 Harold Baines	.20	.09
☐ 27 Damon Buford	.10	.05
☐ 28 Paul Carey	.10	.05
☐ 29 Mike Devereaux	.10	.05
☐ 30 Todd Frohwirth	.10	.05
☐ 31 Leo Gomez	.10	.05
☐ 32 Jeffrey Hammonds	.20	.09
☐ 33 Chris Hoiles	.10	.05
☐ 34 Tim Hulett	.10	.05
☐ 35 Ben McDonald	.10	.05
☐ 36 Mark McLemore	.10	.05
☐ 37 Alan Mills	.10	.05
☐ 38 Mike Mussina	.40	.18
☐ 39 Sherman Obando	.10	.05
☐ 40 Gregg Olson	.10	.05
☐ 41 Mike Pagliarulo	.10	.05
☐ 42 Jim Poole	.10	.05
☐ 43 Harold Reynolds	.10	.05
☐ 44 Cal Ripken	1.50	.70
☐ 45 David Segui	.10	.05
☐ 46 Fernando Valenzuela	.20	.09
☐ 47 Jack Voigt	.10	.05
☐ 48 Scott Bankhead	.10	.05
☐ 49 Roger Clemens	.75	.35
☐ 50 Scott Cooper	.10	.05
☐ 51 Danny Darwin	.10	.05
☐ 52 Andre Dawson	.30	.14
☐ 53 John Dopson	.10	.05
☐ 54 Scott Fletcher	.10	.05
☐ 55 Tony Fossas	.10	.05
☐ 56 Mike Greenwell	.10	.05
☐ 57 Billy Hatcher	.10	.05
☐ 58 Jeff McNeely	.10	.05
☐ 59 Jose Melendez	.10	.05
☐ 60 Tim Naehring	.10	.05
☐ 61 Tony Pena	.10	.05
☐ 62 Carlos Quintana	.10	.05
☐ 63 Paul Quantrill	.10	.05
☐ 64 Luis Rivera	.10	.05
☐ 65 Jeff Russell	.10	.05
☐ 66 Aaron Sele	.10	.05
☐ 67 John Valentin	.20	.09
☐ 68 Mo Vaughn	.50	.23
☐ 69 Frank Viola	.10	.05
☐ 70 Bob Zupcic	.10	.05
☐ 71 Mike Butcher	.10	.05
☐ 72 Rod Correia	.10	.05
☐ 73 Chad Curtis	.10	.05
☐ 74 Chili Davis	.20	.09
☐ 75 Gary DiSarcina	.10	.05
☐ 76 Damion Easley	.10	.05
☐ 77 John Farrell	.10	.05
☐ 78 Chuck Finley	.10	.05
☐ 79 Joe Grahe	.10	.05
☐ 80 Stan Javier	.10	.05
☐ 81 Mark Langston	.10	.05
☐ 82 Phil Leftwich	.10	.05
☐ 83 Torey Lovullo	.10	.05
☐ 84 Joe Magrane	.10	.05
☐ 85 Greg Myers	.10	.05
☐ 86 Eduardo Perez	.10	.05
☐ 87 Luis Polonia	.10	.05
☐ 88 Tim Salmon	.40	.18
☐ 89 J.T. Snow	.10	.05
☐ 90 Kurt Stillwell	.10	.05
☐ 91 Ron Tingley	.10	.05
☐ 92 Chris Turner	.10	.05
☐ 93 Julio Valera	.10	.05
☐ 94 Jose Bautista	.10	.05
☐ 95 Shawn Boskie	.10	.05
☐ 96 Steve Buechele	.10	.05
☐ 97 Frank Castillo	.10	.05
☐ 98 Mark Grace UER	.30	.14
(stats have 98 home runs in 1993; should be 14)		
☐ 99 Jose Guzman	.10	.05
☐ 100 Mike Harkey	.10	.05
☐ 101 Greg Hibbard	.10	.05
☐ 102 Doug Jennings	.10	.05
☐ 103 Derrick May	.10	.05
☐ 104 Mike Morgan	.10	.05
☐ 105 Randy Myers	.10	.05
☐ 106 Karl Rhodes	.10	.05
☐ 107 Kevin Roberson	.10	.05
☐ 108 Rey Sanchez	.10	.05
☐ 109 Ryne Sandberg	.50	.23
☐ 110 Tommy Shields	.10	.05
☐ 111 Dwight Smith	.10	.05
☐ 112 Sammy Sosa	.40	.18
☐ 113 Jose Vizcaino	.10	.05
☐ 114 Turk Wendell	.10	.05
☐ 115 Rick Wilkins	.10	.05
☐ 116 Willie Wilson	.10	.05
☐ 117 Eduardo Zambrano	.10	.05
☐ 118 Wilson Alvarez	.10	.05
☐ 119 Tim Belcher	.10	.05
☐ 120 Jason Bere	.10	.05
☐ 121 Rodney Bolton	.10	.05
☐ 122 Ellis Burks	.20	.09
☐ 123 Joey Cora	.20	.09
☐ 124 Alex Fernandez	.10	.05
☐ 125 Ozzie Guillen	.10	.05
☐ 126 Craig Grebeck	.10	.05
☐ 127 Roberto Hernandez	.10	.05
☐ 128 Bo Jackson	.20	.09
☐ 129 Lance Johnson	.10	.05
☐ 130 Ron Karkovice	.10	.05
☐ 131 Mike LaValliere	.10	.05
☐ 132 Norberto Martin	.10	.05
☐ 133 Kirk McCaskill	.10	.05
☐ 134 Jack McDowell	.10	.05
☐ 135 Scott Radinsky	.10	.05
☐ 136 Tim Raines	.20	.09
☐ 137 Steve Sax	.10	.05
☐ 138 Frank Thomas	1.50	.70
☐ 139 Dan Pasqua	.10	.05
☐ 140 Robin Ventura	.20	.09
☐ 141 Jeff Branson	.10	.05
☐ 142 Tom Browning	.10	.05
☐ 143 Jacob Brumfield	.10	.05
☐ 144 Tim Costo	.10	.05
☐ 145 Rob Dibble	.10	.05
☐ 146 Brian Dorsett	.10	.05
☐ 147 Steve Foster	.10	.05
☐ 148 Cesar Hernandez	.10	.05
☐ 149 Roberto Kelly	.10	.05
☐ 150 Barry Larkin	.30	.14
☐ 151 Larry Luebbers	.10	.05
☐ 152 Kevin Mitchell	.10	.05
☐ 153 Joe Oliver	.10	.05
☐ 154 Tim Pugh	.10	.05
☐ 155 Jeff Reardon	.20	.09
☐ 156 Jose Rijo	.10	.05
☐ 157 Bip Roberts	.10	.05
☐ 158 Chris Sabo	.10	.05
☐ 159 Juan Samuel	.10	.05
☐ 160 Reggie Sanders	.10	.05
☐ 161 John Smiley	.10	.05
☐ 162 Jerry Spradlin	.10	.05
☐ 163 Gary Varsho	.10	.05
☐ 164 Sandy Alomar Jr.	.20	.09
☐ 165 Albert Belle	.50	.23
☐ 166 Carlos Baerga	.10	.05
☐ 167 Mark Clark	.10	.05
☐ 168 Alvaro Espinoza	.10	.05
☐ 169 Felix Fermin	.10	.05
☐ 170 Reggie Jefferson	.10	.05
☐ 171 Wayne Kirby	.10	.05
☐ 172 Tom Kramer	.10	.05
☐ 173 Kenny Lofton	.50	.23
☐ 174 Jesse Levis	.10	.05

☐ 175	Candy Maldonado	.10	.05
☐ 176	Carlos Martinez	.10	.05
☐ 177	Jose Mesa	.10	.05
☐ 178	Jeff Mutis	.10	.05
☐ 179	Charles Nagy	.20	.09
☐ 180	Bob Ojeda	.10	.05
☐ 181	Junior Ortiz	.10	.05
☐ 182	Eric Plunk	.10	.05
☐ 183	Manny Ramirez	.50	.23
☐ 184	Paul Sorrento	.10	.05
☐ 185	Jeff Treadway	.10	.05
☐ 186	Bill Wertz	.10	.05
☐ 187	Freddie Benavides	.10	.05
☐ 188	Dante Bichette	.20	.09
☐ 189	Willie Blair	.10	.05
☐ 190	Daryl Boston	.10	.05
☐ 191	Pedro Castellano	.10	.05
☐ 192	Vinny Castilla	.20	.09
☐ 193	Jerald Clark	.10	.05
☐ 194	Alex Cole	.10	.05
☐ 195	Andres Galarraga	.40	.18
☐ 196	Joe Girardi	.10	.05
☐ 197	Charlie Hayes	.10	.05
☐ 198	Darren Holmes	.10	.05
☐ 199	Chris Jones	.10	.05
☐ 200	Curt Leskanic	.10	.05
☐ 201	Roberto Mejia	.10	.05
☐ 202	David Nied	.10	.05
☐ 203	J. Owens	.10	.05
☐ 204	Steve Reed	.10	.05
☐ 205	Armando Reynoso	.10	.05
☐ 206	Bruce Ruffin	.10	.05
☐ 207	Keith Shepherd	.10	.05
☐ 208	Jim Tatum	.10	.05
☐ 209	Eric Young	.10	.05
☐ 210	Skeeter Barnes	.10	.05
☐ 211	Danny Bautista	.10	.05
☐ 212	Tom Bolton	.10	.05
☐ 213	Eric Davis	.20	.09
☐ 214	Storm Davis	.10	.05
☐ 215	Cecil Fielder	.20	.09
☐ 216	Travis Fryman	.20	.09
☐ 217	Kirk Gibson	.20	.09
☐ 218	Dan Gladden	.10	.05
☐ 219	John Doherty	.10	.05
☐ 220	Chris Gomez	.10	.05
☐ 221	David Haas	.10	.05
☐ 222	Bill Krueger	.10	.05
☐ 223	Chad Kreuter	.10	.05
☐ 224	Mark Leiter	.10	.05
☐ 225	Bob MacDonald	.10	.05
☐ 226	Mike Moore	.10	.05
☐ 227	Tony Phillips	.10	.05
☐ 228	Rich Rowland	.10	.05
☐ 229	Mickey Tettleton	.10	.05
☐ 230	Alan Trammell	.30	.14
☐ 231	David Wells	.10	.05
☐ 232	Lou Whitaker	.20	.09
☐ 233	Luis Aquino	.10	.05
☐ 234	Alex Arias	.10	.05
☐ 235	Jack Armstrong	.10	.05
☐ 236	Ryan Bowen	.10	.05
☐ 237	Chuck Carr	.10	.05
☐ 238	Matias Carrillo	.10	.05
☐ 239	Jeff Conine	.20	.09
☐ 240	Henry Cotto	.10	.05
☐ 241	Orestes Destrade	.10	.05
☐ 242	Chris Hammond	.10	.05
☐ 243	Bryan Harvey	.10	.05
☐ 244	Charlie Hough	.10	.05
☐ 245	Richie Lewis	.10	.05
☐ 246	Mitch Lyden	.10	.05
☐ 247	Dave Magadan	.10	.05
☐ 248	Bob Natal	.10	.05
☐ 249	Benito Santiago	.10	.05
☐ 250	Gary Sheffield	.40	.18
☐ 251	Matt Turner	.10	.05
☐ 252	David Weathers	.10	.05
☐ 253	Walt Weiss	.10	.05
☐ 254	Darrell Whitmore	.10	.05
☐ 255	Nigel Wilson	.10	.05
☐ 256	Eric Anthony	.10	.05
☐ 257	Jeff Bagwell	.75	.35
☐ 258	Kevin Bass	.10	.05
☐ 259	Craig Biggio	.30	.14
☐ 260	Ken Caminiti	.30	.14
☐ 261	Andujar Cedeno	.10	.05
☐ 262	Chris Donnels	.10	.05
☐ 263	Doug Drabek	.10	.05
☐ 264	Tom Edens	.10	.05
☐ 265	Steve Finley	.10	.05
☐ 266	Luis Gonzalez	.10	.05
☐ 267	Pete Harnisch	.10	.05
☐ 268	Xavier Hernandez	.10	.05
☐ 269	Todd Jones	.10	.05
☐ 270	Darryl Kile	.20	.09
☐ 271	Al Osuna	.10	.05
☐ 272	Rick Parker	.10	.05
☐ 273	Mark Portugal	.10	.05
☐ 274	Scott Servais	.10	.05
☐ 275	Greg Swindell	.10	.05
☐ 276	Eddie Taubensee	.10	.05
☐ 277	Jose Uribe	.10	.05
☐ 278	Brian Williams	.10	.05
☐ 279	Kevin Appier	.20	.09
☐ 280	Billy Brewer	.10	.05
☐ 281	David Cone	.20	.09
☐ 282	Greg Gagne	.10	.05
☐ 283	Tom Gordon	.10	.05
☐ 284	Chris Gwynn	.10	.05
☐ 285	John Habyan	.10	.05
☐ 286	Chris Haney	.10	.05
☐ 287	Phil Hiatt	.10	.05
☐ 288	David Howard	.10	.05
☐ 289	Felix Jose	.10	.05
☐ 290	Wally Joyner	.20	.09
☐ 291	Kevin Koslofski	.10	.05
☐ 292	Jose Lind	.10	.05
☐ 293	Brent Mayne	.10	.05
☐ 294	Mike Macfarlane	.10	.05
☐ 295	Brian McRae	.10	.05
☐ 296	Kevin McReynolds	.10	.05
☐ 297	Keith Miller	.10	.05
☐ 298	Jeff Montgomery	.10	.05
☐ 299	Hipolito Pichardo	.10	.05
☐ 300	Rico Rossy	.10	.05
☐ 301	Curtis Wilkerson	.10	.05
☐ 302	Pedro Astacio	.10	.05
☐ 303	Rafael Bournigal	.10	.05
☐ 304	Brett Butler	.20	.09
☐ 305	Tom Candiotti	.10	.05
☐ 306	Omar Daal	.10	.05
☐ 307	Jim Gott	.10	.05
☐ 308	Kevin Gross	.10	.05
☐ 309	Dave Hansen	.10	.05
☐ 310	Carlos Hernandez	.10	.05
☐ 311	Orel Hershiser	.20	.09
☐ 312	Eric Karros	.20	.09
☐ 313	Pedro Martinez	.40	.18
☐ 314	Ramon Martinez	.20	.09
☐ 315	Roger McDowell	.10	.05
☐ 316	Raul Mondesi	.40	.18
☐ 317	Jose Offerman	.10	.05
☐ 318	Mike Piazza	1.25	.55
☐ 319	Jody Reed	.10	.05
☐ 320	Henry Rodriguez	.10	.05
☐ 321	Cory Snyder	.10	.05
☐ 322	Darryl Strawberry	.20	.09
☐ 323	Tim Wallach	.10	.05
☐ 324	Steve Wilson	.10	.05
☐ 325	Juan Bell	.10	.05
☐ 326	Ricky Bones	.10	.05
☐ 327	Alex Diaz	.10	.05
☐ 328	Cal Eldred	.20	.09
☐ 329	Darryl Hamilton	.10	.05
☐ 330	Doug Henry	.10	.05
☐ 331	John Jaha	.10	.05
☐ 332	Pat Listach	.10	.05
☐ 333	Graeme Lloyd	.10	.05
☐ 334	Carlos Maldonado	.10	.05
☐ 335	Angel Miranda	.10	.05
☐ 336	Jaime Navarro	.10	.05
☐ 337	Dave Nilsson	.10	.05
☐ 338	Rafael Novoa	.10	.05
☐ 339	Troy O'Leary	.10	.05
☐ 340	Jesse Orosco	.10	.05
☐ 341	Kevin Seitzer	.10	.05
☐ 342	Bill Spiers	.10	.05
☐ 343	William Suero	.10	.05
☐ 344	B.J. Surhoff	.10	.05
☐ 345	Dickie Thon	.10	.05
☐ 346	Jose Valentin	.10	.05
☐ 347	Greg Vaughn	.10	.05
☐ 348	Robin Yount	.30	.14
☐ 349	Willie Banks	.10	.05
☐ 350	Bernardo Brito	.10	.05
☐ 351	Scott Erickson	.10	.05
☐ 352	Mark Guthrie	.10	.05
☐ 353	Chip Hale	.10	.05
☐ 354	Brian Harper	.10	.05
☐ 355	Kent Hrbek	.20	.09
☐ 356	Terry Jorgensen	.10	.05
☐ 357	Chuck Knoblauch	.40	.18
☐ 358	Gene Larkin	.10	.05
☐ 359	Scott Leius	.10	.05
☐ 360	Shane Mack	.10	.05
☐ 361	David McCarty	.10	.05
☐ 362	Pat Meares	.10	.05
☐ 363	Pedro Munoz	.10	.05
☐ 364	Derek Parks	.10	.05
☐ 365	Kirby Puckett	.75	.35
☐ 366	Jeff Reboulet	.10	.05
☐ 367	Kevin Tapani	.10	.05
☐ 368	Mike Trombley	.10	.05
☐ 369	George Tsamis	.10	.05
☐ 370	Carl Willis	.10	.05
☐ 371	Dave Winfield	.30	.14
☐ 372	Moises Alou	.20	.09
☐ 373	Brian Barnes	.10	.05
☐ 374	Sean Berry	.10	.05
☐ 375	Frank Bolick	.10	.05
☐ 376	Wil Cordero	.20	.09
☐ 377	Delino DeShields	.10	.05
☐ 378	Jeff Fassero	.10	.05
☐ 379	Darrin Fletcher	.10	.05
☐ 380	Cliff Floyd	.20	.09
☐ 381	Lou Frazier	.10	.05
☐ 382	Marquis Grissom	.20	.09
☐ 383	Gil Heredia	.10	.05
☐ 384	Mike Lansing	.20	.09
☐ 385	Oreste Marrero	.10	.05
☐ 386	Dennis Martinez	.20	.09
☐ 387	Curtis Pride	.10	.05
☐ 388	Mel Rojas	.10	.05
☐ 389	Kirk Rueter	.10	.05
☐ 390	Joe Siddall	.10	.05
☐ 391	John Vander Wal	.10	.05
☐ 392	Larry Walker	.40	.18
☐ 393	John Wetteland	.10	.05
☐ 394	Rondell White	.30	.14
☐ 395	Tim Bogar	.10	.05
☐ 396	Bobby Bonilla	.20	.09
☐ 397	Jeromy Burnitz	.20	.09
☐ 398	Mike Draper	.10	.05
☐ 399	Sid Fernandez	.10	.05
☐ 400	John Franco	.20	.09
☐ 401	Dave Gallagher	.10	.05
☐ 402	Dwight Gooden	.20	.09
☐ 403	Eric Hillman	.10	.05
☐ 404	Todd Hundley	.20	.09
☐ 405	Butch Huskey	.10	.05
☐ 406	Jeff Innis	.10	.05
☐ 407	Howard Johnson	.10	.05
☐ 408	Jeff Kent	.20	.09
☐ 409	Ced Landrum	.10	.05
☐ 410	Mike Maddux	.10	.05
☐ 411	Josias Manzanillo	.10	.05
☐ 412	Jeff McKnight	.10	.05
☐ 413	Eddie Murray	.40	.18
☐ 414	Tito Navarro	.10	.05
☐ 415	Joe Orsulak	.10	.05
☐ 416	Bret Saberhagen	.10	.05
☐ 417	Dave Telgheder	.10	.05
☐ 418	Ryan Thompson	.10	.05
☐ 419	Chico Walker	.10	.05
☐ 420	Jim Abbott	.10	.05
☐ 421	Wade Boggs	.40	.18
☐ 422	Mike Gallego	.10	.05
☐ 423	Mark Hutton	.10	.05
☐ 424	Dion James	.10	.05
☐ 425	Domingo Jean	.10	.05
☐ 426	Pat Kelly	.10	.05
☐ 427	Jimmy Key	.20	.09
☐ 428	Jim Leyritz	.10	.05
☐ 429	Kevin Maas	.10	.05
☐ 430	Don Mattingly	.60	.25
☐ 431	Bobby Munoz	.10	.05
☐ 432	Matt Nokes	.10	.05

☐ 433 Paul O'Neill	.20	.09
☐ 434 Spike Owen	.10	.05
☐ 435 Melido Perez	.10	.05
☐ 436 Lee Smith	.20	.09
☐ 437 Andy Stankiewicz	.10	.05
☐ 438 Mike Stanley	.10	.05
☐ 439 Danny Tartabull	.10	.05
☐ 440 Randy Velarde	.10	.05
☐ 441 Bernie Williams	.40	.18
☐ 442 Gerald Williams	.10	.05
☐ 443 Mike Witt	.10	.05
☐ 444 Marcos Armas	.10	.05
☐ 445 Lance Blankenship	.10	.05
☐ 446 Mike Bordick	.10	.05
☐ 447 Ron Darling UER	.10	.05
Reversed negative on front		
☐ 448 Dennis Eckersley	.20	.09
☐ 449 Brent Gates	.10	.05
☐ 450 Goose Gossage	.20	.09
☐ 451 Scott Hemond	.10	.05
☐ 452 Dave Henderson	.10	.05
☐ 453 Shawn Hillegas	.10	.05
☐ 454 Rick Honeycutt	.10	.05
☐ 455 Scott Lydy	.10	.05
☐ 456 Mark McGwire	.75	.35
☐ 457 Henry Mercedes	.10	.05
☐ 458 Mike Mohler	.10	.05
☐ 459 Troy Neel	.10	.05
☐ 460 Edwin Nunez	.10	.05
☐ 461 Craig Paquette	.10	.05
☐ 462 Ruben Sierra	.10	.05
☐ 463 Terry Steinbach	.10	.05
☐ 464 Todd Van Poppel	.10	.05
☐ 465 Bob Welch	.10	.05
☐ 466 Bobby Witt	.10	.05
☐ 467 Ruben Amaro	.10	.05
☐ 468 Larry Andersen	.10	.05
☐ 469 Kim Batiste	.10	.05
☐ 470 Wes Chamberlain	.10	.05
☐ 471 Darren Daulton	.20	.09
☐ 472 Mariano Duncan	.10	.05
☐ 473 Len Dykstra	.20	.09
☐ 474 Jim Eisenreich	.10	.05
☐ 475 Tommy Greene	.10	.05
☐ 476 Dave Hollins	.10	.05
☐ 477 Pete Incaviglia	.10	.05
☐ 478 Danny Jackson	.10	.05
☐ 479 John Kruk	.20	.09
☐ 480 Tony Longmire	.10	.05
☐ 481 Jeff Manto	.10	.05
☐ 482 Mickey Morandini	.10	.05
☐ 483 Terry Mulholland	.10	.05
☐ 484 Todd Pratt	.10	.05
☐ 485 Ben Rivera	.10	.05
☐ 486 Curt Schilling	.20	.09
☐ 487 Kevin Stocker	.10	.05
☐ 488 Milt Thompson	.10	.05
☐ 489 David West	.10	.05
☐ 490 Mitch Williams	.10	.05
☐ 491 Jeff Ballard	.10	.05
☐ 492 Jay Bell	.20	.09
☐ 493 Scott Bullett	.10	.05
☐ 494 Dave Clark	.10	.05
☐ 495 Steve Cooke	.10	.05
☐ 496 Midre Cummings	.10	.05
☐ 497 Mark Dewey	.10	.05
☐ 498 Carlos Garcia	.10	.05
☐ 499 Jeff King	.10	.05
☐ 500 Al Martin	.10	.05
☐ 501 Lloyd McClendon	.10	.05
☐ 502 Orlando Merced	.10	.05
☐ 503 Blas Minor	.10	.05
☐ 504 Denny Neagle	.20	.09
☐ 505 Tom Prince	.10	.05
☐ 506 Don Slaught	.10	.05
☐ 507 Zane Smith	.10	.05
☐ 508 Randy Tomlin	.10	.05
☐ 509 Andy Van Slyke	.20	.09
☐ 510 Paul Wagner	.10	.05
☐ 511 Tim Wakefield	.10	.05
☐ 512 Bob Walk	.10	.05
☐ 513 John Wehner	.10	.05
☐ 514 Kevin Young	.10	.05
☐ 515 Billy Bean	.10	.05
☐ 516 Andy Benes	.20	.09
☐ 517 Derek Bell	.10	.05

☐ 518 Doug Brocail	.10	.05
☐ 519 Jarvis Brown	.10	.05
☐ 520 Phil Clark	.10	.05
☐ 521 Mark Davis	.10	.05
☐ 522 Jeff Gardner	.10	.05
☐ 523 Pat Gomez	.10	.05
☐ 524 Ricky Gutierrez	.10	.05
☐ 525 Tony Gwynn	1.00	.45
☐ 526 Gene Harris	.10	.05
☐ 527 Kevin Higgins	.10	.05
☐ 528 Trevor Hoffman	.10	.05
☐ 529 Luis Lopez	.10	.05
☐ 530 Pedro A.Martinez	.10	.05
☐ 531 Melvin Nieves	.10	.05
☐ 532 Phil Plantier	.10	.05
☐ 533 Frank Seminara	.10	.05
☐ 534 Craig Shipley	.10	.05
☐ 535 Tim Teufel	.10	.05
☐ 536 Guillermo Velasquez	.10	.05
☐ 537 Wally Whitehurst	.10	.05
☐ 538 Rod Beck	.10	.05
☐ 539 Todd Benzinger	.10	.05
☐ 540 Barry Bonds	.50	.23
☐ 541 Jeff Brantley	.10	.05
☐ 542 Dave Burba	.10	.05
☐ 543 John Burkett	.10	.05
☐ 544 Will Clark	.30	.14
☐ 545 Royce Clayton	.10	.05
☐ 546 Bryan Hickerson	.10	.05
☐ 547 Mike Jackson	.10	.05
☐ 548 Darren Lewis	.10	.05
☐ 549 Kirt Manwaring	.10	.05
☐ 550 Dave Martinez	.10	.05
☐ 551 Willie McGee	.10	.05
☐ 552 Jeff Reed	.10	.05
☐ 553 Dave Righetti	.10	.05
☐ 554 Kevin Rogers	.10	.05
☐ 555 Steve Scarsone	.10	.05
☐ 556 Bill Swift	.10	.05
☐ 557 Robby Thompson	.10	.05
☐ 558 Salomon Torres	.10	.05
☐ 559 Matt Williams	.30	.14
☐ 560 Trevor Wilson	.10	.05
☐ 561 Rich Amaral	.10	.05
☐ 562 Mike Blowers	.10	.05
☐ 563 Chris Bosio	.10	.05
☐ 564 Jay Buhner	.30	.14
☐ 565 Norm Charlton	.10	.05
☐ 566 Jim Converse	.10	.05
☐ 567 Rich DeLucia	.10	.05
☐ 568 Mike Felder	.10	.05
☐ 569 Dave Fleming	.10	.05
☐ 570 Ken Griffey Jr.	2.00	.90
☐ 571 Bill Haselman	.10	.05
☐ 572 Dwayne Henry	.10	.05
☐ 573 Brad Holman	.10	.05
☐ 574 Randy Johnson	.40	.18
☐ 575 Greg Litton	.10	.05
☐ 576 Edgar Martinez	.30	.14
☐ 577 Tino Martinez	.40	.18
☐ 578 Jeff Nelson	.10	.05
☐ 579 Marc Newfield	.20	.09
☐ 580 Roger Salkeld	.10	.05
☐ 581 Mackey Sasser	.10	.05
☐ 582 Brian Turang	.10	.05
☐ 583 Omar Vizquel	.20	.09
☐ 584 Dave Valle	.10	.05
☐ 585 Luis Alicea	.10	.05
☐ 586 Rene Arocha	.10	.05
☐ 587 Rheal Cormier	.10	.05
☐ 588 Tripp Cromer	.10	.05
☐ 589 Bernard Gilkey	.10	.05
☐ 590 Lee Guetterman	.10	.05
☐ 591 Gregg Jefferies	.10	.05
☐ 592 Tim Jones	.10	.05
☐ 593 Paul Kilgus	.10	.05
☐ 594 Les Lancaster	.10	.05
☐ 595 Omar Olivares	.10	.05
☐ 596 Jose Oquendo	.10	.05
☐ 597 Donovan Osborne	.10	.05
☐ 598 Tom Pagnozzi	.10	.05
☐ 599 Erik Pappas	.10	.05
☐ 600 Geronimo Pena	.10	.05
☐ 601 Mike Perez	.10	.05
☐ 602 Gerald Perry	.10	.05
☐ 603 Stan Royer	.10	.05

☐ 604 Ozzie Smith	.50	.23
☐ 605 Bob Tewksbury	.10	.05
☐ 606 Allen Watson	.10	.05
☐ 607 Mark Whiten	.10	.05
☐ 608 Todd Zeile	.10	.05
☐ 609 Jeff Bronkey	.10	.05
☐ 610 Kevin Brown	.20	.09
☐ 611 Jose Canseco	.30	.14
☐ 612 Doug Dascenzo	.10	.05
☐ 613 Butch Davis	.10	.05
☐ 614 Mario Diaz	.10	.05
☐ 615 Julio Franco	.10	.05
☐ 616 Benji Gil	.10	.05
☐ 617 Juan Gonzalez	1.00	.45
☐ 618 Tom Henke	.10	.05
☐ 619 Jeff Huson	.10	.05
☐ 620 David Hulse	.10	.05
☐ 621 Craig Lefferts	.10	.05
☐ 622 Rafael Palmeiro	.30	.14
☐ 623 Dean Palmer	.10	.05
☐ 624 Bob Patterson	.10	.05
☐ 625 Roger Pavlik	.10	.05
☐ 626 Gary Redus	.10	.05
☐ 627 Ivan Rodriguez	.50	.23
☐ 628 Kenny Rogers	.10	.05
☐ 629 Jon Shave	.10	.05
☐ 630 Doug Strange	.10	.05
☐ 631 Matt Whiteside	.10	.05
☐ 632 Roberto Alomar	.40	.18
☐ 633 Pat Borders	.10	.05
☐ 634 Scott Brow	.10	.05
☐ 635 Rob Butler	.10	.05
☐ 636 Joe Carter	.20	.09
☐ 637 Tony Castillo	.10	.05
☐ 638 Mark Eichhorn	.10	.05
☐ 639 Tony Fernandez	.10	.05
☐ 640 Huck Flener	.10	.05
☐ 641 Alfredo Griffin	.10	.05
☐ 642 Juan Guzman	.10	.05
☐ 643 Rickey Henderson	.30	.14
☐ 644 Pat Hentgen	.20	.09
☐ 645 Randy Knorr	.10	.05
☐ 646 Al Leiter	.10	.05
☐ 647 Domingo Martinez	.10	.05
☐ 648 Paul Molitor	.40	.18
☐ 649 Jack Morris	.20	.09
☐ 650 John Olerud	.20	.09
☐ 651 Ed Sprague	.10	.05
☐ 652 Dave Stewart	.20	.09
☐ 653 Devon White	.10	.05
☐ 654 Woody Williams	.10	.05
☐ 655 Barry Bonds MVP	.30	.14
☐ 656 Greg Maddux CY	.60	.25
☐ 657 Jack McDowell CY	.10	.05
☐ 658 Mike Piazza ROY	.60	.25
☐ 659 Tim Salmon ROY	.20	.09
☐ 660 Frank Thomas MVP	.75	.35

1994 Pacific All-Latino

Randomly inserted in Pacific purple foil packs at a rate of one in 25, this 20-card standard-size set spotlights the greatest Latin players chosen by the Pacific staff. Print run was limited to 8,000 sets. The fronts feature a full-bleed color player photo with gold foil stamping. The player's name in gold foil appears on the bottom of the photo. Superimposed on the player's native country's flag, the horizontal backs show a close-up color player photo on the left, while 1993 highlights, printed in English and Spanish, appear on the right. The set subdivides into National League

ball field, the horizontal backs show a close-up color player photo on the left, while the number of home runs the player hit in 1993 is highlighted on a large baseball icon on the right. The set subdivides into American League (1-10) and National League (11-20) players.

	MINT	NRMT
COMPLETE SET (20)	90.00	40.00
COMMON CARD (1-20)	1.50	.70

RANDOM INSERTS IN PURPLE PACKS

		MINT	NRMT
☐ 1	Juan Gonzalez	12.00	5.50
☐ 2	Ken Griffey Jr.	25.00	11.00
☐ 3	Frank Thomas	20.00	9.00
☐ 4	Albert Belle	6.00	2.70
☐ 5	Rafael Palmeiro	3.00	1.35
☐ 6	Joe Carter	2.00	.90
☐ 7	Dean Palmer	1.50	.70
☐ 8	Mickey Tettleton	1.50	.70
☐ 9	Tim Salmon	4.00	1.80
☐ 10	Danny Tartabull	1.50	.70
☐ 11	Barry Bonds	6.00	2.70
☐ 12	Dave Justice	4.00	1.80
☐ 13	Matt Williams	3.00	1.35
☐ 14	Fred McGriff	3.00	1.35
☐ 15	Ron Gant	2.00	.90
☐ 16	Mike Piazza	15.00	6.75
☐ 17	Bobby Bonilla	2.00	.90
☐ 18	Phil Plantier	1.50	.70
☐ 19	Sammy Sosa	4.00	1.80
☐ 20	Rick Wilkins	1.50	.70

TRIANGULAR INSERTS IN PURPLE PACKS
COMP.CIRCULAR SET (36) 60.00 27.00
*CIRCULAR STARS: .25X TO 1.5X BASE CARD HI
ONE CIRCULAR PER BLACK RETAIL PACK

		MINT	NRMT
☐ 1	Robin Yount	3.00	1.35
☐ 2	Juan Gonzalez	10.00	4.50
☐ 3	Rafael Palmeiro	3.00	1.35
☐ 4	Paul Molitor	4.00	1.80
☐ 5	Roberto Alomar	4.00	1.80
☐ 6	John Olerud	2.00	.90
☐ 7	Randy Johnson	4.00	1.80
☐ 8	Ken Griffey Jr.	20.00	9.00
☐ 9	Wade Boggs	4.00	1.80
☐ 10	Don Mattingly	6.00	2.70
☐ 11	Kirby Puckett	8.00	3.60
☐ 12	Tim Salmon	4.00	1.80
☐ 13	Frank Thomas	15.00	6.75
☐ 14	Fernando Valenzuela	2.00	.90
☐ 15	Cal Ripken	15.00	6.75
☐ 16	Carlos Baerga	1.00	.45
☐ 17	Kenny Lofton	5.00	2.20
☐ 18	Cecil Fielder	2.00	.90
☐ 19	John Burkett	1.00	.45
☐ 20	Andres Galarraga	4.00	1.80
☐ 21	Charlie Hayes	1.00	.45
☐ 22	Orestes Destrade	1.00	.45
☐ 23	Jeff Conine	2.00	.90
☐ 24	Jeff Bagwell	8.00	3.60
☐ 25	Mark Grace	3.00	1.35
☐ 26	Ryne Sandberg	5.00	2.20
☐ 27	Gregg Jefferies	1.00	.45
☐ 28	Barry Bonds	5.00	2.20
☐ 29	Mike Piazza	12.00	5.50
☐ 30	Greg Maddux	12.00	5.50
☐ 31	Darren Daulton	2.00	.90
☐ 32	John Kruk	2.00	.90
☐ 33	Lenny Dykstra	2.00	.90
☐ 34	Orlando Merced	1.00	.45
☐ 35	Tony Gwynn	10.00	4.50
☐ 36	Robby Thompson	1.00	.45

(1-10) and American League (11-20) players.

	MINT	NRMT
COMPLETE SET (20)	25.00	11.00
COMMON CARD (1-20)	1.00	.45

RANDOM INSERTS IN PURPLE PACKS

		MINT	NRMT
☐ 1	Benito Santiago	1.00	.45
☐ 2	Dave Magadan	1.00	.45
☐ 3	Andres Galarraga	5.00	2.20
☐ 4	Luis Gonzalez	1.00	.45
☐ 5	Jose Offerman	1.00	.45
☐ 6	Bobby Bonilla	2.00	.90
☐ 7	Dennis Martinez	2.00	.90
☐ 8	Mariano Duncan	1.00	.45
☐ 9	Orlando Merced	1.00	.45
☐ 10	Jose Rijo	1.00	.45
☐ 11	Danny Tartabull	1.00	.45
☐ 12	Ruben Sierra	1.00	.45
☐ 13	Ivan Rodriguez	6.00	2.70
☐ 14	Juan Gonzalez	12.00	5.50
☐ 15	Jose Canseco	3.00	1.35
☐ 16	Rafael Palmeiro	3.00	1.35
☐ 17	Roberto Alomar	5.00	2.20
☐ 18	Eduardo Perez	1.00	.45
☐ 19	Alex Fernandez	1.00	.45
☐ 20	Omar Vizquel	2.00	.90

1994 Pacific Silver Prisms

Randomly inserted in Pacific foil packs, this 36-card standard-size set is also known as "Jewels of the Crown." The triangular versions were randomly inserted in purple packs and the more common circular one per black retail pack. The print run was reportedly limited to 8,000 sets. The set divides into American League (1-18) and National League (19-36) players. The cards measure the standard size. The fronts feature a cut-out color player photo against a prism background that is either circular or triangular. The player's name appears at the bottom, highlighted in team colors.

	MINT	NRMT
COMPLETE SET (36)	125.00	55.00
COMMON CARD (1-36)	1.00	.45

1994 Pacific Gold Prisms

Randomly inserted in Pacific purple foil packs at a rate of one in 25, this 20-card standard-size prismatic "Home Run Leaders" set honors the top 1993 home run leaders. Print run was reportedly limited to 8,000 sets. The fronts feature a cut-out color player photo against a gold prism background. The player's name appears at the bottom, highlighted in team colors. Superimposed on a base-

1995 Pacific

This 450-card standard-size set was issued in one series. The full-bleed fronts have action photos; the "Pacific Collection" logo is on the upper left and the player's name is at the bottom. The horizontal backs have a player photo on the left with 1994 stats and some career highlights on the right. The career highlights are in both English and Spanish. The cards are numbered in the lower right corner. The cards are grouped alphabetically within teams and checklisted below alphabetically according to teams for each league. There are no key Rookie Cards in this set.

	MINT	NRMT
COMPLETE SET (450)	30.00	13.50
COMMON CARD (1-450)	.10	.05

	MINOR STARS	.20	.09
	UNLISTED STARS	.40	.18
☐ 1	Steve Avery	.10	.05
☐ 2	Rafael Belliard	.05	.05
☐ 3	Jeff Blauser	.20	.09
☐ 4	Tom Glavine	.20	.09
☐ 5	David Justice	.40	.18
☐ 6	Mike Kelly	.10	.05
☐ 7	Roberto Kelly	.10	.05
☐ 8	Ryan Klesko	.30	.14
☐ 9	Mark Lemke	.10	.05
☐ 10	Javier Lopez	.20	.09
☐ 11	Greg Maddux	1.25	.55
☐ 12	Fred McGriff	.30	.14
☐ 13	Greg McMichael	.10	.05
☐ 14	Jose Oliva	.10	.05
☐ 15	John Smoltz	.20	.09
☐ 16	Tony Tarasco	.10	.05
☐ 17	Brady Anderson	.30	.14
☐ 18	Harold Baines	.20	.09
☐ 19	Armando Benitez	.10	.05
☐ 20	Mike Devereaux	.10	.05
☐ 21	Leo Gomez	.10	.05
☐ 22	Jeffrey Hammonds	.20	.09
☐ 23	Chris Hoiles	.10	.05
☐ 24	Ben McDonald	.10	.05
☐ 25	Mark McLemore	.10	.05
☐ 26	Jamie Moyer	.10	.05
☐ 27	Mike Mussina	.40	.18
☐ 28	Rafael Palmeiro	.30	.14
☐ 29	Jim Poole	.10	.05
☐ 30	Cal Ripken Jr.	1.50	.70
☐ 31	Lee Smith	.20	.09
☐ 32	Mark Smith	.10	.05
☐ 33	Jose Canseco	.30	.14
☐ 34	Roger Clemens	.75	.35
☐ 35	Scott Cooper	.10	.05
☐ 36	Andre Dawson	.30	.14
☐ 37	Tony Fossas	.10	.05
☐ 38	Mike Greenwell	.10	.05
☐ 39	Chris Howard	.10	.05
☐ 40	Jose Melendez	.10	.05
☐ 41	Nate Minchey	.10	.05
☐ 42	Tim Naehring	.10	.05
☐ 43	Otis Nixon	.10	.05
☐ 44	Carlos Rodriguez	.10	.05
☐ 45	Aaron Sele	.10	.05
☐ 46	Lee Tinsley	.10	.05
☐ 47	Sergio Valdez	.10	.05
☐ 48	John Valentin	.10	.05
☐ 49	Mo Vaughn	.50	.23
☐ 50	Brian Anderson	.20	.09
☐ 51	Garret Anderson	.30	.14
☐ 52	Rod Correia	.10	.05
☐ 53	Chad Curtis	.10	.05
☐ 54	Mark Dalesandro	.10	.05
☐ 55	Chili Davis	.20	.09
☐ 56	Gary DiSarcina	.10	.05
☐ 57	Damion Easley	.10	.05
☐ 58	Jim Edmonds	.30	.14
☐ 59	Jorge Fabregas	.10	.05
☐ 60	Chuck Finley	.10	.05
☐ 61	Bo Jackson	.20	.09
☐ 62	Mark Langston	.10	.05
☐ 63	Eduardo Perez	.10	.05
☐ 64	Tim Salmon	.40	.18
☐ 65	J.T. Snow	.20	.09
☐ 66	Willie Banks	.10	.05
☐ 67	Jose Bautista	.10	.05
☐ 68	Shawon Dunston	.10	.05
☐ 69	Kevin Foster	.10	.05
☐ 70	Mark Grace	.30	.14
☐ 71	Jose Guzman	.10	.05
☐ 72	Jose Hernandez	.10	.05
☐ 73	Blaise Ilsley	.10	.05
☐ 74	Derrick May	.10	.05
☐ 75	Randy Myers	.10	.05
☐ 76	Karl Rhodes	.10	.05
☐ 77	Kevin Roberson	.10	.05
☐ 78	Rey Sanchez	.10	.05
☐ 79	Sammy Sosa	.40	.18
☐ 80	Steve Trachsel	.10	.05
☐ 81	Eddie Zambrano	.10	.05
☐ 82	Wilson Alvarez	.10	.05
☐ 83	Jason Bere	.10	.05
☐ 84	Joey Cora	.20	.09
☐ 85	Jose DeLeon	.10	.05
☐ 86	Alex Fernandez	.10	.05
☐ 87	Julio Franco	.10	.05
☐ 88	Ozzie Guillen	.10	.05
☐ 89	Joe Hall	.10	.05
☐ 90	Roberto Hernandez	.10	.05
☐ 91	Darrin Jackson	.10	.05
☐ 92	Lance Johnson	.10	.05
☐ 93	Norberto Martin	.10	.05
☐ 94	Jack McDowell	.10	.05
☐ 95	Tim Raines	.20	.09
☐ 96	Olmedo Saenz	.10	.05
☐ 97	Frank Thomas	1.50	.70
☐ 98	Robin Ventura	.20	.09
☐ 99	Bret Boone	.10	.05
☐ 100	Jeff Brantley	.10	.05
☐ 101	Jacob Brumfield	.10	.05
☐ 102	Hector Carrasco	.10	.05
☐ 103	Brian Dorsett	.10	.05
☐ 104	Tony Fernandez	.10	.05
☐ 105	Willie Greene	.10	.05
☐ 106	Erik Hanson	.10	.05
☐ 107	Kevin Jarvis	.10	.05
☐ 108	Barry Larkin	.30	.14
☐ 109	Kevin Mitchell	.10	.05
☐ 110	Hal Morris	.10	.05
☐ 111	Jose Rijo	.10	.05
☐ 112	Johnny Ruffin	.10	.05
☐ 113	Deion Sanders	.20	.09
☐ 114	Reggie Sanders	.10	.05
☐ 115	Sandy Alomar Jr.	.20	.09
☐ 116	Ruben Amaro	.10	.05
☐ 117	Carlos Baerga	.20	.09
☐ 118	Albert Belle	.50	.23
☐ 119	Alvaro Espinoza	.10	.05
☐ 120	Dennis Eckersley	.20	.09
☐ 121	Wayne Kirby	.10	.05
☐ 122	Kenny Lofton	.50	.23
☐ 123	Candy Maldonado	.10	.05
☐ 124	Dennis Martinez	.20	.09
☐ 125	Eddie Murray	.40	.18
☐ 126	Charles Nagy	.20	.09
☐ 127	Tony Pena	.10	.05
☐ 128	Manny Ramirez	.40	.18
☐ 129	Paul Sorrento	.10	.05
☐ 130	Jim Thoma	.40	.18
☐ 131	Omar Vizquel	.20	.09
☐ 132	Dante Bichette	.20	.09
☐ 133	Ellis Burks	.20	.09
☐ 134	Vinny Castilla	.20	.09
☐ 135	Marvin Freeman	.10	.05
☐ 136	Andres Galarraga	.40	.18
☐ 137	Joe Girardi	.10	.05
☐ 138	Charlie Hayes	.10	.05
☐ 139	Mike Kingery	.10	.05
☐ 140	Nelson Liriano	.10	.05
☐ 141	Roberto Mejia	.10	.05
☐ 142	David Nied	.10	.05
☐ 143	Steve Reed	.10	.05
☐ 144	Armando Reynoso	.10	.05
☐ 145	Bruce Ruffin	.10	.05
☐ 146	John VanderWal	.10	.05
☐ 147	Walt Weiss	.10	.05
☐ 148	Skeeter Barnes	.10	.05
☐ 149	Tim Belcher	.10	.05
☐ 150	Junior Felix	.10	.05
☐ 151	Cecil Fielder	.20	.09
☐ 152	Travis Fryman	.20	.09
☐ 153	Kirk Gibson	.10	.05
☐ 154	Chris Gomez	.10	.05
☐ 155	Buddy Groom	.10	.05
☐ 156	Chad Kreuter	.10	.05
☐ 157	Mike Moore	.10	.05
☐ 158	Tony Phillips	.10	.05
☐ 159	Juan Samuel	.10	.05
☐ 160	Mickey Tettleton	.10	.05
☐ 161	Alan Trammell	.30	.14
☐ 162	David Wells	.10	.05
☐ 163	Lou Whitaker	.20	.09
☐ 164	Kurt Abbott	.10	.05
☐ 165	Luis Aquino	.10	.05
☐ 166	Alex Arias	.10	.05
☐ 167	Bret Barberie	.10	.05
☐ 168	Jerry Browne	.10	.05
☐ 169	Chuck Carr	.10	.05
☐ 170	Matias Carrillo	.10	.05
☐ 171	Greg Colbrunn	.10	.05
☐ 172	Jeff Conine	.20	.09
☐ 173	Carl Everett	.10	.05
☐ 174	Robb Nen	.10	.05
☐ 175	Yorkis Perez	.10	.05
☐ 176	Pat Rapp	.10	.05
☐ 177	Benito Santiago	.10	.05
☐ 178	Gary Sheffield	.40	.18
☐ 179	Darrell Whitmore	.10	.05
☐ 180	Jeff Bagwell	.75	.35
☐ 181	Kevin Bass	.10	.05
☐ 182	Craig Biggio	.30	.14
☐ 183	Andujar Cedeno	.10	.05
☐ 184	Doug Drabek	.10	.05
☐ 185	Tony Eusebio	.10	.05
☐ 186	Steve Finley	.20	.09
☐ 187	Luis Gonzalez	.10	.05
☐ 188	Pete Harnisch	.10	.05
☐ 189	John Hudek	.10	.05
☐ 190	Orlando Miller	.10	.05
☐ 191	James Mouton	.10	.05
☐ 192	Roberto Petagine	.10	.05
☐ 193	Shane Reynolds	.10	.05
☐ 194	Greg Swindell	.10	.05
☐ 195	Dave Veres	.10	.05
☐ 196	Kevin Appier	.20	.09
☐ 197	Stan Belinda	.10	.05
☐ 198	Vince Coleman	.10	.05
☐ 199	David Cone	.20	.09
☐ 200	Gary Gaetti	.10	.05
☐ 201	Greg Gagne	.10	.05
☐ 202	Mark Gubicza	.10	.05
☐ 203	Bob Hamelin	.10	.05
☐ 204	Dave Henderson	.10	.05
☐ 205	Felix Jose	.10	.05
☐ 206	Wally Joyner	.20	.09
☐ 207	Jose Lind	.10	.05
☐ 208	Mike Macfarlane	.10	.05
☐ 209	Brian McRae	.10	.05
☐ 210	Jeff Montgomery	.10	.05
☐ 211	Hipolito Pichardo	.10	.05
☐ 212	Pedro Astacio	.10	.05
☐ 213	Brett Butler	.20	.09
☐ 214	Omar Daal	.10	.05
☐ 215	Delino DeShields	.20	.09
☐ 216	Darren Dreifort	.10	.05
☐ 217	Carlos Hernandez	.10	.05
☐ 218	Orel Hershiser	.20	.09
☐ 219	Garey Ingram	.10	.05
☐ 220	Eric Karros	.20	.09
☐ 221	Ramon Martinez	.20	.09
☐ 222	Raul Mondesi	.30	.14
☐ 223	Jose Offerman	.10	.05
☐ 224	Mike Piazza	1.25	.55
☐ 225	Henry Rodriguez	.10	.05
☐ 226	Ismael Valdes	.30	.14
☐ 227	Tim Wallach	.20	.09
☐ 228	Jeff Cirillo	.20	.09
☐ 229	Alex Diaz	.10	.05
☐ 230	Cal Eldred	.10	.05
☐ 231	Mike Fetters	.10	.05
☐ 232	Brian Harper	.10	.05
☐ 233	Ted Higuera	.10	.05
☐ 234	John Jaha	.10	.05
☐ 235	Graeme Lloyd	.10	.05
☐ 236	Jose Mercedes	.10	.05
☐ 237	Jaime Navarro	.10	.05
☐ 238	Dave Nilsson	.10	.05
☐ 239	Jesse Orosco	.10	.05
☐ 240	Jody Reed	.10	.05
☐ 241	Jose Valentin	.10	.05
☐ 242	Greg Vaughn	.10	.05
☐ 243	Turner Ward	.10	.05
☐ 244	Rick Aguilera	.10	.05
☐ 245	Rich Becker	.10	.05
☐ 246	Jim Deshaies	.10	.05
☐ 247	Steve Dunn	.10	.05
☐ 248	Scott Erickson	.10	.05
☐ 249	Kent Hrbek	.20	.09
☐ 250	Chuck Knoblauch	.40	.18
☐ 251	Scott Leius	.10	.05
☐ 252	David McCarty	.10	.05
☐ 253	Pat Meares	.10	.05
☐ 254	Pedro Munoz	.10	.05
☐ 255	Kirby Puckett	.75	.35

☐ 256	Carlos Pulido	.10	.05	☐ 342	Steve Cooke	.10	.05	☐ 428	Rick Honeycutt	.10	.05

1995 Pacific Gold Crown Die Cuts

Inserted approximately one in every 18 packs, these cards are in a diecut design. The player photo goes to the full-bleed bottom borders while the top has a gold crown. The player is identified on the bottom. The back of the card features a gold crown, player information in both English and Spanish, and a player photo against a blue background. The cards are sequenced in alphabetical order according to team name.

		MINT	NRMT
☐ 18	Juan Gonzalez	20.00	9.00
☐ 19	Roberto Alomar	8.00	3.60
☐ 20	Carlos Delgado	4.00	1.80

1995 Pacific Gold Prisms

This 36-card standard-size set was inserted approximately one in every 12 packs. The fronts feature a player photo set against a gold metallic background. The player is identified on the bottom of the card. The horizontal backs feature a player photo set against a group of baseballs on the left side. Another photo is on the right along with the player's name, his career totals and some brief information in English and Spanish.

		MINT	NRMT
COMPLETE SET (36)		150.00	70.00
COMMON CARD (1-36)		1.50	.70
STATED ODDS 1:12			
☐ 1	Jose Canseco	4.00	1.80
☐ 2	Gregg Jefferies	1.50	.70
☐ 3	Fred McGriff	4.00	1.80
☐ 4	Joe Carter	2.50	1.10
☐ 5	Tim Salmon	5.00	2.20
☐ 6	Wade Boggs	5.00	2.20
☐ 7	Dave Winfield	4.00	1.80
☐ 8	Bob Hamelin	1.50	.70
☐ 9	Cal Ripken Jr.	20.00	9.00
☐ 10	Don Mattingly	10.00	4.50
☐ 11	Juan Gonzalez	12.00	5.50
☐ 12	Carlos Delgado	2.50	1.10
☐ 13	Barry Bonds	5.00	2.20
☐ 14	Albert Belle	6.00	2.70
☐ 15	Raul Mondesi	4.00	1.80
☐ 16	Jeff Bagwell	10.00	4.50
☐ 17	Mike Piazza	15.00	6.75
☐ 18	Rafael Palmeiro	4.00	1.80
☐ 19	Frank Thomas	20.00	9.00
☐ 20	Matt Williams	4.00	1.80
☐ 21	Ken Griffey Jr.	25.00	11.00
☐ 22	Will Clark	4.00	1.80
☐ 23	Bobby Bonilla	2.50	1.10
☐ 24	Kenny Lofton	5.00	2.20
☐ 25	Paul Molitor	5.00	2.20
☐ 26	Kirby Puckett	10.00	4.50
☐ 27	David Justice	5.00	2.20
☐ 28	Jeff Conine	2.50	1.10
☐ 29	Bret Boone	1.50	.70
☐ 30	Larry Walker	5.00	2.20
☐ 31	Cecil Fielder	2.50	1.10
☐ 32	Manny Ramirez	5.00	2.20
☐ 33	Javier Lopez	2.50	1.10
☐ 34	Jimmy Key	2.50	1.10
☐ 35	Andres Galarraga	5.00	2.20
☐ 36	Tony Gwynn	12.00	5.50

1995 Pacific Latinos Destacados

Moises Alou

This 36-card standard size set was inserted approximately one in every nine packs. A literal translation for this set is Hot Hispanics and features only Spanish players. The full-bleed fronts feature color photos with the player's name at the bottom along with a fire design. The backs have the player's name spelled vertically in the upper left with a sentence in both English and Spanish. The bottom left has the team logo while the right side had a player photo. The cards are numbered and arranged in alphabetical order.

		MINT	NRMT
COMPLETE SET (36)		50.00	22.00
COMMON CARD (1-36)		1.00	.45
STATED ODDS 1:9			
☐ 1	Roberto Alomar	4.00	1.80
☐ 2	Moises Alou	2.00	.90
☐ 3	Wilson Alvarez	1.00	.45
☐ 4	Carlos Baerga	1.00	.45
☐ 5	Geronimo Berroa	1.00	.45
☐ 6	Jose Canseco	2.50	1.10
☐ 7	Hector Carrasco	1.00	.45
☐ 8	Wil Cordero	1.00	.45
☐ 9	Carlos Delgado	2.00	.90
☐ 10	Damion Easley	1.00	.45
☐ 11	Tony Eusebio	1.00	.45
☐ 12	Hector Fajardo	1.00	.45
☐ 13	Andres Galarraga	4.00	1.80
☐ 14	Carlos Garcia	1.00	.45
☐ 15	Chris Gomez	1.00	.45
☐ 16	Alex Gonzalez	1.00	.45
☐ 17	Juan Gonzalez	10.00	4.50
☐ 18	Luis Gonzalez	1.00	.45
☐ 19	Felix Jose	1.00	.45
☐ 20	Javier Lopez	2.00	.90
☐ 21	Luis Lopez	1.00	.45
☐ 22	Dennis Martinez	2.00	.90
☐ 23	Orlando Miller	1.00	.45
☐ 24	Raul Mondesi	2.50	1.10
☐ 25	Jose Oliva	1.00	.45
☐ 26	Rafael Palmeiro	2.50	1.10
☐ 27	Yorkis Perez	1.00	.45
☐ 28	Manny Ramirez	4.00	1.80
☐ 29	Jose Rijo	1.00	.45
☐ 30	Alex Rodriguez	15.00	6.75
☐ 31	Ivan Rodriguez	5.00	2.20
☐ 32	Carlos Rodriguez	1.00	.45
☐ 33	Sammy Sosa	4.00	1.80
☐ 34	Tony Tarasco	1.00	.45
☐ 35	Ismael Valdes	2.50	1.10
☐ 36	Bernie Williams	4.00	1.80

1996 Pacific

This 450-card set was issued in 12-card packs. The fronts feature borderless color action player photos with double-etched gold foil printing. The horizontal backs carry a color player portrait with player information in both English and Spanish and 1995 season player statistics.

		MINT	NRMT
COMPLETE SET (450)		35.00	16.00
COMMON CARD (1-450)		.10	.05
MINOR STARS		.20	.09
UNLISTED STARS		.40	.18
SUBSET CARDS HALF VALUE OF BASE CARDS			
☐ 1	Steve Avery	.10	.05
☐ 2	Ryan Klesko	.30	.14
☐ 3	Pedro Borbon	.10	.05
☐ 4	Chipper Jones	1.25	.55
☐ 5	Kent Mercker	.10	.05
☐ 6	Greg Maddux	1.25	.55
☐ 7	Greg McMichael	.10	.05
☐ 8	Mark Wohlers	.10	.05
☐ 9	Fred McGriff	.30	.14
☐ 10	John Smoltz	.20	.09
☐ 11	Rafael Belliard	.10	.05
☐ 12	Mark Lemke	.10	.05
☐ 13	Tom Glavine	.20	.09
☐ 14	Javier Lopez	.20	.09
☐ 15	Jeff Blauser	.10	.05
☐ 16	David Justice	.40	.18
☐ 17	Marquis Grissom	.20	.09
☐ 18	Greg Maddux CY	.60	.25
☐ 19	Randy Myers	.10	.05
☐ 20	Scott Servais	.10	.05
☐ 21	Sammy Sosa	.40	.18
☐ 22	Kevin Foster	.10	.05
☐ 23	Jose Hernandez	.10	.05
☐ 24	Jim Bullinger	.10	.05
☐ 25	Mike Perez	.10	.05
☐ 26	Shawon Dunston	.10	.05
☐ 27	Rey Sanchez	.10	.05
☐ 28	Frank Castillo	.10	.05
☐ 29	Jaime Navarro	.10	.05
☐ 30	Brian McRae	.10	.05
☐ 31	Mark Grace	.30	.14
☐ 32	Roberto Rivera	.10	.05
☐ 33	Luis Gonzalez	.10	.05
☐ 34	Hector Carrasco	.10	.05
☐ 35	Bret Boone	.10	.05
☐ 36	Thomas Howard	.10	.05
☐ 37	Hal Morris	.10	.05
☐ 38	John Smiley	.10	.05
☐ 39	Jeff Brantley	.10	.05
☐ 40	Barry Larkin	.30	.14
☐ 41	Mariano Duncan	.10	.05
☐ 42	Xavier Hernandez	.10	.05
☐ 43	Pete Schourek	.10	.05
☐ 44	Reggie Sanders	.10	.05
☐ 45	Dave Burba	.10	.05
☐ 46	Jeff Branson	.10	.05
☐ 47	Mark Portugal	.10	.05
☐ 48	Ron Gant	.20	.09

49	Benito Santiago	.10	.05
50	Barry Larkin MVP	.20	.09
51	Steve Reed	.10	.05
52	Kevin Ritz	.10	.05
53	Dante Bichette	.20	.09
54	Darren Holmes	.10	.05
55	Ellis Burks	.20	.09
56	Walt Weiss	.10	.05
57	Armando Reynoso	.10	.05
58	Vinny Castilla	.20	.09
59	Jason Bates	.10	.05
60	Mike Kingery	.10	.05
61	Bryan Rekar	.10	.05
62	Curtis Leskanic	.10	.05
63	Bret Saberhagen	.10	.05
64	Andres Galarraga	.40	.18
65	Larry Walker	.40	.18
66	Joe Girardi	.10	.05
67	Quilvio Veras	.10	.05
68	Robb Nen	.10	.05
69	Mario Diaz	.10	.05
70	Chuck Carr	.10	.05
71	Alex Arias	.10	.05
72	Pat Rapp	.10	.05
73	Rich Garces	.10	.05
74	Kurt Abbott	.10	.05
75	Andre Dawson	.30	.14
76	Greg Colbrunn	.10	.05
77	John Burkett	.10	.05
78	Terry Pendleton	.10	.05
79	Jesus Tavarez	.10	.05
80	Charles Johnson	.20	.09
81	Yorkis Perez	.10	.05
82	Jeff Conine	.20	.09
83	Gary Sheffield	.40	.18
84	Brian L. Hunter	.20	.09
85	Derrick May	.10	.05
86	Greg Swindell	.10	.05
87	Derek Bell	.10	.05
88	Dave Veres	.10	.05
89	Jeff Bagwell	.75	.35
90	Todd Jones	.10	.05
91	Orlando Miller	.10	.05
92	Pedro A. Martinez	.10	.05
93	Tony Eusebio	.10	.05
94	Craig Biggio	.30	.14
95	Shane Reynolds	.10	.05
96	James Mouton	.10	.05
97	Doug Drabek	.10	.05
98	Dave Magadan	.10	.05
99	Ricky Gutierrez	.10	.05
100	Hideo Nomo	1.00	.45
101	Delino DeShields	.10	.05
102	Tom Candiotti	.10	.05
103	Mike Piazza	1.25	.55
104	Ramon Martinez	.20	.09
105	Pedro Astacio	.10	.05
106	Chad Fonville	.10	.05
107	Raul Mondesi	.30	.14
108	Ismael Valdes	.20	.09
109	Jose Offerman	.10	.05
110	Todd Worrell	.10	.05
111	Eric Karros	.20	.09
112	Brett Butler	.20	.09
113	Juan Castro	.10	.05
114	Roberto Kelly	.10	.05
115	Omar Daal	.10	.05
116	Antonio Osuna	.10	.05
117	Hideo Nomo ROY	.50	.23
118	Mike Lansing	.10	.05
119	Mel Rojas	.10	.05
120	Sean Berry	.10	.05
121	David Segui	.10	.05
122	Tavo Alvarez	.10	.05
123	Pedro J. Martinez	.40	.18
124	F.P. Santangelo	.10	.05
125	Rondell White	.20	.09
126	Cliff Floyd	.10	.05
127	Henry Rodriguez	.10	.05
128	Tony Tarasco	.10	.05
129	Yamil Benitez	.20	.09
130	Carlos Perez	.10	.05
131	Wil Cordero	.10	.05
132	Jeff Fassero	.10	.05
133	Moises Alou	.20	.09
134	John Franco	.20	.09
135	Rico Brogna	.10	.05
136	Dave Mlicki	.10	.05
137	Bill Pulsipher	.10	.05
138	Jose Vizcaino	.10	.05
139	Carl Everett	.10	.05
140	Edgardo Alfonzo	.30	.14
141	Bobby Jones	.10	.05
142	Alberto Castillo	.10	.05
143	Joe Orsulak	.10	.05
144	Jeff Kent	.10	.05
145	Ryan Thompson	.10	.05
146	Jason Isringhausen	.10	.05
147	Todd Hundley	.20	.09
148	Alex Ochoa	.10	.05
149	Charlie Hayes	.10	.05
150	Michael Mimbs	.10	.05
151	Darren Daulton	.20	.09
152	Toby Borland	.10	.05
153	Andy Van Slyke	.20	.09
154	Mickey Morandini	.10	.05
155	Sid Fernandez	.10	.05
156	Tom Marsh	.10	.05
157	Kevin Stocker	.10	.05
158	Paul Quantrill	.10	.05
159	Gregg Jefferies	.10	.05
160	Ricky Bottalico	.10	.05
161	Lenny Dykstra	.20	.09
162	Mark Whiten	.10	.05
163	Tyler Green	.10	.05
164	Jim Eisenreich	.10	.05
165	Heathcliff Slocumb	.10	.05
166	Esteban Loaiza	.10	.05
167	Rich Aude	.10	.05
168	Jason Christiansen	.10	.05
169	Ramon Morel	.10	.05
170	Orlando Merced	.10	.05
171	Paul Wagner	.10	.05
172	Jeff King	.10	.05
173	Jay Bell	.20	.09
174	Jacob Brumfield	.10	.05
175	Nelson Liriano	.10	.05
176	Dan Miceli	.10	.05
177	Carlos Garcia	.10	.05
178	Denny Neagle	.20	.09
179	Angelo Encarnacion	.10	.05
180	Al Martin	.10	.05
181	Midre Cummings	.10	.05
182	Eddie Williams	.10	.05
183	Roberto Petagine	.10	.05
184	Tony Gwynn	1.00	.45
185	Andy Ashby	.10	.05
186	Melvin Nieves	.10	.05
187	Phil Clark	.10	.05
188	Brad Ausmus	.10	.05
189	Bip Roberts	.10	.05
190	Fernando Valenzuela	.20	.09
191	Marc Newfield	.10	.05
192	Steve Finley	.20	.09
193	Trevor Hoffman	.10	.05
194	Andujar Cedeno	.10	.05
195	Jody Reed	.10	.05
196	Ken Caminiti	.30	.14
197	Joey Hamilton	.20	.09
198	Tony Gwynn BAC	.50	.23
199	Shawn Barton	.10	.05
200	Deion Sanders	.20	.09
201	Rikkert Faneyte	.10	.05
202	Barry Bonds	.50	.23
203	Matt Williams	.30	.14
204	Jose Bautista	.10	.05
205	Mark Leiter	.10	.05
206	Mark Carreon	.10	.05
207	Robby Thompson	.10	.05
208	Terry Mulholland	.10	.05
209	Rod Beck	.10	.05
210	Royce Clayton	.10	.05
211	J.R. Phillips	.10	.05
212	Kirt Manwaring	.10	.05
213	Glenallen Hill	.10	.05
214	William VanLandingham	.10	.05
215	Scott Cooper	.10	.05
216	Bernard Gilkey	.10	.05
217	Allen Watson	.10	.05
218	Donovan Osborne	.10	.05
219	Ray Lankford	.10	.05
220	Tony Fossas	.10	.05
221	Tom Pagnozzi	.10	.05
222	John Mabry	.10	.05
223	Tripp Cromer	.10	.05
224	Mark Petkovsek	.10	.05
225	Mike Morgan	.10	.05
226	Ozzie Smith	.50	.23
227	Tom Henke	.10	.05
228	Jose Oquendo	.10	.05
229	Brian Jordan	.20	.09
230	Cal Ripken	1.50	.70
231	Scott Erickson	.10	.05
232	Harold Baines	.20	.09
233	Jeff Manto	.10	.05
234	Jesse Orosco	.10	.05
235	Jeffrey Hammonds	.10	.05
236	Brady Anderson	.30	.14
237	Manny Alexander	.10	.05
238	Chris Hoiles	.10	.05
239	Rafael Palmeiro	.30	.14
240	Ben McDonald	.10	.05
241	Curtis Goodwin	.10	.05
242	Bobby Bonilla	.20	.09
243	Mike Mussina	.40	.18
244	Kevin Brown	.20	.09
245	Armando Benitez	.10	.05
246	Jose Canseco	.30	.14
247	Erik Hanson	.10	.05
248	Mo Vaughn	.50	.23
249	Tim Naehring	.10	.05
250	Vaughn Eshelman	.10	.05
251	Mike Greenwell	.10	.05
252	Troy O'Leary	.10	.05
253	Tim Wakefield	.10	.05
254	Dwayne Hosey	.10	.05
255	John Valentin	.10	.05
256	Rick Aguilera	.10	.05
257	Mike Macfarlane	.10	.05
258	Roger Clemens	.75	.35
259	Luis Alicea	.10	.05
260	Mo Vaughn MVP	.30	.14
261	Mark Langston	.20	.09
262	Jim Edmonds	.30	.14
263	Rod Correia	.10	.05
264	Tim Salmon	.40	.18
265	J.T. Snow	.20	.09
266	Orlando Palmeiro	.10	.05
267	Jorge Fabregas	.10	.05
268	Jim Abbott	.10	.05
269	Eduardo Perez	.10	.05
270	Lee Smith	.20	.09
271	Gary DiSarcina	.10	.05
272	Damion Easley	.10	.05
273	Tony Phillips	.10	.05
274	Garret Anderson	.20	.09
275	Chuck Finley	.10	.05
276	Chili Davis	.20	.09
277	Lance Johnson	.10	.05
278	Alex Fernandez	.10	.05
279	Robin Ventura	.20	.09
280	Chris Snopek	.10	.05
281	Brian Keyser	.10	.05
282	Lyle Mouton	.10	.05
283	Luis Andujar	.10	.05
284	Tim Raines	.20	.09
285	Larry Thomas	.10	.05
286	Ozzie Guillen	.10	.05
287	Frank Thomas	1.50	.70
288	Roberto Hernandez	.10	.05
289	Dave Martinez	.10	.05
290	Ray Durham	.10	.05
291	Ron Karkovice	.10	.05
292	Wilson Alvarez	.10	.05
293	Omar Vizquel	.20	.09
294	Eddie Murray	.40	.18
295	Sandy Alomar Jr.	.20	.09
296	Orel Hershiser	.20	.09
297	Jose Mesa	.10	.05
298	Julian Tavarez	.10	.05
299	Dennis Martinez	.20	.09
300	Carlos Baerga	.20	.09
301	Manny Ramirez	.40	.18
302	Jim Thome	.40	.18
303	Kenny Lofton	.50	.23
304	Tony Pena	.10	.05
305	Alvaro Espinoza	.10	.05
306	Paul Sorrento	.10	.05

	MINT	NRMT
307 Albert Belle	.50	.23
308 Danny Bautista	.10	.05
309 Chris Gomez	.10	.05
310 Jose Lima	.10	.05
311 Phil Nevin	.10	.05
312 Alan Trammell	.30	.14
313 Chad Curtis	.10	.05
314 John Flaherty	.10	.05
315 Travis Fryman	.20	.09
316 Todd Steverson	.10	.05
317 Brian Bohanon	.10	.05
318 Lou Whitaker	.20	.09
319 Bobby Higginson	.20	.09
320 Steve Rodriguez	.10	.05
321 Cecil Fielder	.20	.09
322 Felipe Lira	.10	.05
323 Juan Samuel	.10	.05
324 Bob Hamelin	.10	.05
325 Tom Goodwin	.10	.05
326 Johnny Damon	.20	.09
327 Hipolito Pichardo	.10	.05
328 Dilson Torres	.10	.05
329 Kevin Appier	.10	.05
330 Mark Gubicza	.10	.05
331 Jon Nunnally	.10	.05
332 Gary Gaetti	.10	.05
333 Brent Mayne	.10	.05
334 Brent Cookson	.10	.05
335 Tom Gordon	.10	.05
336 Wally Joyner	.20	.09
337 Greg Gagne	.10	.05
338 Fernando Vina	.10	.05
339 Joe Oliver	.10	.05
340 John Jaha	.10	.05
341 Jeff Cirillo	.20	.09
342 Pat Listach	.10	.05
343 Dave Nilsson	.10	.05
344 Steve Sparks	.10	.05
345 Ricky Bones	.10	.05
346 David Hulse	.10	.05
347 Scott Karl	.10	.05
348 Darryl Hamilton	.10	.05
349 B.J. Surhoff	.10	.05
350 Angel Miranda	.10	.05
351 Sid Roberson	.10	.05
352 Matt Mieske	.10	.05
353 Jose Valentin	.10	.05
354 Matt Lawton	.30	.14
355 Eddie Guardado	.10	.05
356 Brad Radke	.20	.09
357 Pedro Munoz	.10	.05
358 Scott Stahoviak	.10	.05
359 Erik Schullstrom	.10	.05
360 Pat Meares	.10	.05
361 Marty Cordova	.20	.09
362 Scott Leius	.10	.05
363 Matt Walbeck	.10	.05
364 Rich Becker	.10	.05
365 Kirby Puckett	.75	.35
366 Oscar Munoz	.10	.05
367 Chuck Knoblauch	.40	.18
368 Marty Cordova ROY	.10	.05
369 Bernie Williams	.40	.18
370 Mike Stanley	.10	.05
371 Andy Pettitte	.50	.23
372 Jack McDowell	.10	.05
373 Sterling Hitchcock	.10	.05
374 David Cone	.20	.09
375 Randy Velarde	.10	.05
376 Don Mattingly	.60	.25
377 Melido Perez	.10	.05
378 Wade Boggs	.40	.18
379 Ruben Sierra	.10	.05
380 Tony Fernandez	.10	.05
381 John Wetteland	.10	.05
382 Mariano Rivera	.30	.14
383 Derek Jeter	1.25	.55
384 Paul O'Neill	.20	.09
385 Mark McGwire	.75	.35
386 Scott Brosius	.10	.05
387 Don Wengert	.10	.05
388 Terry Steinbach	.10	.05
389 Brent Gates	.10	.05
390 Craig Paquette	.10	.05
391 Mike Bordick	.10	.05
392 Ariel Prieto	.10	.05
393 Dennis Eckersley	.20	.09
394 Carlos Reyes	.10	.05
395 Todd Stottlemyre	.10	.05
396 Rickey Henderson	.30	.14
397 Geronimo Berroa	.10	.05
398 Steve Ontiveros	.10	.05
399 Mike Gallego	.10	.05
400 Stan Javier	.10	.05
401 Randy Johnson	.40	.18
402 Norm Charlton	.10	.05
403 Mike Blowers	.10	.05
404 Tino Martinez	.40	.18
405 Dan Wilson	.10	.05
406 Andy Benes	.20	.09
407 Alex Diaz	.10	.05
408 Edgar Martinez	.30	.14
409 Chris Bosio	.10	.05
410 Ken Griffey, Jr.	2.00	.90
411 Luis Sojo	.10	.05
412 Bob Wolcott	.10	.05
413 Vince Coleman	.10	.05
414 Rich Amaral	.10	.05
415 Jay Buhner	.30	.14
416 Alex Rodriguez	1.25	.55
417 Joey Cora	.20	.09
418 Randy Johnson CY	.20	.09
419 Edgar Martinez BAC	.20	.09
420 Ivan Rodriguez	.50	.23
421 Mark McLemore	.10	.05
422 Mickey Tettleton	.10	.05
423 Juan Gonzalez	1.00	.45
424 Will Clark	.30	.14
425 Kevin Gross	.10	.05
426 Dean Palmer	.10	.05
427 Kenny Rogers	.10	.05
428 Bob Tewksbury	.10	.05
429 Benji Gil	.10	.05
430 Jeff Russell	.10	.05
431 Rusty Greer	.20	.09
432 Roger Pavlik	.10	.05
433 Esteban Beltre	.10	.05
434 Otis Nixon	.10	.05
435 Paul Molitor	.40	.18
436 Carlos Delgado	.20	.09
437 Ed Sprague	.10	.05
438 Juan Guzman	.10	.05
439 Domingo Cedeno	.10	.05
440 Pat Hentgen	.20	.09
441 Tomas Perez	.10	.05
442 John Olerud	.20	.09
443 Shawn Green	.10	.05
444 Al Leiter	.10	.05
445 Joe Carter	.20	.09
446 Robert Perez	.10	.05
447 Devon White	.10	.05
448 Tony Castillo	.10	.05
449 Alex Gonzalez	.10	.05
450 Roberto Alomar	.40	.18

1996 Pacific Cramer's Choice

Randomly inserted in packs at a rate of one in 721, this 10-card set features the top Major League Baseball players as chosen by Pacific President and CEO, Michael Cramer. The fronts display a color player cut-out on a pyramid diecut shaped background. The backs carry information about why the player was selected for this set in both English and Spanish.

	MINT	NRMT
COMPLETE SET (10)	1200.00	550.00
COMMON CARD (CC1-CC10)	40.00	18.00
STATED ODDS 1:721		
CC1 Roberto Alomar	50.00	22.00
CC2 Wade Boggs	40.00	18.00
CC3 Cal Ripken	200.00	90.00
CC4 Greg Maddux	150.00	70.00
CC5 Frank Thomas	200.00	90.00
CC6 Tony Gwynn	120.00	55.00
CC7 Mike Piazza	150.00	70.00
CC8 Ken Griffey Jr.	250.00	110.00
CC9 Manny Ramirez	50.00	22.00
CC10 Edgar Martinez	40.00	18.00

1996 Pacific Estrellas Latinas

Randomly inserted in packs at a rate of four in 37, this 36-card set salutes the great Latino players in the major leagues today. The fronts feature color player action cut-outs on a black and gold foil background. The horizontal backs carry a player portrait with information about the player in both English and Spanish.

	MINT	NRMT
COMPLETE SET (36)	50.00	22.00
COMMON CARD (EL1-EL36)	1.00	.45
STATED ODDS 1:9		
EL1 Roberto Alomar	2.50	1.10
EL2 Moises Alou	1.50	.70
EL3 Carlos Baerga	1.00	.45
EL4 Geronimo Berroa	1.00	.45
EL5 Ricky Bones	1.00	.45
EL6 Bobby Bonilla	1.50	.70
EL7 Jose Canseco	2.00	.90
EL8 Vinny Castilla	1.50	.70
EL9 Pedro Martinez	2.50	1.10
EL10 John Valentin	1.00	.45
EL11 Andres Galarraga	2.50	1.10
EL12 Juan Gonzalez	8.00	3.60
EL13 Ozzie Guillen	1.00	.45
EL14 Esteban Loaiza	1.00	.45
EL15 Javier Lopez	1.50	.70
EL16 Dennis Martinez	1.50	.70
EL17 Edgar Martinez	2.00	.90
EL18 Tino Martinez	2.50	1.10
EL19 Orlando Merced	1.00	.45
EL20 Jose Mesa	1.00	.45
EL21 Raul Mondesi	2.00	.90

☐ EL22	Jaime Navarro	1.00	.45
☐ EL23	Rafael Palmeiro	2.00	.90
☐ EL24	Carlos Perez	1.00	.45
☐ EL25	Manny Ramirez	2.50	1.10
☐ EL26	Alex Rodriguez	10.00	4.50
☐ EL27	Ivan Rodriguez	4.00	1.80
☐ EL28	David Segui	1.00	.45
☐ EL29	Ruben Sierra	1.00	.45
☐ EL30	Sammy Sosa	2.50	1.10
☐ EL31	Julian Tavarez	1.00	.45
☐ EL32	Ismael Valdes	1.50	.70
☐ EL33	Ferrnando Valenzuela	1.50	.70
☐ EL34	Quilvio Veras	1.00	.45
☐ EL35	Omar Vizquel	1.50	.70
☐ EL36	Bernie Williams	2.50	1.10

1996 Pacific Gold Crown Die Cuts

Randomly inserted in packs at a rate of one in 37, this 36-card set features 1996 Major League Baseball Super Stars. The fronts display color action player photos with a diecut gold crown at the top and gold foil printing. The backs carry a color player portrait and information about the player in English and Spanish.

	MINT	NRMT
COMPLETE SET (36)	450.00	200.00
COMMON CARD (DC1-DC36)	3.00	1.35
SEMISTARS	5.00	2.20
UNLISTED STARS	8.00	3.60
STATED ODDS 1:37		

☐ DC1	Roberto Alomar	8.00	3.60
☐ DC2	Will Clark	5.00	2.20
☐ DC3	Johnny Damon	4.00	1.80
☐ DC4	Don Mattingly	12.00	5.50
☐ DC5	Edgar Martinez	5.00	2.20
☐ DC6	Manny Ramirez	8.00	3.60
☐ DC7	Mike Piazza	25.00	11.00
☐ DC8	Quilvio Veras	3.00	1.35
☐ DC9	Rickey Henderson	5.00	2.20
☐ DC10	Jeff Bagwell	15.00	6.75
☐ DC11	Andres Galarraga	8.00	3.60
☐ DC12	Tim Salmon	8.00	3.60
☐ DC13	Ken Griffey Jr.	40.00	18.00
☐ DC14	Sammy Sosa	8.00	3.60
☐ DC15	Cal Ripken	30.00	13.50
☐ DC16	Raul Mondesi	5.00	2.20
☐ DC17	Jose Canseco	5.00	2.20
☐ DC18	Frank Thomas	30.00	13.50
☐ DC19	Hideo Nomo	20.00	9.00
☐ DC20	Wade Boggs	8.00	3.60
☐ DC21	Reggie Sanders	3.00	1.35
☐ DC22	Carlos Baerga	3.00	1.35
☐ DC23	Mo Vaughn	10.00	4.50
☐ DC24	Ivan Rodriguez	10.00	4.50
☐ DC25	Kirby Puckett	15.00	6.75
☐ DC26	Albert Belle	10.00	4.50
☐ DC27	Vinny Castilla	4.00	1.80
☐ DC28	Greg Maddux	25.00	11.00

☐ DC29	Dante Bichette	4.00	1.80
☐ DC30	Deion Sanders	4.00	1.80
☐ DC31	Chipper Jones	25.00	11.00
☐ DC32	Cecil Fielder	4.00	1.80
☐ DC33	Randy Johnson	8.00	3.60
☐ DC34	Mark McGwire	15.00	6.75
☐ DC35	Tony Gwynn	20.00	9.00
☐ DC36	Barry Bonds	10.00	4.50

1996 Pacific Hometowns

Randomly inserted in packs at a rate of two in 37, this 20-card set features color action player photos with a gold foil border on the left and gold foil printing. The backs carry the player's hometown or city and country and player information printed in both English and Spanish.

	MINT	NRMT
COMPLETE SET (20)	120.00	55.00
COMMON CARD (HP1-HP20)	1.00	.45
STATED ODDS 1:18		

☐ HP1	Mike Piazza	12.00	5.50
☐ HP2	Greg Maddux	12.00	5.50
☐ HP3	Tony Gwynn	10.00	4.50
☐ HP4	Carlos Baerga	1.00	.45
☐ HP5	Don Mattingly	6.00	2.70
☐ HP6	Cal Ripken	15.00	6.75
☐ HP7	Chipper Jones	12.00	5.50
☐ HP8	Andres Galarraga	4.00	1.80
☐ HP9	Manny Ramirez	4.00	1.80
☐ HP10	Roberto Alomar	4.00	1.80
☐ HP11	Ken Griffey Jr.	20.00	9.00
☐ HP12	Jose Canseco	2.50	1.10
☐ HP13	Frank Thomas	15.00	6.75
☐ HP14	Vinny Castilla	2.00	.90
☐ HP15	Roberto Kelly	1.00	.45
☐ HP16	Dennis Martinez	2.00	.90
☐ HP17	Kirby Puckett	8.00	3.60
☐ HP18	Raul Mondesi	2.50	1.10
☐ HP19	Hideo Nomo	10.00	4.50
☐ HP20	Edgar Martinez	2.50	1.10

1996 Pacific Milestones

Randomly inserted in packs at a rate of one in 37, this 10-card set denotes the outstanding milestone and record-breaking achievements of baseball's superstars in 1995. The fronts feature a color action player cut-out on a blue foil background with embossed symbols represting the team logo, baseball, and the milestone or achievement. The backs carry a

player portrait with the milestone or achievement printed in both English and Spanish.

	MINT	NRMT
COMPLETE SET (10)	75.00	34.00
COMMON CARD (M1-M10)	2.00	.90
STATED ODDS 1:37		

☐ M1	Albert Belle	5.00	2.20
☐ M2	Don Mattingly	6.00	2.70
☐ M3	Tony Gwynn	10.00	4.50
☐ M4	Jose Canseco	3.00	1.35
☐ M5	Marty Cordova	2.00	.90
☐ M6	Wade Boggs	4.00	1.80
☐ M7	Greg Maddux	12.00	5.50
☐ M8	Eddie Murray	4.00	1.80
☐ M9	Ken Griffey Jr.	20.00	9.00
☐ M10	Cal Ripken	15.00	6.75

1996 Pacific October Moments

Randomly inserted in packs at a rate of one in 37, this 20-card set highlights 1995 postseason heroics and the players involved. The fronts feature borderless color player action photos with a bronze foil background and printing. The backs carry a player portrait with the heroic action printed in both English and Spanish.

	MINT	NRMT
COMPLETE SET (20)	150.00	70.00
COMMON CARD (OM1-OM20)	2.00	.90
SEMISTARS	4.00	1.80
UNLISTED STARS	6.00	2.70
STATED ODDS 1:37		

☐ OM1	Carlos Baerga	2.00	.90
☐ OM2	Albert Belle	8.00	3.60
☐ OM3	Dante Bichette	3.00	1.35
☐ OM4	Jose Canseco	4.00	1.80

OM5 Tom Glavine	3.00	1.35		
OM6 Ken Griffey Jr.	30.00	13.50		
OM7 Randy Johnson	6.00	2.70		
OM8 Chipper Jones	20.00	9.00		
OM9 David Justice	6.00	2.70		
OM10 Ryan Klesko	4.00	1.80		
OM11 Kenny Lofton	8.00	3.60		
OM12 Javier Lopez	3.00	1.35		
OM13 Greg Maddux	20.00	9.00		
OM14 Edgar Martinez	4.00	1.80		
OM15 Don Mattingly	10.00	4.50		
OM16 Hideo Nomo	15.00	6.75		
OM17 Mike Piazza	20.00	9.00		
OM18 Manny Ramirez	6.00	2.70		
OM19 Reggie Sanders	2.00	.90		
OM20 Jim Thome	6.00	2.70		

1997 Pacific

This 450-card set was issued in one series and distributed in 12-card packs. The fronts feature color action player photos foiled in gold. The backs carry player information in both English and Spanish with player statistics.

	MINT	NRMT
COMPLETE SET (450)	40.00	18.00
COMMON CARD (1-450)	.15	.07
MINOR STARS	.30	.14
UNLISTED STARS	.60	.25
COMP.LT.BLUE SET (450)	300.00	135.00
COMMON LT.BLUE (1-450)	.25	.11

*LT.BLUE STARS: 4X TO 8X HI COLUMN
*LT.BLUE YOUNG STARS: 3X TO 6X HI
ONE LT.BLUE PER WAL-MART PACK

COMP.SILVER SET (450)	8000.00	3600.00
COMMON SILVER (1-450)	12.00	5.50

*SILVER STARS: 60X TO 100X HI COLUMN
*SILVER YOUNG STARS: 50X TO 80X HI
SILVER STATED ODDS 1:73
SILVER STATED PRINT RUN 67 SETS

1 Garret Anderson	.30	.14	22 Scott Erickson	.15	.07	108 Hipolito Pichardo	.15	.07
2 George Arias	.15	.07	23 Jeffrey Hammonds	.15	.07	109 Joe Randa	.15	.07
3 Chili Davis	.30	.14	24 Chris Hoiles	.15	.07	110 Bip Roberts	.15	.07
4 Gary DiSarcina	.15	.07	25 Eddie Murray	.60	.25	111 Chris Stynes	.15	.07
5 Jim Edmonds	.40	.18	26 Mike Mussina	.25	.11	112 Mike Sweeney	.30	.14
6 Darin Erstad	1.00	.45	27 Randy Myers	.15	.07	113 Joe Vitiello	.15	.07
7 Jorge Fabregas	.15	.07	28 Rafael Palmeiro	.40	.18	114 Jeromy Burnitz	.15	.07
8 Chuck Finley	.15	.07	29 Cal Ripken	2.50	1.10	115 Chuck Carr	.15	.07
9 Rex Hudler	.15	.07	30 B.J. Surhoff	.15	.07	116 Jeff Cirillo	.30	.14
10 Mark Langston	.15	.07	31 Tony Tarasco	.15	.07	117 Mike Fetters	.15	.07
11 Orlando Palmeiro	.15	.07	32 Esteban Beltre	.15	.07	118 David Hulse	.15	.07
12 Troy Percival	.15	.07	33 Darren Bragg	.15	.07	119 John Jaha	.15	.07
13 Tim Salmon	.60	.25	34 Jose Canseco	.40	.18	120 Scott Karl	.15	.07
14 J.T. Snow	.30	.14	35 Roger Clemens	1.25	.55	121 Jesse Levis	.15	.07
15 Randy Velarde	.15	.07	36 Wil Cordero	.15	.07	122 Mark Loretta	.15	.07
16 Manny Alexander	.15	.07	37 Alex Delgado	.15	.07	123 Mike Matheny	.15	.07
17 Roberto Alomar	.60	.25	38 Jeff Frye	.15	.07	124 Ben McDonald	.15	.07
18 Brady Anderson	.40	.18	39 Nomar Garciaparra	2.00	.90	125 Matt Mieske	.15	.07
19 Armando Benitez	.15	.07	40 Tom Gordon	.15	.07	126 Angel Miranda	.15	.07
20 Bobby Bonilla	.30	.14	41 Mike Greenwell	.15	.07	127 Dave Nilsson	.15	.07
21 Rocky Coppinger	.15	.07	42 Reggie Jefferson	.15	.07	128 Jose Valentin	.15	.07
			43 Tim Naehring	.15	.07	129 Fernando Vina	.15	.07
			44 Troy O'Leary	.15	.07	130 Ron Villone	.15	.07
			45 Heathcliff Slocumb	.15	.07	131 Gerald Williams	.15	.07
			46 Lee Tinsley	.15	.07	132 Rick Aguilera	.15	.07
			47 John Valentin	.15	.07	133 Rich Becker	.15	.07
			48 Mo Vaughn	.75	.35	134 Ron Coomer	.15	.07
			49 Wilson Alvarez	.15	.07	135 Marty Cordova	.30	.14
			50 Harold Baines	.30	.14	136 Eddie Guardado	.15	.07
			51 Ray Durham	.15	.07	137 Denny Hocking	.15	.07
			52 Alex Fernandez	.30	.14	138 Roberto Kelly	.15	.07
			53 Ozzie Guillen	.15	.07	139 Chuck Knoblauch	.60	.25
			54 Roberto Hernandez	.15	.07	140 Matt Lawton	.15	.07
			55 Ron Karkovice	.15	.07	141 Pat Meares	.15	.07
			56 Darren Lewis	.15	.07	142 Paul Molitor	.60	.25
			57 Norberto Martin	.15	.07	143 Greg Myers	.15	.07
			58 Dave Martinez	.15	.07	144 Jeff Reboulet	.15	.07
			59 Lyle Mouton	.15	.07	145 Scott Stahoviak	.15	.07
			60 Jose Munoz	.15	.07	146 Todd Walker	.30	.14
			61 Tony Phillips	.15	.07	147 Wade Boggs	.60	.25
			62 Kevin Tapani	.15	.07	148 David Cone	.30	.14
			63 Danny Tartabull	.15	.07	149 Mariano Duncan	.15	.07
			64 Frank Thomas	2.50	1.10	150 Cecil Fielder	.30	.14
			65 Robin Ventura	.30	.14	151 Dwight Gooden	.30	.14
			66 Sandy Alomar Jr.	.30	.14	152 Derek Jeter	2.00	.90
			67 Albert Belle	.75	.35	153 Jim Leyritz	.15	.07
			68 Julio Franco	.15	.07	154 Tino Martinez	.60	.25
			69 Brian Giles	.15	.07	155 Paul O'Neill	.30	.14
			70 Danny Graves	.15	.07	156 Andy Pettitte	.60	.25
			71 Orel Hershiser	.30	.14	157 Tim Raines	.30	.14
			72 Jeff Kent	.15	.07	158 Mariano Rivera	.30	.14
			73 Kenny Lofton	.75	.35	159 Ruben Rivera	.30	.14
			74 Dennis Martinez	.30	.14	160 Kenny Rogers	.15	.07
			75 Jack McDowell	.15	.07	161 Darryl Strawberry	.30	.14
			76 Jose Mesa	.15	.07	162 John Wetteland	.15	.07
			77 Charles Nagy	.30	.14	163 Bernie Williams	.60	.25
			78 Manny Ramirez	.60	.25	164 Tony Batista	.15	.07
			79 Julian Tavarez	.15	.07	165 Geronimo Berroa	.15	.07
			80 Jim Thome	.60	.25	166 Mike Bordick	.15	.07
			81 Jose Vizcaino	.15	.07	167 Scott Brosius	.15	.07
			82 Omar Vizquel	.30	.14	168 Brent Gates	.15	.07
			83 Brad Ausmus	.15	.07	169 Jason Giambi	.30	.14
			84 Kimera Bartee	.15	.07	170 Jose Herrera	.15	.07
			85 Raul Casanova	.15	.07	171 Brian Lesher	.15	.07
			86 Tony Clark	.60	.25	172 Damon Mashore	.15	.07
			87 Travis Fryman	.30	.14	173 Mark McGwire	1.25	.55
			88 Bobby Higginson	.30	.14	174 Ariel Prieto	.15	.07
			89 Mark Lewis	.15	.07	175 Carlos Reyes	.15	.07
			90 Jose Lima	.15	.07	176 Matt Stairs	.15	.07
			91 Felipe Lira	.15	.07	177 Terry Steinbach	.15	.07
			92 Phil Nevin	.15	.07	178 John Wasdin	.15	.07
			93 Melvin Nieves	.15	.07	179 Ernie Young	.15	.07
			94 Curtis Pride	.15	.07	180 Rich Amaral	.15	.07
			95 Ruben Sierra	.15	.07	181 Bobby Ayala	.15	.07
			96 Alan Trammell	.30	.14	182 Jay Buhner	.40	.18
			97 Kevin Appier	.30	.14	183 Rafael Carmona	.15	.07
			98 Tim Belcher	.15	.07	184 Norm Charlton	.15	.07
			99 Johnny Damon	.15	.07	185 Joey Cora	.15	.07
			100 Tom Goodwin	.15	.07	186 Ken Griffey Jr.	3.00	1.35
			101 Bob Hamelin	.15	.07	187 Sterling Hitchcock	.15	.07
			102 David Howard	.15	.07	188 Dave Hollins	.15	.07
			103 Jason Jacome	.15	.07	189 Randy Johnson	.60	.25
			104 Keith Lockhart	.15	.07	190 Edgar Martinez	.40	.18
			105 Mike Macfarlane	.15	.07	191 Jamie Moyer	.15	.07
			106 Jeff Montgomery	.15	.07	192 Alex Rodriguez	2.00	.90
			107 Jose Offerman	.15	.07	193 Paul Sorrento	.15	.07

#	Name			#	Name			#	Name		
194	Salomon Torres	.15	.07	280	Ellis Burks	.30	.14	366	Butch Huskey	.30	.14
195	Bob Wells	.15	.07	281	Vinny Castilla	.30	.14	367	Jason Isringhausen	.15	.07
196	Dan Wilson	.15	.07	282	Andres Galarraga	.60	.25	368	Bobby Jones	.15	.07
197	Will Clark	.40	.18	283	Quinton McCracken	.15	.07	369	Lance Johnson	.15	.07
198	Kevin Elster	.15	.07	284	Jayhawk Owens	.15	.07	370	Brent Mayne	.15	.07
199	Rene Gonzales	.15	.07	285	Jeff Reed	.15	.07	371	Alex Ochoa	.15	.07
200	Juan Gonzalez	1.50	.70	286	Bryan Rekar	.15	.07	372	Rey Ordonez	.15	.07
201	Rusty Greer	.30	.14	287	Armando Reynoso	.15	.07	373	Ron Blazier	.15	.07
202	Darryl Hamilton	.15	.07	288	Kevin Ritz	.15	.07	374	Ricky Bottalico	.15	.07
203	Mike Henneman	.15	.07	289	Bruce Ruffin	.15	.07	375	David Doster	.15	.07
204	Ken Hill	.15	.07	290	John Vander Wal	.15	.07	376	Lenny Dykstra	.30	.14
205	Mark McLemore	.15	.07	291	Larry Walker	.60	.25	377	Jim Eisenreich	.15	.07
206	Darren Oliver	.15	.07	292	Walt Weiss	.15	.07	378	Bobby Estalella	.30	.14
207	Dean Palmer	.15	.07	293	Eric Young	.15	.07	379	Gregg Jefferies	.15	.07
208	Roger Pavlik	.15	.07	294	Kurt Abbott	.15	.07	380	Kevin Jordan	.15	.07
209	Ivan Rodriguez	.75	.35	295	Alex Arias	.15	.07	381	Ricardo Jordan	.15	.07
210	Kurt Stillwell	.15	.07	296	Miguel Batista	.15	.07	382	Mickey Morandini	.15	.07
211	Mickey Tettleton	.15	.07	297	Kevin Brown	.30	.14	383	Ricky Otero	.15	.07
212	Bobby Witt	.15	.07	298	Luis Castillo	.30	.14	384	Benito Santiago	.15	.07
213	Tilson Brito	.15	.07	299	Greg Colbrunn	.15	.07	385	Gene Schall	.15	.07
214	Jacob Brumfield	.15	.07	300	Jeff Conine	.30	.14	386	Curt Schilling	.30	.14
215	Miguel Cairo	.30	.14	301	Charles Johnson	.30	.14	387	Kevin Selcik	.15	.07
216	Joe Carter	.30	.14	302	Al Leiter	.15	.07	388	Kevin Stocker	.15	.07
217	Felipe Crespo	.15	.07	303	Robb Nen	.15	.07	389	Jermaine Allensworth	.15	.07
218	Carlos Delgado	.30	.14	304	Joe Orsulak	.15	.07	390	Jay Bell	.30	.14
219	Alex Gonzalez	.15	.07	305	Yorkis Perez	.15	.07	391	Jason Christiansen	.15	.07
220	Shawn Green	.15	.07	306	Edgar Renteria	.30	.14	392	Francisco Cordova	.15	.07
221	Juan Guzman	.15	.07	307	Gary Sheffield	.60	.25	393	Mark Johnson	.15	.07
222	Pat Hentgen	.30	.14	308	Jesus Tavarez	.15	.07	394	Jason Kendall	.30	.14
223	Charlie O'Brien	.15	.07	309	Quilvio Veras	.15	.07	395	Jeff King	.15	.07
224	John Olerud	.30	.14	310	Devon White	.15	.07	396	Jon Lieber	.15	.07
225	Robert Perez	.15	.07	311	Jeff Bagwell	1.25	.55	397	Nelson Liriano	.15	.07
226	Tomas Perez	.15	.07	312	Derek Bell	.15	.07	398	Esteban Loaiza	.15	.07
227	Juan Samuel	.15	.07	313	Sean Berry	.15	.07	399	Al Martin	.15	.07
228	Ed Sprague	.15	.07	314	Craig Biggio	.40	.18	400	Orlando Merced	.15	.07
229	Mike Timlin	.15	.07	315	Doug Drabek	.15	.07	401	Ramon Morel	.15	.07
230	Rafael Belliard	.15	.07	316	Tony Eusebio	.15	.07	402	Luis Alicea	.15	.07
231	Jermaine Dye	.15	.07	317	Ricky Gutierrez	.15	.07	403	Alan Benes	.30	.14
232	Tom Glavine	.30	.14	318	Xavier Hernandez	.15	.07	404	Andy Benes	.30	.14
233	Marquis Grissom	.30	.14	319	Brian L. Hunter	.30	.14	405	Terry Bradshaw	.15	.07
234	Andruw Jones	1.50	.70	320	Darryl Kile	.30	.14	406	Royce Clayton	.15	.07
235	Chipper Jones	2.00	.90	321	Derrick May	.15	.07	407	Dennis Eckersley	.30	.14
236	David Justice	.60	.25	322	Orlando Miller	.15	.07	408	Gary Gaetti	.15	.07
237	Ryan Klesko	.40	.18	323	James Mouton	.15	.07	409	Mike Gallego	.15	.07
238	Mark Lemke	.15	.07	324	Bill Spiers	.15	.07	410	Ron Gant	.30	.14
239	Javier Lopez	.30	.14	325	Pedro Astacio	.15	.07	411	Brian Jordan	.30	.14
240	Greg Maddux	2.00	.90	326	Brett Butler	.30	.14	412	Ray Lankford	.30	.14
241	Fred McGriff	.40	.18	327	Juan Castro	.15	.07	413	John Mabry	.15	.07
242	Denny Neagle	.30	.14	328	Roger Cedeno	.15	.07	414	Willie McGee	.15	.07
243	Eddie Perez	.15	.07	329	Delino DeShields	.15	.07	415	Tom Pagnozzi	.15	.07
244	John Smoltz	.30	.14	330	Karim Garcia	.30	.14	416	Ozzie Smith	.75	.35
245	Mark Wohlers	.15	.07	331	Todd Hollandsworth	.15	.07	417	Todd Stottlemyre	.15	.07
246	Brant Brown	.15	.07	332	Eric Karros	.30	.14	418	Mark Sweeney	.15	.07
247	Scott Bullett	.15	.07	333	Oreste Marrero	.15	.07	419	Andy Ashby	.15	.07
248	Leo Gomez	.15	.07	334	Ramon Martinez	.30	.14	420	Ken Caminiti	.40	.18
249	Luis Gonzalez	.15	.07	335	Raul Mondesi	.40	.18	421	Archi Cianfrocco	.15	.07
250	Mark Grace	.40	.18	336	Hideo Nomo	1.50	.70	422	Steve Finley	.30	.14
251	Jose Hernandez	.15	.07	337	Antonio Osuna	.15	.07	423	Chris Gomez	.15	.07
252	Brooks Kieschnick	.15	.07	338	Chan Ho Park	.60	.25	424	Tony Gwynn	1.50	.70
253	Brian McRae	.15	.07	339	Mike Piazza	2.00	.90	425	Joey Hamilton	.30	.14
254	Jaime Navarro	.15	.07	340	Ismael Valdes	.30	.14	426	Rickey Henderson	.40	.18
255	Mike Perez	.15	.07	341	Moises Alou	.30	.14	427	Trevor Hoffman	.15	.07
256	Rey Sanchez	.15	.07	342	Omar Daal	.15	.07	428	Brian Johnson	.15	.07
257	Ryne Sandberg	.75	.35	343	Jeff Fassero	.15	.07	429	Wally Joyner	.30	.14
258	Scott Servais	.15	.07	344	Cliff Floyd	.15	.07	430	Scott Livingstone	.15	.07
259	Sammy Sosa	.60	.25	345	Mark Grudzielanek	.15	.07	431	Jody Reed	.15	.07
260	Pedro Valdes	.15	.07	346	Mike Lansing	.15	.07	432	Craig Shipley	.15	.07
261	Turk Wendell	.15	.07	347	Pedro Martinez	.60	.25	433	Fernando Valenzuela	.30	.14
262	Bret Boone	.15	.07	348	Sherman Obando	.15	.07	434	Greg Vaughn	.15	.07
263	Jeff Branson	.15	.07	349	Jose Paniagua	.15	.07	435	Rich Aurilia	.15	.07
264	Jeff Brantley	.15	.07	350	Henry Rodriguez	.15	.07	436	Kim Batiste	.15	.07
265	Dave Burba	.15	.07	351	Mel Rojas	.15	.07	437	Jose Bautista	.15	.07
266	Hector Carrasco	.15	.07	352	F.P. Santangelo	.15	.07	438	Rod Beck	.15	.07
267	Eric Davis	.30	.14	353	David Segui	.15	.07	439	Marvin Benard	.15	.07
268	Willie Greene	.15	.07	354	Dave Silvestri	.15	.07	440	Barry Bonds	.75	.35
269	Lenny Harris	.15	.07	355	Ugueth Urbina	.15	.07	441	Shawon Dunston	.15	.07
270	Thomas Howard	.15	.07	356	Rondell White	.30	.14	442	Shawn Estes	.30	.14
271	Barry Larkin	.40	.18	357	Edgardo Alfonzo	.30	.14	443	Osvaldo Fernandez	.15	.07
272	Hal Morris	.15	.07	358	Carlos Baerga	.15	.07	444	Stan Javier	.15	.07
273	Joe Oliver	.15	.07	359	Tim Bogar	.15	.07	445	David McCarty	.15	.07
274	Eric Owens	.15	.07	360	Ricco Brogna	.15	.07	446	Bill Mueller	.15	.07
275	Jose Rijo	.15	.07	361	Alvaro Espinoza	.15	.07	447	Steve Scarsone	.15	.07
276	Reggie Sanders	.15	.07	362	Carl Everett	.15	.07	448	Robby Thompson	.15	.07
277	Eddie Taubensee	.15	.07	363	John Franco	.30	.14	449	Rick Wilkins	.15	.07
278	Jason Bates	.15	.07	364	Bernard Gilkey	.15	.07	450	Matt Williams	.40	.18
279	Dante Bichette	.30	.14	365	Todd Hundley	.30	.14				

1997 Pacific Card-Supials

Randomly inserted in packs at a rate of one in 37, this 36-paired-card insert set features color action player photos of some of the greatest players in the Major Leagues. A smaller card was made to pair with the regular size card of the same player. The backs carry a slot for insertion of the small card.

	MINT	NRMT
COMPLETE SET (72)	550.00	250.00
COMP.LARGE SET (36)	350.00	160.00
COMMON LARGE (1-36)	3.00	1.35
LARGE UNLISTED STARS	6.00	2.70
COMP.MINI SET (36)	200.00	90.00
*MINIS: .25X TO .6X HI COLUMN		
STATED ODDS 1:37		

		MINT	NRMT
☐ 1	Roberto Alomar	6.00	2.70
☐ 2	Brady Anderson	4.00	1.80
☐ 3	Eddie Murray	6.00	2.70
☐ 4	Cal Ripken	25.00	11.00
☐ 5	Jose Canseco	4.00	1.80
☐ 6	Mo Vaughn	8.00	3.60
☐ 7	Frank Thomas	25.00	11.00
☐ 8	Albert Belle	8.00	3.60
☐ 9	Omar Vizquel	3.00	1.35
☐ 10	Chuck Knoblauch	6.00	2.70
☐ 11	Paul Molitor	6.00	2.70
☐ 12	Wade Boggs	6.00	2.70
☐ 13	Derek Jeter	15.00	6.75
☐ 14	Andy Pettitte	6.00	2.70
☐ 15	Mark McGwire	12.00	5.50
☐ 16	Jay Buhner	4.00	1.80
☐ 17	Ken Griffey Jr.	30.00	13.50
☐ 18	Alex Rodriguez	20.00	9.00
☐ 19	Juan Gonzalez	15.00	6.75
☐ 20	Ivan Rodriguez	8.00	3.60
☐ 21	Andruw Jones	15.00	6.75
☐ 22	Chipper Jones	20.00	9.00
☐ 23	Ryan Klesko	4.00	1.80
☐ 24	Greg Maddux	20.00	9.00
☐ 25	Ryne Sandberg	8.00	3.60
☐ 26	Andres Galarraga	6.00	2.70
☐ 27	Gary Sheffield	6.00	2.70
☐ 28	Jeff Bagwell	12.00	5.50
☐ 29	Todd Hollandsworth	3.00	1.35
☐ 30	Hideo Nomo	15.00	6.75
☐ 31	Mike Piazza	20.00	9.00
☐ 32	Todd Hundley	3.00	1.35
☐ 33	Dennis Eckersley	3.00	1.35
☐ 34	Ken Caminiti	4.00	1.80
☐ 35	Tony Gwynn	15.00	6.75
☐ 36	Barry Bonds	8.00	3.60

1997 Pacific Cramer's Choice

Randomly inserted in packs at a rate of one in 721, this 10-card

set features the top Major League Baseball players as chosen by Pacific President and CEO, Michael Cramer. The fronts display a color player cut-out on a pyramid die-cut shaped background. The backs carry information about why the player was selected for this set in both English and Spanish.

	MINT	NRMT
COMPLETE SET (10)	900.00	400.00
COMMON CARD (1-10)	30.00	13.50
STATED ODDS 1:721		

		MINT	NRMT
☐ 1	Roberto Alomar	40.00	18.00
☐ 2	Frank Thomas	150.00	70.00
☐ 3	Albert Belle	50.00	22.00
☐ 4	Andy Pettitte	40.00	18.00
☐ 5	Ken Griffey Jr.	200.00	90.00
☐ 6	Alex Rodriguez	120.00	55.00
☐ 7	Chipper Jones	100.00	45.00
☐ 8	John Smoltz	30.00	13.50
☐ 9	Mike Piazza	120.00	55.00
☐ 10	Tony Gwynn	100.00	45.00

1997 Pacific Fireworks Die Cuts

Randomly inserted in packs at a rate of one in 73, this 20-card set features color action player photos on a fireworks die-cut background. The backs carry player information in both English and Spanish.

	MINT	NRMT
COMPLETE SET (20)	400.00	180.00
COMMON CARD (1-20)	5.00	2.20
UNLISTED STARS	10.00	4.50
STATED ODDS 1:73		

		MINT	NRMT
☐ 1	Roberto Alomar	10.00	4.50
☐ 2	Brady Anderson	6.00	2.70
☐ 3	Eddie Murray	10.00	4.50
☐ 4	Cal Ripken	40.00	18.00
☐ 5	Frank Thomas	40.00	18.00
☐ 6	Albert Belle	12.00	5.50
☐ 7	Derek Jeter	25.00	11.00
☐ 8	Andy Pettitte	10.00	4.50
☐ 9	Bernie Williams	10.00	4.50
☐ 10	Mark McGwire	20.00	9.00
☐ 11	Ken Griffey Jr.	50.00	22.00
☐ 12	Alex Rodriguez	30.00	13.50
☐ 13	Juan Gonzalez	25.00	11.00
☐ 14	Andruw Jones	20.00	9.00
☐ 15	Chipper Jones	30.00	13.50
☐ 16	Hideo Nomo	25.00	11.00
☐ 17	Mike Piazza	30.00	13.50
☐ 18	Henry Rodriguez	5.00	2.20
☐ 19	Tony Gwynn	25.00	11.00
☐ 20	Barry Bonds	12.00	5.50

1997 Pacific Gold Crown Die Cuts

Randomly inserted in packs at a rate of one in 37, this 36-card set honors some of Major League Baseball's Super Stars of today. The fronts feature color action player photos with a die-cut gold crown at the top and gold foil printing. The backs carry player information in both English and Spanish.

	MINT	NRMT
COMPLETE SET (36)	400.00	180.00
COMMON CARD (1-36)	4.00	1.80
UNLISTED STARS	8.00	3.60
STATED ODDS 1:37		

		MINT	NRMT
☐ 1	Roberto Alomar	8.00	3.60
☐ 2	Brady Anderson	5.00	2.20
☐ 3	Mike Mussina	8.00	3.60
☐ 4	Eddie Murray	8.00	3.60
☐ 5	Cal Ripken	30.00	13.50
☐ 6	Jose Canseco	5.00	2.20
☐ 7	Frank Thomas	30.00	13.50
☐ 8	Albert Belle	10.00	4.50
☐ 9	Omar Vizquel	4.00	1.80
☐ 10	Wade Boggs	8.00	3.60
☐ 11	Derek Jeter	20.00	9.00
☐ 12	Andy Pettitte	8.00	3.60
☐ 13	Mariano Rivera	4.00	1.80
☐ 14	Bernie Williams	8.00	3.60
☐ 15	Mark McGwire	15.00	6.75
☐ 16	Ken Griffey Jr.	40.00	18.00
☐ 17	Edgar Martinez	5.00	2.20
☐ 18	Alex Rodriguez	25.00	11.00
☐ 19	Juan Gonzalez	20.00	9.00
☐ 20	Ivan Rodriguez	10.00	4.50
☐ 21	Andruw Jones	15.00	6.75
☐ 22	Chipper Jones	25.00	11.00
☐ 23	Ryan Klesko	5.00	2.20
☐ 24	John Smoltz	4.00	1.80
☐ 25	Ryne Sandberg	10.00	4.50
☐ 26	Andres Galarraga	8.00	3.60
☐ 27	Edgar Renteria	4.00	1.80
☐ 28	Jeff Bugwell	15.00	6.75
☐ 29	Todd Hollandsworth	4.00	1.80
☐ 30	Hideo Nomo	20.00	9.00

		MINT	NRMT
☐ 31	Mike Piazza	25.00	11.00
☐ 32	Todd Hundley	4.00	1.80
☐ 33	Brian Jordan	4.00	1.80
☐ 34	Ken Caminiti	5.00	2.20
☐ 35	Tony Gwynn	20.00	9.00
☐ 36	Barry Bonds	10.00	4.50

1997 Pacific Latinos of the Major Leagues

Randomly inserted in packs at a rate of two in 37, this 36-card set salutes the great Latino players in the Major Leagues today. The fronts feature color player action images on a gold foil background of their name. The backs carry player information in both English and Spanish.

		MINT	NRMT
COMPLETE SET (36)		80.00	36.00
COMMON CARD (1-36)		1.00	.45
MINOR STARS		2.00	.90
UNLISTED STARS		4.00	1.80
STATED ODDS 1:18			

		MINT	NRMT
☐ 1	George Arias	1.00	.45
☐ 2	Roberto Alomar	4.00	1.80
☐ 3	Rafael Palmeiro	2.50	1.10
☐ 4	Bobby Bonilla	2.00	.90
☐ 5	Jose Canseco	2.50	1.10
☐ 6	Wilson Alvarez	1.00	.45
☐ 7	Dave Martinez	1.00	.45
☐ 8	Julio Franco	2.00	.90
☐ 9	Manny Ramirez	4.00	1.80
☐ 10	Omar Vizquel	2.00	.90
☐ 11	Marty Cordova	2.00	.90
☐ 12	Roberto Kelly	1.00	.45
☐ 13	Tino Martinez	4.00	1.80
☐ 14	Mariano Rivera	2.00	.90
☐ 15	Ruben Rivera	2.00	.90
☐ 16	Bernie Williams	4.00	1.80
☐ 17	Geronimo Berroa	1.00	.45
☐ 18	Joey Cora	2.00	.90
☐ 19	Edgar Martinez	2.50	1.10
☐ 20	Alex Rodriguez	12.00	5.50
☐ 21	Juan Gonzalez	10.00	4.50
☐ 22	Ivan Rodriguez	5.00	2.20
☐ 23	Andruw Jones	10.00	4.50
☐ 24	Javier Lopez	2.00	.90
☐ 25	Sammy Sosa	4.00	1.80
☐ 26	Vinny Castilla	2.00	.90
☐ 27	Andres Galarraga	4.00	1.80
☐ 28	Ramon Martinez	2.00	.90
☐ 29	Raul Mondesi	2.50	1.10
☐ 30	Ismael Valdes	2.00	.90
☐ 31	Pedro Martinez	4.00	1.80
☐ 32	Henry Rodriguez	1.00	.45
☐ 33	Carlos Baerga	1.00	.45
☐ 34	Rey Ordonez	1.00	.45
☐ 35	Fernando Valenzuela	2.00	.90
☐ 36	Osvaldo Fernandez	1.00	.45

1997 Pacific Triple Crown Die Cuts

Randomly inserted in packs at a rate of one in 145, this 20-card set features color player images over a gold foil diamond-shaped background with a die-cut gold crown at the top. The backs carry player information in both English and Spanish.

		MINT	NRMT
COMPLETE SET (20)		600.00	275.00
COMMON CARD (1-20)		8.00	3.60
SEMISTARS		10.00	4.50
UNLISTED STARS		15.00	6.75
STATED ODDS 1:145			

		MINT	NRMT
☐ 1	Brady Anderson	10.00	4.50
☐ 2	Rafael Palmeiro	10.00	4.50
☐ 3	Mo Vaughn	20.00	9.00
☐ 4	Frank Thomas	60.00	27.00
☐ 5	Albert Belle	20.00	9.00
☐ 6	Jim Thome	15.00	6.75
☐ 7	Cecil Fielder	8.00	3.60
☐ 8	Mark McGwire	30.00	13.50
☐ 9	Ken Griffey Jr.	80.00	36.00
☐ 10	Alex Rodriguez	50.00	22.00
☐ 11	Juan Gonzalez	40.00	18.00
☐ 12	Andruw Jones	30.00	13.50
☐ 13	Chipper Jones	50.00	22.00
☐ 14	Dante Bichette	8.00	3.60
☐ 15	Ellis Burks	8.00	3.60
☐ 16	Andres Galarraga	15.00	6.75
☐ 17	Jeff Bagwell	30.00	13.50
☐ 18	Mike Piazza	50.00	22.00
☐ 19	Ken Caminiti	10.00	4.50
☐ 20	Barry Bonds	20.00	9.00

1998 Pacific

The 1998 Pacific set was issued in one series totalling 450 cards and distributed in 12-card packs with a suggested retail price of $2.49. The fronts features borderless color player photos with gold foil highlights. The backs carry player information in both Spanish and English.

		MINT	NRMT
COMPLETE SET (450)		50.00	22.00
COMMON CARD (1-450)		.15	.07
MINOR STARS		.30	.14
UNLISTED STARS		.60	.25
COMP.RED SET (450)		300.00	135.00
COMMON RED (1-450)		.30	.14
*RED STARS: 3X TO 6X HI COLUMN			
*RED YOUNG STARS: 2.5X TO 5X HI			
ONE RED PER WAL-MART PACK			
COMP.SILVER SET (450)		250.00	110.00
COMMON SILVER (1-450)		.25	.11
*SILVER STARS: 2.5X TO 5X HI COLUMN			
*SILVER YOUNG STARS: 2X TO 4X HI			
ONE SILVER PER HOBBY PACK			

		MINT	NRMT
☐ 1	Luis Alicea	.15	.07
☐ 2	Garret Anderson	.30	.14
☐ 3	Jason Dickson	.30	.14
☐ 4	Gary DiSarcina	.15	.07
☐ 5	Jim Edmonds	.40	.18
☐ 6	Darin Erstad	.75	.35
☐ 7	Chuck Finley	.15	.07
☐ 8	Shigetoshi Hasegawa	.30	.14
☐ 9	Rickey Henderson	.40	.18
☐ 10	Dave Hollins	.15	.07
☐ 11	Mark Langston	.15	.07
☐ 12	Orlando Palmeiro	.15	.07
☐ 13	Troy Percival	.15	.07
☐ 14	Tony Phillips	.15	.07
☐ 15	Tim Salmon	.60	.25
☐ 16	Allen Watson	.15	.07
☐ 17	Roberto Alomar	.60	.25
☐ 18	Brady Anderson	.40	.18
☐ 19	Harold Baines	.30	.14
☐ 20	Armando Benitez	.15	.07
☐ 21	Geronimo Berroa	.15	.07
☐ 22	Mike Bordick	.15	.07
☐ 23	Eric Davis	.30	.14
☐ 24	Scott Erickson	.15	.07
☐ 25	Chris Hoiles	.15	.07
☐ 26	Jimmy Key	.30	.14
☐ 27	Aaron Ledesma	.15	.07
☐ 28	Mike Mussina	.60	.25
☐ 29	Randy Myers	.15	.07
☐ 30	Jesse Orosco	.15	.07
☐ 31	Rafael Palmeiro	.40	.18
☐ 32	Jeff Reboulet	.15	.07
☐ 33	Cal Ripken	2.50	1.10
☐ 34	B.J. Surhoff	.15	.07
☐ 35	Steve Avery	.15	.07
☐ 36	Darren Bragg	.15	.07
☐ 37	Wil Cordero	.15	.07
☐ 38	Jeff Frye	.15	.07
☐ 39	Nomar Garciaparra	2.00	.90
☐ 40	Tom Gordon	.15	.07
☐ 41	Bill Haselman	.15	.07
☐ 42	Scott Hatteberg	.15	.07
☐ 43	Butch Henry	.15	.07
☐ 44	Reggie Jefferson	.15	.07
☐ 45	Tim Naehring	.15	.07
☐ 46	Troy O'Leary	.15	.07
☐ 47	Jeff Suppan	.15	.07
☐ 48	John Valentin	.15	.07
☐ 49	Mo Vaughn	.75	.35
☐ 50	Tim Wakefield	.15	.07
☐ 51	James Baldwin	.15	.07
☐ 52	Albert Belle	.75	.35
☐ 53	Tony Castillo	.15	.07
☐ 54	Doug Drabek	.15	.07
☐ 55	Ray Durham	.15	.07
☐ 56	Jorge Fabregas	.15	.07
☐ 57	Ozzie Guillen	.15	.07
☐ 58	Matt Karchner	.15	.07
☐ 59	Norberto Martin	.15	.07
☐ 60	Dave Martinez	.15	.07
☐ 61	Lyle Mouton	.15	.07
☐ 62	Jaime Navarro	.15	.07
☐ 63	Frank Thomas	2.50	1.10
☐ 64	Mario Valdez	.30	.14
☐ 65	Robin Ventura	.30	.14

#	Player			#	Player			#	Player		
66	Sandy Alomar Jr.	.30	.14	152	Tino Martinez	.60	.25	238	Kenny Lofton	.75	.35
67	Paul Assenmacher	.15	.07	153	Ramiro Mendoza	.30	.14	239	Javier Lopez	.30	.14
68	Tony Fernandez	.15	.07	154	Paul O'Neill	.30	.14	240	Fred McGriff	.40	.18
69	Brian Giles	.15	.07	155	Andy Pettitte	.60	.25	241	Greg Maddux	2.00	.90
70	Marquis Grissom	.30	.14	156	Jorge Posada	.15	.07	242	Denny Neagle	.30	.14
71	Orel Hershiser	.30	.14	157	Mariano Rivera	.30	.14	243	John Smoltz	.30	.14
72	Mike Jackson	.15	.07	158	Rey Sanchez	.15	.07	244	Michael Tucker	.15	.07
73	David Justice	.60	.25	159	Luis Sojo	.15	.07	245	Mark Wohlers	.15	.07
74	Albie Lopez	.15	.07	160	David Wells	.15	.07	246	Manny Alexander	.15	.07
75	Jose Mesa	.15	.07	161	Bernie Williams	.60	.25	247	Miguel Batista	.15	.07
76	Charles Nagy	.30	.14	162	Rafael Bournigal	.15	.07	248	Mark Clark	.15	.07
77	Chad Ogea	.15	.07	163	Scott Brosius	.15	.07	249	Doug Glanville	.15	.07
78	Manny Ramirez	.60	.25	164	Jose Canseco	.40	.18	250	Jeremi Gonzalez	.30	.14
79	Jim Thome	.60	.25	165	Jason Giambi	.30	.14	251	Mark Grace	.40	.18
80	Omar Vizquel	.30	.14	166	Ben Grieve	1.25	.55	252	Jose Hernandez	.15	.07
81	Matt Williams	.40	.18	167	Dave Magadan	.15	.07	253	Lance Johnson	.15	.07
82	Jaret Wright	1.50	.70	168	Brent Mayne	.15	.07	254	Brooks Kieschnick	.15	.07
83	Willie Blair	.15	.07	169	Jason McDonald	.15	.07	255	Kevin Orie	.30	.14
84	Raul Casanova	.15	.07	170	Izzy Molina	.15	.07	256	Ryne Sandberg	.75	.35
85	Tony Clark	.60	.25	171	Ariel Prieto	.15	.07	257	Scott Servais	.15	.07
86	Deivi Cruz	.15	.07	172	Carlos Reyes	.15	.07	258	Sammy Sosa	.60	.25
87	Damion Easley	.15	.07	173	Scott Spiezio	.30	.14	259	Kevin Tapani	.15	.07
88	Travis Fryman	.30	.14	174	Matt Stairs	.15	.07	260	Ramon Tatis	.15	.07
89	Bobby Higginson	.30	.14	175	Bill Taylor	.15	.07	261	Bret Boone	.15	.07
90	Brian L. Hunter	.30	.14	176	Dave Telgheder	.15	.07	262	Dave Burba	.15	.07
91	Todd Jones	.15	.07	177	Steve Wojciechowski	.15	.07	263	Brook Fordyce	.15	.07
92	Dan Miceli	.15	.07	178	Rich Amaral	.15	.07	264	Willie Greene	.15	.07
93	Brian Moehler	.15	.07	179	Bobby Ayala	.15	.07	265	Barry Larkin	.40	.18
94	Mel Nieves	.15	.07	180	Jay Buhner	.40	.18	266	Pedro A. Martinez	.15	.07
95	Jody Reed	.15	.07	181	Rafael Carmona	.15	.07	267	Hal Morris	.15	.07
96	Justin Thompson	.30	.14	182	Ken Cloude	.30	.14	268	Joe Oliver	.15	.07
97	Bubba Trammell	.30	.14	183	Joey Cora	.30	.14	269	Eduardo Perez	.15	.07
98	Kevin Appier	.30	.14	184	Russ Davis	.15	.07	270	Pokey Reese	.15	.07
99	Jay Bell	.30	.14	185	Jeff Fassero	.15	.07	271	Felix Rodriguez	.15	.07
100	Yamil Benitez	.15	.07	186	Ken Griffey Jr.	3.00	1.35	272	Deion Sanders	.30	.14
101	Johnny Damon	.15	.07	187	Raul Ibanez	.15	.07	273	Reggie Sanders	.15	.07
102	Chili Davis	.30	.14	188	Randy Johnson	.60	.25	274	Jeff Shaw	.15	.07
103	Jermaine Dye	.15	.07	189	Roberto Kelly	.15	.07	275	Scott Sullivan	.15	.07
104	Jed Hansen	.15	.07	190	Edgar Martinez	.40	.18	276	Brett Tomko	.30	.14
105	Jeff King	.15	.07	191	Jamie Moyer	.15	.07	277	Roger Bailey	.15	.07
106	Mike Macfarlane	.15	.07	192	Omar Olivares	.15	.07	278	Dante Bichette	.30	.14
107	Felix Martinez	.15	.07	193	Alex Rodriguez	2.00	.90	279	Ellis Burks	.30	.14
108	Jeff Montgomery	.15	.07	194	Heathcliff Slocumb	.15	.07	280	Vinny Castilla	.30	.14
109	Jose Offerman	.15	.07	195	Paul Sorrento	.15	.07	281	Frank Castillo	.15	.07
110	Dean Palmer	.15	.07	196	Dan Wilson	.15	.07	282	Mike DeJean	.30	.14
111	Hipolito Pichardo	.15	.07	197	Scott Bailes	.15	.07	283	Andres Galarraga	.60	.25
112	Jose Rosado	.15	.07	198	John Burkett	.15	.07	284	Darren Holmes	.15	.07
113	Jeromy Burnitz	.15	.07	199	Domingo Cedeno	.15	.07	285	Kirt Manwaring	.15	.07
114	Jeff Cirillo	.30	.14	200	Will Clark	.40	.18	286	Quinton McCracken	.15	.07
115	Cal Eldred	.15	.07	201	Hanley Frias	.30	.14	287	Neifi Perez	.30	.14
116	John Jaha	.15	.07	202	Juan Gonzalez	1.50	.70	288	Steve Reed	.15	.07
117	Doug Jones	.15	.07	203	Tom Goodwin	.15	.07	289	John Thomson	.15	.07
118	Scott Karl	.15	.07	204	Rusty Greer	.30	.14	290	Larry Walker	.60	.25
119	Jesse Levis	.15	.07	205	Wilson Heredia	.15	.07	291	Walt Weiss	.15	.07
120	Mark Loretta	.15	.07	206	Darren Oliver	.15	.07	292	Kurt Abbott	.15	.07
121	Ben McDonald	.15	.07	207	Bill Ripken	.15	.07	293	Antonio Alfonseca	.15	.07
122	Jose Mercedes	.15	.07	208	Ivan Rodriguez	.60	.25	294	Moises Alou	.30	.14
123	Matt Mieske	.15	.07	209	Lee Stevens	.15	.07	295	Alex Arias	.15	.07
124	Dave Nilsson	.15	.07	210	Fernando Tatis	.60	.25	296	Bobby Bonilla	.30	.14
125	Jose Valentin	.15	.07	211	John Wetteland	.15	.07	297	Kevin Brown	.30	.14
126	Fernando Vina	.15	.07	212	Bobby Witt	.15	.07	298	Craig Counsell	.15	.07
127	Gerald Williams	.15	.07	213	Jacob Brumfield	.15	.07	299	Darren Daulton	.30	.14
128	Rick Aguilera	.15	.07	214	Joe Carter	.30	.14	300	Jim Eisenreich	.15	.07
129	Rich Becker	.15	.07	215	Roger Clemens	1.25	.55	301	Alex Fernandez	.15	.07
130	Ron Coomer	.15	.07	216	Felipe Crespo	.15	.07	302	Felix Heredia	.15	.07
131	Marty Cordova	.30	.14	217	Jose Cruz Jr.	2.50	1.10	303	Livan Hernandez	.40	.18
132	Eddie Guardado	.15	.07	218	Carlos Delgado	.30	.14	304	Charles Johnson	.30	.14
133	LaTroy Hawkins	.15	.07	219	Mariano Duncan	.15	.07	305	Al Leiter	.30	.14
134	Denny Hocking	.15	.07	220	Carlos Garcia	.15	.07	306	Robb Nen	.15	.07
135	Chuck Knoblauch	.60	.25	221	Alex Gonzalez	.15	.07	307	Edgar Renteria	.30	.14
136	Matt Lawton	.15	.07	222	Juan Guzman	.15	.07	308	Gary Sheffield	.60	.25
137	Pat Meares	.15	.07	223	Pat Hentgen	.30	.14	309	Devon White	.15	.07
138	Paul Molitor	.60	.25	224	Orlando Merced	.15	.07	310	Bob Abreu	.30	.14
139	David Ortiz	.30	.14	225	Tomas Perez	.15	.07	311	Brad Ausmus	.15	.07
140	Brad Radke	.30	.14	226	Paul Quantrill	.15	.07	312	Jeff Bagwell	1.25	.55
141	Terry Steinbach	.15	.07	227	Benito Santiago	.15	.07	313	Derek Bell	.15	.07
142	Bob Tewksbury	.15	.07	228	Woody Williams	.15	.07	314	Sean Berry	.15	.07
143	Javier Valentin	.15	.07	229	Rafael Belliard	.15	.07	315	Craig Biggio	.40	.18
144	Wade Boggs	.60	.25	230	Jeff Blauser	.30	.14	316	Ramon Garcia	.15	.07
145	David Cone	.30	.14	231	Pedro Borbon	.15	.07	317	Luis Gonzalez	.15	.07
146	Chad Curtis	.15	.07	232	Tom Glavine	.30	.14	318	Ricky Gutierrez	.15	.07
147	Cecil Fielder	.30	.14	233	Tony Graffanino	.15	.07	319	Mike Hampton	.15	.07
148	Joe Girardi	.15	.07	234	Andruw Jones	1.25	.55	320	Richard Hidalgo	.30	.14
149	Dwight Gooden	.30	.14	235	Chipper Jones	2.00	.90	321	Thomas Howard	.15	.07
150	Hideki Irabu	.30	.14	236	Ryan Klesko	.40	.18	322	Darryl Kile	.30	.14
151	Derek Jeter	1.50	.70	237	Mark Lemke	.15	.07	323	Jose Lima	.15	.07

		MINT	NRMT

□ 324 Shane Reynolds .15 .07
□ 325 Bill Spiers .15 .07
□ 326 Tom Candiotti .15 .07
□ 327 Roger Cedeno .15 .07
□ 328 Greg Gagne .15 .07
□ 329 Karim Garcia .30 .14
□ 330 Wilton Guerrero .15 .07
□ 331 Todd Hollandsworth .15 .07
□ 332 Eric Karros .30 .14
□ 333 Ramon Martinez .30 .14
□ 334 Raul Mondesi .40 .18
□ 335 Otis Nixon .15 .07
□ 336 Hideo Nomo 1.50 .70
□ 337 Antonio Osuna .15 .07
□ 338 Chan Ho Park .60 .25
□ 339 Mike Piazza 2.00 .90
□ 340 Dennis Reyes .30 .14
□ 341 Ismael Valdes .30 .14
□ 342 Todd Worrell .15 .07
□ 343 Todd Zeile .15 .07
□ 344 Darrin Fletcher .15 .07
□ 345 Mark Grudzielanek .15 .07
□ 346 Vladimir Guerrero 1.00 .45
□ 347 Dustin Hermanson .15 .07
□ 348 Mike Lansing .15 .07
□ 349 Pedro Martinez .60 .25
□ 350 Ryan McGuire .15 .07
□ 351 Jose Paniagua .15 .07
□ 352 Carlos Perez .15 .07
□ 353 Henry Rodriguez .15 .07
□ 354 F.P. Santangelo .15 .07
□ 355 David Segui .15 .07
□ 356 Ugueth Urbina .15 .07
□ 357 Marc Valdes .15 .07
□ 358 Jose Vidro .30 .14
□ 359 Rondell White .30 .14
□ 360 Juan Acevedo .15 .07
□ 361 Edgardo Alfonzo .30 .14
□ 362 Carlos Baerga .15 .07
□ 363 Carl Everett .15 .07
□ 364 John Franco .30 .14
□ 365 Bernard Gilkey .15 .07
□ 366 Todd Hundley .30 .14
□ 367 Butch Huskey .30 .14
□ 368 Bobby Jones .15 .07
□ 369 Takashi Kashiwada .60 .25
□ 370 Greg McMichael .15 .07
□ 371 Brian McRae .15 .07
□ 372 Alex Ochoa .15 .07
□ 373 John Olerud .30 .14
□ 374 Rey Ordonez .15 .07
□ 375 Turk Wendell .15 .07
□ 376 Ricky Bottalico .15 .07
□ 377 Rico Brogna .15 .07
□ 378 Len Dykstra .30 .14
□ 379 Bobby Estalella .30 .14
□ 380 Wayne Gomes .15 .07
□ 381 Tyler Green .15 .07
□ 382 Gregg Jefferies .15 .07
□ 383 Mark Leiter .15 .07
□ 384 Mike Lieberthal .15 .07
□ 385 Mickey Morandini .15 .07
□ 386 Scott Rolen 1.50 .70
□ 387 Curt Schilling .30 .14
□ 388 Kevin Stocker .15 .07
□ 389 Danny Tartabull .15 .07
□ 390 Jermaine Allensworth .15 .07
□ 391 Adrian Brown .15 .07
□ 392 Jason Christiansen .15 .07
□ 393 Steve Cooke .15 .07
□ 394 Francisco Cordova .15 .07
□ 395 Jose Guillen .60 .25
□ 396 Jason Kendall .30 .14
□ 397 Jon Lieber .15 .07
□ 398 Esteban Loaiza .15 .07
□ 399 Al Martin .15 .07
□ 400 Kevin Polcovich .15 .07
□ 401 Joe Randa .15 .07
□ 402 Ricardo Rincon .15 .07
□ 403 Tony Womack .15 .07
□ 404 Kevin Young .15 .07
□ 405 Andy Benes .30 .14
□ 406 Royce Clayton .15 .07
□ 407 Delino DeShields .15 .07
□ 408 Mike Difelice .15 .07
□ 409 Dennis Eckersley .30 .14

□ 410 John Frascatore .15 .07
□ 411 Gary Gaetti .15 .07
□ 412 Ron Gant .30 .14
□ 413 Brian Jordan .30 .14
□ 414 Ray Lankford .30 .14
□ 415 Willie McGee .15 .07
□ 416 Mark McGwire 1.50 .70
□ 417 Matt Morris .30 .14
□ 418 Luis Ordaz .15 .07
□ 419 Todd Stottlemyre .15 .07
□ 420 Andy Ashby .15 .07
□ 421 Jim Bruske .15 .07
□ 422 Ken Caminiti .40 .18
□ 423 Will Cunnane .15 .07
□ 424 Steve Finley .30 .14
□ 425 John Flaherty .15 .07
□ 426 Chris Gomez .15 .07
□ 427 Tony Gwynn 1.50 .70
□ 428 Joey Hamilton .30 .14
□ 429 Carlos Hernandez .15 .07
□ 430 Sterling Hitchcock .15 .07
□ 431 Trevor Hoffman .15 .07
□ 432 Wally Joyner .30 .14
□ 433 Greg Vaughn .15 .07
□ 434 Quilvio Veras .15 .07
□ 435 Wilson Alvarez .15 .07
□ 436 Rod Beck .15 .07
□ 437 Barry Bonds .75 .35
□ 438 Jacob Cruz .30 .14
□ 439 Shawn Estes .30 .14
□ 440 Darryl Hamilton .15 .07
□ 441 Roberto Hernandez .15 .07
□ 442 Glenallen Hill .15 .07
□ 443 Stan Javier .15 .07
□ 444 Brian Johnson .15 .07
□ 445 Jeff Kent .15 .07
□ 446 Bill Mueller .15 .07
□ 447 Kirk Rueter .15 .07
□ 448 J.T. Snow .30 .14
□ 449 Julian Tavarez .15 .07
□ 450 Jose Vizcaino .15 .07

1998 Pacific Platinum Blue

Randomly inserted in packs at the rate of one in 73, this 450 card set is parallel to the base set and is similar in design. The difference is found in the platinum blue foil highlights. According to the manufacturer, only 67 sets were produced.

	MINT	NRMT
COMPLETE SET (450)	8000.00	3600.00
COMMON CARD (1-450)	15.00	6.75
MINOR STARS	25.00	11.00
SEMISTARS	40.00	18.00
UNLISTED STARS	60.00	27.00
*STARS 50X TO 100X HI COLUMN		
*YOUNG STARS: 40X TO 80X HI		
STATED ODDS 1:73		
STATED PRINT RUN 67 SETS ..		

□ 33 Cal Ripken 250.00 110.00
□ 39 Nomar Garciaparra 150.00 70.00
□ 63 Frank Thomas 250.00 110.00
□ 82 Jaret Wright 120.00 55.00
□ 151 Derek Jeter 150.00 70.00
□ 186 Ken Griffey Jr. 300.00 135.00
□ 193 Alex Rodriguez 200.00 90.00
□ 202 Juan Gonzalez 150.00 70.00
□ 215 Roger Clemens 120.00 55.00
□ 217 Jose Cruz Jr. 200.00 90.00
□ 235 Chipper Jones 150.00 70.00
□ 241 Greg Maddux 200.00 90.00
□ 312 Jeff Bagwell 120.00 55.00
□ 336 Hideo Nomo 200.00 90.00
□ 339 Mike Piazza 200.00 90.00
□ 386 Scott Rolen 120.00 55.00
□ 416 Mark McGwire 150.00 70.00
□ 427 Tony Gwynn 150.00 70.00

1998 Pacific Cramer's Choice

Randomly inserted in packs at the rate of one in 721, this 10-card set features top Major League players as chosen by Michael Cramer. The fronts display a color player cut-out on a pyramid die-cut shaped background. The backs carry information about why the player was selected for this set in both Spanish and English.

	MINT	NRMT
COMPLETE SET (10)	900.00	400.00
COMMON CARD (1-10)	40.00	18.00
STATED ODDS 1:721		

□ 1 Greg Maddux 120.00 55.00
□ 2 Roberto Alomar 40.00 18.00
□ 3 Cal Ripken 150.00 70.00
□ 4 Nomar Garciaparra 100.00 45.00
□ 5 Larry Walker 40.00 18.00
□ 6 Mike Piazza 120.00 55.00
□ 7 Mark McGwire 100.00 45.00
□ 8 Tony Gwynn 100.00 45.00
□ 9 Ken Griffey Jr. 200.00 90.00
□ 10 Roger Clemens 80.00 36.00

1998 Pacific Gold Crown Die Cuts

Randomly inserted in packs at the rate of one in 37, this 36-card set features color action player photos with a die-cut crown at the top printed on a holographic silver foil background and gold etching on the trim. The backs carry player information in both Spanish and English.

	MINT	NRMT
COMPLETE SET (36)	450.00	200.00
COMMON CARD (1-36)	4.00	1.80

	MINT	NRMT
SEMISTARS	5.00	2.20
UNLISTED STARS	8.00	3.60
STATED ODDS 1:37		

		MINT	NRMT
☐ 1	Chipper Jones	20.00	9.00
☐ 2	Greg Maddux	25.00	11.00
☐ 3	Denny Neagle	4.00	1.80
☐ 4	Roberto Alomar	8.00	3.60
☐ 5	Rafael Palmeiro	5.00	2.20
☐ 6	Cal Ripken	30.00	13.50
☐ 7	Nomar Garciaparra	20.00	9.00
☐ 8	Mo Vaughn	10.00	4.50
☐ 9	Frank Thomas	30.00	13.50
☐ 10	Sandy Alomar Jr.	4.00	1.80
☐ 11	David Justice	8.00	3.60
☐ 12	Manny Ramirez	8.00	3.60
☐ 13	Andres Galarraga	8.00	3.60
☐ 14	Larry Walker	8.00	3.60
☐ 15	Moises Alou	4.00	1.80
☐ 16	Livan Hernandez	5.00	2.20
☐ 17	Gary Sheffield	8.00	3.60
☐ 18	Jeff Bagwell	15.00	6.75
☐ 19	Raul Mondesi	5.00	2.20
☐ 20	Hideo Nomo	20.00	9.00
☐ 21	Mike Piazza	25.00	11.00
☐ 22	Derek Jeter	20.00	9.00
☐ 23	Tino Martinez	8.00	3.60
☐ 24	Bernie Williams	8.00	3.60
☐ 25	Ben Grieve	12.00	5.50
☐ 26	Mark McGwire	20.00	9.00
☐ 27	Tony Gwynn	20.00	9.00
☐ 28	Barry Bonds	10.00	4.50
☐ 29	Ken Griffey Jr.	40.00	18.00
☐ 30	Randy Johnson	8.00	3.60
☐ 31	Edgar Martinez	5.00	2.20
☐ 32	Alex Rodriguez	25.00	11.00
☐ 33	Juan Gonzalez	20.00	9.00
☐ 34	Ivan Rodriguez	10.00	4.50
☐ 35	Roger Clemens	15.00	6.75
☐ 36	Jose Cruz Jr.	25.00	11.00

1998 Pacific Home Run Hitters

Randomly inserted in packs at the rate of one in 73, this 20-card set features color player cut-outs of top home run hitters printed on full-foil cards with the number of home runs they hit in 1997 embossed in the background. The backs carry player information in both Spanish and English.

	MINT	NRMT
COMPLETE SET (20)	300.00	135.00
COMMON CARD (1-20)	5.00	2.20
SEMISTARS	6.00	2.70
UNLISTED STARS	10.00	4.50
STATED ODDS 1:73		

		MINT	NRMT
☐ 1	Rafael Palmeiro	6.00	2.70
☐ 2	Mo Vaughn	12.00	5.50
☐ 3	Sammy Sosa	10.00	4.50
☐ 4	Albert Belle	12.00	5.50

		MINT	NRMT
☐ 5	Frank Thomas	40.00	18.00
☐ 6	David Justice	10.00	4.50
☐ 7	Jim Thome	10.00	4.50
☐ 8	Matt Williams	6.00	2.70
☐ 9	Vinny Castilla	5.00	2.20
☐ 10	Andres Galarraga	10.00	4.50
☐ 11	Larry Walker	10.00	4.50
☐ 12	Jeff Bagwell	20.00	9.00
☐ 13	Mike Piazza	30.00	13.50
☐ 14	Tino Martinez	10.00	4.50
☐ 15	Mark McGwire	25.00	11.00
☐ 16	Barry Bonds	12.00	5.50
☐ 17	Jay Buhner	6.00	2.70
☐ 18	Ken Griffey Jr.	50.00	22.00
☐ 19	Alex Rodriguez	30.00	13.50
☐ 20	Juan Gonzalez	25.00	11.00

1998 Pacific In The Cage

Randomly inserted in packs at the rate of one in 145, this 20-card set features color player cut-outs of the league's best hitters printed on a die-cut card with a laser-cut batting cage as the background. The backs carry player information in both Spanish and English.

	MINT	NRMT
COMPLETE SET (20)	600.00	275.00
COMMON CARD (1-20)	8.00	3.60
SEMISTARS	10.00	4.50
UNLISTED STARS	15.00	6.75
STATED ODDS 1:145		

		MINT	NRMT
☐ 1	Chipper Jones	40.00	18.00
☐ 2	Roberto Alomar	15.00	6.75
☐ 3	Cal Ripken	60.00	27.00
☐ 4	Nomar Garciaparra	60.00	27.00
☐ 5	Frank Thomas	60.00	27.00
☐ 6	Sandy Alomar Jr.	8.00	3.60
☐ 7	David Justice	15.00	6.75
☐ 8	Larry Walker	15.00	6.75
☐ 9	Bobby Bonilla	8.00	3.60
☐ 10	Mike Piazza	50.00	22.00
☐ 11	Tino Martinez	15.00	6.75
☐ 12	Bernie Williams	15.00	6.75
☐ 13	Mark McGwire	40.00	18.00
☐ 14	Tony Gwynn	40.00	18.00
☐ 15	Barry Bonds	20.00	9.00
☐ 16	Ken Griffey Jr.	80.00	36.00
☐ 17	Edgar Martinez	10.00	4.50
☐ 18	Alex Rodriguez	50.00	22.00
☐ 19	Juan Gonzalez	40.00	18.00
☐ 20	Ivan Rodriguez	20.00	9.00

1998 Pacific Latinos of the Major Leagues

Randomly inserted in packs at the rate of two in 37, this 36-

card set features color action photos of top players of Hispanic decent printed on foil cards with images of South and North America, the player's team logo, and the United States Flag in the background. The backs carry player information in both Spanish and English.

	MINT	NRMT
COMPLETE SET (36)	80.00	36.00
COMMON CARD (1-36)	1.00	.45
MINOR STARS	2.00	.90
SEMISTARS	2.50	1.10
UNLISTED STARS	4.00	1.80
STATED ODDS 2:37		

		MINT	NRMT
☐ 1	Andruw Jones	6.00	2.70
☐ 2	Javier Lopez	2.00	.90
☐ 3	Roberto Alomar	4.00	1.80
☐ 4	Geronimo Berroa	1.00	.45
☐ 5	Rafael Palmeiro	2.50	1.10
☐ 6	Nomar Garciaparra	10.00	4.50
☐ 7	Sammy Sosa	4.00	1.80
☐ 8	Ozzie Guillen	1.00	.45
☐ 9	Sandy Alomar Jr.	2.00	.90
☐ 10	Manny Ramirez	4.00	1.80
☐ 11	Omar Vizquel	2.00	.90
☐ 12	Vinny Castilla	2.00	.90
☐ 13	Andres Galarraga	4.00	1.80
☐ 14	Moises Alou	2.00	.90
☐ 15	Bobby Bonilla	2.00	.90
☐ 16	Livan Hernandez	2.50	1.10
☐ 17	Edgar Renteria	2.00	.90
☐ 18	Wilton Guerrero	1.00	.45
☐ 19	Raul Mondesi	2.50	1.10
☐ 20	Ismael Valdes	2.00	.90
☐ 21	Fernando Vina	1.00	.45
☐ 22	Pedro Martinez	4.00	1.80
☐ 23	Edgardo Alfonzo	2.00	.90
☐ 24	Carlos Baerga	1.00	.45
☐ 25	Rey Ordonez	1.00	.45
☐ 26	Tino Martinez	4.00	1.80
☐ 27	Mariano Rivera	2.00	.90
☐ 28	Bernie Williams	4.00	1.80
☐ 29	Jose Canseco	2.50	1.10
☐ 30	Joey Cora	2.00	.90
☐ 31	Roberto Kelly	1.00	.45
☐ 32	Edgar Martinez	2.50	1.10
☐ 33	Alex Rodriguez	12.00	5.50
☐ 34	Juan Gonzalez	10.00	4.50
☐ 35	Ivan Rodriguez	5.00	2.20
☐ 36	Jose Cruz Jr.	12.00	5.50

1998 Pacific Team Checklists

Randomly inserted in packs at the rate of one in 37, this 30-card set features color player photos printed on a die-cut card in the shape of the end of a baseball bat with a laser cut team logo. The two 1998

expansion teams, the Arizona Diamondbacks and the Tampa Bay Devil Rays, are included in these checklists.

	MINT	NRMT
COMPLETE SET (30)	300.00	135.00
COMMON CARD (1-30)	2.00	.90
MINOR STARS	3.00	1.35
SEMISTARS	4.00	1.80
UNLISTED STARS	6.00	2.70
STATED ODDS 1:37		

☐ 1 Tim Salmon	6.00	2.70
Jim Edmonds		
☐ 2 Cal Ripken	25.00	11.00
Roberto Alomar		
☐ 3 Nomar Garciaparra	15.00	6.75
Mo Vaughn		
☐ 4 Frank Thomas	25.00	11.00
Albert Belle		
☐ 5 Sandy Alomar Jr.	6.00	2.70
Manny Ramirez		
☐ 6 Justin Thompson	6.00	2.70
Tony Clark		
☐ 7 Johnny Damon	2.00	.90
Jermaine Dye		
☐ 8 Dave Nilsson	3.00	1.35
Jeff Cirillo		
☐ 9 Paul Molitor	6.00	2.70
Chuck Knoblauch		
☐ 10 Tino Martinez	15.00	6.75
Derek Jeter		
☐ 11 Ben Grieve	10.00	4.50
Jose Canseco		
☐ 12 Ken Griffey Jr.	40.00	18.00
Alex Rodriguez		
☐ 13 Juan Gonzalez	15.00	6.75
Ivan Rodriguez		
☐ 14 Jose Cruz Jr.	25.00	11.00
Roger Clemens		
☐ 15 Greg Maddux	25.00	11.00
Chipper Jones		
☐ 16 Sammy Sosa	6.00	2.70
Mark Grace		
☐ 17 Barry Larkin	4.00	1.80
Deion Sanders		
☐ 18 Larry Walker	6.00	2.70
Andres Galarraga		
☐ 19 Moises Alou	3.00	1.35
Bobby Bonilla		
☐ 20 Jeff Bagwell	12.00	5.50
Craig Biggio		
☐ 21 Mike Piazza	25.00	11.00
Hideo Nomo		
☐ 22 Pedro Martinez	6.00	2.70
Henry Rodriguez		
☐ 23 Rey Ordonez	2.00	.90
Carlos Baerga		
☐ 24 Curt Schilling	12.00	5.50
Scott Rolen		
☐ 25 Al Martin	2.00	.90
Tony Womack		
☐ 26 Mark McGwire	15.00	6.75
Dennis Eckersley		
☐ 27 Tony Gwynn	15.00	6.75
Wally Joyner		
☐ 28 Barry Bonds	8.00	3.60

J.T. Snow
☐ 29 Matt Williams	4.00	1.80
Jay Bell		
☐ 30 Fred McGriff	4.00	1.80
Roberto Hernandez		

1995 Pacific Prisms

This 144-card standard-size set was issued for the first time as a stand alone set instead as an insert alone. Total production of this product was 2,999 individually numbered cases that contained 20 boxes of 36 packs. The full-bleed fronts feature a player photo against a silver prismatic background with the player's name on the bottom. The backs have a full-color photo with some biographical information. The cards are grouped alphabetically according to teams for each league with AL and NL intermingled. There are no key Rookie Cards in this set. A checklist or team logo card was seeded into every pack.

	MINT	NRMT
COMPLETE SET (144)	150.00	70.00
COMMON CARD (1-144)	1.00	.45
SEMISTARS	2.00	.90
UNLISTED STARS	3.00	1.35
COMP.TEAM LOGO SET (28)	5.00	2.20
ONE CL OR TEAM LOGO PER PACK		

☐ 1 David Justice	3.00	1.35
☐ 2 Ryan Klesko	2.00	.90
☐ 3 Javier Lopez	1.50	.70
☐ 4 Greg Maddux	10.00	4.50
☐ 5 Fred McGriff	2.00	.90
☐ 6 Tony Tarasco	1.00	.45
☐ 7 Jeffrey Hammonds	1.50	.70
☐ 8 Mike Mussina	3.00	1.35
☐ 9 Rafael Palmeiro	2.00	.90
☐ 10 Cal Ripken	12.00	5.50
☐ 11 Lee Smith	1.50	.70
☐ 12 Roger Clemens	6.00	2.70
☐ 13 Scott Cooper	1.00	.45
☐ 14 Mike Greenwell	1.50	.70
☐ 15 Carlos Rodriguez	1.00	.45
☐ 16 Mo Vaughn	4.00	1.80
☐ 17 Chili Davis	1.50	.70
☐ 18 Jim Edmonds	2.00	.90
☐ 19 Jorge Fabregas	1.00	.45
☐ 20 Bo Jackson	1.50	.70
☐ 21 Tim Salmon	3.00	1.35
☐ 22 Mark Grace	2.00	.90
☐ 23 Jose Guzman	1.00	.45
☐ 24 Randy Myers	1.00	.45
☐ 25 Rey Sanchez	1.00	.45
☐ 26 Sammy Sosa	3.00	1.35
☐ 27 Wilson Alvarez	1.00	.45

☐ 28 Julio Franco	1.00	.45
☐ 29 Ozzie Guillen	1.00	.45
☐ 30 Jack McDowell	1.00	.45
☐ 31 Frank Thomas	12.00	5.50
☐ 32 Bret Boone	1.00	.45
☐ 33 Barry Larkin	2.00	.90
☐ 34 Hal Morris	1.00	.45
☐ 35 Jose Rijo	1.00	.45
☐ 36 Deion Sanders	1.50	.70
☐ 37 Carlos Baerga	1.00	.45
☐ 38 Albert Belle	4.00	1.80
☐ 39 Kenny Lofton	4.00	1.80
☐ 40 Dennis Martinez	1.50	.70
☐ 41 Manny Ramirez	3.00	1.35
☐ 42 Omar Vizquel	1.50	.70
☐ 43 Dante Bichette	1.50	.70
☐ 44 Marvin Freeman	1.00	.45
☐ 45 Andres Galarraga	3.00	1.35
☐ 46 Mike Kingery	1.00	.45
☐ 47 Danny Bautista	1.00	.45
☐ 48 Cecil Fielder	1.50	.70
☐ 49 Travis Fryman	1.50	.70
☐ 50 Tony Phillips	1.00	.45
☐ 51 Alan Trammell	2.00	.90
☐ 52 Lou Whitaker	1.50	.70
☐ 53 Alex Arias	1.00	.45
☐ 54 Bret Barberie	1.00	.45
☐ 55 Jeff Conine	1.50	.70
☐ 56 Charles Johnson	1.50	.70
☐ 57 Gary Sheffield	3.00	1.35
☐ 58 Jeff Bagwell	6.00	2.70
☐ 59 Craig Biggio	2.00	.90
☐ 60 Doug Drabek	1.00	.45
☐ 61 Tony Eusebio	1.00	.45
☐ 62 Luis Gonzalez	1.50	.70
☐ 63 David Cone	1.50	.70
☐ 64 Bob Hamelin	1.00	.45
☐ 65 Felix Jose	1.00	.45
☐ 66 Wally Joyner	1.50	.70
☐ 67 Brian McRae	1.00	.45
☐ 68 Brett Butler	1.50	.70
☐ 69 Garey Ingram	1.00	.45
☐ 70 Ramon Martinez	1.50	.70
☐ 71 Raul Mondesi	2.00	.90
☐ 72 Mike Piazza	10.00	4.50
☐ 73 Henry Rodriguez	1.50	.70
☐ 74 Ricky Bones	1.00	.45
☐ 75 Pat Listach	1.00	.45
☐ 76 Dave Nilsson	1.00	.45
☐ 77 Jose Valentin	1.00	.45
☐ 78 Rick Aguilera	1.00	.45
☐ 79 Denny Hocking	1.00	.45
☐ 80 Shane Mack	1.00	.45
☐ 81 Pedro Munoz	1.00	.45
☐ 82 Kirby Puckett	6.00	2.70
☐ 83 Dave Winfield	2.00	.90
☐ 84 Moises Alou	1.50	.70
☐ 85 Wil Cordero	1.00	.45
☐ 86 Cliff Floyd	1.00	.45
☐ 87 Marquis Grissom	1.50	.70
☐ 88 Pedro J. Martinez	3.00	1.35
☐ 89 Larry Walker	3.00	1.35
☐ 90 Bobby Bonilla	1.50	.70
☐ 91 Jeromy Burnitz	1.00	.45
☐ 92 John Franco	1.00	.45
☐ 93 Jeff Kent	1.00	.45
☐ 94 Jose Vizcaino	1.00	.45
☐ 95 Wade Boggs	3.00	1.35
☐ 96 Jimmy Key	1.50	.70
☐ 97 Don Mattingly	6.00	2.70
☐ 98 Paul O'Neill	1.50	.70
☐ 99 Luis Polonia	1.00	.45
☐ 100 Danny Tartabull	1.00	.45
☐ 101 Geronimo Berroa	1.00	.45
☐ 102 Rickey Henderson	2.00	.90
☐ 103 Ruben Sierra	1.00	.45
☐ 104 Terry Steinbach	1.00	.45
☐ 105 Darren Daulton	1.00	.70
☐ 106 Mariano Duncan	1.00	.45
☐ 107 Lenny Dykstra	1.50	.70
☐ 108 Mike Lieberthal	1.00	.45
☐ 109 Tony Longmire	1.00	.45
☐ 110 Tom Marsh	1.00	.45
☐ 111 Jay Bell	1.50	.70
☐ 112 Carlos Garcia	1.00	.45
☐ 113 Orlando Merced	1.00	.45

		MINT	NRMT
☐ 114	Andy Van Slyke	1.50	.70
☐ 115	Derek Bell	1.00	.45
☐ 116	Tony Gwynn	8.00	3.60
☐ 117	Luis Lopez	1.00	.45
☐ 118	Bip Roberts	1.00	.45
☐ 119	Rod Beck	1.00	.45
☐ 120	Barry Bonds	4.00	1.80
☐ 121	Darryl Strawberry	1.50	.70
☐ 122	Wm. Van Landingham	1.00	.45
☐ 123	Matt Williams	2.00	.90
☐ 124	Jay Buhner	2.00	.90
☐ 125	Felix Fermin	1.00	.45
☐ 126	Ken Griffey Jr.	15.00	6.75
☐ 127	Randy Johnson	3.00	1.35
☐ 128	Edgar Martinez	2.00	.90
☐ 129	Alex Rodriguez	12.00	5.50
☐ 130	Rene Arocha	1.00	.45
☐ 131	Gregg Jefferies	1.00	.45
☐ 132	Mike Perez	1.00	.45
☐ 133	Ozzie Smith	4.00	1.80
☐ 134	Jose Canseco	2.00	.90
☐ 135	Will Clark	2.00	.90
☐ 136	Juan Gonzalez	8.00	3.60
☐ 137	Ivan Rodriguez	4.00	1.80
☐ 138	Roberto Alomar	3.00	1.35
☐ 139	Joe Carter	1.50	.70
☐ 140	Carlos Delgado	1.50	.70
☐ 141	Alex Gonzalez	1.00	.45
☐ 142	Juan Guzman	1.00	.45
☐ 143	Paul Molitor	3.00	1.35
☐ 144	John Olerud	1.50	.70
☐ CL1	Checklist	.25	.11
☐ CL2	Checklist	.25	.11

1996 Pacific Prisms

This 144-card set features a color action player cut-out over a double-etched silver foil prismatic background. The backs carry a color player portrait with information about the player in both English and Spanish.

	MINT	NRMT
COMPLETE SET (144)	150.00	70.00
COMMON CARD (1-144)	.75	.35
MINOR STARS	1.25	.55
SEMISTARS	2.00	.90
UNLISTED STARS	3.00	1.35
COMP.GOLD SET (144)	600.00	275.00
COMMON GOLD (1-144)	3.00	1.35
*GOLD: 2X TO 4X HI COLUMN		
GOLD STATED ODDS 1:18		

		MINT	NRMT
☐ P1	Tom Glavine	1.25	.55
☐ P2	Chipper Jones	10.00	4.50
☐ P3	David Justice	3.00	1.35
☐ P4	Ryan Klesko	2.00	.90
☐ P5	Javy Lopez	1.25	.55
☐ P6	Greg Maddux	10.00	4.50
☐ P7	Fred McGriff	2.00	.90
☐ P8	Frank Castillo	.75	.35
☐ P9	Luis Gonzalez	.75	.35
☐ P10	Mark Grace	2.00	.90
☐ P11	Brian McRae	.75	.35
☐ P12	Jaime Navarro	.75	.35
☐ P13	Sammy Sosa	3.00	1.35
☐ P14	Bret Boone	.75	.35
☐ P15	Ron Gant	1.25	.55
☐ P16	Barry Larkin	2.00	.90
☐ P17	Reggie Sanders	.75	.35
☐ P18	Benito Santiago	.75	.35
☐ P19	Dante Bichette	1.25	.55
☐ P20	Vinny Castilla	1.25	.55
☐ P21	Andres Galarraga	3.00	1.35
☐ P22	Bryan Rekar	.75	.35
☐ P23	Roberto Alomar	3.00	1.35
☐ P24	Jeff Conine	1.25	.55
☐ P25	Andre Dawson	2.00	.90
☐ P26	Charles Johnson	1.25	.55
☐ P27	Gary Sheffield	3.00	1.35
☐ P28	Quilvio Veras	.75	.35
☐ P29	Jeff Bagwell	6.00	2.70
☐ P30	Derek Bell	.75	.35
☐ P31	Craig Biggio	2.00	.90
☐ P32	Tony Eusebio	.75	.35
☐ P33	Karim Garcia	2.00	.90
☐ P34	Eric Karros	1.25	.55
☐ P35	Ramon Martinez	1.25	.55
☐ P36	Raul Mondesi	2.00	.90
☐ P37	Hideo Nomo	8.00	3.60
☐ P38	Mike Piazza	10.00	4.50
☐ P39	Ismael Valdes	1.25	.55
☐ P40	Moises Alou	1.25	.55
☐ P41	Wil Cordero	.75	.35
☐ P42	Pedro Martinez	3.00	1.35
☐ P43	Mel Rojas	.75	.35
☐ P44	David Segui	.75	.35
☐ P45	Edfardo Alfonzo	2.00	.90
☐ P46	Rico Brogna	.75	.35
☐ P47	John Franco	1.25	.55
☐ P48	Jason Isringhausen	.75	.35
☐ P49	Jose Vizcaino	.75	.35
☐ P50	Ricky Bottalico	.75	.35
☐ P51	Darren Daulton	1.25	.55
☐ P52	Lenny Dykstra	1.25	.55
☐ P53	Tyler Green	.75	.35
☐ P54	Gregg Jefferies	.75	.35
☐ P55	Jay Bell	1.25	.55
☐ P56	Jason Christiansen	.75	.35
☐ P57	Carlos Garcia	.75	.35
☐ P58	Esteban Loaiza	.75	.35
☐ P59	Orlando Merced	.75	.35
☐ P60	Andujar Cedeno	.75	.35
☐ P61	Tony Gwynn	8.00	3.60
☐ P62	Melvin Nieves	.75	.35
☐ P63	Phil Plantier	.75	.35
☐ P64	Fernando Valenzuela	1.25	.55
☐ P65	Barry Bonds	4.00	1.80
☐ P66	J.R. Phillips	.75	.35
☐ P67	Deion Sanders	1.25	.55
☐ P68	Matt Williams	2.00	.90
☐ P69	Bernard Gilkey	.75	.35
☐ P70	Tom Henke	.75	.35
☐ P71	Brian Jordan	1.25	.55
☐ P72	Ozzie Smith	4.00	1.80
☐ P73	Manny Alexander	.75	.35
☐ P74	Bobby Bonilla	1.25	.55
☐ P75	Mike Mussina	3.00	1.35
☐ P76	Rafael Palmeiro	2.00	.90
☐ P77	Cal Ripken	12.00	5.50
☐ P78	Jose Canseco	2.00	.90
☐ P79	Roger Clemens	6.00	2.70
☐ P80	John Valentin	.75	.35
☐ P81	Mo Vaughn	4.00	1.80
☐ P82	Tim Wakefield	.75	.35
☐ P83	Garret Anderson	1.25	.55
☐ P84	Damion Easley	.75	.35
☐ P85	Jim Edmonds	2.00	.90
☐ P86	Tim Salmon	3.00	1.35
☐ P87	Wilson Alvarez	.75	.35
☐ P88	Alex Fernandez	.75	.35
☐ P89	Ozzie Guillen	.75	.35
☐ P90	Roberto Hernandez	.75	.35
☐ P91	Frank Thomas	12.00	5.50
☐ P92	Robin Ventura	1.25	.55
☐ P93	Carlos Baerga	.75	.35
☐ P94	Albert Belle	4.00	1.80
☐ P95	Kenny Lofton	4.00	1.80
☐ P96	Dennis Martinez	1.25	.55
☐ P97	Eddie Murray	3.00	1.35
☐ P98	Manny Ramirez	3.00	1.35
☐ P99	Omar Vizquel	1.25	.55
☐ P100	Chad Curtis	.75	.35
☐ P101	Cecil Fielder	1.25	.55
☐ P102	Felipe Lira	.75	.35
☐ P103	Alan Trammell	2.00	.90
☐ P104	Kevin Appier	1.25	.55
☐ P105	Johnny Damon	1.25	.55
☐ P106	Gary Gaetti	.75	.35
☐ P107	Wally Joyner	1.25	.55
☐ P108	Ricky Bones	.75	.35
☐ P109	John Jaha	.75	.35
☐ P110	B.J. Surhoff	.75	.35
☐ P111	Jose Valentin	.75	.35
☐ P112	Fernando Vina	.75	.35
☐ P113	Marty Cordova	1.25	.55
☐ P114	Chuck Knoblauch	3.00	1.35
☐ P115	Scott Leius	.75	.35
☐ P116	Pedro Munoz	.75	.35
☐ P117	Kirby Puckett	6.00	2.70
☐ P118	Wade Boggs	3.00	1.35
☐ P119	Don Mattingly	5.00	2.20
☐ P120	Jack McDowell	1.25	.55
☐ P121	Paul O'Neill	1.25	.55
☐ P122	Ruben Rivera	.75	.35
☐ P123	Bernie Williams	3.00	1.35
☐ P124	Geronimo Berroa	.75	.35
☐ P125	Rickey Henderson	2.00	.90
☐ P126	Mark McGwire	6.00	2.70
☐ P127	Terry Steinbach	.75	.35
☐ P128	Danny Tartabull	.75	.35
☐ P129	Jay Buhner	2.00	.90
☐ P130	Joey Cora	1.25	.55
☐ P131	Ken Griffey Jr.	15.00	6.75
☐ P132	Randy Johnson	3.00	1.35
☐ P133	Edgar Martinez	2.00	.90
☐ P134	Tino Martinez	3.00	1.35
☐ P135	Will Clark	2.00	.90
☐ P136	Juan Gonzalez	8.00	3.60
☐ P137	Dean Palmer	.75	.35
☐ P138	Ivan Rodriguez	4.00	1.80
☐ P139	Mickey Tettleton	.75	.35
☐ P140	Larry Walker	3.00	1.35
☐ P141	Joe Carter	1.25	.55
☐ P142	Carlos Delgado	1.25	.55
☐ P143	Alex Gonzalez	.75	.35
☐ P144	Paul Molitor	3.00	1.35

1996 Pacific Prisms Fence Busters

Randomly inserted in packs at a rate of one in 37, this 20-card set highlights 20 of baseball's hardest hitters. The fronts feature an embossed color player action cut-out with a borderless foil baseball field as background. The backs carry a player photo with information as to why the player was selected for this set in both English and Spanish.

	MINT	NRMT
COMPLETE SET (20)	180.00	80.00
COMMON CARD (1-20)	4.00	1.80
SEMISTARS	5.00	2.20
UNLISTED STARS	8.00	3.60
STATED ODDS 1:37		

		MINT	NRMT
☐ FB1	Albert Belle	10.00	4.50
☐ FB2	Dante Bichette	4.00	1.80
☐ FB3	Barry Bonds	10.00	4.50
☐ FB4	Jay Buhner	5.00	2.20
☐ FB5	Jose Canseco	5.00	2.20
☐ FB6	Ken Griffey Jr.	40.00	18.00
☐ FB7	Chipper Jones	25.00	11.00
☐ FB8	Dave Justice	8.00	3.60
☐ FB9	Eric Karros	4.00	1.80
☐ FB10	Edgar Martinez	5.00	2.20
☐ FB11	Mark McGwire	15.00	6.75
☐ FB12	Eddie Murray	8.00	3.60
☐ FB13	Mike Piazza	25.00	11.00
☐ FB14	Kirby Puckett	15.00	6.75
☐ FB15	Cal Ripken	30.00	13.50
☐ FB16	Tim Salmon	8.00	3.60
☐ FB17	Sammy Sosa	8.00	3.60
☐ FB18	Frank Thomas	30.00	13.50
☐ FB19	Mo Vaughn	10.00	4.50
☐ FB20	Larry Walker	8.00	3.60

1996 Pacific Prisms Flame Throwers

Randomly inserted in packs at a rate of one in 73, this 10-card set features 10 of Major League Baseball's hardest throwing pitchers. The fronts display a color action player photo printed on a diecut baseball-shaped card with gold foil flames indicating the force of the thrown ball. The backs carry another player photo with information of why the player was selected for this set printed in both English and Spanish.

	MINT	NRMT
COMPLETE SET (10)	150.00	70.00
COMMON CARD (1-10)	5.00	2.20
MINOR STARS	8.00	3.60
SEMISTARS	12.00	5.50
STATED ODDS 1:73		

		MINT	NRMT
☐ FT1	Randy Johnson	20.00	9.00
☐ FT2	Mike Mussina	20.00	9.00
☐ FT3	Roger Clemens	40.00	18.00
☐ FT4	Tom Glavine	8.00	3.60
☐ FT5	Hideo Nomo	50.00	22.00
☐ FT6	Jose Rijo	5.00	2.20

		MINT	NRMT
☐ FT7	Greg Maddux	60.00	27.00
☐ FT8	David Cone	8.00	3.60
☐ FT9	Ramon Martinez	8.00	3.60
☐ FT10	Jose Mesa	5.00	2.20

1996 Pacific Prisms Red Hot Stars

Randomly inserted in packs at a rate of one in 37, this 20-card set features 20 of Major League Baseball's hottest stars. The fronts display a color action player cut-out on a red foil background. The backs carry a color player photo with information about the player printed in both English and Spanish.

	MINT	NRMT
COMPLETE SET (20)	250.00	110.00
COMMON CARD (1-20)	5.00	2.20
UNLISTED STARS	8.00	3.60
STATED ODDS 1:37		

		MINT	NRMT
☐ RH1	Roberto Alomar	8.00	3.60
☐ RH2	Jose Canseco	5.00	2.20
☐ RH3	Chipper Jones	25.00	11.00
☐ RH4	Mike Piazza	25.00	11.00
☐ RH5	Tim Salmon	8.00	3.60
☐ RH6	Jeff Bagwell	15.00	6.75
☐ RH7	Ken Griffey Jr.	40.00	18.00
☐ RH8	Greg Maddux	25.00	11.00
☐ RH9	Kirby Puckett	15.00	6.75
☐ RH10	Frank Thomas	30.00	13.50
☐ RH11	Albert Belle	10.00	4.50
☐ RH12	Tony Gwynn	20.00	9.00
☐ RH13	Edgar Martinez	5.00	2.20
☐ RH14	Manny Ramirez	8.00	3.60
☐ RH15	Barry Bonds	10.00	4.50
☐ RH16	Wade Boggs	8.00	3.60
☐ RH17	Randy Johnson	8.00	3.60
☐ RH18	Don Mattingly	12.00	5.50
☐ RH19	Cal Ripken	40.00	18.00
☐ RH20	Mo Vaughn	10.00	4.50

1997 Pacific Prisms

The 1997 Pacific Prism set was issued in one series totalling 150 cards and displays color action photos of many of the top players from last season. Foiled in gold, the set features a visually stunning inlaid transparent cel on each card. The backs carry player information in both Spanish and English.

	MINT	NRMT
COMPLETE SET (150)	180.00	80.00
COMMON CARD (1-150)	1.00	.45
SEMISTARS	2.00	.90
UNLISTED STARS	2.50	1.10
COMP.LT.BLUE SET (150)	900.00	400.00
COMMON LT.BLUE (1-150)	6.00	2.70
*LT.BLUE STARS: 3X TO 6X HI COLUMN		
LT.BLUE STAT.ODDS 1:18 WAL-MART/SAM'S		
COMP.PLAT.SET (150)	750.00	350.00
COMMON PLAT. (1-150)	5.00	2.20
*PLATINUM STARS: 2.5X TO 5X HI COLUMN		
PLATINUM STATED ODDS 1:18 HOBBY		

		MINT	NRMT
☐ 1	Chili Davis	1.50	.70
☐ 2	Jim Edmonds	2.00	.90
☐ 3	Darin Erstad	5.00	2.20
☐ 4	Orlando Palmeiro	1.00	.45
☐ 5	Tim Salmon	2.50	1.10
☐ 6	J.T. Snow	1.50	.70
☐ 7	Roberto Alomar	3.00	1.35
☐ 8	Brady Anderson	2.00	.90
☐ 9	Eddie Murray	3.00	1.35
☐ 10	Mike Mussina	3.00	1.35
☐ 11	Rafael Palmeiro	2.00	.90
☐ 12	Cal Ripken	12.00	5.50
☐ 13	Jose Canseco	2.00	.90
☐ 14	Roger Clemens	6.00	2.70
☐ 15	Nomar Garciaparra	10.00	4.50
☐ 16	Reggie Jefferson	1.00	.45
☐ 17	Mo Vaughn	4.00	1.80
☐ 18	Wilson Alvarez	1.00	.45
☐ 19	Harold Baines	1.50	.70
☐ 20	Alex Fernandez	1.50	.70
☐ 21	Danny Tartabull	1.00	.45
☐ 22	Frank Thomas	12.00	5.50
☐ 23	Robin Ventura	1.50	.70
☐ 24	Sandy Alomar Jr.	1.50	.70
☐ 25	Albert Belle	4.00	1.80
☐ 26	Kenny Lofton	4.00	1.80
☐ 27	Jim Thome	3.00	1.35
☐ 28	Omar Vizquel	1.50	.70
☐ 29	Raul Casanova	1.00	.45
☐ 30	Tony Clark	2.50	1.10
☐ 31	Travis Fryman	1.50	.70
☐ 32	Bobby Higginson	1.50	.70
☐ 33	Melvin Nieves	1.00	.45
☐ 34	Justin Thompson	1.50	.70
☐ 35	Johnny Damon	1.00	.45
☐ 36	Tom Goodwin	1.00	.45
☐ 37	Jeff Montgomery	1.00	.45
☐ 38	Jose Offerman	1.00	.45
☐ 39	John Jaha	1.00	.45
☐ 40	Jeff Cirillo	1.50	.70
☐ 41	Dave Nilsson	1.00	.45
☐ 42	Jose Valentin	1.00	.45
☐ 43	Fernando Vina	1.00	.45
☐ 44	Marty Cordova	1.50	.70
☐ 45	Roberto Kelly	1.00	.45
☐ 46	Chuck Knoblauch	2.50	1.10
☐ 47	Paul Molitor	3.00	1.35
☐ 48	Todd Walker	1.50	.70
☐ 49	Wade Boggs	2.50	1.10
☐ 50	Cecil Fielder	1.50	.70
☐ 51	Derek Jeter	10.00	4.50
☐ 52	Tino Martinez	2.50	1.10
☐ 53	Andy Pettitte	3.00	1.35
☐ 54	Mariano Rivera	1.50	.70

55	Bernie Williams	2.50	1.10
56	Tony Batista	1.00	.45
57	Geronimo Berroa	1.00	.45
58	Jason Giambi	1.50	.70
59	Mark McGwire	6.00	2.70
60	Terry Steinbach	1.00	.45
61	Jay Buhner	2.00	.90
62	Joey Cora	1.50	.70
63	Ken Griffey Jr.	15.00	6.75
64	Edgar Martinez	2.00	.90
65	Alex Rodriguez	12.00	5.50
66	Paul Sorrento	1.00	.45
67	Will Clark	2.00	.90
68	Juan Gonzalez	8.00	3.60
69	Rusty Greer	1.50	.70
70	Dean Palmer	1.00	.45
71	Ivan Rodriguez	4.00	1.80
72	Joe Carter	1.50	.70
73	Carlos Delgado	1.50	.70
74	Juan Guzman	1.00	.45
75	Pat Hentgen	1.50	.70
76	Ed Sprague	1.00	.45
77	Jermaine Dye	1.00	.45
78	Andruw Jones	8.00	3.60
79	Chipper Jones	10.00	4.50
80	Ryan Klesko	2.00	.90
81	Javier Lopez	1.50	.70
82	Greg Maddux	10.00	4.50
83	John Smoltz	1.50	.70
84	Mark Grace	2.00	.90
85	Luis Gonzalez	1.00	.45
86	Brooks Kieschnick	1.00	.45
87	Jaime Navarro	1.00	.45
88	Ryne Sandberg	4.00	1.80
89	Sammy Sosa	2.50	1.10
90	Bret Boone	1.00	.45
91	Jeff Brantley	1.00	.45
92	Eric Davis	1.50	.70
93	Barry Larkin	2.00	.90
94	Reggie Sanders	1.00	.45
95	Ellis Burks	1.50	.70
96	Dante Bichette	1.50	.70
97	Vinny Castilla	1.50	.70
98	Andres Galarraga	2.00	1.10
99	Eric Young	1.00	.45
100	Kevin Brown	1.50	.70
101	Jeff Conine	1.50	.70
102	Charles Johnson	1.50	.70
103	Edgar Renteria	1.50	.70
104	Gary Sheffield	2.50	1.10
105	Jeff Bagwell	6.00	2.70
106	Derek Bell	1.00	.45
107	Sean Berry	1.00	.45
108	Craig Biggio	2.00	.90
109	Shane Reynolds	1.00	.45
110	Karim Garcia	1.50	.70
111	Todd Hollandsworth	1.00	.45
112	Ramon Martinez	1.50	.70
113	Raul Mondesi	2.00	.90
114	Hideo Nomo	8.00	3.60
115	Mike Piazza	10.00	4.50
116	Ismael Valdes	1.50	.70
117	Moises Alou	1.50	.70
118	Mark Grudzielanek	1.00	.45
119	Pedro Martinez	2.50	1.10
120	Henry Rodriguez	1.00	.45
121	F.P. Santangelo	1.00	.45
122	Carlos Baerga	1.00	.45
123	Bernard Gilkey	1.00	.45
124	Todd Hundley	1.50	.70
125	Lance Johnson	1.00	.45
126	Alex Ochoa	1.00	.45
127	Rey Ordonez	1.00	.45
128	Lenny Dykstra	1.50	.70
129	Gregg Jefferies	1.00	.45
130	Ricky Otero	1.00	.45
131	Benito Santiago	1.00	.45
132	Jermaine Allensworth	1.00	.45
133	Francisco Cordova	1.00	.45
134	Carlos Garcia	1.00	.45
135	Jason Kendall	1.50	.70
136	Al Martin	1.00	.45
137	Dennis Eckersley	1.50	.70
138	Ron Gant	1.50	.70
139	Brian Jordan	1.50	.70
140	John Mabry	1.00	.45
141	Ozzie Smith	4.00	1.80
142	Ken Caminiti	2.00	.90
143	Steve Finley	1.50	.70
144	Tony Gwynn	8.00	3.60
145	Wally Joyner	1.50	.70
146	Fernando Valenzuela	1.50	.70
147	Barry Bonds	4.00	1.80
148	Jacob Cruz	1.50	.70
149	Osvaldo Fernandez	1.00	.45
150	Matt Williams	2.00	.90

1997 Pacific Prisms Gate Attractions

Randomly inserted in packs at a rate of one in 73, this 32-card set features some of the league's current most popular players. The fronts display a player image on a baseball inside a borderless photo of the inside of a baseball glove as background. The backs contain player information in both Spanish and English.

		MINT	NRMT
COMPLETE SET (32)		600.00	275.00
COMMON CARD (GA1-GA32)		6.00	2.70
UNLISTED STARS		12.00	5.50
STATED ODDS 1:73			
GA1	Roberto Alomar	12.00	5.50
GA2	Brady Anderson	8.00	3.60
GA3	Cal Ripken	50.00	22.00
GA4	Frank Thomas	50.00	22.00
GA5	Kenny Lofton	15.00	6.75
GA6	Omar Vizquel	6.00	2.70
GA7	Paul Molitor	12.00	5.50
GA8	Wade Boggs	12.00	5.50
GA9	Derek Jeter	30.00	13.50
GA10	Andy Pettitte	12.00	5.50
GA11	Bernie Williams	12.00	5.50
GA12	Geronimo Berroa	6.00	2.70
GA13	Mark McGwire	25.00	11.00
GA14	Ken Griffey Jr.	60.00	27.00
GA15	Alex Rodriguez	40.00	18.00
GA16	Juan Gonzalez	30.00	13.50
GA17	Andruw Jones	25.00	11.00
GA18	Chipper Jones	40.00	18.00
GA19	Greg Maddux	40.00	18.00
GA20	Ryne Sandberg	15.00	6.75
GA21	Sammy Sosa	12.00	5.50
GA22	Andres Galarraga	12.00	5.50
GA23	Jeff Bagwell	25.00	11.00
GA24	Todd Hollandsworth	6.00	2.70
GA25	Hideo Nomo	30.00	13.50
GA26	Mike Piazza	40.00	18.00
GA27	Todd Hundley	6.00	2.70
GA28	Lance Johnson	6.00	2.70
GA29	Ozzie Smith	15.00	6.75
GA30	Ken Caminiti	8.00	3.60
GA31	Tony Gwynn	30.00	13.50
GA32	Barry Bonds	15.00	6.75

1997 Pacific Prisms Gems of the Diamond

Randomly inserted at the rate of approximately two per pack, this 220 card bonus set features color action photos with the player's name printed in the bottom gold border. A diamond replica displays the name of the player's team. The backs carry player information in both Spanish and English.

		MINT	NRMT
COMPLETE SET (220)		60.00	27.00
COMMON CARD (GD1-GD220)		.25	.11
MINOR STARS		.50	.23
UNLISTED STARS		1.00	.45
STATED ODDS 2:1			
GD1	Jim Abbott	.25	.11
GD2	Shawn Boskie	.25	.11
GD3	Gary Disarcina	.25	.11
GD4	Jim Edmonds	.75	.35
GD5	Todd Greene	.50	.23
GD6	Jack Howell	.25	.11
GD7	Jeff Schmidt	.25	.11
GD8	Shad Williams	.25	.11
GD9	Roberto Alomar	1.00	.45
GD10	Cesar Devarez	.25	.11
GD11	Alan Mills	.25	.11
GD12	Eddie Murray	1.00	.45
GD13	Jesse Orosco	.25	.11
GD14	Arthur Rhodes	.25	.11
GD15	Bill Ripken	.25	.11
GD16	Cal Ripken	4.00	1.80
GD17	Mark Smith	.25	.11
GD18	Roger Clemens	2.00	.90
GD19	Vaughn Eshelman	.25	.11
GD20	Rich Garces	.25	.11
GD21	Bill Haselman	.25	.11
GD22	Dwayne Hosey	.25	.11
GD23	Mike Maddux	.25	.11
GD24	Jose Malave	.25	.11
GD25	Aaron Sele	.25	.11
GD26	James Baldwin	.25	.11
GD27	Pat Borders	.25	.11
GD28	Mike Cameron	.75	.35
GD29	Tony Castillo	.25	.11
GD30	Domingo Cedeno	.25	.11
GD31	Greg Norton	.25	.11
GD32	Frank Thomas	4.00	1.80
GD33	Albert Belle	1.25	.55
GD34	Edgar Blanco	.25	.11
GD35	Alan Embree	.25	.11
GD36	Albie Lopez	.25	.11
GD37	Chad Ogea	.25	.11
GD38	Tony Pena	.25	.11
GD39	Joe Roa	.25	.11
GD40	Fausto Cruz	.25	.11
GD41	Joey Eischen	.25	.11
GD42	Travis Fryman	.50	.23
GD43	Mike Myers	.25	.11
GD44	A.J. Sager	.25	.11

☐ GD45 Duane Singleton	.25	.11
☐ GD46 Justin Thompson	.50	.23
☐ GD47 Jeff Granger	.25	.11
☐ GD48 Les Norman	.25	.11
☐ GD49 Jon Nunnally	.25	.11
☐ GD50 Craig Paquette	.25	.11
☐ GD51 Michael Tucker	.50	.23
☐ GD52 Julio Valera	.25	.11
☐ GD53 Kevin Young	.25	.11
☐ GD54 Cal Eldred	.25	.11
☐ GD55 Ramon Garcia	.25	.11
☐ GD56 Marc Newfield	.25	.11
☐ GD57 Al Reyes	.25	.11
☐ GD58 Tim Unroe	.25	.11
☐ GD59 Tim Vanegmond	.25	.11
☐ GD60 Turner Ward	.25	.11
☐ GD61 Bob Wickman	.25	.11
☐ GD62 Chuck Knoblauch	1.00	.45
☐ GD63 Paul Molitor	1.00	.45
☐ GD64 Kirby Puckett	2.00	.90
☐ GD65 Tom Quinlan	.25	.11
☐ GD66 Rich Robertson	.25	.11
☐ GD67 Dave Stevens	.25	.11
☐ GD68 Matt Walbeck	.25	.11
☐ GD69 Wade Boggs	1.00	.45
☐ GD70 Tony Fernandez	.25	.11
☐ GD71 Andy Fox	.25	.11
☐ GD72 Joe Girardi	.25	.11
☐ GD73 Charlie Hayes	.25	.11
☐ GD74 Pat Kelly	.25	.11
☐ GD75 Jeff Nelson	.25	.11
☐ GD76 Melido Perez	.25	.11
☐ GD77 Mark Acre	.25	.11
☐ GD78 Allen Battle	.25	.11
☐ GD79 Rafael Bournigal	.25	.11
☐ GD80 Mark McGwire	2.00	.90
☐ GD81 Pedro Munoz	.25	.11
☐ GD82 Scott Spiezio	.50	.23
☐ GD83 Don Wengert	.25	.11
☐ GD84 Steve Wojciechowski	.25	.11
☐ GD85 Alex Diaz	.25	.11
☐ GD86 Ken Griffey Jr.	5.00	2.20
☐ GD87 Raul Ibanez	.25	.11
☐ GD88 Mike Jackson	.25	.11
☐ GD89 John Marzano	.25	.11
☐ GD90 Greg McCarthy	.25	.11
☐ GD91 Alex Rodriguez	3.00	1.35
☐ GD92 Andy Sheets	.25	.11
☐ GD93 Mac Suzuki	.25	.11
☐ GD94 Benji Gil	.25	.11
☐ GD95 Juan Gonzalez	2.50	1.10
☐ GD96 Kevin Gross	.25	.11
☐ GD97 Gil Heredia	.25	.11
☐ GD98 Luis Ortiz	.25	.11
☐ GD99 Jeff Russell	.25	.11
☐ GD100 Dave Valle	.25	.11
☐ GD101 Marty Janzen	.25	.11
☐ GD102 Sandy Martinez	.25	.11
☐ GD103 Julio Mosquera	.25	.11
☐ GD104 Otis Nixon	.25	.11
☐ GD105 Paul Spoljaric	.25	.11
☐ GD106 Shannon Stewart	.50	.23
☐ GD107 Woody Williams	.25	.11
☐ GD108 Steve Avery	.25	.11
☐ GD109 Mike Bielecki	.25	.11
☐ GD110 Pedro Borbon	.25	.11
☐ GD111 Ed Giovanola	.25	.11
☐ GD112 Chipper Jones	3.00	1.35
☐ GD113 Greg Maddux	3.00	1.35
☐ GD114 Mike Mordecai	.25	.11
☐ GD115 Terrell Wade	.25	.11
☐ GD116 Terry Adams	.25	.11
☐ GD117 Brian Dorsett	.25	.11
☐ GD118 Doug Glanville	.25	.11
☐ GD119 Tyler Houston	.25	.11
☐ GD120 Robin Jennings	.25	.11
☐ GD121 Ryne Sandberg	1.25	.55
☐ GD122 Terry Shumpert	.25	.11
☐ GD123 Amaury Telemaco	.25	.11
☐ GD124 Steve Trachsel	.25	.11
☐ GD125 Curtis Goodwin	.25	.11
☐ GD126 Mike Kelly	.25	.11
☐ GD127 Chad Mottola	.25	.11
☐ GD128 Mark Portugal	.25	.11
☐ GD129 Roger Salkeld	.25	.11
☐ GD130 John Smiley	.25	.11

☐ GD131 Lee Smith	.50	.23
☐ GD132 Roger Bailey	.25	.11
☐ GD133 Andres Galarraga	1.00	.45
☐ GD134 Darren Holmes	.25	.11
☐ GD135 Curtis Leskanic	.25	.11
☐ GD136 Mike Munoz	.25	.11
☐ GD137 Jeff Reed	.25	.11
☐ GD138 Mark Thompson	.25	.11
☐ GD139 Jamey Wright	.25	.11
☐ GD140 Andre Dawson	.75	.35
☐ GD141 Craig Grebeck	.25	.11
☐ GD142 Matt Mantei	.25	.11
☐ GD143 Billy McMillon	.25	.11
☐ GD144 Kurt Miller	.25	.11
☐ GD145 Ralph Milliard	.25	.11
☐ GD146 Bob Natal	.25	.11
☐ GD147 Joe Siddall	.25	.11
☐ GD148 Bob Abreu	.50	.23
☐ GD149 Doug Brocail	.25	.11
☐ GD150 Danny Darwin	.25	.11
☐ GD151 Mike Hampton	.25	.11
☐ GD152 Todd Jones	.25	.11
☐ GD153 Kirt Manwaring	.25	.11
☐ GD154 Alvin Morman	.25	.11
☐ GD155 Billy Ashley	.25	.11
☐ GD156 Tom Candiotti	.25	.11
☐ GD157 Darren Dreifort	.25	.11
☐ GD158 Greg Gagne	.25	.11
☐ GD159 Wilton Guerrero	.25	.11
☐ GD160 Hideo Nomo	2.50	1.10
☐ GD161 Mike Piazza	3.00	1.35
☐ GD162 Tom Prince	.25	.11
☐ GD163 Todd Worrell	.25	.11
☐ GD164 Moises Alou	.50	.23
☐ GD165 Shane Andrews	.25	.11
☐ GD166 Derek Aucoin	.25	.11
☐ GD167 Raul Chavez	.25	.11
☐ GD168 Darrin Fletcher	.25	.11
☐ GD169 Mark Leiter	.25	.11
☐ GD170 Henry Rodriguez	.25	.11
☐ GD171 Dave Veres	.25	.11
☐ GD172 Paul Byrd	.25	.11
☐ GD173 Alberto Castillo	.25	.11
☐ GD174 Mark Clark	.25	.11
☐ GD175 Rey Ordonez	.25	.11
☐ GD176 Roberto Petagine	.25	.11
☐ GD177 Andy Tomberlin	.25	.11
☐ GD178 Derek Wallace	.25	.11
☐ GD179 Paul Wilson	.25	.11
☐ GD180 Ruben Amaro Jr.	.25	.11
☐ GD181 Toby Borland	.25	.11
☐ GD182 Rich Hunter	.25	.11
☐ GD183 Tony Longmire	.25	.11
☐ GD184 Wendell Magee	.25	.11
☐ GD185 Bobby Munoz	.25	.11
☐ GD186 Scott Rolen	2.50	1.10
☐ GD187 Mike Williams	.25	.11
☐ GD188 Trey Beamon	.25	.11
☐ GD189 Jason Christiansen	.25	.11
☐ GD190 Elmer Dessens	.25	.11
☐ GD191 Angelo Encarnacion	.25	.11
☐ GD192 Carlos Garcia	.25	.11
☐ GD193 Mike Kingery	.25	.11
☐ GD194 Chris Peters	.25	.11
☐ GD195 Tony Womack	.75	.35
☐ GD196 Brian Barber	.25	.11
☐ GD197 David Bell	.25	.11
☐ GD198 Tony Fossas	.25	.11
☐ GD199 Rick Honeycutt	.25	.11
☐ GD200 T.J. Mathews	.25	.11
☐ GD201 Miguel Mejia	.25	.11
☐ GD202 Donovan Osborne	.25	.11
☐ GD203 Ozzie Smith	1.25	.55
☐ GD204 Andres Berumen	.25	.11
☐ GD205 Ken Caminiti	.75	.35
☐ GD206 Chris Gwynn	.25	.11
☐ GD207 Tony Gwynn	2.50	1.10
☐ GD208 Rickey Henderson	.75	.35
☐ GD209 Scott Sanders	.25	.11
☐ GD210 Jason Thompson	.25	.11
☐ GD211 Fernando Valenzuela	.50	.23
☐ GD212 Tim Worrell	.25	.11
☐ GD213 Barry Bonds	1.25	.55
☐ GD214 Jay Canizaro	.25	.11
☐ GD215 Doug Creek	.25	.11
☐ GD216 Jacob Cruz	.50	.23

☐ GD217 Glenallen Hill	.25	.11
☐ GD218 Tom Lampkin	.25	.11
☐ GD219 Jim Poole	.25	.11
☐ GD220 Desi Wilson	.25	.11

1997 Pacific Prisms Sizzling Lumber

Randomly inserted in packs at a rate of one in 37, this 36-card set features color photos of three top hitters from each of twelve major league teams. The die-cut cards display red-and-gold foil flames coming from a portion of a baseball bat. The three player cards from the same team form a complete bat on fire when laid top to bottom according to the letters found after the card number. Information is printed in both Spanish and English.

	MINT	NRMT
COMPLETE SET (36)	400.00	180.00
COMMON CARD (SL1A-SL12C)	4.00	1.80
UNLISTED STARS	8.00	3.60
STATED ODDS 1:37		
☐ SL1A Cal Ripken	30.00	13.50
☐ SL1B Rafael Palmeiro	5.00	2.20
☐ SL1C Roberto Alomar	8.00	3.60
☐ SL2A Frank Thomas	30.00	13.50
☐ SL2B Robin Ventura	4.00	1.80
☐ SL2C Harold Baines	4.00	1.80
☐ SL3A Albert Belle	10.00	4.50
☐ SL3B Manny Ramirez	8.00	3.60
☐ SL3C Kenny Lofton	10.00	4.50
☐ SL4A Derek Jeter	20.00	9.00
☐ SL4B Bernie Williams	8.00	3.60
☐ SL4C Wade Boggs	8.00	3.60
☐ SL5A Mark McGwire	15.00	6.75
☐ SL5B Jason Giambi	4.00	1.80
☐ SL5C Geronimo Berroa	4.00	1.80
☐ SL6A Ken Griffey Jr.	40.00	18.00
☐ SL6B Alex Rodriguez	25.00	11.00
☐ SL6C Jay Buhner	5.00	2.20
☐ SL7A Juan Gonzalez	20.00	9.00
☐ SL7B Dean Palmer	4.00	1.80
☐ SL7C Ivan Rodriguez	10.00	4.50
☐ SL8A Ryan Klesko	5.00	2.20
☐ SL8B Chipper Jones	25.00	11.00
☐ SL8C Andruw Jones	15.00	6.75
☐ SL9A Dante Bichette	4.00	1.80
☐ SL9B Andres Galarraga	8.00	3.60
☐ SL9C Vinny Castilla	4.00	1.80
☐ SL10A Jeff Bagwell	15.00	6.75
☐ SL10B Craig Biggio	5.00	2.20
☐ SL10C Derek Bell	4.00	1.80
☐ SL11A Mike Piazza	25.00	11.00
☐ SL11B Raul Mondesi	5.00	2.20
☐ SL11C Karim Garcia	4.00	1.80
☐ SL12A Tony Gwynn	20.00	9.00

☐ SL12B Ken Caminiti	5.00	2.20
☐ SL12C Greg Vaughn	4.00	1.80

1997 Pacific Prisms Sluggers and Hurlers

black background accented by thin white borders. An anti-counterfeit device appears in the bottom border of each card back. A special ribbed plastic lenticular detector card was made available that allowed the user to view the anti-counterfeit device and unscramble the coding with the word "Pinnacle" appearing. Special subsets featured include '92 Rookie Prospects (52, 55, 168, 247-261, 263-280), Idols (281-286/584-591), Sidelines (287-294/592-596), Draft Picks (295-304), Shades (305-310/601-605), Grips (606-612), and Technicians (614-620). Rookie Cards in the set include Brian Jordan and Manny Ramirez.

Randomly inserted in packs at a rate of one in 145, cards from this 24-card set feature top hitters and pitchers for a dozen teams printed in a two-card puzzle style matching the hitter and pitcher from the same team to form a complete background picture displaying the team's name.

	MINT	NRMT
COMPLETE SET (24)	900.00	400.00
COMMON CARD (SH1A-SH12B)	5.00	2.20
MINOR STARS	8.00	3.60
SEMISTARS	12.00	5.50
UNLISTED STARS	20.00	9.00
STATED ODDS 1:145		

		MINT	NRMT
☐ SH1A	Cal Ripken	80.00	36.00
☐ SH1B	Mike Mussina	20.00	9.00
☐ SH2A	Jose Canseco	12.00	5.50
☐ SH2B	Roger Clemens	40.00	18.00
☐ SH3A	Frank Thomas	80.00	36.00
☐ SH3B	Wilson Alvarez	5.00	2.20
☐ SH4A	Kenny Lofton	25.00	11.00
☐ SH4B	Orel Hershiser	8.00	3.60
☐ SH5A	Derek Jeter	50.00	22.00
☐ SH5B	Andy Pettitte	20.00	9.00
☐ SH6A	Ken Griffey Jr.	100.00	45.00
☐ SH6B	Randy Johnson	20.00	9.00
☐ SH7A	Alex Rodriguez	60.00	27.00
☐ SH7B	Jamie Moyer	5.00	2.20
☐ SH8A	Andruw Jones	40.00	18.00
☐ SH8B	Greg Maddux	60.00	27.00
☐ SH9A	Chipper Jones	60.00	27.00
☐ SH9B	John Smoltz	8.00	3.60
☐ SH10A	Jeff Bagwell	40.00	18.00
☐ SH10B	Shane Reynolds	5.00	2.20
☐ SH11A	Mike Piazza	60.00	27.00
☐ SH11B	Hideo Nomo	50.00	22.00
☐ SH12A	Tony Gwynn	50.00	22.00
☐ SH12B	Fernando Valenzuela	8.00	3.60

1992 Pinnacle

The 1992 Pinnacle set (issued by Score) consists of two series each with 310 standard-size cards. Cards were distributed in first and second series 16-card foil packs and 27-card cello packs. The card fronts feature glossy color player photos, on a

	MINT	NRMT
COMPLETE SET (620)	40.00	18.00
COMPLETE SERIES 1 (310)	25.00	11.00
COMPLETE SERIES 2 (310)	15.00	6.75
COMMON CARD (1-620)	.10	.05
MINOR STARS	.20	.09
UNLISTED STARS	.40	.18
SUBSET CARDS HALF VALUE OF BASE CARDS		

		MINT	NRMT
☐ 1	Frank Thomas	2.00	.90
☐ 2	Benito Santiago	.10	.05
☐ 3	Carlos Baerga	.10	.05
☐ 4	Cecil Fielder	.20	.09
☐ 5	Barry Larkin	.30	.14
☐ 6	Ozzie Smith	.50	.23
☐ 7	Willie McGee	.10	.05
☐ 8	Paul Molitor	.40	.18
☐ 9	Andy Van Slyke	.20	.09
☐ 10	Ryne Sandberg	.50	.23
☐ 11	Kevin Seitzer	.10	.05
☐ 12	Len Dykstra	.20	.09
☐ 13	Edgar Martinez	.30	.14
☐ 14	Ruben Sierra	.10	.05
☐ 15	Howard Johnson	.10	.05
☐ 16	Dave Henderson	.10	.05
☐ 17	Devon White	.10	.05
☐ 18	Terry Pendleton	.20	.09
☐ 19	Steve Finley	.20	.09
☐ 20	Kirby Puckett	.75	.35
☐ 21	Orel Hershiser	.20	.09
☐ 22	Hal Morris	.10	.05
☐ 23	Don Mattingly	.60	.25
☐ 24	Delino DeShields	.10	.05
☐ 25	Dennis Eckersley	.20	.09
☐ 26	Ellis Burks	.20	.09
☐ 27	Jay Buhner	.30	.14
☐ 28	Matt Williams	.30	.14
☐ 29	Lou Whitaker	.20	.09
☐ 30	Alex Fernandez	.20	.09
☐ 31	Albert Belle	.50	.23
☐ 32	Todd Zeile	.10	.05
☐ 33	Tony Pena	.10	.05
☐ 34	Jay Bell	.20	.09
☐ 35	Rafael Palmeiro	.30	.14
☐ 36	Wes Chamberlain	.10	.05
☐ 37	George Bell	.10	.05
☐ 38	Robin Yount	.30	.14
☐ 39	Vince Coleman	.10	.05
☐ 40	Bruce Hurst	.10	.05
☐ 41	Harold Baines	.20	.09
☐ 42	Chuck Finley	.10	.05
☐ 43	Ken Caminiti	.30	.14
☐ 44	Ben McDonald	.10	.05
☐ 45	Roberto Alomar	.40	.18
☐ 46	Chili Davis	.20	.09
☐ 47	Bill Doran	.10	.05
☐ 48	Jerald Clark	.10	.05
☐ 49	Jose Lind	.10	.05
☐ 50	Nolan Ryan	1.50	.70
☐ 51	Phil Plantier	.10	.05
☐ 52	Gary DiSarcina	.10	.05
☐ 53	Kevin Bass	.10	.05
☐ 54	Pat Kelly	.10	.05
☐ 55	Mark Wohlers	.30	.14
☐ 56	Walt Weiss	.10	.05
☐ 57	Lenny Harris	.10	.05
☐ 58	Ivan Calderon	.10	.05
☐ 59	Harold Reynolds	.10	.05
☐ 60	George Brett	.75	.35
☐ 61	Gregg Olson	.10	.05
☐ 62	Orlando Merced	.10	.05
☐ 63	Steve Decker	.10	.05
☐ 64	John Franco	.20	.09
☐ 65	Greg Maddux	1.25	.55
☐ 66	Alex Cole	.10	.05
☐ 67	Dave Hollins	.10	.05
☐ 68	Kent Hrbek	.20	.09
☐ 69	Tom Pagnozzi	.10	.05
☐ 70	Jeff Bagwell	1.25	.55
☐ 71	Jim Gantner	.10	.05
☐ 72	Matt Nokes	.10	.05
☐ 73	Brian Harper	.10	.05
☐ 74	Andy Benes	.20	.09
☐ 75	Tom Glavine	.30	.14
☐ 76	Terry Steinbach	.20	.09
☐ 77	Dennis Martinez	.20	.09
☐ 78	John Olerud	.20	.09
☐ 79	Ozzie Guillen	.10	.05
☐ 80	Darryl Strawberry	.20	.09
☐ 81	Gary Gaetti	.10	.05
☐ 82	Doug Drabek	.10	.05
☐ 83	Chris Hoiles	.10	.05
☐ 84	Andujar Cedeno	.10	.05
☐ 85	Jack Clark	.20	.09
☐ 86	David Howard	.10	.05
☐ 87	Bill Gullickson	.10	.05
☐ 88	Bernard Gilkey	.10	.05
☐ 89	Kevin Elster	.10	.05
☐ 90	Kevin Maas	.10	.05
☐ 91	Mark Lewis	.10	.05
☐ 92	Greg Vaughn	.10	.05
☐ 93	Bret Barberie	.10	.05
☐ 94	Dave Smith	.10	.05
☐ 95	Roger Clemens	.75	.35
☐ 96	Doug Drabek	.20	.09
☐ 97	Omar Vizquel	.20	.09
☐ 98	Jose Guzman	.10	.05
☐ 99	Juan Samuel	.10	.05
☐ 100	Dave Justice	.40	.18
☐ 101	Tom Browning	.10	.05
☐ 102	Mark Gubicza	.10	.05
☐ 103	Mickey Morandini	.10	.05
☐ 104	Ed Whitson	.10	.05
☐ 105	Lance Parrish	.10	.05
☐ 106	Scott Erickson	.20	.09
☐ 107	Jack McDowell	.20	.09
☐ 108	Dave Stieb	.10	.05
☐ 109	Mike Moore	.10	.05
☐ 110	Travis Fryman	.20	.09
☐ 111	Dwight Gooden	.20	.09
☐ 112	Fred McGriff	.30	.14
☐ 113	Alan Trammell	.30	.14
☐ 114	Roberto Kelly	.10	.05
☐ 115	Andre Dawson	.30	.14
☐ 116	Bill Landrum	.10	.05
☐ 117	Brian McRae	.10	.05
☐ 118	B.J. Surhoff	.10	.05
☐ 119	Chuck Knoblauch	.40	.18
☐ 120	Steve Olin	.10	.05
☐ 121	Robin Ventura	.20	.09
☐ 122	Will Clark	.30	.14
☐ 123	Tino Martinez	.40	.18

□ 374	Kal Daniels	.10	.05
□ 375	Dave Winfield	.40	.18
□ 376	Brook Jacoby	.10	.05
□ 377	Mariano Duncan	.10	.05
□ 378	Ron Darling	.10	.05
□ 379	Randy Johnson	.40	.18
□ 380	Chito Martinez	.10	.05
□ 381	Andres Galarraga	.40	.18
□ 382	Willie Randolph	.20	.09
□ 383	Charles Nagy	.20	.09
□ 384	Tim Belcher	.10	.05
□ 385	Duane Ward	.10	.05
□ 386	Vicente Palacios	.10	.05
□ 387	Mike Gallego	.10	.05
□ 388	Rich DeLucia	.10	.05
□ 389	Scott Radinsky	.10	.05
□ 390	Damon Berryhill	.10	.05
□ 391	Kirk McCaskill	.10	.05
□ 392	Pedro Guerrero	.10	.05
□ 393	Kevin Mitchell	.20	.09
□ 394	Dickie Thon	.10	.05
□ 395	Bobby Bonilla	.20	.09
□ 396	Bill Wegman	.10	.05
□ 397	Dave Martinez	.10	.05
□ 398	Rick Sutcliffe	.10	.05
□ 399	Larry Andersen	.10	.05
□ 400	Tony Gwynn	1.00	.45
□ 401	Rickey Henderson	.30	.14
□ 402	Greg Cadaret	.10	.05
□ 403	Keith Miller	.10	.05
□ 404	Bip Roberts	.10	.05
□ 405	Kevin Brown	.20	.09
□ 406	Mitch Williams	.10	.05
□ 407	Frank Viola	.10	.05
□ 408	Darren Lewis	.10	.05
□ 409	Bob Welch	.10	.05
□ 410	Bob Walk	.10	.05
□ 411	Todd Frohwirth	.10	.05
□ 412	Brian Hunter	.10	.05
□ 413	Ron Karkovice	.10	.05
□ 414	Mike Morgan	.10	.05
□ 415	Joe Hesketh	.10	.05
□ 416	Don Slaught	.10	.05
□ 417	Tom Henke	.10	.05
□ 418	Kurt Stillwell	.10	.05
□ 419	Hector Villanueva	.10	.05
□ 420	Glenallen Hill	.10	.05
□ 421	Pat Borders	.10	.05
□ 422	Charlie Hough	.10	.05
□ 423	Charlie Leibrandt	.10	.05
□ 424	Eddie Murray	.40	.18
□ 425	Jesse Barfield	.10	.05
□ 426	Mark Lemke	.10	.05
□ 427	Kevin McReynolds	.10	•.05
□ 428	Gilberto Reyes	.10	.05
□ 429	Ramon Martinez	.20	.09
□ 430	Steve Buechele	.10	.05
□ 431	David Wells	.10	.05
□ 432	Kyle Abbott	.10	.05
□ 433	John Habyan	.10	.05
□ 434	Kevin Appier	.20	.09
□ 435	Gene Larkin	.10	.05
□ 436	Sandy Alomar Jr	.20	.09
□ 437	Mike Jackson	.10	.05
□ 438	Todd Benzinger	.10	.05
□ 439	Teddy Higuera	.10	.05
□ 440	Reggie Sanders	.20	.09
□ 441	Mark Carreon	.10	.05
□ 442	Bret Saberhagen	.10	.05
□ 443	Gene Nelson	.10	.05
□ 444	Jay Howell	.10	.05
□ 445	Roger McDowell	.10	.05
□ 446	Sid Bream	.10	.05
□ 447	Mackey Sasser	.10	.05
□ 448	Bill Swift	.10	.05
□ 449	Hubie Brooks	.10	.05
□ 450	David Cone	.20	.09
□ 451	Bobby Witt	.10	.05
□ 452	Brady Anderson	.30	.14
□ 453	Lee Stevens	.10	.05
□ 454	Luis Aquino	.10	.05
□ 455	Carney Lansford	.20	.09
□ 456	Carlos Hernandez	.10	.05
□ 457	Danny Jackson	.10	.05
□ 458	Gerald Young	.10	.05
□ 459	Tom Candiotti	.10	.05
□ 460	Billy Hatcher	.10	.05
□ 461	John Wetteland	.20	.09
□ 462	Mike Bordick	.10	.05
□ 463	Don Robinson	.10	.05
□ 464	Jeff Johnson	.10	.05
□ 465	Lonnie Smith	.10	.05
□ 466	Paul Assenmacher	.10	.05
□ 467	Alvin Davis	.10	.05
□ 468	Jim Eisenreich	.10	.05
□ 469	Brent Mayne	.10	.05
□ 470	Jeff Brantley	.10	.05
□ 471	Tim Burke	.10	.05
□ 472	Pat Mahomes	.10	.05
□ 473	Ryan Bowen	.10	.05
□ 474	Bryn Smith	.10	.05
□ 475	Mike Flanagan	.10	.05
□ 476	Reggie Jefferson	.20	.09
□ 477	Jeff Blauser	.10	.05
□ 478	Craig Lefferts	.10	.05
□ 479	Todd Worrell	.10	.05
□ 480	Scott Scudder	.10	.05
□ 481	Kirk Gibson	.20	.09
□ 482	Kenny Rogers	.10	.05
□ 483	Jack Morris	.20	.09
□ 484	Russ Swan	.10	.05
□ 485	Mike Huff	.10	.05
□ 486	Ken Hill	.10	.05
□ 487	Geronimo Pena	.10	.05
□ 488	Charlie O'Brien	.10	.05
□ 489	Mike Maddux	.10	.05
□ 490	Scott Livingstone	.10	.05
□ 491	Carl Willis	.10	.05
□ 492	Kelly Downs	.10	.05
□ 493	Dennis Cook	.10	.05
□ 494	Joe Magrane	.10	.05
□ 495	Bob Kipper	.10	.05
□ 496	Jose Mesa	.10	.05
□ 497	Charlie Hayes	.10	.05
□ 498	Joe Girardi	.10	.05
□ 499	Doug Jones	.10	.05
□ 500	Barry Bonds	.50	.23
□ 501	Bill Krueger	.10	.05
□ 502	Glenn Braggs	.10	.05
□ 503	Eric King	.10	.05
□ 504	Frank Castillo	.10	.05
□ 505	Mike Gardiner	.10	.05
□ 506	Cory Snyder	.10	.05
□ 507	Steve Howe	.10	.05
□ 508	Jose Rijo	.10	.05
□ 509	Sid Fernandez	.10	.05
□ 510	Archi Cianfrocco	.10	.05
□ 511	Mark Guthrie	.10	.05
□ 512	Bob Ojeda	.10	.05
□ 513	John Doherty	.10	.05
□ 514	Dante Bichette	.30	.14
□ 515	Juan Berenguer	.10	.05
□ 516	Jeff M. Robinson	.10	.05
□ 517	Mike Macfarlane	.10	.05
□ 518	Matt Young	.10	.05
□ 519	Otis Nixon	.20	.09
□ 520	Brian Holman	.10	.05
□ 521	Chris Haney	.10	.05
□ 522	Jeff Kent	.40	.18
□ 523	Chad Curtis	.40	.18
□ 524	Vince Horsman	.10	.05
□ 525	Rod Nichols	.10	.05
□ 526	Peter Hoy	.10	.05
□ 527	Shawn Boskie	.10	.05
□ 528	Alejandro Pena	.10	.05
□ 529	Dave Burba	.10	.05
□ 530	Ricky Jordan	.10	.05
□ 531	Dave Silvestri	.10	.05
□ 532	John Patterson UER	.10	.05

(Listed as being born in 1960; should be 1967)

□ 533	Jeff Branson	.10	.05
□ 534	Derrick May	.10	.05
□ 535	Esteban Beltre	.10	.05
□ 536	Jose Melendez	.10	.05
□ 537	Wally Joyner	.20	.09
□ 538	Eddie Taubensee	.10	.05
□ 539	Jim Abbott	.40	.18
□ 540	Brian Williams	.10	.05
□ 541	Donovan Osborne	.10	.05
□ 542	Patrick Lennon	.10	.05
□ 543	Mike Groppuso	.10	.05
□ 544	Jarvis Brown	.10	.05
□ 545	Shawn Livsey	.10	.05
□ 546	Jeff Ware	.10	.05
□ 547	Danny Tartabull	.10	.05
□ 548	Bobby Jones	.40	.18
□ 549	Ken Griffey Jr.	2.50	1.10
□ 550	Rey Sanchez	.10	.05
□ 551	Pedro Astacio	.20	.09
□ 552	Juan Guerrero	.10	.05
□ 553	Jacob Brumfield	.10	.05
□ 554	Ben Rivera	.10	.05
□ 555	Brian Jordan	.50	.23
□ 556	Denny Neagle	.30	.14
□ 557	Cliff Brantley	.10	.05
□ 558	Anthony Young	.10	.05
□ 559	John Vander Wal	.10	.05
□ 560	Monty Fariss	.10	.05
□ 561	Russ Springer	.10	.05
□ 562	Pat Listach	.40	.18
□ 563	Pat Hentgen	.40	.18
□ 564	Andy Stankiewicz	.10	.05
□ 565	Mike Perez	.10	.05
□ 566	Mike Bielecki	.10	.05
□ 567	Butch Henry	.10	.05
□ 568	Dave Nilsson	.20	.09
□ 569	Scott Hatteberg	.10	.05
□ 570	Ruben Amaro Jr.	.10	.05
□ 571	Todd Hundley	.30	.14
□ 572	Moises Alou	.30	.14
□ 573	Hector Fajardo	.10	.05
□ 574	Todd Van Poppel	.10	.05
□ 575	Willie Banks	.10	.05
□ 576	Bob Zupcic	.10	.05
□ 577	J.J. Johnson	.20	.09
□ 578	John Burkett	.10	.05
□ 579	Trever Miller	.10	.05
□ 580	Scott Bankhead	.10	.05
□ 581	Rich Amaral	.10	.05
□ 582	Kenny Lofton	1.50	.70
□ 583	Matt Stairs	.10	.05
□ 584	Don Mattingly Rod Carew IDOLS	.40	.18
□ 585	Steve Avery Jack Morris IDOLS	.10	.05
□ 586	Roberto Alomar Sandy Alomar SR. IDOLS	.30	.14
□ 587	Scott Sanderson Catfish Hunter IDOLS	.20	.09
□ 588	Dave Justice Willie Stargell IDOLS	.40	.18
□ 589	Rex Hudler Roger Staubach IDOLS	.40	.18
□ 590	David Cone Jackie Gleason IDOLS	.20	.09
□ 591	Tony Gwynn Willie Davis IDOLS	.40	.18
□ 592	Orel Hershiser SIDE	.10	.05
□ 593	John Wetteland SIDE	.10	.05
□ 594	Tom Glavine SIDE	.20	.09
□ 595	Randy Johnson SIDE	.20	.09
□ 596	Jim Gott SIDE	.10	.05
□ 597	Donald Harris	.10	.05
□ 598	Shawn Hare	.10	.05
□ 599	Chris Gardner	.10	.05
□ 600	Rusty Meacham	.10	.05
□ 601	Benito Santiago	.10	.05
□ 602	Eric Davis SHADE	.10	.05
□ 603	Jose Lind SHADE	.10	.05
□ 604	Dave Justice SHADE	.20	.09
□ 605	Tim Raines SHADE	.20	.09
□ 606	Randy Tomlin GRIP	.10	.05
□ 607	Jack McDowell GRIP	.10	.05
□ 608	Greg Maddux GRIP	.60	.25
□ 609	Charles Nagy GRIP	.10	.05
□ 610	Tom Candiotti GRIP	.10	.05
□ 611	David Cone GRIP	.10	.05
□ 612	Steve Avery GRIP	.10	.05
□ 613	Rod Beck GRIP	.20	.09
□ 614	Rickey Henderson TECH	.20	.09
□ 615	Benito Santiago TECH	.10	.05
□ 616	Ruben Sierra TECH	.10	.05
□ 617	Ryne Sandberg TECH	.40	.18
□ 618	Nolan Ryan TECH	.75	.35
□ 619	Brett Butler TECH	.10	.05
□ 620	Dave Justice TECH	.20	.09

1992 Pinnacle Rookie Idols

This 18-card insert set is a spin-off on the Idols subset featured in the regular series. The cards were randomly inserted in Series II wax packs. The set features full-bleed color photos of 18 rookies along with their pick of sports figures or other individuals who had the greatest impact on their careers. Both sides of the cards are horizontally oriented. The fronts carry a close-up photo of the rookie superimposed on an action game shot of his idol.

	MINT	NRMT
COMPLETE SET (18)	120.00	55.00
COMMON PAIR (1-18)	3.00	1.35
UNLISTED STARS	6.00	2.70
RANDOM INSERTS IN SER.2 FOIL PACKS		

		MINT	NRMT
☐ 1	Reggie Sanders and Eric Davis	4.00	1.80
☐ 2	Hector Fajardo and Jim Abbott	3.00	1.35
☐ 3	Gary Cooper and George Brett	12.00	5.50
☐ 4	Mark Wohlers and Roger Clemens	12.00	5.50
☐ 5	Luis Mercedes and Julio Franco	3.00	1.35
☐ 6	Willie Banks and Doc Gooden	3.00	1.35
☐ 7	Kenny Lofton and Rickey Henderson	25.00	11.00
☐ 8	Keith Mitchell and Dave Henderson	3.00	1.35
☐ 9	Kim Batiste and Barry Larkin	5.00	2.20
☐ 10	Todd Hundley and Thurman Munson	8.00	3.60
☐ 11	Eddie Zosky and Cal Ripken	25.00	11.00
☐ 12	Todd Van Poppel and Nolan Ryan	25.00	11.00
☐ 13	Jim Thome and Ryne Sandberg	25.00	11.00
☐ 14	Dave Fleming and Bobby Murcer	3.00	1.35
☐ 15	Royce Clayton and Ozzie Smith	8.00	3.60
☐ 16	Donald Harris and Darryl Strawberry	3.00	1.35
☐ 17	Chad Curtis and Alan Trammell	5.00	2.20
☐ 18	Derek Bell and Dave Winfield	6.00	2.70

1992 Pinnacle Slugfest

This 15-card set highlights the games top sluggers. The cards

were issued exclusively as an one per pack insert in specially marked cello packs. The horizontally oriented fronts feature glossy photos of players at bat. The player's name is printed in gold and the word "Slugfest" is printed in red in a black border across the bottom of the picture.

	MINT	NRMT
COMPLETE SET (15)	40.00	18.00
COMMON CARD (1-15)	.75	.35
ONE PER SLUGFEST JUMBO PACK		

		MINT	NRMT
☐ 1	Cecil Fielder	1.00	.45
☐ 2	Mark McGwire	3.00	1.35
☐ 3	Jose Canseco	1.25	.55
☐ 4	Barry Bonds	2.00	.90
☐ 5	David Justice	1.50	.70
☐ 6	Bobby Bonilla	1.00	.45
☐ 7	Ken Griffey Jr.	10.00	4.50
☐ 8	Ron Gant	1.00	.45
☐ 9	Ryne Sandberg	2.00	.90
☐ 10	Ruben Sierra	.75	.35
☐ 11	Frank Thomas	8.00	3.60
☐ 12	Will Clark	1.25	.55
☐ 13	Kirby Puckett	4.00	1.80
☐ 14	Cal Ripken	6.00	2.70
☐ 15	Jeff Bagwell	5.00	2.20

1992 Pinnacle Team 2000

This 80-card standard-size set focuses on young players who were projected to be stars in the year 2000. Cards 1-40 were inserted in Series 1 jumbo packs while cards 41-80 were featured in Series 2 jumbo packs. The insertion rate was three per jumbo pack in either

series. The fronts features action color player photos. The cards are bordered by a 1/2" black stripe that runs along the left edge and bottom forming a right angle. The two ends of the black stripe are sloped. The words "Team 2000" and the player's name appear in gold foil in the stripe. The team logo is displayed in the lower left corner.

	MINT	NRMT
COMPLETE SET (80)	30.00	13.50
COMPLETE SERIES 1 (40)	20.00	9.00
COMPLETE SERIES 2 (40)	10.00	4.50
COMMON CARD (1-80)	.15	.07
THREE PER JUMBO PACK		

		MINT	NRMT
☐ 1	Mike Mussina	1.50	.70
☐ 2	Phil Plantier	.15	.07
☐ 3	Frank Thomas	5.00	2.20
☐ 4	Travis Fryman	.25	.11
☐ 5	Kevin Appier	.25	.11
☐ 6	Chuck Knoblauch	.60	.25
☐ 7	Pat Kelly	.15	.07
☐ 8	Ivan Rodriguez	2.00	.90
☐ 9	Dave Justice	.60	.25
☐ 10	Jeff Bagwell	2.00	.90
☐ 11	Marquis Grissom	.25	.11
☐ 12	Andy Benes	.25	.11
☐ 13	Gregg Olson	.15	.07
☐ 14	Kevin Morton	.15	.07
☐ 15	Tim Naehring	.25	.11
☐ 16	Dave Hollins	.25	.11
☐ 17	Sandy Alomar Jr.	.25	.11
☐ 18	Albert Belle	1.25	.55
☐ 19	Charles Nagy	.25	.11
☐ 20	Brian McRae	.15	.07
☐ 21	Larry Walker	.60	.25
☐ 22	Delino DeShields	.15	.07
☐ 23	Jeff Johnson	.15	.07
☐ 24	Bernie Williams	.60	.25
☐ 25	Jose Offerman	.15	.07
☐ 26	Juan Gonzalez	3.00	1.35
☐ 27A	Juan Guzman (Pinnacle logo at top)	.25	.11
☐ 27B	Juan Guzman (Pinnacle logo at bottom)	.25	.11
☐ 28	Eric Anthony	.15	.07
☐ 29	Brian Hunter	.15	.07
☐ 30	John Smoltz	.40	.18
☐ 31	Deion Sanders	.25	.11
☐ 32	Greg Maddux	3.00	1.35
☐ 33	Andujar Cedeno	.15	.07
☐ 34	Royce Clayton	.15	.07
☐ 35	Kenny Lofton	4.00	1.80
☐ 36	Cal Eldred	.15	.07
☐ 37	Jim Thome	3.00	1.35
☐ 38	Gary DiSarcina	.15	.07
☐ 39	Brian Jordan	.60	.25
☐ 40	Chad Curtis	.60	.25
☐ 41	Ben McDonald	.15	.07
☐ 42	Jim Abbott	.15	.07
☐ 43	Robin Ventura	.25	.11
☐ 44	Milt Cuyler	.15	.07
☐ 45	Gregg Jefferies	.15	.07
☐ 46	Scott Radinsky	.15	.07
☐ 47	Ken Griffey Jr.	6.00	2.70
☐ 48	Roberto Alomar	.60	.25
☐ 49	Ramon Martinez	.25	.11
☐ 50	Bret Barberie	.15	.07
☐ 51	Ray Lankford	.60	.25
☐ 52	Leo Gomez	.15	.07
☐ 53	Tommy Greene	.15	.07
☐ 54	Mo Vaughn	1.50	.70
☐ 55	Sammy Sosa	.60	.25
☐ 56	Carlos Baerga	.15	.07
☐ 57	Mark Lewis	.15	.07
☐ 58	Tom Gordon	.15	.07
☐ 59	Gary Sheffield	.60	.25
☐ 60	Scott Erickson	.25	.11
☐ 61	Pedro Munoz	.15	.07
☐ 62	Tino Martinez	.60	.25
☐ 63	Darren Lewis	.15	.07

☐ 64 Dean Palmer	.25	.11
☐ 65 John Olerud	.25	.11
☐ 66 Steve Avery	.15	.07
☐ 67 Pete Harnisch	.15	.07
☐ 68 Luis Gonzalez	.15	.07
☐ 69 Kim Batiste	.15	.07
☐ 70 Reggie Sanders	.25	.11
☐ 71 Luis Mercedes	.15	.07
☐ 72 Todd Van Poppel	.15	.07
☐ 73 Gary Scott	.15	.07
☐ 74 Monty Fariss	.15	.07
☐ 75 Kyle Abbott	.15	.07
☐ 76 Eric Karros	.40	.18
☐ 77 Mo Sanford	.15	.07
☐ 78 Todd Hundley	.40	.18
☐ 79 Reggie Jefferson	.25	.11
☐ 80 Pat Mahomes	.15	.07

1992 Pinnacle Team Pinnacle

This 12-card, double-sided insert set features the National League and American League All-Star team as selected by Pinnacle. The standard-size cards were randomly inserted in Series 1 wax packs. The cards feature illustrations by sports artist Chris Greco with the National League All-Star on one side and the corresponding American League All-Star by position on the other. The words "Team Pinnacle" are printed vertically down the left side of the card in red for American League on one side and blue for National League on the other.

	MINT	NRMT
COMPLETE SET (12)	80.00	36.00
COMMON PAIR (1-12)	3.00	1.35
RANDOM INSERTS IN SER.1 FOIL PACKS		

☐ 1 Roger Clemens and Ramon Martinez	10.00	4.50
☐ 2 Jim Abbott and Steve Avery	3.00	1.35
☐ 3 Ivan Rodriguez and Benito Santiago	8.00	3.60
☐ 4 Frank Thomas and Will Clark	20.00	9.00
☐ 5 Roberto Alomar and Ryne Sandberg	6.00	2.70
☐ 6 Robin Ventura and Matt Williams	4.00	1.80
☐ 7 Cal Ripken and Barry Larkin	20.00	9.00
☐ 8 Danny Tartabull and Barry Bonds	6.00	2.70
☐ 9 Ken Griffey Jr. and Brett Butler	25.00	11.00
☐ 10 Ruben Sierra	3.00	1.35

and Dave Justice

☐ 11 Dennis Eckersley and Rob Dibble	3.00	1.35
☐ 12 Scott Radinsky and John Franco	3.00	1.35

1992 Pinnacle Rookies

This 30-card boxed set features top rookies of the 1992 season, with at least one player from each team. A total of 180,000 sets were produced. The fronts feature full-bleed color action player photos except at the bottom where a team-color coded bar carries the player's name (in gold foil lettering) and a black bar has the words "1992 Rookie." The team logo appears in a gold foil circle at the lower right corner.

	MINT	NRMT
COMP.FACT.SET (30)	5.00	2.20
COMMON CARD (1-30)	.15	.07
MINOR STARS	.40	.18
UNLISTED STARS	.75	.35

☐ 1 Luis Mercedes	.15	.07
☐ 2 Scott Cooper	.15	.07
☐ 3 Kenny Lofton	4.00	1.80
☐ 4 John Doherty	.15	.07
☐ 5 Pat Listach	.15	.07
☐ 6 Andy Stankiewicz	.15	.07
☐ 7 Derek Bell	.40	.18
☐ 8 Gary DiSarcina	.15	.07
☐ 9 Roberto Hernandez	.75	.35
☐ 10 Joel Johnston	.15	.07
☐ 11 Pat Mahomes	.15	.07
☐ 12 Todd Van Poppel	.15	.07
☐ 13 Dave Fleming	.15	.07
☐ 14 Monty Fariss	.15	.07
☐ 15 Gary Scott	.15	.07
☐ 16 Moises Alou	.60	.25
☐ 17 Todd Hundley	.60	.25
☐ 18 Kim Batiste	.15	.07
☐ 19 Denny Neagle	.60	.25
☐ 20 Donovan Osborne	.15	.07
☐ 21 Mark Wohlers	.60	.25
☐ 22 Reggie Sanders	.40	.18
☐ 23 Brian Williams	.15	.07
☐ 24 Eric Karros	.60	.25
☐ 25 Frank Seminara	.15	.07
☐ 26 Royce Clayton	.15	.07
☐ 27 Dave Nilsson	.40	.18
☐ 28 Matt Stairs	.15	.07
☐ 29 Chad Curtis	.75	.35
☐ 30 Carlos Hernandez	.15	.07

1993 Pinnacle

The 1993 Pinnacle set (by Score) contains 620 standard-

size cards issued in two series of 310 cards each. Cards were distributed in hobby and retail foil packs and 27-card jumbo superpacks. The fronts feature color action player photos bordered in white and set on a black card face. The player's name appears below the photo, the player's team is above. The set includes the following topical subsets: Rookies (238-288, 575-620), Now and Then (289-296, 470-476), Idols (297-303, 477-483), Hometown Heroes (304-310, 484-490), and Draft Picks (455-469). Rookie Cards in this set include Derek Jeter and Jason Kendall.

	MINT	NRMT
COMPLETE SET (620)	50.00	22.00
COMPLETE SERIES 1 (310)	25.00	11.00
COMPLETE SERIES 2 (310)	25.00	11.00
COMMON CARD (1-620)	.15	.07
MINOR STARS	.30	.14
UNLISTED STARS	.60	.25
SUBSET CARDS HALF VALUE OF BASE CARDS		
COMP.TRIBUTE SET (10)	75.00	34.00
COMMON BRETT TRIB (1-5)	5.00	2.20
COMMON RYAN TRIB (6-10)	10.00	4.50
TRIBUTE SER.2 STATED ODDS 1:24		

☐ 1 Gary Sheffield	.60	.25
☐ 2 Cal Eldred	.15	.07
☐ 3 Larry Walker	.60	.25
☐ 4 Deion Sanders	.30	.14
☐ 5 Dave Fleming	.15	.07
☐ 6 Carlos Baerga	.30	.14
☐ 7 Bernie Williams	.60	.25
☐ 8 John Kruk	.30	.14
☐ 9 Jimmy Key	.30	.14
☐ 10 Jeff Bagwell	1.25	.55
☐ 11 Jim Abbott	.15	.07
☐ 12 Terry Steinbach	.15	.07
☐ 13 Bob Tewksbury	.15	.07
☐ 14 Eric Karros	.30	.14
☐ 15 Ryne Sandberg	.75	.35
☐ 16 Will Clark	.40	.18
☐ 17 Edgar Martinez	.40	.18
☐ 18 Eddie Murray	.60	.25
☐ 19 Andy Van Slyke	.30	.14
☐ 20 Cal Ripken Jr.	2.50	1.10
☐ 21 Ivan Rodriguez	.75	.35
☐ 22 Barry Larkin	.40	.18
☐ 23 Don Mattingly	1.00	.45
☐ 24 Gregg Jefferies	.15	.07
☐ 25 Roger Clemens	1.25	.55
☐ 26 Cecil Fielder	.30	.14
☐ 27 Kent Hrbek	.30	.14
☐ 28 Robin Ventura	.30	.14
☐ 29 Rickey Henderson	.40	.18
☐ 30 Roberto Alomar	.60	.25
☐ 31 Luis Polonia	.15	.07
☐ 32 Andujar Cedeno	.15	.07
☐ 33 Pat Listach	.15	.07
☐ 34 Mark Grace	.40	.18
☐ 35 Otis Nixon	.15	.07

36	Felix Jose	.15	.07
37	Mike Sharperson	.15	.07
38	Dennis Martinez	.30	.14
39	Willie McGee	.15	.07
40	Kenny Lofton	1.25	.55
41	Randy Johnson	.60	.25
42	Andy Benes	.30	.14
43	Bobby Bonilla	.30	.14
44	Mike Mussina	.60	.25
45	Len Dykstra	.30	.14
46	Ellis Burks	.30	.14
47	Chris Sabo	.15	.07
48	Jay Bell	.30	.14
49	Jose Canseco	.40	.18
50	Craig Biggio	.40	.18
51	Wally Joyner	.30	.14
52	Mickey Tettleton	.15	.07
53	Tim Raines	.30	.14
54	Brian Harper	.15	.07
55	Rene Gonzales	.15	.07
56	Mark Langston	.15	.07
57	Jack Morris	.30	.14
58	Mark McGwire	1.25	.55
59	Ken Caminiti	.40	.18
60	Terry Pendleton	.30	.14
61	Dave Nilsson	.30	.14
62	Tom Pagnozzi	.15	.07
63	Mike Morgan	.15	.07
64	Darryl Strawberry	.30	.14
65	Charles Nagy	.30	.14
66	Ken Hill	.15	.07
67	Matt Williams	.40	.18
68	Jay Buhner	.40	.18
69	Vince Coleman	.15	.07
70	Brady Anderson	.40	.18
71	Fred McGriff	.40	.18
72	Ben McDonald	.15	.07
73	Terry Mulholland	.15	.07
74	Randy Tomlin	.15	.07
75	Nolan Ryan	2.50	1.10
76	Frank Viola UER	.15	.07
	(Card incorrectly states he has a surgically repaired elbow)		
77	Jose Rijo	.15	.07
78	Shane Mack	.15	.07
79	Travis Fryman	.30	.14
80	Jack McDowell	.15	.07
81	Mark Gubicza	.15	.07
82	Matt Nokes	.15	.07
83	Bert Blyleven	.30	.14
84	Eric Anthony	.15	.07
85	Mike Bordick	.15	.07
86	John Olerud	.15	.07
87	B.J.Surhoff	.30	.14
88	Bernard Gilkey	.30	.14
89	Shawon Dunston	.15	.07
90	Tom Glavine	.40	.18
91	Brett Butler	.30	.14
92	Moises Alou	.30	.14
93	Albert Belle	.75	.35
94	Darren Lewis	.15	.07
95	Omar Vizquel	.30	.14
96	Dwight Gooden	.30	.14
97	Gregg Olson	.15	.07
98	Tony Gwynn	1.50	.70
99	Darren Daulton	.30	.14
100	Dennis Eckersley	.30	.14
101	Rob Dibble	.15	.07
102	Mike Greenwell	.15	.07
103	Jose Lind	.15	.07
104	Julio Franco	.15	.07
105	Tom Gordon	.15	.07
106	Scott Livingstone	.15	.07
107	Chuck Knoblauch	.60	.25
108	Frank Thomas	2.50	1.10
109	Melido Perez	.15	.07
110	Ken Griffey Jr.	3.00	1.35
111	Harold Baines	.30	.14
112	Gary Gaetti	.15	.07
113	Pete Harnisch	.15	.07
114	David Wells	.15	.07
115	Charlie Leibrandt	.15	.07
116	Ray Lankford	.40	.18
117	Kevin Seitzer	.15	.07
118	Robin Yount	.40	.18
119	Lenny Harris	.15	.07
120	Chris James	.15	.07
121	Delino DeShields	.15	.07
122	Kirt Manwaring	.15	.07
123	Glenallen Hill	.15	.07
124	Hensley Meulens	.15	.07
125	Darrin Jackson	.15	.07
126	Todd Hundley	.40	.18
127	Dave Hollins	.15	.07
128	Sam Horn	.15	.07
129	Roberto Hernandez	.30	.14
130	Vicente Palacios	.15	.07
131	George Brett	1.25	.55
132	Dave Martinez	.15	.07
133	Kevin Appier	.30	.14
134	Pat Kelly	.15	.07
135	Pedro Munoz	.15	.07
136	Mark Carreon	.15	.07
137	Lance Johnson	.15	.07
138	Devon White	.15	.07
139	Julio Valera	.15	.07
140	Eddie Taubensee	.15	.07
141	Willie Wilson	.15	.07
142	Stan Belinda	.15	.07
143	John Smoltz	.30	.14
144	Darryl Hamilton	.15	.07
145	Sammy Sosa	.60	.25
146	Carlos Hernandez	.15	.07
147	Tom Candiotti	.15	.07
148	Mike Felder	.15	.07
149	Rusty Meacham	.15	.07
150	Ivan Calderon	.15	.07
151	Pete O'Brien	.15	.07
152	Erik Hanson	.15	.07
153	Billy Ripken	.15	.07
154	Kurt Stillwell	.15	.07
155	Jeff Kent	.30	.14
156	Mickey Morandini	.15	.07
157	Randy Milligan	.15	.07
158	Reggie Sanders	.30	.14
159	Luis Rivera	.15	.07
160	Orlando Merced	.15	.07
161	Dean Palmer	.15	.07
162	Mike Perez	.15	.07
163	Scott Erickson	.15	.07
164	Kevin McReynolds	.15	.07
165	Kevin Maas	.15	.07
166	Ozzie Guillen	.15	.07
167	Rob Deer	.15	.07
168	Danny Tartabull	.15	.07
169	Lee Stevens	.15	.07
170	Dave Henderson	.15	.07
171	Derek Bell	.30	.14
172	Steve Finley	.30	.14
173	Greg Olson	.15	.07
174	Geronimo Pena	.15	.07
175	Paul Quantrill	.15	.07
176	Steve Buechele	.15	.07
177	Kevin Gross	.15	.07
178	Tim Wallach	.15	.07
179	Dave Valle	.15	.07
180	Dave Silvestri	.15	.07
181	Bud Black	.15	.07
182	Henry Rodriguez	.30	.14
183	Tim Teufel	.15	.07
184	Mark McLemore	.15	.07
185	Bret Saberhagen	.15	.07
186	Chris Hoiles	.15	.07
187	Ricky Jordan	.15	.07
188	Don Slaught	.15	.07
189	Mo Vaughn	.75	.35
190	Joe Oliver	.15	.07
191	Juan Gonzalez	1.50	.70
192	Scott Leius	.15	.07
193	Milt Cuyler	.15	.07
194	Chris Haney	.15	.07
195	Ron Karkovice	.15	.07
196	Steve Farr	.15	.07
197	John Orton	.15	.07
198	Kelly Gruber	.15	.07
199	Ron Darling	.15	.07
200	Ruben Sierra	.30	.14
201	Chuck Finley	.15	.07
202	Mike Moore	.15	.07
203	Pat Borders	.15	.07
204	Sid Bream	.15	.07
205	Todd Zeile	.15	.07
206	Rick Wilkins	.15	.07
207	Jim Gantner	.15	.07
208	Frank Castillo	.15	.07
209	Dave Hansen	.15	.07
210	Trevor Wilson	.15	.07
211	Sandy Alomar Jr.	.30	.14
212	Sean Berry	.15	.07
213	Tino Martinez	.60	.25
214	Chito Martinez	.15	.07
215	Dan Walters	.15	.07
216	John Franco	.30	.14
217	Glenn Davis	.15	.07
218	Mariano Duncan	.15	.07
219	Mike LaValliere	.15	.07
220	Rafael Palmeiro	.40	.18
221	Jack Clark	.15	.07
222	Hal Morris	.15	.07
223	Ed Sprague	.15	.07
224	John Valentin	.30	.14
225	Sam Militello	.15	.07
226	Bob Wickman	.15	.07
227	Damion Easley	.15	.07
228	John Jaha	.30	.14
229	Bob Ayrault	.15	.07
230	Mo Sanford	.15	.07
231	Walt Weiss	.15	.07
232	Dante Bichette	.40	.18
233	Steve Decker	.15	.07
234	Jerald Clark	.15	.07
235	Bryan Harvey	.15	.07
236	Joe Girardi	.15	.07
237	Dave Magadan	.15	.07
238	David Nied	.30	.14
239	Eric Wedge	.15	.07
240	Rico Brogna	.30	.14
241	J.T.Bruett	.15	.07
242	Jonathan Hurst	.15	.07
243	Bret Boone	.15	.07
244	Manny Alexander	.15	.07
245	Scooter Tucker	.15	.07
246	Troy Neel	.15	.07
247	Eddie Zosky	.15	.07
248	Melvin Nieves	.30	.14
249	Ryan Thompson	.15	.07
250	Shawn Barton	.15	.07
251	Ryan Klesko	.75	.35
252	Mike Piazza	3.00	1.35
253	Steve Hosey	.15	.07
254	Shane Reynolds	.30	.14
255	Dan Wilson	.30	.14
256	Tom Marsh	.15	.07
257	Barry Manuel	.15	.07
258	Paul Miller	.15	.07
259	Pedro Martinez	.60	.25
260	Steve Cooke	.15	.07
261	Johnny Guzman	.15	.07
262	Mike Butcher	.15	.07
263	Bien Figueroa	.15	.07
264	Rich Rowland	.15	.07
265	Shawn Jeter	.15	.07
266	Gerald Williams	.15	.07
267	Derek Parks	.15	.07
268	Henry Mercedes	.15	.07
269	David Hulse	.15	.07
270	Tim Pugh	.15	.07
271	William Suero	.15	.07
272	Ozzie Canseco	.15	.07
273	Fernando Ramsey	.15	.07
274	Bernardo Brito	.15	.07
275	Dave Mlicki	.15	.07
276	Tim Salmon	.75	.35
277	Mike Raczka	.15	.07
278	Ken Ryan	.15	.07
279	Rafael Bournigal	.15	.07
280	Wil Cordero	.15	.07
281	Billy Ashley	.15	.07
282	Paul Wagner	.15	.07
283	Blas Minor	.15	.07
284	Rick Trlicek	.15	.07
285	Willie Greene	.30	.14
286	Ted Wood	.15	.07
287	Phil Clark	.15	.07
288	Jesse Levis	.15	.07
289	Tony Gwynn NT	.60	.25
290	Nolan Ryan NT	1.25	.55

291	Dennis Martinez NT	.15	.07
292	Eddie Murray NT	.30	.14
293	Robin Yount NT	.30	.14
294	George Brett NT	.60	.25
295	Dave Winfield NT	.30	.14
296	Bert Blyleven NT	.15	.07
297	Jeff Bagwell / Carl Yastrzemski	.60	.25
298	John Smoltz / Jack Morris	.30	.14
299	Larry Walker / Mike Bossy	.60	.25
300	Gary Sheffield / Barry Larkin	.30	.14
301	Ivan Rodriguez / Carlton Fisk	.30	.14
302	Delino DeShields / Malcolm X	.60	.25
303	Tim Salmon / Dwight Evans	.40	.18
304	Bernard Gilkey HH	.15	.07
305	Cal Ripken Jr. HH	1.25	.55
306	Barry Larkin HH	.40	.18
307	Kent Hrbek HH	.15	.07
308	Rickey Henderson HH	.30	.14
309	Darryl Strawberry HH	.15	.07
310	John Franco HH	.15	.07
311	Todd Stottlemyre	.15	.07
312	Luis Gonzalez	.15	.07
313	Tommy Greene	.15	.07
314	Randy Velarde	.15	.07
315	Steve Avery	.15	.07
316	Jose Oquendo	.15	.07
317	Rey Sanchez	.15	.07
318	Greg Vaughn	.15	.07
319	Orel Hershiser	.30	.14
320	Paul Sorrento	.15	.07
321	Royce Clayton	.15	.07
322	John Vander Wal	.15	.07
323	Henry Cotto	.15	.07
324	Pete Schourek	.15	.07
325	David Segui	.15	.07
326	Arthur Rhodes	.15	.07
327	Bruce Hurst	.15	.07
328	Wes Chamberlain	.15	.07
329	Ozzie Smith	.75	.35
330	Scott Cooper	.15	.07
331	Felix Fermin	.15	.07
332	Mike Macfarlane	.15	.07
333	Dan Gladden	.15	.07
334	Kevin Tapani	.15	.07
335	Steve Sax	.15	.07
336	Jeff Montgomery	.30	.14
337	Gary DiSarcina	.15	.07
338	Lance Blankenship	.15	.07
339	Brian Williams	.15	.07
340	Duane Ward	.15	.07
341	Chuck McElroy	.15	.07
342	Joe Magrane	.15	.07
343	Jaime Navarro	.15	.07
344	Dave Justice	.60	.25
345	Jose Offerman	.15	.07
346	Marquis Grissom	.30	.14
347	Bill Swift	.15	.07
348	Jim Thome	1.25	.55
349	Archi Cianfrocco	.15	.07
350	Anthony Young	.15	.07
351	Leo Gomez	.15	.07
352	Bill Gullickson	.15	.07
353	Alan Trammell	.40	.18
354	Dan Pasqua	.15	.07
355	Jeff King	.30	.14
356	Kevin Brown	.30	.14
357	Tim Belcher	.15	.07
358	Bip Roberts	.15	.07
359	Brent Mayne	.15	.07
360	Rheal Cormier	.15	.07
361	Mark Guthrie	.15	.07
362	Craig Grebeck	.15	.07
363	Andy Stankiewicz	.15	.07
364	Juan Guzman	.15	.07
365	Bobby Witt	.15	.07
366	Mark Portugal	.15	.07
367	Brian McRae	.15	.07
368	Mark Lemke	.15	.07
369	Bill Wegman	.15	.07
370	Donovan Osborne	.15	.07
371	Derrick May	.15	.07
372	Carl Willis	.15	.07
373	Chris Nabholz	.15	.07
374	Mark Lewis	.15	.07
375	John Burkett	.15	.07
376	Luis Mercedes	.15	.07
377	Ramon Martinez	.30	.14
378	Kyle Abbott	.15	.07
379	Mark Wohlers	.15	.07
380	Bob Walk	.15	.07
381	Kenny Rogers	.15	.07
382	Tim Naehring	.15	.07
383	Alex Fernandez	.30	.14
384	Keith Miller	.15	.07
385	Mike Henneman	.15	.07
386	Rick Aguilera	.15	.07
387	George Bell	.15	.07
388	Mike Gallego	.15	.07
389	Howard Johnson	.15	.07
390	Kim Batiste	.15	.07
391	Jerry Browne	.15	.07
392	Damon Berryhill	.15	.07
393	Ricky Bones	.15	.07
394	Omar Olivares	.15	.07
395	Mike Harkey	.15	.07
396	Pedro Astacio	.15	.07
397	John Wetteland	.30	.14
398	Rod Beck	.30	.14
399	Thomas Howard	.15	.07
400	Mike Devereaux	.15	.07
401	Tim Wakefield	.30	.14
402	Curt Schilling	.15	.07
403	Zane Smith	.15	.07
404	Bob Zupcic	.15	.07
405	Tom Browning	.15	.07
406	Tony Phillips	.15	.07
407	John Doherty	.15	.07
408	Pat Mahomes	.15	.07
409	John Habyan	.15	.07
410	Steve Olin	.15	.07
411	Chad Curtis	.30	.14
412	Joe Grahe	.15	.07
413	John Patterson	.15	.07
414	Brian Hunter	.15	.07
415	Doug Henry	.15	.07
416	Lee Smith	.30	.14
417	Bob Scanlan	.15	.07
418	Kent Mercker	.15	.07
419	Mel Rojas	.15	.07
420	Mark Whiten	.15	.07
421	Carlton Fisk	.50	.25
422	Candy Maldonado	.15	.07
423	Doug Drabek	.15	.07
424	Wade Boggs	.60	.25
425	Mark Davis	.15	.07
426	Kirby Puckett	1.25	.55
427	Joe Carter	.30	.14
428	Paul Molitor	.60	.25
429	Eric Davis	.30	.14
430	Darryl Kile	.15	.07
431	Jeff Parrett	.15	.07
432	Jeff Blauser	.15	.07
433	Dan Plesac	.15	.07
434	Andres Galarraga	.60	.25
435	Jim Gott	.15	.07
436	Jose Mesa	.15	.07
437	Ben Rivera	.15	.07
438	Dave Winfield	.40	.18
439	Norm Charlton	.15	.07
440	Chris Bosio	.15	.07
441	Wilson Alvarez	.30	.14
442	Dave Stewart	.30	.14
443	Doug Jones	.15	.07
444	Jeff Russell	.15	.07
445	Ron Gant	.30	.14
446	Paul O'Neill	.30	.14
447	Charlie Hayes	.15	.07
448	Joe Hesketh	.15	.07
449	Chris Hammond	.15	.07
450	Hipolito Pichardo	.15	.07
451	Scott Radinsky	.15	.07
452	Bobby Thigpen	.15	.07
453	Xavier Hernandez	.15	.07
454	Lonnie Smith	.15	.07
455	Jamie Arnold DP	.30	.14
456	B.J. Wallace DP	.15	.07
457	Derek Jeter DP	6.00	2.70
458	Jason Kendall DP	1.00	.45
459	Rick Helling DP	.30	.14
460	Derek Wallace DP	.15	.07
461	Sean Lowe DP	.15	.07
462	Shannon Stewart DP	.75	.35
463	Benji Grigsby DP	.15	.07
464	Todd Steverson DP	.30	.14
465	Dan Serafini DP	.40	.18
466	Michael Tucker DP	.60	.25
467	Chris Roberts DP	.30	.14
468	Pete Janicki DP	.15	.07
469	Jeff Schmidt DP	.15	.07
470	Don Mattingly NT	.60	.25
471	Cal Ripken Jr. NT	1.25	.55
472	Jack Morris NT	.15	.07
473	Terry Pendleton NT	.15	.07
474	Dennis Eckersley NT	.15	.07
475	Carlton Fisk NT	.30	.14
476	Wade Boggs NT	.60	.25
477	Len Dykstra / Ken Stabler	.30	.14
478	Danny Tartabull / Jose Tartabull	.15	.07
479	Jeff Conine / Dale Murphy	.30	.14
480	Gregg Jefferies / Ron Cey	.15	.07
481	Paul Molitor / Harmon Killebrew	.40	.18
482	John Valentin / Dave Concepcion	.15	.07
483	Alex Arias / Dave Winfield	.30	.14
484	Barry Bonds HH	.40	.18
485	Doug Drabek HH	.15	.07
486	Dave Winfield HH	.30	.14
487	Brett Butler HH	.15	.07
488	Harold Baines HH	.15	.07
489	David Cone HH	.15	.07
490	Willie McGee HH	.15	.07
491	Robby Thompson	.15	.07
492	Pete Incaviglia	.15	.07
493	Manuel Lee	.15	.07
494	Rafael Belliard	.15	.07
495	Scott Fletcher	.15	.07
496	Jeff Frye	.15	.07
497	Andre Dawson	.40	.18
498	Mike Scioscia	.15	.07
499	Spike Owen	.15	.07
500	Sid Fernandez	.15	.07
501	Joe Orsulak	.15	.07
502	Benito Santiago	.15	.07
503	Dale Murphy	.40	.18
504	Barry Bonds	.75	.35
505	Jose Guzman	.15	.07
506	Tony Pena	.15	.07
507	Greg Swindell	.15	.07
508	Mike Pagliarulo	.15	.07
509	Lou Whitaker	.30	.14
510	Greg Gagne	.15	.07
511	Butch Henry	.15	.07
512	Jeff Brantley	.15	.07
513	Jack Armstrong	.15	.07
514	Danny Jackson	.15	.07
515	Junior Felix	.15	.07
516	Milt Thompson	.15	.07
517	Greg Maddux	2.00	.90
518	Eric Young	.60	.25
519	Jody Reed	.15	.07
520	Roberto Kelly	.15	.07
521	Darren Holmes	.15	.07
522	Craig Lefferts	.15	.07
523	Charlie Hough	.15	.07
524	Bo Jackson	.30	.14
525	Bill Spiers	.15	.07
526	Orestes Destrade	.15	.07
527	Greg Hibbard	.15	.07
528	Roger McDowell	.15	.07
529	Cory Snyder	.15	.07
530	Harold Reynolds	.15	.07
531	Kevin Reimer	.15	.07
532	Rick Sutcliffe	.15	.07
533	Tony Fernandez	.15	.07
534	Tom Brunansky	.15	.07

□ 535 Jeff Reardon	.30	.14
□ 536 Chili Davis	.30	.14
□ 537 Bob Ojeda	.15	.07
□ 538 Greg Colbrunn	.15	.07
□ 539 Phil Plantier	.15	.07
□ 540 Brian Jordan	.30	.14
□ 541 Pete Smith	.15	.07
□ 542 Frank Tanana	.15	.07
□ 543 John Smiley	.15	.07
□ 544 David Cone	.30	.14
□ 545 Daryl Boston	.15	.07
□ 546 Tom Henke	.15	.07
□ 547 Bill Krueger	.15	.07
□ 548 Freddie Benavides	.15	.07
□ 549 Randy Myers	.30	.14
□ 550 Reggie Jefferson	.15	.07
□ 551 Kevin Mitchell	.30	.14
□ 552 Dave Stieb	.15	.07
□ 553 Bret Barberie	.15	.07
□ 554 Tim Crews	.15	.07
□ 555 Doug Dascenzo	.15	.07
□ 556 Alex Cole	.15	.07
□ 557 Jeff Innis	.15	.07
□ 558 Carlos Garcia	.15	.07
□ 559 Steve Howe	.15	.07
□ 560 Kirk McCaskill	.15	.07
□ 561 Frank Seminara	.15	.07
□ 562 Cris Carpenter	.15	.07
□ 563 Mike Stanley	.15	.07
□ 564 Carlos Quintana	.15	.07
□ 565 Mitch Williams	.15	.07
□ 566 Juan Bell	.15	.07
□ 567 Eric Fox	.15	.07
□ 568 Al Leiter	.30	.14
□ 569 Mike Stanton	.15	.07
□ 570 Scott Kamieniecki	.15	.07
□ 571 Ryan Bowen	.15	.07
□ 572 Andy Ashby	.15	.07
□ 573 Bob Welch	.15	.07
□ 574 Scott Sanderson	.15	.07
□ 575 Joe Kmak	.15	.07
□ 576 Scott Pose	.15	.07
□ 577 Ricky Gutierrez	.15	.07
□ 578 Mike Trombley	.15	.07
□ 579 Sterling Hitchcock	.30	.14
□ 580 Rodney Bolton	.15	.07
□ 581 Tyler Green	.15	.07
□ 582 Tim Costo	.15	.07
□ 583 Tim Laker	.15	.07
□ 584 Steve Reed	.15	.07
□ 585 Tom Kramer	.15	.07
□ 586 Robb Nen	.40	.18
□ 587 Jim Tatum	.15	.07
□ 588 Frank Bolick	.15	.07
□ 589 Kevin Young	.15	.07
□ 590 Matt Whiteside	.15	.07
□ 591 Cesar Hernandez	.15	.07
□ 592 Mike Mohler	.15	.07
□ 593 Alan Embree	.15	.07
□ 594 Terry Jorgensen	.15	.07
□ 595 John Cummings	.15	.07
□ 596 Domingo Martinez	.15	.07
□ 597 Benji Gil	.15	.07
□ 598 Todd Pratt	.15	.07
□ 599 Rene Arocha	.15	.07
□ 600 Dennis Moeller	.15	.07
□ 601 Jeff Conine	.30	.14
□ 602 Trevor Hoffman	.40	.18
□ 603 Daniel Smith	.15	.07
□ 604 Lee Tinsley	.30	.14
□ 605 Dan Peltier	.15	.07
□ 606 Billy Brewer	.15	.07
□ 607 Matt Walbeck	.15	.07
□ 608 Richie Lewis	.15	.07
□ 609 J.T. Snow	.75	.35
□ 610 Pat Gomez	.15	.07
□ 611 Phil Hiatt	.15	.07
□ 612 Alex Arias	.15	.07
□ 613 Kevin Rogers	.15	.07
□ 614 Al Martin	.30	.14
□ 615 Greg Gohr	.15	.07
□ 616 Graeme Lloyd	.15	.07
□ 617 Kent Bottenfield	.15	.07
□ 618 Chuck Carr	.15	.07
□ 619 Darrell Sherman	.15	.07
□ 620 Mike Lansing	.30	.14

1993 Pinnacle Expansion Opening Day

This nine-card standard-size dual-sided set was issued to commemorate opening day for the two 1993 expansion teams, the Colorado Rockies and the Florida Marlins. The cards were inserted on top of sealed series two hobby boxes. These cards were also available through a mail-in offer. The full-bleed fronts feature glossy color action player images. Across the bottom is a team color-coded bar containing the player's name, position, and opening day date. A logo for the Expansion Draft is printed in the lower right corner. An anti-counterfeit device is printed in the bottom black border. The backs carry the same design as the fronts with a player from the Rockies appearing on one side and a Marlin's player on the flip side. The cards are numbered on both sides.

	MINT	NRMT
COMPLETE SET (9)	25.00	11.00
COMMON PAIR (1-9)	1.50	.70
MINOR STARS	4.00	1.80
ONE CARD PER SEALED SER.2 HOBBY BOX		
□ 1 Charlie Hough	4.00	1.80
David Nied		
□ 2 Benito Santiago	1.50	.70
Joe Girardi		
□ 3 Orestes Destrade	8.00	3.60
Andres Galarraga		
□ 4 Bret Barberie	4.00	1.80
Eric Young		
□ 5 Dave Magadan	1.50	.70
Charlie Hayes		
□ 6 Walt Weiss	1.50	.70
Freddie Benavides		
□ 7 Jeff Conine	6.00	2.70
Jerald Clark		
□ 8 Scott Pose	1.50	.70
Alex Cole		
□ 9 Junior Felix	8.00	3.60
Dante Bichette		

1993 Pinnacle Rookie Team Pinnacle

Cards from this 10-card standard-size set were randomly inserted into one in every 90

series 2 foil packs and each features an American League rookie on one side and a National League rookie on the other. Each double-sided card displays paintings by artist Christopher Greco encased by a bold black border. The cards are numbered on the front and back.

	MINT	NRMT
COMPLETE SET (10)	100.00	45.00
COMMON PAIR (1-10)	4.00	1.80
SEMISTARS	8.00	3.60
SER.2 STATED ODDS 1:90		
□ 1 Pedro Martinez	10.00	4.50
Mike Trombley		
□ 2 Kevin Rogers	4.00	1.80
Sterling Hitchcock		
□ 3 Mike Piazza	50.00	22.00
Jesse Levis		
□ 4 Ryan Klesko	12.00	5.50
J.T. Snow		
□ 5 John Patterson	4.00	1.80
Bret Boone		
□ 6 Kevin Young	4.00	1.80
Domingo Martinez		
□ 7 Wil Cordero	4.00	1.80
Manny Alexander		
□ 8 Steve Hosey	15.00	6.75
Tim Salmon		
□ 9 Ryan Thompson	4.00	1.80
Gerald Williams		
□ 10 Melvin Nieves	6.00	2.70
David Hulse		

1993 Pinnacle Slugfest

These 30 standard-size cards salute baseball's top hitters and were inserted one per series 2 jumbo superpacks. The fronts feature color player action shots that are borderless, except at the bottom, where a black stripe carries the player's name in white lettering. The set's title appears below in black lettering within a gold foil stripe.

	MINT	NRMT
COMPLETE SET (30)	60.00	27.00
COMMON CARD (1-30)		
ONE PER SER.2 JUMBO PACK..		
□ 1 Juan Gonzalez	8.00	3.60
□ 2 Mark McGwire	6.00	2.70
□ 3 Cecil Fielder	1.50	.70
□ 4 Joe Carter	1.50	.70
□ 5 Fred McGriff	2.00	.90
□ 6 Barry Bonds	4.00	1.80
□ 7 Gary Sheffield	3.00	1.35
□ 8 Dave Hollins	1.00	.45
□ 9 Frank Thomas	12.00	5.50
□ 10 Danny Tartabull	1.00	.45
□ 11 Albert Belle	4.00	1.80
□ 12 Ruben Sierra	1.00	.45
□ 13 Larry Walker	3.00	1.35
□ 14 Jeff Bagwell	6.00	2.70
□ 15 David Justice	3.00	1.35
□ 16 Kirby Puckett	6.00	2.70
□ 17 John Kruk	1.50	.70
□ 18 Howard Johnson	1.00	.45
□ 19 Darryl Strawberry	1.50	.70
□ 20 Will Clark	2.00	.90
□ 21 Kevin Mitchell	1.00	.45
□ 22 Mickey Tettleton	1.00	.45
□ 23 Don Mattingly	5.00	2.20
□ 24 Jose Canseco	2.00	.90
□ 25 George Bell	1.00	.45
□ 26 Andre Dawson	2.00	.90
□ 27 Ryne Sandberg	4.00	1.80
□ 28 Ken Griffey Jr.	15.00	6.75
□ 29 Carlos Baerga	1.00	.45
□ 30 Travis Fryman	1.50	.70

1993 Pinnacle Team 2001

This 30-card standard-size set salutes players expected to be stars in the year 2001. The cards were inserted one per pack in first series jumbo super-packs and feature color player action shots on their fronts. These photos are borderless at the top and right, and black-bordered on the bottom and left. The player's name appears in gold-foil in the bottom margin, and his gold-foil-encircled team logo rests in the bottom left.

	MINT	NRMT
COMPLETE SET (30)	40.00	18.00
COMMON CARD (1-30)	.75	.35
ONE PER SER.1 JUMBO PACK..		
□ 1 Wil Cordero	.75	.35
□ 2 Cal Eldred	.75	.35
□ 3 Mike Mussina	2.50	1.10
□ 4 Chuck Knoblauch	2.50	1.10
□ 5 Melvin Nieves	1.00	.45
□ 6 Tim Wakefield	.75	.35
□ 7 Carlos Baerga	.75	.35
□ 8 Bret Boone	.75	.35
□ 9 Jeff Bagwell	6.00	2.70
□ 10 Travis Fryman	1.00	.45
□ 11 Royce Clayton	.75	.35
□ 12 Delino DeShields	.75	.35
□ 13 Juan Gonzalez	8.00	3.60
□ 14 Pedro Martinez	2.50	1.10
□ 15 Bernie Williams	2.50	1.10
□ 16 Billy Ashley	.75	.35
□ 17 Marquis Grissom	1.00	.45
□ 18 Kenny Lofton	6.00	2.70
□ 19 Ray Lankford	1.50	.70
□ 20 Tim Salmon	4.00	1.80
□ 21 Steve Hosey	.75	.35
□ 22 Charles Nagy	1.00	.45
□ 23 Dave Fleming	1.00	.45
□ 24 Reggie Sanders	1.00	.45
□ 25 Sam Militello	.75	.35
□ 26 Eric Karros	1.00	.45
□ 27 Ryan Klesko	4.00	1.80
□ 28 Dean Palmer	.75	.35
□ 29 Ivan Rodriguez	4.00	1.80
□ 30 Sterling Hitchcock	.75	.35

1993 Pinnacle Team Pinnacle

Cards from this ten-card dual-sided set, featuring a selection of top stars paired by position, were randomly inserted into one in every 24 first series foil packs. Each double-sided card displays paintings by artist Christopher Greco. A special bonus Team Pinnacle card (11) was available to collectors only through a mail-in offer for ten 1993 Pinnacle baseball wrappers plus $1.50 for shipping and handling. Moreover, hobby dealers who ordered Pinnacle received two bonus cards and an advertisement display promoting the offer.

	MINT	NRMT
COMPLETE SET (10)	90.00	40.00
COMMON PAIR (1-10/B11)	3.00	1.35
SEMISTARS	6.00	2.70
UNLISTED STARS	8.00	3.60
RANDOM INSERTS IN SER.1 PACKS		
B11 DISTRIBUTED ONLY BY MAIL		
□ 1 Greg Maddux	25.00	11.00
Mike Mussina		
□ 2 Tom Glavine	6.00	2.70
John Smiley		
□ 3 Darren Daulton	10.00	4.50
Ivan Rodriguez		
□ 4 Fred McGriff	30.00	13.50
Frank Thomas		
□ 5 Delino DeShields	4.00	1.80
Carlos Baerga		
□ 6 Gary Sheffield	8.00	3.60
Edgar Martinez		
□ 7 Ozzie Smith	10.00	4.50
Pat Listach		
□ 8 Barry Bonds	20.00	9.00
Juan Gonzalez		
□ 9 Andy Van Slyke	15.00	6.75
Kirby Puckett		
□ 10 Larry Walker	8.00	3.60
Joe Carter		
□ B11 Rob Dibble	3.00	1.35
Rick Aguilera		

1994 Pinnacle

The 540-card 1994 Pinnacle standard-size set was issued in two series of 270. Cards were issued in hobby and retail foil-wrapped packs. The card fronts feature full-bleed color action player photos with a small foil logo and players name at the base. Subsets include Rookie Prospects (224-261) and Draft Picks (262-270/430-438). Notable Rookie Cards include Derrek Lee, Chan Ho Park and Billy Wagner. A Carlos Delgado Super Rookie one shot insert was put into packs at a rate of one in 360. It is labeled SR1 and is listed at the end of the set.

	MINT	NRMT
COMPLETE SET (540)	20.00	9.00
COMPLETE SERIES 1 (270)	10.00	4.50
COMPLETE SERIES 2 (270)	10.00	4.50
COMMON CARD (1-540)	.10	.05
MINOR STARS	.25	.11
UNLISTED STARS	.50	.23
COMP.AP SET (540)	2000.00	900.00
COMP.AP SER.1 (270)	1400.00	650.00
COMP.AP SER.2 (270)	600.00	275.00
COMMON AP (1-540)	3.00	1.35
*AP STARS: 12.5X TO 30X HI COLUMN		
*AP YOUNG STARS: 10X TO 25X HI		
*AP ROOKIES: 8X TO 20X HI		
AP STATED ODDS 1:26 HOB, 1:22 RET		
COMP.MUSEUM SET (540)	600.00	275.00
COMP.MUSEUM SER.1 (270)	400.00	180.00
COMP.MUSEUM SER.2 (270)	200.00	90.00
COMMON MUSEUM (1-540)	1.00	.45
MUS.TRADE (279/313/328)..	3.00	1.35
MUS.TRADE (382/387)	3.00	1.35
*MUSEUM STARS: 6X TO 12X HI COLUMN		
*MUSEUM YOUNG STARS: 5X TO 10X HI		
*MUSEUM ROOKIES: 4X TO 8X HI		
MUSEUM STAT.ODDS 1:4H, 1:3R, 1:4J		
DEL GADO SR STATED ODDS 1:360		
□ 1 Frank Thomas	2.00	.90
□ 2 Carlos Baerga	.10	.05
□ 3 Sammy Sosa	.50	.23

4	Tony Gwynn	1.25	.55
5	John Olerud	.25	.11
6	Ryne Sandberg	.60	.25
7	Moises Alou	.25	.11
8	Steve Avery	.10	.05
9	Tim Salmon	.50	.23
10	Cecil Fielder	.25	.11
11	Greg Maddux	1.50	.70
12	Barry Larkin	.30	.14
13	Mike Devereaux	.10	.05
14	Charlie Hayes	.10	.05
15	Albert Belle	.60	.25
16	Andy Van Slyke	.25	.11
17	Mo Vaughn	.60	.25
18	Brian McRae	.10	.05
19	Cal Eldred	.10	.05
20	Craig Biggio	.30	.14
21	Kirby Puckett	1.00	.45
22	Derek Bell	.10	.05
23	Don Mattingly	.75	.35
24	John Burkett	.10	.05
25	Roger Clemens	1.00	.45
26	Barry Bonds	.60	.25
27	Paul Molitor	.50	.23
28	Mike Piazza	1.50	.70
29	Robin Ventura	.25	.11
30	Jeff Conine	.10	.05
31	Wade Boggs	.50	.23
32	Dennis Eckersley	.25	.11
33	Bobby Bonilla	.25	.11
34	Lenny Dykstra	.25	.11
35	Manny Alexander	.10	.05
36	Ray Lankford	.25	.11
37	Greg Vaughn	.10	.05
38	Chuck Finley	.10	.05
39	Todd Benzinger	.10	.05
40	Dave Justice	.50	.23
41	Rob Dibble	.10	.05
42	Tom Henke	.10	.05
43	David Nied	.10	.05
44	Sandy Alomar Jr	.25	.11
45	Pete Harnisch	.10	.05
46	Jeff Russell	.10	.05
47	Terry Mulholland	.10	.05
48	Kevin Appier	.25	.11
49	Randy Tomlin	.10	.05
50	Cal Ripken Jr	2.00	.90
51	Andy Benes	.25	.11
52	Jimmy Key	.25	.11
53	Kirt Manwaring	.10	.05
54	Kevin Tapani	.10	.05
55	Jose Guzman	.10	.05
56	Todd Stottlemyre	.10	.05
57	Jack McDowell	.25	.11
58	Orel Hershiser	.25	.11
59	Chris Hammond	.10	.05
60	Chris Nabholz	.10	.05
61	Ruben Sierra	.25	.11
62	Dwight Gooden	.25	.11
63	John Kruk	.25	.11
64	Omar Vizquel	.25	.11
65	Tim Naehring	.10	.05
66	Dwight Smith	.10	.05
67	Mickey Tettleton	.10	.05
68	J.T. Snow	.50	.23
69	Greg McMichael	.10	.05
70	Kevin Mitchell	.10	.05
71	Kevin Brown	.25	.11
72	Scott Cooper	.10	.05
73	Jim Thome	.60	.25
74	Joe Girardi	.10	.05
75	Eric Anthony	.10	.05
76	Orlando Merced	.10	.05
77	Felix Jose	.10	.05
78	Tommy Greene	.10	.05
79	Bernard Gilkey	.10	.05
80	Phil Plantier	.10	.05
81	Danny Tartabull	.10	.05
82	Trevor Wilson	.10	.05
83	Chuck Knoblauch	.50	.23
84	Rick Wilkins	.10	.05
85	Devon White	.10	.05
86	Lance Johnson	.10	.05
87	Eric Karros	.25	.11
88	Gary Sheffield	.50	.23
89	Wil Cordero	.10	.05
90	Ron Darling	.10	.05
91	Darren Daulton	.25	.11
92	Joe Orsulak	.10	.05
93	Steve Cooke	.10	.05
94	Darryl Hamilton	.10	.05
95	Aaron Sele	.10	.05
96	John Doherty	.10	.05
97	Gary DiSarcina	.10	.05
98	Jeff Blauser	.25	.11
99	John Smiley	.10	.05
100	Ken Griffey Jr	2.50	1.10
101	Dean Palmer	.10	.05
102	Felix Fermin	.10	.05
103	Jerald Clark	.10	.05
104	Doug Drabek	.10	.05
105	Curt Schilling	.25	.11
106	Jeff Montgomery	.10	.05
107	Rene Arocha	.10	.05
108	Carlos Garcia	.10	.05
109	Wally Whitehurst	.10	.05
110	Jim Abbott	.10	.05
111	Royce Clayton	.10	.05
112	Chris Hoiles	.10	.05
113	Mike Morgan	.10	.05
114	Joe Magrane	.10	.05
115	Tom Candiotti	.10	.05
116	Ron Karkovice	.10	.05
117	Ryan Bowen	.10	.05
118	Rod Beck	.10	.05
119	John Wetteland	.10	.05
120	Terry Steinbach	.10	.05
121	Dave Hollins	.10	.05
122	Jeff Kent	.10	.05
123	Ricky Bones	.10	.05
124	Brian Jordan	.25	.11
125	Chad Kreuter	.10	.05
126	John Valentin	.25	.11
127	Hilly Hathaway	.10	.05
128	Wilson Alvarez	.10	.05
129	Tino Martinez	.50	.23
130	Rodney Bolton	.10	.05
131	David Segui	.10	.05
132	Wayne Kirby	.10	.05
133	Eric Young	.10	.05
134	Scott Servais	.10	.05
135	Scott Radinsky	.10	.05
136	Bret Barberie	.10	.05
137	John Roper	.10	.05
138	Ricky Gutierrez	.10	.05
139	Bernie Williams	.50	.23
140	Bud Black	.10	.05
141	Jose Vizcaino	.10	.05
142	Gerald Williams	.10	.05
143	Duane Ward	.10	.05
144	Danny Jackson	.10	.05
145	Allen Watson	.10	.05
146	Scott Fletcher	.10	.05
147	Delino DeShields	.25	.11
148	Shane Mack	.10	.05
149	Jim Eisenreich	.10	.05
150	Troy Neel	.10	.05
151	Jay Bell	.25	.11
152	B.J. Surhoff	.10	.05
153	Mark Whiten	.10	.05
154	Mike Henneman	.10	.05
155	Todd Hundley	.25	.11
156	Greg Myers	.10	.05
157	Ryan Klesko	.50	.23
158	Dave Fleming	.10	.05
159	Mickey Morandini	.10	.05
160	Blas Minor	.10	.05
161	Reggie Jefferson	.10	.05
162	David Hulse	.10	.05
163	Greg Swindell	.10	.05
164	Roberto Hernandez	.10	.05
165	Brady Anderson	.30	.14
166	Jack Armstrong	.10	.05
167	Phil Clark	.10	.05
168	Melido Perez	.10	.05
169	Darren Lewis	.10	.05
170	Sam Horn	.10	.05
171	Mike Harkey	.10	.05
172	Juan Samuel	.10	.05
173	Bob Natal	.10	.05
174	Deion Sanders	.25	.11
175	Carlos Quintana	.10	.05
176	Mel Rojas	.10	.05
177	Willie Banks	.10	.05
178	Ben Rivera	.10	.05
179	Kenny Lofton	.60	.25
180	Leo Gomez	.10	.05
181	Roberto Mejia	.10	.05
182	Mike Perez	.10	.05
183	Travis Fryman	.25	.11
184	Ben McDonald	.10	.05
185	Steve Frey	.10	.05
186	Kevin Young	.10	.05
187	Dave Magadan	.10	.05
188	Bobby Munoz	.10	.05
189	Pat Rapp	.10	.05
190	Jose Offerman	.10	.05
191	Vinny Castilla	.25	.11
192	Ivan Calderon	.10	.05
193	Ken Caminiti	.30	.14
194	Benji Gil	.10	.05
195	Chuck Carr	.10	.05
196	Derrick May	.10	.05
197	Pat Kelly	.10	.05
198	Jeff Brantley	.10	.05
199	Jose Lind	.10	.05
200	Steve Buechele	.10	.05
201	Wes Chamberlain	.10	.05
202	Eduardo Perez	.10	.05
203	Bret Saberhagen	.10	.05
204	Gregg Jefferies	.10	.05
205	Darrin Fletcher	.10	.05
206	Kent Hrbek	.25	.11
207	Kim Batiste	.10	.05
208	Jeff King	.10	.05
209	Donovan Osborne	.10	.05
210	Dave Nilsson	.10	.05
211	Al Martin	.10	.05
212	Mike Moore	.10	.05
213	Sterling Hitchcock	.10	.05
214	Geronimo Pena	.10	.05
215	Kevin Higgins	.10	.05
216	Norm Charlton	.10	.05
217	Don Slaught	.10	.05
218	Mitch Williams	.10	.05
219	Derek Lilliquist	.10	.05
220	Armando Reynoso	.10	.05
221	Kenny Rogers	.10	.05
222	Doug Jones	.10	.05
223	Luis Aquino	.10	.05
224	Mike Oquist	.10	.05
225	Darryl Scott	.10	.05
226	Kurt Abbott	.10	.05
227	Andy Tomberlin	.10	.05
228	Norberto Martin	.10	.05
229	Pedro Castellano	.10	.05
230	Curtis Pride	.10	.05
231	Jeff McNeely	.10	.05
232	Scott Lydy	.10	.05
233	Darren Oliver	.50	.23
234	Danny Bautista	.10	.05
235	Butch Huskey	.25	.11
236	Chipper Jones	1.50	.70
237	Eddie Zambrano	.10	.05
238	Domingo Jean	.10	.05
239	Javier Lopez	.30	.14
240	Nigel Wilson	.10	.05
241	Drew Denson	.10	.05
242	Raul Mondesi	.50	.23
243	Luis Ortiz	.10	.05
244	Manny Ramirez	.60	.25
245	Greg Blosser	.10	.05
246	Rondell White	.30	.14
247	Steve Karsay	.10	.05
248	Scott Stahoviak	.10	.05
249	Jose Valentin	.10	.05
250	Marc Newfield	.25	.11
251	Keith Kessinger	.10	.05
252	Carl Everett	.10	.05
253	John O'Donoghue	.10	.05
254	Turk Wendell	.10	.05
255	Scott Ruffcorn	.10	.05
256	Tony Tarasco	.10	.05
257	Andy Cook	.10	.05
258	Matt Mieske	.10	.05
259	Luis Lopez	.10	.05
260	Ramon Caraballo	.10	.05
261	Salomon Torres	.10	.05

No.	Name			No.	Name			No.	Name		
262	Brooks Kieschnick	.50	.23	348	Frank Viola	.10	.05	434	Wayne Gomes	.10	.05
263	Daron Kirkreit	.10	.05	349	Ivan Rodriguez	.60	.25	435	Jay Powell	.25	.11
264	Bill Wagner	1.00	.45	350	Juan Gonzalez	1.25	.55	436	Kirk Presley	.25	.11
265	Matt Drews	.25	.11	351	Steve Finley	.10	.05	437	Jon Ratliff	.10	.05
266	Scott Christman	.25	.11	352	Mike Felder	.10	.05	438	Derrek Lee	1.50	.70
267	Torii Hunter	.30	.14	353	Ramon Martinez	.25	.11	439	Tom Pagnozzi	.10	.05
268	Jamey Wright	.50	.23	354	Greg Gagne	.10	.05	440	Kent Mercker	.10	.05
269	Jeff Granger	.10	.05	355	Ken Hill	.10	.05	441	Phil Leftwich	.10	.05
270	Trot Nixon	.25	.11	356	Pedro Munoz	.10	.05	442	Jamie Moyer	.10	.05
271	Randy Myers	.10	.05	357	Todd Van Poppel	.10	.05	443	John Flaherty	.10	.05
272	Trevor Hoffman	.10	.05	358	Marquis Grissom	.25	.11	444	Mark Wohlers	.10	.05
273	Bob Wickman	.10	.05	359	Milt Cuyler	.10	.05	445	Jose Bautista	.10	.05
274	Willie McGee	.10	.05	360	Reggie Sanders	.10	.05	446	Andres Galarraga	.50	.23
275	Hipolito Pichardo	.10	.05	361	Scott Erickson	.10	.05	447	Mark Lemke	.10	.05
276	Bobby Witt	.10	.05	362	Billy Hatcher	.10	.05	448	Tim Wakefield	.10	.05
277	Gregg Olson	.10	.05	363	Gene Harris	.10	.05	449	Pat Listach	.10	.05
278	Randy Johnson	.50	.23	364	Rene Gonzales	.10	.05	450	Rickey Henderson	.30	.14
279	Robb Nen	.10	.05	365	Kevin Rogers	.10	.05	451	Mike Gallego	.10	.05
280	Paul O'Neill	.25	.11	366	Eric Plunk	.10	.05	452	Bob Tewksbury	.10	.05
281	Lou Whitaker	.25	.11	367	Todd Zeile	.25	.11	453	Kirk Gibson	.25	.11
282	Chad Curtis	.10	.05	368	John Franco	.25	.11	454	Pedro Astacio	.10	.05
283	Doug Henry	.10	.05	369	Brett Butler	.25	.11	455	Mike Lansing	.25	.11
284	Tom Glavine	.25	.11	370	Bill Spiers	.10	.05	456	Sean Berry	.10	.05
285	Mike Greenwell	.10	.05	371	Terry Pendleton	.25	.11	457	Bob Walk	.10	.05
286	Roberto Kelly	.10	.05	372	Chris Bosio	.10	.05	458	Chili Davis	.25	.11
287	Roberto Alomar	.50	.23	373	Orestes Destrade	.10	.05	459	Ed Sprague	.10	.05
288	Charlie Hough	.10	.05	374	Dave Stewart	.25	.11	460	Kevin Stocker	.10	.05
289	Alex Fernandez	.10	.05	375	Darren Holmes	.10	.05	461	Mike Stanton	.10	.05
290	Jeff Bagwell	1.00	.45	376	Doug Strange	.10	.05	462	Tim Raines	.25	.11
291	Wally Joyner	.10	.05	377	Brian Turang	.10	.05	463	Mike Bordick	.10	.05
292	Andujar Cedeno	.10	.05	378	Carl Willis	.10	.05	464	David Wells	.10	.05
293	Rick Aguilera	.10	.05	379	Mark McLemore	.10	.05	465	Tim Laker	.10	.05
294	Darryl Strawberry	.25	.11	380	Bobby Jones	.25	.11	466	Cory Snyder	.10	.05
295	Mike Mussina	.50	.23	381	Scott Sanders	.10	.05	467	Alex Cole	.10	.05
296	Jeff Gardner	.10	.05	382	Kirk Rueter	.10	.05	468	Pete Incaviglia	.10	.05
297	Chris Gwynn	.10	.05	383	Randy Velarde	.10	.05	469	Roger Pavlik	.10	.05
298	Matt Williams	.30	.14	384	Fred McGriff	.30	.14	470	Greg W. Harris	.10	.05
299	Brent Gates	.10	.05	385	Charles Nagy	.25	.11	471	Xavier Hernandez	.10	.05
300	Mark McGwire	1.00	.45	386	Rich Amaral	.10	.05	472	Erik Hanson	.10	.05
301	Jim Deshaies	.10	.05	387	Geronimo Berroa	.10	.05	473	Jesse Orosco	.10	.05
302	Edgar Martinez	.30	.14	388	Eric Davis	.25	.11	474	Greg Colbrunn	.10	.05
303	Danny Darwin	.10	.05	389	Ozzie Smith	.60	.25	475	Harold Reynolds	.10	.05
304	Pat Meares	.10	.05	390	Alex Arias	.10	.05	476	Greg A. Harris	.10	.05
305	Benito Santiago	.10	.05	391	Brad Ausmus	.10	.05	477	Pat Borders	.10	.05
306	Jose Canseco	.30	.14	392	Cliff Floyd	.25	.11	478	Melvin Nieves	.10	.05
307	Jim Gott	.10	.05	393	Roger Salkeld	.10	.05	479	Mariano Duncan	.10	.05
308	Paul Sorrento	.10	.05	394	Jim Edmonds	.50	.23	480	Greg Hibbard	.10	.05
309	Scott Kamieniecki	.10	.05	395	Jeromy Burnitz	.10	.05	481	Tim Pugh	.10	.05
310	Larry Walker	.50	.23	396	Dave Staton	.10	.05	482	Bobby Ayala	.10	.05
311	Mark Langston	.10	.05	397	Rob Butler	.10	.05	483	Sid Fernandez	.10	.05
312	John Jaha	.10	.05	398	Marcos Armas	.10	.05	484	Tim Wallach	.10	.05
313	Stan Javier	.10	.05	399	Darrell Whitmore	.10	.05	485	Randy Milligan	.10	.05
314	Hal Morris	.10	.05	400	Ryan Thompson	.10	.05	486	Walt Weiss	.10	.05
315	Robby Thompson	.10	.05	401	Ross Powell	.10	.05	487	Matt Walbeck	.10	.05
316	Pat Hentgen	.25	.11	402	Joe Oliver	.10	.05	488	Mike Macfarlane	.10	.05
317	Tom Gordon	.10	.05	403	Paul Carey	.10	.05	489	Jerry Browne	.10	.05
318	Joey Cora	.25	.11	404	Bob Hamelin	.10	.05	490	Chris Sabo	.10	.05
319	Luis Alicea	.10	.05	405	Chris Turner	.10	.05	491	Tim Belcher	.10	.05
320	Andre Dawson	.30	.14	406	Nate Minchey	.10	.05	492	Spike Owen	.10	.05
321	Darryl Kile	.25	.11	407	Lonnie Maclin	.10	.05	493	Rafael Palmeiro	.30	.14
322	Jose Rijo	.10	.05	408	Harold Baines	.25	.11	494	Brian Harper	.10	.05
323	Luis Gonzalez	.10	.05	409	Brian Williams	.10	.05	495	Eddie Murray	.50	.23
324	Billy Ashley	.10	.05	410	Johnny Ruffin	.10	.05	496	Ellis Burks	.25	.11
325	David Cone	.25	.11	411	Julian Tavarez	.25	.11	497	Karl Rhodes	.10	.05
326	Bill Swift	.10	.05	412	Mark Hutton	.10	.05	498	Otis Nixon	.10	.05
327	Phil Hiatt	.10	.05	413	Carlos Delgado	.30	.14	499	Lee Smith	.25	.11
328	Craig Paquette	.10	.05	414	Chris Gomez	.10	.05	500	Bip Roberts	.10	.05
329	Bob Welch	.10	.05	415	Mike Hampton	.25	.11	501	Pedro Martinez	.50	.23
330	Tony Phillips	.10	.05	416	Alex Diaz	.10	.05	502	Brian Hunter	.10	.05
331	Archi Cianfrocco	.10	.05	417	Jeffrey Hammonds	.25	.11	503	Tyler Green	.10	.05
332	Dave Winfield	.30	.14	418	Jayhawk Owens	.10	.05	504	Bruce Hurst	.10	.05
333	David McCarty	.10	.05	419	J.R. Phillips	.10	.05	505	Alex Gonzalez	.25	.11
334	Al Leiter	.10	.05	420	Cory Bailey	.10	.05	506	Mark Portugal	.10	.05
335	Tom Browning	.10	.05	421	Denny Hocking	.10	.05	507	Bob Ojeda	.10	.05
336	Mark Grace	.30	.14	422	Jon Shave	.10	.05	508	Dave Henderson	.10	.05
337	Jose Mesa	.10	.05	423	Damon Buford	.10	.05	509	Bo Jackson	.25	.11
338	Mike Stanley	.10	.05	424	Troy O'Leary	.10	.05	510	Bret Boone	.10	.05
339	Roger McDowell	.10	.05	425	Tripp Cromer	.10	.05	511	Mark Eichhorn	.10	.05
340	Damion Easley	.10	.05	426	Albie Lopez	.10	.05	512	Luis Polonia	.10	.05
341	Angel Miranda	.10	.05	427	Tony Fernandez	.10	.05	513	Will Clark	.30	.14
342	John Smoltz	.25	.11	428	Ozzie Guillen	.10	.05	514	Dave Valle	.10	.05
343	Jay Buhner	.30	.14	429	Alan Trammell	.30	.14	515	Dan Wilson	.25	.11
344	Bryan Harvey	.10	.05	430	John Wasdin	.10	.05	516	Dennis Martinez	.25	.11
345	Joe Carter	.25	.11	431	Marc Valdes	.10	.05	517	Jim Leyritz	.10	.05
346	Dante Bichette	.25	.11	432	Brian Anderson	.25	.23	518	Howard Johnson	.10	.05
347	Jason Bere	.10	.05	433	Matt Brunson	.10	.05	519	Jody Reed	.10	.05

☐ 520 Julio Franco	.10	.05
☐ 521 Jeff Reardon	.25	.11
☐ 522 Willie Greene	.10	.05
☐ 523 Shawon Dunston	.10	.05
☐ 524 Keith Mitchell	.10	.05
☐ 525 Rick Helling	.10	.05
☐ 526 Mark Kiefer	.10	.05
☐ 527 Chan Ho Park	1.50	.70
☐ 528 Tony Longmire	.10	.05
☐ 529 Rich Becker	.10	.05
☐ 530 Tim Hyers	.10	.05
☐ 531 Darrin Jackson	.10	.05
☐ 532 Jack Morris	.25	.11
☐ 533 Rick White	.10	.05
☐ 534 Mike Kelly	.10	.05
☐ 535 James Mouton	.10	.05
☐ 536 Steve Trachsel	.25	.11
☐ 537 Tony Eusebio	.10	.05
☐ 538 Kelly Stinnett	.10	.05
☐ 539 Paul Spoljaric	.10	.05
☐ 540 Darren Dreifort	.25	.11
☐ SR1 C.Delgado.Super Rook.	4.00	1.80

1994 Pinnacle Rookie Team Pinnacle

*These nine double-front stan-
dard-size cards of the "Rookie
Team Pinnacle" set feature a
top AL and a top NL rookie
prospect by position. The insertion rate for these is one per 48
first series packs. These special portrait cards were painted
by artists Christopher Greco
and Ron DeFelice. The front
features the National League
player and card number. Both
sides contain a gold Rookie
Team Pinnacle logo.*

	MINT	NRMT
COMPLETE SET (9)	80.00	36.00
COMMON PAIR (1-9)	5.00	2.20
MINOR STARS	8.00	3.60
SER.1 STATED ODDS 1:90 HOB, 1:72 RET		

☐ 1 Carlos Delgado	12.00	5.50
Javier Lopez		
☐ 2 Bob Hamelin	5.00	2.20
J.R. Phillips		
☐ 3 Jon Shave	5.00	2.20
Keith Kessinger		
☐ 4 Luis Ortiz	8.00	3.60
Butch Huskey		
☐ 5 Kurt Abbott	40.00	18.00
Chipper Jones		
☐ 6 Manny Ramirez	12.00	5.50
Rondell White		
☐ 7 Jeffrey Hammonds	10.00	4.50
Cliff Floyd		
☐ 8 Marc Newfield	5.00	2.20
Nigel Wilson		

☐ 9 Mark Hutton	5.00	2.20
Salomon Torres		

1994 Pinnacle Run Creators

*Randomly inserted in either
series Pinnacle packs at an
approximate rate of one in four
jumbo packs, this 44-card standard-size set spotlights top run
producers. The player stands
out from a solid background on
front. His last name and the
Pinnacle logo run up the right
border in gold foil. The Run
Creators logo is at bottom center. A solid colored back contains the team logo as background to statistical highlights
including runs created.*

	MINT	NRMT
COMPLETE SET (44)	100.00	45.00
COMPLETE SERIES 1 (22)	60.00	27.00
COMPLETE SERIES 2 (22)	40.00	18.00
COMMON CARD (RC1-RC44)	1.00	.45
STATED ODDS 1:4 JUMBO		

☐ RC1 John Olerud	1.50	.70
☐ RC2 Frank Thomas	15.00	6.75
☐ RC3 Ken Griffey Jr.	20.00	9.00
☐ RC4 Paul Molitor	4.00	1.80
☐ RC5 Rafael Palmeiro	2.50	1.10
☐ RC6 Roberto Alomar	4.00	1.80
☐ RC7 Juan Gonzalez	10.00	4.50
☐ RC8 Albert Belle	4.00	1.80
☐ RC9 Travis Fryman	1.50	.70
☐ RC10 Rickey Henderson	2.50	1.10
☐ RC11 Tony Phillips	1.00	.45
☐ RC12 Mo Vaughn	4.00	1.80
☐ RC13 Tim Salmon	4.00	1.80
☐ RC14 Kenny Lofton	6.00	2.70
☐ RC15 Carlos Baerga	1.00	.45
☐ RC16 Greg Vaughn	1.00	.45
☐ RC17 Jay Buhner	2.50	1.10
☐ RC18 Chris Hoiles	1.00	.45
☐ RC19 Mickey Tettleton	1.00	.45
☐ RC20 Kirby Puckett	8.00	3.60
☐ RC21 Danny Tartabull	1.00	.45
☐ RC22 Devon White	1.00	.45
☐ RC23 Barry Bonds	5.00	2.20
☐ RC24 Lenny Dykstra	1.50	.70
☐ RC25 John Kruk	1.50	.70
☐ RC26 Fred McGriff	2.50	1.10
☐ RC27 Gregg Jefferies	1.00	.45
☐ RC28 Mike Piazza	12.00	5.50
☐ RC29 Jeff Blauser	1.50	.70
☐ RC30 Andres Galarraga	4.00	1.80
☐ RC31 Darren Daulton	1.50	.70
☐ RC32 Dave Justice	4.00	1.80
☐ RC33 Craig Biggio	2.50	1.10
☐ RC34 Mark Grace	2.50	1.10
☐ RC35 Tony Gwynn	8.00	3.60
☐ RC36 Jeff Bagwell	8.00	3.60
☐ RC37 Jay Bell	1.50	.70

☐ RC38 Marquis Grissom	1.50	.70
☐ RC39 Matt Williams	2.50	1.10
☐ RC40 Charlie Hayes	1.00	.45
☐ RC41 Dante Bichette	1.50	.70
☐ RC42 Bernard Gilkey	1.00	.45
☐ RC43 Brett Butler	1.50	.70
☐ RC44 Rick Wilkins	1.00	.45

1994 Pinnacle Team Pinnacle

*Identical in design to the Rookie
Team Pinnacle set, these double-front cards feature top players from each of the nine positions. Randomly inserted in second series hobby and retail
packs at a rate of one in 48,
these special portrait cards
were painted by artists
Christopher Greco and Ron
DeFelice. The front features the
National League player and
card number. Both sides contain a gold Team Pinnacle logo.*

	MINT	NRMT
COMPLETE SET (9)	180.00	80.00
COMMON PAIR (1-9)	8.00	3.60
SER.2 STATED ODDS 1:90 HOB/RET		

☐ 1 Jeff Bagwell	40.00	18.00
Frank Thomas		
☐ 2 Carlos Baerga	8.00	3.60
Robby Thompson		
☐ 3 Matt Williams	10.00	4.50
Dean Palmer		
☐ 4 Cal Ripken Jr.	30.00	13.50
Jay Bell		
☐ 5 Ivan Rodriguez	25.00	11.00
Mike Piazza		
☐ 6 Lenny Dykstra	40.00	18.00
Ken Griffey Jr.		
☐ 7 Juan Gonzalez	25.00	11.00
Barry Bonds		
☐ 8 Tim Salmon	20.00	9.00
Dave Justice		
☐ 9 Greg Maddux	25.00	11.00
Jack McDowell		

1994 Pinnacle Tribute

*Randomly inserted in hobby
packs at a rate of one in 18, this
18-card set was issued in two
series of nine. Showcasing
some of the top superstar veterans, the fronts have a color
player photo with "Tribute" up
the left border in a black stripe.
The player's name appears at
the bottom with a notation given*

to describe the player. The backs are primarily black with a close-up photo of the player. The cards are numbered with a "TR" prefix.

	MINT	NRMT
COMPLETE SET (18)	100.00	45.00
COMPLETE SERIES 1 (9)	30.00	13.50
COMPLETE SERIES 2 (9)	70.00	32.00
COMMON CARD (TR1-TR18)	1.50	.70
STATED ODDS 1:18 HOBBY		

		MINT	NRMT
☐ TR1	Paul Molitor	4.00	1.80
☐ TR2	Jim Abbott	1.50	.70
☐ TR3	Dave Winfield	2.50	1.10
☐ TR4	Bo Jackson	1.50	.70
☐ TR5	David Justice	4.00	1.80
☐ TR6	Len Dykstra	1.50	.70
☐ TR7	Mike Piazza	12.00	5.50
☐ TR8	Barry Bonds	5.00	2.20
☐ TR9	Randy Johnson	4.00	1.80
☐ TR10	Ozzie Smith	5.00	2.20
☐ TR11	Mark Whiten	1.00	.45
☐ TR12	Greg Maddux	12.00	5.50
☐ TR13	Cal Ripken Jr.	15.00	6.75
☐ TR14	Frank Thomas	15.00	6.75
☐ TR15	Juan Gonzalez	10.00	4.50
☐ TR16	Roberto Alomar	4.00	1.80
☐ TR17	Ken Griffey Jr.	20.00	9.00
☐ TR18	Lee Smith	1.50	.70

1995 Pinnacle

This 450-card standard-size set was issued in two series of 225 cards. They were released in 12-card packs, 24 packs to a box and 18 boxes in a case. The full-bleed fronts feature action photos. The player's last name is printed in black ink against a dramatic gold foil background at the base of the card. There are no notable Rookie Cards in this set.

	MINT	NRMT
COMPLETE SET (450)	30.00	13.50
COMPLETE SERIES 1 (225)	15.00	6.75

		MINT	NRMT
COMPLETE SERIES 2 (225)	15.00	6.75
COMMON CARD (1-450)	.15	.07
MINOR STARS	.30	.14
UNLISTED STARS	.60	.25
SUBSET CARDS HALF VALUE OF BASE CARDS		
COMP. AP SET (450)	2000.00	900.00
COMP. AP SER.1 (225)	1000.00	450.00
COMP. AP SER.2 (225)	1000.00	450.00
COMMON AP (1-450)	3.00	1.35
*AP STARS: 10X TO 25X HI COLUMN		
*AP YOUNG STARS: 8X TO 20X HI		
*AP ROOKIES: 6X TO 15X HI		
AP SER.1 STATED ODDS 1:36 HOB/RET		
AP SER.2 STATED ODDS 1:26 HOB/RET		
COMP.MUSEUM SET (450)	600.00	275.00
COMP.MUSEUM SER.1 (225)	300.00	135.00
COMP.MUSEUM SER.2 (225)	300.00	135.00
COMMON MUSEUM (1-450)	1.00	.45
TRADE (410/413/416/420)	3.00	1.35
TRADE (423/426/444)	3.00	1.35
*MUSEUM STARS: 4X TO 10X HI COLUMN		
*MUSEUM YOUNG STARS: 3X TO 8X HI		
*MUSEUM ROOKIES: 2.5X TO 6X HI		
MUSEUM STATED ODDS 1:4 H/R/J, 1:3ANCO		

		MINT	NRMT
☐ 1	Jeff Bagwell	1.25	.55
☐ 2	Roger Clemens	1.25	.55
☐ 3	Mark Whiten	.15	.07
☐ 4	Shawon Dunston	.15	.07
☐ 5	Bobby Bonilla	.30	.14
☐ 6	Kevin Tapani	.15	.07
☐ 7	Eric Karros	.30	.14
☐ 8	Cliff Floyd	.15	.07
☐ 9	Pat Kelly	.15	.07
☐ 10	Jeffrey Hammonds	.30	.14
☐ 11	Jeff Conine	.15	.07
☐ 12	Fred McGriff	.40	.18
☐ 13	Chris Bosio	.15	.07
☐ 14	Mike Mussina	.60	.25
☐ 15	Danny Bautista	.15	.07
☐ 16	Mickey Morandini	.15	.07
☐ 17	Chuck Finley	.15	.07
☐ 18	Jim Thome	.60	.25
☐ 19	Luis Ortiz	.15	.07
☐ 20	Walt Weiss	.15	.07
☐ 21	Don Mattingly	1.00	.45
☐ 22	Bob Hamelin	.15	.07
☐ 23	Melido Perez	.15	.07
☐ 24	Keith Mitchell	.15	.07
☐ 25	John Smoltz	.30	.14
☐ 26	Hector Carrasco	.15	.07
☐ 27	Pat Hentgen	.30	.14
☐ 28	Derrick May	.15	.07
☐ 29	Mike Kingery	.15	.07
☐ 30	Chuck Carr	.15	.07
☐ 31	Billy Ashley	.15	.07
☐ 32	Todd Hundley	.30	.14
☐ 33	Luis Gonzalez	.15	.07
☐ 34	Marquis Grissom	.30	.14
☐ 35	Jeff King	.15	.07
☐ 36	Eddie Williams	.15	.07
☐ 37	Tom Pagnozzi	.15	.07
☐ 38	Chris Hoiles	.15	.07
☐ 39	Sandy Alomar Jr.	.30	.14
☐ 40	Mike Greenwell	.15	.07
☐ 41	Lance Johnson	.15	.07
☐ 42	Junior Felix	.15	.07
☐ 43	Felix Jose	.15	.07
☐ 44	Scott Leius	.15	.07
☐ 45	Ruben Sierra	.15	.07
☐ 46	Kevin Seitzer	.15	.07
☐ 47	Wade Boggs	.60	.25
☐ 48	Reggie Jefferson	.15	.07
☐ 49	Jose Canseco	.40	.18
☐ 50	David Justice	.60	.25
☐ 51	John Smiley	.15	.07
☐ 52	Joe Carter	.30	.14
☐ 53	Rick Wilkins	.15	.07
☐ 54	Ellis Burks	.30	.14
☐ 55	Dave Weathers	.15	.07
☐ 56	Pedro Astacio	.15	.07
☐ 57	Ryan Thompson	.15	.07
☐ 58	James Mouton	.15	.07
☐ 59	Mel Rojas	.15	.07
☐ 60	Orlando Merced	.15	.07
☐ 61	Matt Williams	.40	.18

		MINT	NRMT
☐ 62	Bernard Gilkey	.15	.07
☐ 63	J.R. Phillips	.15	.07
☐ 64	Lee Smith	.30	.14
☐ 65	Jim Edmonds	.40	.18
☐ 66	Darrin Jackson	.15	.07
☐ 67	Scott Cooper	.15	.07
☐ 68	Ron Karkovice	.15	.07
☐ 69	Chris Gomez	.15	.07
☐ 70	Kevin Appier	.30	.14
☐ 71	Bobby Jones	.15	.07
☐ 72	Doug Drabek	.15	.07
☐ 73	Matt Mieske	.15	.07
☐ 74	Sterling Hitchcock	.15	.07
☐ 75	John Valentin	.15	.07
☐ 76	Reggie Sanders	.15	.07
☐ 77	Wally Joyner	.30	.14
☐ 78	Turk Wendell	.15	.07
☐ 79	Charlie Hayes	.15	.07
☐ 80	Bret Barberie	.15	.07
☐ 81	Troy Neel	.15	.07
☐ 82	Ken Caminiti	.40	.18
☐ 83	Milt Thompson	.15	.07
☐ 84	Paul Sorrento	.15	.07
☐ 85	Trevor Hoffman	.15	.07
☐ 86	Jay Bell	.30	.14
☐ 87	Mark Portugal	.15	.07
☐ 88	Sid Fernandez	.15	.07
☐ 89	Charles Nagy	.15	.07
☐ 90	Jeff Montgomery	.15	.07
☐ 91	Chuck Knoblauch	.60	.25
☐ 92	Jeff Frye	.15	.07
☐ 93	Tony Gwynn	1.50	.70
☐ 94	John Olerud	.30	.14
☐ 95	David Nied	.15	.07
☐ 96	Chris Hammond	.15	.07
☐ 97	Edgar Martinez	.40	.18
☐ 98	Kevin Stocker	.15	.07
☐ 99	Jeff Fassero	.15	.07
☐ 100	Curt Schilling	.30	.14
☐ 101	Dave Clark	.15	.07
☐ 102	Delino DeShields	.15	.07
☐ 103	Leo Gomez	.15	.07
☐ 104	Dave Hollins	.15	.07
☐ 105	Tim Naehring	.15	.07
☐ 106	Otis Nixon	.15	.07
☐ 107	Ozzie Guillen	.15	.07
☐ 108	Jose Lind	.15	.07
☐ 109	Stan Javier	.15	.07
☐ 110	Greg Vaughn	.15	.07
☐ 111	Chipper Jones	2.00	.90
☐ 112	Ed Sprague	.15	.07
☐ 113	Mike MacFarlane	.15	.07
☐ 114	Steve Finley	.30	.14
☐ 115	Ken Hill	.15	.07
☐ 116	Carlos Garcia	.15	.07
☐ 117	Lou Whitaker	.30	.14
☐ 118	Todd Zeile	.15	.07
☐ 119	Gary Sheffield	.60	.25
☐ 120	Ben McDonald	.15	.07
☐ 121	Pete Harnisch	.15	.07
☐ 122	Ivan Rodriguez	.75	.35
☐ 123	Wilson Alvarez	.15	.07
☐ 124	Travis Fryman	.30	.14
☐ 125	Pedro Munoz	.15	.07
☐ 126	Mark Lemke	.15	.07
☐ 127	Jose Valentin	.15	.07
☐ 128	Ken Griffey Jr.	3.00	1.35
☐ 129	Omar Vizquel	.30	.14
☐ 130	Milt Cuyler	.15	.07
☐ 131	Steve Trachsel	.15	.07
☐ 132	Alex Rodriguez	2.50	1.10
☐ 133	Garret Anderson	.40	.18
☐ 134	Armando Benitez	.15	.07
☐ 135	Shawn Green	.30	.14
☐ 136	Jorge Fabregas	.15	.07
☐ 137	Orlando Miller	.15	.07
☐ 138	Rikkert Faneyte	.15	.07
☐ 139	Ismael Valdes	.40	.18
☐ 140	Jose Oliva	.15	.07
☐ 141	Aaron Small	.15	.07
☐ 142	Tim Davis	.15	.07
☐ 143	Ricky Bottalico	.30	.14
☐ 144	Mike Matheny	.15	.07
☐ 145	Roberto Petagine	.15	.07
☐ 146	Fausto Cruz	.15	.07
☐ 147	Bryce Florie	.15	.07

#	Player	Price	Price2
148	Jose Lima	.15	.07
149	John Hudek	.15	.07
150	Duane Singleton	.15	.07
151	John Mabry	.30	.14
152	Robert Eenhoorn	.15	.07
153	Jon Lieber	.15	.07
154	Garey Ingram	.15	.07
155	Paul Shuey	.15	.07
156	Mike Lieberthal	.15	.07
157	Steve Dunn	.15	.07
158	Charles Johnson	.30	.14
159	Ernie Young	.15	.07
160	Jose Martinez	.15	.07
161	Kurt Miller	.15	.07
162	Joey Eischen	.15	.07
163	Dave Stevens	.15	.07
164	Brian L.Hunter	.40	.18
165	Jeff Cirillo	.30	.14
166	Mark Smith	.15	.07
167	McKay Christensen	.30	.14
168	C.J. Nitkowski	.15	.07
169	Antone Williamson	.40	.18
170	Paul Konerko	3.00	1.35
171	Scott Elarton	.75	.35
172	Jacob Shumate	.30	.14
173	Terrence Long	.40	.18
174	Mark Johnson	.15	.07
175	Ben Grieve	4.00	1.80
176	Jayson Peterson	.30	.14
177	Checklist	.15	.07
178	Checklist	.15	.07
179	Checklist	.15	.07
180	Checklist	.15	.07
181	Brian Anderson	.30	.14
182	Steve Buechele	.15	.07
183	Mark Clark	.15	.07
184	Cecil Fielder	.30	.14
185	Steve Avery	.15	.07
186	Devon White	.15	.07
187	Craig Shipley	.15	.07
188	Brady Anderson	.40	.18
189	Kenny Lofton	.75	.35
190	Alex Cole	.15	.07
191	Brent Gates	.15	.07
192	Dean Palmer	.15	.07
193	Alex Gonzalez	.15	.07
194	Steve Cooke	.15	.07
195	Ray Lankford	.30	.14
196	Mark McGwire	1.25	.55
197	Marc Newfield	.15	.07
198	Pat Rapp	.15	.07
199	Darren Lewis	.15	.07
200	Carlos Baerga	.15	.07
201	Rickey Henderson	.40	.18
202	Kurt Abbott	.15	.07
203	Kirt Manwaring	.15	.07
204	Cal Ripken	2.50	1.10
205	Darren Daulton	.30	.14
206	Greg Colbrunn	.15	.07
207	Darryl Hamilton	.15	.07
208	Bo Jackson	.30	.14
209	Tony Phillips	.15	.07
210	Geronimo Berroa	.15	.07
211	Rich Becker	.15	.07
212	Tony Tarasco	.15	.07
213	Karl Rhodes	.15	.07
214	Phil Plantier	.15	.07
215	J.T. Snow	.30	.14
216	Mo Vaughn	.75	.35
217	Greg Gagne	.15	.07
218	Ricky Bones	.15	.07
219	Mike Bordick	.15	.07
220	Chad Curtis	.15	.07
221	Royce Clayton	.15	.07
222	Roberto Alomar	.60	.25
223	Jose Rijo	.15	.07
224	Ryan Klesko	.40	.18
225	Mark Langston	.15	.07
226	Frank Thomas	2.50	1.10
227	Juan Gonzalez	1.50	.70
228	Ron Gant	.30	.14
229	Javier Lopez	.30	.14
230	Sammy Sosa	.60	.25
231	Kevin Brown	.30	.14
232	Gary DiSarcina	.15	.07
233	Albert Belle	.75	.35
234	Jay Buhner	.40	.18
235	Pedro J.Martinez	.60	.25
236	Bob Tewksbury	.15	.07
237	Mike Piazza	2.00	.90
238	Darryl Kile	.30	.14
239	Bryan Harvey	.15	.07
240	Andres Galarraga	.60	.25
241	Jeff Blauser	.30	.14
242	Jeff Kent	.15	.07
243	Bobby Munoz	.15	.07
244	Greg Maddux	2.00	.90
245	Paul O'Neill	.30	.14
246	Lenny Dykstra	.30	.14
247	Todd Van Poppel	.15	.07
248	Bernie Williams	.60	.25
249	Glenallen Hill	.15	.07
250	Duane Ward	.15	.07
251	Dennis Eckersley	.30	.14
252	Pat Mahomes	.15	.07
253	Rusty Greer	.60	.25
254	Roberto Kelly	.15	.07
255	Randy Myers	.15	.07
256	Scott Ruffcorn	.15	.07
257	Robin Ventura	.30	.14
258	Eduardo Perez	.15	.07
259	Aaron Sele	.15	.07
260	Paul Molitor	.60	.25
261	Juan Guzman	.15	.07
262	Darren Oliver	.30	.14
263	Mike Stanley	.15	.07
264	Tom Glavine	.30	.14
265	Rico Brogna	.15	.07
266	Craig Biggio	.40	.18
267	Darrell Whitmore	.15	.07
268	Jimmy Key	.30	.14
269	Will Clark	.40	.18
270	David Cone	.30	.14
271	Brian Jordan	.30	.14
272	Barry Bonds	.75	.35
273	Danny Tartabull	.15	.07
274	Ramon J.Martinez	.30	.14
275	Al Martin	.15	.07
276	Fred McGriff SM	.30	.14
277	Carlos Delgado SM	.15	.07
278	Juan Gonzalez SM	.75	.35
279	Shawn Green SM	.15	.07
280	Carlos Baerga SM	.15	.07
281	Cliff Floyd SM	.15	.07
282	Ozzie Smith SM	.60	.25
283	Alex Rodriguez SM	1.25	.55
284	Kenny Lofton SM	.40	.18
285	Dave Justice SM	.30	.14
286	Tim Salmon SM	.30	.14
287	Manny Ramirez SM	.30	.14
288	Will Clark SM	.30	.14
289	Garret Anderson SM	.15	.07
290	Billy Ashley SM	.15	.07
291	Tony Gwynn SM	.60	.25
292	Raul Mondesi SM	.30	.14
293	Rafael Palmeiro SM	.30	.14
294	Matt Williams SM	.30	.14
295	Don Mattingly SM	.40	.18
296	Kirby Puckett SM	.60	.25
297	Paul Molitor SM	.30	.14
298	Albert Belle SM	.40	.18
299	Barry Bonds SM	.40	.18
300	Mike Piazza SM	1.00	.45
301	Jeff Bagwell SM	.60	.25
302	Frank Thomas SM	1.25	.55
303	Chipper Jones SM	1.00	.45
304	Ken Griffey Jr. SM	1.50	.70
305	Cal Ripken Jr. SM	1.25	.55
306	Eric Anthony	.15	.07
307	Todd Benzinger	.15	.07
308	Jacob Brumfield	.15	.07
309	Wes Chamberlain	.15	.07
310	Tino Martinez	.60	.25
311	Roberto Mejia	.15	.07
312	Jose Offerman	.15	.07
313	David Segui	.15	.07
314	Eric Young	.15	.07
315	Rey Sanchez	.15	.07
316	Raul Mondesi	.40	.18
317	Bret Boone	.15	.07
318	Andre Dawson	.40	.18
319	Brian McRae	.15	.07
320	Dave Nilsson	.15	.07
321	Moises Alou	.30	.14
322	Don Slaught	.15	.07
323	Dave McCarty	.15	.07
324	Mike Huff	.15	.07
325	Rick Aguilera	.15	.07
326	Rod Beck	.15	.07
327	Kenny Rogers	.15	.07
328	Andy Benes	.30	.14
329	Allen Watson	.15	.07
330	Randy Johnson	.60	.25
331	Willie Greene	.15	.07
332	Hal Morris	.15	.07
333	Ozzie Smith	.75	.35
334	Jason Bere	.15	.07
335	Scott Erickson	.15	.07
336	Dante Bichette	.30	.14
337	Willie Banks	.15	.07
338	Eric Davis	.30	.14
339	Rondell White	.30	.14
340	Kirby Puckett	1.25	.55
341	Deion Sanders	.30	.14
342	Eddie Murray	.60	.25
343	Mike Harkey	.15	.07
344	Joey Hamilton	.30	.14
345	Roger Salkeld	.15	.07
346	Wil Cordero	.15	.07
347	John Wetteland	.15	.07
348	Geronimo Pena	.15	.07
349	Kirk Gibson	.30	.14
350	Manny Ramirez	.60	.25
351	Wm.VanLandingham	.15	.07
352	B.J. Surhoff	.15	.07
353	Ken Ryan	.15	.07
354	Terry Steinbach	.15	.07
355	Bret Saberhagen	.15	.07
356	John Jaha	.15	.07
357	Joe Girardi	.15	.07
358	Steve Karsay	.15	.07
359	Alex Fernandez	.15	.07
360	Salomon Torres	.15	.07
361	John Burkett	.15	.07
362	Derek Bell	.15	.07
363	Tom Henke	.15	.07
364	Gregg Jefferies	.15	.07
365	Jack McDowell	.15	.07
366	Andujar Cedeno	.15	.07
367	Dave Winfield	.40	.18
368	Carl Everett	.15	.07
369	Danny Jackson	.15	.07
370	Jeromy Burnitz	.15	.07
371	Mark Grace	.40	.18
372	Larry Walker	.60	.25
373	Bill Swift	.15	.07
374	Dennis Martinez	.30	.14
375	Mickey Tettleton	.15	.07
376	Mel Nieves	.15	.07
377	Cal Eldred	.15	.07
378	Orel Hershiser	.30	.14
379	David Wells	.15	.07
380	Gary Gaetti	.15	.07
381	Jeromy Burnitz	.15	.07
382	Barry Larkin	.40	.18
383	Jason Jacome	.15	.07
384	Tim Wallach	.15	.07
385	Robby Thompson	.15	.07
386	Frank Viola	.15	.07
387	Dave Stewart	.30	.14
388	Bip Roberts	.15	.07
389	Ron Darling	.15	.07
390	Carlos Delgado	.30	.14
391	Tim Salmon	.60	.25
392	Alan Trammell	.40	.18
393	Kevin Foster	.15	.07
394	Jim Abbott	.15	.07
395	John Kruk	.30	.14
396	Andy Van Slyke	.30	.14
397	Dave Magadan	.15	.07
398	Rafael Palmeiro	.40	.18
399	Mike Devereaux	.15	.07
400	Benito Santiago	.15	.07
401	Brett Butler	.30	.14
402	John Franco	.30	.14
403	Matt Walbeck	.15	.07
404	Terry Pendleton	.15	.07
405	Chris Sabo	.15	.07

☐ 406	Andrew Lorraine	.15	.07
☐ 407	Dan Wilson	.15	.07
☐ 408	Mike Lansing	.15	.07
☐ 409	Ray McDavid	.15	.07
☐ 410	Shane Andrews	.15	.07
☐ 411	Tom Gordon	.15	.07
☐ 412	Chad Ogea	.15	.07
☐ 413	James Baldwin	.15	.07
☐ 414	Russ Davis	.15	.07
☐ 415	Ray Holbert	.15	.07
☐ 416	Ray Durham	.30	.14
☐ 417	Matt Nokes	.15	.07
☐ 418	Rod Henderson	.15	.07
☐ 419	Gabe White	.15	.07
☐ 420	Todd Hollandsworth	.30	.14
☐ 421	Midre Cummings	.15	.07
☐ 422	Harold Baines	.30	.14
☐ 423	Troy Percival	.15	.07
☐ 424	Joe Vitiello	.15	.07
☐ 425	Andy Ashby	.15	.07
☐ 426	Michael Tucker	.30	.14
☐ 427	Mark Gubicza	.15	.07
☐ 428	Jim Bullinger	.15	.07
☐ 429	Jose Malave	.15	.07
☐ 430	Pete Schourek	.15	.07
☐ 431	Bobby Ayala	.15	.07
☐ 432	Marvin Freeman	.15	.07
☐ 433	Pat Listach	.15	.07
☐ 434	Eddie Taubensee	.15	.07
☐ 435	Steve Howe	.15	.07
☐ 436	Kent Mercker	.15	.07
☐ 437	Hector Fajardo	.15	.07
☐ 438	Scott Kamieniecki	.15	.07
☐ 439	Robb Nen	.15	.07
☐ 440	Mike Kelly	.15	.07
☐ 441	Tom Candiotti	.15	.07
☐ 442	Albie Lopez	.15	.07
☐ 443	Jeff Granger	.15	.07
☐ 444	Rich Aude	.15	.07
☐ 445	Luis Polonia	.15	.07
☐ 446	Frank Thomas CL	1.25	.55
☐ 447	Ken Griffey Jr. CL	1.50	.70
☐ 448	Mike Piazza CL	1.00	.45
☐ 449	Jeff Bagwell CL	.60	.25
☐ 450	Jeff Bagwell CL	1.50	.70
	Frank Thomas		
	Ken Griffey Jr.		
	Mike Piazza		

1995 Pinnacle ETA

This six-card standard-sized set was randomly inserted approximately one in every 24 first series hobby packs. This set features players who were among the leading prospects for major league stardom. The fronts feature a player photo as well as a quick information bit. The player's name is located on the top. The busy full-bleed backs feature a player photo and some quick comments. On the bottom is the player's name and the card is numbered with an "ETA" prefix in the upper left corner.

	MINT	NRMT
COMPLETE SET (6)	25.00	11.00
COMMON CARD (1-6)	2.00	.90
SER.1 STATED ODDS 1:24 HOBBY		

☐ 1	Ben Grieve	15.00	6.75
☐ 2	Alex Ochoa	2.00	.90
☐ 3	Joe Vitiello	2.00	.90
☐ 4	Johnny Damon	3.00	1.35
☐ 5	Trey Beamon	2.00	.90
☐ 6	Brooks Kieschnick	3.00	1.35

1995 Pinnacle Gate Attractions

This 18-card standard-size set was inserted approximately one every 12 second series jumbo packs. The fronts feature two photos, with the words "Gate Attraction" at the bottom left. The player is identified on the top. The horizontal full-bleed backs have the player's name on the left, a player photo in the middle and some career information in the lower right.

	MINT	NRMT
COMPLETE SET (18)	120.00	55.00
COMMON CARD (GA1-GA18)		
SER.2 STATED ODDS 1:12 JUMBO		

☐ GA1	Ken Griffey Jr.	25.00	11.00
☐ GA2	Frank Thomas	20.00	9.00
☐ GA3	Cal Ripken	20.00	9.00
☐ GA4	Jeff Bagwell	10.00	4.50
☐ GA5	Mike Piazza	15.00	6.75
☐ GA6	Barry Bonds	6.00	2.70
☐ GA7	Kirby Puckett	10.00	4.50
☐ GA8	Albert Belle	6.00	2.70
☐ GA9	Tony Gwynn	12.00	5.50
☐ GA10	Raul Mondesi	4.00	1.80
☐ GA11	Will Clark	4.00	1.80
☐ GA12	Don Mattingly	8.00	3.60
☐ GA13	Roger Clemens	10.00	4.50
☐ GA14	Paul Molitor	5.00	2.20
☐ GA15	Matt Williams	4.00	1.80
☐ GA16	Greg Maddux	15.00	6.75
☐ GA17	Kenny Lofton	6.00	2.70
☐ GA18	Cliff Floyd	2.00	.90

1995 Pinnacle New Blood

This nine-card standard-size set was inserted approximately one in every 90 second series hobby and retail packs. This set features nine players who were leading prospects entering the

1995 season. The Dufex enhanced fronts feature two player photos. One photo is a color shot while the other one is a black and white background photo. The words "New Blood" and player's name are on the bottom. The full-bleed backs feature two more photos. Player information is set against these photos.

	MINT	NRMT
COMPLETE SET (9)	100.00	45.00
COMMON CARD (NB1-NB9)	3.00	1.35
SEMISTARS	6.00	2.70
UNLISTED STARS	10.00	4.50
SER.2 STAT.ODDS 1:90 HOB/RET, 1:72 ANCO		

☐ NB1	Alex Rodriguez	40.00	18.00
☐ NB2	Shawn Green	4.00	1.80
☐ NB3	Brian Hunter	6.00	2.70
☐ NB4	Garret Anderson	6.00	2.70
☐ NB5	Charles Johnson	4.00	1.80
☐ NB6	Chipper Jones	30.00	13.50
☐ NB7	Carlos Delgado	4.00	1.80
☐ NB8	Billy Ashley	3.00	1.35
☐ NB9	J.R. Phillips UER	3.00	1.35
	Dodgers logo on back		
	Phillips plays for the Giants		

1995 Pinnacle Performers

These 18 standard-size cards were randomly inserted approximately one in every 12 first series jumbo packs. The full-bleed fronts feature a player photo against a shiny background. The player's name is in white lettering in the upper right corner. The backs have two photos: one a color portrait with the other one being a shaded black and white. There is also some text pertaining to that player.

	MINT	NRMT
COMPLETE SET (18)	100.00	45.00
COMMON CARD (PP1-PP18)	2.00	.90
SER.1 STATED ODDS 1:12 JUMBO		

		MINT	NRMT
☐ PP1	Frank Thomas	25.00	11.00
☐ PP2	Albert Belle	8.00	3.60
☐ PP3	Barry Bonds	8.00	3.60
☐ PP4	Juan Gonzalez	15.00	6.75
☐ PP5	Andres Galarraga	6.00	1.80
☐ PP6	Raul Mondesi	4.00	1.80
☐ PP7	Paul Molitor	6.00	2.70
☐ PP8	Tim Salmon	6.00	2.70
☐ PP9	Mike Piazza	20.00	9.00
☐ PP10	Gregg Jefferies	2.00	.90
☐ PP11	Will Clark	4.00	1.80
☐ PP12	Greg Maddux	20.00	9.00
☐ PP13	Manny Ramirez	6.00	2.70
☐ PP14	Kirby Puckett	12.00	5.50
☐ PP15	Shawn Green	3.00	1.35
☐ PP16	Rafael Palmeiro	4.00	1.80
☐ PP17	Paul O'Neill	3.00	1.35
☐ PP18	Jason Bere	2.00	.90

1995 Pinnacle Pin Redemption

This 18-card standard-size set was randomly inserted in all second series packs. Printed odds indicate that these cards were inserted approximately one every in 48 hobby and retail packs and one in every 36 jumbo packs. The horizontal full-bleed fronts feature an action photo, a team logo and another small player photo. The backs explain the rules for ordering the "Team Pinnacle" Collector Pin. The offer expired on November 15, 1995.

	MINT	NRMT
COMPLETE SET (18)	80.00	36.00
COMMON CARD (1-18)	1.50	.70
SER.2 STAT.ODDS 1:48 H/R, 1:36 JUM/ANCO		
COMP.PIN SET (18)	80.00	36.00
*PINS: 1X BASIC REDEMPTION		
ONE PIN VIA MAIL PER REDEMPTION CARD		

		MINT	NRMT
☐ 1	Greg Maddux	10.00	4.50
☐ 2	Mike Mussina	3.00	1.35
☐ 3	Mike Piazza	10.00	4.50
☐ 4	Carlos Delgado	1.50	.70
☐ 5	Jeff Bagwell	6.00	2.70
☐ 6	Frank Thomas	12.00	5.50
☐ 7	Craig Biggio	2.00	.90
☐ 8	Roberto Alomar	3.00	1.35
☐ 9	Ozzie Smith	4.00	1.80
☐ 10	Cal Ripken Jr.	12.00	5.50
☐ 11	Matt Williams	2.00	.90
☐ 12	Travis Fryman	1.50	.70
☐ 13	Barry Bonds	4.00	1.80
☐ 14	Ken Griffey Jr.	15.00	6.75
☐ 15	Dave Justice	3.00	1.35

		MINT	NRMT
☐ 16	Albert Belle	4.00	1.80
☐ 17	Tony Gwynn	8.00	3.60
☐ 18	Kirby Puckett	6.00	2.70

1995 Pinnacle Red Hot

Cards from this 25-card standard-size set were randomly inserted into second series hobby and retail packs. The fronts feature a player photo on the right, with his name, an inset portrait and the words "Red Hot" on the left.

	MINT	NRMT
COMPLETE SET (25)	80.00	36.00
COMMON CARD (RH1-RH25)	1.00	.45
SER.2 STAT.ODDS 1:16 HOB/RET, 1:12 ANCO		
COMP.WHITE SET (25)	300.00	135.00
COMMON WHITE (WH1-WH25)	4.00	1.80
*WHITE HOT: 2X TO 4X BASE CARD HI		
W.HOT SER.2 STATED ODDS 1:36 HOBBY		

		MINT	NRMT
☐ RH1	Cal Ripken Jr.	12.00	5.50
☐ RH2	Ken Griffey Jr.	15.00	6.75
☐ RH3	Frank Thomas	12.00	5.50
☐ RH4	Jeff Bagwell	6.00	2.70
☐ RH5	Mike Piazza	10.00	4.50
☐ RH6	Barry Bonds	4.00	1.80
☐ RH7	Albert Belle	4.00	1.80
☐ RH8	Tony Gwynn	8.00	3.60
☐ RH9	Kirby Puckett	6.00	2.70
☐ RH10	Don Mattingly	6.00	2.70
☐ RH11	Matt Williams	2.00	.90
☐ RH12	Greg Maddux	10.00	4.50
☐ RH13	Raul Mondesi	2.00	.90
☐ RH14	Paul Molitor	2.50	1.10
☐ RH15	Manny Ramirez	2.50	1.10
☐ RH16	Joe Carter	1.50	.70
☐ RH17	Will Clark	2.00	.90
☐ RH18	Roger Clemens	6.00	2.70
☐ RH19	Tim Salmon	2.50	1.10
☐ RH20	Dave Justice	2.50	1.10
☐ RH21	Kenny Lofton	4.00	1.80
☐ RH22	Deion Sanders	1.50	.70
☐ RH23	Roberto Alomar	2.50	1.10
☐ RH24	Cliff Floyd	1.00	.45
☐ RH25	Carlos Baerga	1.00	.45

1995 Pinnacle Team Pinnacle

Randomly inserted in series one hobby and retail packs at a rate of one in 90, this nine-card standard-size set showcases the game's top players in an etched-foil design. A player photo is superimposed over the player's team logo. The Team Pinnacle logo, player's name and position are printed in silver

foil on a black strip at the bottom left of the card. Cards are numbered with the prefix "TP." All cards were intentionally issued with two variations, whereby one side of the card or the other had the Dufex effect. Regional premiums of up to 25% may exist for the player with the enhanced side.

	MINT	NRMT
COMPLETE SET (9)	250.00	110.00
COMMON CARD (TP1-TP9)	5.00	2.20
UNLISTED STARS	10.00	4.50
SER.1 STAT.ODDS 1:90 HOB/RET, 1:72 ANCO		

		MINT	NRMT
☐ TP1	Mike Mussina Greg Maddux	30.00	13.50
☐ TP2	Carlos Delgado Mike Piazza	30.00	13.50
☐ TP3	Frank Thomas Jeff Bagwell	40.00	18.00
☐ TP4	Roberto Alomar Craig Biggio	10.00	4.50
☐ TP5	Cal Ripken Ozzie Smith	40.00	18.00
☐ TP6	Travis Fryman Matt Williams	5.00	2.20
☐ TP7	Ken Griffey Jr. Barry Bonds	50.00	22.00
☐ TP8	Albert Belle David Justice	12.00	5.50
☐ TP9	Kirby Puckett Tony Gwynn	30.00	13.50

1995 Pinnacle Upstarts

Top young players are featured in this 30-card standard-size set. The cards were randomly inserted in series one hobby and retail packs at a rate of one in eight. Multi-colored foil fronts feature the player in a action cutout set against a star background. The player's name is

wrapped around the "Upstarts" logo which is printed on the lower left of the front. The player's team logo is printed on the top right of the front. Backs are full-bleed color action photos of the player and are numbered at the top right with the prefix "US". A gold polygonal box encloses the player's name and '94 stats along with the team logo. The Pinnacle and '95 Upstarts logo are printed on the top left of the back.

	MINT	NRMT
COMPLETE SET (30)	60.00	27.00
COMMON CARD (US1-US30)	1.00	.45
SER.1 STATED ODDS 1:6 HOB/RET, 1:6 ANCO		

		MINT	NRMT
☐ US1	Frank Thomas	15.00	6.75
☐ US2	Roberto Alomar	4.00	1.80
☐ US3	Mike Piazza	12.00	5.50
☐ US4	Javier Lopez	1.50	.70
☐ US5	Albert Belle	4.00	1.80
☐ US6	Carlos Delgado	1.50	.70
☐ US7	Brent Gates	1.00	.45
☐ US8	Tim Salmon	4.00	1.80
☐ US9	Raul Mondesi	2.50	1.10
☐ US10	Juan Gonzalez	10.00	4.50
☐ US11	Manny Ramirez	4.00	1.80
☐ US12	Sammy Sosa	1.00	.45
☐ US13	Jeff Kent	1.00	.45
☐ US14	Melvin Nieves	1.00	.45
☐ US15	Rondell White	1.50	.70
☐ US16	Shawn Green	1.50	.70
☐ US17	Bernie Williams	4.00	1.80
☐ US18	Aaron Sele	1.00	.45
☐ US19	Jason Bere	1.00	.45
☐ US20	Joey Hamilton	1.50	.70
☐ US21	Mike Kelly	1.00	.45
☐ US22	Wil Cordero	1.00	.45
☐ US23	Moises Alou	1.50	.70
☐ US24	Roberto Kelly	1.00	.45
☐ US25	Deion Sanders	1.50	.70
☐ US26	Steve Karsay	1.00	.45
☐ US27	Bret Boone	1.00	.45
☐ US28	Willie Greene	1.00	.45
☐ US29	Billy Ashley	1.00	.45
☐ US30	Brian Anderson	1.50	.70

1996 Pinnacle

The 1996 Pinnacle set was issued in two separate series of 200 cards each. The 10-card packs retailed for $2.49. On 20-point card stock, the fronts feature full-bleed color action photos, bordered at the bottom by a gold foil triangle. The backs carry a color closeup photo, biography, and statistics. The Series I set features the following topical subsets: The

---

Naturals (134-163), '95 Rookies (164-193) and Checklists (194-200). Series II set features these subsets: Hardball Heroes (30 cards), 300 Series (17 cards), Rookies (25 cards), and Checklists (7 cards). Numbering for the 300 Series subset was based on player's career batting average. At that time, both Paul Molitor and Jeff Bagwell had identical career batting averages of .305, thus Pinnacle numbered both of their 300 Series subset cards as 305. Due to this quirky numbering, the set only runs through card 399, but actually contains 400 cards. A special Cal Ripken Jr. Tribute card was inserted in first series packs at the rate of one in 150.

	MINT	NRMT
COMPLETE SET (400)	30.00	13.50
COMPLETE SERIES 1 (200)	15.00	6.75
COMPLETE SERIES 2 (200)	15.00	6.75
COMMON CARD (1-399)	.15	.07
MINOR STARS	.30	.14
UNLISTED STARS	.60	.25
SUBSET CARDS HALF VALUE OF BASE CARDS		
COMP.FOIL SET (200)	25.00	11.00
COMMON FOIL (201-399)	.15	.07
*FOIL: .75X TO 1.5X HI COLUMN		
FOIL VALS IN SER.2 RETAIL SUPER PACKS		
COMP.STARBURST SET (200)	500.00	220.00
COMP.STAR.SER.1 (100)	250.00	110.00
COMP.STAR.SER.2 (100)	250.00	110.00
COMMON STARBURST (1-200)	1.00	.45
*STARBURST STARS: 4X TO 10X HI COLUMN		
*STARBURST YOUNG STARS: 3X TO 8X HI		
STARB.ODDS 1:7 H/R, 1:6 JUM, 1:10 MAG		
COMP.STAR.AP SET (200)	1500.00	700.00
COMP.STAR.AP SER.1 (100)	750.00	350.00
COMP.STAR.AP SER.2 (100)	750.00	350.00
COMMON STAR.AP (1-200)	3.00	1.35
*STAR.AP STARS: 10X TO 25X HI COLUMN		
*STAR.AP YOUNG STARS: 8X TO 20X HI		
STAR.AP ODDS 1:47 H/R, 1:39 JUM, 1:67 MAG		
RIPKEN TRIB.SER.1 STATED ODDS 1:150		

		MINT	NRMT
☐ 1	Greg Maddux	2.00	.90
☐ 2	Bill Pulsipher	.15	.07
☐ 3	Dante Bichette	.30	.14
☐ 4	Mike Piazza	2.00	.90
☐ 5	Garret Anderson	.30	.14
☐ 6	Steve Finley	.30	.14
☐ 7	Andy Benes	.30	.14
☐ 8	Chuck Knoblauch	.60	.25
☐ 9	Tom Gordon	.15	.07
☐ 10	Jeff Bagwell	1.25	.55
☐ 11	Wil Cordero	.15	.07
☐ 12	John Mabry	.15	.07
☐ 13	Jeff Frye	.15	.07
☐ 14	Travis Fryman	.30	.14
☐ 15	John Wetteland	.15	.07
☐ 16	Jason Bates	.15	.07
☐ 17	Danny Tartabull	.15	.07
☐ 18	Charles Nagy	.30	.14
☐ 19	Robin Ventura	.30	.14
☐ 20	Reggie Sanders	.15	.07
☐ 21	Dave Clark	.15	.07
☐ 22	Jaime Navarro	.15	.07
☐ 23	Joey Hamilton	.30	.14
☐ 24	Al Leiter	.15	.07
☐ 25	Deion Sanders	.30	.14
☐ 26	Tim Salmon	.60	.25
☐ 27	Tino Martinez	.60	.25
☐ 28	Mike Greenwell	.15	.07
☐ 29	Phil Plantier	.15	.07
☐ 30	Bobby Bonilla	.30	.14
☐ 31	Kenny Rogers	.15	.07
☐ 32	Chili Davis	.30	.14
☐ 33	Joe Carter	.30	.14
☐ 34	Mike Mussina	.60	.25
☐ 35	Matt Mieske	.15	.07

		MINT	NRMT
☐ 36	Jose Canseco	.40	.18
☐ 37	Brad Radke	.30	.14
☐ 38	Juan Gonzalez	1.50	.70
☐ 39	David Segui	.15	.07
☐ 40	Alex Fernandez	.15	.07
☐ 41	Jeff Kent	.15	.07
☐ 42	Todd Zeile	.15	.07
☐ 43	Darryl Strawberry	.30	.14
☐ 44	Jose Rijo	.15	.07
☐ 45	Ramon Martinez	.30	.14
☐ 46	Manny Ramirez	.60	.25
☐ 47	Gregg Jefferies	.15	.07
☐ 48	Bryan Rekar	.15	.07
☐ 49	Jeff King	.15	.07
☐ 50	John Olerud	.30	.14
☐ 51	Marc Newfield	.15	.07
☐ 52	Charles Johnson	.30	.14
☐ 53	Robby Thompson	.15	.07
☐ 54	Brian L. Hunter	.30	.14
☐ 55	Mike Blowers	.15	.07
☐ 56	Keith Lockhart	.15	.07
☐ 57	Ray Lankford	.30	.14
☐ 58	Tim Wallach	.15	.07
☐ 59	Ivan Rodriguez	.75	.35
☐ 60	Ed Sprague	.15	.07
☐ 61	Paul Molitor	.60	.25
☐ 62	Eric Karros	.30	.14
☐ 63	Glenallen Hill	.15	.07
☐ 64	Jay Bell	.30	.14
☐ 65	Tom Pagnozzi	.15	.07
☐ 66	Greg Colbrunn	.15	.07
☐ 67	Edgar Martinez	.40	.18
☐ 68	Paul Sorrento	.15	.07
☐ 69	Kirt Manwaring	.15	.07
☐ 70	Pete Schourek	.15	.07
☐ 71	Orlando Merced	.15	.07
☐ 72	Shawon Dunston	.15	.07
☐ 73	Ricky Bottalico	.15	.07
☐ 74	Brady Anderson	.40	.18
☐ 75	Steve Ontiveros	.15	.07
☐ 76	Jim Abbott	.15	.07
☐ 77	Carl Everett	.15	.07
☐ 78	Mo Vaughn	.75	.35
☐ 79	Pedro Martinez	.60	.25
☐ 80	Harold Baines	.30	.14
☐ 81	Alan Trammell	.40	.18
☐ 82	Steve Avery	.15	.07
☐ 83	Jeff Cirillo	.30	.14
☐ 84	John Valentin	.15	.07
☐ 85	Bernie Williams	.60	.25
☐ 86	Andre Dawson	.40	.18
☐ 87	Dave Winfield	.40	.18
☐ 88	B.J. Surhoff	.15	.07
☐ 89	Jeff Blauser	.30	.14
☐ 90	Barry Larkin	.40	.18
☐ 91	Cliff Floyd	.15	.07
☐ 92	Sammy Sosa	.60	.25
☐ 93	Andres Galarraga	.60	.25
☐ 94	Dave Nilsson	.15	.07
☐ 95	James Mouton	.15	.07
☐ 96	Marquis Grissom	.30	.14
☐ 97	Matt Williams	.40	.18
☐ 98	John Jaha	.15	.07
☐ 99	Don Mattingly	1.00	.45
☐ 100	Tim Naehring	.30	.14
☐ 101	Kevin Appier	.30	.14
☐ 102	Bobby Higginson	.30	.14
☐ 103	Andy Pettitte	.75	.35
☐ 104	Ozzie Smith	.75	.35
☐ 105	Kenny Lofton	.75	.35
☐ 106	Ken Caminiti	.40	.18
☐ 107	Walt Weiss	.15	.07
☐ 108	Jack McDowell	.15	.07
☐ 109	Brian McRae	.15	.07
☐ 110	Gary Gaetti	.15	.07
☐ 111	Curtis Goodwin	.15	.07
☐ 112	Dennis Martinez	.30	.14
☐ 113	Omar Vizquel	.30	.14
☐ 114	Chipper Jones	2.00	.90
☐ 115	Mark Gubicza	.15	.07
☐ 116	Ruben Sierra	.15	.07
☐ 117	Eddie Murray	.60	.25
☐ 118	Chad Curtis	.15	.07
☐ 119	Hal Morris	.15	.07
☐ 120	Ben McDonald	.15	.07
☐ 121	Marty Cordova	.30	.14

Card	Price 1	Price 2
☐ 122 Ken Griffey Jr. UER .. 3.00	1.35
Card says Ken homered from both sides		
He is only a left hitter		
☐ 123 Gary Sheffield 60	.25
☐ 124 Charlie Hayes 15	.07
☐ 125 Shawn Green 15	.07
☐ 126 Jason Giambi 30	.14
☐ 127 Mark Langston 15	.07
☐ 128 Mark Whiten 15	.07
☐ 129 Greg Vaughn 15	.07
☐ 130 Mark McGwire 1.25	.55
☐ 131 Hideo Nomo 1.50	.70
☐ 132 Eric Karros 75	.35
Mike Piazza		
Raul Mondesi		
Hideo Nomo		
☐ 133 Jason Bere 15	.07
☐ 134 Ken Griffey Jr. NAT .. 1.50	.70
☐ 135 Frank Thomas NAT .. 1.25	.55
☐ 136 Cal Ripken NAT 1.25	.55
☐ 137 Albert Belle NAT 40	.18
☐ 138 Mike Piazza NAT .. 1.00	.45
☐ 139 Dante Bichette NAT 15	.07
☐ 140 Sammy Sosa NAT 30	.14
☐ 141 Mo Vaughn NAT 40	.18
☐ 142 Tim Salmon NAT 30	.14
☐ 143 Reggie Sanders NAT ..15	.07
☐ 144 Cecil Fielder NAT 15	.07
☐ 145 Jim Edmonds NAT 30	.14
☐ 146 Rafael Palmeiro NAT ..30	.14
☐ 147 Edgar Martinez NAT ..30	.14
☐ 148 Barry Bonds NAT 40	.18
☐ 149 Manny Ramirez NAT ..30	.14
☐ 150 Larry Walker NAT 30	.14
☐ 151 Jeff Bagwell NAT 60	.25
☐ 152 Ron Gant NAT 15	.07
☐ 153 Andres Galarraga NAT .30	.14
☐ 154 Eddie Murray NAT 30	.14
☐ 155 Kirby Puckett NAT 60	.25
☐ 156 Will Clark NAT 30	.14
☐ 157 Don Mattingly NAT 40	.18
☐ 158 Mark McGwire NAT ...60	.25
☐ 159 Dean Palmer NAT 15	.07
☐ 160 Matt Williams NAT 30	.14
☐ 161 Fred McGriff NAT 30	.14
☐ 162 Joe Carter NAT 15	.07
☐ 163 Juan Gonzalez NAT 75	.35
☐ 164 Alex Ochoa 15	.07
☐ 165 Ruben Rivera 30	.14
☐ 166 Tony Clark 60	.25
☐ 167 Brian Barber 15	.07
☐ 168 Matt Lawton 40	.18
☐ 169 Terrell Wade 15	.07
☐ 170 Johnny Damon 30	.14
☐ 171 Derek Jeter 2.00	.90
☐ 172 Phil Nevin 15	.07
☐ 173 Robert Perez 15	.07
☐ 174 C.J. Nitkowski 15	.07
☐ 175 Joe Vitiello 15	.07
☐ 176 Roger Cedeno 15	.07
☐ 177 Ron Coomer 15	.07
☐ 178 Chris Widger 15	.07
☐ 179 Jimmy Haynes 15	.07
☐ 180 Mike Sweeney 60	.25
☐ 181 Howard Battle 15	.07
☐ 182 John Wasdin 15	.07
☐ 183 Jim Pittsley 30	.14
☐ 184 Bob Wolcott 15	.07
☐ 185 LaTroy Hawkins 15	.07
☐ 186 Nigel Wilson 15	.07
☐ 187 Dustin Hermanson 15	.07
☐ 188 Chris Snopek 15	.07
☐ 189 Mariano Rivera 40	.18
☐ 190 Jose Herrera 15	.07
☐ 191 Chris Stynes 15	.07
☐ 192 Larry Thomas 15	.07
☐ 193 David Bell 15	.07
☐ 194 Frank Thomas CL .. 1.25	.55
☐ 195 Ken Griffey Jr. CL .. 1.50	.70
☐ 196 Cal Ripken CL 1.25	.55
☐ 197 Jeff Bagwell CL 60	.25
☐ 198 Mike Piazza CL 1.00	.45
☐ 199 Barry Bonds CL 40	.18
☐ 200 Garret Anderson CL ...60	.25
Chipper Jones		
☐ 201 Frank Thomas 2.50	1.10
☐ 202 Michael Tucker 30	.14
☐ 203 Kirby Puckett 1.25	.55
☐ 204 Alex Gonzalez 15	.07
☐ 205 Tony Gwynn 1.50	.70
☐ 206 Moises Alou 30	.14
☐ 207 Albert Belle 75	.35
☐ 208 Barry Bonds 75	.35
☐ 209 Fred McGriff 40	.18
☐ 210 Dennis Eckersley 30	.14
☐ 211 Craig Biggio 40	.18
☐ 212 David Cone 30	.14
☐ 213 Will Clark 40	.18
☐ 214 Cal Ripken 2.50	1.10
☐ 215 Wade Boggs 60	.25
☐ 216 Pete Schourek 15	.07
☐ 217 Darren Daulton 30	.14
☐ 218 Carlos Baerga 15	.07
☐ 219 Larry Walker 60	.25
☐ 220 Denny Neagle 30	.14
☐ 221 Jim Edmonds 40	.18
☐ 222 Lee Smith 30	.14
☐ 223 Jason Isringhausen ...15	.07
☐ 224 Jay Buhner 40	.18
☐ 225 John Olerud 30	.14
☐ 226 Jeff Conine 30	.14
☐ 227 Dean Palmer 15	.07
☐ 228 Jim Abbott 15	.07
☐ 229 Raul Mondesi 40	.18
☐ 230 Tom Glavine 30	.14
☐ 231 Kevin Seitzer 15	.07
☐ 232 Lenny Dykstra 30	.14
☐ 233 Brian Jordan 30	.14
☐ 234 Rondell White 30	.14
☐ 235 Bret Boone 15	.07
☐ 236 Randy Johnson 60	.25
☐ 237 Paul O'Neill 30	.14
☐ 238 Jim Thome 60	.25
☐ 239 Edgardo Alfonzo 40	.18
☐ 240 Terry Pendleton 15	.07
☐ 241 Harold Baines 15	.07
☐ 242 Roberto Alomar 60	.25
☐ 243 Mark Grace 40	.18
☐ 244 Derek Bell 15	.07
☐ 245 Vinny Castilla 30	.14
☐ 246 Cecil Fielder 30	.14
☐ 247 Roger Clemens 1.25	.55
☐ 248 Orel Hershiser 30	.14
☐ 249 J.T. Snow 30	.14
☐ 250 Rafael Palmeiro 40	.18
☐ 251 Bret Saberhagen 15	.07
☐ 252 Todd Hollandsworth ..15	.07
☐ 253 Ryan Klesko 40	.18
☐ 254 Greg Maddux HH .. 1.00	.45
☐ 255 Ken Griffey Jr. HH .. 1.50	.70
☐ 256 Hideo Nomo HH 75	.35
☐ 257 Frank Thomas HH .. 1.25	.55
☐ 258 Cal Ripken HH 1.25	.55
☐ 259 Jeff Bagwell HH 60	.25
☐ 260 Barry Bonds HH 40	.18
☐ 261 Mo Vaughn HH 40	.18
☐ 262 Albert Belle HH 40	.18
☐ 263 Sammy Sosa HH 30	.14
☐ 264 Reggie Sanders HH ...15	.07
☐ 265 Mike Piazza HH 1.00	.45
☐ 266 Chipper Jones HH .. 1.00	.45
☐ 267 Tony Gwynn HH 75	.35
☐ 268 Kirby Puckett HH 60	.25
☐ 269 Wade Boggs HH 30	.14
☐ 270 Will Clark HH 30	.14
☐ 271 Gary Sheffield HH 30	.14
☐ 272 Dante Bichette HH 15	.07
☐ 273 Randy Johnson HH ...30	.14
☐ 274 Matt Williams HH 30	.14
☐ 275 Alex Rodriguez HH .. 1.00	.45
☐ 276 Tim Salmon HH 30	.14
☐ 277 Johnny Damon HH ...15	.07
☐ 278 Manny Ramirez HH ...30	.14
☐ 279 Derek Jeter HH 1.00	.45
☐ 280 Eddie Murray HH 30	.14
☐ 281 Ozzie Smith HH 40	.18
☐ 282 Garret Anderson HH ..15	.07
☐ 283 Raul Mondesi HH 30	.14
☐ 284 Terry Steinbach 15	.07
☐ 285 Carlos Garcia 15	.07
☐ 286 Dave Justice 60	.25
☐ 287 Eric Anthony 15	.07
☐ 288 Benji Gil 15	.07
☐ 289 Bob Hamelin 15	.07
☐ 290 Dwayne Hosey 15	.07
☐ 291 Andy Pettitte HH 30	.14
☐ 292 Rod Beck 15	.07
☐ 293 Shane Andrews 15	.07
☐ 294 Julian Tavarez 15	.07
☐ 295 Willie Greene 15	.07
☐ 296 Ismael Valdes 30	.14
☐ 297 Glenallen Hill 15	.07
☐ 298 Troy Percival 30	.14
☐ 299 Ray Durham 15	.07
☐ 300 Jeff Conine 300 15	.07
☐ 301 Ken Griffey Jr. 300 .. 1.50	.70
☐ 302 Will Clark 300 30	.14
☐ 303 Mike Greenwell 300 ..15	.07
☐ 304 Carlos Baerga 300 15	.07
☐ 305A Paul Molitor 300 30	.14
☐ 305B Jeff Bagwell 300 60	.25
☐ 306 Mark Grace 300 30	.14
☐ 307 Don Mattingly 300 ...40	.18
☐ 308 Hal Morris 300 15	.07
☐ 309 Butch Huskey 15	.07
☐ 310 Ozzie Guillen 15	.07
☐ 311 Erik Hanson 15	.07
☐ 312 Kenny Lofton 300 40	.18
☐ 313 Edgar Martinez 300 ..30	.14
☐ 314 Kurt Abbott 15	.07
☐ 315 John Smoltz 30	.14
☐ 316 Ariel Prieto 15	.07
☐ 317 Mark Carreon 15	.07
☐ 318 Kirby Puckett 300 60	.25
☐ 319 Carlos Perez 15	.07
☐ 320 Gary DiSarcina 15	.07
☐ 321 Trevor Hoffman 15	.07
☐ 322 Mike Piazza 300 .. 1.00	.45
☐ 323 Frank Thomas 300 . 1.25	.55
☐ 324 Juan Acevedo 15	.07
☐ 325 Bip Roberts 15	.07
☐ 326 Javier Lopez 30	.14
☐ 327 Benito Santiago 15	.07
☐ 328 Mark Lewis 15	.07
☐ 329 Royce Clayton 15	.07
☐ 330 Tom Gordon 15	.07
☐ 331 Ben McDonald 15	.07
☐ 332 Dan Wilson 15	.07
☐ 333 Ron Gant 30	.14
☐ 334 Wade Boggs 300 30	.14
☐ 335 Paul Molitor 60	.25
☐ 336 Tony Gwynn 300 75	.35
☐ 337 Sean Berry 15	.07
☐ 338 Rickey Henderson 40	.18
☐ 339 Wil Cordero 15	.07
☐ 340 Kent Mercker 15	.07
☐ 341 Kenny Rogers 15	.07
☐ 342 Ryne Sandberg 75	.35
☐ 343 Charlie Hayes 15	.07
☐ 344 Andy Benes 30	.14
☐ 345 Sterling Hitchcock 15	.07
☐ 346 Bernard Gilkey 15	.07
☐ 347 Julio Franco 15	.07
☐ 348 Ken Hill 15	.07
☐ 349 Russ Davis 15	.07
☐ 350 Mike Blowers 15	.07
☐ 351 B.J. Surhoff 15	.07
☐ 352 Lance Johnson 15	.07
☐ 353 Darryl Hamilton 15	.07
☐ 354 Shawon Dunston 15	.07
☐ 355 Rick Aguilera 15	.07
☐ 356 Danny Tartabull 15	.07
☐ 357 Todd Stottlemyre 15	.07
☐ 358 Mike Bordick 15	.07
☐ 359 Jack McDowell 15	.07
☐ 360 Todd Zeile 15	.07
☐ 361 Tino Martinez 60	.25
☐ 362 Greg Gagne 15	.07
☐ 363 Mike Kelly 15	.07
☐ 364 Tim Raines 30	.14
☐ 365 Ernie Young 15	.07
☐ 366 Mike Stanley 15	.07
☐ 367 Wally Joyner 30	.14
☐ 368 Karim Garcia 40	.18
☐ 369 Paul Wilson 15	.07
☐ 370 Sal Fasano 15	.07
☐ 371 Jason Schmidt 30	.14
☐ 372 Livan Hernandez .. 2.00	.90

□ 373 George Arias	.15	.07
□ 374 Steve Gibralter	.15	.07
□ 375 Jermaine Dye	.30	.14
□ 376 Jason Kendall	.40	.18
□ 377 Brooks Kieschnick	.30	.14
□ 378 Jeff Ware	.15	.07
□ 379 Alan Benes	.30	.14
□ 380 Rey Ordonez	.30	.14
□ 381 Jay Powell	.15	.07
□ 382 Osvaldo Fernandez	.30	.14
□ 383 Wilton Guerrero	.60	.25
□ 384 Eric Owens	.15	.07
□ 385 George Williams	.15	.07
□ 386 Chan Ho Park	.60	.25
□ 387 Jeff Suppan	.30	.14
□ 388 F.P. Santangelo	.15	.07
□ 389 Terry Adams	.15	.07
□ 390 Bob Abreu	.40	.18
□ 391 Quinton McCracken	.15	.07
□ 392 Mike Busby	.15	.07
□ 393 Cal Ripken CL	1.25	.55
□ 394 Ken Griffey Jr. CL	1.50	.70
□ 395 Frank Thomas CL	1.25	.55
□ 396 Chipper Jones CL	1.00	.45
□ 397 Greg Maddux CL	1.00	.45
□ 398 Mike Piazza CL	1.00	.45
□ 399 Ken Griffey Jr CL	1.50	.70
Cal Ripken Jr.		
Chipper Jones		
Frank Thomas		
Greg Maddux		
Mike Piazza		
□ CR1 Cal Ripken Tribute	20.00	9.00

1996 Pinnacle Christie Brinkley Collection

Randomly inserted at the rate of one in 23 packs, this 16-card set features the 1995 World Series participants captured by the lens of supermodel and photographer Christie Brinkley. The fronts feature color player photos in various poses with different backgrounds. The backs carry a color portrait of the player and Ms. Brinkley with an explanation as to why she posed them as she did.

	MINT	NRMT
COMPLETE SET (16)	75.00	34.00
COMMON CARD (1-30)	1.00	.45
SER.2 STATED ODDS 1:23H/R, 1:19J, 1:32 M		

□ 1 Greg Maddux	15.00	6.75
□ 2 Ryan Klesko	3.00	1.35
□ 3 Dave Justice	5.00	2.20
□ 4 Tom Glavine	2.00	.90
□ 5 Chipper Jones	15.00	6.75
□ 6 Fred McGriff	3.00	1.35
□ 7 Javier Lopez	2.00	.90
□ 8 Marquis Grissom	2.00	.90

□ 9 Jason Schmidt	2.00	.90
□ 10 Albert Belle	6.00	2.70
□ 11 Manny Ramirez	5.00	2.20
□ 12 Carlos Baerga	1.00	.45
□ 13 Sandy Alomar	2.00	.90
□ 14 Jim Thome	5.00	2.20
□ 15 Julio Franco	1.00	.45
□ 16 Kenny Lofton	6.00	2.70
□ PCB Christie Brinkley Promo	6.00	2.70
On the Beach		

1996 Pinnacle Essence of the Game

Randomly inserted in hobby packs only at a rate of one in 23, this 18-card standard-size set takes a unique perspective, photographically capturing the persona of 18 of the game's most popular icons. Using a micro-etched print technology, the fronts display a color player cutout on an acetate card studded with stars, with "Essence of the Game" appearing on a holographic design across the top. On the back, this holographic design carries a highlight.

	MINT	NRMT
COMPLETE SET (18)	150.00	70.00
COMMON CARD (1-18)	1.50	.70
SER.1 STATED ODDS 1:23 HOBBY		

□ 1 Cal Ripken	20.00	9.00
□ 2 Greg Maddux	15.00	6.75
□ 3 Frank Thomas	20.00	9.00
□ 4 Matt Williams	3.00	1.35
□ 5 Chipper Jones	15.00	6.75
□ 6 Reggie Sanders	1.50	.70
□ 7 Ken Griffey Jr.	25.00	11.00
□ 8 Kirby Puckett	10.00	4.50
□ 9 Hideo Nomo	12.00	5.50
□ 10 Mike Piazza	15.00	6.75
□ 11 Jeff Bagwell	10.00	4.50
□ 12 Mo Vaughn	6.00	2.70
□ 13 Albert Belle	6.00	2.70
□ 14 Tim Salmon	5.00	2.20
□ 15 Don Mattingly	8.00	3.60
□ 16 Will Clark	3.00	1.35
□ 17 Eddie Murray	5.00	2.20
□ 18 Barry Bonds	6.00	2.70

1996 Pinnacle First Rate

Randomly inserted in retail packs only at a rate of one in 23, this 18-card set features former first-round draft picks who have become major league superstars done in Dufex print.

	MINT	NRMT
COMPLETE SET (18)	120.00	55.00
COMMON CARD (1-18)	2.00	.90
SEMISTARS	3.00	1.35
UNLISTED STARS	6.00	2.70
SER.1 STATED ODDS 1:23 RETAIL		

□ 1 Ken Griffey Jr.	30.00	13.50
□ 2 Frank Thomas	25.00	11.00
□ 3 Mo Vaughn	8.00	3.60
□ 4 Chipper Jones	20.00	9.00
□ 5 Alex Rodriguez	20.00	9.00
□ 6 Kirby Puckett	12.00	5.50
□ 7 Gary Sheffield	6.00	2.70
□ 8 Matt Williams	3.00	1.35
□ 9 Barry Bonds	8.00	3.60
□ 10 Craig Biggio	3.00	1.35
□ 11 Robin Ventura	3.00	1.35
□ 12 Michael Tucker	3.00	1.35
□ 13 Derek Jeter	15.00	6.75
□ 14 Manny Ramirez	6.00	2.70
□ 15 Barry Larkin	3.00	1.35
□ 16 Shawn Green	2.00	.90
□ 17 Will Clark	3.00	1.35
□ 18 Mark McGwire	12.00	5.50

1996 Pinnacle Power

Randomly inserted in packs at a rate of one in 35 retail and hobby packs, or one in 29 jumbo packs, this 20-card set highlights the league's top long-ball hitters in die-cut holographic foil technology. On a black card face, the fronts have a color player cutout superposed over a holographic homeplate. All printing on the front, including the player's name, is stamped in gold foil. The horizontal backs present a color closeup on the left and a player profile on the right.

	MINT	NRMT
COMPLETE SET (20)	120.00	55.00
COMMON CARD (1-20)	2.00	.90

SEMISTARS 3.00 1.35
UNLISTED STARS 6.00 2.70
SER.1 STATED ODDS 1:35...

		MINT	NRMT
☐ 1	Frank Thomas	25.00	11.00
☐ 2	Mo Vaughn	8.00	3.60
☐ 3	Ken Griffey Jr.	30.00	13.50
☐ 4	Matt Williams	3.00	1.35
☐ 5	Barry Bonds	8.00	3.60
☐ 6	Reggie Sanders	2.00	.90
☐ 7	Mike Piazza	20.00	9.00
☐ 8	Jim Edmonds	3.00	1.35
☐ 9	Dante Bichette	2.50	1.10
☐ 10	Sammy Sosa	6.00	2.70
☐ 11	Jeff Bagwell	12.00	5.50
☐ 12	Fred McGriff	3.00	1.35
☐ 13	Albert Belle	8.00	3.60
☐ 14	Tim Salmon	6.00	2.70
☐ 15	Joe Carter	2.50	1.10
☐ 16	Manny Ramirez	6.00	2.70
☐ 17	Eddie Murray	6.00	2.70
☐ 18	Cecil Fielder	2.50	1.10
☐ 19	Larry Walker	6.00	2.70
☐ 20	Juan Gonzalez	15.00	6.75

1996 Pinnacle Project Stardom

This 18-card set was randomly inserted in hobby packs at the rate of one in 35. The fronts feature a color action player photo on a blue foil background with a player portrait framed by silver foil rays depicting a star shining. The backs carry another player portrait with rays coming from behind his head to give the impression of a shining star, and information about the player is printed on the side.

	MINT	NRMT
COMPLETE SET (18)	150.00	70.00
COMMON CARD (1-18)	3.00	1.35
SEMISTARS	6.00	2.70
UNLISTED STARS	10.00	4.50
SER.2 STATED ODDS 1:35...		

		MINT	NRMT
☐ 1	Paul Wilson	3.00	1.35
☐ 2	Derek Jeter	25.00	11.00
☐ 3	Karim Garcia	6.00	2.70
☐ 4	Johnny Damon	4.00	1.80
☐ 5	Alex Rodriguez	30.00	13.50
☐ 6	Chipper Jones	30.00	13.50
☐ 7	Charles Johnson	4.00	1.80
☐ 8	Bob Abreu	6.00	2.70
☐ 9	Alan Benes	4.00	1.80
☐ 10	Richard Hidalgo	10.00	4.50
☐ 11	Brooks Kieschnick	4.00	1.80
☐ 12	Garret Anderson	4.00	1.80
☐ 13	Livan Hernandez	15.00	6.75
☐ 14	Manny Ramirez	10.00	4.50
☐ 15	Jermaine Dye	4.00	1.80
☐ 16	Todd Hollandsworth	3.00	1.35
☐ 17	Raul Mondesi	6.00	2.70
☐ 18	Ryan Klesko	6.00	2.70

1996 Pinnacle Skylines

Randomly inserted in magazine packs at the rate of one in 29, this 18-card set features baseball's best players pictured against their city's skyline and printed on clear plastic stock. The backs carry the same player portrait with information about the player and the city printed below.

	MINT	NRMT
COMPLETE SET (18)	250.00	110.00
COMMON CARD (1-18)	6.00	2.70
UNLISTED STARS	10.00	4.50
SER.2 STATED ODDS 1:29 JUM, 1:50 MAG		

		MINT	NRMT
☐ 1	Ken Griffey Jr.	50.00	22.00
☐ 2	Frank Thomas	40.00	18.00
☐ 3	Greg Maddux	30.00	13.50
☐ 4	Cal Ripken	40.00	18.00
☐ 5	Albert Belle	12.00	5.50
☐ 6	Mo Vaughn	12.00	5.50
☐ 7	Mike Piazza	30.00	13.50
☐ 8	Wade Boggs	10.00	4.50
☐ 9	Will Clark	6.00	2.70
☐ 10	Barry Bonds	12.00	5.50
☐ 11	Gary Sheffield	10.00	4.50
☐ 12	Hideo Nomo	25.00	11.00
☐ 13	Tony Gwynn	25.00	11.00
☐ 14	Kirby Puckett	20.00	9.00
☐ 15	Chipper Jones	30.00	13.50
☐ 16	Jeff Bagwell	20.00	9.00
☐ 17	Manny Ramirez	10.00	4.50
☐ 18	Raul Mondesi	6.00	2.70

1996 Pinnacle Slugfest

Randomly inserted exclusively into one in every 35 series 2 retail packs, cards from this 18 cards set feature a selection of baseball's top slugging stars. The fronts carry a color action player photo on a silver foil star-burst background. The backs display a color player photo in a wooden bat with player information on the side.

	MINT	NRMT
COMPLETE SET (18)	200.00	90.00
COMMON CARD (1-18)	3.00	1.35
SEMISTARS	5.00	2.20
UNLISTED STARS	8.00	3.60
SER.2 RETAIL STATED ODDS 1:35		

		MINT	NRMT
☐ 1	Frank Thomas	30.00	13.50
☐ 2	Ken Griffey Jr.	40.00	18.00
☐ 3	Jeff Bagwell	15.00	6.75
☐ 4	Barry Bonds	10.00	4.50
☐ 5	Mo Vaughn	10.00	4.50
☐ 6	Albert Belle	10.00	4.50
☐ 7	Mike Piazza	25.00	11.00
☐ 8	Matt Williams	5.00	2.20
☐ 9	Dante Bichette	4.00	1.80
☐ 10	Sammy Sosa	8.00	3.60
☐ 11	Gary Sheffield	8.00	3.60
☐ 12	Reggie Sanders	3.00	1.35
☐ 13	Manny Ramirez	8.00	3.60
☐ 14	Eddie Murray	8.00	3.60
☐ 15	Juan Gonzalez	20.00	9.00
☐ 16	Dean Palmer	3.00	1.35
☐ 17	Rafael Palmeiro	5.00	2.20
☐ 18	Cecil Fielder	4.00	1.80

1996 Pinnacle Team Pinnacle

Randomly inserted in series one packs at a rate of one in 72, this 9-card set spotlights double-front all-foil Dufex card designs featuring nine top AL and NL players, by position, back-to-back. On a gold foil background displaying a baseball, the fronts present a color player cutout extending beyond the picture frame. "Team Pinnacle," the player's name, and an abbreviation for his position is printed in the bottom border. Only one side of each card is Dufexed.

	MINT	NRMT
COMPLETE SET (9)	150.00	70.00
COMMON CARD (1-9)	4.00	1.80
SER.1 STATED ODDS 1:72...		

		MINT	NRMT
☐ 1	Frank Thomas	25.00	11.00
	Jeff Bagwell		
☐ 2	Chuck Knoblauch	7.00	3.10
	Craig Biggio		
☐ 3	Jim Thome	7.00	3.10
	Matt Williams		

		MINT	NRMT
☐ 4	Barry Larkin	25.00	11.00
	Cal Ripken		
☐ 5	Barry Bonds	8.00	3.60
	Tim Salmon		
☐ 6	Ken Griffey Jr.	30.00	13.50
	Reggie Sanders		
☐ 7	Albert Belle	8.00	3.60
	Sammy Sosa		
☐ 8	Ivan Rodriguez	20.00	9.00
	Mike Piazza		
☐ 9	Greg Maddux	20.00	9.00
	Randy Johnson		

1996 Pinnacle Team Spirit

Randomly inserted in series two packs at the rate of one in 72, this 12-card set features color action player images in holographic foil stamping over a silver foil ball outlined in baseball stitching. The backs carry two player photos and player information.

	MINT	NRMT
COMPLETE SET (12)	250.00	110.00
COMMON CARD (1-12)	5.00	2.20
SER.2 STAT.ODDS 1:72H/R, 1:60J, 1:103M		

		MINT	NRMT
☐ 1	Greg Maddux	25.00	11.00
☐ 2	Ken Griffey Jr.	40.00	18.00
☐ 3	Derek Jeter	20.00	9.00
☐ 4	Mike Piazza	25.00	11.00
☐ 5	Cal Ripken	30.00	13.50
☐ 6	Frank Thomas	30.00	13.50
☐ 7	Jeff Bagwell	15.00	6.75
☐ 8	Mo Vaughn	10.00	4.50
☐ 9	Albert Belle	10.00	4.50
☐ 10	Chipper Jones	25.00	11.00
☐ 11	Johnny Damon	7.00	3.10
☐ 12	Barry Bonds	10.00	4.50

1996 Pinnacle Team Tomorrow

Randomly inserted in series one jumbo packs at a rate of one in 19, this 10-card set is a jumbo exclusive and features the next crop of superstars. The fronts are printed in an all-foil Dufex design with two of the same color player action cutouts—one close up and the other full-length. The backs carry a color player portrait and information about the player.

	MINT	NRMT
COMPLETE SET (10)	100.00	45.00
COMMON CARD (1-10)	3.00	1.35

	MINT	NRMT
SEMISTARS	6.00	2.70
UNLISTED STARS	8.00	3.60
SER.1 STATED ODDS 1:19 JUMBO		

		MINT	NRMT
☐ 1	Ruben Rivera	4.00	1.80
☐ 2	Johnny Damon	4.00	1.80
☐ 3	Raul Mondesi	6.00	2.70
☐ 4	Manny Ramirez	8.00	3.60
☐ 5	Hideo Nomo	20.00	9.00
☐ 6	Chipper Jones	25.00	11.00
☐ 7	Garret Anderson	4.00	1.80
☐ 8	Alex Rodriguez	25.00	11.00
☐ 9	Derek Jeter	20.00	9.00
☐ 10	Karim Garcia	6.00	2.70

1997 Pinnacle

The 1997 Pinnacle set was issued as one series of 200 cards. Cards were distributed in 10-card hobby and retail packs (SRP $2.49) and 7-card magazine packs. This set was released in February, 1997. The set contains the following subsets: Rookies (156-185), Clout (186-197) and Checklists (198-200). Basic card fronts feature full color action shots with dramatic gold foil treatment across the bottom. A conglomeration of legendary players, locales and other regional names of interest related to the specified team of the featured player run in small type within the gold foil borders. Backs feature a small, color mug-shot along with various statistics and information. There are no key Rookie Cards in this set.

	MINT	NRMT
COMPLETE SET (200)	20.00	9.00
COMMON CARD (1-200)	.15	.07
MINOR STARS	.30	.14

	MINT	NRMT
UNLISTED STARS	.60	.25
COMP.MUSEUM SET (200)	600.00	275.00
COMMON MUSEUM (1-200)	1.50	.70
*MUSEUM STARS: 6X TO 12X HI COLUMN		
*MUSEUM YOUNG STARS: 5X TO 10X HI		
MUSEUM STATED ODDS 1:9....		

		MINT	NRMT
☐ 1	Cecil Fielder	.30	.14
☐ 2	Garret Anderson	.30	.14
☐ 3	Charles Nagy	.30	.14
☐ 4	Darryl Hamilton	.15	.07
☐ 5	Greg Myers	.15	.07
☐ 6	Eric Davis	.30	.14
☐ 7	Jeff Frye	.15	.07
☐ 8	Marquis Grissom	.30	.14
☐ 9	Curt Schilling	.30	.14
☐ 10	Jeff Fassero	.15	.07
☐ 11	Alan Benes	.30	.14
☐ 12	Orlando Miller	.15	.07
☐ 13	Alex Fernandez	.30	.14
☐ 14	Andy Pettitte	.60	.25
☐ 15	Andre Dawson	.40	.18
☐ 16	Mark Grudzielanek	.15	.07
☐ 17	Joe Vitiello	.15	.07
☐ 18	Juan Gonzalez	1.50	.70
☐ 19	Mark Whiten	.15	.07
☐ 20	Lance Johnson	.15	.07
☐ 21	Trevor Hoffman	.15	.07
☐ 22	Marc Newfield	.15	.07
☐ 23	Jim Eisenreich	.15	.07
☐ 24	Joe Carter	.30	.14
☐ 25	Jose Canseco	.40	.18
☐ 26	Bill Swift	.15	.07
☐ 27	Ellis Burks	.30	.14
☐ 28	Ben McDonald	.15	.07
☐ 29	Edgar Martinez	.40	.18
☐ 30	Jamie Moyer	.15	.07
☐ 31	Chan Ho Park	.60	.25
☐ 32	Carlos Delgado	.30	.14
☐ 33	Kevin Mitchell	.15	.07
☐ 34	Carlos Garcia	.15	.07
☐ 35	Darryl Strawberry	.30	.14
☐ 36	Jim Thome	.60	.25
☐ 37	Jose Offerman	.15	.07
☐ 38	Ryan Klesko	.40	.18
☐ 39	Ruben Sierra	.15	.07
☐ 40	Devon White	.15	.07
☐ 41	Brian Jordan	.30	.14
☐ 42	Tony Gwynn	1.50	.70
☐ 43	Rafael Palmeiro	.40	.18
☐ 44	Dante Bichette	.30	.14
☐ 45	Scott Stahoviak	.15	.07
☐ 46	Roger Cedeno	.15	.07
☐ 47	Ivan Rodriguez	.75	.35
☐ 48	Bob Abreu	.30	.14
☐ 49	Darryl Kile	.30	.14
☐ 50	Darren Dreifort	.15	.07
☐ 51	Shawon Dunston	.15	.07
☐ 52	Mark McGwire	1.25	.55
☐ 53	Tim Salmon	.60	.25
☐ 54	Gene Schall	.15	.07
☐ 55	Roger Clemens	1.25	.55
☐ 56	Rondell White	.30	.14
☐ 57	Ed Sprague	.15	.07
☐ 58	Craig Paquette	.15	.07
☐ 59	David Segui	.15	.07
☐ 60	Jaime Navarro	.15	.07
☐ 61	Tom Glavine	.30	.14
☐ 62	Jeff Brantley	.15	.07
☐ 63	Kimera Bartee	.15	.07
☐ 64	Fernando Vina	.15	.07
☐ 65	Eddie Murray	.60	.25
☐ 66	Lenny Dykstra	.30	.14
☐ 67	Kevin Elster	.15	.07
☐ 68	Vinny Castilla	.30	.14
☐ 69	Mike Fetters	.15	.07
☐ 70	Brett Butler	.30	.14
☐ 71	Robby Thompson	.15	.07
☐ 72	Reggie Jefferson	.15	.07
☐ 73	Todd Hundley	.30	.14
☐ 74	Jeff King	.15	.07
☐ 75	Ernie Young	.15	.07
☐ 76	Jeff Bagwell	1.25	.55
☐ 77	Dan Wilson	.15	.07
☐ 78	Paul Molitor	.60	.25
☐ 79	Kevin Seitzer	.15	.07

☐ 80 Kevin Brown	.30	.14
☐ 81 Ron Gant	.30	.14
☐ 82 Dwight Gooden	.30	.14
☐ 83 Todd Stottlemyre	.15	.07
☐ 84 Ken Caminiti	.40	.18
☐ 85 James Baldwin	.15	.07
☐ 86 Jermaine Dye	.15	.07
☐ 87 Harold Baines	.30	.14
☐ 88 Pat Hentgen	.30	.14
☐ 89 Frank Rodriguez	.15	.07
☐ 90 Mark Johnson	.15	.07
☐ 91 Jason Kendall	.30	.14
☐ 92 Alex Rodriguez	2.00	.90
☐ 93 Alan Trammell	.30	.14
☐ 94 Scott Brosius	.15	.07
☐ 95 Delino DeShields	.15	.07
☐ 96 Chipper Jones	2.00	.90
☐ 97 Barry Bonds	.75	.35
☐ 98 Brady Anderson	.40	.18
☐ 99 Ryne Sandberg	.75	.35
☐ 100 Albert Belle	.75	.35
☐ 101 Jeff Cirillo	.30	.14
☐ 102 Frank Thomas	2.50	1.10
☐ 103 Mike Piazza	2.00	.90
☐ 104 Rickey Henderson	.40	.18
☐ 105 Rey Ordonez	.15	.07
☐ 106 Mark Grace	.40	.18
☐ 107 Terry Steinbach	.15	.07
☐ 108 Ray Durham	.15	.07
☐ 109 Barry Larkin	.40	.18
☐ 110 Tony Clark	.60	.25
☐ 111 Bernie Williams	.60	.25
☐ 112 John Smoltz	.30	.14
☐ 113 Moises Alou	.30	.14
☐ 114 Alex Gonzalez	.15	.07
☐ 115 Rico Brogna	.15	.07
☐ 116 Eric Karros	.30	.14
☐ 117 Jeff Conine	.15	.07
☐ 118 Todd Hollandsworth	.15	.07
☐ 119 Troy Percival	.15	.07
☐ 120 Paul Wilson	.15	.07
☐ 121 Orel Hershiser	.30	.14
☐ 122 Ozzie Smith	.75	.35
☐ 123 Dave Hollins	.15	.07
☐ 124 Ken Hill	.15	.07
☐ 125 Rick Wilkins	.15	.07
☐ 126 Scott Servais	.15	.07
☐ 127 Fernando Valenzuela	.30	.14
☐ 128 Mariano Rivera	.30	.14
☐ 129 Mark Loretta	.15	.07
☐ 130 Shane Reynolds	.15	.07
☐ 131 Darren Oliver	.15	.07
☐ 132 Steve Trachsel	.15	.07
☐ 133 Darren Bragg	.15	.07
☐ 134 Jason Dickson	.30	.14
☐ 135 Darrin Fletcher	.15	.07
☐ 136 Gary Gaetti	.15	.07
☐ 137 Joey Cora	.30	.14
☐ 138 Terry Pendleton	.15	.07
☐ 139 Derek Jeter	2.00	.90
☐ 140 Danny Tartabull	.15	.07
☐ 141 John Flaherty	.15	.07
☐ 142 B.J. Surhoff	.15	.07
☐ 143 Mike Sweeney	.30	.14
☐ 144 Chad Mottola	.15	.07
☐ 145 Andujar Cedeno	.15	.07
☐ 146 Tim Belcher	.15	.07
☐ 147 Mark Thompson	.15	.07
☐ 148 Rafael Bournigal	.15	.07
☐ 149 Marty Cordova	.30	.14
☐ 150 Osvaldo Fernandez	.15	.07
☐ 151 Mike Stanley	.15	.07
☐ 152 Ricky Bottalico	.15	.07
☐ 153 Donne Wall	.15	.07
☐ 154 Omar Vizquel	.30	.14
☐ 155 Mike Mussina	.60	.25
☐ 156 Brant Brown	.15	.07
☐ 157 F.P. Santangelo	.15	.07
☐ 158 Ryan Hancock	.15	.07
☐ 159 Jeff D'Amico	.15	.07
☐ 160 Luis Castillo	.30	.14
☐ 161 Darin Erstad	1.00	.45
☐ 162 Ugueth Urbina	.15	.07
☐ 163 Andruw Jones	1.50	.70
☐ 164 Steve Gibralter	.15	.07
☐ 165 Robin Jennings	.15	.07
☐ 166 Mike Cameron	.40	.18
☐ 167 George Arias	.15	.07
☐ 168 Chris Stynes	.15	.07
☐ 169 Justin Thompson	.30	.14
☐ 170 Jamey Wright	.15	.07
☐ 171 Todd Walker	.30	.14
☐ 172 Nomar Garciaparra	2.00	.90
☐ 173 Jose Paniagua	.15	.07
☐ 174 Marvin Benard	.15	.07
☐ 175 Rocky Coppinger	.15	.07
☐ 176 Quinton McCracken	.15	.07
☐ 177 Amaury Telemaco	.15	.07
☐ 178 Neifi Perez	.30	.14
☐ 179 Todd Greene	.30	.14
☐ 180 Jason Thompson	.15	.07
☐ 181 Wilton Guerrero	.15	.07
☐ 182 Edgar Renteria	.30	.14
☐ 183 Billy Wagner	.30	.14
☐ 184 Alex Ochoa	.15	.07
☐ 185 Dmitri Young	.15	.07
☐ 186 Kenny Lofton CT	.75	.35
☐ 187 Andres Galarraga CT	.60	.25
☐ 188 Chuck Knoblauch CT	.60	.25
☐ 189 Greg Maddux CT	2.00	.90
☐ 190 Mo Vaughn CT	.75	.35
☐ 191 Cal Ripken CT	2.50	1.10
☐ 192 Hideo Nomo CT	1.50	.70
☐ 193 Ken Griffey Jr. CT	3.00	1.35
☐ 194 Sammy Sosa CT	.60	.25
☐ 195 Jay Buhner CT	.40	.18
☐ 196 Manny Ramirez CT	.60	.25
☐ 197 Matt Williams CT	.40	.18
☐ 198 Andruw Jones CT	.75	.35
☐ 199 Darin Erstad CL	.40	.18
☐ 200 Trey Beamon CL	.15	.07

1997 Pinnacle Artist's Proofs

After three years of producing Artist's Proofs cards, Pinnacle decided to add some changes to their line of scarce parallel cards. Instead of the typical one per box parallel with a little foil logo on front the set was completely redesigned in 1997. Following a similar promotion run in the 1996 Finest brand, the 200-card first series set was broken down into three different groups of cards; 125 bronze, 50 silver and 25 gold. One in every 47 first series packs contained either a bronze, silver or gold Artist's Proofs card. The gold cards are scarcest (only 300 of each were produced), and silver cards are scarcer than bronze cards. Print runs for the bronze and silver cards were never announced. Each group of cards is easy to identify by their

bold color-specific backgrounds (i.e. gold cards have gold backgrounds). All three groups share the same Artist's Proof logo on front.

	MINT	NRMT
COMPLETE SET (200)	3000.00	1350.00
COMP.BRONZE SET (125)	800.00	350.00
COMMON BRONZE	6.00	2.70
COMP.SILVER SET (50)	1000.00	450.00
COMMON SILVER	8.00	3.60
COMP.GOLD SET (25)	1200.00	550.00
COMMON GOLD	12.00	5.50
STATED ODDS 1:47 HOB/RET, 1:55 MAG		

☐ 1 Cecil Fielder B	10.00	4.50
☐ 2 Garret Anderson B	10.00	4.50
☐ 3 Charles Nagy B	10.00	4.50
☐ 4 Darryl Hamilton B	6.00	2.70
☐ 5 Greg Myers B	6.00	2.70
☐ 6 Eric Davis B	10.00	4.50
☐ 7 Jeff Frye B	6.00	2.70
☐ 8 Marquis Grissom S	12.00	5.50
☐ 9 Curt Schilling B	10.00	4.50
☐ 10 Jeff Fassero B	6.00	2.70
☐ 11 Alan Benes S	12.00	5.50
☐ 12 Orlando Miller B	6.00	2.70
☐ 13 Alex Fernandez B	10.00	4.50
☐ 14 Andy Pettitte G	40.00	18.00
☐ 15 Andre Dawson B	15.00	6.75
☐ 16 Mark Grudzielanek B	6.00	2.70
☐ 17 Joe Vitiello B	6.00	2.70
☐ 18 Juan Gonzalez G	100.00	45.00
☐ 19 Mark Whiten B	6.00	2.70
☐ 20 Lance Johnson B	6.00	2.70
☐ 21 Trevor Hoffman B	6.00	2.70
☐ 22 Marc Newfield B	6.00	2.70
☐ 23 Jim Eisenreich B	6.00	2.70
☐ 24 Joe Carter S	12.00	5.50
☐ 25 Jose Canseco S	20.00	9.00
☐ 26 Bill Swift B	6.00	2.70
☐ 27 Ellis Burks B	10.00	4.50
☐ 28 Ben McDonald B	6.00	2.70
☐ 29 Edgar Martinez S	20.00	9.00
☐ 30 Jamie Moyer B	6.00	2.70
☐ 31 Chan Ho Park S	30.00	13.50
☐ 32 Carlos Delgado S	12.00	5.50
☐ 33 Kevin Mitchell B	6.00	2.70
☐ 34 Carlos Garcia B	6.00	2.70
☐ 35 Darryl Strawberry G	15.00	6.75
☐ 36 Jim Thome G	40.00	18.00
☐ 37 Jose Offerman B	6.00	2.70
☐ 38 Ryan Klesko S	20.00	9.00
☐ 39 Ruben Sierra B	6.00	2.70
☐ 40 Devon White B	6.00	2.70
☐ 41 Brian Jordan G	15.00	6.75
☐ 42 Tony Gwynn S	80.00	36.00
☐ 43 Rafael Palmeiro S	20.00	9.00
☐ 44 Dante Bichette B	10.00	4.50
☐ 45 Scott Stahoviak B	6.00	2.70
☐ 46 Roger Cedeno B	6.00	2.70
☐ 47 Ivan Rodriguez G	50.00	22.00
☐ 48 Bob Abreu S	12.00	5.50
☐ 49 Darryl Kile B	10.00	4.50
☐ 50 Darren Dreifort B	6.00	2.70
☐ 51 Shawon Dunston B	6.00	2.70
☐ 52 Mark McGwire S	60.00	27.00
☐ 53 Tim Salmon S	30.00	13.50
☐ 54 Gene Schall B	6.00	2.70
☐ 55 Roger Clemens B	50.00	22.00
☐ 56 Rondell White S	12.00	5.50
☐ 57 Ed Sprague B	6.00	2.70
☐ 58 Craig Paquette B	6.00	2.70
☐ 59 David Segui B	6.00	2.70
☐ 60 Jaime Navarro B	6.00	2.70
☐ 61 Tom Glavine S	12.00	5.50
☐ 62 Jeff Brantley B	6.00	2.70
☐ 63 Kimera Bartee B	6.00	2.70
☐ 64 Fernando Vina B	6.00	2.70
☐ 65 Eddie Murray S	30.00	13.50
☐ 66 Lenny Dykstra B	10.00	4.50
☐ 67 Kevin Elster B	6.00	2.70
☐ 68 Vinny Castilla B	10.00	4.50
☐ 69 Mike Fetters S	8.00	3.60
☐ 70 Brett Butler B	10.00	4.50

☐ 71	Robby Thompson B	6.00	2.70
☐ 72	Reggie Jefferson B	6.00	2.70
☐ 73	Todd Hundley S	12.00	5.50
☐ 74	Jeff King B	6.00	2.70
☐ 75	Ernie Young S	8.00	3.60
☐ 76	Jeff Bagwell G	80.00	36.00
☐ 77	Dan Wilson B	10.00	4.50
☐ 78	Paul Molitor S	40.00	18.00
☐ 79	Kevin Seitzer B	6.00	2.70
☐ 80	Kevin Brown S	12.00	5.50
☐ 81	Ron Gant S	12.00	5.50
☐ 82	Dwight Gooden S	12.00	5.50
☐ 83	Todd Stottlemyre B	6.00	2.70
☐ 84	Ken Caminiti G	25.00	11.00
☐ 85	James Baldwin B	6.00	2.70
☐ 86	Jermaine Dye S	8.00	3.60
☐ 87	Harold Baines B	10.00	4.50
☐ 88	Pat Hentgen B	10.00	4.50
☐ 89	Frank Rodriguez B	6.00	2.70
☐ 90	Mark Johnson B	6.00	2.70
☐ 91	Jason Kendall S	12.00	5.50
☐ 92	Alex Rodriguez G	120.00	55.00
☐ 93	Alan Trammell B	10.00	4.50
☐ 94	Scott Brosius B	6.00	2.70
☐ 95	Delino DeShields B	6.00	2.70
☐ 96	Chipper Jones S	80.00	36.00
☐ 97	Barry Bonds S	40.00	18.00
☐ 98	Brady Anderson S	20.00	9.00
☐ 99	Ryne Sandberg G	40.00	18.00
☐ 100	Albert Belle G	50.00	22.00
☐ 101	Jeff Cirillo B	10.00	4.50
☐ 102	Frank Thomas G	150.00	70.00
☐ 103	Mike Piazza S	100.00	45.00
☐ 104	Rickey Henderson B	15.00	6.75
☐ 105	Rey Ordonez S	8.00	3.60
☐ 106	Mark Grace S	20.00	9.00
☐ 107	Terry Steinbach B	6.00	2.70
☐ 108	Ray Durham B	6.00	2.70
☐ 109	Barry Larkin S	20.00	9.00
☐ 110	Tony Clark S	30.00	13.50
☐ 111	Bernie Williams G	40.00	18.00
☐ 112	John Smoltz G	15.00	6.75
☐ 113	Moises Alou B	10.00	4.50
☐ 114	Alex Gonzalez B	6.00	2.70
☐ 115	Rico Brogna B	6.00	2.70
☐ 116	Eric Karros B	10.00	4.50
☐ 117	Jeff Conine S	12.00	5.50
☐ 118	Todd Hollandsworth G	12.00	5.50
☐ 119	Troy Percival S	8.00	3.60
☐ 120	Paul Wilson S	8.00	3.60
☐ 121	Orel Hershiser B	10.00	4.50
☐ 122	Ozzie Smith S	40.00	18.00
☐ 123	Dave Hollins B	6.00	2.70
☐ 124	Ken Hill B	6.00	2.70
☐ 125	Rick Wilkins B	6.00	2.70
☐ 126	Scott Servais B	6.00	2.70
☐ 127	Fernando Valenzuela B	10.00	4.50
☐ 128	Mariano Rivera G	15.00	6.75
☐ 129	Mark Loretta B	6.00	2.70
☐ 130	Shane Reynolds S	8.00	3.60
☐ 131	Darren Oliver B	6.00	2.70
☐ 132	Steve Trachsel B	6.00	2.70
☐ 133	Darren Bragg B	6.00	2.70
☐ 134	Jason Dickson B	10.00	4.50
☐ 135	Darren Fletcher B	6.00	2.70
☐ 136	Gary Gaetti B	6.00	2.70
☐ 137	Joey Cora B	6.00	2.70
☐ 138	Terry Pendleton B	6.00	2.70
☐ 139	Derek Jeter G	100.00	45.00
☐ 140	Danny Tartabull B	6.00	2.70
☐ 141	John Flaherty B	6.00	2.70
☐ 142	B.J. Surhoff B	6.00	2.70
☐ 143	Mark Sweeney B	6.00	2.70
☐ 144	Chad Mottola B	6.00	2.70
☐ 145	Andujar Cedeno B	6.00	2.70
☐ 146	Tim Belcher B	6.00	2.70
☐ 147	Mark Thompson B	6.00	2.70
☐ 148	Rafael Bournigal B	6.00	2.70
☐ 149	Marty Cordova S	12.00	5.50
☐ 150	Osvaldo Fernandez B	6.00	2.70
☐ 151	Mike Stanley B	6.00	2.70
☐ 152	Ricky Bottalico B	6.00	2.70
☐ 153	Donne Wall B	6.00	2.70
☐ 154	Omar Vizquel B	10.00	4.50
☐ 155	Mike Mussina S	30.00	13.50
☐ 156	Brant Brown B	6.00	2.70

☐ 157	F.P. Santangelo S	8.00	3.60
☐ 158	Ryan Hancock B	6.00	2.70
☐ 159	Jeff D'Amico B	6.00	2.70
☐ 160	Luis Castillo B	10.00	4.50
☐ 161	Darin Erstad G	50.00	22.00
☐ 162	Ugueth Urbina B	6.00	2.70
☐ 163	Andruw Jones G	80.00	36.00
☐ 164	Steve Gibralter B	6.00	2.70
☐ 165	Robin Jennings S	8.00	3.60
☐ 166	Mike Cameron B	15.00	6.75
☐ 167	George Arias S	8.00	3.60
☐ 168	Chris Stynes B	6.00	2.70
☐ 169	Justin Thompson B	10.00	4.50
☐ 170	Jamey Wright B	6.00	2.70
☐ 171	Todd Walker G	15.00	6.75
☐ 172	Nomar Garciaparra B	60.00	27.00
☐ 173	Jose Paniagua B	6.00	2.70
☐ 174	Marvin Benard B	6.00	2.70
☐ 175	Rocky Coppinger B	6.00	2.70
☐ 176	Quinton McCracken B	6.00	2.70
☐ 177	Amaury Telemaco B	6.00	2.70
☐ 178	Neifi Perez B	10.00	4.50
☐ 179	Todd Greene B	10.00	4.50
☐ 180	Jason Thompson B	6.00	2.70
☐ 181	Wilton Guerrero B	6.00	2.70
☐ 182	Edgar Renteria S	12.00	5.50
☐ 183	Billy Wagner S	12.00	5.50
☐ 184	Alex Ochoa G	12.00	5.50
☐ 185	Dmitri Young B	6.00	2.70
☐ 186	Kenny Lofton CT B	30.00	13.50
☐ 187	Andres Galarraga CT B	25.00	11.00
☐ 188	Chuck Knoblauch CT G	40.00	18.00
☐ 189	Greg Maddux CT S	100.00	45.00
☐ 190	Mo Vaughn CT S	40.00	18.00
☐ 191	Cal Ripken CT G	150.00	70.00
☐ 192	Hideo Nomo CT S	100.00	45.00
☐ 193	Ken Griffey Jr. CT G	200.00	90.00
☐ 194	Sammy Sosa CT S	30.00	13.50
☐ 195	Jay Buhner CT S	20.00	9.00
☐ 196	Manny Ramirez CT G	40.00	18.00
☐ 197	Matt Williams CT B	15.00	6.75
☐ 198	Andruw Jones CL B	40.00	18.00
☐ 199	Darin Erstad CL B	25.00	11.00
☐ 200	Trey Beamon CL B	6.00	2.70

1997 Pinnacle Cardfrontations

Randomly inserted in hobby packs only at a rate of one in 23, this 20-card set displays color player photos on rainbow holographic foil. The card design features a top pitcher on one side with a top home run hitter on the flip side. Both sides are covered with an opaque peel and reveal protective cover.

	MINT	NRMT
COMPLETE SET (20)	250.00	110.00
COMMON CARD (1-20)	5.00	2.20
UNLISTED STARS	8.00	3.60
SER.1 STATED ODDS 1:23 HOBBY		

☐ 1	Greg Maddux	25.00	11.00
	Mike Piazza		
☐ 2	Tom Glavine	5.00	2.20
	Ken Caminiti		
☐ 3	Randy Johnson	30.00	13.50
	Cal Ripken		
☐ 4	Kevin Appier	15.00	6.75
	Mark McGwire		
☐ 5	Andy Pettitte	20.00	9.00
	Juan Gonzalez		
☐ 6	Pat Hentgen	12.00	5.50
	Albert Belle		
☐ 7	Hideo Nomo	25.00	11.00
	Chipper Jones		
☐ 8	Ismael Valdes	8.00	3.60
	Sammy Sosa		
☐ 9	Mike Mussina	8.00	3.60
	Manny Ramirez		
☐ 10	David Cone	5.00	2.20
	Jay Buhner		
☐ 11	Mark Wohlers	8.00	3.60
	Gary Sheffield		
☐ 12	Alan Benes	10.00	4.50
	Barry Bonds		
☐ 13	Roger Clemens	12.00	5.50
	Ivan Rodriguez		
☐ 14	Mariano Rivera	40.00	18.00
	Ken Griffey Jr.		
☐ 15	Dwight Gooden	30.00	13.50
	Frank Thomas		
☐ 16	John Wetteland	12.00	5.50
	Darin Erstad		
☐ 17	John Smoltz	5.00	2.20
	Brian Jordan		
☐ 18	Kevin Brown	15.00	6.75
	Jeff Bagwell		
☐ 19	Jack McDowell	30.00	13.50
	Alex Rodriguez		
☐ 20	Charles Nagy	8.00	3.60
	Bernie Williams		

1997 Pinnacle Home/Away

Randomly inserted in only jumbo packs at a rate of one in 33, this 24-card set features color player photos on die-cut cards. The cards were designed and shaped to resemble a player's actual jersey.

	MINT	NRMT
COMPLETE SET (24)	400.00	180.00
COMMON CARD (1-24)	8.00	3.60
SER.1 STATED ODDS 1:33 JUMBO		

☐ 1	Chipper Jones Away	20.00	9.00
☐ 2	Chipper Jones Home	30.00	9.00
☐ 3	Ken Griffey Jr. Away	30.00	13.50
☐ 4	Ken Griffey Jr. Home	30.00	13.50
☐ 5	Mike Piazza Away	20.00	9.00
☐ 6	Mike Piazza Home	20.00	9.00
☐ 7	Frank Thomas Away	25.00	11.00
☐ 8	Frank Thomas Home	40.00	11.00
☐ 9	Jeff Bagwell Away	12.00	5.50
☐ 10	Jeff Bagwell Home	20.00	5.50
☐ 11	Alex Rodriguez Away	20.00	9.00
☐ 12	Alex Rodriguez Home	30.00	9.00

		MINT	NRMT
☐ 13	Barry Bonds Away	8.00	3.60
☐ 14	Barry Bonds Home	8.00	3.60
☐ 15	Mo Vaughn Away	8.00	3.60
☐ 16	Mo Vaughn Home	12.00	3.60
☐ 17	Derek Jeter Away	15.00	6.75
☐ 18	Derek Jeter Home	25.00	6.75
☐ 19	Mark McGwire Away	12.00	5.50
☐ 20	Mark McGwire Home	20.00	5.50
☐ 21	Cal Ripken Away	25.00	11.00
☐ 22	Cal Ripken Home	40.00	11.00
☐ 23	Albert Belle Away	8.00	3.60
☐ 24	Albert Belle Home	12.00	3.60

1997 Pinnacle Passport to the Majors

Randomly inserted in all first series packs at a rate of one in 36, this 25-card set features color player photos on a book-fold miniature passport card design and honors the rise to fame of some of the League's most high profile superstars.

	MINT	NRMT
COMPLETE SET (25)	300.00	135.00
COMMON CARD (1-25)	4.00	1.80
UNLISTED STARS	8.00	3.60
SER.1 STAT.ODDS 1:36 HOB/RET, 1:51 MAG		

		MINT	NRMT
☐ 1	Greg Maddux	25.00	11.00
☐ 2	Ken Griffey Jr.	40.00	18.00
☐ 3	Frank Thomas	30.00	13.50
☐ 4	Cal Ripken	30.00	13.50
☐ 5	Mike Piazza	25.00	11.00
☐ 6	Alex Rodriguez	25.00	11.00
☐ 7	Mo Vaughn	10.00	4.50
☐ 8	Chipper Jones	25.00	11.00
☐ 9	Roberto Alomar	8.00	3.60
☐ 10	Edgar Martinez	5.00	2.20
☐ 11	Javier Lopez	4.00	1.80
☐ 12	Ivan Rodriguez	10.00	4.50
☐ 13	Juan Gonzalez	20.00	9.00
☐ 14	Carlos Baerga	4.00	1.80
☐ 15	Sammy Sosa	8.00	3.60
☐ 16	Manny Ramirez	8.00	3.60
☐ 17	Raul Mondesi	5.00	2.20
☐ 18	Henry Rodriguez	4.00	1.80
☐ 19	Rafael Palmeiro	5.00	2.20
☐ 20	Rey Ordonez	4.00	1.80
☐ 21	Hideo Nomo	20.00	9.00
☐ 22	Mac Suzuki	4.00	1.80
☐ 23	Chan Ho Park	8.00	3.60
☐ 24	Larry Walker	8.00	3.60
☐ 25	Ruben Rivera	4.00	1.80

1997 Pinnacle Shades

Randomly inserted in magazine packs at a rate of one in 23, this 10-card set features color

upclose photos of some of the league's best players wearing their favorite pair of sunglasses. The cards have a die-cut design and mirror mylar finish.

	MINT	NRMT
COMPLETE SET (10)	120.00	55.00
COMMON CARD (1-10)	2.50	1.10
UNLISTED STARS	4.00	1.80
SER.1 STATED ODDS 1:23 MAGAZINE		

		MINT	NRMT
☐ 1	Ken Griffey Jr.	25.00	11.00
☐ 2	Juan Gonzalez	12.00	5.50
☐ 3	John Smoltz	2.50	1.10
☐ 4	Gary Sheffield	4.00	1.80
☐ 5	Cal Ripken	20.00	9.00
☐ 6	Mo Vaughn	6.00	2.70
☐ 7	Brian Jordan	2.50	1.10
☐ 8	Mike Piazza	15.00	6.75
☐ 9	Frank Thomas	20.00	9.00
☐ 10	Alex Rodriguez	15.00	6.75

1997 Pinnacle Team Pinnacle

Randomly inserted in packs at a rate of one in 90, this 10-card set matches color player photos of the top American and National League players by position on double-fronted, all-foil Dufex cards. The tenth card is a computer design that makes a full Team Pinnacle picture.

	MINT	NRMT
COMPLETE SET (10)	300.00	135.00
COMMON CARD (1-10)	10.00	4.50
UNLISTED STARS	12.00	5.50
SER.1 STAT.ODDS 1:90 HOB/RET, 1:107 MAG		

		MINT	NRMT
☐ 1	Frank Thomas	40.00	18.00
	Jeff Bagwell		
☐ 2	Chuck Knoblauch	12.00	5.50
	Eric Young		
☐ 3	Ken Caminiti	12.00	5.50
	Jim Thome		
☐ 4	Alex Rodriguez	50.00	22.00
	Chipper Jones		
☐ 5	Mike Piazza	40.00	18.00

		MINT	NRMT
	Ivan Rodriguez		
☐ 6	Albert Belle	20.00	9.00
	Barry Bonds		
☐ 7	Ken Griffey Jr.	50.00	22.00
	Ellis Burks		
☐ 8	Juan Gonzalez	30.00	13.50
	Gary Sheffield		
☐ 9	John Smoltz	12.00	5.50
	Andy Pettitte		
☐ 10	Frank Thomas	40.00	18.00
	Jeff Bagwell		
	Chuck Knoblauch		
	Eric Young		
	Ken Caminiti		
	Jim Thome		
	Alex Rodriguez		
	Chipper Jones		
	Mike Piazza		
	Ivan Rodriguez		
	Albert Belle		
	Barry Bonds		
	Ken Griffey Jr.		
	Ellis Burks		
	Juan Gonzalez		
	Gary Sheffield		
	John Smoltz		
	Andy Pettit7		

1998 Pinnacle

The 1998 Pinnacle set was issued in one series totalling 200 cards and was distributed in 10-card packs with a suggested retail price of $2.99. The fronts feature borderless color player photos with player information on the backs. The set contains the following subsets: Rookies (158-181), Field of Vision (182-187), Goin' Jake (188-197) and Checklists (198-200). Three variations of each card 1-157 were issued. The cards have home, away or seasonal stats on the back and were all produced in equal quantities.

	MINT	NRMT
COMPLETE SET (200)	30.00	13.50
COMMON CARD (1-200)	.15	.07
MINOR STARS	.30	.14
UNLISTED STARS	.60	.25
COMP.AP SET (100)	1500.00	700.00
COMMON AP (1-100)	5.00	2.20
*AP STARS: 15X TO 30X HI COLUMN		
*AP YOUNG STARS: 12.5X TO 25X HI		
AP STATED ODDS 1:39		
COMP.MUSEUM SET (100)	600.00	275.00
COMMON MUSEUM (1-100)	2.00	.90
*MUSEUM STARS: 6X TO 12X HI COLUMN		
*MUSEUM YOUNG STARS: 5X TO 10X HI		
MUSEUM STATED ODDS 1:9...		

		MINT	NRMT
☐ 1	Tony Gwynn	1.50	.70
☐ 2	Pedro Martinez	.60	.25
☐ 3	Kenny Lofton	.75	.35

☐ 4 Curt Schilling	.30	.14
☐ 5 Shawn Estes	.30	.14
☐ 6 Tom Glavine	.30	.14
☐ 7 Mike Piazza	2.00	.90
☐ 8 Ray Lankford	.30	.14
☐ 9 Barry Larkin	.40	.18
☐ 10 Tony Womack	.15	.07
☐ 11 Jeff Blauser	.15	.07
☐ 12 Rod Beck	.15	.07
☐ 13 Larry Walker	.60	.25
☐ 14 Greg Maddux	2.00	.90
☐ 15 Mark Grace	.40	.18
☐ 16 Ken Caminiti	.40	.18
☐ 17 Bobby Bonilla	.15	.07
☐ 18 Chipper Jones	2.00	.90
☐ 19 Javier Lopez	.30	.14
☐ 20 Moises Alou	.30	.14
☐ 21 Royce Clayton	.15	.07
☐ 22 Darryl Kile	.30	.14
☐ 23 Barry Bonds	.75	.35
☐ 24 Steve Finley	.30	.14
☐ 25 Andres Galarraga	.60	.25
☐ 26 Denny Neagle	.30	.14
☐ 27 Todd Hundley	.30	.14
☐ 28 Jeff Bagwell	1.25	.55
☐ 29 Andy Pettitte	.60	.25
☐ 30 Darin Erstad	.75	.35
☐ 31 Carlos Delgado	.30	.14
☐ 32 Matt Williams	.40	.18
☐ 33 Will Clark	.40	.18
☐ 34 Vinny Castilla	.30	.14
☐ 35 Brad Radke	.30	.14
☐ 36 John Olerud	.30	.14
☐ 37 Andruw Jones	1.25	.55
☐ 38 Jason Giambi	.30	.14
☐ 39 Scott Rolen	1.50	.70
☐ 40 Gary Sheffield	.60	.25
☐ 41 Jimmy Key	.30	.14
☐ 42 Kevin Appier	.30	.14
☐ 43 Wade Boggs	.60	.25
☐ 44 Hideo Nomo	1.50	.70
☐ 45 Manny Ramirez	.60	.25
☐ 46 Wilton Guerrero	.15	.07
☐ 47 Travis Fryman	.30	.14
☐ 48 Chili Davis	.15	.07
☐ 49 Jeromy Burnitz	.15	.07
☐ 50 Craig Biggio	.60	.25
☐ 51 Tim Salmon	.60	.25
☐ 52 Jose Cruz Jr.	2.50	1.10
☐ 53 Sammy Sosa	.60	.25
☐ 54 Hideki Irabu	.30	.14
☐ 55 Chan Ho Park	.60	.25
☐ 56 Robin Ventura	.30	.14
☐ 57 Jose Guillen	.60	.25
☐ 58 Deion Sanders	.30	.14
☐ 59 Jose Canseco	.40	.18
☐ 60 Jay Buhner	.30	.14
☐ 61 Rafael Palmeiro	.40	.18
☐ 62 Vladimir Guerrero	1.00	.45
☐ 63 Mark McGwire	1.50	.70
☐ 64 Derek Jeter	1.50	.70
☐ 65 Bobby Bonilla	.30	.14
☐ 66 Raul Mondesi	.40	.18
☐ 67 Paul Molitor	.60	.25
☐ 68 Joe Carter	.30	.14
☐ 69 Marquis Grissom	.15	.07
☐ 70 Juan Gonzalez	1.50	.70
☐ 71 Kevin Orie	.30	.14
☐ 72 Rusty Greer	.15	.07
☐ 73 Henry Rodriguez	.15	.07
☐ 74 Fernando Tatis	.60	.25
☐ 75 John Valentin	.15	.07
☐ 76 Matt Morris	.30	.14
☐ 77 Ray Durham	.15	.07
☐ 78 Geronimo Berroa	.15	.07
☐ 79 Scott Brosius	.15	.07
☐ 80 Willie Greene	.15	.07
☐ 81 Rondell White	.30	.14
☐ 82 Doug Drabek	.15	.07
☐ 83 Derek Bell	.30	.14
☐ 84 Butch Huskey	.30	.14
☐ 85 Doug Jones	.15	.07
☐ 86 Jeff Kent	.30	.14
☐ 87 Jim Edmonds	.40	.18
☐ 88 Mark McLemore	.15	.07
☐ 89 Todd Zeile	.15	.07
☐ 90 Edgardo Alfonso	.30	.14
☐ 91 Carlos Baerga	.15	.07
☐ 92 Jorge Fabregas	.15	.07
☐ 93 Alan Benes	.30	.14
☐ 94 Troy Percival	.15	.07
☐ 95 Edgar Renteria	.15	.07
☐ 96 Jeff Fassero	.15	.07
☐ 97 Reggie Sanders	.15	.07
☐ 98 Dean Palmer	.15	.07
☐ 99 J.T. Snow	.30	.14
☐ 100 Dave Nilsson	.30	.14
☐ 101 Dan Wilson	.15	.07
☐ 102 Robb Nen	.15	.07
☐ 103 Damion Easley	.15	.07
☐ 104 Kevin Foster	.15	.07
☐ 105 Jose Offerman	.15	.07
☐ 106 Steve Cooke	.15	.07
☐ 107 Matt Stairs	.15	.07
☐ 108 Darryl Hamilton	.15	.07
☐ 109 Steve Karsay	.15	.07
☐ 110 Gary DiSarcina	.15	.07
☐ 111 Dante Bichette	.30	.14
☐ 112 Billy Wagner	.30	.14
☐ 113 David Segui	.15	.07
☐ 114 Bobby Higginson	.30	.14
☐ 115 Jeffrey Hammonds	.15	.07
☐ 116 Kevin Brown	.30	.14
☐ 117 Paul Sorrento	.15	.07
☐ 118 Mark Leiter	.15	.07
☐ 119 Charles Nagy	.30	.14
☐ 120 Danny Patterson	.15	.07
☐ 121 Brian McRae	.15	.07
☐ 122 Jay Bell	.30	.14
☐ 123 Jamie Moyer	.15	.07
☐ 124 Carl Everett	.15	.07
☐ 125 Greg Colbrunn	.15	.07
☐ 126 Jason Kendall	.30	.14
☐ 127 Luis Sojo	.15	.07
☐ 128 Mike Lieberthal	.15	.07
☐ 129 Reggie Jefferson	.15	.07
☐ 130 Cal Eldred	.15	.07
☐ 131 Orel Hershiser	.30	.14
☐ 132 Doug Glanville	.15	.07
☐ 133 Willie Blair	.15	.07
☐ 134 Neifi Perez	.30	.14
☐ 135 Sean Berry	.15	.07
☐ 136 Chuck Finley	.15	.07
☐ 137 Alex Gonzalez	.15	.07
☐ 138 Dennis Eckersley	.30	.14
☐ 139 Kenny Rogers	.15	.07
☐ 140 Troy O'Leary	.15	.07
☐ 141 Roger Bailey	.15	.07
☐ 142 Yamil Benitez	.15	.07
☐ 143 Wally Joyner	.15	.07
☐ 144 Bobby Witt	.15	.07
☐ 145 Pete Schourek	.15	.07
☐ 146 Terry Steinbach	.15	.07
☐ 147 B.J. Surhoff	.15	.07
☐ 148 Esteban Loaiza	.15	.07
☐ 149 Heathcliff Slocumb	.15	.07
☐ 150 Ed Sprague	.15	.07
☐ 151 Gregg Jefferies	.15	.07
☐ 152 Scott Erickson	.15	.07
☐ 153 Jaime Navarro	.15	.07
☐ 154 David Wells	.15	.07
☐ 155 Alex Fernandez	.15	.07
☐ 156 Tim Belcher	.15	.07
☐ 157 Mark Grudzielanek	.15	.07
☐ 158 Scott Hatteberg	.15	.07
☐ 159 Paul Konerko	1.00	.45
☐ 160 Ben Grieve	1.25	.55
☐ 161 Abraham Nunez	.30	.14
☐ 162 Shannon Stewart	.30	.14
☐ 163 Jaret Wright	1.50	.70
☐ 164 Derek Lee	.40	.18
☐ 165 Todd Dunwoody	.30	.14
☐ 166 Steve Woodard	.15	.07
☐ 167 Ryan McGuire	.15	.07
☐ 168 Jeremi Gonzalez	.15	.07
☐ 169 Mark Kotsay	.60	.25
☐ 170 Brett Tomko	.30	.14
☐ 171 Bobby Estalella	.30	.14
☐ 172 Livan Hernandez	.40	.18
☐ 173 Todd Helton	.75	.35
☐ 174 Garrett Stephenson	.15	.07
☐ 175 Pokey Reese	.15	.07
☐ 176 Tony Saunders	.30	.14
☐ 177 Antone Williamson	.15	.07
☐ 178 Bartolo Colon	.30	.14
☐ 179 Karim Garcia	.30	.14
☐ 180 Juan Encarnacion	.60	.25
☐ 181 Jacob Cruz	.30	.14
☐ 182 Alex Rodriguez FV	1.00	.45
☐ 183 Cal Ripken FV	.75	.35
Roberto Alomar		
☐ 184 Roger Clemens FV	.60	.25
☐ 185 Derek Jeter FV	.75	.35
☐ 186 Frank Thomas FV	1.25	.55
☐ 187 Ken Griffey Jr. FV	1.50	.70
☐ 188 Mark McGwire GJ	.75	.35
☐ 189 Tino Martinez GJ	.30	.14
☐ 190 Larry Walker GJ	.30	.14
☐ 191 Brady Anderson GJ	.30	.14
☐ 192 Jeff Bagwell GJ	.60	.25
☐ 193 Ken Griffey Jr. GJ	1.50	.70
☐ 194 Chipper Jones GJ	1.00	.45
☐ 195 Ray Lankford GJ	.30	.14
☐ 196 Jim Thome GJ	.30	.14
☐ 197 Nomar Garciaparra GJ	1.00	.45
☐ 198 AS Home Run Contestants	.75	.35
Brady Anderson		
Jeff Bagwell		
Nomar Garciaparra		
Ken Griffey Jr.		
Chipper Jones		
Ray Lankford		
Tino Martinez		
Mark McGwire		
Jim Thome		
Larry Walker		
☐ 199 Tino Martinez CL	.30	.14
☐ 200 Jacob's Field CL	.15	.07
☐ P5 Barry Bonds PROMO	1.25	.55
☐ P9 Juan Gonzalez PROMO	2.50	1.10
☐ P10 Jeff Bagwell PROMO	2.00	.90

1998 Pinnacle Epix

Randomly inserted in Pinnacle packs at the rate of one in 21, this 24-card set features color photos of top players' most memorable games, plays, seasons and moments on Dot Matrix Hologram cards. To obtain all the cards for each player in this fractured insert set, the collector had to open not only Pinnacle Epix packs, but also Score, Pinnacle Certified and Pinnacle Zenith packs.

	MINT	NRMT
COMMON CARD (E1-E24)	6.00	2.70

*PURPLE CARDS: .75X TO 1.5X ORANGE
*EMERALD CARDS: 1.5X TO 3X ORANGE
STATED ODDS 1:21
LESS THAN 30 EMERALD MOMENTS PRINTED
ONLY ORANGE CARDS LISTED BELOW!
USE MULTIPLIERS FOR EMERALD/PURPLE

☐ E1 Ken Griffey Jr. GAME	50.00	22.00
☐ E2 Juan Gonzalez GAME	25.00	11.00

☐ E3 Jeff Bagwell GAME ..	20.00	9.00
☐ E4 Ivan Rodriguez GAME	12.00	5.50
☐ E5 Nomar Garciaparra GAME	25.00	11.00
☐ E6 Ryne Sandberg GAME	12.00	5.50
☐ E7 Frank Thomas SEA ..	80.00	36.00
☐ E8 Derek Jeter SEA	50.00	22.00
☐ E9 Tony Gwynn SEA....	50.00	22.00
☐ E10 Albert Belle SEA	25.00	11.00
☐ E11 Scott Rolen SEA	40.00	18.00
☐ E12 Barry Larkin SEA	12.00	5.50
☐ E13 Alex Rodriguez MOM	100.00	45.00
☐ E14 Cal Ripken MOM ..	120.00	55.00
☐ E15 Chipper Jones MOM	80.00	36.00
☐ E16 Roger Clemens MOM	60.00	27.00
☐ E17 Mo Vaughn MOM ..	40.00	18.00
☐ E18 Mark McGwire MOM	80.00	36.00
☐ E19 Mike Piazza PLAY ..	20.00	9.00
☐ E20 Andruw Jones PLAY	10.00	4.50
☐ E21 Greg Maddux PLAY	20.00	9.00
☐ E22 Barry Bonds PLAY...	8.00	3.60
☐ E23 Paul Molitor PLAY	6.00	2.70
☐ E24 Eddie Murray PLAY ..	6.00	2.70

1998 Pinnacle Hit It Here

Randomly inserted one in 19 retail and magazine first series packs, and one in 17 first series hobby packs, this 10-card set features color player cut-outs of hot hitters in the league printed on micro-etched silver foil cards with a target in the background. If one of these hitters hit for the cycle on opening day, one lucky collector holding that specific player's card could win $1 million. Each card back featured a special serial number that would be entered into a drawing to determine the winner.

	MINT	NRMT
COMPLETE SET (10)	80.00	36.00
COMMON CARD (1-10)	3.00	1.35
UNLISTED STARS	4.00	1.80
STATED ODDS 1:17		

☐ 1 Larry Walker	4.00	1.80
☐ 2 Ken Griffey Jr.	20.00	9.00
☐ 3 Mike Piazza	12.00	5.50
☐ 4 Frank Thomas	15.00	6.75
☐ 5 Barry Bonds	5.00	2.20
☐ 6 Albert Belle	5.00	2.20
☐ 7 Tino Martinez	3.00	1.35
☐ 8 Mark McGwire	10.00	4.50
☐ 9 Juan Gonzalez	10.00	4.50
☐ 10 Jeff Bagwell	8.00	3.60

1998 Pinnacle Spellbound

Randomly inserted in hobby packs only at the rate of one in

17, this 50-card set features game action color photos of nine top players printed on full-foil, micro-etched cards and superimposed over one of the letters of the player's name or nickname. All the cards of the same player needed to be collected in order to spell out the player's name when laid side-by-side.

	MINT	NRMT
COMPLETE SET (50)	600.00	275.00
COMMON M.McGWIRE	12.00	5.50
COMMON R.CLEMENS....	10.00	4.50
COMMON F.THOMAS......	20.00	9.00
COMMON S.ROLEN	10.00	4.50
COMMON K.GRIFFEY......	25.00	11.00
COMMON L.WALKER........	5.00	2.20
COMMON N.GARCIAPARRA	12.00	5.50
COMMON C.RIPKEN........	20.00	9.00
COMMON T.GWYNN........	12.00	5.50
STATED ODDS 1:17		

1996 Pinnacle Aficionado

The 1996 Aficionado set was issued in one series totalling 200 cards. The five-card packs retailed for $3.99 and had a special bubble gum scent which was released when the packs were opened. The fronts feature action player photos in sepia tone for players who have played in the Major League for over five years and in color for those who have played less than five years. A heliographic player head print and the player's name printed in gold foil on a wood-look bar round out the front. The backs carry positional comparison statistics between the player and the league average at that position in different eras. Cards numbered 151-160 are a subset titled "Global Reach" and feature color action player cut-outs of international players on a background of a map, a global baseball, and their country's flag.

	MINT	NRMT
COMPLETE SET (200)	50.00	22.00
COMMON CARD (1-200) ..	.25	.11
MINOR STARS	.50	.23
UNLISTED STARS	1.00	.45
SUBSET CARDS HALF VALUE OF BASE CARDS		
COMP.AP SET (200)	2000.00	900.00
COMMON ART.PRF. (1-200)	4.00	1.80
*ART.PRF.STARS: 15X TO 30X HI COLUMN		
*ART.PRF.YOUNG STARS: 12.5X TO 25X HI		
AP STATED ODDS 1:35		

☐ 1 Jack McDowell	.25	.11
☐ 2 Jay Bell	.50	.23
☐ 3 Rafael Palmeiro	.75	.35
☐ 4 Wally Joyner	.50	.23
☐ 5 Ozzie Smith	1.25	.55
☐ 6 Mark McGwire..........	2.00	.90
☐ 7 Kevin Seitzer	.25	.11
☐ 8 Fred McGriff	.75	.35
☐ 9 Roger Clemens	2.00	.90
☐ 10 Randy Johnson	1.00	.45
☐ 11 Cecil Fielder	.50	.23
☐ 12 David Cone	.50	.23
☐ 13 Chili Davis	.25	.11
☐ 14 Andres Galarraga	1.00	.45
☐ 15 Joe Carter	.50	.23
☐ 16 Ryne Sandberg	1.25	.55
☐ 17 Paul O'Neill	.50	.23
☐ 18 Cal Ripken	4.00	1.80
☐ 19 Wade Boggs	1.00	.45
☐ 20 Greg Gagne	.25	.11
☐ 21 Edgar Martinez	.75	.35
☐ 22 Greg Maddux..........	3.00	1.35
☐ 23 Ken Caminiti	.75	.35
☐ 24 Kirby Puckett	2.00	.90
☐ 25 Craig Biggio..........	.75	.35
☐ 26 Will Clark	.50	.23
☐ 27 Ron Gant	.25	.11
☐ 28 Eddie Murray	1.00	.45
☐ 29 Lance Johnson	.25	.11
☐ 30 Tony Gwynn	2.50	1.10
☐ 31 Dante Bichette	.50	.23
☐ 32 Darren Daulton	.50	.23
☐ 33 Danny Tartabull	.25	.11
☐ 34 Jeff King	.25	.11
☐ 35 Tom Glavine	.50	.23
☐ 36 Rickey Henderson	.75	.35
☐ 37 Jose Canseco	.75	.35
☐ 38 Barry Larkin	.75	.35
☐ 39 Dennis Martinez	.50	.23
☐ 40 Ruben Sierra	.25	.11
☐ 41 Bobby Bonilla	.50	.23
☐ 42 Jeff Conine	.50	.23
☐ 43 Lee Smith	.25	.11
☐ 44 Charlie Hayes	.25	.11
☐ 45 Walt Weiss	.25	.11
☐ 46 Jay Buhner	.75	.35
☐ 47 Kenny Rogers	.25	.11
☐ 48 Paul Molitor	1.00	.45
☐ 49 Hal Morris	.25	.11
☐ 50 Todd Stottlemyre	.25	.11
☐ 51 Mike Stanley	.25	.11
☐ 52 Mark Grace	.75	.35
☐ 53 Lenny Dykstra	.50	.23
☐ 54 Andre Dawson	.75	.35
☐ 55 Dennis Eckersley	.50	.23
☐ 56 Ben McDonald	.25	.11
☐ 57 Ray Lankford	.50	.23
☐ 58 Mo Vaughn	1.25	.55
☐ 59 Frank Thomas	4.00	1.80
☐ 60 Julio Franco	.25	.11
☐ 61 Jim Abbott	.25	.11
☐ 62 Greg Vaughn	.25	.11
☐ 63 Marquis Grissom	.50	.23
☐ 64 Tino Martinez	1.00	.45
☐ 65 Kevin Appier	.25	.11
☐ 66 Matt Williams	.75	.35

☐ 67	Sammy Sosa	1.00	.45
☐ 68	Larry Walker	1.00	.45
☐ 69	Ivan Rodriguez	1.25	.55
☐ 70	Eric Karros	.50	.23
☐ 71	Bernie Williams	1.00	.45
☐ 72	Carlos Baerga	.25	.11
☐ 73	Jeff Bagwell	2.00	.90
☐ 74	Pete Schourek	.25	.11
☐ 75	Ken Griffey Jr.	5.00	2.20
☐ 76	Bernard Gilkey	.25	.11
☐ 77	Albert Belle	1.25	.55
☐ 78	Chuck Knoblauch	1.00	.45
☐ 79	John Smoltz	.50	.23
☐ 80	Barry Bonds	1.25	.55
☐ 81	Vinny Castilla	.50	.23
☐ 82	John Olerud	.50	.23
☐ 83	Mike Mussina	1.00	.45
☐ 84	Alex Fernandez	.25	.11
☐ 85	Shawon Dunston	.25	.11
☐ 86	Travis Fryman	.50	.23
☐ 87	Moises Alou	.50	.23
☐ 88	Dean Palmer	.25	.11
☐ 89	Gregg Jefferies	.25	.11
☐ 90	Jim Thome	1.00	.45
☐ 91	Dave Justice	1.00	.45
☐ 92	B.J. Surhoff	.25	.11
☐ 93	Ramon Martinez	.50	.23
☐ 94	Gary Sheffield	1.00	.45
☐ 95	Andy Benes	.50	.23
☐ 96	Reggie Sanders	.50	.23
☐ 97	Roberto Alomar	1.00	.45
☐ 98	Omar Vizquel	.50	.23
☐ 99	Juan Gonzalez	2.50	1.10
☐ 100	Robin Ventura	.50	.23
☐ 101	Jason Isringhausen	.25	.11
☐ 102	Greg Colbrunn	.25	.11
☐ 103	Brian Jordan	.50	.23
☐ 104	Shawn Green	.25	.11
☐ 105	Brian Hunter	.50	.23
☐ 106	Rondell White	.50	.23
☐ 107	Ryan Klesko	.75	.35
☐ 108	Sterling Hitchcock	.25	.11
☐ 109	Manny Ramirez	1.00	.45
☐ 110	Bret Boone	.25	.11
☐ 111	Michael Tucker	.50	.23
☐ 112	Julian Tavarez	.25	.11
☐ 113	Benji Gil	.25	.11
☐ 114	Kenny Lofton	1.25	.55
☐ 115	Mike Kelly	.25	.11
☐ 116	Ray Durham	.25	.11
☐ 117	Trevor Hoffman	.25	.11
☐ 118	Butch Huskey	.50	.23
☐ 119	Phil Nevin	.25	.11
☐ 120	Pedro Martinez	1.00	.45
☐ 121	Wil Cordero	.25	.11
☐ 122	Tim Salmon	1.00	.45
☐ 123	Jim Edmonds	.75	.35
☐ 124	Mike Piazza	3.00	1.35
☐ 125	Rico Brogna	.25	.11
☐ 126	John Mabry	.25	.11
☐ 127	Chipper Jones	3.00	1.35
☐ 128	Johnny Damon	.50	.23
☐ 129	Raul Mondesi	.75	.35
☐ 130	Denny Neagle	.50	.23
☐ 131	Marc Newfield	.25	.11
☐ 132	Hideo Nomo	2.50	1.10
☐ 133	Joe Vitiello	.25	.11
☐ 134	Garret Anderson	.50	.23
☐ 135	Dave Nilsson	.25	.11
☐ 136	Alex Rodriguez	3.00	1.35
☐ 137	Russ Davis	.25	.11
☐ 138	Frank Rodriguez	.25	.11
☐ 139	Royce Clayton	.25	.11
☐ 140	John Valentin	.25	.11
☐ 141	Marty Cordova	.50	.23
☐ 142	Alex Gonzalez	.25	.11
☐ 143	Carlos Delgado	.50	.23
☐ 144	Willie Greene	.25	.11
☐ 145	Cliff Floyd	.25	.11
☐ 146	Bobby Higginson	.50	.23
☐ 147	J.T. Snow	.50	.23
☐ 148	Derek Bell	.25	.11
☐ 149	Edgardo Alfonzo	.75	.35
☐ 150	Charles Johnson	.50	.23
☐ 151	Hideo Nomo GR	1.25	.55
☐ 152	Larry Walker GR	.50	.23

☐ 153	Bob Abreu GR	.50	.23
☐ 154	Karim Garcia GR	.50	.23
☐ 155	Dave Nilsson GR	.25	.11
☐ 156	Chan Ho Park GR	.25	.11
☐ 157	Dennis Martinez GR	.25	.11
☐ 158	Sammy Sosa GR	.50	.23
☐ 159	Rey Ordonez GR	.25	.11
☐ 160	Roberto Alomar GR	.50	.23
☐ 161	George Arias	.25	.11
☐ 162	Jason Schmidt	.50	.23
☐ 163	Derek Jeter	3.00	1.35
☐ 164	Chris Snopek	.25	.11
☐ 165	Todd Hollandsworth	.25	.11
☐ 166	Sal Fasano	.25	.11
☐ 167	Jay Powell	.25	.11
☐ 168	Paul Wilson	.25	.11
☐ 169	Jim Pittsley	.50	.23
☐ 170	LaTroy Hawkins	.25	.11
☐ 171	Bob Abreu	.75	.35
☐ 172	Mike Grace	.25	.11
☐ 173	Karim Garcia	.75	.35
☐ 174	Richard Hidalgo	1.00	.45
☐ 175	Felipe Crespo	.25	.11
☐ 176	Terrell Wade	.25	.11
☐ 177	Steve Gibralter	.25	.11
☐ 178	Jermaine Dye	.50	.23
☐ 179	Alan Benes	.50	.23
☐ 180	Wilton Guerrero	1.00	.45
☐ 181	Brooks Kieschnick	.50	.23
☐ 182	Roger Cedeno	.25	.11
☐ 183	Osvaldo Fernandez	.50	.23
☐ 184	Matt Lawton	.75	.35
☐ 185	George Williams	.25	.11
☐ 186	Jimmy Haynes	.25	.11
☐ 187	Mike Busby	.25	.11
☐ 188	Chan Ho Park	1.00	.45
☐ 189	Marc Barcelo	.25	.11
☐ 190	Jason Kendall	.75	.35
☐ 191	Rey Ordonez	.50	.23
☐ 192	Tyler Houston	.25	.11
☐ 193	John Wasdin	.25	.11
☐ 194	Jeff Suppan	.50	.23
☐ 195	Jeff Ware	.25	.11
☐ 196	Ken Griffey Jr. CL	2.50	1.10
☐ 197	Albert Belle CL	.75	.35
☐ 198	Mike Piazza CL	1.50	.70
☐ 199	Greg Maddux CL	1.50	.70
☐ 200	Frank Thomas CL	2.00	.90

1996 Pinnacle Aficionado Magic Numbers

Randomly inserted in packs at a rate of one in 72, this 10-card set is printed on actual maple wood and features ten of today's top superstars. The fronts feature an embossed color action player cut-out on a wood background. The backs carry trivia regarding the player's jersey number and those players from the past and present who share this same jersey number.

	MINT	NRMT
COMPLETE SET (10)	250.00	110.00
COMMON CARD (1-10)	6.00	2.70
UNLISTED STARS	8.00	3.60
STATED ODDS 1:72		

		MINT	NRMT
☐ 1	Ken Griffey Jr.	50.00	22.00
☐ 2	Greg Maddux	30.00	13.50
☐ 3	Frank Thomas	40.00	18.00
☐ 4	Mo Vaughn	12.00	5.50
☐ 5	Jeff Bagwell	20.00	9.00
☐ 6	Chipper Jones	30.00	13.50
☐ 7	Albert Belle	12.00	5.50
☐ 8	Cal Ripken	40.00	18.00
☐ 9	Matt Williams	6.00	2.70
☐ 10	Sammy Sosa	8.00	3.60

1996 Pinnacle Aficionado Rivals

Randomly inserted in packs at a rate of one in 24, this 24-card set features two spot embossed color player photos of rival players. The backs carry a head photo of each and candid player comments on each other.

	MINT	NRMT
COMPLETE SET (24)	300.00	135.00
COMMON CARD (1-24)	10.00	4.50
STATED ODDS 1:24		

		MINT	NRMT
☐ 1	Ken Griffey / Frank Thomas	25.00	11.00
☐ 2	Frank Thomas / Cal Ripken	20.00	9.00
☐ 3	Cal Ripken / Mo Vaughn	10.00	4.50
☐ 4	Mo Vaughn / Ken Griffey Jr.	15.00	6.75
☐ 5	Ken Griffey Jr. / Cal Ripken	25.00	11.00
☐ 6	Frank Thomas / Mo Vaughn	12.00	5.50
☐ 7	Cal Ripken / Ken Griffey Jr.	25.00	11.00
☐ 8	Mo Vaughn / Frank Thomas	12.00	5.50
☐ 9	Ken Griffey Jr. / Mo Vaughn	15.00	6.75
☐ 10	Frank Thomas / Ken Griffey Jr.	25.00	11.00
☐ 11	Cal Ripken / Frank Thomas	20.00	9.00
☐ 12	Mo Vaughn / Jeff Bagwell	10.00	4.50
☐ 13	Mike Piazza / Jeff Bagwell	10.00	4.50
☐ 14	Jeff Bagwell / Barry Bonds	10.00	4.50
☐ 15	Jeff Bagwell / Mike Piazza	10.00	4.50
☐ 16	Tony Gwynn / Mike Piazza	10.00	4.50
☐ 17	Mike Piazza / Barry Bonds	10.00	4.50

		MINT	NRMT
☐ 18	Jeff Bagwell...............Tony Gwynn	10.00	4.50
☐ 19	Barry Bonds................Mike Piazza	10.00	4.50
☐ 20	Tony Gwynn................Jeff Bagwell	10.00	4.50
☐ 21	Mike Piazza................Tony Gwynn	10.00	4.50
☐ 22	Barry Bonds................Jeff Bagwell	10.00	4.50
☐ 23	Tony Gwynn................Barry Bonds	10.00	4.50
☐ 24	Barry Bonds................Tony Gwynn	10.00	4.50

1996 Pinnacle Aficionado Slick Picks

Randomly inserted in packs at a rate of one in 10, this 32-card set honors 32 draft picks for their future all-star abilities. Printed using a spectroetch print technology, the fronts feature a color action player photo on a black background on one side with a black-and-white player portrait on the other. A small simulated autograph and team name are printed below the portrait. The backs carry another color player portrait on a white background with a three-sided black border and information about when the player was drafted printed over a gray number indicating the round the player was selected in.

		MINT	NRMT
COMPLETE SET (32)		200.00	90.00
COMMON CARD (1-32)		1.50	.70
STATED ODDS 1:10			

		MINT	NRMT
☐ 1	Mike Piazza.....................	15.00	6.75
☐ 2	Cal Ripken.......................	20.00	9.00
☐ 3	Ken Griffey Jr..................	25.00	11.00
☐ 4	Paul Wilson.....................	1.50	.70
☐ 5	Frank Thomas..................	20.00	9.00
☐ 6	Mo Vaughn.....................	6.00	2.70
☐ 7	Barry Bonds....................	6.00	2.70
☐ 8	Albert Belle....................	6.00	2.70
☐ 9	Jeff Bagwell...................	10.00	4.50
☐ 10	Dante Bichette...............	2.50	1.10
☐ 11	Hideo Nomo...................	12.00	5.50
☐ 12	Raul Mondesi.................	3.00	1.35
☐ 13	Manny Ramirez...............	5.00	2.20
☐ 14	Greg Maddux..................	15.00	6.75
☐ 15	Tony Gwynn...................	12.00	5.50
☐ 16	Ryne Sandberg...............	6.00	2.70
☐ 17	Reggie Sanders..............	1.50	.70
☐ 18	Derek Jeter....................	15.00	6.75
☐ 19	Johnny Damon...............	2.50	1.10
☐ 20	Alex Rodriguez...............	15.00	6.75

		MINT	NRMT
☐ 21	Ryan Klesko...................	3.00	1.35
☐ 22	Jim Thome.....................	5.00	2.20
☐ 23	Kenny Lofton..................	6.00	2.70
☐ 24	Tino Martinez.................	5.00	2.20
☐ 25	Randy Johnson...............	5.00	2.20
☐ 26	Wade Boggs..................	5.00	2.20
☐ 27	Juan Gonzalez...............	12.00	5.50
☐ 28	Kirby Puckett.................	10.00	4.50
☐ 29	Tim Salmon...................	5.00	2.20
☐ 30	Chipper Jones................	15.00	6.75
☐ 31	Garret Anderson.............	2.50	1.10
☐ 32	Eddie Murray..................	5.00	2.20

1997 Pinnacle Certified

This 150-card set was distributed in six-card hobby only packs with a suggested price of $4.99 and features color action player photos with side triangular silver mylar borders and black-and-white center backgrounds. The backs carry another player photo with player information and statistics. The set is divided into the following subsets: Rookie (106-135) and Certified Stars (136-150) which display a color player image on a background of stars. A Jose Cruz Exchange card was randomly seeded into packs. The deadline to redeem the card was March 31, 1998. Collectors who exchanged this cards received a Cruz card featuring him in a Blue Jay uniform. This #151 card is not considered part of the complete set. Some of these cards are also known to have a "Mirror Black" finish. These cards, while not officially released have surfaced in the secondary market and are very scarce. Please refer to upcoming issues of Beckett Baseball Card Monthly for information as it becomes available on key cards.

		MINT	NRMT
COMPLETE SET (150)		40.00	18.00
COMMON CARD (1-150)		.25	.11
MINOR STARS		.50	.23
UNLISTED STARS		1.00	.45
COMP.SET EXCLUDES CRUZ JR. (151)			
CRUZ EXCH.DEADLINE: 3/31/98			
COMP.RED SET (150)		600.00	275.00
COMMON RED (1-150)		2.00	.90
*RED STARS: 3X TO 8X HI COLUMN			
*RED YOUNG STARS: 2.5X TO 6X HI			
RED STATED ODDS 1:5			

		MINT	NRMT
☐ 1	Barry Bonds...................	1.25	.55
☐ 2	Mo Vaughn....................	1.25	.55
☐ 3	Matt Williams.................	.75	.35

		MINT	NRMT
☐ 4	Ryne Sandberg...............	1.25	.55
☐ 5	Jeff Bagwell...................	2.00	.90
☐ 6	Alan Benes....................	.50	.23
☐ 7	John Wetteland..............	.25	.11
☐ 8	Fred McGriff..................	.75	.35
☐ 9	Craig Biggio..................	.75	.35
☐ 10	Bernie Williams..............	1.00	.45
☐ 11	Brian Hunter.................	.50	.23
☐ 12	Sandy Alomar Jr............	.50	.23
☐ 13	Ray Lankford.................	.50	.23
☐ 14	Ryan Klesko..................	.75	.35
☐ 15	Jermaine Dye...............	.25	.11
☐ 16	Andy Benes..................	.50	.23
☐ 17	Albert Belle..................	1.25	.55
☐ 18	Tony Clark...................	1.00	.45
☐ 19	Dean Palmer................	.25	.11
☐ 20	Bernard Gilkey..............	.25	.11
☐ 21	Ken Caminiti................	.75	.35
☐ 22	Alex Rodriguez.............	3.00	1.35
☐ 23	Tim Salmon..................	1.00	.45
☐ 24	Larry Walker.................	1.00	.45
☐ 25	Barry Larkin.................	.75	.35
☐ 26	Mike Piazza.................	3.00	1.35
☐ 27	Brady Anderson............	.75	.35
☐ 28	Cal Ripken..................	4.00	1.80
☐ 29	Charles Nagy...............	.50	.23
☐ 30	Paul Molitor................	1.00	.45
☐ 31	Darin Erstad................	1.50	.70
☐ 32	Rey Ordonez................	.25	.11
☐ 33	Wally Joyner................	.50	.23
☐ 34	David Cone..................	.50	.23
☐ 35	Sammy Sosa................	1.00	.45
☐ 36	Dante Bichette..............	.50	.23
☐ 37	Eric Karros..................	.50	.23
☐ 38	Omar Vizquel................	.50	.23
☐ 39	Roger Clemens..............	2.00	.90
☐ 40	Joe Carter...................	.50	.23
☐ 41	Frank Thomas...............	4.00	1.80
☐ 42	Javy Lopez..................	.50	.23
☐ 43	Mike Mussina...............	1.00	.45
☐ 44	Gary Sheffield..............	1.00	.45
☐ 45	Tony Gwynn.................	2.50	1.10
☐ 46	Jason Kendall...............	.50	.23
☐ 47	Jim Thome...................	1.00	.45
☐ 48	Andres Galarraga...........	1.00	.45
☐ 49	Mark McGwire...............	2.00	.90
☐ 50	Troy Percival................	.25	.11
☐ 51	Derek Jeter..................	3.00	1.35
☐ 52	Todd Hollandsworth........	.25	.11
☐ 53	Ken Griffey Jr...............	5.00	2.20
☐ 54	Randy Johnson.............	1.00	.45
☐ 55	Pat Hentgen................	.50	.23
☐ 56	Rusty Greer.................	.50	.23
☐ 57	John Jaha...................	.25	.11
☐ 58	Kenny Lofton................	1.25	.55
☐ 59	Chipper Jones..............	3.00	1.35
☐ 60	Robb Nen....................	.50	.11
☐ 61	Rafael Palmeiro.............	.75	.35
☐ 62	Mariano Rivera..............	.50	.23
☐ 63	Hideo Nomo.................	2.50	1.10
☐ 64	Greg Vaughn................	.25	.11
☐ 65	Ron Gant....................	.50	.23
☐ 66	Eddie Murray................	1.00	.45
☐ 67	John Smoltz.................	.50	.23
☐ 68	Manny Ramirez..............	1.00	.45
☐ 69	Juan Gonzalez..............	2.50	1.10
☐ 70	F.P. Santangelo............	.25	.11
☐ 71	Moises Alou.................	.50	.23
☐ 72	Alex Ochoa..................	.25	.11
☐ 73	Chuck Knoblauch...........	1.00	.45
☐ 74	Raul Mondesi...............	.75	.35
☐ 75	J.T. Snow...................	.50	.23
☐ 76	Rickey Henderson..........	.75	.35
☐ 77	Bobby Bonilla...............	.50	.23
☐ 78	Wade Boggs................	1.00	.45
☐ 79	Ivan Rodriguez..............	1.25	.55
☐ 80	Brian Jordan................	.50	.23
☐ 81	Al Leiter...................	.25	.11
☐ 82	Jay Buhner..................	.75	.35
☐ 83	Greg Maddux................	3.00	1.35
☐ 84	Edgar Martinez..............	.75	.35
☐ 85	Kevin Brown.................	.50	.23
☐ 86	Eric Young...................	.25	.11
☐ 87	Todd Hundley................	.50	.23
☐ 88	Ellis Burks..................	.50	.23
☐ 89	Marquis Grissom............	.50	.23

	MINT	NRMT
□ 90 Jose Canseco	.75	.35
□ 91 Henry Rodriguez	.25	.11
□ 92 Andy Pettitte	1.00	.45
□ 93 Mark Grudzielanek	.25	.11
□ 94 Dwight Gooden	.50	.23
□ 95 Roberto Alomar	1.00	.45
□ 96 Paul Wilson	.25	.11
□ 97 Will Clark	.75	.35
□ 98 Rondell White	.50	.23
□ 99 Charles Johnson	.50	.23
□ 100 Jim Edmonds	.75	.35
□ 101 Jason Giambi	.50	.23
□ 102 Billy Wagner	.50	.23
□ 103 Edgar Renteria	.50	.23
□ 104 Johnny Damon	.25	.11
□ 105 Jason Isringhausen	.25	.11
□ 106 Andruw Jones	2.50	1.10
□ 107 Jose Guillen	1.25	.55
□ 108 Kevin Orie	.50	.23
□ 109 Brian Giles	.25	.11
□ 110 Danny Patterson	.25	.11
□ 111 Vladimir Guerrero	2.00	.90
□ 112 Scott Rolen	2.50	1.10
□ 113 Damon Mashore	.25	.11
□ 114 Nomar Garciaparra	3.00	1.35
□ 115 Todd Walker	.25	.11
□ 116 Wilton Guerrero	.25	.11
□ 117 Bob Abreu	.25	.11
□ 118 Brooks Kieschnick	.25	.11
□ 119 Pokey Reese	.25	.11
□ 120 Todd Greene	.50	.23
□ 121 Dmitri Young	.25	.11
□ 122 Raul Casanova	.25	.11
□ 123 Glendon Rusch	.25	.11
□ 124 Jason Dickson	.50	.23
□ 125 Jorge Posada	.25	.11
□ 126 Rod Myers	.25	.11
□ 127 Bubba Trammell	1.00	.45
□ 128 Scott Spiezio	.50	.23
□ 129 Hideki Irabu	.25	.45
□ 130 Wendell Magee	.25	.11
□ 131 Bartolo Colon	.50	.23
□ 132 Chris Holt	.25	.11
□ 133 Calvin Maduro	.25	.11
□ 134 Ray Montgomery	.25	.11
□ 135 Shannon Stewart	.50	.23
□ 136 Ken Griffey Jr. CERT	2.50	1.10
□ 137 Vladimir Guerrero CERT	1.00	.45
□ 138 Roger Clemens CERT	1.00	.45
□ 139 Mark McGwire CERT	1.00	.45
□ 140 Albert Belle CERT	.75	.35
□ 141 Derek Jeter CERT	1.50	.70
□ 142 Juan Gonzalez CERT	1.25	.55
□ 143 Greg Maddux CERT	1.50	.70
□ 144 Alex Rodriguez CERT	1.50	.70
□ 145 Jeff Bagwell CERT	1.00	.45
□ 146 Cal Ripken CERT	2.00	.90
□ 147 Tony Gwynn CERT	1.25	.55
□ 148 Frank Thomas CERT	2.00	.90
□ 149 Hideo Nomo CERT	1.25	.55
□ 150 Andruw Jones CERT	1.25	.55
□ 151 Jose Cruz Jr. Blue Jays	30.00	13.50

1997 Pinnacle Certified Mirror Blue

Randomly inserted in packs at the rate of one in 199, this 150-card set is parallel to the base Pinnacle Certified set. The difference is found in the blue design element.

	MINT	NRMT
COMMON CARD (1-150)	25.00	11.00
MINOR STARS	40.00	18.00
SEMISTARS	60.00	27.00
UNLISTED STARS	100.00	45.00

*STARS: 50X TO 100X COLUMN
*YOUNG STARS: 40X TO 80X HI

*ROOKIES: 25X TO 50X HI
STATED ODDS 1:199

	MINT	NRMT
□ 1 Barry Bonds	150.00	70.00
□ 2 Mo Vaughn	120.00	55.00
□ 4 Ryne Sandberg	120.00	55.00
□ 5 Jeff Bagwell	200.00	90.00
□ 17 Albert Belle	120.00	55.00
□ 22 Alex Rodriguez	300.00	135.00
□ 26 Mike Piazza	300.00	135.00
□ 28 Cal Ripken	400.00	180.00
□ 31 Darin Erstad	120.00	55.00
□ 39 Roger Clemens	200.00	90.00
□ 41 Frank Thomas	500.00	220.00
□ 45 Tony Gwynn	250.00	110.00
□ 49 Mark McGwire	200.00	90.00
□ 51 Derek Jeter	250.00	110.00
□ 53 Ken Griffey Jr.	600.00	275.00
□ 58 Kenny Lofton	120.00	55.00
□ 59 Chipper Jones	250.00	110.00
□ 63 Hideo Nomo	400.00	180.00
□ 69 Juan Gonzalez	250.00	110.00
□ 79 Ivan Rodriguez	120.00	55.00
□ 83 Greg Maddux	300.00	135.00
□ 106 Andruw Jones	200.00	90.00
□ 111 Vladimir Guerrero	150.00	70.00
□ 112 Scott Rolen	200.00	90.00
□ 114 Nomar Garciaparra	250.00	110.00
□ 136 Ken Griffey Jr. CERT	250.00	110.00
□ 143 Greg Maddux CERT	120.00	55.00
□ 144 Alex Rodriguez CERT	120.00	55.00
□ 146 Cal Ripken CERT	150.00	70.00
□ 148 Frank Thomas CERT	200.00	90.00

1997 Pinnacle Certified Mirror Gold

Randomly inserted in packs at the rate of one in 299, this 150-card set is parallel to the base Pinnacle Certified set. The difference is found in the gold design element.

	MINT	NRMT
COMMON CARD (1-150)	80.00	36.00
MINOR STARS	150.00	70.00
SEMISTARS	250.00	110.00

*STARS: 200X TO 400X HI COLUMN
*YOUNG STARS: 150X TO 300X HI
*ROOKIES: 100X TO 200X HI
STATED ODDS 1:299

	MINT	NRMT
□ 1 Barry Bonds	500.00	220.00
□ 2 Mo Vaughn	400.00	180.00
□ 4 Ryne Sandberg	500.00	220.00
□ 5 Jeff Bagwell	800.00	350.00
□ 10 Bernie Williams	300.00	135.00
□ 17 Albert Belle	500.00	220.00
□ 18 Tony Clark	300.00	135.00
□ 21 Ken Caminiti	300.00	135.00
□ 22 Alex Rodriguez	1200.00	550.00
□ 24 Larry Walker	400.00	180.00
□ 26 Mike Piazza	1200.00	550.00
□ 28 Cal Ripken	1500.00	700.00
□ 30 Paul Molitor	500.00	220.00
□ 31 Darin Erstad	500.00	220.00
□ 35 Sammy Sosa	300.00	135.00
□ 39 Roger Clemens	800.00	350.00
□ 41 Frank Thomas	1800.00	800.00
□ 43 Mike Mussina	400.00	180.00
□ 44 Gary Sheffield	300.00	135.00
□ 45 Tony Gwynn	1000.00	450.00
□ 47 Jim Thome	400.00	180.00
□ 49 Mark McGwire	800.00	350.00
□ 51 Derek Jeter	800.00	350.00
□ 53 Ken Griffey Jr.	2500.00	1100.00
□ 54 Randy Johnson	400.00	180.00
□ 58 Kenny Lofton	400.00	180.00
□ 59 Chipper Jones	1000.00	450.00
□ 63 Hideo Nomo	1200.00	550.00
□ 66 Eddie Murray	400.00	180.00
□ 68 Manny Ramirez	400.00	180.00
□ 69 Juan Gonzalez	1000.00	450.00
□ 73 Chuck Knoblauch	300.00	135.00
□ 78 Wade Boggs	300.00	135.00
□ 79 Ivan Rodriguez	500.00	220.00
□ 83 Greg Maddux	1200.00	550.00
□ 92 Andy Pettitte	400.00	180.00
□ 95 Roberto Alomar	400.00	180.00
□ 106 Andruw Jones	800.00	350.00
□ 107 Jose Guillen	400.00	180.00
□ 111 Vladimir Guerrero	600.00	275.00
□ 112 Scott Rolen	800.00	350.00
□ 114 Nomar Garciaparra	1000.00	450.00
□ 129 Hideki Irabu	250.00	110.00
□ 136 Ken Griffey Jr. CERT	1000.00	450.00
□ 137 Vlad.Guerrero CERT	250.00	110.00
□ 138 Roger Clemens CERT	300.00	135.00
□ 139 Mark McGwire CERT	300.00	135.00
□ 141 Derek Jeter CERT	300.00	135.00
□ 142 Juan Gonzalez CERT	400.00	180.00
□ 143 Greg Maddux CERT	500.00	220.00
□ 144 Alex Rodriguez CERT	500.00	220.00
□ 145 Jeff Bagwell CERT	300.00	135.00
□ 146 Cal Ripken CERT	600.00	275.00
□ 147 Tony Gwynn CERT	400.00	180.00
□ 148 Frank Thomas CERT	800.00	350.00
□ 149 Hideo Nomo CERT	300.00	135.00
□ 150 Andruw Jones CERT	300.00	135.00

1997 Pinnacle Certified Mirror Red

Randomly inserted in packs at the rate of one in 99, this 150-card set is parallel to the base Pinnacle Certified set. The difference is found in the red design element.

	MINT	NRMT
COMMON CARD (1-150)	12.00	5.50
MINOR STARS	20.00	9.00
SEMISTARS	30.00	13.50
UNLISTED STARS	50.00	22.00

*STARS: 25X TO 50X HI
*YOUNG STARS: 20X TO 40X HI
*ROOKIES: 12.5X TO 25X HI
STATED ODDS 1:99

	MINT	NRMT
□ 1 Barry Bonds	60.00	27.00
□ 2 Mo Vaughn	60.00	27.00
□ 4 Ryne Sandberg	60.00	27.00
□ 5 Jeff Bagwell	100.00	45.00
□ 17 Albert Belle	60.00	27.00
□ 22 Alex Rodriguez	150.00	70.00
□ 26 Mike Piazza	150.00	70.00
□ 28 Cal Ripken	200.00	90.00
□ 31 Darin Erstad	60.00	27.00
□ 39 Roger Clemens	100.00	45.00
□ 41 Frank Thomas	200.00	90.00
□ 45 Tony Gwynn	120.00	55.00
□ 49 Mark McGwire	100.00	45.00
□ 51 Derek Jeter	100.00	45.00
□ 53 Ken Griffey Jr.	250.00	110.00
□ 58 Kenny Lofton	60.00	27.00
□ 59 Chipper Jones	120.00	55.00
□ 63 Hideo Nomo	200.00	90.00
□ 69 Juan Gonzalez	120.00	55.00
□ 83 Greg Maddux	150.00	70.00
□ 106 Andruw Jones	100.00	45.00
□ 111 Vladimir Guerrero	80.00	36.00
□ 112 Scott Rolen	100.00	45.00
□ 114 Nomar Garciaparra	120.00	55.00
□ 136 Ken Griffey Jr. CERT	150.00	70.00
□ 143 Greg Maddux CERT	60.00	27.00
□ 144 Alex Rodriguez CERT	60.00	27.00
□ 146 Cal Ripken CERT	80.00	36.00
□ 148 Frank Thomas CERT	100.00	45.00

1997 Pinnacle Certified Certified Team

Randomly inserted in hobby packs at the rate of one in 19, this 20-card set features color player photos on silver-frosted mirror mylar.

	MINT	NRMT
COMPLETE SET (20)	300.00	135.00
COMMON CARD (1-20)	5.00	2.20
UNLISTED STARS	8.00	3.60
STATED ODDS 1:19 HOBBY		
COMP.GOLD SET (20)	1200.00	550.00
COMMON GOLD (1-20)	20.00	9.00
*GOLD TEAM: 1.5X TO 4X HI COLUMN		
GOLD TEAM STATED ODDS 1:119 HOBBY		
GOLD TEAM PRINT RUN 500 SERIAL #'d SETS		
*MIRROR GOLD: 20X TO 40X HI		
MIR.GOLD: RANDOM INSERTS IN PACKS		
MIR.GOLD PRINT RUN 25 SETS		

☐ 1 Frank Thomas	30.00	13.50
☐ 2 Jeff Bagwell	15.00	6.75
☐ 3 Derek Jeter	20.00	9.00
☐ 4 Chipper Jones	25.00	11.00
☐ 5 Alex Rodriguez	25.00	11.00
☐ 6 Ken Caminiti	5.00	2.20
☐ 7 Cal Ripken	30.00	13.50
☐ 8 Mo Vaughn	10.00	4.50
☐ 9 Ivan Rodriguez	10.00	4.50
☐ 10 Mike Piazza	25.00	11.00
☐ 11 Juan Gonzalez	20.00	9.00
☐ 12 Barry Bonds	10.00	4.50
☐ 13 Ken Griffey Jr.	40.00	18.00
☐ 14 Andruw Jones	15.00	6.75
☐ 15 Albert Belle	10.00	4.50
☐ 16 Gary Sheffield	8.00	3.60
☐ 17 Andy Pettitte	8.00	3.60
☐ 18 Hideo Nomo	25.00	11.00
☐ 19 Greg Maddux	25.00	11.00
☐ 20 John Smoltz	5.00	2.20
☐ G18 H.Nomo Mirror Gold	1200.00	550.00

1997 Pinnacle Certified Lasting Impressions

Randomly inserted in packs at the rate of one in 19, this 20-card set features color action photos of top veteran stars printed on die-cut Mirror Mylar.

	MINT	NRMT
COMPLETE SET (20)	225.00	100.00
COMMON CARD (1-20)	4.00	1.80

SEMISTARS	6.00	2.70
UNLISTED STARS	8.00	3.60
STATED ODDS 1:19 HOBBY		

☐ 1 Cal Ripken	30.00	13.50
☐ 2 Ken Griffey Jr.	40.00	18.00
☐ 3 Mo Vaughn	10.00	4.50
☐ 4 Brian Jordan	4.00	1.80
☐ 5 Mark McGwire	15.00	6.75
☐ 6 Chuck Knoblauch	8.00	3.60
☐ 7 Sammy Sosa	8.00	3.60
☐ 8 Brady Anderson	6.00	2.70
☐ 9 Frank Thomas	30.00	13.50
☐ 10 Tony Gwynn	20.00	9.00
☐ 11 Roger Clemens	15.00	6.75
☐ 12 Alex Rodriguez	25.00	11.00
☐ 13 Paul Molitor	8.00	3.60
☐ 14 Kenny Lofton	10.00	4.50
☐ 15 John Smoltz	4.00	1.80
☐ 16 Roberto Alomar	8.00	3.60
☐ 17 Randy Johnson	8.00	3.60
☐ 18 Ryne Sandberg	10.00	4.50
☐ 19 Manny Ramirez	8.00	3.60
☐ 20 Mike Mussina	8.00	3.60

1997 Pinnacle Inside

The 1997 Pinnacle Inside set was issued in one series totalling 150 cards and was distributed inside 24 different collectible player cans with a suggested retail price of $2.99 for a 10-card can. Printed on 14 pt. stock, the fronts feature a color player photo with a thin black-and-white photo as a side border. The backs carry the black-and-white photo and information about the player's favorite off-the-field activities with a small color activity head shot in the center near the top of the card. The set contains a Rookie sub-

set (128-147) and a checklist subset (148-150). The three checklists display black-and-white player photos of American and National League pairings of the 1996 Rookies of the Year, Cy Young winners, and MVPs.

	MINT	NRMT
COMPLETE SET (150)	40.00	18.00
COMMON CARD (1-150)	.20	.09
MINOR STARS	.40	.18
UNLISTED STARS	.75	.35
COMP.CLUB EDIT.(150)	600.00	275.00
COMMON CLUB EDIT (1-200)	2.00	.90
*CLUB EDIT.STARS: 6X TO 12X HI COLUMN		
*CLUB EDITION YOUNG STARS: 5X TO 10X HI		
CLUB EDIT.STATED ODDS 1:7..		

☐ 1 David Cone	.40	.18
☐ 2 Sammy Sosa	.75	.35
☐ 3 Joe Carter	.40	.18
☐ 4 Juan Gonzalez	2.00	.90
☐ 5 Hideo Nomo	2.00	.90
☐ 6 Moises Alou	.40	.18
☐ 7 Marc Newfield	.20	.09
☐ 8 Alex Rodriguez	2.50	1.10
☐ 9 Kimera Bartee	.20	.09
☐ 10 Chuck Knoblauch	.75	.35
☐ 11 Jason Isringhausen	.20	.09
☐ 12 Jermaine Allensworth	.20	.09
☐ 13 Frank Thomas	3.00	1.35
☐ 14 Paul Molitor	.75	.35
☐ 15 John Mabry	.20	.09
☐ 16 Greg Maddux	2.50	1.10
☐ 17 Rafael Palmeiro	.50	.23
☐ 18 Brian Jordan	.40	.18
☐ 19 Ken Griffey Jr.	4.00	1.80
☐ 20 Brady Anderson	.50	.23
☐ 21 Ruben Sierra	.20	.09
☐ 22 Travis Fryman	.40	.18
☐ 23 Cal Ripken	3.00	1.35
☐ 24 Will Clark	.50	.23
☐ 25 Todd Hollandsworth	.20	.09
☐ 26 Kevin Brown	.40	.18
☐ 27 Mike Piazza	2.50	1.10
☐ 28 Craig Biggio	.50	.23
☐ 29 Paul Wilson	.20	.09
☐ 30 Andres Galarraga	.75	.35
☐ 31 Chipper Jones	2.50	1.10
☐ 32 Jason Giambi	.40	.18
☐ 33 Ernie Young	.20	.09
☐ 34 Marty Cordova	.40	.18
☐ 35 Albert Belle	1.00	.45
☐ 36 Roger Clemens	1.50	.70
☐ 37 Ryne Sandberg	1.00	.45
☐ 38 Henry Rodriguez	.20	.09
☐ 39 Jay Buhner	.50	.23
☐ 40 Raul Mondesi	.50	.23
☐ 41 Jeff Fassero	.20	.09
☐ 42 Edgar Martinez	.50	.23
☐ 43 Trey Beamon	.20	.09
☐ 44 Mo Vaughn	1.00	.45
☐ 45 Gary Sheffield	.75	.35
☐ 46 Ray Durham	.20	.09
☐ 47 Brett Butler	.40	.18
☐ 48 Ivan Rodriguez	1.00	.45
☐ 49 Fred McGriff	.50	.23
☐ 50 Dean Palmer	.20	.09
☐ 51 Rickey Henderson	.50	.23
☐ 52 Andy Pettitte	.75	.35
☐ 53 Bobby Bonilla	.40	.18
☐ 54 Shawn Green	.20	.09
☐ 55 Tino Martinez	.75	.35
☐ 56 Tony Gwynn	2.00	.90
☐ 57 Tom Glavine	.40	.18
☐ 58 Eric Young	.20	.09
☐ 59 Kevin Appier	.40	.18
☐ 60 Barry Bonds	1.00	.45
☐ 61 Wade Boggs	.75	.35
☐ 62 Jason Kendall	.40	.18
☐ 63 Jeff Bagwell	1.50	.70
☐ 64 Jeff Conine	.40	.18
☐ 65 Greg Maddux	.20	.09
☐ 66 Eric Karros	.40	.18
☐ 67 Manny Ramirez	.75	.35

☐ 68	John Smoltz	.40	.18
☐ 69	Terrell Wade	.20	.09
☐ 70	John Wetteland	.20	.09
☐ 71	Kenny Lofton	1.00	.45
☐ 72	Jim Thome	.75	.35
☐ 73	Bill Pulsipher	.20	.09
☐ 74	Darryl Strawberry	.40	.18
☐ 75	Roberto Alomar	.75	.35
☐ 76	Bobby Higginson	.40	.18
☐ 77	James Baldwin	.20	.09
☐ 78	Mark McGwire	1.50	.70
☐ 79	Jose Canseco	.50	.23
☐ 80	Mark Grudzielanek	.50	.23
☐ 81	Ryan Klesko	.50	.23
☐ 82	Javy Lopez	.40	.18
☐ 83	Ken Caminiti	.50	.23
☐ 84	Dave Nilsson	.20	.09
☐ 85	Tim Salmon	.75	.35
☐ 86	Cecil Fielder	.40	.18
☐ 87	Derek Jeter	2.50	1.10
☐ 88	Garret Anderson	.40	.18
☐ 89	Dwight Gooden	.40	.18
☐ 90	Carlos Delgado	.40	.18
☐ 91	Ugueth Urbina	.20	.09
☐ 92	Chan Ho Park	.75	.35
☐ 93	Eddie Murray	.75	.35
☐ 94	Alex Ochoa	.20	.09
☐ 95	Rusty Greer	.40	.18
☐ 96	Mark Grace	.50	.23
☐ 97	Pat Hentgen	.20	.09
☐ 98	John Jaha	.20	.09
☐ 99	Charles Johnson	.40	.18
☐ 100	Jermaine Dye	.20	.09
☐ 101	Quinton McCracken	.20	.09
☐ 102	Troy Percival	.20	.09
☐ 103	Shane Reynolds	.20	.09
☐ 104	Rondell White	.40	.18
☐ 105	Charles Nagy	.40	.18
☐ 106	Alan Benes	.40	.18
☐ 107	Tom Goodwin	.20	.09
☐ 108	Ron Gant	.40	.18
☐ 109	Dan Wilson	.20	.09
☐ 110	Darin Erstad	1.25	.55
☐ 111	Matt Williams	.50	.23
☐ 112	Barry Larkin	.50	.23
☐ 113	Mariano Rivera	.40	.18
☐ 114	Larry Walker	.75	.35
☐ 115	Jim Edmonds	.50	.23
☐ 116	Michael Tucker	.40	.18
☐ 117	Todd Hundley	.40	.18
☐ 118	Alex Fernandez	.40	.18
☐ 119	J.T. Snow	.40	.18
☐ 120	Ellis Burks	.40	.18
☐ 121	Steve Finley	.20	.09
☐ 122	Mike Mussina	.75	.35
☐ 123	Curtis Pride	.20	.09
☐ 124	Derek Bell	.20	.09
☐ 125	Dante Bichette	.40	.18
☐ 126	Terry Steinbach	.20	.09
☐ 127	Randy Johnson	.75	.35
☐ 128	Andruw Jones	2.00	.90
☐ 129	Vladimir Guerrero	1.50	.70
☐ 130	Ruben Rivera	.40	.18
☐ 131	Billy Wagner	.40	.18
☐ 132	Scott Rolen	2.00	.90
☐ 133	Rey Ordonez	.20	.09
☐ 134	Karim Garcia	.40	.18
☐ 135	George Arias	.20	.09
☐ 136	Todd Greene	.40	.18
☐ 137	Robin Jennings	.20	.09
☐ 138	Raul Casanova	.20	.09
☐ 139	Steve Gibralter	.20	.09
☐ 140	Edgar Renteria	.40	.18
☐ 141	Chad Mottola	.20	.09
☐ 142	Dmitri Young	.20	.09
☐ 143	Tony Clark	.75	.35
☐ 144	Todd Walker	.40	.18
☐ 145	Kevin Brown	.40	.18
☐ 146	Nomar Garciaparra	2.50	1.10
☐ 147	Neifi Perez	.40	.18
☐ 148	Derek Jeter CL	.75	.35
	Todd Hollandsworth		
☐ 149	Pat Hentgen CL	.20	.09
	John Smoltz		
☐ 150	Juan Gonzalez CL	.75	.35
	Ken Caminiti		

1997 Pinnacle Inside Diamond Edition

Randomly inserted in packs at a rate of one in 63, this 150-card set is a parallel version of the regular Pinnacle Inside set and is printed on silver foil board with a gold holographic stamp and a die-cut design.

	MINT	NRMT
COMMON CARD (1-150)	20.00	9.00
*STARS: 60X TO 100X HI COLUMN		
*YOUNG STARS: 50X TO 80X HI		
STATED ODDS 1:63		

☐ 4	Juan Gonzalez	200.00	90.00
☐ 5	Hideo Nomo	250.00	110.00
☐ 8	Alex Rodriguez	300.00	135.00
☐ 13	Frank Thomas	400.00	180.00
☐ 16	Greg Maddux	250.00	110.00
☐ 19	Ken Griffey Jr.	500.00	220.00
☐ 23	Cal Ripken	300.00	135.00
☐ 27	Mike Piazza	250.00	110.00
☐ 35	Albert Belle	200.00	90.00
☐ 36	Roger Clemens	150.00	70.00
☐ 37	Ryne Sandberg	100.00	45.00
☐ 44	Mo Vaughn	100.00	45.00
☐ 48	Ivan Rodriguez	100.00	45.00
☐ 56	Tony Gwynn	200.00	90.00
☐ 60	Barry Bonds	100.00	45.00
☐ 63	Jeff Bagwell	150.00	70.00
☐ 71	Kenny Lofton	100.00	45.00
☐ 78	Mark McGwire	150.00	70.00
☐ 87	Derek Jeter	250.00	110.00
☐ 110	Darin Erstad	100.00	45.00
☐ 128	Andruw Jones	150.00	70.00
☐ 129	Vladimir Guerrero	120.00	55.00
☐ 132	Scott Rolen	150.00	70.00
☐ 146	Nomar Garciaparra	200.00	90.00

1997 Pinnacle Inside 40 Something

Randomly inserted in packs at a rate of one in 47, this 16-card set features color player photos of some of the most powerful hitters in the league who have the best chance of pushing past the 40-homer level..

	MINT	NRMT
COMPLETE SET (16)	400.00	180.00
COMMON CARD (1-16)	8.00	3.60

UNLISTED STARS	15.00	6.75
STATED ODDS 1:47:		

☐ 1	Juan Gonzalez	50.00	22.00
☐ 2	Barry Bonds	25.00	11.00
☐ 3	Ken Caminiti	12.00	5.50
☐ 4	Mark McGwire	40.00	18.00
☐ 5	Todd Hundley	8.00	3.60
☐ 6	Albert Belle	25.00	11.00
☐ 7	Ellis Burks	8.00	3.60
☐ 8	Jay Buhner	12.00	5.50
☐ 9	Brady Anderson	12.00	5.50
☐ 10	Vinny Castilla	8.00	3.60
☐ 11	Mo Vaughn	25.00	11.00
☐ 12	Ken Griffey Jr.	100.00	45.00
☐ 13	Sammy Sosa	15.00	6.75
☐ 14	Andres Galarraga	15.00	6.75
☐ 15	Gary Sheffield	15.00	6.75
☐ 16	Frank Thomas	80.00	36.00

1997 Pinnacle Inside Cans

This set features replicas of 24 great player cards from the regular Pinnacle Inside set reproduced on the can labels and is painted directly on the metal. Inside each can is information about an opportunity to win a trip to visit a team during their 1998 Spring Training.

	MINT	NRMT
COMPLETE SET (24)	25.00	11.00
COMMON CAN (1-24)	.30	.14
COMMON SEALED CAN	3.00	1.35
*SEALED: 1X TO 2X BASE HI ON 1.50+ CANS		

☐ 1	Kenny Lofton	.75	.35
☐ 2	Frank Thomas	2.50	1.10
☐ 3	John Smoltz	.30	.14
☐ 4	Manny Ramirez	.60	.25
☐ 5	Alex Rodriguez	2.00	.90
☐ 6	Barry Bonds	.75	.35
☐ 7	Mo Vaughn	.75	.35
☐ 8	Ken Griffey Jr.	3.00	1.35
☐ 9	Albert Belle	.75	.35
☐ 10	Greg Maddux	2.00	.90
☐ 11	Juan Gonzalez	1.50	.70
☐ 12	Andy Pettitte	.60	.25
☐ 13	Jeff Bagwell	1.25	.55
☐ 14	Ryan Klesko	.40	.18
☐ 15	Chipper Jones	2.00	.90
☐ 16	Derek Jeter	2.00	.90
☐ 17	Ivan Rodriguez	.75	.35
☐ 18	Andruw Jones	1.50	.70
☐ 19	Mike Piazza	2.00	.90
☐ 20	Hideo Nomo	1.50	.70
☐ 21	Ken Caminiti	.40	.18
☐ 22	Cal Ripken	2.50	1.10
☐ 23	Mark McGwire	1.25	.55
☐ 24	Tony Gwynn	1.50	.70

1997 Pinnacle Inside Dueling Dugouts

Randomly inserted in packs at a rate of one in 23, this 20-card set features a color photo of a star player on both sides of the card with a spinning wheel that lines up to reveal comparative statistics.

	MINT	NRMT
COMPLETE SET (20)	500.00	220.00
COMMON CARD (1-20)	10.00	4.50
STATED ODDS 1:23		
☐ 1 Alex Rodriguez	60.00	27.00
Cal Ripken		
☐ 2 Jeff Bagwell	25.00	11.00
Ken Caminiti		
☐ 3 Barry Bonds	25.00	11.00
Albert Belle		
☐ 4 Mike Piazza	30.00	13.50
Ivan Rodriguez		
☐ 5 Chuck Knoblauch	15.00	6.75
Roberto Alomar		
☐ 6 Ken Griffey Jr.	60.00	27.00
Andruw Jones		
☐ 7 Chipper Jones	30.00	13.50
Jim Thome		
☐ 8 Frank Thomas	40.00	18.00
Mo Vaughn		
☐ 9 Fred McGriff	25.00	11.00
Mark McGwire		
☐ 10 Brian Jordan	25.00	11.00
Tony Gwynn		
☐ 11 Barry Larkin	25.00	11.00
Derek Jeter		
☐ 12 Kenny Lofton	15.00	6.75
Bernie Williams		
☐ 13 Juan Gonzalez	25.00	11.00
Manny Ramirez		
☐ 14 Will Clark	10.00	4.50
Rafael Palmeiro		
☐ 15 Greg Maddux	30.00	13.50
Roger Clemens		
☐ 16 John Smoltz	10.00	4.50
Andy Pettitte		
☐ 17 Mariano Rivera	10.00	4.50
John Wetteland		
☐ 18 Hideo Nomo	25.00	11.00
Mike Mussina		
☐ 19 Todd Hollandsworth	12.00	5.50
Darin Erstad		
☐ 20 Vladimir Guerrero	15.00	6.75
Karim Garcia		

1997 Pinnacle Mint

The 1997 Pinnacle Mint set was issued in one series totalling 30 cards and was distributed in

packs of three cards and two coins for a suggested retail price of $3.99. The challenge was to fit the coins with the die-cut cards that pictured the same player on the minted coin. Two die-cut cards were inserted in each pack. Either one bronze, silver or gold card was also included in each pack. The fronts featured color action player images on a sepia player portrait background and a cut-out area for the matching coin. Ryan Klesko's die cut card was distributed to dealers as a promo. Die cut cards are listed below.

	MINT	NRMT
COMP.DIE CUT SET (30)	20.00	9.00
COMMON DIE CUT (1-30)	.25	.11
DIE CUT UNLISTED STARS	.50	.23
TWO DIE CUT CARDS PER PACK		
COMP.BRONZE SET (30)	40.00	18.00
COMMON BRONZE (1-30)	.50	.23
*BRONZE: .75X TO 2X HI COLUMN		
ONE BRONZE CARD PER PACK		
COMP.SILVER SET (30)	250.00	110.00
COMMON SILVER (1-30)	3.00	1.35
*SILVER: 5X TO 12X HI COLUMN		
SILVER STATED ODDS 1:15		
COMP.GOLD SET (30)	500.00	220.00
COMMON GOLD (1-30)	6.00	2.70
*GOLD: 10X TO 25X HI COLUMN		
GOLD STATED ODDS 1:48		
DIE CUT CARDS LISTED BELOW		
☐ 1 Ken Griffey Jr.	2.50	1.10
☐ 2 Frank Thomas	2.00	.90
☐ 3 Alex Rodriguez	1.50	.70
☐ 4 Cal Ripken	2.00	.90
☐ 5 Mo Vaughn	.60	.25
☐ 6 Juan Gonzalez	1.25	.55
☐ 7 Mike Piazza	1.50	.70
☐ 8 Albert Belle	.60	.25
☐ 9 Chipper Jones	1.50	.70
☐ 10 Andruw Jones	1.25	.55
☐ 11 Greg Maddux	1.50	.70
☐ 12 Hideo Nomo	1.25	.55
☐ 13 Jeff Bagwell	1.00	.45
☐ 14 Manny Ramirez	.50	.23
☐ 15 Mark McGwire	1.00	.45
☐ 16 Derek Jeter	1.50	.70
☐ 17 Sammy Sosa	.50	.23
☐ 18 Barry Bonds	.60	.25
☐ 19 Chuck Knoblauch	.50	.23
☐ 20 Dante Bichette	.25	.11
☐ 21 Tony Gwynn	1.25	.55
☐ 22 Ken Caminiti	.40	.18
☐ 23 Gary Sheffield	.50	.23
☐ 24 Tim Salmon	.50	.23
☐ 25 Ivan Rodriguez	.60	.25
☐ 26 Henry Rodriguez	.25	.11
☐ 27 Barry Larkin	.40	.18
☐ 28 Ryan Klesko	.40	.18
☐ 29 Brian Jordan	.25	.11

☐ 30 Jay Buhner	.40	.18
☐ P28 Ryan Klesko Promo	3.00	1.35

1997 Pinnacle Mint Coins Brass

Each pack of Pinnacle Mint contained two coins (a mixture of Brass, Nickel and Gold Plated). The Brass coins were the most common. This set features coins minted in brass with embossed player heads and were made to be matched with the die-cut card version of the same player. Two versions of the Manny Ramirez - Brass coin were distributed - an erroneous version with the words "fine silver" printed on back, and a corrected version. Judging from market observations, the "fine silver" version appears to be about four times tougher to find than the corrected. In addition to being inserted in packs, Ryan Klesko's card was distributed to dealers as a promo.

	MINT	NRMT
COMP.BRASS SET (30)	60.00	27.00
COMMON BRASS (1-30)	.75	.35
BRASS UNLISTED STARS	1.50	.70
TWO BRASS COINS PER PACK		
COMP.NICKEL SET (30)	300.00	135.00
COMMON NICKEL (1-30)	4.00	1.80
*NICKEL: 2X TO 5X HI COLUMN		
NICKEL STATED ODDS 1:20		
COMP.GOLD PLTD.SET (30)	750.00	350.00
COMMON GOLD PLTD. (1-30)	10.00	4.50
*GOLD PLATED: 5X TO 12X HI COLUMN		
GOLD PLATED STATED ODDS 1:48		
BRASS COINS LISTED BELOW		
RAMIREZ ERROR NOT PART OF BASIC SET		
☐ 1 Ken Griffey Jr.	8.00	3.60
☐ 2 Frank Thomas	6.00	2.70
☐ 3 Alex Rodriguez	5.00	2.20
☐ 4 Cal Ripken	6.00	2.70
☐ 5 Mo Vaughn	2.00	.90
☐ 6 Juan Gonzalez	4.00	1.80
☐ 7 Mike Piazza	5.00	2.20
☐ 8 Albert Belle	2.50	1.10
☐ 9 Chipper Jones	5.00	2.20
☐ 10 Andruw Jones	4.00	1.80
☐ 11 Greg Maddux	5.00	2.20
☐ 12 Hideo Nomo	4.00	1.80
☐ 13 Jeff Bagwell	3.00	1.35
☐ 14A Manny Ramirez COR	1.50	.70
☐ 14B Manny Ramirez ERR	10.00	4.50
	says "fine Silver" on back	
☐ 15 Mark McGwire	3.00	1.35
☐ 16 Derek Jeter	5.00	2.20
☐ 17 Sammy Sosa	1.50	.70
☐ 18 Barry Bonds	2.00	.90
☐ 19 Chuck Knoblauch	1.50	.70
☐ 20 Dante Bichette	.75	.35
☐ 21 Tony Gwynn	4.00	1.80
☐ 22 Ken Caminiti	1.00	.45
☐ 23 Gary Sheffield	1.50	.70
☐ 24 Tim Salmon	1.50	.70

□ 25 Ivan Rodriguez	2.00	.90
□ 26 Henry Rodriguez	.75	.35
□ 27 Barry Larkin	1.00	.45
□ 28 Ryan Klesko	1.00	.45
□ 29 Brian Jordan	.75	.35
□ 30 Jay Buhner	1.00	.45

1997 Pinnacle Totally Certified Platinum Gold

□ 111 Vladimir Guerrero	500.00	220.00
□ 112 Scott Rolen	600.00	275.00
□ 114 Nomar Garciaparra	800.00	350.00
□ 136 Ken Griffey Jr. CERT	1000.00	450.00
□ 137 Vladimir Guerrero CERT	250.00	110.00
□ 138 Roger Clemens CERT	300.00	135.00
□ 139 Mark McGwire CERT	300.00	135.00
□ 141 Derek Jeter CERT	400.00	180.00
□ 142 Juan Gonzalez CERT	400.00	180.00
□ 143 Greg Maddux CERT	500.00	220.00
□ 144 Alex Rodriguez CERT	500.00	220.00
□ 145 Jeff Bagwell CERT	300.00	135.00
□ 146 Cal Ripken CERT	600.00	275.00
□ 147 Tony Gwynn CERT	400.00	180.00
□ 148 Frank Thomas CERT	800.00	350.00
□ 149 Hideo Nomo CERT	600.00	275.00
□ 150 Andruw Jones CERT	300.00	135.00

1997 Pinnacle Totally Certified Platinum Red

This 150-card set is a parallel version of the 1997 Pinnacle Totally Certified Platinum Red set. Platinum Gold cards were randomly seeded into one in every 79 packs. The fronts feature color action player images utilizing full micro-etched, holographic mylar foil, highlighted with gold vignette accents and foil stamping. Only 30 sets were produced and each card is sequentially numbered on back.

	MINT	NRMT
COMMON CARD (1-150)	80.00	36.00
MINOR STARS	120.00	55.00
SEMISTARS	200.00	90.00
UNLISTED STARS	250.00	110.00
GOLD STATED ODDS 1:79 PACKS		
GOLD STATED PRINT RUN 30 SETS		

□ 1 Barry Bonds	400.00	180.00
□ 2 Mo Vaughn	400.00	180.00
□ 4 Ryne Sandberg	400.00	180.00
□ 5 Jeff Bagwell	600.00	275.00
□ 17 Albert Belle	400.00	180.00
□ 22 Alex Rodriguez	1000.00	450.00
□ 24 Larry Walker	300.00	135.00
□ 26 Mike Piazza	1000.00	450.00
□ 28 Cal Ripken	1200.00	550.00
□ 30 Paul Molitor	300.00	180.00
□ 31 Darin Erstad	400.00	180.00
□ 39 Roger Clemens	600.00	275.00
□ 41 Frank Thomas	1500.00	700.00
□ 43 Mike Mussina	300.00	135.00
□ 45 Tony Gwynn	800.00	350.00
□ 47 Jim Thome	300.00	135.00
□ 49 Mark McGwire	600.00	275.00
□ 51 Derek Jeter	800.00	350.00
□ 53 Ken Griffey Jr.	2000.00	900.00
□ 54 Randy Johnson	400.00	180.00
□ 58 Kenny Lofton	400.00	180.00
□ 59 Chipper Jones	800.00	350.00
□ 63 Hideo Nomo	1200.00	550.00
□ 66 Eddie Murray	300.00	135.00
□ 68 Manny Ramirez	300.00	135.00
□ 69 Juan Gonzalez	800.00	350.00
□ 79 Ivan Rodriguez	400.00	180.00
□ 83 Greg Maddux	1000.00	450.00
□ 92 Andy Pettitte	300.00	135.00
□ 95 Roberto Alomar	300.00	135.00
□ 106 Andruw Jones	600.00	275.00
□ 107 Jose Guillen	300.00	135.00

This 150-card set is a quasi-parallel version of the 1997 Pinnacle Certified set. The checklist and player content is identical, but the photos are all different and the cards are designed a little differently. The fronts feature color action player images utilizing full micro-etched, holographic mylar print technology, highlighted with red vignette accent and foil stamping. The product was distributed in three-card packs with a suggested retail price of $6.99. Platinum Red cards were seeded at a rate of two per pack. Only 3,999 Platinum Red sets were produced and each card is sequentially numbered on back.

	MINT	NRMT
COMPLETE SET (150)	500.00	220.00
COMMON CARD (1-150)	1.50	.70
MINOR STARS	3.00	1.35
UNLISTED STARS	6.00	2.70
RED PRINT RUN 3,999 SERIAL #'d SETS		
COMP.BLUE SET (150)	1000.00	450.00
COMMON BLUE (1-150)	3.00	1.35
*BLUE STARS: .75X TO 2X HI COLUMN		
BLUE STATED ODDS ONE PER PACK		
BLUE PRINT RUN 1,999 SERIAL #'d SETS		

□ 1 Barry Bonds	8.00	3.60
□ 2 Mo Vaughn	8.00	3.60
□ 3 Matt Williams	4.00	1.80
□ 4 Ryne Sandberg	8.00	3.60
□ 5 Jeff Bagwell	12.00	5.50
□ 6 Alan Benes	3.00	1.35
□ 7 John Wetteland	1.50	.70
□ 8 Fred McGriff	4.00	1.80
□ 9 Craig Biggio	4.00	1.80
□ 10 Bernie Williams	6.00	2.70

□ 11 Brian Hunter	3.00	1.35
□ 12 Sandy Alomar Jr.	3.00	1.35
□ 13 Ray Lankford	3.00	1.35
□ 14 Ryan Klesko	4.00	1.80
□ 15 Jermaine Dye	1.50	.70
□ 16 Andy Benes	3.00	1.35
□ 17 Albert Belle	8.00	3.60
□ 18 Tony Clark	6.00	2.70
□ 19 Dean Palmer	1.50	.70
□ 20 Bernard Gilkey	1.50	.70
□ 21 Ken Caminiti	4.00	1.80
□ 22 Alex Rodriguez	20.00	9.00
□ 23 Tim Salmon	6.00	2.70
□ 24 Larry Walker	6.00	2.70
□ 25 Barry Larkin	4.00	1.80
□ 26 Mike Piazza	20.00	9.00
□ 27 Brady Anderson	4.00	1.80
□ 28 Cal Ripken	25.00	11.00
□ 29 Charles Nagy	3.00	1.35
□ 30 Paul Molitor	6.00	2.70
□ 31 Darin Erstad	8.00	3.60
□ 32 Rey Ordonez	1.50	.70
□ 33 Wally Joyner	3.00	1.35
□ 34 David Cone	3.00	1.35
□ 35 Sammy Sosa	6.00	2.70
□ 36 Dante Bichette	3.00	1.35
□ 37 Eric Karros	3.00	1.35
□ 38 Omar Vizquel	3.00	1.35
□ 39 Roger Clemens	12.00	5.50
□ 40 Joe Carter	3.00	1.35
□ 41 Frank Thomas	25.00	11.00
□ 42 Javy Lopez	3.00	1.35
□ 43 Mike Mussina	6.00	2.70
□ 44 Gary Sheffield	6.00	2.70
□ 45 Tony Gwynn	15.00	6.75
□ 46 Jason Kendall	3.00	1.35
□ 47 Jim Thome	6.00	2.70
□ 48 Andres Galarraga	6.00	2.70
□ 49 Mark McGwire	12.00	5.50
□ 50 Troy Percival	1.50	.70
□ 51 Derek Jeter	15.00	6.75
□ 52 Todd Hollandsworth	1.50	.70
□ 53 Ken Griffey Jr.	30.00	13.50
□ 54 Randy Johnson	6.00	2.70
□ 55 Pat Hentgen	3.00	1.35
□ 56 Rusty Greer	3.00	1.35
□ 57 John Jaha	1.50	.70
□ 58 Kenny Lofton	8.00	3.60
□ 59 Chipper Jones	20.00	9.00
□ 60 Robb Nen	1.50	.70
□ 61 Rafael Palmeiro	4.00	1.80
□ 62 Mariano Rivera	3.00	1.35
□ 63 Hideo Nomo	15.00	6.75
□ 64 Greg Vaughn	1.50	.70
□ 65 Ron Gant	3.00	1.35
□ 66 Eddie Murray	6.00	2.70
□ 67 John Smoltz	3.00	1.35
□ 68 Manny Ramirez	6.00	2.70
□ 69 Juan Gonzalez	15.00	6.75
□ 70 F.P. Santangelo	1.50	.70
□ 71 Moises Alou	3.00	1.35
□ 72 Alex Ochoa	1.50	.70
□ 73 Chuck Knoblauch	6.00	2.70
□ 74 Raul Mondesi	4.00	1.80
□ 75 J.T. Snow	3.00	1.35
□ 76 Rickey Henderson	4.00	1.80
□ 77 Bobby Bonilla	3.00	1.35
□ 78 Wade Boggs	6.00	2.70
□ 79 Ivan Rodriguez	8.00	3.60
□ 80 Brian Jordan	3.00	1.35
□ 81 Al Leiter	1.50	.70
□ 82 Jay Buhner	4.00	1.80
□ 83 Greg Maddux	20.00	9.00
□ 84 Edgar Martinez	4.00	1.80
□ 85 Kevin Brown	3.00	1.35
□ 86 Eric Young	1.50	.70
□ 87 Todd Hundley	3.00	1.35
□ 88 Ellis Burks	3.00	1.35
□ 89 Marquis Grissom	3.00	1.35
□ 90 Jose Canseco	4.00	1.80
□ 91 Henry Rodriguez	1.50	.70
□ 92 Andy Pettitte	6.00	2.70
□ 93 Mark Grudzielanek	1.50	.70
□ 94 Dwight Gooden	3.00	1.35
□ 95 Roberto Alomar	6.00	2.70
□ 96 Paul Wilson	1.50	.70

#	Player	MINT	NRMT
97	Will Clark	4.00	1.80
98	Rondell White	3.00	1.35
99	Charles Johnson	3.00	1.35
100	Jim Edmonds	4.00	1.80
101	Jason Giambi	3.00	1.35
102	Billy Wagner	3.00	1.35
103	Edgar Renteria	3.00	1.35
104	Johnny Damon	1.50	.70
105	Jason Isringhausen	1.50	.70
106	Andruw Jones	12.00	5.50
107	Jose Guillen	6.00	2.70
108	Kevin Orie	3.00	1.35
109	Brian Giles	1.50	.70
110	Danny Patterson	1.50	.70
111	Vladimir Guerrero	10.00	4.50
112	Scott Rolen	12.00	5.50
113	Damon Mashore	1.50	.70
114	Nomar Garciaparra	15.00	6.75
115	Todd Walker	3.00	1.35
116	Wilton Guerrero	1.50	.70
117	Bob Abreu	3.00	1.35
118	Brooks Kieschnick	1.50	.70
119	Pokey Reese	1.50	.70
120	Todd Greene	3.00	1.35
121	Dmitri Young	1.50	.70
122	Raul Casanova	1.50	.70
123	Glendon Rusch	1.50	.70
124	Jason Dickson	3.00	1.35
125	Jorge Posada	1.50	.70
126	Rod Myers	3.00	1.35
127	Bubba Trammell	6.00	2.70
128	Scott Spiezio	3.00	1.35
129	Hideki Irabu	6.00	2.70
130	Wendell Magee	1.50	.70
131	Bartolo Colon	3.00	1.35
132	Chris Holt	1.50	.70
133	Calvin Maduro	1.50	.70
134	Ray Montgomery	1.50	.70
135	Shannon Stewart	3.00	1.35
136	Ken Griffey Jr. CERT	15.00	6.75
137	Vladimir Guerrero CERT	6.00	2.70
138	Roger Clemens CERT	6.00	2.70
139	Mark McGwire CERT	6.00	2.70
140	Albert Belle CERT	4.00	1.80
141	Derek Jeter CERT	8.00	3.60
142	Juan Gonzalez CERT	8.00	3.60
143	Greg Maddux CERT	10.00	4.50
144	Alex Rodriguez CERT	10.00	4.50
145	Jeff Bagwell CERT	6.00	2.70
146	Cal Ripken CERT	12.00	5.50
147	Tony Gwynn CERT	8.00	3.60
148	Frank Thomas CERT	12.00	5.50
149	Hideo Nomo CERT	8.00	3.60
150	Andruw Jones CERT	6.00	2.70

1997 Pinnacle X-Press

The 1997 Pinnacle X-Press set was issued in one series totalling 150 cards and was distributed in two different kinds of packs. The eight-card packs retailed for $1.99. X-Press Metal Works home plate-shaped retail boxes carried a suggested retail price of $14.99 and contained an eight-card regular pack along with a master deck that had eight more cards, plus one Metal Works card. The set contains the topical subsets: Rookies (116-137), Peak Performers (138-147), and Checklists (148-150).

	MINT	NRMT
COMPLETE SET (150)	20.00	9.00
COMMON CARD (1-150)	.10	.05
MINOR STARS	.20	.09
UNLISTED STARS	.20	.18
SUBSET CARDS HALF VALUE OF BASE CARDS		
COMP SUMMER SET (150)	500.00	220.00
COMMON SUMMER (1-150)	2.00	.90

*SUMMER STARS: 8X TO 20X HI COLUMN
*SUMMER YOUNG STARS: 6X TO 15X HI
*SUMMER ROOKIES: 4X TO 10X HI
MEN OF SUMMER ODDS 1:7 HOBBY
MEN OF SUMMER 1 PER MASTER DECK

#	Player	MINT	NRMT
1	Larry Walker	.40	.18
2	Andy Pettitte	.40	.18
3	Matt Williams	.30	.14
4	Juan Gonzalez	1.00	.45
5	Frank Thomas	1.50	.70
6	Kenny Lofton	.50	.23
7	Ken Griffey Jr.	2.00	.90
8	Andres Galarraga	.40	.18
9	Greg Maddux	1.25	.55
10	Hideo Nomo	1.00	.45
11	Cecil Fielder	.20	.09
12	Jose Canseco	.30	.14
13	Tony Gwynn	1.00	.45
14	Eddie Murray	.40	.18
15	Alex Rodriguez	1.25	.55
16	Mike Piazza	1.25	.55
17	Ken Hill	.10	.05
18	Chuck Knoblauch	.20	.09
19	Ellis Burks	.20	.09
20	Rafael Palmeiro	.30	.14
21	Vinny Castilla	.20	.09
22	Rusty Greer	.20	.09
23	Chipper Jones	1.25	.55
24	Rey Ordonez	.20	.09
25	Mariano Rivera	.20	.09
26	Garret Anderson	.20	.09
27	Edgar Martinez	.30	.14
28	Dante Bichette	.20	.09
29	Todd Hundley	.20	.09
30	Barry Bonds	.50	.23
31	Barry Larkin	.30	.14
32	Derek Jeter	1.25	.55
33	Marquis Grissom	.20	.09
34	Dave Justice	.40	.18
35	Ivan Rodriguez	.50	.23
36	Jay Buhner	.30	.14
37	Fred McGriff	.30	.14
38	Brady Anderson	.30	.14
39	Tony Clark	.40	.18
40	Eric Young	.10	.05
41	Charles Nagy	.20	.09
42	Mark McGwire	.75	.35
43	Paul O'Neill	.20	.09
44	Tino Martinez	.40	.18
45	Ryne Sandberg	.50	.23
46	Bernie Williams	.40	.18
47	Albert Belle	.50	.23
48	Jeff Cirillo	.20	.09
49	Tim Salmon	.40	.18
50	Steve Finley	.20	.09
51	Lance Johnson	.10	.05
52	John Smoltz	.20	.09
53	Javier Lopez	.20	.09
54	Roger Clemens	.75	.35
55	Kevin Appier	.20	.09
56	Ken Caminiti	.30	.14
57	Cal Ripken	1.50	.70
58	Moises Alou	.20	.09
59	Marty Cordova	.20	.09
60	David Cone	.20	.09
61	Manny Ramirez	.40	.18
62	Ray Durham	.10	.05
63	Jermaine Dye	.10	.05
64	Craig Biggio	.30	.14
65	Will Clark	.30	.14
66	Omar Vizquel	.20	.09
67	Bernard Gilkey	.10	.05
68	Greg Vaughn	.10	.05
69	Wade Boggs	.40	.18
70	Dave Nilsson	.10	.05
71	Mark Grace	.30	.14
72	Dean Palmer	.10	.05
73	Sammy Sosa	.40	.18
74	Mike Mussina	.40	.18
75	Alex Fernandez	.20	.09
76	Henry Rodriguez	.10	.05
77	Travis Fryman	.20	.09
78	Jeff Bagwell	.75	.35
79	Pat Hentgen	.20	.09
80	Gary Sheffield	.40	.18
81	Jim Edmonds	.30	.14
82	Darin Erstad	.60	.25
83	Mark Grudzielanek	.10	.05
84	Jim Thome	.40	.18
85	Bobby Higginson	.20	.09
86	Al Martin	.10	.05
87	Jason Giambi	.20	.09
88	Mo Vaughn	.50	.23
89	Jeff Conine	.20	.09
90	Edgar Renteria	.20	.09
91	Andy Ashby	.10	.05
92	Ryan Klesko	.30	.14
93	John Jaha	.10	.05
94	Paul Molitor	.40	.18
95	Brian Hunter	.20	.09
96	Randy Johnson	.40	.18
97	Joey Hamilton	.20	.09
98	Billy Wagner	.20	.09
99	John Wetteland	.10	.05
100	Jeff Fassero	.10	.05
101	Rondell White	.20	.09
102	Kevin Brown	.20	.09
103	Andy Benes	.20	.09
104	Raul Mondesi	.30	.14
105	Todd Hollandsworth	.10	.05
106	Alex Ochoa	.10	.05
107	Bobby Bonilla	.20	.09
108	Brian Jordan	.20	.09
109	Tom Glavine	.20	.09
110	Ron Gant	.20	.09
111	Jason Kendall	.20	.09
112	Roberto Alomar	.40	.18
113	Troy Percival	.20	.09
114	Michael Tucker	.20	.09
115	Joe Carter	.20	.09
116	Andruw Jones	1.00	.45
117	Nomar Garciaparra	1.25	.55
118	Todd Walker	.20	.09
119	Jose Guillen	1.00	.45
120	Bubba Trammell	.40	.18
121	Wilton Guerrero	.10	.05
122	Bob Abreu	.20	.09
123	Vladimir Guerrero	.75	.35
124	Dmitri Young	.10	.05
125	Kevin Orie	.10	.05
126	Jose Cruz Jr.	3.00	1.35
127	Brooks Kieschnick	.10	.05
128	Scott Spiezio	.20	.09
129	Brian Giles	.10	.05
130	Jason Dickson	.20	.09
131	Damon Mashore	.10	.05
132	Wendell Magee	.10	.05
133	Matt Morris	.20	.09
134	Scott Rolen	1.00	.45
135	Shannon Stewart	.20	.09
136	Deivi Cruz	.30	.14
137	Hideki Irabu	.40	.18
138	Larry Walker PP	.20	.09
139	Ken Griffey Jr. PP	1.00	.45
140	Frank Thomas PP	.75	.35
141	Ivan Rodriguez PP	.20	.09
142	Randy Johnson PP	.20	.09
143	Mark McGwire PP	.40	.18
144	Tino Martinez PP	.20	.09
145	Tony Clark PP	.20	.09
146	Mike Piazza PP	.60	.25
147	Alex Rodriguez PP	.60	.25
148	Roger Clemens CL	.40	.18

	MINT	NRMT
☐ 149 Greg Maddux CL	.60	.25
☐ 150 Hideo Nomo CL	.50	.23

1997 Pinnacle X-Press Far and Away

Randomly inserted in regular packs at the rate of one in 19 and one in five in Master Decks, this 18-card set features color photos of the league's top long-ball hitters. The cards are printed with Dufex hand-etched all-foil highlights.

	MINT	NRMT
COMPLETE SET (18)	120.00	55.00
COMMON CARD (1-18)	2.00	.90
UNLISTED STARS	4.00	1.80
STAT.ODDS 1:19 HOB, 1:5 MAST.DECK		

		MINT	NRMT
☐ 1	Albert Belle	5.00	2.20
☐ 2	Mark McGwire	8.00	3.60
☐ 3	Frank Thomas	15.00	6.75
☐ 4	Mo Vaughn	5.00	2.20
☐ 5	Jeff Bagwell	8.00	3.60
☐ 6	Juan Gonzalez	10.00	4.50
☐ 7	Mike Piazza	12.00	5.50
☐ 8	Andruw Jones	10.00	4.50
☐ 9	Chipper Jones	12.00	5.50
☐ 10	Gary Sheffield	4.00	1.80
☐ 11	Sammy Sosa	4.00	1.80
☐ 12	Darin Erstad	6.00	2.70
☐ 13	Jay Buhner	2.50	1.10
☐ 14	Ken Griffey Jr.	20.00	9.00
☐ 15	Ken Caminiti	2.50	1.10
☐ 16	Brady Anderson	2.50	1.10
☐ 17	Manny Ramirez	4.00	1.80
☐ 18	Alex Rodriguez	12.00	5.50

1997 Pinnacle X-Press Melting Pot

Randomly inserted in regular packs at the rate of one in 288 and one in 189 in Master Decks, this 20-card set features color photos of top players. The set tracks the players' origins on foil board with heligram raised ink printing. The fronts carry a portrait of the player with his country's flag as the background. The backs display another player photo, player information, team logo and his native country. Only 500 of this set were produced and are sequentially numbered.

	MINT	NRMT
COMPLETE SET (20)	800.00	350.00
COMMON CARD (1-20)	8.00	3.60
MINOR STARS	12.00	5.50
UNLISTED STARS	20.00	9.00
STAT.ODDS 1:288 HOB, 1:189 MAST.DECK		
STATED PRINT RUN 500 SERIAL #'d SETS		

		MINT	NRMT
☐ 1	Jose Guillen	25.00	11.00
☐ 2	Vladimir Guerrero	40.00	18.00
☐ 3	Andruw Jones	50.00	22.00
☐ 4	Larry Walker	25.00	11.00
☐ 5	Manny Ramirez	25.00	11.00
☐ 6	Ken Griffey Jr.	120.00	55.00
☐ 7	Alex Rodriguez	80.00	36.00
☐ 8	Frank Thomas	100.00	45.00
☐ 9	Juan Gonzalez	60.00	27.00
☐ 10	Ivan Rodriguez	30.00	13.50
☐ 11	Hideo Nomo	80.00	36.00
☐ 12	Rafael Palmeiro	15.00	6.75
☐ 13	Dave Nilsson	8.00	3.60
☐ 14	Nomar Garciaparra	60.00	27.00
☐ 15	Wilton Guerrero	8.00	3.60
☐ 16	Sammy Sosa	20.00	9.00
☐ 17	Edgar Renteria	12.00	5.50
☐ 18	Cal Ripken	100.00	45.00
☐ 19	Derek Jeter	60.00	27.00
☐ 20	Rey Ordonez	8.00	3.60
☐ P7	Alex Rodriguez SAMPLE	2.50	1.10

1997 Pinnacle X-Press Metal Works

Inserted one in every Home Plate Box, this 20-card bronze set features color photos of top players printed on very thick metal stock. The redemption cards below have no expiration date. They are valid until supplies run out.

	MINT	NRMT
COMPLETE SET (20)	200.00	90.00
COMMON CARD (1-20)	5.00	2.20
ONE BRONZE PER MASTER DECK		
SILVER ODDS 1:54 MASTER DECKS		
*SILVER: 3X TO 8X HI COLUMN		
SILVER REDEMPTION ODDS 1:470 HOBBY		
SILVER PRINT RUN 200 SERIAL #'d SETS		
*GOLD: 7.5X TO 15X HI COLUMN		
GOLD ODDS 1:108 MASTER DECKS		
GOLD REDEMPTION ODDS 1:950 HOBBY		
GOLD PRINT RUN 200 SERIAL #'d SETS		
REDEMPTION CARDS GOOD THROUGH 1999		
OR UNTIL SUPPLIES LAST		
BRONZE CARDS PRICED BELOW		

		MINT	NRMT
☐ 1	Ken Griffey Jr.	25.00	11.00
☐ 2	Frank Thomas	20.00	9.00
☐ 3	Andruw Jones	12.00	5.50
☐ 4	Alex Rodriguez	15.00	6.75
☐ 5	Derek Jeter	15.00	6.75
☐ 6	Cal Ripken	20.00	9.00
☐ 7	Mike Piazza	15.00	6.75
☐ 8	Chipper Jones	15.00	6.75
☐ 9	Juan Gonzalez	12.00	5.50
☐ 10	Greg Maddux	15.00	6.75
☐ 11	Tony Gwynn	12.00	5.50
☐ 12	Jeff Bagwell	10.00	4.50
☐ 13	Albert Belle	6.00	2.70
☐ 14	Mark McGwire	10.00	4.50
☐ 15	Nomar Garciaparra	15.00	6.75
☐ 16	Mo Vaughn	6.00	2.70
☐ 17	Andy Pettitte	5.00	2.20
☐ 18	Manny Ramirez	5.00	2.20
☐ 19	Kenny Lofton	6.00	2.70
☐ 20	Roger Clemens	10.00	4.50
☐ NNO	Gold Redemption Card	80.00	36.00
☐ NNO	Silver Redemption Card	40.00	18.00

1997 Pinnacle X-Press Swing for the Fences

Randomly inserted in packs at the rate of one in two, cards from this 60-card unnumbered set feature color photos of baseball's top long-distance hitters and are the player cards for the Swing for the Fences Game in which collectors accumulated points in order to win prizes. The object was to find the Home Run Champion from either the National or American League and match it with the exact number of home runs hit during the 1997 season by using a combination of Booster Number Point cards and one Base Number Home Run card. A Booster card was inserted one in every two packs and carried a plus or minus point total that allowed collectors to add or subtract points to get the winning homer total. The Base Number Home Run Card was found in the Home Plate Master Deck packs only and carried a predetermined number of Home Runs (between 20 and 42) assigned to each player. The first 1,000 winners received an autographed card of Andruw Jones of the Atlanta Braves. The next 3,000 winners received random 10-card packs of Upgraded Swing For the Fences cards produced on thicker card stock and printed with a special foil prize-winner stamp. After all redemptions were done, a drawing was held for the grand prize of a trip for two to the 1998 Pinnacle All-Star FanFest with tickets to the All-Star Game in Denver, Colorado. Five runner-up winners received a box of all Pinnacle Trading Cards baseball products for a full year. Since Mark McGwire led the majors in homers, his card was also deemed to be a winner although he did not lead either league in homers.

	MINT	NRMT
COMPLETE SET (60)	60.00	27.00
COMMON CARD	.25	.11

MINOR STARS	.50	.23
UNLISTED STARS	1.00	.45
STATED ODDS 1:2		
COMP.UPGRADE SET (60)	200.00	90.00
COMMON UPGRADE	1.50	.70
*UP.STARS: 2.5X TO 6X HI COLUMN		
*UPG.YOUNG STARS: 2X TO 5X HI		
TEN UPGRADES VIA MAIL PER WINNER		
UPGRADE EXCH.DEADLINE: 3/1/98		
NNO CARDS LISTED IN ALPH.ORDER		

☐ 1 Sandy Alomar Jr.	.50	.23
☐ 2 Moises Alou	.50	.23
☐ 3 Brady Anderson	.75	.35
☐ 4 Jeff Bagwell	2.00	.90
☐ 5 Derek Bell	.25	.11
☐ 6 Jay Bell	.50	.23
☐ 7 Albert Belle	1.25	.55
☐ 8 Geronimo Berroa	.25	.11
☐ 9 Dante Bichette	.50	.23
☐ 10 Barry Bonds	1.25	.55
☐ 11 Bobby Bonilla	.50	.23
☐ 12 Jay Buhner	.75	.35
☐ 13 Ellis Burks	.50	.23
☐ 14 Ken Caminiti	.75	.35
☐ 15 Jose Canseco	.75	.35
☐ 16 Joe Carter	.50	.23
☐ 17 Vinny Castilla	.50	.23
☐ 18 Tony Clark	1.00	.45
☐ 19 Carlos Delgado	.50	.23
☐ 20 Jim Edmonds	.75	.35
☐ 21 Cecil Fielder	.50	.23
☐ 22 Andres Galarraga	1.00	.45
☐ 23 Ron Gant	.50	.23
☐ 24 Bernard Gilkey	.25	.11
☐ 25 Juan Gonzalez	2.50	1.10
☐ 26 Ken Griffey Jr. W	15.00	6.75
☐ 27 Vladimir Guerrero	2.00	.90
☐ 28 Todd Hundley	.50	.23
☐ 29 John Jaha	.25	.11
☐ 30 Andruw Jones	1.00	.45
☐ 31 Chipper Jones	3.00	1.35
☐ 32 David Justice	1.00	.45
☐ 33 Jeff Kent	.25	.11
☐ 34 Ryan Klesko	.75	.35
☐ 35 Barry Larkin	.75	.35
☐ 36 Mike Lieberthal	.25	.11
☐ 37 Javier Lopez	.50	.23
☐ 38 Edgar Martinez	.75	.35
☐ 39 Tino Martinez	1.00	.45
☐ 40 Fred McGriff	.75	.35
☐ 41 Mark McGwire W	10.00	4.50
☐ 42 Raul Mondesi	.75	.35
☐ 43 Tim Naehring	.25	.11
☐ 44 Dave Nilsson	.25	.11
☐ 45 Rafael Palmeiro	.75	.35
☐ 46 Dean Palmer	.25	.11
☐ 47 Mike Piazza	3.00	1.35
☐ 48 Cal Ripken	4.00	1.80
☐ 49 Henry Rodriguez	.25	.11
☐ 50 Tim Salmon	1.00	.45
☐ 51 Gary Sheffield	1.00	.45
☐ 52 Sammy Sosa	1.00	.45
☐ 53 Terry Steinbach	.25	.11
☐ 54 Frank Thomas	4.00	1.80
☐ 55 Jim Thome	1.00	.45
☐ 56 Mo Vaughn	1.25	.55
☐ 57 Larry Walker	8.00	3.60
☐ 58 Rondell White	.50	.23
☐ 59 Matt Williams	.75	.35
☐ 60 Todd Zeile	.25	.11
☐U26 Ken Griffey Jr. UPG	30.00	13.50
☐U41 Mark McGwire UPG	12.00	5.40
☐U57 Lary Walker UPG	6.00	2.70
☐ NNO A.Jones AU EXCH	40.00	18.00

1988 Score

This set consists of 660 standard-size cards. The set was distributed by Major League Marketing and features six dis-

tinctive border colors on the front. Subsets include Reggie Jackson Tribute (500-504), Highlights (652-660) and Rookie Prospects (623-647). Card number 501, showing Reggie as a member of the Baltimore Orioles, is one of the few opportunities collectors have to visually remember Reggie's one-year stay with the Orioles. The set is distinguished by the fact that each card back shows a full-color picture of the player. Rookie Cards in this set include Ellis Burks, Ken Caminiti, Ron Gant, Tom Glavine, Gregg Jefferies, Jeff Montgomery, and Matt Williams.

	MINT	NRMT
COMPLETE SET (660)	10.00	4.50
COMMON CARD (1-660)	.05	.02
MINOR STARS	.10	.05
UNLISTED STARS	.20	.09

☐ 1 Don Mattingly	.30	.14
☐ 2 Wade Boggs	.20	.09
☐ 3 Tim Raines	.10	.05
☐ 4 Andre Dawson	.20	.09
☐ 5 Mark McGwire	.60	.25
☐ 6 Kevin Seitzer	.10	.05
☐ 7 Wally Joyner	.20	.09
☐ 8 Jesse Barfield	.05	.02
☐ 9 Pedro Guerrero	.10	.05
☐ 10 Eric Davis	.10	.05
☐ 11 George Brett	.40	.18
☐ 12 Ozzie Smith	.25	.11
☐ 13 Rickey Henderson	.20	.09
☐ 14 Jim Rice	.10	.05
☐ 15 Matt Nokes	.05	.02
☐ 16 Mike Schmidt	.25	.11
☐ 17 Dave Parker	.10	.05
☐ 18 Eddie Murray	.20	.09
☐ 19 Andres Galarraga	.20	.09
☐ 20 Tony Fernandez	.05	.02
☐ 21 Kevin McReynolds	.05	.02
☐ 22 B.J. Surhoff	.05	.02
☐ 23 Pat Tabler	.05	.02
☐ 24 Kirby Puckett	.40	.18
☐ 25 Benny Santiago	.05	.02
☐ 26 Ryne Sandberg	.25	.11
☐ 27 Kelly Downs	.10	.05
(Will Clark in background, out of focus)		
☐ 28 Jose Cruz	.05	.02
☐ 29 Pete O'Brien	.05	.02
☐ 30 Mark Langston	.05	.02
☐ 31 Lee Smith	.10	.05
☐ 32 Juan Samuel	.05	.02
☐ 33 Kevin Bass	.05	.02
☐ 34 R.J. Reynolds	.05	.02
☐ 35 Steve Sax	.10	.05
☐ 36 John Kruk	.10	.05
☐ 37 Alan Trammell	.10	.05
☐ 38 Chris Bosio	.05	.02
☐ 39 Brook Jacoby	.05	.02
☐ 40 Willie McGee UER	.05	.02
(Excited misspelled as excitd)		
☐ 41 Dave Magadan	.05	.02
☐ 42 Fred Lynn	.05	.02
☐ 43 Kent Hrbek	.10	.05
☐ 44 Brian Downing	.05	.02
☐ 45 Jose Canseco	.20	.09
☐ 46 Jim Presley	.05	.02
☐ 47 Mike Stanley	.10	.05
☐ 48 Tony Pena	.05	.02
☐ 49 David Cone	.20	.09
☐ 50 Rick Sutcliffe	.05	.02
☐ 51 Doug Drabek	.05	.02
☐ 52 Bill Doran	.05	.02
☐ 53 Mike Scioscia	.05	.02
☐ 54 Candy Maldonado	.05	.02
☐ 55 Dave Winfield	.20	.09
☐ 56 Lou Whitaker	.10	.05
☐ 57 Tom Henke	.05	.02
☐ 58 Ken Gerhart	.05	.02
☐ 59 Glenn Braggs	.05	.02
☐ 60 Julio Franco	.05	.02
☐ 61 Charlie Leibrandt	.05	.02
☐ 62 Gary Gaetti	.05	.02
☐ 63 Bob Boone	.10	.05
☐ 64 Luis Polonia	.10	.05
☐ 65 Dwight Evans	.10	.05
☐ 66 Phil Bradley	.05	.02
☐ 67 Mike Boddicker	.05	.02
☐ 68 Vince Coleman	.05	.02
☐ 69 Howard Johnson	.05	.02
☐ 70 Tim Wallach	.05	.02
☐ 71 Keith Moreland	.05	.02
☐ 72 Barry Larkin	.20	.09
☐ 73 Alan Ashby	.05	.02
☐ 74 Rick Rhoden	.05	.02
☐ 75 Darrell Evans	.10	.05
☐ 76 Dave Stieb	.05	.02
☐ 77 Dan Plesac	.05	.02
☐ 78 Will Clark UER	.25	.11
(Born 3/17/64, should be 3/13/64)		
☐ 79 Frank White	.10	.05
☐ 80 Joe Carter	.20	.09
☐ 81 Mike Witt	.05	.02
☐ 82 Terry Steinbach	.10	.05
☐ 83 Alvin Davis	.05	.02
☐ 84 Tommy Herr	.05	.02
(Will Clark shown sliding into second)		
☐ 85 Vance Law	.05	.02
☐ 86 Kal Daniels	.05	.02
☐ 87 Rick Honeycutt UER	.05	.02
(Wrong years for stats on back)		
☐ 88 Alfredo Griffin	.05	.02
☐ 89 Bret Saberhagen	.05	.02
☐ 90 Bert Blyleven	.10	.05
☐ 91 Jeff Reardon	.10	.05
☐ 92 Cory Snyder	.05	.02
☐ 93A Greg Walker ERR	2.00	.90
(93 of 66)		
☐ 93B Greg Walker COR	.05	.02
(93 of 660)		
☐ 94 Joe Magrane	.05	.02
☐ 95 Rob Deer	.05	.02
☐ 96 Ray Knight	.05	.02
☐ 97 Casey Candaele	.05	.02
☐ 98 John Cerutti	.05	.02
☐ 99 Buddy Bell	.10	.05
☐ 100 Jack Clark	.10	.05
☐ 101 Eric Bell	.05	.02
☐ 102 Willie Wilson	.05	.02
☐ 103 Dave Schmidt	.05	.02
☐ 104 Dennis Eckersley UER	10.00	4.50
(Complete games stats are wrong)		
☐ 105 Don Sutton	.20	.09
☐ 106 Danny Tartabull	.20	.09
☐ 107 Fred McGriff	.20	.09
☐ 108 Les Straker	.05	.02
☐ 109 Lloyd Moseby	.05	.02
☐ 110 Roger Clemens	.40	.18
☐ 111 Glenn Hubbard	.05	.02
☐ 112 Ken Williams	.05	.02
☐ 113 Ruben Sierra	.05	.02

114	Stan Jefferson	.05	.02
115	Milt Thompson	.05	.02
116	Bobby Bonilla	.10	.05
117	Wayne Tolleson	.05	.02
118	Matt Williams	.60	.25
119	Chet Lemon	.05	.02
120	Dale Sveum	.05	.02
121	Dennis Boyd	.05	.02
122	Brett Butler	.10	.05
123	Terry Kennedy	.05	.02
124	Jack Howell	.05	.02
125	Curt Young	.05	.02
126A	Dave Valle ERR (Misspelled Dale on card front)	.10	.05
126B	Dave Valle COR	.05	.02
127	Curt Wilkerson	.05	.02
128	Tim Teufel	.05	.02
129	Ozzie Virgil	.05	.02
130	Brian Fisher	.05	.02
131	Lance Parrish	.05	.02
132	Tom Browning	.05	.02
133A	Larry Andersen ERR (Misspelled Anderson on card front)	.10	.05
133B	Larry Andersen COR	.05	.02
134A	Bob Brenly ERR (Misspelled Brenley on card front)	.10	.05
134B	Bob Brenly COR	.05	.02
135	Mike Marshall	.05	.02
136	Gerald Perry	.05	.02
137	Bobby Meacham	.05	.02
138	Larry Herndon	.05	.02
139	Fred Manrique	.05	.02
140	Charlie Hough	.10	.05
141	Ron Darling	.05	.02
142	Herm Winningham	.05	.02
143	Mike Diaz	.05	.02
144	Mike Jackson	.10	.05
145	Denny Walling	.05	.02
146	Robby Thompson	.05	.02
147	Franklin Stubbs	.05	.02
148	Albert Hall	.05	.02
149	Bobby Witt	.05	.02
150	Lance McCullers	.05	.02
151	Scott Bradley	.05	.02
152	Mark McLemore	.05	.02
153	Tim Laudner	.05	.02
154	Greg Swindell	.05	.02
155	Marty Barrett	.05	.02
156	Mike Heath	.05	.02
157	Gary Ward	.05	.02
158A	Lee Mazzilli ERR (Misspelled Mazilli on card front)	.10	.05
158B	Lee Mazzilli COR	.05	.02
159	Tom Foley	.05	.02
160	Robin Yount	.20	.09
161	Steve Bedrosian	.05	.02
162	Bob Walk	.05	.02
163	Nick Esasky	.05	.02
164	Ken Caminiti	.75	.35
165	Jose Uribe	.05	.02
166	Dave Anderson	.05	.02
167	Ed Whitson	.05	.02
168	Ernie Whitt	.05	.02
169	Cecil Cooper	.10	.05
170	Mike Pagliarulo	.05	.02
171	Pat Sheridan	.05	.02
172	Chris Bando	.05	.02
173	Lee Lacy	.05	.02
174	Steve Lombardozzi	.05	.02
175	Mike Greenwell	.10	.05
176	Greg Minton	.05	.02
177	Moose Haas	.05	.02
178	Mike Kingery	.05	.02
179	Greg A. Harris	.05	.02
180	Bo Jackson	.20	.09
181	Carmelo Martinez	.05	.02
182	Alex Trevino	.05	.02
183	Ron Oester	.05	.02
184	Danny Darwin	.05	.02
185	Mike Krukow	.05	.02
186	Rafael Palmeiro	.20	.09
187	Tim Burke	.05	.02
188	Roger McDowell	.05	.02
189	Garry Templeton	.05	.02
190	Terry Pendleton	.10	.05
191	Larry Parrish	.05	.02
192	Rey Quinones	.05	.02
193	Joaquin Andujar	.05	.02
194	Tom Brunansky	.05	.02
195	Donnie Moore	.05	.02
196	Dan Pasqua	.05	.02
197	Jim Gantner	.05	.02
198	Mark Eichhorn	.05	.02
199	John Grubb	.05	.02
200	Bill Ripken	.10	.05
201	Sam Horn	.05	.02
202	Todd Worrell	.10	.05
203	Terry Leach	.05	.02
204	Garth Iorg	.05	.02
205	Brian Dayett	.05	.02
206	Bo Diaz	.05	.02
207	Craig Reynolds	.05	.02
208	Brian Holton	.05	.02
209	Marvell Wynne UER (Misspelled Marvelle on card front)	.05	.02
210	Dave Concepcion	.10	.05
211	Mike Davis	.05	.02
212	Devon White	.10	.05
213	Mickey Brantley	.05	.02
214	Greg Gagne	.05	.02
215	Oddibe McDowell	.05	.02
216	Jimmy Key	.10	.05
217	Dave Bergman	.05	.02
218	Calvin Schiraldi	.05	.02
219	Larry Sheets	.05	.02
220	Mike Easler	.05	.02
221	Kurt Stillwell	.05	.02
222	Chuck Jackson	.05	.02
223	Dave Martinez	.05	.02
224	Tim Leary	.05	.02
225	Steve Garvey	.10	.05
226	Greg Mathews	.05	.02
227	Doug Sisk	.05	.02
228	Dave Henderson (Wearing Red Sox uniform; Red Sox logo on back)	.05	.02
229	Jimmy Dwyer	.05	.02
230	Larry Owen	.05	.02
231	Andre Thornton	.10	.05
232	Mark Salas	.05	.02
233	Tom Brookens	.05	.02
234	Greg Brock	.05	.02
235	Rance Mulliniks	.05	.02
236	Bob Brower	.05	.02
237	Joe Niekro	.05	.02
238	Scott Bankhead	.05	.02
239	Doug DeCinces	.05	.02
240	Tommy John	.10	.05
241	Rich Gedman	.05	.02
242	Ted Power	.05	.02
243	Dave Meads	.05	.02
244	Jim Sundberg	.05	.02
245	Ken Oberkfell	.05	.02
246	Jimmy Jones	.05	.02
247	Ken Landreaux	.05	.02
248	Jose Oquendo	.05	.02
249	John Mitchell	.05	.02
250	Don Baylor	.10	.05
251	Scott Fletcher	.05	.02
252	Al Newman	.05	.02
253	Carney Lansford	.05	.02
254	Johnny Ray	.05	.02
255	Gary Pettis	.05	.02
256	Ken Phelps	.05	.02
257	Rick Leach	.05	.02
258	Tim Stoddard	.05	.02
259	Ed Romero	.05	.02
260	Sid Bream	.05	.02
261A	Tom Niedenfuer ERR (Misspelled Neidenfuer on card front)	.10	.05
261B	Tom Niedenfuer COR	.05	.02
262	Rick Dempsey	.05	.02
263	Lonnie Smith	.05	.02
264	Bob Forsch	.05	.02
265	Barry Bonds	.50	.23
266	Willie Randolph	.10	.05
267	Mike Ramsey	.05	.02
268	Don Slaught	.05	.02
269	Mickey Tettleton	.10	.05
270	Jerry Reuss	.05	.02
271	Marc Sullivan	.05	.02
272	Jim Morrison	.05	.02
273	Steve Balboni	.05	.02
274	Dick Schofield	.05	.02
275	John Tudor	.05	.02
276	Gene Larkin	.05	.02
277	Harold Reynolds	.05	.02
278	Jerry Browne	.05	.02
279	Willie Upshaw	.05	.02
280	Ted Higuera	.05	.02
281	Terry McGriff	.05	.02
282	Terry Puhl	.05	.02
283	Mark Wasinger	.05	.02
284	Luis Salazar	.05	.02
285	Ted Simmons	.10	.05
286	John Shelby	.05	.02
287	John Smiley	.10	.05
288	Curt Ford	.05	.02
289	Steve Crawford	.05	.02
290	Dan Quisenberry	.05	.02
291	Alan Wiggins	.05	.02
292	Randy Bush	.05	.02
293	John Candelaria	.05	.02
294	Tony Phillips	.05	.02
295	Mike Morgan	.05	.02
296	Bill Wegman	.05	.02
297A	Terry Francona ERR (Misspelled Franconia on card front)	.10	.05
297B	Terry Francona COR	.05	.02
298	Mickey Hatcher	.05	.02
299	Andres Thomas	.05	.02
300	Bob Stanley	.05	.02
301	Al Pedrique	.05	.02
302	Jim Lindeman	.05	.02
303	Wally Backman	.05	.02
304	Paul O'Neill	.10	.05
305	Hubie Brooks	.05	.02
306	Steve Buechele	.05	.02
307	Bobby Thigpen	.05	.02
308	George Hendrick	.05	.02
309	John Moses	.05	.02
310	Ron Guidry	.10	.05
311	Bill Schroeder	.05	.02
312	Jose Nunez	.05	.02
313	Bud Black	.05	.02
314	Joe Sambito	.05	.02
315	Scott McGregor	.05	.02
316	Rafael Santana	.05	.02
317	Frank Williams	.05	.02
318	Mike Fitzgerald	.05	.02
319	Rick Mahler	.05	.02
320	Jim Gott	.05	.02
321	Mariano Duncan	.05	.02
322	Jose Guzman	.05	.02
323	Lee Guetterman	.05	.02
324	Dan Gladden	.05	.02
325	Gary Carter	.10	.05
326	Tracy Jones	.05	.02
327	Floyd Youmans	.05	.02
328	Bill Dawley	.05	.02
329	Paul Noce	.05	.02
330	Angel Salazar	.05	.02
331	Goose Gossage	.10	.05
332	George Frazier	.05	.02
333	Ruppert Jones	.05	.02
334	Billy Joe Robidoux	.05	.02
335	Mike Scott	.05	.02
336	Randy Myers	.10	.05
337	Bob Sebra	.05	.02
338	Eric Show	.05	.02
339	Mitch Williams	.10	.05
340	Paul Molitor	.20	.09
341	Gus Polidor	.05	.02
342	Steve Trout	.05	.02
343	Jerry Don Gleaton	.05	.02
344	Bob Knepper	.05	.02
345	Mitch Webster	.05	.02
346	John Morris	.05	.02
347	Andy Hawkins	.05	.02
348	Dave Leiper	.05	.02
349	Ernest Riles	.05	.02

350	Dwight Gooden	.10	.05
351	Dave Righetti	.10	.05
352	Pat Dodson	.05	.02
353	John Habyan	.05	.02
354	Jim Deshaies	.05	.02
355	Butch Wynegar	.05	.02
356	Bryn Smith	.05	.02
357	Matt Young	.05	.02
358	Tom Pagnozzi	.10	.05
359	Floyd Rayford	.05	.02
360	Darryl Strawberry	.10	.05
361	Sal Butera	.05	.02
362	Domingo Ramos	.05	.02
363	Chris Brown	.05	.02
364	Jose Gonzalez	.05	.02
365	Dave Smith	.05	.02
366	Andy McGaffigan	.05	.02
367	Stan Javier	.05	.02
368	Henry Cotto	.05	.02
369	Mike Birkbeck	.05	.02
370	Len Dykstra	.10	.05
371	Dave Collins	.05	.02
372	Spike Owen	.05	.02
373	Geno Petralli	.05	.02
374	Ron Karkovice	.05	.02
375	Shane Rawley	.05	.02
376	DeWayne Buice	.05	.02
377	Bill Pecota	.05	.02
378	Leon Durham	.05	.02
379	Ed Olwine	.05	.02
380	Dave Hurst	.05	.02
381	Bob McClure	.05	.02
382	Mark Thurmond	.05	.02
383	Buddy Biancalana	.05	.02
384	Tim Conroy	.05	.02
385	Tony Gwynn	.50	.23
386	Greg Gross	.05	.02
387	Barry Lyons	.05	.02
388	Mike Felder	.05	.02
389	Pat Clements	.05	.02
390	Ken Griffey	.05	.02
391	Mark Davis	.05	.02
392	Jose Rijo	.05	.02
393	Mike Young	.05	.02
394	Willie Fraser	.05	.02
395	Dion James	.05	.02
396	Steve Shields	.05	.02
397	Randy St.Claire	.05	.02
398	Danny Jackson	.05	.02
399	Cecil Fielder	.10	.05
400	Keith Hernandez	.10	.05
401	Don Carman	.05	.02
402	Chuck Crim	.05	.02
403	Rob Woodward	.05	.02
404	Junior Ortiz	.05	.02
405	Glenn Wilson	.05	.02
406	Ken Howell	.05	.02
407	Jeff Kunkel	.05	.02
408	Jeff Reed	.05	.02
409	Chris James	.05	.02
410	Zane Smith	.05	.02
411	Ken Dixon	.05	.02
412	Ricky Horton	.05	.02
413	Frank DiPino	.05	.02
414	Shane Mack	.05	
415	Danny Cox	.05	
416	Andy Van Slyke	.10	.05
417	Danny Heep	.05	.02
418	John Cangelosi	.05	.02
419A	John Christensen ERR (Christiansen on card front)	.10	.05
419B	John Christensen COR	.05	.02
420	Joey Cora	.25	.11
421	Mike LaValliere	.05	.02
422	Kelly Gruber	.05	.02
423	Bruce Benedict	.05	.02
424	Len Matuszek	.05	.02
425	Kent Tekulve	.05	.02
426	Rafael Ramirez	.05	.02
427	Mike Flanagan	.05	.02
428	Mike Gallego	.05	.02
429	Juan Castillo	.05	.02
430	Neal Heaton	.05	.02
431	Phil Garner	.05	.02
432	Mike Dunne	.05	.02
433	Wallace Johnson	.05	.02
434	Jack O'Connor	.05	.02
435	Steve Jeltz	.05	.02
436	Donell Nixon	.05	.02
437	Jack Lazorko	.05	.02
438	Keith Comstock	.05	.02
439	Jeff D. Robinson	.05	.02
440	Graig Nettles	.10	.05
441	Mel Hall	.05	.02
442	Gerald Young	.05	.02
443	Gary Redus	.05	.02
444	Charlie Moore	.05	.02
445	Bill Madlock	.10	.05
446	Mark Clear	.05	.02
447	Greg Booker	.05	.02
448	Rick Schu	.05	.02
449	Ron Kittle	.05	.02
450	Dale Murphy	.20	.09
451	Bob Dernier	.05	.02
452	Dale Mohorcic	.05	.02
453	Rafael Belliard	.05	.02
454	Charlie Puleo	.05	.02
455	Dwayne Murphy	.05	.02
456	Jim Eisenreich	.20	.09
457	David Palmer	.05	.02
458	Dave Stewart	.10	.05
459	Pascual Perez	.05	.02
460	Glenn Davis	.05	.02
461	Dan Petry	.05	.02
462	Jim Winn	.05	.02
463	Darrell Miller	.05	.02
464	Mike Moore	.05	.02
465	Mike LaCoss	.05	.02
466	Steve Farr	.05	.02
467	Jerry Mumphrey	.05	.02
468	Kevin Gross	.05	.02
469	Bruce Bochy	.05	.02
470	Orel Hershiser	.10	.05
471	Eric King	.05	.02
472	Ellis Burks	.30	.14
473	Darren Daulton	.10	.05
474	Mookie Wilson	.05	.02
475	Frank Viola	.05	.02
476	Ron Robinson	.05	.02
477	Bob Melvin	.05	.02
478	Jeff Musselman	.05	.02
479	Charlie Kerfeld	.05	.02
480	Richard Dotson	.05	.02
481	Kevin Mitchell	.10	.05
482	Gary Roenicke	.05	.02
483	Tim Flannery	.05	.02
484	Rich Yett	.05	.02
485	Pete Incaviglia	.05	.02
486	Rick Cerone	.05	.02
487	Tony Armas	.05	.02
488	Jerry Reed	.05	.02
489	Dave Lopes	.10	.05
490	Frank Tanana	.05	.02
491	Mike Loynd	.05	.02
492	Bruce Ruffin	.05	.02
493	Chris Speier	.05	.02
494	Tom Hume	.05	.02
495	Jesse Orosco	.05	
496	Robbie Wine UER (Misspelled Robby on card front)	.05	.02
497	Jeff Montgomery	.20	.09
498	Jeff Dedmon	.05	.02
499	Luis Aguayo	.05	.02
500	Reggie Jackson (Oakland A's)	.20	.09
501	Reggie Jackson (Baltimore Orioles)	.20	.09
502	Reggie Jackson (New York Yankees)	.20	.09
503	Reggie Jackson (California Angels)	.20	.09
504	Reggie Jackson (Oakland A's)	.20	.09
505	Billy Hatcher	.05	.02
506	Ed Lynch	.05	.02
507	Willie Hernandez	.05	.02
508	Jose DeLeon	.05	.02
509	Joel Youngblood	.05	.02
510	Bob Welch	.05	.02
511	Steve Ontiveros	.05	.02
512	Randy Ready	.05	.02
513	Juan Nieves	.05	.02
514	Jeff Russell	.05	.02
515	Von Hayes	.05	.02
516	Mark Gubicza	.05	.02
517	Ken Dayley	.05	.02
518	Don Aase	.05	.02
519	Rick Reuschel	.05	.02
520	Mike Henneman	.10	.05
521	Rick Aguilera	.10	.05
522	Jay Howell	.05	.02
523	Ed Correa	.05	.02
524	Manny Trillo	.05	.02
525	Kirk Gibson	.10	.05
526	Wally Ritchie	.05	.02
527	Al Nipper	.05	.02
528	Atlee Hammaker	.05	.02
529	Shawon Dunston	.05	.02
530	Jim Clancy	.05	.02
531	Tom Paciorek	.05	.02
532	Joel Skinner	.05	.02
533	Scott Garrelts	.05	.02
534	Tom O'Malley	.05	.02
535	John Franco	.10	.05
536	Paul Kilgus	.05	.02
537	Darrell Porter	.05	.02
538	Walt Terrell	.05	.02
539	Bill Long	.05	.02
540	George Bell	.05	.02
541	Jeff Sellers	.05	.02
542	Joe Boever	.05	.02
543	Steve Howe	.05	.02
544	Scott Sanderson	.05	.02
545	Jack Morris	.10	.05
546	Todd Benzinger	.05	.02
547	Steve Henderson	.05	.02
548	Eddie Milner	.05	.02
549	Jeff M. Robinson	.05	.02
550	Cal Ripken	.75	.35
551	Jody Davis	.05	.02
552	Kirk McCaskill	.05	.02
553	Craig Lefferts	.05	.02
554	Darnell Coles	.05	.02
555	Phil Niekro	.20	.09
556	Mike Aldrete	.05	.02
557	Pat Perry	.05	.02
558	Juan Agosto	.05	.02
559	Rob Murphy	.05	.02
560	Dennis Rasmussen	.05	.02
561	Manny Lee	.05	.02
562	Jeff Blauser	.25	.11
563	Bob Ojeda	.05	.02
564	Dave Dravecky	.10	.05
565	Gene Garber	.05	.02
566	Ron Roenicke	.05	.02
567	Tommy Hinzo	.05	.02
568	Eric Nolte	.05	.02
569	Ed Hearn	.05	.02
570	Mark Davidson	.05	.02
571	Jim Walewander	.05	.02
572	Donnie Hill UER (84 Stolen Base total listed as 7)	.05	.02
573	Jamie Moyer	.05	.02
574	Ken Schrom	.05	.02
575	Nolan Ryan	.75	.35
576	Jim Acker	.05	.02
577	Jamie Quirk	.05	.02
578	Jay Aldrich	.05	.02
579	Claudell Washington	.05	.02
580	Jeff Leonard	.05	.02
581	Carmen Castillo	.05	.02
582	Daryl Boston	.05	.02
583	Jeff DeWillis	.05	.02
584	John Marzano	.05	.02
585	Bill Gullickson	.05	.02
586	Andy Allanson	.05	.02
587	Lee Tunnell UER (1987 stat line reads .4.84 ERA)	.05	.02
588	Gene Nelson	.05	.02
589	Dave LaPoint	.05	.02
590	Harold Baines	.10	.05
591	Bill Buckner	.10	.05
592	Carlton Fisk	.20	.09
593	Rick Manning	.05	.02

	MINT	NRMT
594 Doug Jones	.20	.09
595 Tom Candiotti	.05	.02
596 Steve Lake	.05	.02
597 Jose Lind	.05	.02
598 Ross Jones	.05	.02
599 Gary Matthews	.05	.02
600 Fernando Valenzuela	.05	.05
601 Dennis Martinez	.10	.05
602 Les Lancaster	.05	.02
603 Ozzie Guillen	.05	.02
604 Tony Bernazard	.05	.02
605 Chili Davis	.10	.05
606 Roy Smalley	.05	.02
607 Ivan Calderon	.05	.02
608 Jay Tibbs	.05	.02
609 Guy Hoffman	.05	.02
610 Doyle Alexander	.05	.02
611 Mike Bielecki	.05	.02
612 Shawn Hillegas	.05	.02
613 Keith Atherton	.05	.02
614 Eric Plunk	.05	.02
615 Sid Fernandez	.05	.02
616 Dennis Lamp	.05	.02
617 Dave Engle	.05	.02
618 Harry Spilman	.05	.02
619 Don Robinson	.05	.02
620 John Farrell	.05	.02
621 Nelson Liriano	.05	.02
622 Floyd Bannister	.05	.02
623 Randy Milligan	.05	.05
624 Kevin Elster	.10	.05
625 Jody Reed	.10	.05
626 Shawn Abner	.05	.02
627 Kirt Manwaring	.10	.05
628 Pete Stanicek	.05	.02
629 Rob Ducey	.05	.02
630 Steve Kiefer	.05	.02
631 Gary Thurman	.05	.02
632 Darrel Akerfelds	.05	.02
633 Dave Clark	.05	.02
634 Roberto Kelly	.20	.09
635 Keith Hughes	.05	.02
636 John Davis	.05	.02
637 Mike Devereaux	.50	.23
638 Tom Glavine	.50	.23
639 Keith A. Miller	.05	.02
640 Chris Gwynn UER (Wrong batting and throwing on back)	.10	.05
641 Tim Crews	.05	.02
642 Mackey Sasser	.05	.02
643 Vicente Palacios	.05	.02
644 Kevin Romine	.05	.02
645 Gregg Jefferies	.25	.11
646 Jeff Treadway	.05	.02
647 Ron Gant	.15	.07
648 Mark McGwire and Matt Nokes (Rookie Sluggers)	.20	.09
649 Eric Davis and Tim Raines (Speed and Power)	.10	.05
650 Don Mattingly and Jack Clark	.10	.05
651 Tony Fernandez, Alan Trammell, and Cal Ripken	.25	.11
652 Vince Coleman HL 100 Stolen Bases	.05	.02
653 Kirby Puckett HL 10 Hits in a Row	.20	.09
654 Benito Santiago HL Hitting Streak	.05	.02
655 Juan Nieves HL No Hitter	.05	.02
656 Steve Bedrosian HL Saves Record	.05	.02
657 Mike Schmidt HL 500 Homers	.10	.05
658 Don Mattingly HL Home Run Streak	.10	.05
659 Mark McGwire HL Rookie HR Record	.30	.14
660 Paul Molitor HL Hitting Streak	.10	.05

1988 Score Rookie/Traded

This 110-card standard-size set features traded players (1-65) and rookies (66-110) for the 1988 season. The cards are distinguishable from the regular Score set by the orange borders and by the fact that the numbering on the back has a T suffix. The cards were distributed exclusively in factory form along with some trivia cards. Apparently Score's first attempt at a Rookie/Traded set was produced very conservatively, resulting in a set which is now recognized as being much tougher to find than the other Rookie/Traded sets from the other major companies of that year. Extended Rookie Cards in this set include Roberto Alomar, Brady Anderson, Craig Biggio, Jay Buhner, Mark Grace, Darryl Hamilton, Jack McDowell, Todd Stottlemyre and Walt Weiss.

	MINT	NRMT
COMP.FACT.SET (110)	50.00	22.00
COMMON CARD (1T-110T)	.25	.11
MINOR STARS	.75	.35
SEMISTARS	1.50	.70
UNLISTED STARS	3.00	1.35
1T Jack Clark	.75	.35
2T Danny Jackson	.25	.11
3T Brett Butler	.75	.35
4T Kurt Stillwell	.25	.11
5T Tom Brunansky	.25	.11
6T Dennis Lamp	.25	.11
7T Jose DeLeon	.25	.11
8T Tom Herr	.25	.11
9T Keith Moreland	.25	.11
10T Kirk Gibson	3.00	1.35
11T Bud Black	.25	.11
12T Rafael Ramirez	.25	.11
13T Luis Salazar	.25	.11
14T Goose Gossage	1.50	.70
15T Bob Welch	.25	.11
16T Vance Law	.25	.11
17T Ray Knight	.25	.11
18T Dan Quisenberry	.25	.11
19T Don Slaught	.25	.11
20T Lee Smith	.75	.35
21T Rick Cerone	.25	.11
22T Pat Tabler	.25	.11
23T Larry McWilliams	.25	.11
24T Ricky Horton	.25	.11
25T Graig Nettles	.75	.35
26T Dan Petry	.25	.11
27T Jose Rijo	.25	.11
28T Chili Davis	1.50	.70
29T Dickie Thon	.25	.11
30T Mackey Sasser	.25	.11
31T Mickey Tettleton	.75	.35
32T Rick Dempsey	.25	.11
33T Ron Hassey	.25	.11
34T Phil Bradley	.25	.11
35T Jay Howell	.25	.11
36T Bill Buckner	.75	.35
37T Alfredo Griffin	.25	.11
38T Gary Pettis	.25	.11
39T Calvin Schiraldi	.25	.11
40T John Candelaria	.25	.11
41T Joe Orsulak	.25	.11
42T Willie Upshaw	.25	.11
43T Herm Winningham	.25	.11
44T Ron Kittle	.25	.11
45T Bob Dernier	.25	.11
46T Steve Balboni	.25	.11
47T Steve Shields	.25	.11
48T Henry Cotto	.25	.11
49T Dave Henderson	.25	.11
50T Dave Parker	.75	.35
51T Mike Young	.25	.11
52T Mark Salas	.25	.11
53T Mike Davis	.25	.11
54T Rafael Santana	.25	.11
55T Don Baylor	.75	.35
56T Dan Pasqua	.25	.11
57T Ernest Riles	.25	.11
58T Glenn Hubbard	.25	.11
59T Mike Smithson	.25	.11
60T Richard Dotson	.25	.11
61T Jerry Reuss	.25	.11
62T Mike Jackson	.75	.35
63T Floyd Bannister	.25	.11
64T Jesse Orosco	.25	.11
65T Larry Parrish	.25	.11
66T Jeff Bittiger	.25	.11
67T Ray Hayward	.25	.11
68T Ricky Jordan	.75	.35
69T Tommy Gregg	.25	.11
70T Brady Anderson	8.00	3.60
71T Jeff Montgomery	3.00	1.35
72T Darryl Hamilton	.75	.35
73T Cecil Espy	.25	.11
74T Greg Briley	.25	.11
75T Joey Meyer	.25	.11
76T Mike Macfarlane	.75	.35
77T Oswald Peraza	.25	.11
78T Jack Armstrong	.25	.11
79T Don Heinkel	.25	.11
80T Mark Grace	8.00	3.60
81T Steve Curry	.25	.11
82T Damon Berryhill	.25	.11
83T Steve Ellsworth	.25	.11
84T Pete Smith	.75	.35
85T Jack McDowell	3.00	1.35
86T Rob Dibble	.75	.35
87T Bryan Harvey UER (Games Pitched 47, Innings 5)	.75	.35
88T John Dopson	.25	.11
89T Dave Gallagher	.25	.11
90T Todd Stottlemyre	3.00	1.35
91T Mike Schooler	.25	.11
92T Don Gordon	.25	.11
93T Sil Campusano	.25	.11
94T Jeff Pico	.25	.11
95T Jay Buhner	8.00	3.60
96T Nelson Santovenia	.25	.11
97T Al Leiter	3.00	1.35
98T Luis Alicea	.75	.35
99T Pat Borders	.75	.35
100T Chris Sabo	.75	.35
101T Tim Belcher	.75	.35
102T Walt Weiss	1.50	.70
103T Craig Biggio	8.00	3.60
104T Don August	.25	.11
105T Roberto Alomar	25.00	11.00
106T Todd Burns	.25	.11
107T John Costello	.25	.11
108T Melido Perez	.75	.35
109T Darrin Jackson	.25	.11
110T Orestes Destrade	.75	.35

1989 Score

This 660-card standard-size set was distributed by Major

League Marketing. Cards were issued primarily in fin-wrapped plastic packs and factory sets. Cards feature six distinctive inner border (inside a white outer border) colors on the front. Subsets include Highlights (652-660) and Rookie Prospects (621-651). Rookie Cards in this set include Sandy Alomar Jr., Brady Anderson, Craig Biggio, Charlie Hayes, Randy Johnson, Ramon Martinez, Gary Sheffield, and John Smoltz.

	MINT	NRMT
COMPLETE SET (660)	8.00	3.60
COMMON CARD (1-660)	.05	.02
MINOR STARS	.10	.05
UNLISTED STARS	.20	.09

		MINT	NRMT
☐ 1	Jose Canseco	.20	.09
☐ 2	Andre Dawson	.20	.09
☐ 3	Mark McGwire UER	.40	.18
☐ 4	Benito Santiago	.05	.02
☐ 5	Rick Reuschel	.05	.02
☐ 6	Fred McGriff	.20	.09
☐ 7	Kal Daniels	.05	.02
☐ 8	Gary Gaetti	.05	.02
☐ 9	Ellis Burks	.10	.05
☐ 10	Darryl Strawberry	.10	.05
☐ 11	Julio Franco	.05	.02
☐ 12	Lloyd Moseby	.05	.02
☐ 13	Jeff Pico	.05	.02
☐ 14	Johnny Ray	.05	.02
☐ 15	Cal Ripken	.75	.35
☐ 16	Dick Schofield	.05	.02
☐ 17	Mel Hall	.05	.02
☐ 18	Bill Ripken	.05	.02
☐ 19	Brook Jacoby	.05	.02
☐ 20	Kirby Puckett	.40	.18
☐ 21	Bill Doran	.05	.02
☐ 22	Pete O'Brien	.05	.02
☐ 23	Matt Nokes	.05	.02
☐ 24	Brian Fisher	.05	.02
☐ 25	Jack Clark	.10	.05
☐ 26	Gary Pettis	.05	.02
☐ 27	Dave Valle	.05	.02
☐ 28	Willie Wilson	.05	.02
☐ 29	Curt Young	.05	.02
☐ 30	Dale Murphy	.20	.09
☐ 31	Barry Larkin	.20	.09
☐ 32	Dave Stewart	.10	.05
☐ 33	Mike LaValliere	.05	.02
☐ 34	Glenn Hubbard	.05	.02
☐ 35	Ryne Sandberg	.25	.11
☐ 36	Tony Pena	.05	.02
☐ 37	Greg Walker	.05	.02
☐ 38	Von Hayes	.05	.02
☐ 39	Kevin Mitchell	.10	.05
☐ 40	Tim Raines	.10	.05
☐ 41	Keith Hernandez	.10	.05
☐ 42	Keith Moreland	.05	.02
☐ 43	Ruben Sierra	.05	.02
☐ 44	Chet Lemon	.05	.02
☐ 45	Willie Randolph	.10	.05
☐ 46	Andy Allanson	.05	.02
☐ 47	Candy Maldonado	.05	.02
☐ 48	Sid Bream	.05	.02
☐ 49	Denny Walling	.05	.02
☐ 50	Dave Winfield	.20	.09
☐ 51	Alvin Davis	.05	.02
☐ 52	Cory Snyder	.05	.02
☐ 53	Hubie Brooks	.05	.02
☐ 54	Chili Davis	.10	.05
☐ 55	Kevin Seitzer	.05	.02
☐ 56	Jose Uribe	.05	.02
☐ 57	Tony Fernandez	.05	.02
☐ 58	Tim Teufel	.05	.02
☐ 59	Oddibe McDowell	.05	.02
☐ 60	Les Lancaster	.05	.02
☐ 61	Billy Hatcher	.05	.02
☐ 62	Dan Gladden	.05	.02
☐ 63	Marty Barrett	.05	.02
☐ 64	Nick Esasky	.05	.02
☐ 65	Wally Joyner	.05	.02
☐ 66	Mike Greenwell	.05	.02
☐ 67	Ken Williams	.05	.02
☐ 68	Bob Horner	.05	.02
☐ 69	Steve Sax	.05	.02
☐ 70	Rickey Henderson	.20	.09
☐ 71	Mitch Webster	.05	.02
☐ 72	Rob Deer	.05	.02
☐ 73	Jim Presley	.05	.02
☐ 74	Albert Hall	.05	.02
☐ 75	George Brett COR (At age 35)	.40	.18
☐ 75A	George Brett ERR (At age 33)	.75	.35
☐ 76	Brian Downing	.05	.02
☐ 77	Dave Martinez	.05	.02
☐ 78	Scott Fletcher	.05	.02
☐ 79	Phil Bradley	.05	.02
☐ 80	Ozzie Smith	.25	.11
☐ 81	Larry Sheets	.05	.02
☐ 82	Mike Aldrete	.05	.02
☐ 83	Darnell Coles	.05	.02
☐ 84	Len Dykstra	.10	.05
☐ 85	Jim Rice	.10	.05
☐ 86	Jeff Treadway	.05	.02
☐ 87	Jose Lind	.05	.02
☐ 88	Willie McGee	.10	.05
☐ 89	Mickey Brantley	.05	.02
☐ 90	Tony Gwynn	.50	.23
☐ 91	R.J. Reynolds	.05	.02
☐ 92	Milt Thompson	.05	.02
☐ 93	Kevin McReynolds	.05	.02
☐ 94	Eddie Murray UER ('86 batting .205, should be .305)	.20	.09
☐ 95	Lance Parrish	.05	.02
☐ 96	Ron Kittle	.05	.02
☐ 97	Gerald Young	.05	.02
☐ 98	Ernie Whitt	.05	.02
☐ 99	Jeff Reed	.05	.02
☐ 100	Don Mattingly	.30	.14
☐ 101	Gerald Perry	.05	.02
☐ 102	Vance Law	.05	.02
☐ 103	John Shelby	.05	.02
☐ 104	Chris Sabo	.05	.02
☐ 105	Danny Tartabull	.05	.02
☐ 106	Glenn Wilson	.05	.02
☐ 107	Mark Davidson	.05	.02
☐ 108	Dave Parker	.10	.05
☐ 109	Eric Davis	.10	.05
☐ 110	Alan Trammell	.05	.02
☐ 111	Ozzie Virgil	.05	.02
☐ 112	Frank Tanana	.05	.02
☐ 113	Rafael Ramirez	.05	.02
☐ 114	Dennis Martinez	.10	.05
☐ 115	Jose DeLeon	.05	.02
☐ 116	Bob Ojeda	.05	.02
☐ 117	Doug Drabek	.05	.02
☐ 118	Andy Hawkins	.05	.02
☐ 119	Greg Maddux	.75	.35
☐ 120	Cecil Fielder UER Reversed photo on back	.05	.02
☐ 121	Mike Scioscia	.05	.02
☐ 122	Dan Petry	.05	.02
☐ 123	Terry Kennedy	.05	.02
☐ 124	Kelly Downs	.05	.02
☐ 125	Greg Gross UER (Gregg on back)	.05	.02
☐ 126	Fred Lynn	.05	.02
☐ 127	Barry Bonds	.40	.18
☐ 128	Harold Baines	.10	.05
☐ 129	Doyle Alexander	.05	.02
☐ 130	Kevin Elster	.05	.02
☐ 131	Mike Heath	.05	.02
☐ 132	Teddy Higuera	.05	.02
☐ 133	Charlie Leibrandt	.05	.02
☐ 134	Tim Laudner	.05	.02
☐ 135A	Ray Knight ERR (Reverse negative)	.20	.09
☐ 135B	Ray Knight COR	.05	.02
☐ 136	Howard Johnson	.05	.02
☐ 137	Terry Pendleton	.10	.05
☐ 138	Andy McGaffigan	.05	.02
☐ 139	Ken Oberkfell	.05	.02
☐ 140	Butch Wynegar	.05	.02
☐ 141	Rob Murphy	.05	.02
☐ 142	Rich Renteria	.05	.02
☐ 143	Jose Guzman	.05	.02
☐ 144	Andres Galarraga	.20	.09
☐ 145	Ricky Horton	.05	.02
☐ 146	Frank DiPino	.05	.02
☐ 147	Glenn Braggs	.05	.02
☐ 148	John Kruk	.10	.05
☐ 149	Mike Schmidt	.25	.11
☐ 150	Lee Smith	.10	.05
☐ 151	Robin Yount	.20	.09
☐ 152	Mark Eichhorn	.05	.02
☐ 153	DeWayne Buice	.05	.02
☐ 154	B.J. Surhoff	.10	.05
☐ 155	Vince Coleman	.05	.02
☐ 156	Tony Phillips	.05	.02
☐ 157	Willie Fraser	.05	.02
☐ 158	Lance McCullers	.05	.02
☐ 159	Greg Gagne	.05	.02
☐ 160	Jesse Barfield	.05	.02
☐ 161	Mark Langston	.05	.02
☐ 162	Kurt Stillwell	.05	.02
☐ 163	Dion James	.05	.02
☐ 164	Glenn Davis	.05	.02
☐ 165	Walt Weiss	.05	.02
☐ 166	Dave Concepcion	.10	.05
☐ 167	Alfredo Griffin	.05	.02
☐ 168	Don Heinkel	.05	.02
☐ 169	Luis Rivera	.05	.02
☐ 170	Shane Rawley	.05	.02
☐ 171	Darrell Evans	.10	.05
☐ 172	Robby Thompson	.05	.02
☐ 173	Jody Davis	.05	.02
☐ 174	Andy Van Slyke	.10	.05
☐ 175	Wade Boggs UER (Bio says .364, should be .356)	.20	.09
☐ 176	Garry Templeton ('85 stats off-centered)	.05	.02
☐ 177	Gary Redus	.05	.02
☐ 178	Craig Lefferts	.05	.02
☐ 179	Carney Lansford	.10	.05
☐ 180	Ron Darling	.05	.02
☐ 181	Kirk McCaskill	.05	.02
☐ 182	Tony Armas	.05	.02
☐ 183	Steve Farr	.05	.02
☐ 184	Tom Brunansky	.05	.02
☐ 185	Bryan Harvey UER ('87 games 47, should be 3)	.10	.05
☐ 186	Mike Marshall	.05	.02
☐ 187	Bo Diaz	.05	.02
☐ 188	Willie Upshaw	.05	.02
☐ 189	Mike Pagliarulo	.05	.02
☐ 190	Mike Krukow	.05	.02
☐ 191	Tommy Herr	.05	.02
☐ 192	Jim Pankovits	.05	.02
☐ 193	Dwight Evans	.10	.05
☐ 194	Kelly Gruber	.05	.02
☐ 195	Bobby Bonilla	.05	.02
☐ 196	Wallace Johnson	.05	.02
☐ 197	Dave Stieb	.05	.02
☐ 198	Pat Borders	.10	.05
☐ 199	Rafael Palmeiro	.20	.09
☐ 200	Dwight Gooden	.10	.05
☐ 201	Pete Incaviglia	.10	.05
☐ 202	Chris James	.05	.02
☐ 203	Marvell Wynne	.05	.02
☐ 204	Pat Sheridan	.05	.02

205	Don Baylor	.10	.05
206	Paul O'Neill	.10	.05
207	Pete Smith	.05	.02
208	Mark McLemore	.05	.02
209	Henry Cotto	.05	.02
210	Kirk Gibson	.10	.05
211	Claudell Washington	.05	.02
212	Randy Bush	.05	.02
213	Joe Carter	.20	.09
214	Bill Buckner	.10	.05
215	Bert Blyleven UER (Wrong birth year)	.10	.05
216	Brett Butler	.05	.02
217	Lee Mazzilli	.05	.02
218	Spike Owen	.05	.02
219	Bill Swift	.05	.02
220	Tim Wallach	.05	.02
221	David Cone	.20	.09
222	Don Carman	.05	.02
223	Rich Gossage	.10	.05
224	Bob Walk	.05	.02
225	Dave Righetti	.05	.02
226	Kevin Bass	.05	.02
227	Kevin Gross	.05	.02
228	Tim Burke	.05	.02
229	Rick Mahler	.05	.02
230	Lou Whitaker UER (252 games in '85, should be 152)	.10	.05
231	Luis Alicea	.05	.02
232	Roberto Alomar	.30	.14
233	Bob Boone	.10	.05
234	Dickie Thon	.05	.02
235	Shawon Dunston	.05	.02
236	Pete Stanicek	.05	.02
237	Craig Biggio (Inconsistent design, portrait on front)	.50	.23
238	Dennis Boyd	.05	.02
239	Tom Candiotti	.05	.02
240	Gary Carter	.20	.09
241	Mike Stanley	.05	.02
242	Ken Phelps	.05	.02
243	Chris Bosio	.05	.02
244	Les Straker	.05	.02
245	Dave Smith	.05	.02
246	John Candelaria	.05	.02
247	Joe Orsulak	.05	.02
248	Storm Davis	.05	.02
249	Floyd Bannister UER (ML Batting Record)	.05	.02
250	Jack Morris	.10	.05
251	Bret Saberhagen	.05	.02
252	Tom Niedenfuer	.05	.02
253	Neal Heaton	.05	.02
254	Eric Show	.05	.02
255	Juan Samuel	.05	.02
256	Dale Sveum	.05	.02
257	Jim Gott	.05	.02
258	Scott Garrelts	.05	.02
259	Larry McWilliams	.05	.02
260	Steve Bedrosian	.05	.02
261	Jack Howell	.05	.02
262	Jay Tibbs	.05	.02
263	Jamie Moyer	.05	.02
264	Doug Sisk	.05	.02
265	Todd Worrell	.05	.02
266	John Farrell	.05	.02
267	Dave Collins	.05	.02
268	Sid Fernandez	.05	.02
269	Tom Brookens	.05	.02
270	Shane Mack	.05	.02
271	Paul Kilgus	.05	.02
272	Chuck Crim	.05	.02
273	Bob Knepper	.05	.02
274	Mike Moore	.05	.02
275	Guillermo Hernandez	.05	.02
276	Dennis Eckersley	.10	.05
277	Graig Nettles	.10	.05
278	Rich Dotson	.05	.02
279	Larry Herndon	.05	.02
280	Gene Larkin	.05	.02
281	Roger McDowell	.05	.02
282	Greg Swindell	.05	.02
283	Juan Agosto	.05	.02
284	Jeff M. Robinson	.05	.02
285	Mike Dunne	.05	.02
286	Greg Mathews	.05	.02
287	Kent Tekulve	.05	.02
288	Jerry Mumphrey	.05	.02
289	Jack McDowell	.10	.05
290	Frank Viola	.05	.02
291	Mark Gubicza	.05	.02
292	Dave Schmidt	.05	.02
293	Mike Henneman	.05	.02
294	Jimmy Jones	.05	.02
295	Charlie Hough	.10	.05
296	Rafael Santana	.05	.02
297	Chris Speier	.05	.02
298	Mike Witt	.05	.02
299	Pascual Perez	.05	.02
300	Nolan Ryan	.75	.35
301	Mitch Williams	.05	.02
302	Mookie Wilson	.10	.05
303	Mackey Sasser	.05	.02
304	John Cerutti	.05	.02
305	Jeff Reardon	.05	.02
306	Randy Myers UER (6 hits in '87, should be 61)	.10	.05
307	Greg Brock	.05	.02
308	Bob Welch	.05	.02
309	Jeff D. Robinson	.05	.02
310	Harold Reynolds	.05	.02
311	Jim Walewander	.05	.02
312	Dave Magadan	.05	.02
313	Jim Gantner	.05	.02
314	Walt Terrell	.05	.02
315	Wally Backman	.05	.02
316	Luis Salazar	.05	.02
317	Rick Rhoden	.05	.02
318	Tom Henke	.05	.02
319	Mike Macfarlane	.10	.05
320	Dan Plesac	.05	.02
321	Calvin Schiraldi	.05	.02
322	Stan Javier	.05	.02
323	Devon White	.05	.02
324	Scott Bradley	.05	.02
325	Bruce Hurst	.05	.02
326	Manny Lee	.05	.02
327	Rick Aguilera	.10	.05
328	Bruce Ruffin	.05	.02
329	Ed Whitson	.05	.02
330	Bo Jackson	.20	.09
331	Ivan Calderon	.05	.02
332	Mickey Hatcher	.05	.02
333	Barry Jones	.05	.02
334	Ron Hassey	.05	.02
335	Bill Wegman	.05	.02
336	Damon Berryhill	.05	.02
337	Steve Ontiveros	.05	.02
338	Dan Pasqua	.05	.02
339	Bill Pecota	.05	.02
340	Greg Cadaret	.05	.02
341	Scott Bankhead	.05	.02
342	Ron Guidry	.10	.05
343	Danny Heep	.05	.02
344	Bob Brower	.05	.02
345	Rich Gedman	.05	.02
346	Nelson Santovenia	.05	.02
347	George Bell	.05	.02
348	Ted Power	.05	.02
349	Mark Grant	.05	.02
350	Roger Clemens COR (78 career wins)	.40	.18
350A	Roger Clemens ERR (778 career wins)	2.00	.90
351	Bill Long	.05	.02
352	Jay Bell	.10	.05
353	Steve Balboni	.05	.02
354	Bob Kipper	.05	.02
355	Steve Jeltz	.05	.02
356	Jesse Orosco	.05	.02
357	Bob Dernier	.05	.02
358	Mickey Tettleton	.10	.05
359	Duane Ward	.05	.02
360	Darrin Jackson	.05	.02
361	Rey Quinones	.05	.02
362	Mark Grace	.20	.09
363	Steve Lake	.05	.02
364	Pat Perry	.05	.02
365	Terry Steinbach	.10	.05
366	Alan Ashby	.05	.02
367	Jeff Montgomery	.10	.05
368	Steve Buechele	.05	.02
369	Chris Brown	.05	.02
370	Orel Hershiser	.10	.05
371	Todd Benzinger	.05	.02
372	Ron Gant	.10	.05
373	Paul Assenmacher	.05	.02
374	Joey Meyer	.05	.02
375	Neil Allen	.05	.02
376	Mike Davis	.05	.02
377	Jeff Parrett	.05	.02
378	Jay Howell	.05	.02
379	Rafael Bellard	.05	.02
380	Luis Polonia UER (2 triples in '87, should be 10)	.05	.02
381	Keith Atherton	.05	.02
382	Kent Hrbek	.05	.02
383	Bob Stanley	.05	.02
384	Dave LaPoint	.05	.02
385	Rance Mulliniks	.05	.02
386	Melido Perez	.05	.02
387	Doug Jones	.05	.02
388	Steve Lyons	.05	.02
389	Alejandro Pena	.05	.02
390	Frank White	.05	.02
391	Pat Tabler	.05	.02
392	Eric Plunk	.05	.02
393	Mike Maddux	.05	.02
394	Allan Anderson	.05	.02
395	Bob Brenly	.05	.02
396	Rick Cerone	.05	.02
397	Scott Terry	.05	.02
398	Mike Jackson	.05	.02
399	Bobby Thigpen UER (Bio says 37 saves in '88, should be 34)	.05	.02
400	Don Sutton	.20	.09
401	Cecil Espy	.05	.02
402	Junior Ortiz	.05	.02
403	Mike Smithson	.05	.02
404	Bud Black	.05	.02
405	Tom Foley	.05	.02
406	Andres Thomas	.05	.02
407	Rick Sutcliffe	.05	.02
408	Brian Harper	.05	.02
409	John Smiley	.05	.02
410	Juan Nieves	.05	.02
411	Shawn Abner	.05	.02
412	Wes Gardner	.05	.02
413	Darren Daulton	.10	.05
414	Juan Berenguer	.05	.02
415	Charles Hudson	.05	.02
416	Rick Honeycutt	.05	.02
417	Greg Booker	.05	.02
418	Tim Belcher	.05	.02
419	Don August	.05	.02
420	Dale Mohorcic	.05	.02
421	Steve Lombardozzi	.05	.02
422	Atlee Hammaker	.05	.02
423	Jerry Don Gleaton	.05	.02
424	Scott Bailes	.05	.02
425	Bruce Sutter	.10	.05
426	Randy Ready	.05	.02
427	Jerry Reed	.05	.02
428	Bryn Smith	.05	.02
429	Tim Leary	.05	.02
430	Mark Clear	.05	.02
431	Terry Leach	.05	.02
432	John Moses	.05	.02
433	Ozzie Guillen	.05	.02
434	Gene Nelson	.05	.02
435	Gary Ward	.05	.02
436	Luis Aguayo	.05	.02
437	Fernando Valenzuela	.10	.05
438	Jeff Russell UER (Saves total does not add up correctly)	.05	.02
439	Cecilio Guante	.05	.02
440	Don Robinson	.05	.02
441	Rick Anderson	.05	.02
442	Tom Glavine	.20	.09
443	Daryl Boston	.05	.02
444	Joe Price	.05	.02
445	Stewart Cliburn	.05	.02

□	446	Manny Trillo	.05	.02
□	447	Joel Skinner	.05	.02
□	448	Charlie Puleo	.05	.02
□	449	Carlton Fisk	.20	.09
□	450	Will Clark	.20	.09
□	451	Otis Nixon	.10	.05
□	452	Rick Schu	.05	.02
□	453	Todd Stottlemyre UER	.10	.05
		(ML Batting Record)		
□	454	Tim Birtsas	.05	.02
□	455	Dave Gallagher	.05	.02
□	456	Barry Lyons	.05	.02
□	457	Fred Manrique	.05	.02
□	458	Ernest Riles	.05	.02
□	459	Doug Jennings	.05	.02
□	460	Joe Magrane	.05	.02
□	461	Jamie Quirk	.05	.02
□	462	Jack Armstrong	.05	.02
□	463	Bobby Witt	.05	.02
□	464	Keith A. Miller	.05	.02
□	465	Todd Burns	.05	.02
□	466	John Dopson	.05	.02
□	467	Rich Yett	.05	.02
□	468	Craig Reynolds	.05	.02
□	469	Dave Bergman	.05	.02
□	470	Rex Hudler	.05	.02
□	471	Eric King	.05	.02
□	472	Joaquin Andujar	.05	.02
□	473	Sil Campusano	.05	.02
□	474	Terry Mulholland	.05	.02
□	475	Mike Flanagan	.05	.02
□	476	Greg A. Harris	.05	.02
□	477	Tommy John	.10	.05
□	478	Dave Anderson	.05	.02
□	479	Fred Toliver	.05	.02
□	480	Jimmy Key	.10	.05
□	481	Donell Nixon	.05	.02
□	482	Mark Portugal	.05	.02
□	483	Tom Pagnozzi	.05	.02
□	484	Jeff Kunkel	.05	.02
□	485	Frank Williams	.05	.02
□	486	Jody Reed	.05	.02
□	487	Roberto Kelly	.10	.05
□	488	Shawn Hillegas UER	.05	.02
		(165 innings in '87, should be 162.2)		
□	489	Jerry Reuss	.05	.02
□	490	Mark Davis	.05	.02
□	491	Jeff Sellers	.05	.02
□	492	Zane Smith	.05	.02
□	493	Al Newman	.05	.02
□	494	Mike Young	.05	.02
□	495	Larry Parrish	.05	.02
□	496	Herm Winningham	.05	.02
□	497	Carmen Castillo	.05	.02
□	498	Joe Hesketh	.05	.02
□	499	Darrell Miller	.05	.02
□	500	Mike LaCoss	.05	.02
□	501	Charlie Lea	.05	.02
□	502	Bruce Benedict	.05	.02
□	503	Chuck Finley	.10	.05
□	504	Brad Wellman	.05	.02
□	505	Tim Crews	.05	.02
□	506	Ken Gerhart	.05	.02
□	507A	Brian Holton ERR	.05	.02
		(Born 1/25/65 Denver, should be 11/29/59 in McKeesport)		
□	507B	Brian Holton COR	2.00	.90
□	508	Dennis Lamp	.05	.02
□	509	Bobby Meacham UER	.05	.02
		('84 games .099)		
□	510	Tracy Jones	.05	.02
□	511	Mike R. Fitzgerald	.05	.02
□	512	Jeff Bittiger	.05	.02
□	513	Tim Flannery	.05	.02
□	514	Ray Hayward	.05	.02
□	515	Dave Leiper	.05	.02
□	516	Rod Scurry	.05	.02
□	517	Carmelo Martinez	.05	.02
□	518	Curtis Wilkerson	.05	.02
□	519	Stan Jefferson	.05	.02
□	520	Dan Quisenberry	.05	.02
□	521	Lloyd McClendon	.05	.02
□	522	Steve Trout	.05	.02
□	523	Larry Andersen	.05	.02

□	524	Don Aase	.05	.02
□	525	Bob Forsch	.05	.02
□	526	Geno Petralli	.05	.02
□	527	Angel Salazar	.05	.02
□	528	Mike Schooler	.05	.02
□	529	Jose Oquendo	.05	.02
□	530	Jay Buhner UER	.20	.09
		(Wearing 43 on front, listed as 34 on back)		
□	531	Tom Bolton	.05	.02
□	532	Al Nipper	.05	.02
□	533	Dave Henderson	.05	.02
□	534	John Costello	.05	.02
□	535	Donnie Moore	.05	.02
□	536	Mike Laga	.05	.02
□	537	Mike Gallego	.05	.02
□	538	Jim Clancy	.05	.02
□	539	Joel Youngblood	.05	.02
□	540	Rick Leach	.05	.02
□	541	Kevin Romine	.05	.02
□	542	Mark Salas	.05	.02
□	543	Greg Minton	.05	.02
□	544	Dave Palmer	.05	.02
□	545	Dwayne Murphy UER	.05	.02
		(Game-sinning)		
□	546	Jim Deshaies	.05	.02
□	547	Don Gordon	.05	.02
□	548	Ricky Jordan	.10	.05
□	549	Mike Boddicker	.05	.02
□	550	Mike Scott	.05	.02
□	551	Jeff Ballard	.05	.02
□	552A	Jose Rijo ERR	.20	.09
		(Uniform listed as 27 on back)		
□	552B	Jose Rijo COR	.20	.09
		(Uniform listed as 24 on back)		
□	553	Danny Darwin	.05	.02
□	554	Tom Browning	.05	.02
□	555	Danny Jackson	.05	.02
□	556	Rick Dempsey	.05	.02
□	557	Jeffrey Leonard	.05	.02
□	558	Jeff Musselman	.05	.02
□	559	Ron Robinson	.05	.02
□	560	John Tudor	.05	.02
□	561	Don Slaught UER	.05	.02
		(237 games in 1987)		
□	562	Dennis Rasmussen	.05	.02
□	563	Brady Anderson	.50	.23
□	564	Pedro Guerrero	.10	.05
□	565	Paul Molitor	.20	.09
□	566	Terry Clark	.05	.02
□	567	Terry Puhl	.05	.02
□	568	Mike Campbell	.05	.02
□	569	Paul Mirabella	.05	.02
□	570	Jeff Hamilton	.05	.02
□	571	Oswald Peraza	.05	.02
□	572	Bob McClure	.05	.02
□	573	Jose Bautista	.05	.02
□	574	Alex Trevino	.05	.02
□	575	John Franco	.05	.02
□	576	Mark Parent	.05	.02
□	577	Nelson Liriano	.05	.02
□	578	Steve Shields	.05	.02
□	579	Odell Jones	.05	.02
□	580	Al Leiter	.20	.09
□	581	Dave Stapleton	.05	.02
□	582	World Series '88	.10	.05
		Orel Hershiser Jose Canseco Dave Stewart		
□	583	Donnie Hill	.05	.02
□	584	Chuck Jackson	.05	.02
□	585	Rene Gonzales	.05	.02
□	586	Tracy Woodson	.05	.02
□	587	Jim Adduci	.05	.02
□	588	Mario Soto	.05	.02
□	589	Jeff Blauser	.10	.05
□	590	Jim Traber	.05	.02
□	591	Jon Perlman	.05	.02
□	592	Mark Williamson	.05	.02
□	593	Dave Meads	.05	.02
□	594	Jim Eisenreich	.05	.02
□	595A	Paul Gibson P1	1.00	.45
□	595B	Paul Gibson P2	.05	.02

		(Airbrushed leg on player in background)		
□	596	Mike Birkbeck	.05	.02
□	597	Terry Francona	.05	.02
□	598	Paul Zuvella	.05	.02
□	599	Franklin Stubbs	.05	.02
□	600	Gregg Jefferies	.05	.02
□	601	John Cangelosi	.05	.02
□	602	Mike Sharperson	.05	.02
□	603	Mike Diaz	.05	.02
□	604	Gary Varsho	.05	.02
□	605	Terry Blocker	.05	.02
□	606	Charlie O'Brien	.05	.02
□	607	Jim Eppard	.05	.02
□	608	John Davis	.05	.02
□	609	Ken Griffey Sr.	.05	.02
□	610	Buddy Bell	.10	.05
□	611	Ted Simmons UER	.10	.05
		('78 stats Cardinal)		
□	612	Matt Williams	.20	.09
□	613	Danny Cox	.05	.02
□	614	Al Pedrique	.05	.02
□	615	Ron Oester	.05	.02
□	616	John Smoltz	.50	.23
□	617	Bob Melvin	.05	.02
□	618	Rob Dibble	.10	.05
□	619	Kirt Manwaring	.05	.02
□	620	Felix Fermin	.05	.02
□	621	Doug Dascenzo	.05	.02
□	622	Bill Brennan	.05	.02
□	623	Carlos Quintana	.05	.02
□	624	Mike Harkey UER	.05	.02
		(13 and 31 walks in '88, should be 35 and 33)		
□	625	Gary Sheffield	.75	.35
□	626	Tom Prince	.05	.02
□	627	Steve Searcy	.05	.02
□	628	Charlie Hayes	.20	.09
		(Listed as outfielder)		
□	629	Felix Jose UER	.05	.02
		(Modesto misspelled as Modesta)		
□	630	Sandy Alomar Jr.	.50	.23
		(Inconsistent design, portrait on front)		
□	631	Derek Lilliquist	.05	.02
□	632	Geronimo Berroa	.10	.05
□	633	Luis Medina	.05	.02
□	634	Tom Gordon UER	.20	.09
		(Height 6'0")		
□	635	Ramon Martinez	.25	.11
□	636	Craig Worthington	.05	.02
□	637	Edgar Martinez	.20	.09
□	638	Chad Kreuter	.05	.02
□	639	Ron Jones	.05	.02
□	640	Van Snider	.05	.02
□	641	Lance Blankenship	.05	.02
□	642	Dwight Smith UER	.10	.05
		(10 HR's in '87, should be 18)		
□	643	Cameron Drew	.05	.02
□	644	Jerald Clark	.05	.02
□	645	Randy Johnson	1.00	.45
□	646	Norm Charlton	.10	.05
□	647	Todd Frohwirth UER	.05	.02
		(Southpaw on back)		
□	648	Luis De Los Santos	.05	.02
□	649	Tim Jones	.05	.02
□	650	Dave West UER	.05	.02
		(ML hits 3, should be 6)		
□	651	Bob Milacki	.05	.02
□	652	Wrigley Field HL	.10	.05
		(Let There Be Lights)		
□	653	Orel Hershiser HL	.10	.05
		(The Streak)		
□	654A	Wade Boggs HL ERR	1.50	.70
		(Wade Whacks 'Em) ('seaason' on back)		
□	654B	Wade Boggs HL COR	.10	.05
		(Wade Whacks 'Em)		
□	655	Jose Canseco HL	.10	.05
		(One of a Kind)		
□	656	Doug Jones HL	.05	.02
		(Doug Sets Saves)		

☐ 657 Rickey Henderson HL .10 .05
   (Rickey Rocks 'Em)
☐ 658 Tom Browning HL...... .05 .02
   (Tom Perfect Pitches)
☐ 659 Mike Greenwell HL .05 .02
   (Greenwell Gamers)
☐ 660 Boston Red Sox HL... .05 .02
   (Joe Morgan MG,
   Sox Sock 'Em)

1989 Score Rookie/Traded

RAFAEL PALMEIRO

The 1989 Score Rookie and Traded set contains 110 standard-size cards. The set was issued exclusively in factory set form through hobby dealers. The set was distributed in a blue box with 10 Magic Motion trivia cards. The fronts have coral green borders with pink diamonds at the bottom. Cards 1-80 feature traded players; cards 81-110 feature 1989 rookies. Rookie Cards in this set include Jim Abbott, Joey (Albert) Belle, Ken Griffey Jr., Ken Hill and John Wetteland.

	MINT	NRMT
COMP.FACT.SET (110)	10.00	4.50
COMMON CARD (1T-110T)	.05	.02
MINOR STARS	.10	.05
UNLISTED STARS	.20	.09

☐ 1T Rafael Palmeiro ..... .20 .09
☐ 2T Nolan Ryan .... 1.50 .70
☐ 3T Jack Clark .... .10 .05
☐ 4T Dave LaPoint ...... .05 .02
☐ 5T Mike Moore .... .05 .02
☐ 6T Pete O'Brien .... .05 .02
☐ 7T Jeffrey Leonard .... .05 .02
☐ 8T Rob Murphy .... .05 .02
☐ 9T Tom Herr .... .05 .02
☐ 10T Claudell Washington .. .05 .02
☐ 11T Mike Pagliarulo .... .05 .02
☐ 12T Steve Lake .... .05 .02
☐ 13T Spike Owen ...... .05 .02
☐ 14T Andy Hawkins .... .05 .02
☐ 15T Todd Benzinger ... .05 .02
☐ 16T Mookie Wilson .... .05 .02
☐ 17T Bert Blyleven ..... .10 .05
☐ 18T Jeff Treadway .... .05 .02
☐ 19T Bruce Hurst ...... .05 .02
☐ 20T Steve Sax .... .05 .02
☐ 21T Juan Samuel ..... .05 .02
☐ 22T Jesse Barfield .... .05 .02
☐ 23T Carmen Castillo .. .05 .02
☐ 24T Terry Leach ...... .05 .02
☐ 25T Mark Langston .... .05 .02
☐ 26T Eric King .... .05 .02
☐ 27T Steve Balboni .... .05 .02
☐ 28T Len Dykstra ...... .10 .05
☐ 29T Keith Moreland ... .05 .02
☐ 30T Terry Kennedy .... .05 .02

☐ 31T Eddie Murray....... .20 .09
☐ 32T Mitch Williams ..... .05 .02
☐ 33T Jeff Parrett .... .05 .02
☐ 34T Wally Backman .... .05 .02
☐ 35T Julio Franco ...... .05 .02
☐ 36T Lance Parrish ..... .05 .02
☐ 37T Nick Esasky ...... .05 .02
☐ 38T Luis Polonia ...... .05 .02
☐ 39T Kevin Gross ...... .05 .02
☐ 40T John Dopson ..... .05 .02
☐ 41T Willie Randolph .... .10 .05
☐ 42T Jim Clancy .... .05 .02
☐ 43T Tracy Jones ...... .05 .02
☐ 44T Phil Bradley ...... .05 .02
☐ 45T Milt Thompson .... .05 .02
☐ 46T Chris James ...... .05 .02
☐ 47T Scott Fletcher .... .05 .02
☐ 48T Kal Daniels .... .05 .02
☐ 49T Steve Bedrosian .. .05 .02
☐ 50T Rickey Henderson .. .20 .09
☐ 51T Dion James ...... .05 .02
☐ 52T Tim Leary .... .05 .02
☐ 53T Roger McDowell .. .05 .02
☐ 54T Mel Hall .... .05 .02
☐ 55T Dickie Thon ...... .05 .02
☐ 56T Zane Smith ...... .05 .02
☐ 57T Danny Heep ..... .05 .02
☐ 58T Bob McClure .... .05 .02
☐ 59T Brian Holton ..... .05 .02
☐ 60T Randy Ready .... .05 .02
☐ 61T Bob Melvin ...... .05 .02
☐ 62T Harold Baines .... .10 .05
☐ 63T Lance McCullers .. .05 .02
☐ 64T Jody Davis....... .05 .02
☐ 65T Darrell Evans .... .10 .05
☐ 66T Joel Youngblood .. .05 .02
☐ 67T Frank Viola ...... .05 .02
☐ 68T Mike Aldrete .... .05 .02
☐ 69T Greg Cadaret ... .05 .02
☐ 70T John Kruk .... .10 .05
☐ 71T Pat Sheridan .... .05 .02
☐ 72T Oddibe McDowell .. .05 .02
☐ 73T Tom Brookens ... .05 .02
☐ 74T Bob Boone ...... .10 .05
☐ 75T Walt Terrell ..... .05 .02
☐ 76T Joel Skinner .... .05 .02
☐ 77T Randy Johnson .. 1.00 .45
☐ 78T Felix Fermin .... .05 .02
☐ 79T Rick Mahler ..... .05 .02
☐ 80T Richard Dotson .. .05 .02
☐ 81T Cris Carpenter ... .05 .02
☐ 82T Bill Spiers ...... .05 .02
☐ 83T Junior Felix ..... .05 .02
☐ 84T Joe Girardi...... .20 .09
☐ 85T Jerome Walton .. .20 .09
☐ 86T Greg Litton ..... .05 .02
☐ 87T Greg W.Harris .. .05 .02
☐ 88T Jim Abbott...... .20 .09
☐ 89T Kevin Brown .... .20 .09
☐ 90T John Wetteland .. .25 .11
☐ 91T Gary Wayne .... .05 .02
☐ 92T Rich Monteleone .. .05 .02
☐ 93T Bob Geren ..... .05 .02
☐ 94T Clay Parker .... .05 .02
☐ 95T Steve Finley .... .25 .11
☐ 96T Gregg Olson .... .10 .05
☐ 97T Ken Patterson .. .05 .02
☐ 98T Ken Hill .... .20 .09
☐ 99T Scott Scudder ... .05 .02
☐ 100T Ken Griffey Jr... 6.00 2.70
☐ 101T Jeff Brantley .... .05 .02
☐ 102T Donn Pall....... .05 .02
☐ 103T Carlos Martinez .. .05 .02
☐ 104T Joe Oliver ...... .10 .05
☐ 105T Omar Vizquel.... .40 .18
☐ 106T Joey Belle ...... 2.00 .90
☐ 107T Kenny Rogers ... .10 .05
☐ 108T Mark Carreon ... .05 .02
☐ 109T Rolando Roomes .. .05 .02
☐ 110T Pete Harnisch ... .10 .05

1990 Score

The 1990 Score set contains 704 standard-size cards. The

front borders are red, blue, green or white. The vertically oriented backs are white with borders that match the fronts, and feature color mugshots. Subsets include Draft Picks (661-682) and Dream Team (683-695). Rookie Cards of note include Juan Gonzalez, Marquis Grissom, Dave Justice, Chuck Knoblauch, Ben McDonald, Dean Palmer, Sammy Sosa, Frank Thomas, Mo Vaughn, Larry Walker and Bernie Williams. A ten-card set of Dream Team Rookies was inserted into each hobby factory set, but was not included in retail factory sets.

	MINT	NRMT
COMPLETE SET (704)	10.00	4.50
COMP.HOBBY SET (714)	12.00	5.50
COMMON CARD (1-704)	.05	.02
MINOR STARS	.10	.05
UNLISTED STARS	.20	.09
SUBSET CARDS HALF VALUE OF BASE CARDS		

☐ 1 Don Mattingly ...... .30 .14
☐ 2 Cal Ripken .... .75 .35
☐ 3 Dwight Evans ..... .10 .05
☐ 4 Barry Bonds ...... .25 .11
☐ 5 Kevin McReynolds .. .05 .02
☐ 6 Ozzie Guillen ..... .05 .02
☐ 7 Terry Kennedy .... .05 .02
☐ 8 Bryan Harvey ..... .05 .02
☐ 9 Alan Trammell .... .15 .07
☐ 10 Cory Snyder ..... .05 .02
☐ 11 Jody Reed .... .05 .02
☐ 12 Roberto Alomar .. .25 .11
☐ 13 Pedro Guerrero .. .05 .02
☐ 14 Gary Redus ..... .05 .02
☐ 15 Marty Barrett .... .05 .02
☐ 16 Ricky Jordan .... .05 .02
☐ 17 Joe Magrane .... .05 .02
☐ 18 Sid Fernandez ... .05 .02
☐ 19 Richard Dotson ... .05 .02
☐ 20 Jack Clark ...... .10 .05
☐ 21 Bob Walk .... .05 .02
☐ 22 Ron Karkovice ... .05 .02
☐ 23 Lenny Harris .... .05 .02
☐ 24 Phil Bradley ..... .05 .02
☐ 25 Andres Galarraga .. .20 .09
☐ 26 Brian Downing ... .05 .02
☐ 27 Dave Martinez ... .05 .02
☐ 28 Eric King .... .05 .02
☐ 29 Barry Lyons ..... .05 .02
☐ 30 Dave Schmidt ... .05 .02
☐ 31 Mike Boddicker .. .05 .02
☐ 32 Tom Foley ...... .05 .02
☐ 33 Brady Anderson .. .20 .09
☐ 34 Jim Presley ..... .05 .02
☐ 35 Lance Parrish ... .05 .02
☐ 36 Von Hayes ...... .05 .02
☐ 37 Lee Smith ...... .10 .05
☐ 38 Herm Winningham .. .05 .02
☐ 39 Alejandro Pena ... .05 .02
☐ 40 Mike Scott ...... .05 .02

#	Player	Price 1	Price 2
41	Joe Orsulak	.05	.02
42	Rafael Ramirez	.05	.02
43	Gerald Young	.05	.02
44	Dick Schofield	.05	.02
45	Dave Smith	.05	.02
46	Dave Magadan	.05	.02
47	Dennis Martinez	.10	.05
48	Greg Minton	.05	.02
49	Milt Thompson	.05	.02
50	Orel Hershiser	.10	.05
51	Bip Roberts	.05	.02
52	Jerry Browne	.05	.02
53	Bob Ojeda	.05	.02
54	Fernando Valenzuela	.10	.05
55	Matt Nokes	.05	.02
56	Brook Jacoby	.05	.02
57	Frank Tanana	.05	.02
58	Scott Fletcher	.05	.02
59	Ron Oester	.05	.02
60	Bob Boone	.10	.05
61	Dan Gladden	.05	.02
62	Darnell Coles	.05	.02
63	Gregg Olson	.05	.02
64	Todd Burns	.05	.02
65	Todd Benzinger	.05	.02
66	Dale Murphy	.20	.09
67	Mike Flanagan	.05	.02
68	Jose Oquendo	.05	.02
69	Cecil Espy	.05	.02
70	Chris Sabo	.05	.02
71	Shane Rawley	.05	.02
72	Tom Brunansky	.05	.02
73	Vance Law	.05	.02
74	B.J. Surhoff	.10	.05
75	Lou Whitaker	.10	.05
76	Ken Caminiti UER (Euclid, Ohio should be Hanford, California)	.20	.09
77	Nelson Liriano	.05	.02
78	Tommy Gregg	.05	.02
79	Don Slaught	.05	.02
80	Eddie Murray	.20	.09
81	Joe Boever	.05	.02
82	Charlie Leibrandt	.05	.02
83	Jose Lind	.05	.02
84	Tony Phillips	.05	.02
85	Mitch Webster	.05	.02
86	Dan Plesac	.05	.02
87	Rick Mahler	.05	.02
88	Steve Lyons	.05	.02
89	Tony Fernandez	.05	.02
90	Ryne Sandberg	.25	.11
91	Nick Esasky	.05	.02
92	Luis Salazar	.05	.02
93	Pete Incaviglia	.05	.02
94	Ivan Calderon	.05	.02
95	Jeff Treadway	.05	.02
96	Kurt Stillwell	.05	.02
97	Gary Sheffield	.25	.11
98	Jeffrey Leonard	.05	.02
99	Andres Thomas	.05	.02
100	Roberto Kelly	.05	.02
101	Alvaro Espinoza	.05	.02
102	Greg Gagne	.05	.02
103	John Farrell	.05	.02
104	Willie Wilson	.05	.02
105	Glenn Braggs	.05	.02
106	Chet Lemon	.05	.02
107A	Jamie Moyer ERR (Scintillating)	.05	.02
107B	Jamie Moyer COR (Scintillating)	.10	.05
108	Chuck Crim	.05	.02
109	Dave Valle	.05	.02
110	Walt Weiss	.05	.02
111	Larry Sheets	.05	.02
112	Don Robinson	.05	.02
113	Danny Heep	.05	.02
114	Carmelo Martinez	.05	.02
115	Dave Gallagher	.05	.02
116	Mike LaValliere	.05	.02
117	Bob McClure	.05	.02
118	Rene Gonzales	.05	.02
119	Mark Parent	.05	.02
120	Wally Joyner	.10	.05
121	Mark Gubicza	.05	.02
122	Tony Pena	.05	.02
123	Carmen Castillo	.05	.02
124	Howard Johnson	.05	.02
125	Steve Sax	.05	.02
126	Tim Belcher	.05	.02
127	Tim Burke	.05	.02
128	Al Newman	.05	.02
129	Dennis Rasmussen	.05	.02
130	Doug Jones	.05	.02
131	Fred Lynn	.05	.02
132	Jeff Hamilton	.05	.02
133	German Gonzalez	.05	.02
134	John Morris	.05	.02
135	Dave Parker	.10	.05
136	Gary Pettis	.05	.02
137	Dennis Boyd	.05	.02
138	Candy Maldonado	.05	.02
139	Rick Cerone	.05	.02
140	George Brett	.40	.18
141	Dave Clark	.05	.02
142	Dickie Thon	.05	.02
143	Junior Ortiz	.05	.02
144	Don August	.05	.02
145	Gary Gaetti	.05	.02
146	Kirt Manwaring	.05	.02
147	Jeff Reed	.05	.02
148	Jose Alvarez	.05	.02
149	Mike Schooler	.05	.02
150	Mark Grace	.20	.09
151	Geronimo Berroa	.10	.05
152	Barry Jones	.05	.02
153	Geno Petralli	.05	.02
154	Jim Deshaies	.05	.02
155	Barry Larkin	.20	.09
156	Alfredo Griffin	.05	.02
157	Tom Henke	.05	.02
158	Mike Jeffcoat	.05	.02
159	Bob Welch	.05	.02
160	Julio Franco	.05	.02
161	Henry Cotto	.05	.02
162	Terry Steinbach	.10	.05
163	Damon Berryhill	.05	.02
164	Tim Crews	.05	.02
165	Tom Browning	.05	.02
166	Fred Manrique	.05	.02
167	Harold Reynolds	.05	.02
168A	Ron Hassey ERR (27 on back)	.05	.02
168B	Ron Hassey COR (24 on back)	.50	.23
169	Shawon Dunston	.05	.02
170	Bobby Bonilla	.10	.05
171	Tommy Herr	.05	.02
172	Mike Heath	.05	.02
173	Rich Gedman	.05	.02
174	Bill Ripken	.05	.02
175	Pete O'Brien	.05	.02
176A	Lloyd McClendon ERR (Uniform number on back listed as 1)	.50	.23
176B	Lloyd McClendon COR (Uniform number on back listed as 10)	.05	.02
177	Brian Holton	.05	.02
178	Jeff Blauser	.10	.05
179	Jim Eisenreich	.05	.02
180	Bert Blyleven	.10	.05
181	Rob Murphy	.05	.02
182	Bill Doran	.05	.02
183	Curt Ford	.05	.02
184	Mike Henneman	.05	.02
185	Eric Davis	.10	.05
186	Lance McCullers	.05	.02
187	Steve Davis	.05	.02
188	Bill Wegman	.05	.02
189	Brian Harper	.05	.02
190	Mike Moore	.05	.02
191	Dale Mohorcic	.05	.02
192	Tim Wallach	.05	.02
193	Keith Hernandez	.10	.05
194	Dave Righetti	.05	.02
195A	Bret Saberhagen ERR (Joke)	.10	.05
195B	Bret Saberhagen COR (Joke)	.10	.05
196	Paul Kilgus	.05	.02
197	Bud Black	.05	.02
198	Juan Samuel	.05	.02
199	Kevin Seitzer	.05	.02
200	Darryl Strawberry	.10	.05
201	Dave Stieb	.05	.02
202	Charlie Hough	.05	.02
203	Jack Morris	.10	.05
204	Rance Mulliniks	.05	.02
205	Alvin Davis	.05	.02
206	Jack Howell	.05	.02
207	Ken Patterson	.05	.02
208	Terry Pendleton	.10	.05
209	Craig Lefferts	.05	.02
210	Kevin Brown UER (First mention of '89 Rangers should be '88)	.20	.09
211	Dan Petry	.05	.02
212	Dave Leiper	.05	.02
213	Daryl Boston	.05	.02
214	Kevin Hickey	.05	.02
215	Mike Krukow	.05	.02
216	Terry Francona	.05	.02
217	Kirk McCaskill	.05	.02
218	Scott Bailes	.05	.02
219	Bob Forsch	.05	.02
220A	Mike Aldrete ERR (25 on back)	.05	.02
220B	Mike Aldrete COR (24 on back)	.10	.05
221	Steve Buechele	.05	.02
222	Jesse Barfield	.05	.02
223	Juan Berenguer	.05	.02
224	Andy McGaffigan	.05	.02
225	Pete Smith	.05	.02
226	Mike Witt	.05	.02
227	Jay Howell	.05	.02
228	Scott Bradley	.05	.02
229	Jerome Walton	.05	.02
230	Greg Swindell	.05	.02
231	Atlee Hammaker	.05	.02
232A	Mike Devereaux ERR (RF on front)	.05	.02
232B	Mike Devereaux COR (CF on front)	.50	.23
233	Ken Hill	.15	.07
234	Craig Worthington	.05	.02
235	Scott Terry	.05	.02
236	Brett Butler	.10	.05
237	Doyle Alexander	.05	.02
238	Dave Anderson	.05	.02
239	Bob Milacki	.05	.02
240	Dwight Smith	.05	.02
241	Otis Nixon	.10	.05
242	Pat Tabler	.05	.02
243	Derek Lilliquist	.05	.02
244	Danny Tartabull	.05	.02
245	Wade Boggs	.20	.09
246	Scott Garrelts (Should say Relief Pitcher on front)	.05	.02
247	Spike Owen	.05	.02
248	Norm Charlton	.05	.02
249	Gerald Perry	.05	.02
250	Nolan Ryan	.75	.35
251	Kevin Gross	.05	.02
252	Randy Milligan	.05	.02
253	Mike LaCoss	.05	.02
254	Dave Bergman	.05	.02
255	Tony Gwynn	.50	.23
256	Felix Fermin	.05	.02
257	Greg W. Harris	.05	.02
258	Junior Felix	.05	.02
259	Mark Davis	.05	.02
260	Vince Coleman	.05	.02
261	Paul Gibson	.05	.02
262	Mitch Williams	.05	.02
263	Jeff Russell	.05	.02
264	Omar Vizquel	.20	.09
265	Andre Dawson	.20	.09
266	Storm Davis	.05	.02
267	Guillermo Hernandez	.05	.02
268	Mike Felder	.05	.02
269	Tom Candiotti	.05	.02
270	Bruce Hurst	.05	.02
271	Fred McGriff	.20	.09
272	Glenn Davis	.05	.02

□ 273	John Franco	.10	.05
□ 274	Rich Yett	.05	.02
□ 275	Craig Biggio	.20	.09
□ 276	Gene Larkin	.05	.02
□ 277	Rob Dibble	.05	.02
□ 278	Randy Bush	.05	.02
□ 279	Kevin Bass	.05	.02
□ 280A	Bo Jackson ERR (Watham)	.20	.09
□ 280B	Bo Jackson COR (Watham)	.20	.09
□ 281	Wally Backman	.05	.02
□ 282	Larry Andersen	.05	.02
□ 283	Chris Bosio	.05	.02
□ 284	Juan Agosto	.05	.02
□ 285	Ozzie Smith	.25	.11
□ 286	George Bell	.05	.02
□ 287	Rex Hudler	.05	.02
□ 288	Pat Borders	.05	.02
□ 289	Danny Jackson	.05	.02
□ 290	Carlton Fisk	.20	.09
□ 291	Tracy Jones	.05	.02
□ 292	Allan Anderson	.05	.02
□ 293	Johnny Ray	.05	.02
□ 294	Lee Guetterman	.05	.02
□ 295	Paul O'Neill	.10	.05
□ 296	Carney Lansford	.05	.02
□ 297	Tom Brookens	.05	.02
□ 298	Claudell Washington	.05	.02
□ 299	Hubie Brooks	.05	.02
□ 300	Will Clark	.20	.09
□ 301	Kenny Rogers	.05	.02
□ 302	Darrell Evans	.10	.05
□ 303	Greg Briley	.05	.02
□ 304	Donn Pall	.05	.02
□ 305	Teddy Higuera	.05	.02
□ 306	Dan Pasqua	.05	.02
□ 307	Dave Winfield	.20	.09
□ 308	Dennis Powell	.05	.02
□ 309	Jose DeLeon	.05	.02
□ 310	Roger Clemens UER (Dominate, should say dominant)	.40	.18
□ 311	Melido Perez	.05	.02
□ 312	Devon White	.05	.02
□ 313	Dwight Gooden	.10	.05
□ 314	Carlos Martinez	.05	.02
□ 315	Dennis Eckersley	.10	.05
□ 316	Clay Parker UER (Height 6'11")	.05	.02
□ 317	Rick Honeycutt	.05	.02
□ 318	Tim Laudner	.05	.02
□ 319	Joe Carter	.10	.05
□ 320	Robin Yount	.20	.09
□ 321	Felix Jose	.05	.02
□ 322	Mickey Tettleton	.10	.05
□ 323	Mike Gallego	.05	.02
□ 324	Edgar Martinez	.20	.09
□ 325	Dave Henderson	.05	.02
□ 326	Chili Davis	.10	.05
□ 327	Steve Balboni	.05	.02
□ 328	Jody Davis	.05	.02
□ 329	Shawn Hillegas	.05	.02
□ 330	Jim Abbott	.10	.05
□ 331	John Dopson	.05	.02
□ 332	Mark Williamson	.05	.02
□ 333	Jeff D. Robinson	.05	.02
□ 334	John Smiley	.05	.02
□ 335	Bobby Thigpen	.05	.02
□ 336	Garry Templeton	.05	.02
□ 337	Marvell Wynne	.05	.02
□ 338A	Ken Griffey Sr. ERR. (Uniform number on back listed as 25)	.05	.02
□ 338B	Ken Griffey Sr. COR (Uniform number on back listed as 30)	.50	.23
□ 339	Steve Finley	.20	.09
□ 340	Ellis Burks	.15	.07
□ 341	Frank Williams	.05	.02
□ 342	Mike Morgan	.05	.02
□ 343	Kevin Mitchell	.10	.05
□ 344	Joel Youngblood	.05	.02
□ 345	Mike Greenwell	.05	.02
□ 346	Glenn Wilson	.05	.02
□ 347	John Costello	.05	.02
□ 348	Wes Gardner	.05	.02
□ 349	Jeff Ballard	.05	.02
□ 350	Mark Thurmond UER (ERA is 192, should be 1.92)	.05	.02
□ 351	Randy Myers	.10	.05
□ 352	Shawn Abner	.05	.02
□ 353	Jesse Orosco	.05	.02
□ 354	Greg Walker	.05	.02
□ 355	Pete Harnisch	.05	.02
□ 356	Steve Farr	.05	.02
□ 357	Dave LaPoint	.05	.02
□ 358	Willie Fraser	.05	.02
□ 359	Mickey Hatcher	.05	.02
□ 360	Rickey Henderson	.20	.09
□ 361	Mike Fitzgerald	.05	.02
□ 362	Bill Schroeder	.05	.02
□ 363	Mark Carreon	.05	.02
□ 364	Ron Jones	.05	.02
□ 365	Jeff Montgomery	.10	.05
□ 366	Bill Krueger	.05	.02
□ 367	John Cangelosi	.05	.02
□ 368	Jose Gonzalez	.05	.02
□ 369	Greg Hibbard	.05	.02
□ 370	John Smoltz	.20	.09
□ 371	Jeff Brantley	.05	.02
□ 372	Frank White	.10	.05
□ 373	Ed Whitson	.05	.02
□ 374	Willie McGee	.10	.05
□ 375	Jose Canseco	.20	.09
□ 376	Randy Ready	.05	.02
□ 377	Don Aase	.05	.02
□ 378	Tony Armas	.05	.02
□ 379	Steve Bedrosian	.05	.02
□ 380	Chuck Finley	.10	.05
□ 381	Kent Hrbek	.10	.05
□ 382	Jim Gantner	.05	.02
□ 383	Mel Hall	.05	.02
□ 384	Mike Marshall	.05	.02
□ 385	Mark McGwire	.40	.18
□ 386	Wayne Tolleson	.05	.02
□ 387	Brian Holman	.05	.02
□ 388	John Wetteland	.20	.09
□ 389	Darren Daulton	.10	.05
□ 390	Rob Deer	.05	.02
□ 391	John Moses	.05	.02
□ 392	Todd Worrell	.05	.02
□ 393	Chuck Cary	.05	.02
□ 394	Stan Javier	.05	.02
□ 395	Willie Randolph	.10	.05
□ 396	Bill Buckner	.05	.02
□ 397	Robby Thompson	.05	.02
□ 398	Mike Scioscia	.05	.02
□ 399	Lonnie Smith	.05	.02
□ 400	Kirby Puckett	.40	.18
□ 401	Mark Langston	.05	.02
□ 402	Danny Darwin	.05	.02
□ 403	Greg Maddux	.60	.25
□ 404	Lloyd Moseby	.05	.02
□ 405	Rafael Palmeiro	.20	.09
□ 406	Chad Kreuter	.05	.02
□ 407	Jimmy Key	.10	.05
□ 408	Tim Birtsas	.05	.02
□ 409	Tim Raines	.10	.05
□ 410	Dave Stewart	.10	.05
□ 411	Eric Yelding	.05	.02
□ 412	Kent Anderson	.05	.02
□ 413	Les Lancaster	.05	.02
□ 414	Rick Dempsey	.05	.02
□ 415	Randy Johnson	.30	.14
□ 416	Gary Carter	.20	.09
□ 417	Rolando Roomes	.05	.02
□ 418	Dan Schatzeder	.05	.02
□ 419	Bryn Smith	.05	.02
□ 420	Ruben Sierra	.20	.09
□ 421	Steve Jeltz	.05	.02
□ 422	Ken Oberkfell	.05	.02
□ 423	Sid Bream	.05	.02
□ 424	Jim Clancy	.05	.02
□ 425	Kelly Gruber	.05	.02
□ 426	Rick Leach	.05	.02
□ 427	Len Dykstra	.10	.05
□ 428	Jeff Pico	.05	.02
□ 429	John Cerutti	.05	.02
□ 430	David Cone	.20	.09
□ 431	Jeff Kunkel	.05	.02
□ 432	Luis Aquino	.05	.02
□ 433	Ernie Whitt	.05	.02
□ 434	Bo Diaz	.05	.02
□ 435	Steve Lake	.05	.02
□ 436	Pat Perry	.05	.02
□ 437	Mike Davis	.05	.02
□ 438	Cecilio Guante	.05	.02
□ 439	Duane Ward	.05	.02
□ 440	Andy Van Slyke	.10	.05
□ 441	Gene Nelson	.05	.02
□ 442	Luis Polonia	.05	.02
□ 443	Kevin Elster	.05	.02
□ 444	Keith Moreland	.05	.02
□ 445	Roger McDowell	.05	.02
□ 446	Ron Darling	.05	.02
□ 447	Ernest Riles	.05	.02
□ 448	Mookie Wilson	.05	.02
□ 449A	Billy Spiers ERR (No birth year)	.20	.09
□ 449B	Billy Spiers COR (Born in 1966)	.05	.02
□ 450	Rick Sutcliffe	.05	.02
□ 451	Nelson Santovenia	.05	.02
□ 452	Andy Allanson	.05	.02
□ 453	Bob Melvin	.05	.02
□ 454	Benito Santiago	.05	
□ 455	Jose Uribe		
□ 456	Bill Landrum	.05	.02
□ 457	Bobby Witt	.05	
□ 458	Kevin Romine	.05	.02
□ 459	Lee Mazzilli	.05	.02
□ 460	Paul Molitor	.20	.09
□ 461	Ramon Martinez	.15	.07
□ 462	Frank DiPino	.05	.02
□ 463	Walt Terrell	.05	.02
□ 464	Bob Geren	.05	.02
□ 465	Rick Reuschel	.05	.02
□ 466	Mark Grant	.05	.02
□ 467	John Kruk	.10	.05
□ 468	Gregg Jefferies	.10	.05
□ 469	R.J. Reynolds	.05	.02
□ 470	Harold Baines	.15	.07
□ 471	Dennis Lamp	.05	.02
□ 472	Tom Gordon	.05	.02
□ 473	Terry Puhl	.05	.02
□ 474	Curt Wilkerson	.05	.02
□ 475	Dan Quisenberry	.05	.02
□ 476	Oddibe McDowell	.05	.02
□ 477A	Zane Smith ERR (Career ERA .393)	.05	.02
□ 477B	Zane Smith COR (career ERA 3.93)	.05	.02
□ 478	Franklin Stubbs	.05	.02
□ 479	Wallace Johnson	.05	.02
□ 480	Jay Tibbs	.05	.02
□ 481	Tom Glavine	.20	.09
□ 482	Manny Lee	.05	.02
□ 483	Joe Hesketh UER (Says Rookiess on back, should say Rookies)	.05	.02
□ 484	Mike Bielecki	.05	.02
□ 485	Greg Brock	.05	.02
□ 486	Pascual Perez	.05	.02
□ 487	Kirk Gibson	.10	.05
□ 488	Scott Sanderson	.05	.02
□ 489	Domingo Ramos	.05	.02
□ 490	Kal Daniels	.05	.02
□ 491A	David Wells ERR (Reverse negative photo on card back)	.50	.23
□ 491B	David Wells COR	.05	.02
□ 492	Jerry Reed	.05	.02
□ 493	Eric Show	.05	.02
□ 494	Mike Pagliarulo	.05	.02
□ 495	Ron Robinson	.05	.02
□ 496	Brad Komminsk	.05	.02
□ 497	Greg Litton	.05	.02
□ 498	Chris James	.05	.02
□ 499	Luis Quinones	.05	.02
□ 500	Frank Viola	.05	.02
□ 501	Tim Teufel UER (Twins '85, the s is lower case, should be upper case)	.05	.02
□ 502	Terry Leach	.05	.02
□ 503	Matt Williams UER	.20	.09

(Wearing 10 on front, listed as 9 on back)		
☐ 504 Tim Leary	.05	.02
☐ 505 Doug Drabek	.05	.02
☐ 506 Mariano Duncan	.05	.02
☐ 507 Charlie Hayes	.05	.02
☐ 508 Joey Belle	.50	.23
☐ 509 Pat Sheridan	.05	.02
☐ 510 Mackey Sasser	.05	.02
☐ 511 Jose Rijo	.05	.02
☐ 512 Mike Smithson	.05	.02
☐ 513 Gary Ward	.05	.02
☐ 514 Dion James	.05	.02
☐ 515 Jim Gott	.05	.02
☐ 516 Drew Hall	.05	.02
☐ 517 Doug Bair	.05	.02
☐ 518 Scott Scudder	.05	.02
☐ 519 Rick Aguilera	.10	.05
☐ 520 Rafael Belliard	.05	.02
☐ 521 Jay Buhner	.20	.09
☐ 522 Jeff Reardon	.10	.05
☐ 523 Steve Rosenberg	.05	.02
☐ 524 Randy Velarde	.05	.02
☐ 525 Jeff Musselman	.05	.02
☐ 526 Bill Long	.05	.02
☐ 527 Gary Wayne	.05	.02
☐ 528 Dave Johnson (P)	.05	.02
☐ 529 Ron Kittle	.05	.02
☐ 530 Erik Hanson UER	.05	.02
(5th line on back says seson, should say season)		
☐ 531 Steve Wilson	.05	.02
☐ 532 Joey Meyer	.05	.02
☐ 533 Curt Young	.05	.02
☐ 534 Kelly Downs	.05	.02
☐ 535 Joe Girardi	.10	.05
☐ 536 Lance Blankenship	.05	.02
☐ 537 Greg Mathews	.05	.02
☐ 538 Donell Nixon	.05	.02
☐ 539 Mark Knudson	.05	.02
☐ 540 Jeff Wetherby	.05	.02
☐ 541 Darrin Jackson	.05	.02
☐ 542 Terry Mulholland	.05	.02
☐ 543 Eric Hetzel	.05	.02
☐ 544 Rick Reed	.05	.02
☐ 545 Dennis Cook	.05	.02
☐ 546 Mike Jackson	.05	.02
☐ 547 Brian Fisher	.05	.02
☐ 548 Gene Harris	.05	.02
☐ 549 Jeff King	.10	.05
☐ 550 Dave Dravecky	.20	.09
☐ 551 Randy Kutcher	.05	.02
☐ 552 Mark Portugal	.05	.02
☐ 553 Jim Corsi	.05	.02
☐ 554 Todd Stottlemyre	.10	.05
☐ 555 Scott Bankhead	.05	.02
☐ 556 Ken Dayley	.05	.02
☐ 557 Rick Wrona	.05	.02
☐ 558 Sammy Sosa	.75	.35
☐ 559 Keith Miller	.05	.02
☐ 560 Ken Griffey Jr.	1.50	.70
☐ 561A Ryne Sandberg HL ERR	6.00	2.70
(Position on front listed as 3B)		
☐ 561B Ryne Sandberg HL COR	.20	.09
☐ 562 Billy Hatcher	.05	.02
☐ 563 Jay Bell	.10	.05
☐ 564 Jack Daugherty	.05	.02
☐ 565 Rich Monteleone	.05	.02
☐ 566 Bo Jackson AS-MVP	.20	.09
☐ 567 Tony Fossas	.05	.02
☐ 568 Roy Smith	.05	.02
☐ 569 Jaime Navarro	.05	.02
☐ 570 Lance Johnson	.05	.02
☐ 571 Mike Dyer	.05	.02
☐ 572 Kevin Ritz	.05	.02
☐ 573 Dave West	.05	.02
☐ 574 Gary Mielke	.05	.02
☐ 575 Scott Lusader	.05	.02
☐ 576 Joe Oliver	.05	.02
☐ 577 Sandy Alomar Jr.	.20	.09
☐ 578 Andy Benes UER	.20	.09
(Extra comma between day and year)		
☐ 579 Tim Jones	.05	.02

☐ 580 Randy McCament	.05	.02
☐ 581 Curt Schilling	.20	.09
☐ 582 John Orton	.05	.02
☐ 583A Milt Cuyler ERR	.50	.23
(998 games)		
☐ 583B Milt Cuyler COR	.05	.02
(98 games; the extra 9 was ghosted out and may still be visible)		
☐ 584 Eric Anthony	.10	.05
☐ 585 Greg Vaughn	.10	.05
☐ 586 Deion Sanders	.20	.09
☐ 587 Jose DeJesus	.05	.02
☐ 588 Chip Hale	.05	.02
☐ 589 John Olerud	.20	.09
☐ 590 Steve Olin	.10	.05
☐ 591 Marquis Grissom	.40	.18
☐ 592 Moises Alou	.50	.23
☐ 593 Mark Lemke	.05	.02
☐ 594 Dean Palmer	.25	.11
☐ 595 Robin Ventura	.20	.09
☐ 596 Tino Martinez	.40	.18
☐ 597 Mike Huff	.05	.02
☐ 598 Scott Hemond	.05	.02
☐ 599 Wally Whitehurst	.05	.02
☐ 600 Todd Zeile	.10	.05
☐ 601 Glenallen Hill	.05	.02
☐ 602 Hal Morris	.05	.02
☐ 603 Juan Bell	.05	.02
☐ 604 Bobby Rose	.05	.02
☐ 605 Matt Merullo	.05	.02
☐ 606 Kevin Maas	.10	.05
☐ 607 Randy Nosek	.05	.02
☐ 608A Billy Bates	.05	.02
(Text mentions 12 triples in tenth line)		
☐ 608B Billy Bates	.05	.02
(Text has no mention of triples)		
☐ 609 Mike Stanton	.05	.02
☐ 610 Mauro Gozzo	.05	.02
☐ 611 Charles Nagy	.20	.09
☐ 612 Scott Coolbaugh	.05	.02
☐ 613 Jose Vizcaino	.20	.09
☐ 614 Greg Smith	.05	.02
☐ 615 Jeff Huson	.05	.02
☐ 616 Mickey Weston	.05	.02
☐ 617 John Pawlowski	.05	.02
☐ 618A Joe Skalski ERR	.05	.02
(27 on back)		
☐ 618B Joe Skalski COR	.50	.23
(67 on back)		
☐ 619 Bernie Williams	.75	.35
☐ 620 Shawn Holman	.05	.02
☐ 621 Gary Eave	.05	.02
☐ 622 Darrin Fletcher UER	.10	.05
(Elmherst, should be Elmhurst)		
☐ 623 Pat Combs	.05	.02
☐ 624 Mike Blowers	.20	.09
☐ 625 Kevin Appier	.20	.09
☐ 626 Pat Austin	.05	.02
☐ 627 Kelly Mann	.05	.02
☐ 628 Matt Kinzer	.05	.02
☐ 629 Chris Hammond	.05	.02
☐ 630 Dean Wilkins	.05	.02
☐ 631 Larry Walker UER	1.00	.45
(Uniform number 55 on front and 33 on back; Home is Maple Ridge, not Maple River)		
☐ 632 Blaine Beatty	.05	.02
☐ 633A Tommy Barrett ERR	.05	.02
(29 on back)		
☐ 633B Tommy Barrett COR	.50	.23
(14 on back)		
☐ 634 Stan Belinda	.05	.02
☐ 635 Mike (Tex) Smith	.05	.02
☐ 636 Hensley Meulens	.05	.02
☐ 637 Juan Gonzalez UER	2.00	.90
(Sarasots on back, should be Sarasota)		
☐ 638 Lenny Webster	.05	.02
☐ 639 Mark Gardner	.05	.02
☐ 640 Tommy Greene	.05	.02
☐ 641 Mike Hartley	.05	.02

☐ 642 Phil Stephenson	.05	.02
☐ 643 Kevin Mmahat	.05	.02
☐ 644 Ed Whited	.05	.02
☐ 645 Delino DeShields	.20	.09
☐ 646 Kevin Blankenship	.05	.02
☐ 647 Paul Sorrento	.20	.09
☐ 648 Mike Roesler	.05	.02
☐ 649 Jason Grimsley	.05	.02
☐ 650 Dave Justice	.75	.35
☐ 651 Scott Cooper	.05	.02
☐ 652 Dave Eiland	.05	.02
☐ 653 Mike Munoz	.05	.02
☐ 654 Jeff Fischer	.05	.02
☐ 655 Terry Jorgensen	.05	.02
☐ 656 George Canale	.05	.02
☐ 657 Brian DuBois UER	.05	.02
(Misspelled Dubois on card)		
☐ 658 Carlos Quintana	.05	.02
☐ 659 Luis de los Santos	.05	.02
☐ 660 Jerald Clark	.05	.02
☐ 661 Donald Harris DC	.05	.02
☐ 662 Paul Coleman DC	.05	.02
☐ 663 Frank Thomas DC	4.00	1.80
☐ 664 Brent Mayne DC	.05	.02
☐ 665 Eddie Zosky DC	.05	.02
☐ 666 Steve Hosey DC	.05	.02
☐ 667 Scott Bryant DC	.05	.02
☐ 668 Tom Goodwin DC	.20	.09
☐ 669 Cal Eldred DC	.20	.09
☐ 670 Earl Cunningham DC	.05	.02
☐ 671 Alan Zinter DC	.05	.02
☐ 672 Chuck Knoblauch DC	.75	.35
☐ 673 Kyle Abbott DC	.05	.02
☐ 674 Roger Salkeld DC	.05	.02
☐ 675 Maurice Vaughn DC	1.25	.55
☐ 676 Keith(Kiki) Jones DC	.05	.02
☐ 677 Tyler Houston DC	.20	.09
☐ 678 Jeff Jackson DC	.05	.02
☐ 679 Greg Gohr DC	.05	.02
☐ 680 Ben McDonald DC	.15	.07
☐ 681 Greg Blosser DC	.05	.02
☐ 682 Willie Greene DC UER	.15	.07
Name spelled as Green		
☐ 683A Wade Boggs DT ERR	.10	.05
(Text says 215 hits in '89, should be 205)		
☐ 683B Wade Boggs DT	.10	.05
(Text says 205 hits in '89)		
☐ 684 Will Clark DT	.20	.09
☐ 685 Tony Gwynn DT UER	.25	.11
(Text reads battling instead of batting)		
☐ 686 Rickey Henderson DT	.10	.05
☐ 687 Bo Jackson DT	.20	.09
☐ 688 Mark Langston DT	.05	.02
☐ 689 Barry Larkin DT	.10	.05
☐ 690 Kirby Puckett DT	.20	.09
☐ 691 Ryne Sandberg DT	.20	.09
☐ 692 Mike Scott DT	.05	.02
☐ 693A Terry Steinbach DT	.05	.02
ERR (cathers)		
☐ 693B Terry Steinbach DT	.05	.02
COR (catchers)		
☐ 694 Bobby Thigpen DT	.05	.02
☐ 695 Mitch Williams DT	.05	.02
☐ 696 Nolan Ryan HL	.40	.18
☐ 697 Bo Jackson FB/BB	.50	.23
☐ 698 Rickey Henderson	.10	.05
ALCS-MVP		
☐ 699 Will Clark	.20	.09
NLCS-MVP		
☐ 700 WS Games 1/2	.10	.05
(Dave Stewart Mike Moore)		
☐ 701 Lights Out	.20	.09
Candlestick 5:04pm (10/17/89)		
☐ 702 WS Game 3	.20	.09
Bashers Blast Giants (Carney Lansford, Rickey Henderson, Jose Canseco, Dave Henderson)		
☐ 703 WS Game 4/Wrap-up	.05	.02
A's Sweep Battle of		

of the Bay
(A's Celebrate)
☐ 704 Wade Boggs HL .... .10   .05
Wade Raps 200

1990 Score Rookie Dream Team

A ten-card set of Dream Team Rookies was inserted only into hobby factory sets. These standard size cards carry a B prefix on the card number and include a player at each position plus a commemorative card honoring the late Baseball Commissioner A. Bartlett Giamatti.

	MINT	NRMT
COMPLETE SET (10)	4.00	1.80
COMMON CARD (B1-10)	.25	.11
ONE SET PER HOBBY FACTORY SET		
☐ B1 A.Bartlett Giamatti	.50	.23
COMM MEM		
☐ B2 Pat Combs	.25	.11
☐ B3 Todd Zeile	.30	.14
☐ B4 Luis de los Santos	.25	.11
☐ B5 Mark Lemke	.25	.11
☐ B6 Robin Ventura	.50	.23
☐ B7 Jeff Huson	.25	.11
☐ B8 Greg Vaughn	.30	.14
☐ B9 Marquis Grissom	1.50	.70
☐ B10 Eric Anthony	.25	.11

1990 Score Rookie/Traded

The standard-size 110-card 1990 Score Rookie and Traded set marked the third consecutive year Score had issued an end of the year set to note trades and give rookies early cards. The set was issued through hobby accounts and only in factory set form. The first

66 cards are traded players while the last 44 cards are rookie cards. Hockey star Eric Lindros is included in this set. Rookie cards in the set include Carlos Baerga, Derek Bell, Todd Hundley and Ray Lankford.

	MINT	NRMT
COMPLETE SET (110)	6.00	2.70
COMMON CARD (1T-110T)	.05	.02
MINOR STARS	.10	.05
UNLISTED STARS	.20	.09
☐ 1T Dave Winfield	.20	.09
☐ 2T Kevin Bass	.05	.02
☐ 3T Nick Esasky	.05	.02
☐ 4T Mitch Webster	.05	.02
☐ 5T Pascual Perez	.05	.02
☐ 6T Gary Pettis	.05	.02
☐ 7T Tony Pena	.05	.02
☐ 8T Candy Maldonado	.05	.02
☐ 9T Cecil Fielder	.10	.05
☐ 10T Carmelo Martinez	.05	.02
☐ 11T Mark Langston	.05	.02
☐ 12T Dave Parker	.10	.05
☐ 13T Don Slaught	.05	.02
☐ 14T Tony Phillips	.05	.02
☐ 15T John Franco	.10	.05
☐ 16T Randy Myers	.10	.05
☐ 17T Jeff Reardon	.10	.05
☐ 18T Sandy Alomar Jr.	.20	.09
☐ 19T Joe Carter	.20	.09
☐ 20T Fred Lynn	.05	.02
☐ 21T Storm Davis	.05	.02
☐ 22T Craig Lefferts	.05	.02
☐ 23T Pete O'Brien	.05	.02
☐ 24T Dennis Boyd	.05	.02
☐ 25T Lloyd Moseby	.05	.02
☐ 26T Mark Davis	.05	.02
☐ 27T Tim Leary	.05	.02
☐ 28T Gerald Perry	.05	.02
☐ 29T Don Aase	.05	.02
☐ 30T Ernie Whitt	.05	.02
☐ 31T Dale Murphy	.20	.09
☐ 32T Alejandro Pena	.05	.02
☐ 33T Juan Samuel	.05	.02
☐ 34T Hubie Brooks	.05	.02
☐ 35T Gary Carter	.20	.09
☐ 36T Jim Presley	.05	.02
☐ 37T Wally Backman	.05	.02
☐ 38T Matt Nokes	.05	.02
☐ 39T Dan Petry	.05	.02
☐ 40T Franklin Stubbs	.05	.02
☐ 41T Jeff Huson	.05	.02
☐ 42T Billy Hatcher	.05	.02
☐ 43T Terry Leach	.05	.02
☐ 44T Phil Bradley	.05	.02
☐ 45T Claudell Washington	.05	.02
☐ 46T Luis Polonia	.05	.02
☐ 47T Daryl Boston	.05	.02
☐ 48T Lee Smith	.10	.05
☐ 49T Tom Brunansky	.05	.02
☐ 50T Mike Witt	.05	.02
☐ 51T Willie Randolph	.10	.05
☐ 52T Stan Javier	.05	.02
☐ 53T Brad Komminsk	.05	.02
☐ 54T John Candelaria	.05	.02
☐ 55T Bryn Smith	.05	.02
☐ 56T Glenn Braggs	.05	.02
☐ 57T Keith Hernandez	.10	.05
☐ 58T Ken Oberkfell	.05	.02
☐ 59T Steve Jeltz	.05	.02
☐ 60T Chris James	.05	.02
☐ 61T Scott Sanderson	.05	.02
☐ 62T Bill Long	.05	.02
☐ 63T Rick Cerone	.05	.02
☐ 64T Scott Bailes	.05	.02
☐ 65T Larry Sheets	.05	.02
☐ 66T Junior Ortiz	.05	.02
☐ 67T Francisco Cabrera	.05	.02
☐ 68T DiSarcina	.20	.09
☐ 69T Greg Olson	.05	.02
☐ 70T Beau Allred	.05	.02
☐ 71T Oscar Azocar	.05	.02

☐ 72T Kent Mercker	.10	.05
☐ 73T John Burkett	.10	.05
☐ 74T Carlos Baerga	.25	.11
☐ 75T Dave Hollins	.20	.09
☐ 76T Todd Hundley	.40	.18
☐ 77T Rick Parker	.05	.02
☐ 78T Steve Cummings	.05	.02
☐ 79T Bill Sampen	.05	.02
☐ 80T Jerry Kutzler	.05	.02
☐ 81T Derek Bell	.25	.11
☐ 82T Kevin Tapani	.10	.05
☐ 83T Jim Leyritz	.20	.09
☐ 84T Ray Lankford	.50	.23
☐ 85T Wayne Edwards	.05	.02
☐ 86T Frank Thomas	4.00	1.80
☐ 87T Tim Naehring	.20	.09
☐ 88T Willie Blair	.05	.02
☐ 89T Alan Mills	.05	.02
☐ 90T Scott Radinsky	.05	.02
☐ 91T Howard Farmer	.05	.02
☐ 92T Julio Machado	.05	.02
☐ 93T Rafael Valdez	.05	.02
☐ 94T Shawn Boskie	.05	.02
☐ 95T David Segui	.20	.09
☐ 96T Chris Hoiles	.20	.09
☐ 97T D.J. Dozier	.10	.05
☐ 98T Hector Villanueva	.05	.02
☐ 99T Eric Gunderson	.05	.02
☐ 100T Eric Lindros	1.50	.70
☐ 101T Dave Otto	.05	.02
☐ 102T Dana Kiecker	.05	.02
☐ 103T Tim Drummond	.05	.02
☐ 104T Mickey Pina	.05	.02
☐ 105T Craig Grebeck	.05	.02
☐ 106T Bernard Gilkey	.25	.11
☐ 107T Tim Layana	.05	.02
☐ 108T Scott Chiamparino	.05	.02
☐ 109T Steve Avery	.05	.02
☐ 110T Terry Shumpert	.05	.02

1991 Score

The 1991 Score set contains 893 standard-size cards issued in two separate series of 441 and 452 cards each. This set marks the fourth consecutive year that Score has issued a major set but the first time Score issued the set in two series. Cards were distributed in plastic-wrap packs, blister packs and factory sets. The card fronts feature one of four different solid color borders (black, blue, teal and white) framing the full-color photo of the cards. Subsets include Rookie Prospects (331-379), First Draft Picks (380-391, 671-682), AL All-Stars (392-401), Master Blasters (402-406, 689-693), K-Men (407-411, 684-688), Rifleman (412-416, 694-698), NL All-Stars (661-670), No-Hitters (699-707), Franchise (849-874), Award Winners (875-

881) and Dream Team (882-893). An American Flag card (737) was issued to honor the American soldiers involved in Desert Storm. Rookie Cards in the set include Jeff Conine, Chipper Jones, Brian McRae, Mike Mussina and Rondell White. There are a number of pitchers whose card backs show Innings Pitched totals which do not equal the added year-by-year total; the following card numbers were affected, 4, 24, 29, 30, 51, 81, 109, 111, 118, 141, 150, 156, 177, 204, 218, 232, 235, 255, 287, 289, 311, and 328.

	MINT	NRMT
COMPLETE SET (893)	10.00	4.50
COMP.FACT.SET (900)	20.00	9.00
COMMON CARD (1-893)	.05	.02
MINOR STARS	.10	.05
UNLISTED STARS	.20	.09
SUBSET CARDS HALF VALUE OF BASE CARDS		
COMP.MANTLE SET (7)	250.00	110.00
COMMON MANTLE (1-7)	40.00	18.00
MANTLE AUTO (AU)	500.00	220.00
MANTLE: RANDOM INSERTS IN SER.2 PACKS		

☐ 1 Jose Canseco .15 .07
☐ 2 Ken Griffey Jr. 1.50 .70
☐ 3 Ryne Sandberg .25 .11
☐ 4 Nolan Ryan .75 .35
☐ 5 Bo Jackson .15 .07
☐ 6 Bret Saberhagen UER .05 .02
(In bio, missed misspelled as mised)
☐ 7 Will Clark .20 .09
☐ 8 Ellis Burks .10 .05
☐ 9 Joe Carter .10 .05
☐ 10 Rickey Henderson .20 .09
☐ 11 Ozzie Guillen .05 .02
☐ 12 Wade Boggs .20 .09
☐ 13 Jerome Walton .05 .02
☐ 14 John Franco .10 .05
☐ 15 Ricky Jordan UER .05 .02
(League misspelled as legue)
☐ 16 Wally Backman .05 .02
☐ 17 Rob Dibble .05 .02
☐ 18 Glenn Braggs .05 .02
☐ 19 Cory Snyder .05 .02
☐ 20 Kal Daniels .05 .02
☐ 21 Mark Langston .05 .02
☐ 22 Kevin Gross .05 .02
☐ 23 Don Mattingly UER .30 .14
(First line, ' is missing from Yankee)
☐ 24 Dave Righetti .05 .02
☐ 25 Roberto Alomar .20 .09
☐ 26 Robby Thompson .05 .02
☐ 27 Jack McDowell .05 .02
☐ 28 Bip Roberts UER .05 .02
(Bio reads playd)
☐ 29 Jay Howell .05 .02
☐ 30 Dave Stieb UER .05 .02
(17 wins in bio, 18 in stats)
☐ 31 Johnny Ray .05 .02
☐ 32 Steve Sax .05 .02
☐ 33 Terry Mulholland .05 .02
☐ 34 Lee Guetterman .05 .02
☐ 35 Tim Raines .10 .05
☐ 36 Scott Fletcher .05 .02
☐ 37 Lance Parrish .05 .02
☐ 38 Tony Phillips UER .05 .02
(Born 4/15, should be 4/25)
☐ 39 Todd Stottlemyre .05 .02
☐ 40 Alan Trammell .15 .07
☐ 41 Todd Burns .05 .02
☐ 42 Mookie Wilson .10 .05
☐ 43 Chris Bosio .05 .02
☐ 44 Jeffrey Leonard .05 .02

☐ 45 Doug Jones .05 .02
☐ 46 Mike Scott UER .05 .02
(In first line, dominate should read dominating)
☐ 47 Andy Hawkins .05 .02
☐ 48 Harold Reynolds .05 .02
☐ 49 Paul Molitor .20 .09
☐ 50 John Farrell .05 .02
☐ 51 Danny Darwin .05 .02
☐ 52 Jeff Blauser .05 .02
☐ 53 John Tudor UER .05 .02
(41 wins in '81)
☐ 54 Milt Thompson .05 .02
☐ 55 Dave Justice .25 .11
☐ 56 Greg Olson .05 .02
☐ 57 Willie Blair .05 .02
☐ 58 Rick Parker .05 .02
☐ 59 Shawn Boskie .05 .02
☐ 60 Kevin Tapani .05 .02
☐ 61 Dave Hollins .05 .02
☐ 62 Scott Radinsky .05 .02
☐ 63 Francisco Cabrera .05 .02
☐ 64 Tim Layana .05 .02
☐ 65 Jim Leyritz .10 .05
☐ 66 Wayne Edwards .05 .02
☐ 67 Lee Stevens .05 .02
☐ 68 Bill Sampen UER .05 .02
(Fourth line, long is spelled along)
☐ 69 Craig Grebeck UER .05 .02
(Born in Cerritos, not Johnstown)
☐ 70 John Burkett .05 .02
☐ 71 Hector Villanueva .05 .02
☐ 72 Oscar Azocar .05 .02
☐ 73 Alan Mills .05 .02
☐ 74 Carlos Baerga .10 .05
☐ 75 Charles Nagy .20 .09
☐ 76 Tim Drummond .05 .02
☐ 77 Dana Kiecker .05 .02
☐ 78 Tom Edens .05 .02
☐ 79 Kent Mercker .05 .02
☐ 80 Steve Avery .15 .07
☐ 81 Lee Smith .10 .05
☐ 82 Dave Martinez .05 .02
☐ 83 Dave Winfield .20 .09
☐ 84 Bill Spiers .05 .02
☐ 85 Dan Pasqua .05 .02
☐ 86 Randy Milligan .05 .02
☐ 87 Tracy Jones .05 .02
☐ 88 Greg Myers .05 .02
☐ 89 Keith Hernandez .10 .05
☐ 90 Todd Benzinger .05 .02
☐ 91 Mike Jackson .05 .02
☐ 92 Mike Stanley .05 .02
☐ 93 Candy Maldonado .05 .02
☐ 94 John Kruk UER .10 .05
(No decimal point before 1990 BA)
☐ 95 Cal Ripken UER .75 .35
(Genius spelled genuis)
☐ 96 Willie Fraser .05 .02
☐ 97 Mike Felder .05 .02
☐ 98 Bill Landrum .05 .02
☐ 99 Chuck Crim .05 .02
☐ 100 Chuck Finley .10 .05
☐ 101 Kent Manwaring .05 .02
☐ 102 Jaime Navarro .05 .02
☐ 103 Dickie Thon .05 .02
☐ 104 Brian Downing .05 .02
☐ 105 Jim Abbott .05 .02
☐ 106 Tom Brookens .05 .02
☐ 107 Darryl Hamilton UER .05 .02
(Bio info is for Jeff Hamilton)
☐ 108 Bryan Harvey .05 .02
☐ 109 Greg A. Harris UER .05 .02
(Shown pitching lefty, bio says righty)
☐ 110 Gregg Swindell .05 .02
☐ 111 Juan Berenguer .05 .02
☐ 112 Mike Heath .05 .02
☐ 113 Scott Bradley .05 .02
☐ 114 Jack Morris .10 .05
☐ 115 Barry Jones .05 .02

☐ 116 Kevin Romine .05 .02
☐ 117 Garry Templeton .05 .02
☐ 118 Scott Sanderson .05 .02
☐ 119 Roberto Kelly .05 .02
☐ 120 George Brett .40 .18
☐ 121 Oddibe McDowell .05 .02
☐ 122 Jim Acker .05 .02
☐ 123 Bill Swift UER .05 .02
(Born 12/27/61, should be 10/27)
☐ 124 Eric King .05 .02
☐ 125 Jay Buhner .20 .09
☐ 126 Matt Young .05 .02
☐ 127 Alvaro Espinoza .05 .02
☐ 128 Greg Hibbard .05 .02
☐ 129 Jeff M. Robinson .05 .02
☐ 130 Mike Greenwell .05 .02
☐ 131 Dion James .05 .02
☐ 132 Donn Pall UER .05 .02
(1988 ERA in stats 0.00)
☐ 133 Lloyd Moseby .05 .02
☐ 134 Randy Velarde .05 .02
☐ 135 Allan Anderson .05 .02
☐ 136 Mark Davis .05 .02
☐ 137 Eric Davis .10 .05
☐ 138 Phil Stephenson .05 .02
☐ 139 Felix Fermin .05 .02
☐ 140 Pedro Guerrero .05 .02
☐ 141 Charlie Hough .05 .02
☐ 142 Mike Henneman .05 .02
☐ 143 Jeff Montgomery .10 .05
☐ 144 Lenny Harris .05 .02
☐ 145 Bruce Hurst .05 .02
☐ 146 Eric Anthony .05 .02
☐ 147 Paul Assenmacher .05 .02
☐ 148 Jesse Barfield .05 .02
☐ 149 Carlos Quintana .05 .02
☐ 150 Dave Stewart .10 .05
☐ 151 Roy Smith .05 .02
☐ 152 Paul Gibson .05 .02
☐ 153 Mickey Hatcher .05 .02
☐ 154 Jim Eisenreich .05 .02
☐ 155 Kenny Rogers .05 .02
☐ 156 Dave Schmidt .05 .02
☐ 157 Lance Johnson .05 .02
☐ 158 Dave West .05 .02
☐ 159 Steve Balboni .05 .02
☐ 160 Jeff Brantley .05 .02
☐ 161 Craig Biggio .20 .09
☐ 162 Brook Jacoby .05 .02
☐ 163 Dan Gladden .05 .02
☐ 164 Jeff Reardon UER .10 .05
(Total IP shown as 943.2, should be 943.1)
☐ 165 Mark Carreon .05 .02
☐ 166 Mel Hall .05 .02
☐ 167 Gary Mielke .05 .02
☐ 168 Cecil Fielder .05 .02
☐ 169 Darrin Jackson .05 .02
☐ 170 Rick Aguilera .10 .05
☐ 171 Walt Weiss .05 .02
☐ 172 Steve Farr .05 .02
☐ 173 Jody Reed .05 .02
☐ 174 Mike Jeffcoat .05 .02
☐ 175 Mark Grace .20 .09
☐ 176 Larry Sheets .05 .02
☐ 177 Bill Gullickson .05 .02
☐ 178 Chris Gwynn .05 .02
☐ 179 Melido Perez .05 .02
☐ 180 Sid Fernandez UER .05 .02
(779 runs in 1990)
☐ 181 Tim Burke .05 .02
☐ 182 Gary Pettis .05 .02
☐ 183 Rob Murphy .05 .02
☐ 184 Craig Lefferts .05 .02
☐ 185 Howard Johnson .05 .02
☐ 186 Ken Caminiti .20 .09
☐ 187 Tim Belcher .05 .02
☐ 188 Greg Cadaret .05 .02
☐ 189 Matt Williams .20 .09
☐ 190 Dave Magadan .05 .02
☐ 191 Geno Petralli .05 .02
☐ 192 Jeff D. Robinson .05 .02
☐ 193 Jim Deshaies .05 .02
☐ 194 Willie Randolph .10 .05
☐ 195 George Bell .05 .02

☐ 196	Hubie Brooks	.05	.02
☐ 197	Tom Gordon	.05	.02
☐ 198	Mike Fitzgerald	.05	.02
☐ 199	Mike Pagliarulo	.05	.02
☐ 200	Kirby Puckett	.40	.18
☐ 201	Shawon Dunston	.05	.02
☐ 202	Dennis Boyd	.05	.02
☐ 203	Junior Felix UER	.05	.02
	(Text has him in NL)		
☐ 204	Alejandro Pena	.05	.02
☐ 205	Pete Smith	.05	.02
☐ 206	Tom Glavine UER	.20	.09
	(Lefty spelled leftie)		
☐ 207	Luis Salazar	.05	.02
☐ 208	John Smoltz	.20	.09
☐ 209	Doug Dascenzo	.05	.02
☐ 210	Tim Wallach	.05	.02
☐ 211	Greg Gagne	.05	.02
☐ 212	Mark Gubicza	.05	.02
☐ 213	Mark Parent	.05	.02
☐ 214	Ken Oberkfell	.05	.02
☐ 215	Gary Carter	.20	.09
☐ 216	Rafael Palmeiro	.20	.09
☐ 217	Tom Niedenfuer	.05	.02
☐ 218	Dave LaPoint	.05	.02
☐ 219	Jeff Treadway	.05	.02
☐ 220	Mitch Williams UER	.05	.02
	('89 ERA shown as 2.76, should be 2.64)		
☐ 221	Jose DeLeon	.05	.02
☐ 222	Mike LaValliere	.05	.02
☐ 223	Darrel Akerfelds	.05	.02
☐ 224A	Kent Anderson ERR	.10	.05
	(First line, flachy should read flashy)		
☐ 224B	Kent Anderson COR	.10	.05
	(Corrected in factory sets)		
☐ 225	Dwight Evans	.10	.05
☐ 226	Gary Redus	.05	.02
☐ 227	Paul O'Neill	.10	.05
☐ 228	Marty Barrett	.05	.02
☐ 229	Tom Browning	.05	.02
☐ 230	Terry Pendleton	.10	.05
☐ 231	Jack Armstrong	.05	.02
☐ 232	Mike Boddicker	.05	.02
☐ 233	Neal Heaton	.05	.02
☐ 234	Marquis Grissom	.20	.09
☐ 235	Bert Blyleven	.10	.05
☐ 236	Curt Young	.05	.02
☐ 237	Don Carman	.05	.02
☐ 238	Charlie Hayes	.05	.02
☐ 239	Mark Knudson	.05	.02
☐ 240	Todd Zeile	.10	.05
☐ 241	Larry Walker UER	.30	.14
	(Maple River, should be Maple Ridge)		
☐ 242	Jerald Clark	.05	.02
☐ 243	Jeff Ballard	.05	.02
☐ 244	Jeff King	.10	.05
☐ 245	Tom Brunansky	.05	.02
☐ 246	Darren Daulton	.10	.05
☐ 247	Scott Terry	.05	.02
☐ 248	Rob Deer	.05	.02
☐ 249	Brady Anderson UER	.20	.09
	(1990 Hagerstown 1 hit, should say 13 hits)		
☐ 250	Len Dykstra	.10	.05
☐ 251	Greg W. Harris	.05	.02
☐ 252	Mike Hartley	.05	.02
☐ 253	Joey Cora	.15	.07
☐ 254	Ivan Calderon	.05	.02
☐ 255	Ted Power	.05	.02
☐ 256	Sammy Sosa	.25	.11
☐ 257	Steve Buechele	.05	.02
☐ 258	Mike Devereaux UER	.05	.02
	(No comma between city and state)		
☐ 259	Brad Komminsk UER	.05	.02
	(Last text line, Ba should be BA)		
☐ 260	Teddy Higuera	.05	.02
☐ 261	Shawn Abner	.05	.02
☐ 262	Dave Valle	.05	.02
☐ 263	Jeff Huson	.05	.02
☐ 264	Edgar Martinez	.20	.09
☐ 265	Carlton Fisk	.20	.09
☐ 266	Steve Finley	.20	.09
☐ 267	John Wetteland	.20	.09
☐ 268	Kevin Appier	.20	.09
☐ 269	Steve Lyons	.05	.02
☐ 270	Mickey Tettleton	.10	.05
☐ 271	Luis Rivera	.05	.02
☐ 272	Steve Jeltz	.05	.02
☐ 273	R.J. Reynolds	.05	.02
☐ 274	Carlos Martinez	.05	.02
☐ 275	Dan Plesac	.05	.02
☐ 276	Mike Morgan UER	.05	.02
	(Total IP shown as 1149.1, should be 1149)		
☐ 277	Jeff Russell	.05	.02
☐ 278	Pete Incaviglia	.05	.02
☐ 279	Kevin Seitzer UER	.05	.02
	(Bio has 200 hits twice and 300 four hits, should be once and three times)		
☐ 280	Bobby Thigpen	.05	.02
☐ 281	Stan Javier UER	.05	.02
	(Born 1/9, should say 9/1)		
☐ 282	Henry Cotto	.05	.02
☐ 283	Gary Wayne	.05	.02
☐ 284	Shane Mack	.05	.02
☐ 285	Brian Holman	.05	.02
☐ 286	Gerald Perry	.05	.02
☐ 287	Steve Crawford	.05	.02
☐ 288	Nelson Liriano	.05	.02
☐ 289	Don Aase	.05	.02
☐ 290	Randy Johnson	.25	.11
☐ 291	Harold Baines	.10	.05
☐ 292	Kent Hrbek	.10	.05
☐ 293A	Les Lancaster ERR	.05	.02
	(No comma between Dallas and Texas)		
☐ 293B	Les Lancaster COR	.05	.02
	(Corrected in factory sets)		
☐ 294	Jeff Musselman	.05	.02
☐ 295	Kurt Stillwell	.05	.02
☐ 296	Stan Belinda	.05	.02
☐ 297	Lou Whitaker	.10	.05
☐ 298	Glenn Wilson	.05	.02
☐ 299	Omar Vizquel UER	.20	.09
	(Born 5/15, should be 4/24, there is a decimal before GP total for '90)		
☐ 300	Ramon Martinez	.10	.05
☐ 301	Dwight Smith	.05	.02
☐ 302	Tim Crews	.05	.02
☐ 303	Lance Blankenship	.05	.02
☐ 304	Sid Bream	.05	.02
☐ 305	Rafael Ramirez	.05	.02
☐ 306	Steve Wilson	.05	.02
☐ 307	Mackey Sasser	.05	.02
☐ 308	Franklin Stubbs	.05	.02
☐ 309	Jack Daugherty UER	.05	.02
	(Born 6/3/60, should say July)		
☐ 310	Eddie Murray	.20	.09
☐ 311	Bob Welch	.05	.02
☐ 312	Brian Harper	.05	.02
☐ 313	Lance McCullers	.05	.02
☐ 314	Dave Smith	.05	.02
☐ 315	Bobby Bonilla	.10	.05
☐ 316	Jerry Don Gleaton	.05	.02
☐ 317	Greg Maddux	.60	.25
☐ 318	Keith Miller	.05	.02
☐ 319	Mark Portugal	.05	.02
☐ 320	Robin Ventura	.20	.09
☐ 321	Bob Ojeda	.05	.02
☐ 322	Mike Harkey	.05	.02
☐ 323	Jay Bell	.10	.05
☐ 324	Mark McGwire	.40	.18
☐ 325	Gary Gaetti	.05	.02
☐ 326	Jeff Pico	.05	.02
☐ 327	Kevin McReynolds	.05	.02
☐ 328	Frank Tanana	.05	.02
☐ 329	Eric Yelding UER	.05	.02
	(Listed as 6'3" should be 5'11")		
☐ 330	Barry Bonds	.25	.11
☐ 331	Brian McRae UER	.20	.09
	(No comma between city and state)		
☐ 332	Pedro Munoz	.05	.02
☐ 333	Daryl Irvine	.05	.02
☐ 334	Chris Hoiles	.05	.02
☐ 335	Thomas Howard	.05	.02
☐ 336	Jeff Schulz	.05	.02
☐ 337	Jeff Manto	.05	.02
☐ 338	Beau Allred	.05	.02
☐ 339	Mike Bordick	.20	.09
☐ 340	Todd Hundley	.20	.09
☐ 341	Jim Vatcher UER	.05	.02
	(Height 6'9", should be 5'9")		
☐ 342	Luis Sojo	.05	.02
☐ 343	Jose Offerman UER	.05	.02
	(Born 1969, should say 1968)		
☐ 344	Pete Coachman	.05	.02
☐ 345	Mike Benjamin	.05	.02
☐ 346	Ozzie Canseco	.05	.02
☐ 347	Tim McIntosh	.05	.02
☐ 348	Phil Plantier	.10	.05
☐ 349	Terry Shumpert	.05	.02
☐ 350	Darren Lewis	.05	.02
☐ 351	David Walsh	.05	.02
☐ 352A	Scott Chiamparino	.10	.05
	ERR (Bats left, should be right)		
☐ 352B	Scott Chiamparino	.10	.05
	COR (corrected in factory sets)		
☐ 353	Julio Valera	.05	.02
	UER (Progressed misspelled as progressed)		
☐ 354	Anthony Telford	.05	.02
☐ 355	Kevin Wickander	.05	.02
☐ 356	Tim Naehring	.10	.05
☐ 357	Jim Poole	.05	.02
☐ 358	Mark Whiten UER	.05	.02
	(Shown hitting lefty, bio says righty)		
☐ 359	Terry Wells	.05	.02
☐ 360	Rafael Valdez	.05	.02
☐ 361	Mel Stottlemyre Jr.	.05	.02
☐ 362	David Segui	.10	.05
☐ 363	Paul Abbott	.05	.02
☐ 364	Steve Howard	.05	.02
☐ 365	Karl Rhodes	.05	.02
☐ 366	Rafael Novoa	.05	.02
☐ 367	Joe Grahe	.05	.02
☐ 368	Darren Reed	.05	.02
☐ 369	Jeff McKnight	.05	.02
☐ 370	Scott Leius	.05	.02
☐ 371	Mark Dewey	.05	.02
☐ 372	Mark Lee UER	.05	.02
	(Shown hitting lefty, bio says righty, born in Dakota, should say North Dakota)		
☐ 373	Rosario Rodriguez	.05	.02
	(Shown hitting lefty, bio says righty) UER		
☐ 374	Chuck McElroy	.05	.02
☐ 375	Mike Bell	.05	.02
☐ 376	Mickey Morandini	.05	.02
☐ 377	Bill Haselman	.05	.02
☐ 378	Dave Pavlas	.05	.02
☐ 379	Derrick May	.05	.02
☐ 380	Jeromy Burnitz FDP	.15	.07
☐ 381	Donald Peters FDP	.05	.02
☐ 382	Alex Fernandez FDP	.10	.05
☐ 383	Mike Mussina FDP	1.00	.45
☐ 384	Dan Smith FDP	.05	.02
☐ 385	Lance Dickson FDP	.05	.02
☐ 386	Carl Everett FDP	.15	.07
☐ 387	Thomas Nevers FDP	.05	.02
☐ 388	Adam Hyzdu FDP	.05	.02
☐ 389	Todd Van Poppel FDP	.30	.14
☐ 390	Rondell White FDP	.05	.02
☐ 391	Marc Newfield FDP	.15	.07
☐ 392	Julio Franco AS	.05	.02
☐ 393	Wade Boggs AS	.10	.05
☐ 394	Ozzie Guillen AS	.05	.02
☐ 395	Cecil Fielder AS	.05	.02

□			
396	Ken Griffey Jr. AS	.75	.35
397	Rickey Henderson AS	.10	.05
398	Jose Canseco AS	.05	.02
399	Roger Clemens AS	.20	.09
400	Sandy Alomar Jr. AS	.05	.02
401	Bobby Thigpen AS	.05	.02
402	Bobby Bonilla MB	.05	.02
403	Eric Davis MB	.05	.02
404	Fred McGriff MB	.10	.05
405	Glenn Davis MB	.05	.02
406	Kevin Mitchell MB	.05	.02
407	Rob Dibble KM	.05	.02
408	Ramon Martinez KM	.05	.02
409	David Cone KM	.05	.02
410	Bobby Witt KM	.05	.02
411	Mark Langston KM	.05	.02
412	Bo Jackson RIF	.10	.05
413	Shawon Dunston RIF	.05	.02
	UER (In the baseball, should say in baseball)		
414	Jesse Barfield RIF	.05	.02
415	Ken Caminiti RIF	.05	.01
416	Benito Santiago RIF	.05	.02
417	Nolan Ryan HL	.40	.18
418	Bobby Thigpen HL UER	.05	.02
	(Back refers to Hal McRae Jr., should say Brian McRae)		
419	Ramon Martinez HL	.05	.02
420	Bo Jackson HL	.10	.05
421	Carlton Fisk HL	.10	.05
422	Jimmy Key	.10	.05
423	Junior Noboa	.05	.02
424	Al Newman	.05	.02
425	Pat Borders	.05	.02
426	Von Hayes	.05	.02
427	Tim Teufel	.05	.02
428	Eric Plunk UER	.05	.02
	(Text says Eric's had, no apostrophe needed)		
429	John Moses	.05	.02
430	Mike Witt	.05	.02
431	Otis Nixon	.10	.05
432	Tony Fernandez	.05	.02
433	Rance Mulliniks	.05	.02
434	Dan Petry	.05	.02
435	Bob Geren	.05	.02
436	Steve Frey	.05	.02
437	Jamie Moyer	.05	.02
438	Junior Ortiz	.05	.02
439	Tom O'Malley	.05	.02
440	Pat Combs	.05	.02
441	Jose Canseco DT	.10	.05
442	Alfredo Griffin	.05	.02
443	Andres Galarraga	.20	.09
444	Bryn Smith	.05	.02
445	Andre Dawson	.05	.02
446	Juan Samuel	.05	.02
447	Mike Aldrete	.05	.02
448	Ron Gant	.05	.02
449	Fernando Valenzuela	.10	.05
450	Vince Coleman UER	.05	.02
	(Should say topped majors in steals four times, not three times)		
451	Kevin Mitchell	.10	.05
452	Spike Owen	.05	.02
453	Mike Bielecki	.05	.02
454	Dennis Martinez	.10	.05
455	Brett Butler	.05	.02
456	Ron Darling	.05	.02
457	Dennis Rasmussen	.05	.02
458	Ken Howell	.05	.02
459	Steve Bedrosian	.05	.02
460	Frank Viola	.05	.02
461	Jose Lind	.05	.02
462	Chris Sabo	.05	.02
463	Dante Bichette	.20	.09
464	Rick Mahler	.05	.02
465	John Smiley	.05	.02
466	Devon White	.05	.02
467	John Orton	.05	.02
468	Mike Stanton	.05	.02
469	Billy Hatcher	.05	.02
470	Wally Joyner	.05	.02
471	Gene Larkin	.05	.02

□			
472	Doug Drabek	.05	.02
473	Gary Sheffield	.20	.09
474	David Wells	.05	.02
475	Andy Van Slyke	.10	.05
476	Mike Gallego	.05	.02
477	B.J. Surhoff	.10	.05
478	Gene Nelson	.05	.02
479	Mariano Duncan	.05	.02
480	Fred McGriff	.20	.09
481	Jerry Browne	.05	.02
482	Alvin Davis	.05	.02
483	Bill Wegman	.05	.02
484	Dave Parker	.10	.05
485	Dennis Eckersley	.10	.05
486	Erik Hanson UER	.05	.02
	(Basketball misspelled as basketball)		
487	Bill Ripken	.05	.02
488	Tom Candiotti	.05	.02
489	Mike Schooler	.05	.02
490	Gregg Olson	.05	.02
491	Chris James	.05	.02
492	Pete Harnisch	.05	.02
493	Julio Franco	.05	.02
494	Greg Briley	.05	.02
495	Ruben Sierra	.20	.09
496	Steve Olin	.05	.02
497	Mike Fetters	.05	.02
498	Mark Williamson	.05	.02
499	Bob Tewksbury	.05	.02
500	Tony Gwynn	.50	.23
501	Randy Myers	.05	.02
502	Keith Comstock	.05	.02
503	Craig Worthington UER	.05	.02
	(DeCinces misspelled DiCinces on back)		
504	Mark Eichhorn UER	.05	.02
	(Stats incomplete, doesn't have '89 Braves stint)		
505	Barry Larkin	.15	.07
506	Dave Johnson	.05	.02
507	Bobby Witt	.05	.02
508	Joe Orsulak	.05	.02
509	Pete O'Brien	.05	.02
510	Brad Arnsberg	.05	.02
511	Storm Davis	.05	.02
512	Bob Milacki	.05	.02
513	Bill Pecota	.05	.02
514	Glenallen Hill	.05	.02
515	Danny Tartabull	.05	.02
516	Mike Moore	.05	.02
517	Ron Robinson UER	.05	.02
	(577 K's in 1990)		
518	Mark Gardner	.05	.02
519	Rick Wrona	.05	.02
520	Mike Scioscia	.05	.02
521	Frank Wills	.05	.02
522	Greg Brock	.05	.02
523	Jack Clark	.10	.05
524	Bruce Ruffin	.05	.02
525	Robin Yount	.20	.09
526	Tom Foley	.05	.02
527	Pat Perry	.05	.02
528	Greg Vaughn	.05	.02
529	Wally Whitehurst	.05	.02
530	Norm Charlton	.05	.02
531	Marvell Wynne	.05	.02
532	Jim Gantner	.05	.02
533	Greg Litton	.05	.02
534	Manny Lee	.05	.02
535	Scott Bailes	.05	.02
536	Charlie Leibrandt	.05	.02
537	Roger McDowell	.05	.02
538	Andy Benes	.10	.05
539	Rick Honeycutt	.05	.02
540	Dwight Gooden	.10	.05
541	Scott Garrelts	.05	.02
542	Dave Clark	.05	.02
543	Lonnie Smith	.05	.02
544	Rick Reuschel	.05	.02
545	Delino DeShields UER	.05	.02
	(Rockford misspelled as Rock Ford in '88)		
546	Mike Sharperson	.05	.02
547	Mike Kingery	.05	.02

□			
548	Terry Kennedy	.05	.02
549	David Cone	.10	.05
550	Orel Hershiser	.10	.05
551	Matt Nokes	.05	.02
552	Eddie Williams	.05	.02
553	Frank DiPino	.05	.02
554	Fred Lynn	.05	.02
555	Alex Cole	.05	.02
556	Terry Leach	.05	.02
557	Chet Lemon	.05	.02
558	Paul Mirabella	.05	.02
559	Bill Long	.05	.02
560	Phil Bradley	.05	.02
561	Duane Ward	.05	.02
562	Dave Bergman	.05	.02
563	Eric Show	.05	.02
564	Xavier Hernandez	.05	.02
565	Jeff Parrett	.05	.02
566	Chuck Cary	.05	.02
567	Ken Hill	.10	.05
568	Bob Welch Hand	.05	.02
	(Complement should be compliment) UER		
569	John Mitchell	.05	.02
570	Travis Fryman	.20	.09
571	Derek Lilliquist	.05	.02
572	Steve Lake	.05	.02
573	John Barfield	.05	.02
574	Randy Bush	.05	.02
575	Joe Magrane	.05	.02
576	Eddie Diaz	.05	.02
577	Casey Candaele	.05	.02
578	Jesse Orosco	.05	.02
579	Tom Henke	.05	.02
580	Rick Cerone UER	.05	.02
	(Actually his third go-round with Yankees)		
581	Drew Hall	.05	.02
582	Tony Castillo	.05	.02
583	Jimmy Jones	.05	.02
584	Rick Reed	.05	.02
585	Joe Girardi	.10	.05
586	Jeff Gray	.05	.02
587	Luis Polonia	.05	.02
588	Joe Klink	.05	.02
589	Rex Hudler	.05	.02
590	Kirk McCaskill	.05	.02
591	Juan Agosto	.05	.02
592	Wes Gardner	.05	.02
593	Rich Rodriguez	.05	.02
594	Mitch Webster	.05	.02
595	Kelly Gruber	.05	.02
596	Dale Mohorcic	.05	.02
597	Willie McGee	.05	.02
598	Bill Krueger	.05	.02
599	Bob Walk UER	.05	.02
	(Cards says he's 33, but actually he's 34)		
600	Kevin Maas	.05	.02
601	Danny Jackson	.05	.02
602	Craig McMurtry UER	.05	.02
	(Anonymously misspelled anonimously)		
603	Curtis Wilkerson	.05	.02
604	Adam Peterson	.05	.02
605	Sam Horn	.05	.02
606	Tommy Gregg	.05	.02
607	Ken Dayley	.05	.02
608	Carmelo Castillo	.05	.02
609	John Shelby	.05	.02
610	Don Slaught	.05	.02
611	Calvin Schiraldi	.05	.02
612	Dennis Lamp	.05	.02
613	Andres Thomas	.05	.02
614	Jose Gonzalez	.05	.02
615	Randy Ready	.05	.02
616	Kevin Bass	.05	.02
617	Mike Marshall	.05	.02
618	Daryl Boston	.05	.02
619	Andy McGaffigan	.05	.02
620	Joe Oliver	.05	.02
621	Jim Gott	.05	.02
622	Jose Oquendo	.05	.02
623	Jose DeJesus	.05	.02
624	Mike Brumley	.05	.02
625	John Olerud	.10	.05

☐ 626	Ernest Riles	.05	.02
☐ 627	Gene Harris	.05	.02
☐ 628	Jose Uribe	.05	.02
☐ 629	Darnell Coles	.05	.02
☐ 630	Carney Lansford	.10	.05
☐ 631	Tim Leary	.05	.02
☐ 632	Tim Hulett	.05	.02
☐ 633	Kevin Elster	.05	.02
☐ 634	Tony Fossas	.05	.02
☐ 635	Francisco Oliveras	.05	.02
☐ 636	Bob Patterson	.05	.02
☐ 637	Gary Ward	.05	.02
☐ 638	Rene Gonzales	.05	.02
☐ 639	Don Robinson	.05	.02
☐ 640	Darryl Strawberry	.10	.05
☐ 641	Dave Anderson	.05	.02
☐ 642	Scott Scudder	.05	.02
☐ 643	Reggie Harris UER	.05	.02
	(Hepatitis misspelled as hepititis)		
☐ 644	Dave Henderson	.05	.02
☐ 645	Ben McDonald	.05	.02
☐ 646	Bob Kipper	.05	.02
☐ 647	Hal Morris UER	.05	.02
	(It's should be its)		
☐ 648	Tim Birtsas	.05	.02
☐ 649	Steve Searcy	.05	.02
☐ 650	Dale Murphy	.20	.09
☐ 651	Ron Oester	.05	.02
☐ 652	Mike LaCoss	.05	.02
☐ 653	Ron Jones	.05	.02
☐ 654	Kelly Downs	.05	.02
☐ 655	Roger Clemens	.40	.18
☐ 656	Herm Winningham	.05	.02
☐ 657	Trevor Wilson	.05	.02
☐ 658	Jose Rijo	.05	.02
☐ 659	Dann Bilardello UER	.05	.02
	(Bio has 13 games, 1 hit, and 32 AB, stats show 19, 2, and 37)		
☐ 660	Gregg Jefferies	.05	.02
☐ 661	Doug Drabek AS	.05	.02
	(Through is mis-spelled though)		
☐ 662	Randy Myers AS	.05	.02
☐ 663	Benny Santiago AS	.05	.02
☐ 664	Will Clark AS	.10	.05
☐ 665	Ryne Sandberg AS	.20	.09
☐ 666	Barry Larkin AS UER	.10	.05
	(Line 13, coolly misspelled cooly)		
☐ 667	Matt Williams AS	.10	.05
☐ 668	Barry Bonds AS	.25	.11
☐ 669	Eric Davis AS	.05	.02
☐ 670	Bobby Bonilla AS	.05	.02
☐ 671	Chipper Jones FDP	3.00	1.35
☐ 672	Eric Christopherson FDP	.05	.02
☐ 673	Robbie Beckett FDP	.05	.02
☐ 674	Shane Andrews FDP	.05	.02
☐ 675	Steve Karsay FDP	.10	.05
☐ 676	Aaron Holbert FDP	.05	.02
☐ 677	Donovan Osborne FDP	.20	.09
☐ 678	Todd Ritchie FDP	.05	.02
☐ 679	Ron Walden FDP	.05	.02
☐ 680	Tim Costo FDP	.05	.02
☐ 681	Dan Wilson FDP	.25	.11
☐ 682	Kurt Miller FDP	.05	.02
☐ 683	Mike Lieberthal FDP	.15	.07
☐ 684	Roger Clemens KM	.20	.09
☐ 685	Doc Gooden KM	.05	.02
☐ 686	Nolan Ryan KM	.40	.18
☐ 687	Frank Viola KM	.05	.02
☐ 688	Erik Hanson KM	.05	.02
☐ 689	Matt Williams MB	.10	.05
☐ 690	Jose Canseco MB UER	.10	.05
	(Mammoth misspelled as monmouth)		
☐ 691	Darryl Strawberry MB	.05	.02
☐ 692	Bo Jackson MB	.10	.05
☐ 693	Cecil Fielder MB	.05	.02
☐ 694	Sandy Alomar Jr. RF	.10	.05
☐ 695	Cory Snyder RF	.05	.02
☐ 696	Eric Davis RF	.05	.02
☐ 697	Ken Griffey Jr. RF	.75	.35
☐ 698	Andy Van Slyke RF UER	.05	.02
	(Line 2, outfielders does not need)		
☐ 699	Mark Langston NH Mike Witt	.05	.02
☐ 700	Randy Johnson NH	.20	.09
☐ 701	Nolan Ryan NH	.40	.18
☐ 702	Dave Stewart NH	.05	.02
☐ 703	Fernando Valenzuela NH	.05	.02
☐ 704	Andy Hawkins NH	.05	.02
☐ 705	Melido Perez NH	.05	.02
☐ 706	Terry Mulholland NH	.05	.02
☐ 707	Dave Stieb NH	.05	.02
☐ 708	Brian Barnes	.05	.02
☐ 709	Bernard Gilkey	.10	.05
☐ 710	Steve Decker	.05	.02
☐ 711	Paul Faries	.05	.02
☐ 712	Paul Marak	.05	.02
☐ 713	Wes Chamberlain	.05	.02
☐ 714	Kevin Belcher	.05	.02
☐ 715	Dan Boone UER	.05	.02
	(IP adds up to 101, but card has 101.2)		
☐ 716	Steve Adkins	.05	.02
☐ 717	Geronimo Pena	.05	.02
☐ 718	Howard Farmer	.05	.02
☐ 719	Mark Leonard	.05	.02
☐ 720	Tom Lampkin	.05	.02
☐ 721	Mike Gardiner	.05	.02
☐ 722	Jeff Conine	.25	.11
☐ 723	Efrain Valdez	.05	.02
☐ 724	Chuck Malone	.05	.02
☐ 725	Leo Gomez	.05	.02
☐ 726	Paul McClellan	.05	.02
☐ 727	Mark Leiter	.05	.02
☐ 728	Rich DeLucia UER	.05	.02
	(Line 2, all told is written alltold)		
☐ 729	Mel Rojas	.20	.09
☐ 730	Hector Wagner	.05	.02
☐ 731	Ray Lankford	.20	.09
☐ 732	Turner Ward	.05	.02
☐ 733	Gerald Alexander	.05	.02
☐ 734	Scott Anderson	.05	.02
☐ 735	Tony Perezchica	.05	.02
☐ 736	Jimmy Kremers	.05	.02
☐ 737	American Flag	.20	.09
	(Pray for Peace)		
☐ 738	Mike York	.05	.02
☐ 739	Mike Rochford	.05	.02
☐ 740	Scott Aldred	.05	.02
☐ 741	Rico Brogna	.10	.05
☐ 742	Dave Burba	.05	.02
☐ 743	Ray Stephens	.05	.02
☐ 744	Eric Gunderson	.05	.02
☐ 745	Troy Afenir	.05	.02
☐ 746	Jeff Shaw	.05	.02
☐ 747	Orlando Merced	.10	.05
☐ 748	Omar Olivares UER	.05	.02
	(Line 9, league is misspelled legaue)		
☐ 749	Jerry Kutzler	.05	.02
☐ 750	Mo Vaughn UER	.40	.18
	(44 SB's in 1990)		
☐ 751	Matt Stark	.05	.02
☐ 752	Randy Hennis	.05	.02
☐ 753	Andujar Cedeno	.05	.02
☐ 754	Kelvin Torve	.05	.02
☐ 755	Joe Kraemer	.05	.02
☐ 756	Phil Clark	.05	.02
☐ 757	Ed Vosberg	.05	.02
☐ 758	Mike Perez	.05	.02
☐ 759	Scott Lewis	.05	.02
☐ 760	Steve Chitren	.05	.02
☐ 761	Ray Young	.05	.02
☐ 762	Andres Santana	.05	.02
☐ 763	Rodney McCray	.05	.02
☐ 764	Sean Berry UER	.10	.05
	(Name misspelled Barry on card front)		
☐ 765	Brent Mayne	.05	.02
☐ 766	Mike Simms	.05	.02
☐ 767	Glenn Sutko	.05	.02
☐ 768	Gary DiSarcina	.05	.02
☐ 769	George Brett HL	.20	.09
☐ 770	Cecil Fielder HL	.05	.02
☐ 771	Jim Presley	.05	.02
☐ 772	John Dopson	.05	.02
☐ 773	Bo Jackson Breaker	.15	.07
☐ 774	Brent Knackert UER	.05	.02
	(Born in 1954, shown throwing righty, but bio says lefty)		
☐ 775	Bill Doran UER	.05	.02
	(Reds in NL East)		
☐ 776	Dick Schofield	.05	.02
☐ 777	Nelson Santovenia	.05	.02
☐ 778	Mark Guthrie	.05	.02
☐ 779	Mark Lemke	.05	.02
☐ 780	Terry Steinbach	.10	.05
☐ 781	Tom Bolton	.05	.02
☐ 782	Randy Tomlin	.05	.02
☐ 783	Jeff Kunkel	.05	.02
☐ 784	Felix Jose	.05	.02
☐ 785	Rick Sutcliffe	.05	.02
☐ 786	John Cerutti	.05	.02
☐ 787	Jose Vizcaino UER	.05	.02
	(Offerman, not Opperman)		
☐ 788	Curt Schilling	.20	.09
☐ 789	Ed Whitson	.05	.02
☐ 790	Tony Pena	.05	.02
☐ 791	John Candelaria	.05	.02
☐ 792	Carmelo Martinez	.05	.02
☐ 793	Sandy Alomar Jr. UER	.10	.05
	(Indian's should say Indians')		
☐ 794	Jim Neidlinger	.05	.02
☐ 795	Barry Larkin WS and Chris Sabo	.10	.05
☐ 796	Paul Sorrento	.05	.02
☐ 797	Tom Pagnozzi	.05	.02
☐ 798	Tino Martinez	.20	.09
☐ 799	Scott Ruskin UER	.05	.02
	(Text says first three seasons but lists averages for four)		
☐ 800	Kirk Gibson	.10	.05
☐ 801	Walt Terrell	.05	.02
☐ 802	John Russell	.05	.02
☐ 803	Chili Davis	.10	.05
☐ 804	Chris Nabholz	.05	.02
☐ 805	Juan Gonzalez	.75	.35
☐ 806	Ron Hassey	.05	.02
☐ 807	Todd Worrell	.05	.02
☐ 808	Tommy Greene	.05	.02
☐ 809	Joel Skinner UER	.05	.02
	(Joel, not Bob, was drafted in 1979)		
☐ 810	Benito Santiago	.05	.02
☐ 811	Pat Tabler UER	.05	.02
	(Line 3, always misspelled alway)		
☐ 812	Scott Erickson UER	.10	.05
	(Record spelled rcord)		
☐ 813	Moises Alou	.20	.09
☐ 814	Dale Sveum	.05	.02
☐ 815	Ryne Sandberg MANYR	.20	.09
☐ 816	Rick Dempsey	.05	.02
☐ 817	Scott Bankhead	.05	.02
☐ 818	Jason Grimsley	.05	.02
☐ 819	Doug Jennings	.05	.02
☐ 820	Tom Herr	.05	.02
☐ 821	Rob Ducey	.05	.02
☐ 822	Luis Quinones	.05	.02
☐ 823	Greg Minton	.05	.02
☐ 824	Mark Grant	.05	.02
☐ 825	Ozzie Smith UER	.25	.11
	(Shortstop misspelled shortstop)		
☐ 826	Dave Eiland	.05	.02
☐ 827	Danny Heep	.05	.02
☐ 828	Hensley Meulens	.05	.02
☐ 829	Charlie O'Brien	.05	.02
☐ 830	Glenn Davis	.05	.02
☐ 831	John Marzano UER	.05	.02
	(International mis-spelled Internaional)		
☐ 832	Steve Ontiveros	.05	.02
☐ 833	Ron Karkovice	.05	.02
☐ 834	Jerry Goff	.05	.02
☐ 835	Ken Griffey Sr.	.05	.02
☐ 836	Kevin Reimer	.05	.02
☐ 837	Randy Kutcher UER	.05	.02

		MINT	NRMT
(Infectious mis- spelled infectous)			
☐ 838	Mike Blowers .... .05	.02	
☐ 839	Mike Macfarlane ... .05	.02	
☐ 840	Frank Thomas UER .. 1.50	.70	
	(1989 Sarasota stats, 15 games but 188 AB)		
☐ 841	The Griffeys .... .75	.35	
	Ken Griffey Jr. Ken Griffey Sr.		
☐ 842	Jack Howell .... .05	.02	
☐ 843	Goose Gozzo .... .05	.02	
☐ 844	Gerald Young .... .05	.02	
☐ 845	Zane Smith .... .05	.02	
☐ 846	Kevin Brown .... .10	.05	
☐ 847	Sil Campusano .... .05	.02	
☐ 848	Larry Andersen .... .05	.02	
☐ 849	Cal Ripken FRAN .... .40	.18	
☐ 850	Roger Clemens FRAN .20	.09	
☐ 851	Sandy Alomar Jr. FRAN.10	.05	
☐ 852	Alan Trammell FRAN .. .10	.05	
☐ 853	George Brett FRAN ... .20	.09	
☐ 854	Robin Yount FRAN ... .10	.05	
☐ 855	Kirby Puckett FRAN ... .20	.09	
☐ 856	Don Mattingly FRAN .. .20	.09	
☐ 857	Rickey Henderson FRAN.10	.05	
☐ 858	Ken Griffey Jr. FRAN .. .75	.35	
☐ 859	Ruben Sierra FRAN .... .10	.05	
☐ 860	John Olerud FRAN ..... .10	.05	
☐ 861	Dave Justice FRAN ... .10	.05	
☐ 862	Ryne Sandberg FRAN .20	.09	
☐ 863	Eric Davis FRAN ...... .05	.02	
☐ 864	Darryl Strawberry FRAN .05	.02	
☐ 865	Tim Wallach FRAN .... .05	.02	
☐ 866	Doc Gooden FRAN .... .05	.02	
☐ 867	Len Dykstra FRAN .... .05	.02	
☐ 868	Barry Bonds FRAN .... .20	.09	
☐ 869	Todd Zeile FRAN UER .05	.02	
	(Powerful misspelled as powerly)		
☐ 870	Benito Santiago FRAN .05	.02	
☐ 871	Will Clark FRAN ...... .10	.05	
☐ 872	Craig Biggio FRAN .... .05	.02	
☐ 873	Wally Joyner FRAN .... .05	.02	
☐ 874	Frank Thomas FRAN ... .75	.35	
☐ 875	Rickey Henderson MVP.10	.05	
☐ 876	Barry Bonds MVP ..... .20	.09	
☐ 877	Bob Welch CY .... .05	.02	
☐ 878	Doug Drabek CY ...... .05	.02	
☐ 879	Sandy Alomar Jr ROY .10	.05	
☐ 880	Dave Justice ROY ..... .10	.05	
☐ 881	Damon Berryhill ...... .05	.02	
☐ 882	Frank Viola DT .... .05	.02	
☐ 883	Dave Stewart DT ...... .05	.02	
☐ 884	Doug Jones DT .... .05	.02	
☐ 885	Randy Myers DT ...... .05	.02	
☐ 886	Will Clark DT .... .10	.05	
☐ 887	Roberto Alomar DT .... .10	.05	
☐ 888	Barry Larkin DT .... .10	.05	
☐ 889	Wade Boggs DT .... .10	.05	
☐ 890	Rickey Henderson DT .. .10	.05	
☐ 891	Kirby Puckett DT ...... .40	.18	
☐ 892	Ken Griffey Jr DT 1.50	.70	
☐ 893	Benny Santiago .... .05	.02	

1991 Score Cooperstown

This seven-card standard-size set was available only in complete set form as an insert with 1991 Score factory sets. The card design is not like the regular 1991 Score cards. The card front features a portrait of the player in an oval on a white background. The words "Cooperstown Card" are prominently displayed on the front. The cards are numbered on the back with a B prefix.

BARRY LARKIN

	MINT	NRMT
COMPLETE SET (7)	10.00	4.50
COMMON CARD (B1-B7)	.75	.35
ONE PER FACTORY SET		
☐ B1 Wade Boggs	1.25	.55
☐ B2 Barry Larkin	.75	.35
☐ B3 Ken Griffey Jr.	6.00	2.70
☐ B4 Rickey Henderson	1.25	.55
☐ B5 George Brett	1.50	.70
☐ B6 Will Clark	1.25	.55
☐ B7 Nolan Ryan	3.00	1.35

1991 Score Hot Rookies

FRANK THOMAS

This ten-card standard-size set was inserted in the one per 1991 Score 100-card blister pack. The front features a color action player photo, with white borders and the words "Hot Rookie" in yellow above the picture. The card background shades from orange to yellow to orange as one moves down the card face. In a horizontal format, the left half of the back has a color head shot, while the right half has career summary.

	MINT	NRMT
COMPLETE SET (10)	15.00	6.75
COMMON CARD (1-10)	.50	.23
SEMISTARS	1.00	.45
UNLISTED STARS	1.50	.70
ONE PER BLISTER PACK		
☐ 1 Dave Justice	2.00	.90
☐ 2 Kevin Maas	.50	.23
☐ 3 Hal Morris	.50	.23
☐ 4 Frank Thomas	10.00	4.50
☐ 5 Jeff Conine	1.50	.70
☐ 6 Sandy Alomar Jr.	1.00	.45
☐ 7 Ray Lankford	1.50	.70
☐ 8 Steve Decker	.50	.23
☐ 9 Juan Gonzalez	5.00	2.20
☐ 10 Jose Offerman	.50	.23

1991 Score Rookie/Traded

The 1991 Score Rookie and Traded contains 110 standard-size player cards and was issued exclusively in factory set form along with 10 "World Series II" magic motion trivia cards through hobby dealers. The front design is identical to the regular issue 1991 Score set except for the distinctive mauve borders and T-suffixed numbering. Cards 1T-80T feature traded players, while cards 81T-110T focus on rookies. Rookie Cards in the set include Jeff Bagwell and Ivan Rodriguez.

	MINT	NRMT
COMPLETE SET (110)	4.00	1.80
COMMON CARD (1T-110T)	.05	.02
MINOR STARS	.10	.05
UNLISTED STARS	.20	.09
☐ 1T Bo Jackson	.15	.07
☐ 2T Mike Flanagan	.05	.02
☐ 3T Pete Incaviglia	.05	.02
☐ 4T Jack Clark	.10	.05
☐ 5T Hubie Brooks	.05	.02
☐ 6T Ivan Calderon	.05	.02
☐ 7T Glenn Davis	.05	.02
☐ 8T Wally Backman	.05	.02
☐ 9T Dave Smith	.05	.02
☐ 10T Tim Raines	.10	.05
☐ 11T Joe Carter	.10	.05
☐ 12T Sid Bream	.05	.02
☐ 13T George Bell	.05	.02
☐ 14T Steve Bedrosian	.05	.02
☐ 15T Willie Wilson	.05	.02
☐ 16T Darryl Strawberry	.10	.05
☐ 17T Danny Jackson	.05	.02
☐ 18T Kirk Gibson	.10	.05
☐ 19T Willie McGee	.10	.05
☐ 20T Junior Felix	.05	.02
☐ 21T Steve Farr	.05	.02
☐ 22T Pat Tabler	.05	.02
☐ 23T Brett Butler	.10	.05
☐ 24T Danny Darwin	.05	.02
☐ 25T Mickey Tettleton	.05	.02
☐ 26T Gary Carter	.20	.09
☐ 27T Mitch Williams	.05	.02
☐ 28T Candy Maldonado	.05	.02
☐ 29T Otis Nixon	.10	.05
☐ 30T Brian Downing	.05	.02
☐ 31T Tom Candiotti	.05	.02
☐ 32T John Candelaria	.05	.02
☐ 33T Rob Murphy	.05	.02
☐ 34T Deion Sanders	.10	.05
☐ 35T Willie Randolph	.10	.05
☐ 36T Pete Harnisch	.05	.02
☐ 37T Dante Bichette	.20	.09
☐ 38T Garry Templeton	.05	.02
☐ 39T Gary Gaetti	.05	.02
☐ 40T John Cerutti	.05	.02

☐ 41T Rick Cerone	.05	.02
☐ 42T Mike Pagliarulo	.05	.02
☐ 43T Ron Hassey	.05	.02
☐ 44T Roberto Alomar	.20	.09
☐ 45T Mike Boddicker	.05	.02
☐ 46T Bud Black	.05	.02
☐ 47T Rob Deer	.05	.02
☐ 48T Devon White	.05	.02
☐ 49T Luis Sojo	.05	.02
☐ 50T Terry Pendleton	.10	.05
☐ 51T Kevin Gross	.05	.02
☐ 52T Mike Huff	.05	.02
☐ 53T Dave Righetti	.05	.02
☐ 54T Matt Young	.05	.02
☐ 55T Earnest Riles	.05	.02
☐ 56T Bill Gullickson	.05	.02
☐ 57T Vince Coleman	.05	.02
☐ 58T Fred McGriff	.20	.09
☐ 59T Franklin Stubbs	.05	.02
☐ 60T Eric King	.05	.02
☐ 61T Cory Snyder	.05	.02
☐ 62T Dwight Evans	.10	.05
☐ 63T Gerald Perry	.05	.02
☐ 64T Eric Show	.05	.02
☐ 65T Shawn Hillegas	.05	.02
☐ 66T Tony Fernandez	.05	.02
☐ 67T Tim Teufel	.05	.02
☐ 68T Mitch Webster	.05	.02
☐ 69T Mike Heath	.05	.02
☐ 70T Chili Davis	.10	.05
☐ 71T Larry Andersen	.05	.02
☐ 72T Gary Varsho	.05	.02
☐ 73T Juan Berenguer	.05	.02
☐ 74T Jack Morris	.10	.05
☐ 75T Barry Jones	.05	.02
☐ 76T Rafael Belliard	.05	.02
☐ 77T Steve Buechele	.05	.02
☐ 78T Scott Sanderson	.05	.02
☐ 79T Bob Ojeda	.05	.02
☐ 80T Curt Schilling	.20	.09
☐ 81T Brian Drahman	.05	.02
☐ 82T Ivan Rodriguez	1.50	.70
☐ 83T David Howard	.05	.02
☐ 84T Heathcliff Slocumb	.20	.09
☐ 85T Mike Timlin	.05	.02
☐ 86T Darryl Kile	.20	.09
☐ 87T Pete Schourek	.10	.05
☐ 88T Bruce Walton	.05	.02
☐ 89T Al Osuna	.05	.02
☐ 90T Gary Scott	.05	.02
☐ 91T Doug Simons	.05	.02
☐ 92T Chris Jones	.05	.02
☐ 93T Chuck Knoblauch	.25	.11
☐ 94T Dana Allison	.05	.02
☐ 95T Erik Pappas	.05	.02
☐ 96T Jeff Bagwell	2.50	1.10
☐ 97T Kirk Dressendorfer	.05	.02
☐ 98T Freddie Benavides	.05	.02
☐ 99T Luis Gonzalez	.20	.09
☐ 100T Wade Taylor	.05	.02
☐ 101T Ed Sprague	.05	.02
☐ 102T Bob Scanlan	.05	.02
☐ 103T Rick Wilkins	.05	.02
☐ 104T Chris Donnels	.05	.02
☐ 105T Joe Slusarski	.05	.02
☐ 106T Mark Lewis	.05	.02
☐ 107T Pat Kelly	.10	.05
☐ 108T John Briscoe	.05	.02
☐ 109T Luis Lopez	.05	.02
☐ 110T Jeff Johnson	.05	.02

1992 Score

The 1992 Score set marked the second year that Score released their set in two different series. The first series contains 442 cards while the second series contains 451 cards. Cards were distributed in plastic wrapped packs, blister packs, jumbo packs and factory sets. Each pack included a special "World Series II" trivia card. The glossy color action photos on

the basic card fronts are bordered above and below by stripes of the same color, and a thicker, different color stripe runs the length of the card to one side of the picture. Topical subsets include Rookie Prospects (395-424/736-772/814-877), No-Hit Club (425-428/784-787), Highlights (429-430), with color montages displaying Chris Greco's player caricatures), Dream Team (441-442/883-893), NL All-Stars (773-782), Highlights (783, 795-797), Draft Picks (799-810), and Memorabilia (878-882). All of the Rookie Prospects (736-772) can be found with or without the Rookie Prospect stripe. Rookie Cards in the set include Vinny Castilla and Manny Ramirez. Chuck Knoblauch, 1991 American League Rookie of the Year, autographed 3,000 of his own 1990 Score Draft Pick cards (card number 672) in gold ink, 2,989 were randomly inserted in Series 2 poly packs, while the other 11 were given away in a sweepstakes. The backs of these Knoblauch autograph cards have special holograms to differentiate them.

	MINT	NRMT
COMPLETE SET (893)	15.00	6.75
COMP.FACT.SET (910)	20.00	9.00
COMPLETE SERIES 1 (442)	8.00	3.60
COMPLETE SERIES 2 (451)	8.00	3.60
COMMON CARD (1-893)	.05	.02
MINOR STARS	.10	
UNLISTED STARS	.20	.09
SUBSET CARDS HALF VALUE OF BASE CARDS		
COMP.DIMAGGIO SET (5)	150.00	70.00
COMMON DIMAGGIO (1-5)	30.00	13.50
CERTIFIED DIMAGGIO AUTO	550.00	250.00
DIMAGGIO: RANDOM INS.IN SER.1 PACKS		

☐ 1 Ken Griffey Jr.	1.25	.55
☐ 2 Nolan Ryan	.75	.35
☐ 3 Will Clark	.15	.07
☐ 4 Dave Justice	.20	.09
☐ 5 Dave Henderson	.05	.02
☐ 6 Bret Saberhagen	.05	.02
☐ 7 Fred McGriff	.15	.07
☐ 8 Erik Hanson	.05	.02
☐ 9 Darryl Strawberry	.10	.05
☐ 10 Dwight Gooden	.10	.05
☐ 11 Juan Gonzalez	.60	.25
☐ 12 Mark Langston	.05	.02
☐ 13 Lonnie Smith	.05	.02
☐ 14 Jeff Montgomery	.10	.05
☐ 15 Roberto Alomar	.20	.09
☐ 16 Delino DeShields	.05	.02
☐ 17 Steve Bedrosian	.05	.02
☐ 18 Terry Pendleton	.10	.05
☐ 19 Mark Carreon	.05	.02
☐ 20 Mark McGwire	.40	.18
☐ 21 Roger Clemens	.40	.18
☐ 22 Chuck Crim	.05	.02
☐ 23 Don Mattingly	.30	.14
☐ 24 Dickie Thon	.05	.02
☐ 25 Ron Gant	.10	.05
☐ 26 Milt Cuyler	.05	.02
☐ 27 Mike Macfarlane	.05	.02
☐ 28 Dan Gladden	.05	.02
☐ 29 Melido Perez	.05	.02
☐ 30 Willie Randolph	.10	.05
☐ 31 Albert Belle	.25	.11
☐ 32 Dave Winfield	.20	.09
☐ 33 Jimmy Jones	.05	.02
☐ 34 Kevin Gross	.05	.02
☐ 35 Andres Galarraga	.20	.09
☐ 36 Mike Devereaux	.05	.02
☐ 37 Chris Bosio	.05	.02
☐ 38 Mike LaValliere	.05	.02
☐ 39 Gary Gaetti	.05	.02
☐ 40 Felix Jose	.05	.02
☐ 41 Alvaro Espinoza	.05	.02
☐ 42 Rick Aguilera	.05	.02
☐ 43 Mike Gallego	.05	.02
☐ 44 Eric Davis	.10	.05
☐ 45 George Bell	.05	.02
☐ 46 Tom Brunansky	.05	.02
☐ 47 Steve Farr	.05	.02
☐ 48 Duane Ward	.05	.02
☐ 49 David Wells	.05	.02
☐ 50 Cecil Fielder	.10	.05
☐ 51 Walt Weiss	.05	.02
☐ 52 Todd Zeile	.05	.02
☐ 53 Doug Jones	.05	.02
☐ 54 Bob Walk	.05	.02
☐ 55 Rafael Palmeiro	.15	.07
☐ 56 Rob Deer	.05	.02
☐ 57 Paul O'Neill	.10	.05
☐ 58 Jeff Reardon	.10	.05
☐ 59 Randy Ready	.05	.02
☐ 60 Scott Erickson	.10	.05
☐ 61 Paul Molitor	.20	.09
☐ 62 Jack McDowell	.10	.05
☐ 63 Jim Acker	.05	.02
☐ 64 Jay Buhner	.15	.07
☐ 65 Travis Fryman	.10	.05
☐ 66 Marquis Grissom	.10	.05
☐ 67 Mike Harkey	.05	.02
☐ 68 Luis Polonia	.05	.02
☐ 69 Ken Caminiti	.15	.07
☐ 70 Chris Sabo	.05	.02
☐ 71 Gregg Olson	.05	.02
☐ 72 Carlton Fisk	.20	.09
☐ 73 Juan Samuel	.05	.02
☐ 74 Todd Stottlemyre	.05	.02
☐ 75 Andre Dawson	.15	.07
☐ 76 Alvin Davis	.05	.02
☐ 77 Bill Doran	.05	.02
☐ 78 B.J. Surhoff	.05	.02
☐ 79 Kirk McCaskill	.05	.02
☐ 80 Dale Murphy	.20	.09
☐ 81 Jose DeLeon	.05	.02
☐ 82 Alex Fernandez	.10	.05
☐ 83 Ivan Calderon	.05	.02
☐ 84 Brent Mayne	.05	.02
☐ 85 Jody Reed	.05	.02
☐ 86 Randy Tomlin	.05	.02
☐ 87 Randy Milligan	.05	.02
☐ 88 Pascual Perez	.05	.02
☐ 89 Hensley Meulens	.05	.02
☐ 90 Joe Carter	.10	.05
☐ 91 Mike Moore	.05	.02
☐ 92 Ozzie Guillen	.05	.02
☐ 93 Shawn Hillegas	.05	.02
☐ 94 Chili Davis	.10	.05
☐ 95 Vince Coleman	.05	.02
☐ 96 Jimmy Key	.10	.05
☐ 97 Billy Ripken	.05	.02
☐ 98 Dave Smith	.05	.02
☐ 99 Tom Bolton	.05	.02
☐ 100 Barry Larkin	.15	.07
☐ 101 Kenny Rogers	.05	.02
☐ 102 Mike Boddicker	.05	.02
☐ 103 Kevin Elster	.05	.02
☐ 104 Ken Hill	.05	.02

105	Charlie Leibrandt	.05	.02
106	Pat Combs	.05	.02
107	Hubie Brooks	.05	.02
108	Julio Franco	.05	.02
109	Vicente Palacios	.05	.02
110	Kal Daniels	.05	.02
111	Bruce Hurst	.05	.02
112	Willie McGee	.05	.02
113	Ted Power	.05	.02
114	Milt Thompson	.05	.02
115	Doug Drabek	.05	.02
116	Rafael Belliard	.05	.02
117	Scott Garrelts	.05	.02
118	Terry Mulholland	.05	.02
119	Jay Howell	.05	.02
120	Danny Jackson	.05	.02
121	Scott Ruskin	.05	.02
122	Robin Ventura	.10	.05
123	Bip Roberts	.05	.02
124	Jeff Russell	.05	.02
125	Hal Morris	.05	.02
126	Teddy Higuera	.05	.02
127	Luis Sojo	.05	.02
128	Carlos Baerga	.05	.02
129	Jeff Ballard	.05	.02
130	Tom Gordon	.05	.02
131	Sid Bream	.05	.02
132	Rance Mulliniks	.05	.02
133	Andy Benes	.10	.05
134	Mickey Tettleton	.05	.02
135	Rich DeLucia	.05	.02
136	Tom Pagnozzi	.05	.02
137	Harold Baines	.10	.05
138	Danny Darwin	.05	.02
139	Kevin Bass	.05	.02
140	Chris Nabholz	.05	.02
141	Pete O'Brien	.05	.02
142	Jeff Treadway	.05	.02
143	Mickey Morandini	.05	.02
144	Eric King	.05	.02
145	Danny Tartabull	.05	.02
146	Lance Johnson	.05	.02
147	Casey Candaele	.05	.02
148	Felix Fermin	.05	.02
149	Rich Rodriguez	.05	.02
150	Dwight Evans	.10	.05
151	Joe Klink	.05	.02
152	Kevin Reimer	.05	.02
153	Orlando Merced	.05	.02
154	Mel Hall	.05	.02
155	Randy Myers	.10	.05
156	Greg A. Harris	.05	.02
157	Jeff Brantley	.05	.02
158	Jim Eisenreich	.05	.02
159	Luis Rivera	.05	.02
160	Cris Carpenter	.05	.02
161	Bruce Ruffin	.05	.02
162	Omar Vizquel	.10	.05
163	Gerald Alexander	.05	.02
164	Mark Guthrie	.05	.02
165	Scott Lewis	.05	.02
166	Bill Sampen	.05	.02
167	Dave Anderson	.05	.02
168	Kevin McReynolds	.05	.02
169	Jose Vizcaino	.05	.02
170	Bob Geren	.05	.02
171	Mike Morgan	.05	.02
172	Jim Gott	.05	.02
173	Mike Pagliarulo	.05	.02
174	Mike Jeffcoat	.05	.02
175	Craig Lefferts	.05	.02
176	Steve Finley	.10	.05
177	Wally Backman	.05	.02
178	Kent Mercker	.05	.02
179	John Cerutti	.05	.02
180	Jay Bell	.10	.05
181	Dale Sveum	.05	.02
182	Greg Gagne	.05	.02
183	Donnie Hill	.05	.02
184	Rex Hudler	.05	.02
185	Pat Kelly	.05	.02
186	Jeff D. Robinson	.05	.02
187	Jeff Gray	.05	.02
188	Jerry Willard	.05	.02
189	Carlos Quintana	.05	.02
190	Dennis Eckersley	.10	.05
191	Kelly Downs	.05	.02
192	Gregg Jefferies	.05	.02
193	Darrin Fletcher	.05	.02
194	Mike Jackson	.05	.02
195	Eddie Murray	.20	.09
196	Bill Landrum	.05	.02
197	Eric Yelding	.05	.02
198	Devon White	.05	.02
199	Larry Walker	.20	.09
200	Ryne Sandberg	.25	.11
201	Dave Magadan	.05	.02
202	Steve Chitren	.05	.02
203	Scott Fletcher	.05	.02
204	Dwayne Henry	.05	.02
205	Scott Coolbaugh	.05	.02
206	Tracy Jones	.05	.02
207	Von Hayes	.05	.02
208	Bob Melvin	.05	.02
209	Scott Scudder	.05	.02
210	Luis Gonzalez	.05	.02
211	Scott Sanderson	.05	.02
212	Chris Donnels	.05	.02
213	Heathcliff Slocumb	.05	.02
214	Mike Timlin	.05	.02
215	Brian Harper	.05	.02
216	Juan Berenguer UER (Decimal point missing in IP total)	.05	.02
217	Mike Henneman	.05	.02
218	Bill Spiers	.05	.02
219	Scott Terry	.05	.02
220	Frank Viola	.05	.02
221	Mark Eichhorn	.05	.02
222	Ernest Riles	.05	.02
223	Ray Lankford	.20	.09
224	Pete Harnisch	.05	.02
225	Bobby Bonilla	.10	.05
226	Mike Scioscia	.05	.02
227	Joel Skinner	.05	.02
228	Brian Holman	.05	.02
229	Gilberto Reyes	.05	.02
230	Matt Williams	.15	.07
231	Jaime Navarro	.05	.02
232	Jose Rijo	.05	.02
233	Atlee Hammaker	.05	.02
234	Tim Teufel	.05	.02
235	John Kruk	.10	.05
236	Kurt Stillwell	.05	.02
237	Dan Pasqua	.05	.02
238	Tim Crews	.05	.02
239	Dave Gallagher	.05	.02
240	Leo Gomez	.05	.02
241	Steve Avery	.05	.02
242	Bill Gullickson	.05	.02
243	Mark Portugal	.05	.02
244	Lee Guetterman	.05	.02
245	Benito Santiago	.05	.02
246	Jim Gantner	.05	.02
247	Robby Thompson	.05	.02
248	Terry Shumpert	.05	.02
249	Mike Bell	.05	.02
250	Harold Reynolds	.05	.02
251	Mike Felder	.05	.02
252	Bill Pecota	.05	.02
253	Bill Krueger	.05	.02
254	Alfredo Griffin	.05	.02
255	Lou Whitaker	.10	.05
256	Roy Smith	.05	.02
257	Jerald Clark	.05	.02
258	Sammy Sosa	.20	.09
259	Tim Naehring	.10	.05
260	Dave Righetti	.05	.02
261	Paul Gibson	.05	.02
262	Chris James	.05	.02
263	Larry Andersen	.05	.02
264	Storm Davis	.05	.02
265	Jose Lind	.05	.02
266	Greg Hibbard	.05	.02
267	Norm Charlton	.05	.02
268	Paul Kilgus	.05	.02
269	Greg Maddux	.60	.25
270	Ellis Burks	.10	.05
271	Frank Tanana	.05	.02
272	Gene Larkin	.05	.02
273	Ron Hassey	.05	.02
274	Ron M. Robinson	.05	.02
275	Steve Howe	.05	.02
276	Daryl Boston	.05	.02
277	Mark Lee	.05	.02
278	Jose Segura	.05	.02
279	Lance Blankenship	.05	.02
280	Don Slaught	.05	.02
281	Russ Swan	.05	.02
282	Bob Tewksbury	.05	.02
283	Geno Petralli	.05	.02
284	Shane Mack	.05	.02
285	Bob Scanlan	.05	.02
286	Tim Leary	.05	.02
287	John Smoltz	.15	.07
288	Pat Borders	.05	.02
289	Mark Davidson	.05	.02
290	Sam Horn	.05	.02
291	Lenny Harris	.05	.02
292	Franklin Stubbs	.05	.02
293	Thomas Howard	.05	.02
294	Steve Lyons	.05	.02
295	Francisco Oliveras	.05	.02
296	Terry Leach	.05	.02
297	Barry Jones	.05	.02
298	Lance Parrish	.05	.02
299	Wally Whitehurst	.05	.02
300	Bob Welch	.05	.02
301	Charlie Hayes	.05	.02
302	Charlie Hough	.05	.02
303	Gary Redus	.05	.02
304	Scott Bradley	.05	.02
305	Jose Oquendo	.05	.02
306	Pete Incaviglia	.05	.02
307	Marvin Freeman	.05	.02
308	Gary Pettis	.05	.02
309	Joe Slusarski	.05	.02
310	Kevin Seitzer	.05	.02
311	Jeff Reed	.05	.02
312	Pat Tabler	.05	.02
313	Mike Maddux	.05	.02
314	Bob Milacki	.05	.02
315	Eric Anthony	.05	.02
316	Dante Bichette	.15	.07
317	Steve Decker	.05	.02
318	Jack Clark	.10	.05
319	Doug Dascenzo	.05	.02
320	Scott Leius	.05	.02
321	Jim Lindeman	.05	.02
322	Bryan Harvey	.05	.02
323	Spike Owen	.05	.02
324	Roberto Kelly	.05	.02
325	Stan Belinda	.05	.02
326	Joey Cora	.10	.05
327	Jeff Innis	.05	.02
328	Willie Wilson	.05	.02
329	Juan Agosto	.05	.02
330	Charles Nagy	.10	.05
331	Scott Bailes	.05	.02
332	Pete Schourek	.05	.02
333	Mike Flanagan	.05	.02
334	Omar Olivares	.05	.02
335	Dennis Lamp	.05	.02
336	Tommy Greene	.05	.02
337	Randy Velarde	.05	.02
338	Tom Lampkin	.05	.02
339	John Russell	.05	.02
340	Bob Kipper	.05	.02
341	Todd Burns	.05	.02
342	Ron Jones	.05	.02
343	Dave Valle	.05	.02
344	Mike Heath	.05	.02
345	John Olerud	.10	.05
346	Gerald Young	.05	.02
347	Ken Patterson	.05	.02
348	Les Lancaster	.05	.02
349	Steve Crawford	.05	.02
350	John Candelaria	.05	.02
351	Mike Aldrete	.05	.02
352	Mariano Duncan	.05	.02
353	Julio Machado	.05	.02
354	Ken Williams	.05	.02
355	Walt Terrell	.05	.02
356	Mitch Williams	.05	.02
357	Al Newman	.05	.02
358	Bud Black	.05	.02
359	Joe Hesketh	.05	.02
360	Paul Assenmacher	.05	.02

361 Bo Jackson	.10	.05
362 Jeff Blauser	.05	.02
363 Mike Brumley	.05	.02
364 Jim Deshaies	.05	.02
365 Brady Anderson	.15	.07
366 Chuck McElroy	.05	.02
367 Matt Merullo	.05	.02
368 Tim Belcher	.05	.02
369 Luis Aquino	.05	.02
370 Joe Oliver	.05	.02
371 Greg Swindell	.05	.02
372 Lee Stevens	.05	.02
373 Mark Knudson	.05	.02
374 Bill Wegman	.05	.02
375 Jerry Don Gleaton	.05	.02
376 Pedro Guerrero	.05	.02
377 Randy Bush	.05	.02
378 Greg W. Harris	.05	.02
379 Eric Plunk	.05	.02
380 Jose DeJesus	.05	.02
381 Bobby Witt	.05	.02
382 Curtis Wilkerson	.05	.02
383 Gene Nelson	.05	.02
384 Wes Chamberlain	.05	.02
385 Tom Henke	.05	.02
386 Mark Lemke	.05	.02
387 Greg Briley	.05	.02
388 Rafael Ramirez	.05	.02
389 Tony Fossas	.05	.02
390 Henry Cotto	.05	.02
391 Tim Hulett	.05	.02
392 Dean Palmer	.10	.05
393 Glenn Braggs	.05	.02
394 Mark Salas	.05	.02
395 Rusty Meacham	.05	.02
396 Andy Ashby	.05	.02
397 Jose Melendez	.05	.02
398 Warren Newson	.05	.02
399 Frank Castillo	.05	.02
400 Chito Martinez	.05	.02
401 Bernie Williams	.20	.09
402 Derek Bell	.10	.05
403 Javier Ortiz	.05	.02
404 Tim Sherrill	.05	.02
405 Rob MacDonald	.05	.02
406 Phil Plantier	.10	.05
407 Troy Afenir	.05	.02
408 Gino Minutelli	.05	.02
409 Reggie Jefferson	.10	.05
410 Mike Remlinger	.05	.02
411 Carlos Rodriguez	.05	.02
412 Joe Redfield	.05	.02
413 Alonzo Powell	.05	.02
414 Scott Livingstone UER (Travis Fryman, not Woody, should be referenced on back)	.05	.02
415 Scott Kamieniecki	.05	.02
416 Tim Spehr	.05	.02
417 Brian Hunter	.05	.02
418 Ced Landrum	.05	.02
419 Bret Barberie	.05	.02
420 Kevin Morton	.05	.02
421 Doug Henry	.05	.02
422 Doug Piatt	.05	.02
423 Pat Rice	.05	.02
424 Juan Guzman	.05	.02
425 Nolan Ryan NH	.40	.18
426 Tommy Greene NH	.05	.02
427 Bob Milacki and Mike Flanagan NH (Mark Williamson and Gregg Olson)	.05	.02
428 Wilson Alvarez NH	.05	.02
429 Otis Nixon HL	.05	.02
430 Rickey Henderson HL	.10	.05
431 Cecil Fielder AS	.05	.02
432 Julio Franco AS	.05	.02
433 Cal Ripken AS	.20	.09
434 Wade Boggs AS	.20	.09
435 Joe Carter AS	.05	.02
436 Ken Griffey Jr. AS	.60	.25
437 Ruben Sierra AS	.05	.02
438 Scott Erickson AS	.05	.02
439 Tom Henke AS	.05	.02
440 Terry Steinbach AS	.05	.02
441 Rickey Henderson DT	.10	.05
442 Ryne Sandberg DT	.25	.11
443 Otis Nixon	.10	.05
444 Scott Radinsky	.05	.02
445 Mark Grace	.15	.07
446 Tony Pena	.05	.02
447 Billy Hatcher	.05	.02
448 Glenallen Hill	.05	.02
449 Chris Gwynn	.05	.02
450 Tom Glavine	.15	.07
451 John Habyan	.05	.02
452 Al Osuna	.05	.02
453 Tony Phillips	.05	.02
454 Greg Cadaret	.05	.02
455 Rob Dibble	.05	.02
456 Rick Honeycutt	.05	.02
457 Jerome Walton	.05	.02
458 Mookie Wilson	.05	.02
459 Mark Gubicza	.05	.02
460 Craig Biggio	.15	.07
461 Dave Cochrane	.05	.02
462 Keith Miller	.05	.02
463 Alex Cole	.05	.02
464 Pete Smith	.05	.02
465 Brett Butler	.10	.05
466 Jeff Huson	.05	.02
467 Steve Lake	.05	.02
468 Lloyd Moseby	.05	.02
469 Tim McIntosh	.05	.02
470 Dennis Martinez	.10	.05
471 Greg Myers	.05	.02
472 Mackey Sasser	.05	.02
473 Junior Ortiz	.05	.02
474 Greg Olson	.05	.02
475 Steve Sax	.05	.02
476 Ricky Jordan	.05	.02
477 Max Venable	.05	.02
478 Brian McRae	.05	.02
479 Doug Simons	.05	.02
480 Rickey Henderson	.15	.07
481 Gary Varsho	.05	.02
482 Carl Willis	.05	.02
483 Rick Wilkins	.05	.02
484 Donn Pall	.05	.02
485 Edgar Martinez	.15	.07
486 Tom Foley	.05	.02
487 Mark Williamson	.05	.02
488 Jack Armstrong	.05	.02
489 Gary Carter	.20	.09
490 Ruben Sierra	.15	.07
491 Gerald Perry	.05	.02
492 Rob Murphy	.05	.02
493 Zane Smith	.05	.02
494 Darryl Kile	.10	.05
495 Kelly Gruber	.05	.02
496 Jerry Browne	.05	.02
497 Darryl Hamilton	.05	.02
498 Mike Stanton	.05	.02
499 Mark Leonard	.05	.02
500 Jose Canseco	.15	.07
501 Dave Martinez	.05	.02
502 Jose Guzman	.05	.02
503 Terry Kennedy	.05	.02
504 Ed Sprague	.05	.02
505 Frank Thomas UER (His Gulf Coast League stats are wrong)	1.00	.45
506 Darren Daulton	.10	.05
507 Kevin Tapani	.05	.02
508 Luis Salazar	.05	.02
509 Paul Faries	.05	.02
510 Sandy Alomar Jr.	.10	.05
511 Jeff King	.05	.02
512 Gary Thurman	.05	.02
513 Chris Hammond	.05	.02
514 Pedro Munoz	.05	.02
515 Alan Trammell	.15	.07
516 Geronimo Pena	.05	.02
517 Rodney McCray UER (Stole 6 bases in 1990, not 5; career totals are correct at 7)	.05	.02
518 Manny Lee	.05	.02
519 Junior Felix	.05	.02
520 Kirk Gibson	.10	.05
521 Darrin Jackson	.05	.02
522 John Burkett	.05	.02
523 Jeff Johnson	.05	.02
524 Jim Corsi	.05	.02
525 Robin Yount	.15	.07
526 Jamie Quirk	.05	.02
527 Bob Ojeda	.05	.02
528 Mark Lewis	.05	.02
529 Bryn Smith	.05	.02
530 Kent Hrbek	.10	.05
531 Dennis Boyd	.05	.02
532 Ron Karkovice	.05	.02
533 Don August	.05	.02
534 Todd Frohwirth	.05	.02
535 Wally Joyner	.10	.05
536 Dennis Rasmussen	.05	.02
537 Andy Allanson	.05	.02
538 Goose Gossage	.10	.05
539 John Marzano	.05	.02
540 Cal Ripken UER	.75	.35
541 Bill Swift UER (Brewers logo on front)	.05	.02
542 Kevin Appier	.10	.05
543 Dave Bergman	.05	.02
544 Bernard Gilkey	.10	.05
545 Mike Greenwell	.05	.02
546 Jose Uribe	.05	.02
547 Jesse Orosco	.05	.02
548 Bob Patterson	.05	.02
549 Mike Stanley	.05	.02
550 Howard Johnson	.05	.02
551 Joe Orsulak	.05	.02
552 Dick Schofield	.05	.02
553 Dave Hollins	.05	.02
554 David Segui	.05	.02
555 Barry Bonds	.25	.11
556 Mo Vaughn	.30	.14
557 Craig Wilson	.05	.02
558 Bobby Rose	.05	.02
559 Rod Nichols	.05	.02
560 Len Dykstra	.10	.05
561 Craig Grebeck	.05	.02
562 Darren Lewis	.05	.02
563 Todd Benzinger	.05	.02
564 Ed Whitson	.05	.02
565 Jesse Barfield	.05	.02
566 Lloyd McClendon	.05	.02
567 Dan Plesac	.05	.02
568 Danny Cox	.05	.02
569 Skeeter Barnes	.05	.02
570 Bobby Thigpen	.05	.02
571 Deion Sanders	.10	.05
572 Chuck Knoblauch	.20	.09
573 Matt Nokes	.05	.02
574 Herm Winningham	.05	.02
575 Tom Candiotti	.05	.02
576 Jeff Bagwell	.60	.25
577 Brook Jacoby	.05	.02
578 Chico Walker	.05	.02
579 Brian Downing	.05	.02
580 Dave Stewart	.10	.05
581 Francisco Cabrera	.05	.02
582 Rene Gonzales	.05	.02
583 Stan Javier	.05	.02
584 Randy Johnson	.20	.09
585 Chuck Finley	.05	.02
586 Mark Gardner	.05	.02
587 Mark Whiten	.05	.02
588 Garry Templeton	.05	.02
589 Gary Sheffield	.20	.09
590 Ozzie Smith	.25	.11
591 Candy Maldonado	.05	.02
592 Mike Sharperson	.05	.02
593 Carlos Martinez	.05	.02
594 Scott Bankhead	.05	.02
595 Tim Wallach	.10	.05
596 Tino Martinez	.20	.09
597 Roger McDowell	.05	.02
598 Cory Snyder	.05	.02
599 Andujar Cedeno	.20	.09
600 Kirby Puckett	.40	.18
601 Rick Parker	.05	.02
602 Todd Hundley	.15	.07
603 Greg Litton	.05	.02
604 Dave Johnson	.05	.02
605 John Franco	.10	.05
606 Mike Fetters	.05	.02

607	Luis Alicea	.05	.02
608	Trevor Wilson	.05	.02
609	Rob Ducey	.05	.02
610	Ramon Martinez	.10	.05
611	Dave Burba	.05	.02
612	Dwight Smith	.05	.02
613	Kevin Maas	.05	.02
614	John Costello	.05	.02
615	Glenn Davis	.05	.02
616	Shawn Abner	.05	.02
617	Scott Hemond	.05	.02
618	Tom Prince	.05	.02
619	Wally Ritchie	.05	.02
620	Jim Abbott	.05	.02
621	Charlie O'Brien	.05	.02
622	Jack Daugherty	.05	.02
623	Tommy Gregg	.05	.02
624	Jeff Shaw	.05	.02
625	Tony Gwynn	.50	.23
626	Mark Leiter	.05	.02
627	Jim Clancy	.05	.02
628	Tim Layana	.05	.02
629	Jeff Schaefer	.05	.02
630	Lee Smith	.10	.05
631	Wade Taylor	.05	.02
632	Mike Simms	.05	.02
633	Terry Steinbach	.10	.05
634	Shawon Dunston	.05	.02
635	Tim Raines	.10	.05
636	Kirt Manwaring	.05	.02
637	Warren Cromartie	.05	.02
638	Luis Quinones	.05	.02
639	Greg Vaughn	.05	.02
640	Kevin Mitchell	.10	.05
641	Chris Hoiles	.05	.02
642	Tom Browning	.05	.02
643	Mitch Webster	.05	.02
644	Steve Olin	.05	.02
645	Tony Fernandez	.05	.02
646	Juan Bell	.05	.02
647	Joe Boever	.05	.02
648	Carney Lansford	.10	.05
649	Mike Benjamin	.05	.02
650	George Brett	.40	.18
651	Tim Burke	.05	.02
652	Jack Morris	.10	.05
653	Orel Hershiser	.10	.05
654	Mike Schooler	.05	.02
655	Andy Van Slyke	.10	.05
656	Dave Stieb	.05	.02
657	Dave Clark	.05	.02
658	Ben McDonald	.05	.02
659	John Smiley	.05	.02
660	Wade Boggs	.20	.09
661	Eric Bullock	.05	.02
662	Eric Show	.05	.02
663	Lenny Webster	.05	.02
664	Mike Huff	.05	.02
665	Rick Sutcliffe	.05	.02
666	Jeff Manto	.05	.02
667	Mike Fitzgerald	.05	.02
668	Matt Young	.05	.02
669	Dave West	.05	.02
670	Mike Hartley	.05	.02
671	Curt Schilling	.15	.07
672	Brian Bohanon	.05	.02
673	Cecil Espy	.05	.02
674	Joe Grahe	.05	.02
675	Sid Fernandez	.05	.02
676	Edwin Nunez	.05	.02
677	Hector Villanueva	.05	.02
678	Sean Berry	.05	.02
679	Dave Eiland	.05	.02
680	Dave Cone	.10	.05
681	Mike Bordick	.05	.02
682	Tony Castillo	.05	.02
683	John Barfield	.05	.02
684	Jeff Hamilton	.05	.02
685	Ken Dayley	.05	.02
686	Carmelo Martinez	.05	.02
687	Mike Capel	.05	.02
688	Scott Chiamparino	.05	.02
689	Rich Gedman	.05	.02
690	Rich Monteleone	.05	.02
691	Alejandro Pena	.05	.02
692	Oscar Azocar	.05	.02
693	Jim Poole	.05	.02
694	Mike Gardiner	.05	.02
695	Steve Buechele	.05	.02
696	Rudy Seanez	.05	.02
697	Paul Abbott	.05	.02
698	Steve Searcy	.05	.02
699	Jose Offerman	.05	.02
700	Ivan Rodriguez	.40	.18
701	Joe Girardi	.05	.02
702	Tony Perezchica	.05	.02
703	Paul McClellan	.05	.02
704	David Howard	.05	.02
705	Dan Petry	.05	.02
706	Jack Howell	.05	.02
707	Jose Mesa	.05	.02
708	Randy St. Claire	.05	.02
709	Kevin Brown	.10	.05
710	Ron Darling	.05	.02
711	Jason Grimsley	.05	.02
712	John Orton	.05	.02
713	Shawn Boskie	.05	.02
714	Pat Clements	.05	.02
715	Brian Barnes	.05	.02
716	Luis Lopez	.05	.02
717	Bob McClure	.05	.02
718	Mark Davis	.05	.02
719	Dann Bilardello	.05	.02
720	Tom Edens	.05	.02
721	Willie Fraser	.05	.02
722	Curt Young	.05	.02
723	Neal Heaton	.05	.02
724	Craig Worthington	.05	.02
725	Mel Rojas	.10	.05
726	Daryl Irvine	.05	.02
727	Roger Mason	.05	.02
728	Kirk Dressendorfer	.05	.02
729	Scott Aldred	.05	.02
730	Willie Blair	.05	.02
731	Allan Anderson	.05	.02
732	Dana Kiecker	.05	.02
733	Jose Gonzalez	.05	.02
734	Brian Drahman	.05	.02
735	Brad Komminsk	.05	.02
736	Arthur Rhodes	.05	.02
737	Terry Mathews	.05	.02
738	Jeff Fassero	.05	.02
739	Mike Magnante	.05	.02
740	Kip Gross	.05	.02
741	Jim Hunter	.05	.02
742	Jose Mota	.05	.02
743	Joe Bitker	.05	.02
744	Tim Mauser	.05	.02
745	Ramon Garcia	.05	.02
746	Rod Beck	.20	.09
747	Jim Austin	.05	.02
748	Keith Mitchell	.05	.02
749	Wayne Rosenthal	.05	.02
750	Bryan Hickerson	.05	.02
751	Bruce Egloff	.05	.02
752	John Wehner	.05	.02
753	Darren Holmes	.05	.02
754	Dave Hansen	.05	.02
755	Mike Mussina	.30	.14
756	Anthony Young	.05	.02
757	Ron Tingley	.05	.02
758	Ricky Bones	.05	.02
759	Mark Wohlers	.15	.07
760	Wilson Alvarez	.10	.05
761	Harvey Pulliam	.05	.02
762	Ryan Bowen	.05	.02
763	Terry Bross	.05	.02
764	Joel Johnston	.05	.02
765	Terry McDaniel	.05	.02
766	Esteban Beltre	.05	.02
767	Rob Maurer	.05	.02
768	Ted Wood	.05	.02
769	Mo Sanford	.05	.02
770	Jeff Carter	.05	.02
771	Gil Heredia	.05	.02
772	Monty Fariss	.05	.02
773	Will Clark AS	.10	.05
774	Ryne Sandberg AS	.20	.09
775	Barry Larkin AS	.15	.07
776	Howard Johnson AS	.05	.02
777	Barry Bonds AS	.20	.09
778	Brett Butler AS	.05	.02
779	Tony Gwynn AS	.25	.11
780	Ramon Martinez AS	.05	.02
781	Lee Smith AS	.05	.02
782	Mike Scioscia AS	.05	.02
783	Dennis Martinez HL UER (Card has both 13th and 15th perfect game in Major League history)	.05	.02
784	Dennis Martinez NH	.05	.02
785	Mark Gardner NH	.05	.02
786	Bret Saberhagen NH	.05	.02
787	Kent Mercker NH Mark Wohlers Alejandro Pena	.05	.02
788	Cal Ripken MVP	.20	.09
789	Terry Pendleton MVP	.05	.02
790	Roger Clemens CY	.20	.09
791	Tom Glavine CY	.10	.05
792	Chuck Knoblauch ROY	.10	.05
793	Jeff Bagwell ROY	.30	.14
794	Cal Ripken MANYR	.20	.09
795	David Cone HL	.05	.02
796	Kirby Puckett HL	.20	.09
797	Steve Avery HL	.05	.02
798	Jack Morris HL	.05	.02
799	Allen Watson DC	.05	.02
800	Manny Ramirez DC	1.25	.55
801	Cliff Floyd DC	.20	.09
802	Al Shirley DC	.10	.05
803	Brian Barber DC	.10	.05
804	Jon Farrell DC	.05	.02
805	Brent Gates DC	.05	.02
806	Scott Ruffcorn DC	.05	.02
807	Tyrone Hill DC	.05	.02
808	Benji Gil DC	.10	.05
809	Aaron Sele DC	.10	.05
810	Tyler Green DC	.10	.05
811	Chris Jones	.05	.02
812	Steve Wilson	.05	.02
813	Freddie Benavides	.05	.02
814	Don Wakamatsu	.05	.02
815	Mike Humphreys	.05	.02
816	Scott Servais	.05	.02
817	Rico Rossy	.05	.02
818	John Ramos	.05	.02
819	Rob Mallicoat	.05	.02
820	Milt Hill	.05	.02
821	Carlos Garcia	.05	.02
822	Stan Royer	.05	.02
823	Jeff Plympton	.05	.02
824	Braulio Castillo	.05	.02
825	David Haas	.05	.02
826	Luis Mercedes	.05	.02
827	Eric Karros	.15	.07
828	Shawn Hare	.05	.02
829	Reggie Sanders	.10	.05
830	Tom Goodwin	.10	.05
831	Dan Gakeler	.05	.02
832	Stacy Jones	.05	.02
833	Kim Batiste	.05	.02
834	Cal Eldred	.05	.02
835	Chris George	.05	.02
836	Wayne Housie	.05	.02
837	Mike Ignasiak	.05	.02
838	Josias Manzanillo	.05	.02
839	Jim Olander	.05	.02
840	Gary Cooper	.05	.02
841	Royce Clayton	.05	.02
842	Hector Fajardo	.05	.02
843	Blaine Beatty	.05	.02
844	Jorge Pedre	.05	.02
845	Kenny Lofton	.75	.35
846	Scott Brosius	.05	.02
847	Chris Cron	.05	.02
848	Denis Boucher	.05	.02
849	Kyle Abbott	.05	.02
850	Robert Zupcic	.05	.02
851	Rheal Cormier	.05	.02
852	Jim Lewis	.05	.02
853	Anthony Telford	.05	.02
854	Cliff Brantley	.05	.02
855	Kevin Campbell	.05	.02
856	Craig Shipley	.05	.02
857	Chuck Carr	.05	.02
858	Tony Eusebio	.05	.02
859	Jim Thome	.60	.25

			MINT	NRMT
☐	860	Vinny Castilla	.50	.23
☐	861	Dann Howitt	.05	.02
☐	862	Kevin Ward	.05	.02
☐	863	Steve Wapnick	.05	.02
☐	864	Rod Brewer	.05	.02
☐	865	Todd Van Poppel	.50	.23
☐	866	Jose Hernandez	.05	.02
☐	867	Amalio Carreno	.05	.02
☐	868	Calvin Jones	.05	.02
☐	869	Jeff Gardner	.05	.02
☐	870	Jarvis Brown	.05	.02
☐	871	Eddie Taubensee	.05	.02
☐	872	Andy Mota	.05	.02
☐	873	Chris Haney	.05	.02
☐	874	Roberto Hernandez	.20	.09
☐	875	Laddie Renfroe	.05	.02
☐	876	Scott Cooper	.05	.02
☐	877	Armando Reynoso	.05	.02
☐	878	Ty Cobb MEMO	.25	.11
☐	879	Babe Ruth MEMO	.40	.18
☐	880	Honus Wagner MEMO	.20	.09
☐	881	Lou Gehrig MEMO	.25	.11
☐	882	Satchel Paige MEMO	.20	.09
☐	883	Will Clark DT	.10	.45
☐	884	Cal Ripken DT	2.00	.90
☐	885	Wade Boggs DT	.10	.05
☐	886	Kirby Puckett DT	.40	.18
☐	887	Tony Gwynn DT	.50	.23
☐	888	Craig Biggio DT	.10	.05
☐	889	Scott Erickson DT	.05	.02
☐	890	Tom Glavine DT	.10	.05
☐	891	Rob Dibble DT	.05	.02
☐	892	Mitch Williams DT	.05	.02
☐	893	Frank Thomas DT	1.00	.45
☐	X672	Chuck Knoblauch AU	60.00	27.00
		(1990 Score card,		
		autographed with		
		special hologram on back)		

1992 Score Factory Inserts

Game 2

This 17-card insert standard-size set was distributed only in 1992 Score factory sets and consists of four topical subsets. Cards B1-B7 capture a moment from each game of the 1991 World Series. Cards B8-B11 are Cooperstown cards, honoring future Hall of Famers. Cards B12-B14 form a "Joe D" subset paying tribute to Joe DiMaggio. Cards B15-B17, subtitled "Yaz," conclude the set by commemorating Carl Yastrzemski's heroic feats twenty-five years ago in winning the Triple Crown and lifting the Red Sox to their last American League pennant in 21 years. Each subset displayed a different front design. The World Series cards carry full-bleed color action photos except for a blue stripe at the bottom, while the Cooperstown

cards have a color portrait on a white card face. Both the DiMaggio and Yastrzemski subsets have action photos with silver borders; they differ in that the DiMaggio photos are black and white, the Yastrzemski photos color. The DiMaggio and Yastrzemski subsets are numbered on the back within each subset (e.g., "1 of 3") and as a part of the 17-card insert set (e.g., "B1"). In the DiMaggio and Yastrzemski subsets, Score varied the insert set slightly in retail versus hobby factory sets. In the hobby set, the DiMaggio cards display different black-and-white photos that are bordered beneath by a dark blue stripe (the stripe is green in the retail factory insert). On the backs, these hobby inserts have a red stripe at the bottom; the same stripe is dark blue on the retail inserts. The Yastrzemski cards in the hobby set have different color photos on their fronts than the retail inserts.

		MINT	NRMT
COMPLETE SET (17)		6.00	2.70
COMMON CARD (B1-B7)		.25	.11
COM.COOPERSTOWN (B8-B11)		.75	.35
COMMON DIMAGGIO (B12-B14)		1.50	.70
COMMON YAZ (B15-B17)		.25	.11
*SINGLES: 3X TO 8X BASE CARD HI			
ONE SET PER FACTORY SET ...			

☐	B1	Greg Gagne WS	.25	.11
☐	B2	Scott Leius WS	.25	.11
☐	B3	Mark Lemke WS	.25	.11
		David Justice		
☐	B4	Lonnie Smith WS	.25	.11
		Brian Harper		
☐	B5	David Justice		
☐	B6	Kirby Puckett WS	3.00	1.35
☐	B7	Gene Larkin WS	.25	.11
☐	B8	Carlton Fisk	.75	.35
☐	B9	Ozzie Smith	2.00	.90
☐	B10	Dave Winfield	.75	.35
☐	B11	Robin Yount	.75	.35
☐	B12	Joe DiMaggio	1.50	.70
☐	B13	Joe DiMaggio	1.50	.70
☐	B14	Joe DiMaggio	1.50	.70
☐	B15	Carl Yastrzemski	.25	.11
☐	B16	Carl Yastrzemski	.25	.11
☐	B17	Carl Yastrzemski	.25	.11

1992 Score Franchise

This four-card standard-size set features three all-time greats, Stan Musial, Mickey Mantle, and Carl Yastrzemski. Each for-

mer player autographed 2,000 of his 1992 Score cards, and 500 of the combo cards were signed by all three. In addition to these signed cards, Score produced 150,000 of each Franchise card, and both signed and unsigned cards were randomly inserted in 1992 Score Series II poly packs, blister packs, and cello packs. The first three cards feature color action photos of each player. The fourth is horizontally oriented and pictures each player in a batting stance. A forest green stripe borders the top and bottom. The words "The Franchise" and the Score logo appear at the top, and the player's name is printed on the green stripe at the bottom. The backs of the first three cards have a close-up photo and a career summary. The fourth card is a combo card, summarizing the career of all three players.

		MINT	NRMT
COMPLETE SET (4)		30.00	13.50
COMMON CARD (1-4)		4.00	1.80
RANDOM INSERTS IN SER.2 PACKS			

☐	1	Stan Musial	5.00	2.20
☐	2	Mickey Mantle	12.00	5.50
☐	3	Carl Yastrzemski	4.00	1.80
☐	4	The Franchise Players	10.00	4.50
		Stan Musial		
		Mickey Mantle		
		Carl Yastrzemski		
☐	AU1	Stan Musial	200.00	90.00
		(Autographed with		
		certified signature)		
☐	AU2	Mickey Mantle	550.00	250.00
		(Autographed with		
		certified signature)		
☐	AU3	Carl Yastrzemski	150.00	70.00
		(Autographed with		
		certified signature)		
☐	AU4	Franchise Players	1600.00	700.00
		Stan Musial		
		Mickey Mantle		
		Carl Yastrzemski		
		(Autographed with		
		certified signatures		
		of all three)		

1992 Score Hot Rookies

TODD HUNDLEY

This ten-card standard-size set features color action player photos on a white face. These cards were inserted one per blister pack. The words "Hot Rookie" appear in orange and *yellow vertically along the left edge of the photo, and the team logo is in the lower left corner. The player's name is printed in yellow on a red box accented with a shadow detail.*

	MINT	NRMT
COMPLETE SET (10)	15.00	6.75
COMMON CARD (1-10)	.50	.23
MINOR STARS	1.00	.45
SEMISTARS	2.00	.90
ONE PER BLISTER PACK		

		MINT	NRMT
☐ 1	Cal Eldred	.50	.23
☐ 2	Royce Clayton	.50	.23
☐ 3	Kenny Lofton	10.00	4.50
☐ 4	Todd Van Poppel	.50	.23
☐ 5	Scott Cooper	.50	.23
☐ 6	Todd Hundley	2.00	.90
☐ 7	Tino Martinez	3.00	1.35
☐ 8	Anthony Telford	.50	.23
☐ 9	Derek Bell	1.00	.45
☐ 10	Reggie Jefferson	1.00	.45

1992 Score Impact Players

Gary Cooper · 3B

The 1992 Score Impact Players insert set was issued in two series each with 45 standard-size cards with the respective series of the 1992 regular issue Score cards. Five of these cards were inserted in each 1992 Score jumbo pack. The fronts feature full-bleed color action player photos. The pictures are enhanced by a wide vertical stripe running near the left edge containing the words "90s Impact Player" and a narrower stripe at the bottom printed with the player's name.

	MINT	NRMT
COMPLETE SET (90)	20.00	9.00
COMPLETE SERIES 1 (45)	14.00	6.25
COMPLETE SERIES 2 (45)	6.00	2.70
COMMON CARD (1-90)	.10	.05
FIVE PER JUMBO PACK		

		MINT	NRMT
☐ 1	Chuck Knoblauch	.40	.18
☐ 2	Jeff Bagwell	2.00	.90
☐ 3	Juan Guzman	.10	.05
☐ 4	Milt Cuyler	.10	.05
☐ 5	Ivan Rodriguez	1.25	.55
☐ 6	Rich DeLucia	.10	.05
☐ 7	Orlando Merced	.10	.05
☐ 8	Ray Lankford	.40	.18
☐ 9	Brian Hunter	.10	.05
☐ 10	Roberto Alomar	.40	.18
☐ 11	Wes Chamberlain	.10	.05
☐ 12	Steve Avery	.10	.05
☐ 13	Scott Erickson	.10	.05
☐ 14	Jim Abbott	.10	.05

☐ 15	Mark Whiten	.10	.05
☐ 16	Leo Gomez	.10	.05
☐ 17	Doug Henry	.10	.05
☐ 18	Brent Mayne	.10	.05
☐ 19	Charles Nagy	.20	.09
☐ 20	Phil Plantier	.10	.05
☐ 21	Mo Vaughn	1.00	.45
☐ 22	Craig Biggio	.30	.14
☐ 23	Derek Bell	.20	.09
☐ 24	Royce Clayton	.10	.05
☐ 25	Gary Cooper	.10	.05
☐ 26	Scott Cooper	.10	.05
☐ 27	Juan Gonzalez	2.00	.90
☐ 28	Ken Griffey Jr.	4.00	1.80
☐ 29	Larry Walker	.40	.18
☐ 30	John Smoltz	.30	.14
☐ 31	Todd Hundley	.30	.14
☐ 32	Kenny Lofton	2.00	.90
☐ 33	Andy Mota	.10	.05
☐ 34	Todd Zeile	.10	.05
☐ 35	Arthur Rhodes	.10	.05
☐ 36	Jim Thome	2.00	.90
☐ 37	Todd Van Poppel	.10	.05
☐ 38	Mark Wohlers	.30	.14
☐ 39	Anthony Young	.10	.05
☐ 40	Sandy Alomar Jr.	.20	.09
☐ 41	John Olerud	.20	.09
☐ 42	Robin Ventura	.40	.18
☐ 43	Frank Thomas	3.00	1.35
☐ 44	Dave Justice	.40	.18
☐ 45	Hal Morris	.10	.05
☐ 46	Ruben Sierra	.20	.09
☐ 47	Travis Fryman	.20	.09
☐ 48	Mike Mussina	1.00	.45
☐ 49	Tom Glavine	.30	.14
☐ 50	Barry Larkin	.30	.14
☐ 51	Will Clark UER	.30	.14
	Career Totals spelled To als		
☐ 52	Jose Canseco	.30	.14
☐ 53	Bo Jackson	.20	.09
☐ 54	Dwight Gooden	.20	.09
☐ 55	Barry Bonds	.75	.35
☐ 56	Fred McGriff	.30	.14
☐ 57	Roger Clemens	1.25	.55
☐ 58	Benito Santiago	.10	.05
☐ 59	Darryl Strawberry	.20	.09
☐ 60	Cecil Fielder	.20	.09
☐ 61	John Franco	.10	.05
☐ 62	Matt Williams	.30	.14
☐ 63	Marquis Grissom	.20	.09
☐ 64	Danny Tartabull	.10	.05
☐ 65	Ron Gant	.20	.09
☐ 66	Paul O'Neill	.10	.05
☐ 67	Devon White	.10	.05
☐ 68	Rafael Palmeiro	.30	.14
☐ 69	Tom Gordon	.10	.05
☐ 70	Shawon Dunston	.10	.05
☐ 71	Rob Dibble	.10	.05
☐ 72	Eddie Zosky	.10	.05
☐ 73	Jack McDowell	.20	.09
☐ 74	Len Dykstra	.10	.05
☐ 75	Ramon Martinez	.20	.09
☐ 76	Reggie Sanders	.20	.09
☐ 77	Greg Maddux	2.00	.90
☐ 78	Ellis Burks	.20	.09
☐ 79	John Smiley	.10	.05
☐ 80	Roberto Kelly	.10	.05
☐ 81	Ben McDonald	.20	.09
☐ 82	Mark Lewis	.10	.05
☐ 83	Jose Rijo	.10	.05
☐ 84	Ozzie Guillen	.10	.05
☐ 85	Lance Dickson	.10	.05
☐ 86	Kim Batiste	.10	.05
☐ 87	Gregg Olson	.10	.05
☐ 88	Andy Benes	.20	.09
☐ 89	Cal Eldred	.20	.09
☐ 90	David Cone	.20	.09

1992 Score Rookie/Traded

The 1992 Score Rookie and Traded set contains 110 stan

dard-size cards featuring traded veterans and rookies. This set was issued in complete set form and was released through hobby dealers. The fronts display color action player photos edged on one side by an orange stripe that fades to white as one moves down the card face. The player's name appears in a purple bar above the picture, while his position is printed in a purple bar below the picture. The set is arranged numerically such that cards 1T-79T are traded players and cards 80T-110T feature rookies. The only notable Rookie Card in this set features Brian Jordan.

	MINT	NRMT
COMP.FACT.SET (110)	20.00	9.00
COMMON CARD (1T-110T)	.15	.07
MINOR STARS	.30	.14
UNLISTED STARS	.60	.25

		MINT	NRMT
☐ 1T	Gary Sheffield	.60	.25
☐ 2T	Kevin Seitzer	.15	.07
☐ 3T	Danny Tartabull	.15	.07
☐ 4T	Steve Sax	.15	.07
☐ 5T	Bobby Bonilla	.30	.14
☐ 6T	Frank Viola	.15	.07
☐ 7T	Dave Winfield	.60	.25
☐ 8T	Rick Sutcliffe	.15	.07
☐ 9T	Jose Canseco	.40	.18
☐ 10T	Greg Swindell	.15	.07
☐ 11T	Eddie Murray	.60	.25
☐ 12T	Randy Myers	.30	.14
☐ 13T	Wally Joyner	.30	.14
☐ 14T	Kenny Lofton	8.00	3.60
☐ 15T	Jack Morris	.30	.14
☐ 16T	Charlie Hayes	.15	.07
☐ 17T	Pete Incaviglia	.15	.07
☐ 18T	Kevin Mitchell	.30	.14
☐ 19T	Kurt Stillwell	.15	.07
☐ 20T	Bret Saberhagen	.15	.07
☐ 21T	Steve Buechele	.15	.07
☐ 22T	John Smiley	.15	.07
☐ 23T	Sammy Sosa	.75	.35
☐ 24T	George Bell	.15	.07
☐ 25T	Curt Schilling	1.00	.45
☐ 26T	Dick Schofield	.15	.07
☐ 27T	David Cone	.30	.14
☐ 28T	Dan Gladden	.15	.07
☐ 29T	Kirk McCaskill	.15	.07
☐ 30T	Mike Gallego	.15	.07
☐ 31T	Kevin McReynolds	.15	.07
☐ 32T	Bill Swift	.15	.07
☐ 33T	Dave Martinez	.15	.07
☐ 34T	Storm Davis	.15	.07
☐ 35T	Willie Randolph	.30	.14
☐ 36T	Melido Perez	.15	.07
☐ 37T	Mark Carreon	.15	.07
☐ 38T	Doug Jones	.15	.07
☐ 39T	Gregg Jefferies	.15	.07
☐ 40T	Mike Jackson	.15	.07
☐ 41T	Dickie Thon	.15	.07
☐ 42T	Eric King	.15	.07

		MINT	NRMT
☐ 43T	Herm Winningham	.15	.07
☐ 44T	Derek Lilliquist	.15	.07
☐ 45T	Dave Anderson	.15	.07
☐ 46T	Jeff Reardon	.30	.14
☐ 47T	Scott Bankhead	.15	.07
☐ 48T	Cory Snyder	.15	.07
☐ 49T	Al Newman	.15	.07
☐ 50T	Keith Miller	.15	.07
☐ 51T	Dave Burba	.15	.07
☐ 52T	Bill Pecota	.15	.07
☐ 53T	Chuck Crim	.15	.07
☐ 54T	Mariano Duncan	.15	.07
☐ 55T	Dave Gallagher	.15	.07
☐ 56T	Chris Gwynn	.15	.07
☐ 57T	Scott Ruskin	.15	.07
☐ 58T	Jack Armstrong	.15	.07
☐ 59T	Gary Carter	.60	.25
☐ 60T	Andres Galarraga	.25	.25
☐ 61T	Ken Hill	.15	.07
☐ 62T	Eric Davis	.30	.14
☐ 63T	Ruben Sierra	.15	.07
☐ 64T	Darrin Fletcher	.15	.07
☐ 65T	Tim Belcher	.15	.07
☐ 66T	Mike Morgan	.15	.07
☐ 67T	Scott Scudder	.15	.07
☐ 68T	Tom Candiotti	.15	.07
☐ 69T	Hubie Brooks	.15	.07
☐ 70T	Kal Daniels	.15	.07
☐ 71T	Bruce Ruffin	.15	.07
☐ 72T	Billy Hatcher	.15	.07
☐ 73T	Bob Melvin	.15	.07
☐ 74T	Lee Guetterman	.15	.07
☐ 75T	Rene Gonzales	.15	.07
☐ 76T	Kevin Bass	.15	.07
☐ 77T	Tom Bolton	.15	.07
☐ 78T	John Wetteland	.30	.14
☐ 79T	Bip Roberts	.15	.07
☐ 80T	Pat Listach	.15	.07
☐ 81T	John Doherty	.15	.07
☐ 82T	Sam Militello	.15	.07
☐ 83T	Brian Jordan	1.50	.70
☐ 84T	Jeff Kent	.75	.35
☐ 85T	Dave Fleming	.15	.07
☐ 86T	Jeff Tackett	.15	.07
☐ 87T	Chad Curtis	.60	.25
☐ 88T	Eric Fox	.15	.07
☐ 89T	Denny Neagle	1.50	.70
☐ 90T	Donovan Osborne	.15	.07
☐ 91T	Carlos Hernandez	.15	.07
☐ 92T	Tim Wakefield	.60	.25
☐ 93T	Tim Salmon	5.00	2.20
☐ 94T	Dave Nilsson	.30	.14
☐ 95T	Mike Perez	.15	.07
☐ 96T	Pat Hentgen	.60	.25
☐ 97T	Frank Seminara	.15	.07
☐ 98T	Ruben Amaro Jr.	.15	.07
☐ 99T	Archi Cianfrocco	.15	.07
☐ 100T	Andy Stankiewicz	.15	.07
☐ 101T	Jim Bullinger	.15	.07
☐ 102T	Pat Mahomes	.15	.07
☐ 103T	Hipolito Pichardo	.15	.07
☐ 104T	Bret Boone	.30	.14
☐ 105T	John Vander Wal	.15	.07
☐ 106T	Vince Horsman	.15	.07
☐ 107T	James Austin	.15	.07
☐ 108T	Brian Williams	.15	.07
☐ 109T	Dan Walters	.15	.07
☐ 110T	Wil Cordero	.15	.07

1993 Score

The 1993 Score baseball set consists of 660 standard-size cards issued in one single series. The cards were distributed in 16-card poly packs and 35-card jumbo superpacks. The fronts feature color action player photos surrounded by white borders. The player's name appears in the bottom white border, while the team name and position appear in a team color-coded stripe that edges the left side of the picture.

Topical subsets featured are Award Winners (481-486), Draft Picks (487-501), All-Star Caricature (502-512 [AL], 522-531 [NL]), Highlights (513-519), World Series Highlights (520-521), Dream Team (532-542) and Rookies (sprinkled throughout the set). Rookie Cards in this set include Derek Jeter and Jason Kendall.

		MINT	NRMT
COMPLETE SET (660)		40.00	18.00
COMMON CARD (1-660)		.10	.05
MINOR STARS		.20	.09
SEMISTARS		.30	.14
UNLISTED STARS		.40	.18
SUBSET CARDS HALF VALUE OF BASE CARDS			
☐ 1	Ken Griffey Jr.	2.00	.90
☐ 2	Gary Sheffield	.40	.18
☐ 3	Frank Thomas	1.50	.70
☐ 4	Ryne Sandberg	.50	.23
☐ 5	Larry Walker	.40	.18
☐ 6	Cal Ripken Jr.	1.50	.70
☐ 7	Roger Clemens	.75	.35
☐ 8	Bobby Bonilla	.20	.09
☐ 9	Carlos Baerga	.10	.05
☐ 10	Darren Daulton	.20	.09
☐ 11	Travis Fryman	.20	.09
☐ 12	Andy Van Slyke	.20	.09
☐ 13	Jose Canseco	.30	.14
☐ 14	Roberto Alomar	.40	.18
☐ 15	Tom Glavine	.30	.14
☐ 16	Barry Larkin	.30	.14
☐ 17	Gregg Jefferies	.10	.05
☐ 18	Craig Biggio	.30	.14
☐ 19	Shane Mack	.10	.05
☐ 20	Brett Butler	.20	.09
☐ 21	Dennis Eckersley	.20	.09
☐ 22	Will Clark	.30	.14
☐ 23	Don Mattingly	.60	.25
☐ 24	Tony Gwynn	1.00	.45
☐ 25	Ivan Rodriguez	.50	.23
☐ 26	Shawon Dunston	.10	.05
☐ 27	Mike Mussina	.40	.18
☐ 28	Marquis Grissom	.20	.09
☐ 29	Charles Nagy	.20	.09
☐ 30	Len Dykstra	.20	.09
☐ 31	Cecil Fielder	.20	.09
☐ 32	Jay Bell	.20	.09
☐ 33	B.J. Surhoff	.20	.09
☐ 34	Bob Tewksbury	.10	.05
☐ 35	Danny Tartabull	.10	.05
☐ 36	Terry Pendleton	.20	.09
☐ 37	Jack Morris	.20	.09
☐ 38	Hal Morris	.10	.05
☐ 39	Luis Polonia	.10	.05
☐ 40	Ken Caminiti	.30	.14
☐ 41	Robin Ventura	.20	.09
☐ 42	Darryl Strawberry	.20	.09
☐ 43	Wally Joyner	.20	.09
☐ 44	Fred McGriff	.30	.14
☐ 45	Kevin Tapani	.10	.05
☐ 46	Matt Williams	.30	.14
☐ 47	Robin Yount	.30	.14
☐ 48	Ken Hill	.10	.05
☐ 49	Edgar Martinez	.30	.14
☐ 50	Mark Grace	.30	.14
☐ 51	Juan Gonzalez	1.00	.45
☐ 52	Curt Schilling	.20	.09
☐ 53	Dwight Gooden	.20	.09
☐ 54	Chris Hoiles	.10	.05
☐ 55	Frank Viola	.10	.05
☐ 56	Ray Lankford	.30	.14
☐ 57	George Brett	.75	.35
☐ 58	Kenny Lofton	.75	.35
☐ 59	Nolan Ryan	1.50	.70
☐ 60	Mickey Tettleton	.10	.05
☐ 61	John Smoltz	.20	.09
☐ 62	Howard Johnson	.10	.05
☐ 63	Eric Karros	.20	.09
☐ 64	Rick Aguilera	.10	.05
☐ 65	Steve Finley	.20	.09
☐ 66	Mark Langston	.10	.05
☐ 67	Bill Swift	.10	.05
☐ 68	John Olerud	.10	.05
☐ 69	Kevin McReynolds	.10	.05
☐ 70	Jack McDowell	.10	.05
☐ 71	Rickey Henderson	.30	.14
☐ 72	Brian Harper	.10	.05
☐ 73	Mike Morgan	.10	.05
☐ 74	Rafael Palmeiro	.30	.14
☐ 75	Dennis Martinez	.20	.09
☐ 76	Tino Martinez	.40	.18
☐ 77	Eddie Murray	.40	.18
☐ 78	Ellis Burks	.20	.09
☐ 79	John Kruk	.20	.09
☐ 80	Gregg Olson	.10	.05
☐ 81	Bernard Gilkey	.10	.05
☐ 82	Milt Cuyler	.10	.05
☐ 83	Mike LaValliere	.10	.05
☐ 84	Albert Belle	.50	.23
☐ 85	Bip Roberts	.10	.05
☐ 86	Melido Perez	.10	.05
☐ 87	Otis Nixon	.10	.05
☐ 88	Bill Spiers	.10	.05
☐ 89	Jeff Bagwell	.75	.35
☐ 90	Orel Hershiser	.20	.09
☐ 91	Andy Benes	.20	.09
☐ 92	Devon White	.10	.05
☐ 93	Willie McGee	.10	.05
☐ 94	Ozzie Guillen	.10	.05
☐ 95	Ivan Calderon	.10	.05
☐ 96	Keith Miller	.10	.05
☐ 97	Steve Buechele	.10	.05
☐ 98	Kent Hrbek	.20	.09
☐ 99	Dave Hollins	.10	.05
☐ 100	Mike Bordick	.10	.05
☐ 101	Randy Tomlin	.10	.05
☐ 102	Omar Vizquel	.20	.09
☐ 103	Lee Smith	.20	.09
☐ 104	Leo Gomez	.10	.05
☐ 105	Jose Rijo	.10	.05
☐ 106	Mark Whiten	.10	.05
☐ 107	Dave Justice	.40	.18
☐ 108	Eddie Taubensee	.10	.05
☐ 109	Lance Johnson	.10	.05
☐ 110	Felix Jose	.10	.05
☐ 111	Mike Harkey	.10	.05
☐ 112	Randy Milligan	.10	.05
☐ 113	Anthony Young	.10	.05
☐ 114	Rico Brogna	.20	.09
☐ 115	Bret Saberhagen	.10	.05
☐ 116	Sandy Alomar	.20	.09
☐ 117	Terry Mulholland	.10	.05
☐ 118	Darryl Hamilton	.10	.05
☐ 119	Todd Zeile	.10	.05
☐ 120	Bernie Williams	.40	.18
☐ 121	Zane Smith	.10	.05
☐ 122	Derek Bell	.20	.09
☐ 123	Deion Sanders	.30	.14
☐ 124	Luis Sojo	.10	.05
☐ 125	Joe Oliver	.10	.05
☐ 126	Craig Grebeck	.10	.05
☐ 127	Andujar Cedeno	.10	.05
☐ 128	Brian McRae	.10	.05
☐ 129	Jose Offerman	.10	.05
☐ 130	Pedro Munoz	.10	.05
☐ 131	Bud Black	.10	.05
☐ 132	Mo Vaughn	.50	.23
☐ 133	Bruce Hurst	.10	.05
☐ 134	Dave Henderson	.10	.05

☐ 135	Tom Pagnozzi	.10	.05
☐ 136	Erik Hanson	.10	.05
☐ 137	Orlando Merced	.10	.05
☐ 138	Dean Palmer	.10	.05
☐ 139	John Franco	.20	.09
☐ 140	Brady Anderson	.30	.14
☐ 141	Ricky Jordan	.10	.05
☐ 142	Jeff Blauser	.10	.05
☐ 143	Sammy Sosa	.40	.18
☐ 144	Bob Walk	.10	.05
☐ 145	Delino DeShields	.10	.05
☐ 146	Kevin Brown	.20	.09
☐ 147	Mark Lemke	.10	.05
☐ 148	Chuck Knoblauch	.40	.18
☐ 149	Chris Sabo	.10	.05
☐ 150	Bobby Witt	.10	.05
☐ 151	Luis Gonzalez	.10	.05
☐ 152	Ron Karkovice	.10	.05
☐ 153	Jeff Brantley	.10	.05
☐ 154	Kevin Appier	.20	.09
☐ 155	Darrin Jackson	.10	.05
☐ 156	Kelly Gruber	.10	.05
☐ 157	Royce Clayton	.10	.05
☐ 158	Chuck Finley	.10	.05
☐ 159	Jeff King	.20	.09
☐ 160	Greg Vaughn	.10	.05
☐ 161	Geronimo Pena	.10	.05
☐ 162	Steve Farr	.10	.05
☐ 163	Jose Oquendo	.10	.05
☐ 164	Mark Lewis	.10	.05
☐ 165	John Wetteland	.20	.09
☐ 166	Mike Henneman	.10	.05
☐ 167	Todd Hundley	.30	.14
☐ 168	Wes Chamberlain	.10	.05
☐ 169	Steve Avery	.10	.05
☐ 170	Mike Devereaux	.10	.05
☐ 171	Reggie Sanders	.20	.09
☐ 172	Jay Buhner	.30	.14
☐ 173	Eric Anthony	.10	.05
☐ 174	John Burkett	.10	.05
☐ 175	Tom Candiotti	.10	.05
☐ 176	Phil Plantier	.10	.05
☐ 177	Doug Henry	.10	.05
☐ 178	Scott Leius	.10	.05
☐ 179	Kirt Manwaring	.10	.05
☐ 180	Jeff Parrett	.10	.05
☐ 181	Don Slaught	.10	.05
☐ 182	Scott Radinsky	.10	.05
☐ 183	Luis Alicea	.10	.05
☐ 184	Tom Gordon	.10	.05
☐ 185	Rick Wilkins	.10	.05
☐ 186	Todd Stottlemyre	.10	.05
☐ 187	Moises Alou	.20	.09
☐ 188	Joe Grahe	.10	.05
☐ 189	Jeff Kent	.20	.09
☐ 190	Bill Wegman	.10	.05
☐ 191	Kim Batiste	.10	.05
☐ 192	Matt Nokes	.10	.05
☐ 193	Mark Wohlers	.20	.09
☐ 194	Paul Sorrento	.10	.05
☐ 195	Chris Hammond	.10	.05
☐ 196	Scott Livingstone	.10	.05
☐ 197	Doug Jones	.10	.05
☐ 198	Scott Cooper	.10	.05
☐ 199	Ramon Martinez	.20	.09
☐ 200	Dave Valle	.10	.05
☐ 201	Mariano Duncan	.10	.05
☐ 202	Ben McDonald	.10	.05
☐ 203	Darren Lewis	.10	.05
☐ 204	Kenny Rogers	.10	.05
☐ 205	Manuel Lee	.10	.05
☐ 206	Scott Erickson	.10	.05
☐ 207	Dan Gladden	.10	.05
☐ 208	Bob Welch	.10	.05
☐ 209	Greg Olson	.10	.05
☐ 210	Dan Pasqua	.10	.05
☐ 211	Tim Wallach	.10	.05
☐ 212	Jeff Montgomery	.20	.09
☐ 213	Derrick May	.10	.05
☐ 214	Ed Sprague	.10	.05
☐ 215	David Haas	.10	.05
☐ 216	Darrin Fletcher	.10	.05
☐ 217	Brian Jordan	.20	.09
☐ 218	Jaime Navarro	.10	.05
☐ 219	Randy Velarde	.10	.05
☐ 220	Ron Gant	.20	.09
☐ 221	Paul Quantrill	.10	.05
☐ 222	Damion Easley	.10	.05
☐ 223	Charlie Hough	.10	.05
☐ 224	Brad Brink	.10	.05
☐ 225	Barry Manuel	.10	.05
☐ 226	Kevin Koslofski	.10	.05
☐ 227	Ryan Thompson	.30	.14
☐ 228	Mike Munoz	.10	.05
☐ 229	Dan Wilson	.20	.09
☐ 230	Peter Hoy	.10	.05
☐ 231	Pedro Astacio	.10	.05
☐ 232	Matt Stairs	.10	.05
☐ 233	Jeff Reboulet	.10	.05
☐ 234	Manny Alexander	.10	.05
☐ 235	Willie Banks	.10	.05
☐ 236	John Jaha	.20	.09
☐ 237	Scooter Tucker	.10	.05
☐ 238	Russ Springer	.10	.05
☐ 239	Paul Miller	.10	.05
☐ 240	Dan Peltier	.10	.05
☐ 241	Ozzie Canseco	.10	.05
☐ 242	Ben Rivera	.10	.05
☐ 243	John Valentin	.20	.09
☐ 244	Henry Rodriguez	.20	.09
☐ 245	Derek Parks	.10	.05
☐ 246	Carlos Garcia	.10	.05
☐ 247	Tim Pugh	.10	.05
☐ 248	Melvin Nieves	.20	.09
☐ 249	Rich Amaral	.10	.05
☐ 250	Willie Greene	.20	.09
☐ 251	Tim Scott	.10	.05
☐ 252	Dave Silvestri	.10	.05
☐ 253	Rob Mallicoat	.10	.05
☐ 254	Donald Harris	.10	.05
☐ 255	Craig Colbert	.10	.05
☐ 256	Jose Guzman	.10	.05
☐ 257	Domingo Martinez	.10	.05
☐ 258	William Suero	.10	.05
☐ 259	Juan Guerrero	.10	.05
☐ 260	J.T. Snow	.50	.23
☐ 261	Tony Pena	.10	.05
☐ 262	Tim Fortugno	.10	.05
☐ 263	Tom Marsh	.10	.05
☐ 264	Kurt Knudsen	.10	.05
☐ 265	Tim Costo	.10	.05
☐ 266	Steve Shifflett	.10	.05
☐ 267	Billy Ashley	.10	.05
☐ 268	Jerry Nielsen	.10	.05
☐ 269	Pete Young	.10	.05
☐ 270	Johnny Guzman	.10	.05
☐ 271	Greg Colbrunn	.10	.05
☐ 272	Jeff Nelson	.10	.05
☐ 273	Kevin Young	.10	.05
☐ 274	Jeff Frye	.10	.05
☐ 275	J.T. Bruett	.10	.05
☐ 276	Todd Pratt	.10	.05
☐ 277	Mike Butcher	.10	.05
☐ 278	John Flaherty	.10	.05
☐ 279	John Patterson	.10	.05
☐ 280	Eric Hillman	.10	.05
☐ 281	Bien Figueroa	.10	.05
☐ 282	Shane Reynolds	.20	.09
☐ 283	Rich Rowland	.10	.05
☐ 284	Steve Foster	.10	.05
☐ 285	Dave Mlicki	.10	.05
☐ 286	Mike Piazza	2.00	.90
☐ 287	Mike Trombley	.10	.05
☐ 288	Jim Pena	.10	.05
☐ 289	Bob Ayrault	.10	.05
☐ 290	Henry Mercedes	.10	.05
☐ 291	Bob Wickman	.10	.05
☐ 292	Jacob Brumfield	.10	.05
☐ 293	David Hulse	.10	.05
☐ 294	Ryan Klesko	.50	.23
☐ 295	Doug Linton	.10	.05
☐ 296	Steve Cooke	.10	.05
☐ 297	Eddie Zosky	.10	.05
☐ 298	Gerald Williams	.10	.05
☐ 299	Jonathan Hurst	.10	.05
☐ 300	Larry Carter	.10	.05
☐ 301	William Pennyfeather	.10	.05
☐ 302	Cesar Hernandez	.10	.05
☐ 303	Steve Hosey	.10	.05
☐ 304	Blas Minor	.10	.05
☐ 305	Jeff Grotewald	.10	.05
☐ 306	Bernardo Brito	.10	.05
☐ 307	Rafael Bournigal	.10	.05
☐ 308	Jeff Branson	.10	.05
☐ 309	Tom Quinlan	.10	.05
☐ 310	Pat Gomez	.10	.05
☐ 311	Sterling Hitchcock	.20	.09
☐ 312	Kent Bottenfield	.10	.05
☐ 313	Alan Trammell	.30	.14
☐ 314	Cris Colon	.10	.05
☐ 315	Paul Wagner	.10	.05
☐ 316	Matt Maysey	.10	.05
☐ 317	Mike Stanton	.10	.05
☐ 318	Rick Trlicek	.10	.05
☐ 319	Kevin Rogers	.10	.05
☐ 320	Mark Clark	.10	.05
☐ 321	Pedro Martinez	.40	.18
☐ 322	Al Martin	.20	.09
☐ 323	Mike Macfarlane	.10	.05
☐ 324	Rey Sanchez	.10	.05
☐ 325	Roger Pavlik	.10	.05
☐ 326	Troy Neel	.10	.05
☐ 327	Kerry Woodson	.10	.05
☐ 328	Wayne Kirby	.10	.05
☐ 329	Ken Ryan	.10	.05
☐ 330	Jesse Levis	.10	.05
☐ 331	James Austin	.10	.05
☐ 332	Dan Walters	.10	.05
☐ 333	Brian Williams	.10	.05
☐ 334	Wil Cordero	.10	.05
☐ 335	Bret Boone	.10	.05
☐ 336	Hipolito Pichardo	.10	.05
☐ 337	Pat Mahomes	.10	.05
☐ 338	Andy Stankiewicz	.10	.05
☐ 339	Jim Bullinger	.10	.05
☐ 340	Archi Cianfrocco	.10	.05
☐ 341	Ruben Amaro Jr.	.10	.05
☐ 342	Frank Seminara	.10	.05
☐ 343	Pat Hentgen	.30	.14
☐ 344	Dave Nilsson	.20	.09
☐ 345	Mike Perez	.10	.05
☐ 346	Tim Salmon	.50	.23
☐ 347	Tim Wakefield	.20	.09
☐ 348	Carlos Hernandez	.10	.05
☐ 349	Donovan Osborne	.10	.05
☐ 350	Denny Neagle	.20	.09
☐ 351	Sam Militello	.10	.05
☐ 352	Eric Fox	.10	.05
☐ 353	John Doherty	.10	.05
☐ 354	Chad Curtis	.20	.09
☐ 355	Jeff Tackett	.10	.05
☐ 356	Dave Fleming	.10	.05
☐ 357	Pat Listach	.10	.05
☐ 358	Kevin Wickander	.10	.05
☐ 359	John Vander Wal	.10	.05
☐ 360	Arthur Rhodes	.10	.05
☐ 361	Bob Scanlan	.10	.05
☐ 362	Bob Zupcic	.10	.05
☐ 363	Mel Rojas	.20	.09
☐ 364	Jim Thome	.75	.35
☐ 365	Bill Pecota	.10	.05
☐ 366	Mark Carreon	.10	.05
☐ 367	Mitch Williams	.10	.05
☐ 368	Cal Eldred	.10	.05
☐ 369	Stan Belinda	.10	.05
☐ 370	Pat Kelly	.10	.05
☐ 371	Rheal Cormier	.10	.05
☐ 372	Juan Guzman	.10	.05
☐ 373	Damon Berryhill	.10	.05
☐ 374	Gary DiSarcina	.10	.05
☐ 375	Norm Charlton	.10	.05
☐ 376	Roberto Hernandez	.20	.09
☐ 377	Scott Kamieniecki	.10	.05
☐ 378	Rusty Meacham	.10	.05
☐ 379	Kurt Stillwell	.10	.05
☐ 380	Lloyd McClendon	.10	.05
☐ 381	Mark Leonard	.10	.05
☐ 382	Jerry Browne	.10	.05
☐ 383	Glenn Davis	.10	.05
☐ 384	Randy Johnson	.40	.18
☐ 385	Mike Greenwell	.10	.05
☐ 386	Scott Chiamparino	.10	.05
☐ 387	George Bell	.10	.05
☐ 388	Steve Olin	.10	.05
☐ 389	Chuck McElroy	.10	.05
☐ 390	Mark Gardner	.10	.05
☐ 391	Rod Beck	.20	.09
☐ 392	Dennis Rasmussen	.10	.05

393	Charlie Leibrandt	.10	.05
394	Julio Franco	.10	.05
395	Pete Harnisch	.10	.05
396	Sid Bream	.10	.05
397	Milt Thompson	.10	.05
398	Glenallen Hill	.10	.05
399	Chico Walker	.10	.05
400	Alex Cole	.10	.05
401	Trevor Wilson	.10	.05
402	Jeff Conine	.20	.09
403	Kyle Abbott	.10	.05
404	Tom Browning	.10	.05
405	Jerald Clark	.10	.05
406	Vince Horsman	.10	.05
407	Kevin Mitchell	.20	.09
408	Pete Smith	.10	.05
409	Jeff Innis	.10	.05
410	Mike Timlin	.10	.05
411	Charlie Hayes	.10	.05
412	Alex Fernandez	.20	.09
413	Jeff Russell	.10	.05
414	Jody Reed	.10	.05
415	Mickey Morandini	.10	.05
416	Darnell Coles	.10	.05
417	Xavier Hernandez	.10	.05
418	Steve Sax	.10	.05
419	Joe Girardi	.10	.05
420	Mike Fetters	.10	.05
421	Danny Jackson	.10	.05
422	Jim Gott	.10	.05
423	Tim Belcher	.10	.05
424	Jose Mesa	.10	.05
425	Junior Felix	.10	.05
426	Thomas Howard	.10	.05
427	Julio Valera	.10	.05
428	Dante Bichette	.30	.14
429	Mike Sharperson	.10	.05
430	Darryl Kile	.20	.09
431	Lonnie Smith	.10	.05
432	Monty Fariss	.10	.05
433	Reggie Jefferson	.10	.05
434	Bob McClure	.10	.05
435	Craig Lefferts	.10	.05
436	Duane Ward	.10	.05
437	Shawn Abner	.10	.05
438	Roberto Kelly	.10	.05
439	Paul O'Neill	.20	.09
440	Alan Mills	.10	.05
441	Roger Mason	.10	.05
442	Gary Pettis	.10	.05
443	Steve Lake	.10	.05
444	Gene Larkin	.10	.05
445	Larry Andersen	.10	.05
446	Doug Dascenzo	.10	.05
447	Daryl Boston	.10	.05
448	John Candelaria	.10	.05
449	Storm Davis	.10	.05
450	Tom Edens	.10	.05
451	Mike Maddux	.10	.05
452	Tim Naehring	.10	.05
453	John Orton	.10	.05
454	Joey Cora	.10	.05
455	Chuck Crim	.10	.05
456	Dan Plesac	.10	.05
457	Mike Bielecki	.10	.05
458	Terry Jorgensen	.10	.05
459	John Habyan	.10	.05
460	Pete O'Brien	.10	.05
461	Jeff Treadway	.10	.05
462	Frank Castillo	.10	.05
463	Jimmy Jones	.10	.05
464	Tommy Greene	.10	.05
465	Tracy Woodson	.10	.05
466	Rich Rodriguez	.10	.05
467	Joe Hesketh	.10	.05
468	Greg Myers	.10	.05
469	Kirk McCaskill	.10	.05
470	Ricky Bones	.10	.05
471	Lenny Webster	.10	.05
472	Francisco Cabrera	.10	.05
473	Turner Ward	.10	.05
474	Dwayne Henry	.10	.05
475	Al Osuna	.10	.05
476	Craig Wilson	.10	.05
477	Chris Nabholz	.10	.05
478	Rafael Belliard	.10	.05
479	Terry Leach	.10	.05
480	Tim Teufel	.10	.05
481	Dennis Eckersley AW	.10	.05
482	Barry Bonds AW	.30	.14
483	Dennis Eckersley AW	.10	.05
484	Greg Maddux AW	.60	.25
485	Pat Listach AW	.10	.05
486	Eric Karros AW	.10	.05
487	Jamie Arnold DP	.20	.09
488	B.J. Wallace DP	.10	.05
489	Derek Jeter DP	4.00	1.80
490	Jason Kendall DP	.60	.25
491	Rick Helling DP	.20	.09
492	Derek Wallace DP	.10	.05
493	Sean Lowe DP	.10	.05
494	Shannon Stewart DP	.50	.23
495	Benji Grigsby DP	.10	.05
496	Todd Steverson DP	.20	.09
497	Dan Serafini DP	.30	.14
498	Michael Tucker DP	.40	.18
499	Chris Roberts DP	.20	.09
500	Pete Janicki DP	.10	.05
501	Jeff Schmidt DP	.10	.05
502	Edgar Martinez AS	.20	.09
503	Omar Vizquel AS	.20	.09
504	Ken Griffey Jr. AS	1.00	.45
505	Kirby Puckett AS	.40	.18
506	Joe Carter AS	.10	.05
507	Ivan Rodriguez AS	.40	.18
508	Jack Morris AS	.10	.05
509	Dennis Eckersley AS	.10	.05
510	Frank Thomas AS	.75	.35
511	Roberto Alomar AS	.40	.18
512	Mickey Morandini AS	.10	.05
513	Dennis Eckersley HL	.10	.05
514	Jeff Reardon HL	.10	.05
515	Danny Tartabull HL	.10	.05
516	Bip Roberts HL	.10	.05
517	George Brett HL	.40	.18
518	Robin Yount HL	.30	.14
519	Kevin Gross HL	.10	.05
520	Ed Sprague WS	.10	.05
521	Dave Winfield WS	.20	.09
522	Ozzie Smith AS	.40	.18
523	Barry Bonds AS	.40	.18
524	Andy Van Slyke AS	.10	.05
525	Tony Gwynn AS	.40	.18
526	Darren Daulton AS	.10	.05
527	Greg Maddux AS	.60	.25
528	Fred McGriff AS	.30	.14
529	Lee Smith AS	.10	.05
530	Ryne Sandberg AS	.30	.14
531	Gary Sheffield AS	.20	.09
532	Ozzie Smith DT	.40	.18
533	Kirby Puckett DT	.40	.18
534	Gary Sheffield DT	.20	.09
535	Andy Van Slyke DT	.10	.05
536	Ken Griffey Jr. DT	1.00	.45
537	Ivan Rodriguez DT	.40	.18
538	Charles Nagy DT	.10	.05
539	Tom Glavine DT	.20	.09
540	Dennis Eckersley DT	.10	.05
541	Frank Thomas DT	.75	.35
542	Roberto Alomar DT	.20	.09
543	Sean Berry	.10	.05
544	Mike Schooler	.10	.05
545	Chuck Carr	.10	.05
546	Lenny Harris	.10	.05
547	Gary Scott	.10	.05
548	Derek Lilliquist	.10	.05
549	Brian Hunter	.10	.05
550	Kirby Puckett MOY	.40	.18
551	Jim Eisenreich	.10	.05
552	Andre Dawson	.30	.14
553	David Nied	.10	.05
554	Spike Owen	.10	.05
555	Greg Gagne	.10	.05
556	Sid Fernandez	.10	.05
557	Mark McGwire	.75	.35
558	Bryan Harvey	.10	.05
559	Harold Reynolds	.10	.05
560	Barry Bonds	.50	.23
561	Eric Wedge	.10	.05
562	Ozzie Smith	.50	.23
563	Rick Sutcliffe	.10	.05
564	Jeff Reardon	.20	.09
565	Alex Arias	.10	.05
566	Greg Swindell	.10	.05
567	Brook Jacoby	.10	.05
568	Pete Incaviglia	.10	.05
569	Butch Henry	.10	.05
570	Eric Davis	.20	.09
571	Kevin Seitzer	.10	.05
572	Tony Fernandez	.10	.05
573	Steve Reed	.10	.05
574	Cory Snyder	.10	.05
575	Joe Carter	.20	.09
576	Greg Maddux	1.25	.55
577	Bert Blyleven UER	.20	.09
	(Should say 3701 career strikeouts)		
578	Kevin Bass	.10	.05
579	Carlton Fisk	.40	.18
580	Doug Drabek	.10	.05
581	Mark Gubicza	.10	.05
582	Bobby Thigpen	.10	.05
583	Chili Davis	.20	.09
584	Scott Bankhead	.10	.05
585	Harold Baines	.20	.09
586	Eric Young	.40	.18
587	Lance Parrish	.10	.05
588	Juan Bell	.10	.05
589	Bob Ojeda	.10	.05
590	Joe Orsulak	.10	.05
591	Benito Santiago	.10	.05
592	Wade Boggs	.40	.18
593	Robby Thompson	.10	.05
594	Eric Plunk	.10	.05
595	Hensley Meulens	.10	.05
596	Lou Whitaker	.20	.09
597	Dale Murphy	.30	.14
598	Paul Molitor	.40	.18
599	Greg W. Harris	.10	.05
600	Darren Holmes	.10	.05
601	Dave Martinez	.10	.05
602	Tom Henke	.10	.05
603	Mike Benjamin	.10	.05
604	Rene Gonzales	.10	.05
605	Roger McDowell	.10	.05
606	Kirby Puckett	.75	.35
607	Randy Myers	.20	.09
608	Ruben Sierra	.20	.09
609	Wilson Alvarez	.10	.05
610	David Segui	.10	.05
611	Juan Samuel	.10	.05
612	Tom Brunansky	.10	.05
613	Willie Randolph	.20	.09
614	Tony Phillips	.10	.05
615	Candy Maldonado	.10	.05
616	Chris Bosio	.10	.05
617	Bret Barberie	.10	.05
618	Scott Sanderson	.10	.05
619	Ron Darling	.10	.05
620	Dave Winfield	.30	.14
621	Mike Felder	.10	.05
622	Greg Hibbard	.10	.05
623	Mike Scioscia	.10	.05
624	John Smiley	.10	.05
625	Alejandro Pena	.10	.05
626	Terry Steinbach	.10	.05
627	Freddie Benavides	.10	.05
628	Kevin Reimer	.10	.05
629	Braulio Castillo	.10	.05
630	Dave Stieb	.10	.05
631	Dave Magadan	.10	.05
632	Scott Fletcher	.10	.05
633	Cris Carpenter	.10	.05
634	Kevin Maas	.10	.05
635	Todd Worrell	.10	.05
636	Rob Deer	.10	.05
637	Dwight Smith	.10	.05
638	Chito Martinez	.10	.05
639	Jimmy Key	.20	.09
640	Greg A. Harris	.10	.05
641	Mike Moore	.10	.05
642	Pat Borders	.10	.05
643	Bill Gullickson	.10	.05
644	Gary Gaetti	.10	.05
645	David Howard	.10	.05
646	Jim Abbott	.20	.09
647	Willie Wilson	.10	.05
648	David Wells	.10	.05

		MINT	NRMT
☐	649 Andres Galarraga	.40	.18
☐	650 Vince Coleman	.10	.05
☐	651 Rob Dibble	.10	.05
☐	652 Frank Tanana	.10	.05
☐	653 Steve Decker	.10	.05
☐	654 David Cone	.20	.09
☐	655 Jack Armstrong	.10	.05
☐	656 Dave Stewart	.20	.09
☐	657 Billy Hatcher	.10	.05
☐	658 Tim Raines	.20	.09
☐	659 Walt Weiss	.10	.05
☐	660 Jose Lind	.10	.05

1993 Score Boys of Summer

Randomly inserted exclusively into one in every four 1993 Score 35-card super packs, cards from this standard-size set feature 30 rookies expected to be the best in their class. The fronts are borderless with a color action player photo superimposed over an illustration of the sun. The player's name appears in cursive lettering within a greenish stripe across the bottom. An early Mike Piazza card highlights this set.

		MINT	NRMT
	COMPLETE SET (30)	60.00	27.00
	COMMON CARD (1-30)	1.00	.45
	MINOR STARS	2.00	.90
	RANDOM INSERTS IN JUMBO PACKS		
☐	1 Billy Ashley	1.00	.45
☐	2 Tim Salmon	8.00	3.60
☐	3 Pedro Martinez	8.00	3.60
☐	4 Luis Mercedes	1.00	.45
☐	5 Mike Piazza	30.00	13.50
☐	6 Troy Neel	1.00	.45
☐	7 Melvin Nieves	2.00	.90
☐	8 Ryan Klesko	8.00	3.60
☐	9 Ryan Thompson	1.00	.45
☐	10 Kevin Young	1.00	.45
☐	11 Gerald Williams	1.00	.45
☐	12 Willie Greene	2.00	.90
☐	13 John Patterson	1.00	.45
☐	14 Carlos Garcia	1.00	.45
☐	15 Ed Zosky	1.00	.45
☐	16 Sean Berry	1.00	.45
☐	17 Rico Brogna	2.00	.90
☐	18 Larry Carter	1.00	.45
☐	19 Bobby Ayala	1.00	.45
☐	20 Alan Embree	1.00	.45
☐	21 Donald Harris	1.00	.45
☐	22 Sterling Hitchcock	1.00	.45
☐	23 David Nied	1.00	.45
☐	24 Henry Mercedes	1.00	.45
☐	25 Ozzie Canseco	1.00	.45
☐	26 David Hulse	1.00	.45
☐	27 Al Martin	2.00	.90
☐	28 Dan Wilson	2.00	.90
☐	29 Paul Miller	1.00	.45
☐	30 Rich Rowland	1.00	.45

1993 Score Franchise

This 28-card set honors the top player on each of the major league teams. These cards were randomly inserted into one in every 24 16-card packs. The full-bleed, color action photos on the fronts have the background darkened so that the player appears in white lettering within a team color-coded bar near the bottom, which conjoins with the set logo in the lower left.

		MINT	NRMT
	COMPLETE SET (28)	120.00	55.00
	COMMON CARD (1-28)	1.50	.70
	STATED ODDS 1:24		
☐	1 Cal Ripken	25.00	11.00
☐	2 Roger Clemens	10.00	4.50
☐	3 Mark Langston	1.50	.70
☐	4 Frank Thomas	25.00	11.00
☐	5 Carlos Baerga	1.50	.70
☐	6 Cecil Fielder	3.00	1.35
☐	7 Gregg Jefferies	1.50	.70
☐	8 Robin Yount	4.00	1.80
☐	9 Kirby Puckett	12.00	5.50
☐	10 Don Mattingly	12.00	5.50
☐	11 Dennis Eckersley	3.00	1.35
☐	12 Ken Griffey Jr.	30.00	13.50
☐	13 Juan Gonzalez	15.00	6.75
☐	14 Roberto Alomar	6.00	2.70
☐	15 Terry Pendleton	1.50	.70
☐	16 Ryne Sandberg	6.00	2.70
☐	17 Barry Larkin	4.00	1.80
☐	18 Jeff Bagwell	12.00	5.50
☐	19 Brett Butler	1.50	.70
☐	20 Larry Walker	6.00	2.70
☐	21 Bobby Bonilla	3.00	1.35
☐	22 Darren Daulton	3.00	1.35
☐	23 Andy Van Slyke	1.50	.70
☐	24 Ray Lankford	4.00	1.80
☐	25 Gary Sheffield	6.00	2.70
☐	26 Will Clark	4.00	1.80
☐	27 Bryan Harvey	1.50	.70
☐	28 David Nied	1.50	.70

1993 Score Gold Dream Team

Cards from this 12-card standard-size set feature Score's selection of the best players in baseball at each position. The cards were available only through a mail-in offer. Each card front features sepia tone photos of the players out of uniform, with the exception of Griffey's (of whom is pictured in his Mariners togs). The

FRANK THOMAS

photo edges are rounded with an airbrush effect. The words "Dream Team" are printed in gold lettering at the top. The player's name is printed in sepia tones on the bottom edge.

		MINT	NRMT
	COMPLETE SET (12)	5.00	2.20
	COMMON CARD (1-11/NNO)	.25	.11
	SETS DISTRIBUTED VIA MAIL-IN OFFER		
☐	1 Ozzie Smith	.50	.23
☐	2 Kirby Puckett	.75	.35
☐	3 Gary Sheffield	.50	.23
☐	4 Andy Van Slyke	.25	.11
☐	5 Ken Griffey Jr.	2.50	1.10
☐	6 Ivan Rodriguez	.50	.23
☐	7 Charles Nagy	.25	.11
☐	8 Tom Glavine	.40	.18
☐	9 Dennis Eckersley	.25	.11
☐	10 Frank Thomas	1.50	.70
☐	11 Roberto Alomar	.50	.23
☐	NNO Header Card	.25	.11

1994 Score

The 1994 Score set of 660 standard-size cards was issued in two series of 330. Cards were distributed in 14-card hobby and retail packs. Each pack contained 13 basic cards plus one Gold Rush parallel card. Cards were also distributed in retail Jumbo packs. 4,875 cases of 1994 Score baseball were printed for the hobby. This figure does not take into account additional product printed for retail outlets. The navy blue bordered card fronts feature color action photos with the player's name and team name appearing on two team color-coded stripes across the bottom. Among the subsets are

American League stadiums (317-330) and National League stadiums (647-660). Notable Rookie Cards include Derrek Lee and Billy Wagner.

	MINT	NRMT
COMPLETE SET (660)	24.00	11.00
COMPLETE SERIES 1 (330)	12.00	5.50
COMPLETE SERIES 2 (330)	12.00	5.50
COMMON CARD (1-660)	.10	.05
MINOR STARS	.20	.09
UNLISTED STARS	.40	.18
SUBSET CARDS HALF VALUE OF BASE CARDS		
COMP.G.RUSH SET (660)	160.00	70.00
COMP.G.RUSH SER.1 (330)	80.00	36.00
COMP.G.RUSH SER.2 (330)	80.00	36.00
COMMON G.RUSH (1-660)	.25	.11

*G.RUSH STARS: 1.5X TO 4X HI COLUMN
*G.RUSH YOUNG STARS: 1.25X TO 3X HI
ONE GOLD RUSH PER PACK

☐ 1 Barry Bonds	.50	.23	
☐ 2 John Olerud	.20	.09	
☐ 3 Ken Griffey Jr.	2.00	.90	
☐ 4 Jeff Bagwell	.75	.35	
☐ 5 John Burkett	.10	.05	
☐ 6 Jack McDowell	.10	.05	
☐ 7 Albert Belle	.50	.23	
☐ 8 Andres Galarraga	.40	.18	
☐ 9 Mike Mussina	.40	.18	
☐ 10 Will Clark	.30	.14	
☐ 11 Travis Fryman	.20	.09	
☐ 12 Tony Gwynn	1.00	.45	
☐ 13 Robin Yount	.30	.14	
☐ 14 Dave Magadan	.10	.05	
☐ 15 Paul O'Neill	.20	.09	
☐ 16 Ray Lankford	.20	.09	
☐ 17 Damion Easley	.10	.05	
☐ 18 Andy Van Slyke	.20	.09	
☐ 19 Brian McRae	.10	.05	
☐ 20 Ryne Sandberg	.50	.23	
☐ 21 Kirby Puckett	.75	.35	
☐ 22 Dwight Gooden	.20	.09	
☐ 23 Don Mattingly	.60	.25	
☐ 24 Kevin Mitchell	.10	.05	
☐ 25 Roger Clemens	.75	.35	
☐ 26 Eric Karros	.20	.09	
☐ 27 Juan Gonzalez	1.00	.45	
☐ 28 John Kruk	.20	.09	
☐ 29 Gregg Jefferies	.10	.05	
☐ 30 Tom Glavine	.20	.09	
☐ 31 Ivan Rodriguez	.50	.23	
☐ 32 Jay Bell	.20	.09	
☐ 33 Randy Johnson	.40	.18	
☐ 34 Darren Daulton	.20	.09	
☐ 35 Rickey Henderson	.30	.14	
☐ 36 Eddie Murray	.40	.18	
☐ 37 Brian Harper	.10	.05	
☐ 38 Delino DeShields	.10	.05	
☐ 39 Jose Lind	.10	.05	
☐ 40 Benito Santiago	.10	.05	
☐ 41 Frank Thomas	1.50	.70	
☐ 42 Mark Grace	.30	.14	
☐ 43 Roberto Alomar	.40	.18	
☐ 44 Andy Benes	.20	.09	
☐ 45 Luis Polonia	.10	.05	
☐ 46 Brett Butler	.20	.09	
☐ 47 Terry Steinbach	.10	.05	
☐ 48 Craig Biggio	.30	.14	
☐ 49 Greg Vaughn	.20	.09	
☐ 50 Charlie Hayes	.10	.05	
☐ 51 Mickey Tettleton	.10	.05	
☐ 52 Jose Rijo	.10	.05	
☐ 53 Carlos Baerga	.20	.09	
☐ 54 Jeff Blauser	.20	.09	
☐ 55 Leo Gomez	.10	.05	
☐ 56 Bob Tewksbury	.10	.05	
☐ 57 Mo Vaughn	.50	.23	
☐ 58 Orlando Merced	.10	.05	
☐ 59 Tino Martinez	.40	.18	
☐ 60 Lenny Dykstra	.20	.09	
☐ 61 Jose Canseco	.30	.14	
☐ 62 Tony Fernandez	.10	.05	
☐ 63 Donovan Osborne	.10	.05	
☐ 64 Ken Hill	.10	.05	
☐ 65 Kent Hrbek	.20	.09	
☐ 66 Bryan Harvey	.10	.05	
☐ 67 Wally Joyner	.20	.09	
☐ 68 Derrick May	.10	.05	
☐ 69 Lance Johnson	.10	.05	
☐ 70 Willie McGee	.10	.05	
☐ 71 Mark Langston	.10	.05	
☐ 72 Terry Pendleton	.10	.05	
☐ 73 Joe Carter	.20	.09	
☐ 74 Barry Larkin	.30	.14	
☐ 75 Jimmy Key	.10	.09	
☐ 76 Joe Girardi	.10	.05	
☐ 77 B.J. Surhoff	.10	.05	
☐ 78 Pete Harnisch	.10	.05	
☐ 79 Lou Whitaker UER	.20	.09	
(Milt Cuyler			
pictured on front)			
☐ 80 Cory Snyder	.10	.05	
☐ 81 Kenny Lofton	.50	.23	
☐ 82 Fred McGriff	.30	.14	
☐ 83 Mike Greenwell	.10	.05	
☐ 84 Mike Perez	.10	.05	
☐ 85 Cal Ripken	1.50	.70	
☐ 86 Don Slaught	.10	.05	
☐ 87 Omar Vizquel	.20	.09	
☐ 88 Curt Schilling	.20	.09	
☐ 89 Chuck Knoblauch	.40	.18	
☐ 90 Moises Alou	.20	.09	
☐ 91 Greg Gagne	.10	.05	
☐ 92 Bret Saberhagen	.10	.05	
☐ 93 Ozzie Guillen	.10	.05	
☐ 94 Matt Williams	.30	.14	
☐ 95 Chad Curtis	.10	.05	
☐ 96 Mike Harkey	.10	.05	
☐ 97 Devon White	.10	.05	
☐ 98 Walt Weiss	.10	.05	
☐ 99 Kevin Brown	.20	.09	
☐ 100 Gary Sheffield	.40	.18	
☐ 101 Wade Boggs	.40	.18	
☐ 102 Orel Hershiser	.20	.09	
☐ 103 Tony Phillips	.10	.05	
☐ 104 Andujar Cedeno	.10	.05	
☐ 105 Bill Spiers	.10	.05	
☐ 106 Otis Nixon	.10	.05	
☐ 107 Felix Fermin	.10	.05	
☐ 108 Bip Roberts	.10	.05	
☐ 109 Dennis Eckersley	.20	.09	
☐ 110 Dante Bichette	.20	.09	
☐ 111 Ben McDonald	.10	.05	
☐ 112 Jim Poole	.10	.05	
☐ 113 John Dopson	.10	.05	
☐ 114 Rob Dibble	.10	.05	
☐ 115 Jeff Treadway	.10	.05	
☐ 116 Ricky Jordan	.10	.05	
☐ 117 Mike Henneman	.10	.05	
☐ 118 Willie Blair	.10	.05	
☐ 119 Doug Henry	.10	.05	
☐ 120 Gerald Perry	.10	.05	
☐ 121 Greg Myers	.10	.05	
☐ 122 John Franco	.20	.09	
☐ 123 Roger Mason	.10	.05	
☐ 124 Chris Hammond	.10	.05	
☐ 125 Hubie Brooks	.10	.05	
☐ 126 Kent Mercker	.10	.05	
☐ 127 Jim Abbott	.20	.09	
☐ 128 Kevin Bass	.10	.05	
☐ 129 Rick Aguilera	.10	.05	
☐ 130 Mitch Webster	.10	.05	
☐ 131 Eric Plunk	.10	.05	
☐ 132 Mark Carreon	.10	.05	
☐ 133 Dave Stewart	.20	.09	
☐ 134 Willie Wilson	.10	.05	
☐ 135 Dave Fleming	.10	.05	
☐ 136 Jeff Tackett	.10	.05	
☐ 137 Geno Petralli	.10	.05	
☐ 138 Gene Harris	.10	.05	
☐ 139 Scott Bankhead	.10	.05	
☐ 140 Trevor Wilson	.10	.05	
☐ 141 Alvaro Espinoza	.10	.05	
☐ 142 Ryan Bowen	.10	.05	
☐ 143 Mike Moore	.10	.05	
☐ 144 Bill Pecota	.10	.05	
☐ 145 Jaime Navarro	.10	.05	
☐ 146 Jack Daugherty	.10	.05	
☐ 147 Bob Wickman	.10	.05	
☐ 148 Chris Jones	.10	.05	
☐ 149 Todd Stottlemyre	.10	.05	
☐ 150 Brian Williams	.10	.05	
☐ 151 Chuck Finley	.10	.05	
☐ 152 Lenny Harris	.10	.05	
☐ 153 Alex Fernandez	.10	.05	
☐ 154 Candy Maldonado	.10	.05	
☐ 155 Jeff Montgomery	.10	.05	
☐ 156 David West	.10	.05	
☐ 157 Mark Williamson	.10	.05	
☐ 158 Milt Thompson	.10	.05	
☐ 159 Ron Darling	.10	.05	
☐ 160 Stan Belinda	.10	.05	
☐ 161 Henry Cotto	.10	.05	
☐ 162 Mel Rojas	.10	.05	
☐ 163 Doug Strange	.10	.05	
☐ 164 Rene Arocha	.10	.05	
☐ 165 Tim Hulett	.10	.05	
☐ 166 Steve Avery	.20	.09	
☐ 167 Jim Thome	.50	.23	
☐ 168 Tom Browning	.10	.05	
☐ 169 Mario Diaz	.10	.05	
☐ 170 Steve Reed	.10	.05	
☐ 171 Scott Livingstone	.10	.05	
☐ 172 Chris Donnels	.10	.05	
☐ 173 John Jaha	.10	.05	
☐ 174 Carlos Hernandez	.10	.05	
☐ 175 Dion James	.10	.05	
☐ 176 Bud Black	.10	.05	
☐ 177 Tony Castillo	.10	.05	
☐ 178 Jose Guzman	.10	.05	
☐ 179 Torey Lovullo	.10	.05	
☐ 180 John Vander Wal	.10	.05	
☐ 181 Mike LaValliere	.10	.05	
☐ 182 Sid Fernandez	.10	.05	
☐ 183 Brent Mayne	.10	.05	
☐ 184 Terry Mulholland	.10	.05	
☐ 185 Willie Banks	.10	.05	
☐ 186 Steve Cooke	.10	.05	
☐ 187 Brent Gates	.10	.05	
☐ 188 Erik Pappas	.10	.05	
☐ 189 Bill Haselman	.10	.05	
☐ 190 Fernando Valenzuela	.20	.09	
☐ 191 Gary Redus	.10	.05	
☐ 192 Danny Darwin	.10	.05	
☐ 193 Mark Portugal	.10	.05	
☐ 194 Derek Lilliquist	.10	.05	
☐ 195 Charlie O'Brien	.10	.05	
☐ 196 Matt Nokes	.10	.05	
☐ 197 Danny Sheaffer	.10	.05	
☐ 198 Bill Gullickson	.10	.05	
☐ 199 Alex Arias	.10	.05	
☐ 200 Mike Fetters	.10	.05	
☐ 201 Brian Jordan	.20	.09	
☐ 202 Joe Grahe	.10	.05	
☐ 203 Tom Candiotti	.10	.05	
☐ 204 Jeremy Hernandez	.10	.05	
☐ 205 Mike Stanton	.10	.05	
☐ 206 David Howard	.10	.05	
☐ 207 Darren Holmes	.10	.05	
☐ 208 Rick Honeycutt	.10	.05	
☐ 209 Danny Jackson	.10	.05	
☐ 210 Rich Amaral	.10	.05	
☐ 211 Blas Minor	.10	.05	
☐ 212 Kenny Rogers	.10	.05	
☐ 213 Jim Leyritz	.10	.05	
☐ 214 Mike Morgan	.10	.05	
☐ 215 Dan Gladden	.10	.05	
☐ 216 Randy Velarde	.10	.05	
☐ 217 Mitch Williams	.10	.05	
☐ 218 Hipolito Pichardo	.10	.05	
☐ 219 Dave Burba	.10	.05	
☐ 220 Wilson Alvarez	.10	.05	
☐ 221 Bob Zupcic	.10	.05	
☐ 222 Francisco Cabrera	.10	.05	
☐ 223 Julio Valera	.10	.05	
☐ 224 Paul Assenmacher	.10	.05	
☐ 225 Jeff Branson	.10	.05	
☐ 226 Todd Frohwirth	.10	.05	
☐ 227 Armando Reynoso	.10	.05	
☐ 228 Rich Rowland	.10	.05	
☐ 229 Freddie Benavides	.10	.05	
☐ 230 Wayne Kirby	.10	.05	
☐ 231 Darryl Kile	.20	.09	
☐ 232 Skeeter Barnes	.10	.05	
☐ 233 Ramon Martinez	.20	.09	
☐ 234 Tom Gordon	.10	.05	

☐ 235	Dave Gallagher	.10	.05	☐ 319	California Angels CL	.10	.05	☐ 405	David Cone	.20	.09
☐ 236	Ricky Bones	.10	.05	☐ 320	Chicago White Sox CL	.10	.05	☐ 406	Robby Thompson	.10	.05
☐ 237	Larry Andersen	.10	.05	☐ 321	Cleveland Indians CL	.10	.05	☐ 407	Dave Winfield	.30	.14
☐ 238	Pat Meares	.10	.05	☐ 322	Detroit Tigers CL	.10	.05	☐ 408	Dwight Smith	.10	.05
☐ 239	Zane Smith	.10	.05	☐ 323	Kansas City Royals CL	.10	.05	☐ 409	Ruben Sierra	.10	.05
☐ 240	Tim Leary	.10	.05	☐ 324	Milwaukee Brewers CL	.10	.05	☐ 410	Jack Armstrong	.10	.05
☐ 241	Phil Clark	.10	.05	☐ 325	Minnesota Twins CL	.10	.05	☐ 411	Mike Felder	.10	.05
☐ 242	Danny Cox	.10	.05	☐ 326	New York Yankees CL	.10	.05	☐ 412	Wil Cordero	.10	.05
☐ 243	Mike Jackson	.10	.05	☐ 327	Oakland Athletics CL	.10	.05	☐ 413	Julio Franco	.10	.05
☐ 244	Mike Gallego	.10	.05	☐ 328	Seattle Mariners CL	.10	.05	☐ 414	Howard Johnson	.10	.05
☐ 245	Lee Smith	.20	.09	☐ 329	Texas Rangers CL	.10	.05	☐ 415	Mark McLemore	.10	.05
☐ 246	Todd Jones	.10	.05	☐ 330	Toronto Blue Jays CL	.10	.05	☐ 416	Pete Incaviglia	.10	.05
☐ 247	Steve Bedrosian	.10	.05	☐ 331	Frank Viola	.10	.05	☐ 417	John Valentin	.20	.09
☐ 248	Troy Neel	.10	.05	☐ 332	Ron Gant	.20	.09	☐ 418	Tim Wakefield	.10	.05
☐ 249	Jose Bautista	.10	.05	☐ 333	Charles Nagy	.20	.09	☐ 419	Jose Mesa	.10	.05
☐ 250	Steve Frey	.10	.05	☐ 334	Roberto Kelly	.10	.05	☐ 420	Bernard Gilkey	.10	.05
☐ 251	Jeff Reardon	.20	.09	☐ 335	Brady Anderson	.30	.14	☐ 421	Kirk Gibson	.20	.09
☐ 252	Stan Javier	.10	.05	☐ 336	Alex Cole	.10	.05	☐ 422	Dave Justice	.40	.18
☐ 253	Mo Sanford	.10	.05	☐ 337	Alan Trammell	.30	.14	☐ 423	Tom Brunansky	.10	.05
☐ 254	Steve Sax	.10	.05	☐ 338	Derek Bell	.10	.05	☐ 424	John Smiley	.10	.05
☐ 255	Luis Aquino	.10	.05	☐ 339	Bernie Williams	.40	.18	☐ 425	Kevin Maas	.10	.05
☐ 256	Domingo Jean	.10	.05	☐ 340	Jose Offerman	.10	.05	☐ 426	Doug Drabek	.10	.05
☐ 257	Scott Servais	.10	.05	☐ 341	Bill Wegman	.10	.05	☐ 427	Paul Molitor	.40	.18
☐ 258	Brad Pennington	.10	.05	☐ 342	Ken Caminiti	.30	.14	☐ 428	Darryl Strawberry	.20	.09
☐ 259	Dave Hansen	.10	.05	☐ 343	Pat Borders	.10	.05	☐ 429	Tim Naehring	.10	.05
☐ 260	Goose Gossage	.20	.09	☐ 344	Kirt Manwaring	.10	.05	☐ 430	Bill Swift	.10	.05
☐ 261	Jeff Fassero	.10	.05	☐ 345	Chili Davis	.20	.09	☐ 431	Ellis Burks	.20	.09
☐ 262	Junior Ortiz	.10	.05	☐ 346	Steve Buechele	.10	.05	☐ 432	Greg Hibbard	.10	.05
☐ 263	Anthony Young	.10	.05	☐ 347	Robin Ventura	.20	.09	☐ 433	Felix Jose	.10	.05
☐ 264	Chris Bosio	.10	.05	☐ 348	Teddy Higuera	.10	.05	☐ 434	Bret Barberie	.10	.05
☐ 265	Ruben Amaro Jr.	.10	.05	☐ 349	Jerry Browne	.10	.05	☐ 435	Pedro Munoz	.10	.05
☐ 266	Mark Eichhorn	.10	.05	☐ 350	Scott Kamieniecki	.10	.05	☐ 436	Darrin Fletcher	.10	.05
☐ 267	Dave Clark	.10	.05	☐ 351	Kevin Tapani	.10	.05	☐ 437	Bobby Witt	.10	.05
☐ 268	Gary Thurman	.10	.05	☐ 352	Marquis Grissom	.20	.09	☐ 438	Wes Chamberlain	.10	.05
☐ 269	Les Lancaster	.10	.05	☐ 353	Jay Buhner	.30	.14	☐ 439	Mackey Sasser	.10	.05
☐ 270	Jamie Moyer	.10	.05	☐ 354	Dave Hollins	.10	.05	☐ 440	Mark Whiten	.10	.05
☐ 271	Ricky Gutierrez	.10	.05	☐ 355	Dan Wilson	.20	.09	☐ 441	Harold Reynolds	.10	.05
☐ 272	Greg A.Harris	.10	.05	☐ 356	Bob Walk	.10	.05	☐ 442	Greg Olson	.10	.05
☐ 273	Mike Benjamin	.10	.05	☐ 357	Chris Hoiles	.10	.05	☐ 443	Billy Hatcher	.10	.05
☐ 274	Gene Nelson	.10	.05	☐ 358	Todd Zeile	.10	.05	☐ 444	Joe Oliver	.10	.05
☐ 275	Damon Berryhill	.10	.05	☐ 359	Kevin Appier	.20	.09	☐ 445	Sandy Alomar Jr	.20	.09
☐ 276	Scott Radinsky	.10	.05	☐ 360	Chris Sabo	.10	.05	☐ 446	Tim Wallach	.10	.05
☐ 277	Mike Aldrete	.10	.05	☐ 361	David Segui	.10	.05	☐ 447	Karl Rhodes	.10	.05
☐ 278	Jerry DiPoto	.10	.05	☐ 362	Jerald Clark	.10	.05	☐ 448	Royce Clayton	.10	.05
☐ 279	Chris Haney	.10	.05	☐ 363	Tony Pena	.10	.05	☐ 449	Cal Eldred	.10	.05
☐ 280	Richie Lewis	.10	.05	☐ 364	Steve Finley	.20	.09	☐ 450	Rick Wilkins	.10	.05
☐ 281	Jarvis Brown	.10	.05	☐ 365	Roger Pavlik	.10	.05	☐ 451	Mike Stanley	.10	.05
☐ 282	Juan Bell	.10	.05	☐ 366	John Smoltz	.20	.09	☐ 452	Charlie Hough	.10	.05
☐ 283	Joe Klink	.10	.05	☐ 367	Scott Fletcher	.10	.05	☐ 453	Jack Morris	.20	.09
☐ 284	Graeme Lloyd	.10	.05	☐ 368	Jody Reed	.10	.05	☐ 454	Jon Ratliff	.10	.05
☐ 285	Casey Candaele	.10	.05	☐ 369	David Wells	.10	.05	☐ 455	Rene Gonzales	.10	.05
☐ 286	Bob MacDonald	.10	.05	☐ 370	Jose Vizcaino	.10	.05	☐ 456	Eddie Taubensee	.10	.05
☐ 287	Mike Sharperson	.10	.05	☐ 371	Pat Listach	.10	.05	☐ 457	Roberto Hernandez	.10	.05
☐ 288	Gene Larkin	.10	.05	☐ 372	Orestes Destrade	.10	.05	☐ 458	Todd Hundley	.20	.09
☐ 289	Brian Barnes	.10	.05	☐ 373	Danny Tartabull	.10	.05	☐ 459	Mike Macfarlane	.10	.05
☐ 290	David McCarty	.10	.05	☐ 374	Greg W. Harris	.10	.05	☐ 460	Mickey Morandini	.10	.05
☐ 291	Jeff Innis	.10	.05	☐ 375	Juan Guzman	.10	.05	☐ 461	Scott Erickson	.10	.05
☐ 292	Bob Patterson	.10	.05	☐ 376	Larry Walker	.40	.18	☐ 462	Lonnie Smith	.10	.05
☐ 293	Ben Rivera	.10	.05	☐ 377	Gary DiSarcina	.10	.05	☐ 463	Dave Henderson	.10	.05
☐ 294	John Habyan	.10	.05	☐ 378	Bobby Bonilla	.20	.09	☐ 464	Ryan Klesko	.40	.18
☐ 295	Rich Rodriguez	.10	.05	☐ 379	Tim Raines	.20	.09	☐ 465	Edgar Martinez	.30	.14
☐ 296	Edwin Nunez	.10	.05	☐ 380	Tommy Greene	.10	.05	☐ 466	Tom Pagnozzi	.10	.05
☐ 297	Rod Brewer	.10	.05	☐ 381	Chris Gwynn	.10	.05	☐ 467	Charlie Leibrandt	.10	.05
☐ 298	Mike Timlin	.10	.05	☐ 382	Jeff King	.10	.05	☐ 468	Brian Anderson	.40	.18
☐ 299	Jesse Orosco	.10	.05	☐ 383	Shane Mack	.10	.05	☐ 469	Harold Baines	.20	.09
☐ 300	Gary Gaetti	.10	.05	☐ 384	Ozzie Smith	.50	.23	☐ 470	Tim Belcher	.10	.05
☐ 301	Todd Benzinger	.10	.05	☐ 385	Eddie Zambrano	.10	.05	☐ 471	Andre Dawson	.30	.14
☐ 302	Jeff Nelson	.10	.05	☐ 386	Mike Devereaux	.10	.05	☐ 472	Eric Young	.10	.05
☐ 303	Rafael Belliard	.10	.05	☐ 387	Erik Hanson	.10	.05	☐ 473	Paul Sorrento	.10	.05
☐ 304	Matt Whiteside	.10	.05	☐ 388	Scott Cooper	.10	.05	☐ 474	Luis Gonzalez	.10	.05
☐ 305	Vinny Castilla	.20	.09	☐ 389	Dean Palmer	.10	.05	☐ 475	Rob Deer	.10	.05
☐ 306	Matt Turner	.10	.05	☐ 390	John Wetteland	.10	.05	☐ 476	Mike Piazza	1.25	.55
☐ 307	Eduardo Perez	.10	.05	☐ 391	Reggie Jefferson	.10	.05	☐ 477	Kevin Reimer	.10	.05
☐ 308	Joel Johnston	.10	.05	☐ 392	Mark Lemke	.10	.05	☐ 478	Jeff Gardner	.10	.05
☐ 309	Chris Gomez	.10	.05	☐ 393	Cecil Fielder	.20	.09	☐ 479	Melido Perez	.10	.05
☐ 310	Pat Rapp	.10	.05	☐ 394	Reggie Sanders	.10	.05	☐ 480	Darren Lewis	.10	.05
☐ 311	Jim Tatum	.10	.05	☐ 395	Darryl Hamilton	.10	.05	☐ 481	Duane Ward	.10	.05
☐ 312	Kirk Rueter	.10	.05	☐ 396	Daryl Boston	.10	.05	☐ 482	Rey Sanchez	.10	.05
☐ 313	John Flaherty	.10	.05	☐ 397	Pat Kelly	.10	.05	☐ 483	Mark Lewis	.10	.05
☐ 314	Tom Kramer	.10	.05	☐ 398	Joe Orsulak	.10	.05	☐ 484	Jeff Conine	.20	.09
☐ 315	Mark Whiten	.10	.05	☐ 399	Ed Sprague	.10	.05	☐ 485	Joey Cora	.20	.09
☐ 316	Chris Bosio	.10	.05	☐ 400	Eric Anthony	.10	.05	☐ 486	Trot Nixon	.20	.09
☐ 317	Baltimore Orioles CL	.10	.05	☐ 401	Scott Sanderson	.10	.05	☐ 487	Kevin McReynolds	.10	.05
☐ 318	Boston Red Sox CL UER	.10	.05	☐ 402	Jim Gott	.10	.05	☐ 488	Mike Lansing	.20	.09
	(Viola listed as 316; should be 331)			☐ 403	Ron Karkovice	.10	.05	☐ 489	Mike Pagliarulo	.10	.05
				☐ 404	Phil Plantier	.10	.05	☐ 490	Mariano Duncan	.10	.05

□		MINT	NRMT
491	Mike Bordick	.10	.05
492	Kevin Young	.10	.05
493	Dave Valle	.10	.05
494	Wayne Gomes	.10	.05
495	Rafael Palmeiro	.30	.14
496	Deion Sanders	.20	.09
497	Rick Sutcliffe	.10	.05
498	Randy Milligan	.10	.05
499	Carlos Quintana	.10	.05
500	Chris Turner	.10	.05
501	Thomas Howard	.10	.05
502	Greg Swindell	.10	.05
503	Chad Kreuter	.10	.05
504	Eric Davis	.20	.09
505	Dickie Thon	.10	.05
506	Matt Drews	.20	.09
507	Spike Owen	.10	.05
508	Rod Beck	.10	.05
509	Pat Hentgen	.20	.09
510	Sammy Sosa	.40	.18
511	J.T. Snow	.40	.18
512	Chuck Carr	.10	.05
513	Bo Jackson	.20	.09
514	Dennis Martinez	.20	.09
515	Phil Hiatt	.10	.05
516	Jeff Kent	.10	.05
517	Brooks Kieschnick	.40	.18
518	Kirk Presley	.20	.09
519	Kevin Seitzer	.10	.05
520	Carlos Garcia	.10	.05
521	Mike Blowers	.10	.05
522	Luis Alicea	.10	.05
523	David Hulse	.10	.05
524	Greg Maddux UER	1.25	.55

(career strikeout totals listed as 113; should be 1134)

□		MINT	NRMT
525	Gregg Olson	.10	.05
526	Hal Morris	.10	.05
527	Daron Kirkreit	.10	.05
528	David Nied	.10	.05
529	Jeff Russell	.10	.05
530	Kevin Gross	.10	.05
531	John Doherty	.10	.05
532	Matt Brunson	.10	.05
533	Dave Nilsson	.10	.05
534	Randy Myers	.10	.05
535	Steve Farr	.10	.05
536	Billy Wagner	.75	.35
537	Darnell Coles	.10	.05
538	Frank Tanana	.10	.05
539	Tim Salmon	.40	.18
540	Kim Batiste	.10	.05
541	George Bell	.10	.05
542	Tom Henke	.10	.05
543	Sam Horn	.10	.05
544	Doug Jones	.10	.05
545	Scott Leius	.10	.05
546	Al Martin	.10	.05
547	Bob Welch	.10	.05
548	Scott Christman	.20	.09
549	Norm Charlton	.10	.05
550	Mark McGwire	.75	.35
551	Greg McMichael	.10	.05
552	Tim Costo	.10	.05
553	Rodney Bolton	.10	.05
554	Pedro Martinez	.40	.18
555	Marc Valdes	.10	.05
556	Darrell Whitmore	.10	.05
557	Tim Bogar	.10	.05
558	Steve Karsay	.10	.05
559	Danny Bautista	.10	.05
560	Jeffrey Hammonds	.20	.09
561	Aaron Sele	.10	.05
562	Russ Springer	.10	.05
563	Jason Bere	.10	.05
564	Billy Brewer	.10	.05
565	Sterling Hitchcock	.10	.05
566	Bobby Munoz	.10	.05
567	Craig Paquette	.10	.05
568	Bret Boone	.10	.05
569	Dan Peltier	.10	.05
570	Jeromy Burnitz	.10	.05
571	John Wasdin	.20	.09
572	Chipper Jones	1.25	.55
573	Jamey Wright	.40	.18
574	Jeff Granger	.10	.05
575	Jay Powell	.20	.09
576	Ryan Thompson	.10	.05
577	Lou Frazier	.10	.05
578	Paul Wagner	.10	.05
579	Brad Ausmus	.10	.05
580	Jack Voigt	.10	.05
581	Kevin Rogers	.10	.05
582	Damon Buford	.10	.05
583	Paul Quantrill	.10	.05
584	Marc Newfield	.20	.09
585	Derek Lee	1.25	.55
586	Shane Reynolds	.10	.05
587	Cliff Floyd	.20	.09
588	Jeff Schwarz	.10	.05
589	Ross Powell	.10	.05
590	Gerald Williams	.10	.05
591	Mike Trombley	.10	.05
592	Ken Ryan	.10	.05
593	John O'Donoghue	.10	.05
594	Rod Correia	.10	.05
595	Darrell Sherman	.10	.05
596	Steve Scarsone	.10	.05
597	Sherman Obando	.10	.05
598	Kurt Abbott	.10	.05
599	Dave Telgheder	.10	.05
600	Rick Trlicek	.10	.05
601	Carl Everett	.10	.05
602	Luis Ortiz	.10	.05
603	Larry Luebbers	.10	.05
604	Kevin Roberson	.10	.05
605	Butch Huskey	.20	.09
606	Benji Gil	.10	.05
607	Todd Van Poppel	.10	.05
608	Mark Hutton	.10	.05
609	Chip Hale	.10	.05
610	Matt Maysey	.10	.05
611	Scott Ruffcorn	.10	.05
612	Hilly Hathaway	.10	.05
613	Allen Watson	.10	.05
614	Carlos Delgado	.30	.14
615	Roberto Mejia	.10	.05
616	Turk Wendell	.10	.05
617	Tony Tarasco	.10	.05
618	Raul Mondesi	.40	.18
619	Kevin Stocker	.10	.05
620	Javier Lopez	.30	.14
621	Keith Kessinger	.10	.05
622	Bob Hamelin	.10	.05
623	John Roper	.10	.05
624	Lenny Dykstra WS	.10	.05
625	Joe Carter WS	.10	.05
626	Jim Abbott HL	.10	.05
627	Lee Smith HL	.10	.05
628	Ken Griffey Jr. HL	1.00	.45
629	Dave Winfield HL	.10	.09
630	Darryl Kile HL	.10	.05
631	Frank Thomas AL MVP	.75	.35
632	Barry Bonds NL MVP	.60	.14
633	Jack McDowell AL CY	.10	.05
634	Greg Maddux NL CY	.60	.25
635	Tim Salmon AL ROY	.20	.09
636	Mike Piazza NL ROY	.60	.25
637	Brian Turang	.10	.05
638	Rondell White	.30	.14
639	Nigel Wilson	.10	.05
640	Torii Hunter	.30	.14
641	Salomon Torres	.10	.05
642	Kevin Higgins	.10	.05
643	Eric Wedge	.10	.05
644	Roger Salkeld	.10	.05
645	Manny Ramirez	.50	.23
646	Jeff McNeely	.10	.05
647	Atlanta Braves CL	.10	.05
648	Chicago Cubs CL	.10	.05
649	Cincinnati Reds CL	.10	.05
650	Colorado Rockies CL	.10	.05
651	Florida Marlins CL	.10	.05
652	Houston Astros CL	.10	.05
653	Los Angeles Dodgers CL	.10	.05
654	Montreal Expos CL	.10	.05
655	New York Mets CL	.10	.05
656	Philadelphia Phillies CL	.10	.05
657	Pittsburgh Pirates CL	.10	.05
658	St. Louis Cardinals CL	.10	.05
659	San Diego Padres CL	.10	.05
660	San Francisco Giants CL	.10	.05

1994 Score Boys of Summer

Randomly inserted in super packs at a rate of one in four, this 60-card set features top young stars and hopefuls. The set was issued in two series of 30 cards. The fronts have a color player photo that is outlined by what resembles static electricity. The backgrounds are blurred and the player's name and Boys of Summer logo appear up the right-hand side. An orange band contains a player photo and text.

		MINT	NRMT
COMPLETE SET (60)		120.00	55.00
COMPLETE SERIES 1 (30)		50.00	22.00
COMPLETE SERIES 2 (30)		70.00	32.00
COMMON CARD (1-60)		1.50	.70
MINOR STARS		3.00	1.35
STATED ODDS 1:4 SUPER PACKS			

□		MINT	NRMT
1	Jeff Conine	3.00	1.35
2	Aaron Sele	1.50	.70
3	Kevin Stocker	1.50	.70
4	Pat Meares	1.50	.70
5	Jeromy Burnitz	1.50	.70
6	Mike Piazza	25.00	11.00
7	Allen Watson	1.50	.70
8	Jeffrey Hammonds	3.00	1.35
9	Kevin Roberson	1.50	.70
10	Hilly Hathaway	1.50	.70
11	Kirk Rueter	1.50	.70
12	Eduardo Perez	1.50	.70
13	Ricky Gutierrez	1.50	.70
14	Domingo Jean	1.50	.70
15	David Nied	1.50	.70
16	Wayne Kirby	1.50	.70
17	Mike Lansing	3.00	1.35
18	Jason Bere	1.50	.70
19	Brent Gates	1.50	.70
20	Javier Lopez	5.00	2.20
21	Greg McMichael	1.50	.70
22	David Hulse	1.50	.70
23	Roberto Mejia	1.50	.70
24	Tim Salmon	6.00	2.70
25	Rene Arocha	1.50	.70
26	Bret Boone	1.50	.70
27	David McCarty	1.50	.70
28	Todd Van Poppel	1.50	.70
29	Lance Painter	1.50	.70
30	Erik Pappas	1.50	.70
31	Chuck Carr	1.50	.70
32	Mark Hutton	1.50	.70
33	Jeff McNeely	1.50	.70
34	Willie Greene	1.50	.70
35	Nigel Wilson	1.50	.70
36	Rondell White	5.00	2.20
37	Brian Turang	1.50	.70
38	Manny Ramirez	10.00	4.50
39	Salomon Torres	1.50	.70
40	Melvin Nieves	1.50	.70
41	Ryan Klesko	6.00	2.70

		MINT	NRMT
□ 42	Keith Kessinger	1.50	.70
□ 43	Brad Ausmus	1.50	.70
□ 44	Bob Hamelin	1.50	.70
□ 45	Carlos Delgado	5.00	2.20
□ 46	Marc Newfield	3.00	1.35
□ 47	Raul Mondesi	6.00	2.70
□ 48	Tim Costo	1.50	.70
□ 49	Pedro Martinez	6.00	2.70
□ 50	Steve Karsay	1.50	.70
□ 51	Danny Bautista	1.50	.70
□ 52	Butch Huskey	3.00	1.35
□ 53	Kurt Abbott	1.50	.70
□ 54	Darrell Sherman	1.50	.70
□ 55	Damon Buford	1.50	.70
□ 56	Ross Powell	1.50	.70
□ 57	Darrell Whitmore	1.50	.70
□ 58	Chipper Jones	25.00	11.00
□ 59	Jeff Granger	1.50	.70
□ 60	Cliff Floyd	3.00	1.35

1994 Score Cycle

This 20-card set was randomly inserted in second series foil at a rate of one in 72 and jumbo packs at a rate of one in 36. The set is arranged according to players with the most singles (1-5), doubles (6-10), triples (11-15) and home runs (16-20). The front contains an oval player photo with "The Cycle" at top and the players name at the bottom. Also at the bottom, is the number of that particular base hit the player accumulated in 1993. A small baseball diamond appears beneath the oval photo. The back lists the top five of the given base hit category. A dark blue border surrounds both sides. The cards are numbered with a TC prefix.

		MINT	NRMT
COMPLETE SET (20)		150.00	70.00
COMMON CARD (TC1-TC20)		2.50	1.10
SEMISTARS		6.00	
UNLISTED STARS		10.00	4.50
SER.2 STATED ODDS 1:72, 1:36 JUM			

		MINT	NRMT
□ TC1	Brett Butler	3.00	1.35
□ TC2	Kenny Lofton	12.00	5.50
□ TC3	Paul Molitor	10.00	4.50
□ TC4	Carlos Baerga	2.50	1.10
□ TC5	Gregg Jefferies	2.50	1.10
	Tony Phillips		
□ TC6	John Olerud	3.00	1.35
□ TC7	Charlie Hayes	2.50	1.10
□ TC8	Lenny Dykstra	3.00	1.35
□ TC9	Dante Bichette	3.00	1.35
□ TC10	Devon White	2.50	1.10
□ TC11	Lance Johnson	2.50	1.10
□ TC12	Joey Cora	2.50	1.10
	Steve Finley		
□ TC13	Tony Fernandez	2.50	1.10
□ TC14	David Hulse	2.50	1.10
	Brett Butler		
□ TC15	Jay Bell	2.50	1.10
	Brian McRae		
	Mickey Morandini		
□ TC16	Juan Gonzalez	20.00	9.00
	Barry Bonds		
□ TC17	Ken Griffey Jr.	50.00	22.00
□ TC18	Frank Thomas	40.00	18.00
□ TC19	Dave Justice	10.00	4.50
□ TC20	Matt Williams	6.00	2.70
	Albert Belle		

1994 Score Dream Team

Randomly inserted in first series foil and jumbo packs at a rate of one in 72, this ten-card set feature's baseball's Dream Team as selected by Pinnacle Brands. Banded by forest green stripes above and below, the player photos on the fronts feature ten of baseball's best players sporting historical team uniforms from the 1930s. The set title and player's name appear in gold foil lettering on black bars above and below the picture. The backs carry a color head shot and brief player profile.

		MINT	NRMT
COMPLETE SET (10)		60.00	27.00
COMMON CARD (1-10)		2.50	1.10
SEMISTARS		6.00	2.70
UNLISTED STARS		10.00	4.50
SER.1 STATED ODDS 1:72, 1:36 JUM			

		MINT	NRMT
□ 1	Mike Mussina	10.00	4.50
□ 2	Tom Glavine	4.00	1.80
□ 3	Don Mattingly	15.00	6.75
□ 4	Carlos Baerga	2.50	1.10
□ 5	Barry Larkin	6.00	2.70
□ 6	Matt Williams	6.00	2.70
□ 7	Juan Gonzalez	25.00	11.00
□ 8	Andy Van Slyke	4.00	1.80
□ 9	Larry Walker	10.00	4.50
□ 10	Mike Stanley	2.50	1.10

1994 Score Gold Stars

Randomly inserted at a rate of one in every 18 hobby packs, this 60-card set features National and American stars. Split into two series of 30 cards, the first series (1-30) comprises of National League players and the second series (31-60) American Leaguers. The fronts feature a color action player photo cut out and superimposed on a foil background. At the bottom, a navy blue triangle

carries the set title and the player's name appears in a white bar. The backs have a color close-up shot and a player profile.

		MINT	NRMT
COMPLETE SET (60)		250.00	110.00
COMPLETE NL SERIES (30)		100.00	45.00
COMPLETE AL SERIES (30)		150.00	70.00
COMMON CARD (1-60)		2.00	.90
STATED ODDS 1:18 HOBBY			

		MINT	NRMT
□ 1	Barry Bonds	6.00	2.70
□ 2	Orlando Merced	2.00	.90
□ 3	Mark Grace	4.00	1.80
□ 4	Darren Daulton	3.00	1.35
□ 5	Jeff Blauser	3.00	1.35
□ 6	Deion Sanders	3.00	1.35
□ 7	John Kruk	3.00	1.35
□ 8	Jeff Bagwell	12.00	5.50
□ 9	Gregg Jefferies	2.00	.90
□ 10	Matt Williams	4.00	1.80
□ 11	Andres Galarraga	5.00	2.20
□ 12	Jay Bell	3.00	1.35
□ 13	Mike Piazza	20.00	9.00
□ 14	Ron Gant	3.00	1.35
□ 15	Barry Larkin	4.00	1.80
□ 16	Tom Glavine	3.00	1.35
□ 17	Lenny Dykstra	3.00	1.35
□ 18	Fred McGriff	4.00	1.80
□ 19	Andy Van Slyke	3.00	1.35
□ 20	Gary Sheffield	5.00	2.20
□ 21	John Burkett	2.00	.90
□ 22	Dante Bichette	3.00	1.35
□ 23	Tony Gwynn	15.00	6.75
□ 24	Dave Justice	5.00	2.20
□ 25	Marquis Grissom	3.00	1.35
□ 26	Bobby Bonilla	3.00	1.35
□ 27	Larry Walker	5.00	2.20
□ 28	Brett Butler	3.00	1.35
□ 29	Robby Thompson	2.00	.90
□ 30	Jeff Conine	3.00	1.35
□ 31	Joe Carter	3.00	1.35
□ 32	Ken Griffey Jr.	30.00	13.50
□ 33	Juan Gonzalez	15.00	6.75
□ 34	Rickey Henderson	4.00	1.80
□ 35	Bo Jackson	3.00	1.35
□ 36	Cal Ripken	25.00	11.00
□ 37	John Olerud	3.00	1.35
□ 38	Carlos Baerga	2.00	.90
□ 39	Jack McDowell	2.00	.90
□ 40	Cecil Fielder	3.00	1.35
□ 41	Kenny Lofton	6.00	2.70
□ 42	Roberto Alomar	5.00	2.20
□ 43	Randy Johnson	5.00	2.20
□ 44	Tim Salmon	5.00	2.20
□ 45	Frank Thomas	25.00	11.00
□ 46	Albert Belle	8.00	3.60
□ 47	Greg Vaughn	2.00	.90
□ 48	Travis Fryman	3.00	1.35
□ 49	Don Mattingly	10.00	4.50
□ 50	Wade Boggs	5.00	2.20
□ 51	Mo Vaughn	6.00	2.70
□ 52	Kirby Puckett	12.00	5.50
□ 53	Devon White	2.00	.90
□ 54	Tony Phillips	2.00	.90
□ 55	Brian Harper	2.00	.90

□ 56 Chad Curtis .... 2.00 .90
□ 57 Paul Molitor 5.00 2.20
□ 58 Ivan Rodriguez 8.00 3.60
□ 59 Rafael Palmeiro 4.00 1.80
□ 60 Brian McRae .... 2.00 .90

1994 Score Rookie/Traded

The 1994 Score Rookie and Traded set consists of 165 standard-size cards featuring rookie standouts, traded players, and new young prospects. The set is delineated by traded players (RT1-RT70) and rookies/young prospects (RT71-RT163). The set closes with checklists (RT164-RT165). Each foil pack contained one Gold Rush card. The cards are numbered on the back with an "RT" prefix. Several leading dealers are under the belief that Jose Lima's card (#RT158) was short-printed. A special unnumbered September Call-Up Redemption card could be exchanged for an Alex Rodriguez card. The expiration date was January 31, 1995. Odds of finding a redemption card are approximately one in 240 retail and hobby packs. Rookie Cards include John Mabry and Chan Ho Park.

	MINT	NRMT
COMPLETE SET (165)	10.00	4.50
COMMON CARD (RT1-RT165)	.10	.05
MINOR STARS	.20	.09
UNLISTED STARS	.40	.18
COMP.G.RUSH SET (165) ..	50.00	22.00
COMMON G.RUSH (1-165)	.25	.11

*G.RUSH STARS: 1.5X TO 4X HI COLUMN
*G.RUSH YOUNG STARS: 1.25X TO 3X HI
GOLD RUSH STATED ODDS 1:1
A.ROD CALL UP STATED ODDS 1:240

□ RT1 Will Clark .... .30 .14
□ RT2 Lee Smith .... .20 .09
□ RT3 Bo Jackson .... .20 .09
□ RT4 Ellis Burks .... .20 .09
□ RT5 Eddie Murray .... .40 .18
□ RT6 Delino DeShields .. .10 .05
□ RT7 Erik Hanson .... .10 .05
□ RT8 Rafael Palmeiro ... .30 .14
□ RT9 Luis Polonia .... .10 .05
□ RT10 Omar Vizquel ..... .20 .09
□ RT11 Kurt Abbott .... .10 .05
□ RT12 Vince Coleman .... .10 .05
□ RT13 Rickey Henderson .30 .14
□ RT14 Terry Mulholland . .10 .05
□ RT15 Greg Hibbard ...... .10 .05
□ RT16 Walt Weiss .... .10 .05

□ RT17 Chris Sabo .... .10 .05
□ RT18 Dave Henderson .. .10 .05
□ RT19 Rick Sutcliffe ...... .10 .05
□ RT20 Harold Reynolds .. .10 .05
□ RT21 Jack Morris .... .20 .09
□ RT22 Dan Wilson .... .20 .09
□ RT23 Dave Magadan ... .10 .05
□ RT24 Dennis Martinez .. .20 .09
□ RT25 Wes Chamberlain .10 .05
□ RT26 Otis Nixon .... .10 .05
□ RT27 Eric Anthony ...... .10 .05
□ RT28 Randy Milligan ... .10 .05
□ RT29 Julio Franco .... .10 .05
□ RT30 Kevin McReynolds .10 .05
□ RT31 Anthony Young .... .10 .05
□ RT32 Brian Harper ...... .10 .05
□ RT33 Gene Harris .... .10 .05
□ RT34 Eddie Taubensee . .10 .05
□ RT35 David Segui .... .10 .05
□ RT36 Stan Javier .... .10 .05
□ RT37 Felix Fermin .... .10 .05
□ RT38 Darrin Jackson ... .10 .05
□ RT39 Tony Fernandez ... .10 .05
□ RT40 Jose Vizcaino ..... .10 .05
□ RT41 Willie Banks .... .10 .05
□ RT42 Brian Hunter ...... .10 .05
□ RT43 Reggie Jefferson . .10 .05
□ RT44 Junior Felix .... .10 .05
□ RT45 Jack Armstrong ... .10 .05
□ RT46 Bip Roberts .... .10 .05
□ RT47 Jerry Browne ...... .10 .05
□ RT48 Marvin Freeman .. .10 .05
□ RT49 Jody Reed .... .10 .05
□ RT50 Alex Cole .... .10 .05
□ RT51 Sid Fernandez ..... .10 .05
□ RT52 Pete Smith .... .10 .05
□ RT53 Xavier Hernandez . .10 .05
□ RT54 Scott Sanderson .. .10 .05
□ RT55 Turner Ward .... .10 .05
□ RT56 Rex Hudler .... .10 .05
□ RT57 Deion Sanders .... .20 .09
□ RT58 Sid Bream .... .10 .05
□ RT59 Tony Pena .... .10 .05
□ RT60 Bret Boone .... .10 .05
□ RT61 Bobby Ayala .... .10 .05
□ RT62 Pedro Martinez .... .40 .18
□ RT63 Howard Johnson .. .10 .05
□ RT64 Mark Portugal ..... .10 .05
□ RT65 Rondell Reilly ...... .10 .05
□ RT66 Spike Owen .... .10 .05
□ RT67 Jeff Treadway ..... .10 .05
□ RT68 Mike Harkey .... .10 .05
□ RT69 Doug Jones .... .10 .05
□ RT70 Steve Farr .... .10 .05
□ RT71 Billy Taylor .... .10 .05
□ RT72 Manny Ramirez .... .50 .23
□ RT73 Bob Hamelin .... .10 .05
□ RT74 Steve Karsay .... .10 .05
□ RT75 Ryan Klesko .... .40 .18
□ RT76 Cliff Floyd .... .20 .09
□ RT77 Jeffrey Hammonds .20 .09
□ RT78 Javier Lopez .... .30 .14
□ RT79 Roger Salkeld ..... .10 .05
□ RT80 Hector Carrasco .. .10 .05
□ RT81 Gerald Williams ... .10 .05
□ RT82 Raul Mondesi ...... .40 .18
□ RT83 Sterling Hitchcock .10 .05
□ RT84 Danny Bautista .... .10 .05
□ RT85 Chris Turner .... .10 .05
□ RT86 Shane Reynolds ... .10 .05
□ RT87 Rondell White ..... .30 .14
□ RT88 Salomon Torres ... .10 .05
□ RT89 Turk Wendell ...... .10 .05
□ RT90 Tony Tarasco ...... .10 .05
□ RT91 Shawn Green ...... .20 .09
□ RT92 Greg Colbrunn .... .10 .05
□ RT93 Eddie Zambrano .. .10 .05
□ RT94 Rich Becker .... .10 .05
□ RT95 Chris Gomez .... .10 .05
□ RT96 John Patterson .... .10 .05
□ RT97 Derek Parks .... .10 .05
□ RT98 Rich Rowland ...... .10 .05
□ RT99 James Mouton ..... .10 .05
□ RT100 Tim Hyers .... .10 .05
□ RT101 Jose Valentin .... .10 .05
□ RT102 Carlos Delgado .. .30 .14

□ RT103 Robert Eenhoorn .10 .05
□ RT104 John Hudek ...... .10 .05
□ RT105 Domingo Cedeno .10 .05
□ RT106 Denny Hocking .. .10 .05
□ RT107 Greg Pirkl .... .10 .05
□ RT108 Mark Smith ...... .10 .05
□ RT109 Paul Shuey .... .10 .05
□ RT110 Jorge Fabregas .. .10 .05
□ RT111 Rikkert Faneyte . .10 .05
□ RT112 Rob Butler .... .10 .05
□ RT113 Darren Oliver .... .40 .18
□ RT114 Troy O'Leary ..... .10 .05
□ RT115 Scott Brow .... .10 .05
□ RT116 Tony Eusebio .... .10 .05
□ RT117 Carlos Reyes ..... .10 .05
□ RT118 J.R. Phillips ...... .10 .05
□ RT119 Alex Diaz .... .10 .05
□ RT120 Charles Johnson .30 .14
□ RT121 Nate Minchey .... .10 .05
□ RT122 Scott Sanders .... .10 .05
□ RT123 Daryl Boston ..... .10 .05
□ RT124 Joey Hamilton ... .40 .18
□ RT125 Brian Anderson . .40 .18
□ RT126 Dan Miceli .... .10 .05
□ RT127 Tom Brunansky .. .10 .05
□ RT128 Dave Staton ...... .10 .05
□ RT129 Mike Oquist ...... .10 .05
□ RT130 John Mabry ...... .40 .18
□ RT131 Norberto Martin . .10 .05
□ RT132 Hector Fajardo .. .10 .05
□ RT133 Mark Hutton ..... .10 .05
□ RT134 Fernando Vina ... .10 .05
□ RT135 Lee Tinsley .... .10 .05
□ RT136 Chan Ho Park ... 1.25 .55
□ RT137 Paul Spoljaric ... .10 .05
□ RT138 Matias Carrillo .. .10 .05
□ RT139 Mark Kiefer ...... .10 .05
□ RT140 Stan Royer .... .10 .05
□ RT141 Bryan Eversgerd .10 .05
□ RT142 Brian L.Hunter .. .40 .18
□ RT143 Joe Hall .... .10 .05
□ RT144 Johnny Ruffin .... .10 .05
□ RT145 Alex Gonzalez ... .20 .09
□ RT146 Keith Lockhart ... .10 .05
□ RT147 Tom Marsh .... .10 .05
□ RT148 Tony Longmire .. .10 .05
□ RT149 Keith Mitchell .... .10 .05
□ RT150 Melvin Nieves ... .10 .05
□ RT151 Kelly Stinnett .... .10 .05
□ RT152 Miguel Jimenez . .10 .05
□ RT153 Jeff Juden .... .10 .05
□ RT154 Matt Walbeck .... .10 .05
□ RT155 Marc Newfield ... .20 .09
□ RT156 Matt Mieske ...... .10 .05
□ RT157 Marcus Moore ... .10 .05
□ RT158 Jose Lima SP .... 1.00 .45
□ RT159 Mike Kelly .... .10 .05
□ RT160 Jim Edmonds .... .40 .18
□ RT161 Steve Trachsel ... .20 .09
□ RT162 Greg Blosser ..... .10 .05
□ RT163 Marc Acre .... .10 .05
□ RT164 AL Checklist ..... .10 .05
□ RT165 NL Checklist ..... .10 .05
□ HC1 Alex Rodriguez ... 50.00 22.00
Call-Up Redemption

1994 Score Rookie/Traded Changing Places

Randomly inserted in both retail and hobby packs at a rate of one in 36 Rookie/Traded packs, this 10-card standard-size set focuses on ten veteran superstar players who were traded prior to or during the 1994 season. Cards fronts feature a color photo with a slanted design. The backs have a short write-up and a distorted photo.

	MINT	NRMT
COMPLETE SET (10)	30.00	13.50
COMMON CARD (CP1-CP10)	2.50	1.10
STATED ODDS 1:36 HOB/RET		

		MINT	
☐ CP1 Will Clark	4.00	1.80
☐ CP2 Rafael Palmeiro	4.00	1.80
☐ CP3 Roberto Kelly	2.50	1.10
☐ CP4 Bo Jackson	3.00	1.35
☐ CP5 Otis Nixon	2.50	1.10
☐ CP6 Rickey Henderson	4.00	1.80
☐ CP7 Ellis Burks	3.00	1.35
☐ CP8 Lee Smith	3.00	1.35
☐ CP9 Delino DeShields	2.50	1.10
☐ CP10 Deion Sanders	3.00	1.35

1994 Score Rookie/Traded Super Rookies

Randomly inserted in hobby packs at a rate of one in 36, this 18-card standard-size set focuses on top rookies of 1994. Odds of finding one of these cards is approximately one in 36 hobby packs. Designed much like the Gold Rush, the cards have an all-foil design. The fronts have a player photo and the backs have a photo that serves as background to the Super Rookies logo and text.

	MINT	NRMT
COMPLETE SET (18)	60.00	27.00
COMMON CARD (SU1-SU18)	2.50	1.10
MINOR STARS	4.00	1.80
STATED ODDS 1:36 HOBBY		

☐ SU1 Carlos Delgado	6.00	2.70
☐ SU2 Manny Ramirez	12.00	5.50
☐ SU3 Ryan Klesko	8.00	3.60
☐ SU4 Raul Mondesi	8.00	3.60
☐ SU5 Bob Hamelin	2.50	1.10
☐ SU6 Steve Karsay	2.50	1.10
☐ SU7 Jeffrey Hammonds	4.00	1.80
☐ SU8 Cliff Floyd	4.00	1.80

☐ SU9 Kurt Abbott	2.50	1.10
☐ SU10 Marc Newfield	4.00	1.80
☐ SU11 Javier Lopez	6.00	2.70
☐ SU12 Rich Becker	2.50	1.10
☐ SU13 Greg Pirkl	2.50	1.10
☐ SU14 Rondell White	6.00	2.70
☐ SU15 James Mouton	2.50	1.10
☐ SU16 Tony Tarasco	2.50	1.10
☐ SU17 Brian Anderson	8.00	3.60
☐ SU18 Jim Edmonds	8.00	3.60

1995 Score

The 1995 Score set consists of 605 standard-size cards issued in hobby, retail and jumbo packs. The horizontal and vertical fronts feature color action player shots with irregular dark green and sand brown borders. The player's name, position and the team logo appear in a blue bar under the photo. The horizontal backs have the same design as the fronts. They carry another small color headshot on the left, with the player's name, short biography, career highlights and statistics on the right. Hobby packs featured a special signed Ryan Klesko (RG1) card. Retail packs also had a Klesko card (SG1) but these were not signed. There are no key Rookie Cards in this set.

	MINT	NRMT
COMPLETE SET (605)	24.00	11.00
COMPLETE SERIES 1 (330)	12.00	5.50
COMPLETE SERIES 2 (275)	12.00	5.50
COMMON CARD (1-605)	.10	.05
MINOR STARS	.20	.09
UNLISTED STARS	.40	.18
SUBSET CARDS HALF VALUE OF BASE CARDS		
COMP.G.RUSH SET (605)	120.00	55.00
COMP.G.RUSH SER.1 (330)	60.00	27.00
COMP.G.RUSH SER.2 (275)	60.00	27.00
GOLD RUSH COMMON (1-605)	.15	.07
*G.RUSH STARS: 3X TO 6X HI COLUMN		
*G.RUSH YOUNG STARS: 2.5X TO 5X HI		
ONE GOLD RUSH PER PACK		
COMP.PLAT.SET (587)	300.00	135.00
COMP.PLAT.SER.1 (316)	200.00	90.00
COMP.PLAT.SER.2 (271)	100.00	45.00
*PLATINUM STARS: 5X TO 10X HI COLUMN		
*PLATINUM YOUNG STARS: 4X TO 8X HI		
ONE PLAT.TEAM VIA MAIL PER G.RUSH TEAM		
COMP.YOU TRADE SET (11)	1.50	.70
*YTE CARDS: 1X TO 2X HI COLUMN		
ONE YTE SET VIA MAIL PER YTE TRADE CARD		
KLESKO RG1 SER.1 STATED ODDS 1:720 RET		
KLESKO SG1 SER.1 STATED ODDS 1:720 HOB		

☐ 1 Frank Thomas	1.50	.70
☐ 2 Roberto Alomar	.40	.18
☐ 3 Cal Ripken	1.50	.70
☐ 4 Jose Canseco	.30	.14

☐ 5 Matt Williams	.30	.14
☐ 6 Esteban Beltre	.10	.05
☐ 7 Domingo Cedeno	.10	.05
☐ 8 John Valentin	.10	.05
☐ 9 Glenallen Hill	.10	.05
☐ 10 Rafael Belliard	.10	.05
☐ 11 Randy Myers	.10	.05
☐ 12 Mo Vaughn	.50	.23
☐ 13 Hector Carrasco	.10	.05
☐ 14 Chili Davis	.20	.09
☐ 15 Dante Bichette	.20	.09
☐ 16 Darrin Jackson	.10	.05
☐ 17 Mike Piazza	1.25	.55
☐ 18 Junior Felix	.10	.05
☐ 19 Moises Alou	.20	.09
☐ 20 Mark Gubicza	.10	.05
☐ 21 Bret Saberhagen	.10	.05
☐ 22 Lenny Dykstra	.20	.09
☐ 23 Steve Howe	.10	.05
☐ 24 Mark Dewey	.10	.05
☐ 25 Brian Harper	.10	.05
☐ 26 Ozzie Smith	.50	.23
☐ 27 Scott Erickson	.10	.05
☐ 28 Tony Gwynn	1.00	.45
☐ 29 Bob Welch	.10	.05
☐ 30 Barry Bonds	.50	.23
☐ 31 Leo Gomez	.10	.05
☐ 32 Greg Maddux	1.25	.55
☐ 33 Mike Greenwell	.10	.05
☐ 34 Sammy Sosa	.40	.18
☐ 35 Darnell Coles	.10	.05
☐ 36 Tommy Greene	.10	.05
☐ 37 Will Clark	.30	.14
☐ 38 Steve Ontiveros	.10	.05
☐ 39 Stan Javier	.10	.05
☐ 40 Bip Roberts	.10	.05
☐ 41 Paul O'Neill	.20	.09
☐ 42 Bill Haselman	.10	.05
☐ 43 Shane Mack	.10	.05
☐ 44 Orlando Merced	.10	.05
☐ 45 Kevin Seitzer	.10	.05
☐ 46 Trevor Hoffman	.10	.05
☐ 47 Greg Gagne	.10	.05
☐ 48 Jeff Kent	.10	.05
☐ 49 Tony Phillips	.10	.05
☐ 50 Ken Hill	.10	.05
☐ 51 Carlos Baerga	.20	.09
☐ 52 Henry Rodriguez	.10	.05
☐ 53 Scott Sanderson	.10	.05
☐ 54 Jeff Conine	.20	.09
☐ 55 Chris Turner	.10	.05
☐ 56 Ken Caminiti	.30	.14
☐ 57 Harold Baines	.20	.09
☐ 58 Charlie Hayes	.10	.05
☐ 59 Roberto Kelly	.10	.05
☐ 60 John Olerud	.20	.09
☐ 61 Tim Davis	.10	.05
☐ 62 Rich Rowland	.10	.05
☐ 63 Rey Sanchez	.10	.05
☐ 64 Junior Ortiz	.10	.05
☐ 65 Ricky Gutierrez	.10	.05
☐ 66 Rex Hudler	.10	.05
☐ 67 Johnny Ruffin	.10	.05
☐ 68 Jay Buhner	.30	.14
☐ 69 Tom Pagnozzi	.10	.05
☐ 70 Julio Franco	.10	.05
☐ 71 Eric Young	.10	.05
☐ 72 Mike Bordick	.10	.05
☐ 73 Don Slaught	.10	.05
☐ 74 Goose Gossage	.20	.09
☐ 75 Lonnie Smith	.10	.05
☐ 76 Jimmy Key	.10	.05
☐ 77 Dave Hollins	.10	.05
☐ 78 Mickey Tettleton	.10	.05
☐ 79 Luis Gonzalez	.10	.05
☐ 80 Dave Winfield	.30	.14
☐ 81 Ryan Thompson	.10	.05
☐ 82 Felix Jose	.10	.05
☐ 83 Rusty Meacham	.10	.05
☐ 84 Darryl Hamilton	.10	.05
☐ 85 John Wetteland	.10	.05
☐ 86 Tom Brunansky	.10	.05
☐ 87 Mark Lemke	.10	.05
☐ 88 Spike Owen	.10	.05
☐ 89 Shawon Dunston	.10	.05
☐ 90 Wilson Alvarez	.10	.05

91	Lee Smith	.20	.09
92	Scott Kamieniecki	.10	.05
93	Jacob Brumfield	.10	.05
94	Kirk Gibson	.20	.09
95	Joe Girardi	.10	.05
96	Mike Macfarlane	.10	.05
97	Greg Colbrunn	.10	.05
98	Ricky Bones	.10	.05
99	Delino DeShields	.10	.05
100	Pat Meares	.10	.05
101	Jeff Fassero	.10	.05
102	Jim Leyritz	.10	.05
103	Gary Redus	.10	.05
104	Terry Steinbach	.10	.05
105	Kevin McReynolds	.10	.05
106	Felix Fermin	.10	.05
107	Danny Jackson	.10	.05
108	Chris James	.10	.05
109	Jeff King	.10	.05
110	Pat Hentgen	.10	.05
111	Gerald Perry	.10	.05
112	Tim Raines	.10	.05
113	Eddie Williams	.10	.05
114	Jamie Moyer	.10	.05
115	Bud Black	.10	.05
116	Chris Gomez	.10	.05
117	Luis Lopez	.10	.05
118	Roger Clemens	.75	.35
119	Javier Lopez	.20	.09
120	Dave Nilsson	.10	.05
121	Karl Rhodes	.10	.05
122	Rick Aguilera	.10	.05
123	Tony Fernandez	.10	.05
124	Bernie Williams	.40	.18
125	James Mouton	.10	.05
126	Mark Langston	.10	.05
127	Mike Lansing	.10	.05
128	Tino Martinez	.40	.18
129	Joe Orsulak	.10	.05
130	David Hulse	.10	.05
131	Pete Incaviglia	.10	.05
132	Mark Clark	.10	.05
133	Tony Eusebio	.10	.05
134	Chuck Finley	.10	.05
135	Lou Frazier	.10	.05
136	Craig Grebeck	.10	.05
137	Kelly Stinnett	.10	.05
138	Paul Shuey	.10	.05
139	David Nied	.10	.05
140	Billy Brewer	.10	.05
141	Dave Weathers	.10	.05
142	Scott Leius	.10	.05
143	Brian Jordan	.20	.09
144	Melido Perez	.10	.05
145	Tony Tarasco	.10	.05
146	Dan Wilson	.10	.05
147	Rondell White	.20	.09
148	Mike Henneman	.10	.05
149	Brian Johnson	.10	.05
150	Tom Henke	.10	.05
151	John Patterson	.10	.05
152	Bobby Witt	.10	.05
153	Eddie Taubensee	.10	.05
154	Pat Borders	.10	.05
155	Ramon Martinez	.20	.09
156	Mike Kingery	.10	.05
157	Zane Smith	.10	.05
158	Benito Santiago	.10	.05
159	Matias Carrillo	.10	.05
160	Scott Brosius	.10	.05
161	Dave Clark	.10	.05
162	Mark McLemore	.10	.05
163	Curt Schilling	.20	.09
164	J.T. Snow	.20	.09
165	Rod Beck	.10	.05
166	Scott Fletcher	.10	.05
167	Bob Tewksbury	.10	.05
168	Mike LaValliere	.10	.05
169	Dave Hansen	.10	.05
170	Pedro Martinez	.40	.18
171	Kirk Rueter	.10	.05
172	Jose Lind	.10	.05
173	Luis Alicea	.10	.05
174	Mike Moore	.10	.05
175	Andy Ashby	.10	.05
176	Jody Reed	.10	.05
177	Darryl Kile	.20	.09
178	Carl Willis	.10	.05
179	Jeromy Burnitz	.10	.05
180	Mike Gallego	.10	.05
181	Bill VanLandingham	.10	.05
182	Sid Fernandez	.10	.05
183	Kim Batiste	.10	.05
184	Greg Myers	.10	.05
185	Steve Avery	.10	.05
186	Steve Farr	.10	.05
187	Robb Nen	.10	.05
188	Dan Pasqua	.10	.05
189	Bruce Ruffin	.10	.05
190	Jose Valentin	.10	.05
191	Willie Banks	.10	.05
192	Mike Aldrete	.10	.05
193	Randy Milligan	.10	.05
194	Steve Karsay	.10	.05
195	Mike Stanley	.10	.05
196	Jose Mesa	.10	.05
197	Tom Browning	.10	.05
198	John Vander Wal	.10	.05
199	Kevin Brown	.20	.09
200	Mike Oquist	.10	.05
201	Greg Swindell	.10	.05
202	Eddie Zambrano	.10	.05
203	Joe Boever	.10	.05
204	Gary Varsho	.10	.05
205	Chris Gwynn	.10	.05
206	David Howard	.10	.05
207	Jerome Walton	.10	.05
208	Danny Darwin	.10	.05
209	Darryl Strawberry	.20	.09
210	Todd Van Poppel	.10	.05
211	Scott Livingstone	.10	.05
212	Dave Fleming	.10	.05
213	Todd Worrell	.10	.05
214	Carlos Delgado	.20	.09
215	Bill Pecota	.10	.05
216	Jim Lindeman	.10	.05
217	Rick White	.10	.05
218	Jose Oquendo	.10	.05
219	Tony Castillo	.10	.05
220	Fernando Vina	.10	.05
221	Jeff Bagwell	.75	.35
222	Randy Johnson	.40	.18
223	Albert Belle	.50	.23
224	Chuck Carr	.10	.05
225	Mark Leiter	.10	.05
226	Hal Morris	.10	.05
227	Robin Ventura	.20	.09
228	Mike Munoz	.10	.05
229	Jim Thome	.40	.18
230	Mario Diaz	.10	.05
231	John Doherty	.10	.05
232	Bobby Jones	.10	.05
233	Raul Mondesi	.30	.14
234	Ricky Jordan	.10	.05
235	John Jaha	.10	.05
236	Carlos Garcia	.10	.05
237	Kirby Puckett	.75	.35
238	Orel Hershiser	.20	.09
239	Don Mattingly	.60	.25
240	Sid Bream	.10	.05
241	Brent Gates	.10	.05
242	Tony Longmire	.10	.05
243	Robby Thompson	.10	.05
244	Rick Sutcliffe	.10	.05
245	Dean Palmer	.10	.05
246	Marquis Grissom	.20	.09
247	Paul Molitor	.40	.18
248	Mark Carreon	.10	.05
249	Jack Voigt	.10	.05
250	Greg McMichael UER (photo on front is Mike Stanton)	.10	.05
251	Damon Berryhill	.10	.05
252	Brian Dorsett	.10	.05
253	Jim Edmonds	.30	.14
254	Barry Larkin	.30	.14
255	Jack McDowell	.10	.05
256	Wally Joyner	.20	.09
257	Eddie Murray	.40	.18
258	Lenny Webster	.10	.05
259	Milt Cuyler	.10	.05
260	Todd Benzinger	.10	.05
261	Vince Coleman	.10	.05
262	Todd Stottlemyre	.10	.05
263	Turner Ward	.10	.05
264	Ray Lankford	.20	.09
265	Matt Walbeck	.10	.05
266	Deion Sanders	.20	.09
267	Gerald Williams	.10	.05
268	Jim Gott	.10	.05
269	Jeff Frye	.10	.05
270	Jose Rijo	.10	.05
271	Dave Justice	.40	.18
272	Ismael Valdes	.30	.14
273	Ben McDonald	.10	.05
274	Darren Lewis	.10	.05
275	Graeme Lloyd	.10	.05
276	Luis Ortiz	.10	.05
277	Julian Tavarez	.10	.05
278	Mark Dalesandro	.10	.05
279	Brett Merriman	.10	.05
280	Ricky Bottalico	.20	.09
281	Robert Eenhoorn	.10	.05
282	Rikkert Faneyte	.10	.05
283	Mike Welch	.10	.05
284	Mark Smith	.10	.05
285	Turk Wendell	.10	.05
286	Greg Blosser	.10	.05
287	Garey Ingram	.10	.05
288	Jorge Fabregas	.10	.05
289	Blaise Ilsley	.10	.05
290	Joe Hall	.10	.05
291	Orlando Miller	.10	.05
292	Jose Lima	.10	.05
293	Greg O'Halloran	.10	.05
294	Mark Kiefer	.10	.05
295	Jose Oliva	.10	.05
296	Rich Becker	.10	.05
297	Brian L. Hunter	.30	.14
298	Dave Silvestri	.10	.05
299	Armando Benitez	.10	.05
300	Darren Dreifort	.10	.05
301	John Mabry	.20	.09
302	Greg Pirkl	.10	.05
303	J.R. Phillips	.10	.05
304	Shawn Green	.20	.09
305	Roberto Petagine	.10	.05
306	Keith Lockhart	.10	.05
307	Jonathan Hurst	.10	.05
308	Paul Spoljaric	.10	.05
309	Mike Lieberthal	.10	.05
310	Garret Anderson	.30	.14
311	John Johnstone	.10	.05
312	Alex Rodriguez	1.50	.70
313	Kent Mercker HL	.10	.05
314	John Valentin HL	.10	.05
315	Kenny Rogers HL	.10	.05
316	Fred McGriff HL	.20	.09
317	Team Checklists	.10	.05
318	Team Checklists	.10	.05
319	Team Checklists	.10	.05
320	Team Checklists	.10	.05
321	Team Checklists	.10	.05
322	Team Checklists	.10	.05
323	Team Checklists	.10	.05
324	Team Checklists	.10	.05
325	Team Checklists	.10	.05
326	Team Checklists	.10	.05
327	Team Checklists	.10	.05
328	Team Checklists	.10	.05
329	Team Checklists	.10	.05
330	Team Checklists	.10	.05
331	Pedro Munoz	.10	.05
332	Ryan Klesko	.30	.14
333	Andre Dawson	.30	.14
334	Derrick May	.10	.05
335	Aaron Sele	.10	.05
336	Kevin Mitchell	.10	.05
337	Steve Trachsel	.10	.05
338	Andres Galarraga	.40	.18
339	Terry Pendleton	.10	.05
340	Gary Sheffield	.40	.18
341	Travis Fryman	.20	.09
342	Bo Jackson	.20	.09
343	Gary Gaetti	.10	.05
344	Brett Butler	.20	.09
345	B.J. Surhoff	.10	.05
346	Larry Walker	.40	.18
347	Kevin Tapani	.10	.05

348	Rick Wilkins	.10	.05
349	Wade Boggs	.40	.18
350	Mariano Duncan	.10	.05
351	Ruben Sierra	.10	.05
352	Andy Van Slyke	.20	.09
353	Reggie Jefferson	.10	.05
354	Gregg Jefferies	.10	.05
355	Tim Naehring	.10	.05
356	John Roper	.10	.05
357	Joe Carter	.20	.09
358	Kurt Abbott	.10	.05
359	Lenny Harris	.10	.05
360	Lance Johnson	.10	.05
361	Brian Anderson	.20	.09
362	Jim Eisenreich	.10	.05
363	Jerry Browne	.10	.05
364	Mark Grace	.30	.14
365	Devon White	.10	.05
366	Reggie Sanders	.10	.05
367	Ivan Rodriguez	.50	.23
368	Kirt Manwaring	.10	.05
369	Pat Kelly	.10	.05
370	Ellis Burks	.20	.09
371	Charles Nagy	.10	.05
372	Kevin Bass	.10	.05
373	Lou Whitaker	.20	.09
374	Rene Arocha	.10	.05
375	Derek Parks	.10	.05
376	Mark Whiten	.10	.05
377	Mark McGwire	.75	.35
378	Doug Drabek	.10	.05
379	Greg Vaughn	.10	.05
380	Al Martin	.10	.05
381	Ron Darling	.10	.05
382	Tim Wallach	.10	.05
383	Alan Trammell	.30	.14
384	Randy Velarde	.10	.05
385	Chris Sabo	.10	.05
386	Wil Cordero	.10	.05
387	Darrin Fletcher	.10	.05
388	David Segui	.10	.05
389	Steve Buechele	.10	.05
390	Dave Gallagher	.10	.05
391	Thomas Howard	.10	.05
392	Chad Curtis	.10	.05
393	Cal Eldred	.10	.05
394	Jason Bere	.10	.05
395	Bret Barberie	.10	.05
396	Paul Sorrento	.10	.05
397	Steve Finley	.20	.09
398	Cecil Fielder	.20	.09
399	Eric Karros	.20	.09
400	Jeff Montgomery	.10	.05
401	Cliff Floyd	.10	.05
402	Matt Mieske	.10	.05
403	Brian Hunter	.10	.05
404	Alex Cole	.10	.05
405	Kevin Stocker	.10	.05
406	Eric Davis	.20	.09
407	Marvin Freeman	.10	.05
408	Dennis Eckersley	.20	.09
409	Todd Zeile	.10	.05
410	Keith Mitchell	.10	.05
411	Andy Benes	.20	.09
412	Juan Bell	.10	.05
413	Royce Clayton	.10	.05
414	Ed Sprague	.10	.05
415	Mike Mussina	.40	.18
416	Todd Hundley	.20	.09
417	Pat Listach	.10	.05
418	Joe Oliver	.10	.05
419	Rafael Palmeiro	.30	.14
420	Tim Salmon	.40	.18
421	Brady Anderson	.30	.14
422	Kenny Lofton	.50	.23
423	Craig Biggio	.30	.14
424	Bobby Bonilla	.20	.09
425	Kenny Rogers	.10	.05
426	Derek Bell	.10	.05
427	Scott Cooper	.10	.05
428	Ozzie Guillen	.10	.05
429	Omar Vizquel	.20	.09
430	Phil Plantier	.10	.05
431	Chuck Knoblauch	.40	.18
432	Darren Daulton	.20	.09
433	Bob Hamelin	.10	.05
434	Tom Glavine	.20	.09
435	Walt Weiss	.10	.05
436	Jose Vizcaino	.10	.05
437	Ken Griffey Jr.	2.00	.90
438	Jay Bell	.20	.09
439	Juan Gonzalez	1.00	.45
440	Jeff Blauser	.20	.09
441	Rickey Henderson	.30	.14
442	Bobby Ayala	.10	.05
443	David Cone	.20	.09
444	Pedro J. Martinez	.40	.18
445	Manny Ramirez	.40	.18
446	Mark Portugal	.10	.05
447	Damion Easley	.10	.05
448	Gary DiSarcina	.10	.05
449	Roberto Hernandez	.10	.05
450	Jeffrey Hammonds	.20	.09
451	Jeff Treadway	.10	.05
452	Jim Abbott	.10	.05
453	Carlos Rodriguez	.10	.05
454	Joey Cora	.10	.05
455	Bret Boone	.10	.05
456	Danny Tartabull	.10	.05
457	John Franco	.10	.05
458	Roger Salkeld	.10	.05
459	Fred McGriff	.30	.14
460	Pedro Astacio	.10	.05
461	Jon Lieber	.10	.05
462	Luis Polonia	.10	.05
463	Geronimo Pena	.10	.05
464	Tom Gordon	.10	.05
465	Brad Ausmus	.10	.05
466	Willie McGee	.10	.05
467	Doug Jones	.10	.05
468	John Smoltz	.20	.09
469	Troy Neel	.10	.05
470	Luis Sojo	.10	.05
471	John Smiley	.10	.05
472	Rafael Bournigal	.10	.05
473	Bill Taylor	.10	.05
474	Juan Guzman	.10	.05
475	Dave Magadan	.10	.05
476	Mike Devereaux	.10	.05
477	Andujar Cedeno	.10	.05
478	Edgar Martinez	.30	.14
479	Milt Thompson	.10	.05
480	Allen Watson	.10	.05
481	Ron Karkovice	.10	.05
482	Joey Hamilton	.20	.09
483	Vinny Castilla	.20	.09
484	Tim Belcher	.10	.05
485	Bernard Gilkey	.10	.05
486	Scott Servais	.10	.05
487	Cory Snyder	.10	.05
488	Mel Rojas	.10	.05
489	Carlos Reyes	.10	.05
490	Chip Hale	.10	.05
491	Bill Swift	.20	.09
492	Pat Rapp	.10	.05
493	Brian McRae	.10	.05
494	Mickey Morandini	.10	.05
495	Tony Pena	.10	.05
496	Danny Bautista	.10	.05
497	Armando Reynoso	.10	.05
498	Ken Ryan	.10	.05
499	Billy Ripken	.10	.05
500	Pat Mahomes	.10	.05
501	Mark Acre	.10	.05
502	Geronimo Berroa	.10	.05
503	Norberto Martin	.10	.05
504	Chad Kreuter	.10	.05
505	Howard Johnson	.10	.05
506	Eric Anthony	.10	.05
507	Mark Wohlers	.10	.05
508	Scott Sanders	.10	.05
509	Pete Harnisch	.10	.05
510	Wes Chamberlain	.10	.05
511	Tom Candiotti	.10	.05
512	Albie Lopez	.10	.05
513	Denny Neagle	.20	.09
514	Sean Berry	.10	.05
515	Billy Hatcher	.10	.05
516	Todd Jones	.10	.05
517	Wayne Kirby	.10	.05
518	Butch Henry	.10	.05
519	Sandy Alomar Jr.	.20	.09
520	Kevin Appier	.20	.09
521	Roberto Mejia	.10	.05
522	Steve Cooke	.10	.05
523	Terry Shumpert	.10	.05
524	Mike Jackson	.10	.05
525	Kent Mercker	.10	.05
526	David Wells	.10	.05
527	Juan Samuel	.10	.05
528	Salomon Torres	.10	.05
529	Duane Ward	.10	.05
530	Rob Dibble	.10	.05
531	Mike Blowers	.10	.05
532	Mark Eichhorn	.10	.05
533	Alex Diaz	.10	.05
534	Dan Miceli	.10	.05
535	Jeff Branson	.20	.09
536	Dave Stevens	.10	.05
537	Charlie O'Brien	.10	.05
538	Shane Reynolds	.10	.05
539	Rich Amaral	.10	.05
540	Rusty Greer	.40	.18
541	Alex Arias	.10	.05
542	Eric Plunk	.10	.05
543	John Hudek	.10	.05
544	Kirk McCaskill	.10	.05
545	Jeff Reboulet	.10	.05
546	Sterling Hitchcock	.10	.05
547	Warren Newson	.10	.05
548	Bryan Harvey	.10	.05
549	Mike Huff	.10	.05
550	Lance Parrish	.10	.05
551	Ken Griffey Jr. HIT	1.00	.45
552	Matt Williams HIT	.20	.09
553	Roberto Alomar HIT UER	.20	.09
	(Card says he's a NL All-Star He plays in the AL)		
554	Jeff Bagwell HIT	.40	.18
555	Dave Justice HIT	.20	.09
556	Cal Ripken Jr. HIT	.75	.35
557	Albert Belle HIT	.40	.18
558	Mike Piazza HIT	.60	.25
559	Kirby Puckett HIT	.40	.18
560	Wade Boggs HIT	.20	.09
561	Tony Gwynn HIT UER	.50	.23
	card has him winning AL batting titles he's played whole career in the NL		
562	Barry Bonds HIT	.30	.14
563	Mo Vaughn HIT	.30	.14
564	Don Mattingly HIT	.30	.14
565	Carlos Baerga HIT	.10	.05
566	Paul Molitor HIT	.20	.09
567	Raul Mondesi HIT	.20	.09
568	Manny Ramirez HIT	.20	.09
569	Alex Rodriguez HIT	.75	.35
570	Will Clark HIT	.20	.09
571	Frank Thomas HIT	.75	.35
572	Moises Alou HIT	.10	.05
573	Jeff Conine HIT	.10	.05
574	Joe Ausanio	.10	.05
575	Charles Johnson	.20	.09
576	Ernie Young	.10	.05
577	Jeff Granger	.10	.05
578	Robert Perez	.10	.05
579	Melvin Nieves	.10	.05
580	Gar Finnvold	.10	.05
581	Duane Singleton	.10	.05
582	Chan Ho Park	.40	.18
583	Fausto Cruz	.10	.05
584	Dave Staton	.10	.05
585	Denny Hocking	.10	.05
586	Nate Minchey	.10	.05
587	Marc Newfield	.10	.05
588	Jayhawk Owens UER	.10	.05
	Front Photo is Jim Tatum		
589	Darren Bragg	.20	.09
590	Kevin King	.10	.05
591	Kurt Miller	.10	.05
592	Aaron Small	.10	.05
593	Troy O'Leary	.10	.05
594	Phil Stidham	.10	.05
595	Steve Dunn	.10	.05
596	Cory Bailey	.10	.05
597	Alex Gonzalez	.10	.05
598	Jim Bowie	.10	.05
599	Jeff Cirillo	.20	.09
600	Mark Hutton	.10	.05

			MINT	NRMT
☐ 601	Russ Davis	.10	.05
☐ 602	Checklist	.10	.05
☐ 603	Checklist	.10	.05
☐ 604	Checklist	.10	.05
☐ 605	Checklist	.10	.05
☐ RG1	R.Klesko Rook Greatness	4.00	1.80
☐ SG1	Ryan Klesko AU6100	20.00	9.00
☐ NNO	Trade Hall of Gold	1.00	.45

1995 Score Airmail

This 18-card set was randomly inserted in series two jumbo packs at a rate of one in 24. The fronts have a color photo of the player in a home run swing with the sky in the background. Broken red and blue inner borders frame the player. A gold stamp with the words "Air Mail" is prominent in upper left. The backs have a color photo with player information including how many home runs per at-bats he averaged. A sunset serves as background.

		MINT	NRMT
COMPLETE SET (18)		50.00	22.00
COMMON CARD (AM1-AM18)		2.00	.90
SEMISTARS		4.00	1.80
UNLISTED STARS		6.00	2.70
SER.2 STATED ODDS 1:24 JUMBO			
☐ AM1	Bob Hamelin	2.00	.90
☐ AM2	John Mabry	3.00	1.35
☐ AM3	Marc Newfield	2.00	.90
☐ AM4	Jose Oliva	2.00	.90
☐ AM5	Charles Johnson	3.00	1.35
☐ AM6	Russ Davis	2.00	.90
☐ AM7	Ernie Young	2.00	.90
☐ AM8	Billy Ashley	2.00	.90
☐ AM9	Ryan Klesko	4.00	1.80
☐ AM10	J.R. Phillips	2.00	.90
☐ AM11	Cliff Floyd	2.00	.90
☐ AM12	Carlos Delgado	3.00	1.35
☐ AM13	Melvin Nieves	2.00	.90
☐ AM14	Raul Mondesi	4.00	1.80
☐ AM15	Manny Ramirez	6.00	2.70
☐ AM16	Mike Kelly	2.00	.90
☐ AM17	Alex Rodriguez	30.00	13.50
☐ AM18	Rusty Greer	6.00	2.70

1995 Score Double Gold Champs

This 12-card set was randomly inserted in second series hobby packs at a rate of one in 36. Horizontally-designed fronts have a color action photo with the words "Double Gold Champs" in gold-foil at the bottom above the player's name.

The backs have a color photo and a list of the player's accomplishments.

		MINT	NRMT
COMPLETE SET (12)		100.00	45.00
COMMON CARD (GC1-GC12)		5.00	2.20
SER.2 STATED ODDS 1:36 HOBBY			
☐ GC1	Frank Thomas	15.00	6.75
☐ GC2	Ken Griffey Jr.	20.00	9.00
☐ GC3	Barry Bonds	5.00	2.20
☐ GC4	Tony Gwynn	10.00	4.50
☐ GC5	Don Mattingly	8.00	3.60
☐ GC6	Greg Maddux	12.00	5.50
☐ GC7	Roger Clemens	8.00	3.60
☐ GC8	Kenny Lofton	5.00	2.20
☐ GC9	Jeff Bagwell	8.00	3.60
☐ GC10	Matt Williams	3.00	1.35
☐ GC11	Kirby Puckett	8.00	3.60
☐ GC12	Cal Ripken	15.00	6.75

1995 Score Draft Picks

Randomly inserted in first series hobby packs at a rate of one in 36. This 18-card set takes a look at top picks selected in June of 1994. Horizontal fronts have two player photos on a white background. Vertical backs have a player photo and 1994 season's highlights. The cards are numbered with a DP prefix.

		MINT	NRMT
COMPLETE SET (18)		50.00	22.00
COMMON CARD (DP1-DP18)		1.00	.45
MINOR STARS		1.50	.70
SER.1 STATED ODDS 1:36 HOBBY			
☐ DP1	McKay Christensen	1.50	.70
☐ DP2	Bret Wagner	1.00	.45
☐ DP3	Paul Wilson	1.50	.70
☐ DP4	C.J. Nitkowski	1.00	.45
☐ DP5	Josh Booty	2.00	.90
☐ DP6	Antone Williamson	1.00	.45
☐ DP7	Paul Konerko	15.00	6.75
☐ DP8	Scott Elarton	2.50	1.10
☐ DP9	Jacob Shumate	1.50	.70
☐ DP10	Terrance Long	1.50	.70
☐ DP11	Mark Johnson	1.00	.45
☐ DP12	Ben Grieve	20.00	9.00
☐ DP13	Doug Million	1.00	.45
☐ DP14	Jayson Peterson	1.50	.70
☐ DP15	Dustin Hermanson	1.50	.70
☐ DP16	Matt Smith	1.00	.45
☐ DP17	Kevin Witt	4.00	1.80
☐ DP18	Brian Buchanan	1.00	.45

1995 Score Dream Team

Randomly inserted in first series hobby and retail packs at a rate of one in 72 packs, this 12-card hologram set showcases top performers from the 1994 season. The holographic fronts have two player images. The horizontal backs are not holographic. They are multi-colored with a small player close-up and a brief write-up. The cards are numbered with a DG prefix.

		MINT	NRMT
COMPLETE SET (12)		150.00	70.00
COMMON CARD (DG1-DG12)		2.50	1.10
SEMISTARS		5.00	2.20
UNLISTED STARS		8.00	3.60
SER.1 STATED ODDS 1:72			
☐ DG1	Frank Thomas	30.00	13.50
☐ DG2	Roberto Alomar	8.00	3.60
☐ DG3	Cal Ripken	30.00	13.50
☐ DG4	Matt Williams	5.00	2.20
☐ DG5	Mike Piazza	25.00	11.00
☐ DG6	Albert Belle	10.00	4.50
☐ DG7	Ken Griffey Jr.	40.00	18.00
☐ DG8	Tony Gwynn	20.00	9.00
☐ DG9	Paul Molitor	8.00	3.60
☐ DG10	Jimmy Key	4.00	1.80
☐ DG11	Greg Maddux	25.00	11.00
☐ DG12	Lee Smith	4.00	1.80

1995 Score Hall of Gold

Randomly inserted in packs at a rate one in six, this 110-card multi-series set is a collection of top stars and young hopefuls. Metallic fronts are presented in shades of silver and gold that overlay a player photo. The Hall of Gold logo appears in the upper right-hand corner. Black backs contain a brief write-up and a player photo.

KEN GRIFFEY JR.

	MINT	NRMT
COMPLETE SET (110)	80.00	36.00
COMPLETE SERIES 1 (55)	50.00	22.00
COMPLETE SERIES 2 (55)	30.00	13.50
COMMON CARD (HG1-HG110)	.50	.23

STATED ODDS 1:6H/R, 1:4J, 1:3ANCO
COMP.YOU TRADE EM SET (5) 4.00 1.80
*YTE CARDS: .4X TO 1X BASE CARD HI
ONE YTE SET VIA MAIL PER YTE TRADE CARD

☐ HG1 Ken Griffey Jr.	12.00	5.50
☐ HG2 Matt Williams	1.50	.70
☐ HG3 Roberto Alomar	2.50	1.10
☐ HG4 Jeff Bagwell	5.00	2.20
☐ HG5 Dave Justice	2.50	1.10
☐ HG6 Cal Ripken	10.00	4.50
☐ HG7 Randy Johnson	2.50	1.10
☐ HG8 Barry Larkin	1.50	.70
☐ HG9 Albert Belle	3.00	1.35
☐ HG10 Mike Piazza	8.00	3.60
☐ HG11 Kirby Puckett	5.00	2.20
☐ HG12 Moises Alou	1.00	.45
☐ HG13 Jose Canseco	1.50	.70
☐ HG14 Tony Gwynn	6.00	2.70
☐ HG15 Roger Clemens	4.00	1.80
☐ HG16 Barry Bonds	3.00	1.35
☐ HG17 Mo Vaughn	3.00	1.35
☐ HG18 Greg Maddux	8.00	3.60
☐ HG19 Dante Bichette	1.00	.45
☐ HG20 Will Clark	1.50	.70
☐ HG21 Lenny Dykstra	1.00	.45
☐ HG22 Don Mattingly	4.00	1.80
☐ HG23 Carlos Baerga	.50	.23
☐ HG24 Ozzie Smith	3.00	1.35
☐ HG25 Paul Molitor	2.50	1.10
☐ HG26 Paul O'Neill	1.00	.45
☐ HG27 Deion Sanders	1.00	.45
☐ HG28 Jeff Conine	1.00	.45
☐ HG29 John Olerud	1.00	.45
☐ HG30 Jose Rijo	.50	.23
☐ HG31 Sammy Sosa	2.50	1.10
☐ HG32 Robin Ventura	1.00	.45
☐ HG33 Raul Mondesi	1.50	.70
☐ HG34 Eddie Murray	2.50	1.10
☐ HG35 Marquis Grissom	1.00	.45
☐ HG36 Darryl Strawberry	1.00	.45
☐ HG37 Dave Nilsson	.50	.23
☐ HG38 Manny Ramirez	2.50	1.10
☐ HG39 Delino DeShields	.50	.23
☐ HG40 Lee Smith	1.00	.45
☐ HG41 Alex Rodriguez	10.00	4.50
☐ HG42 Julio Franco	.50	.23
☐ HG43 Bret Saberhagen	.50	.23
☐ HG44 Ken Hill	.50	.23
☐ HG45 Roberto Kelly	.50	.23
☐ HG46 Hal Morris	.50	.23
☐ HG47 Jimmy Key	1.00	.45
☐ HG48 Terry Steinbach	.50	.23
☐ HG49 Mickey Tettleton	.50	.23
☐ HG50 Tony Phillips	.50	.23
☐ HG51 Carlos Garcia	.50	.23
☐ HG52 Jim Edmonds	1.50	.70
☐ HG53 Rod Beck	.50	.23
☐ HG54 Shane Mack	.50	.23
☐ HG55 Ken Caminiti	1.50	.70
☐ HG56 Frank Thomas	10.00	4.50
☐ HG57 Kenny Lofton	3.00	1.35
☐ HG58 Juan Gonzalez	6.00	2.70

1995 Score Rookie Dream Team

This 12-card set was randomly inserted in second series retail and hobby packs at a rate of one in 12. The fronts contain a color photo with a metallic background. The "Rookie Dream Team" title occupy two of the borders. The playeris name is at the bottom in gold-foil. The backs are horizontally designed,

☐ HG59 Jason Bere	.50	.23
☐ HG60 Joe Carter	1.00	.45
☐ HG61 Gary Sheffield	2.50	1.10
☐ HG62 Andres Galarraga	2.50	1.10
☐ HG63 Ellis Burks	1.00	.45
☐ HG64 Bobby Bonilla	1.00	.45
☐ HG65 Tom Glavine	1.00	.45
☐ HG66 John Smoltz	1.00	.45
☐ HG67 Fred McGriff	1.50	.70
☐ HG68 Craig Biggio	1.50	.70
☐ HG69 Reggie Sanders	.50	.23
☐ HG70 Kevin Mitchell	.50	.23
☐ HG71 Larry Walker	2.50	1.10
☐ HG72 Carlos Delgado	1.00	.45
☐ HG73 Alex Gonzalez	.50	.23
☐ HG74 Ivan Rodriguez	3.00	1.35
☐ HG75 Ryan Klesko	1.50	.70
☐ HG76 John Kruk	1.00	.45
☐ HG77 Brian McRae	.50	.23
☐ HG78 Tim Salmon	2.50	1.10
☐ HG79 Travis Fryman	1.00	.45
☐ HG80 Chuck Knoblauch	2.50	1.10
☐ HG81 Jay Bell	.50	.23
☐ HG82 Cecil Fielder	1.00	.45
☐ HG83 Cliff Floyd	.50	.23
☐ HG84 Ruben Sierra	.50	.23
☐ HG85 Mike Mussina	2.50	1.10
☐ HG86 Mark Grace	1.50	.70
☐ HG87 Dennis Eckersley	1.00	.45
☐ HG88 Dennis Martinez	1.00	.45
☐ HG89 Rafael Palmeiro	1.50	.70
☐ HG90 Ben McDonald	.50	.23
☐ HG91 Dave Hollins	.50	.23
☐ HG92 Steve Avery	.50	.23
☐ HG93 David Cone	1.00	.45
☐ HG94 Darren Daulton	.50	.23
☐ HG95 Bret Boone	.50	.23
☐ HG96 Wade Boggs	2.50	1.10
☐ HG97 Doug Drabek	.50	.23
☐ HG98 Andy Benes	.50	.23
☐ HG99 Jim Thome	2.50	1.10
☐ HG100 Chili Davis	1.00	.45
☐ HG101 Jeffrey Hammonds	.50	.23
☐ HG102 Rickey Henderson	1.50	.70
☐ HG103 Brett Butler	1.00	.45
☐ HG104 Tim Wallach	.50	.23
☐ HG105 Wil Cordero	.50	.23
☐ HG106 Mark Whiten	.50	.23
☐ HG107 Bob Hamelin	.50	.23
☐ HG108 Rondell White	1.00	.45
☐ HG109 Devon White	.50	.23
☐ HG110 Tony Tarasco	.50	.23

have a head shot and player information with the sky serving as a background. The cards are numbered with a RDT prefix.

	MINT	NRMT
COMPLETE SET (12)	60.00	27.00
COMMON CARD (RDT1-RDT12)	2.50	1.10
SEMISTARS	5.00	2.20
UNLISTED STARS	8.00	3.60
SER.2 STAT.ODDS 1:72 HOB/RET, 1:43 ANCO		

☐ RDT1 J.R. Phillips	2.50	1.10
☐ RDT2 Alex Gonzalez	2.50	1.10
☐ RDT3 Alex Rodriguez	40.00	18.00
☐ RDT4 Jose Oliva	2.50	1.10
☐ RDT5 Charles Johnson	4.00	1.80
☐ RDT6 Shawn Green	4.00	1.80
☐ RDT7 Brian Hunter	5.00	2.20
☐ RDT8 Garret Anderson	5.00	2.20
☐ RDT9 Julian Tavarez	2.50	1.10
☐ RDT10 Jose Lima	2.50	1.10
☐ RDT11 Armando Benitez	2.50	1.10
☐ RDT12 Ricky Bottalico	4.00	1.80

1995 Score Rules

Randomly inserted in first series jumbo packs, this 30-card stan-dard-size set features top big league players. Card fronts offer a player photo to the left. At right, the player's name is spelled vertically within a green vapor trail left by a baseball that is at the top. A horizontally designed back features three images of the player and a brief write-up. The cards are num-bered with an "SR" prefix.

	MINT	NRMT
COMPLETE SET (30)	120.00	55.00
COMMON CARD (SR1-SR30)	1.50	.70
SER.1 STATED ODDS 1:8 JUMBO		

☐ SR1 Ken Griffey Jr	20.00	9.00
☐ SR2 Frank Thomas	15.00	6.75
☐ SR3 Mike Piazza	12.00	5.50
☐ SR4 Jeff Bagwell	8.00	3.60
☐ SR5 Alex Rodriguez	15.00	6.75
☐ SR6 Albert Belle	5.00	2.20
☐ SR7 Matt Williams	3.00	1.35
☐ SR8 Roberto Alomar	4.00	1.80
☐ SR9 Barry Bonds	5.00	2.20
☐ SR10 Raul Mondesi	3.00	1.35
☐ SR11 Jose Canseco	3.00	1.35
☐ SR12 Kirby Puckett	8.00	3.60
☐ SR13 Fred McGriff	3.00	1.35
☐ SR14 Kenny Lofton	5.00	2.20
☐ SR15 Greg Maddux	12.00	5.50
☐ SR16 Juan Gonzalez	10.00	4.50
☐ SR17 Cliff Floyd	1.50	.70
☐ SR18 Cal Ripken Jr.	15.00	6.75
☐ SR19 Will Clark	3.00	1.35
☐ SR20 Tim Salmon	4.00	1.80
☐ SR21 Paul O'Neill	2.00	.90

□ SR22 Jason Bere 1.50 .70
□ SR23 Tony Gwynn 12.00 5.50
□ SR24 Manny Ramirez 4.00 1.80
□ SR25 Don Mattingly 8.00 3.60
□ SR26 Dave Justice 4.00 1.80
□ SR27 Javier Lopez 2.00 .90
□ SR28 Ryan Klesko 3.00 1.35
□ SR29 Carlos Delgado 2.00 .90
□ SR30 Mike Mussina 4.00 1.80

1996 Score

This set consists of 517 standard-size cards. These cards were issued in packs of 10 that retailed for 99 cents per pack. The fronts feature an action photo surrounded by white borders. The "Score 96" logo is in the upper left, while the player is identified on the bottom. The backs have season and career stats as well as a player photo and some text. A Cal Ripken tribute card was issued at a rate of 1 every 300 packs.

	MINT	NRMT
COMPLETE SET (517)	24.00	11.00
COMPLETE SERIES 1 (275)	12.00	5.50
COMPLETE SERIES 2 (242)	12.00	5.50
COMMON CARD (1-517)	.10	.05
MINOR STARS	.20	.09
UNLISTED STARS	.40	.18
SUBSET CARDS HALF VALUE OF BASE CARDS		
RIPKEN 2131 ODDS 1:300 H/R, 1:150 JUM		

□ 1 Will Clark .30 .14
□ 2 Rich Becker .30 .14
□ 3 Ryan Klesko .30 .14
□ 4 Jim Edmonds .30 .14
□ 5 Barry Larkin .30 .14
□ 6 Jim Thome .40 .18
□ 7 Raul Mondesi .30 .14
□ 8 Don Mattingly .60 .25
□ 9 Jeff Conine .20 .09
□ 10 Rickey Henderson .30 .14
□ 11 Chad Curtis .10 .05
□ 12 Darren Daulton .20 .09
□ 13 Larry Walker .40 .18
□ 14 Carlos Garcia .10 .05
□ 15 Carlos Baerga .10 .05
□ 16 Tony Gwynn 1.00 .45
□ 17 Jon Nunnally .10 .05
□ 18 Deion Sanders .20 .09
□ 19 Mark Grace .30 .14
□ 20 Alex Rodriguez 1.25 .55
□ 21 Frank Thomas 1.50 .70
□ 22 Brian Jordan .20 .09
□ 23 J.T. Snow .20 .09
□ 24 Shawn Green .10 .05
□ 25 Tim Wakefield .10 .05
□ 26 Curtis Goodwin .10 .05
□ 27 John Smoltz .20 .09
□ 28 Devon White .10 .05
□ 29 Johnny Damon .20 .09
□ 30 Tim Salmon .40 .18
□ 31 Rafael Palmeiro .30 .14
□ 32 Bernard Gilkey .10 .05
□ 33 John Valentin .10 .05
□ 34 Randy Johnson .40 .18
□ 35 Garret Anderson .20 .09
□ 36 Rikkert Faneyte .10 .05
□ 37 Ray Durham .10 .05
□ 38 Bip Roberts .10 .05
□ 39 Jaime Navarro .10 .05
□ 40 Mark Johnson .10 .05
□ 41 Darren Lewis .10 .05
□ 42 Tyler Green .10 .05
□ 43 Bill Pulsipher .10 .05
□ 44 Jason Giambi .20 .09
□ 45 Kevin Ritz .10 .05
□ 46 Jack McDowell .10 .05
□ 47 Felipe Lira .10 .05
□ 48 Rico Brogna .10 .05
□ 49 Terry Pendleton .10 .05
□ 50 Rondell White .20 .09
□ 51 Andre Dawson .30 .14
□ 52 Kirby Puckett .75 .35
□ 53 Wally Joyner .20 .09
□ 54 B.J. Surhoff .10 .05
□ 55 Randy Velarde .10 .05
□ 56 Greg Vaughn .10 .05
□ 57 Roberto Alomar .40 .18
□ 58 David Justice .40 .18
□ 59 Kevin Seitzer .10 .05
□ 60 Cal Ripken 1.50 .70
□ 61 Ozzie Smith .50 .23
□ 62 Mo Vaughn .50 .23
□ 63 Ricky Bones .10 .05
□ 64 Gary DiSarcina .10 .05
□ 65 Matt Williams .30 .14
□ 66 Wilson Alvarez .10 .05
□ 67 Lenny Dykstra .20 .09
□ 68 Brian McRae .10 .05
□ 69 Todd Stottlemyre .10 .05
□ 70 Bret Boone .10 .05
□ 71 Sterling Hitchcock .10 .05
□ 72 Albert Belle .50 .23
□ 73 Todd Hundley .20 .09
□ 74 Vinny Castilla .20 .09
□ 75 Moises Alou .20 .09
□ 76 Cecil Fielder .20 .09
□ 77 Brad Radke .20 .09
□ 78 Quilvio Veras .10 .05
□ 79 Eddie Murray .40 .18
□ 80 James Mouton .10 .05
□ 81 Pat Listach .10 .05
□ 82 Mark Gubicza .10 .05
□ 83 Dave Winfield .30 .14
□ 84 Fred McGriff .30 .14
□ 85 Darryl Hamilton .10 .05
□ 86 Jeffrey Hammonds .10 .05
□ 87 Pedro Munoz .10 .05
□ 88 Craig Biggio .30 .14
□ 89 Cliff Floyd .10 .05
□ 90 Tim Naehring .10 .05
□ 91 Brett Butler .20 .09
□ 92 Kevin Foster .10 .05
□ 93 Pat Kelly .10 .05
□ 94 John Smiley .10 .05
□ 95 Terry Steinbach .10 .05
□ 96 Orel Hershiser .20 .09
□ 97 Darrin Fletcher .10 .05
□ 98 Walt Weiss .10 .05
□ 99 John Wetteland .10 .05
□ 100 Alan Trammell .30 .14
□ 101 Steve Avery .10 .05
□ 102 Tony Eusebio .10 .05
□ 103 Sandy Alomar Jr .20 .09
□ 104 Joe Girardi .10 .05
□ 105 Rick Aguilera .10 .05
□ 106 Tony Tarasco .10 .05
□ 107 Chris Hammond .10 .05
□ 108 Mike Macfarlane .10 .05
□ 109 Doug Drabek .10 .05
□ 110 Derek Bell .20 .09
□ 111 Ed Sprague .10 .05
□ 112 Todd Hollandsworth .10 .05
□ 113 Otis Nixon .10 .05
□ 114 Keith Lockhart .10 .05
□ 115 Donovan Osborne .10 .05
□ 116 Dave Magadan .10 .05
□ 117 Edgar Martinez .30 .14
□ 118 Chuck Carr .10 .05
□ 119 J.R. Phillips .10 .05
□ 120 Sean Bergman .10 .05
□ 121 Andujar Cedeno .10 .05
□ 122 Eric Young .10 .05
□ 123 Al Martin .10 .05
□ 124 Mark Lemke .10 .05
□ 125 Jim Eisenreich .10 .05
□ 126 Benito Santiago .10 .05
□ 127 Ariel Prieto .10 .05
□ 128 Jim Bullinger .10 .05
□ 129 Russ Davis .10 .05
□ 130 Jim Abbott .10 .05
□ 131 Jason Isringhausen .10 .05
□ 132 Carlos Perez .10 .05
□ 133 David Segui .10 .05
□ 134 Troy O'Leary .10 .05
□ 135 Pat Meares .10 .05
□ 136 Chris Hoiles .20 .09
□ 137 Ismael Valdes .20 .09
□ 138 Jose Oliva .10 .05
□ 139 Carlos Delgado .20 .09
□ 140 Tom Goodwin .10 .05
□ 141 Bob Tewksbury .10 .05
□ 142 Chris Gomez .10 .05
□ 143 Jose Oquendo .10 .05
□ 144 Mark Lewis .10 .05
□ 145 Salomon Torres .10 .05
□ 146 Luis Gonzalez .10 .05
□ 147 Mark Carreon .10 .05
□ 148 Lance Johnson .10 .05
□ 149 Melvin Nieves .10 .05
□ 150 Lee Smith .20 .09
□ 151 Jacob Brumfield .10 .05
□ 152 Armando Benitez .10 .05
□ 153 Curt Schilling .20 .09
□ 154 Javier Lopez .20 .09
□ 155 Frank Rodriguez .10 .05
□ 156 Alex Gonzalez .10 .05
□ 157 Todd Worrell .10 .05
□ 158 Benji Gil .10 .05
□ 159 Greg Gagne .10 .05
□ 160 Tom Henke .10 .05
□ 161 Randy Myers .10 .05
□ 162 Joey Cora .20 .09
□ 163 Scott Ruffcorn .10 .05
□ 164 W. VanLandingham .10 .05
□ 165 Tony Phillips .10 .05
□ 166 Eddie Williams .10 .05
□ 167 Bobby Bonilla .20 .09
□ 168 Denny Neagle .20 .09
□ 169 Troy Percival .10 .05
□ 170 Billy Ashley .10 .05
□ 171 Andy Van Slyke .20 .09
□ 172 Jose Offerman .10 .05
□ 173 Mark Parent .10 .05
□ 174 Edgardo Alfonzo .30 .14
□ 175 Trevor Hoffman .10 .05
□ 176 David Cone .20 .09
□ 177 Dan Wilson .10 .05
□ 178 Steve Ontiveros .10 .05
□ 179 Dean Palmer .10 .05
□ 180 Mike Kelly .10 .05
□ 181 Jim Leyritz .10 .05
□ 182 Ron Karkovice .10 .05
□ 183 Kevin Brown .20 .09
□ 184 Jose Valentin .10 .05
□ 185 Jorge Fabregas .10 .05
□ 186 Jose Mesa .10 .05
□ 187 Brent Mayne .10 .05
□ 188 Carl Everett .10 .05
□ 189 Paul Sorrento .10 .05
□ 190 Pete Schourek .10 .05
□ 191 Scott Kamieniecki .10 .05
□ 192 Roberto Hernandez .10 .05
□ 193 Randy Johnson RR .20 .09
□ 194 Greg Maddux RR .60 .25
□ 195 Hideo Nomo RR .50 .23
□ 196 David Cone RR .10 .05
□ 197 Mike Mussina RR .20 .09
□ 198 Andy Benes RR .10 .05
□ 199 Kevin Appier RR .10 .05
□ 200 John Smoltz RR .10 .05
□ 201 John Wetteland RR .10 .05
□ 202 Mark Wohlers RR .10 .05

203	Stan Belinda	.10	.05
204	Brian Anderson	.10	.05
205	Mike Devereaux	.10	.05
206	Mark Wohlers	.10	.05
207	Omar Vizquel	.20	.09
208	Jose Rijo	.10	.05
209	Willie Blair	.10	.05
210	Jamie Moyer	.10	.05
211	Craig Shipley	.10	.05
212	Shane Reynolds	.10	.05
213	Chad Fonville	.10	.05
214	Jose Vizcaino	.10	.05
215	Sid Fernandez	.10	.05
216	Andy Ashby	.10	.05
217	Frank Castillo	.10	.05
218	Kevin Tapani	.10	.05
219	Kent Mercker	.10	.05
220	Karim Garcia	.30	.14
221	Antonio Osuna	.10	.05
222	Tim Unroe	.10	.05
223	Johnny Damon	.20	.09
224	LaTroy Hawkins	.10	.05
225	Mariano Rivera	.30	.14
226	Jose Alberro	.10	.05
227	Angel Martinez	.10	.05
228	Jason Schmidt	.20	.09
229	Tony Clark	.40	.18
230	Kevin Jordan UER	.10	.05

Ricky Jordan pictured on both sides

231	Mark Thompson	.10	.05
232	Jim Dougherty	.10	.05
233	Roger Cedeno	.10	.05
234	Ugueth Urbina	.10	.05
235	Ricky Otero	.10	.05
236	Mark Smith	.10	.05
237	Brian Barber	.10	.05
238	Kevin Flora	.10	.05
239	Joe Rosselli	.10	.05
240	Derek Jeter	1.25	.55
241	Michael Tucker	.20	.09
242	Ben Blomdahl	.10	.05
243	Joe Vitiello	.10	.05
244	Todd Steverson	.10	.05
245	James Baldwin	.10	.05
246	Alan Embree	.10	.05
247	Shannon Penn	.10	.05
248	Chris Stynes	.10	.05
249	Oscar Munoz	.10	.05
250	Jose Herrera	.10	.05
251	Scott Sullivan	.10	.05
252	Reggie Williams	.10	.05
253	Mark Grudzielanek	.20	.09
254	Steve Rodriguez	.10	.05
255	Terry Bradshaw	.10	.05
256	F.P. Santangelo	.10	.05
257	Lyle Mouton	.10	.05
258	George Williams	.10	.05
259	Larry Thomas	.10	.05
260	Rudy Pemberton	.10	.05
261	Jim Pittsley	.20	.09
262	Les Norman	.10	.05
263	Ruben Rivera	.20	.09
264	Cesar Devarez	.10	.05
265	Greg Zaun	.10	.05
266	Dustin Hermanson	.10	.05
267	John Frascatore	.10	.05
268	Joe Randa	.10	.05
269	Jeff Bagwell CL	.40	.18
270	Mike Piazza CL	.60	.25
271	Dante Bichette CL	.10	.05
272	Frank Thomas CL	.75	.35
273	Ken Griffey Jr. CL	1.00	.45
274	Cal Ripken CL	.75	.35
275	Greg Maddux CL / Albert Belle	.50	.23
276	Greg Maddux	1.25	.55
277	Pedro Martinez	.40	.18
278	Bobby Higginson	.20	.09
279	Ray Lankford	.10	.05
280	Shawn Dunston	.10	.05
281	Gary Sheffield	.40	.18
282	Ken Griffey Jr.	2.00	.90
283	Paul Molitor	.40	.18
284	Kevin Appier	.20	.09
285	Chuck Knoblauch	.40	.18
286	Alex Fernandez	.10	.05
287	Steve Finley	.20	.09
288	Jeff Blauser	.20	.09
289	Charles Johnson	.20	.09
290	John Franco	.20	.09
291	Mark Langston	.10	.05
292	Bret Saberhagen	.10	.05
293	John Mabry	.10	.05
294	Ramon Martinez	.20	.09
295	Mike Blowers	.10	.05
296	Paul O'Neill	.20	.09
297	Dave Nilsson	.10	.05
298	Dante Bichette	.20	.09
299	Marty Cordova	.20	.09
300	Jay Bell	.20	.09
301	Mike Mussina	.40	.18
302	Ivan Rodriguez	.50	.23
303	Jose Canseco	.30	.14
304	Jeff Bagwell	.75	.35
305	Manny Ramirez	.40	.18
306	Dennis Martinez	.10	.05
307	Charlie Hayes	.10	.05
308	Joe Carter	.20	.09
309	Travis Fryman	.20	.09
310	Mark McGwire	.75	.35
311	Reggie Sanders UER	.10	.05

Photo on front is John Roper

312	Julian Tavarez	.10	.05
313	Jeff Montgomery	.10	.05
314	Andy Benes	.20	.09
315	John Jaha	.10	.05
316	Jeff Kent	.10	.05
317	Mike Piazza	1.25	.55
318	Erik Hanson	.10	.05
319	Kenny Rogers	.10	.05
320	Hideo Nomo	1.00	.45
321	Gregg Jefferies	.10	.05
322	Chipper Jones	1.25	.55
323	Jay Buhner	.30	.14
324	Dennis Eckersley	.20	.09
325	Kenny Lofton	.50	.23
326	Robin Ventura	.20	.09
327	Tom Glavine	.20	.09
328	Tim Salmon	.40	.18
329	Andres Galarraga	.40	.18
330	Hal Morris	.10	.05
331	Brady Anderson	.30	.14
332	Chili Davis	.20	.09
333	Roger Clemens	.75	.35
334	Marquis Grissom	.20	.09
335	Mike Greenwell UER	.10	.05

Name spelled Jeff on Front

336	Sammy Sosa	.40	.18
337	Ron Gant	.20	.09
338	Ken Caminiti	.30	.14
339	Danny Tartabull	.10	.05
340	Barry Bonds	.50	.23
341	Ben McDonald	.10	.05
342	Ruben Sierra	.10	.05
343	Bernie Williams	.40	.18
344	Wil Cordero	.10	.05
345	Wade Boggs	.40	.18
346	Gary Gaetti	.10	.05
347	Greg Colbrunn	.10	.05
348	Juan Gonzalez	1.00	.45
349	Marc Newfield	.10	.05
350	Charles Nagy	.20	.09
351	Robby Thompson	.10	.05
352	Roberto Petagine	.10	.05
353	Darryl Strawberry	.20	.09
354	Tino Martinez	.40	.18
355	Eric Karros	.20	.09
356	Cal Ripken SS	.75	.35
357	Cecil Fielder SS	.10	.05
358	Kirby Puckett SS	.40	.18
359	Jim Edmonds SS	.20	.09
360	Matt Williams SS	.20	.09
361	Alex Rodriguez SS	.60	.25
362	Barry Larkin SS	.20	.09
363	Rafael Palmeiro SS	.20	.09
364	David Cone SS	.10	.05
365	Roberto Alomar SS	.20	.09
366	Eddie Murray SS	.20	.09
367	Randy Johnson SS	.20	.09
368	Ryan Klesko SS	.20	.09
369	Raul Mondesi SS	.20	.09
370	Mo Vaughn SS	.30	.14
371	Will Clark SS	.20	.09
372	Carlos Baerga SS	.10	.05
373	Frank Thomas SS	.75	.35
374	Larry Walker SS	.20	.09
375	Garret Anderson SS	.10	.05
376	Edgar Martinez SS	.20	.09
377	Don Mattingly SS	.30	.14
378	Tony Gwynn SS	.50	.23
379	Albert Belle SS	.30	.14
380	Jason Isringhausen SS	.10	.05
381	Ruben Rivera SS	.10	.05
382	Johnny Damon SS	.10	.05
383	Karim Garcia SS	.20	.09
384	Derek Jeter SS	.60	.25
385	David Justice SS	.20	.09
386	Royce Clayton	.10	.05
387	Mark Whiten	.10	.05
388	Mickey Tettleton	.10	.05
389	Steve Trachsel	.10	.05
390	Danny Bautista	.10	.05
391	Midre Cummings	.10	.05
392	Scott Leius	.10	.05
393	Manny Alexander	.10	.05
394	Brent Gates	.10	.05
395	Rey Sanchez	.10	.05
396	Andy Pettitte	.50	.23
397	Jeff Cirillo	.20	.09
398	Kurt Abbott	.10	.05
399	Lee Tinsley	.10	.05
400	Paul Assenmacher	.10	.05
401	Scott Erickson	.10	.05
402	Todd Zeile	.10	.05
403	Tom Pagnozzi	.10	.05
404	Ozzie Guillen	.10	.05
405	Jeff Frye	.10	.05
406	Kirt Manwaring	.10	.05
407	Chad Ogea	.10	.05
408	Harold Baines	.20	.09
409	Jason Bere	.10	.05
410	Chuck Finley	.10	.05
411	Jeff Fassero	.10	.05
412	Joey Hamilton	.20	.09
413	John Olerud	.20	.09
414	Kevin Stocker	.10	.05
415	Eric Anthony	.10	.05
416	Aaron Sele	.10	.05
417	Chris Bosio	.10	.05
418	Michael Mimbs	.10	.05
419	Orlando Miller	.10	.05
420	Stan Javier	.10	.05
421	Matt Mieske	.10	.05
422	Jason Bates	.10	.05
423	Orlando Merced	.10	.05
424	John Flaherty	.10	.05
425	Reggie Jefferson	.10	.05
426	Scott Stahoviak	.10	.05
427	John Burkett	.10	.05
428	Rod Beck	.10	.05
429	Bill Swift	.10	.05
430	Scott Cooper	.10	.05
431	Mel Rojas	.10	.05
432	Todd Van Poppel	.10	.05
433	Bobby Jones	.10	.05
434	Mike Harkey	.10	.05
435	Sean Berry	.10	.05
436	Glenallen Hill	.10	.05
437	Ryan Thompson	.10	.05
438	Luis Alicea	.10	.05
439	Esteban Loaiza	.10	.05
440	Jeff Reboulet	.10	.05
441	Vince Coleman	.10	.05
442	Ellis Burks	.20	.09
443	Allen Battle	.10	.05
444	Jimmy Key	.20	.09
445	Ricky Bottalico	.10	.05
446	Delino DeShields	.20	.09
447	Albie Lopez	.10	.05
448	Mark Petkovsek	.10	.05
449	Tim Raines	.20	.09
450	Bryan Harvey	.10	.05
451	Pat Hentgen	.20	.09
452	Tim Laker	.10	.05
453	Tom Gordon	.10	.05
454	Phil Plantier	.10	.05
455	Ernie Young	.10	.05
456	Pete Harnisch	.10	.05

		MINT	NRMT
☐ 457	Roberto Kelly	.10	.05
☐ 458	Mark Portugal	.10	.05
☐ 459	Mark Leiter	.10	.05
☐ 460	Tony Pena	.10	.05
☐ 461	Roger Pavlik	.10	.05
☐ 462	Jeff King	.10	.05
☐ 463	Bryan Rekar	.10	.05
☐ 464	Al Leiter	.10	.05
☐ 465	Phil Nevin	.10	.05
☐ 466	Jose Lima	.10	.05
☐ 467	Mike Stanley	.10	.05
☐ 468	David McCarty	.10	.05
☐ 469	Herb Perry	.10	.05
☐ 470	Geronimo Berroa	.10	.05
☐ 471	David Wells	.10	.05
☐ 472	Vaughn Eshelman	.10	.05
☐ 473	Greg Swindell	.10	.05
☐ 474	Steve Sparks	.10	.05
☐ 475	Luis Sojo	.10	.05
☐ 476	Derrick May	.10	.05
☐ 477	Joe Oliver	.10	.05
☐ 478	Alex Arias	.10	.05
☐ 479	Brad Ausmus	.10	.05
☐ 480	Gabe White	.10	.05
☐ 481	Pat Rapp	.10	.05
☐ 482	Damon Buford	.10	.05
☐ 483	Turk Wendell	.10	.05
☐ 484	Jeff Brantley	.10	.05
☐ 485	Curtis Leskanic	.10	.05
☐ 486	Robb Nen	.10	.05
☐ 487	Lou Whitaker	.20	.09
☐ 488	Melido Perez	.10	.05
☐ 489	Luis Polonia	.10	.05
☐ 490	Scott Brosius	.10	.05
☐ 491	Robert Perez	.10	.05
☐ 492	Mike Sweeney	.40	.18
☐ 493	Mark Loretta	.10	.05
☐ 494	Alex Ochoa	.10	.05
☐ 495	Matt Lawton	.30	.14
☐ 496	Shawn Estes	.30	.14
☐ 497	John Wasdin	.10	.05
☐ 498	Marc Kroon	.10	.05
☐ 499	Chris Snopek	.10	.05
☐ 500	Jeff Suppan	.20	.09
☐ 501	Terrell Wade	.10	.05
☐ 502	Marvin Benard	.10	.05
☐ 503	Chris Widger	.10	.05
☐ 504	Quinton McCracken	.10	.05
☐ 505	Bob Wolcott	.10	.05
☐ 506	C.J. Nitkowski	.10	.05
☐ 507	Aaron Ledesma	.10	.05
☐ 508	Scott Hatteberg	.10	.05
☐ 509	Jimmy Haynes	.10	.05
☐ 510	Howard Battle	.10	.05
☐ 511	Marty Cordova CL	.10	.05
☐ 512	Randy Johnson CL	.20	.09
☐ 513	Mo Vaughn CL	.30	.14
☐ 514	Chan Ho Park CL	.20	.09
☐ 515	Greg Maddux CL	.60	.25
☐ 516	Barry Larkin CL	.20	.09
☐ 517	Tom Glavine CL	.10	.05
☐ NNO	Cal Ripken 2131	20.00	9.00

1996 Score All-Stars

Randomly inserted in second series jumbo packs at a rate of one in nine, this 20-card set was printed in rainbow holographic prismatic foil.

		MINT	NRMT
COMPLETE SET (20)		80.00	36.00
COMMON CARD (1-20)		1.00	.45
SER.2 STATED ODDS 1:9 JUMBO			
☐ 1	Frank Thomas	12.00	5.50
☐ 2	Albert Belle	4.00	1.80
☐ 3	Ken Griffey Jr.	15.00	6.75
☐ 4	Cal Ripken	12.00	5.50
☐ 5	Mo Vaughn	4.00	1.80
☐ 6	Matt Williams	2.50	1.10
☐ 7	Barry Bonds	4.00	1.80

		MINT	NRMT
☐ 8	Dante Bichette	1.50	.70
☐ 9	Tony Gwynn	8.00	3.60
☐ 10	Greg Maddux	10.00	4.50
☐ 11	Randy Johnson	3.00	1.35
☐ 12	Hideo Nomo	8.00	3.60
☐ 13	Tim Salmon	3.00	1.35
☐ 14	Jeff Bagwell	6.00	2.70
☐ 15	Edgar Martinez	2.50	1.10
☐ 16	Reggie Sanders	1.00	.45
☐ 17	Larry Walker	3.00	1.35
☐ 18	Chipper Jones	10.00	4.50
☐ 19	Manny Ramirez	3.00	1.35
☐ 20	Eddie Murray	3.00	1.35

1996 Score Big Bats

This 20-card set was randomly inserted in retail packs at a rate of approximately one in 31. The fronts feature a player photo set against a gold-foil background. The words "Big Bats" as well as the player's name is printed in white at the bottom. The backs feature a photo against a multi-colored background. The cards are numbered "X" of 20 in the upper left corner.

		MINT	NRMT
COMPLETE SET (20)		120.00	55.00
COMMON CARD (1-20)		1.50	.70
SER.1 STATED ODDS 1:31 RETAIL			
☐ 1	Cal Ripken	20.00	9.00
☐ 2	Ken Griffey Jr.	25.00	11.00
☐ 3	Frank Thomas	20.00	9.00
☐ 4	Jeff Bagwell	10.00	4.50
☐ 5	Mike Piazza	15.00	6.75
☐ 6	Barry Bonds	6.00	2.70
☐ 7	Matt Williams	3.00	1.35
☐ 8	Raul Mondesi	3.00	1.35
☐ 9	Tony Gwynn	12.00	5.50
☐ 10	Albert Belle	6.00	2.70
☐ 11	Manny Ramirez	3.00	1.35
☐ 12	Carlos Baerga	1.50	.70
☐ 13	Mo Vaughn	6.00	2.70
☐ 14	Derek Bell	1.50	.70
☐ 15	Larry Walker	5.00	2.20
☐ 16	Kenny Lofton	6.00	2.70
☐ 17	Edgar Martinez	3.00	1.35
☐ 18	Reggie Sanders	1.50	.70
☐ 19	Eddie Murray	5.00	2.20
☐ 20	Chipper Jones	15.00	6.75

1996 Score Diamond Aces

This 30-card set features some of baseball's best players. These cards were inserted approximately one every eight jumbo packs. The fronts display a color player cutout on a com

puter-generated background with gold foil accenting. On a similar background, the backs carry a color closeup.

		MINT	NRMT
COMPLETE SET (30)		120.00	55.00
COMMON CARD (1-30)		1.50	.70
SER.1 STATED ODDS 1:8 JUMBO			
☐ 1	Hideo Nomo	12.00	5.50
☐ 2	Brian L.Hunter	2.50	1.10
☐ 3	Ray Durham	1.50	.70
☐ 4	Frank Thomas	20.00	9.00
☐ 5	Cal Ripken	20.00	9.00
☐ 6	Barry Bonds	6.00	2.70
☐ 7	Greg Maddux	15.00	6.75
☐ 8	Chipper Jones	15.00	6.75
☐ 9	Raul Mondesi	4.00	1.80
☐ 10	Mike Piazza	15.00	6.75
☐ 11	Derek Jeter	15.00	6.75
☐ 12	Bill Pulsipher	1.50	.70
☐ 13	Larry Walker	5.00	2.20
☐ 14	Ken Griffey Jr.	25.00	11.00
☐ 15	Alex Rodriguez	20.00	9.00
☐ 16	Manny Ramirez	5.00	2.20
☐ 17	Mo Vaughn	6.00	2.70
☐ 18	Reggie Sanders	1.50	.70
☐ 19	Derek Bell	1.50	.70
☐ 20	Jim Edmonds	4.00	1.80
☐ 21	Albert Belle	6.00	2.70
☐ 22	Eddie Murray	5.00	2.20
☐ 23	Tony Gwynn	12.00	5.50
☐ 24	Jeff Bagwell	10.00	4.50
☐ 25	Carlos Baerga	1.50	.70
☐ 26	Matt Williams	4.00	1.80
☐ 27	Garret Anderson	2.50	1.10
☐ 28	Todd Hollandsworth	1.50	.70
☐ 29	Johnny Damon	2.50	1.10
☐ 30	Tim Salmon	5.00	2.20

1996 Score Dream Team

This nine-card set was randomly inserted in approximately one in 72 packs. This set features a leading player at each position. The fronts feature a player *photo set against a holographic foil background. The words "1995 Dream Team" as well as his name and team are printed on the bottom of the card. The horizontal backs feature a player photo and some text. The cards are numbered in the upper right as "X" of nine.*

	MINT	NRMT
COMPLETE SET (9)	100.00	45.00
COMMON CARD (1-9)	1.00	.45
SER.1 STATED ODDS 1:72 HOB/RET		

		MINT	NRMT
☐ 1	Cal Ripken	20.00	9.00
☐ 2	Frank Thomas	20.00	9.00
☐ 3	Carlos Baerga	1.00	.45
☐ 4	Matt Williams	4.00	1.80
☐ 5	Mike Piazza	15.00	6.75
☐ 6	Barry Bonds	6.00	2.70
☐ 7	Ken Griffey Jr.	25.00	11.00
☐ 8	Manny Ramirez	5.00	2.20
☐ 9	Greg Maddux	15.00	6.75

1996 Score Dugout Collection

This set is a mini-parallel to the regular issue. Only 110 cards of each Series 1 and Series 2 were selected. Randomly inserted approximately one in every three packs, these cards have all gold foil printing that gives them a shiny copper cast. The words "Dugout Collection" are printed on the back.

	MINT	NRMT
COMPLETE SERIES 1 (110)	50.00	22.00
COMPLETE SERIES 2 (110)	50.00	22.00
COMMON CARD (A1-B110)	.25	.11
STATED ODDS 1:3 HOB/RET		
COMP AP SER.1 (110)	350.00	160.00
COMP AP SER.2 (110)	350.00	160.00
*AP STARS: 2.5X TO 16X BASE CARD DUGOUT		
*AP YOUNG STARS: 2X TO 5X BASE DUGOUT		
AP STATED ODDS 1:36 HOB/RET		

		MINT	NRMT
☐ A1	Will Clark	1.00	.45
☐ A2	Rich Becker	.25	.11
☐ A3	Ryan Klesko	1.00	.45
☐ A4	Jim Edmonds	1.00	.45
☐ A5	Barry Larkin	1.00	.45
☐ A6	Jim Thome	1.50	.70
☐ A7	Raul Mondesi	1.00	.45
☐ A8	Don Mattingly	2.50	1.10
☐ A9	Jeff Conine	.50	.23
☐ A10	Rickey Henderson	1.00	.45
☐ A11	Chad Curtis	.25	.11
☐ A12	Darren Daulton	.50	.23
☐ A13	Larry Walker	1.50	.70
☐ A14	Carlos Baerga	.25	.11
☐ A15	Tony Gwynn	4.00	1.80
☐ A16	Jon Nunnally	.25	.11
☐ A17	Deion Sanders	.50	.23
☐ A18	Mark Grace	1.00	.45
☐ A19	Alex Rodriguez	5.00	2.20
☐ A20	Frank Thomas	6.00	2.70
☐ A21	Brian Jordan	.25	.23
☐ A22	J.T. Snow	.50	.23
☐ A23	Shawn Green	.25	.11
☐ A24	Tim Wakefield	.25	.11
☐ A25	Curtis Goodwin	.25	.11
☐ A26	John Smoltz	.50	.23
☐ A27	Devon White	.25	.11
☐ A28	Brian L.Hunter	.50	.23
☐ A29	Rusty Greer	.25	.23
☐ A30	Rafael Palmeiro	1.00	.45
☐ A31	Bernard Gilkey	.25	.11
☐ A32	John Valentin	.25	.11
☐ A33	Randy Johnson	1.50	.70
☐ A34	Garret Anderson	.50	.23
☐ A35	Ray Durham	.25	.11
☐ A36	Bip Roberts	.25	.11
☐ A37	Tyler Green	.25	.11
☐ A38	Bill Pulsipher	.25	.11
☐ A39	Jason Giambi	.50	.23
☐ A40	Jack McDowell	.25	.11
☐ A41	Rico Brogna	.25	.11
☐ A42	Terry Pendleton	.25	.11
☐ A43	Rondell White	.50	.23
☐ A44	Andre Dawson	1.00	.45
☐ A45	Kirby Puckett	3.00	1.35
☐ A46	Wally Joyner	.50	.23
☐ A47	B.J. Surhoff	.25	.11
☐ A48	Randy Velarde	.25	.11
☐ A49	Greg Vaughn	.25	.11
☐ A50	Roberto Alomar	1.50	.70
☐ A51	David Justice	1.50	.70
☐ A52	Cal Ripken	6.00	2.70
☐ A53	Ozzie Smith	2.00	.90
☐ A54	Mo Vaughn	2.00	.90
☐ A55	Gary DiSarcina	.25	.11
☐ A56	Matt Williams	1.00	.45
☐ A57	Lenny Dykstra	.50	.23
☐ A58	Bret Boone	.25	.11
☐ A59	Albert Belle	2.00	.90
☐ A60	Vinny Castilla	.50	.23
☐ A61	Moises Alou	.50	.23
☐ A62	Cecil Fielder	.50	.23
☐ A63	Brad Radke	.50	.23
☐ A64	Quivlio Veras	.25	.11
☐ A65	Eddie Murray	1.50	.70
☐ A66	Dave Winfield	1.00	.45
☐ A67	Fred McGriff	1.00	.45
☐ A68	Craig Biggio	1.00	.45
☐ A69	Cliff Floyd	.25	.11
☐ A70	Tim Naehring	.25	.11
☐ A71	John Wetteland	.25	.11
☐ A72	Alan Trammell	1.00	.45
☐ A73	Steve Avery	.25	.11
☐ A74	Rick Aguilera	.25	.11
☐ A75	Derek Bell	.25	.11
☐ A76	Todd Hollandsworth	.25	.11
☐ A77	Edgar Martinez	1.00	.45
☐ A78	Mark Lemke	.25	.11
☐ A79	Ariel Prieto	.25	.11
☐ A80	Russ Davis	.25	.11
☐ A81	Jim Abbott	.50	.23
☐ A82	Jason Isringhausen	.25	.11
☐ A83	Carlos Perez	.25	.11
☐ A84	David Segui	.25	.11
☐ A85	Troy O'Leary	.25	.11
☐ A86	Ismael Valdes	.50	.23
☐ A87	Carlos Delgado	.50	.23
☐ A88	Lee Smith	.50	.23
☐ A89	Javier Lopez	.50	.23
☐ A90	Frank Rodriguez	.25	.11
☐ A91	Alex Gonzalez	.25	.11
☐ A92	Benji Gil	.25	.11
☐ A93	Greg Gagne	.25	.11
☐ A94	Randy Myers	.25	.11
☐ A95	Bobby Bonilla	.50	.23
☐ A96	Billy Ashley	.25	.11
☐ A97	Andy Van Slyke	.50	.23
☐ A98	Edgardo Alfonzo	1.00	.45
☐ A99	David Cone	.50	.23
☐ A100	Dean Palmer	.25	.11
☐ A101	Jose Mesa	.25	.11
☐ A102	Karim Garcia	1.00	.45
☐ A103	Johnny Damon	.50	.23
☐ A104	LaTroy Hawkins	.25	.11
☐ A105	Mark Smith	.25	.11
☐ A106	Derek Jeter	4.00	1.80
☐ A107	Michael Tucker	.50	.23
☐ A108	Joe Vitiello	.25	.11
☐ A109	Ruben Rivera	.50	.23
☐ A110	Greg Zaun	.25	.11
☐ B1	Greg Maddux	5.00	2.20
☐ B2	Pedro Martinez	1.50	.70
☐ B3	Bobby Higginson	.50	.23
☐ B4	Ray Lankford	.50	.23
☐ B5	Shawon Dunston	.25	.11
☐ B6	Gary Sheffield	1.50	.70
☐ B7	Ken Griffey Jr.	8.00	3.60
☐ B8	Paul Molitor	1.50	.70
☐ B9	Kevin Appier	.50	.23
☐ B10	Chuck Knoblauch	1.50	.70
☐ B11	Alex Fernandez	.25	.11
☐ B12	Steve Finley	.50	.23
☐ B13	Jeff Blauser	.50	.23
☐ B14	Charles Johnson	.50	.23
☐ B15	John Franco	.50	.23
☐ B16	Mark Langston	.25	.11
☐ B17	Bret Saberhagen	.25	.11
☐ B18	John Mabry	.25	.11
☐ B19	Ramon Martinez	.50	.23
☐ B20	Mike Blowers	.25	.11
☐ B21	Paul O'Neill	.50	.23
☐ B22	Dave Nilsson	.25	.11
☐ B23	Dante Bichette	.50	.23
☐ B24	Marty Cordova	.50	.23
☐ B25	Jay Bell	.25	.23
☐ B26	Mike Mussina	1.50	.70
☐ B27	Ivan Rodriguez	1.50	.70
☐ B28	Jose Canseco	1.00	.45
☐ B29	Jeff Bagwell	3.00	1.35
☐ B30	Manny Ramirez	1.50	.70
☐ B31	Dennis Martinez	.50	.23
☐ B32	Charlie Hayes	.50	.23
☐ B33	Joe Carter	.50	.23
☐ B34	Travis Fryman	.50	.23
☐ B35	Mark McGwire	3.00	1.35
☐ B36	Reggie Sanders	.25	.11
☐ B37	Julian Tavarez	.25	.11
☐ B38	Jeff Montgomery	.25	.11
☐ B39	Andy Benes	.50	.23
☐ B40	John Jaha	.25	.11
☐ B41	Jeff Kent	.25	.11
☐ B42	Mike Piazza	5.00	2.20
☐ B43	Erik Hanson	.25	.11
☐ B44	Kenny Rogers	.25	.11
☐ B45	Hideo Nomo	4.00	1.80
☐ B46	Gregg Jefferies	.25	.11
☐ B47	Chipper Jones	5.00	2.20
☐ B48	Jay Buhner	1.00	.45
☐ B49	Dennis Eckersley	.50	.23
☐ B50	Kenny Lofton	2.00	.90
☐ B51	Robin Ventura	.50	.23
☐ B52	Tom Glavine	.50	.23
☐ B53	Tim Salmon	1.50	.70
☐ B54	Andres Galarraga	1.50	.70
☐ B55	Hal Morris	.25	.11
☐ B56	Brady Anderson	1.00	.45
☐ B57	Chili Davis	.50	.23
☐ B58	Roger Clemens	3.00	1.35
☐ B59	Marquis Grissom	.50	.23
☐ B60	Mike Greenwell UER	.25	.11
	(Front says Jeff Greenwell		
☐ B61	Sammy Sosa	1.50	.70
☐ B62	Ron Gant	.50	.23
☐ B63	Ken Caminiti	1.00	.45
☐ B64	Danny Tartabull	.25	.11
☐ B65	Barry Bonds	2.00	.90
☐ B66	Ben McDonald	.25	.11
☐ B67	Ruben Sierra	.50	.11
☐ B68	Bernie Williams	1.50	.70
☐ B69	Wil Cordero	.25	.11
☐ B70	Wade Boggs	1.50	.70
☐ B71	Gary Gaetti	.25	.11
☐ B72	Greg Colbrunn	.25	.11
☐ B73	Juan Gonzalez	4.00	1.80
☐ B74	Marc Newfield	.25	.11
☐ B75	Charles Nagy	.50	.23
☐ B76	Robby Thompson	.25	.11
☐ B77	Roberto Petagine	.25	.11

		MINT	NRMT
☐ B78	Darryl Strawberry	.50	.23
☐ B79	Tino Martinez	1.50	.70
☐ B80	Eric Karros	.50	.23
☐ B81	Cal Ripken SS	3.00	1.35
☐ B82	Cecil Fielder SS	.25	.11
☐ B83	Kirby Puckett SS	1.50	.70
☐ B84	Jim Edmonds SS	.50	.23
☐ B85	Matt Williams SS	.50	.23
☐ B86	Alex Rodriguez SS	2.50	1.10
☐ B87	Barry Larkin SS	.50	.23
☐ B88	Rafael Palmeiro SS	.50	.23
☐ B89	David Cone SS	.25	.11
☐ B90	Roberto Alomar SS	.50	.23
☐ B91	Eddie Murray SS	.50	.23
☐ B92	Randy Johnson SS	.50	.23
☐ B93	Ryan Klesko SS	.50	.23
☐ B94	Raul Mondesi SS	.50	.23
☐ B95	Mo Vaughn SS	1.00	.45
☐ B96	Will Clark SS	.50	.23
☐ B97	Carlos Baerga SS	.25	.11
☐ B98	Frank Thomas SS	3.00	1.35
☐ B99	Larry Walker SS	.50	.23
☐ B100	Garret Anderson SS	.25	.11
☐ B101	Edgar Martinez SS	.50	.23
☐ B102	Don Mattingly SS	1.25	.55
☐ B103	Tony Gwynn SS	2.00	.90
☐ B104	Albert Belle SS	1.00	.45
☐ B105	Jason Isringhausen SS	.25	.11
☐ B106	Ruben Rivera SS	.25	.11
☐ B107	Johnny Damon SS	.25	.11
☐ B108	Karim Garcia SS	.50	.23
☐ B109	Derek Jeter SS	2.00	.90
☐ B110	David Justice SS	.50	.23

1996 Score Future Franchise

Randomly inserted in retail packs at a rate of one in 72, this 16-card set honors young stars of the game. The fronts feature a color action player cutout on a special holographic foil printed background. The backs carry another player color photo with player information.

	MINT	NRMT
COMPLETE SET (16)	120.00	55.00
COMMON CARD (1-16)	3.00	1.35
SEMISTARS	5.00	2.20
UNLISTED STARS	8.00	3.60
SER.2 STATED ODDS 1:72 HOB/RET		

			NRMT
☐ 1	Jason Isringhausen		1.35
☐ 2	Chipper Jones	25.00	11.00
☐ 3	Derek Jeter	20.00	9.00
☐ 4	Alex Rodriguez	25.00	11.00
☐ 5	Alex Ochoa	3.00	1.35
☐ 6	Manny Ramirez	8.00	3.60
☐ 7	Johnny Damon	4.00	1.80
☐ 8	Ruben Rivera	4.00	1.80
☐ 9	Karim Garcia	5.00	2.20
☐ 10	Garret Anderson	4.00	1.80
☐ 11	Marty Cordova	4.00	1.80
☐ 12	Bill Pulsipher	3.00	1.35

		MINT	NRMT
☐ 13	Hideo Nomo	20.00	9.00
☐ 14	Marc Newfield	3.00	1.35
☐ 15	Charles Johnson	4.00	1.80
☐ 16	Raul Mondesi	5.00	2.20

1996 Score Gold Stars

Randomly inserted in packs at a rate of one in 15, this 30-card set features borderless color action player photos with a special sepia player cutout inserted behind a gold foil stamp designating the star player. The backs display another player photo with player information.

	MINT	NRMT
COMPLETE SET (30)	60.00	27.00
COMMON CARD (1-30)	.50	.23
SER.2 STATED ODDS 1:15 HOB/RET		

		MINT	NRMT
☐ 1	Ken Griffey Jr.	10.00	4.50
☐ 2	Frank Thomas	8.00	3.60
☐ 3	Reggie Sanders	.50	.23
☐ 4	Tim Salmon	2.00	.90
☐ 5	Mike Piazza	6.00	2.70
☐ 6	Tony Gwynn	5.00	2.20
☐ 7	Gary Sheffield	2.00	.90
☐ 8	Matt Williams	1.50	.70
☐ 9	Bernie Williams	2.00	.90
☐ 10	Jason Isringhausen	.50	.23
☐ 11	Albert Belle	2.50	1.10
☐ 12	Chipper Jones	6.00	2.70
☐ 13	Edgar Martinez	1.50	.70
☐ 14	Barry Larkin	1.50	.70
☐ 15	Barry Bonds	2.50	1.10
☐ 16	Jeff Bagwell	4.00	1.80
☐ 17	Greg Maddux	6.00	2.70
☐ 18	Mo Vaughn	2.50	1.10
☐ 19	Ryan Klesko	1.50	.70
☐ 20	Sammy Sosa	2.00	.90
☐ 21	Darren Daulton	1.00	.45
☐ 22	Ivan Rodriguez	2.50	1.10
☐ 23	Dante Bichette	1.00	.45
☐ 24	Hideo Nomo	5.00	2.20
☐ 25	Cal Ripken	8.00	3.60
☐ 26	Rafael Palmeiro	1.50	.70
☐ 27	Larry Walker	2.00	.90
☐ 28	Carlos Baerga	.50	.23
☐ 29	Randy Johnson	2.00	.90
☐ 30	Manny Ramirez	2.00	.90

1996 Score Numbers Game

This 30-card set was inserted approximately one in every 15 packs. The fronts feature two player photos. The player's name is spelled vertically on the right while the words "Numbers Game" are printed against a gold-foil background. The backs

contain five quick information bytes that feature that player's accomplishments. The cards are numbered as "X" of 30 in the upper left corner.

	MINT	NRMT
COMPLETE SET (30)	60.00	27.00
COMMON CARD (1-30)	.50	.23
SER.1 STATED ODDS 1:15 HOB/RET		

		MINT	NRMT
☐ 1	Cal Ripken	8.00	3.60
☐ 2	Frank Thomas	8.00	3.60
☐ 3	Ken Griffey Jr.	10.00	4.50
☐ 4	Mike Piazza	6.00	2.70
☐ 5	Barry Bonds	2.50	1.10
☐ 6	Greg Maddux	6.00	2.70
☐ 7	Jeff Bagwell	4.00	1.80
☐ 8	Derek Bell	.50	.23
☐ 9	Tony Gwynn	5.00	2.20
☐ 10	Hideo Nomo	5.00	2.20
☐ 11	Raul Mondesi	1.25	.55
☐ 12	Manny Ramirez	2.00	.90
☐ 13	Albert Belle	2.50	1.10
☐ 14	Matt Williams	1.25	.55
☐ 15	Jim Edmonds	1.25	.55
☐ 16	Edgar Martinez	1.25	.55
☐ 17	Mo Vaughn	2.50	1.10
☐ 18	Reggie Sanders	.50	.23
☐ 19	Chipper Jones	6.00	2.70
☐ 20	Larry Walker	2.00	.90
☐ 21	Juan Gonzalez	5.00	2.20
☐ 22	Kenny Lofton	2.50	1.10
☐ 23	Don Mattingly	4.00	1.80
☐ 24	Ivan Rodriguez	2.50	1.10
☐ 25	Randy Johnson	2.00	.90
☐ 26	Derek Jeter	6.00	2.70
☐ 27	J.T. Snow	1.00	.45
☐ 28	Will Clark	1.25	.55
☐ 29	Rafael Palmeiro	1.25	.55
☐ 30	Alex Rodriguez	6.00	2.70

1996 Score Power Pace

Randomly inserted in retail packs at a rate of one in 31, this 18-card set features homerun

hitters. The fronts display color action player cutouts on a gold foil background. The backs carry another player photo with player information including how frequently he can be expected to hit a homerun based on his career at-bats.

	MINT	NRMT
COMPLETE SET (18)	90.00	40.00
COMMON CARD (1-18)	2.00	.90
SER.2 STATED ODDS 1:31 RETAIL		

		MINT	NRMT
☐ 1	Mark McGwire	10.00	4.50
☐ 2	Albert Belle	6.00	2.70
☐ 3	Jay Buhner	4.00	1.80
☐ 4	Frank Thomas	20.00	9.00
☐ 5	Matt Williams	4.00	1.80
☐ 6	Gary Sheffield	5.00	2.20
☐ 7	Mike Piazza	15.00	6.75
☐ 8	Larry Walker	5.00	2.20
☐ 9	Mo Vaughn	6.00	2.70
☐ 10	Rafael Palmeiro	4.00	1.80
☐ 11	Dante Bichette	2.00	.90
☐ 12	Ken Griffey Jr.	25.00	11.00
☐ 13	Barry Bonds	6.00	2.70
☐ 14	Manny Ramirez	5.00	2.20
☐ 15	Sammy Sosa	5.00	2.20
☐ 16	Tim Salmon	5.00	2.20
☐ 17	Dave Justice	5.00	2.20
☐ 18	Eric Karros	2.00	.90

1996 Score Reflexions

This 20-card set was randomly inserted approximately one in every 31 hobby packs. Two players per card are featured, a veteran player and a younger star playing the same position. These cards feature a mirror effect on the front.

	MINT	NRMT
COMPLETE SET (20)	120.00	55.00
COMMON CARD (1-20)	2.00	.90
UNLISTED STARS	5.00	2.20
SER.1 STATED ODDS 1:15 HOBBY		

		MINT	NRMT
☐ 1	Cal Ripken	25.00	11.00
	Chipper Jones		
☐ 2	Ken Griffey Jr.	30.00	13.50
	Alex Rodriguez		
☐ 3	Frank Thomas	20.00	9.00
	Mo Vaughn		
☐ 4	Kenny Lofton	6.00	2.70
	Brian L.Hunter		
☐ 5	Don Mattingly	6.00	2.70
	J.T.Snow		
☐ 6	Manny Ramirez	5.00	2.20
	Raul Mondesi		
☐ 7	Tony Gwynn	10.00	4.50
	Garret Anderson		

		MINT	NRMT
☐ 8	Roberto Alomar	5.00	2.20
	Carlos Baerga		
☐ 9	Andre Dawson	3.00	1.35
	Larry Walker		
☐ 10	Barry Larkin	12.00	5.50
	Derek Jeter		
☐ 11	Barry Bonds	6.00	2.70
	Reggie Sanders		
☐ 12	Mike Piazza	15.00	6.75
	Albert Belle		
☐ 13	Wade Boggs	5.00	2.20
	Edgar Martinez		
☐ 14	David Cone	2.00	.90
	John Smoltz		
☐ 15	Will Clark	10.00	4.50
	Jeff Bagwell		
☐ 16	Mark McGwire	10.00	4.50
	Cecil Fielder		
☐ 17	Greg Maddux	15.00	6.75
	Mike Mussina		
☐ 18	Randy Johnson	12.00	5.50
	Hideo Nomo		
☐ 19	Jim Thome	5.00	2.20
	Dean Palmer		
☐ 20	Chuck Knoblauch	5.00	2.20
	Craig Biggio		

1996 Score Titanic Taters

Randomly inserted in hobby packs at a rate of one in 31, this 18-card set features long home run hitters. The fronts display a color action player cutout on a gold foil background of a baseball park. The backs carry another player photo with information about the player's longest home run and the park where it was hit.

	MINT	NRMT
COMPLETE SET (18)	100.00	45.00
COMMON CARD (1-18)	2.00	.90
SER.2 STATED ODDS 1:31 HOBBY		

		MINT	NRMT
☐ 1	Albert Belle	6.00	2.70
☐ 2	Frank Thomas	20.00	9.00
☐ 3	Mo Vaughn	4.00	1.80
☐ 4	Ken Griffey Jr.	25.00	11.00
☐ 5	Matt Williams	3.00	1.35
☐ 6	Mark McGwire	10.00	4.50
☐ 7	Dante Bichette	2.00	.90
☐ 8	Tim Salmon	4.00	1.80
☐ 9	Jeff Bagwell	10.00	4.50
☐ 10	Rafael Palmeiro	3.00	1.35
☐ 11	Mike Piazza	15.00	6.75
☐ 12	Cecil Fielder	2.00	.90
☐ 13	Larry Walker	4.00	1.80
☐ 14	Sammy Sosa	4.00	1.80
☐ 15	Manny Ramirez	4.00	1.80
☐ 16	Gary Sheffield	4.00	1.80
☐ 17	Barry Bonds	4.00	1.80
☐ 18	Jay Buhner	3.00	1.35

1997 Score

The 1997 Score set has a total of 550 cards. The 10-card Series 1 packs and the 12-card Series 2 packs carried a suggested retail price of $.99 each and were distributed exclusively to retail outlets. The fronts feature color player action photos in a white border. The backs carry player information and career statistics. The Hideki Irabu card (#551A and B) is shortprinted (about twice as tough to pull as a basic card). One final note on the Irabu card, in the retail packs and factory sets, the card text is in English. In the Hobby Reserve packs, text is in Japanese.

	MINT	NRMT
COMPLETE SET (551)	50.00	22.00
COMP.FACT.SET (551)	50.00	22.00
COMPLETE SERIES 1 (330)	20.00	9.00
COMPLETE SERIES 2 (221)	30.00	13.50
COMMON CARD (1-551)	.10	.05
MINOR STARS	.20	.09
UNLISTED STARS	.40	.18
SUBSET CARDS HALF VALUE OF BASE CARDS		
IRABU ENGLISH IN FACT.SET/RETAIL PACKS		
COMP.PRM.ST.SET (551)	80.00	36.00
COMP.PRM.ST.SER.1 (330)	40.00	18.00
COMP.PRM.ST.SER.2 (221)	40.00	18.00
COMMON PRM.STOCK (1-551)	.20	.09
*PREM.STOCK: 1X TO 2X HI COLUMN		
*PREM.STOCK: .5X TO 1X HI		
PRM.STOCK ONLY AVAIL.TO HOBBY		
IRABU JAPANESE IN HOBBY RESERVE PACKS		
PRM.ST.CALLED HOBBY RESERVE IN SER.2		
COMP.RES'V.SER.2 (221)	600.00	275.00
COMMON RESERVE (331-551)	2.00	.90
*RESERVE STARS: 10X TO 20X HI COL.		
*RESERVE YOUNG STARS: 7.5X TO 15X HI		
*RESERVE ROOKIES: 4X TO 8X HI		
*RESERVE IRABU: 1.5X TO 3X HI		
SER.2 RESERVE ODDS 1:11 HOBBY		
COMP.SHOW.SET (551)	450.00	200.00
COMP.SHOW.SER.1 (330)	250.00	110.00
COMP.SHOW.SER.2 (221)	200.00	90.00
COMMON SHOWCASE (1-551)	.75	.35
*SHOWCASE STARS: 4X TO 8X HI COLUMN		
*SHOWCASE YOUNG STARS: 3X TO 6X HI		
*SHOWCASE ROOKIES: 2X TO 4X HI		
*SHOWCASE IRABU: .6X TO 1.25X HI		
SER.1 SHOW.ODDS		
1:7H/R,1:2JUM,1:4MAG.		
SER.2 SHOW.ODDS 1:5 HOBBY, 1:7 RETAIL		
COMP.SHOW.AP SET (551)	1800.00	800.00
COMP.SHOW.AP SER.1 (330)	1000.00	450.00
COMP.SHOW.AP SER.2 (221)	800.00	350.00
COMMON SHOW.AP (1-551)	3.00	1.35
*SHOW.AP STARS: 15X TO 30X HI COLUMN		
*SHOW.AP YOUNG STARS: 10X TO 20X HI		
*SHOW.AP ROOKIES: 5X TO 10X HI		
*SHOW.AP IRABU: 2X TO 4X HI		

SER.1 AP ODDS 1:35H/R, 1:7JUM, 1:17MAG
SER.2 AP ODDS 1:23 HOBBY, 1:35 RETAIL

1	Jeff Bagwell	.75	.35
2	Mickey Tettleton	.10	.05
3	Johnny Damon	.10	.05
4	Jeff Conine	.20	.09
5	Bernie Williams	.40	.18
6	Will Clark	.30	.14
7	Ryan Klesko	.30	.14
8	Cecil Fielder	.20	.09
9	Paul Wilson	.10	.05
10	Gregg Jefferies	.10	.05
11	Chili Davis	.10	.05
12	Albert Belle	.50	.23
13	Ken Hill	.10	.05
14	Cliff Floyd	.10	.05
15	Jaime Navarro	.10	.05
16	Ismael Valdes	.10	.09
17	Jeff King	.10	.05
18	Chris Bosio	.10	.05
19	Reggie Sanders	.10	.05
20	Darren Daulton	.20	.09
21	Ken Caminiti	.30	.14
22	Mike Piazza	1.25	.55
23	Chad Mottola	.10	.05
24	Darin Erstad	.60	.25
25	Dante Bichette	.20	.09
26	Frank Thomas	1.50	.70
27	Ben McDonald	.10	.05
28	Raul Casanova	.10	.05
29	Kevin Ritz	.10	.05
30	Garret Anderson	.20	.09
31	Jason Kendall	.20	.09
32	Billy Wagner	.20	.09
33	Dave Justice	.40	.18
34	Marty Cordova	.20	.09
35	Derek Jeter	1.25	.55
36	Trevor Hoffman	.10	.05
37	Geronimo Berroa	.10	.05
38	Walt Weiss	.10	.05
39	Kirt Manwaring	.10	.05
40	Alex Gonzalez	.10	.05
41	Sean Berry	.10	.05
42	Kevin Appier	.20	.09
43	Rusty Greer	.20	.09
44	Pete Incaviglia	.10	.05
45	Rafael Palmeiro	.30	.14
46	Eddie Murray	.40	.18
47	Moises Alou	.20	.09
48	Mark Lewis	.10	.05
49	Hal Morris	.10	.05
50	Edgar Renteria	.20	.09
51	Rickey Henderson	.30	.14
52	Pat Listach	.10	.05
53	John Wrasdin	.10	.05
54	James Baldwin	.10	.05
55	Brian Jordan	.20	.09
56	Edgar Martinez	.30	.14
57	Wil Cordero	.10	.05
58	Danny Tartabull	.10	.05
59	Keith Lockhart	.10	.05
60	Rico Brogna	.10	.05
61	Ricky Bottalico	.10	.05
62	Terry Pendleton	.10	.05
63	Bret Boone	.10	.05
64	Charlie Hayes	.10	.05
65	Marc Newfield	.10	.05
66	Sterling Hitchcock	.10	.05
67	Roberto Alomar	.40	.18
68	John Jaha	.10	.05
69	Greg Colbrunn	.10	.05
70	Sal Fasano	.10	.05
71	Brooks Kieschnick	.40	.18
72	Pedro Martinez	.40	.18
73	Kevin Elster	.10	.05
74	Ellis Burks	.20	.09
75	Chuck Finley	.10	.05
76	John Olerud	.20	.09
77	Jay Bell	.20	.09
78	Allen Watson	.10	.05
79	Darryl Strawberry	.20	.09
80	Orlando Miller	.10	.05
81	Jose Herrera	.10	.05
82	Andy Pettitte	.40	.18
83	Juan Guzman	.10	.05
84	Alan Benes	.20	.09
85	Jack McDowell	.10	.05
86	Ugueth Urbina	.10	.05
87	Rocky Coppinger	.10	.05
88	Jeff Cirillo	.20	.09
89	Tom Glavine	.20	.09
90	Robby Thompson	.10	.05
91	Barry Bonds	.50	.23
92	Carlos Delgado	.20	.09
93	Mo Vaughn	.50	.23
94	Ryne Sandberg	.50	.23
95	Alex Rodriguez	1.25	.55
96	Brady Anderson	.30	.14
97	Scott Brosius	.10	.05
98	Dennis Eckersley	.20	.09
99	Brian McRae	.10	.05
100	Rey Ordonez	.10	.05
101	John Valentin	.10	.05
102	Brett Butler	.20	.09
103	Eric Karros	.20	.09
104	Harold Baines	.20	.09
105	Javier Lopez	.20	.09
106	Alan Trammell	.20	.09
107	Jim Thome	.40	.18
108	Frank Rodriguez	.10	.05
109	Bernard Gilkey	.10	.05
110	Reggie Jefferson	.10	.05
111	Scott Stahoviak	.10	.05
112	Steve Gibralter	.10	.05
113	Todd Hollandsworth	.10	.05
114	Ruben Rivera	.20	.09
115	Dennis Martinez	.20	.09
116	Mariano Rivera	.20	.09
117	John Smoltz	.20	.09
118	John Mabry	.10	.05
119	Tom Gordon	.10	.05
120	Alex Ochoa	.10	.05
121	Jamey Wright	.10	.05
122	Dave Nilsson	.10	.05
123	Bobby Bonilla	.20	.09
124	Al Leiter	.10	.05
125	Rick Aguilera	.10	.05
126	Jeff Brantley	.10	.05
127	Kevin Brown	.20	.09
128	George Arias	.10	.05
129	Darren Oliver	.10	.05
130	Bill Pulsipher	.10	.05
131	Roberto Hernandez	.10	.05
132	Delino DeShields	.10	.05
133	Mark Grudzielanek	.10	.05
134	John Wetteland	.10	.05
135	Carlos Baerga	.10	.05
136	Paul Sorrento	.10	.05
137	Leo Gomez	.10	.05
138	Andy Ashby	.10	.05
139	Julio Franco	.20	.09
140	Brian Hunter	.10	.05
141	Jermaine Dye	.10	.05
142	Tony Clark	.40	.18
143	Ruben Sierra	.20	.09
144	Donovan Osborne	.10	.05
145	Mark McLemore	.10	.05
146	Terry Steinbach	.10	.05
147	Bob Wells	.10	.05
148	Chan Ho Park	.40	.18
149	Tim Salmon	.40	.18
150	Paul O'Neill	.20	.09
151	Cal Ripken	1.50	.70
152	Wally Joyner	.20	.09
153	Omar Vizquel	.20	.09
154	Mike Mussina	.40	.18
155	Andres Galarraga	2.00	.90
156	Ken Griffey Jr.	2.00	.90
157	Kenny Lofton	.50	.23
158	Ray Durham	.10	.05
159	Hideo Nomo	1.00	.45
160	Ozzie Guillen	.10	.05
161	Roger Pavlik	.10	.05
162	Manny Ramirez	.40	.18
163	Mark Lemke	.10	.05
164	Mark Stanley	.10	.05
165	Chuck Knoblauch	.40	.18
166	Kimera Bartee	.10	.05
167	Wade Boggs	.40	.18
168	Jay Buhner	.30	.14
169	Eric Young	.10	.05
170	Jose Canseco	.30	.14
171	Dwight Gooden	.20	.09
172	Fred McGriff	.30	.14
173	Sandy Alomar Jr	.20	.09
174	Andy Benes	.20	.09
175	Dean Palmer	.10	.05
176	Larry Walker	.40	.18
177	Charles Nagy	.20	.09
178	David Cone	.20	.09
179	Mark Grace	.30	.14
180	Robin Ventura	.20	.09
181	Roger Clemens	.75	.35
182	Bobby Witt	.10	.05
183	Vinny Castilla	.20	.09
184	Gary Sheffield	.40	.18
185	Dan Wilson	.10	.05
186	Roger Cedeno	.10	.05
187	Mark McGwire	.75	.35
188	Darren Bragg	.10	.05
189	Quinton McCracken	.10	.05
190	Randy Myers	.10	.05
191	Jeromy Burnitz	.10	.05
192	Randy Johnson	.40	.18
193	Chipper Jones	1.25	.55
194	Greg Vaughn	.10	.05
195	Travis Fryman	.20	.09
196	Tim Naehring	.10	.05
197	B.J. Surhoff	.10	.05
198	Juan Gonzalez	1.00	.45
199	Terrell Wade	.10	.05
200	Jeff Frye	.10	.05
201	Joey Cora	.10	.05
202	Raul Mondesi	.30	.14
203	Ivan Rodriguez	.50	.23
204	Armando Reynoso	.10	.05
205	Jeffrey Hammonds	.10	.05
206	Darren Dreifort	.10	.05
207	Kevin Seitzer	.10	.05
208	Tino Martinez	.40	.18
209	Jim Bruske	.10	.05
210	Jeff Suppan	.20	.09
211	Mark Carreon	.10	.05
212	Wilson Alvarez	.10	.05
213	John Burkett	.10	.05
214	Tony Phillips	.10	.05
215	Greg Maddux	1.25	.55
216	Mark Whiten	.10	.05
217	Curtis Pride	.10	.05
218	Lyle Mouton	.10	.05
219	Todd Hundley	.20	.09
220	Greg Gagne	.10	.05
221	Rich Amaral	.10	.05
222	Tom Goodwin	.10	.05
223	Chris Hoiles	.10	.05
224	Jayhawk Owens	.10	.05
225	Kenny Rogers	.10	.05
226	Mike Greenwell	.10	.05
227	Mark Wohlers	.10	.05
228	Henry Rodriguez	.10	.05
229	Robert Perez	.10	.05
230	Jeff Kent	.10	.05
231	Darryl Hamilton	.10	.05
232	Alex Fernandez	.20	.09
233	Ron Karkovice	.10	.05
234	Jimmy Haynes	.10	.05
235	Craig Biggio	.30	.14
236	Ray Lankford	.20	.09
237	Lance Johnson	.10	.05
238	Matt Williams	.30	.14
239	Chad Curtis	.10	.05
240	Mark Thompson	.10	.05
241	Jason Giambi	.20	.09
242	Barry Larkin	.30	.14
243	Paul Molitor	.40	.18
244	Sammy Sosa	.40	.18
245	Kevin Tapani	.10	.05
246	Marquis Grissom	.20	.09
247	Joe Carter	.20	.09
248	Ramon Martinez	.20	.09
249	Tony Gwynn	1.00	.45
250	Andy Fox	.10	.05
251	Troy O'Leary	.10	.05
252	Warren Newson	.10	.05
253	Troy Percival	.10	.05
254	Jamie Moyer	.10	.05
255	Danny Graves	.10	.05

256	David Wells	.10	.05
257	Todd Zeile	.10	.05
258	Raul Ibanez	.10	.05
259	Tyler Houston	.10	.05
260	LaTroy Hawkins	.10	.05
261	Joey Hamilton	.20	.09
262	Mike Sweeney	.20	.09
263	Brant Brown	.10	.05
264	Pat Hentgen	.20	.09
265	Mark Johnson	.10	.05
266	Robb Nen	.10	.05
267	Justin Thompson	.20	.09
268	Ron Gant	.20	.09
269	Jeff D'Amico	.20	.09
270	Shawn Estes	.20	.09
271	Derek Bell	.10	.05
272	Fernando Valenzuela	.20	.09
273	Tom Pagnozzi	.10	.05
274	John Burke	.10	.05
275	Ed Sprague	.10	.05
276	F.P. Santangelo	.10	.05
277	Todd Greene	.20	.09
278	Butch Huskey	.20	.09
279	Steve Finley	.20	.09
280	Eric Davis	.20	.09
281	Shawn Green	.20	.09
282	Al Martin	.10	.05
283	Michael Tucker	.20	.09
284	Shane Reynolds	.10	.05
285	Matt Mieske	.10	.05
286	Jose Rosado	.20	.09
287	Mark Langston	.10	.05
288	Ralph Milliard	.10	.05
289	Mike Lansing	.10	.05
290	Scott Servais	.10	.05
291	Royce Clayton	.10	.05
292	Mike Grace	.10	.05
293	James Mouton	.10	.05
294	Charles Johnson	.20	.09
295	Gary Gaetti	.10	.05
296	Kevin Mitchell	.10	.05
297	Carlos Garcia	.10	.05
298	Desi Relaford	.10	.05
299	Jason Thompson	.10	.05
300	Osvaldo Fernandez	.10	.05
301	Fernando Vina	.10	.05
302	Jose Offerman	.10	.05
303	Yamil Benitez	.10	.05
304	J.T. Snow	.20	.09
305	Rafael Bournigal	.10	.05
306	Jason Isringhausen	.10	.05
307	Bobby Higginson	.20	.09
308	Nerio Rodriguez	.25	.11
309	Brian Giles	.10	.05
310	Andruw Jones	1.00	.45
311	Tony Graffanino	.10	.05
312	Arquimedez Pozo	.10	.05
313	Jermaine Allensworth	.10	.05
314	Jeff Darwin	.10	.05
315	George Williams	.10	.05
316	Karim Garcia	.20	.09
317	Trey Beamon	.10	.05
318	Mac Suzuki	.10	.05
319	Robin Jennings	.10	.05
320	Danny Patterson	.10	.05
321	Damon Mashore	.10	.05
322	Wendell Magee	.10	.05
323	Dax Jones	.10	.05
324	Kevin Brown	.20	.09
325	Marvin Benard	.10	.05
326	Mike Cameron	.30	.14
327	Manos Jensen	.10	.05
328	Eddie Murray CL	.20	.09
329	Paul Molitor CL	.20	.09
330	Todd Hundley CL	.10	.05
331	Norm Charlton	.10	.05
332	Bruce Ruffin	.10	.05
333	John Wetteland	.10	.05
334	Marquis Grissom	.20	.09
335	Sterling Hitchcock	.10	.05
336	John Olerud	.20	.09
337	David Wells	.20	.09
338	Chili Davis	.20	.09
339	Mark Lewis	.10	.05
340	Kenny Lofton	.50	.23
341	Alex Fernandez	.20	.09
342	Ruben Sierra	.10	.05
343	Delino DeShields	.10	.05
344	John Wasdin	.10	.05
345	Dennis Martinez	.20	.09
346	Kevin Elster	.10	.05
347	Bobby Bonilla	.20	.09
348	Jaime Navarro	.10	.05
349	Chad Curtis	.10	.05
350	Terry Steinbach	.10	.05
351	Ariel Prieto	.10	.05
352	Jeff Kent	.10	.05
353	Carlos Garcia	.10	.05
354	Mark Whiten	.10	.05
355	Todd Zeile	.10	.05
356	Eric Davis	.20	.09
357	Greg Colbrunn	.10	.05
358	Moises Alou	.20	.09
359	Allen Watson	.10	.05
360	Jose Canseco	.30	.14
361	Matt Williams	.30	.14
362	Jeff King	.10	.05
363	Darryl Hamilton	.10	.05
364	Mark Clark	.10	.05
365	J.T. Snow	.20	.09
366	Kevin Mitchell	.10	.05
367	Orlando Miller	.10	.05
368	Rico Brogna	.10	.05
369	Mike James	.10	.05
370	Brad Ausmus	.10	.05
371	Darryl Kile	.20	.09
372	Edgardo Alfonzo	.20	.09
373	Julian Tavarez	.10	.05
374	Darren Lewis	.10	.05
375	Steve Karsay	.10	.05
376	Lee Stevens	.10	.05
377	Albie Lopez	.10	.05
378	Orel Hershiser	.20	.09
379	Lee Smith	.20	.09
380	Rick Helling	.10	.05
381	Carlos Perez	.10	.05
382	Tony Tarasco	.10	.05
383	Melvin Nieves	.10	.05
384	Benji Gil	.10	.05
385	Devon White	.10	.05
386	Armando Benitez	.10	.05
387	Bill Swift	.10	.05
388	John Smiley	.10	.05
389	Midre Cummings	.10	.05
390	Tim Belcher	.10	.05
391	Tim Raines	.20	.09
392	Todd Worrell	.10	.05
393	Quilvio Veras	.10	.05
394	Matt Lawton	.10	.05
395	Aaron Sele	.10	.05
396	Bip Roberts	.10	.05
397	Denny Neagle	.20	.09
398	Tyler Green	.10	.05
399	Hipolito Pichardo	.10	.05
400	Scott Erickson	.10	.05
401	Bobby Jones	.10	.05
402	Jim Edmonds	.30	.14
403	Chad Ogea	.10	.05
404	Cal Eldred	.10	.05
405	Pat Listach	.10	.05
406	Todd Stottlemyre	.10	.05
407	Phil Nevin	.10	.05
408	Otis Nixon	.10	.05
409	Billy Ashley	.10	.05
410	Jimmy Key	.20	.09
411	Mike Timlin	.10	.05
412	Joe Vitiello	.10	.05
413	Rondell White	.20	.09
414	Jeff Fassero	.10	.05
415	Rex Hudler	.10	.05
416	Curt Schilling	.20	.09
417	Rich Becker	.10	.05
418	William Van Landingham	.10	.05
419	Chris Snopek	.10	.05
420	David Segui	.10	.05
421	Eddie Murray	.40	.18
422	Shane Andrews	.10	.05
423	Gary DiSarcina	.10	.05
424	Brian Hunter	.20	.09
425	Willie Greene	.10	.05
426	Felipe Crespo	.10	.05
427	Jason Bates	.10	.05
428	Albert Belle	.50	.23
429	Rey Sanchez	.10	.05
430	Roger Clemens	.75	.35
431	Deion Sanders	.20	.09
432	Ernie Young	.10	.05
433	Jay Bell	.20	.09
434	Jeff Blauser	.20	.09
435	Lenny Dykstra	.20	.09
436	Chuck Carr	.10	.05
437	Russ Davis	.10	.05
438	Carl Everett	.10	.05
439	Damion Easley	.10	.05
440	Pat Kelly	.10	.05
441	Pat Rapp	.10	.05
442	Dave Justice	.40	.18
443	Graeme Lloyd	.10	.05
444	Damon Buford	.10	.05
445	Jose Valentin	.10	.05
446	Jason Schmidt	.10	.05
447	Dave Martinez	.10	.05
448	Danny Tartabull	.10	.05
449	Jose Vizcaino	.10	.05
450	Steve Avery	.10	.05
451	Mike Devereaux	.10	.05
452	Jim Eisenreich	.10	.05
453	Mark Leiter	.10	.05
454	Roberto Kelly	.10	.05
455	Benito Santiago	.10	.05
456	Steve Trachsel	.10	.05
457	Gerald Williams	.10	.05
458	Pete Schourek	.10	.05
459	Esteban Loaiza	.10	.05
460	Mel Rojas	.10	.05
461	Tim Wakefield	.10	.05
462	Tony Fernandez	.10	.05
463	Doug Drabek	.10	.05
464	Joe Girardi	.10	.05
465	Mike Bordick	.10	.05
466	Jim Leyritz	.10	.05
467	Erik Hanson	.10	.05
468	Michael Tucker	.20	.09
469	Tony Womack	.30	.14
470	Doug Glanville	.10	.05
471	Rudy Pemberton	.10	.05
472	Keith Lockhart	.10	.05
473	Nomar Garciaparra	1.25	.55
474	Scott Rolen	1.00	.45
475	Jason Dickson	.20	.09
476	Glendon Rusch	.10	.05
477	Todd Walker	.20	.09
478	Dmitri Young	.10	.05
479	Rod Myers	.20	.09
480	Wilton Guerrero	.10	.05
481	Jorge Posada	.10	.05
482	Brant Brown	.10	.05
483	Bubba Trammell	.40	.18
484	Jose Guillen	.50	.23
485	Scott Spiezio	.20	.09
486	Bob Abreu	.20	.09
487	Chris Holt	.10	.05
488	Deivi Cruz	.30	.14
489	Vladimir Guerrero	.75	.35
490	Julio Santana	.10	.05
491	Ray Montgomery	.10	.05
492	Kevin Orie	.20	.09
493	Todd Hundley GY	.10	.05
494	Tim Salmon GY	.20	.09
495	Albert Belle GY	.30	.14
496	Manny Ramirez GY	.20	.09
497	Rafael Palmeiro GY	.20	.09
498	Juan Gonzalez GY	.50	.23
499	Ken Griffey Jr. GY	1.00	.45
500	Andruw Jones GY	.50	.23
501	Mike Piazza GY	.60	.25
502	Jeff Bagwell GY	.40	.18
503	Bernie Williams GY	.20	.09
504	Barry Bonds GY	.30	.14
505	Ken Caminiti GY	.20	.09
506	Darin Erstad GY	.40	.18
507	Alex Rodriguez GY	.60	.25
508	Frank Thomas GY	.75	.35
509	Chipper Jones GY	.60	.25
510	Mo Vaughn GY	.30	.14
511	Mark McGwire GY	.40	.18
512	Fred McGriff GY	.20	.09
513	Jay Buhner GY	.20	.09

☐ 514 Jim Thome GY	.20	.09
☐ 515 Gary Sheffield GY	.20	.09
☐ 516 Dean Palmer GY	.10	.05
☐ 517 Henry Rodriguez GY	.10	.05
☐ 518 Andy Pettitte RF	.20	.09
☐ 519 Mike Mussina RF	.20	.09
☐ 520 Greg Maddux RF	.60	.25
☐ 521 John Smoltz RF	.10	.05
☐ 522 Hideo Nomo RF	.50	.23
☐ 523 Troy Percival RF	.10	.05
☐ 524 John Wetteland RF	.10	.05
☐ 525 Roger Clemens RF	.40	.18
☐ 526 Charles Nagy RF	.10	.05
☐ 527 Mariano Rivera RF	.10	.05
☐ 528 Tom Glavine RF	.20	.09
☐ 529 Randy Johnson RF	.20	.09
☐ 530 Jason Isringhausen RF	.10	.05
☐ 531 Alex Fernandez RF	.10	.05
☐ 532 Kevin Brown RF	.10	.05
☐ 533 Chuck Knoblauch TG	.20	.09
☐ 534 Rusty Greer TG	.10	.05
☐ 535 Tony Gwynn TG	.50	.23
☐ 536 Ryan Klesko TG	.20	.09
☐ 537 Ryne Sandberg TG	.30	.14
☐ 538 Barry Larkin TG	.20	.09
☐ 539 Will Clark TG	.20	.09
☐ 540 Kenny Lofton TG	.30	.14
☐ 541 Paul Molitor TG	.20	.09
☐ 542 Roberto Alomar TG	.20	.09
☐ 543 Rey Ordonez TG	.10	.05
☐ 544 Jason Giambi TG	.10	.05
☐ 545 Derek Jeter TG	.60	.25
☐ 546 Cal Ripken TG	.75	.35
☐ 547 Ivan Rodriguez TG	.30	.14
☐ 548 Ken Griffey Jr. CL	1.00	.45
☐ 549 Frank Thomas CL	.75	.35
☐ 550 Mike Piazza CL	.60	.25
☐ 551A Hideki Irabu SP	15.00	6.75
☐ 551B Hideki Irabu Japanese SP	15.00	6.75

1997 Score Blast Masters

Randomly inserted in second series packs at a rate of 1:35 (retail) and 1:23 (hobby reserve), this 18-card set features color player photos on a gold prismatic foil card.

	MINT	NRMT
COMPLETE SET (18)	150.00	70.00
COMMON CARD (1-18)	2.50	1.10
UNLISTED STARS	4.00	1.80
SER.2 ODDS 1:35 RETAIL, 1:23 HOBBY		

☐ 1 Mo Vaughn	6.00	2.70
☐ 2 Mark McGwire	10.00	4.50
☐ 3 Juan Gonzalez	12.00	5.50
☐ 4 Albert Belle	6.00	2.70
☐ 5 Barry Bonds	6.00	2.70
☐ 6 Ken Griffey Jr.	25.00	11.00
☐ 7 Andruw Jones	12.00	5.50
☐ 8 Chipper Jones	15.00	6.75
☐ 9 Mike Piazza	15.00	6.75
☐ 10 Jeff Bagwell	10.00	4.50

☐ 11 Dante Bichette	2.50	1.10
☐ 12 Alex Rodriguez	15.00	6.75
☐ 13 Gary Sheffield	4.00	1.80
☐ 14 Ken Caminiti	3.00	1.35
☐ 15 Sammy Sosa	4.00	1.80
☐ 16 Vladimir Guerrero	10.00	4.50
☐ 17 Brian Jordan	2.50	1.10
☐ 18 Tim Salmon	4.00	1.80

1997 Score Franchise

Randomly inserted in series one hobby packs only at a rate of one in 72, this nine-card set honors superstar players for their irreplaceable contribution to their team. The fronts display sepia player portraits on a white baseball replica background. The backs carry an action player photo with a sentence about the player which explains why he was selected for this set.

	MINT	NRMT
COMPLETE SET (9)	120.00	55.00
COMMON CARD (1-9)	4.00	1.80
UNLISTED STARS	6.00	2.70
SER.1 ODDS 1:72 H/R, 1:17 JUM, 1:35 MAG		
COMP.GLOWING SET (9)	300.00	135.00
COMMON GLOWING (1-9)	12.00	5.50
*GLOWING: 1.25X TO 2X HI COLUMN		
GLOW.SER.1 ODDS 1:240H/R, 1:79J, 1:120M		

☐ 1 Ken Griffey Jr.	30.00	13.50
☐ 2 John Smoltz	4.00	1.80
☐ 3 Cal Ripken	25.00	11.00
☐ 4 Chipper Jones	20.00	9.00
☐ 5 Mike Piazza	20.00	9.00
☐ 6 Albert Belle	8.00	3.60
☐ 7 Frank Thomas	25.00	11.00
☐ 8 Sammy Sosa	12.00	5.50
☐ 9 Roberto Alomar	6.00	2.70

1997 Score Heart of the Order

Randomly inserted in packs at a rate of 1:23 (retail) and 1:15 (hobby reserve), this 36-card set features color photos of players on six teams with a panorama of the stadium in the background. Each team's three cards form one collectible unit. Eighteen of these cards are found in retail packs, and eighteen in Hobby Reserve packs.

	MINT	NRMT
COMPLETE SET (36)	120.00	55.00
COMMON CARD (1-36)	1.50	.70
SEMISTARS	2.50	1.10
UNLISTED STARS	4.00	1.80

CARDS 1-18 RETAIL, 19-36 HOBBY
STATED ODDS 1:23 RETAIL, 1:15 HOBBY

☐ 1 Will Clark	2.50	1.10
☐ 2 Ivan Rodriguez	5.00	2.20
☐ 3 Juan Gonzalez	10.00	4.50
☐ 4 Frank Thomas	15.00	6.75
☐ 5 Albert Belle	5.00	2.20
☐ 6 Robin Ventura	1.50	.70
☐ 7 Alex Rodriguez	12.00	5.50
☐ 8 Jay Buhner	2.50	1.10
☐ 9 Ken Griffey Jr.	20.00	9.00
☐ 10 Rafael Palmeiro	2.50	1.10
☐ 11 Roberto Alomar	4.00	1.80
☐ 12 Cal Ripken	15.00	6.75
☐ 13 Manny Ramirez	4.00	1.80
☐ 14 Matt Williams	2.50	1.10
☐ 15 Jim Thome	4.00	1.80
☐ 16 Derek Jeter	10.00	4.50
☐ 17 Wade Boggs	4.00	1.80
☐ 18 Bernie Williams	4.00	1.80
☐ 19 Chipper Jones	12.00	5.50
☐ 20 Andruw Jones	10.00	4.50
☐ 21 Ryan Klesko	2.50	1.10
☐ 22 Mike Piazza	12.00	5.50
☐ 23 Wilton Guerrero	1.50	.70
☐ 24 Raul Mondesi	2.50	1.10
☐ 25 Tony Gwynn	10.00	4.50
☐ 26 Greg Vaughn	1.50	.70
☐ 27 Ken Caminiti	2.50	1.10
☐ 28 Brian Jordan	1.50	.70
☐ 29 Ron Gant	1.50	.70
☐ 30 Dmitri Young	1.50	.70
☐ 31 Darin Erstad	6.00	2.70
☐ 32 Tim Salmon	4.00	1.80
☐ 33 Jim Edmonds	2.50	1.10
☐ 34 Chuck Knoblauch	4.00	1.80
☐ 35 Paul Molitor	4.00	1.80
☐ 36 Todd Walker	1.50	.70

1997 Score Highlight Zone

Randomly inserted in series one hobby packs only at a rate of one in 35, this 18-card set honors those mega-stars who have the incredible ability to consistently make the highlight films. The set is printed on thicker card stock with special foil stamping and a dot matrix holographic background.

	MINT	NRMT
COMPLETE SET (18)	200.00	90.00
COMMON CARD (1-18)	4.00	1.80
UNLISTED STARS	6.00	2.70
SER.1 ODDS 1:35 HOBBY, 1:9 JUMBO PS		

			MINT	NRMT
□ 1	Frank Thomas		25.00	11.00
□ 2	Ken Griffey Jr.		30.00	13.50
□ 3	Mo Vaughn		8.00	3.60
□ 4	Albert Belle		8.00	3.60
□ 5	Mike Piazza		20.00	9.00
□ 6	Barry Bonds		8.00	3.60
□ 7	Greg Maddux		20.00	9.00
□ 8	Sammy Sosa		6.00	2.70
□ 9	Jeff Bagwell		12.00	5.50
□ 10	Alex Rodriguez		20.00	9.00
□ 11	Chipper Jones		20.00	9.00
□ 12	Brady Anderson		4.00	1.80
□ 13	Ozzie Smith		8.00	3.60
□ 14	Edgar Martinez		4.00	1.80
□ 15	Cal Ripken		25.00	11.00
□ 16	Ryan Klesko		4.00	1.80
□ 17	Randy Johnson		6.00	2.70
□ 18	Eddie Murray		6.00	2.70

1997 Score Pitcher Perfect

Randomly inserted in series one packs at a rate of one in 23, this 15-card set features players photographed by Randy Johnson in unique poses and foil stamping. The backs carry player information.

	MINT	NRMT
COMPLETE SET (15)	70.00	32.00
COMMON CARDS (1-15)	1.50	.70
SER.1 ODDS 1:23 H/R 1:11 MAG, 1:15 JUM PS		

			MINT	NRMT
□ 1	Cal Ripken		12.00	5.50
□ 2	Alex Rodriguez		10.00	4.50
□ 3	Alex Rodriguez		15.00	6.75
	Cal Ripken			
□ 4	Edgar Martinez		2.00	.90
□ 5	Ivan Rodriguez		4.00	1.80
□ 6	Mark McGwire		6.00	2.70
□ 7	Tim Salmon		3.00	1.35
□ 8	Chili Davis		1.50	.70
□ 9	Joe Carter		1.50	.70
□ 10	Frank Thomas		12.00	5.50
□ 11	Will Clark		2.00	.90
□ 12	Mo Vaughn		4.00	1.80
□ 13	Wade Boggs		3.00	1.35
□ 14	Ken Griffey Jr.		15.00	6.75
□ 15	Randy Johnson		3.00	1.35

1997 Score Stand and Deliver

Randomly inserted in series two packs at a rate of 1:71 (retail) and 1:47 (hobby reserve), this 24-card set features color player photos printed on silver foil card stock. The set is broken into six separate 4-card groupings. Groups contain players from the following teams: 1-4 (Braves), 5-8 (Mariners), 9-12 (Yankees), 13-16 (Dodgers), 17-20 (Indians) and 21-24 (Wild Card). The four players featured within the Wild Card group are from "lesser" teams not given a shot at winning the World Series. Each of these cards, unlike cards 1-20, has a "Wild Card" logo stamped on front. Collectors were then supposed to gather up the particular group that won the 1997 World Series, in this case - the Florida Marlins. Since none of the featured teams won, the 4-card Wild Card group was designated as the winner. The winning cards could then be mailed into Pinnacle for a special gold upgrade version of the set, framed in glass.

	MINT	NRMT
COMPLETE SET (24)	350.00	160.00
COMMON CARD (1-24)	4.00	1.80
UNLISTED STARS	10.00	4.50
SER.2 ODDS 1:71 RETAIL, 1:41 HOBBY		

			MINT	NRMT
□ 1	Andruw Jones		20.00	9.00
□ 2	Greg Maddux		30.00	13.50
□ 3	Chipper Jones		30.00	13.50
□ 4	John Smoltz		5.00	2.20
□ 5	Ken Griffey Jr.		50.00	22.00
□ 6	Alex Rodriguez		30.00	13.50
□ 7	Jay Buhner		6.00	2.70
□ 8	Randy Johnson		10.00	4.50
□ 9	Derek Jeter		25.00	11.00
□ 10	Andy Pettitte		10.00	4.50
□ 11	Bernie Williams		10.00	4.50
□ 12	Mariano Rivera		5.00	2.20
□ 13	Mike Piazza		30.00	13.50
□ 14	Hideo Nomo		25.00	11.00
□ 15	Raul Mondesi		6.00	2.70
□ 16	Todd Hollandsworth		4.00	1.80
□ 17	Manny Ramirez		10.00	4.50
□ 18	Jim Thome		10.00	4.50
□ 19	Dave Justice		10.00	4.50
□ 20	Matt Williams		6.00	2.70
□ 21	Juan Gonzalez W		25.00	11.00
□ 22	Jeff Bagwell W		20.00	9.00
□ 23	Cal Ripken W		40.00	18.00
□ 24	Frank Thomas W		40.00	18.00

1997 Score Stellar Season

Randomly inserted in series one at a rate of one in 35, this 18-card set features players who had a star season. The cards are printed using dot matrix holographic printing.

	MINT	NRMT
COMPLETE SET (18)	80.00	36.00
COMMON CARD (1-18)	2.00	.90
UNLISTED STARS	4.00	1.80
SER.1 STATED ODDS 1:35 MAGAZINE		

			MINT	NRMT
□ 1	Juan Gonzalez		10.00	4.50
□ 2	Chuck Knoblauch		4.00	1.80
□ 3	Jeff Bagwell		8.00	3.60
□ 4	John Smoltz		2.00	.90
□ 5	Mark McGwire		8.00	3.60
□ 6	Ken Griffey Jr.		20.00	9.00
□ 7	Frank Thomas		15.00	6.75
□ 8	Alex Rodriguez		12.00	5.50
□ 9	Mike Piazza		12.00	5.50
□ 10	Albert Belle		5.00	2.20
□ 11	Roberto Alomar		4.00	1.80
□ 12	Sammy Sosa		4.00	1.80
□ 13	Mo Vaughn		5.00	2.20
□ 14	Brady Anderson		2.50	1.10
□ 15	Henry Rodriguez		2.00	.90
□ 16	Eric Young		2.00	.90
□ 17	Gary Sheffield		4.00	1.80
□ 18	Ryan Klesko		2.50	1.10

1997 Score Titanic Taters

Randomly inserted in series one retail packs only at a rate of one in 35, this 16-card set honors the long-ball ability of some of the league's top sluggers and uses dot matrix holographic printing.

	MINT	NRMT
COMPLETE SET (18)	125.00	55.00
COMMON CARD (1-18)	2.50	1.10
UNLISTED STARS	4.00	1.80
SER.1 STATED ODDS 1:35 RETAIL		

		MINT	NRMT
□ 1	Mark McGwire	10.00	4.50
□ 2	Mike Piazza	15.00	6.75
□ 3	Ken Griffey Jr.	25.00	11.00
□ 4	Juan Gonzalez	12.00	5.50
□ 5	Frank Thomas	20.00	9.00
□ 6	Albert Belle	5.00	2.20
□ 7	Sammy Sosa	4.00	1.80
□ 8	Jeff Bagwell	10.00	4.50
□ 9	Todd Hundley	2.50	1.10
□ 10	Ryan Klesko	3.00	1.35
□ 11	Brady Anderson	3.00	1.35
□ 12	Mo Vaughn	6.00	2.70
□ 13	Jay Buhner	3.00	1.35
□ 14	Chipper Jones	15.00	6.75
□ 15	Barry Bonds	6.00	2.70
□ 16	Gary Sheffield	4.00	1.80
□ 17	Alex Rodriguez	15.00	6.75
□ 18	Cecil Fielder	2.50	1.10

1998 Score

This 270-card set was distributed in 10-card packs with a suggested retail price of $.99. The fronts feature color player photos in a thin white border. The backs carry player information and statistics.

	MINT	NRMT
COMPLETE SET (270)	20.00	9.00
COMMON CARD (1-270)	.10	.05
MINOR STARS	.20	.09
UNLISTED STARS	.40	.18

□ 1	Andruw Jones	.75	.35
□ 2	Dan Wilson	.10	.05
□ 3	Hideo Nomo	1.00	.45
□ 4	Chuck Carr	.10	.05
□ 5	Barry Bonds	.50	.23
□ 6	Jack McDowell	.10	.05
□ 7	Albert Belle	.50	.23
□ 8	Francisco Cordova	.10	.05
□ 9	Greg Maddux	1.25	.55
□ 10	Alex Rodriguez	1.25	.55
□ 11	Steve Avery	.10	.05
□ 12	Chuck McElroy	.10	.05
□ 13	Larry Walker	.40	.18
□ 14	Hideki Irabu	.20	.09
□ 15	Roberto Alomar	.40	.18
□ 16	Neifi Perez	.20	.09
□ 17	Jim Thome	.40	.18
□ 18	Rickey Henderson	.30	.14
□ 19	Andres Galarraga	.40	.18
□ 20	Jeff Fassero	.10	.05
□ 21	Kevin Young	.10	.05
□ 22	Derek Jeter	1.00	.45
□ 23	Andy Benes	.20	.09
□ 24	Mike Piazza	1.25	.55
□ 25	Todd Stottlemyre	.10	.05
□ 26	Michael Tucker	.20	.09
□ 27	Denny Neagle	.20	.09
□ 28	Javier Lopez	.20	.09
□ 29	Aaron Sele	.10	.05
□ 30	Ryan Klesko	.30	.14
□ 31	Dennis Eckersley	.20	.09
□ 32	Quinton McCracken	.10	.05
□ 33	Brian Anderson	.10	.05
□ 34	Ken Griffey Jr.	2.00	.90
□ 35	Shawn Estes	.20	.09
□ 36	Tim Wakefield	.10	.05
□ 37	Jimmy Key	.20	.09
□ 38	Jeff Bagwell	.75	.35
□ 39	Edgardo Alfonzo	.20	.09
□ 40	Mike Cameron	.20	.09
□ 41	Mark McGwire	1.00	.45
□ 42	Tino Martinez	.40	.18
□ 43	Cal Ripken	1.50	.70
□ 44	Curtis Goodwin	.10	.05
□ 45	Bobby Ayala	.10	.05
□ 46	Sandy Alomar Jr	.20	.09
□ 47	Bobby Jones	.10	.05
□ 48	Omar Vizquel	.20	.09
□ 49	Roger Clemens	.75	.35
□ 50	Tony Gwynn	1.00	.45
□ 51	Chipper Jones	1.25	.55
□ 52	Ron Coomer	.10	.05
□ 53	Dmitri Young	.10	.05
□ 54	Brian Giles	.10	.05
□ 55	Steve Finley	.20	.09
□ 56	David Cone	.20	.09
□ 57	Andy Pettitte	.40	.18
□ 58	Wilton Guerrero	.20	.09
□ 59	Deion Sanders	.20	.09
□ 60	Carlos Delgado	.20	.09
□ 61	Jason Giambi	.20	.09
□ 62	Ozzie Guillen	.20	.09
□ 63	Jay Bell	.20	.09
□ 64	Barry Larkin	.30	.14
□ 65	Sammy Sosa	.40	.18
□ 66	Bernie Williams	.40	.18
□ 67	Terry Steinbach	.10	.05
□ 68	Scott Rolen	1.00	.45
□ 69	Melvin Nieves	.10	.05
□ 70	Craig Biggio	.30	.14
□ 71	Todd Greene	.20	.09
□ 72	Greg Gagne	.10	.05
□ 73	Shigetoshi Hasegawa	.20	.09
□ 74	Mark McLemore	.10	.05
□ 75	Darren Bragg	.10	.05
□ 76	Brett Butler	.20	.09
□ 77	Ron Gant	.20	.09
□ 78	Mike Difelice	.10	.05
□ 79	Charles Nagy	.10	.05
□ 80	Scott Hatteberg	.10	.05
□ 81	Brady Anderson	.30	.14
□ 82	Jay Buhner	.30	.14
□ 83	Todd Hollandsworth	.10	.05
□ 84	Geronimo Berroa	.10	.05
□ 85	Jeff Suppan	.10	.05
□ 86	Pedro Martinez	.40	.18
□ 87	Roger Cedeno	.10	.05
□ 88	Ivan Rodriguez	.50	.23
□ 89	Jaime Navarro	.10	.05
□ 90	Chris Hoiles	.10	.05
□ 91	Nomar Garciaparra	1.25	.55
□ 92	Rafael Palmeiro	.30	.14
□ 93	Darin Erstad	.50	.23
□ 94	Kenny Lofton	.50	.23
□ 95	Mike Timlin	.10	.05
□ 96	Chris Clemons	.10	.05
□ 97	Vinny Castilla	.20	.09
□ 98	Charlie Hayes	.10	.05
□ 99	Lyle Mouton	.10	.05
□ 100	Jason Dickson	.20	.09
□ 101	Justin Thompson	.20	.09
□ 102	Pat Kelly	.10	.05
□ 103	Chan Ho Park	.40	.18
□ 104	Ray Lankford	.20	.09
□ 105	Frank Thomas	1.50	.70
□ 106	Jermaine Allensworth	.10	.05
□ 107	Doug Drabek	.10	.05
□ 108	Todd Hundley	.20	.09
□ 109	Carl Everett	.10	.05
□ 110	Edgar Martinez	.30	.14
□ 111	Robin Ventura	.20	.09
□ 112	John Wetteland	.10	.05
□ 113	Mariano Rivera	.20	.09
□ 114	Jose Rosado	.10	.05
□ 115	Ken Caminiti	.30	.14
□ 116	Paul O'Neill	.20	.09
□ 117	Tim Salmon	.40	.18
□ 118	Eduardo Perez	.10	.05
□ 119	Mike Jackson	.10	.05
□ 120	John Smoltz	.20	.09
□ 121	Brant Brown	.10	.05
□ 122	John Mabry	.10	.05
□ 123	Chuck Knoblauch	.40	.18
□ 124	Reggie Sanders	.10	.05
□ 125	Kon Hill	.10	.05
□ 126	Mike Mussina	.40	.18
□ 127	Chad Curtis	.10	.05
□ 128	Todd Worrell	.10	.05
□ 129	Chris Widger	.10	.05
□ 130	Damon Mashore	.10	.05
□ 131	Kevin Brown	.20	.09
□ 132	Bip Roberts	.10	.05
□ 133	Tim Naehring	.10	.05
□ 134	Dave Martinez	.10	.05
□ 135	Jeff Blauser	.20	.09
□ 136	Dave Justice	.40	.18
□ 137	Dave Hollins	.20	.09
□ 138	Pat Hentgen	.20	.09
□ 139	Darren Daulton	.20	.09
□ 140	Ramon Martinez	.20	.09
□ 141	Raul Casanova	.10	.05
□ 142	Tom Glavine	.20	.09
□ 143	J.T. Snow	.20	.09
□ 144	Tony Graffanino	.10	.05
□ 145	Randy Johnson	.40	.18
□ 146	Orlando Merced	.10	.05
□ 147	Jeff Juden	.10	.05
□ 148	Darryl Kile	.20	.09
□ 149	Ray Durham	.10	.05
□ 150	Alex Fernandez	.10	.05
□ 151	Joey Cora	.20	.09
□ 152	Royce Clayton	.10	.05
□ 153	Randy Myers	.10	.05
□ 154	Charles Johnson	.20	.09
□ 155	Alan Benes	.20	.09
□ 156	Mike Bordick	.10	.05
□ 157	Heathcliff Slocumb	.10	.05
□ 158	Roger Bailey	.10	.05
□ 159	Reggie Jefferson	.10	.05
□ 160	Ricky Bottalico	.10	.05
□ 161	Scott Erickson	.10	.05
□ 162	Matt Williams	.30	.14
□ 163	Robb Nen	.10	.05
□ 164	Matt Stairs	.10	.05
□ 165	Ismael Valdes	.20	.09
□ 166	Lee Stevens	.10	.05
□ 167	Gary DiSarcina	.10	.05
□ 168	Brad Radke	.10	.05
□ 169	Mike Lansing	.10	.05
□ 170	Armando Benitez	.10	.05
□ 171	Mike James	.10	.05
□ 172	Russ Davis	.10	.05
□ 173	Lance Johnson	.10	.05
□ 174	Joey Hamilton	.20	.09
□ 175	John Valentin	.10	.05
□ 176	David Segui	.10	.05
□ 177	David Wells	.20	.09
□ 178	Delino DeShields	.10	.05
□ 179	Eric Karros	.20	.09
□ 180	Jim Leyritz	.10	.05
□ 181	Raul Mondesi	.30	.14
□ 182	Travis Fryman	.20	.09
□ 183	Todd Zeile	.10	.05
□ 184	Brian Jordan	.20	.09
□ 185	Rey Ordonez	.10	.05
□ 186	Jim Edmonds	.30	.14
□ 187	Terrell Wade	.10	.05
□ 188	Marquis Grissom	.20	.09
□ 189	Chris Snopek	.10	.05
□ 190	Shane Reynolds	.10	.05
□ 191	Jeff Frye	.10	.05
□ 192	Paul Sorrento	.10	.05
□ 193	James Baldwin	.10	.05
□ 194	Brian McRae	.10	.05
□ 195	Fred McGriff	.30	.14
□ 196	Troy Percival	.10	.05
□ 197	Rich Amaral	.10	.05

□			
□ 198	Juan Guzman	.10	.05
□ 199	Cecil Fielder	.20	.09
□ 200	Willie Blair	.10	.05
□ 201	Chili Davis	.20	.09
□ 202	Gary Gaetti	.10	.05
□ 203	B.J. Surhoff	.10	.05
□ 204	Steve Cooke	.10	.05
□ 205	Chuck Finley	.10	.05
□ 206	Jeff Kent	.10	.05
□ 207	Ben McDonald	.10	.05
□ 208	Jeffrey Hammonds	.10	.05
□ 209	Tom Goodwin	.10	.05
□ 210	Billy Ashley	.10	.05
□ 211	Wil Cordero	.10	.05
□ 212	Shawon Dunston	.10	.05
□ 213	Tony Phillips	.10	.05
□ 214	Jamie Moyer	.10	.05
□ 215	John Jaha	.10	.05
□ 216	Troy O'Leary	.10	.05
□ 217	Brad Ausmus	.10	.05
□ 218	Garret Anderson	.20	.09
□ 219	Wilson Alvarez	.10	.05
□ 220	Kent Mercker	.10	.05
□ 221	Wade Boggs	.40	.18
□ 222	Mark Wohlers	.10	.05
□ 223	Kevin Appier	.20	.09
□ 224	Tony Fernandez	.10	.05
□ 225	Ugueth Urbina	.10	.05
□ 226	Gregg Jefferies	.10	.05
□ 227	Mo Vaughn	.50	.23
□ 228	Arthur Rhodes	.10	.05
□ 229	Jorge Fabregas	.10	.05
□ 230	Mark Gardner	.10	.05
□ 231	Shane Mack	.10	.05
□ 232	Jorge Posada	.10	.05
□ 233	Jose Cruz Jr.	1.50	.70
□ 234	Paul Konerko	.60	.25
□ 235	Derrek Lee	.30	.14
□ 236	Steve Woodard	.20	.09
□ 237	Todd Dunwoody	.20	.09
□ 238	Fernando Tatis	.40	.18
□ 239	Jacob Cruz	.10	.05
□ 240	Pokey Reese	.10	.05
□ 241	Mark Kotsay	.40	.18
□ 242	Matt Morris	.20	.09
□ 243	Antone Williamson	.10	.05
□ 244	Ben Grieve	.75	.35
□ 245	Ryan McGuire	.10	.05
□ 246	Lou Collier	.10	.05
□ 247	Shannon Stewart	.20	.09
□ 248	Brett Tomko	.20	.09
□ 249	Bobby Estalella	.20	.09
□ 250	Livan Hernandez	.30	.14
□ 251	Todd Helton	.50	.23
□ 252	Jaret Wright	1.00	.45
□ 253	Darryl Hamilton IM	.10	.05
□ 254	Stan Javier IM	.10	.05
□ 255	Glenallen Hill IM	.10	.05
□ 256	Mark Gardner IM	.10	.05
□ 257	Cal Ripken IM	.75	.35
□ 258	Mike Mussina IM	.20	.09
□ 259	Mike Piazza IM	.60	.25
□ 260	Sammy Sosa IM	.50	.23
□ 261	Todd Hundley IM	.10	.05
□ 262	Eric Karros IM	.10	.05
□ 263	Denny Neagle IM	.10	.05
□ 264	Jeromy Burnitz IM	.10	.05
□ 265	Greg Maddux IM	.60	.25
□ 266	Tony Clark IM	.20	.09
□ 267	Vladimir Guerrero IM	.30	.14
□ 268	Cal Ripken Jr. CL	.75	.35
□ 269	Ken Griffey Jr. CL	1.00	.45
□ 270	Mark McGwire CL	.50	.23

1998 Score Showcase Series

Randomly inserted in packs at the rate of one in seven, this 160-card set is an all silver-foil partial parallel rendition of the base set.

		MINT	NRMT
COMPLETE SET (160)		100.00	45.00
COMMON CARD (1-160)		.50	.23
STATED ODDS 1:7			
COMP AP SET (160)		400.00	180.00
COMMON AP (PP1-PP160)		2.00	.90
*AP STARS: 2X TO 4X HI			
*AP YOUNG STARS: 1.5X TO 3X HI			
AP STATED ODDS 1:35			

□			
□ PP1	Andruw Jones	2.00	.90
□ PP2	Dan Wilson	.50	.23
□ PP3	Hideo Nomo	5.00	2.20
□ PP4	Neifi Perez	.75	.35
□ PP5	Jim Thome	2.00	.90
□ PP6	Jeff Fassero	.50	.23
□ PP7	Derek Jeter	5.00	2.20
□ PP8	Andy Benes	.75	.35
□ PP9	Michael Tucker	.75	.35
□ PP10	Ryan Klesko	1.25	.55
□ PP11	Dennis Eckersley	.75	.35
□ PP12	Jimmy Key	.75	.35
□ PP13	Edgardo Alfonzo	.75	.35
□ PP14	Mike Cameron	.75	.35
□ PP15	Omar Vizquel	.75	.35
□ PP16	Ron Coomer	.50	.23
□ PP17	Dmitri Young	.50	.23
□ PP18	Brian Giles	.75	.35
□ PP19	Steve Finley	.75	.35
□ PP20	Andy Pettitte	2.00	.90
□ PP21	Wilton Guerrero	.50	.23
□ PP22	Deion Sanders	.75	.35
□ PP23	Carlos Delgado	.75	.35
□ PP24	Jason Giambi	.75	.35
□ PP25	David Cone	.75	.35
□ PP26	Jay Bell	.75	.35
□ PP27	Sammy Sosa	2.00	.90
□ PP28	Barry Larkin	1.25	.55
□ PP29	Scott Rolen	5.00	2.20
□ PP30	Todd Greene	.75	.35
□ PP31	Bernie Williams	2.00	.90
□ PP32	Brett Butler	.75	.35
□ PP33	Ron Gant	.75	.35
□ PP34	Brady Anderson	1.25	.55
□ PP35	Craig Biggio	1.25	.55
□ PP36	Charles Nagy	.75	.35
□ PP37	Jay Buhner	1.25	.55
□ PP38	Geronimo Berroa	.50	.23
□ PP39	Jeff Suppan	.50	.23
□ PP40	Rafael Palmeiro	1.25	.55
□ PP41	Darin Erstad	2.50	1.10
□ PP42	Mike Timlin	.50	.23
□ PP43	Vinny Castilla	.75	.35
□ PP44	Carl Everett	.50	.23
□ PP45	Robin Ventura	.75	.35
□ PP46	John Wetteland	.50	.23
□ PP47	Paul O'Neill	.75	.35
□ PP48	Tim Salmon	2.00	.90
□ PP49	Mike Jackson	.50	.23
□ PP50	John Smoltz	.75	.35
□ PP51	Brant Brown	.50	.23
□ PP52	Reggie Sanders	.50	.23
□ PP53	Ken Hill	.50	.23
□ PP54	Todd Worrell	.50	.23
□ PP55	Bip Roberts	.50	.23
□ PP56	Tim Naehring	.50	.23
□ PP57	Darren Daulton	.75	.35
□ PP58	Ramon Martinez	.75	.35
□ PP59	Raul Casanova	.50	.23
□ PP60	J.T. Snow	.75	.35
□ PP61	Jeff Juden	.50	.23
□ PP62	Royce Clayton	.50	.23
□ PP63	Charles Johnson	.75	.35
□ PP64	Alan Benes	.75	.35
□ PP65	Reggie Jefferson	.50	.23
□ PP66	Ricky Bottalico	.50	.23
□ PP67	Scott Erickson	.50	.23
□ PP68	Matt Williams	1.25	.55
□ PP69	Robb Nen	.50	.23
□ PP70	Matt Stairs	.50	.23
□ PP71	Ismael Valdes	.75	.35
□ PP72	Brad Radke	.75	.35
□ PP73	Armando Benitez	.50	.23
□ PP74	Russ Davis	.50	.23
□ PP75	Lance Johnson	.50	.23
□ PP76	Joey Hamilton	.75	.35

□			
□ PP77	John Valentin	.50	.23
□ PP78	David Segui	.50	.23
□ PP79	David Wells	.50	.23
□ PP80	Eric Karros	.75	.35
□ PP81	Raul Mondesi	1.25	.55
□ PP82	Travis Fryman	.75	.35
□ PP83	Todd Zeile	.50	.23
□ PP84	Brian Jordan	.75	.35
□ PP85	Rey Ordonez	.50	.23
□ PP86	Jim Edmonds	1.25	.55
□ PP87	Marquis Grissom	.75	.35
□ PP88	Shane Reynolds	.50	.23
□ PP89	Paul Sorrento	.50	.23
□ PP90	Brian McRae	.50	.23
□ PP91	Fred McGriff	1.25	.55
□ PP92	Troy Percival	.50	.23
□ PP93	Juan Guzman	.50	.23
□ PP94	Cecil Fielder	.75	.35
□ PP95	Chili Davis	.75	.35
□ PP96	B.J. Surhoff	.50	.23
□ PP97	Chuck Finley	.50	.23
□ PP98	Jeff Kent	.50	.23
□ PP99	Ben McDonald	.50	.23
□ PP100	Jeffrey Hammonds	.50	.23
□ PP101	Tom Goodwin	.50	.23
□ PP102	Wil Cordero	.50	.23
□ PP103	Tony Phillips	.50	.23
□ PP104	John Jaha	.50	.23
□ PP105	Garret Anderson	.75	.35
□ PP106	Wilson Alvarez	.50	.23
□ PP107	Wade Boggs	2.00	.90
□ PP108	Mark Wohlers	.50	.23
□ PP109	Kevin Appier	.75	.35
□ PP110	Mo Vaughn	2.50	1.10
□ PP111	Ray Durham	.50	.23
□ PP112	Alex Fernandez	.50	.23
□ PP113	Barry Bonds	2.50	1.10
□ PP114	Albert Belle	2.50	1.10
□ PP115	Greg Maddux	6.00	2.70
□ PP116	Alex Rodriguez	6.00	2.70
□ PP117	Larry Walker	2.00	.90
□ PP118	Roberto Alomar	2.00	.90
□ PP119	Andres Galarraga	2.00	.90
□ PP120	Mike Piazza	6.00	2.70
□ PP121	Denny Neagle	.75	.35
□ PP122	Javier Lopez	.75	.35
□ PP123	Ken Griffey Jr.	10.00	4.50
□ PP124	Shawn Estes	.50	.23
□ PP125	Jeff Bagwell	4.00	1.80
□ PP126	Mark McGwire	5.00	2.20
□ PP127	Tino Martinez	2.00	.90
□ PP128	Cal Ripken Jr.	8.00	3.60
□ PP129	Sandy Alomar Jr.	.75	.35
□ PP130	Bobby Jones	.50	.23
□ PP131	Roger Clemens	4.00	1.80
□ PP132	Tony Gwynn	5.00	2.20
□ PP133	Chipper Jones	6.00	2.70
□ PP134	Orlando Merced	.50	.23
□ PP135	Todd Stottlemyre	.50	.23
□ PP136	Delino DeShields	.50	.23
□ PP137	Pedro Martinez	2.00	.90
□ PP138	Ivan Rodriguez	2.50	1.10
□ PP139	Nomar Garciaparra	6.00	2.70
□ PP140	Kenny Lofton	2.50	1.10
□ PP141	Jason Dickson	.75	.35
□ PP142	Justin Thompson	.75	.35
□ PP143	Ray Lankford	.75	.35
□ PP144	Frank Thomas	8.00	3.60
□ PP145	Todd Hundley	.75	.35
□ PP146	Edgar Martinez	1.25	.55
□ PP147	Mariano Rivera	.75	.35
□ PP148	Jose Rosado	.50	.23
□ PP149	Ken Caminiti	1.25	.55
□ PP150	Chuck Knoblauch	2.00	.90
□ PP151	Mike Mussina	2.00	.90
□ PP152	Kevin Brown	.75	.35
□ PP153	Jeff Blauser	.75	.35
□ PP154	Dave Justice	2.00	.90
□ PP155	Pat Hentgen	.75	.35
□ PP156	Tom Glavine	.75	.35
□ PP157	Randy Johnson	2.00	.90
□ PP158	Darryl Kile	.75	.35
□ PP159	Joey Cora	.75	.35
□ PP160	Randy Myers	.50	.23

1998 Score All Score Team

Randomly inserted in packs at the rate of one in 35, this 20-card set features color player images on a metallic foil background. The backs carry a small player head photo with information stating why the player was selected to this appear in this set.

	MINT	NRMT
COMPLETE SET (20)	120.00	55.00
COMMON CARD (1-20)	1.50	.70
SEMISTARS	2.50	1.10
UNLISTED STARS	4.00	1.80
STATED ODDS 1:35		

		MINT	NRMT
☐ 1	Mike Piazza	12.00	5.50
☐ 2	Ivan Rodriguez	5.00	2.20
☐ 3	Frank Thomas	15.00	6.75
☐ 4	Mark McGwire	10.00	4.50
☐ 5	Ryne Sandberg	5.00	2.20
☐ 6	Roberto Alomar	4.00	1.80
☐ 7	Cal Ripken	15.00	6.75
☐ 8	Barry Larkin	2.50	1.10
☐ 9	Paul Molitor	4.00	1.80
☐ 10	Travis Fryman	1.50	.70
☐ 11	Kirby Puckett	8.00	3.60
☐ 12	Tony Gwynn	10.00	4.50
☐ 13	Ken Griffey Jr.	20.00	9.00
☐ 14	Juan Gonzalez	10.00	4.50
☐ 15	Barry Bonds	5.00	2.20
☐ 16	Andruw Jones	6.00	2.70
☐ 17	Roger Clemens	8.00	3.60
☐ 18	Randy Johnson	4.00	1.80
☐ 19	Greg Maddux	12.00	5.50
☐ 20	Dennis Eckersley	1.50	.70

1998 Score Complete Players

Randomly inserted in packs at the rate of one in 23, this 30-card set features three photos

of each of the ten listed players with full holographic foil stamping.

	MINT	NRMT
COMPLETE SET (30)	200.00	90.00
COMMON CARD (1A-10C)	3.00	1.35
STATED ODDS 1:23		
THREE CARDS PER PLAYER		

		MINT	NRMT
☐ 1A	Ken Griffey Jr.	15.00	6.75
☐ 1B	Ken Griffey Jr.	15.00	6.75
☐ 1C	Ken Griffey Jr.	15.00	6.75
☐ 2A	Mark McGwire	8.00	3.60
☐ 2B	Mark McGwire	8.00	3.60
☐ 2C	Mark McGwire	8.00	3.60
☐ 3A	Derek Jeter	8.00	3.60
☐ 3B	Derek Jeter	8.00	3.60
☐ 3C	Derek Jeter	8.00	3.60
☐ 4A	Cal Ripken Jr.	12.00	5.50
☐ 4B	Cal Ripken Jr.	12.00	5.50
☐ 4C	Cal Ripken Jr.	12.00	5.50
☐ 5A	Mike Piazza	10.00	4.50
☐ 5B	Mike Piazza	10.00	4.50
☐ 5C	Mike Piazza	10.00	4.50
☐ 6A	Darin Erstad	3.00	1.35
☐ 6B	Darin Erstad	3.00	1.35
☐ 6C	Darin Erstad	3.00	1.35
☐ 7A	Frank Thomas	12.00	5.50
☐ 7B	Frank Thomas	12.00	5.50
☐ 7C	Frank Thomas	12.00	5.50
☐ 8A	Andruw Jones	5.00	2.20
☐ 8B	Andruw Jones	5.00	2.20
☐ 8C	Andruw Jones	5.00	2.20
☐ 9A	Nomar Garciaparra	8.00	3.60
☐ 9B	Nomar Garciaparra	8.00	3.60
☐ 9C	Nomar Garciaparra	8.00	3.60
☐ 10A	Manny Ramirez	3.00	1.35
☐ 10B	Manny Ramirez	3.00	1.35
☐ 10C	Manny Ramirez	3.00	1.35

1998 Score Epix

Randomly inserted in Score packs at the rate of one in 61, this 24-card set features color photos of top players' most memorable games, plays, seasons and moments on Dot Matrix Hologram cards. Orange, Purple, and Emerald versions of this set were also produced. To obtain all the cards for each player in this fractured insert set, the collector had to open not only Score packs, but also Pinnacle, Pinnacle Certified and Zenith packs.

	MINT	NRMT
COMMON CARD (E1-E24)	6.00	2.70
*PURPLE CARDS: .75X TO 1.5X ORANGE		
*EMERALD CARDS: 1.5X TO 3X ORANGE		
STATED ODDS 1:61		
LESS THAN 30 EMERALD MOMENTS PRINTED		
ONLY ORANGE CARDS LISTED BELOW!		
USE MULTIPLIERS FOR EMERALD/PURPLE		

		MINT	NRMT
☐ E1	Ken Griffey Jr. PLAY	30.00	13.50
☐ E2	Juan Gonzalez PLAY	15.00	6.75
☐ E3	Jeff Bagwell PLAY	12.00	5.50
☐ E4	Ivan Rodriguez PLAY	8.00	3.60
☐ E5	Nomar Garciaparra PLAY	15.00	6.75
☐ E6	Ryne Sandberg PLAY	8.00	3.60
☐ E7	Frank Thomas GAME	40.00	18.00
☐ E8	Derek Jeter GAME	25.00	11.00
☐ E9	Tony Gwynn GAME	25.00	11.00
☐ E10	Albert Belle GAME	12.00	5.50
☐ E11	Scott Rolen GAME	20.00	9.00
☐ E12	Barry Larkin GAME	6.00	2.70
☐ E13	Alex Rodriguez SEAS	60.00	27.00
☐ E14	Cal Ripken Jr. SEAS	80.00	36.00
☐ E15	Chipper Jones SEAS	60.00	27.00
☐ E16	Roger Clemens SEAS	40.00	18.00
☐ E17	Mo Vaughn SEAS	25.00	11.00
☐ E18	Mark McGwire SEAS	50.00	22.00
☐ E19	Mike Piazza MOM	100.00	45.00
☐ E20	Andruw Jones MOM	60.00	27.00
☐ E21	Greg Maddux MOM	100.00	45.00
☐ E22	Barry Bonds MOM	40.00	18.00
☐ E23	Paul Molitor MOM	30.00	13.50
☐ E24	Eddie Murray MOM	30.00	13.50

1993 Select

Seeking a niche in the premium, mid-price market, Score produced a new 405-card standard-size set entitled Select in 1993. The set includes regular players, rookies, and draft picks, and was sold in 15-card hobby and retail packs and 28-card super packs. The front photos, composed either horizontally or vertically, are ultra-violet coated while the two-toned green borders received a matte finish. The player's name appears in mustard-colored lettering in the bottom border. Subset cards include Draft Picks and Rookies, both sprinkled throughout the set. Rookie Cards in this set include Derek Jeter and Jason Kendall.

	MINT	NRMT
COMPLETE SET (405)	30.00	13.50
COMMON CARD (1-405)	.15	.07
MINOR STARS	.30	.14
UNLISTED STARS	.60	.25

		MINT	NRMT
☐ 1	Barry Bonds	.75	.35
☐ 2	Ken Griffey Jr.	3.00	1.35
☐ 3	Will Clark	.40	.18
☐ 4	Kirby Puckett	1.25	.55
☐ 5	Tony Gwynn	1.50	.70
☐ 6	Frank Thomas	2.50	1.10
☐ 7	Tom Glavine	.40	.18
☐ 8	Roberto Alomar	.60	.25
☐ 9	Andre Dawson	.40	.18
☐ 10	Ron Darling	.15	.07
☐ 11	Bobby Bonilla	.30	.14
☐ 12	Danny Tartabull	.15	.07

13	Darren Daulton	.30	.14
14	Roger Clemens	1.25	.55
15	Ozzie Smith	.75	.35
16	Mark McGwire	1.25	.55
17	Terry Pendleton	.30	.14
18	Cal Ripken	2.50	1.10
19	Fred McGriff	.40	.18
20	Cecil Fielder	.30	.14
21	Darryl Strawberry	.30	.14
22	Robin Yount	.40	.18
23	Barry Larkin	.40	.18
24	Don Mattingly	1.00	.45
25	Craig Biggio	.40	.18
26	Sandy Alomar Jr.	.30	.14
27	Larry Walker	.25	.11
28	Junior Felix	.15	.07
29	Eddie Murray	.60	.25
30	Robin Ventura	.30	.14
31	Greg Maddux	2.00	.90
32	Dave Winfield	.40	.18
33	John Kruk	.30	.14
34	Wally Joyner	.30	.14
35	Andy Van Slyke	.30	.14
36	Chuck Knoblauch	.60	.25
37	Tom Pagnozzi	.15	.07
38	Dennis Eckersley	.30	.14
39	Dave Justice	.60	.25
40	Juan Gonzalez	1.50	.70
41	Gary Sheffield	.60	.25
42	Paul Molitor	.60	.25
43	Delino DeShields	.15	.07
44	Travis Fryman	.30	.14
45	Hal Morris	.15	.07
46	Greg Olson	.15	.07
47	Ken Caminiti	.40	.18
48	Wade Boggs	.60	.25
49	Orel Hershiser	.30	.14
50	Albert Belle	.75	.35
51	Bill Swift	.15	.07
52	Mark Langston	.15	.07
53	Joe Girardi	.15	.07
54	Keith Miller	.15	.07
55	Gary Carter	.40	.18
56	Brady Anderson	.40	.18
57	Dwight Gooden	.30	.14
58	Julio Franco	.15	.07
59	Lenny Dykstra	.30	.14
60	Mickey Tettleton	.15	.07
61	Randy Tomlin	.15	.07
62	B.J. Surhoff	.30	.14
63	Todd Zeile	.15	.07
64	Roberto Kelly	.15	.07
65	Rob Dibble	.15	.07
66	Leo Gomez	.15	.07
67	Doug Jones	.15	.07
68	Ellis Burks	.30	.14
69	Mike Scioscia	.15	.07
70	Charles Nagy	.30	.14
71	Cory Snyder	.15	.07
72	Devon White	.15	.07
73	Mark Grace	.40	.18
74	Luis Polonia	.15	.07
75	John Smiley 2X	.15	.07
76	Carlton Fisk	.60	.25
77	Luis Sojo	.15	.07
78	George Brett	1.25	.55
79	Mitch Williams	.15	.07
80	Kent Hrbek	.30	.14
81	Jay Bell	.30	.14
82	Edgar Martinez	.40	.18
83	Lee Smith	.30	.14
84	Deion Sanders	.60	.25
85	Bill Gullickson	.15	.07
86	Paul O'Neill	.30	.14
87	Kevin Seitzer	.15	.07
88	Steve Finley	.15	.07
89	Mel Hall	.15	.07
90	Nolan Ryan	2.50	1.10
91	Eric Davis	.30	.14
92	Mike Mussina	.60	.25
93	Tony Fernandez	.15	.07
94	Frank Viola	.15	.07
95	Matt Williams	.40	.18
96	Joe Carter	.30	.14
97	Ryne Sandberg	.75	.35
98	Jim Abbott	.15	.07
99	Marquis Grissom	.30	.14
100	George Bell	.15	.07
101	Howard Johnson	.15	.07
102	Kevin Appier	.30	.14
103	Dale Murphy	.40	.18
104	Shane Mack	.15	.07
105	Jose Lind	.15	.07
106	Rickey Henderson	.40	.18
107	Bob Tewksbury	.15	.07
108	Kevin Mitchell	.30	.14
109	Steve Avery	.15	.07
110	Candy Maldonado	.15	.07
111	Bip Roberts	.15	.07
112	Lou Whitaker	.30	.14
113	Jeff Bagwell	1.25	.55
114	Dante Bichette	.40	.18
115	Brett Butler	.30	.14
116	Melido Perez	.15	.07
117	Andy Benes	.30	.14
118	Randy Johnson	.60	.25
119	Willie McGee	.15	.07
120	Jody Reed	.15	.07
121	Shawon Dunston	.15	.07
122	Carlos Baerga	.40	.18
123	Bret Saberhagen	.15	.07
124	John Olerud	.15	.07
125	Ivan Calderon	.15	.07
126	Bryan Harvey	.15	.07
127	Terry Mulholland	.15	.07
128	Ozzie Guillen	.15	.07
129	Steve Buechele	.15	.07
130	Kevin Tapani	.15	.07
131	Felix Jose	.15	.07
132	Terry Steinbach	.15	.07
133	Ron Gant	.30	.14
134	Harold Reynolds	.15	.07
135	Chris Sabo	.15	.07
136	Ivan Rodriguez	.75	.35
137	Eric Anthony	.15	.07
138	Mike Henneman	.15	.07
139	Robby Thompson	.15	.07
140	Scott Fletcher	.15	.07
141	Bruce Hurst	.15	.07
142	Kevin Maas	.15	.07
143	Tom Candiotti	.15	.07
144	Chris Hoiles	.15	.07
145	Mike Morgan	.15	.07
146	Mark Whiten	.15	.07
147	Dennis Martinez	.30	.14
148	Tony Pena	.15	.07
149	Dave Magadan	.15	.07
150	Mark Lewis	.15	.07
151	Mariano Duncan	.15	.07
152	Gregg Jefferies	.30	.14
153	Doug Drabek	.15	.07
154	Brian Harper	.15	.07
155	Ray Lankford	.40	.18
156	Carney Lansford	.30	.14
157	Mike Sharperson	.15	.07
158	Jack Morris	.30	.14
159	Otis Nixon	.15	.07
160	Steve Sax	.15	.07
161	Mark Lemke	.15	.07
162	Rafael Palmeiro	.40	.18
163	Jose Rijo	.15	.07
164	Omar Vizquel	.30	.14
165	Sammy Sosa	.60	.25
166	Milt Cuyler	.15	.07
167	John Franco	.30	.14
168	Darryl Hamilton	.15	.07
169	Ken Hill	.15	.07
170	Mike Devereaux	.30	.14
171	Don Slaught	.15	.07
172	Steve Farr	.15	.07
173	Bernard Gilkey	.30	.14
174	Mike Fetters	.15	.07
175	Vince Coleman	.15	.07
176	Kevin McReynolds	.15	.07
177	John Smoltz	.30	.14
178	Greg Gagne	.15	.07
179	Greg Swindell	.15	.07
180	Juan Guzman	.60	.25
181	Kal Daniels	.15	.07
182	Rick Sutcliffe	.15	.07
183	Orlando Merced	.15	.07
184	Bill Wegman	.15	.07
185	Mark Gardner	.15	.07
186	Rob Deer	.15	.07
187	Dave Hollins	.15	.07
188	Jack Clark	.15	.07
189	Brian Hunter	.15	.07
190	Tim Wallach	.15	.07
191	Tim Belcher	.15	.07
192	Walt Weiss	.15	.07
193	Kurt Stillwell	.15	.07
194	Charlie Hayes	.15	.07
195	Willie Randolph	.30	.14
196	Jack McDowell	.30	.14
197	Jose Offerman	.15	.07
198	Chuck Finley	.15	.07
199	Darrin Jackson	.15	.07
200	Kelly Gruber	.15	.07
201	John Wetteland	.30	.14
202	Jay Buhner	.40	.18
203	Mike LaValliere	.15	.07
204	Kevin Brown	.30	.14
205	Luis Gonzalez	.15	.07
206	Rick Aguilera	.15	.07
207	Norm Charlton	.15	.07
208	Mike Bordick	.15	.07
209	Charlie Leibrandt	.15	.07
210	Tom Brunansky	.15	.07
211	Tom Henke	.15	.07
212	Randy Milligan	.15	.07
213	Ramon Martinez	.30	.14
214	Mo Vaughn	.75	.35
215	Randy Myers	.30	.14
216	Greg Hibbard	.15	.07
217	Wes Chamberlain	.15	.07
218	Tony Phillips	.15	.07
219	Pete Harnisch	.15	.07
220	Mike Gallego	.15	.07
221	Bud Black	.15	.07
222	Greg Vaughn	.15	.07
223	Milt Thompson	.15	.07
224	Ben McDonald	.15	.07
225	Billy Hatcher	.15	.07
226	Paul Sorrento	.15	.07
227	Mark Gubicza	.15	.07
228	Mike Greenwell	.15	.07
229	Curt Schilling	.30	.14
230	Alan Trammell	.40	.18
231	Zane Smith	.15	.07
232	Bobby Thigpen	.15	.07
233	Greg Olson	.15	.07
234	Joe Orsulak	.15	.07
235	Joe Oliver	.15	.07
236	Tim Raines	.30	.14
237	Juan Samuel	.15	.07
238	Chili Davis	.30	.14
239	Spike Owen	.15	.07
240	Dave Stewart	.30	.14
241	Jim Eisenreich	.15	.07
242	Phil Plantier	.15	.07
243	Sid Fernandez	.15	.07
244	Dan Gladden	.15	.07
245	Mickey Morandini	.15	.07
246	Tino Martinez	.60	.25
247	Kirt Manwaring	.15	.07
248	Dean Palmer	.15	.07
249	Tom Browning	.15	.07
250	Brian McRae	.15	.07
251	Scott Leius	.15	.07
252	Bert Blyleven	.30	.14
253	Scott Erickson	.15	.07
254	Bob Welch	.15	.07
255	Pat Kelly	.15	.07
256	Felix Fermin	.15	.07
257	Harold Baines	.30	.14
258	Duane Ward	.15	.07
259	Bill Spiers	.15	.07
260	Jaime Navarro	.15	.07
261	Scott Sanderson	.15	.07
262	Gary Gaetti	.15	.07
263	Bob Ojeda	.15	.07
264	Jeff Montgomery	.30	.14
265	Scott Bankhead	.15	.07
266	Lance Johnson	.15	.07
267	Rafael Belliard	.15	.07
268	Kevin Reimer	.15	.07
269	Benito Santiago	.15	.07
270	Mike Moore	.15	.07

☐ 271	Dave Fleming	.15	.07
☐ 272	Moises Alou	.30	.14
☐ 273	Pat Listach	.15	.07
☐ 274	Reggie Sanders	.30	.14
☐ 275	Kenny Lofton	1.25	.55
☐ 276	Donovan Osborne	.15	.07
☐ 277	Rusty Meacham	.15	.07
☐ 278	Eric Karros	.30	.14
☐ 279	Andy Stankiewicz	.15	.07
☐ 280	Brian Jordan	.30	.14
☐ 281	Gary DiSarcina	.15	.07
☐ 282	Mark Wohlers	.30	.14
☐ 283	Dave Nilsson	.15	.07
☐ 284	Anthony Young	.15	.07
☐ 285	Jim Bullinger	.15	.07
☐ 286	Derek Bell	.30	.14
☐ 287	Brian Williams	.15	.07
☐ 288	Julio Valera	.15	.07
☐ 289	Dan Walters	.15	.07
☐ 290	Chad Curtis	.30	.14
☐ 291	Michael Tucker DP	.60	.25
☐ 292	Bob Zupcic	.15	.07
☐ 293	Todd Hundley	.40	.18
☐ 294	Jeff Tackett	.15	.07
☐ 295	Greg Colbrunn	.15	.07
☐ 296	Cal Eldred	.15	.07
☐ 297	Chris Roberts DP	.30	.14
☐ 298	John Doherty	.15	.07
☐ 299	Denny Neagle	.30	.14
☐ 300	Arthur Rhodes	.15	.07
☐ 301	Mark Clark	.15	.07
☐ 302	Scott Cooper	.15	.07
☐ 303	Jamie Arnold DP	.30	.14
☐ 304	Jim Thome	1.25	.55
☐ 305	Frank Seminara	.15	.07
☐ 306	Kurt Knudsen	.15	.07
☐ 307	Tim Wakefield	.30	.14
☐ 308	John Jaha	.30	.14
☐ 309	Pat Hentgen	.40	.18
☐ 310	B.J. Wallace DP	.15	.07
☐ 311	Roberto Hernandez	.30	.14
☐ 312	Hipolito Pichardo	.15	.07
☐ 313	Eric Fox	.15	.07
☐ 314	Willie Banks	.15	.07
☐ 315	Sam Militello	.15	.07
☐ 316	Vince Horsman	.15	.07
☐ 317	Carlos Hernandez	.15	.07
☐ 318	Jeff Kent	.30	.14
☐ 319	Mike Perez	.15	.07
☐ 320	Scott Livingstone	.15	.07
☐ 321	Jeff Conine	.30	.14
☐ 322	James Austin	.15	.07
☐ 323	John Vander Wal	.15	.07
☐ 324	Pat Mahomes	.15	.07
☐ 325	Pedro Astacio	.15	.07
☐ 326	Bret Boone UER	.15	.07
	(Misspelled Brett)		
☐ 327	Matt Stairs	.15	.07
☐ 328	Damion Easley	.15	.07
☐ 329	Ben Rivera	.15	.07
☐ 330	Reggie Jefferson	.15	.07
☐ 331	Luis Mercedes	.15	.07
☐ 332	Kyle Abbott	.15	.07
☐ 333	Eddie Taubensee	.15	.07
☐ 334	Tim McIntosh	.15	.07
☐ 335	Phil Clark	.15	.07
☐ 336	Wil Cordero	.15	.07
☐ 337	Russ Springer	.15	.07
☐ 338	Craig Colbert	.15	.07
☐ 339	Tim Salmon	.75	.35
☐ 340	Braulio Castillo	.15	.07
☐ 341	Donald Harris	.15	.07
☐ 342	Eric Young	.60	.25
☐ 343	Bob Wickman	.15	.07
☐ 344	John Valentin	.30	.14
☐ 345	Dan Wilson	.30	.14
☐ 346	Steve Hosey	.15	.07
☐ 347	Mike Piazza	3.00	1.35
☐ 348	Willie Greene	.30	.14
☐ 349	Tom Goodwin	.15	.07
☐ 350	Eric Hillman	.15	.07
☐ 351	Steve Reed	.15	.07
☐ 352	Dan Serafini DP	.40	.18
☐ 353	Todd Steverson DP	.30	.14
☐ 354	Benji Grigsby DP	.15	.07
☐ 355	Shannon Stewart DP	.75	.35

☐ 356	Sean Lowe DP	.15	.07
☐ 357	Derek Wallace DP	.15	.07
☐ 358	Rick Helling DP	.30	.14
☐ 359	Jason Kendall DP	1.00	.45
☐ 360	Derek Jeter DP	6.00	2.70
☐ 361	David Cone	.30	.14
☐ 362	Jeff Reardon	.30	.14
☐ 363	Bobby Witt	.15	.07
☐ 364	Jose Canseco	.40	.18
☐ 365	Jeff Russell	.15	.07
☐ 366	Ruben Sierra	.15	.07
☐ 367	Alan Mills	.15	.07
☐ 368	Matt Nokes	.15	.07
☐ 369	Pat Borders	.15	.07
☐ 370	Pedro Munoz	.15	.07
☐ 371	Danny Jackson	.15	.07
☐ 372	Geronimo Pena	.15	.07
☐ 373	Craig Lefferts	.15	.07
☐ 374	Joe Grahe	.15	.07
☐ 375	Roger McDowell	.15	.07
☐ 376	Jimmy Key	.30	.14
☐ 377	Steve Olin	.15	.07
☐ 378	Glenn Davis	.15	.07
☐ 379	Rene Gonzales	.15	.07
☐ 380	Manuel Lee	.15	.07
☐ 381	Ron Karkovice	.15	.07
☐ 382	Sid Bream	.15	.07
☐ 383	Gerald Williams	.15	.07
☐ 384	Lenny Harris	.15	.07
☐ 385	J.T. Snow	.75	.35
☐ 386	Dave Stieb	.15	.07
☐ 387	Kirk McCaskill	.15	.07
☐ 388	Lance Parrish	.15	.07
☐ 389	Craig Grebeck	.15	.07
☐ 390	Rick Wilkins	.15	.07
☐ 391	Manny Alexander	.15	.07
☐ 392	Mike Schooler	.15	.07
☐ 393	Bernie Williams	.60	.25
☐ 394	Kevin Koslofski	.15	.07
☐ 395	Willie Wilson	.15	.07
☐ 396	Jeff Parrett	.15	.07
☐ 397	Mike Harkey	.15	.07
☐ 398	Frank Tanana	.15	.07
☐ 399	Doug Henry	.15	.07
☐ 400	Royce Clayton	.15	.07
☐ 401	Eric Wedge	.15	.07
☐ 402	Derrick May	.15	.07
☐ 403	Carlos Garcia	.15	.07
☐ 404	Henry Rodriguez	.30	.14
☐ 405	Ryan Klesko	.75	.35

1993 Select Aces

This 24-card standard-size set features some of the top starting pitchers in both leagues. The cards were randomly inserted into one in every eight 28-card super packs. The fronts display an action player pose cut out and superimposed on a metallic variegated red and silver diamond design. The diamond itself rests on a background consisting of silver metallic streaks that emanate from the center of the card. In imitation of playing card design, the fronts have a large "A" for Ace in upper left and lower right corners. The player's name in the upper right corner rounds out the card face.

	MINT	NRMT
COMPLETE SET (24)	80.00	36.00
COMMON CARD (1-24)	3.00	1.35
SEMISTARS	6.00	2.70
STATED ODDS 1:4 JUMBO		

☐ 1	Roger Clemens	20.00	9.00
☐ 2	Tom Glavine	6.00	2.70
☐ 3	Jack McDowell	3.00	1.35
☐ 4	Greg Maddux	30.00	13.50
☐ 5	Jack Morris	4.00	1.80
☐ 6	Dennis Martinez	4.00	1.80
☐ 7	Kevin Brown	4.00	1.80
☐ 8	Dwight Gooden	4.00	1.80
☐ 9	Kevin Appier	4.00	1.80
☐ 10	Mike Morgan	3.00	1.35
☐ 11	Juan Guzman	4.00	1.80
☐ 12	Charles Nagy	4.00	1.80
☐ 13	John Smiley	3.00	1.35
☐ 14	Ken Hill	3.00	1.35
☐ 15	Bob Tewksbury	3.00	1.35
☐ 16	Doug Drabek	3.00	1.35
☐ 17	John Smoltz	4.00	1.80
☐ 18	Greg Swindell	3.00	1.35
☐ 19	Bruce Hurst	3.00	1.35
☐ 20	Mike Mussina	10.00	4.50
☐ 21	Cal Eldred	3.00	1.35
☐ 22	Melido Perez	3.00	1.35
☐ 23	Dave Fleming	3.00	1.35
☐ 24	Kevin Tapani	3.00	1.35

1993 Select Chase Rookies

This 21-card standard-size set showcases 1992's best rookies. The cards were randomly inserted into one in every eighteen 15-card hobby packs. The fronts exhibit Score's "dufex" printing process, in which a color photo is printed on a metallic base creating an unusual, three-dimensional look. The pictures are tilted slightly to the left and edged on the left and bottom by red metallic borders.

	MINT	NRMT
COMPLETE SET (21)	120.00	55.00
COMMON CARD (1-21)	5.00	2.20
MINOR STARS	10.00	4.50
STATED ODDS 1:18 HOBBY		

☐ 1	Pat Listach	5.00	2.20
☐ 2	Moises Alou	10.00	4.50
☐ 3	Reggie Sanders	10.00	4.50
☐ 4	Kenny Lofton	50.00	22.00

		MINT	NRMT
☐ 5	Eric Karros	10.00	4.50
☐ 6	Brian Williams	5.00	2.20
☐ 7	Donovan Osborne	5.00	2.20
☐ 8	Sam Militello	5.00	2.20
☐ 9	Chad Curtis	10.00	4.50
☐ 10	Bob Zupcic	5.00	2.20
☐ 11	Tim Salmon	30.00	13.50
☐ 12	Jeff Conine	10.00	4.50
☐ 13	Pedro Astacio	5.00	2.20
☐ 14	Arthur Rhodes	5.00	2.20
☐ 15	Cal Eldred	5.00	2.20
☐ 16	Tim Wakefield	10.00	4.50
☐ 17	Andy Stankiewicz	5.00	2.20
☐ 18	Wil Cordero	5.00	2.20
☐ 19	Todd Hundley	12.00	5.50
☐ 20	Dave Fleming	5.00	2.20
☐ 21	Bret Boone	5.00	2.20

1993 Select Chase Stars

This 24-card standard-size set showcases the top players in Major League Baseball. The cards were randomly inserted into one in every regular retail 15-card pack. The fronts exhibit Score's "dufex" printing process, in which a color photo is printed on a metallic base creating an unusual, three-dimensional look. The pictures are tilted slightly to the left and edged on the left and bottom by green metallic borders.

		MINT	NRMT
COMPLETE SET (24)		150.00	70.00
COMMON CARD (1-24)		2.00	.90
SEMISTARS		4.00	1.80
STATED ODDS 1:18 RETAIL			
☐ 1	Fred McGriff	4.00	1.80
☐ 2	Ryne Sandberg	10.00	4.50
☐ 3	Ozzie Smith	10.00	4.50
☐ 4	Gary Sheffield	5.00	2.20
☐ 5	Darren Daulton	3.00	1.35
☐ 6	Andy Van Slyke	2.00	.90
☐ 7	Barry Bonds	10.00	4.50
☐ 8	Tony Gwynn	20.00	9.00
☐ 9	Greg Maddux	25.00	11.00
☐ 10	Tom Glavine	4.00	1.80
☐ 11	John Franco	3.00	1.35
☐ 12	Lee Smith	3.00	1.35
☐ 13	Cecil Fielder	3.00	1.35
☐ 14	Roberto Alomar	5.00	2.20
☐ 15	Cal Ripken	30.00	13.50
☐ 16	Edgar Martinez	4.00	1.80
☐ 17	Ivan Rodriguez	10.00	4.50
☐ 18	Kirby Puckett	15.00	6.75
☐ 19	Ken Griffey Jr.	40.00	18.00
☐ 20	Joe Carter	3.00	1.35
☐ 21	Roger Clemens	15.00	6.75
☐ 22	Dave Fleming	2.00	.90
☐ 23	Paul Molitor	5.00	2.20
☐ 24	Dennis Eckersley	3.00	1.35

1993 Select Stat Leaders

Featuring 45 cards from each league, these 90 Stat Leaders were inserted one per 1993 Score pack in every regular pack and super pack. The fronts feature color player action photos that are borderless on the sides and have oblique green borders at the top and bottom. The player's name appears within an oblique orange stripe across the bottom of the photo. The player appears within the top border, and the set's title appears within the bottom border.

		MINT	NRMT
COMPLETE SET (90)		10.00	4.50
COMMON CARD (1-90)		.10	.05
ONE PER SCORE PACK			
☐ 1	Edgar Martinez	.30	.14
☐ 2	Kirby Puckett	.75	.35
☐ 3	Frank Thomas	1.50	.70
☐ 4	Gary Sheffield	.40	.18
☐ 5	Andy Van Slyke	.20	.09
☐ 6	John Kruk	.20	.09
☐ 7	Kirby Puckett	.75	.35
☐ 8	Carlos Baerga	.10	.05
☐ 9	Paul Molitor	.40	.18
☐ 10	Terry Pendleton	.10	.05
	Andy Van Slyke		
☐ 11	Ryne Sandberg	.50	.23
☐ 12	Mark Grace	.30	.14
☐ 13	Frank Thomas	.75	.35
	Edgar Martinez		
☐ 14	Don Mattingly	.40	.18
	Robin Yount		
☐ 15	Ken Griffey	2.00	.90
☐ 16	Andy Van Slyke	.20	.09
☐ 17	Mariano Duncan	.20	.09
	Will Clark		
	Ray Lankford		
☐ 18	Marquis Grissom	.20	.09
	Terry Pendleton		
☐ 19	Lance Johnson	.10	.05
☐ 20	Mike Devereaux	.10	.05
☐ 21	Brady Anderson	.30	.14
☐ 22	Deion Sanders	.20	.09
☐ 23	Steve Finley	.20	.09
☐ 24	Andy Van Slyke	.20	.09
☐ 25	Juan Gonzalez	1.00	.45
☐ 26	Mark McGwire	.60	.25
☐ 27	Cecil Fielder	.20	.09
☐ 28	Fred McGriff	.30	.14
☐ 29	Barry Bonds	.50	.23
☐ 30	Gary Sheffield	.40	.18
☐ 31	Cecil Fielder	.20	.09
☐ 32	Joe Carter	.20	.09
☐ 33	Frank Thomas	1.50	.70
☐ 34	Darren Daulton	.20	.09
☐ 35	Terry Pendleton	.20	.09
☐ 36	Fred McGriff	.30	.14
☐ 37	Tony Phillips	.10	.05
☐ 38	Frank Thomas	1.50	.70
☐ 39	Roberto Alomar	.40	.18
☐ 40	Barry Bonds	.50	.23
☐ 41	Dave Hollins	.10	.05
☐ 42	Andy Van Slyke	.20	.09
☐ 43	Mark McGwire	.60	.25
☐ 44	Edgar Martinez	.30	.14
☐ 45	Frank Thomas	1.50	.70
☐ 46	Barry Bonds	.50	.23
☐ 47	Gary Sheffield	.40	.18
☐ 48	Fred McGriff	.30	.14
☐ 49	Frank Thomas	1.50	.70
☐ 50	Danny Tartabull	.10	.05
☐ 51	Roberto Alomar	.40	.18
☐ 52	Barry Bonds	.50	.23
☐ 53	John Kruk	.20	.09
☐ 54	Brett Butler	.20	.09
☐ 55	Kenny Lofton	.75	.35
☐ 56	Pat Listach	.10	.05
☐ 57	Brady Anderson	.30	.14
☐ 58	Marquis Grissom	.20	.09
☐ 59	Delino DeShields	.10	.05
☐ 60	Bip Roberts	.10	.05
	Steve Finley		
☐ 61	Jack McDowell	.10	.05
☐ 62	Kevin Brown	.40	.18
	Roger Clemens		
☐ 63	Charles Nagy	.10	.05
	Melido Perez		
☐ 64	Terry Mulholland	.10	.05
☐ 65	Curt Schilling	.10	.05
	Doug Drabek		
☐ 66	Greg Maddux	.75	.35
	John Smoltz		
☐ 67	Dennis Eckersley	.20	.09
☐ 68	Rick Aguilera	.10	.05
☐ 69	Jeff Montgomery	.20	.09
☐ 70	Lee Smith	.20	.09
☐ 71	Randy Myers	.20	.09
☐ 72	John Wetteland	.20	.09
☐ 73	Randy Johnson	.40	.18
☐ 74	Melido Perez	.10	.05
☐ 75	Roger Clemens	1.00	.45
☐ 76	John Smoltz	.20	.09
☐ 77	David Cone	.20	.09
☐ 78	Greg Maddux	1.25	.55
☐ 79	Roger Clemens	1.00	.45
☐ 80	Kevin Appier	.20	.09
☐ 81	Mike Mussina	.40	.18
☐ 82	Bill Swift	.10	.05
☐ 83	Bob Tewksbury	.10	.05
☐ 84	Greg Maddux	1.25	.55
☐ 85	Jack Morris	.20	.09
	Kevin Brown		
☐ 86	Jack McDowell	.10	.05
☐ 87	Roger Clemens	.40	.18
	Mike Mussina		
☐ 88	Tom Glavine	.75	.35
	Greg Maddux		
☐ 89	Ken Hill	.10	.05
	Bob Tewksbury		
☐ 90	Mike Morgan	.10	.05
	Dennis Martinez		

1993 Select Triple Crown

Honoring the three most recent Triple Crown winners since 1993, cards from this 3-card standard-size set were randomly inserted in 15-card hobby packs. The fronts exhibit Score's "dufex" printing process, in which a color photo is printed on a metallic base creating an unusual, three-dimensional look. The color player photos on the fronts have a forest green metallic border. The player's name and the year he won the Triple Crown appear above the picture, while the words "Triple

Crown" are written in script beneath it.

	MINT	NRMT
COMPLETE SET (3)	100.00	45.00
COMMON CARD (1-3)	20.00	9.00
RANDOM INSERTS IN HOBBY PACKS		
☐ 1 Mickey Mantle	80.00	36.00
☐ 2 Carl Yastrzemski	20.00	9.00
☐ 3 Frank Robinson	20.00	9.00

1993 Select Rookie/Traded

These 150 standard-size cards feature rookies and traded veteran players. The production run comprised 1,950 individually numbered cases. Cards were distributed in foil packs. Card design is similar to the regular 1993 Select cards except for the dramatic royal blue borders (instead of emerald green for the regular cards) and T-suffixed numbering. There are no key Rookie Cards in this set. Two Rookie of the Year insert cards and a Nolan Ryan Tribute card were randomly inserted in the foil packs. The chances of finding a Nolan Ryan card was listed at not less than one per 288 packs. The two ROY cards, featuring American League Rookie of the Year, Tim Salmon and National League Rookie of the Year, Mike Piazza were randomly inserted into one in every 576 packs.

	MINT	NRMT
COMPLETE SET (150)	15.00	6.75
COMMON CARD (1T-150T)	.30	.14
MINOR STARS	.50	.23
SEMISTARS	.75	.35
UNLISTED STARS	1.25	.55

RYAN TRIBUTE STATED ODDS 1:288
ROY STATED ODDS 1:576 ....

☐ 1T Rickey Henderson	.75	.35
☐ 2T Rob Deer	.30	.14
☐ 3T Tim Belcher	.30	.14
☐ 4T Gary Sheffield	1.25	.55
☐ 5T Fred McGriff	.75	.35
☐ 6T Mark Whiten	.30	.14
☐ 7T Jeff Russell	.30	.14
☐ 8T Harold Baines	.50	.23
☐ 9T Dave Winfield	.75	.35
☐ 10T Ellis Burks	.50	.23
☐ 11T Andre Dawson	.75	.35
☐ 12T Gregg Jefferies	.30	.14
☐ 13T Jimmy Key	.50	.23
☐ 14T Harold Reynolds	.30	.14
☐ 15T Tom Henke	.30	.14
☐ 16T Paul Molitor	1.25	.55
☐ 17T Wade Boggs	1.25	.55
☐ 18T David Cone	.50	.23
☐ 19T Tony Fernandez	.30	.14
☐ 20T Roberto Kelly	.30	.14
☐ 21T Paul O'Neill	.50	.23
☐ 22T Jose Lind	.30	.14
☐ 23T Barry Bonds	1.50	.70
☐ 24T Dave Stewart	.30	.14
☐ 25T Randy Myers	.50	.23
☐ 26T Benito Santiago	.30	.14
☐ 27T Tim Wallach	.30	.14
☐ 28T Greg Gagne	.30	.14
☐ 29T Kevin Mitchell	.50	.23
☐ 30T Jim Abbott	.30	.14
☐ 31T Lee Smith	.50	.23
☐ 32T Bobby Munoz	.30	.14
☐ 33T Mo Sanford	.30	.14
☐ 34T John Roper	.30	.14
☐ 35T David Hulse	.30	.14
☐ 36T Pedro Martinez	1.50	.70
☐ 37T Chuck Carr	.30	.14
☐ 38T Armando Reynoso	.30	.14
☐ 39T Ryan Thompson	.30	.14
☐ 40T Carlos Garcia	.30	.14
☐ 41T Matt Whiteside	.30	.14
☐ 42T Benji Gil	.30	.14
☐ 43T Rodney Bolton	.30	.14
☐ 44T J.T. Snow	1.25	.55
☐ 45T David McCarty	.30	.14
☐ 46T Paul Quantrill	.30	.14
☐ 47T Al Martin	.50	.23
☐ 48T Lance Painter	.30	.14
☐ 49T Lou Frazier	.30	.14
☐ 50T Eduardo Perez	.30	.14
☐ 51T Kevin Young	.30	.14
☐ 52T Mike Trombley	.30	.14
☐ 53T Sterling Hitchcock	.50	.23
☐ 54T Tim Bogar	.30	.14
☐ 55T Hilly Hathaway	.30	.14
☐ 56T Wayne Kirby	.30	.14
☐ 57T Craig Paquette	.30	.14
☐ 58T Bret Boone	.50	.23
☐ 59T Greg McMichael	.30	.14
☐ 60T Mike Lansing	.50	.23
☐ 61T Brent Gates	.30	.14
☐ 62T Rene Arocha	.30	.14
☐ 63T Ricky Gutierrez	.30	.14
☐ 64T Kevin Rogers	.30	.14
☐ 65T Ken Ryan	.30	.14
☐ 66T Phil Hiatt	.30	.14
☐ 67T Pat Meares	.30	.14
☐ 68T Troy Neel	.30	.14
☐ 69T Steve Cooke	.30	.14
☐ 70T Sherman Obando	.30	.14
☐ 71T Blas Minor	.30	.14
☐ 72T Angel Miranda	.30	.14
☐ 73T Tom Kramer	.30	.14
☐ 74T Chip Hale	.30	.14
☐ 75T Brad Pennington	.30	.14
☐ 76T Graeme Lloyd	.30	.14
☐ 77T Darrell Whitmore	.30	.14
☐ 78T David Nied	.30	.14
☐ 79T Todd Van Poppel	.30	.14
☐ 80T Chris Gomez	.50	.23
☐ 81T Jason Bere	.50	.23
☐ 82T Jeffrey Hammonds	.75	.35
☐ 83T Brad Ausmus	.30	.14

☐ 84T Kevin Stocker	.30	.14
☐ 85T Jeromy Burnitz	.30	.14
☐ 86T Aaron Sele	.50	.23
☐ 87T Roberto Mejia	.30	.14
☐ 88T Kirk Rueter	.30	.14
☐ 89T Kevin Roberson	.30	.14
☐ 90T Allen Watson	.30	.14
☐ 91T Charlie Leibrandt	.30	.14
☐ 92T Eric Davis	.50	.23
☐ 93T Jody Reed	.30	.14
☐ 94T Danny Jackson	.30	.14
☐ 95T Gary Gaetti	.30	.14
☐ 96T Norm Charlton	.30	.14
☐ 97T Doug Drabek	.30	.14
☐ 98T Scott Fletcher	.30	.14
☐ 99T Greg Swindell	.30	.14
☐ 100T John Smiley	.30	.14
☐ 101T Kevin Reimer	.30	.14
☐ 102T Andres Galarraga	1.25	.55
☐ 103T Greg Hibbard	.30	.14
☐ 104T Chris Hammond	.30	.14
☐ 105T Darnell Coles	.30	.14
☐ 106T Mike Felder	.30	.14
☐ 107T Jose Guzman	.30	.14
☐ 108T Chris Bosio	.30	.14
☐ 109T Spike Owen	.30	.14
☐ 110T Felix Jose	.30	.14
☐ 111T Cory Snyder	.30	.14
☐ 112T Craig Lefferts	.30	.14
☐ 113T David Wells	.30	.14
☐ 114T Pete Incaviglia	.30	.14
☐ 115T Mike Pagliarulo	.30	.14
☐ 116T Dave Magadan	.30	.14
☐ 117T Charlie Hough	.30	.14
☐ 118T Ivan Calderon	.30	.14
☐ 119T Manuel Lee	.30	.14
☐ 120T Bob Patterson	.30	.14
☐ 121T Bob Ojeda	.30	.14
☐ 122T Scott Bankhead	.30	.14
☐ 123T Greg Maddux	4.00	1.80
☐ 124T Chili Davis	.50	.23
☐ 125T Milt Thompson	.30	.14
☐ 126T Dave Martinez	.30	.14
☐ 127T Frank Tanana	.30	.14
☐ 128T Phil Plantier	.30	.14
☐ 129T Juan Samuel	.30	.14
☐ 130T Eric Young	1.25	.55
☐ 131T Joe Orsulak	.30	.14
☐ 132T Derek Bell	.50	.23
☐ 133T Darrin Jackson	.30	.14
☐ 134T Tom Brunansky	.30	.14
☐ 135T Jeff Reardon	.50	.23
☐ 136T Kevin Higgins	.30	.14
☐ 137T Joel Johnston	.30	.14
☐ 138T Rick Trlicek	.30	.14
☐ 139T Richie Lewis	.30	.14
☐ 140T Jeff Gardner	.30	.14
☐ 141T Jack Voigt	.30	.14
☐ 142T Rod Correia	.30	.14
☐ 143T Billy Brewer	.30	.14
☐ 144T Terry Jorgensen	.30	.14
☐ 145T Rich Amaral	.30	.14
☐ 146T Sean Berry	.30	.14
☐ 147T Dan Peltier	.30	.14
☐ 148T Paul Wagner	.30	.14
☐ 149T Damon Buford	.30	.14
☐ 150T Wil Cordero	.30	.14
☐ NR1 Nolan Ryan Tribute	100.00	45.00
☐ ROY1 Tim Salmon AL ROY	25.00	11.00
☐ ROY2 Mike Piazza NL ROY	80.00	36.00

1993 Select Rookie/Traded All-Star Rookies

This ten-card standard-size set was randomly inserted in foil packs of 1993 Select Rookie and Traded. The insertion rate was reportedly not less than one in 36 packs. The cards feature on their fronts color player action shots that have a grainy

metallic appearance. These photos are borderless, except at the top, where the silver-colored player's name is displayed upon red and blue metallic stripes. The set's title appears within a metallic silver-colored stripe near the bottom, which has a star-and-baseball icon emblazoned over its center. This combination of the set's title, stripe, and star-and-baseball icon reappears at the top of the non-metallic back, but in a red, white, and blue design. The player's name, position, and team logo are shown on the red-colored right half of the card. His career highlights appear in white lettering on the blue-colored left half.

	MINT	NRMT
COMPLETE SET (10)	120.00	55.00
COMMON CARD (1-10)	4.00	1.80
MINOR STARS	8.00	3.60
STATED ODDS 1:58		

		MINT	NRMT
☐ 1	Jeff Conine	8.00	3.60
☐ 2	Brent Gates	4.00	1.80
☐ 3	Mike Lansing	4.00	1.80
☐ 4	Kevin Stocker	4.00	1.80
☐ 5	Mike Piazza	80.00	36.00
☐ 6	Jeffrey Hammonds	10.00	4.50
☐ 7	David Hulse	4.00	1.80
☐ 8	Tim Salmon	25.00	11.00
☐ 9	Rene Arocha	4.00	1.80
☐ 10	Greg McMichael	4.00	1.80

1994 Select

Measuring the standard size, the 1994 Select set consists of 420 cards that were issued in two series of 210. The horizontal fronts feature a color player action photo and a duo-tone player shot. The backs are vertical and contain a photo, 1993 and career statistics and high-

lights. Special Dave Winfield and Cal Ripken cards were inserted in first series packs. A Paul Molitor MVP card and a Carlos Delgado Rookie of the Year card were inserted in second series packs. The insertion rate for ech card was one in 360 packs. Rookie Cards include Kurt Abbott, Brian Anderson and Chan Ho Park.

	MINT	NRMT
COMPLETE SET (420)	25.00	11.00
COMPLETE SERIES 1 (210)	15.00	6.75
COMPLETE SERIES 2 (210)	10.00	4.50
COMMON CARD (1-420)	.15	.07
MINOR STARS	.30	.14
UNLISTED STARS	.60	.25
SER.1 SALUTE STATED ODDS 1:360		
SER.2 MVP/ROY STATED ODDS 1:360		

		MINT	NRMT
☐ 1	Ken Griffey Jr.	3.00	1.35
☐ 2	Greg Maddux	2.00	.90
☐ 3	Paul Molitor	.60	.25
☐ 4	Mike Piazza	2.00	.90
☐ 5	Jay Bell	.30	.14
☐ 6	Frank Thomas	2.50	1.10
☐ 7	Barry Larkin	.40	.18
☐ 8	Paul O'Neill	.30	.14
☐ 9	Darren Daulton	.30	.14
☐ 10	Mike Greenwell	.15	.07
☐ 11	Chuck Carr	.15	.07
☐ 12	Joe Carter	.30	.14
☐ 13	Lance Johnson	.15	.07
☐ 14	Jeff Blauser	.30	.14
☐ 15	Chris Hoiles	.15	.07
☐ 16	Rick Wilkins	.15	.07
☐ 17	Kirby Puckett	1.25	.55
☐ 18	Larry Walker	.60	.25
☐ 19	Randy Johnson	.60	.25
☐ 20	Bernard Gilkey	.15	.07
☐ 21	Devon White	.15	.07
☐ 22	Randy Myers	.15	.07
☐ 23	Don Mattingly	1.00	.45
☐ 24	John Kruk	.30	.14
☐ 25	Ozzie Guillen	.15	.07
☐ 26	Jeff Conine	.30	.14
☐ 27	Mike Macfarlane	.15	.07
☐ 28	Dave Hollins	.15	.07
☐ 29	Chuck Knoblauch	.60	.25
☐ 30	Ozzie Smith	.75	.35
☐ 31	Harold Baines	.30	.14
☐ 32	Ryne Sandberg	.75	.35
☐ 33	Ron Karkovice	.15	.07
☐ 34	Terry Pendleton	.15	.07
☐ 35	Wally Joyner	.30	.14
☐ 36	Mike Mussina	.60	.25
☐ 37	Felix Jose	.15	.07
☐ 38	Derrick May	.15	.07
☐ 39	Scott Cooper	.15	.07
☐ 40	Jose Rijo	.15	.07
☐ 41	Robin Ventura	.30	.14
☐ 42	Charlie Hayes	.15	.07
☐ 43	Jimmy Key	.30	.14
☐ 44	Eric Karros	.30	.14
☐ 45	Ruben Sierra	.15	.07
☐ 46	Ryan Thompson	.15	.07
☐ 47	Brian McRae	.15	.07
☐ 48	Pat Hentgen	.30	.14
☐ 49	John Valentin	.30	.14
☐ 50	Al Martin	.15	.07
☐ 51	Jose Lind	.15	.07
☐ 52	Kevin Stocker	.15	.07
☐ 53	Mike Gallego	.15	.07
☐ 54	Dwight Gooden	.30	.14
☐ 55	Brady Anderson	.40	.18
☐ 56	Jeff King	.15	.07
☐ 57	Mark McGwire	1.25	.55
☐ 58	Sammy Sosa	.60	.25
☐ 59	Ryan Bowen	.15	.07
☐ 60	Mark Lemke	.15	.07
☐ 61	Roger Clemens	1.25	.55
☐ 62	Brian Jordan	.30	.14
☐ 63	Andres Galarraga	.60	.25
☐ 64	Kevin Appier	.30	.14
☐ 65	Don Slaught	.15	.07
☐ 66	Mike Blowers	.15	.07
☐ 67	Wes Chamberlain	.15	.07
☐ 68	Troy Neel	.15	.07
☐ 69	John Wetteland	.15	.07
☐ 70	Joe Girardi	.15	.07
☐ 71	Reggie Sanders	.15	.07
☐ 72	Edgar Martinez	.40	.18
☐ 73	Todd Hundley	.30	.14
☐ 74	Pat Borders	.15	.07
☐ 75	Roberto Mejia	.15	.07
☐ 76	David Cone	.30	.14
☐ 77	Tony Gwynn	1.50	.70
☐ 78	Jim Abbott	.15	.07
☐ 79	Jay Buhner	.40	.18
☐ 80	Mark McLemore	.15	.07
☐ 81	Wil Cordero	.15	.07
☐ 82	Pedro Astacio	.15	.07
☐ 83	Bob Tewksbury	.15	.07
☐ 84	Dave Winfield	.40	.18
☐ 85	Jeff Kent	.15	.07
☐ 86	Todd Van Poppel	.15	.07
☐ 87	Steve Avery	.15	.07
☐ 88	Mike Lansing	.30	.07
☐ 89	Lenny Dykstra	.15	.14
☐ 90	Jose Guzman	.15	.07
☐ 91	Brian R. Hunter	.30	.14
☐ 92	Tim Raines	.30	.14
☐ 93	Andre Dawson	.40	.18
☐ 94	Joe Orsulak	.15	.07
☐ 95	Ricky Jordan	.15	.07
☐ 96	Billy Hatcher	.15	.07
☐ 97	Jack McDowell	.15	.07
☐ 98	Tom Pagnozzi	.15	.07
☐ 99	Darryl Strawberry	.30	.14
☐ 100	Mike Stanley	.15	.07
☐ 101	Bret Saberhagen	.15	.07
☐ 102	Willie Greene	.15	.07
☐ 103	Bryan Harvey	.15	.07
☐ 104	Tim Bogar	.15	.07
☐ 105	Jack Voigt	.15	.07
☐ 106	Brad Ausmus	.15	.07
☐ 107	Ramon Martinez	.30	.14
☐ 108	Mike Perez	.15	.07
☐ 109	Jeff Montgomery	.15	.07
☐ 110	Danny Darwin	.15	.07
☐ 111	Wilson Alvarez	.15	.07
☐ 112	Kevin Mitchell	.15	.07
☐ 113	David Nied	.15	.07
☐ 114	Rich Amaral	.15	.07
☐ 115	Stan Javier	.15	.07
☐ 116	Mo Vaughn	.75	.35
☐ 117	Ben McDonald	.15	.07
☐ 118	Tom Gordon	.15	.07
☐ 119	Carlos Garcia	.15	.07
☐ 120	Phil Plantier	.15	.07
☐ 121	Mike Morgan	.15	.07
☐ 122	Pat Meares	.15	.07
☐ 123	Kevin Young	.15	.07
☐ 124	Jeff Fassero	.15	.07
☐ 125	Gene Harris	.15	.07
☐ 126	Bob Welch	.15	.07
☐ 127	Walt Weiss	.15	.07
☐ 128	Bobby Witt	.15	.07
☐ 129	Andy Van Slyke	.30	.14
☐ 130	Steve Cooke	.15	.07
☐ 131	Mike Devereaux	.15	.07
☐ 132	Joey Cora	.30	.07
☐ 133	Bret Barberie	.15	.07
☐ 134	Orel Hershiser	.30	.14
☐ 135	Ed Sprague	.15	.07
☐ 136	Shawon Dunston	.15	.07
☐ 137	Alex Arias	.15	.07
☐ 138	Archi Cianfrocco	.15	.07
☐ 139	Tim Wallach	.15	.07
☐ 140	Bernie Williams	.60	.25
☐ 141	Karl Rhodes	.15	.07
☐ 142	Pat Kelly	.15	.07
☐ 143	Dave Magadan	.15	.07
☐ 144	Kevin Tapani	.15	.07
☐ 145	Eric Young	.15	.07
☐ 146	Derek Bell	.15	.07
☐ 147	Dante Bichette	.30	.14
☐ 148	Geronimo Pena	.15	.07
☐ 149	Joe Oliver	.15	.07
☐ 150	Orestes Destrade	.15	.07

#	Player	Val1	Val2
151	Tim Naehring	.15	.07
152	Ray Lankford	.30	.14
153	Phil Clark	.15	.07
154	David McCarty	.15	.07
155	Tommy Greene	.15	.07
156	Wade Boggs	.60	.25
157	Kevin Gross	.15	.07
158	Hal Morris	.15	.07
159	Moises Alou	.30	.14
160	Rick Aguilera	.30	.14
161	Curt Schilling	.30	.14
162	Chip Hale	.15	.07
163	Tino Martinez	.60	.25
164	Mark Whiten	.15	.07
165	Dave Stewart	.30	.14
166	Steve Buechele	.15	.07
167	Bobby Jones	.30	.14
168	Darrin Fletcher	.15	.07
169	John Smiley	.15	.07
170	Cory Snyder	.15	.07
171	Scott Erickson	.15	.07
172	Kirk Rueter	.15	.07
173	Dave Fleming	.15	.07
174	John Smoltz	.30	.14
175	Ricky Gutierrez	.15	.07
176	Mike Bordick	.15	.07
177	Chan Ho Park	1.50	.70
178	Alex Gonzalez	.30	.14
179	Steve Karsay	.15	.07
180	Jeffrey Hammonds	.30	.14
181	Manny Ramirez	.75	.35
182	Salomon Torres	.15	.07
183	Raul Mondesi	.60	.25
184	James Mouton	.15	.07
185	Cliff Floyd	.30	.14
186	Danny Bautista	.15	.07
187	Kurt Abbott	.15	.07
188	Javier Lopez	.40	.18
189	John Patterson	.15	.07
190	Greg Blosser	.15	.07
191	Bob Hamelin	.15	.07
192	Tony Eusebio	.15	.07
193	Carlos Delgado	.40	.18
194	Chris Gomez	.15	.07
195	Kelly Stinnett	.15	.07
196	Shane Reynolds	.15	.07
197	Ryan Klesko	.60	.25
198	Jim Edmonds UER	.60	.25
	Mark Dalesandro pictured on front		
199	James Hurst	.15	.07
200	Dave Staton	.15	.07
201	Rondell White	.40	.18
202	Keith Mitchell	.15	.07
203	Darren Oliver	.60	.25
204	Mike Matheny	.15	.07
205	Chris Turner	.15	.07
206	Matt Mieske	.15	.07
207	NL Team Checklist	.15	.07
208	NL Team Checklist	.15	.07
209	AL Team Checklist	.15	.07
210	AL Team Checklist	.15	.07
211	Barry Bonds	.75	.35
212	Juan Gonzalez	1.50	.70
213	Jim Eisenreich	.15	.07
214	Ivan Rodriguez	.75	.35
215	Tony Phillips	.15	.07
216	John Jaha	.15	.07
217	Lee Smith	.30	.14
218	Bip Roberts	.15	.07
219	Dave Hansen	.15	.07
220	Pat Listach	.15	.07
221	Willie McGee	.15	.07
222	Damion Easley	.15	.07
223	Dean Palmer	.15	.07
224	Mike Moore	.15	.07
225	Brian Harper	.15	.07
226	Gary DiSarcina	.15	.07
227	Delino DeShields	.15	.07
228	Otis Nixon	.15	.07
229	Roberto Alomar	.60	.25
230	Mark Grace	.40	.18
231	Kenny Lofton	.75	.35
232	Gregg Jefferies	.15	.07
233	Cecil Fielder	.30	.14
234	Jeff Bagwell	1.25	.55
235	Albert Belle	.75	.35
236	Dave Justice	.60	.25
237	Tom Henke	.15	.07
238	Bobby Bonilla	.30	.14
239	John Olerud	.30	.14
240	Robby Thompson	.15	.07
241	Dave Valle	.15	.07
242	Marquis Grissom	.30	.14
243	Greg Swindell	.15	.07
244	Todd Zeile	.15	.07
245	Dennis Eckersley	.30	.14
246	Jose Offerman	.15	.07
247	Greg McMichael	.15	.07
248	Tim Belcher	.15	.07
249	Cal Ripken Jr.	2.50	1.10
250	Tom Glavine	.30	.14
251	Luis Polonia	.15	.07
252	Bill Swift	.15	.07
253	Juan Guzman	.15	.07
254	Rickey Henderson	.40	.18
255	Terry Mulholland	.15	.07
256	Gary Sheffield	.60	.25
257	Terry Steinbach	.15	.07
258	Brett Butler	.15	.07
259	Jason Bere	.15	.07
260	Doug Strange	.15	.07
261	Kent Hrbek	.30	.14
262	Graeme Lloyd	.15	.07
263	Lou Frazier	.15	.07
264	Charles Nagy	.30	.14
265	Bret Boone	.15	.07
266	Kirk Gibson	.30	.14
267	Kevin Brown	.30	.14
268	Fred McGriff	.40	.18
269	Matt Williams	.40	.18
270	Greg Gagne	.15	.07
271	Mariano Duncan	.15	.07
272	Jeff Russell	.15	.07
273	Eric Davis	.30	.14
274	Shane Mack	.15	.07
275	Jose Vizcaino	.15	.07
276	Jose Canseco	.40	.18
277	Roberto Hernandez	.15	.07
278	Royce Clayton	.15	.07
279	Carlos Baerga	.30	.14
280	Pete Incaviglia	.15	.07
281	Brent Gates	.15	.07
282	Jeromy Burnitz	.15	.07
283	Chili Davis	.30	.14
284	Pete Harnisch	.15	.07
285	Alan Trammell	.30	.14
286	Eric Anthony	.15	.07
287	Ellis Burks	.30	.14
288	Julio Franco	.15	.07
289	Jack Morris	.30	.14
290	Erik Hanson	.15	.07
291	Chuck Finley	.15	.07
292	Reggie Jefferson	.15	.07
293	Kevin McReynolds	.15	.07
294	Greg Hibbard	.15	.07
295	Travis Fryman	.30	.14
296	Craig Biggio	.40	.18
297	Kenny Rogers	.15	.07
298	Dave Henderson	.15	.07
299	Jim Thome	.75	.35
300	Rene Arocha	.15	.07
301	Pedro Munoz	.15	.07
302	David Hulse	.15	.07
303	Greg Vaughn	.15	.07
304	Darren Lewis	.15	.07
305	Deion Sanders	.30	.14
306	Danny Tartabull	.15	.07
307	Darryl Hamilton	.15	.07
308	Andujar Cedeno	.15	.07
309	Tim Salmon	.60	.25
310	Tony Fernandez	.15	.07
311	Alex Fernandez	.15	.07
312	Roberto Kelly	.15	.07
313	Harold Reynolds	.15	.07
314	Chris Sabo	.15	.07
315	Howard Johnson	.15	.07
316	Mark Portugal	.15	.07
317	Rafael Palmeiro	.40	.18
318	Pete Smith	.15	.07
319	Will Clark	.40	.18
320	Henry Rodriguez	.15	.07
321	Omar Vizquel	.30	.14
322	David Segui	.15	.07
323	Lou Whitaker	.30	.14
324	Felix Fermin	.15	.07
325	Spike Owen	.15	.07
326	Darryl Kile	.30	.14
327	Chad Kreuter	.15	.07
328	Rod Beck	.15	.07
329	Eddie Murray	.60	.25
330	B.J. Surhoff	.15	.07
331	Mickey Tettleton	.15	.07
332	Pedro Martinez	.60	.25
333	Roger Pavlik	.15	.07
334	Eddie Taubensee	.15	.07
335	John Doherty	.15	.07
336	Jody Reed	.15	.07
337	Aaron Sele	.15	.07
338	Leo Gomez	.15	.07
339	Dave Nilsson	.15	.07
340	Rob Dibble	.15	.07
341	John Burkett	.15	.07
342	Wayne Kirby	.15	.07
343	Dan Wilson	.30	.14
344	Armando Reynoso	.15	.07
345	Chad Curtis	.15	.07
346	Dennis Martinez	.30	.14
347	Cal Eldred	.15	.07
348	Luis Gonzalez	.15	.07
349	Doug Drabek	.15	.07
350	Jim Leyritz	.15	.07
351	Mark Langston	.15	.07
352	Darrin Jackson	.15	.07
353	Sid Fernandez	.15	.07
354	Benito Santiago	.15	.07
355	Kevin Seitzer	.15	.07
356	Bo Jackson	.30	.14
357	David Wells	.15	.07
358	Paul Sorrento	.15	.07
359	Ken Caminiti	.40	.18
360	Eduardo Perez	.15	.07
361	Orlando Merced	.15	.07
362	Steve Finley	.30	.14
363	Andy Benes	.30	.14
364	Manuel Lee	.15	.07
365	Todd Benzinger	.15	.07
366	Sandy Alomar Jr.	.30	.14
367	Rex Hudler	.15	.07
368	Mike Henneman	.15	.07
369	Vince Coleman	.15	.07
370	Kirt Manwaring	.15	.07
371	Ken Hill	.30	.14
372	Glenallen Hill	.15	.07
373	Sean Berry	.15	.07
374	Geronimo Berroa	.15	.07
375	Duane Ward	.15	.07
376	Allen Watson	.15	.07
377	Marc Newfield	.30	.14
378	Dan Miceli	.15	.07
379	Denny Hocking	.15	.07
380	Mark Kiefer	.15	.07
381	Tony Tarasco	.15	.07
382	Tony Longmire	.15	.07
383	Brian Anderson	.60	.25
384	Fernando Vina	.15	.07
385	Hector Carrasco	.15	.07
386	Mike Kelly	.15	.07
387	Greg Colbrunn	.15	.07
388	Roger Salkeld	.15	.07
389	Steve Trachsel	.30	.14
390	Rich Becker	.15	.07
391	Billy Taylor	.15	.07
392	Rich Rowland	.15	.07
393	Carl Everett	.15	.07
394	Johnny Ruffin	.15	.07
395	Keith Lockhart	.15	.07
396	J.R. Phillips	.15	.07
397	Sterling Hitchcock	.15	.07
398	Jorge Fabregas	.15	.07
399	Jeff Granger	.15	.07
400	Eddie Zambrano	.15	.07
401	Rikkert Faneyte	.15	.07
402	Gerald Williams	.15	.07
403	Joey Hamilton	.60	.25
404	Joe Hall	.15	.07
405	John Hudek	.15	.07
406	Roberto Petagine	.15	.07
407	Charles Johnson	.40	.18

		MINT	NRMT
☐ 408	Mark Smith	.15	.07
☐ 409	Jeff Juden	.15	.07
☐ 410	Carlos Pulido	.15	.07
☐ 411	Paul Shuey	.15	.07
☐ 412	Rob Butler	.15	.07
☐ 413	Mark Acre	.15	.07
☐ 414	Greg Pirkl	.15	.07
☐ 415	Melvin Nieves	.15	.07
☐ 416	Tim Hyers	.15	.07
☐ 417	NL Checklist	.15	.07
☐ 418	NL Checklist	.15	.07
☐ 419	AL Checklist	.15	.07
☐ 420	AL Checklist	.15	.07
☐ RY1	Carlos Delgado	5.00	2.20
☐ SS1	Cal Ripken Jr. Salute	40.00	18.00
☐ SS2	Dave Winfield Salute	5.00	2.20
☐ MVP1	Paul Molitor	8.00	3.60

1994 Select Crown Contenders

This ten-card set showcases top contenders for various awards such as batting champion, Cy Young Award winner and Most Valuable Player. The cards were inserted in first series packs at a rate of one in 24 and measure the standard size. The horizontal fronts feature color action player shots on a holographic gold foil background. The backs carry a color player close-up photo and highlights. The cards are numbered on the back with a CC prefix.

	MINT	NRMT
COMPLETE SET (10)	80.00	36.00
COMMON CARD (CC1-CC10)	2.00	.90
SER.1 STATED ODDS 1:24		
☐ CC1 Lenny Dykstra	2.00	.90
☐ CC2 Greg Maddux	12.00	5.50
☐ CC3 Roger Clemens	7.50	3.40
☐ CC4 Randy Johnson	5.00	2.20
☐ CC5 Frank Thomas	15.00	6.75
☐ CC6 Barry Bonds	5.00	2.20
☐ CC7 Juan Gonzalez	10.00	4.50
☐ CC8 John Olerud	2.00	.90
☐ CC9 Mike Piazza	12.00	5.50
☐ CC10 Ken Griffey Jr.	20.00	9.00

1994 Select Rookie Surge

This 18-card standard-size set showcased potential top rookies for 1994. The set was divided into two series of nine cards. The cards were randomly inserted in packs at a rate of one in 48. The fronts exhibit

Score's "dufex" printing process, in which a color photo is printed on a metallic base creating an unusual, three-dimensional look. On a multi-colored background, the horizontal backs present a color player headshot. The cards are numbered on the back with an RS prefix.

		MINT	NRMT
COMPLETE SET (18)		80.00	36.00
COMPLETE SERIES 1 (9)		30.00	13.50
COMPLETE SERIES 2 (9)		50.00	22.00
COMMON CARD (RS1-RS18)		2.50	1.10
MINOR STARS		5.00	2.20
STATED ODDS 1:48			
☐ RS1	Cliff Floyd	5.00	2.20
☐ RS2	Bob Hamelin	2.50	1.10
☐ RS3	Ryan Klesko	12.00	5.50
☐ RS4	Carlos Delgado	10.00	4.50
☐ RS5	Jeffrey Hammonds	5.00	2.20
☐ RS6	Rondell White	10.00	4.50
☐ RS7	Salomon Torres	2.50	1.10
☐ RS8	Steve Karsay	2.50	1.10
☐ RS9	Javier Lopez	10.00	4.50
☐ RS10	Manny Ramirez	20.00	9.00
☐ RS11	Tony Tarasco	2.50	1.10
☐ RS12	Kurt Abbott	2.50	1.10
☐ RS13	Chan Ho Park	20.00	9.00
☐ RS14	Rich Becker	2.50	1.10
☐ RS15	James Mouton	2.50	1.10
☐ RS16	Alex Gonzalez	5.00	2.20
☐ RS17	Raul Mondesi	12.00	5.50
☐ RS18	Steve Trachsel	5.00	2.20

1994 Select Skills

This 10-card standard-size set takes an up close look at the leagues top statistical leaders. The cards were randomly inserted in second series packs at a rate of approximately one in 24. A foil front has a holographic appearance that allows the player to stand out. The bottom of the front notes the player as being the best at something.

For example, the front of Barry Bonds' card notes, "Select's Best Run Producer." The back has a small photo with text. The cards are numbered with an "SK" prefix.

		MINT	NRMT
COMPLETE SET (10)		60.00	27.00
COMMON CARD (SK1-SK10)		6.00	2.70
SER.2 STATED ODDS 1:24			
☐ SK1	Randy Johnson	10.00	4.50
☐ SK2	Barry Larkin	8.00	3.60
☐ SK3	Lenny Dykstra	6.00	2.70
☐ SK4	Kenny Lofton	12.00	5.50
☐ SK5	Juan Gonzalez	25.00	11.00
☐ SK6	Barry Bonds	12.00	5.50
☐ SK7	Marquis Grissom	6.00	2.70
☐ SK8	Ivan Rodriguez	12.00	5.50
☐ SK9	Larry Walker	10.00	4.50
☐ SK10	Travis Fryman	6.00	2.70

1995 Select

This 250-card set was issued in 12-card packs with 24 packs per box and 24 boxes per case. There was an announced production run of 4,950 cases. These horizontal cards feature an action photo over most of the card with the player's profile and name on the right side. The "Select 95" logo is in the upper left corner. The vertical backs have a black and white photo on the top. The middle of the card is dedicated to a brief biography as well as seasonal and career stats. A specific important stat is included at the bottom of the card. A special card of Hideo Nomo (#251) was issued to hobby dealers who had bought cases of the Select product.

	MINT	NRMT
COMPLETE SET (250)	15.00	6.75
COMMON CARD (1-250)	.10	.09
MINOR STARS	.20	.09
UNLISTED STARS	.40	.18
SUBSET CARDS HALF VALUE OF BASE CARDS		
COMP.AP SET (250)	2000.00	900.00
COMMON ART.PRF (1-250)	3.00	1.35
*ART.PRF.STARS: 25X TO 50X HI COLUMN		
*ART.PRF.YOUNG STARS: 20X TO 40X HI		
AP STATED ODDS 1:24		
NOMO CARD ISSUED DIRECT TO DEALERS		
☐ 1 Cal Ripken Jr.	1.50	.70
☐ 2 Robin Ventura	.20	.09
☐ 3 Al Martin	.10	.05
☐ 4 Jeff Frye	.10	.05
☐ 5 Darryl Strawberry	.20	.09
☐ 6 Chan Ho Park	.40	.18

7	Steve Avery	.10	.05
8	Bret Boone	.10	.05
9	Danny Tartabull	.10	.05
10	Dante Bichette	.20	.09
11	Rondell White	.20	.09
12	Dave McCarty	.10	.05
13	Bernard Gilkey	.10	.05
14	Mark McGwire	.75	.35
15	Ruben Sierra	.20	.09
16	Wade Boggs	.40	.18
17	Mike Piazza	1.25	.55
18	Jeffrey Hammonds	.20	.09
19	Mike Mussina	.40	.18
20	Darryl Kile	.20	.09
21	Greg Maddux	1.25	.55
22	Frank Thomas	1.50	.70
23	Kevin Appier	.20	.09
24	Jay Bell	.10	.05
25	Kirk Gibson	.20	.09
26	Pat Hentgen	.20	.09
27	Joey Hamilton	.20	.09
28	Bernie Williams	.40	.18
29	Aaron Sele	.10	.05
30	Delino DeShields	.10	.05
31	Danny Bautista	.10	.05
32	Jim Thome	.40	.18
33	Rikkert Faneyte	.10	.05
34	Roberto Alomar	.40	.18
35	Paul Molitor	.40	.18
36	Allen Watson	.10	.05
37	Jeff Bagwell	.75	.35
38	Jay Buhner	.20	.09
39	Marquis Grissom	.20	.09
40	Jim Edmonds	.30	.14
41	Ryan Klesko	.30	.14
42	Fred McGriff	.30	.14
43	Tony Tarasco	.10	.05
44	Darren Daulton	.20	.09
45	Marc Newfield	.10	.05
46	Barry Bonds	.50	.23
47	Bobby Bonilla	.20	.09
48	Greg Pirkl	.10	.05
49	Steve Karsay	.10	.05
50	Bob Hamelin	.20	.09
51	Javier Lopez	.20	.09
52	Barry Larkin	.30	.14
53	Kevin Young	.10	.05
54	Sterling Hitchcock	.10	.05
55	Tom Glavine	.20	.09
56	Carlos Delgado	.20	.09
57	Darren Oliver	.10	.05
58	Cliff Floyd	.10	.05
59	Tim Salmon	.50	.23
60	Albert Belle	.50	.23
61	Salomon Torres	.10	.05
62	Gary Sheffield	.40	.18
63	Ivan Rodriguez	.50	.23
64	Charles Nagy	.10	.05
65	Eduardo Perez	.10	.05
66	Terry Steinbach	.10	.05
67	Dave Justice	.40	.18
68	Jason Bere	.10	.05
69	Dave Nilsson	.10	.05
70	Brian Anderson	.20	.09
71	Billy Ashley	.20	.09
72	Roger Clemens	.75	.35
73	Jimmy Key	.20	.09
74	Wally Joyner	.20	.09
75	Andy Benes	.20	.09
76	Ray Lankford	.20	.09
77	Jeff Kent	.10	.05
78	Moises Alou	.20	.09
79	Kirby Puckett	.75	.35
80	Joe Carter	.20	.09
81	Manny Ramirez	.40	.18
82	J.R. Phillips	.10	.05
83	Matt Mieske	.10	.05
84	John Olerud	.20	.09
85	Andres Galarraga	.40	.18
86	Juan Gonzalez	1.00	.45
87	Pedro Martinez	.40	.18
88	Dean Palmer	.10	.05
89	Ken Griffey Jr.	2.00	.90
90	Brian Jordan	.20	.09
91	Hal Morris	.10	.05
92	Lenny Dykstra	.20	.09
93	Wil Cordero	.10	.05
94	Tony Gwynn	1.00	.45
95	Alex Gonzalez	.10	.05
96	Cecil Fielder	.20	.09
97	Mo Vaughn	.50	.23
98	John Valentin	.10	.05
99	Will Clark	.30	.14
100	Geronimo Pena	.10	.05
101	Don Mattingly	.60	.25
102	Charles Johnson	.20	.09
103	Raul Mondesi	.30	.14
104	Reggie Sanders	.10	.05
105	Royce Clayton	.10	.05
106	Reggie Jefferson	.10	.05
107	Craig Biggio	.30	.14
108	Jack McDowell	.20	.09
109	James Mouton	.10	.05
110	Mike Greenwell	.10	.05
111	David Cone	.20	.09
112	Matt Williams	.30	.14
113	Garret Anderson	.30	.14
114	Carlos Garcia	.10	.05
115	Alex Fernandez	.10	.05
116	Deion Sanders	.20	.09
117	Chili Davis	.20	.09
118	Mike Kelly	.10	.05
119	Jeff Conine	.20	.09
120	Kenny Lofton	.50	.23
121	Rafael Palmeiro	.30	.14
122	Chuck Knoblauch	.20	.09
123	Ozzie Smith	.50	.23
124	Carlos Baerga	.20	.09
125	Brett Butler	.10	.05
126	Sammy Sosa	.40	.18
127	Ellis Burks	.20	.09
128	Bret Saberhagen	.10	.05
129	Doug Drabek	.10	.05
130	Dennis Martinez	.20	.09
131	Paul O'Neill	.20	.09
132	Travis Fryman	.20	.09
133	Brent Gates	.10	.05
134	Rickey Henderson	.30	.14
135	Randy Johnson	.40	.18
136	Mark Langston	.10	.05
137	Greg Colbrunn	.10	.05
138	Jose Rijo	.10	.05
139	Bryan Harvey	.10	.05
140	Dennis Eckersley	.20	.09
141	Ron Gant	.20	.09
142	Carl Everett	.10	.05
143	Jeff Granger	.10	.05
144	Ben McDonald	.10	.05
145	Kurt Abbott UER	.10	.05
	(Mariners logo on front)		
146	Jim Abbott	.10	.05
147	Jason Jacome	.10	.05
148	Rico Brogna	.20	.09
149	Cal Eldred	.10	.05
150	Rich Becker	.10	.05
151	Pete Harnisch	.10	.05
152	Roberto Petagine	.10	.05
153	Jacob Brumfield	.10	.05
154	Todd Hundley	.20	.09
155	Roger Cedeno	.20	.09
156	Harold Baines	.20	.09
157	Steve Dunn	.10	.05
158	Tim Belk	.10	.05
159	Marty Cordova	.50	.23
160	Russ Davis	.10	.05
161	Jose Malave	.10	.05
162	Brian Hunter	.30	.14
163	Andy Pettitte	.60	.25
164	Brooks Kieschnick	.20	.09
165	Midre Cummings	.10	.05
166	Frank Rodriguez	.10	.05
167	Chad Mottola	.10	.05
168	Brian Barber	.10	.05
169	Tim Unroe	.10	.05
170	Shane Andrews	.10	.05
171	Kevin Flora	.10	.05
172	Ray Durham	.20	.09
173	Chipper Jones	1.25	.55
174	Butch Huskey	.10	.05
175	Ray McDavid	.10	.05
176	Jeff Cirillo	.10	.05
177	Terry Pendleton	.10	.05
178	Scott Ruffcorn	.10	.05
179	Ray Holbert	.10	.05
180	Joe Randa	.10	.05
181	Jose Oliva	.10	.05
182	Andy Van Slyke	.20	.09
183	Albie Lopez	.10	.05
184	Chad Curtis	.10	.05
185	Ozzie Guillen	.10	.05
186	Chad Ogea	.10	.05
187	Dan Wilson	.10	.05
188	Tony Fernandez	.10	.05
189	John Smoltz	.20	.09
190	Willie Greene	.10	.05
191	Darren Lewis	.10	.05
192	Orlando Miller	.10	.05
193	Kurt Miller	.10	.05
194	Andrew Lorraine	.10	.05
195	Ernie Young	.10	.05
196	Jimmy Haynes	.20	.09
197	Raul Casanova	.30	.14
198	Joe Vitiello	.10	.05
199	Brad Woodall	.10	.05
200	Juan Acevedo	.10	.05
201	Michael Tucker	.20	.09
202	Shawn Green	.20	.09
203	Alex Rodriguez	1.50	.70
204	Julian Tavarez	.10	.05
205	Jose Lima	.10	.05
206	Wilson Alvarez	.10	.05
207	Rich Aude	.10	.05
208	Armando Benitez	.20	.09
209	Dwayne Hosey	.10	.05
210	Gabe White	.10	.05
211	Joey Eischen	.10	.05
212	Bill Pulsipher	.10	.05
213	Robby Thompson	.10	.05
214	Toby Borland	.10	.05
215	Rusty Greer	.40	.18
216	Fausto Cruz	.10	.05
217	Luis Ortiz	.10	.05
218	Duane Singleton	.10	.05
219	Troy Percival	.10	.05
220	Gregg Jefferies	.10	.05
221	Mark Grace	.30	.14
222	Mickey Tettleton	.10	.05
223	Phil Plantier	.10	.05
224	Larry Walker	.40	.18
225	Ken Caminiti	.30	.14
226	Dave Winfield	.30	.14
227	Brady Anderson	.30	.14
228	Kevin Brown	.20	.09
229	Andujar Cedeno	.10	.05
230	Roberto Kelly	.10	.05
231	Jose Canseco	.30	.14
232	Scott Ruffcorn ST	.10	.05
233	Billy Ashley ST	.10	.05
234	J.R. Phillips ST	.10	.05
235	Chipper Jones ST	.60	.25
236	Charles Johnson ST	.10	.05
237	Midre Cummings ST	.10	.05
238	Brian L.Hunter SH	.20	.09
239	Garret Anderson ST	.20	.09
240	Shawn Green SH	.10	.05
241	Alex Rodriguez ST	.75	.35
242	Frank Thomas CL	.75	.35
243	Ken Griffey Jr. CL	1.00	.45
244	Albert Belle CL	.40	.18
245	Cal Ripken Jr. CL	.75	.35
246	Barry Bonds CL	.30	.14
247	Raul Mondesi CL	.20	.09
248	Mike Piazza CL	.60	.25
249	Jeff Bagwell CL	.40	.18
250	Jeff Bagwell	1.25	.55
	Ken Griffey Jr.		
	Frank Thomas		
	Mike Piazza CL		
251S	Hideo Nomo	2.00	.90

1995 Select Big Sticks

Randomly inserted in packs, these 12 cards feature leading hitters. The fronts picture the

player's photo against a metallic background. The words "Big Sticks 95" as well as the player's name is on the bottom. The player's team is noted in the middle of the background. The backs contain a player photo, personal information as well as some notes about his career. The cards are numbered in the upper right corner with a "BS" prefix.

	MINT	NRMT
COMPLETE SET (12)	150.00	70.00
COMMON CARD (BS1-BS12)	4.00	1.80
STATED ODDS 1:48		

		MINT	NRMT
☐ BS1	Frank Thomas	25.00	11.00
☐ BS2	Ken Griffey Jr.	30.00	13.50
☐ BS3	Cal Ripken Jr.	25.00	11.00
☐ BS4	Mike Piazza	20.00	9.00
☐ BS5	Don Mattingly	10.00	4.50
☐ BS6	Will Clark	4.00	1.80
☐ BS7	Tony Gwynn	15.00	6.75
☐ BS8	Jeff Bagwell	12.00	5.50
☐ BS9	Barry Bonds	8.00	3.60
☐ BS10	Paul Molitor	6.00	2.70
☐ BS11	Matt Williams	4.00	1.80
☐ BS12	Albert Belle	8.00	3.60

1995 Select Can't Miss

These 12 cards featuring promising young players were inserted one per 24 packs. The player is pictured against a wavy red background. His last name is identified on the bottom left with the "Can't Miss" logo directly above the name. In the middle of the "Can't Miss" logo is a drawing of an umpire signaling safe. The backs have a blue background and include an

---

inset photo, some professional information and biographical data. The cards are numbered with a "CM" prefix in the upper right corner.

	MINT	NRMT
COMPLETE SET (12)	50.00	22.00
COMMON CARD (CM1-CM12)	2.00	.90
SEMISTARS	3.00	1.35
UNLISTED STARS	5.00	2.20
STATED ODDS 1:24		

		MINT	NRMT
☐ CM1	Cliff Floyd	2.00	.90
☐ CM2	Ryan Klesko	3.00	1.35
☐ CM3	Charles Johnson	2.50	1.10
☐ CM4	Raul Mondesi	3.00	1.35
☐ CM5	Manny Ramirez	5.00	2.20
☐ CM6	Billy Ashley	2.00	.90
☐ CM7	Alex Gonzalez	2.00	.90
☐ CM8	Carlos Delgado	2.50	1.10
☐ CM9	Garret Anderson	3.00	1.35
☐ CM10	Alex Rodriguez	20.00	9.00
☐ CM11	Chipper Jones	15.00	6.75
☐ CM12	Shawn Green	2.50	1.10

1995 Select Sure Shots

These ten cards were randomly inserted into packs at a rate of one in 90. This set features some of the top 1994 draft picks. The fronts feature the player's photo against a gold metallic background. The phrase "Sure Shots" is printed on gold ink against a blue background on the left. The player is identified in white ink on the bottom. The backs contain some information about the player as well as an inset photo. All this information is set against a blue background with a white light effect. The cards are numbered with an "SS" prefix in the upper right corner.

	MINT	NRMT
COMPLETE SET (10)	70.00	32.00
COMMON CARD (SS1-SS10)	2.00	.90
MINOR STARS	3.00	1.35
STATED ODDS 1:90		

		MINT	NRMT
☐ SS1	Ben Grieve	30.00	13.50
☐ SS2	Kevin Witt	6.00	2.70
☐ SS3	Mark Farris	2.00	.90
☐ SS4	Paul Konerko	25.00	11.00
☐ SS5	Dustin Hermanson	3.00	1.35
☐ SS6	Ramon Castro	3.00	1.35
☐ SS7	McKay Christensen	3.00	1.35
☐ SS8	Brian Buchanan	2.00	.90
☐ SS9	Paul Wilson	3.00	1.35
☐ SS10	Terrence Long	4.00	1.80

1996 Select

The 1996 Select set was issued in one series totalling 200 cards. The 10-card packs retail for $1.99 each. The fronts feature a color action player photo over most of the card with a small player photo framed and name in gold foil printing. The backs carry another player photo, player information and statistics. The set contains the topical subsets: Lineup Leaders (151-160) and Rookies (161-195).

	MINT	NRMT
COMPLETE SET (200)	15.00	6.75
COMMON CARD (1-200)	.10	.05
MINOR STARS	.20	.09
UNLISTED STARS	.40	.18
SUBSET CARDS HALF VALUE OF BASE CARDS		
COMP.AP SET (200)	2000.00	900.00
COMMON ART.PRF. (1-200)	3.00	1.35
*ART.PRF.STARS: 20X TO 40X HI COLUMN		
*ART.PRF.YOUNG STARS: 15X TO 30X HI		
AP STATED ODDS 1:35		

		MINT	NRMT
☐ 1	Wade Boggs	.40	.18
☐ 2	Shawn Green	.10	.05
☐ 3	Andres Galarraga	.40	.18
☐ 4	Bill Pulsipher	.10	.05
☐ 5	Chuck Knoblauch	.40	.18
☐ 6	Ken Griffey Jr.	2.00	.90
☐ 7	Greg Maddux	1.25	.55
☐ 8	Manny Ramirez	.40	.18
☐ 9	Ivan Rodriguez	.50	.23
☐ 10	Tim Salmon	.40	.18
☐ 11	Frank Thomas	1.50	.70
☐ 12	Jeff Bagwell	.75	.35
☐ 13	Travis Fryman	.20	.09
☐ 14	Kenny Lofton	.50	.23
☐ 15	Matt Williams	.30	.14
☐ 16	Jay Bell	.10	.05
☐ 17	Ken Caminiti	.30	.14
☐ 18	Ray Lankford	.20	.09
☐ 19	Cal Ripken	1.50	.70
☐ 20	Roger Clemens	.75	.35
☐ 21	Carlos Baerga	.10	.05
☐ 22	Mike Piazza	1.25	.55
☐ 23	Gregg Jefferies	.10	.05
☐ 24	Reggie Sanders	.10	.05
☐ 25	Rondell White	.20	.09
☐ 26	Sammy Sosa	.40	.18
☐ 27	Kevin Appier	.20	.09
☐ 28	Kevin Seitzer	.10	.05
☐ 29	Gary Sheffield	.40	.18
☐ 30	Mike Mussina	.40	.18
☐ 31	Mark McGwire	.75	.35
☐ 32	Barry Larkin	.30	.14
☐ 33	Marc Newfield	.10	.05
☐ 34	Ismael Valdes	.20	.09
☐ 35	Marty Cordova	.20	.09
☐ 36	Albert Belle	.50	.23
☐ 37	Johnny Damon	.20	.09
☐ 38	Garret Anderson	.20	.09
☐ 39	Cecil Fielder	.20	.09
☐ 40	John Mabry	.10	.05

☐ 41	Chipper Jones	1.25	.55
☐ 42	Omar Vizquel	.20	.09
☐ 43	Jose Rijo	.05	.05
☐ 44	Charles Johnson	.20	.09
☐ 45	Alex Rodriguez	1.25	.55
☐ 46	Rico Brogna	.10	.05
☐ 47	Joe Carter	.20	.09
☐ 48	Mo Vaughn	.50	.23
☐ 49	Moises Alou	.20	.09
☐ 50	Raul Mondesi	.30	.14
☐ 51	Robin Ventura	.20	.09
☐ 52	Jim Thome	.40	.18
☐ 53	David Justice	.40	.18
☐ 54	Jeff King	.10	.05
☐ 55	Brian L. Hunter	.20	.09
☐ 56	Juan Gonzalez	1.00	.45
☐ 57	John Olerud	.20	.09
☐ 58	Rafael Palmeiro	.30	.14
☐ 59	Tony Gwynn	1.00	.45
☐ 60	Eddie Murray	.40	.18
☐ 61	Jason Isringhausen	.10	.05
☐ 62	Dante Bichette	.20	.09
☐ 63	Randy Johnson	.40	.18
☐ 64	Kirby Puckett	.75	.35
☐ 65	Jim Edmonds	.30	.14
☐ 66	David Cone	.20	.09
☐ 67	Ozzie Smith	.50	.23
☐ 68	Fred McGriff	.30	.14
☐ 69	Darren Daulton	.20	.09
☐ 70	Edgar Martinez	.30	.14
☐ 71	J.T. Snow	.20	.09
☐ 72	Butch Huskey	.20	.09
☐ 73	Hideo Nomo	1.00	.45
☐ 74	Pedro Martinez	.40	.18
☐ 75	Bobby Bonilla	.20	.09
☐ 76	Jeff Conine	.20	.09
☐ 77	Ryan Klesko	.30	.14
☐ 78	Bernie Williams	.40	.18
☐ 79	Andre Dawson	.30	.14
☐ 80	Trevor Hoffman	.10	.05
☐ 81	Mark Grace	.30	.14
☐ 82	Benji Gil	.10	.05
☐ 83	Eric Karros	.20	.09
☐ 84	Pete Schourek	.10	.05
☐ 85	Edgardo Alfonzo	.30	.14
☐ 86	Jay Buhner	.30	.14
☐ 87	Vinny Castilla	.20	.09
☐ 88	Bret Boone	.10	.05
☐ 89	Ray Durham	.20	.09
☐ 90	Brian Jordan	.20	.09
☐ 91	Jose Canseco	.30	.14
☐ 92	Paul O'Neill	.20	.09
☐ 93	Chili Davis	.20	.09
☐ 94	Tom Glavine	.20	.09
☐ 95	Julian Tavarez	.10	.05
☐ 96	Derek Bell	.10	.05
☐ 97	Will Clark	.30	.14
☐ 98	Larry Walker	.40	.18
☐ 99	Denny Neagle	.20	.09
☐ 100	Alex Fernandez	.10	.05
☐ 101	Barry Bonds	.50	.23
☐ 102	Ben McDonald	.10	.05
☐ 103	Andy Pettitte	.50	.23
☐ 104	Tino Martinez	.40	.18
☐ 105	Sterling Hitchcock	.10	.05
☐ 106	Royce Clayton	.10	.05
☐ 107	Jim Abbott	.10	.05
☐ 108	Rickey Henderson	.30	.14
☐ 109	Ramon Martinez	.20	.09
☐ 110	Paul Molitor	.40	.18
☐ 111	Dennis Eckersley	.20	.09
☐ 112	Alex Gonzalez	.10	.05
☐ 113	Marquis Grissom	.20	.09
☐ 114	Greg Vaughn	.10	.05
☐ 115	Lance Johnson	.10	.05
☐ 116	Todd Stottlemyre	.10	.05
☐ 117	Jack McDowell	.10	.05
☐ 118	Ruben Sierra	.20	.09
☐ 119	Brady Anderson	.30	.14
☐ 120	Julio Franco	.10	.05
☐ 121	Brooks Kieschnick	.20	.09
☐ 122	Roberto Alomar	.40	.18
☐ 123	Greg Gagne	.10	.05
☐ 124	Wally Joyner	.20	.09
☐ 125	John Smoltz	.20	.09
☐ 126	John Valentin	.10	.05

☐ 127	Russ Davis	.10	.05
☐ 128	Joe Vitiello	.10	.05
☐ 129	Shawon Dunston	.10	.05
☐ 130	Frank Rodriguez	.10	.05
☐ 131	Charlie Hayes	.10	.05
☐ 132	Andy Benes	.20	.09
☐ 133	B.J. Surhoff	.10	.05
☐ 134	Dave Nilsson	.10	.05
☐ 135	Carlos Delgado	.20	.09
☐ 136	Walt Weiss	.10	.05
☐ 137	Mike Stanley	.10	.05
☐ 138	Greg Colbrunn	.10	.05
☐ 139	Mike Kelly	.10	.05
☐ 140	Ryne Sandberg	.50	.23
☐ 141	Lee Smith	.20	.09
☐ 142	Dennis Martinez	.20	.09
☐ 143	Bernard Gilkey	.10	.05
☐ 144	Lenny Dykstra	.20	.09
☐ 145	Danny Tartabull	.10	.05
☐ 146	Dean Palmer	.10	.05
☐ 147	Craig Biggio	.30	.14
☐ 148	Juan Acevedo	.10	.05
☐ 149	Michael Tucker	.20	.09
☐ 150	Bobby Higginson	.20	.09
☐ 151	Ken Griffey Jr. LUL	1.00	.45
☐ 152	Frank Thomas LUL	.75	.35
☐ 153	Cal Ripken LUL	.75	.35
☐ 154	Albert Belle LUL	.30	.14
☐ 155	Mike Piazza LUL	.60	.25
☐ 156	Barry Bonds LUL	.30	.14
☐ 157	Sammy Sosa LUL	.20	.09
☐ 158	Mo Vaughn LUL	.30	.14
☐ 159	Greg Maddux LUL	.60	.25
☐ 160	Jeff Bagwell LUL	.40	.18
☐ 161	Derek Jeter	1.25	.55
☐ 162	Paul Wilson	.10	.05
☐ 163	Chris Snopek	.10	.05
☐ 164	Jason Schmidt	.20	.09
☐ 165	Jimmy Haynes	.10	.05
☐ 166	George Arias	.10	.05
☐ 167	Steve Gibralter	.10	.05
☐ 168	Bob Wolcott	.10	.05
☐ 169	Jason Kendall	.30	.14
☐ 170	Greg Zaun	.10	.05
☐ 171	Quinton McCracken	.10	.05
☐ 172	Alan Benes	.20	.09
☐ 173	Rey Ordonez	.20	.09
☐ 174	Livan Hernandez	1.25	.55
☐ 175	Osvaldo Fernandez	.20	.09
☐ 176	Marc Barcelo	.10	.05
☐ 177	Sal Fasano	.10	.05
☐ 178	Mike Grace	.10	.05
☐ 179	Chan Ho Park	.40	.18
☐ 180	Robert Perez	.10	.05
☐ 181	Todd Hollandsworth	.10	.05
☐ 182	Wilton Guerrero	.20	.09
☐ 183	John Wasdin	.10	.05
☐ 184	Jim Pittsley	.20	.09
☐ 185	LaTroy Hawkins	.10	.05
☐ 186	Jay Powell	.10	.05
☐ 187	Felipe Crespo	.10	.05
☐ 188	Jermaine Dye	.20	.09
☐ 189	Bob Abreu	.30	.14
☐ 190	Matt Luke	.10	.05
☐ 191	Richard Hidalgo	.40	.18
☐ 192	Karim Garcia	.30	.14
☐ 193	Marvin Benard	.10	.05
☐ 194	Andy Fox	.10	.05
☐ 195	Terrell Wade	.10	.05
☐ 196	Frank Thomas CL	.75	.35
☐ 197	Ken Griffey Jr. CL	1.00	.45
☐ 198	Greg Maddux CL	.60	.25
☐ 199	Mike Piazza CL	.60	.25
☐ 200	Cal Ripken CL	.75	.35

enshrine Hall of Famers. The backs carry information about the player's claim to fame. Only 2100 of these sets were produced.

	MINT	NRMT
COMPLETE SET (20)	250.00	110.00
COMMON CARD (1-20)	3.00	1.35
SEMISTARS	5.00	2.20
UNLISTED STARS	8.00	3.60
STATED ODDS 1:72		

☐ 1	Cal Ripken	30.00	13.50
☐ 2	Greg Maddux	25.00	11.00
☐ 3	Ken Griffey Jr.	40.00	18.00
☐ 4	Frank Thomas	30.00	13.50
☐ 5	Mo Vaughn	10.00	4.50
☐ 6	Albert Belle	10.00	4.50
☐ 7	Jeff Bagwell	15.00	6.75
☐ 8	Sammy Sosa	8.00	3.60
☐ 9	Reggie Sanders	3.00	1.35
☐ 10	Hideo Nomo	20.00	9.00
☐ 11	Chipper Jones	25.00	11.00
☐ 12	Mike Piazza	25.00	11.00
☐ 13	Matt Williams	5.00	2.20
☐ 14	Tony Gwynn	20.00	9.00
☐ 15	Johnny Damon	4.00	1.80
☐ 16	Dante Bichette	4.00	1.80
☐ 17	Kirby Puckett	15.00	6.75
☐ 18	Barry Bonds	10.00	4.50
☐ 19	Randy Johnson	8.00	3.60
☐ 20	Eddie Murray	8.00	3.60

1996 Select En Fuego

Randomly inserted in packs at a rate of one in 48, this 25-card set is printed with all-foil Dufex technology, etched highlights and transparent inks that make each card shine. Spanish for "on fire," En Fuego is an expression popularized by ESPN sportscaster Dan Patrick, who provides the commentary for each player on the card back. The fronts feature color action

1996 Select Claim To Fame

Randomly inserted in packs at a rate of one in 72, this 20-card set features potential Hall of Famers. The fronts display a color player portrait on a diecut plaque similar to the ones that player photos while the backs display the more player photos and the commentary.

	MINT	NRMT
COMPLETE SET (25)	250.00	110.00
COMMON CARD (1-25)	2.50	1.10
SEMISTARS	4.00	1.80
UNLISTED STARS	6.00	2.70
STATED ODDS 1:48		

			MINT	NRMT
☐	1	Ken Griffey Jr.	30.00	13.50
☐	2	Frank Thomas	25.00	11.00
☐	3	Cal Ripken	25.00	11.00
☐	4	Greg Maddux	20.00	9.00
☐	5	Jeff Bagwell	12.00	5.50
☐	6	Barry Bonds	8.00	3.60
☐	7	Mo Vaughn	8.00	3.60
☐	8	Albert Belle	8.00	3.60
☐	9	Sammy Sosa	6.00	2.70
☐	10	Reggie Sanders	2.50	1.10
☐	11	Mike Piazza	20.00	9.00
☐	12	Chipper Jones	20.00	9.00
☐	13	Tony Gwynn	15.00	6.75
☐	14	Kirby Puckett	12.00	5.50
☐	15	Wade Boggs	6.00	2.70
☐	16	Dan Patrick	6.00	2.70
☐	17	Gary Sheffield	6.00	2.70
☐	18	Dante Bichette	3.00	1.35
☐	19	Randy Johnson	6.00	2.70
☐	20	Matt Williams	4.00	1.80
☐	21	Alex Rodriguez	20.00	9.00
☐	22	Tim Salmon	6.00	2.70
☐	23	Johnny Damon	3.00	1.35
☐	24	Manny Ramirez	6.00	2.70
☐	25	Hideo Nomo	15.00	6.75

1996 Select Team Nucleus

Randomly inserted in packs at a rate of one in 18, this 28-card set is printed on clear plastic with holographic and micro-etched highlights and gold foil stamping. The fronts feature color pictures of three team players with the backs display-ing the same photos, the play-ers' names, and a sentence stating why these players are special.

			MINT	NRMT
COMPLETE SET (28)			80.00	36.00
COMMON CARD (1-28)			2.00	.90
UNLISTED STARS			3.00	1.35
STATED ODDS 1:18				

☐	1	Albert Belle	4.00	1.80
		Manny Ramirez		
		Carlos Baerga		
☐	2	Ray Lankford	3.00	1.35
		Brian Jordan		
		Ozzie Smith		
☐	3	Jay Bell	2.00	.90

		Jeff King		
		Denny Neagle		
☐	4	Dante Bichette	3.00	1.35
		Andres Galarraga		
		Larry Walker		
☐	5	Mark McGwire	3.00	1.35
		Mike Bordick		
		Terry Steinbach		
☐	6	Bernie Williams	3.00	1.35
		Wade Boggs		
		David Cone		
☐	7	Joe Carter	2.00	.90
		Alex Gonzalez		
		Shawn Green		
☐	8	Roger Clemens	6.00	2.70
		Mo Vaughn		
		Jose Canseco		
☐	9	Ken Griffey Jr.	15.00	6.75
		Edgar Martinez		
		Randy Johnson		
☐	10	Gregg Jefferies	2.00	.90
		Darren Daulton		
		Len Dykstra		
☐	11	Mike Piazza	12.00	5.50
		Raul Mondesi		
		Hideo Nomo		
☐	12	Greg Maddux	15.00	6.75
		Chipper Jones		
		Ryan Klesko		
☐	13	Cecil Fielder	2.00	.90
		Travis Fryman		
		Phil Nevin		
☐	14	Ivan Rodriguez	8.00	3.60
		Will Clark		
		Juan Gonzalez		
☐	15	Ryne Sandberg	4.00	1.80
		Sammy Sosa		
		Mark Grace		
☐	16	Gary Sheffield	3.00	1.35
		Charles Johnson		
		Andre Dawson		
☐	17	Johnny Damon	2.00	.90
		Michael Tucker		
		Kevin Appier		
☐	18	Barry Bonds	3.00	1.35
		Matt Williams		
		Rod Beck		
☐	19	Kirby Puckett	6.00	2.70
		Chuck Knoblauch		
		Marty Cordova		
☐	20	Cal Ripken	12.00	5.50
		Barry Bonilla		
		Mike Mussina		
☐	21	Jason Isringhausen	2.00	.90
		Bill Pulsipher		
		Rico Brogna		
☐	22	Tony Gwynn	6.00	2.70
		Ken Caminiti		
		Mark Newfield		
☐	23	Tim Salmon	3.00	1.35
		Garret Anderson		
		Jim Edmonds		
☐	24	Moises Alou	2.00	.90
		Rondell White		
		Cliff Floyd		
☐	25	Barry Larkin	2.50	1.10
		Reggie Sanders		
		Bret Boone		
☐	26	Jeff Bagwell	6.00	2.70
		Craig Biggio		
		Derek Bell		
☐	27	Frank Thomas	12.00	5.50
		Robin Ventura		
		Alex Fernandez		
☐	28	John Jaha	2.00	.90
		Greg Vaughn		
		Kevin Seitzer		

1997 Select

The 1997 Select set was issued in two series totalling 200 cards and was distributed in hobby only six-card packs with a sug-gested retail price of $2.99. The

---

fronts display a color action player photo over most of the card with a small player photo at the bottom. The backs carry another player photo, player information and statistics. Each card featues a distinctive silver-foil treatment with either a red or blue foil accent. The red cards are twice as easy to find than the blue cards.

	MINT	NRMT
COMPLETE SET (200)	80.00	36.00
COMPLETE SERIES 1 (150)	50.00	22.00
COMMON RED (1-150)	.15	.07
RED MINOR STARS	.30	.14
RED UNLISTED STAR	.60	.25
COMMON BLUE (1-150)	.30	.14
BLUE MINOR STARS	.60	.25
BLUE UNLISTED STAR	1.25	.55
COMPLETE HI SERIES (50)	30.00	13.50
COMMON HI SERIES (151-200)	.30	.14
HI SERIES MINOR STARS	.60	.25
HI SERIES UNLISTED STARS	1.25	.55
SUBSET CARDS HALF VALUE OF BASE CARDS		
ALL HI SERIES FRONTS ERRONEOUSLY		
HAVE "SELECT COMPANY" TEXT ON THEM		
COMP.AP SET (150)	5000.00	2200.00
COMMON AP RED (1-150)	6.00	2.70
COMMON AP BLUE (1-150)	15.00	6.75
*AP STARS: 25X TO 50X HI COLUMN		
*AP YOUNG STARS: 20X TO 40X HI		
AP STATED ODDS 1:71 RED, 1:355 BLUE		
COMP.COMPANY SET (200)	250.00	110.00
COMMON COMPANY (1-200)	.75	.35
*CMPY.RED STARS: 2.5X TO 5X HI COLUMN		
*CMPY.BLUE STARS: 1.25X TO 2.5X HI		
*CMPY.HI SERIES STARS: 1.25X TO 2.5X HI		
ONE COMPANY PER HI SERIES PACK		
COMPANY FRONTS HAVE COARSE FINISH		
COMP.REG.GOLD SET (150)	1000.00	450.00
COMMON RG RED (1-150)	1.50	.70
COMMON RG BLUE (1-150)	3.00	1.35
*REG.GOLD: 5X TO 10X HI COLUMN		
*REG.GOLD YOUNG STARS: 4X TO 8X HI		
REG.GOLD ODDS 1:11 RED, 1:47 BLUE		

			MINT	NRMT
☐	1	Juan Gonzalez B	3.00	1.35
☐	2	Mo Vaughn B	1.50	.70
☐	3	Tony Gwynn R	1.50	.70
☐	4	Manny Ramirez B	1.25	.55
☐	5	Jose Canseco R	.40	.18
☐	6	David Cone R	.30	.14
☐	7	Chan Ho Park R	.60	.25
☐	8	Frank Thomas B	5.00	2.20
☐	9	Todd Hollandsworth R	.15	.07
☐	10	Marty Cordova R	.30	.14
☐	11	Gary Sheffield B	1.25	.55
☐	12	John Smoltz B	.60	.25
☐	13	Mark Grudzielanek R	.15	.07
☐	14	Sammy Sosa B	1.25	.55
☐	15	Paul Molitor R	.60	.25
☐	16	Kevin Brown R	.30	.14
☐	17	Albert Belle B	1.50	.70
☐	18	Eric Young R	.15	.07
☐	19	John Wetteland R	.15	.07
☐	20	Ryan Klesko B	.75	.35

#	Player		MINT	NRMT
21	Joe Carter B		.30	.14
22	Alex Ochoa R		.15	.07
23	Greg Maddux B		4.00	1.80
24	Roger Clemens B		2.50	1.10
25	Ivan Rodriguez B		1.50	.70
26	Barry Bonds B		1.50	.70
27	Kenny Lofton B		1.50	.70
28	Javy Lopez R		.30	.14
29	Hideo Nomo B		3.00	1.35
30	Rusty Greer R		.30	.14
31	Rafael Palmeiro R		.40	.18
32	Mike Piazza B		4.00	1.80
33	Ryne Sandberg		.75	.35
34	Wade Boggs R		.60	.25
35	Jim Thome B		1.25	.55
36	Ken Caminiti B		1.25	.55
37	Mark Grace R		.40	.18
38	Brian Jordan B		1.25	.55
39	Craig Biggio R		.40	.18
40	Henry Rodriguez R		.15	.07
41	Dean Palmer R		.15	.07
42	Jason Kendall R		.30	.14
43	Bill Pulsipher R		.15	.07
44	Tim Salmon B		1.25	.55
45	Marc Newfield R		.15	.07
46	Pat Hentgen R		.30	.14
47	Ken Griffey Jr. B		6.00	2.70
48	Paul Wilson R		.15	.07
49	Jay Buhner R		.75	.35
50	Rickey Henderson R		.40	.18
51	Jeff Bagwell B		2.50	1.10
52	Cecil Fielder R		.30	.14
53	Alex Rodriguez B		4.00	1.80
54	John Jaha R		.15	.07
55	Brady Anderson B		.75	.35
56	Andres Galarraga R		.60	.25
57	Raul Mondesi R		.40	.18
58	Andy Pettitte R		.60	.25
59	Roberto Alomar B		1.25	.55
60	Derek Jeter B		4.00	1.80
61	Charles Johnson R		.30	.14
62	Travis Fryman R		.30	.14
63	Chipper Jones B		4.00	1.80
64	Edgar Martinez R		.40	.18
65	Bobby Bonilla R		.30	.14
66	Greg Vaughn R		.15	.07
67	Bobby Higginson R		.30	.14
68	Garret Anderson R		.30	.14
69	Chuck Knoblauch B		1.25	.55
70	Jermaine Dye R		.15	.07
71	Cal Ripken B		5.00	2.20
72	Jason Giambi R		.30	.14
73	Trey Beamon R		.15	.07
74	Shawn Green R		.15	.07
75	Mark McGwire B		2.50	1.10
76	Carlos Delgado R		.30	.14
77	Jason Isringhausen R		.15	.07
78	Randy Johnson B		1.25	.55
79	Troy Percival R		.30	.14
80	Ron Gant R		.30	.14
81	Ellis Burks R		.30	.14
82	Mike Mussina B		1.25	.55
83	Todd Hundley R		.30	.14
84	Jim Edmonds R		.40	.18
85	Charles Nagy R		.30	.14
86	Dante Bichette B		.60	.25
87	Mariano Rivera R		.30	.14
88	Matt Williams R		.75	.35
89	Rondell White R		.30	.14
90	Steve Finley R		.30	.14
91	Alex Fernandez R		.30	.14
92	Barry Larkin R		.40	.18
93	Tom Goodwin R		.15	.07
94	Will Clark R		.40	.18
95	Michael Tucker R		.30	.14
96	Derek Bell R		.30	.14
97	Larry Walker R		.60	.25
98	Alan Benes R		.30	.14
99	Tom Glavine R		.30	.14
100	Darin Erstad B		2.00	.90
101	Andruw Jones B		3.00	1.35
102	Scott Rolen		1.50	.70
103	Todd Walker B		.60	.25
104	Dmitri Young R		.15	.07
105	Vladimir Guerrero B		2.50	1.10
106	Nomar Garciaparra		2.00	.90
107	Danny Patterson R		.15	.07
108	Karim Garcia R		.30	.14
109	Todd Greene R		.30	.14
110	Ruben Rivera R		.30	.14
111	Raul Casanova R		.15	.07
112	Mike Cameron R		.40	.18
113	Bartolo Colon R		.30	.14
114	Rod Myers R		.30	.14
115	Todd Dunn R		.15	.07
116	Torii Hunter R		.15	.07
117	Jason Dickson R		.30	.14
118	Eugene Kingsale R		.15	.07
119	Rafael Medina R		.30	.14
120	Raul Ibanez R		.15	.07
121	Bobby Henley R		.15	.07
122	Scott Spiezio R		.30	.14
123	Bobby Smith R		.15	.07
124	J.J. Johnson R		.15	.07
125	Bubba Trammell R RC		.60	.25
126	Jeff Abbott R		.15	.07
127	Neifi Perez R		.30	.14
128	Derrek Lee R		.40	.18
129	Kevin Brown C R		.15	.07
130	Mendy Lopez R		.15	.07
131	Kevin Orie R		.30	.14
132	Ryan Jones R		.15	.07
133	Juan Encarnacion R		.60	.25
134	Jose Guillen B		1.50	.70
135	Greg Norton R		.15	.07
136	Richie Sexson R		.30	.14
137	Jay Payton R		.15	.07
138	Bob Abreu R		.30	.14
139	Ron Belliard R		.15	.07
140	Wilton Guerrero R		.30	.14
141	Alex Rodriguez SS B		2.00	.90
142	Juan Gonzalez SS B		1.50	.70
143	Ken Caminiti SS B		.30	.14
144	Frank Thomas SS B		2.50	1.10
145	Ken Griffey Jr. SS B		3.00	1.35
146	John Smoltz SS B		.30	.14
147	Mike Piazza SS B		2.00	.90
148	Derek Jeter SS B		2.00	.90
149	Frank Thomas CL R		1.25	.55
150	Ken Griffey Jr. CL R		1.50	.70
151	Jose Cruz Jr.		12.00	5.50
152	Moises Alou		.60	.25
153	Hideki Irabu		1.50	.70
154	Glendon Rusch		.30	.14
155	Ron Coomer		.30	.14
156	Jeremi Gonzalez		1.00	.45
157	Fernando Tatis		3.00	1.35
158	John Olerud		.75	.35
159	Rickey Henderson		.75	.35
160	Shannon Stewart		.60	.25
161	Kevin Polcovich		.30	.14
162	Jose Rosado		.60	.25
163	Ray Lankford		.60	.25
164	David Justice		1.25	.55
165	Mark Kotsay		.75	.35
166	Deivi Cruz		1.00	.45
167	Billy Wagner		.60	.25
168	Jacob Cruz		.60	.25
169	Matt Morris		.60	.25
170	Brian Banks		.30	.14
171	Brett Tomko		.60	.25
172	Todd Helton		2.00	.90
173	Eric Young		.30	.14
174	Bernie Williams		1.25	.55
175	Jeff Fassero		.30	.14
176	Ryan McGuire		.30	.14
177	Darryl Kile		.30	.14
178	Kelvim Escobar		.50	.23
179	Dave Nilsson		.30	.14
180	Geronimo Berroa		.30	.14
181	Livan Hernandez		.75	.35
182	Tony Womack		1.00	.45
183	Deion Sanders		.60	.25
184	Jeff Kent		.30	.14
185	Brian Hunter		.30	.14
186	Jose Malave		.30	.14
187	Steve Woodard		.50	.23
188	Brad Radke		.60	.25
189	Todd Dunwoody		.75	.35
190	Joey Hamilton		.60	.25
191	Denny Neagle		.30	.14
192	Bobby Jones		.30	.14
193	Tony Clark		1.25	.55
194	Jaret Wright		8.00	3.60
195	Matt Stairs		.30	.14
196	Francisco Cordova		.30	.14
197	Justin Thompson		.60	.25
198	Pokey Reese		.30	.14
199	Garrett Stephenson		.30	.14
200	Carl Everett		.30	.14
P3	Tony Gwynn PROMO		2.00	.90
P23	Greg Maddux PROMO		2.50	1.10
P47	Ken Griffey Jr. PROMO		3.00	1.35

1997 Select Rookie Autographs

This four-card set features color player photos of four potential Rookie of the Year candidates with their autographs. Each player signed 3000 cards except for Andruw Jones who only signed 2500.

	MINT	NRMT
COMPLETE SET (4)	120.00	55.00
COMMON CARD	12.00	5.50
3000 OF EACH EXCEPT A.JONES (2500)		
1 Jose Guillen	30.00	13.50
2 Wilton Guerrero	12.00	5.50
3 Andruw Jones	60.00	27.00
4 Todd Walker	20.00	9.00

1997 Select Rookie Revolution

Randomly inserted in packs at a rate of one in 56, this 20-card set features color photos of top rookies on a micro-etched, full mylar card. Each card is sequentially numbered.

	MINT	NRMT
COMPLETE SET (20)	150.00	70.00
COMMON CARD (1-20)	4.00	1.80

		MINT	NRMT
	UNLISTED STARS	8.00	3.60
	STATED ODDS 1:56		
☐	1 Andruw Jones	25.00	11.00
☐	2 Derek Jeter	30.00	13.50
☐	3 Todd Hollandsworth	4.00	1.80
☐	4 Edgar Renteria	5.00	2.20
☐	5 Jason Kendall	5.00	2.20
☐	6 Rey Ordonez	4.00	1.80
☐	7 F.P. Santangelo	4.00	1.80
☐	8 Jermaine Dye	4.00	1.80
☐	9 Alex Ochoa	4.00	1.80
☐	10 Vladimir Guerrero	20.00	9.00
☐	11 Dmitri Young	4.00	1.80
☐	12 Todd Walker	5.00	2.20
☐	13 Scott Rolen	25.00	11.00
☐	14 Nomar Garciaparra	30.00	13.50
☐	15 Ruben Rivera	5.00	2.20
☐	16 Darin Erstad	15.00	6.75
☐	17 Todd Greene	5.00	2.20
☐	18 Mariano Rivera	5.00	2.20
☐	19 Trey Beamon	4.00	1.80
☐	20 Karim Garcia	5.00	2.20

1997 Select Tools of the Trade

Randomly inserted in packs at a rate of one in nine, this 25-card set matches color photos of 25 young players with 25 veteran superstars printed back-to-back on a double-fronted full silver foil card stock with gold foil stamping.

		MINT	NRMT
	COMPLETE SET (25)	150.00	70.00
	COMMON CARD (1-25)	1.50	.70
	UNLISTED STARS	3.00	1.35
	STATED ODDS 1:9		
	COMP.MIRROR BLUE (25)	1200.00	550.00
	COMMON MIR.BLUE (1-25)	15.00	6.75
	*MIRROR BLUE: 5X TO 10X HI COLUMN		
	MIRROR BLUE STATED ODDS 1:240		
☐	1 Ken Griffey Jr.	20.00	9.00
	Andruw Jones		
☐	2 Greg Maddux	10.00	4.50
	Andy Pettitte		
☐	3 Cal Ripken	15.00	6.75
	Chipper Jones		
☐	4 Mike Piazza	10.00	4.50
	Jason Kendall		
☐	5 Albert Belle	4.00	1.80
	Karim Garcia		
☐	6 Mo Vaughn	4.00	1.80
	Dmitri Young		
☐	7 Juan Gonzalez	10.00	4.50
	Vladimir Guerrero		
☐	8 Tony Gwynn	8.00	3.60
	Jermaine Dye		
☐	9 Barry Bonds	4.00	1.80
	Alex Ochoa		
☐	10 Jeff Bagwell	6.00	2.70
	Jason Giambi		

☐	11 Kenny Lofton	4.00	1.80
	Darin Erstad		
☐	12 Gary Sheffield	3.00	1.35
	Manny Ramirez		
☐	13 Tim Salmon	3.00	1.35
	Todd Hollandsworth		
☐	14 Sammy Sosa	3.00	1.35
	Ruben Rivera		
☐	15 Paul Molitor	3.00	1.35
	George Arias		
☐	16 Jim Thome	3.00	1.35
	Todd Walker		
☐	17 Wade Boggs	6.00	2.70
	Scott Rolen		
☐	18 Ryne Sandberg	4.00	1.80
	Chuck Knoblauch		
☐	19 Mark McGwire	15.00	6.75
	Frank Thomas		
☐	20 Ivan Rodriguez	4.00	1.80
	Charles Johnson		
☐	21 Brian Jordan	1.50	.70
	Rusty Greer		
☐	22 Roger Clemens	6.00	2.70
	Troy Percival		
☐	23 John Smoltz	3.00	1.35
	Mike Mussina		
☐	24 Alex Rodriguez	10.00	4.50
	Rey Ordonez		
☐	25 Derek Jeter	12.00	5.50
	Nomar Garciaparra.		

1995 Select Certified

This 135-card standard-size set was issued through hobby outlets only. This product was issued in six-card packs. The cards are made with 24-point stock and are all metallic and double laminated. The fronts feature a player photo, his name in the lower right and the "Select '95 Certified" logo in the upper right. The horizontal backs feature a team by team seasonal summary and a player photo. The cards are numbered in the upper right corner. Rookie Cards in this set include Bobby Higginson and Hideo Nomo. Card #18 was never printed; Cal Ripken is featured on a special card numbered 2131, which is included in the complete set of 135.

		MINT	NRMT
	COMPLETE SET (135)	40.00	18.00
	COMMON CARD (1-135)	.25	.11
	MINOR STARS	.50	.23
	UNLISTED STARS	1.00	.45
	SET INCLUDES CARD 2131		
	CARD NUMBER 18 DOES NOT EXIST		
	COMP.MIRROR SET (135)	900.00	400.00
	COMMON MIRROR (1-135)	2.00	.90

		MINT	NRMT
	*MIRROR STARS: 6X TO 15X HI COLUMN		
	*MIRROR YOUNG STARS: 5X TO 12X HI		
	MIRROR STATED ODDS 1:5		
	COMP. CHECKLIST SET (7)	4.00	1.80
	CL: RANDOM INSERTS IN PACKS		
☐	1 Barry Bonds	1.25	.55
☐	2 Reggie Sanders	.25	.11
☐	3 Terry Steinbach	.25	.11
☐	4 Eduardo Perez	.25	.11
☐	5 Frank Thomas	4.00	1.80
☐	6 Wil Cordero	.25	.11
☐	7 John Olerud	.50	.23
☐	8 Deion Sanders	.50	.23
☐	9 Mike Mussina	1.00	.45
☐	10 Mo Vaughn	1.25	.55
☐	11 Will Clark	.75	.35
☐	12 Chili Davis	.50	.23
☐	13 Jimmy Key	.50	.23
☐	14 Eddie Murray	1.00	.45
☐	15 Bernard Gilkey	.25	.11
☐	16 David Cone	.50	.23
☐	17 Tim Salmon	1.00	.45
☐	19 Steve Ontiveros	.25	.11
☐	20 Andres Galarraga	1.00	.45
☐	21 Don Mattingly	1.50	.70
☐	22 Kevin Appier	.50	.23
☐	23 Paul Molitor	1.00	.45
☐	24 Edgar Martinez	.75	.35
☐	25 Andy Benes	.50	.23
☐	26 Rafael Palmeiro	.75	.35
☐	27 Barry Larkin	.75	.35
☐	28 Gary Sheffield	1.00	.45
☐	29 Wally Joyner	.50	.23
☐	30 Wade Boggs	1.00	.45
☐	31 Rico Brogna	.25	.11
☐	32 Eddie Murray 3000th Hit	.50	.23
☐	33 Kirby Puckett	2.00	.90
☐	34 Bobby Bonilla	.50	.23
☐	35 Hal Morris	.25	.11
☐	36 Moises Alou	.50	.23
☐	37 Javier Lopez	.50	.23
☐	38 Chuck Knoblauch	1.00	.45
☐	39 Mike Piazza	3.00	1.35
☐	40 Travis Fryman	.50	.23
☐	41 Rickey Henderson	.75	.35
☐	42 Jim Thome	1.00	.45
☐	43 Carlos Baerga	.25	.11
☐	44 Dean Palmer	.25	.11
☐	45 Kirk Gibson	.50	.23
☐	46 Bret Saberhagen	.25	.11
☐	47 Cecil Fielder	.50	.23
☐	48 Manny Ramirez	1.00	.45
☐	49 Derek Bell	.25	.11
☐	50 Mark McGwire	2.00	.90
☐	51 Jim Edmonds	.75	.35
☐	52 Robin Ventura	.50	.23
☐	53 Ryan Klesko	.75	.35
☐	54 Jeff Bagwell	2.00	.90
☐	55 Ozzie Smith	1.25	.55
☐	56 Albert Belle	1.25	.55
☐	57 Darren Daulton	.50	.23
☐	58 Jeff Conine	.50	.23
☐	59 Greg Maddux	3.00	1.35
☐	60 Lenny Dykstra	.50	.23
☐	61 Randy Johnson	1.00	.45
☐	62 Fred McGriff	.75	.35
☐	63 Ray Lankford	.50	.23
☐	64 David Justice	1.00	.45
☐	65 Paul O'Neill	.50	.23
☐	66 Tony Gwynn	2.50	1.10
☐	67 Matt Williams	.75	.35
☐	68 Dante Bichette	.50	.23
☐	69 Craig Biggio	.75	.35
☐	70 Ken Griffey Jr.	5.00	2.20
☐	71 J.T. Snow	.50	.23
☐	72 Cal Ripken	4.00	1.80
☐	73 Jay Bell	.50	.23
☐	74 Joe Carter	.50	.23
☐	75 Roberto Alomar	1.00	.45
☐	76 Benji Gil	.25	.11
☐	77 Ivan Rodriguez	1.25	.55
☐	78 Raul Mondesi	.75	.35
☐	79 Cliff Floyd	.25	.11
☐	80 Eric Karros	1.00	.45
	Mike Piazza		

Raul Mondesi

		MINT	NRMT
☐ 81	Royce Clayton	.25	.11
☐ 82	Billy Ashley	.25	.11
☐ 83	Joey Hamilton	.50	.23
☐ 84	Sammy Sosa	1.00	.45
☐ 85	Jason Bere	.25	.11
☐ 86	Dennis Martinez	.50	.23
☐ 87	Greg Vaughn	.25	.11
☐ 88	Roger Clemens	2.00	.90
☐ 89	Larry Walker	1.00	.45
☐ 90	Mark Grace	.75	.35
☐ 91	Kenny Lofton	1.25	.55
☐ 92	Carlos Perez	.50	.23
☐ 93	Roger Cedeno	.50	.23
☐ 94	Scott Ruffcorn	.25	.11
☐ 95	Jim Pittsley	.50	.23
☐ 96	Andy Pettitte	1.50	.70
☐ 97	James Baldwin	.25	.11
☐ 98	Hideo Nomo	5.00	2.20
☐ 99	Ismael Valdes	.75	.35
☐ 100	Armando Benitez	.25	.11
☐ 101	Jose Malave	.25	.11
☐ 102	Bob Higginson	1.50	.70
☐ 103	LaTroy Hawkins	.25	.11
☐ 104	Russ Davis	.25	.11
☐ 105	Shawn Green	.50	.23
☐ 106	Jose Vitiello	.25	.11
☐ 107	Chipper Jones	3.00	1.35
☐ 108	Shane Andrews	.25	.11
☐ 109	Jose Oliva	.25	.11
☐ 110	Ray Durham	.50	.23
☐ 111	Jon Nunnally	.25	.11
☐ 112	Alex Gonzalez	.25	.11
☐ 113	Vaughn Eshelman	.25	.11
☐ 114	Marty Cordova	.50	.23
☐ 115	Mark Grudzielanek	.75	.35
☐ 116	Brian L.Hunter	.75	.35
☐ 117	Charles Johnson	.50	.23
☐ 118	Alex Rodriguez	4.00	1.80
☐ 119	David Bell	.25	.11
☐ 120	Todd Hollandsworth	.50	.23
☐ 121	Joe Randa	.25	.11
☐ 122	Derek Jeter	3.00	1.35
☐ 123	Frank Rodriguez	.25	.11
☐ 124	Curtis Goodwin	.25	.11
☐ 125	Bill Pulsipher	.25	.11
☐ 126	John Mabry	.50	.23
☐ 127	Julian Tavarez	.25	.11
☐ 128	Edgardo Alfonzo	1.00	.45
☐ 129	Orlando Miller	.25	.11
☐ 130	Juan Acevedo	.25	.11
☐ 131	Jeff Cirillo	.25	.23
☐ 132	Roberto Petagine	.25	.11
☐ 133	Antonio Osuna	.25	.11
☐ 134	Michael Tucker	.50	.23
☐ 135	Garret Anderson	.75	.35
☐ 2131	Cal Ripken TRIB	5.00	2.20

1995 Select Certified Future

This ten-card set was inserted approximately one in every 19 packs. Ten leading 1995 rookie players are included in this set. These cards were produced using Pinnacle's Dufex technology. The fronts feature a player photo with his name on the bottom. The words "Certified Future" are spelled vertically on the right. The horizontal backs feature some textual information and a player photo.

		MINT	NRMT
COMPLETE SET (10)		60.00	27.00
COMMON CARD (1-10)		2.00	.90
UNLISTED STARS		5.00	2.20
STATED ODDS 1:19			
☐ 1	Chipper Jones	15.00	6.75
☐ 2	Curtis Goodwin	2.00	.90
☐ 3	Hideo Nomo	15.00	6.75
☐ 4	Shawn Green	3.00	1.35
☐ 5	Ray Durham	3.00	1.35
☐ 6	Todd Hollandsworth	3.00	1.35
☐ 7	Brian L.Hunter	4.00	1.80
☐ 8	Carlos Delgado	3.00	1.35
☐ 9	Michael Tucker UER	3.00	1.35
	(front photo is Jon Nunnally)		
☐ 10	Alex Rodriguez	20.00	9.00

1995 Select Certified Gold Team

This 12-card was inserted approximately one in every 41 packs. This set features some of the leading players in baseball. These cards feature double-sided all-gold-foil Dufex technology.

		MINT	NRMT
COMPLETE SET (12)		300.00	135.00
COMMON CARD (1-12)		8.00	3.60
STATED ODDS 1:41			
☐ 1	Ken Griffey Jr.	60.00	27.00
☐ 2	Frank Thomas	50.00	22.00
☐ 3	Cal Ripken	50.00	22.00
☐ 4	Jeff Bagwell	25.00	11.00
☐ 5	Mike Piazza	40.00	18.00
☐ 6	Barry Bonds	15.00	6.75
☐ 7	Matt Williams	8.00	3.60
☐ 8	Don Mattingly	20.00	9.00
☐ 9	Will Clark	8.00	3.60
☐ 10	Tony Gwynn	30.00	13.50
☐ 11	Kirby Puckett	25.00	11.00
☐ 12	Jose Canseco	8.00	3.60

1995 Select Certified Potential Unlimited 1975

Cards from this 20-card set were randomly inserted into one

in every 29 packs. The cards feature Pinnacle's all-foil Dufex printing technology. The fronts have a player photo in the middle. The words "Potential Unlimited" appear in the upper left and the player's name appears in the bottom left. The horizontal back has a player photo and some text set against a background of a baseball. Only 1,975 sets were made and each card is numbered 1 of 1,975 at the bottom right.

		MINT	NRMT
COMPLETE SET (20)		250.00	110.00
COMMON CARD (1-20)		5.00	2.20
SEMISTARS		10.00	4.50
STATED ODDS 1:32			
STATED PRINT RUN 1975 SETS			
COMP.903 SET (20)		300.00	135.00
*903 CARDS: .5X TO 1.2X HI COLUMN			
ONE 903 CARD PER SEALED BOX			
STATED PRINT RUN 903 SETS			
☐ 1	Cliff Floyd	5.00	2.20
☐ 2	Manny Ramirez	15.00	6.75
☐ 3	Raul Mondesi	10.00	4.50
☐ 4	Scott Ruffcorn	5.00	2.20
☐ 5	Billy Ashley	5.00	2.20
☐ 6	Alex Gonzalez	5.00	2.20
☐ 7	Midre Cummings	5.00	2.20
☐ 8	Charles Johnson	8.00	3.60
☐ 9	Garret Anderson	10.00	4.50
☐ 10	Hideo Nomo	50.00	22.00
☐ 11	Chipper Jones	50.00	22.00
☐ 12	Curtis Goodwin	5.00	2.20
☐ 13	Frank Rodriguez	5.00	2.20
☐ 14	Shawn Green	8.00	3.60
☐ 15	Ray Durham	8.00	3.60
☐ 16	Todd Hollandsworth	8.00	3.60
☐ 17	Brian L.Hunter	10.00	4.50
☐ 18	Carlos Delgado	8.00	3.60
☐ 19	Michael Tucker	8.00	3.60
☐ 20	Alex Rodriguez	60.00	27.00

1996 Select Certified

The 1996 Select Certified hobby only set was issued in one series totalling 144 cards. Each six-card pack carried a suggested retail price of $4.99. Printed on special 24-point silver mirror mylar card stock, the fronts feature a color player photo on a gray and black background. The backs carry another color player photo with information about his playing abilities.

	MINT	NRMT
COMPLETE SET (144)	40.00	18.00
COMMON CARD (1-144)	.25	.11

MINOR STARS	.50	.23
UNLISTED STARS	1.00	.45
COMP.AP SET (144)	2000.00	900.00
COMMON ART.PRF. (1-144)	3.00	1.35
*AP STARS: 8X TO 20X HI COLUMN		
*AP YOUNG STARS: 6X TO 15X HI		
*AP ROOKIES: 3X TO 8X HI		
AP STATED ODDS 1:18		
COMP.BLUE SET (144)	4000.00	1800.00
COMMON BLUE (1-144)	6.00	2.70
*BLUE STARS: 20X TO 40X HI COLUMN		
*BLUE YOUNG STARS: 15X TO 30X HI		
*BLUE ROOKIES: 7.5X TO 15X HI		
BLUE STATED ODDS 1:50		
COMP.RED SET (144)	600.00	275.00
COMMON RED (1-144)	1.00	.45
*RED STARS: 3X TO 8X HI COLUMN		
*RED YOUNG STARS: 2.5X TO 6X HI		
*RED ROOKIES: 1.25X TO 3X HI		
RED STATED ODDS 1:5		

☐ 1 Frank Thomas	4.00	1.80
☐ 2 Tino Martinez	1.00	.45
☐ 3 Gary Sheffield	1.00	.45
☐ 4 Kenny Lofton	1.25	.55
☐ 5 Joe Carter	.50	.23
☐ 6 Alex Rodriguez	3.00	1.35
☐ 7 Chipper Jones	3.00	1.35
☐ 8 Roger Clemens	2.00	.90
☐ 9 Jay Bell	.50	.23
☐ 10 Eddie Murray	1.00	.45
☐ 11 Will Clark	.75	.35
☐ 12 Mike Mussina	1.00	.45
☐ 13 Hideo Nomo	2.50	1.10
☐ 14 Andres Galarraga	1.00	.45
☐ 15 Marc Newfield	.25	.11
☐ 16 Jason Isringhausen	.25	.11
☐ 17 Randy Johnson	1.00	.45
☐ 18 Chuck Knoblauch	1.00	.45
☐ 19 J.T. Snow	.50	.23
☐ 20 Mark McGwire	2.00	.90
☐ 21 Tony Gwynn	2.50	1.10
☐ 22 Albert Belle	1.25	.55
☐ 23 Gregg Jefferies	.25	.11
☐ 24 Reggie Sanders	.25	.11
☐ 25 Bernie Williams	1.00	.45
☐ 26 Ray Lankford	.50	.23
☐ 27 Johnny Damon	.50	.23
☐ 28 Ryne Sandberg	1.25	.55
☐ 29 Rondell White	.50	.23
☐ 30 Mike Piazza	3.00	1.35
☐ 31 Barry Bonds	1.25	.55
☐ 32 Greg Maddux	3.00	1.35
☐ 33 Craig Biggio	.75	.35
☐ 34 John Valentin	.25	.11
☐ 35 Ivan Rodriguez	1.25	.55
☐ 36 Rico Brogna	.25	.11
☐ 37 Tim Salmon	1.00	.45
☐ 38 Sterling Hitchcock	.25	.11
☐ 39 Charles Johnson	.50	.23
☐ 40 Travis Fryman	.50	.23
☐ 41 Barry Larkin	.75	.35
☐ 42 Tom Glavine	.50	.23
☐ 43 Marty Cordova	.50	.23
☐ 44 Shawn Green	.25	.11
☐ 45 Ben McDonald	.25	.11
☐ 46 Robin Ventura	.50	.23
☐ 47 Ken Griffey Jr.	5.00	2.20

☐ 48 Orlando Merced	.25	.11
☐ 49 Paul O'Neill	.50	.23
☐ 50 Ozzie Smith	1.25	.55
☐ 51 Manny Ramirez	1.00	.45
☐ 52 Ismael Valdes	.50	.23
☐ 53 Cal Ripken	4.00	1.80
☐ 54 Jeff Bagwell	2.00	.90
☐ 55 Greg Vaughn	.25	.11
☐ 56 Juan Gonzalez	2.50	1.10
☐ 57 Raul Mondesi	.75	.35
☐ 58 Carlos Baerga	.25	.11
☐ 59 Sammy Sosa	1.00	.45
☐ 60 Mike Kelly	.25	.11
☐ 61 Edgar Martinez	.75	.35
☐ 62 Kirby Puckett	2.00	.90
☐ 63 Cecil Fielder	.50	.23
☐ 64 David Cone	.50	.23
☐ 65 Moises Alou	.50	.23
☐ 66 Fred McGriff	.75	.35
☐ 67 Mo Vaughn	1.25	.55
☐ 68 Edgardo Alfonzo	.75	.35
☐ 69 Jim Thome	1.00	.45
☐ 70 Rickey Henderson	.75	.35
☐ 71 Dante Bichette	.50	.23
☐ 72 Lenny Dykstra	.50	.23
☐ 73 Benji Gil	.25	.11
☐ 74 Wade Boggs	1.00	.45
☐ 75 Jim Edmonds	.75	.35
☐ 76 Michael Tucker	.50	.23
☐ 77 Carlos Delgado	.50	.23
☐ 78 Butch Huskey	.50	.23
☐ 79 Billy Ashley	.25	.11
☐ 80 Dean Palmer	.25	.11
☐ 81 Paul Molitor	1.00	.45
☐ 82 Ryan Klesko	.75	.35
☐ 83 Brian L.Hunter	.50	.23
☐ 84 Jay Buhner	.75	.35
☐ 85 Larry Walker	1.00	.45
☐ 86 Mike Bordick	.25	.11
☐ 87 Matt Williams	.75	.35
☐ 88 Jack McDowell	.25	.11
☐ 89 Hal Morris	.25	.11
☐ 90 Brian Jordan	.50	.23
☐ 91 Andy Pettitte	1.25	.55
☐ 92 Melvin Nieves	.25	.11
☐ 93 Pedro Martinez	1.00	.45
☐ 94 Mark Grace	.75	.35
☐ 95 Garret Anderson	.50	.23
☐ 96 Andre Dawson	.75	.35
☐ 97 Ray Durham	.25	.11
☐ 98 Jose Canseco	.75	.35
☐ 99 Roberto Alomar	1.00	.45
☐ 100 Derek Jeter	3.00	1.35
☐ 101 Alan Benes	.50	.23
☐ 102 Karim Garcia	.75	.35
☐ 103 Robin Jennings	.25	.11
☐ 104 Bob Abreu	.75	.35
☐ 105 Sal Fasano UER	.25	.11
(name on front is Livan Hernandez)		
☐ 106 Steve Gibralter	.25	.11
☐ 107 Jermaine Dye	.50	.23
☐ 108 Jason Kendall	.75	.35
☐ 109 Mike Grace	.25	.11
☐ 110 Jason Schmidt	.50	.23
☐ 111 Paul Wilson	.50	.23
☐ 112 Rey Ordonez	.50	.23
☐ 113 Wilton Guerrero	1.00	.45
☐ 114 Brooks Kieschnick	.50	.23
☐ 115 George Arias	.25	.11
☐ 116 Osvaldo Fernandez	.50	.23
☐ 117 Todd Hollandsworth	.50	.23
☐ 118 John Wasdin	.25	.11
☐ 119 Eric Owens	.25	.11
☐ 120 Chan Ho Park	1.00	.45
☐ 121 Mark Loretta	.25	.11
☐ 122 Richard Hidalgo	1.00	.45
☐ 123 Jeff Suppan	.50	.23
☐ 124 Jim Pittsley	.50	.23
☐ 125 LaTroy Hawkins	.25	.11
☐ 126 Chris Snopek	.25	.11
☐ 127 Justin Thompson	.25	.11
☐ 128 Jay Powell	.25	.11
☐ 129 Alex Ochoa	.25	.11
☐ 130 Felipe Crespo	.25	.11
☐ 131 Matt Lawton	.75	.35
☐ 132 Jimmy Haynes	.25	.11

☐ 133 Terrell Wade	.25	.11
☐ 134 Ruben Rivera	.50	.23
☐ 135 Frank Thomas PP	2.00	.90
☐ 136 Ken Griffey Jr. PP	2.50	1.10
☐ 137 Greg Maddux PP	1.50	.70
☐ 138 Mike Piazza PP	1.50	.70
☐ 139 Cal Ripken PP	2.00	.90
☐ 140 Albert Belle PP	.75	.35
☐ 141 Mo Vaughn PP	.75	.35
☐ 142 Chipper Jones PP	1.50	.70
☐ 143 Hideo Nomo PP	1.25	.55
☐ 144 Ryan Klesko PP	.50	.23

1996 Select Certified Mirror Blue

Randomly inserted in packs at a rate of one in 200, this 144-card set is parallel to the base set with only 45 sets being produced. This set is a blue holographic foil rendition of the base set. No set price has been provided due to scarcity.

	MINT	NRMT
COMMON CARD (1-144)	30.00	13.50
MINOR STARS	50.00	22.00
SEMISTARS	80.00	36.00
UNLISTED STARS	120.00	55.00
*STARS: 60X TO 120X HI COLUMN		
*YOUNG STARS: 50X TO 100X HI		
*ROOKIES: 30X TO 60X HI		
STATED ODDS 1:200		
STATED PRINT RUN 45 SETS		

☐ 1 Frank Thomas	600.00	275.00
☐ 4 Kenny Lofton	150.00	70.00
☐ 6 Alex Rodriguez	500.00	220.00
☐ 7 Chipper Jones	300.00	135.00
☐ 8 Roger Clemens	300.00	135.00
☐ 13 Hideo Nomo	500.00	220.00
☐ 20 Mark McGwire	250.00	110.00
☐ 21 Tony Gwynn	300.00	135.00
☐ 22 Albert Belle	150.00	70.00
☐ 28 Ryne Sandberg	150.00	70.00
☐ 30 Mike Piazza	400.00	180.00
☐ 31 Barry Bonds	200.00	90.00
☐ 32 Greg Maddux	400.00	180.00
☐ 35 Ivan Rodriguez	150.00	70.00
☐ 47 Ken Griffey Jr.	800.00	350.00
☐ 50 Ozzie Smith	150.00	70.00
☐ 53 Cal Ripken	500.00	220.00
☐ 54 Jeff Bagwell	250.00	110.00
☐ 56 Juan Gonzalez	300.00	135.00
☐ 62 Kirby Puckett	250.00	110.00
☐ 67 Mo Vaughn	150.00	70.00
☐ 100 Derek Jeter	300.00	135.00
☐ 135 Frank Thomas PP	250.00	110.00
☐ 136 Ken Griffey Jr. PP	300.00	135.00
☐ 137 Greg Maddux PP	150.00	70.00
☐ 138 Mike Piazza PP	150.00	70.00
☐ 139 Cal Ripken PP	200.00	90.00
☐ 143 Hideo Nomo PP	200.00	90.00

1996 Select Certified Mirror Gold

Randomly inserted in packs at a rate of one in 300, this 144-card set is parallel to the base set with only 30 sets being produced. This set is a gold holographic foil rendition of the base set. No sale price has been provided due to scarcity.

	MINT	NRMT
COMMON CARD (1-144) ..	100.00	45.00
MINOR STARS	200.00	90.00
*STARS: 300X TO 500X HI COLUMN		
*YOUNG STARS: 250X TO 400X HI		
*ROOKIES: 125X TO 200X BASIC CARDS		
STATED ODDS 1:300		
STATED PRINT RUN 30 SETS ..		

		MINT	NRMT
☐ 1	Frank Thomas	2500.00	1100.00
☐ 2	Tino Martinez	500.00	220.00
☐ 3	Gary Sheffield	350.00	160.00
☐ 4	Kenny Lofton	600.00	275.00
☐ 6	Alex Rodriguez	2000.00	900.00
☐ 7	Chipper Jones	1200.00	550.00
☐ 8	Roger Clemens	1500.00	700.00
☐ 10	Eddie Murray	800.00	350.00
☐ 11	Will Clark	350.00	160.00
☐ 12	Mike Mussina	500.00	220.00
☐ 13	Hideo Nomo	2000.00	900.00
☐ 14	Andres Galarraga..	300.00	135.00
☐ 17	Randy Johnson	800.00	350.00
☐ 18	Chuck Knoblauch ..	400.00	180.00
☐ 20	Mark McGwire	1200.00	550.00
☐ 21	Tony Gwynn	1500.00	700.00
☐ 22	Albert Belle	1200.00	550.00
☐ 25	Bernie Williams	350.00	160.00
☐ 28	Ryne Sandberg	600.00	275.00
☐ 30	Mike Piazza	2000.00	900.00
☐ 31	Barry Bonds	900.00	400.00
☐ 32	Greg Maddux	2000.00	900.00
☐ 33	Craig Biggio	250.00	110.00
☐ 35	Ivan Rodriguez	800.00	350.00
☐ 37	Tim Salmon	400.00	180.00
☐ 39	Charles Johnson ...	250.00	110.00
☐ 41	Barry Larkin	250.00	110.00
☐ 47	Ken Griffey Jr.	4000.00	1800.00
☐ 50	Ozzie Smith	600.00	275.00
☐ 51	Manny Ramirez	500.00	220.00
☐ 53	Cal Ripken	2500.00	1100.00
☐ 54	Jeff Bagwell	1500.00	700.00
☐ 56	Juan Gonzalez	1600.00	700.00
☐ 57	Raul Mondesi	300.00	135.00
☐ 59	Sammy Sosa	350.00	160.00
☐ 61	Edgar Martinez	250.00	110.00
☐ 62	Kirby Puckett	1500.00	700.00
☐ 65	Moises Alou	250.00	110.00
☐ 66	Fred McGriff	250.00	110.00
☐ 67	Mo Vaughn	500.00	220.00
☐ 69	Jim Thome	500.00	220.00
☐ 70	Rickey Henderson ..	300.00	135.00
☐ 74	Wade Boggs	400.00	180.00
☐ 75	Jim Edmonds	300.00	135.00
☐ 81	Paul Molitor	500.00	220.00
☐ 82	Ryan Klesko	300.00	135.00
☐ 84	Jay Buhner	300.00	135.00
☐ 85	Larry Walker	600.00	275.00
☐ 87	Matt Williams	350.00	160.00
☐ 91	Andy Pettitte	600.00	275.00
☐ 93	Pedro Martinez	350.00	160.00
☐ 94	Mark Grace	250.00	110.00
☐ 98	Jose Canseco	300.00	135.00
☐ 99	Roberto Alomar.....	500.00	220.00
☐ 100	Derek Jeter	1200.00	550.00
☐ 102	Karim Garcia	250.00	110.00
☐ 120	Chan Ho Park	350.00	160.00
☐ 122	Richard Hidalgo.....	250.00	110.00
☐ 127	Justin Thompson ...	250.00	110.00
☐ 134	Ruben Rivera	250.00	110.00
☐ 135	Frank Thomas PP ..	600.00	275.00
☐ 136	Ken Griffey Jr. PP	3000.00	1350.00
☐ 137	Greg Maddux PP ..	500.00	220.00
☐ 138	Mike Piazza PP	500.00	220.00
☐ 139	Cal Ripken PP	600.00	275.00
☐ 140	Albert Belle PP	300.00	135.00
☐ 142	Chipper Jones PP ..	300.00	135.00
☐ 143	Hideo Nomo PP	600.00	275.00

1996 Select Certified Mirror Red

Randomly inserted in packs at a rate of one in 100, this 144-card set is parallel to the base set with only 90 sets being produced. This set is a red holographic foil rendition of the base set. No sale price has been provided due to scarcity.

	MINT	NRMT
COMMON CARD (1-144) ..	15.00	6.75
MINOR STARS	25.00	11.00
SEMISTARS	40.00	18.00
UNLISTED STARS	60.00	27.00
*STARS: 30X TO 60X HI COLUMN		
*YOUNG STARS: 25X TO 50X HI		
*ROOKIES: 15X TO 30X BASIC CARDS		
STATED ODDS 1:100		
STATED PRINT RUN 90 SETS ..		

		MINT	NRMT
☐ 1	Frank Thomas	300.00	135.00
☐ 4	Kenny Lofton	80.00	36.00
☐ 6	Alex Rodriguez	250.00	110.00
☐ 7	Chipper Jones	150.00	70.00
☐ 8	Roger Clemens	150.00	70.00
☐ 13	Hideo Nomo	250.00	110.00
☐ 20	Mark McGwire	120.00	55.00
☐ 21	Tony Gwynn	150.00	70.00
☐ 22	Albert Belle	80.00	36.00
☐ 28	Ryne Sandberg	80.00	36.00
☐ 30	Mike Piazza	200.00	90.00
☐ 31	Barry Bonds	100.00	45.00
☐ 32	Greg Maddux	200.00	90.00
☐ 35	Ivan Rodriguez	80.00	36.00
☐ 47	Ken Griffey Jr.	350.00	160.00
☐ 50	Ozzie Smith	80.00	36.00
☐ 53	Cal Ripken	250.00	110.00
☐ 54	Jeff Bagwell	120.00	55.00
☐ 56	Juan Gonzalez	150.00	70.00
☐ 62	Kirby Puckett	120.00	55.00
☐ 67	Mo Vaughn	80.00	36.00
☐ 100	Derek Jeter	150.00	70.00
☐ 135	Frank Thomas PP ..	120.00	55.00
☐ 136	Ken Griffey Jr. PP	150.00	70.00
☐ 137	Greg Maddux PP ..	80.00	36.00
☐ 138	Mike Piazza PP	80.00	36.00
☐ 139	Cal Ripken PP	100.00	45.00
☐ 143	Hideo Nomo PP	100.00	45.00

1996 Select Certified Interleague Preview

Randomly inserted in packs at a rate of one in 42, this 25-card set gets ready for the start of interleague play in the 1997 season. Printed on Silver Prime Frost foil stock with gold lettering, the fronts feature color player cutouts of two opposing players. The backs carry another color cutout of the two players with information as to why they are a great matchup.

	MINT	NRMT
COMPLETE SET (25)	300.00	135.00
COMMON CARD (1-25)	6.00	2.70
STATED ODDS 1:42		

		MINT	NRMT
☐ 1	Ken Griffey Jr. .... Hideo Nomo	50.00	22.00
☐ 2	Greg Maddux .... Mo Vaughn	25.00	11.00
☐ 3	Frank Thomas .... Sammy Sosa	30.00	13.50
☐ 4	Mike Piazza .... Jim Edmonds	25.00	11.00
☐ 5	Ryan Klesko .... Roger Clemens	15.00	6.75
☐ 6	Derek Jeter .... Rey Ordonez	20.00	9.00
☐ 7	Johnny Damon .... Ray Lankford	6.00	2.70
☐ 8	Manny Ramirez .... Reggie Sanders	10.00	4.50
☐ 9	Barry Bonds .... Jay Buhner	10.00	4.50
☐ 10	Jason Isringhausen.... Wade Boggs	6.00	2.70
☐ 11	David Cone .... Chipper Jones	25.00	11.00
☐ 12	Jeff Bagwell .... Will Clark	15.00	6.75
☐ 13	Tony Gwynn .... Randy Johnson	20.00	9.00
☐ 14	Cal Ripken .... Tom Glavine	30.00	13.50
☐ 15	Kirby Puckett .... Andy Benes	15.00	6.75
☐ 16	Gary Sheffield .... Mike Mussina	10.00	4.50
☐ 17	Raul Mondesi .... Tim Salmon	10.00	4.50
☐ 18	Rondell White .... Carlos Delgado	6.00	2.70
☐ 19	Cecil Fielder .... Ryne Sandberg	10.00	4.50
☐ 20	Kenny Lofton .... Brian L.Hunter	10.00	4.50
☐ 21	Paul Wilson .... Paul O'Neill	6.00	2.70

		MINT	NRMT
□ 22	Ismael Valdes	6.00	2.70
	Edgar Martinez		
□ 23	Matt Williams	15.00	6.75
	Mark McGwire		
□ 24	Albert Belle	10.00	4.50
	Barry Larkin		
□ 25	Brady Anderson	8.00	3.60
	Marquis Grissom		
□ P4	Mike Piazza	6.00	2.70
	Jim Edmonds		
	Promo		

1996 Select Certified Select Few

Randomly inserted in packs at a rate of one in 60, this 18-card set honors superstar athletes with unmatched playing field talents. Utilizing the all-new Dot Matrix hologram technology, the fronts feature color action player cutouts. The backs carry player information. Several of the cards were erroneously printed without player's name on the front. These uncorrected errors are worth the same as the corrected cards.

		MINT	NRMT
COMPLETE SET (18)		250.00	110.00
COMMON CARD (1-18)		5.00	2.20
UNLISTED STARS		8.00	3.60
STATED ODDS 1:60			
□ 1	Sammy Sosa	8.00	3.60
□ 2	Derek Jeter	20.00	9.00
□ 3	Ken Griffey Jr.	40.00	18.00
□ 4	Albert Belle	10.00	4.50
□ 5	Cal Ripken	30.00	13.50
□ 6	Greg Maddux	25.00	11.00
□ 7	Frank Thomas	30.00	13.50
□ 8	Mo Vaughn	10.00	4.50
□ 9	Chipper Jones	25.00	11.00
□ 10	Mike Piazza	25.00	11.00
□ 11	Ryan Klesko	6.00	2.70
□ 12	Hideo Nomo	20.00	9.00
□ 13	Alan Benes	5.00	2.20
□ 14	Manny Ramirez	8.00	3.60
□ 15	Gary Sheffield	8.00	3.60
□ 16	Barry Bonds	10.00	4.50
□ 17	Matt Williams	6.00	2.70
□ 18	Johnny Damon	5.00	2.20

1997 SkyBox E-X2000

This 100-card set was distributed in two-card foil packs with a suggested retail price of $3.99. The fronts feature SkyView insert technology utiliz-

ing a die-cut holofoil border with an interior die-cut player image silhouetted in front of a transparent window with a variety of sky patterns. The backs display a modified mirror image of the front with player information and career statistics in a concise, easy-to-read table. An oversized Alex Rodriguez card shipped in its own holder was mailed to dealers who ordered E-X 2000 cases. They are numbered out of 3,000 and priced below. Also priced below is the redemptiokn card for a baseball signed by Rodriguez. 100 of these cards were produced and the redemption deadline was May 1, 1998.

		MINT	NRMT
COMPLETE SET (100)		100.00	45.00
COMMON CARD (1-100)		1.00	.45
SEMISTARS		1.50	.70
UNLISTED STARS		2.00	.90
COMP.CRED.SET (100)		3000.00	1350.00
COMMON CRED. (1-100)		10.00	4.50
*CRED.STARS: 10X TO 20X HI COLUMN			
*CRED.YOUNG.STARS: 7.5X TO 15X HI			
CREDENTIALS RANDOM INSERTS IN PACKS			
CRED.PRINT RUN LESS THAN 299 SETS			
A.ROD.BASEBALL EXCH: 5/1/98			
□ 1	Jim Edmonds	1.50	.70
□ 2	Darin Erstad	3.00	1.35
□ 3	Eddie Murray	2.00	.90
□ 4	Roberto Alomar	2.00	.90
□ 5	Brady Anderson	1.50	.70
□ 6	Mike Mussina	2.00	.90
□ 7	Rafael Palmeiro	1.50	.70
□ 8	Cal Ripken	8.00	3.60
□ 9	Steve Avery	1.00	.45
□ 10	Nomar Garciaparra	6.00	2.70
□ 11	Mo Vaughn	2.50	1.10
□ 12	Albert Belle	2.50	1.10
□ 13	Mike Cameron	1.50	.70
□ 14	Ray Durham	1.00	.45
□ 15	Frank Thomas	8.00	3.60
□ 16	Robin Ventura	2.00	.90
□ 17	Manny Ramirez	2.00	.90
□ 18	Jim Thome	2.00	.90
□ 19	Matt Williams	1.50	.70
□ 20	Tony Clark	2.00	.90
□ 21	Travis Fryman	1.00	.45
□ 22	Bob Higginson	1.00	.45
□ 23	Kevin Appier	1.00	.45
□ 24	Johnny Damon	1.00	.45
□ 25	Jermaine Dye	1.00	.45
□ 26	Jeff Cirillo	1.00	.45
□ 27	Ben McDonald	1.00	.45
□ 28	Chuck Knoblauch	2.00	.90
□ 29	Paul Molitor	2.00	.90
□ 30	Todd Walker	1.00	.45
□ 31	Wade Boggs	2.00	.90
□ 32	Cecil Fielder	1.00	.45
□ 33	Derek Jeter	6.00	2.70
□ 34	Andy Pettitte	2.00	.90
□ 35	Ruben Rivera	1.00	.45
□ 36	Bernie Williams	2.00	.90
□ 37	Jose Canseco	1.50	.70
□ 38	Mark McGwire	4.00	1.80
□ 39	Jay Buhner	1.50	.70
□ 40	Ken Griffey Jr.	10.00	4.50
□ 41	Randy Johnson	2.00	.90
□ 42	Edgar Martinez	1.50	.70
□ 43	Alex Rodriguez	6.00	2.70
□ 44	Dan Wilson	1.00	.45
□ 45	Will Clark	1.50	.70
□ 46	Juan Gonzalez	5.00	2.20
□ 47	Ivan Rodriguez	2.50	1.10
□ 48	Joe Carter	1.00	.45
□ 49	Roger Clemens	4.00	1.80
□ 50	Juan Guzman	1.00	.45
□ 51	Pat Hentgen	1.00	.45
□ 52	Tom Glavine	1.00	.45
□ 53	Andruw Jones	5.00	2.20
□ 54	Chipper Jones	6.00	2.70
□ 55	Ryan Klesko	1.50	.70
□ 56	Kenny Lofton	2.50	1.10
□ 57	Greg Maddux	6.00	2.70
□ 58	Fred McGriff	1.50	.70
□ 59	John Smoltz	1.00	.45
□ 60	Mark Wohlers	1.00	.45
□ 61	Mark Grace	1.50	.70
□ 62	Ryne Sandberg	2.50	1.10
□ 63	Sammy Sosa	2.00	.90
□ 64	Barry Larkin	1.50	.70
□ 65	Deion Sanders	2.00	.90
□ 66	Reggie Sanders	1.00	.45
□ 67	Dante Bichette	1.00	.45
□ 68	Ellis Burks	1.00	.45
□ 69	Andres Galarraga	2.00	.90
□ 70	Moises Alou	1.00	.45
□ 71	Kevin Brown	1.00	.45
□ 72	Cliff Floyd	1.00	.45
□ 73	Edgar Renteria	1.00	.45
□ 74	Gary Sheffield	2.00	.90
□ 75	Bob Abreu	1.00	.45
□ 76	Jeff Bagwell	4.00	1.80
□ 77	Craig Biggio	1.50	.70
□ 78	Todd Hollandsworth	1.00	.45
□ 79	Eric Karros	1.00	.45
□ 80	Raul Mondesi	1.50	.70
□ 81	Hideo Nomo	5.00	2.20
□ 82	Mike Piazza	6.00	2.70
□ 83	Vladimir Guerrero	4.00	1.80
□ 84	Henry Rodriguez	1.00	.45
□ 85	Todd Hundley	1.00	.45
□ 86	Alex Ochoa	1.00	.45
□ 87	Rey Ordonez	1.00	.45
□ 88	Gregg Jefferies	1.00	.45
□ 89	Scott Rolen	5.00	2.20
□ 90	Jermaine Allensworth	1.00	.45
□ 91	Jason Kendall	1.00	.45
□ 92	Ken Caminiti	1.50	.70
□ 93	Tony Gwynn	5.00	2.20
□ 94	Rickey Henderson	1.50	.70
□ 95	Barry Bonds	2.50	1.10
□ 96	J.T. Snow	1.00	.45
□ 97	Dennis Eckersley	1.00	.45
□ 98	Ron Gant	1.00	.45
□ 99	Brian Jordan	1.00	.45
□ 100	Ray Lankford	1.00	.45
□ 101	Checklist	1.00	.45
□ 102	Checklist	1.00	.45
□ P43	Alex Rodriguez	3.00	1.35
	Three card promo strip		
□ S43	Alex Rodriguez	20.00	9.00
	Mailed to Dealers who ordered Cases		
	Card is numbered out of 3,000		

1997 SkyBox E-X2000 Essential Credentials

Randomly inserted in packs at the rate of one in 200, this 100-card set is parallel to the base set with an etched refractive holographic foil border. Less than 99 sets were produced and are sequentially numbered.

	MINT	NRMT
COMMON CARD (1-100)	30.00	13.50
MINOR STARS	40.00	18.00
SEMISTARS	60.00	27.00
UNLISTED STARS	80.00	36.00
RANDOM INSERTS IN PACKS		
STATED PRINT RUN LESS THAN 99 SETS		

		MINT	NRMT
☐ 2	Darin Erstad	150.00	70.00
☐ 3	Eddie Murray	100.00	45.00
☐ 4	Roberto Alomar	120.00	55.00
☐ 6	Mike Mussina	120.00	55.00
☐ 8	Cal Ripken	400.00	180.00
☐ 10	Nomar Garciaparra	300.00	135.00
☐ 11	Mo Vaughn	120.00	55.00
☐ 12	Albert Belle	150.00	70.00
☐ 15	Frank Thomas	400.00	180.00
☐ 17	Manny Ramirez	100.00	45.00
☐ 18	Jim Thome	100.00	45.00
☐ 29	Paul Molitor	100.00	45.00
☐ 33	Derek Jeter	300.00	135.00
☐ 34	Andy Pettitte	120.00	55.00
☐ 38	Mark McGwire	200.00	90.00
☐ 40	Ken Griffey Jr.	500.00	220.00
☐ 41	Randy Johnson	120.00	55.00
☐ 43	Alex Rodriguez	300.00	135.00
☐ 46	Juan Gonzalez	250.00	110.00
☐ 47	Ivan Rodriguez	150.00	70.00
☐ 49	Roger Clemens	200.00	90.00
☐ 53	Andruw Jones	250.00	110.00
☐ 54	Chipper Jones	250.00	110.00
☐ 56	Kenny Lofton	120.00	55.00
☐ 57	Greg Maddux	300.00	135.00
☐ 62	Ryne Sandberg	150.00	70.00
☐ 76	Jeff Bagwell	200.00	90.00
☐ 81	Hideo Nomo	400.00	180.00
☐ 82	Mike Piazza	300.00	135.00
☐ 83	Vladimir Guerrero	200.00	90.00
☐ 89	Scott Rolen	250.00	110.00
☐ 93	Tony Gwynn	250.00	110.00
☐ 95	Barry Bonds	150.00	70.00

1997 SkyBox E-X2000 A Cut Above

Randomly inserted in packs at the rate of one in 288, this 10-card set features color images of "power hitters" on a holographic foil, die-cut sawblade background.

	MINT	NRMT
COMPLETE SET (10)	500.00	220.00
COMMON CARD (1-10)	15.00	6.75
UNLISTED STARS	25.00	11.00
STATED ODDS 1:288		

		MINT	NRMT
☐ 1	Frank Thomas	100.00	45.00
☐ 2	Ken Griffey Jr.	120.00	55.00
☐ 3	Alex Rodriguez	80.00	36.00
☐ 4	Albert Belle	30.00	13.50

		MINT	NRMT
☐ 5	Juan Gonzalez	60.00	27.00
☐ 6	Mark McGwire	50.00	22.00
☐ 7	Mo Vaughn	30.00	13.50
☐ 8	Manny Ramirez	25.00	11.00
☐ 9	Barry Bonds	30.00	13.50
☐ 10	Fred McGriff	15.00	6.75

1997 SkyBox E-X2000 Emerald Autographs

This six-card set features autographed color player photos of some of the hottest young stars in baseball. In addition to an authentic black-ink autograph, each card is embossed with a SkyBox logo about the size of a quarter. These cards were obtained by exchanging a redemption card by mail before the May 1, 1998, deadline.

	MINT	NRMT
COMPLETE SET (6)	400.00	180.00
COMMON CARD	15.00	6.75
ONE CARD VIA MAIL PER EXCH.CARD		

		MINT	NRMT
☐ 2	Darin Erstad	80.00	36.00
☐ 30	Todd Walker	25.00	11.00
☐ 43	Alex Rodriguez	200.00	90.00
☐ 78	Todd Hollandsworth	20.00	9.00
☐ 86	Alex Ochoa	15.00	6.75
☐ 89	Scott Rolen	100.00	45.00

1997 SkyBox E-X2000 Hall or Nothing

Randomly inserted in packs at the rate of one in 20, this 20-card set features color images

of future Cooperstown Hall of Fame candidates printed on 30-pt. acrylic card stock with etched cooper foil borders and gold foil stamping.

	MINT	NRMT
COMPLETE SET (20)	300.00	135.00
COMMON CARD (1-20)	3.00	1.35
SEMISTARS	5.00	2.20
UNLISTED STARS	8.00	3.60
STATED ODDS 1:20		

		MINT	NRMT
☐ 1	Frank Thomas	30.00	13.50
☐ 2	Ken Griffey Jr.	40.00	18.00
☐ 3	Eddie Murray	8.00	3.60
☐ 4	Cal Ripken	30.00	13.50
☐ 5	Ryne Sandberg	10.00	4.50
☐ 6	Wade Boggs	8.00	3.60
☐ 7	Roger Clemens	15.00	6.75
☐ 8	Tony Gwynn	20.00	9.00
☐ 9	Alex Rodriguez	30.00	13.50
☐ 10	Mark McGwire	15.00	6.75
☐ 11	Barry Bonds	10.00	4.50
☐ 12	Greg Maddux	25.00	11.00
☐ 13	Juan Gonzalez	20.00	9.00
☐ 14	Albert Belle	12.00	5.50
☐ 15	Mike Piazza	25.00	11.00
☐ 16	Jeff Bagwell	15.00	6.75
☐ 17	Dennis Eckersley	3.00	1.35
☐ 18	Mo Vaughn	10.00	4.50
☐ 19	Roberto Alomar	8.00	3.60
☐ 20	Kenny Lofton	10.00	4.50

1997 SkyBox E-X2000 Star Date 2000

Randomly inserted in packs at the rate of one in nine, this 15-card set features color images of young star players printed on holographic foil with swirls of spot glitter coating.

	MINT	NRMT
COMPLETE SET (15)	60.00	27.00
COMMON CARD (1-15)	.75	.35
STATED ODDS 1:9		

		MINT	NRMT
☐ 1	Alex Rodriguez	10.00	4.50
☐ 2	Andruw Jones	8.00	3.60
☐ 3	Andy Pettitte	3.00	1.35
☐ 4	Brooks Kieschnick	.75	.35
☐ 5	Chipper Jones	10.00	4.50
☐ 6	Darin Erstad	5.00	2.20
☐ 7	Derek Jeter	10.00	4.50
☐ 8	Jason Kendall	1.50	.70
☐ 9	Jermaine Dye	.75	.35
☐ 10	Neifi Perez	1.50	.70
☐ 11	Scott Rolen	8.00	3.60
☐ 12	Todd Hollandsworth	.75	.35
☐ 13	Todd Walker	1.50	.70
☐ 14	Tony Clark	3.00	1.35
☐ 15	Vladimir Guerrero	6.00	2.70

1993 SP

This 290-card standard-size set features fronts with action color player photos. The player's name and position appear within a team-colored stripe at the bottom edge that shades from dark to light, left to right. A team color-checkered stripe is in the upper left and the team name in a gold-lettered arc appears at the top with a gold underline that extends down the right side. The copper foil-stamped SP logo appears at the bottom right. The back displays an action shot of the player in the top half with a team color-checkered stripe in the upper right. The bottom half carries the player's biography, statistics, and career highlights. Special subsets include All Star players (1-18) and Foil Prospects (271-290). Cards 19-270 are in alphabetical order by team nickname. Notable Rookie Cards include Johnny Damon and Derek Jeter.

	MINT	NRMT
COMPLETE SET (290)	80.00	36.00
COMMON CARD (1-270)	.25	.11
FOIL PROSPECTS (271-290)	.50	.23
MINOR STARS	.50	.23
SEMISTARS	1.00	.45
UNLISTED STARS	1.50	.70
FOIL CARDS ARE CONDITION SENSITIVE		

□ 1 Roberto Alomar AS	1.50	.70
□ 2 Wade Boggs AS	1.50	.70
□ 3 Joe Carter AS	.25	.11
□ 4 Ken Griffey Jr. AS	8.00	3.60
□ 5 Mark Langston AS	.25	.11
□ 6 John Olerud AS	.25	.11
□ 7 Kirby Puckett AS	3.00	1.35
□ 8 Cal Ripken Jr. AS	6.00	2.70
□ 9 Ivan Rodriguez AS	2.00	.90
□ 10 Barry Bonds AS	2.00	.90
□ 11 Darren Daulton AS	.25	.11
□ 12 Marquis Grissom AS	.25	.11
□ 13 David Justice AS	1.50	.70
□ 14 John Kruk AS	.50	.23
□ 15 Barry Larkin AS	1.00	.45
□ 16 Terry Mulholland AS	.25	.11
□ 17 Ryne Sandberg AS	2.00	.90
□ 18 Gary Sheffield AS	.50	.23
□ 19 Chad Curtis	.25	.11
□ 20 Chili Davis	.50	.23
□ 21 Gary DiSarcina	.25	.11
□ 22 Damion Easley	.25	.11
□ 23 Chuck Finley	.25	.11
□ 24 Luis Polonia	.25	.11
□ 25 Tim Salmon	2.00	.90
□ 26 J.T. Snow	2.00	.90
□ 27 Russ Springer	.25	.11
□ 28 Jeff Bagwell	3.00	1.35
□ 29 Craig Biggio	1.00	.45

□ 30 Ken Caminiti	1.00	.45
□ 31 Andujar Cedeno	.25	.11
□ 32 Doug Drabek	.25	.11
□ 33 Steve Finley	.50	.23
□ 34 Luis Gonzalez	.25	.11
□ 35 Pete Harnisch	.25	.11
□ 36 Darryl Kile	.50	.23
□ 37 Mike Bordick	.25	.11
□ 38 Dennis Eckersley	.50	.23
□ 39 Brent Gates	.25	.11
□ 40 Rickey Henderson	1.00	.45
□ 41 Mark McGwire	3.00	1.35
□ 42 Craig Paquette	.25	.11
□ 43 Ruben Sierra	.25	.11
□ 44 Terry Steinbach	.25	.11
□ 45 Todd Van Poppel	.25	.11
□ 46 Pat Borders	.25	.11
□ 47 Tony Fernandez	.25	.11
□ 48 Juan Guzman	.25	.11
□ 49 Pat Hentgen	.25	.11
□ 50 Paul Molitor	1.50	.70
□ 51 Jack Morris	.50	.23
□ 52 Ed Sprague	.25	.11
□ 53 Duane Ward	.25	.11
□ 54 Devon White	.25	.11
□ 55 Steve Avery	.25	.11
□ 56 Jeff Blauser	.25	.11
□ 57 Ron Gant	.50	.23
□ 58 Tom Glavine	1.00	.45
□ 59 Greg Maddux	5.00	2.20
□ 60 Fred McGriff	1.00	.45
□ 61 Terry Pendleton	.50	.23
□ 62 Deion Sanders	.50	.23
□ 63 John Smoltz	.50	.23
□ 64 Cal Eldred	.25	.11
□ 65 Darryl Hamilton	.25	.11
□ 66 John Jaha	.50	.23
□ 67 Pat Listach	.25	.11
□ 68 Jaime Navarro	.25	.11
□ 69 Kevin Reimer	.25	.11
□ 70 B.J. Surhoff	.25	.11
□ 71 Greg Vaughn	.25	.11
□ 72 Robin Yount	1.00	.45
□ 73 Rene Arocha	.25	.11
□ 74 Bernard Gilkey	.25	.11
□ 75 Gregg Jefferies	.25	.11
□ 76 Ray Lankford	1.00	.45
□ 77 Tom Pagnozzi	.25	.11
□ 78 Lee Smith	.50	.23
□ 79 Ozzie Smith	2.00	.90
□ 80 Bob Tewksbury	.25	.11
□ 81 Mark Whiten	.25	.11
□ 82 Steve Buechele	.25	.11
□ 83 Mark Grace	1.00	.45
□ 84 Jose Guzman	.25	.11
□ 85 Derrick May	.25	.11
□ 86 Mike Morgan	.25	.11
□ 87 Randy Myers	.50	.23
□ 88 Kevin Roberson	.50	.23
□ 89 Sammy Sosa	1.50	.70
□ 90 Rick Wilkins	.25	.11
□ 91 Brett Butler	.50	.23
□ 92 Eric Davis	.50	.23
□ 93 Orel Hershiser	.50	.23
□ 94 Eric Karros	.50	.23
□ 95 Ramon Martinez	.50	.23
□ 96 Raul Mondesi	2.00	.90
□ 97 Jose Offerman	.25	.11
□ 98 Mike Piazza	8.00	3.60
□ 99 Darryl Strawberry	.50	.23
□ 100 Moises Alou	.50	.23
□ 101 Wil Cordero	.25	.11
□ 102 Delino DeShields	.25	.11
□ 103 Darrin Fletcher	.25	.11
□ 104 Ken Hill	.25	.11
□ 105 Mike Lansing	.25	.11
□ 106 Dennis Martinez	.50	.23
□ 107 Larry Walker	1.50	.70
□ 108 John Wetteland	.50	.23
□ 109 Rod Beck	.50	.23
□ 110 John Burkett	.25	.11
□ 111 Will Clark	1.00	.45
□ 112 Royce Clayton	.25	.11
□ 113 Darren Lewis	.25	.11
□ 114 Willie McGee	.25	.11
□ 115 Bill Swift	.25	.11

□ 116 Robby Thompson	.25	.11
□ 117 Matt Williams	1.00	.45
□ 118 Sandy Alomar Jr.	.50	.23
□ 119 Carlos Baerga	.25	.11
□ 120 Albert Belle	2.00	.90
□ 121 Reggie Jefferson	.25	.11
□ 122 Wayne Kirby	.25	.11
□ 123 Kenny Lofton	2.50	1.10
□ 124 Carlos Martinez	.25	.11
□ 125 Charles Nagy	.50	.23
□ 126 Paul Sorrento	.25	.11
□ 127 Rich Amaral	.25	.11
□ 128 Jay Buhner	1.00	.45
□ 129 Norm Charlton	.25	.11
□ 130 Dave Fleming	.25	.11
□ 131 Erik Hanson	.25	.11
□ 132 Randy Johnson	1.50	.70
□ 133 Edgar Martinez	1.00	.45
□ 134 Tino Martinez	1.50	.70
□ 135 Omar Vizquel	.50	.23
□ 136 Bret Barberie	.25	.11
□ 137 Chuck Carr	.25	.11
□ 138 Jeff Conine	.50	.23
□ 139 Orestes Destrade	.25	.11
□ 140 Chris Hammond	.25	.11
□ 141 Bryan Harvey	.25	.11
□ 142 Benito Santiago	.25	.11
□ 143 Walt Weiss	.25	.11
□ 144 Darrell Whitmore	.25	.11
□ 145 Tim Bogar	.25	.11
□ 146 Bobby Bonilla	.50	.23
□ 147 Jeromy Burnitz	.25	.11
□ 148 Vince Coleman	.25	.11
□ 149 Dwight Gooden	.50	.23
□ 150 Todd Hundley	1.00	.45
□ 151 Howard Johnson	.25	.11
□ 152 Eddie Murray	1.50	.70
□ 153 Bret Saberhagen	.25	.11
□ 154 Brady Anderson	1.00	.45
□ 155 Mike Devereaux	.25	.11
□ 156 Jeffrey Hammonds	1.00	.45
□ 157 Chris Hoiles	.25	.11
□ 158 Ben McDonald	.25	.11
□ 159 Mark McLemore	.25	.11
□ 160 Mike Mussina	1.50	.70
□ 161 Gregg Olson	.25	.11
□ 162 David Segui	.25	.11
□ 163 Derek Bell	.50	.23
□ 164 Andy Benes	.50	.23
□ 165 Archi Cianfrocco	.25	.11
□ 166 Ricky Gutierrez	.25	.11
□ 167 Tony Gwynn	4.00	1.80
□ 168 Gene Harris	.25	.11
□ 169 Trevor Hoffman	1.00	.45
□ 170 Ray McDavid	.25	.11
□ 171 Phil Plantier	.25	.11
□ 172 Mariano Duncan	.25	.11
□ 173 Len Dykstra	.50	.23
□ 174 Tommy Greene	.25	.11
□ 175 Dave Hollins	.25	.11
□ 176 Pete Incaviglia	.25	.11
□ 177 Mickey Morandini	.25	.11
□ 178 Curt Schilling	.50	.23
□ 179 Kevin Stocker	.25	.11
□ 180 Mitch Williams	.25	.11
□ 181 Stan Belinda	.25	.11
□ 182 Jay Bell	.50	.23
□ 183 Steve Cooke	.25	.11
□ 184 Carlos Garcia	.25	.11
□ 185 Jeff King	.50	.23
□ 186 Orlando Merced	.25	.11
□ 187 Don Slaught	.25	.11
□ 188 Andy Van Slyke	.50	.23
□ 189 Kevin Young	.25	.11
□ 190 Kevin Brown	.50	.23
□ 191 Jose Canseco	1.00	.45
□ 192 Julio Franco	.25	.11
□ 193 Benji Gil	.25	.11
□ 194 Juan Gonzalez	4.00	1.80
□ 195 Tom Henke	.25	.11
□ 196 Rafael Palmeiro	1.00	.45
□ 197 Dean Palmer	.25	.11
□ 198 Nolan Ryan	6.00	2.70
□ 199 Roger Clemens	3.00	1.35
□ 200 Scott Cooper	.25	.11
□ 201 Andre Dawson	1.00	.45

☐ 202 Mike Greenwell	.25	.11
☐ 203 Carlos Quintana	.25	.11
☐ 204 Jeff Russell	.25	.11
☐ 205 Aaron Sele	.50	.23
☐ 206 Mo Vaughn	2.00	.90
☐ 207 Frank Viola	.25	.11
☐ 208 Rob Dibble	.25	.11
☐ 209 Roberto Kelly	.25	.11
☐ 210 Kevin Mitchell	.50	.23
☐ 211 Hal Morris	.25	.11
☐ 212 Joe Oliver	.25	.11
☐ 213 Jose Rijo	.25	.11
☐ 214 Bip Roberts	.25	.11
☐ 215 Chris Sabo	.25	.11
☐ 216 Reggie Sanders	.50	.23
☐ 217 Dante Bichette	1.00	.45
☐ 218 Jerald Clark	.25	.11
☐ 219 Alex Cole	.25	.11
☐ 220 Andres Galarraga	1.50	.70
☐ 221 Joe Girardi	.25	.11
☐ 222 Charlie Hayes	.25	.11
☐ 223 Roberto Mejia	.25	.11
☐ 224 Armando Reynoso	.25	.11
☐ 225 Eric Young	1.50	.70
☐ 226 Kevin Appier	.50	.23
☐ 227 George Brett	3.00	1.35
☐ 228 David Cone	.25	.11
☐ 229 Phil Hiatt	.25	.11
☐ 230 Felix Jose	.25	.11
☐ 231 Wally Joyner	.50	.23
☐ 232 Mike Macfarlane	.25	.11
☐ 233 Brian McRae	.25	.11
☐ 234 Jeff Montgomery	.50	.23
☐ 235 Rob Deer	.25	.11
☐ 236 Cecil Fielder	.50	.23
☐ 237 Travis Fryman	.50	.23
☐ 238 Mike Henneman	.25	.11
☐ 239 Tony Phillips	.25	.11
☐ 240 Mickey Tettleton	.25	.11
☐ 241 Alan Trammell	1.00	.45
☐ 242 David Wells	.25	.11
☐ 243 Lou Whitaker	.50	.23
☐ 244 Rick Aguilera	.25	.11
☐ 245 Scott Erickson	.25	.11
☐ 246 Brian Harper	.25	.11
☐ 247 Kent Hrbek	.50	.23
☐ 248 Chuck Knoblauch	1.50	.70
☐ 249 Shane Mack	.25	.11
☐ 250 David McCarty	.25	.11
☐ 251 Pedro Munoz	.25	.11
☐ 252 Dave Winfield	1.00	.45
☐ 253 Alex Fernandez	.50	.23
☐ 254 Ozzie Guillen	.25	.11
☐ 255 Bo Jackson	.50	.23
☐ 256 Lance Johnson	.25	.11
☐ 257 Ron Karkovice	.25	.11
☐ 258 Jack McDowell	.25	.11
☐ 259 Tim Raines	.50	.23
☐ 260 Frank Thomas	6.00	2.70
☐ 261 Robin Ventura	.50	.23
☐ 262 Jim Abbott	.25	.11
☐ 263 Steve Farr	.25	.11
☐ 264 Jimmy Key	.50	.23
☐ 265 Don Mattingly	2.50	1.10
☐ 266 Paul O'Neill	.25	.11
☐ 267 Mike Stanley	.25	.11
☐ 268 Danny Tartabull	.50	.23
☐ 269 Bob Wickman	.25	.11
☐ 270 Bernie Williams	1.50	.70
☐ 271 Jason Bere FOIL	.50	.23
☐ 272 Roger Cedeno FOIL	1.50	.70
☐ 273 Johnny Damon FOIL	3.00	1.35
☐ 274 Russ Davis FOIL	2.00	.90
☐ 275 Carlos Delgado FOIL	2.00	.90
☐ 276 Carl Everett FOIL	.50	.23
☐ 277 Cliff Floyd FOIL	.50	.23
☐ 278 Alex Gonzalez FOIL	.50	.23
☐ 279 Derek Jeter FOIL	25.00	11.00
☐ 280 Chipper Jones FOIL	10.00	4.50
☐ 281 Javier Lopez FOIL	2.00	.90
☐ 282 Chad Mottola FOIL	.50	.23
☐ 283 Marc Newfield FOIL	.50	.23
☐ 284 Eduardo Perez FOIL	.50	.23
☐ 285 Manny Ramirez FOIL	4.00	1.80
☐ 286 Todd Steverson FOIL	.50	.23
☐ 287 Michael Tucker FOIL	.50	.23

☐ 288 Allen Watson FOIL	.50	.23
☐ 289 Rondell White FOIL	.50	.23
☐ 290 Dmitri Young FOIL	2.00	.90

1993 SP Platinum Power

Cards from this 20-card standard-size were inserted one every pack and feature power hitters from the American and National Leagues. The color action cut-out shot is superimposed on a royal blue background that contains lettering for Upper Deck Platinum Power and about the player. The top edge of the front is cut out in an arc with a copper foil stripe containing the player's name. The copper foil-stamped Platinum Power logo appears in the lower right. The back displays a color action player photo over the same royal blue background as depicted on the front. On a white background below the player photo is a career summary. The cards are numbered on the back with a "PP" prefix alphabetically by player's name.

	MINT	NRMT
COMPLETE SET (20)	120.00	55.00
COMMON CARD (PP1-PP20)	3.00	1.35
STATED ODDS 1:9		

☐ PP1 Albert Belle	10.00	4.50
☐ PP2 Barry Bonds	10.00	4.50
☐ PP3 Joe Carter	4.00	1.80
☐ PP4 Will Clark	5.00	2.20
☐ PP5 Darren Daulton	4.00	1.80
☐ PP6 Cecil Fielder	4.00	1.80
☐ PP7 Ron Gant	4.00	1.80
☐ PP8 Juan Gonzalez	15.00	6.75
☐ PP9 Ken Griffey Jr.	30.00	13.50
☐ PP10 Dave Hollins	3.00	1.35
☐ PP11 David Justice	6.00	2.70
☐ PP12 Fred McGriff	5.00	2.20
☐ PP13 Mark McGwire	12.00	5.50
☐ PP14 Dean Palmer	3.00	1.35
☐ PP15 Mike Piazza	30.00	13.50
☐ PP16 Tim Salmon	8.00	3.60
☐ PP17 Ryne Sandberg	8.00	3.60
☐ PP18 Gary Sheffield	6.00	2.70
☐ PP19 Frank Thomas	25.00	11.00
☐ PP20 Matt Williams	5.00	2.20

1994 SP Previews

These 15 cards were distributed regionally as inserts in second series Upper Deck hobby packs. They were inserted at a rate of one in 35. The manner of distri-

bution was five cards per Central, East and West region. The cards are nearly identical to the basic SP issue. Card fronts differ in that the region is at bottom right where the team name is located on the SP cards.

	MINT	NRMT
COMPLETE SET (15)	180.00	80.00
COMPLETE CENTRAL (5)	80.00	36.00
COMPLETE EAST (5)	40.00	18.00
COMPLETE WEST (5)	60.00	27.00
COMMON CARD (CR1-CR5)	3.00	1.35
STATED ODDS 1:35 REG'L SER.2 UD HOBBY		

☐ CR1 Jeff Bagwell	12.00	5.50
☐ CR2 Michael Jordan	30.00	13.50
☐ CR3 Kirby Puckett	12.00	5.50
☐ CR4 Manny Ramirez	5.00	2.20
☐ CR5 Frank Thomas	25.00	11.00
☐ ER1 Roberto Alomar	5.00	2.20
☐ ER2 Cliff Floyd	3.00	1.35
☐ ER3 Javier Lopez	4.00	1.80
☐ ER4 Don Mattingly	10.00	4.50
☐ ER5 Cal Ripken	25.00	11.00
☐ WR1 Barry Bonds	8.00	3.60
☐ WR2 Juan Gonzalez	15.00	6.75
☐ WR3 Ken Griffey Jr.	30.00	13.50
☐ WR4 Mike Piazza	20.00	9.00
☐ WR5 Tim Salmon	5.00	2.20

1994 SP

This 200-card standard-size set primarily contains the game's top players and prospects. The first 20 cards in the set are Foil Prospects which are brighter and more metallic than the rest of the set. Cards 21-200 are in alphabetical order by team nickname. In either case, card fronts have a metallic finish with color player photos and a gold righthand border. The backs contain a color player photo, 1993, career and best season statistics. The left side has a black border. The Upper Deck hologram on back is gold. Rookie Cards include Brad Fullmer, Derrek Lee, Chan Ho Park and Alex Rodriguez.

	MINT	NRMT
COMPLETE SET (200)	70.00	32.00
COMMON FOIL (1-20)	.50	.23
COMMON CARD (21-200)	.20	.09
MINOR STARS	.40	.18
UNLISTED STARS	.75	.35
COMP.DIE CUT SET (200)	150.00	70.00
COMMON DIE CUT (1-200)	.30	.14

*DIE CUT STARS: 1.5X TO 3X HI COLUMN
*DIE CUT YOUNG STARS: 1X TO 2X HI
ONE DIE CUT PER PACK
FOIL CARDS CONDITION SENSITIVE

1	Mike Bell FOIL	.75	.35
2	D.J. Boston FOIL	.20	.09
3	Johnny Damon FOIL	.75	.35
4	Brad Fullmer FOIL	3.00	1.35
5	Joey Hamilton FOIL	.75	.35
6	Todd Hollandsworth FOIL	.60	.25
7	Brian L. Hunter FOIL	.75	.35
8	LaTroy Hawkins FOIL	.40	.18
9	Brooks Kieschnick FOIL	.75	.35
10	Derrek Lee FOIL	5.00	2.20
11	Trot Nixon FOIL	.40	.18
12	Alex Ochoa FOIL	.20	.09
13	Chan Ho Park FOIL	5.00	2.20
14	Kirk Presley FOIL	.40	.18
15	Alex Rodriguez FOIL	30.00	13.50
16	Jose Silva FOIL	.40	.18
17	Terrell Wade FOIL	.40	.18
18	Billy Wagner FOIL	2.50	1.10
19	Glenn Williams FOIL	.75	.35
20	Preston Wilson FOIL	.75	.35
21	Brian Anderson	.75	.35
22	Chad Curtis	.20	.09
23	Chili Davis	.40	.18
24	Bo Jackson	.40	.18
25	Mark Langston	.20	.09
26	Tim Salmon	.75	.35
27	Jeff Bagwell	1.50	.70
28	Craig Biggio	.60	.25
29	Ken Caminiti	.60	.25
30	Doug Drabek	.20	.09
31	John Hudek	.20	.09
32	Greg Swindell	.20	.09
33	Brent Gates	.20	.09
34	Rickey Henderson	.60	.25
35	Steve Karsay	.20	.09
36	Mark McGwire	1.50	.70
37	Ruben Sierra	.20	.09
38	Terry Steinbach	.20	.09
39	Roberto Alomar	.75	.35
40	Joe Carter	.40	.18
41	Carlos Delgado	.60	.25
42	Alex Gonzalez	.40	.18
43	Juan Guzman	.20	.09
44	Paul Molitor	.75	.35
45	John Olerud	.40	.18
46	Devon White	.20	.09
47	Steve Avery	.20	.09
48	Jeff Blauser	.40	.18
49	Tom Glavine	.40	.18
50	David Justice	.75	.35
51	Roberto Kelly	.20	.09
52	Ryan Klesko	.75	.35
53	Javier Lopez	.60	.25
54	Greg Maddux	2.50	1.10
55	Fred McGriff	.60	.25
56	Ricky Bones	.20	.09
57	Cal Eldred	.20	.09
58	Brian Harper	.20	.09
59	Pat Listach	.20	.09
60	B.J. Surhoff	.20	.09
61	Greg Vaughn	.20	.09
62	Bernard Gilkey	.20	.09
63	Gregg Jefferies	.20	.09
64	Ray Lankford	.40	.18
65	Ozzie Smith	1.00	.45
66	Bob Tewksbury	.20	.09
67	Mark Whiten	.20	.09
68	Todd Zeile	.20	.09
69	Mark Grace	.60	.25
70	Randy Myers	.20	.09
71	Ryne Sandberg	1.00	.45
72	Sammy Sosa	.75	.35
73	Steve Trachsel	.40	.18
74	Rick Wilkins	.20	.09
75	Brett Butler	.40	.18
76	Delino DeShields	.20	.09
77	Orel Hershiser	.40	.18
78	Eric Karros	.40	.18
79	Raul Mondesi	.75	.35
80	Mike Piazza	2.50	1.10
81	Tim Wallach	.20	.09
82	Moises Alou	.40	.18
83	Cliff Floyd	.40	.18
84	Marquis Grissom	.40	.18
85	Pedro J. Martinez	.75	.35
86	Larry Walker	.75	.35
87	John Wetteland	.20	.09
88	Rondell White	.60	.25
89	Rod Beck	.20	.09
90	Barry Bonds	1.00	.45
91	John Burkett	.20	.09
92	Royce Clayton	.20	.09
93	Billy Swift	.20	.09
94	Robby Thompson	.20	.09
95	Matt Williams	.60	.25
96	Carlos Baerga	.20	.09
97	Albert Belle	1.00	.45
98	Kenny Lofton	1.00	.45
99	Dennis Martinez	.40	.18
100	Eddie Murray	.75	.35
101	Manny Ramirez	1.00	.45
102	Eric Anthony	.20	.09
103	Chris Bosio	.20	.09
104	Jay Buhner	.40	.18
105	Ken Griffey Jr.	4.00	1.80
106	Randy Johnson	.75	.35
107	Edgar Martinez	.60	.25
108	Chuck Carr	.20	.09
109	Jeff Conine	.40	.18
110	Carl Everett	.20	.09
111	Chris Hammond	.20	.09
112	Bryan Harvey	.20	.09
113	Charles Johnson	.60	.25
114	Gary Sheffield	.75	.35
115	Bobby Bonilla	.40	.18
116	Dwight Gooden	.40	.18
117	Todd Hundley	.40	.18
118	Bobby Jones	.40	.18
119	Jeff Kent	.20	.09
120	Bret Saberhagen	.20	.09
121	Jeffrey Hammonds	.40	.18
122	Chris Hoiles	.20	.09
123	Ben McDonald	.20	.09
124	Mike Mussina	.75	.35
125	Rafael Palmeiro	.60	.25
126	Cal Ripken Jr.	3.00	1.35
127	Lee Smith	.20	.18
128	Derek Bell	.20	.09
129	Andy Benes	.20	.09
130	Tony Gwynn	2.00	.90
131	Trevor Hoffman	.20	.09
132	Phil Plantier	.20	.09
133	Bip Roberts	.20	.09
134	Darren Daulton	.40	.18
135	Lenny Dykstra	.40	.18
136	Dave Hollins	.20	.09
137	Danny Jackson	.20	.09
138	John Kruk	.40	.18
139	Kevin Stocker	.20	.09
140	Jay Bell	.40	.18
141	Carlos Garcia	.20	.09
142	Jeff King	.20	.09
143	Orlando Merced	.20	.09
144	Andy Van Slyke	.40	.18
145	Rick White	.20	.09
146	Jose Canseco	.60	.25
147	Will Clark	.60	.25
148	Juan Gonzalez	2.00	.90
149	Rick Helling	.20	.09
150	Dean Palmer	.20	.09
151	Ivan Rodriguez	1.00	.45
152	Roger Clemens	1.50	.70
153	Scott Cooper	.20	.09
154	Andre Dawson	.60	.25
155	Mike Greenwell	.20	.09
156	Aaron Sele	.20	.09
157	Mo Vaughn	1.00	.45
158	Bret Boone	.20	.09
159	Barry Larkin	.60	.25
160	Kevin Mitchell	.20	.09
161	Jose Rijo	.20	.09
162	Deion Sanders	.40	.18
163	Reggie Sanders	.20	.09
164	Dante Bichette	.40	.18
165	Ellis Burks	.40	.18
166	Andres Galarraga	.75	.35
167	Charlie Hayes	.20	.09
168	David Nied	.20	.09
169	Walt Weiss	.20	.09
170	Kevin Appier	.40	.18
171	David Cone	.40	.18
172	Jeff Granger	.20	.09
173	Felix Jose	.20	.09
174	Wally Joyner	.20	.09
175	Brian McRae	.20	.09
176	Cecil Fielder	.40	.18
177	Travis Fryman	.40	.18
178	Mike Henneman	.20	.09
179	Tony Phillips	.20	.09
180	Mickey Tettleton	.20	.09
181	Alan Trammell	.40	.18
182	Rick Aguilera	.20	.09
183	Rich Becker	.20	.09
184	Scott Erickson	.20	.09
185	Chuck Knoblauch	.75	.35
186	Kirby Puckett	1.50	.70
187	Dave Winfield	.60	.25
188	Wilson Alvarez	.20	.09
189	Jason Bere	.20	.09
190	Alex Fernandez	.20	.09
191	Julio Franco	.20	.09
192	Jack McDowell	.20	.09
193	Frank Thomas	3.00	1.35
194	Robin Ventura	.40	.18
195	Jim Abbott	.20	.09
196	Wade Boggs	.75	.35
197	Jimmy Key	.40	.18
198	Don Mattingly	1.25	.55
199	Paul O'Neill	.40	.18
200	Danny Tartabull	.20	.09
P24	Ken Griffey Jr. Promo	3.00	1.35

1994 SP Holoviews

Randomly inserted in SP foil packs at a rate of one in five, this 38-card set contains top stars and prospects. Card fronts have a color player photo with a black and blue border to the right with which the player's name appears. A player hologram that runs the width of the card is at the bottom. The backs are primarily blue with a player photo and text.

	MINT	NRMT
COMPLETE SET (38)	150.00	70.00
COMMON CARD (1-38)	2.00	.90
SEMISTARS	4.00	1.80

		MINT	NRMT
UNLISTED STARS	6.00		2.70
STATED ODDS 1:5			
COMP.HOLO.DC SET (38)	1500.00		700.00
*DIE CUT STARS: 3X TO 6X HI COLUMN			
DIE CUT STATED ODDS 1:75 ...			

		MINT	NRMT
☐ 1 Roberto Alomar	6.00		2.70
☐ 2 Kevin Appier	3.00		1.35
☐ 3 Jeff Bagwell	12.00		5.50
☐ 4 Jose Canseco	4.00		1.80
☐ 5 Roger Clemens	12.00		5.50
☐ 6 Carlos Delgado	4.00		1.80
☐ 7 Cecil Fielder	3.00		1.35
☐ 8 Cliff Floyd	3.00		1.35
☐ 9 Travis Fryman	3.00		1.35
☐ 10 Andres Galarraga	6.00		2.70
☐ 11 Juan Gonzalez	15.00		6.75
☐ 12 Ken Griffey Jr.	30.00		13.50
☐ 13 Tony Gwynn	15.00		6.75
☐ 14 Jeffrey Hammonds	3.00		1.35
☐ 15 Bo Jackson	3.00		1.35
☐ 16 Michael Jordan	40.00		18.00
☐ 17 David Justice	6.00		2.70
☐ 18 Steve Karsay	2.00		.90
☐ 19 Jeff Kent	2.00		.90
☐ 20 Brooks Kieschnick	6.00		2.70
☐ 21 Ryan Klesko	6.00		2.70
☐ 22 John Kruk	3.00		1.35
☐ 23 Barry Larkin	4.00		1.80
☐ 24 Pat Listach	2.00		.90
☐ 25 Don Mattingly	10.00		4.50
☐ 26 Mark McGwire	12.00		5.50
☐ 27 Raul Mondesi	6.00		2.70
☐ 28 Trot Nixon	3.00		1.35
☐ 29 Mike Piazza	20.00		9.00
☐ 30 Kirby Puckett	12.00		5.50
☐ 31 Manny Ramirez	8.00		3.60
☐ 32 Cal Ripken	25.00		11.00
☐ 33 Alex Rodriguez	30.00		13.50
☐ 34 Tim Salmon	6.00		2.70
☐ 35 Gary Sheffield	6.00		2.70
☐ 36 Ozzie Smith	8.00		3.60
☐ 37 Sammy Sosa	6.00		2.70
☐ 38 Andy Van Slyke	3.00		1.35

1995 SP

This set consists of 207 cards being sold in eight-card, hobby-only packs with a suggested retail price of $3.99. The fronts have full-bleed photos and a chevron consists of the left. The chevron consists of red and gold foil for American League players and blue and gold for National Leaguers. The backs have a photo with player information and statistics at the bottom. The backs also have a gold hologram to prevent counterfeiting. Subsets featured are Salute (1-4) and Premier Prospects (5-24). The only notable Rookie Card in this set is Hideo Nomo. Dealers who ordered a certain quantity of

		MINT	NRMT
Upper Deck baseball cases received as a bonus, a certified autographed SP card of Ken Griffey Jr.			
COMPLETE SET (207)	40.00		18.00
COMMON CARD (1-207)	.20		.09
FOIL PROSPECTS (5-24)	.25		.11
MINOR STARS	.40		.18
UNLISTED STARS	.75		.35
COMP.SILVER SET (207)	100.00		45.00
COMMON SILVER (1-207)	.25		.11
*SILVER STARS: 1.5X TO 3X HI COLUMN			
*SILVER YOUNG STARS: 1.25X TO 2.5X HI			
ONE SILVER PER PACK			

		MINT	NRMT
☐ 1 Cal Ripken Salute	3.00		1.35
☐ 2 Nolan Ryan Salute	3.00		1.35
☐ 3 George Brett Salute	1.50		.70
☐ 4 Mike Schmidt Salute	1.00		.45
☐ 5 Dustin Hermanson FOIL	.40		.18
☐ 6 Antonio Osuna FOIL	.25		.11
☐ 7 Mark Grudzielanek FOIL	.60		.25
☐ 8 Ray Durham FOIL	.40		.18
☐ 9 Ugueth Urbina FOIL	.20		.09
☐ 10 Ruben Rivera FOIL	.75		.35
☐ 11 Curtis Goodwin FOIL	.25		.11
☐ 12 Jimmy Hurst FOIL	.20		.09
☐ 13 Jose Malave FOIL	.25		.11
☐ 14 Hideo Nomo FOIL	4.00		1.80
☐ 15 Juan Acevedo FOIL	.25		.11
☐ 16 Tony Clark FOIL	1.00		.45
☐ 17 Jim Pittsley FOIL	.40		.18
☐ 18 Freddy Garcia FOIL	.60		.25
☐ 19 Carlos Perez FOIL	.40		.18
☐ 20 Raul Casanova FOIL	.50		.23
☐ 21 Quilvio Veras FOIL	.40		.18
☐ 22 Edgardo Alfonzo FOIL	.75		.35
☐ 23 Marty Cordova FOIL	.40		.18
☐ 24 C.J. Nitkowski FOIL	.25		.11
☐ 25 Wade Boggs CL	.40		.18
☐ 26 Dave Winfield CL	.40		.18
☐ 27 Eddie Murray CL	.40		.18
☐ 28 David Justice	.75		.35
☐ 29 Marquis Grissom	.40		.18
☐ 30 Fred McGriff	.60		.25
☐ 31 Greg Maddux	2.50		1.10
☐ 32 Tom Glavine	.40		.18
☐ 33 Steve Avery	.20		.09
☐ 34 Chipper Jones	2.50		1.10
☐ 35 Sammy Sosa	.75		.35
☐ 36 Jaime Navarro	.20		.09
☐ 37 Randy Myers	.20		.09
☐ 38 Mark Grace	.60		.25
☐ 39 Todd Zeile	.20		.09
☐ 40 Brian McRae	.20		.09
☐ 41 Reggie Sanders	.40		.18
☐ 42 Ron Gant	.40		.18
☐ 43 Deion Sanders	.40		.18
☐ 44 Bret Boone	.20		.09
☐ 45 Barry Larkin	.60		.25
☐ 46 Jose Rijo	.20		.09
☐ 47 Jason Bates	.20		.09
☐ 48 Andres Galarraga	.75		.35
☐ 49 Bill Swift	.20		.09
☐ 50 Larry Walker	.75		.35
☐ 51 Vinny Castilla	.40		.18
☐ 52 Dante Bichette	.40		.18
☐ 53 Jeff Conine	.40		.18
☐ 54 John Burkett	.20		.09
☐ 55 Gary Sheffield	.75		.35
☐ 56 Andre Dawson	.60		.25
☐ 57 Terry Pendleton	.20		.09
☐ 58 Charles Johnson	.40		.18
☐ 59 Brian L. Hunter	.60		.25
☐ 60 Jeff Bagwell	1.50		.70
☐ 61 Craig Biggio	.60		.25
☐ 62 Phil Nevin	.20		.09
☐ 63 Doug Drabek	.20		.09
☐ 64 Derek Bell	.20		.09
☐ 65 Raul Mondesi	.60		.25
☐ 66 Eric Karros	.40		.18
☐ 67 Roger Cedeno	.40		.18
☐ 68 Delino DeShields	.20		.09
☐ 69 Ramon Martinez	.40		.18

		MINT	NRMT
☐ 70 Mike Piazza	2.50		1.10
☐ 71 Billy Ashley	.20		.09
☐ 72 Jeff Fassero	.20		.09
☐ 73 Shane Andrews	.20		.09
☐ 74 Wil Cordero	.20		.09
☐ 75 Tony Tarasco	.20		.09
☐ 76 Rondell White	.40		.18
☐ 77 Pedro J. Martinez	.75		.35
☐ 78 Moises Alou	.40		.18
☐ 79 Rico Brogna	.20		.09
☐ 80 Bobby Bonilla	.40		.18
☐ 81 Jeff Kent	.20		.09
☐ 82 Brett Butler	.20		.09
☐ 83 Bobby Jones	.20		.09
☐ 84 Bill Pulsipher	.20		.09
☐ 85 Bret Saberhagen	.20		.09
☐ 86 Gregg Jefferies	.20		.09
☐ 87 Lenny Dykstra	.40		.18
☐ 88 Dave Hollins	.20		.09
☐ 89 Charlie Hayes	.20		.09
☐ 90 Darren Daulton	.40		.18
☐ 91 Curt Schilling	.40		.18
☐ 92 Heathcliff Slocumb	.20		.09
☐ 93 Carlos Garcia	.20		.09
☐ 94 Denny Neagle	.40		.18
☐ 95 Jay Bell	.40		.18
☐ 96 Orlando Merced	.20		.09
☐ 97 Dave Clark	.20		.09
☐ 98 Bernard Gilkey	.20		.09
☐ 99 Scott Cooper	.20		.09
☐ 100 Ozzie Smith	1.00		.45
☐ 101 Tom Henke	.20		.09
☐ 102 Ken Hill	.20		.09
☐ 103 Brian Jordan	.40		.18
☐ 104 Ray Lankford	.40		.18
☐ 105 Tony Gwynn	2.00		.90
☐ 106 Andy Benes	.40		.18
☐ 107 Ken Caminiti	.60		.25
☐ 108 Steve Finley	.20		.09
☐ 109 Joey Hamilton	.40		.18
☐ 110 Bip Roberts	.20		.09
☐ 111 Eddie Williams	.20		.09
☐ 112 Rod Beck	.20		.09
☐ 113 Matt Williams	.60		.25
☐ 114 Glenallen Hill	.20		.09
☐ 115 Barry Bonds	1.00		.45
☐ 116 Robby Thompson	.20		.09
☐ 117 Mark Portugal	.20		.09
☐ 118 Brady Anderson	.60		.25
☐ 119 Mike Mussina	.75		.35
☐ 120 Rafael Palmeiro	.60		.25
☐ 121 Chris Hoiles	.20		.09
☐ 122 Harold Baines	.40		.18
☐ 123 Jeffrey Hammonds	.40		.18
☐ 124 Tim Naehring	.20		.09
☐ 125 Mo Vaughn	1.00		.45
☐ 126 Mike Macfarlane	.20		.09
☐ 127 Roger Clemens	1.50		.70
☐ 128 John Valentin	.20		.09
☐ 129 Aaron Sele	.20		.09
☐ 130 Jose Canseco	.60		.25
☐ 131 J.T. Snow	.40		.18
☐ 132 Mark Langston	.20		.09
☐ 133 Chili Davis	.40		.18
☐ 134 Chuck Finley	.20		.09
☐ 135 Tim Salmon	.75		.35
☐ 136 Tony Phillips	.20		.09
☐ 137 Jason Bere	.20		.09
☐ 138 Robin Ventura	.40		.18
☐ 139 Tim Raines	.40		.18
☐ 140 Frank Thomas COR	3.00		1.35
☐ 140A Frank Thomas ERR	8.00		3.60
☐ 141 Alex Fernandez	.20		.09
☐ 142 Jim Abbott	.20		.09
☐ 143 Wilson Alvarez	.20		.09
☐ 144 Carlos Baerga	.20		.09
☐ 145 Albert Belle	1.00		.45
☐ 146 Jim Thome	.75		.35
☐ 147 Dennis Martinez	.40		.18
☐ 148 Eddie Murray	.75		.35
☐ 149 Dave Winfield	.60		.25
☐ 150 Kenny Lofton	1.00		.45
☐ 151 Manny Ramirez	.75		.35
☐ 152 Chad Curtis	.20		.09
☐ 153 Lou Whitaker	.40		.18
☐ 154 Alan Trammell	.60		.25

☐ 155 Cecil Fielder	.40	.18
☐ 156 Kirk Gibson	.40	.18
☐ 157 Michael Tucker	.40	.18
☐ 158 Jon Nunnally	.20	.09
☐ 159 Wally Joyner	.40	.18
☐ 160 Kevin Appier	.40	.18
☐ 161 Jeff Montgomery	.20	.09
☐ 162 Greg Gagne	.20	.09
☐ 163 Ricky Bones	.20	.09
☐ 164 Cal Eldred	.20	.09
☐ 165 Greg Vaughn	.20	.09
☐ 166 Kevin Seitzer	.20	.09
☐ 167 Jose Valentin	.20	.09
☐ 168 Joe Oliver	.20	.09
☐ 169 Rick Aguilera	.20	.09
☐ 170 Kirby Puckett	1.50	.70
☐ 171 Scott Stahoviak	.20	.09
☐ 172 Kevin Tapani	.20	.09
☐ 173 Chuck Knoblauch	.75	.35
☐ 174 Rich Becker	.20	.09
☐ 175 Don Mattingly	1.25	.55
☐ 176 Jack McDowell	.20	.09
☐ 177 Jimmy Key	.40	.18
☐ 178 Paul O'Neill	.40	.18
☐ 179 John Wetteland	.20	.09
☐ 180 Wade Boggs	.75	.35
☐ 181 Derek Jeter	2.50	1.10
☐ 182 Rickey Henderson	.60	.25
☐ 183 Terry Steinbach	.20	.09
☐ 184 Ruben Sierra	.20	.09
☐ 185 Mark McGwire	1.50	.70
☐ 186 Todd Stottlemyre	.20	.09
☐ 187 Dennis Eckersley	.40	.18
☐ 188 Alex Rodriguez	3.00	1.35
☐ 189 Randy Johnson	.75	.35
☐ 190 Ken Griffey Jr.	4.00	1.80
☐ 191 Tino Martinez UER	.40	.18
Mike Blowers pictured on back		
☐ 192 Jay Buhner	.60	.25
☐ 193 Edgar Martinez	.60	.25
☐ 194 Mickey Tettleton	.20	.09
☐ 195 Juan Gonzalez	2.00	.90
☐ 196 Benji Gil	.20	.09
☐ 197 Dean Palmer	.20	.09
☐ 198 Ivan Rodriguez	1.00	.45
☐ 199 Kenny Rogers	.20	.09
☐ 200 Will Clark	.60	.25
☐ 201 Roberto Alomar	.75	.35
☐ 202 David Cone	.40	.18
☐ 203 Paul Molitor	.75	.35
☐ 204 Shawn Green	.40	.18
☐ 205 Joe Carter	.40	.18
☐ 206 Alex Gonzalez	.20	.09
☐ 207 Pat Hentgen	.40	.18
☐ AU190 Ken Griffey Jr. AU	200.00	90.00

1995 SP Platinum Power

This 20-card set was randomly inserted in packs at a rate of one in five. This die-cut set is comprised of the top home run hitters in baseball. The fronts have an action photo with a bronze background and rays of

light coming out of the "SP" emblem at bottom right. The backs have a player photo in a box at the middle of the card with player statistics at the bottom. The set is sequenced in alphabetical order.

	MINT	NRMT
COMPLETE SET (20)	20.00	9.00
COMMON CARD (PP1-PP20)	.75	.35
STATED ODDS 1:5		
☐ PP1 Jeff Bagwell	2.00	.90
☐ PP2 Barry Bonds	1.25	.55
☐ PP3 Ron Gant	.50	.23
☐ PP4 Fred McGriff	.75	.35
☐ PP5 Raul Mondesi	.75	.35
☐ PP6 Mike Piazza	3.00	1.35
☐ PP7 Larry Walker	1.00	.45
☐ PP8 Matt Williams	.75	.35
☐ PP9 Albert Belle	1.25	.55
☐ PP10 Cecil Fielder	.50	.23
☐ PP11 Juan Gonzalez	2.50	1.10
☐ PP12 Ken Griffey Jr.	5.00	2.20
☐ PP13 Mark McGwire	2.00	.90
☐ PP14 Eddie Murray	1.00	.45
☐ PP15 Manny Ramirez	1.00	.45
☐ PP16 Cal Ripken	4.00	1.80
☐ PP17 Tim Salmon	1.00	.45
☐ PP18 Frank Thomas	4.00	1.80
☐ PP19 Jim Thome	1.00	.45
☐ PP20 Mo Vaughn	1.25	.55

1995 SP Special FX

This 48-card set was randomly inserted in packs at a rate of one in 75. The set is comprised of the top names in baseball. The fronts have an action photo on a sky-colored foil background. There is a hologram of the player's face that allows you to see a 50-degree, 3-D image. The backs have a photo with player information and statistics. The cards are numbered on the back "X/48."

	MINT	NRMT
COMPLETE SET (48)	1000.00	450.00
COMMON CARD (1-48)	8.00	3.60
SEMISTARS	15.00	6.75
UNLISTED STARS	25.00	11.00
STATED ODDS 1:75		
☐ 1 Jose Canseco	15.00	6.75
☐ 2 Roger Clemens	50.00	22.00
☐ 3 Mo Vaughn	30.00	13.50
☐ 4 Tim Salmon	25.00	11.00
☐ 5 Chuck Finley	8.00	3.60
☐ 6 Robin Ventura	12.00	5.50
☐ 7 Jason Bere	8.00	3.60
☐ 8 Carlos Baerga	8.00	3.60
☐ 9 Albert Belle	30.00	13.50
☐ 10 Kenny Lofton	30.00	13.50

☐ 11 Manny Ramirez	25.00	11.00
☐ 12 Jeff Montgomery	8.00	3.60
☐ 13 Kirby Puckett	50.00	22.00
☐ 14 Wade Boggs	25.00	11.00
☐ 15 Don Mattingly	40.00	18.00
☐ 16 Cal Ripken	100.00	45.00
☐ 17 Ruben Sierra	8.00	3.60
☐ 18 Ken Griffey Jr.	120.00	55.00
☐ 19 Randy Johnson	25.00	11.00
☐ 20 Alex Rodriguez	100.00	45.00
☐ 21 Will Clark	15.00	6.75
☐ 22 Juan Gonzalez	60.00	27.00
☐ 23 Roberto Alomar	25.00	11.00
☐ 24 Joe Carter	12.00	5.50
☐ 25 Alex Gonzalez	8.00	3.60
☐ 26 Paul Molitor	25.00	11.00
☐ 27 Ryan Klesko	15.00	6.75
☐ 28 Fred McGriff	15.00	6.75
☐ 29 Greg Maddux	80.00	36.00
☐ 30 Sammy Sosa	25.00	11.00
☐ 31 Bret Boone	8.00	3.60
☐ 32 Barry Larkin	15.00	6.75
☐ 33 Reggie Sanders	8.00	3.60
☐ 34 Dante Bichette	12.00	5.50
☐ 35 Andres Galarraga	25.00	11.00
☐ 36 Charles Johnson	12.00	5.50
☐ 37 Gary Sheffield	25.00	11.00
☐ 38 Jeff Bagwell	50.00	22.00
☐ 39 Craig Biggio	15.00	6.75
☐ 40 Eric Karros	12.00	5.50
☐ 41 Billy Ashley	8.00	3.60
☐ 42 Raul Mondesi	15.00	6.75
☐ 43 Mike Piazza	80.00	36.00
☐ 44 Rondell White	12.00	5.50
☐ 45 Bret Saberhagen	8.00	3.60
☐ 46 Tony Gwynn	60.00	27.00
☐ 47 Melvin Nieves	8.00	3.60
☐ 48 Matt Williams	15.00	6.75

1996 SP

The 1996 SP set was issued in one series totalling 188 cards. The eight-card packs retail for $4.19 each. Cards number 1-20 feature color action player photos with "Premier Prospects" printed in silver foil across the top and the player's name and team at the bottom in the border. The backs carry player information and statistics. Cards number 21-185 display unique player photos with an outer wood-grain border and inner thin platinum foil border as well as a small inset player shot. The backs carry another color player photo with unique player statistics depending on his position. The only notable Rookie Card in this set is Darin Erstad.

	MINT	NRMT
COMPLETE SET (188)	40.00	18.00
COMMON CARDS (1-188)	.20	.09
MINOR STARS	.40	.18

UNLISTED STARS .75 .35
SUBSET CARDS HALF VALUE OF BASE CARDS

□ 1 Rey Ordonez FOIL .40 .18
□ 2 George Arias FOIL .20 .09
□ 3 Osvaldo Fernandez FOIL .40 .18
□ 4 Darin Erstad FOIL 6.00 2.70
□ 5 Paul Wilson FOIL .20 .09
□ 6 Richard Hidalgo FOIL .75 .35
□ 7 Justin Thompson FOIL .60 .25
□ 8 Jimmy Haynes FOIL .20 .09
□ 9 Edgar Renteria FOIL .60 .25
□ 10 Ruben Rivera FOIL .40 .18
□ 11 Chris Snopek FOIL .20 .09
□ 12 Billy Wagner FOIL .40 .18
□ 13 Mike Grace FOIL .20 .09
□ 14 Todd Greene FOIL .60 .25
□ 15 Karim Garcia FOIL .60 .25
□ 16 John Wasdin FOIL .20 .09
□ 17 Jason Kendall FOIL .60 .25
□ 18 Bob Abreu FOIL .60 .25
□ 19 Jermaine Dye FOIL .40 .18
□ 20 Jason Schmidt FOIL .40 .18
□ 21 Javy Lopez .40 .18
□ 22 Ryan Klesko .60 .25
□ 23 Tom Glavine .40 .18
□ 24 John Smoltz .40 .18
□ 25 Greg Maddux 2.50 1.10
□ 26 Chipper Jones 2.50 1.10
□ 27 Fred McGriff .60 .25
□ 28 David Justice .75 .35
□ 29 Roberto Alomar .75 .35
□ 30 Cal Ripken 3.00 1.35
□ 31 B.J. Surhoff .20 .09
□ 32 Bobby Bonilla .40 .18
□ 33 Mike Mussina .75 .35
□ 34 Randy Myers .20 .09
□ 35 Rafael Palmeiro .60 .25
□ 36 Brady Anderson .60 .25
□ 37 Tim Naehring .20 .09
□ 38 Jose Canseco .60 .25
□ 39 Roger Clemens 1.50 .70
□ 40 Mo Vaughn 1.00 .45
□ 41 Jose Valentin .20 .09
□ 42 Kevin Mitchell .20 .09
□ 43 Chili Davis .40 .18
□ 44 Garret Anderson .40 .18
□ 45 Tim Salmon .75 .35
□ 46 Chuck Finley .20 .09
□ 47 Troy Percival .40 .18
□ 48 Jim Abbott .20 .09
□ 49 J.T. Snow .40 .18
□ 50 Jim Edmonds .60 .25
□ 51 Sammy Sosa .75 .35
□ 52 Brian McRae .20 .09
□ 53 Ryne Sandberg 1.00 .45
□ 54 Jaime Navarro .20 .09
□ 55 Mark Grace .60 .25
□ 56 Harold Baines .40 .18
□ 57 Robin Ventura .40 .18
□ 58 Tony Phillips .20 .09
□ 59 Alex Fernandez .20 .09
□ 60 Frank Thomas 3.00 1.35
□ 61 Ray Durham .20 .09
□ 62 Bret Boone .20 .09
□ 63 Reggie Sanders .20 .09
□ 64 Pete Schourek .20 .09
□ 65 Barry Larkin .60 .25
□ 66 John Smiley .20 .09
□ 67 Carlos Baerga .20 .09
□ 68 Jim Thome .75 .35
□ 69 Eddie Murray .75 .35
□ 70 Albert Belle 1.00 .45
□ 71 Dennis Martinez .40 .18
□ 72 Jack McDowell .20 .09
□ 73 Kenny Lofton 1.00 .45
□ 74 Manny Ramirez .75 .35
□ 75 Dante Bichette .40 .18
□ 76 Vinny Castilla .20 .09
□ 77 Andres Galarraga .75 .35
□ 78 Walt Weiss .20 .09
□ 79 Ellis Burks .40 .18
□ 80 Larry Walker .75 .35
□ 81 Cecil Fielder .40 .18
□ 82 Melvin Nieves .20 .09
□ 83 Travis Fryman .40 .18

□ 84 Chad Curtis .20 .09
□ 85 Alan Trammell .60 .25
□ 86 Gary Sheffield .75 .35
□ 87 Charles Johnson .40 .18
□ 88 Andre Dawson .60 .25
□ 89 Jeff Conine .40 .18
□ 90 Greg Colbrunn .20 .09
□ 91 Derek Bell .20 .09
□ 92 Brian L. Hunter .40 .18
□ 93 Doug Drabek .20 .09
□ 94 Craig Biggio .60 .25
□ 95 Jeff Bagwell 1.50 .70
□ 96 Kevin Appier .40 .18
□ 97 Jeff Montgomery .20 .09
□ 98 Michael Tucker .40 .18
□ 99 Bip Roberts .20 .09
□ 100 Johnny Damon .40 .18
□ 101 Eric Karros .40 .18
□ 102 Raul Mondesi .60 .25
□ 103 Ramon Martinez .40 .18
□ 104 Ismael Valdes .40 .18
□ 105 Mike Piazza 2.50 1.10
□ 106 Hideo Nomo 2.00 .90
□ 107 Chan Ho Park .75 .35
□ 108 Ben McDonald .20 .09
□ 109 Kevin Seitzer .20 .09
□ 110 Greg Vaughn .20 .09
□ 111 Jose Valentin .20 .09
□ 112 Rick Aguilera .20 .09
□ 113 Marty McGwire .40 .18
□ 114 Brad Radke .40 .18
□ 115 Kirby Puckett 1.50 .70
□ 116 Chuck Knoblauch .75 .35
□ 117 Paul Molitor .75 .35
□ 118 Pedro Martinez .75 .35
□ 119 Mike Lansing .20 .09
□ 120 Rondell White .40 .18
□ 121 Moises Alou .40 .18
□ 122 Mark Grudzielanek .40 .18
□ 123 Jeff Fassero .20 .09
□ 124 Rico Brogna .20 .09
□ 125 Jason Isringhausen .20 .09
□ 126 Jeff Kent .20 .09
□ 127 Bernard Gilkey .20 .09
□ 128 Todd Hundley .40 .18
□ 129 David Cone .40 .18
□ 130 Andy Pettitte 1.00 .45
□ 131 Wade Boggs .75 .35
□ 132 Paul O'Neill .40 .18
□ 133 Ruben Sierra .20 .09
□ 134 John Wetteland .20 .09
□ 135 Derek Jeter 2.50 1.10
□ 136 Geronimo Berroa .20 .09
□ 137 Terry Steinbach .20 .09
□ 138 Ariel Prieto .20 .09
□ 139 Scott Brosius .20 .09
□ 140 Mark McGwire 1.50 .70
□ 141 Lenny Dykstra .40 .18
□ 142 Todd Zeile .20 .09
□ 143 Benito Santiago .20 .09
□ 144 Mickey Morandini .20 .09
□ 145 Gregg Jefferies .20 .09
□ 146 Denny Neagle .40 .18
□ 147 Orlando Merced .20 .09
□ 148 Charlie Hayes .20 .09
□ 149 Carlos Garcia .20 .09
□ 150 Jay Bell .40 .18
□ 151 Ray Lankford .40 .18
□ 152 Alan Benes .40 .18
   Andy Benes .09
□ 153 Dennis Eckersley .40 .18
□ 154 Gary Gaetti .20 .09
□ 155 Ozzie Smith 1.00 .45
□ 156 Ron Gant .40 .18
□ 157 Brian Jordan .40 .18
□ 158 Ken Caminiti .40 .18
□ 159 Rickey Henderson .60 .25
□ 160 Tony Gwynn 1.50 .70
□ 161 Wally Joyner .20 .09
□ 162 Andy Ashby .20 .09
□ 163 Steve Finley .40 .18
□ 164 Glenallen Hill .20 .09
□ 165 Matt Williams .60 .25
□ 166 Barry Bonds 1.00 .45
□ 167 William VanLandingham .20 .09
□ 168 Rod Beck .20 .09

□ 169 Randy Johnson .75 .35
□ 170 Ken Griffey Jr. 4.00 1.80
□ 171 Alex Rodriguez 2.50 1.10
□ 172 Edgar Martinez .60 .25
□ 173 Jay Buhner .60 .25
□ 174 Russ Davis .20 .09
□ 175 Juan Gonzalez 2.00 .90
□ 176 Mickey Tettleton .20 .09
□ 177 Will Clark .60 .25
□ 178 Ken Hill .20 .09
□ 179 Dean Palmer .20 .09
□ 180 Ivan Rodriguez 1.00 .45
□ 181 Carlos Delgado .40 .18
□ 182 Alex Gonzalez .20 .09
□ 183 Shawn Green .20 .09
□ 184 Juan Guzman .20 .09
□ 185 Joe Carter .40 .18
□ 186 Hideo Nomo CL 1.00 .45
□ 187 Cal Ripken CL 1.50 .70
□ 188 Ken Griffey Jr. CL 2.00 .90

1996 SP Baseball Heroes

This 10-card set was randomly inserted at the rate of one in 96 packs. It continues the insert set that was started in 1990 featuring ten of the top players in baseball. The fronts feature color action player photos with the team logo on an embossed foil background. The backs carry another color player photo, player information and statistics.

	MINT	NRMT
COMPLETE SET (10)	250.00	110.00
COMMON CARD (82-90/HDR)	12.00	5.50
STATED ODDS 1:96		

□ 82 Frank Thomas 40.00 18.00
□ 83 Albert Belle 12.00 5.50
□ 84 Barry Bonds 12.00 5.50
□ 85 Chipper Jones 30.00 13.50
□ 86 Hideo Nomo 25.00 11.00
□ 87 Mike Piazza 30.00 13.50
□ 88 Manny Ramirez 12.00 5.50
□ 89 Greg Maddux 30.00 13.50
□ 90 Ken Griffey Jr. 30.00 13.50
□ NNO Ken Griffey Jr. HDR 50.00 22.00

1996 SP Marquee Matchups

Randomly inserted at the rate of one in five packs, this 20-card set highlights two superstars' cards with a common matching stadium background photograph in a blue border. Each card features double foil stamping and embossed player images. The backs carry player information.

COMPLETE SET (20) ..... MINT 40.00 / NRMT 18.00
COMMON CARD (MM1-MM20) 1.25 .55
STATED ODDS 1:5
COMP.DIE CUT SET (20) .. 200.00 90.00
*DIE CUT STARS: 2X TO 5X BASIC MARQUEE
DC STATED ODDS 1:61

		MINT	NRMT
☐ MM1	Ken Griffey Jr.	8.00	3.60
☐ MM2	Hideo Nomo	4.00	1.80
☐ MM3	Derek Jeter	5.00	2.20
☐ MM4	Rey Ordonez	1.25	.55
☐ MM5	Tim Salmon	1.50	.70
☐ MM6	Mike Piazza	5.00	2.20
☐ MM7	Mark McGwire	3.00	1.35
☐ MM8	Barry Bonds	1.50	.70
☐ MM9	Cal Ripken	6.00	2.70
☐ MM10	Greg Maddux	5.00	2.20
☐ MM11	Albert Belle	2.00	.90
☐ MM12	Barry Larkin	1.25	.55
☐ MM13	Jeff Bagwell	3.00	1.35
☐ MM14	Juan Gonzalez	3.00	1.35
☐ MM15	Frank Thomas	6.00	2.70
☐ MM16	Sammy Sosa	1.50	.70
☐ MM17	Mike Mussina	1.50	.70
☐ MM18	Chipper Jones	5.00	2.20
☐ MM19	Roger Clemens	3.00	1.35
☐ MM20	Fred McGriff	1.25	.55

1996 SP Special FX

Randomly inserted at the rate of one in 5 packs, this 48-card set features a color action player cutout on a gold foil background with a holoview diamond shaped insert containing a black-and-white player portrait. A wide blue border runs vertically down one side of the card. The backs carry player information and statistics at home and away in baseball field designs on a blue background.

	MINT	NRMT
COMPLETE SET (48)	175.00	80.00
COMMON CARD (1-48)	1.00	.45
STATED ODDS 1:5		
COMP.DIE CUT SET (48) ..	800.00	350.00

*DIE CUT STARS: 1.5X TO 4X BASIC SPECIAL
DC STATED ODDS 1:75 ....

☐ 1	Greg Maddux	12.00	5.50
☐ 2	Eric Karros	2.00	.90
☐ 3	Mike Piazza	12.00	5.50
☐ 4	Raul Mondesi	2.50	1.10
☐ 5	Hideo Nomo	10.00	4.50
☐ 6	Jim Edmonds	2.50	1.10
☐ 7	Jason Isringhausen ...	1.00	.45
☐ 8	Jay Buhner	2.50	1.10
☐ 9	Barry Larkin	2.50	1.10
☐ 10	Ken Griffey Jr.	20.00	9.00
☐ 11	Gary Sheffield	4.00	1.80
☐ 12	Craig Biggio	2.50	1.10
☐ 13	Paul Wilson	1.00	.45
☐ 14	Rondell White	2.00	.90
☐ 15	Chipper Jones	12.00	5.50
☐ 16	Kirby Puckett	8.00	3.60
☐ 17	Ron Gant	2.00	.90
☐ 18	Wade Boggs	4.00	1.80
☐ 19	Fred McGriff	2.50	1.10
☐ 20	Cal Ripken	15.00	6.75
☐ 21	Jason Kendall	2.50	1.10
☐ 22	Johnny Damon	2.00	.90
☐ 23	Kenny Lofton	5.00	2.20
☐ 24	Roberto Alomar	5.00	2.20
☐ 25	Barry Bonds	5.00	2.20
☐ 26	Dante Bichette	2.00	.90
☐ 27	Mark McGwire	8.00	3.60
☐ 28	Rafael Palmeiro	2.50	1.10
☐ 29	Juan Gonzalez	10.00	4.50
☐ 30	Albert Belle	5.00	2.20
☐ 31	Randy Johnson	4.00	1.80
☐ 32	Jose Canseco	2.50	1.10
☐ 33	Sammy Sosa	4.00	1.80
☐ 34	Eddie Murray	4.00	1.80
☐ 35	Frank Thomas	15.00	6.75
☐ 36	Tom Glavine	2.00	.90
☐ 37	Matt Williams	2.50	1.10
☐ 38	Roger Clemens	8.00	3.60
☐ 39	Paul Molitor	4.00	1.80
☐ 40	Tony Gwynn	8.00	3.60
☐ 41	Mo Vaughn	5.00	2.20
☐ 42	Tim Salmon	4.00	1.80
☐ 43	Manny Ramirez	4.00	1.80
☐ 44	Jeff Bagwell	6.00	2.70
☐ 45	Edgar Martinez	2.50	1.10
☐ 46	Rey Ordonez	2.00	.90
☐ 47	Osvaldo Fernandez	2.00	.90
☐ 48	Derek Jeter	12.00	5.50

1997 SP

The 1997 SP set was issued in one series totalling 183 cards and was distributed in eight-card packs with a suggested retail of $4.39. The fronts feature color player photos with foil highlights. The backs carry player information and career statistics. Although unconfirmed by the manufacturer, it is widely perceived in collecting circles that cards numbered between 160 and 180 are in slightly

shorter supply. There are Jose Cruz and Hideki Irabu Rookie Cards in this set.

	MINT	NRMT
COMPLETE SET (184) ...	60.00	27.00
COMMON CARD (1-184) ..	.20	.09
MINOR STARS	.40	.18
UNLISTED STARS	.75	.35
COMP.GRIFFEY SET (10) .	250.00	110.00
COMMON GRIFFEY (91-100)	30.00	13.50
GRIFFEY PRINT RUN 2000 SERIAL #'d SETS		
GRIFFEY HEROES CONDITION SENSITIVE		

☐ 1	Andruw Jones FOIL	2.00	.90
☐ 2	Kevin Orie FOIL	.40	.18
☐ 3	Nomar Garciaparra FOIL	2.50	1.10
☐ 4	Jose Guillen FOIL	1.00	.45
☐ 5	Todd Walker FOIL	.40	.18
☐ 6	Derrick Gibson FOIL	.50	.23
☐ 7	Aaron Boone FOIL	.20	.09
☐ 8	Bartolo Colon FOIL	.40	.18
☐ 9	Derrek Lee FOIL	.50	.23
☐ 10	Vladimir Guerrero FOIL	1.50	.70
☐ 11	Wilton Guerrero FOIL ...	.20	.09
☐ 12	Luis Castillo FOIL	.40	.18
☐ 13	Jason Dickson FOIL	.40	.18
☐ 14	Bubba Trammell FOIL ..	1.00	.45
☐ 15	Jose Cruz Jr. FOIL	8.00	3.60
☐ 16	Eddie Murray	.75	.35
☐ 17	Darin Erstad	1.25	.55
☐ 18	Garret Anderson	.40	.18
☐ 19	Jim Edmonds	.50	.23
☐ 20	Tim Salmon	.75	.35
☐ 21	Chuck Finley	.20	.09
☐ 22	John Smoltz	.40	.18
☐ 23	Greg Maddux	2.50	1.10
☐ 24	Kenny Lofton	1.00	.45
☐ 25	Chipper Jones	2.50	1.10
☐ 26	Ryan Klesko	.50	.23
☐ 27	Javier Lopez	.40	.18
☐ 28	Fred McGriff	.50	.23
☐ 29	Roberto Alomar	.75	.35
☐ 30	Rafael Palmeiro	.50	.23
☐ 31	Mike Mussina	.75	.35
☐ 32	Brady Anderson	.50	.23
☐ 33	Rocky Coppinger	.20	.09
☐ 34	Cal Ripken	3.00	1.35
☐ 35	Mo Vaughn	1.00	.45
☐ 36	Steve Avery	.20	.09
☐ 37	Tom Gordon	.20	.09
☐ 38	Tim Naehring	.20	.09
☐ 39	Troy O'Leary	.20	.09
☐ 40	Sammy Sosa	.75	.35
☐ 41	Brian McRae	.20	.09
☐ 42	Mel Rojas	.20	.09
☐ 43	Ryne Sandberg	1.00	.45
☐ 44	Mark Grace	.50	.23
☐ 45	Albert Belle	1.00	.45
☐ 46	Robin Ventura	.40	.18
☐ 47	Roberto Hernandez	.20	.09
☐ 48	Ray Durham	.20	.09
☐ 49	Harold Baines	.40	.18
☐ 50	Frank Thomas	3.00	1.35
☐ 51	Bret Boone	.20	.09
☐ 52	Reggie Sanders	.20	.09
☐ 53	Deion Sanders	.40	.18
☐ 54	Hal Morris	.20	.09
☐ 55	Barry Larkin	.50	.23
☐ 56	Jim Thome	.75	.35
☐ 57	Marquis Grissom	.40	.18
☐ 58	David Justice	.75	.35
☐ 59	Charles Nagy	.40	.18
☐ 60	Manny Ramirez	.75	.35
☐ 61	Matt Williams	.50	.23
☐ 62	Jack McDowell	.20	.09
☐ 63	Vinny Castilla	.40	.18
☐ 64	Dante Bichette	.40	.18
☐ 65	Andres Galarraga	.75	.35
☐ 66	Ellis Burks	.40	.18
☐ 67	Larry Walker	.75	.35
☐ 68	Eric Young	.20	.09
☐ 69	Brian L. Hunter	.40	.18
☐ 70	Travis Fryman	.40	.18
☐ 71	Tony Clark	.75	.35
☐ 72	Bobby Higginson	.40	.18

□ 73	Melvin Nieves	.20	.09
□ 74	Jeff Conine	.40	.18
□ 75	Gary Sheffield	.75	.35
□ 76	Moises Alou	.40	.18
□ 77	Edgar Renteria	.40	.18
□ 78	Alex Fernandez	.40	.18
□ 79	Charles Johnson	.40	.18
□ 80	Bobby Bonilla	.40	.18
□ 81	Darryl Kile	.40	.18
□ 82	Derek Bell	.20	.09
□ 83	Shane Reynolds	.20	.09
□ 84	Craig Biggio	.50	.23
□ 85	Jeff Bagwell	1.50	.70
□ 86	Billy Wagner	.40	.18
□ 87	Chili Davis	.40	.18
□ 88	Kevin Appier	.40	.18
□ 89	Jay Bell	.40	.18
□ 90	Johnny Damon	.20	.09
□ 91	Jeff King	.20	.09
□ 92	Hideo Nomo	2.00	.90
□ 93	Todd Hollandsworth	.20	.09
□ 94	Eric Karros	.40	.18
□ 95	Mike Piazza	2.50	1.10
□ 96	Ramon Martinez	.40	.18
□ 97	Todd Worrell	.20	.09
□ 98	Raul Mondesi	.50	.23
□ 99	Dave Nilsson	.20	.09
□ 100	John Jaha	.20	.09
□ 101	Jose Valentin	.20	.09
□ 102	Jeff Cirillo	.40	.18
□ 103	Jeff D'Amico	.20	.09
□ 104	Ben McDonald	.20	.09
□ 105	Paul Molitor	.75	.35
□ 106	Rich Becker	.20	.09
□ 107	Frank Rodriguez	.20	.09
□ 108	Marty Cordova	.40	.18
□ 109	Terry Steinbach	.20	.09
□ 110	Chuck Knoblauch	.75	.35
□ 111	Mark Grudzielanek	.20	.09
□ 112	Mike Lansing	.20	.09
□ 113	Pedro J. Martinez	.75	.35
□ 114	Henry Rodriguez	.20	.09
□ 115	Rondell White	.40	.18
□ 116	Rey Ordonez	.20	.09
□ 117	Carlos Baerga	.20	.09
□ 118	Lance Johnson	.20	.09
□ 119	Bernard Gilkey	.20	.09
□ 120	Todd Hundley	.40	.18
□ 121	John Franco	.40	.18
□ 122	Bernie Williams	.75	.35
□ 123	David Cone	.40	.18
□ 124	Cecil Fielder	.40	.18
□ 125	Derek Jeter	2.50	1.10
□ 126	Tino Martinez	.75	.35
□ 127	Mariano Rivera	.40	.18
□ 128	Andy Pettitte	.75	.35
□ 129	Wade Boggs	.75	.35
□ 130	Mark McGwire	1.50	.70
□ 131	Jose Canseco	.50	.23
□ 132	Geronimo Berroa	.20	.09
□ 133	Jason Giambi	.40	.18
□ 134	Ernie Young	.20	.09
□ 135	Scott Rolen	2.00	.90
□ 136	Ricky Bottalico	.20	.09
□ 137	Curt Schilling	.40	.18
□ 138	Gregg Jefferies	.20	.09
□ 139	Mickey Morandini	.20	.09
□ 140	Jason Kendall	.40	.18
□ 141	Kevin Elster	.20	.09
□ 142	Al Martin	.20	.09
□ 143	Joe Randa	.20	.09
□ 144	Jason Schmidt	.20	.09
□ 145	Ray Lankford	.40	.18
□ 146	Brian Jordan	.40	.18
□ 147	Andy Benes	.40	.18
□ 148	Alan Benes	.40	.18
□ 149	Gary Gaetti	.20	.09
□ 150	Ron Gant	.40	.18
□ 151	Dennis Eckersley	.40	.18
□ 152	Rickey Henderson	.50	.23
□ 153	Joey Hamilton	.40	.18
□ 154	Ken Caminiti	.50	.23
□ 155	Tony Gwynn	2.00	.90
□ 156	Steve Finley	.40	.18
□ 157	Trevor Hoffman	.20	.09
□ 158	Greg Vaughn	.20	.09

□ 159	J.T. Snow	.40	.18
□ 160	Barry Bonds	1.00	.45
□ 161	Glenalien Hill	.20	.09
□ 162	William VanLandingham	.20	.09
□ 163	Jeff Kent	.20	.09
□ 164	Jay Buhner	.50	.23
□ 165	Ken Griffey Jr.	4.00	1.80
□ 166	Alex Rodriguez	2.50	1.10
□ 167	Randy Johnson	.75	.35
□ 168	Edgar Martinez	.50	.23
□ 169	Dan Wilson	.20	.09
□ 170	Ivan Rodriguez	1.00	.45
□ 171	Roger Pavlik	.20	.09
□ 172	Will Clark	.50	.23
□ 173	Dean Palmer	.20	.09
□ 174	Rusty Greer	.40	.18
□ 175	Juan Gonzalez	2.00	.90
□ 176	John Wetteland	.20	.09
□ 177	Joe Carter	.40	.18
□ 178	Ed Sprague	.20	.09
□ 179	Carlos Delgado	.40	.18
□ 180	Roger Clemens	1.50	.70
□ 181	Juan Guzman	.20	.09
□ 182	Pat Hentgen	.40	.18
□ 183	Ken Griffey Jr. CL	.75	.35
□ 184	Hideki Irabu	1.00	.45

	MINT	NRMT
COMPLETE SET (25)	300.00	135.00
COMMON CARD (1-25)	4.00	1.80
UNLISTED STARS	6.00	2.70
ONE PER SEALED BOX		

□ 1	Ken Griffey Jr.	30.00	13.50
□ 2	Mark McGwire	12.00	5.50
□ 3	Kenny Lofton	8.00	3.60
□ 4	Paul Molitor	6.00	2.70
□ 5	Frank Thomas	25.00	11.00
□ 6	Greg Maddux	20.00	9.00
□ 7	Mo Vaughn	8.00	3.60
□ 8	Cal Ripken	25.00	11.00
□ 9	Jeff Bagwell	12.00	5.50
□ 10	Alex Rodriguez	20.00	9.00
□ 11	John Smoltz	4.00	1.80
□ 12	Manny Ramirez	6.00	2.70
□ 13	Sammy Sosa	6.00	2.70
□ 14	Vladimir Guerrero	10.00	4.50
□ 15	Albert Belle	8.00	3.60
□ 16	Mike Piazza	20.00	9.00
□ 17	Derek Jeter	15.00	6.75
□ 18	Scott Rolen	12.00	5.50
□ 19	Tony Gwynn	15.00	6.75
□ 20	Barry Bonds	8.00	3.60
□ 21	Ken Caminiti	4.00	1.80
□ 22	Chipper Jones	20.00	9.00
□ 23	Juan Gonzalez	15.00	6.75
□ 24	Roger Clemens	12.00	5.50
□ 25	Andruw Jones	12.00	5.50

1997 SP Game Film

Randomly inserted in packs, this 10-card set features actual game film that highlights the accomplishments of some of the League's greatest players. Only 500 of each card in this crash numbered, limited edition set were produced.

	MINT	NRMT
COMPLETE SET (10)	1200.00	550.00
COMMON CARD (GF1-GF10)	50.00	22.00
RANDOM INSERTS IN PACKS		
STATED PRINT RUN 500 SERIAL #'d SETS		

□ GF1	Alex Rodriguez	120.00	55.00
□ GF2	Frank Thomas	150.00	70.00
□ GF3	Andruw Jones	80.00	36.00
□ GF4	Cal Ripken	150.00	70.00
□ GF5	Mike Piazza	120.00	55.00
□ GF6	Derek Jeter	100.00	45.00
□ GF7	Mark McGwire	80.00	36.00
□ GF8	Chipper Jones	100.00	45.00
□ GF9	Barry Bonds	50.00	22.00
□ GF10	Ken Griffey Jr.	200.00	90.00

1997 SP Inside Info

Inserted one in every 30-pack box, this 25-card set features color player photos on original cards with an exclusive pull-out panel that details the accomplishments of the League's brightest stars.

1997 SP Marquee Matchups

Randomly inserted in packs at a rate of one in five, this 20-card set features color player images on die-cut cards that match-up the best pitchers and hitters from around the League.

	MINT	NRMT
COMPLETE SET (20)	50.00	22.00
COMMON CARD (MM1-MM20)	1.00	.45
STATED ODDS 1:5		

| □ MM1 | Ken Griffey Jr. | 8.00 | 3.60 |
| □ MM2 | Andres Galarraga | 1.50 | .70 |

☐ MM3	Barry Bonds	2.00	.90
☐ MM4	Mark McGwire	3.00	1.35
☐ MM5	Mike Piazza	5.00	2.20
☐ MM6	Tim Salmon	1.50	.70
☐ MM7	Tony Gwynn	4.00	1.80
☐ MM8	Alex Rodriguez	5.00	2.20
☐ MM9	Chipper Jones	5.00	2.20
☐ MM10	Derek Jeter	5.00	2.20
☐ MM11	Manny Ramirez	1.50	.70
☐ MM12	Jeff Bagwell	3.00	1.35
☐ MM13	Greg Maddux	5.00	2.20
☐ MM14	Cal Ripken	6.00	2.70
☐ MM15	Mo Vaughn	2.00	.90
☐ MM16	Gary Sheffield	1.50	.70
☐ MM17	Jim Thome	1.50	.70
☐ MM18	Barry Larkin	1.00	.45
☐ MM19	Frank Thomas	6.00	2.70
☐ MM20	Sammy Sosa	1.50	.70

☐ 31	Eric Karros	2.50	1.10
☐ 32	Tim Salmon	5.00	2.20
☐ 33	Jay Buhner	3.00	1.35
☐ 34	Andy Pettitte	5.00	2.20
☐ 35	Jim Thome	5.00	2.20
☐ 36	Ryne Sandberg	5.00	2.70
☐ 37	Matt Williams	3.00	1.35
☐ 38	Ryan Klesko	3.00	1.35
☐ 39	Jose Canseco	3.00	1.35
☐ 40	Paul Molitor	5.00	2.20
☐ 41	Eddie Murray	5.00	2.20
☐ 42	Darin Erstad	6.00	2.70
☐ 43	Todd Walker	2.50	1.10
☐ 44	Wade Boggs	5.00	2.20
☐ 45	Andruw Jones	10.00	4.50
☐ 46	Scott Rolen	10.00	4.50
☐ 47	Vladimir Guerrero	8.00	3.60
☐ 49	Alex Rodriguez '96	20.00	9.00

	Roberto Alomar		
	Ivan Rodriguez		
☐ 9	Tony Gwynn	100.00	45.00
	Wade Boggs		
	Eddie Murray		
	Paul Molitor		
☐ 10	Andruw Jones	100.00	45.00
	Vladimir Guerrero		
	Todd Walker		
	Scott Rolen		

1997 SP Special FX

Randomly inserted in packs at a rate of one in nine, this 48-card set features color player photos on Holoview cards with the Special F/X die-cut design. Cards #1-47 are from 1997 with card #49 featuring a design from 1996. There is no card #48.

	MINT	NRMT
COMPLETE SET (48)	300.00	135.00
COMMON CARD (1-47/49)	2.50	1.10
UNLISTED STARS	5.00	2.20
STATED ODDS 1:9		

☐ 1	Ken Griffey Jr.	25.00	11.00
☐ 2	Frank Thomas	20.00	9.00
☐ 3	Barry Bonds	6.00	2.70
☐ 4	Albert Belle	6.00	2.70
☐ 5	Mike Piazza	15.00	6.75
☐ 6	Greg Maddux	15.00	6.75
☐ 7	Chipper Jones	15.00	6.75
☐ 8	Cal Ripken	20.00	9.00
☐ 9	Jeff Bagwell	10.00	4.50
☐ 10	Alex Rodriguez	15.00	6.75
☐ 11	Mark McGwire	10.00	4.50
☐ 12	Kenny Lofton	6.00	2.70
☐ 13	Juan Gonzalez	12.00	5.50
☐ 14	Mo Vaughn	6.00	2.70
☐ 15	John Smoltz	2.50	1.10
☐ 16	Derek Jeter	12.00	5.50
☐ 17	Tony Gwynn	12.00	5.50
☐ 18	Ivan Rodriguez	6.00	2.70
☐ 19	Barry Larkin	3.00	1.35
☐ 20	Sammy Sosa	5.00	2.20
☐ 21	Mike Mussina	5.00	2.20
☐ 22	Gary Sheffield	5.00	2.20
☐ 23	Brady Anderson	3.00	1.35
☐ 24	Roger Clemens	10.00	4.50
☐ 25	Ken Caminiti	3.00	1.35
☐ 26	Roberto Alomar	5.00	2.20
☐ 27	Hideo Nomo	12.00	5.50
☐ 28	Bernie Williams	5.00	2.20
☐ 29	Todd Hundley	2.50	1.10
☐ 30	Manny Ramirez	5.00	2.20

1997 SP SPx Force

Randomly inserted in packs, this 10-card die-cut set features head photos of four of the very best players on each card with an "X" in the background and players' and teams' names on one side. Only 500 of each card in this crash numbered, limited edition set were produced.

	MINT	NRMT
COMPLETE SET (10)	1200.00	550.00
COMMON CARD (1-10)	60.00	27.00
RANDOM INSERTS IN PACKS		
STATED PRINT RUN 500 SERIAL #'d SETS		

☐ 1	Ken Griffey Jr.	200.00	90.00
	Jay Buhner		
	Andres Galarraga		
	Dante Bichette		
☐ 2	Albert Belle	80.00	36.00
	Brady Anderson		
	Mark McGwire		
	Cecil Fielder		
☐ 3	Mo Vaughn	150.00	70.00
	Ken Caminiti		
	Frank Thomas		
	Jeff Bagwell		
☐ 4	Gary Sheffield	60.00	27.00
	Sammy Sosa		
	Barry Bonds		
	Jose Canseco		
☐ 5	Greg Maddux	150.00	70.00
	Roger Clemens		
	John Smoltz		
	Randy Johnson		
☐ 6	Alex Rodriguez	150.00	70.00
	Derek Jeter		
	Chipper Jones		
	Cal Ripken		
☐ 7	Todd Hollandsworth	100.00	45.00
	Mike Piazza		
	Raul Mondesi		
	Hideo Nomo		
☐ 8	Juan Gonzalez	100.00	45.00
	Manny Ramirez		

1997 SP SPx Force Autographs

Randomly inserted in packs, this 10-card set is an autographed parallel version of the regular SPx Force set. Only 100 of each card in this crash numbered, limited edition set were produced.

	MINT	NRMT
COMPLETE SET (10)	3000.00	1350.00
COMMON CARD (1-10)	120.00	55.00
RANDOM INSERTS IN PACKS		
STATED PRINT RUN 100 SERIAL #'d SETS		

☐ 1	Ken Griffey Jr. AU	1000.00	450.00
☐ 2	Albert Belle AU	200.00	90.00
☐ 3	Mo Vaughn AU EXCH	200.00	90.00
☐ 4	Gary Sheffield AU	150.00	70.00
☐ 5	Greg Maddux AU	500.00	220.00
☐ 6	Alex Rodriguez AU	500.00	220.00
☐ 7	Todd Hollandsworth AU	120.00	55.00
☐ 8	Roberto Alomar AU	200.00	90.00
☐ 9	Tony Gwynn AU	400.00	180.00
☐ 10	Andruw Jones AU	250.00	110.00

1997 SP Vintage Autographs

Randomly inserted in packs, this 31-card set features authenticated original 1993-1996 SP cards that have been autographed by the pictured player. The print runs are listed after year following the player's name in the checklist below. Some of the very short printed autographs are listed but not priced.

	MINT	NRMT
COMMON CARD (1-31)	25.00	11.00
RANDOM INSERTS IN PACKS		
PRINT RUNS LISTED AFTER YEAR BELOW		

☐ 1	Jeff Bagwell '93/7		
☐ 2	Jeff Bagwell '95/173	200.00	90.00
☐ 3	Jeff Bagwell '96/292	150.00	70.00
☐ 4	Jeff Bagwell '96 MM/23	500.00	220.00
☐ 5	Jay Buhner '95/57	100.00	45.00
☐ 6	Jay Buhner '96/79	100.00	45.00

☐ 7 Jay Buhner '96 FX/27 150.00 70.00
☐ 8 Ken Griffey Jr. '93/16 2500.00 1100.00
☐ 9 Ken Griffey Jr. '93 PP/5....
☐ 10 Ken Griffey Jr. '94/103 1000.00 450.00
☐ 11 Ken Griffey Jr. '95/38 1500.00 700.00
☐ 12 Ken Griffey Jr. '96/312 500.00 220.00
☐ 13 Tony Gwynn '93/17 800.00 350.00
☐ 14 Tony Gwynn '94/367 200.00 90.00
☐ 15 Tony Gwynn '94 HV/31 500.00 220.00
☐ 16 Tony Gwynn '95/64 400.00 180.00
☐ 17 Tony Gwynn '96/20 600.00 275.00
☐ 18 Todd Hollandsworth '94/167 25.00 11.00
☐ 19 Chipper Jones '93/34 500.00 220.00
☐ 20 Chipper Jones '95/60 400.00 180.00
☐ 21 Chipper Jones '96/102 300.00 135.00
☐ 22 R.Ordonez '96/111 . 30.00 13.50
☐ 23 Rey Ordonez '96 MM/40 50.00 22.00
☐ 24 Alex Rodriguez '94/94 400.00 180.00
☐ 25 Alex Rodriguez '95/63 500.00 220.00
☐ 26 Alex Rodriguez '96/73 500.00 220.00
☐ 27 Gary Sheffield '94/130 100.00 45.00
☐ 28 Gary Sheffield '94 HVDC/4
☐ 29 Gary Sheffield '95/221 80.00 36.00
☐ 30 Gary Sheffield '96/58 120.00 55.00
☐ 31 Mo Vaughn '97 EXCH/250 80.00 36.00

1995 SP Championship

This set contains 200 cards that were sold in six-card retail packs for a suggested price of $2.99. The fronts have a full-bleed action photo with the words "SP Championship Series" in gold-foil in the bottom left-hand corner. In the bottom right-hand corner is the team's name in blue (National League) and red (American League) foil. The backs have a small head shot and player information. Statistics and team name are also on the back in blue or red just like on the front. Subsets featured are Diamonds in the Rough (1-20), October Legends (100-114) and Major League Profiles. Rookie Cards in this set include Bobby Higginson and Hideo Nomo.

	MINT	NRMT
COMPLETE SET (200)	40.00	18.00
COMMON CARD (1-200)	.20	.09
MINOR STARS	.40	.18
UNLISTED STARS	.75	.35
SUBSET CARDS HALF VALUE OF BASE CARDS		
COMP.DIE CUT SET (200)	150.00	70.00
COMMON DIE CUT (1-200)	.30	.14
*DIE CUT STARS: 1.5X TO 3X HI COLUMN		
*DIE CUT YOUNG STARS: 1.25X TO 2.5X HI		
ONE DIE CUT PER PACK		

☐ 1 Hideo Nomo 4.00 1.80
☐ 2 Roger Cedeno .40 .18

☐ 3 Curtis Goodwin .20 .09
☐ 4 Jon Nunnally .20 .09
☐ 5 Bill Pulsipher .20 .09
☐ 6 Garret Anderson .60 .25
☐ 7 Dustin Hermanson .40 .18
☐ 8 Marty Cordova .40 .18
☐ 9 Ruben Rivera .75 .35
☐ 10 Ariel Prieto .40 .18
☐ 11 Edgardo Alfonzo .75 .35
☐ 12 Ray Durham .40 .18
☐ 13 Quilvio Veras .20 .09
☐ 14 Ugueth Urbina .40 .18
☐ 15 Carlos Perez .40 .18
☐ 16 Glenn Dishman .40 .18
☐ 17 Jeff Suppan .60 .25
☐ 18 Jason Bates .20 .09
☐ 19 Jason Isringhausen .40 .18
☐ 20 Derek Jeter 2.50 1.10
☐ 21 Fred McGriff MLP .60 .25
☐ 22 Marquis Grissom .40 .18
☐ 23 Fred McGriff .60 .25
☐ 24 Tom Glavine .40 .18
☐ 25 Greg Maddux 2.50 1.10
☐ 26 Chipper Jones 2.50 1.10
☐ 27 Sammy Sosa MLP .40 .18
☐ 28 Randy Myers .20 .09
☐ 29 Mark Grace .60 .25
☐ 30 Sammy Sosa .75 .35
☐ 31 Todd Zeile .20 .09
☐ 32 Brian McRae .20 .09
☐ 33 Ron Gant MLP .20 .09
☐ 34 Reggie Sanders .40 .18
☐ 35 Ron Gant .40 .18
☐ 36 Barry Larkin .60 .25
☐ 37 Bret Boone .20 .09
☐ 38 John Smiley .20 .09
☐ 39 Larry Walker MLP .40 .18
☐ 40 Andres Galarraga .75 .35
☐ 41 Bill Swift .20 .09
☐ 42 Larry Walker .75 .35
☐ 43 Vinny Castilla .40 .18
☐ 44 Dante Bichette .40 .18
☐ 45 Jeff Conine MLP .20 .09
☐ 46 Charles Johnson .40 .18
☐ 47 Gary Sheffield .75 .35
☐ 48 Andre Dawson .60 .25
☐ 49 Jeff Conine .40 .18
☐ 50 Jeff Bagwell MLP .75 .35
☐ 51 Phil Nevin .20 .09
☐ 52 Craig Biggio .60 .25
☐ 53 Brian L. Hunter .25 .11
☐ 54 Doug Drabek .20 .09
☐ 55 Jeff Bagwell 1.50 .70
☐ 56 Derek Bell .20 .09
☐ 57 Mike Piazza MLP 1.25 .55
☐ 58 Raul Mondesi .60 .25
☐ 59 Eric Karros .40 .18
☐ 60 Mike Piazza 2.50 1.10
☐ 61 Ramon Martinez .40 .18
☐ 62 Billy Ashley .20 .09
☐ 63 Rondell White MLP .20 .09
☐ 64 Jeff Fassero .20 .09
☐ 65 Moises Alou .40 .18
☐ 66 Tony Tarasco .20 .09
☐ 67 Rondell White .40 .18
☐ 68 Pedro J. Martinez .75 .35
☐ 69 Bobby Jones MLP .20 .09
☐ 70 Bobby Bonilla .40 .18
☐ 71 Bobby Jones .20 .09
☐ 72 Bret Saberhagen .20 .09
☐ 73 Darren Daulton MLP .20 .09
☐ 74 Darren Daulton .40 .18
☐ 75 Gregg Jefferies .20 .09
☐ 76 Tyler Green .20 .09
☐ 77 Heathcliff Slocumb .20 .09
☐ 78 Lenny Dykstra .40 .18
☐ 79 Jay Bell MLP .20 .09
☐ 80 Denny Neagle .40 .18
☐ 81 Orlando Merced .20 .09
☐ 82 Jay Bell .40 .18
☐ 83 Ozzie Smith MLP .40 .18
☐ 84 Ken Hill .20 .09
☐ 85 Ozzie Smith 1.00 .45
☐ 86 Bernard Gilkey .20 .09
☐ 87 Ray Lankford .40 .18
☐ 88 Tony Gwynn MLP .75 .35

☐ 89 Ken Caminiti .60 .25
☐ 90 Tony Gwynn 2.00 .90
☐ 91 Joey Hamilton .40 .18
☐ 92 Bip Roberts .20 .09
☐ 93 Deion Sanders MLP .20 .09
☐ 94 Glenallen Hill .20 .09
☐ 95 Matt Williams .60 .25
☐ 96 Barry Bonds 1.00 .45
☐ 97 Rod Beck .20 .09
☐ 98 Eddie Murray CL .40 .18
☐ 99 Cal Ripken Jr. CL 1.50 .70
☐ 100 Roberto Alomar OL .75 .35
☐ 101 George Brett OL 1.50 .70
☐ 102 Joe Carter OL .20 .09
☐ 103 Will Clark OL .40 .18
☐ 104 Dennis Eckersley OL .. .20 .09
☐ 105 Whitey Ford OL .75 .35
☐ 106 Steve Garvey OL .40 .18
☐ 107 Kirk Gibson OL .20 .09
☐ 108 Orel Hershiser OL .40 .18
☐ 109 Reggie Jackson OL .75 .35
☐ 110 Paul Molitor OL .40 .18
☐ 111 Kirby Puckett OL .75 .35
☐ 112 Mike Schmidt OL .75 .35
☐ 113 Dave Stewart OL .20 .09
☐ 114 Alan Trammell OL .60 .25
☐ 115 Cal Ripken Jr. MLP 1.50 .70
☐ 116 Brady Anderson .60 .25
☐ 117 Mike Mussina .75 .35
☐ 118 Rafael Palmeiro .60 .25
☐ 119 Chris Hoiles .20 .09
☐ 120 Cal Ripken 3.00 1.35
☐ 121 Mo Vaughn MLP .60 .25
☐ 122 Roger Clemens 1.50 .70
☐ 123 Tim Naehring .20 .09
☐ 124 John Valentin .20 .09
☐ 125 Mo Vaughn 1.00 .45
☐ 126 Tim Wakefield .20 .09
☐ 127 Jose Canseco .60 .25
☐ 128 Rick Aguilera .20 .09
☐ 129 Chili Davis MLP .20 .09
☐ 130 Lee Smith .40 .18
☐ 131 Jim Edmonds .60 .25
☐ 132 Chuck Finley .20 .09
☐ 133 Chili Davis .20 .09
☐ 134 J.T. Snow .40 .18
☐ 135 Tim Salmon .75 .35
☐ 136 Frank Thomas MLP . 1.50 .70
☐ 137 Jason Bere .20 .09
☐ 138 Robin Ventura .40 .18
☐ 139 Tim Raines .40 .18
☐ 140 Frank Thomas 3.00 1.35
☐ 141 Alex Fernandez .20 .09
☐ 142 Eddie Murray MLP .40 .18
☐ 143 Carlos Baerga .20 .09
☐ 144 Eddie Murray .75 .35
☐ 145 Albert Belle 1.00 .45
☐ 146 Jim Thome .75 .35
☐ 147 Dennis Martinez .40 .18
☐ 148 Dave Winfield .60 .25
☐ 149 Kenny Lofton 1.00 .45
☐ 150 Manny Ramirez .75 .35
☐ 151 Cecil Fielder MLP .20 .09
☐ 152 Lou Whitaker .40 .18
☐ 153 Alan Trammell .40 .18
☐ 154 Kirk Gibson .40 .18
☐ 155 Cecil Fielder .40 .18
☐ 156 Bobby Higginson 1.25 .55
☐ 157 Kevin Appier MLP .20 .09
☐ 158 Wally Joyner .40 .18
☐ 159 Jeff Montgomery .20 .09
☐ 160 Kevin Appier .20 .09
☐ 161 Gary Gaetti .20 .09
☐ 162 Greg Gagne .20 .09
☐ 163 Ricky Bones .20 .09
☐ 164 Greg Vaughn .20 .09
☐ 165 Kevin Seitzer .20 .09
☐ 166 Ricky Bones .20 .09
☐ 167 Kirby Puckett MLP .75 .35
☐ 168 Pedro Munoz .20 .09
☐ 169 Chuck Knoblauch .75 .35
☐ 170 Kirby Puckett 1.50 .70
☐ 171 Don Mattingly MLP .60 .25
☐ 172 Wade Boggs .75 .35
☐ 173 Paul O'Neill .40 .18
☐ 174 John Wetteland .20 .09

☐ 175	Don Mattingly	1.25	.55
☐ 176	Jack McDowell	.20	.09
☐ 177	Mark McGwire MLP	.75	.35
☐ 178	Rickey Henderson	.60	.25
☐ 179	Terry Steinbach	.20	.09
☐ 180	Ruben Sierra	.20	.09
☐ 181	Mark McGwire	1.50	.70
☐ 182	Dennis Eckersley	.40	.18
☐ 183	Ken Griffey Jr. MLP	2.00	.90
☐ 184	Alex Rodriguez	3.00	1.35
☐ 185	Ken Griffey Jr.	4.00	1.80
☐ 186	Randy Johnson	.75	.35
☐ 187	Jay Buhner	.60	.25
☐ 188	Edgar Martinez	.60	.25
☐ 189	Will Clark MLP	.40	.18
☐ 190	Juan Gonzalez	2.00	.90
☐ 191	Benji Gil	.20	.09
☐ 192	Ivan Rodriguez	1.00	.45
☐ 193	Kenny Rogers	.20	.09
☐ 194	Will Clark	.60	.25
☐ 195	Paul Molitor MLP	.40	.18
☐ 196	Roberto Alomar	.75	.35
☐ 197	David Cone	.40	.18
☐ 198	Paul Molitor	.75	.35
☐ 199	Shawn Green	.40	.18
☐ 200	Joe Carter	.40	.18
☐ CR1	Cal Ripken, Jr. Tribute	25.00	11.00
☐ CR1	Cal Ripken 2131 DC	80.00	36.00

1995 SP Championship Classic Performances

Cards from this 10-card set were randomly inserted in packs at a rate of one in 15. The set consists of 10 of the most memorable highlights since the 1969 Miracle Mets. The fronts have a series action photo highlighted with the words "Classic Performances" at the top in gold-foil enclosed by red. The backs have a color head shot with information and statistics from the series.

		MINT	NRMT
	COMPLETE SET (10)	40.00	18.00
	COMMON CARD (CP1-CP10)	2.00	.90
	UNLISTED STARS	4.00	1.80
	STATED ODDS 1:15		
	COMP.DIE CUT SET (10)	200.00	90.00
	*DIE CUTS: 2X TO 5X HI COLUMN		
	DC STATED ODDS 1:75		

☐ CP1	Reggie Jackson	5.00	2.20
☐ CP2	Nolan Ryan	15.00	6.75
☐ CP3	Kirk Gibson	2.50	1.10
☐ CP4	Joe Carter	2.50	1.10
☐ CP5	George Brett	8.00	3.60
☐ CP6	Roberto Alomar	4.00	1.80
☐ CP7	Ozzie Smith	5.00	2.20

☐ CP8	Kirby Puckett	8.00	3.60
☐ CP9	Bret Saberhagen	2.00	.90
☐ CP10	Steve Garvey	2.50	1.10

1995 SP Championship Fall Classic

This nine-card set was randomly inserted in packs at a rate of one in 40. The set is comprised of players who had never been to the World Series prior to the 1995 Fall Classic. The fronts have a color-action photo with the game background in foil. There is a grain-colored border with the word "Destination" at the top in bronze-foil and "Fall Classic" underneath in black. The backs have a small, color picture inside a black box with player information underneath. Diecut versions were inserted at a rate of one in 72 packs and are valued at 1.5X to 3X the prices below.

		MINT	NRMT
	COMPLETE SET (9)	120.00	55.00
	*SINGLES: 3X TO 8X BASE CARD HI		
	STATED ODDS 1:40		
	COMP.DIE CUT SET (9)	250.00	110.00
	*DIE CUTS: .75X TO 2X BASIC FALL		
	DC STATED ODDS 1:75		

☐ 1	Ken Griffey Jr.	30.00	13.50
☐ 2	Frank Thomas	25.00	11.00
☐ 3	Albert Belle	8.00	3.60
☐ 4	Mike Piazza	20.00	9.00
☐ 5	Don Mattingly	10.00	4.50
☐ 6	Hideo Nomo	30.00	13.50
☐ 7	Greg Maddux	20.00	9.00
☐ 8	Fred McGriff	4.00	1.80
☐ 9	Barry Bonds	6.00	2.70

1994 Sportflics

After a three-year hiatus, Pinnacle resumed producing these lenticular "three-dimensional" cards, issued in hobby and retail packs. Each of the 193 "Magic Motion" cards features two images, which alternate when the card is viewed from different angles and creates the illusion of movement. Cards 176-193 are Starflics featuring top stars. The two commemorative cards, featuring Cliff Floyd and Paul Molitor, were inserted at a rate of one in every 360 packs.

		MINT	NRMT
	COMPLETE SET (193)	25.00	11.00
	COMMON CARD (1-193)	.15	.07
	MINOR STARS	.30	.14
	UNLISTED STARS	.60	.25
	SUBSET CARDS HALF VALUE OF BASE CARDS		
	SPECIAL CARDS STATED ODDS 1:360		

☐ 1	Lenny Dykstra	.30	.14
☐ 2	Mike Stanley	.15	.07
☐ 3	Alex Fernandez	.15	.07
☐ 4	Mark McGwire UER	1.25	.55
	(name spelled McGuire on front)		
☐ 5	Eric Karros	.30	.14
☐ 6	Dave Justice	.60	.25
☐ 7	Jeff Bagwell	1.25	.55
☐ 8	Darren Lewis	.15	.07
☐ 9	David McCarty	.15	.07
☐ 10	Albert Belle	.75	.35
☐ 11	Ben McDonald	.15	.07
☐ 12	Joe Carter	.30	.14
☐ 13	Benito Santiago	.15	.07
☐ 14	Rob Dibble	.15	.07
☐ 15	Roger Clemens	1.25	.55
☐ 16	Travis Fryman	.30	.14
☐ 17	Doug Drabek	.15	.07
☐ 18	Jay Buhner	.40	.18
☐ 19	Orlando Merced	.15	.07
☐ 20	Ryan Klesko	.60	.25
☐ 21	Chuck Finley	.15	.07
☐ 22	Dante Bichette	.30	.14
☐ 23	Wally Joyner	.30	.14
☐ 24	Robin Yount	.40	.18
☐ 25	Tony Gwynn	1.50	.70
☐ 26	Allen Watson	.15	.07
☐ 27	Rick Wilkins	.15	.07
☐ 28	Gary Sheffield	.60	.25
☐ 29	John Burkett	.15	.07
☐ 30	Randy Johnson	.60	.25
☐ 31	Roberto Alomar	.60	.25
☐ 32	Fred McGriff	.40	.18
☐ 33	Ozzie Guillen	.15	.07
☐ 34	Jimmy Key	.30	.14
☐ 35	Juan Gonzalez	1.50	.70
☐ 36	Wil Cordero	.15	.07
☐ 37	Aaron Sele	.15	.07
☐ 38	Mark Langston	.15	.07
☐ 39	David Cone	.30	.14
☐ 40	John Jaha	.15	.07
☐ 41	Ozzie Smith	.75	.35
☐ 42	Kirby Puckett	1.25	.55
☐ 43	Kenny Lofton	.75	.35
☐ 44	Mike Mussina	.60	.25
☐ 45	Ryne Sandberg	.75	.35
☐ 46	Robby Thompson	.15	.07
☐ 47	Bryan Harvey	.15	.07
☐ 48	Marquis Grissom	.30	.14
☐ 49	Bobby Bonilla	.30	.14
☐ 50	Dennis Eckersley	.30	.14
☐ 51	Curt Schilling	.30	.14
☐ 52	Andy Benes	.30	.14
☐ 53	Greg Maddux	2.00	.90
☐ 54	Bill Swift	.15	.07
☐ 55	Andres Galarraga	.60	.25
☐ 56	Tony Phillips	.15	.07
☐ 57	Darryl Hamilton	.15	.07
☐ 58	Duane Ward	.15	.07
☐ 59	Bernie Williams	.60	.25

☐ 60 Steve Avery	.15	.07
☐ 61 Eduardo Perez	.15	.07
☐ 62 Jeff Conine	.30	.14
☐ 63 Dave Winfield	.40	.18
☐ 64 Phil Plantier	.15	.07
☐ 65 Ray Lankford	.30	.14
☐ 66 Robin Ventura	.30	.14
☐ 67 Mike Piazza	2.00	.90
☐ 68 Jason Bere	.15	.07
☐ 69 Cal Ripken	2.50	1.10
☐ 70 Frank Thomas	2.50	1.10
☐ 71 Carlos Baerga	.15	.07
☐ 72 Darryl Kile	.30	.14
☐ 73 Ruben Sierra	.15	.07
☐ 74 Gregg Jefferies UER	.15	.07
Name spelled Jeffries on front		
☐ 75 John Olerud	.30	.14
☐ 76 Andy Van Slyke	.30	.14
☐ 77 Larry Walker	.60	.25
☐ 78 Cecil Fielder	.30	.14
☐ 79 Andre Dawson	.40	.18
☐ 80 Tom Glavine	.30	.14
☐ 81 Sammy Sosa	.60	.25
☐ 82 Charlie Hayes	.15	.07
☐ 83 Chuck Knoblauch	.60	.25
☐ 84 Kevin Appier	.30	.14
☐ 85 Dean Palmer	.15	.07
☐ 86 Royce Clayton	.15	.07
☐ 87 Moises Alou	.30	.14
☐ 88 Ivan Rodriguez	.75	.35
☐ 89 Tim Salmon	.60	.25
☐ 90 Ron Gant	.30	.14
☐ 91 Barry Bonds	.75	.35
☐ 92 Jack McDowell	.15	.07
☐ 93 Alan Trammell	.40	.18
☐ 94 Doc Gooden	.30	.14
☐ 95 Jay Bell	.30	.14
☐ 96 Devon White	.15	.07
☐ 97 Wilson Alvarez	.15	.07
☐ 98 Jim Thome	.75	.35
☐ 99 Ramon Martinez	.30	.14
☐ 100 Kent Hrbek	.30	.14
☐ 101 John Kruk	.30	.14
☐ 102 Wade Boggs	.60	.25
☐ 103 Greg Vaughn	.15	.07
☐ 104 Tom Henke	.15	.07
☐ 105 Brian Jordan	.40	.18
☐ 106 Paul Molitor	.60	.25
☐ 107 Cal Eldred	.15	.07
☐ 108 Deion Sanders	.30	.14
☐ 109 Barry Larkin	.40	.18
☐ 110 Mike Greenwell	.15	.07
☐ 111 Jeff Blauser	.30	.14
☐ 112 Jose Rijo	.15	.07
☐ 113 Pete Harnisch	.15	.07
☐ 114 Chris Hoiles	.15	.07
☐ 115 Edgar Martinez	.40	.18
☐ 116 Juan Guzman	.15	.07
☐ 117 Todd Zeile	.15	.07
☐ 118 Danny Tartabull	.15	.07
☐ 119 Chad Curtis	.15	.07
☐ 120 Mark Grace	.40	.18
☐ 121 J.T. Snow	.60	.25
☐ 122 Mo Vaughn	.75	.35
☐ 123 Lance Johnson	.15	.07
☐ 124 Eric Davis	.30	.14
☐ 125 Orel Hershiser	.15	.07
☐ 126 Kevin Mitchell	.15	.07
☐ 127 Don Mattingly	1.00	.45
☐ 128 Darren Daulton	.30	.14
☐ 129 Rod Beck	.15	.07
☐ 130 Charles Nagy	.30	.14
☐ 131 Mickey Tettleton	.15	.07
☐ 132 Kevin Brown	.30	.14
☐ 133 Pat Hentgen	.30	.14
☐ 134 Terry Mulholland	.15	.07
☐ 135 Steve Finley	.30	.14
☐ 136 John Smoltz	.30	.14
☐ 137 Frank Viola	.15	.07
☐ 138 Jim Abbott	.30	.14
☐ 139 Matt Williams	.40	.18
☐ 140 Bernard Gilkey	.15	.07
☐ 141 Jose Canseco	.40	.18
☐ 142 Mark Whiten	.15	.07
☐ 143 Ken Griffey Jr.	3.00	1.35
☐ 144 Rafael Palmeiro	.40	.18

☐ 145 Dave Hollins	.15	.07
☐ 146 Will Clark	.40	.18
☐ 147 Paul O'Neill	.30	.14
☐ 148 Bobby Jones	.30	.14
☐ 149 Butch Huskey	.30	.14
☐ 150 Jeffrey Hammonds	.30	.14
☐ 151 Manny Ramirez	.75	.35
☐ 152 Bob Hamelin	.15	.07
☐ 153 Kurt Abbott	.15	.07
☐ 154 Scott Stahoviak	.15	.07
☐ 155 Steve Hosey	.15	.07
☐ 156 Salomon Torres	.15	.07
☐ 157 Sterling Hitchcock	.15	.07
☐ 158 Nigel Wilson	.15	.07
☐ 159 Luis Lopez	.15	.07
☐ 160 Chipper Jones	2.00	.90
☐ 161 Norberto Martin	.15	.07
☐ 162 Raul Mondesi	.60	.25
☐ 163 Steve Karsay	.15	.07
☐ 164 J.R. Phillips	.15	.07
☐ 165 Marc Newfield	.30	.14
☐ 166 Mark Hutton	.15	.07
☐ 167 Curtis Pride	.15	.07
☐ 168 Carl Everett	.15	.07
☐ 169 Scott Ruffcorn	.15	.07
☐ 170 Turk Wendell	.15	.07
☐ 171 Jeff McNeely	.15	.07
☐ 172 Javier Lopez	.40	.18
☐ 173 Cliff Floyd	.30	.14
☐ 174 Rondell White	.40	.18
☐ 175 Scott Lydy	.15	.07
☐ 176 Frank Thomas AS	1.25	.55
☐ 177 Roberto Alomar AS	.30	.14
☐ 178 Travis Fryman AS	.15	.07
☐ 179 Cal Ripken AS	1.25	.55
☐ 180 Chris Hoiles AS	.15	.07
☐ 181 Ken Griffey Jr. AS	1.50	.70
☐ 182 Juan Gonzalez AS	.75	.35
☐ 183 Joe Carter AS	.15	.07
☐ 184 Jack McDowell AS	.15	.07
☐ 185 Fred McGriff AS	.30	.14
☐ 186 Robby Thompson AS	.15	.07
☐ 187 Matt Williams AS	.30	.14
☐ 188 Jay Bell AS	.15	.07
☐ 189 Mike Piazza AS	1.00	.45
☐ 190 Barry Bonds AS	.40	.18
☐ 191 Lenny Dykstra AS	.30	.14
☐ 192 Dave Justice AS	.30	.14
☐ 193 Greg Maddux AS	1.00	.45
☐ NNO0 Cliff Floyd Special	2.00	.90
☐ NNO0 Paul Molitor Special	10.00	4.50

	MINT	NRMT
COMPLETE SET (12)	50.00	22.00
COMMON CARD (MM1-MM12)	1.00	.45
STATED ODDS 1:24 RETAIL		
☐ MM1 Gregg Jefferies	1.00	.45
☐ MM2 Ryne Sandberg	8.00	3.60
☐ MM3 Cecil Fielder	2.00	.90
☐ MM4 Kirby Puckett	10.00	4.50
☐ MM5 Tony Gwynn	12.00	5.50
☐ MM6 Andres Galarraga	5.00	2.20
☐ MM7 Sammy Sosa	5.00	2.20
☐ MM8 Rickey Henderson	3.00	1.35
☐ MM9 Don Mattingly	8.00	3.60
☐ MM10 Joe Carter	2.00	.90
☐ MM11 Carlos Baerga	1.00	.45
☐ MM12 Lenny Dykstra	2.00	.90

1994 Sportflics Shakers

These 12 standard-size chase cards were randomly inserted in hobby foil packs and picture baseball's elite young players. The insertion rate was one in every 24 foil packs. Fronts feature the dual image effect with the player's name also appearing as dual image. The name "Shakers" appears in a circular design off to the left of the player's name.

	MINT	NRMT
COMPLETE SET (12)	70.00	32.00
COMMON CARD (SH1-SH12)	2.00	.90
STATED ODDS 1:24 HOBBY		
☐ SH1 Kenny Lofton	8.00	3.60
☐ SH2 Tim Salmon	6.00	2.70
☐ SH3 Jeff Bagwell	15.00	6.75
☐ SH4 Jason Bere	2.00	.90
☐ SH5 Salomon Torres	2.00	.90
☐ SH6 Rondell White	4.00	1.80
☐ SH7 Javier Lopez	4.00	1.80
☐ SH8 Dean Palmer	2.00	.90
☐ SH9 Jim Thome	8.00	3.60
☐ SH10 J.T. Snow	6.00	2.70
☐ SH11 Mike Piazza	20.00	9.00
☐ SH12 Manny Ramirez	8.00	3.60

1994 Sportflics Movers

These 12 standard-size chase cards were randomly inserted in retail foil packs and picture the game's top veterans. The insertion rate was one in every 24 packs. Fronts feature the dual image effect with the player's name appearing in dual image. The name "Movers" appears in a circular design off to the left of the player's name.

1994 Sportflics Rookie/Traded

This set of 150 standard-size cards was distributed in five-card retail packs at a suggested price of $1.89. The set features top rookies and traded players. This set was released only through retail (non-hobby) outlets. The fronts feature the "Magic Motion" printing with two action views of the player which

change with the tilting of the card. The player's name is printed in red and expands and contracts with the tilting of the card. Numbered backs include a player biography and career stats and the 1994 performance of the rookie or how the player was acquired in a trade. A full-color photo of the player is framed at an angle with a red and black background. Rookie Cards in this set include Chan Ho Park and Alex Rodriguez.

	MINT	NRMT
COMPLETE SET (150)	25.00	11.00
COMMON CARD (1-150)	.25	.11
MINOR STARS	.50	.23
UNLISTED STARS	1.00	.45
ROY STATED ODDS 1:360		

☐ 1 Will Clark	.75	.35
☐ 2 Sid Fernandez	.25	.11
☐ 3 Joe Magrane	.25	.11
☐ 4 Pete Smith	.25	.11
☐ 5 Roberto Kelly	.25	.11
☐ 6 Delino DeShields	.25	.11
☐ 7 Brian Harper	.25	.11
☐ 8 Darrin Jackson	.25	.11
☐ 9 Omar Vizquel	.50	.23
☐ 10 Luis Polonia	.25	.11
☐ 11 Reggie Jefferson	.25	.11
☐ 12 Geronimo Berroa	.25	.11
☐ 13 Mike Harkey	.25	.11
☐ 14 Bret Boone	.25	.11
☐ 15 Dave Henderson	.25	.11
☐ 16 Pedro J.Martinez	1.00	.45
☐ 17 Jose Vizcaino	.25	.11
☐ 18 Xavier Hernandez	.25	.11
☐ 19 Eddie Taubensee	.25	.11
☐ 20 Ellis Burks	.50	.23
☐ 21 Turner Ward	.25	.11
☐ 22 Terry Mulholland	.25	.11
☐ 23 Howard Johnson	.25	.11
☐ 24 Vince Coleman	.25	.11
☐ 25 Deion Sanders	.50	.23
☐ 26 Rafael Palmeiro	.75	.35
☐ 27 Dave Weathers	.25	.11
☐ 28 Kent Mercker	.25	.11
☐ 29 Gregg Olson	.25	.11
☐ 30 Cory Bailey	.25	.11
☐ 31 Brian L.Hunter	1.00	.45
☐ 32 Garey Ingram	.25	.11
☐ 33 Daniel Smith	.25	.11
☐ 34 Denny Hocking	.25	.11
☐ 35 Charles Johnson	.75	.35
☐ 36 Otis Nixon	.25	.11
☐ 37 Hector Fajardo	.25	.11
☐ 38 Lee Smith	.50	.23
☐ 39 Phil Stidham	.25	.11
☐ 40 Melvin Nieves	.25	.11
☐ 41 Julio Franco	.25	.11
☐ 42 Greg Gohr	.25	.11
☐ 43 Steve Dunn	.25	.11
☐ 44 Tony Fernandez	.25	.11
☐ 45 Toby Borland	.25	.11
☐ 46 Paul Shuey	.25	.11
☐ 47 Shawn Hare	.25	.11
☐ 48 Shawn Green	.50	.23
☐ 49 Julian Tavarez	.25	.11
☐ 50 Ernie Young	.25	.11
☐ 51 Chris Sabo	.25	.11
☐ 52 Greg O'Halloran	.25	.11
☐ 53 Donnie Elliott	.25	.11
☐ 54 Jim Converse	.25	.11
☐ 55 Ray Holbert	.25	.11
☐ 56 Keith Lockhart	.25	.11
☐ 57 Tony Longmire	.25	.11
☐ 58 Jorge Fabregas	.25	.11
☐ 59 Ravelo Manzanillo	.25	.11
☐ 60 Marcus Moore	.25	.11
☐ 61 Carlos Rodriguez	.25	.11
☐ 62 Mark Portugal	.25	.11
☐ 63 Yorkis Perez	.25	.11
☐ 64 Dan Miceli	.25	.11
☐ 65 Chris Turner	.25	.11
☐ 66 Mike Oquist	.25	.11
☐ 67 Tom Quinlan	.25	.11
☐ 68 Matt Walbeck	.25	.11
☐ 69 Dave Staton	.25	.11
☐ 70 Wm.VanLandingham	.50	.23
☐ 71 Dave Stevens	.25	.11
☐ 72 Domingo Cedeno	.25	.11
☐ 73 Alex Diaz	.25	.11
☐ 74 Darren Bragg	.50	.23
☐ 75 James Hurst	.25	.11
☐ 76 Alex Gonzalez	.50	.23
☐ 77 Steve Dreyer	.25	.11
☐ 78 Robert Eenhoorn	.25	.11
☐ 79 Derek Parks	.25	.11
☐ 80 Jose Valentin	.25	.11
☐ 81 Wes Chamberlain	.25	.11
☐ 82 Tony Tarasco	.25	.11
☐ 83 Steve Traschel	.50	.23
☐ 84 Willie Banks	.25	.11
☐ 85 Rob Butler	.25	.11
☐ 86 Miguel Jimenez	.25	.11
☐ 87 Gerald Williams	.25	.11
☐ 88 Aaron Small	.25	.11
☐ 89 Matt Mieske	.25	.11
☐ 90 Tim Hyers	.25	.11
☐ 91 Eddie Murray	1.00	.45
☐ 92 Dennis Martinez	.50	.23
☐ 93 Tony Eusebio	.25	.11
☐ 94 Brian Anderson	1.00	.45
☐ 95 Blaise Ilsley	.25	.11
☐ 96 Johnny Ruffin	.25	.11
☐ 97 Carlos Reyes	.25	.11
☐ 98 Greg Pirkl	.25	.11
☐ 99 Jack Morris	.50	.23
☐ 100 John Mabry	1.00	.45
☐ 101 Mike Kelly	.25	.11
☐ 102 Rich Becker	.25	.11
☐ 103 Chris Gomez	.25	.11
☐ 104 Jim Edmonds	1.00	.45
☐ 105 Rich Rowland	.25	.11
☐ 106 Damon Buford	.25	.11
☐ 107 Mark Kiefer	.25	.11
☐ 108 Matias Carrillo	.25	.11
☐ 109 James Mouton	.25	.11
☐ 110 Kelly Stinnett	.25	.11
☐ 111 Billy Ashley	.25	.11
☐ 112 Fausto Cruz	.25	.11
☐ 113 Roberto Petagine	.25	.11
☐ 114 Joe Hall	.25	.11
☐ 115 Brian Johnson	.25	.11
☐ 116 Kevin Jarvis	.25	.11
☐ 117 Tim Davis	.25	.11
☐ 118 John Patterson	.25	.11
☐ 119 Stan Royer	.25	.11
☐ 120 Jeff Juden	.25	.11
☐ 121 Bryan Eversgerd	.25	.11
☐ 122 Chan Ho Park	2.50	1.10
☐ 123 Shane Reynolds	.25	.11
☐ 124 Danny Bautista	.25	.11
☐ 125 Rikkert Faneyte	.25	.11
☐ 126 Carlos Pulido	.25	.11
☐ 127 Mike Matheny	.25	.11
☐ 128 Hector Carrasco	.25	.11
☐ 129 Eddie Zambrano	.25	.11
☐ 130 Lee Tinsley	.25	.11
☐ 131 Roger Salkeld	.25	.11
☐ 132 Carlos Delgado	.75	.35
☐ 133 Troy O'Leary	.25	.11
☐ 134 Keith Mitchell	.25	.11
☐ 135 Lance Painter	.25	.11
☐ 136 Nate Minchey	.25	.11
☐ 137 Eric Anthony	.25	.11
☐ 138 Rafael Bournigal	.25	.11
☐ 139 Joey Hamilton	1.00	.45
☐ 140 Bobby Munoz	.25	.11
☐ 141 Rex Hudler	.25	.11
☐ 142 Alex Cole	.25	.11
☐ 143 Stan Javier	.25	.11
☐ 144 Jose Oliva	.25	.11
☐ 145 Tom Brunansky	.25	.11
☐ 146 Greg Colbrunn	.25	.11
☐ 147 Luis S.Lopez	.25	.11
☐ 148 Alex Rodriguez	10.00	4.50
☐ 149 Darryl Strawberry	.50	.23
☐ 150 Bo Jackson	.50	.23
☐ R01 R.Klesko ROY	8.00	3.60
M.Ramirez		

1994 Sportflics Rookie/Traded Artist's Proofs

This set of cards parallels the 150 regular issue Rookie/Traded cards and are embellished with the gold foil "Artist's Proof" stamp. They were randomly inserted in at a rate of one in 24 packs.

	MINT	NRMT
COMPLETE SET (150)	2000.00	900.00
COMMON CARD (1-150)	10.00	4.50
MINOR STARS	20.00	9.00
STATED ODDS 1:24		

☐ 1 Will Clark	50.00	22.00
☐ 16 Pedro Martinez	60.00	27.00
☐ 26 Rafael Palmeiro	40.00	18.00
☐ 31 Brian L.Hunter	40.00	18.00
☐ 91 Eddie Murray	80.00	36.00
☐ 104 Jim Edmonds	60.00	27.00
☐ 122 Chan Ho Park	100.00	45.00
☐ 132 Carlos Delgado	40.00	18.00
☐ 139 Joey Hamilton	40.00	18.00
☐ 148 Alex Rodriguez	400.00	180.00

1994 Sportflics Rookie/Traded Going Going Gone

Randomly inserted in packs at a rate of one in 18, this 12-card set features big hitters. Sportflics used its "Magic Mirror" technology to produce two images when the card is tilted. The Going, Going, Gone logo is placed at the top left of the front and a gold strip runs vertically on the left side. The player's name is printed in black on top of the gold strip. It expands and contracts when the card is moved. Borderless backs are numbered with the prefix "GG" and have a dark background containing a blurred stadium. The player's close-up picture is bordered with a biography box and name on the left. The player's slugging percentage, number of home runs and RBI totals are printed on the right side of the back with a shadow effect.

	MINT	NRMT
COMPLETE SET (12)	90.00	40.00
COMMON CARD (GG1-GG12)	2.50	1.10
STATED ODDS 1:18		
☐ GG1 Gary Sheffield	5.00	2.20
☐ GG2 Matt Williams	4.00	1.80
☐ GG3 Juan Gonzalez	12.00	5.50
☐ GG4 Ken Griffey Jr.	25.00	11.00
☐ GG5 Mike Piazza	15.00	6.75
☐ GG6 Frank Thomas	20.00	9.00
☐ GG7 Tim Salmon	5.00	2.20
☐ GG8 Barry Bonds	6.00	2.70
☐ GG9 Fred McGriff	4.00	1.80
☐ GG10 Cecil Fielder	2.50	1.10
☐ GG11 Albert Belle	6.00	2.70
☐ GG12 Joe Carter	2.50	1.10

1994 Sportflics Rookie/Traded Rookie Starflics

Randomly inserted in packs at a rate of one in 36, these 3-D cards highlight the rookie sensations of 1994. Horizontal fronts feature the player in a full-color action shot with a smaller, mirror image of the player set off in the blue background. The Starflics logo, player's name and team logo are printed on the left side of the front. Backs are borderless and carry full-color action shots of the player. The player's name is printed in gold foil and a player background is printed with reverse type on gold foil.

	MINT	NRMT
COMPLETE SET (18)	150.00	70.00
COMMON CARD (TR1-TR18)	5.00	2.20
MINOR STARS	8.00	3.60
STATED ODDS 1:36		
☐ TR1 John Hudek	5.00	2.20
☐ TR2 Manny Ramirez	25.00	11.00
☐ TR3 Jeffrey Hammonds	8.00	3.60
☐ TR4 Carlos Delgado	12.00	5.50
☐ TR5 Javier Lopez	12.00	5.50
☐ TR6 Alex Gonzalez	8.00	3.60
☐ TR7 Raul Mondesi	15.00	6.75
☐ TR8 Bob Hamelin	5.00	2.20
☐ TR9 Ryan Klesko	15.00	6.75
☐ TR10 Brian Anderson	15.00	6.75
☐ TR11 Alex Rodriguez	80.00	36.00
☐ TR12 Cliff Floyd	8.00	3.60
☐ TR13 Chan Ho Park	20.00	9.00
☐ TR14 Steve Karsay	5.00	2.20
☐ TR15 Rondell White	12.00	5.50
☐ TR16 Shawn Green	8.00	3.60
☐ TR17 Rich Becker	5.00	2.20
☐ TR18 Charles Johnson	12.00	5.50

1995 Sportflix

This 170 card standard-size set was released by Pinnacle brands. The set was issued in 5 card packs that had a suggested retail price of $1.89 per pack. Thirty-six of these packs are contained in a full box. Jumbo packs were also issued: these packs contained 8 cards per pack and had 36 packs in a box. Card fronts feature Pinnacle's "Magic Motion" printing which shows the player in two different action shots when the card is tilted. The player's position is printed diagonally on the top right with the team logo underneath. Horizontal backs feature a full-color player photo on the right. Subsets include a rookies section (141-165) and a checklist grouping (166-170). There are no key Rookie Cards in this set.

	MINT	NRMT
COMPLETE SET (170)	20.00	9.00
COMMON CARD (1-170)	.15	.07
MINOR STARS	.30	.14
UNLISTED STARS	.60	.25
SUBSET CARDS HALF VALUE OF BASE CARDS		
COMP.AP SET (170)	1000.00	450.00
COMMON ART.PRF. (1-170)	2.50	1.10
*ART.PRF.STARS: 10X TO 25X HI COLUMN		
*ART.PRF.YOUNG STARS: 8X TO 20X HI		
AP STATED ODDS 1:36		
☐ 1 Ken Griffey Jr.	3.00	1.35
☐ 2 Jeffrey Hammonds	.30	.14
☐ 3 Fred McGriff	.40	.18
☐ 4 Rickey Henderson	.40	.18
☐ 5 Derrick May	.15	.07
☐ 6 Robin Ventura	.30	.14
☐ 7 Royce Clayton	.15	.07
☐ 8 Paul Molitor	.60	.25
☐ 9 Charlie Hayes	.15	.07
☐ 10 David Nied	.15	.07
☐ 11 Ellis Burks	.30	.14
☐ 12 Bernard Gilkey	.15	.07
☐ 13 Don Mattingly	1.00	.45
☐ 14 Albert Belle	.75	.35
☐ 15 Doug Drabek	.15	.07
☐ 16 Tony Gwynn	1.50	.70
☐ 17 Delino DeShields	.15	.07
☐ 18 Bobby Bonilla	.30	.14
☐ 19 Cliff Floyd	.15	.07
☐ 20 Frank Thomas	2.50	1.10
☐ 21 Raul Mondesi	.40	.18
☐ 22 Dave Nilsson	.15	.07
☐ 23 Todd Zeile	.15	.07
☐ 24 Bernie Williams	.60	.25
☐ 25 Kirby Puckett	1.25	.55
☐ 26 David Cone	.30	.14
☐ 27 Darren Daulton	.30	.14
☐ 28 Marquis Grissom	.30	.14
☐ 29 Randy Johnson	.60	.25
☐ 30 Jeff Kent	.15	.07
☐ 31 Orlando Merced	.15	.07
☐ 32 Dave Justice	.60	.25
☐ 33 Ivan Rodriguez	.75	.35
☐ 34 Kirk Gibson	.30	.14
☐ 35 Alex Fernandez	.15	.07
☐ 36 Rick Wilkins	.15	.07
☐ 37 Andy Benes	.30	.14
☐ 38 Bret Saberhagen	.15	.07
☐ 39 Billy Ashley	.15	.07
☐ 40 Jose Rijo	.15	.07
☐ 41 Matt Williams	.40	.18
☐ 42 Lenny Dykstra	.30	.14
☐ 43 Jay Bell	.15	.07
☐ 44 Reggie Jefferson	.15	.07
☐ 45 Greg Maddux	2.00	.90
☐ 46 Gary Sheffield	.60	.25
☐ 47 Bret Boone	.15	.07
☐ 48 Jeff Bagwell	1.25	.55
☐ 49 Ben McDonald	.15	.07
☐ 50 Eric Karros	.30	.14
☐ 51 Roger Clemens	1.25	.55
☐ 52 Sammy Sosa	.60	.25
☐ 53 Barry Bonds	.75	.35
☐ 54 Joey Hamilton	.30	.14
☐ 55 Brian Jordan	.30	.14
☐ 56 Wil Cordero	.15	.07
☐ 57 Aaron Sele	.15	.07
☐ 58 Paul O'Neill	.30	.14
☐ 59 Carlos Garcia	.15	.07
☐ 60 Mike Mussina	.60	.25
☐ 61 John Olerud	.30	.14
☐ 62 Kevin Appier	.30	.14
☐ 63 Matt Mieske	.15	.07
☐ 64 Carlos Baerga	.30	.14
☐ 65 Ryan Klesko	.40	.18
☐ 66 Jimmy Key	.30	.14
☐ 67 James Mouton	.15	.07
☐ 68 Tim Salmon	.60	.25
☐ 69 Hal Morris	.15	.07
☐ 70 Albie Lopez	.15	.07
☐ 71 Dave Hollins	.15	.07
☐ 72 Greg Colbrunn	.15	.07
☐ 73 Juan Gonzalez	1.50	.70
☐ 74 Wally Joyner	.15	.07
☐ 75 Bob Hamelin	.15	.07
☐ 76 Brady Anderson	.40	.18
☐ 77 Deion Sanders	.30	.14
☐ 78 Javier Lopez	.30	.14
☐ 79 Brian McRae	.15	.07
☐ 80 Craig Biggio	.40	.18
☐ 81 Kenny Lofton	.75	.35
☐ 82 Cecil Fielder	.30	.14
☐ 83 Mike Piazza	2.00	.90
☐ 84 Rafael Palmeiro	.40	.18
☐ 85 Jim Thome	.60	.25
☐ 86 Ruben Sierra	.15	.07
☐ 87 Mark Langston	.15	.07
☐ 88 John Valentin	.15	.07
☐ 89 Shawon Dunston	.15	.07
☐ 90 Travis Fryman	.30	.14
☐ 91 Chuck Knoblauch	.60	.25
☐ 92 Dean Palmer	.15	.07
☐ 93 Robby Thompson	.15	.07
☐ 94 Barry Larkin	.40	.18
☐ 95 Darren Lewis	.15	.07
☐ 96 Andres Galarraga	.60	.25
☐ 97 Tony Phillips	.15	.07

□ 98 Mo Vaughn	.75	.35
□ 99 Pedro Martinez	.60	.25
□ 100 Chad Curtis	.15	.07
□ 101 Brent Gates	.15	.07
□ 102 Pat Hentgen	.30	.14
□ 103 Rico Brogna	.15	.07
□ 104 Carlos Delgado	.30	.14
□ 105 Manny Ramirez	.60	.25
□ 106 Mike Greenwell	.15	.07
□ 107 Wade Boggs	.60	.25
□ 108 Ozzie Smith	.75	.35
□ 109 Rusty Greer	.60	.25
□ 110 Willie Greene	.15	.07
□ 111 Chili Davis	.30	.14
□ 112 Reggie Sanders	.15	.07
□ 113 Roberto Kelly	.15	.07
□ 114 Tom Glavine	.30	.14
□ 115 Moises Alou	.30	.14
□ 116 Dennis Eckersley	.30	.14
□ 117 Danny Tartabull	.15	.07
□ 118 Jeff Conine	.30	.14
□ 119 Will Clark	.40	.18
□ 120 Joe Carter	.30	.14
□ 121 Mark McGwire	1.25	.55
□ 122 Cal Ripken Jr.	2.50	1.10
□ 123 Danny Jackson	.15	.07
□ 124 Phil Plantier	.15	.07
□ 125 Dante Bichette	.30	.14
□ 126 Jack McDowell	.15	.07
□ 127 Jose Canseco	.40	.18
□ 128 Roberto Alomar	.60	.25
□ 129 Rondell White	.30	.14
□ 130 Ray Lankford	.15	.07
□ 131 Ryan Thompson	.15	.07
□ 132 Ken Caminiti	.40	.18
□ 133 Gregg Jefferies	.30	.14
□ 134 Omar Vizquel	.30	.14
□ 135 Mark Grace	.40	.18
□ 136 Derek Bell	.15	.07
□ 137 Mickey Tettleton	.15	.07
□ 138 Wilson Alvarez	.15	.07
□ 139 Larry Walker	.60	.25
□ 140 Bo Jackson	.30	.14
□ 141 Alex Rodriguez	2.50	1.10
□ 142 Orlando Miller	.15	.07
□ 143 Shawn Green	.15	.14
□ 144 Steve Dunn	.15	.07
□ 145 Midre Cummings	.15	.07
□ 146 Chan Ho Park	.60	.25
□ 147 Jose Oliva	.15	.07
□ 148 Armando Benitez	.15	.07
□ 149 J.R. Phillips	.15	.07
□ 150 Charles Johnson	.30	.14
□ 151 Garret Anderson	.40	.18
□ 152 Russ Davis	.15	.07
□ 153 Brian L.Hunter	.40	.18
□ 154 Ernie Young	.15	.07
□ 155 Marc Newfield	.15	.07
□ 156 Greg Pirkl	.15	.07
□ 157 Scott Ruffcorn	.15	.07
□ 158 Rikkert Faneyte	.15	.07
□ 159 Duane Singleton	.15	.07
□ 160 Gabe White	.15	.07
□ 161 Alex Gonzalez	.15	.07
□ 162 Chipper Jones	2.00	.90
□ 163 Mike Kelly	.15	.07
□ 164 Kurt Miller	.15	.07
□ 165 Roberto Petagine	.15	.07
□ 166 Jeff Bagwell CL	.60	.25
□ 167 Mike Piazza CL	1.00	.45
□ 168 Ken Griffey Jr. CL	1.50	.70
□ 169 Frank Thomas CL	1.25	.55
□ 170 Barry Bonds CL	1.25	.55
Cal Ripken		

1995 Sportflix Detonators

Randomly inserted in packs at a rate of one in 16, this nine-card set highlights power hitters. The player is featured in a full-color cutout action shot atop a gold column with his name inscribed.

The background is set back and is lit up with fireworks. The player's team logo and a rocket with the word "Detonators" is printed along the bottom of the card. A blue-sky with a Greek column serves as a backdrop for the borderless backs. A full-color shot of the player is pictured in the column and a short synopsis of the player's '94 performance is printed in black type on the right side of the back. Backs are numbered with the prefix "DE."

	MINT	NRMT
COMPLETE SET (9)	30.00	13.50
COMMON CARD (DE1-DE9)	1.00	.45
STATED ODDS 1:16		

□ DE1 Jeff Bagwell	4.00	1.80
□ DE2 Matt Williams	1.50	.70
□ DE3 Ken Griffey Jr.	10.00	4.50
□ DE4 Frank Thomas	8.00	3.60
□ DE5 Mike Piazza	6.00	2.70
□ DE6 Barry Bonds	2.50	1.10
□ DE7 Albert Belle	2.00	.90
□ DE8 Cliff Floyd	1.00	.45
□ DE9 Juan Gonzalez	5.00	2.20

1995 Sportflix Double Take

Randomly inserted in packs at a rate of one in 16, this 12-card set features two stars in one see-through 3-D card. Fronts feature the Sportflix "Magic Motion" process that allows the viewer to see two different images when the card is tilted. The players' names are reverse-printed across a red bar with the corresponding team logo on the bottom right. When the card is tilted, the player's picture, name and team logo appear. "Double Take" is print-

ed vertically on the left side of the card. Backs are see through and contain only the card number.

	MINT	NRMT
COMPLETE SET (12)	150.00	70.00
COMMON CARD (1-12)	4.00	1.80
STATED ODDS 1:48		

□ 1 Jeff Bagwell	25.00	11.00
Frank Thomas		
□ 2 Will Clark	4.00	1.80
Fred McGriff		
□ 3 Roberto Alomar	4.00	1.80
Jeff Kent		
□ 4 Matt Williams	4.00	1.80
Wade Boggs		
□ 5 Cal Ripken Jr.	20.00	9.00
Ozzie Smith		
□ 6 Alex Rodriguez	20.00	9.00
Wil Cordero		
□ 7 Mike Piazza	15.00	6.75
Carlos Delgado		
□ 8 Kenny Lofton	6.00	2.70
Dave Justice		
□ 9 Barry Bonds	25.00	11.00
Ken Griffey Jr.		
□ 10 Albert Belle	6.00	2.70
Raul Mondesi		
□ 11 Tony Gwynn	15.00	6.75
Kirby Puckett		
□ 12 Jimmy Key	12.00	5.50
Greg Maddux		

1995 Sportflix Hammer Team

This 18-card set was inserted randomly in packs at a rate of one in 48 and looks at the league's top hitters. The 3-D fronts feature a full-color cutout of the player in action set against a backdrop of blue sky and basepaths. Sledgehammers are placed in the foreground and background of the fronts, while the player's name is printed at the bottom of the card against a green grass background. Full-bleed, horizontal backs are numbered with the prefix "HT" and picture the player in full color. A swinging sledgehammer is in motion against a backdrop of green grass while a 1994 player synopsis is printed in white type underneath the hammer.

	MINT	NRMT
COMPLETE SET (18)	25.00	11.00
COMMON CARD (HT1-HT18)	.75	.35
STATED ODDS 1:4		

☐ HT1 Ken Griffey Jr.	5.00	2.20
☐ HT2 Frank Thomas	4.00	1.80
☐ HT3 Jeff Bagwell	2.00	.90
☐ HT4 Mike Piazza	3.00	1.35
☐ HT5 Cal Ripken Jr.	4.00	1.80
☐ HT6 Albert Belle	1.25	.55
☐ HT7 Barry Bonds	1.25	.55
☐ HT8 Don Mattingly	2.00	.90
☐ HT9 Will Clark	.75	.35
☐ HT10 Tony Gwynn	2.00	.90
☐ HT11 Matt Williams	.75	.35
☐ HT12 Kirby Puckett	2.00	.90
☐ HT13 Manny Ramirez	1.00	.45
☐ HT14 Fred McGriff	.75	.35
☐ HT15 Juan Gonzalez	2.50	1.10
☐ HT16 Kenny Lofton	1.25	.55
☐ HT17 Raul Mondesi	.75	.35
☐ HT18 Tim Salmon	1.00	.45

1995 Sportflix ProMotion

Randomly inserted in jumbo packs at a rate of one in 18, this 12-card set features top stars in the "Magic Motion" technology. Card fronts are coordinated in team colors and depict the player in a full-color action photo. The player's team logo is displayed when tilted. The horizontal backs feature the player in an action shot and are numbered with the prefix "PM." The player's name appears in white type across the top while the "Pro-Motion" logo is printed in black across the bottom of the back.

	MINT	NRMT
COMPLETE SET (12)	150.00	70.00
COMMON CARD (PM1-PM12)	5.00	2.20
STATED ODDS 1:18 JUMBO		
☐ PM1 Ken Griffey Jr.	40.00	18.00
☐ PM2 Frank Thomas	30.00	13.50
☐ PM3 Cal Ripken Jr.	30.00	13.50
☐ PM4 Jeff Bagwell	15.00	6.75
☐ PM5 Mike Piazza	25.00	11.00
☐ PM6 Matt Williams	5.00	2.20
☐ PM7 Albert Belle	10.00	4.50
☐ PM8 Jose Canseco	5.00	2.20
☐ PM9 Don Mattingly	12.00	5.50
☐ PM10 Barry Bonds	10.00	4.50
☐ PM11 Will Clark	5.00	2.20
☐ PM12 Kirby Puckett	15.00	6.75

1996 Sportflix

With retail only distribution, this 144 card set comes in five card packs that retail for $1.99. Regular cards picture two different pieces of photography. By flicking the wrist, one image dis-appears and another appears. Some cards use two different photos, and others use sequence action photography to create the illusion of animation. The wording in the bottom border also changes with movement. The set contains the UC3 Subset (97-120), Rookies Subset (121-141), and Checklists (142-144). The UC3 Subset features veteran superstars in 3-D animation. The 21-card Rookie subset carries color player photos on a background of part of a baseball that changes into a wooden baseball bat section when moved. Eight of the Rookies subset cards were made in jumbo (5 X 7") format, renumbered out of eight, and inserted as "chiptoppers" in retail boxes. These cards are valued at 15 times the corresponding basic card.

	MINT	NRMT
COMPLETE SET (144)	25.00	11.00
COMMON CARD (1-144)	.15	.07
MINOR STARS	.30	.14
UNLISTED STARS	.60	.25
SUBSET CARDS HALF OF BASE CARDS		
COMP AP SET (144)	1000.00	450.00
COMMON ART.PRF. (1-144)	3.00	1.35
*AP STARS: 10X TO 25X HI COLUMN		
*AP STATED ODDS 1:48		
☐ 1 Wade Boggs	.60	.25
☐ 2 Tim Salmon	.60	.25
☐ 3 Will Clark	.40	.18
☐ 4 Dante Bichette	.30	.14
☐ 5 Barry Bonds	.75	.35
☐ 6 Kirby Puckett	1.25	.55
☐ 7 Albert Belle	.75	.35
☐ 8 Greg Maddux	2.00	.90
☐ 9 Tony Gwynn	1.50	.70
☐ 10 Mike Piazza	2.00	.90
☐ 11 Ivan Rodriguez	.75	.35
☐ 12 Marty Cordova	.30	.14
☐ 13 Frank Thomas	2.50	1.10
☐ 14 Raul Mondesi	.40	.18
☐ 15 Johnny Damon	.30	.14
☐ 16 Mark McGwire	1.25	.55
☐ 17 Len Dykstra	.30	.14
☐ 18 Ken Griffey Jr.	3.00	1.35
☐ 19 Chipper Jones	2.00	.90
☐ 20 Alex Rodriguez	2.00	.90
☐ 21 Jeff Bagwell	1.25	.55
☐ 22 Jim Edmonds	.40	.18
☐ 23 Edgar Martinez	.40	.18
☐ 24 David Cone	.30	.14
☐ 25 Tom Glavine	.30	.14
☐ 26 Eddie Murray	.60	.25
☐ 27 Paul Molitor	.60	.25
☐ 28 Ryan Klesko	.40	.18
☐ 29 Rafael Palmeiro	.40	.18
☐ 30 Manny Ramirez	.60	.25
☐ 31 Mo Vaughn	.75	.35
☐ 32 Rico Brogna	.15	.07
☐ 33 Marc Newfield	.15	.07
☐ 34 J.T. Snow	.30	.14
☐ 35 Reggie Sanders	.15	.07
☐ 36 Fred McGriff	.40	.18
☐ 37 Craig Biggio	.40	.18
☐ 38 Jeff King	.15	.07
☐ 39 Kenny Lofton	.75	.35
☐ 40 Gary Gaetti	.15	.07
☐ 41 Eric Karros	.30	.14
☐ 42 Jason Isringhausen	.15	.07
☐ 43 B.J. Surhoff	.15	.07
☐ 44 Michael Tucker	.30	.14
☐ 45 Gary Sheffield	.60	.25
☐ 46 Chili Davis	.30	.14
☐ 47 Bobby Bonilla	.30	.14
☐ 48 Hideo Nomo	1.50	.70
☐ 49 Ray Durham	.15	.07
☐ 50 Phil Nevin	.15	.07
☐ 51 Randy Johnson	.60	.25
☐ 52 Bill Pulsipher	.15	.07
☐ 53 Ozzie Smith	.75	.35
☐ 54 Cal Ripken	2.50	1.10
☐ 55 Cecil Fielder	.30	.14
☐ 56 Matt Williams	.40	.18
☐ 57 Sammy Sosa	.60	.25
☐ 58 Roger Clemens	1.25	.55
☐ 59 Brian L.Hunter	.30	.14
☐ 60 Barry Larkin	.40	.18
☐ 61 Charles Johnson	.30	.14
☐ 62 David Justice	.60	.25
☐ 63 Garret Anderson	.30	.14
☐ 64 Rondell White	.30	.14
☐ 65 Derek Bell	.15	.07
☐ 66 Andres Galarraga	.60	.25
☐ 67 Moises Alou	.30	.14
☐ 68 Travis Fryman	.30	.14
☐ 69 Pedro J. Martinez	.60	.25
☐ 70 Carlos Baerga	.15	.07
☐ 71 John Valentin	.15	.07
☐ 72 Larry Walker	.60	.25
☐ 73 Roberto Alomar	.60	.25
☐ 74 Mike Mussina	.60	.25
☐ 75 Kevin Appier	.30	.14
☐ 76 Bernie Williams	.60	.25
☐ 77 Ray Lankford	.30	.14
☐ 78 Gregg Jefferies	.15	.07
☐ 79 Robin Ventura	.30	.14
☐ 80 Kenny Rogers	.15	.07
☐ 81 Paul O'Neill	.30	.14
☐ 82 Mark Grace	.40	.18
☐ 83 Deion Sanders	.30	.14
☐ 84 Tino Martinez	.60	.25
☐ 85 Joe Carter	.30	.14
☐ 86 Pete Schourek	.15	.07
☐ 87 Jack McDowell	.15	.07
☐ 88 John Mabry	.15	.07
☐ 89 Darren Daulton	.30	.14
☐ 90 Jim Thome	.60	.25
☐ 91 Jay Buhner	.40	.18
☐ 92 Jay Bell	.30	.14
☐ 93 Kevin Seitzer	.15	.07
☐ 94 Jose Canseco	.40	.18
☐ 95 Juan Gonzalez	1.50	.70
☐ 96 Jeff Conine	.30	.14
☐ 97 Chipper Jones UC3	1.00	.45
☐ 98 Ken Griffey Jr. UC3	1.50	.70
☐ 99 Frank Thomas UC3	1.25	.55
☐ 100 Cal Ripken UC3	1.25	.55
☐ 101 Albert Belle UC3	.40	.18
☐ 102 Mike Piazza UC3	1.00	.45
☐ 103 Dante Bichette UC3	.30	.14
☐ 104 Sammy Sosa UC3	.30	.14
☐ 105 Mo Vaughn UC3	.40	.18
☐ 106 Tim Salmon UC3	.30	.14
☐ 107 Reggie Sanders UC3	.15	.07
☐ 108 Gary Sheffield UC3	.30	.14
☐ 109 Ruben Rivera UC3	.15	.07
☐ 110 Rafael Palmeiro UC3	.30	.14
☐ 111 Edgar Martinez UC3	.30	.14
☐ 112 Barry Bonds UC3	.40	.18
☐ 113 Manny Ramirez UC3	.30	.14
☐ 114 Larry Walker UC3	.30	.14
☐ 115 Jeff Bagwell UC3	.60	.25
☐ 116 Matt Williams UC3	.30	.14

☐ 117 Mark McGwire UC3	.60	.25
☐ 118 Johnny Damon UC3	.15	.07
☐ 119 Eddie Murray UC3	.30	.14
☐ 120 Jay Buhner UC3	.30	.14
☐ 121 Tim Unroe	.15	.07
☐ 122 Todd Hollandsworth	.15	.07
☐ 123 Tony Clark	.60	.25
☐ 124 Roger Cedeno	.15	.07
☐ 125 Jim Pittsley	.30	.14
☐ 126 Ruben Rivera	.30	.14
☐ 127 Bob Wolcott	.15	.07
☐ 128 Chan Ho Park	.60	.25
☐ 129 Chris Snopek	.15	.07
☐ 130 Alex Ochoa	.15	.07
☐ 131 Yamil Benitez	.30	.14
☐ 132 Jimmy Haynes	.15	.07
☐ 133 Dustin Hermanson	.15	.07
☐ 134 Shawn Estes	.40	.18
☐ 135 Howard Battle	.15	.07
☐ 136 Matt Lawton	.40	.18
☐ 137 Terrell Wade	.15	.07
☐ 138 Jason Schmidt	.30	.14
☐ 139 Derek Jeter	2.00	.90
☐ 140 Shannon Stewart	.30	.14
☐ 141 Chris Stynes	.15	.07
☐ 142 Ken Griffey Jr. CL	1.50	.70
☐ 143 Greg Maddux CL	1.00	.45
☐ 144 Cal Ripken CL	1.25	.55

1996 Sportflix Double Take

Randomly inserted in jumbo packs, this 12-card set features color player photos of 2 players per card that play the same position.

	MINT	NRMT
COMPLETE SET (12)	120.00	55.00
COMMON CARD (1-12)	5.00	2.20
STATED ODDS 1:22 JUMBO	....	

☐ 1 Barry Larkin	15.00	6.75
Cal Ripken		
☐ 2 Roberto Alomar	5.00	2.20
Craig Biggio		
☐ 3 Chipper Jones	12.00	5.50
Matt Williams		
☐ 4 Ken Griffey	20.00	9.00
Ruben Rivera		
☐ 5 Greg Maddux	12.00	5.50
Hideo Nomo		
☐ 6 Frank Thomas	15.00	6.75
Mo Vaughn		
☐ 7 Ivan Rodriguez	12.00	5.50
Mike Piazza		
☐ 8 Albert Belle	6.00	2.70
Barry Bonds		
☐ 9 Alex Rodriguez	20.00	9.00
Derek Jeter		
☐ 10 Kirby Puckett	15.00	6.75
Tony Gwynn		
☐ 11 Manny Ramirez	5.00	2.20
Sammy Sosa		

☐ 12 Jeff Bagwell	6.00	2.70
Rico Brogna		

1996 Sportflix Hit Parade

With an insertion rate of one in 35, this 16-card set features color player photos of hitters in 3D with a background scene in full-motion animation.

	MINT	NRMT
COMPLETE SET (16)	120.00	55.00
COMMON CARD (1-16)	2.00	.90
STATED ODDS 1:35		

☐ 1 Ken Griffey Jr.	20.00	9.00
☐ 2 Cal Ripken	15.00	6.75
☐ 3 Frank Thomas	15.00	6.75
☐ 4 Mike Piazza	12.00	5.50
☐ 5 Mo Vaughn	5.00	2.20
☐ 6 Albert Belle	5.00	2.20
☐ 7 Jeff Bagwell	8.00	3.60
☐ 8 Matt Williams	2.50	1.10
☐ 9 Sammy Sosa	4.00	1.80
☐ 10 Kirby Puckett	8.00	3.60
☐ 11 Dante Bichette	2.00	.90
☐ 12 Gary Sheffield	4.00	1.80
☐ 13 Tony Gwynn	10.00	4.50
☐ 14 Wade Boggs	4.00	1.80
☐ 15 Chipper Jones	12.00	5.50
☐ 16 Barry Bonds	5.00	2.20

1996 Sportflix Power Surge

With an insertion rate of one in 35, this retail only 24-card set is pinted on clear plastic and is a 3-D parallel rendition of the UC3 subset found in the regular Sportflix set.

	MINT	NRMT
COMPLETE SET (24)	200.00	90.00
COMMON CARD (1-24)	3.00	1.35
SEMISTARS	6.00	2.70
STATED ODDS 1:35 RETAIL	....	

☐ 1 Chipper Jones	25.00	11.00
☐ 2 Ken Griffey Jr.	40.00	18.00
☐ 3 Frank Thomas	30.00	13.50
☐ 4 Cal Ripken	30.00	13.50
☐ 5 Albert Belle	10.00	4.50
☐ 6 Mike Piazza	25.00	11.00
☐ 7 Dante Bichette	4.00	1.80
☐ 8 Sammy Sosa	6.00	2.70
☐ 9 Mo Vaughn	10.00	4.50
☐ 10 Tim Salmon	5.00	2.20
☐ 11 Reggie Sanders	3.00	1.35
☐ 12 Gary Sheffield	6.00	2.70
☐ 13 Ruben Rivera	4.00	1.80
☐ 14 Rafael Palmeiro	6.00	2.70
☐ 15 Edgar Martinez	6.00	2.70
☐ 16 Barry Bonds	10.00	4.50
☐ 17 Manny Ramirez	8.00	3.60
☐ 18 Larry Walker	8.00	3.60
☐ 19 Jeff Bagwell	15.00	6.75
☐ 20 Matt Williams	6.00	2.70
☐ 21 Mark McGwire	15.00	6.75
☐ 22 Johnny Damon	4.00	1.80
☐ 23 Eddie Murray	8.00	3.60
☐ 24 Jay Buhner	6.00	2.70

1996 Sportflix ProMotion

Inserted at the rate of one in 17, this 20-card set uses morphing technology and multi-phase animation to turn a player's photo into a bat, a ball, a glove, or a catcher's mask.

	MINT	NRMT
COMPLETE SET (20)	100.00	45.00
COMMON CARD (1-20)	1.50	.70
STATED ODDS 1:17		

☐ 1 Cal Ripken	12.00	5.50
☐ 2 Greg Maddux	10.00	4.50
☐ 3 Mo Vaughn	4.00	1.80
☐ 4 Albert Belle	4.00	1.80
☐ 5 Mike Piazza	10.00	4.50
☐ 6 Ken Griffey Jr.	15.00	6.75
☐ 7 Frank Thomas	12.00	5.50
☐ 8 Jeff Bagwell	6.00	2.70
☐ 9 Hideo Nomo	8.00	3.60
☐ 10 Chipper Jones	10.00	4.50
☐ 11 Tony Gwynn	8.00	3.60
☐ 12 Don Mattingly	5.00	2.20
☐ 13 Dante Bichette	1.50	.70
☐ 14 Matt Williams	2.00	.90
☐ 15 Manny Ramirez	3.00	1.35
☐ 16 Barry Bonds	4.00	1.80
☐ 17 Reggie Sanders	1.00	.45
☐ 18 Tim Salmon	3.00	1.35
☐ 19 Ruben Rivera	1.50	.70
☐ 20 Garret Anderson	1.50	.70

1997 Sports Illustrated

The 1997 Sports Illustrated set was issued in one series totalling 180 cards. Each pack contained six cards and carried a $1.99 SRP. The fronts feature Sports Illustrated action player photos with player stories on the backs. The set contains the topical subsets: Fresh Faces (1-27), Season Highlights (28-36), Inside Baseball (37-54), S.I.BER Vision 55-72) and Classic Covers (169-180). An unnumbered Jose Cruz Jr. fold-out checklist was also seeded in approximately 1:4 packs.

	MINT	NRMT
COMPLETE SET (180)	40.00	18.00
COMMON CARD (1-180)	.15	.07
MINOR STARS	.30	.14
UNLISTED STARS	.60	.25
SUBSET CARDS HALF VALUE OF BASE CARDS		

		MINT	NRMT
☐ 1	Bob Abreu	.30	.14
☐ 2	Jaime Bluma	.15	.07
☐ 3	Emil Brown	.40	.18
☐ 4	Jose Cruz Jr.	5.00	2.20
☐ 5	Jason Dickson	.30	.14
☐ 6	Nomar Garciaparra	2.00	.90
☐ 7	Todd Greene	.30	.14
☐ 8	Vladimir Guerrero	1.25	.55
☐ 9	Wilton Guerrero	.15	.07
☐ 10	Jose Guillen	.75	.35
☐ 11	Hideki Irabu	.60	.25
☐ 12	Russ Johnson	.15	.07
☐ 13	Andruw Jones	1.50	.70
☐ 14	Damon Mashore	.15	.07
☐ 15	Jason McDonald	.15	.07
☐ 16	Ryan McGuire	.15	.07
☐ 17	Matt Morris	.30	.14
☐ 18	Kevin Orie	.30	.14
☐ 19	Dante Powell	.15	.07
☐ 20	Pokey Reese	.15	.07
☐ 21	Joe Roa	.15	.07
☐ 22	Scott Rolen	1.50	.70
☐ 23	Glendon Rusch	.15	.07
☐ 24	Scott Spiezio	.30	.14
☐ 25	Bubba Trammell	.60	.25
☐ 26	Todd Walker	.30	.14
☐ 27	Jamey Wright	.15	.07
☐ 28	Ken Griffey Jr. SH	1.50	.70
☐ 29	Tino Martinez SH	.30	.14
☐ 30	Roger Clemens SH	.60	.25
☐ 31	Hideki Irabu SH	.60	.25
☐ 32	Kevin Brown SH	.15	.07
☐ 33	Chipper Jones SH	1.25	.55
	Cal Ripken		
☐ 34	Sandy Alomar SH	.30	.14
☐ 35	Ken Caminiti SH	.30	.14
☐ 36	Randy Johnson SH	.30	.14
☐ 37	Andy Ashby IB	.15	.07
☐ 38	Jay Buhner IB	.30	.14
☐ 39	Joe Carter IB	.15	.07
☐ 40	Darren Daulton IB	.15	.07
☐ 41	Jeff Fassero IB	.15	.07
☐ 42	Andres Galarraga IB	.30	.14
☐ 43	Rusty Greer IB	.15	.07
☐ 44	Marquis Grissom IB	.15	.07
☐ 45	Joey Hamilton IB	.15	.07
☐ 46	Jimmy Key IB	.15	.07
☐ 47	Ryan Klesko IB	.30	.14
☐ 48	Eddie Murray IB	.30	.14
☐ 49	Charles Nagy IB	.15	.07
☐ 50	Dave Nilsson IB	.15	.07
☐ 51	Ricardo Rincon IB	.15	.07
☐ 52	Billy Wagner IB	.15	.07
☐ 53	Dan Wilson IB	.15	.07
☐ 54	Dmitri Young IB	.15	.07
☐ 55	Roberto Alomar SIV	.30	.14
☐ 56	Sandy Alomar Jr. SIV	.15	.07
☐ 57	Scott Brosius SIV	.15	.07
☐ 58	Tony Clark SIV	.30	.14
☐ 59	Carlos Delgado SIV	.15	.07
☐ 60	Jermaine Dye SIV	.15	.07
☐ 61	Darin Erstad SIV	.40	.18
☐ 62	Derek Jeter SIV	1.00	.45
☐ 63	Jason Kendall SIV	.15	.07
☐ 64	Hideo Nomo SIV	.75	.35
☐ 65	Rey Ordonez SIV	.15	.07
☐ 66	Andy Pettitte SIV	.30	.14
☐ 67	Manny Ramirez SIV	.30	.14
☐ 68	Edgar Renteria SIV	.15	.07
☐ 69	Shane Reynolds SIV	.15	.07
☐ 70	Alex Rodriguez SIV	1.00	.45
☐ 71	Ivan Rodriguez SIV	.40	.18
☐ 72	Jose Rosado SIV	.15	.07
☐ 73	John Smoltz	.30	.14
☐ 74	Tom Glavine	.30	.14
☐ 75	Greg Maddux	2.00	.90
☐ 76	Chipper Jones	2.00	.90
☐ 77	Kenny Lofton	.75	.35
☐ 78	Fred McGriff	.40	.18
☐ 79	Kevin Brown	.30	.14
☐ 80	Alex Fernandez	.15	.07
☐ 81	Al Leiter	.15	.07
☐ 82	Bobby Bonilla	.30	.14
☐ 83	Gary Sheffield	.60	.25
☐ 84	Moises Alou	.30	.14
☐ 85	Henry Rodriguez	.15	.07
☐ 86	Mark Grudzielanek	.15	.07
☐ 87	Pedro Martinez	.60	.25
☐ 88	Todd Hundley	.30	.14
☐ 89	Bernard Gilkey	.15	.07
☐ 90	Bobby Jones	.15	.07
☐ 91	Curt Schilling	.30	.14
☐ 92	Ricky Bottalico	.15	.07
☐ 93	Mike Lieberthal	.15	.07
☐ 94	Sammy Sosa	.60	.25
☐ 95	Ryne Sandberg	.75	.35
☐ 96	Mark Grace	.40	.18
☐ 97	Deion Sanders	.30	.14
☐ 98	Reggie Sanders	.15	.07
☐ 99	Barry Larkin	.40	.18
☐ 100	Craig Biggio	.40	.18
☐ 101	Jeff Bagwell	1.25	.55
☐ 102	Derek Bell	.15	.07
☐ 103	Brian Jordan	.30	.14
☐ 104	Ray Lankford	.30	.14
☐ 105	Ron Gant	.30	.14
☐ 106	Al Martin	.15	.07
☐ 107	Kevin Elster	.15	.07
☐ 108	Jermaine Allensworth	.15	.07
☐ 109	Vinny Castilla	.30	.14
☐ 110	Dante Bichette	.30	.14
☐ 111	Larry Walker	.60	.25
☐ 112	Mike Piazza	2.00	.90
☐ 113	Eric Karros	.30	.14
☐ 114	Todd Hollandsworth	.15	.07
☐ 115	Raul Mondesi	.40	.18
☐ 116	Hideo Nomo	1.50	.70
☐ 117	Ramon Martinez	.30	.14
☐ 118	Ken Caminiti	.30	.14
☐ 119	Tony Gwynn	1.50	.70
☐ 120	Steve Finley	.15	.07
☐ 121	Barry Bonds	.75	.35
☐ 122	J.T. Snow	.30	.14
☐ 123	Rod Beck	.15	.07
☐ 124	Cal Ripken	2.50	1.10
☐ 125	Mike Mussina	.60	.25
☐ 126	Brady Anderson	.40	.18
☐ 127	Bernie Williams	.60	.25
☐ 128	Derek Jeter	2.00	.90
☐ 129	Tino Martinez	.60	.25
☐ 130	Andy Pettitte	.60	.25
☐ 131	David Cone	.30	.14
☐ 132	Mariano Rivera	.30	.14
☐ 133	Roger Clemens	1.25	.55
☐ 134	Pat Hentgen	.30	.14
☐ 135	Juan Guzman	.15	.07
☐ 136	Bob Higginson	.30	.14
☐ 137	Tony Clark	.60	.25
☐ 138	Travis Fryman	.30	.14
☐ 139	Mo Vaughn	.75	.35
☐ 140	Tim Naehring	.15	.07
☐ 141	John Valentin	.15	.07
☐ 142	Matt Williams	.30	.14
☐ 143	David Justice	.60	.25
☐ 144	Jim Thome	.60	.25
☐ 145	Chuck Knoblauch	.60	.25
☐ 146	Paul Molitor	.60	.25
☐ 147	Marty Cordova	.30	.14
☐ 148	Frank Thomas	2.50	1.10
☐ 149	Albert Belle	.75	.35
☐ 150	Robin Ventura	.30	.14
☐ 151	John Jaha	.15	.07
☐ 152	Jeff Cirillo	.30	.14
☐ 153	Jose Valentin	.15	.07
☐ 154	Jay Bell	.30	.14
☐ 155	Jeff King	.15	.07
☐ 156	Kevin Appier	.30	.14
☐ 157	Ken Griffey Jr.	3.00	1.35
☐ 158	Alex Rodriguez	2.00	.90
☐ 159	Randy Johnson	.60	.25
☐ 160	Juan Gonzalez	1.50	.70
☐ 161	Will Clark	.40	.18
☐ 162	Dean Palmer	.15	.07
☐ 163	Tim Salmon	.60	.25
☐ 164	Jim Edmonds	.30	.14
☐ 165	Jim Leyritz	.15	.07
☐ 166	Jose Canseco	.40	.18
☐ 167	Jason Giambi	.30	.14
☐ 168	Mark McGwire	1.25	.55
☐ 169	Barry Bonds CC	.40	.18
☐ 170	Alex Rodriguez CC	1.00	.45
☐ 171	Roger Clemens CC	.60	.25
☐ 172	Ken Griffey Jr. CC	1.50	.70
☐ 173	Greg Maddux CC	1.00	.45
☐ 174	Mike Piazza CC	1.00	.45
☐ 175	Will Clark CC	.60	.25
	Mark McGwire		
☐ 176	Hideo Nomo CC	.75	.35
☐ 177	Cal Ripken CC	1.25	.55
	Frank Thomas		
☐ 178	Ken Griffey Jr. CC	1.25	.55
☐ 179	Alex Rodriguez CC	1.25	.55
	Derek Jeter		
☐ 180	John Wetteland CC	.15	.07
☐ P158	Alex Rodriguez Promo	1.00	.45
☐ NNO	Jose Cruz Jr. CL	.50	.23

1997 Sports Illustrated Extra Edition

Randomly inserted in packs, this 180-card set if parallel to the base set with etched holofoil accents. Only 500 of each card were produced and are sequentially numbered.

	MINT	NRMT
COMPLETE SET (180)	2500.00	1100.00
COMMON CARD (1-180)	5.00	2.20
MINOR STARS	8.00	3.60
SEMISTARS	12.00	5.50
UNLISTED STARS	20.00	9.00
*STARS: 15X TO 30X HI COLUMN		
*YOUNG STARS: 12.5X TO 25X HI		
*ROOKIES: 7.5X TO 15X HI		
RANDOM INSERTS IN PACKS		
STATED PRINT RUN 500 SERIAL #'d SETS		

		MINT	NRMT
□ 4	Jose Cruz Jr.	80.00	36.00
□ 6	Nomar Garciaparra	50.00	22.00
□ 13	Andruw Jones	40.00	18.00
□ 22	Scott Rolen	40.00	18.00
□ 28	Ken Griffey Jr.SH	60.00	27.00
□ 33	Chipper Jones SH	50.00	22.00
	Cal Ripken		
□ 70	Alex Rodriguez SIV	40.00	18.00
□ 75	Greg Maddux	60.00	27.00
□ 76	Chipper Jones	60.00	27.00
□ 101	Jeff Bagwell	40.00	18.00
□ 112	Mike Piazza	60.00	27.00
□ 116	Hideo Nomo	50.00	22.00
□ 119	Tony Gwynn	50.00	22.00
□ 124	Cal Ripken	80.00	36.00
□ 128	Derek Jeter	50.00	22.00
□ 133	Roger Clemens	40.00	18.00
□ 148	Frank Thomas	80.00	36.00
□ 157	Ken Griffey Jr.	100.00	45.00
□ 158	Alex Rodriguez	60.00	27.00
□ 160	Juan Gonzalez	50.00	22.00
□ 168	Mark McGwire	40.00	18.00
□ 170	Alex Rodriguez CC..	40.00	18.00
□ 172	Ken Griffey Jr. CC .	60.00	27.00
□ 173	Greg Maddux CC ..	40.00	18.00
□ 174	Mike Piazza CC ...	40.00	18.00
□ 177	Cal Ripken CC	50.00	22.00
□ 178	Ken Griffey Jr. CC	100.00	45.00
	Frank Thomas		
□ 179	Alex Rodriguez CC..	50.00	22.00
	Derek Jeter		

1997 Sports Illustrated Autographed Mini-Covers

Randomly inserted in packs, this six-card set features color photos of three current and three retired players on miniature SI covers. Only 250 of each card was produced and serially numbered and autographed.

		MINT	NRMT
COMPLETE SET (6)		1000.00	450.00
COMMON CARD (1-6)		80.00	36.00
RANDOM INSERTS IN PACKS ..			
STATED PRINT RUN 250 SETS			

□ 1	Alex Rodriguez	250.00	110.00
□ 2	Cal Ripken	300.00	135.00
□ 3	Kirby Puckett	150.00	70.00
□ 4	Willie Mays	200.00	90.00
□ 5	Frank Robinson	80.00	36.00
□ 6	Hank Aaron	150.00	70.00

1997 Sports Illustrated Cooperstown Collection

Randomly inserted in packs at the rate of one in 12, this 12-card set features classic Sports Illustrated baseball covers with a description of the issue on the back.

		MINT	NRMT
COMPLETE SET (12)		60.00	27.00
COMMON CARD (1-12)		5.00	2.20
STATED ODDS 1:12			

□ 1	Hank Aaron	10.00	4.50
□ 2	Yogi Berra	6.00	2.70
□ 3	Lou Brock	5.00	2.20
□ 4	Rod Carew	5.00	2.20

□ 5	Juan Marichal	5.00	2.20
□ 6	Al Kaline	6.00	2.70
□ 7	Joe Morgan	5.00	2.20
□ 8	Brooks Robinson	5.00	2.20
□ 9	Willie Stargell	5.00	2.20
□ 10	Kirby Puckett	10.00	4.50
□ 11	Willie Mays	12.00	5.50
□ 12	Frank Robinson	5.00	2.20

1997 Sports Illustrated Great Shots

Randomly inserted one per pack, this 25-card set showcases some of the greatest photography in Sports Illustrated history and features color player photos that unfold into mini posters. When unfolded the posters measure 5" by 7".

		MINT	NRMT
COMPLETE SET (25)		8.00	3.60
COMMON CARD (1-25)		.30	.14
STATED ODDS ONE PER PACK			

□ 1	Chipper Jones	1.25	.55
□ 2	Ryan Klesko	.30	.14
□ 3	Kenny Lofton	.50	.23
□ 4	Greg Maddux	1.25	.55
□ 5	John Smoltz	.20	.09
□ 6	Roberto Alomar	.40	.18
□ 7	Cal Ripken	1.50	.70
□ 8	Mo Vaughn	.50	.23
□ 9	Albert Belle	.50	.23
□ 10	Frank Thomas	1.50	.70
□ 11	Ryne Sandberg	.50	.23
□ 12	Deion Sanders	.20	.09
□ 13	Vinny Castilla	.30	.14
	Andres Galarraga		
□ 14	Eric Karros	.20	.09
□ 15	Mike Piazza	1.25	.55
□ 16	Derek Jeter	1.25	.55
□ 17	Mark McGwire	.75	.35
□ 18	Darren Daulton	.20	.09
□ 19	Andy Ashby	.20	.09
□ 20	Barry Bonds	.50	.23
□ 21	Jay Buhner	.30	.14
□ 22	Randy Johnson	.40	.18
□ 23	Alex Rodriguez	1.25	.55
□ 24	Juan Gonzalez	1.00	.45
□ 25	Ken Griffey Jr.	2.00	.90

1996 SPx

This 1996 SPx set was issued in one series totalling 60 cards. The one-card packs had a suggested retail price of $3.49. Printed on 32 pt. card stock with Holoview technology and a perimeter diecut design, the set features color player photos with a Holography background on the fronts and decorative foil stamping on the back. Two special cards are included in the set: a Ken Griffey Jr. Commemorative card was inserted in every 75 packs and a Mike Piazza Tribute card inserted in every 95 packs. An autographed version of each of these cards was inserted at the rate of one in 2,000.

		MINT	NRMT
COMPLETE SET (60)		80.00	36.00
COMMON CARD (1-60)		1.00	.45
SEMISTARS		1.50	.70
UNLISTED STARS		2.00	.90
COMP.GOLD SET (60)		300.00	135.00
COMMON GOLD (1-60)		4.00	1.80
*GOLD STARS: 1.5X TO 4X HI COLUMN			
GOLD STATED ODDS 1:7			
GRIFFEY KG1 STATED ODDS 1:75			
PIAZZA MP1 STATED ODDS 1:95			
GRIFFEY AUTO STATED ODDS 1:2000			
PIAZZA AUTO STATED ODDS 1:2000			

□ 1	Greg Maddux	6.00	2.70
□ 2	Chipper Jones	6.00	2.70
□ 3	Fred McGriff	1.50	.70
□ 4	Tom Glavine	1.25	.55
□ 5	Cal Ripken	8.00	3.60
□ 6	Roberto Alomar	2.00	.90
□ 7	Rafael Palmeiro	1.50	.70
□ 8	Jose Canseco	1.50	.70
□ 9	Roger Clemens	4.00	1.80
□ 10	Mo Vaughn	2.50	1.10
□ 11	Jim Edmonds	1.50	.70
□ 12	Tim Salmon	2.00	.90
□ 13	Sammy Sosa	2.00	.90
□ 14	Ryne Sandberg	2.50	1.10
□ 15	Mark Grace	1.50	.70
□ 16	Frank Thomas	8.00	3.60
□ 17	Barry Larkin	1.50	.70
□ 18	Kenny Lofton	2.50	1.10
□ 19	Albert Belle	2.50	1.10
□ 20	Eddie Murray	2.00	.90
□ 21	Manny Ramirez	2.00	.90
□ 22	Dante Bichette	1.25	.55
□ 23	Larry Walker	2.00	.90
□ 24	Vinny Castilla	1.25	.55
□ 25	Andres Galarraga	2.00	.90
□ 26	Cecil Fielder	1.25	.55
□ 27	Gary Sheffield	2.00	.90
□ 28	Craig Biggio	1.50	.70

		MINT	NRMT
☐ 29	Jeff Bagwell	4.00	1.80
☐ 30	Derek Bell	1.00	.45
☐ 31	Johnny Damon	1.25	.55
☐ 32	Eric Karros	1.25	.55
☐ 33	Mike Piazza	6.00	2.70
☐ 34	Raul Mondesi	1.50	.70
☐ 35	Hideo Nomo	5.00	2.20
☐ 36	Kirby Puckett	4.00	1.80
☐ 37	Paul Molitor	2.00	.90
☐ 38	Marty Cordova	1.25	.55
☐ 39	Rondell White	1.25	.55
☐ 40	Jason Isringhausen	1.00	.45
☐ 41	Paul Wilson	1.00	.45
☐ 42	Rey Ordonez	1.25	.55
☐ 43	Derek Jeter	6.00	2.70
☐ 44	Wade Boggs	2.00	.90
☐ 45	Mark McGwire	4.00	1.80
☐ 46	Jason Kendall	1.50	.70
☐ 47	Ron Gant	1.25	.55
☐ 48	Ozzie Smith	2.50	1.10
☐ 49	Tony Gwynn	5.00	2.20
☐ 50	Ken Caminiti	1.50	.70
☐ 51	Barry Bonds	2.50	1.10
☐ 52	Matt Williams	1.50	.70
☐ 53	Osvaldo Fernandez	1.25	.55
☐ 54	Jay Buhner	1.25	.55
☐ 55	Ken Griffey Jr.	10.00	4.50
☐ 56	Randy Johnson	2.00	.90
☐ 57	Alex Rodriguez	6.00	2.70
☐ 58	Juan Gonzalez	5.00	2.20
☐ 59	Joe Carter	1.25	.55
☐ 60	Carlos Delgado	1.25	.55
☐ KG1	Ken Griffey Jr. Comm.	15.00	6.75
☐ MP1	Mike Piazza Trib.	8.00	3.60
☐ KGAU	Ken Griffey Jr. Auto.	350.00	160.00
☐ MPAU	Mike Piazza Auto.	225.00	100.00

1996 SPx Bound for Glory

Randomly inserted in packs at a rate of one in 24, this 10-card set features players with a chance to be long remembered. The fronts display color player photos with a diecut perimeter design and a Holography background. The words, "Bound for Glory" are printed at the top. The backs carry decorative foil stamping.

		MINT	NRMT
COMPLETE SET (10)		150.00	70.00
COMMON CARD (1-10)		6.00	2.70
STATED ODDS 1:24			

☐ 1	Ken Griffey Jr.	30.00	13.50
☐ 2	Frank Thomas	25.00	11.00
☐ 3	Barry Bonds	8.00	3.60
☐ 4	Cal Ripken	25.00	11.00
☐ 5	Greg Maddux	20.00	9.00
☐ 6	Chipper Jones	20.00	9.00
☐ 7	Roberto Alomar	6.00	2.70
☐ 8	Manny Ramirez	6.00	2.70
☐ 9	Tony Gwynn	15.00	6.75
☐ 10	Mike Piazza	20.00	9.00

1997 SPx

The 1997 SPx set was issued in one series totalling 50 cards and was distributed in three-card hobby only packs with a suggested retail price of $5.99. The fronts feature color player images on a Holoview perimeter die cut design. The backs feature a player photo, player information, and career statistics.

	MINT	NRMT
COMPLETE SET (50)	60.00	27.00
COMMON CARD (1-50)	.50	.23
SEMISTARS	.75	.35
UNLISTED STARS	1.25	.55
COMP.STEEL SET (50)	120.00	55.00
COMMON STEEL (1-50)	1.00	.45
*STEEL CARDS: 1X TO 2X HI COLUMN		
*STEEL ROOKIES: .75X TO 1.5X HI		
STEEL RANDOM INSERTS IN PACKS		
COMP.BRONZE SET (50)	200.00	90.00
COMMON BRONZE (1-50)	1.50	.70
*BRONZE CARDS: 1.5X TO 3X HI COLUMN		
*BRONZE ROOKIES: 1X TO 2X HI		
BRONZE RANDOM INSERTS IN PACKS		
COMP.SILVER SET (50)	300.00	135.00
COMMON SILVER (1-50)	2.50	1.10
*SILVER CARDS: 2.5X TO 5X HI COLUMN		
*SILVER ROOKIES: 1.5X TO 3X HI		
SILVER RANDOM INSERTS IN PACKS		
COMP.GOLD SET (50)	800.00	350.00
COMMON GOLD (1-50)	5.00	2.20
*GOLD STARS: 5X TO 10X HI COLUMN		
*GOLD YOUNG STARS: 4X TO 8X HI		
*GOLD ROOKIES: 3X TO 6X HI		
GOLD STATED ODDS 1:17		
GOLD: SILVER HOLOVIEW IMAGE ON FRONT		

☐ 1	Eddie Murray	1.25	.55
☐ 2	Darin Erstad	2.00	.90
☐ 3	Tim Salmon	1.25	.55
☐ 4	Andruw Jones	3.00	1.35
☐ 5	Chipper Jones	4.00	1.80
☐ 6	John Smoltz	.50	.23
☐ 7	Greg Maddux	4.00	1.80
☐ 8	Kenny Lofton	1.50	.70
☐ 9	Roberto Alomar	1.25	.55
☐ 10	Rafael Palmeiro	.75	.35
☐ 11	Brady Anderson	.75	.35
☐ 12	Cal Ripken	5.00	2.20
☐ 13	Nomar Garciaparra	4.00	1.80
☐ 14	Mo Vaughn	1.50	.70
☐ 15	Ryne Sandberg	1.50	.70
☐ 16	Sammy Sosa	1.25	.55
☐ 17	Frank Thomas	5.00	2.20
☐ 18	Albert Belle	1.50	.70
☐ 19	Barry Larkin	.75	.35
☐ 20	Deion Sanders	.50	.23
☐ 21	Manny Ramirez	1.25	.55
☐ 22	Jim Thome	1.25	.55
☐ 23	Dante Bichette	.50	.23
☐ 24	Andres Galarraga	1.25	.55
☐ 25	Larry Walker	1.25	.55
☐ 26	Gary Sheffield	1.25	.55
☐ 27	Jeff Bagwell	2.50	1.10

☐ 28	Raul Mondesi	.75	.35
☐ 29	Hideo Nomo	3.00	1.35
☐ 30	Mike Piazza	4.00	1.80
☐ 31	Paul Molitor	1.25	.55
☐ 32	Todd Walker	.50	.23
☐ 33	Vladimir Guerrero	2.50	1.10
☐ 34	Todd Hundley	.50	.23
☐ 35	Andy Pettitte	1.25	.55
☐ 36	Derek Jeter	4.00	1.80
☐ 37	Jose Canseco	.75	.35
☐ 38	Mark McGwire	2.50	1.10
☐ 39	Scott Rolen	3.00	1.35
☐ 40	Ron Gant	.50	.23
☐ 41	Ken Caminiti	.75	.35
☐ 42	Tony Gwynn	3.00	1.35
☐ 43	Barry Bonds	1.50	.70
☐ 44	Jay Buhner	.75	.35
☐ 45	Ken Griffey Jr.	6.00	2.70
☐ 46	Alex Rodriguez	4.00	1.80
☐ 47	Jose Cruz Jr.	12.00	5.50
☐ 48	Juan Gonzalez	3.00	1.35
☐ 49	Ivan Rodriguez	1.50	.70
☐ 50	Roger Clemens	2.50	1.10
☐ S45	Ken Griffey Jr. SAMPLE	3.00	1.35

1997 SPx Grand Finale

Randomly inserted in packs, cards from this 50-card set are an extremely limited edition parallel version of the base set and features an all gold holoview image. Only 50 of each card was produced. The set was entitled Grand Finale to signify the fact that this would be the last baseball product Upper Deck would ever use the holoview technology on.

	MINT	NRMT
COMPLETE SET (50)	7500.00	3400.00
COMMON CARD (1-50)	25.00	11.00
MINOR STARS	40.00	18.00
SEMISTARS	60.00	27.00
UNLISTED STARS	100.00	45.00
RANDOM INSERTS IN PACKS		
STATED PRINT RUN 50 SETS		
GOLD HOLOVIEW IMAGE ON FRONT		

☐ 2	Darin Erstad	120.00	55.00
☐ 4	Andruw Jones	200.00	90.00
☐ 5	Chipper Jones	250.00	110.00
☐ 7	Greg Maddux	300.00	135.00
☐ 8	Kenny Lofton	120.00	55.00
☐ 12	Cal Ripken	400.00	180.00
☐ 13	Nomar Garciaparra	250.00	110.00
☐ 14	Mo Vaughn	120.00	55.00
☐ 15	Ryne Sandberg	120.00	55.00
☐ 17	Frank Thomas	500.00	220.00
☐ 18	Albert Belle	120.00	55.00
☐ 27	Jeff Bagwell	200.00	90.00
☐ 29	Hideo Nomo	300.00	135.00
☐ 30	Mike Piazza	300.00	135.00
☐ 33	Vladimir Guerrero	150.00	70.00
☐ 36	Derek Jeter	250.00	110.00
☐ 38	Mark McGwire	200.00	90.00
☐ 39	Scott Rolen	200.00	90.00
☐ 42	Tony Gwynn	250.00	110.00
☐ 43	Barry Bonds	120.00	55.00
☐ 45	Ken Griffey Jr.	600.00	275.00
☐ 46	Alex Rodriguez	300.00	135.00
☐ 47	Jose Cruz Jr.	300.00	135.00
☐ 48	Juan Gonzalez	250.00	110.00
☐ 49	Ivan Rodriguez	120.00	55.00
☐ 50	Roger Clemens	200.00	90.00

1997 SPx Bound for Glory

Randomly inserted in packs, this 20-card set features color photos of promising great play

	MINT	NRMT
☐ 1 Jeff Bagwell	200.00	90.00
☐ 2 Ken Griffey Jr.	500.00	220.00
☐ 3 Andruw Jones	200.00	90.00
☐ 4 Alex Rodriguez	300.00	135.00
☐ 5 Gary Sheffield	80.00	36.00

1997 SPx
Cornerstones of
the Game

Randomly inserted in packs, cards from this 10-card set display color photos of 20 top players. Two players are featured on each card using double Holoview technology. Only 500 of each card are produced and are sequentially numbered on back.

	MINT	NRMT
COMPLETE SET (10)	700.00	325.00
COMMON CARD (1-10)	50.00	22.00
RANDOM INSERTS IN PACKS ..		
STATED PRINT RUN 500 SERIAL #'d SETS		

		MINT	NRMT
☐ 1 Ken Griffey Jr. Barry Bonds		120.00	55.00
☐ 2 Frank Thomas Albert Belle		100.00	45.00
☐ 3 Chipper Jones Greg Maddux		80.00	36.00
☐ 4 Tony Gwynn Paul Molitor		50.00	22.00
☐ 5 Andruw Jones Vladimir Guerrero		50.00	22.00
☐ 6 Jeff Bagwell Ryne Sandberg		50.00	22.00
☐ 7 Mike Piazza Ivan Rodriguez		60.00	27.00
☐ 8 Cal Ripken Eddie Murray		80.00	36.00
☐ 9 Mo Vaughn Mark McGwire		50.00	22.00
☐ 10 Alex Rodriguez Derek Jeter		80.00	36.00

1991 Stadium Club

This 600-card standard size set marked Topps first premium quality set. The set was issued in two separate series of 300 cards each. Cards were distributed in plastic wrapped packs. Series II cards were also available at McDonald's restaurants in the Northeast at three cards per pack. The set created a stir in the hobby upon release with dazzling full-color borderless photos and slick, glossy card stock. The back of each card has the basic biographical information as well as making use of the Fastball BARS system and an inset photo of the player's Topps rookie card. Rookie

Cards include Jeff Bagwell, Jeff Conine and Brian McRae.

	MINT	NRMT
COMPLETE SET (600)	100.00	45.00
COMPLETE SERIES 1 (300)	60.00	27.00
COMPLETE SERIES 2 (300)	40.00	18.00
COMMON CARD (1-600)	.25	.11
MINOR STARS	.50	.23
UNLISTED STARS	1.00	.45

		MINT	NRMT
☐ 1 Dave Stewart TUX		.75	.35
☐ 2 Wally Joyner		.50	.23
☐ 3 Shawon Dunston		.25	.11
☐ 4 Darren Daulton		.50	.23
☐ 5 Will Clark		1.00	.45
☐ 6 Sammy Sosa		1.25	.55
☐ 7 Dan Plesac		.25	.11
☐ 8 Marquis Grissom		1.00	.45
☐ 9 Erik Hanson		.25	.11
☐ 10 Geno Petralli		.25	.11
☐ 11 Jose Rijo		.25	.11
☐ 12 Carlos Quintana		.25	.11
☐ 13 Junior Ortiz		.25	.11
☐ 14 Bob Walk		.25	.11
☐ 15 Mike Macfarlane		.25	.11
☐ 16 Eric Yelding		.25	.11
☐ 17 Bryn Smith		.25	.11
☐ 18 Bip Roberts		.25	.11
☐ 19 Mike Scioscia		.25	.11
☐ 20 Mark Williamson		.25	.11
☐ 21 Don Mattingly		1.50	.70
☐ 22 John Franco		.50	.23
☐ 23 Chet Lemon		.25	.11
☐ 24 Tom Henke		.25	.11
☐ 25 Jerry Browne		.25	.11
☐ 26 Dave Justice		1.25	.55
☐ 27 Mark Langston		.25	.11
☐ 28 Damon Berryhill		.25	.11
☐ 29 Kevin Bass		.25	.11
☐ 30 Scott Fletcher		.25	.11
☐ 31 Moises Alou		2.00	.90
☐ 32 Dave Valle		.25	.11
☐ 33 Jody Reed		.25	.11
☐ 34 Dave West		.25	.11
☐ 35 Kevin McReynolds		.25	.11
☐ 36 Pat Combs		.25	.11
☐ 37 Eric Davis		.50	.23
☐ 38 Bret Saberhagen		.25	.11
☐ 39 Stan Javier		.25	.11
☐ 40 Chuck Cary		.25	.11
☐ 41 Tony Phillips		.25	.11
☐ 42 Lee Smith		.50	.23
☐ 43 Tim Teufel		.25	.11
☐ 44 Lance Dickson		.25	.11
☐ 45 Greg Litton		.25	.11
☐ 46 Teddy Higuera		.25	.11
☐ 47 Edgar Martinez		1.00	.45
☐ 48 Steve Avery		.25	.11
☐ 49 Walt Weiss		.25	.11
☐ 50 David Segui		.50	.23
☐ 51 Andy Benes		.50	.23
☐ 52 Karl Rhodes		.25	.11
☐ 53 Neal Heaton		.25	.11
☐ 54 Danny Gladden		.25	.11
☐ 55 Luis Rivera		.25	.11
☐ 56 Kevin Brown		.50	.23
☐ 57 Frank Thomas		8.00	3.60

ers on a Holoview die cut card design. Only 1,500 of each card was produced and are sequentially numbered.

	MINT	NRMT
COMPLETE SET (20)	500.00	220.00
COMMON CARD (1-20)	10.00	4.50
UNLISTED STARS	12.00	5.50
RANDOM INSERTS IN PACKS ..		
STATED PRINT RUN 1500 SERIAL #'d SETS		

		MINT	NRMT
☐ 1 Andruw Jones		25.00	11.00
☐ 2 Chipper Jones		40.00	18.00
☐ 3 Greg Maddux		40.00	18.00
☐ 4 Kenny Lofton		15.00	6.75
☐ 5 Cal Ripken		50.00	22.00
☐ 6 Mo Vaughn		15.00	6.75
☐ 7 Frank Thomas		50.00	22.00
☐ 8 Albert Belle		15.00	6.75
☐ 9 Manny Ramirez		12.00	5.50
☐ 10 Gary Sheffield		12.00	5.50
☐ 11 Jeff Bagwell		25.00	11.00
☐ 12 Mike Piazza		40.00	18.00
☐ 13 Derek Jeter		30.00	13.50
☐ 14 Mark McGwire		25.00	11.00
☐ 15 Tony Gwynn		30.00	13.50
☐ 16 Ken Caminiti		10.00	4.50
☐ 17 Barry Bonds		15.00	6.75
☐ 18 Alex Rodriguez		40.00	18.00
☐ 19 Ken Griffey Jr.		60.00	27.00
☐ 20 Juan Gonzalez		30.00	13.50

1997 SPx Bound
for Glory Supreme
Signatures

Randomly inserted in packs, this five-card set features autographed Bound for Glory cards. Only 250 of each card were produced and are signed and are sequentially numbered.

	MINT	NRMT
COMPLETE SET (5)	1200.00	550.00
COMMON CARD (1-5)	80.00	36.00
RANDOM INSERTS IN PACKS ..		
STATED PRINT RUN 250 SERIAL #'d SETS		

58	Terry Mulholland	.25	.11
59	Dick Schofield	.25	.11
60	Ron Darling	.25	.11
61	Sandy Alomar Jr.	.75	.35
62	Dave Stieb	.25	.11
63	Alan Trammell	.75	.35
64	Matt Nokes	.25	.11
65	Lenny Harris	.25	.11
66	Milt Thompson	.25	.11
67	Storm Davis	.25	.11
68	Joe Oliver	.25	.11
69	Andres Galarraga	1.00	.45
70	Ozzie Guillen	.25	.11
71	Ken Howell	.25	.11
72	Garry Templeton	.25	.11
73	Derrick May	.25	.11
74	Xavier Hernandez	.25	.11
75	Dave Parker	.50	.23
76	Rick Aguilera	.25	.11
77	Robby Thompson	.25	.11
78	Pete Incaviglia	.25	.11
79	Bob Welch	.25	.11
80	Randy Milligan	.25	.11
81	Chuck Finley	.50	.23
82	Alvin Davis	.25	.11
83	Tim Naehring	.50	.23
84	Jay Bell	.50	.23
85	Joe Magrane	.25	.11
86	Howard Johnson	.25	.11
87	Jack McDowell	.25	.11
88	Kevin Seitzer	.25	.11
89	Bruce Ruffin	.25	.11
90	Fernando Valenzuela	.50	.23
91	Terry Kennedy	.25	.11
92	Barry Larkin	.75	.35
93	Larry Walker	1.50	.70
94	Luis Salazar	.25	.11
95	Gary Sheffield	1.00	.45
96	Bobby Witt	.25	.11
97	Lonnie Smith	.25	.11
98	Bryan Harvey	.25	.11
99	Mookie Wilson	.50	.23
100	Dwight Gooden	.50	.23
101	Lou Whitaker	.50	.23
102	Ron Karkovice	.25	.11
103	Jesse Barfield	.25	.11
104	Jose DeJesus	.25	.11
105	Benito Santiago	.25	.11
106	Brian Holman	.25	.11
107	Rafael Ramirez	.25	.11
108	Ellis Burks	.50	.23
109	Mike Bielecki	.25	.11
110	Kirby Puckett	2.00	.90
111	Terry Shumpert	.25	.11
112	Chuck Crim	.25	.11
113	Todd Benzinger	.25	.11
114	Brian Barnes	.25	.11
115	Carlos Baerga	.50	.23
116	Kal Daniels	.25	.11
117	Dave Johnson	.25	.11
118	Andy Van Slyke	.50	.23
119	John Burkett	.25	.11
120	Rickey Henderson	1.00	.45
121	Tim Jones	.25	.11
122	Daryl Irvine	.25	.11
123	Ruben Sierra	.25	.11
124	Jim Abbott	.25	.11
125	Daryl Boston	.25	.11
126	Greg Maddux	3.00	1.35
127	Von Hayes	.25	.11
128	Mike Fitzgerald	.25	.11
129	Wayne Edwards	.25	.11
130	Greg Briley	.25	.11
131	Rob Dibble	.25	.11
132	Gene Larkin	.25	.11
133	David Wells	.25	.11
134	Steve Balboni	.25	.11
135	Greg Vaughn	.50	.23
136	Mark Davis	.25	.11
137	Dave Rhode	.25	.11
138	Eric Show	.25	.11
139	Bobby Bonilla	.50	.23
140	Dana Kiecker	.25	.11
141	Gary Pettis	.25	.11
142	Dennis Boyd	.25	.11
143	Mike Benjamin	.25	.11
144	Luis Polonia	.25	.11
145	Doug Jones	.25	.11
146	Al Newman	.25	.11
147	Alex Fernandez	1.50	.70
148	Bill Doran	.25	.11
149	Kevin Elster	.25	.11
150	Len Dykstra	.50	.23
151	Mike Gallego	.25	.11
152	Tim Belcher	.25	.11
153	Jay Buhner	1.00	.45
154	Ozzie Smith UER (Rookie card is 1979, but card back says '78)	1.25	.55
155	Jose Canseco	.75	.35
156	Gregg Olson	.25	.11
157	Charlie O'Brien	.25	.11
158	Frank Tanana	.25	.11
159	George Brett	2.00	.90
160	Jeff Huson	.25	.11
161	Kevin Tapani	.25	.11
162	Jerome Walton	.25	.11
163	Charlie Hayes	.25	.11
164	Chris Bosio	.25	.11
165	Chris Sabo	.25	.11
166	Lance Parrish	.25	.11
167	Don Robinson	.25	.11
168	Manny Lee	.25	.11
169	Dennis Rasmussen	.25	.11
170	Wade Boggs	1.00	.45
171	Bob Geren	.25	.11
172	Mackey Sasser	.25	.11
173	Julio Franco	.25	.11
174	Otis Nixon	.50	.23
175	Bert Blyleven	.50	.23
176	Craig Biggio	1.00	.45
177	Eddie Murray	1.00	.45
178	Randy Tomlin	.25	.11
179	Tino Martinez	1.00	.45
180	Carlton Fisk	1.00	.45
181	Dwight Smith	.25	.11
182	Scott Garrelts	.25	.11
183	Jim Gantner	.25	.11
184	Dickie Thon	.25	.11
185	John Farrell	.25	.11
186	Cecil Fielder	.50	.23
187	Glenn Braggs	.25	.11
188	Allan Anderson	.25	.11
189	Kurt Stillwell	.25	.11
190	Jose Oquendo	.25	.11
191	Joe Orsulak	.25	.11
192	Ricky Jordan	.25	.11
193	Kelly Downs	.25	.11
194	Delino DeShields	.25	.11
195	Omar Vizquel	1.00	.45
196	Mark Carreon	.25	.11
197	Mike Harkey	.25	.11
198	Jack Howell	.25	.11
199	Lance Johnson	.25	.11
200	Nolan Ryan TUX	4.00	1.80
201	John Marzano	.25	.11
202	Doug Drabek	.25	.11
203	Mark Lemke	.25	.11
204	Steve Sax	.25	.11
205	Greg Harris	.25	.11
206	B.J. Surhoff	.50	.23
207	Todd Burns	.25	.11
208	Jose Gonzalez	.25	.11
209	Mike Scott	.25	.11
210	Dave Magadan	.25	.11
211	Dante Bichette	1.00	.45
212	Trevor Wilson	.25	.11
213	Hector Villanueva	.25	.11
214	Dan Pasqua	.25	.11
215	Greg Colbrunn	.25	.11
216	Mike Jeffcoat	.25	.11
217	Harold Reynolds	.25	.11
218	Paul O'Neill	.50	.23
219	Mark Guthrie	.25	.11
220	Barry Bonds	1.25	.55
221	Jimmy Key	.25	.11
222	Billy Ripken	.25	.11
223	Tom Pagnozzi	.25	.11
224	Bo Jackson	.75	.35
225	Sid Fernandez	.25	.11
226	Mike Marshall	.25	.11
227	John Kruk	.50	.23
228	Mike Fetters	.25	.11
229	Eric Anthony	.25	.11
230	Ryne Sandberg	1.25	.55
231	Carney Lansford	.50	.23
232	Melido Perez	.25	.11
233	Jose Lind	.25	.11
234	Darryl Hamilton	.25	.11
235	Tom Browning	.25	.11
236	Spike Owen	.25	.11
237	Juan Gonzalez	8.00	3.60
238	Felix Fermin	.25	.11
239	Keith Miller	.25	.11
240	Mark Gubicza	.25	.11
241	Kent Anderson	.25	.11
242	Alvaro Espinoza	.25	.11
243	Dale Murphy	1.00	.45
244	Orel Hershiser	.50	.23
245	Paul Molitor	1.00	.45
246	Eddie Whitson	.25	.11
247	Joe Girardi	.50	.23
248	Kent Hrbek	.50	.23
249	Bill Sampen	.25	.11
250	Kevin Mitchell	.50	.23
251	Mariano Duncan	.25	.11
252	Scott Bradley	.25	.11
253	Mike Greenwell	.25	.11
254	Tom Gordon	.25	.11
255	Todd Zeile	.50	.23
256	Bobby Thigpen	.25	.11
257	Gregg Jefferies	.25	.11
258	Kenny Rogers	.25	.11
259	Shane Mack	.25	.11
260	Zane Smith	.25	.11
261	Mitch Williams	.25	.11
262	Jim Deshaies	.25	.11
263	Dave Winfield	1.00	.45
264	Ben McDonald	.25	.11
265	Randy Ready	.25	.11
266	Pat Borders	.25	.11
267	Jose Uribe	.25	.11
268	Derek Lilliquist	.25	.11
269	Greg Brock	.25	.11
270	Ken Griffey Jr.	8.00	3.60
271	Jeff Gray	.25	.11
272	Danny Tartabull	.25	.11
273	Denny Martinez	.50	.23
274	Robin Ventura	1.00	.45
275	Randy Myers	.25	.11
276	Jack Daugherty	.25	.11
277	Greg Gagne	.25	.11
278	Jay Howell	.25	.11
279	Mike LaValliere	.25	.11
280	Rex Hudler	.25	.11
281	Mike Simms	.25	.11
282	Kevin Maas	.25	.11
283	Jeff Ballard	.25	.11
284	Dave Henderson	.25	.11
285	Pete O'Brien	.25	.11
286	Brook Jacoby	.25	.11
287	Mike Henneman	.25	.11
288	Greg Olson	.25	.11
289	Greg Myers	.25	.11
290	Mark Grace	1.00	.45
291	Shawn Abner	.25	.11
292	Frank Viola	.25	.11
293	Lee Stevens	.25	.11
294	Jason Grimsley	.25	.11
295	Matt Williams	1.00	.45
296	Ron Robinson	.25	.11
297	Tom Brunansky	.25	.11
298	Checklist 1-100	.25	.11
299	Checklist 101-200	.25	.11
300	Checklist 201-300	.25	.11
301	Darryl Strawberry	.50	.23
302	Bud Black	.25	.11
303	Harold Baines	.50	.23
304	Roberto Alomar	1.00	.45
305	Norm Charlton	.25	.11
306	Gary Thurman	.25	.11
307	Mike Felder	.25	.11
308	Tony Gwynn	2.50	1.10
309	Roger Clemens	2.00	.90
310	Andre Dawson	1.00	.45
311	Scott Radinsky	.25	.11
312	Bob Melvin	.25	.11
313	Kirk McCaskill	.25	.11

314	Pedro Guerrero	.25	.11
315	Walt Terrell	.25	.11
316	Sam Horn	.25	.11
317	Wes Chamberlain UER	.25	.11
	(Card listed as 1989 Debut card, should be 1990)		
318	Pedro Munoz	.25	.11
319	Roberto Kelly	.25	.11
320	Mark Portugal	.25	.11
321	Tim McIntosh	.25	.11
322	Jesse Orosco	.25	.11
323	Gary Green	.25	.11
324	Greg Harris	.25	.11
325	Hubie Brooks	.25	.11
326	Chris Nabholz	.25	.11
327	Terry Pendleton	.50	.23
328	Eric King	.25	.11
329	Chili Davis	.50	.23
330	Anthony Telford	.25	.11
331	Kelly Gruber	.25	.11
332	Dennis Eckersley	.50	.23
333	Mel Hall	.25	.11
334	Bob Kipper	.25	.11
335	Willie McGee	.25	.11
336	Steve Olin	.25	.11
337	Steve Buechele	.25	.11
338	Scott Leius	.25	.11
339	Hal Morris	.25	.11
340	Jose Offerman	.25	.11
341	Kent Mercker	.25	.11
342	Ken Griffey Sr	.25	.11
343	Pete Harnisch	.25	.11
344	Kirk Gibson	.50	.23
345	Dave Smith	.25	.11
346	Dave Martinez	.25	.11
347	Atlee Hammaker	.25	.11
348	Brian Downing	.25	.11
349	Todd Hundley	1.50	.70
350	Candy Maldonado	.25	.11
351	Dwight Evans	.50	.23
352	Steve Searcy	.25	.11
353	Gary Gaetti	.25	.11
354	Jeff Reardon	.50	.23
355	Travis Fryman	1.50	.70
356	Dave Righetti	.25	.11
357	Fred McGriff	1.00	.45
358	Don Slaught	.25	.11
359	Gene Nelson	.25	.11
360	Billy Spiers	.25	.11
361	Lee Guetterman	.25	.11
362	Darren Lewis	.25	.11
363	Duane Ward	.25	.11
364	Lloyd Moseby	.25	.11
365	John Smoltz	1.00	.45
366	Felix Jose	.25	.11
367	David Cone	.50	.23
368	Wally Backman	.25	.11
369	Jeff Montgomery	.50	.23
370	Rich Garces	.25	.11
371	Billy Hatcher	.25	.11
372	Bill Swift	.25	.11
373	Jim Eisenreich	.25	.11
374	Rob Ducey	.25	.11
375	Tim Crews	.25	.11
376	Steve Finley	1.00	.45
377	Jeff Blauser	.25	.11
378	Willie Wilson	.25	.11
379	Gerald Perry	.25	.11
380	Jose Mesa	.25	.11
381	Pat Kelly	.25	.11
382	Matt Merullo	.25	.11
383	Ivan Calderon	.25	.11
384	Scott Chiamparino	.25	.11
385	Lloyd McClendon	.25	.11
386	Dave Bergman	.25	.11
387	Ed Sprague	.25	.11
388	Jeff Bagwell	6.00	2.70
389	Brett Butler	.50	.23
390	Larry Andersen	.25	.11
391	Glenn Davis	.25	.11
392	Alex Cole UER	.25	.11
	(Front photo actually Otis Nixon)		
393	Mike Heath	.25	.11
394	Danny Darwin	.25	.11
395	Steve Lake	.25	.11
396	Tim Layana	.25	.11
397	Terry Leach	.25	.11
398	Bill Wegman	.25	.11
399	Mark McGwire	2.00	.90
400	Mike Boddicker	.25	.11
401	Steve Howe	.25	.11
402	Bernard Gilkey	.50	.23
403	Thomas Howard	.25	.11
404	Rafael Belliard	.25	.11
405	Tom Candiotti	.25	.11
406	Rene Gonzales	.25	.11
407	Chuck McElroy	.25	.11
408	Paul Sorrento	.50	.23
409	Randy Johnson	1.25	.55
410	Brady Anderson	1.00	.45
411	Dennis Cook	.25	.11
412	Mickey Tettleton	.50	.23
413	Mike Stanton	.25	.11
414	Ken Oberkfell	.25	.11
415	Rick Honeycutt	.25	.11
416	Nelson Santovenia	.25	.11
417	Bob Tewksbury	.25	.11
418	Brent Mayne	.25	.11
419	Steve Farr	.25	.11
420	Phil Stephenson	.25	.11
421	Jeff Russell	.25	.11
422	Chris James	.25	.11
423	Tim Leary	.25	.11
424	Gary Carter	1.00	.45
425	Glenallen Hill	.25	.11
426	Matt Young UER	.25	.11
	(Card mentions 83T/Tr as RC, but 84T shown)		
427	Sid Bream	.25	.11
428	Greg Swindell	.25	.11
429	Scott Aldred	.25	.11
430	Cal Ripken	4.00	1.80
431	Bill Landrum	.25	.11
432	Earnest Riles	.25	.11
433	Danny Jackson	.25	.11
434	Casey Candaele	.25	.11
435	Ken Hill	.50	.23
436	Jaime Navarro	.25	.11
437	Lance Blankenship	.25	.11
438	Randy Velarde	.25	.11
439	Frank DiPino	.25	.11
440	Carl Nichols	.25	.11
441	Jeff M. Robinson	.25	.11
442	Deion Sanders	.50	.23
443	Vicente Palacios	.25	.11
444	Devon White	.25	.11
445	John Cerutti	.25	.11
446	Tracy Jones	.25	.11
447	Jack Morris	.50	.23
448	Mitch Webster	.25	.11
449	Bob Ojeda	.25	.11
450	Oscar Azocar	.25	.11
451	Luis Aquino	.25	.11
452	Mark Whiten	.25	.11
453	Stan Belinda	.25	.11
454	Ron Gant	.50	.23
455	Jose DeLeon	.25	.11
456	Mark Salas UER	.25	.11
	(Back has 85T photo, but calls it 86T)		
457	Junior Felix	.25	.11
458	Wally Whitehurst	.25	.11
459	Phil Plantier	.50	.23
460	Juan Berenguer	.25	.11
461	Franklin Stubbs	.25	.11
462	Joe Boever	.25	.11
463	Tim Wallach	.25	.11
464	Mike Moore	.25	.11
465	Albert Belle	1.50	.70
466	Mike Witt	.25	.11
467	Craig Worthington	.25	.11
468	Jerald Clark	.25	.11
469	Scott Terry	.25	.11
470	Milt Cuyler	.25	.11
471	Jim Gantner	.25	.11
472	Charles Nagy	1.00	.45
473	Alan Mills	.25	.11
474	John Russell	.25	.11
475	Bruce Hurst	.25	.11
476	Andujar Cedeno	.25	.11
477	Dave Eiland	.25	.11
478	Brian McRae	1.00	.45
479	Mike LaCoss	.25	.11
480	Chris Gwynn	.25	.11
481	Jamie Moyer	.25	.11
482	John Olerud	.50	.23
483	Efrain Valdez	.25	.11
484	Sil Campusano	.25	.11
485	Pascual Perez	.25	.11
486	Gary Redus	.25	.11
487	Andy Hawkins	.25	.11
488	Cory Snyder	.25	.11
489	Chris Hoiles	.25	.11
490	Ron Hassey	.25	.11
491	Gary Wayne	.25	.11
492	Mark Lewis	.25	.11
493	Scott Coolbaugh	.25	.11
494	Gerald Young	.25	.11
495	Juan Samuel	.25	.11
496	Willie Fraser	.25	.11
497	Jeff Treadway	.25	.11
498	Vince Coleman	.25	.11
499	Cris Carpenter	.25	.11
500	Jack Clark	.50	.23
501	Kevin Appier	1.00	.45
502	Rafael Palmeiro	1.00	.45
503	Hensley Meulens	.25	.11
504	George Bell	.25	.11
505	Tony Pena	.25	.11
506	Roger McDowell	.25	.11
507	Luis Sojo	.25	.11
508	Mike Schooler	.25	.11
509	Robin Yount	1.00	.45
510	Jack Armstrong	.25	.11
511	Rick Cerone	.25	.11
512	Curt Wilkerson	.25	.11
513	Joe Carter	.50	.23
514	Tim Burke	.25	.11
515	Tony Fernandez	.25	.11
516	Ramon Martinez	.50	.23
517	Tim Hulett	.25	.11
518	Terry Steinbach	.50	.23
519	Pete Smith	.25	.11
520	Ken Caminiti	1.00	.45
521	Shawn Boskie	.25	.11
522	Mike Pagliarulo	.25	.11
523	Tim Raines	.50	.23
524	Alfredo Griffin	.25	.11
525	Henry Cotto	.25	.11
526	Mike Stanley	.25	.11
527	Charlie Leibrandt	.25	.11
528	Jeff King	.50	.23
529	Eric Plunk	.25	.11
530	Tom Lampkin	.25	.11
531	Steve Bedrosian	.25	.11
532	Tom Herr	.25	.11
533	Craig Lefferts	.25	.11
534	Jeff Reed	.25	.11
535	Mickey Morandini	.25	.11
536	Greg Cadaret	.25	.11
537	Ray Lankford	2.00	.90
538	John Candelaria	.25	.11
539	Rob Deer	.25	.11
540	Brad Arnsberg	.25	.11
541	Mike Sharperson	.25	.11
542	Jeff D. Robinson	.25	.11
543	Mo Vaughn	5.00	2.20
544	Jeff Parrett	.25	.11
545	Willie Randolph	.50	.23
546	Herm Winningham	.25	.11
547	Jeff Innis	.25	.11
548	Chuck Knoblauch	3.00	1.35
549	Tommy Greene UER	.25	.11
	(Born in North Carolina, not South Carolina)		
550	Jeff Hamilton	.25	.11
551	Barry Jones	.25	.11
552	Ken Dayley	.25	.11
553	Rick Dempsey	.25	.11
554	Greg Smith	.25	.11
555	Mike Devereaux	.25	.11
556	Keith Comstock	.25	.11
557	Paul Faries	.25	.11
558	Tom Glavine	1.00	.45
559	Craig Grebeck	.25	.11
560	Scott Erickson	.50	.23
561	Joel Skinner	.25	.11

☐ 562 Mike Morgan	.25	.11
☐ 563 Dave Gallagher	.25	.11
☐ 564 Todd Stottlemyre	.25	.11
☐ 565 Rich Rodriguez	.25	.11
☐ 566 Craig Wilson	.25	.11
☐ 567 Jeff Brantley	.25	.11
☐ 568 Scott Kamieniecki	.25	.11
☐ 569 Steve Decker	.25	.11
☐ 570 Juan Agosto	.25	.11
☐ 571 Tommy Gregg	.25	.11
☐ 572 Kevin Wickander	.25	.11
☐ 573 Jamie Quirk UER	.25	.11
(Rookie card is 1976,		
but card back is 1990)		
☐ 574 Jerry Don Gleaton	.25	.11
☐ 575 Chris Hammond	.25	.11
☐ 576 Luis Gonzalez	1.00	.45
☐ 577 Russ Swan	.25	.11
☐ 578 Jeff Conine	1.00	.45
☐ 579 Charlie Hough	.25	.11
☐ 580 Jeff Kunkel	.25	.11
☐ 581 Darrel Akerfelds	.25	.11
☐ 582 Jeff Manto	.25	.11
☐ 583 Alejandro Pena	.25	.11
☐ 584 Mark Davidson	.25	.11
☐ 585 Bob MacDonald	.25	.11
☐ 586 Paul Assenmacher	.25	.11
☐ 587 Dan Wilson	1.00	.45
☐ 588 Tom Bolton	.25	.11
☐ 589 Brian Harper	.25	.11
☐ 590 John Habyan	.25	.11
☐ 591 John Orton	.25	.11
☐ 592 Mark Gardner	.25	.11
☐ 593 Turner Ward	.25	.11
☐ 594 Bob Patterson	.25	.11
☐ 595 Ed Nunez	.25	.11
☐ 596 Gary Scott UER	.25	.11
(Major League Batting		
Record should be		
Minor League)		
☐ 597 Scott Bankhead	.25	.11
☐ 598 Checklist 301-400	.25	.11
☐ 599 Checklist 401-500	.25	.11
☐ 600 Checklist 501-600	.25	.11

1992 Stadium Club Dome

The 1992 Stadium Club Dome set (issued by Topps) features 100 top draft picks, 56 1991 All-Star Game cards, 25 1991 Team U.S.A. cards, and 19 1991 Championship and World Series cards, all packaged in a factory set box inside a molded-plastic SkyDome display. Topps actually references this set as a 1991 set and the copyright lines on the card backs say 1991, but the set was released well into 1992. The standard-size cards display full-bleed glossy player photos on the fronts. The player's name appears in an sky-blue stripe that is accented by parallel gold stripes. Rookie Cards in this set include Shawn Green, Todd Hollandsworth, Alex Ochoa and Manny Ramirez.

	MINT	NRMT
COMP.FACT.SET (200)	10.00	4.50
COMMON CARD (1-200)	.10	.05
MINOR STARS	.20	.09
UNLISTED STARS	.40	.18

☐ 1 Terry Adams	.20	.09
☐ 2 Tommy Adams	.10	.05
☐ 3 Rick Aguilera	.10	.05
☐ 4 Ron Allen	.10	.05
☐ 5 Roberto Alomar	.40	.18
☐ 6 Sandy Alomar	.10	.05
☐ 7 Greg Anthony	.10	.05
☐ 8 James Austin	.10	.05
☐ 9 Steve Avery	.10	.05
☐ 10 Harold Baines	.20	.09
☐ 11 Brian Barber	.20	.09
☐ 12 Jon Barnes	.10	.05
☐ 13 George Bell	.10	.05
☐ 14 Doug Bennett	.10	.05
☐ 15 Sean Bergman	.20	.09
☐ 16 Craig Biggio	.30	.14
☐ 17 Bill Bliss	.10	.05
☐ 18 Wade Boggs	.40	.18
☐ 19 Bobby Bonilla	.20	.09
☐ 20 Russell Brock	.10	.05
☐ 21 Tarrik Brock	.10	.05
☐ 22 Tom Browning	.10	.05
☐ 23 Brett Butler	.20	.09
☐ 24 Ivan Calderon	.10	.05
☐ 25 Joe Carter	.20	.09
☐ 26 Joe Caruso	.10	.05
☐ 27 Dan Cholowsky	.10	.05
☐ 28 Will Clark	.30	.14
☐ 29 Roger Clemens	.75	.35
☐ 30 Shawn Curran	.10	.05
☐ 31 Chris Curtis	.10	.05
☐ 32 Chili Davis	.20	.09
☐ 33 Andre Dawson	.30	.14
☐ 34 Joe DeBerry	.10	.05
☐ 35 John Dettmer	.10	.05
☐ 36 Rob Dibble	.10	.05
☐ 37 John Donati	.10	.05
☐ 38 Dave Doorneweerd	.10	.05
☐ 39 Darren Dreifort	.20	.09
☐ 40 Mike Durant	.10	.05
☐ 41 Chris Durkin	.10	.05
☐ 42 Dennis Eckersley	.20	.09
☐ 43 Brian Edmondson	.10	.05
☐ 44 Vaughn Eshelman	.10	.05
☐ 45 Shawn Estes	.75	.35
☐ 46 Jorge Fabregas	.10	.05
☐ 47 Jon Farrell	.10	.05
☐ 48 Cecil Fielder	.20	.09
☐ 49 Carlton Fisk	.40	.18
☐ 50 Tim Flannelly	.10	.05
☐ 51 Cliff Floyd	.40	.18
☐ 52 Julio Franco	.10	.05
☐ 53 Greg Gagne	.10	.05
☐ 54 Chris Gambs	.10	.05
☐ 55 Ron Gant	.20	.09
☐ 56 Brent Gates	.10	.05
☐ 57 Dwayne Gerald	.10	.05
☐ 58 Jason Giambi	.50	.23
☐ 59 Benji Gil	.20	.09
☐ 60 Mark Gipner	.10	.05
☐ 61 Danny Gladden	.10	.05
☐ 62 Tom Glavine	.30	.14
☐ 63 Jimmy Gonzalez	.10	.05
☐ 64 Jeff Granger	.20	.09
☐ 65 Dan Grapenthien	.10	.05
☐ 66 Dennis Gray	.10	.05
☐ 67 Shawn Green	.50	.23
☐ 68 Tyler Green	.20	.09
☐ 69 Todd Greene	.75	.35
☐ 70 Ken Griffey Jr.	2.00	.90
☐ 71 Kelly Gruber	.10	.05
☐ 72 Ozzie Guillen	.10	.05
☐ 73 Tony Gwynn	1.00	.45
☐ 74 Shane Halter	.10	.05
☐ 75 Jeffrey Hammonds	.40	.18
☐ 76 Larry Hanlon	.10	.05

☐ 77 Pete Harnisch	.10	.05
☐ 78 Mike Harrison	.10	.05
☐ 79 Bryan Harvey	.10	.05
☐ 80 Scott Hatteberg	.10	.05
☐ 81 Rick Helling	.10	.05
☐ 82 Dave Henderson	.10	.05
☐ 83 Rickey Henderson	.30	.14
☐ 84 Tyrone Hill	.10	.05
☐ 85 Todd Hollandsworth	.50	.23
☐ 86 Brian Holliday	.10	.05
☐ 87 Terry Horn	.10	.05
☐ 88 Jeff Hostetler	.10	.05
☐ 89 Kent Hrbek	.20	.09
☐ 90 Mark Hubbard	.10	.05
☐ 91 Charles Johnson	1.00	.45
☐ 92 Howard Johnson	.10	.05
☐ 93 Todd Johnson	.10	.05
☐ 94 Bobby Jones	.40	.18
☐ 95 Dan Jones	.10	.05
☐ 96 Felix Jose	.10	.05
☐ 97 David Justice	.40	.18
☐ 98 Jimmy Key	.20	.09
☐ 99 Marc Kroon	.10	.05
☐ 100 John Kruk	.20	.09
☐ 101 Mark Langston	.10	.05
☐ 102 Barry Larkin	.30	.14
☐ 103 Mike LaValliere	.10	.05
☐ 104 Scott Leius	.10	.05
☐ 105 Mark Lemke	.10	.05
☐ 106 Donnie Leshnock	.10	.05
☐ 107 Jimmy Lewis	.10	.05
☐ 108 Shane Livesy	.10	.05
☐ 109 Ryan Long	.10	.05
☐ 110 Trevor Mallory	.10	.05
☐ 111 Denny Martinez	.20	.09
☐ 112 Justin Mashore	.10	.05
☐ 113 Jason McDonald	.20	.09
☐ 114 Jack McDowell	.10	.05
☐ 115 Tom McKinnon	.10	.05
☐ 116 Billy McMillon	.20	.09
☐ 117 Buck McNabb	.20	.09
☐ 118 Jim Mecir	.10	.05
☐ 119 Dan Melendez	.10	.05
☐ 120 Shawn Miller	.20	.09
☐ 121 Trever Miller	.10	.05
☐ 122 Paul Molitor	.40	.18
☐ 123 Vincent Moore	.10	.05
☐ 124 Mike Morgan	.10	.05
☐ 125 Jack Morris WS	.10	.05
☐ 126 Jack Morris AS	.10	.05
☐ 127 Sean Mulligan	.10	.05
☐ 128 Eddie Murray AS	.40	.18
☐ 129 Mike Neill	.10	.05
☐ 130 Phil Nevin	.20	.09
☐ 131 Mark O'Brien	.10	.05
☐ 132 Alex Ochoa	.40	.18
☐ 133 Chad Ogea	.50	.23
☐ 134 Greg Olson	.10	.05
☐ 135 Paul O'Neill	.20	.09
☐ 136 Jared Osentowski	.10	.05
☐ 137 Mike Pagliarulo	.10	.05
☐ 138 Rafael Palmeiro	.30	.14
☐ 139 Rodney Pedraza	.10	.05
☐ 140 Tony Phillips (P)	.10	.05
☐ 141 Scott Pisciotta	.10	.05
☐ 142 Christopher Pritchett	.10	.05
☐ 143 Jason Pruitt	.10	.05
☐ 144 Kirby Puckett WS UER	.75	.35
(Championship series		
AB and BA is wrong)		
☐ 145 Kirby Puckett AS	.75	.35
☐ 146 Manny Ramirez	2.50	1.10
☐ 147 Eddie Ramos	.10	.05
☐ 148 Mark Ratekin	.10	.05
☐ 149 Jeff Reardon	.20	.09
☐ 150 Sean Rees	.10	.05
☐ 151 Calvin Reese	.30	.14
☐ 152 Desmond Relaford	.40	.18
☐ 153 Eric Richardson	.10	.05
☐ 154 Cal Ripken	1.50	.70
☐ 155 Chris Roberts	.20	.09
☐ 156 Mike Robertson	.10	.05
☐ 157 Steve Rodriguez	.20	.09
☐ 158 Mike Rossiter	.10	.05
☐ 159 Scott Ruffcorn	.10	.05
☐ 160 Chris Sabo	.10	.05

□ 161 Juan Samuel .10 / .05
□ 162 Ryne Sandberg UER .50 / .23
  (On 5th line, prior misspelled as prilor)
□ 163 Scott Sanderson .10 / .05
□ 164 Benny Santiago .10 / .05
□ 165 Gene Schall .10 / .05
□ 166 Chad Schoenvogel .10 / .05
□ 167 Chris Seelbach .20 / .09
□ 168 Aaron Sele .20 / .09
□ 169 Basil Shabazz .10 / .05
□ 170 Al Shirley .20 / .05
□ 171 Paul Shuey .10 / .05
□ 172 Ruben Sierra .10 / .05
□ 173 John Smiley .10 / .05
□ 174 Lee Smith .20 / .05
□ 175 Ozzie Smith .50 / .23
□ 176 Tim Smith .10 / .05
□ 177 Zane Smith .10 / .05
□ 178 John Smoltz .30 / .14
□ 179 Scott Stahoviak .20 / .09
□ 180 Kennie Steenstra .10 / .05
□ 181 Kevin Stocker .10 / .05
□ 182 Chris Stynes .40 / .18
□ 183 Danny Tartabull .10 / .05
□ 184 Brien Taylor .10 / .05
□ 185 Todd Taylor .10 / .05
□ 186 Larry Thomas .10 / .05
□ 187 Ozzie Timmons .20 / .05
  (See also 188)
□ 188 David Tuttle UER .10 / .05
  (Mistakenly numbered as 187 on card)
□ 189 Andy Van Slyke .20 / .09
□ 190 Frank Viola .10 / .05
□ 191 Michael Walkden .10 / .05
□ 192 Jeff Ware .10 / .05
□ 193 Allen Watson .20 / .09
□ 194 Steve Whitaker .10 / .05
□ 195 Jerry Willard .10 / .05
□ 196 Craig Wilson .10 / .05
□ 197 Chris Wimmer .10 / .05
□ 198 Steve Wojciechowski .10 / .05
□ 199 Joel Wolfe .10 / .05
□ 200 Ivan Zweig .10 / .05

1992 Stadium Club

The 1992 Stadium Club baseball card set consists of 900 standard-size cards issued in three series of 300 cards each. Cards were issued in plastic wrapped packs. A card-like application form for membership in Topps Stadium Club was inserted in each pack. The fronts are full-bleed. The glossy color player photos on the fronts are full-bleed. The "Topps Stadium Club" logo is superimposed at the bottom of the card face, with the player's name appearing immediately below the logo. Some cards in the set have the Stadium Club logo printed upside down. The backs display a mini reprint of the player's rookie card and

"BARS" (Baseball Analysis and Reporting System) statistics. Card numbers 591-610 form a "Members Choice" subset.

	MINT	NRMT
COMPLETE SET (900)	50.00	22.00
COMPLETE SERIES 1 (300)	18.00	8.00
COMPLETE SERIES 2 (300)	18.00	8.00
COMPLETE SERIES 3 (300)	18.00	8.00
COMMON CARD (1-900)	.10	.05
MINOR STARS	.20	.09
UNLISTED STARS	.40	.18
SUBSET CARDS HALF VALUE OF BASE CARDS		

□ 1 Cal Ripken UER 1.50 / .70
  (Misspelled Ripkin on card back)
□ 2 Eric Yelding .10 / .05
□ 3 Geno Petralli .10 / .05
□ 4 Wally Backman .10 / .05
□ 5 Milt Cuyler .10 / .05
□ 6 Kevin Bass .10 / .05
□ 7 Dante Bichette .30 / .14
□ 8 Ray Lankford .40 / .18
□ 9 Mel Hall .10 / .05
□ 10 Joe Carter .20 / .09
□ 11 Juan Samuel .10 / .05
□ 12 Jeff Montgomery .20 / .09
□ 13 Glenn Braggs .10 / .05
□ 14 Henry Cotto .10 / .05
□ 15 Deion Sanders .20 / .09
□ 16 Dick Schofield .10 / .05
□ 17 David Cone .20 / .09
□ 18 Chili Davis .10 / .05
□ 19 Tom Foley .10 / .05
□ 20 Ozzie Guillen .10 / .05
□ 21 Luis Salazar .10 / .05
□ 22 Terry Steinbach .20 / .09
□ 23 Chris James .10 / .05
□ 24 Jeff King .20 / .09
□ 25 Carlos Quintana .10 / .05
□ 26 Mike Maddux .10 / .05
□ 27 Tommy Greene .10 / .05
□ 28 Jeff Russell .10 / .05
□ 29 Steve Finley .20 / .09
□ 30 Mike Flanagan .10 / .05
□ 31 Darren Lewis .10 / .05
□ 32 Mark Lee .10 / .05
□ 33 Willie Fraser .10 / .05
□ 34 Mike Henneman .10 / .05
□ 35 Kevin Maas .10 / .05
□ 36 Dave Hansen .10 / .05
□ 37 Erik Hanson .10 / .05
□ 38 Bill Doran .10 / .05
□ 39 Mike Boddicker .10 / .05
□ 40 Vince Coleman .10 / .05
□ 41 Devon White .10 / .05
□ 42 Mark Gardner .10 / .05
□ 43 Scott Lewis .10 / .05
□ 44 Juan Berenguer .10 / .05
□ 45 Carney Lansford .20 / .09
□ 46 Curt Wilkerson .10 / .05
□ 47 Shane Mack .10 / .05
□ 48 Bip Roberts .10 / .05
□ 49 Greg A. Harris .10 / .05
□ 50 Ryne Sandberg .50 / .23
□ 51 Mark Whiten .10 / .05
□ 52 Jack McDowell .10 / .05
□ 53 Jimmy Jones .10 / .05
□ 54 Steve Lake .10 / .05
□ 55 Bud Black .10 / .05
□ 56 Dave Valle .10 / .05
□ 57 Kevin Reimer .10 / .05
□ 58 Rich Gedman UER .10 / .05
  (Wrong BARS chart used)
□ 59 Travis Fryman .20 / .09
□ 60 Steve Avery .20 / .09
□ 61 Francisco de la Rosa .10 / .05
□ 62 Scott Hemond .10 / .05
□ 63 Hal Morris .10 / .05
□ 64 Hensley Meulens .10 / .05
□ 65 Frank Castillo .10 / .05
□ 66 Gene Larkin .10 / .05
□ 67 Jose DeLeon .10 / .05
□ 68 Al Osuna .10 / .05

□ 69 Dave Cochrane .10 / .05
□ 70 Robin Ventura .20 / .09
□ 71 John Cerutti .10 / .05
□ 72 Kevin Gross .10 / .05
□ 73 Ivan Calderon .10 / .05
□ 74 Mike Macfarlane .10 / .05
□ 75 Stan Belinda .10 / .05
□ 76 Shawn Hillegas .10 / .05
□ 77 Pat Borders .10 / .05
□ 78 Jim Vatcher .10 / .05
□ 79 Bobby Rose .10 / .05
□ 80 Roger Clemens .75 / .35
□ 81 Craig Worthington .10 / .05
□ 82 Jeff Treadway .10 / .05
□ 83 Jamie Quirk .10 / .05
□ 84 Randy Bush .10 / .05
□ 85 Anthony Young .10 / .05
□ 86 Trevor Wilson .10 / .05
□ 87 Jaime Navarro .10 / .05
□ 88 Les Lancaster .10 / .05
□ 89 Pat Kelly .10 / .05
□ 90 Alvin Davis .10 / .05
□ 91 Larry Andersen .10 / .05
□ 92 Rob Deer .10 / .05
□ 93 Mike Sharperson .10 / .05
□ 94 Lance Parrish .10 / .05
□ 95 Cecil Espy .10 / .05
□ 96 Tim Spehr .10 / .05
□ 97 Dave Stieb .10 / .05
□ 98 Terry Mulholland .10 / .05
□ 99 Dennis Boyd .10 / .05
□ 100 Barry Larkin .30 / .14
□ 101 Ryan Bowen .10 / .05
□ 102 Felix Fermin .10 / .05
□ 103 Luis Alicea .10 / .05
□ 104 Tim Hulett .10 / .05
□ 105 Rafael Belliard .10 / .05
□ 106 Mike Gallego .10 / .05
□ 107 Dave Righetti .10 / .05
□ 108 Jeff Schaefer .10 / .05
□ 109 Ricky Bones .10 / .05
□ 110 Scott Erickson .20 / .09
□ 111 Matt Nokes .10 / .05
□ 112 Bob Scanlan .10 / .05
□ 113 Tom Candiotti .10 / .05
□ 114 Sean Berry .10 / .05
□ 115 Kevin Morton .10 / .05
□ 116 Scott Fletcher .10 / .05
□ 117 B.J. Surhoff .20 / .09
□ 118 Dave Magadan UER .10 / .05
  (Born Tampa, not Tamps)
□ 119 Bill Gullickson .10 / .05
□ 120 Marquis Grissom .20 / .09
□ 121 Lenny Harris .10 / .05
□ 122 Wally Joyner .10 / .05
□ 123 Kevin Brown .20 / .09
□ 124 Braulio Castillo .10 / .05
□ 125 Eric King .10 / .05
□ 126 Mark Portugal .10 / .05
□ 127 Calvin Jones .10 / .05
□ 128 Mike Heath .10 / .05
□ 129 Todd Van Poppel .10 / .05
□ 130 Benny Santiago .10 / .05
□ 131 Gary Thurman .10 / .05
□ 132 Joe Girardi .10 / .05
□ 133 Dave Eiland .10 / .05
□ 134 Orlando Merced .10 / .05
□ 135 Joe Orsulak .10 / .05
□ 136 John Burkett .10 / .05
□ 137 Ken Dayley .10 / .05
□ 138 Ken Hill .10 / .05
□ 139 Walt Terrell .10 / .05
□ 140 Mike Scioscia .10 / .05
□ 141 Junior Felix .10 / .05
□ 142 Ken Caminiti .30 / .14
□ 143 Carlos Baerga .10 / .05
□ 144 Tony Fossas .10 / .05
□ 145 Craig Grebeck .10 / .05
□ 146 Scott Bradley .10 / .05
□ 147 Kent Mercker .10 / .05
□ 148 Derrick May .10 / .05
□ 149 Jerald Clark .10 / .05
□ 150 George Brett .75 / .35
□ 151 Luis Quinones .10 / .05
□ 152 Mike Pagliarulo .10 / .05
□ 153 Jose Guzman .10 / .05

□ 154	Charlie O'Brien	.10	.05
□ 155	Darren Holmes	.10	.05
□ 156	Joe Boever	.10	.05
□ 157	Rich Monteleone	.10	.05
□ 158	Reggie Harris	.10	.05
□ 159	Roberto Alomar	.40	.18
□ 160	Robby Thompson	.10	.05
□ 161	Chris Hoiles	.10	.05
□ 162	Tom Pagnozzi	.10	.05
□ 163	Omar Vizquel	.20	.09
□ 164	John Candelaria	.10	.05
□ 165	Terry Shumpert	.10	.05
□ 166	Andy Mota	.10	.05
□ 167	Scott Bailes	.10	.05
□ 168	Jeff Blauser	.10	.05
□ 169	Steve Olin	.10	.05
□ 170	Doug Drabek	.10	.05
□ 171	Dave Bergman	.10	.05
□ 172	Eddie Whitson	.10	.05
□ 173	Gilberto Reyes	.10	.05
□ 174	Mark Grace	.30	.14
□ 175	Paul O'Neill	.10	.09
□ 176	Greg Cadaret	.10	.05
□ 177	Mark Williamson	.10	.05
□ 178	Casey Candaele	.10	.05
□ 179	Candy Maldonado	.10	.05
□ 180	Lee Smith	.20	.09
□ 181	Harold Reynolds	.10	.05
□ 182	David Justice	.40	.18
□ 183	Lenny Webster	.10	.05
□ 184	Donn Pall	.10	.05
□ 185	Gerald Alexander	.10	.05
□ 186	Jack Clark	.10	.09
□ 187	Stan Javier	.10	.05
□ 188	Ricky Jordan	.10	.05
□ 189	Franklin Stubbs	.10	.05
□ 190	Dennis Eckersley	.20	.09
□ 191	Danny Tartabull	.10	.05
□ 192	Pete O'Brien	.10	.05
□ 193	Mark Lewis	.10	.05
□ 194	Mike Felder	.10	.05
□ 195	Mickey Tettleton	.10	.05
□ 196	Dwight Smith	.10	.05
□ 197	Shawn Abner	.10	.05
□ 198	Jim Leyritz UER (Career totals less than 1991 totals)	.10	.05
□ 199	Mike Devereaux	.10	.05
□ 200	Craig Biggio	.30	.14
□ 201	Kevin Elster	.10	.05
□ 202	Rance Mulliniks	.10	.05
□ 203	Tony Fernandez	.10	.05
□ 204	Allan Anderson	.10	.05
□ 205	Herm Winningham	.10	.05
□ 206	Tim Jones	.10	.05
□ 207	Ramon Martinez	.20	.09
□ 208	Teddy Higuera	.10	.05
□ 209	John Kruk	.20	.09
□ 210	Jim Abbott	.20	.09
□ 211	Dean Palmer	.20	.09
□ 212	Mark Davis	.10	.05
□ 213	Jay Buhner	.30	.14
□ 214	Jesse Barfield	.20	.09
□ 215	Kevin Mitchell	.20	.09
□ 216	Mike LaValliere	.10	.05
□ 217	Mark Wohlers	.30	.14
□ 218	Dave Henderson	.10	.05
□ 219	Dave Smith	.10	.05
□ 220	Albert Belle	.50	.23
□ 221	Spike Owen	.10	.05
□ 222	Jeff Gray	.10	.05
□ 223	Paul Gibson	.10	.05
□ 224	Bobby Thigpen	.10	.05
□ 225	Mike Mussina	.60	.25
□ 226	Darrin Jackson	.10	.05
□ 227	Luis Gonzalez	.20	.09
□ 228	Greg Briley	.10	.05
□ 229	Brent Mayne	.10	.05
□ 230	Paul Molitor	.40	.18
□ 231	Al Leiter	.10	.05
□ 232	Andy Van Slyke	.20	.09
□ 233	Ron Tingley	.10	.05
□ 234	Bernard Gilkey	.20	.09
□ 235	Kent Hrbek	.20	.09
□ 236	Eric Karros	.30	.14
□ 237	Randy Velarde	.10	.05
□ 238	Andy Allanson	.10	.05
□ 239	Willie McGee	.10	.05
□ 240	Juan Gonzalez	1.25	.55
□ 241	Karl Rhodes	.10	.05
□ 242	Luis Mercedes	.10	.05
□ 243	Billy Swift	.10	.05
□ 244	Tommy Gregg	.10	.05
□ 245	David Howard	.10	.05
□ 246	Dave Hollins	.10	.05
□ 247	Kip Gross	.10	.05
□ 248	Walt Weiss	.10	.05
□ 249	Mackey Sasser	.10	.05
□ 250	Cecil Fielder	.20	.09
□ 251	Jerry Browne	.10	.05
□ 252	Doug Dascenzo	.10	.05
□ 253	Darryl Hamilton	.10	.05
□ 254	Dann Bilardello	.10	.05
□ 255	Luis Rivera	.10	.05
□ 256	Larry Walker	.40	.18
□ 257	Ron Karkovice	.10	.05
□ 258	Bob Tewksbury	.10	.05
□ 259	Jimmy Key	.20	.09
□ 260	Bernie Williams	.40	.18
□ 261	Gary Wayne	.10	.05
□ 262	Mike Simms UER (Reversed negative)	.10	.05
□ 263	John Orton	.10	.05
□ 264	Marvin Freeman	.10	.05
□ 265	Mike Jeffcoat	.10	.05
□ 266	Roger Mason	.10	.05
□ 267	Edgar Martinez	.30	.14
□ 268	Henry Rodriguez	.40	.18
□ 269	Sam Horn	.10	.05
□ 270	Brian McRae	.10	.05
□ 271	Kirt Manwaring	.10	.05
□ 272	Mike Bordick	.10	.05
□ 273	Chris Sabo	.10	.05
□ 274	Jim Olander	.10	.05
□ 275	Greg W. Harris	.10	.05
□ 276	Dan Gakeler	.10	.05
□ 277	Bill Sampen	.10	.05
□ 278	Joel Skinner	.10	.05
□ 279	Curt Schilling	.30	.14
□ 280	Dale Murphy	.40	.18
□ 281	Lee Stevens	.10	.05
□ 282	Lonnie Smith	.10	.05
□ 283	Manuel Lee	.10	.05
□ 284	Shawn Boskie	.10	.05
□ 285	Kevin Seitzer	.10	.05
□ 286	Stan Royer	.10	.05
□ 287	John Dopson	.10	.05
□ 288	Scott Bullett	.10	.05
□ 289	Ken Patterson	.10	.05
□ 290	Todd Hundley	.30	.14
□ 291	Tim Leary	.10	.05
□ 292	Brett Butler	.20	.09
□ 293	Gregg Olson	.10	.05
□ 294	Jeff Brantley	.10	.05
□ 295	Brian Holman	.10	.05
□ 296	Brian Harper	.10	.05
□ 297	Brian Bohanon	.10	.05
□ 298	Checklist 1-100	.10	.05
□ 299	Checklist 101-200	.10	.05
□ 300	Checklist 201-300	.10	.05
□ 301	Frank Thomas	2.00	.90
□ 302	Lloyd McClendon	.10	.05
□ 303	Brady Anderson	.30	.14
□ 304	Julio Valera	.10	.05
□ 305	Mike Aldrete	.10	.05
□ 306	Joe Oliver	.10	.05
□ 307	Todd Stottlemyre	.10	.05
□ 308	Rey Sanchez	.10	.05
□ 309	Gary Sheffield UER (Listed as 5'1", should be 5'11")	.40	.18
□ 310	Andujar Cedeno	.10	.05
□ 311	Kenny Rogers	.10	.05
□ 312	Bruce Hurst	.10	.05
□ 313	Mike Schooler	.10	.05
□ 314	Mike Benjamin	.10	.05
□ 315	Chuck Finley	.10	.05
□ 316	Mark Lemke	.10	.05
□ 317	Scott Livingstone	.10	.05
□ 318	Chris Nabholz	.10	.05
□ 319	Mike Humphreys	.10	.05
□ 320	Pedro Guerrero	.10	.05
□ 321	Willie Banks	.10	.05
□ 322	Tom Goodwin	.20	.09
□ 323	Hector Wagner	.10	.05
□ 324	Wally Ritchie	.10	.05
□ 325	Mo Vaughn	.60	.25
□ 326	Joe Klink	.10	.05
□ 327	Cal Eldred	.10	.05
□ 328	Daryl Boston	.10	.05
□ 329	Mike Huff	.10	.05
□ 330	Jeff Bagwell	1.25	.55
□ 331	Bob Milacki	.10	.05
□ 332	Tom Prince	.10	.05
□ 333	Pat Tabler	.10	.05
□ 334	Ced Landrum	.10	.05
□ 335	Reggie Jefferson	.20	.09
□ 336	Mo Sanford	.10	.05
□ 337	Kevin Ritz	.10	.05
□ 338	Gerald Perry	.10	.05
□ 339	Jeff Hamilton	.10	.05
□ 340	Tim Wallach	.10	.05
□ 341	Jeff Huson	.10	.05
□ 342	Jose Melendez	.10	.05
□ 343	Willie Wilson	.10	.05
□ 344	Mike Stanton	.10	.05
□ 345	Joel Johnston	.10	.05
□ 346	Lee Guetterman	.10	.05
□ 347	Francisco Oliveras	.10	.05
□ 348	Dave Burba	.10	.05
□ 349	Tim Crews	.10	.05
□ 350	Scott Leius	.10	.05
□ 351	Danny Cox	.10	.05
□ 352	Wayne Housie	.10	.05
□ 353	Chris Donnels	.10	.05
□ 354	Chris George	.10	.05
□ 355	Gerald Young	.10	.05
□ 356	Roberto Hernandez	.40	.18
□ 357	Neal Heaton	.10	.05
□ 358	Todd Frohwirth	.10	.05
□ 359	Jose Vizcaino	.10	.05
□ 360	Jim Thome	1.25	.55
□ 361	Craig Wilson	.10	.05
□ 362	Dave Haas	.10	.05
□ 363	Billy Hatcher	.10	.05
□ 364	John Barfield	.10	.05
□ 365	Luis Aquino	.10	.05
□ 366	Charlie Leibrandt	.10	.05
□ 367	Howard Farmer	.10	.05
□ 368	Bryn Smith	.10	.05
□ 369	Mickey Morandini	.10	.05
□ 370	Jose Canseco (See also 597)	.30	.14
□ 371	Jose Uribe	.10	.05
□ 372	Bob MacDonald	.10	.05
□ 373	Luis Sojo	.10	.05
□ 374	Craig Shipley	.10	.05
□ 375	Scott Bankhead	.10	.05
□ 376	Greg Gagne	.10	.05
□ 377	Scott Cooper	.10	.05
□ 378	Jose Offerman	.10	.05
□ 379	Billy Spiers	.10	.05
□ 380	John Smiley	.10	.05
□ 381	Jeff Carter	.10	.05
□ 382	Heathcliff Slocumb	.10	.05
□ 383	Jeff Tackett	.10	.05
□ 384	John Kiely	.10	.05
□ 385	John Vander Wal	.10	.05
□ 386	Omar Olivares	.10	.05
□ 387	Ruben Sierra	.10	.05
□ 388	Tom Gordon	.10	.05
□ 389	Charles Nagy	.20	.09
□ 390	Dave Stewart	.20	.09
□ 391	Pete Harnisch	.10	.05
□ 392	Tim Burke	.10	.05
□ 393	Roberto Kelly	.10	.05
□ 394	Freddie Benavides	.10	.05
□ 395	Tom Glavine	.30	.14
□ 396	Wes Chamberlain	.10	.05
□ 397	Eric Gunderson	.10	.05
□ 398	Dave West	.10	.05
□ 399	Ellis Burks	.20	.09
□ 400	Ken Griffey Jr.	2.50	1.10
□ 401	Thomas Howard	.10	.05
□ 402	Juan Guzman	.10	.05
□ 403	Mitch Webster	.10	.05
□ 404	Matt Merullo	.10	.05
□ 405	Steve Buechele	.10	.05

406	Danny Jackson	.10	.05
407	Felix Jose	.10	.05
408	Doug Piatt	.10	.05
409	Jim Eisenreich	.10	.05
410	Bryan Harvey	.10	.05
411	Jim Austin	.10	.05
412	Jim Poole	.10	.05
413	Glenallen Hill	.10	.05
414	Gene Nelson	.10	.05
415	Ivan Rodriguez	.75	.35
416	Frank Tanana	.10	.05
417	Steve Decker	.10	.05
418	Jason Grimsley	.10	.05
419	Tim Layana	.10	.05
420	Don Mattingly	.60	.25
421	Jerome Walton	.10	.05
422	Rob Ducey	.10	.05
423	Andy Benes	.20	.09
424	John Marzano	.10	.05
425	Gene Harris	.10	.05
426	Tim Raines	.20	.09
427	Bret Barberie	.10	.05
428	Harvey Pulliam	.10	
429	Cris Carpenter	.10	.05
430	Howard Johnson	.10	.05
431	Orel Hershiser	.20	.09
432	Brian Hunter	.10	.05
433	Kevin Tapani	.10	.05
434	Rick Reed	.10	.05
435	Ron Witmeyer	.20	.09
436	Gary Gaetti	.10	.05
437	Alex Cole	.10	.05
438	Chito Martinez	.10	.05
439	Greg Litton	.10	.05
440	Julio Franco	.10	.05
441	Mike Munoz	.10	.05
442	Erik Pappas	.10	.05
443	Pat Combs	.10	.05
444	Lance Johnson	.10	.05
445	Ed Sprague	.10	.05
446	Mike Greenwell	.10	.05
447	Milt Thompson	.10	.05
448	Mike Magnante	.10	.05
449	Chris Haney	.10	.05
450	Robin Yount	.30	.14
451	Rafael Ramirez	.10	.05
452	Gino Minutelli	.10	.05
453	Tom Lampkin	.10	.05
454	Tony Perezchica	.10	.05
455	Dwight Gooden	.20	.09
456	Mark Guthrie	.10	.05
457	Jay Howell	.10	.05
458	Gary DiSarcina	.10	.05
459	John Smoltz	.30	.14
460	Will Clark	.30	.14
461	Dave Otto	.10	.05
462	Rob Maurer	.10	.05
463	Dwight Evans	.20	.09
464	Tom Brunansky	.10	.05
465	Shawn Hare	.10	.05
466	Geronimo Pena	.10	.05
467	Alex Fernandez	.20	.09
468	Greg Myers	.10	.05
469	Jeff Fassero	.10	.05
470	Len Dykstra	.20	.09
471	Jeff Johnson	.10	.05
472	Russ Swan	.10	.05
473	Archie Corbin	.10	.05
474	Chuck McElroy	.10	.05
475	Mark McGwire	.75	.35
476	Wally Whitehurst	.10	.05
477	Tim McIntosh	.10	.05
478	Sid Bream	.10	.05
479	Jeff Juden	.10	.05
480	Carlton Fisk	.40	.18
481	Jeff Plympton	.10	.05
482	Carlos Martinez	.10	.05
483	Jim Gott	.10	.05
484	Bob McClure	.10	.05
485	Tim Teufel	.10	.05
486	Vicente Palacios	.10	.05
487	Jeff Reed	.10	.05
488	Tony Phillips	.10	.05
489	Mel Rojas	.20	.09
490	Ben McDonald	.10	.05
491	Andres Santana	.10	.05
492	Chris Beasley	.10	.05
493	Mike Timlin	.10	.05
494	Brian Downing	.10	.05
495	Kirk Gibson	.20	.09
496	Scott Sanderson	.10	.05
497	Nick Esasky	.10	.05
498	Johnny Guzman	.10	.05
499	Mitch Williams	.10	.05
500	Kirby Puckett	.75	.35
501	Mike Harkey	.10	.05
502	Jim Gantner	.10	.05
503	Bruce Egloff	.10	.05
504	Josias Manzanillo	.10	.05
505	Delino DeShields	.10	.05
506	Rheal Cormier	.10	.05
507	Jay Bell	.20	.09
508	Rich Rowland	.10	.05
509	Scott Servais	.10	.05
510	Terry Pendleton	.20	.09
511	Rich DeLucia	.10	.05
512	Warren Newson	.10	.05
513	Paul Faries	.10	.05
514	Kal Daniels	.10	.05
515	Jarvis Brown	.10	.05
516	Rafael Palmeiro	.30	.14
517	Kelly Downs	.10	.05
518	Steve Chitren	.10	.05
519	Moises Alou	.30	.14
520	Wade Boggs	.40	.18
521	Pete Schourek	.10	.05
522	Scott Terry	.10	.05
523	Kevin Appier	.20	.09
524	Gary Redus	.10	.05
525	George Bell	.20	.09
526	Jeff Kaiser	.10	.05
527	Alvaro Espinoza	.10	.05
528	Luis Sojo	.10	.05
529	Darren Daulton	.20	.09
530	Norm Charlton	.10	.05
531	John Olerud	.20	.09
532	Dan Plesac	.10	.05
533	Billy Ripken	.10	.05
534	Rod Nichols	.10	.05
535	Joey Cora	.20	.09
536	Harold Baines	.20	.09
537	Bob Ojeda	.10	.05
538	Mark Leonard	.10	.05
539	Danny Darwin	.10	.05
540	Shawon Dunston	.10	.05
541	Pedro Munoz	.10	.05
542	Mark Gubicza	.10	.05
543	Kevin Baez	.10	.05
544	Todd Zeile	.10	.05
545	Don Slaught	.10	.05
546	Tony Eusebio	.10	.05
547	Alonzo Powell	.10	.05
548	Gary Pettis	.10	.05
549	Brian Barnes	.10	.05
550	Lou Whitaker	.20	.09
551	Keith Mitchell	.10	.05
552	Oscar Azocar	.10	.05
553	Stu Cole	.10	.05
554	Steve Wapnick	.10	.05
555	Derek Bell	.20	.09
556	Luis Lopez	.10	.05
557	Anthony Telford	.10	.05
558	Tim Mauser	.10	.05
559	Glen Sutko	.10	.05
560	Darryl Strawberry	.20	.09
561	Tom Bolton	.10	.05
562	Cliff Young	.10	.05
563	Bruce Walton	.10	.05
564	Chico Walker	.10	.05
565	John Franco	.20	.09
566	Paul McClellan	.10	.05
567	Paul Abbott	.10	.05
568	Gary Varsho	.10	.05
569	Carlos Maldonado	.10	.05
570	Kelly Gruber	.10	.05
571	Jose Oquendo	.10	.05
572	Steve Frey	.10	.05
573	Tino Martinez	.40	.18
574	Bill Haselman	.10	.05
575	Eric Anthony	.10	.05
576	John Habyan	.10	.05
577	Jeff McNeely	.10	.05
578	Chris Bosio	.10	.05
579	Joe Grahe	.10	.05
580	Fred McGriff	.30	.14
581	Rick Honeycutt	.10	.05
582	Matt Williams	.30	.14
583	Cliff Brantley	.10	.05
584	Rob Dibble	.10	.05
585	Skeeter Barnes	.10	.05
586	Greg Hibbard	.10	.05
587	Randy Milligan	.10	.05
588	Checklist 301-400	.10	.05
589	Checklist 401-500	.10	.05
590	Checklist 501-600	.10	.05
591	Frank Thomas MC	1.00	.45
592	David Justice MC	.20	.09
593	Roger Clemens MC	.40	.18
594	Steve Avery MC	.10	.05
595	Cal Ripken MC	1.25	.55
596	Barry Larkin MC UER (Ranked in AL, should be NL)	.20	.09
597	Jose Canseco MC UER (Mistakenly numbered 370 on card back)	.20	.09
598	Will Clark MC	.20	.09
599	Cecil Fielder MC	.10	.05
600	Ryne Sandberg MC	.40	.18
601	Chuck Knoblauch MC	.20	.09
602	Dwight Gooden MC	.10	.05
603	Ken Griffey Jr. MC	1.25	.55
604	Barry Bonds MC	.40	.18
605	Nolan Ryan MC	1.25	.55
606	Jeff Bagwell MC	.60	.25
607	Robin Yount MC	.20	.09
608	Bobby Bonilla MC	.10	.05
609	George Brett MC	.40	.18
610	Howard Johnson MC	.10	.05
611	Esteban Beltre	.10	.05
612	Mike Christopher	.10	.05
613	Troy Afenir	.10	.05
614	Mariano Duncan	.10	.05
615	Doug Henry	.10	.05
616	Doug Jones	.10	.05
617	Alvin Davis	.10	.05
618	Craig Lefferts	.10	.05
619	Kevin McReynolds	.10	.05
620	Barry Bonds	.50	.23
621	Turner Ward	.10	.05
622	Joe Magrane	.10	.05
623	Mark Parent	.10	.05
624	Tom Browning	.10	.05
625	John Smiley	.10	.05
626	Steve Wilson	.10	.05
627	Mike Gallego	.10	.05
628	Sammy Sosa	.40	.18
629	Rico Rossy	.10	.05
630	Royce Clayton	.10	.05
631	Clay Parker	.10	.05
632	Pete Smith	.10	.05
633	Jeff McKnight	.10	.05
634	Jack Daugherty	.10	.05
635	Steve Sax	.10	.05
636	Joe Hesketh	.10	.05
637	Vince Horsman	.10	.05
638	Eric King	.10	.05
639	Joe Boever	.10	.05
640	Jack Morris	.20	.09
641	Arthur Rhodes	.10	.05
642	Bob Melvin	.10	.05
643	Rick Wilkins	.10	.05
644	Scott Scudder	.10	.05
645	Bip Roberts	.10	.05
646	Julio Valera	.10	.05
647	Kevin Campbell	.10	.05
648	Steve Searcy	.10	.05
649	Scott Kamieniecki	.10	.05
650	Kurt Stillwell	.10	.05
651	Bob Welch	.10	.05
652	Andres Galarraga	.40	.18
653	Mike Jackson	.10	.05
654	Bo Jackson	.20	.09
655	Sid Fernandez	.10	.05
656	Mike Bielecki	.10	.05
657	Jeff Reardon	.20	.09
658	Wayne Rosenthal	.10	.05
659	Eric Bullock	.10	.05

□ 660 Eric Davis	.20	.09
□ 661 Randy Tomlin	.10	.05
□ 662 Tom Edens	.10	.05
□ 663 Rob Murphy	.10	.05
□ 664 Leo Gomez	.15	.05
□ 665 Greg Maddux	1.25	.55
□ 666 Greg Vaughn	.25	.11
□ 667 Wade Taylor	.10	.05
□ 668 Brad Arnsberg	.10	.05
□ 669 Mike Moore	.10	.05
□ 670 Mark Langston	.10	.05
□ 671 Barry Jones	.10	.05
□ 672 Bill Landrum	.10	.05
□ 673 Greg Swindell	.10	.05
□ 674 Wayne Edwards	.10	.05
□ 675 Greg Olson	.10	.05
□ 676 Bill Pulsipher	.40	.18
□ 677 Bobby Witt	.10	.05
□ 678 Mark Carreon	.10	.05
□ 679 Patrick Lennon	.10	.05
□ 680 Ozzie Smith	.50	.23
□ 681 John Briscoe	.10	.05
□ 682 Matt Young	.10	.05
□ 683 Jeff Conine	.30	.14
□ 684 Phil Stephenson	.10	.05
□ 685 Ron Darling	.10	.05
□ 686 Bryan Hickerson	.10	.05
□ 687 Dale Sveum	.10	.05
□ 688 Kirk McCaskill	.10	.05
□ 689 Rich Amaral	.10	.05
□ 690 Danny Tartabull	.10	.05
□ 691 Donald Harris	.10	.05
□ 692 Doug Davis	.10	.05
□ 693 John Farrell	.10	.05
□ 694 Paul Gibson	.10	.05
□ 695 Kenny Lofton	1.50	.70
□ 696 Mike Fetters	.10	.05
□ 697 Rosario Rodriguez	.10	.05
□ 698 Chris Jones	.10	.05
□ 699 Jeff Manto	.10	.05
□ 700 Rick Sutcliffe	.10	.05
□ 701 Scott Bankhead	.10	.05
□ 702 Donnie Hill	.10	.05
□ 703 Todd Worrell	.10	.05
□ 704 Rene Gonzales	.10	.05
□ 705 Rick Cerone	.10	.05
□ 706 Tony Pena	.10	.05
□ 707 Paul Sorrento	.10	.05
□ 708 Gary Scott	.10	.05
□ 709 Junior Noboa	.10	.05
□ 710 Wally Joyner	.20	.09
□ 711 Charlie Hayes	.10	.05
□ 712 Rich Rodriguez	.10	.05
□ 713 Rudy Seanez	.10	.05
□ 714 Jim Bullinger	.10	.05
□ 715 Jeff M. Robinson	.10	.05
□ 716 Jeff Branson	.10	.05
□ 717 Andy Ashby	.10	.05
□ 718 Dave Burba	.10	.05
□ 719 Rich Gossage	.20	.09
□ 720 Randy Johnson	.40	.18
□ 721 David Wells	.10	.05
□ 722 Paul Kilgus	.10	.05
□ 723 Dave Martinez	.10	.05
□ 724 Denny Neagle	.30	.14
□ 725 Andy Stankiewicz	.10	.05
□ 726 Rick Aguilera	.10	.05
□ 727 Junior Ortiz	.10	.05
□ 728 Storm Davis	.10	.05
□ 729 Don Robinson	.10	.05
□ 730 Ron Gant	.20	.09
□ 731 Paul Assenmacher	.10	.05
□ 732 Mike Gardiner	.10	.05
□ 733 Milt Hill	.10	.05
□ 734 Jeremy Hernandez	.10	.05
□ 735 Ken Hill	.10	.05
□ 736 Xavier Hernandez	.10	.05
□ 737 Gregg Jefferies	.10	.05
□ 738 Dick Schofield	.10	.05
□ 739 Ron Robinson	.10	.05
□ 740 Sandy Alomar	.20	.09
□ 741 Mike Stanley	.10	.05
□ 742 Butch Henry	.10	.05
□ 743 Floyd Bannister	.10	.05
□ 744 Brian Drahman	.10	.05
□ 745 Dave Winfield	.40	.18

□ 746 Bob Walk	.10	.05
□ 747 Chris James	.10	.05
□ 748 Don Prybylinski	.10	.05
□ 749 Dennis Rasmussen	.10	.05
□ 750 Rickey Henderson	.30	.14
□ 751 Chris Hammond	.10	.05
□ 752 Bob Kipper	.10	.05
□ 753 Dave Rohde	.10	.05
□ 754 Hubie Brooks	.10	.05
□ 755 Bret Saberhagen	.10	.05
□ 756 Jeff D. Robinson	.10	.05
□ 757 Pat Listach	.10	.05
□ 758 Bill Wegman	.10	.05
□ 759 John Wetteland	.20	.09
□ 760 Phil Plantier	.10	.05
□ 761 Wilson Alvarez	.20	.09
□ 762 Scott Aldred	.10	.05
□ 763 Armando Reynoso	.10	.05
□ 764 Todd Benzinger	.10	.05
□ 765 Kevin Mitchell	.20	.09
□ 766 Gary Sheffield	.40	.18
□ 767 Allan Anderson	.10	.05
□ 768 Rusty Meacham	.10	.05
□ 769 Rick Parker	.10	.05
□ 770 Nolan Ryan	1.50	.70
□ 771 Jeff Ballard	.10	.05
□ 772 Cory Snyder	.10	.05
□ 773 Denis Boucher	.10	.05
□ 774 Jose Guzman	.10	.05
□ 775 Juan Guerrero	.10	.05
□ 776 Ed Nunez	.10	.05
□ 777 Scott Ruskin	.10	.05
□ 778 Terry Leach	.10	.05
□ 779 Carl Willis	.10	.05
□ 780 Bobby Bonilla	.20	.09
□ 781 Duane Ward	.10	.05
□ 782 Joe Slusarski	.10	.05
□ 783 David Segui	.10	.05
□ 784 Kirk Gibson	.20	.09
□ 785 Frank Viola	.10	.05
□ 786 Keith Miller	.10	.05
□ 787 Mike Morgan	.10	.05
□ 788 Kim Batiste	.10	.05
□ 789 Sergio Valdez	.10	.05
□ 790 Eddie Taubensee	.10	.05
□ 791 Jack Armstrong	.10	.05
□ 792 Scott Fletcher	.10	.05
□ 793 Steve Farr	.10	.05
□ 794 Dan Pasqua	.10	.05
□ 795 Eddie Murray	.40	.18
□ 796 John Morris	.10	.05
□ 797 Francisco Cabrera	.10	.05
□ 798 Mike Perez	.10	.05
□ 799 Ted Wood	.10	.05
□ 800 Jose Rijo	.10	.05
□ 801 Danny Gladden	.10	.05
□ 802 Archi Cianfrocco	.10	.05
□ 803 Monty Fariss	.10	.05
□ 804 Roger McDowell	.10	.05
□ 805 Randy Myers	.20	.09
□ 806 Kirk Dressendorfer	.10	.05
□ 807 Zane Smith	.10	.05
□ 808 Glenn Davis	.10	.05
□ 809 Torey Lovullo	.10	.05
□ 810 Andre Dawson	.30	.14
□ 811 Bill Pecota	.10	.05
□ 812 Ted Power	.10	.05
□ 813 Willie Blair	.10	.05
□ 814 Dave Fleming	.10	.05
□ 815 Chris Gwynn	.10	.05
□ 816 Jody Reed	.10	.05
□ 817 Mark Dewey	.10	.05
□ 818 Kyle Abbott	.10	.05
□ 819 Tom Henke	.10	.05
□ 820 Kevin Seitzer	.10	.05
□ 821 Al Newman	.10	.05
□ 822 Tim Sherrill	.10	.05
□ 823 Chuck Crim	.10	.05
□ 824 Darren Reed	.10	.05
□ 825 Tony Gwynn	1.00	.45
□ 826 Steve Foster	.10	.05
□ 827 Steve Howe	.10	.05
□ 828 Brock Jacoby	.10	.05
□ 829 Rodney McCray	.10	.05
□ 830 Chuck Knoblauch	.40	.18
□ 831 John Wehner	.10	.05

□ 832 Scott Garrelts	.10	.05
□ 833 Alejandro Pena	.10	.05
□ 834 Jeff Parrett UER	.10	.05
(Kentucky)		
□ 835 Juan Bell	.10	.05
□ 836 Lance Dickson	.10	.05
□ 837 Darryl Kile	.20	.09
□ 838 Efrain Valdez	.10	.05
□ 839 Bob Zupcic	.10	.05
□ 840 George Bell	.10	.05
□ 841 Dave Gallagher	.10	.05
□ 842 Tim Belcher	.10	.05
□ 843 Jeff Shaw	.10	.05
□ 844 Mike Fitzgerald	.10	.05
□ 845 Gary Carter	.40	.18
□ 846 John Russell	.10	.05
□ 847 Eric Hillman	.10	.05
□ 848 Mike Witt	.10	.05
□ 849 Curt Wilkerson	.10	.05
□ 850 Alan Trammell	.20	.09
□ 851 Rex Hudler	.10	.05
□ 852 Mike Walkden	.10	.05
□ 853 Kevin Ward	.10	.05
□ 854 Tim Naehring	.20	.09
□ 855 Bill Swift	.10	.05
□ 856 Damon Berryhill	.10	.05
□ 857 Mark Eichhorn	.10	.05
□ 858 Hector Villanueva	.10	.05
□ 859 Jose Lind	.10	.05
□ 860 Denny Martinez	.20	.09
□ 861 Bill Krueger	.10	.05
□ 862 Mike Kingery	.10	.05
□ 863 Jeff Innis	.10	.05
□ 864 Derek Lilliquist	.10	.05
□ 865 Reggie Sanders	.20	.09
□ 866 Ramon Garcia	.10	.05
□ 867 Bruce Ruffin	.10	.05
□ 868 Dickie Thon	.10	.05
□ 869 Melido Perez	.10	.05
□ 870 Ruben Amaro	.10	.05
□ 871 Alan Mills	.10	.05
□ 872 Matt Sinatro	.10	.05
□ 873 Eddie Zosky	.10	.05
□ 874 Pete Incaviglia	.10	.05
□ 875 Tom Candiotti	.10	.05
□ 876 Bob Patterson	.10	.05
□ 877 Neal Heaton	.10	.05
□ 878 Terrel Hansen	.10	.05
□ 879 Dave Eiland	.10	.05
□ 880 Von Hayes	.10	.05
□ 881 Tim Scott	.10	.05
□ 882 Otis Nixon	.20	.09
□ 883 Herm Winningham	.10	.05
□ 884 Dion James	.10	.05
□ 885 Dave Wainhouse	.10	.05
□ 886 Frank DiPino	.10	.05
□ 887 Dennis Cook	.10	.05
□ 888 Jose Mesa	.10	.05
□ 889 Mark Leiter	.10	.05
□ 890 Willie Randolph	.20	.09
□ 891 Craig Colbert	.10	.05
□ 892 Dwayne Henry	.10	.05
□ 893 Jim Lindeman	.10	.05
□ 894 Charlie Hough	.10	.05
□ 895 Gil Heredia	.10	.05
□ 896 Scott Chiamparino	.10	.05
□ 897 Lance Blankenship	.10	.05
□ 898 Checklist 601-700	.10	.05
□ 899 Checklist 701-800	.10	.05
□ 900 Checklist 801-900	.10	.05

1992 Stadium Club First Draft Picks

This three-card standard-size set, featuring Major League Baseball's Number 1 draft pick for 1990, 1991, and 1992, was randomly inserted into 1992 Stadium Club Series III packs at an approximate rate of 1:72. One card also was mailed to each member of Topps Stadium Club. The cards feature on the

fronts full-bleed posed color player photos. The player's draft year is printed on an orange circle in the upper right corner and is accented by gold foil stripes of varying lengths that run vertically down the right edge of the card. The player's name appears on the Stadium Club logo at the bottom. The number "1" is gold-foil stamped in a black diamond at the lower left and is followed by a red stripe gold-foil stamped with the words "Draft Pick of the '90s." The back design features color photos on a black and red background with the player's signature gold-foil stamped across the bottom of the photo and gold foil bars running down the right edge of the picture. The team name and biographical information is included in a yellow and white box.

	MINT	NRMT
COMPLETE SET (3)	16.00	7.25
COMMON CARD (1-3)	1.00	.45

RANDOM INSERTS IN SER.3 PACKS
ONE CARD SENT TO EACH ST.CLUB MEMBER

			MINT	NRMT
☐ 1	Chipper Jones		15.00	6.75
☐ 2	Brien Taylor		1.00	.45
☐ 3	Phil Nevin			.90

1993 Stadium Club Murphy

This 200-card boxed set features 1992 All-Star Game cards, 1992 Team USA cards, and 1992 Championship and World Series cards. Topps actually refers to this set as a 1992 issue, but the set was released in 1993. The standard-size cards display full-bleed posed and action color player shots on

the fronts. The player's name appears below the Topps Stadium Club logo in the lower right with parallel gold foil stripes intersecting the logo. The horizontal back presents the player's biography, statistics, and highlights on a ghosted photo. This set is housed in a replica of San Diego's Jack Murphy Stadium, site of the 1992 All-Star Game. Production was limited to 8,000 cases, with 16 boxes per case. The set includes 100 Draft Pick cards, 56 All-Star cards, 25 Team USA cards, and 19 cards commemorating the 1992 National and American League Championship Series and the World Series. Notable Rookie Cards in this set include Derek Jeter, Jason Kendall, and Preston Wilson.

		MINT	NRMT
COMP.FACT.SET (212)	30.00	13.50
COMPLETE SET (200)	25.00	11.00
COMMON CARD (1-200)	.15	.07
MINOR STARS	.30	.14
UNLISTED STARS	.40	.25
COMP.MAST.PHOTO SET (12)	5.00	2.20

*MASTER PHOTOS: .5X TO 1X HI COLUMN
ONE MP SET PER FACTORY SET

			MINT	NRMT
☐ 1	Dave Winfield		.40	.18
☐ 2	Juan Guzman		.15	.07
☐ 3	Tony Gwynn		1.50	.70
☐ 4	Chris Roberts		.30	.14
☐ 5	Benny Santiago		.15	.07
☐ 6	Sherard Clinkscales		.15	.07
☐ 7	Jon Nunnally		.30	.14
☐ 8	Chuck Knoblauch		.60	.25
☐ 9	Bob Wolcott		.30	.14
☐ 10	Steve Rodriguez		.15	.07
☐ 11	Mark Williams		.15	.07
☐ 12	Danny Clyburn		1.00	.45
☐ 13	Darren Dreifort		.15	.07
☐ 14	Andy Van Slyke		.30	.14
☐ 15	Wade Boggs		.60	.25
☐ 16	Scott Patton		.15	.07
☐ 17	Gary Sheffield		.60	.25
☐ 18	Ron Villone		.15	.07
☐ 19	Roberto Alomar		.60	.25
☐ 20	Marc Valdes		.15	.07
☐ 21	Daron Kirkreit		.15	.07
☐ 22	Jeff Granger		.15	.07
☐ 23	Levon Largusa		.15	.07
☐ 24	Jimmy Key		.30	.14
☐ 25	Kevin Pearson		.15	.07
☐ 26	Michael Moore		.15	.07
☐ 27	Preston Wilson		1.50	.70
☐ 28	Kirby Puckett		1.25	.55
☐ 29	Tim Crabtree		.15	.07
☐ 30	Bip Roberts		.15	.07
☐ 31	Kelly Gruber		.15	.07
☐ 32	Tony Fernandez		.15	.07
☐ 33	Jason Angel		.15	.07
☐ 34	Calvin Murray		.15	.07
☐ 35	Chad McConnell		.15	.07
☐ 36	Jason Moler		.15	.07
☐ 37	Mark Lemke		.15	.07
☐ 38	Tom Knauss		.15	.07
☐ 39	Larry Mitchell		.15	.07
☐ 40	Doug Mirabelli		.15	.07
☐ 41	Everett Stull II		.15	.07
☐ 42	Chris Wimmer		.15	.07
☐ 43	Dan Serafini		.50	.23
☐ 44	Ryne Sandberg		.75	.35
☐ 45	Steve Lyons		.15	.07
☐ 46	Ryan Freeburg		.15	.07
☐ 47	Ruben Sierra		.30	.14
☐ 48	David Mysel		.15	.07
☐ 49	Joe Hamilton		.15	.07
☐ 50	Steve Rodriguez		.15	.07
☐ 51	Tim Wakefield		.30	.14
☐ 52	Scott Gentile		.15	.07
☐ 53	Doug Jones		.15	.07
☐ 54	Willie Brown		.15	.07
☐ 55	Chad Mottola		.15	.07
☐ 56	Ken Griffey Jr.		3.00	1.35
☐ 57	Jon Lieber		.15	.07
☐ 58	Denny Martinez		.30	.14
☐ 59	Joe Petcka		.15	.07
☐ 60	Benji Simonton		.15	.07
☐ 61	Brett Backlund		.15	.07
☐ 62	Damon Berryhill		.15	.07
☐ 63	Juan Guzman		.15	.07
☐ 64	Doug Hecker		.15	.07
☐ 65	Jamie Arnold		.30	.14
☐ 66	Bob Tewksbury		.15	.07
☐ 67	Tim Leger		.15	.07
☐ 68	Todd Etler		.15	.07
☐ 69	Lloyd McClendon		.15	.07
☐ 70	Kurt Ehmann		.15	.07
☐ 71	Rick Magdaleno		.30	.14
☐ 72	Tom Pagnozzi		.15	.07
☐ 73	Jeffrey Hammonds		.40	.18
☐ 74	Joe Carter		.30	.14
☐ 75	Chris Holt		.15	.07
☐ 76	Charles Johnson		1.00	.45
☐ 77	Bob Walk		.15	.07
☐ 78	Fred McGriff		.40	.18
☐ 79	Tom Evans		.75	.35
☐ 80	Scott Klingenbeck		.15	.07
☐ 81	Chad McConnell		.15	.07
☐ 82	Chris Eddy		.15	.07
☐ 83	Phil Nevin		.15	.07
☐ 84	John Kruk		.30	.14
☐ 85	Tony Sheffield		.15	.07
☐ 86	John Smoltz		.30	.14
☐ 87	Trevor Humphry		.15	.07
☐ 88	Charles Nagy		.30	.14
☐ 89	Sean Runyan		.15	.07
☐ 90	Mike Galan		.15	.07
☐ 91	Darren Daulton		.30	.14
☐ 92	Otis Nixon		.15	.07
☐ 93	Nomar Garciaparra		10.00	4.50
☐ 94	Larry Walker		.60	.25
☐ 95	Hut Smith		.15	.07
☐ 96	Rick Helling		.15	.07
☐ 97	Roger Clemens		1.25	.55
☐ 98	Ron Gant		.30	.14
☐ 99	Kenny Felder		.15	.07
☐ 100	Steve Murphy		.15	.07
☐ 101	Mike Smith		.15	.07
☐ 102	Terry Pendleton		.30	.14
☐ 103	Tim Davis		.15	.07
☐ 104	Jeff Patzke		.40	.18
☐ 105	Craig Wilson		.15	.07
☐ 106	Tom Glavine		.40	.18
☐ 107	Mark Langston		.15	.07
☐ 108	Mark Thompson		.15	.07
☐ 109	Eric Owens		.15	.07
☐ 110	Keith Johnson		.15	.07
☐ 111	Robin Ventura		.30	.14
☐ 112	Ed Sprague		.15	.07
☐ 113	Jeff Schmidt		.15	.07
☐ 114	Don Wengert		.15	.07
☐ 115	Craig Biggio		.40	.18
☐ 116	Kenny Carlyle		.15	.07
☐ 117	Derek Jeter		8.00	3.60
☐ 118	Manuel Lee		.15	.07
☐ 119	Jeff Haas		.15	.07
☐ 120	Roger Bailey		.15	.07
☐ 121	Sean Lowe		.15	.07
☐ 122	Rick Aguilera		.15	.07
☐ 123	Sandy Alomar		.30	.14
☐ 124	Derek Wallace		.15	.07
☐ 125	B.J. Wallace		.15	.07
☐ 126	Greg Maddux		2.00	.90
☐ 127	Tim Moore		.15	.07
☐ 128	Lee Smith		.30	.14
☐ 129	Todd Stevenson		.30	.14
☐ 130	Chris Widger		.15	.07
☐ 131	Paul Molitor		.60	.25
☐ 132	Chris Smith		.15	.07
☐ 133	Chris Gomez		.40	.18
☐ 134	Jimmy Baron		.15	.07
☐ 135	John Smoltz		.30	.14
☐ 136	Pat Borders		.15	.07
☐ 137	Donnie Leshnock		.15	.07

☐ 138 Gus Gandarillas	.15	.07
☐ 139 Will Clark	.40	.18
☐ 140 Ryan Luzinski	.15	.07
☐ 141 Cal Ripken	2.50	1.10
☐ 142 B.J. Wallace	.15	.07
☐ 143 Trey Beamon	.50	.23
☐ 144 Norm Charlton	.15	.07
☐ 145 Mike Mussina	.60	.25
☐ 146 Billy Owens	.15	.07
☐ 147 Ozzie Smith	.75	.35
☐ 148 Jason Kendall	2.00	.90
☐ 149 Mike Matthews	.80	.14
☐ 150 David Spykstra	.15	.07
☐ 151 Benji Grigsby	.15	.07
☐ 152 Sean Smith	.30	.14
☐ 153 Mark McGwire	1.25	.55
☐ 154 David Cone	.30	.14
☐ 155 Shon Walker	.30	.14
☐ 156 Jason Giambi	.60	.25
☐ 157 Jack McDowell	.15	.07
☐ 158 Paxton Briley	.15	.07
☐ 159 Edgar Martinez	.40	.18
☐ 160 Brian Sackinsky	.15	.07
☐ 161 Barry Bonds	.75	.35
☐ 162 Roberto Kelly	.15	.07
☐ 163 Jeff Alkire	.15	.07
☐ 164 Mike Sharperson	.15	.07
☐ 165 Jamie Taylor	.15	.07
☐ 166 John Saffer	.15	.07
☐ 167 Jerry Browne	.15	.07
☐ 168 Travis Fryman	.30	.14
☐ 169 Brady Anderson	.40	.18
☐ 170 Chris Roberts	.30	.14
☐ 171 Lloyd Peever	.15	.07
☐ 172 Francisco Cabrera	.15	.07
☐ 173 Ramiro Martinez	.15	.07
☐ 174 Jeff Alkire	.15	.07
☐ 175 Ivan Rodriguez	.75	.35
☐ 176 Kevin Brown	.30	.14
☐ 177 Chad Roper	.15	.07
☐ 178 Rod Henderson	.15	.07
☐ 179 Dennis Eckersley	.30	.14
☐ 180 Shannon Stewart	1.50	.70
☐ 181 DeShawn Warren	.15	.07
☐ 182 Lonnie Smith	.15	.07
☐ 183 Willie Adams	.15	.07
☐ 184 Jeff Montgomery	.30	.14
☐ 185 Damon Hollins	.50	.23
☐ 186 Byron Mathews	.15	.07
☐ 187 Harold Baines	.15	.07
☐ 188 Rick Greene	.15	.07
☐ 189 Carlos Baerga	.15	.07
☐ 190 Brandon Cromer	.15	.07
☐ 191 Roberto Alomar	.60	.25
☐ 192 Rich Ireland	.15	.07
☐ 193 Steve Montgomery	.15	.07
☐ 194 Brant Brown	.50	.23
☐ 195 Ritchie Moody	.15	.07
☐ 196 Michael Tucker	.60	.25
☐ 197 Jason Varitek	.60	.25
☐ 198 David Manning	.15	.07
☐ 199 Marquis Riley	.15	.07
☐ 200 Jason Giambi	.60	.25

1993 Stadium Club

The 1993 Stadium Club baseball set consists of 750 standard-size cards issued in three series of 300, 300, and 150 cards respectively. The fronts display full-bleed glossy color player photos. A red stripe carrying the player's name and edged on the bottom by a gold stripe cuts across the bottom of the picture. A white baseball icon with gold motion streaks rounds out the front. Award Winner and League Leader cards are studded with gold foil stars. On a background consisting of an artistic drawing of a baseball player's arm extended with ball in glove, the backs

carry a second color action photo, biographical information, 1992 Stats Player Profile, the player's ranking (either on his team and/or in the AL or NL), statistics, and a miniature reproduction of his Topps rookie card. Each series closes with a Members Choice subset (291-300, 591-600, and 746-750.

	MINT	NRMT
COMPLETE SET (750)	60.00	27.00
COMPLETE SERIES 1 (300)	20.00	9.00
COMPLETE SERIES 2 (300)	25.00	11.00
COMPLETE SERIES 3 (150)	15.00	6.75
COMMON CARD (1-750)	.15	.07
MINOR STARS	.30	.14
UNLISTED STARS	.60	.25
SUBSET CARDS HALF OF BASE CARDS		
COMP.1ST DAY SET (750)	2000.00	900.00
COMP.1ST DAY SER.1 (300)	700.00	325.00
COMP.1ST DAY SER.2 (300)	800.00	350.00
COMP.1ST DAY SER.3 (150)	500.00	220.00
COMMON 1ST DAY (1-750)	2.00	.90
*1ST DAY STARS: 10X TO ...X HI COLUMN		
1ST DAY STAT.ODDS 1:24 ... 3, 1:15 JUM		

☐ 1 Pat Borders	.15	.07
☐ 2 Greg Maddux	2.00	.90
☐ 3 Daryl Boston	.15	.07
☐ 4 Bob Ayrault	.15	.07
☐ 5 Tony Phillips IF	.15	.07
☐ 6 Damion Easley	.15	.07
☐ 7 Kip Gross	.15	.07
☐ 8 Jim Thome	1.25	.55
☐ 9 Tim Belcher	.15	.07
☐ 10 Gary Wayne	.15	.07
☐ 11 Sam Militello	.15	.07
☐ 12 Mike Magnante	.15	.07
☐ 13 Tim Wakefield	.30	.14
☐ 14 Tim Hulett	.15	.07
☐ 15 Rheal Cormier	.15	.07
☐ 16 Juan Guerrero	.15	.07
☐ 17 Rich Gossage	.30	.14
☐ 18 Tim Laker	.15	.07
☐ 19 Darrin Jackson	.15	.07
☐ 20 Jack Clark	.15	.07
☐ 21 Roberto Hernandez	.30	.14
☐ 22 Dean Palmer	.15	.07
☐ 23 Harold Reynolds	.15	.07
☐ 24 Dan Plesac	.15	.07
☐ 25 Brent Mayne	.15	.07
☐ 26 Pat Hentgen	.40	.18
☐ 27 Luis Sojo	.15	.07
☐ 28 Ron Gant	.30	.14
☐ 29 Paul Gibson	.15	.07
☐ 30 Bip Roberts	.15	.07
☐ 31 Mickey Tettleton	.15	.07
☐ 32 Randy Velarde	.15	.07
☐ 33 Brian McRae	.15	.07
☐ 34 Wes Chamberlain	.15	.07
☐ 35 Wayne Kirby	.15	.07
☐ 36 Rey Sanchez	.15	.07
☐ 37 Jesse Orosco	.15	.07
☐ 38 Mike Stanton	.15	.07
☐ 39 Royce Clayton	.15	.07
☐ 40 Cal Ripken UER	2.50	1.10

(Place of birth Havre de Grave; should be Havre de Grace)		
☐ 41 John Dopson	.15	.07
☐ 42 Gene Larkin	.15	.07
☐ 43 Tim Raines	.30	.14
☐ 44 Randy Myers	.30	.14
☐ 45 Clay Parker	.15	.07
☐ 46 Mike Scioscia	.15	.07
☐ 47 Pete Incaviglia	.15	.07
☐ 48 Todd Van Poppel	.15	.07
☐ 49 Ray Lankford	.30	.18
☐ 50 Eddie Murray	.60	.25
☐ 51 Barry Bonds COR	.75	.35
☐ 51A Barry Bonds ERR	.75	.35
(Missing four stars over name to indicate NL MVP)		
☐ 52 Gary Thurman	.15	.07
☐ 53 Bob Wickman	.15	.07
☐ 54 Joey Cora	.30	.14
☐ 55 Kenny Rogers	.15	.07
☐ 56 Mike Devereaux	.15	.07
☐ 57 Kevin Seitzer	.15	.07
☐ 58 Rafael Belliard	.15	.07
☐ 59 David Wells	.15	.07
☐ 60 Mark Clark	.15	.07
☐ 61 Carlos Baerga	.15	.07
☐ 62 Scott Brosius	.15	.07
☐ 63 Jeff Grotewold	.15	.07
☐ 64 Rick Wrona	.15	.07
☐ 65 Kurt Knudsen	.15	.07
☐ 66 Lloyd McClendon	.15	.07
☐ 67 Omar Vizquel	.30	.14
☐ 68 Jose Vizcaino	.15	.07
☐ 69 Rob Ducey	.15	.07
☐ 70 Casey Candaele	.15	.07
☐ 71 Ramon Martinez	.30	.14
☐ 72 Todd Hundley	.40	.18
☐ 73 John Marzano	.15	.07
☐ 74 Derek Parks	.15	.07
☐ 75 Jack McDowell	.15	.07
☐ 76 Tim Scott	.15	.07
☐ 77 Mike Mussina	.60	.25
☐ 78 Delino DeShields	.15	.07
☐ 79 Chris Bosio	.15	.07
☐ 80 Mike Bordick	.15	.07
☐ 81 Rod Beck	.30	.14
☐ 82 Ted Power	.15	.07
☐ 83 John Kruk	.30	.14
☐ 84 Steve Shifflett	.15	.07
☐ 85 Danny Tartabull	.15	.07
☐ 86 Mike Greenwell	.15	.07
☐ 87 Jose Melendez	.15	.07
☐ 88 Craig Wilson	.15	.07
☐ 89 Melvin Nieves	.30	.14
☐ 90 Ed Sprague	.15	.07
☐ 91 Willie McGee	.15	.07
☐ 92 Joe Orsulak	.15	.07
☐ 93 Jeff King	.30	.14
☐ 94 Dan Pasqua	.15	.07
☐ 95 Brian Harper	.15	.07
☐ 96 Joe Oliver	.15	.07
☐ 97 Shane Turner	.15	.07
☐ 98 Lenny Harris	.15	.07
☐ 99 Jeff Parrett	.15	.07
☐ 100 Luis Polonia	.15	.07
☐ 101 Kent Bottenfield	.15	.07
☐ 102 Albert Belle	.75	.35
☐ 103 Mike Maddux	.15	.07
☐ 104 Randy Tomlin	.15	.07
☐ 105 Andy Stankiewicz	.15	.07
☐ 106 Rico Rossy	.15	.07
☐ 107 Joe Hesketh	.15	.07
☐ 108 Dennis Powell	.15	.07
☐ 109 Derrick May	.15	.07
☐ 110 Pete Harnisch	.15	.07
☐ 111 Kent Mercker	.15	.07
☐ 112 Scott Fletcher	.15	.07
☐ 113 Rex Hudler	.15	.07
☐ 114 Chico Walker	.15	.07
☐ 115 Rafael Palmeiro	.40	.18
☐ 116 Mark Leiter	.15	.07
☐ 117 Pedro Munoz	.15	.07
☐ 118 Jim Bullinger	.15	.07
☐ 119 Ivan Calderon	.15	.07
☐ 120 Mike Timlin	.15	.07
☐ 121 Rene Gonzales	.15	.07

122	Greg Vaughn	.15	.07
123	Mike Flanagan	.15	.07
124	Mike Hartley	.15	.07
125	Jeff Montgomery	.30	.14
126	Mike Gallego	.15	.07
127	Don Slaught	.15	.07
128	Charlie O'Brien	.15	.07
129	Jose Offerman	.15	.07
	(Can be found with home town missing on back)		
130	Mark Wohlers	.30	.14
131	Eric Fox	.15	.07
132	Doug Strange	.15	.07
133	Jeff Frye	.15	.07
134	Wade Boggs UER	.60	.25
	(Redundantly lists lefty breakdown)		
135	Lou Whitaker	.30	.14
136	Craig Grebeck	.15	.07
137	Rich Rodriguez	.15	.07
138	Jay Bell	.30	.14
139	Felix Fermin	.15	.07
140	Denny Martinez	.30	.14
141	Eric Anthony	.15	.07
142	Roberto Alomar	.60	.25
143	Darren Lewis	.15	.07
144	Mike Blowers	.15	.07
145	Scott Bankhead	.15	.07
146	Jeff Reboulet	.15	.07
147	Frank Viola	.15	.07
148	Bill Pecota	.15	.07
149	Carlos Hernandez	.15	.07
150	Bobby Witt	.15	.07
151	Sid Bream	.15	.07
152	Todd Zeile	.15	.07
153	Dennis Cook	.15	.07
154	Brian Bohanon	.15	.07
155	Pat Kelly	.15	.07
156	Milt Cuyler	.15	.07
157	Juan Bell	.15	.07
158	Randy Milligan	.15	.07
159	Mark Gardner	.15	.07
160	Pat Tabler	.15	.07
161	Jeff Reardon	.30	.14
162	Ken Patterson	.15	.07
163	Bobby Bonilla	.30	.14
164	Tony Pena	.15	.07
165	Greg Swindell	.15	.07
166	Kirk McCaskill	.15	.07
167	Doug Drabek	.15	.07
168	Franklin Stubbs	.15	.07
169	Ron Tingley	.15	.07
170	Willie Banks	.15	.07
171	Sergio Valdez	.15	.07
172	Mark Lemke	.15	.07
173	Robin Yount	.40	.18
174	Storm Davis	.15	.07
175	Dan Walters	.15	.07
176	Steve Farr	.15	.07
177	Curt Wilkerson	.15	.07
178	Luis Alicea	.15	.07
179	Russ Swan	.15	.07
180	Mitch Williams	.15	.07
181	Wilson Alvarez	.30	.14
182	Carl Willis	.15	.07
183	Craig Biggio	.40	.18
184	Sean Berry	.15	.07
185	Trevor Wilson	.15	.07
186	Jeff Tackett	.15	.07
187	Ellis Burks	.30	.14
188	Jeff Branson	.15	.07
189	Matt Nokes	.15	.07
190	John Smiley	.15	.07
191	Danny Cox	.15	.07
192	Mike Boddicker	.15	.07
193	Roger Pavlik	.15	.07
194	Paul Sorrento	.15	.07
195	Vince Coleman	.15	.07
196	Gary DiSarcina	.15	.07
197	Rafael Bournigal	.15	.07
198	Mike Schooler	.15	.07
199	Scott Ruskin	.15	.07
200	Frank Thomas	2.50	1.10
201	Kyle Abbott	.15	.07
202	Mike Perez	.15	.07
203	Andre Dawson	.40	.18
204	Bill Swift	.15	.07
205	Alejandro Pena	.15	.07
206	Dave Winfield	.40	.18
207	Andujar Cedeno	.15	.07
208	Terry Steinbach	.15	.07
209	Chris Hammond	.15	.07
210	Todd Burns	.15	.07
211	Hipolito Pichardo	.15	.07
212	John Kiely	.15	.07
213	Tim Teufel	.15	.07
214	Lee Guetterman	.15	.07
215	Geronimo Pena	.15	.07
216	Brett Butler	.30	.14
217	Bryan Hickerson	.15	.07
218	Rick Trlicek	.15	.07
219	Lee Stevens	.15	.07
220	Roger Clemens	1.25	.55
221	Carlton Fisk	.60	.25
222	Chili Davis	.30	.14
223	Walt Terrell	.15	.07
224	Jim Eisenreich	.15	.07
225	Ricky Bones	.15	.07
226	Henry Rodriguez	.30	.14
227	Ken Hill	.15	.07
228	Rick Wilkins	.15	.07
229	Ricky Jordan	.15	.07
230	Bernard Gilkey	.30	.14
231	Tim Fortugno	.15	.07
232	Geno Petralli	.15	.07
233	Jose Rijo	.15	.07
234	Jim Leyritz	.15	.07
235	Kevin Campbell	.15	.07
236	Al Osuna	.15	.07
237	Pete Smith	.15	.07
238	Pete Schourek	.15	.07
239	Moises Alou	.30	.14
240	Donn Pall	.15	.07
241	Dan Peltier	.30	.14
242	Dan Peltier	.15	.07
243	Scott Scudder	.15	.07
244	Juan Guzman	.60	.25
245	Dave Burba	.15	.07
246	Rick Sutcliffe	.15	.07
247	Tony Fossas	.15	.07
248	Mike Munoz	.15	.07
249	Tim Salmon	.75	.35
250	Rob Murphy	.15	.07
251	Roger McDowell	.15	.07
252	Lance Parrish	.15	.07
253	Cliff Brantley	.15	.07
254	Scott Leius	.15	.07
255	Carlos Martinez	.15	.07
256	Vince Horsman	.15	.07
257	Oscar Azocar	.15	.07
258	Craig Shipley	.15	.07
259	Ben McDonald	.15	.07
260	Jeff Brantley	.15	.07
261	Damon Berryhill	.15	.07
262	Joe Grahe	.15	.07
263	Dave Hansen	.15	.07
264	Rich Amaral	.15	.07
265	Tim Pugh	.15	.07
266	Dion James	.15	.07
267	Frank Tanana	.15	.07
268	Stan Belinda	.15	.07
269	Jeff Kent	.30	.14
270	Bruce Ruffin	.15	.07
271	Xavier Hernandez	.15	.07
272	Darrin Fletcher	.15	.07
273	Tino Martinez	.60	.25
274	Benny Santiago	.15	.07
275	Scott Radinsky	.15	.07
276	Mariano Duncan	.15	.07
277	Kenny Lofton	1.25	.55
278	Dwight Smith	.15	.07
279	Joe Carter	.30	.14
280	Tim Jones	.15	.07
281	Jeff Hudson	.15	.07
282	Phil Plantier	.15	.07
283	Kirby Puckett	1.25	.55
284	Johnny Guzman	.15	.07
285	Mike Morgan	.15	.07
286	Chris Sabo	.15	.07
287	Matt Williams	.40	.18
288	Checklist 1-100	.15	.07
289	Checklist 101-200	.15	.07
290	Checklist 201-300	.15	.07
291	Dennis Eckersley MC	.15	.07
292	Eric Karros MC	.15	.07
293	Pat Listach MC	.15	.07
294	Andy Van Slyke MC	.15	.07
295	Robin Ventura MC	.30	.14
296	Tom Glavine MC	.30	.14
297	Juan Gonzalez MC UER	.75	.35
	(Misspelled Gonzales)		
298	Travis Fryman MC	.15	.07
299	Larry Walker MC	.60	.25
300	Gary Sheffield MC	.30	.14
301	Chuck Finley	.15	.07
302	Luis Gonzalez	.15	.07
303	Darryl Hamilton	.15	.07
304	Bien Figueroa	.15	.07
305	Ron Darling	.15	.07
306	Jonathan Hurst	.15	.07
307	Mike Sharperson	.15	.07
308	Mike Christopher	.15	.07
309	Marvin Freeman	.15	.07
310	Jay Buhner	.40	.18
311	Butch Henry	.15	.07
312	Greg W. Harris	.15	.07
313	Darren Daulton	.30	.14
314	Chuck Knoblauch	.60	.25
315	Greg A. Harris	.15	.07
316	John Franco	.30	.14
317	John Wehner	.15	.07
318	Donald Harris	.15	.07
319	Benny Santiago	.15	.07
320	Larry Walker	.60	.25
321	Randy Knorr	.15	.07
322	Ramon Martinez	.30	.14
323	Mike Stanley	.15	.07
324	Bill Wegman	.15	.07
325	Tom Candiotti	.15	.07
326	Glenn Davis	.15	.07
327	Chuck Crim	.15	.07
328	Scott Livingstone	.15	.07
329	Eddie Taubensee	.15	.07
330	George Bell	.15	.07
331	Edgar Martinez	.40	.18
332	Paul Assenmacher	.15	.07
333	Steve Hosey	.15	.07
334	Mo Vaughn	.75	.35
335	Bret Saberhagen	.15	.07
336	Mike Trombley	.15	.07
337	Mark Lewis	.15	.07
338	Terry Pendleton	.30	.14
339	Dave Hollins	.15	.07
340	Jeff Conine	.30	.14
341	Bob Tewksbury	.15	.07
342	Billy Ashley	.15	.07
343	Zane Smith	.15	.07
344	John Wetteland	.30	.14
345	Chris Hoiles	.15	.07
346	Frank Castillo	.15	.07
347	Bruce Hurst	.15	.07
348	Kevin McReynolds	.15	.07
349	Dave Henderson	.15	.07
350	Ryan Bowen	.15	.07
351	Sid Fernandez	.15	.07
352	Mark Whiten	.15	.07
353	Nolan Ryan	2.50	1.10
354	Rick Aguilera	.15	.07
355	Mark Langston	.15	.07
356	Jack Morris	.30	.14
357	Rob Deer	.15	.07
358	Dave Fleming	.15	.07
359	Lance Johnson	.15	.07
360	Joe Millette	.15	.07
361	Wil Cordero	.15	.07
362	Chito Martinez	.15	.07
363	Scott Servais	.15	.07
364	Bernie Williams	.60	.25
365	Pedro Martinez	.60	.25
366	Ryne Sandberg	.75	.35
367	Brad Ausmus	.15	.07
368	Scott Cooper	.15	.07
369	Rob Dibble	.15	.07
370	Walt Weiss	.15	.07
371	Mark Davis	.15	.07
372	Orlando Merced	.15	.07
373	Mike Jackson	.15	.07
374	Kevin Appier	.30	.14

No.	Player	Mint	VG
375	Esteban Beltre	.15	.07
376	Joe Slusarski	.15	.07
377	William Suero	.15	.07
378	Pete O'Brien	.15	.07
379	Alan Embree	.15	.07
380	Lenny Webster	.15	.07
381	Eric Davis	.30	.14
382	Duane Ward	.15	.07
383	John Habyan	.15	.07
384	Jeff Bagwell	1.25	.55
385	Ruben Amaro	.15	.07
386	Julio Valera	.15	.07
387	Robin Ventura	.30	.14
388	Archi Cianfrocco	.15	.07
389	Skeeter Barnes	.15	.07
390	Tim Costo	.15	.07
391	Luis Mercedes	.15	.07
392	Jeremy Hernandez	.15	.07
393	Shawon Dunston	.15	.07
394	Andy Van Slyke	.30	.14
395	Kevin Maas	.15	.07
396	Kevin Brown	.30	.14
397	J.T. Bruett	.15	.07
398	Darryl Strawberry	.30	.14
399	Tom Pagnozzi	.15	.07
400	Sandy Alomar Jr	.30	.14
401	Keith Miller	.15	.07
402	Rich DeLucia	.15	.07
403	Shawn Abner	.15	.07
404	Howard Johnson	.15	.07
405	Mike Benjamin	.15	.07
406	Roberto Mejia	.15	.07
407	Mike Butcher	.15	.07
408	Deion Sanders UER	.30	.14
	(Braves on front and Yankees on back)		
409	Todd Stottlemyre	.15	.07
410	Scott Kamieniecki	.15	.07
411	Doug Jones	.15	.07
412	John Burkett	.15	.07
413	Lance Blankenship	.15	.07
414	Jeff Parrett	.15	.07
415	Barry Larkin	.40	.18
416	Alan Trammell	.40	.18
417	Mark Kiefer	.15	.07
418	Gregg Olson	.15	.07
419	Mark Grace	.40	.18
420	Shane Mack	.15	.07
421	Bob Walk	.15	.07
422	Curt Schilling	.30	.14
423	Erik Hanson	.15	.07
424	George Brett	1.25	.55
425	Reggie Jefferson	.15	.07
426	Mark Portugal	.15	.07
427	Ron Karkovice	.15	.07
428	Matt Young	.15	.07
429	Troy Neel	.15	.07
430	Hector Fajardo	.15	.07
431	Dave Righetti	.15	.07
432	Pat Listach	.15	.07
433	Jeff Innis	.15	.07
434	Bob MacDonald	.15	.07
435	Brian Jordan	.30	.14
436	Jeff Blauser	.15	.07
437	Mike Myers	.15	.07
438	Frank Seminara	.15	.07
439	Rusty Meacham	.15	.07
440	Greg Briley	.15	.07
441	Derek Lilliquist	.15	.07
442	John Vander Wal	.15	.07
443	Scott Erickson	.15	.07
444	Bob Scanlan	.15	.07
445	Todd Frohwirth	.15	.07
446	Tom Goodwin	.15	.07
447	William Pennyfeather	.15	.07
448	Travis Fryman	.30	.14
449	Mickey Morandini	.15	.07
450	Greg Olson	.15	.07
451	Trevor Hoffman	.40	.18
452	Dave Magadan	.15	.07
453	Shawn Jeter	.15	.07
454	Andres Galarraga	.60	.25
455	Ted Wood	.15	.07
456	Freddie Benavides	.15	.07
457	Junior Felix	.15	.07
458	Alex Cole	.15	.07
459	John Orton	.15	.07
460	Eddie Zosky	.15	.07
461	Dennis Eckersley	.30	.14
462	Lee Smith	.30	.14
463	John Smoltz	.30	.14
464	Ken Caminiti	.40	.18
465	Melido Perez	.15	.07
466	Tom Marsh	.15	.07
467	Jeff Nelson	.15	.07
468	Jesse Levis	.15	.07
469	Chris Nabholz	.15	.07
470	Mike Macfarlane	.15	.07
471	Reggie Sanders	.30	.14
472	Chuck McElroy	.15	.07
473	Kevin Gross	.15	.07
474	Matt Whiteside	.15	.07
475	Cal Eldred	.15	.07
476	Dave Gallagher	.15	.07
477	Len Dykstra	.30	.14
478	Mark McGwire	1.25	.55
479	David Segui	.15	.07
480	Mike Henneman	.15	.07
481	Bret Barberie	.15	.07
482	Steve Sax	.15	.07
483	Dave Valle	.15	.07
484	Danny Darwin	.15	.07
485	Devon White	.15	.07
486	Eric Plunk	.15	.07
487	Jim Gott	.15	.07
488	Scooter Tucker	.15	.07
489	Omar Olivares	.15	.07
490	Greg Myers	.15	.07
491	Brian Hunter	.15	.07
492	Kevin Tapani	.15	.07
493	Rich Monteleone	.15	.07
494	Steve Buechele	.15	.07
495	Bo Jackson	.30	.14
496	Mike LaValliere	.15	.07
497	Mark Leonard	.15	.07
498	Daryl Boston	.15	.07
499	Jose Canseco	.40	.18
500	Brian Barnes	.15	.07
501	Randy Johnson	.60	.25
502	Tim McIntosh	.15	.07
503	Cecil Fielder	.30	.14
504	Derek Bell	.30	.14
505	Kevin Koslofski	.15	.07
506	Darren Holmes	.15	.07
507	Brady Anderson	.40	.18
508	John Valentin	.30	.14
509	Jerry Browne	.15	.07
510	Fred McGriff	.40	.18
511	Pedro Astacio	.15	.07
512	Gary Gaetti	.15	.07
513	John Burke	.15	.07
514	Dwight Gooden	.30	.14
515	Thomas Howard	.15	.07
516	Darrell Whitmore UER	.15	.07
	(11 games played in 1992; should be 121)		
517	Ozzie Guillen	.15	.07
518	Darryl Kile	.30	.14
519	Rich Rowland	.15	.07
520	Carlos Delgado	.60	.25
521	Doug Henry	.15	.07
522	Greg Colbrunn	.15	.07
523	Tom Gordon	.15	.07
524	Ivan Rodriguez	.75	.35
525	Kent Hrbek	.30	.14
526	Eric Young	.25	.11
527	Rod Brewer	.15	.07
528	Eric Karros	.30	.14
529	Marquis Grissom	.30	.14
530	Rico Brogna	.15	.07
531	Sammy Sosa	.60	.25
532	Bret Boone	.25	.07
533	Luis Rivera	.15	.07
534	Hal Morris	.15	.07
535	Monty Fariss	.15	.07
536	Leo Gomez	.15	.07
537	Wally Joyner	.30	.14
538	Tony Gwynn	1.50	.70
539	Mike Williams	.15	.07
540	Juan Gonzalez	1.50	.70
541	Ryan Klesko	.75	.35
542	Ryan Thompson	.15	.07
543	Chad Curtis	.30	.14
544	Orel Hershiser	.30	.14
545	Carlos Garcia	.15	.07
546	Bob Welch	.15	.07
547	Vinny Castilla	.60	.25
548	Ozzie Smith	.75	.35
549	Luis Salazar	.15	.07
550	Mark Guthrie	.15	.07
551	Charles Nagy	.30	.14
552	Alex Fernandez	.30	.14
553	Mel Rojas	.30	.14
554	Orestes Destrade	.15	.07
555	Mark Gubicza	.15	.07
556	Steve Finley	.30	.14
557	Don Mattingly	1.00	.45
558	Rickey Henderson	.40	.18
559	Tommy Greene	.15	.07
560	Arthur Rhodes	.15	.07
561	Alfredo Griffin	.15	.07
562	Will Clark	.40	.18
563	Bob Zupcic	.15	.07
564	Chuck Carr	.15	.07
565	Henry Cotto	.15	.07
566	Billy Spiers	.15	.07
567	Jack Armstrong	.15	.07
568	Kurt Stillwell	.15	.07
569	David McCarty	.15	.07
570	Joe Vitiello	.15	.07
571	Gerald Williams	.15	.07
572	Dale Murphy	.40	.18
573	Scott Aldred	.15	.07
574	Bill Gullickson	.15	.07
575	Bobby Thigpen	.15	.07
576	Glenallen Hill	.15	.07
577	Dwayne Henry	.15	.07
578	Calvin Jones	.15	.07
579	Al Martin	.30	.14
580	Ruben Sierra	.30	.14
581	Andy Benes	.30	.14
582	Anthony Young	.15	.07
583	Shawn Boskie	.15	.07
584	Scott Pose	.15	.07
585	Mike Piazza	3.00	1.35
586	Donovan Osborne	.15	.07
587	James Austin	.15	.07
588	Checklist 301-400	.15	.07
589	Checklist 401-500	.15	.07
590	Checklist 501-600	.15	.07
591	Ken Griffey Jr. MC	1.50	.70
592	Ivan Rodriguez MC	.60	.25
593	Carlos Baerga MC	.15	.07
594	Fred McGriff MC	.30	.14
595	Mark McGwire MC	.60	.25
596	Roberto Alomar MC	.30	.14
597	Kirby Puckett MC	.60	.25
598	Marquis Grissom MC	.15	.07
599	John Smoltz MC	.15	.07
600	Ryne Sandberg MC	.40	.18
601	Wade Boggs	.60	.25
602	Jeff Reardon	.30	.14
603	Billy Ripken	.15	.07
604	Bryan Harvey	.15	.07
605	Carlos Quintana	.15	.07
606	Greg Hibbard	.15	.07
607	Ellis Burks	.30	.14
608	Greg Swindell	.15	.07
609	Dave Winfield	.40	.18
610	Charlie Hough	.15	.07
611	Chili Davis	.30	.14
612	Jody Reed	.15	.07
613	Mark Williamson	.15	.07
614	Phil Plantier	.15	.07
615	Jim Abbott	.15	.07
616	Dante Bichette	.40	.18
617	Mark Eichhorn	.15	.07
618	Gary Sheffield	.60	.25
619	Richie Lewis	.15	.07
620	Joe Girardi	.15	.07
621	Jaime Navarro	.15	.07
622	Willie Wilson	.15	.07
623	Scott Fletcher	.15	.07
624	Bud Black	.15	.07
625	Tom Brunansky	.15	.07
626	Steve Avery	.30	.14
627	Paul Molitor	.60	.25
628	Gregg Jefferies	.15	.07
629	Dave Stewart	.30	.14

		MINT	NRMT
☐ 630	Javier Lopez	.60	.25
☐ 631	Greg Gagne	.15	.07
☐ 632	Roberto Kelly	.15	.07
☐ 633	Mike Fetters	.15	.07
☐ 634	Ozzie Canseco	.15	.07
☐ 635	Jeff Russell	.15	.07
☐ 636	Pete Incaviglia	.15	.07
☐ 637	Tom Henke	.15	.07
☐ 638	Chipper Jones	3.00	1.35
☐ 639	Jimmy Key	.30	.14
☐ 640	Dave Martinez	.15	.07
☐ 641	Dave Stieb	.15	.07
☐ 642	Milt Thompson	.15	.07
☐ 643	Alan Mills	.15	.07
☐ 644	Jim Fernandez	.15	.07
☐ 645	Randy Bush	.15	.07
☐ 646	Joe Magrane	.15	.07
☐ 647	Ivan Calderon	.15	.07
☐ 648	Jose Guzman	.15	.07
☐ 649	John Olerud	.15	.07
☐ 650	Tom Glavine	.40	.18
☐ 651	Julio Franco	.15	.07
☐ 652	Armando Reynoso	.15	.07
☐ 653	Felix Jose	.15	.07
☐ 654	Ben Rivera	.15	.07
☐ 655	Andre Dawson	.40	.18
☐ 656	Mike Harkey	.15	.07
☐ 657	Kevin Seitzer	.15	.07
☐ 658	Lonnie Smith	.15	.07
☐ 659	Norm Charlton	.15	.07
☐ 660	David Justice	.60	.25
☐ 661	Fernando Valenzuela	.30	.14
☐ 662	Dan Wilson	.30	.14
☐ 663	Mark Gardner	.15	.07
☐ 664	Doug Dascenzo	.15	.07
☐ 665	Greg Maddux	2.00	.90
☐ 666	Harold Baines	.30	.14
☐ 667	Randy Myers	.30	.14
☐ 668	Harold Reynolds	.15	.07
☐ 669	Candy Maldonado	.15	.14
☐ 670	Al Leiter	.30	.14
☐ 671	Jerald Clark	.15	.07
☐ 672	Doug Drabek	.15	.07
☐ 673	Kirk Gibson	.30	.14
☐ 674	Steve Reed	.15	.07
☐ 675	Mike Felder	.15	.07
☐ 676	Ricky Gutierrez	.15	.07
☐ 677	Spike Owen	.15	.07
☐ 678	Otis Nixon	.15	.07
☐ 679	Scott Sanderson	.15	.07
☐ 680	Mark Carreon	.15	.07
☐ 681	Troy Percival	.30	.14
☐ 682	Kevin Stocker	.15	.07
☐ 683	Jim Converse	.15	.07
☐ 684	Barry Bonds	.75	.35
☐ 685	Greg Gohr	.15	.07
☐ 686	Tim Wallach	.30	.14
☐ 687	Matt Mieske	.30	.14
☐ 688	Robby Thompson	.15	.07
☐ 689	Brien Taylor	.15	.07
☐ 690	Kirt Manwaring	.15	.14
☐ 691	Mike Lansing	.30	.14
☐ 692	Steve Decker	.15	.07
☐ 693	Mike Moore	.15	.14
☐ 694	Kevin Mitchell	.30	.14
☐ 695	Phil Hiatt	.15	.07
☐ 696	Tony Tarasco	.15	.07
☐ 697	Benji Gil	.15	.07
☐ 698	Jeff Juden	.15	.07
☐ 699	Kevin Reimer	.15	.07
☐ 700	Andy Ashby	.15	.07
☐ 701	John Jaha	.30	.14
☐ 702	Tim Bogar	.15	.07
☐ 703	David Cone	.30	.14
☐ 704	Willie Greene	.15	.14
☐ 705	David Hulse	.15	.07
☐ 706	Cris Carpenter	.15	.07
☐ 707	Ken Griffey Jr.	3.00	1.35
☐ 708	Steve Bedrosian	.15	.07
☐ 709	Dave Nilsson	.30	.14
☐ 710	Paul Wagner	.15	.07
☐ 711	B.J. Surhoff	.30	.14
☐ 712	Rene Arocha	.15	.07
☐ 713	Manuel Lee	.15	.07
☐ 714	Brian Williams	.15	.07
☐ 715	Sherman Obando	.15	.07
☐ 716	Terry Mulholland	.15	.07
☐ 717	Paul O'Neill	.30	.14
☐ 718	David Nied	.15	.07
☐ 719	J.T. Snow	.75	.35
☐ 720	Nigel Wilson	.15	.07
☐ 721	Mike Bielecki	.15	.07
☐ 722	Kevin Young	.15	.07
☐ 723	Charlie Leibrandt	.15	.07
☐ 724	Frank Bolick	.15	.07
☐ 725	Jon Shave	.15	.07
☐ 726	Steve Cooke	.15	.07
☐ 727	Domingo Martinez	.15	.07
☐ 728	Todd Worrell	.15	.07
☐ 729	Jose Lind	.15	.07
☐ 730	Jim Tatum	.15	.07
☐ 731	Mike Hampton	.40	.18
☐ 732	Mike Draper	.15	.07
☐ 733	Henry Mercedes	.15	.07
☐ 734	John Johnstone	.15	.07
☐ 735	Mitch Webster	.15	.07
☐ 736	Russ Springer	.15	.07
☐ 737	Rob Natal	.15	.07
☐ 738	Steve Howe	.15	.07
☐ 739	Darrell Sherman	.15	.07
☐ 740	Pat Mahomes	.15	.07
☐ 741	Alex Arias	.15	.07
☐ 742	Damon Buford	.15	.07
☐ 743	Charlie Hayes	.15	.07
☐ 744	Guillermo Velasquez	.15	.07
☐ 745	Checklist 601-750 UER	.15	.07
	(650 Tom Glavine)		
☐ 746	Frank Thomas MC	1.25	.55
☐ 747	Barry Bonds MC	.40	.18
☐ 748	Roger Clemens MC	.60	.25
☐ 749	Joe Carter MC	.15	.07
☐ 750	Greg Maddux MC	1.00	.45

1993 Stadium Club Inserts

This 10-card set was randomly inserted in all series of Stadium Club packs, the first four in series 1, the second four in series 2 and the last two in series 3. The themes of the standard-size cards differ from series to series, but the basic design -- borderless color action shots on the fronts -- remains the same throughout. The series 1 and 3 cards are numbered on the back, the series 2 cards are unnumbered. No matter what series, all of these inserts were inserted one every 15 packs.

	MINT	NRMT
COMPLETE SET (10)	16.00	7.25
COMPLETE SERIES 1 (4)	5.00	2.20
COMPLETE SERIES 2 (4)	10.00	4.50
COMPLETE SERIES 3 (2)	2.00	.90
COMMON CARD (A1-C2)	.50	.23
A1-A4 SER.1 STATED ODDS 1:15		
B1-B4 SER.2 STATED ODDS 1:15		
C1-C2 SER.3 STATED ODDS 1:15		

		MINT	NRMT
☐ A1	Robin Yount 3000 Hit Club	1.00	.45
☐ A2	George Brett 3000 Hit Club	4.00	1.80
☐ A3	David Nied First Draft Pick of the Rockies	.50	.23
☐ A4	Nigel Wilson 1st DP Marlins	.50	.23
☐ B1	Will Clark Mark McGwire Pacific Terrific	1.25	.55
☐ B2	Dwight Gooden Don Mattingly Broadway Stars NY	1.25	.55
☐ B3	Ryne Sandberg Frank Thomas Second City Sluggers	4.00	1.80
☐ B4	Darryl Strawberry Ken Griffey Jr. Pacific Terrific	4.00	1.80
☐ C1	David Nied UER Colorado Rockies Firsts (Misspelled pitch- hitter on back)	.50	.23
☐ C2	Charlie Hough Florida Marlins Firsts	.50	.23

1993 Stadium Club Master Photos

Each of the three Stadium Club series features Master Photos, uncropped versions of the regular Stadium Club cards. Each Master Photo is inlaid in a 5" by 7" white frame and bordered with a prismatic foil trim. The Master Photos were made available to the public in two ways. First, one in every 24 packs included a Master Photo winner card redeemable for a group of three Master Photos until Jan. 31, 1994. Second, each hobby box contained one Master Photo. The cards are unnumbered and checklisted below in alphabetical order within series I (1-12), II (13-24), and III (25-30). Two different versions of these master photos were issued, one with and one without the "Members Only" gold foil seal at the upper right corner. The "Members Only" Master Photos were only available with the direct-mail solicited 750-card Stadium Club Members Only set.

	MINT	NRMT
COMPLETE SET (30)	24.00	11.00
COMPLETE SERIES 1 (12)	6.00	2.70
COMPLETE SERIES 2 (12)	8.00	3.60
COMPLETE SERIES 3 (6)	10.00	4.50

COMMON CARD (1-30) .... .25 .11
STATED ODDS 1:24 HOB/RET, 1:15 JUM
COMP.JUMBO SET (30)..... 24.00 11.00
*JUMBOS: .6X TO 1.5X BASE CARD HI
THREE JUMBOS VIA MAIL PER WINNER CARD
ONE JUMBO PER HOBBY BOX.

		MINT	NRMT
□ 1	Carlos Baerga	.25	.11
□ 2	Delino DeShields	.25	.11
□ 3	Brian McRae	.25	.11
□ 4	Sam Militello	.25	.11
□ 5	Joe Oliver	.25	.11
□ 6	Kirby Puckett	2.00	.90
□ 7	Cal Ripken	4.00	1.80
□ 8	Bip Roberts	.25	.11
□ 9	Mike Scioscia	.25	.11
□ 10	Rick Sutcliffe	.25	.11
□ 11	Danny Tartabull	.25	.11
□ 12	Tim Wakefield	.25	.11
□ 13	George Brett	2.00	.90
□ 14	Jose Canseco	.75	.35
□ 15	Will Clark	.75	.35
□ 16	Travis Fryman	.50	.23
□ 17	Dwight Gooden	.50	.23
□ 18	Mark Grace	.75	.35
□ 19	Rickey Henderson	.75	.35
□ 20	Mark McGwire MC	2.00	.90
□ 21	Nolan Ryan	4.00	1.80
□ 22	Ruben Sierra	.25	.11
□ 23	Darryl Strawberry	.50	.23
□ 24	Larry Walker	1.00	.45
□ 25	Barry Bonds	1.25	.55
□ 26	Ken Griffey Jr	5.00	2.20
□ 27	Greg Maddux	3.00	1.35
□ 28	David Nied	.25	.11
□ 29	J.T. Snow	1.00	.45
□ 30	Brien Taylor	.25	.11

1994 Stadium Club

The 720 standard-size cards comprising this set were issued two series of 270 and a third series of 180. Card fronts feature borderless color player action photos. The player's last name appears in white lettering within a red-foil-stamped rectangle at the bottom. His first name appears alongside in black "typewritten" lettering within a division color-coded "tearaway." The red-foil-stamped Stadium Club logo appears in an upper corner. The back carries a color player action cutout superimposed upon a blue and black background. The player's name, team, biography, career highlights and statistics appear in lettering of several different colors and typefaces. There are a number of subsets including

Home Run Club (258-268), Tale of Two Players (525/526), Division Leaders (527-532), Quick Starts (533-538), Career Contributors (541-543), Rookie Rocker (626-630), Rookie Rocket (631-634) and Fantastic Finishes (714-719). The only notable Rookie Card is Chan Ho Park.

	MINT	NRMT
COMPLETE SET (720)	55.00	25.00
COMPLETE SERIES 1 (270)	20.00	9.00
COMPLETE SERIES 2 (270)	20.00	9.00
COMPLETE SERIES 3 (180)	15.00	6.75
COMMON CARD (1-720)	.15	.07
MINOR STARS	.30	.14
UNLISTED STARS	.60	.25
SUBSET CARDS HALF VALUE OF BASE CARDS		
COMP.1ST DAY SET (720)	2300.00	1050.00
COMP.1ST DAY SER.1 (270)	1000.00	450.00
COMP.1ST DAY SER.2 (270)	800.00	350.00
COMP.1ST DAY SER.3 (180)	500.00	220.00
COMMON 1ST DAY (1-720)..	2.00	.90
*1ST DAY STARS: 10X TO 25X HI COLUMN		
*1ST DAY YOUNG STARS: 8X TO 20X HI		
1ST DAY ODDS 1:24 H/R, 1:15 JUM		
COMP.RAINBOW (720)	170.00	75.00
COMP.RAINBOW SER.1 (270)	65.00	29.00
COMP.RAINBOW SER.2 (270)	65.00	29.00
COMP.RAINBOW SER.3 (180)	40.00	18.00
COMMON RAINBOW (1-720)..	.25	.11
*RAINBOW STARS: 1.5X TO 4X HI COLUMN		
*RAINBOW YOUNG STARS: 1.25X TO 3X HI		
ONE RAINBOW PER PACK		

□ 1	Robin Yount	.40	.18
□ 2	Rick Wilkins	.15	.07
□ 3	Steve Scarsone	.15	.07
□ 4	Gary Sheffield	.60	.25
□ 5	George Brett UER	1.25	.55
	(birthdate listed as 1963; should be 1953)		
□ 6	Al Martin	.15	.07
□ 7	Joe Oliver	.15	.07
□ 8	Stan Belinda	.15	.07
□ 9	Denny Hocking	.15	.07
□ 10	Roberto Alomar	.60	.25
□ 11	Luis Polonia	.15	.07
□ 12	Scott Hemond	.15	.07
□ 13	Jody Reed	.15	.07
□ 14	Mel Rojas	.15	.07
□ 15	Junior Ortiz	.15	.07
□ 16	Harold Baines	.30	.14
□ 17	Brad Pennington	.15	.07
□ 18	Jay Bell	.30	.14
□ 19	Tom Henke	.15	.07
□ 20	Jeff Branson	.15	.07
□ 21	Roberto Mejia	.15	.07
□ 22	Pedro Munoz	.15	.07
□ 23	Matt Nokes	.15	.07
□ 24	Jack McDowell	.15	.07
□ 25	Cecil Fielder	.30	.14
□ 26	Tony Fossas	.15	.07
□ 27	Jim Eisenreich	.15	.07
□ 28	Anthony Young	.15	.07
□ 29	Chuck Carr	.15	.07
□ 30	Jeff Treadway	.15	.07
□ 31	Chris Nabholz	.15	.07
□ 32	Tom Candiotti	.15	.07
□ 33	Mike Maddux	.15	.07
□ 34	Nolan Ryan	2.50	1.10
□ 35	Luis Gonzalez	.15	.07
□ 36	Tim Salmon	.60	.25
□ 37	Mark Whiten	.15	.07
□ 38	Roger McDowell	.15	.07
□ 39	Royce Clayton	.15	.07
□ 40	Troy Neel	.15	.07
□ 41	Mike Harkey	.15	.07
□ 42	Darrin Fletcher	.15	.07
□ 43	Wayne Kirby	.15	.07
□ 44	Rich Amaral	.15	.07
□ 45	Robb Nen UER	.15	.07
	(Nenn on back)		
□ 46	Tim Teufel	.15	.07

□ 47	Steve Cooke	.15	.07
□ 48	Jeff McNeely	.15	.07
□ 49	Jeff Montgomery	.15	.07
□ 50	Skeeter Barnes	.15	.07
□ 51	Scott Stahoviak	.15	.07
□ 52	Pat Kelly	.15	.07
□ 53	Brady Anderson	.40	.18
□ 54	Mariano Duncan	.15	.07
□ 55	Brian Bohanon	.15	.07
□ 56	Jerry Spradlin	.15	.07
□ 57	Ron Karkovice	.15	.07
□ 58	Jeff Gardner	.15	.07
□ 59	Bobby Bonilla	.30	.14
□ 60	Tino Martinez	.60	.25
□ 61	Todd Benzinger	.15	.07
□ 62	Steve Trachsel	.30	.14
□ 63	Brian Jordan	.30	.14
□ 64	Steve Bedrosian	.15	.07
□ 65	Brent Gates	.15	.07
□ 66	Shawn Green	.30	.14
□ 67	Sean Berry	.15	.07
□ 68	Joe Klink	.15	.07
□ 69	Fernando Valenzuela	.30	.14
□ 70	Andy Tomberlin	.15	.07
□ 71	Tony Pena	.15	.07
□ 72	Eric Young	.15	.07
□ 73	Chris Gomez	.15	.07
□ 74	Paul O'Neill	.30	.14
□ 75	Ricky Gutierrez	.15	.07
□ 76	Brad Holman	.15	.07
□ 77	Lance Painter	.15	.07
□ 78	Mike Butcher	.15	.07
□ 79	Sid Bream	.15	.07
□ 80	Sammy Sosa	.60	.25
□ 81	Felix Fermin	.15	.07
□ 82	Todd Hundley	.30	.14
□ 83	Kevin Higgins	.15	.07
□ 84	Todd Pratt	.15	.07
□ 85	Ken Griffey Jr.	3.00	1.35
□ 86	John O'Donoghue	.15	.07
□ 87	Rick Renteria	.15	.07
□ 88	John Burkett	.15	.07
□ 89	Jose Vizcaino	.15	.07
□ 90	Kevin Seitzer	.15	.07
□ 91	Bobby Witt	.15	.07
□ 92	Chris Turner	.15	.07
□ 93	Omar Vizquel	.30	.14
□ 94	David Justice	.60	.25
□ 95	David Segui	.15	.07
□ 96	Dave Hollins	.15	.07
□ 97	Doug Strange	.15	.07
□ 98	Jerald Clark	.15	.07
□ 99	Mike Moore	.15	.07
□ 100	Joey Cora	.30	.14
□ 101	Scott Kamieniecki	.15	.07
□ 102	Andy Benes	.30	.14
□ 103	Chris Bosio	.15	.07
□ 104	Rey Sanchez	.15	.07
□ 105	John Jaha	.15	.07
□ 106	Otis Nixon	.15	.07
□ 107	Rickey Henderson	.40	.18
□ 108	Jeff Bagwell	1.25	.55
□ 109	Gregg Jefferies	.15	.07
□ 110	Roberto Alomar	.40	.18
	Paul Molitor		
	John Olerud		
□ 111	Ron Gant	.30	.14
	David Justice		
	Fred McGriff		
□ 112	Juan Gonzalez	.40	.18
	Rafael Palmeiro		
	Dean Palmer		
□ 113	Greg Swindell	.15	.07
□ 114	Bill Haselman	.15	.07
□ 115	Phil Plantier	.15	.07
□ 116	Ivan Rodriguez	.75	.35
□ 117	Kevin Tapani	.15	.07
□ 118	Mike LaValliere	.15	.07
□ 119	Tim Costo	.15	.07
□ 120	Mickey Morandini	.15	.07
□ 121	Brett Butler	.30	.14
□ 122	Tom Pagnozzi	.15	.07
□ 123	Ron Gant	.30	.14
□ 124	Damion Easley	.15	.07
□ 125	Dennis Eckersley	.30	.14
□ 126	Matt Mieske	.15	.07

127	Cliff Floyd	.30	.14
128	Julian Tavarez	.30	.14
129	Arthur Rhodes	.15	.07
130	Dave West	.15	.07
131	Tim Naehring	.15	.07
132	Freddie Benavides	.15	.07
133	Paul Assenmacher	.15	.07
134	David McCarty	.15	.07
135	Jose Lind	.15	.07
136	Reggie Sanders	.15	.07
137	Don Slaught	.15	.07
138	Andujar Cedeno	.15	.07
139	Rob Deer	.15	.07
140	Mike Piazza UER (listed as outfielder)	2.00	.90
141	Moises Alou	.30	.14
142	Tom Foley	.15	.07
143	Benito Santiago	.15	.07
144	Sandy Alomar	.30	.14
145	Carlos Hernandez	.15	.07
146	Luis Alicea	.15	.07
147	Tom Lampkin	.15	.07
148	Ryan Klesko	.60	.25
149	Juan Guzman	.15	.07
150	Scott Servais	.15	.07
151	Tony Gwynn	1.50	.70
152	Tim Wakefield	.15	.07
153	David Nied	.15	.07
154	Chris Haney	.15	.07
155	Danny Bautista	.15	.07
156	Randy Velarde	.15	.07
157	Darrin Jackson	.15	.07
158	J.R. Phillips	.15	.07
159	Greg Gagne	.15	.07
160	Luis Aquino	.15	.07
161	John Vander Wal	.15	.07
162	Randy Myers	.15	.07
163	Ted Power	.15	.07
164	Scott Brosius	.15	.07
165	Len Dykstra	.30	.14
166	Jacob Brumfield	.15	.07
167	Bo Jackson	.30	.14
168	Eddie Taubensee	.15	.07
169	Carlos Baerga	.15	.07
170	Tim Bogar	.15	.07
171	Jose Canseco	.40	.18
172	Greg Blosser UER (Gregg on front)	.15	.07
173	Chili Davis	.30	.14
174	Randy Knorr	.15	.07
175	Mike Perez	.15	.07
176	Henry Rodriguez	.15	.07
177	Brian Turang	.15	.07
178	Roger Pavlik	.15	.07
179	Aaron Sele	.15	.07
180	Fred McGriff / Gary Sheffield	.40	.18
181	J.T. Snow / Tim Salmon	.60	.25
182	Roberto Hernandez	.15	.07
183	Jeff Reboulet	.15	.07
184	John Doherty	.15	.07
185	Danny Sheaffer	.15	.07
186	Bip Roberts	.15	.07
187	Denny Martinez	.30	.14
188	Darryl Hamilton	.15	.07
189	Eduardo Perez	.15	.07
190	Pete Harnisch	.15	.07
191	Rich Gossage	.30	.14
192	Mickey Tettleton	.15	.07
193	Lenny Webster	.15	.07
194	Lance Johnson	.15	.07
195	Don Mattingly	1.00	.45
196	Gregg Olson	.15	.07
197	Mark Gubicza	.15	.07
198	Scott Fletcher	.15	.07
199	Jon Shave	.15	.07
200	Tim Mauser	.15	.07
201	Jeromy Burnitz	.15	.07
202	Rob Dibble	.15	.07
203	Will Clark	.40	.18
204	Steve Buechele	.15	.07
205	Brian Williams	.15	.07
206	Carlos Garcia	.15	.07
207	Mark Clark	.15	.07
208	Rafael Palmeiro	.40	.18
209	Eric Davis	.30	.14
210	Pat Meares	.15	.07
211	Chuck Finley	.15	.07
212	Jason Bere	.15	.07
213	Gary DiSarcina	.15	.07
214	Tony Fernandez	.15	.07
215	B.J. Surhoff	.15	.07
216	Lee Guetterman	.15	.07
217	Tim Wallach	.15	.07
218	Kirt Manwaring	.15	.07
219	Albert Belle	.35	.15
220	Doc Gooden	.30	.14
221	Archi Cianfrocco	.15	.07
222	Terry Mulholland	.15	.07
223	Hipolito Pichardo	.15	.07
224	Kent Hrbek	.30	.14
225	Craig Grebeck	.15	.07
226	Todd Jones	.15	.07
227	Mike Bordick	.15	.07
228	John Olerud	.30	.14
229	Jeff Blauser	.30	.14
230	Alex Arias	.15	.07
231	Bernard Gilkey	.15	.07
232	Denny Neagle	.30	.14
233	Pedro Borbon	.15	.07
234	Dick Schofield	.15	.07
235	Matias Carrillo	.15	.07
236	Juan Bell	.15	.07
237	Mike Hampton	.30	.14
238	Barry Bonds	.75	.35
239	Cris Carpenter	.15	.07
240	Eric Karros	.30	.14
241	Greg McMichael	.15	.07
242	Pat Hentgen	.30	.14
243	Tim Pugh	.15	.07
244	Vinny Castilla	.30	.14
245	Charlie Hough	.15	.07
246	Bobby Munoz	.15	.07
247	Kevin Baez	.15	.07
248	Todd Frohwirth	.15	.07
249	Charlie Hayes	.15	.07
250	Mike Macfarlane	.15	.07
251	Danny Darwin	.15	.07
252	Ben Rivera	.15	.07
253	Dave Henderson	.15	.07
254	Steve Avery	.30	.14
255	Tim Belcher	.15	.07
256	Dan Plesac	.15	.07
257	Jim Thome	.75	.35
258	Albert Belle HR	.40	.18
259	Barry Bonds HR	.40	.18
260	Ron Gant HR	.15	.07
261	Juan Gonzalez HR	.75	.35
262	Ken Griffey Jr. HR	1.50	.70
263	David Justice HR	.30	.14
264	Fred McGriff HR	.30	.14
265	Rafael Palmeiro HR	.30	.14
266	Mike Piazza HR	1.00	.45
267	Frank Thomas HR	1.25	.55
268	Matt Williams HR	.30	.14
269	Checklist 1-135	.15	.07
270	Checklist 136-270	.15	.07
271	Mike Stanley	.15	.07
272	Tony Tarasco	.15	.07
273	Teddy Higuera	.15	.07
274	Ryan Thompson	.15	.07
275	Rick Aguilera	.15	.07
276	Ramon Martinez	.30	.14
277	Orlando Merced	.15	.07
278	Guillermo Velasquez	.15	.07
279	Mark Hutton	.15	.07
280	Larry Walker	.60	.25
281	Kevin Gross	.15	.07
282	Jose Offerman	.15	.07
283	Jim Leyritz	.15	.07
284	Jamie Moyer	.15	.07
285	Frank Thomas	2.50	1.10
286	Derek Bell	.15	.07
287	Derrick May	.15	.07
288	Dave Winfield	.40	.18
289	Curt Schilling	.30	.14
290	Carlos Quintana	.15	.07
291	Bob Natal	.15	.07
292	David Cone	.30	.14
293	Al Osuna	.15	.07
294	Bob Hamelin	.15	.07
295	Chad Curtis	.15	.07
296	Danny Jackson	.15	.07
297	Bob Welch	.15	.07
298	Felix Jose	.15	.07
299	Jay Buhner	.40	.18
300	Joe Carter	.30	.14
301	Kenny Lofton	.75	.35
302	Kirk Rueter	.15	.07
303	Kim Batiste	.15	.07
304	Mike Morgan	.15	.07
305	Pat Borders	.15	.07
306	Rene Arocha	.15	.07
307	Ruben Sierra	.15	.07
308	Steve Finley	.30	.14
309	Travis Fryman	.30	.14
310	Zane Smith	.15	.07
311	Willie Wilson	.15	.07
312	Trevor Hoffman	.15	.07
313	Terry Pendleton	.15	.07
314	Salomon Torres	.15	.07
315	Robin Ventura	.30	.14
316	Randy Tomlin	.15	.07
317	Dave Stewart	.30	.14
318	Mike Benjamin	.15	.07
319	Matt Turner	.15	.07
320	Manny Ramirez	.75	.35
321	Kevin Young	.15	.07
322	Ken Caminiti	.40	.18
323	Joe Girardi	.15	.07
324	Jeff McKnight	.15	.07
325	Gene Harris	.15	.07
326	Devon White	.15	.07
327	Darryl Kile	.30	.14
328	Craig Paquette	.15	.07
329	Cal Eldred	.30	.14
330	Bill Swift	.15	.07
331	Alan Trammell	.40	.18
332	Armando Reynoso	.15	.07
333	Brent Mayne	.15	.07
334	Chris Donnels	.15	.07
335	Darryl Strawberry	.30	.14
336	Dean Palmer	.15	.07
337	Frank Castillo	.15	.07
338	Jeff King	.15	.07
339	John Franco	.30	.14
340	Kevin Appier	.30	.14
341	Lance Blankenship	.15	.07
342	Mark McLemore	.15	.07
343	Pedro Astacio	.15	.07
344	Rich Batchelor	.15	.07
345	Ryan Bowen	.15	.07
346	Terry Steinbach	.15	.07
347	Troy O'Leary	.15	.07
348	Willie Blair	.15	.07
349	Wade Boggs	.60	.25
350	Tim Raines	.30	.14
351	Scott Livingstone	.15	.07
352	Rod Correia	.15	.07
353	Ray Lankford	.30	.14
354	Pat Listach	.15	.07
355	Milt Thompson	.15	.07
356	Miguel Jimenez	.15	.07
357	Marc Newfield	.30	.14
358	Mark McGwire	1.25	.55
359	Kirby Puckett	1.25	.55
360	Kent Mercker	.15	.07
361	John Kruk	.30	.14
362	Jeff Kent	.15	.07
363	Hal Morris	.15	.07
364	Edgar Martinez	.40	.18
365	Dave Magadan	.15	.07
366	Dante Bichette	.30	.14
367	Chris Hammond	.15	.07
368	Bret Saberhagen	.15	.07
369	Billy Ripken	.15	.07
370	Bill Gullickson	.15	.07
371	Andre Dawson	.40	.18
372	Roberto Kelly	.15	.07
373	Cal Ripken	2.50	1.10
374	Craig Biggio	.40	.18
375	Dan Pasqua	.15	.07
376	Dave Nilsson	.15	.07
377	Duane Ward	.15	.07
378	Greg Vaughn	.15	.07
379	Jeff Fassero	.15	.07
380	Jerry DiPoto	.15	.07

381	John Patterson	.15	.07
382	Kevin Brown	.30	.14
383	Kevin Roberson	.15	.07
384	Joe Orsulak	.15	.07
385	Hilly Hathaway	.15	.07
386	Mike Greenwell	.15	.07
387	Orestes Destrade	.15	.07
388	Mike Gallego	.15	.07
389	Ozzie Guillen	.15	.07
390	Raul Mondesi	.60	.25
391	Scott Lydy	.15	.07
392	Tom Urbani	.15	.07
393	Wil Cordero	.15	.07
394	Tony Longmire	.15	.07
395	Todd Zeile	.15	.07
396	Scott Cooper	.15	.07
397	Ryne Sandberg	.75	.35
398	Ricky Bones	.15	.07
399	Phil Clark	.15	.07
400	Orel Hershiser	.30	.14
401	Mike Henneman	.15	.07
402	Mark Lemke	.15	.07
403	Mark Grace	.40	.18
404	Ken Ryan	.15	.07
405	John Smoltz	.30	.14
406	Jeff Conine	.30	.14
407	Greg Harris	.15	.07
408	Doug Drabek	.15	.07
409	Dave Fleming	.15	.07
410	Danny Tartabull	.15	.07
411	Chad Kreuter	.15	.07
412	Brad Ausmus	.15	.07
413	Ben McDonald	.15	.07
414	Barry Larkin	.40	.18
415	Bret Barberie	.15	.07
416	Chuck Knoblauch	.60	.25
417	Ozzie Smith	.75	.35
418	Ed Sprague	.15	.07
419	Matt Williams	.40	.18
420	Jeremy Hernandez	.15	.07
421	Jose Bautista	.15	.07
422	Kevin Mitchell	.15	.07
423	Manuel Lee	.15	.07
424	Mike Devereaux	.15	.07
425	Omar Olivares	.15	.07
426	Rafael Belliard	.15	.07
427	Richie Lewis	.15	.07
428	Ron Darling	.15	.07
429	Shane Mack	.15	.07
430	Tim Hulett	.15	.07
431	Wally Joyner	.30	.14
432	Wes Chamberlain	.15	.07
433	Tom Browning	.15	.07
434	Scott Radinsky	.15	.07
435	Rondell White	.40	.18
436	Rod Beck	.15	.07
437	Rheal Cormier	.15	.07
438	Randy Johnson	.60	.25
439	Pete Schourek	.15	.07
440	Mo Vaughn	.75	.35
441	Mike Timlin	.15	.07
442	Mark Langston	.15	.07
443	Lou Whitaker	.30	.14
444	Kevin Stocker	.15	.07
445	Ken Hill	.15	.07
446	John Wetteland	.15	.07
447	J.T. Snow	.60	.25
448	Erik Pappas	.15	.07
449	David Hulse	.15	.07
450	Darren Daulton	.30	.14
451	Chris Hoiles	.15	.07
452	Bryan Harvey	.15	.07
453	Darren Lewis	.15	.07
454	Andres Galarraga	.60	.25
455	Joe Hesketh	.15	.07
456	Jose Valentin	.15	.07
457	Dan Peltier	.15	.07
458	Joe Boever	.15	.07
459	Kevin Rogers	.15	.07
460	Craig Shipley	.15	.07
461	Alvaro Espinoza	.15	.07
462	Wilson Alvarez	.15	.07
463	Cory Snyder	.15	.07
464	Candy Maldonado	.15	.07
465	Blas Minor	.15	.07
466	Rod Bolton	.15	.07
467	Kenny Rogers	.15	.07
468	Greg Myers	.15	.07
469	Jimmy Key	.30	.14
470	Tony Castillo	.15	.07
471	Mike Stanton	.15	.07
472	Deion Sanders	.30	.14
473	Tito Navarro	.15	.07
474	Mike Gardiner	.15	.07
475	Steve Reed	.15	.07
476	John Roper	.15	.07
477	Mike Trombley	.15	.07
478	Charles Nagy	.30	.14
479	Larry Casian	.15	.07
480	Eric Hillman	.15	.07
481	Bill Wertz	.15	.07
482	Jeff Schwarz	.15	.07
483	John Valentin	.30	.14
484	Carl Willis	.15	.07
485	Gary Gaetti	.15	.07
486	Bill Pecota	.15	.07
487	John Smiley	.15	.07
488	Mike Mussina	.60	.25
489	Mike Ignasiak	.15	.07
490	Billy Brewer	.15	.07
491	Jack Voigt	.15	.07
492	Mike Munoz	.15	.07
493	Lee Tinsley	.15	.07
494	Bob Wickman	.15	.07
495	Roger Salkeld	.15	.07
496	Thomas Howard	.15	.07
497	Mark Davis	.15	.07
498	Dave Clark	.15	.07
499	Turk Wendell	.15	.07
500	Rafael Bournigal	.15	.07
501	Chip Hale	.15	.07
502	Matt Whiteside	.15	.07
503	Brian Koelling	.15	.07
504	Jeff Reed	.15	.07
505	Paul Wagner	.15	.07
506	Torey Lovullo	.15	.07
507	Curtis Leskanic	.15	.07
508	Derek Lilliquist	.15	.07
509	Joe Magrane	.15	.07
510	Mackey Sasser	.15	.07
511	Lloyd McClendon	.15	.07
512	Jayhawk Owens	.15	.07
513	Woody Williams	.15	.07
514	Gary Redus	.15	.07
515	Tim Spehr	.15	.07
516	Jim Abbott	.15	.07
517	Lou Frazier	.15	.07
518	Erik Plantenberg	.15	.07
519	Tim Worrell	.15	.07
520	Brian McRae	.15	.07
521	Chan Ho Park	2.00	.90
522	Mark Wohlers	.15	.07
523	Geronimo Pena	.15	.07
524	Andy Ashby	.15	.07
525	Tim Raines TALE	.15	.07
526	Paul Molitor TALE	.30	.14
527	Joe Carter DL	.15	.07
528	Frank Thomas DL UER	1.25	.55
	(listed as third in RBI in 1993; was actually second)		
529	Ken Griffey Jr. DL	1.50	.70
530	David Justice DL	.30	.14
531	Gregg Jefferies DL	.15	.07
532	Barry Bonds DL	.40	.18
533	John Kruk QS	.15	.07
534	Roger Clemens QS	.60	.25
535	Cecil Fielder QS	.15	.07
536	Ruben Sierra QS	.15	.07
537	Tony Gwynn QS	.75	.35
538	Tom Glavine QS	.15	.07
539	Checklist 271-405 UER	.15	.07
	(number on back is 269)		
540	Checklist 406-540 UER	.15	.07
	(numbered 270 on back)		
541	Ozzie Smith ATL	.60	.25
542	Eddie Murray ATL	.30	.14
543	Lee Smith ATL	.15	.07
544	Greg Maddux	2.00	.90
545	Denis Boucher	.15	.07
546	Mark Gardner	.15	.07
547	Bo Jackson	.30	.14
548	Eric Anthony	.15	.07
549	Delino DeShields	.15	.07
550	Turner Ward	.15	.07
551	Scott Sanderson	.15	.07
552	Hector Carrasco	.15	.07
553	Tony Phillips	.15	.07
554	Melido Perez	.15	.07
555	Mike Felder	.15	.07
556	Jack Morris	.30	.14
557	Rafael Palmeiro	.40	.18
558	Shane Reynolds	.15	.07
559	Pete Incaviglia	.15	.07
560	Greg Harris	.15	.07
561	Matt Walbeck	.15	.07
562	Todd Van Poppel	.15	.07
563	Todd Stottlemyre	.15	.07
564	Ricky Bones	.15	.07
565	Mike Jackson	.15	.07
566	Kevin McReynolds	.15	.07
567	Melvin Nieves	.15	.07
568	Juan Gonzalez	1.50	.70
569	Frank Viola	.15	.07
570	Vince Coleman	.15	.07
571	Brian Anderson	.60	.25
572	Omar Vizquel	.30	.14
573	Bernie Williams	.60	.25
574	Tom Glavine	.30	.14
575	Mitch Williams	.15	.07
576	Shawon Dunston	.15	.07
577	Mike Lansing	.30	.14
578	Greg Pirkl	.15	.07
579	Sid Fernandez	.15	.07
580	Doug Jones	.15	.07
581	Walt Weiss	.15	.07
582	Tim Belcher	.15	.07
583	Alex Fernandez	.15	.07
584	Alex Cole	.15	.07
585	Greg Cadaret	.15	.07
586	Bob Tewksbury	.15	.07
587	Dave Hansen	.15	.07
588	Kurt Abbott	.15	.07
589	Rick White	.15	.07
590	Kevin Bass	.15	.07
591	Geronimo Berroa	.15	.07
592	Jaime Navarro	.15	.07
593	Steve Farr	.15	.07
594	Jack Armstrong	.15	.07
595	Steve Howe	.15	.07
596	Jose Rijo	.15	.07
597	Otis Nixon	.15	.07
598	Robby Thompson	.15	.07
599	Kelly Stinnett	.15	.07
600	Carlos Delgado	.40	.18
601	Brian Johnson	.15	.07
602	Gregg Olson	.15	.07
603	Jim Edmonds	.60	.25
604	Mike Blowers	.15	.07
605	Lee Smith	.30	.14
606	Pat Rapp	.15	.07
607	Mike Magnante	.15	.07
608	Karl Rhodes	.15	.07
609	Jeff Juden	.15	.07
610	Rusty Meacham	.15	.07
611	Pedro Martinez	.60	.25
612	Todd Worrell	.15	.07
613	Stan Javier	.15	.07
614	Mike Hampton	.30	.14
615	Jose Guzman	.15	.07
616	Xavier Hernandez	.15	.07
617	David Wells	.15	.07
618	John Habyan	.15	.07
619	Chris Nabholz	.15	.07
620	Bobby Jones	.30	.14
621	Chris James	.15	.07
622	Ellis Burks	.30	.14
623	Erik Hanson	.15	.07
624	Pat Meares	.15	.07
625	Harold Reynolds	.15	.07
626	Bob Hamelin RR	.15	.07
627	Manny Ramirez RR	.30	.14
628	Ryan Klesko RR	.30	.14
629	Carlos Delgado RR	.30	.14
630	Javier Lopez RR	.30	.14
631	Steve Karsay RR	.15	.07
632	Rick Helling RR	.15	.07
633	Steve Trachsel RR	.15	.07
634	Hector Carrasco RR	.15	.07

☐ 635 Andy Stankiewicz	.15	.07
☐ 636 Paul Sorrento	.15	.07
☐ 637 Scott Erickson	.15	.07
☐ 638 Chipper Jones	2.00	.90
☐ 639 Luis Polonia	.15	.07
☐ 640 Howard Johnson	.15	.07
☐ 641 John Dopson	.15	.07
☐ 642 Jody Reed	.15	.07
☐ 643 Lonnie Smith	.15	.07
☐ 644 Mark Portugal	.15	.07
☐ 645 Paul Molitor	.60	.25
☐ 646 Paul Assenmacher	.15	.07
☐ 647 Hubie Brooks	.15	.07
☐ 648 Gary Wayne	.15	.07
☐ 649 Sean Berry	.15	.07
☐ 650 Roger Clemens	1.25	.55
☐ 651 Brian L.Hunter	.60	.25
☐ 652 Wally Whitehurst	.15	.07
☐ 653 Allen Watson	.15	.07
☐ 654 Rickey Henderson	.40	.18
☐ 655 Sid Bream	.15	.07
☐ 656 Dan Wilson	.30	.14
☐ 657 Ricky Jordan	.15	.07
☐ 658 Sterling Hitchcock	.15	.07
☐ 659 Darrin Jackson	.15	.07
☐ 660 Junior Felix	.15	.07
☐ 661 Tom Brunansky	.15	.07
☐ 662 Jose Vizcaino	.15	.07
☐ 663 Mark Leiter	.15	.07
☐ 664 Gil Heredia	.15	.07
☐ 665 Fred McGriff	.40	.18
☐ 666 Will Clark	.40	.18
☐ 667 Al Leiter	.15	.07
☐ 668 James Mouton	.15	.07
☐ 669 Billy Bean	.15	.07
☐ 670 Scott Leius	.15	.07
☐ 671 Bret Boone	.15	.07
☐ 672 Darren Holmes	.15	.07
☐ 673 Dave Weathers	.15	.07
☐ 674 Eddie Murray	.60	.25
☐ 675 Felix Fermin	.15	.07
☐ 676 Chris Sabo	.15	.07
☐ 677 Billy Spiers	.15	.07
☐ 678 Aaron Sele	.15	.07
☐ 679 Juan Samuel	.15	.07
☐ 680 Julio Franco	.15	.07
☐ 681 Heathcliff Slocumb	.15	.07
☐ 682 Denny Martinez	.30	.14
☐ 683 Jerry Browne	.15	.07
☐ 684 Pedro Martinez	.60	.25
☐ 685 Rex Hudler	.15	.07
☐ 686 Willie McGee	.15	.07
☐ 687 Andy Van Slyke	.30	.14
☐ 688 Pat Mahomes	.15	.07
☐ 689 Dave Henderson	.15	.07
☐ 690 Tony Eusebio	.15	.07
☐ 691 Rick Sutcliffe	.15	.07
☐ 692 Willie Banks	.15	.07
☐ 693 Alan Mills	.15	.07
☐ 694 Jeff Treadway	.15	.07
☐ 695 Alex Gonzalez	.30	.14
☐ 696 David Segui	.15	.07
☐ 697 Rick Helling	.15	.07
☐ 698 Bip Roberts	.15	.07
☐ 699 Jeff Cirillo	.50	.23
☐ 700 Terry Mulholland	.15	.07
☐ 701 Marvin Freeman	.15	.07
☐ 702 Jason Bere	.15	.07
☐ 703 Javier Lopez	.40	.18
☐ 704 Greg Hibbard	.15	.07
☐ 705 Tommy Greene	.15	.07
☐ 706 Marquis Grissom	.30	.14
☐ 707 Brian Harper	.15	.07
☐ 708 Steve Karsay	.15	.07
☐ 709 Jeff Brantley	.15	.07
☐ 710 Jeff Russell	.15	.07
☐ 711 Bryan Hickerson	.15	.07
☐ 712 Jim Pittsley	.50	.23
☐ 713 Bobby Ayala	.15	.07
☐ 714 John Smoltz	.30	.14
☐ 715 Jose Rijo	.15	.07
☐ 716 Greg Maddux	1.00	.45
☐ 717 Matt Williams	.40	.18
☐ 718 Frank Thomas	1.25	.55
☐ 719 Ryne Sandberg	.60	.25
☐ 720 Checklist	.15	.07

1994 Stadium Club Dugout Dirt

Randomly inserted at a rate of one per six packs, these standard-size cards feature some of baseball's most popular and colorful players by sports cartoonists Daniel Guidera and Steve Benson. The cards resemble basic Stadium Club cards except for a Dugout Dirt logo at the bottom. Backs contain a cartoon. Cards 1-4 were found in first series packs with cards 5-8 and 9-12 were inserted in second series and third series packs respectively.

	MINT	NRMT
COMPLETE SET (12)	10.00	4.50
COMPLETE SERIES 1 (4)	5.00	2.20
COMPLETE SERIES 2 (4)	3.00	1.35
COMPLETE SERIES 3 (4)	3.00	1.35
COMMON CARD (DD1-DD12)	.15	.07
STATED ODDS 1:6 H/R, 1:3 JUM		

☐ DD1 Mike Piazza	2.00	.90
☐ DD2 Dave Winfield	.40	.18
☐ DD3 John Kruk	.15	.07
☐ DD4 Cal Ripken	2.50	1.10
☐ DD5 Jack McDowell	.15	.07
☐ DD6 Barry Bonds	.75	.35
☐ DD7 Ken Griffey Jr.	3.00	1.35
☐ DD8 Tim Salmon	.60	.25
☐ DD9 Frank Thomas	2.50	1.10
☐ DD10 Jeff Kent	.15	.07
☐ DD11 Randy Johnson	.60	.25
☐ DD12 Darren Daulton	.25	.11

1994 Stadium Club Finest

This set contains 10 standard-size metallic cards of top players. They were randomly inserted one in 6 third series packs.

The fronts feature a color player photo with a red and yellow background. Backs contain a color player photo with 1993 and career statistics. Jumbo versions measuring approximately five inches by seven inches were issued for retail repacks.

	MINT	NRMT
COMPLETE SET (10)	30.00	13.50
COMMON CARD (F1-F10)	1.00	.45
SER.3 STATED ODDS 1:6		

☐ F1 Jeff Bagwell	4.00	1.80
☐ F2 Albert Belle	2.50	1.10
☐ F3 Barry Bonds	2.50	1.10
☐ F4 Juan Gonzalez	5.00	2.20
☐ F5 Ken Griffey Jr.	10.00	4.50
☐ F6 Marquis Grissom	1.00	.45
☐ F7 David Justice	2.00	.90
☐ F8 Mike Piazza	6.00	2.70
☐ F9 Tim Salmon	2.00	.90
☐ F10 Frank Thomas	8.00	3.60

1994 Stadium Club Super Teams

Randomly inserted at a rate of one per 24 first series packs only, this 28-card standard-size set features one card for each of the 28 MLB teams. Collectors holding team cards could redeem them for special prizes if those teams won a division title, a league championship, or the World Series. But, since the strike affected the 1994 season, Topps postponed the promotion until the 1995 season. The expiration was pushed back to January 31, 1996.

	MINT	NRMT
COMPLETE SET (28)	50.00	22.00
COMMON TEAM (1-28)	1.00	.45
SEMISTARS	1.50	.70
UNLISTED STARS	2.00	.90
SER.1 STAT.ODDS 1:24 HOB/RET, 1:15 JUM		
CONTEST APPLIED TO 1995 SEASON		

☐ ST1 Atlanta Braves (Jeff Blauser Terry Pendleton)	10.00	4.50
☐ ST2 Chicago Cubs (Sammy Sosa Derrick May)	1.00	.45
☐ ST3 Cincinnati Reds (Reggie Sanders Barry Larkin)	2.00	.90
☐ ST4 Colorado Rockies (Vinny Castilla Eric Young)	1.00	.45
☐ ST5 Florida Marlins	1.00	.45

(Alex Arias)
☐ ST6 Houston Astros .... 1.00 .45
(Eric Anthony
Steve Finley)
☐ ST7 Los Angeles Dodgers 6.00 2.70
(Mike Piazza)
☐ ST8 Montreal Expos .... 1.00 .45
(Marquis Grissom)
☐ ST9 New York Mets .... 1.00 .45
(Bobby Bonilla)
☐ ST10 Philadelphia Phillies 1.00 .45
(Mickey Morandini)
☐ ST11 Pittsburgh Pirates.. 1.00 .45
(Andy Van Slyke
Jay Bell)
☐ ST12 St. Louis Cardinals 1.00 .45
(Todd Zeile
Gregg Jefferies)
☐ ST13 San Diego Padres .. 1.00 .45
(Ricky Gutierrez)
☐ ST14 San Francisco Giants 2.00 .90
(Matt Williams
Kirt Manwaring)
☐ ST15 Baltimore Orioles .. 8.00 3.60
(Cal Ripken)
☐ ST16 Boston Red Sox .... 2.00 .90
(Luis Rivera
John Valentin)
☐ ST17 California Angels .... 1.00 .45
(Tim Salmon)
☐ ST18 Chicago White Sox 1.00 .45
(Joey Cora)
☐ ST19 Cleveland Indians .. 5.00 2.20
(Kenny Lofton
Carlos Baerga
Albert Belle)
☐ ST20 Detroit Tigers .... 1.00 .45
(Alan Trammell
Tony Phillips)
☐ ST21 Kansas City Royals .. 1.00 .45
(Jose Lind
Curt Wilkerson)
☐ ST22 Milwaukee Brewers .... 1.00 .45
(Julio Navarro
John Jaha
Cal Eldred)
☐ ST23 Minnesota Twins 4.00 1.80
(Kirby Puckett
Kent Hrbek)
☐ ST24 New York Yankees 3.00 1.35
(Don Mattingly
Bernie Williams)
☐ ST25 Oakland Athletics .. 1.00 .45
(Mike Bordick
Brent Gates)
☐ ST26 Seattle Mariners .... 2.00 .90
(Jay Buhner
Mike Blowers)
☐ ST27 Texas Rangers 5.00 2.20
(Ivan Rodriguez
Dean Palmer
Jose Canseco
Juan Gonzalez)
☐ ST28 Toronto Blue Jays .. 1.00 .45
(John Olerud)

1995 Stadium Club

The 1995 Stadium Club base-ball card collection was issued in three series of 270, 225 and 135 standard-size cards for a total of 630. The cards were dis-tributed in 14-card packs at a suggested retail price of $2.50 and contained 24 packs per box. Cards feature players in full-bleed action photos with team logo and player's name in gold foil at the bottom of the

card. Backs feature statistical bar graphs and action photos of players. Notable Rookie Cards include Mark Grudzielanek, Bobby Higginson and Hideo Nomo.

	MINT	NRMT
COMPLETE SET (630)	60.00	27.00
COMPLETE SERIES 1 (270)	25.00	11.00
COMPLETE SERIES 2 (225)	20.00	9.00
COMPLETE SERIES 3 (135)	15.00	6.75
COMMON CARD (1-630)	.15	.07
MINOR STARS	.30	.14
UNLISTED STARS	.60	.25

SUBSET CARDS HALF VALUE OF BASE CARDS
COMP.1ST DAY SET (270) 275.00 125.00
COMMON 1ST DAY (1-270).. 1.00 .45
*1ST DAY STARS: 7.5X TO 15X HI COLUMN
*1ST DAY YOUNG STARS: 6X TO 12X HI
*1ST DAY DP STARS: 2X TO 4X HI
1ST DAY: RANDOM INS.IN TOPPS SER.2
1ST DAY DP'S ALSO IN TOPPS SER.1
TEN 1ST DAY PER TOPPS FACTORY SET
COMP.SUP.TM.SET (585) 100.00 45.00
COMP.SUP.TM.EC/TA SET (45) 15.00 6.75
*SUP.TM.STARS: 1X TO 2X HI COLUMN
*SUP.TM.YOUNG STARS: .75X TO 1.5X HI
ONE SET VIA MAIL PER 94 BRAVES SUP.TM
SER.3 EC/TA SUBSETS SHIPPED LATER
COMP.VI.REAL.SET (270) 100.00 45.00
COMP.VI.REAL.SER.1 (135) 50.00 22.00
COMP.VI.REAL.SER.2 (135) 50.00 22.00
*VIRT.REAL.STARS: 1X TO 2X HI COLUMN
*VIRT.REAL.YOUNG STARS: .75X TO 1.5X HI
ONE VIRTUAL REALITY CARD PER PACK

☐ 1 Cal Ripken 2.50 1.10
☐ 2 Bo Jackson .... .30 .14
☐ 3 Bryan Harvey .... .15 .07
☐ 4 Curt Schilling .... .30 .14
☐ 5 Bruce Ruffin .... .15 .07
☐ 6 Travis Fryman .... .30 .14
☐ 7 Jim Abbott .... .15 .07
☐ 8 David McCarty .... .15 .07
☐ 9 Gary Gaetti .... .15 .07
☐ 10 Roger Clemens .... 1.25 .55
☐ 11 Carlos Garcia .... .15 .07
☐ 12 Lee Smith .... .30 .14
☐ 13 Bobby Ayala .... .15 .07
☐ 14 Charles Nagy .... .30 .14
☐ 15 Lou Frazier .... .15 .07
☐ 16 Rene Arocha .... .15 .07
☐ 17 Carlos Delgado .... .30 .14
☐ 18 Steve Finley .... .30 .14
☐ 19 Ryan Klesko .... .40 .18
☐ 20 Cal Eldred .... .15 .07
☐ 21 Rey Sanchez .... .15 .07
☐ 22 Kevin Roth .... .15 .07
☐ 23 Benito Santiago ...... .15 .07
☐ 24 Julian Tavarez .... .15 .07
☐ 25 Jose Vizcaino .... .15 .07
☐ 26 Andy Benes .... .30 .14
☐ 27 Mariano Duncan .... .15 .07
☐ 28 Checklist A .... .15 .07
☐ 29 Shawon Dunston .... .15 .07
☐ 30 Rafael Palmeiro ...... .40 .18
☐ 31 Dean Palmer .... .15 .07
☐ 32 Andres Galarraga ..... .60 .25
☐ 33 Joey Cora .... .30 .14
☐ 34 Mickey Tettleton ..... .15 .07
☐ 35 Barry Larkin .... .40 .18
☐ 36 Carlos Baerga .... .15 .07
☐ 37 Orel Hershiser .... .30 .14
☐ 38 Jody Reed .... .15 .07
☐ 39 Paul Molitor .... .60 .25
☐ 40 Jim Edmonds .... .40 .18
☐ 41 Bob Tewksbury .... .15 .07
☐ 42 John Patterson .... .15 .07
☐ 43 Ray McDavid .... .15 .07
☐ 44 Zane Smith .... .15 .07
☐ 45 Bret Saberhagen SE ... .15 .07
☐ 46 Greg Maddux SE .... 1.00 .45
☐ 47 Frank Thomas SE ...... 1.25 .55
☐ 48 Carlos Baerga SE ..... .15 .07
☐ 49 Billy Spiers .... .15 .07
☐ 50 Stan Javier .... .15 .07
☐ 51 Rex Hudler .... .15 .07
☐ 52 Denny Hocking .... .15 .07
☐ 53 Todd Worrell .... .15 .07
☐ 54 Mark Clark .... .15 .07
☐ 55 Hipolito Pichardo .... .15 .07
☐ 56 Bob Wickman .... .15 .07
☐ 57 Raul Mondesi .... .40 .18
☐ 58 Steve Cooke .... .15 .07
☐ 59 Rod Beck .... .15 .07
☐ 60 Tim Davis .... .15 .07
☐ 61 Jeff Kent .... .15 .07
☐ 62 John Valentin .... .15 .07
☐ 63 Alex Arias .... .15 .07
☐ 64 Steve Reed .... .15 .07
☐ 65 Ozzie Smith .... .75 .35
☐ 66 Terry Pendleton ...... .15 .07
☐ 67 Kenny Rogers .... .15 .07
☐ 68 Vince Coleman .... .15 .07
☐ 69 Tom Pagnozzi .... .15 .07
☐ 70 Roberto Alomar .... .60 .25
☐ 71 Darrin Jackson .... .15 .07
☐ 72 Dennis Eckersley ..... .30 .14
☐ 73 Jay Buhner .... .40 .18
☐ 74 Darren Lewis .... .15 .07
☐ 75 Dave Weathers .... .15 .07
☐ 76 Matt Walbeck .... .15 .07
☐ 77 Brad Ausmus .... .15 .07
☐ 78 Danny Bautista .... .15 .07
☐ 79 Bob Hamelin .... .15 .07
☐ 80 Steve Trachsel .... .15 .07
☐ 81 Ken Ryan .... .15 .07
☐ 82 Chris Turner .... .15 .07
☐ 83 David Segui .... .15 .07
☐ 84 Ben McDonald .... .15 .07
☐ 85 Wade Boggs .... .60 .25
☐ 86 John VanderWal .... .15 .07
☐ 87 Sandy Alomar Jr ...... .30 .14
☐ 88 Ron Karkovice .... .15 .07
☐ 89 Doug Jones .... .15 .07
☐ 90 Gary Sheffield .... .60 .25
☐ 91 Ken Caminiti .... .40 .18
☐ 92 Chris Bosio .... .15 .07
☐ 93 Kevin Tapani .... .15 .07
☐ 94 Walt Weiss .... .15 .07
☐ 95 Erik Hanson .... .15 .07
☐ 96 Ruben Sierra .... .15 .07
☐ 97 Nomar Garciaparra 4.00 1.80
☐ 98 Terrence Long .... .40 .18
☐ 99 Jacob Shumate .... .30 .14
☐ 100 Paul Wilson .... .30 .14
☐ 101 Kevin Witt .... .75 .35
☐ 102 Paul Konerko 3.00 1.35
☐ 103 Ben Grieve 4.00 1.80
☐ 104 Mark Johnson .... .15 .07
☐ 105 Cade Gaspar .... .30 .14
☐ 106 Mark Farris .... .30 .14
☐ 107 Dustin Hermanson .... .30 .14
☐ 108 Scott Elarton .... .75 .35
☐ 109 Doug Million .... .15 .07
☐ 110 Matt Smith .... .15 .07
☐ 111 Brian Buchanan ...... .30 .14
☐ 112 Jayson Peterson ..... .30 .14
☐ 113 Bret Wagner .... .15 .07
☐ 114 C.J. Nitkowski ...... .15 .07
☐ 115 Ramon Castro .... .30 .14
☐ 116 Rafael Bournigal .... .15 .07
☐ 117 Jeff Fassero .... .15 .07

☐ 118	Bobby Bonilla	.30	.14
☐ 119	Ricky Gutierrez	.15	.07
☐ 120	Roger Pavlik	.15	.07
☐ 121	Mike Greenwell	.15	.07
☐ 122	Deion Sanders	.30	.14
☐ 123	Charlie Hayes	.15	.07
☐ 124	Paul O'Neill	.30	.14
☐ 125	Jay Bell	.30	.14
☐ 126	Royce Clayton	.15	.07
☐ 127	Willie Banks	.15	.07
☐ 128	Mark Wohlers	.15	.07
☐ 129	Todd Jones	.15	.07
☐ 130	Todd Stottlemyre	.15	.07
☐ 131	Will Clark	.40	.18
☐ 132	Wilson Alvarez	.15	.07
☐ 133	Chili Davis	.30	.14
☐ 134	Dave Burba	.15	.07
☐ 135	Chris Hoiles	.15	.07
☐ 136	Jeff Blauser	.30	.14
☐ 137	Jeff Reboulet	.15	.07
☐ 138	Bret Saberhagen	.15	.07
☐ 139	Kirk Rueter	.15	.07
☐ 140	Dave Nilsson	.15	.07
☐ 141	Pat Borders	.15	.07
☐ 142	Ron Darling	.15	.07
☐ 143	Derek Bell	.15	.07
☐ 144	Dave Hollins	.15	.07
☐ 145	Juan Gonzalez	1.50	.70
☐ 146	Andre Dawson	.40	.18
☐ 147	Jim Thome	.60	.25
☐ 148	Larry Walker	.60	.25
☐ 149	Mike Piazza	2.00	.90
☐ 150	Mike Perez	.15	.07
☐ 151	Steve Avery	.15	.07
☐ 152	Dan Wilson	.15	.07
☐ 153	Andy Van Slyke	.30	.14
☐ 154	Junior Felix	.15	.07
☐ 155	Jack McDowell	.15	.07
☐ 156	Danny Tartabull	.15	.07
☐ 157	Willie Blair	.15	.07
☐ 158	Wm.VanLandingham	.15	.07
☐ 159	Robb Nen	.15	.07
☐ 160	Lee Tinsley	.15	.07
☐ 161	Ismael Valdes	.40	.18
☐ 162	Juan Guzman	.30	.14
☐ 163	Scott Servais	.15	.07
☐ 164	Cliff Floyd	.15	.07
☐ 165	Allen Watson	.15	.07
☐ 166	Eddie Taubensee	.15	.07
☐ 167	Scott Hemond	.15	.07
☐ 168	Jeff Tackett	.15	.07
☐ 169	Chad Curtis	.15	.07
☐ 170	Rico Brogna	.15	.07
☐ 171	Luis Polonia	.15	.07
☐ 172	Checklist B	.15	.07
☐ 173	Lance Johnson	.15	.07
☐ 174	Sammy Sosa	.60	.25
☐ 175	Mike Macfarlane	.15	.07
☐ 176	Darryl Hamilton	.15	.07
☐ 177	Rick Aguilera	.15	.07
☐ 178	Dave West	.15	.07
☐ 179	Mike Gallego	.15	.07
☐ 180	Marc Newfield	.15	.07
☐ 181	Steve Buechele	.15	.07
☐ 182	David Wells	.15	.07
☐ 183	Tom Glavine	.30	.14
☐ 184	Joe Girardi	.15	.07
☐ 185	Craig Biggio	.40	.18
☐ 186	Eddie Murray	.60	.25
☐ 187	Kevin Gross	.15	.07
☐ 188	Sid Fernandez	.15	.07
☐ 189	John Franco	.30	.14
☐ 190	Bernard Gilkey	.15	.07
☐ 191	Matt Williams	.40	.18
☐ 192	Darrin Fletcher	.15	.07
☐ 193	Jeff Conine	.30	.14
☐ 194	Ed Sprague	.15	.07
☐ 195	Eduardo Perez	.15	.07
☐ 196	Scott Livingstone	.15	.07
☐ 197	Ivan Rodriguez	.75	.35
☐ 198	Orlando Merced	.15	.07
☐ 199	Ricky Bones	.15	.07
☐ 200	Javier Lopez	.30	.14
☐ 201	Miguel Jimenez	.15	.07
☐ 202	Terry McGriff	.15	.07
☐ 203	Mike Lieberthal	.15	.07
☐ 204	David Cone	.30	.14
☐ 205	Todd Hundley	.30	.14
☐ 206	Ozzie Guillen	.15	.07
☐ 207	Alex Cole	.15	.07
☐ 208	Tony Phillips	.15	.07
☐ 209	Jim Eisenreich	.15	.07
☐ 210	Greg Vaughn BES	.15	.07
☐ 211	Barry Larkin BES	.30	.14
☐ 212	Don Mattingly BES	.40	.18
☐ 213	Mark Grace BES	.30	.14
☐ 214	Jose Canseco BES	.30	.14
☐ 215	Joe Carter BES	.15	.07
☐ 216	David Cone BES	.15	.07
☐ 217	Sandy Alomar Jr. BES	.15	.07
☐ 218	Al Martin BES	.15	.07
☐ 219	Roberto Kelly BES	.15	.07
☐ 220	Paul Sorrento	.15	.07
☐ 221	Tony Fernandez	.15	.07
☐ 222	Stan Belinda	.15	.07
☐ 223	Mike Stanley	.15	.07
☐ 224	Doug Drabek	.15	.07
☐ 225	Todd Van Poppel	.15	.07
☐ 226	Matt Mieske	.15	.07
☐ 227	Tino Martinez	.60	.25
☐ 228	Andy Ashby	.15	.07
☐ 229	Midre Cummings	.15	.07
☐ 230	Jeff Frye	.15	.07
☐ 231	Hal Morris	.15	.07
☐ 232	Jose Lind	.15	.07
☐ 233	Shawn Green	.30	.14
☐ 234	Rafael Belliard	.15	.07
☐ 235	Randy Myers	.15	.07
☐ 236	Frank Thomas CE	1.25	.55
☐ 237	Darren Daulton CE	.15	.07
☐ 238	Sammy Sosa CE	.30	.14
☐ 239	Cal Ripken CE	1.25	.55
☐ 240	Jeff Bagwell CE	.60	.25
☐ 241	Ken Griffey Jr.	3.00	1.35
☐ 242	Brett Butler	.30	.14
☐ 243	Derrick May	.15	.07
☐ 244	Pat Listach	.15	.07
☐ 245	Mike Bordick	.15	.07
☐ 246	Mark Langston	.15	.07
☐ 247	Randy Velarde	.15	.07
☐ 248	Julio Franco	.15	.07
☐ 249	Chuck Knoblauch	.60	.25
☐ 250	Bill Gullickson	.15	.07
☐ 251	Dave Henderson	.15	.07
☐ 252	Bret Boone	.15	.07
☐ 253	Al Martin	.15	.07
☐ 254	Armando Benitez	.15	.07
☐ 255	Wil Cordero	.15	.07
☐ 256	Al Leiter	.15	.07
☐ 257	Luis Gonzalez	.15	.07
☐ 258	Charlie O'Brien	.15	.07
☐ 259	Tim Wallach	.15	.07
☐ 260	Scott Sanders	.15	.07
☐ 261	Tom Henke	.15	.07
☐ 262	Otis Nixon	.15	.07
☐ 263	Darren Daulton	.30	.14
☐ 264	Manny Ramirez	.60	.25
☐ 265	Bret Barberie	.15	.07
☐ 266	Mel Rojas	.15	.07
☐ 267	John Burkett	.15	.07
☐ 268	Brady Anderson	.40	.18
☐ 269	John Roper	.15	.07
☐ 270	Shane Reynolds	.15	.07
☐ 271	Barry Bonds	.75	.35
☐ 272	Alex Fernandez	.15	.07
☐ 273	Brian McRae	.15	.07
☐ 274	Todd Zeile	.15	.07
☐ 275	Greg Swindell	.15	.07
☐ 276	Johnny Ruffin	.15	.07
☐ 277	Troy Neel	.15	.07
☐ 278	Eric Karros	.30	.14
☐ 279	John Hudek	.15	.07
☐ 280	Thomas Howard	.15	.07
☐ 281	Joe Carter	.30	.14
☐ 282	Mike Devereaux	.15	.07
☐ 283	Butch Henry	.15	.07
☐ 284	Reggie Jefferson	.15	.07
☐ 285	Mark Lemke	.15	.07
☐ 286	Jeff Montgomery	.15	.07
☐ 287	Ryan Thompson	.15	.07
☐ 288	Paul Shuey	.15	.07
☐ 289	Mark McGwire	1.25	.55
☐ 290	Bernie Williams	.60	.25
☐ 291	Mickey Morandini	.15	.07
☐ 292	Scott Leius	.15	.07
☐ 293	David Hulse	.15	.07
☐ 294	Greg Gagne	.15	.07
☐ 295	Moises Alou	.30	.14
☐ 296	Geronimo Berroa	.15	.07
☐ 297	Eddie Zambrano	.15	.07
☐ 298	Alan Trammell	.40	.18
☐ 299	Don Slaught	.15	.07
☐ 300	Jose Rijo	.15	.07
☐ 301	Joe Ausanio	.15	.07
☐ 302	Tim Raines	.30	.14
☐ 303	Melido Perez	.15	.07
☐ 304	Kent Mercker	.15	.07
☐ 305	James Mouton	.15	.07
☐ 306	Luis Lopez	.15	.07
☐ 307	Mike Kingery	.15	.07
☐ 308	Willie Greene	.15	.07
☐ 309	Cecil Fielder	.30	.14
☐ 310	Scott Kamieniecki	.15	.07
☐ 311	Mike Greenwell BES	.15	.07
☐ 312	Bobby Bonilla BES	.15	.07
☐ 313	Andres Galarraga BES	.30	.14
☐ 314	Cal Ripken BES	1.25	.55
☐ 315	Matt Williams BES	.30	.14
☐ 316	Tom Pagnozzi BES	.15	.07
☐ 317	Len Dykstra BES	.15	.07
☐ 318	Frank Thomas BES	1.25	.55
☐ 319	Kirby Puckett BES	.60	.25
☐ 320	Mike Piazza BES	1.00	.45
☐ 321	Jason Jacome	.15	.07
☐ 322	Brian Hunter	.15	.07
☐ 323	Brent Gates	.15	.07
☐ 324	Jim Converse	.15	.07
☐ 325	Damion Easley	.15	.07
☐ 326	Dante Bichette	.30	.14
☐ 327	Kurt Abbott	.15	.07
☐ 328	Scott Cooper	.15	.07
☐ 329	Mike Henneman	.15	.07
☐ 330	Orlando Miller	.15	.07
☐ 331	John Kruk	.30	.14
☐ 332	Jose Oliva	.15	.07
☐ 333	Reggie Sanders	.15	.07
☐ 334	Omar Vizquel	.30	.14
☐ 335	Devon White	.15	.07
☐ 336	Mike Morgan	.15	.07
☐ 337	J.R. Phillips	.15	.07
☐ 338	Gary DiSarcina	.15	.07
☐ 339	Joey Hamilton	.30	.14
☐ 340	Randy Johnson	.60	.25
☐ 341	Jim Leyritz	.15	.07
☐ 342	Bobby Jones	.15	.07
☐ 343	Jaime Navarro	.15	.07
☐ 344	Bip Roberts	.15	.07
☐ 345	Steve Karsay	.15	.07
☐ 346	Kevin Stocker	.15	.07
☐ 347	Jose Canseco	.40	.18
☐ 348	Bill Wegman	.15	.07
☐ 349	Rondell White	.30	.14
☐ 350	Mo Vaughn	.75	.35
☐ 351	Joe Orsulak	.15	.07
☐ 352	Pat Meares	.15	.07
☐ 353	Albie Lopez	.15	.07
☐ 354	Edgar Martinez	.40	.18
☐ 355	Brian Jordan	.30	.14
☐ 356	Tommy Greene	.15	.07
☐ 357	Chuck Carr	.15	.07
☐ 358	Pedro Astacio	.15	.07
☐ 359	Russ Davis	.15	.07
☐ 360	Chris Hammond	.15	.07
☐ 361	Gregg Jefferies	.15	.07
☐ 362	Shane Mack	.15	.07
☐ 363	Fred McGriff	.40	.18
☐ 364	Pat Rapp	.15	.07
☐ 365	Bill Swift	.15	.07
☐ 366	Checklist	.15	.07
☐ 367	Robin Ventura	.30	.14
☐ 368	Bobby Witt	.15	.07
☐ 369	Karl Rhodes	.15	.07
☐ 370	Eddie Williams	.15	.07
☐ 371	John Jaha	.15	.07
☐ 372	Steve Howe	.15	.07
☐ 373	Leo Gomez	.15	.07
☐ 374	Hector Fajardo	.15	.07
☐ 375	Jeff Bagwell	1.25	.55

376	Mark Acre	.15	.07
377	Wayne Kirby	.15	.07
378	Mark Portugal	.15	.07
379	Jesus Tavarez	.15	.07
380	Jim Lindeman	.15	.07
381	Don Mattingly	1.00	.45
382	Trevor Hoffman	.15	.07
383	Chris Gomez	.15	.07
384	Garret Anderson	.40	.18
385	Bobby Munoz	.15	.07
386	Jon Lieber	.15	.07
387	Rick Helling	.15	.07
388	Marvin Freeman	.15	.07
389	Juan Castillo	.15	.07
390	Jeff Cirillo	.30	.14
391	Sean Berry	.15	.07
392	Hector Carrasco	.15	.07
393	Mark Grace	.40	.18
394	Pat Kelly	.15	.07
395	Tim Naehring	.15	.07
396	Greg Pirkl	.15	.07
397	John Smoltz	.30	.14
398	Robby Thompson	.15	.07
399	Rick White	.15	.07
400	Frank Thomas	2.50	1.10
401	Jeff Conine CS	.15	.07
402	Jose Valentin CS	.15	.07
403	Carlos Baerga CS	.15	.07
404	Rick Aguilera CS	.15	.07
405	Wilson Alvarez CS	.15	.07
406	Juan Gonzalez CS	.75	.35
407	Barry Larkin CS	.30	.14
408	Ken Hill CS	.15	.07
409	Chuck Carr CS	.15	.07
410	Tim Raines CS	.15	.07
411	Bryan Eversgerd	.15	.07
412	Phil Plantier	.15	.07
413	Josias Manzanillo	.15	.07
414	Roberto Kelly	.15	.07
415	Rickey Henderson	.40	.18
416	John Smiley	.15	.07
417	Kevin Brown	.30	.14
418	Jimmy Key	.30	.14
419	Wally Joyner	.30	.14
420	Roberto Hernandez	.15	.07
421	Felix Fermin	.15	.07
422	Checklist	.15	.07
423	Greg Vaughn	.15	.07
424	Ray Lankford	.30	.14
425	Greg Maddux	2.00	.90
426	Mike Mussina	.60	.25
427	Geronimo Pena	.15	.07
428	David Nied	.15	.07
429	Scott Erickson	.15	.07
430	Kevin Mitchell	.15	.07
431	Mike Lansing	.15	.07
432	Brian Anderson	.30	.14
433	Jeff King	.15	.07
434	Ramon Martinez	.30	.14
435	Kevin Seitzer	.15	.07
436	Salomon Torres	.15	.07
437	Brian L.Hunter	.40	.18
438	Melvin Nieves	.15	.07
439	Mike Kelly	.15	.07
440	Marquis Grissom	.30	.14
441	Chuck Finley	.15	.07
442	Len Dykstra	.30	.14
443	Ellis Burks	.15	.07
444	Harold Baines	.30	.14
445	Kevin Appier	.30	.14
446	David Justice	.60	.25
447	Darryl Kile	.30	.14
448	John Olerud	.30	.14
449	Greg McMichael	.15	.07
450	Kirby Puckett	1.25	.55
451	Jose Valentin	.15	.07
452	Rick Wilkins	.15	.07
453	Arthur Rhodes	.15	.07
454	Pat Hentgen	.30	.14
455	Tom Gordon	.15	.07
456	Tom Candiotti	.15	.07
457	Jason Bere	.15	.07
458	Wes Chamberlain	.15	.07
459	Greg Colbrunn	.15	.07
460	John Doherty	.15	.07
461	Kevin Foster	.15	.07
462	Mark Whiten	.15	.07
463	Terry Steinbach	.15	.07
464	Aaron Sele	.15	.07
465	Kirt Manwaring	.15	.07
466	Darren Hall	.15	.07
467	Delino DeShields	.15	.07
468	Andujar Cedeno	.15	.07
469	Billy Ashley	.15	.07
470	Kenny Lofton	.75	.35
471	Pedro Munoz	.15	.07
472	John Wetteland	.15	.07
473	Tim Salmon	.60	.25
474	Denny Neagle	.30	.14
475	Tony Gwynn	1.50	.70
476	Vinny Castilla	.30	.14
477	Steve Dreyer	.15	.07
478	Jeff Shaw	.15	.07
479	Chad Ogea	.15	.07
480	Scott Ruffcorn	.15	.07
481	Lou Whitaker	.30	.14
482	J.T. Snow	.30	.14
483	Rich Rowland	.15	.07
484	Denny Martinez	.30	.14
485	Pedro Martinez	.60	.25
486	Rusty Greer	.60	.25
487	Dave Fleming	.15	.07
488	John Dettmer	.15	.07
489	Albert Belle	.75	.35
490	Ravelo Manzanillo	.15	.07
491	Henry Rodriguez	.15	.07
492	Andrew Lorraine	.15	.07
493	Dwayne Hosey	.15	.07
494	Mike Blowers	.15	.07
495	Turner Ward	.15	.07
496	Fred McGriff EC	.30	.14
497	Sammy Sosa EC	.30	.14
498	Barry Larkin EC	.30	.14
499	Andres Galarraga EC	.30	.14
500	Gary Sheffield EC	.30	.14
501	Jeff Bagwell EC	.60	.25
502	Mike Piazza EC	1.00	.45
503	Moises Alou EC	.15	.07
504	Bobby Bonilla EC	.15	.07
505	Darren Daulton EC	.15	.07
506	Jeff King EC	.15	.07
507	Ray Lankford EC	.15	.07
508	Tony Gwynn EC	.75	.35
509	Barry Bonds EC	.40	.18
510	Cal Ripken EC	1.25	.55
511	Mo Vaughn EC	.40	.18
512	Tim Salmon EC	.30	.14
513	Frank Thomas EC	1.25	.55
514	Albert Belle EC	.60	.25
515	Cecil Fielder EC	.15	.07
516	Kevin Appier EC	.15	.07
517	Greg Vaughn EC	.15	.07
518	Kirby Puckett EC	.60	.25
519	Paul O'Neill EC	.15	.07
520	Ruben Sierra EC	.15	.07
521	Ken Griffey Jr. EC	1.50	.70
522	Will Clark EC	.30	.14
523	Joe Carter EC	.15	.07
524	Antonio Osuna	.15	.07
525	Glenallen Hill	.15	.07
526	Alex Gonzalez	.30	.14
527	Dave Stewart	.30	.14
528	Ron Gant	.30	.14
529	Jason Bates	.15	.07
530	Mike Macfarlane	.15	.07
531	Esteban Loaiza	.15	.07
532	Joe Randa	.15	.07
533	Dave Winfield	.40	.18
534	Danny Darwin	.15	.07
535	Pete Harnisch	.15	.07
536	Joey Cora	.30	.14
537	Jaime Navarro	.15	.07
538	Marty Cordova	.30	.14
539	Andujar Cedeno	.15	.07
540	Mickey Tettleton	.15	.07
541	Andy Van Slyke	.30	.14
542	Carlos Perez	.30	.14
543	Chipper Jones	2.00	.90
544	Tony Fernandez	.15	.07
545	Tom Henke	.15	.07
546	Pat Borders	.15	.07
547	Chad Curtis	.15	.07
548	Ray Durham	.30	.14
549	Joe Oliver	.15	.07
550	Jose Mesa	.15	.07
551	Steve Finley	.30	.14
552	Otis Nixon	.15	.07
553	Jacob Brumfield	.15	.07
554	Bill Swift	.15	.07
555	Quilvio Veras	.15	.07
556	Hideo Nomo UER Wins and IP totals reversed	3.00	1.35
557	Joe Vitiello	.15	.07
558	Mike Perez	.15	.07
559	Charlie Hayes	.15	.07
560	Brad Radke	.75	.35
561	Darren Bragg	.30	.14
562	Orel Hershiser	.30	.14
563	Edgardo Alfonzo	.60	.25
564	Doug Jones	.15	.07
565	Andy Pettitte	1.00	.45
566	Benito Santiago	.15	.07
567	John Burkett	.15	.07
568	Brad Clontz	.15	.07
569	Jim Abbott	.15	.07
570	Joe Rosselli	.15	.07
571	Mark Grudzielanek	.50	.23
572	Dustin Hermanson	.30	.14
573	Benji Gil	.15	.07
574	Mark Whiten	.15	.07
575	Mike Ignasiak	.15	.07
576	Kevin Ritz	.15	.07
577	Paul Quantrill	.15	.07
578	Andre Dawson	.40	.18
579	Jerald Clark	.15	.07
580	Frank Rodriguez	.15	.07
581	Mark Kiefer	.15	.07
582	Trevor Wilson	.15	.07
583	Gary Wilson	.15	.07
584	Andy Stankiewicz	.15	.07
585	Felipe Lira	.15	.07
586	Mike Mimbs	.15	.07
587	Jon Nunnally	.15	.07
588	Tomas Perez	.30	.14
589	Checklist	.15	.07
590	Todd Hollandsworth	.30	.14
591	Roberto Petagine	.15	.07
592	Mariano Rivera	.60	.25
593	Mark McLemore	.15	.07
594	Bobby Witt	.15	.07
595	Jose Offerman	.15	.07
596	Jason Christiansen	.15	.07
597	Jeff Manto	.15	.07
598	Jim Dougherty	.15	.07
599	Juan Acevedo	.15	.07
600	Troy O'Leary	.15	.07
601	Ron Villone	.15	.07
602	Tripp Cromer	.15	.07
603	Steve Scarsone	.15	.07
604	Lance Parrish	.15	.07
605	Ozzie Timmons	.15	.07
606	Ray Holbert	.15	.07
607	Tony Phillips	.15	.07
608	Phil Plantier	.15	.07
609	Shane Andrews	.15	.07
610	Heathcliff Slocumb	.15	.07
611	Bobby Higginson	1.00	.45
612	Bob Tewksbury	.15	.07
613	Terry Pendleton	.15	.07
614	Scott Cooper TA	.15	.07
615	John Wetteland TA	.15	.07
616	Ken Hill TA	.15	.07
617	Marquis Grissom TA	.15	.07
618	Larry Walker TA	.30	.14
619	Derek Bell TA	.15	.07
620	David Cone TA	.15	.07
621	Ken Caminiti TA	.30	.14
622	Jack McDowell TA	.15	.07
623	Vaughn Eshelman TA	.15	.07
624	Brian McRae TA	.15	.07
625	Gregg Jefferies TA	.15	.07
626	Kevin Brown TA	.15	.07
627	Lee Smith TA	.15	.07
628	Tony Tarasco TA	.15	.07
629	Brett Butler TA	.15	.07
630	Jose Canseco TA	.30	.14

1995 Stadium Club Clear Cut

Randomly inserted at a rate of one in 24 hobby and retail packs, this 28-card set features a full color action photo of the player against a clear acetate background with the player's name printed vertically. Backs highlight the season achievement of the player on a thin horizontal strip.

	MINT	NRMT
COMPLETE SET (28)	80.00	36.00
COMPLETE SERIES 1 (14)	40.00	18.00
COMPLETE SERIES 2 (14)	40.00	18.00
COMMON CARD (CC1-CC28)	1.50	.70
STATED ODDS 1:24 HOB/RET,1:10 RACK		

		MINT	NRMT
☐	CC1 Mike Piazza	15.00	6.75
☐	CC2 Ruben Sierra	1.50	.70
☐	CC3 Tony Gwynn	12.00	5.50
☐	CC4 Frank Thomas	20.00	9.00
☐	CC5 Fred McGriff	4.00	1.80
☐	CC6 Rafael Palmeiro	4.00	1.80
☐	CC7 Bobby Bonilla	2.50	1.10
☐	CC8 Chili Davis	2.50	1.10
☐	CC9 Hal Morris	1.50	.70
☐	CC10 Jose Canseco	4.00	1.80
☐	CC11 Jay Bell	2.50	1.10
☐	CC12 Kirby Puckett	10.00	4.50
☐	CC13 Gary Sheffield	5.00	2.20
☐	CC14 Bob Hamelin	1.50	.70
☐	CC15 Jeff Bagwell	10.00	4.50
☐	CC16 Albert Belle	6.00	2.70
☐	CC17 Sammy Sosa	5.00	2.20
☐	CC18 Ken Griffey Jr.	25.00	11.00
☐	CC19 Todd Zeile	1.50	.70
☐	CC20 Mo Vaughn	6.00	2.70
☐	CC21 Moises Alou	2.50	1.10
☐	CC22 Paul O'Neill	2.50	1.10
☐	CC23 Andres Galarraga	5.00	2.20
☐	CC24 Greg Vaughn	1.50	.70
☐	CC25 Len Dykstra	2.50	1.10
☐	CC26 Joe Carter	2.50	1.10
☐	CC27 Barry Bonds	6.00	2.70
☐	CC28 Cecil Fielder	2.50	1.10

1995 Stadium Club Crunch Time

This 20-card standard-size set features home run hitters and was randomly inserted in first series rack packs. Fronts are action illustrations of players on gold foil paper with the Crunch Time logo and player's name printed in gold foil at the bottom of the card. The horizontal backs include a pie chart and statistics of player offensive output and player action photos.

The cards are numbered as "X" of 20 in the upper right corner.

	MINT	NRMT
COMPLETE SET (20)	40.00	18.00
COMMON CARD (1-10)	.50	.23
ONE PER SER.1 RACK PACK		

		MINT	NRMT
☐	1 Jeff Bagwell	4.00	1.80
☐	2 Kirby Puckett	4.00	1.80
☐	3 Frank Thomas	8.00	3.60
☐	4 Albert Belle	2.50	1.10
☐	5 Julio Franco	.50	.23
☐	6 Jose Canseco	1.50	.70
☐	7 Paul Molitor	2.00	.90
☐	8 Joe Carter	1.00	.45
☐	9 Ken Griffey Jr.	10.00	4.50
☐	10 Larry Walker	2.00	.90
☐	11 Dante Bichette	1.00	.45
☐	12 Carlos Baerga	.50	.23
☐	13 Fred McGriff	1.50	.70
☐	14 Ruben Sierra	.50	.23
☐	15 Will Clark	1.50	.70
☐	16 Moises Alou	1.00	.45
☐	17 Rafael Palmeiro	1.50	.70
☐	18 Travis Fryman	1.00	.45
☐	19 Barry Bonds	2.50	1.10
☐	20 Cal Ripken	8.00	3.60

1995 Stadium Club Crystal Ball

This 15-card standard-size set was inserted into series three packs at a rate of one in 24. Fifteen leading 1995 rookies and prospects were featured in this set. The fronts feature a player photo in the middle with the words "Crystal Ball" on the top with the player's name on the bottom. The backs have season-by-season stats with a sentence about the player's accomplishments during that season. A player photo in the

upper right is set in a crystal ball. The player is identified on the top and the cards are numbered with a "CB" prefix in the upper left corner.

	MINT	NRMT
COMPLETE SET (15)	60.00	27.00
COMMON CARD (CB1-CB15)	2.00	.90
SEMISTARS	4.00	1.80
SER.3 STATED ODDS 1:24		

		MINT	NRMT
☐	CB1 Chipper Jones	25.00	11.00
☐	CB2 Dustin Hermanson	3.00	1.35
☐	CB3 Ray Durham	3.00	1.35
☐	CB4 Phil Nevin	2.00	.90
☐	CB5 Billy Ashley	2.00	.90
☐	CB6 Shawn Green	3.00	1.35
☐	CB7 Jason Bates	2.00	.90
☐	CB8 Benji Gil	2.00	.90
☐	CB9 Marty Cordova	3.00	1.35
☐	CB10 Quilvio Veras	2.00	.90
☐	CB11 Mark Grudzielanek	4.00	1.80
☐	CB12 Ruben Rivera	6.00	2.70
☐	CB13 Bill Pulsipher	2.00	.90
☐	CB14 Derek Jeter	25.00	11.00
☐	CB15 LaTroy Hawkins	2.00	.90

1995 Stadium Club Power Zone

This 12-card standard-size set was inserted into series three packs at a rate of one in 24. The fronts feature a player photo and his name on the right. The left side of the card has the bat powering through an explosion. The words "Power Zone" are on the bottom. The horizontal backs feature a close-up photo, some vital information as well as some seasonal highlights. The cards are numbered in the upper right corner with a "PZ" prefix. The set is sequenced in alphabetical order.

	MINT	NRMT
COMPLETE SET (12)	90.00	40.00
COMMON CARD (PZ1-PZ12)	3.00	1.35
SER.3 STATED ODDS 1:24		

		MINT	NRMT
☐	PZ1 Jeff Bagwell	12.00	5.50
☐	PZ2 Albert Belle	6.00	2.70
☐	PZ3 Barry Bonds	8.00	3.60
☐	PZ4 Joe Carter	3.00	1.35
☐	PZ5 Cecil Fielder	3.00	1.35
☐	PZ6 Andres Galarraga	6.00	2.70
☐	PZ7 Ken Griffey Jr.	30.00	13.50
☐	PZ8 Paul Molitor	6.00	2.70
☐	PZ9 Fred McGriff	4.00	1.80
☐	PZ10 Rafael Palmeiro	4.00	1.80
☐	PZ11 Frank Thomas	25.00	11.00
☐	PZ12 Matt Williams	4.00	1.80

1995 Stadium Club Ring Leaders

Randomly inserted in packs, this set features players who have won various awards or titles. This set was also redeemable as a prize with winning regular phone cards. This set features Stadium Club's *"Power Matrix Technology,"* which makes the cards shine and glow. The horizontal fronts feature a player photo, rings in both upper corners as well as other designs that make for a very busy front. The backs have information on how the player earned his rings, along with a player photo and some other pertinent information.

	MINT	NRMT
COMPLETE SET (40)	175.00	80.00
COMPLETE SERIES 1 (20)	65.00	29.00
COMPLETE SERIES 2 (20)	100.00	45.00
COMMON CARD (RL1-RL40)	2.00	.90
STATED ODDS 1:24 HOB/RET,1:10 RACK		
ONE SET VIA MAIL PER PHONE WINNER		

		MINT	NRMT
☐ RL1	Jeff Bagwell	12.00	5.50
☐ RL2	Mark McGwire	12.00	5.50
☐ RL3	Ozzie Smith	8.00	3.60
☐ RL4	Paul Molitor	6.00	2.70
☐ RL5	Darryl Strawberry	3.00	1.35
☐ RL6	Eddie Murray	6.00	2.70
☐ RL7	Tony Gwynn	15.00	6.75
☐ RL8	Jose Canseco	4.00	1.80
☐ RL9	Howard Johnson	2.00	.90
☐ RL10	Andre Dawson	4.00	1.80
☐ RL11	Matt Williams	4.00	1.80
☐ RL12	Tim Raines	3.00	1.35
☐ RL13	Fred McGriff	4.00	1.80
☐ RL14	Ken Griffey Jr.	30.00	13.50
☐ RL15	Gary Sheffield	6.00	2.70
☐ RL16	Dennis Eckersley	3.00	1.35
☐ RL17	Kevin Mitchell	2.00	.90
☐ RL18	Will Clark	4.00	1.80
☐ RL19	Darren Daulton	3.00	4.35
☐ RL20	Paul O'Neill	3.00	1.35
☐ RL21	Julio Franco	2.00	.90
☐ RL22	Albert Belle	8.00	3.60
☐ RL23	Juan Gonzalez	15.00	6.75
☐ RL24	Kirby Puckett	12.00	5.50
☐ RL25	Joe Carter	3.00	1.35
☐ RL26	Frank Thomas	25.00	11.00
☐ RL27	Cal Ripken	25.00	11.00
☐ RL28	John Olerud	3.00	1.35
☐ RL29	Ruben Sierra	2.00	.90
☐ RL30	Barry Bonds	6.00	2.70
☐ RL31	Cecil Fielder	3.00	1.35
☐ RL32	Roger Clemens	12.00	5.50
☐ RL33	Don Mattingly	12.00	5.50
☐ RL34	Terry Pendleton	2.00	.90
☐ RL35	Rickey Henderson	4.00	1.80
☐ RL36	Dave Winfield	4.00	1.80
☐ RL37	Edgar Martinez	4.00	1.80
☐ RL38	Wade Boggs	6.00	2.70
☐ RL39	Willie McGee	2.00	.90
☐ RL40	Andres Galarraga	6.00	2.70

1995 Stadium Club Super Skills

This 20-card set was randomly inserted into hobby packs. The full-bleed front features a player photo against a multi-colored background. The background was enhanced using Stadium Club's *"Power Matrix"* Technology. The "Super Skills" logo is in the lower left corner. The backs have a full-bleed photo with a description of the player's special skill. The cards are numbered in the upper left as "X" of 9.

		MINT	NRMT
COMPLETE SET (20)		70.00	32.00
COMPLETE SERIES 1 (9)		30.00	13.50
COMPLETE SERIES 2 (11)		40.00	18.00
COMMON CARD (SS1-SS20)		1.50	.70
STATED ODDS 1:24 HOBBY			

		MINT	NRMT
☐ SS1	Roberto Alomar	5.00	2.20
☐ SS2	Barry Bonds	6.00	2.70
☐ SS3	Jay Buhner	4.00	1.80
☐ SS4	Chuck Carr	1.50	.70
☐ SS5	Don Mattingly	8.00	3.60
☐ SS6	Raul Mondesi	4.00	1.80
☐ SS7	Tim Salmon	5.00	2.20
☐ SS8	Deion Sanders	2.50	1.10
☐ SS9	Devon White	1.50	.70
☐ SS10	Mark Whiten	1.50	.70
☐ SS11	Ken Griffey Jr.	25.00	11.00
☐ SS12	Marquis Grissom	2.50	1.10
☐ SS13	Paul O'Neill	2.50	1.10
☐ SS14	Kenny Lofton	6.00	2.70
☐ SS15	Larry Walker	5.00	2.20
☐ SS16	Scott Cooper	1.50	.70
☐ SS17	Barry Larkin	4.00	1.80
☐ SS18	Matt Williams	4.00	1.80
☐ SS19	John Wetteland	1.50	.70
☐ SS20	Randy Johnson	5.00	2.20

1995 Stadium Club Virtual Extremists

This 10-card set was inserted randomly into second series rack packs. The fronts feature a player photo against a baseball backdrop. The words *"VR Extremist"* are spelled vertically down the right side while the player name is in silver foil on the bottom. All of this is surrounded by blue and purple borders. The horizontal backs feature projected full-season 1994

stats. The cards are numbered with a "VRE" prefix in the upper right corner.

		MINT	NRMT
COMPLETE SET (10)		120.00	55.00
COMMON CARD (VRE1-VRE10)		2.50	1.10
SEMISTARS		5.00	2.20
SER.2 STATED ODDS 1:10 RACK			

		MINT	NRMT
☐ VRE1	Barry Bonds	10.00	4.50
☐ VRE2	Ken Griffey Jr.	40.00	18.00
☐ VRE3	Jeff Bagwell	15.00	6.75
☐ VRE4	Albert Belle	10.00	4.50
☐ VRE5	Frank Thomas	30.00	13.50
☐ VRE6	Tony Gwynn	20.00	9.00
☐ VRE7	Kenny Lofton	10.00	4.50
☐ VRE8	Deion Sanders	4.00	1.80
☐ VRE9	Ken Hill	2.50	1.10
☐ VRE10	Jimmy Key	4.00	1.80

1996 Stadium Club

The 1996 Stadium Club set consists of 450 cards. The product was primarily distributed in first and second series foil-wrapped packs. There was also a factory set, which included the Mantle insert cards, packaged in cereal box type cartons and made available through retail outlets. Card fronts feature glossy, full-bleed color action photos. At the bottom, the player's name is gold foil stamped on a team color-coded nameplate that is highlighted by gold foil stamping. The colorful backs carry biography, highlights, and the TSC Skills Matrix. The set includes a Team TSC subset (181-270). These subset cards were slightly shortprinted in comparison to the other cards in the set.

	MINT	NRMT
COMPLETE SET (450)	80.00	36.00
COMP.CEREAL SET (454)	80.00	36.00

COMPLETE SERIES 1 (225)	40.00	18.00
COMPLETE SERIES 2 (225)	40.00	18.00
COMMON (1-180/271-450)	.15	.07
MINOR STARS	.30	.14
UNLISTED STARS	.60	.25
COMMON TSC SP (181-270)	.25	.11
TSC SP MINOR STARS	.40	.18
TSC SP SEMISTARS	.50	.23
TSC SP UNLISTED STARS	.75	.35
COMP.MANTLE SET (19)	170.00	75.00
COMP.MANTLE SER.1 (9)	110.00	50.00
COMP.MANTLE SER.2 (10)	60.00	27.00
COMMON MANTLE (1-9)	15.00	6.75
COMMON MANTLE (10-19)	8.00	3.60
MANTLE SER.1 STATED ODDS 1:24		
MANTLE SER.2 STATED ODDS 1:12		

1	Hideo Nomo	1.50	.70
2	Paul Molitor	.60	.25
3	Garret Anderson	.30	.14
4	Jose Mesa	.15	.07
5	Vinny Castilla	.30	.14
6	Mike Mussina	.60	.25
7	Ray Durham	.15	.07
8	Jack McDowell	.15	.07
9	Juan Gonzalez	1.50	.70
10	Chipper Jones	2.00	.90
11	Deion Sanders	.30	.14
12	Rondell White	.30	.14
13	Tom Henke	.15	.07
14	Derek Bell	.15	.07
15	Randy Myers	.15	.07
16	Randy Johnson	.60	.25
17	Len Dykstra	.30	.14
18	Bill Pulsipher	.15	.07
19	Greg Colbrunn	.15	.07
20	David Wells	.15	.07
21	Chad Curtis	.15	.07
22	Roberto Hernandez	.15	.07
23	Kirby Puckett	1.25	.55
24	Joe Vitiello	.15	.07
25	Roger Clemens	1.25	.55
26	Al Martin	.15	.07
27	Chad Ogea	.15	.07
28	David Segui	.15	.07
29	Joey Hamilton	.30	.14
30	Dan Wilson	.15	.07
31	Chad Fonville	.15	.07
32	Bernard Gilkey	.15	.07
33	Kevin Seitzer	.15	.07
34	Shawn Green	.15	.07
35	Rick Aguilera	.15	.07
36	Gary DiSarcina	.15	.07
37	Jaime Navarro	.15	.07
38	Doug Jones	.15	.07
39	Brent Gates	.15	.07
40	Dean Palmer	.15	.07
41	Pat Rapp	.15	.07
42	Tony Clark	.60	.25
43	Bill Swift	.15	.07
44	Randy Velarde	.15	.07
45	Matt Williams	.40	.18
46	John Mabry	.15	.07
47	Mike Fetters	.15	.07
48	Orlando Miller	.15	.07
49	Tom Glavine	.30	.14
50	Delino DeShields	.15	.07
51	Scott Erickson	.15	.07
52	Andy Van Slyke	.30	.14
53	Jim Bullinger	.15	.07
54	Lyle Mouton	.15	.07
55	Bret Saberhagen	.15	.07
56	Benito Santiago	.15	.07
57	Dan Miceli	.15	.07
58	Carl Everett	.15	.07
59	Rod Beck	.15	.07
60	Phil Nevin	.15	.07
61	Jason Giambi	.30	.14
62	Paul Menhart	.15	.07
63	Eric Karros	.30	.14
64	Allen Watson	.15	.07
65	Jeff Cirillo	.30	.14
66	Lee Smith	.30	.14
67	Sean Berry	.15	.07
68	Luis Sojo	.15	.07
69	Jeff Montgomery	.15	.07
70	Todd Hundley	.30	.14
71	John Burkett	.15	.07
72	Mark Gubicza	.15	.07
73	Don Mattingly	1.00	.45
74	Jeff Brantley	.15	.07
75	Matt Walbeck	.15	.07
76	Steve Parris	.15	.07
77	Ken Caminiti	.40	.18
78	Kirt Manwaring	.15	.07
79	Greg Vaughn	.15	.07
80	Pedro Martinez	.60	.25
81	Benji Gil	.15	.07
82	Heathcliff Slocumb	.15	.07
83	Joe Girardi	.15	.07
84	Sean Bergman	.15	.07
85	Matt Karchner	.15	.07
86	Butch Huskey	.30	.14
87	Mike Morgan	.15	.07
88	Todd Worrell	.15	.07
89	Mike Bordick	.15	.07
90	Bip Roberts	.15	.07
91	Mike Hampton	.15	.07
92	Troy O'Leary	.15	.07
93	Wally Joyner	.30	.14
94	Dave Stevens	.15	.07
95	Cecil Fielder	.30	.14
96	Wade Boggs	.60	.25
97	Hal Morris	.15	.07
98	Mickey Tettleton	.15	.07
99	Jeff Kent	.15	.07
100	Denny Martinez	.30	.14
101	Luis Gonzalez	.15	.07
102	John Jaha	.15	.07
103	Javier Lopez	.30	.14
104	Mark McGwire	1.25	.55
105	Ken Griffey Jr.	3.00	1.35
106	Darren Daulton	.30	.14
107	Bryan Rekar	.15	.07
108	Mike Macfarlane	.15	.07
109	Gary Gaetti	.15	.07
110	Shane Reynolds	.15	.07
111	Pat Meares	.15	.07
112	Jason Schmidt	.30	.14
113	Otis Nixon	.15	.07
114	John Franco	.30	.14
115	Marc Newfield	.15	.07
116	Andy Benes	.30	.14
117	Ozzie Guillen	.15	.07
118	Brian Jordan	.30	.14
119	Terry Pendleton	.15	.07
120	Chuck Finley	.15	.07
121	Scott Stahoviak	.15	.07
122	Sid Fernandez	.15	.07
123	Derek Jeter	2.00	.90
124	John Smiley	.15	.07
125	David Bell	.15	.07
126	Brett Butler	.30	.14
127	Doug Drabek	.15	.07
128	J.T. Snow	.30	.14
129	Joe Carter	.30	.14
130	Dennis Eckersley	.30	.14
131	Marty Cordova	.30	.14
132	Greg Maddux	2.00	.90
133	Tom Goodwin	.15	.07
134	Andy Ashby	.15	.07
135	Paul Sorrento	.15	.07
136	Ricky Bones	.15	.07
137	Shawon Dunston	.15	.07
138	Moises Alou	.30	.14
139	Mickey Morandini	.15	.07
140	Ramon Martinez	.30	.14
141	Royce Clayton	.15	.07
142	Brad Ausmus	.15	.07
143	Kenny Rogers	.15	.07
144	Tim Naehring	.15	.07
145	Chris Gomez	.15	.07
146	Bobby Bonilla	.30	.14
147	Wilson Alvarez	.15	.07
148	Johnny Damon	.30	.14
149	Pat Hentgen	.30	.14
150	Andres Galarraga	.60	.25
151	David Cone	.30	.14
152	Lance Johnson	.15	.07
153	Carlos Garcia	.15	.07
154	Doug Johns	.15	.07
155	Midre Cummings	.15	.07
156	Steve Sparks	.15	.07
157	Sandy Martinez	.15	.07
158	Wm. Van Landingham	.15	.07
159	David Justice	.60	.25
160	Mark Grace	.40	.18
161	Robb Nen	.15	.07
162	Mike Greenwell	.15	.07
163	Brad Radke	.30	.14
164	Edgardo Alfonzo	.40	.18
165	Mark Lemke	.15	.07
166	Walt Weiss	.15	.07
167	Mel Rojas	.15	.07
168	Bret Boone	.15	.07
169	Ricky Bottalico	.15	.07
170	Bobby Higginson	.30	.14
171	Trevor Hoffman	.15	.07
172	Jay Bell	.30	.14
173	Gabe White	.15	.07
174	Curtis Goodwin	.15	.07
175	Tyler Green	.15	.07
176	Roberto Alomar	.60	.25
177	Sterling Hitchcock	.15	.07
178	Ryan Klesko	.40	.18
179	Donne Wall	.15	.07
180	Brian McRae	.15	.07
181	Will Clark TSC SP	.40	.18
182	Frank Thomas TSC SP	3.00	1.35
183	Jeff Bagwell TSC SP	1.50	.70
184	Mo Vaughn TSC SP	1.00	.45
185	Tino Martinez TSC SP	.75	.35
186	Craig Biggio TSC SP	.50	.23
187	Chuck Knoblauch TSC SP	.75	.35
188	Carlos Baerga TSC SP	.25	.11
189	Quilvio Veras TSC SP	.25	.11
190	Luis Alicea TSC SP	.25	.11
191	Jim Thome TSC SP	.75	.35
192	Mike Blowers TSC SP	.25	.11
193	Robin Ventura TSC SP	.40	.18
194	Jeff King TSC SP	.25	.11
195	Tony Phillips TSC SP	.25	.11
196	John Valentin TSC SP	.25	.11
197	Barry Larkin TSC SP	.50	.23
198	Cal Ripken TSC SP	3.00	1.35
199	Omar Vizquel TSC SP	.40	.18
200	Kurt Abbott TSC SP	.25	.11
201	Albert Belle TSC SP	1.00	.45
202	Barry Bonds TSC SP	1.00	.45
203	Ron Gant TSC SP	.40	.18
204	Dante Bichette TSC SP	.40	.18
205	Jeff Conine TSC SP	.40	.18
206	Jim Edmonds TSC SP UER	.50	.23
	Greg Myers pictured on front		
207	Stan Javier TSC SP	.25	.11
208	Kenny Lofton TSC SP	1.00	.45
209	Ray Lankford TSC SP	.40	.18
210	Bernie Williams TSC SP	.75	.35
211	Jay Buhner TSC SP	.40	.18
212	Paul O'Neill TSC SP	.40	.18
213	Tim Salmon TSC SP	.75	.35
214	Reggie Sanders TSC SP	.25	.11
215	Manny Ramirez TSC SP	.75	.35
216	Mike Piazza TSC SP	2.50	1.10
217	Mike Stanley TSC SP	.25	.11
218	Tony Eusebio TSC SP	.25	.11
219	Chris Hoiles TSC SP	.25	.11
220	Ron Karkovice TSC SP	.25	.11
221	Edgar Martinez TSC SP	.50	.23
222	Chili Davis TSC SP	.40	.18
223	Jose Canseco TSC SP	.50	.23
224	Eddie Murray TSC SP	.75	.35
225	Geronimo Berroa TSC SP	.25	.11
226	Chipper Jones TSC SP	2.50	1.10
227	Garret Anderson TSC SP	.40	.18
228	Marty Cordova TSC SP	.40	.18
229	Jon Nunnally TSC SP	.25	.11
230	Brian L.Hunter TSC SP	.40	.18
231	Shawn Green TSC SP	.25	.11
232	Ray Durham TSC SP	.25	.11
233	Alex Gonzalez TSC SP	.25	.11
234	Bobby Higginson TSC SP	.40	.18
235	Randy Johnson TSC SP	.75	.35
236	Al Leiter TSC SP	.25	.11
237	Tom Glavine TSC SP	.40	.18
238	Kenny Rogers TSC SP	.25	.11
239	Mike Hampton TSC SP	.25	.11
240	David Wells TSC SP	.25	.11

□ 241 Jim Abbott TSC SP	.25	.11
□ 242 Denny Neagle TSC SP	.40	.18
□ 243 Wilson Alvarez TSC SP	.25	.11
□ 244 John Smiley TSC SP	.25	.11
□ 245 Greg Maddux TSC SP	2.50	1.10
□ 246 Andy Ashby TSC SP	.25	.11
□ 247 Hideo Nomo TSC SP	2.00	.90
□ 248 Pat Rapp TSC SP	.25	.11
□ 249 Tim Wakefield TSC SP	.40	.18
□ 250 John Smoltz TSC SP	.40	.18
□ 251 Joey Hamilton TSC SP	.40	.18
□ 252 Frank Castillo TSC SP	.25	.11
□ 253 Denny Martinez TSC SP	.40	.18
□ 254 Jaime Navarro TSC SP	.25	.11
□ 255 Karim Garcia TSC SP	.50	.23
□ 256 Bob Abreu TSC SP	.50	.23
□ 257 Butch Huskey TSC SP	.40	.18
□ 258 Ruben Rivera TSC SP	.40	.18
□ 259 Johnny Damon TSC SP	.40	.18
□ 260 Derek Jeter TSC SP	2.50	1.10
□ 261 Dennis Eckersley TSC SP	.40	.18
□ 262 Jose Mesa TSC SP	.25	.11
□ 263 Tom Henke TSC SP	.25	.11
□ 264 Rick Aguilera TSC SP	.25	.11
□ 265 Randy Myers TSC SP	.25	.11
□ 266 John Franco TSC SP	.40	.18
□ 267 Jeff Brantley TSC SP	.25	.11
□ 268 John Wetteland TSC SP	.25	.11
□ 269 Mark Wohlers TSC SP	.25	.11
□ 270 Rod Beck TSC SP	.25	.11
□ 271 Barry Larkin	.40	.18
□ 272 Paul O'Neil	.30	.14
□ 273 Bobby Jones	.15	.07
□ 274 Will Clark	.40	.18
□ 275 Steve Avery	.15	.07
□ 276 Jim Edmonds	.40	.18
□ 277 John Olerud	.30	.14
□ 278 Carlos Perez	.15	.07
□ 279 Chris Hoiles	.15	.07
□ 280 Jeff Conine	.30	.14
□ 281 Jim Eisenreich	.15	.07
□ 282 Jason Jacome	.15	.07
□ 283 Ray Lankford	.30	.14
□ 284 John Wasdin	.15	.07
□ 285 Frank Thomas	2.50	1.10
□ 286 Jason Isringhausen	.15	.07
□ 287 Glenallen Hill	.15	.07
□ 288 Esteban Loaiza	.15	.07
□ 289 Bernie Williams	.60	.25
□ 290 Curtis Leskanic	.15	.07
□ 291 Scott Cooper	.15	.07
□ 292 Curt Schilling	.30	.14
□ 293 Eddie Murray	.60	.25
□ 294 Rick Krivda	.15	.07
□ 295 Domingo Cedeno	.15	.07
□ 296 Jeff Fassero	.15	.07
□ 297 Albert Belle	.75	.35
□ 298 Craig Biggio	.40	.18
□ 299 Fernando Vina	.15	.07
□ 300 Edgar Martinez	.40	.18
□ 301 Tony Gwynn	1.50	.70
□ 302 Felipe Lira	.15	.07
□ 303 Mo Vaughn	.75	.35
□ 304 Alex Fernandez	.15	.07
□ 305 Keith Lockhart	.15	.07
□ 306 Roger Pavlik	.15	.07
□ 307 Lee Tinsley	.15	.07
□ 308 Omar Vizquel	.30	.14
□ 309 Scott Servais	.15	.07
□ 310 Danny Tartabull	.15	.07
□ 311 Chili Davis	.30	.14
□ 312 Cal Eldred	.15	.07
□ 313 Roger Cedeno	.15	.07
□ 314 Chris Hammond	.15	.07
□ 315 Rusty Greer	.30	.14
□ 316 Brady Anderson	.40	.18
□ 317 Ron Villone	.15	.07
□ 318 Mark Carreon	.15	.07
□ 319 Larry Walker	.60	.25
□ 320 Pete Harnisch	.15	.07
□ 321 Robin Ventura	.30	.14
□ 322 Tim Belcher	.15	.07
□ 323 Tony Tarasco	.15	.07
□ 324 Juan Guzman	.15	.07
□ 325 Kenny Lofton	.75	.35
□ 326 Kevin Foster	.15	.07

□ 327 Wil Cordero	.15	.07
□ 328 Troy Percival	.15	.07
□ 329 Turk Wendell	.15	.07
□ 330 Thomas Howard	.15	.07
□ 331 Carlos Baerga	.15	.07
□ 332 B.J. Surhoff	.15	.07
□ 333 Jay Buhner	.40	.18
□ 334 Anduiar Cedeno	.15	.07
□ 335 Jeff King	.15	.07
□ 336 Dante Bichette	.30	.14
□ 337 Alan Trammell	.40	.18
□ 338 Scott Leius	.15	.07
□ 339 Chris Snopek	.15	.07
□ 340 Roger Bailey	.15	.07
□ 341 Jacob Brumfield	.15	.07
□ 342 Jose Canseco	.40	.18
□ 343 Rafael Palmeiro	.40	.18
□ 344 Quilvio Veras	.15	.07
□ 345 Darrin Fletcher	.15	.07
□ 346 Carlos Delgado	.30	.14
□ 347 Tony Eusebio	.15	.07
□ 348 Ismael Valdes	.30	.14
□ 349 Terry Steinbach	.15	.07
□ 350 Orel Hershiser	.30	.14
□ 351 Kurt Abbott	.15	.07
□ 352 Jody Reed	.15	.07
□ 353 David Howard	.15	.07
□ 354 Ruben Sierra	.15	.07
□ 355 John Ericks	.15	.07
□ 356 Buck Showalter MG	.15	.07
□ 357 Jim Thome	.60	.25
□ 358 Geronimo Berroa	.15	.07
□ 359 Robby Thompson	.15	.07
□ 360 Jose Vizcaino	.15	.07
□ 361 Jeff Frye	.15	.07
□ 362 Kevin Appier	.30	.14
□ 363 Pat Kelly	.15	.07
□ 364 Ron Gant	.30	.14
□ 365 Luis Alicea	.15	.07
□ 366 Armando Benitez	.15	.07
□ 367 Rico Brogna	.15	.07
□ 368 Manny Ramirez	.60	.25
□ 369 Mike Lansing	.15	.07
□ 370 Sammy Sosa	.60	.25
□ 371 Don Wengert	.15	.07
□ 372 Dave Nilsson	.15	.07
□ 373 Sandy Alomar	.30	.14
□ 374 Joey Cora	.15	.07
□ 375 Larry Thomas	.15	.07
□ 376 John Valentin	.15	.07
□ 377 Kevin Ritz	.15	.07
□ 378 Steve Finley	.30	.14
□ 379 Frank Rodriguez	.15	.07
□ 380 Ivan Rodriguez	.75	.35
□ 381 Alex Ochoa	.15	.07
□ 382 Mark Lemke	.15	.07
□ 383 Scott Brosius	.15	.07
□ 384 James Mouton	.15	.07
□ 385 Mark Langston	.15	.07
□ 386 Ed Sprague	.15	.07
□ 387 Joe Oliver	.15	.07
□ 388 Steve Ontiveros	.15	.07
□ 389 Rey Sanchez	.15	.07
□ 390 Mike Henneman	.15	.07
□ 391 Jose Valentin	.15	.07
□ 392 Tom Candiotti	.15	.07
□ 393 Damon Buford	.15	.07
□ 394 Erik Hanson	.15	.07
□ 395 Mark Smith	.15	.07
□ 396 Pete Schourek	.15	.07
□ 397 John Flaherty	.15	.07
□ 398 Dave Martinez	.15	.07
□ 399 Tommy Greene	.15	.07
□ 400 Gary Sheffield	.60	.25
□ 401 Glenn Dishman	.15	.07
□ 402 Barry Bonds	.75	.35
□ 403 Tom Pagnozzi	.15	.07
□ 404 Todd Stottlemyre	.15	.07
□ 405 Tim Salmon	.60	.25
□ 406 John Hudek	.15	.07
□ 407 Fred McGriff	.40	.18
□ 408 Orlando Merced	.15	.07
□ 409 Brian Barber	.15	.07
□ 410 Ryan Thompson	.15	.07
□ 411 Mariano Rivera	.40	.18
□ 412 Eric Young	.15	.07

□ 413 Chris Bosio	.15	.07
□ 414 Chuck Knoblauch	.60	.25
□ 415 Jamie Moyer	.15	.07
□ 416 Chan Ho Park	.60	.25
□ 417 Mark Portugal	.15	.07
□ 418 Tim Raines	.30	.14
□ 419 Antonio Osuna	.15	.07
□ 420 Todd Zeile	.15	.07
□ 421 Steve Wojciechowski	.15	.07
□ 422 Marquis Grissom	.30	.14
□ 423 Norm Charlton	.15	.07
□ 424 Cal Ripken	2.50	1.10
□ 425 Gregg Jefferies	.15	.07
□ 426 Mike Stanton	.15	.07
□ 427 Tony Fernandez	.15	.07
□ 428 Jose Rijo	.15	.07
□ 429 Jeff Bagwell	1.25	.55
□ 430 Raul Mondesi	.40	.18
□ 431 Travis Fryman	.30	.14
□ 432 Ron Karkovice	.15	.07
□ 433 Alan Benes	.30	.14
□ 434 Tony Phillips	.15	.07
□ 435 Reggie Sanders	.15	.07
□ 436 Andy Pettitte	.75	.35
□ 437 Matt Lawton	.40	.18
□ 438 Jeff Blauser	.15	.07
□ 439 Michael Tucker	.30	.14
□ 440 Mark Loretta	.15	.07
□ 441 Charlie Hayes	.15	.07
□ 442 Mike Piazza	2.00	.90
□ 443 Shane Andrews	.15	.07
□ 444 Jeff Suppan	.30	.14
□ 445 Steve Rodriguez	.15	.07
□ 446 Mike Matheny	.15	.07
□ 447 Trenidad Hubbard	.15	.07
□ 448 Denny Hocking	.15	.07
□ 449 Mark Grudzielanek	.30	.14
□ 450 Joe Randa	.15	.07

1996 Stadium Club Bash and Burn

Randomly inserted in packs at a rate of one in 29 (retail) and one in 48 (hobby), this ten card set features power/speed players. The fronts carry photos of the players hitting with a baseball background. The backs display photos of the same players running down the baseline on a background of flames.

	MINT	NRMT
COMPLETE SET (10)	30.00	13.50
COMMON CARD (BB1-BB10)	2.00	.90
SEMISTARS	4.00	1.80
UNLISTED STARS	8.00	3.60
SER.2 STATED ODDS 1:48 HOB, 1:24 RET		

□ BB1 Sammy Sosa	8.00	3.60
□ BB2 Barry Bonds	12.00	5.50
□ BB3 Reggie Sanders	2.00	.90
□ BB4 Craig Biggio	4.00	1.80
□ BB5 Raul Mondesi	4.00	1.80

☐ BB6	Ron Gant	3.00	1.35
☐ BB7	Ray Lankford	3.00	1.35
☐ BB8	Glenallen Hill	2.00	.90
☐ BB9	Chad Curtis	2.00	.90
☐ BB10	John Valentin	2.00	.90

1996 Stadium Club Extreme Players Bronze

One hundred and seventy nine different players were featured on Extreme Player game cards randomly issued in 1996 Stadium Club first and second series packs. Each player has three versions: Bronze, Silver and Gold. All of these cards parallel their corresponding regular issue card except for the Bronze foil "Extreme Players" logo on each card front and the "EP" suffix on the card number, thus creating a skip-numbered set. The Bronze cards listed below were seeded at a rate of 1:12 packs. At the conclusion of the 1996 regular season, an Extreme Player from each of ten positions was identified as a winner based on scores calculated from their actual playing statistics. The 10 winning players are noted with a "W" below. Prior to the December 31, 1996 deadline, each of the ten winning Extreme Players Bronze cards was redeemable for a 10-card set of Extreme Winners Bronze.

	MINT	NRMT
COMP.BRONZE SET (179)	250.00	110.00
COMP.BRONZE SER.1 (90)	125.00	55.00
COMP.BRONZE SER.2 (89)	125.00	55.00
COMMON BRONZE	.75	.35
BRONZE STATED ODDS 1:12	1.50	.70
*SILVER SINGLES: 6X TO 1.5X BASIC BRONZE		
*SILVER WIN: .75X TO 1.5X BRONZE WIN		
SILVER STATED ODDS 1:24		
*GOLD SINGLES: 1.2X TO 3X BASIC BRONZE		
*GOLD WIN: 1.5X TO 3X BRONZE WIN		
GOLD STATED ODDS 1:48		
BRONZE WINNERS LISTED BELOW		
SKIP-NUMBERED SET		

☐ 1	Hideo Nomo	5.00	2.20
☐ 3	Garret Anderson	1.50	.70
☐ 4	Jose Mesa	.75	.35
☐ 5	Vinny Castilla	1.50	.70
☐ 6	Mike Mussina	3.00	1.35
☐ 7	Ray Durham	.75	.35
☐ 8	Jack McDowell	.75	.35

☐ 9	Juan Gonzalez	8.00	3.60
☐ 10	Chipper Jones	10.00	4.50
☐ 11	Deion Sanders	1.50	.70
☐ 12	Rondell White	1.50	.70
☐ 13	Tom Henke	.75	.35
☐ 14	Derek Bell	.75	.35
☐ 15	Randy Myers	.75	.35
☐ 16	Randy Johnson	3.00	1.35
☐ 17	Len Dykstra	1.50	.70
☐ 18	Bill Pulsipher	.75	.35
☐ 21	Chad Curtis	.75	.35
☐ 22	Roberto Hernandez	.75	.35
☐ 23	Kirby Puckett	6.00	2.70
☐ 25	Roger Clemens	6.00	2.70
☐ 31	Chad Fonville	.75	.35
☐ 32	Bernard Gilkey	.75	.35
☐ 34	Shawn Green	.75	.35
☐ 35	Rick Aguilera	.75	.35
☐ 40	Dean Palmer	.75	.35
☐ 45	Matt Williams	2.00	.90
☐ 49	Tom Glavine	1.50	.70
☐ 50	Delino DeShields	.75	.35
☐ 56	Benito Santiago	.75	.35
☐ 59	Rod Beck	.75	.35
☐ 63	Eric Karros	1.50	.70
☐ 66	Lee Smith	1.50	.70
☐ 69	Jeff Montgomery	.75	.35
☐ 70	Todd Hundley	1.50	.70
☐ 73	Don Mattingly	5.00	2.20
☐ 77	Ken Caminiti W	4.00	1.80
☐ 80	Pedro Martinez	3.00	1.35
☐ 82	Heathcliff Slocumb	.75	.35
☐ 83	Joe Girardi	.75	.35
☐ 88	Todd Worrell W	1.50	.70
☐ 90	Bip Roberts	.75	.35
☐ 95	Cecil Fielder	1.50	.70
☐ 96	Wade Boggs	3.00	1.35
☐ 98	Mickey Tettleton	.75	.35
☐ 99	Jeff Kent	.75	.35
☐ 100	Denny Martinez	1.50	.70
☐ 101	Luis Gonzalez	.75	.35
☐ 103	Javy Lopez	1.50	.70
☐ 104	Mark McGwire	6.00	2.70
☐ 105	Ken Griffey Jr. W	30.00	13.50
☐ 106	Darren Daulton	.75	.35
☐ 108	Mike Macfarlane	.75	.35
☐ 110	Shane Reynolds	.75	.35
☐ 114	John Franco	1.50	.70
☐ 116	Andy Benes	1.50	.70
☐ 118	Brian Jordan	1.50	.70
☐ 119	Terry Pendleton	.75	.35
☐ 120	Chuck Finley	.75	.35
☐ 123	Derek Jeter	10.00	4.50
☐ 124	John Smiley	.75	.35
☐ 126	Brett Butler	1.50	.70
☐ 127	Doug Drabek	.75	.35
☐ 128	J.T. Snow	1.50	.70
☐ 129	Joe Carter	1.50	.70
☐ 130	Dennis Eckersley	1.50	.70
☐ 131	Marty Cordova	1.50	.70
☐ 132	Greg Maddux W	20.00	9.00
☐ 135	Paul Sorrento	.75	.35
☐ 137	Shawon Dunston	.75	.35
☐ 138	Moises Alou	1.50	.70
☐ 140	Ramon Martinez	.75	.35
☐ 141	Royce Clayton	.75	.35
☐ 143	Kenny Rogers	.75	.35
☐ 144	Tim Naehring	.75	.35
☐ 145	Chris Gomez	.75	.35
☐ 146	Bobby Bonilla	1.50	.70
☐ 148	Johnny Damon	1.50	.70
☐ 150	Andres Galarraga W	5.00	2.20
☐ 151	David Cone	1.50	.70
☐ 152	Lance Johnson	.75	.35
☐ 159	David Justice	3.00	1.35
☐ 160	Mark Grace	2.00	.90
☐ 161	Robb Nen	.75	.35
☐ 162	Mike Greenwell	.75	.35
☐ 167	Mel Rojas	.75	.35
☐ 168	Bret Boone	.75	.35
☐ 172	Jay Bell	1.50	.70
☐ 176	Roberto Alomar	3.00	1.35
☐ 178	Ryan Klesko	2.00	.90
☐ 271	Barry Larkin W	4.00	1.80
☐ 272	Paul O'Neill	1.50	.70
☐ 274	Will Clark	2.00	.90

☐ 275	Steve Avery	.75	.35
☐ 276	Jim Edmonds	2.00	.90
☐ 277	John Olerud	1.50	.70
☐ 279	Chris Hoiles	.75	.35
☐ 280	Jeff Conine	1.50	.70
☐ 283	Ray Lankford	1.50	.70
☐ 285	Frank Thomas	12.00	5.50
☐ 286	Jason Isringhausen	.75	.35
☐ 287	Glenallen Hill	.75	.35
☐ 289	Bernie Williams	3.00	1.35
☐ 290	Eddie Murray	3.00	1.35
☐ 296	Jeff Fassero	.75	.35
☐ 297	Albert Belle	4.00	1.80
☐ 298	Craig Biggio	2.00	.90
☐ 300	Edgar Martinez	2.00	.90
☐ 301	Tony Gwynn	8.00	3.60
☐ 303	Mo Vaughn	4.00	1.80
☐ 304	Alex Fernandez	.75	.35
☐ 308	Omar Vizquel	1.50	.70
☐ 310	Danny Tartabull	.75	.35
☐ 316	Brady Anderson	2.00	.90
☐ 319	Larry Walker	3.00	1.35
☐ 321	Robin Ventura	1.50	.70
☐ 325	Kenny Lofton	4.00	1.80
☐ 327	Wil Cordero	.75	.35
☐ 328	Troy Percival	.75	.35
☐ 331	Carlos Baerga	.75	.35
☐ 333	Jay Buhner	2.00	.90
☐ 335	Jeff King	.75	.35
☐ 336	Dante Bichette	1.50	.70
☐ 337	Alan Trammell	2.00	.90
☐ 342	Jose Canseco	2.00	.90
☐ 343	Rafael Palmeiro	2.00	.90
☐ 344	Quivio Veras	.75	.35
☐ 345	Darrin Fletcher	.75	.35
☐ 347	Tony Eusebio	.75	.35
☐ 348	Ismael Valdes	1.50	.70
☐ 349	Terry Steinbach	.75	.35
☐ 350	Orel Hershiser	1.50	.70
☐ 351	Kurt Abbott	.75	.35
☐ 354	Ruben Sierra	.75	.35
☐ 357	Jim Thome	3.00	1.35
☐ 358	Geronimo Berroa	.75	.35
☐ 359	Robby Thompson	.75	.35
☐ 360	Jose Vizcaino	.75	.35
☐ 362	Kevin Appier	1.50	.70
☐ 364	Ron Gant	1.50	.70
☐ 367	Rico Brogna	.75	.35
☐ 368	Manny Ramirez	3.00	1.35
☐ 370	Sammy Sosa	3.00	1.35
☐ 373	Sandy Alomar	1.50	.70
☐ 378	Steve Finley	1.50	.70
☐ 380	Ivan Rodriguez	3.00	1.35
☐ 382	Mark Lemke	.75	.35
☐ 385	Mark Langston	.75	.35
☐ 386	Ed Sprague	.75	.35
☐ 388	Steve Ontiveros	.75	.35
☐ 392	Tom Candiotti	.75	.35
☐ 394	Erik Hanson	.75	.35
☐ 396	Pete Schourek	.75	.35
☐ 400	Gary Sheffield W	5.00	2.20
☐ 402	Barry Bonds W	8.00	3.60
☐ 403	Tom Pagnozzi	.75	.35
☐ 404	Todd Stottlemyre	.75	.35
☐ 405	Tim Salmon	3.00	1.35
☐ 407	Fred McGriff	2.00	.90
☐ 408	Orlando Merced	.75	.35
☐ 412	Eric Young	.75	.35
☐ 414	Chuck Knoblauch W	5.00	2.20
☐ 417	Mark Portugal	.75	.35
☐ 418	Tim Raines	1.50	.70
☐ 420	Todd Zeile	.75	.35
☐ 422	Marquis Grissom	1.50	.70
☐ 423	Norm Charlton	.75	.35
☐ 424	Cal Ripken	12.00	5.50
☐ 425	Gregg Jefferies	.75	.35
☐ 428	Jose Rijo	.75	.35
☐ 429	Jeff Bagwell	6.00	2.70
☐ 430	Raul Mondesi	2.00	.90
☐ 433	Travis Fryman	1.50	.70
☐ 434	Tony Phillips	.75	.35
☐ 435	Reggie Sanders	.75	.35
☐ 436	Andy Pettitte	3.00	1.35
☐ 438	Jeff Blauser	1.50	.70
☐ 441	Charlie Hayes	.75	.35
☐ 442	Mike Piazza W	20.00	9.00

1996 Stadium Club Extreme Winners Bronze

This 10-card skip-numbered set was only available to collectors who redeemed one of the ten winning Bronze Extreme Players cards before the December 31, 1996 deadline. The cards parallel the Extreme Players cards inserted in Stadium Club packs except for their distinctive diffraction foil fronts.

	MINT	NRMT
COMPLETE SET (10)	25.00	11.00
OMMON CARD (EW1-EW10)	.50	.23
ONE SET VIA MAIL PER BRONZE WINNER		
COMP.SILVER SET (10)	80.00	36.00
*SILVER SINGLES: 1.5X TO 3X BASIC WINNERS		
ONE SILV.SET VIA MAIL PER SILV.WINNER		
COMP.GOLD SET (10)	400.00	180.00
*GOLD SINGLES: 7.5X TO 15X BASIC WINNERS		
ONE GOLD CARD VIA MAIL PER GOLD WNR.		

		MINT	NRMT
☐ EW1	Greg Maddux	6.00	2.70
☐ EW2	Mike Piazza	6.00	2.70
☐ EW3	Andres Galarraga	.90	.90
☐ EW4	Chuck Knoblauch	2.00	.90
☐ EW5	Ken Caminiti	1.50	.70
☐ EW6	Barry Larkin	1.50	.70
☐ EW7	Barry Bonds	2.50	1.10
☐ EW8	Ken Griffey Jr.	10.00	4.50
☐ EW9	Gary Sheffield	1.50	.70
☐ EW10	Todd Worrell	.50	.23

1996 Stadium Club Megaheroes

Randomly inserted at a rate of one in every 48 hobby and 24 retail packs, this 10-card set features super-heroic players matched with a comic book-

style illustration depicting their nicknames. The fronts display a color player cutout superposed on diffraction foilboard illustrating the player's nickname. On a textured background, the backs present a closeup photo (in an oval format) and a career highlight in the form of an etymology of his nickname.

		MINT	NRMT
COMPLETE SET (10)		50.00	22.00
COMMON CARD (MH1-MH10)		1.00	.45
SER.1 STATED ODDS 1:48 HOB, 1:24 RET			

		MINT	NRMT
☐ MH1	Frank Thomas	15.00	6.75
☐ MH2	Ken Griffey Jr.	20.00	9.00
☐ MH3	Hideo Nomo	10.00	4.50
☐ MH4	Ozzie Smith	5.00	2.20
☐ MH5	Will Clark	2.50	1.10
☐ MH6	Jack McDowell	1.00	.45
☐ MH7	Andres Galarraga	2.50	1.10
☐ MH8	Roger Clemens	6.00	2.70
☐ MH9	Deion Sanders	2.00	.90
☐ MH10	Mo Vaughn	5.00	2.20

1996 Stadium Club Metalists

Randomly inserted in packs at a rate of one in 96 (retail) and one in 48 (hobby), this eight-card set features players with two or more MLB awards and is printed on laser-cut foil board.

		MINT	NRMT
COMPLETE SET (8)		50.00	22.00
COMMON CARD (MH1-MH8)		2.00	.90
SER.2 STATED ODDS 1:48 HOB, 1:96 RET			

		MINT	NRMT
☐ M1	Jeff Bagwell	8.00	3.60
☐ M2	Barry Bonds	5.00	2.20
☐ M3	Jose Canseco	3.00	1.35
☐ M4	Roger Clemens	6.00	2.70
☐ M5	Dennis Eckersley	2.00	.90
☐ M6	Greg Maddux	12.00	5.50
☐ M7	Cal Ripken	15.00	6.75
☐ M8	Frank Thomas	15.00	6.75

1996 Stadium Club Midsummer Matchups

Randomly inserted at a rate of one in every 48 hobby and 24 retail packs, this 10-card set salutes 1995 National League and American League All-Stars as they are matched back-to-back by position on these two-sided etched foil cards. Each side features a color player

cutout on a screened background of 1995 All-Star game emblems. On each side, the lower right corner is peeled back to reveal space for the American or National League logo.

		MINT	NRMT
COMPLETE SET (10)		60.00	27.00
COMMON CARD (M1-M10)		2.00	.90
SER.1 STATED ODDS 1:48 HOB, 1:24 RET			

		MINT	NRMT
☐ MM1	Hideo Nomo	10.00	4.50
	Randy Johnson		
☐ MM2	Mike Piazza	12.00	5.50
	Ivan Rodriguez		
☐ MM3	Fred McGriff	15.00	6.75
	Frank Thomas		
☐ MM4	Craig Biggio	2.00	.90
	Carlos Baerga		
☐ MM5	Vinny Castilla	2.50	1.10
	Wade Boggs		
☐ MM6	Barry Larkin	15.00	6.75
	Cal Ripken		
☐ MM7	Barry Bonds	8.00	3.60
	Albert Belle		
☐ MM8	Len Dykstra	5.00	2.20
	Kenny Lofton		
☐ MM9	Tony Gwynn	15.00	6.75
	Kirby Puckett		
☐ MM10	Ron Gant	2.50	1.10
	Edgar Martinez		

1996 Stadium Club Power Packed

Randomly inserted in packs at a rate of one in 48, this 15-card set features the biggest, most powerful hitters in the League. Printed on Power Matrix, the cards carry diagrams showing where the players hit the ball over the fence and how far.

	MINT	NRMT
COMPLETE SET (15)	80.00	36.00
COMMON CARD (PP1-PP15)	2.50	1.10
SER.2 STATED ODDS 1:48 RETAIL		

		MINT	NRMT
☐ PP1	Albert Belle	6.00	2.70
☐ PP2	Mark McGwire	10.00	4.50
☐ PP3	Jose Canseco	3.00	1.35
☐ PP4	Mike Piazza	15.00	6.75
☐ PP5	Ron Gant	2.50	1.10
☐ PP6	Ken Griffey Jr.	25.00	11.00
☐ PP7	Mo Vaughn	6.00	2.70
☐ PP8	Cecil Fielder	2.50	1.10
☐ PP9	Tim Salmon	4.00	1.80
☐ PP10	Frank Thomas	20.00	9.00
☐ PP11	Juan Gonzalez	12.00	5.50
☐ PP12	Andres Galarraga	3.00	1.35
☐ PP13	Fred McGriff	3.00	1.35
☐ PP14	Jay Buhner	3.00	1.35
☐ PP15	Dante Bichette	2.50	1.10

1996 Stadium Club Prime Cuts

Randomly inserted at a rate of one in every 36 hobby and 72 retail packs, this 8-card set highlights eight hitters with the purest swings. These laser-cut cards feature diffraction gold foil. The cards are numbered on the back with a "PC" prefix.

	MINT	NRMT
COMPLETE SET (8)	60.00	27.00
COMMON CARD (PC1-PC8)	2.50	1.10
SER.1 STATED ODDS 1:36 HOB, 1:72 RET		

		MINT	NRMT
☐ PC1	Albert Belle	5.00	2.20
☐ PC2	Barry Bonds	5.00	2.20
☐ PC3	Ken Griffey Jr.	20.00	9.00
☐ PC4	Tony Gwynn	10.00	4.50
☐ PC5	Edgar Martinez	2.50	1.10
☐ PC6	Rafael Palmeiro	2.50	1.10
☐ PC7	Mike Piazza	12.00	5.50
☐ PC8	Frank Thomas	15.00	6.75

1996 Stadium Club TSC Awards

Randomly inserted in packs at a rate of one in 24 (retail) and one in 48 (hobby), this ten-card set features players whom TSC baseball experts voted on for various awards and is printed on diffraction foil.

	MINT	NRMT
COMPLETE SET (10)	40.00	18.00
COMMON CARD (1-10)	1.00	.45
SER.2 STATED ODDS 1:48 HOB, 1:24 RET		

		MINT	NRMT
☐ 1	Cal Ripken	12.00	5.50
☐ 2	Albert Belle	4.00	1.80
☐ 3	Tom Glavine	1.50	.70
☐ 4	Jeff Conine	1.50	.70
☐ 5	Ken Griffey Jr.	15.00	6.75

1996 Stadium Club Power Streak

Randomly inserted at a rate of one in every 24 hobby packs and 48 retail packs, this 15-card set spotlights baseball's most awesome power hitters and strikeout artists. The cards feature Topps' Power Matrix technology. The fronts display a color player cutout on a silver metallic and holographic background featuring a baseball. The backs carry a small color photo and biography; in addition, the player's batting prowess is presented under three topics: 1995 Power Profile, Power Stroke, and Power Zone.

	MINT	NRMT
COMPLETE SET (15)	60.00	27.00
COMMON CARD (PS1-PS15)	1.00	.45
SER.1 STATED ODDS 1:24 HOB, 1:48 RET		

		MINT	NRMT
☐ PS1	Randy Johnson	4.00	1.80
☐ PS2	Hideo Nomo	12.00	5.50
☐ PS3	Albert Belle	6.00	2.70
☐ PS4	Dante Bichette	2.00	.90
☐ PS5	Jay Buhner	3.00	1.35
☐ PS6	Frank Thomas	20.00	9.00
☐ PS7	Mark McGwire	10.00	4.50
☐ PS8	Rafael Palmeiro	3.00	1.35
☐ PS9	Mo Vaughn	6.00	2.70
☐ PS10	Sammy Sosa	4.00	1.80
☐ PS11	Larry Walker	4.00	1.80
☐ PS12	Gary Gaetti	1.00	.45
☐ PS13	Tim Salmon	4.00	1.80
☐ PS14	Barry Bonds	6.00	2.70
☐ PS15	Jim Edmonds	3.00	1.35

	MINT	NRMT
☐ 6 Hideo Nomo	6.00	2.70
☐ 7 Greg Maddux	10.00	4.50
☐ 8 Chipper Jones	10.00	4.50
☐ 9 Randy Johnson	3.00	1.35
☐ 10 Jose Mesa	1.00	.45

1997 Stadium Club

Cards from this 390 card set were distributed in eight-card hobby and retail packs (SRP $3) and 13-card hobby collector packs (SRP $5). Card fronts feature color action player photos printed on 20 pt. card stock with Topps Super Color processing, Hi-gloss laminating, embossing and double foil stamping. The backs carry player information and statistics. In addition to the standard selection of major leaguers, the set contains a 15-card TSC 2000 subset (181-195) featuring a selection of top young prospects. These subset cards were inserted one in every two eight-card first series packs and one per 13-card first series pack. First series cards were released in February 1997. The 195-card Series 2 set was issued in six-card packs with a suggested retail price of $2 and in nine-card hobby packs with a suggested retail price of $3. The second series set features a 15-card Stadium Sluggers subset (376-390) with an insertion rate of one in every two hobby and three retail Series 2 packs. Second series cards were released in April 1997.

	MINT	NRMT
COMPLETE SET (390)	80.00	36.00
COMPLETE SERIES 1 (195)	40.00	18.00
COMPLETE SERIES 2 (195)	40.00	18.00
COMMON (1-180/196-375)	.15	.07
MINOR STARS	.30	.14
UNLISTED STARS	.60	.25
COM.SP (181-195/376-390)	.30	.14
SP MINOR STARS	.50	
SP SEMISTARS	.75	
SP UNLISTED STARS	1.25	
CARDS 361 AND 374 DON´T EXIST		
SWEENEY AND PAGNOZZI NUMBERED 274		
J.DYE AND B.BROWN NUMBERED 351		
COMP.MATRIX SET (120)	500.00	220.00
COMP.MATRIX SER.1 (60)	250.00	110.00
COMP.MATRIX SER.2 (60)	250.00	110.00
*MATRIX STARS: 6X TO 12X HI COLUMN		
*MATRIX YOUNG STARS: 5X TO 10X HI		
MATRIX ODDS 1:12H/R, 1:18ANCO, 1:6HCP		

#	Player	Price 1	Price 2
1	Chipper Jones	2.00	.90
2	Gary Sheffield	.60	.25
3	Kenny Lofton	.75	.35
4	Brian Jordan	.30	.14
5	Mark McGwire	1.25	.55
6	Charles Nagy	.30	.14
7	Tim Salmon	.60	.25
8	Cal Ripken	2.50	1.10
9	Jeff Conine	.30	.14
10	Paul Molitor	.60	.25
11	Mariano Rivera	.30	.14
12	Pedro Martinez	.60	.25
13	Jeff Bagwell	1.25	.55
14	Bobby Bonilla	.30	.14
15	Barry Bonds	.75	.35
16	Ryan Klesko	.40	.18
17	Barry Larkin	.40	.18
18	Jim Thome	.60	.25
19	Jay Buhner	.40	.18
20	Juan Gonzalez	1.50	.70
21	Mike Mussina	.60	.25
22	Kevin Appier	.30	.14
23	Eric Karros	.30	.14
24	Steve Finley	.30	.14
25	Ed Sprague	.15	.07
26	Bernard Gilkey	.15	.07
27	Tony Phillips	.15	.07
28	Henry Rodriguez	.15	.07
29	John Smoltz	.30	.14
30	Dante Bichette	.30	.14
31	Mike Piazza	2.00	.90
32	Paul O'Neill	.30	.14
33	Billy Wagner	.30	.14
34	Reggie Sanders	.15	.07
35	John Jaha	.15	.07
36	Eddie Murray	.60	.25
37	Eric Young	.15	.07
38	Roberto Hernandez	.15	.07
39	Pat Hentgen	.30	.14
40	Sammy Sosa	.60	.25
41	Todd Hundley	.30	.14
42	Mo Vaughn	.75	.35
43	Robin Ventura	.30	.14
44	Mark Grudzielanek	.15	.07
45	Shane Reynolds	.15	.07
46	Andy Pettitte	.60	.25
47	Fred McGriff	.60	.18
48	Rey Ordonez	.15	.07
49	Will Clark	.40	.18
50	Ken Griffey Jr.	3.00	1.35
51	Todd Worrell	.15	.07
52	Rusty Greer	.30	.14
53	Mark Grace	.40	.18
54	Tom Glavine	.30	.14
55	Derek Jeter	2.00	.90
56	Rafael Palmeiro	.40	.18
57	Bernie Williams	.60	.25
58	Marty Cordova	.30	.14
59	Andres Galarraga	.60	.25
60	Ken Caminiti	.40	.18
61	Garret Anderson	.30	.14
62	Denny Martinez	.30	.14
63	Mike Greenwell	.15	.07
64	David Segui	.15	.07
65	Julio Franco	.30	.14
66	Rickey Henderson	.40	.18
67	Ozzie Guillen	.15	.07
68	Pete Harnisch	.15	.07
69	Chan Ho Park	.60	.25
70	Harold Baines	.30	.14
71	Mark Clark	.15	.07
72	Steve Avery	.15	.07
73	Brian Hunter	.30	.14
74	Pedro Astacio	.15	.07
75	Jack McDowell	.15	.07
76	Gregg Jefferies	.15	.07
77	Jason Kendall	.30	.14
78	Todd Walker	.30	.14
79	B.J. Surhoff	.15	.07
80	Moises Alou	.30	.14
81	Fernando Vina	.15	.07
82	Darryl Strawberry	.30	.14
83	Jose Rosado	.30	.14
84	Chris Gomez	.15	.07
85	Chili Davis	.30	.14
86	Alan Benes	.30	.14
87	Todd Hollandsworth	.15	.07
88	Jose Vizcaino	.15	.07
89	Edgardo Alfonzo	.30	.14
90	Ruben Rivera	.30	.14
91	Donovan Osborne	.15	.07
92	Doug Glanville	.15	.07
93	Gary DiSarcina	.15	.07
94	Brooks Kieschnick	.15	.07
95	Bobby Jones	.15	.07
96	Raul Casanova	.15	.07
97	Jermaine Allensworth	.15	.07
98	Kenny Rogers	.15	.07
99	Mark McLemore	.15	.07
100	Jeff Fassero	.15	.07
101	Sandy Alomar Jr.	.30	.14
102	Chuck Finley	.15	.07
103	Eric Owens	.15	.07
104	Billy McMillon	.15	.07
105	Dwight Gooden	.30	.14
106	Sterling Hitchcock	.15	.07
107	Doug Drabek	.15	.07
108	Paul Wilson	.15	.07
109	Chris Snopek	.15	.07
110	Al Leiter	.15	.07
111	Bob Tewksbury	.15	.07
112	Todd Greene	.30	.14
113	Jose Valentin	.15	.07
114	Delino DeShields	.15	.07
115	Mike Bordick	.15	.07
116	Pat Meares	.15	.07
117	Mariano Duncan	.15	.07
118	Steve Trachsel	.15	.07
119	Luis Castillo	.30	.14
120	Andy Benes	.30	.14
121	Dorne Wall	.15	.07
122	Alex Gonzalez	.15	.07
123	Dan Wilson	.15	.07
124	Omar Vizquel	.30	.14
125	Devon White	.15	.07
126	Darryl Hamilton	.15	.07
127	Orlando Merced	.15	.07
128	Royce Clayton	.15	.07
129	William VanLandingham	.15	.07
130	Terry Steinbach	.30	.14
131	Jeff Blauser	.30	.14
132	Jeff Cirillo	.30	.14
133	Roger Clemens	1.25	.55
134	Danny Tartabull	.15	.07
135	Jeff Montgomery	.15	.07
136	Bobby Higginson	.30	.14
137	Mike Grace	.15	.07
138	Kevin Elster	.15	.07
139	Brian Giles	.15	.07
140	Rod Beck	.15	.07
141	Ismael Valdes	.30	.14
142	Scott Brosius	.15	.07
143	Mike Fetters	.15	.07
144	Gary Gaetti	.15	.07
145	Mike Lansing	.15	.07
146	Glenallen Hill	.15	.07
147	Shawn Green	.15	.07
148	Mel Rojas	.15	.07
149	Joey Cora	.30	.14
150	John Smiley	.15	.07
151	Marvin Benard	.15	.07
152	Curt Schilling	.30	.14
153	Dave Nilsson	.15	.07
154	Edgar Renteria	.30	.14
155	Joey Hamilton	.30	.14
156	Carlos Garcia	.15	.07
157	Nomar Garciaparra	2.00	.90
158	Kevin Ritz	.15	.07
159	Keith Lockhart	.15	.07
160	Justin Thompson	.30	.14
161	Terry Adams	.15	.07
162	Jamey Wright	.15	.07
163	Otis Nixon	.15	.07
164	Michael Tucker	.30	.14
165	Mike Stanley	.15	.07
166	Ben McDonald	.15	.07
167	John Mabry	.15	.07
168	Troy O'Leary	.15	.07
169	Mel Nieves	.15	.07
170	Bret Boone	.15	.07
171	Mike Timlin	.15	.07
172	Scott Rolen	1.50	.70
173	Reggie Jefferson	.15	.07
174	Neil Perez	.30	.14
175	Brian McRae	.15	.07
176	Tom Goodwin	.15	.07
177	Aaron Sele	.15	.07
178	Benito Santiago	.15	.07
179	Frank Rodriguez	.15	.07
180	Eric Davis	.30	.14
181	Andruw Jones 2000 SP	3.00	1.35
182	Todd Walker 2000 SP	1.00	.45
183	Wes Helms 2000 SP	.75	.35
184	Nelson Figueroa 2000 SP	.50	.23
185	Vladimir Guerrero 2000 SP	2.50	1.10
186	Billy McMillon 2000	.30	.14
187	Todd Helton 2000 SP	2.50	1.10
188	Nomar Garciaparra 2000 SP	4.00	1.80
189	Katsuhiro Maeda 2000	.50	.23
190	Russell Branyan 2000 SP	2.00	.90
191	Glendon Rusch 2000	.30	.14
192	Bartolo Colon 2000	.50	.23
193	Scott Rolen 2000 SP	3.00	1.35
194	Angel Echevarria 2000	.30	.14
195	Bob Abreu 2000	.50	.23
196	Greg Maddux	2.00	.90
197	Joe Carter	.30	.14
198	Alex Ochoa	.15	.07
199	Ellis Burks	.30	.14
200	Ivan Rodriguez	.75	.35
201	Marquis Grissom	.30	.14
202	Trevor Hoffman	.15	.07
203	Matt Williams	.40	.18
204	Carlos Delgado	.30	.14
205	Ramon Martinez	.30	.14
206	Chuck Knoblauch	.60	.25
207	Juan Guzman	.15	.07
208	Derek Bell	.15	.07
209	Roger Clemens	1.25	.55
210	Vladimir Guerrero	1.25	.55
211	Cecil Fielder	.30	.14
212	Hideo Nomo	1.25	.55
213	Frank Thomas	2.50	1.10
214	Greg Vaughn	.15	.07
215	Javy Lopez	.30	.14
216	Raul Mondesi	.40	.18
217	Wade Boggs	.60	.25
218	Carlos Baerga	.15	.07
219	Tony Gwynn	1.50	.70
220	Tino Martinez	.60	.25
221	Vinny Castilla	.30	.14
222	Lance Johnson	.15	.07
223	David Justice	.60	.25
224	Rondell White	.30	.14
225	Dean Palmer	.15	.07
226	Jim Edmonds	.40	.18
227	Albert Belle	1.00	.45
228	Alex Fernandez	.30	.14
229	Ryne Sandberg	.75	.35
230	Jose Mesa	.15	.07
231	David Cone	.30	.14
232	Troy Percival	.15	.07
233	Edgar Martinez	.40	.18
234	Jose Canseco	.40	.18
235	Kevin Brown	.30	.14
236	Ray Lankford	.30	.14
237	Karim Garcia	.30	.14
238	J.T. Snow	.30	.14
239	Dennis Eckersley	.30	.14
240	Roberto Alomar	.60	.25
241	John Valentin	.15	.07
242	Ron Gant	.30	.14
243	Geronimo Berroa	.15	.07
244	Manny Ramirez	.60	.25
245	Travis Fryman	.30	.14
246	Denny Neagle	.30	.14
247	Randy Johnson	.60	.25
248	Darin Erstad	1.00	.45
249	Mark Wohlers	.15	.07
250	Ken Hill	.15	.07
251	Larry Walker	.60	.25
252	Craig Biggio	.40	.18
253	Brady Anderson	.40	.18
254	John Wetteland	.15	.07
255	Andruw Jones	1.50	.70
256	Turk Wendell	.15	.07
257	Jason Isringhausen	.15	.07
258	Jaime Navarro	.15	.07

☐ 259	Sean Berry	.15	.07
☐ 260	Albie Lopez	.15	.07
☐ 261	Jay Bell	.30	.14
☐ 262	Bobby Witt	.15	.07
☐ 263	Tony Clark	.60	.25
☐ 264	Tim Wakefield	.15	.07
☐ 265	Brad Radke	.30	.14
☐ 266	Tim Belcher	.15	.07
☐ 267	Nerio Rodriguez	.50	.23
☐ 268	Roger Cedeno	.15	.07
☐ 269	Tim Naehring	.15	.07
☐ 270	Kevin Tapani	.15	.07
☐ 271	Joe Randa	.15	.07
☐ 272	Randy Myers	.15	.07
☐ 273	Dave Burba	.15	.07
☐ 274	Mike Sweeney	.30	.14
☐ 275	Danny Graves	.15	.07
☐ 276	Chad Mottola	.15	.07
☐ 277	Ruben Sierra	.15	.07
☐ 278	Norm Charlton	.15	.07
☐ 279	Scott Servais	.15	.07
☐ 280	Jacob Cruz	.30	.14
☐ 281	Mike Macfarlane	.15	.07
☐ 282	Rich Becker	.15	.07
☐ 283	Shannon Stewart	.30	.14
☐ 284	Gerald Williams	.15	.07
☐ 285	Jody Reed	.15	.07
☐ 286	Jeff D'Amico	.15	.07
☐ 287	Walt Weiss	.15	.07
☐ 288	Jim Leyritz	.15	.07
☐ 289	Francisco Cordova	.15	.07
☐ 290	F.P. Santangelo	.15	.07
☐ 291	Scott Erickson	.15	.07
☐ 292	Hal Morris	.15	.07
☐ 293	Ray Durham	.15	.07
☐ 294	Andy Ashby	.15	.07
☐ 295	Darryl Kile	.30	.14
☐ 296	Jose Paniagua	.15	.07
☐ 297	Mickey Tettleton	.15	.07
☐ 298	Joe Girardi	.15	.07
☐ 299	Rocky Coppinger	.15	.07
☐ 300	Bob Abreu	.30	.14
☐ 301	John Olerud	.30	.14
☐ 302	Paul Shuey	.15	.07
☐ 303	Jeff Brantley	.15	.07
☐ 304	Bob Wells	.15	.07
☐ 305	Kevin Seitzer	.15	.07
☐ 306	Shawon Dunston	.15	.07
☐ 307	Jose Herrera	.15	.07
☐ 308	Butch Huskey	.30	.14
☐ 309	Jose Offerman	.15	.07
☐ 310	Rick Aguilera	.15	.07
☐ 311	Greg Gagne	.15	.07
☐ 312	John Burkett	.15	.07
☐ 313	Mark Thompson	.15	.07
☐ 314	Alvaro Espinoza	.15	.07
☐ 315	Todd Stottlemyre	.15	.07
☐ 316	Al Martin	.15	.07
☐ 317	James Baldwin	.15	.07
☐ 318	Cal Eldred	.15	.07
☐ 319	Sid Fernandez	.15	.07
☐ 320	Mickey Morandini	.15	.07
☐ 321	Robb Nen	.15	.07
☐ 322	Mark Lemke	.15	.07
☐ 323	Pete Schourek	.15	.07
☐ 324	Marcus Jensen	.15	.07
☐ 325	Rich Aurilla	.15	.07
☐ 326	Jeff King	.15	.07
☐ 327	Scott Stahoviak	.15	.07
☐ 328	Ricky Otero	.15	.07
☐ 329	Antonio Osuna	.15	.07
☐ 330	Chris Hoiles	.15	.07
☐ 331	Luis Gonzalez	.15	.07
☐ 332	Wil Cordero	.15	.07
☐ 333	Johnny Damon	.15	.07
☐ 334	Mark Langston	.15	.07
☐ 335	Orlando Miller	.15	.07
☐ 336	Jason Giambi	.30	.14
☐ 337	Damian Jackson	.15	.07
☐ 338	David Wells	.15	.07
☐ 339	Bip Roberts	.15	.07
☐ 340	Matt Ruebel	.15	.07
☐ 341	Tom Candiotti	.15	.07
☐ 342	Wally Joyner	.30	.14
☐ 343	Jimmy Key	.15	.07
☐ 344	Tony Batista	.15	.07

☐ 345	Paul Sorrento	.15	.07
☐ 346	Ron Karkovice	.15	.07
☐ 347	Wilson Alvarez	.15	.07
☐ 348	John Flaherty	.15	.07
☐ 349	Rey Sanchez	.15	.07
☐ 350	John Vander Wal	.15	.07
☐ 351	Jermaine Dye	.15	.07
☐ 352	Mike Hampton	.15	.07
☐ 353	Greg Colbrunn	.15	.07
☐ 354	Heathcliff Slocumb	.15	.07
☐ 355	Ricky Bottalico	.15	.07
☐ 356	Marty Janzen	.15	.07
☐ 357	Orel Hershiser	.30	.14
☐ 358	Rex Hudler	.15	.07
☐ 359	Amaury Telemaco	.15	.07
☐ 360	Darrin Fletcher	.15	.07
☐ 361	Brant Brown UER	.15	.07
	Card numbered 351		
☐ 362	Russ Davis	.15	.07
☐ 363	Allen Watson	.15	.07
☐ 364	Mike Lieberthal	.15	.07
☐ 365	Dave Stevens	.15	.07
☐ 366	Jay Powell	.15	.07
☐ 367	Tony Fossas	.15	.07
☐ 368	Bob Wolcott	.15	.07
☐ 369	Mark Loretta	.15	.07
☐ 370	Shawn Estes	.30	.14
☐ 371	Sandy Martinez	.15	.07
☐ 372	Wendell Magee Jr.	.15	.07
☐ 373	John Franco	.30	.14
☐ 374	Tom Pagnozzi UER	.15	.07
	misnumbered as 274		
☐ 375	Willie Adams	.15	.07
☐ 376	Chipper Jones SS SP	4.00	1.80
☐ 377	Mo Vaughn SS SP	1.25	.55
☐ 378	Frank Thomas SS SP	5.00	2.20
☐ 379	Albert Belle SS SP	1.50	.70
☐ 380	Andres Galarraga SS SP	1.25	.55
☐ 381	Gary Sheffield SS SP	1.25	.55
☐ 382	Jeff Bagwell SS SP	2.50	1.10
☐ 383	Mike Piazza SS SP	4.00	1.80
☐ 384	Mark McGwire SS SP	2.50	1.10
☐ 385	Ken Griffey Jr. SS SP	6.00	2.70
☐ 386	Barry Bonds SS SP	1.50	.70
☐ 387	Juan Gonzalez SS SP	3.00	1.35
☐ 388	Brady Anderson SS SP	.75	.35
☐ 389	Ken Caminiti SS SP	.75	.35
☐ 390	Jay Buhner SS SP	.75	.35

1997 Stadium Club Co-Signers

Randomly inserted in first series eight-card hobby packs at a rate of one in 96 and first series 13-card hobby collector packs at a rate of one in 96, cards (CO1-CO5) from this dual-sided, dual-player set feature color action player photos printed on 20pt. card stock with authentic signatures of two major league standouts per card. The last five cards (CO6-CO10) were randomly inserted in second series 10-card hobby packs with a rate

of one in 168 and inserted with a rate of one in 96 hobby collector packs.

	MINT	NRMT
COMPLETE SET (10)	700.00	325.00
COMPLETE SERIES 1 (5)	350.00	160.00
COMPLETE SERIES 2 (5)	350.00	160.00
COMMON CARD (CO1-CO10)	30.00	13.50
STATED ODDS 1:168 HOBBY, 1:96 HCP		

☐ CO1	Andy Pettitte	150.00	70.00
	Derek Jeter		
☐ CO2	Paul Wilson	30.00	13.50
	Todd Hundley		
☐ CO3	Jermaine Dye	30.00	13.50
	Mark Wohlers		
☐ CO4	Scott Rolen	100.00	45.00
	Gregg Jefferies		
☐ CO5	Todd Hollandsworth	40.00	18.00
	Jason Kendall		
☐ CO6	Alan Benes	50.00	22.00
	Robin Ventura		
☐ CO7	Eric Karros	60.00	27.00
	Raul Mondesi		
☐ CO8	Rey Ordonez	120.00	55.00
	Nomar Garciaparra		
☐ CO9	Rondell White	40.00	18.00
	Marty Cordova		
☐ CO10	Tony Gwynn	120.00	55.00
	Karim Garcia		

1997 Stadium Club Firebrand Redemption

Randomly inserted exclusively into first series eight-card retail packs at a rate of one in 36, these redemption cards feature a selection of the leagues top sluggers. Due to circumstances beyond the manufacturers control, they were not able to insert the actual etched-wood cards into packs and had to resort to these redemption cards.

	MINT	NRMT
COMPLETE SET (12)	150.00	70.00
COMMON CARD (F1-F12)	4.00	1.80
SER.1 STAT.ODDS 1:24 HOB/RET,1:36 ANCO		
*WOOD CARDS: 1.25X BASIC CARDS		
ONE WOOD CARD VIA MAIL PER EXCH.CARD		

☐ F1	Jeff Bagwell	12.00	5.50
☐ F2	Albert Belle	8.00	3.60
☐ F3	Barry Bonds	8.00	3.60
☐ F4	Andres Galarraga	5.00	2.20
☐ F5	Ken Griffey Jr.	30.00	13.50
☐ F6	Brady Anderson	4.00	1.80
☐ F7	Mark McGwire	12.00	5.50
☐ F8	Chipper Jones	20.00	9.00
☐ F9	Frank Thomas	25.00	11.00
☐ F10	Mike Piazza	20.00	9.00

	MINT	NRMT
☐ F11 Mo Vaughn	8.00	3.60
☐ F12 Juan Gonzalez	15.00	6.75

1997 Stadium Club Instavision

The first ten cards of this 22-card set were randomly inserted in first series eight-card packs at a rate of one in 24 and first series 13-card packs at a rate of 1:12. The last 12 cards were inserted in series two packs at the rate of one in 24 and one in 12 in hobby collector packs. The set highlights some of the 1996 season's most exciting moments through exclusive holographic video action.

	MINT	NRMT
COMPLETE SET (22)	80.00	36.00
COMPLETE SERIES 1 (10)	30.00	13.50
COMPLETE SERIES 2 (12)	50.00	22.00
COMMON CARD (I1-I22)	2.50	1.10
UNLISTED STARS	5.00	2.20
STATED ODDS 1:24 HOB/RET, 1:36 ANCO

		MINT	NRMT
☐ I1	Eddie Murray	5.00	2.20
☐ I2	Paul Molitor	5.00	2.20
☐ I3	Todd Hundley	2.50	1.10
☐ I4	Roger Clemens	10.00	4.50
☐ I5	Barry Bonds	6.00	2.70
☐ I6	Mark McGwire	10.00	4.50
☐ I7	Brady Anderson	3.00	1.35
☐ I8	Barry Larkin	3.00	1.35
☐ I9	Ken Caminiti	3.00	1.35
☐ I10	Hideo Nomo	12.00	5.50

1997 Stadium Club Millennium

Randomly inserted in first and second series eight-card packs at a rate of one in 24 and 13-card packs at a rate of 1:12, this 40-card set features color play-

er photos of 40 breakthrough stars of Major League Baseball reproduced using state-of-the-art advanced embossed holographic technology.

	MINT	NRMT
COMPLETE SET (40)	250.00	110.00
COMPLETE SERIES 1 (20)	100.00	45.00
COMPLETE SERIES 2 (20)	150.00	70.00
COMMON CARD (M1-M40)	3.00	1.35
UNLISTED STARS	8.00	3.60
STATED ODDS 1:24H/R, 1:36ANCO, 1:12HCP

		MINT	NRMT
☐ M1	Derek Jeter	20.00	9.00
☐ M2	Mark Grudzielanek	3.00	1.35
☐ M3	Jacob Cruz	4.00	1.80
☐ M4	Ray Durham	3.00	1.35
☐ M5	Tony Clark	8.00	3.60
☐ M6	Chipper Jones	25.00	11.00
☐ M7	Luis Castillo	4.00	1.80
☐ M8	Carlos Delgado	4.00	1.80
☐ M9	Brant Brown	3.00	1.35
☐ M10	Jason Kendall	4.00	1.80
☐ M11	Alan Benes	4.00	1.80
☐ M12	Rey Ordonez	3.00	1.35
☐ M13	Justin Thompson	4.00	1.80
☐ M14	Jermaine Allensworth	3.00	1.35
☐ M15	Brian Hunter	4.00	1.80
☐ M16	Marty Cordova	4.00	1.80
☐ M17	Edgar Renteria	4.00	1.80
☐ M18	Karim Garcia	4.00	1.80
☐ M19	Todd Greene	4.00	1.80
☐ M20	Paul Wilson	3.00	1.35

1997 Stadium Club Patent Leather

Randomly inserted in second series retail packs only at a rate of one in 36, this 13-card set features action player images standing in a baseball glove background with an inner die-cut glove printed on leather card stock.

	MINT	NRMT
COMPLETE SET (13)	125.00	55.00
COMMON CARD (PL1-PL13)	3.00	1.35
UNLISTED STARS	8.00	3.60
SER.2 STATED ODDS 1:36 RETAIL

		MINT	NRMT
☐ PL1	Ivan Rodriguez	10.00	4.50
☐ PL2	Ken Caminiti	5.00	2.20
☐ PL3	Barry Bonds	10.00	4.50
☐ PL4	Ken Griffey Jr	40.00	18.00
☐ PL5	Greg Maddux	25.00	11.00
☐ PL6	Craig Biggio	5.00	2.20
☐ PL7	Andres Galarraga	8.00	3.60
☐ PL8	Kenny Lofton	10.00	4.50
☐ PL9	Barry Larkin	5.00	2.20
☐ PL10	Mark Grace	5.00	2.20
☐ PL11	Rey Ordonez	3.00	1.35
☐ PL12	Roberto Alomar	8.00	3.60
☐ PL13	Derek Jeter	20.00	9.00

1997 Stadium Club Pure Gold

Randomly inserted in first and second series eight-card packs at a rate of one in 72 and 13-card packs at a rate of one in 36, this 20-card set features color action star player photos reproduced on 20 pt. embossed gold mirror foilboard.

	MINT	NRMT
COMPLETE SET (20)	450.00	200.00
COMPLETE SERIES 1 (10)	200.00	90.00
COMPLETE SERIES 2 (10)	250.00	110.00
COMMON CARD (PG1-PG20)	8.00	3.60
UNLISTED STARS	10.00	4.50
STATED ODDS 1:72H/R, 1:108ANCO, 1:36HCP

		MINT	NRMT
☐ PG1	Brady Anderson	8.00	3.60
☐ PG2	Albert Belle	15.00	6.75
☐ PG3	Dante Bichette	8.00	3.60
☐ PG4	Barry Bonds	15.00	6.75
☐ PG5	Jay Buhner	8.00	3.60
☐ PG6	Tony Gwynn	30.00	13.50
☐ PG7	Chipper Jones	40.00	18.00
☐ PG8	Mark McGwire	25.00	11.00
☐ PG9	Gary Sheffield		
☐ PG10	Frank Thomas	50.00	22.00
☐ PG11	Juan Gonzalez	30.00	13.50
☐ PG12	Ken Caminiti	8.00	3.60
☐ PG13	Kenny Lofton	15.00	6.75
☐ PG14	Jeff Bagwell	25.00	11.00
☐ PG15	Ken Griffey Jr	60.00	27.00
☐ PG16	Cal Ripken	50.00	22.00
☐ PG17	Mo Vaughn	15.00	6.75
☐ PG18	Mike Piazza	40.00	18.00
☐ PG19	Derek Jeter	30.00	13.50
☐ PG20	Andres Galarraga	10.00	4.50

1998 Stadium Club

The 1998 Stadium Club first series was issued with a total of 200 cards and distributed in seven-card packs with a suggested retail price of $2, 10-

card hobby packs for $3, and 16-card collector packs for $5. The fronts feature action color player photos with player information displayed on the backs. The Series 1 set included odd numbered cards only. The set contains the topical subsets: Future Stars (361-379), and Draft Picks (381-399).

	MINT	NRMT
COMPLETE SERIES 1 (200)	40.00	18.00
COMMON CARD (1-360)	.15	.07
MINOR STARS	.30	.14
UNLISTED STARS	.60	.25
COMMON FS/DP (361-399)	.30	.14
FS/DP MINOR STARS	.50	.23
FS/DP SEMISTARS	.75	.35
FS/DP UNLISTED STARS	1.25	.55
SKIP-NUMBERED SET		
ONE RIPKEN SOUND CHIP PER HTA BOX		

☐ 1 Chipper Jones	2.00	.90			
☐ 3 Vladimir Guerrero	1.00	.45			
☐ 5 John Franco	.30	.14			
☐ 7 Rusty Greer	.30	.14			
☐ 9 Brett Tomko	.30	.14			
☐ 11 Mike Cameron	.30	.14			
☐ 13 Bernie Williams	.60	.25			
☐ 15 Jason Dickson	.30	.14			
☐ 17 Brian Jordan	.30	.14			
☐ 19 Scott Spiezio	.30	.14			
☐ 21 Jim Thome	.60	.25			
☐ 23 Livan Hernandez	.30	.14			
☐ 25 Chris Gomez	.15	.07			
☐ 27 Willie Greene	.15	.07			
☐ 29 Johnny Damon	.15	.07			
☐ 31 Chuck Knoblauch	.60	.25			
☐ 33 Tony Clark	.60	.25			
☐ 35 Vinny Castilla	.30	.14			
☐ 37 Reggie Jefferson	.15	.07			
☐ 39 Jermaine Allensworth	.15	.07			
☐ 41 Heathcliff Slocumb	.15	.07			
☐ 43 Barry Bonds	.75	.35			
☐ 45 Chan Ho Park	.60	.25			
☐ 47 Jeff Cirillo	.30	.14			
☐ 49 Craig Biggio	.40	.18			
☐ 51 Mark Clark	.15	.07			
☐ 53 F.P. Santangelo	.15	.07			
☐ 55 Edgar Renteria	.30	.14			
☐ 57 Jimmy Key	.30	.14			
☐ 59 Curt Schilling	.30	.14			
☐ 61 Andy Ashby	.15	.07			
☐ 63 Orel Hershiser	.30	.14			
☐ 65 Scott Servais	.15	.07			
☐ 67 Javy Lopez	.30	.14			
☐ 69 Miguel Tejada	.75	.35			
☐ 71 Reggie Sanders	.15	.07			
☐ 73 Dean Palmer	.15	.07			
☐ 75 David Wells	.15	.07			
☐ 77 Albert Belle	.75	.35			
☐ 79 Brian Hunter	.30	.14			
☐ 81 Darren Oliver	.15	.07			
☐ 83 Cal Ripken	2.50	1.10			
☐ 85 Derrek Lee	.40	.18			
☐ 87 Rey Ordonez	.15	.07			
☐ 89 Jeff Kent	.15	.07			
☐ 91 Manny Ramirez	.60	.25			
☐ 93 Doug Glanville	.15	.07			
☐ 95 Andy Benes	.30	.14			
☐ 97 Mike Matheny	.15	.07			
☐ 99 Keith Lockhart	.15	.07			
☐ 101 Roger Clemens	1.25	.55			
☐ 103 Mark Bellhorn	.30	.14			
☐ 105 Darin Erstad	.75	.35			
☐ 107 Wilson Alvarez	.15	.07			
☐ 109 George Williams	.15	.07			
☐ 111 Shawn Estes	.30	.14			
☐ 113 Tony Gwynn	1.50	.70			
☐ 115 Terry Steinbach	.15	.07			
☐ 117 Andy Pettitte	.60	.25			
☐ 119 Deivi Cruz	.15	.07			
☐ 121 Scott Hatteberg	.15	.07			
☐ 123 Todd Dunwoody	.30	.14			
☐ 125 Royce Clayton	.15	.07			

☐ 127 Tom Glavine	.30	.14			
☐ 129 Terry Adams	.15	.07			
☐ 131 Dan Wilson	.15	.07			
☐ 133 Mickey Morandini	.15	.07			
☐ 135 Juan Encarnacion	.60	.25			
☐ 137 Magglio Ordonez	.75	.35			
☐ 139 Todd Helton	.75	.35			
☐ 141 Esteban Loaiza	.15	.07			
☐ 143 Jeff Fassero	.15	.07			
☐ 145 Butch Huskey	.30	.14			
☐ 147 Brian Giles	.15	.07			
☐ 149 John Smoltz	.30	.14			
☐ 151 Jose Valentin	.15	.07			
☐ 153 Ed Sprague	.15	.07			
☐ 155 Carlos Perez	.15	.07			
☐ 157 Bobby Bonilla	.30	.14			
☐ 159 Jeffrey Hammonds	.15	.07			
☐ 161 Rich Loiselle	.40	.18			
☐ 163 Larry Walker	.60	.25			
☐ 165 Jeff Montgomery	.15	.07			
☐ 167 James Baldwin	.15	.07			
☐ 169 Kevin Appier	.30	.14			
☐ 171 Nomar Garciaparra	2.00	.90			
☐ 173 Armando Benitez	.15	.07			
☐ 175 Ismael Valdes	.30	.14			
☐ 177 Paul Sorrento	.15	.07			
☐ 179 Kevin Elster	.15	.07			
☐ 181 Carlos Baerga	.15	.07			
☐ 183 Ryan McGuire	.30	.14			
☐ 185 Ron Gant	.30	.14			
☐ 187 Scott Karl	.15	.07			
☐ 189 Randall Simon	.30	.14			
☐ 191 Jaret Wright	1.50	.70			
☐ 193 John Valentin	.15	.07			
☐ 195 Mike Sweeney	.15	.07			
☐ 197 Jaime Navarro	.15	.07			
☐ 199 Ken Griffey Jr.	3.00	1.35			
☐ 201 Billy Wagner	.30	.14			
☐ 203 Mark McGwire	1.50	.70			
☐ 205 Rico Brogna	.15	.07			
☐ 207 Chad Curtis	.15	.07			
☐ 209 Neifi Perez	.30	.14			
☐ 211 Quilvio Veras	.15	.07			
☐ 213 Kirk Rueter	.15	.07			
☐ 215 Cal Eldred	.15	.07			
☐ 217 Todd Greene	.30	.14			
☐ 219 Ricky Bottalico	.15	.07			
☐ 221 Rich Becker	.15	.07			
☐ 223 Ivan Rodriguez	.75	.35			
☐ 225 Deion Sanders	.30	.14			
☐ 227 Mark Kotsay	.60	.25			
☐ 229 Ryan Klesko	.40	.18			
☐ 231 Luis Gonzalez	.15	.07			
☐ 233 Michael Tucker	.15	.07			
☐ 235 Ariel Prieto	.15	.07			
☐ 237 Omar Vizquel	.30	.14			
☐ 239 Justin Thompson	.30	.14			
☐ 241 Derek Jeter	1.50	.70			
☐ 243 Jose Offerman	.15	.07			
☐ 245 Jason Kendall	.30	.14			
☐ 247 Mike Bordick	.15	.07			
☐ 249 Darrin Fletcher	.15	.07			
☐ 251 Ramon Martinez	.30	.14			
☐ 253 Mark Grace	.40	.18			
☐ 255 Jose Cruz Jr.	2.50	1.10			
☐ 257 Brad Ausmus	.15	.07			
☐ 259 Doug Jones	.15	.07			
☐ 261 Chuck Finley	.15	.07			
☐ 263 David Segui	.15	.07			
☐ 265 Tim Salmon	.60	.25			
☐ 267 Alex Fernandez	.30	.14			
☐ 269 B.J. Surhoff	.15	.07			
☐ 271 Edgar Martinez	.40	.18			
☐ 273 Eduardo Perez	.15	.07			
☐ 275 Kevin Young	.15	.07			
☐ 277 Brad Radke	.30	.14			
☐ 279 Joe Girardi	.15	.07			
☐ 281 Jeff Frye	.15	.07			
☐ 283 Scott Erickson	.15	.07			
☐ 285 Shigetoshi Hasegawa	.30	.14			
☐ 287 Willie McGee	.15	.07			
☐ 289 Ugueth Urbina	.15	.07			
☐ 291 Fernando Tatis	.60	.25			
☐ 293 Bernard Gilkey	.15	.07			
☐ 295 Matt Karchner	.15	.07			
☐ 297 Damion Easley	.15	.07			

☐ 299 Ellis Burks	.30	.14			
☐ 301 Jermaine Dye	.15	.07			
☐ 303 Ron Coomer	.15	.07			
☐ 305 Bobby Higginson	.30	.14			
☐ 307 Jon Nunnally	.15	.07			
☐ 309 Jason Schmidt	.15	.07			
☐ 311 Sterling Hitchcock	.15	.07			
☐ 313 Shane Reynolds	.15	.07			
☐ 315 Scott Rolen	1.50	.70			
☐ 317 David Justice	.60	.25			
☐ 319 Bobby Jones	.15	.07			
☐ 321 Tim Wakefield	.15	.07			
☐ 323 David Cone	.30	.14			
☐ 325 Jose Canseco	.40	.18			
☐ 327 Gerald Williams	.15	.07			
☐ 329 Mark Gardner	.15	.07			
☐ 331 Kevin Brown	.30	.14			
☐ 333 Jed Hansen	.15	.07			
☐ 335 John Thomson	.15	.07			
☐ 337 Mike Piazza	2.00	.90			
☐ 339 Ray Durham	.15	.07			
☐ 341 Kevin Polcovich	.15	.07			
☐ 343 Darryl Hamilton	.15	.07			
☐ 345 Kevin Orie	.30	.14			
☐ 347 Juan Guzman	.15	.07			
☐ 349 Rick Aguilera	.15	.07			
☐ 351 Bobby Witt	.15	.07			
☐ 353 Matt Morris	.30	.14			
☐ 355 Todd Zeile	.15	.07			
☐ 357 Alex Gonzalez	.15	.07			
☐ 359 Joey Cora	.30	.14			
☐ 361 Adrian Beltre	4.00	1.80			
☐ 363 A.J. Hinch	1.50	.70			
☐ 365 Alex Gonzalez	.50	.23			
☐ 367 Mike Stoner	1.50	.70			
☐ 369 Kevin McGlinchy	.50	.23			
☐ 371 Kris Benson	1.00	.45			
☐ 373 Dermal Brown	1.25	.55			
☐ 375 Eric Milton	.50	.23			
☐ 377 Preston Wilson	.50	.23			
☐ 379 Travis Lee	5.00	2.20			
☐ 381 Vernon Wells	1.25	.55			
☐ 383 J.J. Davis	1.00	.45			
☐ 385 Michael Cuddyer	1.00	.45			
☐ 387 Chris Enochs	1.00	.45			
☐ 389 Jason Dellaero	.50	.23			
☐ 391 Mark Mangum	.30	.14			
☐ 393 Adam Kennedy	.50	.23			
☐ 395 Jack Cust	1.00	.45			
☐ 397 Jon Garland	.50	.23			
☐ 399 Aaron Akin	.30	.14			
☐ NNO Cal Ripken Sound Chip	15.00	6.75			

1998 Stadium Club One Of A Kind

Randomly inserted one in every 21 hobby packs, this 200-card set parallels the Series 1 base set. Only 150 of this set were produced.

	MINT	NRMT
COMMON CARD (1-399)	10.00	4.50
MINOR STARS	15.00	6.75
SEMISTARS	25.00	11.00
UNLISTED STARS	40.00	18.00
*STARS: 30X TO 60X HI COLUMN		
*YOUNG STARS: 25X TO 50X HI		
*ROOKIES/PROSPECTS: 12.5X TO 25X HI		
SER.1 STATED ODDS 1:21 HOB, 1:13 HTA		
STATED PRINT RUN 150 SERIAL #'d SETS		
SKIP-NUMBERED SET		

1998 Stadium Club Bowman Previews

Randomly inserted in Series 1 packs at the rate of one in 12, this 10-card set is a sneak preview of the Bowman series and features color photos of top

players. The cards are numbered with a BP prefix on the backs.

	MINT	NRMT
COMPLETE SET (10)	40.00	18.00
COMMON CARD (BP1-BP10)	1.50	.70
SER.1 STATED ODDS 1:12 H/R, 1:4 HTA		

		MINT	NRMT
☐ BP1	Nomar Garciaparra	6.00	2.70
☐ BP2	Scott Rolen	5.00	2.20
☐ BP3	Ken Griffey Jr.	10.00	4.50
☐ BP4	Frank Thomas	8.00	3.60
☐ BP5	Larry Walker	2.00	.90
☐ BP6	Mike Piazza	6.00	2.70
☐ BP7	Chipper Jones	6.00	2.70
☐ BP8	Tino Martinez	1.50	.70
☐ BP9	Mark McGwire	5.00	2.20
☐ BP10	Barry Bonds	2.50	1.10

1998 Stadium Club Co-Signers

Randomly inserted in hobby packs only at the rate of one in 109, this 18-card set features color player photos of two great players on each card along with their autographs. Each autograph card is coded A, B or C. The A cards are currently not priced.

	MINT	NRMT
COMMON CARD (CS1-CS18)	80.00	36.00
GROUP A ODDS 1:4372 HOB, 1:2623 HTA		
GROUP B ODDS 1:1457 HOB, 1:874 HTA		
GROUP C ODDS 1:121 HOB, 1:73 HTA		

		MINT	NRMT
☐ CS1	Nomar Garciaparra A .. Scott Rolen		
☐ CS2	Nomar Garciaparra B Derek Jeter	300.00	135.00
☐ CS3	Nomar Garciaparra C Eric Karros	120.00	55.00
☐ CS4	Scott Rolen C Derek Jeter	150.00	70.00
☐ CS5	Scott Rolen B Eric Karros	200.00	90.00

		MINT	NRMT
☐ CS6	Derek Jeter A Eric Karros		
☐ CS7	Travis Lee B Jose Cruz Jr.	300.00	135.00
☐ CS8	Travis Lee C Mark Kotsay	150.00	70.00
☐ CS9	Travis Lee A Paul Konerko		
☐ CS10	Jose Cruz Jr A. Mark Kotsay		
☐ CS11	Jose Cruz Jr C.. Paul Konerko	150.00	70.00
☐ CS12	Mark Kotsay B Paul Konerko	150.00	70.00
☐ CS13	Tony Gwynn A Larry Walker		
☐ CS14	Tony Gwynn C Mark Grudzielanek	120.00	55.00
☐ CS15	Tony Gwynn B Andres Galarraga	250.00	110.00
☐ CS16	Larry Walker B Mark Grudzielanek	100.00	45.00
☐ CS17	Larry Walker C Andres Galarraga	80.00	36.00
☐ CS18	Mark Grudzielanek A.. Andres Galarraga		

1998 Stadium Club In The Wings

Randomly inserted in Series 1 packs at the rate of one in 36, this 15-card set features color photos of some of the top young players in the league.

	MINT	NRMT
COMPLETE SET (15)	100.00	45.00
COMMON CARD (W1-W15)	3.00	1.35
SER.1 STATED ODDS 1:36 H/R, 1:12 HTA		

		MINT	NRMT
☐ W1	Juan Encarnacion	6.00	2.70
☐ W2	Brad Fullmer	4.00	1.80
☐ W3	Ben Grieve	15.00	6.75
☐ W4	Todd Helton	10.00	4.50
☐ W5	Richard Hidalgo	4.00	1.80
☐ W6	Russ Johnson	3.00	1.35
☐ W7	Paul Konerko	12.00	5.50
☐ W8	Mark Kotsay	8.00	3.60
☐ W9	Derrek Lee	5.00	2.20
☐ W10	Travis Lee	25.00	11.00
☐ W11	Eli Marrero	4.00	1.80
☐ W12	David Ortiz	4.00	1.80
☐ W13	Randall Simon	4.00	1.80
☐ W14	Shannon Stewart	3.00	1.35
☐ W15	Fernando Tatis	8.00	3.60

1998 Stadium Club Never Compromise

Randomly inserted in Series 1 packs at the rate of one in 12, this 20-card set features color photos of top players who never compromise in their game play.

The card backs are numbered with a "NC" prefix.

	MINT	NRMT
COMPLETE SET (20)	100.00	45.00
COMMON CARD (NC1-NC20)	2.00	.90
SER.1 STATED ODDS 1:12 H/R, 1:4 HTA		

		MINT	NRMT
☐ NC1	Cal Ripken	12.00	5.50
☐ NC2	Ivan Rodriguez	4.00	1.80
☐ NC3	Ken Griffey Jr	15.00	6.75
☐ NC4	Frank Thomas	12.00	5.50
☐ NC5	Tony Gwynn	8.00	3.60
☐ NC6	Mike Piazza	10.00	4.50
☐ NC7	Randy Johnson	3.00	1.35
☐ NC8	Greg Maddux	10.00	4.50
☐ NC9	Roger Clemens	6.00	2.70
☐ NC10	Derek Jeter	8.00	3.60
☐ NC11	Chipper Jones	10.00	4.50
☐ NC12	Barry Bonds	4.00	1.80
☐ NC13	Larry Walker	3.00	1.35
☐ NC14	Jeff Bagwell	6.00	2.70
☐ NC15	Barry Larkin	2.00	.90
☐ NC16	Ken Caminiti	2.00	.90
☐ NC17	Mark McGwire	8.00	3.60
☐ NC18	Manny Ramirez	3.00	1.35
☐ NC19	Tim Salmon	2.50	1.10
☐ NC20	Paul Molitor	3.00	1.35

1991 Studio Previews

This 18-card preview set was issued four at a time within 1991 Donruss retail factory sets in order to show dealers and collectors the look of their new Studio cards. The standard-size cards are exactly the same style as those in the Studio series, with black and white player photos bordered in mauve and player information on the backs.

	MINT	NRMT
COMPLETE SET (18)	20.00	9.00
COMMON CARD (1-17)	1.00	.45
MINOR STARS	2.00	.90

SEMISTARS 3.00   1.35
FOUR PER DONRUSS RETAIL FACTORY SET

- □ 1 Juan Bell .... 1.00   .45
- □ 2 Roger Clemens 10.00   4.50
- □ 3 Dave Parker .... 2.00   .90
- □ 4 Tim Raines .... 2.00   .90
- □ 5 Kevin Seitzer .... 1.00   .45
- □ 6 Ted Higuera .... 1.00   .45
- □ 7 Bernie Williams 8.00   3.60
- □ 8 Harold Baines .... 2.00   .90
- □ 9 Gary Pettis .... 1.00   .45
- □ 10 Dave Justice 5.00   2.20
- □ 11 Eric Davis .... 2.00   .90
- □ 12 Andujar Cedeno .... 1.00   .45
- □ 13 Tom Foley .... 1.00   .45
- □ 14 Dwight Gooden ...... 2.00   .90
- □ 15 Doug Drabek .... 1.00   .45
- □ 16 Steve Decker .... 1.00   .45
- □ 17 Joe Torre MG .... 2.00   .90
- □ NNO Title card .... 1.00   .45

1991 Studio

The 1991 Studio set, issued by Donruss/Leaf, contains 264 standard-size cards issued in one series. Cards were distributed in foil packs each of which contained one of 21 different Rod Carew puzzle panels. The Studio card fronts feature posed black and white head-and-shoulders player photos with mauve borders. The team logo, player's name, and position appear along the bottom of the card face. The cards are ordered alphabetically within and according to teams for each league in the set with American League teams preceding National League. Rookie Cards in the set include Jeff Bagwell, Jeff Conine and Brian McRae.

	MINT	NRMT
COMPLETE SET (264)	15.00	6.75
COMMON CARD (1-263)	.10	.05
MINOR STARS	.20	.09
UNLISTED STARS	.40	.18

- □ 1 Glenn Davis .... .10   .05
- □ 2 Dwight Evans .... .20   .09
- □ 3 Leo Gomez .... .20   .09
- □ 4 Chris Hoiles .... .20   .09
- □ 5 Sam Horn .... .10   .05
- □ 6 Ben McDonald .... .20   .09
- □ 7 Randy Milligan .... .10   .05
- □ 8 Gregg Olson .... .10   .05
- □ 9 Cal Ripken .... 1.50   .70
- □ 10 Dave Segui .... .20   .09
- □ 11 Wade Boggs .... .40   .18
- □ 12 Ellis Burks .... .20   .09
- □ 13 Jack Clark .... .20   .09
- □ 14 Roger Clemens ...... .75   .35
- □ 15 Mike Greenwell ..... .10   .05

- □ 16 Tim Naehring .... .20   .09
- □ 17 Tony Pena .... .10   .05
- □ 18 Phil Plantier .... .20   .09
- □ 19 Jeff Reardon .... .20   .09
- □ 20 Mo Vaughn .... .75   .35
- □ 21 Jimmy Reese CO .... .20   .09
- □ 22 Jim Abbott UER ..... .10   .05
  (Born in 1967, not 1969)
- □ 23 Bert Blyleven .... .20   .09
- □ 24 Chuck Finley .... .10   .05
- □ 25 Gary Gaetti .... .10   .05
- □ 26 Wally Joyner .... .20   .09
- □ 27 Mark Langston ...... .10   .05
- □ 28 Kirk McCaskill .... .10   .05
- □ 29 Lance Parrish .... .10   .05
- □ 30 Dave Winfield .... .40   .18
- □ 31 Alex Fernandez ..... .20   .09
- □ 32 Carlton Fisk .... .40   .18
- □ 33 Scott Fletcher .... .10   .05
- □ 34 Greg Hibbard .... .10   .05
- □ 35 Charlie Hough .... .10   .05
- □ 36 Jack McDowell ...... .20   .09
- □ 37 Tim Raines .... .20   .09
- □ 38 Sammy Sosa .... .50   .23
- □ 39 Bobby Thigpen ...... .10   .05
- □ 40 Frank Thomas 3.00   1.35
- □ 41 Sandy Alomar Jr .... .30   .14
- □ 42 John Farrell .... .10   .05
- □ 43 Glenallen Hill .... .10   .05
- □ 44 Brook Jacoby .... .10   .05
- □ 45 Chris James .... .10   .05
- □ 46 Doug Jones .... .10   .05
- □ 47 Eric King .... .10   .05
- □ 48 Mark Lewis .... .10   .05
- □ 49 Greg Swindell UER .. .10   .05
  (Photo actually Turner Ward)
- □ 50 Mark Whiten .... .10   .05
- □ 51 Milt Cuyler .... .10   .05
- □ 52 Rob Deer .... .10   .05
- □ 53 Cecil Fielder .... .20   .09
- □ 54 Travis Fryman .... .40   .18
- □ 55 Bill Gullickson .... .10   .05
- □ 56 Lloyd Moseby .... .10   .05
- □ 57 Frank Tanana .... .10   .05
- □ 58 Mickey Tettleton .... .20   .09
- □ 59 Alan Trammell .... .30   .14
- □ 60 Lou Whitaker .... .20   .09
- □ 61 Mike Boddicker ...... .10   .05
- □ 62 George Brett .... .75   .35
- □ 63 Jim Eisenreich .... .50   .23
- □ 64 Warren Cromartie ... .10   .05
- □ 65 Storm Davis .... .10   .05
- □ 66 Kirk Gibson .... .20   .09
- □ 67 Mark Gubicza .... .10   .05
- □ 68 Brian McRae .... .40   .18
- □ 69 Bret Saberhagen .... .20   .09
- □ 70 Kurt Stillwell .... .10   .05
- □ 71 Tim McIntosh .... .10   .05
- □ 72 Candy Maldonado ... .10   .05
- □ 73 Paul Molitor .... .40   .18
- □ 74 Willie Randolph ...... .20   .09
- □ 75 Ron Robinson .... .10   .05
- □ 76 Gary Sheffield .... .40   .18
- □ 77 Franklin Stubbs ..... .10   .05
- □ 78 B.J. Surhoff .... .20   .09
- □ 79 Greg Vaughn .... .20   .09
- □ 80 Robin Yount .... .40   .18
- □ 81 Rick Aguilera .... .20   .09
- □ 82 Steve Bedrosian ..... .10   .05
- □ 83 Scott Erickson .... .20   .09
- □ 84 Greg Gagne .... .10   .05
- □ 85 Dan Gladden .... .10   .05
- □ 86 Brian Harper .... .10   .05
- □ 87 Kent Hrbek .... .20   .09
- □ 88 Shane Mack .... .10   .05
- □ 89 Jack Morris .... .20   .09
- □ 90 Kirby Puckett .... .75   .35
- □ 91 Jesse Barfield .... .10   .05
- □ 92 Steve Farr .... .10   .05
- □ 93 Steve Howe .... .10   .05
- □ 94 Roberto Kelly .... .20   .09
- □ 95 Tim Leary .... .10   .05
- □ 96 Kevin Maas .... .10   .05
- □ 97 Don Mattingly .... .60   .25
- □ 98 Hensley Meulens .... .10   .05

- □ 99 Scott Sanderson .... .10   .05
- □ 100 Steve Sax .... .10   .05
- □ 101 Jose Canseco ...... .30   .14
- □ 102 Dennis Eckersley .. .20   .09
- □ 103 Dave Henderson ... .10   .05
- □ 104 Rickey Henderson . .40   .18
- □ 105 Rick Honeycutt .... .10   .05
- □ 106 Mark McGwire ..... .75   .35
- □ 107 Dave Stewart UER . .10   .05
  (No-hitter against Toronto, not Texas)
- □ 108 Eric Show .... .10   .05
- □ 109 Todd Van Poppel .. .10   .05
- □ 110 Bob Welch .... .10   .05
- □ 111 Alvin Davis .... .10   .05
- □ 112 Ken Griffey Jr. 3.00   1.35
- □ 113 Ken Griffey Sr. .... .10   .05
- □ 114 Erik Hanson UER .. .10   .05
  (Misspelled Eric)
- □ 115 Brian Holman ...... .10   .05
- □ 116 Randy Johnson .... .50   .23
- □ 117 Edgar Martinez .... .40   .18
- □ 118 Tino Martinez ...... .40   .18
- □ 119 Harold Reynolds ... .10   .05
- □ 120 David Valle .... .10   .05
- □ 121 Kevin Belcher ...... .10   .05
- □ 122 Scott Chiamparino . .10   .05
- □ 123 Julio Franco .... .10   .05
- □ 124 Juan Gonzalez ..... 1.50   .70
- □ 125 Rich Gossage ...... .20   .09
- □ 126 Jeff Kunkel .... .10   .05
- □ 127 Rafael Palmeiro ... .40   .18
- □ 128 Nolan Ryan .... 1.50   .70
- □ 129 Ruben Sierra .... .10   .05
- □ 130 Bobby Witt .... .10   .05
- □ 131 Roberto Alomar .... .40   .18
- □ 132 Tom Candiotti ...... .10   .05
- □ 133 Joe Carter .... .20   .09
- □ 134 Ken Dayley .... .10   .05
- □ 135 Kelly Gruber .... .10   .05
- □ 136 John Olerud .... .20   .09
- □ 137 Dave Stieb .... .10   .05
- □ 138 Turner Ward .... .10   .05
- □ 139 Devon White .... .10   .05
- □ 140 Mookie Wilson ..... .20   .09
- □ 141 Steve Avery .... .40   .18
- □ 142 Sid Bream .... .10   .05
- □ 143 Nick Esasky UER .. .10   .05
  (Homers abbreviated RH)
- □ 144 Ron Gant .... .20   .09
- □ 145 Tom Glavine .... .40   .18
- □ 146 David Justice ...... .50   .23
- □ 147 Kelly Mann .... .10   .05
- □ 148 Terry Pendleton ... .20   .09
- □ 149 John Smoltz .... .40   .18
- □ 150 Jeff Treadway ..... .10   .05
- □ 151 George Bell .... .10   .05
- □ 152 Shawn Boskie ...... .10   .05
- □ 153 Andre Dawson ..... .40   .18
- □ 154 Lance Dickson ..... .10   .05
- □ 155 Shawon Dunston .. .10   .05
- □ 156 Joe Girardi .... .20   .09
- □ 157 Mark Grace .... .40   .18
- □ 158 Ryne Sandberg .... .50   .23
- □ 159 Gary Scott .... .10   .05
- □ 160 Dave Smith .... .10   .05
- □ 161 Tom Browning ..... .10   .05
- □ 162 Eric Davis .... .20   .09
- □ 163 Rob Dibble .... .10   .05
- □ 164 Mariano Duncan ... .10   .05
- □ 165 Chris Hammond .... .10   .05
- □ 166 Billy Hatcher ...... .10   .05
- □ 167 Barry Larkin .... .30   .14
- □ 168 Hal Morris .... .10   .05
- □ 169 Paul O'Neill .... .20   .09
- □ 170 Chris Sabo .... .10   .05
- □ 171 Eric Anthony .... .10   .05
- □ 172 Jeff Bagwell 3.00   1.35
- □ 173 Craig Biggio .... .40   .18
- □ 174 Ken Caminiti .... .10   .05
- □ 175 Jim Deshaies ...... .10   .05
- □ 176 Steve Finley .... .10   .05
- □ 177 Pete Harnisch ..... .10   .05
- □ 178 Darryl Kile .... .40   .18
- □ 179 Curt Schilling ...... .40   .18
- □ 180 Mike Scott .... .10   .05

☐ 181	Brett Butler	.20	.09
☐ 182	Gary Carter	.40	.18
☐ 183	Orel Hershiser	.20	.09
☐ 184	Ramon Martinez	.20	.09
☐ 185	Eddie Murray	.40	.18
☐ 186	Jose Offerman	.10	.05
☐ 187	Bob Ojeda	.10	.05
☐ 188	Juan Samuel	.10	.05
☐ 189	Mike Scioscia	.10	.05
☐ 190	Darryl Strawberry	.20	.09
☐ 191	Moises Alou	.40	.18
☐ 192	Brian Barnes	.10	.05
☐ 193	Oil Can Boyd	.10	.05
☐ 194	Ivan Calderon	.10	.05
☐ 195	Delino DeShields	.10	.05
☐ 196	Mike Fitzgerald	.10	.05
☐ 197	Andres Galarraga	.40	.18
☐ 198	Marquis Grissom	.40	.18
☐ 199	Bill Sampen	.10	.05
☐ 200	Tim Wallach	.10	.05
☐ 201	Daryl Boston	.10	.05
☐ 202	Vince Coleman	.10	.05
☐ 203	John Franco	.20	.09
☐ 204	Dwight Gooden	.20	.09
☐ 205	Tom Herr	.10	.05
☐ 206	Gregg Jefferies	.10	.05
☐ 207	Howard Johnson	.10	.05
☐ 208	Dave Magadan UER	.10	.05
	(Born 1862, should be 1962)		
☐ 209	Kevin McReynolds	.10	.05
☐ 210	Frank Viola	.10	.05
☐ 211	Wes Chamberlain	.10	.05
☐ 212	Darren Daulton	.20	.09
☐ 213	Len Dykstra	.20	.09
☐ 214	Charlie Hayes	.10	.05
☐ 215	Ricky Jordan	.10	.05
☐ 216	Steve Lake	.20	.09
	(Pictured with parrot on his shoulder)		
☐ 217	Roger McDowell	.10	.05
☐ 218	Mickey Morandini	.10	.05
☐ 219	Terry Mulholland	.10	.05
☐ 220	Dale Murphy	.40	.18
☐ 221	Jay Bell	.20	.09
☐ 222	Barry Bonds	.50	.23
☐ 223	Bobby Bonilla	.20	.09
☐ 224	Doug Drabek	.10	.05
☐ 225	Bill Landrum	.10	.05
☐ 226	Mike LaValliere	.10	.05
☐ 227	Jose Lind	.10	.05
☐ 228	Don Slaught	.10	.05
☐ 229	John Smiley	.10	.05
☐ 230	Andy Van Slyke	.20	.09
☐ 231	Bernard Gilkey	.20	.09
☐ 232	Pedro Guerrero	.10	.05
☐ 233	Rex Hudler	.10	.05
☐ 234	Ray Lankford	.40	.18
☐ 235	Joe Magrane	.10	.05
☐ 236	Jose Oquendo	.10	.05
☐ 237	Lee Smith	.20	.09
☐ 238	Ozzie Smith	.50	.23
☐ 239	Milt Thompson	.10	.05
☐ 240	Todd Zeile	.20	.09
☐ 241	Larry Andersen	.10	.05
☐ 242	Andy Benes	.20	.09
☐ 243	Paul Faries	.10	.05
☐ 244	Tony Fernandez	.10	.05
☐ 245	Tony Gwynn	1.00	.45
☐ 246	Atlee Hammaker	.10	.05
☐ 247	Fred McGriff	.40	.18
☐ 248	Bip Roberts	.10	.05
☐ 249	Bento Santiago	.10	.05
☐ 250	Ed Whitson	.10	.05
☐ 251	Dave Anderson	.10	.05
☐ 252	Mike Benjamin	.10	.05
☐ 253	John Burkett UER	.10	.05
	(Front photo actually Trevor Wilson)		
☐ 254	Will Clark	.40	.18
☐ 255	Scott Garrelts	.10	.05
☐ 256	Willie McGee	.10	.05
☐ 257	Kevin Mitchell	.20	.09
☐ 258	Dave Righetti	.10	.05
☐ 259	Matt Williams	.40	.18
☐ 260	Bud Black	.10	.05

	Steve Decker		
☐ 261	Sparky Anderson MG CL	.20	.09
☐ 262	Tom Lasorda MG CL	.30	.14
☐ 263	Tony LaRussa MG CL	.20	.09
☐ NNO	Title Card	.10	.05

1992 Studio

The 1992 Studio set consists of ten players from each of the 26 major league teams, three checklists, and an introduction card for a total of 264 standard-size cards. Inside champagne color metallic borders, the fronts carry a color close-up shot superimposed on a black and white action player photo. The backs focus on the personal side of each player by providing an up-close look, and unusual statistics show the batter or pitcher each player "Loves to Face" or "Hates to Face." The key Rookie Cards in this set are Chad Curtis and Brian Jordan.

	MINT	NRMT
COMPLETE SET (264)	15.00	6.75
COMMON CARD (1-264)	.05	.02
MINOR STARS	.10	.05
UNLISTED STARS	.30	.14

☐ 1	Steve Avery	.05	.02
☐ 2	Sid Bream	.05	.02
☐ 3	Ron Gant	.10	.05
☐ 4	Tom Glavine	.20	.09
☐ 5	David Justice	.30	.14
☐ 6	Mark Lemke	.05	.02
☐ 7	Greg Olson	.05	.02
☐ 8	Terry Pendleton	.05	.02
☐ 9	Deion Sanders	.10	.05
☐ 10	John Smoltz	.20	.09
☐ 11	Doug Dascenzo	.05	.02
☐ 12	Andre Dawson	.20	.09
☐ 13	Joe Girardi	.05	.02
☐ 14	Mark Grace	.20	.09
☐ 15	Greg Maddux	1.00	.45
☐ 16	Chuck McElroy	.05	.02
☐ 17	Mike Morgan	.05	.02
☐ 18	Ryne Sandberg	.40	.18
☐ 19	Gary Scott	.05	.02
☐ 20	Sammy Sosa	.30	.14
☐ 21	Norm Charlton	.05	.02
☐ 22	Rob Dibble	.05	.02
☐ 23	Barry Larkin	.20	.09
☐ 24	Hal Morris	.05	.02
☐ 25	Paul O'Neill	.10	.05
☐ 26	Jose Rijo	.05	.02
☐ 27	Bip Roberts	.05	.02
☐ 28	Chris Sabo	.05	.02
☐ 29	Reggie Sanders	.10	.05
☐ 30	Greg Swindell	.05	.02
☐ 31	Jeff Bagwell	1.00	.45
☐ 32	Craig Biggio	.20	.09
☐ 33	Ken Caminiti	.20	.09
☐ 34	Andujar Cedeno	.05	.02

☐ 35	Steve Finley	.10	.05
☐ 36	Pete Harnisch	.05	.02
☐ 37	Butch Henry	.05	.02
☐ 38	Doug Jones	.05	.02
☐ 39	Darryl Kile	.10	.05
☐ 40	Eddie Taubensee	.05	.02
☐ 41	Brett Butler	.10	.05
☐ 42	Tom Candiotti	.05	.02
☐ 43	Eric Davis	.05	.02
☐ 44	Orel Hershiser	.10	.05
☐ 45	Eric Karros	.20	.09
☐ 46	Ramon Martinez	.05	.02
☐ 47	Jose Offerman	.05	.02
☐ 48	Mike Scioscia	.05	.02
☐ 49	Mike Sharperson	.05	.02
☐ 50	Darryl Strawberry	.10	.05
☐ 51	Bret Barberie	.05	.02
☐ 52	Ivan Calderon	.05	.02
☐ 53	Gary Carter	.30	.14
☐ 54	Delino DeShields	.05	.02
☐ 55	Marquis Grissom	.10	.05
☐ 56	Ken Hill	.05	.02
☐ 57	Dennis Martinez	.10	.05
☐ 58	Spike Owen	.05	.02
☐ 59	Larry Walker	.30	.14
☐ 60	Tim Wallach	.05	.02
☐ 61	Bobby Bonilla	.10	.05
☐ 62	Tim Burke	.05	.02
☐ 63	Vince Coleman	.05	.02
☐ 64	John Franco	.10	.05
☐ 65	Dwight Gooden	.10	.05
☐ 66	Todd Hundley	.20	.09
☐ 67	Howard Johnson	.05	.02
☐ 68	Eddie Murray UER	.30	.14
	(He's not all-time switch homer leader, but he has most games with homers from both sides)		
☐ 69	Bret Saberhagen	.05	.02
☐ 70	Anthony Young	.05	.02
☐ 71	Kim Batiste	.05	.02
☐ 72	Wes Chamberlain	.05	.02
☐ 73	Darren Daulton	.10	.05
☐ 74	Mariano Duncan	.05	.02
☐ 75	Len Dykstra	.10	.05
☐ 76	John Kruk	.10	.05
☐ 77	Mickey Morandini	.05	.02
☐ 78	Terry Mulholland	.05	.02
☐ 79	Dale Murphy	.30	.14
☐ 80	Mitch Williams	.05	.02
☐ 81	Jay Bell	.10	.05
☐ 82	Barry Bonds	.40	.18
☐ 83	Steve Buechele	.05	.02
☐ 84	Doug Drabek	.05	.02
☐ 85	Mike LaValliere	.05	.02
☐ 86	Jose Lind	.05	.02
☐ 87	Denny Neagle	.20	.09
☐ 88	Randy Tomlin	.05	.02
☐ 89	Andy Van Slyke	.10	.05
☐ 90	Gary Varsho	.05	.02
☐ 91	Pedro Guerrero	.05	.02
☐ 92	Rex Hudler	.05	.02
☐ 93	Brian Jordan	.40	.18
☐ 94	Felix Jose	.05	.02
☐ 95	Donovan Osborne	.20	.09
☐ 96	Tom Pagnozzi	.05	.02
☐ 97	Lee Smith	.10	.05
☐ 98	Ozzie Smith	.40	.18
☐ 99	Todd Worrell	.05	.02
☐ 100	Todd Zeile	.05	.02
☐ 101	Andy Benes	.10	.05
☐ 102	Jerald Clark	.05	.02
☐ 103	Tony Fernandez	.05	.02
☐ 104	Tony Gwynn	.75	.35
☐ 105	Greg W. Harris	.05	.02
☐ 106	Fred McGriff	.20	.09
☐ 107	Benito Santiago	.05	.02
☐ 108	Gary Sheffield	.30	.14
☐ 109	Kurt Stillwell	.05	.02
☐ 110	Tim Teufel	.05	.02
☐ 111	Kevin Bass	.05	.02
☐ 112	Jeff Brantley	.05	.02
☐ 113	John Burkett	.05	.02
☐ 114	Will Clark	.20	.09
☐ 115	Royce Clayton	.05	.02
☐ 116	Mike Jackson	.05	.02

☐ 117	Darren Lewis	.05	.02	☐ 203	Greg Gagne	.05	.02
☐ 118	Bill Swift	.05	.02	☐ 204	Brian Harper	.05	.02
☐ 119	Robby Thompson	.05	.02	☐ 205	Kent Hrbek	.10	.05
☐ 120	Matt Williams	.20	.09	☐ 206	Scott Leius	.05	.02
☐ 121	Brady Anderson	.20	.09	☐ 207	Shane Mack	.05	.02
☐ 122	Glenn Davis	.05	.02	☐ 208	Pat Mahomes	.05	.02
☐ 123	Mike Devereaux	.05	.02	☐ 209	Kirby Puckett	.60	.25
☐ 124	Chris Hoiles	.05	.02	☐ 210	John Smiley	.05	.02
☐ 125	Sam Horn	.05	.02	☐ 211	Mike Gallego	.05	.02
☐ 126	Ben McDonald	.05	.02	☐ 212	Charlie Hayes	.05	.02
☐ 127	Mike Mussina	.50	.23	☐ 213	Pat Kelly	.05	.02
☐ 128	Gregg Olson	.05	.02	☐ 214	Roberto Kelly	.05	.02
☐ 129	Cal Ripken Jr.	1.25	.55	☐ 215	Kevin Maas	.05	.02
☐ 130	Rick Sutcliffe	.05	.02	☐ 216	Don Mattingly	.50	.23
☐ 131	Wade Boggs	.30	.14	☐ 217	Matt Nokes	.05	.02
☐ 132	Roger Clemens	.60	.25	☐ 218	Melido Perez	.05	.02
☐ 133	Greg A. Harris	.05	.02	☐ 219	Scott Sanderson	.05	.02
☐ 134	Tim Naehring	.05	.02	☐ 220	Danny Tartabull	.05	.02
☐ 135	Tony Pena	.05	.02	☐ 221	Harold Baines	.10	.05
☐ 136	Phil Plantier	.05	.02	☐ 222	Jose Canseco	.20	.09
☐ 137	Jeff Reardon	.10	.05	☐ 223	Dennis Eckersley	.10	.05
☐ 138	Jody Reed	.05	.02	☐ 224	Dave Henderson	.05	.02
☐ 139	Mo Vaughn	.50	.23	☐ 225	Carney Lansford	.10	.05
☐ 140	Frank Viola	.05	.02	☐ 226	Mark McGwire	.60	.25
☐ 141	Jim Abbott	.05	.02	☐ 227	Mike Moore	.05	.02
☐ 142	Hubie Brooks	.05	.02	☐ 228	Randy Ready	.05	.02
☐ 143	Chad Curtis	.30	.14	☐ 229	Terry Steinbach	.10	.05
☐ 144	Gary DiSarcina	.05	.02	☐ 230	Dave Stewart	.10	.05
☐ 145	Chuck Finley	.05	.02	☐ 231	Jay Buhner	.20	.09
☐ 146	Bryan Harvey	.05	.02	☐ 232	Ken Griffey Jr.	2.00	.90
☐ 147	Von Hayes	.05	.02	☐ 233	Erik Hanson	.05	.02
☐ 148	Mark Langston	.05	.02	☐ 234	Randy Johnson	.30	.14
☐ 149	Lance Parrish	.05	.02	☐ 235	Edgar Martinez	.20	.09
☐ 150	Lee Stevens	.05	.02	☐ 236	Tino Martinez	.30	.14
☐ 151	George Bell	.05	.02	☐ 237	Kevin Mitchell	.05	.02
☐ 152	Alex Fernandez	.10	.05	☐ 238	Pete O'Brien	.05	.02
☐ 153	Greg Hibbard	.05	.02	☐ 239	Harold Reynolds	.05	.02
☐ 154	Lance Johnson	.05	.02	☐ 240	David Valle	.05	.02
☐ 155	Kirk McCaskill	.05	.02	☐ 241	Julio Franco	.05	.02
☐ 156	Tim Raines	.10	.05	☐ 242	Juan Gonzalez	1.00	.45
☐ 157	Steve Sax	.05	.02	☐ 243	Jose Guzman	.05	.02
☐ 158	Bobby Thigpen	.05	.02	☐ 244	Rafael Palmeiro	.20	.09
☐ 159	Frank Thomas	1.50	.70	☐ 245	Dean Palmer	.10	.05
☐ 160	Robin Ventura	.10	.05	☐ 246	Ivan Rodriguez	.60	.25
☐ 161	Sandy Alomar Jr.	.05	.02	☐ 247	Jeff Russell	.05	.02
☐ 162	Jack Armstrong	.05	.02	☐ 248	Nolan Ryan	1.25	.55
☐ 163	Carlos Baerga	.05	.02	☐ 249	Ruben Sierra	.05	.02
☐ 164	Albert Belle	.40	.18	☐ 250	Dickie Thon	.05	.02
☐ 165	Alex Cole	.05	.02	☐ 251	Roberto Alomar	.30	.14
☐ 166	Glenallen Hill	.05	.02	☐ 252	Derek Bell	.10	.05
☐ 167	Mark Lewis	.05	.02	☐ 253	Pat Borders	.05	.02
☐ 168	Kenny Lofton	1.25	.55	☐ 254	Joe Carter	.10	.05
☐ 169	Paul Sorrento	.05	.02	☐ 255	Kelly Gruber	.05	.02
☐ 170	Mark Whiten	.05	.02	☐ 256	Juan Guzman	.05	.02
☐ 171	Milt Cuyler	.05	.02	☐ 257	Jack Morris	.10	.05
☐ 172	Rob Deer	.05	.02	☐ 258	John Olerud	.05	.02
☐ 173	Cecil Fielder	.10	.05	☐ 259	Devon White	.05	.02
☐ 174	Travis Fryman	.05	.02	☐ 260	Dave Winfield	.30	.14
☐ 175	Mike Henneman	.05	.02	☐ 261	Checklist	.05	.02
☐ 176	Tony Phillips	.05	.02	☐ 262	Checklist	.05	.02
☐ 177	Frank Tanana	.05	.02	☐ 263	Checklist	.05	.02
☐ 178	Mickey Tettleton	.05	.02	☐ 264	History Card	.05	.02
☐ 179	Alan Trammell	.20	.09				
☐ 180	Lou Whitaker	.10	.05				
☐ 181	George Brett	.60	.25				
☐ 182	Tom Gordon	.05	.02				
☐ 183	Mark Gubicza	.05	.02				
☐ 184	Gregg Jefferies	.05	.02				
☐ 185	Wally Joyner	.10	.05				
☐ 186	Brent Mayne	.05	.02				
☐ 187	Brian McRae	.05	.02				
☐ 188	Kevin McReynolds	.05	.02				
☐ 189	Keith Miller	.05	.02				
☐ 190	Jeff Montgomery	.05	.02				
☐ 191	Dante Bichette	.20	.09				
☐ 192	Ricky Bones	.05	.02				
☐ 193	Scott Fletcher	.05	.02				
☐ 194	Paul Molitor	.30	.14				
☐ 195	Jaime Navarro	.05	.02				
☐ 196	Franklin Stubbs	.05	.02				
☐ 197	B.J. Surhoff	.05	.02				
☐ 198	Greg Vaughn	.05	.02				
☐ 199	Bill Wegman	.05	.02				
☐ 200	Robin Yount	.20	.09				
☐ 201	Rick Aguilera	.05	.02				
☐ 202	Scott Erickson	.10	.05				

Within a bronze picture frame design on dark turquoise, the backs give a brief history of the team with special reference to the year of the vintage uniform. The cards are numbered on the back with a "BC" prefix.

	MINT	NRMT
COMPLETE SET (14)	25.00	11.00
COMP.FOIL SET (8)	15.00	6.75
COMP.JUMBO SET (6)	10.00	4.50
COMMON CARD (BC1-BC14)	.75	.35
FOIL: RAND.INSERTS IN FOIL PACKS		
JUMBO'S: ONE PER JUMBO PACK		

		MINT	NRMT
☐ BC1	Ryne Sandberg	2.00	.90
☐ BC2	Carlton Fisk	1.50	.70
☐ BC3	Wade Boggs	1.50	.70
☐ BC4	Jose Canseco	1.25	.55
☐ BC5	Don Mattingly	2.50	1.10
☐ BC6	Darryl Strawberry	.75	.35
☐ BC7	Cal Ripken	6.00	2.70
☐ BC8	Will Clark	1.25	.55
☐ BC9	Andre Dawson	1.25	.55
☐ BC10	Andy Van Slyke	.75	.35
☐ BC11	Paul Molitor	1.50	.70
☐ BC12	Jeff Bagwell	5.00	2.20
☐ BC13	Darren Daulton	1.00	.45
☐ BC14	Kirby Puckett	3.00	1.35

1993 Studio

1992 Studio Heritage

The 1992 Studio Heritage standard-size insert set presents today's star players dressed in vintage uniforms. Cards numbered 1-8 were randomly inserted in 12-card foil packs while cards numbered 9-14 were inserted one per pack in 28-card jumbo packs. The fronts display sepia-toned portraits of the players dressed in vintage uniforms of their current teams. The pictures are bordered by dark turquoise and have bronze foil picture holders at each corner. The set title "Heritage Series" also appears in bronze foil lettering above the pictures.

The 220 standard-size cards comprising this set feature borderless fronts with posed color player photos that are cut out and superposed upon a closeup of an embroidered team logo. A facsimile player autograph appears in prismatic gold foil across the lower portion of the photo. The borderless black backs carry another posed color player photo shunted to the right side, with the player's name, position, team, biography, and personal profile appearing in white lettering on the left side. The key Rookie Card in this set is J.T. Snow.

	MINT	NRMT
COMPLETE SET (220)	20.00	9.00
COMMON CARD (1-220)	.10	.05
MINOR STARS	.25	.11
UNLISTED STARS	.50	.23
COMP.F.THOMAS SET (5)	30.00	13.50
COMMON THOMAS (1-5)	6.00	2.70
THOMAS: RANDOM INSERTS IN ALL PACKS		

□ 1 Dennis Eckersley .25 .11
□ 2 Chad Curtis .25 .11
□ 3 Eric Anthony .10 .05
□ 4 Roberto Alomar .50 .23
□ 5 Steve Avery .10 .05
□ 6 Cal Eldred .10 .05
□ 7 Bernard Gilkey .25 .11
□ 8 Steve Buechele .10 .05
□ 9 Brett Butler .25 .11
□ 10 Terry Mulholland .10 .05
□ 11 Moises Alou .25 .11
□ 12 Barry Bonds .60 .25
□ 13 Sandy Alomar Jr. .25 .11
□ 14 Chris Bosio .10 .05
□ 15 Scott Sanderson .10 .05
□ 16 Bobby Bonilla .25 .11
□ 17 Brady Anderson .30 .14
□ 18 Derek Bell .25 .11
□ 19 Wes Chamberlain .10 .05
□ 20 Jay Bell .25 .11
□ 21 Kevin Brown .25 .11
□ 22 Roger Clemens 1.00 .45
□ 23 Roberto Kelly .25 .11
□ 24 Dante Bichette .30 .14
□ 25 George Brett 1.00 .45
□ 26 Rob Deer .10 .05
□ 27 Brian Harper .10 .05
□ 28 George Bell .10 .05
□ 29 Jim Abbott .10 .05
□ 30 Dave Henderson .10 .05
□ 31 Wade Boggs .50 .23
□ 32 Chili Davis .25 .11
□ 33 Ellis Burks .25 .11
□ 34 Jeff Bagwell 1.00 .45
□ 35 Kent Hrbek .25 .11
□ 36 Pat Borders .10 .05
□ 37 Cecil Fielder .25 .11
□ 38 Sid Bream .10 .05
□ 39 Greg Gagne .10 .05
□ 40 Darryl Hamilton .10 .05
□ 41 Jerald Clark .10 .05
□ 42 Mark Grace .30 .14
□ 43 Barry Larkin .30 .14
□ 44 John Burkett .10 .05
□ 45 Scott Cooper .10 .05
□ 46 Mike Lansing .25 .11
□ 47 Jose Canseco .30 .14
□ 48 Will Clark .30 .14
□ 49 Carlos Garcia .10 .05
□ 50 Carlos Baerga .10 .05
□ 51 Darren Daulton .25 .11
□ 52 Jay Buhner .30 .14
□ 53 Andy Benes .25 .11
□ 54 Jeff Conine .25 .11
□ 55 Mike Devereaux .10 .05
□ 56 Vince Coleman .10 .05
□ 57 Terry Steinbach .10 .05
□ 58 J.T. Snow .60 .25
□ 59 Greg Swindell .10 .05
□ 60 Devon White .10 .05
□ 61 John Smoltz .25 .11
□ 62 Todd Zeile .10 .05
□ 63 Rick Wilkins .10 .05
□ 64 Tim Wallach .10 .05
□ 65 John Wetteland .25 .11
□ 66 Matt Williams .30 .14
□ 67 Paul Sorrento .10 .05
□ 68 David Valle .10 .05
□ 69 Walt Weiss .10 .05
□ 70 John Franco .25 .11
□ 71 Nolan Ryan 2.00 .90
□ 72 Frank Viola .10 .05
□ 73 Chris Sabo .10 .05
□ 74 David Nied .10 .05

□ 75 Kevin McReynolds .10 .05
□ 76 Lou Whitaker .25 .11
□ 77 Dave Winfield .30 .14
□ 78 Robin Ventura .25 .11
□ 79 Spike Owen .10 .05
□ 80 Cal Ripken Jr. 2.00 .90
□ 81 Dan Walters .10 .05
□ 82 Mitch Williams .10 .05
□ 83 Tim Wakefield .25 .11
□ 84 Rickey Henderson .30 .14
□ 85 Gary DiSarcina .10 .05
□ 86 Craig Biggio .30 .14
□ 87 Joe Carter .25 .11
□ 88 Ron Gant .25 .11
□ 89 John Jaha .25 .11
□ 90 Gregg Jefferies .10 .05
□ 91 Jose Guzman .10 .05
□ 92 Eric Karros .25 .11
□ 93 Wil Cordero .10 .05
□ 94 Royce Clayton .10 .05
□ 95 Albert Belle .60 .25
□ 96 Ken Griffey Jr. 2.50 1.10
□ 97 Orestes Destrade .10 .05
□ 98 Tony Fernandez .10 .05
□ 99 Leo Gomez .10 .05
□ 100 Tony Gwynn 1.25 .55
□ 101 Len Dykstra .25 .11
□ 102 Jeff King .10 .05
□ 103 Julio Franco .10 .05
□ 104 Andre Dawson .30 .14
□ 105 Randy Milligan .10 .05
□ 106 Alex Cole .10 .05
□ 107 Phil Hiatt .10 .05
□ 108 Travis Fryman .25 .11
□ 109 Chuck Knoblauch .50 .23
□ 110 Bo Jackson .25 .11
□ 111 Pat Kelly .10 .05
□ 112 Bret Saberhagen .10 .05
□ 113 Ruben Sierra .10 .05
□ 114 Tim Salmon .60 .25
□ 115 Doug Jones .10 .05
□ 116 Ed Sprague .10 .05
□ 117 Terry Pendleton .25 .11
□ 118 Robin Yount .30 .14
□ 119 Mark Whiten .10 .05
□ 120 Checklist 1-110 .10 .05
□ 121 Sammy Sosa .50 .23
□ 122 Darryl Strawberry .25 .11
□ 123 Larry Walker .50 .23
□ 124 Robby Thompson .10 .05
□ 125 Carlos Martinez .10 .05
□ 126 Edgar Martinez .30 .14
□ 127 Benito Santiago .10 .05
□ 128 Howard Johnson .10 .05
□ 129 Harold Reynolds .10 .05
□ 130 Craig Shipley .10 .05
□ 131 Curt Schilling .25 .11
□ 132 Andy Van Slyke .25 .11
□ 133 Ivan Rodriguez .60 .25
□ 134 Mo Vaughn .60 .25
□ 135 Bip Roberts .10 .05
□ 136 Charlie Hayes .10 .05
□ 137 Brian McRae .10 .05
□ 138 Mickey Tettleton .10 .05
□ 139 Frank Thomas 2.00 .90
□ 140 Paul O'Neill .25 .11
□ 141 Mark McGwire 1.00 .45
□ 142 Damion Easley .10 .05
□ 143 Ken Caminiti .30 .14
□ 144 Juan Guzman .10 .05
□ 145 Tom Glavine .30 .14
□ 146 Pat Listach .25 .11
□ 147 Lee Smith .25 .11
□ 148 Derrick May .10 .05
□ 149 Ramon Martinez .25 .11
□ 150 Delino DeShields .10 .05
□ 151 Kirt Manwaring .10 .05
□ 152 Reggie Jefferson .10 .05
□ 153 Randy Johnson .50 .23
□ 154 Dave Magadan .10 .05
□ 155 Dwight Gooden .25 .11
□ 156 Chris Hoiles .10 .05
□ 157 Fred McGriff .30 .14
□ 158 Dave Hollins .25 .11
□ 159 Al Martin .10 .05
□ 160 Juan Gonzalez 1.25 .55

□ 161 Mike Greenwell .10 .05
□ 162 Kevin Mitchell .25 .11
□ 163 Andres Galarraga .50 .23
□ 164 Wally Joyner .25 .11
□ 165 Kirk Gibson .25 .11
□ 166 Pedro Munoz .10 .05
□ 167 Ozzie Guillen .10 .05
□ 168 Jimmy Key .25 .11
□ 169 Kevin Seitzer .10 .05
□ 170 Luis Polonia .10 .05
□ 171 Luis Gonzalez .10 .05
□ 172 Paul Molitor .50 .23
□ 173 David Justice .50 .23
□ 174 B.J. Surhoff .25 .11
□ 175 Ray Lankford .30 .14
□ 176 Ryne Sandberg .60 .25
□ 177 Jody Reed .10 .05
□ 178 Marquis Grissom .25 .11
□ 179 Willie McGee .10 .05
□ 180 Kenny Lofton 1.00 .45
□ 181 Junior Felix .10 .05
□ 182 Jose Offerman .10 .05
□ 183 John Kruk .25 .11
□ 184 Orlando Merced .10 .05
□ 185 Rafael Palmeiro .30 .14
□ 186 Billy Hatcher .10 .05
□ 187 Joe Oliver .10 .05
□ 188 Joe Girardi .10 .05
□ 189 Jose Lind .10 .05
□ 190 Harold Baines .25 .11
□ 191 Mike Pagliarulo .10 .05
□ 192 Lance Johnson .10 .05
□ 193 Don Mattingly .75 .35
□ 194 Doug Drabek .10 .05
□ 195 John Olerud .10 .05
□ 196 Greg Maddux 1.50 .70
□ 197 Greg Vaughn .10 .05
□ 198 Tom Pagnozzi .10 .05
□ 199 Willie Wilson .10 .05
□ 200 Jack McDowell .10 .05
□ 201 Mike Piazza 2.50 1.10
□ 202 Mike Mussina .50 .23
□ 203 Charles Nagy .25 .11
□ 204 Tino Martinez .50 .23
□ 205 Charlie Hough .10 .05
□ 206 Todd Hundley .30 .14
□ 207 Gary Sheffield .50 .23
□ 208 Mickey Morandini .10 .05
□ 209 Don Slaught .10 .05
□ 210 Dean Palmer .25 .11
□ 211 Jose Rijo .10 .05
□ 212 Vinny Castilla .50 .23
□ 213 Tony Phillips .10 .05
□ 214 Kirby Puckett 1.00 .45
□ 215 Tim Raines .25 .11
□ 216 Otis Nixon .10 .05
□ 217 Ozzie Smith .60 .25
□ 218 Jose Vizcaino .10 .05
□ 219 Randy Tomlin .10 .05
□ 220 Checklist 111-220 .10 .05

1993 Studio Heritage

This 12-card standard-size set was randomly inserted in all 1993 Leaf Studio foil packs, and features sepia-toned portraits of current players in vintage team uniforms. The pictures are bordered in turquoise blue and have bronze-foil simulated picture holders at each corner. The set title appears in white lettering above the picture, and the player's name is printed in white below. The horizontal and turquoise-blue-bordered back shades from beige to red from top to bottom, and carries a posed sepia-toned player picture on the right within an oval set off by red and black lines. His name appears in white lettering at the top within a black arc. A brief story of the team represented by the player's vintage uniform follows below.

	MINT	NRMT
COMPLETE SET (12)	30.00	13.50
COMMON CARD (1-12)	1.00	.45
RANDOM INSERTS IN ALL PACKS		

		MINT	NRMT
☐ 1	George Brett	6.00	2.70
☐ 2	Juan Gonzalez	8.00	3.60
☐ 3	Roger Clemens	6.00	2.70
☐ 4	Mark McGwire	6.00	2.70
☐ 5	Mark Grace	2.00	.90
☐ 6	Ozzie Smith	4.00	1.80
☐ 7	Barry Larkin	2.00	.90
☐ 8	Frank Thomas	12.00	5.50
☐ 9	Carlos Baerga	1.00	.45
☐ 10	Eric Karros	1.50	.70
☐ 11	J.T. Snow	1.50	.70
☐ 12	John Kruk	1.00	.45

1993 Studio Silhouettes

The 1993 Studio Silhouettes 10-card standard-size set was inserted one per 20-card Studio jumbo pack. Full-bleed sharp fronts display posed color photos of star players against action silhouettes. The set's title is printed across the top and the player's name appears along the bottom within a darker gray area. The borderless and grayish back features a color player action photo on one side and a personal profile on the other.

	MINT	NRMT
COMPLETE SET (10)	25.00	11.00
COMMON CARD (1-10)	.50	.23
ONE PER JUMBO PACK		

		MINT	NRMT
☐ 1	Frank Thomas	6.00	2.70
☐ 2	Barry Bonds	2.00	.90

		MINT	NRMT
☐ 3	Jeff Bagwell	3.00	1.35
☐ 4	Juan Gonzalez	4.00	1.80
☐ 5	Travis Fryman	.75	.35
☐ 6	J.T. Snow	1.00	.45
☐ 7	John Kruk	.75	.35
☐ 8	Jeff Blauser	.50	.23
☐ 9	Mike Piazza	8.00	3.60
☐ 10	Nolan Ryan	6.00	2.70

1993 Studio Superstars on Canvas

This ten-card standard-size set was randomly inserted in 1993 Studio hobby and retail foil packs. The set features players in gray-bordered portraits that blend photography and artwork. The design of each front simulates a canvas painting of a player displayed on an artist's easel. The player's name appears in copper foil across the easel's base near the bottom. The set's title appears in white lettering beneath. The horizontal back carries a cutout color action player photo on one side and the player's name and career highlights within a black rectangle on the other, all superposed upon an abstract team color-coded design.

	MINT	NRMT
COMPLETE SET (10)	35.00	16.00
COMMON CARD (1-10)	1.50	.70
RANDOM INSERTS IN HOBBY/RETAIL PACKS		

		MINT	NRMT
☐ 1	Ken Griffey Jr.	15.00	6.75
☐ 2	Jose Canseco	2.00	.90
☐ 3	Mark McGwire	6.00	2.70
☐ 4	Mike Mussina	3.00	1.35
☐ 5	Joe Carter	1.50	.70
☐ 6	Frank Thomas	12.00	5.50
☐ 7	Darren Daulton	1.50	.70
☐ 8	Mark Grace	2.00	.90
☐ 9	Andres Galarraga	3.00	1.35
☐ 10	Barry Bonds	4.00	1.80

1994 Studio

The 1994 Studio set consists of 220 full-bleed, standard-size cards. Card fronts offer a player photo with his jersey hanging in a locker room setting in the background. Backs contain statistics and a small photo. The set is grouped alphabetically within teams.

	MINT	NRMT
COMPLETE SET (220)	15.00	6.75
COMMON CARD (1-220)	.15	.07
MINOR STARS	.30	.14
UNLISTED STARS	.60	.25

		MINT	NRMT
☐ 1	Dennis Eckersley	.30	.14
☐ 2	Brent Gates	.15	.07
☐ 3	Rickey Henderson	.40	.18
☐ 4	Mark McGwire	1.25	.55
☐ 5	Troy Neel	.15	.07
☐ 6	Ruben Sierra	.15	.07
☐ 7	Terry Steinbach	.15	.07
☐ 8	Chad Curtis	.15	.07
☐ 9	Chili Davis	.30	.14
☐ 10	Gary DiSarcina	.15	.07
☐ 11	Damion Easley	.15	.07
☐ 12	Bo Jackson	.30	.14
☐ 13	Mark Langston	.15	.07
☐ 14	Eduardo Perez	.15	.07
☐ 15	Tim Salmon	.60	.25
☐ 16	Jeff Bagwell	1.25	.55
☐ 17	Craig Biggio	.40	.18
☐ 18	Ken Caminiti	.40	.18
☐ 19	Andujar Cedeno	.15	.07
☐ 20	Doug Drabek	.15	.07
☐ 21	Steve Finley	.30	.14
☐ 22	Luis Gonzalez	.15	.07
☐ 23	Darryl Kile	.30	.14
☐ 24	Roberto Alomar	.60	.25
☐ 25	Pat Borders	.15	.07
☐ 26	Joe Carter	.30	.14
☐ 27	Carlos Delgado	.40	.18
☐ 28	Pat Hentgen	.30	.14
☐ 29	Paul Molitor	.60	.25
☐ 30	John Olerud	.30	.14
☐ 31	Ed Sprague	.15	.07
☐ 32	Devon White	.15	.07
☐ 33	Steve Avery	.15	.07
☐ 34	Tom Glavine	.30	.14
☐ 35	David Justice	.60	.25
☐ 36	Roberto Kelly	.15	.07
☐ 37	Ryan Klesko	.60	.25
☐ 38	Javier Lopez	.40	.18
☐ 39	Greg Maddux	2.00	.90
☐ 40	Fred McGriff	.40	.18
☐ 41	Terry Pendleton	.15	.07
☐ 42	Ricky Bones	.15	.07
☐ 43	Darryl Hamilton	.15	.07
☐ 44	Brian Harper	.15	.07
☐ 45	John Jaha	.15	.07
☐ 46	Dave Nilsson	.15	.07
☐ 47	Kevin Seitzer	.15	.07
☐ 48	Greg Vaughn	.15	.07
☐ 49	Turner Ward	.15	.07
☐ 50	Bernard Gilkey	.15	.07
☐ 51	Gregg Jefferies	.15	.07
☐ 52	Ray Lankford	.30	.14
☐ 53	Tom Pagnozzi	.15	.07
☐ 54	Ozzie Smith	.75	.35
☐ 55	Bob Tewksbury	.15	.07
☐ 56	Mark Whiten	.15	.07
☐ 57	Todd Zeile	.15	.07
☐ 58	Steve Buechele	.15	.07
☐ 59	Shawon Dunston	.15	.07
☐ 60	Mark Grace	.40	.18
☐ 61	Derrick May	.15	.07
☐ 62	Karl Rhodes	.15	.07

		MINT	NRMT
☐ 63	Ryne Sandberg	.75	.35
☐ 64	Sammy Sosa	.60	.25
☐ 65	Rick Wilkins	.15	.07
☐ 66	Brett Butler	.30	.14
☐ 67	Delino DeShields	.15	.07
☐ 68	Orel Hershiser	.30	.14
☐ 69	Eric Karros	.30	.14
☐ 70	Raul Mondesi	.60	.25
☐ 71	Jose Offerman	.15	.07
☐ 72	Mike Piazza	2.00	.90
☐ 73	Tim Wallach	.15	.07
☐ 74	Moises Alou	.30	.14
☐ 75	Sean Berry	.15	.07
☐ 76	Wil Cordero	.15	.07
☐ 77	Cliff Floyd	.30	.14
☐ 78	Marquis Grissom	.30	.14
☐ 79	Ken Hill	.15	.07
☐ 80	Larry Walker	.15	.07
☐ 81	John Wetteland	.15	.07
☐ 82	Rod Beck	.15	.07
☐ 83	Barry Bonds	.75	.35
☐ 84	Royce Clayton	.15	.07
☐ 85	Darren Lewis	.15	.07
☐ 86	Willie McGee	.15	.07
☐ 87	Bill Swift	.15	.07
☐ 88	Robby Thompson	.15	.07
☐ 89	Matt Williams	.40	.18
☐ 90	Sandy Alomar Jr.	.30	.14
☐ 91	Carlos Baerga	.15	.07
☐ 92	Albert Belle	.75	.35
☐ 93	Kenny Lofton	.75	.35
☐ 94	Eddie Murray	.60	.25
☐ 95	Manny Ramirez	.75	.35
☐ 96	Paul Sorrento	.15	.07
☐ 97	Jim Thome	.75	.35
☐ 98	Rich Amaral	.15	.07
☐ 99	Eric Anthony	.15	.07
☐ 100	Jay Buhner	.30	.14
☐ 101	Ken Griffey Jr.	3.00	1.35
☐ 102	Randy Johnson	.60	.25
☐ 103	Edgar Martinez	.40	.18
☐ 104	Tino Martinez	.60	.25
☐ 105	Kurt Abbott	.15	.07
☐ 106	Bret Barberie	.15	.07
☐ 107	Chuck Carr	.15	.07
☐ 108	Jeff Conine	.30	.14
☐ 109	Chris Hammond	.15	.07
☐ 110	Bryan Harvey	.15	.07
☐ 111	Benito Santiago	.15	.07
☐ 112	Gary Sheffield	.60	.25
☐ 113	Bobby Bonilla	.30	.14
☐ 114	Dwight Gooden	.30	.14
☐ 115	Todd Hundley	.30	.14
☐ 116	Bobby Jones	.30	.14
☐ 117	Jeff Kent	.15	.07
☐ 118	Kevin McReynolds	.15	.07
☐ 119	Bret Saberhagen	.15	.07
☐ 120	Ryan Thompson	.15	.07
☐ 121	Harold Baines	.30	.14
☐ 122	Mike Devereaux	.15	.07
☐ 123	Jeffrey Hammonds	.30	.14
☐ 124	Ben McDonald	.15	.07
☐ 125	Mike Mussina	.60	.25
☐ 126	Rafael Palmeiro	.40	.18
☐ 127	Cal Ripken Jr.	2.50	1.10
☐ 128	Lee Smith	.30	.14
☐ 129	Brad Ausmus	.15	.07
☐ 130	Derek Bell	.15	.07
☐ 131	Andy Benes	.30	.14
☐ 132	Tony Gwynn	1.50	.70
☐ 133	Trevor Hoffman	.15	.07
☐ 134	Scott Livingstone	.15	.07
☐ 135	Phil Plantier	.15	.07
☐ 136	Darren Daulton	.30	.14
☐ 137	Mariano Duncan	.15	.07
☐ 138	Lenny Dykstra	.30	.14
☐ 139	Dave Hollins	.15	.07
☐ 140	Pete Incaviglia	.15	.07
☐ 141	Danny Jackson	.15	.07
☐ 142	John Kruk	.30	.14
☐ 143	Kevin Stocker	.15	.07
☐ 144	Jay Bell	.30	.14
☐ 145	Carlos Garcia	.15	.07
☐ 146	Jeff King	.15	.07
☐ 147	Al Martin	.15	.07
☐ 148	Orlando Merced	.15	.07
☐ 149	Don Slaught	.15	.07
☐ 150	Andy Van Slyke	.30	.14
☐ 151	Kevin Brown	.15	.07
☐ 152	Jose Canseco	.40	.18
☐ 153	Will Clark	.40	.18
☐ 154	Juan Gonzalez	1.50	.70
☐ 155	David Hulse	.15	.07
☐ 156	Dean Palmer	.15	.07
☐ 157	Ivan Rodriguez	.75	.35
☐ 158	Kenny Rogers	.15	.07
☐ 159	Roger Clemens	1.25	.55
☐ 160	Scott Cooper	.15	.07
☐ 161	Andre Dawson	.40	.18
☐ 162	Mike Greenwell	.15	.07
☐ 163	Otis Nixon	.15	.07
☐ 164	Aaron Sele	.15	.07
☐ 165	John Valentin	.30	.14
☐ 166	Mo Vaughn	.75	.35
☐ 167	Bret Boone	.15	.07
☐ 168	Barry Larkin	.40	.18
☐ 169	Kevin Mitchell	.15	.07
☐ 170	Hal Morris	.15	.07
☐ 171	Jose Rijo	.15	.07
☐ 172	Deion Sanders	.30	.14
☐ 173	Reggie Sanders	.15	.07
☐ 174	John Smiley	.15	.07
☐ 175	Dante Bichette	.30	.14
☐ 176	Ellis Burks	.15	.07
☐ 177	Andres Galarraga	.60	.25
☐ 178	Joe Girardi	.15	.07
☐ 179	Charlie Hayes	.15	.07
☐ 180	Roberto Mejia	.15	.07
☐ 181	Walt Weiss	.15	.07
☐ 182	David Cone	.30	.14
☐ 183	Gary Gaetti	.15	.07
☐ 184	Greg Gagne	.15	.07
☐ 185	Felix Jose	.15	.07
☐ 186	Wally Joyner	.30	.14
☐ 187	Mike Macfarlane	.15	.07
☐ 188	Brian McRae	.15	.07
☐ 189	Eric Davis	.30	.14
☐ 190	Cecil Fielder	.30	.14
☐ 191	Travis Fryman	.30	.14
☐ 192	Tony Phillips	.15	.07
☐ 193	Mickey Tettleton	.15	.07
☐ 194	Alan Trammell	.40	.18
☐ 195	Lou Whitaker	.30	.14
☐ 196	Kent Hrbek	.30	.14
☐ 197	Chuck Knoblauch	.60	.25
☐ 198	Shane Mack	.15	.07
☐ 199	Pat Meares	.15	.07
☐ 200	Kirby Puckett	1.25	.55
☐ 201	Matt Walbeck	.15	.07
☐ 202	Dave Winfield	.40	.18
☐ 203	Wilson Alvarez	.15	.07
☐ 204	Alex Fernandez	.15	.07
☐ 205	Julio Franco	.15	.07
☐ 206	Ozzie Guillen	.15	.07
☐ 207	Jack McDowell	.15	.07
☐ 208	Tim Raines	.30	.14
☐ 209	Frank Thomas	2.50	1.10
☐ 210	Robin Ventura	.30	.14
☐ 211	Jim Abbott	.30	.14
☐ 212	Wade Boggs	.60	.25
☐ 213	Pat Kelly	.15	.07
☐ 214	Jimmy Key	.30	.14
☐ 215	Don Mattingly	1.00	.45
☐ 216	Paul O'Neill	.30	.14
☐ 217	Mike Stanley	.15	.07
☐ 218	Danny Tartabull	.15	.07
☐ 219	Checklist	.15	.07
☐ 220	Checklist	.15	.07

		MINT	NRMT
COMPLETE SET (8)		40.00	18.00
COMMON CARD (1-8)		2.00	.90
STATED ODDS 1:36			
☐ 1	Barry Bonds	4.00	1.80
☐ 2	Frank Thomas	12.00	5.50
☐ 3	Ken Griffey Jr.	15.00	6.75
☐ 4	Andres Galarraga	3.00	1.35
☐ 5	Juan Gonzalez	8.00	3.60
☐ 6	Tim Salmon	3.00	1.35
☐ 7	Paul O'Neill	2.00	.90
☐ 8	Mike Piazza	10.00	4.50

1994 Studio Heritage

Each player in this eight-card insert set (randomly inserted in foil packs at a rate of one in nine) is modelling a vintage uniform of his team. The year of the uniform is noted at the top with a gold lettering logo at the bottom. A black and white photo of the stadium that the team used from the era of the depicted uniform serves as background. The back has a small photo a team highlight from that year.

		MINT	NRMT
COMPLETE SET (8)		15.00	6.75
COMMON CARD (1-8)		.50	.23
STATED ODDS 1:9			
☐ 1	Barry Bonds	2.00	.90
☐ 2	Frank Thomas	6.00	2.70
☐ 3	Joe Carter	.75	.35
☐ 4	Don Mattingly	2.50	1.10
☐ 5	Ryne Sandberg	1.00	.45
☐ 6	Javier Lopez	1.00	.45
☐ 7	Gregg Jefferies	.50	.23
☐ 8	Mike Mussina	1.50	.70

1994 Studio Editor's Choice

This eight-card standard-sized set was randomly inserted in foil packs at a rate of one in 36. These cards are acetate and were designed much like a film strip with black borders. The fronts have various stop-action shots of the player and no back.

1994 Studio Series Stars

This 10-card acetate set show-cases top stars and was limited to 10,000 of each card. They were randomly inserted in foil packs at a rate of one in 60. The player cutout is surrounded by a small circle of stars with the player's name at the top. The team name, limited edition nota-tion and the Series Stars logo are at the bottom. The back of the cutout contains a photo. Gold versions of this set were more difficult to obtain in packs (one in 120, 5,000 total).

	MINT	NRMT
COMPLETE SET (10)	150.00	70.00
COMMON CARD (1-10)	3.00	1.35
SILVER STATED ODDS 1:60		
SILVER STATED PRINT RUN 10,000 SETS		
COMP.GOLD SET (10)	300.00	135.00
*GOLD: 1X TO 2X SILVER		
GOLD STATED ODDS 1:120		
GOLD PRINT RUN 5000 SERIAL #'d SETS		

☐ 1	Tony Gwynn	15.00	6.75
☐ 2	Barry Bonds	8.00	3.60
☐ 3	Frank Thomas	25.00	11.00
☐ 4	Ken Griffey Jr	30.00	13.50
☐ 5	Joe Carter	3.00	1.35
☐ 6	Mike Piazza	20.00	9.00
☐ 7	Cal Ripken Jr.	25.00	11.00
☐ 8	Greg Maddux	20.00	9.00
☐ 9	Juan Gonzalez	15.00	6.75
☐ 10	Don Mattingly	10.00	4.50

1995 Studio

This 200-card horizontal set was issued by Donruss for the fifth consecutive year. Using a different design than past Studio issues, these cards were designed similarly to credit cards. The cards were issued in five-card packs with a suggest-ed retail price of $1.49. The fronts have a player photo on the right with holographic team logo in the right corner. The rest of the card has the player iden-tified in the upper left. Underneath that information are 1994 stats as well as various vital statistics. There is also the "Studio" logo in the upper left corner. The horizontal backs have an action photo on the left. The right has the player's signa-ture along with a pertinent fact and his career statistics. There are no Rookie Cards in this set.

	MINT	NRMT
COMPLETE SET (200)	60.00	27.00
COMMON CARD (1-200)	.20	.09
MINOR STARS	.40	.18
UNLISTED STARS	.75	.35
COMP.GOLD SET (50)	30.00	13.50
COMMON GOLD (1-50)	.50	.23
*GOLD STARS: .6X TO 1.2X HI COLUMN		
ONE GOLD PER PACK		
COMP.PLATINUM SET (25)	150.00	70.00
COMMON PLATINUM (1-25)	2.00	.90
*PLAT.STARS: 3X TO 6X HI COLUMN		
PLATINUM STATED ODDS 1:10		

☐ 1	Frank Thomas	3.00	1.35
☐ 2	Jeff Bagwell	1.50	.70
☐ 3	Don Mattingly	1.25	.55
☐ 4	Mike Piazza	2.50	1.10
☐ 5	Ken Griffey Jr.	4.00	1.80
☐ 6	Greg Maddux	2.50	1.10
☐ 7	Barry Bonds	1.00	.45
☐ 8	Cal Ripken Jr.	3.00	1.35
☐ 9	Jose Canseco	.60	.25
☐ 10	Paul Molitor	.75	.35
☐ 11	Kenny Lofton	1.00	.45
☐ 12	Will Clark	.60	.25
☐ 13	Tim Salmon	.75	.35
☐ 14	Joe Carter	.40	.18
☐ 15	Albert Belle	1.00	.45
☐ 16	Roger Clemens	1.50	.70
☐ 17	Roberto Alomar	.75	.35
☐ 18	Alex Rodriguez	3.00	1.35
☐ 19	Raul Mondesi	.60	.25
☐ 20	Deion Sanders	.40	.18
☐ 21	Juan Gonzalez	2.00	.90
☐ 22	Kirby Puckett	1.50	.70
☐ 23	Fred McGriff	.60	.25
☐ 24	Matt Williams	.60	.25
☐ 25	Tony Gwynn	2.00	.90
☐ 26	Cliff Floyd	.20	.09
☐ 27	Travis Fryman	.40	.18
☐ 28	Shawn Green	.40	.18
☐ 29	Mike Mussina	.75	.35
☐ 30	Bob Hamelin	.20	.09
☐ 31	David Justice	.75	.35
☐ 32	Manny Ramirez	.75	.35
☐ 33	David Cone	.40	.18
☐ 34	Marquis Grissom	.40	.18
☐ 35	Moises Alou	.40	.18
☐ 36	Carlos Baerga	.20	.09
☐ 37	Barry Larkin	.60	.25
☐ 38	Robin Ventura	.40	.18
☐ 39	Mo Vaughn	1.00	.45
☐ 40	Jeffrey Hammonds	.20	.09
☐ 41	Ozzie Smith	1.00	.45
☐ 42	Andres Galarraga	.75	.35
☐ 43	Carlos Delgado	.40	.18
☐ 44	Lenny Dykstra	.40	.18
☐ 45	Cecil Fielder	.40	.18
☐ 46	Wade Boggs	.75	.35
☐ 47	Gregg Jefferies	.20	.09
☐ 48	Randy Johnson	.75	.35
☐ 49	Rafael Palmeiro	.60	.25
☐ 50	Craig Biggio	.60	.25
☐ 51	Steve Avery	.20	.09
☐ 52	Ricky Bottalico	.40	.18
☐ 53	Chris Gomez	.20	.09
☐ 54	Carlos Garcia	.20	.09
☐ 55	Brian Anderson	.40	.18
☐ 56	Wilson Alvarez	.20	.09
☐ 57	Roberto Kelly	.20	.09
☐ 58	Larry Walker	.75	.35
☐ 59	Dean Palmer	.20	.09
☐ 60	Rick Aguilera	.20	.09
☐ 61	Javier Lopez	.40	.18
☐ 62	Shawon Dunston	.20	.09
☐ 63	Wm. VanLandingham	.20	.09
☐ 64	Jeff Kent	.20	.09
☐ 65	David McCarty	.20	.09
☐ 66	Armando Benitez	.20	.09
☐ 67	Brett Butler	.40	.18
☐ 68	Bernard Gilkey	.20	.09
☐ 69	Joey Hamilton	.40	.18
☐ 70	Chad Curtis	.20	.09
☐ 71	Dante Bichette	.40	.18
☐ 72	Chuck Carr	.20	.09
☐ 73	Pedro Martinez	.75	.35
☐ 74	Ramon Martinez	.40	.18
☐ 75	Rondell White	.40	.18
☐ 76	Alex Fernandez	.20	.09
☐ 77	Dennis Martinez	.40	.18
☐ 78	Sammy Sosa	.75	.35
☐ 79	Bernie Williams	.75	.35
☐ 80	Lou Whitaker	.40	.18
☐ 81	Kurt Abbott	.20	.09
☐ 82	Tino Martinez	.75	.35
☐ 83	Willie Greene	.20	.09
☐ 84	Garret Anderson	.60	.25
☐ 85	Jose Rijo	.20	.09
☐ 86	Jeff Montgomery	.20	.09
☐ 87	Mark Langston	.20	.09
☐ 88	Reggie Sanders	.20	.09
☐ 89	Rusty Greer	.75	.35
☐ 90	Delino DeShields	.20	.09
☐ 91	Jason Bere	.20	.09
☐ 92	Lee Smith	.40	.18
☐ 93	Devon White	.20	.09
☐ 94	John Wetteland	.20	.09
☐ 95	Luis Gonzalez	.20	.09
☐ 96	Greg Vaughn	.20	.09
☐ 97	Lance Johnson	.20	.09
☐ 98	Alan Trammell	.60	.25
☐ 99	Bret Saberhagen	.20	.09
☐ 100	Jack McDowell	.20	.09
☐ 101	Trevor Hoffman	.20	.09
☐ 102	Dave Nilsson	.20	.09
☐ 103	Bryan Harvey	.20	.09
☐ 104	Chuck Knoblauch	.75	.35
☐ 105	Bobby Bonilla	.40	.18
☐ 106	Hal Morris	.20	.09
☐ 107	Mark Whiten	.20	.09
☐ 108	Phil Plantier	.20	.09
☐ 109	Ryan Klesko	.60	.25
☐ 110	Greg Gagne	.20	.09
☐ 111	Ruben Sierra	.20	.09
☐ 112	J.R. Phillips	.20	.09
☐ 113	Terry Steinbach	.20	.09
☐ 114	Jay Buhner	.60	.25
☐ 115	Ken Caminiti	.60	.25
☐ 116	Gary DiSarcina	.20	.09
☐ 117	Ivan Rodriguez	1.00	.45
☐ 118	Bip Roberts	.20	.09
☐ 119	Jay Bell	.40	.18
☐ 120	Ken Hill	.20	.09
☐ 121	Mike Greenwell	.20	.09
☐ 122	Rick Wilkins	.20	.09
☐ 123	Rickey Henderson	.60	.25
☐ 124	Dave Hollins	.20	.09
☐ 125	Terry Pendleton	.20	.09
☐ 126	Rich Becker	.20	.09
☐ 127	Billy Ashley	.20	.09
☐ 128	Derek Bell	.20	.09
☐ 129	Dennis Eckersley	.40	.18
☐ 130	Andujar Cedeno	.20	.09
☐ 131	John Jaha	.20	.09
☐ 132	Chuck Finley	.20	.09
☐ 133	Steve Finley	.40	.18
☐ 134	Danny Tartabull	.20	.09
☐ 135	Jeff Conine	.40	.18
☐ 136	Jon Lieber	.20	.09
☐ 137	Jim Abbott	.20	.09
☐ 138	Steve Trachsel	.20	.09
☐ 139	Bret Boone	.20	.09

		MINT	NRMT
☐ 140	Charles Johnson	.40	.18
☐ 141	Mark McGwire	1.50	.70
☐ 142	Eddie Murray	.75	.35
☐ 143	Doug Drabek	.20	.09
☐ 144	Steve Cooke	.20	.09
☐ 145	Kevin Seitzer	.20	.09
☐ 146	Rod Beck	.20	.09
☐ 147	Eric Karros	.40	.18
☐ 148	Tim Raines	.40	.18
☐ 149	Joe Girardi	.20	.09
☐ 150	Aaron Sele	.20	.09
☐ 151	Robby Thompson	.20	.09
☐ 152	Chan Ho Park	.75	.35
☐ 153	Ellis Burks	.40	.18
☐ 154	Brian McRae	.20	.09
☐ 155	Jimmy Key	.40	.18
☐ 156	Rico Brogna	.20	.09
☐ 157	Ozzie Guillen	.20	.09
☐ 158	Chili Davis	.40	.18
☐ 159	Darren Daulton	.40	.18
☐ 160	Chipper Jones	2.50	1.10
☐ 161	Walt Weiss	.20	.09
☐ 162	Paul O'Neill	.40	.18
☐ 163	Al Martin	.20	.09
☐ 164	John Valentin	.20	.09
☐ 165	Tim Wallach	.20	.09
☐ 166	Scott Erickson	.20	.09
☐ 167	Ryan Thompson	.20	.09
☐ 168	Todd Zeile	.20	.09
☐ 169	Scott Cooper	.20	.09
☐ 170	Matt Mieske	.20	.09
☐ 171	Allen Watson	.20	.09
☐ 172	Brian L. Hunter	.60	.25
☐ 173	Kevin Stocker	.20	.09
☐ 174	Cal Eldred	.20	.09
☐ 175	Tony Phillips	.20	.09
☐ 176	Ben McDonald	.20	.09
☐ 177	Mark Grace	.60	.25
☐ 178	Midre Cummings	.20	.09
☐ 179	Orlando Merced	.20	.09
☐ 180	Jeff King	.20	.09
☐ 181	Gary Sheffield	.75	.35
☐ 182	Tom Glavine	.40	.18
☐ 183	Edgar Martinez	.60	.25
☐ 184	Steve Karsay	.20	.09
☐ 185	Pat Listach	.20	.09
☐ 186	Wil Cordero	.20	.09
☐ 187	Brady Anderson	.60	.25
☐ 188	Bobby Jones	.20	.09
☐ 189	Andy Benes	.40	.18
☐ 190	Ray Lankford	.40	.18
☐ 191	John Doherty	.20	.09
☐ 192	Wally Joyner	.40	.18
☐ 193	Jim Thome	.75	.35
☐ 194	Royce Clayton	.20	.09
☐ 195	John Olerud	.40	.18
☐ 196	Steve Buechele	.20	.09
☐ 197	Harold Baines	.40	.18
☐ 198	Geronimo Berroa	.20	.09
☐ 199	Checklist	.20	.09
☐ 200	Checklist	.20	.09

1996 Studio

The 1996 Studio set was issued in one series totalling 150 cards. and distributed in seven-card

packs. The fronts feature color action player photos with a player portrait in the background. The backs carry another player photo, biographical information, with a head photo and vital statistics printed on the letters of the card's name.

	MINT	NRMT
COMPLETE SET (150)	15.00	6.75
COMMON CARD (1-150)		.07
MINOR STARS	.25	.11
UNLISTED STARS	.50	.23
COMP.BRZ.PP SET (150)	400.00	180.00
COMMON BRZ.PP (1-150)	1.00	.45
*BRONZE PP STARS: 5X TO 12X HI COLUMN		
*BRONZE PP YOUNG STARS: 4X TO 10X HI		
BRONZE PP STATED ODDS 1:6		
BRONZE PP STATED PRINT RUN 2000 SETS		
COMP.GOLD PP SET (150)	1500.00	700.00
COMMON GOLD PP (1-150)	4.00	1.80
*GOLD PP STARS: 25X TO 50X HI COLUMN		
*GOLD PP YOUNG STARS: 20X TO 40X HI		
GOLD PP STATED ODDS 1:24		
GOLD PP STATED PRINT RUN 500 SETS		
COMP.SILVER PP SET (150)	3000.00	1350.00
COMMON SILV.PP (1-150)	10.00	4.50
*SILVER PP STARS: 50X TO 100X HI COLUMN		
*SILVER PP YOUNG STARS: 40X TO 80X HI		
SILVER: RANDOM INS.IN MAGAZINE PACKS		
SILVER STATED PRINT RUN 100 SETS		

☐ 1	Cal Ripken	2.00	.90
☐ 2	Alex Gonzalez	.15	.07
☐ 3	Roger Cedeno	.15	.07
☐ 4	Todd Hollandsworth	.15	.07
☐ 5	Gregg Jefferies	.15	.07
☐ 6	Ryne Sandberg	.60	.25
☐ 7	Eric Karros	.25	.11
☐ 8	Jeff Conine	.25	.11
☐ 9	Rafael Palmeiro	.40	.18
☐ 10	Bip Roberts	.15	.07
☐ 11	Roger Clemens	1.00	.45
☐ 12	Tom Glavine	.25	.11
☐ 13	Jason Giambi	.25	.11
☐ 14	Rey Ordonez	.25	.11
☐ 15	Chan Ho Park	.50	.23
☐ 16	Vinny Castilla	.25	.11
☐ 17	Butch Huskey	.25	.11
☐ 18	Greg Maddux	1.50	.70
☐ 19	Bernard Gilkey	.15	.07
☐ 20	Marquis Grissom	.25	.11
☐ 21	Chuck Knoblauch	.50	.23
☐ 22	Ozzie Smith	.60	.25
☐ 23	Garret Anderson	.25	.11
☐ 24	J.T. Snow	.25	.11
☐ 25	John Valentin	.15	.07
☐ 26	Barry Larkin	.40	.18
☐ 27	Bobby Bonilla	.25	.11
☐ 28	Todd Zeile	.15	.07
☐ 29	Roberto Alomar	.50	.23
☐ 30	Ramon Martinez	.25	.11
☐ 31	Jeff King	.15	.07
☐ 32	Dennis Eckersley	.25	.11
☐ 33	Derek Jeter	1.50	.70
☐ 34	Edgar Martinez	.40	.18
☐ 35	Geronimo Berroa	.15	.07
☐ 36	Hal Morris	.15	.07
☐ 37	Troy Percival	.15	.07
☐ 38	Jason Isringhausen	.15	.07
☐ 39	Greg Vaughn	.15	.07
☐ 40	Robin Ventura	.25	.11
☐ 41	Craig Biggio	.40	.18
☐ 42	Will Clark	.40	.18
☐ 43	Sammy Sosa	.50	.23
☐ 44	Bernie Williams	.50	.23
☐ 45	Kenny Lofton	.60	.25
☐ 46	Wade Boggs	.50	.23
☐ 47	Javy Lopez	.25	.11
☐ 48	Reggie Sanders	.15	.07
☐ 49	Jeff Bagwell	1.00	.45
☐ 50	Fred McGriff	.25	.11
☐ 51	Charles Johnson	.25	.11
☐ 52	Darren Daulton	.25	.11
☐ 53	Jose Canseco	.40	.18
☐ 54	Cecil Fielder	.25	.11
☐ 55	Hideo Nomo	1.25	.55
☐ 56	Tim Salmon	.50	.23
☐ 57	Carlos Delgado	.25	.11
☐ 58	David Cone	.25	.11
☐ 59	Tim Raines	.25	.11
☐ 60	Lyle Mouton	.15	.07
☐ 61	Wally Joyner	.25	.11
☐ 62	Bret Boone	.15	.07
☐ 63	Raul Mondesi	.40	.18
☐ 64	Gary Sheffield	.50	.23
☐ 65	Alex Rodriguez	1.50	.70
☐ 66	Russ Davis	.15	.07
☐ 67	Checklist	.15	.07
☐ 68	Marty Cordova	.25	.11
☐ 69	Ruben Sierra	.15	.07
☐ 70	Jose Mesa	.15	.07
☐ 71	Matt Williams	.40	.18
☐ 72	Chipper Jones	1.50	.70
☐ 73	Randy Johnson	.50	.23
☐ 74	Kirby Puckett	1.00	.45
☐ 75	Jim Edmonds	.40	.18
☐ 76	Barry Bonds	.60	.25
☐ 77	David Segui	.15	.07
☐ 78	Larry Walker	.50	.23
☐ 79	Jason Kendall	.40	.18
☐ 80	Mike Piazza	1.50	.70
☐ 81	Brian L.Hunter	.25	.11
☐ 82	Julio Franco	.15	.07
☐ 83	Jay Bell	.25	.11
☐ 84	Kevin Seitzer	.15	.07
☐ 85	John Smoltz	.25	.11
☐ 86	Joe Carter	.25	.11
☐ 87	Ray Durham	.15	.07
☐ 88	Carlos Baerga	.15	.07
☐ 89	Ron Gant	.25	.11
☐ 90	Orlando Merced	.15	.07
☐ 91	Lee Smith	.25	.11
☐ 92	Pedro Martinez	.50	.23
☐ 93	Frank Thomas	2.00	.90
☐ 94	Al Martin	.15	.07
☐ 95	Chad Curtis	.15	.07
☐ 96	Eddie Murray	.50	.23
☐ 97	Rusty Greer	.25	.11
☐ 98	Jay Buhner	.40	.18
☐ 99	Rico Brogna	.15	.07
☐ 100	Todd Hundley	.25	.11
☐ 101	Moises Alou	.25	.11
☐ 102	Chili Davis	.25	.11
☐ 103	Ismael Valdes	.15	.07
☐ 104	Mo Vaughn	.60	.25
☐ 105	Juan Gonzalez	1.25	.55
☐ 106	Mark Grudzielanek	.25	.11
☐ 107	Derek Bell	.15	.07
☐ 108	Shawn Green	.15	.07
☐ 109	David Justice	.50	.23
☐ 110	Paul O'Neill	.25	.11
☐ 111	Kevin Appier	.15	.07
☐ 112	Ray Lankford	.25	.11
☐ 113	Travis Fryman	.25	.11
☐ 114	Manny Ramirez	.50	.23
☐ 115	Brooks Kieschnick	.25	.11
☐ 116	Ken Griffey Jr.	2.50	1.10
☐ 117	Jeffrey Hammonds	.15	.07
☐ 118	Mark McGwire	1.00	.45
☐ 119	Denny Neagle	.25	.11
☐ 120	Quilvio Veras	.15	.07
☐ 121	Alan Benes	.25	.11
☐ 122	Rondell White	.25	.11
☐ 123	Osvaldo Fernandez	.25	.11
☐ 124	Andres Galarraga	.50	.23
☐ 125	Johnny Damon	.25	.11
☐ 126	Lenny Dykstra	.25	.11
☐ 127	Jason Schmidt	.25	.11
☐ 128	Mike Mussina	.50	.23
☐ 129	Ken Caminiti	.40	.18
☐ 130	Michael Tucker	.25	.11
☐ 131	LaTroy Hawkins	.15	.07
☐ 132	Checklist	.15	.07
☐ 133	Delino DeShields	.15	.07
☐ 134	Dave Nilsson	.15	.07
☐ 135	Jack McDowell	.15	.07
☐ 136	Joey Hamilton	.25	.11
☐ 137	Dante Bichette	.25	.11
☐ 138	Paul Molitor	.50	.23
☐ 139	Ivan Rodriguez	.60	.25

☐ 140 Mark Grace	.40	.18
☐ 141 Paul Wilson	.15	.07
☐ 142 Orel Hershiser	.25	.11
☐ 143 Albert Belle	.60	.25
☐ 144 Tino Martinez	.50	.23
☐ 145 Tony Gwynn	1.25	.55
☐ 146 George Arias	.15	.07
☐ 147 Brian Jordan	.25	.11
☐ 148 Brian McRae	.15	.07
☐ 149 Rickey Henderson	.40	.18
☐ 150 Ryan Klesko	.40	.18

1996 Studio Hit Parade

Randomly inserted in packs at a rate of 1:48, cards from this ten-card set feature some of the League's top long-ball hitters. The fronts feature color action player photos on a die-cut record design in the background. The backs carry the player's batting average breakdown. Each card is serial numbered of 5,000 on back.

	MINT	NRMT
COMPLETE SET (10)	100.00	45.00
COMMON CARD (1-10)	5.00	2.20
STATED ODDS 1:48 HOBBY		
STATED PRINT RUN 5000 SERIAL #'d SETS		

☐ 1 Tony Gwynn	12.00	5.50
☐ 2 Ken Griffey Jr.	25.00	11.00
☐ 3 Frank Thomas	20.00	9.00
☐ 4 Jeff Bagwell	10.00	4.50
☐ 5 Kirby Puckett	10.00	4.50
☐ 6 Mike Piazza	15.00	6.75
☐ 7 Barry Bonds	6.00	2.70
☐ 8 Albert Belle	6.00	2.70
☐ 9 Tim Salmon	5.00	2.20
☐ 10 Mo Vaughn	6.00	2.70

1996 Studio Masterstrokes

Randomly inserted in packs, this eight-card set features some of the League's most popular stars. Printed with brushed embossed technologies, the cards display color action player images in simulated oil painting detail. Each card from this set was also produced in a promo form.

	MINT	NRMT
COMPLETE SET (8)	150.00	70.00
COMMON CARD (1-8)	8.00	3.60
STATED ODDS 1:96		
STATED PRINT RUN 5000 SERIAL #'d SETS		

☐ 1 Tony Gwynn	20.00	9.00
☐ 2 Mike Piazza	25.00	11.00
☐ 3 Jeff Bagwell	15.00	6.75
☐ 4 Manny Ramirez	8.00	3.60
☐ 5 Cal Ripken	30.00	13.50
☐ 6 Frank Thomas	30.00	13.50
☐ 7 Ken Griffey Jr.	40.00	18.00
☐ 8 Greg Maddux	25.00	11.00
☐ P2 Mike Piazza Promo	5.00	2.20

1996 Studio Stained Glass Stars

Randomly inserted in packs, this 12-card set honors some of the league's hottest superstars. The cards feature color player images on a genuine-look stained glass background and were printed with a clear plastic, die-cut technology.

	MINT	NRMT
COMPLETE SET (12)	100.00	45.00
COMMON CARD (1-12)	3.00	1.35
STATED ODDS 1:24		

☐ 1 Cal Ripken	12.00	5.50
☐ 2 Ken Griffey Jr.	15.00	6.75
☐ 3 Frank Thomas	12.00	5.50
☐ 4 Greg Maddux	10.00	4.50
☐ 5 Chipper Jones	10.00	4.50
☐ 6 Mike Piazza	10.00	4.50
☐ 7 Albert Belle	4.00	1.80
☐ 8 Jeff Bagwell	6.00	2.70
☐ 9 Hideo Nomo	8.00	3.60
☐ 10 Barry Bonds	4.00	1.80
☐ 11 Manny Ramirez	3.00	1.35
☐ 12 Kenny Lofton	4.00	1.80

1997 Studio

The 1997 Studio set was issued in one series totalling 165 cards and was distributed in five-card packs with an 8x10 Studio

Portrait for a suggested retail price of $2.49. The fronts feature color player portraits, while the backs carry player information. It is believed that the following cards: 112, 133, 137, 147 and 161 were short printed.

	MINT	NRMT
COMPLETE SET (165)	60.00	27.00
COMMON CARD (1-165)	.15	.07
SP's (112,133,137,147,161)	2.00	.90
SEMISTARS	.40	.18
UNLISTED STARS	.60	.25
SUBSET CARDS HALF VALUE OF BASE CARDS		
COMP.SILV.PP SET (165)	600.00	275.00
COMMON SILVER PP (1-165)	2.00	.90
*SILVER PP STARS: 6X TO 12X HI COLUMN		
*SILVER PP YOUNG STARS: 5X TO 10X HI		
SILVER PP STATED PRINT RUN 1500 SETS		
COMP.GOLD PP SET (165)	2000.00	900.00
COMMON GOLD PP (1-165)	5.00	2.20
*GOLD PP STARS: 15X TO 30X HI COLUMN		
*GOLD PP YOUNG STARS: 12.5X TO 25X HI		
GOLD PP STATED PRINT RUN 500 SETS		
PRESS PROOFS: RANDOM INS.IN PACKS		

☐ 1 Frank Thomas	2.50	1.10
☐ 2 Gary Sheffield	.60	.25
☐ 3 Jason Isringhausen	.15	.07
☐ 4 Ron Gant	.30	.14
☐ 5 Andy Pettitte	.60	.25
☐ 6 Todd Hollandsworth	.15	.07
☐ 7 Troy Percival	.15	.07
☐ 8 Mark McGwire	1.25	.55
☐ 9 Barry Larkin	.40	.18
☐ 10 Ken Caminiti	.40	.18
☐ 11 Paul Molitor	.60	.25
☐ 12 Travis Fryman	.30	.14
☐ 13 Kevin Brown	.30	.14
☐ 14 Robin Ventura	.30	.14
☐ 15 Andres Galarraga	.60	.25
☐ 16 Ken Griffey Jr.	3.00	1.35
☐ 17 Roger Clemens	1.25	.55
☐ 18 Alan Benes	.30	.14
☐ 19 Dave Justice	.60	.25
☐ 20 Damon Buford	.15	.07
☐ 21 Mike Piazza	2.00	.90
☐ 22 Ray Durham	.15	.07
☐ 23 Billy Wagner	.30	.14
☐ 24 Dean Palmer	.15	.07
☐ 25 David Cone	.30	.14
☐ 26 Ruben Sierra	.15	.07
☐ 27 Henry Rodriguez	.15	.07
☐ 28 Ray Lankford	.30	.14
☐ 29 Jamey Wright	.15	.07
☐ 30 Brady Anderson	.40	.18
☐ 31 Tino Martinez	.60	.25
☐ 32 Manny Ramirez	.60	.25
☐ 33 Jeff Conine	.30	.14
☐ 34 Dante Bichette	.30	.14
☐ 35 Jose Canseco	.40	.18
☐ 36 Mo Vaughn	.75	.35
☐ 37 Sammy Sosa	.60	.25
☐ 38 Mark Grudzielanek	.15	.07
☐ 39 Mike Mussina	.60	.25
☐ 40 Bill Pulsipher	.15	.07
☐ 41 Ryne Sandberg	.75	.35

☐ 42	Rickey Henderson	.40	.18
☐ 43	Alex Rodriguez	2.00	.90
☐ 44	Eddie Murray	.60	.25
☐ 45	Ernie Young	.15	.07
☐ 46	Joey Hamilton	.30	.14
☐ 47	Wade Boggs	.60	.25
☐ 48	Rusty Greer	.30	.14
☐ 49	Carlos Delgado	.30	.14
☐ 50	Ellis Burks	.30	.14
☐ 51	Cal Ripken	2.50	1.10
☐ 52	Alex Fernandez	.30	.14
☐ 53	Wally Joyner	.30	.14
☐ 54	James Baldwin	.15	.07
☐ 55	Juan Gonzalez	1.50	.70
☐ 56	John Smoltz	.30	.14
☐ 57	Omar Vizquel	.30	.14
☐ 58	Shane Reynolds	.15	.07
☐ 59	Barry Bonds	.75	.35
☐ 60	Jason Kendall	.30	.14
☐ 61	Marty Cordova	.30	.14
☐ 62	Charles Johnson	.30	.14
☐ 63	John Jaha	.15	.07
☐ 64	Chan Ho Park	.50	.25
☐ 65	Jermaine Allensworth	.15	.07
☐ 66	Mark Grace	.40	.18
☐ 67	Tim Salmon	.60	.25
☐ 68	Edgar Martinez	.40	.18
☐ 69	Marquis Grissom	.30	.14
☐ 70	Craig Biggio	.30	.18
☐ 71	Bobby Higginson	.30	.14
☐ 72	Kevin Seitzer	.15	.07
☐ 73	Hideo Nomo	1.50	.70
☐ 74	Dennis Eckersley	.30	.14
☐ 75	Bobby Bonilla	.30	.14
☐ 76	Dwight Gooden	.30	.14
☐ 77	Jeff Cirillo	.30	.14
☐ 78	Brian McRae	.15	.07
☐ 79	Chipper Jones	2.00	.90
☐ 80	Jeff Fassero	.15	.07
☐ 81	Fred McGriff	.40	.18
☐ 82	Garret Anderson	.30	.14
☐ 83	Eric Karros	.30	.14
☐ 84	Derek Bell	.15	.07
☐ 85	Kenny Lofton	.75	.35
☐ 86	John Mabry	.15	.07
☐ 87	Pat Hentgen	.30	.14
☐ 88	Greg Maddux	2.00	.90
☐ 89	Jason Giambi	.30	.14
☐ 90	Al Martin	.15	.07
☐ 91	Derek Jeter	2.00	.90
☐ 92	Rey Ordonez	.15	.07
☐ 93	Will Clark	.40	.18
☐ 94	Kevin Appier	.30	.14
☐ 95	Roberto Alomar	.60	.25
☐ 96	Joe Carter	.30	.14
☐ 97	Bernie Williams	.60	.25
☐ 98	Albert Belle	.75	.35
☐ 99	Greg Vaughn	.15	.07
☐ 100	Tony Clark	.60	.25
☐ 101	Matt Williams	.40	.18
☐ 102	Jeff Bagwell	1.25	.55
☐ 103	Reggie Sanders	.15	.07
☐ 104	Mariano Rivera	.30	.14
☐ 105	Larry Walker	.60	.25
☐ 106	Shawn Green	.15	.07
☐ 107	Alex Ochoa	.15	.07
☐ 108	Ivan Rodriguez	.75	.35
☐ 109	Eric Young	.15	.07
☐ 110	Javier Lopez	.30	.14
☐ 111	Brian Hunter	.15	.07
☐ 112	Raul Mondesi SP	2.50	1.10
☐ 113	Randy Johnson	.60	.25
☐ 114	Tony Phillips	.15	.07
☐ 115	Carlos Garcia	.15	.07
☐ 116	Moises Alou	.30	.14
☐ 117	Paul O'Neill	.30	.14
☐ 118	Jim Thome	.60	.25
☐ 119	Jermaine Dye	.15	.07
☐ 120	Wilson Alvarez	.15	.07
☐ 121	Rondell White	.30	.14
☐ 122	Michael Tucker	.15	.07
☐ 123	Mike Lansing	.15	.07
☐ 124	Tony Gwynn	1.50	.70
☐ 125	Ryan Klesko	.40	.18
☐ 126	Jim Edmonds	.40	.18
☐ 127	Chuck Knoblauch	.60	.25

☐ 128	Rafael Palmeiro	.40	.18
☐ 129	Jay Buhner	.40	.18
☐ 130	Tom Glavine	.30	.14
☐ 131	Julio Franco	.30	.14
☐ 132	Cecil Fielder	.30	.14
☐ 133	Paul Wilson SP	2.00	.90
☐ 134	Deion Sanders	.30	.14
☐ 135	Alex Gonzalez	.15	.07
☐ 136	Charles Nagy	.30	.14
☐ 137	Andy Ashby SP	2.00	.90
☐ 138	Edgar Renteria	.30	.14
☐ 139	Pedro Martinez	.60	.25
☐ 140	Brian Jordan	.30	.14
☐ 141	Todd Hundley	.30	.14
☐ 142	Marc Newfield	.15	.07
☐ 143	Darryl Strawberry	.30	.14
☐ 144	Dan Wilson	.15	.07
☐ 145	Brian Giles	.15	.07
☐ 146	F.P. Santangelo	.15	.07
☐ 147	Shannon Stewart SP	2.00	.90
☐ 148	Scott Spiezio	.30	.14
☐ 149	Andruw Jones	1.50	.70
☐ 150	Karim Garcia	.30	.14
☐ 151	Vladimir Guerrero	1.25	.55
☐ 152	George Arias	.15	.07
☐ 153	Brooks Kieschnick	.15	.07
☐ 154	Todd Walker	.30	.14
☐ 155	Scott Rolen	1.50	.70
☐ 156	Todd Greene	.30	.14
☐ 157	Dmitri Young	.15	.07
☐ 158	Ruben Rivera	.30	.14
☐ 159	Bartolo Colon	.30	.14
☐ 160	Nomar Garciaparra	2.00	.90
☐ 161	Bob Abreu SP	2.00	.90
☐ 162	Darin Erstad	1.00	.45
☐ 163	Ken Griffey Jr. CL	1.50	.70
☐ 164	Frank Thomas CL	1.25	.55
☐ 165	Alex Rodriguez CL	1.00	.45

1997 Studio Autographs

Randomly inserted in packs, this three-card set features autographed 8x10 Studio Portraits of the three players checklisted below. Only a limited number of portraits were signed by each player. The amount each player signed is listed next to his name.

	MINT	NRMT
COMPLETE SET (3)	250.00	110.00
COMMON CARD (1-3)	30.00	13.50
RANDOM INSERTS IN PACKS ..		

☐ 1	Vladimir Guerrero/500	120.00	55.00
☐ 2	Scott Rolen/1000	100.00	45.00
☐ 3	Todd Walker/1250	30.00	13.50

1997 Studio Hard Hats

Randomly inserted in packs, this 24-card set features color player images of 24 major league superstars on a unique clear plastic, foil-stamped, die cut batting helmet design. Only 5000 of each card was produced and is sequentially numbered.

	MINT	NRMT
COMPLETE SET (24)	250.00	110.00
COMMON CARD (1-24)	2.50	1.10
UNLISTED STARS	6.00	2.70
RANDOM INSERTS IN PACKS ..		
STATED PRINT RUN 5000 SERIAL #'d SETS		

☐ 1	Ivan Rodriguez	8.00	3.60
☐ 2	Albert Belle	8.00	3.60
☐ 3	Ken Griffey Jr.	30.00	13.50
☐ 4	Chuck Knoblauch	6.00	2.70
☐ 5	Frank Thomas	25.00	11.00
☐ 6	Cal Ripken	25.00	11.00
☐ 7	Todd Walker	2.50	1.10
☐ 8	Alex Rodriguez	20.00	9.00
☐ 9	Jim Thome	6.00	2.70
☐ 10	Mike Piazza	20.00	9.00
☐ 11	Barry Larkin	4.00	1.80
☐ 12	Chipper Jones	20.00	9.00
☐ 13	Derek Jeter	15.00	6.75
☐ 14	Matt Williams	4.00	1.80
☐ 15	Jason Giambi	2.50	1.10
☐ 16	Tim Salmon	6.00	2.70
☐ 17	Brady Anderson	4.00	1.80
☐ 18	Rondell White	2.50	1.10
☐ 19	Bernie Williams	6.00	2.70
☐ 20	Juan Gonzalez	15.00	6.75
☐ 21	Karim Garcia	2.50	1.10
☐ 22	Scott Rolen	15.00	6.75
☐ 23	Darin Erstad	10.00	4.50
☐ 24	Brian Jordan	2.50	1.10

1997 Studio Master Strokes

Randomly inserted in packs, this 24-card set features color photos of superstar players on all canvas card stock with gold foil stamping. Only 2,000 of each card was produced and is sequentially numbered.

	MINT	NRMT
COMPLETE SET (24)	600.00	275.00
COMMON CARD (1-24)	10.00	4.50
UNLISTED STARS	12.00	5.50
RANDOM INSERTS IN PACKS		
STATED PRINT RUN 2000 SERIAL #'d SETS		
COMP. 8 X 10 SET (24)	250.00	110.00
COMMON 8 X 10 (1-24)	4.00	1.80
*8 X 10'S: .2X TO .4X HI COLUMN		

8 X 10: RANDOM INSERTS IN PACKS
8 X 10 PRINT RUN 5000 SERIAL #'d SETS

☐ 1	Derek Jeter	30.00	13.50
☐ 2	Jeff Bagwell	25.00	11.00
☐ 3	Ken Griffey Jr.	60.00	27.00
☐ 4	Barry Bonds	15.00	6.75
☐ 5	Frank Thomas	50.00	22.00
☐ 6	Andy Pettitte	12.00	5.50
☐ 7	Mo Vaughn	15.00	6.75
☐ 8	Alex Rodriguez	40.00	18.00
☐ 9	Andruw Jones	25.00	11.00
☐ 10	Kenny Lofton	15.00	6.75
☐ 11	Cal Ripken	50.00	22.00
☐ 12	Greg Maddux	40.00	18.00
☐ 13	Manny Ramirez	12.00	5.50
☐ 14	Mike Piazza	40.00	18.00
☐ 15	Vladimir Guerrero	20.00	9.00
☐ 16	Albert Belle	20.00	9.00
☐ 17	Chipper Jones	20.00	9.00
☐ 18	Hideo Nomo	30.00	13.50
☐ 19	Sammy Sosa	10.00	4.50
☐ 20	Tony Gwynn	30.00	13.50
☐ 21	Gary Sheffield	10.00	4.50
☐ 22	Mark McGwire	25.00	11.00
☐ 23	Juan Gonzalez	30.00	13.50
☐ 24	Paul Molitor	12.00	5.50

1997 Studio Portraits 8x10

Inserted one per pack, this 24-card set is a partial parallel version of the base set and features full-color portraits of star players measuring approximately 8" by 10" with a signable UV coating.

	MINT	NRMT
COMPLETE SET (24)	25.00	11.00
COMMON CARD (1-24)	.50	.23
ONE PER PACK		

☐ 1	Ken Griffey Jr.	6.00	2.70
☐ 2	Frank Thomas	5.00	2.20
☐ 3	Alex Rodriguez	4.00	1.80
☐ 4	Andruw Jones	3.00	1.35
☐ 5	Cal Ripken	5.00	2.20
☐ 6	Greg Maddux	4.00	1.80
☐ 7	Mike Piazza	4.00	1.80
☐ 8	Chipper Jones	4.00	1.80
☐ 9	Albert Belle	1.50	.70
☐ 10	Derek Jeter	4.00	1.80
☐ 11	Juan Gonzalez	3.00	1.35
☐ 12	Todd Walker	.50	.23
☐ 13	Mark McGwire	2.50	1.10
☐ 14	Barry Bonds	1.50	.70
☐ 15	Jeff Bagwell	2.50	1.10
☐ 16	Manny Ramirez	1.25	.55
☐ 17	Kenny Lofton	1.50	.70
☐ 18	Mo Vaughn	1.50	.70
☐ 19	Hideo Nomo	3.00	1.35
☐ 20	Tony Gwynn	3.00	1.35
☐ 21	Vladimir Guerrero	2.50	1.10
☐ 22	Gary Sheffield	1.25	.55
☐ 23	Ryne Sandberg	1.50	.70
☐ 24	Scott Rolen	3.00	1.35

1995 Summit

This set contains 200 standard-size cards and was sold in seven-card retail packs for a suggested price of $1.99. This set is a premium product issued by Pinnacle Brands and produced on thicker paper than the regular set. The fronts have an action photo on a white background with the player's name and team emblem at the bottom in gold-foil. The backs have a player color photo on the left side with a baseball diamond on the right that gives the player's statistics month by month for the season. Subsets featured are Rookies (112-173), Bat Speed (174-188) and Special Delivery (189-193). Notable Rookie Cards in this set include Bobby Higginson and Hideo Nomo.

	MINT	NRMT
COMPLETE SET (200)	20.00	9.00
COMMON CARD (1-200)	.10	.05
MINOR STARS	.25	.11
UNLISTED STARS	.50	.23
SUBSET CARDS HALF VALUE OF BASE CARDS		
COMP.NTH DEG.SET (200)	400.00	180.00
COMMON NTH DEGREE (1-200)	1.00	.45
*NTH DEGREE STARS: 6X TO 12X HI COLUMN		
*NTH DEGREE YOUNG STARS: 5X TO 10X HI		
NTH DEGREE ODDS 1:4		

☐ 1	Ken Griffey Jr.	2.50	1.10
☐ 2	Alex Fernandez	.10	.05
☐ 3	Fred McGriff	.40	.18
☐ 4	Ben McDonald	.10	.05
☐ 5	Rafael Palmeiro	.40	.18
☐ 6	Tony Gwynn	1.25	.55
☐ 7	Jim Thome	.50	.23
☐ 8	Ken Hill	.10	.05
☐ 9	Barry Bonds	.60	.25
☐ 10	Barry Larkin	.40	.18
☐ 11	Albert Belle	.50	.25
☐ 12	Billy Ashley	.10	.05
☐ 13	Matt Williams	.40	.18
☐ 14	Andy Benes	.25	.11
☐ 15	Midre Cummings	.10	.05
☐ 16	J.R. Phillips	.10	.05
☐ 17	Edgar Martinez	.40	.18
☐ 18	Manny Ramirez	.50	.23
☐ 19	Jose Canseco	.40	.18
☐ 20	Chili Davis	.25	.11
☐ 21	Don Mattingly	.75	.35
☐ 22	Bernie Williams	.50	.23
☐ 23	Tom Glavine	.25	.11
☐ 24	Robin Ventura	.25	.11
☐ 25	Jeff Conine	.25	.11
☐ 26	Mark Grace	.40	.18
☐ 27	Mark McGwire	1.00	.45
☐ 28	Carlos Delgado	.25	.11
☐ 29	Greg Colbrunn	.10	.05
☐ 30	Greg Maddux	1.50	.70
☐ 31	Craig Biggio	.40	.18
☐ 32	Kirby Puckett	1.00	.45
☐ 33	Derek Bell	.10	.05
☐ 34	Lenny Dykstra	.25	.11
☐ 35	Tim Salmon	.50	.23
☐ 36	Deion Sanders	.25	.11
☐ 37	Moises Alou	.25	.11
☐ 38	Ray Lankford	.25	.11
☐ 39	Willie Greene	.10	.05
☐ 40	Ozzie Smith	.60	.25
☐ 41	Roger Clemens	1.00	.45
☐ 42	Andres Galarraga	.50	.23
☐ 43	Gary Sheffield	.50	.23
☐ 44	Sammy Sosa	.50	.23
☐ 45	Larry Walker	.50	.23
☐ 46	Kevin Appier	.25	.11
☐ 47	Raul Mondesi	.40	.18
☐ 48	Kenny Lofton	.60	.25
☐ 49	Darryl Hamilton	.10	.05
☐ 50	Roberto Alomar	.50	.23
☐ 51	Hal Morris	.10	.05
☐ 52	Cliff Floyd	.10	.05
☐ 53	Brent Gates	.10	.05
☐ 54	Rickey Henderson	.50	.23
☐ 55	John Olerud	.25	.11
☐ 56	Gregg Jefferies	.10	.05
☐ 57	Cecil Fielder	.25	.11
☐ 58	Paul Molitor	.50	.23
☐ 59	Bret Boone	.10	.05
☐ 60	Greg Vaughn	.10	.05
☐ 61	Wally Joyner	.25	.11
☐ 62	Jeffrey Hammonds	.25	.11
☐ 63	James Mouton	.10	.05
☐ 64	Omar Vizquel	.25	.11
☐ 65	Wade Boggs	.50	.23
☐ 66	Terry Steinbach	.10	.05
☐ 67	Wil Cordero	.10	.05
☐ 68	Joey Hamilton	.25	.11
☐ 69	Rico Brogna	.10	.05
☐ 70	Darren Daulton	.25	.11
☐ 71	Chuck Knoblauch	.50	.23
☐ 72	Bob Hamelin	.10	.05
☐ 73	Carl Everett	.10	.05
☐ 74	Joe Carter	.25	.11
☐ 75	Dave Winfield	.40	.18
☐ 76	Bobby Bonilla	.25	.11
☐ 77	Paul O'Neill	.25	.11
☐ 78	Javier Lopez	.25	.11
☐ 79	Cal Ripken	2.00	.90
☐ 80	David Cone	.25	.11
☐ 81	Bernard Gilkey	.10	.05
☐ 82	Ivan Rodriguez	.60	.25
☐ 83	Dean Palmer	.10	.05
☐ 84	Jason Bere	.10	.05
☐ 85	Will Clark	.40	.18
☐ 86	Scott Cooper	.10	.05
☐ 87	Royce Clayton	.10	.05
☐ 88	Mike Piazza	1.50	.70
☐ 89	Ryan Klesko	.40	.18
☐ 90	Juan Gonzalez	1.25	.55
☐ 91	Travis Fryman	.25	.11
☐ 92	Frank Thomas	2.00	.90
☐ 93	Eduardo Perez	.10	.05
☐ 94	Mo Vaughn	.60	.25
☐ 95	Jay Bell	.25	.11
☐ 96	Jeff Bagwell	1.00	.45
☐ 97	Randy Johnson	.50	.23
☐ 98	Jimmy Key	.25	.11
☐ 99	Dennis Eckersley	.25	.11
☐ 100	Carlos Baerga	.10	.05
☐ 101	Eddie Murray	.50	.23
☐ 102	Mike Mussina	.50	.23
☐ 103	Brian Anderson	.25	.11
☐ 104	Jeff Cirillo	.25	.11
☐ 105	Dante Bichette	.25	.11
☐ 106	Bret Saberhagen	.10	.05
☐ 107	Jeff Kent	.10	.05
☐ 108	Ruben Sierra	.10	.05
☐ 109	Kirk Gibson	.25	.11
☐ 110	Steve Karsay	.10	.05
☐ 111	David Justice	.50	.23
☐ 112	Benji Gil	.10	.05
☐ 113	Vaughn Eshelman	.10	.05
☐ 114	Carlos Perez	.25	.11
☐ 115	Chipper Jones	1.50	.70
☐ 116	Shane Andrews	.10	.05

		MINT	NRMT
☐ 117	Orlando Miller	.10	.05
☐ 118	Scott Ruffcorn	.10	.05
☐ 119	Jose Oliva	.10	.05
☐ 120	Joe Vitiello	.10	.05
☐ 121	Jon Nunnally	.10	.05
☐ 122	Garret Anderson	.40	.18
☐ 123	Curtis Goodwin	.10	.05
☐ 124	Mark Grudzielanek	.40	.18
☐ 125	Alex Gonzalez	.10	.05
☐ 126	David Bell	.10	.05
☐ 127	Dustin Hermanson	.25	.11
☐ 128	Dave Nilsson	.10	.05
☐ 129	Wilson Heredia	.10	.05
☐ 130	Charles Johnson	.25	.11
☐ 131	Frank Rodriguez	.10	.05
☐ 132	Alex Ochoa	.10	.05
☐ 133	Alex Rodriguez	2.00	.90
☐ 134	Bobby Higginson	.75	.35
☐ 135	Edgardo Alfonzo	.50	.23
☐ 136	Armando Benitez	.10	.05
☐ 137	Rich Aude	.10	.05
☐ 138	Tim Naehring	.10	.05
☐ 139	Joe Randa	.10	.05
☐ 140	Quilvio Veras	.10	.05
☐ 141	Hideo Nomo	2.50	1.10
☐ 142	Ray Holbert	.10	.05
☐ 143	Michael Tucker	.25	.11
☐ 144	Chad Mottola	.10	.05
☐ 145	John Valentin	.10	.05
☐ 146	James Baldwin	.10	.05
☐ 147	Esteban Loaiza	.25	.11
☐ 148	Marty Cordova	.25	.11
☐ 149	Juan Acevedo	.10	.05
☐ 150	Tim Unroe UER	.10	.05
	Cardinals logo		
☐ 151	Brad Clontz UER	.10	.05
	A's logo		
☐ 152	Steve Rodriguez UER	.10	.05
	Yankees logo		
☐ 153	Rudy Pemberton UER	.10	.05
	Dodgers logo		
☐ 154	Ozzie Timmons UER ...	.10	.05
	Tigers logo		
☐ 155	Ricky Otero	.10	.05
☐ 156	Allen Battle	.10	.05
☐ 157	Joe Rosselli	.10	.05
☐ 158	Roberto Petagine	.10	.05
☐ 159	Todd Hollandsworth	.25	.11
☐ 160	Shannon Penn UER	.10	.05
	Cubs logo		
☐ 161	Antonio Osuna UER	.10	.05
	Tigers logo		
☐ 162	Russ Davis UER	.10	.05
	Red Sox logo		
☐ 163	Jason Giambi UER	.50	.23
	two errors: front photo actually Brent Gates		
☐ 164	also Braves logo Terry Bradshaw UER ..	.10	.05
	Brewers logo		
☐ 165	Ray Durham	.25	.11
☐ 166	Todd Steverson	.10	.05
☐ 167	Tim Belk	.10	.05
☐ 168	Andy Pettitte	.75	.35
☐ 169	Roger Cedeno	.25	.11
☐ 170	Jose Parra	.25	.11
☐ 171	Scott Sullivan	.10	.05
☐ 172	LaTroy Hawkins	.10	.05
☐ 173	Jeff McCurry	.10	.05
☐ 174	Ken Griffey Jr. BS	1.25	.55
☐ 175	Frank Thomas BS	1.00	.45
☐ 176	Cal Ripken Jr. BS	1.00	.45
☐ 177	Jeff Bagwell BS	.50	.23
☐ 178	Mike Piazza BS	.75	.35
☐ 179	Barry Bonds BS	.40	.18
☐ 180	Matt Williams BS	.25	.11
☐ 181	Don Mattingly BS	.40	.18
☐ 182	Will Clark BS	.25	.11
☐ 183	Tony Gwynn BS	.60	.25
☐ 184	Kirby Puckett BS	.50	.23
☐ 185	Jose Canseco BS	.25	.11
☐ 186	Paul Molitor BS	.25	.11
☐ 187	Albert Belle BS	.50	.23
☐ 188	Joe Carter BS	.10	.05
☐ 189	Greg Maddux SD	.75	.35
☐ 190	Roger Clemens SD	.50	.23

		MINT	NRMT
☐ 191	David Cone SD	.10	.05
☐ 192	Mike Mussina SD	.25	.11
☐ 193	Randy Johnson SD	.25	.11
☐ 194	Frank Thomas CL	1.00	.45
☐ 195	Ken Griffey Jr. CL	1.25	.55
☐ 196	Cal Ripken CL	1.00	.45
☐ 197	Jeff Bagwell CL	.60	.25
☐ 198	Mike Piazza CL	.75	.35
☐ 199	Barry Bonds CL	.40	.18
☐ 200	Mo Vaughn CL	.40	.18
	Matt Williams		

1995 Summit Big Bang

This 20-card set was randomly inserted in packs at a rate of one in 72. The set is comprised of the best home run hitters in the game. The set uses a process called "Spectrotech" which allows the card to be made of foil and have a holographic image. The fronts have an action photo with a game background which also shows the player. The backs have a player photo and information on his power exploits.

	MINT	NRMT
COMPLETE SET (20)	400.00	180.00
COMMON CARD (BB1-BB20)	6.00	2.70
SEMISTARS	8.00	3.60
UNLISTED STARS	12.00	5.50
STATED ODDS 1:72		

		MINT	NRMT
☐ BB1	Ken Griffey Jr.	60.00	27.00
☐ BB2	Frank Thomas	50.00	22.00
☐ BB3	Cal Ripken	50.00	22.00
☐ BB4	Jeff Bagwell	25.00	11.00
☐ BB5	Mike Piazza	40.00	18.00
☐ BB6	Barry Bonds	15.00	6.75
☐ BB7	Matt Williams	8.00	3.60
☐ BB8	Don Mattingly	20.00	9.00
☐ BB9	Will Clark	8.00	3.60
☐ BB10	Tony Gwynn	30.00	13.50
☐ BB11	Kirby Puckett	25.00	11.00
☐ BB12	Jose Canseco	8.00	3.60
☐ BB13	Paul Molitor	12.00	5.50
☐ BB14	Albert Belle	15.00	6.75
☐ BB15	Joe Carter	6.00	2.70
☐ BB16	Rafael Palmeiro	8.00	3.60
☐ BB17	Fred McGriff	8.00	3.60
☐ BB18	David Justice	12.00	5.50
☐ BB19	Tim Salmon	12.00	5.50
☐ BB20	Mo Vaughn	15.00	6.75

1995 Summit New Age

This 15-card set was randomly inserted in packs at a rate of one in 18. The set is comprised 15 of the best young players in

baseball. The fronts are horizontally designed and have a color-action photo with a background of a baseball stadium with a red and gray background. The backs have a photo and player information and the words "New Age" at the bottom in red and white.

	MINT	NRMT
COMPLETE SET (15)	60.00	27.00
COMMON CARD (NA1-NA15)	1.50	.70
SEMISTARS	3.00	1.35
UNLISTED STARS	6.00	2.70
STATED ODDS 1:18		

		MINT	NRMT
☐ NA1	Cliff Floyd	1.50	.70
☐ NA2	Manny Ramirez	6.00	2.70
☐ NA3	Raul Mondesi	3.00	1.35
☐ NA4	Alex Rodriguez	25.00	11.00
☐ NA5	Billy Ashley	1.50	.70
☐ NA6	Alex Gonzalez	1.50	.70
☐ NA7	Michael Tucker	2.00	.90
☐ NA8	Charles Johnson	2.00	.90
☐ NA9	Carlos Delgado	2.00	.90
☐ NA10	Benji Gil	1.50	.70
☐ NA11	Chipper Jones	20.00	9.00
☐ NA12	Todd Hollandsworth	2.00	.90
☐ NA13	Frankie Rodriguez..	1.50	.70
☐ NA14	Shawn Green	2.00	.90
☐ NA15	Ray Durham	2.00	.90

1995 Summit 21 Club

This nine-card set was randomly inserted in packs at a rate of one in 36. The set is comprised of young players with bright futures. Both sides of the cards are done in foil with the front having a color photo with a gold background with "21 Club" in gray and red in the bottom right hand corner. The backs are laid out horizontally with a player head shot and information done in foil.

	MINT	NRMT
COMPLETE SET (9)	30.00	13.50
COMMON CARD (TC1-TC9)	3.00	1.35
STATED ODDS 1:36		

□ TC1 Bob Abreu	5.00	2.20
□ TC2 Pokey Reese	3.00	1.35
□ TC3 Edgardo Alfonzo	4.00	1.80
□ TC4 Jim Pittsley	4.00	1.80
□ TC5	4.00	1.80
□ TC6 Chan Ho Park	8.00	3.60
□ TC6 Chan Ho Park	4.00	1.80
□ TC7 Julian Tavarez	3.00	1.35
□ TC8 Ismael Valdes	4.00	1.80
□ TC9 Dmitri Young	3.00	1.35

1996 Summit

The 1996 Summit set was issued in one series totalling 200 cards. The seven-card packs had a suggested retail of $2.99 each. The fronts feature color player photos on a gold striped background. The backs carry another player photo and statistics.

	MINT	NRMT
COMPLETE SET (200)	25.00	11.00
COMMON CARD (1-200)	.15	.07
MINOR STARS	.30	.14
UNLISTED STARS	.60	.25
SUBSET CARDS HALF VALUE OF BASE CARDS		
COMP.ABV/BYND.SET (200)	500.00	220.00
COMMON ABV/BYND (1-200)	1.50	.70
*ABV/BYND.STARS: 6X TO 12X HI COLUMN		
*ABV/BYND.YOUNG STARS: 5X TO 10X HI		
ABV.BYND.STATED ODDS 1:4		
COMP.AP SET(200)	2500.00	1100.00
COMMON ART.PRF. (1-200)	4.00	1.80
*ART.PRF.STARS: 25X TO 40X HI COLUMN		
*ART.PRF.YOUNG STARS: 20X TO 30X HI		
AP STATED ODDS 1:36		
COMP.FOIL SET (200)	50.00	22.00
COMMON FOIL (1-200)	.15	.07
*FOIL: .75X TO 1.5X HI COLUMN		
FOIL CARDS AVAIL.IN RETAIL SUPER PACKS		

□ 1 Mike Piazza	2.00	.90
□ 2 Matt Williams	.40	.18
□ 3 Tino Martinez	.60	.25
□ 4 Reggie Sanders	.15	.07
□ 5 Ray Durham	.15	.07
□ 6 Brad Radke	.30	.14
□ 7 Jeff Bagwell	1.25	.55
□ 8 Ron Gant	.30	.14
□ 9 Lance Johnson	.15	.07
□ 10 Kevin Seitzer	.15	.07
□ 11 Dante Bichette	.30	.14
□ 12 Ivan Rodriguez	.75	.35
□ 13 Jim Abbott	.15	.07
□ 14 Greg Colbrun	.15	.07
□ 15 Rondell White	.30	.14
□ 16 Shawn Green	.15	.07

□ 17 Gregg Jefferies	.15	.07
□ 18 Omar Vizquel	.30	.14
□ 19 Cal Ripken	2.50	1.10
□ 20 Mark McGwire	1.25	.55
□ 21 Wally Joyner	.30	.14
□ 22 Chili Davis	.30	.14
□ 23 Jose Canseco	.40	.18
□ 24 Royce Clayton	.15	.07
□ 25 Jay Bell	.30	.14
□ 26 Travis Fryman	.30	.14
□ 27 Jeff King	.15	.07
□ 28 Todd Hundley	.30	.14
□ 29 Joe Vitiello	.15	.07
□ 30 Russ Davis	.15	.07
□ 31 Mo Vaughn	.75	.35
□ 32 Raul Mondesi	.40	.18
□ 33 Ray Lankford	.30	.14
□ 34 Mike Stanley	.15	.07
□ 35 B.J. Surhoff	.15	.07
□ 36 Greg Vaughn	.15	.07
□ 37 Todd Stottlemyre	.15	.07
□ 38 Carlos Delgado	.30	.14
□ 39 Kenny Lofton	.75	.35
□ 40 Hideo Nomo	1.50	.70
□ 41 Sterling Hitchcock	.15	.07
□ 42 Pete Schourek	.15	.07
□ 43 Edgardo Alfonzo	.40	.18
□ 44 Ken Hill	.15	.07
□ 45 Ken Caminiti	.40	.18
□ 46 Bobby Higginson	.30	.14
□ 47 Michael Tucker	.30	.14
□ 48 David Cone	.30	.14
□ 49 Cecil Fielder	.30	.14
□ 50 Brian L. Hunter	.30	.14
□ 51 Charles Johnson	.30	.14
□ 52 Bobby Bonilla	.30	.14
□ 53 Eddie Murray	.60	.25
□ 54 Kenny Rogers	.15	.07
□ 55 Jim Edmonds	.40	.18
□ 56 Trevor Hoffman	.15	.07
□ 57 Kevin Mitchell UER	.15	.07
□ 58 Ruben Sierra	.15	.07
□ 59 Benji Gil	.15	.07
□ 60 Juan Gonzalez	1.50	.70
□ 61 Larry Walker	.60	.25
□ 62 Jack McDowell	.15	.07
□ 63 Shawon Dunston	.15	.07
□ 64 Andy Benes	.30	.14
□ 65 Jay Buhner	.40	.18
□ 66 Rickey Henderson	.40	.18
□ 67 Alex Gonzalez	.15	.07
□ 68 Mike Kelly	.15	.07
□ 69 Fred McGriff	.40	.18
□ 70 Ryne Sandberg	.75	.35
□ 71 Ernie Young	.15	.07
□ 72 Kevin Appier	.30	.14
□ 73 Moises Alou	.30	.14
□ 74 John Jaha	.15	.07
□ 75 J.T. Snow	.30	.14
□ 76 Jim Thome	.60	.25
□ 77 Kirby Puckett	1.25	.55
□ 78 Hal Morris	.15	.07
□ 79 Robin Ventura	.30	.14
□ 80 Ben McDonald	.15	.07
□ 81 Tim Salmon	.60	.25
□ 82 Albert Belle	.75	.35
□ 83 Marquis Grissom	.30	.14
□ 84 Alex Rodriguez	2.00	.90
□ 85 Manny Ramirez	.60	.25
□ 86 Ken Griffey Jr.	3.00	1.35
□ 87 Sammy Sosa	.60	.25
□ 88 Frank Thomas	2.50	1.10
□ 89 Lee Smith	.30	.14
□ 90 Manty Cordova	.30	.14
□ 91 Greg Maddux	2.00	.90
□ 92 Lenny Dykstra	.30	.14
□ 93 Butch Huskey	.15	.07
□ 94 Garret Anderson	.30	.14
□ 95 Mike Bordick	.15	.07
□ 96 Dave Justice	.60	.25
□ 97 Chad Curtis	.15	.07
□ 98 Carlos Baerga	.15	.07
□ 99 Jason Isringhausen	.15	.07
□ 100 Gary Sheffield	.60	.25
□ 101 Roger Clemens	1.25	.55
□ 102 Ozzie Smith	.75	.35

□ 103 Ramon Martinez	.30	.14
□ 104 Paul O'Neill	.30	.14
□ 105 Will Clark	.40	.18
□ 106 Tom Glavine	.30	.14
□ 107 Barry Bonds	.75	.35
□ 108 Barry Larkin	.40	.18
□ 109 Derek Bell	.15	.07
□ 110 Randy Johnson	.60	.25
□ 111 Jeff Conine	.30	.14
□ 112 John Mabry	.15	.07
□ 113 Julian Tavarez	.15	.07
□ 114 Gary DiSarcina	.15	.07
□ 115 Andres Galarraga	.40	.18
□ 116 Marc Newfield	.15	.07
□ 117 Frank Rodriguez	.15	.07
□ 118 Brady Anderson	.40	.18
□ 119 Mike Mussina	.60	.25
□ 120 Orlando Merced	.15	.07
□ 121 Melvin Nieves	.15	.07
□ 122 Brian Jordan	.30	.14
□ 123 Rafael Palmeiro	.40	.18
□ 124 Johnny Damon	.30	.14
□ 125 Wil Cordero	.15	.07
□ 126 Chipper Jones	2.00	.90
□ 127 Eric Karros	.30	.14
□ 128 Darren Daulton	.30	.14
□ 129 Vinny Castilla	.30	.14
□ 130 Joe Carter	.30	.14
□ 131 Bernie Williams	.60	.25
□ 132 Bernard Gilkey	.15	.07
□ 133 Bret Boone	.15	.07
□ 134 Tony Gwynn	1.50	.70
□ 135 Dave Nilsson	.15	.07
□ 136 Ryan Klesko	.40	.18
□ 137 Paul Molitor	.60	.25
□ 138 John Olerud	.30	.14
□ 139 Craig Biggio	.40	.18
□ 140 John Valentin	.15	.07
□ 141 Chuck Knoblauch	.60	.25
□ 142 Edgar Martinez	.40	.18
□ 143 Rico Brogna	.15	.07
□ 144 Dean Palmer	.15	.07
□ 145 Mark Grace	.40	.18
□ 146 Roberto Alomar	.60	.25
□ 147 Alex Fernandez	.15	.07
□ 148 Andre Dawson	.40	.18
□ 149 Wade Boggs	.60	.25
□ 150 Mark Lewis	.15	.07
□ 151 Gary Gaetti	.15	.07
□ 152 Paul Wilson	.40	.18
Roger Clemens		
□ 153 Rey Ordonez	.30	.14
Ozzie Smith		
□ 154 Derek Jeter	1.00	.45
Cal Ripken		
□ 155 Andy Benes	.15	.07
Alan Benes		
□ 156 Jason Kendall	.75	.35
Mike Piazza		
□ 157 Ryan Klesko	.75	.35
Frank Thomas		
□ 158 Johnny Damon	1.00	.45
Ken Griffey Jr.		
□ 159 Karim Garcia	.30	.14
Sammy Sosa		
□ 160 Raul Mondesi	.30	.14
Tim Salmon		
□ 161 Chipper Jones	.75	.35
Matt Williams		
□ 162 Rey Ordonez	.30	.14
□ 163 Bob Wolcott	.15	.07
□ 164 Brooks Kieschnick	.30	.14
□ 165 Steve Gibralter	.15	.07
□ 166 Bob Abreu	.40	.18
□ 167 Greg Zaun	.15	.07
□ 168 Tavo Alvarez	.15	.07
□ 169 Sal Fasano	.15	.07
□ 170 George Arias	.15	.07
□ 171 Derek Jeter	2.00	.90
□ 172 Livan Hernandez	2.00	.90
□ 173 Alan Benes	.30	.14
□ 174 George Williams	.15	.07
□ 175 John Wasdin	.15	.07
□ 176 Chan Ho Park	.60	.25
□ 177 Paul Wilson	.15	.07
□ 178 Jeff Suppan	.30	.14

		MINT	NRMT
☐ 179	Quinton McCracken	.15	.07
☐ 180	Wilton Guerrero	.60	.25
☐ 181	Eric Owens	.15	.07
☐ 182	Felipe Crespo	.15	.07
☐ 183	LaTroy Hawkins	.15	.07
☐ 184	Jason Schmidt	.30	.14
☐ 185	Terrell Wade	.15	.07
☐ 186	Mike Grace	.15	.07
☐ 187	Chris Snopek	.15	.07
☐ 188	Jason Kendall	.40	.18
☐ 189	Todd Hollandsworth	.15	.07
☐ 190	Jim Pittsley	.30	.14
☐ 191	Jermaine Dye	.30	.14
☐ 192	Mike Busby	.15	.07
☐ 193	Richard Hidalgo	.60	.25
☐ 194	Tyler Houston	.15	.07
☐ 195	Jimmy Haynes	.15	.07
☐ 196	Karim Garcia	.40	.18
☐ 197	Ken Griffey Jr. CL	1.50	.70
☐ 198	Frank Thomas CL	1.25	.55
☐ 199	Greg Maddux CL	1.00	.45
☐ 200	Cal Ripken CL	1.25	.55

1996 Summit Ballparks

Randomly inserted in packs at a rate of one in seven, this 18-card set features color action player photos on picture back-grounds of their home ballparks. The backs carry the name of the ballparks and players statistics. Eight thousand of these sets were produced and each card was serial numbered on the back.

		MINT	NRMT
COMPLETE SET (18)		150.00	70.00
COMMON CARD (1-18)		2.00	.90

STATED ODDS 1:18
STATED PRINT RUN 8000 SERIAL #'d SETS

☐ 1	Cal Ripken	20.00	9.00
☐ 2	Albert Belle	6.00	2.70
☐ 3	Dante Bichette	2.50	1.10
☐ 4	Mo Vaughn	6.00	2.70
☐ 5	Ken Griffey Jr.	25.00	11.00
☐ 6	Derek Jeter	15.00	6.75
☐ 7	Juan Gonzalez	12.00	5.50
☐ 8	Greg Maddux	15.00	6.75
☐ 9	Frank Thomas	20.00	9.00
☐ 10	Ryne Sandberg	6.00	2.70
☐ 11	Mike Piazza	15.00	6.75
☐ 12	Johnny Damon	2.50	1.10
☐ 13	Barry Bonds	6.00	2.70
☐ 14	Jeff Bagwell	10.00	4.50
☐ 15	Paul Wilson	2.00	.90
☐ 16	Tim Salmon	5.00	2.20
☐ 17	Kirby Puckett	10.00	4.50
☐ 18	Tony Gwynn	12.00	5.50

1996 Summit Big Bang

Randomly inserted in packs at a rate of one in 72, this 16-card set features the League's big hitters on Spectroetched back-grounds with etched foil high-lights. Only 600 sets were pro-duced and each card is individually numbered of 600 on back. The backs carry a player portrait in a diamond with a faded version of the front as a background and information about the player.

		MINT	NRMT
COMPLETE SET (16)		750.00	350.00
COMMON CARD (1-16)		10.00	4.50
SEMISTARS		15.00	6.75
UNLISTED STARS		25.00	11.00

STATED ODDS 1:72
STATED PRINT RUN 600 SERIAL #'d SETS
*MIRAGE: 1X BASIC CARDS ....
MIRAGE STATED ODDS 1:72....
MIRAGE STATED PRINT RUN 600 SERIAL #'d SETS

☐ 1	Frank Thomas	100.00	45.00
☐ 2	Ken Griffey Jr.	120.00	55.00
☐ 3	Albert Belle	30.00	13.50
☐ 4	Mo Vaughn	30.00	13.50
☐ 5	Barry Bonds	30.00	13.50
☐ 6	Cal Ripken	100.00	45.00
☐ 7	Jeff Bagwell	50.00	22.00
☐ 8	Mike Piazza	80.00	36.00
☐ 9	Ryan Klesko	15.00	6.75
☐ 10	Manny Ramirez	25.00	11.00
☐ 11	Tim Salmon	25.00	11.00
☐ 12	Dante Bichette	10.00	4.50
☐ 13	Sammy Sosa	25.00	11.00
☐ 14	Raul Mondesi	15.00	6.75
☐ 15	Chipper Jones	80.00	36.00
☐ 16	Garret Anderson	10.00	4.50

1996 Summit Hitters Inc.

Randomly inserted in packs at a rate of one in 36, this 16-card set features color action player images with embossed high-lights on an enlarged photo of the player's eyes for back-ground. The backs carry infor-mation about the player's bat-ting ability. Four thousand of these sets were produced and individually serially numbered on the back.

		MINT	NRMT
COMPLETE SET (16)		250.00	110.00
COMMON CARD (1-16)		5.00	2.20
UNLISTED STARS		8.00	3.60

STATED ODDS 1:36 ....
STATED PRINT RUN 4000 SERIAL #'d SETS

☐ 1	Tony Gwynn	20.00	9.00
☐ 2	Mo Vaughn	10.00	4.50
☐ 3	Tim Salmon	8.00	3.60
☐ 4	Ken Griffey Jr.	40.00	18.00
☐ 5	Sammy Sosa	8.00	3.60
☐ 6	Frank Thomas	30.00	13.50
☐ 7	Wade Boggs	8.00	3.60
☐ 8	Albert Belle	10.00	4.50
☐ 9	Cal Ripken	30.00	13.50
☐ 10	Manny Ramirez	8.00	3.60
☐ 11	Ryan Klesko	6.00	2.70
☐ 12	Dante Bichette	5.00	2.20
☐ 13	Mike Piazza	25.00	11.00
☐ 14	Chipper Jones	25.00	11.00
☐ 15	Ryne Sandberg	10.00	4.50
☐ 16	Matt Williams	6.00	2.70

1996 Summit Positions

Randomly inserted in Magazine packs only at the rate of one in 50, this nine-card set honors the best players at each playing position. The fronts feature color action player images on a baseball diamond background with head photos of the players at the bottom. The backs carry information about how well the players perform at their position.

		MINT	NRMT
COMPLETE SET (9)		325.00	145.00
COMMON CARD (1-9)		20.00	9.00

STATED ODDS 1:50 MAGAZINE

☐ 1	Jeff Bagwell	50.00	22.00
	Mo Vaughn		
	Frank Thomas		
☐ 2	Roberto Alomar	20.00	9.00
	Craig Biggio		
	Chuck Knoblauch		
☐ 3	Matt Williams	40.00	18.00
	Jim Thome		
	Chipper Jones		

		NRMT	VG-E
☐ 4	Barry Larkin	80.00	36.00
	Cal Ripken		
	Alex Rodriguez		
☐ 5	Mike Piazza	40.00	18.00
	Ivan Rodriguez		
	Charles Johnson		
☐ 6	Hideo Nomo	50.00	22.00
	Greg Maddux		
	Randy Johnson		
☐ 7	Barry Bonds	25.00	11.00
	Albert Belle		
	Ryan Klesko		
☐ 8	Johnny Damon	50.00	22.00
	Jim Edmonds		
	Ken Griffey Jr.		
☐ 9	Manny Ramirez	20.00	9.00
	Gary Sheffield		
	Sammy Sosa		

1952 Topps

The cards in this 407-card set measure approximately 2 5/8" by 3 3/4". The 1952 Topps set is Topps' first truly major set. Card numbers 1 to 80 were issued with red or black backs, both of which are less plentiful than card numbers 81 to 250. In fact, the first series is considered the most difficult with respect to finding perfect condition cards. Card number 48 (Joe Page) and number 49 (Johnny Sain) can be found with each other's write-up on their back. However, many dealers today believe that all cards numbered 1-250 are valued the same. Card numbers 251 to 310 are somewhat scarce and numbers 311 to 407 are quite scarce. Cards 281-300 were single printed compared to the other cards in the next to last series. Cards 311-313 were double printed on the last high number printing sheet. The key card in the set is obviously Mickey Mantle, number 311. Mickey's first of many Topps cards. A really obscure variation on cards from 311 through 313 is that they exist with the stitching on the number circle in the back either clockwise or counter clockwise. There is no price differential for either variation. Card #307, Frank Campos has been discovered to have a black star next to the words "Topps Baseball" on the back. This card is very scarce but since it is rarely traded in the secondary market -- no value can be established at this time. Many collectors are not aware of this variation. In the early

1980's, Topps issued a standard-size reprint set of the 52 Topps set. These cards were issued only as a factory set and have a current market value of between two and three hundred dollars. Five people portrayed in the regular set: Billy Loes (#20), Dom DiMaggio (#22), Saul Rogovin (#159), Solly Hemus (#196) and Tommy Holmes (#289) are not in the reprint set. Although rarely seen, there exist salesman sample panels of three cards containing the fronts of regular cards with ad information on the back. Two such panels seen are Bob Mahoney/Robin Roberts/Sid Hudson and Wally Westlake/Dizzy Trout/Irv Noren. The cards were issued in one-card penny packs and six-card nickel packs. The key Rookie Cards in this set are Billy Martin, Eddie Mathews (the last card in the set), and Hoyt Wilhelm.

		NRMT	VG-E
COMPLETE SET (407)		65000.00	29200.00
COMMON CARD (1-80)		50.00	22.00
MINOR STARS 1-80		60.00	27.00
SEMISTARS 1-80		80.00	36.00
*RED/BLACK BACKS 1-80 SAME VALUE			
COMMON CARD (81-250)		35.00	16.00
MINOR STARS 81-250		50.00	22.00
SEMISTARS 81-250		60.00	27.00
UNLISTED STARS 81-250		80.00	36.00
COMMON CARD (251-310)		50.00	22.00
MINOR STARS (251-310)		60.00	27.00
SEMISTARS 251-310		80.00	36.00
COMMON CARD (311-407)		250.00	110.00
MINOR STARS 311-407		300.00	135.00
*UNLISTED DODGER/YANKEE: 1.25X VALUE			
CARDS PRICED IN NM CONDITION !			

		NRMT	VG-E
☐ 1	Andy Pafko	1300.00	130.00
☐ 2	Pete Runnels	100.00	45.00
☐ 3	Hank Thompson	60.00	27.00
☐ 4	Don Lenhardt	50.00	22.00
☐ 5	Larry Jansen	60.00	27.00
☐ 6	Grady Hatton	50.00	22.00
☐ 7	Wayne Terwilliger	50.00	22.00
☐ 8	Fred Marsh	50.00	22.00
☐ 9	Robert Hogue	50.00	22.90
☐ 10	Al Rosen	60.00	27.00
☐ 11	Phil Rizzuto	200.00	90.00
☐ 12	Monty Basgall	50.00	22.00
☐ 13	Johnny Wyrostek	50.00	22.00
☐ 14	Bob Elliott	60.00	27.00
☐ 15	Johnny Pesky	60.00	27.00
☐ 16	Gene Hermanski	50.00	22.00
☐ 17	Jim Hegan	60.00	27.00
☐ 18	Merrill Combs	50.00	22.00
☐ 19	Johnny Bucha	50.00	22.00
☐ 20	Billy Loes	120.00	55.00
☐ 21	Ferris Fain	60.00	27.00
☐ 22	Dom DiMaggio	80.00	36.00
☐ 23	Billy Goodman	60.00	27.00
☐ 24	Luke Easter	60.00	27.00
☐ 25	Johnny Groth	50.00	22.00
☐ 26	Monte Irvin	100.00	45.00
☐ 27	Sam Jethroe	60.00	27.00
☐ 28	Jerry Priddy	50.00	22.00
☐ 29	Ted Kluszewski	100.00	45.00
☐ 30	Mel Parnell	60.00	27.00
☐ 31	Gus Zernial	80.00	36.00
	Posed with seven baseballs		
☐ 32	Eddie Robinson	50.00	22.00
☐ 33	Warren Spahn	200.00	90.00
☐ 34	Elmer Valo	50.00	22.00
☐ 35	Hank Sauer	60.00	27.00
☐ 36	Gil Hodges	175.00	80.00
☐ 37	Duke Snider	250.00	110.00
☐ 38	Wally Westlake	50.00	22.00
☐ 39	Dizzy Trout	60.00	27.00

		NRMT	VG-E
☐ 40	Irv Noren	60.00	27.00
☐ 41	Bob Wellman	50.00	22.00
☐ 42	Lou Kretlow	50.00	22.00
☐ 43	Ray Scarborough	50.00	22.00
☐ 44	Con Dempsey	50.00	22.00
☐ 45	Eddie Joost	50.00	22.00
☐ 46	Gordon Goldsberry	50.00	22.00
☐ 47	Willie Jones	60.00	27.00
☐ 48A	Joe Page COR	75.00	34.00
☐ 48B	Joe Page ERR	275.00	125.00
	(Bio for Sain)		
☐ 49A	Johnny Sain COR	75.00	34.00
☐ 49B	Johnny Sain ERR	275.00	125.00
	(Bio for Page)		
☐ 50	Marv Rickert	50.00	22.00
☐ 51	Jim Russell	50.00	22.00
☐ 52	Don Mueller	60.00	27.00
☐ 53	Chris Van Cuyk	50.00	22.00
☐ 54	Leo Kiely	50.00	22.00
☐ 55	Ray Boone	60.00	27.00
☐ 56	Tommy Glaviano	50.00	22.00
☐ 57	Ed Lopat	80.00	36.00
☐ 58	Bob Mahoney	50.00	22.00
☐ 59	Robin Roberts	150.00	70.00
☐ 60	Sid Hudson	50.00	22.00
☐ 61	Tookie Gilbert	50.00	22.00
☐ 62	Chuck Stobbs	50.00	22.00
☐ 63	Howie Pollet	50.00	22.00
☐ 64	Roy Sievers	60.00	27.00
☐ 65	Enos Slaughter	150.00	70.00
☐ 66	Preacher Roe	80.00	36.00
☐ 67	Allie Reynolds	80.00	36.00
☐ 68	Cliff Chambers	50.00	22.00
☐ 69	Virgil Stallcup	50.00	22.00
☐ 70	Al Zarilla	50.00	22.00
☐ 71	Tom Upton	50.00	22.00
☐ 72	Karl Olson	50.00	22.00
☐ 73	Bill Werle	50.00	22.00
☐ 74	Andy Hansen	50.00	22.00
☐ 75	Wes Westrum	60.00	27.00
☐ 76	Eddie Stanky	60.00	27.00
☐ 77	Bob Kennedy	60.00	27.00
☐ 78	Ellis Kinder	50.00	22.00
☐ 79	Gerry Staley	50.00	22.00
☐ 80	Herman Wehmeier	50.00	22.00
☐ 81	Vernon Law	50.00	22.00
☐ 82	Duane Pillette	35.00	16.00
☐ 83	Billy Johnson	35.00	16.00
☐ 84	Vern Stephens	50.00	22.00
☐ 85	Bob Kuzava	50.00	22.00
☐ 86	Ted Gray	35.00	16.00
☐ 87	Dale Coogan	35.00	16.00
☐ 88	Bob Feller	200.00	90.00
☐ 89	Johnny Lipon	35.00	16.00
☐ 90	Mickey Grasso	35.00	16.00
☐ 91	Red Schoendienst	80.00	36.00
☐ 92	Dale Mitchell	50.00	22.00
☐ 93	Al Sima	35.00	16.00
☐ 94	Sam Mele	50.00	16.00
☐ 95	Ken Holcombe	35.00	16.00
☐ 96	Willard Marshall	35.00	16.00
☐ 97	Earl Torgeson	35.00	16.00
☐ 98	Billy Pierce	50.00	22.00
☐ 99	Gene Woodling	60.00	27.00
☐ 100	Del Rice	35.00	16.00
☐ 101	Max Lanier	35.00	16.00
☐ 102	Bill Kennedy	35.00	16.00
☐ 103	Cliff Mapes	35.00	16.00
☐ 104	Don Kolloway	35.00	16.00
☐ 105	Johnny Pramesa	35.00	16.00
☐ 106	Mickey Vernon	60.00	27.00
☐ 107	Connie Ryan	35.00	16.00
☐ 108	Jim Konstanty	60.00	27.00
☐ 109	Ted Wilks	35.00	16.00
☐ 110	Dutch Leonard	35.00	16.00
☐ 111	Peanuts Lowrey	35.00	16.00
☐ 112	Hank Majeski	35.00	16.00
☐ 113	Dick Sisler	50.00	22.00
☐ 114	Willard Ramsdell	35.00	16.00
☐ 115	Red Munger	35.00	16.00
☐ 116	Carl Scheib	35.00	16.00
☐ 117	Sherm Lollar	50.00	22.00
☐ 118	Ken Raffensberger	35.00	16.00
☐ 119	Mickey McDermott	35.00	16.00
☐ 120	Bob Chakales	35.00	16.00
☐ 121	Gus Niarhos	35.00	16.00

122	Jackie Jensen	80.00	36.00
123	Eddie Yost	50.00	22.00
124	Monte Kennedy	35.00	16.00
125	Bill Rigney	50.00	16.00
126	Fred Hutchinson	50.00	22.00
127	Paul Minner	35.00	16.00
128	Don Bollweg	35.00	16.00
129	Johnny Mize	90.00	40.00
130	Sheldon Jones	35.00	16.00
131	Morrie Martin	35.00	16.00
132	Clyde Kluttz	35.00	16.00
133	Al Widmar	35.00	16.00
134	Joe Tipton	35.00	16.00
135	Dixie Howell	35.00	16.00
136	Johnny Schmitz	35.00	16.00
137	Roy McMillan	50.00	16.00
138	Bill MacDonald	35.00	16.00
139	Ken Wood	35.00	16.00
140	Johnny Antonelli	50.00	22.00
141	Clint Hartung	35.00	16.00
142	Harry Perkowski	35.00	16.00
143	Les Moss	35.00	16.00
144	Ed Blake	35.00	16.00
145	Joe Haynes	35.00	16.00
146	Frank House	35.00	16.00
147	Bob Young	35.00	16.00
148	Johnny Klippstein	35.00	16.00
149	Dick Kryhoski	35.00	16.00
150	Ted Beard	35.00	16.00
151	Wally Post	50.00	22.00
152	Al Evans	35.00	16.00
153	Bob Rush	35.00	16.00
154	Joe Muir	35.00	16.00
155	Frank Overmire	35.00	16.00
156	Frank Hiller	35.00	16.00
157	Bob Usher	35.00	16.00
158	Eddie Waitkus	35.00	16.00
159	Saul Rogovin	35.00	16.00
160	Owen Friend	35.00	16.00
161	Bud Byerly	35.00	16.00
162	Del Crandall	50.00	22.00
163	Stan Rojek	35.00	16.00
164	Walt Dubiel	35.00	16.00
165	Eddie Kazak	35.00	16.00
166	Paul LaPalme	35.00	16.00
167	Bill Howerton	35.00	16.00
168	Charlie Silvera	60.00	27.00
169	Howie Judson	35.00	16.00
170	Gus Bell	50.00	22.00
171	Ed Erautt	35.00	16.00
172	Eddie Miksis	35.00	16.00
173	Roy Smalley	35.00	16.00
174	Clarence Marshall	35.00	16.00
175	Billy Martin	300.00	135.00
176	Hank Edwards	35.00	16.00
177	Bill Wight	35.00	16.00
178	Cass Michaels	35.00	16.00
179	Frank Smith	35.00	16.00
180	Charlie Maxwell	50.00	22.00
181	Bob Swift	35.00	16.00
182	Billy Hitchcock	35.00	16.00
183	Erv Dusak	35.00	16.00
184	Bob Ramazzotti	35.00	16.00
185	Bill Nicholson	50.00	22.00
186	Walt Masterson	35.00	16.00
187	Bob Miller	35.00	16.00
188	Clarence Podbielan	35.00	16.00
189	Pete Reiser	60.00	27.00
190	Don Johnson	35.00	16.00
191	Yogi Berra	350.00	160.00
192	Myron Ginsberg	35.00	16.00
193	Harry Simpson	35.00	22.00
194	Joe Hatton	35.00	16.00
195	Minnie Minoso	150.00	70.00
196	Solly Hemus	35.00	27.00
197	George Strickland	35.00	16.00
198	Phil Haugstad	35.00	16.00
199	George Zuverink	35.00	16.00
200	Ralph Houk	80.00	36.00
201	Alex Kellner	35.00	16.00
202	Joe Collins	65.00	29.00
203	Curt Simmons	60.00	27.00
204	Ron Northey	35.00	16.00
205	Clyde King	35.00	16.00
206	Joe Ostrowski	35.00	16.00
207	Mickey Harris	35.00	16.00
208	Marlin Stuart	35.00	16.00
209	Howie Fox	35.00	16.00
210	Dick Fowler	35.00	16.00
211	Ray Coleman	35.00	16.00
212	Ned Garver	35.00	16.00
213	Nippy Jones	35.00	16.00
214	Johnny Hopp	50.00	22.00
215	Hank Bauer	65.00	29.00
216	Richie Ashburn	175.00	80.00
217	Snuffy Stirnweiss	50.00	22.00
218	Clyde McCullough	35.00	16.00
219	Bobby Shantz	60.00	27.00
220	Joe Presko	35.00	16.00
221	Granny Hamner	35.00	16.00
222	Hoot Evers	35.00	16.00
223	Del Ennis	50.00	22.00
224	Bruce Edwards	35.00	16.00
225	Frank Baumholtz	35.00	16.00
226	Dave Philley	35.00	16.00
227	Joe Garagiola	80.00	36.00
228	Al Brazle	35.00	16.00
229	Gene Bearden UER	35.00	16.00
	(Misspelled Beardon)		
230	Matt Batts	35.00	16.00
231	Sam Zoldak	35.00	16.00
232	Billy Cox	50.00	22.00
233	Bob Friend	60.00	27.00
234	Steve Souchock	35.00	16.00
235	Walt Dropo	50.00	16.00
236	Ed Fitzgerald	35.00	16.00
237	Jerry Coleman	65.00	29.00
238	Art Houtteman	35.00	16.00
239	Rocky Bridges	50.00	22.00
240	Jack Phillips	35.00	16.00
241	Tommy Byrne	50.00	16.00
242	Tom Poholsky	35.00	16.00
243	Larry Doby	80.00	36.00
244	Vic Wertz	35.00	16.00
245	Sherry Robertson	35.00	16.00
246	George Kell	80.00	36.00
247	Randy Gumpert	35.00	16.00
248	Frank Shea	35.00	16.00
249	Bobby Adams	35.00	16.00
250	Carl Erskine	90.00	40.00
251	Chico Carrasquel	50.00	22.00
252	Vern Bickford	35.00	16.00
253	Johnny Berardino	75.00	34.00
254	Joe Dobson	35.00	16.00
255	Clyde Vollmer	35.00	16.00
256	Pete Suder	35.00	16.00
257	Bobby Avila	60.00	27.00
258	Steve Gromek	35.00	16.00
259	Bob Addis	35.00	16.00
260	Pete Castiglione	35.00	16.00
261	Willie Mays	2500.00	1100.00
262	Virgil Trucks	60.00	27.00
263	Harry Brecheen	60.00	27.00
264	Roy Hartsfield	35.00	22.00
265	Chuck Diering	50.00	22.00
266	Murry Dickson	50.00	22.00
267	Sid Gordon	35.00	16.00
268	Bob Lemon	150.00	70.00
269	Willard Nixon	35.00	16.00
270	Lou Brissie	50.00	22.00
271	Jim Delsing	35.00	16.00
272	Mike Garcia	60.00	22.00
273	Erv Palica	35.00	22.00
274	Ralph Branca	120.00	55.00
275	Pat Mullin	35.00	16.00
276	Jim Wilson	35.00	16.00
277	Early Wynn	150.00	70.00
278	Allie Clark	35.00	16.00
279	Eddie Stewart	35.00	22.00
280	Cloyd Boyer	35.00	16.00
281	Tommy Brown SP	60.00	27.00
282	Birdie Tebbetts SP	80.00	36.00
283	Phil Masi SP	60.00	27.00
284	Hank Arft SP	60.00	27.00
285	Cliff Fannin SP	60.00	27.00
286	Joe DeMaestri SP	60.00	27.00
287	Steve Bilko SP	60.00	27.00
288	Chet Nichols SP	60.00	27.00
289	Tommy Holmes SP	75.00	34.00
290	Joe Astroth SP	60.00	27.00
291	Gil Coan SP	60.00	27.00
292	Floyd Baker SP	60.00	27.00
293	Sibby Sisti SP	60.00	27.00
294	Walker Cooper SP	60.00	27.00
295	Phil Cavarretta SP	75.00	34.00
296	Red Rolfe MG SP	60.00	27.00
297	Andy Seminick SP	60.00	27.00
298	Bob Ross SP	60.00	27.00
299	Ray Murray SP	60.00	27.00
300	Barney McCosky SP	60.00	27.00
301	Bob Porterfield	50.00	22.00
302	Max Surkont	50.00	22.00
303	Harry Dorish	50.00	22.00
304	Sam Dente	50.00	22.00
305	Paul Richards MG	60.00	27.00
306	Lou Sleater	50.00	22.00
307	Frank Campos	50.00	22.00
308	Luis Aloma	50.00	22.00
309	Jim Busby	50.00	22.00
310	George Metkovich	60.00	27.00
311	Mickey Mantle	23000.00	10400.00
312	Jackie Robinson DP	1400.00	650.00
313	Bobby Thomson DP	300.00	135.00
314	Roy Campanella	2000.00	900.00
315	Leo Durocher MG	375.00	170.00
316	Dave Williams	300.00	135.00
317	Conrado Marrero	300.00	110.00
318	Harold Gregg	250.00	110.00
319	Al Walker	250.00	110.00
320	John Rutherford	300.00	135.00
321	Joe Black	350.00	160.00
322	Randy Jackson	250.00	110.00
323	Bubba Church	250.00	110.00
324	Warren Hacker	250.00	110.00
325	Bill Serena	250.00	110.00
326	George Shuba	400.00	180.00
327	Al Wilson	250.00	110.00
328	Bob Borkowski	250.00	110.00
329	Ike Delock	250.00	110.00
330	Turk Lown	250.00	110.00
331	Tom Morgan	250.00	110.00
332	Anthony Bartirome	250.00	110.00
333	Pee Wee Reese	1500.00	700.00
334	Wilmer Mizell	300.00	135.00
335	Ted Lepcio	250.00	110.00
336	Dave Koslo	250.00	110.00
337	Jim Hearn	250.00	110.00
338	Sal Yvars	250.00	110.00
339	Russ Meyer	250.00	110.00
340	Bob Hooper	250.00	110.00
341	Hal Jeffcoat	250.00	110.00
342	Clem Labine	400.00	180.00
343	Dick Gernert	250.00	110.00
344	Ewell Blackwell	300.00	135.00
345	Sammy White	250.00	110.00
346	George Spencer	250.00	110.00
347	Joe Adcock	300.00	135.00
348	Robert Kelly	250.00	110.00
349	Bob Cain	250.00	110.00
350	Cal Abrams	250.00	110.00
351	Alvin Dark	300.00	135.00
352	Karl Drews	250.00	110.00
353	Bobby Del Greco	250.00	110.00
354	Fred Hatfield	250.00	110.00
355	Bobby Morgan	250.00	110.00
356	Toby Atwell	250.00	110.00
357	Smoky Burgess	300.00	135.00
358	John Kucab	250.00	110.00
359	Dee Fondy	250.00	110.00
360	George Crowe	300.00	135.00
361	William Posedel CO	250.00	110.00
362	Ken Heintzelman	250.00	110.00
363	Dick Rozek	250.00	110.00
364	Clyde Sukeforth CO	250.00	110.00
365	Cookie Lavagetto CO	375.00	170.00
366	Dave Madison	250.00	110.00
367	Ben Thorpe	250.00	110.00
368	Ed Wright	250.00	110.00
369	Dick Groat	350.00	160.00
370	Billy Hoeft	250.00	110.00
371	Bobby Hofman	250.00	110.00
372	Gil McDougald	375.00	170.00
373	Jim Turner CO	400.00	180.00
374	John Benton	250.00	110.00
375	John Merson	250.00	110.00
376	Faye Throneberry	250.00	110.00
377	Chuck Dressen MG	375.00	170.00
378	Leroy Fusselman	250.00	110.00

		NRMT	VG-E
☐ 379	Joe Rossi	250.00	110.00
☐ 380	Clem Koshorek	250.00	110.00
☐ 381	Milton Stock CO	250.00	110.00
☐ 382	Sam Jones	350.00	160.00
☐ 383	Del Wilber	250.00	110.00
☐ 384	Frank Crosetti CO	400.00	180.00
☐ 385	Herman Franks CO	250.00	110.00
☐ 386	John Yuhas	250.00	110.00
☐ 387	Billy Meyer MG	250.00	110.00
☐ 388	Bob Chipman	250.00	110.00
☐ 389	Ben Wade	250.00	110.00
☐ 390	Glenn Nelson	250.00	110.00
☐ 391	Ben Chapman UER	250.00	110.00
	(Photo actually Sam Chapman)		
☐ 392	Hoyt Wilhelm	700.00	325.00
☐ 393	Ebba St.Claire	250.00	110.00
☐ 394	Billy Herman CO	400.00	180.00
☐ 395	Jake Pitler CO	325.00	145.00
☐ 396	Dick Williams	400.00	180.00
☐ 397	Forrest Main	250.00	110.00
☐ 398	Hal Rice	250.00	110.00
☐ 399	Jim Fridley	250.00	110.00
☐ 400	Bill Dickey CO	800.00	350.00
☐ 401	Bob Schultz	250.00	110.00
☐ 402	Earl Harrist	250.00	110.00
☐ 403	Bill Miller	250.00	110.00
☐ 404	Dick Brodowski	250.00	110.00
☐ 405	Eddie Pellagrini	250.00	110.00
☐ 406	Joe Nuxhall	350.00	160.00
☐ 407	Eddie Mathews	4000.00	1000.00

1953 Topps

BOB FELLER
CLEVELAND INDIANS

The cards in this 274-card set measure 2 5/8" by 3 3/4". Although the last card is numbered 280, there are only 274 cards in the set since numbers 253, 261, 267, 268, 271, and 275 were never issued. The 1953 Topps series contains line drawings of players in full color. The name and team panel at the card base is easily damaged, making it very difficult to complete a mint set. The high number series, 221 to 280, was produced in shorter supply late in the year and hence is more difficult to complete than the lower numbers. The key cards in the set are Mickey Mantle (82) and Willie Mays (244). The key Rookie Cards in this set are Roy Face, Jim Gilliam, and Johnny Podres, all from the last series. There are a number of double-printed cards (actually not double but 50 percent more of each of these numbers are printed compared to the other cards in the series) indicated by DP in the checklist below. There were five players (10 Smoky Burgess, 44 Ellis Kinder, 61 Early Wynn, 72 Fred

Hutchinson, and 81 Joe Black) held out of the first run of 1-85 (but printed in numbers 86-165), who are each marked by SP in the checklist below. In addition, there are five numbers which were printed with the more plentiful series 166-220; these cards (94, 107, 131, 145, and 156) are also indicated by DP in the checklist below. The cards were issued in one-card penny packs or six-card nickel packs. There were some three-card advertising panels produced by Topps; the players include Johnny Mize/Clem Koshorek/Toby Atwell and Mickey Mantle/Johnny Wyrostek/Sal Yvars. When cut apart, these advertising cards are distinguished by the card back, i.e., part of an advertisement for the 1953 Topps set instead of the typical statistics and biographical information about the player pictured.

	NRMT	VG-E
COMPLETE SET (274) ..	13500.00	6100.00
COMMON CARD (1-165) ..	30.00	13.50
COMMON CARD (166-220)	25.00	11.00
COMMON DP (1-220)	15.00	6.75
MINOR STARS 1-220	40.00	18.00
SEMISTARS 1-220	60.00	27.00
UNLISTED STARS 1-220 ..	80.00	36.00
COMMON CARD (221-280)	100.00	45.00
COMMON DP (221-280)	50.00	22.00
MINOR STARS 221-280 ..	120.00	55.00
SEMISTARS 221-280	150.00	70.00
NOT ISSUED (253/261/267).....		
NOT ISSUED (268/271/275).....		
*UNLISTED DODGER/YANKEE: 1.25X VALUE		
CARDS PRICED IN NM CONDITION !		

☐ 1	Jackie Robinson DP	500.00	140.00
☐ 2	Luke Easter DP	20.00	9.00
☐ 3	George Crowe	30.00	13.50
☐ 4	Ben Wade	30.00	13.50
☐ 5	Joe Dobson	30.00	13.50
☐ 6	Sam Jones	40.00	18.00
☐ 7	Bob Borkowski DP	15.00	6.75
☐ 8	Clem Koshorek DP	15.00	6.75
☐ 9	Joe Collins	40.00	18.00
☐ 10	Smoky Burgess SP	75.00	32.00
☐ 11	Sal Yvars	30.00	13.50
☐ 12	Howie Judson DP	15.00	6.75
☐ 13	Conrado Marrero DP	15.00	6.75
☐ 14	Clem Labine DP	20.00	9.00
☐ 15	Bobo Newsom DP	30.00	13.50
☐ 16	Peanuts Lowrey DP	15.00	6.75
☐ 17	Billy Hitchcock	30.00	13.50
☐ 18	Ted Lepcio DP	30.00	13.50
☐ 19	Mel Parnell DP	30.00	13.50
☐ 20	Hank Thompson	40.00	18.00
☐ 21	Billy Johnson	30.00	13.50
☐ 22	Howie Fox	30.00	13.50
☐ 23	Toby Atwell DP	15.00	6.75
☐ 24	Ferris Fain	40.00	18.00
☐ 25	Ray Boone	40.00	18.00
☐ 26	Dale Mitchell DP	20.00	9.00
☐ 27	Roy Campanella DP	175.00	80.00
☐ 28	Eddie Pellagrini	30.00	13.50
☐ 29	Hal Jeffcoat	30.00	13.50
☐ 30	Willard Nixon	30.00	13.50
☐ 31	Ewell Blackwell	50.00	22.00
☐ 32	Clyde Vollmer	30.00	13.50
☐ 33	Bob Kennedy DP	15.00	6.75
☐ 34	George Shuba	40.00	18.00
☐ 35	Irv Noren DP	15.00	6.75
☐ 36	Johnny Groth DP	15.00	6.75
☐ 37	Eddie Mathews DP	100.00	45.00
☐ 38	Jim Hearn DP	15.00	6.75
☐ 39	Eddie Miksis	30.00	13.50
☐ 40	John Lipon	30.00	13.50
☐ 41	Enos Slaughter	80.00	36.00
☐ 42	Gus Zernial DP	30.00	13.50
☐ 43	Gil McDougald	50.00	22.00
☐ 44	Ellis Kinder SP	35.00	16.00
☐ 45	Grady Hatton DP	15.00	6.75
☐ 46	Johnny Klippstein DP	15.00	6.75
☐ 47	Bubba Church DP	15.00	6.75
☐ 48	Bob Del Greco DP	15.00	6.75
☐ 49	Faye Throneberry DP	15.00	6.75
☐ 50	Chuck Dressen MG DP	22.50	10.00
☐ 51	Frank Campos DP	15.00	6.75
☐ 52	Ted Gray DP	15.00	6.75
☐ 53	Sherm Lollar DP	30.00	13.50
☐ 54	Bob Feller DP	100.00	45.00
☐ 55	Maurice McDermott DP	15.00	6.75
☐ 56	Gerry Staley DP	15.00	6.75
☐ 57	Carl Scheib	30.00	13.50
☐ 58	George Metkovich	30.00	13.50
☐ 59	Karl Drews DP	15.25	6.75
☐ 60	Cloyd Boyer DP	15.00	6.75
☐ 61	Early Wynn SP	90.00	40.00
☐ 62	Monte Irvin DP	35.00	16.00
☐ 63	Gus Niarhos DP	15.00	6.75
☐ 64	Dave Philley	30.00	13.50
☐ 65	Earl Harrist	30.00	13.50
☐ 66	Minnie Minoso	50.00	22.00
☐ 67	Roy Sievers DP	30.00	13.50
☐ 68	Del Rice	30.00	13.50
☐ 69	Dick Brodowski	30.00	13.50
☐ 70	Ed Yuhas	30.00	13.50
☐ 71	Tony Bartirome	30.00	13.50
☐ 72	Fred Hutchinson MG SP	50.00	22.00
☐ 73	Eddie Robinson	30.00	13.50
☐ 74	Joe Rossi	30.00	13.50
☐ 75	Mike Garcia	40.00	18.00
☐ 76	Pee Wee Reese	150.00	70.00
☐ 77	Johnny Mize DP	50.00	22.00
☐ 78	Red Schoendienst	60.00	27.00
☐ 79	Johnny Wyrostek	30.00	13.50
☐ 80	Jim Hegan	40.00	18.00
☐ 81	Joe Black SP	70.00	32.00
☐ 82	Mickey Mantle	3000.00	1350.00
☐ 83	Howie Pollet	30.00	13.50
☐ 84	Bob Hooper DP	15.00	6.75
☐ 85	Bobby Morgan DP	15.00	6.75
☐ 86	Billy Martin	125.00	55.00
☐ 87	Ed Lopat	50.00	22.00
☐ 88	Willie Jones DP	15.00	6.75
☐ 89	Chuck Stobbs DP	15.00	6.75
☐ 90	Hank Edwards DP	15.00	6.75
☐ 91	Ebba St.Claire DP	15.00	6.75
☐ 92	Paul Minner DP	15.00	6.75
☐ 93	Hal Rice DP	15.00	6.75
☐ 94	Bill Kennedy DP	15.00	6.75
☐ 95	Willard Marshall DP	15.00	6.75
☐ 96	Virgil Trucks	40.00	18.00
☐ 97	Don Kolloway DP	15.00	6.75
☐ 98	Cal Abrams DP	15.00	6.75
☐ 99	Dave Madison	30.00	13.50
☐ 100	Bill Miller	30.00	13.50
☐ 101	Ted Wilks	30.00	13.50
☐ 102	Connie Ryan DP	15.00	6.75
☐ 103	Joe Astroth DP	15.00	6.75
☐ 104	Yogi Berra	200.00	90.00
☐ 105	Joe Nuxhall DP	30.00	13.50
☐ 106	Johnny Antonelli	40.00	18.00
☐ 107	Danny O'Connell DP	15.00	6.75
☐ 108	Bob Porterfield DP	15.00	6.75
☐ 109	Alvin Dark	40.00	18.00
☐ 110	Herman Wehmeier DP	15.00	6.75
☐ 111	Hank Sauer DP	20.00	9.00
☐ 112	Ned Garver DP	15.00	6.75
☐ 113	Jerry Priddy	30.00	13.50
☐ 114	Phil Rizzuto	160.00	70.00
☐ 115	George Spencer	30.00	13.50
☐ 116	Frank Smith DP	15.00	6.75
☐ 117	Sid Gordon DP	15.00	6.75
☐ 118	Gus Bell DP	20.00	9.00
☐ 119	Johnny Sain SP	50.00	22.00
☐ 120	Davey Williams	40.00	18.00
☐ 121	Walt Dropo	40.00	18.00
☐ 122	Elmer Valo	30.00	13.50
☐ 123	Tommy Byrne DP	15.00	6.75
☐ 124	Sibby Sisti DP	15.00	6.75
☐ 125	Dick Williams DP	22.50	10.00
☐ 126	Bill Connelly DP	15.00	6.75

☐ 127 Clint Courtney DP	15.00	6.75	
☐ 128 Wilmer Mizell DP	20.00	9.00	
(Inconsistent design, logo on front with black birds)			
☐ 129 Keith Thomas	30.00	13.50	
☐ 130 Turk Lown DP	15.00	6.75	
☐ 131 Harry Byrd DP	15.00	6.75	
☐ 132 Tom Morgan	30.00	13.50	
☐ 133 Gil Coan	30.00	13.50	
☐ 134 Rube Walker	40.00	18.00	
☐ 135 Al Rosen DP	25.00	11.00	
☐ 136 Ken Heintzelman DP	15.00	6.75	
☐ 137 John Rutherford DP	15.00	6.75	
☐ 138 George Kell	60.00	27.00	
☐ 139 Sammy White	30.00	13.50	
☐ 140 Tommy Glaviano	30.00	13.50	
☐ 141 Allie Reynolds DP	25.00	11.00	
☐ 142 Vic Wertz	40.00	18.00	
☐ 143 Billy Pierce !	50.00	22.00	
☐ 144 Bob Schultz DP	15.00	6.75	
☐ 145 Harry Dorish DP	15.00	6.75	
☐ 146 Granny Hamner	30.00	13.50	
☐ 147 Warren Spahn	150.00	70.00	
☐ 148 Mickey Grasso	30.00	13.50	
☐ 149 Dom DiMaggio DP	35.00	16.00	
☐ 150 Harry Simpson DP	15.00	6.75	
☐ 151 Hoyt Wilhelm	80.00	36.00	
☐ 152 Bob Adams DP	15.00	6.75	
☐ 153 Andy Seminick DP	15.00	6.75	
☐ 154 Dick Groat	40.00	18.00	
☐ 155 Dutch Leonard	30.00	13.50	
☐ 156 Jim Rivera DP	30.00	13.50	
☐ 157 Bob Addis DP	15.00	6.75	
☐ 158 Johnny Logan	35.00	16.00	
☐ 159 Wayne Terwilliger DP	15.00	6.75	
☐ 160 Bob Young	30.00	13.50	
☐ 161 Vern Bickford DP	15.00	6.75	
☐ 162 Ted Kluszewski	50.00	22.00	
☐ 163 Fred Hatfield DP	15.00	6.75	
☐ 164 Frank Shea DP	15.00	6.75	
☐ 165 Billy Hoeft	30.00	13.50	
☐ 166 Billy Hunter	25.00	11.00	
☐ 167 Art Schult	25.00	11.00	
☐ 168 Willard Schmidt	25.00	11.00	
☐ 169 Dizzy Trout	40.00	18.00	
☐ 170 Bill Werle	25.00	11.00	
☐ 171 Bill Glynn	25.00	11.00	
☐ 172 Rip Repulski	25.00	11.00	
☐ 173 Preston Ward	25.00	11.00	
☐ 174 Billy Loes	40.00	18.00	
☐ 175 Ron Kline	25.00	11.00	
☐ 176 Don Hoak	40.00	18.00	
☐ 177 Jim Dyck	25.00	11.00	
☐ 178 Jim Waugh	25.00	11.00	
☐ 179 Gene Hermanski	25.00	11.00	
☐ 180 Virgil Stallcup	25.00	11.00	
☐ 181 Al Zarilla	25.00	11.00	
☐ 182 Bobby Hofman	25.00	11.00	
☐ 183 Stu Miller	40.00	18.00	
☐ 184 Hal Brown	25.00	11.00	
☐ 185 Jim Pendleton	25.00	11.00	
☐ 186 Charlie Bishop	25.00	11.00	
☐ 187 Jim Fridley	25.00	11.00	
☐ 188 Andy Carey	40.00	18.00	
☐ 189 Ray Jablonski	25.00	11.00	
☐ 190 Dixie Walker CO	40.00	18.00	
☐ 191 Ralph Kiner	80.00	36.00	
☐ 192 Wally Westlake	25.00	11.00	
☐ 193 Mike Clark	25.00	11.00	
☐ 194 Eddie Kazak	25.00	11.00	
☐ 195 Ed McGhee	25.00	11.00	
☐ 196 Bob Keegan	25.00	11.00	
☐ 197 Del Crandall	40.00	18.00	
☐ 198 Forrest Main	25.00	11.00	
☐ 199 Marion Fricano	25.00	11.00	
☐ 200 Gordon Goldsberry	25.00	11.00	
☐ 201 Paul LaPalme	25.00	11.00	
☐ 202 Carl Sawatski	25.00	11.00	
☐ 203 Cliff Fannin	25.00	11.00	
☐ 204 Dick Bokelman	25.00	11.00	
☐ 205 Vern Benson	25.00	11.00	
☐ 206 Ed Bailey	25.00	11.00	
☐ 207 Whitey Ford	160.00	70.00	
☐ 208 Jim Wilson	25.00	11.00	
☐ 209 Jim Greengrass	25.00	11.00	

☐ 210 Bob Cerv	40.00	18.00	
☐ 211 J.W. Porter	25.00	11.00	
☐ 212 Jack Dittmer	25.00	11.00	
☐ 213 Ray Scarborough	25.00	11.00	
☐ 214 Bill Bruton	40.00	18.00	
☐ 215 Gene Conley	40.00	18.00	
☐ 216 Jim Hughes	25.00	11.00	
☐ 217 Murray Wall	25.00	11.00	
☐ 218 Les Fusselman	25.00	11.00	
☐ 219 Pete Runnels UER	40.00	18.00	
(Photo actually Don Johnson)			
☐ 220 Satchel Paige UER	450.00	200.00	
(Misspelled Satchell on card front)			
☐ 221 Bob Milliken	100.00	45.00	
☐ 222 Vic Janowicz DP	60.00	27.00	
☐ 223 Johnny O'Brien DP	50.00	22.00	
☐ 224 Lou Sleater DP	100.00	45.00	
☐ 225 Bobby Shantz	120.00	55.00	
☐ 226 Ed Erautt	100.00	45.00	
☐ 227 Morrie Martin	100.00	45.00	
☐ 228 Hal Newhouser	150.00	70.00	
☐ 229 Rocky Krsnich	100.00	45.00	
☐ 230 Johnny Lindell DP	50.00	22.00	
☐ 231 Solly Hemus DP	50.00	22.00	
☐ 232 Dick Kokos	100.00	45.00	
☐ 233 Al Aber	100.00	45.00	
☐ 234 Ray Murray DP	50.00	22.00	
☐ 235 John Hetki DP	50.00	22.00	
☐ 236 Harry Perkowski DP	50.00	22.00	
☐ 237 Bud Podbielan DP	50.00	22.00	
☐ 238 Cal Hogue DP	50.00	22.00	
☐ 239 Jim Delsing	100.00	45.00	
☐ 240 Fred Marsh	100.00	45.00	
☐ 241 Al Sima DP	50.00	22.00	
☐ 242 Charlie Silvera	120.00	55.00	
☐ 243 Carlos Bernier DP	50.00	22.00	
☐ 244 Willie Mays	2700.00	1200.00	
☐ 245 Bill Norman CO	100.00	45.00	
☐ 246 Roy Face DP	80.00	36.00	
☐ 247 Mike Sandlock DP	50.00	22.00	
☐ 248 Gene Stephens DP	50.00	22.00	
☐ 249 Eddie O'Brien	100.00	45.00	
☐ 250 Bob Wilson	100.00	45.00	
☐ 251 Sid Hudson	100.00	45.00	
☐ 252 Hank Foiles	100.00	45.00	
☐ 253 Does not exist			
☐ 254 Preacher Roe DP	80.00	36.00	
☐ 255 Dixie Howell	100.00	45.00	
☐ 256 Les Peden	100.00	45.00	
☐ 257 Bob Boyd	100.00	45.00	
☐ 258 Jim Gilliam	300.00	135.00	
☐ 259 Roy McMillan DP	100.00	45.00	
☐ 260 Sam Calderone	100.00	45.00	
☐ 261 Does not exist			
☐ 262 Bob Oldis	100.00	45.00	
☐ 263 Johnny Podres	275.00	125.00	
☐ 264 Gene Woodling DP	100.00	45.00	
☐ 265 Jackie Jensen	125.00	55.00	
☐ 266 Bob Cain	100.00	45.00	
☐ 267 Does not exist			
☐ 268 Does not exist			
☐ 269 Duane Pillette	100.00	45.00	
☐ 270 Vern Stephens	120.00	55.00	
☐ 271 Does not exist			
☐ 272 Bill Antonello	100.00	45.00	
☐ 273 Harvey Haddix	125.00	55.00	
☐ 274 John Riddle CO	100.00	45.00	
☐ 275 Does not exist			
☐ 276 Ken Raffensberger	100.00	45.00	
☐ 277 Don Lund	100.00	45.00	
☐ 278 Willie Miranda	100.00	45.00	
☐ 279 Joe Coleman DP	50.00	22.00	
☐ 280 Milt Bolling	300.00	50.00	

against a color background. The cards were issued in one-card penny packs or five-card nickel packs. This set contains the Rookie Cards of Hank Aaron, Ernie Banks, and Al Kaline and two separate cards of Ted Williams (number 1 and number 250). Conspicuous by his absence is Mickey Mantle who apparently was the exclusive property of Bowman during 1954 (and 1955). The first two issues of Sports Illustrated magazine contained "card" inserts on regular paper stock. The first issue showed actual cards in the set in color, while the second issue showed some created cards of New York Yankees players in black and white, including Mickey Mantle.

	NRMT	VG-E
COMPLETE SET (250)	7500.00	3400.00
COMMON (1-50/76-250)	15.00	6.75
MINOR STARS 1-50/76-250	25.00	11.00
SEMISTARS 1-50/76-250	40.00	18.00
UNL.STARS 1-50/76-250	50.00	22.00
COMMON CARD (51-75)	25.00	11.00
MINOR STARS 51-75	30.00	13.50
SEMISTARS 51-75	50.00	22.00
UNLISTED STARS 51-75	60.00	27.00
*UNLISTED DODGER/YANKEE: 1.25X VALUE		
CARDS PRICED IN NM CONDITION !		

1954 Topps

The cards in this 250-card set measure approximately 2 5/8" by 3 3/4". Each of the cards in the 1954 Topps set contains a large "head" shot of the player in color plus a smaller full-length photo in black and white set

☐ 1 Ted Williams	650.00	230.00	
☐ 2 Gus Zernial	25.00	11.00	
☐ 3 Monte Irvin	40.00	18.00	
☐ 4 Hank Sauer	25.00	11.00	
☐ 5 Ed Lopat	25.00	11.00	
☐ 6 Pete Runnels	25.00	11.00	
☐ 7 Ted Kluszewski	40.00	18.00	
☐ 8 Bob Young	15.00	6.75	
☐ 9 Harvey Haddix	25.00	11.00	
☐ 10 Jackie Robinson	300.00	135.00	
☐ 11 Paul Leslie Smith	15.00	6.75	
☐ 12 Del Crandall	25.00	11.00	
☐ 13 Billy Martin	60.00	27.00	
☐ 14 Preacher Roe	25.00	11.00	
☐ 15 Al Rosen	25.00	11.00	
☐ 16 Vic Janowicz	25.00	11.00	
☐ 17 Phil Rizzuto	75.00	34.00	
☐ 18 Walt Dropo	25.00	11.00	
☐ 19 Johnny Lipon	15.00	6.75	
☐ 20 Warren Spahn	75.00	34.00	
☐ 21 Bobby Shantz	25.00	11.00	
☐ 22 Jim Greengrass	15.00	6.75	
☐ 23 Luke Easter	25.00	11.00	
☐ 24 Granny Hamner	15.00	6.75	
☐ 25 Harvey Kuenn	40.00	18.00	
☐ 26 Ray Jablonski	15.00	6.75	
☐ 27 Ferris Fain	25.00	11.00	
☐ 28 Paul Minner	15.00	6.75	
☐ 29 Jim Hegan	25.00	11.00	
☐ 30 Eddie Mathews	75.00	34.00	
☐ 31 Johnny Klippstein	15.00	6.75	
☐ 32 Duke Snider	125.00	55.00	

□ 33 Johnny Schmitz........ 15.00 6.75
□ 34 Jim Rivera................ 15.00 6.75
□ 35 Jim Gilliam 40.00 18.00
□ 36 Hoyt Wilhelm............ 50.00 22.00
□ 37 Whitey Ford........... 100.00 45.00
□ 38 Eddie Stanky MG...... 25.00 11.00
□ 39 Sherm Lollar 25.00 11.00
□ 40 Mel Parnell 25.00 11.00
□ 41 Willie Jones.............. 15.00 6.75
□ 42 Don Mueller.............. 25.00 11.00
□ 43 Dick Groat 25.00 11.00
□ 44 Ned Garver 15.00 6.75
□ 45 Richie Ashburn 70.00 32.00
□ 46 Ken Raffensberger.... 15.00 6.75
□ 47 Ellis Kinder 15.00 6.75
□ 48 Billy Hunter 25.00 11.00
□ 49 Ray Murray 15.00 6.75
□ 50 Yogi Berra 150.00 70.00
□ 51 Johnny Lindell........... 25.00 11.00
□ 52 Vic Power 35.00 16.00
□ 53 Jack Dittmer 25.00 11.00
□ 54 Vern Stephens.......... 30.00 13.50
□ 55 Phil Cavarretta MG .. 30.00 13.50
□ 56 Willie Miranda 25.00 11.00
□ 57 Luis Aloma 25.00 11.00
□ 58 Bob Wilson 25.00 11.00
□ 59 Gene Conley 30.00 13.50
□ 60 Frank Baumholtz 25.00 11.00
□ 61 Bob Cain 25.00 11.00
□ 62 Eddie Robinson 25.00 11.00
□ 63 Johnny Pesky 30.00 13.50
□ 64 Hank Thompson 25.00 11.00
□ 65 Bob Swift CO........... 25.00 11.00
□ 66 Ted Lepcio................ 25.00 11.00
□ 67 Jim Willis 25.00 11.00
□ 68 Sam Calderone 25.00 11.00
□ 69 Bud Podbielan.......... 25.00 11.00
□ 70 Larry Doby 50.00 22.00
□ 71 Frank Smith.............. 25.00 11.00
□ 72 Preston Ward 25.00 11.00
□ 73 Wayne Terwilliger 25.00 11.00
□ 74 Bill Taylor 25.00 11.00
□ 75 Fred Haney MG 25.00 11.00
□ 76 Bob Scheffing CO 15.00 6.75
□ 77 Ray Boone................ 25.00 11.00
□ 78 Ted Kazanski 15.00 6.75
□ 79 Andy Pafko 25.00 11.00
□ 80 Jackie Jensen 25.00 11.00
□ 81 Dave Hoskins 15.00 6.75
□ 82 Milt Bolling 15.00 6.75
□ 83 Joe Collins................ 25.00 11.00
□ 84 Dick Cole.................. 15.00 6.75
□ 85 Bob Turley................ 30.00 13.50
□ 86 Billy Herman CO 25.00 11.00
□ 87 Roy Face 25.00 11.00
□ 88 Matt Batts 15.00 6.75
□ 89 Howie Pollet 15.00 6.75
□ 90 Willie Mays 500.00 220.00
□ 91 Bob Oldis.................. 15.00 6.75
□ 92 Wally Westlake 15.00 6.75
□ 93 Sid Hudson 15.00 6.75
□ 94 Ernie Banks 750.00 350.00
□ 95 Hal Rice.................... 15.00 6.75
□ 96 Charlie Silvera 25.00 11.00
□ 97 Jerald Hal Lane 15.00 6.75
□ 98 Joe Black.................. 30.00 13.50
□ 99 Bobby Hofman 15.00 6.75
□ 100 Bob Keegan............ 15.00 6.75
□ 101 Gene Woodling 25.00 11.00
□ 102 Gil Hodges............. 70.00 32.00
□ 103 Jim Lemon 15.00 6.75
□ 104 Mike Sandlock........ 15.00 6.75
□ 105 Andy Carey 25.00 11.00
□ 106 Dick Kokos 15.00 6.75
□ 107 Duane Pillette 15.00 6.75
□ 108 Thornton Kipper 15.00 6.75
□ 109 Bill Bruton 25.00 11.00
□ 110 Harry Dorish 15.00 6.75
□ 111 Jim Delsing 15.00 6.75
□ 112 Bill Renna 15.00 6.75
□ 113 Bob Boyd................ 15.00 6.75
□ 114 Dean Stone 15.00 6.75
□ 115 Rip Repulski 15.00 6.75
□ 116 Steve Bilko 15.00 6.75
□ 117 Solly Hemus 15.00 6.75
□ 118 Carl Scheib 15.00 6.75
□ 119 Johnny Antonelli 25.00 11.00
□ 120 Roy McMillan 25.00 11.00
□ 121 Clem Labine 25.00 11.00
□ 122 Johnny Logan 25.00 11.00
□ 123 Bobby Adams 15.00 6.75
□ 124 Marion Fricano 15.00 6.75
□ 125 Harry Perkowski 15.00 6.75
□ 126 Ben Wade 15.00 6.75
□ 127 Steve O'Neill MG 15.00 6.75
□ 128 Hank Aaron 1500.00 700.00
□ 129 Forrest Jacobs........ 15.00 6.75
□ 130 Hank Bauer 25.00 11.00
□ 131 Reno Bertoia 15.00 6.75
□ 132 Tommy Lasorda .. 200.00 90.00
□ 133 Dave Baker CO 15.00 6.75
□ 134 Cal Hogue 15.00 6.75
□ 135 Joe Presko.............. 15.00 6.75
□ 136 Connie Ryan 15.00 6.75
□ 137 Wally Moon............ 30.00 13.50
□ 138 Bob Borkowski 15.00 6.75
□ 139 The O'Briens 40.00 18.00
Johnny O'Brien
Eddie O'Brien
□ 140 Tom Wright............ 15.00 6.75
□ 141 Joey Jay 25.00 11.00
□ 142 Tom Poholsky 15.00 6.75
□ 143 Rollie Hemsley CO.. 15.00 6.75
□ 144 Bill Werle................ 15.00 6.75
□ 145 Elmer Valo.............. 15.00 6.75
□ 146 Don Johnson.......... 15.00 6.75
□ 147 Johnny Riddle CO .. 15.00 6.75
□ 148 Bob Trice................ 15.00 6.75
□ 149 Al Robertson 15.00 6.75
□ 150 Dick Kryhoski 15.00 6.75
□ 151 Alex Grammas........ 15.00 6.75
□ 152 Michael Blyzka....... 15.00 6.75
□ 153 Al Walker................ 15.00 6.75
□ 154 Mike Fornieles........ 15.00 6.75
□ 155 Bob Kennedy.......... 25.00 11.00
□ 156 Joe Coleman 15.00 6.75
□ 157 Don Lenhardt 15.00 6.75
□ 158 Peanuts Lowrey...... 15.00 6.75
□ 159 Dave Philley............ 15.00 6.75
□ 160 Ralph Kress CO 15.00 6.75
□ 161 John Hetki.............. 15.00 6.75
□ 162 Herman Wehmeier 15.00 6.75
□ 163 Frank House 15.00 6.75
□ 164 Stu Miller................ 25.00 11.00
□ 165 Jim Pendleton 15.00 6.75
□ 166 Johnny Podres 30.00 13.50
□ 167 Don Lund 15.00 6.75
□ 168 Morrie Martin 15.00 6.75
□ 169 Jim Hughes............ 25.00 11.00
□ 170 James(Dusty) Rhodes 25.00 11.00
□ 171 Leo Kiely 15.00 6.75
□ 172 Harold Brown 15.00 6.75
□ 173 Jack Harshman 15.00 6.75
□ 174 Tom Qualters.......... 15.00 6.75
□ 175 Frank Leja 25.00 11.00
□ 176 Robert Keely CO 15.00 6.75
□ 177 Bob Milliken 15.00 6.75
□ 178 Bill Glynn................ 15.00 6.75
□ 179 Gair Allie 15.00 6.75
□ 180 Wes Westrum 25.00 11.00
□ 181 Mel Roach.............. 15.00 6.75
□ 182 Chuck Harmon 15.00 6.75
□ 183 Earle Combs CO 25.00 11.00
□ 184 Ed Bailey 15.00 6.75
□ 185 Chuck Stobbs 15.00 6.75
□ 186 Karl Olson 15.00 6.75
□ 187 Heinie Manush CO.. 25.00 11.00
□ 188 Dave Jolly 15.00 6.75
□ 189 Bob Ross................ 15.00 6.75
□ 190 Ray Herbert............ 15.00 6.75
□ 191 John(Dick) Schofield 25.00 11.00
□ 192 Ellis Deal CO 15.00 6.75
□ 193 Johnny Hopp CO 25.00 11.00
□ 194 Bill Sarni 15.00 6.75
□ 195 Billy Consolo 15.00 6.75
□ 196 Stan Jok 15.00 6.75
□ 197 Lynwood Rowe CO 25.00 11.00
("Schoolboy")
□ 198 Carl Sawatski.......... 15.00 6.75
□ 199 Glenn(Rocky) Nelson 15.00 6.75
□ 200 Larry Jansen 25.00 11.00
□ 201 Al Kaline 750.00 350.00
□ 202 Bob Purkey 25.00 11.00
□ 203 Harry Brecheen CO 25.00 11.00
□ 204 Angel Scull 15.00 6.75
□ 205 Johnny Sain 30.00 13.50
□ 206 Ray Crone 15.00 6.75
□ 207 Tom Oliver CO........ 15.00 6.75
□ 208 Grady Hatton.......... 15.00 6.75
□ 209 Chuck Thompson .. 15.00 6.75
□ 210 Bob Buhl 25.00 11.00
□ 211 Don Hoak 25.00 11.00
□ 212 Bob Micelotta 15.00 6.75
□ 213 Johnny Fitzpatrick CO 15.00 6.75
□ 214 Arnie Portocarrero.. 15.00 6.75
□ 215 Ed McGhee 15.00 6.75
□ 216 Al Sima 15.00 6.75
□ 217 Paul Schreiber CO .. 15.00 6.75
□ 218 Fred Marsh 15.00 6.75
□ 219 Chuck Kress 15.00 6.75
□ 220 Ruben Gomez 25.00 11.00
□ 221 Dick Brodowski 15.00 6.75
□ 222 Bill Wilson.............. 15.00 6.75
□ 223 Joe Haynes CO 15.00 6.75
□ 224 Dick Weik 15.00 6.75
□ 225 Don Liddle.............. 15.00 6.75
□ 226 Jehosie Heard 15.00 6.75
□ 227 Colonel Mills CO 15.00 6.75
□ 228 Gene Hermanski 15.00 6.75
□ 229 Bob Talbot.............. 15.00 6.75
□ 230 Bob Kuzava 25.00 11.00
□ 231 Roy Smalley 15.00 6.75
□ 232 Lou Limmer............ 15.00 6.75
□ 233 Augie Galan CO 15.00 6.75
□ 234 Jerry Lynch 15.00 6.75
□ 235 Vern Law................ 25.00 11.00
□ 236 Paul Penson 15.00 6.75
□ 237 Mike Ryba CO 15.00 6.75
□ 238 Al Aber 15.00 6.75
□ 239 Bill Skowron 100.00 45.00
□ 240 Sam Mele 25.00 11.00
□ 241 Robert Miller 15.00 6.75
□ 242 Curt Roberts 15.00 6.75
□ 243 Ray Blades CO........ 15.00 6.75
□ 244 Leroy Wheat 15.00 6.75
□ 245 Roy Sievers............ 25.00 11.00
□ 246 Howie Fox 15.00 6.75
□ 247 Ed Mayo CO 15.00 6.75
□ 248 Al Smith 25.00 11.00
□ 249 Wilmer Mizell 25.00 11.00
□ 250 Ted Williams 750.00 300.00

1955 Topps

HANK SAUER
outfield CHICAGO CUBS

The cards in this 206-card set measure approximately 2 5/8" by 3 3/4". Both the large "head" shot and the smaller full-length photos used on each card of the 1955 Topps set are in color. The card fronts were designed horizontally for the first time in Topps' history. The first card features Dusty Rhodes, hitting star and MVP in the New York Giants' 1954 World Series sweep over the Cleveland Indians. A "high" series, 161 to 210, is more difficult to find than cards 1 to 160. Numbers 175, 186, 203, and 188 were never issued. To fill in for the four cards not issued in the high number series, Topps double printed four players, those appearing on cards 170, 172, 184, and 188. Cards were issued in one-card penny packs or six-card nickel packs. Although rarely seen, there exist salesman sample panels of three cards containing the fronts of regular cards with ad information for the 1955 Topps regular and the 1955 Topps Doubleheaders on the back. One such ad panel depicts (from top to bottom) Danny Schell, Jake Thies, and Howie Poliet. The key Rookie Cards in this set are Ken Boyer, Roberto Clemente, Harmon Killebrew, and Sandy Koufax.

	NRMT	VG-E
COMPLETE SET (206)	7200.00	3200.00
COMMON CARD (1-150)	12.00	5.50
MINOR STARS 1-150	15.00	6.75
SEMISTARS 1-150	25.00	11.00
UNLISTED STARS 1-150	40.00	18.00
COMMON CARD (151-160)	20.00	9.00
MINOR STARS 151-160	25.00	11.00
SEMISTARS 151-160	40.00	18.00
COMMON CARD (161-210)	30.00	13.50
DP (170/172/184/188)	15.00	6.75
MINOR STARS 161-210	40.00	18.00
SEMISTARS 161-210	60.00	27.00
NOT ISSUED (175/186/203/209)		

*UNLISTED DODGER/YANKEE: 1.25X VALUE
CARDS PRICED IN NM CONDITION !

#	Player	NRMT	VG-E
1	Dusty Rhodes	50.00	10.00
2	Ted Williams	475.00	210.00
3	Art Fowler	12.00	6.75
4	Al Kaline	175.00	80.00
5	Jim Gilliam	25.00	11.00
6	Stan Hack MG	18.00	8.00
7	Jim Hegan	15.00	6.75
8	Harold Smith	12.00	5.50
9	Robert Miller	12.00	5.50
10	Bob Keegan	12.00	5.50
11	Ferris Fain	15.00	6.75
12	Vernon(Jake) Thies	12.00	5.50
13	Fred Marsh	12.00	5.50
14	Jim Finigan	12.00	5.50
15	Jim Pendleton	12.00	5.50
16	Roy Sievers	15.00	6.75
17	Bobby Hofman	12.00	5.50
18	Russ Kemmerer	12.00	5.50
19	Billy Herman CO	18.00	8.00
20	Andy Carey	15.00	6.75
21	Alex Grammas	12.00	5.50
22	Bill Skowron	20.00	9.00
23	Jack Parks	12.00	5.50
24	Hal Newhouser	18.00	8.00
25	Johnny Podres	20.00	9.00
26	Dick Groat	18.00	8.00
27	Billy Gardner	15.00	6.75
28	Ernie Banks	175.00	80.00
29	Herman Wehmeier	12.00	5.50
30	Vic Power	15.00	6.75
31	Warren Spahn	90.00	40.00
32	Warren McGhee	12.00	5.50
33	Tom Qualters	12.00	5.50
34	Wayne Terwilliger	12.00	5.50
35	Dave Jolly	12.00	5.50
36	Leo Kiely	12.00	5.50
37	Joe Cunningham	15.00	6.75
38	Bob Turley	18.00	8.00
39	Bill Glynn	12.00	5.50
40	Don Hoak	15.00	6.75
41	Chuck Stobbs	12.00	5.50
42	John(Windy) McCall	12.00	5.50
43	Harvey Haddix	18.00	8.00
44	Harold Valentine	12.00	5.50
45	Hank Sauer	18.00	8.00
46	Ted Kazanski	12.00	5.50
47	Hank Aaron UER	350.00	160.00
	(Birth incorrectly listed as 2/10)		
48	Bob Kennedy	15.00	6.75
49	J.W. Porter	12.00	5.50
50	Jackie Robinson	300.00	135.00
51	Jim Hughes	15.00	6.75
52	Bill Tremel	12.00	5.50
53	Bill Taylor	12.00	5.50
54	Lou Limmer	12.00	5.50
55	Rip Repulski	12.00	5.50
56	Ray Jablonski	12.00	5.50
57	Billy O'Dell	12.00	5.50
58	Jim Rivera	12.00	5.50
59	Gair Allie	12.00	5.50
60	Dean Stone	12.00	5.50
61	Forrest Jacobs	12.00	5.50
62	Thornton Kipper	12.00	5.50
63	Joe Collins	15.00	6.75
64	Gus Triandos	18.00	8.00
65	Ray Boone	18.00	8.00
66	Ron Jackson	12.00	5.50
67	Wally Moon	18.00	8.00
68	Jim Davis	12.00	5.50
69	Ed Bailey	15.00	6.75
70	Al Rosen	18.00	8.00
71	Ruben Gomez	12.00	5.50
72	Karl Olson	12.00	5.50
73	Jack Shepard	12.00	5.50
74	Bob Borkowski	12.00	5.50
75	Sandy Amoros	30.00	13.50
76	Howie Pollet	12.00	5.50
77	Arnie Portocarrero	12.00	5.50
78	Gordon Jones	12.00	5.50
79	Clyde(Danny) Schell	12.00	5.50
80	Bob Grim	18.00	8.00
81	Gene Conley	15.00	6.75
82	Chuck Harmon	12.00	5.50
83	Tom Brewer	12.00	5.50
84	Camilo Pascual	18.00	8.00
85	Don Mossi	18.00	8.00
86	Bill Wilson	12.00	5.50
87	Frank House	12.00	5.50
88	Bob Skinner	18.00	8.00
89	Joe Frazier	15.00	6.75
90	Karl Spooner	15.00	6.75
91	Milt Bolling	12.00	5.50
92	Don Zimmer	30.00	13.50
93	Steve Bilko	12.00	5.50
94	Reno Bertoia	12.00	5.50
95	Preston Ward	12.00	5.50
96	Chuck Bishop	12.00	5.50
97	Carlos Paula	12.00	5.50
98	John Riddle CO	12.00	5.50
99	Frank Laga	12.00	5.50
100	Monte Irvin	35.00	16.00
101	Johnny Gray	12.00	5.50
102	Wally Westlake	12.00	5.50
103	Chuck White	12.00	5.50
104	Jack Harshman	12.00	5.50
105	Chuck Diering	12.00	5.50
106	Frank Sullivan	12.00	5.50
107	Curt Roberts	12.00	5.50
108	Al Walker	15.00	6.75
109	Ed Lopat	18.00	8.00
110	Gus Zernial	15.00	6.75
111	Bob Milliken	12.00	5.50
112	Nelson King	12.00	5.50
113	Harry Brecheen CO	15.00	6.75
114	Louis Ortiz	12.00	5.50
115	Ellis Kinder	12.00	5.50
116	Tom Hurd	12.00	5.50
117	Mel Roach	12.00	5.50
118	Bob Purkey	12.00	5.50
119	Bob Lennon	12.00	5.50
120	Ted Kluszewski	40.00	18.00
121	Bill Renna	12.00	5.50
122	Carl Sawatski	12.00	5.50
123	Sandy Koufax	900.00	400.00
124	Harmon Killebrew	250.00	110.00
125	Ken Boyer	60.00	27.00
126	Dick Hall	12.00	5.50
127	Dale Long	18.00	8.00
128	Ted Lepcio	12.00	5.50
129	Elvin Tappe	12.00	5.50
130	Mayo Smith MG	12.00	5.50
131	Grady Hatton	12.00	5.50
132	Bob Trice	12.00	5.50
133	Dave Hoskins	12.00	5.50
134	Joey Jay	15.00	6.75
135	Johnny O'Brien	15.00	6.75
136	Veston(Bunky) Stewart	12.00	5.50
137	Harry Elliott	12.00	5.50
138	Ray Herbert	12.00	5.50
139	Steve Kraly	12.00	5.50
140	Mel Parnell	15.00	6.75
141	Tom Wright	12.00	5.50
142	Jerry Lynch	15.00	6.75
143	John(Dick) Schofield	15.00	6.75
144	John(Joe) Amalfitano	12.00	5.50
145	Elmer Valo	12.00	5.50
146	Dick Donovan	12.00	5.50
147	Hugh Pepper	12.00	5.50
148	Hector Brown	12.00	5.50
149	Ray Crone	12.00	5.50
150	Mike Higgins MG	12.00	5.50
151	Ralph Kress CO	20.00	9.00
152	Harry Agganis	70.00	32.00
153	Bud Podbielan	20.00	9.00
154	Willie Miranda	20.00	9.00
155	Eddie Mathews	90.00	40.00
156	Joe Black	35.00	16.00
157	Robert Miller	20.00	9.00
158	Tommy Carroll	20.00	9.00
159	Johnny Schmitz	20.00	9.00
160	Ray Narleski	20.00	9.00
161	Chuck Tanner	35.00	16.00
162	Joe Coleman	30.00	13.50
163	Faye Throneberry	30.00	13.50
164	Roberto Clemente	2200.00	1000.00
165	Don Johnson	30.00	13.50
166	Hank Bauer	45.00	20.00
167	Thomas Casagrande	30.00	13.50
168	Duane Pillette	30.00	13.50
169	Bob Oldis	30.00	13.50
170	Jim Pearce DP	15.00	6.75
171	Dick Brodowski	30.00	13.50
172	Frank Baumholtz DP	15.00	6.75
173	Bob Kline	30.00	13.50
174	Rudy Minarcin	30.00	13.50
175	Does not exist		
176	Norm Zauchin	30.00	13.50
177	Al Robertson	30.00	13.50
178	Bobby Adams	30.00	13.50
179	Jim Bolger	30.00	13.50
180	Clem Labine	45.00	20.00
181	Roy McMillan	40.00	18.00
182	Humberto Robinson	30.00	13.50
183	Anthony Jacobs	30.00	13.50
184	Harry Perkowski DP	15.00	6.75
185	Don Ferrarese	30.00	13.50
186	Does not exist		
187	Gil Hodges	125.00	55.00
188	Charlie Silvera DP	15.00	6.75
189	Phil Rizzuto	125.00	55.00
190	Gene Woodling	40.00	18.00
191	Eddie Stanky MG	40.00	18.00
192	Jim Delsing	30.00	13.50
193	Johnny Sain	45.00	20.00
194	Willie Mays	400.00	180.00
195	Ed Roebuck	45.00	20.00
196	Gale Wade	30.00	13.50
197	Al Smith	40.00	18.00
198	Yogi Berra	200.00	90.00
199	Odbert Hamric	40.00	18.00
200	Jackie Jensen	35.00	16.00
201	Sherman Lollar !	40.00	18.00
202	Jim Owens	30.00	13.50
203	Does not exist		
204	Frank Smith	30.00	13.50
205	Gene Freese	30.00	13.50
206	Pete Daley	30.00	13.50
207	Billy Consolo	30.00	13.50
208	Ray Moore	30.00	13.50
209	Does not exist		
210	Duke Snider	450.00	135.00

1956 Topps

The cards in this 340-card set measure approximately 2 5/8" by 3 3/4". Following up with another horizontally-oriented card in 1956, Topps improved the format by layering the color "head" shot onto an actual action sequence involving the player. Cards 1 to 180 come with either white or gray backs: in the 1 to 100 sequence, gray backs are less common (worth about 10 percent more) and in the 101 to 180 sequence, white backs are less common (worth 30 percent more). The team cards, used for the first time in a regular set by Topps, are found dated 1955, or undated, with the team name appearing on either side. The dated team cards in the first series were not printed on the gray stock. The two unnumbered checklist cards are highly prized (must be unmarked to qualify as excellent or mint). The complete set price below does not include the unnumbered checklist cards or any of the variations. The set was issued in one-card penny packs or six-card nickel packs. Both types of packs included a piece of bubble gum. The key Rookie Cards in this set are Walt Alston, Luis Aparicio, and Roger Craig. There are ten double-printed cards in the first series as evidenced by the discovery of an uncut sheet of 110 cards (10 by 11); these DP's are listed below.

	NRMT	VG-E
COMPLETE SET (340)	7000.00	3200.00
COMMON CARD (1-100)	10.00	4.50
COMMON CARD (101-180)	12.00	5.50
COMMON CARD (261-340)	12.00	5.50
DP (9/21/46/60/75/80/86)	9.00	4.00
MINOR STARS 1-180/261-340	15.00	6.75
SEMISTARS 1-180/261-340	25.00	11.00
UNL.STARS 1-180/261-340	40.00	18.00
COMMON CARD (181-260)	15.00	6.75
MINOR STARS 181-260	20.00	9.00
SEMISTARS 181-260	30.00	13.50
UNLISTED STARS 181-260	50.00	22.00
*UNLISTED DODGER/YANKEE: 1.25X VALUE		
CARDS PRICED IN NM CONDITION !		

☐ 1	William Harridge PRES	100.00	28.00
☐ 2	Warren Giles PRES	25.00	11.00
☐ 3	Elmer Valo	10.00	4.50
☐ 4	Carlos Paula	10.00	4.50
☐ 5	Ted Williams	325.00	145.00
☐ 6	Ray Boone	16.00	7.25
☐ 7	Ron Negray	10.00	4.50
☐ 8	Walter Alston MG	40.00	18.00
☐ 9	Ruben Gomez DP	9.00	4.00
☐ 10	Warren Spahn	70.00	32.00
☐ 11A	Chicago Cubs (Centered)	30.00	13.50
☐ 11B	Cubs Team (Dated 1955)	80.00	36.00
☐ 11C	Cubs Team (Name at far left)	30.00	13.50
☐ 12	Andy Carey	15.00	6.75
☐ 13	Roy Face	16.00	7.25
☐ 14	Ken Boyer DP	16.00	7.25
☐ 15	Ernie Banks DP	80.00	36.00
☐ 16	Hector Lopez	16.00	7.25
☐ 17	Gene Conley	15.00	6.75
☐ 18	Dick Donovan	10.00	4.50
☐ 19	Chuck Diering	10.00	4.50
☐ 20	Al Kaline	90.00	40.00
☐ 21	Joe Collins DP	15.00	6.75
☐ 22	Jim Finigan	10.00	4.50
☐ 23	Fred Marsh	10.00	4.50
☐ 24	Dick Groat	16.00	7.25
☐ 25	Ted Kluszewski	35.00	16.00
☐ 26	Grady Hatton	10.00	4.50
☐ 27	Nelson Burbrink	10.00	4.50
☐ 28	Bobby Hofman	10.00	4.50
☐ 29	Jack Harshman	10.00	4.50
☐ 30	Jackie Robinson DP	175.00	80.00
☐ 31	Hank Aaron UER (Small photo actually Willie Mays)	275.00	125.00
☐ 32	Frank House	10.00	4.50
☐ 33	Roberto Clemente	450.00	200.00
☐ 34	Tom Brewer	10.00	4.50
☐ 35	Al Rosen	16.00	7.25
☐ 36	Rudy Minarcin	10.00	4.50
☐ 37	Alex Grammas	10.00	4.50
☐ 38	Bob Kennedy	15.00	6.75
☐ 39	Don Mossi	15.00	6.75
☐ 40	Bob Turley	16.00	7.25
☐ 41	Hank Sauer	16.00	7.25
☐ 42	Sandy Amoros	16.00	7.25
☐ 43	Ray Moore	10.00	4.50
☐ 44	Windy McCall	10.00	4.50
☐ 45	Gus Zernial	15.00	6.75
☐ 46	Gene Freese DP	9.00	4.00
☐ 47	Art Fowler	10.00	4.50
☐ 48	Jim Hegan	15.00	6.75
☐ 49	Pedro Ramos	10.00	4.50
☐ 50	Dusty Rhodes	16.00	7.25
☐ 51	Ernie Oravetz	10.00	4.50
☐ 52	Bob Grim	15.00	6.75
☐ 53	Arnie Portocarrero	10.00	4.50
☐ 54	Bob Keegan	10.00	4.50
☐ 55	Wally Moon	16.00	7.25
☐ 56	Dale Long	15.00	6.75
☐ 57	Duke Maas	10.00	4.50
☐ 58	Ed Roebuck	15.00	6.75
☐ 59	Jose Santiago	10.00	4.50
☐ 60	Mayo Smith MG DP	9.00	4.00
☐ 61	Bill Skowron	16.00	7.25
☐ 62	Hal Smith	10.00	4.50
☐ 63	Roger Craig	16.00	7.25
☐ 64	Luis Arroyo	10.00	4.50
☐ 65	Johnny O'Brien	15.00	6.75
☐ 66	Bob Speake	10.00	4.50
☐ 67	Vic Power	15.00	6.75
☐ 68	Chuck Stobbs	10.00	4.50
☐ 69	Chuck Tanner	16.00	7.25
☐ 70	Jim Rivera	10.00	4.50
☐ 71	Frank Sullivan	10.00	4.50
☐ 72A	Phillies Team (Centered)	30.00	13.50
☐ 72B	Phillies Team (Dated 1955)	80.00	36.00
☐ 72C	Phillies Team (Name at far left)	30.00	13.50
☐ 73	Wayne Terwilliger	10.00	4.50
☐ 74	Jim King	10.00	4.50
☐ 75	Roy Sievers DP	15.00	6.75
☐ 76	Ray Crone	10.00	4.50
☐ 77	Harvey Haddix	16.00	7.25
☐ 78	Herman Wehmeier	10.00	4.50
☐ 79	Sandy Koufax	350.00	160.00
☐ 80	Gus Triandos DP	10.00	4.50
☐ 81	Wally Westlake	10.00	4.50
☐ 82	Bill Renna	10.00	4.50
☐ 83	Karl Spooner	15.00	6.75
☐ 84	Babe Birrer	10.00	4.50
☐ 85A	Cleveland Indians (Centered)	30.00	13.50
☐ 85B	Indians Team (Dated 1955)	80.00	36.00
☐ 85C	Indians Team (Name at far left)	30.00	13.50
☐ 86	Ray Jablonski DP	9.00	4.00
☐ 87	Dean Stone	10.00	4.50
☐ 88	Johnny Kucks	15.00	6.75
☐ 89	Norm Zauchin	10.00	4.50
☐ 90A	Cincinnati Redlegs Team (Centered)	30.00	13.50
☐ 90B	Reds Team (Dated 1955)	80.00	36.00
☐ 90C	Reds Team (Name at far left)	30.00	13.50
☐ 91	Gail Harris	10.00	4.50
☐ 92	Bob(Red) Wilson	10.00	4.50
☐ 93	George Susce	10.00	4.50
☐ 94	Ron Kline	10.00	4.50
☐ 95A	Milwaukee Braves Team (Centered)	42.00	19.00
☐ 95B	Braves Team (Dated 1955)	80.00	36.00
☐ 95C	Braves Team (Name at far left)	42.00	19.00
☐ 96	Bill Tremel	10.00	4.50
☐ 97	Jerry Lynch	15.00	6.75
☐ 98	Camilo Pascual	15.00	6.75
☐ 99	Don Zimmer	15.00	6.75
☐ 100A	Baltimore Orioles Team (centered)	35.00	16.00
☐ 100B	Orioles Team (Dated 1955)	80.00	36.00
☐ 100C	Orioles Team (Name at far left)	35.00	16.00
☐ 101	Roy Campanella	150.00	70.00
☐ 102	Jim Davis	12.00	5.50
☐ 103	Willie Miranda	12.00	5.50
☐ 104	Bob Lennon	12.00	5.50
☐ 105	Al Smith	12.00	5.50
☐ 106	Joe Astroth	12.00	5.50
☐ 107	Eddie Mathews	70.00	32.00
☐ 108	Laurin Pepper	12.00	5.50
☐ 109	Enos Slaughter	35.00	16.00
☐ 110	Yogi Berra	150.00	70.00
☐ 111	Boston Red Sox Team Card	40.00	18.00
☐ 112	Dee Fondy	12.00	5.50
☐ 113	Phil Rizzuto	100.00	45.00
☐ 114	Jim Owens	12.00	5.50
☐ 115	Jackie Jensen	15.00	6.75
☐ 116	Eddie O'Brien	12.00	5.50
☐ 117	Virgil Trucks	15.00	6.75
☐ 118	Nellie Fox	50.00	22.00
☐ 119	Larry Jackson	15.00	6.75
☐ 120	Richie Ashburn	50.00	22.00
☐ 121	Pittsburgh Pirates Team Card	25.00	11.00
☐ 122	Willard Nixon	12.00	5.50
☐ 123	Roy McMillan	12.00	5.50
☐ 124	Don Kaiser	12.00	5.50
☐ 125	Minnie Minoso	35.00	16.00
☐ 126	Jim Brady	12.00	5.50
☐ 127	Willie Jones	15.00	6.75
☐ 128	Eddie Yost	15.00	6.75
☐ 129	Jake Martin	12.00	5.50
☐ 130	Willie Mays	300.00	135.00
☐ 131	Bob Roselli	12.00	5.50
☐ 132	Bobby Avila	12.00	5.50
☐ 133	Ray Narleski	12.00	5.50
☐ 134	St. Louis Cardinals Team Card	25.00	11.00
☐ 135	Mickey Mantle	1400.00	650.00
☐ 136	Johnny Logan	15.00	6.75
☐ 137	Al Silvera	12.00	5.50
☐ 138	Johnny Antonelli	15.00	6.75
☐ 139	Tommy Carroll	12.00	5.50
☐ 140	Herb Score	60.00	27.00
☐ 141	Joe Frazier	12.00	5.50
☐ 142	Gene Baker	12.00	5.50
☐ 143	Jim Piersall	15.00	6.75
☐ 144	Leroy Powell	12.00	5.50

□ 145	Gil Hodges	50.00	22.00
□ 146	Washington Nationals Team Card	25.00	11.00
□ 147	Earl Torgeson	12.00	5.50
□ 148	Alvin Dark	16.00	7.25
□ 149	Dixie Howell	12.00	5.50
□ 150	Duke Snider	90.00	40.00
□ 151	Spook Jacobs	12.00	6.75
□ 152	Billy Hoeft	15.00	6.75
□ 153	Frank Thomas	15.00	6.75
□ 154	Dave Pope	12.00	5.50
□ 155	Harvey Kuenn	16.00	7.25
□ 156	Wes Westrum	15.00	6.75
□ 157	Dick Brodowski	12.00	5.50
□ 158	Wally Post	15.00	6.75
□ 159	Clint Courtney	12.00	5.50
□ 160	Billy Pierce	15.00	6.75
□ 161	Joe DeMaestri	12.00	5.50
□ 162	Dave(Gus) Bell	15.00	6.75
□ 163	Gene Woodling	15.00	6.75
□ 164	Harmon Killebrew	100.00	45.00
□ 165	Red Schoendienst	35.00	16.00
□ 166	Brooklyn Dodgers Team Card	250.00	110.00
□ 167	Harry Dorish	12.00	5.50
□ 168	Sammy White	12.00	5.50
□ 169	Bob Nelson	12.00	5.50
□ 170	Bill Virdon	15.00	6.75
□ 171	Jim Wilson	12.00	5.50
□ 172	Frank Torre	15.00	6.75
□ 173	Johnny Podres	22.50	10.00
□ 174	Glen Gorbous	12.00	5.50
□ 175	Del Crandall	15.00	6.75
□ 176	Alex Kellner	12.00	5.50
□ 177	Hank Bauer	22.50	10.00
□ 178	Joe Black	16.00	7.25
□ 179	Harry Chiti	12.00	5.50
□ 180	Robin Roberts	40.00	18.00
□ 181	Billy Martin	60.00	27.00
□ 182	Paul Minner	15.00	6.75
□ 183	Stan Lopata	15.00	6.75
□ 184	Don Bessent	15.00	6.75
□ 185	Bill Bruton	20.00	9.00
□ 186	Ron Jackson	15.00	6.75
□ 187	Early Wynn	40.00	18.00
□ 188	Chicago White Sox Team Card	40.00	18.00
□ 189	Ned Garver	15.00	6.75
□ 190	Carl Furillo	35.00	16.00
□ 191	Frank Lary	20.00	9.00
□ 192	Smoky Burgess	20.00	9.00
□ 193	Wilmer Mizell	15.00	9.00
□ 194	Monte Irvin	35.00	16.00
□ 195	George Kell	35.00	16.00
□ 196	Tom Poholsky	15.00	6.75
□ 197	Granny Hamner	15.00	6.75
□ 198	Ed Fitzgerald	15.00	6.75
□ 199	Hank Thompson	20.00	9.00
□ 200	Bob Feller	100.00	45.00
□ 201	Rip Repulski	15.00	6.75
□ 202	Jim Hearn	15.00	6.75
□ 203	Bill Tuttle	15.00	6.75
□ 204	Art Swanson	15.00	6.75
□ 205	Whitey Lockman	20.00	9.00
□ 206	Erv Palica	15.00	6.75
□ 207	Jim Small	15.00	6.75
□ 208	Elston Howard	50.00	22.00
□ 209	Max Surkont	15.00	6.75
□ 210	Mike Garcia	20.00	9.00
□ 211	Murry Dickson	15.00	6.75
□ 212	Johnny Temple	15.00	6.75
□ 213	Detroit Tigers Team Card	60.00	27.00
□ 214	Bob Rush	15.00	6.75
□ 215	Tommy Byrne	20.00	9.00
□ 216	Jerry Schoonmaker	15.00	6.75
□ 217	Billy Klaus	15.00	6.75
□ 218	Joe Nuxhall UER (Misspelled Nuxall)	20.00	9.00
□ 219	Lew Burdette	20.00	9.00
□ 220	Del Ennis	20.00	9.00
□ 221	Bob Friend	20.00	9.00
□ 222	Dave Philley	15.00	6.75
□ 223	Randy Jackson	15.00	6.75
□ 224	Bud Podbielan	15.00	6.75
□ 225	Gil McDougald	30.00	13.50

□ 226	New York Giants Team Card	80.00	36.00
□ 227	Russ Meyer	15.00	6.75
□ 228	Mickey Vernon	20.00	9.00
□ 229	Harry Brecheen CO	20.00	9.00
□ 230	Chico Carrasquel	15.00	6.75
□ 231	Bob Hale	15.00	6.75
□ 232	Toby Atwell	15.00	6.75
□ 233	Carl Erskine	35.00	16.00
□ 234	Pete Runnels	15.00	6.75
□ 235	Don Newcombe	50.00	22.00
□ 236	Kansas City Athletics Team Card	30.00	13.50
□ 237	Jose Valdivielso	15.00	6.75
□ 238	Walt Dropo	20.00	9.00
□ 239	Harry Simpson	15.00	6.75
□ 240	Whitey Ford	100.00	45.00
□ 241	Don Mueller UER (8" full)	20.00	9.00
□ 242	Hershell Freeman	15.00	6.75
□ 243	Sherm Lollar	20.00	9.00
□ 244	Bob Buhl	20.00	9.00
□ 245	Billy Goodman	20.00	9.00
□ 246	Tom Gorman	15.00	6.75
□ 247	Bill Sarni	15.00	6.75
□ 248	Bob Porterfield	15.00	6.75
□ 249	Johnny Klippstein	15.00	6.75
□ 250	Larry Doby	35.00	16.00
□ 251	New York Yankees Team Card UER (Don Larsen misspelled as Larson on front)	275.00	125.00
□ 252	Vern Law	20.00	9.00
□ 253	Irv Noren	15.00	6.75
□ 254	George Crowe	15.00	6.75
□ 255	Bob Lemon	35.00	16.00
□ 256	Tom Hurd	15.00	6.75
□ 257	Bobby Thomson	35.00	16.00
□ 258	Art Ditmar	15.00	6.75
□ 259	Sam Jones	20.00	9.00
□ 260	Pee Wee Reese	120.00	55.00
□ 261	Bobby Shantz	15.00	6.75
□ 262	Howie Pollet	12.00	5.50
□ 263	Bob Miller	12.00	5.50
□ 264	Ray Monzant	12.00	5.50
□ 265	Sandy Consuegra	12.00	5.50
□ 266	Don Ferrarese	12.00	5.50
□ 267	Bob Nieman	12.00	5.50
□ 268	Dale Mitchell	16.00	7.25
□ 269	Jack Meyer	12.00	5.50
□ 270	Billy Loes	15.00	6.75
□ 271	Foster Castleman	12.00	5.50
□ 272	Danny O'Connell	12.00	5.50
□ 273	Walker Cooper	12.00	5.50
□ 274	Frank Baumholtz	12.00	5.50
□ 275	Jim Greengrass	12.00	5.50
□ 276	George Zuverink	12.00	5.50
□ 277	Daryl Spencer	12.00	5.50
□ 278	Chet Nichols	12.00	5.50
□ 279	Johnny Groth	12.00	5.50
□ 280	Jim Gilliam	35.00	16.00
□ 281	Art Houtteman	12.00	5.50
□ 282	Warren Hacker	12.00	5.50
□ 283	Hal Smith	12.00	5.50
□ 284	Ike Delock	12.00	5.50
□ 285	Eddie Miksis	12.00	5.50
□ 286	Bill Wight	12.00	5.50
□ 287	Bobby Adams	12.00	5.50
□ 288	Bob Cerv	40.00	18.00
□ 289	Hal Jeffcoat	12.00	5.50
□ 290	Curt Simmons	15.00	5.50
□ 291	Frank Kellert	150.00	70.00
□ 292	Luis Aparicio	150.00	70.00
□ 293	Stu Miller	15.00	6.75
□ 294	Ernie Johnson	15.00	6.75
□ 295	Clem Labine	18.00	8.00
□ 296	Andy Seminick	12.00	5.50
□ 297	Bob Skinner	15.00	6.75
□ 298	Johnny Schmitz	12.00	5.50
□ 299	Charlie Neal	35.00	16.00
□ 300	Vic Wertz	16.00	7.25
□ 301	Marv Grissom	12.00	5.50
□ 302	Eddie Robinson	12.00	5.50
□ 303	Jim Dyck	12.00	5.50
□ 304	Frank Malzone	16.00	7.25
□ 305	Brooks Lawrence	12.00	5.50

□ 306	Curt Roberts	12.00	5.50
□ 307	Hoyt Wilhelm	35.00	16.00
□ 308	Chuck Harmon	12.00	5.50
□ 309	Don Blasingame	16.00	7.25
□ 310	Steve Gromek	12.00	5.50
□ 311	Hal Naragon	12.00	5.50
□ 312	Andy Pafko	16.00	7.25
□ 313	Gene Stephens	12.00	5.50
□ 314	Hobie Landrith	12.00	5.50
□ 315	Milt Bolling	12.00	5.50
□ 316	Jerry Coleman	18.00	8.00
□ 317	Al Aber	12.00	5.50
□ 318	Fred Hatfield	12.00	5.50
□ 319	Jack Crimian	12.00	5.50
□ 320	Joe Adcock	16.00	7.25
□ 321	Jim Konstanty	15.00	6.75
□ 322	Karl Olson	12.00	5.50
□ 323	Willard Schmidt	12.00	5.50
□ 324	Rocky Bridges	15.00	6.75
□ 325	Don Liddle	12.00	5.50
□ 326	Connie Johnson	12.00	5.50
□ 327	Bob Wiesler	12.00	5.50
□ 328	Preston Ward	12.00	5.50
□ 329	Lou Berberet	12.00	5.50
□ 330	Jim Busby	12.00	5.50
□ 331	Dick Hall	12.00	5.50
□ 332	Don Larsen	60.00	27.00
□ 333	Rube Walker	12.00	5.50
□ 334	Bob Miller	12.00	5.50
□ 335	Don Hoak	15.00	6.75
□ 336	Ellis Kinder	12.00	5.50
□ 337	Bobby Morgan	12.00	5.50
□ 338	Jim Delsing	12.00	5.50
□ 339	Rance Pless	12.00	5.50
□ 340	Mickey McDermott	60.00	12.00
□ NNO	Checklist 2/4	300.00	95.00
□ NNO	Checklist 1/3	300.00	95.00

1957 Topps

RICHIE Ashburn
PHILADELPHIA PHILLIES O.F.

The cards in this 407-card set measure 2 1/2" by 3 1/2". In 1957, Topps returned to the vertical obverse, adopted what we now call the standard card size, and used a large, uncluttered color photo for the first time since 1952. Cards in the series 265 through 352 and the unnumbered checklist cards are scarcer than other cards in the set. However within this scarce series (265-352) there are 22 cards which were printed in double the quantity of the other cards in the series; these 22 double prints are indicated by DP in the checklist below. The first star combination cards, cards 400 and 407, are quite popular with collectors. They feature the big stars of the previous season's World Series teams, the Dodgers (Furillo, Hodges, Campanella, and Snider) and Yankees (Berra and Mantle). The complete set *price below does not include the unnumbered checklist cards. Confirmed packaging includes one-cent penny packs and six-card nickel packs. Cello packs are definately known to exist and some collectors remember buyikng rack packs of 57's as well. The key Rookie Cards in this set are Jim Bunning, Rocky Colavito, Don Drysdale, Whitey Herzog, Tony Kubek, Bill Mazeroski, Bobby Richardson, Brooks Robinson, and Frank Robinson.*

	NRMT	VG-E
COMPLETE SET (407)	7000.00	3200.00
COMMON CARD (1-88)	10.00	4.50
COMMON CARD (89-176) ..	8.00	3.60
COMMON CARD (177-264) ..	8.00	3.60
COMMON CARD (265-352)	20.00	9.00
COMMON CARD (353-407) ..	8.00	3.60
MINOR STARS 1-264/353-407	15.00	6.75
SEMISTARS 1-264/353-407	20.00	9.00
UNL.STARS 1-264/353-407	30.00	13.50
COMMON DP (265-352)	14.00	6.25
MINOR STARS 265-352....	30.00	13.50
SEMISTARS 265-352....	40.00	18.00

*UNLISTED DODGER/YANKEE: 1.25X VALUE
CARDS PRICED IN NM CONDITION

#	Player	NRMT	VG-E
☐ 1	Ted Williams	500.00	150.00
☐ 2	Yogi Berra	125.00	55.00
☐ 3	Dale Long	15.00	6.75
☐ 4	Johnny Logan	15.00	6.75
☐ 5	Sal Maglie	18.00	8.00
☐ 6	Hector Lopez	15.00	6.75
☐ 7	Luis Aparicio	35.00	16.00
☐ 8	Don Mossi	15.00	6.75
☐ 9	Johnny Temple	15.00	6.75
☐ 10	Willie Mays	225.00	100.00
☐ 11	George Zuverink	10.00	4.50
☐ 12	Dick Groat	14.00	6.25
☐ 13	Wally Burnette	10.00	4.50
☐ 14	Bob Nieman	10.00	4.50
☐ 15	Robin Roberts	35.00	16.00
☐ 16	Walt Moryn	10.00	4.50
☐ 17	Billy Gardner	10.00	4.50
☐ 18	Don Drysdale	200.00	90.00
☐ 19	Bob Wilson	10.00	4.50
☐ 20	Hank Aaron UER	200.00	90.00
	(Reverse negative photo on front)		
☐ 21	Frank Sullivan	10.00	4.50
☐ 22	Jerry Snyder UER	10.00	4.50
	(Photo actually Ed Fitzgerald)		
☐ 23	Sherm Lollar	15.00	6.75
☐ 24	Bill Mazeroski	75.00	34.00
☐ 25	Whitey Ford	70.00	32.00
☐ 26	Bob Boyd	10.00	4.50
☐ 27	Ted Kazanski	10.00	4.50
☐ 28	Gene Conley	15.00	6.75
☐ 29	Whitey Herzog	25.00	11.00
☐ 30	Pee Wee Reese	65.00	29.00
☐ 31	Ron Northey	10.00	4.50
☐ 32	Hershell Freeman	10.00	4.50
☐ 33	Jim Small	10.00	4.50
☐ 34	Tom Sturdivant	15.00	6.75
☐ 35	Frank Robinson	200.00	90.00
☐ 36	Bob Grim	10.00	4.50
☐ 37	Frank Torre	15.00	6.75
☐ 38	Nellie Fox	45.00	20.00
☐ 39	Al Worthington	10.00	4.50
☐ 40	Early Wynn	30.00	13.50
☐ 41	Hal W. Smith	10.00	4.50
☐ 42	Dee Fondy	10.00	4.50
☐ 43	Connie Johnson	10.00	4.50
☐ 44	Joe DeMaestri	10.00	4.50
☐ 45	Carl Furillo	20.00	9.00
☐ 46	Robert J. Miller	10.00	4.50
☐ 47	Don Blasingame	10.00	4.50
☐ 48	Bill Virdon	15.00	6.75
☐ 49	Daryl Spencer	10.00	4.50
☐ 50	Herb Score	20.00	9.00
☐ 51	Clint Courtney	10.00	4.50
☐ 52	Lee Walls	10.00	4.50
☐ 53	Clem Labine	18.00	8.00
☐ 54	Elmer Valo	10.00	4.50
☐ 55	Ernie Banks	120.00	55.00
☐ 56	Dave Sisler	10.00	4.50
☐ 57	Jim Lemon	15.00	6.75
☐ 58	Ruben Gomez	10.00	4.50
☐ 59	Dick Williams	14.00	6.25
☐ 60	Billy Hoeft	15.00	6.75
☐ 61	Dusty Rhodes	14.00	6.25
☐ 62	Billy Martin	45.00	20.00
☐ 63	Ike Delock	10.00	4.50
☐ 64	Pete Runnels	15.00	6.75
☐ 65	Wally Moon	14.00	6.25
☐ 66	Brooks Lawrence	10.00	4.50
☐ 67	Chico Carrasquel	10.00	4.50
☐ 68	Ray Crone	10.00	4.50
☐ 69	Roy McMillan	15.00	6.75
☐ 70	Richie Ashburn	45.00	20.00
☐ 71	Murry Dickson	10.00	4.50
☐ 72	Bill Tuttle	10.00	4.50
☐ 73	George Crowe	10.00	4.50
☐ 74	Vito Valentinetti	10.00	4.50
☐ 75	Jimmy Piersall	14.00	6.25
☐ 76	Roberto Clemente	300.00	135.00
☐ 77	Paul Foytack	10.00	4.50
☐ 78	Vic Wertz	14.00	6.25
☐ 79	Lindy McDaniel	14.00	6.25
☐ 80	Gil Hodges	45.00	20.00
☐ 81	Herman Wehmeier	10.00	4.50
☐ 82	Elston Howard	20.00	9.00
☐ 83	Lou Skizas	10.00	4.50
☐ 84	Moe Drabowsky	15.00	6.75
☐ 85	Larry Doby	20.00	9.00
☐ 86	Bill Sarni	10.00	4.50
☐ 87	Tom Gorman	10.00	4.50
☐ 88	Harvey Kuenn	14.00	6.25
☐ 89	Roy Sievers	15.00	6.75
☐ 90	Warren Spahn	70.00	32.00
☐ 91	Mack Burk	8.00	3.60
☐ 92	Mickey Vernon	15.00	6.75
☐ 93	Hal Jeffcoat	8.00	3.60
☐ 94	Bobby Del Greco	8.00	3.60
☐ 95	Mickey Mantle	1000.00	450.00
☐ 96	Hank Aguirre	8.00	3.60
☐ 97	New York Yankees Team Card	80.00	36.00
☐ 98	Alvin Dark	14.00	6.25
☐ 99	Bob Keegan	8.00	3.60
☐ 100	League Presidents Warren Giles Will Harridge	14.00	6.25
☐ 101	Chuck Stobbs	8.00	3.60
☐ 102	Ray Boone	14.00	6.25
☐ 103	Joe Nuxhall	14.00	6.25
☐ 104	Hank Foiles	8.00	3.60
☐ 105	Johnny Antonelli	14.00	6.25
☐ 106	Ray Moore	8.00	3.60
☐ 107	Jim Rivera	8.00	3.60
☐ 108	Tommy Byrne	15.00	6.75
☐ 109	Hank Thompson	8.00	3.60
☐ 110	Bill Virdon	15.00	6.75
☐ 111	Hal R. Smith	8.00	3.60
☐ 112	Tom Brewer	8.00	3.60
☐ 113	Wilmer Mizell	15.00	6.75
☐ 114	Milwaukee Braves Team Card	22.00	10.00
☐ 115	Jim Gilliam	14.00	6.25
☐ 116	Mike Fornieles	8.00	3.60
☐ 117	Joe Adcock	14.00	6.25
☐ 118	Bob Porterfield	8.00	3.60
☐ 119	Stan Lopata	8.00	3.60
☐ 120	Bob Lemon	25.00	11.00
☐ 121	Clete Boyer	20.00	9.00
☐ 122	Ken Boyer	18.00	8.00
☐ 123	Steve Ridzik	8.00	3.60
☐ 124	Dave Philley	8.00	3.60
☐ 125	Al Kaline	100.00	45.00
☐ 126	Bob Wiesler	8.00	3.60
☐ 127	Bob Buhl	15.00	6.75
☐ 128	Ed Bailey	15.00	6.75
☐ 129	Saul Rogovin	8.00	3.60
☐ 130	Don Newcombe	20.00	9.00
☐ 131	Milt Bolling	8.00	3.60
☐ 132	Art Ditmar	15.00	6.75
☐ 133	Del Crandall	15.00	6.75
☐ 134	Don Kaiser	8.00	3.60
☐ 135	Bill Skowron	18.00	8.00
☐ 136	Jim Hegan	15.00	6.75
☐ 137	Bob Rush	8.00	3.60
☐ 138	Minnie Minoso	20.00	9.00
☐ 139	Lou Kretlow	8.00	3.60
☐ 140	Frank Thomas	15.00	6.75
☐ 141	Al Aber	8.00	3.60
☐ 142	Charley Thompson	8.00	3.60
☐ 143	Andy Pafko	14.00	6.25
☐ 144	Ray Narleski	8.00	3.60
☐ 145	Al Smith	8.00	3.60
☐ 146	Don Ferrarese	8.00	3.60
☐ 147	Al Walker	8.00	3.60
☐ 148	Don Mueller	15.00	6.75
☐ 149	Bob Kennedy	15.00	6.75
☐ 150	Bob Friend	14.00	6.25
☐ 151	Willie Miranda	8.00	3.60
☐ 152	Jack Harshman	8.00	3.60
☐ 153	Karl Olson	8.00	3.60
☐ 154	Red Schoendienst	25.00	11.00
☐ 155	Jim Brosnan	15.00	6.75
☐ 156	Gus Triandos	15.00	6.75
☐ 157	Wally Post	15.00	6.75
☐ 158	Curt Simmons	15.00	6.75
☐ 159	Solly Drake	8.00	3.60
☐ 160	Billy Pierce	15.00	6.75
☐ 161	Pittsburgh Pirates Team Card	20.00	9.00
☐ 162	Jack Meyer	8.00	3.60
☐ 163	Sammy White	8.00	3.60
☐ 164	Tommy Carroll	8.00	3.60
☐ 165	Ted Kluszewski	50.00	22.00
☐ 166	Roy Face	15.00	6.75
☐ 167	Vic Power	15.00	6.75
☐ 168	Frank Lary	15.00	6.75
☐ 169	Herb Plews	8.00	3.60
☐ 170	Duke Snider	100.00	45.00
☐ 171	Boston Red Sox Team Card	20.00	9.00
☐ 172	Gene Woodling	15.00	6.75
☐ 173	Roger Craig	14.00	6.25
☐ 174	Willie Jones	8.00	3.60
☐ 175	Don Larsen	25.00	11.00
☐ 176A	Gene Baker ERR (Misspelled Bakep on card back)	350.00	160.00
☐ 176B	Gene Baker COR	15.00	6.75
☐ 177	Eddie Yost	15.00	6.75
☐ 178	Don Bessent	8.00	3.60
☐ 179	Ernie Oravetz	8.00	3.60
☐ 180	Gus Bell	15.00	6.75
☐ 181	Dick Donovan	8.00	3.60
☐ 182	Hobie Landrith	8.00	3.60
☐ 183	Chicago Cubs Team Card	20.00	9.00
☐ 184	Tito Francona	8.00	3.60
☐ 185	Johnny Kucks	15.00	6.75
☐ 186	Jim King	8.00	3.60
☐ 187	Virgil Trucks	15.00	6.75
☐ 188	Felix Mantilla	15.00	6.75
☐ 189	Willard Nixon	8.00	3.60
☐ 190	Randy Jackson	8.00	3.60
☐ 191	Joe Margoneri	8.00	3.60
☐ 192	Jerry Coleman	15.00	6.75
☐ 193	Del Rice	8.00	3.60
☐ 194	Hal Brown	8.00	3.60
☐ 195	Bobby Avila	15.00	6.75
☐ 196	Larry Jackson	15.00	6.75
☐ 197	Hank Sauer	15.00	6.75
☐ 198	Detroit Tigers Team Card	20.00	9.00
☐ 199	Vern Law	15.00	6.75
☐ 200	Gil McDougald	18.00	8.00
☐ 201	Sandy Amoros	15.00	6.75
☐ 202	Dick Gernert	8.00	3.60
☐ 203	Hoyt Wilhelm	25.00	11.00
☐ 204	Kansas City Athletics Team Card	20.00	9.00
☐ 205	Charlie Maxwell	15.00	6.75
☐ 206	Willard Schmidt	8.00	3.60
☐ 207	Gordon(Billy) Hunter	8.00	3.60
☐ 208	Lou Burdette	14.00	6.25
☐ 209	Bob Skinner	15.00	6.75
☐ 210	Roy Campanella	125.00	55.00

211	Camilo Pascual	15.00	6.75
212	Rocky Colavito	160.00	70.00
213	Les Moss	8.00	3.60
214	Philadelphia Phillies Team Card	20.00	9.00
215	Enos Slaughter	25.00	11.00
216	Marv Grissom	8.00	3.60
217	Gene Stephens	8.00	3.60
218	Ray Jablonski	8.00	3.60
219	Tom Acker	8.00	3.60
220	Jackie Jensen	15.00	6.75
221	Dixie Howell	8.00	3.60
222	Alex Grammas	8.00	3.60
223	Frank House	8.00	3.60
224	Marv Blaylock	8.00	3.60
225	Harry Simpson	8.00	3.60
226	Preston Ward	8.00	3.60
227	Gerry Staley	8.00	3.60
228	Smoky Burgess UER (Misspelled Smokey on card back)	15.00	6.75
229	George Susce	8.00	3.60
230	George Kell	25.00	11.00
231	Solly Hemus	8.00	3.60
232	Whitey Lockman	15.00	6.75
233	Art Fowler	8.00	3.60
234	Dick Cole	8.00	3.60
235	Tom Poholsky	8.00	3.60
236	Joe Ginsberg	8.00	3.60
237	Foster Castleman	8.00	3.60
238	Eddie Robinson	8.00	3.60
239	Tom Morgan	8.00	3.60
240	Hank Bauer	14.00	6.25
241	Joe Lonnett	8.00	3.60
242	Charlie Neal	14.00	6.25
243	St. Louis Cardinals Team Card	20.00	9.00
244	Billy Loes	15.00	6.75
245	Rip Repulski	8.00	3.60
246	Jose Valdivielso	8.00	3.60
247	Turk Lown	8.00	3.60
248	Jim Finigan	8.00	3.60
249	Dave Pope	8.00	3.60
250	Eddie Mathews	45.00	20.00
251	Baltimore Orioles Team Card	15.00	6.75
252	Carl Erskine	14.00	6.25
253	Gus Zernial	15.00	6.75
254	Ron Negray	8.00	3.60
255	Charlie Silvera	15.00	6.75
256	Ron Kline	8.00	3.60
257	Walt Dropo	8.00	3.60
258	Steve Gromek	8.00	3.60
259	Eddie O'Brien	8.00	3.60
260	Del Ennis	15.00	6.75
261	Bob Chakales	8.00	3.60
262	Bobby Thomson	15.00	6.75
263	George Strickland	8.00	3.60
264	Bob Turley	15.00	6.75
265	Harvey Haddix DP	14.00	6.25
266	Ken Kuhn DP	14.00	6.25
267	Danny Kravitz	20.00	9.00
268	Jack Collum	20.00	9.00
269	Bob Cerv	25.00	11.00
270	Washington Senators Team Card	50.00	22.00
271	Danny O'Connell DP	14.00	6.25
272	Bobby Shantz	25.00	11.00
273	Jim Davis	20.00	9.00
274	Don Hoak	20.00	9.00
275	Cleveland Indians Team Card UER (Text on back credits Tribe with winning AL title in '28. The Yankees won that year.)	50.00	22.00
276	Jim Pyburn	20.00	9.00
277	Johnny Podres DP	45.00	20.00
278	Fred Hatfield DP	14.00	6.25
279	Bob Thurman	20.00	9.00
280	Alex Kellner	20.00	9.00
281	Gail Harris	20.00	9.00
282	Jack Dittmer DP	14.00	6.25
283	Wes Covington DP	14.00	6.25
284	Don Zimmer	35.00	16.00
285	Ned Garver	20.00	9.00
286	Bobby Richardson	120.00	55.00
287	Sam Jones	20.00	9.00
288	Ted Lepcio	20.00	9.00
289	Jim Bolger DP	14.00	6.25
290	Andy Carey DP	30.00	13.50
291	Windy McCall	20.00	9.00
292	Billy Klaus	20.00	9.00
293	Ted Abernathy	20.00	9.00
294	Rocky Bridges DP	14.00	6.25
295	Joe Collins DP	30.00	13.50
296	Johnny Klippstein	20.00	9.00
297	Jack Crimian	20.00	9.00
298	Irv Noren DP	14.00	6.25
299	Chuck Harmon	20.00	9.00
300	Mike Garcia	30.00	13.50
301	Sammy Esposito DP	20.00	9.00
302	Sandy Koufax DP	250.00	110.00
303	Billy Goodman	30.00	13.50
304	Joe Cunningham	30.00	13.50
305	Chico Fernandez	20.00	9.00
306	Darrell Johnson DP	14.00	6.25
307	Jack D. Phillips DP	14.00	6.25
308	Dick Hall	20.00	9.00
309	Jim Busby DP	14.00	6.25
310	Max Surkont DP	14.00	6.25
311	Al Pilarcik DP	14.00	6.25
312	Tony Kubek DP	65.00	29.00
313	Mel Parnell	15.00	6.75
314	Ed Bouchee DP	14.00	6.25
315	Lou Berberet DP	14.00	6.25
316	Billy O'Dell	20.00	9.00
317	New York Giants Team Card	50.00	22.00
318	Mickey McDermott	20.00	9.00
319	Gino Cimoli	20.00	9.00
320	Neil Chrisley	20.00	9.00
321	John(Red) Murff	20.00	9.00
322	Cincinnati Reds Team Card	50.00	22.00
323	Wes Westrum	30.00	13.50
324	Brooklyn Dodgers Team Card	125.00	55.00
325	Frank Bolling	20.00	9.00
326	Pedro Ramos	20.00	9.00
327	Jim Pendleton	20.00	9.00
328	Brooks Robinson	400.00	180.00
329	Chicago White Sox Team Card	50.00	22.00
330	Jim Wilson	20.00	9.00
331	Ray Katt	20.00	9.00
332	Bob Bowman	20.00	9.00
333	Ernie Johnson	20.00	9.00
334	Jerry Schoonmaker	20.00	9.00
335	Granny Hamner	20.00	9.00
336	Haywood Sullivan	25.00	11.00
337	Rene Valdes	20.00	9.00
338	Jim Bunning	130.00	57.50
339	Bob Speake	20.00	9.00
340	Bill Wight	20.00	9.00
341	Don Gross	20.00	9.00
342	Gene Mauch	25.00	11.00
343	Taylor Phillips	20.00	9.00
344	Paul LaPalme	20.00	9.00
345	Paul Smith	20.00	9.00
346	Dick Littlefield	20.00	9.00
347	Hal Naragon	20.00	9.00
348	Jim Hearn	20.00	9.00
349	Nellie King	20.00	9.00
350	Eddie Miksis	20.00	9.00
351	Dave Hillman	20.00	9.00
352	Ellis Kinder	20.00	9.00
353	Cal Neeman	8.00	3.60
354	W. (Rip) Coleman	8.00	3.60
355	Frank Malzone	15.00	6.75
356	Faye Throneberry	8.00	3.60
357	Earl Torgeson	8.00	3.60
358	Jerry Lynch	15.00	6.75
359	Tom Cheney	8.00	3.60
360	Johnny Groth	8.00	3.60
361	Curt Barclay	8.00	3.60
362	Roman Mejias	8.00	3.60
363	Eddie Kasko	8.00	3.60
364	Cal McLish	15.00	6.75
365	Ozzie Virgil	8.00	3.60
366	Ken Lehman	8.00	3.60
367	Ed Fitzgerald	8.00	3.60
368	Bob Purkey	8.00	3.60
369	Milt Graff	8.00	3.60
370	Warren Hacker	8.00	3.60
371	Bob Lennon	8.00	3.60
372	Norm Zauchin	8.00	3.60
373	Pete Whisenant	8.00	3.60
374	Don Cardwell	8.00	3.60
375	Jim Landis	15.00	6.75
376	Don Elston	8.00	3.60
377	Andre Rodgers	8.00	3.60
378	Elmer Singleton	8.00	3.60
379	Don Lee	8.00	3.60
380	Walker Cooper	8.00	3.60
381	Dean Stone	8.00	3.60
382	Jim Bridweiser	8.00	3.60
383	Juan Pizarro	8.00	3.60
384	Bobby G. Smith	8.00	3.60
385	Art Houtteman	8.00	3.60
386	Lyle Luttrell	8.00	3.60
387	Jack Sanford	15.00	6.75
388	Pete Daley	8.00	3.60
389	Dave Jolly	8.00	3.60
390	Reno Bertoia	8.00	3.60
391	Ralph Terry	15.00	6.75
392	Chuck Tanner	14.00	6.25
393	Raul Sanchez	8.00	3.60
394	Luis Arroyo	14.00	6.75
395	Bubba Phillips	8.00	3.60
396	Casey Wise	8.00	3.60
397	Roy Smalley	8.00	3.60
398	Al Cicotte	15.00	6.75
399	Billy Consolo	8.00	3.60
400	Dodgers' Sluggers Carl Furillo Gil Hodges Roy Campanella Duke Snider	250.00	110.00
401	Earl Battey	14.00	6.25
402	Jim Pisoni	8.00	3.60
403	Dick Hyde	8.00	3.60
404	Harry Anderson	8.00	3.60
405	Duke Maas	8.00	3.60
406	Bob Hale	8.00	3.60
407	Yankee Power Hitters Mickey Mantle Yogi Berra	500.00	150.00
NNO1	Checklist 1/2	250.00	75.00
NNO2	Checklist 2/3	400.00	100.00
NNO3	Checklist 3/4	750.00	170.00
NNO4	Checklist 4/5	900.00	200.00
NNO5	Saturday, May 4th Boston Red Sox vs. Cleveland Indians Cincinnati Redlegs vs. New York Giants	80.00	20.00
NNO6	Saturday, May 25th Detroit Tigers vs. Kansas City Athletics Pittsburgh Pirates vs. Philadelphia Phillies	80.00	20.00
NNO7	Saturday, June 22nd Brooklyn Dodgers vs. St. Louis Cardinals Chicago White Sox vs. New York Yankees	100.00	25.00
NNO8	Saturday, July 19th Milwaukee Braves vs. New York Giants Baltimore Orioles vs. Kansas City Athletics	100.00	25.00
NNO9	Lucky Penny Charm and Key Chain offer card	80.00	36.00

1958 Topps

This is a 494-card standard-size set. Card number 145, which was supposedly to be Ed Bouchee, was not issued. The 1958 Topps set contains the first Sport Magazine All-Star Selection series (475-495) and expanded use of combination cards. For the first time team cards carried series checklists

Bob Clemente — PITTSBURGH PIRATES

on back (Milwaukee, Detroit, Baltimore, and Cincinnati are also found with players listed alphabetically). In the first series some cards were issued with yellow name (YL) or team (YT) lettering, as opposed to the common white lettering. They are explicitly noted below. Cards were issued in one-card penny packs or six-card nickel packs. In the last series, All-Star cards of Stan Musial and Mickey Mantle were triple printed; the cards they replaced (443, 446, 450, and 462) on the printing sheet were hence printed in shorter supply than other cards in the last series and are marked with an SP in the list below. The All-Star card of Musial marked his first appearance on a Topps card. Technically the New York Giants team card (19) is an error as the Giants had already moved to San Francisco. The key Rookie Cards in this set are Orlando Cepeda, Curt Flood, Roger Maris, and Vada Pinson.

	NRMT	VG-E
COMPLETE SET (494)	4800.00	2200.00
COMMON CARD (1-110)	12.00	5.50
YELLOW LETTER 1-110	45.00	20.00
YELLOW TEAM 1-110	45.00	20.00
MINOR STARS 1-110	15.00	6.75
SEMISTARS 1-110	20.00	9.00
UNLISTED STARS 1-110	30.00	13.50
COMMON CARD (111-495)	8.00	3.60
MINOR STARS 111-495	10.00	4.50
SEMISTARS 111-495	15.00	6.75
UNLISTED STARS 111-495	25.00	11.00
NOT ISSUED (145)		

*UNLISTED DODGER/YANKEE: 1.25X VALUE
CARDS PRICED IN NM CONDITION

		NRMT	VG-E
☐	1 Ted Williams	425.00	150.00
☐	2A Bob Lemon	30.00	16.00
☐	2B Bob Lemon YT	60.00	27.00
☐	3 Alex Kellner	12.00	5.50
☐	4 Hank Foiles	12.00	5.50
☐	5 Willie Mays	225.00	100.00
☐	6 George Zuverink	12.00	5.50
☐	7 Dale Long	15.00	6.75
☐	8A Eddie Kasko	12.00	5.50
☐	8B Eddie Kasko YL	45.00	20.00
☐	9 Hank Bauer	15.00	6.75
☐	10 Lou Burdette	15.00	6.75
☐	11A Jim Rivera	12.00	5.50
☐	11B Jim Rivera YT	45.00	20.00
☐	12 George Crowe	12.00	5.50
☐	13A Billy Hoeft	12.00	5.50
☐	13B Billy Hoeft YL	45.00	20.00
☐	14 Rip Repulski	12.00	5.50
☐	15 Jim Lemon	15.00	6.75
☐	16 Charlie Neal	15.00	6.75
☐	17 Felix Mantilla	12.00	5.50
☐	18 Frank Sullivan	12.00	5.50
☐	19 New York Giants Team Card (Checklist on back)	40.00	8.00
☐	20A Gil McDougald	18.00	8.00
☐	20B Gil McDougald YL	60.00	27.00
☐	21 Curt Barclay	12.00	5.50
☐	22 Hal Naragon	12.00	5.50
☐	23A Bill Tuttle	12.00	5.50
☐	23B Bill Tuttle YL	45.00	20.00
☐	24A Hobie Landrith	12.00	5.50
☐	24B Hobie Landrith YL	45.00	20.00
☐	25 Don Drysdale	85.00	38.00
☐	26 Ron Jackson	12.00	5.50
☐	27 Bud Freeman	12.00	5.50
☐	28 Jim Bugby	12.00	5.50
☐	29 Ted Lepcio	12.00	5.50
☐	30A Hank Aaron	200.00	90.00
☐	30B Hank Aaron YL	425.00	190.00
☐	31 Tex Clevenger	12.00	5.50
☐	32A J.W. Porter	12.00	5.50
☐	32B J.W. Porter YL	45.00	20.00
☐	33A Cal Neeman	12.00	5.50
☐	33B Cal Neeman YT	45.00	20.00
☐	34 Bob Thurman	12.00	5.50
☐	35A Don Mossi	15.00	6.75
☐	35B Don Mossi YT	45.00	20.00
☐	36 Ted Kazanski	12.00	5.50
☐	37 Mike McCormick UER (Photo actually Ray Monzant)	15.00	6.75
☐	38 Dick Gernert	12.00	5.50
☐	39 Bob Martyn	12.00	5.50
☐	40 George Kell	18.00	8.00
☐	41 Dave Hillman	12.00	5.50
☐	42 John Roseboro	24.00	11.00
☐	43 Sal Maglie	15.00	6.75
☐	44 Washington Senators Team Card (Checklist on back)	20.00	4.00
☐	45 Dick Groat	15.00	6.75
☐	46A Lou Sleater	12.00	5.50
☐	46B Lou Sleater YL	45.00	20.00
☐	47 Roger Maris	425.00	190.00
☐	48 Chuck Harmon	12.00	5.50
☐	49 Smoky Burgess	15.00	6.75
☐	50A Billy Pierce	15.00	6.75
☐	50B Billy Pierce YT	50.00	22.00
☐	51 Del Rice	12.00	5.50
☐	52A Bob Clemens	275.00	125.00
☐	52B Bob Clemente YT	450.00	200.00
☐	53A Morrie Martin	12.00	5.50
☐	53B Morrie Martin YL	45.00	20.00
☐	54 Norm Siebern	20.00	9.00
☐	55 Chico Carrasquel	12.00	5.50
☐	56 Bill Fischer	12.00	5.50
☐	57A Tim Thompson	12.00	5.50
☐	57B Tim Thompson YL	45.00	20.00
☐	58A Art Schult	12.00	5.50
☐	58B Art Schult YT	45.00	20.00
☐	59 Dave Sisler	12.00	5.50
☐	60A Del Ennis	15.00	6.75
☐	60B Del Ennis YL	50.00	22.00
☐	61A Darrell Johnson	12.00	5.50
☐	61B Darrell Johnson YL	45.00	20.00
☐	62 Joe DeMaestri	12.00	5.50
☐	63 Joe Nuxhall	15.00	6.75
☐	64 Joe Lonnett	12.00	5.50
☐	65A Von McDaniel	12.00	5.50
☐	65B Von McDaniel YL	45.00	20.00
☐	66 Lee Walls	12.00	5.50
☐	67 Joe Ginsberg	12.00	5.50
☐	68 Daryl Spencer	12.00	5.50
☐	69 Wally Burnette	12.00	5.50
☐	70A Al Kaline	100.00	45.00
☐	70B Al Kaline YL	180.00	80.00
☐	71 Dodgers Team (Checklist on back)	60.00	
☐	72 Bud Byerly	12.00	5.50
☐	73 Pete Daley	12.00	5.50
☐	74 Roy Face	15.00	6.75
☐	75 Gus Bell	15.00	6.75
☐	76A Dick Farrell	12.00	5.50
☐	76B Dick Farrell YT	45.00	20.00
☐	77A Don Zimmer	15.00	6.75
☐	77B Don Zimmer YT	50.00	22.00
☐	78A Ernie Johnson	15.00	6.75
☐	78B Ernie Johnson YL	50.00	22.00
☐	79A Dick Williams	15.00	6.75
☐	79B Dick Williams YT	50.00	22.00
☐	80 Dick Drott	12.00	5.50
☐	81A Steve Boros	12.00	5.50
☐	81B Steve Boros YT	45.00	20.00
☐	82 Ron Kline	12.00	5.50
☐	83 Bob Hazle	12.00	5.50
☐	84 Billy O'Dell	12.00	5.50
☐	85A Luis Aparicio	30.00	13.50
☐	85B Luis Aparicio YT	70.00	32.00
☐	86 Valmy Thomas	12.00	5.50
☐	87 Johnny Kucks	12.00	5.50
☐	88 Duke Snider	75.00	34.00
☐	89 Billy Klaus	12.00	5.50
☐	90 Robin Roberts	30.00	13.50
☐	91 Chuck Tanner	15.00	6.75
☐	92A Clint Courtney	12.00	5.50
☐	92B Clint Courtney YL	45.00	20.00
☐	93 Sandy Amoros	15.00	6.75
☐	94 Bob Skinner	12.00	5.50
☐	95 Frank Bolling	12.00	5.50
☐	96 Joe Durham	12.00	5.50
☐	97A Larry Jackson	12.00	5.50
☐	97B Larry Jackson YL	45.00	20.00
☐	98A Billy Hunter	12.00	5.50
☐	98B Billy Hunter YL	45.00	20.00
☐	99 Bobby Adams	12.00	5.50
☐	100A Early Wynn	25.00	11.00
☐	100B Early Wynn YT	60.00	27.00
☐	101A Bobby Richardson	24.00	11.00
☐	101B Bobby Richardson YL	55.00	25.00
☐	102 George Strickland	12.00	5.50
☐	103 Jerry Lynch	15.00	6.75
☐	104 Jim Pendleton	12.00	5.50
☐	105 Billy Gardner	12.00	5.50
☐	106 Dick Schofield	15.00	6.75
☐	107 Ossie Virgil	12.00	5.50
☐	108A Jim Landis	12.00	5.50
☐	108B Jim Landis YL	45.00	20.00
☐	109 Herb Plews	12.00	5.50
☐	110 Johnny Logan	15.00	6.75
☐	111 Stu Miller	10.00	4.50
☐	112 Gus Zernial	10.00	4.50
☐	113 Jerry Walker	8.00	3.60
☐	114 Irv Noren	10.00	4.50
☐	115 Jim Bunning	25.00	11.00
☐	116 Dave Philley	8.00	3.60
☐	117 Frank Torre	10.00	4.50
☐	118 Harvey Haddix	10.00	4.50
☐	119 Harry Chiti	8.00	3.60
☐	120 Johnny Podres	12.00	5.50
☐	121 Eddie Miksis	8.00	3.60
☐	122 Walt Moryn	8.00	3.60
☐	123 Dick Tomanek	8.00	3.60
☐	124 Bobby Usher	8.00	3.60
☐	125 Alvin Dark	10.00	4.50
☐	126 Stan Palys	8.00	3.60
☐	127 Tom Sturdivant	10.00	4.50
☐	128 Willie Kirkland	8.00	3.60
☐	129 Jim Derrington	8.00	3.60
☐	130 Jackie Jensen	10.00	4.50
☐	131 Bob Henrich	8.00	3.60
☐	132 Vern Law	10.00	4.50
☐	133 Russ Nixon	8.00	3.60
☐	134 Philadelphia Phillies Team Card (Checklist on back)	15.00	3.00
☐	135 Mike(Moe) Drabowsky	10.00	4.50
☐	136 Jim Finigan	8.00	3.60
☐	137 Russ Kemmerer	8.00	3.60
☐	138 Earl Torgeson	8.00	3.60
☐	139 George Brunet	8.00	3.60
☐	140 Wes Covington	10.00	4.50
☐	141 Ken Lehman	8.00	3.60
☐	142 Enos Slaughter	25.00	11.00
☐	143 Billy Muffett	8.00	3.60
☐	144 Bobby Morgan	8.00	3.60
☐	145 Never issued		
☐	146 Dick Gray	8.00	3.60
☐	147 Don McMahon	8.00	3.60
☐	148 Billy Consolo	8.00	3.60
☐	149 Tom Acker	8.00	3.60
☐	150 Mickey Mantle	800.00	350.00
☐	151 Buddy Pritchard	8.00	3.60

No.	Player	Price 1	Price 2
152	Johnny Antonelli	10.00	4.50
153	Les Moss	8.00	3.60
154	Harry Byrd	8.00	3.60
155	Hector Lopez	10.00	4.50
156	Dick Hyde	8.00	3.60
157	Dee Fondy	8.00	3.60
158	Cleveland Indians Team Card (Checklist on back)	15.00	3.00
159	Taylor Phillips	8.00	3.60
160	Don Hoak	10.00	4.50
161	Don Larsen	14.00	6.25
162	Gil Hodges	30.00	13.50
163	Jim Wilson	8.00	3.60
164	Bob Taylor	8.00	3.60
165	Bob Nieman	8.00	3.60
166	Danny O'Connell	8.00	3.60
167	Frank Baumann	8.00	3.60
168	Joe Cunningham	8.00	3.60
169	Ralph Terry	10.00	4.50
170	Vic Wertz	10.00	4.50
171	Harry Anderson	8.00	3.60
172	Don Gross	8.00	3.60
173	Eddie Yost	8.00	3.60
174	Athletics Team (Checklist on back)	15.00	3.00
175	Marv Throneberry	16.00	7.25
176	Bob Buhl	10.00	4.50
177	Al Smith	8.00	3.60
178	Ted Kluszewski	16.00	7.25
179	Willie Miranda	8.00	3.60
180	Lindy McDaniel	10.00	4.50
181	Willie Jones	8.00	3.60
182	Joe Caffie	8.00	3.60
183	Dave Jolly	8.00	3.60
184	Elvin Tappe	8.00	3.60
185	Ray Boone	10.00	4.50
186	Jack Meyer	8.00	3.60
187	Sandy Koufax	225.00	100.00
188	Milt Bolling UER (Photo actually Lou Berberet)	8.00	3.60
189	George Susce	8.00	3.60
190	Red Schoendienst	18.00	8.00
191	Art Ceccarelli	8.00	3.60
192	Milt Graff	8.00	3.60
193	Jerry Lumpe	8.00	3.60
194	Roger Craig	10.00	4.50
195	Whitey Lockman	10.00	4.50
196	Mike Garcia	10.00	4.50
197	Haywood Sullivan	10.00	4.50
198	Bill Virdon	10.00	4.50
199	Don Blasingame	8.00	3.60
200	Bob Keegan	8.00	3.60
201	Jim Bolger	8.00	3.60
202	Woody Held	8.00	3.60
203	Al Walker	8.00	3.60
204	Leo Kiely	8.00	3.60
205	Johnny Temple	10.00	4.50
206	Bob Shaw	8.00	3.60
207	Solly Hemus	8.00	3.60
208	Cal McLish	8.00	3.60
209	Bob Anderson	8.00	3.60
210	Wally Moon	10.00	4.50
211	Pete Burnside	8.00	3.60
212	Bubba Phillips	8.00	3.60
213	Red Wilson	8.00	3.60
214	Willard Schmidt	8.00	3.60
215	Jim Gilliam	14.00	6.25
216	St. Louis Cardinals Team Card (Checklist on back)	15.00	3.00
217	Jack Harshman	8.00	3.60
218	Dick Rand	8.00	3.60
219	Camilo Pascual	10.00	4.50
220	Tom Brewer	8.00	3.60
221	Jerry Kindall	8.00	3.60
222	Bud Daley	8.00	3.60
223	Andy Pafko	10.00	4.50
224	Bob Grim	10.00	4.50
225	Billy Goodman	10.00	4.50
226	Bob Smith	8.00	3.60
227	Gene Stephens	8.00	3.60
228	Duke Maas	8.00	3.60
229	Frank Zupo	8.00	3.60
230	Richie Ashburn	30.00	13.50
231	Lloyd Merritt	8.00	3.60
232	Reno Bertoia	8.00	3.60
233	Mickey Vernon	10.00	4.50
234	Carl Sawatski	8.00	3.60
235	Tom Gorman	8.00	3.60
236	Ed Fitzgerald	8.00	3.60
237	Bill Wight	8.00	3.60
238	Bill Mazeroski	24.00	11.00
239	Chuck Stobbs	8.00	3.60
240	Bill Skowron	16.00	7.25
241	Dick Littlefield	8.00	3.60
242	Johnny Klippstein	8.00	3.60
243	Larry Raines	8.00	3.60
244	Don Demeter	8.00	3.60
245	Frank Lary	10.00	4.50
246	New York Yankees Team Card (Checklist on back)	90.00	18.00
247	Casey Wise	8.00	3.60
248	Herman Wehmeier	8.00	3.60
249	Ray Moore	8.00	3.60
250	Roy Sievers	10.00	4.50
251	Warren Hacker	8.00	3.60
252	Bob Trowbridge	8.00	3.60
253	Don Mueller	10.00	4.50
254	Alex Grammas	8.00	3.60
255	Bob Turley	10.00	4.50
256	Chicago White Sox Team Card (Checklist on back)	15.00	3.00
257	Hal Smith	8.00	3.60
258	Carl Erskine	14.00	6.25
259	Al Pilarcik	8.00	3.60
260	Frank Malzone	10.00	4.50
261	Turk Lown	8.00	3.60
262	Johnny Groth	8.00	3.60
263	Eddie Bressoud	10.00	4.50
264	Jack Sanford	10.00	4.50
265	Pete Runnels	10.00	4.50
266	Connie Johnson	8.00	3.60
267	Sherm Lollar	10.00	4.50
268	Granny Hamner	8.00	3.60
269	Paul Smith	8.00	3.60
270	Warren Spahn	50.00	22.00
271	Billy Martin	30.00	13.50
272	Ray Crone	8.00	3.60
273	Hal Smith	8.00	3.60
274	Rocky Bridges	8.00	3.60
275	Elston Howard	16.00	7.25
276	Bobby Avila	8.00	3.60
277	Virgil Trucks	10.00	4.50
278	Mack Burk	8.00	3.60
279	Bob Boyd	8.00	3.60
280	Jim Piersall	10.00	4.50
281	Sammy Taylor	8.00	3.60
282	Paul Foytack	8.00	3.60
283	Ray Shearer	8.00	3.60
284	Ray Katt	8.00	3.60
285	Frank Robinson	100.00	45.00
286	Gino Cimoli	8.00	3.60
287	Sam Jones	10.00	4.50
288	Harmon Killebrew	85.00	38.00
289	Lou Burdette / Bobby Shantz	10.00	4.50
290	Dick Donovan	8.00	3.60
291	Don Landrum	8.00	3.60
292	Ned Garver	8.00	3.60
293	Gene Freese	8.00	3.60
294	Hal Jeffcoat	8.00	3.60
295	Minnie Minoso	14.00	6.25
296	Ryne Duren	16.00	7.25
297	Don Buddin	8.00	3.60
298	Jim Hearn	8.00	3.60
299	Harry Simpson	8.00	3.60
300	Will Harridge PRES / Warren Giles	14.00	6.25
301	Randy Jackson	8.00	3.60
302	Mike Baxes	8.00	3.60
303	Neil Chrisley	8.00	3.60
304	Harvey Haddix / Al Kaline	20.00	9.00
305	Clem Labine	8.00	4.50
306	Whammy Douglas	8.00	3.60
307	Brooks Robinson	100.00	45.00
308	Paul Giel	10.00	4.50
309	Gail Harris	8.00	3.60
310	Ernie Banks	100.00	45.00
311	Bob Purkey	8.00	3.60
312	Boston Red Sox Team Card (Checklist on back)	15.00	3.00
313	Bob Rush	8.00	3.60
314	Duke Snider / Walt Alston MG	30.00	13.50
315	Bob Friend	10.00	4.50
316	Tito Francona	10.00	4.50
317	Albie Pearson	10.00	4.50
318	Frank House	8.00	3.60
319	Lou Skizas	8.00	3.60
320	Whitey Ford	50.00	22.00
321	Sluggers Supreme / Ted Kluszewski / Ted Williams	70.00	32.00
322	Harding Peterson	10.00	4.50
323	Elmer Valo	8.00	3.60
324	Hoyt Wilhelm	18.00	8.00
325	Joe Adcock	10.00	4.50
326	Bob Miller	8.00	3.60
327	Chicago Cubs Team Card (Checklist on back)	15.00	3.00
328	Ike Delock	8.00	3.60
329	Bob Cerv	10.00	4.50
330	Ed Bailey	10.00	4.50
331	Pedro Ramos	8.00	3.60
332	Jim King	8.00	3.60
333	Andy Carey	10.00	4.50
334	Bob Friend / Billy Pierce	10.00	4.50
335	Ruben Gomez	8.00	3.60
336	Bert Hamric	8.00	3.60
337	Hank Aguirre	8.00	3.60
338	Walt Dropo	10.00	4.50
339	Fred Hatfield	8.00	3.60
340	Don Newcombe	14.00	6.25
341	Pittsburgh Pirates Team Card (Checklist on back)	15.00	3.00
342	Jim Brosnan	10.00	4.50
343	Orlando Cepeda	90.00	40.00
344	Bob Porterfield	8.00	3.60
345	Jim Hegan	10.00	4.50
346	Steve Bilko	8.00	3.60
347	Don Rudolph	8.00	3.60
348	Chico Fernandez	8.00	3.60
349	Murry Dickson	8.00	3.60
350	Ken Boyer	16.00	7.25
351	Braves Fence Busters / Del Crandall / Eddie Mathews / Hank Aaron / Joe Adcock	35.00	16.00
352	Herb Score	14.00	6.25
353	Stan Lopata	8.00	3.60
354	Art Ditmar	10.00	4.50
355	Bill Bruton	10.00	4.50
356	Bob Malkmus	8.00	3.60
357	Danny McDevitt	8.00	3.60
358	Gene Baker	8.00	3.60
359	Billy Loes	10.00	4.50
360	Roy McMillan	10.00	4.50
361	Mike Fornieles	8.00	3.60
362	Ray Jablonski	8.00	3.60
363	Don Elston	8.00	3.60
364	Earl Battey	8.00	3.60
365	Tom Morgan	8.00	3.60
366	Gene Green	8.00	3.60
367	Jack Urban	8.00	3.60
368	Rocky Colavito	50.00	22.00
369	Ralph Lumenti	8.00	3.60
370	Yogi Berra	90.00	40.00
371	Marty Keough	8.00	3.60
372	Don Cardwell	8.00	3.60
373	Joe Pignatano	8.00	3.60
374	Brooks Lawrence	8.00	3.60
375	Pee Wee Reese	50.00	22.00
376	Charley Rabe	8.00	3.60
377A	Milwaukee Braves Team Card (Alphabetical)	15.00	6.75
377B	Milwaukee Team numerical checklist	100.00	20.00

□	#	Name	NRMT	VG-E
□	378	Hank Sauer	10.00	4.50
□	379	Ray Herbert	8.00	3.60
□	380	Charlie Maxwell	10.00	4.50
□	381	Hal Brown	8.00	3.60
□	382	Al Cicotte	8.00	3.60
□	383	Lou Berberet	8.00	3.60
□	384	John Goryl	8.00	3.60
□	385	Wilmer Mizell	10.00	4.50
□	386	Birdie's Sluggers	14.00	6.25
		Ed Bailey		
		Birdie Tebbetts MG		
		Frank Robinson		
□	387	Wally Post	10.00	4.50
□	388	Billy Moran	8.00	3.60
□	389	Bill Taylor	8.00	3.60
□	390	Del Crandall	10.00	4.50
□	391	Dave Melton	8.00	3.60
□	392	Bennie Daniels	8.00	3.60
□	393	Tony Kubek	18.00	8.00
□	394	Jim Grant	8.00	3.60
□	395	Willard Nixon	8.00	3.60
□	396	Dutch Dotterer	8.00	3.60
□	397A	Detroit Tigers	15.00	6.75
		Team Card		
		(Alphabetical)		
□	397B	Detroit Team	100.00	20.00
		numerical checklist		
□	398	Gene Woodling	10.00	4.50
□	399	Marv Grissom	8.00	3.60
□	400	Nellie Fox	30.00	13.50
□	401	Don Bessent	8.00	3.60
□	402	Bobby Gene Smith	8.00	3.60
□	403	Steve Korcheck	8.00	3.60
□	404	Curt Simmons	10.00	4.50
□	405	Ken Aspromonte	8.00	3.60
□	406	Vic Power	10.00	4.50
□	407	Carlton Willey	10.00	4.50
□	408A	Baltimore Orioles	15.00	6.75
		Team Card		
		(Alphabetical)		
□	408B	Baltimore Team	100.00	20.00
		numerical checklist		
□	409	Frank Thomas	10.00	4.50
□	410	Murray Wall	8.00	3.60
□	411	Tony Taylor	10.00	4.50
□	412	Gerry Staley	8.00	3.60
□	413	Jim Davenport	8.00	3.60
□	414	Sammy White	8.00	3.60
□	415	Bob Bowman	8.00	3.60
□	416	Foster Castleman	8.00	3.60
□	417	Carl Furillo	14.00	6.25
□	418	Mickey Mantle	275.00	125.00
		Hank Aaron		
□	419	Bobby Shantz	10.00	4.50
□	420	Vada Pinson	40.00	18.00
□	421	Dixie Howell	8.00	3.60
□	422	Norm Zauchin	8.00	3.60
□	423	Phil Clark	8.00	3.60
□	424	Larry Doby	14.00	6.25
□	425	Sammy Esposito	8.00	3.60
□	426	Johnny O'Brien	10.00	4.50
□	427	Al Worthington	8.00	3.60
□	428A	Cincinnati Reds	15.00	6.75
		Team Card		
		(Alphabetical)		
□	428B	Cincinnati Team	100.00	20.00
		numerical checklist		
□	429	Gus Triandos	10.00	4.50
□	430	Bobby Thomson	10.00	4.50
□	431	Gene Conley	10.00	4.50
□	432	John Powers	8.00	3.60
□	433A	Pancho Herrer ERR	650.00	300.00
□	433B	Pancho Herrera COR	10.00	4.50
□	434	Harvey Kuenn	10.00	4.50
□	435	Ed Roebuck	10.00	4.50
□	436	Willie Mays	75.00	34.00
		Duke Snider		
□	437	Bob Speake	8.00	3.60
□	438	Whitey Herzog	10.00	4.50
□	439	Ray Narleski	8.00	3.60
□	440	Eddie Mathews	40.00	18.00
□	441	Jim Marshall	10.00	4.50
□	442	Phil Paine	8.00	3.60
□	443	Billy Harrell SP	20.00	9.00
□	444	Danny Kravitz	8.00	3.60
□	445	Bob Smith	8.00	3.60
□	446	Carroll Hardy SP	20.00	9.00
□	447	Ray Monzant	8.00	3.60
□	448	Charlie Lau	12.00	5.50
□	449	Gene Fodge	8.00	3.60
□	450	Preston Ward SP	20.00	9.00
□	451	Joe Taylor	8.00	3.60
□	452	Roman Mejias	8.00	3.60
□	453	Tom Qualters	8.00	3.60
□	454	Harry Hanebrink	8.00	3.60
□	455	Hal Griggs	8.00	3.60
□	456	Dick Brown	8.00	3.60
□	457	Milt Pappas	12.00	5.50
□	458	Julio Becquer	8.00	3.60
□	459	Ron Blackburn	8.00	3.60
□	460	Chuck Essegian	8.00	3.60
□	461	Ed Mayer	8.00	3.60
□	462	Gary Geiger SP	20.00	9.00
□	463	Vito Valentinetti	8.00	3.60
□	464	Curt Flood	30.00	13.50
□	465	Arnie Portocarrero	8.00	3.60
□	466	Pete Whisenant	8.00	3.60
□	467	Glen Hobbie	8.00	3.60
□	468	Bob Schmidt	8.00	3.60
□	469	Don Ferrarese	8.00	3.60
□	470	R.C. Stevens	8.00	3.60
□	471	Lenny Green	8.00	3.60
□	472	Joey Jay	10.00	4.50
□	473	Bill Renna	8.00	3.60
□	474	Roman Semproch	8.00	3.60
□	475	Fred Haney AS MG and	20.00	6.00
		Casey Stengel AS MG		
		(Checklist back)		
□	476	Stan Musial AS TP	40.00	18.00
□	478	Johnny Temple AS	8.00	3.60
□	479	Nellie Fox AS	18.00	8.00
□	480	Eddie Mathews AS	20.00	9.00
□	481	Frank Malzone AS	8.00	3.60
□	482	Ernie Banks AS	35.00	16.00
□	483	Luis Aparicio AS	18.00	8.00
□	484	Frank Robinson AS	24.00	11.00
□	485	Ted Williams AS	125.00	55.00
□	486	Willie Mays AS	50.00	22.00
□	487	Mickey Mantle AS TP	200.00	90.00
□	488	Hank Aaron AS	50.00	22.00
□	489	Jackie Jensen AS	10.00	4.50
□	490	Ed Bailey AS	8.00	3.60
□	491	Sherm Lollar AS	8.00	3.60
□	492	Bob Friend AS	8.00	3.60
□	493	Bob Turley AS	10.00	4.50
□	494	Warren Spahn AS	24.00	11.00
□	495	Herb Score AS	8.00	3.20
□	xx	Contest Cards	60.00	27.00

more difficult to obtain. Several cards in the 300s exist with or without an extra traded or option line on the back of the card. Cards 199 to 286 exist with either white or gray backs. There is no price differential for either colored back. Cards 461 to 470 contain "Highlights" while cards 116 to 146 give an alphabetically ordered listing of "Rookie Prospects." These Rookie Prospects (RP) are Topps' first organized inclusion of untested "Rookie" cards. Card 440 features Lew Burdette erroneously posing as a left-handed pitcher. Cards were issued in one-card penny packs or six-card nickel packs. There were some three-card advertising panels produced by Topps; the players included are from the first series. One advertising panel shows Don McMahon, Red Wilson and Bob Boyd on the front with Ted Kluszewski's card back on the back of the panel. Other panels are: Joe Pignatano, Sam Jones and Jack Urban also with Kluszewski's card back on back, Billy Hunter, Chuck Stobbs and Carl Sawatski on the front with the back of Nellie Fox's card on the back, Vito Valentinetti, Ken Lehman and Ed Bouchee on the front with Fox's card back on back and Mel Roach, Brooks Lawrence and Warren Spahn also with Fox on back. When separated, these advertising cards are distinguished by the non-standard card back, i.e., part of an advertisement for the 1959 Topps set instead of the typical statistics and biographical information about the player pictured. The key Rookie Cards in this set are Felipe Alou, Sparky Anderson (called George on the card), Norm Cash, Bob Gibson, and Bill White.

1959 Topps

yogi berra

NEW YORK YANKEES
CATCHER

The cards in this 572-card set measure 2 1/2" by 3 1/2". The 1959 Topps set contains bust pictures of the players in a colored circle. Card numbers 551 to 572 are Sporting News All-Star Selections. High numbers 507 to 572 have the card number in a black background on the reverse rather than a green background as in the lower numbers. The high numbers are

	NRMT	VG-E
COMPLETE SET (572)	4500.00	2000.00
COMMON CARD (1-110)	6.00	2.70
COMMON CARD (111-506)	4.00	1.80
MINOR STARS 1-506	8.00	3.60
SEMISTARS 1-506	12.00	5.50
UNLISTED STARS 1-506	20.00	9.00
COMMON CARD (507-572)	16.00	7.25
MINOR STARS 507-572	20.00	9.00
SEMISTARS 507-572	30.00	13.50
*UNLISTED DODGER/YANKEE: 1.25X VALUE		
CARDS PRICED IN NM CONDITION		

□	#	Name	NRMT	VG-E
□	1	Ford Frick COMM	50.00	13.50
□	2	Eddie Yost	8.00	3.60
□	3	Don McMahon	8.00	3.60
□	4	Albie Pearson	8.00	3.60
□	5	Dick Donovan	6.00	2.70
□	6	Alex Grammas	6.00	2.70
□	7	Al Pilarcik	6.00	2.70
□	8	Phillies Team	65.00	13.00
		(Checklist on back)		
□	9	Paul Giel	8.00	3.60
□	10	Mickey Mantle	600.00	275.00
□	11	Billy Hunter	8.00	3.60
□	12	Vern Law	8.00	3.60
□	13	Dick Gernert	6.00	2.70
□	14	Pete Whisenant	6.00	2.70
□	15	Dick Drott	6.00	2.70
□	16	Joe Pignatano	6.00	2.70
□	17	Frank Thomas	8.00	3.60

Danny Murtaugh MG
Ted Kluszewski

☐ 18	Jack Urban	6.00	2.70
☐ 19	Eddie Bressoud	6.00	2.70
☐ 20	Duke Snider	50.00	22.00
☐ 21	Connie Johnson	6.00	2.70
☐ 22	Al Smith	8.00	3.60
☐ 23	Murry Dickson	8.00	3.60
☐ 24	Red Wilson	6.00	2.70
☐ 25	Don Hoak	8.00	3.60
☐ 26	Chuck Stobbs	6.00	2.70
☐ 27	Andy Pafko	8.00	3.60
☐ 28	Al Worthington	6.00	2.70
☐ 29	Jim Bolger	6.00	2.70
☐ 30	Nellie Fox	30.00	13.50
☐ 31	Ken Lehman	6.00	2.70
☐ 32	Don Buddin	6.00	2.70
☐ 33	Ed Fitzgerald	6.00	2.70
☐ 34	Al Kaline	20.00	9.00
	Charley Maxwell		
☐ 35	Ted Kluszewski	16.00	7.25
☐ 36	Hank Aguirre	6.00	2.70
☐ 37	Gene Green	6.00	2.70
☐ 38	Morrie Martin	6.00	2.70
☐ 39	Ed Bouchee	6.00	2.70
☐ 40A	Warren Spahn ERR (Born 1931)	75.00	34.00
☐ 40B	Warren Spahn ERR (Born 1931, but three is partially obscured)	100.00	45.00
☐ 40C	Warren Spahn COR (Born 1921)	50.00	22.00
☐ 41	Bob Martyn	6.00	2.70
☐ 42	Murray Wall	6.00	2.70
☐ 43	Steve Bilko	6.00	2.70
☐ 44	Vito Valentinetti	6.00	2.70
☐ 45	Andy Carey	8.00	3.60
☐ 46	Bill R. Henry	6.00	2.70
☐ 47	Jim Finigan	6.00	2.70
☐ 48	Orioles Team (Checklist on back)	25.00	5.00
☐ 49	Bill Hall	6.00	2.70
☐ 50	Willie Mays	125.00	55.00
☐ 51	Rip Coleman	6.00	2.70
☐ 52	Coot Veal	6.00	2.70
☐ 53	Stan Williams	8.00	3.60
☐ 54	Mel Roach	6.00	2.70
☐ 55	Tom Brewer	6.00	2.70
☐ 56	Carl Sawatski	6.00	2.70
☐ 57	Al Cicotte	6.00	2.70
☐ 58	Eddie Miksis	6.00	2.70
☐ 59	Irv Noren	8.00	3.60
☐ 60	Bob Turley	8.00	3.60
☐ 61	Dick Brown	6.00	2.70
☐ 62	Tony Taylor	8.00	3.60
☐ 63	Jim Hearn	6.00	2.70
☐ 64	Joe DeMaestri	6.00	2.70
☐ 65	Frank Torre	8.00	3.60
☐ 66	Joe Ginsberg	6.00	2.70
☐ 67	Brooks Lawrence	6.00	2.70
☐ 68	Dick Schofield	8.00	3.60
☐ 69	Giants Team (Checklist on back)	25.00	5.00
☐ 70	Harvey Kuenn	8.00	3.60
☐ 71	Don Bessent	6.00	2.70
☐ 72	Bill Renna	6.00	2.70
☐ 73	Ron Jackson	8.00	3.60
☐ 74	Jim Lemon	8.00	3.60
	Cookie Lavagetto MG		
	Roy Sievers		
☐ 75	Sam Jones	8.00	3.60
☐ 76	Bobby Richardson	20.00	9.00
☐ 77	John Goryl	6.00	2.70
☐ 78	Pedro Ramos	6.00	2.70
☐ 79	Harry Chiti	6.00	2.70
☐ 80	Minnie Minoso	10.00	4.50
☐ 81	Hal Jeffcoat	6.00	2.70
☐ 82	Bob Boyd	6.00	2.70
☐ 83	Bob Smith	6.00	2.70
☐ 84	Reno Bertoia	6.00	2.70
☐ 85	Harry Anderson	6.00	2.70
☐ 86	Bob Keegan	8.00	3.60
☐ 87	Danny O'Connell	6.00	2.70
☐ 88	Herb Score	10.00	4.50
☐ 89	Billy Gardner	6.00	2.70
☐ 90	Bill Skowron	16.00	7.25
☐ 91	Herb Moford	6.00	2.70
☐ 92	Dave Philley	6.00	2.70
☐ 93	Julio Becquer	6.00	2.70
☐ 94	White Sox Team (Checklist on back)	40.00	8.00
☐ 95	Carl Willey	6.00	2.70
☐ 96	Lou Berberet	6.00	2.70
☐ 97	Jerry Lynch	8.00	3.60
☐ 98	Arnie Portocarrero	6.00	2.70
☐ 99	Ted Kazanski	6.00	2.70
☐ 100	Bob Cerv	8.00	3.60
☐ 101	Alex Kellner	6.00	2.70
☐ 102	Felipe Alou	30.00	13.50
☐ 103	Billy Goodman	8.00	3.60
☐ 104	Del Rice	6.00	2.70
☐ 105	Lee Walls	6.00	2.70
☐ 106	Hal Woodeshick	6.00	2.70
☐ 107	Norm Larker	8.00	3.60
☐ 108	Zack Monroe	6.00	2.70
☐ 109	Bob Schmidt	6.00	2.70
☐ 110	George Witt	8.00	3.60
☐ 111	Redlegs Team (Checklist on back)	12.00	2.40
☐ 112	Billy Consolo	4.00	1.80
☐ 113	Taylor Phillips	4.00	1.80
☐ 114	Earl Battey	8.00	3.60
☐ 115	Mickey Vernon	8.00	3.60
☐ 116	Bob Allison RP	12.00	5.50
☐ 117	John Blanchard RP	4.00	1.80
☐ 118	John Buzhardt RP	4.00	1.80
☐ 119	John Callison RP	12.00	5.50
☐ 120	Chuck Coles RP	4.00	1.80
☐ 121	Bob Conley RP	4.00	1.80
☐ 122	Bennie Daniels RP	4.00	1.80
☐ 123	Don Dillard RP	4.00	1.80
☐ 124	Dan Dobbek RP	4.00	1.80
☐ 125	Ron Fairly RP	8.00	3.60
☐ 126	Ed Haas RP	4.00	1.80
☐ 127	Kent Hadley RP	4.00	1.80
☐ 128	Bob Hartman RP	4.00	1.80
☐ 129	Frank Herrera RP	4.00	1.80
☐ 130	Lou Jackson RP	4.00	1.80
☐ 131	Deron Johnson RP	8.00	3.60
☐ 132	Don Lee RP	4.00	1.80
☐ 133	Bob Lillis RP	4.00	1.80
☐ 134	Jim McDaniel RP	4.00	1.80
☐ 135	Gene Oliver RP	4.00	1.80
☐ 136	Jim O'Toole RP	4.00	1.80
☐ 137	Dick Ricketts RP	4.00	1.80
☐ 138	John Romano RP	4.00	1.80
☐ 139	Ed Sadowski RP	4.00	1.80
☐ 140	Charlie Secrest RP	4.00	1.80
☐ 141	Joe Shipley RP	4.00	1.80
☐ 142	Dick Stigman RP	4.00	1.80
☐ 143	Willie Tasby RP	4.00	1.80
☐ 144	Jerry Walker RP	4.00	1.80
☐ 145	Dom Zanni RP	4.00	1.80
☐ 146	Jerry Zimmerman RP	4.00	1.80
☐ 147	Cubs Clubbers	25.00	11.00
	Dale Long		
	Ernie Banks		
	Walt Moryn		
☐ 148	Mike McCormick	8.00	3.60
☐ 149	Jim Bunning	20.00	9.00
☐ 150	Stan Musial	125.00	55.00
☐ 151	Bob Malkmus	4.00	1.80
☐ 152	Johnny Klippstein	4.00	1.80
☐ 153	Jim Marshall	4.00	1.80
☐ 154	Ray Herbert	4.00	1.80
☐ 155	Enos Slaughter	20.00	9.00
☐ 156	Ace Hurlers	12.00	5.50
	Billy Pierce		
	Robin Roberts		
☐ 157	Felix Mantilla	4.00	1.80
☐ 158	Walt Dropo	4.00	1.80
☐ 159	Bob Shaw	8.00	3.60
☐ 160	Dick Groat	8.00	3.60
☐ 161	Frank Baumann	4.00	1.80
☐ 162	Bobby G. Smith	4.00	1.80
☐ 163	Sandy Koufax	150.00	70.00
☐ 164	Johnny Groth	4.00	1.80
☐ 165	Bill Bruton	8.00	3.60
☐ 166	Destruction Crew	25.00	11.00
	Minnie Minoso		
	Rocky Colavito (Misspelled Colovito on card back)		
	Larry Doby		
☐ 167	Duke Maas	4.00	1.80
☐ 168	Carroll Hardy	4.00	1.80
☐ 169	Ted Abernathy	4.00	1.80
☐ 170	Gene Woodling	8.00	3.60
☐ 171	Willard Schmidt	4.00	1.80
☐ 172	Athletics Team (Checklist on back)	12.00	2.40
☐ 173	Bill Monbouquette	8.00	3.60
☐ 174	Jim Pendleton	4.00	1.80
☐ 175	Dick Farrell	8.00	3.60
☐ 176	Preston Ward	4.00	1.80
☐ 177	John Briggs	4.00	1.80
☐ 178	Ruben Amaro	8.00	3.60
☐ 179	Don Rudolph	4.00	1.80
☐ 180	Yogi Berra	75.00	34.00
☐ 181	Bob Porterfield	4.00	1.80
☐ 182	Milt Graff	4.00	1.80
☐ 183	Stu Miller	8.00	3.60
☐ 184	Harvey Haddix	8.00	3.60
☐ 185	Jim Busby	8.00	3.60
☐ 186	Mudcat Grant	8.00	3.60
☐ 187	Bubba Phillips	8.00	3.60
☐ 188	Juan Pizarro	4.00	1.80
☐ 189	Neil Chrisley	4.00	1.80
☐ 190	Bill Virdon	8.00	3.60
☐ 191	Russ Kemmerer	4.00	1.80
☐ 192	Charlie Beamon	4.00	1.80
☐ 193	Sammy Taylor	4.00	1.80
☐ 194	Jim Brosnan	8.00	3.60
☐ 195	Rip Repulski	4.00	1.80
☐ 196	Billy Moran	4.00	1.80
☐ 197	Ray Semproch	4.00	1.80
☐ 198	Jim Davenport	8.00	3.60
☐ 199	Leo Kiely	4.00	1.80
☐ 200	Warren Giles NL PRES	8.00	3.60
☐ 201	Tom Acker	4.00	1.80
☐ 202	Roger Maris	100.00	45.00
☐ 203	Ossie Virgil	4.00	1.80
☐ 204	Casey Wise	4.00	1.80
☐ 205	Don Larsen	8.00	3.60
☐ 206	Carl Furillo	8.00	3.60
☐ 207	George Strickland	4.00	1.80
☐ 208	Willie Jones	4.00	1.80
☐ 209	Lenny Green	4.00	1.80
☐ 210	Ed Bailey	4.00	1.80
☐ 211	Bob Blaylock	4.00	1.80
☐ 212	Hank Aaron	75.00	34.00
	Eddie Mathews		
☐ 213	Jim Rivera	8.00	3.60
☐ 214	Marcelino Solis	4.00	1.80
☐ 215	Jim Lemon	8.00	3.60
☐ 216	Andre Rodgers	4.00	1.80
☐ 217	Carl Erskine	8.00	3.60
☐ 218	Roman Mejias	4.00	1.80
☐ 219	George Zuverink	4.00	1.80
☐ 220	Frank Malzone	8.00	3.60
☐ 221	Bob Bowman	4.00	1.80
☐ 222	Bobby Shantz	4.00	1.80
☐ 223	Cardinals Team (Checklist on back)	12.00	2.40
☐ 224	Claude Osteen	8.00	3.60
☐ 225	Johnny Logan	8.00	3.60
☐ 226	Art Ceccarelli	4.00	1.80
☐ 227	Hal W. Smith	4.00	1.80
☐ 228	Don Gross	4.00	1.80
☐ 229	Vic Power	8.00	3.60
☐ 230	Bill Fischer	4.00	1.80
☐ 231	Ellis Burton	4.00	1.80
☐ 232	Eddie Kasko	4.00	1.80
☐ 233	Paul Foytack	4.00	1.80
☐ 234	Chuck Tanner	8.00	3.60
☐ 235	Valmy Thomas	4.00	1.80
☐ 236	Ted Bowsfield	4.00	1.80
☐ 237	Run Preventers	12.00	5.50
	Gil McDougald		
	Bob Turley		
	Bobby Richardson		
☐ 238	Gene Baker	4.00	1.80
☐ 239	Bob Trowbridge	4.00	1.80
☐ 240	Hank Bauer	8.00	3.60
☐ 241	Billy Muffett	4.00	1.80
☐ 242	Ron Samford	4.00	1.80
☐ 243	Marv Grissom	4.00	1.80
☐ 244	Ted Gray	4.00	1.80

#	Player	Price 1	Price 2
245	Ned Garver	4.00	1.80
246	J.W. Porter	4.00	1.80
247	Don Ferrarese	4.00	1.80
248	Red Sox Team	12.00	2.40
	(Checklist on back)		
249	Bobby Adams	4.00	1.80
250	Billy O'Dell	4.00	1.80
251	Clete Boyer	8.00	3.60
252	Ray Boone	8.00	3.60
253	Seth Morehead	4.00	1.80
254	Zeke Bella	4.00	1.80
255	Del Ennis	8.00	3.60
256	Jerry Davie	4.00	1.80
257	Leon Wagner	8.00	3.60
258	Fred Kipp	4.00	1.80
259	Jim Pisoni	4.00	1.80
260	Early Wynn UER	16.00	7.25
	(1957 Cleevland)		
261	Gene Stephens	4.00	1.80
262	Johnny Podres	16.00	7.25
	Clem Labine		
	Don Drysdale		
263	Bud Daley	4.00	1.80
264	Chico Carrasquel	4.00	1.80
265	Ron Kline	4.00	1.80
266	Woody Held	4.00	1.80
267	John Romonosky	4.00	1.80
268	Tito Francona	8.00	3.60
269	Jack Meyer	4.00	1.80
270	Gil Hodges	25.00	11.00
271	Orlando Pena	4.00	1.80
272	Jerry Lumpe	4.00	1.80
273	Joey Jay	4.00	1.80
274	Jerry Kindall	8.00	3.60
275	Jack Sanford	4.00	1.80
276	Pete Daley	4.00	1.80
277	Turk Lown	8.00	3.60
278	Chuck Essegian	4.00	1.80
279	Ernie Johnson	4.00	1.80
280	Frank Bolling	4.00	1.80
281	Walt Craddock	4.00	1.80
282	R.C. Stevens	4.00	1.80
283	Russ Heman	4.00	1.80
284	Steve Korcheck	4.00	1.80
285	Joe Cunningham	4.00	1.80
286	Dean Stone	4.00	1.80
287	Don Zimmer	8.00	3.60
288	Dutch Dotterer	4.00	1.80
289	Johnny Kucks	8.00	3.60
290	Wes Covington	4.00	1.80
291	Pedro Ramos	4.00	1.80
	Camilo Pascual		
292	Dick Williams	8.00	3.60
293	Ray Moore	4.00	1.80
294	Hank Foiles	4.00	1.80
295	Billy Martin	25.00	11.00
296	Ernie Broglio	4.00	1.80
297	Jackie Brandt	4.00	1.80
298	Tex Clevenger	4.00	1.80
299	Billy Klaus	4.00	1.80
300	Richie Ashburn	25.00	11.00
301	Earl Averill	4.00	1.80
302	Don Mossi	8.00	3.60
303	Marty Keough	4.00	1.80
304	Cubs Team	12.00	2.40
	(Checklist on back)		
305	Curt Raydon	4.00	1.80
306	Jim Gilliam	8.00	3.60
307	Curt Barclay	4.00	1.80
308	Norm Siebern	4.00	1.80
309	Sal Maglie	8.00	3.60
310	Luis Aparicio	20.00	9.00
311	Norm Zauchin	4.00	1.80
312	Don Newcombe	8.00	3.60
313	Frank House	4.00	1.80
314	Don Cardwell	4.00	1.80
315	Joe Adcock	8.00	3.60
316A	Ralph Lumenti UER	4.00	1.80
	(Option)		
	(Photo actually		
	Camilo Pascual)		
316B	Ralph Lumenti UER	80.00	36.00
	(No option)		
	(Photo actually		
	Camilo Pascual)		
317	Willie Mays	70.00	32.00
	Richie Ashburn		
318	Rocky Bridges	4.00	1.80
319	Dave Hillman	4.00	1.80
320	Bob Skinner	8.00	3.60
321A	Bob Giallombardo ..	4.00	1.80
	(Option)		
321B	Bob Giallombardo	80.00	36.00
	(No option)		
322A	Harry Hanebrink	4.00	1.80
	(Traded)		
322B	Harry Hanebrink ..	80.00	36.00
	(No trade)		
323	Frank Sullivan	4.00	1.80
324	Don Demeter	4.00	1.80
325	Ken Boyer	10.00	4.50
326	Marv Throneberry	8.00	3.60
327	Gary Bell	4.00	1.80
328	Lou Skizas	4.00	1.80
329	Tigers Team	12.00	2.40
	(Checklist on back)		
330	Gus Triandos	8.00	3.60
331	Steve Boros	4.00	1.80
332	Ray Monzant	4.00	1.80
333	Harry Simpson	4.00	1.80
334	Glen Hobbie	4.00	1.80
335	Johnny Temple	8.00	3.60
336A	Billy Loes	8.00	3.60
	(With traded line)		
336B	Billy Loes	80.00	36.00
	(No trade)		
337	George Crowe	4.00	1.80
338	Sparky Anderson	65.00	29.00
339	Roy Face	8.00	3.60
340	Roy Sievers	8.00	3.60
341	Tom Qualters	4.00	1.80
342	Ray Jablonski	4.00	1.80
343	Billy Hoeft	4.00	1.80
344	Russ Nixon	4.00	1.80
345	Gil McDougald	8.00	3.60
346	Dave Sisler	4.00	1.80
	Tom Brewer		
347	Bob Buhl	4.00	1.80
348	Ted Lepcio	4.00	1.80
349	Hoyt Wilhelm	16.00	7.25
350	Ernie Banks	75.00	34.00
351	Earl Torgeson	4.00	1.80
352	Robin Roberts	20.00	9.00
353	Curt Flood	8.00	3.60
354	Pete Burnside	4.00	1.80
355	Jimmy Piersall	8.00	3.60
356	Bob Mabe	4.00	1.80
357	Dick Stuart	8.00	3.60
358	Ralph Terry	8.00	3.60
359	Bill White	20.00	9.00
360	Al Kaline	65.00	29.00
361	Willard Nixon	4.00	1.80
362A	Dolan Nichols	4.00	1.80
	(With option line)		
362B	Dolan Nichols	80.00	36.00
	(No option)		
363	Bobby Avila	4.00	1.80
364	Danny McDevitt	4.00	1.80
365	Gus Bell	8.00	3.60
366	Humberto Robinson	4.00	1.80
367	Cal Neeman	4.00	1.80
368	Don Mueller	8.00	3.60
369	Dick Tomanek	4.00	1.80
370	Pete Runnels	8.00	3.60
371	Dick Brodowski	4.00	1.80
372	Jim Hegan	8.00	3.60
373	Herb Plews	4.00	1.80
374	Art Ditmar	8.00	3.60
375	Bob Nieman	4.00	1.80
376	Hal Naragon	4.00	1.80
377	John Antonelli	8.00	3.60
378	Gail Harris	4.00	1.80
379	Bob Miller	4.00	1.80
380	Hank Aaron	125.00	55.00
381	Mike Baxes	4.00	1.80
382	Curt Simmons	8.00	3.60
383	Words of Wisdom ..	14.00	6.25
	Don Larsen		
	Casey Stengel MG		
384	Dave Sisler	4.00	1.80
385	Sherm Lollar	8.00	3.60
386	Jim Delsing	4.00	1.80
387	Don Drysdale	35.00	16.00
388	Bob Will	4.00	1.80
389	Joe Nuxhall	8.00	3.60
390	Orlando Cepeda	16.00	7.25
391	Milt Pappas	8.00	3.60
392	Whitey Herzog	8.00	3.60
393	Frank Lary	8.00	3.60
394	Randy Jackson	4.00	1.80
395	Elston Howard	10.00	4.50
396	Bob Rush	4.00	1.80
397	Senators Team	12.00	2.40
	(Checklist on back)		
398	Wally Post	8.00	3.60
399	Larry Jackson	4.00	1.80
400	Jackie Jensen	8.00	3.60
401	Ron Blackburn	4.00	1.80
402	Hector Lopez	8.00	3.60
403	Clem Labine	8.00	3.60
404	Hank Sauer	8.00	3.60
405	Roy McMillan	8.00	3.60
406	Solly Drake	4.00	1.80
407	Moe Drabowsky	8.00	3.60
408	Nellie Fox	35.00	16.00
	Luis Aparicio		
409	Gus Zernial	8.00	3.60
410	Billy Pierce	8.00	3.60
411	Whitey Lockman	4.00	1.80
412	Stan Lopata	4.00	1.80
413	Camilo Pascual UER	8.00	3.60
	(Listed as Camillo		
	on front and Pasqual		
	on back)		
414	Dale Long	8.00	3.60
415	Bill Mazeroski	12.00	5.50
416	Haywood Sullivan	8.00	3.60
417	Virgil Trucks	8.00	3.60
418	Gino Cimoli	4.00	1.80
419	Braves Team	12.00	2.40
	(Checklist on back)		
420	Rocky Colavito	30.00	13.50
421	Herman Wehmeier	4.00	1.80
422	Hobie Landrith	4.00	1.80
423	Bob Grim	8.00	3.60
424	Ken Aspromonte	4.00	1.80
425	Del Crandall	8.00	3.60
426	Gerry Staley	8.00	3.60
427	Charlie Neal	8.00	3.60
428	Ron Kline	4.00	1.80
	Bob Friend		
	Vernon Law		
	Roy Face		
429	Bobby Thomson	8.00	3.60
430	Whitey Ford	50.00	22.00
431	Whammy Douglas	4.00	1.80
432	Smoky Burgess	8.00	3.60
433	Billy Harrell	4.00	1.80
434	Hal Griggs	4.00	1.80
435	Frank Robinson	50.00	22.00
436	Granny Hamner	4.00	1.80
437	Ike Delock	4.00	1.80
438	Sammy Esposito	4.00	1.80
439	Brooks Robinson	50.00	22.00
440	Lou Burdette	8.00	3.60
	(Posing as if		
	lefthanded)		
441	John Roseboro	8.00	3.60
442	Ray Narleski	4.00	1.80
443	Daryl Spencer	4.00	1.80
444	Ron Hansen	8.00	3.60
445	Cal McLish	4.00	1.80
446	Rocky Nelson	4.00	1.80
447	Bob Anderson	4.00	1.80
448	Vada Pinson UER	10.00	4.50
	(Born: 8/8/38		
	should be 8/11/38)		
449	Tom Gorman	4.00	1.80
450	Eddie Mathews	35.00	16.00
451	Jimmy Constable	4.00	1.80
452	Chico Fernandez	4.00	1.80
453	Les Moss	4.00	1.80
454	Phil Clark	4.00	1.80
455	Larry Doby	8.00	3.60
456	Jerry Casale	4.00	1.80
457	Dodgers Team	30.00	6.00
	(Checklist on back)		
458	Gordon Jones	4.00	1.80

		NRMT	VG-E
☐ 459	Bill Tuttle	4.00	1.80
☐ 460	Bob Friend	8.00	3.60
☐ 461	Mickey Mantle HL	130.00	57.50
☐ 462	Rocky Colavito HL	16.00	7.25
☐ 463	Al Kaline HL	25.00	11.00
☐ 464	Willie Mays HL	40.00	18.00
	54 World Series Catch		
☐ 465	Roy Sievers HL	8.00	3.60
☐ 466	Billy Pierce HL	8.00	3.60
☐ 467	Hank Aaron HL	30.00	13.50
☐ 468	Duke Snider HL	18.00	8.00
☐ 469	Ernie Banks HL	18.00	8.00
☐ 470	Stan Musial HL	25.00	11.00
	3,000 Hits		
☐ 471	Tom Sturdivant	4.00	1.80
☐ 472	Gene Freese	4.00	1.80
☐ 473	Mike Fornieles	4.00	1.80
☐ 474	Moe Thacker	4.00	1.80
☐ 475	Jack Harshman	4.00	1.80
☐ 476	Indians Team	12.00	2.40
	(Checklist on back)		
☐ 477	Barry Latman	4.00	1.80
☐ 478	Bob Clemente	225.00	100.00
☐ 479	Lindy McDaniel	8.00	3.60
☐ 480	Red Schoendienst	16.00	7.25
☐ 481	Charlie Maxwell	8.00	3.60
☐ 482	Russ Meyer	4.00	1.80
☐ 483	Clint Courtney	4.00	1.80
☐ 484	Willie Kirkland	4.00	1.80
☐ 485	Ryne Duren	8.00	3.60
☐ 486	Sammy White	4.00	1.80
☐ 487	Hal Brown	4.00	1.80
☐ 488	Walt Moryn	4.00	1.80
☐ 489	John Powers	4.00	1.80
☐ 490	Frank Thomas	8.00	3.60
☐ 491	Don Blasingame	4.00	1.80
☐ 492	Gene Conley	8.00	3.60
☐ 493	Jim Landis	8.00	3.60
☐ 494	Don Pavletich	8.00	3.60
☐ 495	Johnny Podres	8.00	3.60
☐ 496	Wayne Terwilliger UER	4.00	1.80
	(Athletics on front)		
☐ 497	Hal R. Smith	4.00	1.80
☐ 498	Dick Hyde	4.00	1.80
☐ 499	Johnny O'Brien	8.00	3.60
☐ 500	Vic Wertz	8.00	3.60
☐ 501	Bob Tiefenauer	4.00	1.80
☐ 502	Alvin Dark	8.00	3.60
☐ 503	Jim Owens	4.00	1.80
☐ 504	Ossie Alvarez	4.00	1.80
☐ 505	Tony Kubek	12.00	5.50
☐ 506	Bob Purkey	4.00	1.80
☐ 507	Bob Hale	16.00	7.25
☐ 508	Art Fowler	16.00	7.25
☐ 509	Norm Cash	65.00	29.00
☐ 510	Yankees Team	125.00	25.00
	(Checklist on back)		
☐ 511	George Susce	16.00	7.25
☐ 512	George Altman	16.00	7.25
☐ 513	Tommy Carroll	16.00	7.25
☐ 514	Bob Gibson	250.00	110.00
☐ 515	Harmon Killebrew	125.00	55.00
☐ 516	Mike Garcia	20.00	9.00
☐ 517	Joe Koppe	16.00	7.25
☐ 518	Mike Cuellar UER	30.00	13.50
	(Sic, Cuellar)		
☐ 519	Pete Runnels	20.00	9.00
	Dick Gernert		
	Frank Malzone		
☐ 520	Don Elston	16.00	7.25
☐ 521	Gary Geiger	16.00	7.25
☐ 522	Gene Snyder	16.00	7.25
☐ 523	Harry Bright	16.00	7.25
☐ 524	Larry Osborne	16.00	7.25
☐ 525	Jim Coates	20.00	9.00
☐ 526	Bob Speake	16.00	7.25
☐ 527	Solly Hemus	16.00	7.25
☐ 528	Pirates Team	65.00	13.00
	(Checklist on back)		
☐ 529	George Bamberger	25.00	11.00
☐ 530	Wally Moon	16.00	7.25
☐ 531	Ray Webster	16.00	7.25
☐ 532	Mark Freeman	16.00	7.25
☐ 533	Darrell Johnson	20.00	9.00
☐ 534	Faye Throneberry	16.00	7.25
☐ 535	Ruben Gomez	16.00	7.25

☐ 536	Danny Kravitz	16.00	7.25
☐ 537	Rudolph Arias	16.00	7.25
☐ 538	Chick King	16.00	7.25
☐ 539	Gary Blaylock	16.00	7.25
☐ 540	Willie Miranda	16.00	7.25
☐ 541	Bob Thurman	16.00	7.25
☐ 542	Jim Perry	30.00	13.50
☐ 543	Bob Skinner	175.00	80.00
	Bill Virdon		
	Roberto Clemente		
☐ 544	Lee Tate	16.00	7.25
☐ 545	Tom Morgan	16.00	7.25
☐ 546	Al Schroll	16.00	7.25
☐ 547	Jim Baxes	16.00	7.25
☐ 548	Elmer Singleton	16.00	7.25
☐ 549	Howie Nunn	16.00	7.25
☐ 550	Roy Campanella	160.00	70.00
	(Symbol of Courage)		
☐ 551	Fred Haney AS MG	16.00	7.25
☐ 552	Casey Stengel AS MG	30.00	13.50
☐ 553	Orlando Cepeda AS	25.00	11.00
☐ 554	Bill Skowron AS	25.00	11.00
☐ 555	Bill Mazeroski AS	25.00	11.00
☐ 556	Nellie Fox AS	40.00	18.00
☐ 557	Ken Boyer AS	25.00	11.00
☐ 558	Frank Malzone AS	16.00	7.25
☐ 559	Ernie Banks AS	65.00	29.00
☐ 560	Luis Aparicio AS	30.00	13.50
☐ 561	Hank Aaron AS	125.00	55.00
☐ 562	Al Kaline AS	65.00	29.00
☐ 563	Willie Mays AS	125.00	55.00
☐ 564	Mickey Mantle AS	300.00	135.00
☐ 565	Wes Covington AS	16.00	7.25
☐ 566	Roy Sievers AS	16.00	7.25
☐ 567	Del Crandall AS	16.00	7.25
☐ 568	Gus Triandos AS	16.00	7.25
☐ 569	Bob Friend AS	16.00	7.25
☐ 570	Bob Turley AS	16.00	7.25
☐ 571	Warren Spahn AS	40.00	18.00
☐ 572	Billy Pierce AS	30.00	9.50

1960 Topps

The cards in this 572-card set measure 2 1/2" by 3 1/2". The 1960 Topps set is the only Topps standard size issue to use a horizontally oriented front. World Series cards appeared for the first time (385 to 391), and there is a Rookie Prospect (RP) series (117-148), the most famous of which is Carl Yastrzemski, and a Sport Magazine All-Star Selection (AS) series (553-572). There are 16 manager cards listed alphabetically from 212 through 227. The 1959 Topps All-Rookie team is featured on cards 316-325. The coaching staff of each team was also afforded their own card in a 16-card subset (455-470). Cards 375 to 440 come with either gray or white backs. There is no price differential for either color back. The high series (507-572) were printed on a more limited basis than the rest of the set. The team cards have series checklists on the reverse. Cards were issued in one-card penny packs and six-card nickel packs. The key Rookie Cards in this set are Jim Kaat, Willie McCovey and Carl Yastrzemski.

	NRMT	VG-E
COMPLETE SET (572)	3500.00	1600.00
COMMON CARD (1-440)	4.00	1.80
MINOR STARS 1-440	6.00	2.70
SEMISTARS 1-440	10.00	4.50
UNLISTED STARS 1-440	15.00	6.75
COMMON CARD (441-506)	7.00	3.10
MINOR STARS 441-506	10.00	4.50
SEMISTARS 441-506	15.00	6.75
UNLISTED STARS 441-506	25.00	11.00
COMMON CARD (507-572)	16.00	7.25
MINOR STARS 507-572	20.00	9.00
SEMISTARS 507-572	25.00	11.00
*UNLISTED DODGER/YANKEE: 1.25X VALUE		
CARDS PRICED IN NM CONDITION		

☐ 1	Early Wynn	30.00	7.50
☐ 2	Roman Mejias	4.00	1.80
☐ 3	Joe Adcock	6.00	2.70
☐ 4	Bob Purkey	4.00	1.80
☐ 5	Wally Moon	6.00	2.70
☐ 6	Lou Berberet	4.00	1.80
☐ 7	Master and Mentor	25.00	11.00
	Willie Mays		
	Bill Rigney MG		
☐ 8	Bud Daley	4.00	1.80
☐ 9	Faye Throneberry	4.00	1.80
☐ 10	Ernie Banks	50.00	22.00
☐ 11	Norm Siebern	4.00	1.80
☐ 12	Milt Pappas	6.00	2.70
☐ 13	Wally Post	6.00	2.70
☐ 14	Jim Grant	6.00	2.70
☐ 15	Pete Runnels	6.00	2.70
☐ 16	Ernie Broglio	6.00	2.70
☐ 17	Johnny Callison	6.00	2.70
☐ 18	Dodgers Team	50.00	10.00
	(Checklist on back)		
☐ 19	Felix Mantilla	4.00	1.80
☐ 20	Roy Face	6.00	2.70
☐ 21	Dutch Dotterer	4.00	1.80
☐ 22	Rocky Bridges	4.00	1.80
☐ 23	Eddie Fisher	4.00	1.80
☐ 24	Dick Gray	4.00	1.80
☐ 25	Roy Sievers	6.00	2.70
☐ 26	Wayne Terwilliger	4.00	1.80
☐ 27	Dick Drott	4.00	1.80
☐ 28	Brooks Robinson	50.00	22.00
☐ 29	Clem Labine	6.00	2.70
☐ 30	Tito Francona	4.00	1.80
☐ 31	Sammy Esposito	4.00	1.80
☐ 32	Sophomore Stalwarts	4.00	1.80
	Jim O'Toole		
	Vada Pinson		
☐ 33	Tom Morgan	4.00	1.80
☐ 34	Sparky Anderson	14.00	6.25
☐ 35	Whitey Ford	50.00	22.00
☐ 36	Russ Nixon	4.00	1.80
☐ 37	Bill Bruton	4.00	1.80
☐ 38	Jerry Casale	4.00	1.80
☐ 39	Earl Averill	4.00	1.80
☐ 40	Joe Cunningham	4.00	1.80
☐ 41	Barry Latman	4.00	1.80
☐ 42	Hobie Landrith	4.00	1.80
☐ 43	Senators Team	9.00	1.80
	(Checklist on back)		
☐ 44	Bobby Locke	4.00	1.80
☐ 45	Roy McMillan	6.00	2.70
☐ 46	Jerry Fisher	4.00	1.80
☐ 47	Don Zimmer	6.00	2.70
☐ 48	Hal W. Smith	4.00	1.80
☐ 49	Curt Raydon	4.00	1.80
☐ 50	Al Kaline	50.00	22.00
☐ 51	Jim Coates	6.00	2.70
☐ 52	Dave Philley	4.00	1.80
☐ 53	Jackie Brandt	4.00	1.80

#	Card	Price	Price
54	Mike Fornieles	4.00	1.80
55	Bill Mazeroski	10.00	4.50
56	Steve Korcheck	4.00	1.80
57	Win Savers	4.00	1.80
	Turk Lown		
	Gerry Staley		
58	Gino Cimoli	4.00	1.80
59	Juan Pizarro	4.00	1.80
60	Gus Triandos	6.00	2.70
61	Eddie Kasko	4.00	1.80
62	Roger Craig	6.00	2.70
63	George Strickland	4.00	1.80
64	Jack Meyer	4.00	1.80
65	Elston Howard	7.00	3.10
66	Bob Trowbridge	4.00	1.80
67	Jose Pagan	4.00	1.80
68	Dave Hillman	4.00	1.80
69	Billy Goodman	6.00	2.70
70	Lew Burdette	6.00	2.70
71	Marty Keough	4.00	1.80
72	Tigers Team	20.00	4.00
	(Checklist on back)		
73	Bob Gibson	50.00	22.00
74	Walt Moryn	4.00	1.80
75	Vic Power	6.00	2.70
76	Bill Fischer	4.00	1.80
77	Hank Foiles	4.00	1.80
78	Bob Grim	4.00	1.80
79	Walt Dropo	4.00	1.80
80	Johnny Antonelli	6.00	2.70
81	Russ Snyder	4.00	1.80
82	Ruben Gomez	4.00	1.80
83	Tony Kubek	7.00	3.10
84	Hal R. Smith	4.00	1.80
85	Frank Lary	6.00	2.70
86	Dick Gernert	4.00	1.80
87	John Romonosky	4.00	1.80
88	John Roseboro	6.00	2.70
89	Hal Brown	4.00	1.80
90	Bobby Avila	4.00	1.80
91	Bennie Daniels	4.00	1.80
92	Whitey Herzog	6.00	2.70
93	Art Schult	4.00	1.80
94	Leo Kiely	4.00	1.80
95	Frank Thomas	6.00	2.70
96	Ralph Terry	6.00	2.70
97	Ted Lepcio	4.00	1.80
98	Gordon Jones	4.00	1.80
99	Lenny Green	4.00	1.80
100	Nellie Fox	20.00	9.00
101	Bob Miller	4.00	1.80
102	Kent Hadley	4.00	1.80
103	Dick Farrell	6.00	2.70
104	Dick Schofield	6.00	2.70
105	Larry Sherry	6.00	2.70
106	Billy Gardner	4.00	1.80
107	Carlton Willey	4.00	1.80
108	Pete Daley	4.00	1.80
109	Clete Boyer	6.00	2.70
110	Cal McLish	4.00	1.80
111	Vic Wertz	6.00	2.70
112	Jack Harshman	4.00	1.80
113	Bob Skinner	4.00	1.80
114	Ken Aspromonte	4.00	1.80
115	Fork and Knuckler	7.00	3.10
	Roy Face		
	Hoyt Wilhelm		
116	Jim Rivera	4.00	1.80
117	Tom Borland RP	4.00	1.80
118	Bob Bruce RP	4.00	1.80
119	Chico Cardenas RP	6.00	2.70
120	Duke Carmel RP	4.00	1.80
121	Camilo Carreon RP	4.00	1.80
122	Don Dillard RP	4.00	1.80
123	Dan Dobbek RP	4.00	1.80
124	Jim Donohue RP	4.00	1.80
125	Dick Ellsworth RP	6.00	2.70
126	Chuck Estrada RP	4.00	1.80
127	Ron Hansen RP	6.00	2.70
128	Bill Harris RP	4.00	1.80
129	Bob Hartman RP	4.00	1.80
130	Frank Herrera RP	4.00	1.80
131	Ed Hobaugh RP	4.00	1.80
132	Frank Howard RP	25.00	11.00
133	Manuel Javier RP	6.00	2.70
	(Sic, Julian)		
134	Deron Johnson RP	6.00	2.70
135	Ken Johnson RP	4.00	1.80
136	Jim Kaat RP	40.00	18.00
137	Lou Klimchock RP	4.00	1.80
138	Art Mahaffey RP	6.00	2.70
139	Carl Mathias RP	4.00	1.80
140	Julio Navarro RP	4.00	1.80
141	Jim Proctor RP	4.00	1.80
142	Bill Short RP	4.00	1.80
143	Al Spangler RP	4.00	1.80
144	Al Stieglitz RP	4.00	1.80
145	Jim Umbricht RP	4.00	1.80
146	Ted Wieand RP	4.00	1.80
147	Bob Will RP	4.00	1.80
148	Carl Yastrzemski RP	125.00	55.00
149	Bob Nieman	4.00	1.80
150	Billy Pierce	6.00	2.70
151	Giants Team	9.00	1.80
	(Checklist on back)		
152	Gail Harris	4.00	1.80
153	Bobby Thomson	6.00	2.70
154	Jim Davenport	6.00	2.70
155	Charlie Neal	6.00	2.70
156	Art Ceccarelli	4.00	1.80
157	Rocky Nelson	6.00	2.70
158	Wes Covington	6.00	2.70
159	Jim Piersall	6.00	2.70
160	Rival All-Stars	140.00	65.00
	Mickey Mantle		
	Ken Boyer		
161	Ray Narleski	4.00	1.80
162	Sammy Taylor	4.00	1.80
163	Hector Lopez	6.00	2.70
164	Reds Team	9.00	1.80
	(Checklist on back)		
165	Jack Sanford	6.00	2.70
166	Chuck Essegian	4.00	1.80
167	Valmy Thomas	4.00	1.80
168	Alex Grammas	4.00	1.80
169	Jake Striker	4.00	1.80
170	Del Crandall	6.00	2.70
171	Johnny Groth	4.00	1.80
172	Willie Kirkland	4.00	1.80
173	Billy Martin	20.00	9.00
174	Indians Team	9.00	1.80
	(Checklist on back)		
175	Pedro Ramos	4.00	1.80
176	Vada Pinson	6.00	2.70
177	Johnny Kucks	4.00	1.80
178	Woody Held	4.00	1.80
179	Rip Coleman	4.00	1.80
180	Harry Simpson	4.00	1.80
181	Billy Loes	6.00	2.70
182	Glen Hobbie	4.00	1.80
183	Eli Grba	4.00	1.80
184	Gary Geiger	4.00	1.80
185	Jim Owens	4.00	1.80
186	Dave Sisler	4.00	1.80
187	Jay Hook	4.00	1.80
188	Dick Williams	6.00	2.70
189	Don McMahon	4.00	1.80
190	Gene Woodling	6.00	2.70
191	Johnny Klippstein	4.00	1.80
192	Danny O'Connell	4.00	1.80
193	Dick Hyde	4.00	1.80
194	Bobby Gene Smith	4.00	1.80
195	Lindy McDaniel	6.00	2.70
196	Andy Carey	6.00	2.70
197	Ron Kline	4.00	1.80
198	Jerry Lynch	6.00	2.70
199	Dick Donovan	6.00	2.70
200	Willie Mays	90.00	40.00
201	Larry Osborne	4.00	1.80
202	Fred Kipp	4.00	1.80
203	Sammy White	4.00	1.80
204	Ryne Duren	6.00	2.70
205	Johnny Logan	6.00	2.70
206	Claude Osteen	6.00	2.70
207	Bob Boyd	4.00	1.80
208	White Sox Team	9.00	1.80
	(Checklist on back)		
209	Ron Blackburn	4.00	1.80
210	Harmon Killebrew	25.00	11.00
211	Taylor Phillips	4.00	1.80
212	Walter Alston MG	12.00	5.50
213	Chuck Dressen MG	6.00	2.70
214	Jimmy Dykes MG	6.00	2.70
215	Bob Elliott MG	6.00	2.70
216	Joe Gordon MG	6.00	2.70
217	Charlie Grimm MG	6.00	2.70
218	Solly Hemus MG	4.00	1.80
219	Fred Hutchinson MG	6.00	2.70
220	Billy Jurges MG	4.00	1.80
221	Cookie Lavagetto MG	4.00	1.80
222	Al Lopez MG	6.00	2.70
223	Danny Murtaugh MG	6.00	2.70
224	Paul Richards MG	6.00	2.70
225	Bill Rigney MG	4.00	1.80
226	Eddie Sawyer MG	4.00	1.80
227	Casey Stengel MG	15.00	6.75
228	Ernie Johnson	6.00	2.70
229	Joe M. Morgan	4.00	1.80
230	Mound Magicians	12.00	5.50
	Lou Burdette		
	Warren Spahn		
	Bob Buhl		
231	Hal Naragon	4.00	1.80
232	Jim Busby	4.00	1.80
233	Don Elston	4.00	1.80
234	Don Demeter	4.00	1.80
235	Gus Bell	6.00	2.70
236	Dick Ricketts	4.00	1.80
237	Elmer Valo	4.00	1.80
238	Danny Kravitz	4.00	1.80
239	Joe Shipley	4.00	1.80
240	Luis Aparicio	15.00	6.75
241	Albie Pearson	6.00	2.70
242	Cardinals Team	9.00	1.80
	(Checklist on back)		
243	Bubba Phillips	4.00	1.80
244	Hal Griggs	4.00	1.80
245	Eddie Yost	6.00	2.70
246	Lee Maye	6.00	2.70
247	Gil McDougald	6.00	2.70
248	Del Rice	4.00	1.80
249	Earl Wilson	6.00	2.70
250	Stan Musial	80.00	36.00
251	Bob Malkmus	4.00	1.80
252	Ray Herbert	4.00	1.80
253	Eddie Bressoud	4.00	1.80
254	Arnie Portocarrero	4.00	1.80
255	Jim Gilliam	6.00	2.70
256	Dick Brown	4.00	1.80
257	Gordy Coleman	6.00	2.70
258	Dick Groat	6.00	2.70
259	George Altman	4.00	1.80
260	Power Plus	14.00	6.25
	Rocky Colavito		
	Tito Francona		
261	Pete Burnside	4.00	1.80
262	Hank Bauer	6.00	2.70
263	Darrell Johnson	4.00	1.80
264	Robin Roberts	15.00	6.75
265	Rip Repulski	4.00	1.80
266	Joey Jay	6.00	2.70
267	Jim Marshall	4.00	1.80
268	Al Worthington	4.00	1.80
269	Gene Green	4.00	1.80
270	Bob Turley	6.00	2.70
271	Julio Becquer	4.00	1.80
272	Fred Green	6.00	2.70
273	Neil Chrisley	4.00	1.80
274	Tom Acker	4.00	1.80
275	Curt Flood	6.00	2.70
276	Ken McBride	4.00	1.80
277	Harry Bright	4.00	1.80
278	Stan Williams	6.00	2.70
279	Chuck Tanner	6.00	2.70
280	Frank Sullivan	4.00	1.80
281	Ray Boone	6.00	2.70
282	Joe Nuxhall	6.00	2.70
283	John Blanchard	6.00	2.70
284	Don Gross	4.00	1.80
285	Harry Anderson	4.00	1.80
286	Ray Semproch	4.00	1.80
287	Felipe Alou	6.00	2.70
288	Bob Mabe	4.00	1.80
289	Willie Jones	4.00	1.80
290	Jerry Lumpe	4.00	1.80
291	Bob Keegan	4.00	1.80
292	Dodger Backstops	6.00	2.70
	Joe Pignatano		

John Roseboro

☐ 293	Gene Conley	6.00	2.70
☐ 294	Tony Taylor	6.00	2.70
☐ 295	Gil Hodges	20.00	9.00
☐ 296	Nelson Chittum	4.00	1.80
☐ 297	Reno Bertoia	4.00	1.80
☐ 298	George Witt	4.00	1.80
☐ 299	Earl Torgeson	4.00	1.80
☐ 300	Hank Aaron	80.00	36.00
☐ 301	Jerry Davie	4.00	1.80
☐ 302	Phillies Team	9.00	1.80
	(Checklist on back)		
☐ 303	Billy O'Dell	4.00	1.80
☐ 304	Joe Ginsberg	4.00	1.80
☐ 305	Richie Ashburn	20.00	9.00
☐ 306	Frank Baumann	4.00	1.80
☐ 307	Gene Oliver	4.00	1.80
☐ 308	Dick Hall	4.00	1.80
☐ 309	Bob Hale	4.00	1.80
☐ 310	Frank Malzone	6.00	2.70
☐ 311	Raul Sanchez	4.00	1.80
☐ 312	Charley Lau	6.00	2.70
☐ 313	Turk Lown	4.00	1.80
☐ 314	Chico Fernandez	4.00	1.80
☐ 315	Bobby Shantz	6.00	2.70
☐ 316	Willie McCovey	115.00	52.50
☐ 317	Pumpsie Green	6.00	2.70
☐ 318	Jim Baxes	6.00	2.70
☐ 319	Joe Koppe	6.00	2.70
☐ 320	Bob Allison	6.00	2.70
☐ 321	Ron Fairly	6.00	2.70
☐ 322	Willie Tasby	6.00	2.70
☐ 323	John Romano	6.00	2.70
☐ 324	Jim Perry	6.00	2.70
☐ 325	Jim O'Toole	6.00	2.70
☐ 326	Bob Clemente	225.00	100.00
☐ 327	Ray Sadecki	4.00	1.80
☐ 328	Earl Battey	4.00	1.80
☐ 329	Zack Monroe	4.00	1.80
☐ 330	Harvey Kuenn	6.00	2.70
☐ 331	Henry Mason	4.00	1.80
☐ 332	Yankees Team	80.00	16.00
	(Checklist on back)		
☐ 333	Danny McDevitt	4.00	1.80
☐ 334	Ted Abernathy	4.00	1.80
☐ 335	Red Schoendienst	12.00	5.50
☐ 336	Ike Delock	4.00	1.80
☐ 337	Cal Neeman	4.00	1.80
☐ 338	Ray Monzant	4.00	1.80
☐ 339	Harry Chiti	4.00	1.80
☐ 340	Harvey Haddix	6.00	2.70
☐ 341	Carroll Hardy	4.00	1.80
☐ 342	Casey Wise	4.00	1.80
☐ 343	Sandy Koufax	175.00	80.00
☐ 344	Clint Courtney	4.00	1.80
☐ 345	Don Newcombe	6.00	2.70
☐ 346	J.C. Martin UER	6.00	2.70
	(Face actually Gary Peters)		
☐ 347	Ed Bouchee	4.00	1.80
☐ 348	Barry Shetrone	4.00	1.80
☐ 349	Moe Drabowsky	6.00	2.70
☐ 350	Mickey Mantle	475.00	210.00
☐ 351	Don Nottebart	4.00	1.80
☐ 352	Cincy Clouters	8.00	3.60
	Gus Bell		
	Frank Robinson		
	Jerry Lynch		
☐ 353	Don Larsen	6.00	2.70
☐ 354	Bob Lillis	4.00	1.80
☐ 355	Bill White	6.00	2.70
☐ 356	Joe Amalfitano	4.00	1.80
☐ 357	Al Schroll	4.00	1.80
☐ 358	Joe DeMaestri	4.00	1.80
☐ 359	Buddy Gilbert	4.00	1.80
☐ 360	Herb Score	6.00	2.70
☐ 361	Bob Oldis	4.00	1.80
☐ 362	Russ Kemmerer	4.00	1.80
☐ 363	Gene Stephens	4.00	1.80
☐ 364	Paul Foytack	4.00	1.80
☐ 365	Minnie Minoso	7.00	3.10
☐ 366	Dallas Green	8.00	3.60
☐ 367	Bill Tuttle	4.00	1.80
☐ 368	Daryl Spencer	4.00	1.80
☐ 369	Billy Hoeft	4.00	1.80
☐ 370	Bill Skowron	7.00	3.10
☐ 371	Bud Byerly	4.00	1.80
☐ 372	Frank House	4.00	1.80
☐ 373	Don Hoak	6.00	2.70
☐ 374	Bob Buhl	6.00	2.70
☐ 375	Dale Long	6.00	2.70
☐ 376	John Briggs	4.00	1.80
☐ 377	Roger Maris	80.00	36.00
☐ 378	Stu Miller	6.00	2.70
☐ 379	Red Wilson	4.00	1.80
☐ 380	Bob Shaw	4.00	1.80
☐ 381	Braves Team	9.00	1.80
	(Checklist on back)		
☐ 382	Ted Bowsfield	4.00	1.80
☐ 383	Leon Wagner	4.00	1.80
☐ 384	Don Cardwell	4.00	1.80
☐ 385	Charlie Neal WS	6.00	2.70
☐ 386	Charlie Neal WS	6.00	2.70
☐ 387	Carl Furillo WS	6.00	2.70
☐ 388	Gil Hodges WS	10.00	4.50
☐ 389	Luis Aparicio WS	12.00	5.50
	Maury Wills		
☐ 390	World Series Game 6	6.00	2.70
☐ 391	World Series Summary	6.00	2.70
	The Champs Celebrate		
☐ 392	Tex Clevenger	4.00	1.80
☐ 393	Smoky Burgess	6.00	2.70
☐ 394	Norm Larker	6.00	2.70
☐ 395	Hoyt Wilhelm	15.00	6.75
☐ 396	Steve Bilko	4.00	1.80
☐ 397	Don Blasingame	4.00	1.80
☐ 398	Mike Cuellar	6.00	2.70
☐ 399	Young Hill Stars	6.00	2.70
	Milt Pappas		
	Jack Fisher		
	Jerry Walker		
☐ 400	Rocky Colavito	20.00	9.00
☐ 401	Bob Duliba	4.00	1.80
☐ 402	Dick Stuart	6.00	2.70
☐ 403	Ed Sadowski	4.00	1.80
☐ 404	Bob Rush	4.00	1.80
☐ 405	Bobby Richardson	14.00	6.25
☐ 406	Billy Klaus	4.00	1.80
☐ 407	Gary Peters UER	6.00	2.70
	(Face actually J.C. Martin)		
☐ 408	Carl Furillo	6.00	2.70
☐ 409	Ron Samford	4.00	1.80
☐ 410	Sam Jones	6.00	2.70
☐ 411	Ed Bailey	4.00	1.80
☐ 412	Bob Anderson	4.00	1.80
☐ 413	Athletics Team	9.00	1.80
	(Checklist on back)		
☐ 414	Don Williams	4.00	1.80
☐ 415	Bob Cerv	4.00	1.80
☐ 416	Humberto Robinson	4.00	1.80
☐ 417	Chuck Cottier	4.00	1.80
☐ 418	Don Mossi	6.00	2.70
☐ 419	George Crowe	4.00	1.80
☐ 420	Eddie Mathews	30.00	13.50
☐ 421	Duke Maas	4.00	1.80
☐ 422	John Powers	4.00	1.80
☐ 423	Ed Fitzgerald	4.00	1.80
☐ 424	Pete Whisenant	4.00	1.80
☐ 425	Johnny Podres	6.00	2.70
☐ 426	Ron Jackson	4.00	1.80
☐ 427	Al Grunwald	4.00	1.80
☐ 428	Al Smith	4.00	1.80
☐ 429	AL Kings	12.00	5.50
	Nellie Fox		
	Harvey Kuenn		
☐ 430	Art Ditmar	4.00	1.80
☐ 431	Andre Rodgers	4.00	1.80
☐ 432	Chuck Stobbs	4.00	1.80
☐ 433	Irv Noren	4.00	1.80
☐ 434	Brooks Lawrence	4.00	1.80
☐ 435	Gene Freese	4.00	1.80
☐ 436	Marv Throneberry	6.00	2.70
☐ 437	Bob Friend	6.00	2.70
☐ 438	Jim Coker	4.00	1.80
☐ 439	Tom Brewer	4.00	1.80
☐ 440	Jim Lemon	6.00	2.70
☐ 441	Gary Bell	7.00	3.10
☐ 442	Joe Pignatano	7.00	3.10
☐ 443	Charlie Maxwell	7.00	3.10
☐ 444	Jerry Kindall	7.00	3.10
☐ 445	Warren Spahn	50.00	22.00
☐ 446	Ellis Burton	7.00	3.10
☐ 447	Ray Moore	7.00	3.10
☐ 448	Jim Gentile	20.00	9.00
☐ 449	Jim Brosnan	7.00	3.10
☐ 450	Orlando Cepeda	18.00	8.00
☐ 451	Curt Simmons	7.00	3.10
☐ 452	Ray Webster	7.00	3.10
☐ 453	Vern Law	10.00	4.50
☐ 454	Hal Woodeshick	7.00	3.10
☐ 455	Baltimore Coaches	7.00	3.10
	Eddie Robinson		
	Harry Brecheen		
	Luman Harris		
☐ 456	Red Sox Coaches	10.00	4.50
	Rudy York		
	Billy Herman		
	Sal Maglie		
	Del Baker		
☐ 457	Cubs Coaches	7.00	3.10
	Charlie Root		
	Lou Klein		
	Elvin Tappe		
☐ 458	White Sox Coaches	7.00	3.10
	Johnny Cooney		
	Don Gutteridge		
	Tony Cuccinello		
	Ray Berres		
☐ 459	Reds Coaches	7.00	3.10
	Reggie Otero		
	Cot Deal		
	Wally Moses		
☐ 460	Indians Coaches	10.00	4.50
	Mel Harder		
	Jo-Jo White		
	Bob Lemon		
	Ralph(Red) Kress		
☐ 461	Tigers Coaches	10.00	4.50
	Tom Ferrick		
	Luke Appling		
	Billy Hitchcock		
☐ 462	Athletics Coaches	7.00	3.10
	Fred Fitzsimmons		
	Don Heffner		
	Walker Cooper		
☐ 463	Dodgers Coaches	7.00	3.10
	Bobby Bragan		
	Pete Reiser		
	Joe Becker		
	Greg Mulleavy		
☐ 464	Braves Coaches	7.00	3.10
	Bob Scheffing		
	Whitlow Wyatt		
	Andy Pafko		
	George Myatt		
☐ 465	Yankees Coaches	12.00	5.50
	Bill Dickey		
	Ralph Houk		
	Frank Crosetti		
	Ed Lopat		
☐ 466	Phillies Coaches	7.00	3.10
	Ken Silvestri		
	Dick Carter		
	Andy Cohen		
☐ 467	Pirates Coaches	7.00	3.10
	Mickey Vernon		
	Frank Oceak		
	Sam Narron		
	Bill Burwell		
☐ 468	Cardinals Coaches	7.00	3.10
	Johnny Keane		
	Howie Pollet		
	Ray Katt		
	Harry Walker		
☐ 469	Giants Coaches	7.00	3.10
	Wes Westrum		
	Salty Parker		
	Bill Posedel		
☐ 470	Senators Coaches	7.00	3.10
	Bob Swift		
	Ellis Clary		
	Sam Mele		
☐ 471	Ned Garver	7.00	3.10
☐ 472	Alvin Dark	7.00	3.10
☐ 473	Al Cicotte	7.00	3.10
☐ 474	Haywood Sullivan	7.00	3.10
☐ 475	Don Drysdale	35.00	16.00

☐ 476 Lou Johnson	7.00	3.10
☐ 477 Don Ferrarese	7.00	3.10
☐ 478 Frank Torre	7.00	3.10
☐ 479 Georges Maranda	7.00	3.10
☐ 480 Yogi Berra	70.00	32.00
☐ 481 Wes Stock	7.00	3.10
☐ 482 Frank Bolling	7.00	3.10
☐ 483 Camilo Pascual	7.00	3.10
☐ 484 Pirates Team	50.00	10.00
(Checklist on back)		
☐ 485 Ken Boyer	14.00	6.25
☐ 486 Bobby Del Greco	7.00	3.10
☐ 487 Tom Sturdivant	7.00	3.10
☐ 488 Norm Cash	20.00	9.00
☐ 489 Steve Ridzik	7.00	3.10
☐ 490 Frank Robinson	50.00	22.00
☐ 491 Mel Roach	7.00	3.10
☐ 492 Larry Jackson	7.00	3.10
☐ 493 Duke Snider	50.00	22.00
☐ 494 Orioles Team	25.00	5.00
(Checklist on back)		
☐ 495 Sherm Lollar	7.00	3.10
☐ 496 Bill Virdon	10.00	4.50
☐ 497 John Tsitouris	7.00	3.10
☐ 498 Al Pilarcik	7.00	3.10
☐ 499 Johnny James	7.00	3.10
☐ 500 Johnny Temple	7.00	3.10
☐ 501 Bob Schmidt	7.00	3.10
☐ 502 Jim Bunning	20.00	9.00
☐ 503 Don Lee	7.00	3.10
☐ 504 Seth Morehead	7.00	3.10
☐ 505 Ted Kluszewski	20.00	9.00
☐ 506 Lee Walls	7.00	3.10
☐ 507 Dick Stigman	16.00	7.25
☐ 508 Billy Consolo	16.00	7.25
☐ 509 Tommy Davis	25.00	11.00
☐ 510 Gerry Staley	16.00	7.25
☐ 511 Ken Walters	16.00	7.25
☐ 512 Joe Gibbon	16.00	7.25
☐ 513 Chicago Cubs	30.00	6.00
Team Card		
(Checklist on back)		
☐ 514 Steve Barber	16.00	7.25
☐ 515 Stan Lopata	16.00	7.25
☐ 516 Marty Kutyna	16.00	7.25
☐ 517 Charlie James	16.00	7.25
☐ 518 Tony Gonzalez	16.00	7.25
☐ 519 Ed Roebuck	16.00	7.25
☐ 520 Don Buddin	16.00	7.25
☐ 521 Mike Lee	16.00	7.25
☐ 522 Ken Hunt	20.00	9.00
☐ 523 Clay Dalrymple	16.00	7.25
☐ 524 Bill Henry	16.00	7.25
☐ 525 Marv Breeding	16.00	7.25
☐ 526 Paul Giel	16.00	7.25
☐ 527 Jose Valdivielso	16.00	7.25
☐ 528 Ben Johnson	16.00	7.25
☐ 529 Norm Sherry	20.00	9.00
☐ 530 Mike McCormick	16.00	7.25
☐ 531 Sandy Amoros	16.00	7.25
☐ 532 Mike Garcia	16.00	7.25
☐ 533 Lu Clinton	16.00	7.25
☐ 534 Ken MacKenzie	16.00	7.25
☐ 535 Whitey Lockman	16.00	7.25
☐ 536 Wynn Hawkins	16.00	7.25
☐ 537 Boston Red Sox	30.00	6.00
Team Card		
(Checklist on back)		
☐ 538 Frank Barnes	16.00	7.25
☐ 539 Gene Baker	16.00	7.25
☐ 540 Jerry Walker	16.00	7.25
☐ 541 Tony Curry	16.00	7.25
☐ 542 Ken Hamlin	16.00	7.25
☐ 543 Elio Chacon	16.00	7.25
☐ 544 Bill Monbouquette	16.00	7.25
☐ 545 Carl Sawatski	16.00	7.25
☐ 546 Hank Aguirre	16.00	7.25
☐ 547 Bob Aspromonte	16.00	7.25
☐ 548 Don Mincher	16.00	7.25
☐ 549 John Buzhardt	16.00	7.25
☐ 550 Jim Landis	16.00	7.25
☐ 551 Ed Rakow	16.00	7.25
☐ 552 Walt Bond	16.00	7.25
☐ 553 Bill Skowron AS	20.00	9.00
☐ 554 Willie McCovey AS	30.00	13.50
☐ 555 Nellie Fox AS	30.00	13.50

☐ 556 Charlie Neal AS	16.00	7.25
☐ 557 Frank Malzone AS	16.00	7.25
☐ 558 Eddie Mathews AS	30.00	13.50
☐ 559 Luis Aparicio AS	30.00	13.50
☐ 560 Ernie Banks AS	60.00	27.00
☐ 561 Al Kaline AS	60.00	27.00
☐ 562 Joe Cunningham AS	16.00	7.25
☐ 563 Mickey Mantle AS	325.00	145.00
☐ 564 Willie Mays AS	125.00	55.00
☐ 565 Roger Maris AS	80.00	36.00
☐ 566 Hank Aaron AS	115.00	52.50
☐ 567 Sherm Lollar AS	16.00	7.25
☐ 568 Del Crandall AS	16.00	7.25
☐ 569 Camilo Pascual AS	16.00	7.25
☐ 570 Don Drysdale AS	30.00	13.50
☐ 571 Billy Pierce AS	16.00	7.25
☐ 572 Johnny Antonelli AS	30.00	13.50
☐ NNO Iron-on team transfer	4.00	1.80

1961 Topps

The cards in this 587-card set measure 2 1/2" by 3 1/2". In 1961, Topps returned to the vertical obverse format. Introduced for the first time were "League Leaders" (41-50) and separate, numbered checklist cards. Two number 463s exist: the Braves team card carrying that number was meant to be number 426. There are three versions of the second series checklist card number 98; the variations are distinguished by the color of the "CHECKLIST" headline on the front of the card, the color of the printing of the card number on the bottom of the reverse, and the presence of the copyright notice running vertically on the card back. There are two groups of managers (131-139/219-226) as well as separate subsets of World Series cards (306-313), Baseball Thrills (401-410), MVP's of the 1950's (AL 471-478/NL 479-486) and Sporting News All-Stars (566-589). The usual late series scarcity (523-589) exists. Some collectors believe that 61 high numbers are the toughest of all the Topps hi numbers. The set actually totals 587 cards since numbers 587 and 588 were never issued. Cards were issued in one-card penny packs as well as five-card nickel packs. The key Rookie Cards in this set are Juan Marichal, Ron Santo and Billy Williams.

	NRMT	VG-E
COMPLETE SET (587)	4800.00	2200.00
COMMON CARD (1-370)	3.00	1.35

COMMON CARD (371-446)	4.00	1.80
MINOR STARS 1-446	6.00	2.70
SEMISTARS 1-446	8.00	3.60
UNLISTED STARS 1-446	12.00	5.50
COMMON CARD (447-522)	7.00	3.10
MINOR STARS 447-522	10.00	4.50
SEMISTARS 447-522	15.00	6.75
UNLISTED STARS 447-522	25.00	11.00
COMMON CARD (523-589)	30.00	13.50
MINOR STARS 523-589	40.00	18.00
NOT ISSUED (587/588)	30.00	
*UNLISTED DODGER/YANKEE: 1.25X VALUE		
CARDS PRICED IN NM CONDITION		

☐ 1 Dick Groat	30.00	6.00
☐ 2 Roger Maris	150.00	70.00
☐ 3 John Buzhardt	3.00	1.35
☐ 4 Lenny Green	3.00	1.35
☐ 5 John Romano	3.00	1.35
☐ 6 Ed Roebuck	3.00	1.35
☐ 7 White Sox Team	8.00	3.60
☐ 8 Dick Williams	6.00	2.70
☐ 9 Bob Purkey	3.00	1.35
☐ 10 Brooks Robinson	40.00	18.00
☐ 11 Curt Simmons	6.00	2.70
☐ 12 Moe Thacker	3.00	1.35
☐ 13 Chuck Cottier	3.00	1.35
☐ 14 Don Mossi	6.00	2.70
☐ 15 Willie Kirkland	3.00	1.35
☐ 16 Billy Muffett	3.00	1.35
☐ 17 Checklist 1	12.00	2.40
☐ 18 Jim Grant	6.00	2.70
☐ 19 Clete Boyer	7.00	3.10
☐ 20 Robin Roberts	15.00	6.75
☐ 21 Zorro Versalles UER	7.00	3.10
(First name should		
be Zoilo)		
☐ 22 Clem Labine	6.00	2.70
☐ 23 Don Demeter	3.00	1.35
☐ 24 Ken Johnson	3.00	1.35
☐ 25 Reds' Heavy Artillery	8.00	3.60
Vada Pinson		
Gus Bell		
Frank Robinson		
☐ 26 Wes Stock	3.00	1.35
☐ 27 Jerry Kindall	3.00	1.35
☐ 28 Hector Lopez	6.00	2.70
☐ 29 Don Nottebart	3.00	1.35
☐ 30 Nellie Fox	16.00	7.25
☐ 31 Bob Schmidt	3.00	1.35
☐ 32 Ray Sadecki	3.00	1.35
☐ 33 Gary Geiger	3.00	1.35
☐ 34 Wynn Hawkins	3.00	1.35
☐ 35 Ron Santo	40.00	18.00
☐ 36 Jack Kralick	3.00	1.35
☐ 37 Charley Maxwell	6.00	2.70
☐ 38 Bob Lillis	3.00	1.35
☐ 39 Leo Posada	3.00	1.35
☐ 40 Bob Turley	6.00	2.70
☐ 41 NL Batting Leaders	35.00	16.00
Dick Groat		
Norm Larker		
Willie Mays		
Roberto Clemente		
☐ 42 AL Batting Leaders	8.00	3.60
Pete Runnels		
Al Smith		
Minnie Minoso		
Bill Skowron		
☐ 43 NL Home Run Leaders	30.00	13.50
Ernie Banks		
Hank Aaron		
Ed Mathews		
Ken Boyer		
☐ 44 AL Home Run Leaders	120.00	55.00
Mickey Mantle		
Roger Maris		
Jim Lemon		
Rocky Colavito		
☐ 45 NL ERA Leaders	8.00	3.60
Mike McCormick		
Ernie Broglio		
Don Drysdale		
Bob Friend		
Stan Williams		
☐ 46 AL ERA Leaders	8.00	3.60

	Frank Baumann		
	Jim Bunning		
	Art Ditmar		
	Hal Brown		
☐ 47	NL Pitching Leaders	8.00	3.60
	Ernie Broglio		
	Warren Spahn		
	Vern Law		
	Lou Burdette		
☐ 48	AL Pitching Leaders	8.00	3.60
	Chuck Estrada		
	Jim Perry UER		
	(Listed as an Oriole)		
	Bud Daley		
	Art Ditmar		
	Frank Lary		
	Milt Pappas		
☐ 49	NL Strikeout Leaders	20.00	9.00
	Don Drysdale		
	Sandy Koufax		
	Sam Jones		
	Ernie Broglio		
☐ 50	AL Strikeout Leaders	8.00	3.60
	Jim Bunning		
	Pedro Ramos		
	Early Wynn		
	Frank Lary		
☐ 51	Detroit Tigers	8.00	3.60
	Team Card		
☐ 52	George Crowe	3.00	1.35
☐ 53	Russ Nixon	3.00	1.35
☐ 54	Earl Francis	3.00	1.35
☐ 55	Jim Davenport	6.00	2.70
☐ 56	Russ Kemmerer	3.00	1.35
☐ 57	Marv Throneberry	7.00	3.10
☐ 58	Joe Schaffernoth	3.00	1.35
☐ 59	Jim Woods	3.00	1.35
☐ 60	Woody Held	3.00	1.35
☐ 61	Ron Piche	3.00	1.35
☐ 62	Al Pilarcik	3.00	1.35
☐ 63	Jim Kaat	8.00	3.60
☐ 64	Alex Grammas	3.00	1.35
☐ 65	Ted Kluszewski	8.00	3.60
☐ 66	Bill Henry	3.00	1.35
☐ 67	Ossie Virgil	3.00	1.35
☐ 68	Deron Johnson	6.00	2.70
☐ 69	Earl Wilson	6.00	2.70
☐ 70	Bill Virdon	6.00	2.70
☐ 71	Jerry Adair	3.00	1.35
☐ 72	Stu Miller	6.00	2.70
☐ 73	Al Spangler	3.00	1.35
☐ 74	Joe Pignatano	3.00	1.35
☐ 75	Lindy Shows Larry	6.00	2.70
	Lindy McDaniel		
	Larry Jackson		
☐ 76	Harry Anderson	3.00	1.35
☐ 77	Dick Stigman	3.00	1.35
☐ 78	Lee Walls	3.00	1.35
☐ 79	Joe Ginsberg	3.00	1.35
☐ 80	Harmon Killebrew	20.00	9.00
☐ 81	Tracy Stallard	3.00	1.35
☐ 82	Joe Christopher	3.00	1.35
☐ 83	Bob Bruce	3.00	1.35
☐ 84	Lee Maye	3.00	1.35
☐ 85	Jerry Walker	3.00	1.35
☐ 86	Los Angeles Dodgers	8.00	3.60
	Team Card		
☐ 87	Joe Amalfitano	3.00	1.35
☐ 88	Richie Ashburn	16.00	7.25
☐ 89	Billy Martin	16.00	7.25
☐ 90	Gerry Staley	3.00	1.35
☐ 91	Walt Moryn	3.00	1.35
☐ 92	Hal Naragon	3.00	1.35
☐ 93	Tony Gonzalez	3.00	1.35
☐ 94	Johnny Kucks	3.00	1.35
☐ 95	Norm Cash	7.00	3.10
☐ 96	Billy O'Dell	3.00	1.35
☐ 97	Jerry Lynch	6.00	2.70
☐ 98A	Checklist 2	70.00	14.00
	(Red 'Checklist'		
	98 black on white)		
☐ 98B	Checklist 2	70.00	14.00
	(Yellow 'Checklist'		
	98 black on white)		
☐ 98C	Checklist 2	70.00	14.00
	(Yellow 'Checklist'		
	98 white on black		
	no copyright)		
	(66 HR's)		
☐ 99	Don Buddin UER	3.00	1.35
☐ 100	Harvey Haddix	7.00	3.10
☐ 101	Bubba Phillips	3.00	1.35
☐ 102	Gene Stephens	3.00	1.35
☐ 103	Ruben Amaro	3.00	1.35
☐ 104	John Blanchard	6.00	2.70
☐ 105	Carl Willey	3.00	1.35
☐ 106	Whitey Herzog	3.00	1.35
☐ 107	Seth Morehead	3.00	1.35
☐ 108	Dan Dobbek	3.00	1.35
☐ 109	Johnny Podres	7.00	3.10
☐ 110	Vada Pinson	7.00	3.10
☐ 111	Jack Meyer	3.00	1.35
☐ 112	Chico Fernandez	3.00	1.35
☐ 113	Mike Fornieles	3.00	1.35
☐ 114	Hobie Landrith	3.00	1.35
☐ 115	Johnny Antonelli	6.00	2.70
☐ 116	Joe DeMaestri	3.00	1.35
☐ 117	Dale Long	6.00	2.70
☐ 118	Chris Cannizzaro	3.00	1.35
☐ 119	A's Big Armor	6.00	2.70
	Norm Siebern		
	Hank Bauer		
	Jerry Lumpe		
☐ 120	Eddie Mathews	30.00	13.50
☐ 121	Eli Grba	6.00	2.70
☐ 122	Chicago Cubs	8.00	3.60
	Team Card		
☐ 123	Billy Gardner	3.00	1.35
☐ 124	J.C. Martin	3.00	1.35
☐ 125	Steve Barber	3.00	1.35
☐ 126	Dick Stuart	6.00	2.70
☐ 127	Ron Kline	3.00	1.35
☐ 128	Rip Repulski	3.00	1.35
☐ 129	Ed Hobaugh	3.00	1.35
☐ 130	Norm Larker	3.00	1.35
☐ 131	Paul Richards MG	6.00	2.70
☐ 132	Al Lopez MG	6.00	2.70
☐ 133	Ralph Houk MG	6.00	2.70
☐ 134	Mickey Vernon MG	6.00	2.70
☐ 135	Fred Hutchinson MG	6.00	2.70
☐ 136	Walter Alston MG	7.00	3.10
☐ 137	Chuck Dressen MG	6.00	2.70
☐ 138	Danny Murtaugh MG	7.00	3.10
☐ 139	Solly Hemus MG	6.00	2.70
☐ 140	Gus Triandos	6.00	2.70
☐ 141	Billy Williams	60.00	27.00
☐ 142	Luis Arroyo	6.00	2.70
☐ 143	Russ Snyder	3.00	1.35
☐ 144	Jim Coker	3.00	1.35
☐ 145	Bob Buhl	6.00	2.70
☐ 146	Marty Keough	3.00	1.35
☐ 147	Ed Rakow	3.00	1.35
☐ 148	Julian Javier	6.00	2.70
☐ 149	Bob Oldis	3.00	1.35
☐ 150	Willie Mays	100.00	45.00
☐ 151	Jim Donohue	3.00	1.35
☐ 152	Earl Torgeson	3.00	1.35
☐ 153	Don Lee	3.00	1.35
☐ 154	Bobby Del Greco	3.00	1.35
☐ 155	Johnny Temple	6.00	2.70
☐ 156	Ken Hunt	6.00	2.70
☐ 157	Cal McLish	3.00	1.35
☐ 158	Pete Daley	3.00	1.35
☐ 159	Orioles Team	8.00	3.60
☐ 160	Whitey Ford UER	40.00	18.00
	(Incorrectly listed		
	as 5'0" tall)		
☐ 161	Sherman Jones UER	3.00	1.35
	(Photo actually		
	Eddie Fisher)		
☐ 162	Jay Hook	3.00	1.35
☐ 163	Ed Sadowski	3.00	1.35
☐ 164	Felix Mantilla	3.00	1.35
☐ 165	Gino Cimoli	3.00	1.35
☐ 166	Danny Kravitz	3.00	1.35
☐ 167	San Francisco Giants	8.00	3.60
	Team Card		
☐ 168	Tommy Davis	7.00	3.10
☐ 169	Don Elston	3.00	1.35
☐ 170	Al Smith	3.00	1.35
☐ 171	Paul Foytack	3.00	1.35
☐ 172	Don Dillard	3.00	1.35
☐ 173	Beantown Bombers	6.00	2.70
	Frank Malzone		
	Vic Wertz		
	Jackie Jensen		
☐ 174	Ray Semproch	3.00	1.35
☐ 175	Gene Freese	3.00	1.35
☐ 176	Ken Aspromonte	3.00	1.35
☐ 177	Don Larsen	7.00	3.10
☐ 178	Bob Nieman	3.00	1.35
☐ 179	Joe Koppe	3.00	1.35
☐ 180	Bobby Richardson	12.00	5.50
☐ 181	Fred Green	3.00	1.35
☐ 182	Dave Nicholson	3.00	1.35
☐ 183	Andre Rodgers	3.00	1.35
☐ 184	Steve Bilko	6.00	2.70
☐ 185	Herb Score	7.00	3.10
☐ 186	Elmer Valo	6.00	2.70
☐ 187	Billy Klaus	3.00	1.35
☐ 188	Jim Marshall	3.00	1.35
☐ 189A	Checklist 3	70.00	14.00
	(Copyright symbol		
	almost adjacent to		
	263 Ken Hamlin)		
☐ 189B	Checklist 3	70.00	14.00
	(Copyright symbol		
	adjacent to		
	264 Glen Hobbie)		
☐ 190	Stan Williams	6.00	2.70
☐ 191	Mike de la Hoz	3.00	1.35
☐ 192	Dick Brown	3.00	1.35
☐ 193	Gene Conley	6.00	2.70
☐ 194	Gordy Coleman	6.00	2.70
☐ 195	Jerry Casale	3.00	1.35
☐ 196	Ed Bouchee	3.00	1.35
☐ 197	Dick Hall	3.00	1.35
☐ 198	Carl Sawatski	3.00	1.35
☐ 199	Bob Boyd	3.00	1.35
☐ 200	Warren Spahn	30.00	13.50
☐ 201	Pete Whisenant	3.00	1.35
☐ 202	Al Neiger	3.00	1.35
☐ 203	Eddie Bressoud	3.00	1.35
☐ 204	Bob Skinner	6.00	2.70
☐ 205	Billy Pierce	6.00	2.70
☐ 206	Gene Green	3.00	1.35
☐ 207	Dodger Southpaws	30.00	13.50
	Sandy Koufax		
	Johnny Podres		
☐ 208	Larry Osborne	3.00	1.35
☐ 209	Ken McBride	3.00	1.35
☐ 210	Pete Runnels	6.00	2.70
☐ 211	Bob Gibson	40.00	18.00
☐ 212	Haywood Sullivan	6.00	2.70
☐ 213	Bill Stafford	3.00	1.35
☐ 214	Danny Murphy	3.00	1.35
☐ 215	Gus Bell	6.00	2.70
☐ 216	Ted Bowsfield	3.00	1.35
☐ 217	Mel Roach	3.00	1.35
☐ 218	Hal Brown	3.00	1.35
☐ 219	Gene Mauch MG	6.00	2.70
☐ 220	Alvin Dark MG	6.00	2.70
☐ 221	Mike Higgins MG	3.00	1.35
☐ 222	Jimmy Dykes MG	6.00	2.70
☐ 223	Bob Scheffing MG	3.00	1.35
☐ 224	Joe Gordon MG	6.00	2.70
☐ 225	Bill Rigney MG	6.00	2.70
☐ 226	Cookie Lavagetto MG	6.00	2.70
☐ 227	Juan Pizarro	3.00	1.35
☐ 228	New York Yankees	70.00	32.00
	Team Card		
☐ 229	Rudy Hernandez	3.00	1.35
☐ 230	Don Hoak	6.00	2.70
☐ 231	Dick Drott	3.00	1.35
☐ 232	Bill White	7.00	3.10
☐ 233	Joey Jay	6.00	2.70
☐ 234	Ted Lepcio	3.00	1.35
☐ 235	Camilo Pascual	6.00	2.70
☐ 236	Don Gile	3.00	1.35
☐ 237	Billy Loes	6.00	2.70
☐ 238	Jim Gilliam	7.00	3.10
☐ 239	Dave Sisler	3.00	1.35
☐ 240	Ron Hansen	3.00	1.35
☐ 241	Al Cicotte	3.00	1.35
☐ 242	Hal Smith	3.00	1.35
☐ 243	Frank Lary	6.00	2.70
☐ 244	Chico Cardenas	6.00	2.70
☐ 245	Joe Adcock	7.00	3.10

246	Bob Davis	3.00	1.35
247	Billy Goodman	6.00	2.70
248	Ed Keegan	3.00	1.35
249	Cincinnati Reds Team Card	6.00	2.70
250	Buc Hill Aces Vern Law Roy Face	6.00	2.70
251	Bill Bruton	3.00	1.35
252	Bill Short	3.00	1.35
253	Sammy Taylor	3.00	1.35
254	Ted Sadowski	3.00	1.35
255	Vic Power	6.00	2.70
256	Billy Hoeft	3.00	1.35
257	Carroll Hardy	3.00	1.35
258	Jack Sanford	6.00	2.70
259	John Schaive	3.00	1.35
260	Don Drysdale	30.00	13.50
261	Charlie Lau	6.00	2.70
262	Tony Curry	3.00	1.35
263	Ken Hamlin	3.00	1.35
264	Glen Hobbie	3.00	1.35
265	Tony Kubek	8.00	3.60
266	Lindy McDaniel	6.00	2.70
267	Norm Siebern	3.00	1.35
268	Ike Delock	3.00	1.35
269	Harry Chiti	3.00	1.35
270	Bob Friend	7.00	3.10
271	Jim Landis	3.00	1.35
272	Tom Morgan	3.00	1.35
273A	Checklist 4 (Copyright symbol adjacent to 336 Don Mincher)	16.00	3.20
273B	Checklist 4 (Copyright symbol adjacent to 339 Gene Baker)	16.00	3.20
274	Gary Bell	3.00	1.35
275	Gene Woodling	6.00	2.70
276	Ray Rippelmeyer	3.00	1.35
277	Hank Foiles	3.00	1.35
278	Don McMahon	3.00	1.35
279	Jose Pagan	3.00	1.35
280	Frank Howard	8.00	3.60
281	Frank Sullivan	3.00	1.35
282	Faye Throneberry	3.00	1.35
283	Bob Anderson	3.00	1.35
284	Dick Gernert	3.00	1.35
285	Sherm Lollar	6.00	2.70
286	George Witt	3.00	1.35
287	Carl Yastrzemski	50.00	22.00
288	Albie Pearson	6.00	2.70
289	Ray Moore	3.00	1.35
290	Stan Musial	100.00	45.00
291	Tex Clevenger	3.00	1.35
292	Jim Baumer	3.00	1.35
293	Tom Sturdivant	3.00	1.35
294	Don Blasingame	3.00	1.35
295	Milt Pappas	6.00	2.70
296	Wes Covington	6.00	2.70
297	Athletics Team	16.00	7.25
298	Jim Golden	3.00	1.35
299	Clay Dalrymple	3.00	1.35
300	Mickey Mantle	500.00	220.00
301	Chet Nichols	3.00	1.35
302	Al Heist	3.00	1.35
303	Gary Peters	6.00	2.70
304	Rocky Nelson	3.00	1.35
305	Mike McCormick	6.00	2.70
306	Bill Virdon WS	8.00	3.60
307	Mickey Mantle WS	100.00	45.00
308	Bobby Richardson WS	12.00	5.50
309	Gino Cimoli WS	8.00	3.60
310	Roy Face WS	8.00	3.60
311	Whitey Ford WS	16.00	7.25
312	Bill Mazeroski WS Mazeroski Homer Wins it	20.00	9.00
313	World Series Summary Pirates Celebrate	16.00	7.25
314	Bob Miller	3.00	1.35
315	Earl Battey	6.00	2.70
316	Bobby Gene Smith	3.00	1.35
317	Jim Brewer	3.00	1.35
318	Danny O'Connell	3.00	1.35
319	Valmy Thomas	3.00	1.35
320	Lou Burdette	7.00	3.10
321	Marv Breeding	3.00	1.35
322	Bill Kunkel	6.00	2.70
323	Sammy Esposito	3.00	1.35
324	Hank Aguirre	3.00	1.35
325	Wally Moon	6.00	2.70
326	Dave Hillman	3.00	1.35
327	Matty Alou	10.00	4.50
328	Jim O'Toole	6.00	2.70
329	Julio Becquer	3.00	1.35
330	Rocky Colavito	20.00	9.00
331	Ned Garver	3.00	1.35
332	Dutch Dotterer UER.. (Photo actually Tommy Dotterer Dutch's brother)	3.00	1.35
333	Fritz Brickell	3.00	1.35
334	Walt Bond	3.00	1.35
335	Frank Bolling	3.00	1.35
336	Don Mincher	6.00	2.70
337	Al's Aces Early Wynn Al Lopez Herb Score	7.00	3.10
338	Don Landrum	3.00	1.35
339	Gene Baker	3.00	1.35
340	Vic Wertz	6.00	2.70
341	Jim Owens	3.00	1.35
342	Clint Courtney	3.00	1.35
343	Earl Robinson	3.00	1.35
344	Sandy Koufax	125.00	55.00
345	Jimmy Piersall	7.00	3.10
346	Howie Nunn	3.00	1.35
347	St. Louis Cardinals Team Card	6.00	2.70
348	Steve Boros	3.00	1.35
349	Danny McDevitt	3.00	1.35
350	Ernie Banks	45.00	20.00
351	Jim King	3.00	1.35
352	Bob Shaw	3.00	1.35
353	Howie Bedell	3.00	1.35
354	Billy Harrell	3.00	1.35
355	Bob Allison	7.00	3.10
356	Ryne Duren	6.00	2.70
357	Daryl Spencer	3.00	1.35
358	Earl Averill	6.00	2.70
359	Dallas Green	3.00	1.35
360	Frank Robinson	40.00	18.00
361A	Checklist 5 (No ad on back)	10.00	2.00
361B	Checklist 5 (Special Feature ad on back)	10.00	2.00
362	Frank Funk	3.00	1.35
363	John Roseboro	7.00	3.10
364	Moe Drabowsky	6.00	2.70
365	Jerry Lumpe	3.00	1.35
366	Eddie Fisher	3.00	1.35
367	Jim Rivera	3.00	1.35
368	Bennie Daniels	3.00	1.35
369	Dave Philley	3.00	1.35
370	Roy Face	6.00	2.70
371	Bill Skowron SP	60.00	27.00
372	Bob Hendley	4.00	1.80
373	Boston Red Sox Team Card	6.00	2.70
374	Paul Giel	4.00	1.80
375	Ken Boyer	10.00	4.50
376	Mike Roarke	4.00	1.80
377	Ruben Gomez	4.00	1.80
378	Wally Post	6.00	2.70
379	Bobby Shantz	4.00	1.80
380	Minnie Minoso	8.00	3.60
381	Dave Wickersham	4.00	1.80
382	Frank Thomas	6.00	2.70
383	Frisco First Liners Mike McCormick Jack Sanford Billy O'Dell	6.00	2.70
384	Chuck Essegian	4.00	1.80
385	Jim Perry	6.00	2.70
386	Joe Hicks	4.00	1.80
387	Duke Maas	4.00	1.80
388	Bob Clemente	200.00	90.00
389	Ralph Terry	6.00	2.70
390	Del Crandall	4.00	2.70
391	Winston Brown	4.00	1.80
392	Reno Bertoia	4.00	1.80
393	Batter Bafflers Don Cardwell Glen Hobbie	4.00	1.80
394	Ken Walters	4.00	1.80
395	Chuck Estrada	6.00	2.70
396	Bob Aspromonte	4.00	1.80
397	Hal Woodeshick	4.00	1.80
398	Hank Bauer	7.00	3.10
399	Cliff Cook	4.00	1.80
400	Vern Law	6.00	2.70
401	Babe Ruth HL 60th HR	50.00	22.00
402	Don Larsen HL SP WS Perfect Game	30.00	13.50
403	Joe Oeschger HL Leon Cadore 26 Inning Tie	6.00	2.70
404	Rogers Hornsby HL .424 Season BA	10.00	4.50
405	Lou Gehrig HL Consecutive Game Streak	80.00	36.00
406	Mickey Mantle HL 565 foot HR	100.00	45.00
407	Jack Chesbro HL 41 victories	6.00	2.70
408	Christy Mathewson HL SP 267 Strikeouts	20.00	9.00
409	Walter Johnson SL 3 Shutouts in 4 days	12.00	5.50
410	Harvey Haddix HL 12 Perfect Innings	6.00	2.70
411	Tony Taylor	6.00	2.70
412	Larry Sherry	6.00	2.70
413	Eddie Yost	6.00	2.70
414	Dick Donovan	6.00	2.70
415	Hank Aaron	90.00	40.00
416	Dick Howser	10.00	4.50
417	Juan Marichal SP	125.00	55.00
418	Ed Bailey	6.00	2.70
419	Tom Borland	4.00	1.80
420	Ernie Broglio	6.00	2.70
421	Ty Cline SP	9.00	4.00
422	Bud Daley	4.00	1.80
423	Charlie Neal SP	9.00	4.00
424	Turk Lown	4.00	1.80
425	Yogi Berra	80.00	36.00
426	Milwaukee Braves Team Card (Back numbered 463)	12.00	5.50
427	Dick Ellsworth	6.00	2.70
428	Ray Barker SP	9.00	4.00
429	Al Kaline	45.00	20.00
430	Bill Mazeroski SP	60.00	27.00
431	Chuck Stobbs	4.00	1.80
432	Coot Veal	6.00	2.70
433	Art Mahaffey	4.00	1.80
434	Tom Brewer	4.00	1.80
435	Orlando Cepeda UER (San Francis on card front)	14.00	6.25
436	Jim Maloney SP	20.00	9.00
437A	Checklist 6 440 Louis Aparicio	10.00	2.00
437B	Checklist 6 440 Luis Aparicio	10.00	2.00
438	Curt Flood	8.00	3.60
439	Phil Regan	6.00	2.70
440	Luis Aparicio	15.00	6.75
441	Dick Bertell	4.00	1.80
442	Gordon Jones	4.00	1.80
443	Duke Snider	40.00	18.00
444	Joe Nuxhall	6.00	2.70
445	Frank Malzone	6.00	2.70
446	Bob Taylor	4.00	1.80
447	Harry Bright	4.00	1.80
448	Del Rice	7.00	3.10
449	Bob Bolin	7.00	3.10
450	Jim Lemon	7.00	3.10
451	Power for Ernie Daryl Spencer Bill White Ernie Broglio	7.00	3.10
452	Bob Allen	7.00	3.10
453	Dick Schofield	7.00	3.10

No.	Player	NRMT	VG-E
454	Pumpsie Green	7.00	3.10
455	Early Wynn	15.00	6.75
456	Hal Bevan	7.00	3.10
457	Johnny James	7.00	3.10
	(Listed as Angel, but wearing Yankee uniform and cap)		
458	Willie Tasby	7.00	3.10
459	Terry Fox	7.00	3.10
460	Gil Hodges	20.00	9.00
461	Smoky Burgess	10.00	4.50
462	Lou Klimchock	7.00	3.10
463	Jack Fisher	7.00	3.10
	(See also 426)		
464	Lee Thomas	10.00	4.50
	(Pictured with Yankee cap but listed as Los Angeles Angel)		
465	Roy McMillan	7.00	3.10
466	Ron Moeller	7.00	3.10
467	Cleveland Indians Team Card	7.50	3.40
468	John Callison	10.00	4.50
469	Ralph Lumenti	7.00	3.10
470	Roy Sievers	10.00	4.50
471	Phil Rizzuto MVP	20.00	9.00
472	Yogi Berra MVP	60.00	27.00
473	Bob Shantz MVP	7.00	3.10
474	Al Rosen MVP	10.00	4.50
475	Mickey Mantle MVP	200.00	90.00
476	Jackie Jensen MVP	10.00	4.50
477	Nellie Fox MVP	18.00	8.00
478	Roger Maris MVP	50.00	22.00
479	Jim Konstanty MVP	7.00	3.10
480	Roy Campanella MVP	35.00	16.00
481	Hank Sauer MVP	7.00	3.10
482	Willie Mays MVP	50.00	22.00
483	Don Newcombe MVP	10.00	4.50
484	Hank Aaron MVP	50.00	22.00
485	Ernie Banks MVP	35.00	16.00
486	Dick Groat MVP	10.00	4.50
487	Gene Oliver	7.00	3.10
488	Joe McClain	10.00	4.50
489	Walt Dropo	7.00	3.10
490	Jim Bunning	16.00	7.25
491	Philadelphia Phillies Team Card	7.50	3.40
492	Ron Fairly	10.00	4.50
493	Don Zimmer UER (Brooklyn A.L.)	10.00	4.50
494	Tom Cheney	7.00	3.10
495	Elston Howard	12.00	5.50
496	Ken MacKenzie	7.00	3.10
497	Willie Jones	7.00	3.10
498	Ray Herbert	7.00	3.10
499	Chuck Schilling	7.00	3.10
500	Harvey Kuenn	10.00	4.50
501	John DeMerit	7.00	3.10
502	Clarence Coleman	7.00	3.10
503	Tito Francona	7.00	3.10
504	Billy Consolo	7.00	3.10
505	Red Schoendienst	14.00	6.25
506	Willie Davis	16.00	7.25
507	Pete Burnside	7.00	3.10
508	Rocky Bridges	7.00	3.10
509	Camilo Carreon	7.00	3.10
510	Art Ditmar	7.00	3.10
511	Joe M. Morgan	7.00	3.10
512	Bob Will	7.00	3.10
513	Jim Brosnan	7.00	3.10
514	Jake Wood	7.00	3.10
515	Jackie Brandt	7.00	3.10
516	Checklist 7	10.00	2.00
517	Willie McCovey	50.00	22.00
518	Andy Carey	7.00	3.10
519	Jim Pagliaroni	7.00	3.10
520	Joe Cunningham	7.00	3.10
521	Brother Battery Norm Sherry Larry Sherry	7.00	3.10
522	Dick Farrell UER (Phillies cap but listed on Dodgers)	7.00	3.10
523	Joe Gibbon	30.00	13.50
524	Johnny Logan	30.00	13.50
525	Ron Perranoski	40.00	18.00
526	R.C. Stevens	30.00	13.50
527	Gene Leek	30.00	13.50
528	Pedro Ramos	30.00	13.50
529	Bob Roselli	30.00	13.50
530	Bob Malkmus	30.00	13.50
531	Jim Coates	40.00	18.00
532	Bob Hale	30.00	13.50
533	Jack Curtis	30.00	13.50
534	Eddie Kasko	30.00	13.50
535	Larry Jackson	30.00	13.50
536	Bill Tuttle	30.00	13.50
537	Bobby Locke	30.00	13.50
538	Chuck Hiller	30.00	13.50
539	Johnny Klippstein	30.00	13.50
540	Jackie Jensen	40.00	18.00
541	Roland Sheldon	40.00	18.00
542	Minnesota Twins Team Card	70.00	32.00
543	Roger Craig	40.00	18.00
544	George Thomas	30.00	13.50
545	Hoyt Wilhelm	50.00	22.00
546	Marty Kutyna	30.00	13.50
547	Leon Wagner	30.00	13.50
548	Ted Wills	30.00	13.50
549	Hal R. Smith	30.00	13.50
550	Frank Baumann	30.00	13.50
551	George Altman	30.00	13.50
552	Jim Archer	30.00	13.50
553	Bill Fischer	30.00	13.50
554	Pittsburgh Pirates Team Card	70.00	32.00
555	Sam Jones	30.00	13.50
556	Ken R. Hunt	30.00	13.50
557	Jose Valdivielso	30.00	13.50
558	Don Ferrarese	30.00	13.50
559	Jim Gentile	60.00	27.00
560	Barry Latman	30.00	13.50
561	Charley James	30.00	13.50
562	Bill Monbouquette	30.00	13.50
563	Bob Cerv	45.00	20.00
564	Don Cardwell	30.00	13.50
565	Felipe Alou	40.00	18.00
566	Paul Richards AS MG	30.00	13.50
567	Danny Murtaugh AS MG	30.00	13.50
568	Bill Skowron AS	45.00	20.00
569	Frank Herrera AS	30.00	13.50
570	Nellie Fox AS	50.00	22.00
571	Bill Mazeroski AS	45.00	20.00
572	Brooks Robinson AS	90.00	40.00
573	Ken Boyer AS	45.00	20.00
574	Luis Aparicio AS	45.00	20.00
575	Ernie Banks AS	90.00	40.00
576	Roger Maris AS	160.00	70.00
577	Hank Aaron AS	160.00	70.00
578	Mickey Mantle AS	450.00	200.00
579	Willie Mays AS	160.00	70.00
580	Al Kaline AS	90.00	40.00
581	Frank Robinson AS	90.00	40.00
582	Earl Battey AS	30.00	13.50
583	Del Crandall AS	30.00	13.50
584	Jim Perry AS	30.00	13.50
585	Bob Friend AS	30.00	13.50
586	Whitey Ford AS	90.00	40.00
589	Warren Spahn AS	100.00	30.00

1962 Topps

The cards in this 598-card set measure 2 1/2" by 3 1/2". The 1962 Topps set contains a mini-series spotlighting Babe Ruth (135-144). Other subsets in the set include League Leaders (51-60), World Series cards (232-237), In Action cards (311-319), NL All Stars (390-399), AL All Stars (466-475), and Rookie Prospects (591-598). The All-Star selections were again provided by Sport Magazine, as in 1958 and 1960. The second series had two distinct printings which are distinguishable by numerous color and pose variations. Those cards with a dis-

ROBERTS

tinctive "green tint" are valued at a slight premium as they are basically the result of a flawed printing process occurring early in the second series run. Card number 139 exists as A: Babe Ruth Special card, B: Hal Reniff with arms over head, or C: Hal Reniff in the same pose as card number 159. In addition, two poses exist for these cards: 129, 132, 134, 147, 174, 176, and 190. The high number series, 523 to 598, is somewhat more difficult to obtain than other cards in the set. Within the last series (523-598) there are 43 cards which were printed in lesser quantities; these are marked SP in the checklist below. In particular, the Rookie Parade subset (591-598) of this last series is even more difficult. This was the first year Topps produced multi-player Rookie Cards. The set price listed does not include the pose variations (see checklist below for individual values). Cards were issued in one-cent penny packs as well as five-card nickel packs. The key Rookie Cards in this set are Lou Brock, Tim McCarver, Gaylord Perry, and Bob Uecker.

	NRMT	VG-E
COMPLETE SET (598)	4600.00	2100.00
COMMON CARD (1-370)	5.00	2.20
COMMON CARD (371-446)	6.00	2.70
BABE RUTH STORY (135-144)	20.00	9.00
MINOR STARS 1-446	8.00	3.60
SEMISTARS 1-446	10.00	4.50
UNLISTED STARS 1-446	15.00	6.75
COMMON CARD (447-522)	12.00	5.50
MINOR STARS 447-522	15.00	6.75
SEMISTARS 447-522	20.00	9.00
COMMON CARD (523-598)	20.00	9.00
COMMON SP (523-598)	32.00	14.50
MINOR STARS 523-598	30.00	13.50
SEMISTARS 523-598	40.00	18.00
COMMON POSE VAR	25.00	11.00

*UNLISTED DODG/MET/YANK: 1.25X VALUE
CARDS PRICED IN NM CONDITION !

No.	Player	NRMT	VG-E
1	Roger Maris	200.00	50.00
2	Jim Brosnan	5.00	2.20
3	Pete Runnels	5.00	2.20
4	John DeMerit	8.00	3.60
5	Sandy Koufax UER (Struck ou 18)	175.00	80.00
6	Marv Breeding	5.00	2.20
7	Frank Thomas	10.00	4.50
8	Ray Herbert	5.00	2.20
9	Jim Davenport	8.00	3.60
10	Bob Clemente	250.00	110.00
11	Tom Morgan	5.00	2.20
12	Harry Craft MG	8.00	3.60
13	Dick Howser	8.00	3.60

☐ 14	Bill White	8.00	3.60
☐ 15	Dick Donovan	5.00	2.20
☐ 16	Darrell Johnson	5.00	2.20
☐ 17	Johnny Callison	8.00	3.60
☐ 18	Managers' Dream	200.00	90.00
	Mickey Mantle		
	Willie Mays		
☐ 19	Ray Washburn	5.00	2.20
☐ 20	Rocky Colavito	15.00	6.75
☐ 21	Jim Kaat	8.00	3.60
☐ 22A	Checklist 1 ERR	12.00	2.40
	(121-176 on back)		
☐ 22B	Checklist 1 COR	12.00	2.40
☐ 23	Norm Larker	5.00	2.20
☐ 24	Tigers Team	10.00	4.50
☐ 25	Ernie Banks	45.00	20.00
☐ 26	Chris Cannizzaro	8.00	3.60
☐ 27	Chuck Cottier	5.00	2.20
☐ 28	Minnie Minoso	10.00	4.50
☐ 29	Casey Stengel MG	20.00	9.00
☐ 30	Eddie Mathews	25.00	11.00
☐ 31	Tom Tresh	20.00	9.00
☐ 32	John Roseboro	8.00	3.60
☐ 33	Don Larsen	8.00	3.60
☐ 34	Johnny Temple	8.00	3.60
☐ 35	Don Schwall	8.00	3.60
☐ 36	Don Leppert	5.00	2.20
☐ 37	Tribe Hill Trio	5.00	2.20
	Barry Latman		
	Dick Stigman		
	Jim Perry		
☐ 38	Gene Stephens	5.00	2.20
☐ 39	Joe Koppe	5.00	2.20
☐ 40	Orlando Cepeda	14.00	6.25
☐ 41	Cliff Cook	5.00	2.20
☐ 42	Jim King	5.00	2.20
☐ 43	Los Angeles Dodgers	10.00	4.50
	Team Card		
☐ 44	Don Taussig	5.00	2.20
☐ 45	Brooks Robinson	45.00	20.00
☐ 46	Jack Baldschun	5.00	2.20
☐ 47	Bob Will	5.00	2.20
☐ 48	Ralph Terry	8.00	3.60
☐ 49	Hal Jones	5.00	2.20
☐ 50	Stan Musial	100.00	45.00
☐ 51	AL Batting Leaders	8.00	3.60
	Norm Cash		
	Jim Piersall		
	Al Kaline		
	Elston Howard		
☐ 52	NL Batting Leaders	18.00	8.00
	Bob Clemente		
	Vada Pinson		
	Ken Boyer		
	Wally Moon		
☐ 53	AL Home Run Leaders	110.00	50.00
	Roger Maris		
	Mickey Mantle		
	Jim Gentile		
	Harmon Killebrew		
☐ 54	NL Home Run Leaders	18.00	8.00
	Orlando Cepeda		
	Willie Mays		
	Frank Robinson		
☐ 55	AL ERA Leaders	8.00	3.60
	Dick Donovan		
	Bill Stafford		
	Don Mossi		
	Milt Pappas		
☐ 56	NL ERA Leaders	8.00	3.60
	Warren Spahn		
	Jim O'Toole		
	Curt Simmons		
	Mike McCormick		
☐ 57	AL Wins Leaders	8.00	3.60
	Whitey Ford		
	Frank Lary		
	Steve Barber		
	Jim Bunning		
☐ 58	NL Wins Leaders	8.00	3.60
	Warren Spahn		
	Joe Jay		
	Jim O'Toole		
☐ 59	AL Strikeout Leaders	8.00	3.60
	Camilo Pascual		
	Whitey Ford		
	Jim Bunning		
	Juan Pizzaro		
☐ 60	NL Strikeout Leaders	18.00	8.00
	Sandy Koufax		
	Stan Williams		
	Don Drysdale		
	Jim O'Toole		
☐ 61	Cardinals Team	10.00	4.50
☐ 62	Steve Boros	5.00	2.20
☐ 63	Tony Cloninger	8.00	3.60
☐ 64	Russ Snyder	5.00	2.20
☐ 65	Bobby Richardson	12.00	5.50
☐ 66	Cuno Barragan	5.00	2.20
☐ 67	Harvey Haddix	8.00	3.60
☐ 68	Ken Hunt	5.00	2.20
☐ 69	Phil Ortega	5.00	2.20
☐ 70	Harmon Killebrew	25.00	11.00
☐ 71	Dick LeMay	5.00	2.20
☐ 72	Bob's Pupils	5.00	2.20
	Steve Boros		
	Bob Scheffing MG		
	Jake Wood		
☐ 73	Nellie Fox	20.00	9.00
☐ 74	Bob Lillis	8.00	3.60
☐ 75	Milt Pappas	8.00	3.60
☐ 76	Howie Bedell	5.00	2.20
☐ 77	Tony Taylor	8.00	3.60
☐ 78	Gene Green	5.00	2.20
☐ 79	Ed Hobaugh	5.00	2.20
☐ 80	Vada Pinson	8.00	3.60
☐ 81	Jim Pagliaroni	5.00	2.20
☐ 82	Deron Johnson	8.00	3.60
☐ 83	Larry Jackson	5.00	2.20
☐ 84	Lenny Green	5.00	2.20
☐ 85	Gil Hodges	20.00	9.00
☐ 86	Donn Clendenon	8.00	3.60
☐ 87	Mike Roarke	5.00	2.20
☐ 88	Ralph Houk MG	8.00	3.60
	(Berra in background)		
☐ 89	Barney Schultz	5.00	2.20
☐ 90	Jimmy Piersall	8.00	3.60
☐ 91	J.C. Martin	5.00	2.20
☐ 92	Sam Jones	5.00	2.20
☐ 93	John Blanchard	8.00	3.60
☐ 94	Jay Hook	8.00	3.60
☐ 95	Don Hoak	8.00	3.60
☐ 96	Eli Grba	5.00	2.20
☐ 97	Tito Francona	5.00	2.20
☐ 98	Checklist 2	12.00	2.40
☐ 99	John (Boog) Powell	30.00	13.50
☐ 100	Warren Spahn	30.00	13.50
☐ 101	Carroll Hardy	5.00	2.20
☐ 102	Al Schroll	5.00	2.20
☐ 103	Don Blasingame	5.00	2.20
☐ 104	Ted Savage	5.00	2.20
☐ 105	Don Mossi	8.00	3.60
☐ 106	Carl Sawatski	5.00	2.20
☐ 107	Mike McCormick	8.00	3.60
☐ 108	Willie Davis	8.00	3.60
☐ 109	Bob Shaw	5.00	2.20
☐ 110	Bill Skowron	8.00	3.60
☐ 111	Dallas Green	8.00	3.60
☐ 112	Hank Foiles	5.00	2.20
☐ 113	Chicago White Sox	10.00	4.50
	Team Card		
☐ 114	Howie Koplitz	5.00	2.20
☐ 115	Bob Skinner	8.00	3.60
☐ 116	Herb Score	8.00	3.60
☐ 117	Gary Geiger	5.00	2.20
☐ 118	Julian Javier	8.00	3.60
☐ 119	Danny Murphy	5.00	2.20
☐ 120	Bob Purkey	5.00	2.20
☐ 121	Billy Hitchcock MG	5.00	2.20
☐ 122	Norm Bass	5.00	2.20
☐ 123	Mike de la Hoz	5.00	2.20
☐ 124	Bill Pleis	5.00	2.20
☐ 125	Gene Woodling	8.00	3.60
☐ 126	Al Cicotte	5.00	2.20
☐ 127	Pride of A's	5.00	2.20
	Norm Siebern		
	Hank Bauer MG		
	Jerry Lumpe		
☐ 128	Art Fowler	5.00	2.20
☐ 129A	Lee Walls	5.00	2.20
	(Facing right)		
☐ 129B	Lee Walls	25.00	11.00
	(Facing left)		
☐ 130	Frank Bolling	5.00	2.20
☐ 131	Pete Richert	5.00	2.20
☐ 132A	Angels Team	10.00	4.50
	(Without photo)		
☐ 132B	Angels Team	25.00	11.00
	(With photo)		
☐ 133	Felipe Alou	8.00	3.60
☐ 134A	Billy Hoeft	5.00	2.20
	(Facing right)		
☐ 134B	Billy Hoeft	25.00	11.00
	(Facing straight)		
☐ 135	Babe Ruth Special 1	20.00	9.00
	Babe as a Boy		
☐ 136	Babe Ruth Special 2	20.00	9.00
	Babe Joins Yanks		
☐ 137	Babe Ruth Special 3	20.00	9.00
	With Miller Huggins		
☐ 138	Babe Ruth Special 4	20.00	9.00
	Famous Slugger		
☐ 139A	Babe Ruth Special 5	30.00	13.50
	Babe Hits 60		
☐ 139B	Hal Reniff PORT	12.00	5.50
☐ 139C	Hal Reniff	65.00	29.00
	(Pitching)		
☐ 140	Babe Ruth Special 6	50.00	22.00
	With Lou Gehrig		
☐ 141	Babe Ruth Special 7	20.00	9.00
	Twilight Years		
☐ 142	Babe Ruth Special 8	20.00	9.00
	Coaching Dodgers		
☐ 143	Babe Ruth Special 9	20.00	9.00
	Greatest Sports Hero		
☐ 144	Babe Ruth Special 10	20.00	9.00
	Farewell Speech		
☐ 145	Barry Latman	5.00	2.20
☐ 146	Don Demeter	5.00	2.20
☐ 147A	Hal Kunkel PORT	5.00	2.20
☐ 147B	Bill Kunkel	25.00	11.00
	(Pitching pose)		
☐ 148	Wally Post	5.00	2.20
☐ 149	Bob Duliba	5.00	2.20
☐ 150	Al Kaline	45.00	20.00
☐ 151	Johnny Klippstein	5.00	2.20
☐ 152	Mickey Vernon MG	8.00	3.60
☐ 153	Pumpsie Green	6.00	2.70
☐ 154	Lee Thomas	6.00	2.70
☐ 155	Stu Miller	6.00	2.70
☐ 156	Merritt Ranew	5.00	2.20
☐ 157	Wes Covington	8.00	3.60
☐ 158	Braves Team	10.00	4.50
☐ 159	Hal Reniff	8.00	3.60
☐ 160	Dick Stuart	8.00	3.60
☐ 161	Frank Baumann	5.00	2.20
☐ 162	Sammy Drake	5.00	2.20
☐ 163	Hot Corner Guard	8.00	3.60
	Billy Gardner		
	Cletis Boyer		
☐ 164	Hal Naragon	5.00	2.20
☐ 165	Jackie Brandt	5.00	2.20
☐ 166	Don Lee	5.00	2.20
☐ 167	Tim McCarver	30.00	13.50
☐ 168	Leo Posada	5.00	2.20
☐ 169	Bob Cerv	8.00	3.60
☐ 170	Ron Santo	14.00	6.25
☐ 171	Dave Sisler	5.00	2.20
☐ 172	Fred Hutchinson MG	8.00	3.60
☐ 173	Chico Fernandez	5.00	2.20
☐ 174A	Carl Willey	5.00	2.20
	(Capless)		
☐ 174B	Carl Willey	25.00	11.00
	(With cap)		
☐ 175	Frank Howard	8.00	3.60
☐ 176A	Eddie Yost PORT	5.00	2.20
☐ 176B	Eddie Yost BATTING	25.00	11.00
☐ 177	Bobby Shantz	8.00	3.60
☐ 178	Camilo Carreon	5.00	2.20
☐ 179	Tom Sturdivant	5.00	2.20
☐ 180	Bob Allison	8.00	3.60
☐ 181	Paul Brown	5.00	2.20
☐ 182	Bob Nieman	5.00	2.20
☐ 183	Roger Craig	8.00	3.60
☐ 184	Haywood Sullivan	8.00	3.60
☐ 185	Roland Sheldon	5.00	2.20
☐ 186	Mack Jones	5.00	2.20
☐ 187	Gene Conley	5.00	2.20

No.	Player	Price 1	Price 2
188	Chuck Hiller	5.00	2.20
189	Dick Hall	5.00	2.20
190A	Wally Moon PORT..	5.00	2.20
190B	Wally Moon BATTING	28.00	12.50
191	Jim Brewer	5.00	2.20
192A	Checklist 3 (Without comma)	12.00	2.40
192B	Checklist 3 (Comma after Checklist)	16.00	3.20
193	Eddie Kasko	5.00	2.20
194	Dean Chance	8.00	3.60
195	Joe Cunningham	5.00	2.20
196	Terry Fox	5.00	2.20
197	Daryl Spencer	5.00	2.20
198	Johnny Keane MG	5.00	2.20
199	Gaylord Perry	80.00	36.00
200	Mickey Mantle	450.00	200.00
201	Ike Delock	5.00	2.20
202	Carl Warwick	5.00	2.20
203	Jack Fisher	5.00	2.20
204	Johnny Weekly	5.00	2.20
205	Gene Freese	5.00	2.20
206	Senators Team	10.00	4.50
207	Pete Burnside	5.00	2.20
208	Billy Martin	20.00	9.00
209	Jim Fregosi	14.00	6.25
210	Roy Face	8.00	3.60
211	Midway Masters Frank Bolling Roy McMillan	5.00	2.20
212	Jim Owens	5.00	2.20
213	Richie Ashburn	20.00	9.00
214	Dom Zanni	5.00	2.20
215	Woody Held	5.00	2.20
216	Ron Kline	5.00	2.20
217	Walter Alston MG	8.00	3.60
218	Joe Torre	40.00	18.00
219	Al Downing	8.00	3.60
220	Roy Sievers	5.00	2.20
221	Bill Short	5.00	2.20
222	Jerry Zimmerman	5.00	2.20
223	Alex Grammas	5.00	2.20
224	Don Rudolph	5.00	2.20
225	Frank Malzone	5.00	2.20
226	San Francisco Giants Team Card	10.00	4.50
227	Bob Tiefenauer	5.00	2.20
228	Dale Long	8.00	3.60
229	Jesus McFarlane	5.00	2.20
230	Camilo Pascual	8.00	3.60
231	Ernie Bowman	5.00	2.20
232	World Series Game 1 Yanks win opener	10.00	4.50
233	Joey Jay WS	10.00	4.50
234	Roger Maris WS	20.00	9.00
235	Whitey Ford WS sets new mark	10.00	4.50
236	World Series Game 5 Yanks clinch Reds	10.00	4.50
237	World Series Summary Yanks celebrate	10.00	4.50
238	Norm Sherry	5.00	2.20
239	Cecil Butler	5.00	2.20
240	George Altman	5.00	2.20
241	Johnny Kucks	5.00	2.20
242	Mel McGaha MG	5.00	2.20
243	Robin Roberts	15.00	6.75
244	Don Gile	5.00	2.20
245	Ron Hansen	5.00	2.20
246	Art Ditmar	5.00	2.20
247	Joe Pignatano	5.00	2.20
248	Bob Aspromonte	8.00	3.60
249	Ed Keegan	5.00	2.20
250	Norm Cash	8.00	3.60
251	New York Yankees Team Card	60.00	27.00
252	Earl Francis	5.00	2.20
253	Harry Chiti MG	5.00	2.20
254	Gordon Windhorn	5.00	2.20
255	Juan Pizarro	5.00	2.20
256	Elio Chacon	8.00	3.60
257	Jack Spring	5.00	2.20
258	Marty Keough	5.00	2.20
259	Lou Klimchock	5.00	2.20
260	Billy Pierce	8.00	3.60
261	George Alusik	5.00	2.20
262	Bob Schmidt	5.00	2.20
263	The Right Pitch Bob Purkey Jim Turner CO Joe Jay	5.00	2.20
264	Dick Ellsworth	8.00	3.60
265	Joe Adcock	8.00	3.60
266	John Anderson	5.00	2.20
267	Dan Dobbek	5.00	2.20
268	Ken McBride	5.00	2.20
269	Bob Oldis	5.00	2.20
270	Dick Groat	8.00	3.60
271	Ray Rippelmeyer	5.00	2.20
272	Earl Robinson	5.00	2.20
273	Gary Bell	5.00	2.20
274	Sammy Taylor	5.00	2.20
275	Norm Siebern	5.00	2.20
276	Hal Kolstad	5.00	2.20
277	Checklist 4	16.00	3.20
278	Ken Johnson	8.00	3.60
279	Hobie Landrith UER.. (Wrong birthdate)	8.00	3.60
280	Johnny Podres	8.00	3.60
281	Jake Gibbs	8.00	3.60
282	Dave Hillman	5.00	2.20
283	Charlie Smith	5.00	2.20
284	Ruben Amaro	5.00	2.20
285	Curt Simmons	8.00	3.60
286	Al Lopez MG	8.00	3.60
287	George Witt	5.00	2.20
288	Billy Williams	30.00	13.50
289	Mike Krsnich	5.00	2.20
290	Jim Gentile	8.00	3.60
291	Hal Stowe	5.00	2.20
292	Jerry Kindall	5.00	2.20
293	Bob Miller	8.00	3.60
294	Phillies Team	10.00	4.50
295	Vern Law	8.00	3.60
296	Ken Hamlin	5.00	2.20
297	Ron Perranoski	8.00	3.60
298	Bill Tuttle	5.00	2.20
299	Don Wert	5.00	2.20
300	Willie Mays	150.00	70.00
301	Galen Cisco	5.00	2.20
302	Johnny Edwards	5.00	2.20
303	Frank Torre	8.00	3.60
304	Dick Farrell	8.00	3.60
305	Jerry Lumpe	5.00	2.20
306	Redbird Rippers Lindy McDaniel Larry Jackson	5.00	2.20
307	Jim Grant	8.00	3.60
308	Neil Chrisley	5.00	2.20
309	Moe Morhardt	5.00	2.20
310	Whitey Ford	45.00	20.00
311	Tony Kubek IA	8.00	3.60
312	Warren Spahn IA	14.00	6.25
313	Roger Maris IA Blasts 61st	35.00	16.00
314	Rocky Colavito IA	12.00	5.50
315	Whitey Ford IA	15.00	6.75
316	Harmon Killebrew IA	15.00	6.75
317	Stan Musial IA	20.00	9.00
318	Mickey Mantle IA..	175.00	80.00
319	Mike McCormick IA..	5.00	2.20
320	Hank Aaron	140.00	65.00
321	Lee Stange	5.00	2.20
322	Alvin Dark MG	8.00	3.60
323	Don Landrum	5.00	2.20
324	Joe McClain	5.00	2.20
325	Luis Aparicio	15.00	6.75
326	Tom Parsons	5.00	2.20
327	Ozzie Virgil	5.00	2.20
328	Ken Walters	5.00	2.20
329	Bob Bolin	5.00	2.20
330	John Romano	5.00	2.20
331	Moe Drabowsky	8.00	3.60
332	Don Buddin	5.00	2.20
333	Frank Cipriani	5.00	2.20
334	Boston Red Sox Team Card	10.00	4.50
335	Bill Bruton	5.00	2.20
336	Billy Muffett	5.00	2.20
337	Jim Marshall	8.00	3.60
338	Billy Gardner	5.00	2.20
339	Jose Valdivielso	5.00	2.20
340	Don Drysdale	40.00	18.00
341	Mike Hershberger	5.00	2.20
342	Ed Rakow	5.00	2.20
343	Albie Pearson	8.00	3.60
344	Ed Bauta	5.00	2.20
345	Chuck Schilling	5.00	2.20
346	Jack Kralick	5.00	2.20
347	Chuck Hinton	5.00	2.20
348	Larry Burright	8.00	3.60
349	Paul Foytack	5.00	2.20
350	Frank Robinson	45.00	20.00
351	Braves' Backstops Joe Torre Del Crandall	8.00	3.60
352	Frank Sullivan	5.00	2.20
353	Bill Mazeroski	10.00	4.50
354	Roman Mejias	8.00	3.60
355	Steve Barber	5.00	2.20
356	Tom Haller	5.00	2.20
357	Jerry Walker	5.00	2.20
358	Tommy Davis	8.00	3.60
359	Bobby Locke	5.00	2.20
360	Yogi Berra	75.00	34.00
361	Bob Hendley	5.00	2.20
362	Ty Cline	5.00	2.20
363	Bob Roselli	5.00	2.20
364	Ken Hunt	5.00	2.20
365	Charlie Neal	8.00	3.60
366	Phil Regan	8.00	3.60
367	Checklist 5	16.00	3.20
368	Bob Tillman	5.00	2.20
369	Ted Bowsfield	5.00	2.20
370	Ken Boyer	8.00	3.60
371	Earl Battey	6.00	2.70
372	Jack Curtis	6.00	2.70
373	Al Heist	6.00	2.70
374	Gene Mauch MG	10.00	4.50
375	Ron Fairly	10.00	4.50
376	Bud Daley	6.00	2.70
377	John Orsino	6.00	2.70
378	Bennie Daniels	6.00	2.70
379	Chuck Essegian	6.00	2.70
380	Lou Burdette	10.00	4.50
381	Chico Cardenas	10.00	4.50
382	Dick Williams	8.00	3.60
383	Ray Sadecki	6.00	2.70
384	K.C. Athletics Team Card	10.00	4.50
385	Early Wynn	15.00	6.75
386	Don Mincher	8.00	3.60
387	Lou Brock	125.00	55.00
388	Ryne Duren	8.00	3.60
389	Smoky Burgess	10.00	4.50
390	Orlando Cepeda AS	10.00	4.50
391	Bill Mazeroski AS	10.00	4.50
392	Ken Boyer AS	10.00	4.50
393	Roy McMillan AS	6.00	2.70
394	Hank Aaron AS	45.00	20.00
395	Willie Mays AS	50.00	22.00
396	Frank Robinson AS	16.00	7.25
397	John Roseboro AS	6.00	2.70
398	Don Drysdale AS	16.00	7.25
399	Warren Spahn AS	16.00	7.25
400	Elston Howard	10.00	4.50
401	AL/NL Homer Kings Roger Maris Orlando Cepeda	60.00	27.00
402	Gino Cimoli	6.00	2.70
403	Chet Nichols	6.00	2.70
404	Tim Harkness	6.00	2.70
405	Jim Perry	8.00	3.60
406	Bob Taylor	6.00	2.70
407	Hank Aguirre	6.00	2.70
408	Gus Bell	8.00	3.60
409	Pittsburgh Pirates Team Card	10.00	4.50
410	Al Smith	6.00	2.70
411	Danny O'Connell	6.00	2.70
412	Charlie James	6.00	2.70
413	Matty Alou	10.00	4.50
414	Joe Gaines	6.00	2.70
415	Bill Virdon	10.00	4.50
416	Bob Scheffing MG	6.00	2.70
417	Joe Azcue	6.00	2.70
418	Andy Carey	6.00	2.70

□ 419 Bob Bruce	8.00	3.60	
□ 420 Gus Triandos	8.00	3.60	
□ 421 Ken MacKenzie	8.00	3.60	
□ 422 Steve Bilko	6.00	2.70	
□ 423 Rival League	10.00	4.50	
Relief Aces:			
Roy Face			
Hoyt Wilhelm			
□ 424 Al McBean	6.00	2.70	
□ 425 Carl Yastrzemski	125.00	55.00	
□ 426 Bob Farley	6.00	2.70	
□ 427 Jake Wood	6.00	2.70	
□ 428 Joe Hicks	6.00	2.70	
□ 429 Billy O'Dell	6.00	2.70	
□ 430 Tony Kubek	10.00	4.50	
□ 431 Bob Rodgers	8.00	3.60	
□ 432 Jim Pendleton	6.00	2.70	
□ 433 Jim Archer	6.00	2.70	
□ 434 Clay Dalrymple	6.00	2.70	
□ 435 Larry Sherry	8.00	3.60	
□ 436 Felix Mantilla	8.00	3.60	
□ 437 Ray Moore	6.00	2.70	
□ 438 Dick Brown	6.00	2.70	
□ 439 Jerry Buchek	6.00	2.70	
□ 440 Joey Jay	6.00	2.70	
□ 441 Checklist 6	16.00	7.25	
□ 442 Wes Stock	6.00	2.70	
□ 443 Del Crandall	8.00	3.60	
□ 444 Ted Wills	6.00	2.70	
□ 445 Vic Power	8.00	3.60	
□ 446 Don Elston	6.00	2.70	
□ 447 Willie Kirkland	12.00	5.50	
□ 448 Joe Gibbon	12.00	5.50	
□ 449 Jerry Adair	12.00	5.50	
□ 450 Jim O'Toole	15.00	6.75	
□ 451 Jose Tartabull	16.00	7.25	
□ 452 Earl Averill Jr.	12.00	5.50	
□ 453 Cal McLish	12.00	5.50	
□ 454 Floyd Robinson	15.00	6.75	
□ 455 Luis Arroyo	15.00	6.75	
□ 456 Joe Amalfitano	15.00	6.75	
□ 457 Lou Clinton	12.00	5.50	
□ 458A Bob Buhl	15.00	6.75	
(Braves emblem			
on cap)			
□ 458B Bob Buhl	50.00	22.00	
(No emblem on cap)			
□ 459 Ed Bailey	12.00	5.50	
□ 460 Jim Bunning	18.00	8.00	
□ 461 Ken Hubbs	35.00	16.00	
□ 462A Willie Tasby	12.00	5.50	
(Senators emblem			
on cap)			
□ 462B Willie Tasby	50.00	22.00	
(No emblem on cap)			
□ 463 Hank Bauer MG	16.00	7.25	
□ 464 Al Jackson	12.00	5.50	
□ 465 Reds Team	20.00	9.00	
□ 466 Norm Cash AS	15.00	6.75	
□ 467 Chuck Schilling AS	12.00	5.50	
□ 468 Brooks Robinson AS	25.00	11.00	
□ 469 Luis Aparicio AS	16.00	7.25	
□ 470 Al Kaline AS	25.00	11.00	
□ 471 Mickey Mantle AS	200.00	90.00	
□ 472 Rocky Colavito AS	16.00	7.25	
□ 473 Elston Howard AS	20.00	9.00	
□ 474 Frank Lary AS	12.00	5.50	
□ 475 Whitey Ford AS	16.00	7.25	
□ 476 Orioles Team	20.00	9.00	
□ 477 Andre Rodgers	12.00	5.50	
□ 478 Don Zimmer	20.00	9.00	
(Shown with Mets cap,			
but listed as with			
Cincinnati)			
□ 479 Joel Horlen	12.00	5.50	
□ 480 Harvey Kuenn	16.00	7.25	
□ 481 Vic Wertz	16.00	7.25	
□ 482 Sam Mele MG	12.00	5.50	
□ 483 Don McMahon	12.00	5.50	
□ 484 Dick Schofield	12.00	5.50	
□ 485 Pedro Ramos	12.00	5.50	
□ 486 Jim Gilliam	16.00	7.25	
□ 487 Jerry Lynch	12.00	5.50	
□ 488 Hal Brown	12.00	5.50	
□ 489 Julio Gotay	12.00	5.50	
□ 490 Clete Boyer UER	16.00	7.25	

Reversed Negative			
□ 491 Leon Wagner	12.00	5.50	
□ 492 Hal W. Smith	15.00	6.75	
□ 493 Danny McDevitt	12.00	5.50	
□ 494 Sammy White	12.00	5.50	
□ 495 Don Cardwell	12.00	5.50	
□ 496 Wayne Causey	12.00	5.50	
□ 497 Ed Bouchee	15.00	6.75	
□ 498 Jim Donohue	12.00	5.50	
□ 499 Zoilo Versalles	15.00	6.75	
□ 500 Duke Snider	50.00	22.00	
□ 501 Claude Osteen	15.00	6.75	
□ 502 Hector Lopez	15.00	6.75	
□ 503 Danny Murtaugh MG	15.00	6.75	
□ 504 Eddie Bressoud	12.00	5.50	
□ 505 Juan Marichal	45.00	20.00	
□ 506 Charlie Maxwell	15.00	6.75	
□ 507 Ernie Broglio	15.00	6.75	
□ 508 Gordy Coleman	15.00	6.75	
□ 509 Dave Giusti	16.00	7.25	
□ 510 Jim Lemon	12.00	5.50	
□ 511 Bubba Phillips	12.00	5.50	
□ 512 Mike Fornieles	12.00	5.50	
□ 513 Whitey Herzog	16.00	7.25	
□ 514 Sherm Lollar	15.00	6.75	
□ 515 Stan Williams	15.00	6.75	
□ 516 Checklist 7	45.00	9.00	
□ 517 Dave Wickersham	12.00	5.50	
□ 518 Lee Maye	12.00	5.50	
□ 519 Bob Johnson	12.00	5.50	
□ 520 Bob Friend	16.00	7.25	
□ 521 Jackie Davis UER	12.00	5.50	
(Listed as OF on			
front and P on back)			
□ 522 Lindy McDaniel	15.00	6.75	
□ 523 Russ Nixon SP	32.00	14.50	
□ 524 Howie Nunn SP	32.00	14.50	
□ 525 George Thomas	20.00	9.00	
□ 526 Hal Woodeshick SP	32.00	14.50	
□ 527 Dick McAuliffe	25.00	11.00	
□ 528 Turk Lown	20.00	9.00	
□ 529 John Schaive SP	32.00	14.50	
□ 530 Bob Gibson SP	150.00	70.00	
□ 531 Bobby G. Smith	20.00	9.00	
□ 532 Dick Stigman	20.00	9.00	
□ 533 Charley Lau SP	35.00	16.00	
□ 534 Tony Gonzalez SP	32.00	14.50	
□ 535 Ed Roebuck	20.00	9.00	
□ 536 Dick Gernert	20.00	9.00	
□ 537 Cleveland Indians	50.00	22.00	
Team Card			
□ 538 Jack Sanford	20.00	9.00	
□ 539 Billy Moran	20.00	9.00	
□ 540 Jim Landis SP	32.00	14.50	
□ 541 Don Nottebart SP	32.00	14.50	
□ 542 Dave Philley	20.00	9.00	
□ 543 Bob Allen SP	32.00	14.50	
□ 544 Willie McCovey SP	115.00	52.50	
□ 545 Hoyt Wilhelm SP	50.00	22.00	
□ 546 Moe Thacker SP	32.00	14.50	
□ 547 Don Ferrarese	20.00	9.00	
□ 548 Bobby Del Greco	20.00	9.00	
□ 549 Bill Rigney MG SP	32.00	14.50	
□ 550 Art Mahaffey SP	32.00	14.50	
□ 551 Harry Bright	20.00	9.00	
□ 552 Chicago Cubs SP	60.00	27.00	
Team Card			
□ 553 Jim Coates	20.00	9.00	
□ 554 Bubba Morton SP	32.00	14.50	
□ 555 John Buzhardt SP	32.00	14.50	
□ 556 Al Spangler	20.00	9.00	
□ 557 Bob Anderson SP	32.00	14.50	
□ 558 John Goryl	20.00	9.00	
□ 559 Mike Higgins MG	20.00	9.00	
□ 560 Chuck Estrada SP	32.00	14.50	
□ 561 Gene Oliver SP	32.00	14.50	
□ 562 Bill Henry	20.00	9.00	
□ 563 Ken Aspromonte	20.00	9.00	
□ 564 Bob Grim	20.00	9.00	
□ 565 Jose Pagan	20.00	9.00	
□ 566 Marty Kutyna SP	32.00	14.50	
□ 567 Tracy Stallard SP	32.00	14.50	
□ 568 Jim Golden	20.00	9.00	
□ 569 Ed Sadowski SP	32.00	14.50	
□ 570 Bill Stafford SP	32.00	14.50	
□ 571 Billy Klaus SP	32.00	14.50	

□ 572 Bob G. Miller SP	35.00	16.00	
□ 573 Johnny Logan	20.00	9.00	
□ 574 Dean Stone	20.00	9.00	
□ 575 Red Schoendienst SP	50.00	22.00	
□ 576 Russ Kemmerer SP	32.00	14.50	
□ 577 Dave Nicholson SP	32.00	14.50	
□ 578 Jim Duffalo	20.00	9.00	
□ 579 Jim Schaffer SP	32.00	14.50	
□ 580 Bill Monbouquette	20.00	9.00	
□ 581 Mel Roach	20.00	9.00	
□ 582 Ron Piche	20.00	9.00	
□ 583 Larry Osborne	20.00	9.00	
□ 584 Minnesota Twins SP	60.00	27.00	
Team Card			
□ 585 Glen Hobbie SP	32.00	14.50	
□ 586 Sammy Esposito SP	32.00	14.50	
□ 587 Frank Funk SP	32.00	14.50	
□ 588 Birdie Tebbetts MG	20.00	9.00	
□ 589 Bob Turley	30.00	13.50	
□ 590 Curt Flood	30.00	13.50	
□ 591 Rookie Pitchers SP	70.00	32.00	
Sam McDowell			
Ron Taylor			
Ron Nischwitz			
Art Quirk			
Dick Radatz			
□ 592 Rookie Pitchers SP	70.00	32.00	
Dan Pfister			
Bo Belinsky			
Dave Stenhouse			
Jim Bouton			
Joe Bonikowski			
□ 593 Rookie Pitchers SP	40.00	18.00	
Jack Lamabe			
Craig Anderson			
Jack Hamilton			
Bob Moorhead			
Bob Veale			
□ 594 Rookie Catchers SP	75.00	34.00	
Doc Edwards			
Ken Retzer			
Bob Uecker			
Doug Camilli			
Don Pavletich			
□ 595 Rookie Infielders SP	40.00	18.00	
Bob Sadowski			
Felix Torres			
Marlan Coughtry			
Ed Charles			
□ 596 Rookie Infielders SP	70.00	32.00	
Bernie Allen			
Joe Pepitone			
Phil Linz			
Rich Rollins			
□ 597 Rookie Infielders SP	40.00	18.00	
Jim McKnight			
Rod Kanehl			
Amado Samuel			
Denis Menke			
□ 598 Rookie Outfielders SP	80.00	23.00	
Al Luplow			
Manny Jimenez			
Howie Goss			
Jim Hickman			
Ed Olivares			

1963 Topps

The cards in this 576-card set measure 2 1/2" by 3 1/2". The sharp color photographs on the 1963 set are a vivid contrast to the drab pictures of 1962. In addition to the "League Leaders" series (1-10) and World Series cards (142-148), the seventh and last series of cards (523-576) contains seven rookie cards (each depicting four players). Cards were issued, among other ways, in one-card penny packs and five-card nickel packs. There were some three-card advertising panels produced by Topps; the

players included are from the first series; one player shows Hoyt Wilhelm, Don Lock, and Bob Duliba on the front with a Stan Musial ad/endorsement on one of the backs. Key Rookie Cards in this set are Bill Freehan, Tony Oliva, Pete Rose, Willie Stargell and Rusty Staub.

	NRMT	VG-E
COMPLETE SET (576)	5000.00	2200.00
COMMON CARD (1-196)	4.00	1.80
COMMON CARD (197-283)	5.00	2.20
COMMON CARD (284-370)	5.00	2.20
COMMON CARD (371-446)	5.00	2.20
MINOR STARS 1-446	8.00	3.60
SEMISTARS 1-446	10.00	4.50
UNLISTED STARS 1-446	15.00	6.75
COMMON CARD (447-522)	25.00	11.00
MINOR STARS 447-522	30.00	13.50
SEMISTARS 447-522	40.00	18.00
COMMON CARD (523-576)	15.00	6.75
MINOR STARS 523-576	20.00	9.00
SEMISTARS 523-576	30.00	13.50

*UNLISTED DODGER/YANKEE: 1.25X VALUE CARDS PRICED IN NM CONDITION !

			NRMT	VG-E
☐	1	NL Batting Leaders	40.00	8.00
		Tommy Davis		
		Frank Robinson		
		Stan Musial		
		Hank Aaron		
		Bill White		
☐	2	AL Batting Leaders	50.00	22.00
		Pete Runnels		
		Mickey Mantle		
		Floyd Robinson		
		Norm Siebern		
		Chuck Hinton		
☐	3	NL Home Run Leaders	30.00	13.50
		Willie Mays		
		Hank Aaron		
		Frank Robinson		
		Orlando Cepeda		
		Ernie Banks		
☐	4	AL Home Run Leaders	18.00	8.00
		Harmon Killebrew		
		Norm Cash		
		Rocky Colavito		
		Roger Maris		
		Jim Gentile		
		Leon Wagner		
☐	5	NL ERA Leaders	20.00	9.00
		Sandy Koufax		
		Bob Shaw		
		Bob Purkey		
		Bob Gibson		
		Don Drysdale		
☐	6	AL ERA Leaders	10.00	4.50
		Hank Aguirre		
		Robin Roberts		
		Whitey Ford		
		Eddie Fisher		
		Dean Chance		
☐	7	NL Pitching Leaders	10.00	4.50
		Don Drysdale		

			NRMT	VG-E
		Jack Sanford		
		Bob Purkey		
		Billy O'Dell		
		Art Mahaffey		
		Joe Jay		
☐	8	AL Pitching Leaders	8.00	3.60
		Ralph Terry		
		Dick Donovan		
		Ray Herbert		
		Jim Bunning		
		Camilo Pascual		
☐	9	NL Strikeout Leaders	20.00	9.00
		Don Drysdale		
		Sandy Koufax		
		Bob Gibson		
		Billy O'Dell		
		Dick Farrell		
☐	10	AL Strikeout Leaders	8.00	3.60
		Camilo Pascual		
		Jim Bunning		
		Ralph Terry		
		Juan Pizarro		
		Jim Kaat		
☐	11	Lee Walls	4.00	1.80
☐	12	Steve Barber	4.00	1.80
☐	13	Philadelphia Phillies	8.00	3.60
		Team Card		
☐	14	Pedro Ramos	4.00	1.80
☐	15	Ken Hubbs UER	10.00	4.50
		(No position listed		
		on front of card)		
☐	16	Al Smith	4.00	1.80
☐	17	Ryne Duren	8.00	3.60
☐	18	Buc Blasters	70.00	32.00
		Smoky Burgess		
		Dick Stuart		
		Bob Clemente		
		Bob Skinner		
☐	19	Pete Burnside	4.00	1.80
☐	20	Tony Kubek	8.00	3.60
☐	21	Marty Keough	4.00	1.80
☐	22	Curt Simmons	8.00	3.60
☐	23	Ed Lopat MG	8.00	3.60
☐	24	Bob Bruce	4.00	1.80
☐	25	Al Kaline	45.00	20.00
☐	26	Ray Moore	4.00	1.80
☐	27	Choo Choo Coleman	8.00	3.60
☐	28	Mike Fornieles	4.00	1.80
☐	29A	1962 Rookie Stars	8.00	3.60
		Sammy Ellis		
		Ray Culp		
		John Boozer		
		Jesse Gonder		
☐	29B	1963 Rookie Stars	4.00	1.80
		Sammy Ellis		
		Ray Culp		
		John Boozer		
		Jesse Gonder		
☐	30	Harvey Kuenn	8.00	3.60
☐	31	Cal Koonce	4.00	1.80
☐	32	Tony Gonzalez	4.00	1.80
☐	33	Bo Belinsky	8.00	3.60
☐	34	Dick Schofield	4.00	1.80
☐	35	John Buzhardt	4.00	1.80
☐	36	Jerry Kindall	4.00	1.80
☐	37	Jerry Lynch	4.00	1.80
☐	38	Bud Daley	8.00	3.60
☐	39	Angels Team	8.00	3.60
☐	40	Vic Power	8.00	3.60
☐	41	Charley Lau	8.00	3.60
☐	42	Stan Williams	8.00	3.60
		(Listed as Yankee on		
		card but LA cap)		
☐	43	Veteran Masters	8.00	3.60
		Casey Stengel MG		
		Gene Woodling		
☐	44	Terry Fox	4.00	1.80
☐	45	Bob Aspromonte	4.00	1.80
☐	46	Tommie Aaron	8.00	3.60
☐	47	Don Lock	4.00	1.80
☐	48	Birdie Tebbetts MG	8.00	1.80
☐	49	Dal Maxvill	8.00	3.60
☐	50	Billy Pierce	8.00	3.60
☐	51	George Alusik	4.00	1.80
☐	52	Chuck Schilling	4.00	1.80
☐	53	Joe Moeller	8.00	3.60

			NRMT	VG-E
☐	54A	1962 Rookie Stars	15.00	6.75
		Nelson Mathews		
		Harry Fanok		
		Jack Cullen		
		Dave DeBusschere		
☐	54B	1963 Rookie Stars	8.00	3.60
		Nelson Mathews		
		Harry Fanok		
		Jack Cullen		
		Dave DeBusschere		
☐	55	Bill Virdon	8.00	3.60
☐	56	Dennis Bennett	4.00	1.80
☐	57	Billy Moran	4.00	1.80
☐	58	Bob Will	4.00	1.80
☐	59	Craig Anderson	4.00	1.80
☐	60	Elston Howard	8.00	3.60
☐	61	Ernie Bowman	4.00	1.80
☐	62	Bob Hendley	4.00	1.80
☐	63	Reds Team	8.00	3.60
☐	64	Dick McAuliffe	8.00	3.60
☐	65	Jackie Brandt	4.00	1.80
☐	66	Mike Joyce	4.00	1.80
☐	67	Ed Charles	4.00	1.80
☐	68	Friendly Foes	25.00	11.00
		Duke Snider		
		Gil Hodges		
☐	69	Bud Zipfel	4.00	1.80
☐	70	Jim O'Toole	8.00	3.60
☐	71	Bobby Wine	8.00	3.60
☐	72	Johnny Romano	4.00	1.80
☐	73	Bobby Bragan MG	8.00	3.60
☐	74	Denny Lemaster	4.00	1.80
☐	75	Bob Allison	8.00	3.60
☐	76	Earl Wilson	8.00	3.60
☐	77	Al Spangler	4.00	1.80
☐	78	Marv Throneberry	8.00	3.60
☐	79	Checklist 1	10.00	2.00
☐	80	Jim Gilliam	8.00	3.60
☐	81	Jim Schaffer	4.00	1.80
☐	82	Ed Rakow	4.00	1.80
☐	83	Charley James	4.00	1.80
☐	84	Ron Kline	4.00	1.80
☐	85	Tom Haller	8.00	3.60
☐	86	Charley Maxwell	4.00	1.80
☐	87	Bob Veale	8.00	3.60
☐	88	Ron Hansen	4.00	1.80
☐	89	Dick Stigman	4.00	1.80
☐	90	Gordy Coleman	8.00	3.60
☐	91	Dallas Green	8.00	3.60
☐	92	Hector Lopez	8.00	3.60
☐	93	Galen Cisco	4.00	1.80
☐	94	Bob Schmidt	4.00	1.80
☐	95	Larry Jackson	4.00	1.80
☐	96	Lou Clinton	4.00	1.80
☐	97	Bob Duliba	4.00	1.80
☐	98	George Thomas	4.00	1.80
☐	99	Jim Umbricht	4.00	1.80
☐	100	Joe Cunningham	4.00	1.80
☐	101	Joe Gibbon	4.00	1.80
☐	102A	Checklist 2	10.00	2.00
		(Red on yellow)		
☐	102B	Checklist 2	10.00	2.00
		(White on red)		
☐	103	Chuck Essegian	4.00	1.80
☐	104	Lew Krausse	4.00	1.80
☐	105	Ron Fairly	8.00	3.60
☐	106	Bobby Bolin	4.00	1.80
☐	107	Jim Hickman	8.00	3.60
☐	108	Hoyt Wilhelm	10.00	4.50
☐	109	Lee Maye	4.00	1.80
☐	110	Rich Rollins	8.00	3.60
☐	111	Al Jackson	4.00	1.80
☐	112	Dick Brown	4.00	1.80
☐	113	Don Landrum UER	4.00	1.80
		(Photo actually		
		Ron Santo)		
☐	114	Dan Osinski	4.00	1.80
☐	115	Carl Yastrzemski	40.00	18.00
☐	116	Jim Brosnan	8.00	3.60
☐	117	Jacke Davis	4.00	1.80
☐	118	Sherm Lollar	8.00	3.60
☐	119	Bob Lillis	4.00	1.80
☐	120	Roger Maris	45.00	20.00
☐	121	Jim Hannan	4.00	1.80
☐	122	Julio Gotay	4.00	1.80
☐	123	Frank Howard	8.00	3.60

No.	Card	NM	EX
124	Dick Howser	8.00	3.60
125	Robin Roberts	14.00	6.25
126	Bob Uecker	14.00	6.25
127	Bill Tuttle	4.00	1.80
128	Matty Alou	8.00	3.60
129	Gary Bell	4.00	1.80
130	Dick Groat	8.00	3.60
131	Washington Senators Team Card	8.00	3.60
132	Jack Hamilton	4.00	1.80
133	Gene Freese	4.00	1.80
134	Bob Scheffing MG	4.00	1.80
135	Richie Ashburn	20.00	9.00
136	Ike Delock	4.00	1.80
137	Mack Jones	4.00	1.80
138	Pride of NL — Willie Mays, Stan Musial	70.00	32.00
139	Earl Averill	4.00	1.80
140	Frank Lary	8.00	3.60
141	Manny Mota	8.00	3.60
142	Whitey Ford WS	10.00	4.50
143	Jack Sanford WS	8.00	3.60
144	Roger Maris WS	12.00	5.50
145	Chuck Hiller WS	8.00	3.60
146	Tom Tresh WS	8.00	3.60
147	Billy Pierce WS	8.00	3.60
148	Ralph Terry WS	8.00	3.60
149	Marv Breeding	4.00	1.80
150	Johnny Podres	8.00	3.60
151	Pirates Team	8.00	3.60
152	Ron Nischwitz	4.00	1.80
153	Hal Smith	4.00	1.80
154	Walter Alston MG	8.00	3.60
155	Bill Stafford	4.00	1.80
156	Roy McMillan	8.00	3.60
157	Diego Segui	8.00	3.60
158	Rookie Stars — Rogelio Alvares, Dave Roberts, Tommy Harper, Bob Saverine	8.00	3.60
159	Jim Pagliaroni	4.00	1.80
160	Juan Pizarro	4.00	1.80
161	Frank Torre	8.00	3.60
162	Twins Team	8.00	3.60
163	Don Larsen	8.00	3.60
164	Bubba Morton	4.00	1.80
165	Jim Kaat	8.00	3.60
166	Johnny Keane MG	4.00	1.80
167	Jim Fregosi	8.00	3.60
168	Russ Nixon	4.00	1.80
169	Rookie Stars — Dick Egan, Julio Navarro, Tommie Sisk, Gaylord Perry	25.00	11.00
170	Joe Adcock	8.00	3.60
171	Steve Hamilton	4.00	1.80
172	Gene Oliver	4.00	1.80
173	Bombers' Best — Tom Tresh, Mickey Mantle, Bobby Richardson	200.00	90.00
174	Larry Burright	4.00	1.80
175	Bob Buhl	8.00	3.60
176	Jim King	4.00	1.80
177	Bubba Phillips	4.00	1.80
178	Johnny Edwards	4.00	1.80
179	Ron Piche	4.00	1.80
180	Bill Skowron	8.00	3.60
181	Sammy Esposito	4.00	1.80
182	Albie Pearson	4.00	1.80
183	Joe Pepitone	8.00	3.60
184	Vern Law	8.00	3.60
185	Chuck Hiller	4.00	1.80
186	Jerry Zimmerman	4.00	1.80
187	Willie Kirkland	4.00	1.80
188	Eddie Bressoud	4.00	1.80
189	Dave Giusti	8.00	3.60
190	Minnie Minoso	8.00	3.60
191	Checklist 3	10.00	2.00
192	Clay Dalrymple	4.00	1.80
193	Andre Rodgers	4.00	1.80
194	Joe Nuxhall	8.00	3.60
195	Manny Jimenez	4.00	1.80
196	Doug Camilli	4.00	1.80
197	Roger Craig	8.00	3.60
198	Lenny Green	5.00	2.20
199	Joe Amalfitano	5.00	2.20
200	Mickey Mantle	550.00	250.00
201	Cecil Butler	5.00	2.20
202	Boston Red Sox Team Card	8.00	3.60
203	Chico Cardenas	8.00	3.60
204	Don Nottebart	5.00	2.20
205	Luis Aparicio	15.00	6.75
206	Ray Washburn	5.00	2.20
207	Ken Hunt	5.00	2.20
208	Rookie Stars — Ron Herbel, John Miller, Wally Wolf, Ron Taylor	5.00	2.20
209	Hobie Landrith	5.00	2.20
210	Sandy Koufax !	175.00	80.00
211	Fred Whitfield	5.00	2.20
212	Glen Hobbie	5.00	2.20
213	Billy Hitchcock MG	5.00	2.20
214	Orlando Pena	5.00	2.20
215	Bob Skinner	8.00	3.60
216	Gene Conley	8.00	3.60
217	Joe Christopher	5.00	2.20
218	Tiger Twirlers — Frank Lary, Don Mossi, Jim Bunning	8.00	3.60
219	Chuck Cottier	5.00	2.20
220	Camilo Pascual	8.00	3.60
221	Cookie Rojas	8.00	3.60
222	Cubs Team	8.00	3.60
223	Eddie Fisher	5.00	2.20
224	Mike Roarke	5.00	2.20
225	Joey Jay	5.00	2.20
226	Julian Javier	8.00	3.60
227	Jim Grant	8.00	3.60
228	Rookie Stars — Max Alvis, Bob Bailey, Tony Oliva (Listed as Pedro), Ed Kranepool	40.00	18.00
229	Willie Davis	8.00	3.60
230	Pete Runnels	8.00	3.60
231	Eli Grba UER (Large photo is Ryne Duren)	5.00	2.20
232	Frank Malzone	8.00	3.60
233	Casey Stengel MG	20.00	9.00
234	Dave Nicholson	5.00	2.20
235	Billy O'Dell	5.00	2.20
236	Bill Bryan	5.00	2.20
237	Jim Coates	8.00	3.60
238	Lou Johnson	5.00	2.20
239	Harvey Haddix	8.00	3.60
240	Rocky Colavito	15.00	6.75
241	Bob Smith	5.00	2.20
242	Power Plus — Ernie Banks, Hank Aaron	60.00	27.00
243	Don Leppert	5.00	2.20
244	John Tsitouris	5.00	2.20
245	Gil Hodges	20.00	9.00
246	Lee Stange	5.00	2.20
247	Yankees Team	40.00	18.00
248	Tito Francona	5.00	2.20
249	Leo Burke	5.00	2.20
250	Stan Musial	125.00	55.00
251	Jack Lamabe	5.00	2.20
252	Ron Santo	10.00	4.50
253	Rookie Stars — Len Gabrielson, Pete Jernigan, John Wojcik, Deacon Jones	5.00	2.20
254	Mike Hershberger	5.00	2.20
255	Bob Shaw	5.00	2.20
256	Jerry Lumpe	5.00	2.20
257	Hank Aguirre	5.00	2.20
258	Alvin Dark MG	8.00	3.60
259	Johnny Logan	8.00	3.60
260	Jim Gentile	8.00	3.60
261	Bob Miller	5.00	2.20
262	Ellis Burton	5.00	2.20
263	Dave Stenhouse	5.00	2.20
264	Phil Linz	5.00	2.20
265	Vada Pinson	8.00	3.60
266	Bob Allen	5.00	2.20
267	Carl Sawatski	5.00	2.20
268	Don Demeter	5.00	2.20
269	Don Mincher	5.00	2.20
270	Felipe Alou	8.00	3.60
271	Dean Stone	5.00	2.20
272	Danny Murphy	5.00	2.20
273	Sammy Taylor	5.00	2.20
274	Checklist 4	10.00	2.00
275	Eddie Mathews	20.00	9.00
276	Barry Shetrone	5.00	2.20
277	Dick Farrell	5.00	2.20
278	Chico Fernandez	5.00	2.20
279	Wally Moon	8.00	3.60
280	Bob Rodgers	5.00	2.20
281	Tom Sturdivant	5.00	2.20
282	Bobby Del Greco	5.00	2.20
283	Roy Sievers	8.00	3.60
284	Dave Sisler	5.00	2.20
285	Dick Stuart	8.00	3.60
286	Stu Miller	5.00	2.20
287	Dick Bertell	5.00	2.20
288	Chicago White Sox Team Card	8.00	3.60
289	Hal Brown	5.00	2.20
290	Bill White	8.00	3.60
291	Don Rudolph	5.00	2.20
292	Pumpsie Green	8.00	3.60
293	Bill Pleis	5.00	2.20
294	Bill Rigney MG	5.00	2.20
295	Ed Roebuck	5.00	2.20
296	Doc Edwards	5.00	2.20
297	Jim Golden	5.00	2.20
298	Don Dillard	5.00	2.20
299	Rookie Stars — Dave Morehead, Bob Dustal, Tom Butters, Dan Schneider	8.00	3.60
300	Willie Mays	135.00	60.00
301	Bill Fischer	5.00	2.20
302	Whitey Herzog	8.00	3.60
303	Earl Francis	5.00	2.20
304	Harry Bright	5.00	2.20
305	Don Hoak	5.00	2.20
306	Star Receivers — Earl Battey, Elston Howard	8.00	3.60
307	Chet Nichols	5.00	2.20
308	Camilo Carreon	5.00	2.20
309	Jim Brewer	5.00	2.20
310	Tommy Davis	8.00	3.60
311	Joe McClain	5.00	2.20
312	Houston Colts Team Card	25.00	11.00
313	Ernie Broglio	5.00	2.20
314	John Goryl	5.00	2.20
315	Ralph Terry	8.00	3.60
316	Norm Sherry	8.00	3.60
317	Sam McDowell	8.00	3.60
318	Gene Mauch MG	8.00	3.60
319	Joe Gaines	5.00	2.20
320	Warren Spahn	40.00	18.00
321	Gino Cimoli	5.00	2.20
322	Bob Turley	8.00	3.60
323	Bill Mazeroski	10.00	4.50
324	Rookie Stars — George Williams, Pete Ward, Phil Roof, Vic Davalillo	8.00	3.60
325	Jack Sanford	5.00	2.20
326	Hank Foiles	5.00	2.20
327	Paul Foytack	5.00	2.20
328	Dick Williams	8.00	3.60
329	Lindy McDaniel	5.00	2.20
330	Chuck Hinton	8.00	3.60
331	Series Foes — Bill Stafford, Bill Pierce	8.00	3.60
332	Joel Horlen	8.00	3.60

333 Carl Warwick	5.00	2.20
334 Wynn Hawkins	5.00	2.20
335 Leon Wagner	5.00	2.20
336 Ed Bauta	5.00	2.20
337 Dodgers Team	25.00	11.00
338 Russ Kemmerer	5.00	2.20
339 Ted Bowsfield	5.00	2.20
340 Yogi Berra P/CO	70.00	32.00
341 Jack Baldschun	5.00	2.20
342 Gene Woodling	8.00	3.60
343 Johnny Pesky MG	8.00	3.60
344 Don Schwall	5.00	2.20
345 Brooks Robinson	60.00	27.00
346 Billy Hoeft	5.00	2.20
347 Joe Torre	14.00	6.25
348 Vic Wertz	8.00	3.60
349 Zoilo Versalles	8.00	3.60
350 Bob Purkey	5.00	2.20
351 Al Luplow	5.00	2.20
352 Ken Johnson	5.00	2.20
353 Billy Williams	30.00	13.50
354 Dom Zanni	5.00	2.20
355 Dean Chance	8.00	3.60
356 John Schaive	5.00	2.20
357 George Altman	5.00	2.20
358 Milt Pappas	8.00	3.60
359 Haywood Sullivan	8.00	3.60
360 Don Drysdale	40.00	18.00
361 Clete Boyer	8.00	3.60
362 Checklist 5	10.00	2.00
363 Dick Radatz	8.00	3.60
364 Howie Goss	5.00	2.20
365 Jim Bunning	15.00	6.75
366 Tony Taylor	8.00	3.60
367 Tony Cloninger	5.00	2.20
368 Ed Bailey	5.00	2.20
369 Jim Lemon	5.00	2.20
370 Dick Donovan	5.00	2.20
371 Rod Kanehl	8.00	3.60
372 Don Lee	5.00	2.20
373 Jim Campbell	5.00	2.20
374 Claude Osteen	8.00	3.60
375 Ken Boyer	8.00	3.60
376 John Wyatt	5.00	2.20
377 Baltimore Orioles	10.00	4.50
Team Card		
378 Bill Henry	5.00	2.20
379 Bob Anderson	5.00	2.20
380 Ernie Banks UER	75.00	34.00
(Back has career Major		
and Minor, but he		
never played in Minors)		
381 Frank Baumann	5.00	2.20
382 Ralph Houk MG	8.00	3.60
383 Pete Richert	5.00	2.20
384 Bob Tillman	5.00	2.20
385 Art Mahaffey	5.00	2.20
386 Rookie Stars	5.00	2.20
Ed Kirkpatrick		
John Bateman		
Larry Bearnarth		
Garry Roggenburk		
387 Al McBean	5.00	2.20
388 Jim Davenport	8.00	3.60
389 Frank Sullivan	5.00	2.20
390 Hank Aaron	125.00	55.00
391 Bill Dailey	5.00	2.20
392 Tribe Thumpers	5.00	2.20
Johnny Romano		
Tito Francona		
393 Ken MacKenzie	8.00	3.60
394 Tim McCarver	14.00	6.25
395 Don McMahon	5.00	2.20
396 Joe Koppe	5.00	2.20
397 Kansas City Athletics	8.00	3.60
Team Card		
398 Boog Powell	25.00	11.00
399 Dick Ellsworth	5.00	2.20
400 Frank Robinson	60.00	27.00
401 Jim Bouton	14.00	6.25
402 Mickey Vernon MG	8.00	3.60
403 Ron Perranoski	8.00	3.60
404 Bob Oldis	5.00	2.20
405 Floyd Robinson	5.00	2.20
406 Howie Koplitz	5.00	2.20
407 Rookie Stars	5.00	2.20

Frank Kostro		
Chico Ruiz		
Larry Elliot		
Dick Simpson		
408 Billy Gardner	5.00	2.20
409 Roy Face	8.00	3.60
410 Earl Battey	5.00	2.20
411 Jim Constable	5.00	2.20
412 Dodger Big Three	40.00	18.00
Johnny Podres		
Don Drysdale		
Sandy Koufax		
413 Jerry Walker	5.00	2.20
414 Ty Cline	5.00	2.20
415 Bob Gibson	60.00	27.00
416 Alex Grammas	5.00	2.20
417 Giants Team	8.00	3.60
418 John Orsino	5.00	2.20
419 Tracy Stallard	5.00	2.20
420 Bobby Richardson	14.00	6.25
421 Tom Morgan	5.00	2.20
422 Fred Hutchinson MG	8.00	3.60
423 Ed Hobaugh	5.00	2.20
424 Charlie Smith	5.00	2.20
425 Smoky Burgess	8.00	3.60
426 Barry Latman	5.00	2.20
427 Bernie Allen	5.00	2.20
428 Carl Boles	5.00	2.20
429 Lou Burdette	8.00	3.60
430 Norm Siebern	5.00	2.20
431A Checklist 6	10.00	2.00
(White on red)		
431B Checklist 6	30.00	6.00
(Black on orange)		
432 Roman Mejias	5.00	2.20
433 Denis Menke	5.00	2.20
434 John Callison	8.00	3.60
435 Woody Held	5.00	2.20
436 Tim Harkness	5.00	2.20
437 Bill Bruton	5.00	2.20
438 Wes Stock	5.00	2.20
439 Don Zimmer	8.00	3.60
440 Juan Marichal	30.00	13.50
441 Lee Thomas	8.00	3.60
442 J.C. Hartman	5.00	2.20
443 Jimmy Piersall	8.00	3.60
444 Jim Maloney	8.00	3.60
445 Norm Cash	8.00	3.60
446 Whitey Ford	40.00	18.00
447 Felix Mantilla	25.00	11.00
448 Jack Kralick	25.00	11.00
449 Jose Tartabull	25.00	11.00
450 Bob Friend	30.00	13.50
451 Indians Team	40.00	18.00
452 Barney Schultz	25.00	11.00
453 Jake Wood	25.00	11.00
454A Art Fowler	25.00	11.00
(Card number on		
white background)		
454B Art Fowler	30.00	13.50
(Card number on		
orange background)		
455 Ruben Amaro	25.00	11.00
456 Jim Coker	25.00	11.00
457 Tex Clevenger	25.00	11.00
458 Al Lopez MG	30.00	13.50
459 Dick LeMay	25.00	11.00
460 Del Crandall	30.00	13.50
461 Norm Bass	25.00	11.00
462 Wally Post	25.00	11.00
463 Joe Schaffernoth	25.00	11.00
464 Ken Aspromonte	25.00	11.00
465 Chuck Estrada	25.00	11.00
466 Rookie Stars SP	60.00	27.00
Nate Oliver		
Tony Martinez		
Bill Freehan		
Jerry Robinson		
467 Phil Ortega	25.00	11.00
468 Carroll Hardy	30.00	13.50
469 Jay Hook	30.00	13.50
470 Tom Tresh SP	60.00	27.00
471 Ken Retzer	25.00	11.00
472 Lou Brock	100.00	45.00
473 New York Mets	100.00	45.00
Team Card		

474 Jack Fisher	25.00	11.00
475 Gus Triandos	30.00	13.50
476 Frank Funk	25.00	11.00
477 Donn Clendenon	30.00	13.50
478 Paul Brown	25.00	11.00
479 Ed Brinkman	25.00	11.00
480 Bill Monbouquette	25.00	11.00
481 Bob Taylor	25.00	11.00
482 Felix Torres	25.00	11.00
483 Jim Owens UER	25.00	11.00
(Stat column for Wins		
has an R instead)		
484 Dale Long SP	30.00	13.50
485 Jim Landis	25.00	11.00
486 Ray Sadecki	25.00	11.00
487 John Roseboro	30.00	13.50
488 Jerry Adair	25.00	11.00
489 Paul Toth	25.00	11.00
490 Willie McCovey	125.00	55.00
491 Harry Craft MG	25.00	11.00
492 Dave Wickersham	25.00	11.00
493 Walt Bond	25.00	11.00
494 Phil Regan	25.00	11.00
495 Frank Thomas SP	30.00	13.50
496 Rookie Stars	30.00	13.50
Steve Dalkowski		
Fred Newman		
Jack Smith		
Carl Bouldin		
497 Bennie Daniels	25.00	11.00
498 Eddie Kasko	25.00	11.00
499 J.C. Martin	25.00	11.00
500 Harmon Killebrew SP	150.00	70.00
501 Joe Azcue	25.00	11.00
502 Daryl Spencer	25.00	11.00
503 Braves Team	40.00	18.00
504 Bob Johnson	25.00	11.00
505 Curt Flood	30.00	13.50
506 Gene Green	25.00	11.00
507 Roland Sheldon	30.00	13.50
508 Ted Savage	25.00	11.00
509A Checklist 7	40.00	8.00
(Checklist centered)		
509B Checklist 7	40.00	8.00
(Copyright to right)		
510 Ken McBride	25.00	11.00
511 Charlie Neal	30.00	13.50
512 Cal McLish	25.00	11.00
513 Gary Geiger	25.00	11.00
514 Larry Osborne	25.00	11.00
515 Don Elston	25.00	11.00
516 Purnell Goldy	25.00	11.00
517 Hal Woodeshick	25.00	11.00
518 Don Blasingame	25.00	11.00
519 Claude Raymond	25.00	11.00
520 Orlando Cepeda	30.00	13.50
521 Dan Pfister	25.00	11.00
522 Rookie Stars	30.00	13.50
Mel Nelson		
Gary Peters		
Jim Roland		
Art Quirk		
523 Bill Kunkel	15.00	6.75
524 Cardinals Team	30.00	13.50
525 Nellie Fox	50.00	22.00
526 Dick Hall	15.00	6.75
527 Ed Sadowski	15.00	6.75
528 Carl Willey	15.00	6.75
529 Wes Covington	15.00	6.75
530 Don Mossi	20.00	9.00
531 Sam Mele MG	15.00	6.75
532 Steve Boros	15.00	6.75
533 Bobby Shantz	20.00	9.00
534 Ken Walters	15.00	6.75
535 Jim Perry	20.00	9.00
536 Norm Larker	15.00	6.75
537 Rookie Stars	1000.00	450.00
Pedro Gonzalez		
Ken McMullen		
Al Weis		
Pete Rose		
538 George Brunet	15.00	6.75
539 Wayne Causey	15.00	6.75
540 Bob Clemente	375.00	170.00
541 Ron Moeller	15.00	6.75
542 Lou Klimchock	15.00	6.75

☐ 543	Russ Snyder	15.00	6.75
☐ 544	Rookie Stars	40.00	18.00
	Duke Carmel		
	Bill Haas		
	Rusty Staub		
	Dick Phillips		
☐ 545	Jose Pagan	15.00	6.75
☐ 546	Hal Reniff	20.00	9.00
☐ 547	Gus Bell	15.00	6.75
☐ 548	Tom Satriano	15.00	6.75
☐ 549	Rookie Stars	15.00	6.75
	Marcelino Lopez		
	Pete Lovrich		
	Paul Ratliff		
	Elmo Plaskett		
☐ 550	Duke Snider	75.00	34.00
☐ 551	Billy Klaus	15.00	6.75
☐ 552	Detroit Tigers	50.00	22.00
	Team Card		
☐ 553	Rookie Stars	125.00	55.00
	Brock Davis		
	Jim Gosger		
	Willie Stargell		
	John Herrnstein		
☐ 554	Hank Fischer	15.00	6.75
☐ 555	John Blanchard	20.00	9.00
☐ 556	Al Worthington	15.00	6.75
☐ 557	Cuno Barragan	15.00	6.75
☐ 558	Rookie Stars	20.00	9.00
	Bill Faul		
	Ron Hunt		
	Al Moran		
	Bob Lipski		
☐ 559	Danny Murtaugh MG	15.00	6.75
☐ 560	Ray Herbert	15.00	6.75
☐ 561	Mike De La Hoz	15.00	6.75
☐ 562	Rookie Stars	25.00	11.00
	Randy Cardinal		
	Dave McNally		
	Ken Rowe		
	Don Rowe		
☐ 563	Mel McCormick	15.00	6.75
☐ 564	George Banks	15.00	6.75
☐ 565	Larry Sherry	15.00	6.75
☐ 566	Cliff Cook	15.00	6.75
☐ 567	Jim Duffalo	15.00	6.75
☐ 568	Bob Sadowski	15.00	6.75
☐ 569	Luis Arroyo	20.00	9.00
☐ 570	Frank Bolling	15.00	6.75
☐ 571	Johnny Klippstein	15.00	6.75
☐ 572	Jack Spring	15.00	6.75
☐ 573	Coot Veal	15.00	6.75
☐ 574	Hal Kolstad	15.00	6.75
☐ 575	Don Cardwell	15.00	6.75
☐ 576	Johnny Temple	25.00	9.50

1964 Topps

The cards in this 587-card set measure 2 1/2" by 3 1/2". Players in the 1964 Topps baseball series were easy to sort by team due to the giant block lettering found at the top of each card. The name and position of the player are found underneath the picture, and the

card is numbered in a ball design on the orange-colored back. The usual last series scarcity holds for this set (523 to 587). Subsets within this set include League Leaders (1-12) and World Series cards (136-140). Among other vehicles, cards were issued in one-card penny packs as well as five-card nickel packs. There were some three-card advertising panels produced by Topps; the players included are from the first series; one panel shows Walt Alston, Bill Henry, and Vada Pinson on the front with a Mickey Mantle card back on one of the backs. Another panel shows Carl Willey, White Sox Rookies, and Bob Friend on the front with a Mickey Mantle card back on one of the backs. The key Rookie Cards in this set are Richie Allen, Tony Conigliaro, Tommy John, Tony LaRussa, Phil Niekro and Lou Piniella.

	NRMT	VG-E
COMPLETE SET (587)	3000.00	1350.00
COMMON CARD (1-196)	3.00	1.35
COMMON CARD (197-370)	4.00	1.80
MINOR STARS 1-370	6.00	2.70
SEMISTARS 1-370	8.00	3.60
UNLISTED STARS 1-370	12.00	5.50
COMMON CARD (371-522)	7.00	3.10
MINOR STARS 371-522	10.00	4.50
SEMISTARS 371-522	15.00	6.75
UNLISTED STARS 371-522	25.00	11.00
COMMON CARD (523-587)	16.00	7.25
MINOR STARS 523-587	20.00	9.00
SEMISTARS 523-587	30.00	13.50
*UNLISTED DODGER/YANKEE: 1.25X VALUE
CARDS PRICED IN NM CONDITION

☐ 1	NL ERA Leaders	30.00	9.00
	Sandy Koufax		
	Dick Ellsworth		
	Bob Friend		
☐ 2	AL ERA Leaders	6.00	2.70
	Gary Peters		
	Juan Pizarro		
	Camilo Pascual		
☐ 3	NL Pitching Leaders	18.00	8.00
	Sandy Koufax		
	Juan Marichal		
	Warren Spahn		
	Jim Maloney		
☐ 4	AL Pitching Leaders	10.00	4.50
	Whitey Ford		
	Camilo Pascual		
	Jim Bouton		
☐ 5	NL Strikeout Leaders	15.00	6.75
	Sandy Koufax		
	Jim Maloney		
	Don Drysdale		
☐ 6	AL Strikeout Leaders	6.00	2.70
	Camilo Pascual		
	Jim Bunning		
	Dick Stigman		
☐ 7	NL Batting Leaders	20.00	9.00
	Tommy Davis		
	Bob Clemente		
	Dick Groat		
	Hank Aaron		
☐ 8	AL Batting Leaders	15.00	6.75
	Carl Yastrzemski		
	Al Kaline		
	Rich Rollins		
☐ 9	NL Home Run Leaders	30.00	13.50
	Hank Aaron		
	Willie McCovey		
	Willie Mays		
	Orlando Cepeda		
☐ 10	AL Home Run Leaders	10.00	4.50
	Harmon Killebrew		
	Dick Stuart		
	Bob Allison		
☐ 11	NL RBI Leaders	15.00	6.75
	Hank Aaron		
	Ken Boyer		
	Bill White		
☐ 12	AL RBI Leaders	10.00	4.50
	Dick Stuart		
	Al Kaline		
	Harmon Killebrew		
☐ 13	Hoyt Wilhelm	10.00	4.50
☐ 14	Dodgers Rookies	3.00	1.35
	Dick Nen		
	Nick Willhite		
☐ 15	Zoilo Versalles	6.00	2.70
☐ 16	John Boozer	3.00	1.35
☐ 17	Willie Kirkland	3.00	1.35
☐ 18	Billy O'Dell	3.00	1.35
☐ 19	Don Wert	3.00	1.35
☐ 20	Bob Friend	6.00	2.70
☐ 21	Yogi Berra MG	30.00	13.50
☐ 22	Jerry Adair	3.00	1.35
☐ 23	Chris Zachary	3.00	1.35
☐ 24	Carl Sawatski	3.00	1.35
☐ 25	Bill Monbouquette	3.00	1.35
☐ 26	Gino Cimoli	3.00	1.35
☐ 27	New York Mets	8.00	3.60
	Team Card		
☐ 28	Claude Osteen	6.00	2.70
☐ 29	Lou Brock	35.00	16.00
☐ 30	Ron Perranoski	6.00	2.70
☐ 31	Dave Nicholson	3.00	1.35
☐ 32	Dean Chance	6.00	2.70
☐ 33	Reds Rookies	6.00	2.70
	Sammy Ellis		
	Mel Queen		
☐ 34	Jim Perry	6.00	2.70
☐ 35	Eddie Mathews	20.00	9.00
☐ 36	Hal Reniff	3.00	1.35
☐ 37	Smoky Burgess	6.00	2.70
☐ 38	Jim Wynn	7.00	3.10
☐ 39	Hank Aguirre	3.00	1.35
☐ 40	Dick Groat	6.00	2.70
☐ 41	Friendly Foes	8.00	3.60
	Willie McCovey		
	Leon Wagner		
☐ 42	Moe Drabowsky	6.00	2.70
☐ 43	Roy Sievers	6.00	2.70
☐ 44	Duke Carmel	3.00	1.35
☐ 45	Milt Pappas	6.00	2.70
☐ 46	Ed Brinkman	3.00	1.35
☐ 47	Giants Rookies	6.00	2.70
	Jesus Alou		
	Ron Herbel		
☐ 48	Bob Perry	3.00	1.35
☐ 49	Bill Henry	3.00	1.35
☐ 50	Mickey Mantle	300.00	135.00
☐ 51	Pete Richert	3.00	1.35
☐ 52	Chuck Hinton	3.00	1.35
☐ 53	Denis Menke	3.00	1.35
☐ 54	Sam Mele MG	3.00	1.35
☐ 55	Ernie Banks	35.00	16.00
☐ 56	Hal Brown	3.00	1.35
☐ 57	Tim Harkness	3.00	1.35
☐ 58	Don Demeter	3.00	1.35
☐ 59	Ernie Broglio	3.00	1.35
☐ 60	Frank Malzone	6.00	2.70
☐ 61	Angel Backstops	6.00	2.70
	Bob Rodgers		
	Ed Sadowski		
☐ 62	Ted Savage	3.00	1.35
☐ 63	John Orsino	3.00	1.35
☐ 64	Ted Abernathy	3.00	1.35
☐ 65	Felipe Alou	6.00	2.70
☐ 66	Eddie Fisher	3.00	1.35
☐ 67	Tigers Team	8.00	3.60
☐ 68	Willie Davis	6.00	2.70
☐ 69	Clete Boyer	6.00	2.70
☐ 70	Joe Torre	8.00	3.60
☐ 71	Jack Spring	3.00	1.35
☐ 72	Chico Cardenas	6.00	2.70
☐ 73	Jimmie Hall	6.00	2.70
☐ 74	Pirates Rookies	3.00	1.35
	Bob Priddy		
	Tom Butters		
☐ 75	Wayne Causey	3.00	1.35

76	Checklist 1	8.00	1.60
77	Jerry Walker	3.00	1.35
78	Merritt Ranew	3.00	1.35
79	Bob Heffner	3.00	1.35
80	Vada Pinson	6.00	2.70
81	All-Star Vets	10.00	4.50
	Nellie Fox		
	Harmon Killebrew		
82	Jim Davenport	6.00	2.70
83	Gus Triandos	6.00	2.70
84	Carl Willey	3.00	1.35
85	Pete Ward	3.00	1.35
86	Al Downing	6.00	2.70
87	St. Louis Cardinals	8.00	3.60
	Team Card		
88	John Roseboro	6.00	2.70
89	Boog Powell	6.00	2.70
90	Earl Battey	3.00	1.35
91	Bob Bailey	6.00	2.70
92	Steve Ridzik	3.00	1.35
93	Gary Geiger	3.00	1.35
94	Braves Rookies	3.00	1.35
	Jim Britton		
	Larry Maxie		
95	George Altman	3.00	1.35
96	Bob Buhl	6.00	2.70
97	Jim Fregosi	6.00	2.70
98	Bill Bruton	3.00	1.35
99	Al Stanek	3.00	1.35
100	Elston Howard	6.00	2.70
101	Walt Alston MG	6.00	2.70
102	Checklist 2	8.00	1.60
103	Curt Flood	6.00	2.70
104	Art Mahaffey	6.00	2.70
105	Woody Held	3.00	1.35
106	Joe Nuxhall	6.00	2.70
107	White Sox Rookies	3.00	1.35
	Bruce Howard		
	Frank Kreutzer		
108	John Wyatt	3.00	1.35
109	Rusty Staub	6.00	2.70
110	Albie Pearson	6.00	2.70
111	Don Elston	3.00	1.35
112	Bob Tillman	3.00	1.35
113	Grover Powell	3.00	1.35
114	Don Lock	3.00	1.35
115	Frank Bolling	3.00	1.35
116	Twins Rookies	12.00	5.50
	Jay Ward		
	Tony Oliva		
117	Earl Francis	3.00	1.35
118	John Blanchard	6.00	2.70
119	Gary Kolb	3.00	1.35
120	Don Drysdale	20.00	9.00
121	Pete Runnels	6.00	2.70
122	Don McMahon	3.00	1.35
123	Jose Pagan	3.00	1.35
124	Orlando Pena	3.00	1.35
125	Pete Rose	150.00	70.00
126	Russ Snyder	3.00	1.35
127	Angels Rookies	3.00	1.35
	Aubrey Gatewood		
	Dick Simpson		
128	Mickey Lolich	20.00	9.00
129	Amado Samuel	3.00	1.35
130	Gary Peters	6.00	2.70
131	Steve Boros	3.00	1.35
132	Braves Team	8.00	3.60
133	Jim Grant	6.00	2.70
134	Don Zimmer	6.00	2.70
135	Johnny Callison	6.00	2.70
136	Sandy Koufax WS	18.00	8.00
	strikes out 15		
137	Tommy Davis WS	8.00	3.60
138	Ron Fairly WS	8.00	3.60
139	Frank Howard WS	8.00	3.60
140	World Series Summary	8.00	3.60
	Dodgers celebrate		
141	Danny Murtaugh MG	6.00	2.70
142	John Bateman	3.00	1.35
143	Bubba Phillips	3.00	1.35
144	Al Worthington	3.00	1.35
145	Norm Siebern	3.00	1.35
146	Indians Rookies	30.00	13.50
	Tommy John		
	Bob Chance		
147	Ray Sadecki	3.00	1.35
148	J.C. Martin	3.00	1.35
149	Paul Foytack	3.00	1.35
150	Willie Mays	100.00	45.00
151	Athletics Team	8.00	3.60
152	Denny Lemaster	3.00	1.35
153	Dick Williams	6.00	2.70
154	Dick Tracewski	6.00	2.70
155	Duke Snider	30.00	13.50
156	Bill Dailey	3.00	1.35
157	Gene Mauch MG	6.00	2.70
158	Ken Johnson	3.00	1.35
159	Charlie Dees	3.00	1.35
160	Ken Boyer	6.00	2.70
161	Dave McNally	6.00	2.70
162	Hitting Area	6.00	2.70
	Dick Sisler CO		
	Vada Pinson		
163	Donn Clendenon	6.00	2.70
164	Bud Daley	3.00	1.35
165	Jerry Lumpe	3.00	1.35
166	Marty Keough	3.00	1.35
167	Senators Rookies	30.00	13.50
	Mike Brumley		
	Lou Piniella		
168	Al Weis	3.00	1.35
169	Del Crandall	6.00	2.70
170	Dick Radatz	6.00	2.70
171	Ty Cline	3.00	1.35
172	Indians Team	8.00	3.60
173	Ryne Duren	6.00	2.70
174	Doc Edwards	3.00	1.35
175	Billy Williams	12.00	5.50
176	Tracy Stallard	3.00	1.35
177	Harmon Killebrew	20.00	9.00
178	Hank Bauer MG	6.00	2.70
179	Carl Warwick	3.00	1.35
180	Tommy Davis	6.00	2.70
181	Dave Wickersham	3.00	1.35
182	Sox Sockers	15.00	6.75
	Carl Yastrzemski		
	Chuck Schilling		
183	Ron Taylor	3.00	1.35
184	Al Luplow	3.00	1.35
185	Jim O'Toole	6.00	2.70
186	Roman Mejias	3.00	1.35
187	Ed Roebuck	3.00	1.35
188	Checklist 3	8.00	1.60
189	Bob Hendley	3.00	1.35
190	Bobby Richardson	8.00	3.60
191	Clay Dalrymple	6.00	2.70
192	Cubs Rookies	3.00	1.35
	John Boccabella		
	Billy Cowan		
193	Jerry Lynch	3.00	1.35
194	John Goryl	3.00	1.35
195	Floyd Robinson	3.00	1.35
196	Jim Gentile	6.00	2.70
197	Frank Lary	6.00	2.70
198	Len Gabrielson	4.00	1.80
199	Joe Azcue	4.00	1.80
200	Sandy Koufax	100.00	45.00
201	Orioles Rookies	6.00	2.70
	Sam Bowens		
	Wally Bunker		
202	Galen Cisco	6.00	2.70
203	John Kennedy	6.00	2.70
204	Matty Alou	6.00	2.70
205	Nellie Fox	14.00	6.25
206	Steve Hamilton	6.00	2.70
207	Fred Hutchinson MG	6.00	2.70
208	Wes Covington	6.00	2.70
209	Bob Allen	4.00	1.80
210	Carl Yastrzemski	35.00	16.00
211	Jim Coker	4.00	1.80
212	Pete Lovrich	4.00	1.80
213	Angels Team	8.00	3.60
214	Ken McMullen	6.00	2.70
215	Ray Herbert	4.00	1.80
216	Mike de la Hoz	4.00	1.80
217	Jim King	4.00	1.80
218	Hank Fischer	4.00	1.80
219	Young Aces	6.00	2.70
	Al Downing		
	Jim Bouton		
220	Dick Ellsworth	6.00	2.70
221	Bob Saverine	4.00	1.80
222	Billy Pierce	6.00	2.70
223	George Banks	4.00	1.80
224	Tommie Sisk	4.00	1.80
225	Roger Maris	50.00	22.00
226	Colts Rookies	7.00	3.10
	Jerry Grote		
	Larry Yellen		
227	Barry Latman	4.00	1.80
228	Felix Mantilla	4.00	1.80
229	Charley Lau	6.00	2.70
230	Brooks Robinson	35.00	16.00
231	Dick Calmus	4.00	1.80
232	Al Lopez MG	6.00	2.70
233	Hal Smith	4.00	1.80
234	Gary Bell	4.00	1.80
235	Ron Hunt	4.00	1.80
236	Bill Faul	4.00	1.80
237	Cubs Team	8.00	3.60
238	Roy McMillan	6.00	2.70
239	Herm Starrette	4.00	1.80
240	Bill White	6.00	2.70
241	Jim Owens	4.00	1.80
242	Harvey Kuenn	6.00	2.70
243	Phillies Rookies	30.00	13.50
	Richie Allen		
	John Herrnstein		
244	Tony LaRussa	30.00	13.50
245	Dick Stigman	4.00	1.80
246	Manny Mota	6.00	2.70
247	Dave DeBusschere	6.00	2.70
248	Johnny Pesky MG	6.00	2.70
249	Doug Camilli	4.00	1.80
250	Al Kaline	40.00	18.00
251	Choo Choo Coleman	6.00	2.70
252	Ken Aspromonte	4.00	1.80
253	Wally Post	6.00	2.70
254	Don Hoak	6.00	2.70
255	Lee Thomas	6.00	2.70
256	Johnny Weekly	4.00	1.80
257	San Francisco Giants	8.00	3.60
	Team Card		
258	Garry Roggenburk	4.00	1.80
259	Harry Bright	4.00	1.80
260	Frank Robinson	35.00	16.00
261	Jim Hannan	4.00	1.80
262	Cards Rookies	8.00	3.60
	Mike Shannon		
	Harry Fanok		
263	Chuck Estrada	4.00	1.80
264	Jim Landis	4.00	1.80
265	Jim Bunning	14.00	6.25
266	Gene Freese	4.00	1.80
267	Wilbur Wood	7.00	3.10
268	Bill's Got It	6.00	2.70
	Danny Murtaugh MG		
	Bill Virdon		
269	Ellis Burton	4.00	1.80
270	Rich Rollins	6.00	2.70
271	Bob Sadowski	4.00	1.80
272	Jake Wood	4.00	1.80
273	Mel Nelson	4.00	1.80
274	Checklist 4	8.00	1.60
275	John Tsitouris	4.00	1.80
276	Jose Tartabull	6.00	2.70
277	Ken Retzer	4.00	1.80
278	Bobby Shantz	6.00	2.70
279	Joe Koppe UER	4.00	1.80
	(Glove on wrong hand)		
280	Juan Marichal	12.00	5.50
281	Yankees Rookies	6.00	2.70
	Jake Gibbs		
	Tom Metcalf		
282	Bob Bruce	4.00	1.80
283	Tom McGraw	4.00	1.80
284	Dick Schofield	4.00	1.80
285	Robin Roberts	14.00	6.25
286	Don Landrum	4.00	1.80
287	Red Sox Rookies	50.00	22.00
	Tony Conigliaro		
	Bill Spanswick		
288	Al Moran	4.00	1.80
289	Frank Funk	4.00	1.80
290	Bob Allison	6.00	2.70
291	Phil Ortega	4.00	1.80
292	Mike Roarke	4.00	1.80

293	Phillies Team	8.00	3.60
294	Ken L. Hunt	4.00	1.80
295	Roger Craig	6.00	2.70
296	Ed Kirkpatrick	4.00	1.80
297	Ken MacKenzie	4.00	1.80
298	Harry Craft MG	4.00	1.80
299	Bill Stafford	4.00	1.80
300	Hank Aaron	90.00	40.00
301	Larry Brown	4.00	1.80
302	Dan Pfister	4.00	1.80
303	Jim Campbell	4.00	1.80
304	Bob Johnson	4.00	1.80
305	Jack Lamabe	4.00	1.80
306	Giant Gunners	35.00	16.00
	Willie Mays		
	Orlando Cepeda		
307	Joe Gibbon	4.00	1.80
308	Gene Stephens	4.00	1.80
309	Paul Toth	4.00	1.80
310	Jim Gilliam	6.00	2.70
311	Tom Brown	6.00	2.70
312	Tigers Rookies	4.00	1.80
	Fritz Fisher		
	Fred Gladding		
313	Chuck Hiller	4.00	1.80
314	Jerry Buchek	4.00	1.80
315	Bo Belinsky	6.00	2.70
316	Gene Oliver	4.00	1.80
317	Al Smith	4.00	1.80
318	Minnesota Twins	8.00	3.60
	Team Card		
319	Paul Brown	4.00	1.80
320	Rocky Colavito	14.00	6.25
321	Bob Lillis	4.00	1.80
322	George Brunet	4.00	1.80
323	John Buzhardt	4.00	1.80
324	Casey Stengel MG	15.00	6.75
325	Hector Lopez	6.00	2.70
326	Ron Brand	4.00	1.80
327	Don Blasingame	4.00	1.80
328	Bob Shaw	4.00	1.80
329	Russ Nixon	4.00	1.80
330	Tommy Harper	6.00	2.70
331	AL Bombers	175.00	80.00
	Roger Maris		
	Norm Cash		
	Mickey Mantle		
	Al Kaline		
332	Ray Washburn	4.00	1.80
333	Billy Moran	4.00	1.80
334	Lew Krausse	4.00	1.80
335	Don Mossi	6.00	2.70
336	Andre Rodgers	4.00	1.80
337	Dodgers Rookies	6.00	2.70
	Al Ferrara		
	Jeff Torborg		
338	Jack Kralick	4.00	1.80
339	Walt Bond	4.00	1.80
340	Joe Cunningham	4.00	1.80
341	Jim Roland	4.00	1.80
342	Willie Stargell	30.00	13.50
343	Senators Team	8.00	3.60
344	Phil Linz	6.00	2.70
345	Frank Thomas	6.00	2.70
346	Joey Jay	4.00	1.80
347	Bobby Wine	6.00	2.70
348	Ed Lopat MG	6.00	2.70
349	Art Fowler	4.00	1.80
350	Willie McCovey	20.00	9.00
351	Dan Schneider	4.00	1.80
352	Eddie Bressoud	4.00	1.80
353	Wally Moon	6.00	2.70
354	Dave Giusti	4.00	1.80
355	Vic Power	6.00	2.70
356	Reds Rookies	6.00	2.70
	Bill McCool		
	Chico Ruiz		
357	Charley James	4.00	1.80
358	Ron Kline	4.00	1.80
359	Jim Schaffer	4.00	1.80
360	Joe Pepitone	7.00	3.10
361	Jay Hook	4.00	1.80
362	Checklist 5	8.00	1.60
363	Dick McAuliffe	6.00	2.70
364	Joe Gaines	4.00	1.80
365	Cal McLish	6.00	2.70
366	Nelson Mathews	4.00	1.80
367	Fred Whitfield	4.00	1.80
368	White Sox Rookies	6.00	2.70
	Fritz Ackley		
	Don Buford		
369	Jerry Zimmerman	4.00	1.80
370	Hal Woodeshick	4.00	1.80
371	Frank Howard	10.00	4.50
372	Howie Koplitz	7.00	3.10
373	Pirates Team	15.00	6.75
374	Bobby Bolin	7.00	3.10
375	Ron Santo	10.00	4.50
376	Dave Morehead	7.00	3.10
377	Bob Skinner	7.00	3.10
378	Braves Rookies	10.00	4.50
	Woody Woodward		
	Jack Smith		
379	Tony Gonzalez	7.00	3.10
380	Whitey Ford	35.00	16.00
381	Bob Taylor	7.00	3.10
382	Wes Stock	7.00	3.10
383	Bill Rigney MG	7.00	3.10
384	Ron Hansen	7.00	3.10
385	Curt Simmons	10.00	4.50
386	Lenny Green	7.00	3.10
387	Terry Fox	7.00	3.10
388	A's Rookies	10.00	4.50
	John O'Donoghue		
	George Williams		
389	Jim Umbricht	10.00	4.50
	(Card back mentions		
	his death)		
390	Orlando Cepeda	10.00	4.50
391	Sam McDowell	10.00	4.50
392	Jim Pagliaroni	7.00	3.10
393	Casey Teaches	10.00	4.50
	Casey Stengel MG		
	Ed Kranepool		
394	Bob Miller	7.00	3.10
395	Tom Tresh	10.00	4.50
396	Dennis Bennett	7.00	3.10
397	Chuck Cottier	7.00	3.10
398	Mets Rookies	7.00	3.10
	Bill Haas		
	Dick Smith		
399	Jackie Brandt	7.00	3.10
400	Warren Spahn	40.00	18.00
401	Charlie Maxwell	7.00	3.10
402	Tom Sturdivant	7.00	3.10
403	Reds Team	15.00	6.75
404	Tony Martinez	7.00	3.10
405	Ken McBride	7.00	3.10
406	Al Spangler	7.00	3.10
407	Bill Freehan	10.00	4.50
408	Cubs Rookies	7.00	3.10
	Jim Stewart		
	Fred Burdette		
409	Bill Fischer	7.00	3.10
410	Dick Stuart	10.00	4.50
411	Lee Walls	7.00	3.10
412	Ray Culp	10.00	4.50
413	Johnny Keane MG	7.00	3.10
414	Jack Sanford	7.00	3.10
415	Tony Kubek	10.00	4.50
416	Lee Maye	7.00	3.10
417	Don Cardwell	7.00	3.10
418	Orioles Rookies	10.00	4.50
	Darold Knowles		
	Les Narum		
419	Ken Harrelson	14.00	6.25
420	Jim Maloney	10.00	4.50
421	Camilo Carreon	7.00	3.10
422	Jack Fisher	7.00	3.10
423	Tops in NL...	125.00	55.00
	Hank Aaron		
	Willie Mays		
424	Dick Bertell	7.00	3.10
425	Norm Cash	10.00	4.50
426	Bob Rodgers	7.00	3.10
427	Don Rudolph	7.00	3.10
428	Red Sox Rookies	7.00	3.10
	Archie Skeen		
	Pete Smith		
	(Back states Archie		
	has retired)		
429	Tim McCarver	10.00	4.50
430	Juan Pizarro	7.00	3.10
431	George Alusik	7.00	3.10
432	Ruben Amaro	10.00	4.50
433	Yankees Team	40.00	18.00
434	Don Nottebart	7.00	3.10
435	Vic Davalillo	7.00	3.10
436	Charlie Neal	10.00	4.50
437	Ed Bailey	7.00	3.10
438	Checklist 6	25.00	5.00
439	Harvey Haddix	10.00	4.50
440	Bob Clemente UER	250.00	110.00
	(1960 Pittsburfh)		
441	Bob Duliba	7.00	3.10
442	Pumpsie Green	10.00	4.50
443	Chuck Dressen MG	10.00	4.50
444	Larry Jackson	7.00	3.10
445	Bill Skowron	10.00	4.50
446	Julian Javier	10.00	4.50
447	Ted Bowsfield	7.00	3.10
448	Cookie Rojas	10.00	4.50
449	Deron Johnson	10.00	4.50
450	Steve Barber	7.00	3.10
451	Joe Amalfitano	7.00	3.10
452	Giants Rookies	10.00	4.50
	Gil Garrido		
	Jim Ray Hart		
453	Frank Baumann	7.00	3.10
454	Tommie Aaron	10.00	4.50
455	Bernie Allen	7.00	3.10
456	Dodgers Rookies	10.00	4.50
	Wes Parker		
	John Werhas		
457	Jesse Gonder	7.00	3.10
458	Ralph Terry	10.00	4.50
459	Red Sox Rookies	7.00	3.10
	Pete Charton		
	Dalton Jones		
460	Bob Gibson	35.00	16.00
461	George Thomas	7.00	3.10
462	Birdie Tebbetts MG	7.00	3.10
463	Don Leppert	7.00	3.10
464	Dallas Green	10.00	4.50
465	Mike Hershberger	7.00	3.10
466	A's Rookies	10.00	4.50
	Dick Green		
	Aurelio Monteagudo		
467	Bob Aspromonte	7.00	3.10
468	Gaylord Perry	40.00	18.00
469	Cubs Rookies	10.00	4.50
	Fred Norman		
	Sterling Slaughter		
470	Jim Bouton	10.00	4.50
471	Gates Brown	10.00	4.50
472	Vern Law	10.00	4.50
473	Baltimore Orioles..	15.00	6.75
	Team Card		
474	Larry Sherry	10.00	4.50
475	Ed Charles	7.00	3.10
476	Braves Rookies	14.00	6.25
	Rico Carty		
	Dick Kelley		
477	Mike Joyce	7.00	3.10
478	Dick Howser	10.00	4.50
479	Cardinals Rookies	7.00	3.10
	Dave Bakenhaster		
	Johnny Lewis		
480	Bob Purkey	7.00	3.10
481	Chuck Schilling	7.00	3.10
482	Phillies Rookies	10.00	4.50
	John Briggs		
	Danny Cater		
483	Fred Valentine	7.00	3.10
484	Bill Pleis	7.00	3.10
485	Tom Haller	7.00	3.10
486	Bob Kennedy MG	7.00	3.10
487	Mike McCormick	7.00	3.10
488	Yankees Rookies	10.00	4.50
	Pete Mikkelsen		
	Bob Meyer		
489	Julio Navarro	7.00	3.10
490	Ron Fairly	10.00	4.50
491	Ed Rakow	7.00	3.10
492	Colts Rookies	7.00	3.10
	Jim Beauchamp		
	Mike White		
493	Don Lee	7.00	3.10

☐ 494 Al Jackson	7.00	3.10
☐ 495 Bill Virdon	10.00	4.50
☐ 496 White Sox Team	15.00	6.75
☐ 497 Jeoff Long	7.00	3.10
☐ 498 Dave Stenhouse	7.00	3.10
☐ 499 Indians Rookies	7.00	3.10
Chico Salmon		
Gordon Seyfried		
☐ 500 Camilo Pascual	10.00	4.50
☐ 501 Bob Veale	10.00	4.50
☐ 502 Angels Rookies	7.00	3.10
Bobby Knoop		
Bob Lee		
☐ 503 Earl Wilson	7.00	3.10
☐ 504 Claude Raymond	7.00	3.10
☐ 505 Stan Williams	7.00	3.10
☐ 506 Bobby Bragan MG	7.00	3.10
☐ 507 Johnny Edwards	7.00	3.10
☐ 508 Diego Segui	7.00	3.10
☐ 509 Pirates Rookies	10.00	4.50
Gene Alley		
Orlando McFarlane		
☐ 510 Lindy McDaniel	10.00	4.50
☐ 511 Lou Jackson	10.00	4.50
☐ 512 Tigers Rookies	14.00	6.25
Willie Horton		
Joe Sparma		
☐ 513 Don Larsen	10.00	4.50
☐ 514 Jim Hickman	10.00	4.50
☐ 515 Johnny Romano	7.00	3.10
☐ 516 Twins Rookies	7.00	3.10
Jerry Arrigo		
Dwight Siebler		
☐ 517A Checklist 7 ERR	25.00	5.00
(Incorrect numbering		
sequence on back)		
☐ 517B Checklist 7 COR	15.00	3.00
(Correct numbering		
on back)		
☐ 518 Carl Bouldin	7.00	3.10
☐ 519 Charlie Smith	7.00	3.10
☐ 520 Jack Baldschun	10.00	4.50
☐ 521 Tom Satriano	7.00	3.10
☐ 522 Bob Tiefenauer	7.00	3.10
☐ 523 Lou Burdette UER	20.00	9.00
(Pitching lefty)		
☐ 524 Reds Rookies	16.00	7.25
Jim Dickson		
Bobby Klaus		
☐ 525 Al McBean	16.00	7.25
☐ 526 Lou Clinton	16.00	7.25
☐ 527 Larry Bearnarth	16.00	7.25
☐ 528 A's Rookies	20.00	9.00
Dave Duncan		
Tommie Reynolds		
☐ 529 Alvin Dark MG	20.00	9.00
☐ 530 Leon Wagner	16.00	7.25
☐ 531 Los Angeles Dodgers	25.00	11.00
Team Card		
☐ 532 Twins Rookies	16.00	7.25
Bud Bloomfield		
(Bloomfield photo		
actually Jay Ward)		
Joe Nossek		
☐ 533 Johnny Klippstein	16.00	7.25
☐ 534 Gus Bell	16.00	7.25
☐ 535 Phil Regan	16.00	7.25
☐ 536 Mets Rookies	16.00	7.25
Larry Elliot		
John Stephenson		
☐ 537 Dan Osinski	16.00	7.25
☐ 538 Minnie Minoso	20.00	9.00
☐ 539 Roy Face	20.00	9.00
☐ 540 Luis Aparicio	25.00	11.00
☐ 541 Braves Rookies	100.00	45.00
Phil Roof		
Phil Niekro		
☐ 542 Don Mincher	16.00	7.25
☐ 543 Bob Uecker	40.00	18.00
☐ 544 Colts Rookies	16.00	7.25
Steve Hertz		
Joe Hoerner		
☐ 545 Max Alvis	16.00	7.25
☐ 546 Joe Christopher	16.00	7.25
☐ 547 Gil Hodges MG	25.00	11.00
☐ 548 NL Rookies	16.00	7.25

Wayne Schurr		
Paul Speckenbach		
☐ 549 Joe Moeller	16.00	7.25
☐ 550 Ken Hubbs MEM	35.00	16.00
☐ 551 Billy Hoeft	16.00	7.25
☐ 552 Indians Rookies	16.00	7.25
Tom Kelley		
Sonny Siebert		
☐ 553 Jim Brewer	16.00	7.25
☐ 554 Hank Foiles	16.00	7.25
☐ 555 Lee Stange	16.00	7.25
☐ 556 Mets Rookies	16.00	7.25
Steve Dillon		
Ron Locke		
☐ 557 Leo Burke	16.00	7.25
☐ 558 Don Schwall	16.00	7.25
☐ 559 Dick Phillips	16.00	7.25
☐ 560 Dick Farrell	16.00	7.25
☐ 561 Phillies Rookies UER	20.00	9.00
Dave Bennett		
(19... is 18)		
Rick Wise		
☐ 562 Pedro Ramos	16.00	7.25
☐ 563 Dal Maxvill	16.00	7.25
☐ 564 AL Rookies	16.00	7.25
Joe McCabe		
Jerry McNertney		
☐ 565 Stu Miller	16.00	7.25
☐ 566 Ed Kranepool	20.00	9.00
☐ 567 Jim Kaat	20.00	9.00
☐ 568 NL Rookies	16.00	7.25
Phil Gagliano		
Cap Peterson		
☐ 569 Fred Newman	16.00	7.25
☐ 570 Bill Mazeroski	20.00	9.00
☐ 571 Gene Conley	16.00	7.25
☐ 572 AL Rookies	16.00	7.25
Dave Gray		
Dick Egan		
☐ 573 Jim Duffalo	16.00	7.25
☐ 574 Manny Jimenez	16.00	7.25
☐ 575 Tony Cloninger	16.00	7.25
☐ 576 Mets Rookies	16.00	7.25
Jerry Hinsley		
Bill Wakefield		
☐ 577 Gordy Coleman	16.00	7.25
☐ 578 Glen Hobbie	16.00	7.25
☐ 579 Red Sox Team	25.00	11.00
☐ 580 Johnny Podres	20.00	9.00
☐ 581 Yankees Rookies	20.00	9.00
Pedro Gonzalez		
Archie Moore		
☐ 582 Rod Kanehl	20.00	9.00
☐ 583 Tito Francona	16.00	7.25
☐ 584 Joe Koppe	16.00	7.25
☐ 585 Tony Taylor	16.00	7.25
☐ 586 Jimmy Piersall	20.00	9.00
☐ 587 Bennie Daniels !	18.00	8.00

1965 Topps

The cards in this 598-card set measure 2 1/2" by 3 1/2". The cards comprising the 1965 Topps set have team names located within a distinctive pennant design below the picture.

The cards have blue borders on the reverse and were issued by series. Within this last series (523-598) there are 44 cards that were printed in lesser quantities than the other cards in that series; these shorter-printed cards are marked by SP in the checklist below. Featured subsets within this set include League Leaders (1-12) and World Series cards (132-139). This was the last year Topps issued one-card penny packs. Card were also issued in five-card nickel packs. The key Rookie Cards in this set are Steve Carlton, Jim "Catfish" Hunter, Joe Morgan, Mansori Murakami and Tony Perez.

	NRMT	VG-E
COMPLETE SET (598)	3500.00	1600.00
COMMON CARD (1-196)	2.00	.90
COMMON CARD (197-283)	2.50	1.10
MINOR STARS 1-283	4.00	1.80
SEMISTARS 1-283	6.00	2.70
UNLISTED STARS 1-283	10.00	4.50
COMMON CARD (284-370)	4.00	1.80
MINOR STARS 284-370	6.00	2.70
SEMISTARS 284-370	10.00	4.50
UNLISTED STARS 284-370	15.00	6.75
COMMON CARD (371-598)	7.00	3.10
COMMON SP (371-598)	12.00	5.50
MINOR STARS 371-598	15.00	6.75
SEMISTARS 371-598	25.00	11.00
*UNLISTED DODGER/YANKEE: 1.25X VALUE		
CARDS PRICED IN NM CONDITION		

☐ 1 AL Batting Leaders	20.00	6.00
Tony Oliva		
Elston Howard		
Brooks Robinson		
☐ 2 NL Batting Leaders	25.00	11.00
Bob Clemente		
Hank Aaron		
Rico Carty		
☐ 3 AL Home Run Leaders	40.00	18.00
Harmon Killebrew		
Mickey Mantle		
Boog Powell		
☐ 4 NL Home Run Leaders	15.00	6.75
Willie Mays		
Billy Williams		
Jim Ray Hart		
Orlando Cepeda		
Johnny Callison		
☐ 5 AL RBI Leaders	40.00	18.00
Brooks Robinson		
Harmon Killebrew		
Mickey Mantle		
Dick Stuart		
☐ 6 NL RBI Leaders	12.00	5.50
Ken Boyer		
Willie Mays		
Ron Santo		
☐ 7 AL ERA Leaders	4.00	1.80
Dean Chance		
Joel Horlen		
☐ 8 NL ERA Leaders	20.00	9.00
Sandy Koufax		
Don Drysdale		
☐ 9 AL Pitching Leaders	4.00	1.80
Dean Chance		
Gary Peters		
Dave Wickersham		
Juan Pizarro		
Wally Bunker		
☐ 10 NL Pitching Leaders	4.00	1.80
Larry Jackson		
Ray Sadecki		
Juan Marichal		
☐ 11 AL Strikeout Leaders	4.00	1.80
Al Downing		
Dean Chance		
Camilo Pascual		

No.	Card	Price	Price
☐ 12	NL Strikeout Leaders..	8.00	3.60
	Bob Veale		
	Don Drysdale		
	Bob Gibson		
☐ 13	Pedro Ramos	4.00	1.80
☐ 14	Len Gabrielson	2.00	.90
☐ 15	Robin Roberts	10.00	4.50
☐ 16	Houston Rookie DP	70.00	32.00
	Joe Morgan		
	Sonny Jackson		
☐ 17	Johnny Romano	2.00	.90
☐ 18	Bill McCool	2.00	.90
☐ 19	Gates Brown	4.00	1.80
☐ 20	Jim Bunning	10.00	4.50
☐ 21	Don Blasingame	2.00	.90
☐ 22	Charlie Smith	2.00	.90
☐ 23	Bob Tiefenauer	2.00	.90
☐ 24	Minnesota Twins	4.00	1.80
	Team Card		
☐ 25	Al McBean	2.00	.90
☐ 26	Bobby Knoop	2.00	.90
☐ 27	Dick Bertell	2.00	.90
☐ 28	Barney Schultz	2.00	.90
☐ 29	Felix Mantilla	2.00	.90
☐ 30	Jim Bouton	6.00	2.70
☐ 31	Mike White	2.00	.90
☐ 32	Herman Franks MG	2.00	.90
☐ 33	Jackie Brandt	2.00	.90
☐ 34	Cal Koonce	2.00	.90
☐ 35	Ed Charles	2.00	.90
☐ 36	Bobby Wine	2.00	.90
☐ 37	Fred Gladding	2.00	.90
☐ 38	Jim King	2.00	.90
☐ 39	Gerry Arrigo	2.00	.90
☐ 40	Frank Howard	5.00	2.20
☐ 41	White Sox Rookies	2.00	.90
	Bruce Howard		
	Marv Staehle		
☐ 42	Earl Wilson	4.00	1.80
☐ 43	Mike Shannon	4.00	1.80
	(Name in red, other		
	Cardinals in yellow)		
☐ 44	Wade Blasingame	2.00	.90
☐ 45	Roy McMillan	4.00	1.80
☐ 46	Bob Lee	2.00	.90
☐ 47	Tommy Harper	4.00	1.80
☐ 48	Claude Raymond	4.00	1.80
☐ 49	Orioles Rookies	4.00	1.80
	Curt Blefary		
	John Miller		
☐ 50	Juan Marichal	10.00	4.50
☐ 51	Bill Bryan	2.00	.90
☐ 52	Ed Roebuck	2.00	.90
☐ 53	Dick McAuliffe	4.00	1.80
☐ 54	Joe Gibbon	2.00	.90
☐ 55	Tony Conigliaro	15.00	6.75
☐ 56	Ron Kline	2.00	.90
☐ 57	Cardinals Team	4.00	1.80
☐ 58	Fred Talbot	2.00	.90
☐ 59	Nate Oliver	2.00	.90
☐ 60	Jim O'Toole	4.00	1.80
☐ 61	Chris Cannizzaro	2.00	.90
☐ 62	Jim Kaat UER DP	6.00	2.70
	(Misspelled Katt)		
☐ 63	Ty Cline	2.00	.90
☐ 64	Lou Burdette	5.00	2.20
☐ 65	Tony Kubek	5.00	2.20
☐ 66	Bill Rigney MG	2.00	.90
☐ 67	Harvey Haddix	4.00	1.80
☐ 68	Del Crandall	4.00	1.80
☐ 69	Bill Virdon	4.00	1.80
☐ 70	Bill Skowron	5.00	2.20
☐ 71	John O'Donoghue	2.00	.90
☐ 72	Tony Gonzalez	2.00	.90
☐ 73	Dennis Ribant	2.00	.90
☐ 74	Red Sox Rookies	10.00	4.50
	Rico Petrocelli		
	Jerry Stephenson		
☐ 75	Deron Johnson	4.00	1.80
☐ 76	Sam McDowell	4.00	1.80
☐ 77	Doug Camilli	2.00	.90
☐ 78	Dal Maxvill	2.00	.90
☐ 79A	Checklist 1	10.00	2.00
	(61 Cannizzaro)		
☐ 79B	Checklist 1	10.00	2.00
	(61 C.Cannizzaro)		
☐ 80	Turk Farrell	2.00	.90
☐ 81	Don Buford	4.00	1.80
☐ 82	Braves Rookies	6.00	2.70
	Santos Alomar		
	John Braun		
☐ 83	George Thomas	2.00	.90
☐ 84	Ron Herbel	2.00	.90
☐ 85	Willie Smith	2.00	.90
☐ 86	Les Narum	2.00	.90
☐ 87	Nelson Mathews	2.00	.90
☐ 88	Jack Lamabe	2.00	.90
☐ 89	Mike Hershberger	2.00	.90
☐ 90	Rich Rollins	4.00	1.80
☐ 91	Cubs Team	4.00	1.80
☐ 92	Dick Howser	4.00	1.80
☐ 93	Jack Fisher	2.00	.90
☐ 94	Charlie Lau	4.00	1.80
☐ 95	Bill Mazeroski DP	5.00	2.20
☐ 96	Sonny Siebert	4.00	1.80
☐ 97	Pedro Gonzalez	2.00	.90
☐ 98	Bob Miller	2.00	.90
☐ 99	Gil Hodges MG	7.00	3.10
☐ 100	Ken Boyer	5.00	2.20
☐ 101	Fred Newman	2.00	.90
☐ 102	Steve Boros	2.00	.90
☐ 103	Harvey Kuenn	4.00	1.80
☐ 104	Checklist 2	10.00	2.00
☐ 105	Chico Salmon	2.00	.90
☐ 106	Gene Oliver	2.00	.90
☐ 107	Phillies Rookies	4.00	1.80
	Pat Corrales		
	Costen Shockley		
☐ 108	Don Mincher	2.00	.90
☐ 109	Walt Bond	2.00	.90
☐ 110	Ron Santo	6.00	2.70
☐ 111	Lee Thomas	4.00	1.80
☐ 112	Derrell Griffith	2.00	.90
☐ 113	Steve Barber	2.00	.90
☐ 114	Jim Hickman	4.00	1.80
☐ 115	Bobby Richardson	6.00	2.70
☐ 116	Cardinals Rookies	4.00	1.80
	Dave Dowling		
	Bob Tolan		
☐ 117	Wes Stock	2.00	.90
☐ 118	Hal Lanier	4.00	1.80
☐ 119	John Kennedy	2.00	.90
☐ 120	Frank Robinson	35.00	16.00
☐ 121	Gene Alley	4.00	1.80
☐ 122	Bill Pleis	2.00	.90
☐ 123	Frank Thomas	4.00	1.80
☐ 124	Tom Satriano	2.00	.90
☐ 125	Juan Pizarro	2.00	.90
☐ 126	Dodgers Team	6.00	2.70
☐ 127	Frank Lary	2.00	.90
☐ 128	Vic Davalillo	2.00	.90
☐ 129	Bennie Daniels	2.00	.90
☐ 130	Al Kaline	35.00	16.00
☐ 131	Johnny Keane MG	2.00	.90
☐ 132	Mike Shannon WS	6.00	2.70
☐ 133	Mel Stottlemyre WS	6.00	2.70
☐ 134	Mickey Mantle WS	75.00	34.00
	Mantle's Clutch HR		
☐ 135	Ken Boyer WS	6.00	2.70
☐ 136	Tim McCarver WS	6.00	2.70
☐ 137	Jim Bouton WS	6.00	2.70
☐ 138	Bob Gibson WS	12.00	5.50
☐ 139	World Series Summary	4.00	1.80
	Cards celebrate		
☐ 140	Dean Chance	5.00	2.20
☐ 141	Charlie James	2.00	.90
☐ 142	Bill Monbouquette	2.00	.90
☐ 143	Pirates Rookies	2.00	.90
	John Gelnar		
	Jerry May		
☐ 144	Ed Kranepool	4.00	1.80
☐ 145	Luis Tiant	12.00	5.50
☐ 146	Ron Hansen	2.00	.90
☐ 147	Dennis Bennett	2.00	.90
☐ 148	Willie Kirkland	2.00	.90
☐ 149	Wayne Schurr	2.00	.90
☐ 150	Brooks Robinson	35.00	16.00
☐ 151	Athletics Team	4.00	1.80
☐ 152	Phil Ortega	2.00	.90
☐ 153	Norm Cash	5.00	2.20
☐ 154	Bob Humphreys	2.00	.90
☐ 155	Roger Maris	40.00	18.00
☐ 156	Bob Sadowski	2.00	.90
☐ 157	Zoilo Versalles	4.00	1.80
☐ 158	Dick Sisler	2.00	.90
☐ 159	Jim Duffalo	2.00	.90
☐ 160	Bob Clemente UER	160.00	70.00
	(1960 Pittsburh)		
☐ 161	Frank Baumann	2.00	.90
☐ 162	Russ Nixon	2.00	.90
☐ 163	Johnny Briggs	2.00	.90
☐ 164	Al Spangler	2.00	.90
☐ 165	Dick Ellsworth	2.00	.90
☐ 166	Indians Rookies	5.00	2.20
	George Culver		
	Tommie Agee		
☐ 167	Bill Wakefield	2.00	.90
☐ 168	Dick Green	2.00	.90
☐ 169	Dave Vineyard	2.00	.90
☐ 170	Hank Aaron	90.00	40.00
☐ 171	Jim Roland	2.00	.90
☐ 172	Jimmy Piersall	5.00	2.20
☐ 173	Detroit Tigers	4.00	1.80
	Team Card		
☐ 174	Joey Jay	2.00	.90
☐ 175	Bob Aspromonte	2.00	.90
☐ 176	Willie McCovey	20.00	9.00
☐ 177	Pete Mikkelsen	2.00	.90
☐ 178	Dalton Jones	2.00	.90
☐ 179	Hal Woodeshick	2.00	.90
☐ 180	Bob Allison	4.00	1.80
☐ 181	Senators Rookies	2.00	.90
	Don Loun		
	Joe McCabe		
☐ 182	Mike de la Hoz	2.00	.90
☐ 183	Dave Nicholson	2.00	.90
☐ 184	John Boozer	2.00	.90
☐ 185	Max Alvis	2.00	.90
☐ 186	Billy Cowan	2.00	.90
☐ 187	Casey Stengel MG	15.00	6.75
☐ 188	Sam Bowens	2.00	.90
☐ 189	Checklist 3	10.00	2.00
☐ 190	Bill White	5.00	2.20
☐ 191	Phil Regan	4.00	1.80
☐ 192	Jim Coker	2.00	.90
☐ 193	Gaylord Perry	18.00	8.00
☐ 194	Rookie Stars	2.00	.90
	Bill Kelso		
	Rick Reichardt		
☐ 195	Bob Veale	4.00	1.80
☐ 196	Ron Fairly	5.00	2.20
☐ 197	Diego Segui	2.50	1.10
☐ 198	Smoky Burgess	4.00	1.80
☐ 199	Bob Heffner	2.50	1.10
☐ 200	Joe Torre	6.00	2.70
☐ 201	Twins Rookies	4.00	1.80
	Sandy Valdespino		
	Cesar Tovar		
☐ 202	Leo Burke	2.50	1.10
☐ 203	Dallas Green	4.00	1.80
☐ 204	Russ Snyder	2.50	1.10
☐ 205	Warren Spahn	30.00	13.50
☐ 206	Willie Horton	4.00	1.80
☐ 207	Pete Rose	140.00	65.00
☐ 208	Tommy John	8.00	3.60
☐ 209	Pirates Team	6.00	2.70
☐ 210	Jim Fregosi	5.00	2.20
☐ 211	Steve Ridzik	2.50	1.10
☐ 212	Ron Brand	2.50	1.10
☐ 213	Jim Davenport	2.50	1.10
☐ 214	Bob Purkey	2.50	1.10
☐ 215	Pete Ward	2.50	1.10
☐ 216	Al Worthington	2.50	1.10
☐ 217	Walter Alston MG	5.00	2.20
☐ 218	Dick Schofield	2.50	1.10
☐ 219	Bob Meyer	2.50	1.10
☐ 220	Billy Williams	10.00	4.50
☐ 221	John Tsitouris	2.50	1.10
☐ 222	Bob Tillman	2.50	1.10
☐ 223	Dan Osinski	2.50	1.10
☐ 224	Bob Chance	2.50	1.10
☐ 225	Bo Belinsky	4.00	1.80
☐ 226	Yankees Rookies	4.00	1.80
	Elvio Jimenez		
	Jake Gibbs		
☐ 227	Bobby Klaus	2.50	1.10
☐ 228	Jack Sanford	2.50	1.10
☐ 229	Lou Clinton	2.50	1.10

230	Ray Sadecki	2.50	1.10
231	Jerry Adair	2.50	1.10
232	Steve Blass	4.00	1.80
233	Don Zimmer	4.00	1.80
234	White Sox Team	4.00	1.80
235	Chuck Hinton	2.50	1.10
236	Denny McLain	30.00	13.50
237	Bernie Allen	2.50	1.10
238	Joe Moeller	2.50	1.10
239	Doc Edwards	2.50	1.10
240	Bob Bruce	2.50	1.10
241	Mack Jones	2.50	1.10
242	George Brunet	2.50	1.10
243	Reds Rookies	4.00	1.80
	Ted Davidson		
	Tommy Helms		
244	Lindy McDaniel	4.00	1.80
245	Joe Pepitone	3.50	1.55
246	Tom Butters	4.00	1.80
247	Wally Moon	4.00	1.80
248	Gus Triandos	4.00	1.80
249	Dave McNally	4.00	1.80
250	Willie Mays	100.00	45.00
251	Billy Herman MG	5.00	2.20
252	Pete Richert	2.50	1.10
253	Danny Cater	2.50	1.10
254	Roland Sheldon	2.50	1.10
255	Camilo Pascual	4.00	1.80
256	Tito Francona	2.50	1.10
257	Jim Wynn	5.00	2.20
258	Larry Bearnarth	2.50	1.10
259	Tigers Rookies	7.00	3.10
	Jim Northrup		
	Ray Oyler		
260	Don Drysdale	20.00	9.00
261	Duke Carmel	2.50	1.10
262	Bud Daley	2.50	1.10
263	Marty Keough	2.50	1.10
264	Bob Buhl	4.00	1.80
265	Jim Pagliaroni	2.50	1.10
266	Bert Campaneris	10.00	4.50
267	Senators Team	4.00	1.80
268	Ken McBride	2.50	1.10
269	Frank Bolling	2.50	1.10
270	Milt Pappas	4.00	1.80
271	Don Wert	2.50	1.10
272	Chuck Schilling	2.50	1.10
273	Checklist 4	10.00	2.00
274	Lum Harris MG	2.50	1.10
275	Dick Groat	5.00	2.20
276	Hoyt Wilhelm	10.00	4.50
277	Johnny Lewis	2.50	1.10
278	Ken Retzer	2.50	1.10
279	Dick Tracewski	2.50	1.10
280	Dick Stuart	4.00	1.80
281	Bill Stafford	2.50	1.10
282	Giants Rookies	40.00	18.00
	Dick Estelle		
	Masanori Murakami		
283	Fred Whitfield	2.50	1.10
284	Nick Willhite	4.00	1.80
285	Ron Hunt	4.00	1.80
286	Athletics Rookies	4.00	1.80
	Jim Dickson		
	Aurelio Monteagudo		
287	Gary Kolb	4.00	1.80
288	Jack Hamilton	4.00	1.80
289	Gordy Coleman	6.00	2.70
290	Wally Bunker	6.00	2.70
291	Jerry Lynch	4.00	1.80
292	Larry Yellen	4.00	1.80
293	Angels Team	10.00	4.50
294	Tim McCarver	8.00	3.60
295	Dick Radatz	6.00	2.70
296	Tony Taylor	6.00	2.70
297	Dave DeBusschere	8.00	3.60
298	Jim Stewart	4.00	1.80
299	Jerry Zimmerman	4.00	1.80
300	Sandy Koufax	120.00	55.00
301	Birdie Tebbetts MG	6.00	2.70
302	Al Stanek	4.00	1.80
303	John Orsino	4.00	1.80
304	Dave Stenhouse	4.00	1.80
305	Rico Carty	6.00	2.70
306	Bubba Phillips	4.00	1.80
307	Barry Latman	4.00	1.80
308	Mets Rookies	6.00	2.70
	Cleon Jones		
	Tom Parsons		
309	Steve Hamilton	6.00	2.70
310	Johnny Callison	6.00	2.70
311	Orlando Pena	4.00	1.80
312	Joe Nuxhall	4.00	1.80
313	Jim Schaffer	4.00	1.80
314	Sterling Slaughter	4.00	1.80
315	Frank Malzone	6.00	2.70
316	Reds Team	10.00	4.50
317	Don McMahon	4.00	1.80
318	Matty Alou	8.00	3.60
319	Ken McMullen	4.00	1.80
320	Bob Gibson	40.00	18.00
321	Rusty Staub	8.00	3.60
322	Rick Wise	6.00	2.70
323	Hank Bauer MG	6.00	2.70
324	Bobby Locke	4.00	1.80
325	Donn Clendenon	6.00	2.70
326	Dwight Siebler	4.00	1.80
327	Denis Menke	4.00	1.80
328	Eddie Fisher	4.00	1.80
329	Hawk Taylor	4.00	1.80
330	Whitey Ford	35.00	16.00
331	Dodgers Rookies	6.00	2.70
	Al Ferrara		
	John Purdin		
332	Ted Abernathy	4.00	1.80
333	Tom Reynolds	4.00	1.80
334	Vic Roznovsky	4.00	1.80
335	Mickey Lolich	8.00	3.60
336	Woody Held	4.00	1.80
337	Mike Cuellar	6.00	2.70
338	Philadelphia Phillies	10.00	4.50
	Team Card		
339	Ryne Duren	6.00	2.70
340	Tony Oliva	20.00	9.00
341	Bob Bolin	4.00	1.80
342	Bob Rodgers	4.00	1.80
343	Mike McCormick	6.00	2.70
344	Wes Parker	6.00	2.70
345	Floyd Robinson	4.00	1.80
346	Bobby Bragan MG	4.00	1.80
347	Roy Face	6.00	2.70
348	George Banks	4.00	1.80
349	Larry Miller	4.00	1.80
350	Mickey Mantle	550.00	250.00
351	Jim Perry	6.00	2.70
352	Alex Johnson	6.00	2.70
353	Jerry Lumpe	4.00	1.80
354	Cubs Rookies	4.00	1.80
	Billy Ott		
	Jack Warner		
355	Vada Pinson	8.00	3.60
356	Bill Spanswick	4.00	1.80
357	Carl Warwick	4.00	1.80
358	Albie Pearson	6.00	2.70
359	Ken Johnson	4.00	1.80
360	Orlando Cepeda	8.00	3.60
361	Checklist 5	15.00	3.00
362	Don Schwall	4.00	1.80
363	Bob Johnson	4.00	1.80
364	Galen Cisco	4.00	1.80
365	Jim Gentile	6.00	2.70
366	Dan Schneider	4.00	1.80
367	Leon Wagner	4.00	1.80
368	White Sox Rookies	4.00	2.70
	Ken Berry		
	Joel Gibson		
369	Phil Linz	6.00	2.70
370	Tommy Davis	6.00	2.70
371	Frank Kreutzer	7.00	3.10
372	Clay Dalrymple	7.00	3.10
373	Curt Simmons	7.00	3.10
374	Angels Rookies	7.00	3.10
	Jose Cardenal		
	Dick Simpson		
375	Dave Wickersham	7.00	3.10
376	Jim Landis	7.00	3.10
377	Willie Stargell	30.00	13.50
378	Chuck Estrada	7.00	3.10
379	Giants Team	15.00	6.75
380	Rocky Colavito	18.00	8.00
381	Al Jackson	7.00	3.10
382	J.C. Martin	7.00	3.10
383	Felipe Alou	10.00	4.50
384	Johnny Klippstein	7.00	3.10
385	Carl Yastrzemski	70.00	32.00
386	Cubs Rookies	7.00	3.10
	Paul Jaeckel		
	Fred Norman		
387	Johnny Podres	10.00	4.50
388	John Blanchard	15.00	6.75
389	Don Larsen	10.00	4.50
390	Bill Freehan	10.00	4.50
391	Mel McGaha MG	7.00	3.10
392	Bob Friend	15.00	6.75
393	Ed Kirkpatrick	7.00	3.10
394	Jim Hannan	7.00	3.10
395	Jim Ray Hart	7.00	3.10
396	Frank Bertaina	7.00	3.10
397	Jerry Buchek	7.00	3.10
398	Reds Rookies	15.00	6.75
	Dan Neville		
	Art Shamsky		
399	Ray Herbert	7.00	3.10
400	Harmon Killebrew	40.00	18.00
401	Carl Willey	7.00	3.10
402	Joe Amalfitano	7.00	3.10
403	Boston Red Sox	15.00	6.75
	Team Card		
404	Stan Williams	7.00	3.10
	(Listed as Indian		
	but Yankee cap)		
405	John Roseboro	15.00	6.75
406	Ralph Terry	15.00	6.75
407	Lee Maye	7.00	3.10
408	Larry Sherry	7.00	3.10
409	Astros Rookies	10.00	4.50
	Jim Beauchamp		
	Larry Dierker		
410	Luis Aparicio	12.00	5.50
411	Roger Craig	15.00	6.75
412	Bob Bailey	7.00	3.10
413	Hal Reniff	7.00	3.10
414	Al Lopez MG	10.00	4.50
415	Curt Flood	10.00	4.50
416	Jim Brewer	7.00	3.10
417	Ed Brinkman	7.00	3.10
418	Johnny Edwards	7.00	3.10
419	Ruben Amaro	7.00	3.10
420	Larry Jackson	7.00	3.10
421	Twins Rookies	7.00	3.10
	Gary Dotter		
	Jay Ward		
422	Aubrey Gatewood	7.00	3.10
423	Jesse Gonder	7.00	3.10
424	Gary Bell	7.00	3.10
425	Wayne Causey	7.00	3.10
426	Braves Team	25.00	11.00
427	Bob Saverine	7.00	3.10
428	Bob Shaw	7.00	3.10
429	Don Demeter	7.00	3.10
430	Gary Peters	7.00	3.10
431	Cards Rookies	10.00	4.50
	Nelson Briles		
	Wayne Spiezio		
432	Jim Grant	15.00	6.75
433	John Bateman	7.00	3.10
434	Dave Morehead	7.00	3.10
435	Willie Davis	10.00	4.50
436	Don Elston	7.00	3.10
437	Chico Cardenas	15.00	6.75
438	Harry Walker MG	7.00	3.10
439	Moe Drabowsky	15.00	6.75
440	Tom Tresh	10.00	4.50
441	Denny Lemaster	7.00	3.10
442	Vic Power	7.00	3.10
443	Checklist 6	25.00	5.00
444	Bob Hendley	7.00	3.10
445	Don Lock	7.00	3.10
446	Art Mahaffey	7.00	3.10
447	Julian Javier	15.00	6.75
448	Lee Stange	7.00	3.10
449	Mets Rookies	15.00	6.75
	Jerry Hinsley		
	Gary Kroll		
450	Elston Howard	10.00	4.50
451	Jim Owens	7.00	3.10
452	Gary Geiger	7.00	3.10
453	Dodgers Rookies	15.00	6.75

	Willie Crawford		
	John Werhas		
☐ 454	Ed Rakow	7.00	3.10
☐ 455	Norm Siebern	7.00	3.10
☐ 456	Bill Henry	7.00	3.10
☐ 457	Bob Kennedy MG	15.00	6.75
☐ 458	John Buzhardt	7.00	3.10
☐ 459	Frank Kostro	7.00	3.10
☐ 460	Richie Allen	40.00	18.00
☐ 461	Braves Rookies	60.00	27.00
	Clay Carroll		
	Phil Niekro		
☐ 462	Lew Krausse UER	7.00	3.10
	(Photo actually		
	Pete Lovrich)		
☐ 463	Manny Mota	10.00	4.50
☐ 464	Ron Piche	7.00	3.10
☐ 465	Tom Haller	15.00	6.75
☐ 466	Senators Rookies	7.00	3.10
	Pete Craig		
	Dick Nen		
☐ 467	Ray Washburn	7.00	3.10
☐ 468	Larry Brown	7.00	3.10
☐ 469	Don Nottebart	7.00	3.10
☐ 470	Yogi Berra P/CO	50.00	22.00
☐ 471	Billy Hoeft	7.00	3.10
☐ 472	Don Pavletich UER	7.00	3.10
	Listed as a pitcher		
☐ 473	Orioles Rookies	16.00	7.25
	Paul Blair		
	Dave Johnson		
☐ 474	Cookie Rojas	15.00	6.75
☐ 475	Clete Boyer	10.00	4.50
☐ 476	Billy O'Dell	7.00	3.10
☐ 477	Cards Rookies	250.00	110.00
	Fritz Ackley		
	Steve Carlton		
☐ 478	Wilbur Wood	10.00	4.50
☐ 479	Ken Harrelson	10.00	4.50
☐ 480	Joel Horlen	7.00	3.10
☐ 481	Cleveland Indians	25.00	11.00
	Team Card		
☐ 482	Bob Priddy	7.00	3.10
☐ 483	George Smith	7.00	3.10
☐ 484	Ron Perranoski	15.00	6.75
☐ 485	Nellie Fox P/CO	16.00	7.25
☐ 486	Angels Rookies	7.00	3.10
	Tom Egan		
	Pat Rogan		
☐ 487	Woody Woodward	15.00	6.75
☐ 488	Ted Wills	7.00	3.10
☐ 489	Gene Mauch MG	15.00	6.75
☐ 490	Earl Battey	7.00	3.10
☐ 491	Tracy Stallard	7.00	3.10
☐ 492	Gene Freese	7.00	3.10
☐ 493	Tigers Rookies	7.00	3.10
	Bill Roman		
	Bruce Brubaker		
☐ 494	Jay Ritchie	7.00	3.10
☐ 495	Joe Christopher	7.00	3.10
☐ 496	Joe Cunningham	7.00	3.10
☐ 497	Giants Rookies	15.00	6.75
	Ken Henderson		
	Jack Hiatt		
☐ 498	Gene Stephens	7.00	3.10
☐ 499	Stu Miller	15.00	6.75
☐ 500	Eddie Mathews	35.00	16.00
☐ 501	Indians Rookies	7.00	3.10
	Ralph Gagliano		
	Jim Rittwage		
☐ 502	Don Cardwell	7.00	3.10
☐ 503	Phil Gagliano	7.00	3.10
☐ 504	Jerry Grote	15.00	6.75
☐ 505	Ray Culp	7.00	3.10
☐ 506	Sam Mele MG	7.00	3.10
☐ 507	Sammy Ellis	7.00	3.10
☐ 508	Checklist 7	25.00	3.10
☐ 509	Red Sox Rookies	7.00	3.10
	Bob Guindon		
	Gerry Vezendy		
☐ 510	Ernie Banks	80.00	36.00
☐ 511	Ron Locke	7.00	3.10
☐ 512	Cap Peterson	7.00	3.10
☐ 513	New York Yankees	40.00	18.00
	Team Card		
☐ 514	Joe Azcue	7.00	3.10
☐ 515	Vern Law	15.00	6.75
☐ 516	Al Weis	7.00	3.10
☐ 517	Angels Rookies	15.00	6.75
	Paul Schaal		
	Jack Warner		
☐ 518	Ken Rowe	7.00	3.10
☐ 519	Bob Uecker UER	30.00	13.50
	(Posing as a left-		
	handed batter)		
☐ 520	Tony Cloninger	7.00	3.10
☐ 521	Phillies Rookies	7.00	3.10
	Dave Bennett		
	Morrie Stevens		
☐ 522	Hank Aguirre	7.00	3.10
☐ 523	Mike Brumley SP	12.00	5.50
☐ 524	Dave Giusti SP	12.00	5.50
☐ 525	Eddie Bressoud	7.00	3.10
☐ 526	Athletics Rookies SP	80.00	36.00
	Rene Lachemann		
	Johnny Odom		
	Jim Hunter UER		
	(Tim on back)		
	Skip Lockwood		
☐ 527	Jeff Torborg SP	16.00	7.25
☐ 528	George Altman	7.00	3.10
☐ 529	Jerry Fosnow SP	12.00	5.50
☐ 530	Jim Maloney	15.00	6.75
☐ 531	Chuck Hiller	7.00	3.10
☐ 532	Hector Lopez	15.00	6.75
☐ 533	Mets Rookies SP	25.00	11.00
	Dan Napoleon		
	Ron Swoboda		
	Tug McGraw		
	Jim Bethke		
☐ 534	John Herrnstein	7.00	3.10
☐ 535	Jack Kralick SP	12.00	5.50
☐ 536	Andre Rodgers SP	12.00	5.50
☐ 537	Angels Rookies	7.00	3.10
	Marcelino Lopez		
	Phil Roof		
	Rudy May		
☐ 538	Chuck Dressen SP MG	15.00	6.75
☐ 539	Herm Starrette	7.00	3.10
☐ 540	Lou Brock SP	50.00	22.00
☐ 541	White Sox Rookies	7.00	3.10
	Greg Bollo		
	Bob Locker		
☐ 542	Lou Klimchock	7.00	3.10
☐ 543	Ed Connolly SP	12.00	5.50
☐ 544	Howie Reed	7.00	3.10
☐ 545	Jesus Alou SP	14.00	6.25
☐ 546	Indians Rookies	7.00	3.10
	Bill Davis		
	Mike Hedlund		
	Ray Barker		
	Floyd Weaver		
☐ 547	Jake Wood SP	12.00	5.50
☐ 548	Dick Stigman	7.00	3.10
☐ 549	Cubs Rookies SP	20.00	9.00
	Roberto Pena		
	Glenn Beckert		
☐ 550	Mel Stottlemyre SP	30.00	13.50
☐ 551	New York Mets SP	30.00	13.50
	Team Card		
☐ 552	Julio Gotay	7.00	3.10
☐ 553	Astros Rookies	7.00	3.10
	Dan Coombs		
	Gene Ratliff		
	Jack McClure		
☐ 554	Chico Ruiz SP	12.00	5.50
☐ 555	Jack Baldschun SP	12.00	5.50
☐ 556	Red Schoendienst	24.00	11.00
	SP MG		
☐ 557	Jose Santiago	7.00	3.10
☐ 558	Tommie Sisk	7.00	3.10
☐ 559	Ed Bailey SP	12.00	5.50
☐ 560	Boog Powell SP	24.00	11.00
☐ 561	Dodgers Rookies	10.00	4.50
	Dennis Daboll		
	Mike Kekich		
	Hector Valle		
	Jim Lefebvre		
☐ 562	Billy Moran	7.00	3.10
☐ 563	Julio Navarro	7.00	3.10
☐ 564	Mel Nelson	7.00	3.10
☐ 565	Ernie Broglio SP	12.00	5.50
☐ 566	Yankees Rookies SP	15.00	6.75
	Gil Blanco		
	Ross Moschitto		
	Art Lopez		
☐ 567	Tommie Aaron	7.00	3.10
☐ 568	Ron Taylor SP	12.00	5.50
☐ 569	Gino Cimoli SP	12.00	5.50
☐ 570	Claude Osteen SP	15.00	6.75
☐ 571	Ossie Virgil SP	12.00	5.50
☐ 572	Baltimore Orioles SP	30.00	13.50
	Team Card		
☐ 573	Red Sox Rookies SP	24.00	11.00
	Jim Lonborg		
	Gerry Moses		
	Bill Schlesinger		
	Mike Ryan		
☐ 574	Roy Sievers	15.00	6.75
☐ 575	Jose Pagan	7.00	3.10
☐ 576	Terry Fox SP	12.00	5.50
☐ 577	AL Rookie Stars SP	15.00	6.75
	Darold Knowles		
	Don Buschhorn		
	Richie Scheinblum		
☐ 578	Camilo Carreon SP	12.00	5.50
☐ 579	Dick Smith SP	12.00	5.50
☐ 580	Jimmie Hall SP	12.00	5.50
☐ 581	NL Rookie Stars SP	100.00	45.00
	Tony Perez		
	Dave Ricketts		
	Kevin Collins		
☐ 582	Bob Schmidt SP	12.00	5.50
☐ 583	Wes Covington SP	12.00	5.50
☐ 584	Harry Bright	15.00	6.75
☐ 585	Hank Fischer	7.00	3.10
☐ 586	Tom McCraw SP	12.00	5.50
☐ 587	Joe Sparma	7.00	3.10
☐ 588	Lenny Green	7.00	3.10
☐ 589	Giants Rookies SP	12.00	5.50
	Frank Linzy		
	Bob Schroder		
☐ 590	John Wyatt	7.00	3.10
☐ 591	Bob Skinner SP	12.00	5.50
☐ 592	Frank Bork SP	12.00	5.50
☐ 593	Tigers Rookies SP	12.00	5.50
	Jackie Moore		
	John Sullivan		
☐ 594	Joe Gaines	7.00	3.10
☐ 595	Don Lee	7.00	3.10
☐ 596	Don Landrum SP	12.00	5.50
☐ 597	Twins Rookies	7.00	3.10
	Joe Nossek		
	John Sevcik		
	Dick Reese		
☐ 598	Al Downing SP	24.00	7.25

1966 Topps

PHIL NIEKRO   pitcher

The cards in this 598-card set measure 2 1/2" by 3 1/2". There are the same number of cards as in the 1965 set. Once again, the seventh series cards (523 to 598) are considered more difficult to obtain than the cards of any other series in the set. Within this last series there are 43 cards that were printed in lesser quantities than the other cards in that series; these short-er-printed cards are marked by SP in the checklist below. Among other ways, cards were issued in five-card nickel packs. The only featured subset within this set is League Leaders (215-226). Noteworthy Rookie Cards in the set include Jim Palmer (126), Ferguson Jenkins (254), and Don Sutton (288). Jim Palmer is described in the bio (on his card back) as a left-hander.

	NRMT	VG-E
COMPLETE SET (598)	4000.00	1800.00
COMMON CARD (1-109)	1.50	.70
COMMON CARD (110-283)	2.00	.90
MINOR STARS 1-283	4.00	1.80
SEMISTARS 1-283	6.00	2.70
UNLISTED STARS 1-283	8.00	3.60
COMMON CARD (284-370)	3.00	1.35
MINOR STARS 284-370	5.00	2.20
SEMISTARS 284-370	8.00	3.60
UNLISTED STARS 284-370	12.00	5.50
COMMON CARD (371-446)	5.00	2.20
MINOR STARS 371-446	8.00	3.60
SEMISTARS 371-446	10.00	4.50
UNLISTED STARS 371-446	15.00	6.75
COMMON CARD (447-522)	9.00	4.00
MINOR STARS 447-522	15.00	6.75
SEMISTARS 447-522	25.00	11.00
COMMON CARD (523-598)	15.00	6.75
COMMON SP (523-598)	30.00	13.50
MINOR STARS 523-598	25.00	11.00

*UNLISTED DODGER/YANKEE: 1.25X VALUE
CARDS PRICED IN NM CONDITION
LAST SERIES CONDITION SENSITIVE*

☐ 1 Willie Mays	135.00	42.50
☐ 2 Ted Abernathy	1.50	.70
☐ 3 Sam Mele MG	1.50	.70
☐ 4 Ray Culp	1.50	.70
☐ 5 Jim Fregosi	4.00	1.80
☐ 6 Chuck Schilling	1.50	.70
☐ 7 Tracy Stallard	1.50	.70
☐ 8 Floyd Robinson	1.50	.70
☐ 9 Clete Boyer	4.00	1.80
☐ 10 Tony Cloninger	1.50	.70
☐ 11 Senators Rookies	1.50	.70
Brant Alyea		
Pete Craig		
☐ 12 John Tsitouris	1.50	.70
☐ 13 Lou Johnson	4.00	1.80
☐ 14 Norm Siebern	1.50	.70
☐ 15 Vern Law	4.00	1.80
☐ 16 Larry Brown	1.50	.70
☐ 17 John Stephenson	1.50	.70
☐ 18 Roland Sheldon	1.50	.70
☐ 19 San Francisco Giants	6.00	2.70
Team Card		
☐ 20 Willie Horton	4.00	1.80
☐ 21 Don Nottebart	1.50	.70
☐ 22 Joe Nossek	1.50	.70
☐ 23 Jack Sanford	1.50	.70
☐ 24 Don Kessinger	6.00	2.70
☐ 25 Pete Ward	1.50	.70
☐ 26 Ray Sadecki	1.50	.70
☐ 27 Orioles Rookies	1.50	.70
Darold Knowles		
Andy Etchebarren		
☐ 28 Phil Niekro	20.00	9.00
☐ 29 Mike Brumley	1.50	.70
☐ 30 Pete Rose DP	35.00	16.00
☐ 31 Jack Cullen	4.00	1.80
☐ 32 Adolfo Phillips	1.50	.70
☐ 33 Jim Pagliaroni	1.50	.70
☐ 34 Checklist 1	6.00	1.20
☐ 35 Ron Swoboda	4.00	1.80
☐ 36 Jim Hunter UER	20.00	9.00
(Stats say 1963 and 1964, should be 1964 and 1965)		
☐ 37 Billy Herman MG	4.00	1.80

☐ 38 Ron Nischwitz	1.50	.70
☐ 39 Ken Henderson	1.50	.70
☐ 40 Jim Grant	1.50	.70
☐ 41 Don LeJohn	1.50	.70
☐ 42 Aubrey Gatewood	1.50	.70
☐ 43A Don Landrum	4.00	1.80
(Dark button on pants showing)		
☐ 43B Don Landrum	20.00	9.00
(Button on pants partially airbrushed)		
☐ 43C Don Landrum	4.00	1.80
(Button on pants not showing)		
☐ 44 Indians Rookies	1.50	.70
Bill Davis		
Tom Kelley		
☐ 45 Jim Gentile	4.00	1.80
☐ 46 Howie Koplitz	1.50	.70
☐ 47 J.C. Martin	1.50	.70
☐ 48 Paul Blair	4.00	1.80
☐ 49 Woody Woodward	4.00	1.80
☐ 50 Mickey Mantle DP	200.00	90.00
☐ 51 Gordon Richardson	1.50	.70
☐ 52 Power Plus	4.00	1.80
Wes Covington		
Johnny Callison		
☐ 53 Bob Duliba	1.50	.70
☐ 54 Jose Pagan	1.50	.70
☐ 55 Ken Harrelson	4.00	1.80
☐ 56 Sandy Valdespino	1.50	.70
☐ 57 Jim Lefebvre	4.00	1.80
☐ 58 Dave Wickersham	1.50	.70
☐ 59 Reds Team	6.00	2.70
☐ 60 Curt Flood	4.00	1.80
☐ 61 Bob Bolin	1.50	.70
☐ 62A Merritt Ranew	1.50	.70
(With sold line)		
☐ 62B Merritt Ranew	30.00	13.50
(Without sold line)		
☐ 63 Jim Stewart	1.50	.70
☐ 64 Bob Bruce	1.50	.70
☐ 65 Leon Wagner	1.50	.70
☐ 66 Al Weis	1.50	.70
☐ 67 Mets Rookies	4.00	1.80
Cleon Jones		
Dick Selma		
☐ 68 Hal Reniff	1.50	.70
☐ 69 Ken Hamlin	1.50	.70
☐ 70 Carl Yastrzemski	25.00	11.00
☐ 71 Frank Carpin	1.50	.70
☐ 72 Tony Perez	25.00	11.00
☐ 73 Jerry Zimmerman	1.50	.70
☐ 74 Don Mossi	4.00	1.80
☐ 75 Tommy Davis	4.00	1.80
☐ 76 Red Schoendienst MG	4.00	1.80
☐ 77 John Orsino	1.50	.70
☐ 78 Frank Linzy	1.50	.70
☐ 79 Joe Pepitone	2.50	1.10
☐ 80 Richie Allen	5.00	2.20
☐ 81 Ray Oyler	1.50	.70
☐ 82 Bob Hendley	1.50	.70
☐ 83 Albie Pearson	4.00	1.80
☐ 84 Braves Rookies	1.50	.70
Jim Beauchamp		
Dick Kelley		
☐ 85 Eddie Fisher	1.50	.70
☐ 86 John Bateman	1.50	.70
☐ 87 Dan Napoleon	1.50	.70
☐ 88 Fred Whitfield	1.50	.70
☐ 89 Ted Davidson	1.50	.70
☐ 90 Luis Aparicio	7.00	3.10
☐ 91A Bob Uecker TR	12.00	5.50
☐ 91B Bob Uecker NTR	40.00	18.00
☐ 92 Yankees Team	14.00	6.25
☐ 93 Jim Lonborg	4.00	1.80
☐ 94 Matty Alou	4.00	1.80
☐ 95 Pete Richert	1.50	.70
☐ 96 Felipe Alou	4.00	1.80
☐ 97 Jim Merritt	1.50	.70
☐ 98 Don Demeter	1.50	.70
☐ 99 Buc Belters	6.00	2.70
Willie Stargell		
Donn Clendenon		
☐ 100 Sandy Koufax	75.00	34.00
☐ 101A Checklist 2	16.00	3.20

(115 W. Spahn) ERR		
☐ 101B Checklist 2	10.00	2.00
(115 Bill Henry) COR		
☐ 102 Ed Kirkpatrick	1.50	.70
☐ 103A Dick Groat TR	4.00	1.80
☐ 103B Dick Groat NTR	40.00	18.00
☐ 104A Alex Johnson TR	4.00	1.80
☐ 104B Alex Johnson NTR	30.00	13.50
☐ 105 Milt Pappas	4.00	1.80
☐ 106 Rusty Staub	4.00	1.80
☐ 107 A's Rookies	1.50	.70
Larry Stahl		
Ron Tompkins		
☐ 108 Bobby Klaus	1.50	.70
☐ 109 Ralph Terry	4.00	1.80
☐ 110 Ernie Banks	30.00	13.50
☐ 111 Gary Peters	2.00	.90
☐ 112 Manny Mota	4.00	1.80
☐ 113 Hank Aguirre	2.00	.90
☐ 114 Jim Gosger	2.00	.90
☐ 115 Bill Henry	2.00	.90
☐ 116 Walter Alston MG	4.00	1.80
☐ 117 Jake Gibbs	2.00	.90
☐ 118 Mike McCormick	4.00	1.80
☐ 119 Art Shamsky	2.00	.90
☐ 120 Harmon Killebrew	16.00	7.25
☐ 121 Ray Herbert	2.00	.90
☐ 122 Joe Gaines	2.00	.90
☐ 123 Pirates Rookies	2.00	.90
Frank Bork		
Jerry May		
☐ 124 Tug McGraw	4.00	1.80
☐ 125 Lou Brock	20.00	9.00
☐ 126 Jim Palmer UER	100.00	45.00
(Described as a lefthander on card back)		
☐ 127 Ken Berry	2.00	.90
☐ 128 Jim Landis	2.00	.90
☐ 129 Jack Kralick	2.00	.90
☐ 130 Joe Torre	4.00	1.80
☐ 131 Angels Team	6.00	2.70
☐ 132 Orlando Cepeda	5.00	2.20
☐ 133 Don McMahon	2.00	.90
☐ 134 Wes Parker	4.00	1.80
☐ 135 Dave Morehead	2.00	.90
☐ 136 Woody Held	2.00	.90
☐ 137 Pat Corrales	4.00	1.80
☐ 138 Roger Repoz	2.00	.90
☐ 139 Cubs Rookies	2.00	.90
Byron Browne		
Don Young		
☐ 140 Jim Maloney	4.00	1.80
☐ 141 Tom McCraw	2.00	.90
☐ 142 Don Dennis	2.00	.90
☐ 143 Jose Tartabull	4.00	1.80
☐ 144 Don Schwall	2.00	.90
☐ 145 Bill Freehan	4.00	1.80
☐ 146 George Altman	2.00	.90
☐ 147 Lum Harris MG	2.00	.90
☐ 148 Bob Johnson	2.00	.90
☐ 149 Dick Nen	2.00	.90
☐ 150 Rocky Colavito	8.00	3.60
☐ 151 Gary Wagner	2.00	.90
☐ 152 Frank Malzone	4.00	1.80
☐ 153 Rico Carty	4.00	1.80
☐ 154 Chuck Hiller	2.00	.90
☐ 155 Marcelino Lopez	2.00	.90
☐ 156 Double Play Combo.	2.00	.90
Dick Schofield		
Hal Lanier		
☐ 157 Rene Lachemann	2.00	.90
☐ 158 Jim Brewer	2.00	.90
☐ 159 Chico Ruiz	2.00	.90
☐ 160 Whitey Ford	25.00	11.00
☐ 161 Jerry Lumpe	2.00	.90
☐ 162 Lee Maye	2.00	.90
☐ 163 Tito Francona	2.00	.90
☐ 164 White Sox Rookies	4.00	1.80
Tommie Agee		
Marv Staehle		
☐ 165 Don Lock	2.00	.90
☐ 166 Chris Krug	2.00	.90
☐ 167 Boog Powell	5.00	2.20
☐ 168 Dan Osinski	2.00	.90
☐ 169 Duke Sims	2.00	.90

☐ 170	Cookie Rojas	4.00	1.80
☐ 171	Nick Willhite	2.00	.90
☐ 172	Mets Team	6.00	2.70
☐ 173	Al Spangler	2.00	.90
☐ 174	Ron Taylor	2.00	.90
☐ 175	Bert Campaneris	4.00	1.80
☐ 176	Jim Davenport	2.00	.90
☐ 177	Hector Lopez	2.00	.90
☐ 178	Bob Tillman	2.00	.90
☐ 179	Cards Rookies	4.00	1.80
	Dennis Aust		
	Bob Tolan		
☐ 180	Vada Pinson	4.00	1.80
☐ 181	Al Worthington	2.00	.90
☐ 182	Jerry Lynch	2.00	.90
☐ 183A	Checklist 3	8.00	1.60
	(Large print on front)		
☐ 183B	Checklist 3	8.00	1.60
	(Small print on front)		
☐ 184	Denis Menke	2.00	.90
☐ 185	Bob Buhl	4.00	1.80
☐ 186	Ruben Amaro	2.00	.90
☐ 187	Chuck Dressen MG	4.00	1.80
☐ 188	Al Luplow	2.00	.90
☐ 189	John Roseboro	4.00	1.80
☐ 190	Jimmie Hall	2.00	.90
☐ 191	Darrell Sutherland	2.00	.90
☐ 192	Vic Power	4.00	1.80
☐ 193	Dave McNally	4.00	1.80
☐ 194	Senators Team	6.00	2.70
☐ 195	Joe Morgan	14.00	6.25
☐ 196	Don Pavletich	2.00	.90
☐ 197	Sonny Siebert	2.00	.90
☐ 198	Mickey Stanley	4.00	1.80
☐ 199	Chisox Clubbers	4.00	1.80
	Bill Skowron		
	Johnny Romano		
	Floyd Robinson		
☐ 200	Eddie Mathews	14.00	6.25
☐ 201	Jim Dickson	2.00	.90
☐ 202	Clay Dalrymple	2.00	.90
☐ 203	Jose Santiago	2.00	.90
☐ 204	Cubs Team	6.00	2.70
☐ 205	Tom Tresh	4.00	1.80
☐ 206	Al Jackson	2.00	.90
☐ 207	Frank Quilici	2.00	.90
☐ 208	Bob Miller	2.00	.90
☐ 209	Tigers Rookies	4.00	1.80
	Fritz Fisher		
	John Hiller		
☐ 210	Bill Mazeroski	5.00	2.20
☐ 211	Frank Kreutzer	2.00	.90
☐ 212	Ed Kranepool	4.00	1.80
☐ 213	Fred Newman	2.00	.90
☐ 214	Tommy Harper	4.00	1.80
☐ 215	NL Batting Leaders	50.00	22.00
	Bob Clemente		
	Hank Aaron		
	Willie Mays		
☐ 216	AL Batting Leaders	6.00	2.70
	Tony Oliva		
	Carl Yastrzemski		
	Vic Davalillo		
☐ 217	NL Home Run Leaders	20.00	9.00
	Willie Mays		
	Willie McCovey		
	Billy Williams		
☐ 218	AL Home Run Leaders	4.00	1.80
	Tony Conigliaro		
	Norm Cash		
	Willie Horton		
☐ 219	NL RBI Leaders	12.00	5.50
	Deron Johnson		
	Frank Robinson		
	Willie Mays		
☐ 220	AL RBI Leaders	4.00	1.80
	Rocky Colavito		
	Willie Horton		
	Tony Oliva		
☐ 221	NL ERA Leaders	12.00	5.50
	Sandy Koufax		
	Juan Marichal		
	Vern Law		
☐ 222	AL ERA Leaders	4.00	1.80
	Sam McDowell		
	Eddie Fisher		
	Sonny Siebert		
☐ 223	NL Pitching Leaders	12.00	5.50
	Sandy Koufax		
	Tony Cloninger		
	Don Drysdale		
☐ 224	AL Pitching Leaders	4.00	1.80
	Mel Stottlemyre		
	Jim Kaat		
☐ 225	NL Strikeout Leaders	12.00	5.50
	Sandy Koufax		
	Bob Veale		
	Bob Gibson		
☐ 226	AL Strikeout Leaders	4.00	1.80
	Sam McDowell		
	Mickey Lolich		
	Dennis McLain		
	Sonny Siebert		
☐ 227	Russ Nixon	2.00	.90
☐ 228	Larry Dierker	4.00	1.80
☐ 229	Hank Bauer MG	4.00	1.80
☐ 230	Johnny Callison	4.00	1.80
☐ 231	Floyd Weaver	2.00	.90
☐ 232	Glenn Beckert	4.00	1.80
☐ 233	Dom Zanni	2.00	.90
☐ 234	Yankees Rookies	8.00	3.60
	Rich Beck		
	Roy White		
☐ 235	Don Cardwell	2.00	.90
☐ 236	Mike Hershberger	2.00	.90
☐ 237	Billy O'Dell	2.00	.90
☐ 238	Dodgers Team	6.00	2.70
☐ 239	Orlando Pena	2.00	.90
☐ 240	Earl Battey	2.00	.90
☐ 241	Dennis Ribant	2.00	.90
☐ 242	Jesus Alou	2.00	.90
☐ 243	Nelson Briles	4.00	1.80
☐ 244	Astros Rookies	2.00	.90
	Chuck Harrison		
	Sonny Jackson		
☐ 245	John Buzhardt	2.00	.90
☐ 246	Ed Bailey	2.00	.90
☐ 247	Carl Warwick	2.00	.90
☐ 248	Pete Mikkelsen	2.00	.90
☐ 249	Bill Rigney MG	2.00	.90
☐ 250	Sammy Ellis	2.00	.90
☐ 251	Ed Brinkman	2.00	.90
☐ 252	Denny Lemaster	2.00	.90
☐ 253	Don Wert	2.00	.90
☐ 254	Phillies Rookies	80.00	36.00
	Ferguson Jenkins		
	Bill Sorrell		
☐ 255	Willie Stargell	20.00	9.00
☐ 256	Lew Krausse	2.00	.90
☐ 257	Jeff Torborg	4.00	1.80
☐ 258	Dave Giusti	2.00	.90
☐ 259	Boston Red Sox	6.00	2.70
	Team Card		
☐ 260	Bob Shaw	2.00	.90
☐ 261	Ron Hansen	2.00	.90
☐ 262	Jack Hamilton	2.00	.90
☐ 263	Tom Egan	2.00	.90
☐ 264	Twins Rookies	2.00	.90
	Andy Kosco		
	Ted Uhlaender		
☐ 265	Stu Miller	4.00	1.80
☐ 266	Pedro Gonzalez UER	2.00	.90
	(Misspelled Gonzales on card back)		
☐ 267	Joe Sparma	2.00	.90
☐ 268	John Blanchard	2.00	.90
☐ 269	Don Heffner MG	2.00	.90
☐ 270	Claude Osteen	4.00	1.80
☐ 271	Hal Lanier	2.00	.90
☐ 272	Jack Baldschun	2.00	.90
☐ 273	Astro Aces	4.00	1.80
	Bob Aspromonte		
	Rusty Staub		
☐ 274	Buster Narum	2.00	.90
☐ 275	Tim McCarver	4.00	1.80
☐ 276	Jim Bouton	4.00	1.80
☐ 277	George Thomas	2.00	.90
☐ 278	Cal Koonce	2.00	.90
☐ 279A	Checklist 4	8.00	1.60
	(Player's cap black)		
☐ 279B	Checklist 4	8.00	1.60
	(Player's cap red)		
☐ 280	Bobby Knoop	2.00	.90
☐ 281	Bruce Howard	2.00	.90
☐ 282	Johnny Lewis	2.00	.90
☐ 283	Jim Perry	4.00	1.80
☐ 284	Bobby Wine	3.00	1.35
☐ 285	Luis Tiant	6.00	2.70
☐ 286	Gary Geiger	3.00	1.35
☐ 287	Jack Aker	3.00	1.35
☐ 288	Dodgers Rookies	50.00	22.00
	Bill Singer		
	Don Sutton		
☐ 289	Larry Sherry	3.00	1.35
☐ 290	Ron Santo	6.00	2.70
☐ 291	Moe Drabowsky	5.00	2.20
☐ 292	Jim Coker	3.00	1.35
☐ 293	Mike Shannon	5.00	2.20
☐ 294	Steve Ridzik	3.00	1.35
☐ 295	Jim Ray Hart	5.00	2.20
☐ 296	Johnny Keane MG	5.00	2.20
☐ 297	Jim Owens	3.00	1.35
☐ 298	Rico Petrocelli	6.00	2.70
☐ 299	Lou Burdette	6.00	2.70
☐ 300	Bob Clemente	150.00	70.00
☐ 301	Greg Bollo	3.00	1.35
☐ 302	Ernie Bowman	3.00	1.35
☐ 303	Cleveland Indians	5.00	2.20
	Team Card		
☐ 304	John Herrnstein	3.00	1.35
☐ 305	Camilo Pascual	5.00	2.20
☐ 306	Ty Cline	3.00	1.35
☐ 307	Clay Carroll	5.00	2.20
☐ 308	Tom Haller	5.00	2.20
☐ 309	Diego Segui	3.00	1.35
☐ 310	Frank Robinson	30.00	13.50
☐ 311	Reds Rookies	5.00	2.20
	Tommy Helms		
	Dick Simpson		
☐ 312	Bob Saverine	3.00	1.35
☐ 313	Chris Zachary	3.00	1.35
☐ 314	Hector Valle	3.00	1.35
☐ 315	Norm Cash	6.00	2.70
☐ 316	Jack Fisher	3.00	1.35
☐ 317	Dalton Jones	3.00	1.35
☐ 318	Harry Walker MG	3.00	1.35
☐ 319	Gene Freese	3.00	1.35
☐ 320	Bob Gibson	25.00	11.00
☐ 321	Rick Reichardt	3.00	1.35
☐ 322	Bill Faul	3.00	1.35
☐ 323	Ray Barker	3.00	1.35
☐ 324	John Boozer	3.00	1.35
☐ 325	Vic Davalillo	3.00	1.35
☐ 326	Braves Team	5.00	2.20
☐ 327	Bernie Allen	3.00	1.35
☐ 328	Jerry Grote	5.00	2.20
☐ 329	Pete Charton	3.00	1.35
☐ 330	Ron Fairly	5.00	2.20
☐ 331	Ron Herbel	3.00	1.35
☐ 332	Bill Bryan	3.00	1.35
☐ 333	Senators Rookies	3.00	1.35
	Joe Coleman		
	Jim French		
☐ 334	Marty Keough	3.00	1.35
☐ 335	Juan Pizarro	3.00	1.35
☐ 336	Gene Alley	5.00	2.20
☐ 337	Fred Gladding	3.00	1.35
☐ 338	Dal Maxvill	3.00	1.35
☐ 339	Del Crandall	5.00	2.20
☐ 340	Dean Chance	5.00	2.20
☐ 341	Wes Westrum MG	5.00	2.20
☐ 342	Bob Humphreys	3.00	1.35
☐ 343	Joe Christopher	3.00	1.35
☐ 344	Steve Blass	5.00	2.20
☐ 345	Bob Allison	5.00	2.20
☐ 346	Mike de la Hoz	3.00	1.35
☐ 347	Phil Regan	5.00	2.20
☐ 348	Orioles Team	8.00	3.60
☐ 349	Cap Peterson	3.00	1.35
☐ 350	Mel Stottlemyre	6.00	2.70
☐ 351	Fred Valentine	3.00	1.35
☐ 352	Bob Aspromonte	3.00	1.35
☐ 353	Al McBean	3.00	1.35
☐ 354	Smoky Burgess	5.00	2.20
☐ 355	Wade Blasingame	3.00	1.35

☐ 356	Red Sox Rookies	3.00	1.35
	Owen Johnson		
	Ken Sanders		
☐ 357	Gerry Arrigo	3.00	1.35
☐ 358	Charlie Smith	3.00	1.35
☐ 359	Johnny Briggs	3.00	1.35
☐ 360	Ron Hunt	3.00	1.35
☐ 361	Tom Satriano	3.00	1.35
☐ 362	Gates Brown	5.00	2.20
☐ 363	Checklist 5	8.00	1.60
☐ 364	Nate Oliver	3.00	1.35
☐ 365	Roger Maris	35.00	16.00
☐ 366	Wayne Causey	3.00	1.35
☐ 367	Mel Nelson	3.00	1.35
☐ 368	Charlie Lau	5.00	2.20
☐ 369	Jim King	3.00	1.35
☐ 370	Chico Cardenas	3.00	1.35
☐ 371	Lee Stange	5.00	2.20
☐ 372	Harvey Kuenn	8.00	3.60
☐ 373	Giants Rookies	8.00	3.60
	Jack Hiatt		
	Dick Estelle		
☐ 374	Bob Locker	5.00	2.20
☐ 375	Donn Clendenon	8.00	3.60
☐ 376	Paul Schaal	5.00	2.20
☐ 377	Turk Farrell	5.00	2.20
☐ 378	Dick Tracewski	5.00	2.20
☐ 379	Cardinal Team	10.00	4.50
☐ 380	Tony Conigliaro	10.00	4.50
☐ 381	Hank Fischer	5.00	2.20
☐ 382	Phil Roof	5.00	2.20
☐ 383	Jackie Brandt	5.00	2.20
☐ 384	Al Downing	8.00	3.60
☐ 385	Ken Boyer	8.00	3.60
☐ 386	Gil Hodges MG	8.00	3.60
☐ 387	Howie Reed	5.00	2.20
☐ 388	Don Mincher	5.00	2.20
☐ 389	Jim O'Toole	5.00	2.20
☐ 390	Brooks Robinson	45.00	20.00
☐ 391	Chuck Hinton	5.00	2.20
☐ 392	Cubs Rookies	8.00	3.60
	Bill Hands		
	Randy Hundley		
☐ 393	George Brunet	5.00	2.20
☐ 394	Ron Brand	5.00	2.20
☐ 395	Len Gabrielson	5.00	2.20
☐ 396	Jerry Stephenson	5.00	2.20
☐ 397	Bill White	8.00	3.60
☐ 398	Danny Cater	5.00	2.20
☐ 399	Ray Washburn	5.00	2.20
☐ 400	Zoilo Versalles	8.00	3.60
☐ 401	Ken McMullen	5.00	2.20
☐ 402	Jim Hickman	5.00	2.20
☐ 403	Fred Talbot	5.00	2.20
☐ 404	Pittsburgh Pirates	10.00	4.50
	Team Card		
☐ 405	Elston Howard	8.00	3.60
☐ 406	Joey Jay	5.00	2.20
☐ 407	John Kennedy	5.00	2.20
☐ 408	Lee Thomas	8.00	3.60
☐ 409	Billy Hoeft	5.00	2.20
☐ 410	Al Kaline	35.00	16.00
☐ 411	Gene Mauch MG	5.00	2.20
☐ 412	Sam Bowens	5.00	2.20
☐ 413	Johnny Romano	5.00	2.20
☐ 414	Dan Coombs	5.00	2.20
☐ 415	Max Alvis	5.00	2.20
☐ 416	Phil Ortega	5.00	2.20
☐ 417	Angels Rookies	5.00	2.20
	Jim McGlothlin		
	Ed Sukla		
☐ 418	Phil Gagliano	5.00	2.20
☐ 419	Mike Ryan	5.00	2.20
☐ 420	Juan Marichal	14.00	6.25
☐ 421	Roy McMillan	8.00	3.60
☐ 422	Ed Charles	5.00	2.20
☐ 423	Ernie Broglio	5.00	2.20
☐ 424	Reds Rookies	10.00	4.50
	Lee May		
	Darrell Osteen		
☐ 425	Bob Veale	8.00	3.60
☐ 426	White Sox Team	8.00	3.60
☐ 427	John Miller	5.00	2.20
☐ 428	Sandy Alomar	8.00	3.60
☐ 429	Bill Monbouquette	5.00	2.20
☐ 430	Don Drysdale	20.00	9.00

☐ 431	Walt Bond	5.00	2.20
☐ 432	Bob Heffner	5.00	2.20
☐ 433	Alvin Dark MG	8.00	3.60
☐ 434	Willie Kirkland	5.00	2.20
☐ 435	Jim Bunning	14.00	6.25
☐ 436	Julian Javier	8.00	3.60
☐ 437	Al Stanek	5.00	2.20
☐ 438	Willie Smith	5.00	2.20
☐ 439	Pedro Ramos	5.00	2.20
☐ 440	Deron Johnson	8.00	3.60
☐ 441	Tommie Sisk	5.00	2.20
☐ 442	Orioles Rookies	5.00	2.20
	Ed Barnowski		
	Eddie Watt		
☐ 443	Bill Wakefield	5.00	2.20
☐ 444	Checklist 6	8.00	1.60
☐ 445	Jim Kaat	10.00	4.50
☐ 446	Mack Jones	5.00	2.20
☐ 447	Dick Ellsworth UER	12.00	5.50
	(Photo actually		
	Ken Hubbs)		
☐ 448	Eddie Stanky MG	9.00	4.00
☐ 449	Joe Moeller	9.00	4.00
☐ 450	Tony Oliva	12.00	5.50
☐ 451	Barry Latman	9.00	4.00
☐ 452	Joe Azcue	9.00	4.00
☐ 453	Ron Kline	9.00	4.00
☐ 454	Jerry Buchek	9.00	4.00
☐ 455	Mickey Lolich	12.00	5.50
☐ 456	Red Sox Rookies	9.00	4.00
	Darrell Brandon		
	Joe Foy		
☐ 457	Joe Gibbon	9.00	4.00
☐ 458	Manny Jiminez	9.00	4.00
☐ 459	Bill McCool	9.00	4.00
☐ 460	Curt Blefary	9.00	4.00
☐ 461	Roy Face	15.00	6.75
☐ 462	Bob Rodgers	9.00	4.00
☐ 463	Philadelphia Phillies	15.00	6.75
	Team Card		
☐ 464	Larry Bearnarth	9.00	4.00
☐ 465	Don Buford	9.00	4.00
☐ 466	Ken Johnson	9.00	4.00
☐ 467	Vic Roznovsky	9.00	4.00
☐ 468	Johnny Podres	12.00	5.50
☐ 469	Yankees Rookies	25.00	11.00
	Bobby Murcer		
	Dooley Womack		
☐ 470	Sam McDowell	15.00	6.75
☐ 471	Bob Skinner	9.00	4.00
☐ 472	Terry Fox	9.00	4.00
☐ 473	Rich Rollins	9.00	4.00
☐ 474	Dick Schofield	9.00	4.00
☐ 475	Dick Radatz	9.00	4.00
☐ 476	Bobby Bragan MG	9.00	4.00
☐ 477	Steve Barber	9.00	4.00
☐ 478	Tony Gonzalez	9.00	4.00
☐ 479	Jim Hannan	9.00	4.00
☐ 480	Dick Stuart	9.00	4.00
☐ 481	Bob Lee	9.00	4.00
☐ 482	Cubs Rookies	9.00	4.00
	John Boccabella		
	Dave Dowling		
☐ 483	Joe Nuxhall	9.00	4.00
☐ 484	Wes Covington	9.00	4.00
☐ 485	Bob Bailey	9.00	4.00
☐ 486	Tommy John	12.00	5.50
☐ 487	Al Ferrara	9.00	4.00
☐ 488	George Banks	9.00	4.00
☐ 489	Curt Simmons	9.00	4.00
☐ 490	Bobby Richardson	12.00	5.50
☐ 491	Dennis Bennett	9.00	4.00
☐ 492	Athletics Team	15.00	6.75
☐ 493	Johnny Klippstein	9.00	4.00
☐ 494	Gordy Coleman	9.00	4.00
☐ 495	Dick McAuliffe	15.00	6.75
☐ 496	Lindy McDaniel	9.00	4.00
☐ 497	Chris Cannizzaro	9.00	4.00
☐ 498	Pirates Rookies	9.00	4.00
	Luke Walker		
	Woody Fryman		
☐ 499	Wally Bunker	9.00	4.00
☐ 500	Hank Aaron	125.00	55.00
☐ 501	John O'Donoghue	9.00	4.00
☐ 502	Lenny Green UER	9.00	4.00
	(Born: aJn. 6. 1933)		

☐ 503	Steve Hamilton	15.00	6.75
☐ 504	Grady Hatton MG	9.00	4.00
☐ 505	Jose Cardenal	9.00	4.00
☐ 506	Bo Belinsky	15.00	6.75
☐ 507	Johnny Edwards	9.00	4.00
☐ 508	Steve Hargan	9.00	4.00
☐ 509	Jake Wood	9.00	4.00
☐ 510	Hoyt Wilhelm	16.00	7.25
☐ 511	Giants Rookies	9.00	4.00
	Bob Barton		
	Tito Fuentes		
☐ 512	Dick Stigman	9.00	4.00
☐ 513	Camilo Carreon	9.00	4.00
☐ 514	Hal Woodeshick	9.00	4.00
☐ 515	Frank Howard	14.00	6.25
☐ 516	Eddie Bressoud	9.00	4.00
☐ 517A	Checklist 7	15.00	3.00
	529 White Sox Rookies		
	544 Cardinals Rookies		
☐ 517B	Checklist 7	15.00	3.00
	529 W. Sox Rookies		
	544 Cards Rookies		
☐ 518	Braves Rookies	9.00	4.00
	Herb Hippauf		
	Arnie Umbach		
☐ 519	Bob Friend	15.00	6.75
☐ 520	Jim Wynn	15.00	6.75
☐ 521	John Wyatt	9.00	4.00
☐ 522	Phil Linz	9.00	4.00
☐ 523	Bob Sadowski	15.00	6.75
☐ 524	Giants Rookies SP	30.00	13.50
	Ollie Brown		
	Don Mason		
☐ 525	Gary Bell SP	30.00	13.50
☐ 526	Twins Team SP	100.00	45.00
☐ 527	Julio Navarro	15.00	6.75
☐ 528	Jesse Gonder SP	30.00	13.50
☐ 529	White Sox Rookies	15.00	6.75
	Lee Elia		
	Dennis Higgins		
	Bill Voss		
☐ 530	Robin Roberts	60.00	27.00
☐ 531	Joe Cunningham	15.00	6.75
☐ 532	Aurelio Monteagudo SP		30.00
☐ 533	Jerry Adair SP	30.00	13.50
☐ 534	Mets Rookies	15.00	6.75
	Dave Eilers		
	Rob Gardner		
☐ 535	Willie Davis SP	40.00	18.00
☐ 536	Dick Egan	15.00	6.75
☐ 537	Herman Franks MG	15.00	6.75
☐ 538	Bob Allen SP	30.00	13.50
☐ 539	Astros Rookies	15.00	6.75
	Bill Heath		
	Carroll Sembera		
☐ 540	Denny McLain SP	80.00	36.00
☐ 541	Gene Oliver SP	30.00	13.50
☐ 542	George Smith	15.00	6.75
☐ 543	Roger Craig SP	35.00	16.00
☐ 544	Cardinals Rookies SP	30.00	13.50
	Joe Hoerner		
	George Kernek		
	Jimy Williams UER		
	(Misspelled Jimmy		
	on card)		
☐ 545	Dick Green SP	30.00	13.50
☐ 546	Dwight Siebler	15.00	6.75
☐ 547	Horace Clarke SP	40.00	18.00
☐ 548	Gary Kroll SP	30.00	13.50
☐ 549	Senators Rookies	15.00	6.75
	Al Closter		
	Casey Cox		
☐ 550	Willie McCovey SP	90.00	40.00
☐ 551	Bob Purkey SP	30.00	13.50
☐ 552	Birdie Tebbetts	30.00	13.50
	MG SP		
☐ 553	Rookie Stars	15.00	6.75
	Pat Garrett		
	Jackie Warner		
☐ 554	Jim Northrup SP	30.00	13.50
☐ 555	Ron Perranoski SP	30.00	13.50
☐ 556	Mel Queen SP	30.00	13.50
☐ 557	Felix Mantilla SP	30.00	13.50
☐ 558	Red Sox Rookies	20.00	9.00
	Guido Grilli		

Pete Magrini
George Scott
☐ 559 Roberto Pena SP 30.00 13.50
☐ 560 Joel Horlen 8.00 3.60
☐ 561 ChooChoo Coleman SP 35.00 16.00
☐ 562 Russ Snyder 15.00 6.75
☐ 563 Twins Rookies 15.00 6.75
Pete Cimino
Cesar Tovar
☐ 564 Bob Chance SP 30.00 13.50
☐ 565 Jimmy Piersall SP 40.00 18.00
☐ 566 Mike Cuellar SP 35.00 16.00
☐ 567 Dick Howser SP 40.00 18.00
☐ 568 Athletics Rookies 15.00 6.75
Paul Lindblad
Ron Stone
☐ 569 Orlando McFarlane SP 30.00 13.50
☐ 570 Art Mahaffey SP 30.00 13.50
☐ 571 Dave Roberts SP 30.00 13.50
☐ 572 Bob Priddy 15.00 6.75
☐ 573 Derrell Griffith 15.00 6.75
☐ 574 Mets Rookies 15.00 6.75
Bill Hepler
Bill Murphy
☐ 575 Earl Wilson 15.00 6.75
☐ 576 Dave Nicholson SP 30.00 13.50
☐ 577 Jack Lamabe SP 30.00 13.50
☐ 578 Chi Chi Olivo SP 30.00 13.50
☐ 579 Orioles Rookies 20.00 9.00
Frank Bertaina
Gene Brabender
Dave Johnson
☐ 580 Billy Williams SP 70.00 32.00
☐ 581 Tony Martinez 15.00 6.75
☐ 582 Garry Roggenburk 15.00 6.75
☐ 583 Tigers Team SP UER 125.00 55.00
(Text on back states Tigers finished third in 1966 instead of fourth.)
☐ 584 Yankees Rookies 15.00 6.75
Frank Fernandez
Fritz Peterson
☐ 585 Tony Taylor 25.00 11.00
☐ 586 Claude Raymond SP 30.00 13.50
☐ 587 Dick Bertell 15.00 6.75
☐ 588 Athletics Rookies 15.00 6.75
Chuck Dobson
Ken Suarez
☐ 589 Lou Klimchock SP ... 35.00 16.00
☐ 590 Bill Skowron SP 40.00 18.00
☐ 591 NL Rookies SP 40.00 18.00
Bart Shirley
Grant Jackson
☐ 592 Andre Rodgers 15.00 6.75
☐ 593 Doug Camilli SP 30.00 13.50
☐ 594 Chico Salmon 15.00 6.75
☐ 595 Larry Jackson 15.00 6.75
☐ 596 Astros Rookies SP 35.00 16.00
Nate Colbert
Greg Sims
☐ 597 John Sullivan 15.00 6.75
☐ 598 Gaylord Perry SP.. 190.00 55.00

1967 Topps

CURT FLOOD · OUTFIELD

The cards in this 609-card set measure 2 1/2" by 3 1/2". The

1967 Topps series is considered by some collectors to be one of the company's finest accomplishments in baseball card production. Excellent color photographs are combined with easy-to-read backs. Cards 458 to 533 are slightly harder to find than numbers 1 to 457, and the inevitable high series (534 to 609) exists. Each checklist card features a small circular picture of a popular player included in that series. Printing discrepancies resulted in some high series cards being in shorter supply. The checklist below identifies (by DP) 22 double-printed high numbers; of the 76 cards in the last series, 54 cards were short printed and the other 22 cards are much more plentiful. Featured subsets within this set include World Series cards (151-155) and League Leaders (233-244). A limited number of "proof" Roger Maris cards were produced. These cards are blank backed and Maris is listed as a New York Yankee on it. The Maris card is currently valued between $500 and $1000. Some Bob Bolin cards: #252 have a white smear in between his names. Another tough variation that has been recently discovered is a variation on card #58 Paul Schaal. The tough version has a green bar above his name. The key Rookie Cards in the set are high number cards of Rod Carew and Tom Seaver. Confirmed methods of selling these cards include five-cent nickel wax packs. Although rarely seen, there exists a salesman's sample panel of three cards that pictures Earl Battey, Manny Mota, and Gene Brabender with ad information on the back about the "new" Topps cards.

	NRMT	VG-E
COMPLETE SET (609)	4600.00	2100.00
COMMON CARD (1-109)	1.50	.70
COMMON CARD (110-283)	2.00	.90
MINOR STARS 1-283	4.00	1.80
SEMISTARS 1-283	6.00	2.70
UNLISTED STARS 1-283	8.00	3.60
COMMON CARD (284-370)	2.50	1.10
MINOR STARS 284-370	5.00	2.20
SEMISTARS 284-370	8.00	3.60
UNLISTED STARS 284-370	10.00	4.50
COMMON CARD (371-457)	4.00	1.80
MINOR STARS 371-457	8.00	3.60
SEMISTARS 371-457	12.00	5.50
UNLISTED STARS 371-457	15.00	6.75
COMMON CARD (458-533)	6.00	2.70
MINOR STARS 458-533	12.00	5.50
SEMISTARS 458-533	20.00	9.00
COMMON CARD (534-609)	16.00	7.25
COMMON DP (534-609)	9.00	4.00
MINOR STARS 534-609	25.00	11.00
SEMISTARS 534-609	40.00	18.00

*UNLISTED DODGER/YANKEE: 1.25X VALUE
CARDS PRICED IN NM CONDITION

☐ 1 The Champs DP 20.00 6.00
Frank Robinson
Hank Bauer MG
Brooks Robinson
☐ 2 Jack Hamilton .... 1.50 .70
☐ 3 Duke Sims .... 1.50 .70
☐ 4 Hal Lanier .... 1.50 .70
☐ 5 Whitey Ford UER 20.00 9.00

(1953 listed as
1933 in stats on back)
☐ 6 Dick Simpson .... 1.50 .70
☐ 7 Don McMahon .... 1.50 .70
☐ 8 Chuck Harrison .... 1.50 .70
☐ 9 Ron Hansen .... 1.50 .70
☐ 10 Matty Alou 2.50 1.10
☐ 11 Barry Moore .... 1.50 .70
☐ 12 Dodgers Rookies 2.50 1.10
Jim Campanis
Bill Singer
☐ 13 Joe Sparma .... 1.50 .70
☐ 14 Phil Linz 4.00 1.80
☐ 15 Earl Battey .... 1.50 .70
☐ 16 Bill Hands .... 1.50 .70
☐ 17 Jim Gosger .... 1.50 .70
☐ 18 Gene Oliver .... 1.50 .70
☐ 19 Jim McGlothlin .... 1.50 .70
☐ 20 Orlando Cepeda 6.00 2.70
☐ 21 Dave Bristol MG .... 1.50 .70
☐ 22 Gene Brabender .... 1.50 .70
☐ 23 Larry Elliot .... 1.50 .70
☐ 24 Bob Allen................. 1.50 .70
☐ 25 Elston Howard 4.00 1.80
☐ 26A Bob Priddy NTR 30.00 13.50
☐ 26B Bob Priddy TR.... 4.00 1.80
☐ 27 Bob Saverine .... 1.50 .70
☐ 28 Barry Latman .... 1.50 .70
☐ 29 Tom McCraw .... 1.50 .70
☐ 30 Al Kaline DP 16.00 7.25
☐ 31 Jim Brewer .... 1.50 .70
☐ 32 Bob Bailey 4.00 1.80
☐ 33 Athletic Rookies 5.00 2.20
Sal Bando
Randy Schwartz
☐ 34 Pete Cimino .... 1.50 .70
☐ 35 Rico Carty 4.00 1.80
☐ 36 Bob Tillman .... 1.50 .70
☐ 37 Rick Wise 4.00 1.80
☐ 38 Bob Johnson .... 1.50 .70
☐ 39 Curt Simmons 2.50 1.10
☐ 40 Rick Reichardt .... 1.50 .70
☐ 41 Joe Hoerner .... 1.50 .70
☐ 42 Mets Team 10.00 4.50
☐ 43 Chico Salmon .... 1.50 .70
☐ 44 Joe Nuxhall 4.00 1.80
☐ 45 Roger Maris 30.00 13.50
☐ 46 Lindy McDaniel 4.00 1.80
☐ 47 Ken McMullen .... 1.50 .70
☐ 48 Bill Freehan 2.50 1.10
☐ 49 Roy Face 2.50 1.10
☐ 50 Tony Oliva 6.00 2.70
☐ 51 Astros Rookies .... 1.50 .70
Dave Adlesh
Wes Bales
☐ 52 Dennis Higgins .... 1.50 .70
☐ 53 Clay Dalrymple .... 1.50 .70
☐ 54 Dick Green .... 1.50 .70
☐ 55 Don Drysdale 16.00 7.25
☐ 56 Jose Tartabull 4.00 1.80
☐ 57 Pat Jarvis .... 1.50 .70
☐ 58 Paul Schaal .... 1.50 .70
☐ 59 Ralph Terry 4.00 1.80
☐ 60 Luis Aparicio 6.00 2.70
☐ 61 Gordy Coleman .... 1.50 .70
☐ 62 Frank Robinson CL 30.00 6.00
☐ 63 Cards' Clubbers 10.00 4.50
Lou Brock
Curt Flood
☐ 64 Fred Valentine .... 1.50 .70
☐ 65 Tom Haller 4.00 1.80
☐ 66 Manny Mota 2.50 1.10
☐ 67 Ken Berry .... 1.50 .70
☐ 68 Bob Buhl 4.00 1.80
☐ 69 Vic Davalillo .... 1.50 .70
☐ 70 Ron Santo 4.00 1.80
☐ 71 Camilo Pascual 2.50 1.10
☐ 72 Tigers Rookies .... 1.50 .70
George Korince
(Photo actually
James Murray Brown)
John (Tom) Matchick
☐ 73 Rusty Staub 4.00 1.80
☐ 74 Wes Stock .... 1.50 .70
☐ 75 George Scott 2.50 1.10
☐ 76 Jim Barbieri .... 1.50 .70

No.	Name	Price	Price
77	Dooley Womack	4.00	1.80
78	Pat Corrales	4.00	1.80
79	Bubba Morton	1.50	.70
80	Jim Maloney	4.00	1.80
81	Eddie Stanky MG	2.50	1.10
82	Steve Barber	1.50	.70
83	Ollie Brown	1.50	.70
84	Tommie Sisk	1.50	.70
85	Johnny Callison	2.50	1.10
86A	Mike McCormick NTR	30.00	13.50
	(Senators on front and Senators on back)		
86B	Mike McCormick TR	4.00	1.80
	(Traded line at end of bio; Senators on front, but Giants on back)		
87	George Altman	1.50	.70
88	Mickey Lolich	4.00	1.80
89	Felix Millan	2.50	1.10
90	Jim Nash	1.50	.70
91	Johnny Lewis	1.50	.70
92	Ray Washburn	1.50	.70
93	Yankees Rookies	4.00	1.80
	Stan Bahnsen		
	Bobby Murcer		
94	Ron Fairly	2.50	1.10
95	Sonny Siebert	1.50	.70
96	Art Shamsky	1.50	.70
97	Mike Cuellar	4.00	1.80
98	Rich Rollins	1.50	.70
99	Lee Stange	1.50	.70
100	Frank Robinson DP	14.00	6.25
101	Ken Johnson	1.50	.70
102	Philadelphia Phillies Team Card	4.00	1.80
103	Mickey Mantle CL	16.00	3.20
104	Minnie Rojas	1.50	.70
105	Ken Boyer	2.50	1.10
106	Randy Hundley	4.00	1.80
107	Joel Horlen	1.50	.70
108	Alex Johnson	4.00	1.80
109	Tribe Thumpers	5.00	2.20
	Rocky Colavito		
	Leon Wagner		
110	Jack Aker	4.00	1.80
111	John Kennedy	2.00	.90
112	Dave Wickersham	2.00	.90
113	Dave Nicholson	2.00	.90
114	Jack Baldschun	2.00	.90
115	Paul Casanova	2.00	.90
116	Herman Franks MG	2.00	.90
117	Darrell Brandon	2.00	.90
118	Bernie Allen	2.00	.90
119	Wade Blasingame	2.00	.90
120	Floyd Robinson	2.00	.90
121	Eddie Bressoud	2.00	.90
122	George Brunet	2.00	.90
123	Pirates Rookies	2.00	.90
	Jim Price		
	Luke Walker		
124	Jim Stewart	2.00	.90
125	Moe Drabowsky	4.00	.90
126	Tony Taylor	2.00	.90
127	John O'Donoghue	2.00	.90
128	Ed Spiezio	2.00	.90
129	Phil Roof	2.00	.90
130	Phil Regan	4.00	1.80
131	Yankees Team	10.00	4.50
132	Ozzie Virgil	2.00	.90
133	Ron Kline	2.00	.90
134	Gates Brown	3.00	1.35
135	Deron Johnson	4.00	1.80
136	Carroll Sembera	2.00	.90
137	Twins Rookies	2.00	.90
	Ron Clark		
	Jim Ollum		
138	Dick Kelley	2.00	.90
139	Dalton Jones	4.00	1.80
140	Willie Stargell	20.00	9.00
141	John Miller	2.00	.90
142	Jackie Brandt	2.00	.90
143	Sox Sockers	2.00	.90
	Pete Ward		
	Don Buford		
144	Bill Hepler	2.00	.90
145	Larry Brown	2.00	.90
146	Steve Carlton	70.00	32.00
147	Tom Egan	2.00	.90
148	Adolfo Phillips	2.00	.90
149	Joe Moeller	2.00	.90
150	Mickey Mantle	300.00	135.00
151	Moe Drabowsky WS	4.00	1.80
152	Jim Palmer WS	8.00	3.60
153	Paul Blair WS	4.00	1.80
154	Brooks Robinson WS	4.00	1.80
	Dave McNally		
155	World Series Summary	4.00	1.80
	Winners celebrate		
156	Ron Herbel	2.00	.90
157	Danny Cater	2.00	.90
158	Jimmie Coker	2.00	.90
159	Bruce Howard	2.00	.90
160	Willie Davis	3.00	1.35
161	Dick Williams MG	3.00	1.35
162	Billy O'Dell	2.00	.90
163	Vic Roznovsky	2.00	.90
164	Dwight Siebler UER	2.00	.90
	(Last line of stats shows 1960 Minnesota)		
165	Cleon Jones	4.00	1.80
166	Eddie Mathews	16.00	7.25
167	Senators Rookies	2.00	.90
	Joe Coleman		
	Tim Cullen		
168	Ray Culp	2.00	.90
169	Horace Clarke	4.00	1.80
170	Dick McAuliffe	3.00	1.35
171	Cal Koonce	2.00	.90
172	Bill Heath	2.00	.90
173	St. Louis Cardinals Team Card	4.00	1.80
174	Dick Radatz	4.00	1.80
175	Bobby Knoop	2.00	.90
176	Sammy Ellis	2.00	.90
177	Tito Fuentes	2.00	.90
178	John Buzhardt	2.00	.90
179	Braves Rookies	2.00	.90
	Charles Vaughan		
	Cecil Upshaw		
180	Curt Blefary	2.00	.90
181	Terry Fox	2.00	.90
182	Ed Charles	2.00	.90
183	Jim Pagliaroni	2.00	.90
184	George Thomas	2.00	.90
185	Ken Holtzman	3.00	1.35
186	Mets Maulers	3.00	1.35
	Ed Kranepool		
	Ron Swoboda		
187	Pedro Ramos	2.00	.90
188	Ken Harrelson	3.00	1.35
189	Chuck Hinton	2.00	.90
190	Turk Farrell	2.00	.90
191A	Willie Mays CL	10.00	2.00
	214 Tom Kelley		
191B	Willie Mays CL	12.00	2.40
	214 Dick Kelley		
192	Fred Gladding	2.00	.90
193	Jose Cardenal	3.00	1.35
194	Bob Allison	3.00	1.35
195	Al Jackson	2.00	.90
196	Johnny Romano	2.00	.90
197	Ron Perranoski	3.00	1.35
198	Chuck Hiller	2.00	.90
199	Billy Hitchcock MG	2.00	.90
200	Willie Mays UER	85.00	38.00
	('63 Sna Francisco on card back stats)		
201	Hal Reniff	4.00	1.80
202	Johnny Edwards	2.00	.90
203	Al McBean	2.00	.90
204	Orioles Rookies	3.00	1.35
	Mike Epstein		
	Tom Phoebus		
205	Dick Groat	3.00	1.35
206	Dennis Bennett	2.00	.90
207	John Orsino	2.00	.90
208	Jack Lamabe	2.00	.90
209	Joe Nossek	2.00	.90
210	Bob Gibson	20.00	9.00
211	Twins Team	4.00	1.80
212	Chris Zachary	2.00	.90
213	Jay Johnstone	3.00	1.35
214	Dick Kelley	2.00	.90
215	Ernie Banks	20.00	9.00
216	Bengal Belters	10.00	4.50
	Norm Cash		
	Al Kaline		
217	Rob Gardner	2.00	.90
218	Wes Parker	3.00	1.35
219	Clay Carroll	4.00	1.80
220	Jim Ray Hart	3.00	1.35
221	Woody Fryman	4.00	1.80
222	Reds Rookies	3.00	1.35
	Darrell Osteen		
	Lee May		
223	Mike Ryan	4.00	1.80
224	Walt Bond	2.00	.90
225	Mel Stottlemyre	3.00	1.35
226	Julian Javier	3.00	1.35
227	Paul Lindblad	2.00	.90
228	Gil Hodges MG	5.00	2.20
229	Larry Jackson	2.00	.90
230	Boog Powell	6.00	2.70
231	John Bateman	2.00	.90
232	Don Buford	2.00	.90
233	AL ERA Leaders	4.00	1.80
	Gary Peters		
	Joel Horlen		
	Steve Hargan		
234	NL ERA Leaders	15.00	6.75
	Sandy Koufax		
	Mike Cuellar		
	Juan Marichal		
235	AL Pitching Leaders	6.00	2.70
	Jim Kaat		
	Denny McLain		
	Earl Wilson		
236	NL Pitching Leaders	25.00	11.00
	Sandy Koufax		
	Juan Marichal		
	Bob Gibson		
	Gaylord Perry		
237	AL Strikeout Leaders	6.00	2.70
	Sam McDowell		
	Jim Kaat		
	Earl Wilson		
238	NL Strikeout Leaders	12.00	5.50
	Sandy Koufax		
	Jim Bunning		
	Bob Veale		
239	AL Batting Leaders	9.00	4.00
	Frank Robinson		
	Tony Oliva		
	Al Kaline		
240	NL Batting Leaders	6.00	2.70
	Matty Alou		
	Felipe Alou		
	Rico Carty		
241	AL RBI Leaders	9.00	4.00
	Frank Robinson		
	Harmon Killebrew		
	Boog Powell		
242	NL RBI Leaders	24.00	11.00
	Hank Aaron		
	Bob Clemente		
	Richie Allen		
243	AL Home Run Leaders	9.00	4.00
	Frank Robinson		
	Harmon Killebrew		
	Boog Powell		
244	NL Home Run Leaders	20.00	9.00
	Hank Aaron		
	Richie Allen		
	Willie Mays		
245	Curt Flood	3.00	1.35
246	Jim Perry	3.00	1.35
247	Jerry Lumpe	2.00	.90
248	Gene Mauch MG	3.00	1.35
249	Nick Willhite	2.00	.90
250	Hank Aaron UER	80.00	36.00
	(Second 1961 in stats should be 1962)		
251	Woody Held	2.00	.90
252	Bob Bolin	2.00	.90
253	Indians Rookies	2.00	.90
	Bill Davis		
	Gus Gil		

Card	Player	Price	Price
254	Milt Pappas	3.00	1.35
	(No facsimile autograph on card front)		
255	Frank Howard	4.00	1.80
256	Bob Hendley	2.00	.90
257	Charlie Smith	2.00	.90
258	Lee Maye	2.00	.90
259	Don Dennis	2.00	.90
260	Jim Lefebvre	3.00	1.35
261	John Wyatt	2.00	.90
262	Athletics Team	4.00	1.80
263	Hank Aguirre	2.00	.90
264	Ron Swoboda	3.00	1.35
265	Lou Burdette	3.00	1.35
266	Pitt Power	5.00	2.20
	Willie Stargell		
	Donn Clendenon		
267	Don Schwall	2.00	.90
268	Johnny Briggs	2.00	.90
269	Don Nottebart	2.00	.90
270	Zoilo Versalles	2.00	.90
271	Eddie Watt	2.00	.90
272	Cubs Rookies	4.00	1.80
	Bill Connors		
	Dave Dowling		
273	Dick Lines	2.00	.90
274	Bob Aspromonte	2.00	.90
275	Fred Whitfield	2.00	.90
276	Bruce Brubaker	2.00	.90
277	Steve Whitaker	4.00	1.80
278	Jim Kaat CL	30.00	6.00
279	Frank Linzy	2.00	.90
280	Tony Conigliaro	10.00	4.50
281	Bob Rodgers	2.00	.90
282	John Odom	2.00	.90
283	Gene Alley	4.00	1.80
284	Johnny Podres	3.00	1.35
285	Lou Brock	20.00	9.00
286	Wayne Causey	2.50	1.10
287	Mets Rookies	2.50	1.10
	Greg Goossen		
	Bart Shirley		
288	Denny Lemaster	2.50	1.10
289	Tom Tresh	3.50	1.55
290	Bill White	3.00	1.35
291	Jim Hannan	2.50	1.10
292	Don Pavletich	2.50	1.10
293	Ed Kirkpatrick	2.50	1.10
294	Walter Alston MG	4.00	1.80
295	Sam McDowell	5.00	2.20
296	Glenn Beckert	5.00	2.20
297	Dave Morehead	5.00	2.20
298	Ron Davis	2.50	1.10
299	Norm Siebern	2.50	1.10
300	Jim Kaat	6.00	2.70
301	Jesse Gonder	2.50	1.10
302	Orioles Team	6.00	2.70
303	Gil Blanco	2.50	1.10
304	Phil Gagliano	2.50	1.10
305	Earl Wilson	5.00	2.20
306	Bud Harrelson	6.00	2.70
307	Jim Beauchamp	2.50	1.10
308	Al Downing	5.00	2.20
309	Hurlers Beware	5.00	2.20
	Johnny Callison		
	Richie Allen		
310	Gary Peters	2.50	1.10
311	Ed Brinkman	2.50	1.10
312	Don Mincher	2.50	1.10
313	Bob Lee	2.50	1.10
314	Red Sox Rookies	8.00	3.60
	Mike Andrews		
	Reggie Smith		
315	Billy Williams	10.00	4.50
316	Jack Kralick	2.50	1.10
317	Cesar Tovar	3.00	1.35
318	Dave Giusti	2.50	1.10
319	Paul Blair	5.00	2.20
320	Gaylord Perry	14.00	6.25
321	Mayo Smith MG	2.00	1.10
322	Jose Pagan	2.50	1.10
323	Mike Hershberger	2.50	1.10
324	Hal Woodeshick	2.50	1.10
325	Chico Cardenas	5.00	2.20
326	Bob Uecker	10.00	4.50
327	California Angels	6.00	2.70
	Team Card		
328	Clete Boyer UER	5.00	2.20
	(Stats only go up through 1965)		
329	Charlie Lau	5.00	2.20
330	Claude Osteen	5.00	2.20
331	Joe Foy	5.00	2.20
332	Jesus Alou	2.50	1.10
333	Ferguson Jenkins	18.00	8.00
334	Twin Terrors	6.00	2.70
	Bob Allison		
	Harmon Killebrew		
335	Bob Veale	5.00	2.20
336	Joe Azcue	2.50	1.10
337	Joe Morgan	14.00	6.25
338	Bob Locker	2.50	1.10
339	Chico Ruiz	2.50	1.10
340	Joe Pepitone	3.50	1.55
341	Giants Rookies	2.50	1.10
	Dick Dietz		
	Bill Sorrell		
342	Hank Fischer	2.50	1.10
343	Tom Satriano	2.50	1.10
344	Ossie Chavarria	2.50	1.10
345	Stu Miller	5.00	2.20
346	Jim Hickman	2.50	1.10
347	Grady Hatton MG	2.50	1.10
348	Tug McGraw	9.00	1.35
349	Bob Chance	2.50	1.10
350	Joe Torre	5.00	2.20
351	Vern Law	5.00	2.20
352	Ray Oyler	2.50	1.10
353	Bill McCool	2.50	1.10
354	Cubs Team	6.00	2.70
355	Carl Yastrzemski	50.00	22.00
356	Larry Jaster	2.50	1.10
357	Bill Skowron	3.00	1.35
358	Ruben Amaro	2.50	1.10
359	Dick Ellsworth	2.50	1.10
360	Leon Wagner	2.50	1.10
361	Roberto Clemente CL	14.00	2.80
362	Donald Knowles	2.50	1.10
363	Dave Johnson	5.00	2.20
364	Claude Raymond	2.50	1.10
365	John Roseboro	5.00	2.20
366	Andy Kosco	2.50	1.10
367	Angels Rookies	2.50	1.10
	Bill Kelso		
	Don Wallace		
368	Jack Hiatt	2.50	1.10
369	Jim Hunter	18.00	8.00
370	Tommy Davis	3.00	1.35
371	Jim Lonborg	8.00	3.60
372	Mike de la Hoz	4.00	1.80
373	White Sox Rookies DP	4.00	1.80
	Duane Josephson		
	Fred Klages		
374A	Mel Queen ERR DP	20.00	9.00
	(Incomplete stat line on back)		
374B	Mel Queen COR DP	4.00	1.80
	(Complete stat line on back)		
375	Jake Gibbs	8.00	3.60
376	Don Lock DP	4.00	1.80
377	Luis Tiant	8.00	3.60
378	Detroit Tigers	8.00	3.60
	Team Card UER		
	(Willie Horton with 262 RBI's in 1966)		
379	Jerry May DP	4.00	1.80
380	Dean Chance DP	4.00	1.80
381	Dick Schofield DP	4.00	1.80
382	Dave McNally	8.00	3.60
383	Ken Henderson DP	4.00	1.80
384	Cardinals Rookies	4.00	1.80
	Jim Cosman		
	Dick Hughes		
385	Jim Fregosi	8.00	3.60
	(Batting wrong)		
386	Dick Selma DP	4.00	1.80
387	Cap Peterson DP	4.00	1.80
388	Arnold Earley DP	4.00	1.80
389	Alvin Dark MG DP	8.00	3.60
390	Jim Wynn DP	8.00	3.60
391	Wilbur Wood DP	8.00	3.60
392	Tommy Harper DP	8.00	3.60
393	Jim Bouton DP	8.00	3.60
394	Jake Wood DP	4.00	1.80
395	Chris Short	8.00	3.60
396	Atlanta Aces	4.00	1.80
	Denis Menke		
	Tony Cloninger		
397	Willie Smith DP	4.00	1.80
398	Jeff Torborg	8.00	3.60
399	Al Worthington DP	4.00	1.80
400	Bob Clemente DP	100.00	45.00
401	Jim Coates	4.00	1.80
402A	Phillies Rookies DP	20.00	9.00
	Grant Jackson		
	Billy Wilson		
	Incomplete stat line		
402B	Phillies Rookies DP	8.00	3.60
	Grant Jackson		
	Billy Wilson		
403	Dick Nen	4.00	1.80
404	Nelson Briles	8.00	3.60
405	Russ Snyder	4.00	1.80
406	Lee Elia DP	4.00	1.80
407	Reds Team	8.00	3.60
408	Jim Northrup DP	8.00	3.60
409	Ray Sadecki	4.00	1.80
410	Lou Johnson DP	4.00	1.80
411	Dick Howser DP	4.00	1.80
412	Astros Rookies	8.00	3.60
	Norm Miller		
	Doug Rader		
413	Jerry Grote	4.00	1.80
414	Casey Cox	4.00	1.80
415	Sonny Jackson	4.00	1.80
416	Roger Repoz	4.00	1.80
417A	Bob Bruce ERR DP	30.00	13.50
	(RBAVES on back)		
417B	Bob Bruce COR DP	4.00	1.80
418	Sam Mele MG	4.00	1.80
419	Don Kessinger DP	8.00	3.60
420	Denny McLain	6.00	2.70
421	Dal Maxvill DP	4.00	1.80
422	Hoyt Wilhelm	10.00	4.50
423	Fence Busters DP	25.00	11.00
	Willie Mays		
	Willie McCovey		
424	Pedro Gonzalez	4.00	1.80
425	Pete Mikkelsen	4.00	1.80
426	Lou Clinton	4.00	1.80
427A	Ruben Gomez ERR DP	20.00	9.00
	(Incomplete stat line on back)		
427B	Ruben Gomez COR DP	4.00	1.80
	(Complete stat line on back)		
428	Dodgers Rookies DP	8.00	3.60
	Tom Hutton		
	Gene Michael		
429	Garry Roggenburk DP	4.00	1.80
430	Pete Rose	80.00	36.00
431	Ted Uhlaender	4.00	1.80
432	Jimmie Hall DP	4.00	1.80
433	Al Luplow DP	4.00	1.80
434	Eddie Fisher DP	4.00	1.80
435	Mack Jones DP	4.00	1.80
436	Pete Ward	4.00	1.80
437	Senators Team	8.00	3.60
438	Chuck Dobson	4.00	1.80
439	Byron Browne	4.00	1.80
440	Steve Hargan	4.00	1.80
441	Jim Davenport	4.00	1.80
442	Yankees Rookies DP	8.00	3.60
	Bill Robinson		
	Joe Verbanic		
443	Tito Francona	4.00	1.80
444	George Smith	4.00	1.80
445	Don Sutton	25.00	11.00
446	Russ Nixon DP	4.00	1.80
447A	Bo Belinsky ERR	5.00	2.20
	(Incomplete stat line on back)		
447B	Bo Belinsky COR DP	8.00	3.60
	(Complete stat line on back)		
448	Harry Walker DP MG	4.00	1.80
449	Orlando Pena	4.00	1.80

450 Richie Allen	9.00	4.00
451 Fred Newman DP	4.00	1.80
452 Ed Kranepool	8.00	3.60
453 Aurelio Monteagudo DP	4.00	1.80
454A Juan Marichal CL	8.00	1.60
Missing left ear		
454B Juan Marichal CL	8.00	1.60
left ear showing		
455 Tommie Agee	8.00	3.60
456 Phil Niekro	16.00	7.25
457 Andy Etchebarren DP	8.00	3.60
458 Lee Thomas	6.00	2.70
459 Senators Rookies	6.00	2.70
Dick Bosman		
Pete Craig		
460 Harmon Killebrew	60.00	27.00
461 Bob Miller	6.00	2.70
462 Bob Barton	6.00	2.70
463 Hill Aces	12.00	5.50
Sam McDowell		
Sonny Siebert		
464 Dan Coombs	6.00	2.70
465 Willie Horton	12.00	5.50
466 Bobby Wine	6.00	2.70
467 Jim O'Toole	6.00	2.70
468 Ralph Houk MG	6.00	2.70
469 Len Gabrielson	6.00	2.70
470 Bob Shaw	6.00	2.70
471 Rene Lachemann	6.00	2.70
472 Rookies Pirates	6.00	2.70
John Gelnar		
George Spriggs		
473 Jose Santiago	6.00	2.70
474 Bob Tolan	6.00	2.70
475 Jim Palmer	90.00	40.00
476 Tony Perez SP	70.00	32.00
477 Braves Team	15.00	6.75
478 Bob Humphreys	6.00	2.70
479 Gary Bell	6.00	2.70
480 Willie McCovey	35.00	16.00
481 Leo Durocher MG	15.00	6.75
482 Bill Monbouquette	6.00	2.70
483 Jim Landis	6.00	2.70
484 Jerry Adair	6.00	2.70
485 Tim McCarver	20.00	9.00
486 Twins Rookies	6.00	2.70
Rich Reese		
Bill Whitby		
487 Tommie Reynolds	6.00	2.70
488 Gerry Arrigo	6.00	2.70
489 Doug Clemens	6.00	2.70
490 Tony Cloninger	6.00	2.70
491 Sam Bowens	6.00	2.70
492 Pittsburgh Pirates	15.00	6.75
Team Card		
493 Phil Ortega	6.00	2.70
494 Bill Rigney MG	6.00	2.70
495 Fritz Peterson	6.00	2.70
496 Orlando McFarlane	6.00	2.70
497 Ron Campbell	6.00	2.70
498 Larry Dierker	12.00	5.50
499 Indians Rookies	6.00	2.70
George Culver		
Jose Vidal		
500 Juan Marichal	25.00	11.00
501 Jerry Zimmerman	6.00	2.70
502 Derrell Griffith	6.00	2.70
503 Los Angeles Dodgers	15.00	6.75
Team Card		
504 Orlando Martinez	6.00	2.70
505 Tommy Helms	12.00	5.50
506 Smoky Burgess	6.00	2.70
507 Orioles Rookies	6.00	2.70
Ed Barnowski		
Larry Haney		
508 Dick Hall	6.00	2.70
509 Jim King	6.00	2.70
510 Bill Mazeroski	15.00	6.75
511 Don Wert	6.00	2.70
512 Red Schoendienst MG	15.00	6.75
513 Marcelino Lopez	6.00	2.70
514 John Werhas	6.00	2.70
515 Bert Campaneris	9.00	4.00
516 Giants Team	15.00	6.75
517 Fred Talbot	6.00	2.70
518 Denis Menke	6.00	2.70
519 Ted Davidson	6.00	2.70
520 Max Alvis	6.00	2.70
521 Bird Bombers	12.00	5.50
Boog Powell		
Curt Blefary		
522 John Stephenson	6.00	2.70
523 Jim Merritt	6.00	2.70
524 Felix Mantilla	6.00	2.70
525 Ron Hunt	6.00	2.70
526 Tigers Rookies	6.00	2.70
Pat Dobson		
George Korince		
(See 67T-72)		
527 Dennis Ribant	6.00	2.70
528 Rico Petrocelli	10.00	4.50
529 Gary Wagner	6.00	2.70
530 Felipe Alou	12.00	5.50
531 Brooks Robinson CL	14.00	2.80
532 Jim Hicks	6.00	2.70
533 Jack Fisher	6.00	2.70
534 Hank Bauer MG DP	9.00	4.00
535 Donn Clendenon	18.00	8.00
536 Cubs Rookies	35.00	16.00
Joe Niekro		
Paul Popovich		
537 Chuck Estrada DP	9.00	4.00
538 J.C. Martin	16.00	7.25
539 Dick Egan DP	9.00	4.00
540 Norm Cash	35.00	16.00
541 Joe Gibbon	16.00	7.25
542 Athletics Rookies DP	15.00	6.75
Rick Monday		
Tony Pierce		
543 Dan Schneider	16.00	7.25
544 Cleveland Indians	30.00	13.50
Team Card		
545 Jim Stewart	16.00	7.25
546 Woody Woodward	18.00	8.00
547 Red Sox Rookies DP	9.00	4.00
Russ Gibson		
Bill Rohr		
548 Tony Gonzalez DP	9.00	4.00
549 Jack Sanford	16.00	7.25
550 Vada Pinson DP	10.00	4.50
551 Doug Camilli DP	9.00	4.00
552 Ted Savage	16.00	7.25
553 Yankees Rookies	30.00	13.50
Mike Hegan		
Thad Tillotson		
554 Andre Rodgers DP	9.00	4.00
555 Don Cardwell	18.00	8.00
556 Al Weis DP	9.00	4.00
557 Al Ferrara	16.00	7.25
558 Orioles Rookies	50.00	22.00
Mark Belanger		
Bill Dillman		
559 Dick Tracewski DP	9.00	4.00
560 Jim Bunning	70.00	32.00
561 Sandy Alomar	20.00	9.00
562 Steve Blass DP	9.00	4.00
563 Joe Adcock	20.00	9.00
564 Astros Rookies DP	9.00	4.00
Alonzo Harris		
Aaron Pointer		
565 Lew Krausse	16.00	7.25
566 Gary Geiger DP	9.00	4.00
567 Steve Hamilton	25.00	11.00
568 John Sullivan	25.00	11.00
569 AL Rookies DP	250.00	110.00
Rod Carew		
Hank Allen		
570 Maury Wills	85.00	38.00
571 Larry Sherry	16.00	7.25
572 Don Demeter	16.00	7.25
573 Chicago White Sox	30.00	13.50
Team Card UER		
(Indians team		
stats on back)		
574 Jerry Buchek	16.00	7.25
575 Dave Boswell	16.00	7.25
576 NL Rookies	25.00	11.00
Ramon Hernandez		
Norm Gigon		
577 Bill Short	16.00	7.25
578 John Boccabella	16.00	7.25
579 Bill Henry	16.00	7.25
580 Rocky Colavito	100.00	45.00
581 Mets Rookies	850.00	375.00
Bill Denehy		
Tom Seaver		
582 Jim Owens DP	9.00	4.00
583 Ray Barker	25.00	11.00
584 Jimmy Piersall	35.00	16.00
585 Wally Bunker	16.00	7.25
586 Manny Jimenez	16.00	7.25
587 NL Rookies	35.00	16.00
Don Shaw		
Gary Sutherland		
588 Johnny Klippstein DP	9.00	4.00
589 Dave Ricketts DP	9.00	4.00
590 Pete Richert	16.00	7.25
591 Ty Cline	16.00	7.25
592 NL Rookies	25.00	11.00
Jim Shellenback		
Ron Willis		
593 Wes Westrum MG	25.00	11.00
594 Dan Osinski	18.00	8.00
595 Cookie Rojas	18.00	8.00
596 Galen Cisco DP	10.00	4.50
597 Ted Abernathy	16.00	7.25
598 White Sox Rookies	18.00	8.00
Walt Williams		
Ed Stroud		
599 Bob Duliba DP	9.00	4.00
600 Brooks Robinson	275.00	125.00
601 Bill Bryan DP	9.00	4.00
602 Juan Pizarro	25.00	11.00
603 Athletics Rookies	25.00	11.00
Tim Talton		
Ramon Webster		
604 Red Sox Team	125.00	55.00
605 Mike Shannon	50.00	22.00
606 Ron Taylor	18.00	8.00
607 Mickey Stanley	40.00	18.00
608 Cubs Rookies	9.00	4.00
Rich Nye		
John Upham		
609 Tommy John	70.00	23.00

1968 Topps

The cards in this 598-card set measure 2 1/2" by 3 1/2". The 1968 Topps set includes Sporting News All-Star Selections as card numbers 361 to 380. Other subsets in the set include League Leaders (1-12) and World Series cards (151-158). The front of each checklist card features a picture of a popular player inside a circle. Higher numbers 458 to 598 are slightly more difficult to obtain. The first series looks different from the other series, as it has a lighter, white mesh background on the card front. The later series all has a much darker, finer mesh pattern. Among other fashions, cards were issued in five-card nickel packs. The key Rookie Cards in the set *are Johnny Bench and Nolan Ryan.*

	NRMT	VG-E
COMPLETE SET (598)	3000.00	1350.00
COMMON CARD (1-457)	1.75	.80
MINOR STARS 1-457	4.00	1.80
SEMISTARS 1-457	6.00	2.70
UNLISTED STARS 1-457	8.00	3.60
COMMON CARD (458-598)	3.50	1.55
MINOR STARS 458-598	6.00	2.70
SEMISTARS 458-598	10.00	4.50
UNLISTED STARS 458-598	12.00	5.50

UNLISTED DODGER/YANKEE: 1.25X VALUE
CARDS PRICED IN NM CONDITION

		NRMT	VG-E
☐ 1	NL Batting Leaders	30.00	12.00
	Bob Clemente		
	Tony Gonzalez		
	Matty Alou		
☐ 2	AL Batting Leaders	14.00	6.25
	Carl Yastrzemski		
	Frank Robinson		
	Al Kaline		
☐ 3	NL RBI Leaders	20.00	9.00
	Orlando Cepeda		
	Bob Clemente		
	Hank Aaron		
☐ 4	AL RBI Leaders	12.00	5.50
	Carl Yastrzemski		
	Harmon Killebrew		
	Frank Robinson		
☐ 5	NL Home Run Leaders	8.00	3.60
	Hank Aaron		
	Jim Wynn		
	Ron Santo		
	Willie McCovey		
☐ 6	AL Home Run Leaders	8.00	3.60
	Carl Yastrzemski		
	Harmon Killebrew		
	Frank Howard		
☐ 7	NL ERA Leaders	3.50	1.55
	Phil Niekro		
	Jim Bunning		
	Chris Short		
☐ 8	AL ERA Leaders	3.50	1.55
	Joel Horlen		
	Gary Peters		
	Sonny Siebert		
☐ 9	NL Pitching Leaders	5.00	2.20
	Mike McCormick		
	Ferguson Jenkins		
	Jim Bunning		
	Claude Osteen		
☐ 10A	AL Pitching Leaders	4.00	1.80
	Jim Lonborg ERR		
	(Misspelled Lonberg		
	on card back)		
	Earl Wilson		
	Dean Chance		
☐ 10B	AL Pitching Leaders	4.00	1.80
	Jim Lonborg COR		
	Earl Wilson		
	Dean Chance		
☐ 11	NL Strikeout Leaders	6.00	2.70
	Jim Bunning		
	Ferguson Jenkins		
	Gaylord Perry		
☐ 12	AL Strikeout Leaders	3.50	1.55
	Jim Lonborg UER		
	(Misspelled Longberg		
	on card back)		
	Sam McDowell		
	Dean Chance		
☐ 13	Chuck Hartenstein	1.75	.80
☐ 14	Jerry McNertney	1.75	.80
☐ 15	Ron Hunt	1.75	.80
☐ 16	Indians Rookies	5.00	2.20
	Lou Piniella		
	Richie Scheinblum		
☐ 17	Dick Hall	1.75	.80
☐ 18	Mike Hershberger	1.75	.80
☐ 19	Juan Pizarro	1.75	.80
☐ 20	Brooks Robinson	25.00	11.00
☐ 21	Ron Davis	1.75	.80
☐ 22	Pat Dobson	4.00	1.80

		NRMT	VG-E
☐ 23	Chico Cardenas	4.00	1.80
☐ 24	Bobby Locke	1.75	.80
☐ 25	Julian Javier	4.00	1.80
☐ 26	Darrell Brandon	1.75	.80
☐ 27	Gil Hodges MG	8.00	3.60
☐ 28	Ted Uhlaender	1.75	.80
☐ 29	Joe Verbanic	1.75	.80
☐ 30	Joe Torre	5.00	2.20
☐ 31	Ed Stroud	1.75	.80
☐ 32	Joe Gibbon	1.75	.80
☐ 33	Pete Ward	1.75	.80
☐ 34	Al Ferrara	1.75	.80
☐ 35	Steve Hargan	1.75	.80
☐ 36	Pirates Rookies	4.00	1.80
	Bob Moose		
	Bob Robertson		
☐ 37	Billy Williams	8.00	3.60
☐ 38	Tony Pierce	1.75	.80
☐ 39	Cookie Rojas	4.00	1.80
☐ 40	Denny McLain	10.00	4.50
☐ 41	Julio Gotay	1.75	.80
☐ 42	Larry Haney	1.75	.80
☐ 43	Gary Bell	1.75	.80
☐ 44	Frank Kostro	1.75	.80
☐ 45	Tom Seaver	50.00	22.00
☐ 46	Dave Ricketts	1.75	.80
☐ 47	Ralph Houk MG	4.00	1.80
☐ 48	Ted Davidson	1.75	.80
☐ 49A	Eddie Brinkman	1.75	.80
	(White team name)		
☐ 49B	Eddie Brinkman	50.00	22.00
	(Yellow team name)		
☐ 50	Willie Mays	65.00	29.00
☐ 51	Bob Locker	1.75	.80
☐ 52	Hawk Taylor	1.75	.80
☐ 53	Gene Alley	4.00	1.80
☐ 54	Stan Williams	4.00	1.80
☐ 55	Felipe Alou	5.00	2.20
☐ 56	Orioles Rookies	1.75	.80
	Dave Leonhard		
	Dave May		
☐ 57	Dan Schneider	1.75	.80
☐ 58	Eddie Mathews	16.00	7.25
☐ 59	Don Lock	1.75	.80
☐ 60	Ken Holtzman	4.00	1.80
☐ 61	Reggie Smith	3.00	1.35
☐ 62	Chuck Dobson	1.75	.80
☐ 63	Dick Kenworthy	1.75	.80
☐ 64	Jim Merritt	1.75	.80
☐ 65	John Roseboro	4.00	1.80
☐ 66A	Casey Cox	1.75	.80
	(White team name)		
☐ 66B	Casey Cox	100.00	45.00
	(Yellow team name)		
☐ 67	Jim Kaat CL	6.00	1.20
☐ 68	Ron Willis	1.75	.80
☐ 69	Tom Tresh	2.50	1.10
☐ 70	Bob Veale	1.75	.80
☐ 71	Vern Fuller	1.75	.80
☐ 72	Tommy John	6.00	2.70
☐ 73	Jim Ray Hart	4.00	1.80
☐ 74	Milt Pappas	4.00	1.80
☐ 75	Don Mincher	1.75	.80
☐ 76	Braves Rookies	4.00	1.80
	Jim Britton		
	Ron Reed		
☐ 77	Don Wilson	4.00	1.80
☐ 78	Jim Northrup	5.00	2.20
☐ 79	Ted Kubiak	1.75	.80
☐ 80	Rod Carew	50.00	22.00
☐ 81	Larry Jackson	1.75	.80
☐ 82	Sam Bowens	1.75	.80
☐ 83	John Stephenson	1.75	.80
☐ 84	Bob Tolan	4.00	1.80
☐ 85	Gaylord Perry	8.00	3.60
☐ 86	Willie Stargell	8.00	3.60
☐ 87	Dick Williams MG	4.00	1.80
☐ 88	Phil Regan	4.00	1.80
☐ 89	Jake Gibbs	1.75	.80
☐ 90	Vada Pinson	3.00	1.35
☐ 91	Jim Ollom	1.75	.80
☐ 92	Ed Kranepool	4.00	1.80
☐ 93	Tony Cloninger	1.75	.80
☐ 94	Lee Maye	1.75	.80
☐ 95	Bob Aspromonte	1.75	.80
☐ 96	Senator Rookies	1.75	.80

		NRMT	VG-E
	Frank Coggins		
	Dick Nold		
☐ 97	Tom Phoebus	1.75	.80
☐ 98	Gary Sutherland	1.75	.80
☐ 99	Rocky Colavito	8.00	3.60
☐ 100	Bob Gibson	25.00	11.00
☐ 101	Glenn Beckert	4.00	1.80
☐ 102	Jose Cardenal	4.00	1.80
☐ 103	Don Sutton	6.00	2.70
☐ 104	Dick Dietz	1.75	.80
☐ 105	Al Downing	4.00	1.80
☐ 106	Dalton Jones	1.75	.80
☐ 107A	Juan Marichal CL	6.00	1.20
	Tan wide mesh		
☐ 107B	Juan Marichal CL	6.00	1.20
	Brown fine mesh		
☐ 108	Don Pavletich	1.75	.80
☐ 109	Bert Campaneris	4.00	1.80
☐ 110	Hank Aaron	60.00	27.00
☐ 111	Rich Reese	1.75	.80
☐ 112	Woody Fryman	1.75	.80
☐ 113	Tigers Rookies	2.50	1.10
	Tom Matchick		
	Daryl Patterson		
☐ 114	Ron Swoboda	4.00	1.80
☐ 115	Sam McDowell	4.00	1.80
☐ 116	Ken McMullen	1.75	.80
☐ 117	Larry Jaster	1.75	.80
☐ 118	Mark Belanger	4.00	1.80
☐ 119	Ted Savage	1.75	.80
☐ 120	Mel Stottlemyre	5.00	2.20
☐ 121	Jimmie Hall	1.75	.80
☐ 122	Gene Mauch MG	4.00	1.80
☐ 123	Jose Santiago	1.75	.80
☐ 124	Nate Oliver	1.75	.80
☐ 125	Joel Horlen	1.75	.80
☐ 126	Bobby Etheridge	1.75	.80
☐ 127	Paul Lindblad	1.75	.80
☐ 128	Astros Rookies	1.75	.80
	Tom Dukes		
	Alonzo Harris		
☐ 129	Mickey Stanley	5.00	2.20
☐ 130	Tony Perez	8.00	3.60
☐ 131	Frank Bertaina	1.75	.80
☐ 132	Bud Harrelson	4.00	1.80
☐ 133	Fred Whitfield	1.75	.80
☐ 134	Pat Jarvis	1.75	.80
☐ 135	Paul Blair	4.00	1.80
☐ 136	Randy Hundley	4.00	1.80
☐ 137	Twins Team	4.00	1.80
☐ 138	Ruben Amaro	1.75	.80
☐ 139	Chris Short	1.75	.80
☐ 140	Tony Conigliaro	8.00	3.60
☐ 141	Dal Maxvill	1.75	.80
☐ 142	White Sox Rookies	1.75	.80
	Buddy Bradford		
	Bill Voss		
☐ 143	Pete Cimino	1.75	.80
☐ 144	Joe Morgan	12.00	5.50
☐ 145	Don Drysdale	12.00	5.50
☐ 146	Sal Bando	4.00	1.80
☐ 147	Frank Linzy	1.75	.80
☐ 148	Dave Bristol MG	1.75	.80
☐ 149	Bob Saverine	1.75	.80
☐ 150	Bob Clemente	70.00	32.00
☐ 151	Lou Brock WS	10.00	4.50
☐ 152	Carl Yastrzemski WS	10.00	4.50
☐ 153	Nellie Briles WS	4.50	2.00
☐ 154	Bob Gibson WS	10.00	4.50
☐ 155	Jim Lonborg WS	4.50	2.00
☐ 156	Rico Petrocelli WS	4.50	2.00
☐ 157	World Series Game 7	4.50	2.00
	St. Louis wins it		
☐ 158	World Series Summary	4.50	2.00
	Cardinals celebrate		
☐ 159	Don Kessinger	4.00	1.80
☐ 160	Earl Wilson	4.00	1.80
☐ 161	Norm Miller	1.75	.80
☐ 162	Cards Rookies	4.00	1.80
	Hal Gilson		
	Mike Torrez		
☐ 163	Gene Brabender	1.75	.80
☐ 164	Ramon Webster	1.75	.80
☐ 165	Tony Oliva	5.00	2.20
☐ 166	Claude Raymond	1.75	.80
☐ 167	Elston Howard	5.00	2.20

☐ 168	Dodgers Team	4.00	1.80
☐ 169	Bob Bolin	1.75	.80
☐ 170	Jim Fregosi	4.00	1.80
☐ 171	Don Nottebart	1.75	.80
☐ 172	Walt Williams	1.75	.80
☐ 173	John Boozer	1.75	.80
☐ 174	Bob Tillman	1.75	.80
☐ 175	Maury Wills	6.00	2.70
☐ 176	Bob Allen	1.75	.80
☐ 177	Mets Rookies	900.00	400.00
	Jerry Koosman		
	Nolan Ryan		
☐ 178	Don Wert	4.00	1.80
☐ 179	Bill Stoneman	1.75	.80
☐ 180	Curt Flood	3.00	1.35
☐ 181	Jerry Zimmerman	1.75	.80
☐ 182	Dave Giusti	1.75	.80
☐ 183	Bob Kennedy MG	4.00	1.80
☐ 184	Lou Johnson	4.00	1.80
☐ 185	Tom Haller	1.75	.80
☐ 186	Eddie Watt	1.75	.80
☐ 187	Sonny Jackson	1.75	.80
☐ 188	Cap Peterson	1.75	.80
☐ 189	Bill Landis	1.75	.80
☐ 190	Bill White	3.00	1.35
☐ 191	Dan Frisella	1.75	.80
☐ 192A	Carl Yastrzemski CL	8.00	1.60
	Special Baseball Playing Card		
☐ 192B	Carl Yastrzemski CL	8.00	1.60
	Special Baseball Playing Card Game		
☐ 193	Jack Hamilton	1.75	.80
☐ 194	Don Buford	1.75	.80
☐ 195	Joe Pepitone	2.50	1.10
☐ 196	Gary Nolan	4.00	1.80
☐ 197	Larry Brown	1.75	.80
☐ 198	Roy Face	4.00	1.80
☐ 199	A's Rookies	1.75	.80
	Roberto Rodriquez		
	Darrell Osteen		
☐ 200	Orlando Cepeda	6.00	2.70
☐ 201	Mike Marshall	3.00	1.35
☐ 202	Adolfo Phillips	1.75	.80
☐ 203	Dick Kelley	1.75	.80
☐ 204	Andy Etchebarren	1.75	.80
☐ 205	Juan Marichal	8.00	3.60
☐ 206	Cal Ermer MG	1.75	.80
☐ 207	Carroll Sembera	1.75	.80
☐ 208	Willie Davis	2.50	1.10
☐ 209	Tim Cullen	1.75	.80
☐ 210	Gary Peters	1.75	.80
☐ 211	J.C. Martin	1.75	.80
☐ 212	Dave Morehead	1.75	.80
☐ 213	Chico Ruiz	1.75	.80
☐ 214	Yankees Rookies	4.00	1.80
	Stan Bahnsen		
	Frank Fernandez		
☐ 215	Jim Bunning	7.00	3.10
☐ 216	Bubba Morton	1.75	.80
☐ 217	Dick Farrell	1.75	.80
☐ 218	Ken Suarez	1.75	.80
☐ 219	Rob Gardner	1.75	.80
☐ 220	Harmon Killebrew	14.00	6.25
☐ 221	Braves Team	4.00	1.80
☐ 222	Jim Hardin	1.75	.80
☐ 223	Ollie Brown	1.75	.80
☐ 224	Jack Aker	1.75	.80
☐ 225	Richie Allen	6.00	2.70
☐ 226	Jimmie Price	1.75	.80
☐ 227	Joe Hoerner	1.75	.80
☐ 228	Dodgers Rookies	4.00	1.80
	Jack Billingham		
	Jim Fairey		
☐ 229	Fred Klages	1.75	.80
☐ 230	Pete Rose	35.00	16.00
☐ 231	Dave Baldwin	1.75	.80
☐ 232	Denis Menke	1.75	.80
☐ 233	George Scott	4.00	1.80
☐ 234	Bill Monbouquette	1.75	.80
☐ 235	Ron Santo	5.00	2.20
☐ 236	Tug McGraw	5.00	2.20
☐ 237	Alvin Dark MG	4.00	1.80
☐ 238	Tom Satriano	1.75	.80
☐ 239	Bill Henry	1.75	.80
☐ 240	Al Kaline	25.00	11.00
☐ 241	Felix Millan	1.75	.80
☐ 242	Moe Drabowsky	4.00	1.80
☐ 243	Rich Rollins	1.75	.80
☐ 244	John Donaldson	1.75	.80
☐ 245	Tony Gonzalez	1.75	.80
☐ 246	Fritz Peterson	4.00	1.80
☐ 247	Reds Rookies	125.00	55.00
	Johnny Bench		
	Ron Tompkins		
☐ 248	Fred Valentine	1.75	.80
☐ 249	Bill Singer	4.00	1.80
☐ 250	Carl Yastrzemski	25.00	11.00
☐ 251	Manny Sanguillen	6.00	2.70
☐ 252	Angels Team	4.00	1.80
☐ 253	Dick Hughes	1.75	.80
☐ 254	Cleon Jones	1.75	.80
☐ 255	Dean Chance	4.00	1.80
☐ 256	Norm Cash	6.00	2.70
☐ 257	Phil Niekro	8.00	3.60
☐ 258	Cubs Rookies	1.75	.80
	Jose Arcia		
	Bill Schlesinger		
☐ 259	Ken Boyer	3.00	1.35
☐ 260	Jim Wynn	4.00	1.80
☐ 261	Dave Duncan	4.00	1.80
☐ 262	Rick Wise	4.00	1.80
☐ 263	Horace Clarke	4.00	1.80
☐ 264	Ted Abernathy	1.75	.80
☐ 265	Tommy Davis	4.00	1.80
☐ 266	Paul Popovich	1.75	.80
☐ 267	Herman Franks MG	1.75	.80
☐ 268	Bob Humphreys	1.75	.80
☐ 269	Bob Tiefenauer	1.75	.80
☐ 270	Matty Alou	4.00	1.80
☐ 271	Bobby Knoop	1.75	.80
☐ 272	Ray Culp	1.75	.80
☐ 273	Dave Johnson	4.00	1.80
☐ 274	Mike Cuellar	4.00	1.80
☐ 275	Tim McCarver	5.00	2.20
☐ 276	Jim Roland	1.75	.80
☐ 277	Jerry Buchek	1.75	.80
☐ 278	Orlando Cepeda CL	6.00	1.20
☐ 279	Bill Hands	1.75	.80
☐ 280	Mickey Mantle	250.00	110.00
☐ 281	Jim Campanis	1.75	.80
☐ 282	Rick Monday	4.00	1.80
☐ 283	Mel Queen	1.75	.80
☐ 284	Johnny Briggs	1.75	.80
☐ 285	Dick McAuliffe	4.00	1.80
☐ 286	Cecil Upshaw	1.75	.80
☐ 287	White Sox Rookies	1.75	.80
	Mickey Abarbanel		
	Cisco Carlos		
☐ 288	Dave Wickersham	1.75	.80
☐ 289	Woody Held	1.75	.80
☐ 290	Willie McCovey	12.00	5.50
☐ 291	Dick Lines	1.75	.80
☐ 292	Art Shamsky	1.75	.80
☐ 293	Bruce Howard	1.75	.80
☐ 294	Red Schoendienst MG	5.00	2.20
☐ 295	Sonny Siebert	1.75	.80
☐ 296	Byron Browne	1.75	.80
☐ 297	Russ Gibson	1.75	.80
☐ 298	Jim Brewer	1.75	.80
☐ 299	Gene Michael	4.00	1.80
☐ 300	Rusty Staub	3.00	1.35
☐ 301	Twins Rookies	1.75	.80
	George Mitterwald		
	Rick Renick		
☐ 302	Gerry Arrigo	1.75	.80
☐ 303	Dick Green	4.00	1.80
☐ 304	Sandy Valdespino	1.75	.80
☐ 305	Minnie Rojas	1.75	.80
☐ 306	Mike Ryan	1.75	.80
☐ 307	John Hiller	4.00	1.80
☐ 308	Pirates Team	4.00	1.80
☐ 309	Ken Henderson	1.75	.80
☐ 310	Luis Aparicio	7.00	3.10
☐ 311	Jack Lamabe	1.75	.80
☐ 312	Curt Blefary	1.75	.80
☐ 313	Al Weis	1.75	.80
☐ 314	Red Sox Rookies	1.75	.80
	Bill Rohr		
	George Spriggs		
☐ 315	Zoilo Versalles	1.75	.80
☐ 316	Steve Barber	1.75	.80
☐ 317	Ron Brand	1.75	.80
☐ 318	Chico Salmon	1.75	.80
☐ 319	George Culver	1.75	.80
☐ 320	Frank Howard	5.00	2.20
☐ 321	Leo Durocher MG	5.00	2.20
☐ 322	Dave Boswell	1.75	.80
☐ 323	Deron Johnson	4.00	1.80
☐ 324	Jim Nash	1.75	.80
☐ 325	Manny Mota	4.00	1.80
☐ 326	Dennis Ribant	1.75	.80
☐ 327	Tony Taylor	4.00	1.80
☐ 328	Angels Rookies	1.75	.80
	Chuck Vinson		
	Jim Weaver		
☐ 329	Duane Josephson	1.75	.80
☐ 330	Roger Maris	30.00	13.50
☐ 331	Dan Osinski	1.75	.80
☐ 332	Doug Rader	4.00	1.80
☐ 333	Ron Herbel	1.75	.80
☐ 334	Orioles Team	4.00	1.80
☐ 335	Bob Allison	4.00	1.80
☐ 336	John Purdin	1.75	.80
☐ 337	Bill Robinson	4.00	1.80
☐ 338	Bob Johnson	1.75	.80
☐ 339	Rich Nye	4.00	1.80
☐ 340	Max Alvis	1.75	.80
☐ 341	Jim Lemon MG	1.75	.80
☐ 342	Ken Johnson	1.75	.80
☐ 343	Jim Gosger	1.75	.80
☐ 344	Donn Clendenon	4.00	1.80
☐ 345	Bob Hendley	1.75	.80
☐ 346	Jerry Adair	1.75	.80
☐ 347	George Brunet	1.75	.80
☐ 348	Phillies Rookies	1.75	.80
	Larry Colton		
	Dick Thoenen		
☐ 349	Ed Spiezio	1.75	.80
☐ 350	Hoyt Wilhelm	7.00	3.10
☐ 351	Bob Barton	1.75	.80
☐ 352	Jackie Hernandez	1.75	.80
☐ 353	Mack Jones	1.75	.80
☐ 354	Pete Richert	1.75	.80
☐ 355	Ernie Banks	25.00	11.00
☐ 356A	Ken Holtzman CL	6.00	1.20
	Head centered within circle		
☐ 356B	Ken Holtzman	6.00	1.20
	Head shifted right within circle		
☐ 357	Len Gabrielson	1.75	.80
☐ 358	Mike Epstein	1.75	.80
☐ 359	Joe Moeller	1.75	.80
☐ 360	Willie Horton	5.00	2.20
☐ 361	Harmon Killebrew AS	8.00	3.60
☐ 362	Orlando Cepeda AS	4.00	1.80
☐ 363	Rod Carew AS	8.00	3.60
☐ 364	Joe Morgan AS	8.00	3.60
☐ 365	Brooks Robinson AS	8.00	3.60
☐ 366	Ron Santo AS	3.00	1.35
☐ 367	Jim Fregosi AS	4.00	1.80
☐ 368	Gene Alley AS	4.00	1.80
☐ 369	Carl Yastrzemski AS	10.00	4.50
☐ 370	Hank Aaron AS	20.00	9.00
☐ 371	Tony Oliva AS	3.00	1.35
☐ 372	Lou Brock AS	8.00	3.60
☐ 373	Frank Robinson AS	8.00	3.60
☐ 374	Bob Clemente AS	30.00	13.50
☐ 375	Bill Freehan AS	3.00	1.35
☐ 376	Tim McCarver AS	4.00	1.80
☐ 377	Joel Horlen AS	4.00	1.80
☐ 378	Bob Gibson AS	8.00	3.60
☐ 379	Gary Peters AS	4.00	1.80
☐ 380	Ken Holtzman AS	4.00	1.80
☐ 381	Boog Powell	5.00	2.20
☐ 382	Ramon Hernandez	1.75	.80
☐ 383	Steve Whitaker	1.75	.80
☐ 384	Reds Rookies	6.00	2.70
	Bill Henry		
	Hal McRae		
☐ 385	Jim Hunter	12.00	5.50
☐ 386	Greg Goossen	1.75	.80
☐ 387	Joe Foy	1.75	.80
☐ 388	Ray Washburn	1.75	.80
☐ 389	Jay Johnstone	4.00	1.80
☐ 390	Bill Mazeroski	5.00	2.20
☐ 391	Bob Priddy	1.75	.80
☐ 392	Grady Hatton MG	1.75	.80
☐ 393	Jim Perry	4.00	1.80

☐ 394 Tommie Aaron 4.00 1.80
☐ 395 Camilo Pascual 4.00 1.80
☐ 396 Bobby Wine .... 1.75 .80
☐ 397 Vic Davalillo .... 1.75 .80
☐ 398 Jim Grant .... 1.75 .80
☐ 399 Ray Oyler 4.00 1.80
☐ 400A Mike McCormick 4.00 1.80
  (Yellow letters)
☐ 400B Mike McCormick ... 150.00 70.00
  (Team name in
  white letters)
☐ 401 Mets Team 3.50 1.55
☐ 402 Mike Hegan 4.00 1.80
☐ 403 John Buzhardt .... 1.75 .80
☐ 404 Floyd Robinson .... 1.75 .80
☐ 405 Tommy Helms 4.00 1.80
☐ 406 Dick Ellsworth .... 1.75 .80
☐ 407 Gary Kolb .... 1.75 .80
☐ 408 Steve Carlton 30.00 13.50
☐ 409 Orioles Rookies .... 1.75 .80
  Frank Peters
  Ron Stone
☐ 410 Ferguson Jenkins .. 10.00 4.50
☐ 411 Ron Hansen 4.00 1.80
☐ 412 Clay Carroll 4.00 1.80
☐ 413 Tom McCraw .... 1.75 .80
☐ 414 Mickey Lolich 8.00 3.60
☐ 415 Johnny Callison 4.00 1.80
☐ 416 Bill Rigney MG .... 1.75 .80
☐ 417 Willie Crawford .... 1.75 .80
☐ 418 Eddie Fisher .... 1.75 .80
☐ 419 Jack Hiatt .... 1.75 .80
☐ 420 Cesar Tovar .... 1.75 .80
☐ 421 Ron Taylor .... 1.75 .80
☐ 422 Rene Lachemann .... 1.75 .80
☐ 423 Fred Gladding .... 1.75 .80
☐ 424 Chicago White Sox .. 3.50 1.55
  Team Card
☐ 425 Jim Maloney 4.00 1.80
☐ 426 Hank Allen .... 1.75 .80
☐ 427 Dick Calmus .... 1.75 .80
☐ 428 Vic Roznovsky .... 1.75 .80
☐ 429 Tommie Sisk .... 1.75 .80
☐ 430 Rico Petrocelli 4.00 1.80
☐ 431 Dooley Womack .... 1.75 .80
☐ 432 Indians Rookies .... 1.75 .80
  Bill Davis
  Jose Vidal
☐ 433 Bob Rodgers .... 1.75 .80
☐ 434 Ricardo Joseph .... 1.75 .80
☐ 435 Ron Perranoski 4.00 1.80
☐ 436 Hal Lanier .... 1.75 .80
☐ 437 Don Cardwell .... 1.75 .80
☐ 438 Lee Thomas 4.00 1.80
☐ 439 Lum Harris MG .... 1.75 .80
☐ 440 Claude Osteen 4.00 1.80
☐ 441 Alex Johnson 4.00 1.80
☐ 442 Dick Bosman .... 1.75 .80
☐ 443 Joe Azcue .... 1.75 .80
☐ 444 Jack Fisher .... 1.75 .80
☐ 445 Mike Shannon 4.00 1.80
☐ 446 Ron Kline .... 1.75 .80
☐ 447 Tigers Rookies 4.00 1.80
  George Korince
  Fred Lasher
☐ 448 Gary Wagner .... 1.75 .80
☐ 449 Gene Oliver .... 1.75 .80
☐ 450 Jim Kaat 6.00 2.70
☐ 451 Al Spangler .... 1.75 .80
☐ 452 Jesus Alou .... 1.75 .80
☐ 453 Sammy Ellis .... 1.75 .80
☐ 454A Frank Robinson CL .. 6.00 1.20
  Cap complete within circle
☐ 454B Frank Robinson CL .. 6.00 1.20
  Cap partially within circle
☐ 455 Rico Carty 1.80
☐ 456 John D'Donoghue .... 1.75 .80
☐ 457 Jim Lefebvre 4.00 1.80
☐ 458 Lew Krausse 6.00 2.70
☐ 459 Dick Simpson 3.50 1.55
☐ 460 Jim Lonborg 6.00 2.70
☐ 461 Chuck Hiller 3.50 1.55
☐ 462 Barry Moore 3.50 1.55
☐ 463 Jim Schaffer 3.50 1.55
☐ 464 Don McMahon 3.50 1.55
☐ 465 Tommie Agee 4.00 1.80

☐ 466 Bill Dillman 3.50 1.55
☐ 467 Dick Howser 6.00 2.70
☐ 468 Larry Sherry 3.50 1.55
☐ 469 Ty Cline 3.50 1.55
☐ 470 Bill Freehan 6.00 2.70
☐ 471 Orlando Pena 3.50 1.55
☐ 472 Walter Alston MG 6.00 2.70
☐ 473 Al Worthington 3.50 1.55
☐ 474 Paul Schaal 3.50 1.55
☐ 475 Joe Niekro 5.00 2.20
☐ 476 Woody Woodward 3.50 1.55
☐ 477 Philadelphia Phillies .. 6.00 2.70
  Team Card
☐ 478 Dave McNally 6.00 2.70
☐ 479 Phil Gagliano 3.50 1.55
☐ 480 Manager's Dream 80.00 36.00
  Tony Oliva
  Chico Cardenas
  Bob Clemente
☐ 481 John Wyatt 3.50 1.55
☐ 482 Jose Pagan 3.50 1.55
☐ 483 Darold Knowles 3.50 1.55
☐ 484 Phil Roof 3.50 1.55
☐ 485 Ken Berry 3.50 1.55
☐ 486 Cal Koonce 3.50 1.55
☐ 487 Lee May 4.00 1.80
☐ 488 Dick Tracewski 4.50 2.00
☐ 489 Wally Bunker 3.50 1.55
☐ 490 Super Stars 175.00 80.00
  Harmon Killebrew
  Willie Mays
  Mickey Mantle
☐ 491 Denny Lemaster 3.50 1.55
☐ 492 Jeff Torborg 6.00 2.70
☐ 493 Jim McGlothlin 3.50 1.55
☐ 494 Ray Sadecki 3.50 1.55
☐ 495 Leon Wagner 3.50 1.55
☐ 496 Steve Hamilton 3.50 1.55
☐ 497 Cardinals Team 7.00 3.10
☐ 498 Bill Bryan 3.50 1.55
☐ 499 Steve Blass 6.00 2.70
☐ 500 Frank Robinson 30.00 13.50
☐ 501 John Odom 6.00 2.70
☐ 502 Mike Andrews 3.50 1.55
☐ 503 Al Jackson 3.50 1.55
☐ 504 Russ Snyder 3.50 1.55
☐ 505 Joe Sparma 10.00 4.50
☐ 506 Clarence Jones 4.00 1.80
☐ 507 Wade Blasingame 3.50 1.55
☐ 508 Duke Sims 3.50 1.55
☐ 509 Dennis Higgins 3.50 1.55
☐ 510 Ron Fairly 4.00 1.80
☐ 511 Bill Kelso 3.50 1.55
☐ 512 Grant Jackson 3.50 1.55
☐ 513 Hank Bauer MG 6.00 2.70
☐ 514 Al McBean 3.50 1.55
☐ 515 Russ Nixon 3.50 1.55
☐ 516 Pete Mikkelsen 3.50 1.55
☐ 517 Diego Segui 6.00 2.70
☐ 518A Clete Boyer CL ERR .. 12.00 2.40
  539 AL Rookies
☐ 518B Clete Boyer CL COR .. 12.00 2.40
  539 NL Rookies
☐ 519 Jerry Stephenson 3.50 1.55
☐ 520 Lou Brock 25.00 11.00
☐ 521 Don Shaw 3.50 1.55
☐ 522 Wayne Causey 3.50 1.55
☐ 523 John Tsitouris 3.50 1.55
☐ 524 Andy Kosco 3.50 1.55
☐ 525 Jim Davenport 3.50 1.55
☐ 526 Bill Denehy 3.50 1.55
☐ 527 Tito Francona 3.50 1.55
☐ 528 Tigers Team 70.00 32.00
☐ 529 Bruce Von Hoff 3.50 1.55
☐ 530 Bird Belters 40.00 18.00
  Brooks Robinson
  Frank Robinson
☐ 531 Chuck Hinton 3.50 1.55
☐ 532 Luis Tiant 6.00 2.70
☐ 533 Wes Parker 4.50 2.00
☐ 534 Bob Miller 3.50 1.55
☐ 535 Danny Cater 6.00 2.70
☐ 536 Bill Short 3.50 1.55
☐ 537 Norm Siebern 3.50 1.55
☐ 538 Manny Jimenez 3.50 1.55
☐ 539 Major League Rookies 3.50 1.55

  Jim Ray
  Mike Ferraro
☐ 540 Nelson Briles 6.00 2.70
☐ 541 Sandy Alomar 6.00 2.70
☐ 542 John Boccabella 3.50 1.55
☐ 543 Bob Lee 3.50 1.55
☐ 544 Mayo Smith MG 8.00 3.60
☐ 545 Lindy McDaniel 6.00 2.70
☐ 546 Roy White 4.50 2.00
☐ 547 Dan Coombs 3.50 1.55
☐ 548 Bernie Allen 3.50 1.55
☐ 549 Orioles Rookies 3.50 1.55
  Curt Motton
  Roger Nelson
☐ 550 Clete Boyer 6.00 2.70
☐ 551 Darrell Sutherland 3.50 1.55
☐ 552 Ed Kirkpatrick 3.50 1.55
☐ 553 Hank Aguirre 3.50 1.55
☐ 554 A's Team 8.00 3.60
☐ 555 Jose Tartabull 6.00 2.70
☐ 556 Dick Selma 3.50 1.55
☐ 557 Frank Quilici 3.50 1.55
☐ 558 Johnny Edwards 3.50 1.55
☐ 559 Pirates Rookies 3.50 1.55
  Carl Taylor
  Luke Walker
☐ 560 Paul Casanova 3.50 1.55
☐ 561 Lee Elia 3.50 1.55
☐ 562 Jim Bouton 6.00 2.70
☐ 563 Ed Charles 3.50 1.55
☐ 564 Eddie Stanky MG 6.00 2.70
☐ 565 Larry Dierker 6.00 2.70
☐ 566 Ken Harrelson 6.00 2.70
☐ 567 Clay Dalrymple 3.50 1.55
☐ 568 Willie Smith 3.50 1.55
☐ 569 NL Rookies 3.50 1.55
  Ivan Murrell
  Les Rohr
☐ 570 Rick Reichardt 3.50 1.55
☐ 571 Tony LaRussa 12.00 5.50
☐ 572 Don Bosch 3.50 1.55
☐ 573 Joe Coleman 3.50 1.55
☐ 574 Cincinnati Reds 8.00 3.60
  Team Card
☐ 575 Jim Palmer 35.00 16.00
☐ 576 Dave Adlesh 3.50 1.55
☐ 577 Fred Talbot 3.50 1.55
☐ 578 Orlando Martinez 3.50 1.55
☐ 579 NL Rookies 6.00 2.70
  Larry Hisle
  Mike Lum
☐ 580 Bob Bailey 3.50 1.55
☐ 581 Garry Roggenburk 3.50 1.55
☐ 582 Jerry Grote 6.00 2.70
☐ 583 Gates Brown 8.00 3.60
☐ 584 Larry Shepard MG 3.50 1.55
☐ 585 Wilbur Wood 6.00 2.70
☐ 586 Jim Pagliaroni 6.00 2.70
☐ 587 Roger Repoz 3.50 1.55
☐ 588 Dick Schofield 3.50 1.55
☐ 589 Twins Rookies 3.50 1.55
  Ron Clark
  Moe Ogier
☐ 590 Tommy Harper 4.00 1.80
☐ 591 Dick Nen 3.50 1.55
☐ 592 John Bateman 3.50 1.55
☐ 593 Lee Stange 3.50 1.55
☐ 594 Phil Linz 6.00 2.70
☐ 595 Phil Ortega 3.50 1.55
☐ 596 Charlie Smith 3.50 1.55
☐ 597 Bill McCool 3.50 1.55
☐ 598 Jerry May 7.00 2.20

1969 Topps

The cards in this 664-card set measure 2 1/2" by 3 1/2". The 1969 Topps set includes Sporting News All-Star Selections as card numbers 416 to 435. Other popular subsets within this set include League Leaders (1-12) and World Series cards (162-169). The fifth series contains several

variations; the more difficult variety consists of cards with the player's first name, last name, and/or position in white letters instead of lettering in some other color. These are designated in the checklist below by WL (white letters). Each checklist card features a different popular player's picture inside a circle on the front of the checklist card. Two different team identifications of Clay Dalrymple and Donn Clendenon exist, as indicated in the checklist. The key Rookie Cards in this set are Rollie Fingers, Reggie Jackson, and Graig Nettles. This was the last year that Topps issued multi-player special star cards, ending a 13-year tradition, which they had begun in 1957. There were cropping differences in checklist cards 57, 214, and 412, due to their each being printed with two different series. The differences are difficult to explain and have not been greatly sought by collectors; hence they are not listed explicitly in the list below. The All-Star cards 426-435, when turned over and placed together, form a puzzle back of Pete Rose. This would turn out to be the final year that Topps issued cards in five-card nickel wax packs.

	NRMT	VG-E
COMPLETE SET (664)	2200.00	1000.00
COMMON (1-218/328-512)	1.50	.70
MNR. STARS 1-218/328-512	2.50	1.10
SEMISTARS 1-218/328-512	4.00	1.80
UNL. STARS 1-218/328-512	6.00	2.70
COMMON CARD (219-327)	2.50	1.10
MINOR STARS 219-327	4.00	1.80
SEMISTARS 219-327	6.00	2.70
UNLISTED STARS 219-327	10.00	4.50
COMMON CARD (513-588)	2.00	.90
MINOR STARS 513-588	3.00	1.35
SEMISTARS 513-588	5.00	2.20
UNLISTED STARS 513-588	8.00	3.60
COMMON CARD (589-664)	3.00	1.35
MINOR STARS 589-664	5.00	2.20
SEMISTARS 589-664	8.00	3.60
UNLISTED STARS 589-664	12.00	5.50
COMMON WHITE LTR	20.00	9.00

*UNLISTED DODGER/YANKEE: 1.25X VALUE
CARDS PRICED IN NM CONDITION

☐ 1	AL Batting Leaders	14.00	5.00
	Carl Yastrzemski		
	Danny Cater		
	Tony Oliva		
☐ 2	NL Batting Leaders	7.00	3.10
	Pete Rose		
	Matty Alou		
☐ 3	AL RBI Leaders	3.50	1.55
	Ken Harrelson		
	Frank Howard		
	Jim Northrup		
☐ 4	NL RBI Leaders	6.00	2.70
	Willie McCovey		
	Ron Santo		
	Billy Williams		
☐ 5	AL Home Run Leaders	3.50	1.55
	Frank Howard		
	Willie Horton		
	Ken Harrelson		
☐ 6	NL Home Run Leaders	6.00	2.70
	Willie McCovey		
	Richie Allen		
	Ernie Banks		
☐ 7	AL ERA Leaders	3.50	1.55
	Luis Tiant		
	Sam McDowell		
	Dave McNally		
☐ 8	NL ERA Leaders	5.00	2.20
	Bob Gibson		
	Bobby Bolin		
	Bob Veale		
☐ 9	AL Pitching Leaders	3.50	1.55
	Denny McLain		
	Dave McNally		
	Luis Tiant		
	Mel Stottlemyre		
☐ 10	NL Pitching Leaders	7.00	3.10
	Juan Marichal		
	Bob Gibson		
	Fergie Jenkins		
☐ 11	AL Strikeout Leaders	3.50	1.55
	Sam McDowell		
	Denny McLain		
	Luis Tiant		
☐ 12	NL Strikeout Leaders	4.00	1.80
	Bob Gibson		
	Fergie Jenkins		
	Bill Singer		
☐ 13	Mickey Stanley	2.50	1.10
☐ 14	Al McBean	1.50	.70
☐ 15	Boog Powell	3.50	1.55
☐ 16	Giants Rookies	1.50	.70
	Cesar Gutierrez		
	Rich Robertson		
☐ 17	Mike Marshall	2.50	1.10
☐ 18	Dick Schofield	1.50	.70
☐ 19	Ken Suarez	1.50	.70
☐ 20	Ernie Banks	18.00	8.00
☐ 21	Jose Santiago	1.50	.70
☐ 22	Jesus Alou	2.50	1.10
☐ 23	Lew Krausse	1.50	.70
☐ 24	Walt Alston MG	4.00	1.80
☐ 25	Roy White	2.50	1.10
☐ 26	Clay Carroll	2.50	1.10
☐ 27	Bernie Allen	1.50	.70
☐ 28	Mike Ryan	1.50	.70
☐ 29	Dave Morehead	1.50	.70
☐ 30	Bob Allison	2.50	1.10
☐ 31	Mets Rookies	2.50	1.10
	Gary Gentry		
	Amos Otis		
☐ 32	Sammy Ellis	1.50	.70
☐ 33	Wayne Causey	1.50	.70
☐ 34	Gary Peters	1.50	.70
☐ 35	Joe Morgan	10.00	4.50
☐ 36	Luke Walker	1.50	.70
☐ 37	Curt Motton	1.50	.70
☐ 38	Zoilo Versalles	2.50	1.10
☐ 39	Dick Hughes	1.50	.70
☐ 40	Mayo Smith MG	1.50	.70
☐ 41	Bob Barton	1.50	.70
☐ 42	Tommy Harper	2.50	1.10
☐ 43	Joe Niekro	2.50	1.10
☐ 44	Danny Cater	1.50	.70
☐ 45	Maury Wills	3.00	1.35
☐ 46	Fritz Peterson	2.50	1.10
☐ 47A	Paul Popovich	1.50	.70
	(No helmet emblem)		
☐ 47B	Paul Popovich	25.00	11.00
	(C emblem on helmet)		
☐ 48	Brant Alyea	1.50	.70
☐ 49A	Royals Rookies ERR	25.00	11.00
	Steve Jones		
	E. Rodriguez		
☐ 49B	Royals Rookies COR	1.50	.70
	Steve Jones		
	E. Rodriguez		
☐ 50	Bob Clemente UER	50.00	22.00
	(Bats Right listed twice)		
☐ 51	Woody Fryman	1.50	.70
☐ 52	Mike Andrews	1.50	.70
☐ 53	Sonny Jackson	1.50	.70
☐ 54	Cisco Carlos	1.50	.70
☐ 55	Jerry Grote	2.50	1.10
☐ 56	Rich Reese	1.50	.70
☐ 57	Denny McLain CL	6.00	1.20
☐ 58	Fred Gladding	1.50	.70
☐ 59	Jay Johnstone	2.50	1.10
☐ 60	Nelson Briles	2.50	1.10
☐ 61	Jimmie Hall	1.50	.70
☐ 62	Chico Salmon	1.50	.70
☐ 63	Jim Hickman	2.50	1.10
☐ 64	Bill Monbouquette	1.50	.70
☐ 65	Willie Davis	2.50	1.10
☐ 66	Orioles Rookies	1.50	.70
	Mike Adamson		
	Merv Rettenmund		
☐ 67	Bill Stoneman	2.50	1.10
☐ 68	Dave Duncan	2.50	1.10
☐ 69	Steve Hamilton	2.50	1.10
☐ 70	Tommy Helms	2.50	1.10
☐ 71	Steve Whitaker	2.50	1.10
☐ 72	Ron Taylor	1.50	.70
☐ 73	Johnny Briggs	1.50	.70
☐ 74	Preston Gomez MG	2.50	1.10
☐ 75	Luis Aparicio	5.00	2.20
☐ 76	Norm Miller	1.50	.70
☐ 77A	Ron Perranoski	2.50	1.10
	(No emblem on cap)		
☐ 77B	Ron Perranoski	25.00	11.00
	(LA on cap)		
☐ 78	Tom Satriano	1.50	.70
☐ 79	Milt Pappas	2.50	1.10
☐ 80	Norm Cash	2.50	1.10
☐ 81	Mel Queen	1.50	.70
☐ 82	Pirates Rookies	8.00	3.60
	Rich Hebner		
	Al Oliver		
☐ 83	Mike Ferraro	2.50	1.10
☐ 84	Bob Humphreys	1.50	.70
☐ 85	Lou Brock	20.00	9.00
☐ 86	Pete Richert	1.50	.70
☐ 87	Horace Clarke	2.50	1.10
☐ 88	Rich Nye	1.50	.70
☐ 89	Russ Gibson	1.50	.70
☐ 90	Jerry Koosman	2.50	1.10
☐ 91	Alvin Dark MG	2.50	1.10
☐ 92	Jack Billingham	2.50	1.10
☐ 93	Joe Foy	2.50	1.10
☐ 94	Hank Aguirre	1.50	.70
☐ 95	Johnny Bench	45.00	20.00
☐ 96	Denny Lemaster	1.50	.70
☐ 97	Buddy Bradford	1.50	.70
☐ 98	Dave Giusti	1.50	.70
☐ 99A	Twins Rookies	16.00	7.25
	Danny Morris		
	Graig Nettles		
	(No loop)		
☐ 99B	Twins Rookies	16.00	7.25
	Danny Morris		
	Graig Nettles		
	(Errant loop in upper left corner of obverse)		
☐ 100	Hank Aaron	35.00	16.00
☐ 101	Daryl Patterson	1.50	.70
☐ 102	Jim Davenport	1.50	.70
☐ 103	Roger Repoz	1.50	.70
☐ 104	Steve Blass	2.50	1.10
☐ 105	Rick Monday	2.50	1.10
☐ 106	Jim Hannan	1.50	.70
☐ 107A	Bob Gibson CL ERR	6.00	1.20
	161 John Purdin		
☐ 107B	Bob Gibson CL COR	7.50	1.50
	161 John Purdin		
☐ 108	Tony Taylor	2.50	1.10
☐ 109	Jim Lonborg	2.50	1.10

110	Mike Shannon	2.50	1.10
111	Johnny Morris	1.50	.70
112	J.C. Martin	1.50	.70
113	Dave May	1.50	.70
114	Yankees Rookies	2.50	1.10
	Alan Closter		
	John Cumberland		
115	Bill Hands	1.50	.70
116	Chuck Harrison	1.50	.70
117	Jim Fairey	1.50	.70
118	Stan Williams	1.50	.70
119	Doug Rader	2.50	1.10
120	Pete Rose	18.00	8.00
121	Joe Grzenda	1.50	.70
122	Ron Fairly	2.50	1.10
123	Wilbur Wood	2.50	1.10
124	Hank Bauer MG	2.50	1.10
125	Ray Sadecki	1.50	.70
126	Dick Tracewski	1.50	.70
127	Kevin Collins	1.50	.70
128	Tommie Aaron	2.50	1.10
129	Bill McCool	1.50	.70
130	Carl Yastrzemski	18.00	8.00
131	Chris Cannizzaro	1.50	.70
132	Dave Baldwin	1.50	.70
133	Johnny Callison	2.50	1.10
134	Jim Weaver	1.50	.70
135	Tommy Davis	2.50	1.10
136	Cards Rookies	1.50	.70
	Steve Huntz		
	Mike Torrez		
137	Wally Bunker	1.50	.70
138	John Bateman	1.50	.70
139	Andy Kosco	1.50	.70
140	Jim Lefebvre	2.50	1.10
141	Bill Dillman	1.50	.70
142	Woody Woodward	2.50	1.10
143	Joe Nossek	1.50	.70
144	Bob Hendley	1.50	.70
145	Max Alvis	1.50	.70
146	Jim Perry	2.50	1.10
147	Leo Durocher MG	4.00	1.80
148	Lee Stange	1.50	.70
149	Ollie Brown	2.50	1.10
150	Denny McLain	4.00	1.80
151A	Clay Dalrymple	1.50	.70
	Portrait, Orioles		
151B	Clay Dalrymple	16.00	7.25
	Catching, Phillies		
152	Tommie Sisk	1.50	.70
153	Ed Brinkman	1.50	.70
154	Jim Britton	1.50	.70
155	Pete Ward	1.50	.70
156	Houston Rookies	1.50	.70
	Hal Gilson		
	Leon McFadden		
157	Bob Rodgers	2.50	1.10
158	Joe Gibbon	1.50	.70
159	Jerry Adair	1.50	.70
160	Vada Pinson	2.50	1.10
161	John Purdin	1.50	.70
162	Bob Gibson WS	8.00	3.60
	Fans 17		
163	Willie Horton WS	6.00	2.70
164	Tim McCarver WS	8.00	3.60
	Roger Maris		
165	Lou Brock WS	8.00	3.60
166	Al Kaline WS	8.00	3.60
167	Jim Northrup WS	6.00	2.70
168	Mickey Lolich WS	8.00	3.60
	Bob Gibson		
169	Dick McAuliffe WS	6.00	2.70
	Denny McLain		
	Willie Horton		
170	Frank Howard	3.00	1.35
171	Glenn Beckert	2.50	1.10
172	Jerry Stephenson	1.50	.70
173	White Sox Rookies	1.50	.70
	Bob Christian		
	Gerry Nyman		
174	Grant Jackson	1.50	.70
175	Jim Bunning	7.00	3.10
176	Joe Azcue	1.50	.70
177	Ron Reed	1.50	.70
178	Ray Oyler	2.50	1.10
179	Don Pavletich	1.50	.70
180	Willie Horton	2.50	1.10
181	Mel Nelson	1.50	.70
182	Bill Rigney MG	1.50	.70
183	Don Shaw	1.50	.70
184	Roberto Pena	1.50	.70
185	Tom Phoebus	1.50	.70
186	Johnny Edwards	1.50	.70
187	Leon Wagner	1.50	.70
188	Rick Wise	2.50	1.10
189	Red Sox Rookies	1.50	.70
	Joe Lahoud		
	John Thibodeau		
190	Willie Mays	45.00	20.00
191	Lindy McDaniel	2.50	1.10
192	Jose Pagan	1.50	.70
193	Don Cardwell	2.50	1.10
194	Ted Uhlaender	1.50	.70
195	John Odom	1.50	.70
196	Lum Harris MG	1.50	.70
197	Dick Selma	1.50	.70
198	Willie Smith	1.50	.70
199	Jim French	1.50	.70
200	Bob Gibson	12.00	5.50
201	Russ Snyder	1.50	.70
202	Don Wilson	2.50	1.10
203	Dave Johnson	2.50	1.10
204	Jack Hiatt	1.50	.70
205	Rick Reichardt	1.50	.70
206	Phillies Rookies	2.50	1.10
	Larry Hisle		
	Barry Lersch		
207	Roy Face	2.50	1.10
208A	John Olendenon... Houston		
208B	John Olendenon...	16.00	7.25
	Expos		
209	Larry Haney UER	1.50	.70
	(Reverse negative)		
210	Felix Millan	1.50	.70
211	Galen Cisco	1.50	.70
212	Tom Tresh	2.50	1.10
213	Gerry Arrigo	1.50	.70
214	Checklist 3	6.00	1.20
	With 69T deckle CL		
	on back (no player)		
215	Rico Petrocelli	2.50	1.10
216	Don Sutton	6.00	2.70
217	John Donaldson	1.50	.70
218	John Roseboro	2.50	1.10
219	Freddie Patek	3.00	1.35
220	Sam McDowell	4.00	1.80
221	Art Shamsky	2.50	1.10
222	Duane Josephson	2.50	1.10
223	Tom Dukes	2.50	1.10
224	Angels Rookies	2.50	1.10
	Bill Harrelson		
	Steve Kealey		
225	Don Kessinger	4.00	1.80
226	Bruce Howard	2.50	1.10
227	Frank Johnson	2.50	1.10
228	Dave Leonhard	2.50	1.10
229	Don Lock	2.50	1.10
230	Rusty Staub UER	4.00	1.80
	For 1966 stats, Houston spelled		
	Huoston		
231	Pat Dobson	4.00	1.80
232	Dave Ricketts	2.50	1.10
233	Steve Barber	4.00	1.80
234	Dave Bristol MG	2.50	1.10
235	Jim Hunter	10.00	4.50
236	Manny Mota	2.50	1.10
237	Bobby Cox	10.00	4.50
238	Ken Johnson	2.50	1.10
239	Bob Taylor	4.00	1.80
240	Ken Harrelson	4.00	1.80
241	Jim Brewer	2.50	1.10
242	Frank Kostro	2.50	1.10
243	Ron Kline	2.50	1.10
244	Indians Rookies	3.00	1.35
	Ray Fosse		
	George Woodson		
245	Ed Charles	4.00	1.80
246	Joe Coleman	2.50	1.10
247	Gene Oliver	2.50	1.10
248	Bob Priddy	2.50	1.10
249	Ed Spiezio	4.00	1.80
250	Frank Robinson	20.00	9.00
251	Ron Herbel	2.50	1.10
252	Chuck Cottier	2.50	1.10
253	Jerry Johnson	2.50	1.10
254	Joe Schultz MG	4.00	1.80
255	Steve Carlton	30.00	13.50
256	Gates Brown	4.00	1.80
257	Jim Ray	2.50	1.10
258	Jackie Hernandez	4.00	1.80
259	Bill Short	2.50	1.10
260	Reggie Jackson	350.00	160.00
261	Bob Johnson	2.50	1.10
262	Mike Kekich	4.00	1.80
263	Jerry May	2.50	1.10
264	Bill Landis	2.50	1.10
265	Chico Cardenas	4.00	1.10
266	Dodger Rookies	4.00	1.80
	Tom Hutton		
	Alan Foster		
267	Vicente Romo	2.50	1.10
268	Al Spangler	2.50	1.10
269	Al Weis	4.00	1.80
270	Mickey Lolich	3.00	1.35
271	Larry Stahl	2.50	1.10
272	Ed Stroud	2.50	1.10
273	Ron Willis	2.50	1.10
274	Clyde King MG	2.50	1.10
275	Vic Davalillo	2.50	1.10
276	Gary Wagner	2.50	1.10
277	Elrod Hendricks	2.50	1.10
278	Gary Geiger UER	2.50	1.10
	(Batting wrong)		
279	Roger Nelson	4.00	1.80
280	Alex Johnson	4.00	1.80
281	Ted Kubiak	2.50	1.10
282	Pat Jarvis	2.50	1.10
283	Sandy Alomar	2.50	1.10
284	Expos Rookies	4.00	1.80
	Jerry Robertson		
	Mike Wegener		
285	Don Mincher	4.00	1.80
286	Dock Ellis	3.00	1.35
287	Jose Tartabull	2.50	1.10
288	Ken Holtzman	4.00	1.80
289	Bart Shirley	2.50	1.10
290	Jim Kaat	4.00	1.80
291	Vern Fuller	2.50	1.10
292	Al Downing	4.00	1.80
293	Dick Dietz	2.50	1.10
294	Jim Lemon MG	2.50	1.10
295	Tony Perez	12.00	5.50
296	Andy Messersmith	4.00	1.80
297	Deron Johnson	2.50	1.10
298	Dave Nicholson	4.00	1.80
299	Mark Belanger	4.00	1.80
300	Felipe Alou	4.00	1.80
301	Darrell Brandon	4.00	1.80
302	Jim Pagliaroni	2.50	1.10
303	Cal Koonce	4.00	1.80
304	Padres Rookies	8.00	3.60
	Bill Davis		
	Clarence Gaston		
305	Dick McAuliffe	4.00	1.80
306	Jim Grant	4.00	1.80
307	Gary Kolb	2.50	1.10
308	Wade Blasingame	2.50	1.10
309	Walt Williams	2.50	1.10
310	Tom Haller	2.50	1.10
311	Sparky Lyle	8.00	3.60
312	Lee Elia	2.50	1.10
313	Bill Robinson	4.00	1.80
314	Don Drysdale CL	6.00	1.20
315	Eddie Fisher	2.50	1.10
316	Hal Lanier	2.50	1.10
317	Bruce Look	2.50	1.10
318	Jack Fisher	2.50	1.10
319	Ken McMullen UER	2.50	1.10
	(Headings on back		
	are for a pitcher)		
320	Dal Maxvill	2.50	1.10
321	Jim McAndrew	4.00	1.80
322	Jose Vidal	2.50	1.10
323	Larry Miller	2.50	1.10
324	Tiger Rookies	4.00	1.80
	Les Cain		
	Dave Campbell		

□ 325 Jose Cardenal	4.00	1.80
□ 326 Gary Sutherland	4.00	1.80
□ 327 Willie Crawford	2.50	1.10
□ 328 Joel Horlen	1.50	.70
□ 329 Rick Joseph	1.50	.70
□ 330 Tony Conigliaro	5.00	2.20
□ 331 Braves Rookies	2.50	1.10
Gil Garrido		
Tom House		
□ 332 Fred Talbot	1.50	.70
□ 333 Ivan Murrell	1.50	.70
□ 334 Phil Roof	1.50	.70
□ 335 Bill Mazeroski	3.00	1.35
□ 336 Jim Roland	1.50	.70
□ 337 Marty Martinez	1.50	.70
□ 338 Del Unser	1.50	.70
□ 339 Reds Rookies	1.50	.70
Steve Mingori		
Jose Pena		
□ 340 Dave McNally	2.50	1.10
□ 341 Dave Adlesh	1.50	.70
□ 342 Bubba Morton	1.50	.70
□ 343 Dan Frisella	1.50	.70
□ 344 Tom Matchick	1.50	.70
□ 345 Frank Linzy	1.50	.70
□ 346 Wayne Comer	1.50	.70
□ 347 Randy Hundley	2.50	1.10
□ 348 Steve Hargan	1.50	.70
□ 349 Dick Williams MG	2.50	1.10
□ 350 Richie Allen	4.00	1.80
□ 351 Carroll Sembera	1.50	.70
□ 352 Paul Schaal	2.50	1.10
□ 353 Jeff Torborg	2.50	1.10
□ 354 Nate Oliver	1.50	.70
□ 355 Phil Niekro	7.00	3.10
□ 356 Frank Quilici	1.50	.70
□ 357 Carl Taylor	1.50	.70
□ 358 Athletics Rookies	1.50	.70
George Lauzerique		
Roberto Rodriquez		
□ 359 Dick Kelley	1.50	.70
□ 360 Jim Wynn	2.50	1.10
□ 361 Gary Holman	1.50	.70
□ 362 Jim Maloney	2.50	1.10
□ 363 Russ Nixon	1.50	.70
□ 364 Tommie Agee	4.00	1.80
□ 365 Jim Fregosi	2.50	1.10
□ 366 Bo Belinsky	2.50	1.10
□ 367 Lou Johnson	2.50	1.10
□ 368 Vic Roznovsky	1.50	.70
□ 369 Bob Skinner MG	1.50	.70
□ 370 Juan Marichal	8.00	3.60
□ 371 Sal Bando	2.50	1.10
□ 372 Adolfo Phillips	1.50	.70
□ 373 Fred Lasher	1.50	.70
□ 374 Bob Tillman	1.50	.70
□ 375 Harmon Killebrew	16.00	7.25
□ 376 Royals Rookies	1.50	.70
Mike Fiore		
Jim Rooker		
□ 377 Gary Bell	2.50	1.10
□ 378 Jose Herrera	1.50	.70
□ 379 Ken Boyer	2.50	1.10
□ 380 Stan Bahnsen	2.50	1.10
□ 381 Ed Kranepool	2.50	1.10
□ 382 Pat Corrales	2.50	1.10
□ 383 Casey Cox	1.50	.70
□ 384 Larry Shepard MG	1.50	.70
□ 385 Orlando Cepeda	3.50	1.55
□ 386 Jim McGlothlin	1.50	.70
□ 387 Bobby Klaus	1.50	.70
□ 388 Tom McCraw	1.50	.70
□ 389 Dan Coombs	1.50	.70
□ 390 Bill Freehan	2.50	1.10
□ 391 Ray Culp	1.50	.70
□ 392 Bob Burda	1.50	.70
□ 393 Gene Brabender	2.50	1.10
□ 394 Pilots Rookies	5.00	2.20
Lou Piniella		
Marv Staehle		
□ 395 Chris Short	1.50	.70
□ 396 Jim Campanis	1.50	.70
□ 397 Chuck Dobson	1.50	.70
□ 398 Tito Francona	1.50	.70
□ 399 Bob Bailey	2.50	1.10
□ 400 Don Drysdale	16.00	7.25
□ 401 Jake Gibbs	2.50	1.10
□ 402 Ken Boswell	2.50	1.10
□ 403 Bob Miller	1.50	.70
□ 404 Cubs Rookies	2.50	1.10
Vic LaRose		
Gary Ross		
□ 405 Lee May	2.50	1.10
□ 406 Phil Ortega	1.50	.70
□ 407 Tom Egan	1.50	.70
□ 408 Nate Colbert	1.50	.70
□ 409 Bob Moose	1.50	.70
□ 410 Al Kaline	25.00	11.00
□ 411 Larry Dierker	2.50	1.10
□ 412 Mickey Mantle CL DP	12.00	2.40
□ 413 Roland Sheldon	2.50	1.10
□ 414 Duke Sims	1.50	.70
□ 415 Ray Washburn	1.50	.70
□ 416 Willie McCovey AS	7.00	3.10
□ 417 Ken Harrelson AS	2.50	1.10
□ 418 Tommy Helms AS	2.50	1.10
□ 419 Rod Carew AS	10.00	4.50
□ 420 Ron Santo AS	4.00	1.80
□ 421 Brooks Robinson AS	7.00	3.10
□ 422 Don Kessinger AS	2.50	1.10
□ 423 Bert Campaneris AS	4.00	1.80
□ 424 Pete Rose AS	14.00	6.25
□ 425 Carl Yastrzemski AS	10.00	4.50
□ 426 Curt Flood AS	4.00	1.80
□ 427 Tony Oliva AS	4.00	1.80
□ 428 Lou Brock AS	6.00	2.70
□ 429 Willie Horton AS	2.50	1.10
□ 430 Johnny Bench AS	10.00	4.50
□ 431 Bill Freehan AS	4.00	1.80
□ 432 Bob Gibson AS	6.00	2.70
□ 433 Denny McLain AS	2.50	1.10
□ 434 Jerry Koosman AS	3.00	1.35
□ 435 Sam McDowell AS	2.50	1.10
□ 436 Gene Alley	2.50	1.10
□ 437 Luis Alcaraz	1.50	.70
□ 438 Gary Waslewski	1.50	.70
□ 439 White Sox Rookies	1.50	.70
Ed Herrmann		
Dan Lazar		
□ 440A Willie McCovey	18.00	8.00
□ 440B Willie McCovey WL	100.00	45.00
(McCovey white)		
□ 441A Dennis Higgins	1.50	.70
□ 441B Dennis Higgins WL	20.00	9.00
(Higgins white)		
□ 442 Ty Cline	2.50	1.10
□ 443 Don Wert	1.50	.70
□ 444A Joe Moeller	1.50	.70
□ 444B Joe Moeller WL	20.00	9.00
(Moeller white)		
□ 445 Bobby Knoop	1.50	.70
□ 446 Claude Raymond	1.50	.70
□ 447A Ralph Houk MG	2.50	1.10
□ 447B Ralph Houk WL	22.00	10.00
MG (Houk white)		
□ 448 Bob Tolan	2.50	1.10
□ 449 Paul Lindblad	1.50	.70
□ 450 Billy Williams	7.00	3.10
□ 451A Rich Rollins	2.50	1.10
□ 451B Rich Rollins WL	20.00	9.00
(Rich and 2B white)		
□ 452A Al Ferrara	1.50	.70
□ 452B Al Ferrara WL	20.00	9.00
(Al and OF white)		
□ 453 Mike Cuellar	2.50	1.10
□ 454A Phillies Rookies	2.50	1.10
Larry Colton		
Don Money		
□ 454B Phillies Rookies WL	22.00	10.00
Larry Colton		
Don Money		
(Names in white)		
□ 455 Sonny Siebert	1.50	.70
□ 456 Bud Harrelson	2.50	1.10
□ 457 Dalton Jones	1.50	.70
□ 458 Curt Blefary	1.50	.70
□ 459 Dave Boswell	1.50	.70
□ 460 Joe Torre	3.50	1.55
□ 461A Mike Epstein	1.50	.70
□ 461B Mike Epstein WL	20.00	9.00
(Epstein white)		
□ 462 Red Schoendienst	2.50	1.10
MG		
□ 463 Dennis Ribant	1.50	.70
□ 464A Dave Marshall	1.50	.70
□ 464B Dave Marshall WL	20.00	9.00
(Marshall white)		
□ 465 Tommy John	4.00	1.80
□ 466 John Boccabella	2.50	1.10
□ 467 Tommie Reynolds	1.50	.70
□ 468A Pirates Rookies	1.50	.70
Bruce Dal Canton		
Bob Robertson		
□ 468B Pirates Rookies WL	20.00	9.00
Bruce Dal Canton		
Bob Robertson		
(Names in white)		
□ 469 Chico Ruiz	1.50	.70
□ 470A Mel Stottlemyre	2.50	1.10
□ 470B Mel Stottlemyre WL	30.00	13.50
(Stottlemyre white)		
□ 471A Ted Savage	1.50	.70
□ 471B Ted Savage WL	20.00	9.00
(Savage white)		
□ 472 Jim Price	1.50	.70
□ 473A Jose Arcia	1.50	.70
□ 473B Jose Arcia WL	20.00	9.00
(Jose and 2B white)		
□ 474 Tom Murphy	1.50	.70
□ 475 Tim McCarver	3.00	1.35
□ 476A Boston Rookies	1.50	1.35
Ken Brett		
Gerry Moses		
□ 476B Boston Rookies WL	30.00	13.50
Ken Brett		
Gerry Moses		
(Names in white)		
□ 477 Jeff James	1.50	.70
□ 478 Don Buford	1.50	.70
□ 479 Richie Scheinblum	1.50	.70
□ 480 Tom Seaver	80.00	36.00
□ 481 Bill Melton	2.50	1.10
□ 482A Jim Gosger	1.50	.70
□ 482B Jim Gosger WL	20.00	9.00
(Jim and OF white)		
□ 483 Ted Abernathy	1.50	.70
□ 484 Joe Gordon MG	2.50	1.10
□ 485A Gaylord Perry	10.00	4.50
□ 485B Gaylord Perry WL	85.00	38.00
(Perry white)		
□ 486A Paul Casanova	1.50	.70
□ 486B Paul Casanova WL	20.00	9.00
(Casanova white)		
□ 487 Denis Menke	1.50	.70
□ 488 Joe Sparma	1.50	.70
□ 489 Clete Boyer	2.50	1.10
□ 490 Matty Alou	2.50	1.10
□ 491A Twins Rookies	1.50	.70
Jerry Crider		
George Mitterwald		
□ 491B Twins Rookies WL	20.00	9.00
Jerry Crider		
George Mitterwald		
(Names in white)		
□ 492 Tony Cloninger	1.50	.70
□ 493A Wes Parker	2.50	1.10
□ 493B Wes Parker WL	22.00	10.00
(Parker white)		
□ 494 Ken Berry	1.50	.70
□ 495 Bert Campaneris	2.50	1.10
□ 496 Larry Jaster	1.50	.70
□ 497 Julian Javier	2.50	1.10
□ 498 Juan Pizarro	2.50	1.10
□ 499 Astro Rookies	1.50	.70
Don Bryant		
Steve Shea		
□ 500A Mickey Mantle UER	350.00	160.00
(No Topps copy-		
right on card back)		
□ 500B Mickey Mantle WL	1000.00	450.00
(Mantle in white;		
no Topps copyright		
on card back) UER		
□ 501A Tony Gonzalez	2.50	1.10
□ 501B Tony Gonzalez WL	22.00	10.00
(Tony and OF white)		
□ 502 Minnie Rojas	1.50	.70
□ 503 Larry Brown	1.50	.70

☐ 504 Brooks Robinson CL	7.00	1.40
☐ 505A Bobby Bolin	1.50	.70
☐ 505B Bobby Bolin WL	22.00	10.00
(Bolin white)		
☐ 506 Paul Blair	2.50	1.10
☐ 507 Cookie Rojas	2.50	1.10
☐ 508 Moe Drabowsky	2.50	1.10
☐ 509 Manny Sanguillen	2.50	1.10
☐ 510 Rod Carew	35.00	16.00
☐ 511A Diego Segui	2.50	1.10
☐ 511B Diego Segui WL	22.00	10.00
(Diego and P white)		
☐ 512 Cleon Jones	2.50	1.10
☐ 513 Camilo Pascual	3.00	1.35
☐ 514 Mike Lum	2.00	.90
☐ 515 Dick Green	2.00	.90
☐ 516 Earl Weaver MG	18.00	8.00
☐ 517 Mike McCormick	3.00	1.35
☐ 518 Fred Whitfield	2.00	.90
☐ 519 Yankees Rookies	2.00	.90
Jerry Kenney		
Len Boehmer		
☐ 520 Bob Veale	3.00	1.35
☐ 521 George Thomas	2.00	.90
☐ 522 Joe Hoerner	2.00	.90
☐ 523 Bob Chance	2.00	.90
☐ 524 Expos Rookies	3.00	1.35
Jose Laboy		
Floyd Wicker		
☐ 525 Earl Wilson	3.00	1.35
☐ 526 Hector Torres	2.00	.90
☐ 527 Al Lopez MG	4.00	1.80
☐ 528 Claude Osteen	3.00	1.35
☐ 529 Ed Kirkpatrick	3.00	1.35
☐ 530 Cesar Tovar	2.00	.90
☐ 531 Dick Farrell	2.00	.90
☐ 532 Bird Hill Aces	3.00	1.35
Tom Phoebus		
Jim Hardin		
Dave McNally		
Mike Cuellar		
☐ 533 Nolan Ryan	425.00	190.00
☐ 534 Jerry McNertney	3.00	1.35
☐ 535 Phil Regan	3.00	1.35
☐ 536 Padres Rookies	2.00	.90
Danny Breeden		
Dave Roberts		
☐ 537 Mike Paul	2.00	.90
☐ 538 Charlie Smith	2.00	.90
☐ 539 Ted Shows How	10.00	4.50
Mike Epstein		
Ted Williams MG		
☐ 540 Curt Flood	3.00	1.35
☐ 541 Joe Verbanic	2.00	.90
☐ 542 Bob Aspromonte	2.00	.90
☐ 543 Fred Newman	2.00	.90
☐ 544 Tigers Rookies	2.00	.90
Mike Kilkenny		
Ron Woods		
☐ 545 Willie Stargell	12.00	5.50
☐ 546 Jim Nash	2.00	.90
☐ 547 Billy Martin MG	6.00	2.70
☐ 548 Bob Locker	2.00	.90
☐ 549 Ron Brand	2.00	.90
☐ 550 Brooks Robinson	30.00	13.50
☐ 551 Wayne Granger	2.00	.90
☐ 552 Dodgers Rookies	3.00	1.35
Ted Sizemore		
Bill Sudakis		
☐ 553 Ron Davis	2.00	.90
☐ 554 Frank Bertaina	2.00	.90
☐ 555 Jim Ray Hart	3.00	1.35
☐ 556 A's Stars	3.00	1.35
Sal Bando		
Bert Campaneris		
Danny Cater		
☐ 557 Frank Fernandez	2.00	.90
☐ 558 Tom Burgmeier	3.00	1.35
☐ 559 Cardinals Rookies	2.00	.90
Joe Hague		
Jim Hicks		
☐ 560 Luis Tiant	3.00	1.35
☐ 561 Ron Clark	2.00	.90
☐ 562 Bob Watson	7.00	3.10
☐ 563 Marty Pattin	3.00	1.35
☐ 564 Gil Hodges MG	10.00	4.50
☐ 565 Hoyt Wilhelm	7.00	3.10
☐ 566 Ron Hansen	2.00	.90
☐ 567 Pirates Rookies	2.00	.90
Elvio Jimenez		
Jim Shellenback		
☐ 568 Cecil Upshaw	2.00	.90
☐ 569 Billy Harris	2.00	.90
☐ 570 Ron Santo	7.00	3.10
☐ 571 Cap Peterson	2.00	.90
☐ 572 Giants Heroes	16.00	7.25
Willie McCovey		
Juan Marichal		
☐ 573 Jim Palmer	35.00	16.00
☐ 574 George Scott	3.00	1.35
☐ 575 Bill Singer	3.00	1.35
☐ 576 Phillies Rookies	2.00	.90
Ron Stone		
Bill Wilson		
☐ 577 Mike Hegan	3.00	1.35
☐ 578 Don Bosch	2.00	.90
☐ 579 Dave Nelson	2.00	.90
☐ 580 Jim Northrup	3.00	1.35
☐ 581 Gary Nolan	3.00	1.35
☐ 582A Tony Oliva CL	5.00	1.00
White circle on back		
☐ 582B Tony Oliva CL	8.00	1.60
Red circle on back		
☐ 583 Clyde Wright	2.00	.90
☐ 584 Don Mason	2.00	.90
☐ 585 Ron Swoboda	3.00	1.35
☐ 586 Tim Cullen	2.00	.90
☐ 587 Joe Rudi	7.00	3.10
☐ 588 Bill White	3.00	1.35
☐ 589 Joe Pepitone	4.00	1.80
☐ 590 Rico Carty	5.00	2.20
☐ 591 Mike Hedlund	3.00	1.35
☐ 592 Padres Rookies	5.00	2.20
Rafael Robles		
Al Santorini		
☐ 593 Don Nottebart	3.00	1.35
☐ 594 Dooley Womack	3.00	1.35
☐ 595 Lee Maye	3.00	1.35
☐ 596 Chuck Hartenstein	3.00	1.35
☐ 597 A.L. Rookies	35.00	16.00
Bob Floyd		
Larry Burchart		
Rollie Fingers		
☐ 598 Ruben Amaro	3.00	1.35
☐ 599 John Boozer	3.00	1.35
☐ 600 Tony Oliva	6.00	2.70
☐ 601 Tug McGraw	7.00	3.10
☐ 602 Cubs Rookies	5.00	2.20
Alec Distaso		
Don Young		
Jim Qualls		
☐ 603 Joe Keough	3.00	1.35
☐ 604 Bobby Etheridge	3.00	1.35
☐ 605 Dick Ellsworth	3.00	1.35
☐ 606 Gene Mauch MG	5.00	2.20
☐ 607 Dick Bosman	3.00	1.35
☐ 608 Dick Simpson	3.00	1.35
☐ 609 Phil Gagliano	3.00	1.35
☐ 610 Jim Hardin	3.00	1.35
☐ 611 Braves Rookies	5.00	2.20
Bob Didier		
Walt Hriniak		
Gary Neibauer		
☐ 612 Jack Aker	5.00	2.20
☐ 613 Jim Beauchamp	3.00	1.35
☐ 614 Houston Rookies	3.00	1.35
Tom Griffin		
Skip Guinn		
☐ 615 Len Gabrielson	3.00	1.35
☐ 616 Don McMahon	3.00	1.35
☐ 617 Jesse Gonder	3.00	1.35
☐ 618 Ramon Webster	3.00	1.35
☐ 619 Royals Rookies	4.00	1.80
Bill Butler		
Pat Kelly		
Juan Rios		
☐ 620 Dean Chance	4.00	1.80
☐ 621 Bill Voss	3.00	1.35
☐ 622 Dan Osinski	3.00	1.35
☐ 623 Hank Allen	3.00	1.35
☐ 624 NL Rookies	4.00	1.80
Darrel Chaney		
Duffy Dyer		
Terry Harmon		
☐ 625 Mack Jones UER	5.00	2.20
(Batting wrong)		
☐ 626 Gene Michael	5.00	2.20
☐ 627 George Stone	3.00	1.35
☐ 628 Red Sox Rookies	4.00	1.80
Bill Conigliaro		
Syd O'Brien		
Fred Wenz		
☐ 629 Jack Hamilton	3.00	1.35
☐ 630 Bobby Bonds	35.00	16.00
☐ 631 John Kennedy	5.00	2.20
☐ 632 Jon Warden	3.00	1.35
☐ 633 Harry Walker MG	3.00	1.35
☐ 634 Andy Etchebarren	3.00	1.35
☐ 635 George Culver	3.00	1.35
☐ 636 Woody Held	3.00	1.35
☐ 637 Padres Rookies	4.00	1.80
Jerry DaVanon		
Frank Reberger		
Clay Kirby		
☐ 638 Ed Sprague	3.00	1.35
☐ 639 Barry Moore	3.00	1.35
☐ 640 Ferguson Jenkins	20.00	9.00
☐ 641 NL Rookies	4.00	1.80
Bobby Darwin		
John Miller		
Tommy Dean		
☐ 642 John Hiller	3.00	1.35
☐ 643 Billy Cowan	3.00	1.35
☐ 644 Chuck Hinton	3.00	1.35
☐ 645 George Brunet	3.00	1.35
☐ 646 Expos Rookies	5.00	2.20
Dan McGinn		
Carl Morton		
☐ 647 Dave Wickersham	3.00	1.35
☐ 648 Bobby Wine	5.00	2.20
☐ 649 Al Jackson	3.00	1.35
☐ 650 Ted Williams MG	18.00	8.00
☐ 651 Gus Gil	3.00	1.35
☐ 652 Eddie Watt	3.00	1.35
☐ 653 Aurelio Rodriguez UER	5.00	2.20
(Photo actually		
Angels' batboy)		
☐ 654 White Sox Rookies	5.00	2.20
Carlos May		
Don Secrist		
Rich Morales		
☐ 655 Mike Hershberger	3.00	1.35
☐ 656 Dan Schneider	3.00	1.35
☐ 657 Bobby Murcer	6.00	2.70
☐ 658 AL Rookies	3.00	1.35
Tom Hall		
Bill Burbach		
Jim Miles		
☐ 659 Johnny Podres	4.00	1.80
☐ 660 Reggie Smith	6.00	2.70
☐ 661 Jim Merritt	3.00	1.35
☐ 662 Royals Rookies	5.00	2.20
Dick Drago		
George Spriggs		
Bob Oliver		
☐ 663 Dick Radatz	5.00	2.20
☐ 664 Ron Hunt	3.00	1.35

1970 Topps

The cards in this 720-card set measure 2 1/2" by 3 1/2". The Topps set for 1970 has color photos surrounded by white frame lines and gray borders. The backs have a blue biographical section and a yellow record section. All-Star selections are featured on cards 450 to 469. Other topical subsets within this set include League Leaders (61-72), Playoffs cards (195-202), and World Series cards (305-310). There are graduations of scarcity, terminating in the high series (634-720), which are outlined in the

Billy Williams OUTFIELD

value summary. Cards were
issued in ten-card dime packs
as well as thirty-three card cello
packs encased in a small Topps
box. The key Rookie Card in
this set is Thurman Munson.

	NRMT	VG-E
COMPLETE SET (720)	1800.00	800.00
COMMON CARD (1-372)	1.00	.45
COMMON CARD (373-459)	1.50	.70
MINOR STARS 1-459	2.00	.90
SEMISTARS 1-459	4.00	1.80
UNLISTED STARS 1-459	6.00	2.70
COMMON CARD (460-546)	2.00	.90
MINOR STARS 460-546	3.00	1.35
SEMISTARS 460-546	5.00	2.20
UNLISTED STARS 460-546	8.00	3.60
COMMON CARD (547-633)	4.00	1.80
MINOR STARS 547-633	6.00	2.70
SEMISTARS 547-633	8.00	3.60
UNLISTED STARS 547-633	12.00	5.50
COMMON CARD (634-720)	10.00	4.50
MINOR STARS 634-720	15.00	6.75
SEMISTARS 634-720	20.00	9.00

CARDS PRICED IN NM CONDITION !

☐ 1 New York Mets	16.00	5.00
	Team Card		
☐ 2 Diego Segui	2.00	.90
☐ 3 Darrel Chaney	1.00	.45
☐ 4 Tom Egan	1.00	.45
☐ 5 Wes Parker	1.50	.70
☐ 6 Grant Jackson	1.00	.45
☐ 7 Indians Rookies	1.00	.45
	Gary Boyd		
	Russ Nagelson		
☐ 8 Jose Martinez	1.00	.45
☐ 9 Checklist 1	12.00	2.40
☐ 10 Carl Yastrzemski	14.00	6.25
☐ 11 Nate Colbert	1.00	.45
☐ 12 John Hiller	1.00	.45
☐ 13 Jack Hiatt	1.00	.45
☐ 14 Hank Allen	1.00	.45
☐ 15 Larry Dierker	1.00	.45
☐ 16 Charlie Metro MG	1.00	.45
☐ 17 Hoyt Wilhelm	5.00	2.20
☐ 18 Carlos May	1.00	.45
☐ 19 John Boccabella	1.00	.45
☐ 20 Dave McNally	1.00	.45
☐ 21 A's Rookies	6.00	2.70
	Vida Blue		
	Gene Tenace		
☐ 22 Ray Washburn	1.00	.45
☐ 23 Bill Robinson	2.00	.90
☐ 24 Dick Selma	1.00	.45
☐ 25 Cesar Tovar	1.00	.45
☐ 26 Tug McGraw	2.00	.90
☐ 27 Chuck Hinton	1.00	.45
☐ 28 Billy Wilson	1.00	.45
☐ 29 Sandy Alomar	2.00	.90
☐ 30 Matty Alou	2.00	.90
☐ 31 Marty Pattin	2.00	.90
☐ 32 Harry Walker MG	1.00	.45
☐ 33 Don Wert	1.00	.45
☐ 34 Willie Crawford	1.00	.45
☐ 35 Joel Horlen	1.00	.45
☐ 36 Red Rookies	2.00	

	Danny Breeden		
	Bernie Carbo		
☐ 37 Dick Drago	1.00	.45
☐ 38 Mack Jones	1.00	.45
☐ 39 Mike Nagy	1.00	.45
☐ 40 Rich Allen	2.00	.90
☐ 41 George Lauzerique	1.00	.45
☐ 42 Tito Fuentes	1.00	.45
☐ 43 Jack Aker	1.00	.45
☐ 44 Roberto Pena	1.00	.45
☐ 45 Dave Johnson	2.00	.90
☐ 46 Ken Rudolph	1.00	.45
☐ 47 Bob Miller	1.00	.45
☐ 48 Gil Garrido	1.00	.45
☐ 49 Tim Cullen	1.00	.45
☐ 50 Tommie Agee	2.00	.90
☐ 51 Bob Christian	1.00	.45
☐ 52 Bruce Dal Canton	1.00	.45
☐ 53 John Kennedy	1.00	.45
☐ 54 Jeff Torborg	2.00	.90
☐ 55 John Odom	1.00	.45
☐ 56 Phillies Rookies	1.00	.45
	Joe Lis		
	Scott Reid		
☐ 57 Pat Kelly	1.00	.45
☐ 58 Dave Marshall	1.00	.45
☐ 59 Dick Ellsworth	1.00	.45
☐ 60 Jim Wynn	2.00	.90
☐ 61 NL Batting Leaders	12.00	5.50
	Pete Rose		
	Bob Clemente		
	Cleon Jones		
☐ 62 AL Batting Leaders	3.50	1.55
	Rod Carew		
	Reggie Smith		
	Tony Oliva		
☐ 63 NL RBI Leaders	4.00	1.80
	Willie McCovey		
	Ron Santo		
	Tony Perez		
☐ 64 AL RBI Leaders	6.00	2.70
	Harmon Killebrew		
	Boog Powell		
	Reggie Jackson		
☐ 65 NL Home Run Leaders	6.00	2.70
	Willie McCovey		
	Hank Aaron		
	Lee May		
☐ 66 AL Home Run Leaders	6.00	2.70
	Harmon Killebrew		
	Frank Howard		
	Reggie Jackson		
☐ 67 NL ERA Leaders	7.00	3.10
	Juan Marichal		
	Steve Carlton		
	Bob Gibson		
☐ 68 AL ERA Leaders	2.00	.90
	Dick Bosman		
	Jim Palmer		
	Mike Cuellar		
☐ 69 NL Pitching Leaders	7.00	3.10
	Tom Seaver		
	Phil Niekro		
	Fergie Jenkins		
	Juan Marichal		
☐ 70 AL Pitching Leaders	2.00	.90
	Dennis McLain		
	Mike Cuellar		
	Dave Boswell		
	Dave McNally		
	Jim Perry		
	Mel Stottlemyre		
☐ 71 NL Strikeout Leaders	4.00	1.80
	Fergie Jenkins		
	Bob Gibson		
	Bill Singer		
☐ 72 AL Strikeout Leaders	2.00	.90
	Sam McDowell		
	Mickey Lolich		
	Andy Messersmith		
☐ 73 Wayne Granger	1.00	.45
☐ 74 Angels Rookies	1.00	.45
	Greg Washburn		
	Wally Wolf		
☐ 75 Jim Kaat	2.00	.90
☐ 76 Carl Taylor	1.00	.45

☐ 77 Frank Linzy	1.00	.45
☐ 78 Joe Lahoud	1.00	.45
☐ 79 Clay Kirby	1.00	.45
☐ 80 Don Kessinger	2.00	.90
☐ 81 Dave May	1.00	.45
☐ 82 Frank Fernandez	1.00	.45
☐ 83 Don Cardwell	1.00	.45
☐ 84 Paul Casanova	1.00	.45
☐ 85 Max Alvis	1.00	.45
☐ 86 Lum Harris MG	1.00	.45
☐ 87 Steve Renko	1.00	.45
☐ 88 Pilots Rookies	2.00	.90
	Miguel Fuentes		
	Dick Baney		
☐ 89 Juan Rios	1.00	.45
☐ 90 Tim McCarver	2.00	.90
☐ 91 Rich Morales	1.00	.45
☐ 92 George Culver	1.00	.45
☐ 93 Rick Renick	1.00	.45
☐ 94 Freddie Patek	2.00	.90
☐ 95 Earl Wilson	1.00	.45
☐ 96 Cardinals Rookies	2.00	.90
	Leron Lee		
	Jerry Reuss		
☐ 97 Joe Moeller	1.00	.45
☐ 98 Gates Brown	2.00	.90
☐ 99 Bobby Pfeil	1.00	.45
☐ 100 Mel Stottlemyre	2.00	.90
☐ 101 Bobby Floyd	1.00	.45
☐ 102 Joe Rudi	2.00	.90
☐ 103 Frank Reberger	1.00	.45
☐ 104 Gerry Moses	1.00	.45
☐ 105 Tony Gonzalez	1.00	.45
☐ 106 Darold Knowles	1.00	.45
☐ 107 Bobby Etheridge	1.00	.45
☐ 108 Tom Burgmeier	1.00	.45
☐ 109 Expos Rookies	1.00	.45
	Garry Jestadt		
	Carl Morton		
☐ 110 Bob Moose	1.00	.45
☐ 111 Mike Hegan	2.00	.90
☐ 112 Dave Nelson	1.00	.45
☐ 113 Jim Ray	1.00	.45
☐ 114 Gene Michael	1.00	.45
☐ 115 Alex Johnson	2.00	.90
☐ 116 Sparky Lyle	2.00	.90
☐ 117 Don Young	1.00	.45
☐ 118 George Mitterwald	1.00	.45
☐ 119 Chuck Taylor	1.00	.45
☐ 120 Sal Bando	2.00	.90
☐ 121 Orioles Rookies	1.00	.45
	Fred Beene		
	Terry Crowley		
☐ 122 George Stone	1.00	.45
☐ 123 Don Gutteridge MG	1.00	.45
☐ 124 Larry Jaster	1.00	.45
☐ 125 Deron Johnson	1.00	.45
☐ 126 Marty Martinez	1.00	.45
☐ 127 Joe Coleman	1.00	.45
☐ 128A Checklist 2 ERR	6.00	1.20
	(226 R Peranoski)		
☐ 128B Checklist 2 COR	6.00	1.20
	(226 R. Perranoski)		
☐ 129 Jimmie Price	1.00	.45
☐ 130 Ollie Brown	1.00	.45
☐ 131 Dodgers Rookies	1.00	.45
	Ray Lamb		
	Bob Stinson		
☐ 132 Jim McGlothlin	1.00	.45
☐ 133 Clay Carroll	1.00	.45
☐ 134 Danny Walton	1.00	.45
☐ 135 Dick Dietz	1.00	.45
☐ 136 Steve Hargan	1.00	.45
☐ 137 Art Shamsky	1.00	.45
☐ 138 Joe Foy	1.00	.45
☐ 139 Rich Nye	1.00	.45
☐ 140 Reggie Jackson	50.00	22.00
☐ 141 Pirates Rookies	2.00	.90
	Dave Cash		
	Johnny Jeter		
☐ 142 Fritz Peterson	1.00	.45
☐ 143 Phil Gagliano	1.00	.45
☐ 144 Ray Culp	1.00	.45
☐ 145 Rico Carty	2.00	.90
☐ 146 Danny Murphy	1.00	.45
☐ 147 Angel Hermoso	1.00	.45

148	Earl Weaver MG	3.00	1.35
149	Billy Champion	1.00	.45
150	Harmon Killebrew	8.00	3.60
151	Dave Roberts	1.00	.45
152	Ike Brown	1.00	.45
153	Gary Gentry	1.00	.45
154	Senators Rookies	1.00	.45
	Jim Miles		
	Jan Dukes		
155	Denis Menke	1.00	.45
156	Eddie Fisher	1.00	.45
157	Manny Mota	2.00	.90
158	Jerry McNertney	1.00	.45
159	Tommy Helms	2.00	.90
160	Phil Niekro	5.00	2.20
161	Richie Scheinblum	1.00	.45
162	Jerry Johnson	1.00	.45
163	Syd O'Brien	1.00	.45
164	Ty Cline	1.00	.45
165	Ed Kirkpatrick	1.00	.45
166	Al Oliver	2.00	.90
167	Bill Burbach	1.00	.45
168	Dave Watkins	1.00	.45
169	Tom Hall	1.00	.45
170	Billy Williams	7.00	3.10
171	Jim Nash	1.00	.45
172	Braves Rookies	2.00	.90
	Garry Hill		
	Ralph Garr		
173	Jim Hicks	1.00	.45
174	Ted Sizemore	2.00	.90
175	Dick Bosman	1.00	.45
176	Jim Ray Hart	1.00	.45
177	Jim Northrup	2.00	.90
178	Denny Lemaster	1.00	.45
179	Ivan Murrell	1.00	.45
180	Tommy John	2.00	.90
181	Sparky Anderson MG	5.00	2.20
182	Dick Hall	1.00	.45
183	Jerry Grote	1.00	.45
184	Ray Fosse	2.00	.45
185	Don Mincher	1.00	.45
186	Rick Joseph	1.00	.45
187	Mike Hedlund	1.00	.45
188	Manny Sanguillen	2.00	.90
189	Yankees Rookies	50.00	22.00
	Thurman Munson		
	Dave McDonald		
190	Joe Torre	2.00	.90
191	Vicente Romo	1.00	.45
192	Jim Qualls	1.00	.45
193	Mike Wegener	1.00	.45
194	Chuck Manuel	1.00	.45
195	Tom Seaver NLCS	15.00	6.75
196	Ken Boswell NLCS	2.00	.90
197	Nolan Ryan NLCS	30.00	13.50
198	NL Playoff Summary	15.00	6.75
	Mets celebrate		
	(Nolan Ryan)		
199	Mike Cuellar ALCS	2.00	.90
200	Boog Powell ALCS	4.00	1.80
201	Boog Powell ALCS	2.00	.90
	Andy Etchebarren		
202	AL Playoff Summary	2.00	.90
	Orioles celebrate		
203	Rudy May	1.00	.45
204	Len Gabrielson	1.00	.45
205	Bert Campaneris	2.00	.90
206	Clete Boyer	2.00	.90
207	Tigers Rookies	1.00	.45
	Norman McRae		
	Bob Reed		
208	Fred Gladding	1.00	.45
209	Ken Suarez	1.00	.45
210	Juan Marichal	7.00	3.10
211	Ted Williams MG	12.00	5.50
212	Al Santorini	1.00	.45
213	Andy Etchebarren	1.00	.45
214	Ken Boswell	1.00	.45
215	Reggie Smith	2.00	.90
216	Chuck Hartenstein	1.00	.45
217	Ron Hansen	1.00	.45
218	Ron Stone	1.00	.45
219	Jerry Kenney	1.00	.45
220	Steve Carlton	15.00	6.75
221	Ron Brand	1.00	.45
222	Jim Rooker	2.00	.90
223	Nate Oliver	1.00	.45
224	Steve Barber	2.00	.90
225	Lee May	2.00	.90
226	Ron Perranoski	1.50	.70
227	Astros Rookies	1.50	.50
	John Mayberry		
	Bob Watkins		
228	Aurelio Rodriguez	1.00	.45
229	Rich Robertson	1.00	.45
230	Brooks Robinson	14.00	6.25
231	Luis Tiant	1.50	.70
232	Bob Didier	1.00	.45
233	Lew Krausse	1.00	.45
234	Tommy Dean	1.00	.45
235	Mike Epstein	1.00	.45
236	Bob Veale	1.00	.45
237	Russ Gibson	1.00	.45
238	Jose Laboy	1.00	.45
239	Ken Berry	1.00	.45
240	Ferguson Jenkins	7.00	3.10
241	Royals Rookies	1.00	.45
	Al Fitzmorris		
	Scott Northey		
242	Walter Alston MG	2.00	.90
243	Joe Sparma	1.00	.45
244A	Checklist 3	6.00	1.20
	(Red dot on front)		
244B	Checklist 3	6.00	1.20
	(Brown bat on front)		
245	Leo Cardenas	1.00	.45
246	Jim McAndrew	1.00	.45
247	Lou Klimchock	1.00	.45
248	Jesus Alou	1.00	.45
249	Bob Locker	1.00	.45
250	Willie McCovey UER	10.00	4.50
	(1963 San Francisci)		
251	Dick Schofield	1.00	.45
252	Lowell Palmer	1.00	.45
253	Ron Woods	1.00	.45
254	Camilo Pascual	1.00	.45
255	Jim Spencer	1.00	.45
256	Vic Davalillo	1.00	.45
257	Dennis Higgins	1.00	.45
258	Paul Popovich	1.00	.45
259	Tommie Reynolds	1.00	.45
260	Claude Osteen	1.00	.45
261	Curt Motton	1.00	.45
262	Padres Rookies	1.00	.45
	Jerry Morales		
	Jim Williams		
263	Duane Josephson	1.00	.45
264	Rich Hebner	1.00	.45
265	Randy Hundley	1.00	.45
266	Wally Bunker	1.00	.45
267	Twins Rookies	1.00	.45
	Herman Hill		
	Paul Ratliff		
268	Claude Raymond	1.00	.45
269	Cesar Gutierrez	1.00	.45
270	Chris Short	1.00	.45
271	Greg Goossen	1.00	.45
272	Hector Torres	1.00	.45
273	Ralph Houk MG	1.50	.70
274	Gerry Arrigo	1.00	.45
275	Duke Sims	1.00	.45
276	Ron Hunt	1.00	.45
277	Paul Doyle	1.00	.45
278	Tommie Aaron	1.00	.45
279	Bill Lee	2.00	.90
280	Donn Clendenon	1.00	.45
281	Casey Cox	1.00	.45
282	Steve Huntz	1.00	.45
283	Angel Bravo	1.00	.45
284	Jack Baldschun	1.00	.45
285	Paul Blair	2.00	.90
286	Dodgers Rookies	6.00	2.70
	Jack Jenkins		
	Bill Buckner		
287	Fred Talbot	1.00	.45
288	Larry Hisle	1.00	.45
289	Gene Brabender	1.00	.45
290	Rod Carew	18.00	8.00
291	Leo Durocher MG	3.00	1.35
292	Eddie Leon	1.00	.45
293	Bob Bailey	1.00	.45
294	Jose Azcue	1.00	.45
295	Cecil Upshaw	1.00	.45
296	Woody Woodward	1.00	.45
297	Curt Blefary	1.00	.45
298	Ken Henderson	1.00	.45
299	Buddy Bradford	1.00	.45
300	Tom Seaver	40.00	18.00
301	Chico Salmon	1.00	.45
302	Jeff James	1.00	.45
303	Brant Alyea	1.00	.45
304	Bill Russell	6.00	2.70
305	Don Buford WS	4.00	1.80
306	Donn Clendenon WS	4.00	1.80
307	Tommie Agee WS	4.00	1.80
308	J.C. Martin WS	1.00	.45
309	Jerry Koosman WS	4.00	1.80
310	World Series Summary	5.00	2.20
	Mets whoop it up		
311	Dick Green	1.00	.45
312	Mike Torrez	1.00	.45
313	Mayo Smith MG	1.00	.45
314	Bill McCool	1.00	.45
315	Luis Aparicio	5.00	2.20
316	Skip Guinn	1.00	.45
317	Red Sox Rookies	1.00	.45
	Billy Conigliaro		
	Luis Alvarado		
318	Willie Smith	1.00	.45
319	Clay Dalrymple	1.00	.45
320	Jim Maloney	1.00	.45
321	Lou Piniella	2.00	.90
322	Luke Walker	1.00	.45
323	Wayne Comer	1.00	.45
324	Tony Taylor	1.00	.45
325	Dave Boswell	1.00	.45
326	Bill Voss	1.00	.45
327	Hal King	1.00	.45
328	George Brunet	1.00	.45
329	Chris Cannizzaro	1.00	.45
330	Lou Brock	10.00	4.50
331	Chuck Dobson	1.00	.45
332	Bobby Wine	1.00	.45
333	Bobby Murcer	2.00	.90
334	Phil Regan	1.00	.45
335	Bill Freehan	2.00	.90
336	Del Unser	1.00	.45
337	Mike McCormick	1.00	.45
338	Paul Schaal	1.00	.45
339	Johnny Edwards	1.00	.45
340	Tony Conigliaro	3.00	1.35
341	Bill Sudakis	1.00	.45
342	Wilbur Wood	1.50	.70
343A	Checklist 4	6.00	1.20
	(Red bat on front)		
343B	Checklist 4	6.00	1.20
	(Brown bat on front)		
344	Marcelino Lopez	1.00	.45
345	Al Ferrara	1.00	.45
346	Red Schoendienst MG	2.00	.90
347	Russ Snyder	1.00	.45
348	Mets Rookies	1.50	.70
	Mike Jorgensen		
	Jesse Hudson		
349	Steve Hamilton	1.00	.45
350	Roberto Clemente	70.00	32.00
351	Tom Murphy	1.00	.45
352	Bob Barton	1.00	.45
353	Stan Williams	1.00	.45
354	Amos Otis	1.50	.70
355	Doug Rader	1.00	.45
356	Fred Lasher	1.00	.45
357	Bob Burda	1.00	.45
358	Pedro Borbon	1.50	.70
359	Phil Roof	1.00	.45
360	Curt Flood	2.00	.90
361	Ray Jarvis	1.00	.45
362	Joe Hague	1.00	.45
363	Tom Shopay	1.00	.45
364	Dan McGinn	1.00	.45
365	Zoilo Versalles	1.00	.45
366	Barry Moore	1.00	.45
367	Mike Lum	1.00	.45
368	Ed Herrmann	1.00	.45
369	Alan Foster	1.00	.45
370	Tommy Harper	2.00	.90
371	Rod Gaspar	1.00	.45

372	Dave Giusti	1.50	.70
373	Roy White	2.00	.90
374	Tommie Sisk	1.50	.70
375	Johnny Callison	2.00	.90
376	Lefty Phillips MG	1.50	.70
377	Bill Butler	1.00	.45
378	Jim Davenport	1.50	.70
379	Tom Tischinski	1.50	.70
380	Tony Perez	1.50	3.10
381	Athletics Rookies	1.50	.70
	Bobby Brooks		
	Mike Olivo		
382	Jack DiLauro	1.50	.70
383	Mickey Stanley	2.00	.90
384	Gary Neibauer	1.50	.70
385	George Scott	2.00	.90
386	Bill Dillman	1.50	.70
387	Baltimore Orioles	4.00	1.80
	Team Card		
388	Byron Browne	1.50	.70
389	Jim Shellenback	1.50	.70
390	Willie Davis	2.00	.90
391	Larry Brown	1.50	.70
392	Walt Hriniak	1.50	.90
393	John Gelnar	1.50	.70
394	Gil Hodges MG	5.00	2.20
395	Walt Williams	1.50	.70
396	Steve Blass	2.00	.90
397	Roger Repoz	1.50	.70
398	Bill Stoneman	2.00	.90
399	New York Yankees	4.00	1.80
	Team Card		
400	Denny McLain	2.00	.90
401	Giants Rookies	1.50	.70
	John Harrell		
	Bernie Williams		
402	Ellie Rodriguez	1.50	.70
403	Jim Bunning	5.00	2.20
404	Rich Reese	1.50	.70
405	Bill Hands	1.50	.70
406	Mike Andrews	1.50	.70
407	Bob Watson	2.00	.90
408	Paul Lindblad	1.50	.70
409	Bob Tolan	2.00	.90
410	Boog Powell	4.00	1.80
411	Los Angeles Dodgers	4.00	1.80
	Team Card		
412	Larry Burchart	1.50	.70
413	Sonny Jackson	1.50	.70
414	Paul Edmondson	1.50	.70
415	Julian Javier	2.00	.90
416	Joe Verbanic	1.50	.70
417	John Bateman	1.50	.70
418	John Donaldson	1.50	.70
419	Ron Taylor	1.50	.70
420	Ken McMullen	2.00	.90
421	Pat Dobson	2.00	.90
422	Royals Team	4.00	1.80
423	Jerry May	1.50	.70
424	Mike Kilkenny	1.50	.70
	(Inconsistent design card number in white circle)		
425	Bobby Bonds	6.00	2.70
426	Bill Rigney MG	1.50	.70
427	Fred Norman	1.50	.70
428	Don Buford	1.50	.70
429	Cubs Rookies	1.50	.70
	Randy Bobb		
	Jim Cosman		
430	Andy Messersmith	2.00	.90
431	Ron Swoboda	2.00	.90
432A	Checklist 5	6.00	1.20
	(Baseball in yellow letters)		
432B	Checklist 5	6.00	1.20
	(Baseball in white letters)		
433	Ron Bryant	1.50	.70
434	Felipe Alou	2.00	.90
435	Nelson Briles	2.00	.90
436	Philadelphia Phillies	4.00	1.80
	Team Card		
437	Danny Cater	1.50	.70
438	Pat Jarvis	1.50	.70
439	Lee Maye	1.50	.70
440	Bill Mazeroski	3.00	1.35
441	John O'Donoghue	1.50	.70
442	Gene Mauch MG	2.00	.90
443	Al Jackson	1.50	.70
444	White Sox Rookies	1.50	.70
	Billy Farmer		
	John Matias		
445	Vada Pinson	2.00	.90
446	Billy Grabarkewitz	1.50	.70
447	Lee Stange	1.50	.70
448	Houston Astros	4.00	1.80
	Team Card		
449	Jim Palmer	12.00	5.50
450	Willie McCovey AS	7.00	3.10
451	Boog Powell AS	4.00	1.80
452	Felix Millan AS	2.00	.90
453	Rod Carew AS	7.00	3.10
454	Ron Santo AS	4.00	1.80
455	Brooks Robinson AS	7.00	3.10
456	Don Kessinger AS	2.00	.90
457	Rico Petrocelli AS	4.00	1.80
458	Pete Rose AS	14.00	6.25
459	Reggie Jackson AS	14.00	6.25
460	Matty Alou AS	3.00	1.35
461	Carl Yastrzemski AS	10.00	4.50
462	Hank Aaron AS	15.00	6.75
463	Frank Robinson AS	7.00	3.10
464	Johnny Bench AS	14.00	6.25
465	Bill Freehan AS	3.00	1.35
466	Juan Marichal AS	4.00	1.80
467	Ron McLain AS	3.00	1.35
468	Jerry Koosman AS	3.00	1.35
469	Sam McDowell AS	3.00	1.35
470	Willie Stargell	10.00	4.50
471	Chris Zachary	2.00	.90
472	Braves Team	3.00	1.35
473	Don Bryant	2.00	.90
474	Dick Kelley	2.00	.90
475	Dick McAuliffe	3.00	1.35
476	Don Shaw	2.00	.90
477	Orioles Rookies	2.00	.90
	Al Severinsen		
	Roger Freed		
478	Bobby Heise	2.00	.90
479	Dick Woodson	2.00	.90
480	Glenn Beckert	3.00	1.35
481	Jose Tartabull	3.00	1.35
482	Tom Hilgendorf	2.00	.90
483	Gail Hopkins	2.00	.90
484	Gary Nolan	3.00	1.35
485	Jay Johnstone	3.00	1.35
486	Terry Harmon	2.00	.90
487	Cisco Carlos	2.00	.90
488	J.C. Martin	2.00	.90
489	Eddie Kasko MG	2.00	.90
490	Bill Singer	3.00	1.35
491	Graig Nettles	6.00	2.70
492	Astros Rookies	2.00	.90
	Keith Lampard		
	Scipio Spinks		
493	Lindy McDaniel	3.00	1.35
494	Larry Stahl	2.00	.90
495	Dave Morehead	2.00	.90
496	Steve Whitaker	2.00	.90
497	Eddie Watt	2.00	.90
498	Al Weis	2.00	.90
499	Skip Lockwood	2.00	1.35
500	Hank Aaron	50.00	22.00
501	Chicago White Sox	5.00	2.20
	Team Card		
502	Rollie Fingers	10.00	4.50
503	Dal Maxvill	2.00	.90
504	Don Pavletich	2.00	.90
505	Ken Holtzman	3.00	1.35
506	Ed Stroud	2.00	.90
507	Pat Corrales	3.00	1.35
508	Joe Niekro	3.00	1.35
509	Montreal Expos	3.00	1.35
	Team Card		
510	Tony Oliva	3.00	1.35
511	Joe Hoerner	2.00	.90
512	Billy Harris	2.00	.90
513	Preston Gomez MG	2.00	.90
514	Steve Hovley	2.00	.90
515	Don Wilson	3.00	1.35
516	Yankees Rookies	2.00	.90
	John Ellis		
	Jim Lyttle		
517	Joe Gibbon	2.00	.90
518	Bill Melton	2.00	.90
519	Don McMahon	2.00	.90
520	Willie Horton	3.00	1.35
521	Cal Koonce	2.00	.90
522	Angels Team	5.00	2.20
523	Jose Pena	2.00	.90
524	Alvin Dark MG	3.00	1.35
525	Jerry Adair	2.00	.90
526	Ron Herbel	2.00	.90
527	Don Bosch	2.00	.90
528	Elrod Hendricks	2.00	.90
529	Bob Aspromonte	2.00	.90
530	Bob Gibson	14.00	6.25
531	Ron Clark	2.00	.90
532	Danny Murtaugh MG	3.00	1.35
533	Buzz Stephen	2.00	.90
534	Minnesota Twins	5.00	2.20
	Team Card		
535	Andy Kosco	2.00	.90
536	Mike Kekich	2.00	.90
537	Joe Morgan	10.00	4.50
538	Bob Humphreys	2.00	.90
539	Phillies Rookies	6.00	2.70
	Denny Doyle		
	Larry Bowa		
540	Gary Peters	2.00	.90
541	Bill Heath	2.00	.90
542	Checklist 6	8.00	1.60
543	Clyde Wright	2.00	.90
544	Cincinnati Reds	2.50	1.10
	Team Card		
545	Ken Harrelson	3.00	1.35
546	Ron Reed	2.00	.90
547	Rick Monday	6.00	2.70
548	Howie Reed	4.00	1.80
549	St. Louis Cardinals	8.00	3.60
	Team Card		
550	Frank Howard	6.00	2.70
551	Dock Ellis	6.00	2.70
552	Royals Rookies	4.00	1.80
	Don O'Riley		
	Dennis Paepke		
	Fred Rico		
553	Jim Lefebvre	6.00	2.70
554	Tom Timmermann	4.00	1.80
555	Orlando Cepeda	6.00	2.70
556	Dave Bristol MG	4.00	1.80
557	Ed Kranepool	6.00	2.70
558	Vern Fuller	4.00	1.80
559	Tommy Davis	6.00	2.70
560	Gaylord Perry	10.00	4.50
561	Tom McCraw	4.00	1.80
562	Ted Abernathy	4.00	1.80
563	Boston Red Sox	8.00	3.60
	Team Card		
564	Johnny Briggs	4.00	1.80
565	Jim Hunter	10.00	4.50
566	Gene Alley	6.00	2.70
567	Bob Oliver	4.00	1.80
568	Stan Bahnsen	4.00	1.80
569	Cookie Rojas	6.00	2.70
570	Jim Fregosi	6.00	2.70
571	Jim Brewer	4.00	1.80
572	Frank Quilici MG	4.00	1.80
573	Padres Rookies	4.00	1.80
	Mike Corkins		
	Rafael Robles		
	Ron Slocum		
574	Bobby Bolin	6.00	2.70
575	Cleon Jones	6.00	2.70
576	Milt Pappas	6.00	2.70
577	Bernie Allen	4.00	1.80
578	Tom Griffin	4.00	1.80
579	Detroit Tigers	8.00	3.60
	Team Card		
580	Pete Rose	50.00	22.00
581	Tom Satriano	4.00	1.80
582	Mike Paul	4.00	1.80
583	Hal Lanier	4.00	1.80
584	Al Downing	6.00	2.70
585	Rusty Staub	8.00	3.60
586	Rickey Clark	4.00	1.80
587	Jose Arcia	4.00	1.80

		NRMT	VG-E
☐ 588A	Checklist 7 ERR ..	12.00	2.40
	(666 Adolfo)		
☐ 588B	Checklist 7 COR ..	12.00	2.40
	(666 Adolpho)		
☐ 589	Joe Keough	4.00	1.80
☐ 590	Mike Cuellar	6.00	2.70
☐ 591	Mike Ryan UER	4.00	1.80
	(Pitching Record		
	header on card back)		
☐ 592	Daryl Patterson	4.00	1.80
☐ 593	Chicago Cubs	8.00	3.60
	Team Card		
☐ 594	Jake Gibbs	4.00	1.80
☐ 595	Maury Wills	8.00	3.60
☐ 596	Mike Hershberger	6.00	2.70
☐ 597	Sonny Siebert	4.00	1.80
☐ 598	Joe Pepitone	6.00	2.70
☐ 599	Senators Rookies	4.00	1.80
	Dick Stelmaszek		
	Gene Martin		
	Dick Such		
☐ 600	Willie Mays	70.00	32.00
☐ 601	Pete Richert	4.00	1.80
☐ 602	Ted Savage	4.00	1.80
☐ 603	Ray Oyler	4.00	1.80
☐ 604	Clarence Gaston	6.00	2.70
☐ 605	Rick Wise	6.00	2.70
☐ 606	Chico Ruiz	4.00	1.80
☐ 607	Gary Waslewski	4.00	1.80
☐ 608	Pittsburgh Pirates	8.00	3.60
	Team Card		
☐ 609	Buck Martinez	6.00	2.70
	(Inconsistent design		
	card number in		
	white circle)		
☐ 610	Jerry Koosman	8.00	3.60
☐ 611	Norm Cash	5.00	2.20
☐ 612	Jim Hickman	6.00	2.70
☐ 613	Dave Baldwin	6.00	2.70
☐ 614	Mike Shannon	6.00	2.70
☐ 615	Mark Belanger	6.00	2.70
☐ 616	Jim Merritt	4.00	1.80
☐ 617	Jim French	4.00	1.80
☐ 618	Billy Wynne	4.00	1.80
☐ 619	Norm Miller	4.00	1.80
☐ 620	Jim Perry	6.00	2.70
☐ 621	Braves Rookies	10.00	4.50
	Mike McQueen		
	Darrell Evans		
	Rick Kester		
☐ 622	Don Sutton	10.00	4.50
☐ 623	Horace Clarke	6.00	2.70
☐ 624	Clyde King MG	4.00	1.80
☐ 625	Dean Chance	4.00	1.80
☐ 626	Dave Ricketts	4.00	1.80
☐ 627	Gary Wagner	4.00	1.80
☐ 628	Wayne Garrett	4.00	1.80
☐ 629	Merv Rettenmund ...	4.00	1.80
☐ 630	Ernie Banks	50.00	22.00
☐ 631	Oakland Athletics ...	8.00	3.60
	Team Card		
☐ 632	Gary Sutherland	4.00	1.80
☐ 633	Roger Nelson	4.00	1.80
☐ 634	Bud Harrelson	15.00	6.75
☐ 635	Bob Allison	15.00	6.75
☐ 636	Jim Stewart	10.00	4.50
☐ 637	Cleveland Indians ...	15.00	6.75
	Team Card		
☐ 638	Frank Bertaina	10.00	4.50
☐ 639	Dave Campbell	10.00	4.50
☐ 640	Al Kaline	50.00	22.00
☐ 641	Al McBean	10.00	4.50
☐ 642	Angels Rookies	10.00	4.50
	Greg Garrett		
	Gordon Lund		
	Jarvis Tatum		
☐ 643	Jose Pagan	10.00	4.50
☐ 644	Gerry Nyman	10.00	4.50
☐ 645	Don Money	15.00	6.75
☐ 646	Jim Britton	10.00	4.50
☐ 647	Tom Matchick	10.00	4.50
☐ 648	Larry Haney	10.00	4.50
☐ 649	Jimmie Hall	10.00	4.50
☐ 650	Sam McDowell	15.00	6.75
☐ 651	Jim Gosger	10.00	4.50
☐ 652	Rich Rollins.........	15.00	6.75

		NRMT	VG-E
☐ 653	Moe Drabowsky	10.00	4.50
☐ 654	NL Rookies	12.00	5.50
	Oscar Gamble		
	Boots Day		
	Angel Mangual		
☐ 655	John Roseboro	15.00	6.75
☐ 656	Jim Hardin...........	10.00	4.50
☐ 657	San Diego Padres	15.00	6.75
	Team Card		
☐ 658	Ken Tatum...........	10.00	4.50
☐ 659	Pete Ward	10.00	4.50
☐ 660	Johnny Bench	100.00	45.00
☐ 661	Jerry Robertson	10.00	4.50
☐ 662	Frank Lucchesi MG ...	10.00	4.50
☐ 663	Tito Francona	10.00	4.50
☐ 664	Bob Robertson	10.00	4.50
☐ 665	Jim Lonborg	15.00	6.75
☐ 666	Adolpho Phillips	10.00	4.50
☐ 667	Bob Meyer	15.00	6.75
☐ 668	Bob Tillman	10.00	4.50
☐ 669	White Sox Rookies ..	10.00	4.50
	Bart Johnson		
	Dan Lazar		
	Mickey Scott		
☐ 670	Ron Santo	12.00	5.50
☐ 671	Jim Campanis	10.00	4.50
☐ 672	Leon McFadden	10.00	4.50
☐ 673	Ted Uhlaender	10.00	4.50
☐ 674	Dave Leonhard	10.00	4.50
☐ 675	Jose Cardenal	15.00	6.75
☐ 676	Washington Senators	20.00	9.00
	Team Card		
☐ 677	Woodie Fryman	10.00	4.50
☐ 678	Dave Duncan	15.00	6.75
☐ 679	Ray Sadecki	10.00	4.50
☐ 680	Rico Petrocelli	15.00	6.75
☐ 681	Bob Garibaldi	10.00	4.50
☐ 682	Dalton Jones	10.00	4.50
☐ 683	Reds Rookies	15.00	6.75
	Vern Geishert		
	Hal McRae		
	Wayne Simpson		
☐ 684	Jack Fisher	10.00	4.50
☐ 685	Tom Haller	10.00	4.50
☐ 686	Jackie Hernandez ..	10.00	4.50
☐ 687	Bob Priddy	10.00	4.50
☐ 688	Ted Kubiak	15.00	6.75
☐ 689	Frank Tepedino	10.00	4.50
☐ 690	Ron Fairly	15.00	6.75
☐ 691	Joe Grzenda	10.00	4.50
☐ 692	Duffy Dyer	10.00	4.50
☐ 693	Bob Johnson	10.00	4.50
☐ 694	Gary Ross	10.00	4.50
☐ 695	Bobby Knoop	10.00	4.50
☐ 696	San Francisco Giants	15.00	6.75
	Team Card		
☐ 697	Jim Hannan	10.00	4.50
☐ 698	Tom Tresh	15.00	6.75
☐ 699	Hank Aguirre	10.00	4.50
☐ 700	Frank Robinson	50.00	22.00
☐ 701	Jack Billingham	10.00	4.50
☐ 702	AL Rookies	10.00	4.50
	Bob Johnson		
	Ron Klimkowski		
	Bill Zepp		
☐ 703	Lou Marone	10.00	4.50
☐ 704	Frank Baker	10.00	4.50
☐ 705	Tony Cloninger UER	10.00	4.50
	(Batter headings		
	on card back)		
☐ 706	John McNamara MG	10.00	4.50
☐ 707	Kevin Collins	10.00	4.50
☐ 708	Jose Santiago	10.00	4.50
☐ 709	Mike Fiore	10.00	4.50
☐ 710	Felix Millan	10.00	4.50
☐ 711	Ed Brinkman	10.00	4.50
☐ 712	Nolan Ryan	375.00	170.00
☐ 713	Seattle Pilots	25.00	11.00
	Team Card		
☐ 714	Al Spangler	10.00	4.50
☐ 715	Mickey Lolich	15.00	6.75
☐ 716	Cardinals Rookies ..	15.00	6.75
	Sal Campisi		
	Reggie Cleveland		
	Santiago Guzman		
☐ 717	Tom Phoebus	10.00	4.50

		NRMT	VG-E
☐ 718	Ed Spiezio	10.00	4.50
☐ 719	Jim Roland	10.00	4.50
☐ 720	Rick Reichardt	14.00	4.70

1971 Topps

The cards in this 752-card set measure 2 1/2" by 3 1/2". The 1971 Topps set is a challenge to complete in strict mint condition because the black obverse border is easily scratched and damaged. An unusual feature of this set is that the player is also pictured in black and white on the back of the card. Featured subsets within this set include League Leaders (61-72), Playoffs cards (195-202), and World Series cards (327-332). Cards 524-643 and the last series (644-752) are somewhat scarce. The last series were printed on two sheets of 132. On the printing sheets 44 cards were printed in 50 percent greater quantity than the other 66 cards. These 66 (slightly) shorter-printed numbers are identified in the checklist below by SP. The key Rookie Cards in this set are the multi-player Rookie Card of Dusty Baker and Don Baylor and the individual cards of Bert Blyleven, Dave Concepcion, Steve Garvey, and Ted Simmons.

	NRMT	VG-E
COMPLETE SET (752)	2000.00	900.00
COMMON CARD (1-393)	1.50	.70
MINOR STARS 1-393	2.00	.90
SEMISTARS 1-393	4.00	1.80
UNLISTED STARS 1-393	6.00	2.70
COMMON CARD (394-523)	2.50	1.10
MINOR STARS 394-523	4.00	1.80
SEMISTARS 394-523	6.00	2.70
UNLISTED STARS 394-523 ...	10.00	4.50
COMMON CARD (524-643)	4.00	1.80
MINOR STARS 524-643	6.00	2.70
SEMISTARS 524-643	8.00	3.60
UNLISTED STARS 524-643 ...	12.00	5.50
COMMON CARD (644-752)	8.00	3.60
COMMON SP (644-752)	12.00	5.50
MINOR STARS 644-752	12.00	5.50
SEMISTARS 644-752	15.00	6.75
CARDS PRICED IN NM CONDITION !		

		NRMT	VG-E
☐ 1	Baltimore Orioles........	15.00	5.00
	Team Card		
☐ 2	Dock Ellis	1.50	.70
☐ 3	Dick McAuliffe	1.50	.70
☐ 4	Vic Davalillo	1.50	.70
☐ 5	Thurman Munson	18.00	8.00
☐ 6	Ed Spiezio	1.50	.70
☐ 7	Jim Holt................	1.50	.70
☐ 8	Mike McQueen	1.50	.70

#	Card	Price	Price
9	George Scott	2.00	.90
10	Claude Osteen	1.50	.70
11	Elliott Maddox	2.00	.90
12	Johnny Callison	2.00	.90
13	White Sox Rookies	1.50	.70
	Charlie Brinkman		
	Dick Moloney		
14	Dave Concepcion	18.00	8.00
15	Andy Messersmith	2.00	.90
16	Ken Singleton	4.00	1.80
17	Billy Sorrell	1.50	.70
18	Norm Miller	1.50	.70
19	Skip Pitlock	1.50	.70
20	Reggie Jackson	25.00	11.00
21	Dan McGinn	1.50	.70
22	Phil Roof	1.50	.70
23	Oscar Gamble	1.50	.70
24	Rich Hand	1.50	.70
25	Clarence Gaston	2.50	1.10
26	Bert Blyleven	8.00	3.60
27	Pirates Rookies	1.50	.70
	Fred Cambria		
	Gene Clines		
28	Ron Klimkowski	1.50	.70
29	Don Buford	1.50	.70
30	Phil Niekro	5.00	2.20
31	Eddie Kasko MG	1.50	.70
32	Jerry DaVanon	1.50	.70
33	Del Unser	1.50	.70
34	Sandy Vance	1.50	.70
35	Lou Piniella	2.50	1.10
36	Dean Chance	1.50	.70
37	Rich McKinney	1.50	.70
38	Jim Colborn	1.50	.70
39	Tiger Rookies	1.50	.70
	Lerrin LaGrow		
	Gene Lamont		
40	Lee May	2.00	.90
41	Rick Austin	1.50	.70
42	Boots Day	1.50	.70
43	Steve Kealey	1.50	.70
44	Johnny Edwards	1.50	.70
45	Jim Hunter	7.00	3.10
46	Dave Campbell	1.50	.70
47	Johnny Jeter	1.50	.70
48	Dave Baldwin	1.50	.70
49	Don Money	1.50	.70
50	Willie McCovey	8.00	3.60
51	Steve Kline	1.50	.70
52	Braves Rookies	1.50	.70
	Oscar Brown		
	Earl Williams		
53	Paul Blair	2.00	.90
54	Checklist 1	6.00	1.20
55	Steve Carlton	15.00	6.75
56	Duane Josephson	1.50	.70
57	Von Joshua	1.50	.70
58	Bill Lee	2.00	.90
59	Gene Mauch MG	2.00	.90
60	Dick Bosman	1.50	.70
61	AL Batting Leaders	3.50	1.55
	Alex Johnson		
	Carl Yastrzemski		
	Tony Oliva		
62	NL Batting Leaders	2.00	.90
	Rico Carty		
	Joe Torre		
	Manny Sanguillen		
63	AL RBI Leaders	2.50	1.10
	Frank Howard		
	Tony Conigliaro		
	Boog Powell		
64	NL RBI Leaders	5.00	2.20
	Johnny Bench		
	Tony Perez		
	Billy Williams		
65	AL HR Leaders	4.00	1.80
	Frank Howard		
	Harmon Killebrew		
	Carl Yastrzemski		
66	NL HR Leaders	6.00	2.70
	Johnny Bench		
	Billy Williams		
	Tony Perez		
67	AL ERA Leaders	3.50	1.55
	Diego Segui		
	Jim Palmer		
	Clyde Wright		
68	NL ERA Leaders	3.50	1.55
	Tom Seaver		
	Wayne Simpson		
	Luke Walker		
69	AL Pitching Leaders	2.00	.90
	Mike Cuellar		
	Dave McNally		
	Jim Perry		
70	NL Pitching Leaders	6.00	2.70
	Bob Gibson		
	Gaylord Perry		
	Fergie Jenkins		
71	AL Strikeout Leaders	2.00	.90
	Sam McDowell		
	Mickey Lolich		
	Bob Johnson		
72	NL Strikeout Leaders	7.00	3.10
	Tom Seaver		
	Bob Gibson		
	Fergie Jenkins		
73	George Brunet	1.50	.70
74	Twins Rookies	1.50	.70
	Pete Hamm		
	Jim Nettles		
75	Gary Nolan	2.00	.90
76	Ted Savage	1.50	.70
77	Mike Compton	1.50	.70
78	Jim Spencer	1.50	.70
79	Wade Blasingame	1.50	.70
80	Bill Melton	1.50	.70
81	Felix Millan	1.50	.70
82	Casey Cox	1.50	.70
83	Met Rookies	1.50	.70
	Tim Foli		
	Randy Bobb		
84	Marcel Lachemann	1.50	.70
85	Billy Grabarkewitz	1.50	.70
86	Mike Kilkenny	1.50	.70
87	Jack Heidemann	1.50	.70
88	Hal King	1.50	.70
89	Ken Brett	1.50	.70
90	Joe Pepitone	2.50	1.10
91	Bob Lemon MG	2.50	1.10
92	Fred Wenz	1.50	.70
93	Senators Rookies	1.50	.70
	Norm McRae		
	Denny Riddleberger		
94	Don Hahn	1.50	.70
95	Luis Tiant	2.50	1.10
96	Joe Hague	1.50	.70
97	Floyd Wicker	1.50	.70
98	Joe Decker	1.50	.70
99	Mark Belanger	2.00	.90
100	Pete Rose	25.00	11.00
101	Les Cain	1.50	.70
102	Astros Rookies	2.00	.90
	Ken Forsch		
	Larry Howard		
103	Rich Severson	1.50	.70
104	Dan Frisella	1.50	.70
105	Tony Conigliaro	2.50	1.10
106	Tom Dukes	1.50	.70
107	Roy Foster	1.50	.70
108	John Cumberland	1.50	.70
109	Steve Hovley	1.50	.70
110	Bill Mazeroski	2.50	1.10
111	Yankee Rookies	1.50	.70
	Loyd Colson		
	Bobby Mitchell		
112	Manny Mota	2.00	.90
113	Jerry Crider	1.50	.70
114	Billy Conigliaro	2.00	.90
115	Donn Clendenon	2.00	.90
116	Ken Sanders	1.50	.70
117	Ted Simmons	8.00	3.60
118	Cookie Rojas	2.00	.90
119	Frank Lucchesi MG	1.50	.70
120	Willie Horton	2.50	1.10
121	Cubs Rookies	1.50	.70
	Jim Dunegan		
	Roe Skidmore		
122	Eddie Watt	1.50	.70
123A	Checklist 2	6.00	1.20
	(Card number at bottom right)		
123B	Checklist 2	6.00	1.20
	(Card number centered)		
124	Don Gullett	2.00	.90
125	Ray Fosse	2.00	.90
126	Danny Coombs	1.50	.70
127	Danny Thompson	2.00	.90
128	Frank Johnson	1.50	.70
129	Aurelio Monteagudo	1.50	.70
130	Denis Menke	1.50	.70
131	Curt Blefary	1.50	.70
132	Jose Laboy	1.50	.70
133	Mickey Lolich	2.50	1.10
134	Jose Arcia	1.50	.70
135	Rick Monday	2.50	1.10
136	Duffy Dyer	1.50	.70
137	Marcelino Lopez	1.50	.70
138	Phillies Rookies	2.00	.90
	Joe Lis		
	Willie Montanez		
139	Paul Casanova	1.50	.70
140	Gaylord Perry	7.00	3.10
141	Frank Quilici	1.50	.70
142	Mack Jones	1.50	.70
143	Steve Blass	2.00	.90
144	Jackie Hernandez	1.50	.70
145	Bill Singer	2.00	.90
146	Ralph Houk MG	2.50	.70
147	Bob Priddy	1.50	.70
148	John Mayberry	2.00	.90
149	Mike Hershberger	1.50	.70
150	Sam McDowell	2.50	1.10
151	Tommy Davis	2.00	.90
152	Angels Rookies	1.50	.70
	Lloyd Allen		
	Winston Llenas		
153	Gary Ross	1.50	.70
154	Cesar Gutierrez	1.50	.70
155	Ken Henderson	1.50	.70
156	Bart Johnson	1.50	.70
157	Bob Bailey	1.50	.70
158	Jerry Reuss	2.00	.90
159	Jarvis Tatum	1.50	.70
160	Tom Seaver	18.00	8.00
161	Coin Checklist	6.00	1.20
162	Jack Billingham	1.50	.70
163	Buck Martinez	2.00	.90
164	Reds Rookies	2.00	.90
	Frank Duffy		
	Milt Wilcox		
165	Cesar Tovar	1.50	.70
166	Joe Hoerner	1.50	.70
167	Tom Grieve	2.50	1.10
168	Bruce Dal Canton	1.50	.70
169	Ed Herrmann	1.50	.70
170	Mike Cuellar	2.00	.90
171	Bobby Wine	1.50	.70
172	Duke Sims	1.50	.70
173	Gil Garrido	1.50	.70
174	Dave LaRoche	1.50	.70
175	Jim Hickman	1.50	.70
176	Red Sox Rookies	2.00	.90
	Bob Montgomery		
	Doug Griffin		
177	Hal McRae	2.50	1.10
178	Dave Duncan	1.50	.70
179	Mike Corkins	1.50	.70
180	Al Kaline UER	18.00	8.00
	(Home instead of Birth)		
181	Hal Lanier	1.50	.70
182	Al Downing	2.00	.90
183	Gil Hodges MG	4.00	1.80
184	Stan Bahnsen	1.50	.70
185	Julian Javier	2.00	.90
186	Bob Spence	1.50	.70
187	Ted Abernathy	1.50	.70
188	Dodgers Rookies	3.00	1.35
	Bob Valentine		
	Mike Strahler		
189	George Mitterwald	1.50	.70
190	Bob Tolan	2.00	.90
191	Mike Andrews	1.50	.70
192	Billy Wilson	1.50	.70
193	Bob Grich	4.00	1.80

194	Mike Lum	1.50	.70
195	Boog Powell ALCS	3.00	1.35
196	Dave McNally ALCS	3.00	1.35
197	Jim Palmer ALCS	5.00	2.20
198	AL Playoff Summary	2.50	1.10
	Orioles celebrate		
199	Ty Cline NLCS	2.50	1.10
200	Bobby Tolan NLCS	2.50	1.10
201	Ty Cline NLCS	2.50	1.10
202	NL Playoff Summary	2.50	1.10
	Reds celebrate		
203	Larry Gura	2.00	.90
204	Brewers Rookies	1.50	.70
	Bernie Smith		
	George Kopacz		
205	Gerry Moses	1.50	.70
206	Checklist 3	6.00	1.20
207	Alan Foster	1.50	.70
208	Billy Martin MG	4.00	1.80
209	Steve Renko	1.50	.70
210	Rod Carew	18.00	8.00
211	Phil Hennigan	1.50	.70
212	Rich Hebner	2.00	.90
213	Frank Baker	1.50	.70
214	Al Ferrara	1.50	.70
215	Diego Segui	1.50	.70
216	Cards Rookies	1.50	.70
	Reggie Cleveland		
	Luis Melendez		
217	Ed Stroud	1.50	.70
218	Tony Cloninger	1.50	.70
219	Elrod Hendricks	1.50	.70
220	Ron Santo	2.50	1.10
221	Dave Morehead	1.50	.70
222	Bob Watson	2.50	1.10
223	Cecil Upshaw	1.50	.70
224	Alan Gallagher	1.50	.70
225	Gary Peters	1.50	.70
226	Bill Russell	2.50	1.10
227	Floyd Weaver	1.50	.70
228	Wayne Garrett	1.50	.70
229	Jim Hannan	1.50	.70
230	Willie Stargell	8.00	3.60
231	Indians Rookies	1.50	.70
	Vince Colbert		
	John Lowenstein		
232	John Strohmayer	1.50	.70
233	Larry Bowa	2.50	1.10
234	Jim Lyttle	1.50	.70
235	Nate Colbert	1.50	.70
236	Bob Humphreys	1.50	.70
237	Cesar Cedeno	3.00	1.35
238	Chuck Dobson	1.50	.70
239	Red Schoendienst MG	2.50	1.10
240	Clyde Wright	1.50	.70
241	Dave Nelson	1.50	.70
242	Jim Ray	1.50	.70
243	Carlos May	2.00	.90
244	Bob Tillman	1.50	.70
245	Jim Kaat	2.50	1.10
246	Tony Taylor	2.00	.90
247	Royals Rookies	2.00	.90
	Jerry Cram		
	Paul Splittorff		
248	Hoyt Wilhelm	4.00	1.80
249	Chico Salmon	1.50	.70
250	Johnny Bench	18.00	8.00
251	Frank Reberger	1.50	.70
252	Eddie Leon	1.50	.70
253	Bill Sudakis	1.50	.70
254	Cal Koonce	1.50	.70
255	Bob Robertson	2.00	.90
256	Tony Gonzalez	1.50	.70
257	Nelson Briles	1.50	.70
258	Dick Green	1.50	.70
259	Dave Marshall	1.50	.70
260	Tommy Harper	2.00	.90
261	Darold Knowles	1.50	.70
262	Padres Rookies	1.50	.70
	Jim Williams		
	Dave Robinson		
263	John Ellis	1.50	.70
264	Joe Morgan	8.00	3.60
265	Jim Northrup	2.00	.90
266	Bill Stoneman	1.50	.70
267	Rich Morales	1.50	.70
268	Philadelphia Phillies	4.00	1.80
	Team Card		
269	Gail Hopkins	1.50	.70
270	Rico Carty	2.50	1.10
271	Bill Zepp	1.50	.70
272	Tommy Helms	2.00	.90
273	Pete Richert	1.50	.70
274	Ron Slocum	1.50	.70
275	Vada Pinson	2.50	1.10
276	Giants Rookies	8.00	3.60
	Mike Davison		
	George Foster		
277	Gary Waslewski	1.50	.70
278	Jerry Grote	1.50	.70
279	Lefty Phillips MG	1.50	.70
280	Ferguson Jenkins	7.00	3.10
281	Danny Walton	1.50	.70
282	Jose Pagan	1.50	.70
283	Dick Such	1.50	.70
284	Jim Gosger	1.50	.70
285	Sal Bando	2.50	1.10
286	Jerry McNertney	1.50	.70
287	Mike Fiore	1.50	.70
288	Joe Moeller	1.50	.70
289	Chicago White Sox	2.00	.90
	Team Card		
290	Tony Oliva	2.50	1.10
291	George Culver	1.50	.70
292	Jay Johnstone	2.00	.90
293	Pat Corrales	2.00	.90
294	Steve Dunning	1.50	.70
295	Bobby Bonds	5.00	2.20
296	Tom Timmermann	1.50	.70
297	Johnny Briggs	1.50	.70
298	Jim Nelson	1.50	.70
299	Ed Kirkpatrick	1.50	.70
300	Brooks Robinson	18.00	8.00
301	Earl Wilson	1.50	.70
302	Phil Gagliano	1.50	.70
303	Lindy McDaniel	2.00	.90
304	Ron Brand	1.50	.70
305	Reggie Smith	2.50	1.10
306	Jim Nash	1.50	.70
307	Don Wert	1.50	.70
308	St. Louis Cardinals	2.00	.90
	Team Card		
309	Dick Ellsworth	1.50	.70
310	Tommie Agee	2.50	1.10
311	Lee Stange	1.50	.70
312	Harry Walker MG	1.50	.70
313	Tom Hall	1.50	.70
314	Jeff Torborg	2.00	.90
315	Ron Fairly	2.50	1.10
316	Fred Scherman	1.50	.70
317	Athletic Rookies	1.50	.70
	Jim Driscoll		
	Angel Mangual		
318	Rudy May	1.50	.70
319	Ty Cline	1.50	.70
320	Dave McNally	2.00	.90
321	Tom Matchick	1.50	.70
322	Jim Beauchamp	1.50	.70
323	Billy Champion	1.50	.70
324	Graig Nettles	2.50	1.10
325	Juan Marichal	7.00	3.10
326	Richie Scheinblum	1.50	.70
327	Boog Powell WS	2.50	1.10
328	Don Buford WS	1.50	.70
329	Frank Robinson WS	5.00	2.20
330	World Series Game 4	2.50	1.10
	Reds stay alive		
331	Brooks Robinson WS	6.00	2.70
	commits robbery		
332	World Series Summary	2.50	1.10
	Orioles celebrate		
333	Clay Kirby	1.50	.70
334	Roberto Pena	1.50	.70
335	Jerry Koosman	2.50	1.10
336	Detroit Tigers	2.00	.90
	Team Card		
337	Jesus Alou	1.50	.70
338	Gene Tenace	2.00	.90
339	Wayne Simpson	1.50	.70
340	Rico Petrocelli	2.50	1.10
341	Steve Garvey	25.00	11.00
342	Frank Tepedino	1.50	.70
343	Pirates Rookies	1.50	.70
	Ed Acosta		
	Milt May		
344	Ellie Rodriguez	1.50	.70
345	Joel Horlen	1.50	.70
346	Lum Harris MG	1.50	.70
347	Ted Uhlaender	1.50	.70
348	Fred Norman	1.50	.70
349	Rich Reese	1.50	.70
350	Billy Williams	7.00	3.10
351	Jim Shellenback	1.50	.70
352	Denny Doyle	1.50	.70
353	Carl Taylor	1.50	.70
354	Don McMahon	1.50	.70
355	Bud Harrelson	3.50	1.55
	(Nolan Ryan in photo)		
356	Bob Locker	1.50	.70
357	Cincinnati Reds	2.00	.90
	Team Card		
358	Danny Cater	1.50	.70
359	Ron Reed	1.50	.70
360	Jim Fregosi	2.00	.90
361	Don Sutton	7.00	3.10
362	Orioles Rookies	1.50	.70
	Mike Adamson		
	Roger Freed		
363	Mike Nagy	1.50	.70
364	Tommy Dean	1.50	.70
365	Bob Johnson	1.50	.70
366	Ron Stone	1.50	.70
367	Dalton Jones	1.50	.70
368	Bob Veale	2.00	.90
369	Checklist 4	6.00	1.20
370	Joe Torre	2.50	1.10
371	Jack Hiatt	1.50	.70
372	Lew Krausse	1.50	.70
373	Tom McCraw	1.50	.70
374	Clete Boyer	2.00	.90
375	Steve Hargan	1.50	.70
376	Expos Rookies	1.50	.70
	Clyde Mashore		
	Ernie McAnally		
377	Greg Garrett	1.50	.70
378	Tito Fuentes	1.50	.70
379	Wayne Granger	1.50	.70
380	Ted Williams MG	10.00	4.50
381	Fred Gladding	1.50	.70
382	Jake Gibbs	1.50	.70
383	Rod Gaspar	1.50	.70
384	Rollie Fingers	6.00	2.70
385	Maury Wills	2.50	1.10
386	Boston Red Sox	2.00	.90
	Team Card		
387	Ron Herbel	1.50	.70
388	Al Oliver	2.50	1.10
389	Ed Brinkman	1.50	.70
390	Glenn Beckert	2.00	.90
391	Twins Rookies	2.00	.90
	Steve Brye		
	Cotton Nash		
392	Grant Jackson	1.50	.70
393	Merv Rettenmund	2.00	.90
394	Clay Carroll	2.50	1.10
395	Roy White	3.00	1.35
396	Dick Schofield	2.50	1.10
397	Alvin Dark MG	3.00	1.35
398	Howie Reed	1.50	.70
399	Jim French	2.50	1.10
400	Hank Aaron	50.00	22.00
401	Tom Murphy	2.50	1.10
402	Los Angeles Dodgers	5.00	2.20
	Team Card		
403	Joe Coleman	2.50	1.10
404	Astros Rookies	2.50	1.10
	Buddy Harris		
	Roger Metzger		
405	Leo Cardenas	2.50	1.10
406	Ray Sadecki	2.50	1.10
407	Joe Rudi	3.00	1.35
408	Rafael Robles	2.50	1.10
409	Don Pavletich	2.50	1.10
410	Ken Holtzman	4.00	1.80
411	George Spriggs	2.50	1.10
412	Jerry Johnson	2.50	1.10
413	Pat Kelly	2.50	1.10
414	Woodie Fryman	2.50	1.10

415	Mike Hegan	2.50	1.10
416	Gene Alley	2.50	1.10
417	Dick Hall	2.50	1.10
418	Adolfo Phillips	2.50	1.10
419	Ron Hansen	2.50	1.10
420	Jim Merritt	2.50	1.10
421	John Stephenson	2.50	1.10
422	Frank Bertaina	2.50	1.10
423	Tigers Rookies	2.50	1.10
	Dennis Saunders		
	Tim Marting		
424	Roberto Rodriquez	2.50	1.10
425	Doug Rader	2.50	1.10
426	Chris Cannizzaro	2.50	1.10
427	Bernie Allen	2.50	1.10
428	Jim McAndrew	2.50	1.10
429	Chuck Hinton	2.50	1.10
430	Wes Parker	2.50	1.10
431	Tom Burgmeier	2.50	1.10
432	Bob Didier	2.50	1.10
433	Skip Lockwood	2.50	1.10
434	Gary Sutherland	2.50	1.10
435	Jose Cardenal	4.00	1.80
436	Wilbur Wood	2.50	1.10
437	Danny Murtaugh MG	3.00	1.35
438	Mike McCormick	4.00	1.80
439	Phillies Rookies	6.00	2.70
	Greg Luzinski		
	Scott Reid		
440	Bert Campaneris	3.00	1.35
441	Milt Pappas	4.00	1.80
442	California Angels	4.00	1.80
	Team Card		
443	Rich Robertson	2.50	1.10
444	Jimmie Price	2.50	1.10
445	Art Shamsky	2.50	1.10
446	Bobby Bolin	2.50	1.10
447	Cesar Geronimo	4.00	1.80
448	Dave Roberts	2.50	1.10
449	Brant Alyea	2.50	1.10
450	Bob Gibson	18.00	8.00
451	Joe Keough	2.50	1.10
452	John Boccabella	2.50	1.10
453	Terry Crowley	2.50	1.10
454	Mike Paul	2.50	1.10
455	Don Kessinger	3.00	1.35
456	Bob Meyer	2.50	1.10
457	Willie Smith	2.50	1.10
458	White Sox Rookies	2.50	1.10
	Ron Lolich		
	Dave Lemonds		
459	Jim Lefebvre	2.50	1.10
460	Fritz Peterson	2.50	1.10
461	Jim Ray Hart	2.50	1.10
462	Washington Senators	5.00	2.20
	Team Card		
463	Tom Kelley	2.50	1.10
464	Aurelio Rodriguez	2.50	1.10
465	Ken McMarver	6.00	2.70
466	Ken Berry	2.50	1.10
467	Al Santorini	2.50	1.10
468	Frank Fernandez	2.50	1.10
469	Bob Aspromonte	2.50	1.10
470	Bob Oliver	2.50	1.10
471	Tom Griffin	2.50	1.10
472	Ken Rudolph	2.50	1.10
473	Gary Wagner	2.50	1.10
474	Jim Fairey	2.50	1.10
475	Ron Perranoski	4.00	1.80
476	Dal Maxvill	2.50	1.10
477	Earl Weaver MG	4.00	1.80
478	Bernie Carbo	2.50	1.10
479	Dennis Higgins	2.50	1.10
480	Manny Sanguillen	3.00	1.35
481	Daryl Patterson	2.50	1.10
482	San Diego Padres	5.00	2.20
	Team Card		
483	Gene Michael	4.00	1.80
484	Don Wilson	2.50	1.10
485	Ken McMullen	2.50	1.10
486	Steve Huntz	2.50	1.10
487	Paul Schaal	2.50	1.10
488	Jerry Stephenson	2.50	1.10
489	Luis Alvarado	2.50	1.10
490	Deron Johnson	4.00	1.80
491	Jim Hardin	2.50	1.10
492	Ken Boswell	2.50	1.10
493	Dave May	2.50	1.10
494	Braves Rookies	4.00	1.80
	Ralph Garr		
	Rick Kester		
495	Felipe Alou	4.00	1.80
496	Woody Woodward	2.50	1.10
497	Horacio Pina	2.50	1.10
498	John Kennedy	2.50	1.10
499	Checklist 5	6.00	1.20
500	Jim Perry	4.00	1.80
501	Andy Etchebarren	2.50	1.10
502	Chicago Cubs	5.00	2.20
	Team Card		
503	Gates Brown	4.00	1.80
504	Ken Wright	2.50	1.10
505	Ollie Brown	2.50	1.10
506	Bobby Knoop	2.50	1.10
507	George Stone	2.50	1.10
508	Roger Repoz	2.50	1.10
509	Jim Grant	2.50	1.10
510	Ken Harrelson	3.00	1.35
511	Chris Short	4.00	1.80
	(Pete Rose leading off second)		
512	Red Sox Rookies	2.50	1.10
	Dick Mills		
	Mike Garman		
513	Nolan Ryan	250.00	110.00
514	Ron Woods	2.50	1.10
515	Carl Morton	2.50	1.10
516	Ted Kubiak	2.50	1.10
517	Charlie Fox MG	2.50	1.10
518	Joe Grzenda	2.50	1.10
519	Willie Crawford	2.50	1.10
520	Tommy John	5.00	2.20
521	Leron Lee	2.50	1.10
522	Minnesota Twins	5.00	2.20
	Team Card		
523	John Odom	2.50	1.10
524	Mickey Stanley	5.00	2.20
525	Ernie Banks	50.00	22.00
526	Ray Jarvis	4.00	1.80
527	Cleon Jones	6.00	2.70
528	Wally Bunker	4.00	1.80
529	NL Rookie Infielders	5.00	2.20
	Enzo Hernandez		
	Bill Buckner		
	Marty Perez		
530	Carl Yastrzemski	40.00	18.00
531	Mike Torrez	4.00	1.80
532	Bill Rigney MG	4.00	1.80
533	Mike Ryan	4.00	1.80
534	Luke Walker	4.00	1.80
535	Curt Flood	5.00	2.20
536	Claude Raymond	5.00	2.20
537	Tom Egan	4.00	1.80
538	Angel Bravo	4.00	1.80
539	Larry Brown	4.00	1.80
540	Larry Dierker	6.00	2.70
541	Bob Burda	4.00	1.80
542	Bob Miller	4.00	1.80
543	New York Yankees	10.00	4.50
	Team Card		
544	Vida Blue	6.00	2.70
545	Dick Dietz	4.00	1.80
546	John Matias	4.00	1.80
547	Pat Dobson	6.00	2.70
548	Don Mason	4.00	1.80
549	Jim Brewer	5.00	2.20
550	Harmon Killebrew	25.00	11.00
551	Frank Linzy	4.00	1.80
552	Buddy Bradford	4.00	1.80
553	Kevin Collins	4.00	1.80
554	Lowell Palmer	4.00	1.80
555	Walt Williams	4.00	1.80
556	Jim McGlothlin	4.00	1.80
557	Tom Satriano	4.00	1.80
558	Hector Torres	4.00	1.80
559	AL Rookie Pitchers	4.00	1.80
	Terry Cox		
	Bill Gogolewski		
	Gary Jones		
560	Rusty Staub	5.00	2.20
561	Syd O'Brien	4.00	1.80
562	Dave Giusti	4.00	1.80
563	San Francisco Giants	8.00	3.60
	Team Card		
564	Al Fitzmorris	4.00	1.80
565	Jim Wynn	5.00	2.20
566	Tim Cullen	4.00	1.80
567	Walt Alston MG	6.00	2.70
568	Sal Campisi	4.00	1.80
569	Ivan Murrell	4.00	1.80
570	Jim Palmer	30.00	13.50
571	Ted Sizemore	4.00	1.80
572	Jerry Kenney	4.00	1.80
573	Ed Kranepool	5.00	2.20
574	Jim Bunning	7.00	3.10
575	Bill Freehan	5.00	2.20
576	Cubs Rookies	4.00	1.80
	Adrian Garrett		
	Brock Davis		
	Garry Jestadt		
577	Jim Lonborg	5.00	2.20
578	Ron Hunt	4.00	1.80
579	Marty Pattin	4.00	1.80
580	Tony Perez	18.00	8.00
581	Roger Nelson	4.00	1.80
582	Dave Cash	6.00	2.70
583	Ron Cook	4.00	1.80
584	Cleveland Indians	8.00	3.60
	Team Card		
585	Willie Davis	5.00	2.20
586	Dick Woodson	4.00	1.80
587	Sonny Jackson	4.00	1.80
588	Tom Bradley	4.00	1.80
589	Bob Barton	4.00	1.80
590	Alex Johnson	6.00	2.70
591	Jackie Brown	4.00	1.80
592	Randy Hundley	6.00	2.70
593	Jack Aker	4.00	1.80
594	Cards Rookies	5.00	2.20
	Bob Chlupsa		
	Bob Stinson		
	Al Hrabosky		
595	Dave Johnson	6.00	2.70
596	Mike Jorgensen	4.00	1.80
597	Ken Suarez	4.00	1.80
598	Rick Wise	6.00	2.70
599	Norm Cash	6.00	2.70
600	Willie Mays	90.00	40.00
601	Ken Tatum	4.00	1.80
602	Marty Martinez	4.00	1.80
603	Pittsburgh Pirates	8.00	3.60
	Team Card		
604	John Gelnar	4.00	1.80
605	Orlando Cepeda	6.00	2.70
606	Chuck Taylor	4.00	1.80
607	Paul Ratliff	4.00	1.80
608	Mike Wegener	4.00	1.80
609	Leo Durocher MG	7.00	3.10
610	Amos Otis	6.00	2.70
611	Tom Phoebus	4.00	1.80
612	Indians Rookies	4.00	1.80
	Lou Camilli		
	Ted Ford		
	Steve Mingori		
613	Pedro Borbon	4.00	1.80
614	Billy Cowan	4.00	1.80
615	Mel Stottlemyre	5.00	2.20
616	Larry Hisle	6.00	2.70
617	Clay Dalrymple	4.00	1.80
618	Tug McGraw	5.00	2.20
619A	Checklist 6 ERR	8.00	1.60
	(No copyright)		
619B	Checklist 6 COR	12.00	2.40
	(Copyright on back)		
620	Frank Howard	5.00	2.20
621	Ron Bryant	4.00	1.80
622	Joe Lahoud	4.00	1.80
623	Pat Jarvis	4.00	1.80
624	Oakland Athletics	8.00	3.60
	Team Card		
625	Lou Brock	30.00	13.50
626	Freddie Patek	6.00	2.70
627	Steve Hamilton	4.00	1.80
628	John Bateman	4.00	1.80
629	John Hiller	6.00	2.70
630	Roberto Clemente	110.00	50.00
631	Eddie Fisher	4.00	1.80
632	Darrel Chaney	4.00	1.80
633	AL Rookie Outfielders	4.00	1.80

Bobby Brooks
Pete Koegel
Scott Northey
- ☐ 634 Phil Regan ... 6.00 2.70
- ☐ 635 Bobby Murcer ... 6.00 2.70
- ☐ 636 Denny Lemaster ... 4.00 1.80
- ☐ 637 Dave Bristol MG ... 4.00 1.80
- ☐ 638 Stan Williams ... 4.00 1.80
- ☐ 639 Tom Haller ... 4.00 1.80
- ☐ 640 Frank Robinson ... 40.00 18.00
- ☐ 641 New York Mets ... 15.00 6.75
  Team Card
- ☐ 642 Jim Roland ... 4.00 1.80
- ☐ 643 Rick Reichardt ... 6.00 2.70
- ☐ 644 Jim Stewart SP ... 12.00 5.50
- ☐ 645 Jim Maloney SP ... 14.00 6.25
- ☐ 646 Bobby Floyd SP ... 12.00 5.50
- ☐ 647 Juan Pizarro ... 8.00 3.60
- ☐ 648 Mets Rookies SP ... 25.00 11.00
  Rich Folkers
  Ted Martinez
  John Matlack
- ☐ 649 Sparky Lyle SP ... 18.00 8.00
- ☐ 650 Rich Allen SP ... 40.00 18.00
- ☐ 651 Jerry Robertson SP ... 12.00 5.50
- ☐ 652 Atlanta Braves ... 8.00 3.60
  Team Card
- ☐ 653 Russ Snyder SP ... 12.00 5.50
- ☐ 654 Don Shaw SP ... 12.00 5.50
- ☐ 655 Mike Epstein SP ... 12.00 5.50
- ☐ 656 Gerry Nyman SP ... 12.00 5.50
- ☐ 657 Jose Azcue ... 8.00 3.60
- ☐ 658 Paul Lindblad SP ... 12.00 5.50
- ☐ 659 Byron Browne SP ... 12.00 5.50
- ☐ 660 Ray Culp ... 8.00 3.60
- ☐ 661 Chuck Tanner MG SP ... 14.00 6.25
- ☐ 662 Mike Hedlund SP ... 12.00 5.50
- ☐ 663 Marv Staehle ... 8.00 3.60
- ☐ 664 Rookie Pitchers SP ... 14.00 6.25
  Archie Reynolds
  Bob Reynolds
  Ken Reynolds
- ☐ 665 Ron Swoboda SP ... 18.00 8.00
- ☐ 666 Gene Brabender SP ... 12.00 5.50
- ☐ 667 Pete Ward ... 8.00 3.60
- ☐ 668 Gary Neibauer ... 8.00 3.60
- ☐ 669 Ike Brown SP ... 14.00 6.25
- ☐ 670 Bill Hands ... 8.00 3.60
- ☐ 671 Bill Voss SP ... 12.00 5.50
- ☐ 672 Ed Crosby SP ... 12.00 5.50
- ☐ 673 Gerry Janeski SP ... 12.00 5.50
- ☐ 674 Montreal Expos ... 12.00 5.50
  Team Card
- ☐ 675 Dave Boswell ... 8.00 3.60
- ☐ 676 Tommie Reynolds ... 8.00 3.60
- ☐ 677 Jack DiLauro SP ... 12.00 5.50
- ☐ 678 George Thomas ... 8.00 3.60
- ☐ 679 Don O'Riley ... 8.00 3.60
- ☐ 680 Don Mincher SP ... 12.00 5.50
- ☐ 681 Bill Butler ... 8.00 3.60
- ☐ 682 Terry Harmon ... 8.00 3.60
- ☐ 683 Bill Burbach SP ... 12.00 5.50
- ☐ 684 Curt Motton ... 8.00 3.60
- ☐ 685 Moe Drabowsky ... 8.00 3.60
- ☐ 686 Chico Ruiz SP ... 12.00 5.50
- ☐ 687 Ron Taylor SP ... 12.00 5.50
- ☐ 688 Sparky Anderson MG SP 40.00 18.00
- ☐ 689 Frank Baker ... 8.00 3.60
- ☐ 690 Bob Mose ... 8.00 3.60
- ☐ 691 Bobby Heise ... 8.00 3.60
- ☐ 692 AL Rookie Pitchers SP 12.00 5.50
  Hal Haydel
  Rogelio Moret
  Wayne Twitchell
- ☐ 693 Jose Pena SP ... 12.00 5.50
- ☐ 694 Rick Renick SP ... 12.00 5.50
- ☐ 695 Joe Niekro ... 9.00 4.00
- ☐ 696 Jerry Morales ... 8.00 3.60
- ☐ 697 Rickey Clark SP ... 12.00 5.50
- ☐ 698 Milwaukee Brewers SP 20.00 9.00
  Team Card
- ☐ 699 Jim Britton ... 8.00 3.60
- ☐ 700 Boog Powell SP ... 30.00 13.50
- ☐ 701 Bob Garibaldi ... 8.00 3.60
- ☐ 702 Milt Ramirez ... 8.00 3.60
- ☐ 703 Mike Kekich ... 8.00 3.60

- ☐ 704 J.C. Martin SP ... 12.00 5.50
- ☐ 705 Dick Selma SP ... 12.00 5.50
- ☐ 706 Joe Foy SP ... 12.00 5.50
- ☐ 707 Fred Lasher ... 8.00 3.60
- ☐ 708 Russ Nagelson SP ... 12.00 5.50
- ☐ 709 Rookie Outfielders SP 90.00 40.00
  Dusty Baker
  Don Baylor
  Tom Paciorek
- ☐ 710 Sonny Siebert ... 8.00 3.60
- ☐ 711 Larry Stahl SP ... 12.00 5.50
- ☐ 712 Jose Martinez ... 8.00 3.60
- ☐ 713 Mike Marshall SP ... 14.00 6.25
- ☐ 714 Dick Williams MG SP 14.00 6.25
- ☐ 715 Horace Clarke SP ... 14.00 6.25
- ☐ 716 Dave Leonhard ... 8.00 3.60
- ☐ 717 Tommie Aaron SP ... 12.00 5.50
- ☐ 718 Billy Wynne ... 8.00 3.60
- ☐ 719 Jerry May SP ... 12.00 5.50
- ☐ 720 Matty Alou ... 9.00 4.00
- ☐ 721 John Morris ... 8.00 3.60
- ☐ 722 Houston Astros SP ... 20.00 9.00
  Team Card
- ☐ 723 Vicente Romo SP ... 12.00 5.50
- ☐ 724 Tom Tischinski SP ... 12.00 5.50
- ☐ 725 Gary Gentry SP ... 12.00 5.50
- ☐ 726 Paul Popovich ... 8.00 3.60
- ☐ 727 Ray Lamb SP ... 12.00 5.50
- ☐ 728 NL Rookie Outfielders 8.00 3.60
  Wayne Redmond
  Keith Lampard
  Bernie Williams
- ☐ 729 Dick Billings ... 8.00 3.60
- ☐ 730 Jim Rooker ... 8.00 3.60
- ☐ 731 Jim Qualls SP ... 12.00 5.50
- ☐ 732 Bob Reed ... 8.00 3.60
- ☐ 733 Lee Maye SP ... 12.00 5.50
- ☐ 734 Rob Gardner SP ... 12.00 5.50
- ☐ 735 Mike Shannon SP ... 14.00 6.25
- ☐ 736 Mel Queen SP ... 12.00 5.50
- ☐ 737 Preston Gomez SP MG 12.00 5.50
- ☐ 738 Russ Gibson SP ... 12.00 5.50
- ☐ 739 Barry Lersch SP ... 12.00 5.50
- ☐ 740 Luis Aparicio SP UER 30.00 13.50
  (Led AL in steals
  from 1965 to 1964,
  should be 1956 to 1964)
- ☐ 741 Skip Guinn ... 8.00 3.60
- ☐ 742 Kansas City Royals 12.00 5.50
  Team Card
- ☐ 743 John O'Donoghue SP 12.00 5.50
- ☐ 744 Chuck Manuel SP ... 12.00 5.50
- ☐ 745 Sandy Alomar SP ... 12.00 5.50
- ☐ 746 Andy Kosco ... 8.00 3.60
- ☐ 747 NL Rookie Pitchers ... 8.00 3.60
  Al Severinsen
  Scipio Spinks
  Balor Moore
- ☐ 748 John Purdin SP ... 12.00 5.50
- ☐ 749 Ken Szotkiewicz ... 8.00 3.60
- ☐ 750 Denny McLain SP ... 25.00 11.00
- ☐ 751 Al Weis SP ... 15.00 6.75
- ☐ 752 Dick Drago ... 12.00 2.90

1972 Topps

The cards in this 787-card set measure 2 1/2" by 3 1/2". The

1972 Topps set contained the most cards ever for a Topps set to that point in time. Features appearing for the first time were "Boyhood Photos" (341-348/491-498), Awards and Trophy cards (621-626), "In Action" (distributed throughout the set), and "Traded Cards" (751-757). Other subsets included League Leaders (85-96), Playoffs cards (221-222), and World Series cards (223-230). The curved lines of the color picture are a departure from the rectangular designs of other years. There is a series of intermediate scarcity (526-656) and the usual high numbers (657-787). The backs of cards 692, 694, 696, 700, 706 and 710 form a picture back of Tom Seaver. The backs of cards 698, 702, 704, 708, 712, 714 form a picture back of Tony Oliva. As in previous years, cards were issued in a variety of ways including ten-card dime wax packs. The key Rookie Card in this set is Carlton Fisk.

	NRMT	VG-E
COMPLETE SET (787)	1700.00	750.00
COMMON CARD (1-132)	.60	.25
CUBS VAR (18B/29B/45B/117B)	5.00	2.20
MINOR STARS 1-132	1.25	.55
SEMISTARS 1-132	2.50	1.10
UNLISTED STARS 1-132	4.00	1.80
COMMON CARD (133-263)	1.00	.45
COMMON CARD (264-394)	1.25	.55
COMMON CARD (395-525)	1.50	.70
MINOR STARS 133-525	2.00	.90
SEMISTARS 133-525	4.00	1.80
UNLISTED STARS 133-525	6.00	2.70
COMMON CARD (526-656)	4.00	1.80
MINOR STARS 526-656	6.00	2.70
SEMISTARS 526-656	8.00	3.60
UNLISTED STARS 526-656	12.00	5.50
COMMON CARD (657-787)	12.00	5.50
MINOR STARS 657-787	15.00	6.75
SEMISTARS 657-787	20.00	9.00
CARDS PRICED IN NM CONDITION		
LAST SERIES CONDITION SENSITIVE		

- ☐ 1 Pittsburgh Pirates 8.00 2.90
  Team Card
- ☐ 2 Ray Culp .60 .25
- ☐ 3 Bob Tolan .60 .25
- ☐ 4 Checklist 1-132 4.00 .80
- ☐ 5 John Bateman .60 .25
- ☐ 6 Fred Scherman .60 .25
- ☐ 7 Enzo Hernandez .60 .25
- ☐ 8 Ron Swoboda 1.25 .55
- ☐ 9 Stan Williams .60 .25
- ☐ 10 Amos Otis 1.25 .55
- ☐ 11 Bobby Valentine 1.00 .45
- ☐ 12 Jose Cardenal .60 .25
- ☐ 13 Joe Grzenda .60 .25
- ☐ 14 Phillies Rookies .60 .25
  Pete Koegel
  Mike Anderson
  Wayne Twitchell
- ☐ 15 Walt Williams .60 .25
- ☐ 16 Mike Jorgensen .60 .25
- ☐ 17 Dave Duncan .60 .25
- ☐ 18A Juan Pizarro .60 .25
  (Yellow underline
  C and S of Cubs)
- ☐ 18B Juan Pizarro 5.00 2.20
  (Green underline
  C and S of Cubs)
- ☐ 19 Billy Cowan .60 .25
- ☐ 20 Don Wilson .60 .25
- ☐ 21 Atlanta Braves 1.25 .55
  Team Card
- ☐ 22 Rob Gardner .60 .25

☐ 23	Ted Kubiak	.60	.25
☐ 24	Ted Ford	.60	.25
☐ 25	Bill Singer	.60	.25
☐ 26	Andy Etchebarren	.60	.25
☐ 27	Bob Johnson	.60	.25
☐ 28	Twins Rookies	.60	.25
	Bob Gebhard		
	Steve Brye		
	Hal Haydel		
☐ 29A	Bill Bonham	.60	.25
	(Yellow underline		
	C and S of Cubs)		
☐ 29B	Bill Bonham	5.00	2.20
	(Green underline		
	C and S of Cubs)		
☐ 30	Rico Petrocelli	1.00	.45
☐ 31	Cleon Jones	1.25	.55
☐ 32	Cleon Jones IA	.60	.25
☐ 33	Billy Martin MG	4.00	1.80
☐ 34	Billy Martin IA	2.00	.90
☐ 35	Jerry Johnson	.60	.25
☐ 36	Jerry Johnson IA	.60	.25
☐ 37	Carl Yastrzemski	10.00	4.50
☐ 38	Carl Yastrzemski IA	6.00	2.70
☐ 39	Bob Barton	.60	.25
☐ 40	Bob Barton IA	.60	.25
☐ 41	Tommy Davis	1.00	.45
☐ 42	Tommy Davis IA	.60	.25
☐ 43	Rick Wise	1.25	.55
☐ 44	Rick Wise IA	.60	.25
☐ 45A	Glenn Beckert	1.25	.55
	(Yellow underline		
	C and S of Cubs)		
☐ 45B	Glenn Beckert	5.00	2.20
	(Green underline		
	C and S of Cubs)		
☐ 46	Glenn Beckert IA	.60	.25
☐ 47	John Ellis	.60	.25
☐ 48	John Ellis IA	.60	.25
☐ 49	Willie Mays	25.00	11.00
☐ 50	Willie Mays IA	14.00	6.25
☐ 51	Harmon Killebrew	7.00	3.10
☐ 52	Harmon Killebrew IA	3.50	1.55
☐ 53	Bud Harrelson	1.00	.45
☐ 54	Bud Harrelson IA	.60	.25
☐ 55	Clyde Wright	.60	.25
☐ 56	Rich Chiles	.60	.25
☐ 57	Bob Oliver	.60	.25
☐ 58	Ernie McAnally	.60	.25
☐ 59	Fred Stanley	.60	.25
☐ 60	Manny Sanguillen	1.00	.45
☐ 61	Cubs Rookies	1.00	.45
	Burt Hooton		
	Gene Hiser		
	Earl Stephenson		
☐ 62	Angel Mangual	.60	.25
☐ 63	Duke Sims	.60	.25
☐ 64	Pete Broberg	.60	.25
☐ 65	Cesar Cedeno	1.00	.45
☐ 66	Ray Corbin	.60	.25
☐ 67	Red Schoendienst MG	1.00	.45
☐ 68	Jim York	.60	.25
☐ 69	Roger Freed	.60	.25
☐ 70	Mike Cuellar	1.25	.55
☐ 71	California Angels	1.50	.70
	Team Card		
☐ 72	Bruce Kison	.60	.25
☐ 73	Steve Huntz	.60	.25
☐ 74	Cecil Upshaw	.60	.25
☐ 75	Bert Campaneris	1.00	.45
☐ 76	Don Carrithers	.60	.25
☐ 77	Ron Theobald	.60	.25
☐ 78	Steve Arlin	.60	.25
☐ 79	Red Sox Rookies	60.00	27.00
	Mike Garman		
	Cecil Cooper		
	Carlton Fisk		
☐ 80	Tony Perez	4.00	1.80
☐ 81	Mike Hedlund	.60	.25
☐ 82	Ron Woods	.60	.25
☐ 83	Dalton Jones	.60	.25
☐ 84	Vince Colbert	.60	.25
☐ 85	NL Batting Leaders	1.75	.80
	Joe Torre		
	Ralph Garr		
	Glenn Beckert		
☐ 86	AL Batting Leaders	1.75	.80
	Tony Oliva		
	Bobby Murcer		
	Merv Rettenmund		
☐ 87	NL RBI Leaders	3.50	1.55
	Joe Torre		
	Willie Stargell		
	Hank Aaron		
☐ 88	AL RBI Leaders	3.00	1.35
	Harmon Killebrew		
	Frank Robinson		
	Reggie Smith		
☐ 89	NL Home Run Leaders	3.00	1.35
	Willie Stargell		
	Hank Aaron		
	Lee May		
☐ 90	AL Home Run Leaders	2.50	1.10
	Bill Melton		
	Norm Cash		
	Reggie Jackson		
☐ 91	NL ERA Leaders	2.50	1.10
	Tom Seaver		
	Dave Roberts UER		
	(Photo actually		
	Danny Coombs)		
	Don Wilson		
☐ 92	AL ERA Leaders	2.50	1.10
	Vida Blue		
	Wilbur Wood		
	Jim Palmer		
☐ 93	NL Pitching Leaders	4.00	1.80
	Fergie Jenkins		
	Steve Carlton		
	Al Downing		
	Tom Seaver		
☐ 94	AL Pitching Leaders	1.75	.80
	Mickey Lolich		
	Vida Blue		
	Wilbur Wood		
☐ 95	NL Strikeout Leaders	3.00	1.35
	Tom Seaver		
	Fergie Jenkins		
	Bill Stoneman		
☐ 96	AL Strikeout Leaders	1.75	.80
	Mickey Lolich		
	Vida Blue		
	Joe Coleman		
☐ 97	Tom Kelley	.60	.25
☐ 98	Chuck Tanner MG	1.00	.45
☐ 99	Ross Grimsley	.60	.25
☐ 100	Frank Robinson	8.00	3.60
☐ 101	Astros Rookies	1.50	.70
	Bill Greif		
	J.R. Richard		
	Ray Busse		
☐ 102	Lloyd Allen	.60	.25
☐ 103	Checklist 133-263	4.00	.80
☐ 104	Toby Harrah	1.50	.70
☐ 105	Gary Waslewski	.60	.25
☐ 106	Milwaukee Brewers	1.25	.55
	Team Card		
☐ 107	Jose Cruz	1.50	.70
☐ 108	Gary Waslewski	.60	.25
☐ 109	Jerry May	.60	.25
☐ 110	Ron Hunt	.60	.25
☐ 111	Jim Grant	.60	.25
☐ 112	Greg Luzinski	1.50	.70
☐ 113	Rogelio Moret	.60	.25
☐ 114	Bill Buckner	1.50	.70
☐ 115	Jim Fregosi	1.00	.45
☐ 116	Ed Farmer	.60	.25
☐ 117A	Cleo James	.60	.25
	(Yellow underline		
	C and S of Cubs)		
☐ 117B	Cleo James	5.00	2.20
	(Green underline		
	C and S of Cubs)		
☐ 118	Skip Lockwood	.60	.25
☐ 119	Marty Perez	.60	.25
☐ 120	Bill Freehan	1.00	.45
☐ 121	Ed Sprague	.60	.25
☐ 122	Larry Biittner	.60	.25
☐ 123	Ed Acosta	.60	.25
☐ 124	Yankees Rookies	.60	.25
	Alan Closter		
	Rusty Torres		
	Roger Hambright		
☐ 125	Dave Cash	1.25	.55
☐ 126	Bart Johnson	.60	.25
☐ 127	Duffy Dyer	.60	.25
☐ 128	Eddie Watt	.60	.25
☐ 129	Charlie Fox MG	.60	.25
☐ 130	Bob Gibson	8.00	3.60
☐ 131	Jim Nettles	.60	.25
☐ 132	Joe Morgan	6.00	2.70
☐ 133	Joe Keough	1.00	.45
☐ 134	Carl Morton	1.00	.45
☐ 135	Vada Pinson	1.50	.70
☐ 136	Darrel Chaney	1.00	.45
☐ 137	Dick Williams MG	1.50	.70
☐ 138	Mike Kekich	1.00	.45
☐ 139	Tim McCarver	2.00	.90
☐ 140	Pat Dobson	2.00	.90
☐ 141	Mets Rookies	2.00	.90
	Buzz Capra		
	Lee Stanton		
	Jon Matlack		
☐ 142	Chris Chambliss	4.00	1.80
☐ 143	Garry Jestadt	1.00	.45
☐ 144	Marty Pattin	1.00	.45
☐ 145	Don Kessinger	1.50	.70
☐ 146	Steve Kealey	1.00	.45
☐ 147	Dave Kingman	5.00	2.20
☐ 148	Dick Billings	1.00	.45
☐ 149	Gary Neibauer	1.00	.45
☐ 150	Norm Cash	2.00	.90
☐ 151	Jim Brewer	1.00	.45
☐ 152	Gene Clines	1.00	.45
☐ 153	Rick Auerbach	1.00	.45
☐ 154	Ted Simmons	3.00	1.35
☐ 155	Larry Dierker	2.00	.90
☐ 156	Minnesota Twins	2.00	.90
	Team Card		
☐ 157	Don Gullett	1.00	.45
☐ 158	Jerry Kenney	1.00	.45
☐ 159	John Boccabella	1.00	.45
☐ 160	Andy Messersmith	2.00	.90
☐ 161	Brock Davis	1.00	.45
☐ 162	Brewers Rookies UER	2.00	.90
	Jerry Bell		
	Darrell Porter		
	Bob Reynolds		
	(Porter and Bell		
	photos switched)		
☐ 163	Tug McGraw	2.00	.90
☐ 164	Tug McGraw IA	2.00	.90
☐ 165	Chris Speier	2.00	.90
☐ 166	Chris Speier IA	2.00	.90
☐ 167	Deron Johnson	1.00	.45
☐ 168	Deron Johnson IA	1.00	.45
☐ 169	Vida Blue	2.00	.90
☐ 170	Vida Blue IA	2.00	.90
☐ 171	Darrell Evans	2.00	.90
☐ 172	Darrell Evans IA	2.00	.90
☐ 173	Clay Kirby	1.00	.45
☐ 174	Clay Kirby IA	1.00	.45
☐ 175	Tom Haller	1.00	.45
☐ 176	Tom Haller IA	1.00	.45
☐ 177	Paul Schaal	1.00	.45
☐ 178	Paul Schaal IA	1.00	.45
☐ 179	Dock Ellis	1.00	.45
☐ 180	Dock Ellis IA	1.00	.45
☐ 181	Ed Kranepool	1.00	.45
☐ 182	Ed Kranepool IA	1.00	.45
☐ 183	Bill Melton	1.00	.45
☐ 184	Bill Melton IA	1.00	.45
☐ 185	Ron Bryant	1.00	.45
☐ 186	Ron Bryant IA	1.00	.45
☐ 187	Gates Brown	1.00	.45
☐ 188	Frank Lucchesi MG	1.00	.45
☐ 189	Gene Tenace	1.50	.70
☐ 190	Dave Giusti	1.00	.45
☐ 191	Jeff Burroughs	2.00	.90
☐ 192	Chicago Cubs	2.00	.90
	Team Card		
☐ 193	Kurt Bevacqua	1.00	.45
☐ 194	Fred Norman	1.00	.45
☐ 195	Orlando Cepeda	2.00	.90
☐ 196	Mel Queen	1.00	.45
☐ 197	Johnny Briggs	1.00	.45
☐ 198	Dodgers Rookies	4.00	1.80
	Charlie Hough		

	Bob O'Brien		
	Mike Strahler		
199	Mike Fiore	1.00	.45
200	Lou Brock	7.00	3.10
201	Phil Roof	1.00	.45
202	Scipio Spinks	1.00	.45
203	Ron Blomberg	1.00	.45
204	Tommy Helms	1.00	.45
205	Dick Drago	1.00	.45
206	Dal Maxvill	1.00	.45
207	Tom Egan	1.00	.45
208	Milt Pappas	2.00	.90
209	Joe Rudi	1.50	.70
210	Denny McLain	1.50	.70
211	Gary Sutherland	1.00	.45
212	Grant Jackson	1.00	.45
213	Angels Rookies	1.00	.45
	Billy Parker		
	Art Kusnyer		
	Tom Silverio		
214	Mike McQueen	1.00	.45
215	Alex Johnson	2.00	.90
216	Joe Niekro	2.00	.90
217	Roger Metzger	1.00	.45
218	Eddie Kasko MG	1.00	.45
219	Rennie Stennett	2.00	.90
220	Jim Perry	2.00	.90
221	NL Playoffs	1.50	.70
	Bucs champs		
222	Brooks Robinson ALCS	3.00	1.35
223	Dave McNally WS	1.75	.80
224	Dave Johnson WS	1.75	.80
	Mark Belanger		
225	Manny Sanguillen WS	1.75	.80
226	Roberto Clemente WS	8.00	3.60
227	Nellie Briles WS	1.75	.80
228	Frank Robinson WS	2.50	1.10
	Manny Sanguillen		
229	Steve Blass WS	1.75	.80
230	World Series Summary	1.75	.80
	(Pirates celebrate)		
231	Casey Cox	1.00	.45
232	Giants Rookies	1.00	.45
	Chris Arnold		
	Jim Barr		
	Dave Rader		
233	Jay Johnstone	2.00	.90
234	Ron Taylor	1.00	.45
235	Merv Rettenmund	1.00	.45
236	Jim McGlothlin	1.00	.45
237	New York Yankees	2.00	.90
	Team Card		
238	Leron Lee	1.00	.45
239	Tom Timmermann	1.00	.45
240	Rich Allen	2.00	.90
241	Rollie Fingers	5.00	2.20
242	Don Mincher	2.00	.90
243	Frank Linzy	1.00	.45
244	Steve Braun	1.00	.45
245	Tommie Agee	1.50	.70
246	Tom Burgmeier	1.00	.45
247	Milt May	1.00	.45
248	Tom Bradley	1.00	.45
249	Harry Walker MG	1.00	.45
250	Boog Powell	2.00	.90
251	Checklist 264-394	6.00	1.20
252	Ken Reynolds	1.00	.45
253	Sandy Alomar	1.50	.70
254	Boots Day	1.00	.45
255	Jim Lonborg	2.00	.90
256	George Foster	2.50	1.10
257	Tigers Rookies	1.00	.45
	Jim Foor		
	Tim Hosley		
	Paul Jata		
258	Randy Hundley	1.50	.70
259	Sparky Lyle	2.00	.90
260	Ralph Garr	2.00	.90
261	Steve Mingori	1.00	.45
262	San Diego Padres	2.00	.90
	Team Card		
263	Felipe Alou	1.50	.70
264	Tommy John	1.50	.70
265	Wes Parker	1.50	.70
266	Bobby Bolin	1.25	.55
267	Dave Concepcion	3.00	1.35
268	A's Rookies	1.25	.55
	Dwain Anderson		
	Chris Floethe		
269	Don Hahn	1.25	.55
270	Jim Palmer	8.00	3.60
271	Ken Rudolph	1.25	.55
272	Mickey Rivers	1.50	.70
273	Bobby Floyd	1.25	.55
274	Al Severinsen	1.25	.55
275	Cesar Tovar	1.25	.55
276	Gene Mauch MG	2.00	.90
277	Elliott Maddox	1.25	.55
278	Dennis Higgins	1.25	.55
279	Larry Brown	1.25	.55
280	Willie McCovey	7.00	3.10
281	Bill Parsons	1.25	.55
282	Houston Astros	2.00	.90
	Team Card		
283	Darrell Brandon	1.25	.55
284	Ike Brown	1.25	.55
285	Gaylord Perry	6.00	2.70
286	Gene Alley	2.00	.90
287	Jim Hardin	1.25	.55
288	Johnny Jeter	1.25	.55
289	Syd O'Brien	1.25	.55
290	Sonny Siebert	1.25	.55
291	Hal McRae	1.50	.70
292	Hal McRae IA	2.00	.90
293	Dan Frisella	1.25	.55
294	Dan Frisella IA	1.25	.55
295	Dick Dietz	1.25	.55
296	Dick Dietz IA	1.25	.55
297	Claude Osteen	2.00	.90
298	Claude Osteen IA	1.25	.55
299	Hank Aaron	40.00	18.00
300	Hank Aaron IA	20.00	9.00
301	George Mitterwald	1.25	.55
302	George Mitterwald IA	1.25	.55
303	Joe Pepitone	1.50	.70
304	Joe Pepitone IA	1.25	.55
305	Ken Boswell	1.25	.55
306	Ken Boswell IA	1.25	.55
307	Steve Renko	1.25	.55
308	Steve Renko IA	1.25	.55
309	Roberto Clemente	50.00	22.00
310	Roberto Clemente IA	25.00	11.00
311	Clay Carroll	1.25	.55
312	Clay Carroll IA	1.25	.55
313	Luis Aparicio	4.00	1.80
314	Luis Aparicio IA	1.75	.80
315	Paul Splittorff	1.25	.55
316	Cardinals Rookies	2.00	.90
	Jim Bibby		
	Jorge Roque		
	Santiago Guzman		
317	Rich Hand	1.25	.55
318	Sonny Jackson	1.25	.55
319	Aurelio Rodriguez	1.25	.55
320	Steve Blass	2.00	.90
321	Joe Lahoud	1.25	.55
322	Jose Pena	1.25	.55
323	Earl Weaver MG	1.50	.70
324	Mike Ryan	1.25	.55
325	Mel Stottlemyre	1.50	.70
326	Pat Kelly	1.25	.55
327	Steve Stone	1.50	.70
328	Boston Red Sox	2.00	.90
	Team Card		
329	Roy Foster	1.25	.55
330	Jim Hunter	4.00	1.80
331	Stan Swanson	1.25	.55
332	Buck Martinez	1.25	.55
333	Steve Barber	1.25	.55
334	Rangers Rookies	1.25	.55
	Bill Fahey		
	Jim Mason		
	Tom Ragland		
335	Bill Hands	1.25	.55
336	Marty Martinez	1.25	.55
337	Mike Kilkenny	1.25	.55
338	Bob Grich	1.50	.70
339	Ron Cook	1.25	.55
340	Roy White	1.50	.70
341	Joe Torre KP	1.25	.55
342	Wilbur Wood KP	1.25	.55
343	Willie Stargell KP	1.50	.70
344	Dave McNally KP	1.25	.55
345	Rick Wise KP	1.25	.55
346	Jim Fregosi KP	1.25	.55
347	Tom Seaver KP	3.00	1.35
348	Sal Bando KP	1.25	.55
349	Al Fitzmorris	1.25	.55
350	Frank Howard	1.50	.70
351	Braves Rookies	2.00	.90
	Tom House		
	Rick Kester		
	Jimmy Britton		
352	Dave LaRoche	1.25	.55
353	Art Shamsky	1.25	.55
354	Tom Murphy	1.25	.55
355	Bob Watson	2.00	.90
356	Gerry Moses	1.25	.55
357	Woody Fryman	1.25	.55
358	Sparky Anderson MG	3.00	1.35
359	Don Pavletich	1.25	.55
360	Dave Roberts	1.25	.55
361	Mike Andrews	1.25	.55
362	New York Mets	2.00	.90
	Team Card		
363	Ron Klimkowski	1.25	.55
364	Johnny Callison	2.00	.90
365	Dick Bosman	1.25	.55
366	Jimmy Rosario	1.25	.55
367	Ron Perranoski	2.00	.90
368	Danny Thompson	1.25	.55
369	Jim Lefebvre	2.00	.90
370	Don Buford	1.25	.55
371	Denny Lemaster	1.25	.55
372	Royals Rookies	1.25	.55
	Lance Clemons		
	Monty Montgomery		
373	John Mayberry	2.00	.90
374	Jack Heidemann	1.25	.55
375	Reggie Cleveland	1.25	.55
376	Andy Kosco	1.25	.55
377	Terry Harmon	1.25	.55
378	Checklist 395-525	4.00	.80
379	Ken Berry	1.25	.55
380	Earl Williams	1.25	.55
381	Chicago White Sox	2.00	.90
	Team Card		
382	Joe Gibbon	1.25	.55
383	Brant Alyea	1.25	.55
384	Dave Campbell	2.00	.90
385	Mickey Stanley	2.00	.90
386	Jim Colborn	1.25	.55
387	Horace Clarke	2.00	.90
388	Charlie Williams	1.25	.55
389	Bill Rigney MG	1.25	.55
390	Willie Davis	1.50	.70
391	Ken Sanders	1.25	.55
392	Pirates Rookies	2.00	.90
	Fred Cambria		
	Richie Zisk		
393	Curt Motton	1.25	.55
394	Ken Forsch	2.00	.90
395	Matty Alou	1.75	.80
396	Paul Lindblad	1.50	.70
397	Philadelphia Phillies	2.00	.90
	Team Card		
398	Larry Hisle	2.00	.90
399	Milt Wilcox	1.50	.70
400	Tony Oliva	1.75	.80
401	Jim Nash	1.50	.70
402	Bobby Heise	1.50	.70
403	John Cumberland	1.50	.70
404	Jeff Torborg	2.00	.90
405	Ron Fairly	2.00	.90
406	George Hendrick	1.75	.80
407	Chuck Taylor	1.00	.45
408	Jim Northrup	2.00	.90
409	Frank Baker	1.00	.45
410	Ferguson Jenkins	6.00	2.70
411	Bob Montgomery	1.00	.45
412	Dick Kelley	1.00	.45
413	White Sox Rookies	1.00	.45
	Don Eddy		
	Dave Lemonds		
414	Bob Miller	1.00	.45
415	Cookie Rojas	2.00	.90
416	Johnny Edwards	1.00	.45
417	Tom Hall	1.00	.45

□	418	Tom Shopay	1.00	.45
□	419	Jim Spencer	1.00	.45
□	420	Steve Carlton	18.00	8.00
□	421	Ellie Rodriguez	1.00	.45
□	422	Ray Lamb	1.00	.45
□	423	Oscar Gamble	2.00	.90
□	424	Bill Gogolewski	1.00	.45
□	425	Ken Singleton	2.00	.90
□	426	Ken Singleton IA	1.00	.45
□	427	Tito Fuentes	1.00	.45
□	428	Tito Fuentes IA	1.00	.45
□	429	Bob Robertson	1.00	.45
□	430	Bob Robertson IA	1.00	.45
□	431	Clarence Gaston	1.75	.80
□	432	Clarence Gaston IA	2.00	.90
□	433	Johnny Bench	25.00	11.00
□	434	Johnny Bench IA	14.00	6.25
□	435	Reggie Jackson	25.00	11.00
□	436	Reggie Jackson IA.	14.00	6.25
□	437	Maury Wills	1.75	.80
□	438	Maury Wills IA	2.00	.90
□	439	Billy Williams	6.00	2.70
□	440	Billy Williams IA	3.00	1.35
□	441	Thurman Munson	15.00	6.75
□	442	Thurman Munson IA	8.00	3.60
□	443	Ken Henderson	1.50	.70
□	444	Ken Henderson IA	1.50	.70
□	445	Tom Seaver	30.00	13.50
□	446	Tom Seaver IA	15.00	6.75
□	447	Willie Stargell	8.00	3.60
□	448	Willie Stargell IA	3.00	1.35
□	449	Bob Lemon MG	1.75	.80
□	450	Mickey Lolich	1.75	.80
□	451	Tony LaRussa	3.00	1.35
□	452	Ed Herrmann	1.50	.70
□	453	Barry Lersch	1.50	.70
□	454	Oakland A's	2.00	.90
		Team Card		
□	455	Tommy Harper	2.00	.90
□	456	Mark Belanger	2.00	.90
□	457	Padres Rookies	1.50	.70
		Darcy Fast		
		Derrel Thomas		
		Mike Ivie		
□	458	Aurelio Monteagudo	1.50	.70
□	459	Rick Renick	1.50	.70
□	460	Al Downing	1.50	.70
□	461	Tim Cullen	1.50	.70
□	462	Rickey Clark	1.50	.70
□	463	Bernie Carbo	1.50	.70
□	464	Jim Roland	1.50	.70
□	465	Gil Hodges MG	4.00	1.80
□	466	Norm Miller	1.50	.70
□	467	Steve Kline	1.50	.70
□	468	Richie Scheinblum	1.50	.70
□	469	Ron Herbel	1.50	.70
□	470	Ray Fosse	1.50	.70
□	471	Luke Walker	1.50	.70
□	472	Phil Gagliano	1.50	.70
□	473	Dan McGinn	1.50	.70
□	474	Orioles Rookies	15.00	6.75
		Don Baylor		
		Roric Harrison		
		Johnny Oates		
□	475	Gary Nolan	2.00	.90
□	476	Lee Richard	1.50	.70
□	477	Tom Phoebus	1.50	.70
□	478	Checklist 526-656	6.00	1.20
□	479	Don Shaw	1.50	.70
□	480	Lee May	2.00	.90
□	481	Billy Conigliaro	1.75	.80
□	482	Joe Hoerner	1.50	.70
□	483	Ken Suarez	1.50	.70
□	484	Lum Harris MG	1.50	.70
□	485	Phil Regan	2.00	.90
□	486	John Lowenstein	1.50	.70
□	487	Detroit Tigers	2.00	.90
		Team Card		
□	488	Mike Nagy	1.50	.70
□	489	Expos Rookies	1.50	.70
		Terry Humphrey		
		Keith Lampard		
□	490	Dave McNally	2.00	.90
□	491	Lou Piniella KP	2.00	.90
□	492	Mel Stottlemyre KP	1.50	.90
□	493	Bob Bailey KP	2.00	.90
□	494	Willie Horton KP	2.00	.90
□	495	Bill Melton KP	2.00	.90
□	496	Bud Harrelson KP	2.00	.90
□	497	Jim Perry KP	2.00	.90
□	498	Brooks Robinson KP	3.00	1.35
□	499	Vicente Romo	1.50	.70
□	500	Joe Torre	1.75	.80
□	501	Pete Hamm	1.50	.70
□	502	Jackie Hernandez	1.50	.70
□	503	Gary Peters	1.50	.70
□	504	Ed Spiezio	1.50	.70
□	505	Mike Marshall	1.75	.80
□	506	Indians Rookies	1.50	.70
		Terry Ley		
		Jim Moyer		
		Dick Tidrow		
□	507	Fred Gladding	1.50	.70
□	508	Elrod Hendricks	1.50	.70
□	509	Don McMahon	1.50	.70
□	510	Ted Williams MG	10.00	4.50
□	511	Tony Taylor	2.00	.90
□	512	Paul Popovich	1.50	.70
□	513	Lindy McDaniel	2.00	.90
□	514	Ted Sizemore	1.50	.70
□	515	Bert Blyleven	3.00	1.35
□	516	Oscar Brown	1.00	.45
□	517	Ken Brett	1.00	.45
□	518	Wayne Garrett	1.00	.45
□	519	Ted Abernathy	1.00	.45
□	520	Larry Bowa	1.75	.80
□	521	Alan Foster	1.00	.45
□	522	Los Angeles Dodgers	3.00	1.35
		Team Card		
□	523	Chuck Dobson	1.00	.45
□	524	Reds Rookies	1.00	.45
		Ed Armbrister		
		Mel Behney		
□	525	Carlos May	2.00	.90
□	526	Bob Bailey	6.00	2.70
□	527	Dave Leonhard	4.00	1.80
□	528	Ron Stone	4.00	1.80
□	529	Dave Nelson	6.00	2.70
□	530	Don Sutton	7.00	3.10
□	531	Freddie Patek	6.00	2.70
□	532	Fred Kendall	4.00	1.80
□	533	Ralph Houk MG	4.50	2.00
□	534	Jim Hickman	6.00	2.70
□	535	Ed Brinkman	4.00	1.80
□	536	Doug Rader	6.00	2.70
□	537	Bob Locker	4.00	1.80
□	538	Charlie Sands	4.00	1.80
□	539	Terry Forster	4.50	2.00
□	540	Felix Millan	4.00	1.80
□	541	Roger Repoz	4.00	1.80
□	542	Jack Billingham	4.00	1.80
□	543	Duane Josephson	4.00	1.80
□	544	Ted Martinez	4.00	1.80
□	545	Wayne Granger	4.00	1.80
□	546	Joe Hague	4.00	1.80
□	547	Cleveland Indians	8.00	3.60
		Team Card		
□	548	Frank Reberger	4.00	1.80
□	549	Dave May	4.00	1.80
□	550	Brooks Robinson	25.00	11.00
□	551	Ollie Brown	4.00	1.80
□	552	Ollie Brown IA	4.00	1.80
□	553	Wilbur Wood	4.50	2.00
□	554	Wilbur Wood IA	4.00	1.80
□	555	Ron Santo	4.50	2.00
□	556	Ron Santo IA	6.00	2.70
□	557	John Odom	4.00	1.80
□	558	John Odom IA	4.00	1.80
□	559	Pete Rose	40.00	18.00
□	560	Pete Rose IA	20.00	9.00
□	561	Leo Cardenas	4.00	1.80
□	562	Leo Cardenas IA	4.00	1.80
□	563	Ray Sadecki	4.00	1.80
□	564	Ray Sadecki IA	4.00	1.80
□	565	Reggie Smith	4.50	2.00
□	566	Reggie Smith IA	4.00	1.80
□	567	Juan Marichal	12.00	5.50
□	568	Juan Marichal IA	6.00	2.70
□	569	Ed Kirkpatrick	4.00	1.80
□	570	Ed Kirkpatrick IA	4.00	1.80
□	571	Nate Colbert	4.00	1.80
□	572	Nate Colbert IA	4.00	1.80
□	573	Fritz Peterson	4.00	1.80
□	574	Fritz Peterson IA	4.00	1.80
□	575	Al Oliver	4.50	2.00
□	576	Leo Durocher MG	5.00	2.20
□	577	Mike Paul	4.00	1.80
□	578	Billy Grabarkewitz	4.00	1.80
□	579	Doyle Alexander	4.50	2.00
□	580	Lou Piniella	5.00	2.20
□	581	Wade Blasingame	4.00	1.80
□	582	Montreal Expos	8.00	3.60
		Team Card		
□	583	Darold Knowles	4.00	1.80
□	584	Jerry McNertney	4.00	1.80
□	585	George Scott	4.50	2.00
□	586	Denis Menke	4.00	1.80
□	587	Billy Wilson	4.00	1.80
□	588	Jim Holt	4.00	1.80
□	589	Hal Lanier	4.00	1.80
□	590	Graig Nettles	4.50	2.00
□	591	Paul Casanova	4.00	1.80
□	592	Lew Krausse	4.00	1.80
□	593	Rich Morales	4.00	1.80
□	594	Jim Beauchamp	4.00	1.80
□	595	Nolan Ryan	225.00	100.00
□	596	Manny Mota	4.50	2.00
□	597	Jim Magnuson	4.00	1.80
□	598	Hal King	6.00	2.70
□	599	Billy Champion	4.00	1.80
□	600	Al Kaline	25.00	11.00
□	601	George Stone	4.00	1.80
□	602	Dave Bristol MG	4.00	1.80
□	603	Jim Ray	4.00	1.80
□	604A	Checklist 657-787	12.00	2.40
		(Copyright on back bottom right)		
□	604B	Checklist 657-787	12.00	2.40
		(Copyright on back bottom left)		
□	605	Nelson Briles	6.00	2.70
□	606	Luis Melendez	4.00	1.80
□	607	Frank Duffy	4.00	1.80
□	608	Mike Corkins	4.00	1.80
□	609	Tom Grieve	6.00	2.70
□	610	Bill Stoneman	6.00	2.70
□	611	Rich Reese	4.00	1.80
□	612	Joe Decker	4.00	1.80
□	613	Mike Ferraro	4.00	1.80
□	614	Ted Uhlaender	4.00	1.80
□	615	Steve Hargan	4.00	1.80
□	616	Joe Ferguson	4.00	1.80
□	617	Kansas City Royals	8.00	3.60
		Team Card		
□	618	Rich Robertson	4.00	1.80
□	619	Rich McKinney	4.00	1.80
□	620	Phil Niekro	10.00	4.50
□	621	Commissioners Award	5.00	2.20
□	622	MVP Award	5.00	2.20
□	623	Cy Young Award	5.00	2.20
□	624	Minor League Player of the Year	5.00	2.20
□	625	Rookie of the Year	5.00	2.20
□	626	Babe Ruth Award	5.00	2.20
□	627	Moe Drabowsky	4.00	1.80
□	628	Terry Crowley	4.00	1.80
□	629	Paul Doyle	4.00	1.80
□	630	Rich Hebner	6.00	2.70
□	631	John Strohmayer	4.00	1.80
□	632	Mike Hegan	4.00	1.80
□	633	Jack Hiatt	4.00	1.80
□	634	Dick Woodson	4.00	1.80
□	635	Don Money	6.00	2.70
□	636	Bill Lee	6.00	2.70
□	637	Preston Gomez MG	4.00	1.80
□	638	Ken Wright	4.00	1.80
□	639	J.C. Martin	4.00	1.80
□	640	Joe Coleman	4.00	1.80
□	641	Mike Lum	4.00	1.80
□	642	Dennis Riddleberger	4.00	1.80
□	643	Russ Gibson	4.00	1.80
□	644	Bernie Allen	4.00	1.80
□	645	Jim Maloney	6.00	2.70
□	646	Chico Salmon	4.00	1.80
□	647	Bob Moose	4.00	1.80
□	648	Jim Lyttle	4.00	1.80
□	649	Pete Richert	4.00	1.80
□	650	Sal Bando	4.50	2.00

☐ 651	Cincinnati Reds Team Card	7.00	3.10		
☐ 652	Marcelino Lopez	4.00	1.80		
☐ 653	Jim Fairey	4.00	1.80		
☐ 654	Horacio Pina	6.00	2.70		
☐ 655	Jerry Grote	4.00	1.80		
☐ 656	Rudy May	4.00	1.80		
☐ 657	Bobby Wine	12.00	5.50		
☐ 658	Steve Dunning	12.00	5.50		
☐ 659	Bob Aspromonte	12.00	5.50		
☐ 660	Paul Blair	15.00	6.75		
☐ 661	Bill Virdon MG	13.00	5.75		
☐ 662	Stan Bahnsen	12.00	5.50		
☐ 663	Fran Healy	15.00	6.75		
☐ 664	Bobby Knoop	12.00	5.50		
☐ 665	Chris Short	12.00	5.50		
☐ 666	Hector Torres	12.00	5.50		
☐ 667	Ray Newman	12.00	5.50		
☐ 668	Texas Rangers Team Card	30.00	13.50		
☐ 669	Willie Crawford	12.00	5.50		
☐ 670	Ken Holtzman	15.00	6.75		
☐ 671	Donn Clendenon	15.00	6.75		
☐ 672	Archie Reynolds	12.00	5.50		
☐ 673	Dave Marshall	12.00	5.50		
☐ 674	John Kennedy	12.00	5.50		
☐ 675	Pat Jarvis	12.00	5.50		
☐ 676	Danny Cater	12.00	5.50		
☐ 677	Ivan Murrell	12.00	5.50		
☐ 678	Steve Luebber	12.00	5.50		
☐ 679	Astros Rookies Bob Fenwick Bob Stinson	12.00	5.50		
☐ 680	Dave Johnson	15.00	6.75		
☐ 681	Bobby Pfeil	12.00	5.50		
☐ 682	Mike McCormick	15.00	6.75		
☐ 683	Steve Hovley	12.00	5.50		
☐ 684	Hal Breeden	12.00	5.50		
☐ 685	Joel Horlen	12.00	5.50		
☐ 686	Steve Garvey	40.00	18.00		
☐ 687	Del Unser	12.00	5.50		
☐ 688	St. Louis Cardinals Team Card	20.00	9.00		
☐ 689	Eddie Fisher	12.00	5.50		
☐ 690	Willie Montanez	15.00	6.75		
☐ 691	Curt Blefary	12.00	5.50		
☐ 692	Curt Blefary IA	12.00	5.50		
☐ 693	Alan Gallagher	12.00	5.50		
☐ 694	Alan Gallagher IA	12.00	5.50		
☐ 695	Rod Carew	75.00	34.00		
☐ 696	Rod Carew IA	35.00	16.00		
☐ 697	Jerry Koosman	15.00	6.75		
☐ 698	Jerry Koosman IA	13.00	5.75		
☐ 699	Bobby Murcer	15.00	6.75		
☐ 700	Bobby Murcer IA	13.00	5.75		
☐ 701	Jose Pagan	12.00	5.50		
☐ 702	Jose Pagan IA	12.00	5.50		
☐ 703	Doug Griffin	12.00	5.50		
☐ 704	Doug Griffin IA	12.00	5.50		
☐ 705	Pat Corrales	15.00	6.75		
☐ 706	Pat Corrales IA	12.00	5.50		
☐ 707	Tim Foli	12.00	5.50		
☐ 708	Tim Foli IA	12.00	5.50		
☐ 709	Jim Kaat	16.00	7.25		
☐ 710	Jim Kaat IA	14.00	6.25		
☐ 711	Bobby Bonds	20.00	9.00		
☐ 712	Bobby Bonds IA	14.00	6.25		
☐ 713	Gene Michael	12.00	5.50		
☐ 714	Gene Michael IA	12.00	5.50		
☐ 715	Mike Epstein	12.00	5.50		
☐ 716	Jesus Alou	12.00	5.50		
☐ 717	Bruce Dal Canton	12.00	5.50		
☐ 718	Del Rice MG	12.00	5.50		
☐ 719	Cesar Geronimo	12.00	5.50		
☐ 720	Sam McDowell	15.00	6.75		
☐ 721	Eddie Leon	12.00	5.50		
☐ 722	Bill Sudakis	12.00	5.50		
☐ 723	Al Santorini	12.00	5.50		
☐ 724	AL Rookie Pitchers John Curtis Rich Hinton Mickey Scott	12.00	5.50		
☐ 725	Dick McAuliffe	15.00	6.75		
☐ 726	Dick Selma	12.00	5.50		
☐ 727	Jose Laboy	12.00	5.50		
☐ 728	Gail Hopkins	12.00	5.50		
☐ 729	Bob Veale	15.00	6.75		
☐ 730	Rick Monday	13.00	5.75		
☐ 731	Baltimore Orioles Team Card	20.00	9.00		
☐ 732	George Culver	12.00	5.50		
☐ 733	Jim Ray Hart	15.00	6.75		
☐ 734	Bob Burda	12.00	5.50		
☐ 735	Diego Segui	12.00	5.50		
☐ 736	Bill Russell	13.00	5.75		
☐ 737	Len Randle	15.00	6.75		
☐ 738	Jim Merritt	12.00	5.50		
☐ 739	Don Mason	12.00	5.50		
☐ 740	Rico Carty	15.00	6.75		
☐ 741	Rookie First Basemen Tom Hutton John Milner Rick Miller	13.00	5.75		
☐ 742	Jim Rooker	12.00	5.50		
☐ 743	Cesar Gutierrez	12.00	5.50		
☐ 744	Jim Slaton	12.00	5.50		
☐ 745	Julian Javier	15.00	6.75		
☐ 746	Lowell Palmer	12.00	5.50		
☐ 747	Jim Stewart	12.00	5.50		
☐ 748	Phil Hennigan	12.00	5.50		
☐ 749	Walter Alston MG	14.00	6.25		
☐ 750	Willie Horton	15.00	6.75		
☐ 751	Steve Carlton TR	50.00	22.00		
☐ 752	Joe Morgan TR	45.00	20.00		
☐ 753	Denny McLain TR	20.00	9.00		
☐ 754	Frank Robinson TR	45.00	20.00		
☐ 755	Jim Fregosi TR	13.00	5.75		
☐ 756	Rick Wise TR	15.00	6.75		
☐ 757	Jose Cardenal TR	15.00	6.75		
☐ 758	Gil Garrido	12.00	5.50		
☐ 759	Chris Cannizzaro	12.00	5.50		
☐ 760	Bill Mazeroski	18.00	8.00		
☐ 761	Rookie Outfielders Ben Oglivie Ron Cey Bernie Williams	25.00	11.00		
☐ 762	Wayne Simpson	12.00	5.50		
☐ 763	Ron Hansen	12.00	5.50		
☐ 764	Dusty Baker	20.00	9.00		
☐ 765	Ken McMullen	12.00	5.50		
☐ 766	Steve Hamilton	12.00	5.50		
☐ 767	Tom McCraw	15.00	6.75		
☐ 768	Denny Doyle	12.00	5.50		
☐ 769	Jack Aker	12.00	5.50		
☐ 770	Jim Wynn	13.00	5.75		
☐ 771	San Francisco Giants Team Card	20.00	9.00		
☐ 772	Ken Tatum	12.00	5.50		
☐ 773	Ron Brand	12.00	5.50		
☐ 774	Luis Alvarado	12.00	5.50		
☐ 775	Jerry Reuss	15.00	6.75		
☐ 776	Bill Voss	12.00	5.50		
☐ 777	Hoyt Wilhelm	25.00	11.00		
☐ 778	Twins Rookies Vic Albury Rick Dempsey Jim Strickland	18.00	8.00		
☐ 779	Tony Cloninger	12.00	5.50		
☐ 780	Dick Green	12.00	5.50		
☐ 781	Jim McAndrew	12.00	5.50		
☐ 782	Larry Stahl	12.00	5.50		
☐ 783	Les Cain	12.00	5.50		
☐ 784	Ken Aspromonte	12.00	5.50		
☐ 785	Vic Davalillo	12.00	5.50		
☐ 786	Chuck Brinkman	12.00	5.50		
☐ 787	Ron Reed	16.00	5.50		

AL KALINE
DETROIT TIGERS OUTFIELD

eliminating the "high number" factor. The set features team leader cards with small individual pictures of the coaching staff members and a larger picture of the manager. The "background" variations below with respect to these leader cards are subtle and are best understood after a side-by-side comparison of the two varieties. An "All-Time Leaders" series (471-478) appeared for the first time in this set. Kid Pictures appeared again for the second year in a row (341-346). Other topical subsets within the set included League Leaders (61-68), Playoffs cards (201-202), World Series cards (203-210), and Rookie Prospects (601-616). For the fourth and final time, cards were issued in ten-card dime packs, cards were also released in 54-card rack packs. The key Rookie Cards in this set are all in the Rookie Prospect series: Bob Boone, Dwight Evans, and Mike Schmidt.

1973 Topps

The cards in this 660-card set measure 2 1/2" by 3 1/2". The 1973 Topps set marked the last year in which Topps marketed baseball cards in consecutive series. The last series (529-660) is more difficult to obtain. In some parts of the country, however, all five series were distributed together. Beginning in 1974, all Topps cards were printed at the same time, thus

	NRMT	VG-E
COMPLETE SET (660)	750.00	350.00
COMMON CARD (1-264)	.50	.23
COMMON CARD (265-396)	.75	.35
MINOR STARS 1-396	1.25	.55
SEMISTARS 1-396	2.50	1.10
UNLISTED STARS 1-396	4.00	1.80
COMMON CARD (397-528)	1.25	.55
MINOR STARS 397-528	2.00	.90
SEMISTARS 397-528	3.00	1.35
UNLISTED STARS 397-528	5.00	2.20
COMMON CARD (529-660)	3.50	1.55
MINOR STARS 529-660	5.00	2.20
SEMISTARS 529-660	8.00	3.60
BLUE TEAM CL !	8.00	2.40
CARDS PRICED IN NM CONDITION !		

☐ 1	All-Time HR Leaders Babe Ruth 714 Hank Aaron 673 Willie Mays 654	40.00	11.50
☐ 2	Rich Hebner	1.25	.55
☐ 3	Jim Lonborg	1.25	.55
☐ 4	John Milner	.50	.23
☐ 5	Ed Brinkman	.50	.23
☐ 6	Mac Scarce	.50	.23
☐ 7	Texas Rangers Team Card	1.25	.55
☐ 8	Tom Hall	.50	.23
☐ 9	Johnny Oates	.50	.23
☐ 10	Don Sutton	1.00	.45
☐ 11	Chris Chambliss	.75	.35
☐ 12A	Padres Leaders Don Zimmer MG Dave Garcia CO Johnny Podres CO Bob Skinner CO	1.25	.55

Whitey Wietelmann CO
(Padres no right ear)

☐ 12B Padres Leaders	2.50	1.10

(Padres has right ear)

☐ 13 George Hendrick	1.25	.55
☐ 14 Sonny Siebert	.50	.23
☐ 15 Ralph Garr	1.25	.55
☐ 16 Steve Braun	.50	.23
☐ 17 Fred Gladding	.50	.23
☐ 18 Leroy Stanton	.50	.23
☐ 19 Tim Foli	.50	.23
☐ 20 Stan Bahnsen	.50	.23
☐ 21 Randy Hundley	1.25	.55
☐ 22 Ted Abernathy	.50	.23
☐ 23 Dave Kingman	1.00	.45
☐ 24 Al Santorini	.50	.23
☐ 25 Roy White	.75	.35
☐ 26 Pittsburgh Pirates	1.25	.55

Team Card

☐ 27 Bill Gogolewski	.50	.23
☐ 28 Hal McRae	1.00	.45
☐ 29 Tony Taylor	1.25	.55
☐ 30 Tug McGraw	.75	.35
☐ 31 Buddy Bell	3.00	1.35
☐ 32 Fred Norman	.50	.23
☐ 33 Jim Breazeale	.50	.23
☐ 34 Pat Dobson	.50	.23
☐ 35 Willie Davis	.75	.35
☐ 36 Steve Barber	.50	.23
☐ 37 Bill Robinson	.50	.55
☐ 38 Mike Epstein	.50	.23
☐ 39 Dave Roberts	.50	.23
☐ 40 Reggie Smith	.75	.35
☐ 41 Tom Walker	.50	.23
☐ 42 Mike Andrews	.50	.23
☐ 43 Randy Moffitt	.50	.23
☐ 44 Rick Monday	.75	.35
☐ 45 Ellie Rodriguez UER	.50	.23

(Photo actually John Felske)

☐ 46 Lindy McDaniel	1.25	.55
☐ 47 Luis Melendez	.50	.23
☐ 48 Paul Splittorff	.50	.23
☐ 49A Twins Leaders	1.25	.55

Frank Quilici MG
Vern Morgan CO
Bob Rodgers CO
Ralph Rowe CO
Al Worthington CO
(Solid backgrounds)

☐ 49B Twins Leaders	2.50	1.10

(Natural backgrounds)

☐ 50 Roberto Clemente	60.00	27.00
☐ 51 Chuck Seelbach	.50	.23
☐ 52 Denis Menke	.50	.23
☐ 53 Steve Dunning	.50	.23
☐ 54 Checklist 1-132	4.00	.80
☐ 55 Jon Matlack	1.25	.55
☐ 56 Merv Rettenmund	.50	.23
☐ 57 Derrel Thomas	.50	.23
☐ 58 Mike Paul	.50	.23
☐ 59 Steve Yeager	1.25	.55
☐ 60 Ken Holtzman	1.25	.55
☐ 61 Batting Leaders	3.00	1.35

Billy Williams
Rod Carew

☐ 62 Home Run Leaders	2.50	1.10

Johnny Bench
Dick Allen

☐ 63 RBI Leaders	2.50	1.10

Johnny Bench
Dick Allen

☐ 64 Stolen Base Leaders	2.00	.90

Lou Brock
Bert Campaneris

☐ 65 ERA Leaders	2.00	.90

Steve Carlton
Luis Tiant

☐ 66 Victory Leaders	2.00	.90

Steve Carlton
Gaylord Perry
Wilbur Wood

☐ 67 Strikeout Leaders	30.00	13.50

Steve Carlton
Nolan Ryan

☐ 68 Leading Firemen	1.25	.55

Clay Carroll
Sparky Lyle

☐ 69 Phil Gagliano	.50	.23
☐ 70 Milt Pappas	1.25	.55
☐ 71 Johnny Briggs	.50	.23
☐ 72 Ron Reed	.50	.23
☐ 73 Ed Herrmann	.50	.23
☐ 74 Billy Champion	.50	.23
☐ 75 Vada Pinson	1.00	.45
☐ 76 Doug Rader	.50	.23
☐ 77 Mike Torrez	1.25	.55
☐ 78 Richie Scheinblum	.50	.23
☐ 79 Jim Willoughby	.50	.23
☐ 80 Tony Oliva UER	1.00	.45

(Minnesota on front)

☐ 81A Cubs Leaders	1.50	.70

Whitey Lockman MG
Hank Aguirre CO
Ernie Banks CO
Larry Jansen CO
Pete Reiser CO
(Solid backgrounds)

☐ 81B Cubs Leaders	2.00	.90

(Natural backgrounds)

☐ 82 Fritz Peterson	.50	.23
☐ 83 Leron Lee	.50	.23
☐ 84 Rollie Fingers	5.00	2.20
☐ 85 Ted Simmons	1.00	.45
☐ 86 Tom McCraw	.50	.23
☐ 87 Ken Boswell	.50	.23
☐ 88 Mickey Stanley	1.25	.55
☐ 89 Jack Billingham	.50	.23
☐ 90 Brooks Robinson	7.00	3.10
☐ 91 Los Angeles Dodgers	1.25	.55

Team Card

☐ 92 Jerry Bell	.50	.23
☐ 93 Jesus Alou	.50	.23
☐ 94 Dick Billings	.50	.23
☐ 95 Steve Blass	1.25	.55
☐ 96 Doug Griffin	.50	.23
☐ 97 Willie Montanez	1.25	.55
☐ 98 Dick Woodson	.50	.23
☐ 99 Carl Taylor	.50	.23
☐ 100 Hank Aaron	25.00	11.00
☐ 101 Ken Henderson	.50	.23
☐ 102 Rudy May	.50	.23
☐ 103 Celerino Sanchez	.50	.23
☐ 104 Reggie Cleveland	.50	.23
☐ 105 Carlos May	.50	.23
☐ 106 Terry Humphrey	.50	.23
☐ 107 Phil Hennigan	.50	.23
☐ 108 Bill Russell	.75	.35
☐ 109 Doyle Alexander	1.25	.55
☐ 110 Bob Watson	1.25	.55
☐ 111 Dave Nelson	.50	.23
☐ 112 Gary Ross	.50	.23
☐ 113 Jerry Grote	.50	.23
☐ 114 Lynn McGlothen	.50	.23
☐ 115 Ron Santo	1.00	.45
☐ 116A Yankees Leaders	1.25	.55

Ralph Houk MG
Jim Hegan CO
Elston Howard CO
Dick Howser CO
(Solid backgrounds)

☐ 116B Yankees Leaders	2.50	1.10

(Natural backgrounds)

☐ 117 Ramon Hernandez	.50	.23
☐ 118 John Mayberry	1.25	.55
☐ 119 Larry Bowa	.75	.35
☐ 120 Joe Coleman	.50	.23
☐ 121 Dave Rader	.50	.23
☐ 122 Jim Strickland	.50	.23
☐ 123 Sandy Alomar	1.25	.55
☐ 124 Jim Hardin	.50	.23
☐ 125 Ron Fairly	1.25	.55
☐ 126 Jim Brewer	.50	.23
☐ 127 Milwaukee Brewers	1.25	.55

Team Card

☐ 128 Ted Sizemore	.50	.23
☐ 129 Terry Forster	1.25	.55
☐ 130 Pete Rose	15.00	6.75
☐ 131A Red Sox Leaders	1.25	.55

Eddie Kasko MG
Doug Camilli CO

Don Lenhardt CO
Eddie Popowski CO
(No right ear)
Lee Stange CO

☐ 131B Red Sox Leaders	2.50	1.10

(Popowski has right ear showing)

☐ 132 Matty Alou	.75	.35
☐ 133 Dave Roberts	.50	.23
☐ 134 Milt Wilcox	.50	.23
☐ 135 Lee May UER	1.25	.55

(Career average .000)

☐ 136A Orioles Leaders	2.00	.90

Earl Weaver MG
George Bamberger CO
Jim Frey CO
Billy Hunter CO
George Staller CO
(Orange backgrounds)

☐ 136B Orioles Leaders	3.00	1.35

(Dark pale backgrounds)

☐ 137 Jim Beauchamp	.50	.23
☐ 138 Horacio Pina	.50	.23
☐ 139 Carmen Fanzone	.50	.23
☐ 140 Lou Piniella	1.00	.45
☐ 141 Bruce Kison	.50	.23
☐ 142 Thurman Munson	6.00	2.70
☐ 143 John Curtis	.50	.23
☐ 144 Marty Perez	.50	.23
☐ 145 Bobby Bonds	1.00	.45
☐ 146 Woodie Fryman	.50	.23
☐ 147 Mike Anderson	.50	.23
☐ 148 Dave Goltz	.50	.23
☐ 149 Ron Hunt	.50	.23
☐ 150 Wilbur Wood	1.25	.55
☐ 151 Wes Parker	1.25	.55
☐ 152 Dave May	.50	.23
☐ 153 Al Hrabosky	1.25	.55
☐ 154 Jeff Torborg	1.25	.55
☐ 155 Sal Bando	1.25	.55
☐ 156 Cesar Geronimo	.50	.23
☐ 157 Denny Riddleberger	.50	.23
☐ 158 Houston Astros	1.25	.55

Team Card

☐ 159 Clarence Gaston	1.00	.45
☐ 160 Jim Palmer	7.00	3.10
☐ 161 Ted Martinez	.50	.23
☐ 162 Pete Broberg	.50	.23
☐ 163 Vic Davalillo	.50	.23
☐ 164 Monty Montgomery	.50	.23
☐ 165 Luis Aparicio	3.00	1.35
☐ 166 Terry Harmon	.50	.23
☐ 167 Steve Stone	1.25	.55
☐ 168 Jim Northrup	1.25	.55
☐ 169 Ron Schueler	.50	.23
☐ 170 Harmon Killebrew	5.00	2.20
☐ 171 Bernie Carbo	.50	.23
☐ 172 Steve Kline	.50	.23
☐ 173 Hal Breeden	.50	.23
☐ 174 Rich Gossage	6.00	2.70
☐ 175 Frank Robinson	7.00	3.10
☐ 176 Chuck Taylor	.50	.23
☐ 177 Bill Plummer	.50	.23
☐ 178 Don Rose	.50	.23
☐ 179A A's Leaders	1.25	.55

Dick Williams MG
Jerry Adair CO
Vern Hoscheit CO
Irv Noren CO
Wes Stock CO
(Hoscheit left ear showing)

☐ 179B A's Leaders	2.50	1.10

(Hoscheit left ear not showing)

☐ 180 Ferguson Jenkins	5.00	2.20
☐ 181 Jack Brohamer	.50	.23
☐ 182 Mike Caldwell	1.25	.55
☐ 183 Don Buford	.50	.23
☐ 184 Jerry Koosman	1.00	.45
☐ 185 Jim Wynn	.75	.35
☐ 186 Bill Fahey	.50	.23
☐ 187 Luke Walker	.50	.23
☐ 188 Cookie Rojas	1.25	.55
☐ 189 Greg Luzinski	1.00	.45

190 Bob Gibson	7.00	3.10
191 Detroit Tigers	1.25	.55
Team Card		
192 Pat Jarvis	.50	.23
193 Carlton Fisk	7.00	3.10
194 Jorge Orta	.50	.23
195 Clay Carroll	.50	.23
196 Ken McMullen	.50	.23
197 Ed Goodson	.50	.23
198 Horace Clarke	.50	.23
199 Bert Blyleven	1.00	.45
200 Billy Williams	5.00	2.20
201 George Hendrick ALCS	1.25	.55
202 George Foster NLCS	1.25	.55
203 Gene Tenace WS	1.25	.55
204 World Series Game 2	1.25	.55
A's two straight		
205 Tony Perez WS	2.50	1.10
206 Gene Tenace WS	1.25	.55
207 John 'Blue Moon' Odom WS	1.25	.55
208 Johnny Bench WS6	5.00	2.20
209 Bert Campaneris WS	1.25	.55
210 World Series Summary	.50	.23
World champions:		
A's Win		
211 Balor Moore	.50	.23
212 Joe Lahoud	.50	.23
213 Steve Garvey	5.00	2.20
214 Steve Hamilton	.50	.23
215 Dusty Baker	1.00	.45
216 Toby Harrah	1.25	.55
217 Don Wilson	.50	.23
218 Aurelio Rodriguez	.50	.23
219 St. Louis Cardinals	1.25	.55
Team Card		
220 Nolan Ryan	100.00	45.00
221 Fred Kendall	.50	.23
222 Rob Gardner	.50	.23
223 Bud Harrelson	1.25	.55
224 Bill Lee	1.25	.55
225 Al Oliver	1.00	.45
226 Ray Fosse	.50	.23
227 Wayne Twitchell	.50	.23
228 Bobby Darwin	.50	.23
229 Roric Harrison	.50	.23
230 Joe Morgan	6.00	2.70
231 Bill Parsons	.50	.23
232 Ken Singleton	1.25	.55
233 Ed Kirkpatrick	.50	.23
234 Bill North	.50	.23
235 Jim Hunter	4.00	1.80
236 Tito Fuentes	.50	.23
237A Braves Leaders	1.50	.70
Eddie Mathews MG		
Lew Burdette CO		
Jim Busby CO		
Roy Hartsfield CO		
Ken Silvestri CO		
(Burdette right ear showing)		
237B Braves Leaders	3.00	1.35
(Burdette right ear not showing)		
238 Tony Muser	.50	.23
239 Pete Richert	.50	.23
240 Bobby Murcer	.75	.35
241 Dwain Anderson	.50	.23
242 George Culver	.50	.23
243 California Angels	1.25	.55
Team Card		
244 Ed Acosta	.50	.23
245 Carl Yastrzemski	8.00	3.60
246 Ken Sanders	.50	.23
247 Del Unser	.50	.23
248 Jerry Johnson	.50	.23
249 Larry Biittner	.50	.23
250 Manny Sanguillen	1.25	.55
251 Roger Nelson	.50	.23
252A Giants Leaders	1.25	.55
Charlie Fox MG		
Joe Amalfitano CO		
Andy Gilbert CO		
Don McMahon CO		
John McNamara CO		
(Orange backgrounds)		
252B Giants Leaders	2.50	1.10
(Dark pale backgrounds)		
253 Mark Belanger	1.25	.55
254 Bill Stoneman	.50	.23
255 Reggie Jackson	15.00	6.75
256 Chris Zachary	.50	.23
257A Mets Leaders	2.50	1.10
Yogi Berra MG		
Roy McMillan CO		
Joe Pignatano CO		
Rube Walker CO		
Eddie Yost CO		
(Orange backgrounds)		
257B Mets Leaders	5.00	2.20
(Dark pale backgrounds)		
258 Tommy John	1.00	.45
259 Jim Holt	.50	.23
260 Gary Nolan	1.25	.55
261 Pat Kelly	.50	.23
262 Jack Aker	.50	.23
263 George Scott	1.25	.55
264 Checklist 133-264	4.00	.80
265 Gene Michael	1.25	.55
266 Mike Lum	.50	.23
267 Lloyd Allen	.50	.23
268 Jerry Morales	.50	.23
269 Tim McCarver	1.00	.45
270 Luis Tiant	1.00	.45
271 Tom Hutton	.50	.23
272 Ed Farmer	.50	.23
273 Chris Speier	.50	.23
274 Darold Knowles	.50	.23
275 Tony Perez	4.00	1.80
276 Joe Lovitto	.50	.23
277 Bob Miller	.50	.23
278 Baltimore Orioles	1.25	.55
Team Card		
279 Mike Strahler	.50	.23
280 Al Kaline	7.00	3.10
281 Mike Jorgensen	.50	.23
282 Steve Hovley	.50	.23
283 Ray Sadecki	.50	.23
284 Glenn Borgmann	.50	.23
285 Don Kessinger	.50	.23
286 Frank Linzy	.50	.23
287 Eddie Leon	.50	.23
288 Gary Gentry	.50	.23
289 Bob Oliver	.50	.23
290 Cesar Cedeno	1.00	.45
291 Rogelio Moret	.50	.23
292 Jose Cruz	1.25	.55
293 Bernie Allen	.50	.23
294 Steve Arlin	.50	.23
295 Bert Campaneris	1.00	.45
296 Reds Leaders	2.50	1.10
Sparky Anderson MG		
Alex Grammas CO		
Ted Kluszewski CO		
George Scherger CO		
Larry Shepard CO		
297 Walt Williams	.50	.23
298 Ron Bryant	.50	.23
299 Ted Ford	.50	.23
300 Steve Carlton	10.00	4.50
301 Billy Grabarkewitz	.50	.23
302 Terry Crowley	.50	.23
303 Nelson Briles	.50	.23
304 Duke Sims	.50	.23
305 Willie Mays	35.00	16.00
306 Tom Burgmeier	.50	.23
307 Boots Day	.50	.23
308 Skip Lockwood	.50	.23
309 Paul Popovich	.50	.23
310 Dick Allen	1.50	.70
311 Joe Decker	.50	.23
312 Oscar Brown	.50	.23
313 Jim Ray	.50	.23
314 Ron Swoboda	.50	.23
315 John Odom	.50	.23
316 San Diego Padres	1.25	.55
Team Card		
317 Danny Cater	.50	.23
318 Jim McGlothlin	.50	.23
319 Jim Spencer	.50	.23
320 Lou Brock	6.00	2.70
321 Rich Hinton	.50	.23
322 Garry Maddox	1.00	.45
323 Tigers Leaders	1.50	.70
Billy Martin MG		
Art Fowler CO		
Charlie Silvera CO		
Dick Tracewski CO		
324 Al Downing	.50	.23
325 Boog Powell	1.00	.45
326 Darrell Brandon	.50	.23
327 John Lowenstein	.50	.23
328 Bill Bonham	.50	.23
329 Ed Kranepool	.50	.23
330 Rod Carew	7.00	3.10
331 Carl Morton	.50	.23
332 John Felske	.50	.23
333 Gene Clines	.50	.23
334 Freddie Patek	.50	.23
335 Bob Tolan	.50	.23
336 Tom Bradley	.50	.23
337 Dave Duncan	.50	.23
338 Checklist 265-396	4.00	.80
339 Dick Tidrow	.50	.23
340 Nate Colbert	.50	.23
341 Jim Palmer KP	1.50	.70
342 Sam McDowell KP	.50	.23
343 Bobby Murcer KP	.50	.23
344 Jim Hunter KP	1.50	.70
345 Chris Speier KP	.50	.23
346 Gaylord Perry KP	1.25	.55
347 Kansas City Royals	1.25	.55
Team Card		
348 Rennie Stennett	.50	.23
349 Dick McAuliffe	.50	.23
350 Tom Seaver	12.00	5.50
351 Jimmy Stewart	.50	.23
352 Don Stanhouse	.50	.23
353 Steve Brye	.50	.23
354 Billy Parker	.50	.23
355 Mike Marshall	1.25	.55
356 White Sox Leaders	.50	.23
Chuck Tanner MG		
Joe Lonnett CO		
Jim Mahoney CO		
Al Monchak CO		
Johnny Sain CO		
357 Ross Grimsley	.50	.23
358 Jim Nettles	.50	.23
359 Cecil Upshaw	.50	.23
360 Joe Rudi UER	1.25	.55
(Photo actually Gene Tenace)		
361 Fran Healy	.50	.23
362 Eddie Watt	.50	.23
363 Jackie Hernandez	.50	.23
364 Rick Wise	.50	.23
365 Rico Petrocelli	1.25	.55
366 Brock Davis	.50	.23
367 Burt Hooton	.50	.23
368 Bill Buckner	1.00	.45
369 Lerrin LaGrow	.50	.23
370 Willie Stargell	5.00	2.20
371 Mike Kekich	.50	.23
372 Oscar Gamble	.50	.23
373 Clyde Wright	.50	.23
374 Darrell Evans	1.00	.45
375 Larry Dierker	1.25	.55
376 Frank Duffy	.50	.23
377 Expos Leaders	.50	.23
Gene Mauch MG		
Dave Bristol CO		
Larry Doby CO		
Cal McLish CO		
Jerry Zimmerman CO		
378 Len Randle	.50	.23
379 Cy Acosta	.50	.23
380 Johnny Bench	12.00	5.50
381 Vicente Romo	.50	.23
382 Mike Hegan	.50	.23
383 Diego Segui	.50	.23
384 Don Baylor	4.00	1.80
385 Jim Perry	1.25	.55
386 Don Money	.50	.23
387 Jim Barr	.50	.23
388 Ben Oglivie	1.25	.55
389 New York Mets	3.00	1.35

Team Card		
☐ 390 Mickey Lolich 1.00	.45	
☐ 391 Lee Lacy .... .50	.23	
☐ 392 Dick Drago .... .50	.23	
☐ 393 Jose Cardenal .... .50	.23	
☐ 394 Sparky Lyle 1.00	.45	
☐ 395 Roger Metzger ...... .50	.23	
☐ 396 Grant Jackson ...... .50	.23	
☐ 397 Dave Cash 1.25	.55	
☐ 398 Rich Hand 1.25	.55	
☐ 399 George Foster 2.00	.90	
☐ 400 Gaylord Perry 5.00	2.20	
☐ 401 Clyde Mashore 1.25	.55	
☐ 402 Jack Hiatt 1.25	.55	
☐ 403 Sonny Jackson 1.25	.55	
☐ 404 Chuck Brinkman ... 1.25	.55	
☐ 405 Cesar Tovar 1.25	.55	
☐ 406 Paul Lindblad 1.25	.55	
☐ 407 Felix Millan 1.25	.55	
☐ 408 Jim Colborn 1.25	.55	
☐ 409 Ivan Murrell 1.25	.55	
☐ 410 Willie McCovey 6.00	2.70	
(Bench behind plate)		
☐ 411 Ray Corbin 1.25	.55	
☐ 412 Manny Mota 2.00	.90	
☐ 413 Tom Timmermann .. 1.25	.55	
☐ 414 Ken Rudolph 1.25	.55	
☐ 415 Marty Pattin 1.25	.55	
☐ 416 Paul Schaal 1.25	.55	
☐ 417 Scipio Spinks 1.25	.55	
☐ 418 Bob Grich 2.00	.90	
☐ 419 Casey Cox 1.25	.55	
☐ 420 Tommie Agee 1.25	.55	
☐ 421A Angels Leaders 2.00	.90	
Bobby Winkles MG		
Tom Morgan CO		
Salty Parker CO		
Jimmie Reese CO		
John Roseboro CO		
(Orange backgrounds)		
☐ 421B Angels Leaders 3.00	1.35	
(Dark pale backgrounds)		
☐ 422 Bob Robertson 1.25	.55	
☐ 423 Johnny Jeter 1.25	.55	
☐ 424 Denny Doyle 1.25	.55	
☐ 425 Alex Johnson 1.25	.55	
☐ 426 Dave LaRoche 1.25	.55	
☐ 427 Rick Auerbach 1.25	.55	
☐ 428 Wayne Simpson 1.25	.55	
☐ 429 Jim Fairey 1.25	.55	
☐ 430 Vida Blue 2.00	.90	
☐ 431 Gerry Moses 1.25	.55	
☐ 432 Dan Frisella 1.25	.55	
☐ 433 Willie Horton 2.00	.90	
☐ 434 San Francisco Giants 3.00	1.35	
Team Card		
☐ 435 Rico Carty 2.00	.90	
☐ 436 Jim McAndrew 1.25	.55	
☐ 437 John Kennedy 1.25	.55	
☐ 438 Enzo Hernandez 1.25	.55	
☐ 439 Eddie Fisher 1.25	.55	
☐ 440 Glenn Beckert 1.25	.55	
☐ 441 Gail Hopkins 1.25	.55	
☐ 442 Dick Dietz 1.25	.55	
☐ 443 Danny Thompson ... 1.25	.55	
☐ 444 Ken Brett 1.25	.55	
☐ 445 Ken Berry 1.25	.55	
☐ 446 Jerry Reuss 2.00	.90	
☐ 447 Joe Hague 1.25	.55	
☐ 448 John Hiller 1.25	.55	
☐ 449A Indians Leaders ... 4.00	1.80	
Ken Aspromonte MG		
Rocky Colavito CO		
Joe Lutz CO		
Warren Spahn CO		
(Spahn's right ear pointed)		
☐ 449B Indians Leaders ... 4.00	1.80	
(Spahn's right ear round)		
☐ 450 Joe Torre 2.00	.90	
☐ 451 John Vukovich 1.25	.55	
☐ 452 Paul Casanova 1.25	.55	
☐ 453 Checklist 397-528 .. 3.00	.60	
☐ 454 Tom Haller 1.25		

☐ 455 Bill Melton 1.25	.55	
☐ 456 Dick Green 1.25	.55	
☐ 457 John Strohmayer 1.25	.55	
☐ 458 Jim Mason 1.25	.55	
☐ 459 Jimmy Howarth 1.25	.55	
☐ 460 Bill Freehan 2.00	.90	
☐ 461 Mike Corkins 1.25	.55	
☐ 462 Ron Blomberg 1.25	.55	
☐ 463 Ken Tatum 1.25	.55	
☐ 464 Chicago Cubs 3.00	1.35	
Team Card		
☐ 465 Dave Giusti 1.25	.55	
☐ 466 Jose Arcia 1.25	.55	
☐ 467 Mike Ryan 1.25	.55	
☐ 468 Tom Griffin 1.25	.55	
☐ 469 Dan Monzon 1.25	.55	
☐ 470 Mike Cuellar 2.00	.90	
☐ 471 Ty Cobb ATL 8.00	3.60	
4191 Hits		
☐ 472 Lou Gehrig ATL 14.00	6.25	
23 Grand Slams		
☐ 473 Hank Aaron ATL 10.00	4.50	
6172 Total Bases		
☐ 474 Babe Ruth ATL 16.00	7.25	
2209 RBI		
☐ 475 Ty Cobb ATL 8.00	3.60	
.367 Batting Average		
☐ 476 Walter Johnson ATL 3.00	1.35	
113 Shutouts		
☐ 477 Cy Young ATL 3.00	1.35	
511 Victories		
☐ 478 Walter Johnson ATL 3.00	1.35	
3508 Strikeouts		
☐ 479 Hal Lanier 1.25	.55	
☐ 480 Juan Marichal 5.00	2.20	
☐ 481 Chicago White Sox .. 3.00	1.35	
Team Card		
☐ 482 Rick Reuschel 3.00	1.35	
☐ 483 Dal Maxvill 1.25	.55	
☐ 484 Ernie McAnally 1.25	.55	
☐ 485 Norm Cash 2.00	.90	
☐ 486A Phillies Leaders ... 2.00	.90	
Danny Ozark MG		
Billy DeMars CO		
Ray Rippelmeyer CO		
Bobby Wine CO		
(Orange backgrounds)		
☐ 486B Phillies Leaders ... 3.00	1.35	
(Dark pale backgrounds)		
☐ 487 Bruce Dal Canton .. 1.25	.55	
☐ 488 Dave Campbell 2.00	.90	
☐ 489 Jeff Burroughs 2.00	.90	
☐ 490 Claude Osteen 1.25	.55	
☐ 491 Bob Montgomery ... 1.25	.55	
☐ 492 Pedro Borbon 1.25	.55	
☐ 493 Duffy Dyer 1.25	.55	
☐ 494 Rich Morales 1.25	.55	
☐ 495 Tommy Helms 1.25	.55	
☐ 496 Ray Lamb 1.25	.55	
☐ 497A Cardinals Leaders .. 2.00	.90	
Red Schoendienst MG		
Vern Benson CO		
George Kissell CO		
Barney Schultz CO		
(Orange backgrounds)		
☐ 497B Cardinals Leaders .. 3.00	1.35	
(Dark pale backgrounds)		
☐ 498 Graig Nettles 3.00	1.35	
☐ 499 Bob Moose 1.25	.55	
☐ 500 Oakland A's 3.00	1.35	
Team Card		
☐ 501 Larry Gura 1.25	.55	
☐ 502 Bobby Valentine 1.25	.55	
☐ 503 Phil Niekro 5.00	2.20	
☐ 504 Earl Williams 1.25	.55	
☐ 505 Bob Bailey 1.25	.55	
☐ 506 Bart Johnson 1.25	.55	
☐ 507 Darrel Chaney 1.25	.55	
☐ 508 Gates Brown 1.25	.55	
☐ 509 Jim Nash 1.25	.55	
☐ 510 Amos Otis 2.00	.90	
☐ 511 Sam McDowell 2.00	.90	
☐ 512 Dalton Jones 1.25	.55	

☐ 513 Dave Marshall 1.25	.55	
☐ 514 Jerry Kenney 1.25	.55	
☐ 515 Andy Messersmith ... 2.00	.90	
☐ 516 Danny Walton 1.25	.55	
☐ 517A Pirates Leaders 2.00	.90	
Bill Virdon MG		
Don Leppert CO		
Bill Mazeroski CO		
Dave Ricketts CO		
Mel Wright CO		
(Mazeroski has no right ear)		
☐ 517B Pirates Leaders 3.00	1.35	
(Mazeroski has right ear)		
☐ 518 Bob Veale 1.25	.55	
☐ 519 Johnny Edwards 1.25	.55	
☐ 520 Mel Stottlemyre 2.00	.90	
☐ 521 Atlanta Braves 3.00	1.35	
Team Card		
☐ 522 Leo Cardenas 1.25	.55	
☐ 523 Wayne Granger 1.25	.55	
☐ 524 Gene Tenace 2.00	.90	
☐ 525 Jim Fregosi 2.00	.90	
☐ 526 Ollie Brown 1.25	.55	
☐ 527 Dan McGinn 1.25	.55	
☐ 528 Paul Blair 1.25	.55	
☐ 529 Milt May 3.50	1.55	
☐ 530 Jim Kaat 5.00	2.20	
☐ 531 Ron Woods 3.50	1.55	
☐ 532 Steve Mingori 3.50	1.55	
☐ 533 Larry Stahl 3.50	1.55	
☐ 534 Dave Lemonds 3.50	1.55	
☐ 535 Johnny Callison 5.00	2.20	
☐ 536 Philadelphia Phillies 5.00	2.20	
Team Card		
☐ 537 Bill Slayback 3.50	1.55	
☐ 538 Jim Ray Hart 5.00	2.20	
☐ 539 Tom Murphy 3.50	1.55	
☐ 540 Cleon Jones 5.00	2.20	
☐ 541 Bob Bolin 3.50	1.55	
☐ 542 Pat Corrales 5.00	2.20	
☐ 543 Alan Foster 3.50	1.55	
☐ 544 Von Joshua 3.50	1.55	
☐ 545 Orlando Cepeda 5.00	2.20	
☐ 546 Jim York 3.50	1.55	
☐ 547 Bobby Heise 3.50	1.55	
☐ 548 Don Durham 3.50	1.55	
☐ 549 Rangers Leaders 5.00	2.20	
Whitey Herzog MG		
Chuck Estrada CO		
Jackie Moore CO		
☐ 550 Dave Johnson 5.00	2.20	
☐ 551 Mike Kilkenny 3.50	1.55	
☐ 552 J.C. Martin 3.50	1.55	
☐ 553 Mickey Scott 3.50	1.55	
☐ 554 Dave Concepcion 5.00	2.20	
☐ 555 Bill Hands 3.50	1.55	
☐ 556 New York Yankees .. 8.00	3.60	
Team Card		
☐ 557 Bernie Williams 3.50	1.55	
☐ 558 Jerry May 3.50	1.55	
☐ 559 Barry Lersch 3.50	1.55	
☐ 560 Frank Howard 4.00	1.80	
☐ 561 Jim Geddes 3.50	1.55	
☐ 562 Wayne Garrett 3.50	1.55	
☐ 563 Larry Haney 3.50	1.55	
☐ 564 Mike Thompson 3.50	1.55	
☐ 565 Jim Hickman 3.50	1.55	
☐ 566 Lew Krausse 3.50	1.55	
☐ 567 Bob Fenwick 3.50	1.55	
☐ 568 Ray Newman 3.50	1.55	
☐ 569 Dodgers Leaders 5.00	2.20	
Walt Alston MG		
Red Adams CO		
Monty Basgall CO		
Jim Gilliam CO		
Tom Lasorda CO		
☐ 570 Bill Singer 5.00	2.20	
☐ 571 Rusty Torres 3.50	1.55	
☐ 572 Gary Sutherland 3.50	1.55	
☐ 573 Fred Beene 3.50	1.55	
☐ 574 Bob Didier 3.50	1.55	
☐ 575 Dock Ellis 3.50	1.55	
☐ 576 Montreal Expos 6.00	2.70	

Team Card			
□ 577 Eric Soderholm	3.50	1.55	
□ 578 Ken Wright	3.50	1.55	
□ 579 Tom Grieve	5.00	2.20	
□ 580 Joe Pepitone	5.00	2.20	
□ 581 Steve Kealey	3.50	1.55	
□ 582 Darrell Porter	5.00	2.20	
□ 583 Bill Grief	3.50	1.55	
□ 584 Chris Arnold	3.50	1.55	
□ 585 Joe Niekro	5.00	2.20	
□ 586 Bill Sudakis	3.50	1.55	
□ 587 Rich McKinney	3.50	1.55	
□ 588 Checklist 529-660	24.00	4.80	
□ 589 Ken Forsch	3.50	1.55	
□ 590 Deron Johnson	5.00	2.20	
□ 591 Mike Hedlund	3.50	1.55	
□ 592 John Boccabella	3.50	1.55	
□ 593 Royals Leaders	3.50	1.55	
Jack McKeon MG			
Galen Cisco CO			
Harry Dunlop CO			
Charlie Lau CO			
□ 594 Vic Harris	3.50	1.55	
□ 595 Don Gullett	5.00	2.20	
□ 596 Boston Red Sox	8.00	3.60	
Team Card			
□ 597 Mickey Rivers	4.00	1.80	
□ 598 Phil Roof	3.50	1.55	
□ 599 Ed Crosby	3.50	1.55	
□ 600 Dave McNally	5.00	2.20	
□ 601 Rookie Catchers	5.00	2.20	
Sergio Robles			
George Pena			
Rick Stelmaszek			
□ 602 Rookie Pitchers	5.00	2.20	
Mel Behney			
Ralph Garcia			
Doug Rau			
□ 603 Rookie 3rd Basemen	5.00	2.20	
Terry Hughes			
Bill McNulty			
Ken Reitz			
□ 604 Rookie Pitchers	5.00	2.20	
Jesse Jefferson			
Dennis O'Toole			
Bob Strampe			
□ 605 Rookie 1st Basemen	5.00	2.20	
Enos Cabell			
Pat Bourque			
Gonzalo Marquez			
□ 606 Rookie Outfielders	5.00	2.20	
Gary Matthews			
Tom Paciorek			
Jorge Roque			
□ 607 Rookie Shortstops	5.00	2.20	
Pepe Frias			
Ray Busse			
Mario Guerrero			
□ 608 Rookie Pitchers	5.00	2.20	
Steve Busby			
Dick Colpaert			
George Medich			
□ 609 Rookie 2nd Basemen	6.00	2.70	
Larvell Blanks			
Pedro Garcia			
Dave Lopes			
□ 610 Rookie Pitchers	5.00	2.20	
Jimmy Freeman			
Charlie Hough			
Hank Webb			
□ 611 Rookie Outfielders	5.00	2.20	
Rich Coggins			
Jim Wohlford			
Richie Zisk			
□ 612 Rookie Pitchers	5.00	2.20	
Steve Lawson			
Bob Reynolds			
Brent Strom			
□ 613 Rookie Catchers	16.00	7.25	
Bob Boone			
Skip Jutze			
Mike Ivie			
□ 614 Rookie Outfielders	16.00	7.25	
Al Bumbry			
Dwight Evans			
Charlie Spikes			

□ 615 Rookie 3rd Basemen	300.00	135.00	
Ron Cey			
John Hilton			
Mike Schmidt			
□ 616 Rookie Pitchers	5.00	2.20	
Norm Angelini			
Steve Blateric			
Mike Garman			
□ 617 Rich Chiles	3.50	1.55	
□ 618 Andy Etchebarren	3.50	1.55	
□ 619 Billy Wilson	3.50	1.55	
□ 620 Tommy Harper	5.00	2.20	
□ 621 Joe Ferguson	5.00	2.20	
□ 622 Larry Hisle	5.00	2.20	
□ 623 Steve Renko	3.50	1.55	
□ 624 Astros Leaders	6.00	2.70	
Preston Gomez CO			
Leo Durocher MG			
Grady Hatton CO			
Hub Kittle CO			
Jim Owens CO			
□ 625 Angel Mangual	3.50	1.55	
□ 626 Bob Barton	3.50	1.55	
□ 627 Luis Alvarado	3.50	1.55	
□ 628 Jim Slaton	3.50	1.55	
□ 629 Cleveland Indians	6.00	2.70	
Team Card			
□ 630 Denny McLain	8.00	3.60	
□ 631 Tom Matchick	3.50	1.55	
□ 632 Dick Selma	3.50	1.55	
□ 633 Ike Brown	3.50	1.55	
□ 634 Alan Closter	3.50	1.55	
□ 635 Gene Alley	5.00	2.20	
□ 636 Rickey Clark	3.50	1.55	
□ 637 Norm Miller	3.50	1.55	
□ 638 Ken Reynolds	3.50	1.55	
□ 639 Willie Crawford	3.50	1.55	
□ 640 Dick Bosman	3.50	1.55	
□ 641 Cincinnati Reds	8.00	3.60	
Team Card			
□ 642 Jose Laboy	3.50	1.55	
□ 643 Al Fitzmorris	3.50	1.55	
□ 644 Jack Heidemann	3.50	1.55	
□ 645 Bob Locker	3.50	1.55	
□ 646 Brewers Leaders	3.50	1.55	
Del Crandall MG			
Harvey Kuenn CO			
Joe Nossek CO			
Bob Shaw CO			
Jim Walton CO			
□ 647 George Stone	3.50	1.55	
□ 648 Tom Egan	3.50	1.55	
□ 649 Rich Folkers	3.50	1.55	
□ 650 Felipe Alou	4.00	1.80	
□ 651 Don Carrithers	3.50	1.55	
□ 652 Ted Kubiak	3.50	1.55	
□ 653 Joe Hoerner	3.50	1.55	
□ 654 Minnesota Twins	5.00	2.20	
Team Card			
□ 655 Clay Kirby	3.50	1.55	
□ 656 John Ellis	3.50	1.55	
□ 657 Bob Johnson	3.50	1.55	
□ 658 Elliott Maddox	3.50	1.55	
□ 659 Jose Pagan	3.50	1.55	
□ 660 Fred Scherman	4.00	1.55	

1974 Topps

The cards in this 660-card set measure 2 1/2" by 3 1/2". This year marked the first time Topps issued all the cards of its baseball set at the same time rather than in series. Among other methods, cards were issued in eight-card dime wax packs and 42 card rack packs. For the first time, factory sets were issued through the JC Penny's catalog. Sales were probably disappointing for it would be several years before factory sets were issued again. Some interesting variations were created by the rumored move of the San Diego

Padres to Washington. Fifteen cards (13 players, the team card, and the rookie card (599) of the Padres were printed either as "San Diego" (SD) or "Washington." The latter are the scarcer variety and are denoted in the checklist below by WAS. Each team's manager and his coaches again have a combined card with small pictures of each coach below the larger photo of the team's manager. The first six cards in the set (1-6) feature Hank Aaron and his illustrious career. Other topical subsets included in the set are League Leaders (201-208), All-Star selections (331-339), Playoffs cards (470-471), World Series cards (472-479), and Rookie Prospects (596-608). The card backs for the All-Stars (331-339) have no statistics, but form a picture puzzle of Bobby Bonds, the 1973 All-Star Game MVP. The key Rookie Cards in this set are Ken Griffey Sr., Dave Parker, and Dave Winfield.

	NRMT	VG-E
COMPLETE SET (660)	600.00	275.00
COMPLETE FACT.SET (660)	625.00	275.00
COMMON CARD (1-660)	.50	.23
AARON SPECIALS (2-6)	7.00	3.10
WASH.VARIATIONS	6.00	2.70
MINOR STARS	1.00	.45
SEMISTARS	2.00	.90
UNLISTED STARS	3.00	1.35
1974-85 PRICED IN NM-MT CONDITION		

□ 1 Hank Aaron	40.00	12.00	
All-Time Home Run King			
(Complete ML record)			
□ 2 Aaron Special 54-57	7.00	3.10	
(Records on back)			
□ 3 Aaron Special 58-61	7.00	3.10	
(Memorable homers)			
□ 4 Aaron Special 62-65	7.00	3.10	
(Life in ML's 1954-63)			
□ 5 Aaron Special 66-69	7.00	3.10	
(Life in ML's 1964-73)			
□ 6 Aaron Special 70-73	7.00	3.10	
(Milestone homers)			
□ 7 Jim Hunter	3.00	1.35	
□ 8 George Theodore	.50	.23	
□ 9 Mickey Lolich	1.00	.45	
□ 10 Johnny Bench	12.00	5.50	
□ 11 Jim Bibby	.50	.23	
□ 12 Dave May	.50	.23	
□ 13 Tom Hilgendorf	.50	.23	
□ 14 Paul Popovich	.50	.23	
□ 15 Joe Torre	2.00	.90	
□ 16 Baltimore Orioles	1.00	.45	
Team Card			
□ 17 Doug Bird	.50	.23	
□ 18 Gary Thomasson	.50	.23	

☐ 19	Gerry Moses	.50	.23
☐ 20	Nolan Ryan	70.00	32.00
☐ 21	Bob Gallagher	.50	.23
☐ 22	Cy Acosta	.50	.23
☐ 23	Craig Robinson	.50	.23
☐ 24	John Hiller	1.00	.45
☐ 25	Ken Singleton	1.00	.45
☐ 26	Bill Campbell	.50	.23
☐ 27	George Scott	1.00	.45
☐ 28	Manny Sanguillen	1.00	.45
☐ 29	Phil Niekro	3.00	1.35
☐ 30	Bobby Bonds	2.00	.90
☐ 31	Astros Leaders	1.00	.45

Preston Gomez MG
Roger Craig CO
Hub Kittle CO
Grady Hatton CO
Bob Lillis CO

☐ 32A	Johnny Grubb SD	1.00	.45
☐ 32B	Johnny Grubb WAS	6.00	2.70
☐ 33	Don Newhauser	.50	.23
☐ 34	Andy Kosco	.50	.23
☐ 35	Gaylord Perry	3.00	1.35
☐ 36	St. Louis Cardinals	1.00	.45

Team Card

☐ 37	Dave Sells	.50	.23
☐ 38	Don Kessinger	1.00	.45
☐ 39	Ken Suarez	.50	.23
☐ 40	Jim Palmer	5.00	2.20
☐ 41	Bobby Floyd	.50	.23
☐ 42	Claude Osteen	1.00	.45
☐ 43	Jim Wynn	1.00	.45
☐ 44	Mel Stottlemyre	1.00	.45
☐ 45	Dave Johnson	1.00	.45
☐ 46	Pat Kelly	.50	.23
☐ 47	Dick Ruthven	.50	.23
☐ 48	Dick Sharon	.50	.23
☐ 49	Steve Renko	.50	.23
☐ 50	Rod Carew	5.00	2.20
☐ 51	Bobby Heise	.50	.23
☐ 52	Al Oliver	1.00	.45
☐ 53A	Fred Kendall SD	1.00	.45
☐ 53B	Fred Kendall WAS	6.00	2.70
☐ 54	Elias Sosa	.50	.23
☐ 55	Frank Robinson	6.00	2.70
☐ 56	New York Mets	1.00	.45

Team Card

☐ 57	Darold Knowles	.50	.23
☐ 58	Charlie Spikes	.50	.23
☐ 59	Ross Grimsley	.50	.23
☐ 60	Lou Brock	5.00	2.20
☐ 61	Luis Aparicio	3.00	1.35
☐ 62	Bob Locker	.50	.23
☐ 63	Bill Sudakis	.50	.23
☐ 64	Doug Rau	.50	.23
☐ 65	Amos Otis	1.00	.45
☐ 66	Sparky Lyle	1.00	.45
☐ 67	Tommy Helms	.50	.23
☐ 68	Grant Jackson	.50	.23
☐ 69	Del Unser	.50	.23
☐ 70	Dick Allen	2.00	.90
☐ 71	Dan Frisella	.50	.23
☐ 72	Aurelio Rodriguez	.50	.23
☐ 73	Mike Marshall	2.00	.90
☐ 74	Minnesota Twins	1.00	.45

Team Card

☐ 75	Jim Colborn	.50	.23
☐ 76	Mickey Rivers	1.00	.45
☐ 77A	Rich Troedson SD	6.00	2.70
☐ 77B	Rich Troedson WAS	1.00	.45
☐ 78	Giants Leaders	.75	.35

Charlie Fox MG
John McNamara CO
Joe Amalfitano CO
Andy Gilbert CO
Don McMahon CO

☐ 79	Gene Tenace	1.00	.45
☐ 80	Tom Seaver	12.00	5.50
☐ 81	Frank Duffy	.50	.23
☐ 82	Dave Giusti	.50	.23
☐ 83	Orlando Cepeda	2.00	.90
☐ 84	Rick Wise	.50	.23
☐ 85	Joe Morgan	5.00	2.20
☐ 86	Joe Ferguson	1.00	.45
☐ 87	Fergie Jenkins	3.00	1.35
☐ 88	Freddie Patek	1.00	.45

☐ 89	Jackie Brown	.50	.23
☐ 90	Bobby Murcer	1.00	.45
☐ 91	Ken Forsch	.50	.23
☐ 92	Paul Blair	1.00	.45
☐ 93	Rod Gilbreath	.50	.23
☐ 94	Detroit Tigers	1.00	.45

Team Card

☐ 95	Steve Carlton	6.00	2.70
☐ 96	Jerry Hairston	.50	.23
☐ 97	Bob Bailey	.50	.23
☐ 98	Bert Blyleven	2.00	.90
☐ 99	Brewers Leaders	1.00	.45

Del Crandall MG
Harvey Kuenn CO
Joe Nossek CO
Jim Walton CO
Al Widmar CO

☐ 100	Willie Stargell	4.00	1.80
☐ 101	Bobby Valentine	1.00	.45
☐ 102A	Bill Greif SD	1.00	.45
☐ 102B	Bill Greif WAS	6.00	2.70
☐ 103	Sal Bando	1.00	.45
☐ 104	Ron Bryant	.50	.23
☐ 105	Carlton Fisk	12.00	5.50
☐ 106	Harry Parker	.50	.23
☐ 107	Alex Johnson	.50	.23
☐ 108	Al Hrabosky	1.00	.45
☐ 109	Bob Grich	1.00	.45
☐ 110	Billy Williams	3.00	1.35
☐ 111	Clay Carroll	.50	.23
☐ 112	Dave Lopes	2.00	.90
☐ 113	Dick Drago	.50	.23
☐ 114	Angels Team	1.00	.45
☐ 115	Willie Horton	1.00	.45
☐ 116	Jerry Reuss	1.00	.45
☐ 117	Ron Blomberg	.50	.23
☐ 118	Bill Lee	1.00	.45
☐ 119	Phillies Leaders	1.00	.45

Danny Ozark MG
Ray Ripplemeyer CO
Bobby Wine CO
Carroll Beringer CO
Billy DeMars CO

☐ 120	Wilbur Wood	.50	.23
☐ 121	Larry Lintz	.50	.23
☐ 122	Jim Holt	.50	.23
☐ 123	Nelson Briles	1.00	.45
☐ 124	Bobby Coluccio	.50	.23
☐ 125A	Nate Colbert SD	1.00	.45
☐ 125B	Nate Colbert WAS	6.00	2.70
☐ 126	Checklist 1-132	3.00	.60
☐ 127	Tom Paciorek	1.00	.45
☐ 128	John Ellis	.50	.23
☐ 129	Chris Speier	.50	.23
☐ 130	Reggie Jackson	15.00	6.75
☐ 131	Bob Boone	2.00	.90
☐ 132	Felix Millan	.50	.23
☐ 133	David Clyde	1.00	.45
☐ 134	Denis Menke	.50	.23
☐ 135	Roy White	1.00	.45
☐ 136	Rick Reuschel	1.00	.45
☐ 137	Al Bumbry	1.00	.45
☐ 138	Eddie Brinkman	.50	.23
☐ 139	Aurelio Monteagudo	.50	.23
☐ 140	Darrell Evans	2.00	.90
☐ 141	Pat Bourque	.50	.23
☐ 142	Pedro Garcia	.50	.23
☐ 143	Dick Woodson	.50	.23
☐ 144	Dodgers Leaders	2.00	.90

Walter Alston MG
Tom Lasorda CO
Jim Gilliam CO
Red Adams CO
Monty Basgall CO

☐ 145	Dock Ellis	.50	.23
☐ 146	Ron Fairly	1.00	.45
☐ 147	Bart Johnson	.50	.23
☐ 148A	Dave Hilton SD	1.00	.45
☐ 148B	Dave Hilton WAS	6.00	2.70
☐ 149	Mac Scarce	.50	.23
☐ 150	John Mayberry	1.00	.45
☐ 151	Diego Segui	.50	.23
☐ 152	Oscar Gamble	1.00	.45
☐ 153	Jon Matlack	1.00	.45
☐ 154	Houston Astros	1.00	.45

Team Card

☐ 155	Bert Campaneris	1.00	.45
☐ 156	Randy Moffitt	.50	.23
☐ 157	Vic Harris	.50	.23
☐ 158	Jack Billingham	.50	.23
☐ 159	Jim Ray Hart	1.00	.45
☐ 160	Brooks Robinson	6.00	2.70
☐ 161	Ray Burris UER	1.00	.45

(Card number is
printed sideways)

☐ 162	Bill Freehan	1.00	.45
☐ 163	Ken Berry	.50	.23
☐ 164	Tom House	1.00	.45
☐ 165	Willie Davis	1.00	.45
☐ 166	Royals Leaders	1.00	.45

Jack McKeon MG
Charlie Lau CO
Harry Dunlop CO
Galen Cisco CO

☐ 167	Luis Tiant	2.00	.90
☐ 168	Danny Thompson	.50	.23
☐ 169	Steve Rogers	2.00	.90
☐ 170	Bill Melton	.50	.23
☐ 171	Eduardo Rodriguez	.50	.23
☐ 172	Gene Clines	.50	.23
☐ 173A	Randy Jones SD	2.00	.90
☐ 173B	Randy Jones WAS	10.00	4.50
☐ 174	Bill Robinson	1.00	.45
☐ 175	Reggie Cleveland	.50	.23
☐ 176	John Lowenstein	.50	.23
☐ 177	Dave Roberts	.50	.23
☐ 178	Garry Maddox	1.00	.45
☐ 179	Mets Leaders	3.00	1.35

Yogi Berra MG
Rube Walker CO
Eddie Yost CO
Roy McMillan CO
Joe Pignatano CO

☐ 180	Ken Holtzman	1.00	.45
☐ 181	Cesar Geronimo	.50	.23
☐ 182	Lindy McDaniel	1.00	.45
☐ 183	Johnny Oates	1.00	.45
☐ 184	Texas Rangers	1.00	.45

Team Card

☐ 185	Jose Cardenal	.50	.23
☐ 186	Fred Scherman	.50	.23
☐ 187	Don Baylor	2.00	.90
☐ 188	Rudy Meoli	.50	.23
☐ 189	Jim Brewer	.50	.23
☐ 190	Tony Oliva	2.00	.90
☐ 191	Al Fitzmorris	.50	.23
☐ 192	Mario Guerrero	.50	.23
☐ 193	Tom Walker	.50	.23
☐ 194	Darrell Porter	1.00	.45
☐ 195	Carlos May	.50	.23
☐ 196	Jim Fregosi	1.00	.45
☐ 197A	Vicente Romo SD	1.00	.45
☐ 197B	Vicente Romo WAS	6.00	2.70
☐ 198	Dave Cash	.50	.23
☐ 199	Mike Kekich	.50	.23
☐ 200	Cesar Cedeno	1.00	.45
☐ 201	Batting Leaders	5.00	2.20

Rod Carew
Pete Rose

☐ 202	Home Run Leaders	5.00	2.20

Reggie Jackson
Willie Stargell

☐ 203	RBI Leaders	5.00	2.20

Reggie Jackson
Willie Stargell

☐ 204	Stolen Base Leaders	2.00	.90

Tommy Harper
Lou Brock

☐ 205	Victory Leaders	1.00	.45

Wilbur Wood
Ron Bryant

☐ 206	ERA Leaders	5.00	2.20

Jim Palmer
Tom Seaver

☐ 207	Strikeout Leaders	20.00	9.00

Nolan Ryan
Tom Seaver

☐ 208	Leading Firemen	1.00	.45

John Hiller
Mike Marshall

☐ 209	Ted Sizemore	.50	.23
☐ 210	Bill Singer	.50	.23

☐ 211 Chicago Cubs Team 1.00 .45
☐ 212 Rollie Fingers 3.00 1.35
☐ 213 Dave Rader .50 .23
☐ 214 Billy Grabarkewitz .50 .23
☐ 215 Al Kaline UER 5.00 2.20
   (No copyright on back)
☐ 216 Ray Sadecki .50 .23
☐ 217 Tim Foli .50 .23
☐ 218 Johnny Briggs .50 .23
☐ 219 Doug Griffin .50 .23
☐ 220 Don Sutton 3.00 1.35
☐ 221 White Sox Leaders 1.00 .45
   Chuck Tanner MG
   Jim Mahoney CO
   Alex Monchak CO
   Johnny Sain CO
   Joe Lonnett CO
☐ 222 Ramon Hernandez .50 .23
☐ 223 Jeff Burroughs 1.00 .45
☐ 224 Roger Metzger .50 .23
☐ 225 Paul Splittorff .50 .23
☐ 226A Padres Team SD 2.00 .90
☐ 226B Padres Team WAS 10.00 4.50
☐ 227 Mike Lum .50 .23
☐ 228 Ted Kubiak .50 .23
☐ 229 Fritz Peterson .50 .23
☐ 230 Tony Perez 3.00 1.35
☐ 231 Dick Tidrow .50 .23
☐ 232 Steve Brye .50 .23
☐ 233 Jim Barr .50 .23
☐ 234 John Milner .50 .23
☐ 235 Dave McNally 1.00 .45
☐ 236 Cardinals Leaders 2.00 .90
   Red Schoendienst MG
   Barney Schultz CO
   George Kissell CO
   Johnny Lewis CO
   Vern Benson CO
☐ 237 Ken Brett .50 .23
☐ 238 Fran Healy HOR 2.00 .90
   (Munson sliding
   in background)
☐ 239 Bill Russell 2.00 .90
☐ 240 Joe Coleman .50 .23
☐ 241A Glenn Beckett SD .75 .35
☐ 241B Glenn Beckett WAS 6.00 2.70
☐ 242 Bill Gogolewski .50 .23
☐ 243 Bob Oliver .50 .23
☐ 244 Carl Morton .50 .23
☐ 245 Cleon Jones 6.00 2.70
☐ 246 Oakland Athletics 2.00 .90
   Team Card
☐ 247 Rick Miller .50 .23
☐ 248 Tom Hall .50 .23
☐ 249 George Mitterwald .50 .23
☐ 250A Willie McCovey SD 6.00 2.70
☐ 250B Willie McCovey WAS 30.00 13.50
☐ 251 Graig Nettles 2.00 .90
☐ 252 Dave Parker 10.00 4.50
☐ 253 John Boccabella .50 .23
☐ 254 Stan Bahnsen .50 .23
☐ 255 Larry Bowa 1.00 .45
☐ 256 Tom Griffin .50 .23
☐ 257 Buddy Bell 2.00 .90
☐ 258 Jerry Morales .50 .23
☐ 259 Bob Reynolds .50 .23
☐ 260 Ted Simmons 2.00 .90
☐ 261 Jerry Bell .50 .23
☐ 262 Ed Kirkpatrick .50 .23
☐ 263 Checklist 133-264 2.50 .50
☐ 264 Joe Rudi 1.00 .45
☐ 265 Tug McGraw 2.00 .90
☐ 266 Jim Northrup 1.00 .45
☐ 267 Andy Messersmith 1.00 .45
☐ 268 Tom Grieve 1.00 .45
☐ 269 Bob Johnson .50 .23
☐ 270 Ron Santo 2.00 .90
☐ 271 Bill Hands .50 .23
☐ 272 Paul Casanova .50 .23
☐ 273 Checklist 265-396 3.00 .60
☐ 274 Fred Beene .50 .23
☐ 275 Ron Hunt .50 .23
☐ 276 Angels Leaders 1.00 .45
   Bobby Winkles MG
   John Roseboro CO
   Tom Morgan CO

Jimmie Reese CO
Salty Parker CO
☐ 277 Gary Nolan 1.00 .45
☐ 278 Cookie Rojas 1.00 .45
☐ 279 Jim Crawford .50 .23
☐ 280 Carl Yastrzemski 6.00 2.70
☐ 281 San Francisco Giants 1.00 .45
   Team Card
☐ 282 Doyle Alexander 1.00 .45
☐ 283 Mike Schmidt 50.00 22.00
☐ 284 Dave Duncan .50 .23
☐ 285 Reggie Smith 1.00 .45
☐ 286 Tony Muser .50 .23
☐ 287 Clay Kirby .50 .23
☐ 288 Gorman Thomas 2.00 .90
☐ 289 Rick Auerbach .50 .23
☐ 290 Vida Blue 1.00 .45
☐ 291 Don Hahn .50 .23
☐ 292 Chuck Seelbach .50 .23
☐ 293 Milt May .50 .23
☐ 294 Steve Foucault .50 .23
☐ 295 Rick Monday 1.00 .45
☐ 296 Ray Corbin .50 .23
☐ 297 Hal Breeden .50 .23
☐ 298 Roric Harrison .50 .23
☐ 299 Gene Michael 1.00 .45
☐ 300 Pete Rose 15.00 6.75
☐ 301 Bob Montgomery .50 .23
☐ 302 Rudy May .50 .23
☐ 303 George Hendrick 1.00 .45
☐ 304 Don Wilson .50 .23
☐ 305 Tito Fuentes .50 .23
☐ 306 Orioles Leaders 2.00 .90
   Earl Weaver MG
   Jim Frey CO
   George Bamberger CO
   Billy Hunter CO
   George Staller CO
☐ 307 Luis Melendez .50 .23
☐ 308 Bruce Dal Canton .50 .23
☐ 309A Dave Roberts SD 1.00 .45
☐ 309B Dave Roberts WAS 7.00 3.10
☐ 310 Terry Forster 1.00 .45
☐ 311 Jerry Grote .50 .23
☐ 312 Deron Johnson 1.00 .45
☐ 313 Barry Lersch .50 .23
☐ 314 Milwaukee Brewers 1.00 .45
   Team Card
☐ 315 Ron Cey 2.00 .90
☐ 316 Jim Perry 1.00 .45
☐ 317 Richie Zisk 1.00 .45
☐ 318 Jim Merritt .50 .23
☐ 319 Randy Hundley 1.00 .45
☐ 320 Dusty Baker 2.00 .90
☐ 321 Steve Braun .50 .23
☐ 322 Ernie McAnally .50 .23
☐ 323 Richie Scheinblum .50 .23
☐ 324 Steve Kline .50 .23
☐ 325 Tommy Harper 2.00 .90
☐ 326 Reds Leaders 3.00 1.35
   Sparky Anderson MG
   Larry Shepard CO
   George Scherger CO
   Alex Grammas CO
   Ted Kluszewski CO
☐ 327 Tom Timmermann .50 .23
☐ 328 Skip Jutze .50 .23
☐ 329 Mark Belanger 1.00 .45
☐ 330 Juan Marichal 3.00 1.35
☐ 331 All-Star Catchers 5.00 2.20
   Carlton Fisk
   Johnny Bench
☐ 332 All-Star 1B 5.00 2.20
   Dick Allen
   Hank Aaron
☐ 333 All-Star 2B 3.00 1.35
   Rod Carew
   Joe Morgan
☐ 334 All-Star 3B 3.00 1.35
   Brooks Robinson
   Ron Santo
☐ 335 All-Star SS 1.00 .45
   Bert Campaneris
   Chris Speier
☐ 336 All-Star LF 3.00 1.35
   Bobby Murcer

Pete Rose
☐ 337 All-Star CF 1.00 .45
   Amos Otis
   Cesar Cedeno
☐ 338 All-Star RF 5.00 2.20
   Reggie Jackson
   Billy Williams
☐ 339 All-Star Pitchers 3.00 1.35
   Jim Hunter
   Rick Wise
☐ 340 Thurman Munson 6.00 2.70
☐ 341 Dan Driessen 1.00 .45
☐ 342 Jim Lonborg 1.00 .45
☐ 343 Royals Team 1.00 .45
☐ 344 Mike Caldwell .50 .23
☐ 345 Bill North .50 .23
☐ 346 Ron Reed .50 .23
☐ 347 Sandy Alomar 1.00 .45
☐ 348 Pete Richert .50 .23
☐ 349 John Vukovich .50 .23
☐ 350 Bob Gibson 5.00 2.20
☐ 351 Dwight Evans 3.00 1.35
☐ 352 Bill Stoneman .50 .23
☐ 353 Rich Coggins .50 .23
☐ 354 Cubs Leaders 1.00 .45
   Whitey Lockman MG
   J.C. Martin CO
   Hank Aguirre CO
   Al Spangler CO
   Jim Marshall CO
☐ 355 Dave Nelson .50 .23
☐ 356 Jerry Koosman 1.00 .45
☐ 357 Buddy Bradford .50 .23
☐ 358 Dal Maxvill .50 .23
☐ 359 Brent Strom .50 .23
☐ 360 Greg Luzinski 2.00 .90
☐ 361 Don Carrithers .50 .23
☐ 362 Hal King .50 .23
☐ 363 New York Yankees 2.00 .90
   Team Card
☐ 364A Cito Gaston SD 2.00 .90
☐ 364B Cito Gaston WAS 8.00 3.60
☐ 365 Steve Busby 1.00 .45
☐ 366 Larry Hisle 1.00 .45
☐ 367 Norm Cash 2.00 .90
☐ 368 Manny Mota 1.00 .45
☐ 369 Paul Lindblad .50 .23
☐ 370 Bob Watson 1.00 .45
☐ 371 Jim Slaton .50 .23
☐ 372 Ken Reitz .50 .23
☐ 373 John Curtis .50 .23
☐ 374 Marty Perez .50 .23
☐ 375 Earl Williams .50 .23
☐ 376 Jorge Orta .50 .23
☐ 377 Ron Woods .50 .23
☐ 378 Burt Hooton 1.00 .45
☐ 379 Rangers Leaders 2.00 .90
   Billy Martin MG
   Frank Lucchesi CO
   Art Fowler CO
   Charlie Silvera CO
   Jackie Moore CO
☐ 380 Bud Harrelson 1.00 .45
☐ 381 Charlie Sands .50 .23
☐ 382 Bob Moose .50 .23
☐ 383 Philadelphia Phillies 1.00 .45
   Team Card
☐ 384 Chris Chambliss 1.00 .45
☐ 385 Don Gullett 1.00 .45
☐ 386 Gary Matthews 2.00 .90
☐ 387A Rich Morales SD 1.00 .45
☐ 387B Rich Morales WAS 7.00 3.10
☐ 388 Phil Roof .50 .23
☐ 389 Gates Brown .50 .23
☐ 390 Lou Piniella 2.00 .90
☐ 391 Billy Champion .50 .23
☐ 392 Dick Green .50 .23
☐ 393 Orlando Pena .50 .23
☐ 394 Ken Henderson .50 .23
☐ 395 Doug Rader .50 .23
☐ 396 Tommy Davis 1.00 .45
☐ 397 George Stone .50 .23
☐ 398 Duke Sims .50 .23
☐ 399 Mike Paul .50 .23
☐ 400 Harmon Killebrew 5.00 2.20
☐ 401 Elliott Maddox .50 .23

☐ 402 Jim Rooker	.50	.23
☐ 403 Red Sox Leaders	1.00	.45
Darrell Johnson MG		
Eddie Popowski CO		
Lee Stange CO		
Don Zimmer CO		
Don Bryant CO		
☐ 404 Jim Howarth	.50	.23
☐ 405 Ellie Rodriguez	.50	.23
☐ 406 Steve Arlin	.50	.23
☐ 407 Jim Wohlford	.50	.23
☐ 408 Charlie Hough	2.00	.90
☐ 409 Ike Brown	.50	.23
☐ 410 Pedro Borbon	.50	.23
☐ 411 Frank Baker	.50	.23
☐ 412 Chuck Taylor	.50	.23
☐ 413 Don Money	1.00	.45
☐ 414 Checklist 397-528	3.00	.60
☐ 415 Gary Gentry	.50	.23
☐ 416 Chicago White Sox	1.00	.45
Team Card		
☐ 417 Rich Folkers	.50	.23
☐ 418 Walt Williams	.50	.23
☐ 419 Wayne Twitchell	.50	.23
☐ 420 Ray Fosse	.50	.23
☐ 421 Dan Fife	.50	.23
☐ 422 Gonzalo Marquez	.50	.23
☐ 423 Fred Stanley	.50	.23
☐ 424 Jim Beauchamp	.50	.23
☐ 425 Pete Broberg	.50	.23
☐ 426 Rennie Stennett	.50	.23
☐ 427 Bobby Bolin	.50	.23
☐ 428 Gary Sutherland	.50	.23
☐ 429 Dick Lange	.50	.23
☐ 430 Matty Alou	1.00	.45
☐ 431 Gene Garber	1.00	.45
☐ 432 Chris Arnold	.50	.23
☐ 433 Lerrin LaGrow	.50	.23
☐ 434 Ken McMullen	.50	.23
☐ 435 Dave Concepcion	2.00	.90
☐ 436 Don Hood	.50	.23
☐ 437 Jim Lyttle	.50	.23
☐ 438 Ed Herrmann	.50	.23
☐ 439 Norm Miller	.50	.23
☐ 440 Jim Kaat	2.00	.90
☐ 441 Tom Ragland	.50	.23
☐ 442 Alan Foster	.50	.23
☐ 443 Tom Hutton	.50	.23
☐ 444 Vic Davalillo	.50	.23
☐ 445 George Medich	.50	.23
☐ 446 Len Randle	.50	.23
☐ 447 Twins Leaders	1.00	.45
Frank Quilici MG		
Ralph Rowe CO		
Bob Rodgers CO		
Vern Morgan CO		
☐ 448 Ron Hodges	.50	.23
☐ 449 Tom McCraw	.50	.23
☐ 450 Rich Hebner	1.00	.45
☐ 451 Tommy John	2.00	.90
☐ 452 Gene Hiser	.50	.23
☐ 453 Balor Moore	.50	.23
☐ 454 Kurt Bevacqua	.50	.23
☐ 455 Tom Bradley	.50	.23
☐ 456 Dave Winfield	100.00	45.00
☐ 457 Chuck Goggin	.50	.23
☐ 458 Jim Ray	.50	.23
☐ 459 Cincinnati Reds	2.00	.90
Team Card		
☐ 460 Boog Powell	2.00	.90
☐ 461 John Odom	.50	.23
☐ 462 Luis Alvarado	.50	.23
☐ 463 Pat Dobson	.50	.23
☐ 464 Jose Cruz	2.00	.90
☐ 465 Dick Bosman	.50	.23
☐ 466 Dick Billings	.50	.23
☐ 467 Winston Llenas	.50	.23
☐ 468 Pepe Frias	.50	.23
☐ 469 Joe Decker	.50	.23
☐ 470 Reggie Jackson ALCS	6.00	2.70
☐ 471 Jon Matlack NLCS	1.00	.45
☐ 472 Darold Knowles WS	1.00	.45
☐ 473 Willie Mays WS	8.00	3.60
☐ 474 Bert Campaneris WS	1.00	.45
☐ 475 Rusty Staub WS	1.00	.45
☐ 476 Cleon Jones WS	1.00	.45

☐ 477 Reggie Jackson WS	6.00	2.70
☐ 478 Bert Campaneris WS	1.00	.45
☐ 479 World Series Summary	1.00	.45
A's celebrate; win		
2nd consecutive		
championship		
☐ 480 Willie Crawford	.50	.23
☐ 481 Jerry Terrell	.50	.23
☐ 482 Bob Didier	.50	.23
☐ 483 Atlanta Braves	1.00	.45
Team Card		
☐ 484 Carmen Fanzone	.50	.23
☐ 485 Felipe Alou	2.00	.90
☐ 486 Steve Stone	1.00	.45
☐ 487 Ted Martinez	.50	.23
☐ 488 Andy Etchebarren	.50	.23
☐ 489 Pirates Leaders	1.00	.45
Danny Murtaugh MG		
Don Osborn CO		
Don Leppert CO		
Bill Mazeroski CO		
Bob Skinner CO		
☐ 490 Vada Pinson	2.00	.90
☐ 491 Roger Nelson	.50	.23
☐ 492 Mike Rogodzinski	.50	.23
☐ 493 Joe Hoerner	.50	.23
☐ 494 Ed Goodson	.50	.23
☐ 495 Dick McAuliffe	1.00	.45
☐ 496 Tom Murphy	.50	.23
☐ 497 Bobby Mitchell	.50	.23
☐ 498 Pat Corrales	1.00	.45
☐ 499 Rusty Torres	.50	.23
☐ 500 Lee May	1.00	.45
☐ 501 Eddie Leon	.50	.23
☐ 502 Dave LaRoche	.50	.23
☐ 503 Eric Soderholm	.50	.23
☐ 504 Joe Niekro	1.00	.45
☐ 505 Bill Buckner	1.00	.45
☐ 506 Ed Farmer	.50	.23
☐ 507 Larry Stahl	.50	.23
☐ 508 Montreal Expos	1.00	.45
Team Card		
☐ 509 Jesse Jefferson	.50	.23
☐ 510 Wayne Garrett	.50	.23
☐ 511 Toby Harrah	1.00	.45
☐ 512 Joe Lahoud	.50	.23
☐ 513 Jim Campanis	.50	.23
☐ 514 Paul Schaal	.50	.23
☐ 515 Willie Montanez	.50	.23
☐ 516 Horacio Pina	.50	.23
☐ 517 Mike Hegan	.50	.23
☐ 518 Derrel Thomas	.50	.23
☐ 519 Bill Sharp	.50	.23
☐ 520 Tim McCarver	2.00	.90
☐ 521 Indians Leaders	1.00	.45
Ken Aspromonte MG		
Clay Bryant CO		
Tony Pacheco CO		
☐ 522 J.R. Richard	2.00	.90
☐ 523 Cecil Cooper	2.00	.90
☐ 524 Bill Plummer	.50	.23
☐ 525 Clyde Wright	.50	.23
☐ 526 Frank Tepedino	.50	.23
☐ 527 Bobby Darwin	.50	.23
☐ 528 Bill Bonham	.50	.23
☐ 529 Horace Clarke	1.00	.45
☐ 530 Mickey Stanley	1.00	.45
☐ 531 Expos Leaders	1.00	.45
Gene Mauch MG		
Dave Bristol CO		
Cal McLish CO		
Larry Doby CO		
Jerry Zimmerman CO		
☐ 532 Skip Lockwood	.50	.23
☐ 533 Mike Phillips	.50	.23
☐ 534 Eddie Watt	.50	.23
☐ 535 Bob Tolan	.50	.23
☐ 536 Duffy Dyer	.50	.23
☐ 537 Steve Mingori	.50	.23
☐ 538 Cesar Tovar	.50	.23
☐ 539 Lloyd Allen	.50	.23
☐ 540 Bob Robertson	.50	.23
☐ 541 Cleveland Indians	1.00	.45
Team Card		
☐ 542 Rich Gossage	2.00	.90
☐ 543 Danny Cater	.50	.23

☐ 544 Ron Schueler	.50	.23
☐ 545 Billy Conigliaro	1.00	.45
☐ 546 Mike Corkins	.50	.23
☐ 547 Glenn Borgmann	.50	.23
☐ 548 Sonny Siebert	.50	.23
☐ 549 Mike Jorgensen	.50	.23
☐ 550 Sam McDowell	1.00	.45
☐ 551 Von Joshua	.50	.23
☐ 552 Denny Doyle	.50	.23
☐ 553 Jim Willoughby	.50	.23
☐ 554 Tim Johnson	.50	.23
☐ 555 Woodie Fryman	.50	.23
☐ 556 Dave Campbell	.50	.23
☐ 557 Jim McGlothlin	.50	.23
☐ 558 Bill Fahey	.50	.23
☐ 559 Darrel Chaney	.50	.23
☐ 560 Mike Cuellar	1.00	.45
☐ 561 Ed Kranepool	1.00	.45
☐ 562 Jack Aker	.50	.23
☐ 563 Hal McRae	1.00	.45
☐ 564 Mike Ryan	.50	.23
☐ 565 Milt Wilcox	.50	.23
☐ 566 Jackie Hernandez	.50	.23
☐ 567 Boston Red Sox	1.00	.45
Team Card		
☐ 568 Mike Torrez	1.00	.45
☐ 569 Rick Dempsey	1.00	.45
☐ 570 Ralph Garr	1.00	.45
☐ 571 Rich Hand	.50	.23
☐ 572 Enzo Hernandez	.50	.23
☐ 573 Mike Adams	.50	.23
☐ 574 Bill Parsons	.50	.23
☐ 575 Steve Garvey	4.00	1.80
☐ 576 Scipio Spinks	.50	.23
☐ 577 Mike Sadek	.50	.23
☐ 578 Ralph Houk MG	1.00	.45
☐ 579 Cecil Upshaw	.50	.23
☐ 580 Jim Spencer	.50	.23
☐ 581 Fred Norman	.50	.23
☐ 582 Bucky Dent	4.00	1.80
☐ 583 Marty Pattin	.50	.23
☐ 584 Ken Rudolph	.50	.23
☐ 585 Merv Rettenmund	.50	.23
☐ 586 Jack Brohamer	.50	.23
☐ 587 Larry Christenson	.50	.23
☐ 588 Hal Lanier	.50	.23
☐ 589 Boots Day	.50	.23
☐ 590 Roger Moret	.50	.23
☐ 591 Sonny Jackson	.50	.23
☐ 592 Ed Brinkman	.50	.23
☐ 593 Steve Yeager	1.00	.45
☐ 594 Leroy Stanton	.50	.23
☐ 595 Steve Blass	1.00	.45
☐ 596 Rookie Pitchers	.50	.23
Wayne Garland		
Fred Holdsworth		
Mark Littell		
Dick Pole		
☐ 597 Rookie Shortstops	.75	.35
Dave Chalk		
John Gamble		
Pete MacKanin		
Manny Trillo		
☐ 598 Rookie Outfielders	12.00	5.50
Dave Augustine		
Ken Griffey		
Steve Ontiveros		
Jim Tyrone		
☐ 599A Rookie Pitchers WAS	2.00	.90
Ron Diorio		
Dave Freisleben		
Frank Riccelli		
Greg Shanahan		
☐ 599B Rookie Pitchers SD	3.00	1.35
(SD in large print)		
☐ 599C Rookie Pitchers SD	5.00	2.20
(SD in small print)		
☐ 600 Rookie Infielders	5.00	2.20
Ron Cash		
Jim Cox		
Bill Madlock		
Reggie Sanders		
☐ 601 Rookie Outfielders	3.00	1.35
Ed Armbrister		
Rich Bladt		
Brian Downing		

Bake McBride
☐ 602	Rookie Pitchers 1.00		.45
	Glen Abbott		
	Rick Henninger		
	Craig Swan		
	Dan Vossler		
☐ 603	Rookie Catchers 1.00		.45
	Barry Foote		
	Tom Lundstedt		
	Charlie Moore		
	Sergio Robles		
☐ 604	Rookie Infielders 5.00		2.20
	Terry Hughes		
	John Knox		
	Andre Thornton		
	Frank White		
☐ 605	Rookie Pitchers 4.00		1.80
	Vic Albury		
	Ken Frailing		
	Kevin Kobel		
	Frank Tanana		
☐ 606	Rookie Outfielders.... 1.00		.45
	Jim Fuller		
	Wilbur Howard		
	Tommy Smith		
	Otto Velez		
☐ 607	Rookie Shortstops.... 1.00		.45
	Leo Foster		
	Tom Heintzelman		
	Dave Rosello		
	Frank Taveras		
☐ 608A	Rookie Pitchers: ERR 2.00		.90
	Bob Apodaco (sic)		
	Dick Baney		
	John D'Acquisto		
	Mike Wallace		
☐ 608B	Rookie Pitchers: COR 1.00		.45
	Bob Apodaca		
	Dick Baney		
	John D'Acquisto		
	Mike Wallace		
☐ 609	Rico Petrocelli 1.00		.45
☐ 610	Dave Kingman 2.00		.90
☐ 611	Rich Stelmaszek .... .50		.23
☐ 612	Luke Walker .... .50		.23
☐ 613	Dan Monzon .... .50		.23
☐ 614	Adrian Devine .... .50		.23
☐ 615	Johnny Jeter UER .... .50		.23
	(Misspelled Johnnie		
	on card back)		
☐ 616	Larry Gura .... .50		.23
☐ 617	Ted Ford .... .50		.23
☐ 618	Jim Mason .... .50		.23
☐ 619	Mike Anderson .... .50		.23
☐ 620	Al Downing .... .50		.23
☐ 621	Bernie Carbo .... .50		.23
☐ 622	Phil Gagliano .... .50		.23
☐ 623	Celerino Sanchez .... .50		.23
☐ 624	Bob Miller .... .50		.23
☐ 625	Ollie Brown .... .50		.23
☐ 626	Pittsburgh Pirates 1.00		.45
	Team Card		
☐ 627	Carl Taylor .... .50		.23
☐ 628	Ivan Murrell................. .50		.23
☐ 629	Rusty Staub................. 2.00		.90
☐ 630	Tommie Agee 1.00		.45
☐ 631	Steve Barber .... .50		.23
☐ 632	George Culver .... .50		.23
☐ 633	Dave Hamilton............. .50		.23
☐ 634	Braves Leaders 2.00		.90
	Eddie Mathews MG		
	Herm Starrette CO		
	Connie Ryan CO		
	Jim Busby CO		
	Ken Silvestri CO		
☐ 635	Johnny Edwards .... .50		.23
☐ 636	Dave Goltz................... .50		.23
☐ 637	Checklist 529-660 .... 3.00		.60
☐ 638	Ken Sanders .... .50		.23
☐ 639	Joe Lovitto .... .50		.23
☐ 640	Milt Pappas 1.00		.45
☐ 641	Chuck Brinkman .... .50		.23
☐ 642	Terry Harmon .... .50		.23
☐ 643	Dodgers Team 1.00		.45
☐ 644	Wayne Granger .... .50		.23
☐ 645	Ken Boswell.................. .50		.23

☐ 646	George Foster 2.00		.90
☐ 647	Juan Beniquez .... .50		.23
☐ 648	Terry Crowley .... .50		.23
☐ 649	Fernando Gonzalez ... .50		.23
☐ 650	Mike Epstein .... .50		.23
☐ 651	Leron Lee .... .50		.23
☐ 652	Gail Hopkins .... .50		.23
☐ 653	Bob Stinson.............. .50		.23
☐ 654A	Jesus Alou ERR 1.00		.45
	(No position)		
☐ 654B	Jesus Alou COR 5.00		2.20
	(Outfield)		
☐ 655	Mike Tyson .... .50		.23
☐ 656	Adrian Garrett .... .50		.23
☐ 657	Jim Shellenback ...... .50		.23
☐ 658	Lee Lacy .... .50		.23
☐ 659	Joe Lis..................... .50		.23
☐ 660	Larry Dierker 2.00		.50

1974 Topps Traded

The cards in this 44-card set measure 2 1/2" by 3 1/2". The 1974 Topps Traded set contains 43 player cards and one unnumbered checklist card. The fronts have the word "traded" in block letters and the backs are designed in newspaper style. Card numbers are the same as in the regular set except they are followed by a "T." No known scarcities exist for this set. The cards were inserted in all packs toward the end of the production run. They were produced in large enough quantity that they are no scarcer than the regular Topps cards.

	NRMT	VG-E
COMPLETE SET (44)	15.00	6.75
COMMON CARD..................	.50	.23
MINOR STARS	.75	.35
SEMISTARS	1.00	.45
INCLUDED IN ALL LATE PACKS		

☐ 23T	Craig Robinson .... .50		.23
☐ 42T	Claude Osteen .... .75		.35
☐ 43T	Jim Wynn .... .75		.35
☐ 51T	Bobby Heise .... .50		.23
☐ 59T	Ross Grimsley........... .50		.23
☐ 62T	Bob Locker .... .50		.23
☐ 63T	Bill Sudakis .... .50		.23
☐ 73T	Mike Marshall .... .75		.35
☐ 123T	Nelson Briles............ .75		.23
☐ 139T	Aurelio Monteagudo ... .50		.23
☐ 151T	Diego Segui.............. .75		.23
☐ 165T	Willie Davis .... .75		.35
☐ 175T	Reggie Cleveland....... .50		.23
☐ 182T	Lindy McDaniel .... .75		.35
☐ 186T	Fred Scherman .... .50		.23
☐ 249T	George Mitterwald...... .50		.23
☐ 262T	Ed Kirkpatrick .... .50		.23
☐ 269T	Bob Johnson............. .50		.23
☐ 270T	Ron Santo 1.00		.45
☐ 313T	Barry Lersch .... .50		.23

☐ 319T	Randy Hundley .... .75		.35
☐ 330T	Juan Marichal 2.00		.90
☐ 348T	Pete Richert............. .50		.23
☐ 373T	John Curtis.............. .50		.23
☐ 390T	Lou Piniella 1.00		.45
☐ 428T	Gary Sutherland ...... .50		.23
☐ 454T	Kurt Bevacqua .... .50		.23
☐ 458T	Jim Ray .... .50		.23
☐ 485T	Felipe Alou 1.00		.45
☐ 486T	Steve Stone .... .75		.35
☐ 496T	Tom Murphy .... .50		.23
☐ 516T	Horacio Pina .... .50		.23
☐ 534T	Eddie Watt .... .50		.23
☐ 538T	Cesar Tovar .... .50		.23
☐ 544T	Ron Schueler .... .50		.23
☐ 579T	Cecil Upshaw............ .50		.23
☐ 585T	Merv Rettenmund ..... .50		.23
☐ 612T	Luke Walker .... .50		.23
☐ 616T	Larry Gura .... .75		.35
☐ 618T	Jim Mason .... .50		.23
☐ 630T	Tommie Agee .... .75		.35
☐ 648T	Terry Crowley .... .50		.23
☐ 649T	Fernando Gonzalez .. .50		.23
☐ NNO	Traded Checklist 1.50		.30

1975 Topps

CARL YASTRZEMSKI

The cards in the 1975 Topps set were issued in two different sizes: a regular standard size (2 1/2" by 3 1/2") and a mini size (2 1/2" by 3 1/8") which was issued as a test in certain areas of the country. The 660-card Topps baseball set for 1975 was radically different in appearance from sets of the preceding years. The most prominent change was the use of a two-color frame surrounding the picture area rather than a single, subdued color. A facsimile autograph appears on the picture, and the backs are printed in red and green on gray. Cards were released in ten-card wax packs as well as in 42-card rack packs. Cards 189-212 depict the MVP's of both leagues from 1951 through 1974. The first seven cards (1-7) feature players (listed in alphabetical order) breaking records or achieving milestones during the previous season. Cards 306-313 picture league leaders in various statistical categories. Cards 459-466 depict the results of post-season action. Team cards feature a checklist back for players on that team and show a small inset photo of the manager on the front. The following players' regular issue cards are explicitly denoted as All-Stars, 1, 50, 80, 140, 170, 180, 260, 320, 350,

390, 400, 420, 440, 470, 530, 570, and 600. This set is quite popular with collectors, at least in part due to the fact that the Rookie Cards of George Brett, Gary Carter, Keith Hernandez, Fred Lynn, Jim Rice and Robin Yount are all in the set. Topps minis have the same checklist and are valued approximately 1.5 times the prices listed below.

	NRMT	VG-E
COMPLETE SET (660)	750.00	350.00
COMMON CARD (1-660)	.50	.23
MINOR STARS	1.00	.45
SEMISTARS	2.00	.90
UNLISTED STARS	3.00	1.35
*MINI: 1.5X BASIC CARDS		
CONDITION SENSITIVE SET		

		NRMT	VG-E
☐ 1	Hank Aaron RB	30.00	10.00
	Sets Homer Mark		
☐ 2	Lou Brock RB	3.00	1.35
	118 Stolen Bases		
☐ 3	Bob Gibson RB	3.00	1.35
	3000th Strikeout		
☐ 4	Al Kaline RB	4.00	1.80
	3000 Hit Club		
☐ 5	Nolan Ryan RB	40.00	18.00
	Fans 300 for		
	3rd Year in a Row		
☐ 6	Mike Marshall RB	1.00	.45
	Hurls 106 Games		
☐ 7	Steve Busby HL	12.00	5.50
	Dick Bosman		
	Nolan Ryan		
☐ 8	Rogelio Moret	.50	.23
☐ 9	Frank Tepedino	.50	.23
☐ 10	Willie Davis	1.00	.45
☐ 11	Bill Melton	.50	.23
☐ 12	David Clyde	.50	.23
☐ 13	Gene Locklear	1.00	.45
☐ 14	Milt Wilcox	.50	.23
☐ 15	Jose Cardenal	1.00	.45
☐ 16	Frank Tanana	2.00	.90
☐ 17	Dave Concepcion	2.00	.90
☐ 18	Tigers: Team/Mgr.	2.00	.40
	Ralph Houk		
	(Checklist back)		
☐ 19	Jerry Koosman	1.00	.45
☐ 20	Thurman Munson	6.00	2.70
☐ 21	Rollie Fingers	3.00	1.35
☐ 22	Dave Cash	.50	.23
☐ 23	Bill Russell	1.00	.45
☐ 24	Al Fitzmorris	.50	.23
☐ 25	Lee May	1.00	.45
☐ 26	Dave McNally	1.00	.45
☐ 27	Ken Reitz	.50	.23
☐ 28	Tom Murphy	.50	.23
☐ 29	Dave Parker	4.00	1.80
☐ 30	Bert Blyleven	2.00	.90
☐ 31	Dave Rader	.50	.23
☐ 32	Reggie Cleveland	.50	.23
☐ 33	Dusty Baker	2.00	.90
☐ 34	Steve Renko	.50	.23
☐ 35	Ron Santo	1.00	.45
☐ 36	Joe Lovitto	.50	.23
☐ 37	Dave Freisleben	.50	.23
☐ 38	Buddy Bell	2.00	.90
☐ 39	Andre Thornton	1.00	.45
☐ 40	Bill Singer	.50	.23
☐ 41	Cesar Geronimo	1.00	.45
☐ 42	Joe Coleman	.50	.23
☐ 43	Cleon Jones	1.00	.45
☐ 44	Pat Dobson	.50	.23
☐ 45	Joe Rudi	1.00	.45
☐ 46	Phillies: Team/Mgr.	2.00	.40
	Danny Ozark UER		
	(Checklist back)		
	(Terry Harmon listed as 339		
	instead of 399)		
☐ 47	Tommy John	2.00	.90
☐ 48	Freddie Patek	1.00	.45
☐ 49	Larry Dierker	.50	.45
☐ 50	Brooks Robinson	6.00	2.70
☐ 51	Bob Forsch	1.00	.45
☐ 52	Darrell Porter	1.00	.45
☐ 53	Dave Giusti	.50	.23
☐ 54	Eric Soderholm	.50	.23
☐ 55	Bobby Bonds	2.00	.90
☐ 56	Rick Wise	1.00	.45
☐ 57	Dave Johnson	1.00	.45
☐ 58	Chuck Taylor	.50	.23
☐ 59	Ken Henderson	.50	.23
☐ 60	Fergie Jenkins	3.00	1.35
☐ 61	Dave Winfield	40.00	18.00
☐ 62	Fritz Peterson	.50	.23
☐ 63	Steve Swisher	.50	.23
☐ 64	Dave Chalk	.50	.23
☐ 65	Don Gullett	1.00	.45
☐ 66	Willie Horton	1.00	.45
☐ 67	Tug McGraw	1.00	.45
☐ 68	Ron Blomberg	.50	.23
☐ 69	John Odom	.50	.23
☐ 70	Mike Schmidt	50.00	22.00
☐ 71	Charlie Hough	1.00	.45
☐ 72	Royals: Team/Mgr.	2.00	.40
	Jack McKeon		
	(Checklist back)		
☐ 73	J.R. Richard	1.00	.45
☐ 74	Mark Belanger	1.00	.45
☐ 75	Ted Simmons	2.00	.90
☐ 76	Ed Sprague	.50	.23
☐ 77	Richie Zisk	1.00	.45
☐ 78	Ray Corbin	.50	.23
☐ 79	Gary Matthews	1.00	.45
☐ 80	Carlton Fisk	10.00	4.50
☐ 81	Ron Reed	.50	.23
☐ 82	Pat Kelly	.50	.23
☐ 83	Jim Merritt	.50	.23
☐ 84	Enzo Hernandez	.50	.23
☐ 85	Bill Bonham	.50	.23
☐ 86	Joe Lis	.50	.23
☐ 87	George Foster	2.00	.90
☐ 88	Tom Egan	.50	.23
☐ 89	Jim Ray	.50	.23
☐ 90	Rusty Staub	.50	.90
☐ 91	Dick Green	.50	.23
☐ 92	Cecil Upshaw	.50	.23
☐ 93	Dave Lopes	2.00	.90
☐ 94	Jim Lonborg	1.00	.45
☐ 95	John Mayberry	1.00	.45
☐ 96	Mike Cosgrove	.50	.23
☐ 97	Earl Williams	.50	.23
☐ 98	Rich Folkers	.50	.23
☐ 99	Mike Hegan	.50	.23
☐ 100	Willie Stargell	4.00	1.80
☐ 101	Expos: Team/Mgr.	2.00	.40
	Gene Mauch		
	(Checklist back)		
☐ 102	Joe Decker	.50	.23
☐ 103	Rick Miller	.50	.23
☐ 104	Bill Madlock	2.00	.90
☐ 105	Buzz Capra	.50	.23
☐ 106	Mike Hargrove	3.00	1.35
☐ 107	Jim Barr	.50	.23
☐ 108	Tom Hall	.50	.23
☐ 109	George Hendrick	1.00	.45
☐ 110	Wilbur Wood	.50	.23
☐ 111	Wayne Garrett	.50	.23
☐ 112	Larry Hardy	.50	.23
☐ 113	Elliott Maddox	.50	.23
☐ 114	Dick Lange	.50	.23
☐ 115	Joe Ferguson	.50	.23
☐ 116	Lerrin LaGrow	.50	.23
☐ 117	Orioles: Team/Mgr.	3.00	.60
	Earl Weaver		
	(Checklist back)		
☐ 118	Mike Anderson	.50	.23
☐ 119	Tommy Helms	.50	.23
☐ 120	Steve Busby UER	1.00	.45
	(Photo actually		
	Fran Healy)		
☐ 121	Bill North	.50	.23
☐ 122	Al Hrabosky	1.00	.45
☐ 123	Johnny Briggs	.50	.23
☐ 124	Jerry Reuss	1.00	.45
☐ 125	Ken Singleton	1.00	.45
☐ 126	Checklist 1-132	3.00	.60
☐ 127	Glenn Borgmann	.50	.23
☐ 128	Bill Lee	1.00	.45
☐ 129	Rick Monday	1.00	.45
☐ 130	Phil Niekro	3.00	1.35
☐ 131	Toby Harrah	1.00	.45
☐ 132	Randy Moffitt	.50	.23
☐ 133	Dan Driessen	1.00	.45
☐ 134	Ron Hodges	.50	.23
☐ 135	Charlie Spikes	.50	.23
☐ 136	Jim Mason	.50	.23
☐ 137	Terry Forster	1.00	.45
☐ 138	Del Unser	.50	.23
☐ 139	Horacio Pina	.50	.23
☐ 140	Steve Garvey	5.00	2.20
☐ 141	Mickey Stanley	.50	.23
☐ 142	Bob Reynolds	.50	.23
☐ 143	Cliff Johnson	1.00	.45
☐ 144	Jim Wohlford	.50	.23
☐ 145	Ken Holtzman	1.00	.45
☐ 146	Padres: Team/Mgr.	2.00	.40
	John McNamara		
	(Checklist back)		
☐ 147	Pedro Garcia	.50	.23
☐ 148	Jim Rooker	.50	.23
☐ 149	Tim Foli	.50	.23
☐ 150	Bob Gibson	5.00	2.20
☐ 151	Steve Brye	.50	.23
☐ 152	Mario Guerrero	.50	.23
☐ 153	Rick Reuschel	1.00	.45
☐ 154	Mike Lum	.50	.23
☐ 155	Jim Bibby	.50	.23
☐ 156	Dave Kingman	2.00	.90
☐ 157	Pedro Borbon	1.00	.45
☐ 158	Jerry Grote	.50	.23
☐ 159	Steve Arlin	.50	.23
☐ 160	Graig Nettles	2.00	.90
☐ 161	Stan Bahnsen	.50	.23
☐ 162	Willie Montanez	.50	.23
☐ 163	Jim Brewer	.50	.23
☐ 164	Mickey Rivers	1.00	.45
☐ 165	Doug Rader	.50	.45
☐ 166	Woodie Fryman	.50	.23
☐ 167	Rich Coggins	.50	.23
☐ 168	Bill Greif	.50	.23
☐ 169	Cookie Rojas	1.00	.45
☐ 170	Bert Campaneris	1.00	.45
☐ 171	Ed Kirkpatrick	.50	.23
☐ 172	Red Sox: Team/Mgr.	3.00	.60
	Darrell Johnson		
	(Checklist back)		
☐ 173	Steve Rogers	1.00	.45
☐ 174	Bake McBride	1.00	.45
☐ 175	Don Money	1.00	.45
☐ 176	Burt Hooton	1.00	.45
☐ 177	Vic Correll	.50	.23
☐ 178	Cesar Tovar	.50	.23
☐ 179	Tom Bradley	.50	.23
☐ 180	Joe Morgan	5.00	2.20
☐ 181	Fred Beene	.50	.23
☐ 182	Don Hahn	.50	.23
☐ 183	Mel Stottlemyre	1.00	.45
☐ 184	Jorge Orta	.50	.23
☐ 185	Steve Carlton	6.00	2.70
☐ 186	Willie Crawford	.50	.23
☐ 187	Denny Doyle	.50	.23
☐ 188	Tom Griffin	.50	.23
☐ 189	1951 MVP's	3.00	1.35
	Larry (Yogi) Berra		
	Roy Campanella		
	(Campy never issued)		
☐ 190	1952 MVP's	2.00	.90
	Bobby Shantz		
	Hank Sauer		
☐ 191	1953 MVP's	2.00	.90
	Al Rosen		
	Roy Campanella		
☐ 192	1954 MVP's	4.00	1.80
	Yogi Berra		
	Willie Mays		
☐ 193	1955 MVP's UER	3.00	1.35
	Yogi Berra		
	Roy Campanella		
	(Campy card never		
	issued, pictured		
	with LA cap)		
☐ 194	1956 MVP's	15.00	6.75
	Mickey Mantle		

Don Newcombe
- ☐ 195 1957 MVP's .... 25.00 — 11.00
  - Mickey Mantle
  - Hank Aaron
- ☐ 196 1958 MVP's .... 2.00 — .90
  - Jackie Jensen
  - Ernie Banks
- ☐ 197 1959 MVP's .... 2.00 — .90
  - Nellie Fox
  - Ernie Banks
- ☐ 198 1960 MVP's .... 2.00 — .90
  - Roger Maris
  - Dick Groat
- ☐ 199 1961 MVP's .... 3.00 — 1.35
  - Roger Maris
  - Frank Robinson
- ☐ 200 1962 MVP's .... 15.00 — 6.75
  - Mickey Mantle
  - Maury Wills
  - (Wills never issued)
- ☐ 201 1963 MVP's .... 2.00 — .90
  - Elston Howard
  - Sandy Koufax
- ☐ 202 1964 MVP's .... 2.00 — .90
  - Brooks Robinson
  - Ken Boyer
- ☐ 203 1965 MVP's .... 2.00 — .90
  - Zoilo Versalles
  - Willie Mays
- ☐ 204 1966 MVP's .... 8.00 — 3.60
  - Frank Robinson
  - Bob Clemente
- ☐ 205 1967 MVP's .... 2.00 — .90
  - Carl Yastrzemski
  - Orlando Cepeda
- ☐ 206 1968 MVP's .... 2.00 — .90
  - Denny McLain
  - Bob Gibson
- ☐ 207 1969 MVP's .... 2.00 — .90
  - Harmon Killebrew
  - Willie McCovey
- ☐ 208 1970 MVP's .... 2.00 — .90
  - Boog Powell
  - Johnny Bench
- ☐ 209 1971 MVP's .... 2.00 — .90
  - Vida Blue
  - Joe Torre
- ☐ 210 1972 MVP's .... 2.00 — .90
  - Rich Allen
  - Johnny Bench
- ☐ 211 1973 MVP's .... 6.00 — 2.70
  - Reggie Jackson
  - Pete Rose
- ☐ 212 1974 MVP's .... 2.00 — .90
  - Jeff Burroughs
  - Steve Garvey
- ☐ 213 Oscar Gamble ...... 1.00 — .45
- ☐ 214 Harry Parker .... .50 — .23
- ☐ 215 Bobby Valentine ... 1.00 — .45
- ☐ 216 Giants: Team/Mgr. .. 2.00 — .40
  - Wes Westrum
  - (Checklist back)
- ☐ 217 Lou Piniella .... 2.00 — .90
- ☐ 218 Jerry Johnson ...... .50 — .23
- ☐ 219 Ed Herrmann .... .50 — .23
- ☐ 220 Don Sutton .... 3.00 — 1.35
- ☐ 221 Aurelio Rodriguez .. .50 — .23
- ☐ 222 Dan Spillner .... .50 — .23
- ☐ 223 Robin Yount .... 80.00 — 36.00
- ☐ 224 Ramon Hernandez .. .50 — .23
- ☐ 225 Bob Grich .... 1.00 — .45
- ☐ 226 Bill Campbell .... .50 — .23
- ☐ 227 Bob Watson .... 1.00 — .45
- ☐ 228 George Brett .... 200.00 — 90.00
- ☐ 229 Barry Foote .... .50 — .23
- ☐ 230 Jim Hunter .... 3.00 — 1.35
- ☐ 231 Mike Tyson .... .50 — .23
- ☐ 232 Diego Segui .... .50 — .23
- ☐ 233 Billy Grabarkewitz .. .50 — .23
- ☐ 234 Tom Grieve .... 1.00 — .45
- ☐ 235 Jack Billingham ..... 1.00 — .45
- ☐ 236 Angels: Team/Mgr. .. 2.00 — .40
  - Dick Williams
  - (Checklist back)
- ☐ 237 Carl Morton .... .50 — .23
- ☐ 238 Dave Duncan .... .50 — .23

- ☐ 239 George Stone .... .50 — .23
- ☐ 240 Garry Maddox ...... 1.00 — .45
- ☐ 241 Dick Tidrow .... .50 — .23
- ☐ 242 Jay Johnstone ...... 1.00 — .45
- ☐ 243 Jim Kaat .... 2.00 — .90
- ☐ 244 Bill Buckner .... 1.00 — .45
- ☐ 245 Mickey Lolich ...... 2.00 — .90
- ☐ 246 Cardinals: Team/Mgr. 2.00 — .40
  - Red Schoendienst
  - (Checklist back)
- ☐ 247 Enos Cabell .... .50 — .23
- ☐ 248 Randy Jones .... 2.00 — .90
- ☐ 249 Danny Thompson ... .50 — .23
- ☐ 250 Ken Brett .... .50 — .23
- ☐ 251 Fran Healy .... .50 — .23
- ☐ 252 Fred Scherman ..... .50 — .23
- ☐ 253 Jesus Alou .... .50 — .23
- ☐ 254 Mike Torrez .... 1.00 — .45
- ☐ 255 Dwight Evans .... 2.00 — .90
- ☐ 256 Billy Champion ..... .50 — .23
- ☐ 257 Checklist: 133-264 .. 3.00 — .60
- ☐ 258 Dave LaRoche ...... .50 — .23
- ☐ 259 Len Randle .... .50 — .23
- ☐ 260 Johnny Bench ...... 12.00 — 5.50
- ☐ 261 Andy Hassler .... .50 — .23
- ☐ 262 Rowland Office ..... .50 — .23
- ☐ 263 Jim Perry .... 1.00 — .45
- ☐ 264 John Milner .... .50 — .23
- ☐ 265 Ron Bryant .... .50 — .23
- ☐ 266 Sandy Alomar ...... 1.00 — .45
- ☐ 267 Dick Ruthven .... .50 — .23
- ☐ 268 Hal McRae .... 1.00 — .45
- ☐ 269 Doug Rau .... .50 — .23
- ☐ 270 Ron Fairly .... 1.00 — .45
- ☐ 271 Gerry Moses .... .50 — .23
- ☐ 272 Lynn McGlothen .... .50 — .23
- ☐ 273 Steve Braun .... .50 — .23
- ☐ 274 Vicente Romo ...... .50 — .23
- ☐ 275 Paul Blair .... 1.00 — .45
- ☐ 276 White Sox Team/Mgr. 2.00 — .40
  - Chuck Tanner
  - (Checklist back)
- ☐ 277 Frank Taveras ...... .50 — .23
- ☐ 278 Paul Lindblad ...... .50 — .23
- ☐ 279 Milt May .... .50 — .23
- ☐ 280 Carl Yastrzemski ... 6.00 — 2.70
- ☐ 281 Jim Slaton .... .50 — .23
- ☐ 282 Jerry Morales .... .50 — .23
- ☐ 283 Steve Foucault ..... .50 — .23
- ☐ 284 Ken Griffey .... 4.00 — 1.80
- ☐ 285 Ellie Rodriguez .... .50 — .23
- ☐ 286 Mike Jorgensen .... .50 — .23
- ☐ 287 Roric Harrison ..... .50 — .23
- ☐ 288 Bruce Ellingsen .... .50 — .23
- ☐ 289 Ken Rudolph .... .50 — .23
- ☐ 290 Jon Matlack .... .50 — .23
- ☐ 291 Bill Sudakis .... .50 — .23
- ☐ 292 Ron Schueler ...... .50 — .23
- ☐ 293 Dick Sharon .... .50 — .23
- ☐ 294 Geoff Zahn .... .50 — .23
- ☐ 295 Vada Pinson .... 2.00 — .90
- ☐ 296 Alan Foster .... .50 — .23
- ☐ 297 Craig Kusick .... .50 — .23
- ☐ 298 Johnny Grubb ...... .50 — .23
- ☐ 299 Bucky Dent .... 2.00 — .90
- ☐ 300 Reggie Jackson .... 15.00 — 6.75
- ☐ 301 Dave Roberts ...... .50 — .23
- ☐ 302 Rick Burleson ...... 1.00 — .45
- ☐ 303 Grant Jackson ..... .50 — .23
- ☐ 304 Pirates: Team/Mgr. .. 2.00 — .40
  - Danny Murtaugh
  - (Checklist back)
- ☐ 305 Jim Colborn .... .50 — .23
- ☐ 306 Batting Leaders .... 2.00 — .90
  - Rod Carew
  - Ralph Garr
- ☐ 307 Home Run Leaders .. 3.00 — 1.35
  - Dick Allen
  - Mike Schmidt
- ☐ 308 RBI Leaders .... 2.00 — .90
  - Jeff Burroughs
  - Johnny Bench
- ☐ 309 Stolen Base Leaders .. 2.00 — .90
  - Bill North
  - Lou Brock
- ☐ 310 Victory Leaders ..... 2.00 — .90

Jim Hunter
Fergie Jenkins
Andy Messersmith
Phil Niekro
- ☐ 311 ERA Leaders .... 2.00 — .90
  - Jim Hunter
  - Buzz Capra
- ☐ 312 Strikeout Leaders .. 20.00 — 9.00
  - Nolan Ryan
  - Steve Carlton
- ☐ 313 Leading Firemen ... 1.00 — .45
  - Terry Forster
  - Mike Marshall
- ☐ 314 Buck Martinez ...... .50 — .23
- ☐ 315 Don Kessinger ..... 1.00 — .45
- ☐ 316 Jackie Brown .... .50 — .23
- ☐ 317 Joe Lahoud .... .50 — .23
- ☐ 318 Ernie McAnally .... .50 — .23
- ☐ 319 Johnny Oates ...... 1.00 — .45
- ☐ 320 Pete Rose .... 15.00 — 6.75
- ☐ 321 Rudy May .... .50 — .23
- ☐ 322 Ed Goodson .... .50 — .23
- ☐ 323 Fred Holdsworth ... .50 — .23
- ☐ 324 Ed Kranepool ...... 1.00 — .45
- ☐ 325 Tony Oliva .... 2.00 — .90
- ☐ 326 Wayne Twitchell ... .50 — .23
- ☐ 327 Jerry Hairston ..... .50 — .23
- ☐ 328 Sonny Siebert ..... .50 — .23
- ☐ 329 Ted Kubiak .... .50 — .23
- ☐ 330 Mike Marshall ..... 1.00 — .45
- ☐ 331 Indians: Team/Mgr. .. 2.00 — .40
  - Frank Robinson
  - (Checklist back)
- ☐ 332 Fred Kendall .... .50 — .23
- ☐ 333 Dick Drago .... .50 — .23
- ☐ 334 Greg Gross .... .50 — .23
- ☐ 335 Jim Palmer .... 5.00 — 2.20
- ☐ 336 Rennie Stennett ... .50 — .23
- ☐ 337 Kevin Kobel .... .50 — .23
- ☐ 338 Rich Stelmaszek ... .50 — .23
- ☐ 339 Jim Fregosi .... 1.00 — .45
- ☐ 340 Paul Splittorff ..... .50 — .23
- ☐ 341 Hal Breeden .... .50 — .23
- ☐ 342 Leroy Stanton ..... .50 — .23
- ☐ 343 Danny Frisella ..... .50 — .23
- ☐ 344 Ben Oglivie .... 1.00 — .45
- ☐ 345 Clay Carroll .... 1.00 — .45
- ☐ 346 Bobby Darwin ..... .50 — .23
- ☐ 347 Mike Caldwell ..... .50 — .23
- ☐ 348 Tony Muser .... .50 — .23
- ☐ 349 Ray Sadecki .... .50 — .23
- ☐ 350 Bobby Murcer ..... 1.00 — .45
- ☐ 351 Bob Boone .... 2.00 — .90
- ☐ 352 Darold Knowles ... .50 — .23
- ☐ 353 Luis Melendez ..... .50 — .23
- ☐ 354 Dick Bosman ...... .50 — .23
- ☐ 355 Chris Cannizzaro .. .50 — .23
- ☐ 356 Rico Petrocelli .... 1.00 — .45
- ☐ 357 Ken Forsch .... .50 — .23
- ☐ 358 Al Bumbry .... 1.00 — .45
- ☐ 359 Paul Popovich ..... .50 — .23
- ☐ 360 George Scott ...... 1.00 — .45
- ☐ 361 Dodgers: Team/Mgr. 2.00 — .40
  - Walter Alston
  - (Checklist back)
- ☐ 362 Steve Hargan ...... .50 — .23
- ☐ 363 Carmen Fanzone .. .50 — .23
- ☐ 364 Doug Bird .... .50 — .23
- ☐ 365 Bob Bailey .... .50 — .23
- ☐ 366 Ken Sanders .... .50 — .23
- ☐ 367 Craig Robinson .... .50 — .23
- ☐ 368 Vic Albury .... .50 — .23
- ☐ 369 Merv Rettenmund .. .50 — .23
- ☐ 370 Tom Seaver .... 12.00 — 5.50
- ☐ 371 Gate Brown .... .50 — .23
- ☐ 372 John D'Acquisto ... .50 — .23
- ☐ 373 Bill Sharp .... .50 — .23
- ☐ 374 Eddie Watt .... .50 — .23
- ☐ 375 Roy White .... 1.00 — .45
- ☐ 376 Steve Yeager ...... 1.00 — .45
- ☐ 377 Tom Hilgendorf .... .50 — .23
- ☐ 378 Derrel Thomas ..... .50 — .23
- ☐ 379 Bernie Carbo ...... .50 — .23
- ☐ 380 Sal Bando .... 1.00 — .45
- ☐ 381 John Curtis .... .50 — .23
- ☐ 382 Don Baylor .... 2.00 — .90

□ 383 Jim York .50 .23
□ 384 Brewers: Team/Mgr. 2.00 .40
   Del Crandall
   (Checklist back)
□ 385 Dock Ellis .50 .23
□ 386 Checklist: 265-396 .. 3.00 .60
□ 387 Jim Spencer .50 .23
□ 388 Steve Stone 1.00 .45
□ 389 Tony Solaita .50 .23
□ 390 Ron Cey 2.00 .90
□ 391 Don DeMola .50 .23
□ 392 Bruce Bochte 1.00 .45
□ 393 Gary Gentry .50 .23
□ 394 Larvell Blanks .50 .23
□ 395 Bud Harrelson 1.00 .45
□ 396 Fred Norman 1.00 .45
□ 397 Bill Freehan 1.00 .45
□ 398 Elias Sosa .50 .23
□ 399 Terry Harmon .50 .23
□ 400 Dick Allen 2.00 .90
□ 401 Mike Wallace .50 .23
□ 402 Bob Tolan .50 .23
□ 403 Tom Buskey .50 .23
□ 404 Ted Sizemore .50 .23
□ 405 John Montague .50 .23
□ 406 Bob Gallagher .50 .23
□ 407 Herb Washington 2.00 .90
□ 408 Clyde Wright .50 .23
□ 409 Bob Robertson .50 .23
□ 410 Mike Cueller UER 1.00 .45
   (Sic, Cuellar)
□ 411 George Mitterwald .50 .23
□ 412 Bill Hands .50 .23
□ 413 Marty Pattin .50 .23
□ 414 Manny Mota 1.00 .45
□ 415 John Hiller 1.00 .45
□ 416 Larry Lintz .50 .23
□ 417 Skip Lockwood .50 .23
□ 418 Leo Foster .50 .23
□ 419 Dave Goltz .50 .23
□ 420 Larry Bowa 2.00 .90
□ 421 Mets: Team/Mgr. 3.00 .60
   Yogi Berra
   (Checklist back)
□ 422 Brian Downing 1.00 .45
□ 423 Clay Kirby .50 .23
□ 424 John Lowenstein .50 .23
□ 425 Tito Fuentes .50 .23
□ 426 George Medich .50 .23
□ 427 Clarence Gaston 1.00 .45
□ 428 Dave Hamilton .50 .23
□ 429 Jim Dwyer .50 .23
□ 430 Luis Tiant 2.00 .90
□ 431 Rod Gilbreath .50 .23
□ 432 Ken Berry .50 .23
□ 433 Larry Demery .50 .23
□ 434 Bob Locker .50 .23
□ 435 Dave Nelson .50 .23
□ 436 Ken Frailing .50 .23
□ 437 Al Cowens 1.00 .45
□ 438 Don Carrithers .50 .23
□ 439 Ed Brinkman .50 .23
□ 440 Andy Messersmith 1.00 .45
□ 441 Bobby Heise .50 .23
□ 442 Maximino Leon .50 .23
□ 443 Twins: Team/Mgr. 2.00 .40
   Frank Quilici
   (Checklist back)
□ 444 Gene Garber 1.00 .45
□ 445 Felix Millan .50 .23
□ 446 Bart Johnson .50 .23
□ 447 Terry Crowley .50 .23
□ 448 Frank Duffy .50 .23
□ 449 Charlie Williams .50 .23
□ 450 Willie McCovey 5.00 2.20
□ 451 Rick Dempsey 1.00 .45
□ 452 Angel Mangual .50 .23
□ 453 Claude Osteen 1.00 .45
□ 454 Doug Griffin .50 .23
□ 455 Don Wilson .50 .23
□ 456 Bob Coluccio .50 .23
□ 457 Mario Mendoza .50 .23
□ 458 Ross Grimsley .50 .23
□ 459 1974 AL Champs. 1.00 .45
   A's over Orioles
   (Second base action
   pictured)
□ 460 Frank Taveras NLCS 2.00 .90
   Steve Garvey
□ 461 Reggie Jackson WS 4.00 1.80
□ 462 World Series Game 2 1.00 .45
   (Dodger dugout)
□ 463 Rollie Fingers WS .... 2.00 .90
□ 464 World Series Game 4 1.00 .45
   (A's batter)
□ 465 Joe Rudi WS 1.00 .45
□ 466 World Series Summary 2.00 .90
   A's do it again;
   win third straight
   (A's group picture)
□ 467 Ed Halicki .50 .23
□ 468 Bobby Mitchell .50 .23
□ 469 Tom Dettore .50 .23
□ 470 Jeff Burroughs 1.00 .45
□ 471 Bob Stinson .50 .23
□ 472 Bruce Dal Canton .50 .23
□ 473 Ken McMullen .50 .23
□ 474 Luke Walker .50 .23
□ 475 Darrell Evans 1.00 .45
□ 476 Ed Figueroa .50 .23
□ 477 Tom Hutton .50 .23
□ 478 Tom Burgmeier .50 .23
□ 479 Ken Boswell .50 .23
□ 480 Carlos May .50 .23
□ 481 Will McEnaney 1.00 .45
□ 482 Tom McCraw .50 .23
□ 483 Steve Ontiveros .50 .23
□ 484 Glenn Beckert 1.00 .45
□ 485 Sparky Lyle 1.00 .45
□ 486 Ray Fosse .50 .23
□ 487 Astros: Team/Mgr. .. 2.00 .40
   Preston Gomez
   (Checklist back)
□ 488 Bill Travers .50 .23
□ 489 Cecil Cooper 2.00 .90
□ 490 Reggie Smith 1.00 .45
□ 491 Doyle Alexander 1.00 .45
□ 492 Rich Hebner 1.00 .45
□ 493 Don Stanhouse .50 .23
□ 494 Pete LaCock .50 .23
□ 495 Nelson Briles 1.00 .45
□ 496 Pepe Frias .50 .23
□ 497 Jim Nettles .50 .23
□ 498 Al Downing .50 .23
□ 499 Marty Perez .50 .23
□ 500 Nolan Ryan 80.00 36.00
□ 501 Bill Robinson 1.00 .45
□ 502 Pat Bourque .50 .23
□ 503 Fred Stanley .50 .23
□ 504 Buddy Bradford .50 .23
□ 505 Chris Speier .50 .23
□ 506 Leron Lee .50 .23
□ 507 Tom Carroll .50 .23
□ 508 Bob Hansen .50 .23
□ 509 Dave Hilton .50 .23
□ 510 Vida Blue 1.00 .45
□ 511 Rangers: Team/Mgr. 2.00 .40
   Billy Martin
   (Checklist back)
□ 512 Larry Milbourne .50 .23
□ 513 Dick Pole .50 .23
□ 514 Jose Cruz 2.00 .90
□ 515 Manny Sanguillen 1.00 .45
□ 516 Don Hood .50 .23
□ 517 Checklist: 397-528 .. 3.00 .60
□ 518 Leo Cardenas .50 .23
□ 519 Jim Todd .50 .23
□ 520 Amos Otis 1.00 .45
□ 521 Dennis Blair .50 .23
□ 522 Gary Sutherland .50 .23
□ 523 Tom Paciorek 1.00 .45
□ 524 John Doherty .50 .23
□ 525 Tom House .50 .23
□ 526 Larry Hisle 1.00 .45
□ 527 Mac Scarce .50 .23
□ 528 Eddie Leon .50 .23
□ 529 Gary Thomasson .50 .23
□ 530 Gaylord Perry 3.00 1.35
□ 531 Reds: Team/Mgr. 4.00 .80
   Sparky Anderson
   (Checklist back)
□ 532 Gorman Thomas 1.00 .45
□ 533 Rudy Meoli .50 .23
□ 534 Alex Johnson .50 .23
□ 535 Gene Tenace 1.00 .45
□ 536 Bob Moose .50 .23
□ 537 Tommy Harper 1.00 .45
□ 538 Duffy Dyer .50 .23
□ 539 Jesse Jefferson .50 .23
□ 540 Lou Brock 5.00 2.20
□ 541 Roger Metzger .50 .23
□ 542 Pete Broberg .50 .23
□ 543 Larry Biittner .50 .23
□ 544 Steve Mingori .50 .23
□ 545 Billy Williams 3.00 1.35
□ 546 John Knox .50 .23
□ 547 Von Joshua .50 .23
□ 548 Charlie Sands .50 .23
□ 549 Bill Butler .50 .23
□ 550 Ralph Garr 1.00 .45
□ 551 Larry Christenson .50 .23
□ 552 Jack Brohamer .50 .23
□ 553 John Boccabella .50 .23
□ 554 Rich Gossage 2.00 .90
□ 555 Al Oliver 2.00 .90
□ 556 Tim Johnson .50 .23
□ 557 Larry Gura .50 .23
□ 558 Dave Roberts .50 .23
□ 559 Bob Montgomery .50 .23
□ 560 Tony Perez 3.00 1.35
□ 561 A's: Team/Mgr. .50 .40
   Alvin Dark
   (Checklist back)
□ 562 Gary Nolan 1.00 .45
□ 563 Wilbur Howard .50 .23
□ 564 Tommy Davis 1.00 .45
□ 565 Joe Torre 2.00 .90
□ 566 Ray Burris .50 .23
□ 567 Jim Sundberg 2.00 .90
□ 568 Dale Murray .50 .23
□ 569 Frank White 1.00 .45
□ 570 Jim Wynn 1.00 .45
□ 571 Dave Lemanczyk .50 .23
□ 572 Roger Nelson .50 .23
□ 573 Orlando Pena .50 .23
□ 574 Tony Taylor 1.00 .45
□ 575 Gene Clines .50 .23
□ 576 Phil Roof .50 .23
□ 577 John Morris .50 .23
□ 578 Dave Tomlin .50 .23
□ 579 Skip Pitlock .50 .23
□ 580 Frank Robinson 6.00 2.70
□ 581 Darrel Chaney .50 .23
□ 582 Eduardo Rodriguez .50 .23
□ 583 Andy Etchebarren .50 .23
□ 584 Mike Garman .50 .23
□ 585 Chris Chambliss 1.00 .45
□ 586 Tim McCarver 2.00 .90
□ 587 Chris Ward .50 .23
□ 588 Rick Auerbach .50 .23
□ 589 Braves: Team/Mgr.. 2.00 .40
   Clyde King
   (Checklist back)
□ 590 Cesar Cedeno 1.00 .45
□ 591 Glenn Abbott .50 .23
□ 592 Balor Moore .50 .23
□ 593 Gene Lamont .50 .23
□ 594 Jim Fuller .50 .23
□ 595 Joe Niekro 1.00 .45
□ 596 Ollie Brown .50 .23
□ 597 Winston Llenas .50 .23
□ 598 Bruce Kison .50 .23
□ 599 Nate Colbert .50 .23
□ 600 Rod Carew 5.00 2.20
□ 601 Juan Beniquez .50 .23
□ 602 John Vukovich .50 .23
□ 603 Lew Krausse .50 .23
□ 604 Oscar Zamora .50 .23
□ 605 John Ellis .50 .23
□ 606 Bruce Miller .50 .23
□ 607 Jim Holt .50 .23
□ 608 Gene Michael 1.00 .45
□ 609 Elrod Hendricks .50 .23
□ 610 Ron Hunt .50 .23
□ 611 Yankees: Team/Mgr. 2.00 .40
   Bill Virdon
   (Checklist back)
□ 612 Terry Hughes .50 .23

☐ 613 Bill Parsons .... .50	.23
☐ 614 Rookie Pitchers .. 1.00	.45

Jack Kucek
Dyar Miller
Vern Ruhle
Paul Siebert

☐ 615 Rookie Pitchers ...... 2.00 .90
Pat Darcy
Dennis Leonard
Tom Underwood
Hank Webb

☐ 616 Rookie Outfielders .. 12.00 5.50
Dave Augustine
Pepe Mangual
Jim Rice
John Scott

☐ 617 Rookie Infielders ...... 2.00 .90
Mike Cubbage
Doug DeCinces
Reggie Sanders
Manny Trillo

☐ 618 Rookie Pitchers ...... 1.00 .45
Jamie Easterly
Tom Johnson
Scott McGregor
Rick Rhoden

☐ 619 Rookie Outfielders .. 1.00 .45
Benny Ayala
Nyls Nyman
Tommy Smith
Jerry Turner

☐ 620 Rookie Catcher/OF.. 20.00 9.00
Gary Carter
Marc Hill
Danny Meyer
Leon Roberts

☐ 621 Rookie Pitchers .... 2.00 .90
John Denny
Rawly Eastwick
Juan Veintidos

☐ 622 Rookie Outfielders .. 6.00 2.70
Ed Armbrister
Fred Lynn
Tom Poquette
Terry Whitfield UER
(Listed as Ney York)

☐ 623 Rookie Infielders 6.00 2.70
Phil Garner
Keith Hernandez UER
(Sic, bats right)
Bob Sheldon
Tom Veryzer

☐ 624 Rookie Pitchers .... 1.00 .45
Doug Konieczny
Gary Lavelle
Jim Otten
Eddie Solomon

☐ 625 Boog Powell .... 2.00 .90
☐ 626 Larry Haney UER .... .50 .23
(Photo actually
Dave Duncan)
☐ 627 Tom Walker .... .50 .23
☐ 628 Ron LeFlore .... 1.00 .45
☐ 629 Joe Hoerner .... .50 .23
☐ 630 Greg Luzinski .... 2.00 .90
☐ 631 Lee Lacy .... .50 .23
☐ 632 Morris Nettles .... .50 .23
☐ 633 Paul Casanova .... .50 .23
☐ 634 Cy Acosta .... .50 .23
☐ 635 Chuck Dobson .... .50 .23
☐ 636 Charlie Moore .... .50 .23
☐ 637 Ted Martinez .... .50 .23
☐ 638 Cubs: Team/Mgr. .... 2.00 .40
Jim Marshall
(Checklist back)
☐ 639 Steve Kline .... .50 .23
☐ 640 Harmon Killebrew 5.00 2.20
☐ 641 Jim Northrup .... .50 .23
☐ 642 Mike Phillips .... .50 .23
☐ 643 Brent Strom .... .50 .23
☐ 644 Bill Fahey .... .50 .23
☐ 645 Danny Cater .... .50 .23
☐ 646 Checklist: 529-660 .. 3.00 .60
☐ 647 Claudell Washington 2.00 .90
☐ 648 Dave Pagan .... .50 .23

☐ 649 Jack Heidemann .... .50 .23
☐ 650 Dave May .... .50 .23
☐ 651 John Morlan .... .50 .23
☐ 652 Lindy McDaniel .... 1.00 .45
☐ 653 Lee Richard UER ...... .50 .23
(Listed as Richards
on card front)
☐ 654 Jerry Terrell .... .50 .23
☐ 655 Rico Carty .... 1.00 .45
☐ 656 Bill Plummer .... .50 .23
☐ 657 Bob Oliver .... .50 .23
☐ 658 Vic Harris .... .50 .23
☐ 659 Bob Apodaca .... .50 .23
☐ 660 Hank Aaron 30.00 9.00

1976 Topps

The 1976 Topps set of 660 standard-size cards is known for its sharp color photographs and interesting presentation of subjects. Team cards feature a checklist back for players on that team and show a small inset photo of the manager on the front. A "Father and Son" series (66-70) spotlights five Major Leaguers whose fathers also made the "Big Show." Other subseries include "All Time All Stars" (341-350), "Record Breakers" from the previous season (1-6), League Leaders (191-205), Post-season cards (461-462), and Rookie Prospects (589-599). The following players' regular issue cards are explicitly denoted as All-Stars, 10, 48, 60, 140, 150, 165, 169, 240, 300, 370, 380, 395, 400, 420, 475, 500, 580, and 650. Cards were issued in 10-card wax packs, 42-card rack packs as well as cello packs and other options. The key Rookie Cards in this set are Dennis Eckersley, Ron Guidry, and Willie Randolph.

	NRMT	VG-E
COMPLETE SET (660)	400.00	180.00
COMMON CARD (1-660)	.40	.18
MINOR STARS	.75	.35
SEMISTARS	1.50	.70
UNLISTED STARS	2.50	1.10

☐ 1 Hank Aaron RB 15.00 4.70
2262 Career RBIs
☐ 2 Bobby Bonds RB ...... 1.50 .70
Most leadoff HR's 32;
plus three seasons
30 homers/30 steals
☐ 3 Mickey Lolich RB ...... .75 .35
Most Lefthanded Strikeouts: 2679
☐ 4 Dave Lopes RB .... .75 .35
Most Consecutive SB's: 38
☐ 5 Tom Seaver RB 4.00 1.80

Most Consecutive seasons
with 200 Strikeouts
☐ 6 Rennie Stennett RB .... .75 .35
7 Hits in a 9 inning game
☐ 7 Jim Umbarger .... .40 .18
☐ 8 Tito Fuentes .... .40 .18
☐ 9 Paul Lindblad .... .40 .18
☐ 10 Lou Brock 4.00 1.80
☐ 11 Jim Hughes .... .40 .18
☐ 12 Richie Zisk .... .75 .35
☐ 13 John Wockenfuss .... .40 .18
☐ 14 Gene Garber .... .75 .35
☐ 15 George Scott .... .75 .35
☐ 16 Bob Apodaca .... .40 .18
☐ 17 New York Yankees .... 1.50 .30
Team Card;
Billy Martin MG
(Checklist back)
☐ 18 Dale Murray .... .40 .18
☐ 19 George Brett 60.00 27.00
☐ 20 Bob Watson .... .75 .35
☐ 21 Dave LaRoche .... .40 .18
☐ 22 Bill Russell .... .75 .35
☐ 23 Brian Downing .... .40 .18
☐ 24 Cesar Geronimo .... .75 .35
☐ 25 Mike Torrez .... .75 .35
☐ 26 Andre Thornton .... .75 .35
☐ 27 Ed Figueroa .... .40 .18
☐ 28 Dusty Baker .... 1.50 .70
☐ 29 Rick Burleson .... .75 .35
☐ 30 John Montefusco .... .75 .35
☐ 31 Len Randle .... .40 .18
☐ 32 Danny Frisella .... .40 .18
☐ 33 Bill North .... .40 .18
☐ 34 Mike Garman .... .40 .18
☐ 35 Tony Oliva .... 1.50 .70
☐ 36 Frank Taveras .... .40 .18
☐ 37 John Hiller .... .75 .35
☐ 38 Garry Maddox .... .75 .35
☐ 39 Pete Broberg .... .40 .18
☐ 40 Dave Kingman .... 1.50 .70
☐ 41 Tippy Martinez .... .75 .35
☐ 42 Barry Foote .... .40 .18
☐ 43 Paul Splittorff .... .40 .18
☐ 44 Doug Rader .... .75 .35
☐ 45 Boog Powell .... 1.50 .70
☐ 46 Los Angeles Dodgers 1.50 .30
Team Card;
Walter Alston MG
(Checklist back)
☐ 47 Jesse Jefferson .... .40 .18
☐ 48 Dave Concepcion ...... 1.50 .70
☐ 49 Dave Duncan .... .40 .18
☐ 50 Fred Lynn .... 1.50 .70
☐ 51 Ray Burris .... .40 .18
☐ 52 Dave Chalk .... .40 .18
☐ 53 Mike Beard .... .40 .18
☐ 54 Dave Rader .... .40 .18
☐ 55 Gaylord Perry 2.50 1.10
☐ 56 Bob Tolan .... .40 .18
☐ 57 Phil Garner .... .75 .35
☐ 58 Ron Reed .... .40 .18
☐ 59 Larry Hisle .... .75 .35
☐ 60 Jerry Reuss .... .75 .35
☐ 61 Ron LeFlore .... .75 .35
☐ 62 Johnny Oates .... .75 .35
☐ 63 Bobby Darwin .... .40 .18
☐ 64 Jerry Koosman .... .75 .35
☐ 65 Chris Chambliss ...... .75 .35
☐ 66 Gus Bell FS .... .75 .35
Buddy Bell
☐ 67 Ray Boone FS .... .75 .35
Bob Boone
☐ 68 Joe Coleman FS .... .40 .18
Joe Coleman Jr.
☐ 69 Jim Hegan FS .... .75 .35
Mike Hegan
☐ 70 Roy Smalley FS .... .75 .35
Roy Smalley Jr.
☐ 71 Steve Rogers .... .75 .35
☐ 72 Hal McRae .... .75 .35
☐ 73 Baltimore Orioles .... 1.50 .30
Team Card;
Earl Weaver MG
(Checklist back)
☐ 74 Oscar Gamble .... .75 .35

□	Card	Price 1	Price 2
□	75 Larry Dierker	.75	.35
□	76 Willie Crawford	.40	.18
□	77 Pedro Borbon	.75	.35
□	78 Cecil Cooper	.75	.35
□	79 Jerry Morales	.40	.18
□	80 Jim Kaat	1.50	.70
□	81 Darrell Evans	.75	.35
□	82 Von Joshua	.40	.18
□	83 Jim Spencer	.40	.18
□	84 Brent Strom	.40	.18
□	85 Mickey Rivers	.75	.35
□	86 Mike Tyson	.40	.18
□	87 Tom Burgmeier	.40	.18
□	88 Duffy Dyer	.40	.18
□	89 Vern Ruhle	.40	.18
□	90 Sal Bando	.75	.35
□	91 Tom Hutton	.40	.18
□	92 Eduardo Rodriguez	.40	.18
□	93 Mike Phillips	.40	.18
□	94 Jim Dwyer	.40	.18
□	95 Brooks Robinson	5.00	2.20
□	96 Doug Bird	.40	.18
□	97 Wilbur Howard	.40	.18
□	98 Dennis Eckersley	40.00	18.00
□	99 Lee Lacy	.40	.18
□	100 Jim Hunter	2.50	1.10
□	101 Pete LaCock	.40	.18
□	102 Jim Willoughby	.40	.18
□	103 Biff Pocoroba	.40	.18
□	104 Cincinnati Reds	2.50	.50
	Team Card; Sparky Anderson MG (Checklist back)		
□	105 Gary Lavelle	.40	.18
□	106 Tom Grieve	.75	.35
□	107 Dave Roberts	.40	.18
□	108 Don Kirkwood	.40	.18
□	109 Larry Lintz	.40	.18
□	110 Carlos May	.40	.18
□	111 Danny Thompson	.40	.18
□	112 Kent Tekulve	1.50	.70
□	113 Gary Sutherland	.40	.18
□	114 Jay Johnstone	.75	.35
□	115 Ken Holtzman	.75	.35
□	116 Charlie Moore	.40	.18
□	117 Mike Jorgensen	.40	.18
□	118 Boston Red Sox	1.50	.30
	Team Card; Darrell Johnson MG (Checklist back)		
□	119 Checklist 1-132	1.50	.30
□	120 Rusty Staub	.75	.35
□	121 Tony Solaita	.40	.18
□	122 Mike Cosgrove	.40	.18
□	123 Walt Williams	.40	.18
□	124 Doug Rau	.40	.18
□	125 Don Baylor	1.50	.70
□	126 Tom Dettore	.40	.18
□	127 Larvell Blanks	.40	.18
□	128 Ken Griffey	2.50	1.10
□	129 Andy Etchebarren	.40	.18
□	130 Luis Tiant	1.50	.70
□	131 Bill Stein	.40	.18
□	132 Don Hood	.40	.18
□	133 Gary Matthews	.75	.35
□	134 Mike Ivie	.40	.18
□	135 Bake McBride	.75	.35
□	136 Dave Goltz	.40	.18
□	137 Bill Robinson	.75	.35
□	138 Lerrin LaGrow	.40	.18
□	139 Gorman Thomas	.75	.35
□	140 Vida Blue	.75	.35
□	141 Larry Parrish	1.50	.70
□	142 Dick Drago	.40	.18
□	143 Jerry Grote	.40	.18
□	144 Al Fitzmorris	.40	.18
□	145 Larry Bowa	.75	.35
□	146 George Medich	.40	.18
□	147 Houston Astros	1.50	.30
	Team Card; Bill Virdon MG (Checklist back)		
□	148 Stan Thomas	.40	.18
□	149 Tommy Davis	.75	.35
□	150 Steve Garvey	4.00	1.80
□	151 Bill Bonham	.40	.18
□	152 Leroy Stanton	.40	.18
□	153 Buzz Capra	.40	.18
□	154 Bucky Dent	.75	.35
□	155 Jack Billingham	.75	.35
□	156 Rico Carty	.75	.35
□	157 Mike Caldwell	.40	.18
□	158 Ken Reitz	.40	.18
□	159 Jerry Terrell	.40	.18
□	160 Dave Winfield	15.00	6.75
□	161 Bruce Kison	.40	.18
□	162 Jack Pierce	.40	.18
□	163 Jim Slaton	.40	.18
□	164 Pepe Mangual	.40	.18
□	165 Gene Tenace	.75	.35
□	166 Skip Lockwood	.40	.18
□	167 Freddie Patek	.75	.35
□	168 Tom Hilgendorf	.40	.18
□	169 Graig Nettles	1.50	.70
□	170 Rick Wise	.40	.18
□	171 Greg Gross	.40	.18
□	172 Texas Rangers	1.50	.30
	Team Card; Frank Lucchesi MG (Checklist back)		
□	173 Steve Swisher	.40	.18
□	174 Charlie Hough	.75	.35
□	175 Ken Singleton	.75	.35
□	176 Dick Lange	.40	.18
□	177 Marty Perez	.40	.18
□	178 Tom Buskey	.40	.18
□	179 George Foster	1.50	.70
□	180 Rich Gossage	1.50	.70
□	181 Willie Montanez	.40	.18
□	182 Harry Rasmussen	.40	.18
□	183 Steve Braun	.40	.18
□	184 Bill Greif	.40	.18
□	185 Dave Parker	1.50	.70
□	186 Tom Walker	.40	.18
□	187 Pedro Garcia	.40	.18
□	188 Fred Scherman	.40	.18
□	189 Claudell Washington	.75	.35
□	190 Jon Matlack	.40	.18
□	191 NL Batting Leaders	.75	.35
	Bill Madlock / Ted Simmons / Manny Sanguillen		
□	192 AL Batting Leaders	2.50	1.10
	Rod Carew / Fred Lynn / Thurman Munson		
□	193 NL Home Run Leaders	3.00	1.35
	Mike Schmidt / Dave Kingman / Greg Luzinski		
□	194 AL Home Run Leaders	2.50	1.10
	Reggie Jackson / George Scott / John Mayberry		
□	195 NL RBI Leaders	1.50	.70
	Greg Luzinski / Johnny Bench / Tony Perez		
□	196 AL RBI Leaders	.75	.35
	George Scott / John Mayberry / Fred Lynn		
□	197 NL Steals Leaders	1.50	
	Dave Lopes / Joe Morgan / Lou Brock		
□	198 AL Steals Leaders	.75	.35
	Mickey Rivers / Claudell Washington / Amos Otis		
□	199 NL Victory Leaders	1.50	.70
	Tom Seaver / Randy Jones / Andy Messersmith		
□	200 AL Victory Leaders	1.50	.70
	Jim Hunter / Jim Palmer / Vida Blue		
□	201 NL ERA Leaders	1.50	.70
	Randy Jones / Andy Messersmith / Tom Seaver		
□	202 AL ERA Leaders	5.00	2.20
	Jim Palmer / Jim Hunter / Dennis Eckersley		
□	203 NL Strikeout Leaders	1.50	.70
	Tom Seaver / John Montefusco / Andy Messersmith		
□	204 AL Strikeout Leaders	.75	.35
	Frank Tanana / Bert Blyleven / Gaylord Perry		
□	205 NL Leading Firemen	.75	.35
	Al Hrabosky / Rich Gossage		
□	206 Manny Trillo	.40	.18
□	207 Andy Hassler	.40	.18
□	208 Mike Lum	.40	.18
□	209 Alan Ashby	.75	.35
□	210 Lee May	.75	.35
□	211 Clay Carroll	.75	.35
□	212 Pat Kelly	.40	.18
□	213 Dave Heaverlo	.40	.18
□	214 Eric Soderholm	.40	.18
□	215 Reggie Smith	.75	.35
□	216 Montreal Expos	1.50	.30
	Team Card; Karl Kuehl MG (Checklist back)		
□	217 Dave Freisleben	.40	.18
□	218 John Knox	.40	.18
□	219 Tom Murphy	.40	.18
□	220 Manny Sanguillen	.75	.35
□	221 Jim Todd	.40	.18
□	222 Wayne Garrett	.40	.18
□	223 Ollie Brown	.40	.18
□	224 Jim York	.40	.18
□	225 Roy White	.75	.35
□	226 Jim Sundberg	.75	.35
□	227 Oscar Zamora	.40	.18
□	228 John Hale	.40	.18
□	229 Jerry Remy	.40	.18
□	230 Carl Yastrzemski	5.00	2.20
□	231 Tom House	.40	.18
□	232 Frank Duffy	.40	.18
□	233 Grant Jackson	.40	.18
□	234 Mike Sadek	.40	.18
□	235 Bert Blyleven	1.50	.70
□	236 Kansas City Royals	1.50	.30
	Team Card; Whitey Herzog MG (Checklist back)		
□	237 Dave Hamilton	.40	.18
□	238 Larry Biittner	.40	.18
□	239 John Curtis	.40	.18
□	240 Pete Rose	12.00	5.50
□	241 Hector Torres	.40	.18
□	242 Dan Meyer	.40	.18
□	243 Jim Rooker	.40	.18
□	244 Bill Sharp	.40	.18
□	245 Felix Millan	.40	.18
□	246 Cesar Tovar	.40	.18
□	247 Terry Harmon	.40	.18
□	248 Dick Tidrow	.40	.18
□	249 Cliff Johnson	.75	.35
□	250 Fergie Jenkins	2.50	1.10
□	251 Rick Monday	.75	.35
□	252 Tim Nordbrook	.40	.18
□	253 Bill Buckner	.75	.35
□	254 Rudy Meoli	.40	.18
□	255 Fritz Peterson	.40	.18
□	256 Rowland Office	.40	.18
□	257 Ross Grimsley	.40	.18
□	258 Nyls Nyman	.40	.18
□	259 Darrel Chaney	.40	.18
□	260 Steve Busby	.40	.18
□	261 Gary Thomasson	.40	.18
□	262 Checklist 133-264	1.50	.30
□	263 Lyman Bostock	1.50	.70
□	264 Steve Renko	.40	.18
□	265 Willie Davis	.75	.35
□	266 Alan Foster	.40	.18
□	267 Aurelio Rodriguez	.40	.18
□	268 Del Unser	.40	.18
□	269 Rick Austin	.40	.18
□	270 Willie Stargell	3.00	1.35

□	#	Name		
□	271	Jim Lonborg	.75	.35
□	272	Rick Dempsey	.75	.35
□	273	Joe Niekro	.75	.35
□	274	Tommy Harper	.75	.35
□	275	Rick Manning	.40	.18
□	276	Mickey Scott	.40	.18
□	277	Chicago Cubs 1.50		.30
		Team Card; Jim Marshall MG (Checklist back)		
□	278	Bernie Carbo	.40	.18
□	279	Roy Howell	.40	.18
□	280	Burt Hooton	.75	.35
□	281	Dave May	.40	.18
□	282	Dan Osborn	.40	.18
□	283	Merv Rettenmund	.40	.18
□	284	Steve Ontiveros	.40	.18
□	285	Mike Cuellar	.75	.35
□	286	Jim Wohlford	.40	.18
□	287	Pete Mackanin	.40	.18
□	288	Bill Campbell	.40	.18
□	289	Enzo Hernandez	.40	.18
□	290	Ted Simmons	.75	.35
□	291	Ken Sanders	.40	.18
□	292	Leon Roberts	.40	.18
□	293	Bill Castro	.40	.18
□	294	Ed Kirkpatrick	.40	.18
□	295	Dave Cash	.40	.18
□	296	Pat Dobson	.40	.18
□	297	Roger Metzger	.40	.18
□	298	Dick Bosman	.40	.18
□	299	Champ Summers	.40	.18
□	300	Johnny Bench	8.00	3.60
□	301	Jackie Brown	.40	.18
□	302	Rick Miller	.40	.18
□	303	Steve Foucault	.40	.18
□	304	California Angels 1.50		.30
		Team Card; Dick Williams MG (Checklist back)		
□	305	Andy Messersmith	.75	.35
□	306	Rod Gilbreath	.40	.18
□	307	Al Bumbry	.75	.35
□	308	Jim Barr	.40	.18
□	309	Bill Melton	.40	.18
□	310	Randy Jones	.75	.35
□	311	Cookie Rojas	.75	.35
□	312	Don Carrithers	.40	.18
□	313	Dan Ford	.40	.18
□	314	Ed Kranepool	.40	.18
□	315	Al Hrabosky	.75	.35
□	316	Robin Yount	30.00	13.50
□	317	John Candelaria	1.50	.70
□	318	Bob Boone	1.50	.70
□	319	Larry Gura	.40	.18
□	320	Willie Horton	.75	.35
□	321	Jose Cruz	1.50	.70
□	322	Glenn Abbott	.40	.18
□	323	Rob Sperring	.40	.18
□	324	Jim Bibby	.40	.18
□	325	Tony Perez	2.50	1.10
□	326	Dick Pole	.40	.18
□	327	Dave Moates	.40	.18
□	328	Carl Morton	.40	.18
□	329	Joe Ferguson	.40	.18
□	330	Nolan Ryan	65.00	29.00
□	331	San Diego Padres 1.50		.30
		Team Card; John McNamara MG (Checklist back)		
□	332	Charlie Williams	.40	.18
□	333	Bob Coluccio	.40	.18
□	334	Dennis Leonard	.75	.35
□	335	Bob Grich	.75	.35
□	336	Vic Albury	.40	.18
□	337	Bud Harrelson	.75	.35
□	338	Bob Bailey	.40	.18
□	339	John Denny	.75	.35
□	340	Jim Rice	5.00	2.20
□	341	Lou Gehrig ATG	12.00	5.50
□	342	Rogers Hornsby ATG	3.00	1.35
□	343	Pie Traynor ATG	1.50	.70
□	344	Honus Wagner ATG	5.00	2.20
□	345	Babe Ruth ATG	15.00	6.75
□	346	Ty Cobb ATG	8.00	3.60
□	347	Ted Williams ATG	10.00	4.50
□	348	Mickey Cochrane ATG 1.50		.70
□	349	Walter Johnson ATG 3.00		1.35
□	350	Lefty Grove ATG	1.50	.70
□	351	Randy Hundley	.75	.35
□	352	Dave Giusti	.40	.18
□	353	Sixto Lezcano	.40	.18
□	354	Ron Blomberg	.40	.18
□	355	Steve Carlton	5.00	2.20
□	356	Ted Martinez	.40	.18
□	357	Ken Forsch	.40	.18
□	358	Buddy Bell	.75	.35
□	359	Rick Reuschel	.75	.35
□	360	Jeff Burroughs	.75	.37
□	361	Detroit Tigers 1.50		.30
		Team Card; Ralph Houk MG (Checklist back)		
□	362	Will McEnaney	.75	.35
□	363	Dave Collins	.75	.35
□	364	Elias Sosa	.40	.18
□	365	Carlton Fisk	6.00	2.70
□	366	Bobby Valentine	.75	.35
□	367	Bruce Miller	.40	.18
□	368	Wilbur Wood	.40	.18
□	369	Frank White	.75	.35
□	370	Ron Cey	.75	.35
□	371	Elrod Hendricks	.40	.18
□	372	Rick Baldwin	.40	.18
□	373	Johnny Briggs	.40	.18
□	374	Dan Warthen	.40	.18
□	375	Ron Fairly	.75	.35
□	376	Rich Hebner	.75	.35
□	377	Mike Hegan	.40	.18
□	378	Steve Stone	.75	.35
□	379	Ken Boswell	.40	.18
□	380	Bobby Bonds	1.50	.70
□	381	Denny Doyle	.40	.18
□	382	Matt Alexander	.40	.18
□	383	John Ellis	.40	.18
□	384	Philadelphia Phillies 1.50		.30
		Team Card; Danny Ozark MG (Checklist back)		
□	385	Mickey Lolich	.75	.35
□	386	Ed Goodson	.40	.18
□	387	Mike Miley	.40	.18
□	388	Stan Perzanowski	.40	.18
□	389	Glenn Adams	.40	.18
□	390	Don Gullett	.75	.35
□	391	Jerry Hairston	.40	.18
□	392	Checklist 265-396	1.50	.30
□	393	Paul Mitchell	.40	.18
□	394	Fran Healy	.40	.18
□	395	Jim Wynn	.75	.35
□	396	Bill Lee	.75	.35
□	397	Tim Foli	.40	.18
□	398	Dave Tomlin	.40	.18
□	399	Luis Melendez	.40	.18
□	400	Rod Carew	4.00	1.80
□	401	Ken Brett	.40	.18
□	402	Don Money	.75	.35
□	403	Geoff Zahn	.40	.18
□	404	Enos Cabell	.40	.18
□	405	Rollie Fingers	2.50	1.10
□	406	Ed Herrmann	.40	.18
□	407	Tom Underwood	.40	.18
□	408	Charlie Spikes	.40	.18
□	409	Dave Lemanczyk	.40	.18
□	410	Ralph Garr	.75	.35
□	411	Bill Singer	.40	.18
□	412	Toby Harrah	.75	.35
□	413	Pete Varney	.40	.18
□	414	Wayne Garland	.40	.18
□	415	Vada Pinson	1.50	.70
□	416	Tommy John	1.50	.70
□	417	Gene Clines	.40	.18
□	418	Jose Morales	.40	.18
□	419	Reggie Cleveland	.40	.18
□	420	Joe Morgan	4.00	1.80
□	421	Oakland A's 1.50		.30
		Team Card; (No MG on front; checklist back)		
□	422	Johnny Grubb	.40	.18
□	423	Ed Halicki	.40	.18
□	424	Phil Roof	.40	.18
□	425	Rennie Stennett	.40	.18
□	426	Bob Forsch	.40	.18
□	427	Kurt Bevacqua	.40	.18
□	428	Jim Crawford	.40	.18
□	429	Fred Stanley	.40	.18
□	430	Jose Cardenal	.75	.35
□	431	Dick Ruthven	.40	.18
□	432	Tom Veryzer	.40	.18
□	433	Rick Waits	.40	.18
□	434	Morris Nettles	.40	.18
□	435	Phil Niekro	2.50	1.10
□	436	Bill Fahey	.40	.18
□	437	Terry Forster	.40	.18
□	438	Doug DeCinces	.75	.35
□	439	Rick Rhoden	.75	.35
□	440	John Mayberry	.75	.35
□	441	Gary Carter	5.00	2.20
□	442	Hank Webb	.40	.18
□	443	San Francisco Giants 1.50		.30
		Team Card; (No MG on front; checklist back)		
□	444	Gary Nolan	.75	.35
□	445	Rico Petrocelli	.75	.35
□	446	Larry Haney	.40	.18
□	447	Gene Locklear	.75	.35
□	448	Tom Johnson	.40	.18
□	449	Bob Robertson	.40	.18
□	450	Jim Palmer	4.00	1.80
□	451	Buddy Bradford	.40	.18
□	452	Tom Hausman	.40	.18
□	453	Lou Piniella	1.50	.70
□	454	Tom Griffin	.40	.18
□	455	Dick Allen	1.50	.70
□	456	Joe Coleman	.40	.18
□	457	Ed Crosby	.40	.18
□	458	Earl Williams	.40	.18
□	459	Jim Brewer	.40	.18
□	460	Cesar Cedeno	.75	.35
□	461	NL and AL Champs	.75	.35
		Reds sweep Bucs, Bosox surprise A's		
□	462	'75 World Series	.75	.35
		Reds Champs		
□	463	Steve Hargan	.40	.18
□	464	Ken Henderson	.40	.18
□	465	Mike Marshall	.75	.35
□	466	Bob Stinson	.40	.18
□	467	Woodie Fryman	.40	.18
□	468	Jesus Alou	.40	.18
□	469	Rawly Eastwick	.75	.35
□	470	Bobby Murcer	.75	.35
□	471	Jim Burton	.40	.18
□	472	Bob Davis	.40	.18
□	473	Paul Blair	.75	.35
□	474	Ray Corbin	.40	.18
□	475	Joe Rudi	.75	.35
□	476	Bob Moose	1.50	.70
□	477	Cleveland Indians 1.50		.30
		Team Card; Frank Robinson MG (Checklist back)		
□	478	Lynn McGlothen	.40	.18
□	479	Bobby Mitchell	.40	.18
□	480	Mike Schmidt	25.00	11.00
□	481	Rudy May	.40	.18
□	482	Tim Hosley	.40	.18
□	483	Mickey Stanley	.40	.18
□	484	Eric Raich	.40	.18
□	485	Mike Hargrove	.75	.35
□	486	Bruce Dal Canton	.40	.18
□	487	Leron Lee	.40	.18
□	488	Claude Osteen	.75	.35
□	489	Skip Jutze	.40	.18
□	490	Frank Tanana	.75	.35
□	491	Terry Crowley	.40	.18
□	492	Marty Pattin	.40	.18
□	493	Derrel Thomas	.40	.18
□	494	Craig Swan	.75	.35
□	495	Nate Colbert	.40	.18
□	496	Juan Beniquez	.40	.18
□	497	Joe McIntosh	.40	.18
□	498	Glenn Borgmann	.40	.18
□	499	Mario Guerrero	.40	.18
□	500	Reggie Jackson	12.00	5.50
□	501	Billy Champion	.40	.18

□ 502 Tim McCarver	1.50	.70
□ 503 Elliott Maddox	.40	.18
□ 504 Pittsburgh Pirates	1.50	.30
Team Card;		
Danny Murtaugh MG		
(Checklist back)		
□ 505 Mark Belanger	.75	.35
□ 506 George Mitterwald	.40	.18
□ 507 Ray Bare	.40	.18
□ 508 Duane Kuiper	.40	.18
□ 509 Bill Hands	.40	.18
□ 510 Amos Otis	.75	.35
□ 511 Jamie Easterley	.40	.18
□ 512 Ellie Rodriguez	.40	.18
□ 513 Bart Johnson	.40	.18
□ 514 Dan Driessen	.75	.35
□ 515 Steve Yeager	.75	.35
□ 516 Wayne Granger	.40	.18
□ 517 John Milner	.40	.18
□ 518 Doug Flynn	.40	.18
□ 519 Steve Brye	.40	.18
□ 520 Willie McCovey	4.00	1.80
□ 521 Jim Colborn	.40	.18
□ 522 Ted Sizemore	.40	.18
□ 523 Bob Montgomery	.40	.18
□ 524 Pete Falcone	.40	.18
□ 525 Billy Williams	2.50	1.10
□ 526 Checklist 397-528	1.50	.30
□ 527 Mike Anderson	.40	.18
□ 528 Dock Ellis	.40	.18
□ 529 Deron Johnson	.75	.35
□ 530 Don Sutton	2.50	1.10
□ 531 New York Mets	1.50	.30
Team Card;		
Joe Frazier MG		
(Checklist back)		
□ 532 Milt May	.40	.18
□ 533 Lee Richard	.40	.18
□ 534 Stan Bahnsen	.40	.18
□ 535 Dave Nelson	.40	.18
□ 536 Mike Thompson	.40	.18
□ 537 Tony Muser	.40	.18
□ 538 Pat Darcy	.40	.18
□ 539 John Balaz	.75	.35
□ 540 Bill Freehan	.75	.35
□ 541 Steve Mingori	.40	.18
□ 542 Keith Hernandez	1.50	.70
□ 543 Wayne Twitchell	.40	.18
□ 544 Pepe Frias	.40	.18
□ 545 Sparky Lyle	.75	.35
□ 546 Dave Rosello	.40	.18
□ 547 Roric Harrison	.40	.18
□ 548 Manny Mota	.75	.35
□ 549 Randy Tate	.40	.18
□ 550 Hank Aaron	25.00	11.00
□ 551 Jerry DaVanon	.40	.18
□ 552 Terry Humphrey	.40	.18
□ 553 Randy Moffitt	.40	.18
□ 554 Ray Fosse	.40	.18
□ 555 Dyar Miller	.40	.18
□ 556 Minnesota Twins	1.50	.30
Team Card;		
Gene Mauch MG		
(Checklist back)		
□ 557 Dan Spillner	.40	.18
□ 558 Clarence Gaston	.75	.35
□ 559 Clyde Wright	.40	.18
□ 560 Jorge Orta	.40	.18
□ 561 Tom Carroll	.40	.18
□ 562 Adrian Garrett	.40	.18
□ 563 Larry Demery	.40	.18
□ 564 Bubble Gum Champ	1.50	.70
Kurt Bevacqua		
□ 565 Tug McGraw	.75	.35
□ 566 Ken McMullen	.40	.18
□ 567 George Stone	.40	.18
□ 568 Rob Andrews	.40	.18
□ 569 Nelson Briles	.75	.35
□ 570 George Hendrick	.75	.35
□ 571 Don DeMola	.40	.18
□ 572 Rich Coggins	.40	.18
□ 573 Bill Travers	.40	.18
□ 574 Don Kessinger	.75	.35
□ 575 Dwight Evans	1.50	.70
□ 576 Maximino Leon	.40	.18
□ 577 Marc Hill	.40	.18

□ 578 Ted Kubiak	.40	.18
□ 579 Clay Kirby	.40	.18
□ 580 Bert Campaneris	.75	.35
□ 581 St. Louis Cardinals	1.50	.30
Team Card;		
Red Schoendienst MG		
(Checklist back)		
□ 582 Mike Kekich	.40	.18
□ 583 Tommy Helms	.40	.18
□ 584 Stan Wall	.40	.18
□ 585 Joe Torre	1.50	.70
□ 586 Ron Schueler	.40	.18
□ 587 Leo Cardenas	.40	.18
□ 588 Kevin Kobel	.40	.18
□ 589 Rookie Pitchers	1.50	.70
Santo Alcala		
Mike Flanagan		
Joe Pactwa		
Pablo Torrealba		
□ 590 Rookie Outfielders	.75	.35
Henry Cruz		
Chet Lemon		
Ellis Valentine		
Terry Whitfield		
□ 591 Rookie Pitchers	.35	
Steve Grilli		
Craig Mitchell		
Jose Sosa		
George Throop		
□ 592 Rookie Infielders	6.00	2.70
Willie Randolph		
Dave McKay		
Jerry Royster		
Roy Staiger		
□ 593 Rookie Pitchers	.75	.35
Larry Anderson		
Ken Crosby		
Mark Littell		
Butch Metzger		
□ 594 Rookie Catchers/OF	.75	.35
Andy Merchant		
Ed Ott		
Royle Stillman		
Jerry White		
□ 595 Rookie Pitchers	.75	.35
Art DeFillips		
Randy Lerch		
Sid Monge		
Steve Barr		
□ 596 Rookie Infielders	.75	.35
Craig Reynolds		
Lamar Johnson		
Johnnie LeMaster		
Jerry Manuel		
□ 597 Rookie Pitchers	.35	
Don Aase		
Jack Kucek		
Frank LaCorte		
Mike Pazik		
□ 598 Rookie Outfielders	.75	.35
Hector Cruz		
Jamie Quirk		
Jerry Turner		
Joe Wallis		
□ 599 Rookie Pitchers	6.00	2.70
Rob Dressler		
Ron Guidry		
Bob McClure		
Pat Zachry		
□ 600 Tom Seaver	8.00	3.60
□ 601 Ken Rudolph	.40	.18
□ 602 Doug Konieczny	.40	.18
□ 603 Jim Holt	.40	.18
□ 604 Joe Lovitto	.40	.18
□ 605 Al Downing	.40	.18
□ 606 Milwaukee Brewers	1.50	.30
Team Card;		
Alex Grammas MG		
(Checklist back)		
□ 607 Rich Hinton	.40	.18
□ 608 Vic Correll	.40	.18
□ 609 Fred Norman	.75	.35
□ 610 Greg Luzinski	1.50	.70
□ 611 Rich Folkers	.40	.18
□ 612 Joe Lahoud	.40	.18
□ 613 Tim Johnson	.40	.18

□ 614 Fernando Arroyo	.40	.18
□ 615 Mike Cubbage	.40	.18
□ 616 Buck Martinez	.40	.18
□ 617 Darold Knowles	.40	.18
□ 618 Jack Brohamer	.40	.18
□ 619 Bill Butler	.40	.18
□ 620 Al Oliver	.75	.35
□ 621 Tom Hall	.40	.18
□ 622 Rick Auerbach	.40	.18
□ 623 Bob Allietta	.40	.18
□ 624 Tony Taylor	.75	.35
□ 625 J.R. Richard	.75	.35
□ 626 Bob Sheldon	.40	.18
□ 627 Bill Plummer	.40	.18
□ 628 John D'Acquisto	.40	.18
□ 629 Sandy Alomar	.75	.35
□ 630 Chris Speier	.40	.18
□ 631 Atlanta Braves	1.50	.30
Team Card;		
Dave Bristol MG		
(Checklist back)		
□ 632 Rogelio Moret	.40	.18
□ 633 John Stearns	.75	.35
□ 634 Larry Christenson	.40	.18
□ 635 Jim Fregosi	.75	.35
□ 636 Joe Decker	.40	.18
□ 637 Bruce Bochte	.40	.18
□ 638 Doyle Alexander	.75	.35
□ 639 Fred Kendall	.40	.18
□ 640 Bill Madlock	1.50	.70
□ 641 Tom Paciorek	.75	.35
□ 642 Dennis Blair	.40	.18
□ 643 Checklist 529-660	1.50	.30
□ 644 Tom Bradley	.40	.18
□ 645 Darrell Porter	.75	.35
□ 646 John Lowenstein	.40	.18
□ 647 Ramon Hernandez	.40	.18
□ 648 Al Cowens	.40	.18
□ 649 Dave Roberts	.40	.18
□ 650 Thurman Munson	5.00	2.20
□ 651 John Odom	.40	.18
□ 652 Ed Armbrister	.40	.18
□ 653 Mike Norris	.75	.35
□ 654 Doug Griffin	.40	.18
□ 655 Mike Vail	.40	.18
□ 656 Chicago White Sox	1.50	.30
Team Card;		
Chuck Tanner MG		
(Checklist back)		
□ 657 Roy Smalley	.75	.35
□ 658 Jerry Johnson	.40	.18
□ 659 Ben Oglivie	.75	.35
□ 660 Dave Lopes	1.50	.30

1976 Topps Traded

The cards in this 44-card set measure 2 1/2" by 3 1/2". The 1976 Topps Traded set contains 43 players and one unnumbered checklist card. The individuals pictured were traded after the Topps regular set was printed. A "Sports Extra" heading design is found on each picture and is also used to introduce the biographical section of the reverse. Each card is numbered according to the player's regular 1976 card with the addition of "T" to indicate his new status. As in 1974, the cards were inserted in all packs toward the end of the production run. According to published reports at the time, they were not released until April, 1976. Because they were produced in large quantities, they are no scarcer than the basic cards. Reports at the time indicated that a dealer could make approximately 35 sets from a vending case. The vending cases included both regular and traded cards.

	NRMT	VG-E
COMPLETE SET (44)	20.00	9.00
COMMON CARD	.25	.11
MINOR STARS	.50	.23
SEMISTARS	.75	.35

INCLUDED IN ALL LATE PACKS

☐ 27T	Ed Figueroa	.25	.11
☐ 28T	Dusty Baker	1.00	.45
☐ 44T	Doug Rader	.50	.23
☐ 58T	Ron Reed	.25	.11
☐ 74T	Oscar Gamble	1.00	.45
☐ 80T	Jim Kaat	1.00	.45
☐ 83T	Jim Spencer	.25	.11
☐ 85T	Mickey Rivers	.50	.23
☐ 99T	Lee Lacy	.25	.11
☐ 120T	Rusty Staub	.50	.23
☐ 127T	Larvell Blanks	.25	.11
☐ 146T	George Medich	.25	.11
☐ 158T	Ken Reitz	.25	.11
☐ 208T	Mike Lum	.25	.11
☐ 211T	Clay Carroll	.25	.11
☐ 231T	Tom House	.25	.11
☐ 250T	Fergie Jenkins	2.50	1.10
☐ 259T	Darrel Chaney	.25	.11
☐ 292T	Leon Roberts	.25	.11
☐ 296T	Pat Dobson	.25	.11
☐ 309T	Bill Melton	.25	.11
☐ 338T	Bob Bailey	.25	.11
☐ 380T	Bobby Bonds	1.00	.45
☐ 383T	John Ellis	.25	.11
☐ 385T	Mickey Lolich	.50	.23
☐ 401T	Ken Brett	.25	.11
☐ 410T	Ralph Garr	.50	.23
☐ 411T	Bill Singer	.25	.11
☐ 428T	Jim Crawford	.25	.11
☐ 434T	Morris Nettles	.25	.11
☐ 464T	Ken Henderson	.25	.11
☐ 497T	Joe McIntosh	.25	.11
☐ 524T	Pete Falcone	.25	.11
☐ 527T	Mike Anderson	.25	.11
☐ 528T	Dock Ellis	.25	.11
☐ 532T	Milt May	.25	.11
☐ 554T	Ray Fosse	.25	.11
☐ 579T	Clay Kirby	.25	.11
☐ 583T	Tommy Helms	.25	.11
☐ 592T	Willie Randolph	4.00	1.80
☐ 618T	Jack Brohamer	.25	.11
☐ 632T	Rogelio Moret	.25	.11
☐ 649T	Dave Roberts	.25	.11
☐ NNO	Traded Checklist	1.50	

1977 Topps

In 1977 for the fifth consecutive year, Topps produced a 660-card standard-size baseball set. Among other fashions, this set was released in 10-card wax packs as well as thirty-nine card rack packs. The player's name, team affiliation, and his position are compactly arranged over the picture area and a facsimile autograph appears on the

photo. Team cards feature a checklist of that team's players in the set and a small picture of the manager on the front of the card. Appearing for the first time are the series "Brothers" (631-634) and "Turn Back the Clock" (433-437). Other subseries in the set are League Leaders (1-8), Record Breakers (231-234), Playoffs cards (276-277), World Series cards (411-413), and Rookie Prospects (472-479/487-494). The following players' regular issue cards are explicitly denoted as All-Stars, 30, 70, 100, 120, 170, 210, 240, 265, 301, 347, 400, 420, 450, 500, 521, 550, 560, and 580. The key Rookie Cards in the set are Jack Clark, Andre Dawson, Mark "The Bird" Fidrych, Dennis Martinez and Dale Murphy. Cards numbered 23 or lower, that feature Yankees and do not follow the numbering checklisted below, are not necessarily error cards. They are undoubtedly Burger King cards, a separate set with its own pricing and mass distribution. Burger King cards are indistinguishable from the corresponding Topps cards except for the card numbering difference and the fact that Burger King cards do not have a printing sheet designation (such as A through F like the regular Topps) anywhere on the card back in very small print. There was an aluminum version of the Dale Murphy rookie card number 476 produced (legally) in the early '80s; proceeds from the sales originally priced at 10.00) of this "card" went to the Huntington's Disease Foundation.

		NRMT	VG-E
COMPLETE SET (660)		300.00	135.00
COMMON CARD (1-660)		.30	.14
MINOR STARS		.60	.25
SEMISTARS		1.25	.55
UNLISTED STARS		2.00	.90

☐ 1	Batting Leaders	8.00	2.30
	George Brett		
	Bill Madlock		
☐ 2	Home Run Leaders	2.00	.90
	Graig Nettles		
	Mike Schmidt		
☐ 3	RBI Leaders	1.25	.55
	Lee May		
	George Foster		
☐ 4	Stolen Base Leaders	.60	.25
	Bill North		
	Dave Lopes		
☐ 5	Victory Leaders	1.25	.55
	Jim Palmer		
	Randy Jones		
☐ 6	Strikeout Leaders	15.00	6.75
	Nolan Ryan		
	Tom Seaver		
☐ 7	ERA Leaders	.60	.25
	Mark Fidrych		
	John Denny		
☐ 8	Leading Firemen	.60	.25
	Bill Campbell		
	Rawly Eastwick		
☐ 9	Doug Rader	.30	.14
☐ 10	Reggie Jackson	10.00	4.50
☐ 11	Rob Dressler	.30	.14
☐ 12	Larry Haney	.30	.14
☐ 13	Luis Gomez	.30	.14
☐ 14	Tommy Smith	.30	.14
☐ 15	Don Gullett	.60	.25
☐ 16	Bob Jones	.30	.14
☐ 17	Steve Stone	.60	.25
☐ 18	Indians Team/Mgr.	1.25	.25
	Frank Robinson		
	(Checklist back)		
☐ 19	John D'Acquisto	.30	.14
☐ 20	Graig Nettles	1.25	.55
☐ 21	Ken Forsch	.30	.14
☐ 22	Bill Freehan	.60	.25
☐ 23	Dan Driessen	.30	.14
☐ 24	Carl Morton	.30	.14
☐ 25	Dwight Evans	1.25	.55
☐ 26	Ray Sadecki	.30	.14
☐ 27	Bill Buckner	.60	.25
☐ 28	Woodie Fryman	.30	.14
☐ 29	Bucky Dent	.60	.25
☐ 30	Greg Luzinski	1.25	.55
☐ 31	Jim Todd	.30	.14
☐ 32	Checklist 1-132	1.25	.25
☐ 33	Wayne Garland	.30	.14
☐ 34	Angels Team/Mgr.	1.25	.25
	Norm Sherry		
	(Checklist back)		
☐ 35	Rennie Stennett	.30	.14
☐ 36	John Ellis	.30	.14
☐ 37	Steve Hargan	.30	.14
☐ 38	Craig Kusick	.30	.14
☐ 39	Tom Griffin	.30	.14
☐ 40	Bobby Murcer	.60	.25
☐ 41	Jim Kern	.30	.14
☐ 42	Jose Cruz	.60	.25
☐ 43	Ray Bare	.30	.14
☐ 44	Bud Harrelson	.60	.25
☐ 45	Rawly Eastwick	.30	.14
☐ 46	Buck Martinez	.30	.14
☐ 47	Lynn McGlothen	.30	.14
☐ 48	Tom Paciorek	.60	.25
☐ 49	Grant Jackson	.30	.14
☐ 50	Ron Cey	.60	.25
☐ 51	Brewers Team/Mgr.	1.25	.25
	Alex Grammas		
	(Checklist back)		
☐ 52	Ellis Valentine	.30	.14
☐ 53	Paul Mitchell	.30	.14
☐ 54	Sandy Alomar	.60	.25
☐ 55	Jeff Burroughs	.60	.25
☐ 56	Rudy May	.30	.14
☐ 57	Marc Hill	.30	.14
☐ 58	Chet Lemon	.30	.14
☐ 59	Larry Christenson	.30	.14
☐ 60	Jim Rice	2.00	.90
☐ 61	Manny Sanguillen	.60	.25
☐ 62	Eric Raich	.30	.14
☐ 63	Tito Fuentes	.30	.14
☐ 64	Larry Biittner	.30	.14
☐ 65	Skip Lockwood	.30	.14
☐ 66	Roy Smalley	.60	.25
☐ 67	Joaquin Andujar	.60	.25
☐ 68	Bruce Bochte	.30	.14
☐ 69	Jim Crawford	.30	.14
☐ 70	Johnny Bench	6.00	2.70
☐ 71	Dock Ellis	.30	.14
☐ 72	Mike Anderson	.30	.14
☐ 73	Charlie Williams	.30	.14
☐ 74	A's Team/Mgr.	1.25	.25
	Jack McKeon		
	(Checklist back)		

75	Dennis Leonard	.60	.25
76	Tim Foli	.30	.14
77	Dyar Miller	.30	.14
78	Bob Davis	.30	.14
79	Don Money	.60	.25
80	Andy Messersmith	.60	.25
81	Juan Beniquez	.30	.14
82	Jim Rooker	.30	.14
83	Kevin Bell	.30	.14
84	Ollie Brown	.30	.14
85	Duane Kuiper	.30	.14
86	Pat Zachry	.30	.14
87	Glenn Borgmann	.30	.14
88	Stan Wall	.30	.14
89	Butch Hobson	.60	.25
90	Cesar Cedeno	.60	.25
91	John Verhoeven	.30	.14
92	Dave Rosello	.30	.14
93	Tom Poquette	.30	.14
94	Craig Swan	.30	.14
95	Keith Hernandez	.60	.25
96	Lou Piniella	.60	.25
97	Dave Heaverlo	.30	.14
98	Milt May	.30	.14
99	Tom Hausman	.30	.14
100	Joe Morgan	3.00	1.35
101	Dick Bosman	.30	.14
102	Jose Morales	.30	.14
103	Mike Bacsik	.30	.14
104	Omar Moreno	.60	.25
105	Steve Yeager	.60	.25
106	Mike Flanagan	.60	.25
107	Bill Melton	.30	.14
108	Alan Foster	.30	.14
109	Jorge Orta	.30	.14
110	Steve Carlton	4.00	1.80
111	Rico Petrocelli	.60	.25
112	Bill Greif	.30	.14
113	Blue Jays Leaders	1.25	.25
	Roy Hartsfield MG		
	Don Leppert CO		
	Bob Miller CO		
	Jackie Moore CO		
	Harry Warner CO		
	(Checklist back)		
114	Bruce Dal Canton	.30	.14
115	Rick Manning	.30	.14
116	Joe Niekro	.60	.25
117	Frank White	.60	.25
118	Rick Jones	.30	.14
119	John Stearns	.30	.14
120	Rod Carew	3.00	1.35
121	Gary Nolan	.30	.14
122	Ben Oglivie	.60	.25
123	Fred Stanley	.30	.14
124	George Mitterwald	.30	.14
125	Bill Travers	.30	.14
126	Rod Gilbreath	.30	.14
127	Ron Fairly	.60	.25
128	Tommy John	1.25	.55
129	Mike Sadek	.30	.14
130	Al Oliver	.60	.25
131	Orlando Ramirez	.30	.14
132	Chip Lang	.30	.14
133	Ralph Garr	.60	.25
134	Padres Team/Mgr.	1.25	.25
	John McNamara		
	(Checklist back)		
135	Mark Belanger	.60	.25
136	Jerry Mumphrey	.60	.25
137	Jeff Terpko	.30	.14
138	Bob Stinson	.30	.14
139	Fred Norman	.30	.14
140	Mike Schmidt	15.00	6.75
141	Mark Littell	.30	.14
142	Steve Dillard	.30	.14
143	Ed Herrmann	.30	.14
144	Bruce Sutter	2.50	1.10
145	Tom Veryzer	.30	.14
146	Dusty Baker	1.25	.55
147	Jackie Brown	.30	.14
148	Fran Healy	.30	.14
149	Mike Cubbage	.30	.14
150	Tom Seaver	6.00	2.70
151	Johnny LeMaster	.30	.14
152	Gaylord Perry	2.00	.90
153	Ron Jackson	.30	.14
154	Dave Giusti	.30	.14
155	Joe Rudi	.60	.25
156	Pete Mackanin	.30	.14
157	Ken Brett	.30	.14
158	Ted Kubiak	.30	.14
159	Bernie Carbo	.30	.14
160	Will McEnaney	.30	.14
161	Garry Templeton	1.25	.55
162	Mike Cuellar	.60	.25
163	Dave Hilton	.30	.14
164	Tug McGraw	.60	.25
165	Jim Wynn	.60	.25
166	Bill Campbell	.30	.14
167	Rich Hebner	.60	.25
168	Charlie Spikes	.30	.14
169	Darold Knowles	.30	.14
170	Thurman Munson	4.00	1.80
171	Ken Sanders	.30	.14
172	John Milner	.30	.14
173	Chuck Scrivener	.30	.14
174	Nelson Briles	.60	.25
175	Butch Wynegar	.60	.25
176	Bob Robertson	.30	.14
177	Bart Johnson	.30	.14
178	Bombo Rivera	.30	.14
179	Paul Hartzell	.30	.14
180	Dave Lopes	.60	.25
181	Ken McMullen	.30	.14
182	Dan Spillner	.30	.14
183	Cardinals Team/Mgr.	1.25	.25
	Vern Rapp		
	(Checklist back)		
184	Bo McLaughlin	.30	.14
185	Sixto Lezcano	.30	.14
186	Doug Flynn	.30	.14
187	Dick Pole	.30	.14
188	Bob Tolan	.30	.14
189	Rick Dempsey	.60	.25
190	Ray Burris	.30	.14
191	Doug Griffin	.30	.14
192	Clarence Gaston	.60	.25
193	Larry Gura	.30	.14
194	Gary Matthews	.60	.25
195	Ed Figueroa	.30	.14
196	Len Randle	.30	.14
197	Ed Ott	.30	.14
198	Wilbur Wood	.30	.14
199	Pepe Frias	.30	.14
200	Frank Tanana	.60	.25
201	Ed Kranepool	.30	.14
202	Tom Johnson	.30	.14
203	Ed Armbrister	.30	.14
204	Jeff Newman	.30	.14
205	Pete Falcone	.30	.14
206	Boog Powell	1.25	.55
207	Glenn Abbott	.30	.14
208	Checklist 133-264	1.25	.25
209	Rob Andrews	.30	.14
210	Fred Lynn	1.25	.12
211	Giants Team/Mgr.	1.25	.55
	Joe Altobelli		
	(Checklist back)		
212	Jim Mason	.30	.14
213	Maximino Leon	.30	.14
214	Darrell Porter	.60	.25
215	Butch Metzger	.30	.14
216	Doug DeCinces	.60	.25
217	Tom Underwood	.30	.14
218	John Wathan	.30	.14
219	Joe Coleman	.30	.14
220	Chris Chambliss	.60	.25
221	Bob Bailey	.30	.14
222	Francisco Barrios	.30	.14
223	Earl Williams	.30	.14
224	Rusty Torres	.30	.14
225	Bob Apodaca	.30	.14
226	Leroy Stanton	.30	.25
227	Joe Sambito	.30	.14
228	Twins Team/Mgr.	1.25	.25
	Gene Mauch		
	(Checklist back)		
229	Don Kessinger	.60	.25
230	Vida Blue	.60	.25
231	George Brett RB	12.00	5.50
	Most consecutive games		
	3 or more hits		
232	Minnie Minoso RB	.60	.25
	Oldest to hit safely		
233	Jose Morales RB	.30	.14
	Most pinch-hits season		
234	Nolan Ryan RB	20.00	9.00
	Most seasons, 300 strikeouts		
235	Cecil Cooper	.60	.25
236	Tom Buskey	.30	.14
237	Gene Clines	.30	.14
238	Tippy Martinez	.60	.25
239	Bill Plummer	.30	.14
240	Ron LeFlore	.60	.25
241	Dave Tomlin	.30	.14
242	Ken Henderson	.30	.14
243	Ron Reed	.30	.14
244	John Mayberry	.60	.25
245	Rick Rhoden	.60	.25
246	Mike Vail	.30	.14
247	Chris Knapp	.30	.14
248	Wilbur Howard	.30	.14
249	Pete Redfern	.30	.14
250	Bill Madlock	.60	.25
251	Tony Muser	.30	.14
252	Dale Murray	.30	.14
253	John Hale	.30	.14
254	Doyle Alexander	.30	.14
255	George Scott	.60	.25
256	Joe Hoerner	.30	.14
257	Mike Miley	.30	.14
258	Luis Tiant	.60	.25
259	Mets Team/Mgr.	1.25	.25
	Joe Frazier		
	(Checklist back)		
260	J.R. Richard	.60	.25
261	Phil Garner	.60	.25
262	Al Cowens	.30	.14
263	Mike Marshall	.60	.25
264	Tom Hutton	.30	.14
265	Mark Fidrych	4.00	1.80
266	Derrel Thomas	.30	.14
267	Ray Fosse	.30	.14
268	Rick Sawyer	.30	.14
269	Joe Lis	.30	.14
270	Dave Parker	1.25	.55
271	Terry Forster	.30	.14
272	Lee Lacy	.30	.14
273	Eric Soderholm	.30	.14
274	Don Stanhouse	.30	.14
275	Mike Hargrove	.60	.25
276	Chris Chambliss ALCS	1.25	.55
	homer decides it		
277	Pete Rose NLCS	2.50	1.10
278	Danny Frisella	.30	.14
279	Joe Wallis	.30	.14
280	Jim Hunter	2.00	.90
281	Roy Staiger	.30	.14
282	Sid Monge	.30	.14
283	Jerry DaVanon	.30	.14
284	Mike Norris	.30	.14
285	Brooks Robinson	4.00	1.80
286	Johnny Grubb	.30	.06
287	Reds Team/Mgr.	1.25	.55
	Sparky Anderson		
	(Checklist back)		
288	Bob Montgomery	.30	.14
289	Gene Garber	.60	.25
290	Amos Otis	.60	.25
291	Jason Thompson	.60	.25
292	Rogelio Moret	.30	.14
293	Jack Brohamer	.30	.14
294	George Medich	.30	.14
295	Gary Carter	2.50	1.10
296	Don Hood	.30	.14
297	Ken Reitz	.30	.14
298	Charlie Hough	.60	.25
299	Otto Velez	.60	.25
300	Jerry Koosman	.60	.25
301	Toby Harrah	.60	.25
302	Mike Garman	.30	.14
303	Gene Tenace	.60	.25
304	Jim Hughes	.30	.14
305	Mickey Rivers	.60	.25
306	Rick Waits	.30	.14

☐ 307 Gary Sutherland .30 .14
☐ 308 Gene Pentz .30 .14
☐ 309 Red Sox Team/Mgr. 1.25 .25
Don Zimmer
(Checklist back)
☐ 310 Larry Bowa .60 .25
☐ 311 Vern Ruhle .30 .14
☐ 312 Rob Belloir .30 .14
☐ 313 Paul Blair .60 .25
☐ 314 Steve Mingori .30 .14
☐ 315 Dave Chalk .30 .14
☐ 316 Steve Rogers .30 .14
☐ 317 Kurt Bevacqua .30 .14
☐ 318 Duffy Dyer .30 .14
☐ 319 Rich Gossage 1.25 .55
☐ 320 Ken Griffey 1.25 .55
☐ 321 Dave Goltz .30 .14
☐ 322 Bill Russell .60 .25
☐ 323 Larry Lintz .30 .14
☐ 324 John Curtis .30 .14
☐ 325 Mike Ivie .30 .14
☐ 326 Jesse Jefferson .30 .14
☐ 327 Astros Team/Mgr. 1.25 .25
Bill Virdon
(Checklist back)
☐ 328 Tommy Boggs .30 .14
☐ 329 Ron Hodges .30 .14
☐ 330 George Hendrick .60 .25
☐ 331 Jim Colborn .30 .14
☐ 332 Elliott Maddox .30 .14
☐ 333 Paul Reuschel .30 .14
☐ 334 Bill Stein .30 .14
☐ 335 Bill Robinson .60 .25
☐ 336 Denny Doyle .30 .14
☐ 337 Ron Schueler .30 .14
☐ 338 Dave Duncan .30 .14
☐ 339 Adrian Devine .30 .14
☐ 340 Hal McRae .60 .25
☐ 341 Joe Kerrigan .30 .14
☐ 342 Jerry Remy .30 .14
☐ 343 Ed Halicki .30 .14
☐ 344 Brian Downing .60 .25
☐ 345 Reggie Smith .60 .25
☐ 346 Bill Singer .30 .14
☐ 347 George Foster 1.25 .55
☐ 348 Brent Strom .30 .14
☐ 349 Jim Holt .30 .14
☐ 350 Larry Dierker .60 .25
☐ 351 Jim Sundberg .60 .25
☐ 352 Mike Phillips .30 .14
☐ 353 Stan Thomas .30 .14
☐ 354 Pirates Team/Mgr. 1.25 .25
Chuck Tanner
(Checklist back)
☐ 355 Lou Brock 3.00 1.35
☐ 356 Checklist 265-396 1.25 .25
☐ 357 Tim McCarver 1.25 .55
☐ 358 Tom House .30 .14
☐ 359 Willie Randolph 1.25 .55
☐ 360 Rick Monday .60 .25
☐ 361 Eduardo Rodriguez .30 .14
☐ 362 Tommy Davis .60 .25
☐ 363 Dave Roberts .30 .14
☐ 364 Vic Correll .30 .14
☐ 365 Mike Torrez .60 .25
☐ 366 Ted Sizemore .30 .14
☐ 367 Dave Hamilton .30 .14
☐ 368 Mike Jorgensen .30 .14
☐ 369 Terry Humphrey .30 .14
☐ 370 John Montefusco .30 .14
☐ 371 Royals Team/Mgr. 1.25 .25
Whitey Herzog
(Checklist back)
☐ 372 Rich Folkers .30 .14
☐ 373 Bert Campaneris .60 .25
☐ 374 Kent Tekulve .60 .25
☐ 375 Larry Hisle .60 .25
☐ 376 Nino Espinosa .30 .14
☐ 377 Dave McKay .30 .14
☐ 378 Jim Umbarger .30 .14
☐ 379 Larry Cox .30 .14
☐ 380 Lee May .60 .25
☐ 381 Bob Forsch .60 .25
☐ 382 Charlie Moore .30 .14
☐ 383 Stan Bahnsen .30 .14
☐ 384 Darrel Chaney .30 .14

☐ 385 Dave LaRoche .30 .14
☐ 386 Manny Mota .60 .25
☐ 387 Yankees Team/Mgr. 2.00 .40
Billy Martin
(Checklist back)
☐ 388 Terry Harmon .30 .14
☐ 389 Ken Kravec .30 .14
☐ 390 Dave Winfield 10.00 4.50
☐ 391 Dan Warthen .30 .14
☐ 392 Phil Roof .30 .14
☐ 393 John Lowenstein .30 .14
☐ 394 Bill Laxton .30 .14
☐ 395 Manny Trillo .30 .14
☐ 396 Tom Murphy .30 .14
☐ 397 Larry Herndon .60 .25
☐ 398 Tom Burgmeier .30 .14
☐ 399 Bruce Boisclair .30 .14
☐ 400 Steve Garvey 2.00 .90
☐ 401 Mickey Scott .30 .14
☐ 402 Tommy Helms .30 .14
☐ 403 Tom Grieve .60 .25
☐ 404 Eric Rasmussen .30 .14
☐ 405 Claudell Washington .60 .25
☐ 406 Tim Johnson .30 .14
☐ 407 Dave Freisleben .30 .14
☐ 408 Cesar Tovar .30 .14
☐ 409 Pete Broberg .30 .14
☐ 410 Willie Montanez .30 .14
☐ 411 Joe Morgan WS 2.00 .90
Johnny Bench
☐ 412 Johnny Bench WS 2.00 .90
☐ 413 World Series Summary .60 .25
Cincy wins 2nd
straight series
☐ 414 Tommy Harper .60 .25
☐ 415 Jay Johnstone .60 .25
☐ 416 Chuck Hartenstein .30 .14
☐ 417 Wayne Garrett .30 .14
☐ 418 White Sox Team/Mgr. 1.25 .25
Bob Lemon
(Checklist back)
☐ 419 Steve Swisher .30 .14
☐ 420 Rusty Staub 1.25 .55
☐ 421 Doug Rau .30 .14
☐ 422 Freddie Patek .60 .25
☐ 423 Gary Lavelle .30 .14
☐ 424 Steve Brye .30 .14
☐ 425 Joe Torre 1.25 .55
☐ 426 Dick Drago .30 .14
☐ 427 Dave Rader .30 .14
☐ 428 Rangers Team/Mgr. 1.25 .25
Frank Lucchesi
(Checklist back)
☐ 429 Ken Boswell .30 .14
☐ 430 Fergie Jenkins 2.00 .90
☐ 431 Dave Collins UER .60 .25
(Photo actually
Bobby Jones)
☐ 432 Buzz Capra .30 .14
☐ 433 Nate Colbert TBC .30 .14
(5 HR, 13 RBI)
☐ 434 Carl Yastrzemski TBC 1.25 .55
'67 Triple Crown
☐ 435 Maury Wills TBC .60 .25
104 steals
☐ 436 Bob Keegan TBC .30 .14
Majors' only no-hitter
☐ 437 Ralph Kiner TBC 1.25 .55
Leads NL in HR's
7th straight year
☐ 438 Marty Perez .30 .14
☐ 439 Gorman Thomas .60 .25
☐ 440 Jon Matlack .30 .14
☐ 441 Larvell Blanks .30 .14
☐ 442 Braves Team/Mgr. 1.25 .25
Dave Bristol
(Checklist back)
☐ 443 Lamar Johnson .30 .14
☐ 444 Wayne Twitchell .30 .14
☐ 445 Ken Singleton .60 .25
☐ 446 Bill Bonham .30 .14
☐ 447 Jerry Turner .30 .14
☐ 448 Ellie Rodriguez .30 .14
☐ 449 Al Fitzmorris .30 .14
☐ 450 Pete Rose 10.00 4.50
☐ 451 Checklist 397-528 1.25 .25

☐ 452 Mike Caldwell .30 .14
☐ 453 Pedro Garcia .30 .14
☐ 454 Andy Etchebarren .30 .14
☐ 455 Rick Wise .30 .14
☐ 456 Leon Roberts .30 .14
☐ 457 Steve Luebber .30 .14
☐ 458 Leo Foster .30 .14
☐ 459 Steve Foucault .30 .14
☐ 460 Willie Stargell 2.50 1.10
☐ 461 Dick Tidrow .30 .14
☐ 462 Don Baylor 1.25 .55
☐ 463 Jamie Quirk .30 .14
☐ 464 Randy Moffitt .30 .14
☐ 465 Rico Carty .60 .25
☐ 466 Fred Holdsworth .30 .14
☐ 467 Phillies Team/Mgr. 1.25 .25
Danny Ozark
(Checklist back)
☐ 468 Ramon Hernandez .30 .14
☐ 469 Pat Kelly .30 .14
☐ 470 Ted Simmons .60 .25
☐ 471 Del Unser .30 .14
☐ 472 Rookie Pitchers .30 .14
Don Aase
Bob McClure
Gil Patterson
Dave Wehrmeister
☐ 473 Rookie Outfielders 40.00 18.00
Andre Dawson
Gene Richards
John Scott
Denny Walling
☐ 474 Rookie Shortstops .60 .25
Bob Bailor
Kiko Garcia
Craig Reynolds
Alex Taveras
☐ 475 Rookie Pitchers .60 .25
Chris Batton
Rick Camp
Scott McGregor
Manny Sarmiento
☐ 476 Rookie Catchers 20.00 9.00
Gary Alexander
Rick Cerone
Dale Murphy
Kevin Pasley
☐ 477 Rookie Infielders .60 .25
Doug Ault
Rich Dauer
Orlando Gonzalez
Phil Mankowski
☐ 478 Rookie Pitchers .60 .25
Jim Gideon
Leon Hooten
Dave Johnson
Mark Lemongello
☐ 479 Rookie Outfielders .60 .25
Brian Asselstine
Wayne Gross
Sam Mejias
Alvis Woods
☐ 480 Carl Yastrzemski 4.00 1.80
☐ 481 Roger Metzger .30 .14
☐ 482 Tony Solaita .30 .14
☐ 483 Richie Zisk .30 .14
☐ 484 Burt Hooton .60 .25
☐ 485 Roy White .60 .25
☐ 486 Ed Bane .30 .14
☐ 487 Rookie Pitchers .60 .25
Larry Anderson
Ed Glynn
Joe Henderson
Greg Terlecky
☐ 488 Rookie Outfielders 4.00 1.80
Jack Clark
Ruppert Jones
Lee Mazzilli
Dan Thomas
☐ 489 Rookie Pitchers .60 .25
Len Barker
Randy Lerch
Greg Minton
Mike Overy
☐ 490 Rookie Shortstops .60 .25
Billy Almon

	Mickey Klutts		
	Tommy McMillan		
	Mark Wagner		
□ 491	Rookie Pitchers	4.00	1.80
	Mike Dupree		
	Dennis Martinez		
	Craig Mitchell		
	Bob Sykes		
□ 492	Rookie Outfielders	.60	.25
	Tony Armas		
	Steve Kemp		
	Carlos Lopez		
	Gary Woods		
□ 493	Rookie Pitchers	.60	.25
	Mike Krukow		
	Jim Otten		
	Gary Wheelock		
	Mike Willis		
□ 494	Rookie Infielders	1.25	.55
	Juan Bernhardt		
	Mike Champion		
	Jim Gantner		
	Bump Wills		
□ 495	Al Hrabosky	.30	.14
□ 496	Gary Thomasson	.30	.14
□ 497	Clay Carroll	.30	.14
□ 498	Sal Bando	.60	.25
□ 499	Pablo Torrealba	.30	.14
□ 500	Dave Kingman	1.25	.55
□ 501	Jim Bibby	.30	.14
□ 502	Randy Hundley	.30	.14
□ 503	Bill Lee	.30	.14
□ 504	Dodgers Team/Mgr.	1.25	.25
	Tom Lasorda		
	(Checklist back)		
□ 505	Oscar Gamble	.60	.25
□ 506	Steve Grilli	.30	.14
□ 507	Mike Hegan	.30	.14
□ 508	Dave Pagan	.30	.14
□ 509	Cookie Rojas	.60	.25
□ 510	John Candelaria	.30	.14
□ 511	Bill Fahey	.30	.14
□ 512	Jack Billingham	.30	.14
□ 513	Jerry Terrell	.30	.14
□ 514	Cliff Johnson	.30	.14
□ 515	Chris Speier	.30	.14
□ 516	Bake McBride	.60	.25
□ 517	Pete Vuckovich	.60	.25
□ 518	Cubs Team/Mgr.	1.25	.25
	Herman Franks		
	(Checklist back)		
□ 519	Don Kirkwood	.30	.14
□ 520	Garry Maddox	.30	.14
□ 521	Bob Grich	.60	.25
□ 522	Enzo Hernandez	.30	.14
□ 523	Rollie Fingers	2.00	.90
□ 524	Rowland Office	.30	.14
□ 525	Dennis Eckersley	6.00	2.70
□ 526	Larry Parrish	.60	.25
□ 527	Dan Meyer	.60	.25
□ 528	Bill Castro	.30	.14
□ 529	Jim Essian	.30	.14
□ 530	Rick Reuschel	.60	.25
□ 531	Lyman Bostock	.60	.25
□ 532	Jim Willoughby	.30	.14
□ 533	Mickey Stanley	.30	.14
□ 534	Paul Splittorff	.30	.14
□ 535	Cesar Geronimo	.30	.14
□ 536	Vic Albury	.30	.14
□ 537	Dave Roberts	.30	.14
□ 538	Frank Taveras	.30	.14
□ 539	Mike Wallace	.30	.14
□ 540	Bob Watson	.60	.25
□ 541	John Denny	.60	.25
□ 542	Frank Duffy	.30	.14
□ 543	Ron Blomberg	.30	.14
□ 544	Gary Ross	.30	.14
□ 545	Bob Boone	.60	.25
□ 546	Orioles Team/Mgr.	1.25	.25
	Earl Weaver		
	(Checklist back)		
□ 547	Willie McCovey	3.00	1.35
□ 548	Joel Youngblood	.30	.14
□ 549	Jerry Royster	.30	.14
□ 550	Randy Jones	.30	.14
□ 551	Bill North	.30	.14
□ 552	Pepe Mangual	.30	.14
□ 553	Jack Heidemann	.30	.14
□ 554	Bruce Kimm	.30	.14
□ 555	Dan Ford	.30	.14
□ 556	Doug Bird	.30	.14
□ 557	Jerry White	.30	.14
□ 558	Elias Sosa	.30	.14
□ 559	Alan Bannister	.30	.14
□ 560	Dave Concepcion	1.25	.55
□ 561	Pete LaCock	.30	.14
□ 562	Checklist 529-660	1.25	.25
□ 563	Bruce Kison	.30	.14
□ 564	Alan Ashby	.60	.25
□ 565	Mickey Lolich	.60	.25
□ 566	Rick Miller	.30	.14
□ 567	Enos Cabell	.30	.14
□ 568	Carlos May	.30	.14
□ 569	Jim Lonborg	.60	.25
□ 570	Bobby Bonds	1.25	.55
□ 571	Darrell Evans	.60	.25
□ 572	Ross Grimsley	.30	.14
□ 573	Joe Ferguson	.30	.14
□ 574	Aurelio Rodriguez	.30	.14
□ 575	Dick Ruthven	.30	.14
□ 576	Fred Kendall	.30	.14
□ 577	Jerry Augustine	.30	.14
□ 578	Bob Randall	.30	.14
□ 579	Don Carrithers	.30	.14
□ 580	George Brett	30.00	13.50
□ 581	Pedro Borbon	.30	.14
□ 582	Ed Kirkpatrick	.30	.14
□ 583	Paul Lindblad	.30	.14
□ 584	Ed Goodson	.30	.14
□ 585	Rick Burleson	.60	.25
□ 586	Steve Renko	.30	.14
□ 587	Rick Baldwin	.30	.14
□ 588	Dave Moates	.30	.14
□ 589	Mike Cosgrove	.30	.14
□ 590	Buddy Bell	.60	.25
□ 591	Chris Arnold	.30	.14
□ 592	Dan Briggs	.30	.14
□ 593	Dennis Blair	.30	.14
□ 594	Biff Pocoroba	.30	.14
□ 595	John Hiller	.60	.25
□ 596	Jerry Martin	.30	.14
□ 597	Mariners Leaders	1.25	.25
	Darrell Johnson MG		
	Don Bryant CO		
	Jim Busby CO		
	Vada Pinson CO		
	Wes Stock CO		
	(Checklist back)		
□ 598	Sparky Lyle	.60	.25
□ 599	Mike Tyson	.30	.14
□ 600	Jim Palmer	3.00	1.35
□ 601	Mike Lum	.30	.14
□ 602	Andy Hassler	.30	.14
□ 603	Willie Davis	.60	.25
□ 604	Jim Slaton	.30	.14
□ 605	Felix Millan	.30	.14
□ 606	Steve Braun	.30	.14
□ 607	Larry Demery	.30	.14
□ 608	Roy Howell	.30	.14
□ 609	Jim Barr	.30	.14
□ 610	Jose Cardenal	.60	.25
□ 611	Dave Lemanczyk	.30	.14
□ 612	Barry Foote	.30	.14
□ 613	Reggie Cleveland	.30	.14
□ 614	Greg Gross	.30	.14
□ 615	Phil Niekro	2.00	.90
□ 616	Tommy Sandt	.30	.14
□ 617	Bobby Darwin	.30	.14
□ 618	Pat Dobson	.30	.14
□ 619	Johnny Oates	.30	.14
□ 620	Don Sutton	2.00	.90
□ 621	Tigers Team/Mgr.	1.25	.25
	Ralph Houk		
	(Checklist back)		
□ 622	Jim Wohlford	.30	.14
□ 623	Jack Kucek	.30	.14
□ 624	Hector Cruz	.30	.14
□ 625	Ken Holtzman	.60	.25
□ 626	Al Bumbry	.30	.25
□ 627	Bob Myrick	.30	.14
□ 628	Mario Guerrero	.30	.14
□ 629	Bobby Valentine	.30	.14
□ 630	Bert Blyleven	1.25	.55
□ 631	George Brett	8.00	3.60
	Ken Brett		
□ 632	Bob Forsch	.60	.25
	Ken Forsch		
□ 633	Lee May	.60	.25
	Carlos May		
□ 634	Paul Reuschel	.60	.25
	Rick Reuschel UER		
	(Photos switched)		
□ 635	Robin Yount	15.00	6.75
□ 636	Santo Alcala	.30	.14
□ 637	Alex Johnson	.30	.14
□ 638	Jim Kaat	1.25	.55
□ 639	Jerry Morales	.30	.14
□ 640	Carlton Fisk	5.00	2.20
□ 641	Dan Larson	.30	.14
□ 642	Willie Crawford	.30	.14
□ 643	Mike Pazik	.30	.14
□ 644	Matt Alexander	.30	.14
□ 645	Jerry Reuss	.60	.25
□ 646	Andres Mora	.30	.14
□ 647	Expos Team/Mgr.	1.25	.25
	Dick Williams		
	(Checklist back)		
□ 648	Jim Spencer	.30	.14
□ 649	Dave Cash	.30	.14
□ 650	Nolan Ryan	50.00	22.00
□ 651	Von Joshua	.30	.14
□ 652	Tom Walker	.30	.14
□ 653	Diego Segui	.60	.25
□ 654	Ron Pruitt	.30	.14
□ 655	Tony Perez	2.00	.90
□ 656	Ron Guidry	1.25	.55
□ 657	Mick Kelleher	.30	.14
□ 658	Marty Pattin	.30	.14
□ 659	Merv Rettenmund	.30	.14
□ 660	Willie Horton	1.25	.25

1978 Topps

The cards in this 726-card set measure 2 1/2" by 3 1/2". The 1978 Topps set experienced an increase in number of cards from the previous five regular issue sets of 660. Card numbers 1 through 7 feature Record Breakers (RB) of the 1977 season. Other subsets within this set include League Leaders (201-208), Post-season cards (411-413), and Rookie Prospects (701-711). The key Rookie Cards in this set are the multi-player Rookie Card of Paul Molitor and Alan Trammell, Jack Morris, Eddie Murray, Lance Parrish, and Lou Whitaker. Almost all of the Molitor/Trammell cards are found with dark printing smudges. The manager cards in the set feature a "then and now" format on the card front showing the manager as he looked during his playing days.

While no scarcities exist, 66 of the cards are more abundant in supply, as they were "double printed." These 66 double-printed cards are noted in the checklist by DP. Team cards again feature a checklist of that team's players in the set on the back. As in previous years, this set was issued in many different ways: some of them include 14-card wax packs and 39-card rack packs. Cards numbered 23 or lower, that feature Astros, Rangers, Tigers, or Yankees and do not follow the numbering checklisted below, are not necessarily error cards. They are undoubtedly Burger King cards, a separate set with its own pricing and mass distribution. Burger King cards are indistinguishable from the corresponding Topps cards except for the card numbering difference and the fact that Burger King cards do not have a printing sheet designation (such as A through F like the regular Topps cards) anywhere on the card back in very small print.

	NRMT	VG-E
COMPLETE SET (726)	250.00	110.00
COMMON CARD (1-726)		.11
MINOR STARS	.50	.23
SEMISTARS	1.00	.45
UNLISTED STARS	1.50	.70

#	Player	NRMT	VG-E
1	Lou Brock RB	2.50	.75
	Most lifetime steals		
2	Sparky Lyle RB	.50	.23
	Most career games pure relief		
3	Willie McCovey RB	1.50	.70
	Most times 2 HR's in inning		
4	Brooks Robinson RB	2.00	.90
	Most consecutive seasons with one club		
5	Pete Rose RB	3.00	1.35
	Most lifetime switch-hitter hits		
6	Nolan Ryan RB	15.00	6.75
	Most games 10 or more strikeouts		
7	Reggie Jackson RB	3.00	1.35
	Most homers, one World Series		
8	Mike Sadek	.25	.11
9	Doug DeCinces	.50	.23
10	Phil Niekro	1.50	.70
11	Rick Manning	.25	.11
12	Don Aase	.25	.11
13	Art Howe	.50	.23
14	Lerrin LaGrow	.25	.11
15	Tony Perez DP	1.00	.45
16	Roy White	.50	.23
17	Mike Krukow	.25	.11
18	Bob Grich	.50	.23
19	Darrell Porter	.50	.23
20	Pete Rose DP	5.00	2.20
21	Steve Kemp	.25	.11
22	Charlie Hough	.50	.23
23	Bump Wills	.25	.11
24	Don Money DP	.15	.07
25	Jon Matlack	.25	.11
26	Rich Hebner	.50	.23
27	Geoff Zahn	.25	.11
28	Ed Ott	.25	.11
29	Bob Lacey	.25	.11
30	George Hendrick	.50	.23
31	Glenn Abbott	.25	.11
32	Garry Templeton	.50	.23
33	Dave Lemanczyk	.25	.11
34	Willie McCovey	2.50	1.10
35	Sparky Lyle	.50	.23
36	Eddie Murray	120.00	55.00
37	Rick Waits	.25	.11
38	Willie Montanez	.25	.11
39	Floyd Bannister	.25	.11
40	Carl Yastrzemski	3.00	1.35
41	Burt Hooton	.50	.23
42	Jorge Orta	.25	.11
43	Bill Atkinson	.25	.11
44	Toby Harrah	.50	.23
45	Mark Fidrych	1.50	.70
46	Al Cowens	.25	.11
47	Jack Billingham	.25	.11
48	Don Baylor	1.00	.45
49	Ed Kranepool	.50	.23
50	Rick Reuschel	.50	.23
51	Charlie Moore DP	.15	.07
52	Jim Lonborg	.25	.11
53	Phil Garner DP	.25	.11
54	Tom Johnson	.25	.11
55	Mitchell Page	.25	.11
56	Randy Jones	.25	.11
57	Dan Meyer	.25	.11
58	Bob Forsch	.25	.11
59	Otto Velez	.25	.11
60	Thurman Munson	3.00	1.35
61	Larvell Blanks	.25	.11
62	Jim Barr	.25	.11
63	Don Zimmer MG	.50	.23
64	Gene Pentz	.25	.11
65	Ken Singleton	.50	.23
66	Chicago White Sox Team Card (Checklist back)	1.00	.20
67	Claudell Washington	.50	.23
68	Steve Foucault DP	.15	.07
69	Mike Vail	.25	.11
70	Rich Gossage	1.00	.45
71	Terry Humphrey	.25	.11
72	Andre Dawson	10.00	4.50
73	Andy Hassler	.25	.11
74	Checklist 1-121	1.00	.20
75	Dick Ruthven	.25	.11
76	Steve Mingori	.25	.11
77	Ed Kirkpatrick	.25	.11
78	Pablo Torrealba	.25	.11
79	Darrell Johnson DP MG	.15	.07
80	Ken Griffey	1.00	.45
81	Pete Redfern	.25	.11
82	San Francisco Giants Team Card (Checklist back)	1.00	.20
83	Bob Montgomery	.25	.11
84	Kent Tekulve	.50	.23
85	Ron Fairly	.50	.23
86	Dave Tomlin	.25	.11
87	John Lowenstein	.25	.11
88	Mike Phillips	.25	.11
89	Ken Clay	.25	.11
90	Larry Bowa	1.00	.45
91	Oscar Zamora	.25	.11
92	Adrian Devine	.25	.11
93	Bob Apodaca	.25	.11
94	Chuck Scrivener	.25	.11
95	Jamie Quirk	.25	.11
96	Baltimore Orioles Team Card (Checklist back)	1.00	.20
97	Stan Bahnsen	.25	.11
98	Jim Essian	.50	.23
99	Willie Hernandez	1.00	.45
100	George Brett	20.00	9.00
101	Sid Monge	.25	.11
102	Matt Alexander	.25	.11
103	Tom Murphy	.25	.11
104	Lee Lacy	.25	.11
105	Reggie Cleveland	.25	.11
106	Bill Plummer	.25	.11
107	Ed Halicki	.25	.11
108	Von Joshua	.25	.11
109	Joe Torre MG	.50	.23
110	Richie Zisk	.25	.11
111	Mike Tyson	.25	.11
112	Houston Astros Team Card (Checklist back)	1.00	.20
113	Don Carrithers	.25	.11
114	Paul Blair	.50	.23
115	Gary Nolan	.25	.11
116	Tucker Ashford	.25	.11
117	John Montague	.25	.11
118	Terry Harmon	.25	.11
119	Dennis Martinez	1.50	.70
120	Gary Carter	1.50	.70
121	Alvis Woods	.25	.11
122	Dennis Eckersley	4.00	1.80
123	Manny Trillo	.25	.11
124	Dave Rozema	.25	.11
125	George Scott	.50	.23
126	Paul Moskau	.25	.11
127	Chet Lemon	.50	.23
128	Bill Russell	.50	.23
129	Jim Colborn	.25	.11
130	Jeff Burroughs	.50	.23
131	Bert Blyleven	1.00	.45
132	Enos Cabell	.25	.11
133	Jerry Augustine	.25	.11
134	Steve Henderson	.25	.11
135	Ron Guidry DP	1.00	.45
136	Ted Sizemore	.25	.11
137	Craig Kusick	.25	.11
138	Larry Demery	.25	.11
139	Wayne Gross	.25	.11
140	Rollie Fingers	1.50	.70
141	Ruppert Jones	.25	.11
142	John Montefusco	.25	.11
143	Keith Hernandez	.50	.23
144	Jesse Jefferson	.25	.11
145	Rick Monday	.50	.23
146	Doyle Alexander	.25	.11
147	Lee Mazzilli	.25	.11
148	Andre Thornton	.50	.23
149	Dale Murray	.25	.11
150	Bobby Bonds	1.00	.45
151	Milt Wilcox	.25	.11
152	Ivan DeJesus	.25	.11
153	Steve Stone	.50	.23
154	Cecil Cooper DP	.25	.11
155	Butch Hobson	.25	.11
156	Andy Messersmith	.50	.23
157	Pete LaCock DP	.15	.07
158	Joaquin Andujar	.50	.23
159	Lou Piniella	.50	.23
160	Jim Palmer	2.50	1.10
161	Bob Boone	1.00	.45
162	Paul Thormodsgard	.25	.11
163	Bill North	.25	.11
164	Bob Owchinko	.25	.11
165	Rennie Stennett	.25	.11
166	Carlos Lopez	.25	.11
167	Tim Foli	.25	.11
168	Reggie Smith	.50	.23
169	Jerry Johnson	.25	.11
170	Lou Brock	2.50	1.10
171	Pat Zachry	.25	.11
172	Mike Hargrove	.50	.23
173	Robin Yount UER (Played for Newark in 1973, not 1971)	10.00	4.50
174	Wayne Garland	.25	.11
175	Jerry Morales	.25	.11
176	Milt May	.25	.11
177	Gene Garber DP	.25	.11
178	Dave Chalk	.25	.11
179	Dick Tidrow	.25	.11
180	Dave Concepcion	1.00	.45
181	Ken Forsch	.25	.11
182	Jim Spencer	.25	.11
183	Doug Bird	.25	.11
184	Checklist 122-242	1.00	.20
185	Ellis Valentine	.25	.11
186	Bob Stanley DP	.25	.11
187	Jerry Royster DP	.15	.07
188	Al Bumbry	.50	.23
189	Tom Lasorda MG	1.50	.70
190	John Candelaria	.50	.23
191	Rodney Scott	.25	.11
192	San Diego Padres Team Card (Checklist back)	1.00	.20
193	Rich Chiles	.25	.11
194	Derrel Thomas	.25	.11
195	Larry Dierker	.50	.23
196	Bob Bailor	.25	.11
197	Nino Espinosa	.25	.11

No.	Player / Card	Price 1	Price 2
198	Ron Pruitt	.25	.11
199	Craig Reynolds	.25	.11
200	Reggie Jackson	8.00	3.60
201	Batting Leaders	1.00	.45
	Dave Parker		
	Rod Carew		
202	Home Run Leaders DP	.50	.23
	George Foster		
	Jim Rice		
203	RBI Leaders	.50	.23
	George Foster		
	Larry Hisle		
204	Steals Leaders DP	.25	.11
	Frank Taveras		
	Freddie Patek		
205	Victory Leaders	1.50	.70
	Steve Carlton		
	Dave Goltz		
	Dennis Leonard		
	Jim Palmer		
206	Strikeout Leaders DP	5.00	2.20
	Phil Niekro		
	Nolan Ryan		
207	ERA Leaders DP	.50	.23
	John Candelaria		
	Frank Tanana		
208	Top Firemen	1.00	.45
	Rollie Fingers		
	Bill Campbell		
209	Dock Ellis	.25	.11
210	Jose Cardenal	.25	.11
211	Earl Weaver MG DP	1.00	.45
212	Mike Caldwell	.25	.11
213	Alan Bannister	.25	.11
214	California Angels	1.00	.20
	Team Card		
	(Checklist back)		
215	Darrell Evans	.50	.23
216	Mike Paxton	.25	.11
217	Rod Gilbreath	.25	.11
218	Marty Pattin	.25	.11
219	Mike Cubbage	.25	.11
220	Pedro Borbon	.25	.11
221	Chris Speier	.25	.11
222	Jerry Martin	.25	.11
223	Bruce Kison	.25	.11
224	Jerry Tabb	.25	.11
225	Don Gullett DP	.25	.11
226	Joe Ferguson	.25	.11
227	Al Fitzmorris	.25	.11
228	Manny Mota DP	.25	.11
229	Leo Foster	.25	.11
230	Al Hrabosky	.25	.11
231	Wayne Nordhagen	.25	.11
232	Mickey Stanley	.25	.11
233	Dick Pole	.25	.11
234	Herman Franks MG	.25	.11
235	Tim McCarver	.50	.23
236	Terry Whitfield	.25	.11
237	Rich Dauer	.25	.11
238	Juan Beniquez	.25	.11
239	Dyar Miller	.25	.11
240	Gene Tenace	.50	.23
241	Pete Vuckovich	.50	.23
242	Barry Bonnell DP	.15	.07
243	Bob McClure	.25	.11
244	Montreal Expos	.50	.10
	Team Card DP		
	(Checklist back)		
245	Rick Burleson	.50	.23
246	Dan Driessen	.25	.11
247	Larry Christenson	.25	.11
248	Frank White DP	.50	.23
249	Dave Goltz DP	.25	.07
250	Graig Nettles DP	.50	.23
251	Don Kirkwood	.25	.11
252	Steve Swisher DP	.15	.07
253	Jim Kern	.25	.11
254	Dave Collins	.25	.23
255	Jerry Reuss	.50	.23
256	Joe Altobelli MG	.25	.11
257	Hector Cruz	.25	.11
258	John Hiller	.25	.11
259	Los Angeles Dodgers	1.00	.20
	Team Card		
	(Checklist back)		
260	Bert Campaneris	.50	.23
261	Tim Hosley	.25	.11
262	Rudy May	.25	.11
263	Danny Walton	.25	.11
264	Jamie Easterly	.25	.11
265	Sal Bando DP	.50	.23
266	Bob Shirley	.25	.11
267	Doug Ault	.25	.11
268	Gil Flores	.25	.11
269	Wayne Twitchell	.25	.11
270	Carlton Fisk	3.00	1.35
271	Randy Lerch DP	.15	.07
272	Royle Stillman	.25	.11
273	Fred Norman	.25	.11
274	Freddie Patek	.50	.23
275	Dan Ford	.25	.11
276	Bill Bonham DP	.15	.07
277	Bruce Boisclair	.25	.11
278	Enrique Romo	.25	.11
279	Bill Virdon MG	.25	.11
280	Buddy Bell	.50	.23
281	Eric Rasmussen DP	.25	.11
282	New York Yankees	1.50	.30
	Team Card		
	(Checklist back)		
283	Omar Moreno	.25	.11
284	Randy Moffitt	.25	.11
285	Steve Yeager DP	.50	.23
286	Ben Oglivie	.25	.23
287	Kiko Garcia	.25	.11
288	Dave Hamilton	.25	.11
289	Checklist 243-363	1.00	.20
290	Willie Horton	.50	.23
291	Gary Ross	.25	.11
292	Gene Richards	.25	.11
293	Mike Willis	.25	.11
294	Larry Parrish	.50	.23
295	Bill Lee	.25	.11
296	Biff Pocoroba	.25	.11
297	Warren Brusstar DP	.15	.07
298	Tony Armas	.50	.23
299	Whitey Herzog MG	.50	.23
300	Joe Morgan	2.50	1.10
301	Buddy Schultz	.25	.11
302	Chicago Cubs	1.00	.20
	Team Card		
	(Checklist back)		
303	Sam Hinds	.25	.11
304	John Milner	.25	.11
305	Rico Carty	.50	.23
306	Joe Niekro	.50	.23
307	Glenn Borgmann	.25	.11
308	Jim Rooker	.25	.11
309	Cliff Johnson	.25	.11
310	Don Sutton	1.50	.70
311	Jose Baez DP	.15	.07
312	Greg Minton	.25	.11
313	Andy Etchebarren	.25	.11
314	Paul Lindblad	.25	.11
315	Mark Belanger	.50	.23
316	Henry Cruz DP	.15	.07
317	Dave Johnson	.25	.11
318	Tom Griffin	.25	.11
319	Alan Ashby	.25	.11
320	Fred Lynn	.50	.23
321	Santo Alcala	.25	.11
322	Tom Paciorek	.25	.23
323	Jim Fregosi DP	.25	.11
324	Vern Rapp MG	.25	.11
325	Bruce Sutter	1.00	.45
326	Mike Lum DP	.15	.07
327	Rick Langford DP	.15	.07
328	Milwaukee Brewers	1.00	.20
	Team Card		
	(Checklist back)		
329	John Verhoeven	.25	.11
330	Bob Watson	.50	.23
331	Mark Littell	.25	.11
332	Duane Kuiper	.25	.11
333	Jim Todd	.25	.11
334	John Stearns	.25	.11
335	Bucky Dent	.50	.23
336	Steve Busby	.25	.11
337	Tom Grieve	.50	.23
338	Dave Heaverlo	.25	.11
339	Mario Guerrero	.25	.11
340	Bake McBride	.50	.23
341	Mike Flanagan	.50	.23
342	Aurelio Rodriguez	.25	.11
343	John Wathan DP	.15	.07
344	Sam Ewing	.25	.11
345	Luis Tiant	.50	.23
346	Larry Biittner	.25	.11
347	Terry Forster	.25	.11
348	Del Unser	.25	.11
349	Rick Camp DP	.15	.07
350	Steve Garvey	1.50	.70
351	Jeff Torborg	.50	.23
352	Tony Scott	.25	.11
353	Doug Bair	.25	.11
354	Cesar Geronimo	.25	.11
355	Bill Travers	.25	.11
356	New York Mets	1.00	.20
	Team Card		
	(Checklist back)		
357	Tom Poquette	.25	.11
358	Mark Lemongello	.25	.11
359	Marc Hill	.25	.11
360	Mike Schmidt	12.00	5.50
361	Chris Knapp	.25	.11
362	Dave May	.25	.11
363	Bob Randall	.25	.11
364	Jerry Turner	.25	.11
365	Ed Figueroa	.25	.11
366	Larry Milbourne DP	.15	.07
367	Rick Dempsey	.50	.23
368	Balor Moore	.25	.11
369	Tim Nordbrook	.25	.11
370	Rusty Staub	1.00	.45
371	Ray Burris	.25	.11
372	Brian Asselstine	.25	.11
373	Jim Willoughby	.25	.11
374	Jose Morales	.25	.11
375	Tommy John	1.00	.45
376	Jim Wohlford	.25	.11
377	Manny Sarmiento	.25	.11
378	Bobby Winkles MG	.25	.11
379	Skip Lockwood	.25	.11
380	Ted Simmons	.50	.23
381	Philadelphia Phillies	1.00	.20
	Team Card		
	(Checklist back)		
382	Joe Lahoud	.25	.11
383	Mario Mendoza	.25	.11
384	Jack Clark	1.00	.45
385	Tito Fuentes	.25	.11
386	Bob Gorinski	.25	.11
387	Ken Holtzman	.50	.23
388	Bill Fahey DP	.15	.07
389	Julio Gonzalez	.25	.11
390	Oscar Gamble	.50	.23
391	Larry Haney	.25	.11
392	Billy Almon	.25	.11
393	Tippy Martinez	.50	.23
394	Roy Howell DP	.15	.07
395	Jim Hughes	.25	.11
396	Bob Stinson DP	.15	.07
397	Greg Gross	.25	.11
398	Don Hood	.25	.11
399	Pete Mackanin	.25	.11
400	Nolan Ryan	40.00	18.00
401	Sparky Anderson MG	.50	.23
402	Dave Campbell	.25	.11
403	Bud Harrelson	.50	.23
404	Detroit Tigers	1.00	.20
	Team Card		
	(Checklist back)		
405	Rawly Eastwick	.25	.11
406	Mike Jorgensen	.25	.11
407	Odell Jones	.25	.11
408	Joe Zdeb	.25	.11
409	Ron Schueler	.25	.11
410	Bill Madlock	.50	.23
411	Willie Randolph ALCS	.50	.23
412	Davey Lopes NLCS	.25	.23
413	Reggie Jackson WS	3.00	1.35
414	Darold Knowles DP	.15	.07
415	Ray Fosse	.25	.11
416	Jack Brohamer	.25	.11
417	Mike Garman DP	.15	.07
418	Tony Muser	.25	.11
419	Jerry Garvin	.25	.11

☐ 420 Greg Luzinski	1.00	.45
☐ 421 Junior Moore	.25	.11
☐ 422 Steve Braun	.25	.11
☐ 423 Dave Rosello	.25	.11
☐ 424 Boston Red Sox	1.00	.20
Team Card		
(Checklist back)		
☐ 425 Steve Rogers DP	.25	.11
☐ 426 Fred Kendall	.25	.11
☐ 427 Mario Soto	.50	.23
☐ 428 Joel Youngblood	.25	.11
☐ 429 Mike Barlow	.25	.11
☐ 430 Al Oliver	.50	.23
☐ 431 Butch Metzger	.25	.11
☐ 432 Terry Bulling	.25	.11
☐ 433 Fernando Gonzalez	.25	.11
☐ 434 Mike Norris	.25	.11
☐ 435 Checklist 364-484	1.00	.10
☐ 436 Vic Harris DP	.15	.07
☐ 437 Bo McLaughlin	.25	.11
☐ 438 John Ellis	.25	.11
☐ 439 Ken Kravec	.25	.11
☐ 440 Dave Lopes	.50	.23
☐ 441 Larry Gura	.25	.11
☐ 442 Elliott Maddox	.25	.11
☐ 443 Darrel Chaney	.25	.11
☐ 444 Roy Hartsfield MG	.25	.11
☐ 445 Mike Ivie	.25	.11
☐ 446 Tug McGraw	.50	.23
☐ 447 Leroy Stanton	.25	.11
☐ 448 Bill Castro	.25	.11
☐ 449 Tim Blackwell DP	.15	.07
☐ 450 Tom Seaver	4.00	1.80
☐ 451 Minnesota Twins	1.00	.20
Team Card		
(Checklist back)		
☐ 452 Jerry Mumphrey	.25	.11
☐ 453 Doug Flynn	.25	.11
☐ 454 Dave LaRoche	.25	.11
☐ 455 Bill Robinson	.50	.23
☐ 456 Vern Ruhle	.25	.11
☐ 457 Bob Bailey	.25	.11
☐ 458 Jeff Newman	.25	.11
☐ 459 Charlie Spikes	.25	.11
☐ 460 Jim Hunter	1.50	.70
☐ 461 Rob Andrews DP	.15	.07
☐ 462 Rogelio Moret	.25	.11
☐ 463 Kevin Bell	.25	.11
☐ 464 Jerry Grote	.25	.11
☐ 465 Hal McRae	.50	.23
☐ 466 Dennis Blair	.25	.11
☐ 467 Alvin Dark MG	.50	.23
☐ 468 Warren Cromartie	.50	.23
☐ 469 Rick Cerone	.50	.23
☐ 470 J.R. Richard	.50	.23
☐ 471 Roy Smalley	.50	.23
☐ 472 Ron Reed	.25	.11
☐ 473 Bill Buckner	.50	.23
☐ 474 Jim Slaton	.25	.11
☐ 475 Gary Matthews	.50	.23
☐ 476 Bill Stein	.25	.11
☐ 477 Doug Capilla	.25	.11
☐ 478 Jerry Remy	.25	.11
☐ 479 St. Louis Cardinals	1.00	.20
Team Card		
(Checklist back)		
☐ 480 Ron LeFlore	.50	.23
☐ 481 Jackson Todd	.25	.11
☐ 482 Rick Miller	.25	.11
☐ 483 Ken Macha	.25	.11
☐ 484 Jim Norris	.25	.11
☐ 485 Chris Chambliss	.50	.23
☐ 486 John Curtis	.25	.11
☐ 487 Jim Tyrone	.25	.11
☐ 488 Dan Spillner	.25	.11
☐ 489 Rudy Meoli	.25	.11
☐ 490 Amos Otis	.50	.23
☐ 491 Scott McGregor	.50	.23
☐ 492 Jim Sundberg	.50	.23
☐ 493 Steve Renko	.25	.11
☐ 494 Chuck Tanner MG	.50	.23
☐ 495 Dave Cash	.25	.11
☐ 496 Jim Clancy DP	.15	.07
☐ 497 Glenn Adams	.25	.11
☐ 498 Joe Sambito	.25	.11
☐ 499 Seattle Mariners	1.00	.11

Team Card		
(Checklist back)		
☐ 500 George Foster	1.00	.45
☐ 501 Dave Roberts	.25	.11
☐ 502 Pat Rockett	.25	.11
☐ 503 Ike Hampton	.25	.11
☐ 504 Roger Freed	.25	.11
☐ 505 Felix Millan	.25	.11
☐ 506 Ron Blomberg	.25	.11
☐ 507 Willie Crawford	.25	.11
☐ 508 Johnny Oates	.25	.23
☐ 509 Brent Strom	.25	.11
☐ 510 Willie Stargell	2.00	.90
☐ 511 Frank Duffy	.25	.11
☐ 512 Larry Herndon	.25	.11
☐ 513 Barry Foote	.25	.11
☐ 514 Rob Sperring	.25	.11
☐ 515 Tim Corcoran	.25	.11
☐ 516 Gary Beare	.25	.11
☐ 517 Andres Mora	.25	.11
☐ 518 Tommy Boggs DP	.15	.07
☐ 519 Brian Downing	.50	.23
☐ 520 Larry Hisle	.25	.11
☐ 521 Steve Staggs	.25	.11
☐ 522 Dick Williams MG	.50	.23
☐ 523 Donnie Moore	.25	.11
☐ 524 Bernie Carbo	.25	.11
☐ 525 Jerry Terrell	.25	.11
☐ 526 Cincinnati Reds	1.00	.20
Team Card		
(Checklist back)		
☐ 527 Vic Correll	.25	.11
☐ 528 Rob Picciolo	.25	.11
☐ 529 Paul Hartzell	.25	.11
☐ 530 Dave Winfield	8.00	3.60
☐ 531 Tom Underwood	.25	.11
☐ 532 Skip Jutze	.25	.11
☐ 533 Sandy Alomar	.50	.23
☐ 534 Wilbur Howard	.25	.11
☐ 535 Checklist 485-605	1.00	.20
☐ 536 Roric Harrison	.25	.11
☐ 537 Bruce Bochte	.25	.11
☐ 538 Johnny LeMaster	.25	.11
☐ 539 Vic Davalillo DP	.15	.07
☐ 540 Steve Carlton	3.00	1.35
☐ 541 Larry Cox	.25	.11
☐ 542 Tim Johnson	.25	.11
☐ 543 Larry Harlow DP	.15	.07
☐ 544 Len Randle DP	.15	.07
☐ 545 Bill Campbell	.25	.11
☐ 546 Ted Martinez	.25	.11
☐ 547 John Scott	.25	.11
☐ 548 Billy Hunter DP MG	.15	.07
☐ 549 Joe Kerrigan	.25	.11
☐ 550 John Mayberry	.25	.23
☐ 551 Atlanta Braves	1.00	.20
Team Card		
(Checklist back)		
☐ 552 Francisco Barrios	.25	.11
☐ 553 Terry Puhl	.50	.23
☐ 554 Joe Coleman	.25	.11
☐ 555 Butch Wynegar	.25	.11
☐ 556 Ed Armbrister	.25	.11
☐ 557 Tony Solaita	.25	.11
☐ 558 Paul Mitchell	.25	.11
☐ 559 Phil Mankowski	.25	.11
☐ 560 Dave Parker	1.00	.45
☐ 561 Charlie Williams	.25	.11
☐ 562 Glenn Burke	.25	.11
☐ 563 Dave Rader	.25	.11
☐ 564 Mick Kelleher	.25	.11
☐ 565 Jerry Koosman	.50	.23
☐ 566 Merv Rettenmund	.25	.11
☐ 567 Dick Drago	.25	.11
☐ 568 Tom Hutton	.25	.11
☐ 569 Lary Sorensen	.25	.11
☐ 570 Dave Kingman	1.00	.45
☐ 571 Buck Martinez	.25	.11
☐ 572 Rick Wise	.25	.11
☐ 573 Luis Gomez	.25	.11
☐ 574 Bob Lemon MG	1.00	.45
☐ 575 Pat Dobson	.25	.11
☐ 576 Sam Mejias	.25	.11
☐ 577 Oakland A's	1.00	.20
Team Card		
(Checklist back)		

☐ 578 Buzz Capra	.25	.11
☐ 579 Rance Mulliniks	.25	.11
☐ 580 Rod Carew	2.50	1.10
☐ 581 Lynn McGlothen	.25	.11
☐ 582 Fran Healy	.25	.11
☐ 583 George Medich	.25	.11
☐ 584 John Hale	.25	.11
☐ 585 Woodie Fryman DP	.15	.07
☐ 586 Ed Goodson	.25	.11
☐ 587 John Urrea	.25	.11
☐ 588 Jim Mason	.25	.11
☐ 589 Bob Knepper	.25	.11
☐ 590 Bobby Murcer	.50	.23
☐ 591 George Zeber	.25	.11
☐ 592 Bob Apodaca	.25	.11
☐ 593 Dave Skaggs	.25	.11
☐ 594 Dave Freisleben	.25	.11
☐ 595 Sixto Lezcano	.25	.11
☐ 596 Gary Wheelock	.25	.11
☐ 597 Steve Dillard	.25	.11
☐ 598 Eddie Solomon	.25	.11
☐ 599 Gary Woods	.25	.11
☐ 600 Frank Tanana	.50	.23
☐ 601 Gene Mauch MG	.50	.23
☐ 602 Eric Soderholm	.25	.11
☐ 603 Will McEnaney	.25	.11
☐ 604 Earl Williams	.25	.11
☐ 605 Rick Rhoden	.50	.23
☐ 606 Pittsburgh Pirates	1.00	.20
Team Card		
(Checklist back)		
☐ 607 Fernando Arroyo	.25	.11
☐ 608 Johnny Grubb	.25	.11
☐ 609 John Denny	.25	.11
☐ 610 Garry Maddox	.50	.23
☐ 611 Pat Scanlon	.25	.11
☐ 612 Ken Henderson	.25	.11
☐ 613 Marty Perez	.25	.11
☐ 614 Joe Wallis	.25	.11
☐ 615 Clay Carroll	.25	.11
☐ 616 Pat Kelly	.25	.11
☐ 617 Joe Nolan	.25	.11
☐ 618 Tommy Helms	.25	.11
☐ 619 Thad Bosley DP	.15	.07
☐ 620 Willie Randolph	1.00	.45
☐ 621 Craig Swan DP	.15	.07
☐ 622 Champ Summers	.25	.11
☐ 623 Eduardo Rodriguez	.25	.11
☐ 624 Gary Alexander DP	.15	.07
☐ 625 Jose Cruz	.50	.23
☐ 626 Toronto Blue Jays	1.00	.20
Team Card		
(Checklist back)		
☐ 627 David Johnson	.25	.11
☐ 628 Ralph Garr	.50	.23
☐ 629 Don Stanhouse	.25	.11
☐ 630 Ron Cey	1.00	.45
☐ 631 Danny Ozark MG	.25	.11
☐ 632 Rowland Office	.25	.11
☐ 633 Tom Veryzer	.25	.11
☐ 634 Len Barker	.25	.11
☐ 635 Joe Rudi	.50	.23
☐ 636 Jim Bibby	.25	.11
☐ 637 Duffy Dyer	.25	.11
☐ 638 Paul Splittorff	.25	.11
☐ 639 Gene Clines	.25	.11
☐ 640 Lee May DP	.25	.11
☐ 641 Doug Rau	.25	.11
☐ 642 Denny Doyle	.25	.11
☐ 643 Tom House	.25	.11
☐ 644 Jim Dwyer	.25	.11
☐ 645 Mike Torrez	.50	.23
☐ 646 Rick Auerbach DP	.15	.07
☐ 647 Steve Dunning	.25	.11
☐ 648 Gary Thomasson	.25	.11
☐ 649 Moose Haas	.25	.11
☐ 650 Cesar Cedeno	.50	.23
☐ 651 Doug Rader	.25	.11
☐ 652 Checklist 606-726	1.00	.20
☐ 653 Ron Hodges DP	.15	.07
☐ 654 Pepe Frias	.25	.11
☐ 655 Lyman Bostock	.50	.23
☐ 656 Dave Garcia MG	.25	.11
☐ 657 Bombo Rivera	.25	.11
☐ 658 Manny Sanguillen	.50	.23
☐ 659 Texas Rangers	1.00	.20

Team Card (Checklist back)

		NRMT	VG-E
□ 660	Jason Thompson	.50	.23
□ 661	Grant Jackson	.25	.11
□ 662	Paul Dade	.25	.11
□ 663	Paul Reuschel	.25	.11
□ 664	Fred Stanley	.25	.11
□ 665	Dennis Leonard	.50	.23
□ 666	Billy Smith	.25	.11
□ 667	Jeff Byrd	.25	.11
□ 668	Dusty Baker	1.00	.45
□ 669	Pete Falcone	.25	.11
□ 670	Jim Rice	1.00	.45
□ 671	Gary Lavelle	.25	.11
□ 672	Don Kessinger	.50	.23
□ 673	Steve Brye	.25	.11
□ 674	Ray Knight	1.50	.70
□ 675	Jay Johnstone	.50	.23
□ 676	Bob Myrick	.25	.11
□ 677	Ed Herrmann	.25	.11
□ 678	Tom Burgmeier	.25	.11
□ 679	Wayne Garrett	.25	.11
□ 680	Vida Blue	.50	.23
□ 681	Rob Belloir	.25	.11
□ 682	Ken Brett	.25	.11
□ 683	Mike Champion	.25	.11
□ 684	Ralph Houk MG	.50	.23
□ 685	Frank Taveras	.25	.11
□ 686	Gaylord Perry	1.50	.70
□ 687	Julio Cruz	.25	.11
□ 688	George Mitterwald	.25	.11
□ 689	Cleveland Indians	1.00	.20

Team Card (Checklist back)

		NRMT	VG-E
□ 690	Mickey Rivers	.50	.23
□ 691	Ross Grimsley	.25	.11
□ 692	Ken Reitz	.25	.11
□ 693	Lamar Johnson	.25	.11
□ 694	Elias Sosa	.25	.11
□ 695	Dwight Evans	1.00	.45
□ 696	Steve Mingori	.25	.11
□ 697	Roger Metzger	.25	.11
□ 698	Juan Bernhardt	.25	.11
□ 699	Jackie Brown	.25	.11
□ 700	Johnny Bench	4.00	1.80
□ 701	Rookie Pitchers	.50	.23

Tom Hume
Larry Landreth
Steve McCatty
Bruce Taylor

		NRMT	VG-E
□ 702	Rookie Catchers	.50	.23

Bill Nahorodny
Kevin Pasley
Rick Sweet
Don Werner

		NRMT	VG-E
□ 703	Rookie Pitchers DP	5.00	2.20

Larry Andersen
Tim Jones
Mickey Mahler
Jack Morris

		NRMT	VG-E
□ 704	Rookie 2nd Basemen	12.00	5.50

Garth Iorg
Dave Oliver
Sam Perlozzo
Lou Whitaker

		NRMT	VG-E
□ 705	Rookie Outfielders	1.00	.45

Dave Bergman
Miguel Dilone
Clint Hurdle
Willie Norwood

		NRMT	VG-E
□ 706	Rookie 1st Basemen	.50	.23

Wayne Cage
Ted Cox
Pat Putnam
Dave Revering

		NRMT	VG-E
□ 707	Rookie Shortstops	100.00	45.00

Mickey Klutts
Paul Molitor
Alan Trammell
U.L. Washington

		NRMT	VG-E
□ 708	Rookie Catchers	5.00	2.20

Bo Diaz
Dale Murphy
Lance Parrish
Ernie Whitt

		NRMT	VG-E
□ 709	Rookie Pitchers	.50	.23

Steve Burke
Matt Keough
Lance Rautzhan
Dan Schatzeder

		NRMT	VG-E
□ 710	Rookie Outfielders	1.00	.45

Dell Alston
Rick Bosetti
Mike Easler
Keith Smith

		NRMT	VG-E
□ 711	Rookie Pitchers DP	.25	.11

Cardell Camper
Dennis Lamp
Craig Mitchell
Roy Thomas

		NRMT	VG-E
□ 712	Bobby Valentine	.50	.23
□ 713	Bob Davis	.25	.11
□ 714	Mike Anderson	.25	.11
□ 715	Jim Kaat	1.00	.45
□ 716	Clarence Gaston	.50	.23
□ 717	Nelson Briles	.25	.11
□ 718	Ron Jackson	.25	.11
□ 719	Randy Elliott	.25	.11
□ 720	Fergie Jenkins	1.50	.70
□ 721	Billy Martin MG	1.00	.45
□ 722	Pete Broberg	.25	.11
□ 723	John Wockenfuss	.25	.11
□ 724	Kansas City Royals	1.00	.20

Team Card (Checklist back)

		NRMT	VG-E
□ 725	Kurt Bevacqua	.25	.11
□ 726	Wilbur Wood	1.00	.22

1979 Topps

The cards in this 726-card set measure 2 1/2" by 3 1/2". Topps continued with the same number of cards as in 1978. Various series spotlight League Leaders (1-8), "Season and Career Record Holders" (411-418), "Record Breakers" (201-206), and one "Prospects" card for each team (701-726). Team cards feature a checklist on back of that team's players in the set and a small picture of the manager on the front of the card. There are 66 cards that were double printed and these are noted in the checklist by the abbreviation DP. Bump Wills (369) was initially depicted in a Ranger uniform but with a Blue Jays affiliation; later printings correctly labeled him with Texas. The set price includes either Wills card. The key Rookie Cards in this set are Pedro Guerrero, Carney Lansford, Ozzie Smith, Bob Welch and Willie Wilson. As in previous years, this set was released in many different formats, among them are 12-card wax packs and 39-card rack packs. Cards numbered 23 or lower, which feature Phillies or Yankees and do not follow the numbering checklisted below, are not necessarily error cards. They are undoubtedly Burger King cards, separate sets for each team each with its own pricing and mass distribution. Burger King cards are indistinguishable from the corresponding Topps cards except for the card numbering difference and the fact that Burger King cards do not have a printing sheet designation (such as A through F like the regular Topps) anywhere on the card back in very small print.

	NRMT	VG-E
COMPLETE SET (726)	200.00	90.00
COMMON CARD (1-726)	.20	.09
MINOR STARS	.40	.18
SEMISTARS	.75	.35
UNLISTED STARS	1.25	.55

		NRMT	VG-E
□ 1	Batting Leaders	2.50	.50

Rod Carew
Dave Parker

		NRMT	VG-E
□ 2	Home Run Leaders	.75	.35

Jim Rice
George Foster

		NRMT	VG-E
□ 3	RBI Leaders	.75	.35

Jim Rice
George Foster

		NRMT	VG-E
□ 4	Stolen Base Leaders	.40	.18

Ron LeFlore
Omar Moreno

		NRMT	VG-E
□ 5	Victory Leaders	.40	.18

Ron Guidry
Gaylord Perry

		NRMT	VG-E
□ 6	Strikeout Leaders	6.00	2.70

Nolan Ryan
J.R. Richard

		NRMT	VG-E
□ 7	ERA Leaders	.40	.18

Ron Guidry
Craig Swan

		NRMT	VG-E
□ 8	Leading Firemen	.75	.35

Rich Gossage
Rollie Fingers

		NRMT	VG-E
□ 9	Dave Campbell	.20	.09
□ 10	Lee May	.40	.18
□ 11	Marc Hill	.20	.09
□ 12	Dick Drago	.20	.09
□ 13	Paul Dade	.20	.09
□ 14	Rafael Landestoy	.20	.09
□ 15	Ross Grimsley	.20	.09
□ 16	Fred Stanley	.20	.09
□ 17	Donnie Moore	.20	.09
□ 18	Tony Solaita	.20	.09
□ 19	Larry Gura DP	.10	.09
□ 20	Joe Morgan DP	1.00	.45
□ 21	Kevin Kobel	.20	.09
□ 22	Mike Jorgensen	.20	.09
□ 23	Terry Forster	.20	.09
□ 24	Paul Molitor	20.00	9.00
□ 25	Steve Carlton	2.50	1.10
□ 26	Jamie Quirk	.20	.09
□ 27	Dave Goltz	.20	.09
□ 28	Steve Brye	.20	.09
□ 29	Rick Langford	.20	.09
□ 30	Dave Winfield	6.00	2.70
□ 31	Tom House DP	.10	.05
□ 32	Jerry Mumphrey	.20	.09
□ 33	Dave Rozema	.20	.09
□ 34	Rob Andrews	.20	.09
□ 35	Ed Figueroa	.20	.09
□ 36	Alan Ashby	.20	.09
□ 37	Joe Kerrigan DP	.10	.05
□ 38	Bernie Carbo	.20	.09
□ 39	Dale Murphy	4.00	1.80
□ 40	Dennis Eckersley	2.00	.90
□ 41	Twins Team/Mgr.	.75	.15

Gene Mauch (Checklist back)

		NRMT	VG-E
□ 42	Ron Blomberg	.20	.09

43	Wayne Twitchell	.20	.09
44	Kurt Bevacqua	.20	.09
45	Al Hrabosky	.20	.09
46	Ron Hodges	.20	.09
47	Fred Norman	.20	.09
48	Merv Rettenmund	.20	.09
49	Vern Ruhle	.20	.09
50	Steve Garvey DP	.75	.35
51	Ray Fosse DP	.10	.05
52	Randy Lerch	.20	.09
53	Mick Kelleher	.20	.09
54	Dell Alston DP	.10	.05
55	Willie Stargell	1.50	.70
56	John Hale	.20	.09
57	Eric Rasmussen	.20	.09
58	Bob Randall DP	.10	.05
59	John Denny DP	.20	.09
60	Mickey Rivers	.40	.18
61	Bo Diaz	.20	.09
62	Randy Moffitt	.20	.09
63	Jack Brohamer	.20	.09
64	Tom Underwood	.20	.09
65	Mark Belanger	.35	.16
66	Tigers Team/Mgr.	.75	.15
	Les Moss		
	(Checklist back)		
67	Jim Mason DP	.10	.05
68	Joe Niekro DP	.20	.09
69	Elliott Maddox	.20	.09
70	John Candelaria	.40	.18
71	Brian Downing	.40	.18
72	Steve Mingori	.20	.09
73	Ken Henderson	.20	.09
74	Shane Rawley	.20	.09
75	Steve Yeager	.40	.18
76	Warren Cromartie	.40	.18
77	Dan Briggs DP	.10	.05
78	Elias Sosa	.20	.09
79	Ted Cox	.20	.09
80	Jason Thompson	.40	.18
81	Roger Erickson	.20	.09
82	Mets Team/Mgr.	.75	.15
	Joe Torre		
	(Checklist back)		
83	Fred Kendall	.20	.09
84	Greg Minton	.20	.09
85	Gary Matthews	.40	.18
86	Rodney Scott	.20	.09
87	Pete Falcone	.20	.09
88	Bob Molinaro	.20	.09
89	Dick Tidrow	.20	.09
90	Bob Boone	.75	.35
91	Terry Crowley	.20	.09
92	Jim Bibby	.20	.09
93	Phil Mankowski	.20	.09
94	Len Barker	.20	.09
95	Robin Yount	8.00	3.60
96	Indians Team/Mgr.	.75	.15
	Jeff Torborg		
	(Checklist back)		
97	Sam Mejias	.20	.09
98	Ray Burris	.20	.09
99	John Wathan	.40	.18
100	Tom Seaver DP	2.00	.90
101	Roy Howell	.20	.09
102	Mike Anderson	.20	.09
103	Jim Todd	.20	.09
104	Johnny Oates DP	.20	.09
105	Rick Camp DP	.10	.05
106	Frank Duffy	.20	.09
107	Jesus Alou DP	.10	.05
108	Eduardo Rodriguez	.20	.09
109	Joel Youngblood	.20	.09
110	Vida Blue	.40	.18
111	Roger Freed	.20	.09
112	Phillies Team/Mgr.	.75	.15
	Danny Ozark		
	(Checklist back)		
113	Pete Redfern	.20	.09
114	Cliff Johnson	.20	.09
115	Nolan Ryan	30.00	13.50
116	Ozzie Smith	100.00	45.00
117	Grant Jackson	.20	.09
118	Bud Harrelson	.20	.18
119	Don Stanhouse	.20	.09
120	Jim Sundberg	.40	.18
121	Checklist 1-121 DP	.40	.08
122	Mike Paxton	.20	.09
123	Lou Whitaker	4.00	1.80
124	Dan Schatzeder	.20	.09
125	Rick Burleson	.20	.09
126	Doug Bair	.20	.09
127	Thad Bosley	.20	.09
128	Ted Martinez	.20	.09
129	Marty Pattin DP	.10	.05
130	Bob Watson DP	.20	.09
131	Jim Clancy	.20	.09
132	Rowland Office	.20	.09
133	Bill Castro	.20	.09
134	Alan Bannister	.20	.09
135	Bobby Murcer	.40	.18
136	Jim Kaat	.40	.18
137	Larry Wolfe DP	.10	.05
138	Mark Lee	.20	.09
139	Luis Pujols	.20	.09
140	Don Gullett	.40	.18
141	Tom Paciorek	.40	.09
142	Charlie Williams	.20	.09
143	Tony Scott	.20	.09
144	Sandy Alomar	.40	.18
145	Rick Rhoden	.20	.09
146	Duane Kuiper	.20	.09
147	Dave Hamilton	.20	.09
148	Bruce Boisclair	.20	.09
149	Manny Sarmiento	.20	.09
150	Wayne Cage	.20	.09
151	John Hiller	.20	.09
152	Rick Cerone	.20	.09
153	Dennis Lamp	.20	.09
154	Jim Gantner DP	.20	.09
155	Dwight Evans	.75	.35
156	Buddy Solomon	.20	.09
157	U.L. Washington UER	.20	.09
	(Sic, bats left,		
	should be right)		
158	Joe Sambito	.20	.09
159	Roy White	.40	.18
160	Mike Flanagan	.75	.35
161	Barry Foote	.20	.09
162	Tom Johnson	.20	.09
163	Glenn Burke	.20	.09
164	Mickey Lolich	.40	.18
165	Frank Taveras	.20	.09
166	Leon Roberts	.20	.09
167	Roger Metzger DP	.10	.05
168	Dave Freisleben	.20	.09
169	Bill Nahorodny	.20	.09
170	Don Sutton	1.25	.55
171	Gene Clines	.20	.09
172	Mike Bruhert	.20	.09
173	John Lowenstein	.20	.09
174	Rick Auerbach	.20	.09
175	George Hendrick	.75	.35
176	Aurelio Rodriguez	.20	.09
177	Ron Reed	.20	.09
178	Alvis Woods	.20	.09
179	Jim Beattie DP	.20	.09
180	Larry Hisle	.20	.09
181	Mike Garman	.20	.09
182	Tim Johnson	.20	.09
183	Paul Splittorff	.20	.09
184	Darrel Chaney	.20	.09
185	Mike Torrez	.40	.18
186	Eric Soderholm	.20	.09
187	Mark Lemongello	.20	.09
188	Pat Kelly	.20	.09
189	Eddie Whitson	.20	.09
190	Ron Cey	.40	.18
191	Mike Norris	.20	.09
192	Cardinals Team/Mgr.	.75	.15
	Ken Boyer		
	(Checklist back)		
193	Glenn Adams	.20	.09
194	Randy Jones	.20	.09
195	Bill Madlock	.40	.18
196	Steve Kemp DP	.20	.09
197	Bob Apodaca	.20	.09
198	Johnny Grubb	.20	.09
199	Larry Milbourne	.20	.09
200	Johnny Bench DP	2.00	.90
201	Mike Edwards RB	.20	.09
202	Ron Guidry RB	.75	.35
203	J.R. Richard RB	.20	.09
204	Pete Rose RB	2.00	.90
205	John Stearns RB	.20	.09
206	Sammy Stewart RB	.20	.09
207	Dave Lemanczyk	.20	.09
208	Clarence Gaston	.40	.18
209	Reggie Cleveland	.20	.09
210	Larry Bowa	.40	.18
211	Denny Martinez	1.25	.55
212	Carney Lansford	1.50	.70
213	Bill Travers	.20	.09
214	Red Sox Team/Mgr.	.75	.15
	Don Zimmer		
	(Checklist back)		
215	Willie McCovey	2.00	.90
216	Wilbur Wood	.20	.09
217	Steve Dillard	.20	.09
218	Dennis Leonard	.40	.18
219	Roy Smalley	.40	.18
220	Cesar Geronimo	.20	.09
221	Jesse Jefferson	.20	.09
222	Bob Beall	.20	.09
223	Kent Tekulve	.40	.18
224	Dave Revering	.20	.09
225	Rich Gossage	.75	.35
226	Ron Pruitt	.20	.09
227	Steve Stone	.40	.18
228	Vic Davalillo	.20	.09
229	Doug Flynn	.20	.09
230	Bob Forsch	.20	.09
231	John Wockenfuss	.20	.09
232	Jimmy Sexton	.20	.09
233	Paul Mitchell	.20	.09
234	Toby Harrah	.40	.18
235	Steve Rogers	.20	.09
236	Jim Dwyer	.20	.09
237	Billy Smith	.20	.09
238	Balor Moore	.20	.09
239	Willie Horton	.40	.18
240	Rick Reuschel	.40	.18
241	Checklist 122-242 DP	.40	.08
242	Pablo Torrealba	.20	.09
243	Buck Martinez DP	.10	.05
244	Pirates Team/Mgr.	.75	.15
	Chuck Tanner		
	(Checklist back)		
245	Jeff Burroughs	.40	.18
246	Darrell Jackson	.20	.09
247	Tucker Ashford DP	.10	.05
248	Pete LaCock	.20	.09
249	Paul Thormodsgard	.20	.09
250	Willie Randolph	.40	.18
251	Jack Morris	2.00	.90
252	Bob Stinson	.20	.09
253	Rick Wise	.20	.09
254	Luis Gomez	.20	.09
255	Tommy John	.75	.35
256	Mike Sadek	.20	.09
257	Adrian Devine	.20	.09
258	Mike Phillips	.20	.09
259	Reds Team/Mgr.	.75	.15
	Sparky Anderson		
	(Checklist back)		
260	Richie Zisk	.20	.09
261	Mario Guerrero	.20	.09
262	Nelson Briles	.20	.09
263	Oscar Gamble	.40	.18
264	Don Robinson	.20	.09
265	Don Money	.20	.09
266	Jim Willoughby	.20	.09
267	Joe Rudi	.40	.18
268	Julio Gonzalez	.20	.09
269	Woodie Fryman	.20	.09
270	Butch Hobson	.40	.18
271	Rawly Eastwick	.20	.09
272	Tim Corcoran	.20	.09
273	Jerry Terrell	.20	.09
274	Willie Norwood	.20	.09
275	Junior Moore	.20	.09
276	Jim Colborn	.20	.09
277	Tom Grieve	.40	.18
278	Andy Messersmith	.40	.18
279	Jerry Grote DP	.10	.05
280	Andre Thornton	.40	.18
281	Vic Correll DP	.10	.05
282	Blue Jays Team/Mgr.	.75	.08

Roy Hartsfield
(Checklist back)

☐ 283	Ken Kravec	.20	.09
☐ 284	Johnnie LeMaster	.20	.09
☐ 285	Bobby Bonds	.75	.35
☐ 286	Duffy Dyer	.20	.09
☐ 287	Andres Mora	.20	.09
☐ 288	Milt Wilcox	.20	.09
☐ 289	Jose Cruz	.75	.35
☐ 290	Dave Lopes	.40	.18
☐ 291	Tom Griffin	.20	.09
☐ 292	Don Reynolds	.20	.09
☐ 293	Jerry Garvin	.20	.09
☐ 294	Pepe Frias	.20	.09
☐ 295	Mitchell Page	.20	.09
☐ 296	Preston Hanna	.20	.09
☐ 297	Ted Sizemore	.20	.09
☐ 298	Rich Gale	.20	.09
☐ 299	Steve Ontiveros	.20	.09
☐ 300	Rod Carew	2.00	.90
☐ 301	Tom Hume	.20	.09
☐ 302	Braves Team/Mgr.	.75	.15

Bobby Cox
(Checklist back)

☐ 303	Lary Sorensen DP	.10	.05
☐ 304	Steve Swisher	.20	.09
☐ 305	Willie Montanez	.20	.09
☐ 306	Floyd Bannister	.20	.09
☐ 307	Larvell Blanks	.20	.09
☐ 308	Bert Blyleven	.75	.35
☐ 309	Ralph Garr	.40	.18
☐ 310	Thurman Munson	2.00	.90
☐ 311	Gary Lavelle	.20	.09
☐ 312	Bob Robertson	.20	.09
☐ 313	Dyar Miller	.20	.09
☐ 314	Larry Harlow	.20	.09
☐ 315	Jon Matlack	.20	.09
☐ 316	Milt May	.20	.09
☐ 317	Jose Cardenal	.20	.18
☐ 318	Bob Welch	1.50	.70
☐ 319	Wayne Garrett	.20	.09
☐ 320	Carl Yastrzemski	2.50	1.10
☐ 321	Gaylord Perry	1.25	.55
☐ 322	Danny Goodwin	.20	.09
☐ 323	Lynn McGlothen	.20	.09
☐ 324	Mike Tyson	.20	.09
☐ 325	Cecil Cooper	.40	.18
☐ 326	Pedro Borbon	.20	.09
☐ 327	Art Howe DP	.20	.09
☐ 328	Oakland A's Team/Mgr.	.75	.15

Jack McKeon
(Checklist back)

☐ 329	Joe Coleman	.20	.09
☐ 330	George Brett	15.00	6.75
☐ 331	Mickey Mahler	.20	.09
☐ 332	Gary Alexander	.20	.09
☐ 333	Chet Lemon	.40	.18
☐ 334	Craig Swan	.20	.09
☐ 335	Chris Chambliss	.40	.18
☐ 336	Bobby Thompson	.20	.09
☐ 337	John Montague	.20	.09
☐ 338	Vic Harris	.20	.09
☐ 339	Ron Jackson	.20	.09
☐ 340	Jim Palmer	2.00	.90
☐ 341	Willie Upshaw	.40	.18
☐ 342	Dave Roberts	.20	.09
☐ 343	Ed Glynn	.20	.09
☐ 344	Jerry Royster	.20	.09
☐ 345	Tug McGraw	.40	.18
☐ 346	Bill Buckner	.40	.18
☐ 347	Doug Rau	.20	.09
☐ 348	Andre Dawson	5.00	2.20
☐ 349	Jim Wright	.20	.09
☐ 350	Garry Templeton	.40	.18
☐ 351	Wayne Nordhagen DP	.10	.05
☐ 352	Steve Renko	.20	.09
☐ 353	Checklist 243-363	.75	.15
☐ 354	Bill Bonham	.20	.09
☐ 355	Lee Mazzilli	.20	.09
☐ 356	Giants Team/Mgr.	.75	.15

Joe Altobelli
(Checklist back)

☐ 357	Jerry Augustine	.20	.09
☐ 358	Alan Trammell	6.00	2.70
☐ 359	Dan Spillner DP	.10	.05
☐ 360	Amos Otis	.40	.18

☐ 361	Tom Dixon	.20	.09
☐ 362	Mike Cubbage	.20	.09
☐ 363	Craig Skok	.20	.09
☐ 364	Gene Richards	.20	.09
☐ 365	Sparky Lyle	.40	.18
☐ 366	Juan Bernhardt	.20	.09
☐ 367	Dave Skaggs	.20	.09
☐ 368	Don Aase	.20	.09
☐ 369A	Bump Wills ERR	3.00	1.35

(Blue Jays)

☐ 369B	Bump Wills COR	3.00	1.35

(Rangers)

☐ 370	Dave Kingman	.75	.35
☐ 371	Jeff Holly	.20	.09
☐ 372	Lamar Johnson	.20	.09
☐ 373	Lance Rautzhan	.20	.09
☐ 374	Ed Herrmann	.20	.09
☐ 375	Bill Campbell	.20	.09
☐ 376	Gorman Thomas	.40	.18
☐ 377	Paul Moskau	.20	.09
☐ 378	Rob Picciolo DP	.10	.05
☐ 379	Dale Murray	.20	.09
☐ 380	John Mayberry	.40	.18
☐ 381	Astros Team/Mgr.	.75	.15

Bill Virdon
(Checklist back)

☐ 382	Jerry Martin	.20	.09
☐ 383	Phil Garner	.40	.18
☐ 384	Tommy Boggs	.20	.09
☐ 385	Dan Ford	.20	.09
☐ 386	Francisco Barrios	.20	.09
☐ 387	Gary Thomasson	.20	.09
☐ 388	Jack Billingham	.20	.09
☐ 389	Joe Zdeb	.20	.09
☐ 390	Rollie Fingers	1.25	.55
☐ 391	Al Oliver	.40	.18
☐ 392	Doug Ault	.20	.09
☐ 393	Scott McGregor	.40	.18
☐ 394	Randy Stein	.20	.09
☐ 395	Dave Cash	.20	.09
☐ 396	Bill Plummer	.20	.09
☐ 397	Sergio Ferrer	.20	.09
☐ 398	Ivan DeJesus	.20	.09
☐ 399	David Clyde	.20	.09
☐ 400	Jim Rice	.75	.35
☐ 401	Ray Knight	.40	.18
☐ 402	Paul Hartzell	.20	.09
☐ 403	Tim Foli	.20	.09
☐ 404	White Sox Team/Mgr	.75	.15

Don Kessinger
(Checklist back)

☐ 405	Butch Wynegar DP	.10	.05
☐ 406	Joe Wallis DP	.10	.05
☐ 407	Pete Vuckovich	.40	.18
☐ 408	Charlie Moore DP	.10	.05
☐ 409	Willie Wilson	1.50	.70
☐ 410	Darrell Evans	.75	.35
☐ 411	George Sisler ATL	1.25	.55

Ty Cobb

☐ 412	Hack Wilson ATL	1.25	.55

Hank Aaron

☐ 413	Roger Maris ATL	1.50	.70

Hank Aaron

☐ 414	Rogers Hornsby ATL	1.25	.55

Ty Cobb

☐ 415	Lou Brock ATL	.75	.35
☐ 416	Jack Chesbro ATL	.40	.18

Cy Young

☐ 417	Nolan Ryan ATL DP..	4.00	1.80

Walter Johnson

☐ 418	Dutch Leonard ATL DP	.20	.09

Walter Johnson

☐ 419	Dick Ruthven	.20	.09
☐ 420	Ken Griffey	.40	.18
☐ 421	Doug DeCinces	.40	.18
☐ 422	Ruppert Jones	.20	.09
☐ 423	Bob Montgomery	.20	.09
☐ 424	Angels Team/Mgr.	.75	.15

Jim Fregosi
(Checklist back)

☐ 425	Rick Manning	.20	.09
☐ 426	Chris Speier	.20	.09
☐ 427	Andy Replogle	.20	.09
☐ 428	Bobby Valentine	.40	.18
☐ 429	John Urrea DP	.10	.05
☐ 430	Dave Parker	.75	.35

☐ 431	Glenn Borgmann	.20	.09
☐ 432	Dave Heaverlo	.20	.09
☐ 433	Larry Biittner	.20	.09
☐ 434	Ken Clay	.20	.09
☐ 435	Gene Tenace	.40	.18
☐ 436	Hector Cruz	.20	.09
☐ 437	Rick Williams	.20	.09
☐ 438	Horace Speed	.20	.09
☐ 439	Frank White	.40	.18
☐ 440	Rusty Staub	.75	.35
☐ 441	Lee Lacy	.20	.09
☐ 442	Doyle Alexander	.20	.09
☐ 443	Bruce Bochte	.20	.09
☐ 444	Aurelio Lopez	.20	.09
☐ 445	Steve Henderson	.20	.09
☐ 446	Jim Lonborg	.40	.18
☐ 447	Manny Sanguillen	.40	.18
☐ 448	Moose Haas	.20	.09
☐ 449	Bombo Rivera	.20	.09
☐ 450	Dave Concepcion	.75	.35
☐ 451	Royals Team/Mgr.	.75	.15

Whitey Herzog
(Checklist back)

☐ 452	Jerry Morales	.20	.09
☐ 453	Chris Knapp	.20	.09
☐ 454	Len Randle	.20	.09
☐ 455	Bill Lee DP	.10	.05
☐ 456	Chuck Baker	.20	.09
☐ 457	Bruce Sutter	.40	.18
☐ 458	Jim Essian	.20	.09
☐ 459	Sid Monge	.20	.09
☐ 460	Graig Nettles	.75	.35
☐ 461	Jim Barr DP	.10	.05
☐ 462	Otto Velez	.20	.09
☐ 463	Steve Comer	.20	.09
☐ 464	Joe Nolan	.20	.09
☐ 465	Reggie Smith	.40	.18
☐ 466	Mark Littell	.20	.09
☐ 467	Don Kessinger DP	.20	.09
☐ 468	Stan Bahnsen DP	.10	.05
☐ 469	Lance Parrish	.75	.35
☐ 470	Garry Maddox DP	.20	.09
☐ 471	Joaquin Andujar	.40	.18
☐ 472	Craig Kusick	.20	.09
☐ 473	Dave Roberts	.20	.09
☐ 474	Dick Davis	.20	.09
☐ 475	Dan Driessen	.20	.09
☐ 476	Tom Poquette	.20	.09
☐ 477	Bob Grich	.40	.18
☐ 478	Juan Beniquez	.20	.09
☐ 479	Padres Team/Mgr.	.75	.15

Roger Craig
(Checklist back)

☐ 480	Fred Lynn	.40	.18
☐ 481	Skip Lockwood	.20	.09
☐ 482	Craig Reynolds	.20	.09
☐ 483	Checklist 364-484 DP	.40	.08
☐ 484	Rick Waits	.20	.09
☐ 485	Bucky Dent	.40	.18
☐ 486	Bob Knepper	.20	.09
☐ 487	Miguel Dilone	.20	.09
☐ 488	Bob Owchinko	.20	.09
☐ 489	Larry Cox UER	.20	.09

(Photo actually Dave Rader)

☐ 490	Al Cowens	.20	.09
☐ 491	Tippy Martinez	.20	.09
☐ 492	Bob Bailor	.20	.09
☐ 493	Larry Christenson	.20	.09
☐ 494	Jerry White	.20	.09
☐ 495	Tony Perez	1.25	.55
☐ 496	Barry Bonnell DP	.10	.05
☐ 497	Glenn Abbott	.20	.09
☐ 498	Rich Chiles	.20	.09
☐ 499	Rangers Team/Mgr.	.75	.15

Pat Corrales
(Checklist back)

☐ 500	Ron Guidry	.40	.18
☐ 501	Junior Kennedy	.20	.09
☐ 502	Steve Braun	.20	.09
☐ 503	Terry Humphrey	.20	.09
☐ 504	Larry McWilliams	.20	.09
☐ 505	Ed Kranepool	.40	.18
☐ 506	John D'Acquisto	.20	.09
☐ 507	Tony Armas	.40	.18
☐ 508	Charlie Hough	.40	.18

☐ 509	Mario Mendoza UER .. (Career BA .278, should say .204)	.20	.09
☐ 510	Ted Simmons	.75	.35
☐ 511	Paul Reuschel DP	.10	.05
☐ 512	Jack Clark	.40	.18
☐ 513	Dave Johnson	.40	.18
☐ 514	Mike Proly	.20	.09
☐ 515	Enos Cabell	.20	.09
☐ 516	Champ Summers DP	.10	.05
☐ 517	Al Bumbry	.40	.18
☐ 518	Jim Umbarger	.20	.09
☐ 519	Ben Oglivie	.40	.18
☐ 520	Gary Carter	1.25	.55
☐ 521	Sam Ewing	.20	.09
☐ 522	Ken Holtzman	.40	.18
☐ 523	John Milner	.20	.09
☐ 524	Tom Burgmeier	.20	.09
☐ 525	Freddie Patek	.20	.09
☐ 526	Dodgers Team/Mgr. Tom Lasorda (Checklist back)	.75	.15
☐ 527	Lerrin LaGrow	.20	.09
☐ 528	Wayne Gross DP	.10	.05
☐ 529	Brian Asselstine	.20	.09
☐ 530	Frank Tanana	.40	.18
☐ 531	Fernando Gonzalez	.20	.09
☐ 532	Buddy Schultz	.20	.09
☐ 533	Leroy Stanton	.20	.09
☐ 534	Ken Forsch	.20	.09
☐ 535	Ellis Valentine	.20	.09
☐ 536	Jerry Reuss	.40	.18
☐ 537	Tom Veryzer	.20	.09
☐ 538	Mike Ivie DP	.10	.05
☐ 539	John Ellis	.20	.09
☐ 540	Greg Luzinski	.40	.18
☐ 541	Jim Slaton	.20	.09
☐ 542	Rick Bosetti	.20	.09
☐ 543	Kiko Garcia	.20	.09
☐ 544	Fergie Jenkins	1.25	.55
☐ 545	John Stearns	.20	.09
☐ 546	Bill Russell	.40	.18
☐ 547	Clint Hurdle	.20	.09
☐ 548	Enrique Romo	.20	.09
☐ 549	Bob Bailey	.20	.09
☐ 550	Sal Bando	.40	.18
☐ 551	Cubs Team/Mgr. Herman Franks (Checklist back)	.75	.15
☐ 552	Jose Morales	.20	.09
☐ 553	Denny Walling	.20	.09
☐ 554	Matt Keough	.20	.09
☐ 555	Biff Pocoroba	.20	.09
☐ 556	Mike Lum	.20	.09
☐ 557	Ken Brett	.20	.09
☐ 558	Jay Johnstone	.40	.18
☐ 559	Greg Pryor	.20	.09
☐ 560	John Montefusco	.20	.09
☐ 561	Ed Ott	.20	.09
☐ 562	Dusty Baker	.75	.35
☐ 563	Roy Thomas	.20	.09
☐ 564	Jerry Turner	.20	.09
☐ 565	Rico Carty	.40	.18
☐ 566	Nino Espinosa	.20	.09
☐ 567	Richie Hebner	.40	.18
☐ 568	Carlos Lopez	.20	.09
☐ 569	Bob Sykes	.20	.09
☐ 570	Cesar Cedeno	.40	.18
☐ 571	Darrell Porter	.40	.18
☐ 572	Rod Gilbreath	.20	.09
☐ 573	Jim Kern	.20	.09
☐ 574	Claudell Washington	.40	.18
☐ 575	Luis Tiant	.40	.18
☐ 576	Mike Parrott	.20	.09
☐ 577	Brewers Team/Mgr. George Bamberger (Checklist back)	.75	.15
☐ 578	Pete Broberg	.20	.09
☐ 579	Greg Gross	.20	.09
☐ 580	Ron Fairly	.40	.18
☐ 581	Darold Knowles	.20	.09
☐ 582	Paul Blair	.40	.18
☐ 583	Julio Cruz	.20	.09
☐ 584	Jim Rooker	.20	.09
☐ 585	Hal McRae	.75	.35
☐ 586	Bob Horner	.75	.35

☐ 587	Ken Reitz	.20	.09
☐ 588	Tom Murphy	.20	.09
☐ 589	Terry Whitfield	.20	.09
☐ 590	J.R. Richard	.40	.18
☐ 591	Mike Hargrove	.40	.18
☐ 592	Mike Krukow	.20	.09
☐ 593	Rick Dempsey	.40	.18
☐ 594	Bob Shirley	.20	.09
☐ 595	Phil Niekro	1.25	.55
☐ 596	Jim Wohlford	.20	.09
☐ 597	Bob Stanley	.20	.09
☐ 598	Mark Wagner	.20	.09
☐ 599	Jim Spencer	.20	.09
☐ 600	George Foster	.40	.18
☐ 601	Dave LaRoche	.20	.09
☐ 602	Checklist 485-605	.75	.15
☐ 603	Rudy May	.20	.09
☐ 604	Jeff Newman	.20	.09
☐ 605	Rick Monday DP	.20	.09
☐ 606	Expos Team/Mgr. Dick Williams (Checklist back)	.75	.15
☐ 607	Omar Moreno	.20	.09
☐ 608	Dave McKay	.20	.09
☐ 609	Silvio Martinez	.20	.09
☐ 610	Mike Schmidt	8.00	3.60
☐ 611	Jim Norris	.20	.09
☐ 612	Rick Honeycutt	.40	.18
☐ 613	Mike Edwards	.20	.09
☐ 614	Willie Hernandez	.40	.18
☐ 615	Ken Singleton	.40	.18
☐ 616	Billy Almon	.20	.09
☐ 617	Terry Puhl	.20	.09
☐ 618	Jerry Remy	.20	.09
☐ 619	Ken Landreaux	.40	.18
☐ 620	Bert Campaneris	.40	.18
☐ 621	Pat Zachry	.20	.09
☐ 622	Dave Collins	.40	.18
☐ 623	Bob McClure	.20	.09
☐ 624	Larry Herndon	.20	.09
☐ 625	Mark Fidrych	1.25	.55
☐ 626	Yankees Team/Mgr. Bob Lemon (Checklist back)	.75	.15
☐ 627	Gary Serum	.20	.09
☐ 628	Del Unser	.20	.09
☐ 629	Gene Garber	.40	.18
☐ 630	Bake McBride	.40	.18
☐ 631	Jorge Orta	.20	.09
☐ 632	Don Kirkwood	.20	.09
☐ 633	Rob Wilfong DP	.10	.05
☐ 634	Paul Lindblad	.20	.09
☐ 635	Don Baylor	.75	.35
☐ 636	Wayne Garland	.20	.09
☐ 637	Bill Robinson	.40	.18
☐ 638	Al Fitzmorris	.20	.09
☐ 639	Manny Trillo	.20	.09
☐ 640	Eddie Murray	20.00	9.00
☐ 641	Bobby Castillo	.20	.09
☐ 642	Wilbur Howard DP	.10	.05
☐ 643	Tom Hausman	.20	.09
☐ 644	Manny Mota	.40	.18
☐ 645	George Scott DP	.20	.09
☐ 646	Rick Sweet	.20	.09
☐ 647	Bob Lacey	.20	.09
☐ 648	Lou Piniella	.40	.18
☐ 649	John Curtis	.20	.09
☐ 650	Pete Rose	5.00	2.20
☐ 651	Mike Caldwell	.20	.09
☐ 652	Stan Papi	.20	.09
☐ 653	Warren Brusstar DP	.10	.05
☐ 654	Rick Miller	.20	.09
☐ 655	Jerry Koosman	.40	.18
☐ 656	Hosken Powell	.20	.09
☐ 657	George Medich	.20	.09
☐ 658	Taylor Duncan	.20	.09
☐ 659	Mariners Team/Mgr. Darrell Johnson (Checklist back)	.75	.15
☐ 660	Ron LeFlore DP	.20	.09
☐ 661	Bruce Kison	.20	.09
☐ 662	Kevin Bell	.20	.09
☐ 663	Mike Vail	.20	.09
☐ 664	Doug Bird	.20	.09
☐ 665	Lou Brock	2.00	.90
☐ 666	Rich Dauer	.20	.09

☐ 667	Don Hood	.20	.09
☐ 668	Bill North	.20	.09
☐ 669	Checklist 606-726	.75	.15
☐ 670	Jim Hunter DP	.75	.35
☐ 671	Joe Ferguson DP	.10	.05
☐ 672	Ed Halicki	.20	.09
☐ 673	Tom Hutton	.20	.09
☐ 674	Dave Tomlin	.20	.09
☐ 675	Tim McCarver	.75	.35
☐ 676	Johnny Sutton	.20	.09
☐ 677	Larry Parrish	.40	.18
☐ 678	Geoff Zahn	.20	.09
☐ 679	Derrel Thomas	.20	.09
☐ 680	Carlton Fisk	2.50	1.10
☐ 681	John Henry Johnson	.20	.09
☐ 682	Dave Chalk	.20	.09
☐ 683	Dan Meyer DP	.10	.05
☐ 684	Jamie Easterly DP	.10	.05
☐ 685	Sixto Lezcano	.20	.09
☐ 686	Ron Schueler DP	.10	.05
☐ 687	Rennie Stennett	.20	.09
☐ 688	Mike Willis	.20	.09
☐ 689	Orioles Team/Mgr. Earl Weaver (Checklist back)	.75	.15
☐ 690	Buddy Bell DP	.20	.09
☐ 691	Dock Ellis DP	.10	.05
☐ 692	Mickey Stanley	.20	.09
☐ 693	Dave Rader	.20	.09
☐ 694	Burt Hooton	.40	.18
☐ 695	Keith Hernandez	.75	.35
☐ 696	Andy Hassler	.20	.09
☐ 697	Dave Bergman	.20	.09
☐ 698	Bill Stein	.20	.09
☐ 699	Hal Dues	.20	.09
☐ 700	Reggie Jackson DP	2.00	.90
☐ 701	Orioles Prospects Mark Corey John Flinn Sammy Stewart	.40	.18
☐ 702	Red Sox Prospects Joel Finch Garry Hancock Allen Ripley		.18
☐ 703	Angels Prospects Jim Anderson Dave Frost Bob Slater	.40	.18
☐ 704	White Sox Prospects Ross Baumgarten Mike Colbern Mike Squires		.18
☐ 705	Indians Prospects Alfredo Griffin Tim Norrid Dave Oliver	.75	.35
☐ 706	Tigers Prospects Dave Stegman Dave Tobik Kip Young	.40	.18
☐ 707	Royals Prospects Randy Bass Jim Gaudet Randy McGilberry	.75	.35
☐ 708	Brewers Prospects Kevin Bass Eddie Romero Ned Yost	.75	.35
☐ 709	Twins Prospects Sam Perlozzo Rick Sofield Kevin Stanfield	.40	.18
☐ 710	Yankees Prospects Brian Doyle Mike Heath Dave Rajsich	.40	.18
☐ 711	A's Prospects Dwayne Murphy Bruce Robinson Alan Wirth	.75	.35
☐ 712	Mariners Prospects Bud Anderson Greg Biercevicz Byron McLaughlin	.40	.18
☐ 713	Rangers Prospects Danny Darwin	.75	.35

	Pat Putnam	
	Billy Sample	
☐ 714	Blue Jays Prospects .. .40	.18
	Victor Cruz	
	Pat Kelly	
	Ernie Whitt	
☐ 715	Braves Prospects ...... .75	.35
	Bruce Benedict	
	Glenn Hubbard	
	Larry Whisenton	
☐ 716	Cubs Prospects .... .40	.18
	Dave Geisel	
	Karl Pagel	
	Scot Thompson	
☐ 717	Reds Prospects .... .40	.18
	Mike LaCoss	
	Ron Oester	
	Harry Spilman	
☐ 718	Astros Prospects .... .40	.18
	Bruce Bochy	
	Mike Fischlin	
	Don Pisker	
☐ 719	Dodgers Prospects .. 1.50	.70
	Pedro Guerrero	
	Rudy Law	
	Joe Simpson	
☐ 720	Expos Prospects .... .75	.35
	Jerry Fry	
	Jerry Pirtle	
	Scott Sanderson	
☐ 721	Mets Prospects .... .40	.18
	Juan Berenguer	
	Dwight Bernard	
	Dan Norman	
☐ 722	Phillies Prospects ...... .75	.35
	Jim Morrison	
	Lonnie Smith	
	Jim Wright	
☐ 723	Pirates Prospects .... .40	.18
	Dale Berra	
	Eugenio Cotes	
	Ben Wiltbank	
☐ 724	Cardinals Prospects .. .75	.35
	Tom Bruno	
	George Frazier	
	Terry Kennedy	
☐ 725	Padres Prospects .... .40	.18
	Jim Beswick	
	Steve Mura	
	Broderick Perkins	
☐ 726	Giants Prospects .... .40	.08
	Greg Johnston	
	Joe Strain	
	John Tamargo	

1980 Topps

The cards in this 726-card set measure the standard size. In 1980 Topps released another set of the same size and number of cards as the previous two years. As with those sets, Topps again produced 66 double-printed cards in the set; they are noted by DP in the checklist below. The player's name

appears over the picture and his position and team are found in pennant design. Every card carries a facsimile autograph. Team cards feature a team checklist of players in the set on the back and the manager's name on the front. Cards 1-6 show Highlights (HL) of the 1979 season, cards 201-207 are League Leaders, and cards 661-686 feature American and National League rookie "Future Stars," one card for each team showing three young prospects. Ways this set was released include 15-card wax packs as well as 42-card rack packs. A special experiment in 1980 was the issuance of a 28-card cello pack with a three-pack of gum at the bottom so no cards would be damaged. The key Rookie Card in this set is Rickey Henderson; other Rookie Cards included in this set are Dan Quisenberry, Dave Stieb and Rick Sutcliffe.

	NRMT	VG-E
COMPLETE SET (726)	120.00	55.00
COMMON CARD (1-726)	.25	.11
MINOR STARS	.75	.35
SEMISTARS	1.50	.70
UNLISTED STARS	2.50	1.10

☐ 1	Lou Brock HL	3.00	.60
	Carl Yastrzemski		
	Enter 3000 hit circle		
☐ 2	Willie McCovey HL ...	2.50	1.10
	512th homer sets new		
	mark for NL lefties		
☐ 3	Manny Mota HL	.75	.35
	All-time pinch-hits, 145		
☐ 4	Pete Rose HL	2.00	.90
	Career Record 10th season		
	with 200 or more hits		
☐ 5	Garry Templeton HL ...	.75	.35
	First with 100 hits		
	from each side of plate		
☐ 6	Del Unser HL	.75	.35
	3 consecutive		
	pinch homers		
☐ 7	Mike Lum	.25	.11
☐ 8	Craig Swan	.25	.11
☐ 9	Steve Braun	.25	.11
☐ 10	Dennis Martinez	1.50	.70
☐ 11	Jimmy Sexton	.25	.11
☐ 12	John Curtis DP	.10	.05
☐ 13	Ron Pruitt	.25	.11
☐ 14	Dave Cash	.25	.11
☐ 15	Bill Campbell	.25	.11
☐ 16	Jerry Narron	.25	.11
☐ 17	Bruce Sutter	.75	.35
☐ 18	Ron Jackson	.25	.11
☐ 19	Balor Moore	.25	.11
☐ 20	Dan Ford	.25	.11
☐ 21	Manny Sarmiento	.25	.11
☐ 22	Pat Putnam	.25	.11
☐ 23	Derrel Thomas	.25	.11
☐ 24	Jim Slaton	.25	.11
☐ 25	Lee Mazzilli	.75	.35
☐ 26	Marty Pattin	.25	.11
☐ 27	Del Unser	.25	.11
☐ 28	Bruce Kison	.25	.11
☐ 29	Mark Wagner	.25	.11
☐ 30	Vida Blue	1.50	.70
☐ 31	Jay Johnstone	.75	.35
☐ 32	Julio Cruz DP	.05	.11
☐ 33	Tony Scott	.25	.11
☐ 34	Jeff Newman DP	.10	.05
☐ 35	Luis Tiant	.75	.35
☐ 36	Rusty Torres	.25	.11
☐ 37	Kiko Garcia	.25	.11
☐ 38	Dan Spillner DP	.10	.05
☐ 39	Rowland Office	.25	.11

☐ 40	Carlton Fisk	2.00	.90
☐ 41	Rangers Team/Mgr. ..	1.50	.30
	Pat Corrales		
	(Checklist back)		
☐ 42	David Palmer	.25	.11
☐ 43	Bombo Rivera	.25	.11
☐ 44	Bill Fahey	.25	.11
☐ 45	Frank White	1.50	.70
☐ 46	Rico Carty	.75	.35
☐ 47	Bill Bonham DP	.10	.05
☐ 48	Rick Miller	.25	.11
☐ 49	Mario Guerrero	.25	.11
☐ 50	J.R. Richard	.75	.35
☐ 51	Joe Ferguson DP	.10	.05
☐ 52	Warren Brusstar	.25	.11
☐ 53	Ben Oglivie	.75	.35
☐ 54	Dennis Lamp	.25	.11
☐ 55	Bill Madlock	.75	.35
☐ 56	Bobby Valentine	.75	.35
☐ 57	Pete Vuckovich	.25	.11
☐ 58	Doug Flynn	.25	.11
☐ 59	Eddy Putman	.25	.11
☐ 60	Bucky Dent	.75	.35
☐ 61	Gary Serum	.25	.11
☐ 62	Mike Ivie	.25	.11
☐ 63	Bob Stanley	.25	.11
☐ 64	Joe Nolan	.25	.11
☐ 65	Al Bumbry	.75	.35
☐ 66	Royals Team/Mgr.	1.50	.30
	Jim Frey		
	(Checklist back)		
☐ 67	Doyle Alexander	.25	.11
☐ 68	Larry Harlow	.25	.11
☐ 69	Rick Williams	.25	.11
☐ 70	Gary Carter	2.50	1.10
☐ 71	John Milner DP	.10	.05
☐ 72	Fred Howard DP	.10	.05
☐ 73	Dave Collins	.25	.11
☐ 74	Sid Monge	.25	.11
☐ 75	Bill Russell	.75	.35
☐ 76	John Stearns	.25	.11
☐ 77	Dave Stieb	2.50	1.10
☐ 78	Ruppert Jones	.25	.11
☐ 79	Bob Owchinko	.25	.11
☐ 80	Ron LeFlore	.75	.35
☐ 81	Ted Sizemore	.25	.11
☐ 82	Astros Team/Mgr.	1.50	.30
	Bill Virdon		
	(Checklist back)		
☐ 83	Steve Trout	.25	.11
☐ 84	Gary Lavelle	.25	.11
☐ 85	Ted Simmons	.75	.35
☐ 86	Dave Hamilton	.25	.11
☐ 87	Pepe Frias	.25	.11
☐ 88	Ken Landreaux	.25	.11
☐ 89	Don Hood	.25	.11
☐ 90	Manny Trillo	.75	.35
☐ 91	Rick Dempsey	.75	.35
☐ 92	Rick Rhoden	.25	.11
☐ 93	Dave Roberts DP	.10	.05
☐ 94	Neil Allen	.75	.35
☐ 95	Cecil Cooper	.75	.35
☐ 96	A's Team/Mgr.	1.50	.30
	Jim Marshall		
	(Checklist back)		
☐ 97	Bill Lee	.75	.35
☐ 98	Jerry Terrell	.25	.11
☐ 99	Victor Cruz	.25	.11
☐ 100	Johnny Bench	3.00	1.35
☐ 101	Aurelio Lopez	.25	.11
☐ 102	Rich Dauer	.25	.11
☐ 103	Bill Caudill	.25	.11
☐ 104	Manny Mota	.75	.35
☐ 105	Frank Tanana	.75	.35
☐ 106	Jeff Leonard	1.50	.70
☐ 107	Francisco Barrios	.25	.11
☐ 108	Bob Horner	.75	.35
☐ 109	Bill Travers	.25	.11
☐ 110	Fred Lynn DP	.75	.35
☐ 111	Bob Knepper	.25	.11
☐ 112	White Sox Team/Mgr.	1.50	.30
	Tony LaRussa		
	(Checklist back)		
☐ 113	Geoff Zahn	.25	.11
☐ 114	Juan Beniquez	.25	.11
☐ 115	Sparky Lyle	.75	.35

116	Larry Cox	.25	.11
117	Dock Ellis	.25	.11
118	Phil Garner	.75	.35
119	Sammy Stewart	.25	.11
120	Greg Luzinski	.75	.35
121	Checklist 1-121	1.50	.30
122	Dave Rosello DP	.25	.05
123	Lynn Jones	.25	.11
124	Dave Lemanczyk	.25	.11
125	Tony Perez	2.50	1.10
126	Dave Tomlin	.25	.11
127	Gary Thomasson	.25	.11
128	Tom Burgmeier	.25	.11
129	Craig Reynolds	.25	.11
130	Amos Otis	.75	.35
131	Paul Mitchell	.25	.11
132	Biff Pocoroba	.25	.11
133	Jerry Turner	.25	.11
134	Matt Keough	.25	.11
135	Bill Buckner	.75	.35
136	Dick Ruthven	.25	.11
137	John Castino	.25	.11
138	Ross Baumgarten	.25	.11
139	Dane Iorg	.25	.11
140	Rich Gossage	1.50	.70
141	Gary Alexander	.25	.11
142	Phil Huffman	.25	.11
143	Bruce Roselle DP	.10	.05
144	Steve Comer	.25	.11
145	Darrell Evans	.75	.35
146	Bob Welch	.75	.35
147	Terry Puhl	.25	.11
148	Manny Sanguillen	.75	.35
149	Tom Hume	.25	.11
150	Jason Thompson	.25	.11
151	Tom Hausman DP	.10	.05
152	John Fulgham	.25	.11
153	Tim Blackwell	.25	.11
154	Lary Sorensen	.25	.11
155	Jerry Remy	.25	.11
156	Tony Brizzolara	.25	.11
157	Willie Wilson DP	.75	.35
158	Rob Picciolo DP	.05	.05
159	Ken Clay	.25	.11
160	Eddie Murray	12.00	5.50
161	Larry Christenson	.25	.11
162	Bob Randall	.25	.11
163	Steve Swisher	.25	.11
164	Greg Pryor	.25	.11
165	Omar Moreno	.25	.11
166	Glenn Abbott	.25	.11
167	Jack Clark	.75	.35
168	Rick Waits	.25	.11
169	Luis Gomez	.25	.11
170	Burt Hooton	.75	.35
171	Fernando Gonzalez	.25	.11
172	Ron Hodges	.25	.11
173	John Henry Johnson	.25	.11
174	Ray Knight	.75	.35
175	Rick Reuschel	.75	.35
176	Champ Summers	.25	.11
177	Dave Heaverlo	.25	.11
178	Tim McCarver	1.50	.70
179	Ron Davis	.25	.11
180	Warren Cromartie	.25	.11
181	Moose Haas	.25	.11
182	Ken Reitz	.25	.11
183	Jim Anderson DP	.10	.05
184	Steve Renko DP	.05	.05
185	Hal McRae	.75	.35
186	Junior Moore	.25	.11
187	Alan Ashby	.25	.11
188	Terry Crowley	.25	.11
189	Kevin Kobel	.25	.11
190	Buddy Bell	.75	.35
191	Ted Martinez	.25	.11
192	Braves Team/Mgr.	1.50	.30
	Bobby Cox (Checklist back)		
193	Dave Goltz	.25	.11
194	Mike Easler	.25	.11
195	John Montefusco	.25	.11
196	Lance Parrish	.75	.35
197	Byron McLaughlin	.25	.11
198	Dell Alston DP	.10	.05
199	Mike LaCoss	.25	.11
200	Jim Rice	.75	.35
201	Batting Leaders	1.50	.70
	Keith Hernandez		
	Fred Lynn		
202	Home Run Leaders	1.50	.70
	Dave Kingman		
	Gorman Thomas		
203	RBI Leaders	2.50	1.10
	Dave Winfield		
	Don Baylor		
204	Stolen Base Leaders	.75	.35
	Omar Moreno		
	Willie Wilson		
205	Victory Leaders	1.50	.70
	Joe Niekro		
	Phil Niekro		
	Mike Flanagan		
206	Strikeout Leaders	5.00	2.20
	J.R. Richard		
	Nolan Ryan		
207	ERA Leaders	1.50	.70
	J.R. Richard		
	Ron Guidry		
208	Wayne Cage	.25	.11
209	Von Joshua	.25	.11
210	Steve Carlton	2.00	.90
211	Dave Skaggs DP	.10	.05
212	Dave Roberts	.25	.11
213	Mike Jorgensen DP	.10	.05
214	Angels Team/Mgr.	1.50	.30
	Jim Fregosi (Checklist back)		
215	Sixto Lezcano	.25	.11
216	Phil Mankowski	.25	.11
217	Ed Halicki	.25	.11
218	Jose Morales	.25	.11
219	Steve Mingori	.25	.11
220	Dave Concepcion	1.50	.70
221	Joe Cannon	.25	.11
222	Ron Hassey	.25	.11
223	Bob Sykes	.25	.11
224	Willie Montanez	.25	.11
225	Lou Piniella	1.50	.70
226	Bill Stein	.25	.11
227	Len Barker	.25	.11
228	Johnny Oates	.75	.35
229	Jim Bibby	.25	.11
230	Dave Winfield	5.00	2.20
231	Steve McCatty	.25	.11
232	Alan Trammell	3.00	1.35
233	LaRue Washington	.25	.11
234	Vern Ruhle	.25	.11
235	Andre Dawson	3.00	1.35
236	Marc Hill	.25	.11
237	Scott McGregor	.25	.11
238	Rob Wilfong	.25	.11
239	Don Aase	.25	.11
240	Dave Kingman	1.50	.70
241	Checklist 122-242	1.50	.30
242	Lamar Johnson	.25	.11
243	Jerry Augustine	.25	.11
244	Cardinals Team/Mgr.	1.50	.30
	Ken Boyer (Checklist back)		
245	Phil Niekro	2.50	1.10
246	Tim Foli DP	.10	.05
247	Frank Riccelli	.25	.11
248	Jamie Quirk	.25	.11
249	Jim Clancy	.25	.11
250	Jim Kaat	1.50	.70
251	Kip Young	.25	.11
252	Ted Cox	.25	.11
253	John Montague	.25	.11
254	Paul Dade DP	.10	.05
255	Dusty Baker DP	.75	.35
256	Roger Erickson	.25	.11
257	Larry Herndon	.25	.11
258	Paul Moskau	.25	.11
259	Mets Team/Mgr.	1.50	.30
	Joe Torre (Checklist back)		
260	Al Oliver	1.50	.70
261	Dave Chalk	.25	.11
262	Steve Mura	.25	.11
263	Dave LaRoche DP	.10	.05
264	Bill Robinson	.25	.11
265	Robin Yount	6.00	2.70
266	Bernie Carbo	.25	.11
267	Dan Schatzeder	.25	.11
268	Rafael Landestoy	.25	.11
269	Dave Tobik	.25	.11
270	Mike Schmidt DP	3.00	1.35
271	Dick Drago DP	.10	.05
272	Ralph Garr	.75	.35
273	Eduardo Rodriguez	.25	.11
274	Dale Murphy	2.50	1.10
275	Jerry Koosman	.75	.35
276	Tom Veryzer	.25	.11
277	Rick Bosetti	.25	.11
278	Jim Spencer	.25	.11
279	Rob Andrews	.25	.11
280	Gaylord Perry	2.50	1.10
281	Paul Blair	.75	.35
282	Mariners Team/Mgr.	1.50	.30
	Darrell Johnson (Checklist back)		
283	John Ellis	.25	.11
284	Larry Murray DP	.10	.05
285	Don Baylor	1.50	.70
286	Darold Knowles DP	.10	.05
287	John Lowenstein	.25	.11
288	Dave Rozema	.25	.11
289	Bruce Bochy	.25	.11
290	Steve Garvey	2.50	1.10
291	Randy Scarberry	.25	.11
292	Dale Berra	.25	.11
293	Elias Sosa	.25	.11
294	Charlie Spikes	.25	.11
295	Larry Gura	.25	.11
296	Dave Rader	.25	.11
297	Tim Johnson	.25	.11
298	Ken Holtzman	.75	.35
299	Steve Henderson	.25	.11
300	Ron Guidry	.75	.35
301	Mike Edwards	.25	.11
302	Dodgers Team/Mgr.	1.50	.30
	Tom Lasorda (Checklist back)		
303	Bill Castro	.25	.11
304	Butch Wynegar	.25	.11
305	Randy Jones	.25	.11
306	Denny Walling	.25	.11
307	Rick Honeycutt	.75	.35
308	Mike Hargrove	.75	.35
309	Larry McWilliams	.25	.11
310	Dave Parker	1.50	.70
311	Roger Metzger	.25	.11
312	Mike Barlow	.25	.11
313	Johnny Grubb	.25	.11
314	Tim Stoddard	.25	.11
315	Steve Kemp	.25	.11
316	Bob Lacey	.25	.11
317	Mike Anderson DP	.10	.05
318	Jerry Reuss	.75	.35
319	Chris Speier	.25	.11
320	Dennis Eckersley	1.50	.70
321	Keith Hernandez	.75	.35
322	Claudell Washington	.75	.35
323	Mick Kelleher	.25	.11
324	Tom Underwood	.25	.11
325	Dan Driessen	.25	.11
326	Bo McLaughlin	.25	.11
327	Ray Fosse DP	.10	.05
328	Twins Team/Mgr.	1.50	.30
	Gene Mauch (Checklist back)		
329	Bert Roberge	.25	.11
330	Al Cowens	.25	.11
331	Richie Hebner	.75	.35
332	Enrique Romo	.25	.11
333	Jim Norris DP	.10	.05
334	Jim Beattie	.25	.11
335	Willie McCovey	1.50	.70
336	George Medich	.25	.11
337	Carney Lansford	.75	.35
338	John Wockenfuss	.25	.11
339	John D'Acquisto	.25	.11
340	Ken Singleton	.75	.35
341	Jim Essian	.25	.11
342	Odell Jones	.25	.11
343	Mike Vail	.25	.11
344	Randy Lerch	.25	.11

345	Larry Parrish	.75	.35
346	Buddy Solomon	.25	.11
347	Harry Chappas	.25	.11
348	Checklist 243-363	1.50	.30
349	Jack Brohamer	.25	.11
350	George Hendrick	.75	.35
351	Bob Davis	.25	.11
352	Dan Briggs	.25	.11
353	Andy Hassler	.25	.11
354	Rick Auerbach	.25	.11
355	Gary Matthews	.75	.35
356	Padres Team/Mgr.	1.50	.30
	Jerry Coleman (Checklist back)		
357	Bob McClure	.25	.11
358	Lou Whitaker	5.00	2.20
359	Randy Moffitt	.25	.11
360	Darrell Porter DP	.25	.11
361	Wayne Garland	.25	.11
362	Danny Goodwin	.25	.11
363	Wayne Gross	.25	.11
364	Ray Burris	.25	.11
365	Bobby Murcer	.75	.35
366	Rob Dressler	.25	.11
367	Billy Smith	.25	.11
368	Willie Aikens	.25	.11
369	Jim Kern	.25	.11
370	Cesar Cedeno	.75	.35
371	Jack Morris	1.50	.70
372	Joel Youngblood	.25	.11
373	Dan Petry DP	.25	.11
374	Jim Gantner	.75	.35
375	Ross Grimsley	.25	.11
376	Gary Allenson	.25	.11
377	Junior Kennedy	.25	.11
378	Jerry Mumphrey	.25	.11
379	Kevin Bell	.25	.11
380	Garry Maddox	.75	.35
381	Cubs Team/Mgr.	1.50	.30
	Preston Gomez (Checklist back)		
382	Dave Freisleben	.25	.11
383	Ed Ott	.25	.11
384	Joey McLaughlin	.25	.11
385	Enos Cabell	.25	.11
386	Darrell Jackson	.25	.11
387A	Fred Stanley YL	2.00	.90
387B	Fred Stanley	.25	.11
	(Red name on front)		
388	Mike Paxton	.25	.11
389	Pete LaCock	.25	.11
390	Fergie Jenkins	2.50	1.10
391	Tony Armas DP	.25	.11
392	Milt Wilcox	.25	.11
393	Ozzie Smith	20.00	9.00
394	Reggie Cleveland	.25	.11
395	Ellis Valentine	.25	.11
396	Dan Meyer	.25	.11
397	Roy Thomas DP	.10	.05
398	Barry Foote	.25	.11
399	Mike Proly DP	.10	.05
400	George Foster	.75	.35
401	Pete Falcone	.25	.11
402	Merv Rettenmund	.25	.11
403	Pete Redfern DP	.10	.05
404	Orioles Team/Mgr.	1.50	.30
	Earl Weaver (Checklist back)		
405	Dwight Evans	.75	.35
406	Paul Molitor	12.00	5.50
407	Tony Solaita	.25	.11
408	Bill North	.25	.11
409	Paul Splittorff	.25	.11
410	Bobby Bonds	1.50	.70
411	Frank LaCorte	.25	.11
412	Thad Bosley	.25	.11
413	Allen Ripley	.25	.11
414	George Scott	.75	.35
415	Bill Atkinson	.25	.11
416	Tom Brookens	.25	.11
417	Craig Chamberlain DP	.10	.05
418	Roger Freed DP	.10	.05
419	Vic Correll	.25	.11
420	Butch Hobson	.75	.35
421	Doug Bird	.25	.11
422	Larry Milbourne	.25	.11
423	Dave Frost	.25	.11
424	Yankees Team/Mgr.	1.50	.30
	Dick Howser (Checklist back)		
425	Mark Belanger	.75	.35
426	Grant Jackson	.25	.11
427	Tom Hutton DP	.10	.05
428	Pat Zachry	.25	.11
429	Duane Kuiper	.25	.11
430	Larry Hisle DP	.10	.05
431	Mike Krukow	.25	.11
432	Willie Norwood	.25	.11
433	Rich Gale	.25	.11
434	Johnnie LeMaster	.25	.11
435	Don Gullett	.75	.35
436	Billy Almon	.25	.11
437	Joe Niekro	.75	.35
438	Dave Revering	.25	.11
439	Mike Phillips	.25	.11
440	Don Sutton	2.50	1.10
441	Eric Soderholm	.25	.11
442	Jorge Orta	.25	.11
443	Mike Parrott	.25	.11
444	Alvis Woods	.25	.11
445	Mark Fidrych	2.50	1.10
446	Duffy Dyer	.25	.11
447	Nino Espinosa	.25	.11
448	Jim Wohlford	.25	.11
449	Doug Bair	.25	.11
450	George Brett	12.00	5.50
451	Indians Team/Mgr.	.75	.15
	Dave Garcia (Checklist back)		
452	Steve Dillard	.25	.11
453	Mike Bacsik	.25	.11
454	Tom Donohue	.25	.11
455	Mike Torrez	.25	.11
456	Frank Taveras	.25	.11
457	Bert Blyleven	1.50	.70
458	Billy Sample	.25	.11
459	Mickey Lolich DP	.25	.11
460	Willie Randolph	.75	.35
461	Dwayne Murphy	.25	.11
462	Mike Sadek DP	.10	.05
463	Jerry Royster	.25	.11
464	John Denny	.25	.11
465	Rick Monday	.25	.11
466	Mike Squires	.25	.11
467	Jesse Jefferson	.25	.11
468	Aurelio Rodriguez	.25	.11
469	Randy Niemann DP	.10	.05
470	Bob Boone	1.50	.70
471	Hosken Powell DP	.10	.05
472	Willie Hernandez	.75	.35
473	Bump Wills	.25	.11
474	Steve Busby	.25	.11
475	Cesar Geronimo	.25	.11
476	Bob Shirley	.25	.11
477	Buck Martinez	.25	.11
478	Gil Flores	.25	.11
479	Expos Team/Mgr.	1.50	.30
	Dick Williams (Checklist back)		
480	Bob Watson	.75	.35
481	Tom Paciorek	.25	.11
482	Rickey Henderson UER	40.00	18.00
	(7 steals at Modesto, should be at Fresno)		
483	Bo Diaz	.25	.11
484	Checklist 364-484	1.50	.30
485	Mickey Rivers	.75	.35
486	Mike Tyson DP	.10	.05
487	Wayne Nordhagen	.25	.11
488	Roy Howell	.25	.11
489	Preston Hanna DP	.10	.05
490	Lee May	.75	.35
491	Steve Mura DP	.10	.05
492	Todd Cruz	.25	.11
493	Jerry Martin	.25	.11
494	Craig Minetto	.25	.11
495	Bake McBride	.25	.11
496	Silvio Martinez	.25	.11
497	Jim Mason	.25	.11
498	Danny Darwin	.75	.35
499	Giants Team/Mgr.	1.50	.30
	Dave Bristol (Checklist back)		
500	Tom Seaver	3.00	1.35
501	Rennie Stennett	.25	.11
502	Rich Wortham DP	.10	.05
503	Mike Cubbage	.25	.11
504	Gene Garber	.75	.35
505	Bert Campaneris	.75	.35
506	Tom Buskey	.25	.11
507	Leon Roberts	.25	.11
508	U.L. Washington	.25	.11
509	Ed Glynn	.25	.11
510	Ron Cey	1.50	.70
511	Eric Wilkins	.25	.11
512	Jose Cardenal	.25	.11
513	Tom Dixon DP	.10	.05
514	Steve Ontiveros	.25	.11
515	Mike Caldwell UER	.25	.11
	1979 loss total reads 96 instead of 6#		
516	Hector Cruz	.25	.11
517	Don Stanhouse	.25	.11
518	Nelson Norman	.25	.11
519	Steve Nicosia	.25	.11
520	Steve Rogers	.25	.11
521	Ken Brett	.25	.11
522	Jim Morrison	.25	.11
523	Ken Henderson	.25	.11
524	Jim Wright DP	.10	.05
525	Clint Hurdle	.25	.11
526	Phillies Team/Mgr.	1.50	.30
	Dallas Green (Checklist back)		
527	Doug Rau DP	.10	.05
528	Adrian Devine	.25	.11
529	Jim Barr	.25	.11
530	Jim Sundberg DP	.25	.11
531	Eric Rasmussen	.25	.11
532	Willie Horton	.75	.35
533	Checklist 485-605	1.50	.30
534	Andre Thornton	.75	.35
535	Bob Forsch	.25	.11
536	Lee Lacy	.25	.11
537	Alex Trevino	.25	.11
538	Joe Strain	.25	.11
539	Rudy May	.25	.11
540	Pete Rose	3.00	1.35
541	Miguel Dilone	.25	.11
542	Joe Coleman	.25	.11
543	Pat Kelly	.25	.11
544	Rick Sutcliffe	2.00	.90
545	Jeff Burroughs	.75	.35
546	Rick Langford	.25	.11
547	John Wathan	.25	.11
548	Dave Rajsich	.25	.11
549	Larry Wolfe	.25	.11
550	Ken Griffey	1.50	.70
551	Pirates Team/Mgr.	1.50	.30
	Chuck Tanner (Checklist back)		
552	Bill Nahorodny	.25	.11
553	Dick Davis	.25	.11
554	Art Howe	.75	.35
555	Ed Figueroa	.25	.11
556	Joe Rudi	.75	.35
557	Mark Lee	.25	.11
558	Alfredo Griffin	.25	.11
559	Dale Murray	.25	.11
560	Dave Lopes	.75	.35
561	Eddie Whitson	.75	.35
562	Joe Wallis	.25	.11
563	Will McEnaney	.25	.11
564	Rick Manning	.25	.11
565	Dennis Leonard	.75	.35
566	Bud Harrelson	.75	.35
567	Skip Lockwood	.25	.11
568	Gary Roenicke	.75	.35
569	Terry Kennedy	.75	.35
570	Roy Smalley	.25	.11
571	Joe Sambito	.25	.11
572	Jerry Morales DP	.10	.05
573	Kent Tekulve	.75	.35
574	Scot Thompson	.25	.11
575	Ken Kravec	.25	.11
576	Jim Dwyer	.25	.11
577	Blue Jays Team/Mgr.	1.50	.30
	Bobby Mattick		

(Checklist back)		
☐ 578 Scott Sanderson	.75	.35
☐ 579 Charlie Moore	.25	.11
☐ 580 Nolan Ryan	20.00	9.00
☐ 581 Bob Bailor	.25	.11
☐ 582 Brian Doyle	.25	.11
☐ 583 Bob Stinson	.25	.11
☐ 584 Kurt Bevacqua	.25	.11
☐ 585 Al Hrabosky	.25	.11
☐ 586 Mitchell Page	.25	.11
☐ 587 Garry Templeton	.25	.11
☐ 588 Greg Minton	.25	.11
☐ 589 Chet Lemon	.75	.35
☐ 590 Jim Palmer	1.50	.70
☐ 591 Rick Cerone	.25	.11
☐ 592 Jon Matlack	.25	.11
☐ 593 Jesus Alou	.25	.11
☐ 594 Dick Tidrow	.25	.11
☐ 595 Don Money	.25	.11
☐ 596 Rick Matula	.25	.11
☐ 597 Tom Poquette	.25	.11
☐ 598 Fred Kendall DP	.10	.05
☐ 599 Mike Norris	.25	.11
☐ 600 Reggie Jackson	3.00	1.35
☐ 601 Buddy Schultz	.25	.11
☐ 602 Brian Downing	.25	.11
☐ 603 Jack Billingham DP	.10	.05
☐ 604 Glenn Adams	.25	.11
☐ 605 Terry Forster	.25	.11
☐ 606 Reds Team/Mgr	1.50	.30
John McNamara		
(Checklist back)		
☐ 607 Woodie Fryman	.25	.11
☐ 608 Alan Bannister	.25	.11
☐ 609 Ron Reed	.25	.11
☐ 610 Willie Stargell	1.25	.55
☐ 611 Jerry Garvin DP	.10	.05
☐ 612 Cliff Johnson	.25	.11
☐ 613 Randy Stein	.25	.11
☐ 614 John Hiller	.25	.11
☐ 615 Doug DeCinces	.75	.35
☐ 616 Gene Richards	.25	.11
☐ 617 Joaquin Andujar	.75	.35
☐ 618 Bob Montgomery DP	.10	.05
☐ 619 Sergio Ferrer	.25	.11
☐ 620 Richie Zisk	.25	.11
☐ 621 Bob Grich	.75	.35
☐ 622 Mario Soto	.25	.11
☐ 623 Gorman Thomas	.75	.35
☐ 624 Lerrin LaGrow	.25	.11
☐ 625 Chris Chambliss	.75	.35
☐ 626 Tigers Team/Mgr.	1.50	.30
Sparky Anderson		
(Checklist back)		
☐ 627 Pedro Borbon	.25	.11
☐ 628 Doug Capilla	.25	.11
☐ 629 Jim Todd	.25	.11
☐ 630 Larry Bowa	.75	.35
☐ 631 Mark Littell	.25	.11
☐ 632 Barry Bonnell	.25	.11
☐ 633 Bob Apodaca	.25	.11
☐ 634 Glenn Borgmann DP	.10	.05
☐ 635 John Candelaria	.75	.35
☐ 636 Toby Harrah	.75	.35
☐ 637 Joe Simpson	.25	.11
☐ 638 Mark Clear	.25	.11
☐ 639 Larry Biittner	.25	.11
☐ 640 Mike Flanagan	.75	.35
☐ 641 Ed Kranepool	.25	.11
☐ 642 Ken Forsch DP	.10	.05
☐ 643 John Mayberry	.75	.35
☐ 644 Charlie Hough	.75	.35
☐ 645 Rick Burleson	.25	.11
☐ 646 Checklist 606-726	1.50	.30
☐ 647 Milt May	.25	.11
☐ 648 Roy White	.25	.11
☐ 649 Tom Griffin	.25	.11
☐ 650 Joe Morgan	1.50	.70
☐ 651 Rollie Fingers	2.50	1.10
☐ 652 Mario Mendoza	.25	.11
☐ 653 Stan Bahnsen	.25	.11
☐ 654 Bruce Boisclair DP	.10	.05
☐ 655 Tug McGraw	.75	.35
☐ 656 Larvell Blanks	.25	.11
☐ 657 Dave Edwards	.25	.11
☐ 658 Chris Knapp	.25	.11

☐ 659 Brewers Team/Mgr	1.50	.30
George Bamberger		
(Checklist back)		
☐ 660 Rusty Staub	.75	.35
☐ 661 Orioles Rookies	.75	.35
Mark Corey		
Dave Ford		
Wayne Krenchicki		
☐ 662 Red Sox Rookies	.75	.35
Joel Finch		
Mike O'Berry		
Chuck Rainey		
☐ 663 Angels Rookies	1.50	.70
Ralph Botting		
Bob Clark		
Dickie Thon		
☐ 664 White Sox Rookies	.75	.35
Mike Colbern		
Guy Hoffman		
Dewey Robinson		
☐ 665 Indians Rookies	1.50	.70
Larry Andersen		
Bobby Cuellar		
Sandy Wihtol		
☐ 666 Tigers Rookies	.75	.35
Mike Chris		
Al Greene		
Bruce Robbins		
☐ 667 Royals Rookies	2.00	.90
Renie Martin		
Bill Paschall		
Dan Quisenberry		
☐ 668 Brewers Rookies	.75	.35
Danny Boitano		
Willie Mueller		
Lenn Sakata		
☐ 669 Twins Rookies	.75	.35
Dan Graham		
Rick Sofield		
Gary Ward		
☐ 670 Yankees Rookies	.75	.35
Bobby Brown		
Brad Gulden		
Darryl Jones		
☐ 671 A's Rookies	2.50	1.10
Derek Bryant		
Brian Kingman		
Mike Morgan		
☐ 672 Mariners Rookies	.75	.35
Charlie Beamon		
Rodney Craig		
Rafael Vasquez		
☐ 673 Rangers Rookies	.75	.35
Brian Allard		
Jerry Don Gleaton		
Greg Mahlberg		
☐ 674 Blue Jays Rookies	.75	.35
Butch Edge		
Pat Kelly		
Ted Wilborn		
☐ 675 Braves Rookies	.75	.35
Bruce Benedict		
Larry Bradford		
Eddie Miller		
☐ 676 Cubs Rookies	.75	.35
Dave Geisel		
Steve Macko		
Karl Pagel		
☐ 677 Reds Rookies	.75	.35
Art DeFreites		
Frank Pastore		
Harry Spilman		
☐ 678 Astros Rookies	.75	.35
Reggie Baldwin		
Alan Knicely		
Pete Ladd		
☐ 679 Dodgers Rookies	1.50	.70
Joe Beckwith		
Mickey Hatcher		
Dave Patterson		
☐ 680 Expos Rookies	1.50	.70
Tony Bernazard		
Randy Miller		
John Tamargo		
☐ 681 Mets Rookies	2.50	1.10
Dan Norman		

Jesse Orosco		
Mike Scott		
☐ 682 Phillies Rookies	.75	.35
Ramon Aviles		
Dickie Noles		
Kevin Saucier		
☐ 683 Pirates Rookies	.75	.35
Dorian Boyland		
Alberto Lois		
Harry Saferight		
☐ 684 Cardinals Rookies	1.50	.70
George Frazier		
Tom Herr		
Dan O'Brien		
☐ 685 Padres Rookies	.75	.35
Tim Flannery		
Brian Greer		
Jim Wilhelm		
☐ 686 Giants Rookies	.75	.35
Greg Johnston		
Dennis Littlejohn		
Phil Nastu		
☐ 687 Mike Heath DP	.10	.05
☐ 688 Steve Stone	.75	.35
☐ 689 Red Sox Team/Mgr.	1.50	.30
Don Zimmer		
(Checklist back)		
☐ 690 Tommy John	1.50	.70
☐ 691 Ivan DeJesus	.25	.11
☐ 692 Rawly Eastwick DP	.10	.05
☐ 693 Craig Kusick	.25	.11
☐ 694 Jim Rooker	.25	.11
☐ 695 Reggie Smith	.75	.35
☐ 696 Julio Gonzalez	.25	.11
☐ 697 David Clyde	.25	.11
☐ 698 Oscar Gamble	.75	.35
☐ 699 Floyd Bannister	.25	.11
☐ 700 Rod Carew DP	1.00	.45
☐ 701 Ken Oberkfell	.25	.11
☐ 702 Ed Farmer	.25	.11
☐ 703 Otto Velez	.25	.11
☐ 704 Gene Tenace	.75	.35
☐ 705 Freddie Patek	.25	.11
☐ 706 Tippy Martinez	.25	.11
☐ 707 Elliott Maddox	.25	.11
☐ 708 Bob Tolan	.25	.11
☐ 709 Pat Underwood	.25	.11
☐ 710 Graig Nettles	1.50	.70
☐ 711 Bob Galasso	.25	.11
☐ 712 Rodney Scott	.25	.11
☐ 713 Terry Whitfield	.25	.11
☐ 714 Fred Norman	.25	.11
☐ 715 Sal Bando	.75	.35
☐ 716 Lynn McGlothen	.25	.11
☐ 717 Mickey Klutts DP	.10	.05
☐ 718 Greg Gross	.25	.11
☐ 719 Don Robinson	.75	.35
☐ 720 Carl Yastrzemski DP	1.50	.70
☐ 721 Paul Hartzell	.25	.11
☐ 722 Jose Cruz	.75	.35
☐ 723 Shane Rawley	.25	.11
☐ 724 Jerry White	.25	.11
☐ 725 Rick Wise	.25	.11
☐ 726 Steve Yeager	1.50	.30

1981 Topps

The cards in this 726-card set measure the standard size.

League Leaders (1-8), Record Breakers (201-208), and Post-season cards (401-404) are the topical subsets. The team cards are all grouped together (661-686) and feature team checklist backs and a very small photo of the team's manager in the upper right corner of the obverse. The obverses carry the player's position and team in a baseball cap design, and the company name is printed in a small baseball. The backs are red and gray. The 66 double-printed cards are noted in the checklist by DP. This set was issued primarily in 15-card wax packs and 50-card rack packs. Notable Rookie Cards in the set include Harold Baines, Kirk Gibson, Tim Raines, Jeff Reardon, and Fernando Valenzuela.

	NRMT	VG-E
COMPLETE SET (726)	50.00	22.00
COMMON CARD (1-726)	.15	.07
MINOR STARS	.40	.18
SEMISTARS	.75	.35
UNLISTED STARS	1.50	.70

☐ 1 Batting Leaders	2.50	1.10	
George Brett			
Bill Buckner			
☐ 2 Home Run Leaders	1.50	.70	
Reggie Jackson			
Ben Oglivie			
Mike Schmidt			
☐ 3 RBI Leaders	1.50	.70	
Cecil Cooper			
Mike Schmidt			
☐ 4 Stolen Base Leaders	1.50	.70	
Rickey Henderson			
Ron LeFlore			
☐ 5 Victory Leaders	1.50	.70	
Steve Stone			
Steve Carlton			
☐ 6 Strikeout Leaders	1.50	.70	
Len Barker			
Steve Carlton			
☐ 7 ERA Leaders	.75	.35	
Rudy May			
Don Sutton			
☐ 8 Leading Firemen	.75	.35	
Dan Quisenberry			
Rollie Fingers			
Tom Hume			
☐ 9 Pete LaCock DP	.10	.05	
☐ 10 Mike Flanagan	.40	.18	
☐ 11 Jim Wohlford DP	.10	.05	
☐ 12 Mark Clear	.15	.07	
☐ 13 Joe Charboneau	1.50	.70	
☐ 14 John Tudor	.40	.18	
☐ 15 Larry Parrish	.15	.07	
☐ 16 Ron Davis	.15	.07	
☐ 17 Cliff Johnson	.15	.07	
☐ 18 Glenn Adams	.15	.07	
☐ 19 Jim Clancy	.15	.07	
☐ 20 Jeff Burroughs	.15	.07	
☐ 21 Ron Oester	.15	.07	
☐ 22 Danny Darwin	.40	.18	
☐ 23 Alex Trevino	.15	.07	
☐ 24 Don Stanhouse	.15	.07	
☐ 25 Sixto Lezcano	.15	.07	
☐ 26 U.L. Washington	.15	.07	
☐ 27 Champ Summers DP	.10	.05	
☐ 28 Enrique Romo	.15	.07	
☐ 29 Gene Tenace	.40	.18	
☐ 30 Jack Clark	.40	.18	
☐ 31 Checklist 1-121 DP	.15	.07	
☐ 32 Ken Oberkfell	.15	.07	
☐ 33 Rick Honeycutt	.15	.07	
☐ 34 Aurelio Rodriguez	.15	.07	
☐ 35 Mitchell Page	.15	.07	
☐ 36 Ed Farmer	.15	.07	
☐ 37 Gary Roenicke	.15	.07	
☐ 38 Win Remmerswaal	.15	.07	
☐ 39 Tom Veryzer	.15	.07	
☐ 40 Tug McGraw	.40	.18	
☐ 41 Ranger Rookies	.15	.07	
Bob Babcock			
John Butcher			
Jerry Don Gleaton			
☐ 42 Jerry White DP	.10	.05	
☐ 43 Jose Morales	.15	.07	
☐ 44 Larry McWilliams	.15	.07	
☐ 45 Enos Cabell	.15	.07	
☐ 46 Rick Bosetti	.15	.07	
☐ 47 Ken Brett	.15	.07	
☐ 48 Dave Skaggs	.15	.07	
☐ 49 Bob Shirley	.15	.07	
☐ 50 Dave Lopes	.40	.18	
☐ 51 Bill Robinson DP	.15	.07	
☐ 52 Hector Cruz	.15	.07	
☐ 53 Kevin Saucier	.15	.07	
☐ 54 Ivan DeJesus	.15	.07	
☐ 55 Mike Norris	.15	.07	
☐ 56 Buck Martinez	.15	.07	
☐ 57 Dave Roberts	.15	.07	
☐ 58 Joel Youngblood	.15	.07	
☐ 59 Dan Petry	.40	.18	
☐ 60 Willie Randolph	.40	.18	
☐ 61 Butch Wynegar	.15	.07	
☐ 62 Joe Pettini	.15	.07	
☐ 63 Steve Renko DP	.10	.05	
☐ 64 Brian Asselstine	.15	.07	
☐ 65 Scott McGregor	.15	.07	
☐ 66 Royals Rookies	.15	.07	
Manny Castillo			
Tim Ireland			
Mike Jones			
☐ 67 Ken Kravec	.15	.07	
☐ 68 Matt Alexander DP	.10	.05	
☐ 69 Ed Halicki	.15	.07	
☐ 70 Al Oliver DP	.40	.18	
☐ 71 Hal Dues	.15	.07	
☐ 72 Barry Evans DP	.10	.05	
☐ 73 Doug Bair	.15	.07	
☐ 74 Mike Hargrove	.40	.18	
☐ 75 Reggie Smith	.40	.18	
☐ 76 Mario Mendoza	.15	.07	
☐ 77 Mike Barlow	.15	.07	
☐ 78 Steve Dillard	.15	.07	
☐ 79 Bruce Robbins	.15	.07	
☐ 80 Rusty Staub	.40	.18	
☐ 81 Dave Stapleton	.15	.07	
☐ 82 Astros Rookies DP	.15	.07	
Danny Heep			
Alan Knicely			
Bobby Sprowl			
☐ 83 Mike Proly	.15	.07	
☐ 84 Johnnie LeMaster	.15	.07	
☐ 85 Mike Caldwell	.15	.07	
☐ 86 Wayne Gross	.15	.07	
☐ 87 Rick Camp	.15	.07	
☐ 88 Joe Lefebvre	.15	.07	
☐ 89 Darrell Jackson	.15	.07	
☐ 90 Bake McBride	.15	.07	
☐ 91 Tim Stoddard DP	.10	.05	
☐ 92 Mike Easler	.15	.07	
☐ 93 Ed Glynn DP	.10	.05	
☐ 94 Harry Spilman DP	.10	.05	
☐ 95 Jim Sundberg	.40	.18	
☐ 96 A's Rookies	.15	.07	
Dave Beard			
Ernie Camacho			
Pat Dempsey			
☐ 97 Chris Speier	.15	.07	
☐ 98 Clint Hurdle	.15	.07	
☐ 99 Eric Wilkins	.15	.07	
☐ 100 Rod Carew	1.25	.55	
☐ 101 Benny Ayala	.15	.07	
☐ 102 Dave Tobik	.15	.07	
☐ 103 Jerry Martin	.15	.07	
☐ 104 Terry Forster	.40	.18	
☐ 105 Jose Cruz	.40	.18	
☐ 106 Don Money	.15	.07	
☐ 107 Rich Wortham	.15	.07	
☐ 108 Bruce Benedict	.15	.07	
☐ 109 Mike Scott	.40	.18	
☐ 110 Carl Yastrzemski	1.50	.70	
☐ 111 Greg Minton	.15	.07	
☐ 112 White Sox Rookies	.15	.07	
Rusty Kuntz			
Fran Mullins			
Leo Sutherland			
☐ 113 Mike Phillips	.15	.07	
☐ 114 Tom Underwood	.15	.07	
☐ 115 Roy Smalley	.15	.07	
☐ 116 Joe Simpson	.15	.07	
☐ 117 Pete Falcone	.15	.07	
☐ 118 Kurt Bevacqua	.15	.07	
☐ 119 Tippy Martinez	.15	.07	
☐ 120 Larry Bowa	.40	.18	
☐ 121 Larry Harlow	.15	.07	
☐ 122 John Denny	.15	.07	
☐ 123 Al Cowens	.15	.07	
☐ 124 Jerry Garvin	.15	.07	
☐ 125 Andre Dawson	2.00	.90	
☐ 126 Charlie Leibrandt	.75	.35	
☐ 127 Rudy Law	.15	.07	
☐ 128 Gary Allenson DP	.10	.05	
☐ 129 Art Howe	.15	.07	
☐ 130 Larry Gura	.15	.07	
☐ 131 Keith Moreland	.40	.18	
☐ 132 Tommy Boggs	.15	.07	
☐ 133 Jeff Cox	.15	.07	
☐ 134 Steve Mura	.15	.07	
☐ 135 Gorman Thomas	.40	.18	
☐ 136 Doug Capilla	.15	.07	
☐ 137 Hosken Powell	.15	.07	
☐ 138 Rich Dotson DP	.15	.07	
☐ 139 Oscar Gamble	.15	.07	
☐ 140 Bob Forsch	.15	.07	
☐ 141 Miguel Dilone	.15	.07	
☐ 142 Jackson Todd	.15	.07	
☐ 143 Dan Meyer	.15	.07	
☐ 144 Allen Ripley	.15	.07	
☐ 145 Mickey Rivers	.40	.18	
☐ 146 Bobby Castillo	.15	.07	
☐ 147 Dale Berra	.15	.07	
☐ 148 Randy Niemann	.15	.07	
☐ 149 Joe Nolan	.15	.07	
☐ 150 Mark Fidrych	1.50	.70	
☐ 151 Claudell Washington	.40	.18	
☐ 152 John Urrea	.15	.07	
☐ 153 Tom Poquette	.15	.07	
☐ 154 Rick Langford	.15	.07	
☐ 155 Chris Chambliss	.40	.18	
☐ 156 Bob McClure	.15	.07	
☐ 157 John Wathan	.15	.07	
☐ 158 Fergie Jenkins	1.50	.70	
☐ 159 Brian Doyle	.15	.07	
☐ 160 Garry Maddox	.15	.07	
☐ 161 Dan Graham	.15	.07	
☐ 162 Doug Corbett	.15	.07	
☐ 163 Bill Almon	.15	.07	
☐ 164 LaMarr Hoyt	.40	.18	
☐ 165 Tony Scott	.15	.07	
☐ 166 Floyd Bannister	.15	.07	
☐ 167 Terry Whitfield	.15	.07	
☐ 168 Don Robinson DP	.10	.05	
☐ 169 John Mayberry	.15	.07	
☐ 170 Ross Grimsley	.15	.07	
☐ 171 Gene Richards	.15	.07	
☐ 172 Gary Woods	.15	.07	
☐ 173 Bump Wills	.15	.07	
☐ 174 Doug Rau	.15	.07	
☐ 175 Dave Collins	.15	.07	
☐ 176 Mike Krukow	.15	.07	
☐ 177 Rick Peters	.15	.07	
☐ 178 Jim Essian DP	.10	.05	
☐ 179 Rudy May	.15	.07	
☐ 180 Pete Rose	2.00	.90	
☐ 181 Elias Sosa	.15	.07	
☐ 182 Bob Grich	.40	.18	
☐ 183 Dick Davis DP	.10	.05	
☐ 184 Jim Dwyer	.15	.07	
☐ 185 Dennis Leonard	.15	.07	
☐ 186 Wayne Nordhagen	.15	.07	
☐ 187 Mike Parrott	.15	.07	
☐ 188 Doug DeCinces	.40	.18	
☐ 189 Craig Swan	.15	.07	
☐ 190 Cesar Cedeno	.40	.18	
☐ 191 Rick Sutcliffe	.40	.18	
☐ 192 Braves Rookies	.40	.18	
Terry Harper			

	Ed Miller		
	Rafael Ramirez		
193	Pete Vuckovich	.40	.18
194	Rod Scurry	.15	.07
195	Rich Murray	.15	.07
196	Duffy Dyer	.15	.07
197	Jim Kern	.15	.07
198	Jerry Dybzinski	.15	.07
199	Chuck Rainey	.15	.07
200	George Foster	.40	.18
201	Johnny Bench RB	1.50	.70
	Most homers catchers		
202	Steve Carlton RB	1.50	.70
	Most strikeouts,		
	lefthander, lifetime		
203	Bill Gullickson RB	.75	.35
	Most SO's, game, rookie		
204	Ron LeFlore RB	.40	.18
	Rodney Scott RB		
	Most stolen bases		
	teammates, season		
205	Pete Rose RB	1.50	.70
	Most cons. seasons		
	600 or more at-bats		
206	Mike Schmidt RB	1.50	.70
	Most homers, 3rd baseman, season		
207	Ozzie Smith RB	2.00	.90
	Most assists,		
	season, shortstop		
208	Willie Wilson RB	.40	.18
	Most AB's season		
209	Dickie Thon DP	.40	.18
210	Jim Palmer	1.00	.45
211	Derrel Thomas	.15	.07
212	Steve Nicosia	.15	.07
213	Al Holland	.15	.07
214	Angels Rookies	.15	.07
	Ralph Botting		
	Jim Dorsey		
	John Harris		
215	Larry Hisle	.15	.07
216	John Henry Johnson	.15	.07
217	Rich Hebner	.15	.07
218	Paul Splittorff	.15	.07
219	Ken Landreaux	.15	.07
220	Tom Seaver	2.00	.90
221	Bob Davis	.15	.07
222	Jorge Orta	.15	.07
223	Roy Lee Jackson	.15	.07
224	Pat Zachry	.15	.07
225	Ruppert Jones	.15	.07
226	Manny Sanguillen DP	.10	.05
227	Fred Martinez	.15	.07
228	Tom Paciorek	.15	.18
229	Rollie Fingers	1.50	.70
230	George Hendrick	.40	.18
231	Joe Beckwith	.15	.07
232	Mickey Klutts	.15	.07
233	Skip Lockwood	.15	.07
234	Lou Whitaker	1.50	.70
235	Scott Sanderson	.15	.07
236	Mike Ivie	.15	.07
237	Charlie Moore	.15	.07
238	Willie Hernandez	.40	.18
239	Rick Miller DP	.10	.05
240	Nolan Ryan	8.00	3.60
241	Checklist 122-242 DP	.15	.07
242	Chet Lemon	.15	.07
243	Sal Butera	.15	.07
244	Cardinals Rookies	.15	.07
	Tito Landrum		
	Al Olmsted		
	Andy Rincon		
245	Ed Figueroa	.15	.07
246	Ed Ott DP	.10	.05
247	Glenn Hubbard DP	.10	.05
248	Joey McLaughlin	.15	.07
249	Larry Cox	.15	.07
250	Ron Guidry	.40	.18
251	Tom Brookens	.15	.07
252	Victor Cruz	.15	.07
253	Dave Bergman	.15	.07
254	Ozzie Smith	6.00	2.70
255	Mark Littell	.15	.07
256	Bombo Rivera	.15	.07
257	Rennie Stennett	.15	.07
258	Joe Price	.15	.07
259	Mets Rookies	1.50	.70
	Juan Berenguer		
	Hubie Brooks		
	Mookie Wilson		
260	Ron Cey	.40	.18
261	Rickey Henderson	4.00	1.80
262	Sammy Stewart	.15	.07
263	Brian Downing	.40	.18
264	Jim Norris	.15	.07
265	John Candelaria	.40	.18
266	Tom Herr	.40	.18
267	Stan Bahnsen	.15	.07
268	Jerry Royster	.15	.07
269	Ken Forsch	.15	.07
270	Greg Luzinski	.40	.18
271	Bill Castro	.15	.07
272	Bruce Kimm	.15	.07
273	Stan Papi	.15	.07
274	Craig Chamberlain	.15	.07
275	Dwight Evans	.75	.35
276	Dan Spillner	.15	.07
277	Alfredo Griffin	.15	.07
278	Rick Sofield	.15	.07
279	Bob Knepper	.15	.07
280	Ken Griffey	.75	.35
281	Fred Stanley	.15	.07
282	Mariners Rookies	.15	.07
	Rick Anderson		
	Greg Biercevicz		
	Rodney Craig		
283	Billy Sample	.15	.07
284	Brian Kingman	.15	.07
285	Jerry Turner	.15	.07
286	Dave Frost	.15	.07
287	Lenn Sakata	.15	.07
288	Bob Clark	.15	.07
289	Mickey Hatcher	.40	.18
290	Bob Boone DP	.40	.18
291	Aurelio Lopez	.15	.07
292	Mike Squires	.15	.07
293	Charlie Lea	.15	.07
294	Mike Tyson DP	.10	.05
295	Hal McRae	.75	.35
296	Bill Nahorodny DP	.10	.05
297	Bob Bailor	.15	.07
298	Buddy Solomon	.15	.07
299	Elliott Maddox	.15	.07
300	Paul Molitor	3.00	1.35
301	Matt Keough	.15	.07
302	Dodgers Rookies	3.00	1.35
	Jack Perconte		
	Mike Scioscia		
	Fernando Valenzuela		
303	Johnny Oates	.40	.18
304	John Castino	.15	.07
305	Ken Clay	.15	.07
306	Juan Beniquez DP	.10	.05
307	Gene Garber	.15	.07
308	Rick Manning	.15	.07
309	Luis Salazar	.15	.07
310	Vida Blue DP	.15	.07
311	Freddie Patek	.15	.07
312	Rick Rhoden	.15	.07
313	Luis Pujols	.15	.07
314	Rich Dauer	.15	.07
315	Kirk Gibson	3.00	1.35
316	Craig Minetto	.15	.07
317	Lonnie Smith	.40	.18
318	Steve Yeager	.15	.07
319	Rowland Office	.15	.07
320	Tom Burgmeier	.15	.07
321	Leon Durham	.40	.18
322	Neil Allen	.15	.07
323	Jim Morrison DP	.10	.05
324	Mike Willis	.15	.07
325	Ray Knight	.40	.18
326	Biff Pocoroba	.15	.07
327	Moose Haas	.15	.07
328	Twins Rookies	.15	.07
	Dave Engle		
	Greg Johnston		
	Gary Ward		
329	Joaquin Andujar	.40	.18
330	Frank White	.40	.18
331	Dennis Lamp	.15	.07
332	Lee Lacy DP	.10	.05
333	Sid Monge	.15	.07
334	Dane Iorg	.15	.07
335	Rick Cerone	.15	.07
336	Eddie Whitson	.15	.07
337	Lynn Jones	.15	.07
338	Checklist 243-363	.75	.35
339	John Ellis	.15	.07
340	Bruce Kison	.15	.07
341	Dwayne Murphy	.15	.07
342	Eric Rasmussen DP	.10	.05
343	Frank Taveras	.15	.07
344	Byron McLaughlin	.15	.07
345	Warren Cromartie	.15	.07
346	Larry Christenson DP	.10	.05
347	Harold Baines	2.50	1.10
348	Bob Sykes	.15	.07
349	Glenn Hoffman	.15	.07
350	J.R. Richard	.40	.18
351	Otto Velez	.15	.07
352	Dick Tidrow DP	.10	.05
353	Terry Kennedy	.15	.07
354	Mario Soto	.15	.07
355	Bob Horner	.40	.18
356	Padres Rookies	.15	.07
	George Stablein		
	Craig Stimac		
	Tom Tellmann		
357	Jim Slaton	.15	.07
358	Mark Wagner	.15	.07
359	Tom Hausman	.15	.07
360	Willie Wilson	.40	.18
361	Joe Strain	.15	.07
362	Bo Diaz	.15	.07
363	Geoff Zahn	.15	.07
364	Mike Davis	.15	.07
365	Graig Nettles DP	.40	.18
366	Mike Ramsey	.15	.07
367	Dennis Martinez	.75	.35
368	Leon Roberts	.15	.07
369	Frank Tanana	.40	.18
370	Dave Winfield	2.50	1.10
371	Charlie Hough	.40	.18
372	Jay Johnstone	.40	.18
373	Pat Underwood	.15	.07
374	Tommy Hutton	.15	.07
375	Dave Concepcion	.40	.18
376	Ron Reed	.15	.07
377	Jerry Morales	.15	.07
378	Dave Rader	.15	.07
379	Lary Sorensen	.15	.07
380	Willie Stargell	1.50	.70
381	Cubs Rookies	.15	.07
	Carlos Lezcano		
	Steve Macko		
	Randy Martz		
382	Paul Mirabella	.15	.07
383	Eric Soderholm DP	.10	.05
384	Mike Sadek	.15	.07
385	Joe Sambito	.15	.07
386	Dave Edwards	.15	.07
387	Phil Niekro	1.50	.70
388	Andre Thornton	.40	.18
389	Marty Pattin	.15	.07
390	Cesar Geronimo	.15	.07
391	Dave Lemanczyk DP	.10	.05
392	Lance Parrish	.40	.18
393	Broderick Perkins	.15	.07
394	Woodie Fryman	.15	.07
395	Scot Thompson	.15	.07
396	Bill Campbell	.15	.07
397	Julio Cruz	.15	.07
398	Ross Baumgarten	.15	.07
399	Orioles Rookies	.15	.70
	Mike Boddicker		
	Mark Corey		
	Floyd Rayford		
400	Reggie Jackson	2.00	.90
401	George Brett ALCS	2.00	.90
402	NL Champs	.75	.35
	Phillies squeak		
	past Astros		
	(Phillies celebrating)		
403	Larry Bowa WS	.75	.35
404	Tug McGraw WS	.75	.35
405	Nino Espinosa	.15	.07

406	Dickie Noles	.15	.07
407	Ernie Whitt	.15	.07
408	Fernando Arroyo	.15	.07
409	Larry Herndon	.15	.07
410	Bert Campaneris	.40	.18
411	Terry Puhl	.15	.07
412	Britt Burns	.15	.07
413	Tony Bernazard	.15	.07
414	John Pacella DP	.05	.05
415	Ben Oglivie	.40	.18
416	Gary Alexander	.15	.07
417	Dan Schatzeder	.15	.07
418	Bobby Brown	.15	.07
419	Tom Hume	.15	.07
420	Keith Hernandez	.40	.18
421	Bob Stanley	.15	.07
422	Dan Ford	.15	.07
423	Shane Rawley	.15	.07
424	Yankees Rookies	.15	.07
	Tim Lollar		
	Bruce Robinson		
	Dennis Werth		
425	Al Bumbry	.40	.18
426	Warren Brusstar	.15	.07
427	John D'Acquisto	.15	.07
428	John Stearns	.15	.07
429	Mick Kelleher	.15	.07
430	Jim Bibby	.15	.07
431	Dave Roberts	.15	.07
432	Len Barker	.15	.07
433	Rance Mulliniks	.15	.07
434	Roger Erickson	.15	.07
435	Jim Spencer	.15	.07
436	Gary Lucas	.15	.07
437	Mike Heath DP	.10	.05
438	John Montefusco	.15	.07
439	Denny Walling	.15	.07
440	Jerry Reuss	.40	.18
441	Ken Reitz	.15	.07
442	Ron Pruitt	.15	.07
443	Jim Beattie DP	.10	.05
444	Garth Iorg	.15	.07
445	Ellis Valentine	.15	.07
446	Checklist 364-484	.75	.35
447	Junior Kennedy DP	.10	.05
448	Tim Corcoran	.15	.07
449	Paul Mitchell	.15	.07
450	Dave Kingman DP	.40	.18
451	Indians Rookies	.15	.07
	Chris Bando		
	Tom Brennan		
	Sandy Wihtol		
452	Renie Martin	.15	.07
453	Rob Wilfong DP	.05	.05
454	Andy Hassler	.15	.07
455	Rick Burleson	.15	.07
456	Jeff Reardon	2.00	.90
457	Mike Lum	.15	.07
458	Randy Jones	.15	.07
459	Greg Gross	.15	.07
460	Rich Gossage	.75	.35
461	Dave McKay	.15	.07
462	Jack Brohamer	.15	.07
463	Milt May	.15	.07
464	Adrian Devine	.15	.07
465	Bill Russell	.40	.18
466	Bob Molinaro	.15	.07
467	Dave Stieb	.40	.18
468	John Wockenfuss	.15	.07
469	Jeff Leonard	.40	.18
470	Manny Trillo	.15	.07
471	Mike Vail	.15	.07
472	Dyar Miller DP	.10	.05
473	Jose Cardenal	.15	.07
474	Mike LaCoss	.15	.07
475	Buddy Bell	.40	.18
476	Jerry Koosman	.15	.18
477	Luis Gomez	.15	.07
478	Juan Eichelberger	.15	.07
479	Expos Rookies	3.00	1.35
	Tim Raines		
	Roberto Ramos		
	Bobby Pate		
480	Carlton Fisk	2.00	.90
481	Bob Lacey DP	.10	.05
482	Jim Gantner	.40	.18
483	Mike Griffin	.15	.07
484	Max Venable DP	.10	.05
485	Garry Templeton	.15	.07
486	Marc Hill	.15	.07
487	Dewey Robinson	.15	.07
488	Damaso Garcia	.15	.07
489	John Littlefield	.15	.07
490	Eddie Murray	3.00	1.35
491	Gordy Pladson	.15	.07
492	Barry Foote	.15	.07
493	Dan Quisenberry	.40	.18
494	Bob Walk	.40	.18
495	Dusty Baker	.75	.35
496	Paul Dade	.15	.07
497	Fred Norman	.15	.07
498	Pat Putnam	.15	.07
499	Frank Pastore	.15	.07
500	Jim Rice	.40	.18
501	Tim Foli DP	.10	.05
502	Giants Rookies	.15	.07
	Chris Bourjos		
	Al Hargesheimer		
	Mike Rowland		
503	Steve McCatty	.15	.07
504	Dale Murphy	1.50	.70
505	Jason Thompson	.15	.07
506	Phil Huffman	.15	.07
507	Jamie Quirk	.15	.07
508	Rob Dressler	.15	.07
509	Pete Mackanin	.15	.07
510	Lee Mazzilli	.15	.07
511	Wayne Garland	.15	.07
512	Gary Thomasson	.15	.07
513	Frank LaCorte	.15	.07
514	George Riley	.15	.07
515	Robin Yount	2.00	.90
516	Doug Bird	.15	.07
517	Richie Zisk	.15	.07
518	Grant Jackson	.15	.07
519	John Tamargo DP	.10	.05
520	Steve Stone	.40	.18
521	Sam Mejias	.15	.07
522	Mike Colbern	.15	.07
523	John Fulgham	.15	.07
524	Willie Aikens	.15	.07
525	Mike Torrez	.15	.07
526	Phillies Rookies	.15	.07
	Marty Bystrom		
	Jay Loviglio		
	Jim Wright		
527	Danny Goodwin	.15	.07
528	Gary Matthews	.40	.18
529	Dave LaRoche	.15	.07
530	Steve Garvey	.75	.35
531	John Curtis	.15	.07
532	Bill Stein	.15	.07
533	Jesus Figueroa	.15	.07
534	Dave Smith	.40	.18
535	Omar Moreno	.15	.07
536	Bob Owchinko DP	.10	.05
537	Ron Hodges	.15	.07
538	Tom Griffin	.15	.07
539	Rodney Scott	.15	.07
540	Mike Schmidt DP	2.00	.90
541	Steve Swisher	.15	.07
542	Larry Bradford DP	.10	.05
543	Terry Crowley	.15	.07
544	Rich Gale	.15	.07
545	Johnny Grubb	.15	.07
546	Paul Moskau	.15	.07
547	Mario Guerrero	.15	.07
548	Dave Goltz	.15	.07
549	Jerry Remy	.15	.07
550	Tommy John	.75	.35
551	Pirates Rookies	1.50	.70
	Vance Law		
	Tony Pena		
	Pascual Perez		
552	Steve Trout	.15	.07
553	Tim Blackwell	.15	.07
554	Bert Blyleven UER	.75	.35
	(1 is missing from		
	1980 on card back)		
555	Cecil Cooper	.40	.18
556	Jerry Mumphrey	.15	.07
557	Chris Knapp	.15	.07
558	Barry Bonnell	.15	.07
559	Willie Montanez	.15	.07
560	Joe Morgan	1.50	.70
561	Dennis Littlejohn	.15	.07
562	Checklist 485-605	.75	.35
563	Jim Kaat	.40	.18
564	Ron Hassey DP	.10	.05
565	Burt Hooton	.15	.07
566	Del Unser	.15	.07
567	Mark Bomback	.15	.07
568	Dave Revering	.15	.07
569	Al Williams DP	.10	.05
570	Ken Singleton	.40	.18
571	Todd Cruz	.15	.07
572	Jack Morris	.75	.35
573	Phil Garner	.40	.18
574	Bill Caudill	.15	.07
575	Tony Perez	1.50	.70
576	Reggie Cleveland	.15	.07
577	Blue Jays Rookies	.15	.07
	Luis Leal		
	Brian Milner		
	Ken Schrom		
578	Bill Gullickson	.75	.35
579	Tim Flannery	.15	.07
580	Don Baylor	.75	.35
581	Roy Howell	.15	.07
582	Gaylord Perry	1.50	.70
583	Larry Milbourne	.15	.07
584	Randy Lerch	.15	.07
585	Amos Otis	.40	.18
586	Silvio Martinez	.15	.07
587	Jeff Newman	.15	.07
588	Gary Lavelle	.15	.07
589	Lamar Johnson	.15	.07
590	Bruce Sutter	.40	.18
591	John Lowenstein	.15	.07
592	Steve Comer	.15	.07
593	Steve Kemp	.15	.07
594	Preston Hanna DP	.10	.05
595	Butch Hobson	.15	.07
596	Jerry Augustine	.15	.07
597	Rafael Landestoy	.15	.07
598	George Vukovich DP	.10	.05
599	Dennis Kinney	.15	.07
600	Johnny Bench	2.00	.90
601	Don Aase	.15	.07
602	Bobby Murcer	.40	.18
603	John Verhoeven	.15	.07
604	Rob Picciolo	.15	.07
605	Don Sutton	1.50	.70
606	Reds Rookies DP	.15	.07
	Bruce Berenyi		
	Geoff Combe		
	Paul Householder		
607	David Palmer	.15	.07
608	Greg Pryor	.15	.07
609	Lynn McGlothen	.15	.07
610	Darrell Porter	.15	.07
611	Rick Matula DP	.10	.05
612	Duane Kuiper	.15	.07
613	Jim Anderson	.15	.07
614	Dave Rozema	.15	.07
615	Rick Dempsey	.40	.18
616	Rick Wise	.15	.07
617	Craig Reynolds	.15	.07
618	John Milner	.15	.07
619	Steve Henderson	.15	.07
620	Dennis Eckersley	1.50	.70
621	Tom Donohue	.15	.07
622	Randy Moffitt	.15	.07
623	Sal Bando	.40	.18
624	Bob Welch	.40	.18
625	Bill Buckner	.40	.18
626	Tigers Rookies	.15	.07
	Dave Steffen		
	Jerry Ujdur		
	Roger Weaver		
627	Luis Tiant	.40	.18
628	Vic Correll	.15	.07
629	Tony Armas	.40	.18
630	Steve Carlton	1.50	.70
631	Ron Jackson	.15	.07
632	Alan Bannister	.15	.07
633	Bill Lee	.40	.18
634	Doug Flynn	.15	.07

635 Bobby Bonds	.40	.18
636 Al Hrabosky	.15	.07
637 Jerry Narron	.15	.07
638 Checklist 606-726	.75	.35
639 Carney Lansford	.40	.18
640 Dave Parker	.40	.18
641 Mark Belanger	.15	.07
642 Vern Ruhle	.15	.07
643 Lloyd Moseby	.40	.18
644 Ramon Aviles DP	.10	.05
645 Rick Reuschel	.40	.18
646 Marvis Foley	.15	.07
647 Dick Drago	.15	.07
648 Darrell Evans	.40	.18
649 Manny Sarmiento	.15	.07
650 Bucky Dent	.40	.18
651 Pedro Guerrero	.75	.35
652 John Montague	.15	.07
653 Bill Fahey	.15	.07
654 Ray Burris	.15	.07
655 Dan Driessen	.15	.07
656 Jon Matlack	.15	.07
657 Mike Cubbage DP	.10	.05
658 Milt Wilcox	.15	.07
659 Brewers Rookies	.15	.07
John Flinn		
Ed Romero		
Ned Yost		
660 Gary Carter	1.50	.70
661 Orioles Team/Mgr.	.75	.35
Earl Weaver		
662 Red Sox Team/Mgr.	.75	.35
Ralph Houk		
663 Angels Team/Mgr.	.75	.35
Jim Fregosi		
664 White Sox Team/Mgr.	.75	.35
Tony LaRussa		
665 Indians Team/Mgr.	.75	.35
Dave Garcia		
666 Tigers Team/Mgr.	.75	.35
Sparky Anderson		
667 Royals Team/Mgr.	.75	.35
Jim Frey		
668 Brewers Team/Mgr.	.75	.35
Bob Rodgers		
669 Twins Team/Mgr.	.75	.35
John Goryl		
670 Yankees Team/Mgr.	.75	.35
Gene Michael		
671 A's Team/Mgr.	.75	.35
Billy Martin		
672 Mariners Team/Mgr.	.75	.35
Maury Wills		
673 Rangers Team/Mgr.	.75	.35
Don Zimmer		
674 Blue Jays Team/Mgr.	.75	.35
Bobby Mattick		
675 Braves Team/Mgr.	.75	.35
Bobby Cox		
676 Cubs Team/Mgr.	.75	.35
Joe Amalfitano		
677 Reds Team/Mgr.	.75	.35
John McNamara		
678 Astros Team/Mgr.	.75	.35
Bill Virdon		
679 Dodgers Team/Mgr.	.75	.35
Tom Lasorda		
680 Expos Team/Mgr.	.75	.35
Dick Williams		
681 Mets Team/Mgr.	.75	.35
Joe Torre		
682 Phillies Team/Mgr.	.75	.35
Dallas Green		
683 Pirates Team/Mgr.	.75	.35
Chuck Tanner		
684 Cardinals Team/Mgr.	.75	.35
Whitey Herzog		
685 Padres Team/Mgr.	.75	.35
Frank Howard		
686 Giants Team/Mgr.	.75	.35
Dave Bristol		
687 Jeff Jones	.15	.07
688 Kiko Garcia	.15	.07
689 Red Sox Rookies	1.50	.70
Bruce Hurst		
Keith MacWhorter		

Reid Nichols		
690 Bob Watson	.40	.18
691 Dick Ruthven	.15	.07
692 Lenny Randle	.15	.07
693 Steve Howe	.40	.18
694 Bud Harrelson DP	.15	.07
695 Kent Tekulve	.40	.18
696 Alan Ashby	.15	.07
697 Rick Waits	.15	.07
698 Mike Jorgensen	.15	.07
699 Glenn Abbott	.15	.07
700 George Brett	4.00	1.80
701 Joe Rudi	.40	.18
702 George Medich	.15	.07
703 Alvis Woods	.15	.07
704 Bill Travers DP	.10	.05
705 Ted Simmons	.40	.18
706 Dave Ford	.15	.07
707 Dave Cash	.15	.07
708 Doyle Alexander	.15	.07
709 Alan Trammell	1.50	.70
710 Ron LeFlore DP	.15	.07
711 Joe Ferguson	.15	.07
712 Bill Bonham	.15	.07
713 Bill North	.15	.07
714 Pete Redfern	.15	.07
715 Bill Madlock	.40	.18
716 Glenn Borgmann	.15	.07
717 Jim Barr DP	.10	.05
718 Larry Biittner	.15	.07
719 Sparky Lyle	.40	.18
720 Fred Lynn	.40	.18
721 Toby Harrah	.40	.18
722 Joe Niekro	.40	.18
723 Bruce Bochte	.15	.07
724 Lou Piniella	.40	.18
725 Steve Rogers	.15	.07
726 Rick Monday	.40	.18

1981 Topps Traded

For the first time since 1976, Topps issued a 132-card factory boxed "traded" set in 1981, issued exclusively through hobby dealers. This set was sequentially numbered, alphabetically, from 727 to 858 and carries the same design as the regular issue 1981 Topps set. There are no key Rookie Cards in this set although Tim Raines, Jeff Reardon, and Fernando Valenzuela are depicted in their rookie year for cards. The key extended Rookie Card in the set is Danny Ainge.

	NRMT	VG-E
COMPLETE SET (132)	30.00	13.50
COMMON CARD (727-858)	.25	.11
MINOR STARS	1.00	.45
SEMISTARS	3.00	1.35
727 Danny Ainge	5.00	2.20
728 Doyle Alexander	.25	.11
729 Gary Alexander	.25	.11

730 Bill Almon	.25	.11
731 Joaquin Andujar	1.00	.45
732 Bob Bailor	.25	.11
733 Juan Beniquez	.25	.11
734 Dave Bergman	.25	.11
735 Tony Bernazard	.25	.11
736 Larry Biittner	.25	.11
737 Doug Bird	.25	.11
738 Bert Blyleven	3.00	1.35
739 Mark Bomback	.25	.11
740 Bobby Bonds	1.00	.45
741 Rick Bosetti	.25	.11
742 Hubie Brooks	1.00	.45
743 Rick Burleson	.25	.11
744 Ray Burris	.25	.11
745 Jeff Burroughs	.25	.11
746 Enos Cabell	.25	.11
747 Ken Clay	.25	.11
748 Mark Clear	.25	.11
749 Larry Cox	.25	.11
750 Hector Cruz	.25	.11
751 Victor Cruz	.25	.11
752 Mike Cubbage	.25	.11
753 Dick Davis	.25	.11
754 Brian Doyle	.25	.11
755 Dick Drago	.25	.11
756 Leon Durham	1.00	.45
757 Jim Dwyer	.25	.11
758 Dave Edwards UER	.25	.11
No birthdate on card		
759 Jim Essian	.25	.11
760 Bill Fahey	.25	.11
761 Rollie Fingers	3.00	1.35
762 Carlton Fisk	5.00	2.20
763 Barry Foote	.25	.11
764 Ken Forsch	.25	.11
765 Kiko Garcia	.25	.11
766 Cesar Geronimo	.25	.11
767 Gary Gray	.25	.11
768 Mickey Hatcher	1.00	.45
769 Steve Henderson	.25	.11
770 Marc Hill	.25	.11
771 Butch Hobson	.25	.11
772 Rick Honeycutt	.25	.11
773 Roy Howell	.25	.11
774 Mike Ivie	.25	.11
775 Roy Lee Jackson	.25	.11
776 Cliff Johnson	.25	.11
777 Randy Jones	.25	.11
778 Ruppert Jones	.25	.11
779 Mick Kelleher	.25	.11
780 Terry Kennedy	.25	.11
781 Dave Kingman	3.00	1.35
782 Bob Knepper	.25	.11
783 Ken Kravec	.25	.11
784 Bob Lacey	.25	.11
785 Dennis Lamp	.25	.11
786 Rafael Landestoy	.25	.11
787 Ken Landreaux	.25	.11
788 Carney Lansford	1.00	.45
789 Dave LaRoche	.25	.11
790 Joe Lefebvre	.25	.11
791 Ron LeFlore	1.00	.45
792 Randy Lerch	.25	.11
793 Sixto Lezcano	.25	.11
794 John Littlefield	.25	.11
795 Mike Lum	.25	.11
796 Greg Luzinski	1.00	.45
797 Fred Lynn	1.00	.45
798 Jerry Martin	.25	.11
799 Buck Martinez	.25	.11
800 Gary Matthews	1.00	.45
801 Mario Mendoza	.25	.11
802 Larry Milbourne	.25	.11
803 Rick Miller	.25	.11
804 John Montefusco	.25	.11
805 Jerry Morales	.25	.11
806 Jose Morales	.25	.11
807 Joe Morgan	4.00	1.80
808 Jerry Mumphrey	.25	.11
809 Gene Nelson	.25	.11
810 Ed Ott	.25	.11
811 Bob Owchinko	.25	.11
812 Gaylord Perry	4.00	1.80
813 Mike Phillips	.25	.11
814 Darrell Porter	.25	.11

☐ 815 Mike Proly	.25	.11
☐ 816 Tim Raines	6.00	2.70
☐ 817 Lenny Randle	.25	.11
☐ 818 Doug Rau	.25	.11
☐ 819 Jeff Reardon	3.00	1.35
☐ 820 Ken Reitz	.25	.11
☐ 821 Steve Renko	.25	.11
☐ 822 Rick Reuschel	1.00	.45
☐ 823 Dave Revering	.25	.11
☐ 824 Dave Roberts	.25	.11
☐ 825 Leon Roberts	.25	.11
☐ 826 Joe Rudi	1.00	.45
☐ 827 Kevin Saucier	.25	.11
☐ 828 Tony Scott	.25	.11
☐ 829 Bob Shirley	.25	.11
☐ 830 Ted Simmons	1.00	.45
☐ 831 Lary Sorensen	.25	.11
☐ 832 Jim Spencer	.25	.11
☐ 833 Harry Spilman	.25	.11
☐ 834 Fred Stanley	.25	.11
☐ 835 Rusty Staub	1.00	.45
☐ 836 Bill Stein	.25	.11
☐ 837 Joe Strain	.25	.11
☐ 838 Bruce Sutter	1.00	.45
☐ 839 Don Sutton	4.00	1.80
☐ 840 Steve Swisher	.25	.11
☐ 841 Frank Tanana	1.00	.45
☐ 842 Gene Tenace	.25	.11
☐ 843 Jason Thompson	.25	.11
☐ 844 Dickie Thon	1.00	.45
☐ 845 Bill Travers	.25	.11
☐ 846 Tom Underwood	.25	.11
☐ 847 John Urrea	.25	.11
☐ 848 Mike Vail	.25	.11
☐ 849 Ellis Valentine	.25	.11
☐ 850 Fernando Valenzuela	2.70	
☐ 851 Pete Vuckovich	1.00	.45
☐ 852 Mark Wagner	.25	.11
☐ 853 Bob Walk	1.00	.45
☐ 854 Claudell Washington	.25	.11
☐ 855 Dave Winfield	5.00	2.20
☐ 856 Geoff Zahn	.25	.11
☐ 857 Richie Zisk	.25	.11
☐ 858 Checklist 727-858	.25	.11

1982 Topps

The cards in this 792-card set measure the standard size. The 1982 baseball series was the first of the largest sets Topps issued at one printing. The 66-card increase from the previous year's total eliminated the "double print" practice, that had occurred in every regular issue since 1978. Cards 1-6 depict Highlights of the strike-shortened 1981 season, cards 161-168 picture League Leaders, and there are subsets of AL (547-557) and NL (337-347) All-Stars (AS). The abbreviation "SA" in the checklist is given for the 40 "Super Action" cards introduced in this set. The team cards are actually Team Leader

(TL) cards picturing the batting average and ERA leader for that team with a checklist back. All 26 of these cards were available from Topps on a perforated sheet through an offer on wax pack wrappers. Cards were primarily distributed in 15-card wax packs and 51-card rack packs. Notable Rookie Cards include Brett Butler, Chili Davis, Cal Ripken Jr., Lee Smith, and Dave Stewart. Be careful when purchasing blank-back Cal Ripken Jr. Rookie Cards. Those cards are undoubtedly counterfeit.

	NRMT	VG-E
COMPLETE SET (792)	120.00	55.00
COMMON CARD (1-792)	.15	.07
MINOR STARS	.30	.14
SEMISTARS	.60	.25
UNLISTED STARS	1.25	.55
SUBSET CARDS HALF VALUE OF BASE CARDS		
BEWARE RIPKEN BLANK-BACK FAKES		

☐ 1 Steve Carlton HL	1.00		.45
	Sets new NL strikeout record		
☐ 2 Ron Davis HL		.30	.14
	Fans 8 straight in relief		
☐ 3 Tim Raines HL	.60		.25
	71 steals as rookie		
☐ 4 Pete Rose HL		1.00	.45
	Sets NL hit mark		
☐ 5 Nolan Ryan HL	3.00		1.35
	Pitches fifth no-hitter		
☐ 6 Fernando Valenzuela HL	.30		.14
	8 shutouts as rookie		
☐ 7 Scott Sanderson		.15	.07
☐ 8 Rich Dauer		.15	.07
☐ 9 Ron Guidry		.30	.14
☐ 10 Ron Guidry SA		.30	.14
☐ 11 Gary Alexander		.15	.07
☐ 12 Moose Haas		.15	.07
☐ 13 Lamar Johnson		.15	.07
☐ 14 Steve Howe		.15	.07
☐ 15 Ellis Valentine		.15	.07
☐ 16 Steve Comer		.15	.07
☐ 17 Darrell Evans		.30	.14
☐ 18 Fernando Arroyo		.15	.07
☐ 19 Ernie Whitt		.15	.07
☐ 20 Garry Maddox		.15	.07
☐ 21 Orioles Rookies	70.00		32.00
	Bob Bonner		
	Cal Ripken		
	Jeff Schneider		
☐ 22 Jim Beattie		.15	.07
☐ 23 Willie Hernandez		.30	.14
☐ 24 Dave Frost		.15	.07
☐ 25 Jerry Remy		.15	.07
☐ 26 Jorge Orta		.15	.07
☐ 27 Tom Herr		.30	.14
☐ 28 John Urrea		.15	.07
☐ 29 Dwayne Murphy		.15	.07
☐ 30 Tom Seaver		1.50	.70
☐ 31 Tom Seaver SA		.60	.25
☐ 32 Gene Garber		.15	.07
☐ 33 Jerry Morales		.15	.07
☐ 34 Joe Sambito		.15	.07
☐ 35 Willie Aikens		.15	.07
☐ 36 Rangers TL	.60		.25
	BA: Al Oliver		
	Pitching: Doc Medich		
☐ 37 Dan Graham		.15	.07
☐ 38 Charlie Lea		.15	.07
☐ 39 Lou Whitaker		1.25	.55
☐ 40 Dave Parker		.30	.14
☐ 41 Dave Parker SA		.30	.14
☐ 42 Rick Sofield		.15	.07
☐ 43 Mike Cubbage		.15	.07
☐ 44 Britt Burns		.15	.07
☐ 45 Rick Cerone		.15	.07
☐ 46 Jerry Augustine		.15	.07
☐ 47 Jeff Leonard		.15	.07
☐ 48 Bobby Castillo		.15	.07

☐ 49 Alvis Woods		.15	.07
☐ 50 Buddy Bell		.30	.14
☐ 51 Cubs Rookies	.60		.25
	Jay Howell		
	Carlos Lezcano		
	Ty Waller		
☐ 52 Larry Andersen		.15	.07
☐ 53 Greg Gross		.15	.07
☐ 54 Ron Hassey		.15	.07
☐ 55 Rick Burleson		.15	.07
☐ 56 Mark Littell		.15	.07
☐ 57 Craig Reynolds		.15	.07
☐ 58 John D'Acquisto		.15	.07
☐ 59 Rich Gedman		.30	.14
☐ 60 Tony Armas		.15	.07
☐ 61 Tommy Boggs		.15	.07
☐ 62 Mike Tyson		.15	.07
☐ 63 Mario Soto		.15	.07
☐ 64 Lynn Jones		.15	.07
☐ 65 Terry Kennedy		.15	.07
☐ 66 Astros TL	.20		.90
	BA: Art Howe		
	Pitching: Nolan Ryan		
☐ 67 Rich Gale		.15	.07
☐ 68 Roy Howell		.15	.07
☐ 69 Al Williams		.15	.07
☐ 70 Tim Raines		1.25	.55
☐ 71 Roy Lee Jackson		.15	.07
☐ 72 Rick Auerbach		.15	.07
☐ 73 Buddy Solomon		.15	.07
☐ 74 Bob Clark		.15	.07
☐ 75 Tommy John	.60		.25
☐ 76 Greg Pryor		.15	.07
☐ 77 Miguel Dilone		.15	.07
☐ 78 George Medich		.15	.07
☐ 79 Bob Bailor		.15	.07
☐ 80 Jim Palmer		1.25	.55
☐ 81 Jim Palmer SA	.60		.25
☐ 82 Bob Welch		.30	.14
☐ 83 Yankees Rookies	.60		.25
	Steve Balboni		
	Andy McGaffigan		
	Andre Robertson		
☐ 84 Rennie Stennett		.15	.07
☐ 85 Lynn McGlothen		.15	.07
☐ 86 Dane Iorg		.15	.07
☐ 87 Matt Keough		.15	.07
☐ 88 Biff Pocoroba		.15	.07
☐ 89 Steve Henderson		.15	.07
☐ 90 Nolan Ryan		6.00	2.70
☐ 91 Carney Lansford		.30	.14
☐ 92 Brad Havens		.15	.07
☐ 93 Larry Hisle		.15	.07
☐ 94 Andy Hassler		.15	.07
☐ 95 Ozzie Smith		3.00	1.35
☐ 96 Royals TL	1.25		.55
	BA: George Brett		
	Pitching: Larry Gura		
☐ 97 Paul Moskau		.15	.07
☐ 98 Terry Bulling		.15	.07
☐ 99 Barry Bonnell		.15	.07
☐ 100 Mike Schmidt		1.50	.70
☐ 101 Mike Schmidt SA		.75	.35
☐ 102 Dan Briggs		.15	.07
☐ 103 Bob Lacey		.15	.07
☐ 104 Rance Mullinicks		.15	.07
☐ 105 Kirk Gibson		1.00	.45
☐ 106 Enrique Romo		.15	.07
☐ 107 Wayne Krenchicki		.15	.07
☐ 108 Bob Sykes		.15	.07
☐ 109 Dave Revering		.15	.07
☐ 110 Carlton Fisk		1.50	.70
☐ 111 Carlton Fisk SA	.60		.25
☐ 112 Billy Sample		.15	.07
☐ 113 Steve McCatty		.15	.07
☐ 114 Ken Landreaux		.15	.07
☐ 115 Gaylord Perry		1.25	.55
☐ 116 Jim Wohlford		.15	.07
☐ 117 Rawly Eastwick		.15	.07
☐ 118 Expos Rookies	.30		.14
	Terry Francona		
	Brad Mills		
	Bryn Smith		
☐ 119 Joe Pittman		.15	.07
☐ 120 Gary Lucas		.15	.07
☐ 121 Ed Lynch		.15	.07

□ 122	Jamie Easterly UER	.15	.07
	(Photo actually		
	Reggie Cleveland)		
□ 123	Danny Goodwin	.15	.07
□ 124	Reid Nichols	.15	.07
□ 125	Danny Ainge	1.50	.70
□ 126	Braves TL	.60	.25
	BA: Claudell Washington		
	Pitching: Rick Mahler		
□ 127	Lonnie Smith	.30	.14
□ 128	Frank Pastore	.15	.07
□ 129	Checklist 1-132	.60	.25
□ 130	Julio Cruz	.15	.07
□ 131	Stan Bahnsen	.15	.07
□ 132	Lee May	.30	.14
□ 133	Pat Underwood	.15	.07
□ 134	Dan Ford	.15	.07
□ 135	Andy Rincon	.15	.07
□ 136	Lenn Sakata	.15	.07
□ 137	George Cappuzzello.....	.15	.07
□ 138	Tony Pena	.30	.14
□ 139	Jeff Jones	.15	.07
□ 140	Ron LeFlore	.30	.14
□ 141	Indians Rookies	.30	.14
	Chris Bando		
	Tom Brennan		
	Von Hayes		
□ 142	Dave LaRoche	.15	.07
□ 143	Mookie Wilson	.30	.14
□ 144	Fred Breining	.15	.07
□ 145	Bob Horner	.30	.14
□ 146	Mike Griffin	.15	.07
□ 147	Denny Walling	.15	.07
□ 148	Mickey Klutts	.15	.07
□ 149	Pat Putnam	.15	.07
□ 150	Ted Simmons	.30	.14
□ 151	Dave Edwards	.15	.07
□ 152	Ramon Aviles	.15	.07
□ 153	Roger Erickson	.15	.07
□ 154	Dennis Werth	.15	.07
□ 155	Otto Velez	.15	.07
□ 156	Oakland A's TL	.60	.25
	BA: Rickey Henderson		
	Pitching: Steve McCatty		
□ 157	Steve Crawford	.15	.07
□ 158	Brian Downing	.15	.07
□ 159	Larry Biittner	.15	.07
□ 160	Luis Tiant	.30	.14
□ 161	Batting Leaders	.30	.14
	Bill Madlock		
	Carney Lansford		
□ 162	Home Run Leaders .	1.25	.55
	Mike Schmidt		
	Tony Armas		
	Dwight Evans		
	Bobby Grich		
	Eddie Murray		
□ 163	RBI Leaders..............	1.25	.55
	Mike Schmidt		
	Eddie Murray		
□ 164	Stolen Base Leaders	1.25	.55
	Tim Raines		
	Rickey Henderson		
□ 165	Victory Leaders	.60	.25
	Tom Seaver		
	Denny Martinez		
	Steve McCatty		
	Jack Morris		
	Pete Vuckovich		
□ 166	Strikeout Leaders	.30	.14
	Fernando Valenzuela		
	Len Barker		
□ 167	ERA Leaders	2.00	.90
	Nolan Ryan		
	Steve McCatty		
□ 168	Leading Firemen	.60	.25
	Bruce Sutter		
	Rollie Fingers		
□ 169	Charlie Leibrandt	.15	.07
□ 170	Jim Bibby	.15	.07
□ 171	Giants Rookies	2.00	.90
	Bob Brenly		
	Chili Davis		
	Bob Tufts		
□ 172	Bill Gullickson	.15	.07
□ 173	Jamie Quirk	.15	.07

□ 174	Dave Ford	.15	.07
□ 175	Jerry Mumphrey	.15	.07
□ 176	Dewey Robinson	.15	.07
□ 177	John Ellis..................	.15	.07
□ 178	Dyar Miller	.15	.07
□ 179	Steve Garvey	.60	.25
□ 180	Steve Garvey SA	.30	.14
□ 181	Silvio Martinez............	.15	.07
□ 182	Larry Herndon	.15	.07
□ 183	Mike Proly	.15	.07
□ 184	Mick Kelleher	.15	.07
□ 185	Phil Niekro................	1.25	.55
□ 186	Cardinals TL	.60	.25
	BA: Keith Hernandez		
	Pitching: Bob Forsch		
□ 187	Jeff Newman	.15	.07
□ 188	Randy Martz	.15	.07
□ 189	Glenn Hoffman	.15	.07
□ 190	J.R. Richard	.30	.14
□ 191	Tim Wallach	1.25	.55
□ 192	Broderick Perkins	.15	.07
□ 193	Darrell Jackson	.15	.07
□ 194	Mike Vail	.15	.07
□ 195	Paul Molitor	2.00	.90
□ 196	Willie Upshaw	.15	.07
□ 197	Shane Rawley	.15	.07
□ 198	Chris Speier	.15	.07
□ 199	Don Aase	.15	.07
□ 200	George Brett	2.50	1.10
□ 201	George Brett SA	1.25	.55
□ 202	Rick Manning	.15	.07
□ 203	Blue Jays Rookies	.60	.25
	Jesse Barfield		
	Brian Milner		
	Boomer Wells		
□ 204	Gary Roenicke............	.15	.07
□ 205	Neil Allen	.15	.07
□ 206	Tony Bernazard	.15	.07
□ 207	Rod Scurry	.15	.07
□ 208	Bobby Murcer	.30	.14
□ 209	Gary Lavelle	.15	.07
□ 210	Keith Hernandez	.30	.14
□ 211	Dan Petry	.15	.07
□ 212	Mario Mendoza	.15	.07
□ 213	Dave Stewart	1.50	.70
□ 214	Brian Asselstine..........	.15	.07
□ 215	Mike Krukow	.15	.07
□ 216	White Sox TL..............	.60	.25
	BA: Chet Lemon		
	Pitching: Dennis Lamp		
□ 217	Bo McLaughlin	.15	.07
□ 218	Dave Roberts	.15	.07
□ 219	John Curtis	.15	.07
□ 220	Manny Trillo	.15	.07
□ 221	Jim Slaton	.15	.07
□ 222	Butch Wynegar	.15	.07
□ 223	Lloyd Moseby	.15	.07
□ 224	Bruce Bochte	.15	.07
□ 225	Mike Torrez	.15	.07
□ 226	Checklist 133-264	.60	.25
□ 227	Ray Burris	.15	.07
□ 228	Sam Mejias	.15	.07
□ 229	Geoff Zahn................	.15	.07
□ 230	Willie Wilson	.30	.14
□ 231	Phillies Rookies..........	.60	.25
	Mark Davis		
	Bob Dernier		
	Ozzie Virgil		
□ 232	Terry Crowley	.15	.07
□ 233	Duane Kuiper..............	.15	.07
□ 234	Ron Hodges	.15	.07
□ 235	Mike Easler	.15	.07
□ 236	John Martin	.15	.07
□ 237	Rusty Kuntz................	.15	.07
□ 238	Kevin Saucier	.15	.07
□ 239	Jon Matlack................	.15	.07
□ 240	Bucky Dent	.30	.14
□ 241	Bucky Dent SA	.15	.07
□ 242	Milt May	.15	.07
□ 243	Bob Owchinko	.15	.07
□ 244	Rufino Linares	.15	.07
□ 245	Ken Reitz..................	.15	.07
□ 246	New York Mets TL.........	.60	.25
	BA: Hubie Brooks		
	Pitching: Mike Scott		
□ 247	Pedro Guerrero	.30	.14

□ 248	Frank LaCorte	.15	.07
□ 249	Tim Flannery	.15	.07
□ 250	Tug McGraw	.30	.14
□ 251	Fred Lynn..................	.30	.14
□ 252	Fred Lynn SA	.15	.07
□ 253	Chuck Baker	.15	.07
□ 254	Jorge Bell	1.25	.55
□ 255	Tony Perez	1.25	.55
□ 256	Tony Perez SA..............	.60	.25
□ 257	Larry Harlow	.15	.07
□ 258	Bo Diaz	.15	.07
□ 259	Rodney Scott..............	.15	.07
□ 260	Bruce Sutter	.30	.14
□ 261	Tigers Rookies UER	.15	.07
	Howard Bailey		
	Marty Castillo		
	Dave Rucker		
	(Rucker photo act-		
	ually Roger Weaver)		
□ 262	Doug Bair	.15	.07
□ 263	Victor Cruz	.15	.07
□ 264	Dan Quisenberry	.30	.14
□ 265	Al Bumbry	.15	.07
□ 266	Rick Leach................	.15	.07
□ 267	Kurt Bevacqua............	.15	.07
□ 268	Rickey Keeton	.15	.07
□ 269	Jim Essian	.15	.07
□ 270	Rusty Staub	.30	.14
□ 271	Larry Bradford............	.15	.07
□ 272	Bump Wills................	.15	.07
□ 273	Doug Bird	.15	.07
□ 274	Bob Ojeda	.60	.25
□ 275	Bob Watson	.30	.14
□ 276	Angels TL..................	.60	.25
	BA: Rod Carew		
	Pitching: Ken Forsch		
□ 277	Terry Puhl	.15	.07
□ 278	John Littlefield............	.15	.07
□ 279	Bill Russell................	.30	.14
□ 280	Ben Oglivie	.15	.07
□ 281	John Verhoeven	.15	.07
□ 282	Ken Macha	.15	.07
□ 283	Brian Allard	.15	.07
□ 284	Bob Grich	.30	.14
□ 285	Sparky Lyle	.30	.14
□ 286	Bill Fahey	.15	.07
□ 287	Alan Bannister	.15	.07
□ 288	Garry Templeton	.15	.07
□ 289	Bob Stanley	.15	.07
□ 290	Ken Singleton	.30	.14
□ 291	Pirates Rookies	.30	.14
	Vance Law		
	Bob Long		
	Johnny Ray		
□ 292	David Palmer	.15	.07
□ 293	Rob Picciolo	.15	.07
□ 294	Mike LaCoss	.15	.07
□ 295	Jason Thompson	.15	.07
□ 296	Bob Walk	.15	.07
□ 297	Clint Hurdle	.15	.07
□ 298	Danny Darwin	.15	.07
□ 299	Steve Trout	.15	.07
□ 300	Reggie Jackson	1.50	.70
□ 301	Reggie Jackson SA	.60	.25
□ 302	Doug Flynn	.15	.07
□ 303	Bill Caudill................	.15	.07
□ 304	Johnnie LeMaster	.15	.07
□ 305	Don Sutton	1.25	.55
□ 306	Don Sutton SA	.60	.25
□ 307	Randy Bass	.15	.07
□ 308	Charlie Moore	.15	.07
□ 309	Pete Redfern	.15	.07
□ 310	Mike Hargrove............	.30	.14
□ 311	Dodgers TL................	.60	.25
	BA: Dusty Baker		
	Pitching: Burt Hooton		
□ 312	Lenny Randle	.15	.07
□ 313	John Harris................	.15	.07
□ 314	Buck Martinez	.15	.07
□ 315	Burt Hooton	.15	.07
□ 316	Steve Braun	.15	.07
□ 317	Dick Ruthven..............	.15	.07
□ 318	Mike Heath	.15	.07
□ 319	Dave Rozema	.15	.07
□ 320	Chris Chambliss	.30	.14
□ 321	Chris Chambliss SA......	.15	.07

322	Garry Hancock	.15	.07
323	Bill Lee	.30	.14
324	Steve Dillard	.15	.07
325	Jose Cruz	.30	.14
326	Pete Falcone	.15	.07
327	Joe Nolan	.15	.07
328	Ed Farmer	.15	.07
329	U.L. Washington	.15	.07
330	Rick Wise	.15	.07
331	Benny Ayala	.15	.07
332	Don Robinson	.15	.07
333	Brewers Rookies	.15	.07
	Frank DiPino		
	Marshall Edwards		
	Chuck Porter		
334	Aurelio Rodriguez	.15	.07
335	Jim Sundberg	.30	.14
336	Mariners TL	.60	.25
	BA: Tom Paciorek		
	Pitching: Glenn Abbott		
337	Pete Rose AS	1.00	.45
338	Dave Lopes AS	.30	.14
339	Mike Schmidt AS	.75	.35
340	Dave Concepcion AS	.30	.14
341	Andre Dawson AS	.60	.25
342A	George Foster AS	.30	.14
	(With autograph)		
342B	George Foster AS	1.25	.55
	(W/o autograph)		
343	Dave Parker AS	.30	.14
344	Gary Carter AS	.30	.14
345	Fernando Valenzuela AS	.30	.14
346	Tom Seaver AS ERR	1.25	.55
	("t ed)		
346B	Tom Seaver AS COR	1.25	.55
	("tied)		
347	Bruce Sutter AS	.30	.14
348	Derrel Thomas	.15	.07
349	George Frazier	.15	.07
350	Thad Bosley	.15	.07
351	Reds Rookies	.15	.07
	Scott Brown		
	Geoff Combe		
	Paul Householder		
352	Dick Davis	.15	.07
353	Jack O'Connor	.15	.07
354	Roberto Ramos	.15	.07
355	Dwight Evans	.60	.25
356	Denny Lewallyn	.15	.07
357	Butch Hobson	.15	.07
358	Mike Parrott	.15	.07
359	Jim Dwyer	.15	.07
360	Len Barker	.15	.07
361	Rafael Landestoy	.15	.07
362	Jim Wright UER	.15	.07
	(Wrong Jim Wright pictured)		
363	Bob Molinaro	.15	.07
364	Doyle Alexander	.15	.07
365	Bill Madlock	.30	.14
366	Padres TL	.60	.25
	BA: Luis Salazar		
	Pitching: Juan Eichelberger		
367	Jim Kaat	.30	.14
368	Alex Trevino	.15	.07
369	Champ Summers	.15	.07
370	Mike Norris	.15	.07
371	Jerry Don Gleaton	.15	.07
372	Luis Gomez	.15	.07
373	Gene Nelson	.15	.07
374	Tim Blackwell	.15	.07
375	Dusty Baker	.60	.25
376	Chris Welsh	.15	.07
377	Kiko Garcia	.15	.07
378	Mike Caldwell	.15	.07
379	Rob Wilfong	.15	.07
380	Dave Stieb	.30	.14
381	Red Sox Rookies	.30	.14
	Bruce Hurst		
	Dave Schmidt		
	Julio Valdez		
382	Joe Simpson	.15	.07
383A	Pascual Perez ERR	8.00	3.60
	(No position on front)		
383B	Pascual Perez COR :.	.30	.14
384	Keith Moreland	.15	.07
385	Ken Forsch	.15	.07
386	Jerry White	.15	.07
387	Tom Veryzer	.15	.07
388	Joe Rudi	.15	.07
389	George Vukovich	.15	.07
390	Eddie Murray	2.00	.90
391	Dave Tobik	.15	.07
392	Rick Bosetti	.15	.07
393	Al Hrabosky	.15	.07
394	Checklist 265-396	.60	.25
395	Omar Moreno	.15	.07
396	Twins TL	.60	.25
	BA: John Castino		
	Fernando Arroyo		
397	Ken Brett	.15	.07
398	Mike Squires	.15	.07
399	Pat Zachry	.15	.07
400	Johnny Bench	1.50	.70
401	Johnny Bench SA	.60	.25
402	Bill Stein	.15	.07
403	Jim Tracy	.15	.07
404	Dickie Thon	.15	.07
405	Rick Reuschel	.30	.14
406	Al Holland	.15	.07
407	Danny Boone	.15	.07
408	Ed Romero	.15	.07
409	Don Cooper	.15	.07
410	Ron Cey	.30	.14
411	Ron Cey SA	.15	.07
412	Luis Leal	.15	.07
413	Dan Meyer	.15	.07
414	Elias Sosa	.15	.07
415	Don Baylor	.60	.25
416	Marty Bystrom	.15	.07
417	Pat Kelly	.15	.07
418	Rangers Rookies	.15	.07
	John Butcher		
	Bobby Johnson		
	Dave Schmidt		
419	Steve Stone	.30	.14
420	George Hendrick	.15	.07
421	Mark Clear	.15	.07
422	Cliff Johnson	.15	.07
423	Stan Papi	.15	.07
424	Bruce Benedict	.15	.07
425	John Candelaria	.15	.07
426	Orioles TL	.60	.25
	BA: Eddie Murray		
	Pitching: Sammy Stewart		
427	Ron Oester	.15	.07
428	LaMarr Hoyt	.15	.07
429	John Wathan	.15	.07
430	Vida Blue	.30	.14
431	Vida Blue SA	.15	.07
432	Mike Scott	.30	.14
433	Alan Ashby	.15	.07
434	Joe Lefebvre	.15	.07
435	Robin Yount	2.00	.90
436	Joe Strain	.15	.07
437	Juan Berenguer	.15	.07
438	Pete Mackanin	.15	.07
439	Dave Righetti	1.25	.55
440	Jeff Burroughs	.15	.07
441	Astros Rookies	.15	.07
	Danny Heep		
	Billy Smith		
	Bobby Sprowl		
442	Bruce Kison	.15	.07
443	Mark Wagner	.15	.07
444	Terry Forster	.15	.07
445	Larry Parrish	.15	.07
446	Wayne Garland	.15	.07
447	Darrell Porter	.30	.14
448	Darrell Porter SA	.15	.07
449	Luis Aguayo	.15	.07
450	Jack Morris	.30	.14
451	Ed Miller	.15	.07
452	Lee Smith	4.00	1.80
453	Art Howe	.15	.07
454	Rick Langford	.15	.07
455	Tom Burgmeier	.15	.07
456	Chicago Cubs TL	.60	.25
	BA: Bill Buckner		
	Pitching: Randy Martz		
457	Tim Stoddard	.15	.07
458	Willie Montanez	.15	.07
459	Bruce Berenyi	.15	.07
460	Jack Clark	.30	.14
461	Rich Dotson	.15	.07
462	Dave Chalk	.15	.07
463	Jim Kern	.15	.07
464	Juan Bonilla	.15	.07
465	Lee Mazzilli	.15	.07
466	Randy Lerch	.15	.07
467	Mickey Hatcher	.15	.07
468	Floyd Bannister	.15	.07
469	Ed Ott	.15	.07
470	John Mayberry	.15	.07
471	Royals Rookies	.15	.07
	Atlee Hammaker		
	Mike Jones		
	Darryl Motley		
472	Oscar Gamble	.15	.07
473	Mike Stanton	.15	.07
474	Ken Oberkfell	.15	.07
475	Alan Trammell	1.25	.55
476	Brian Kingman	.15	.07
477	Steve Yeager	.15	.07
478	Ray Searage	.15	.07
479	Rowland Office	.15	.07
480	Steve Carlton	1.25	.55
481	Steve Carlton SA	.60	.25
482	Glenn Hubbard	.15	.07
483	Gary Woods	.15	.07
484	Ivan DeJesus	.15	.07
485	Kent Tekulve	.30	.14
486	Yankees TL	.30	.14
	BA: Jerry Mumphrey		
	Pitching: Tommy John		
487	Bob McClure	.15	.07
488	Ron Jackson	.15	.07
489	Rick Dempsey	.30	.14
490	Dennis Eckersley	1.25	.55
491	Checklist 397-528	.60	.25
492	Joe Price	.15	.07
493	Chet Lemon	.15	.07
494	Hubie Brooks	.30	.14
495	Dennis Leonard	.15	.07
496	Johnny Grubb	.15	.07
497	Jim Anderson	.15	.07
498	Dave Bergman	.15	.07
499	Paul Mirabella	.15	.07
500	Rod Carew	1.25	.55
501	Rod Carew SA	.60	.25
502	Braves Rookies	2.00	.90
	Steve Bedrosian UER		
	(Photo actually Larry Owen)		
	Brett Butler		
	Larry Owen		
503	Julio Gonzalez	.15	.07
504	Rick Peters	.15	.07
505	Graig Nettles	.30	.14
506	Graig Nettles SA	.15	.07
507	Terry Harper	.15	.07
508	Jody Davis	.15	.07
509	Harry Spilman	.15	.07
510	Fernando Valenzuela	.60	.25
511	Ruppert Jones	.15	.07
512	Jerry Dybzinski	.15	.07
513	Rick Rhoden	.15	.07
514	Joe Ferguson	.15	.07
515	Larry Bowa	.30	.14
516	Larry Bowa SA	.15	.07
517	Mark Brouhard	.15	.07
518	Garth Iorg	.15	.07
519	Glenn Adams	.15	.07
520	Mike Flanagan	.30	.14
521	Bill Almon	.15	.07
522	Chuck Rainey	.15	.07
523	Gary Gray	.15	.07
524	Tom Hausman	.15	.07
525	Ray Knight	.30	.14
526	Expos TL	.60	.25
	BA: Warren Cromartie		
	Pitching: Bill Gullickson		
527	John Henry Johnson	.15	.07
528	Matt Alexander	.15	.07
529	Allen Ripley	.15	.07
530	Dickie Noles	.15	.07

- □ 531 A's Rookies .15 .07
  Rich Bordi
  Mark Budaska
  Kelvin Moore
- □ 532 Toby Harrah .30 .14
- □ 533 Joaquin Andujar .30 .14
- □ 534 Dave McKay .15 .07
- □ 535 Lance Parrish .60 .25
- □ 536 Rafael Ramirez .15 .07
- □ 537 Doug Capilla .15 .07
- □ 538 Lou Piniella .30 .14
- □ 539 Vern Ruhle .15 .07
- □ 540 Andre Dawson 1.25 .55
- □ 541 Barry Evans .15 .07
- □ 542 Ned Yost .15 .07
- □ 543 Bill Robinson .15 .07
- □ 544 Larry Christenson .15 .07
- □ 545 Reggie Smith .30 .14
- □ 546 Reggie Smith SA .15 .07
- □ 547 Rod Carew AS 1.25 .55
- □ 548 Willie Randolph AS .30 .14
- □ 549 George Brett AS 1.25 .55
- □ 550 Bucky Dent AS .30 .14
- □ 551 Reggie Jackson AS .60 .25
- □ 552 Ken Singleton AS .30 .14
- □ 553 Dave Winfield AS .60 .25
- □ 554 Carlton Fisk AS .25 .25
- □ 555 Scott McGregor AS .15 .07
- □ 556 Jack Morris AS .30 .14
- □ 557 Rich Gossage AS .30 .14
- □ 558 John Tudor .30 .14
- □ 559 Indians TL .30 .14
  BA: Mike Hargrove
  Pitching: Bert Blyleven
- □ 560 Doug Corbett .15 .07
- □ 561 Cardinals Rookies .15 .07
  Glenn Brummer
  Luis DeLeon
  Gene Roof
- □ 562 Mike O'Berry .15 .07
- □ 563 Ross Baumgarten .15 .07
- □ 564 Doug DeCinces .30 .14
- □ 565 Jackson Todd .15 .07
- □ 566 Mike Jorgensen .15 .07
- □ 567 Bob Babcock .15 .07
- □ 568 Joe Pettini .15 .07
- □ 569 Willie Randolph .30 .14
- □ 570 Willie Randolph SA .30 .14
- □ 571 Glenn Abbott .15 .07
- □ 572 Juan Beniquez .15 .07
- □ 573 Rick Waits .15 .07
- □ 574 Mike Ramsey .15 .07
- □ 575 Al Cowens .15 .07
- □ 576 Giants TL .60 .25
  BA: Milt May
  Pitching: Vida Blue
- □ 577 Rick Monday .15 .07
- □ 578 Shooty Babitt .15 .07
- □ 579 Rick Mahler .15 .07
- □ 580 Bobby Bonds .30 .14
- □ 581 Ron Reed .15 .07
- □ 582 Luis Pujols .15 .07
- □ 583 Tippy Martinez .15 .07
- □ 584 Hosken Powell .15 .07
- □ 585 Rollie Fingers 1.25 .55
- □ 586 Rollie Fingers SA .60 .25
- □ 587 Tim Lollar .15 .07
- □ 588 Dale Berra .15 .07
- □ 589 Dave Stapleton .15 .07
- □ 590 Al Oliver .30 .14
- □ 591 Al Oliver SA .15 .07
- □ 592 Craig Swan .15 .07
- □ 593 Billy Smith .15 .07
- □ 594 Renie Martin .15 .07
- □ 595 Dave Collins .15 .07
- □ 596 Damaso Garcia .15 .07
- □ 597 Wayne Nordhagen .15 .07
- □ 598 Bob Galasso .15 .07
- □ 599 White Sox Rookies .15 .07
  Jay Loviglio
  Reggie Patterson
  Leo Sutherland
- □ 600 Dave Winfield 2.00 .90
- □ 601 Sid Monge .15 .07
- □ 602 Freddie Patek .15 .07
- □ 603 Rich Hebner .30 .14
- □ 604 Orlando Sanchez .15 .07
- □ 605 Steve Rogers .15 .07
- □ 606 Blue Jays TL .60 .25
  BA: John Mayberry
  Pitching: Dave Stieb
- □ 607 Leon Durham .15 .07
- □ 608 Jerry Royster .15 .07
- □ 609 Rick Sutcliffe .30 .14
- □ 610 Rickey Henderson 2.50 1.10
- □ 611 Joe Niekro .30 .14
- □ 612 Gary Ward .15 .07
- □ 613 Jim Gantner .30 .14
- □ 614 Juan Eichelberger .15 .07
- □ 615 Bob Boone .30 .14
- □ 616 Bob Boone SA .15 .07
- □ 617 Scott McGregor .15 .07
- □ 618 Tim Foli .15 .07
- □ 619 Bill Campbell .15 .07
- □ 620 Ken Griffey .30 .14
- □ 621 Ken Griffey SA .15 .07
- □ 622 Dennis Lamp .15 .07
- □ 623 Mets Rookies .60 .25
  Ron Gardenhire
  Terry Leach
  Tim Leary
- □ 624 Fergie Jenkins .60 .25
- □ 625 Hal McRae .30 .14
- □ 626 Randy Jones .15 .07
- □ 627 Enos Cabell .15 .07
- □ 628 Bill Travers .15 .07
- □ 629 John Wockenfuss .15 .07
- □ 630 Joe Charboneau .15 .07
- □ 631 Gene Tenace .30 .14
- □ 632 Bryan Clark .15 .07
- □ 633 Mitchell Page .15 .07
- □ 634 Checklist 529-660 .60 .07
- □ 635 Ron Davis .15 .07
- □ 636 Phillies TL 1.25 .55
  BA: Pete Rose
  Pitching: Steve Carlton
- □ 637 Rick Camp .15 .07
- □ 638 John Milner .15 .07
- □ 639 Ken Kravec .15 .07
- □ 640 Cesar Cedeno .30 .14
- □ 641 Steve Mura .15 .07
- □ 642 Mike Scioscia .30 .14
- □ 643 Pete Vuckovich .15 .07
- □ 644 John Castino .15 .07
- □ 645 Frank White .30 .14
- □ 646 Frank White SA .15 .07
- □ 647 Warren Brusstar .15 .07
- □ 648 Jose Morales .15 .07
- □ 649 Ken Clay .15 .07
- □ 650 Carl Yastrzemski 1.25 .55
- □ 651 Carl Yastrzemski SA .60 .25
- □ 652 Steve Nicosia .15 .07
- □ 653 Angels Rookies .60 .25
  Tom Brunansky
  Luis Sanchez
  Daryl Sconiers
- □ 654 Jim Morrison .15 .07
- □ 655 Joel Youngblood .15 .07
- □ 656 Eddie Whitson .15 .07
- □ 657 Tom Poquette .15 .07
- □ 658 Tito Landrum .15 .07
- □ 659 Fred Martinez .15 .07
- □ 660 Dave Concepcion .30 .14
- □ 661 Dave Concepcion SA .15 .07
- □ 662 Luis Salazar .15 .07
- □ 663 Hector Cruz .15 .07
- □ 664 Dan Spillner .15 .07
- □ 665 Jim Clancy .15 .07
- □ 666 Tigers TL .60 .25
  BA: Steve Kemp
  Pitching: Dan Petry
- □ 667 Jeff Reardon .60 .25
- □ 668 Dale Murphy 1.25 .55
- □ 669 Larry Milbourne .15 .07
- □ 670 Mike Davis .15 .07
- □ 671 Bob Knepper .15 .07
- □ 672 Bob Knepper .15 .07
- □ 673 Keith Drumwright .15 .07
- □ 674 Dave Goltz .15 .07
- □ 675 Cecil Cooper .30 .14
- □ 676 Sal Butera .15 .07
- □ 677 Alfredo Griffin .15 .07
- □ 678 Tom Paciorek .30 .14
- □ 679 Sammy Stewart .15 .07
- □ 680 Gary Matthews .30 .14
- □ 681 Dodgers Rookies 1.25 .55
  Mike Marshall
  Ron Roenicke
  Steve Sax
- □ 682 Jesse Jefferson .15 .07
- □ 683 Phil Garner .30 .14
- □ 684 Harold Baines 1.25 .55
- □ 685 Bert Blyleven .60 .25
- □ 686 Gary Allenson .15 .07
- □ 687 Greg Minton .15 .07
- □ 688 Leon Roberts .15 .07
- □ 689 Lary Sorensen .15 .07
- □ 690 Dave Kingman .30 .14
- □ 691 Dan Schatzeder .15 .07
- □ 692 Wayne Gross .15 .07
- □ 693 Cesar Geronimo .15 .07
- □ 694 Dave Wehrmeister .15 .07
- □ 695 Warren Cromartie .15 .07
- □ 696 Pirates TL .60 .25
  BA: Bill Madlock
  Pitching: Eddie Solomon
- □ 697 John Montefusco .15 .07
- □ 698 Tony Scott .15 .07
- □ 699 Dick Tidrow .15 .07
- □ 700 George Foster .30 .14
- □ 701 George Foster SA .15 .07
- □ 702 Steve Renko .15 .07
- □ 703 Brewers TL .60 .25
  BA: Cecil Cooper
  Pitching: Pete Vuckovich
- □ 704 Mickey Rivers .15 .07
- □ 705 Mickey Rivers SA .15 .07
- □ 706 Barry Foote .15 .07
- □ 707 Mark Bomback .15 .07
- □ 708 Gene Richards .15 .07
- □ 709 Don Money .15 .07
- □ 710 Jerry Reuss .30 .14
- □ 711 Mariners Rookies .60 .25
  Dave Edler
  Dave Henderson
  Reggie Walton
- □ 712 Dennis Martinez .30 .14
- □ 713 Del Unser .15 .07
- □ 714 Jerry Koosman .30 .14
- □ 715 Willie Stargell 1.25 .55
- □ 716 Willie Stargell SA .60 .25
- □ 717 Rick Miller .15 .07
- □ 718 Charlie Hough .30 .14
- □ 719 Jerry Narron .15 .07
- □ 720 Greg Luzinski .30 .14
- □ 721 Greg Luzinski SA .15 .07
- □ 722 Jerry Martin .15 .07
- □ 723 Junior Kennedy .15 .07
- □ 724 Dave Rosello .15 .07
- □ 725 Amos Otis .30 .14
- □ 726 Amos Otis SA .15 .07
- □ 727 Sixto Lezcano .15 .07
- □ 728 Aurelio Lopez .15 .07
- □ 729 Jim Spencer .15 .07
- □ 730 Gary Carter 1.25 .55
- □ 731 Padres Rookies .15 .07
  Mike Armstrong
  Doug Gwosdz
  Fred Kuhaulua
- □ 732 Mike Lum .15 .07
- □ 733 Larry McWilliams .15 .07
- □ 734 Mike Ivie .15 .07
- □ 735 Rudy May .15 .07
- □ 736 Jerry Turner .15 .07
- □ 737 Reggie Cleveland .15 .07
- □ 738 Dave Engle .15 .07
- □ 739 Joey McLaughlin .15 .07
- □ 740 Dave Lopes .30 .14
- □ 741 Dave Lopes SA .15 .07
- □ 742 Dick Drago .15 .07
- □ 743 John Stearns .15 .07
- □ 744 Mike Witt .30 .14
- □ 745 Bake McBride .15 .07
- □ 746 Andre Thornton .15 .07
- □ 747 John Lowenstein .15 .07
- □ 748 Marc Hill .15 .07
- □ 749 Bob Shirley .15 .07
- □ 750 Jim Rice .60 .25

☐ 751	Rick Honeycutt	.15	.07
☐ 752	Lee Lacy	.15	.07
☐ 753	Tom Brookens	.15	.07
☐ 754	Joe Morgan	1.25	.55
☐ 755	Joe Morgan SA	.60	.25
☐ 756	Reds TL	.60	.25
	BA: Ken Griffey		
	Pitching: Tom Seaver		
☐ 757	Tom Underwood	.15	.07
☐ 758	Claudell Washington	.15	.07
☐ 759	Paul Splittorff	.15	.07
☐ 760	Bill Buckner	.30	.14
☐ 761	Dave Smith	.15	.07
☐ 762	Mike Phillips	.15	.07
☐ 763	Tom Hume	.15	.07
☐ 764	Steve Swisher	.15	.07
☐ 765	Gorman Thomas	.30	.14
☐ 766	Twins Rookies	1.50	.70
	Lenny Faedo		
	Kent Hrbek		
	Tim Laudner		
☐ 767	Roy Smalley	.15	.07
☐ 768	Jerry Garvin	.15	.07
☐ 769	Richie Zisk	.15	.07
☐ 770	Rich Gossage	.60	.25
☐ 771	Rich Gossage SA	.30	.14
☐ 772	Bert Campaneris	.30	.14
☐ 773	John Denny	.15	.07
☐ 774	Jay Johnstone	.30	.14
☐ 775	Bob Forsch	.15	.07
☐ 776	Mark Belanger	.30	.14
☐ 777	Tom Griffin	.15	.07
☐ 778	Kevin Hickey	.15	.07
☐ 779	Grant Jackson	.15	.07
☐ 780	Pete Rose	1.50	.70
☐ 781	Pete Rose SA	.60	.25
☐ 782	Frank Taveras	.15	.07
☐ 783	Greg Harris	.15	.07
☐ 784	Milt Wilcox	.15	.07
☐ 785	Dan Driessen	.15	.07
☐ 786	Red Sox TL	.60	.25
	BA: Carney Lansford		
	Pitching: Mike Torrez		
☐ 787	Fred Stanley	.15	.07
☐ 788	Woodie Fryman	.15	.07
☐ 789	Checklist 661-792	.60	.25
☐ 790	Larry Gura	.15	.07
☐ 791	Bobby Brown	.15	.07
☐ 792	Frank Tanana	.30	.14

1982 Topps Traded

CUBS
FERGIE JENKINS

The cards in this 132-card set measure the standard size. The 1982 Topps Traded or extended series is distinguished by a "T" printed after the number (located on the reverse). This was the first time Topps began a tradition of newly numbering (and alphabetizing) their traded series from 1T to 132T. All 131 player photos used in the set are completely new. Of this total, 112 individuals are seen in the uniform of their new team, 11 youngsters have been ele-

---

vated to single card status from multi-player "Future Stars" cards, and eight more are entirely new to the 1982 Topps lineup. The backs are almost completely red in color with black print. There are no key Rookie Cards in this set. Although the Cal Ripken card is this set's most valuable card, it is not his Rookie Card since he had already been included in the 1982 regular set, albeit on a multi-player card.

		NRMT	VG-E
COMP.FACT.SET (132)		300.00	135.00
COMMON CARD (1T-132T)		.50	.23
MINOR STARS		1.00	.45
SEMISTARS		2.00	.90
UNLISTED STARS		4.00	1.80

☐ 1T	Doyle Alexander	.50	.23
☐ 2T	Jesse Barfield	1.00	.45
☐ 3T	Ross Baumgarten	.50	.23
☐ 4T	Steve Bedrosian	1.00	.45
☐ 5T	Mark Belanger	1.00	.45
☐ 6T	Kurt Bevacqua	.50	.23
☐ 7T	Tim Blackwell	.50	.23
☐ 8T	Vida Blue	1.00	.45
☐ 9T	Bob Boone	1.00	.45
☐ 10T	Larry Bowa	1.00	.45
☐ 11T	Dan Briggs	.50	.23
☐ 12T	Bobby Brown	.50	.23
☐ 13T	Tom Brunansky	1.00	.45
☐ 14T	Jeff Burroughs	.50	.23
☐ 15T	Enos Cabell	.50	.23
☐ 16T	Bill Campbell	.50	.23
☐ 17T	Bobby Castillo	.50	.23
☐ 18T	Bill Caudill	.50	.23
☐ 19T	Cesar Cedeno	1.00	.45
☐ 20T	Dave Collins	1.00	.45
☐ 21T	Doug Corbett	.50	.23
☐ 22T	Al Cowens	.50	.23
☐ 23T	Chili Davis	6.00	2.70
☐ 24T	Dick Davis	.50	.23
☐ 25T	Ron Davis	.50	.23
☐ 26T	Doug DeCinces	1.00	.45
☐ 27T	Ivan DeJesus	.50	.23
☐ 28T	Bob Dernier	.50	.23
☐ 29T	Bo Diaz	.50	.23
☐ 30T	Roger Erickson	.50	.23
☐ 31T	Jim Essian	.50	.23
☐ 32T	Ed Farmer	.50	.23
☐ 33T	Doug Flynn	.50	.23
☐ 34T	Tim Foli	.50	.23
☐ 35T	Dan Ford	.50	.23
☐ 36T	George Foster	1.00	.45
☐ 37T	Dave Frost	.50	.23
☐ 38T	Rich Gale	.50	.23
☐ 39T	Ron Gardenhire	1.00	.45
☐ 40T	Ken Griffey	1.00	.45
☐ 41T	Greg Harris	1.00	.45
☐ 42T	Von Hayes	1.00	.45
☐ 43T	Larry Herndon	.50	.23
☐ 44T	Kent Hrbek	2.00	.90
☐ 45T	Mike Ivie	.50	.23
☐ 46T	Grant Jackson	.50	.23
☐ 47T	Reggie Jackson	10.00	4.50
☐ 48T	Ron Jackson	.50	.23
☐ 49T	Fergie Jenkins	2.00	.90
☐ 50T	Lamar Johnson	.50	.23
☐ 51T	Randy Johnson	.50	.23
☐ 52T	Jay Johnstone	1.00	.45
☐ 53T	Mick Kelleher	.50	.23
☐ 54T	Steve Kemp	.50	.23
☐ 55T	Junior Kennedy	.50	.23
☐ 56T	Jim Kern	.50	.23
☐ 57T	Ray Knight	1.00	.45
☐ 58T	Wayne Krenchicki	.50	.23
☐ 59T	Mike Krukow	.50	.23
☐ 60T	Duane Kuiper	.50	.23
☐ 61T	Mike LaCoss	.50	.23
☐ 62T	Chet Lemon	.50	.23
☐ 63T	Sixto Lezcano	.50	.23
☐ 64T	Dave Lopes	1.00	.45

☐ 65T	Jerry Martin	.50	.23
☐ 66T	Renie Martin	.50	.23
☐ 67T	John Mayberry	.50	.23
☐ 68T	Lee Mazzilli	.50	.23
☐ 69T	Bake McBride	.50	.23
☐ 70T	Dan Meyer	.50	.23
☐ 71T	Larry Milbourne	.50	.23
☐ 72T	Eddie Milner	.50	.23
☐ 73T	Sid Monge	.50	.23
☐ 74T	John Montefusco	.50	.23
☐ 75T	Jose Morales	.50	.23
☐ 76T	Keith Moreland	.50	.23
☐ 77T	Jim Morrison	.50	.23
☐ 78T	Rance Mulliniks	.50	.23
☐ 79T	Steve Mura	.50	.23
☐ 80T	Gene Nelson	.50	.23
☐ 81T	Joe Nolan	.50	.23
☐ 82T	Dickie Noles	.50	.23
☐ 83T	Al Oliver	1.00	.45
☐ 84T	Jorge Orta	.50	.23
☐ 85T	Tom Paciorek	1.00	.45
☐ 86T	Larry Parrish	.50	.23
☐ 87T	Jack Perconte	.50	.23
☐ 88T	Gaylord Perry	2.00	.90
☐ 89T	Rob Picciolo	.50	.23
☐ 90T	Joe Pittman	.50	.23
☐ 91T	Hosken Powell	.50	.23
☐ 92T	Mike Proly	.50	.23
☐ 93T	Greg Pryor	.50	.23
☐ 94T	Charlie Puleo	.50	.23
☐ 95T	Shane Rawley	.50	.23
☐ 96T	Johnny Ray	1.00	.45
☐ 97T	Dave Revering	.50	.23
☐ 98T	Cal Ripken	250.00	110.00
☐ 99T	Allen Ripley	.50	.23
☐ 100T	Bill Robinson	.50	.23
☐ 101T	Aurelio Rodriguez	.50	.23
☐ 102T	Joe Rudi	.50	.23
☐ 103T	Steve Sax	2.00	.90
☐ 104T	Dan Schatzeder	.50	.23
☐ 105T	Bob Shirley	.50	.23
☐ 106T	Eric Show	1.00	.45
☐ 107T	Roy Smalley	.50	.23
☐ 108T	Lonnie Smith	1.00	.45
☐ 109T	Ozzie Smith	25.00	11.00
☐ 110T	Reggie Smith	1.00	.45
☐ 111T	Lary Sorensen	.50	.23
☐ 112T	Elias Sosa	.50	.23
☐ 113T	Mike Stanton	.50	.23
☐ 114T	Steve Stroughter	.50	.23
☐ 115T	Champ Summers	.50	.23
☐ 116T	Rick Sutcliffe	1.00	.45
☐ 117T	Frank Tanana	.50	.23
☐ 118T	Frank Taveras	.50	.23
☐ 119T	Garry Templeton	.50	.23
☐ 120T	Alex Trevino	.50	.23
☐ 121T	Jerry Turner	.50	.23
☐ 122T	Ed VandeBerg	.50	.23
☐ 123T	Tom Veryzer	.50	.23
☐ 124T	Ron Washington	.50	.23
☐ 125T	Bob Watson	1.00	.45
☐ 126T	Dennis Werth	.50	.23
☐ 127T	Eddie Whitson	.50	.23
☐ 128T	Rob Wilfong	.50	.23
☐ 129T	Bump Wills	.50	.23
☐ 130T	Gary Woods	.50	.23
☐ 131T	Butch Wynegar	.50	.23
☐ 132T	Checklist: 1-132	.50	.23

1983 Topps

The cards in this 792-card set measure the standard size. Each player card front features a large action shot with a small cameo portrait at bottom right. There are special series for AL and NL All Stars (386-407), League Leaders (701-708), and Record Breakers (1-6). In addition, there are 34 "Super Veteran" (SV) cards and six numbered checklist cards. The Super Veteran cards are oriented horizontally and show two

pictures of the featured player, a recent picture and a picture showing the player as a rookie. The team cards are actually Team Leader (TL) cards picturing the batting and pitching leader for that team with a checklist back. Cards were primarily issued in 15-card wax packs and 51-card rack packs. Notable Rookie Cards include Wade Boggs, Tony Gwynn and Ryne Sandberg.

	NRMT	VG-E
COMPLETE SET (792)	120.00	55.00
COMMON CARD (1-792)	.15	.07
MINOR STARS	.30	.14
SEMISTARS	.60	.25
UNLISTED STARS	1.25	.55
SUBSET CARDS HALF VALUE OF BASE CARDS		

☐ 1	Tony Armas RB	.60	.25
☐ 2	Rickey Henderson RB	.60	.25
	Sets modern SB record		
☐ 3	Greg Minton RB	.15	.07
	269 1/3 homerless innings streak		
☐ 4	Lance Parrish RB	.30	.14
☐ 5	Manny Trillo RB	.30	.14
	479 consecutive errorless chances, second baseman		
☐ 6	John Wathan RB	.15	.07
	ML catcher steals, season		
☐ 7	Gene Richards	.15	.07
☐ 8	Steve Balboni	.15	.07
☐ 9	Joey McLaughlin	.15	.07
☐ 10	Gorman Thomas	.15	.07
☐ 11	Billy Gardner MG	.15	.07
☐ 12	Paul Mirabella	.15	.07
☐ 13	Larry Herndon	.15	.07
☐ 14	Frank LaCorte	.15	.07
☐ 15	Ron Cey	.30	.14
☐ 16	George Vukovich	.15	.07
☐ 17	Kent Tekulve	.30	.14
☐ 18	Kent Tekulve SV	.15	.07
☐ 19	Oscar Gamble	.15	.07
☐ 20	Carlton Fisk	1.00	.45
☐ 21	Baltimore Orioles TL	.60	.25
	BA: Eddie Murray		
	ERA: Jim Palmer		
☐ 22	Randy Martz	.15	.07
☐ 23	Mike Heath	.15	.07
☐ 24	Steve Mura	.15	.07
☐ 25	Hal McRae	.30	.14
☐ 26	Jerry Royster	.15	.07
☐ 27	Doug Corbett	.15	.07
☐ 28	Bruce Bochte	.15	.07
☐ 29	Randy Jones	.15	.07
☐ 30	Jim Rice	.30	.14
☐ 31	Bill Gullickson	.30	.14
☐ 32	Dave Bergman	.15	.07
☐ 33	Jack O'Connor	.15	.07
☐ 34	Paul Householder	.15	.07
☐ 35	Rollie Fingers	1.25	.55
☐ 36	Rollie Fingers SV	.60	.25

☐ 37	Darrell Johnson MG	.15	.07
☐ 38	Tim Flannery	.15	.07
☐ 39	Terry Puhl	.15	.07
☐ 40	Fernando Valenzuela	1.25	.55
☐ 41	Jerry Turner	.15	.07
☐ 42	Dale Murray	.15	.07
☐ 43	Bob Dernier	.15	.07
☐ 44	Don Robinson	.15	.07
☐ 45	John Mayberry	.15	.07
☐ 46	Richard Dotson	.15	.07
☐ 47	Dave McKay	.15	.07
☐ 48	Lary Sorensen	.15	.07
☐ 49	Willie McGee	1.25	.55
☐ 50	Bob Horner UER	.15	.07
	('82 RBI total 7)		
☐ 51	Chicago Cubs TL	.30	.14
	BA: Leon Durham		
	ERA: Fergie Jenkins		
☐ 52	Onix Concepcion	.15	.07
☐ 53	Mike Witt	.15	.07
☐ 54	Jim Maler	.15	.07
☐ 55	Mookie Wilson	.30	.14
☐ 56	Chuck Rainey	.15	.07
☐ 57	Tim Blackwell	.15	.07
☐ 58	Al Holland	.15	.07
☐ 59	Benny Ayala	.15	.07
☐ 60	Johnny Bench	1.50	.70
☐ 61	Johnny Bench SV	.60	.25
☐ 62	Bob McClure	.15	.07
☐ 63	Rick Monday	.15	.07
☐ 64	Bill Stein	.15	.07
☐ 65	Jack Morris	.30	.14
☐ 66	Bob Lillis MG	.15	.07
☐ 67	Sal Butera	.15	.07
☐ 68	Eric Show	.15	.07
☐ 69	Lee Lacy	.15	.07
☐ 70	Steve Carlton	1.00	.45
☐ 71	Steve Carlton SV	.60	.25
☐ 72	Tom Paciorek	.15	.07
☐ 73	Allen Ripley	.15	.07
☐ 74	Julio Gonzalez	.15	.07
☐ 75	Amos Otis	.30	.14
☐ 76	Rick Mahler	.15	.07
☐ 77	Hosken Powell	.15	.07
☐ 78	Bill Caudill	.15	.07
☐ 79	Mick Kelleher	.15	.07
☐ 80	George Foster	.30	.14
☐ 81	Yankees TL	.30	.14
	BA: Jerry Mumphrey		
	ERA: Dave Righetti		
☐ 82	Bruce Hurst	.30	.14
☐ 83	Ryne Sandberg	25.00	11.00
☐ 84	Milt May	.15	.07
☐ 85	Ken Singleton	.30	.14
☐ 86	Tom Hume	.15	.07
☐ 87	Joe Rudi	.15	.07
☐ 88	Jim Gantner	.30	.14
☐ 89	Leon Roberts	.15	.07
☐ 90	Jerry Reuss	.30	.14
☐ 91	Larry Milbourne	.15	.07
☐ 92	Mike LaCoss	.15	.07
☐ 93	John Castino	.15	.07
☐ 94	Dave Edwards	.15	.07
☐ 95	Alan Trammell	1.25	.55
☐ 96	Dick Howser MG	.15	.07
☐ 97	Ross Baumgarten	.15	.07
☐ 98	Vance Law	.15	.07
☐ 99	Dickie Noles	.15	.07
☐ 100	Pete Rose	1.50	.70
☐ 101	Pete Rose SV	.60	.25
☐ 102	Dave Beard	.15	.07
☐ 103	Darrell Porter	.15	.07
☐ 104	Bob Walk	.15	.07
☐ 105	Don Baylor	.60	.25
☐ 106	Gene Nelson	.15	.07
☐ 107	Mike Jorgensen	.15	.07
☐ 108	Glenn Hoffman	.15	.07
☐ 109	Luis Leal	.15	.07
☐ 110	Ken Griffey	.30	.14
☐ 111	Montreal Expos TL	.30	.14
	BA: Al Oliver		
	ERA: Steve Rogers		
☐ 112	Bob Shirley	.15	.07
☐ 113	Ron Roenicke	.15	.07
☐ 114	Jim Slaton	.15	.07
☐ 115	Chili Davis	1.25	.55

☐ 116	Dave Schmidt	.15	.07
☐ 117	Alan Knicely	.15	.07
☐ 118	Chris Welsh	.15	.07
☐ 119	Tom Brookens	.15	.07
☐ 120	Len Barker	.15	.07
☐ 121	Mickey Hatcher	.15	.07
☐ 122	Jimmy Smith	.15	.07
☐ 123	George Frazier	.15	.07
☐ 124	Marc Hill	.15	.07
☐ 125	Leon Durham	.15	.07
☐ 126	Joe Torre MG	.30	.14
☐ 127	Preston Hanna	.15	.07
☐ 128	Mike Ramsey	.15	.07
☐ 129	Checklist: 1-132	.30	.14
☐ 130	Dave Stieb	.30	.14
☐ 131	Ed Ott	.15	.07
☐ 132	Todd Cruz	.15	.07
☐ 133	Jim Barr	.15	.07
☐ 134	Hubie Brooks	.30	.14
☐ 135	Dwight Evans	.30	.14
☐ 136	Willie Aikens	.15	.07
☐ 137	Woodie Fryman	.15	.07
☐ 138	Rick Dempsey	.15	.07
☐ 139	Bruce Berenyi	.15	.07
☐ 140	Willie Randolph	.30	.14
☐ 141	Indians TL	.30	.14
	BA: Toby Harrah		
	ERA: Rick Sutcliffe		
☐ 142	Mike Caldwell	.15	.07
☐ 143	Joe Pettini	.15	.07
☐ 144	Mark Wagner	.15	.07
☐ 145	Don Sutton	1.25	.55
☐ 146	Don Sutton SV	.60	.25
☐ 147	Rick Leach	.15	.07
☐ 148	Dave Roberts	.15	.07
☐ 149	Johnny Ray	.15	.07
☐ 150	Bruce Sutter	.30	.14
☐ 151	Bruce Sutter SV	.15	.07
☐ 152	Jay Johnstone	.15	.07
☐ 153	Jerry Koosman	.30	.14
☐ 154	Johnnie LeMaster	.15	.07
☐ 155	Dan Quisenberry	.30	.14
☐ 156	Billy Martin MG	.30	.14
☐ 157	Steve Bedrosian	.30	.14
☐ 158	Rob Wilfong	.15	.07
☐ 159	Mike Stanton	.15	.07
☐ 160	Dave Kingman	.60	.25
☐ 161	Dave Kingman SV	.30	.14
☐ 162	Mark Clear	.15	.07
☐ 163	Cal Ripken	15.00	6.75
☐ 164	David Palmer	.15	.07
☐ 165	Dan Driessen	.15	.07
☐ 166	John Pacella	.15	.07
☐ 167	Mark Brouhard	.15	.07
☐ 168	Juan Eichelberger	.15	.07
☐ 169	Doug Flynn	.15	.07
☐ 170	Steve Howe	.15	.07
☐ 171	Giants TL	.60	.25
	BA: Joe Morgan		
	ERA: Bill Laskey		
☐ 172	Vern Ruhle	.15	.07
☐ 173	Jim Morrison	.15	.07
☐ 174	Jerry Ujdur	.15	.07
☐ 175	Bo Diaz	.15	.07
☐ 176	Dave Righetti	.30	.14
☐ 177	Harold Baines	.60	.25
☐ 178	Luis Tiant	.30	.14
☐ 179	Luis Tiant SV	.15	.07
☐ 180	Rickey Henderson	1.50	.70
☐ 181	Terry Felton	.15	.07
☐ 182	Mike Fischlin	.15	.07
☐ 183	Ed VandeBerg	.15	.07
☐ 184	Bob Clark	.15	.07
☐ 185	Tim Lollar	.15	.07
☐ 186	Whitey Herzog MG	.30	.14
☐ 187	Terry Leach	.15	.07
☐ 188	Rick Miller	.15	.07
☐ 189	Dan Schatzeder	.15	.07
☐ 190	Cecil Cooper	.30	.14
☐ 191	Joe Price	.15	.07
☐ 192	Floyd Rayford	.15	.07
☐ 193	Harry Spilman	.15	.07
☐ 194	Cesar Geronimo	.15	.07
☐ 195	Bob Stoddard	.15	.07
☐ 196	Bill Fahey	.15	.07
☐ 197	Jim Eisenreich	1.25	.55

#	Card	Price	Price
198	Kiko Garcia	.15	.07
199	Marty Bystrom	.15	.07
200	Rod Carew	1.25	.55
201	Rod Carew SV	.60	.25
202	Blue Jays TL	.30	.14
	BA: Damaso Garcia		
	ERA: Dave Stieb		
203	Mike Morgan	.15	.07
204	Junior Kennedy	.15	.07
205	Dave Parker	.30	.14
206	Ken Oberkfell	.15	.07
207	Rick Camp	.15	.07
208	Dan Meyer	.15	.07
209	Mike Moore	.30	.14
210	Jack Clark	.30	.14
211	John Denny	.15	.07
212	John Stearns	.15	.07
213	Tom Burgmeier	.15	.07
214	Jerry White	.15	.07
215	Mario Soto	.15	.07
216	Tony LaRussa MG	.30	.14
217	Tim Stoddard	.15	.07
218	Roy Howell	.15	.07
219	Mike Armstrong	.15	.07
220	Dusty Baker	.30	.14
221	Joe Niekro	.30	.14
222	Damaso Garcia	.15	.07
223	John Montefusco	.15	.07
224	Mickey Rivers	.15	.07
225	Enos Cabell	.15	.07
226	Enrique Romo	.15	.07
227	Chris Bando	.15	.07
228	Joaquin Andujar	.15	.07
229	Phillies TL	.60	.25
	BA: Bo Diaz		
	ERA: Steve Carlton		
230	Fergie Jenkins	1.25	.55
231	Fergie Jenkins SV	.60	.25
232	Tom Brunansky	.60	.25
233	Wayne Gross	.15	.07
234	Larry Andersen	.15	.07
235	Claudell Washington	.15	.07
236	Steve Renko	.15	.07
237	Dan Norman	.15	.07
238	Bud Black	.30	.14
239	Dave Stapleton	.15	.07
240	Rich Gossage	.60	.25
241	Rich Gossage SV	.30	.14
242	Joe Nolan	.15	.07
243	Duane Walker	.15	.07
244	Dwight Bernard	.15	.07
245	Steve Sax	.30	.14
246	George Bamberger MG	.15	.07
247	Dave Smith	.15	.07
248	Bake McBride	.15	.07
249	Checklist: 133-264	.30	.14
250	Bill Buckner	.30	.14
251	Alan Wiggins	.15	.07
252	Luis Aguayo	.15	.07
253	Larry McWilliams	.15	.07
254	Rick Cerone	.15	.07
255	Gene Garber	.15	.07
256	Gene Garber SV	.15	.07
257	Jesse Barfield	.30	.14
258	Manny Castillo	.15	.07
259	Jeff Jones	.15	.07
260	Steve Kemp	.15	.07
261	Tigers TL	.30	.14
	BA: Larry Herndon		
	ERA: Dan Petry		
262	Ron Jackson	.15	.07
263	Renie Martin	.15	.07
264	Jamie Quirk	.15	.07
265	Joel Youngblood	.15	.07
266	Paul Boris	.15	.07
267	Terry Francona	.15	.07
268	Storm Davis	.15	.07
269	Ron Oester	.15	.07
270	Dennis Eckersley	1.25	.55
271	Ed Romero	.15	.07
272	Frank Tanana	.30	.14
273	Mark Belanger	.15	.07
274	Terry Kennedy	.15	.07
275	Ray Knight	.30	.14
276	Gene Mauch MG	.15	.07
277	Rance Mulliniks	.15	.07
278	Kevin Hickey	.15	.07
279	Greg Gross	.15	.07
280	Bert Blyleven	1.25	.55
281	Andre Robertson	.15	.07
282	Reggie Smith	1.25	.55
	(Ryne Sandberg ducking back)		
283	Reggie Smith SV	.15	.07
284	Jeff Lahti	.15	.07
285	Lance Parrish	.30	.14
286	Rick Langford	.15	.07
287	Bobby Brown	.15	.07
288	Joe Cowley	.15	.07
289	Jerry Dybzinski	.15	.07
290	Jeff Reardon	.30	.14
291	Pirates TL	.15	.07
	BA: Bill Madlock		
	ERA: John Candelaria		
292	Craig Swan	.15	.07
293	Glenn Gulliver	.15	.07
294	Dave Engle	.15	.07
295	Jerry Remy	.15	.07
296	Greg Harris	.15	.07
297	Ned Yost	.15	.07
298	Floyd Chiffer	.15	.07
299	George Wright	.15	.07
300	Mike Schmidt	1.50	.70
301	Mike Schmidt SV	.60	.25
302	Ernie Whitt	.15	.07
303	Miguel Dilone	.15	.07
304	Dave Rucker	.15	.07
305	Larry Bowa	.30	.14
306	Tom Lasorda MG	.60	.25
307	Lou Piniella	.30	.14
308	Jesus Vega	.15	.07
309	Jeff Leonard	.15	.07
310	Greg Luzinski	.30	.14
311	Glenn Brummer	.15	.07
312	Brian Kingman	.15	.07
313	Gary Gray	.15	.07
314	Ken Dayley	.15	.07
315	Rick Burleson	.15	.07
316	Paul Splittorff	.15	.07
317	Gary Rajsich	.15	.07
318	John Tudor	.15	.07
319	Lenn Sakata	.15	.07
320	Steve Rogers	.15	.07
321	Brewers TL	.60	.25
	BA: Robin Yount		
	ERA: Pete Vuckovich		
322	Dave Van Gorder	.15	.07
323	Luis DeLeon	.15	.07
324	Mike Marshall	.15	.07
325	Von Hayes	.30	.14
326	Garth Iorg	.15	.07
327	Bobby Castillo	.15	.07
328	Craig Reynolds	.15	.07
329	Randy Niemann	.15	.07
330	Buddy Bell	.30	.14
331	Mike Krukow	.15	.07
332	Glenn Wilson	.30	.14
333	Dave LaRoche	.15	.07
334	Dave LaRoche SV	.15	.07
335	Steve Henderson	.15	.07
336	Rene Lachemann MG	.15	.07
337	Tito Landrum	.15	.07
338	Bob Owchinko	.15	.07
339	Terry Harper	.15	.07
340	Larry Gura	.15	.07
341	Doug DeCinces	.30	.14
342	Atlee Hammaker	.15	.07
343	Bob Bailor	.15	.07
344	Roger LaFrancois	.15	.07
345	Jim Clancy	.15	.07
346	Joe Pittman	.15	.07
347	Sammy Stewart	.15	.07
348	Alan Bannister	.15	.07
349	Checklist: 265-396	.30	.14
350	Robin Yount	2.00	.90
351	Reds TL	.15	.07
	BA: Cesar Cedeno		
	ERA: Mario Soto		
352	Mike Scioscia	.30	.14
353	Steve Comer	.15	.07
354	Randy Johnson	.15	.07
355	Jim Bibby	.15	.07
356	Gary Woods	.15	.07
357	Len Matuszek	.15	.07
358	Jerry Garvin	.15	.07
359	Dave Collins	.15	.07
360	Nolan Ryan	6.00	2.70
361	Nolan Ryan SV	4.00	1.80
362	Bill Almon	.15	.07
363	John Stuper	.15	.07
364	Brett Butler	1.25	.55
365	Dave Lopes	.30	.14
366	Dick Williams MG	.15	.07
367	Bud Anderson	.15	.07
368	Richie Zisk	.15	.07
369	Jesse Orosco	.15	.07
370	Gary Carter	1.25	.55
371	Mike Richardt	.15	.07
372	Terry Crowley	.15	.07
373	Kevin Saucier	.15	.07
374	Wayne Krenchicki	.15	.07
375	Pete Vuckovich	.15	.07
376	Ken Landreaux	.15	.07
377	Lee May	.30	.14
378	Lee May SV	.15	.07
379	Guy Sularz	.15	.07
380	Ron Davis	.15	.07
381	Red Sox TL	.30	.14
	BA: Jim Rice		
	ERA: Bob Stanley		
382	Bob Knepper	.15	.07
383	Ozzie Virgil	.15	.07
384	Dave Dravecky	1.25	.55
385	Mike Easler	.15	.07
386	Rod Carew AS	.60	.25
387	Bob Grich AS	.15	.07
388	George Brett AS	1.25	.55
389	Robin Yount AS	.60	.25
390	Reggie Jackson AS	.60	.25
391	Rickey Henderson AS	.60	.25
392	Fred Lynn AS	.30	.14
393	Carlton Fisk AS	.60	.25
394	Pete Vuckovich AS	.15	.07
395	Larry Gura AS	.15	.07
396	Dan Quisenberry AS	.30	.14
397	Pete Rose AS	.60	.25
398	Manny Trillo AS	.15	.07
399	Mike Schmidt AS	.60	.25
400	Dave Concepcion AS	.30	.14
401	Dale Murphy AS	.60	.25
402	Andre Dawson AS	.60	.25
403	Tim Raines AS	.60	.25
404	Gary Carter AS	.60	.25
405	Steve Rogers AS	.15	.07
406	Steve Carlton AS	.60	.25
407	Bruce Sutter AS	.30	.14
408	Rudy May	.15	.07
409	Marvis Foley	.15	.07
410	Phil Niekro	1.25	.55
411	Phil Niekro SV	.60	.25
412	Rangers TL	.30	.14
	BA: Buddy Bell		
	ERA: Charlie Hough		
413	Matt Keough	.15	.07
414	Julio Cruz	.15	.07
415	Bob Forsch	.15	.07
416	Joe Ferguson	.15	.07
417	Tom Hausman	.15	.07
418	Greg Pryor	.15	.07
419	Steve Crawford	.15	.07
420	Al Oliver	.30	.14
421	Al Oliver SV	.15	.07
422	George Cappuzzello	.15	.07
423	Tom Lawless	.15	.07
424	Jerry Augustine	.15	.07
425	Pedro Guerrero	.30	.14
426	Earl Weaver MG	1.25	.55
427	Roy Lee Jackson	.15	.07
428	Champ Summers	.15	.07
429	Eddie Whitson	.15	.07
430	Kirk Gibson	1.25	.55
431	Gary Gaetti	1.25	.55
432	Porfirio Altamirano	.15	.07
433	Dale Berra	.15	.07
434	Dennis Lamp	.15	.07
435	Tony Armas	.15	.07
436	Bill Campbell	.15	.07
437	Rick Sweet	.15	.07

438	Dave LaPoint	.15	.07
439	Rafael Ramirez	.15	.07
440	Ron Guidry	.30	.14
441	Astros TL	.30	.14
	BA: Ray Knight		
	ERA: Joe Niekro		
442	Brian Downing	.15	.07
443	Don Hood	.15	.07
444	Wally Backman	.15	.07
445	Mike Flanagan	.30	.14
446	Reid Nichols	.15	.07
447	Bryn Smith	.15	.07
448	Darrell Evans	.30	.14
449	Eddie Milner	.15	.07
450	Ted Simmons	.30	.14
451	Ted Simmons SV	.15	.07
452	Lloyd Moseby	.15	.07
453	Lamar Johnson	.15	.07
454	Bob Welch	.30	.14
455	Sixto Lezcano	.15	.07
456	Lee Elia MG	.15	.07
457	Milt Wilcox	.15	.07
458	Ron Washington	.15	.07
459	Ed Farmer	.15	.07
460	Roy Smalley	.15	.07
461	Steve Trout	.15	.07
462	Steve Nicosia	.15	.07
463	Gaylord Perry	1.25	.55
464	Gaylord Perry SV	.60	.25
465	Lonnie Smith	.15	.07
466	Tom Underwood	.15	.07
467	Rufino Linares	.15	.07
468	Dave Goltz	.15	.07
469	Ron Gardenhire	.15	.07
470	Greg Minton	.15	.07
471	Kansas City Royals TL	.30	.14
	BA: Willie Wilson		
	ERA: Vida Blue		
472	Gary Allenson	.15	.07
473	John Lowenstein	.15	.07
474	Ray Burris	.15	.07
475	Cesar Cedeno	.30	.14
476	Rob Picciolo	.15	.07
477	Tom Niedenfuer	.15	.07
478	Phil Garner	.30	.14
479	Charlie Hough	.30	.14
480	Toby Harrah	.15	.07
481	Scot Thompson	.15	.07
482	Tony Gwynn UER	60.00	27.00
	(No Topps logo under		
	card number on back)		
483	Lynn Jones	.15	.07
484	Dick Ruthven	.15	.07
485	Omar Moreno	.15	.07
486	Clyde King MG	.15	.07
487	Jerry Hairston	.15	.07
488	Alfredo Griffin	.15	.07
489	Tom Herr	.15	.07
490	Jim Palmer	1.25	.55
491	Jim Palmer SV	.60	.25
492	Paul Serna	.15	.07
493	Steve McCatty	.15	.07
494	Bob Brenly	.15	.07
495	Warren Cromartie	.15	.07
496	Tom Veryzer	.15	.07
497	Rick Sutcliffe	.30	.14
498	Wade Boggs	16.00	7.25
499	Jeff Little	.15	.07
500	Reggie Jackson	1.50	.70
501	Reggie Jackson SV	.60	.25
502	Atlanta Braves TL	.30	.14
	BA: Dale Murphy		
	ERA: Phil Niekro		
503	Moose Haas	.15	.07
504	Don Werner	.15	.07
505	Garry Templeton	.15	.07
506	Jim Gott	.15	.07
507	Tony Scott	.15	.07
508	Tom Filer	.15	.07
509	Lou Whitaker	.60	.25
510	Tug McGraw	.30	.14
511	Tug McGraw SV	.15	.07
512	Doyle Alexander	.15	.07
513	Fred Stanley	.15	.07
514	Rudy Law	.15	.07
515	Gene Tenace	.30	.14
516	Bill Virdon MG	.15	.07
517	Gary Ward	.15	.07
518	Bill Laskey	.15	.07
519	Terry Bulling	.15	.07
520	Fred Lynn	.30	.14
521	Bruce Benedict	.15	.07
522	Pat Zachry	.15	.07
523	Carney Lansford	.30	.14
524	Tom Brennan	.15	.07
525	Frank White	.30	.14
526	Checklist: 397-528	.30	.14
527	Larry Biittner	.15	.07
528	Jamie Easterly	.15	.07
529	Tim Laudner	.15	.07
530	Eddie Murray	1.50	.70
531	Oakland A's TL	.60	.25
	BA: Rickey Henderson		
	ERA: Rick Langford		
532	Dave Stewart	.30	.14
533	Luis Salazar	.15	.07
534	John Butcher	.15	.07
535	Manny Trillo	.15	.07
536	John Wockenfuss	.15	.07
537	Rod Scurry	.15	.07
538	Danny Heep	.15	.07
539	Roger Erickson	.15	.07
540	Ozzie Smith	2.50	1.10
541	Britt Burns	.15	.07
542	Jody Davis	.15	.07
543	Alan Fowlkes	.15	.07
544	Larry Whisenton	.15	.07
545	Floyd Bannister	.15	.07
546	Dave Garcia MG	.15	.07
547	Geoff Zahn	.15	.07
548	Brian Giles	.15	.07
549	Charlie Puleo	.15	.07
550	Carl Yastrzemski	1.25	.55
551	Carl Yastrzemski SV	.60	.25
552	Tim Wallach	.30	.14
553	Dennis Martinez	.30	.14
554	Mike Vail	.15	.07
555	Steve Yeager	.15	.07
556	Willie Upshaw	.15	.07
557	Rick Honeycutt	.15	.07
558	Dickie Thon	.15	.07
559	Pete Redfern	.15	.07
560	Ron LeFlore	.30	.14
561	Cardinals TL	.30	.14
	BA: Lonnie Smith		
	ERA: Joaquin Andujar		
562	Dave Rozema	.15	.07
563	Juan Bonilla	.15	.07
564	Sid Monge	.15	.07
565	Bucky Dent	.30	.14
566	Manny Sarmiento	.15	.07
567	Joe Simpson	.15	.07
568	Willie Hernandez	.30	.14
569	Jack Perconte	.15	.07
570	Vida Blue	.30	.14
571	Mickey Klutts	.15	.07
572	Bob Watson	.30	.14
573	Andy Hassler	.15	.07
574	Glenn Adams	.15	.07
575	Neil Allen	.15	.07
576	Frank Robinson MG	1.25	.55
577	Luis Aponte	.15	.07
578	David Green	.15	.07
579	Rich Dauer	.15	.07
580	Tom Seaver	1.50	.70
581	Tom Seaver SV	.60	.25
582	Marshall Edwards	.15	.07
583	Terry Forster	.15	.07
584	Dave Hostetler	.15	.07
585	Jose Cruz	.30	.14
586	Frank Viola	1.25	.55
587	Ivan DeJesus	.15	.07
588	Pat Underwood	.15	.07
589	Alvis Woods	.15	.07
590	Tony Pena	.15	.07
591	White Sox TL	.30	.14
	BA: Greg Luzinski		
	ERA: LaMarr Hoyt		
592	Shane Rawley	.15	.07
593	Broderick Perkins	.15	.07
594	Eric Rasmussen	.15	.07
595	Tim Raines	1.25	.55
596	Randy Johnson	.15	.07
597	Mike Proly	.15	.07
598	Dwayne Murphy	.15	.07
599	Don Aase	.15	.07
600	George Brett	2.50	1.10
601	Ed Lynch	.15	.07
602	Rich Gedman	.15	.07
603	Joe Morgan	1.25	.55
604	Joe Morgan SV	1.25	.55
605	Gary Roenicke	.15	.07
606	Bobby Cox MG	.30	.14
607	Charlie Leibrandt	.15	.07
608	Don Money	.15	.07
609	Danny Darwin	.15	.07
610	Steve Garvey	.60	.25
611	Bert Roberge	.15	.07
612	Steve Swisher	.15	.07
613	Mike Ivie	.15	.07
614	Ed Glynn	.15	.07
615	Garry Maddox	.15	.07
616	Bill Nahorodny	.15	.07
617	Butch Wynegar	.15	.07
618	LaMarr Hoyt	.30	.14
619	Keith Moreland	.15	.07
620	Mike Norris	.15	.07
621	New York Mets TL	.30	.14
	BA: Mookie Wilson		
	ERA: Craig Swan		
622	Dave Edler	.15	.07
623	Luis Sanchez	.15	.07
624	Glenn Hubbard	.15	.07
625	Ken Forsch	.15	.07
626	Jerry Martin	.15	.07
627	Doug Bair	.15	.07
628	Julio Valdez	.15	.07
629	Charlie Lea	.15	.07
630	Paul Molitor	1.50	.70
631	Tippy Martinez	.15	.07
632	Alex Trevino	.15	.07
633	Vicente Romo	.15	.07
634	Max Venable	.15	.07
635	Graig Nettles	.30	.14
636	Graig Nettles SV	.15	.07
637	Pat Corrales MG	.15	.07
638	Dan Petry	.15	.07
639	Art Howe	.15	.07
640	Andre Thornton	.15	.07
641	Billy Sample	.15	.07
642	Checklist: 529-660	.30	.14
643	Bump Wills	.15	.07
644	Joe Lefebvre	.15	.07
645	Bill Madlock	.30	.14
646	Jim Essian	.15	.07
647	Bobby Mitchell	.15	.07
648	Jeff Burroughs	.15	.07
649	Tommy Boggs	.15	.07
650	George Hendrick	.15	.07
651	Angels TL	.60	.25
	BA: Rod Carew		
	ERA: Mike Witt		
652	Butch Hobson	.15	.07
653	Ellis Valentine	.15	.07
654	Bob Ojeda	.30	.14
655	Al Bumbry	.30	.14
656	Dave Frost	.15	.07
657	Mike Gates	.15	.07
658	Frank Pastore	.15	.07
659	Charlie Moore	.15	.07
660	Mike Hargrove	.30	.14
661	Bill Russell	.30	.14
662	Joe Sambito	.15	.07
663	Tom O'Malley	.15	.07
664	Bob Molinaro	.15	.07
665	Jim Sundberg	.30	.14
666	Sparky Anderson MG	.30	.14
667	Dick Davis	.15	.07
668	Larry Christenson	.15	.07
669	Mike Squires	.15	.07
670	Jerry Mumphrey	.15	.07
671	Lenny Faedo	.15	.07
672	Jim Kaat	.60	.25
673	Jim Kaat SV	.30	.14
674	Kurt Bevacqua	.15	.07
675	Jim Beattie	.15	.07
676	Biff Pocoroba	.15	.07
677	Dave Revering	.15	.07

☐ 678 Juan Beniquez	.15	.07	
☐ 679 Mike Scott	.30	.14	
☐ 680 Andre Dawson	1.25	.55	
☐ 681 Dodgers Leaders	.30	.14	
BA: Pedro Guerrero			
ERA: Fernando Valenzuela			
☐ 682 Bob Stanley	.15	.07	
☐ 683 Dan Ford	.15	.07	
☐ 684 Rafael Landestoy	.15	.07	
☐ 685 Lee Mazzilli	.15	.07	
☐ 686 Randy Lerch	.15	.07	
☐ 687 U.L. Washington	.15	.07	
☐ 688 Jim Wohlford	.15	.07	
☐ 689 Ron Hassey	.15	.07	
☐ 690 Kent Hrbek	.60	.25	
☐ 691 Dave Tobik	.15	.07	
☐ 692 Denny Walling	.15	.07	
☐ 693 Sparky Lyle	.30	.14	
☐ 694 Sparky Lyle SV	.15	.07	
☐ 695 Ruppert Jones	.15	.07	
☐ 696 Chuck Tanner MG	.15	.07	
☐ 697 Barry Foote	.15	.07	
☐ 698 Tony Bernazard	.15	.07	
☐ 699 Lee Smith	2.50	1.10	
☐ 700 Keith Hernandez	.30	.14	
☐ 701 Batting Leaders	.30	.14	
AL: Willie Wilson			
NL: Al Oliver			
☐ 702 Home Run Leaders	.60	.25	
AL: Reggie Jackson			
Gorman Thomas			
NL: Dave Kingman			
☐ 703 RBI Leaders	.30	.14	
AL: Hal McRae			
NL: Dale Murphy			
Al Oliver			
☐ 704 SB Leaders	1.25	.55	
AL: Rickey Henderson			
NL: Tim Raines			
☐ 705 Victory Leaders	.25		
AL: LaMarr Hoyt			
NL: Steve Carlton			
☐ 706 Strikeout Leaders	.60	.25	
AL: Floyd Bannister			
NL: Steve Carlton			
☐ 707 ERA Leaders	.30	.14	
AL: Rick Sutcliffe			
NL: Steve Rogers			
☐ 708 Leading Firemen	.30	.14	
AL: Dan Quisenberry			
NL: Bruce Sutter			
☐ 709 Jimmy Sexton	.15	.07	
☐ 710 Willie Wilson	.30	.14	
☐ 711 Mariners TL	.15	.07	
BA: Bruce Bochte			
ERA: Jim Beattie			
☐ 712 Bruce Kison	.15	.07	
☐ 713 Ron Hodges	.15	.07	
☐ 714 Wayne Nordhagen	.15	.07	
☐ 715 Tony Perez	1.25	.55	
☐ 716 Tony Perez SV	.60	.25	
☐ 717 Scott Sanderson	.15	.07	
☐ 718 Jim Dwyer	.15	.07	
☐ 719 Rich Gale	.15	.07	
☐ 720 Dave Concepcion	.30	.14	
☐ 721 John Martin	.15	.07	
☐ 722 Jorge Orta	.15	.07	
☐ 723 Randy Moffitt	.15	.07	
☐ 724 Johnny Grubb	.15	.07	
☐ 725 Dan Spillner	.15	.07	
☐ 726 Harvey Kuenn MG	.15	.07	
☐ 727 Chet Lemon	.15	.07	
☐ 728 Ron Reed	.15	.07	
☐ 729 Jerry Morales	.15	.07	
☐ 730 Jason Thompson	.15	.07	
☐ 731 Al Williams	.15	.07	
☐ 732 Dave Henderson	.30	.14	
☐ 733 Buck Martinez	.15	.07	
☐ 734 Steve Braun	.15	.07	
☐ 735 Tommy John	.60	.25	
☐ 736 Tommy John SV	.30	.14	
☐ 737 Mitchell Page	.15	.07	
☐ 738 Tim Foli	.15	.07	
☐ 739 Rick Ownbey	.15	.07	
☐ 740 Rusty Staub	.30	.14	
☐ 741 Rusty Staub SV	.15	.07	

☐ 742 Padres TL	.30	.14	
BA: Terry Kennedy			
ERA: Tim Lollar			
☐ 743 Mike Torrez	.15	.07	
☐ 744 Brad Mills	.15	.07	
☐ 745 Scott McGregor	.15	.07	
☐ 746 John Wathan	.15	.07	
☐ 747 Fred Breining	.15	.07	
☐ 748 Derrel Thomas	.15	.07	
☐ 749 Jon Matlack	.15	.07	
☐ 750 Ben Oglivie	.15	.07	
☐ 751 Brad Havens	.15	.07	
☐ 752 Luis Pujols	.15	.07	
☐ 753 Elias Sosa	.15	.07	
☐ 754 Bill Robinson	.15	.07	
☐ 755 John Candelaria	.15	.07	
☐ 756 Russ Nixon MG	.15	.07	
☐ 757 Rick Manning	.15	.07	
☐ 758 Aurelio Rodriguez	.15	.07	
☐ 759 Doug Bird	.15	.07	
☐ 760 Dale Murphy	1.25	.55	
☐ 761 Gary Lucas	.15	.07	
☐ 762 Cliff Johnson	.15	.07	
☐ 763 Al Cowens	.15	.07	
☐ 764 Pete Falcone	.15	.07	
☐ 765 Bob Boone	.30	.14	
☐ 766 Barry Bonnell	.15	.07	
☐ 767 Duane Kuiper	.15	.07	
☐ 768 Chris Speier	.15	.07	
☐ 769 Checklist 661-792	.30	.14	
☐ 770 Dave Winfield	1.25	.55	
☐ 771 Twins TL	.30	.14	
BA: Kent Hrbek			
ERA: Bobby Castillo			
☐ 772 Jim Kern	.15	.07	
☐ 773 Larry Hisle	.15	.07	
☐ 774 Alan Ashby	.15	.07	
☐ 775 Burt Hooton	.15	.07	
☐ 776 Larry Parrish	.15	.07	
☐ 777 John Curtis	.15	.07	
☐ 778 Rich Hebner	.30	.14	
☐ 779 Rick Waits	.15	.07	
☐ 780 Gary Matthews	.30	.14	
☐ 781 Rick Rhoden	.15	.07	
☐ 782 Bobby Murcer	.30	.14	
☐ 783 Bobby Murcer SV	.15	.07	
☐ 784 Jeff Newman	.15	.07	
☐ 785 Dennis Leonard	.15	.07	
☐ 786 Ralph Houk MG	.15	.07	
☐ 787 Dick Tidrow	.15	.07	
☐ 788 Dane Iorg	.15	.07	
☐ 789 Bryan Clark	.15	.07	
☐ 790 Bob Grich	.30	.14	
☐ 791 Gary Lavelle	.15	.07	
☐ 792 Chris Chambliss	.30	.14	

ed in Ireland by the Topps affiliate in that country. The set is numbered alphabetically by player. The Darryl Strawberry card number 108 can be found with either one or two asterisks (in the lower left corner of the reverse). There is no difference in value for either version. The key (extended) Rookie Cards in this set include Julio Franco, Tony Phillips and Darryl Strawberry.

	NRMT	VG-E
COMP.FACT.SET (132)	35.00	16.00
COMMON CARD (1T-132T)	.25	.11
MINOR STARS	1.00	.45
SEMISTARS	2.00	.90

☐ 1T Neil Allen	.25	.11
☐ 2T Bill Almon	.25	.11
☐ 3T Joe Altobelli MG	.25	.11
☐ 4T Tony Armas	.25	.11
☐ 5T Doug Bair	.25	.11
☐ 6T Steve Baker	.25	.11
☐ 7T Floyd Bannister	.25	.11
☐ 8T Don Baylor	2.00	.90
☐ 9T Tony Bernazard	.25	.11
☐ 10T Larry Biittner	.25	.11
☐ 11T Dann Bilardello	.25	.11
☐ 12T Doug Bird	.25	.11
☐ 13T Steve Boros MG	.25	.11
☐ 14T Greg Brock	.25	.11
☐ 15T Mike C. Brown	.25	.11
☐ 16T Tom Burgmeier	.25	.11
☐ 17T Randy Bush	.25	.11
☐ 18T Bert Campaneris	1.00	.45
☐ 19T Ron Cey	.25	.45
☐ 20T Chris Codiroli	.25	.11
☐ 21T Dave Collins	.25	.11
☐ 22T Terry Crowley	.25	.11
☐ 23T Julio Cruz	.25	.11
☐ 24T Mike Davis	.25	.11
☐ 25T Frank DiPino	.25	.11
☐ 26T Bill Doran	1.00	.45
☐ 27T Jerry Dybzinski	.25	.11
☐ 28T Jamie Easterly	.25	.11
☐ 29T Juan Eichelberger	.25	.11
☐ 30T Jim Essian	.25	.11
☐ 31T Pete Falcone	.25	.11
☐ 32T Mike Ferraro MG	.25	.11
☐ 33T Terry Forster	.25	.11
☐ 34T Julio Franco	4.00	1.80
☐ 35T Rich Gale	.25	.11
☐ 36T Kiko Garcia	.25	.11
☐ 37T Steve Garvey	2.00	.90
☐ 38T Johnny Grubb	.25	.11
☐ 39T Mel Hall	1.00	.45
☐ 40T Von Hayes	1.00	.45
☐ 41T Danny Heep	.25	.11
☐ 42T Steve Henderson	.25	.11
☐ 43T Keith Hernandez	2.00	.90
☐ 44T Leo Hernandez	.25	.11
☐ 45T Willie Hernandez	1.00	.45
☐ 46T Al Holland	.25	.11
☐ 47T Frank Howard MG	1.00	.45
☐ 48T Bobby Johnson	.25	.11
☐ 49T Cliff Johnson	.25	.11
☐ 50T Odell Jones	.25	.11
☐ 51T Mike Jorgensen	.25	.11
☐ 52T Bob Kearney	.25	.11
☐ 53T Steve Kemp	.25	.11
☐ 54T Matt Keough	.25	.11
☐ 55T Ron Kittle	1.00	.45
☐ 56T Mickey Klutts	.25	.11
☐ 57T Alan Knicely	.25	.11
☐ 58T Mike Krukow	.25	.11
☐ 59T Rafael Landestoy	.25	.11
☐ 60T Carney Lansford	1.00	.45
☐ 61T Joe Lefebvre	.25	.11
☐ 62T Bryan Little	.25	.11
☐ 63T Aurelio Lopez	.25	.11
☐ 64T Mike Madden	.25	.11
☐ 65T Rick Manning	.25	.11
☐ 66T Billy Martin MG	1.00	.45

1983 Topps Traded

For the third year in a row, Topps issued a 132-card standard-size Traded (or extended) set featuring some of the year's top rookies and players who had changed teams during the year. The cards were available through hobby dealers only in factory set form and were print-

□ 67T Lee Mazzilli .... .25 .11
□ 68T Andy McGaffigan ... .25 .11
□ 69T Craig McMurtry ..... .25 .11
□ 70T John McNamara MG .25 .11
□ 71T Orlando Mercado ... .25 .11
□ 72T Larry Milbourne ...... .25 .11
□ 73T Randy Moffitt .... .25 .11
□ 74T Sid Monge .... .25 .11
□ 75T Jose Morales .... .25 .11
□ 76T Omar Moreno .... .25 .11
□ 77T Joe Morgan ....
□ 78T Mike Morgan .... .25 .11
□ 79T Dale Murray .... .25 .11
□ 80T Jeff Newman .... .25 .11
□ 81T Pete O'Brien .... 1.00 .45
□ 82T Jorge Orta .... .25 .11
□ 83T Alejandro Pena ..... 1.00 .45
□ 84T Pascual Perez .... .25 .11
□ 85T Tony Perez ....
□ 86T Broderick Perkins .. .25 .11
□ 87T Tony Phillips 4.00 1.80
□ 88T Charlie Puleo .... .25 .11
□ 89T Pat Putnam .... .25 .11
□ 90T Jamie Quirk .... .25 .11
□ 91T Doug Rader MG ..... .25 .11
□ 92T Chuck Rainey .... .25 .11
□ 93T Bobby Ramos .... .25 .11
□ 94T Gary Redus .... 1.00 .45
□ 95T Steve Renko .... .25 .11
□ 96T Leon Roberts .... .25 .11
□ 97T Aurelio Rodriguez .. .25 .11
□ 98T Dick Ruthven .... .25 .11
□ 99T Daryl Sconiers ..... .25 .11
□ 100T Mike Scott .... 1.00 .45
□ 101T Tom Seaver 5.00 2.20
□ 102T John Shelby .... .25 .11
□ 103T Bob Shirley .... .25 .11
□ 104T Joe Simpson ...... .25 .11
□ 105T Doug Sisk .... .25 .11
□ 106T Mike Smithson .... .25 .11
□ 107T Elias Sosa .... .25 .11
□ 108T Darryl Strawberry 20.00 9.00
□ 109T Tom Tellmann ..... .25 .11
□ 110T Gene Tenace ...... 1.00 .45
□ 111T Gorman Thomas ... .25 .11
□ 112T Dick Tidrow .... .25 .11
□ 113T Dave Tobik .... .25 .11
□ 114T Wayne Tolleson ... .25 .11
□ 115T Mike Torrez .... .25 .11
□ 116T Manny Trillo .... .25 .11
□ 117T Steve Trout .... .25 .11
□ 118T Lee Tunnell .... .25 .11
□ 119T Mike Vail .... .25 .11
□ 120T Ellis Valentine .... .25 .11
□ 121T Tom Veryzer ...... .25 .11
□ 122T George Vukovich .. .25 .11
□ 123T Rick Waits .... .25 .11
□ 124T Greg Walker ...... 1.00 .45
□ 125T Chris Welsh .... .25 .11
□ 126T Len Whitehouse ... .25 .11
□ 127T Eddie Whitson .... .25 .11
□ 128T Jim Wohlford ..... .25 .11
□ 129T Matt Young .... .25 .11
□ 130T Joel Youngblood .. .25 .11
□ 131T Pat Zachry .... .25 .11
□ 132T Checklist 1T-132T .25 .11

1984 Topps

The cards in this 792-card set
measure the standard size. For
the second year in a row, Topps
utilized a dual picture on the
front of the card. A portrait is
shown in a square inset and an
action shot is featured in the
main photo. Card numbers 1-6
feature 1983 Highlights (HL),
cards 131-138 depict League
Leaders, card numbers 386-407
feature All-Stars, and card numbers 701-718 feature active
Major League career leaders in
various statistical categories.
Each team leader (TL) card fea-

tures the team's leading hitter
and pitcher pictured on the front
with a team checklist back.
There are six numerical checklist cards in the set. The player
cards feature team logos on the
reverse. Cards were primarily
distributed in 15-card wax packs
and 54-card rack packs. The
key Rookie Cards in this set are
Don Mattingly and Darryl
Strawberry. Topps tested a special send-in offer in Michigan
and a few other states whereby
collectors could obtain direct
from Topps ten cards of their
choice. Needless to say most
people ordered the key (most
valuable) players necessitating
the printing of a special sheet to
keep up with the demand. The
special sheet had five cards of
Darryl Strawberry, three cards
of Don Mattingly, etc. The test
was apparently a failure in
Topps' eyes as they have never
tried it again.

	NRMT	VG-E
COMPLETE SET (792)	40.00	18.00
COMMON CARD (1-792)	.10	.05
MINOR STARS	.20	.09
SEMISTARS	.40	.18
UNLISTED STARS	.60	.25
SUBSET CARDS HALF VALUE OF BASE CARDS		

□ 1 Steve Carlton HL ..... .60 .25
   300th win and
   all-time SO king
□ 2 Rickey Henderson HL .40 .18
   100 stolen bases
   three times
□ 3 Dan Quisenberry HL .. .10 .05
   Sets save record
□ 4 Nolan Ryan HL ...... 1.00 .45
   Steve Carlton
   Gaylord Perry
   All surpass Johnson
□ 5 Dave Righetti HL ..... .20 .09
   Bob Forsch
   Mike Warren
   All pitch no-hitters
□ 6 Johnny Bench HL ..... .60 .25
   Gaylord Perry
   Carl Yastrzemski
   Superstars retire
□ 7 Gary Lucas .... .10 .05
□ 8 Don Mattingly 8.00 3.60
□ 9 Jim Gott .... .10 .05
□ 10 Robin Yount .... .60 .25
□ 11 Minnesota Twins TL .20 .09
   Kent Hrbek
   Ken Schrom
□ 12 Billy Sample .... .10 .05
□ 13 Scott Holman .... .10 .05
□ 14 Tom Brookens ...... .20 .09
□ 15 Burt Hooton .... .10 .05

□ 16 Omar Moreno .... .10 .05
□ 17 John Denny .... .10 .05
□ 18 Dale Berra .... .10 .05
□ 19 Ray Fontenot .... .10 .05
□ 20 Greg Luzinski .... .20 .09
□ 21 Joe Altobelli MG .... .10 .05
□ 22 Bryan Clark .... .10 .05
□ 23 Keith Moreland ..... .10 .05
□ 24 John Martin .... .10 .05
□ 25 Glenn Hubbard ..... .10 .05
□ 26 Bud Black .... .10 .05
□ 27 Daryl Sconiers ...... .10 .05
□ 28 Frank Viola .... .40 .18
□ 29 Danny Heep .... .10 .05
□ 30 Wade Boggs .... 1.25 .55
□ 31 Andy McGaffigan ... .10 .05
□ 32 Bobby Ramos ...... .10 .05
□ 33 Tom Burgmeier ..... .10 .05
□ 34 Eddie Milner .... .10 .05
□ 35 Don Sutton .... .60 .25
□ 36 Denny Walling ...... .10 .05
□ 37 Texas Rangers TL .. .20 .09
   Buddy Bell
   Rick Honeycutt
□ 38 Luis DeLeon .... .10 .05
□ 39 Garth Iorg .... .10 .05
□ 40 Dusty Baker .... .40 .18
□ 41 Tony Bernazard ..... .10 .05
□ 42 Johnny Grubb ...... .10 .05
□ 43 Ron Reed .... .10 .05
□ 44 Jim Morrison .... .10 .05
□ 45 Jerry Mumphrey .... .10 .05
□ 46 Ray Smith .... .10 .05
□ 47 Rudy Law .... .10 .05
□ 48 Julio Franco .... .40 .18
□ 49 John Stuper .... .10 .05
□ 50 Chris Chambliss .... .10 .05
□ 51 Jim Frey MG .... .10 .05
□ 52 Paul Splittorff ...... .10 .05
□ 53 Juan Beniquez ...... .10 .05
□ 54 Jesse Orosco .... .10 .05
□ 55 Dave Concepcion ... .20 .09
□ 56 Gary Allenson ...... .10 .05
□ 57 Dan Schatzeder ..... .10 .05
□ 58 Max Venable .... .10 .05
□ 59 Sammy Stewart ..... .10 .05
□ 60 Paul Molitor UER .... .60 .25
   ('83 stats .272, 613,
   167; should be .270,
   608, 164)
□ 61 Chris Codiroli ...... .10 .05
□ 62 Dave Hostetler ..... .10 .05
□ 63 Ed VandeBerg ...... .10 .05
□ 64 Mike Scioscia ...... .10 .05
□ 65 Kirk Gibson .... .60 .25
□ 66 Houston Astros TL .. 1.00 .45
   Jose Cruz
   Nolan Ryan
□ 67 Gary Ward .... .10 .05
□ 68 Luis Salazar .... .10 .05
□ 69 Rod Scurry .... .10 .05
□ 70 Gary Matthews ..... .10 .05
□ 71 Leo Hernandez ..... .10 .05
□ 72 Mike Squires .... .10 .05
□ 73 Jody Davis .... .10 .05
□ 74 Jerry Martin .... .10 .05
□ 75 Bob Forsch .... .10 .05
□ 76 Alfredo Griffin ...... .10 .05
□ 77 Brett Butler .... .60 .25
□ 78 Mike Torrez .... .10 .05
□ 79 Rob Wilfong .... .10 .05
□ 80 Steve Rogers .... .10 .05
□ 81 Billy Martin MG ..... .20 .09
□ 82 Doug Bird .... .10 .05
□ 83 Richie Zisk .... .10 .05
□ 84 Lenny Faedo .... .10 .05
□ 85 Atlee Hammaker .... .10 .05
□ 86 John Shelby .... .10 .05
□ 87 Frank Pastore ...... .10 .05
□ 88 Rob Picciolo .... .10 .05
□ 89 Mike Smithson ..... .10 .05
□ 90 Pedro Guerrero .... .20 .09
□ 91 Dan Spillner .... .10 .05
□ 92 Lloyd Moseby ...... .10 .05
□ 93 Bob Knepper .... .10 .05
□ 94 Mario Ramirez ...... .10 .05

320	Bob Stanley	.10	.05
321	Harvey Kuenn MG	.20	.09
322	Ken Schrom	.10	.05
323	Alan Knicely	.10	.05
324	Alejandro Pena	.20	.09
325	Darrell Evans	.20	.09
326	Bob Kearney	.10	.05
327	Ruppert Jones	.10	.05
328	Vern Ruhle	.10	.05
329	Pat Tabler	.10	.05
330	John Candelaria	.10	.05
331	Bucky Dent	.20	.09
332	Kevin Gross	.10	.09
333	Larry Herndon	.20	.09
334	Chuck Rainey	.10	.05
335	Don Baylor	.40	.18
336	Seattle Mariners TL / Pat Putnam / Matt Young	.20	
337	Kevin Hagen	.10	.05
338	Mike Warren	.10	.05
339	Roy Lee Jackson	.10	.05
340	Hal McRae	.20	.09
341	Dave Tobik	.10	.05
342	Tim Foli	.10	.05
343	Mark Davis	.10	.05
344	Rick Miller	.10	.05
345	Kent Hrbek	.20	.09
346	Kurt Bevacqua	.10	.05
347	Allan Ramirez	.10	.05
348	Toby Harrah	.20	.09
349	Bob L. Gibson	.10	.05
350	George Foster	.20	.09
351	Russ Nixon MG	.10	.05
352	Dave Stewart	.20	.09
353	Jim Anderson	.10	.05
354	Jeff Burroughs	.10	.05
355	Jason Thompson	.10	.05
356	Glenn Abbott	.10	.05
357	Ron Cey	.20	.09
358	Bob Dernier	.10	.05
359	Jim Acker	.10	.05
360	Willie Randolph	.20	.09
361	Dave Smith	.10	.05
362	David Green	.10	.05
363	Tim Laudner	.10	.05
364	Scott Fletcher	.10	.05
365	Steve Bedrosian	.10	.05
366	Padres TL / Terry Kennedy / Dave Dravecky	.20	.09
367	Jamie Easterly	.10	.05
368	Hubie Brooks	.10	.05
369	Steve McCatty	.10	.05
370	Tim Raines	.40	.18
371	Dave Gumpert	.10	.05
372	Gary Roenicke	.10	.05
373	Bill Scherrer	.10	.05
374	Don Money	.10	.05
375	Dennis Leonard	.10	.05
376	Dave Anderson	.10	.05
377	Danny Darwin	.20	.09
378	Bob Brenly	.10	.05
379	Checklist 265-396	.20	.02
380	Steve Garvey	.40	.18
381	Ralph Houk MG	.10	.05
382	Chris Nyman	.10	.05
383	Terry Puhl	.10	.05
384	Lee Tunnell	.10	.05
385	Tony Perez	.60	.25
386	George Hendrick AS	.10	.05
387	Johnny Ray AS	.10	.05
388	Mike Schmidt AS	.40	.18
389	Ozzie Smith AS	.60	.25
390	Tim Raines AS	.20	.09
391	Dale Murphy AS	.40	.18
392	Andre Dawson AS	.40	.18
393	Gary Carter AS	.40	.18
394	Steve Rogers AS	.10	.05
395	Steve Carlton AS	.40	.18
396	Jesse Orosco AS	.10	.05
397	Eddie Murray AS	.40	.18
398	Lou Whitaker AS	.20	.09
399	George Brett AS	.60	.25
400	Cal Ripken AS	2.00	.90
401	Jim Rice AS	.20	.09
402	Dave Winfield AS	.40	.18
403	Lloyd Moseby AS	.10	.05
404	Ted Simmons AS	.20	.09
405	LaMarr Hoyt AS	.10	.05
406	Ron Guidry AS	.20	.09
407	Dan Quisenberry AS	.10	.05
408	Lou Piniella	.20	.09
409	Juan Agosto	.10	.05
410	Claudell Washington	.10	.05
411	Houston Jimenez	.10	.05
412	Doug Rader MG	.10	.05
413	Spike Owen	.20	.09
414	Mitchell Page	.10	.05
415	Tommy John	.40	.18
416	Dane Iorg	.10	.05
417	Mike Armstrong	.10	.05
418	Ron Hodges	.10	.05
419	John Henry Johnson	.10	.05
420	Cecil Cooper	.20	.09
421	Charlie Lea	.10	.05
422	Jose Cruz	.20	.09
423	Mike Morgan	.10	.05
424	Dann Bilardello	.10	.05
425	Steve Howe	.10	.05
426	Orioles TL / Cal Ripken / Mike Boddicker	1.50	.70
427	Rick Leach	.10	.05
428	Fred Breining	.10	.05
429	Randy Bush	.10	.05
430	Rusty Staub	.20	.09
431	Chris Bando	.10	.05
432	Charles Hudson	.10	.05
433	Rich Hebner	.10	.05
434	Harold Baines	.40	.18
435	Neil Allen	.10	.05
436	Rick Peters	.10	.05
437	Mike Proly	.10	.05
438	Biff Pocoroba	.10	.05
439	Bob Stoddard	.10	.05
440	Steve Kemp	.10	.05
441	Bob Lillis MG	.10	.05
442	Byron McLaughlin	.10	.05
443	Benny Ayala	.10	.05
444	Steve Renko	.10	.05
445	Jerry Remy	.10	.05
446	Luis Pujols	.10	.05
447	Tom Brunansky	.20	.09
448	Ben Hayes	.10	.05
449	Joe Pettini	.10	.05
450	Gary Carter	.60	.25
451	Bob Jones	.10	.05
452	Chuck Porter	.10	.05
453	Willie Upshaw	.10	.05
454	Joe Beckwith	.10	.05
455	Terry Kennedy	.10	.05
456	Chicago Cubs TL / Keith Moreland / Fergie Jenkins	.40	.18
457	Dave Rozema	.10	.05
458	Kiko Garcia	.10	.05
459	Kevin Hickey	.10	.05
460	Dave Winfield	1.00	.45
461	Jim Maler	.10	.05
462	Lee Lacy	.10	.05
463	Dave Engle	.10	.05
464	Jeff A. Jones	.10	.05
465	Mookie Wilson	.20	.09
466	Gene Garber	.10	.05
467	Mike Ramsey	.10	.05
468	Geoff Zahn	.10	.05
469	Tom O'Malley	.10	.05
470	Nolan Ryan	4.00	1.80
471	Dick Howser MG	.10	.05
472	Mike G. Brown	.10	.05
473	Jim Dwyer	.10	.05
474	Greg Bargar	.10	.05
475	Gary Redus	.10	.05
476	Tom Tellmann	.10	.05
477	Rafael Landestoy	.10	.05
478	Alan Bannister	.10	.05
479	Frank Tanana	.20	.09
480	Ron Kittle	.20	.09
481	Mark Thurmond	.10	.05
482	Enos Cabell	.10	.05
483	Fergie Jenkins	.60	.25
484	Ozzie Virgil	.10	.05
485	Rick Rhoden	.10	.05
486	N.Y. Yankees TL / Don Baylor / Ron Guidry	.60	.25
487	Ricky Adams	.10	.05
488	Jesse Barfield	.20	.09
489	Dave Von Ohlen	.10	.05
490	Cal Ripken	5.00	2.20
491	Bobby Castillo	.10	.05
492	Tucker Ashford	.10	.05
493	Mike Norris	.10	.05
494	Chili Davis	.40	.18
495	Rollie Fingers	.60	.25
496	Terry Francona	.10	.05
497	Bud Anderson	.10	.05
498	Rich Gedman	.10	.05
499	Mike Witt	.10	.05
500	George Brett	1.25	.55
501	Steve Henderson	.10	.05
502	Joe Torre MG	.20	.09
503	Elias Sosa	.10	.06
504	Mickey Rivers	.10	.05
505	Pete Vuckovich	.10	.05
506	Ernie Whitt	.10	.05
507	Mike LaCoss	.10	.05
508	Mel Hall	.20	.09
509	Brad Havens	.10	.05
510	Alan Trammell	.60	.25
511	Marty Bystrom	.10	.05
512	Oscar Gamble	.10	.05
513	Dave Beard	.10	.05
514	Floyd Rayford	.10	.05
515	Gorman Thomas	.20	.09
516	Montreal Expos TL / Al Oliver / Charlie Lea	.20	.09
517	John Moses	.10	.05
518	Greg Walker	.20	.09
519	Ron Davis	.10	.05
520	Bob Boone	.20	.09
521	Pete Falcone	.10	.05
522	Dave Bergman	.10	.05
523	Glenn Hoffman	.10	.05
524	Carlos Diaz	.10	.05
525	Willie Wilson	.20	.09
526	Ron Oester	.10	.05
527	Checklist 397-528	.20	.02
528	Mark Brouhard	.10	.05
529	Keith Atherton	.10	.05
530	Dan Ford	.10	.05
531	Steve Boros MG	.10	.05
532	Eric Show	.10	.05
533	Ken Landreaux	.10	.05
534	Pete O'Brien	.20	.09
535	Bo Diaz	.10	.05
536	Doug Bair	.10	.05
537	Johnny Ray	.10	.05
538	Kevin Bass	.10	.05
539	George Frazier	.10	.05
540	George Hendrick	.10	.05
541	Dennis Lamp	.10	.05
542	Duane Kuiper	.10	.05
543	Craig McMurtry	.10	.05
544	Cesar Geronimo	.10	.05
545	Bill Buckner	.20	.09
546	Indians TL / Mike Hargrove / Lary Sorensen	.20	.09
547	Mike Moore	.10	.05
548	Ron Jackson	.10	.05
549	Walt Terrell	.10	.05
550	Jim Rice	.20	.09
551	Scott Ullger	.10	.05
552	Ray Burris	.10	.05
553	Joe Nolan	.10	.05
554	Ted Power	.10	.05
555	Greg Brock	.10	.05
556	Joey McLaughlin	.10	.05
557	Wayne Tolleson	.10	.05
558	Mike Davis	.10	.05
559	Mike Scott	.20	.09
560	Carlton Fisk	.75	.35
561	Whitey Herzog MG	.10	.05
562	Manny Castillo	.10	.05
563	Glenn Wilson	.20	.09

564	Al Holland	.10	.05
565	Leon Durham	.10	.05
566	Jim Bibby	.10	.05
567	Mike Heath	.10	.05
568	Pete Filson	.10	.05
569	Bake McBride	.10	.05
570	Dan Quisenberry	.10	.05
571	Bruce Bochy	.10	.05
572	Jerry Royster	.10	.05
573	Dave Kingman	.40	.18
574	Brian Downing	.10	.05
575	Jim Clancy	.10	.05
576	Giants TL	.20	.09
	Jeff Leonard		
	Atlee Hammaker		
577	Mark Clear	.10	.05
578	Lenn Sakata	.10	.05
579	Bob James	.10	.05
580	Lonnie Smith	.10	.05
581	Jose DeLeon	.10	.05
582	Bob McClure	.10	.05
583	Derrel Thomas	.10	.05
584	Dave Schmidt	.10	.05
585	Dan Driessen	.10	.05
586	Joe Niekro	.20	.09
587	Von Hayes	.10	.05
588	Milt Wilcox	.10	.05
589	Mike Easler	.10	.05
590	Dave Stieb	.10	.05
591	Tony LaRussa MG	.20	.09
592	Andre Robertson	.10	.05
593	Jeff Lahti	.10	.05
594	Gene Richards	.10	.05
595	Jeff Reardon	.10	.05
596	Ryne Sandberg	2.00	.90
597	Rick Camp	.10	.05
598	Rusty Kuntz	.10	.05
599	Doug Sisk	.10	.05
600	Rod Carew	.60	.25
601	John Tudor	.10	.05
602	John Wathan	.10	.05
603	Renie Martin	.10	.05
604	John Lowenstein	.10	.05
605	Mike Caldwell	.10	.05
606	Blue Jays TL	.20	.09
	Lloyd Moseby		
	Dave Stieb		
607	Tom Hume	.10	.05
608	Bobby Johnson	.10	.05
609	Dan Meyer	.10	.05
610	Steve Sax	.20	.09
611	Chet Lemon	.10	.05
612	Harry Spilman	.10	.05
613	Greg Gross	.10	.05
614	Len Barker	.10	.05
615	Garry Templeton	.10	.05
616	Don Robinson	.10	.05
617	Rick Cerone	.10	.05
618	Dickie Noles	.10	.05
619	Jerry Dybzinski	.10	.05
620	Al Oliver	.20	.09
621	Frank Howard MG	.20	.09
622	Al Cowens	.10	.05
623	Ron Washington	.10	.05
624	Terry Harper	.10	.05
625	Larry Gura	.10	.05
626	Bob Clark	.10	.05
627	Dave LaPoint	.10	.05
628	Ed Jurak	.10	.05
629	Rick Langford	.10	.05
630	Ted Simmons	.20	.09
631	Dennis Martinez	.20	.09
632	Tom Foley	.10	.05
633	Mike Krukow	.10	.05
634	Mike Marshall	.20	.09
635	Dave Righetti	.20	.09
636	Pat Putnam	.10	.05
637	Phillies TL	.20	.09
	Gary Matthews		
	John Denny		
638	George Vukovich	.10	.05
639	Rick Lysander	.10	.05
640	Lance Parrish	.20	.09
641	Mike Richardt	.10	.05
642	Tom Underwood	.10	.05
643	Mike C. Brown	.10	.05
644	Tim Lollar	.10	.05
645	Tony Pena	.10	.05
646	Checklist 529-660	.20	.09
647	Ron Roenicke	.10	.05
648	Len Whitehouse	.10	.05
649	Tom Herr	.20	.09
650	Phil Niekro	.60	.25
651	John McNamara MG	.10	.05
652	Rudy May	.10	.05
653	Dave Stapleton	.10	.05
654	Bob Bailor	.10	.05
655	Amos Otis	.20	.09
656	Bryn Smith	.10	.05
657	Thad Bosley	.10	.05
658	Jerry Augustine	.10	.05
659	Duane Walker	.10	.05
660	Ray Knight	.20	.09
661	Steve Yeager	.10	.05
662	Tom Brennan	.10	.05
663	Johnnie LeMaster	.10	.05
664	Dave Stegman	.10	.05
665	Buddy Bell	.20	.09
666	Detroit Tigers TL	.60	.25
	Lou Whitaker		
	Jack Morris		
667	Vance Law	.10	.05
668	Larry McWilliams	.10	.05
669	Dave Lopes	.20	.09
670	Rich Gossage	.60	.25
671	Jamie Quirk	.10	.05
672	Ricky Nelson	.10	.05
673	Mike Walters	.10	.05
674	Tim Flannery	.10	.05
675	Pascual Perez	.10	.05
676	Brian Giles	.10	.05
677	Doyle Alexander	.10	.05
678	Chris Speier	.10	.05
679	Art Howe	.10	.05
680	Fred Lynn	.20	.09
681	Tom Lasorda MG	.40	.18
682	Dan Morogiello	.10	.05
683	Marty Barrett	.20	.09
684	Bob Shirley	.10	.05
685	Willie Aikens	.10	.05
686	Joe Price	.10	.05
687	Roy Howell	.10	.05
688	George Wright	.10	.05
689	Mike Fischlin	.10	.05
690	Jack Clark	.20	.09
691	Steve Lake	.10	.05
692	Dickie Thon	.10	.05
693	Alan Wiggins	.10	.05
694	Mike Stanton	.10	.05
695	Lou Whitaker	.60	.25
696	Pirates TL	.20	.09
	Bill Madlock		
	Rick Rhoden		
697	Dale Murray	.10	.05
698	Marc Hill	.10	.05
699	Dave Rucker	.10	.05
700	Mike Schmidt	.75	.35
701	NL Active Batting	.60	.25
	Bill Madlock		
	Pete Rose		
	Dave Parker		
702	NL Active Hits	.60	.25
	Pete Rose		
	Rusty Staub		
	Tony Perez		
703	NL Active Home Run	.60	.25
	Mike Schmidt		
	Tony Perez		
	Dave Kingman		
704	NL Active RBI	.60	.25
	Tony Perez		
	Rusty Staub		
	Al Oliver		
705	NL Active Steals	.60	.25
	Joe Morgan		
	Cesar Cedeno		
	Larry Bowa		
706	NL Active Victory	.60	.25
	Steve Carlton		
	Fergie Jenkins		
	Tom Seaver		
707	NL Active Strikeout	1.50	.70
	Steve Carlton		
	Nolan Ryan		
	Tom Seaver		
708	NL Active ERA	.60	.25
	Tom Seaver		
	Steve Carlton		
	Steve Rogers		
709	NL Active Save	.20	.09
	Bruce Sutter		
	Tug McGraw		
	Gene Garber		
710	AL Active Batting	.60	.25
	Rod Carew		
	George Brett		
	Cecil Cooper		
711	AL Active Hits	.60	.25
	Rod Carew		
	Bert Campaneris		
	Reggie Jackson		
712	AL Active Home Run	.60	.25
	Reggie Jackson		
	Graig Nettles		
	Greg Luzinski		
713	AL Active RBI	.60	.25
	Reggie Jackson		
	Ted Simmons		
	Graig Nettles		
714	AL Active Steals	.20	.09
	Bert Campaneris		
	Dave Lopes		
	Omar Moreno		
715	AL Active Victory	.60	.25
	Jim Palmer		
	Don Sutton		
	Tommy John		
716	AL Active Strikeout	.60	.25
	Don Sutton		
	Bert Blyleven		
	Jerry Koosman		
717	AL Active ERA	.60	.25
	Jim Palmer		
	Rollie Fingers		
	Ron Guidry		
718	AL Active Save	.60	.25
	Rollie Fingers		
	Rich Gossage		
	Dan Quisenberry		
719	Andy Hassler	.10	.05
720	Dwight Evans	.20	.09
721	Del Crandall MG	.10	.05
722	Bob Welch	.10	.05
723	Rich Dauer	.10	.05
724	Eric Rasmussen	.10	.05
725	Cesar Cedeno	.20	.09
726	Brewers TL	.20	.09
	Ted Simmons		
	Moose Haas		
727	Joel Youngblood	.10	.05
728	Tug McGraw	.20	.09
729	Gene Tenace	.20	.09
730	Bruce Sutter	.20	.09
731	Lynn Jones	.10	.05
732	Terry Crowley	.10	.05
733	Dave Collins	.10	.05
734	Odell Jones	.10	.05
735	Rick Burleson	.10	.05
736	Dick Ruthven	.10	.05
737	Jim Essian	.10	.05
738	Bill Schroeder	.10	.05
739	Bob Watson	.20	.09
740	Tom Seaver	.75	.35
741	Wayne Gross	.10	.05
742	Dick Williams MG	.20	.09
743	Don Hood	.10	.05
744	Jamie Allen	.10	.05
745	Dennis Eckersley	.60	.25
746	Mickey Hatcher	.10	.05
747	Pat Zachry	.10	.05
748	Jeff Leonard	.10	.05
749	Doug Flynn	.10	.05
750	Jim Palmer	.60	.25
751	Charlie Moore	.10	.05
752	Phil Garner	.20	.09
753	Doug Gwosdz	.10	.05
754	Kent Tekulve	.20	.09
755	Garry Maddox	.10	.05

☐ 756	Reds TL .20 .09		
	Ron Oester		
	Mario Soto		
☐ 757	Larry Bowa	.20	.09
☐ 758	Bill Stein	.10	.05
☐ 759	Richard Dotson	.10	.05
☐ 760	Bob Horner	.10	.05
☐ 761	John Montefusco	.10	.05
☐ 762	Rance Mulliniks	.10	.05
☐ 763	Craig Swan	.10	.05
☐ 764	Mike Hargrove	.20	.09
☐ 765	Ken Forsch	.10	.05
☐ 766	Mike Vail	.10	.05
☐ 767	Carney Lansford	.20	.09
☐ 768	Champ Summers	.10	.05
☐ 769	Bill Caudill	.10	.05
☐ 770	Ken Griffey	.20	.09
☐ 771	Billy Gardner MG	.10	.05
☐ 772	Jim Slaton	.10	.05
☐ 773	Todd Cruz	.10	.05
☐ 774	Tom Gorman	.10	.05
☐ 775	Dave Parker	.20	.09
☐ 776	Craig Reynolds	.10	.05
☐ 777	Tom Paciorek	.20	.09
☐ 778	Andy Hawkins	.10	.05
☐ 779	Jim Sundberg	.20	.09
☐ 780	Steve Carlton	.75	.35
☐ 781	Checklist 661-792	.20	.09
☐ 782	Steve Balboni	.10	.05
☐ 783	Luis Leal	.10	.05
☐ 784	Leon Roberts	.10	.05
☐ 785	Joaquin Andujar	.10	.05
☐ 786	Red Sox TL .60 .25		
	Wade Boggs		
	Bob Ojeda		
☐ 787	Bill Campbell	.10	.05
☐ 788	Milt May	.10	.05
☐ 789	Bert Blyleven	.20	.09
☐ 790	Doug DeCinces	.10	.05
☐ 791	Terry Forster	.10	.05
☐ 792	Bill Russell	.20	.09

1984 Topps Traded

In now standard procedure, Topps issued its standard-size Traded (or extended) set for the fourth year in a row. Several of 1984's top rookies not contained in the regular set are pictured in the Traded set. Extended Rookie Cards in this set include Dwight Gooden, Jimmy Key, Mark Langston, Jose Rijo, and Bret Saberhagen. Again this year, the Topps affiliate in Ireland printed the cards, and the cards were available through hobby channels only in factory set form. The set numbering is in alphabetical order by player's name.

	NRMT	VG-E
COMP.FACT.SET (132)	40.00	18.00
COMMON CARD (1T-132T)	.25	.11
MINOR STARS	1.00	.45

☐ 1T	Willie Aikens	.25	.11
☐ 2T	Luis Aponte	.25	.11
☐ 3T	Mike Armstrong	.25	.11
☐ 4T	Bob Bailor	.25	.11
☐ 5T	Dusty Baker	1.25	.55
☐ 6T	Steve Balboni	.25	.11
☐ 7T	Alan Bannister	.25	.11
☐ 8T	Dave Beard	.25	.11
☐ 9T	Joe Beckwith	.25	.11
☐ 10T	Bruce Berenyi	.25	.11
☐ 11T	Dave Bergman	.25	.11
☐ 12T	Tony Bernazard	.25	.11
☐ 13T	Yogi Berra MG	2.00	.90
☐ 14T	Barry Bonnell	.25	.11
☐ 15T	Phil Bradley	1.00	.45
☐ 16T	Fred Breining	.25	.11
☐ 17T	Bill Buckner	1.00	.45
☐ 18T	Ray Burris	.25	.11
☐ 19T	John Butcher	.25	.11
☐ 20T	Brett Butler	1.25	.55
☐ 21T	Enos Cabell	.25	.11
☐ 22T	Bill Campbell	.25	.11
☐ 23T	Bill Caudill	.25	.11
☐ 24T	Bob Clark	.25	.11
☐ 25T	Bryan Clark	.25	.11
☐ 26T	Jaime Cocanower	.25	.11
☐ 27T	Ron Darling	1.25	.55
☐ 28T	Alvin Davis	1.00	.45
☐ 29T	Ken Dayley	.25	.11
☐ 30T	Jeff Dedmon	.25	.11
☐ 31T	Bob Dernier	.25	.11
☐ 32T	Carlos Diaz	.25	.11
☐ 33T	Mike Easler	.25	.11
☐ 34T	Dennis Eckersley	2.00	.90
☐ 35T	Jim Essian	.25	.11
☐ 36T	Darrell Evans	1.00	.45
☐ 37T	Mike Fitzgerald	.25	.11
☐ 38T	Tim Foli	.25	.11
☐ 39T	George Frazier	.25	.11
☐ 40T	Rich Gale	.25	.11
☐ 41T	Barbaro Garbey	.25	.11
☐ 42T	Dwight Gooden	10.00	4.50
☐ 43T	Rich Gossage	1.25	.55
☐ 44T	Wayne Gross	.25	.11
☐ 45T	Mark Gubicza	1.00	.45
☐ 46T	Jackie Gutierrez	.25	.11
☐ 47T	Mel Hall	.25	.11
☐ 48T	Toby Harrah	1.00	.45
☐ 49T	Ron Hassey	.25	.11
☐ 50T	Rich Hebner	.25	.11
☐ 51T	Willie Hernandez	1.00	.45
☐ 52T	Ricky Horton	.25	.11
☐ 53T	Art Howe	.25	.11
☐ 54T	Dane Iorg	.25	.11
☐ 55T	Brook Jacoby	1.00	.45
☐ 56T	Mike Jeffcoat	.25	.11
☐ 57T	Dave Johnson MG	1.00	.45
☐ 58T	Lynn Jones	.25	.11
☐ 59T	Ruppert Jones	.25	.11
☐ 60T	Mike Jorgensen	.25	.11
☐ 61T	Bob Kearney	.25	.11
☐ 62T	Jimmy Key	4.00	1.80
☐ 63T	Dave Kingman	1.25	.55
☐ 64T	Jerry Koosman	1.00	.45
☐ 65T	Wayne Krenchicki	.25	.11
☐ 66T	Rusty Kuntz	.25	.11
☐ 67T	Rene Lachemann MG	.25	.11
☐ 68T	Frank LaCorte	.25	.11
☐ 69T	Dennis Lamp	.25	.11
☐ 70T	Mark Langston	2.00	.90
☐ 71T	Rick Leach	.25	.11
☐ 72T	Craig Lefferts	1.00	.45
☐ 73T	Gary Lucas	.25	.11
☐ 74T	Jerry Martin	.25	.11
☐ 75T	Carmelo Martinez	.25	.11
☐ 76T	Mike Mason	.25	.11
☐ 77T	Gary Matthews	1.00	.45
☐ 78T	Andy McGaffigan	.25	.11
☐ 79T	Larry Milbourne	.25	.11
☐ 80T	Sid Monge	.25	.11
☐ 81T	Jackie Moore MG	.25	.11
☐ 82T	Joe Morgan	2.50	1.10
☐ 83T	Graig Nettles	1.25	.55
☐ 84T	Phil Niekro	1.50	.70
☐ 85T	Ken Oberkfell	.25	.11
☐ 86T	Mike O'Berry	.25	.11

☐ 87T	Al Oliver	1.00	.45
☐ 88T	Jorge Orta	.25	.11
☐ 89T	Amos Otis	1.00	.45
☐ 90T	Dave Parker	1.00	.45
☐ 91T	Tony Perez	1.50	.70
☐ 92T	Gerald Perry	1.00	.45
☐ 93T	Gary Pettis	.25	.11
☐ 94T	Rob Picciolo	.25	.11
☐ 95T	Vern Rapp MG	.25	.11
☐ 96T	Floyd Rayford	.25	.11
☐ 97T	Randy Ready	1.00	.45
☐ 98T	Ron Reed	.25	.11
☐ 99T	Gene Richards	.25	.11
☐ 100T	Jose Rijo	1.50	.70
☐ 101T	Jeff D. Robinson	.25	.11
☐ 102T	Ron Romanick	.25	.11
☐ 103T	Pete Rose	5.00	2.20
☐ 104T	Bret Saberhagen	2.00	.90
☐ 105T	Juan Samuel	1.25	.55
☐ 106T	Scott Sanderson	.25	.11
☐ 107T	Dick Schofield	1.00	.45
☐ 108T	Tom Seaver	5.00	2.20
☐ 109T	Jim Slaton	.25	.11
☐ 110T	Mike Smithson	.25	.11
☐ 111T	Lary Sorensen	.25	.11
☐ 112T	Tim Stoddard	.25	.11
☐ 113T	Champ Summers	.25	.11
☐ 114T	Jim Sundberg	1.00	.45
☐ 115T	Rick Sutcliffe	1.00	.45
☐ 116T	Craig Swan	.25	.11
☐ 117T	Tim Teufel	.25	.11
☐ 118T	Derrel Thomas	.25	.11
☐ 119T	Gorman Thomas	.25	.11
☐ 120T	Alex Trevino	.25	.11
☐ 121T	Manny Trillo	.25	.11
☐ 122T	John Tudor	.25	.11
☐ 123T	Tom Underwood	.25	.11
☐ 124T	Mike Vail	.25	.11
☐ 125T	Tom Waddell	.25	.11
☐ 126T	Gary Ward	.25	.11
☐ 127T	Curt Wilkerson	.25	.11
☐ 128T	Frank Williams	.25	.11
☐ 129T	Glenn Wilson	.25	.11
☐ 130T	John Wockenfuss	.25	.11
☐ 131T	Ned Yost	.25	.11
☐ 132T	Checklist 1T-132T	.25	.11

1985 Topps

The 1985 Topps set contains 792 standard-size full-color cards. Cards were primarily distributed in 15-card wax packs and 51-card rack packs. Manager cards feature the team checklist on the reverse. Full color card fronts both the Topps and team logos along with the team name, player's name, and his position. The first ten cards (1-10) are Record Breakers, cards 131-143 are Father and Sons, and cards 701 to 722 portray All-Star selections. Cards 271-282 represent "First Draft Picks" still active in professional baseball and cards

389-404 feature selected members of the 1984 U.S. Olympic Baseball Team. Rookie Cards include Roger Clemens, Eric Davis, Shawon Dunston, Dwight Gooden, Orel Hershiser, Jimmy Key, Mark Langston, Mark McGwire, Terry Pendleton, Kirby Puckett, Jose Rijo and Bret Saberhagen.

	NRMT	VG-E
COMPLETE SET (792)	50.00	22.00
COMMON CARD (1-792)	1.00	.09
MINOR STARS	.20	.09
SEMISTARS	.40	.18
UNLISTED STARS	.60	.25
SUBSET CARDS HALF VALUE OF BASE CARDS		

□ 1	Carlton Fisk RB Longest game by catcher	.20	.09
□ 2	Steve Garvey RB Consecutive error- less games, 1B	.20	.09
□ 3	Dwight Gooden RB Most rookie strikeouts	.60	.25
□ 4	Cliff Johnson RB Most pinch-hit homers	.10	.05
□ 5	Joe Morgan RB Most homers 2B, lifetime	.20	.09
□ 6	Pete Rose RB Most career singles	.40	.18
□ 7	Nolan Ryan RB Most career strikeouts	1.50	.70
□ 8	Juan Samuel RB Most SB's, rookie season	.10	.05
□ 9	Bruce Sutter RB Most NL season saves	.10	.05
□ 10	Don Sutton RB Most seasons 100 or more K's	.20	.09
□ 11	Ralph Houk MG	.10	.05
□ 12	Dave Lopes (Now with Cubs on card front)	.20	.09
□ 13	Tim Lollar	.10	.05
□ 14	Chris Bando	.10	.05
□ 15	Jerry Koosman	.10	.05
□ 16	Bobby Meacham	.10	.05
□ 17	Mike Scott	.10	.05
□ 18	Mickey Hatcher	.10	.05
□ 19	George Frazier	.10	.05
□ 20	Chet Lemon	.10	.05
□ 21	Lee Tunnell	.10	.05
□ 22	Duane Kuiper	.10	.05
□ 23	Bret Saberhagen	.60	.25
□ 24	Jesse Barfield	.10	.05
□ 25	Steve Bedrosian	.10	.05
□ 26	Roy Smalley	.10	.05
□ 27	Bruce Berenyi	.10	.05
□ 28	Dann Bilardello	.10	.05
□ 29	Odell Jones	.10	.05
□ 30	Cal Ripken	3.00	1.35
□ 31	Terry Whitfield	.10	.05
□ 32	Chuck Porter	.10	.05
□ 33	Tito Landrum	.10	.05
□ 34	Ed Nunez	.10	.05
□ 35	Graig Nettles	.20	.09
□ 36	Fred Breining	.10	.05
□ 37	Reid Nichols	.10	.05
□ 38	Jackie Moore MG	.10	.05
□ 39	John Wockenfuss	.10	.05
□ 40	Phil Niekro	.60	.25
□ 41	Mike Fischlin	.10	.05
□ 42	Luis Sanchez	.10	.05
□ 43	Andre David	.10	.05
□ 44	Dickie Thon	.10	.05
□ 45	Greg Minton	.10	.05
□ 46	Gary Woods	.10	.05
□ 47	Dave Rozema	.10	.05
□ 48	Tony Fernandez	.20	.09
□ 49	Butch Davis	.10	.05
□ 50	John Candelaria	.10	.05
□ 51	Bob Watson	.20	.09
□ 52	Jerry Dybzinski	.10	.05
□ 53	Tom Gorman	.10	.05

□ 54	Cesar Cedeno	.20	.09
□ 55	Frank Tanana	.10	.05
□ 56	Jim Dwyer	.10	.05
□ 57	Pat Zachry	.10	.05
□ 58	Orlando Mercado	.10	.05
□ 59	Rick Waits	.10	.05
□ 60	George Hendrick	.10	.05
□ 61	Curt Kaufman	.10	.05
□ 62	Mike Ramsey	.10	.05
□ 63	Steve McCatty	.10	.05
□ 64	Mark Bailey	.10	.05
□ 65	Bill Buckner	.20	.09
□ 66	Dick Williams MG	.20	.09
□ 67	Rafael Santana	.10	.05
□ 68	Von Hayes	.10	.05
□ 69	Jim Winn	.10	.05
□ 70	Don Baylor	.20	.09
□ 71	Tim Laudner	.10	.05
□ 72	Rick Sutcliffe	.10	.05
□ 73	Rusty Kuntz	.10	.05
□ 74	Mike Krukow	.10	.05
□ 75	Willie Upshaw	.10	.05
□ 76	Alan Bannister	.10	.05
□ 77	Joe Beckwith	.10	.05
□ 78	Scott Fletcher	.10	.05
□ 79	Rick Mahler	.10	.05
□ 80	Keith Hernandez	.20	.09
□ 81	Lenn Sakata	.10	.05
□ 82	Joe Price	.10	.05
□ 83	Charlie Moore	.10	.05
□ 84	Spike Owen	.10	.05
□ 85	Mike Marshall	.10	.05
□ 86	Don Aase	.10	.05
□ 87	David Green	.10	.05
□ 88	Bryn Smith	.10	.05
□ 89	Jackie Gutierrez	.10	.05
□ 90	Rich Gossage	.20	.09
□ 91	Jeff Burroughs	.10	.05
□ 92	Paul Owens MG	.10	.05
□ 93	Don Schulze	.10	.05
□ 94	Toby Harrah	.10	.05
□ 95	Jose Cruz	.20	.09
□ 96	Johnny Ray	.10	.05
□ 97	Pete Filson	.10	.05
□ 98	Steve Lake	.10	.05
□ 99	Milt Wilcox	.10	.05
□ 100	George Brett	1.25	.55
□ 101	Jim Acker	.10	.05
□ 102	Tommy Dunbar	.10	.05
□ 103	Randy Lerch	.10	.05
□ 104	Mike Fitzgerald	.10	.05
□ 105	Ron Kittle	.10	.05
□ 106	Pascual Perez	.10	.05
□ 107	Tom Foley	.10	.05
□ 108	Darnell Coles	.10	.05
□ 109	Gary Roenicke	.10	.05
□ 110	Alejandro Pena	.10	.05
□ 111	Doug DeCinces	.10	.05
□ 112	Tom Tellmann	.10	.05
□ 113	Tom Herr	.10	.05
□ 114	Bob James	.10	.05
□ 115	Rickey Henderson	.60	.25
□ 116	Dennis Boyd	.10	.05
□ 117	Greg Gross	.10	.05
□ 118	Eric Show	.10	.05
□ 119	Pat Corrales MG	.10	.05
□ 120	Steve Kemp	.10	.05
□ 121	Checklist: 1-132	.10	.05
□ 122	Tom Brunansky	.20	.09
□ 123	Dave Smith	.10	.05
□ 124	Rich Hebner	.10	.05
□ 125	Kent Tekulve	.10	.05
□ 126	Ruppert Jones	.10	.05
□ 127	Mark Gubicza	.20	.09
□ 128	Ernie Whitt	.10	.05
□ 129	Gene Garber	.10	.05
□ 130	Al Oliver	.20	.09
□ 131	Buddy Bell FS Gus Bell	.20	.09
□ 132	Dale Berra FS Yogi Berra	.20	.09
□ 133	Bob Boone FS Ray Boone	.10	.05
□ 134	Terry Francona FS Tito Francona	.20	.09
□ 135	Terry Kennedy FS	.20	.09

	Bob Kennedy		
□ 136	Jeff Kunkel FS Bill Kunkel	.10	.05
□ 137	Vance Law FS Vern Law	.20	.09
□ 138	Dick Schofield FS Dick Schofield	.10	.05
□ 139	Joel Skinner FS Bob Skinner	.10	.05
□ 140	Roy Smalley Jr. FS Roy Smalley	.20	.09
□ 141	Mike Stenhouse FS Dave Stenhouse	.10	.05
□ 142	Steve Trout FS Dizzy Trout	.10	.05
□ 143	Ozzie Virgil FS Ozzie Virgil	.10	.05
□ 144	Ron Gardenhire	.10	.05
□ 145	Alvin Davis	.20	.09
□ 146	Gary Redus	.10	.05
□ 147	Bill Swaggerty	.10	.05
□ 148	Steve Yeager	.10	.05
□ 149	Dickie Noles	.10	.05
□ 150	Jim Rice	.20	.09
□ 151	Moose Haas	.10	.05
□ 152	Steve Braun	.10	.05
□ 153	Frank LaCorte	.10	.05
□ 154	Argenis Salazar	.10	.05
□ 155	Yogi Berra MG	.40	.18
□ 156	Craig Reynolds	.10	.05
□ 157	Tug McGraw	.20	.09
□ 158	Pat Tabler	.10	.05
□ 159	Carlos Diaz	.10	.05
□ 160	Lance Parrish	.20	.09
□ 161	Ken Schrom	.10	.05
□ 162	Benny Distefano	.10	.05
□ 163	Dennis Eckersley	.60	.25
□ 164	Jorge Orta	.10	.05
□ 165	Dusty Baker	.20	.09
□ 166	Keith Atherton	.10	.05
□ 167	Rufino Linares	.10	.05
□ 168	Garth Iorg	.10	.05
□ 169	Dan Spillner	.10	.05
□ 170	George Foster	.20	.09
□ 171	Bill Stein	.10	.05
□ 172	Jack Perconte	.10	.05
□ 173	Mike Young	.10	.05
□ 174	Rick Honeycutt	.10	.05
□ 175	Dave Parker	.20	.09
□ 176	Bill Schroeder	.10	.05
□ 177	Dave Von Ohlen	.10	.05
□ 178	Miguel Dilone	.10	.05
□ 179	Tommy John	.40	.18
□ 180	Dave Winfield	.60	.25
□ 181	Roger Clemens	8.00	3.60
□ 182	Tim Flannery	.10	.05
□ 183	Larry McWilliams	.10	.05
□ 184	Carmen Castillo	.10	.05
□ 185	Al Holland	.10	.05
□ 186	Bob Lillis MG	.10	.05
□ 187	Mike Walters	.10	.05
□ 188	Greg Pryor	.10	.05
□ 189	Warren Brusstar	.10	.05
□ 190	Rusty Staub	.20	.09
□ 191	Steve Nicosia	.10	.05
□ 192	Howard Johnson	.20	.09
□ 193	Jimmy Key	.75	.35
□ 194	Dave Stegman	.10	.05
□ 195	Glenn Hubbard	.10	.05
□ 196	Pete O'Brien	.10	.05
□ 197	Mike Warren	.10	.05
□ 198	Eddie Milner	.10	.05
□ 199	Dennis Martinez	.20	.09
□ 200	Reggie Jackson	.75	.35
□ 201	Burt Hooton	.10	.05
□ 202	Gorman Thomas	.10	.05
□ 203	Bob McClure	.10	.05
□ 204	Art Howe	.10	.05
□ 205	Steve Rogers	.10	.05
□ 206	Phil Garner	.10	.05
□ 207	Mark Clear	.10	.05
□ 208	Champ Summers	.10	.05
□ 209	Bill Campbell	.10	.05
□ 210	Gary Matthews	.10	.05
□ 211	Clay Christiansen	.10	.05
□ 212	George Vukovich	.10	.05

☐ 213	Billy Gardner MG	.20	.09
☐ 214	John Tudor	.10	.05
☐ 215	Bob Brenly	.10	.05
☐ 216	Jerry Don Gleaton	.10	.05
☐ 217	Leon Roberts	.10	.05
☐ 218	Doyle Alexander	.10	.05
☐ 219	Gerald Perry	.10	.05
☐ 220	Fred Lynn	.20	.09
☐ 221	Ron Reed	.10	.05
☐ 222	Hubie Brooks	.10	.05
☐ 223	Tom Hume	.10	.05
☐ 224	Al Cowens	.10	.05
☐ 225	Mike Boddicker	.10	.05
☐ 226	Juan Beniquez	.10	.05
☐ 227	Danny Darwin	.10	.05
☐ 228	Dion James	.10	.05
☐ 229	Dave LaPoint	.10	.05
☐ 230	Gary Carter	.60	.25
☐ 231	Dwayne Murphy	.10	.05
☐ 232	Dave Beard	.10	.05
☐ 233	Ed Jurak	.10	.05
☐ 234	Jerry Narron	.10	.05
☐ 235	Garry Maddox	.10	.05
☐ 236	Mark Thurmond	.10	.05
☐ 237	Julio Franco	.40	.18
☐ 238	Jose Rijo	.40	.18
☐ 239	Tim Teufel	.10	.05
☐ 240	Dave Stieb	.20	.09
☐ 241	Jim Frey MG	.10	.05
☐ 242	Greg Harris	.10	.05
☐ 243	Barbaro Garbey	.10	.05
☐ 244	Mike Jones	.10	.05
☐ 245	Chili Davis	.20	.09
☐ 246	Mike Norris	.10	.05
☐ 247	Wayne Tolleson	.10	.05
☐ 248	Terry Forster	.10	.05
☐ 249	Harold Baines	.20	.09
☐ 250	Jesse Orosco	.10	.05
☐ 251	Brad Gulden	.10	.05
☐ 252	Dan Ford	.10	.05
☐ 253	Sid Bream	.20	.09
☐ 254	Pete Vuckovich	.10	.05
☐ 255	Lonnie Smith	.10	.05
☐ 256	Mike Stanton	.10	.05
☐ 257	Bryan Little UER	.10	.05
	Name spelled Brian on front		
☐ 258	Mike C. Brown	.10	.05
☐ 259	Gary Allenson	.10	.05
☐ 260	Dave Righetti	.20	.09
☐ 261	Checklist: 133-264	.10	.05
☐ 262	Greg Booker	.10	.05
☐ 263	Mel Hall	.10	.05
☐ 264	Joe Sambito	.10	.05
☐ 265	Juan Samuel	.10	.05
☐ 266	Frank Viola	.20	.09
☐ 267	Henry Cotto	.10	.05
☐ 268	Chuck Tanner MG	.20	.09
☐ 269	Doug Baker	.10	.05
☐ 270	Dan Quisenberry	.20	.09
☐ 271	Tim Foli FDP68	.10	.05
☐ 272	Jeff Burroughs FDP69	.10	.05
☐ 273	Bill Almon FDP74	.10	.05
☐ 274	Floyd Bannister FDP76	.10	.05
☐ 275	Harold Baines FDP77	.10	.05
☐ 276	Bob Horner FDP78	.10	.05
☐ 277	Al Chambers FDP79	.10	.05
☐ 278	Darryl Strawberry	.20	.09
	FDP80		
☐ 279	Mike Moore FDP81	.10	.05
☐ 280	Shawon Dunston FDP82	.60	.25
☐ 281	Tim Belcher FDP83	.60	.25
☐ 282	Shawn Abner FDP84	.10	.05
☐ 283	Fran Mullins	.10	.05
☐ 284	Marty Bystrom	.10	.05
☐ 285	Dan Driessen	.10	.05
☐ 286	Rudy Law	.10	.05
☐ 287	Walt Terrell	.10	.05
☐ 288	Jeff Kunkel	.10	.05
☐ 289	Tom Underwood	.10	.05
☐ 290	Cecil Cooper	.20	.09
☐ 291	Bob Welch	.10	.05
☐ 292	Brad Komminsk	.10	.05
☐ 293	Curt Young	.10	.05
☐ 294	Tom Nieto	.10	.05
☐ 295	Joe Niekro	.10	.05
☐ 296	Ricky Nelson	.10	.05
☐ 297	Gary Lucas	.10	.05
☐ 298	Marty Barrett	.10	.05
☐ 299	Andy Hawkins	.10	.05
☐ 300	Rod Carew	.60	.25
☐ 301	John Montefusco	.10	.05
☐ 302	Tim Corcoran	.10	.05
☐ 303	Mike Jeffcoat	.10	.05
☐ 304	Gary Gaetti	.20	.09
☐ 305	Dale Berra	.10	.05
☐ 306	Rick Reuschel	.10	.05
☐ 307	Sparky Anderson MG	.20	.09
☐ 308	John Wathan	.10	.05
☐ 309	Mike Witt	.10	.05
☐ 310	Manny Trillo	.10	.05
☐ 311	Jim Gott	.10	.05
☐ 312	Marc Hill	.10	.05
☐ 313	Dave Schmidt	.10	.05
☐ 314	Ron Oester	.10	.05
☐ 315	Doug Sisk	.10	.05
☐ 316	John Lowenstein	.10	.05
☐ 317	Jack Lazorko	.10	.05
☐ 318	Ted Simmons	.20	.09
☐ 319	Jeff Jones	.10	.05
☐ 320	Dale Murphy	.60	.25
☐ 321	Ricky Horton	.10	.05
☐ 322	Dave Stapleton	.10	.05
☐ 323	Andy McGaffigan	.10	.05
☐ 324	Bruce Bochy	.10	.05
☐ 325	John Denny	.10	.05
☐ 326	Kevin Bass	.10	.05
☐ 327	Brook Jacoby	.10	.05
☐ 328	Bob Shirley	.10	.05
☐ 329	Ron Washington	.10	.05
☐ 330	Leon Durham	.10	.05
☐ 331	Bill Laskey	.10	.05
☐ 332	Brian Harper	.10	.05
☐ 333	Willie Hernandez	.10	.05
☐ 334	Dick Howser MG	.20	.09
☐ 335	Bruce Benedict	.10	.05
☐ 336	Rance Mulliniks	.10	.05
☐ 337	Billy Sample	.10	.05
☐ 338	Britt Burns	.10	.05
☐ 339	Danny Heep	.10	.05
☐ 340	Robin Yount	.60	.25
☐ 341	Floyd Rayford	.10	.05
☐ 342	Ted Power	.10	.05
☐ 343	Bill Russell	.10	.05
☐ 344	Dave Henderson	.10	.05
☐ 345	Charlie Lea	.10	.05
☐ 346	Terry Pendleton	.60	.25
☐ 347	Rick Langford	.10	.05
☐ 348	Bob Boone	.20	.09
☐ 349	Domingo Ramos	.10	.05
☐ 350	Wade Boggs	.75	.35
☐ 351	Juan Agosto	.10	.05
☐ 352	Joe Morgan	.60	.25
☐ 353	Julio Solano	.10	.05
☐ 354	Andre Robertson	.10	.05
☐ 355	Bert Blyleven	.20	.09
☐ 356	Dave Meier	.10	.05
☐ 357	Rich Bordi	.10	.05
☐ 358	Tony Pena	.10	.05
☐ 359	Pat Sheridan	.10	.05
☐ 360	Steve Carlton	.60	.25
☐ 361	Alfredo Griffin	.10	.05
☐ 362	Craig McMurtry	.10	.05
☐ 363	Ron Hodges	.10	.05
☐ 364	Richard Dotson	.10	.05
☐ 365	Danny Ozark MG	.10	.05
☐ 366	Todd Cruz	.10	.05
☐ 367	Keefe Cato	.10	.05
☐ 368	Dave Bergman	.10	.05
☐ 369	R.J. Reynolds	.10	.05
☐ 370	Bruce Sutter	.20	.09
☐ 371	Mickey Rivers	.10	.05
☐ 372	Roy Howell	.10	.05
☐ 373	Mike Moore	.10	.05
☐ 374	Brian Downing	.10	.05
☐ 375	Jeff Reardon	.20	.09
☐ 376	Jeff Newman	.10	.05
☐ 377	Checklist: 265-396	.10	.05
☐ 378	Alan Wiggins	.10	.05
☐ 379	Charles Hudson	.10	.05
☐ 380	Ken Griffey	.20	.09
☐ 381	Roy Smith	.10	.05
☐ 382	Denny Walling	.10	.05
☐ 383	Rick Lysander	.10	.05
☐ 384	Jody Davis	.10	.05
☐ 385	Jose DeLeon	.10	.05
☐ 386	Dan Gladden	.20	.09
☐ 387	Buddy Biancalana	.10	.05
☐ 388	Bert Roberge	.10	.05
☐ 389	Rod Dedeaux OLY CO	.20	.09
☐ 390	Sid Akins OLY	.10	.05
☐ 391	Flavio Alfaro OLY	.10	.05
☐ 392	Don August OLY	.10	.05
☐ 393	Scott Bankhead OLY	.10	.05
☐ 394	Bob Caffrey OLY	.10	.05
☐ 395	Mike Dunne OLY	.20	.09
☐ 396	Gary Green OLY	.10	.05
☐ 397	John Hoover OLY	.10	.05
☐ 398	Shane Mack OLY	.60	.25
☐ 399	John Marzano OLY	.20	.09
☐ 400	Oddibe McDowell OLY	.20	.09
☐ 401	Mark McGwire OLY	40.00	18.00
☐ 402	Pat Pacillo OLY	.20	.09
☐ 403	Cory Snyder OLY	.40	.18
☐ 404	Billy Swift OLY	.40	.18
☐ 405	Tom Veryzer	.10	.05
☐ 406	Len Whitehouse	.10	.05
☐ 407	Bobby Ramos	.10	.05
☐ 408	Sid Monge	.10	.05
☐ 409	Brad Wellman	.10	.05
☐ 410	Bob Horner	.10	.05
☐ 411	Bobby Cox MG	.10	.05
☐ 412	Bud Black	.10	.05
☐ 413	Vance Law	.10	.05
☐ 414	Gary Ward	.10	.05
☐ 415	Ron Darling UER	.20	.09
	(No trivia answer)		
☐ 416	Wayne Gross	.10	.05
☐ 417	John Franco	.60	.25
☐ 418	Ken Landreaux	.10	.05
☐ 419	Mike Caldwell	.10	.05
☐ 420	Andre Dawson	.60	.25
☐ 421	Dave Rucker	.10	.05
☐ 422	Carney Lansford	.20	.09
☐ 423	Barry Bonnell	.10	.05
☐ 424	Al Nipper	.10	.05
☐ 425	Mike Hargrove	.20	.09
☐ 426	Vern Ruhle	.10	.05
☐ 427	Mario Ramirez	.10	.05
☐ 428	Larry Andersen	.10	.05
☐ 429	Rick Cerone	.10	.05
☐ 430	Ron Davis	.10	.05
☐ 431	U.L. Washington	.10	.05
☐ 432	Thad Bosley	.10	.05
☐ 433	Jim Morrison	.10	.05
☐ 434	Gene Richards	.10	.05
☐ 435	Dan Petry	.10	.05
☐ 436	Willie Aikens	.10	.05
☐ 437	Al Jones	.10	.05
☐ 438	Joe Torre MG	.40	.18
☐ 439	Junior Ortiz	.10	.05
☐ 440	Fernando Valenzuela	.20	.09
☐ 441	Duane Walker	.10	.05
☐ 442	Ken Forsch	.10	.05
☐ 443	George Wright	.10	.05
☐ 444	Tony Phillips	.10	.05
☐ 445	Tippy Martinez	.10	.05
☐ 446	Jim Sundberg	.10	.05
☐ 447	Jeff Lahti	.10	.05
☐ 448	Derrel Thomas	.10	.05
☐ 449	Phil Bradley	.20	.09
☐ 450	Steve Garvey	.40	.18
☐ 451	Bruce Hurst	.10	.05
☐ 452	John Castino	.10	.05
☐ 453	Tom Waddell	.10	.05
☐ 454	Glenn Wilson	.10	.05
☐ 455	Bob Knepper	.10	.05
☐ 456	Tim Foli	.10	.05
☐ 457	Cecilio Guante	.10	.05
☐ 458	Randy Johnson	.10	.05
☐ 459	Charlie Leibrandt	.10	.05
☐ 460	Ryne Sandberg	1.25	.55
☐ 461	Marty Castillo	.10	.05
☐ 462	Gary Lavelle	.10	.05
☐ 463	Dave Collins	.10	.05
☐ 464	Mike Mason	.10	.05
☐ 465	Bob Grich	.20	.09
☐ 466	Tony LaRussa MG	.40	.18
☐ 467	Ed Lynch	.10	.05

□ 468	Wayne Krenchicki	.10	.05
□ 469	Sammy Stewart	.10	.05
□ 470	Steve Sax	.10	.05
□ 471	Pete Ladd	.10	.05
□ 472	Jim Essian	.10	.05
□ 473	Tim Wallach	.20	.09
□ 474	Kurt Kepshire	.10	.05
□ 475	Andre Thornton	.10	.05
□ 476	Jeff Stone	.10	.05
□ 477	Bob Ojeda	.10	.05
□ 478	Kurt Bevacqua	.10	.05
□ 479	Mike Madden	.10	.05
□ 480	Lou Whitaker	.40	.18
□ 481	Dale Murray	.10	.05
□ 482	Harry Spilman	.10	.05
□ 483	Mike Smithson	.10	.05
□ 484	Larry Bowa	.20	.09
□ 485	Matt Young	.20	.09
□ 486	Steve Balboni	.10	.05
□ 487	Frank Williams	.10	.05
□ 488	Joel Skinner	.10	.05
□ 489	Bryan Clark	.10	.05
□ 490	Jason Thompson	.10	.05
□ 491	Rick Camp	.10	.05
□ 492	Dave Johnson MG	.20	.09
□ 493	Orel Hershiser	.75	.35
□ 494	Rich Dauer	.10	.05
□ 495	Mario Soto	.10	.05
□ 496	Donnie Scott	.10	.05
□ 497	Gary Pettis UER	.10	.05
	(Photo actually		
	Gary's little		
	brother Lynn)		
□ 498	Ed Romero	.10	.05
□ 499	Danny Cox	.10	.05
□ 500	Mike Schmidt	.75	.35
□ 501	Dan Schatzeder	.10	.05
□ 502	Rick Miller	.10	.05
□ 503	Tim Conroy	.10	.05
□ 504	Jerry Willard	.10	.05
□ 505	Jim Beattie	.10	.05
□ 506	Franklin Stubbs	.10	.05
□ 507	Ray Fontenot	.10	.05
□ 508	John Shelby	.10	.05
□ 509	Milt May	.10	.05
□ 510	Kent Hrbek	.20	.09
□ 511	Lee Smith	.40	.18
□ 512	Tom Brookens	.10	.05
□ 513	Lynn Jones	.10	.05
□ 514	Jeff Cornell	.10	.05
□ 515	Dave Concepcion	.20	.09
□ 516	Roy Lee Jackson	.10	.05
□ 517	Jerry Martin	.10	.05
□ 518	Chris Chambliss	.10	.05
□ 519	Doug Rader MG	.10	.05
□ 520	LaMarr Hoyt	.10	.05
□ 521	Rick Dempsey	.10	.05
□ 522	Paul Molitor	.60	.25
□ 523	Candy Maldonado	.10	.05
□ 524	Rob Wilfong	.10	.05
□ 525	Darrell Porter	.10	.05
□ 526	David Palmer	.10	.05
□ 527	Checklist: 397-528	.10	.05
□ 528	Bill Krueger	.10	.05
□ 529	Rich Gedman	.10	.05
□ 530	Dave Dravecky	.20	.09
□ 531	Joe Lefebvre	.10	.05
□ 532	Frank DiPino	.10	.05
□ 533	Tony Bernazard	.10	.05
□ 534	Brian Dayett	.10	.05
□ 535	Pat Putnam	.10	.05
□ 536	Kirby Puckett	8.00	3.60
□ 537	Don Robinson	.10	.05
□ 538	Keith Moreland	.10	.05
□ 539	Aurelio Lopez	.10	.05
□ 540	Claudell Washington	.10	.05
□ 541	Mark Davis	.10	.05
□ 542	Don Slaught	.10	.05
□ 543	Mike Squires	.10	.05
□ 544	Bruce Kison	.10	.05
□ 545	Lloyd Moseby	.10	.05
□ 546	Brent Gaff	.10	.05
□ 547	Pete Rose MG	.40	.18
□ 548	Larry Parrish	.10	.05
□ 549	Mike Scioscia	.10	.05
□ 550	Scott McGregor	.10	.05

□ 551	Andy Van Slyke	.40	.18
□ 552	Chris Codiroli	.10	.05
□ 553	Bob Clark	.10	.05
□ 554	Doug Flynn	.10	.05
□ 555	Bob Stanley	.10	.05
□ 556	Sixto Lezcano	.10	.05
□ 557	Len Barker	.10	.05
□ 558	Carmelo Martinez	.10	.05
□ 559	Jay Howell	.10	.05
□ 560	Bill Madlock	.20	.09
□ 561	Darryl Motley	.10	.05
□ 562	Houston Jimenez	.10	.05
□ 563	Dick Ruthven	.10	.05
□ 564	Alan Ashby	.10	.05
□ 565	Kirk Gibson	.20	.09
□ 566	Ed VandeBerg	.10	.05
□ 567	Joel Youngblood	.10	.05
□ 568	Cliff Johnson	.10	.05
□ 569	Ken Oberkfell	.10	.05
□ 570	Darryl Strawberry	.60	.25
□ 571	Charlie Hough	.20	.09
□ 572	Tom Paciorek	.10	.05
□ 573	Jay Tibbs	.10	.05
□ 574	Joe Altobelli MG	.10	.05
□ 575	Pedro Guerrero	.20	.09
□ 576	Jaime Cocanower	.10	.05
□ 577	Chris Speier	.10	.05
□ 578	Terry Francona	.10	.05
□ 579	Ron Romanick	.10	.05
□ 580	Dwight Evans	.20	.09
□ 581	Mark Wagner	.10	.05
□ 582	Ken Phelps	.10	.05
□ 583	Bobby Brown	.10	.05
□ 584	Kevin Gross	.10	.05
□ 585	Butch Wynegar	.10	.05
□ 586	Bill Scherrer	.10	.05
□ 587	Doug Frobel	.10	.05
□ 588	Bobby Castillo	.10	.05
□ 589	Bob Dernier	.10	.05
□ 590	Ray Knight	.10	.05
□ 591	Larry Herndon	.10	.05
□ 592	Jeff D. Robinson	.10	.05
□ 593	Rick Leach	.10	.05
□ 594	Curt Wilkerson	.10	.05
□ 595	Larry Gura	.10	.05
□ 596	Jerry Hairston	.10	.05
□ 597	Brad Lesley	.10	.05
□ 598	Jose Oquendo	.10	.05
□ 599	Storm Davis	.10	.05
□ 600	Pete Rose	.75	.35
□ 601	Tom Lasorda MG	.40	.18
□ 602	Jeff Dedmon	.10	.05
□ 603	Rick Manning	.10	.05
□ 604	Daryl Sconiers	.10	.05
□ 605	Ozzie Smith	.75	.35
□ 606	Rich Gale	.10	.05
□ 607	Bill Almon	.10	.05
□ 608	Craig Lefferts	.10	.05
□ 609	Broderick Perkins	.10	.05
□ 610	Jack Morris	.20	.09
□ 611	Ozzie Virgil	.10	.05
□ 612	Mike Armstrong	.10	.05
□ 613	Terry Puhl	.10	.05
□ 614	Al Williams	.10	.05
□ 615	Marvell Wynne	.10	.05
□ 616	Scott Sanderson	.10	.05
□ 617	Willie Wilson	.10	.05
□ 618	Pete Falcone	.10	.05
□ 619	Jeff Leonard	.10	.05
□ 620	Dwight Gooden	1.50	.70
□ 621	Marvis Foley	.10	.05
□ 622	Luis Leal	.10	.05
□ 623	Greg Walker	.10	.05
□ 624	Benny Ayala	.10	.05
□ 625	Mark Langston	.40	.18
□ 626	German Rivera	.10	.05
□ 627	Eric Davis	.75	.35
□ 628	Rene Lachemann MG	.10	.05
□ 629	Dick Schofield	.10	.05
□ 630	Tim Raines	.20	.09
□ 631	Bob Forsch	.10	.05
□ 632	Bruce Bochte	.10	.05
□ 633	Glenn Hoffman	.10	.05
□ 634	Bill Dawley	.10	.05
□ 635	Terry Kennedy	.10	.05
□ 636	Shane Rawley	.10	.05

□ 637	Brett Butler	.20	.09
□ 638	Mike Pagliarulo	.10	.05
□ 639	Ed Hodge	.10	.05
□ 640	Steve Henderson	.10	.05
□ 641	Rod Scurry	.10	.05
□ 642	Dave Owen	.10	.05
□ 643	Johnny Grubb	.10	.05
□ 644	Mark Huismann	.10	.05
□ 645	Damaso Garcia	.10	.05
□ 646	Scot Thompson	.10	.05
□ 647	Rafael Ramirez	.10	.05
□ 648	Bob Jones	.10	.05
□ 649	Sid Fernandez	.20	.09
□ 650	Greg Luzinski	.20	.09
□ 651	Jeff Russell	.10	.05
□ 652	Joe Nolan	.10	.05
□ 653	Mark Brouhard	.10	.05
□ 654	Dave Anderson	.10	.05
□ 655	Joaquin Andujar	.10	.05
□ 656	Chuck Cottier MG	.10	.05
□ 657	Jim Slaton	.10	.05
□ 658	Mike Stenhouse	.10	.05
□ 659	Checklist: 529-660	.10	.05
□ 660	Tony Gwynn	2.50	1.10
□ 661	Steve Crawford	.10	.05
□ 662	Mike Heath	.10	.05
□ 663	Luis Aguayo	.10	.05
□ 664	Steve Farr	.10	.05
□ 665	Don Mattingly	2.00	.90
□ 666	Mike LaCoss	.10	.05
□ 667	Dave Engle	.10	.05
□ 668	Steve Trout	.10	.05
□ 669	Lee Lacy	.10	.05
□ 670	Tom Seaver	.75	.35
□ 671	Dane Iorg	.10	.05
□ 672	Juan Berenguer	.10	.05
□ 673	Buck Martinez	.10	.05
□ 674	Atlee Hammaker	.10	.05
□ 675	Tony Perez	.60	.25
□ 676	Albert Hall	.10	.05
□ 677	Wally Backman	.10	.05
□ 678	Joey McLaughlin	.10	.05
□ 679	Bob Kearney	.10	.05
□ 680	Jerry Reuss	.10	.05
□ 681	Ben Oglivie	.10	.05
□ 682	Doug Corbett	.10	.05
□ 683	Whitey Herzog MG	.20	.09
□ 684	Bill Doran	.10	.05
□ 685	Bill Caudill	.10	.05
□ 686	Mike Easler	.10	.05
□ 687	Bill Gullickson	.10	.05
□ 688	Len Matuszek	.10	.05
□ 689	Luis DeLeon	.10	.05
□ 690	Alan Trammell	.40	.18
□ 691	Dennis Rasmussen	.10	.05
□ 692	Randy Bush	.10	.05
□ 693	Tim Stoddard	.10	.05
□ 694	Joe Carter	.60	.25
□ 695	Rick Rhoden	.10	.05
□ 696	John Rabb	.10	.05
□ 697	Onix Concepcion	.10	.05
□ 698	Jorge Bell	.20	.09
□ 699	Donnie Moore	.10	.05
□ 700	Eddie Murray	.60	.25
□ 701	Eddie Murray AS	.20	.09
□ 702	Damaso Garcia AS	.10	.05
□ 703	George Brett AS	.60	.25
□ 704	Cal Ripken AS	1.50	.70
□ 705	Dave Winfield AS	.20	.09
□ 706	Rickey Henderson AS	.20	.09
□ 707	Tony Armas AS	.10	.05
□ 708	Lance Parrish AS	.10	.05
□ 709	Mike Boddicker AS	.10	.05
□ 710	Frank Viola AS	.10	.05
□ 711	Dan Quisenberry AS	.10	.05
□ 712	Keith Hernandez AS	.20	.09
□ 713	Ryne Sandberg AS	.60	.25
□ 714	Mike Schmidt AS	.40	.18
□ 715	Ozzie Smith AS	.40	.18
□ 716	Dale Murphy AS	.20	.09
□ 717	Tony Gwynn AS	1.25	.55
□ 718	Jeff Leonard AS	.10	.05
□ 719	Gary Carter AS	.20	.09
□ 720	Rick Sutcliffe AS	.10	.05
□ 721	Bob Knepper AS	.10	.05
□ 722	Bruce Sutter AS	.10	.05

☐ 723	Dave Stewart	.20 .09
☐ 724	Oscar Gamble	.10 .05
☐ 725	Floyd Bannister	.10 .05
☐ 726	Al Bumbry	.10 .05
☐ 727	Frank Pastore	.10 .05
☐ 728	Bob Bailor	.10 .05
☐ 729	Don Sutton	.60 .25
☐ 730	Dave Kingman	.20 .09
☐ 731	Neil Allen	.10 .05
☐ 732	John McNamara MG	.10 .05
☐ 733	Tony Scott	.10 .05
☐ 734	John Henry Johnson	.10 .05
☐ 735	Garry Templeton	.10 .05
☐ 736	Jerry Mumphrey	.10 .05
☐ 737	Bo Diaz	.10 .05
☐ 738	Omar Moreno	.10 .05
☐ 739	Ernie Camacho	.10 .05
☐ 740	Jack Clark	.20 .09
☐ 741	John Butcher	.10 .05
☐ 742	Ron Hassey	.10 .05
☐ 743	Frank White	.20 .09
☐ 744	Doug Bair	.10 .05
☐ 745	Buddy Bell	.20 .09
☐ 746	Jim Clancy	.10 .05
☐ 747	Alex Trevino	.10 .05
☐ 748	Lee Mazzilli	.10 .05
☐ 749	Julio Cruz	.10 .05
☐ 750	Rollie Fingers	.60 .25
☐ 751	Kelvin Chapman	.10 .05
☐ 752	Bob Owchinko	.10 .05
☐ 753	Greg Brock	.10 .05
☐ 754	Larry Milbourne	.10 .05
☐ 755	Ken Singleton	.10 .05
☐ 756	Rob Picciolo	.10 .05
☐ 757	Willie McGee	.20 .09
☐ 758	Ray Burris	.10 .05
☐ 759	Jim Fanning MG	.10 .05
☐ 760	Nolan Ryan	3.00 1.35
☐ 761	Jerry Remy	.10 .05
☐ 762	Eddie Whitson	.10 .05
☐ 763	Kiko Garcia	.10 .05
☐ 764	Jamie Easterly	.10 .05
☐ 765	Willie Randolph	.20 .09
☐ 766	Paul Mirabella	.10 .05
☐ 767	Darrell Brown	.10 .05
☐ 768	Ron Cey	.20 .09
☐ 769	Joe Cowley	.10 .05
☐ 770	Carlton Fisk	.60 .25
☐ 771	Geoff Zahn	.10 .05
☐ 772	Johnnie LeMaster	.10 .05
☐ 773	Hal McRae	.20 .09
☐ 774	Dennis Lamp	.10 .05
☐ 775	Mookie Wilson	.20 .09
☐ 776	Jerry Royster	.10 .05
☐ 777	Ned Yost	.10 .05
☐ 778	Mike Davis	.10 .05
☐ 779	Nick Esasky	.10 .05
☐ 780	Mike Flanagan	.10 .05
☐ 781	Jim Gantner	.10 .05
☐ 782	Tom Niedenfuer	.10 .05
☐ 783	Mike Jorgensen	.10 .05
☐ 784	Checklist: 661-792	.10 .05
☐ 785	Tony Armas	.10 .05
☐ 786	Enos Cabell	.10 .05
☐ 787	Jim Wohlford	.10 .05
☐ 788	Steve Comer	.10 .05
☐ 789	Luis Salazar	.10 .05
☐ 790	Ron Guidry	.20 .09
☐ 791	Ivan DeJesus	.10 .05
☐ 792	Darrell Evans	.20 .09

1985 Topps Traded

In its now standard procedure, Topps issued its standard-size Traded (or extended) set for the fifth year in a row. In addition to the typical factory set hobby distribution, Topps tested the limited issuance of these Traded cards in wax packs. Card design is identical to the regular-issue 1985 Topps set except for whiter card stock and T-suffixed numbering on back. The

set numbering is in alphabetical order by player's name. The key extended Rookie Cards in this set include Vince Coleman, Mariano Duncan, Ozzie Guillen, and Mickey Tettleton.

	NRMT	VG-E
COMP.FACT.SET (132)	12.00	5.50
COMMON CARD (1T-132T)	.15	.07
MINOR STARS	.40	.18
SEMISTARS	.75	.35

☐ 1T	Don Aase	.15 .07
☐ 2T	Bill Almon	.15 .07
☐ 3T	Benny Ayala	.15 .07
☐ 4T	Dusty Baker	.40 .18
☐ 5T	George Bamberger MG	.15 .07
☐ 6T	Dale Berra	.15 .07
☐ 7T	Rich Bordi	.15 .07
☐ 8T	Daryl Boston	.15 .07
☐ 9T	Hubie Brooks	.15 .07
☐ 10T	Chris Brown	.15 .07
☐ 11T	Tom Browning	.40 .18
☐ 12T	Al Bumbry	.15 .07
☐ 13T	Ray Burris	.15 .07
☐ 14T	Jeff Burroughs	.15 .07
☐ 15T	Bill Campbell	.15 .07
☐ 16T	Don Carman	.15 .07
☐ 17T	Gary Carter	.75 .35
☐ 18T	Bobby Castillo	.15 .07
☐ 19T	Bill Caudill	.15 .07
☐ 20T	Rick Cerone	.15 .07
☐ 21T	Bryan Clark	.15 .07
☐ 22T	Jack Clark	.40 .18
☐ 23T	Pat Clements	.15 .07
☐ 24T	Vince Coleman	.75 .35
☐ 25T	Dave Collins	.15 .07
☐ 26T	Danny Darwin	.15 .07
☐ 27T	Jim Davenport MG	.15 .07
☐ 28T	Jerry Davis	.15 .07
☐ 29T	Brian Dayett	.15 .07
☐ 30T	Ivan DeJesus	.15 .07
☐ 31T	Ken Dixon	.15 .07
☐ 32T	Mariano Duncan	.75 .35
☐ 33T	John Felske MG	.15 .07
☐ 34T	Mike Fitzgerald	.15 .07
☐ 35T	Ray Fontenot	.15 .07
☐ 36T	Greg Gagne	.40 .18
☐ 37T	Oscar Gamble	.15 .07
☐ 38T	Scott Garrelts	.15 .07
☐ 39T	Bob L. Gibson	.15 .07
☐ 40T	Jim Gott	.15 .07
☐ 41T	David Green	.15 .07
☐ 42T	Alfredo Griffin	.15 .07
☐ 43T	Ozzie Guillen	1.50 .70
☐ 44T	Eddie Haas MG	.15 .07
☐ 45T	Terry Harper	.15 .07
☐ 46T	Toby Harrah	.15 .07
☐ 47T	Greg Harris	.15 .07
☐ 48T	Ron Hassey	.15 .07
☐ 49T	Rickey Henderson	1.00 .45
☐ 50T	Steve Henderson	.15 .07
☐ 51T	George Hendrick	.15 .07
☐ 52T	Joe Hesketh	.15 .07
☐ 53T	Teddy Higuera	.40 .18
☐ 54T	Donnie Hill	.15 .07
☐ 55T	Al Holland	.15 .07

☐ 56T	Burt Hooton	.15 .07
☐ 57T	Jay Howell	.15 .07
☐ 58T	Ken Howell	.15 .07
☐ 59T	LaMarr Hoyt	.15 .07
☐ 60T	Tim Hulett	.15 .07
☐ 61T	Bob James	.15 .07
☐ 62T	Steve Jeltz	.15 .07
☐ 63T	Cliff Johnson	.15 .07
☐ 64T	Howard Johnson	.40 .18
☐ 65T	Ruppert Jones	.15 .07
☐ 66T	Steve Kemp	.15 .07
☐ 67T	Bruce Kison	.15 .07
☐ 68T	Alan Knicely	.15 .07
☐ 69T	Mike LaCoss	.15 .07
☐ 70T	Lee Lacy	.15 .07
☐ 71T	Dave LaPoint	.15 .07
☐ 72T	Gary Lavelle	.15 .07
☐ 73T	Vance Law	.15 .07
☐ 74T	Johnnie LeMaster	.15 .07
☐ 75T	Sixto Lezcano	.15 .07
☐ 76T	Tim Lollar	.15 .07
☐ 77T	Fred Lynn	.40 .18
☐ 78T	Billy Martin MG	.40 .18
☐ 79T	Ron Mathis	.15 .07
☐ 80T	Len Matuszek	.15 .07
☐ 81T	Gene Mauch MG	.40 .18
☐ 82T	Oddibe McDowell	.40 .18
☐ 83T	Roger McDowell	.40 .18
☐ 84T	John McNamara MG	.15 .07
☐ 85T	Donnie Moore	.15 .07
☐ 86T	Gene Nelson	.15 .07
☐ 87T	Steve Nicosia	.15 .07
☐ 88T	Al Oliver	.40 .18
☐ 89T	Joe Orsulak	.40 .18
☐ 90T	Rob Picciolo	.15 .07
☐ 91T	Chris Pittaro	.15 .07
☐ 92T	Jim Presley	.40 .18
☐ 93T	Rick Reuschel	.15 .07
☐ 94T	Bert Roberge	.15 .07
☐ 95T	Bob Rodgers MG	.15 .07
☐ 96T	Jerry Royster	.15 .07
☐ 97T	Dave Rozema	.15 .07
☐ 98T	Dave Rucker	.15 .07
☐ 99T	Vern Ruhle	.15 .07
☐ 100T	Paul Runge	.15 .07
☐ 101T	Mark Salas	.15 .07
☐ 102T	Luis Salazar	.15 .07
☐ 103T	Joe Sambito	.15 .07
☐ 104T	Rick Schu	.15 .07
☐ 105T	Donnie Scott	.15 .07
☐ 106T	Larry Sheets	.15 .07
☐ 107T	Don Slaught	.15 .07
☐ 108T	Roy Smalley	.15 .07
☐ 109T	Lonnie Smith	.15 .07
☐ 110T	Nate Snell UER	.15 .07
	(Headings on back	
	for a batter)	
☐ 111T	Chris Speier	.15 .07
☐ 112T	Mike Stenhouse	.15 .07
☐ 113T	Tim Stoddard	.15 .07
☐ 114T	Jim Sundberg	.15 .07
☐ 115T	Bruce Sutter	.40 .18
☐ 116T	Don Sutton	.75 .35
☐ 117T	Kent Tekulve	.15 .07
☐ 118T	Tom Tellmann	.15 .07
☐ 119T	Walt Terrell	.15 .07
☐ 120T	Mickey Tettleton	1.00 .45
☐ 121T	Derrel Thomas	.15 .07
☐ 122T	Rich Thompson	.15 .07
☐ 123T	Alex Trevino	.15 .07
☐ 124T	John Tudor	.15 .07
☐ 125T	Jose Uribe	.15 .07
☐ 126T	Bobby Valentine MG	.15 .07
☐ 127T	Dave Von Ohlen	.15 .07
☐ 128T	U.L. Washington	.15 .07
☐ 129T	Earl Weaver MG	.75 .35
☐ 130T	Eddie Whitson	.15 .07
☐ 131T	Herm Winningham	.15 .07
☐ 132T	Checklist 1-132	.15 .07

1986 Topps

This set consists of 792 standard-size cards. Cards were primarily distributed in 15-card

VINCE COLEMAN

wax packs and 48-card rack packs. This was also the first year Topps offered a factory set to hobby dealers. Standard card fronts feature a black and white split border framing a color photo with team name on top and player name on bottom. Subsets include Pete Rose tribute (1-7), Record Breakers (201-207), Turn Back the Clock (401-405), All-Stars (701-722) and Team Leaders (seeded throughout the set). Manager cards feature the team checklist on the reverse. There are two uncorrected errors involving misnumbered cards; see card numbers 51, 57, 141, and 171 in the checklist below. The key Rookie Cards in this set are Darren Daulton, Len Dykstra, Cecil Fielder, and Mickey Tettleton.

	MINT	NRMT
COMPLETE SET (792)	20.00	9.00
COMP.FACT.SET (792)	25.00	11.00
COMMON CARD (1-792)	.05	.02
PETE ROSE SPECIALS (2-7)	.25	.11
MINOR STARS	.10	.05
SEMISTARS	.20	.09
UNLISTED STARS	.40	.18
SUBSET CARDS HALF VALUE OF BASE CARDS		

☐ 1 Pete Rose	.75		.35
☐ 2 Rose Special: '63-'66	.25		.11
☐ 3 Rose Special: '67-'70	.25		.11
☐ 4 Rose Special: '71-'74	.25		.11
☐ 5 Rose Special: '75-'78	.25		.11
☐ 6 Rose Special: '79-'82	.25		.11
☐ 7 Rose Special: '83-'85	.25		.11
☐ 8 Dwayne Murphy	.05		.02
☐ 9 Roy Smith	.05		.02
☐ 10 Tony Gwynn	1.00		.45
☐ 11 Bob Ojeda	.05		.02
☐ 12 Jose Uribe	.05		.02
☐ 13 Bob Kearney	.05		.02
☐ 14 Julio Cruz	.05		.02
☐ 15 Eddie Whitson	.05		.02
☐ 16 Rick Schu	.05		.02
☐ 17 Mike Stenhouse	.05		.02
☐ 18 Brent Gaff	.05		.02
☐ 19 Rich Hebner	.05		.02
☐ 20 Lou Whitaker	.10		.05
☐ 21 George Bamberger MG	.05		.02
☐ 22 Duane Walker	.05		.02
☐ 23 Manny Lee	.05		.02
☐ 24 Len Barker	.05		.02
☐ 25 Willie Wilson	.05		.02
☐ 26 Frank DiPino	.05		.02
☐ 27 Ray Knight	.10		.05
☐ 28 Eric Davis	.20		.09
☐ 29 Tony Phillips	.05		.02
☐ 30 Eddie Murray	.40		.18
☐ 31 Jamie Easterly	.05		.02
☐ 32 Steve Yeager	.05		.02
☐ 33 Jeff Lahti	.05		.02

☐ 34 Ken Phelps	.05		
☐ 35 Jeff Reardon	.10		.05
☐ 36 Lance Parrish TL	.10		
☐ 37 Mark Thurmond	.05		.02
☐ 38 Glenn Hoffman	.05		
☐ 39 Dave Rucker	.05		.02
☐ 40 Ken Griffey	.10		
☐ 41 Brad Wellman	.05		.02
☐ 42 Geoff Zahn	.05		
☐ 43 Dave Engle	.05		.02
☐ 44 Lance McCullers	.05		
☐ 45 Damaso Garcia	.05		.02
☐ 46 Billy Hatcher	.05		
☐ 47 Juan Berenguer	.05		.02
☐ 48 Bill Almon	.05		
☐ 49 Rick Manning	.05		.02
☐ 50 Dan Quisenberry	.05		
☐ 51 Bobby Wine MG ERR	.05		.02
Number of card on back is actually 57)			
☐ 52 Chris Welsh	.05		.02
☐ 53 Len Dykstra	.75		.35
☐ 54 John Franco	.40		.18
☐ 55 Fred Lynn	.10		.05
☐ 56 Tom Niedenfuer	.05		.02
☐ 57 Bill Doran	.05		.02
(See also 51)			
☐ 58 Bill Krueger	.05		.02
☐ 59 Andre Thornton	.05		.02
☐ 60 Dwight Evans	.10		.05
☐ 61 Karl Best	.05		.02
☐ 62 Bob Boone	.10		.05
☐ 63 Ron Roenicke	.05		.02
☐ 64 Floyd Bannister	.05		.02
☐ 65 Dan Driessen	.05		.02
☐ 66 Bob Forsch TL	.05		.02
☐ 67 Carmelo Martinez	.05		.02
☐ 68 Ed Lynch	.05		.02
☐ 69 Luis Aguayo	.05		.02
☐ 70 Dave Winfield	.40		.18
☐ 71 Ken Schrom	.05		.02
☐ 72 Shawon Dunston	.10		.05
☐ 73 Randy O'Neal	.05		.02
☐ 74 Rance Mulliniks	.05		.02
☐ 75 Jose DeLeon	.05		.02
☐ 76 Dion James	.05		.02
☐ 77 Charlie Leibrandt	.05		.02
☐ 78 Bruce Benedict	.05		.02
☐ 79 Dave Schmidt	.05		.02
☐ 80 Darryl Strawberry	.40		.18
☐ 81 Gene Mauch MG	.10		.05
☐ 82 Tippy Martinez	.05		.02
☐ 83 Phil Garner	.05		.02
☐ 84 Curt Young	.05		.02
☐ 85 Tony Perez	.40		.18
(Eric Davis also shown on card)			
☐ 86 Tom Waddell	.05		.02
☐ 87 Candy Maldonado	.05		.02
☐ 88 Tom Nieto	.05		.02
☐ 89 Randy St.Claire	.05		.02
☐ 90 Garry Templeton	.05		.02
☐ 91 Steve Crawford	.05		.02
☐ 92 Al Cowens	.05		.02
☐ 93 Scot Thompson	.05		.02
☐ 94 Rich Bordi	.05		.02
☐ 95 Ozzie Virgil	.05		.02
☐ 96 Jim Clancy TL	.05		.02
☐ 97 Gary Gaetti	.10		.05
☐ 98 Dick Ruthven	.05		.02
☐ 99 Buddy Biancalana	.05		.02
☐ 100 Nolan Ryan	1.50		.70
☐ 101 Dave Bergman	.05		.02
☐ 102 Joe Orsulak	.05		.02
☐ 103 Luis Salazar	.05		.02
☐ 104 Sid Fernandez	.10		.05
☐ 105 Gary Ward	.05		.02
☐ 106 Ray Burris	.05		.02
☐ 107 Rafael Ramirez	.05		.02
☐ 108 Ted Power	.05		.02
☐ 109 Len Matuszek	.05		.02
☐ 110 Scott McGregor	.05		.02
☐ 111 Roger Craig MG	.10		.05
☐ 112 Bill Campbell	.05		.02
☐ 113 U.L. Washington	.05		.02
☐ 114 Mike C. Brown	.05		.02

☐ 115 Jay Howell	.05		.02
☐ 116 Brook Jacoby	.05		.02
☐ 117 Bruce Kison	.05		.02
☐ 118 Jerry Royster	.05		.02
☐ 119 Barry Bonnell	.05		.02
☐ 120 Steve Carlton	.40		.18
☐ 121 Nelson Simmons	.05		.02
☐ 122 Pete Filson	.05		.02
☐ 123 Greg Walker	.05		.02
☐ 124 Luis Sanchez	.05		.02
☐ 125 Dave Lopes	.10		.05
☐ 126 Mookie Wilson TL	.05		.02
☐ 127 Jack Howell	.05		.02
☐ 128 John Wathan	.05		.02
☐ 129 Jeff Dedmon	.05		.02
☐ 130 Alan Trammell	.20		.09
☐ 131 Checklist: 1-132	.10		.05
☐ 132 Razor Shines	.05		.02
☐ 133 Andy McGaffigan	.05		.02
☐ 134 Carney Lansford	.10		.05
☐ 135 Joe Niekro	.05		.02
☐ 136 Mike Hargrove	.05		.02
☐ 137 Charlie Moore	.05		.02
☐ 138 Mark Davis	.05		.02
☐ 139 Daryl Boston	.05		.02
☐ 140 John Candelaria	.05		.02
☐ 141 Chuck Cottier MG	.05		.02
See also 171			
☐ 142 Bob Jones	.05		.02
☐ 143 Dave Van Gorder	.05		.02
☐ 144 Doug Sisk	.05		.02
☐ 145 Pedro Guerrero	.10		.05
☐ 146 Jack Perconte	.05		.02
☐ 147 Larry Sheets	.05		.02
☐ 148 Mike Heath	.05		.02
☐ 149 Brett Butler	.10		.05
☐ 150 Joaquin Andujar	.05		.02
☐ 151 Dave Stapleton	.05		.02
☐ 152 Mike Morgan	.05		.02
☐ 153 Ricky Adams	.05		.02
☐ 154 Bert Roberge	.05		.02
☐ 155 Bob Grich	.10		.05
☐ 156 Richard Dotson TL	.05		.02
☐ 157 Ron Hassey	.05		.02
☐ 158 Derrel Thomas	.05		.02
☐ 159 Orel Hershiser UER	.40		.18
(82 Alburquerque)			
☐ 160 Chet Lemon	.05		.02
☐ 161 Lee Tunnell	.05		.02
☐ 162 Greg Gagne	.05		.02
☐ 163 Pete Ladd	.05		.02
☐ 164 Steve Balboni	.05		.02
☐ 165 Mike Davis	.05		.02
☐ 166 Dickie Thon	.05		.02
☐ 167 Zane Smith	.05		.02
☐ 168 Jeff Burroughs	.05		.02
☐ 169 George Wright	.05		.02
☐ 170 Gary Carter	.40		.18
☐ 171 Bob Rodgers MG ERR	.05		.02
Number of card on back actually 141)			
☐ 172 Jerry Reed	.05		.02
☐ 173 Wayne Gross	.05		.02
☐ 174 Brian Snyder	.05		.02
☐ 175 Steve Sax	.05		.02
☐ 176 Jay Tibbs	.05		.02
☐ 177 Joel Youngblood	.05		.02
☐ 178 Ivan DeJesus	.05		.02
☐ 179 Stu Cliburn	.05		.02
☐ 180 Don Mattingly	.60		.25
☐ 181 Al Nipper	.05		.02
☐ 182 Bobby Brown	.05		.02
☐ 183 Larry Andersen	.05		.02
☐ 184 Tim Laudner	.05		.02
☐ 185 Rollie Fingers	.40		.18
☐ 186 Jose Cruz TL	.05		.02
☐ 187 Scott Fletcher	.05		.02
☐ 188 Bob Dernier	.05		.02
☐ 189 Mike Mason	.05		.02
☐ 190 George Hendrick	.05		.02
☐ 191 Wally Backman	.05		.02
☐ 192 Milt Wilcox	.05		.02
☐ 193 Daryl Sconiers	.05		.02
☐ 194 Craig McMurtry	.05		.02
☐ 195 Dave Concepcion	.10		.05
☐ 196 Doyle Alexander	.05		.02

197	Enos Cabell	.05	.02
198	Ken Dixon	.05	.02
199	Dick Howser MG	.10	.05
200	Mike Schmidt	.50	.23
201	Vince Coleman RB	.10	
	Most SB's rookie season		
202	Dwight Gooden RB	.10	.05
	Youngest 20 game winner		
203	Keith Hernandez RB	.05	
	Most game-winning RBI's		
204	Phil Niekro RB	.10	.05
	Oldest shutout pitcher		
205	Tony Perez RB	.10	.05
	Oldest grand slammer		
206	Pete Rose RB	.40	.18
	Most lifetime hits		
207	Fernando Valenzuela RB	.10	.05
	Most cons. innings start of season, no earned runs		
208	Ramon Romero	.05	.02
209	Randy Ready	.05	.02
210	Calvin Schiraldi	.05	.02
211	Ed Wojna	.05	.02
212	Chris Speier	.05	.02
213	Bob Shirley	.05	.02
214	Randy Bush	.05	.02
215	Frank White	.10	.05
216	Dwayne Murphy TL	.05	.02
217	Bill Scherrer	.05	.02
218	Randy Hunt	.05	.02
219	Dennis Lamp	.05	.02
220	Bob Horner	.05	.02
221	Dave Henderson	.05	.02
222	Craig Gerber	.05	.02
223	Atlee Hammaker	.05	.02
224	Cesar Cedeno	.10	.05
225	Ron Darling	.05	.02
226	Lee Lacy	.05	.02
227	Al Jones	.05	.02
228	Tom Lawless	.05	.02
229	Bill Gullickson	.05	.02
230	Terry Kennedy	.05	.02
231	Jim Frey MG	.10	.05
232	Rick Rhoden	.05	.02
233	Steve Lyons	.05	.02
234	Doug Corbett	.05	.02
235	Butch Wynegar	.05	.02
236	Frank Eufemia	.05	.02
237	Ted Simmons	.10	.05
238	Larry Parrish	.05	.02
239	Joel Skinner	.05	.02
240	Tommy John	.10	.05
241	Tony Fernandez	.05	.02
242	Rich Thompson	.05	.02
243	Johnny Grubb	.05	.02
244	Craig Lefferts	.05	.02
245	Jim Sundberg	.05	.02
246	Steve Carlton	.10	.05
247	Terry Harper	.05	.02
248	Spike Owen	.05	.02
249	Rob Deer	.10	.05
250	Dwight Gooden	.40	.18
251	Rich Dauer	.05	.02
252	Bobby Castillo	.05	.02
253	Dann Bilardello	.05	.02
254	Ozzie Guillen	.20	.09
255	Tony Armas	.05	.02
256	Kurt Kepshire	.05	.02
257	Doug DeCinces	.05	.02
258	Tim Burke	.05	.02
259	Dan Pasqua	.05	.02
260	Tony Pena	.05	.02
261	Bobby Valentine MG	.10	.05
262	Mario Ramirez	.05	.02
263	Checklist: 133-264	.10	.05
264	Darren Daulton	.75	.35
265	Ron Davis	.05	.02
266	Keith Moreland	.05	.02
267	Paul Molitor	.40	.18
268	Mike Scott	.05	.02
269	Dane Iorg	.05	.02
270	Jack Morris	.10	.05
271	Dave Collins	.05	.02
272	Tim Tolman	.05	.02
273	Jerry Willard	.05	.02
274	Ron Gardenhire	.05	.02
275	Charlie Hough	.10	.05
276	Willie Randolph TL	.10	.05
277	Jaime Cocanower	.05	.02
278	Sixto Lezcano	.05	.02
279	Al Pardo	.05	.02
280	Tim Raines	.10	.05
281	Steve Mura	.05	.02
282	Jerry Mumphrey	.05	.02
283	Mike Fischlin	.05	.02
284	Brian Dayett	.05	.02
285	Buddy Bell	.05	.02
286	Luis DeLeon	.05	.02
287	John Christensen	.05	.02
288	Don Aase	.05	.02
289	Johnnie LeMaster	.05	.02
290	Carlton Fisk	.40	.18
291	Tom Lasorda MG	.20	.09
292	Chuck Porter	.05	.02
293	Chris Chambliss	.10	.05
294	Danny Cox	.05	.02
295	Kirk Gibson	.10	.05
296	Geno Petralli	.05	.02
297	Tim Lollar	.05	.02
298	Craig Reynolds	.05	.02
299	Bryn Smith	.05	.02
300	George Brett	.75	.35
301	Dennis Rasmussen	.05	.02
302	Greg Gross	.05	.02
303	Curt Wardle	.05	.02
304	Mike Gallego	.10	.05
305	Phil Bradley	.05	.02
306	Terry Kennedy TL	.05	.02
307	Dave Sax	.05	.02
308	Ray Fontenot	.05	.02
309	John Shelby	.05	.02
310	Greg Minton	.05	.02
311	Dick Schofield	.05	.02
312	Tom Filer	.05	.02
313	Joe DeSa	.05	.02
314	Frank Pastore	.05	.02
315	Mookie Wilson	.10	.05
316	Sammy Khalifa	.05	.02
317	Ed Romero	.05	.02
318	Terry Whitfield	.05	.02
319	Rick Camp	.05	.02
320	Jim Rice	.10	.05
321	Earl Weaver MG	.40	.18
322	Bob Forsch	.05	.02
323	Jerry Davis	.05	.02
324	Dan Schatzeder	.05	.02
325	Juan Beniquez	.05	.02
326	Kent Tekulve	.05	.02
327	Mike Pagliarulo	.05	.02
328	Pete O'Brien	.05	.02
329	Kirby Puckett	1.50	.70
330	Rick Sutcliffe	.05	.02
331	Alan Ashby	.05	.02
332	Darryl Motley	.05	.02
333	Tom Henke	.10	.05
334	Ken Oberkfell	.05	.02
335	Don Sutton	.40	.18
336	Andre Thornton TL	.05	.02
337	Darnell Coles	.05	.02
338	Jorge Bell	.10	.05
339	Bruce Berenyi	.05	.02
340	Cal Ripken	1.50	.70
341	Frank Williams	.05	.02
342	Gary Redus	.05	.02
343	Carlos Diaz	.05	.02
344	Jim Wohlford	.05	.02
345	Donnie Moore	.05	.02
346	Bryan Little	.05	.02
347	Teddy Higuera	.10	.05
348	Cliff Johnson	.05	.02
349	Mark Clear	.05	.02
350	Jack Clark	.10	.05
351	Chuck Tanner MG	.05	.02
352	Harry Spilman	.05	.02
353	Keith Atherton	.05	.02
354	Tony Bernazard	.05	.02
355	Lee Smith	.20	.09
356	Mickey Hatcher	.05	.02
357	Ed VandeBerg	.05	.02
358	Rick Dempsey	.05	.02
359	Mike LaCoss	.05	.02
360	Lloyd Moseby	.05	.02
361	Shane Rawley	.05	.02
362	Tom Paciorek	.10	.05
363	Terry Forster	.05	.02
364	Reid Nichols	.05	.02
365	Mike Flanagan	.05	.02
366	Dave Concepcion TL	.10	.05
367	Aurelio Lopez	.05	.02
368	Greg Brock	.05	.02
369	Al Holland	.05	.02
370	Vince Coleman	.40	.18
371	Bill Stein	.05	.02
372	Ben Oglivie	.05	.02
373	Urbano Lugo	.05	.02
374	Terry Francona	.05	.02
375	Rich Gedman	.05	.02
376	Bill Dawley	.05	.02
377	Joe Carter	.40	.18
378	Bruce Bochte	.05	.02
379	Bobby Meacham	.05	.02
380	LaMarr Hoyt	.05	.02
381	Ray Miller MG	.05	.02
382	Ivan Calderon	.10	.05
383	Chris Brown	.05	.02
384	Steve Trout	.05	.02
385	Cecil Cooper	.10	.05
386	Cecil Fielder	1.00	.45
387	Steve Kemp	.05	.02
388	Dickie Noles	.05	.02
389	Glenn Davis	.10	.05
390	Tom Seaver	.50	.23
391	Julio Franco	.10	.05
392	John Russell	.05	.02
393	Chris Pittaro	.05	.02
394	Checklist: 265-396	.10	.05
395	Scott Garrelts	.05	.02
396	Dwight Evans TL	.10	.05
397	Steve Buechele	.10	.05
398	Earnie Riles	.05	.02
399	Bill Swift	.05	.02
400	Rod Carew	.40	.18
401	Fernando Valenzuela TBC '81	.10	.05
402	Tom Seaver TBC '76	.10	.05
403	Willie Mays TBC '71	.20	.09
404	Frank Robinson TBC '66	.10	.05
405	Roger Maris TBC '61	.10	.05
406	Scott Sanderson	.05	.02
407	Sal Butera	.05	.02
408	Dave Smith	.05	.02
409	Paul Runge	.05	.02
410	Dave Kingman	.10	.05
411	Sparky Anderson MG	.20	.09
412	Jim Clancy	.05	.02
413	Tim Flannery	.05	.02
414	Tom Gorman	.05	.02
415	Hal McRae	.10	.05
416	Dennis Martinez	.10	.05
417	R.J. Reynolds	.05	.02
418	Alan Knicely	.05	.02
419	Frank Wills	.05	.02
420	Von Hayes	.05	.02
421	David Palmer	.05	.02
422	Mike Jorgensen	.05	.02
423	Dan Spillner	.05	.02
424	Rick Miller	.05	.02
425	Larry McWilliams	.05	.02
426	Charlie Moore TL	.05	.02
427	Joe Cowley	.05	.02
428	Max Venable	.05	.02
429	Greg Booker	.05	.02
430	Kent Hrbek	.10	.05
431	George Frazier	.05	.02
432	Mark Bailey	.05	.02
433	Chris Codiroli	.05	.02
434	Curt Wilkerson	.05	.02
435	Bill Caudill	.05	.02
436	Doug Flynn	.05	.02
437	Rick Mahler	.05	.02
438	Clint Hurdle	.05	.02
439	Rick Honeycutt	.05	.02
440	Alvin Davis	.05	.02
441	Whitey Herzog MG	.20	.09
442	Ron Robinson	.05	.02

☐ 443 Bill Buckner	.10	.05
☐ 444 Alex Trevino	.05	.02
☐ 445 Bert Blyleven	.10	.05
☐ 446 Lenn Sakata	.05	.02
☐ 447 Jerry Don Gleaton	.05	.02
☐ 448 Herm Winningham	.05	.02
☐ 449 Rod Scurry	.05	.02
☐ 450 Graig Nettles	.10	.05
☐ 451 Mark Brown	.05	.02
☐ 452 Bob Clark	.05	.02
☐ 453 Steve Jeltz	.05	.02
☐ 454 Burt Hooton	.05	.02
☐ 455 Willie Randolph	.10	.05
☐ 456 Dale Murphy TL	.10	.05
☐ 457 Mickey Tettleton	.40	.18
☐ 458 Kevin Bass	.05	.02
☐ 459 Luis Leal	.05	.02
☐ 460 Leon Durham	.05	.02
☐ 461 Walt Terrell	.05	.02
☐ 462 Domingo Ramos	.05	.02
☐ 463 Jim Gott	.05	.02
☐ 464 Ruppert Jones	.05	.02
☐ 465 Jesse Orosco	.05	.02
☐ 466 Tom Foley	.05	.02
☐ 467 Bob James	.05	.02
☐ 468 Mike Scioscia	.05	.02
☐ 469 Storm Davis	.05	.02
☐ 470 Bill Madlock	.05	.02
☐ 471 Bobby Cox MG	.10	.05
☐ 472 Joe Hesketh	.05	.02
☐ 473 Mark Brouhard	.05	.02
☐ 474 John Tudor	.05	.02
☐ 475 Juan Samuel	.05	.02
☐ 476 Ron Mathis	.05	.02
☐ 477 Mike Easler	.05	.02
☐ 478 Andy Hawkins	.05	.02
☐ 479 Bob Melvin	.05	.02
☐ 480 Oddibe McDowell	.05	.02
☐ 481 Scott Bradley	.05	.02
☐ 482 Rick Lysander	.05	.02
☐ 483 George Vukovich	.05	.02
☐ 484 Donnie Hill	.05	.02
☐ 485 Gary Matthews	.05	.02
☐ 486 Bobby Grich TL	.05	.02
☐ 487 Bret Saberhagen	.10	.05
☐ 488 Lou Thornton	.05	.02
☐ 489 Jim Winn	.05	.02
☐ 490 Jeff Leonard	.05	.02
☐ 491 Pascual Perez	.05	.02
☐ 492 Kelvin Chapman	.05	.02
☐ 493 Gene Nelson	.05	.02
☐ 494 Gary Roenicke	.05	.02
☐ 495 Mark Langston	.05	.02
☐ 496 Jay Johnstone	.10	.05
☐ 497 John Stuper	.05	.02
☐ 498 Tito Landrum	.05	.02
☐ 499 Bob L. Gibson	.05	.02
☐ 500 Rickey Henderson	.40	.18
☐ 501 Dave Johnson MG	.10	.05
☐ 502 Glen Cook	.05	.02
☐ 503 Mike Fitzgerald	.05	.02
☐ 504 Denny Walling	.05	.02
☐ 505 Jerry Koosman	.10	.05
☐ 506 Bill Russell	.10	.05
☐ 507 Steve Ontiveros	.10	.05
☐ 508 Alan Wiggins	.05	.02
☐ 509 Ernie Camacho	.05	.02
☐ 510 Wade Boggs	.40	.18
☐ 511 Ed Nunez	.05	.02
☐ 512 Thad Bosley	.05	.02
☐ 513 Ron Washington	.05	.02
☐ 514 Mike Jones	.05	.02
☐ 515 Darrell Evans	.10	.05
☐ 516 Greg Minton TL	.05	.02
☐ 517 Milt Thompson	.10	.05
☐ 518 Buck Martinez	.05	.02
☐ 519 Danny Darwin	.05	.02
☐ 520 Keith Hernandez	.10	.05
☐ 521 Nate Snell	.05	.02
☐ 522 Bob Bailor	.05	.02
☐ 523 Joe Price	.05	.02
☐ 524 Darrell Miller	.05	.02
☐ 525 Marvell Wynne	.05	.02
☐ 526 Charlie Lea	.05	.02
☐ 527 Checklist: 397-528	.10	.05
☐ 528 Terry Pendleton	.20	.09
☐ 529 Marc Sullivan	.05	.02
☐ 530 Rich Gossage	.10	.05
☐ 531 Tony LaRussa MG	.10	.05
☐ 532 Don Carman	.05	.02
☐ 533 Billy Sample	.05	.02
☐ 534 Jeff Calhoun	.05	.02
☐ 535 Toby Harrah	.05	.02
☐ 536 Jose Rijo	.05	.02
☐ 537 Mark Salas	.05	.02
☐ 538 Dennis Eckersley	.40	.18
☐ 539 Glenn Hubbard	.05	.02
☐ 540 Dan Petry	.05	.02
☐ 541 Jorge Orta	.05	.02
☐ 542 Don Schulze	.05	.02
☐ 543 Jerry Narron	.05	.02
☐ 544 Eddie Milner	.05	.02
☐ 545 Jimmy Key	.40	.18
☐ 546 Dave Henderson TL	.05	.02
☐ 547 Roger McDowell	.10	.05
☐ 548 Mike Young	.05	.02
☐ 549 Bob Welch	.05	.02
☐ 550 Tom Herr	.05	.02
☐ 551 Dave LaPoint	.05	.02
☐ 552 Marc Hill	.05	.02
☐ 553 Jim Morrison	.05	.02
☐ 554 Paul Householder	.05	.02
☐ 555 Hubie Brooks	.05	.02
☐ 556 John Denny	.05	.02
☐ 557 Gerald Perry	.05	.02
☐ 558 Tim Stoddard	.05	.02
☐ 559 Tommy Dunbar	.05	.02
☐ 560 Dave Righetti	.05	.02
☐ 561 Bob Lillis MG	.05	.02
☐ 562 Joe Beckwith	.05	.02
☐ 563 Alejandro Sanchez	.05	.02
☐ 564 Warren Brusstar	.05	.02
☐ 565 Tom Brunansky	.05	.02
☐ 566 Alfredo Griffin	.05	.02
☐ 567 Jeff Barkley	.05	.02
☐ 568 Donnie Scott	.05	.02
☐ 569 Jim Acker	.05	.02
☐ 570 Rusty Staub	.10	.05
☐ 571 Mike Jeffcoat	.05	.02
☐ 572 Paul Zuvella	.05	.02
☐ 573 Tom Hume	.05	.02
☐ 574 Ron Kittle	.05	.02
☐ 575 Mike Boddicker	.05	.02
☐ 576 Andre Dawson TL	.10	.05
☐ 577 Jerry Reuss	.05	.02
☐ 578 Lee Mazzilli	.05	.02
☐ 579 Jim Slaton	.05	.02
☐ 580 Willie McGee	.10	.05
☐ 581 Bruce Hurst	.05	.02
☐ 582 Jim Gantner	.05	.02
☐ 583 Al Bumbry	.05	.02
☐ 584 Brian Fisher	.05	.02
☐ 585 Garry Maddox	.05	.02
☐ 586 Greg Harris	.05	.02
☐ 587 Rafael Santana	.05	.02
☐ 588 Steve Lake	.05	.02
☐ 589 Sid Bream	.05	.02
☐ 590 Bob Knepper	.05	.02
☐ 591 Jackie Moore MG	.05	.02
☐ 592 Frank Tanana	.05	.02
☐ 593 Jesse Barfield	.05	.02
☐ 594 Chris Bando	.05	.02
☐ 595 Dave Parker	.10	.05
☐ 596 Onix Concepcion	.05	.02
☐ 597 Sammy Stewart	.05	.02
☐ 598 Jim Presley	.05	.02
☐ 599 Rick Aguilera	.40	.18
☐ 600 Dale Murphy	.40	.18
☐ 601 Gary Lucas	.05	.02
☐ 602 Mariano Duncan	.40	.18
☐ 603 Bill Laskey	.05	.02
☐ 604 Gary Pettis	.05	.02
☐ 605 Dennis Boyd	.05	.02
☐ 606 Hal McRae TL	.10	.05
☐ 607 Ken Dayley	.05	.02
☐ 608 Bruce Bochy	.05	.02
☐ 609 Barbaro Garbey	.05	.02
☐ 610 Ron Guidry	.10	.05
☐ 611 Gary Woods	.05	.02
☐ 612 Richard Dotson	.05	.02
☐ 613 Roy Smalley	.05	.02
☐ 614 Rick Waits	.05	.02
☐ 615 Johnny Ray	.05	.02
☐ 616 Glenn Brummer	.05	.02
☐ 617 Lonnie Smith	.05	.02
☐ 618 Jim Pankovits	.05	.02
☐ 619 Danny Heep	.05	.02
☐ 620 Bruce Sutter	.10	.05
☐ 621 John Felske MG	.05	.02
☐ 622 Gary Lavelle	.05	.02
☐ 623 Floyd Rayford	.05	.02
☐ 624 Steve McCatty	.05	.02
☐ 625 Bob Brenly	.05	.02
☐ 626 Roy Thomas	.05	.02
☐ 627 Ron Oester	.05	.02
☐ 628 Kirk McCaskill	.10	.05
☐ 629 Mitch Webster	.05	.02
☐ 630 Fernando Valenzuela	.10	.05
☐ 631 Steve Braun	.05	.02
☐ 632 Dave Von Ohlen	.05	.02
☐ 633 Jackie Gutierrez	.05	.02
☐ 634 Roy Lee Jackson	.05	.02
☐ 635 Jason Thompson	.05	.02
☐ 636 Lee Smith TL	.10	.05
☐ 637 Rudy Law	.05	.02
☐ 638 John Butcher	.05	.02
☐ 639 Bo Diaz	.05	.02
☐ 640 Jose Cruz	.10	.05
☐ 641 Wayne Tolleson	.05	.02
☐ 642 Ray Searage	.05	.02
☐ 643 Tom Brookens	.05	.02
☐ 644 Mark Gubicza	.05	.02
☐ 645 Dusty Baker	.10	.05
☐ 646 Mike Moore	.05	.02
☐ 647 Mel Hall	.05	.02
☐ 648 Steve Bedrosian	.05	.02
☐ 649 Ronn Reynolds	.05	.02
☐ 650 Dave Stieb	.05	.02
☐ 651 Billy Martin MG	.10	.05
☐ 652 Tom Browning	.05	.02
☐ 653 Jim Dwyer	.05	.02
☐ 654 Ken Howell	.05	.02
☐ 655 Manny Trillo	.05	.02
☐ 656 Brian Harper	.05	.02
☐ 657 Juan Agosto	.05	.02
☐ 658 Rob Wilfong	.05	.02
☐ 659 Checklist: 529-660	.10	.05
☐ 660 Steve Garvey	.20	.09
☐ 661 Roger Clemens	1.50	.70
☐ 662 Bill Schroeder	.05	.02
☐ 663 Neil Allen	.05	.02
☐ 664 Tim Corcoran	.05	.02
☐ 665 Alejandro Pena	.05	.02
☐ 666 Charlie Hough TL	.10	.05
☐ 667 Tim Teufel	.05	.02
☐ 668 Cecilio Guante	.05	.02
☐ 669 Ron Cey	.10	.05
☐ 670 Willie Hernandez	.05	.02
☐ 671 Lynn Jones	.05	.02
☐ 672 Rob Picciolo	.05	.02
☐ 673 Ernie Whitt	.05	.02
☐ 674 Pat Tabler	.05	.02
☐ 675 Claudell Washington	.05	.02
☐ 676 Matt Young	.05	.02
☐ 677 Nick Esasky	.05	.02
☐ 678 Dan Gladden	.05	.02
☐ 679 Britt Burns	.05	.02
☐ 680 George Foster	.10	.05
☐ 681 Dick Williams MG	.10	.05
☐ 682 Junior Ortiz	.05	.02
☐ 683 Andy Van Slyke	.10	.05
☐ 684 Bob McClure	.05	.02
☐ 685 Tim Wallach	.05	.02
☐ 686 Jeff Stone	.05	.02
☐ 687 Mike Trujillo	.05	.02
☐ 688 Larry Herndon	.05	.02
☐ 689 Dave Stewart	.10	.05
☐ 690 Ryne Sandberg UER (No Topps logo on front)	.50	.23
☐ 691 Mike Madden	.05	.02
☐ 692 Dale Berra	.05	.02
☐ 693 Tom Tellmann	.05	.02
☐ 694 Garth Iorg	.05	.02
☐ 695 Mike Smithson	.05	.02
☐ 696 Bill Russell TL	.10	.05
☐ 697 Bud Black	.05	.02
☐ 698 Brad Komminsk	.05	.02

□			
□ 699 Pat Corrales MG	.05	.02
□ 700 Reggie Jackson	.50	.23
□ 701 Keith Hernandez AS	.05	.02
□ 702 Tom Herr AS	.05	.02
□ 703 Tim Wallach AS	.05	.02
□ 704 Ozzie Smith AS	.20	.09
□ 705 Dale Murphy AS	.10	.05
□ 706 Pedro Guerrero AS	.05	.02
□ 707 Willie McGee AS	.05	.02
□ 708 Gary Carter AS	.10	.05
□ 709 Dwight Gooden AS	.10	.05
□ 710 John Tudor AS	.05	.02
□ 711 Jeff Reardon AS	.05	.02
□ 712 Don Mattingly AS	.40	.18
□ 713 Damaso Garcia AS	.05	.02
□ 714 George Brett AS	.40	.18
□ 715 Cal Ripken AS	.75	.35
□ 716 Rickey Henderson AS	.10	.05
□ 717 Dave Winfield AS	.10	.05
□ 718 George Bell AS	.05	.02
□ 719 Carlton Fisk AS	.10	.05
□ 720 Bret Saberhagen AS	.05	.02
□ 721 Ron Guidry AS	.10	.05
□ 722 Dan Quisenberry AS	.05	.02
□ 723 Marty Bystrom	.05	.02
□ 724 Tim Hulett	.05	.02
□ 725 Mario Soto	.05	.02
□ 726 Rick Dempsey TL	.10	.05
□ 727 David Green	.05	.02
□ 728 Mike Marshall	.05	.02
□ 729 Jim Beattie	.05	.02
□ 730 Ozzie Smith	.50	.23
□ 731 Don Robinson	.05	.02
□ 732 Floyd Youmans	.05	.02
□ 733 Ron Romanick	.05	.02
□ 734 Marty Barrett	.05	.02
□ 735 Dave Dravecky	.10	.05
□ 736 Glenn Wilson	.05	.02
□ 737 Pete Vuckovich	.05	.02
□ 738 Andre Robertson	.05	.02
□ 739 Dave Rozema	.05	.02
□ 740 Lance Parrish	.05	.02
□ 741 Pete Rose MG	.40	.18
□ 742 Frank Viola	.10	.05
□ 743 Pat Sheridan	.05	.02
□ 744 Lary Sorensen	.05	.02
□ 745 Willie Upshaw	.05	.02
□ 746 Denny Gonzalez	.05	.02
□ 747 Rick Cerone	.05	.02
□ 748 Steve Henderson	.05	.02
□ 749 Ed Jurak	.05	.02
□ 750 Gorman Thomas	.05	.02
□ 751 Howard Johnson	.10	.05
□ 752 Mike Krukow	.05	.02
□ 753 Dan Ford	.05	.02
□ 754 Pat Clements	.05	.02
□ 755 Harold Baines	.20	.09
□ 756 Rick Rhoden TL	.05	.02
□ 757 Darrell Porter	.10	.05
□ 758 Dave Anderson	.05	.02
□ 759 Moose Haas	.05	.02
□ 760 Andre Dawson	.40	.18
□ 761 Don Slaught	.05	.02
□ 762 Eric Show	.05	.02
□ 763 Terry Puhl	.05	.02
□ 764 Kevin Gross	.05	.02
□ 765 Don Baylor	.20	.09
□ 766 Rick Langford	.05	.02
□ 767 Jody Davis	.05	.02
□ 768 Vern Ruhle	.05	.02
□ 769 Harold Reynolds	.40	.18
□ 770 Vida Blue	.10	.05
□ 771 John McNamara MG	.05	.02
□ 772 Brian Downing	.05	.02
□ 773 Greg Pryor	.05	.02
□ 774 Terry Leach	.05	.02
□ 775 Al Oliver	.10	.05
□ 776 Gene Garber	.05	.02
□ 777 Wayne Krenchicki	.05	.02
□ 778 Jerry Hairston	.05	.02
□ 779 Rick Reuschel	.05	.02
□ 780 Robin Yount	.40	.18
□ 781 Joe Nolan	.05	.02
□ 782 Ken Landreaux	.05	.02
□ 783 Ricky Horton	.05	.02
□ 784 Alan Bannister	.05	.02

□ 785 Bob Stanley	.05	.02
□ 786 Mickey Hatcher TL	.05	.02
□ 787 Vance Law	.05	.02
□ 788 Marty Castillo	.05	.02
□ 789 Kurt Bevacqua	.05	.02
□ 790 Phil Niekro	.40	.18
□ 791 Checklist: 661-792	.10	.05
□ 792 Charles Hudson	.05	.02

1986 Topps Traded

This 132-card standard-size Traded set was distributed in factory set form in a red and white box through hobby dealers. The cards are identical in style to regular-issue 1986 Topps cards except for whiter stock and t-suffixed numbering. The key extended Rookie Cards in this set are Barry Bonds, Bobby Bonilla, Jose Canseco, Will Clark, Andres Galarraga, Bo Jackson, Wally Joyner, John Kruk, and Kevin Mitchell.

	MINT	NRMT
COMP.FACT.SET (132)	8.00	3.60
COMMON CARD (1T-132T)	.05	.02
MINOR STARS	.10	.05
SEMISTARS	.20	.09
UNLISTED STARS	.40	.18

□ 1T Andy Allanson	.05	.02
□ 2T Neil Allen	.05	.02
□ 3T Joaquin Andujar	.05	.02
□ 4T Paul Assenmacher	.05	.02
□ 5T Scott Bailes	.05	.02
□ 6T Don Baylor	.20	.09
□ 7T Steve Bedrosian	.05	.02
□ 8T Juan Beniquez	.05	.02
□ 9T Juan Berenguer	.05	.02
□ 10T Mike Bielecki	.05	.02
□ 11T Barry Bonds	3.00	1.35
□ 12T Bobby Bonilla	.75	.35
□ 13T Juan Bonilla	.05	.02
□ 14T Rich Bordi	.05	.02
□ 15T Steve Boros MG	.05	.02
□ 16T Rick Burleson	.05	.02
□ 17T Bill Campbell	.05	.02
□ 18T Tom Candiotti	.05	.02
□ 19T John Cangelosi	.05	.02
□ 20T Jose Canseco	1.50	.70
□ 21T Carmen Castillo	.05	.02
□ 22T Rick Cerone	.05	.02
□ 23T John Cerutti	.05	.02
□ 24T Will Clark	1.25	.55
□ 25T Mark Clear	.05	.02
□ 26T Darnell Coles	.05	.02
□ 27T Dave Collins	.05	.02
□ 28T Tim Conroy	.05	.02
□ 29T Joe Cowley	.05	.02
□ 30T Joel Davis	.05	.02
□ 31T Rob Deer	.05	.02
□ 32T John Denny	.05	.02
□ 33T Mike Easler	.05	.02
□ 34T Mark Eichhorn	.05	.02

□ 35T Steve Farr	.05	.02
□ 36T Scott Fletcher	.05	.02
□ 37T Terry Forster	.05	.02
□ 38T Terry Francona	.05	.02
□ 39T Jim Fregosi MG	.05	.02
□ 40T Andres Galarraga	1.50	.70
□ 41T Ken Griffey	.10	.05
□ 42T Bill Gullickson	.05	.02
□ 43T Jose Guzman	.05	.02
□ 44T Moose Haas	.05	.02
□ 45T Billy Hatcher	.05	.02
□ 46T Mike Heath	.05	.02
□ 47T Tom Hume	.05	.02
□ 48T Pete Incaviglia	.40	.18
□ 49T Dane Iorg	.05	.02
□ 50T Bo Jackson	.75	.35
□ 51T Wally Joyner	.40	.18
□ 52T Charlie Kerfeld	.05	.02
□ 53T Eric King	.05	.02
□ 54T Bob Kipper	.05	.02
□ 55T Wayne Krenchicki	.05	.02
□ 56T John Kruk	.40	.18
□ 57T Mike LaCoss	.05	.02
□ 58T Pete Ladd	.05	.02
□ 59T Mike Laga	.05	.02
□ 60T Hal Lanier MG	.05	.02
□ 61T Dave LaPoint	.05	.02
□ 62T Rudy Law	.05	.02
□ 63T Rick Leach	.05	.02
□ 64T Tim Leary	.05	.02
□ 65T Dennis Leonard	.05	.02
□ 66T Jim Leyland MG	.05	.02
□ 67T Steve Lyons	.05	.02
□ 68T Mickey Mahler	.05	.02
□ 69T Candy Maldonado	.05	.02
□ 70T Roger Mason	.05	.02
□ 71T Bob McClure	.05	.02
□ 72T Andy McGaffigan	.05	.02
□ 73T Gene Michael MG	.05	.02
□ 74T Kevin Mitchell	.40	.18
□ 75T Omar Moreno	.05	.02
□ 76T Jerry Mumphrey	.05	.02
□ 77T Phil Niekro	.40	.18
□ 78T Randy Niemann	.05	.02
□ 79T Juan Nieves	.05	.02
□ 80T Otis Nixon	.40	.18
□ 81T Bob Ojeda	.05	.02
□ 82T Jose Oquendo	.05	.02
□ 83T Tom Paciorek	.10	.05
□ 84T David Palmer	.05	.02
□ 85T Frank Pastore	.05	.02
□ 86T Lou Piniella MG	.10	.05
□ 87T Dan Plesac	.10	.05
□ 88T Darrell Porter	.10	.05
□ 89T Rey Quinones	.05	.02
□ 90T Gary Redus	.05	.02
□ 91T Bip Roberts	.40	.18
□ 92T Billy Joe Robidoux	.05	.02
□ 93T Jeff D. Robinson	.05	.02
□ 94T Gary Roenicke	.05	.02
□ 95T Ed Romero	.05	.02
□ 96T Argenis Salazar	.05	.02
□ 97T Joe Sambito	.05	.02
□ 98T Billy Sample	.05	.02
□ 99T Dave Schmidt	.05	.02
□ 100T Ken Schrom	.05	.02
□ 101T Tom Seaver	.50	.23
□ 102T Ted Simmons	.10	.05
□ 103T Sammy Stewart	.05	.02
□ 104T Kurt Stillwell	.05	.02
□ 105T Franklin Stubbs	.05	.02
□ 106T Dale Sveum	.05	.02
□ 107T Chuck Tanner MG	.05	.02
□ 108T Danny Tartabull	.10	.05
□ 109T Tim Teufel	.05	.02
□ 110T Bob Tewksbury	.10	.05
□ 111T Andres Thomas	.05	.02
□ 112T Milt Thompson	.05	.02
□ 113T Robby Thompson	.10	.05
□ 114T Jay Tibbs	.05	.02
□ 115T Wayne Tolleson	.05	.02
□ 116T Alex Trevino	.05	.02
□ 117T Manny Trillo	.05	.02
□ 118T Ed VandeBerg	.05	.02
□ 119T George Virgil	.05	.02
□ 120T Bob Walk	.05	.02

☐ 121T Gene Walter	.05	.02
☐ 122T Claudell Washington	.05	.02
☐ 123T Bill Wegman	.05	.02
☐ 124T Dick Williams MG	.10	.05
☐ 125T Mitch Williams	.10	.05
☐ 126T Bobby Witt	.20	.09
☐ 127T Todd Worrell	.40	.18
☐ 128T George Wright	.05	.02
☐ 129T Ricky Wright	.05	.02
☐ 130T Steve Yeager	.05	.02
☐ 131T Paul Zuvella	.05	.02
☐ 132T Checklist 1T-132T	.05	.02

1987 Topps

This set consists of 792 stan-dard-size cards. Cards were pri-marily issued in 17-card wax packs, 50-card rack packs and factory sets. Card fronts feature wood grain borders encasing a color photo (reminiscent of Topps' classic 1962 baseball set). Subsets include Record Breakers (1-7), Turn Back the Clock (311-315), All-Star selec-tions (595-616) and Team Leaders (scattered throughout the set). The manager cards contain a team checklist on back. The key Rookie Cards in this set are Barry Bonds, Bobby Bonilla, Will Clark, Mike Greenwell, Bo Jackson, Wally Joyner, John Kruk, Barry Larkin, Kevin Mitchell, Rafael Palmeiro, Ruben Sierra, and Devon White.

	MINT	NRMT
COMPLETE SET (792)	12.00	5.50
COMP.FACT.SET (792)	15.00	6.75
COMMON CARD (1-792)	.05	.02
MINOR STARS	.10	.05
UNLISTED STARS	.20	.09
SUBSET CARDS HALF VALUE OF BASE CARDS		

☐ 1 Roger Clemens RB	.20	.09
Most K's 9-inning game		
☐ 2 Jim Deshaies RB	.05	.02
Most cons. K's, start of game		
☐ 3 Dwight Evans RB	.10	.05
Earliest home run		
☐ 4 Davey Lopes RB	.05	.02
Most steals season, 40-year-old		
☐ 5 Dave Righetti RB	.05	.02
Most saves season		
☐ 6 Ruben Sierra RB	.05	.02
Youngest player to switch hit HR's, game		
☐ 7 Todd Worrell RB	.05	.02
Most saves rookie season		
☐ 8 Terry Pendleton	.05	.02
☐ 9 Jay Tibbs	.05	.02
☐ 10 Cecil Cooper	.10	.05
☐ 11 Indians Team	.05	.02

(Mound conference)		
☐ 12 Jeff Sellers	.05	.02
☐ 13 Nick Esasky	.05	.02
☐ 14 Dave Stewart	.10	.05
☐ 15 Claudell Washington	.05	.02
☐ 16 Pat Clements	.05	.02
☐ 17 Pete O'Brien	.05	.02
☐ 18 Dick Howser MG	.10	.05
☐ 19 Matt Young	.05	.02
☐ 20 Gary Carter	.15	.07
☐ 21 Mark Davis	.05	.02
☐ 22 Doug DeCinces	.05	.02
☐ 23 Lee Smith	.15	.07
☐ 24 Tony Walker	.05	.02
☐ 25 Bert Blyleven	.10	.05
☐ 26 Greg Brock	.05	.02
☐ 27 Joe Cowley	.05	.02
☐ 28 Rick Dempsey	.05	.02
☐ 29 Jimmy Key	.15	.07
☐ 30 Tim Raines	.10	.05
☐ 31 Braves Team	.05	.02
(Glenn Hubbard and Rafael Ramirez)		
☐ 32 Tim Leary	.05	.02
☐ 33 Andy Van Slyke	.10	.05
☐ 34 Jose Rijo	.05	.02
☐ 35 Sid Bream	.05	.02
☐ 36 Eric King	.05	.02
☐ 37 Marvell Wynne	.05	.02
☐ 38 Dennis Leonard	.05	.02
☐ 39 Marty Barrett	.05	.02
☐ 40 Dave Righetti	.05	.02
☐ 41 Bo Diaz	.05	.02
☐ 42 Gary Redus	.05	.02
☐ 43 Gene Michael MG	.05	.02
☐ 44 Greg Harris	.05	.02
☐ 45 Jim Presley	.05	.02
☐ 46 Dan Gladden	.05	.02
☐ 47 Dennis Powell	.05	.02
☐ 48 Wally Backman	.05	.02
☐ 49 Terry Harper	.05	.02
☐ 50 Dave Smith	.05	.02
☐ 51 Mel Hall	.05	.02
☐ 52 Keith Atherton	.05	.02
☐ 53 Ruppert Jones	.05	.02
☐ 54 Bill Dawley	.05	.02
☐ 55 Tim Wallach	.05	.02
☐ 56 Brewers Team	.05	.02
(Mound conference)		
☐ 57 Scott Nielsen	.05	.02
☐ 58 Thad Bosley	.05	.02
☐ 59 Ken Dayley	.05	.02
☐ 60 Tony Pena	.05	.02
☐ 61 Bobby Thigpen	.10	.05
☐ 62 Bobby Meacham	.05	.02
☐ 63 Fred Toliver	.05	.02
☐ 64 Harry Spilman	.05	.02
☐ 65 Tom Browning	.05	.02
☐ 66 Marc Sullivan	.05	.02
☐ 67 Bill Swift	.05	.02
☐ 68 Tony LaRussa MG	.10	.05
☐ 69 Lonnie Smith	.05	.02
☐ 70 Charlie Hough	.05	.02
☐ 71 Mike Aldrete	.10	.05
☐ 72 Walt Terrell	.05	.02
☐ 73 Dave Anderson	.05	.02
☐ 74 Dan Pasqua	.05	.02
☐ 75 Ron Darling	.05	.02
☐ 76 Rafael Ramirez	.05	.02
☐ 77 Bryan Oelkers	.05	.02
☐ 78 Tom Foley	.05	.02
☐ 79 Juan Nieves	.05	.02
☐ 80 Wally Joyner	.20	.09
☐ 81 Padres Team	.05	.02
(Andy Hawkins and Terry Kennedy)		
☐ 82 Rob Murphy	.05	.02
☐ 83 Mike Davis	.05	.02
☐ 84 Steve Lake	.05	.02
☐ 85 Kevin Bass	.05	.02
☐ 86 Nate Snell	.05	.02
☐ 87 Mark Salas	.05	.02
☐ 88 Ed Wojna	.05	.02
☐ 89 Ozzie Guillen	.10	.05
☐ 90 Dave Stieb	.05	.02
☐ 91 Harold Reynolds	.05	.02

☐ 92A Urbano Lugo	.20	.09
ERR (no trademark)		
☐ 92B Urbano Lugo COR	.05	.02
☐ 93 Jim Leyland MG	.10	.05
☐ 94 Calvin Schiraldi	.05	.02
☐ 95 Oddibe McDowell	.05	.02
☐ 96 Frank Williams	.05	.02
☐ 97 Glenn Wilson	.05	.02
☐ 98 Bill Scherrer	.05	.02
☐ 99 Darryl Motley	.05	.02
(Now with Braves on card front)		
☐ 100 Steve Garvey	.20	.09
☐ 101 Carl Willis	.05	.02
☐ 102 Paul Zuvella	.05	.02
☐ 103 Rick Aguilera	.10	.05
☐ 104 Billy Sample	.05	.02
☐ 105 Floyd Youmans	.05	.02
☐ 106 Blue Jays Team	.05	.02
(George Bell and Jesse Barfield)		
☐ 107 John Butcher	.05	.02
☐ 108 Jim Gantner UER	.05	.02
(Brewers logo reversed)		
☐ 109 R.J. Reynolds	.05	.02
☐ 110 John Tudor	.05	.02
☐ 111 Alfredo Griffin	.05	.02
☐ 112 Alan Ashby	.05	.02
☐ 113 Neil Allen	.05	.02
☐ 114 Billy Beane	.05	.02
☐ 115 Donnie Moore	.05	.02
☐ 116 Bill Russell	.05	.02
☐ 117 Jim Beattie	.05	.02
☐ 118 Bobby Valentine MG	.05	.02
☐ 119 Ron Robinson	.05	.02
☐ 120 Eddie Murray	.20	.09
☐ 121 Kevin Romine	.05	.02
☐ 122 Jim Clancy	.05	.02
☐ 123 John Kruk	.20	.09
☐ 124 Ray Fontenot	.05	.02
☐ 125 Bob Brenly	.05	.02
☐ 126 Mike Loynd	.05	.02
☐ 127 Vance Law	.05	.02
☐ 128 Checklist 1-132	.05	.02
☐ 129 Rick Cerone	.05	.02
☐ 130 Dwight Gooden	.20	.09
☐ 131 Pirates Team	.05	.02
(Sid Bream and Tony Pena)		
☐ 132 Paul Assenmacher	.05	.02
☐ 133 Jose Oquendo	.05	.02
☐ 134 Rich Yett	.05	.02
☐ 135 Mike Easler	.05	.02
☐ 136 Ron Romanick	.05	.02
☐ 137 Jerry Willard	.05	.02
☐ 138 Roy Lee Jackson	.05	.02
☐ 139 Devon White	.20	.09
☐ 140 Bret Saberhagen	.05	.02
☐ 141 Herm Winningham	.05	.02
☐ 142 Rick Sutcliffe	.05	.02
☐ 143 Steve Boros MG	.05	.02
☐ 144 Mike Scioscia	.05	.02
☐ 145 Charlie Kerfeld	.05	.02
☐ 146 Tracy Jones	.05	.02
☐ 147 Randy Niemann	.05	.02
☐ 148 Dave Collins	.05	.02
☐ 149 Ray Searage	.05	.02
☐ 150 Wade Boggs	.20	.09
☐ 151 Mike LaCoss	.05	.02
☐ 152 Toby Harrah	.05	.02
☐ 153 Duane Ward	.10	.05
☐ 154 Tom O'Malley	.05	.02
☐ 155 Eddie Whitson	.05	.02
☐ 156 Mariners Team	.05	.02
(Mound conference)		
☐ 157 Danny Darwin	.05	.02
☐ 158 Tim Teufel	.05	.02
☐ 159 Ed Olwine	.05	.02
☐ 160 Julio Franco	.05	.02
☐ 161 Steve Ontiveros	.05	.02
☐ 162 Mike LaValliere	.05	.02
☐ 163 Kevin Gross	.05	.02
☐ 164 Sammy Khalifa	.05	.02
☐ 165 Jeff Reardon	.10	.05
☐ 166 Bob Boone	.10	.05

167	Jim Deshaies	.05	.02
168	Lou Piniella MG	.10	.05
169	Ron Washington	.05	.02
170	Bo Jackson	.30	.14
171	Chuck Cary	.05	.02
172	Ron Oester	.05	.02
173	Alex Trevino	.05	.02
174	Henry Cotto	.05	.02
175	Bob Stanley	.05	.02
176	Steve Buechele	.05	.02
177	Keith Moreland	.05	.02
178	Cecil Fielder	.15	.07
179	Bill Wegman	.05	.02
180	Chris Brown	.05	.02
181	Cardinals Team	.05	.02
	(Mound conference)		
182	Lee Lacy	.05	.02
183	Andy Hawkins	.05	.02
184	Bobby Bonilla	.30	.14
185	Roger McDowell	.05	.02
186	Bruce Benedict	.05	.02
187	Mark Huismann	.05	.02
188	Tony Phillips	.05	.02
189	Joe Hesketh	.05	.02
190	Jim Sundberg	.05	.02
191	Charles Hudson	.05	.02
192	Cory Snyder	.05	.02
193	Roger Craig MG	.05	.02
194	Kirk McCaskill	.05	.02
195	Mike Pagliarulo	.05	.02
196	Randy O'Neal UER	.05	.02
	(Wrong ML career W-L totals)		
197	Mark Bailey	.05	.02
198	Lee Mazzilli	.05	.02
199	Mariano Duncan	.05	.02
200	Pete Rose	.25	.11
201	John Cangelosi	.05	.02
202	Ricky Wright	.05	.02
203	Mike Kingery	.10	.05
204	Sammy Stewart	.05	.02
205	Graig Nettles	.10	.05
206	Twins Team	.05	.02
	(Frank Viola and Tim Laudner)		
207	George Frazier	.05	.02
208	John Shelby	.05	.02
209	Rick Schu	.05	.02
210	Lloyd Moseby	.05	.02
211	John Morris	.05	.02
212	Mike Fitzgerald	.05	.02
213	Randy Myers	.20	.09
214	Omar Moreno	.05	.02
215	Mark Langston	.05	.02
216	B.J. Surhoff	.20	.09
217	Chris Codiroli	.05	.02
218	Sparky Anderson MG	.10	.05
219	Cecilio Guante	.05	.02
220	Joe Carter	.20	.09
221	Vern Ruhle	.05	.02
222	Denny Walling	.05	.02
223	Charlie Leibrandt	.05	.02
224	Wayne Tolleson	.05	.02
225	Mike Smithson	.05	.02
226	Max Venable	.05	.02
227	Jamie Moyer	.15	.07
228	Curt Wilkerson	.05	.02
229	Mike Birkbeck	.05	.02
230	Don Baylor	.05	.02
231	Giants Team	.05	.02
	(Bob Brenly and Jim Gott)		
232	Reggie Williams	.05	.02
233	Russ Morman	.05	.02
234	Pat Sheridan	.05	.02
235	Alvin Davis	.05	.02
236	Tommy John	.10	.05
237	Jim Morrison	.05	.02
238	Bill Krueger	.05	.02
239	Juan Espino	.05	.02
240	Steve Balboni	.05	.02
241	Danny Heep	.05	.02
242	Rick Mahler	.05	.02
243	Whitey Herzog MG	.10	.05
244	Dickie Noles	.05	.02
245	Willie Upshaw	.05	.02

246	Jim Dwyer	.05	.02
247	Jeff Reed	.05	.02
248	Gene Walter	.05	.02
249	Jim Pankovits	.05	.02
250	Teddy Higuera	.05	.02
251	Rob Wilfong	.05	.02
252	Dennis Martinez	.10	.05
253	Eddie Milner	.05	.02
254	Bob Tewksbury	.10	.05
255	Juan Samuel	.05	.02
256	Royals Team	.15	.07
	(George Brett and Frank White)		
257	Bob Forsch	.05	.02
258	Steve Yeager	.05	.02
259	Mike Greenwell	.20	.09
260	Vida Blue	.10	.05
261	Ruben Sierra	.20	
262	Jim Winn	.05	.02
263	Stan Javier	.05	.02
264	Checklist 133-264	.05	.02
265	Darrell Evans	.10	.05
266	Jeff Hamilton	.05	.02
267	Howard Johnson	.25	.11
268	Pat Corrales MG	.05	.02
269	Cliff Speck	.05	.02
270	Jody Davis	.05	.02
271	Mike G. Brown	.05	.02
272	Andres Galarraga	.25	.11
273	Gene Nelson	.05	.02
274	Jeff Hearron UER	.05	.02
	(Duplicate 1986 stat line on back)		
275	LaMarr Hoyt	.05	.02
276	Jackie Gutierrez	.05	.02
277	Juan Agosto	.05	.02
278	Gary Pettis	.05	.02
279	Dan Plesac	.05	.02
280	Jeff Leonard	.05	.02
281	Reds Team	.20	.09
	(Pete Rose, Bo Diaz, and Bill Gullickson)		
282	Jeff Calhoun	.05	.02
283	Doug Drabek	.20	.09
284	John Moses	.05	.02
285	Dennis Boyd	.05	.02
286	Mike Woodard	.05	.02
287	Dave Von Ohlen	.05	.02
288	Tito Landrum	.05	.02
289	Bob Kipper	.05	.02
290	Leon Durham	.05	.02
291	Mitch Williams	.10	.05
292	Franklin Stubbs	.05	.02
293	Bob Rodgers MG	.05	.02
294	Steve Jeltz	.05	.02
295	Len Dykstra	.20	.09
296	Andres Thomas	.05	.02
297	Don Schulze	.05	.02
298	Larry Herndon	.05	.02
299	Joel Davis	.05	.02
300	Reggie Jackson	.25	.11
301	Luis Aquino UER	.05	.02
	(No trademark never corrected)		
302	Bill Schroeder	.05	.02
303	Juan Berenguer	.05	.02
304	Phil Garner	.05	.02
305	John Franco	.10	.05
306	Red Sox Team	.10	.05
	(Tom Seaver, John McNamara MG, and Rich Gedman)		
307	Lee Guetterman	.05	.02
308	Don Slaught	.05	.02
309	Mike Young	.05	.02
310	Frank Viola	.05	.02
311	Rickey Henderson	.10	.05
	TBC '82		
312	Reggie Jackson	.20	.09
	TBC '77		
313	Roberto Clemente	.25	.11
	TBC '72		
314	Carl Yastrzemski UER	.20	.09
	TBC '67 (Sic, 112 RBI's on back)		
315	Maury Wills TBC '62	.10	.05

316	Brian Fisher	.05	.02
317	Clint Hurdle	.05	.02
318	Jim Fregosi MG	.05	.02
319	Greg Swindell	.20	
320	Barry Bonds	1.25	.55
321	Mike Laga	.05	.02
322	Chris Bando	.05	.02
323	Al Newman	.05	.02
324	David Palmer	.05	.02
325	Garry Templeton	.05	.02
326	Mark Gubicza	.05	.02
327	Dale Sveum	.05	.02
328	Bob Welch	.05	.02
329	Ron Roenicke	.05	.02
330	Mike Scott	.05	.02
331	Mets Team	.10	.05
	(Gary Carter and Darryl Strawberry)		
332	Joe Price	.05	.02
333	Ken Phelps	.05	.02
334	Ed Correa	.05	.02
335	Candy Maldonado	.05	.02
336	Allan Anderson	.05	.02
337	Darrell Miller	.05	.02
338	Tim Conroy	.05	.02
339	Donnie Hill	.05	.02
340	Roger Clemens	.50	.23
341	Mike C. Brown	.05	.02
342	Bob James	.05	.02
343	Hal Lanier MG	.05	.02
344A	Joe Niekro		
	(Copyright inside righthand border)		
344B	Joe Niekro	.05	.02
	(Copyright outside righthand border)		
345	Andre Dawson	.20	.09
346	Shawon Dunston	.05	.02
347	Mickey Brantley	.05	.02
348	Carmelo Martinez	.05	.02
349	Storm Davis	.05	.02
350	Keith Hernandez	.10	.05
351	Gene Garber	.05	.02
352	Mike Felder	.05	.02
353	Ernie Camacho	.05	.02
354	Jamie Quirk	.05	.02
355	Don Carman	.05	.02
356	White Sox Team	.05	.02
	(Mound conference)		
357	Steve Fireovid	.05	.02
358	Sal Butera	.05	.02
359	Doug Corbett	.05	.02
360	Pedro Guerrero	.10	.05
361	Mark Thurmond	.05	.02
362	Luis Quinones	.05	.02
363	Jose Guzman	.05	.02
364	Randy Bush	.05	.02
365	Rick Rhoden	.05	.02
366	Mark McGwire	1.50	.70
367	Jeff Lahti	.05	.02
368	John McNamara MG	.05	.02
369	Brian Dayett	.05	.02
370	Fred Lynn	.10	.05
371	Mark Eichhorn	.05	.02
372	Jerry Mumphrey	.05	.02
373	Jeff Dedmon	.05	.02
374	Glenn Hoffman	.05	.02
375	Ron Guidry	.10	.05
376	Scott Bradley	.05	.02
377	John Henry Johnson	.05	.02
378	Rafael Santana	.05	.02
379	John Russell	.05	.02
380	Rich Gossage	.10	.05
381	Expos Team	.05	.02
	(Mound conference)		
382	Rudy Law	.05	.02
383	Ron Davis	.05	.02
384	Johnny Grubb	.05	.02
385	Orel Hershiser	.10	.05
386	Dickie Thon	.05	.02
387	T.R. Bryden	.05	.02
388	Geno Petralli	.05	.02
389	Jeff D. Robinson	.05	.02
390	Gary Matthews	.05	.02
391	Jay Howell	.05	.02
392	Checklist 265-396	.05	.02

☐ 393	Pete Rose MG	.15	.07
☐ 394	Mike Bielecki	.05	.02
☐ 395	Damaso Garcia	.05	.02
☐ 396	Tim Lollar	.05	.02
☐ 397	Greg Walker	.05	.02
☐ 398	Brad Havens	.05	.02
☐ 399	Curt Ford	.05	.02
☐ 400	George Brett	.40	.18
☐ 401	Billy Joe Robidoux	.05	.02
☐ 402	Mike Trujillo	.05	.02
☐ 403	Jerry Royster	.05	.02
☐ 404	Doug Sisk	.05	.02
☐ 405	Brook Jacoby	.05	.02
☐ 406	Yankees Team (Rickey Henderson and Don Mattingly)	.20	.09
☐ 407	Jim Acker	.05	.02
☐ 408	John Mizerock	.05	.02
☐ 409	Milt Thompson	.05	.02
☐ 410	Fernando Valenzuela	.10	.05
☐ 411	Darnell Coles	.05	.02
☐ 412	Eric Davis	.15	.07
☐ 413	Moose Haas	.05	.02
☐ 414	Joe Orsulak	.05	.02
☐ 415	Bobby Witt	.10	.05
☐ 416	Tom Nieto	.05	.02
☐ 417	Pat Perry	.05	.02
☐ 418	Dick Williams MG	.10	.05
☐ 419	Mark Portugal	.10	.05
☐ 420	Will Clark	.60	.25
☐ 421	Jose DeLeon	.05	.02
☐ 422	Jack Howell	.05	.02
☐ 423	Jaime Cocanower	.05	.02
☐ 424	Chris Speier	.05	.02
☐ 425	Tom Seaver UER Earned Runs amount is wrong For 86 Red Sox and Career Also the ERA is wrong for 86 and career	.20	.09
☐ 426	Floyd Rayford	.05	.02
☐ 427	Edwin Nunez	.05	.02
☐ 428	Bruce Bochy	.05	.02
☐ 429	Tim Pyznarski	.05	.02
☐ 430	Mike Schmidt	.25	.11
☐ 431	Dodgers Team (Mound conference)	.05	.02
☐ 432	Jim Slaton	.05	.02
☐ 433	Ed Hearn	.05	.02
☐ 434	Mike Fischlin	.05	.02
☐ 435	Bruce Sutter	.05	.02
☐ 436	Andy Allanson	.05	.02
☐ 437	Ted Power	.05	.02
☐ 438	Kelly Downs	.05	.02
☐ 439	Karl Best	.05	.02
☐ 440	Willie McGee	.05	.02
☐ 441	Dave Leiper	.05	.02
☐ 442	Mitch Webster	.05	.02
☐ 443	John Felske MG	.05	.02
☐ 444	Jeff Russell	.05	.02
☐ 445	Dave Lopes	.10	.05
☐ 446	Chuck Finley	.20	.09
☐ 447	Bill Almon	.05	.02
☐ 448	Chris Bosio	.05	.02
☐ 449	Pat Dodson	.05	.02
☐ 450	Kirby Puckett	.50	.23
☐ 451	Joe Sambito	.05	.02
☐ 452	Dave Henderson	.05	.02
☐ 453	Scott Terry	.05	.02
☐ 454	Luis Salazar	.05	.02
☐ 455	Mike Boddicker	.05	.02
☐ 456	A's Team (Mound conference)	.05	.02
☐ 457	Len Matuszek	.05	.02
☐ 458	Kelly Gruber	.05	.02
☐ 459	Dennis Eckersley	.20	.09
☐ 460	Darryl Strawberry	.10	.05
☐ 461	Craig McMurtry	.05	.02
☐ 462	Scott Fletcher	.05	.02
☐ 463	Tom Candiotti	.05	.02
☐ 464	Butch Wynegar	.05	.02
☐ 465	Todd Worrell	.10	.05
☐ 466	Kal Daniels	.05	.02
☐ 467	Randy St.Claire	.05	.02
☐ 468	George Bamberger MG	.10	.05
☐ 469	Mike Diaz	.05	.02
☐ 470	Dave Dravecky	.10	.05
☐ 471	Ronn Reynolds	.05	.02
☐ 472	Bill Doran	.05	.02
☐ 473	Steve Farr	.05	.02
☐ 474	Jerry Narron	.05	.02
☐ 475	Scott Garrelts	.05	.02
☐ 476	Danny Tartabull	.05	.02
☐ 477	Ken Howell	.05	.02
☐ 478	Tim Laudner	.05	.02
☐ 479	Bob Sebra	.05	.02
☐ 480	Jim Rice	.10	.05
☐ 481	Phillies Team (Glenn Wilson Juan Samuel and Von Hayes)	.05	.02
☐ 482	Daryl Boston	.05	.02
☐ 483	Dwight Lowry	.05	.02
☐ 484	Jim Traber	.05	.02
☐ 485	Tony Fernandez	.05	.02
☐ 486	Otis Nixon	.10	.05
☐ 487	Dave Gumpert	.05	.02
☐ 488	Ray Knight	.05	.02
☐ 489	Bill Gullickson	.05	.02
☐ 490	Dale Murphy	.20	.09
☐ 491	Ron Karkovice	.10	.05
☐ 492	Mike McRae	.05	.02
☐ 493	Tom Lasorda MG	.10	.05
☐ 494	Barry Jones	.05	.02
☐ 495	Gorman Thomas	.05	.02
☐ 496	Bruce Bochte	.05	.02
☐ 497	Dale Mohorcic	.05	.02
☐ 498	Bob Kearney	.05	.02
☐ 499	Bruce Ruffin	.05	.02
☐ 500	Don Mattingly	.30	.14
☐ 501	Craig Lefferts	.05	.02
☐ 502	Dick Schofield	.05	.02
☐ 503	Larry Andersen	.05	.02
☐ 504	Mickey Hatcher	.05	.02
☐ 505	Bryn Smith	.05	.02
☐ 506	Orioles Team (Mound conference)	.05	.02
☐ 507	Dave L. Stapleton	.05	.02
☐ 508	Scott Bankhead	.05	.02
☐ 509	Enos Cabell	.05	.02
☐ 510	Tom Henke	.05	.02
☐ 511	Steve Lyons	.05	.02
☐ 512	Dave Magadan	.15	.07
☐ 513	Carmen Castillo	.05	.02
☐ 514	Orlando Mercado	.05	.02
☐ 515	Willie Hernandez	.05	.02
☐ 516	Ted Simmons	.10	.05
☐ 517	Mario Soto	.05	.02
☐ 518	Gene Mauch MG	.10	.05
☐ 519	Curt Young	.05	.02
☐ 520	Jack Clark	.10	.05
☐ 521	Rick Reuschel	.05	.02
☐ 522	Checklist 397-528	.05	.02
☐ 523	Earnie Riles	.05	.02
☐ 524	Bob Shirley	.05	.02
☐ 525	Phil Bradley	.05	.02
☐ 526	Roger Mason	.05	.02
☐ 527	Jim Wohlford	.05	.02
☐ 528	Ken Dixon	.05	.02
☐ 529	Alvaro Espinoza	.05	.02
☐ 530	Tony Gwynn	.50	.23
☐ 531	Astros Team (Yogi Berra conference)	.05	.02
☐ 532	Jeff Stone	.05	.02
☐ 533	Argenis Salazar	.05	.02
☐ 534	Scott Sanderson	.05	.02
☐ 535	Tony Armas	.05	.02
☐ 536	Terry Mulholland	.10	.05
☐ 537	Rance Mulinks	.05	.02
☐ 538	Tom Niedenfuer	.05	.02
☐ 539	Reid Nichols	.05	.02
☐ 540	Terry Kennedy	.05	.02
☐ 541	Rafael Belliard	.05	.02
☐ 542	Ricky Horton	.05	.02
☐ 543	Dave Johnson MG	.05	.02
☐ 544	Zane Smith	.05	.02
☐ 545	Buddy Bell	.10	.05
☐ 546	Mike Morgan	.05	.02
☐ 547	Rob Deer	.05	.02
☐ 548	Bill Mooneyham	.05	.02
☐ 549	Bob Melvin	.05	.02
☐ 550	Pete Incaviglia	.10	.05
☐ 551	Frank Wills	.05	.02
☐ 552	Larry Sheets	.05	.02
☐ 553	Mike Maddux	.05	.02
☐ 554	Buddy Biancalana	.05	.02
☐ 555	Dennis Rasmussen	.05	.02
☐ 556	Angels Team (Rene Lachemann CO, Mike Witt, and Bob Boone)	.05	.02
☐ 557	John Cerutti	.05	.02
☐ 558	Greg Gagne	.05	.02
☐ 559	Lance McCullers	.05	.02
☐ 560	Glenn Davis	.05	.02
☐ 561	Rey Quinones	.05	.02
☐ 562	Bryan Clutterbuck	.05	.02
☐ 563	John Stefero	.05	.02
☐ 564	Larry McWilliams	.05	.02
☐ 565	Dusty Baker	.10	.05
☐ 566	Tim Hulett	.05	.02
☐ 567	Greg Mathews	.05	.02
☐ 568	Earl Weaver MG	.20	.09
☐ 569	Wade Rowdon	.05	.02
☐ 570	Sid Fernandez	.05	.02
☐ 571	Ozzie Virgil	.05	.02
☐ 572	Pete Ladd	.05	.02
☐ 573	Hal McRae	.10	.05
☐ 574	Manny Lee	.05	.02
☐ 575	Pat Tabler	.05	.02
☐ 576	Frank Pastore	.05	.02
☐ 577	Dann Bilardello	.05	.02
☐ 578	Billy Hatcher	.05	.02
☐ 579	Rick Burleson	.05	.02
☐ 580	Mike Krukow	.05	.02
☐ 581	Cubs Team (Ron Cey and Steve Trout)	.05	.02
☐ 582	Bruce Berenyi	.05	.02
☐ 583	Junior Ortiz	.05	.02
☐ 584	Ron Kittle	.05	.02
☐ 585	Scott Bailes	.05	.02
☐ 586	Ben Oglivie	.05	.02
☐ 587	Eric Plunk	.05	.02
☐ 588	Wallace Johnson	.05	.02
☐ 589	Steve Crawford	.05	.02
☐ 590	Vince Coleman	.10	.05
☐ 591	Spike Owen	.05	.02
☐ 592	Chris Welsh	.05	.02
☐ 593	Chuck Tanner MG	.05	.02
☐ 594	Rick Anderson	.05	.02
☐ 595	Keith Hernandez AS	.05	.02
☐ 596	Steve Sax AS	.05	.02
☐ 597	Mike Schmidt AS	.15	.07
☐ 598	Ozzie Smith AS	.05	.02
☐ 599	Tony Gwynn AS	.20	.09
☐ 600	Dave Parker AS	.05	.02
☐ 601	Darryl Strawberry AS	.10	.05
☐ 602	Gary Carter AS	.10	.05
☐ 603A	Dwight Gooden AS ERR (no trademark)	.20	.09
☐ 603B	Dwight Gooden COR	.20	.09
☐ 604	Fernando Valenzuela AS	.10	.05
☐ 605	Todd Worrell AS	.10	.05
☐ 606	Don Mattingly AS COR	.20	.09
☐ 606A	Don Mattingly AS ERR (no trademark)	.75	.35
☐ 607	Tony Bernazard AS	.05	.02
☐ 608	Wade Boggs AS	.10	.05
☐ 609	Cal Ripken AS	.40	.18
☐ 610	Jim Rice AS	.05	.02
☐ 611	Kirby Puckett AS	.20	.09
☐ 612	George Bell AS	.05	.02
☐ 613	Lance Parrish AS UER (Pitcher heading on back)	.10	.05
☐ 614	Roger Clemens AS	.20	.09
☐ 615	Teddy Higuera AS	.05	.02
☐ 616	Dave Righetti AS	.05	.02
☐ 617	Al Nipper AS	.05	.02
☐ 618	Tom Kelly MG	.05	.02
☐ 619	Jerry Reed	.05	.02
☐ 620	Jose Canseco	.40	.18
☐ 621	Danny Cox	.05	.02
☐ 622	Glenn Braggs	.05	.02
☐ 623	Kurt Stillwell	.05	.02
☐ 624	Tim Burke	.05	.02
☐ 625	Mookie Wilson	.10	.05
☐ 626	Joel Skinner	.05	.02

☐ 627 Ken Oberkfell	.05	.02	☐ 705 Bruce Hurst	.05	.02	☐ 791 Lance Parrish UER	.10	.05
☐ 628 Bob Walk	.05	.02	☐ 706 Rick Manning	.05	.02	(No trademark,		
☐ 629 Larry Parrish	.05	.02	☐ 707 Bob McClure	.05	.02	never corrected)		
☐ 630 John Candelaria	.05	.02	☐ 708 Scott McGregor	.05	.02	☐ 792 Checklist 661-792	.05	.02
☐ 631 Tigers Team	.05	.02	☐ 709 Dave Kingman	.10	.05			

(Mound conference) / (Bobby Valentine MG and Ricky Wright)

1987 Topps Traded

This is a 132-card standard-size Traded set was distributed exclusively in factory set form in a special green and white box through hobby dealers. The card fronts are identical in style to the Topps regular issue except for whiter stock and t-suffixed numbering on back. The cards are ordered alphabetically by player's last name. The key extended Rookie Cards in this set are Ellis Burks, David Cone, Greg Maddux, Fred McGriff and Matt Williams.

☐ 632 Rob Woodward	.05	.02	☐ 710 Gary Gaetti	.05	.02
☐ 633 Jose Uribe	.05	.02	☐ 711 Ken Griffey	.10	.05
☐ 634 Rafael Palmeiro	.60	.25	☐ 712 Don Robinson	.05	.02
☐ 635 Ken Schrom	.05	.02	☐ 713 Tom Brookens	.05	.02
☐ 636 Darren Daulton	.15	.07	☐ 714 Dan Quisenberry	.05	.02
☐ 637 Bip Roberts	.20	.09	☐ 715 Bob Dernier	.05	.02
☐ 638 Rich Bordi	.05	.02	☐ 716 Rick Leach	.05	.02
☐ 639 Gerald Perry	.05	.02	☐ 717 Ed VandeBerg	.05	.02
☐ 640 Mark Clear	.05	.02	☐ 718 Steve Carlton	.20	.09
☐ 641 Domingo Ramos	.05	.02	☐ 719 Tom Hume	.05	.02
☐ 642 Al Pulido	.05	.02	☐ 720 Richard Dotson	.05	.02
☐ 643 Ron Shepherd	.05	.02	☐ 721 Tom Herr	.05	.02
☐ 644 John Denny	.05	.02	☐ 722 Bob Knepper	.05	.02
☐ 645 Dwight Evans	.10	.05	☐ 723 Brett Butler	.10	.05
☐ 646 Mike Mason	.05	.02	☐ 724 Greg Minton	.05	.02
☐ 647 Tom Lawless	.05	.02	☐ 725 George Hendrick	.05	.02
☐ 648 Barry Larkin	.60	.25	☐ 726 Frank Tanana	.05	.02
☐ 649 Mickey Tettleton	.10	.05	☐ 727 Mike Moore	.05	.02
☐ 650 Hubie Brooks	.05	.02	☐ 728 Tippy Martinez	.05	.02
☐ 651 Benny Distefano	.05	.02	☐ 729 Tom Paciorek	.05	.02
☐ 652 Terry Forster	.05	.02	☐ 730 Eric Show	.05	.02
☐ 653 Kevin Mitchell	.15	.07	☐ 731 Dave Concepcion	.10	.05
☐ 654 Checklist 529-660	.05	.02	☐ 732 Manny Trillo	.05	.02
☐ 655 Jesse Barfield	.05	.02	☐ 733 Bill Caudill	.05	.02
☐ 656 Rangers Team	.05	.02	☐ 734 Bill Madlock	.10	.05
☐ 657 Tom Waddell	.05	.02	☐ 735 Rickey Henderson	.20	.09
☐ 658 Robby Thompson	.10	.05	☐ 736 Steve Bedrosian	.05	.02
☐ 659 Aurelio Lopez	.05	.02	☐ 737 Floyd Bannister	.05	.02
☐ 660 Bob Horner	.05	.02	☐ 738 Jorge Orta	.05	.02
☐ 661 Lou Whitaker	.10	.05	☐ 739 Chet Lemon	.05	.02
☐ 662 Frank DiPino	.05	.02	☐ 740 Rich Gedman	.05	.02
☐ 663 Cliff Johnson	.05	.02	☐ 741 Paul Molitor	.20	.09
☐ 664 Mike Marshall	.05	.02	☐ 742 Andy McGaffigan	.05	.02
☐ 665 Rod Scurry	.05	.02	☐ 743 Dwayne Murphy	.05	.02
☐ 666 Von Hayes	.05	.02	☐ 744 Roy Smalley	.05	.02
☐ 667 Ron Hassey	.05	.02	☐ 745 Glenn Hubbard	.05	.02
☐ 668 Juan Bonilla	.05	.02	☐ 746 Bob Ojeda	.05	.02
☐ 669 Bud Black	.05	.02	☐ 747 Johnny Ray	.05	.02
☐ 670 Jose Cruz	.10	.05	☐ 748 Mike Flanagan	.05	.02
☐ 671A Ray Soff ERR	.05	.02	☐ 749 Ozzie Smith	.25	.11

(No D* before copyright line)

☐ 671B Ray Soff COR	.05	.02	☐ 750 Steve Trout	.05	.02

(D* before copyright line)

☐ 672 Chili Davis	.15	.07	☐ 751 Garth Iorg	.05	.02
☐ 673 Don Sutton	.20	.09	☐ 752 Dan Petry	.05	.02
☐ 674 Bill Campbell	.05	.02	☐ 753 Rick Honeycutt	.05	.02
☐ 675 Ed Romero	.05	.02	☐ 754 Dave LaPoint	.05	.02
☐ 676 Charlie Moore	.05	.02	☐ 755 Luis Aguayo	.05	.02
☐ 677 Bob Grich	.05	.02	☐ 756 Carlton Fisk	.20	.09
☐ 678 Carney Lansford	.05	.02	☐ 757 Nolan Ryan	.75	.35
☐ 679 Kent Hrbek	.10	.05	☐ 758 Tony Bernazard	.05	.02
☐ 680 Ryne Sandberg	.25	.11	☐ 759 Joel Youngblood	.05	.02
☐ 681 George Bell	.05	.02	☐ 760 Mike Witt	.05	.02
☐ 682 Jerry Reuss	.05	.02	☐ 761 Greg Pryor	.05	.02
☐ 683 Gary Roenicke	.05	.02	☐ 762 Gary Ward	.05	.02
☐ 684 Kent Tekulve	.05	.02	☐ 763 Tim Flannery	.05	.02
☐ 685 Jerry Hairston	.05	.02	☐ 764 Bill Buckner	.10	.05
☐ 686 Doyle Alexander	.05	.02	☐ 765 Kirk Gibson	.10	.05
☐ 687 Alan Trammell	.15	.07	☐ 766 Don Aase	.05	.02
☐ 688 Juan Beniquez	.05	.02	☐ 767 Ron Cey	.10	.05
☐ 689 Darrell Porter	.05	.02	☐ 768 Dennis Lamp	.05	.02
☐ 690 Dane Iorg	.05	.02	☐ 769 Steve Sax	.05	.02
☐ 691 Dave Parker	.10	.05	☐ 770 Dave Winfield	.20	.09
☐ 692 Frank White	.05	.02	☐ 771 Shane Rawley	.05	.02
☐ 693 Terry Puhl	.05	.02	☐ 772 Harold Baines	.10	.05
☐ 694 Phil Niekro	.20	.09	☐ 773 Robin Yount	.20	.09
☐ 695 Chico Walker	.05	.02	☐ 774 Wayne Krenchicki	.05	.02
☐ 696 Gary Lucas	.05	.02	☐ 775 Joaquin Andujar	.05	.02
☐ 697 Ed Lynch	.05	.02	☐ 776 Tom Runnansky	.05	.02
☐ 698 Ernie Whitt	.05	.02	☐ 777 Chris Chambliss	.05	.02
☐ 699 Ken Landreaux	.05	.02	☐ 778 Jack Morris	.10	.05
☐ 700 Dave Bergman	.05	.02	☐ 779 Craig Reynolds	.05	.02
☐ 701 Willie Randolph	.10	.05	☐ 780 Andre Thornton	.05	.02
☐ 702 Greg Gross	.05	.02	☐ 781 Atlee Hammaker	.05	.02
☐ 703 Dave Schmidt	.05	.02	☐ 782 Brian Downing	.05	.02
☐ 704 Jesse Orosco	.05	.02	☐ 783 Willie Wilson	.05	.02
			☐ 784 Cal Ripken	.75	.35
			☐ 785 Terry Francona	.05	.02
			☐ 786 Jerry Willard MG	.05	.02
			☐ 787 Alejandro Pena	.05	.02
			☐ 788 Tim Stoddard	.05	.02
			☐ 789 Dan Schatzeder	.05	.02
			☐ 790 Julio Cruz	.05	.02

	MINT	NRMT
COMP.FACT.SET (132)	8.00	3.60
COMMON CARD (1T-132T)	.05	.02
MINOR STARS	.15	.07
UNLISTED STARS	.30	.14

☐ 1T Bill Almon	.05	.02
☐ 2T Scott Bankhead	.05	.02
☐ 3T Eric Bell	.05	.02
☐ 4T Juan Beniquez	.05	.02
☐ 5T Juan Berenguer	.05	.02
☐ 6T Greg Booker	.05	.02
☐ 7T Thad Bosley	.05	.02
☐ 8T Larry Bowa MG	.15	.07
☐ 9T Greg Brock	.05	.02
☐ 10T Bob Brower	.05	.02
☐ 11T Jerry Browne	.05	.02
☐ 12T Ralph Bryant	.05	.02
☐ 13T DeWayne Buice	.05	.02
☐ 14T Ellis Burks	.50	.23
☐ 15T Ivan Calderon	.05	.02
☐ 16T Jeff Calhoun	.05	.02
☐ 17T Casey Candaele	.05	.02
☐ 18T John Cangelosi	.05	.02
☐ 19T Steve Carlton	.30	.14
☐ 20T Juan Castillo	.05	.02
☐ 21T Rick Cerone	.05	.02
☐ 22T Ron Cey	.15	.07
☐ 23T John Christensen	.05	.02
☐ 24T David Cone	.50	.23
☐ 25T Chuck Crim	.05	.02
☐ 26T Storm Davis	.05	.02
☐ 27T Andre Dawson	.30	.14
☐ 28T Rick Dempsey	.15	.07
☐ 29T Doug Drabek	.30	.14
☐ 30T Mike Dunne	.05	.02
☐ 31T Dennis Eckersley	.30	.14
☐ 32T Lee Elia MG	.05	.02
☐ 33T Brian Fisher	.05	.02
☐ 34T Terry Francona	.05	.02
☐ 35T Willie Fraser	.05	.02
☐ 36T Billy Gardner MG	.05	.02
☐ 37T Ken Gerhart	.05	.02
☐ 38T Dan Gladden	.05	.02

Card		MINT	NRMT
39T	Jim Gott	.05	.02
40T	Cecilio Guante	.05	.02
41T	Albert Hall	.05	.02
42T	Terry Harper	.05	.02
43T	Mickey Hatcher	.05	.02
44T	Brad Havens	.05	.02
45T	Neal Heaton	.05	.02
46T	Mike Henneman	.30	.14
47T	Donnie Hill	.05	.02
48T	Guy Hoffman	.05	.02
49T	Brian Holton	.05	.02
50T	Charles Hudson	.05	.02
51T	Danny Jackson	.05	.02
52T	Reggie Jackson	.40	.18
53T	Chris James	.05	.02
54T	Dion James	.05	.02
55T	Stan Jefferson	.05	.02
56T	Joe Johnson	.05	.02
57T	Terry Kennedy	.05	.02
58T	Mike Kingery	.15	.07
59T	Ray Knight	.05	.02
60T	Gene Larkin	.05	.02
61T	Mike LaValliere	.05	.02
62T	Jack Lazorko	.05	.02
63T	Terry Leach	.05	.02
64T	Tim Leary	.05	.02
65T	Jim Lindeman	.05	.02
66T	Steve Lombardozzi	.05	.02
67T	Bill Long	.05	.02
68T	Barry Lyons	.05	.02
69T	Shane Mack	.15	.07
70T	Greg Maddux	5.00	2.20
71T	Bill Madlock	.15	.07
72T	Joe Magrane	.05	.02
73T	Dave Martinez	.10	.02
74T	Fred McGriff	.40	.18
75T	Mark McLemore	.05	.02
76T	Kevin McReynolds	.05	.02
77T	Dave Meads	.05	.02
78T	Eddie Milner	.05	.02
79T	Greg Minton	.05	.02
80T	John Mitchell	.05	.02
81T	Kevin Mitchell	.10	.02
82T	Charlie Moore	.05	.02
83T	Jeff Musselman	.05	.02
84T	Gene Nelson	.05	.02
85T	Graig Nettles	.15	.07
86T	Al Newman	.05	.02
87T	Reid Nichols	.05	.02
88T	Tom Niedenfuer	.05	.02
89T	Joe Niekro	.05	.02
90T	Tom Nieto	.05	.02
91T	Matt Nokes	.15	.07
92T	Dickie Noles	.05	.02
93T	Pat Pacillo	.05	.02
94T	Lance Parrish	.15	.07
95T	Tony Pena	.05	.02
96T	Luis Polonia	.15	
97T	Randy Ready	.05	.02
98T	Jeff Reardon	.15	.07
99T	Gary Redus	.05	.02
100T	Jeff Reed	.05	.02
101T	Rick Rhoden	.05	.02
102T	Cal Ripken Sr. MG	.05	.02
103T	Wally Ritchie	.05	.02
104T	Jeff M. Robinson	.05	.02
105T	Gary Roenicke	.05	.02
106T	Jerry Royster	.05	.02
107T	Mark Salas	.05	.02
108T	Luis Salazar	.05	.02
109T	Benny Santiago	.15	.07
110T	Dave Schmidt	.05	.02
111T	Kevin Seitzer	.15	.07
112T	John Shelby	.05	.02
113T	Steve Shields	.05	.02
114T	John Smiley	.15	.07
115T	Chris Speier	.05	.02
116T	Mike Stanley	.30	.14
117T	Terry Steinbach	.30	.14
118T	Les Straker	.05	.02
119T	Jim Sundberg	.05	.02
120T	Danny Tartabull	.15	.07
121T	Tom Trebelhorn MG	.05	.02
122T	Dave Valle	.05	.02
123T	Ed VandeBerg	.05	.02
124T	Andy Van Slyke	.15	.07
125T	Gary Ward	.05	.02
126T	Alan Wiggins	.05	.02
127T	Bill Wilkinson	.05	.02
128T	Frank Williams	.05	.02
129T	Matt Williams	2.00	.90
130T	Jim Winn	.05	.02
131T	Matt Young	.05	.02
132T	Checklist 1T-132T	.05	.02

1988 Topps

This set consists of 792 standard-size cards. The cards were primarily issued in 15-card wax packs, 42-card rack packs and factory sets. Card fronts feature white borders encasing a color photo with team name running across the top and player name diagonally across the bottom. Subsets include Record Breakers (1-7), All-Stars (386-407), Turn Back the Clock (661-665), and Team Leaders (scattered throughout the set). The manager cards contain a team checklist on back. The key Rookie Cards in this set are Ellis Burks, Ken Caminiti, Tom Glavine, Jeff Montgomery, and Matt Williams.

	MINT	NRMT
COMPLETE SET (792)	10.00	4.50
COMP.FACT.SET (792)	12.00	5.50
COMMON CARD (1-792)	.05	.02
MINOR STARS	.10	.05
UNLISTED STARS	.20	.09
SUBSET CARDS HALF VALUE OF BASE CARDS		

Card		MINT	NRMT
1	Vince Coleman RB — 100 Steals for Third Cons. Season	.05	.02
2	Don Mattingly RB — Six Grand Slams	.15	.07
3	Mark McGwire RB — Rookie Homer Record (No white spot)	.30	.14
3A	Mark McGwire RB — Rookie Homer Record (White spot behind left foot)	.30	.14
4	Eddie Murray RB — Switch Home Runs, Two Straight Games (No caption on front)	.10	.05
4A	Eddie Murray RB — Switch Home Runs, Two Straight Games (Caption in box on card front)	.40	.18
5	Phil Niekro — Joe Niekro RB Brothers Win Record	.10	.05
6	Nolan Ryan RB — 11th 200 K's Season	.40	.18
7	Benito Santiago RB — 34-Game Hitting Streak Rookie Record	.05	.02
8	Kevin Elster	.10	.05
9	Andy Hawkins	.05	.02
10	Ryne Sandberg	.25	.11
11	Mike Young	.05	.02
12	Bill Schroeder	.05	.02
13	Andres Thomas	.05	.02
14	Sparky Anderson MG	.10	.05
15	Chili Davis	.15	.07
16	Kirk McCaskill	.05	.02
17	Ron Oester	.05	.02
18A	Al Leiter ERR (Photo actually Steve George, right ear visible)	.20	.09
18B	Al Leiter COR (Left ear visible)	.20	.09
19	Mark Davidson	.05	.02
20	Kevin Gross	.05	.02
21	Red Sox TL — Wade Boggs and Spike Owen	.10	.05
22	Greg Swindell	.05	.02
23	Ken Landreaux	.05	.02
24	Jim Deshaies	.05	.02
25	Andres Galarraga	.20	.09
26	Mitch Williams	.10	.05
27	R.J. Reynolds	.05	.02
28	Jose Nunez	.05	.02
29	Argenis Salazar	.05	.02
30	Sid Fernandez	.05	.02
31	Bruce Bochy	.05	.02
32	Mike Morgan	.05	.02
33	Rob Deer	.05	.02
34	Ricky Horton	.05	.02
35	Harold Baines	.15	.07
36	Jamie Moyer	.05	.02
37	Ed Romero	.05	.02
38	Jeff Calhoun	.05	.02
39	Gerald Perry	.05	.02
40	Orel Hershiser	.10	.05
41	Bob Melvin	.05	.02
42	Bill Landrum	.05	.02
43	Dick Schofield	.05	.02
44	Lou Piniella MG	.10	.05
45	Kent Hrbek	.10	.05
46	Darnell Coles	.05	.02
47	Joaquin Andujar	.05	.02
48	Alan Ashby	.05	.02
49	Dave Clark	.05	.02
50	Huble Brooks	.05	.02
51	Orioles TL — Eddie Murray and Cal Ripken	.40	.18
52	Don Robinson	.05	.02
53	Curt Wilkerson	.05	.02
54	Jim Clancy	.05	.02
55	Phil Bradley	.05	.02
56	Ed Hearn	.05	.02
57	Tim Crews	.05	.02
58	Dave Magadan	.05	.02
59	Danny Cox	.05	.02
60	Rickey Henderson	.20	.09
61	Mark Knudson	.05	.02
62	Jeff Hamilton	.05	.02
63	Jimmy Jones	.05	.02
64	Ken Caminiti	.75	.35
65	Leon Durham	.05	.02
66	Shane Rawley	.05	.02
67	Ken Oberkfell	.05	.02
68	Dave Dravecky	.10	.05
69	Mike Hart	.05	.02
70	Roger Clemens	.40	.18
71	Gary Pettis	.05	.02
72	Dennis Eckersley	.10	.05
73	Randy Bush	.05	.02
74	Tom Lasorda MG	.20	.09
75	Joe Carter	.20	.09
76	Dennis Martinez	.10	.05
77	Tom O'Malley	.05	.02
78	Dan Petry	.05	.02
79	Ernie Whitt	.05	.02
80	Mark Langston	.10	.05
81	Reds TL — Ron Robinson	.05	.02

	and John Franco		
☐ 82	Darrel Akerfelds	.05	.02
☐ 83	Jose Oquendo	.05	.02
☐ 84	Cecilio Guante	.05	.02
☐ 85	Howard Johnson	.05	.02
☐ 86	Ron Karkovice	.05	.02
☐ 87	Mike Mason	.05	.02
☐ 88	Earnie Riles	.05	.02
☐ 89	Gary Thurman	.05	.02
☐ 90	Dale Murphy	.20	.09
☐ 91	Joey Cora	.25	.11
☐ 92	Len Matuszek	.05	.02
☐ 93	Bob Sebra	.05	.02
☐ 94	Chuck Jackson	.05	.02
☐ 95	Lance Parrish	.05	.02
☐ 96	Todd Benzinger	.05	.02
☐ 97	Scott Garrelts	.05	.02
☐ 98	Rene Gonzales	.05	.02
☐ 99	Chuck Finley	.05	.02
☐ 100	Jack Clark	.10	.05
☐ 101	Allan Anderson	.05	.02
☐ 102	Barry Larkin	.20	.09
☐ 103	Curt Young	.05	.02
☐ 104	Dick Williams MG	.10	.05
☐ 105	Jesse Orosco	.05	.02
☐ 106	Jim Walewander	.05	.02
☐ 107	Scott Bailes	.05	.02
☐ 108	Steve Lyons	.05	.02
☐ 109	Joel Skinner	.05	.02
☐ 110	Teddy Higuera	.05	.02
☐ 111	Expos TL	.05	.02
	Hubie Brooks and		
	Vance Law		
☐ 112	Les Lancaster	.05	.02
☐ 113	Kelly Gruber	.05	.02
☐ 114	Jeff Russell	.05	.02
☐ 115	Johnny Ray	.05	.02
☐ 116	Jerry Don Gleaton	.05	.02
☐ 117	James Steels	.05	.02
☐ 118	Bob Welch	.05	.02
☐ 119	Robbie Wine	.05	.02
☐ 120	Kirby Puckett	.40	.18
☐ 121	Checklist 1-132	.05	.02
☐ 122	Tony Bernazard	.05	.02
☐ 123	Tom Candiotti	.05	.02
☐ 124	Ray Knight	.05	.02
☐ 125	Bruce Hurst	.05	.02
☐ 126	Steve Jeltz	.05	.02
☐ 127	Jim Gott	.05	.02
☐ 128	Johnny Grubb	.05	.02
☐ 129	Greg Minton	.05	.02
☐ 130	Buddy Bell	.10	.05
☐ 131	Don Schulze	.05	.02
☐ 132	Donnie Hill	.05	.02
☐ 133	Greg Mathews	.05	.02
☐ 134	Chuck Tanner MG	.10	.05
☐ 135	Dennis Rasmussen	.05	.02
☐ 136	Brian Dayett	.05	.02
☐ 137	Chris Bosio	.05	.02
☐ 138	Mitch Webster	.05	.02
☐ 139	Jerry Browne	.05	.02
☐ 140	Jesse Barfield	.05	.02
☐ 141	Royals TL	.20	.09
	George Brett and		
	Bret Saberhagen		
☐ 142	Andy Van Slyke	.10	.05
☐ 143	Mickey Tettleton	.05	.02
☐ 144	Don Gordon	.05	.02
☐ 145	Bill Madlock	.10	.05
☐ 146	Donell Nixon	.05	.02
☐ 147	Bill Buckner	.10	.05
☐ 148	Carmelo Martinez	.05	.02
☐ 149	Ken Howell	.05	.02
☐ 150	Eric Davis	.10	.05
☐ 151	Bob Knepper	.05	.02
☐ 152	Jody Reed	.10	.05
☐ 153	John Habyan	.05	.02
☐ 154	Jeff Stone	.05	.02
☐ 155	Bruce Sutter	.05	.02
☐ 156	Gary Matthews	.05	.02
☐ 157	Atlee Hammaker	.05	.02
☐ 158	Tim Hulett	.05	.02
☐ 159	Brad Arnsberg	.05	.02
☐ 160	Willie McGee	.10	.05
☐ 161	Bryn Smith	.05	.02
☐ 162	Mark McLemore	.05	.02
☐ 163	Dale Mohorcic	.05	.02
☐ 164	Dave Johnson MG	.10	.05
☐ 165	Robin Yount	.20	.09
☐ 166	Rick Rodriguez	.05	.02
☐ 167	Rance Mulliniks	.05	.02
☐ 168	Barry Jones	.05	.02
☐ 169	Ross Jones	.05	.02
☐ 170	Rich Gossage	.10	.05
☐ 171	Cubs TL	.05	.02
	Shawon Dunston		
	and Manny Trillo		
☐ 172	Lloyd McClendon	.05	.02
☐ 173	Eric Plunk	.05	.02
☐ 174	Phil Garner	.05	.02
☐ 175	Kevin Bass	.05	.02
☐ 176	Jeff Reed	.05	.02
☐ 177	Frank Tanana	.05	.02
☐ 178	Dwayne Henry	.05	.02
☐ 179	Charlie Puleo	.05	.02
☐ 180	Terry Kennedy	.05	.02
☐ 181	David Cone	.20	.09
☐ 182	Ken Phelps	.05	.02
☐ 183	Tom Lawless	.05	.02
☐ 184	Ivan Calderon	.05	.02
☐ 185	Rick Rhoden	.05	.02
☐ 186	Rafael Palmeiro	.20	.09
☐ 187	Steve Kiefer	.05	.02
☐ 188	John Russell	.05	.02
☐ 189	Wes Gardner	.05	.02
☐ 190	Candy Maldonado	.05	.02
☐ 191	John Cerutti	.05	.02
☐ 192	Devon White	.10	.05
☐ 193	Brian Fisher	.05	.02
☐ 194	Tom Kelly MG	.05	.02
☐ 195	Dan Quisenberry	.05	.02
☐ 196	Dave Engle	.05	.02
☐ 197	Lance McCullers	.05	.02
☐ 198	Franklin Stubbs	.05	.02
☐ 199	Dave Meads	.05	.02
☐ 200	Wade Boggs	.20	.09
☐ 201	Rangers TL	.05	.02
	Bobby Valentine MG		
	Pete O'Brien,		
	Pete Incaviglia and		
	Steve Buechele		
☐ 202	Glenn Hoffman	.05	.02
☐ 203	Fred Toliver	.05	.02
☐ 204	Paul O'Neill	.15	.07
☐ 205	Nelson Liriano	.05	.02
☐ 206	Domingo Ramos	.05	.02
☐ 207	John Mitchell	.05	.02
☐ 208	Steve Lake	.05	.02
☐ 209	Richard Dotson	.05	.02
☐ 210	Willie Randolph	.10	.05
☐ 211	Frank DiPino	.05	.02
☐ 212	Greg Brock	.05	.02
☐ 213	Albert Hall	.05	.02
☐ 214	Dave Schmidt	.05	.02
☐ 215	Von Hayes	.05	.02
☐ 216	Jerry Reuss	.05	.02
☐ 217	Harry Spilman	.05	.02
☐ 218	Dan Schatzeder	.05	.02
☐ 219	Mike Stanley	.10	.05
☐ 220	Tom Henke	.05	.02
☐ 221	Rafael Belliard	.05	.02
☐ 222	Steve Farr	.05	.02
☐ 223	Stan Jefferson	.05	.02
☐ 224	Tom Trebelhorn MG	.05	.02
☐ 225	Mike Scioscia	.05	.02
☐ 226	Dave Lopes	.10	.05
☐ 227	Ed Correa	.05	.02
☐ 228	Wallace Johnson	.05	.02
☐ 229	Jeff Musselman	.05	.02
☐ 230	Pat Tabler	.05	.02
☐ 231	Pirates TL	.20	.09
	Barry Bonds and		
	Bobby Bonilla		
☐ 232	Bob James	.05	.02
☐ 233	Rafael Santana	.05	.02
☐ 234	Ken Dayley	.05	.02
☐ 235	Gary Ward	.05	.02
☐ 236	Ted Power	.05	.02
☐ 237	Mike Heath	.05	.02
☐ 238	Luis Polonia	.10	.05
☐ 239	Roy Smalley	.05	.02
☐ 240	Lee Smith	.10	.05
☐ 241	Damaso Garcia	.05	.02
☐ 242	Tom Niedenfuer	.05	.02
☐ 243	Mark Ryal	.05	.02
☐ 244	Jeff D. Robinson	.05	.02
☐ 245	Rich Gedman	.05	.02
☐ 246	Mike Campbell	.05	.02
☐ 247	Thad Bosley	.05	.02
☐ 248	Storm Davis	.05	.02
☐ 249	Mike Marshall	.05	.02
☐ 250	Nolan Ryan	.75	.35
☐ 251	Tom Foley	.05	.02
☐ 252	Bob Brower	.05	.02
☐ 253	Checklist 133-264	.05	.02
☐ 254	Lee Elia MG	.05	.02
☐ 255	Mookie Wilson	.10	.05
☐ 256	Ken Schrom	.05	.02
☐ 257	Jerry Royster	.05	.02
☐ 258	Ed Nunez	.05	.02
☐ 259	Ron Kittle	.05	.02
☐ 260	Vince Coleman	.10	.05
☐ 261	Giants TL	.05	.02
	(Five players)		
☐ 262	Drew Hall	.05	.02
☐ 263	Glenn Braggs	.05	.02
☐ 264	Les Straker	.05	.02
☐ 265	Bo Diaz	.05	.02
☐ 266	Paul Assenmacher	.05	.02
☐ 267	Billy Bean	.05	.02
☐ 268	Bruce Ruffin	.05	.02
☐ 269	Ellis Burks	.30	.14
☐ 270	Mike Witt	.05	.02
☐ 271	Ken Gerhart	.05	.02
☐ 272	Steve Ontiveros	.05	.02
☐ 273	Garth Iorg	.05	.02
☐ 274	Junior Ortiz	.05	.02
☐ 275	Kevin Seitzer	.10	.05
☐ 276	Luis Salazar	.05	.02
☐ 277	Alejandro Pena	.05	.02
☐ 278	Jose Cruz	.05	.02
☐ 279	Randy St.Claire	.05	.02
☐ 280	Pete Incaviglia	.05	.02
☐ 281	Jerry Hairston	.05	.02
☐ 282	Pat Perry	.05	.02
☐ 283	Phil Lombardi	.05	.02
☐ 284	Larry Bowa MG	.10	.05
☐ 285	Jim Presley	.05	.02
☐ 286	Chuck Crim	.05	.02
☐ 287	Manny Trillo	.05	.02
☐ 288	Pat Pacillo	.05	.02
	(Chris Sabo in		
	background of photo)		
☐ 289	Dave Bergman	.05	.02
☐ 290	Tony Fernandez	.05	.02
☐ 291	Astros TL	.05	.02
	Billy Hatcher		
	and Kevin Bass		
☐ 292	Carney Lansford	.10	.05
☐ 293	Doug Jones	.20	.09
☐ 294	Al Pedrique	.05	.02
☐ 295	Bert Blyleven	.10	.05
☐ 296	Floyd Rayford	.05	.02
☐ 297	Zane Smith	.05	.02
☐ 298	Milt Thompson	.05	.02
☐ 299	Steve Crawford	.05	.02
☐ 300	Don Mattingly	.30	.14
☐ 301	Bud Black	.05	.02
☐ 302	Jose Uribe	.05	.02
☐ 303	Eric Show	.05	.02
☐ 304	George Hendrick	.05	.02
☐ 305	Steve Sax	.05	.02
☐ 306	Billy Hatcher	.05	.02
☐ 307	Mike Trujillo	.05	.02
☐ 308	Lee Mazzilli	.05	.02
☐ 309	Bill Long	.05	.02
☐ 310	Tom Herr	.05	.02
☐ 311	Scott Sanderson	.05	.02
☐ 312	Joey Meyer	.05	.02
☐ 313	Bob McClure	.05	.02
☐ 314	Jimy Williams MG	.05	.02
☐ 315	Dave Parker	.10	.05
☐ 316	Jose Rijo	.05	.02
☐ 317	Tom Nieto	.05	.02
☐ 318	Mel Hall	.05	.02
☐ 319	Mike Loynd	.05	.02
☐ 320	Alan Trammell	.15	.07
☐ 321	White Sox TL	.10	.05

	Harold Baines and Carlton Fisk		
322	Vicente Palacios	.05	.02
323	Rick Leach	.05	.02
324	Danny Jackson	.05	.02
325	Glenn Hubbard	.05	.02
326	Al Nipper	.05	.02
327	Larry Sheets	.05	.02
328	Greg Cadaret	.05	.02
329	Chris Speier	.05	.02
330	Eddie Whitson	.05	.02
331	Brian Downing	.05	.02
332	Jerry Reed	.05	.02
333	Wally Backman	.05	.02
334	Dave LaPoint	.05	.02
335	Claudell Washington	.05	.02
336	Ed Lynch	.05	.02
337	Jim Gantner	.05	.02
338	Brian Holton UER (1987 ERA .389, should be 3.89)	.05	.02
339	Kurt Stillwell	.05	.02
340	Jack Morris	.15	.07
341	Carmen Castillo	.05	.02
342	Larry Andersen	.05	.02
343	Greg Gagne	.05	.02
344	Tony LaRussa MG	.10	.05
345	Scott Fletcher	.05	.02
346	Vance Law	.05	.02
347	Joe Johnson	.05	.02
348	Jim Eisenreich	.20	.09
349	Bob Walk	.05	.02
350	Will Clark	.20	.09
351	Cardinals TL Red Schoendienst CO and Tony Pena	.10	.05
352	Billy Ripken	.10	.05
353	Ed Olwine	.05	.02
354	Marc Sullivan	.05	.02
355	Roger McDowell	.05	.02
356	Luis Aguayo	.05	.02
357	Floyd Bannister	.05	.02
358	Rey Quinones	.05	.02
359	Tim Stoddard	.05	.02
360	Tony Gwynn	.50	.23
361	Greg Maddux	1.25	.55
362	Juan Castillo	.05	.02
363	Willie Fraser	.05	.02
364	Nick Esasky	.05	.02
365	Floyd Youmans	.05	.02
366	Chet Lemon	.05	.02
367	Tim Leary	.05	.02
368	Gerald Young	.05	.02
369	Greg Harris	.05	.02
370	Jose Canseco	.20	.09
371	Joe Hesketh	.05	.02
372	Matt Williams	.60	.25
373	Checklist 265-396	.05	.02
374	Doc Edwards MG	.05	.02
375	Tom Brunansky	.05	.02
376	Bill Wilkinson	.05	.02
377	Sam Horn	.05	.02
378	Todd Frohwirth	.05	.02
379	Rafael Ramirez	.05	.02
380	Joe Magrane	.05	.02
381	Angels TL Wally Joyner and Jack Howell	.10	.05
382	Keith A. Miller	.05	.02
383	Eric Bell	.05	.02
384	Neil Allen	.05	.02
385	Carlton Fisk	.15	.07
386	Don Mattingly AS	.15	.07
387	Willie Randolph AS	.05	.02
388	Wade Boggs AS	.10	.05
389	Alan Trammell AS	.05	.02
390	George Bell AS	.05	.02
391	Kirby Puckett AS	.20	.09
392	Dave Winfield AS	.20	.09
393	Matt Nokes AS	.05	.02
394	Roger Clemens AS	.20	.09
395	Jimmy Key AS	.05	.02
396	Tom Henke AS	.05	.02
397	Jack Clark AS	.05	.02
398	Juan Samuel AS	.05	.02
399	Tim Wallach AS	.05	.02
400	Ozzie Smith AS	.15	.07
401	Andre Dawson AS	.20	.09
402	Tony Gwynn AS	.25	.11
403	Tim Raines AS	.05	.02
404	Benny Santiago AS	.05	.02
405	Dwight Gooden AS	.10	.05
406	Shane Rawley AS	.05	.02
407	Steve Bedrosian AS	.05	.02
408	Dion James	.05	.02
409	Joel McKeon	.05	.02
410	Tony Pena	.05	.02
411	Wayne Tolleson	.05	.02
412	Randy Myers	.15	.07
413	John Christensen	.05	.02
414	John McNamara MG	.05	.02
415	Don Carman	.05	.02
416	Keith Moreland	.05	.02
417	Mark Ciardi	.05	.02
418	Joel Youngblood	.05	.02
419	Scott McGregor	.05	.02
420	Wally Joyner	.20	.09
421	Ed VandeBerg	.05	.02
422	Dave Concepcion	.10	.05
423	John Smiley	.10	.05
424	Dwayne Murphy	.05	.02
425	Jeff Reardon	.10	.05
426	Randy Ready	.05	.02
427	Paul Kilgus	.05	.02
428	John Shelby	.05	.02
429	Tigers TL Alan Trammell and Kirk Gibson	.10	.05
430	Glenn Davis	.05	.02
431	Casey Candaele	.05	.02
432	Mike Moore	.05	.02
433	Bill Pecota	.05	.02
434	Rick Aguilera	.10	.05
435	Mike Pagliarulo	.05	.02
436	Mike Bielecki	.05	.02
437	Fred Manrique	.05	.02
438	Rob Ducey	.05	.02
439	Dave Martinez	.05	.02
440	Steve Bedrosian	.05	.02
441	Rick Manning	.05	.02
442	Tom Bolton	.05	.02
443	Ken Griffey	.05	.02
444	Cal Ripken Sr. MG UER (two copyrights)	.05	.02
445	Mike Krukow	.05	.02
446	Doug DeCinces (Now with Cardinals on card front)	.05	.02
447	Jeff Montgomery	.20	.09
448	Mike Davis	.05	.02
449	Jeff M. Robinson	.05	.02
450	Barry Bonds	.50	.23
451	Keith Atherton	.05	.02
452	Willie Wilson	.05	.02
453	Dennis Powell	.05	.02
454	Marvell Wynne	.05	.02
455	Shawn Hillegas	.05	.02
456	Dave Anderson	.05	.02
457	Terry Leach	.05	.02
458	Ron Hassey	.05	.02
459	Yankees TL Dave Winfield and Willie Randolph	.20	.09
460	Ozzie Smith	.25	.11
461	Danny Darwin	.05	.02
462	Don Slaught	.05	.02
463	Fred McGriff	.20	.09
464	Jay Tibbs	.05	.02
465	Paul Molitor	.20	.09
466	Jerry Mumphrey	.05	.02
467	Don Aase	.05	.02
468	Darren Daulton	.10	.05
469	Jeff Dedmon	.05	.02
470	Dwight Evans	.10	.05
471	Donnie Moore	.05	.02
472	Robby Thompson	.05	.02
473	Joe Niekro	.05	.02
474	Tom Brookens	.05	.02
475	Pete Rose MG	.25	.11
476	Dave Stewart	.10	.05
477	Jamie Quirk	.05	.02
478	Sid Bream	.05	.02
479	Brett Butler	.10	.05
480	Dwight Gooden	.10	.05
481	Mariano Duncan	.05	.02
482	Mark Davis	.05	.02
483	Rod Booker	.05	.02
484	Pat Clements	.05	.02
485	Harold Reynolds	.05	.02
486	Pat Keedy	.05	.02
487	Jim Pankovits	.05	.02
488	Andy McGaffigan	.05	.02
489	Dodgers TL Pedro Guerrero and Fernando Valenzuela	.05	.02
490	Larry Parrish	.05	.02
491	B.J. Surhoff	.10	.05
492	Doyle Alexander	.05	.02
493	Mike Greenwell	.10	.05
494	Wally Ritchie	.05	.02
495	Eddie Murray	.20	.09
496	Guy Hoffman	.05	.02
497	Kevin Mitchell	.10	.05
498	Bob Boone	.10	.05
499	Eric King	.05	.02
500	Andre Dawson	.20	.09
501	Tim Birtsas	.05	.02
502	Dan Gladden	.05	.02
503	Junior Noboa	.05	.02
504	Bob Rodgers MG	.05	.02
505	Willie Upshaw	.05	.02
506	John Cangelosi	.05	.02
507	Mark Gubicza	.05	.02
508	Tim Teufel	.05	.02
509	Bill Dawley	.05	.02
510	Dave Winfield	.20	.09
511	Joel Davis	.05	.02
512	Alex Trevino	.05	.02
513	Tim Flannery	.05	.02
514	Pat Sheridan	.05	.02
515	Juan Nieves	.05	.02
516	Jim Sundberg	.05	.02
517	Ron Robinson	.05	.02
518	Greg Gross	.05	.02
519	Mariners TL Harold Reynolds and Phil Bradley	.05	.02
520	Dave Smith	.05	.02
521	Jim Dwyer	.05	.02
522	Bob Patterson	.05	.02
523	Gary Roenicke	.05	.02
524	Gary Lucas	.05	.02
525	Marty Barrett	.05	.02
526	Juan Berenguer	.05	.02
527	Steve Henderson	.05	.02
528A	Checklist 397-528 ERR (455 S. Carlton)	.20	.09
528B	Checklist 397-528 COR (455 S. Hillegas)	.10	.05
529	Tim Burke	.05	.02
530	Gary Carter	.15	.07
531	Rich Yett	.05	.02
532	Mike Kingery	.05	.02
533	John Farrell	.05	.02
534	John Wathan MG	.05	.02
535	Ron Guidry	.05	.02
536	John Morris	.05	.02
537	Steve Buechele	.05	.02
538	Bill Wegman	.05	.02
539	Mike LaValliere	.05	.02
540	Bret Saberhagen	.05	.02
541	Juan Beniquez	.05	.02
542	Paul Noce	.05	.02
543	Kent Tekulve	.05	.02
544	Jim Traber	.05	.02
545	Don Baylor	.10	.05
546	John Candelaria	.05	.02
547	Felix Fermin	.05	.02
548	Shane Mack	.05	.02
549	Braves TL Albert Hall, Dale Murphy, Ken Griffey and Dion James	.05	.02
550	Pedro Guerrero	.10	.05
551	Terry Steinbach	.15	.07
552	Mark Thurmond	.05	.02
553	Tracy Jones	.05	.02

554	Mike Smithson	.05	.02
555	Brook Jacoby	.05	.02
556	Stan Clarke	.05	.02
557	Craig Reynolds	.05	.02
558	Bob Ojeda	.05	.02
559	Ken Williams	.05	.02
560	Tim Wallach	.05	.02
561	Rick Cerone	.05	.02
562	Jim Lindeman	.05	.02
563	Jose Guzman	.05	.02
564	Frank Lucchesi MG	.05	.02
565	Lloyd Moseby	.05	.02
566	Charlie O'Brien	.05	.02
567	Mike Diaz	.05	.02
568	Chris Brown	.05	.02
569	Charlie Leibrandt	.05	.02
570	Jeffrey Leonard	.05	.02
571	Mark Williamson	.05	.02
572	Chris James	.05	.02
573	Bob Stanley	.05	.02
574	Graig Nettles	.10	.05
575	Don Sutton	.20	.09
576	Tommy Hinzo	.05	.02
577	Tom Browning	.05	.02
578	Gary Gaetti	.05	.02
579	Mets TL	.10	.05
	Gary Carter and Kevin McReynolds		
580	Mark McGwire	.60	.25
581	Tito Landrum	.05	.02
582	Mike Henneman	.10	.05
583	Dave Valle	.05	.02
584	Steve Trout	.05	.02
585	Ozzie Guillen	.05	.02
586	Bob Forsch	.05	.02
587	Terry Puhl	.05	.02
588	Jeff Parrett	.05	.02
589	Geno Petralli	.05	.02
590	George Bell	.05	.02
591	Doug Drabek	.05	.02
592	Dale Sveum	.05	.02
593	Bob Tewksbury	.05	.02
594	Bobby Valentine MG	.10	.05
595	Frank White	.10	.05
596	John Kruk	.05	.02
597	Gene Garber	.05	.02
598	Lee Lacy	.05	.02
599	Calvin Schiraldi	.05	.02
600	Mike Schmidt	.25	.11
601	Jack Lazorko	.05	.02
602	Mike Aldrete	.05	.02
603	Rob Murphy	.05	.02
604	Chris Bando	.05	.02
605	Kirk Gibson	.10	.05
606	Moose Haas	.05	.02
607	Mickey Hatcher	.05	.02
608	Charlie Kerfeld	.05	.02
609	Twins TL	.05	.02
	Gary Gaetti and Kent Hrbek		
610	Keith Hernandez	.10	.05
611	Tommy John	.10	.05
612	Curt Ford	.05	.02
613	Bobby Thigpen	.05	.02
614	Herm Winningham	.05	.02
615	Jody Davis	.05	.02
616	Jay Aldrich	.05	.02
617	Oddibe McDowell	.05	.02
618	Cecil Fielder	.15	.07
619	Mike Dunne	.05	.02
	(Inconsistent design, black name on front)		
620	Cory Snyder	.05	.02
621	Gene Nelson	.05	.02
622	Kal Daniels	.05	.02
623	Mike Flanagan	.05	.02
624	Jim Leyland MG	.10	.05
625	Frank Viola	.10	.05
626	Glenn Wilson	.05	.02
627	Joe Boever	.05	.02
628	Dave Henderson	.05	.02
629	Kelly Downs	.05	.02
630	Darrell Evans	.10	.05
631	Jack Howell	.05	.02
632	Steve Shields	.05	.02
633	Barry Lyons	.05	.02
634	Jose DeLeon	.05	.02
635	Terry Pendleton	.10	.05
636	Charles Hudson	.05	.02
637	Jay Bell	.25	.11
638	Steve Balboni	.05	.02
639	Brewers TL	.05	.02
	Glenn Braggs and Tony Muser CO		
640	Garry Templeton	.05	.02
	(Inconsistent design, green border)		
641	Rick Honeycutt	.05	.02
642	Bob Dernier	.05	.02
643	Rocky Childress	.05	.02
644	Terry McGriff	.05	.02
645	Matt Nokes	.05	.02
646	Checklist 529-660	.05	.02
647	Pascual Perez	.05	.02
648	Al Newman	.05	.02
649	DeWayne Buice	.05	.02
650	Cal Ripken	.75	.35
651	Mike Jackson	.10	.05
652	Bruce Benedict	.05	.02
653	Jeff Sellers	.05	.02
654	Roger Craig MG	.05	.02
655	Len Dykstra	.10	.05
656	Lee Guetterman	.05	.02
657	Gary Redus	.05	.02
658	Tim Conroy	.05	.02
	(Inconsistent design, name in white)		
659	Bobby Meacham	.05	.02
660	Rick Reuschel	.05	.02
661	Nolan Ryan TBC '83	.40	.18
662	Jim Rice TBC '78	.05	.02
663	Ron Blomberg TBC '73	.05	.02
664	Bob Gibson TBC '68	.20	.09
665	Stan Musial TBC '63	.20	.09
666	Mario Soto	.05	.02
667	Luis Quinones	.05	.02
668	Walt Terrell	.05	.02
669	Phillies TL	.05	.02
	Lance Parrish and Mike Ryan CO		
670	Dan Plesac	.05	.02
671	Tim Laudner	.05	.02
672	John Davis	.05	.02
673	Tony Phillips	.05	.02
674	Mike Fitzgerald	.05	.02
675	Jim Rice	.10	.05
676	Ken Dixon	.05	.02
677	Eddie Milner	.05	.02
678	Jim Acker	.05	.02
679	Darrell Miller	.05	.02
680	Charlie Hough	.10	.05
681	Bobby Bonilla	.15	.07
682	Jimmy Key	.10	.05
683	Julio Franco	.05	.02
684	Hal Lanier MG	.05	.02
685	Ron Darling	.05	.02
686	Terry Francona	.05	.02
687	Mickey Brantley	.05	.02
688	Jim Winn	.05	.02
689	Tom Pagnozzi	.10	.05
690	Jay Howell	.05	.02
691	Dan Pasqua	.05	.02
692	Mike Birkbeck	.05	.02
693	Benito Santiago	.05	.02
694	Eric Nolte	.05	.02
695	Shawon Dunston	.05	.02
696	Duane Ward	.05	.02
697	Steve Lombardozzi	.05	.02
698	Brad Havens	.05	.02
699	Padres TL	.10	.05
	Benito Santiago and Tony Gwynn		
700	George Brett	.40	.18
701	Sammy Stewart	.05	.02
702	Mike Gallego	.05	.02
703	Bob Brenly	.05	.02
704	Dennis Boyd	.05	.02
705	Juan Samuel	.05	.02
706	Rick Mahler	.05	.02
707	Fred Lynn	.05	.02
708	Gus Polidor	.05	.02
709	George Frazier	.05	.02
710	Darryl Strawberry	.10	.05
711	Bill Gullickson	.05	.02
712	John Moses	.05	.02
713	Willie Hernandez	.05	.02
714	Jim Fregosi MG	.05	.02
715	Todd Worrell	.10	.05
716	Lenn Sakata	.05	.02
717	Jay Baller	.05	.02
718	Mike Felder	.05	.02
719	Denny Walling	.05	.02
720	Tim Raines	.10	.05
721	Pete O'Brien	.05	.02
722	Manny Lee	.05	.02
723	Bob Kipper	.05	.02
724	Danny Tartabull	.05	.02
725	Mike Boddicker	.05	.02
726	Alfredo Griffin	.05	.02
727	Greg Booker	.05	.02
728	Andy Allanson	.05	.02
729	Blue Jays TL	.10	.05
	George Bell and Fred McGriff		
730	John Franco	.10	.05
731	Rick Schu	.05	.02
732	David Palmer	.05	.02
733	Spike Owen	.05	.02
734	Craig Lefferts	.05	.02
735	Kevin McReynolds	.05	.02
736	Matt Young	.05	.02
737	Butch Wynegar	.05	.02
738	Scott Bankhead	.05	.02
739	Daryl Boston	.05	.02
740	Rick Sutcliffe	.05	.02
741	Mike Easler	.05	.02
742	Mark Clear	.05	.02
743	Larry Herndon	.05	.02
744	Whitey Herzog MG	.10	.05
745	Bill Doran	.05	.02
746	Gene Larkin	.05	.02
747	Bobby Witt	.05	.02
748	Reid Nichols	.05	.02
749	Mark Eichhorn	.05	.02
750	Bo Jackson	.20	.09
751	Jim Morrison	.05	.02
752	Mark Grant	.05	.02
753	Danny Heep	.05	.02
754	Mike LaCoss	.05	.02
755	Ozzie Virgil	.05	.02
756	Mike Maddux	.05	.02
757	John Marzano	.05	.02
758	Eddie Williams	.10	.05
759	A's TL UER	.30	.14
	Mark McGwire and Jose Canseco (two copyrights)		
760	Mike Scott	.05	.02
761	Tony Armas	.05	.02
762	Scott Bradley	.05	.02
763	Doug Sisk	.05	.02
764	Greg Walker	.05	.02
765	Neal Heaton	.05	.02
766	Henry Cotto	.05	.02
767	Jose Lind	.05	.02
768	Dickie Noles	.05	.02
	(Now with Tigers on card front)		
769	Cecil Cooper	.10	.05
770	Lou Whitaker	.10	.05
771	Ruben Sierra	.05	.02
772	Sal Butera	.05	.02
773	Frank Williams	.05	.02
774	Gene Mauch MG	.10	.05
775	Dave Stieb	.05	.02
776	Checklist 661-792	.05	.02
777	Lonnie Smith	.05	.02
778A	Keith Comstock ERR	2.00	.90
	(White 'Padres')		
778B	Keith Comstock COR	.05	.02
	(Blue 'Padres')		
779	Tom Glavine	.50	.23
780	Fernando Valenzuela	.10	.05
781	Keith Hughes	.05	.02
782	Jeff Ballard	.05	.02
783	Ron Roenicke	.05	.02
784	Joe Sambito	.05	.02
785	Alvin Davis	.05	.02

□ 786 Joe Price	.05	.02
(Inconsistent design, orange team name)		
□ 787 Bill Almon	.05	.02
□ 788 Ray Searage	.05	.02
□ 789 Indians TL	.10	.05
Joe Carter and Cory Snyder		
□ 790 Dave Righetti	.10	.05
□ 791 Ted Simmons	.10	.05
□ 792 John Tudor	.05	.02

1988 Topps Traded

This standard-size 132-card Traded set was distributed exclusively in factory set form in blue and white taped boxes through hobby dealers. The cards are identical in style to the Topps regular issue except for white stock and t-suffixed numbering on back. The cards are ordered alphabetically by player's last name. This set generated additional interest upon release due to the inclusion of members of the 1988 U.S. Olympic baseball team. These Olympians are indicated in the checklist below by OLY. The key extended Rookie Cards in this set are Jim Abbott, Roberto Alomar, Brady Anderson, Andy Benes, Jay Buhner, Ron Gant, Mark Grace, Tino Martinez, Jack McDowell, Charles Nagy, Robin Ventura and Walt Weiss.

	MINT	NRMT
COMP.FACT.SET (132)	12.00	5.50
COMMON CARD (1T-132T)	.05	.05
MINOR STARS	.20	.09
UNLISTED STARS	.40	.18

□ 1T Jim Abbott OLY	.40	.18
□ 2T Juan Agosto	.10	.05
□ 3T Luis Alicea	.20	.09
□ 4T Roberto Alomar	3.00	1.35
□ 5T Brady Anderson	1.50	.70
□ 6T Jack Armstrong	.10	.05
□ 7T Don August	.10	.05
□ 8T Floyd Bannister	.10	.05
□ 9T Bret Barberie OLY	.20	.09
□ 10T Jose Bautista	.10	.05
□ 11T Don Baylor	.20	.09
□ 12T Tim Belcher	.20	.09
□ 13T Buddy Bell	.20	.09
□ 14T Andy Benes OLY	1.00	.45
□ 15T Damon Berryhill	.10	.05
□ 16T Bud Black	.10	.05
□ 17T Pat Borders	.20	.09
□ 18T Phil Bradley	.10	.05
□ 19T Jeff Branson OLY	.20	.09
□ 20T Tom Brunansky	.10	.05
□ 21T Jay Buhner	1.50	.70
□ 22T Brett Butler	.20	.09

□ 23T Jim Campanis OLY	.10	.05
□ 24T Sil Campusano	.10	.05
□ 25T John Candelaria	.10	.05
□ 26T Jose Cecena	.10	.05
□ 27T Rick Cerone	.10	.05
□ 28T Jack Clark	.20	.09
□ 29T Kevin Coffman	.10	.05
□ 30T Pat Combs OLY	.10	.05
□ 31T Henry Cotto	.10	.05
□ 32T Chili Davis	.30	.14
□ 33T Mike Davis	.10	.05
□ 34T Jose DeLeon	.10	.05
□ 35T Richard Dotson	.10	.05
□ 36T Cecil Espy	.10	.05
□ 37T Tom Filer	.10	.05
□ 38T Mike Fiore OLY	.10	.05
□ 39T Ron Gant	.50	.23
□ 40T Kirk Gibson	.40	.18
□ 41T Rich Gossage	.20	.09
□ 42T Mark Grace	1.50	.70
□ 43T Alfredo Griffin	.10	.05
□ 44T Ty Griffin OLY	.10	.05
□ 45T Bryan Harvey	.20	.09
□ 46T Ron Hassey	.10	.05
□ 47T Ray Hayward		.05
□ 48T Dave Henderson	.10	.05
□ 49T Tom Herr	.10	.05
□ 50T Bob Horner	.10	.05
□ 51T Ricky Horton		.05
□ 52T Jay Howell	.10	.05
□ 53T Glenn Hubbard	.10	.05
□ 54T Jeff Innis	.10	.05
□ 55T Danny Jackson	.10	.05
□ 56T Darrin Jackson	.20	.09
□ 57T Roberto Kelly	.40	.18
□ 58T Ron Kittle	.10	.05
□ 59T Ray Knight	.10	.05
□ 60T Vance Law	.10	.05
□ 61T Jeffrey Leonard	.10	.05
□ 62T Mike Macfarlane	.20	.09
□ 63T Scotti Madison	.10	.05
□ 64T Kirt Manwaring	.10	.05
□ 65T Mark Marquess OLY CO	.10	.05
□ 66T Tino Martinez OLY	5.00	2.20
□ 67T Billy Masse OLY	.10	.05
□ 68T Jack McDowell	.40	.18
□ 69T Jack McKeon MG	.10	.05
□ 70T Larry McWilliams	.10	.05
□ 71T Mickey Morandini OLY	.30	.14
□ 72T Keith Moreland	.10	.05
□ 73T Mike Morgan	.10	.05
□ 74T Charles Nagy OLY	1.00	.45
□ 75T Al Nipper	.10	.05
□ 76T Russ Nixon MG	.10	.05
□ 77T Jesse Orosco	.10	.05
□ 78T Joe Orsulak	.10	.05
□ 79T Dave Palmer	.10	.05
□ 80T Mark Parent	.10	.05
□ 81T Dave Parker	.20	.09
□ 82T Dan Pasqua	.10	.05
□ 83T Melido Perez	.10	.05
□ 84T Steve Peters	.10	.05
□ 85T Dan Petry	.10	.05
□ 86T Gary Pettis		.05
□ 87T Jeff Pico		.05
□ 88T Jim Poole OLY	.20	.09
□ 89T Ted Power	.10	.05
□ 90T Rafael Ramirez	.10	.05
□ 91T Dennis Rasmussen	.10	.05
□ 92T Jose Rijo	.10	.05
□ 93T Ernie Riles	.10	.05
□ 94T Luis Rivera	.10	.05
□ 95T Doug Robbins OLY	.10	.05
□ 96T Frank Robinson MG	.30	.14
□ 97T Cookie Rojas MG	.10	.05
□ 98T Chris Sabo	.20	.09
□ 99T Mark Salas	.10	.05
□ 100T Luis Salazar	.10	.05
□ 101T Rafael Santana	.10	.05
□ 102T Nelson Santovenia	.10	.05
□ 103T Mackey Sasser	.10	.05
□ 104T Calvin Schiraldi	.10	.05
□ 105T Mike Schooler		.05
□ 106T Scott Servais OLY	.20	.09
□ 107T Dave Silvestri OLY	.10	.05
□ 108T Don Slaught	.10	.05

□ 109T Joe Slusarski OLY	.10	.05
□ 110T Lee Smith	.20	.09
□ 111T Pete Smith	.10	.05
□ 112T Jim Snyder MG	.10	.05
□ 113T Ed Sprague OLY	.75	.35
□ 114T Pete Stanicek	.10	.05
□ 115T Kurt Stillwell	.10	.05
□ 116T Todd Stottlemyre	.40	.18
□ 117T Bill Swift	.10	.05
□ 118T Pat Tabler	.10	.05
□ 119T Scott Terry	.10	.05
□ 120T Mickey Tettleton	.20	.09
□ 121T Dickie Thon	.10	.05
□ 122T Jeff Treadway	.10	.05
□ 123T Willie Upshaw	.10	.05
□ 124T Robin Ventura OLY	1.50	.70
□ 125T Ron Washington	.10	.05
□ 126T Walt Weiss	.30	.14
□ 127T Bob Welch	.10	.05
□ 128T David Wells	.40	.18
□ 129T Glenn Wilson	.10	.05
□ 130T Ted Wood OLY	.20	.09
□ 131T Don Zimmer MG	.20	.09
□ 132T Checklist 1T-132T	.10	.05

1989 Topps

ERIC DAVIS

This set consists of 792 standard-size cards. Cards were primarily issued in 15-card wax packs, 42-card rack packs and factory sets. Subsets in the set include Record Breakers (1-7), Turn Back the Clock (661-665), All-Star selections (386-407) and First Draft Picks, Future Stars and Team Leaders (all scattered throughout the set). The manager cards contain a team checklist on back. The key Rookie Cards in this set are Jim Abbott, Sandy Alomar Jr., Brady Anderson, Steve Avery, Andy Benes, Dante Bichette, Craig Biggio, Randy Johnson, Ramon Martinez, Gary Sheffield, John Smoltz, and Robin Ventura.

	MINT	NRMT
COMPLETE SET (792)	10.00	4.50
COMP.FACT.SET (792)	12.00	5.50
COMMON CARD (1-792)	.05	.02
MINOR STARS	.10	.05
UNLISTED STARS	.20	.09

□ 1 George Bell RB	.05	.02
Slams 3 Opening Day HR's		
□ 2 Wade Boggs RB	.10	.05
200 Hits 6th Straight Season		
□ 3 Gary Carter RB	.05	.05
Career Putouts Record		
□ 4 Andre Dawson RB	.10	.05
Logs Double Figures in HR and SB		
□ 5 Orel Hershiser RB	.10	.05
59 Scoreless Innings		
□ 6 Doug Jones RB UER	.05	.02

Earns His 15th
Straight Save
(Photo actually
Chris Codiroli)
- [ ] 7 Kevin McReynolds RB..... .05 .02
       Steals 21 Without
       Being Caught
- [ ] 8 Dave Eiland .... .05 .02
- [ ] 9 Tim Teufel .... .05 .02
- [ ] 10 Andre Dawson .... .20 .09
- [ ] 11 Bruce Sutter .... .05 .02
- [ ] 12 Dale Sveum .... .05 .02
- [ ] 13 Doug Sisk .... .05 .02
- [ ] 14 Tom Kelly MG .... .05 .02
- [ ] 15 Robby Thompson .... .05 .02
- [ ] 16 Ron Robinson .... .05 .02
- [ ] 17 Brian Downing .... .05 .02
- [ ] 18 Rick Rhoden .... .05 .02
- [ ] 19 Greg Gagne .... .05 .02
- [ ] 20 Steve Bedrosian .... .05 .02
- [ ] 21 Chicago White Sox TL .. .05 .02
       Greg Walker
- [ ] 22 Tim Crews .... .05 .02
- [ ] 23 Mike Fitzgerald .... .05 .02
- [ ] 24 Larry Andersen .... .05 .02
- [ ] 25 Frank White .... .10 .05
- [ ] 26 Dale Mohorcic .... .05 .02
- [ ] 27A Orestes Destrade....... .05 .02
       (F* next to copyright)
- [ ] 27B Orestes Destrade....... .05 .02
       (E*F* next to
       copyright)
- [ ] 28 Mike Moore .... .05 .02
- [ ] 29 Kelly Gruber .... .05 .02
- [ ] 30 Dwight Gooden .... .10 .05
- [ ] 31 Terry Francona .... .05 .02
- [ ] 32 Dennis Rasmussen ..... .05 .02
- [ ] 33 B.J. Surhoff .... .10 .05
- [ ] 34 Ken Williams .... .05 .02
- [ ] 35 John Tudor UER .... .05 .02
       (With Red Sox in '84, should be
       Pirates)
- [ ] 36 Mitch Webster .... .05 .02
- [ ] 37 Bob Stanley .... .05 .02
- [ ] 38 Paul Runge .... .05 .02
- [ ] 39 Mike Maddux .... .05 .02
- [ ] 40 Steve Sax .... .05 .02
- [ ] 41 Terry Mulholland .... .05 .02
- [ ] 42 Jim Eppard .... .05 .02
- [ ] 43 Guillermo Hernandez ... .05 .02
- [ ] 44 Jim Snyder MG .... .05 .02
- [ ] 45 Kal Daniels .... .05 .02
- [ ] 46 Mark Portugal .... .05 .02
- [ ] 47 Carney Lansford .... .10 .05
- [ ] 48 Tim Burke .... .05 .02
- [ ] 49 Craig Biggio .... .50 .23
- [ ] 50 George Bell .... .05 .02
- [ ] 51 California Angels TL ..... .05 .02
       Mark McLemore
- [ ] 52 Bob Brenly .... .05 .02
- [ ] 53 Ruben Sierra .... .05 .02
- [ ] 54 Steve Trout .... .05 .02
- [ ] 55 Julio Franco .... .05 .02
- [ ] 56 Pat Tabler .... .05 .02
- [ ] 57 Alejandro Pena .... .05 .02
- [ ] 58 Lee Mazzilli .... .05 .02
- [ ] 59 Mark Davis .... .05 .02
- [ ] 60 Tom Brunansky .... .05 .02
- [ ] 61 Neil Allen .... .05 .02
- [ ] 62 Alfredo Griffin .... .05 .02
- [ ] 63 Mark Clear .... .05 .02
- [ ] 64 Alex Trevino .... .05 .02
- [ ] 65 Rick Reuschel .... .05 .02
- [ ] 66 Manny Trillo .... .05 .02
- [ ] 67 Dave Palmer .... .05 .02
- [ ] 68 Darrell Miller .... .05 .02
- [ ] 69 Jeff Ballard .... .05 .02
- [ ] 70 Mark McGwire .... .40 .18
- [ ] 71 Mike Boddicker .... .05 .02
- [ ] 72 John Moses .... .05 .02
- [ ] 73 Pascual Perez .... .05 .02
- [ ] 74 Nick Leyva MG .... .05 .02
- [ ] 75 Tom Henke .... .05 .02
- [ ] 76 Terry Blocker .... .05 .02
- [ ] 77 Doyle Alexander .... .05 .02
- [ ] 78 Jim Sundberg .... .05 .02

- [ ] 79 Scott Bankhead .... .05 .02
- [ ] 80 Cory Snyder .... .05 .02
- [ ] 81 Montreal Expos TL ...... .10 .05
       Tim Raines
- [ ] 82 Dave Leiper .... .05 .02
- [ ] 83 Jeff Blauser .... .10 .05
- [ ] 84 Bill Bene FDP .... .05 .02
- [ ] 85 Kevin McReynolds .... .05 .02
- [ ] 86 Al Nipper .... .05 .02
- [ ] 87 Larry Owen .... .05 .02
- [ ] 88 Darryl Hamilton .... .05 .02
- [ ] 89 Dave LaPoint .... .05 .02
- [ ] 90 Vince Coleman UER ..... .05 .02
       (Wrong birth year)
- [ ] 91 Floyd Youmans .... .05 .02
- [ ] 92 Jeff Kunkel .... .05 .02
- [ ] 93 Ken Howell .... .05 .02
- [ ] 94 Chris Speier .... .05 .02
- [ ] 95 Gerald Young .... .05 .02
- [ ] 96 Rick Cerone .... .05 .02
- [ ] 97 Greg Mathews .... .05 .02
- [ ] 98 Larry Sheets .... .05 .02
- [ ] 99 Sherman Corbett .... .05 .02
- [ ] 100 Mike Schmidt .... .25 .11
- [ ] 101 Les Straker .... .05 .02
- [ ] 102 Mike Gallego .... .05 .02
- [ ] 103 Tim Birtsas .... .05 .02
- [ ] 104 Dallas Green MG ...... .05 .02
- [ ] 105 Ron Darling .... .05 .02
- [ ] 106 Willie Upshaw .... .05 .02
- [ ] 107 Jose DeLeon .... .05 .02
- [ ] 108 Fred Manrique .... .05 .02
- [ ] 109 Hipolito Pena .... .05 .02
- [ ] 110 Paul Molitor .... .20 .09
- [ ] 111 Cincinnati Reds TL .... .05 .02
       Eric Davis
       (Swinging bat)
- [ ] 112 Jim Presley .... .05 .02
- [ ] 113 Lloyd Moseby .... .05 .02
- [ ] 114 Bob Kipper .... .05 .02
- [ ] 115 Jody Davis .... .05 .02
- [ ] 116 Jeff Montgomery .... .10 .05
- [ ] 117 Dave Anderson .... .05 .02
- [ ] 118 Checklist 1-132 .... .05 .02
- [ ] 119 Terry Puhl .... .05 .02
- [ ] 120 Frank Viola .... .05 .02
- [ ] 121 Garry Templeton .... .05 .02
- [ ] 122 Lance Johnson .... .10 .05
- [ ] 123 Spike Owen .... .05 .02
- [ ] 124 Jim Traber .... .05 .02
- [ ] 125 Mike Krukow .... .05 .02
- [ ] 126 Sid Bream .... .05 .02
- [ ] 127 Walt Terrell .... .05 .02
- [ ] 128 Milt Thompson .... .05 .02
- [ ] 129 Terry Clark .... .05 .02
- [ ] 130 Gerald Perry .... .05 .02
- [ ] 131 Dave Otto .... .05 .02
- [ ] 132 Curt Ford .... .05 .02
- [ ] 133 Bill Long .... .05 .02
- [ ] 134 Don Zimmer MG .... .05 .02
- [ ] 135 Jose Rijo .... .05 .02
- [ ] 136 Joey Meyer .... .05 .02
- [ ] 137 Geno Petralli .... .05 .02
- [ ] 138 Wallace Johnson .... .05 .02
- [ ] 139 Mike Flanagan .... .05 .02
- [ ] 140 Shawon Dunston .... .05 .02
- [ ] 141 Cleveland Indians TL .. .05 .02
       Brook Jacoby
- [ ] 142 Mike Diaz .... .05 .02
- [ ] 143 Mike Campbell .... .05 .02
- [ ] 144 Jay Bell .... .10 .05
- [ ] 145 Dave Stewart .... .10 .05
- [ ] 146 Gary Pettis .... .05 .02
- [ ] 147 DeWayne Buice .... .05 .02
- [ ] 148 Bill Pecota .... .05 .02
- [ ] 149 Doug Dascenzo .... .05 .02
- [ ] 150 Fernando Valenzuela .. .10 .05
- [ ] 151 Terry McGriff .... .05 .02
- [ ] 152 Mark Thurmond .... .05 .02
- [ ] 153 Jim Pankovits .... .05 .02
- [ ] 154 Don Carman .... .05 .02
- [ ] 155 Marty Barrett .... .05 .02
- [ ] 156 Dave Gallagher .... .05 .02
- [ ] 157 Tom Glavine .... .20 .09
- [ ] 158 Mike Aldrete .... .05 .02
- [ ] 159 Pat Clements .... .05 .02

- [ ] 160 Jeffrey Leonard .... .05 .02
- [ ] 161 Gregg Olson FDP UER .10 .05
       (Born Scribner, NE,
       should be Omaha, NE)
- [ ] 162 John Davis .... .05 .02
- [ ] 163 Bob Forsch .... .05 .02
- [ ] 164 Hal Lanier MG .... .05 .02
- [ ] 165 Mike Dunne .... .05 .02
- [ ] 166 Doug Jennings .... .05 .02
- [ ] 167 Steve Searcy FS ...... .05 .02
- [ ] 168 Willie Wilson .... .05 .02
- [ ] 169 Mike Jackson .... .05 .02
- [ ] 170 Tony Fernandez .... .05 .02
- [ ] 171 Atlanta Braves TL ..... .05 .02
       Andres Thomas
- [ ] 172 Frank Williams .... .05 .02
- [ ] 173 Mel Hall .... .05 .02
- [ ] 174 Todd Burns .... .05 .02
- [ ] 175 John Shelby .... .05 .02
- [ ] 176 Jeff Parrett .... .05 .02
- [ ] 177 Monty Fariss FDP ..... .05 .02
- [ ] 178 Mark Grant .... .05 .02
- [ ] 179 Ozzie Virgil .... .05 .02
- [ ] 180 Mike Scott .... .05 .02
- [ ] 181 Craig Worthington ..... .05 .02
- [ ] 182 Bob McClure .... .05 .02
- [ ] 183 Oddibe McDowell ...... .05 .02
- [ ] 184 John Costello .... .05 .02
- [ ] 185 Claudell Washington .. .05 .02
- [ ] 186 Pat Perry .... .05 .02
- [ ] 187 Darren Daulton .... .10 .05
- [ ] 188 Dennis Lamp .... .05 .02
- [ ] 189 Kevin Mitchell .... .10 .05
- [ ] 190 Mike Witt .... .05 .02
- [ ] 191 Sil Campusano .... .05 .02
- [ ] 192 Paul Mirabella .... .05 .02
- [ ] 193 Sparky Anderson MG .. .10 .05
       UER (553 Salazer)
- [ ] 194 Greg W. Harris .... .05 .02
- [ ] 195 Ozzie Guillen .... .05 .02
- [ ] 196 Denny Walling .... .05 .02
- [ ] 197 Neal Heaton .... .05 .02
- [ ] 198 Danny Heep .... .05 .02
- [ ] 199 Mike Schooler .... .05 .02
- [ ] 200 George Brett .... .40 .18
- [ ] 201 Blue Jays TL .... .05 .02
       Kelly Gruber
- [ ] 202 Brad Moore .... .05 .02
- [ ] 203 Rob Ducey .... .05 .02
- [ ] 204 Brad Havens .... .05 .02
- [ ] 205 Dwight Evans .... .10 .05
- [ ] 206 Roberto Alomar .... .30 .14
- [ ] 207 Terry Leach .... .05 .02
- [ ] 208 Tom Pagnozzi .... .05 .02
- [ ] 209 Jeff Bittiger .... .05 .02
- [ ] 210 Dale Murphy .... .20 .09
- [ ] 211 Mike Pagliarulo .... .05 .02
- [ ] 212 Scott Sanderson .... .05 .02
- [ ] 213 Rene Gonzales .... .05 .02
- [ ] 214 Charlie O'Brien .... .05 .02
- [ ] 215 Kevin Gross .... .05 .02
- [ ] 216 Jack Howell .... .05 .02
- [ ] 217 Joe Price .... .05 .02
- [ ] 218 Mike LaValliere .... .05 .02
- [ ] 219 Jim Clancy .... .05 .02
- [ ] 220 Gary Gaetti .... .05 .02
- [ ] 221 Cecil Espy .... .05 .02
- [ ] 222 Mark Lewis FDP .... .20 .09
- [ ] 223 Jay Buhner .... .20 .09
- [ ] 224 Tony LaRussa MG ..... .10 .05
- [ ] 225 Ramon Martinez .... .25 .11
- [ ] 226 Bill Doran .... .05 .02
- [ ] 227 John Farrell .... .05 .02
- [ ] 228 Nelson Santovenia .... .05 .02
- [ ] 229 Jimmy Key .... .10 .05
- [ ] 230 Ozzie Smith .... .25 .11
- [ ] 231 San Diego Padres TL .. .20 .09
       Roberto Alomar
       (Gary Carter at plate)
- [ ] 232 Ricky Horton .... .05 .02
- [ ] 233 Gregg Jefferies FS ... .15 .07
- [ ] 234 Tom Browning .... .05 .02
- [ ] 235 John Kruk .... .10 .05
- [ ] 236 Charles Hudson .... .05 .02
- [ ] 237 Glenn Hubbard .... .05 .02
- [ ] 238 Eric King .... .05 .02

239	Tim Laudner	.05	.02
240	Greg Maddux	.75	.35
241	Brett Butler	.10	.05
242	Ed VandeBerg	.05	.02
243	Bob Boone	.10	.05
244	Jim Acker	.05	.02
245	Jim Rice	.10	.05
246	Rey Quinones	.05	.02
247	Shawn Hillegas	.05	.02
248	Tony Phillips	.05	.02
249	Tim Leary	.05	.02
250	Cal Ripken	.75	.35
251	John Dopson	.05	.02
252	Billy Hatcher	.05	.02
253	Jose Alvarez	.05	.02
254	Tom Lasorda MG	.05	.02
255	Ron Guidry	.10	.05
256	Benny Santiago	.05	.02
257	Rick Aguilera	.10	.05
258	Checklist 133-264	.05	.02
259	Larry McWilliams	.05	.02
260	Dave Winfield	.20	.09
261	St.Louis Cardinals TL Tom Brunansky (With Luis Alicea)	.05	.02
262	Jeff Pico	.05	.02
263	Mike Felder	.05	.02
264	Rob Dibble	.10	.05
265	Kent Hrbek	.10	.05
266	Luis Aquino	.05	.02
267	Jeff M. Robinson	.05	.02
268	N. Keith Miller	.05	.02
269	Tom Bolton	.05	.02
270	Wally Joyner	.10	.05
271	Jay Tibbs	.05	.02
272	Ron Hassey	.05	.02
273	Jose Lind	.05	.02
274	Mark Eichhorn	.05	.02
275	Danny Tartabull UER (Born San Juan, PR should be Miami, FL)	.05	.02
276	Paul Kilgus	.05	.02
277	Mike Davis	.05	.02
278	Andy McGaffigan	.05	.02
279	Scott Bradley	.05	.02
280	Bob Knepper	.05	.02
281	Gary Redus	.05	.02
282	Cris Carpenter	.05	.02
283	Andy Allanson	.05	.02
284	Jim Leyland MG	.10	.05
285	John Candelaria	.05	.02
286	Darrin Jackson	.05	.02
287	Juan Nieves	.05	.02
288	Pat Sheridan	.05	.02
289	Ernie Whitt	.05	.02
290	John Franco	.05	.02
291	New York Mets TL Darryl Strawberry (With Keith Hernandez and Kevin McReynolds)	.10	.05
292	Jim Corsi	.05	.02
293	Glenn Wilson	.05	.02
294	Juan Berenguer	.05	.02
295	Scott Fletcher	.05	.02
296	Ron Gant	.10	.05
297	Oswald Peraza	.05	.02
298	Chris James	.05	.02
299	Steve Ellsworth	.05	.02
300	Darryl Strawberry	.10	.05
301	Charlie Leibrandt	.05	.02
302	Gary Ward	.05	.02
303	Felix Fermin	.05	.02
304	Joe Youngblood	.05	.02
305	Dave Smith	.05	.02
306	Tracy Woodson	.05	.02
307	Lance McCullers	.05	.02
308	Ron Karkovice	.05	.02
309	Mario Diaz	.05	.02
310	Rafael Palmeiro	.20	.09
311	Chris Bosio	.05	.02
312	Tom Lawless	.05	.02
313	Dennis Martinez	.10	.05
314	Bobby Valentine MG	.05	.02
315	Greg Swindell	.05	.02
316	Walt Weiss	.05	.02
317	Jack Armstrong	.05	.02
318	Gene Larkin	.05	.02
319	Greg Booker	.05	.02
320	Lou Whitaker	.10	.05
321	Boston Red Sox TL Jody Reed	.05	.02
322	John Smiley	.05	.02
323	Gary Thurman	.05	.02
324	Bob Milacki	.05	.02
325	Jesse Barfield	.05	.02
326	Dennis Boyd	.05	.02
327	Mark Lemke	.15	.07
328	Rick Honeycutt	.05	.02
329	Bob Melvin	.05	.02
330	Eric Davis	.10	.05
331	Curt Wilkerson	.05	.02
332	Tony Armas	.05	.02
333	Bob Ojeda	.05	.02
334	Steve Lyons	.05	.02
335	Dave Righetti	.05	.02
336	Steve Balboni	.05	.02
337	Calvin Schiraldi	.05	.02
338	Jim Adduci	.05	.02
339	Scott Bailes	.05	.02
340	Kirk Gibson	.10	.05
341	Jim Deshaies	.05	.02
342	Tom Brookens	.05	.02
343	Gary Sheffield FS	.75	.35
344	Tom Trebelhorn MG	.05	.02
345	Charlie Hough	.10	.05
346	Rex Hudler	.05	.02
347	John Cerutti	.05	.02
348	Ed Hearn	.05	.02
349	Ron Jones	.05	.02
350	Andy Van Slyke	.10	.05
351	San Fran. Giants TL Bob Melvin (With Bill Fahey CO)	.05	.02
352	Rick Schu	.05	.02
353	Marvell Wynne	.05	.02
354	Larry Parrish	.05	.02
355	Mark Langston	.05	.02
356	Kevin Elster	.05	.02
357	Jerry Reuss	.05	.02
358	Ricky Jordan	.10	.05
359	Tommy John	.10	.05
360	Ryne Sandberg	.25	.11
361	Kelly Downs	.05	.02
362	Jack Lazorko	.05	.02
363	Rich Yett	.05	.02
364	Rob Deer	.05	.02
365	Mike Henneman	.05	.02
366	Herm Winningham	.05	.02
367	Johnny Paredes	.05	.02
368	Brian Holton	.05	.02
369	Ken Caminiti	.20	.09
370	Dennis Eckersley	.10	.05
371	Manny Lee	.05	.02
372	Craig Lefferts	.05	.02
373	Tracy Jones	.05	.02
374	John Wathan MG	.05	.02
375	Terry Pendleton	.10	.05
376	Steve Lombardozzi	.05	.02
377	Mike Smithson	.05	.02
378	Checklist 265-396	.05	.02
379	Tim Flannery	.05	.02
380	Rickey Henderson	.20	.09
381	Baltimore Orioles TL Larry Sheets	.05	.02
382	John Smoltz	.50	.23
383	Howard Johnson	.10	.05
384	Mark Salas	.05	.02
385	Von Hayes	.05	.02
386	Andres Galarraga AS	.05	.02
387	Ryne Sandberg AS	.15	.07
388	Bobby Bonilla AS	.05	.02
389	Ozzie Smith AS	.15	.07
390	Darryl Strawberry AS	.05	.02
391	Andre Dawson AS	.10	.05
392	Andy Van Slyke AS	.05	.02
393	Gary Carter AS	.05	.02
394	Orel Hershiser AS	.05	.02
395	Danny Jackson AS	.05	.02
396	Kirk Gibson AS	.05	.02
397	Don Mattingly AS	.15	.07
398	Julio Franco AS	.05	.02
399	Wade Boggs AS	.10	.05
400	Alan Trammell AS	.10	.05
401	Jose Canseco AS	.10	.05
402	Mike Greenwell AS	.05	.02
403	Kirby Puckett AS	.20	.09
404	Bob Boone AS	.05	.02
405	Roger Clemens AS	.20	.09
406	Frank Viola AS	.05	.02
407	Dave Winfield AS	.10	.05
408	Greg Walker	.05	.02
409	Ken Dayley	.05	.02
410	Jack Clark	.10	.05
411	Mitch Williams	.05	.02
412	Barry Lyons	.05	.02
413	Mike Kingery	.05	.02
414	Jim Fregosi MG	.05	.02
415	Rich Gossage	.10	.05
416	Fred Lynn	.05	.02
417	Mike LaCoss	.05	.02
418	Bob Dernier	.05	.02
419	Tom Filer	.05	.02
420	Joe Carter	.20	.09
421	Kirk McCaskill	.05	.02
422	Bo Diaz	.05	.02
423	Brian Fisher	.05	.02
424	Luis Polonia UER (Wrong birthdate)	.05	.02
425	Jay Howell	.05	.02
426	Dan Gladden	.05	.02
427	Eric Show	.05	.02
428	Craig Reynolds	.05	.02
429	Minnesota Twins TL Greg Gagne (Taking throw at 2nd)	.05	.02
430	Mark Gubicza	.05	.02
431	Luis Rivera	.05	.02
432	Chad Kreuter	.05	.02
433	Albert Hall	.05	.02
434	Ken Patterson	.05	.02
435	Len Dykstra	.10	.05
436	Bobby Meacham	.05	.02
437	Andy Benes FDP	.25	.11
438	Greg Gross	.05	.02
439	Frank DiPino	.05	.02
440	Bobby Bonilla	.15	.07
441	Jerry Reed	.05	.02
442	Jose Oquendo	.05	.02
443	Rod Nichols	.05	.02
444	Moose Stubing MG	.05	.02
445	Matt Nokes	.05	.02
446	Rob Murphy	.05	.02
447	Donell Nixon	.05	.02
448	Eric Plunk	.05	.02
449	Carmelo Martinez	.05	.02
450	Roger Clemens	.40	.18
451	Mark Davidson	.05	.02
452	Israel Sanchez	.05	.02
453	Tom Prince	.05	.02
454	Paul Assenmacher	.05	.02
455	Johnny Ray	.05	.02
456	Tim Belcher	.05	.02
457	Mackey Sasser	.05	.02
458	Donn Pall	.05	.02
459	Seattle Mariners TL Dave Valle	.05	.02
460	Dave Stieb	.05	.02
461	Buddy Bell	.10	.05
462	Jose Guzman	.05	.02
463	Steve Lake	.05	.02
464	Bryn Smith	.05	.02
465	Mark Grace	.20	.09
466	Chuck Crim	.05	.02
467	Jim Walewander	.05	.02
468	Henry Cotto	.05	.02
469	Jose Bautista	.05	.02
470	Lance Parrish	.05	.02
471	Steve Curry	.05	.02
472	Brian Harper	.05	.02
473	Don Robinson	.05	.02
474	Bob Rodgers MG	.05	.02
475	Dave Parker	.10	.05
476	Jon Perlman	.05	.02
477	Dick Schofield	.05	.02
478	Doug Drabek	.05	.02
479	Mike Macfarlane	.05	.02
480	Keith Hernandez	.10	.05
481	Chris Brown	.05	.02

482	Steve Peters	.05	.02
483	Mickey Hatcher	.05	.02
484	Steve Shields	.05	.02
485	Hubie Brooks	.05	.02
486	Jack McDowell	.10	.05
487	Scott Lusader	.05	.02
488	Kevin Coffman	.05	.02
	Now with Cubs		
489	Phila. Phillies TL	.10	.05
	Mike Schmidt		
490	Chris Sabo	.05	.02
491	Mike Birkbeck	.05	.02
492	Alan Ashby	.05	.02
493	Todd Benzinger	.05	.02
494	Shane Rawley	.05	.02
495	Candy Maldonado	.05	.02
496	Dwayne Henry	.05	.02
497	Pete Stanicek	.05	.02
498	Dave Valle	.05	.02
499	Don Heinkel	.05	.02
500	Jose Canseco	.20	.09
501	Vance Law	.05	.02
502	Duane Ward	.05	.02
503	Al Newman	.05	.02
504	Bob Walk	.05	.02
505	Pete Rose MG	.25	.11
506	Kirt Manwaring	.05	.02
507	Steve Farr	.05	.02
508	Wally Backman	.05	.02
509	Bud Black	.05	.02
510	Bob Horner	.05	.02
511	Richard Dotson	.05	.02
512	Donnie Hill	.05	.02
513	Jesse Orosco	.05	.02
514	Chet Lemon	.05	.02
515	Barry Larkin	.20	.09
516	Eddie Whitson	.05	.02
517	Greg Brock	.05	.02
518	Bruce Ruffin	.05	.02
519	New York Yankees TL	.05	.02
	Willie Randolph		
520	Rick Sutcliffe	.05	.02
521	Mickey Tettleton	.10	.05
522	Randy Kramer	.05	.02
523	Andres Thomas	.05	.02
524	Checklist 397-528	.05	.02
525	Chili Davis	.10	.05
526	Wes Gardner	.05	.02
527	Dave Henderson	.05	.02
528	Luis Medina	.05	.02
	(Lower left front has white triangle)		
529	Tom Foley	.05	.02
530	Nolan Ryan	.75	.35
531	Dave Hengel	.05	.02
532	Jerry Browne	.05	.02
533	Andy Hawkins	.05	.02
534	Doc Edwards MG	.05	.02
535	Todd Worrell UER	.05	.02
	(4 wins in 88, should be 5)		
536	Joel Skinner	.05	.02
537	Pete Smith	.05	.02
538	Juan Castillo	.05	.02
539	Barry Jones	.05	.02
540	Bo Jackson	.20	.09
541	Cecil Fielder	.15	.07
542	Todd Frohwirth	.05	.02
543	Damon Berryhill	.05	.02
544	Jeff Sellers	.05	.02
545	Mookie Wilson	.10	.05
546	Mark Williamson	.05	.02
547	Mark McLemore	.05	.02
548	Bobby Witt	.05	.02
549	Chicago Cubs TL	.05	.02
	Jamie Moyer (Pitching)		
550	Orel Hershiser	.10	.05
551	Randy Ready	.05	.02
552	Greg Cadaret	.05	.02
553	Luis Salazar	.05	.02
554	Nick Esasky	.05	.02
555	Bert Blyleven	.10	.05
556	Bruce Fields	.05	.02
557	Keith A. Miller	.05	.02
558	Dan Pasqua	.05	.02
559	Juan Agosto	.05	.02
560	Tim Raines	.10	.05
561	Luis Aguayo	.05	.02
562	Danny Cox	.05	.02
563	Bill Schroeder	.05	.02
564	Russ Nixon MG	.05	.02
565	Jeff Russell	.05	.02
566	Al Pedrique	.05	.02
567	David Wells ER	.05	.02
	(Complete Pitching Recor)		
568	Mickey Brantley	.05	.02
569	German Jimenez	.05	.02
570	Tony Gwynn UER	.50	.23
	('88 average should be italicized as league leader)		
571	Billy Ripken	.05	.02
572	Atlee Hammaker	.05	.02
573	Jim Abbott FDP	.20	.09
574	Dave Clark	.05	.02
575	Juan Samuel	.05	.02
576	Greg Minton	.05	.02
577	Randy Bush	.05	.02
578	John Morris	.05	.02
579	Houston Astros TL	.05	.02
	Glenn Davis (Batting stance)		
580	Harold Reynolds	.05	.02
581	Gene Nelson	.05	.02
582	Mike Marshall	.05	.02
583	Paul Gibson	.05	.02
584	Randy Velarde UER	.05	.02
	(Signed 1935, should be 1985)		
585	Harold Baines	.10	.05
586	Joe Boever	.05	.02
587	Mike Stanley	.05	.02
588	Luis Alicea	.05	.02
589	Dave Meads	.05	.02
590	Andres Galarraga	.20	.09
591	Jeff Musselman	.05	.02
592	John Cangelosi	.05	.02
593	Drew Hall	.05	.02
594	Jimy Williams MG	.05	.02
595	Teddy Higuera	.05	.02
596	Kurt Stillwell	.05	.02
597	Terry Taylor	.05	.02
598	Ken Gerhart	.05	.02
599	Tom Candiotti	.05	.02
600	Wade Boggs	.20	.09
601	Dave Dravecky	.10	.05
602	Devon White	.05	.02
603	Frank Tanana	.05	.02
604	Paul O'Neill	.05	.02
605A	Bob Welch ERR	2.00	.90
	(Missing line on back, "Complete M.L. Pitching Record")		
605B	Bob Welch COR	.05	.02
606	Rick Dempsey	.05	.02
607	Willie Ansley FDP	.05	.02
608	Phil Bradley	.05	.02
609	Detroit Tigers TL	.05	.02
	Frank Tanana (With Alan Trammell and Mike Heath)		
610	Randy Myers	.10	.05
611	Don Slaught	.05	.02
612	Dan Quisenberry	.05	.02
613	Gary Varsho	.05	.02
614	Joe Hesketh	.05	.02
615	Robin Yount	.20	.09
616	Steve Rosenberg	.05	.02
617	Mark Parent	.05	.02
618	Rance Mulliniks	.05	.02
619	Checklist 529-660	.05	.02
620	Barry Bonds	.40	.18
621	Rick Mahler	.05	.02
622	Stan Javier	.05	.02
623	Fred Toliver	.05	.02
624	Jack McKeon MG	.05	.02
625	Eddie Murray	.20	.09
626	Jeff Reed	.05	.02
627	Greg A. Harris	.05	.02
628	Matt Williams	.20	.09
629	Pete O'Brien	.05	.02
630	Mike Greenwell	.05	.02
631	Dave Bergman	.05	.02
632	Bryan Harvey	.10	.05
633	Daryl Boston	.05	.02
634	Marvin Freeman	.05	.02
635	Willie Randolph	.10	.05
636	Bill Wilkinson	.05	.02
637	Carmen Castillo	.05	.02
638	Floyd Bannister	.05	.02
639	Oakland A's TL	.05	.02
	Walt Weiss		
640	Willie McGee	.10	.05
641	Curt Young	.05	.02
642	Argenis Salazar	.05	.02
643	Louie Meadows	.05	.02
644	Lloyd McClendon	.05	.02
645	Jack Morris	.10	.05
646	Kevin Bass	.05	.02
647	Randy Johnson	1.00	.45
648	Sandy Alomar FS	.50	.23
649	Stewart Cliburn	.05	.02
650	Kirby Puckett	.40	.18
651	Tom Niedenfuel	.05	.02
652	Rich Gedman	.05	.02
653	Tommy Barrett	.05	.02
654	Whitey Herzog MG	.10	.05
655	Dave Magadan	.05	.02
656	Ivan Calderon	.05	.02
657	Joe Magrane	.05	.02
658	R.J. Reynolds	.05	.02
659	Al Leiter	.20	.09
660	Will Clark	.20	.09
661	Dwight Gooden TBC84	.05	.02
662	Lou Brock TBC79	.20	.09
663	Hank Aaron TBC74	.20	.09
664	Gil Hodges TBC69	.15	.07
665A	Tony Oliva TBC64	2.00	.90
	ERR (fabricated card is enlarged version of Oliva's 64T card; Topps copyright missing)		
665B	Tony Oliva TBC64	.10	.05
	COR (fabricated card)		
666	Randy St.Claire	.05	.02
667	Dwayne Murphy	.05	.02
668	Mike Bielecki	.05	.02
669	L.A. Dodgers TL	.10	.05
	Orel Hershiser (Mound conference with Mike Scioscia)		
670	Kevin Seitzer	.05	.02
671	Jim Gantner	.05	.02
672	Allan Anderson	.05	.02
673	Don Baylor	.05	.02
674	Otis Nixon	.10	.05
675	Bruce Hurst	.05	.02
676	Ernie Riles	.05	.02
677	Dave Schmidt	.05	.02
678	Dion James	.05	.02
679	Willie Fraser	.05	.02
680	Gary Carter	.20	.09
681	Jeff D. Robinson	.05	.02
682	Rick Leach	.05	.02
683	Jose Cecena	.05	.02
684	Dave Johnson MG	.05	.02
685	Jeff Treadway	.05	.02
686	Scott Terry	.05	.02
687	Alvin Davis	.05	.02
688	Zane Smith	.05	.02
689A	Stan Jefferson	.05	.02
	(Pink triangle on front bottom left)		
689B	Stan Jefferson	.05	.02
	(Violet triangle on front bottom left)		
690	Doug Jones	.05	.02
691	Roberto Kelly UER	.05	.02
	(83 Oneonta)		
692	Steve Ontiveros	.05	.02
693	Pat Borders	.10	.05
694	Les Lancaster	.05	.02
695	Carlton Fisk	.20	.09
696	Don August	.05	.02

☐ 697A Franklin Stubbs .... .05 .02
(Team name on front
in white)
☐ 697B Franklin Stubbs .05 .02
(Team name on front
in gray)
☐ 698 Keith Atherton .... .05 .02
☐ 699 Pittsburgh Pirates TL .05 .02
Al Pedrique
(Tony Gwynn sliding)
☐ 700 Don Mattingly .... .30 .14
☐ 701 Storm Davis .... .05 .02
☐ 702 Jamie Quirk .... .05 .02
☐ 703 Scott Garrelts .... .05 .02
☐ 704 Carlos Quintana .... .05 .02
☐ 705 Terry Kennedy .... .05 .02
☐ 706 Pete Incaviglia .... .10 .05
☐ 707 Steve Jeltz .... .05 .02
☐ 708 Chuck Finley .... .10 .05
☐ 709 Tom Herr .... .05 .02
☐ 710 David Cone .... .20 .09
☐ 711 Candy Sierra .... .05 .02
☐ 712 Bill Swift .... .05 .02
☐ 713 Ty Griffin FDP .... .05 .02
☐ 714 Joe Morgan MG .... .05 .02
☐ 715 Tony Pena .... .05 .02
☐ 716 Wayne Tolleson .... .05 .02
☐ 717 Jamie Moyer .... .05 .02
☐ 718 Glenn Braggs .... .05 .02
☐ 719 Danny Darwin .... .05 .02
☐ 720 Tim Wallach .... .05 .02
☐ 721 Ron Tingley .... .05 .02
☐ 722 Todd Stottlemyre .... .05 .02
☐ 723 Rafael Belliard .... .05 .02
☐ 724 Jerry Don Gleaton .... .05 .02
☐ 725 Terry Steinbach .... .10 .05
☐ 726 Dickie Thon .... .05 .02
☐ 727 Joe Orsulak .... .05 .02
☐ 728 Charlie Puleo .... .05 .02
☐ 729 Texas Rangers TL .... .05 .02
Steve Buechele
(Inconsistent design,
team name on front
surrounded by black,
should be white)
☐ 730 Danny Jackson .... .05 .02
☐ 731 Mike Young .... .05 .02
☐ 732 Steve Buechele .... .05 .02
☐ 733 Randy Bockus .... .05 .02
☐ 734 Jody Reed .... .05 .02
☐ 735 Roger McDowell .... .05 .02
☐ 736 Jeff Hamilton .... .05 .02
☐ 737 Norm Charlton .... .10 .05
☐ 738 Darnell Coles .... .05 .02
☐ 739 Brook Jacoby .... .05 .02
☐ 740 Dan Plesac .... .05 .02
☐ 741 Ken Phelps .... .05 .02
☐ 742 Mike Harkey FS .... .05 .02
☐ 743 Mike Heath .... .05 .02
☐ 744 Roger Craig MG .... .05 .02
☐ 745 Fred McGriff .... .20 .09
☐ 746 German Gonzalez UER .05 .02
(Wrong birthdate)
☐ 747 Wil Tejada .... .05 .02
☐ 748 Jimmy Jones .... .05 .02
☐ 749 Rafael Ramirez .... .05 .02
☐ 750 Bret Saberhagen .... .05 .02
☐ 751 Ken Oberkfell .... .05 .02
☐ 752 Jim Gott .... .05 .02
☐ 753 Jose Uribe .... .05 .02
☐ 754 Bob Brower .... .05 .02
☐ 755 Mike Scioscia .... .05 .02
☐ 756 Scott Medvin .... .05 .02
☐ 757 Brady Anderson .... .50 .23
☐ 758 Gene Walter .... .05 .02
☐ 759 Milwaukee Brewers TL .05 .02
Rob Deer
☐ 760 Lee Smith .... .10 .05
☐ 761 Dante Bichette .... .40 .18
☐ 762 Bobby Thigpen .... .05 .02
☐ 763 Dave Martinez .... .05 .02
☐ 764 Robin Ventura FDP ...... .40 .18
☐ 765 Glenn Davis .... .05 .02
☐ 766 Cecilio Guante .... .05 .02
☐ 767 Mike Capel .... .05 .02
☐ 768 Bill Wegman .... .05 .02

☐ 769 Junior Ortiz .... .05 .02
☐ 770 Alan Trammell .... .15 .07
☐ 771 Ron Kittle .... .05 .02
☐ 772 Ron Oester .... .05 .02
☐ 773 Keith Moreland .... .05 .02
☐ 774 Frank Robinson MG ..... .20 .09
☐ 775 Jeff Reardon .... .10 .05
☐ 776 Nelson Liriano .... .05 .02
☐ 777 Ted Power .... .05 .02
☐ 778 Bruce Benedict .... .05 .02
☐ 779 Craig McMurtry .... .05 .02
☐ 780 Pedro Guerrero .... .10 .05
☐ 781 Greg Briley .... .05 .02
☐ 782 Checklist 661-792 .... .05 .02
☐ 783 Trevor Wilson .... .05 .02
☐ 784 Steve Avery FDP .... .10 .05
☐ 785 Ellis Burks .... .05 .02
☐ 786 Melido Perez .... .05 .02
☐ 787 Dave West .... .05 .02
☐ 788 Mike Morgan .... .05 .02
☐ 789 Kansas City Royals TL .20 .09
Bo Jackson
(Throwing)
☐ 790 Sid Fernandez .... .05 .02
☐ 791 Jim Lindeman .... .05 .02
☐ 792 Rafael Santana .... .05 .02

1989 Topps Traded

The 1989 Topps Traded set contains 132 standard-size cards. The cards were distributed exclusively in factory set form in red and white taped boxes through hobby dealers. The cards are identical to the 1989 Topps regular issue cards except for whiter stock and "T"-suffixed numbering on back. Rookie Cards in this set include Ken Griffey Jr., Ken Hill and Deion Sanders.

	MINT	NRMT
COMP.FACT.SET (132)	8.00	3.60
COMMON CARD (1T-132T)	.05	.02
MINOR STARS	.10	.05
UNLISTED STARS	.20	.09

☐ 1T Don Aase .... .05 .02
☐ 2T Jim Abbott .... .20 .09
☐ 3T Kent Anderson .... .05 .02
☐ 4T Keith Atherton .... .05 .02
☐ 5T Wally Backman .... .05 .02
☐ 6T Steve Balboni .... .05 .02
☐ 7T Jesse Barfield .... .05 .02
☐ 8T Steve Bedrosian .... .05 .02
☐ 9T Todd Benzinger .... .05 .02
☐ 10T Geronimo Berroa ...... .05 .02
☐ 11T Bert Blyleven .... .10 .05
☐ 12T Bob Boone .... .10 .05
☐ 13T Phil Bradley .... .05 .02
☐ 14T Jeff Brantley .... .05 .02
☐ 15T Kevin Brown .... .20 .09
☐ 16T Jerry Browne .... .05 .02
☐ 17T Chuck Cary .... .05 .02
☐ 18T Carmen Castillo .... .05 .02

☐ 19T Jim Clancy .... .05 .02
☐ 20T Jack Clark .... .10 .05
☐ 21T Bryan Clutterbuck ..... .05 .02
☐ 22T Jody Davis .... .05 .02
☐ 23T Mike Devereaux .... .05 .02
☐ 24T Frank DiPino .... .05 .02
☐ 25T Benny Distefano ...... .05 .02
☐ 26T John Dopson .... .05 .02
☐ 27T Len Dykstra .... .10 .05
☐ 28T Jim Eisenreich .... .05 .02
☐ 29T Nick Esasky .... .05 .02
☐ 30T Alvaro Espinoza ...... .05 .02
☐ 31T Darrell Evans UER .... .10 .05
(Stat headings on back
are for a pitcher)
☐ 32T Junior Felix .... .05 .02
☐ 33T Felix Fermin .... .05 .02
☐ 34T Julio Franco .... .05 .02
☐ 35T Terry Francona .... .05 .02
☐ 36T Cito Gaston MG .... .10 .05
☐ 37T Bob Geren UER .... .05 .02
(Photo actually
Mike Fennell)
☐ 38T Tom Gordon .... .20 .09
☐ 39T Tommy Gregg .... .05 .02
☐ 40T Ken Griffey Sr. .... .05 .02
☐ 41T Ken Griffey Jr. 6.00 2.70
☐ 42T Kevin Gross .... .05 .02
☐ 43T Lee Guetterman .... .05 .02
☐ 44T Mel Hall .... .05 .02
☐ 45T Erik Hanson .... .10 .05
☐ 46T Gene Harris .... .05 .02
☐ 47T Andy Hawkins .... .05 .02
☐ 48T Rickey Henderson .... .20 .09
☐ 49T Tom Herr .... .05 .02
☐ 50T Ken Hill .... .20 .09
☐ 51T Brian Holman .... .05 .02
☐ 52T Brian Holton .... .05 .02
☐ 53T Art Howe MG .... .05 .02
☐ 54T Ken Howell .... .05 .02
☐ 55T Bruce Hurst .... .05 .02
☐ 56T Chris James .... .05 .02
☐ 57T Randy Johnson .... 1.00 .45
☐ 58T Jimmy Jones .... .05 .02
☐ 59T Terry Kennedy .... .05 .02
☐ 60T Paul Kilgus .... .05 .02
☐ 61T Eric King .... .05 .02
☐ 62T Ron Kittle .... .05 .02
☐ 63T John Kruk .... .10 .05
☐ 64T Randy Kutcher .... .05 .02
☐ 65T Steve Lake .... .05 .02
☐ 66T Mark Langston .... .05 .02
☐ 67T Dave LaPoint .... .05 .02
☐ 68T Rick Leach .... .05 .02
☐ 69T Terry Leach .... .05 .02
☐ 70T Jim Lefebvre MG ...... .05 .02
☐ 71T Al Leiter .... .20 .09
☐ 72T Jeffrey Leonard .... .05 .02
☐ 73T Derek Lilliquist .... .05 .02
☐ 74T Rick Mahler .... .05 .02
☐ 75T Tom McCarthy .... .05 .02
☐ 76T Lloyd McClendon ...... .05 .02
☐ 77T Lance McCullers ...... .05 .02
☐ 78T Oddibe McDowell ..... .05 .02
☐ 79T Roger McDowell .... .05 .02
☐ 80T Larry McWilliams ..... .05 .02
☐ 81T Randy Milligan .... .05 .02
☐ 82T Mike Moore .... .05 .02
☐ 83T Keith Moreland .... .05 .02
☐ 84T Mike Morgan .... .05 .02
☐ 85T Jamie Moyer .... .05 .02
☐ 86T Rob Murphy .... .05 .02
☐ 87T Eddie Murray .... .20 .09
☐ 88T Pete O'Brien .... .05 .02
☐ 89T Gregg Olson .... .10 .05
☐ 90T Steve Ontiveros ...... .05 .02
☐ 91T Jesse Orosco .... .05 .02
☐ 92T Spike Owen .... .05 .02
☐ 93T Rafael Palmeiro .... .20 .09
☐ 94T Clay Parker .... .05 .02
☐ 95T Jeff Parrett .... .05 .02
☐ 96T Lance Parrish .... .05 .02
☐ 97T Dennis Powell .... .05 .02
☐ 98T Rey Quinones .... .05 .02
☐ 99T Doug Rader MG .... .05 .02
☐ 100T Willie Randolph ...... .10 .05

		MINT	NRMT

□ 101T Shane Rawley .05 .02
□ 102T Randy Ready .05 .02
□ 103T Bip Roberts .10 .05
□ 104T Kenny Rogers .10 .05
□ 105T Ed Romero .05 .02
□ 106T Nolan Ryan 1.50 .70
□ 107T Luis Salazar .05 .02
□ 108T Juan Samuel .05 .02
□ 109T Alex Sanchez .05 .02
□ 110T Deion Sanders .75 .35
□ 111T Steve Sax .05 .02
□ 112T Rick Schu .05 .02
□ 113T Dwight Smith .10 .05
□ 114T Lonnie Smith .05 .02
□ 115T Billy Spiers .05 .02
□ 116T Kent Tekulve .05 .02
□ 117T Walt Terrell .05 .02
□ 118T Milt Thompson .05 .02
□ 119T Dickie Thon .05 .02
□ 120T Jeff Torborg MG .05 .02
□ 121T Jeff Treadway .05 .02
□ 122T Omar Vizquel .40 .18
□ 123T Jerome Walton .20 .09
□ 124T Gary Ward .05 .02
□ 125T Claudell Washington .05 .02
□ 126T Curt Wilkerson .05 .02
□ 127T Eddie Williams .05 .02
□ 128T Frank Williams .05 .02
□ 129T Ken Williams .05 .02
□ 130T Mitch Williams .05 .02
□ 131T Steve Wilson .05 .02
□ 132T Checklist 1T-132T .05 .02

1990 Topps

The 1990 Topps set contains 792 standard-size cards. Cards were issued primarily in wax packs, rack packs and hobby and retail factory sets. Card fronts feature various colored borders with the player's name at the bottom and team name at top. Subsets include All-Stars (385-407), Turn Back the Clock (661-665) and Draft Picks (scattered throughout the set). The key Rookie Cards in this set are Juan Gonzalez, Marquis Grissom, Ben McDonald, Sammy Sosa, Frank Thomas, Larry Walker and Bernie Williams. The Thomas card (414A) was printed without his name on front causing a scarce variation. The card is rarely seen and, for a newer issue, has experienced unprecedented growth as far as value. Be careful when purchasing this card as counterfeits have been produced.

	MINT	NRMT
COMPLETE SET (792)	15.00	6.75
COMP.FACT.SET (792)	15.00	6.75
COMMON CARD (1-792)	.05	.02

RYAN SALUTE (2-5) .40 .18
MINOR STARS .10 .05
UNLISTED STARS .20 .09
SUBSET CARDS HALF VALUE OF BASE CARDS
BEWARE COUNTERFEIT THOMAS NNOF

□ 1 Nolan Ryan .75 .35
□ 2 Nolan Ryan Salute .40 .18
    New York Mets
□ 3 Nolan Ryan Salute .40 .18
    California Angels
□ 4 Nolan Ryan Salute .40 .18
    Houston Astros
□ 5 Nolan Ryan Salute .40 .18
    Texas Rangers UER
    (Says Texas Stadium
    rather than
    Arlington Stadium)
□ 6 Vince Coleman RB .05 .02
    (50 consecutive SB's)
□ 7 Rickey Henderson RB .10 .05
    (40 career leadoff HR's)
□ 8 Cal Ripken RB .40 .18
    (20 or more homers for
    8 consecutive years,
    record for shortstops)
□ 9 Eric Plunk .05 .02
□ 10 Barry Larkin .20 .09
□ 11 Paul Gibson .05 .02
□ 12 Joe Girardi .10 .05
□ 13 Mark Williamson .05 .02
□ 14 Mike Fetters .05 .02
□ 15 Teddy Higuera .05 .02
□ 16 Kent Anderson .05 .02
□ 17 Kelly Downs .05 .02
□ 18 Carlos Quintana .05 .02
□ 19 Al Newman .05 .02
□ 20 Mark Gubicza .05 .02
□ 21 Jeff Torborg MG .05 .02
□ 22 Bruce Ruffin .05 .02
□ 23 Randy Velarde .05 .02
□ 24 Joe Hesketh .05 .02
□ 25 Willie Randolph .10 .05
□ 26 Don Slaught .05 .02
□ 27 Rick Leach .05 .02
□ 28 Duane Ward .05 .02
□ 29 John Cangelosi .05 .02
□ 30 David Cone .20 .09
□ 31 Henry Cotto .05 .02
□ 32 John Farrell .05 .02
□ 33 Greg Walker .05 .02
□ 34 Tony Fossas .05 .02
□ 35 Benito Santiago .05 .02
□ 36 John Costello .05 .02
□ 37 Domingo Ramos .05 .02
□ 38 Wes Gardner .05 .02
□ 39 Curt Ford .05 .02
□ 40 Jay Howell .05 .02
□ 41 Matt Williams .20 .09
□ 42 Jeff M. Robinson .05 .02
□ 43 Dante Bichette .20 .09
□ 44 Roger Salkeld FDP .05 .02
□ 45 Dave Parker UER .10 .05
    (Born in Jackson,
    not Calhoun)
□ 46 Rob Dibble .05 .02
□ 47 Brian Harper .05 .02
□ 48 Zane Smith .05 .02
□ 49 Tom Lawless .05 .02
□ 50 Glenn Davis .05 .02
□ 51 Doug Rader MG .05 .02
□ 52 Jack Daugherty .05 .02
□ 53 Mike LaCoss .05 .02
□ 54 Joel Skinner .05 .02
□ 55 Darrell Evans UER .10 .05
    (HR total should be
    414, not 424)
□ 56 Franklin Stubbs .05 .02
□ 57 Greg Vaughn .10 .05
□ 58 Keith Miller .05 .02
□ 59 Ted Power .05 .02
□ 60 George Brett .40 .18
□ 61 Deion Sanders .20 .09
□ 62 Ramon Martinez .15 .07
□ 63 Mike Pagliarulo .05 .02
□ 64 Danny Darwin .05 .02

□ 65 Devon White .05 .02
□ 66 Greg Litton .05 .02
□ 67 Scott Sanderson .05 .02
□ 68 Dave Henderson .05 .02
□ 69 Todd Frohwirth .05 .02
□ 70 Mike Greenwell .05 .02
□ 71 Allan Anderson .05 .02
□ 72 Jeff Huson .05 .02
□ 73 Bob Milacki .05 .02
□ 74 Jeff Jackson FDP .05 .02
□ 75 Doug Jones .05 .02
□ 76 Dave Valle .05 .02
□ 77 Dave Bergman .05 .02
□ 78 Mike Flanagan .05 .02
□ 79 Ron Kittle .05 .02
□ 80 Jeff Russell .05 .02
□ 81 Bob Rodgers MG .05 .02
□ 82 Scott Terry .05 .02
□ 83 Hensley Meulens .05 .02
□ 84 Ray Searage .05 .02
□ 85 Juan Samuel .05 .02
□ 86 Paul Kilgus .05 .02
□ 87 Rick Luecken .05 .02
□ 88 Glenn Braggs .05 .02
□ 89 Clint Zavaras .05 .02
□ 90 Jack Clark .10 .05
□ 91 Steve Frey .05 .02
□ 92 Mike Stanley .05 .02
□ 93 Shawn Hillegas .05 .02
□ 94 Herm Winningham .05 .02
□ 95 Todd Worrell .05 .02
□ 96 Jody Reed .05 .02
□ 97 Curt Schilling .20 .09
□ 98 Jose Gonzalez .05 .02
□ 99 Rich Monteleone .05 .02
□ 100 Will Clark .20 .09
□ 101 Shane Rawley .05 .02
□ 102 Stan Javier .05 .02
□ 103 Marvin Freeman .05 .02
□ 104 Bob Knepper .05 .02
□ 105 Randy Myers .10 .05
□ 106 Charlie O'Brien .05 .02
□ 107 Fred Lynn .05 .02
□ 108 Rod Nichols .05 .02
□ 109 Roberto Kelly .05 .02
□ 110 Tommy Helms MG .05 .02
□ 111 Ed Whited .05 .02
□ 112 Glenn Wilson .05 .02
□ 113 Manny Lee .05 .02
□ 114 Mike Bielecki .05 .02
□ 115 Tony Pena .05 .02
□ 116 Floyd Bannister .05 .02
□ 117 Mike Sharperson .05 .02
□ 118 Erik Hanson .05 .02
□ 119 Billy Hatcher .05 .02
□ 120 John Franco .10 .05
□ 121 Robin Ventura .20 .09
□ 122 Shawn Abner .05 .02
□ 123 Rich Gedman .05 .02
□ 124 Dave Dravecky .10 .05
□ 125 Kent Hrbek .05 .02
□ 126 Randy Kramer .05 .02
□ 127 Mike Devereaux .05 .02
□ 128 Checklist 1 .05 .02
□ 129 Ron Jones .05 .02
□ 130 Bert Blyleven .10 .05
□ 131 Matt Nokes .05 .02
□ 132 Lance Blankenship .05 .02
□ 133 Ricky Horton .05 .02
□ 134 Earl Cunningham FDP .05 .02
□ 135 Dave Magadan .05 .02
□ 136 Kevin Brown .20 .09
□ 137 Marty Pevey .05 .02
□ 138 Al Leiter .20 .09
□ 139 Greg Brock .05 .02
□ 140 Andre Dawson .20 .09
□ 141 John Hart MG .05 .02
□ 142 Jeff Wetherby .05 .02
□ 143 Rafael Belliard .05 .02
□ 144 Bud Black .10 .05
□ 145 Terry Steinbach .10 .05
□ 146 Rob Richie .05 .02
□ 147 Chuck Finley .10 .05
□ 148 Edgar Martinez .20 .09
□ 149 Steve Farr .05 .02
□ 150 Kirk Gibson .10 .05

151	Rick Mahler	.05	.02
152	Lonnie Smith	.05	.02
153	Randy Milligan	.05	.02
154	Mike Maddux	.05	.02
155	Ellis Burks	.15	.07
156	Ken Patterson	.05	.02
157	Craig Biggio	.20	.09
158	Craig Lefferts	.05	.02
159	Mike Felder	.05	.02
160	Dave Righetti	.05	.02
161	Harold Reynolds	.05	.02
162	Todd Zeile	.10	.05
163	Phil Bradley	.05	.02
164	Jeff Juden FDP	.05	.02
165	Walt Weiss	.05	.02
166	Bobby Witt	.05	.02
167	Kevin Appier	.20	.09
168	Jose Lind	.05	.02
169	Richard Dotson	.05	.02
170	George Bell	.05	.02
171	Russ Nixon MG	.05	.02
172	Tom Lampkin	.05	.02
173	Tim Belcher	.05	.02
174	Jeff Kunkel	.05	.02
175	Mike Moore	.05	.02
176	Luis Quinones	.05	.02
177	Mike Henneman	.05	.02
178	Chris James	.05	.02
179	Brian Holton	.05	.02
180	Tim Raines	.10	.05
181	Juan Agosto	.05	.02
182	Mookie Wilson	.05	.02
183	Steve Lake	.05	.02
184	Danny Cox	.05	.02
185	Ruben Sierra	.25	.11
186	Dave LaPoint	.05	.02
187	Rick Wrona	.05	.02
188	Mike Smithson	.05	.02
189	Dick Schofield	.05	.02
190	Rick Reuschel	.05	.02
191	Pat Borders	.05	.02
192	Don August	.05	.02
193	Andy Benes	.20	.09
194	Glenallen Hill	.05	.02
195	Tim Burke	.05	.02
196	Gerald Young	.05	.02
197	Doug Drabek	.05	.02
198	Mike Marshall	.05	.02
199	Sergio Valdez	.05	.02
200	Don Mattingly	.30	.14
201	Cito Gaston MG	.05	.02
202	Mike Macfarlane	.05	.02
203	Mike Roesler	.05	.02
204	Bob Dernier	.05	.02
205	Mark Davis	.05	.02
206	Nick Esasky	.05	.02
207	Bob Ojeda	.05	.02
208	Brook Jacoby	.05	.02
209	Greg Mathews	.05	.02
210	Ryne Sandberg	.25	.11
211	John Cerutti	.05	.02
212	Joe Orsulak	.05	.02
213	Scott Bankhead	.05	.02
214	Terry Francona	.05	.02
215	Kirk McCaskill	.05	.02
216	Ricky Jordan	.05	.02
217	Don Robinson	.05	.02
218	Wally Backman	.05	.02
219	Donn Pall	.05	.02
220	Barry Bonds	.25	.11
221	Gary Mielke	.05	.02
222	Kurt Stillwell UER	.05	.02
	(Graduate misspelled as gradute)		
223	Tommy Gregg	.05	.02
224	Delino DeShields	.20	.09
225	Jim Deshaies	.05	.02
226	Mickey Hatcher	.05	.02
227	Kevin Tapani	.10	.05
228	Dave Martinez	.05	.02
229	David Wells	.05	.02
230	Keith Hernandez	.10	.05
231	Jack McKeon MG	.05	.02
232	Darnell Coles	.05	.02
233	Ken Hill	.15	.07
234	Mariano Duncan	.05	.02
235	Jeff Reardon	.10	.05
236	Hal Morris	.05	.02
237	Kevin Ritz	.05	.02
238	Felix Jose	.05	.02
239	Eric Show	.05	.02
240	Mark Grace	.20	.09
241	Mike Krukow	.05	.02
242	Fred Manrique	.05	.02
243	Barry Jones	.05	.02
244	Bill Schroeder	.05	.02
245	Roger Clemens	.40	.18
246	Jim Eisenreich	.05	.02
247	Jerry Reed	.05	.02
248	Dave Anderson	.05	.02
249	Mike(Texas) Smith	.05	.02
250	Jose Canseco	.20	.09
251	Jeff Blauser	.10	.05
252	Otis Nixon	.10	.05
253	Mark Portugal	.05	.02
254	Francisco Cabrera	.05	.02
255	Bobby Thigpen	.05	.02
256	Marvell Wynne	.05	.02
257	Jose DeLeon	.05	.02
258	Barry Lyons	.05	.02
259	Lance McCullers	.05	.02
260	Eric Davis	.10	.05
261	Whitey Herzog MG	.10	.05
262	Checklist 2	.05	.02
263	Mel Stottlemyre Jr.	.05	.02
264	Bryan Clutterbuck	.05	.02
265	Pete O'Brien	.05	.02
266	German Gonzalez	.05	.02
267	Mark Davidson	.05	.02
268	Rob Murphy	.05	.02
269	Dickie Thon	.05	.02
270	Dave Stewart	.10	.05
271	Chet Lemon	.05	.02
272	Bryan Harvey	.05	.02
273	Bobby Bonilla	.10	.05
274	Mauro Gozzo	.05	.02
275	Mickey Tettleton	.10	.05
276	Gary Thurman	.05	.02
277	Lenny Harris	.05	.02
278	Pascual Perez	.05	.02
279	Steve Buechele	.05	.02
280	Lou Whitaker	.10	.05
281	Kevin Bass	.05	.02
282	Derek Lilliquist	.05	.02
283	Joey Belle	.50	.23
284	Mark Gardner	.05	.02
285	Willie McGee	.10	.05
286	Lee Guetterman	.05	.02
287	Vance Law	.05	.02
288	Greg Briley	.05	.02
289	Norm Charlton	.05	.02
290	Robin Yount	.20	.09
291	Dave Johnson MG	.10	.05
292	Jim Gott	.05	.02
293	Mike Gallego	.05	.02
294	Craig McMurtry	.05	.02
295	Fred McGriff	.20	.09
296	Jeff Ballard	.05	.02
297	Tommy Herr	.05	.02
298	Dan Gladden	.05	.02
299	Adam Peterson	.05	.02
300	Bo Jackson	.20	.09
301	Don Aase	.05	.02
302	Marcus Lawton	.05	.02
303	Rick Cerone	.05	.02
304	Marty Clary	.05	.02
305	Eddie Murray	.20	.09
306	Tom Niedenfuer	.05	.02
307	Bip Roberts	.05	.02
308	Jose Guzman	.05	.02
309	Eric Yelding	.05	.02
310	Steve Bedrosian	.05	.02
311	Dwight Smith	.05	.02
312	Dan Quisenberry	.05	.02
313	Gus Polidor	.05	.02
314	Donald Harris FDP	.05	.02
315	Bruce Hurst	.05	.02
316	Carney Lansford	.05	.02
317	Mark Guthrie	.05	.02
318	Wallace Johnson	.05	.02
319	Dion James	.05	.02
320	Dave Stieb	.05	.02
321	Joe Morgan MG	.05	.02
322	Junior Ortiz	.05	.02
323	Willie Wilson	.05	.02
324	Pete Harnisch	.05	.02
325	Robby Thompson	.05	.02
326	Tom McCarthy	.05	.02
327	Ken Williams	.05	.02
328	Curt Young	.05	.02
329	Oddibe McDowell	.05	.02
330	Ron Darling	.05	.02
331	Juan Gonzalez	2.00	.90
332	Paul O'Neill	.10	.05
333	Bill Wegman	.05	.02
334	Johnny Ray	.05	.02
335	Andy Hawkins	.05	.02
336	Ken Griffey Jr.	1.50	.70
337	Lloyd McClendon	.05	.02
338	Dennis Lamp	.05	.02
339	Dave Clark	.05	.02
340	Fernando Valenzuela	.10	.05
341	Tom Foley	.05	.02
342	Alex Trevino	.05	.02
343	Frank Tanana	.05	.02
344	George Canale	.05	.02
345	Harold Baines	.10	.05
346	Jim Presley	.05	.02
347	Junior Felix	.05	.02
348	Gary Wayne	.05	.02
349	Steve Finley	.20	.09
350	Bret Saberhagen	.05	.02
351	Roger Craig MG	.05	.02
352	Bryn Smith	.05	.02
353	Sandy Alomar Jr.	.20	.09
	(Not listed as Jr. on card front)		
354	Stan Belinda	.05	.02
355	Marty Barrett	.05	.02
356	Randy Ready	.05	.02
357	Dave West	.05	.02
358	Andres Thomas	.05	.02
359	Jimmy Jones	.05	.02
360	Paul Molitor	.20	.09
361	Randy McCament	.05	.02
362	Damon Berryhill	.05	.02
363	Dan Petry	.05	.02
364	Rolando Roomes	.05	.02
365	Ozzie Guillen	.05	.02
366	Mike Heath	.05	.02
367	Mike Morgan	.05	.02
368	Bill Doran	.05	.02
369	Todd Burns	.05	.02
370	Tim Wallach	.05	.02
371	Jimmy Key	.10	.05
372	Terry Kennedy	.05	.02
373	Alvin Davis	.05	.02
374	Steve Cummings	.05	.02
375	Dwight Evans	.10	.05
376	Checklist 3 UER	.05	.02
	(Higuera misalphabetized in Brewer list)		
377	Mickey Weston	.05	.02
378	Luis Salazar	.05	.02
379	Steve Rosenberg	.05	.02
380	Dave Winfield	.20	.09
381	Frank Robinson MG	.15	.07
382	Jeff Musselman	.05	.02
383	John Morris	.05	.02
384	Pat Combs	.05	.02
385	Fred McGriff AS	.10	.05
386	Julio Franco AS	.05	.02
387	Wade Boggs AS	.10	.05
388	Cal Ripken AS	.40	.18
389	Robin Yount AS	.10	.05
390	Ruben Sierra AS	.05	.02
391	Kirby Puckett AS	.20	.09
392	Carlton Fisk AS	.10	.05
393	Bret Saberhagen AS	.05	.02
394	Jeff Ballard AS	.05	.02
395	Jeff Russell AS	.05	.02
396	A.Bartlett Giamatti COMM MEM	.20	.09
397	Will Clark AS	.20	.09
398	Ryne Sandberg AS	.20	.09
399	Howard Johnson AS	.05	.02
400	Ozzie Smith AS	.20	.09
401	Kevin Mitchell AS	.05	.02

402	Eric Davis AS	.05	.02
403	Tony Gwynn AS	.25	.11
404	Craig Biggio AS	.10	.05
405	Mike Scott AS	.05	.02
406	Joe Magrane AS	.05	.02
407	Mark Davis AS	.05	.02
408	Trevor Wilson	.05	.02
409	Tom Brunansky	.05	.02
410	Joe Boever	.05	.02
411	Ken Phelps	.05	.02
412	Jamie Moyer	.05	.02
413	Brian DuBois	.05	.02
414A	Frank Thomas FDP ERR (Name missing on card front)	1500.00	700.00
414B	Frank Thomas FDP COR	4.00	1.80
415	Shawon Dunston	.05	.02
416	Dave Johnson (P)	.05	.02
417	Jim Gantner	.05	.02
418	Tom Browning	.05	.02
419	Beau Allred	.05	.02
420	Carlton Fisk	.20	.09
421	Greg Minton	.05	.02
422	Pat Sheridan	.05	.02
423	Fred Toliver	.05	.02
424	Jerry Reuss	.05	.02
425	Bill Landrum	.05	.02
426	Jeff Hamilton UER (Stats say he fanned 197 times in 1987, but he only had 147 at bats)	.05	.02
427	Carmen Castillo	.05	.02
428	Steve Davis	.05	.02
429	Tom Kelly MG	.05	.02
430	Pete Incaviglia	.05	.02
431	Randy Johnson	.30	.14
432	Damaso Garcia	.05	.02
433	Steve Olin	.10	.05
434	Mark Carreon	.05	.02
435	Kevin Seitzer	.05	.02
436	Mel Hall	.05	.02
437	Les Lancaster	.05	.02
438	Greg Myers	.05	.02
439	Jeff Parrett	.05	.02
440	Alan Trammell	.15	.07
441	Bob Kipper	.05	.02
442	Jerry Browne	.05	.02
443	Cris Carpenter	.05	.02
444	Kyle Abbott FDP	.05	.02
445	Danny Jackson	.05	.02
446	Dan Pasqua	.05	.02
447	Atlee Hammaker	.05	.02
448	Greg Gagne	.05	.02
449	Dennis Rasmussen	.05	.02
450	Rickey Henderson	.20	.09
451	Mark Lemke	.05	.02
452	Luis DeLosSantos	.05	.02
453	Jody Davis	.05	.02
454	Jeff King	.10	.05
455	Jeffrey Leonard	.05	.02
456	Chris Gwynn	.05	.02
457	Gregg Jefferies	.05	.02
458	Bob McClure	.05	.02
459	Jim Lefebvre MG	.05	.02
460	Mike Scott	.05	.02
461	Carlos Martinez	.05	.02
462	Denny Walling	.05	.02
463	Drew Hall	.05	.02
464	Jerome Walton	.05	.02
465	Kevin Gross	.05	.02
466	Rance Mulliniks	.05	.02
467	Juan Nieves	.05	.02
468	Bill Ripken	.05	.02
469	John Kruk	.10	.05
470	Frank Viola	.05	.02
471	Mike Brumley	.05	.02
472	Jose Uribe	.05	.02
473	Joe Price	.05	.02
474	Rich Thompson	.05	.02
475	Bob Welch	.05	.02
476	Brad Komminsk	.05	.02
477	Willie Fraser	.05	.02
478	Mike LaValliere	.05	.02
479	Frank White	.10	.05
480	Sid Fernandez	.05	.02
481	Garry Templeton	.05	.02
482	Steve Carter	.05	.02
483	Alejandro Pena	.05	.02
484	Mike Fitzgerald	.05	.02
485	John Candelaria	.05	.02
486	Jeff Treadway	.05	.02
487	Steve Searcy	.05	.02
488	Ken Oberkfell	.05	.02
489	Nick Leyva MG	.05	.02
490	Dan Plesac	.05	.02
491	Dave Cochrane	.05	.02
492	Ron Oester	.05	.02
493	Jason Grimsley	.05	.02
494	Terry Puhl	.05	.02
495	Lee Smith	.10	.05
496	Cecil Espy UER ('88 stats have 3 SB's, should be 33)	.05	.02
497	Dave Schmidt	.05	.02
498	Rick Schu	.05	.02
499	Bill Long	.05	.02
500	Kevin Mitchell	.10	.05
501	Matt Young	.05	.02
502	Mitch Webster	.05	.02
503	Randy St.Claire	.05	.02
504	Tom O'Malley	.05	.02
505	Kelly Gruber	.05	.02
506	Tom Glavine	.20	.09
507	Gary Redus	.05	.02
508	Terry Leach	.05	.02
509	Tom Pagnozzi	.05	.02
510	Dwight Gooden	.10	.05
511	Clay Parker	.05	.02
512	Gary Pettis	.05	.02
513	Mark Eichhorn	.05	.02
514	Andy Allanson	.05	.02
515	Len Dykstra	.10	.05
516	Tim Leary	.05	.02
517	Roberto Alomar	.25	.11
518	Bill Krueger	.05	.02
519	Bucky Dent MG	.05	.02
520	Mitch Williams	.05	.02
521	Craig Worthington	.05	.02
522	Mike Dunne	.05	.02
523	Jay Bell	.10	.05
524	Daryl Boston	.05	.02
525	Wally Joyner	.10	.05
526	Checklist 4.	.05	.02
527	Ron Hassey	.05	.02
528	Kevin Wickander UER (Monthly scoreboard strikeout total was 2.2, that was his innings pitched total)	.05	.02
529	Greg A. Harris	.05	.02
530	Mark Langston	.05	.02
531	Ken Caminiti	.20	.09
532	Cecilio Guante	.05	.02
533	Tim Jones	.05	.02
534	Louie Meadows	.05	.02
535	John Smoltz	.20	.09
536	Bob Geren	.05	.02
537	Mark Grant	.05	.02
538	Bill Spiers UER (Photo actually George Canale)	.05	.02
539	Neal Heaton	.05	.02
540	Danny Tartabull	.05	.02
541	Pat Perry	.05	.02
542	Darren Daulton	.10	.05
543	Nelson Liriano	.05	.02
544	Dennis Boyd	.05	.02
545	Kevin McReynolds	.05	.02
546	Kevin Hickey	.05	.02
547	Jack Howell	.05	.02
548	Pat Clements	.05	.02
549	Don Zimmer MG	.05	.02
550	Julio Franco	.05	.02
551	Tim Crews	.05	.02
552	Mike(Miss.) Smith	.05	.02
553	Scott Scudder UER (Cedar Rap1ds)	.05	.02
554	Jay Buhner	.20	.09
555	Jack Morris	.10	.05
556	Gene Larkin	.05	.02
557	Jeff Innis	.05	.02
558	Rafael Ramirez	.05	.02
559	Andy McGaffigan	.05	.02
560	Steve Sax	.05	.02
561	Ken Dayley	.05	.02
562	Chad Kreuter	.05	.02
563	Alex Sanchez	.05	.02
564	Tyler Houston FDP	.20	.09
565	Scott Fletcher	.05	.02
566	Mark Knudson	.05	.02
567	Ron Gant	.10	.05
568	John Smiley	.05	.02
569	Ivan Calderon	.05	.02
570	Cal Ripken	.75	.35
571	Brett Butler	.10	.05
572	Greg W. Harris	.05	.02
573	Danny Heep	.05	.02
574	Bill Swift	.05	.02
575	Lance Parrish	.05	.02
576	Mike Dyer	.05	.02
577	Charlie Hayes	.05	.02
578	Joe Magrane	.05	.02
579	Art Howe MG	.05	.02
580	Joe Carter	.10	.05
581	Ken Griffey Sr.	.05	.02
582	Rick Honeycutt	.05	.02
583	Bruce Benedict	.05	.02
584	Phil Stephenson	.05	.02
585	Kal Daniels	.05	.02
586	Edwin Nunez	.05	.02
587	Lance Johnson	.05	.02
588	Rick Rhoden	.05	.02
589	Mike Aldrete	.05	.02
590	Ozzie Smith	.25	.11
591	Todd Stottlemyre	.05	.02
592	R.J. Reynolds	.05	.02
593	Scott Bradley	.05	.02
594	Luis Sojo	.05	.02
595	Greg Swindell	.05	.02
596	Jose DeJesus	.05	.02
597	Chris Bosio	.05	.02
598	Brady Anderson	.20	.09
599	Frank Williams	.05	.02
600	Darryl Strawberry	.10	.05
601	Luis Rivera	.05	.02
602	Scott Garrelts	.05	.02
603	Tony Armas	.05	.02
604	Ron Robinson	.05	.02
605	Mike Scioscia	.05	.02
606	Storm Davis	.05	.02
607	Steve Jeltz	.05	.02
608	Eric Anthony	.10	.05
609	Sparky Anderson MG	.10	.05
610	Pedro Guerrero	.05	.02
611	Walt Terrell	.05	.02
612	Dave Gallagher	.05	.02
613	Jeff Pico	.05	.02
614	Nelson Santovenia	.05	.02
615	Rob Deer	.05	.02
616	Brian Holman	.05	.02
617	Geronimo Berroa	.10	.05
618	Ed Whitson	.05	.02
619	Rob Ducey	.05	.02
620	Tony Castillo	.05	.02
621	Melido Perez	.05	.02
622	Sid Bream	.05	.02
623	Jim Corsi	.05	.02
624	Darrin Jackson	.05	.02
625	Roger McDowell	.05	.02
626	Bob Melvin	.05	.02
627	Jose Rijo	.05	.02
628	Candy Maldonado	.05	.02
629	Eric Hetzel	.05	.02
630	Gary Gaetti	.05	.02
631	John Wetteland	.20	.09
632	Scott Lusader	.05	.02
633	Dennis Cook	.05	.02
634	Luis Polonia	.05	.02
635	Brian Downing	.05	.02
636	Jesse Orosco	.05	.02
637	Craig Reynolds	.05	.02
638	Jeff Montgomery	.10	.05
639	Tony LaRussa MG	.10	.05
640	Rick Sutcliffe	.05	.02
641	Doug Strange	.05	.02
642	Jack Armstrong	.05	.02
643	Alfredo Griffin	.05	.02
644	Paul Assenmacher	.05	.02

	MINT	NRMT

□ 645 Jose Oquendo .05 .02
□ 646 Checklist 5 .05 .02
□ 647 Rex Hudler .05 .02
□ 648 Jim Clancy .05 .02
□ 649 Dan Murphy .05 .02
□ 650 Mike Witt .05 .02
□ 651 Rafael Santana .05 .02
□ 652 Mike Boddicker .05 .02
□ 653 John Moses .05 .02
□ 654 Paul Coleman FDP .05 .02
□ 655 Gregg Olson .05 .02
□ 656 Mackey Sasser .05 .02
□ 657 Terry Mulholland .05 .02
□ 658 Donell Nixon .05 .02
□ 659 Greg Cadaret .05 .02
□ 660 Vince Coleman .05 .02
□ 661 Dick Howser TBC '85 .05
     UER (Seaver's 300th on 7/11/85, should be 8/4/85)
□ 662 Mike Schmidt TBC '80 .20 .09
□ 663 Fred Lynn TBC '75 .05 .02
□ 664 Johnny Bench TBC '70 .20 .09
□ 665 Sandy Koufax TBC '65 .25 .11
□ 666 Brian Fisher .05 .02
□ 667 Curt Wilkerson .05 .02
□ 668 Joe Oliver .05 .02
□ 669 Tom Lasorda MG .20 .09
□ 670 Dennis Eckersley .10 .05
□ 671 Bob Boone .10 .05
□ 672 Roy Smith .05 .02
□ 673 Joey Meyer .05 .02
□ 674 Spike Owen .05 .02
□ 675 Jim Abbott .10 .05
□ 676 Randy Kutcher .05 .02
□ 677 Jay Tibbs .05 .02
□ 678 Kirt Manwaring UER .05
     ('88 Phoenix stats repeated)
□ 679 Gary Ward .05 .02
□ 680 Howard Johnson .05 .02
□ 681 Mike Schooler .05 .02
□ 682 Dann Bilardello .05 .02
□ 683 Kenny Rogers .05 .02
□ 684 Julio Machado .05 .02
□ 685 Tony Fernandez .05 .02
□ 686 Carmelo Martinez .05 .02
□ 687 Tim Birtsas .05 .02
□ 688 Milt Thompson .05 .02
□ 689 Rich Yett .05 .02
□ 690 Mark McGwire .40 .18
□ 691 Chuck Cary .05 .02
□ 692 Sammy Sosa .75 .35
□ 693 Calvin Schiraldi .05 .02
□ 694 Mike Stanton .05 .02
□ 695 Tom Henke .05 .02
□ 696 B.J. Surhoff .10 .05
□ 697 Mike Davis .05 .02
□ 698 Omar Vizquel .20 .09
□ 699 Jim Leyland MG .05 .02
□ 700 Kirby Puckett .40 .18
□ 701 Bernie Williams .75 .35
□ 702 Tony Phillips .05 .02
□ 703 Jeff Brantley .05 .02
□ 704 Chip Hale .05 .02
□ 705 Claudell Washington .05 .02
□ 706 Geno Petralli .05 .02
□ 707 Luis Aquino .05 .02
□ 708 Larry Sheets .05 .02
□ 709 Juan Berenguer .05 .02
□ 710 Von Hayes .05 .02
□ 711 Rick Aguilera .10 .05
□ 712 Todd Benzinger .05 .02
□ 713 Tim Drummond .05 .02
□ 714 Marquis Grissom .40 .18
□ 715 Greg Maddux .60 .25
□ 716 Steve Balboni .05 .02
□ 717 Ron Karkovice .05 .02
□ 718 Gary Sheffield .25 .11
□ 719 Wally Whitehurst .05 .02
□ 720 Andres Galarraga .20 .09
□ 721 Lee Mazzilli .05 .02
□ 722 Felix Fermin .05 .02
□ 723 Jeff D. Robinson .05 .02
□ 724 Juan Bell .05 .02
□ 725 Terry Pendleton .10 .05

□ 726 Gene Nelson .05 .02
□ 727 Pat Tabler .05 .02
□ 728 Jim Acker .05 .02
□ 729 Bobby Valentine MG .05 .02
□ 730 Tony Gwynn .50 .23
□ 731 Don Carman .05 .02
□ 732 Ernest Riles .05 .02
□ 733 John Dopson .05 .02
□ 734 Kevin Elster .05 .02
□ 735 Charlie Hough .05 .02
□ 736 Rick Dempsey .05 .02
□ 737 Chris Sabo .05 .02
□ 738 Gene Harris .05 .02
□ 739 Dale Sveum .05 .02
□ 740 Jesse Barfield .05 .02
□ 741 Steve Wilson .05 .02
□ 742 Ernie Whitt .05 .02
□ 743 Tom Candiotti .05 .02
□ 744 Kelly Mann .05 .02
□ 745 Hubie Brooks .05 .02
□ 746 Dave Smith .05 .02
□ 747 Randy Bush .05 .02
□ 748 Doyle Alexander .05 .02
□ 749 Mark Parent UER .05 .02
     ('87 BA .80, should be .080)
□ 750 Dale Murphy .20 .09
□ 751 Steve Lyons .05 .02
□ 752 Tom Gordon .05 .02
□ 753 Chris Speier .05 .02
□ 754 Bob Walk .05 .02
□ 755 Rafael Palmeiro .20 .09
□ 756 Ken Howell .05 .02
□ 757 Larry Walker 1.00 .45
□ 758 Mark Thurmond .05 .02
□ 759 Tom Trebelhorn MG .05 .02
□ 760 Wade Boggs .20 .09
□ 761 Mike Jackson .05 .02
□ 762 Doug Dascenzo .05 .02
□ 763 Dennis Martinez .10 .05
□ 764 Tim Teufel .05 .02
□ 765 Chili Davis .10 .05
□ 766 Brian Meyer .05 .02
□ 767 Tracy Jones .05 .02
□ 768 Chuck Crim .05 .02
□ 769 Greg Hibbard .05 .02
□ 770 Cory Snyder .05 .02
□ 771 Pete Smith .05 .02
□ 772 Jeff Reed .05 .02
□ 773 Dave Leiper .05 .02
□ 774 Ben McDonald .15 .07
□ 775 Andy Van Slyke .10 .05
□ 776 Charlie Leibrandt .05 .02
□ 777 Tim Laudner .05 .02
□ 778 Mike Jeffcoat .05 .02
□ 779 Lloyd Moseby .05 .02
□ 780 Orel Hershiser .10 .05
□ 781 Mario Diaz .05 .02
□ 782 Jose Alvarez .05 .02
□ 783 Checklist 6 .05 .02
□ 784 Scott Bailes .05 .02
□ 785 Jim Rice .10 .05
□ 786 Eric King .05 .02
□ 787 Rene Gonzales .05 .02
□ 788 Frank DiPino .05 .02
□ 789 John Wathan MG .05 .02
□ 790 Gary Carter .20 .09
□ 791 Alvaro Espinoza .05 .02
□ 792 Gerald Perry .05 .02

1990 Topps Traded

The 1990 Topps Traded Set was the tenth consecutive year Topps issued a 132-card standard-size set at the end of the year. For the first time, Topps not only issued the set in factory set form but also distributed (on a significant basis) the set via 7-card wax packs. Unlike the factory set cards (which feature the whiter paper stock typical of the previous years Traded sets), the wax pack cards feature gray

paper stock. Gray and white stock cards are equally valued. This set was arranged alphabetically by player and includes a mix of traded players and rookies for whom Topps did not include a card in the regular set. The key Rookie Cards in this set are Carlos Baerga, Travis Fryman, Todd Hundley and Dave Justice.

	MINT	NRMT
COMPLETE SET (132)	3.00	1.35
COMMON CARD (1T-132T)	.05	.02
MINOR STARS	.10	.05
UNLISTED STARS	.20	.09

*GRAY AND WHITE BACKS: SAME VALUE

□ 1T Darrel Akerfelds .05 .02
□ 2T Sandy Alomar Jr. .20 .09
□ 3T Brad Arnsberg .05 .02
□ 4T Steve Avery .75 .35
□ 5T Wally Backman .05 .02
□ 6T Carlos Baerga .25 .11
□ 7T Kevin Bass .05 .02
□ 8T Willie Blair .05 .02
□ 9T Mike Blowers .20 .09
□ 10T Shawn Boskie .05 .02
□ 11T Daryl Boston .05 .02
□ 12T Dennis Boyd .05 .02
□ 13T Glenn Braggs .05 .02
□ 14T Hubie Brooks .05 .02
□ 15T Tom Brunansky .05 .02
□ 16T John Burkett .10 .05
□ 17T Casey Candaele .05 .02
□ 18T John Candelaria .05 .02
□ 19T Gary Carter .20 .09
□ 20T Joe Carter .10 .05
□ 21T Rick Cerone .05 .02
□ 22T Scott Coolbaugh .05 .02
□ 23T Bobby Cox MG .05 .02
□ 24T Mark Davis .05 .02
□ 25T Storm Davis .05 .02
□ 26T Edgar Diaz .05 .02
□ 27T Wayne Edwards .05 .02
□ 28T Mark Eichhorn .05 .02
□ 29T Scott Erickson .25 .11
□ 30T Nick Esasky .05 .02
□ 31T Cecil Fielder .10 .05
□ 32T John Franco .10 .05
□ 33T Travis Fryman .40 .18
□ 34T Bill Gullickson .05 .02
□ 35T Darryl Hamilton .05 .02
□ 36T Mike Harkey .05 .02
□ 37T Bud Harrelson MG .05 .02
□ 38T Billy Hatcher .05 .02
□ 39T Keith Hernandez .10 .05
□ 40T Joe Hesketh .05 .02
□ 41T Dave Hollins .20 .09
□ 42T Sam Horn .05 .02
□ 43T Steve Howard .05 .02
□ 44T Todd Hundley .40 .18
□ 45T Jeff Huson .05 .02
□ 46T Chris James .05 .02
□ 47T Stan Javier .05 .02
□ 48T Dave Justice .75 .35
□ 49T Jeff Kaiser .05 .02

		MINT	NRMT
☐ 50T	Dana Kiecker	.05	.02
☐ 51T	Joe Klink	.05	.02
☐ 52T	Brent Knackert	.05	.02
☐ 53T	Brad Komminsk	.05	.02
☐ 54T	Mark Langston	.05	.02
☐ 55T	Tim Layana	.05	.02
☐ 56T	Rick Leach	.05	.02
☐ 57T	Terry Leach	.05	.02
☐ 58T	Tim Leary	.05	.02
☐ 59T	Craig Lefferts	.05	.02
☐ 60T	Charlie Leibrandt	.05	.02
☐ 61T	Jim Leyritz	.20	.09
☐ 62T	Fred Lynn	.05	.02
☐ 63T	Kevin Maas	.10	.05
☐ 64T	Shane Mack	.05	.02
☐ 65T	Candy Maldonado	.05	.02
☐ 66T	Fred Manrique	.05	.02
☐ 67T	Mike Marshall	.05	.02
☐ 68T	Carmelo Martinez	.05	.02
☐ 69T	John Marzano	.05	.02
☐ 70T	Ben McDonald	.05	.02
☐ 71T	Jack McDowell	.05	.02
☐ 72T	John McNamara MG	.05	.02
☐ 73T	Orlando Mercado	.05	.02
☐ 74T	Stump Merrill MG	.05	.02
☐ 75T	Alan Mills	.05	.02
☐ 76T	Hal Morris	.05	.02
☐ 77T	Lloyd Moseby	.05	.02
☐ 78T	Randy Myers	.10	.05
☐ 79T	Tim Naehring	.20	.09
☐ 80T	Junior Noboa	.05	.02
☐ 81T	Matt Nokes	.05	.02
☐ 82T	Pete O'Brien	.05	.02
☐ 83T	John Olerud	.20	.09
☐ 84T	Greg Olson	.05	.02
☐ 85T	Junior Ortiz	.05	.02
☐ 86T	Dave Parker	.10	.05
☐ 87T	Rick Parker	.05	.02
☐ 88T	Bob Patterson	.05	.02
☐ 89T	Alejandro Pena	.05	.02
☐ 90T	Tony Pena	.05	.02
☐ 91T	Pascual Perez	.05	.02
☐ 92T	Gerald Perry	.05	.02
☐ 93T	Dan Petry	.05	.02
☐ 94T	Gary Pettis	.05	.02
☐ 95T	Tony Phillips	.05	.02
☐ 96T	Lou Piniella MG	.10	.05
☐ 97T	Luis Polonia	.05	.05
☐ 98T	Jim Presley	.05	.02
☐ 99T	Scott Radinsky	.05	.02
☐ 100T	Willie Randolph	.10	.05
☐ 101T	Jeff Reardon	.10	.05
☐ 102T	Greg Riddoch MG	.05	.02
☐ 103T	Jeff Robinson	.05	.02
☐ 104T	Ron Robinson	.05	.02
☐ 105T	Kevin Romine	.05	.02
☐ 106T	Scott Ruskin	.05	.02
☐ 107T	John Russell	.05	.02
☐ 108T	Bill Sampen	.05	.02
☐ 109T	Juan Samuel	.05	.02
☐ 110T	Scott Sanderson	.05	.02
☐ 111T	Jack Savage	.05	.02
☐ 112T	Dave Schmidt	.05	.02
☐ 113T	Red Schoendienst MG	.20	.09
☐ 114T	Terry Shumpert	.05	.02
☐ 115T	Matt Sinatro	.05	.02
☐ 116T	Don Slaught	.05	.02
☐ 117T	Bryn Smith	.05	.02
☐ 118T	Lee Smith	.10	.05
☐ 119T	Paul Sorrento	.20	.09
☐ 120T	Franklin Stubbs UER	.05	.02
	('84 says '99 and has the same stats as '89, '83 stats are missing)		
☐ 121T	Russ Swan	.05	.02
☐ 122T	Bob Tewksbury	.05	.02
☐ 123T	Wayne Tolleson	.05	.02
☐ 124T	John Tudor	.05	.02
☐ 125T	Randy Veres	.05	.02
☐ 126T	Hector Villanueva	.05	.02
☐ 127T	Mitch Webster	.05	.02
☐ 128T	Ernie Whitt	.05	.02
☐ 129T	Frank Wills	.05	.02
☐ 130T	Dave Winfield	.20	.09
☐ 131T	Matt Young	.05	.02
☐ 132T	Checklist 1T-132T	.05	.02

1991 Topps

This set marks Topps tenth consecutive year of issuing a 792-card standard-size set. Cards were primarily issued in wax packs, rack packs and factory sets. The fronts feature a full color player photo with a white border. Topps also commemorated their fortieth anniversary by including a "Topps 40" logo on the front and back of each card. Virtually all of the cards have been discovered without the 40th logo on the back. Subsets include Record Breakers (2-8) and All-Stars (386-407). In addition, First Draft Picks and Future Stars subset cards are scattered throughout the set. The key Rookie Cards include Chipper Jones and Brian McRae. As a special promotion Topps inserted (randomly) in their wax packs one of every previous card they ever issued.

		MINT	NRMT
COMPLETE SET (792)		15.00	6.75
COMP.FACT.SET (792)		15.00	6.75
COMMON CARD (1-792)		.05	.02
MINOR STARS		.10	.05
UNLISTED STARS		.20	.09
SUBSET CARDS HALF VALUE OF BASE CARDS			
☐ 1	Nolan Ryan	.75	.35
☐ 2	George Brett RB	.20	.09
	Batting Title, 3 decades		
☐ 3	Carlton Fisk RB	.10	.05
	Catcher HR Record		
☐ 4	Kevin Maas RB	.05	.02
	Quickest to 10 HR's		
☐ 5	Cal Ripken RB	.40	.18
	Most cons. errorless games		
☐ 6	Nolan Ryan RB	.40	.18
	Oldest pitcher, no-hitter		
☐ 7	Ryne Sandberg RB	.20	.09
	Most cons. errorless games		
☐ 8	Bobby Thigpen RB	.05	.02
	Most saves, season		
☐ 9	Darrin Fletcher	.05	.02
☐ 10	Gregg Olson	.05	.02
☐ 11	Roberto Kelly	.05	.02
☐ 12	Paul Assenmacher	.05	.02
☐ 13	Mariano Duncan	.05	.02
☐ 14	Dennis Lamp	.05	.02
☐ 15	Von Hayes	.05	.02
☐ 16	Mike Heath	.05	.02
☐ 17	Jeff Brantley	.05	.02
☐ 18	Nelson Liriano	.05	.02
☐ 19	Jeff D. Robinson	.05	.02
☐ 20	Pedro Guerrero	.05	.02
☐ 21	Joe Morgan MG	.05	.02
☐ 22	Storm Davis	.05	.02
☐ 23	Jim Gantner	.05	.02
☐ 24	Dave Martinez	.05	.02

		MINT	NRMT
☐ 25	Tim Belcher	.05	.02
☐ 26	Luis Sojo UER	.05	.02
	(Born in Barquisimento, not Carquis)		
☐ 27	Bobby Witt	.05	.02
☐ 28	Alvaro Espinoza	.05	.02
☐ 29	Bob Walk	.05	.02
☐ 30	Gregg Jefferies	.05	.02
☐ 31	Colby Ward	.05	.02
☐ 32	Mike Simms	.05	.02
☐ 33	Barry Jones	.05	.02
☐ 34	Atlee Hammaker	.05	.02
☐ 35	Greg Maddux	.60	.25
☐ 36	Donnie Hill	.05	.02
☐ 37	Tom Bolton	.05	.02
☐ 38	Scott Bradley	.05	.02
☐ 39	Jim Neidlinger	.05	.02
☐ 40	Kevin Mitchell	.10	.05
☐ 41	Ken Dayley	.05	.02
☐ 42	Chris Hoiles	.05	.02
☐ 43	Roger McDowell	.05	.02
☐ 44	Mike Felder	.05	.02
☐ 45	Chris Sabo	.05	.02
☐ 46	Tim Drummond	.05	.02
☐ 47	Brook Jacoby	.05	.02
☐ 48	Dennis Boyd	.05	.02
☐ 49A	Pat Borders ERR	.20	
	(40 steals at Kinston in '86)		
☐ 49B	Pat Borders COR	.05	.02
	(0 steals at Kinston in '86)		
☐ 50	Bob Welch	.05	.02
☐ 51	Art Howe MG	.05	.02
☐ 52	Francisco Oliveras	.05	.02
☐ 53	Mike Sharperson UER	.05	.02
	(Born in 1961, not 1960)		
☐ 54	Gary Mielke	.05	.02
☐ 55	Jeffrey Leonard	.05	.02
☐ 56	Jeff Parrett	.05	.02
☐ 57	Jack Howell	.05	.02
☐ 58	Mel Stottlemyre Jr.	.05	.02
☐ 59	Eric Yelding	.05	.02
☐ 60	Frank Viola	.05	.02
☐ 61	Stan Javier	.05	.02
☐ 62	Lee Guetterman	.05	.02
☐ 63	Milt Thompson	.05	.02
☐ 64	Tom Herr	.05	.02
☐ 65	Bruce Hurst	.05	.02
☐ 66	Terry Kennedy	.05	.02
☐ 67	Rick Honeycutt	.05	.02
☐ 68	Gary Sheffield	.20	.09
☐ 69	Steve Wilson	.05	.02
☐ 70	Ellis Burks	.10	.05
☐ 71	Jim Acker	.05	.02
☐ 72	Junior Ortiz	.05	.02
☐ 73	Craig Worthington	.05	.02
☐ 74	Shane Andrews	.05	.02
☐ 75	Jack Morris	.10	.05
☐ 76	Jerry Browne	.05	.02
☐ 77	Drew Hall	.05	.02
☐ 78	Geno Petralli	.05	.02
☐ 79	Frank Thomas	1.50	.70
☐ 80A	Fernando Valenzuela	.10	
	ERR (104 earned runs in '90 tied for league lead)		
☐ 80B	Fernando Valenzuela	.10	.05
	COR (104 earned runs in '90 led league, 20 CG's in 1986 now italicized)		
☐ 81	Cito Gaston MG	.05	.02
☐ 82	Tom Glavine	.20	.09
☐ 83	Daryl Boston	.05	.02
☐ 84	Bob McClure	.05	.02
☐ 85	Jesse Barfield	.05	.02
☐ 86	Les Lancaster	.05	.02
☐ 87	Tracy Jones	.05	.02
☐ 88	Bob Tewksbury	.05	.02
☐ 89	Darren Daulton	.10	.05
☐ 90	Danny Tartabull	.05	.05
☐ 91	Greg Colbrunn	.05	.02
☐ 92	Danny Jackson	.05	.02
☐ 93	Ivan Calderon	.05	.02
☐ 94	John Dopson	.05	.02

☐ 95 Paul Molitor	.20		.09
☐ 96 Trevor Wilson	.05		.02
☐ 97A Brady Anderson ERR	.25		.11
(September, 2 RBI and			
3 hits, should be 3			
RBI and 14 hits)			
☐ 97B Brady Anderson COR	.20		.09
☐ 98 Sergio Valdez	.05		.02
☐ 99 Chris Gwynn	.05		
☐ 100 Don Mattingly COR	.30		.14
(101 hits in 1990)			
☐ 100A Don Mattingly ERR	1.00		.45
(10 hits in 1990)			
☐ 101 Rob Ducey	.05		.02
☐ 102 Gene Larkin	.05		.02
☐ 103 Tim Costo	.05		.02
☐ 104 Don Robinson	.05		.02
☐ 105 Kevin McReynolds	.05		.02
☐ 106 Ed Nunez	.05		.02
☐ 107 Luis Polonia	.05		.02
☐ 108 Matt Young	.05		.02
☐ 109 Greg Riddoch MG	.05		.02
☐ 110 Tom Henke	.05		.02
☐ 111 Andres Thomas	.05		.02
☐ 112 Frank DiPino	.05		.02
☐ 113 Carl Everett	.15		.07
☐ 114 Lance Dickson	.05		.02
☐ 115 Hubie Brooks	.05		.02
☐ 116 Mark Davis	.05		.02
☐ 117 Dion James	.05		.02
☐ 118 Tom Edens	.05		.02
☐ 119 Carl Nichols	.05		.02
☐ 120 Joe Carter	.10		.05
☐ 121 Eric King	.05		.02
☐ 122 Paul O'Neill	.10		.05
☐ 123 Greg A. Harris	.05		.02
☐ 124 Randy Bush	.05		.02
☐ 125 Steve Bedrosian	.05		.02
☐ 126 Bernard Gilkey	.10		.05
☐ 127 Joe Price	.05		.02
☐ 128 Travis Fryman	.20		.09
(Front has SS			
back has SS-3B)			
☐ 129 Mark Eichhorn	.05		.02
☐ 130 Ozzie Smith	.25		.11
☐ 131A Checklist 1 ERR	.20		.09
727 Phil Bradley			
☐ 131B Checklist 1 COR	.05		
717 Phil Bradley			
☐ 132 Jamie Quirk	.05		.02
☐ 133 Greg Briley	.05		.02
☐ 134 Kevin Elster	.05		.02
☐ 135 Jerome Walton	.05		.02
☐ 136 Dave Schmidt	.05		.02
☐ 137 Randy Ready	.05		.02
☐ 138 Jamie Moyer	.05		.02
☐ 139 Jeff Treadway	.05		.02
☐ 140 Fred McGriff	.20		.09
☐ 141 Nick Leyva MG	.05		.02
☐ 142 Curt Wilkerson	.05		.02
☐ 143 John Smiley	.05		.02
☐ 144 Dave Henderson	.05		.02
☐ 145 Lou Whitaker	.10		.05
☐ 146 Dan Plesac	.05		.02
☐ 147 Carlos Baerga	.10		.05
☐ 148 Rey Palacios	.05		.02
☐ 149 Al Osuna UER	.05		
(Shown throwing right,			
but bio says lefty)			
☐ 150 Cal Ripken	.75		.35
☐ 151 Tom Browning	.05		.02
☐ 152 Mickey Hatcher	.05		.02
☐ 153 Bryan Harvey	.05		.02
☐ 154 Jay Buhner	.20		.09
☐ 155A Dwight Evans ERR	.20		.09
(Led league with			
162 games in '82)			
☐ 155B Dwight Evans COR	.10		.05
(Tied for lead with			
162 games in '82)			
☐ 156 Carlos Martinez	.05		.02
☐ 157 John Smoltz	.20		.09
☐ 158 Jose Uribe	.05		.02
☐ 159 Joe Boever	.05		
☐ 160 Vince Coleman UER	.05		.02
(Wrong birth year,			

born 9/22/60)			
☐ 161 Tim Leary	.05		.02
☐ 162 Ozzie Canseco	.05		.02
☐ 163 Dave Johnson	.05		.02
☐ 164 Edgar Diaz	.05		.02
☐ 165 Sandy Alomar Jr.	.15		.07
☐ 166 Harold Baines	.10		.05
☐ 167A Randy Tomlin ERR	.20		.09
(Harrisburg)			
☐ 167B Randy Tomlin COR	.05		.02
(Harrisburg)			
☐ 168 John Olerud	.10		.05
☐ 169 Luis Aquino	.05		.02
☐ 170 Carlton Fisk	.20		.09
☐ 171 Tony LaRussa MG	.10		.05
☐ 172 Pete Incaviglia	.05		.02
☐ 173 Jason Grimsley	.05		.02
☐ 174 Ken Caminiti	.20		.09
☐ 175 Jack Armstrong	.05		.02
☐ 176 John Orton	.05		.02
☐ 177 Reggie Harris	.05		.02
☐ 178 Dave Valle	.05		.02
☐ 179 Pete Harnisch	.05		.02
☐ 180 Tony Gwynn	.50		.23
☐ 181 Duane Ward	.05		.02
☐ 182 Junior Noboa	.05		.02
☐ 183 Clay Parker	.05		.02
☐ 184 Gary Green	.05		.02
☐ 185 Joe Magrane	.05		.02
☐ 186 Rod Booker	.05		.02
☐ 187 Greg Cadaret	.05		.02
☐ 188 Damon Berryhill	.05		.02
☐ 189 Daryl Irvine	.05		.02
☐ 190 Matt Williams	.20		.09
☐ 191 Willie Blair	.05		.02
☐ 192 Rob Deer	.05		.02
☐ 193 Felix Fermin	.05		.02
☐ 194 Xavier Hernandez	.05		.02
☐ 195 Wally Joyner	.10		.05
☐ 196 Jim Vatcher	.05		.02
☐ 197 Chris Nabholz	.05		.02
☐ 198 R.J. Reynolds	.05		.02
☐ 199 Mike Hartley	.05		.02
☐ 200 Darryl Strawberry	.10		.05
☐ 201 Tom Kelly MG	.05		.02
☐ 202 Jim Leyritz	.05		.02
☐ 203 Gene Harris	.05		.02
☐ 204 Herm Winningham	.05		.02
☐ 205 Mike Perez	.05		.02
☐ 206 Carlos Quintana	.05		.02
☐ 207 Gary Wayne	.05		.02
☐ 208 Willie Wilson	.05		.02
☐ 209 Ken Howell	.05		.02
☐ 210 Lance Parrish	.05		.02
☐ 211 Brian Barnes	.05		.02
☐ 212 Steve Finley	.20		.09
☐ 213 Frank Wills	.05		.02
☐ 214 Joe Girardi	.05		.02
☐ 215 Dave Smith	.05		.02
☐ 216 Greg Gagne	.05		.02
☐ 217 Chris Bosio	.05		.02
☐ 218 Rick Parker	.05		.02
☐ 219 Jack McDowell	.05		.02
☐ 220 Tim Wallach	.05		.02
☐ 221 Don Slaught	.05		.02
☐ 222 Brian McRae	.20		.09
☐ 223 Allan Anderson	.05		.02
☐ 224 Juan Gonzalez	.75		.35
☐ 225 Randy Johnson	.25		.11
☐ 226 Alfredo Griffin	.05		.02
☐ 227 Steve Avery UER	.05		.02
(Pitched 13 games for			
Durham in 1989, not 2)			
☐ 228 Rex Hudler	.05		.02
☐ 229 Rance Mulliniks	.05		.02
☐ 230 Sid Fernandez	.05		.02
☐ 231 Doug Rader MG	.05		.02
☐ 232 Jose DeJesus	.05		.02
☐ 233 Al Leiter	.05		.02
☐ 234 Scott Erickson	.10		.05
☐ 235 Dave Parker	.05		.02
☐ 236A Frank Tanana ERR	.10		.05
(Tied for lead with			
269 K's in '75)			
☐ 236B Frank Tanana COR	.05		.02
(Led league with			

269 K's in '75)			
☐ 237 Rick Cerone	.05		.02
☐ 238 Mike Dunne	.05		.02
☐ 239 Darren Lewis	.05		.02
☐ 240 Mike Scott	.05		.02
☐ 241 Dave Clark UER	.05		.02
(Career totals 19 HR			
and 5 3B, should			
be 22 and 3)			
☐ 242 Mike LaCoss	.05		.02
☐ 243 Lance Johnson	.05		.02
☐ 244 Mike Jeffcoat	.05		.02
☐ 245 Kal Daniels	.05		.02
☐ 246 Kevin Wickander	.05		.02
☐ 247 Jody Reed	.05		.02
☐ 248 Tom Gordon	.05		.02
☐ 249 Bob Melvin	.05		.02
☐ 250 Dennis Eckersley	.10		.05
☐ 251 Mark Lemke	.05		.02
☐ 252 Mel Rojas	.20		.09
☐ 253 Garry Templeton	.05		.02
☐ 254 Shawn Boskie	.05		.02
☐ 255 Brian Downing	.05		.02
☐ 256 Greg Hibbard	.05		.02
☐ 257 Tom O'Malley	.05		.02
☐ 258 Chris Hammond	.05		.02
☐ 259 Hensley Meulens	.05		.02
☐ 260 Harold Reynolds	.05		.02
☐ 261 Bud Harrelson MG	.05		.02
☐ 262 Tim Jones	.05		.02
☐ 263 Checklist 2	.05		.02
☐ 264 Dave Hollins	.05		.02
☐ 265 Mark Gubicza	.05		.02
☐ 266 Carmelo Castillo	.05		.02
☐ 267 Mark Knudson	.05		.02
☐ 268 Tom Brookens	.05		.02
☐ 269 Joe Hesketh	.05		.02
☐ 270 Mark McGwire COR	.40		.18
(1987 Slugging Pctg.			
listed as .618)			
☐ 270A Mark McGwire ERR	.50		.23
(1987 Slugging Pctg.			
listed as 618)			
☐ 271 Omar Olivares	.05		.02
☐ 272 Jeff King	.10		.05
☐ 273 Johnny Ray	.05		.02
☐ 274 Ken Williams	.05		.02
☐ 275 Alan Trammell	.15		.07
☐ 276 Bill Swift	.05		.02
☐ 277 Scott Coolbaugh	.05		.02
☐ 278 Alex Fernandez UER	.10		.05
(No '90 White Sox stats)			
☐ 279A Jose Gonzalez ERR	.05		.02
(Photo actually			
Billy Bean)			
☐ 279B Jose Gonzalez COR	.05		.02
☐ 280 Bret Saberhagen	.05		.02
☐ 281 Larry Sheets	.05		.02
☐ 282 Don Carman	.05		.02
☐ 283 Marquis Grissom	.20		.09
☐ 284 Billy Spiers	.05		.02
☐ 285 Jim Abbott	.05		.02
☐ 286 Ken Oberkfell	.05		.02
☐ 287 Mark Grant	.05		.02
☐ 288 Derrick May	.05		.02
☐ 289 Tim Birtsas	.05		.02
☐ 290 Steve Sax	.05		.02
☐ 291 John Wathan MG	.05		.02
☐ 292 Bud Black	.05		.02
☐ 293 Jay Bell	.10		.05
☐ 294 Mike Moore	.05		.02
☐ 295 Rafael Palmeiro	.20		.09
☐ 296 Mark Williamson	.05		.02
☐ 297 Manny Lee	.05		.02
☐ 298 Omar Vizquel	.20		.09
☐ 299 Scott Radinsky	.05		.02
☐ 300 Kirby Puckett	.40		.18
☐ 301 Steve Farr	.05		.02
☐ 302 Tim Teufel	.05		.02
☐ 303 Mike Boddicker	.05		.02
☐ 304 Kevin Reimer	.05		.02
☐ 305 Mike Scioscia	.05		.02
☐ 306A Lonnie Smith ERR	.20		.09
(136 games in '90)			
☐ 306B Lonnie Smith COR	.05		.02
(135 games in '90)			

☐ 307	Andy Benes	.10	.05
☐ 308	Tom Pagnozzi	.05	.02
☐ 309	Norm Charlton	.05	.02
☐ 310	Gary Carter	.20	.09
☐ 311	Jeff Pico	.05	.02
☐ 312	Charlie Hayes	.05	.02
☐ 313	Ron Robinson	.05	.02
☐ 314	Gary Pettis	.05	.02
☐ 315	Roberto Alomar	.20	.09
☐ 316	Gene Nelson	.05	.02
☐ 317	Mike Fitzgerald	.05	.02
☐ 318	Rick Aguilera	.10	.05
☐ 319	Jeff McKnight	.05	.02
☐ 320	Tony Fernandez	.05	.02
☐ 321	Bob Rodgers MG	.05	.02
☐ 322	Terry Shumpert	.05	.02
☐ 323	Cory Snyder	.05	.02
☐ 324A	Ron Kittle ERR	.20	.09
	(Set another standard ...)		
☐ 324B	Ron Kittle COR	.05	.02
	(Tied another standard ...)		
☐ 325	Brett Butler	.10	.05
☐ 326	Ken Patterson	.05	.02
☐ 327	Ron Hassey	.05	.02
☐ 328	Walt Terrell	.05	.02
☐ 329	Dave Justice UER	.25	.11
	(Drafted third round on card, should say fourth pick)		
☐ 330	Dwight Gooden	.10	.05
☐ 331	Eric Anthony	.05	.02
☐ 332	Kenny Rogers	.05	.02
☐ 333	Chipper Jones FDP	3.00	1.35
☐ 334	Todd Benzinger	.05	.02
☐ 335	Mitch Williams	.05	.02
☐ 336	Matt Nokes	.05	.02
☐ 337A	Keith Comstock ERR	.20	.09
	(Cubs logo on front)		
☐ 337B	Keith Comstock COR	.05	.02
	(Mariners logo on front)		
☐ 338	Luis Rivera	.05	.02
☐ 339	Larry Walker	.30	.14
☐ 340	Ramon Martinez	.10	.05
☐ 341	John Moses	.05	.02
☐ 342	Mickey Morandini	.05	.02
☐ 343	Jose Oquendo	.05	.02
☐ 344	Jeff Russell	.05	.02
☐ 345	Len Dykstra	.10	.05
☐ 346	Jesse Orosco	.05	.02
☐ 347	Greg Vaughn	.05	.02
☐ 348	Todd Stottlemyre	.05	.02
☐ 349	Dave Gallagher	.05	.02
☐ 350	Glenn Davis	.05	.02
☐ 351	Joe Torre MG	.10	.05
☐ 352	Frank White	.05	.02
☐ 353	Tony Castillo	.05	.02
☐ 354	Sid Bream	.05	.02
☐ 355	Chili Davis	.10	.05
☐ 356	Mike Marshall	.05	.02
☐ 357	Jack Savage	.05	.02
☐ 358	Mark Parent	.05	.02
☐ 359	Chuck Cary	.05	.02
☐ 360	Tim Raines	.10	.05
☐ 361	Scott Garrelts	.05	.02
☐ 362	Hector Villanueva	.05	.02
☐ 363	Rick Mahler	.05	.02
☐ 364	Dan Pasqua	.05	.02
☐ 365	Mike Schooler	.05	.02
☐ 366A	Checklist 3 ERR	.20	.09
	19 Carl Nichols		
☐ 366B	Checklist 3 COR	.05	.02
	119 Carl Nichols		
☐ 367	Dave Walsh	.05	.02
☐ 368	Felix Jose	.05	.02
☐ 369	Steve Searcy	.05	.02
☐ 370	Kelly Gruber	.05	.02
☐ 371	Jeff Montgomery	.10	.05
☐ 372	Spike Owen	.05	.02
☐ 373	Darrin Jackson	.05	.02
☐ 374	Larry Casian	.05	.02
☐ 375	Tony Pena	.05	.02
☐ 376	Mike Harkey	.05	.02
☐ 377	Rene Gonzales	.05	.02
☐ 378A	Wilson Alvarez ERR	.50	.23
	('89 Port Charlotte and '90 Birmingham stat lines omitted)		
☐ 378B	Wilson Alvarez COR	.20	.09
	(Text still says 143 K's in 1988, whereas stats say 134)		
☐ 379	Randy Velarde	.05	.02
☐ 380	Willie McGee	.05	.02
☐ 381	Jim Leyland MG	.05	.02
☐ 382	Mackey Sasser	.05	.02
☐ 383	Pete Smith	.05	.02
☐ 384	Gerald Perry	.05	.02
☐ 385	Mickey Tettleton	.10	.05
☐ 386	Cecil Fielder AS	.05	.02
☐ 387	Julio Franco AS	.05	.02
☐ 388	Kelly Gruber AS	.05	.02
☐ 389	Alan Trammell AS	.10	.05
☐ 390	Jose Canseco AS	.10	.05
☐ 391	Rickey Henderson AS	.10	.05
☐ 392	Ken Griffey Jr. AS	.75	.35
☐ 393	Carlton Fisk AS	.05	.02
☐ 394	Bob Welch AS	.05	.02
☐ 395	Chuck Finley AS	.05	.02
☐ 396	Bobby Thigpen AS	.05	.02
☐ 397	Eddie Murray AS	.05	.02
☐ 398	Ryne Sandberg AS	.20	.09
☐ 399	Matt Williams AS	.10	.05
☐ 400	Barry Larkin AS	.10	.05
☐ 401	Barry Bonds AS	.20	.09
☐ 402	Darryl Strawberry AS	.05	.02
☐ 403	Bobby Bonilla AS	.05	.02
☐ 404	Mike Scioscia AS	.05	.02
☐ 405	Doug Drabek AS	.05	.02
☐ 406	Frank Viola AS	.05	.02
☐ 407	John Franco AS	.05	.02
☐ 408	Earnie Riles	.05	.02
☐ 409	Mike Stanley	.05	.02
☐ 410	Dave Righetti	.05	.02
☐ 411	Lance Blankenship	.05	.02
☐ 412	Dave Bergman	.05	.02
☐ 413	Terry Mulholland	.05	.02
☐ 414	Gary Sheffield	.25	.11
☐ 415	Rick Sutcliffe	.05	.02
☐ 416	Randy Milligan	.05	.02
☐ 417	Bill Krueger	.05	.02
☐ 418	Nick Esasky	.05	.02
☐ 419	Jeff Reed	.05	.02
☐ 420	Bobby Thigpen	.05	.02
☐ 421	Alex Cole	.05	.02
☐ 422	Rick Reuschel	.05	.02
☐ 423	Rafael Ramirez UER	.05	.02
	(Born 1959, not 1958)		
☐ 424	Calvin Schiraldi	.05	.02
☐ 425	Andy Van Slyke	.10	.05
☐ 426	Joe Grahe	.05	.02
☐ 427	Rick Dempsey	.05	.02
☐ 428	John Barfield	.05	.02
☐ 429	Stump Merrill MG	.05	.02
☐ 430	Gary Gaetti	.05	.02
☐ 431	Paul Gibson	.05	.02
☐ 432	Delino DeShields	.05	.02
☐ 433	Pat Tabler	.05	.02
☐ 434	Julio Machado	.05	.02
☐ 435	Kevin Maas	.05	.02
☐ 436	Scott Bankhead	.05	.02
☐ 437	Doug Dascenzo	.05	.02
☐ 438	Vicente Palacios	.05	.02
☐ 439	Dickie Thon	.05	.02
☐ 440	George Bell	.05	.02
☐ 441	Zane Smith	.05	.02
☐ 442	Charlie O'Brien	.05	.02
☐ 443	Jeff Innis	.05	.02
☐ 444	Glenn Braggs	.05	.02
☐ 445	Greg Swindell	.05	.02
☐ 446	Craig Grebeck	.05	.02
☐ 447	John Burkett	.05	.02
☐ 448	Craig Lefferts	.05	.02
☐ 449	Juan Berenguer	.05	.02
☐ 450	Wade Boggs	.20	.09
☐ 451	Neal Heaton	.05	.02
☐ 452	Bill Schroeder	.05	.02
☐ 453	Lenny Harris	.05	.02
☐ 454A	Kevin Appier ERR	.20	.09
	('90 Omaha stat line omitted)		
☐ 454B	Kevin Appier COR	.20	.09
☐ 455	Walt Weiss	.05	.02
☐ 456	Charlie Leibrandt	.05	.02
☐ 457	Todd Hundley	.20	.09
☐ 458	Brian Holman	.05	.02
☐ 459	Tom Trebelhorn MG UER	.05	.02
	(Pitching and batting columns switched)		
☐ 460	Dave Stieb	.05	.02
☐ 461	Robin Ventura	.20	.09
☐ 462	Steve Frey	.05	.02
☐ 463	Dwight Smith	.05	.02
☐ 464	Steve Buechele	.05	.02
☐ 465	Ken Griffey Sr.	.05	.02
☐ 466	Charles Nagy	.20	.09
☐ 467	Dennis Cook	.05	.02
☐ 468	Tim Hulett	.05	.02
☐ 469	Chet Lemon	.05	.02
☐ 470	Howard Johnson	.05	.02
☐ 471	Mike Lieberthal	.15	.07
☐ 472	Kirt Manwaring	.05	.02
☐ 473	Curt Young	.05	.02
☐ 474	Phil Plantier	.10	.05
☐ 475	Teddy Higuera	.05	.02
☐ 476	Glenn Wilson	.05	.02
☐ 477	Mike Fetters	.05	.02
☐ 478	Kurt Stillwell	.05	.02
☐ 479	Bob Patterson UER	.05	.02
	(Has a decimal point between 7 and 9)		
☐ 480	Dave Magadan	.05	.02
☐ 481	Eddie Whitson	.05	.02
☐ 482	Tino Martinez	.20	.09
☐ 483	Mike Aldrete	.05	.02
☐ 484	Dave LaPoint	.05	.02
☐ 485	Terry Pendleton	.10	.05
☐ 486	Tommy Greene	.05	.02
☐ 487	Rafael Belliard	.05	.02
☐ 488	Jeff Manto	.05	.02
☐ 489	Bobby Valentine MG	.05	.02
☐ 490	Kirk Gibson	.10	.05
☐ 491	Kurt Miller	.05	.02
☐ 492	Ernie Whitt	.05	.02
☐ 493	Jose Rijo	.05	.02
☐ 494	Chris James	.05	.02
☐ 495	Charlie Hough	.05	.02
☐ 496	Marty Barrett	.05	.02
☐ 497	Ben McDonald	.05	.02
☐ 498	Mark Salas	.05	.02
☐ 499	Melido Perez	.05	.02
☐ 500	Will Clark	.20	.09
☐ 501	Mike Bielecki	.05	.02
☐ 502	Carney Lansford	.10	.05
☐ 503	Roy Smith	.05	.02
☐ 504	Julio Valera	.05	.02
☐ 505	Chuck Finley	.10	.05
☐ 506	Darnell Coles	.05	.02
☐ 507	Steve Jeltz	.05	.02
☐ 508	Mike York	.05	.02
☐ 509	Glenallen Hill	.05	.02
☐ 510	John Franco	.10	.05
☐ 511	Steve Balboni	.05	.02
☐ 512	Jose Mesa	.05	.02
☐ 513	Jerald Clark	.05	.02
☐ 514	Mike Stanton	.05	.02
☐ 515	Alvin Davis	.05	.02
☐ 516	Karl Rhodes	.05	.02
☐ 517	Joe Oliver	.05	.02
☐ 518	Cris Carpenter	.05	.02
☐ 519	Sparky Anderson MG	.05	.02
☐ 520	Mark Grace	.20	.09
☐ 521	Joe Orsulak	.05	.02
☐ 522	Stan Belinda	.05	.02
☐ 523	Rodney McCray	.05	.02
☐ 524	Darrel Akerfelds	.05	.02
☐ 525	Willie Randolph	.10	.05
☐ 526A	Moises Alou ERR	.50	.23
	(37 runs in 2 games for '90 Pirates)		
☐ 526B	Moises Alou COR	.20	.09
	(0 runs in 2 games for '90 Pirates)		
☐ 527A	Checklist 4 ERR	.20	.09
	105 Keith Miller		
	719 Kevin McReynolds		
☐ 527B	Checklist 4 COR	.05	.02

105 Kevin McReynolds
719 Keith Miller

□ 528 Denny Martinez	.10	.05
□ 529 Marc Newfield	.15	.07
□ 530 Roger Clemens	.40	.18
□ 531 Dave Rohde	.05	.02
□ 532 Kirk McCaskill	.05	.02
□ 533 Oddibe McDowell	.05	.02
□ 534 Mike Jackson	.05	.02
□ 535 Ruben Sierra UER	.05	.02
(Back reads 100 Runs amd 100 RBI's)		
□ 536 Mike Witt	.05	.02
□ 537 Jose Lind	.05	.02
□ 538 Bip Roberts	.05	.02
□ 539 Scott Terry	.05	.02
□ 540 George Brett	.40	.18
□ 541 Domingo Ramos	.05	.02
□ 542 Rob Murphy	.05	.02
□ 543 Junior Felix	.05	.02
□ 544 Alejandro Pena	.05	.02
□ 545 Dale Murphy	.20	.09
□ 546 Jeff Ballard	.05	.02
□ 547 Mike Pagliarulo	.05	.02
□ 548 Jaime Navarro	.05	.02
□ 549 John McNamara MG	.05	.02
□ 550 Eric Davis	.10	.05
□ 551 Bob Kipper	.05	.02
□ 552 Jeff Hamilton	.05	.02
□ 553 Joe Klink	.05	.02
□ 554 Brian Harper	.05	.02
□ 555 Turner Ward	.05	.02
□ 556 Gary Ward	.05	.02
□ 557 Wally Whitehurst	.05	.02
□ 558 Otis Nixon	.10	.05
□ 559 Adam Peterson	.05	.02
□ 560 Greg Smith	.05	.02
□ 561 Tim McIntosh	.05	.02
□ 562 Jeff Kunkel	.05	.02
□ 563 Brent Knackert	.05	.02
□ 564 Dante Bichette	.20	.09
□ 565 Craig Biggio	.20	.09
□ 566 Craig Wilson	.05	.02
□ 567 Dwayne Henry	.05	.02
□ 568 Ron Karkovice	.05	.02
□ 569 Curt Schilling	.09	.04
□ 570 Barry Bonds	.25	.11
□ 571 Pat Combs	.05	.02
□ 572 Dave Anderson	.05	.02
□ 573 Rich Rodriguez UER	.05	.02
(Stats say drafted 4th, but bio says 9th round)		
□ 574 John Marzano	.05	.02
□ 575 Robin Yount	.20	.09
□ 576 Jeff Kaiser	.05	.02
□ 577 Bill Doran	.05	.02
□ 578 Dave West	.05	.02
□ 579 Roger Craig MG	.05	.02
□ 580 Dave Stewart	.10	.05
□ 581 Luis Quinones	.05	.02
□ 582 Marty Clary	.05	.02
□ 583 Tony Phillips	.05	.02
□ 584 Kevin Brown	.10	.05
□ 585 Pete O'Brien	.05	.02
□ 586 Fred Lynn	.05	.02
□ 587 Jose Offerman UER	.05	.02
(Text says he signed 7/24/86, but bio says 1988)		
□ 588 Mark Whiten	.05	.02
□ 589 Scott Ruskin	.05	.02
□ 590 Eddie Murray	.20	.09
□ 591 Ken Hill	.05	.02
□ 592 B.J. Surhoff	.10	.05
□ 593A Mike Walker ERR	.20	.09
('90 Canton-Akron stat line omitted)		
□ 593B Mike Walker COR	.05	.02
□ 594 Rich Garces	.05	.02
□ 595 Bill Landrum	.05	.02
□ 596 Ronnie Walden	.05	.02
□ 597 Jerry Don Gleaton	.05	.02
□ 598 Sam Horn	.05	.02
□ 599A Greg Myers ERR	.20	.09
('90 Syracuse stat line omitted)		
□ 599B Greg Myers COR	.05	.02
□ 600 Bo Jackson	.15	.07
□ 601 Bob Ojeda	.05	.02
□ 602 Casey Candaele	.05	.02
□ 603A Wes Chamberlain ERR	.20	.09
(Photo actually Louie Meadows)		
□ 603B Wes Chamberlain COR	.05	.02
□ 604 Billy Hatcher	.05	.02
□ 605 Jeff Reardon	.10	.05
□ 606 Jim Gott	.05	.02
□ 607 Edgar Martinez	.20	.09
□ 608 Todd Burns	.05	.02
□ 609 Jeff Torborg MG	.05	.02
□ 610 Andres Galarraga	.20	.09
□ 611 Dave Eiland	.05	.02
□ 612 Steve Lyons	.05	.02
□ 613 Eric Show	.05	.02
□ 614 Luis Salazar	.05	.02
□ 615 Bert Blyleven	.10	.05
□ 616 Todd Zeile	.10	.05
□ 617 Bill Wegman	.05	.02
□ 618 Sil Campusano	.05	.02
□ 619 David Wells	.05	.02
□ 620 Ozzie Guillen	.05	.02
□ 621 Ted Power	.05	.02
□ 622 Jack Daugherty	.05	.02
□ 623 Jeff Blauser	.05	.02
□ 624 Tom Candiotti	.05	.02
□ 625 Terry Steinbach	.10	.05
□ 626 Gerald Young	.05	.02
□ 627 Tim Layana	.05	.02
□ 628 Greg Litton	.05	.02
□ 629 Wes Gardner	.05	.02
□ 630 Dave Winfield	.20	.09
□ 631 Mike Morgan	.05	.02
□ 632 Lloyd Moseby	.05	.02
□ 633 Kevin Tapani	.05	.02
□ 634 Henry Cotto	.05	.02
□ 635 Andy Hawkins	.05	.02
□ 636 Geronimo Pena	.05	.02
□ 637 Bruce Ruffin	.05	.02
□ 638 Mike Macfarlane	.05	.02
□ 639 Frank Robinson MG	.15	.07
□ 640 Andre Dawson	.20	.09
□ 641 Mike Henneman	.05	.02
□ 642 Hal Morris	.05	.02
□ 643 Jim Presley	.05	.02
□ 644 Chuck Crim	.05	.02
□ 645 Juan Samuel	.05	.02
□ 646 Andujar Cedeno	.05	.02
□ 647 Mark Portugal	.05	.02
□ 648 Lee Stevens	.05	.02
□ 649 Bill Sampen	.05	.02
□ 650 Jack Clark	.10	.05
□ 651 Alan Mills	.05	.02
□ 652 Kevin Romine	.05	.02
□ 653 Anthony Telford	.05	.02
□ 654 Paul Sorrento	.10	.05
□ 655 Erik Hanson	.05	.02
□ 656A Checklist 5 ERR	.20	.09
348 Vicente Palacios		
381 Jose Lind		
537 Mike LaValliere		
665 Jim Leyland		
□ 656B Checklist 5 ERR	.20	.09
433 Vicente Palacios		
(Palacios should be 438)		
537 Jose Lind		
665 Mike LaValliere		
381 Jim Leyland		
□ 656C Checklist 5 COR	.20	.09
438 Vicente Palacios		
537 Jose Lind		
665 Mike LaValliere		
381 Jim Leyland		
□ 657 Mike Kingery	.05	.02
□ 658 Scott Aldred	.05	.02
□ 659 Oscar Azocar	.05	.02
□ 660 Lee Smith	.10	.05
□ 661 Steve Lake	.05	.02
□ 662 Ron Dibble	.05	.02
□ 663 Greg Brock	.05	.02
□ 664 John Farrell	.05	.02
□ 665 Mike LaValliere	.05	.02
□ 666 Danny Darwin	.05	.02
□ 667 Kent Anderson	.05	.02
□ 668 Bill Long	.05	.02
□ 669 Lou Piniella MG	.10	.05
□ 670 Rickey Henderson	.20	.09
□ 671 Andy McGaffigan	.05	.02
□ 672 Shane Mack	.05	.02
□ 673 Greg Olson UER	.05	.02
(6 RBI in '88 at Tidewater and 2 RBI in '87, should be 48 and 15)		
□ 674A Kevin Gross ERR	.20	.09
(89 BB with Phillies in '88 tied for league lead)		
□ 674B Kevin Gross COR	.05	.02
(89 BB with Phillies in '88 led in league)		
□ 675 Tom Brunansky	.05	.02
□ 676 Scott Chiamparino	.05	.02
□ 677 Billy Ripken	.05	.02
□ 678 Mark Davidson	.05	.02
□ 679 Bill Bathe	.05	.02
□ 680 David Cone	.10	.05
□ 681 Jeff Schaefer	.05	.02
□ 682 Ray Lankford	.20	.09
□ 683 Derek Lilliquist	.05	.02
□ 684 Milt Cuyler	.05	.02
□ 685 Doug Drabek	.05	.02
□ 686 Mike Gallego	.05	.02
□ 687A John Cerutti ERR	.20	.09
(4.46 ERA in '90)		
□ 687B John Cerutti COR	.05	.02
(4.76 ERA in '90)		
□ 688 Rosario Rodriguez	.05	.02
□ 689 John Kruk	.10	.05
□ 690 Orel Hershiser	.10	.05
□ 691 Mike Blowers	.05	.02
□ 692A Efrain Valdez ERR	.20	.09
(Born 6/11/66)		
□ 692B Efrain Valdez COR	.05	.02
(Born 7/11/66 and two lines of text added)		
□ 693 Francisco Cabrera	.05	.02
□ 694 Randy Veres	.05	.02
□ 695 Kevin Seitzer	.05	.02
□ 696 Steve Olin	.05	.02
□ 697 Shawn Abner	.05	.02
□ 698 Mark Guthrie	.05	.02
□ 699 Jim Lefebvre MG	.05	.02
□ 700 Jose Canseco	.15	.07
□ 701 Pascual Perez	.05	.02
□ 702 Tim Naehring	.10	.05
□ 703 Juan Agosto	.05	.02
□ 704 Devon White	.05	.02
□ 705 Robby Thompson	.05	.02
□ 706A Brad Arnsberg ERR	.20	.09
(68.2 IP in '90)		
□ 706B Brad Arnsberg COR	.05	.02
(62.2 IP in '90)		
□ 707 Jim Eisenreich	.05	.02
□ 708 John Mitchell	.05	.02
□ 709 Matt Sinatro	.05	.02
□ 710 Kent Hrbek	.10	.05
□ 711 Jose DeLeon	.05	.02
□ 712 Ricky Jordan	.05	.02
□ 713 Scott Scudder	.05	.02
□ 714 Marvell Wynne	.05	.02
□ 715 Tim Burke	.05	.02
□ 716 Bob Geren	.05	.02
□ 717 Phil Bradley	.05	.02
□ 718 Steve Crawford	.05	.02
□ 719 Keith Miller	.05	.02
□ 720 Cecil Fielder	.10	.05
□ 721 Mark Lee	.05	.02
□ 722 Wally Backman	.05	.02
□ 723 Candy Maldonado	.05	.02
□ 724 David Segui	.10	.05
□ 725 Ron Gant	.05	.05
□ 726 Phil Stephenson	.05	.02
□ 727 Mookie Wilson	.10	.05
□ 728 Scott Sanderson	.05	.02
□ 729 Don Zimmer MG	.05	.02
□ 730 Barry Larkin	.15	.07
□ 731 Jeff Gray	.05	.02
□ 732 Franklin Stubbs	.05	.02
□ 733 Kelly Downs	.05	.02

☐ 734 John Russell	.05	.02
☐ 735 Ron Darling	.05	.02
☐ 736 Dick Schofield	.05	.02
☐ 737 Tim Crews	.05	.02
☐ 738 Mel Hall	.05	.02
☐ 739 Russ Swan	.05	.02
☐ 740 Ryne Sandberg	.25	.11
☐ 741 Jimmy Key	.10	.05
☐ 742 Tommy Gregg	.05	.02
☐ 743 Bryn Smith	.05	.02
☐ 744 Nelson Santovenia	.05	.02
☐ 745 Doug Jones	.05	.02
☐ 746 John Shelby	.05	.02
☐ 747 Tony Fossas	.05	.02
☐ 748 Al Newman	.05	.02
☐ 749 Greg W. Harris	.05	.02
☐ 750 Bobby Bonilla	.10	.05
☐ 751 Wayne Edwards	.05	.02
☐ 752 Kevin Bass	.05	.02
☐ 753 Paul Marak UER	.05	.02

(Stats say drafted in Jan. but bio says May)

☐ 754 Bill Pecota	.05	.02
☐ 755 Mark Langston	.05	.02
☐ 756 Jeff Huson	.05	.02
☐ 757 Mark Gardner	.05	.02
☐ 758 Mike Devereaux	.05	.02
☐ 759 Bobby Cox MG	.05	.02
☐ 760 Benny Santiago	.05	.02
☐ 761 Larry Andersen	.05	.02
☐ 762 Mitch Webster	.05	.02
☐ 763 Dana Kiecker	.05	.02
☐ 764 Mark Carreon	.05	.02
☐ 765 Shawon Dunston	.05	.02
☐ 766 Jeff Robinson	.05	.02
☐ 767 Dan Wilson	.25	.11
☐ 768 Don Pall	.05	.02
☐ 769 Tim Sherrill	.05	.02
☐ 770 Jay Howell	.05	.02
☐ 771 Gary Redus UER	.05	.02

(Born in Tanner, should say Athens)

☐ 772 Kent Mercker UER	.05	.02

(Born in Indianapolis, should say Dublin, Ohio)

☐ 773 Tom Foley	.05	.02
☐ 774 Dennis Rasmussen	.05	.02
☐ 775 Julio Franco	.05	.02
☐ 776 Brent Mayne	.05	.02
☐ 777 John Candelaria	.05	.02
☐ 778 Dan Gladden	.05	.02
☐ 779 Carmelo Martinez	.05	.02
☐ 780A Randy Myers ERR	.05	.02

(15 career losses)

☐ 780B Randy Myers COR	.05	.02

(19 career losses)

☐ 781 Darryl Hamilton	.05	.02
☐ 782 Jim Deshaies	.05	.02
☐ 783 Joel Skinner	.05	.02
☐ 784 Willie Fraser	.05	.02
☐ 785 Scott Fletcher	.05	.02
☐ 786 Eric Plunk	.05	.02
☐ 787 Checklist 6	.05	.02
☐ 788 Bob Milacki	.05	.02
☐ 789 Tom Lasorda MG	.15	.07
☐ 790 Ken Griffey Jr.	1.50	.70
☐ 791 Mike Benjamin	.05	.02
☐ 792 Mike Greenwell	.05	.02

1991 Topps Traded

The 1991 Topps Traded set contains 132 standard-size cards. The cards were issued primarily in factory set form through hobby dealers but were also made available on a limited basis in wax packs. The cards in the wax packs (gray backs) and collated factory sets (white backs) are from different card stock. Both versions are valued equally. The card design is identical to the regular issue 1991 Topps cards except for the

whiter stock (for factory set cards) and T-suffixed numbering. The set is numbered in alphabetical order. The set includes a Team U.S.A. subset, featuring 25 of America's top collegiate players. The key Rookie Cards in this set are Jeff Bagwell, Jason Giambi, Todd Greene, Charles Johnson and Ivan Rodriguez.

	MINT	NRMT
COMPLETE SET (132)	5.00	2.20
COMMON CARD (1T-132T)	.05	.02
MINOR STARS	.10	.05
UNLISTED STARS	.20	.09
*GRAY AND WHITE BACKS: SAME VALUE		

☐ 1T Juan Agosto	.05	.02
☐ 2T Roberto Alomar	.20	.09
☐ 3T Wally Backman	.05	.02
☐ 4T Jeff Bagwell	2.50	1.10
☐ 5T Skeeter Barnes	.05	.02
☐ 6T Steve Bedrosian	.05	.02
☐ 7T Derek Bell	.20	.09
☐ 8T George Bell	.05	.02
☐ 9T Rafael Belliard	.05	.02
☐ 10T Dante Bichette	.20	.09
☐ 11T Bud Black	.05	.02
☐ 12T Mike Boddicker	.05	.02
☐ 13T Sid Bream	.05	.02
☐ 14T Hubie Brooks	.05	.02
☐ 15T Brett Butler	.10	.05
☐ 16T Ivan Calderon	.05	.02
☐ 17T John Candelaria	.05	.02
☐ 18T Tom Candiotti	.05	.02
☐ 19T Gary Carter	.20	.09
☐ 20T Joe Carter	.10	.05
☐ 21T Rick Cerone	.05	.02
☐ 22T Jack Clark	.10	.05
☐ 23T Vince Coleman	.05	.02
☐ 24T Scott Coolbaugh	.05	.02
☐ 25T Danny Cox	.05	.02
☐ 26T Danny Darwin	.05	.02
☐ 27T Chili Davis	.10	.05
☐ 28T Glenn Davis	.05	.02
☐ 29T Steve Decker	.05	.02
☐ 30T Rob Deer	.05	.02
☐ 31T Rich DeLucia	.05	.02
☐ 32T John Dettmer USA	.10	.05
☐ 33T Brian Downing	.05	.02
☐ 34T Darren Dreifort USA	.25	.11
☐ 35T Kirk Dressendorfer	.05	.02
☐ 36T Jim Essian MG	.05	.02
☐ 37T Dwight Evans	.10	.05
☐ 38T Steve Farr	.05	.02
☐ 39T Jeff Fassero	.25	.11
☐ 40T Junior Felix	.05	.02
☐ 41T Tony Fernandez	.05	.02
☐ 42T Steve Finley	.05	.02
☐ 43T Jim Fregosi MG	.05	.02
☐ 44T Gary Gaetti	.05	.02
☐ 45T Jason Giambi USA	1.00	.45
☐ 46T Kirk Gibson	.10	.05
☐ 47T Leo Gomez	.05	.02
☐ 48T Luis Gonzalez	.20	.09
☐ 49T Jeff Granger USA	.20	.09

☐ 50T Todd Greene USA	1.50	.70
☐ 51T Jeffrey Hammonds USA	.50	.23
☐ 52T Mike Hargrove MG	.05	.02
☐ 53T Pete Harnisch	.05	.02
☐ 54T Rick Helling USA UER	.10	.05

(Misspelled Hellings on card back)

☐ 55T Glenallen Hill	.05	.02
☐ 56T Charlie Hough	.05	.02
☐ 57T Pete Incaviglia	.05	.02
☐ 58T Bo Jackson	.15	.07
☐ 59T Danny Jackson	.05	.02
☐ 60T Reggie Jefferson	.15	.07
☐ 61T Charles Johnson USA	2.00	.90
☐ 62T Jeff Johnson	.05	.02
☐ 63T Todd Johnson USA	.05	.02
☐ 64T Barry Jones	.05	.02
☐ 65T Chris Jones	.05	.02
☐ 66T Scott Kamieniecki	.05	.02
☐ 67T Pat Kelly	.05	.02
☐ 68T Darryl Kile	.20	.09
☐ 69T Chuck Knoblauch	.25	.11
☐ 70T Bill Krueger	.05	.02
☐ 71T Scott Leius	.05	.02
☐ 72T Donnie Leshnock USA	.05	.02
☐ 73T Mark Lewis	.05	.02
☐ 74T Candy Maldonado	.05	.02
☐ 75T Jason McDonald USA	.20	.09
☐ 76T Willie McGee	.05	.02
☐ 77T Fred McGriff	.20	.09
☐ 78T Billy McMillon USA	.20	.09
☐ 79T Hal McRae MG	.05	.02
☐ 80T Dan Melendez USA	.05	.02
☐ 81T Orlando Merced	.10	.05
☐ 82T Jack Morris	.10	.05
☐ 83T Phil Nevin USA	.20	.09
☐ 84T Otis Nixon	.10	.05
☐ 85T Johnny Oates MG	.05	.02
☐ 86T Bob Ojeda	.05	.02
☐ 87T Mike Pagliarulo	.05	.02
☐ 88T Dean Palmer	.10	.05
☐ 89T Dave Parker	.10	.05
☐ 90T Terry Pendleton	.10	.05
☐ 91T Tony Phillips (P) USA	.05	.02
☐ 92T Doug Piatt	.05	.02
☐ 93T Ron Polk USA CO	.05	.02
☐ 94T Tim Raines	.10	.05
☐ 95T Willie Randolph	.10	.05
☐ 96T Dave Righetti	.05	.02
☐ 97T Ernie Riles	.05	.02
☐ 98T Chris Roberts USA	.20	.09
☐ 99T Jeff D. Robinson	.05	.02
☐ 100T Jeff M. Robinson	.05	.02
☐ 101T Ivan Rodriguez	1.50	.70
☐ 102T Steve Rodriguez USA	.05	.02
☐ 103T Tom Runnells MG	.05	.02
☐ 104T Scott Sanderson	.05	.02
☐ 105T Bob Scanlan	.05	.02
☐ 106T Pete Schourek	.10	.05
☐ 107T Gary Scott	.05	.02
☐ 108T Paul Shuey USA	.20	.09
☐ 109T Doug Simons	.05	.02
☐ 110T Dave Smith	.05	.02
☐ 111T Cory Snyder	.05	.02
☐ 112T Luis Sojo	.05	.02
☐ 113T Kennie Steenstra USA	.05	.02
☐ 114T Darryl Strawberry	.10	.05
☐ 115T Franklin Stubbs	.05	.02
☐ 116T Todd Taylor USA	.05	.02
☐ 117T Wade Taylor	.05	.02
☐ 118T Garry Templeton	.05	.02
☐ 119T Mickey Tettleton	.10	.05
☐ 120T Tim Teufel	.05	.02
☐ 121T Mike Timlin	.05	.02
☐ 122T David Tuttle USA	.05	.02
☐ 123T Mo Vaughn	.40	.18
☐ 124T Walt Weiss USA	.05	.02
☐ 125T Devon White	.05	.02
☐ 126T Mark Whiten	.05	.02
☐ 127T Mitch Williams	.05	.02
☐ 128T Craig Wilson USA	.05	.02
☐ 129T Willie Wilson	.05	.02
☐ 130T Chris Wimmer USA	.05	.02
☐ 131T Ivan Zweig USA	.05	.02
☐ 132T Checklist 1T-132T	.05	.02

1992 Topps

The 1992 Topps set contains 792 standard-size cards. Cards were distributed in plastic wrap packs, jumbo packs, rack packs and factory sets. The fronts have either posed or action color player photos on a white card face. Different color stripes frame the pictures, and the player's name and team name appear in two color stripes respectively at the bottom. Special subsets included are Record Breakers (2-5), Prospects (58, 126, 179, 473, 551, 591, 618, 656, 676), and All-Stars (386-407). The key Rookie Cards in this set are Shawn Green, John Jaha and Manny Ramirez.

	MINT	NRMT
COMPLETE SET (792)	25.00	11.00
COMP.FACT.SET (802)	30.00	13.50
COMP.HOLIDAY SET (811)	35.00	16.00
COMMON CARD (1-792)	.05	.02
MINOR STARS	.10	.05
UNLISTED STARS	.20	.09
SUBSET CARDS HALF VALUE OF BASE CARDS		
COMP.GOLD SET (792)	120.00	55.00
COMP.GOLD FACT.SET (793)	120.00	55.00
COMMON GOLD (1-792)	.25	.11
*GOLD STARS: 7.5X TO 15X HI COLUMN		
*GOLD ROOKIES: 6X TO 12X HI		
GOLD: RANDOM INSERTS IN PACKS		
COMP.GOLD WIN.SET (792)	50.00	22.00
COMMON GOLD WIN. (1-792)	.10	.05
*GOLD WIN.STARS: 1.5X TO 3X HI COLUMN		
*GOLD WIN.ROOKIES: 1.25X TO 2.5X HI		
GOLD WIN: DISTRIBUTED W/GAME CARDS		

☐ 1 Nolan Ryan	.75	.35
☐ 2 Ricky Henderson RB	.10	.05
Most career SB's		
(Some cards have print		
marks that show 1.991		
on the front)		
☐ 3 Jeff Reardon RB	.05	.02
10 seasons, 20 or more saves		
☐ 4 Nolan Ryan RB	.40	.18
22 cons. 100 K seasons		
☐ 5 Dave Winfield RB	.20	.09
Oldest player, cycle		
☐ 6 Brien Taylor	.05	.02
☐ 7 Jim Olander	.05	.02
☐ 8 Bryan Hickerson	.05	.02
☐ 9 Jon Farrell	.05	.02
☐ 10 Wade Boggs	.20	.09
☐ 11 Jack McDowell	.10	.05
☐ 12 Luis Gonzalez	.05	.02
☐ 13 Mike Scioscia	.05	.02
☐ 14 Wes Chamberlain	.05	.02
☐ 15 Dennis Martinez	.10	.05
☐ 16 Jeff Montgomery	.10	.05
☐ 17 Randy Milligan	.05	.02
☐ 18 Greg Cadaret	.05	.02

☐ 19 Jamie Quirk	.05	.02
☐ 20 Bip Roberts	.05	.02
☐ 21 Buck Rodgers MG	.05	.02
☐ 22 Bill Wegman	.05	.02
☐ 23 Chuck Knoblauch	.20	.09
☐ 24 Randy Myers	.10	.05
☐ 25 Ron Gant	.10	.05
☐ 26 Mike Bielecki	.05	.02
☐ 27 Juan Gonzalez	.60	.25
☐ 28 Mike Schooler	.05	.02
☐ 29 Mickey Tettleton	.05	.02
☐ 30 John Kruk	.10	.05
☐ 31 Bryn Smith	.05	.02
☐ 32 Chris Nabholz	.05	.02
☐ 33 Carlos Baerga	.20	.09
☐ 34 Jeff Juden	.05	.02
☐ 35 Dave Righetti	.05	.02
☐ 36 Scott Ruffcorn	.05	.02
☐ 37 Luis Polonia	.05	.02
☐ 38 Tom Candiotti	.05	.02
☐ 39 Greg Olson	.05	.02
☐ 40 Cal Ripken	2.00	.90
☐ 41 Craig Lefferts	.05	.02
☐ 42 Mike Macfarlane	.05	.02
☐ 43 Jose Lind	.05	.02
☐ 44 Rick Aguilera	.05	.02
☐ 45 Gary Carter	.20	.09
☐ 46 Steve Farr	.05	.02
☐ 47 Rex Hudler	.05	.02
☐ 48 Scott Scudder	.05	.02
☐ 49 Damon Berryhill	.05	.02
☐ 50 Ken Griffey Jr.	1.25	.55
☐ 51 Tom Runnells MG	.05	.02
☐ 52 Juan Bell	.05	.02
☐ 53 Tommy Gregg	.05	.02
☐ 54 David Wells	.05	.02
☐ 55 Rafael Palmeiro	.15	.07
☐ 56 Charlie O'Brien	.05	.02
☐ 57 Donn Pall	.05	.02
☐ 58 1992 Prospects C	.20	.09
Brad Ausmus		
Jim Campanis Jr.		
Dave Nilsson		
Doug Robbins		
☐ 59 Mo Vaughn	.30	.14
☐ 60 Tony Fernandez	.05	.02
☐ 61 Paul O'Neill	.10	.05
☐ 62 Gene Nelson	.05	.02
☐ 63 Randy Ready	.05	.02
☐ 64 Bob Kipper	.05	.02
☐ 65 Willie McGee	.05	.02
☐ 66 Scott Stahoviak	.10	.05
☐ 67 Luis Salazar	.05	.02
☐ 68 Marvin Freeman	.05	.02
☐ 69 Kenny Lofton	.75	.35
☐ 70 Gary Gaetti	.05	.02
☐ 71 Erik Hanson	.05	.02
☐ 72 Eddie Zosky	.05	.02
☐ 73 Brian Barnes	.05	.02
☐ 74 Scott Leius	.05	.02
☐ 75 Bret Saberhagen	.05	.02
☐ 76 Mike Gallego	.05	.02
☐ 77 Jack Armstrong	.05	.02
☐ 78 Ivan Rodriguez	.40	.18
☐ 79 Jesse Orosco	.05	.02
☐ 80 David Justice	.20	.09
☐ 81 Ced Landrum	.05	.02
☐ 82 Doug Simons	.05	.02
☐ 83 Tommy Greene	.05	.02
☐ 84 Leo Gomez	.05	.02
☐ 85 Jose Del.eon	.05	.02
☐ 86 Steve Finley	.05	.02
☐ 87 Bob MacDonald	.05	.02
☐ 88 Darrin Jackson	.05	.02
☐ 89 Neal Heaton	.05	.02
☐ 90 Robin Yount	.15	.07
☐ 91 Jeff Reed	.05	.02
☐ 92 Lenny Harris	.05	.02
☐ 93 Reggie Sanders	.10	.05
☐ 94 Sammy Sosa	.20	.09
☐ 95 Scott Bailes	.05	.02
☐ 96 Tom McKinnon	.05	.02
☐ 97 Luis Rivera	.05	.02
☐ 98 Mike Harkey	.05	.02
☐ 99 Jeff Treadway	.05	.02
☐ 100 Jose Canseco	.15	.07

☐ 101 Omar Vizquel	.10	.05
☐ 102 Scott Kamieniecki	.05	.02
☐ 103 Ricky Jordan	.05	.02
☐ 104 Jeff Ballard	.05	.02
☐ 105 Felix Jose	.05	.02
☐ 106 Mike Boddicker	.05	.02
☐ 107 Dan Pasqua	.05	.02
☐ 108 Mike Timlin	.05	.02
☐ 109 Roger Craig MG	.05	.02
☐ 110 Ryne Sandberg	.25	.11
☐ 111 Mark Carreon	.05	.02
☐ 112 Oscar Azocar	.05	.02
☐ 113 Mike Greenwell	.05	.02
☐ 114 Mark Portugal	.05	.02
☐ 115 Terry Pendleton	.10	.05
☐ 116 Willie Randolph	.05	.02
☐ 117 Scott Terry	.05	.02
☐ 118 Chili Davis	.10	.05
☐ 119 Mark Gardner	.05	.02
☐ 120 Alan Trammell	.15	.07
☐ 121 Derek Bell	.10	.05
☐ 122 Gary Varsho	.05	.02
☐ 123 Bob Ojeda	.05	.02
☐ 124 Shawn Livsey	.05	.02
☐ 125 Chris Hoiles	.05	.02
☐ 126 1992 Prospects 1B	.40	.18
Ryan Klesko		
John Jaha		
Rico Brogna		
Dave Staton		
☐ 127 Carlos Quintana	.05	.02
☐ 128 Kurt Stillwell	.05	.02
☐ 129 Melido Perez	.05	.02
☐ 130 Alvin Davis	.05	.02
☐ 131 Checklist 1-132	.05	.02
☐ 132 Eric Show	.05	.02
☐ 133 Rance Mulliniks	.05	.02
☐ 134 Darryl Kile	.10	.05
☐ 135 Von Hayes	.05	.02
☐ 136 Bill Doran	.05	.02
☐ 137 Jeff D. Robinson	.05	.02
☐ 138 Monty Fariss	.05	.02
☐ 139 Jeff Innis	.05	.02
☐ 140 Mark Grace UER	.15	.07
(Home Calie., should		
be Calif.)		
☐ 141 Jim Leyland MG UER	.10	.05
(No closed parenthesis		
after East in 1991)		
☐ 142 Todd Van Poppel	.05	.02
☐ 143 Paul Gibson	.05	.02
☐ 144 Bill Swift	.05	.02
☐ 145 Danny Tartabull	.05	.02
☐ 146 Al Newman	.05	.02
☐ 147 Cris Carpenter	.05	.02
☐ 148 Anthony Young	.05	.02
☐ 149 Brian Bohanon	.05	.02
☐ 150 Roger Clemens UER	.40	.18
(League leading ERA in		
1990 not italicized)		
☐ 151 Jeff Hamilton	.05	.02
☐ 152 Charlie Leibrandt	.05	.02
☐ 153 Ron Karkovice	.05	.02
☐ 154 Hensley Meulens	.05	.02
☐ 155 Scott Bankhead	.05	.02
☐ 156 Manny Ramirez	1.25	.55
☐ 157 Keith Miller	.05	.02
☐ 158 Todd Frohwirth	.05	.02
☐ 159 Darrin Fletcher	.05	.02
☐ 160 Bobby Bonilla	.10	.05
☐ 161 Casey Candaele	.05	.02
☐ 162 Paul Faries	.05	.02
☐ 163 Dana Kiecker	.05	.02
☐ 164 Shane Mack	.05	.02
☐ 165 Mark Langston	.05	.02
☐ 166 Geronimo Pena	.05	.02
☐ 167 Andy Allanson	.05	.02
☐ 168 Dwight Smith	.05	.02
☐ 169 Chuck Crim	.05	.02
☐ 170 Alex Cole	.05	.02
☐ 171 Bill Plummer MG	.05	.02
☐ 172 Juan Berenguer	.05	.02
☐ 173 Brian Downing	.05	.02
☐ 174 Steve Frey	.05	.02
☐ 175 Orel Hershiser	.10	.05
☐ 176 Ramon Garcia	.05	.02

429	Tony LaRussa MG	.10	.05
430	Steve Sax	.05	.02
431	Tom Gordon	.05	.02
432	Billy Hatcher	.05	.02
433	Cal Eldred	.05	
434	Wally Backman	.05	.02
435	Mark Eichhorn	.05	.02
436	Mookie Wilson	.05	.02
437	Scott Servais	.05	.02
438	Mike Maddux	.05	.02
439	Chico Walker	.05	.02
440	Doug Drabek	.05	.02
441	Rob Deer	.05	.02
442	Dave West	.05	.02
443	Spike Owen	.05	.02
444	Tyrone Hill	.05	.02
445	Matt Williams	.15	.07
446	Mark Lewis	.05	.02
447	David Segui	.05	.02
448	Tom Pagnozzi	.05	.02
449	Jeff Johnson	.05	.02
450	Mark McGwire	.40	.18
451	Tom Henke	.05	.02
452	Wilson Alvarez	.10	.05
453	Gary Redus	.05	.02
454	Darren Holmes	.05	.02
455	Pete O'Brien	.05	.02
456	Pat Combs	.05	.02
457	Hubie Brooks	.05	.02
458	Frank Tanana	.05	.02
459	Tom Kelly MG	.05	.02
460	Andre Dawson	.15	.07
461	Doug Jones	.05	.02
462	Rich Rodriguez	.05	.02
463	Mike Simms	.05	.02
464	Mike Jeffcoat	.05	.02
465	Barry Larkin	.15	.07
466	Stan Belinda	.05	.02
467	Lonnie Smith	.05	.02
468	Greg Harris	.05	.02
469	Jim Eisenreich	.05	.02
470	Pedro Guerrero	.05	.02
471	Jose DeJesus	.05	.02
472	Rich Rowland	.05	.02
473	1992 Prospects 3B UER	.20	.09
	Frank Bolick		
	Craig Paquette		
	Tom Redington		
	Paul Russo		
	(Line around top border)		
474	Mike Rossiter	.05	.02
475	Robby Thompson	.05	.02
476	Randy Bush	.05	.02
477	Greg Hibbard	.05	.02
478	Dale Sveum	.05	.02
479	Chito Martinez	.05	.02
480	Scott Sanderson	.05	.02
481	Tino Martinez	.20	.09
482	Jimmy Key	.10	.05
483	Terry Shumpert	.05	.02
484	Mike Hartley	.05	.02
485	Chris Sabo	.05	.02
486	Bob Walk	.05	.02
487	John Cerutti	.05	.02
488	Scott Cooper	.05	.02
489	Bobby Cox MG	.05	.02
490	Julio Franco	.05	.02
491	Jeff Brantley	.05	.02
492	Mike Devereaux	.05	.02
493	Jose Offerman	.05	.02
494	Gary Thurman	.05	.02
495	Carney Lansford	.10	.05
496	Joe Grahe	.05	.02
497	Andy Ashby	.05	.02
498	Gerald Perry	.05	.02
499	Dave Otto	.05	.02
500	Vince Coleman	.05	.02
501	Rob Mallicoat	.05	.02
502	Greg Briley	.05	.02
503	Pascual Perez	.05	.02
504	Aaron Sele	.10	.05
505	Bobby Thigpen	.05	.02
506	Todd Benzinger	.05	.02
507	Candy Maldonado	.05	.02
508	Bill Gullickson	.05	.02
509	Doug Dascenzo	.05	.02
510	Frank Viola	.05	.02
511	Kenny Rogers	.05	.02
512	Mike Heath	.05	.02
513	Kevin Bass	.05	.02
514	Kim Batiste	.05	.02
515	Delino DeShields	.05	.02
516	Ed Sprague Jr.	.05	.02
517	Jim Gott	.05	.02
518	Jose Melendez	.05	.02
519	Hal McRae MG	.05	.02
520	Jeff Bagwell	.60	.25
521	Joe Hesketh	.05	.02
522	Milt Cuyler	.05	.02
523	Shawn Hillegas	.05	.02
524	Don Slaught	.05	.02
525	Randy Johnson	.20	.09
526	Doug Piatt	.05	.02
527	Checklist 397-528	.05	.02
528	Steve Foster	.05	.02
529	Joe Girardi	.05	.02
530	Jim Abbott	.20	.09
531	Larry Walker	.20	.09
532	Mike Huff	.05	.02
533	Mackey Sasser	.05	.02
534	Benji Gil	.10	.05
535	Dave Stieb	.05	.02
536	Willie Wilson	.05	.02
537	Mark Leiter	.05	.02
538	Jose Uribe	.05	.02
539	Thomas Howard	.05	.02
540	Ben McDonald	.05	.02
541	Jose Tolentino	.05	.02
542	Keith Mitchell	.05	.02
543	Jerome Walton	.05	.02
544	Cliff Brantley	.05	.02
545	Andy Van Slyke	.10	.05
546	Paul Sorrento	.05	.02
547	Herm Winningham	.05	.02
548	Mark Guthrie	.05	.02
549	Joe Torre MG	.10	.05
550	Darryl Strawberry	.10	.05
551	1992 Prospects SS UER	1.50	.70
	Wilfredo Cordero		
	Chipper Jones		
	Manny Alexander		
	Alex Arias		
	(No line around top border)		
552	Dave Gallagher	.05	.02
553	Edgar Martinez	.15	.07
554	Donald Harris	.05	.02
555	Frank Thomas	1.00	.45
556	Storm Davis	.05	.02
557	Dickie Thon	.05	.02
558	Scott Garrelts	.05	.02
559	Steve Olin	.05	.02
560	Rickey Henderson	.15	.07
561	Jose Vizcaino	.05	.02
562	Wade Taylor	.05	.02
563	Pat Borders	.05	.02
564	Jimmy Gonzalez	.05	.02
565	Lee Smith	.10	.05
566	Bill Sampen	.05	.02
567	Dean Palmer	.10	.05
568	Bryan Harvey	.05	.02
569	Tony Pena	.05	.02
570	Lou Whitaker	.10	.05
571	Randy Tomlin	.05	.02
572	Greg Vaughn	.05	.02
573	Kelly Downs	.05	.02
574	Steve Avery UER	.05	.02
	(Should be 13 games for Durham in 1989)		
575	Kirby Puckett	.40	.18
576	Heathcliff Slocumb	.05	.02
577	Kevin Seitzer	.05	.02
578	Lee Guetterman	.05	.02
579	Johnny Oates MG	.05	.02
580	Greg Maddux	.60	.25
581	Stan Javier	.05	.02
582	Vicente Palacios	.05	.02
583	Mel Rojas	.10	.05
584	Wayne Rosenthal	.05	.02
585	Lenny Webster	.05	.02
586	Rod Nichols	.05	.02
587	Mickey Morandini	.05	.02
588	Russ Swan	.05	.02
589	Mariano Duncan	.05	.02
590	Howard Johnson	.05	.02
591	1992 Prospects OF	.10	.05
	Jeromy Burnitz		
	Jacob Brumfield		
	Alan Cockrell		
	D.J. Dozier		
592	Denny Neagle	.15	.07
593	Steve Decker	.05	.02
594	Brian Barber	.10	.05
595	Bruce Hurst	.05	.02
596	Kent Mercker	.05	.02
597	Mike Magnante	.05	.02
598	Jody Reed	.05	.02
599	Steve Searcy	.05	.02
600	Paul Molitor	.20	.09
601	Dave Smith	.05	.02
602	Mike Fetters	.05	.02
603	Luis Mercedes	.05	.02
604	Chris Gwynn	.05	.02
605	Scott Erickson	.10	.05
606	Brook Jacoby	.05	.02
607	Todd Stottlemyre	.05	.02
608	Scott Bradley	.05	.02
609	Mike Hargrove MG	.05	.02
610	Eric Davis	.10	.05
611	Brian Hunter	.05	.02
612	Pat Kelly	.05	.02
613	Pedro Munoz	.05	.02
614	Al Osuna	.05	.02
615	Matt Merullo	.05	.02
616	Larry Andersen	.05	.02
617	Junior Ortiz	.05	.02
618	1992 Prospects OF	.05	.02
	Cesar Hernandez		
	Steve Hosey		
	Jeff McNeely		
	Dan Peltier		
619	Danny Jackson	.05	.02
620	George Brett	.40	.18
621	Dan Gakeler	.05	.02
622	Steve Buechele	.05	.02
623	Bob Tewksbury	.05	.02
624	Shawn Estes	.40	.18
625	Kevin McReynolds	.05	.02
626	Chris Haney	.05	.02
627	Mike Sharperson	.05	.02
628	Mark Williamson	.05	.02
629	Wally Joyner	.10	.05
630	Carlton Fisk	.20	.09
631	Armando Reynoso	.05	.02
632	Felix Fermin	.05	.02
633	Mitch Williams	.05	.02
634	Manuel Lee	.05	.02
635	Harold Baines	.10	.05
636	Greg Harris	.05	.02
637	Orlando Merced	.05	.02
638	Chris Bosio	.05	.02
639	Wayne Housie	.05	.02
640	Xavier Hernandez	.05	.02
641	David Howard	.05	.02
642	Tim Crews	.05	.02
643	Rick Cerone	.05	.02
644	Terry Leach	.05	.02
645	Deion Sanders	.10	.05
646	Craig Wilson	.05	.02
647	Marquis Grissom	.10	.05
648	Scott Fletcher	.05	.02
649	Norm Charlton	.05	.02
650	Jesse Barfield	.05	.02
651	Joe Slusarski	.05	.02
652	Bobby Rose	.05	.02
653	Dennis Lamp	.05	.02
654	Allen Watson	.10	.05
655	Brett Butler	.10	.05
656	1992 Prospects OF	.20	.09
	Rudy Pemberton		
	Henry Rodriguez		
	Lee Tinsley		
	Gerald Williams		
657	Dave Johnson	.05	.02
658	Checklist 529-660	.05	.02
659	Brian McRae	.05	.02
660	Fred McGriff	.15	.07
661	Bill Landrum	.05	.02

□ 662	Juan Guzman	.05	.02
□ 663	Greg Gagne	.05	.02
□ 664	Ken Hill	.05	.02
□ 665	Dave Haas	.05	.02
□ 666	Tom Foley	.05	.02
□ 667	Roberto Hernandez	.20	.09
□ 668	Dwayne Henry	.05	.02
□ 669	Jim Fregosi MG	.05	.02
□ 670	Harold Reynolds	.05	.02
□ 671	Mark Whiten	.05	.02
□ 672	Eric Plunk	.05	.02
□ 673	Todd Hundley	.15	.07
□ 674	Mo Sanford	.05	.02
□ 675	Bobby Witt	.05	.02
□ 676	1992 Prospects P	.05	.02
	Sam Militello		
	Pat Mahomes		
	Turk Wendell		
	Roger Salkeld		
□ 677	John Marzano	.05	.02
□ 678	Joe Klink	.05	.02
□ 679	Pete Incaviglia	.05	.02
□ 680	Dale Murphy	.20	.09
□ 681	Rene Gonzales	.05	.02
□ 682	Andy Benes	.10	.05
□ 683	Jim Poole	.05	.02
□ 684	Trever Miller	.05	.02
□ 685	Scott Livingstone	.05	.02
□ 686	Rich DeLucia	.05	.02
□ 687	Harvey Pulliam	.05	.02
□ 688	Tim Belcher	.05	.02
□ 689	Mark Lemke	.05	.02
□ 690	John Franco	.10	.05
□ 691	Walt Weiss	.05	.02
□ 692	Scott Ruskin	.05	.02
□ 693	Jeff King	.10	.05
□ 694	Mike Gardiner	.05	.02
□ 695	Gary Sheffield	.20	.09
□ 696	Joe Boever	.05	.02
□ 697	Mike Felder	.05	.02
□ 698	John Habyan	.05	.02
□ 699	Cito Gaston MG	.05	.02
□ 700	Ruben Sierra	.10	.05
□ 701	Scott Radinsky	.05	.02
□ 702	Lee Stevens	.05	.02
□ 703	Mark Wohlers	.15	.07
□ 704	Curt Young	.05	.02
□ 705	Dwight Evans	.10	.05
□ 706	Rob Murphy	.05	.02
□ 707	Gregg Jefferies	.05	.02
□ 708	Tom Bolton	.05	.02
□ 709	Chris James	.05	.02
□ 710	Kevin Maas	.05	.02
□ 711	Ricky Bones	.05	.02
□ 712	Curt Wilkerson	.05	.02
□ 713	Roger McDowell	.05	.02
□ 714	Calvin Reese	.15	.07
□ 715	Craig Biggio	.15	.07
□ 716	Kirk Dressendorfer	.05	.02
□ 717	Ken Dayley	.05	.02
□ 718	B.J. Surhoff	.10	.05
□ 719	Terry Mulholland	.05	.02
□ 720	Kirk Gibson	.10	.05
□ 721	Mike Pagliarulo	.05	.02
□ 722	Walt Terrell	.05	.02
□ 723	Jose Oquendo	.05	.02
□ 724	Kevin Morton	.05	.02
□ 725	Dwight Gooden	.10	.05
□ 726	Kirt Manwaring	.05	.02
□ 727	Chuck McElroy	.05	.02
□ 728	Dave Burba	.05	.02
□ 729	Art Howe MG	.05	.02
□ 730	Ramon Martinez	.10	.05
□ 731	Donnie Hill	.05	.02
□ 732	Nelson Santovenia	.05	.02
□ 733	Bob Melvin	.05	.02
□ 734	Scott Hatteberg	.05	.02
□ 735	Greg Swindell	.05	.02
□ 736	Lance Johnson	.05	.02
□ 737	Kevin Reimer	.05	.02
□ 738	Dennis Eckersley	.10	.05
□ 739	Rob Ducey	.05	.02
□ 740	Ken Caminiti	.15	.07
□ 741	Mark Gubicza	.05	.02
□ 742	Billy Spiers	.05	.02
□ 743	Darren Lewis	.05	.02

□ 744	Chris Hammond	.05	.02
□ 745	Dave Magadan	.05	.02
□ 746	Bernard Gilkey	.10	.05
□ 747	Willie Banks	.05	.02
□ 748	Matt Nokes	.05	.02
□ 749	Jerald Clark	.05	.02
□ 750	Travis Fryman	.10	.05
□ 751	Steve Wilson	.05	.02
□ 752	Billy Ripken	.05	.02
□ 753	Paul Assenmacher	.05	.02
□ 754	Charlie Hayes	.05	.02
□ 755	Alex Fernandez	.10	.05
□ 756	Gary Pettis	.05	.02
□ 757	Rob Dibble	.05	.02
□ 758	Tim Naehring	.10	.05
□ 759	Jeff Torborg MG	.05	.02
□ 760	Ozzie Smith	.25	.11
□ 761	Mike Fitzgerald	.05	.02
□ 762	John Burkett	.05	.02
□ 763	Kyle Abbott	.05	.02
□ 764	Tyler Green	.10	.05
□ 765	Pete Harnisch	.05	.02
□ 766	Mark Davis	.05	.02
□ 767	Kal Daniels	.05	.02
□ 768	Jim Thome	.60	.25
□ 769	Jack Howell	.05	.02
□ 770	George Bell	.05	.02
□ 771	Arthur Rhodes	.05	.02
□ 772	Garry Templeton UER	.05	.02
	(Stat heading in for pitchers)		
□ 773	Hal Morris	.05	.02
□ 774	Bud Black	.05	.02
□ 775	Ivan Calderon	.05	.02
□ 776	Doug Henry	.05	.02
□ 777	John Olerud	.10	.05
□ 778	Tim Leary	.05	.02
□ 779	Jay Bell	.05	.02
□ 780	Eddie Murray	.20	.09
□ 781	Paul Abbott	.05	.02
□ 782	Phil Plantier	.05	.02
□ 783	Joe Magrane	.05	.02
□ 784	Ken Patterson	.05	.02
□ 785	Albert Belle	.25	.11
□ 786	Royce Clayton	.05	.02
□ 787	Checklist 661-792	.05	.02
□ 788	Mike Stanton	.05	.02
□ 789	Bobby Valentine MG	.05	.02
□ 790	Joe Carter	.05	.02
□ 791	Danny Cox	.05	.02
□ 792	Dave Winfield	.20	.09

1992 Topps Traded

MICHAEL TUCKER

The 1992 Topps Traded set comprises 132 standard-size cards. The set was distributed exclusively in factory set form through hobby dealers. As in past editions, the focuses on promising rookies, new managers, and players who changed teams. The set also includes a Team U.S.A. subset, featuring 25 of America's top college players and the Team U.S.A. coach. Card design is identical to the regular issue

1992 Topps cards except for the T-suffixed numbering. The cards are arranged in alphabetical order by player's last name. The key Rookie Cards in this set are Nomar Garciaparra, Brian Jordan and Michael Tucker.

		MINT	NRMT
COMP.FACT.SET (132)		40.00	18.00
COMMON CARD (1T-132T)		.10	.05
MINOR STARS		.20	.09
UNLISTED STARS		.40	.18
COMP.GOLD FACT.SET (132)		50.00	22.00
*GOLD: .6X TO 1.2X HI COLUMN			
GOLD SOLD ONLY IN FACTORY SET FORM			

□ 1T	Willie Adams USA	.10	.05
□ 2T	Jeff Alkire USA	.10	.05
□ 3T	Felipe Alou MG	.10	.05
□ 4T	Moises Alou	.30	.14
□ 5T	Ruben Amaro	.10	.05
□ 6T	Jack Armstrong	.10	.05
□ 7T	Scott Bankhead	.10	.05
□ 8T	Tim Belcher	.10	.05
□ 9T	George Bell	.10	.05
□ 10T	Freddie Benavides	.10	.05
□ 11T	Todd Benzinger	.10	.05
□ 12T	Joe Boever	.10	.05
□ 13T	Ricky Bones	.10	.05
□ 14T	Bobby Bonilla	.20	.09
□ 15T	Hubie Brooks	.10	.05
□ 16T	Jerry Browne	.10	.05
□ 17T	Jim Bullinger	.10	.05
□ 18T	Dave Burba	.10	.05
□ 19T	Kevin Campbell	.10	.05
□ 20T	Tom Candiotti	.10	.05
□ 21T	Mark Carreon	.10	.05
□ 22T	Gary Carter	.40	.18
□ 23T	Archi Cianfrocco	.10	.05
□ 24T	Phil Clark	.10	.05
□ 25T	Chad Curtis	.40	.18
□ 26T	Eric Davis	.20	.09
□ 27T	Tim Davis USA	.10	.05
□ 28T	Gary DiSarcina	.10	.05
□ 29T	Darren Dreifort USA	.20	.09
□ 30T	Mariano Duncan	.10	.05
□ 31T	Mike Fitzgerald	.10	.05
□ 32T	John Flaherty	.10	.05
□ 33T	Darrin Fletcher	.10	.05
□ 34T	Scott Fletcher	.10	.05
□ 35T	Ron Fraser CO USA	.10	.05
□ 36T	Andres Galarraga	.40	.18
□ 37T	Dave Gallagher	.10	.05
□ 38T	Mike Gallego	.10	.05
□ 39T	Nomar Garciaparra USA	30.00	13.50
□ 40T	Jason Giambi USA	.50	.23
□ 41T	Danny Gladden	.10	.05
□ 42T	Rene Gonzales	.10	.05
□ 43T	Jeff Granger USA	.20	.09
□ 44T	Rick Greene USA	.10	.05
□ 45T	Jeffrey Hammonds USA	.40	.18
□ 46T	Charlie Hayes	.10	.05
□ 47T	Von Hayes	.10	.05
□ 48T	Rick Helling USA	.10	.05
□ 49T	Butch Henry	.10	.05
□ 50T	Carlos Hernandez	.10	.05
□ 51T	Ken Hill	.10	.05
□ 52T	Butch Hobson	.10	.05
□ 53T	Vince Horsman	.10	.05
□ 54T	Pete Incaviglia	.10	.05
□ 55T	Gregg Jefferies	.10	.05
□ 56T	Charles Johnson USA	1.00	.45
□ 57T	Doug Jones	.10	.05
□ 58T	Brian Jordan	.50	.23
□ 59T	Wally Joyner	.20	.09
□ 60T	Daron Kirkreit USA	.20	.09
□ 61T	Bill Krueger	.10	.05
□ 62T	Gene Lamont MG	.10	.05
□ 63T	Jim Lefebvre MG	.10	.05
□ 64T	Danny Leon	.10	.05
□ 65T	Pat Listach	.10	.05
□ 66T	Kenny Lofton	1.50	.70
□ 67T	Dave Martinez	.10	.05
□ 68T	Derrick May	.10	.05

		MINT	NRMT

□ 69T Kirk McCaskill .10 .05
□ 70T Chad McConnell USA .20 .09
□ 71T Kevin McReynolds .10 .05
□ 72T Rusty Meacham .10 .05
□ 73T Keith Miller .10 .05
□ 74T Kevin Mitchell .20 .09
□ 75T Jason Moler USA .10 .05
□ 76T Mike Morgan .10 .05
□ 77T Jack Morris .20 .09
□ 78T Calvin Murray USA .10 .05
□ 79T Eddie Murray .40 .18
□ 80T Randy Myers .20 .09
□ 81T Denny Neagle .30 .14
□ 82T Phil Nevin USA .20 .09
□ 83T Dave Nilsson .20 .09
□ 84T Junior Ortiz .10 .05
□ 85T Donovan Osborne .10 .05
□ 86T Bill Pecota .10 .05
□ 87T Melido Perez .10 .05
□ 88T Mike Perez .10 .05
□ 89T Hipolito Pichardo .10 .05
□ 90T Willie Randolph .20 .09
□ 91T Darren Reed .10 .05
□ 92T Bip Roberts .10 .05
□ 93T Chris Roberts USA .20 .09
□ 94T Steve Rodriguez USA .10 .05
□ 95T Bruce Ruffin .10 .05
□ 96T Scott Ruskin .10 .05
□ 97T Bret Saberhagen .10 .05
□ 98T Rey Sanchez .10 .05
□ 99T Steve Sax .10 .05
□ 100T Curt Schilling .30 .14
□ 101T Dick Schofield .10 .05
□ 102T Gary Scott .10 .05
□ 103T Kevin Seitzer .10 .05
□ 104T Frank Seminara .10 .05
□ 105T Gary Sheffield .40 .18
□ 106T John Smiley .10 .05
□ 107T Cory Snyder .10 .05
□ 108T Paul Sorrento .10 .05
□ 109T Sammy Sosa .40 .18
□ 110T Matt Stairs .10 .05
□ 111T Andy Stankiewicz .10 .05
□ 112T Kurt Stillwell .10 .05
□ 113T Rick Sutcliffe .10 .05
□ 114T Bill Swift .10 .05
□ 115T Jeff Tackett .10 .05
□ 116T Danny Tartabull .10 .05
□ 117T Eddie Taubensee .10 .05
□ 118T Dickie Thon .10 .05
□ 119T Michael Tucker USA 1.00 .45
□ 120T Scooter Tucker .10 .05
□ 121T Marc Valdes USA .10 .05
□ 122T Julio Valera .10 .05
□ 123T Jason Varitek USA .50 .23
□ 124T Ron Villone USA .20 .09
□ 125T Frank Viola .10 .05
□ 126T B.J. Wallace USA .20 .09
□ 127T Dan Walters .10 .05
□ 128T Craig Wilson USA .10 .05
□ 129T Chris Wimmer USA .10 .05
□ 130T Dave Winfield .40 .18
□ 131T Herm Winningham .10 .05
□ 132T Checklist 1T-132T .10 .05

1993 Topps

The 1993 Topps baseball set consists of two series, respectively, of 396 and 429 standard-size cards. A Topps Gold card was inserted in every 15-card pack, and Topps Black Gold cards were randomly inserted throughout the packs. The fronts feature color action player photos with white borders. The player's name appears in a stripe at the bottom of the picture, and this stripe and two short diagonal stripes at the bottom corners of the picture are team color-coded. The backs are colorful and carry a color head shot, biography, complete statistical information, with a career highlight if space permitted. Cards 401-411 comprise an All-Star subset. Rookie Cards in this set include Jim Edmonds, Derek Jeter and Jason Kendall.

	MINT	NRMT
COMPLETE SET (825)	30.00	13.50
COMP.RETAIL.SET (838)	40.00	18.00
COMP.HOBBY.SET (847)	40.00	18.00
COMPLETE SERIES 1 (396)	15.00	6.75
COMPLETE SERIES 2 (429)	15.00	6.75
COMMON CARD (1-825)	.10	.05
MINOR STARS	.20	.09
UNLISTED STARS	.40	.18
COMP.GOLD SET (825)	70.00	32.00
COMP.GOLD SET.1 (396)	40.00	18.00
COMP.GOLD SER.2 (429)	30.00	13.50
COMMON GOLD (1-825)	.15	.07

*GOLD STARS: 2X TO 4X HI COLUMN
*GOLD YOUNG STARS: 1.5X TO 3X HI
ONE GOLD PER PACK
10 GOLD PER FACTORY SET

□ 1 Robin Yount .30 .14
□ 2 Barry Bonds .50 .23
□ 3 Ryne Sandberg .50 .23
□ 4 Roger Clemens .75 .35
□ 5 Tony Gwynn 1.00 .45
□ 6 Jeff Tackett .10 .05
□ 7 Pete Incaviglia .10 .05
□ 8 Mark Wohlers .20 .09
□ 9 Kent Hrbek .20 .09
□ 10 Will Clark .30 .14
□ 11 Eric Karros .20 .09
□ 12 Lee Smith .20 .09
□ 13 Esteban Beltre .10 .05
□ 14 Greg Briley .10 .05
□ 15 Marquis Grissom .20 .09
□ 16 Dan Plesac .10 .05
□ 17 Dave Hollins .10 .05
□ 18 Terry Steinbach .10 .05
□ 19 Ed Nunez .10 .05
□ 20 Tim Salmon .50 .23
□ 21 Luis Salazar .10 .05
□ 22 Jim Eisenreich .10 .05
□ 23 Todd Stottlemyre .10 .05
□ 24 Tim Naehring .10 .05
□ 25 John Franco .20 .09
□ 26 Skeeter Barnes .10 .05
□ 27 Carlos Garcia .10 .05
□ 28 Joe Orsulak .10 .05
□ 29 Dwayne Henry .10 .05
□ 30 Fred McGriff .30 .14
□ 31 Derek Lilliquist .10 .05
□ 32 Don Mattingly .60 .25
□ 33 B.J. Wallace .10 .05
□ 34 Juan Gonzalez 1.00 .45
□ 35 John Smoltz .20 .09
□ 36 Scott Servais .10 .05
□ 37 Lenny Webster .10 .05
□ 38 Chris James .10 .05
□ 39 Roger McDowell .10 .05
□ 40 Ozzie Smith .50 .23
□ 41 Alex Fernandez .20 .09
□ 42 Spike Owen .10 .05
□ 43 Ruben Amaro .10 .05

□ 44 Kevin Seitzer .10 .05
□ 45 Dave Fleming .10 .05
□ 46 Eric Fox .10 .05
□ 47 Bob Scanlan .10 .05
□ 48 Bert Blyleven .20 .09
□ 49 Brian McRae .10 .05
□ 50 Roberto Alomar .40 .18
□ 51 Mo Vaughn .50 .23
□ 52 Bobby Bonilla .20 .09
□ 53 Frank Tanana .10 .05
□ 54 Mike LaValliere .10 .05
□ 55 Mark McLemore .10 .05
□ 56 Chad Mottola .10 .05
□ 57 Norm Charlton .10 .05
□ 58 Jose Melendez .10 .05
□ 59 Carlos Martinez .10 .05
□ 60 Roberto Kelly .10 .05
□ 61 Gene Larkin .10 .05
□ 62 Rafael Belliard .10 .05
□ 63 Al Osuna .10 .05
□ 64 Scott Chiamparino .10 .05
□ 65 Brett Butler .20 .09
□ 66 John Burkett .10 .05
□ 67 Felix Jose .10 .05
□ 68 Omar Vizquel .20 .09
□ 69 John Vander Wal .10 .05
□ 70 Roberto Hernandez .20 .09
□ 71 Ricky Bones .10 .05
□ 72 Jeff Grotewold .10 .05
□ 73 Mike Moore .10 .05
□ 74 Steve Buechele .10 .05
□ 75 Juan Guzman .20 .09
□ 76 Kevin Appier .20 .09
□ 77 Junior Felix .10 .05
□ 78 Greg W. Harris .10 .05
□ 79 Dick Schofield .10 .05
□ 80 Cecil Fielder .20 .09
□ 81 Lloyd McClendon .10 .05
□ 82 David Segui .10 .05
□ 83 Reggie Sanders .20 .09
□ 84 Kurt Stillwell .10 .05
□ 85 Sandy Alomar .20 .09
□ 86 John Habyan .10 .05
□ 87 Kevin Reimer .10 .05
□ 88 Mike Stanton .10 .05
□ 89 Eric Anthony .10 .05
□ 90 Scott Erickson .10 .05
□ 91 Craig Colbert .10 .05
□ 92 Tom Pagnozzi .10 .05
□ 93 Pedro Astacio .10 .05
□ 94 Lance Johnson .10 .05
□ 95 Larry Walker .40 .18
□ 96 Russ Swan .10 .05
□ 97 Scott Fletcher .10 .05
□ 98 Derek Jeter 4.00 1.80
□ 99 Mike Williams .10 .05
□ 100 Mark McGwire .75 .35
□ 101 Jim Bullinger .10 .05
□ 102 Brian Hunter .10 .05
□ 103 Jody Reed .10 .05
□ 104 Mike Butcher .10 .05
□ 105 Gregg Jefferies .10 .05
□ 106 Howard Johnson .10 .05
□ 107 John Kiely .10 .05
□ 108 Jose Lind .10 .05
□ 109 Sam Horn .10 .05
□ 110 Barry Larkin .30 .14
□ 111 Bruce Hurst .10 .05
□ 112 Brian Barnes .10 .05
□ 113 Thomas Howard .10 .05
□ 114 Mel Hall .10 .05
□ 115 Robby Thompson .10 .05
□ 116 Mark Lemke .10 .05
□ 117 Eddie Taubensee .10 .05
□ 118 David Hulse .10 .05
□ 119 Pedro Munoz .10 .05
□ 120 Ramon Martinez .20 .09
□ 121 Todd Worrell .10 .05
□ 122 Joey Cora .10 .05
□ 123 Moises Alou .20 .09
□ 124 Franklin Stubbs .10 .05
□ 125 Pete O'Brien .10 .05
□ 126 Bob Ayrault .10 .05
□ 127 Carney Lansford .20 .09
□ 128 Kal Daniels .10 .05
□ 129 Joe Grahe .10 .05

130	Jeff Montgomery	.20	.09
131	Dave Winfield	.30	.14
132	Preston Wilson	.50	.23
133	Steve Wilson	.10	.05
134	Lee Guetterman	.10	.05
135	Mickey Tettleton	.10	.05
136	Jeff King	.20	.09
137	Alan Mills	.10	.05
138	Joe Oliver	.10	.05
139	Gary Gaetti	.10	.05
140	Gary Sheffield	.40	.18
141	Dennis Cook	.10	.05
142	Charlie Hayes	.10	.05
143	Jeff Huson	.10	.05
144	Kent Mercker	.10	.05
145	Eric Young	.40	.18
146	Scott Leius	.10	.05
147	Bryan Hickerson	.10	.05
148	Steve Finley	.20	.09
149	Rheal Cormier	.10	.05
150	Frank Thomas UER	1.50	.70
	(Categories leading league are italicized but not printed in red)		
151	Archi Cianfrocco	.10	.05
152	Rich DeLucia	.10	.05
153	Greg Vaughn	.10	.05
154	Wes Chamberlain	.10	.05
155	Dennis Eckersley	.20	.09
156	Sammy Sosa	.40	.18
157	Gary DiSarcina	.10	.05
158	Kevin Koslofski	.10	.05
159	Doug Linton	.10	.05
160	Lou Whitaker	.20	.09
161	Chad McConnell	.10	.05
162	Joe Hesketh	.10	.05
163	Tim Wakefield	.20	.09
164	Leo Gomez	.10	.05
165	Jose Rijo	.10	.05
166	Tim Scott	.10	.05
167	Steve Olin UER	.10	.05
	(Born 10/4/65 should say 10/10/65)		
168	Kevin Maas	.10	.05
169	Kenny Rogers	.10	.05
170	David Justice	.40	.18
171	Doug Jones	.10	.05
172	Jeff Reboulet	.10	.05
173	Andres Galarraga	.40	.18
174	Randy Velarde	.10	.05
175	Kirk McCaskill	.10	.05
176	Darren Lewis	.10	.05
177	Lenny Harris	.10	.05
178	Jeff Fassero	.10	.05
179	Ken Griffey Jr.	2.00	.90
180	Darren Daulton	.20	.09
181	John Jaha	.20	.09
182	Ron Darling	.10	.05
183	Greg Maddux	1.25	.55
184	Damion Easley	.10	.05
185	Jack Morris	.20	.09
186	Mike Magnante	.10	.05
187	John Dopson	.10	.05
188	Sid Fernandez	.10	.05
189	Tony Phillips	.10	.05
190	Doug Drabek	.10	.05
191	Sean Lowe	.10	.05
192	Bob Milacki	.10	.05
193	Steve Foster	.10	.05
194	Jerald Clark	.10	.05
195	Pete Harnisch	.10	.05
196	Pat Kelly	.10	.05
197	Jeff Frye	.10	.05
198	Alejandro Pena	.10	.05
199	Junior Ortiz	.10	.05
200	Kirby Puckett	.75	.35
201	Jose Uribe	.10	.05
202	Mike Scioscia	.10	.05
203	Bernard Gilkey	.20	.09
204	Dan Pasqua	.10	.05
205	Gary Carter	.30	.14
206	Henry Cotto	.10	.05
207	Paul Molitor	.40	.18
208	Mike Hartley	.10	.05
209	Jeff Parrett	.10	.05
210	Mark Langston	.10	.05
211	Doug Dascenzo	.10	.05
212	Rick Reed	.10	.05
213	Candy Maldonado	.10	.05
214	Danny Darwin	.10	.05
215	Pat Howell	.10	.05
216	Mark Leiter	.10	.05
217	Kevin Mitchell	.20	.09
218	Ben McDonald	.10	.05
219	Bip Roberts	.10	.05
220	Benny Santiago	.10	.05
221	Carlos Baerga	.40	.18
222	Bernie Williams	.40	.18
223	Roger Pavlik	.10	.05
224	Sid Bream	.10	.05
225	Matt Williams	.30	.14
226	Willie Banks	.10	.05
227	Jeff Bagwell	.75	.35
228	Tom Goodwin	.10	.05
229	Mike Perez	.10	.05
230	Carlton Fisk	.40	.18
231	John Wetteland	.20	.09
232	Tino Martinez	.40	.18
233	Rick Greene	.10	.05
234	Tim McIntosh	.10	.05
235	Mitch Williams	.10	.05
236	Kevin Campbell	.10	.05
237	Jose Vizcaino	.10	.05
238	Chris Donnels	.10	.05
239	Mike Boddicker	.10	.05
240	John Olerud	.20	.09
241	Mike Gardiner	.10	.05
242	Charlie O'Brien	.10	.05
243	Rob Deer	.10	.05
244	Denny Neagle	.20	.09
245	Chris Sabo	.10	.05
246	Gregg Olson	.10	.05
247	Frank Seminara UER	.10	.05
	(Acquired 12/3/98)		
248	Scott Scudder	.10	.05
249	Tim Burke	.10	.05
250	Chuck Knoblauch	.40	.18
251	Mike Bielecki	.10	.05
252	Xavier Hernandez	.10	.05
253	Jose Guzman	.10	.05
254	Cory Snyder	.10	.05
255	Orel Hershiser	.20	.09
256	Wil Cordero	.10	.05
257	Luis Alicea	.10	.05
258	Mike Schooler	.10	.05
259	Craig Grebeck	.10	.05
260	Duane Ward	.10	.05
261	Bill Wegman	.10	.05
262	Mickey Morandini	.10	.05
263	Vince Horsman	.10	.05
264	Paul Sorrento	.10	.05
265	Andre Dawson	.30	.14
266	Rene Gonzales	.10	.05
267	Keith Miller	.10	.05
268	Derek Bell	.20	.09
269	Todd Steverson	.20	.09
270	Frank Viola	.10	.05
271	Wally Whitehurst	.10	.05
272	Kurt Knudsen	.10	.05
273	Dan Walters	.10	.05
274	Rick Sutcliffe	.10	.05
275	Andy Van Slyke	.20	.09
276	Paul O'Neill	.20	.09
277	Mark Whiten	.10	.05
278	Chris Nabholz	.10	.05
279	Todd Burns	.10	.05
280	Tom Glavine	.30	.14
281	Butch Henry	.10	.05
282	Shane Mack	.10	.05
283	Mike Jackson	.10	.05
284	Henry Rodriguez	.20	.09
285	Bob Tewksbury	.10	.05
286	Ron Karkovice	.10	.05
287	Mike Gallego	.10	.05
288	Dave Cochrane	.10	.05
289	Jesse Orosco	.10	.05
290	Dave Stewart	.20	.09
291	Tommy Greene	.10	.05
292	Rey Sanchez	.10	.05
293	Rob Ducey	.10	.05
294	Brent Mayne	.10	.05
295	Dave Stieb	.10	.05
296	Luis Rivera	.10	.05
297	Jeff Innis	.10	.05
298	Scott Livingstone	.10	.05
299	Bob Patterson	.10	.05
300	Cal Ripken	1.50	.70
301	Cesar Hernandez	.10	.05
302	Randy Myers	.20	.09
303	Brook Jacoby	.10	.05
304	Melido Perez	.10	.05
305	Rafael Palmeiro	.30	.14
306	Damon Berryhill	.10	.05
307	Dan Serafini	.30	.14
308	Darryl Kile	.20	.09
309	J.T. Bruett	.10	.05
310	Dave Righetti	.10	.05
311	Jay Howell	.10	.05
312	Geronimo Pena	.10	.05
313	Greg Hibbard	.10	.05
314	Mark Gardner	.10	.05
315	Edgar Martinez	.30	.14
316	Dave Nilsson	.20	.09
317	Kyle Abbott	.10	.05
318	Willie Wilson	.10	.05
319	Paul Assenmacher	.10	.05
320	Tim Fortugno	.10	.05
321	Rusty Meacham	.10	.05
322	Pat Borders	.10	.05
323	Mike Greenwell	.10	.05
324	Willie Randolph	.20	.09
325	Bill Gullickson	.10	.05
326	Gary Varsho	.10	.05
327	Tim Hulett	.10	.05
328	Scott Ruskin	.10	.05
329	Mike Maddux	.10	.05
330	Danny Tartabull	.20	.09
331	Kenny Lofton	.75	.35
332	Geno Petralli	.10	.05
333	Otis Nixon	.10	.05
334	Jason Kendall	.60	.25
335	Mark Portugal	.10	.05
336	Mike Pagliarulo	.10	.05
337	Kent Manwaring	.10	.05
338	Bob Ojeda	.10	.05
339	Mark Clark	.10	.05
340	John Kruk	.20	.09
341	Mel Rojas	.20	.09
342	Erik Hanson	.10	.05
343	Doug Henry	.10	.05
344	Jack McDowell	.20	.09
345	Harold Baines	.20	.09
346	Chuck McElroy	.10	.05
347	Luis Sojo	.10	.05
348	Andy Stankiewicz	.10	.05
349	Hipolito Pichardo	.10	.05
350	Joe Carter	.20	.09
351	Ellis Burks	.20	.09
352	Pete Schourek	.10	.05
353	Bubby Groom	.10	.05
354	Jay Bell	.20	.09
355	Brady Anderson	.30	.14
356	Freddie Benavides	.10	.05
357	Phil Stephenson	.10	.05
358	Kevin Wickander	.10	.05
359	Mike Stanley	.10	.05
360	Ivan Rodriguez	.50	.23
361	Scott Bankhead	.10	.05
362	Luis Gonzalez	.10	.05
363	John Smiley	.10	.05
364	Trevor Wilson	.10	.05
365	Tom Candiotti	.10	.05
366	Craig Wilson	.10	.05
367	Steve Sax	.10	.05
368	Delino DeShields	.20	.09
369	Jaime Navarro	.10	.05
370	Dave Valle	.10	.05
371	Mariano Duncan	.10	.05
372	Rod Nichols	.10	.05
373	Mike Morgan	.10	.05
374	Julio Valera	.10	.05
375	Wally Joyner	.20	.09
376	Tom Henke	.10	.05
377	Herm Winningham	.10	.05
378	Orlando Merced	.10	.05
379	Mike Munoz	.10	.05
380	Todd Hundley	.30	.14
381	Mike Flanagan	.10	.05

382	Tim Belcher	.10	.05
383	Jerry Browne	.10	.05
384	Mike Benjamin	.10	.05
385	Jim Leyritz	.10	.05
386	Ray Lankford	.30	.14
387	Devon White	.10	.05
388	Jeremy Hernandez	.10	.05
389	Brian Harper	.10	.05
390	Wade Boggs	.40	.18
391	Derrick May	.10	.05
392	Travis Fryman	.20	.09
393	Ron Gant	.20	.09
394	Checklist 1-132	.10	.05
395	Checklist 133-264 UER (Eckersley)	.10	.05
396	Checklist 265-396	.10	.05
397	George Brett	.75	.35
398	Bobby Witt	.10	.05
399	Daryl Boston	.10	.05
400	Bo Jackson	.20	.09
401	Fred McGriff / Frank Thomas	.50	.23
402	Ryne Sandberg / Carlos Baerga	.20	.09
403	Gary Sheffield / Edgar Martinez	.20	.09
404	Barry Larkin / Travis Fryman	.20	.09
405	Andy Van Slyke / Ken Griffey Jr.	.50	.23
406	Larry Walker / Kirby Puckett	.40	.18
407	Barry Bonds / Joe Carter	.20	.09
408	Darren Daulton / Brian Harper	.20	.09
409	Greg Maddux / Roger Clemens	.40	.18
410	Tom Glavine / Dave Fleming	.20	.09
411	Lee Smith / Dennis Eckersley	.20	.09
412	Jamie McAndrew	.10	.05
413	Pete Smith	.10	.05
414	Juan Guerrero	.10	.05
415	Todd Frohwirth	.10	.05
416	Randy Tomlin	.10	.05
417	B.J. Surhoff	.10	.05
418	Jim Gott	.10	.05
419	Mark Thompson	.10	.05
420	Kevin Tapani	.10	.05
421	Curt Schilling	.20	.09
422	J.T. Snow	.50	.23
423	1993 Prospects: Ryan Klesko / Ivan Cruz / Bubba Smith / Larry Sutton	.50	.23
424	John Valentin	.20	.09
425	Joe Girardi	.10	.05
426	Nigel Wilson	.10	.05
427	Bob MacDonald	.10	.05
428	Todd Zeile	.10	.05
429	Milt Cuyler	.10	.05
430	Eddie Murray	.40	.18
431	Rich Amaral	.10	.05
432	Pete Young	.10	.05
433	Roger Bailey and Tom Schmidt	.10	.05
434	Jack Armstrong	.10	.05
435	Willie McGee	.10	.05
436	Greg W. Harris	.10	.05
437	Chris Hammond	.10	.05
438	Ritchie Moody	.10	.05
439	Bryan Harvey	.10	.05
440	Ruben Sierra	.10	.05
441	Don Lemon and Todd Pridy	.10	.05
442	Kevin McReynolds	.10	.05
443	Terry Leach	.10	.05
444	David Nied	.10	.05
445	Dale Murphy	.30	.14
446	Luis Mercedes	.10	.05
447	Keith Shepherd	.10	.05
448	Ken Caminiti	.30	.14
449	James Austin	.10	.05
450	Darryl Strawberry	.20	.09
451	1993 Prospects: Ramon Caraballo / Jon Shave / Brent Gates / Quinton McCracken	.20	.09
452	Bob Wickman	.10	.05
453	Victor Cole	.10	.05
454	John Johnstone	.10	.05
455	Chili Davis	.20	.09
456	Scott Taylor	.10	.05
457	Tracy Woodson	.10	.05
458	David Wells	.10	.05
459	Derek Wallace	.10	.05
460	Randy Johnson	.40	.18
461	Steve Reed	.10	.05
462	Felix Fermin	.10	.05
463	Scott Aldred	.10	.05
464	Greg Colbrunn	.10	.05
465	Tony Fernandez	.10	.05
466	Mike Felder	.10	.05
467	Lee Stevens	.10	.05
468	Matt Whiteside	.10	.05
469	Dave Hansen	.10	.05
470	Rob Dibble	.10	.05
471	Dave Gallagher	.10	.05
472	Chris Gwynn	.10	.05
473	Dave Henderson	.10	.05
474	Ozzie Guillen	.10	.05
475	Jeff Reardon	.20	.09
476	Mark Voisard and Will Scalzitti	.10	.05
477	Jimmy Jones	.10	.05
478	Greg Cadaret	.10	.05
479	Todd Pratt	.10	.05
480	Pat Listach	.10	.05
481	Ryan Luzinski	.10	.05
482	Darren Reed	.10	.05
483	Brian Griffiths	.10	.05
484	John Wehner	.10	.05
485	Glenn Davis	.10	.05
486	Eric Wedge	.10	.05
487	Jesse Hollins	.10	.05
488	Manuel Lee	.10	.05
489	Scott Fredrickson	.10	.05
490	Omar Olivares	.10	.05
491	Shawn Hare	.10	.05
492	Tom Lampkin	.10	.05
493	Jeff Nelson	.10	.05
494	1993 Prospects: Kevin Young / Adell Davenport / Eduardo Perez / Lou Lucca	.20	.09
495	Ken Hill	.10	.05
496	Reggie Jefferson	.10	.05
497	Matt Petersen and Willie Brown	.10	.05
498	Bud Black	.10	.05
499	Chuck Crim	.10	.05
500	Jose Canseco	.30	.14
501	Johnny Oates MG / Bobby Cox MG	.20	.09
502	Butch Hobson MG / Jim Lefebvre MG	.10	.05
503	Buck Rodgers MG / Tony Perez MG	.20	.09
504	Gene Lamont MG / Don Baylor MG	.20	.09
505	Mike Hargrove MG / Rene Lachemann MG	.20	.09
506	Sparky Anderson MG / Art Howe MG	.20	.09
507	Hal McRae MG / Tom Lasorda MG	.20	.09
508	Phil Garner MG / Felipe Alou MG	.20	.09
509	Tom Kelly MG / Jeff Torborg MG	.10	.05
510	Buck Showalter MG / Jim Fregosi MG	.20	.09
511	Tony LaRussa MG / Jim Leyland MG	.20	.09
512	Lou Piniella MG / Joe Torre MG	.20	.09
513	Kevin Kennedy MG / Jim Riggleman MG	.10	.05
514	Cito Gaston MG / Dusty Baker MG	.20	.09
515	Greg Swindell	.10	.05
516	Alex Arias	.10	.05
517	Bill Pecota	.10	.05
518	Benji Grigsby UER (Misspelled Bengi on card front)	.10	.05
519	David Howard	.10	.05
520	Charlie Hough	.10	.05
521	Kevin Flora	.10	.05
522	Shane Reynolds	.10	.05
523	Doug Bochtler	.10	.05
524	Chris Hoiles	.10	.05
525	Scott Sanderson	.10	.05
526	Mike Sharperson	.10	.05
527	Mike Fetters	.10	.05
528	Paul Quantrill	.10	.05
529	1993 Prospects: Dave Silvestri / Chipper Jones / Benji Gil / Jeff Patzke	2.00	.90
530	Sterling Hitchcock	.20	.09
531	Joe Millette	.10	.05
532	Tom Brunansky	.10	.05
533	Frank Castillo	.10	.05
534	Randy Knorr	.10	.05
535	Jose Oquendo	.10	.05
536	Dave Haas	.10	.05
537	Jason Hutchins and Ryan Turner	.10	.05
538	Jimmy Baron	.10	.05
539	Kerry Woodson	.10	.05
540	Ivan Calderon	.10	.05
541	Denis Boucher	.10	.05
542	Royce Clayton	.10	.05
543	Reggie Williams	.10	.05
544	Steve Decker	.10	.05
545	Dean Palmer	.10	.05
546	Hal Morris	.10	.05
547	Ryan Thompson	.10	.05
548	Lance Blankenship	.10	.05
549	Hensley Meulens	.10	.05
550	Scott Radinsky	.10	.05
551	Eric Young	.40	.18
552	Jeff Blauser	.10	.05
553	Andujar Cedeno	.10	.05
554	Arthur Rhodes	.10	.05
555	Terry Mulholland	.10	.05
556	Darryl Hamilton	.10	.05
557	Pedro Martinez	.40	.18
558	Ryan Whitman and Mark Skeels	.10	.05
559	Jamie Arnold	.20	.09
560	Zane Smith	.10	.05
561	Matt Nokes	.10	.05
562	Bob Zupcic	.10	.05
563	Shawn Boskie	.10	.05
564	Mike Timlin	.10	.05
565	Jerald Clark	.10	.05
566	Rod Brewer	.10	.05
567	Mark Carreon	.10	.05
568	Andy Benes	.20	.09
569	Shawn Barton	.10	.05
570	Tim Wallach	.10	.05
571	Dave Mlicki	.10	.05
572	Trevor Hoffman	.30	.14
573	John Patterson	.10	.05
574	De Shawn Warren	.10	.05
575	Monty Fariss	.10	.05
576	1993 Prospects: Darrell Sherman / Damon Buford / Cliff Floyd / Michael Moore	.20	.09
577	Tim Costo	.10	.05
578	Dave Magadan	.10	.05
579	Neil Garret and Jason Bates	.20	.09
580	Walt Weiss	.10	.05
581	Chris Haney	.10	.05
582	Shawn Abner	.10	.05
583	Marvin Freeman	.10	.05
584	Casey Candaele	.10	.05

585	Ricky Jordan	.10	.05
586	Jeff Tabaka	.10	.05
587	Manny Alexander	.10	.05
588	Mike Trombley	.10	.05
589	Carlos Hernandez	.10	.05
590	Cal Eldred	.10	.05
591	Alex Cole	.10	.05
592	Phil Plantier	.10	.05
593	Brett Merriman	.10	.05
594	Jerry Nielsen	.10	.05
595	Shawon Dunston	.10	.05
596	Jimmy Key	.20	.09
597	Gerald Perry	.10	.05
598	Rico Brogna	.10	.05
599	Clemente Nunez and Daniel Robinson	.20	.09
600	Bret Saberhagen	.10	.05
601	Craig Shipley	.10	.05
602	Henry Mercedes	.10	.05
603	Jim Thome	.75	.35
604	Rod Beck	.20	.09
605	Chuck Finley	.10	.05
606	J. Owens	.10	.05
607	Dan Smith	.10	.05
608	Bill Doran	.10	.05
609	Lance Parrish	.10	.05
610	Denny Martinez	.20	.09
611	Tom Gordon	.10	.05
612	Byron Mathews	.10	.05
613	Joel Adamson	.10	.05
614	Brian Williams	.10	.05
615	Steve Avery	.10	.05
616	1993 Prospects Matt Mieske Tracy Sanders Midre Cummings Ryan Freeburg	.40	.18
617	Craig Lefferts	.10	.05
618	Tony Pena	.10	.05
619	Billy Spiers	.10	.05
620	Todd Benzinger	.10	.05
621	Mike Kotarski and Greg Boyd	.10	.05
622	Ben Rivera	.10	.05
623	Al Martin	.20	.09
624	Sam Militello UER (Profile says drafted in 1988, bio says drafted in 1990)	.10	.05
625	Rick Aguilera	.10	.05
626	Dan Gladden	.10	.05
627	Andres Berumen	.10	.05
628	Kelly Gruber	.10	.05
629	Cris Carpenter	.10	.05
630	Mark Grace	.30	.14
631	Jeff Brantley	.10	.05
632	Chris Widger	.10	.05
633	Three Russians UER Rudolf Razjigaev Eugneyi Puchkov Ilya Bogatyrev Bogatyrev is a shortstop, card has pitching header	.20	.09
634	Mo Sanford	.10	.05
635	Albert Belle	.50	.23
636	Tim Teufel	.10	.05
637	Greg Myers	.10	.05
638	Brian Bohanon	.10	.05
639	Mike Bordick	.10	.05
640	Dwight Gooden	.20	.09
641	Pat Leahy and Gavin Baugh	.10	.05
642	Milt Hill	.10	.05
643	Luis Aquino	.10	.05
644	Dante Bichette	.30	.14
645	Bobby Thigpen	.10	.05
646	Rich Scheid	.10	.05
647	Brian Sackinsky	.10	.05
648	Ryan Hawblitzel	.10	.05
649	Tom Marsh	.10	.05
650	Terry Pendleton	.20	.09
651	Rafael Bournigal	.10	.05
652	Dave West	.10	.05
653	Steve Hosey	.10	.05
654	Gerald Williams	.10	.05
655	Scott Cooper	.10	.05
656	Gary Scott	.10	.05
657	Mike Harkey	.10	.05
658	1993 Prospects Jeromy Burnitz Melvin Nieves Rich Becker Shon Walker	.30	.14
659	Ed Sprague	.10	.05
660	Alan Trammell	.30	.14
661	Garvin Alston and Michael Case	.20	.09
662	Donovan Osborne	.10	.05
663	Jeff Gardner	.10	.05
664	Calvin Jones	.10	.05
665	Darrin Fletcher	.10	.05
666	Glenallen Hill	.10	.05
667	Jim Rosenbohm	.10	.05
668	Scott Lewis	.10	.05
669	Kip Yaughn	.10	.05
670	Julio Franco	.10	.05
671	Dave Martinez	.10	.05
672	Kevin Baes	.10	.05
673	Todd Van Poppel	.10	.05
674	Mark Gubicza	.10	.05
675	Tim Raines	.20	.09
676	Rudy Seanez	.10	.05
677	Charlie Leibrandt	.10	.05
678	Randy Milligan	.10	.05
679	Kim Batiste	.10	.05
680	Craig Biggio	.30	.14
681	Darren Holmes	.10	.05
682	John Candelaria	.10	.05
683	Jerry Stafford and Eddie Christian	.20	.09
684	Pat Mahomes	.10	.05
685	Bob Walk	.10	.05
686	Russ Springer	.10	.05
687	Tony Sheffield	.10	.05
688	Dwight Smith	.10	.05
689	Eddie Zosky	.10	.05
690	Bien Figueroa	.10	.05
691	Jim Tatum	.10	.05
692	Chad Kreuter	.10	.05
693	Rich Rodriguez	.10	.05
694	Shane Turner	.10	.05
695	Kent Bottenfield	.10	.05
696	Jose Mesa	.10	.05
697	Darrell Whitmore	.10	.05
698	Ted Wood	.10	.05
699	Chad Curtis	.20	.09
700	Nolan Ryan	1.50	.70
701	1993 Prospects Mike Piazza Brook Fordyce Carlos Delgado Donnie Leshnock	2.00	.90
702	Tim Pugh	.10	.05
703	Jeff Kent	.20	.09
704	Jon Goodrich and Danny Figueroa	.20	.09
705	Bob Welch	.10	.05
706	Sherard Clinkscales	.10	.05
707	Donn Pall	.10	.05
708	Greg Olson	.10	.05
709	Jeff Juden	.10	.05
710	Mike Mussina	.40	.18
711	Scott Chiamparino	.10	.05
712	Stan Javier	.10	.05
713	John Doherty	.10	.05
714	Kevin Gross	.10	.05
715	Greg Gagne	.10	.05
716	Steve Cooke	.10	.05
717	Steve Farr	.10	.05
718	Jay Buhner	.30	.14
719	Butch Henry	.10	.05
720	David Cone	.20	.09
721	Rick Wilkins	.10	.05
722	Chuck Carr	.10	.05
723	Kenny Felder	.10	.05
724	Guillermo Velasquez	.10	.05
725	Billy Hatcher	.10	.05
726	Mike Veneziale and Ken Kendrena	.20	.09
727	Juniman Hurst	.10	.05
728	Steve Frey	.10	.05
729	Mark Leonard	.10	.05
730	Charles Nagy	.20	.09
731	Donald Harris	.10	.05
732	Travis Buckley	.10	.05
733	Tom Browning	.10	.05
734	Anthony Young	.10	.05
735	Steve Shifflett	.10	.05
736	Jeff Russell	.10	.05
737	Wilson Alvarez	.20	.09
738	Lance Painter	.10	.05
739	Dave Weathers	.10	.05
740	Len Dykstra	.20	.09
741	Mike Devereaux	.10	.05
742	1993 Prospects Rene Arocha Alan Embree Brien Taylor Tim Crabtree	.20	.09
743	Dave Landaker	.10	.05
744	Chris George	.10	.05
745	Eric Davis	.20	.09
746	Mark Strittmatter and Lamarr Rogers	.20	.09
747	Carl Willis	.10	.05
748	Stan Belinda	.10	.05
749	Scott Kamieniecki	.10	.05
750	Rickey Henderson	.30	.14
751	Eric Hillman	.10	.05
752	Pat Hentgen	.30	.14
753	Jim Corsi	.10	.05
754	Brian Jordan	.20	.09
755	Bill Swift	.10	.05
756	Mike Henneman	.10	.05
757	Harold Reynolds	.10	.05
758	Sean Berry	.10	.05
759	Charlie Hayes	.10	.05
760	Luis Polonia	.10	.05
761	Darrin Jackson	.10	.05
762	Mark Lewis	.10	.05
763	Rob Maurer	.10	.05
764	Willie Greene	.20	.09
765	Vince Coleman	.10	.05
766	Todd Revenig	.10	.05
767	Rich Ireland	.10	.05
768	Mike Macfarlane	.10	.05
769	Francisco Cabrera	.10	.05
770	Robin Ventura	.20	.09
771	Kevin Ritz	.10	.05
772	Chito Martinez	.10	.05
773	Cliff Brantley	.10	.05
774	Curtis Leskanic	.10	.05
775	Chris Bosio	.10	.05
776	Jose Offerman	.10	.05
777	Mark Guthrie	.10	.05
778	Don Slaught	.10	.05
779	Rich Monteleone	.10	.05
780	Jim Abbott	.10	.05
781	Jack Clark	.10	.05
782	Reynol Mendoza and Dan Roman	.20	.09
783	Heathcliff Slocumb	.10	.05
784	Jeff Branson	.10	.05
785	Kevin Brown	.20	.09
786	1993 Prospects Mike Christopher Ken Ryan Aaron Taylor Gus Gandarillas	.20	.09
787	Mike Matthews	.20	.09
788	Mackey Sasser	.10	.05
789	Jeff Conine UER (No inclusion of 1990 stats in career total)	.20	.09
790	George Bell	.10	.05
791	Pat Rapp	.10	.05
792	Joe Boever	.10	.05
793	Jim Poole	.10	.05
794	Andy Ashby	.10	.05
795	Deion Sanders	.20	.09
796	Scott Brosius	.10	.05
797	Brad Pennington	.10	.05
798	Greg Blosser	.10	.05
799	Jim Edmonds	1.00	.45
800	Shawn Jeter	.10	.05
801	Jesse Levis	.10	.05
802	Phil Clark UER (Word 'a' is missing in	.10	.05

sentence beginning with "In 1992 ...")		
☐ 803 Ed Pierce	.10	.05
☐ 804 Jose Valentin	.25	.11
☐ 805 Terry Jorgensen	.10	.05
☐ 806 Mark Hutton	.10	.05
☐ 807 Troy Neel	.10	.05
☐ 808 Bret Boone	.10	.05
☐ 809 Cris Colon	.10	.05
☐ 810 Domingo Martinez	.10	.05
☐ 811 Javier Lopez	.40	.18
☐ 812 Matt Walbeck	.10	.05
☐ 813 Dan Wilson	.20	.09
☐ 814 Scooter Tucker	.10	.05
☐ 815 Billy Ashley	.10	.05
☐ 816 Tim Laker	.10	.05
☐ 817 Bobby Jones	.20	.09
☐ 818 Brad Brink	.10	.05
☐ 819 William Pennyfeather	.10	.05
☐ 820 Stan Royer	.10	.05
☐ 821 Doug Brocail	.10	.05
☐ 822 Kevin Rogers	.10	.05
☐ 823 Checklist 397-540	.10	.05
☐ 824 Checklist 541-691	.10	.05
☐ 825 Checklist 692-825	.10	.05

1993 Topps Black Gold

Topps Black Gold cards 1-22 were randomly inserted in Series I packs while card numbers 23-44 were featured in Series II packs. In packs, cards were also inserted three per factory set. In the packs, the cards were inserted one every 72 hobby or retail packs; one every 12 jumbo packs and one every 24 rack packs. Hobbyists could obtain the set by collecting individual random insert cards or receive 11, 22, or 44 Black Gold cards by mail when they sent in special "You've Just Won" cards, which were randomly inserted in packs. Series I packs featured three different "You've Just Won" cards, entitling the holder to receive Group A (cards 1-11), Group B (cards 12-22), or Groups A and B (Cards 1-22). In a similar fashion, four "You've Just Won" cards were inserted in series II packs and entitled the holder to receive Group C (23-33), Group D (34-44), Groups C and D (23-44), or Groups A-D (1-44). By returning the "You've Just Won" card with $1.50 for postage and handling, the collector received not only the Black Gold cards won but also a special "You've Just Won" card and a congratulatory letter informing the collec-

tor that his/her name has been entered into a drawing for one of 500 uncut sheets of all 44 Topps Black Gold cards in a leatherette frame. These standard-size cards feature different color player photos than either the 1993 Topps regular issue or the Topps Gold issue. The player pictures are cut out and superimposed on a black and gloss background. Inside white borders, gold refractory foil edges the top and bottom of the card face. On a black-and-gray pinstripe pattern inside white borders, the horizontal backs have a a second cut out player photo and a player profile on a blue panel. The player's name appears in gold foil lettering on a blue-and-gray geometric shape. The first 22 cards are National Leaguers while the second 22 cards are American Leaguers. Winner cards C and D were both originally produced erroneously and later corrected; the error versions show the players from Winner A and B on the respective fronts of Winner cards C and D. There is no value difference in the variations at this time. The winner cards were redeemable until January 31, 1994.

	MINT	NRMT
COMPLETE SET (44)	10.00	4.50
COMPLETE SERIES 1 (22)	4.00	1.80
COMPLETE SERIES 2 (22)	6.00	2.70
COMMON CARD(1-44)	.10	.05
STATED ODDS 1:72 H/R, 1:12 J, 1:24 RACK		
THREE PER FACTORY SET		

☐ 1 Barry Bonds	.75	.35
☐ 2 Will Clark	.40	.18
☐ 3 Darren Daulton	.25	.11
☐ 4 Andre Dawson	.40	.18
☐ 5 Delino DeShields	.10	.05
☐ 6 Tom Glavine	.40	.18
☐ 7 Marquis Grissom	.25	.11
☐ 8 Tony Gwynn	1.50	.70
☐ 9 Eric Karros	.25	.11
☐ 10 Ray Lankford	.25	.11
☐ 11 Barry Larkin	.40	.18
☐ 12 Greg Maddux	2.00	.90
☐ 13 Fred McGriff	.40	.18
☐ 14 Joe Oliver	.10	.05
☐ 15 Terry Pendleton	.10	.05
☐ 16 Bip Roberts	.10	.05
☐ 17 Ryne Sandberg	.75	.35
☐ 18 Gary Sheffield	.60	.25
☐ 19 Lee Smith	.25	.11
☐ 20 Ozzie Smith	.60	.25
☐ 21 Andy Van Slyke	.10	.05
☐ 22 Larry Walker	.60	.25
☐ 23 Roberto Alomar	.60	.25
☐ 24 Brady Anderson	.10	.05
☐ 25 Carlos Baerga	.10	.05
☐ 26 Joe Carter	.25	.11
☐ 27 Roger Clemens	1.00	.45
☐ 28 Mike Devereaux	.10	.05
☐ 29 Dennis Eckersley	.25	.11
☐ 30 Cecil Fielder	.25	.11
☐ 31 Travis Fryman	.25	.11
☐ 32 Juan Gonzalez UER	1.50	.70
(No copyright or licensing on card)		
☐ 33 Ken Griffey Jr.	3.00	1.35
☐ 34 Brian Harper	.10	.05
☐ 35 Pat Listach	.10	.05
☐ 36 Kenny Lofton	1.25	.55
☐ 37 Edgar Martinez	.40	.18
☐ 38 Jack McDowell	.10	.05
☐ 39 Mark McGwire	1.00	.45

☐ 40 Kirby Puckett	1.25	.55
☐ 41 Mickey Tettleton	.10	.05
☐ 42 Frank Thomas UER	3.00	1.35
(No copyright or licensing on card)		
☐ 43 Robin Ventura	.25	.11
☐ 44 Dave Winfield	.40	.18
☐ A Winner A 1-11	.50	.23
☐ B Winner B 12-22	.50	.23
☐ C Winner C 23-33	.75	.35
☐ D Winner D 34-44	.75	.35
☐ AB Winner AB 1-22 UER	1.00	.45
(Numbers 10 and 11 have the 1 missing)		
☐ CD Winner C/D 23-44	1.50	.70
☐ ABCD Winner ABCD 1-44	2.50	1.10

1993 Topps Traded

This 132-card standard-size set focuses on promising rookies, new managers, free agents, and players who changed teams. The set also includes 22 members of Team USA. The set has the same design on the front as the regular 1993 Topps issue. The backs are also the same design and carry a head shot, biography, stats, and career highlights. Rookie Cards in this set include Todd Helton, A.J. Hinch, Dante Powell and Todd Walker.

	MINT	NRMT
COMP.FACT.SET (132)	20.00	9.00
COMMON CARD (1T-132T)	.10	.05
MINOR STARS	.20	.09
UNLISTED STARS	.40	.18

☐ 1T Barry Bonds	.50	.23
☐ 2T Rich Renteria	.20	.09
☐ 3T Aaron Sele	.20	.09
☐ 4T Carlton Loewer USA	.20	.09
☐ 5T Erik Pappas	.10	.05
☐ 6T Greg McMichael	.10	.05
☐ 7T Freddie Benavides	.10	.05
☐ 8T Kirk Gibson	.20	.09
☐ 9T Tony Fernandez	.20	.09
☐ 10T Jay Gainer	.10	.05
☐ 11T Orestes Destrade	.10	.05
☐ 12T A.J. Hinch USA	4.00	1.80
☐ 13T Bobby Munoz	.10	.05
☐ 14T Tom Henke	.10	.05
☐ 15T Rob Butler	.10	.05
☐ 16T Gary Wayne	.10	.05
☐ 17T David McCarty	.10	.05
☐ 18T Walt Weiss	.10	.05
☐ 19T Todd Helton USA	12.00	5.50
☐ 20T Mark Whiten	.10	.05
☐ 21T Ricky Gutierrez	.10	.05
☐ 22T Dustin Hermanson USA	.75	.35
☐ 23T Sherman Obando	.10	.05
☐ 24T Mike Piazza	2.00	.90
☐ 25T Jeff Russell	.10	.05
☐ 26T Jason Bere	.20	.09

	MINT	NRMT

☐ 27T Jack Voigt .10 .05
☐ 28T Chris Bosio .10 .05
☐ 29T Phil Hiatt .10 .05
☐ 30T Matt Beaumont USA .40 .18
☐ 31T Andres Galarraga .40 .18
☐ 32T Greg Swindell .10 .05
☐ 33T Vinny Castilla .40 .18
☐ 34T Pat Clougherty USA .10 .05
☐ 35T Greg Briley .10 .05
☐ 36T Dallas Green MG .10 .05
   Davey Johnson MG
☐ 37T Tyler Green .10 .05
☐ 38T Craig Paquette .10 .05
☐ 39T Danny Sheaffer .10 .05
☐ 40T Jim Converse .10 .05
☐ 41T Terry Harvey USA .10 .05
☐ 42T Phil Plantier .10 .05
☐ 43T Doug Saunders .10 .05
☐ 44T Benny Santiago .10 .05
☐ 45T Dante Powell USA 1.50 .70
☐ 46T Jeff Parrett .10 .05
☐ 47T Wade Boggs .40 .18
☐ 48T Paul Molitor .40 .18
☐ 49T Turk Wendell .10 .05
☐ 50T David Wells .10 .05
☐ 51T Gary Sheffield .40 .18
☐ 52T Kevin Young .10 .05
☐ 53T Nelson Liriano .10 .05
☐ 54T Greg Maddux 1.25 .55
☐ 55T Derek Bell .20 .09
☐ 56T Matt Turner .10 .05
☐ 57T Charlie Nelson USA .10 .05
☐ 58T Mike Hampton .30 .14
☐ 59T Troy O'Leary .10 .05
☐ 60T Benji Gil .10 .05
☐ 61T Mitch Lyden .10 .05
☐ 62T J.T. Snow .40 .18
☐ 63T Damon Buford .10 .05
☐ 64T Gene Harris .10 .05
☐ 65T Randy Myers .20 .09
☐ 66T Felix Jose .10 .05
☐ 67T Todd Dunn USA .10 .05
☐ 68T Jimmy Key .20 .09
☐ 69T Pedro Castellano .10 .05
☐ 70T Mark Merila USA .20 .09
☐ 71T Rich Rodriguez .10 .05
☐ 72T Matt Mieske .10 .05
☐ 73T Pete Incaviglia .10 .05
☐ 74T Carl Everett .20 .09
☐ 75T Jim Abbott .10 .05
☐ 76T Luis Aquino .10 .05
☐ 77T Rene Arocha .10 .05
☐ 78T Jon Shave .10 .05
☐ 79T Todd Walker USA 3.00 1.35
☐ 80T Jack Armstrong .10 .05
☐ 81T Jeff Richardson .10 .05
☐ 82T Blas Minor .10 .05
☐ 83T Dave Winfield .30 .14
☐ 84T Paul O'Neill .10 .05
☐ 85T Steve Reich USA .10 .05
☐ 86T Chris Hammond .10 .05
☐ 87T Hilly Hathaway .10 .05
☐ 88T Fred McGriff .30 .14
☐ 89T Dave Telgheder .10 .05
☐ 90T Richie Lewis .10 .05
☐ 91T Brent Gates .20 .09
☐ 92T Andre Dawson .30 .14
☐ 93T Andy Barkett USA .20 .09
☐ 94T Doug Drabek .10 .05
☐ 95T Joe Klink .10 .05
☐ 96T Willie Blair .10 .05
☐ 97T Danny Graves USA .20 .09
☐ 98T Pat Meares .10 .05
☐ 99T Mike Lansing .20 .09
☐ 100T Marcos Armas .10 .05
☐ 101T Darren Grass USA .10 .05
☐ 102T Chris Jones .10 .05
☐ 103T Ken Ryan .10 .05
☐ 104T Ellis Burks .20 .09
☐ 105T Roberto Kelly .10 .05
☐ 106T Dave Magadan .10 .05
☐ 107T Paul Wilson USA .75 .35
☐ 108T Rob Natal .10 .05
☐ 109T Paul Wagner .10 .05
☐ 110T Jeromy Burnitz .10 .05
☐ 111T Monty Fariss .10 .05

☐ 112T Kevin Mitchell .20 .09
☐ 113T Scott Pose .10 .05
☐ 114T Dave Stewart .20 .09
☐ 115T Russ Johnson USA .50 .23
☐ 116T Armando Reynoso .10 .05
☐ 117T Geronimo Berroa .20 .09
☐ 118T Woody Williams .10 .05
☐ 119T Tim Bogar .10 .05
☐ 120T Bob Scata USA .10 .05
☐ 121T Henry Cotto .10 .05
☐ 122T Gregg Jefferies .10 .05
☐ 123T Norm Charlton .10 .05
☐ 124T Bret Wagner USA .40 .18
☐ 125T David Cone .20 .09
☐ 126T Daryl Boston .10 .05
☐ 127T Tim Wallach .10 .05
☐ 128T Mike Martin USA .20 .09
☐ 129T John Cummings .10 .05
☐ 130T Ryan Bowen .10 .05
☐ 131T John Hudek USA .20 .09
☐ 132T Checklist 1-132 .10 .05

1994 Topps

These 792 standard-size cards were issued in two series of 396. Two types of factory sets were also issued. One features the 792 basic cards, ten Topps Gold, three Black Gold and three Finest Pre-Production cards for a total of 808. The other factory set (Bakers Dozen) includes the 792 basic cards, ten Topps Gold, ten Black Gold, ten 1995 Topps Pre-Production cards and a sample pack of three special Topps cards for a total of 818. The standard cards feature glossy color player photos with white borders on the fronts. The player's name is in white cursive lettering at the bottom left, with the team name and player's position printed on a team color-coded bar. There is an inner multicolored border along the left side that extends obliquely across the bottom. The horizontal backs carry an action shot of the player with biography, statistics and highlights. Subsets include Draft Picks (201-210/739-762), All-Stars (384-394) and Stat Twins (601-609). Rookie Cards include Alan Benes, Jeff D'Amico, Brooks Kieschnick, Kirk Presley and Pat Watkins.

	MINT	NRMT
COMPLETE SET (792)	30.00	13.50
COMP.FACT.SET (808)	50.00	22.00
COMP.BAKER SET (818)	50.00	22.00
COMPLETE SERIES 1 (396)	15.00	6.75
COMPLETE SERIES 2 (396)	15.00	6.75

COMMON CARD (1-792) .10 .05
MINOR STARS .20 .09
UNLISTED STARS .40 .18
SUBSET CARDS HALF VALUE OF BASE CARDS
COMP.GOLD SET (792) 80.00 36.00
COMP.GOLD SERIES 1 (396) 40.00 18.00
COMP.GOLD SERIES 2 (396) 40.00 18.00
COMMON GOLD (1-792) .15 .07
*GOLD STARS: 1.5X TO 4X HI COLUMN
*GOLD YOUNG STARS: 1.25X TO 3X HI
ONE GOLD PER PACK
TEN GOLD PER FACTORY SET

☐ 1 Mike Piazza 1.25 .55
☐ 2 Bernie Williams .40 .18
☐ 3 Kevin Rogers .10 .05
☐ 4 Paul Carey .10 .05
☐ 5 Ozzie Guillen .10 .05
☐ 6 Derrick May .10 .05
☐ 7 Jose Mesa .10 .05
☐ 8 Todd Hundley .20 .09
☐ 9 Chris Haney .10 .05
☐ 10 John Olerud .20 .09
☐ 11 Andujar Cedeno .10 .05
☐ 12 John Smiley .10 .05
☐ 13 Phil Plantier .10 .05
☐ 14 Willie Banks .10 .05
☐ 15 Jay Bell .20 .09
☐ 16 Doug Henry .10 .05
☐ 17 Lance Blankenship .10 .05
☐ 18 Greg W. Harris .10 .05
☐ 19 Scott Livingstone .10 .05
☐ 20 Bryan Harvey .10 .05
☐ 21 Wil Cordero .10 .05
☐ 22 Roger Pavlik .10 .05
☐ 23 Mark Lemke .10 .05
☐ 24 Jeff Nelson .10 .05
☐ 25 Todd Zeile .10 .05
☐ 26 Billy Hatcher .10 .05
☐ 27 Joe Magrane .10 .05
☐ 28 Tony Longmire .10 .05
☐ 29 Omar Daal .10 .05
☐ 30 Kirt Manwaring .10 .05
☐ 31 Melido Perez .10 .05
☐ 32 Tim Hulett .10 .05
☐ 33 Jeff Schwartz .10 .05
☐ 34 Nolan Ryan 1.50 .70
☐ 35 Jose Guzman .10 .05
☐ 36 Felix Fermin .10 .05
☐ 37 Jeff Innis .10 .05
☐ 38 Brett Mayne .10 .05
☐ 39 Huck Flener .10 .05
☐ 40 Jeff Bagwell .75 .35
☐ 41 Kevin Wickander .10 .05
☐ 42 Ricky Gutierrez .10 .05
☐ 43 Pat Mahomes .10 .05
☐ 44 Jeff King .10 .05
☐ 45 Cal Eldred .20 .09
☐ 46 Craig Paquette .10 .05
☐ 47 Richie Lewis .10 .05
☐ 48 Tony Phillips .10 .05
☐ 49 Armando Reynoso .10 .05
☐ 50 Moises Alou .20 .09
☐ 51 Manuel Lee .10 .05
☐ 52 Otis Nixon .10 .05
☐ 53 Billy Ashley .10 .05
☐ 54 Mark Whiten .10 .05
☐ 55 Jeff Russell .10 .05
☐ 56 Chad Curtis .10 .05
☐ 57 Kevin Stocker .10 .05
☐ 58 Mike Jackson .10 .05
☐ 59 Matt Nokes .10 .05
☐ 60 Chris Bosio .10 .05
☐ 61 Damon Buford .10 .05
☐ 62 Tim Belcher .10 .05
☐ 63 Glenallen Hill .10 .05
☐ 64 Bill Wertz .10 .05
☐ 65 Eddie Murray .40 .18
☐ 66 Tom Gordon .10 .05
☐ 67 Alex Gonzalez .20 .09
☐ 68 Eddie Taubensee .10 .05
☐ 69 Jacob Brumfield .10 .05
☐ 70 Andy Benes .20 .09
☐ 71 Rich Becker .10 .05
☐ 72 Steve Cooke .10 .05
☐ 73 Billy Spiers .10 .05

☐ 74	Scott Brosius	.10	.05	☐ 156	David McCarty	.10	.05		Curtis Pride
☐ 75	Alan Trammell	.30	.14	☐ 157	Paul Wagner	.10	.05		Shawn Green
☐ 76	Luis Aquino	.10	.05	☐ 158	Shortstop Prospects	1.50	.70		Mark Sweeney
☐ 77	Jerald Clark	.10	.05		Orlando Miller				Eddie Davis
☐ 78	Mel Rojas	.10	.05		Brandon Wilson			☐ 238	Kim Batiste	.10	.05
☐ 79	Outfield Prospects	.30	.14		Derek Jeter			☐ 239	Paul Assenmacher	.10	.05
	Billy Masse				Mike Neal			☐ 240	Will Clark	.30	.14
	Stanton Cameron			☐ 159	Mike Fetters	.10	.05	☐ 241	Jose Offerman	.10	.05
	Tim Clark			☐ 160	Scott Lydy	.10	.05	☐ 242	Todd Frohwirth	.10	.05
	Craig McClure			☐ 161	Darrell Whitmore	.10	.05	☐ 243	Tim Raines	.20	.09
☐ 80	Jose Canseco	.30	.14	☐ 162	Bob MacDonald	.10	.05	☐ 244	Rick Wilkins	.10	.05
☐ 81	Greg McMichael	.10	.05	☐ 163	Vinny Castilla	.20	.09	☐ 245	Bret Saberhagen	.10	.05
☐ 82	Brian Turang	.10	.05	☐ 164	Denis Boucher	.10	.05	☐ 246	Thomas Howard	.10	.05
☐ 83	Tom Urbani	.10	.05	☐ 165	Ivan Rodriguez	.50	.23	☐ 247	Stan Belinda	.10	.05
☐ 84	Garret Anderson	.40	.18	☐ 166	Ron Gant	.20	.09	☐ 248	Rickey Henderson	.30	.14
☐ 85	Tony Pena	.10	.05	☐ 167	Tim Davis	.10	.05	☐ 249	Brian Williams	.10	.05
☐ 86	Ricky Jordan	.10	.05	☐ 168	Steve Dixon	.10	.05	☐ 250	Barry Larkin	.30	.14
☐ 87	Jim Gott	.10	.05	☐ 169	Scott Fletcher	.10	.05	☐ 251	Jose Valentin	.10	.05
☐ 88	Pat Kelly	.10	.05	☐ 170	Terry Mulholland	.10	.05	☐ 252	Lenny Webster	.10	.05
☐ 89	Bud Black	.10	.05	☐ 171	Greg Myers	.10	.05	☐ 253	Blas Minor	.10	.05
☐ 90	Robin Ventura	.20	.09	☐ 172	Brett Butler	.20	.09	☐ 254	Tim Teufel	.10	.05
☐ 91	Rick Sutcliffe	.10	.05	☐ 173	Bob Wickman	.10	.05	☐ 255	Bobby Witt	.10	.05
☐ 92	Jose Bautista	.10	.05	☐ 174	Dave Martinez	.10	.05	☐ 256	Walt Weiss	.10	.05
☐ 93	Bob Ojeda	.10	.05	☐ 175	Fernando Valenzuela	.20	.09	☐ 257	Chad Kreuter	.10	.05
☐ 94	Phil Hiatt	.10	.05	☐ 176	Craig Grebeck	.10	.05	☐ 258	Roberto Mejia	.10	.05
☐ 95	Tim Pugh	.10	.05	☐ 177	Shawn Boskie	.10	.05	☐ 259	Cliff Floyd	.20	.09
☐ 96	Randy Knorr	.10	.05	☐ 178	Alfie Lopez	.10	.05	☐ 260	Julio Franco	.10	.05
☐ 97	Todd Jones	.10	.05	☐ 179	Butch Huskey	.20	.09	☐ 261	Rafael Belliard	.10	.05
☐ 98	Ryan Thompson	.10	.05	☐ 180	George Brett	.75	.35	☐ 262	Marc Newfield	.20	.09
☐ 99	Tim Mauser	.10	.05	☐ 181	Juan Guzman	.10	.05	☐ 263	Gerald Perry	.10	.05
☐ 100	Kirby Puckett	.75	.35	☐ 182	Eric Anthony	.10	.05	☐ 264	Ken Ryan	.10	.05
☐ 101	Mark Dewey	.10	.05	☐ 183	Rob Dibble	.10	.05	☐ 265	Chili Davis	.20	.09
☐ 102	B.J. Surhoff	.10	.05	☐ 184	Craig Shipley	.10	.05	☐ 266	Dave West	.10	.05
☐ 103	Sterling Hitchcock	.10	.05	☐ 185	Kevin Tapani	.10	.05	☐ 267	Royce Clayton	.10	.05
☐ 104	Alex Arias	.10	.05	☐ 186	Marcus Moore	.10	.05	☐ 268	Pedro Martinez	.40	.18
☐ 105	David Wells	.10	.05	☐ 187	Graeme Lloyd	.10	.05	☐ 269	Mark Hutton	.10	.05
☐ 106	Daryl Boston	.10	.05	☐ 188	Mike Bordick	.10	.05	☐ 270	Frank Thomas	1.50	.70
☐ 107	Mike Stanton	.10	.05	☐ 189	Chris Hammond	.10	.05	☐ 271	Brad Pennington	.10	.05
☐ 108	Gary Redus	.10	.05	☐ 190	Cecil Fielder	.20	.09	☐ 272	Mike Harkey	.10	.05
☐ 109	Delino DeShields	.10	.05	☐ 191	Curtis Leskanic	.10	.05	☐ 273	Sandy Alomar	.20	.09
☐ 110	Lee Smith	.20	.09	☐ 192	Lou Frazier	.10	.05	☐ 274	Dave Gallagher	.10	.05
☐ 111	Greg Litton	.10	.05	☐ 193	Steve Dreyer	.10	.05	☐ 275	Wally Joyner	.20	.09
☐ 112	Frankie Rodriguez	.10	.05	☐ 194	Javier Lopez	.30	.14	☐ 276	Ricky Trlicek	.10	.05
☐ 113	Russ Springer	.10	.05	☐ 195	Edgar Martinez	.30	.14	☐ 277	Al Osuna	.10	.05
☐ 114	Mitch Williams	.10	.05	☐ 196	Allen Watson	.10	.05	☐ 278	Calvin Reese	.20	.09
☐ 115	Eric Karros	.20	.09	☐ 197	John Flaherty	.10	.05	☐ 279	Kevin Higgins	.10	.05
☐ 116	Jeff Brantley	.10	.05	☐ 198	Kurt Stillwell	.10	.05	☐ 280	Rick Aguilera	.10	.05
☐ 117	Jack Voigt	.10	.05	☐ 199	Danny Jackson	.10	.05	☐ 281	Orlando Merced	.10	.05
☐ 118	Jason Bere	.10	.05	☐ 200	Cal Ripken	1.50	.70	☐ 282	Mike Mohler	.10	.05
☐ 119	Kevin Roberson	.10	.05	☐ 201	Mike Bell FDP	.40	.18	☐ 283	John Jaha	.10	.05
☐ 120	Jimmy Key	.20	.09	☐ 202	Alan Benes FDP	1.00	.45	☐ 284	Robb Nen	.10	.05
☐ 121	Reggie Jefferson	.10	.05	☐ 203	Matt Farner FDP	.10	.05	☐ 285	Travis Fryman	.20	.09
☐ 122	Jeromy Burnitz	.10	.05	☐ 204	Jeff Granger FDP	.10	.05	☐ 286	Mark Thompson	.10	.05
☐ 123	Billy Brewer	.10	.05	☐ 205	Brooks Kieschnick FDP	.40	.18	☐ 287	Mike Lansing	.20	.09
☐ 124	Willie Canate	.10	.05	☐ 206	Jeremy Lee FDP	.10	.05	☐ 288	Craig Lefferts	.10	.05
☐ 125	Greg Swindell	.10	.05	☐ 207	Charles Peterson FDP	.20	.09	☐ 289	Damon Berryhill	.10	.05
☐ 126	Hal Morris	.10	.05	☐ 208	Alan Rice FDP	.10	.05	☐ 290	Randy Johnson	.40	.18
☐ 127	Brad Ausmus	.10	.05	☐ 209	Billy Wagner FDP	.75	.35	☐ 291	Jeff Reed	.10	.05
☐ 128	George Tsamis	.10	.05	☐ 210	Kelly Wunsch FDP	.10	.05	☐ 292	Danny Darwin	.10	.05
☐ 129	Denny Neagle	.20	.09	☐ 211	Tom Candiotti	.10	.05	☐ 293	J.T. Snow	.40	.18
☐ 130	Pat Listach	.10	.05	☐ 212	Domingo Jean	.10	.05	☐ 294	Tyler Green	.10	.05
☐ 131	Steve Karsay	.10	.05	☐ 213	John Burkett	.10	.05	☐ 295	Chris Hoiles	.10	.05
☐ 132	Bret Barberie	.10	.05	☐ 214	George Bell	.10	.05	☐ 296	Roger McDowell	.10	.05
☐ 133	Mark Leiter	.10	.05	☐ 215	Dan Plesac	.10	.05	☐ 297	Spike Owen	.10	.05
☐ 134	Greg Colbrunn	.10	.05	☐ 216	Manny Ramirez	.50	.23	☐ 298	Salomon Torres	.10	.05
☐ 135	David Nied	.10	.05	☐ 217	Mike Maddux	.10	.05	☐ 299	Wilson Alvarez	.10	.05
☐ 136	Dean Palmer	.10	.05	☐ 218	Kevin McReynolds	.10	.05	☐ 300	Ryne Sandberg	.50	.23
☐ 137	Steve Avery	.10	.05	☐ 219	Pat Borders	.10	.05	☐ 301	Derek Lilliquist	.10	.05
☐ 138	Bill Haselman	.10	.05	☐ 220	Doug Drabek	.10	.05	☐ 302	Howard Johnson	.10	.05
☐ 139	Tripp Cromer	.10	.05	☐ 221	Larry Luebbers	.10	.05	☐ 303	Greg Cadaret	.10	.05
☐ 140	Frank Viola	.10	.05	☐ 222	Trevor Hoffman	.10	.05	☐ 304	Pat Hentgen	.20	.09
☐ 141	Rene Gonzales	.10	.05	☐ 223	Pat Meares	.10	.05	☐ 305	Craig Biggio	.30	.14
☐ 142	Curt Schilling	.20	.09	☐ 224	Danny Miceli	.10	.05	☐ 306	Scott Service	.10	.05
☐ 143	Tim Wallach	.10	.05	☐ 225	Greg Vaughn	.10	.05	☐ 307	Melvin Nieves	.10	.05
☐ 144	Bobby Munoz	.10	.05	☐ 226	Scott Hemond	.10	.05	☐ 308	Mike Trombley	.10	.05
☐ 145	Brady Anderson	.30	.14	☐ 227	Pat Rapp	.10	.05	☐ 309	Carlos Garcia	.10	.05
☐ 146	Rod Beck	.10	.05	☐ 228	Kirk Gibson	.20	.09	☐ 310	Robin Yount UER	.30	.14
☐ 147	Mike LaValliere	.10	.05	☐ 229	Lance Painter	.10	.05		(listed with 111 triples in
☐ 148	Greg Hibbard	.10	.05	☐ 230	Larry Walker	.40	.18		1988; should be 11)
☐ 149	Kenny Lofton	.50	.23	☐ 231	Benji Gil	.10	.05	☐ 311	Marcos Armas	.10	.05
☐ 150	Doc Gooden	.20	.09	☐ 232	Mark Wohlers	.10	.05	☐ 312	Rich Rodriguez	.10	.05
☐ 151	Greg Gagne	.10	.05	☐ 233	Rich Amaral	.10	.05	☐ 313	Justin Thompson	.40	.18
☐ 152	Ray McDavid	.10	.05	☐ 234	Eric Pappas	.10	.05	☐ 314	Danny Sheaffer	.10	.05
☐ 153	Chris Donnels	.10	.05	☐ 235	Scott Cooper	.10	.05	☐ 315	Ken Hill	.10	.05
☐ 154	Dan Wilson	.20	.09	☐ 236	Mike Butcher	.10	.05	☐ 316	Pitching Prospects	.20	.09
☐ 155	Todd Stottlemyre	.10	.05	☐ 237	Outfield Prospects	.20	.09		Chad Ogea

Duff Brumley
Terrell Wade
Chris Michalak
□ 317 Cris Carpenter .... .10 .05
□ 318 Jeff Blauser .... .20 .09
□ 319 Ted Power .... .10 .05
□ 320 Ozzie Smith .... .50 .23
□ 321 John Dopson .... .10 .05
□ 322 Chris Turner .... .10 .05
□ 323 Pete Incaviglia .... .10 .05
□ 324 Alan Mills .... .10 .05
□ 325 Jody Reed .... .10 .05
□ 326 Rich Monteleone .... .10 .05
□ 327 Mark Carreon .... .10 .05
□ 328 Donn Pall .... .10 .05
□ 329 Matt Walbeck .... .10 .05
□ 330 Charles Nagy .... .20 .09
□ 331 Jeff McKnight .... .10 .05
□ 332 Jose Lind .... .10 .05
□ 333 Mike Timlin .... .10 .05
□ 334 Doug Jones .... .10 .05
□ 335 Kevin Mitchell .... .10 .05
□ 336 Luis Lopez .... .10 .05
□ 337 Shane Mack .... .10 .05
□ 338 Randy Tomlin .... .10 .05
□ 339 Matt Mieske .... .10 .05
□ 340 Mark McGwire .... .75 .35
□ 341 Nigel Wilson .... .10 .05
□ 342 Danny Gladden .... .10 .05
□ 343 Mo Sanford .... .10 .05
□ 344 Sean Berry .... .10 .05
□ 345 Kevin Brown .... .20 .09
□ 346 Greg Olson .... .10 .05
□ 347 Dave Magadan .... .10 .05
□ 348 Rene Arocha .... .10 .05
□ 349 Carlos Quintana .... .10 .05
□ 350 Jim Abbott .... .10 .05
□ 351 Gary DiSarcina .... .10 .05
□ 352 Ben Rivera .... .10 .05
□ 353 Carlos Hernandez .... .10 .05
□ 354 Darren Lewis .... .10 .05
□ 355 Harold Reynolds .... .10 .05
□ 356 Scott Ruffcorn .... .10 .05
□ 357 Mark Gubicza .... .10 .05
□ 358 Paul Sorrento .... .10 .05
□ 359 Anthony Young .... .10 .05
□ 360 Mark Grace .... .30 .14
□ 361 Rob Butler .... .10 .05
□ 362 Kevin Bass .... .10 .05
□ 363 Eric Helfand .... .10 .05
□ 364 Derek Bell .... .10 .05
□ 365 Scott Erickson .... .10 .05
□ 366 Al Martin .... .10 .05
□ 367 Ricky Bones .... .10 .05
□ 368 Jeff Branson .... .10 .05
□ 369 Third Base Prospects .40 .18
Luis Ortiz
David Bell
Jason Giambi
George Arias
□ 370 Benito Santiago .... .10 .05
(See also 379)
□ 371 John Doherty .... .10 .05
□ 372 Joe Girardi .... .10 .05
□ 373 Tim Scott .... .10 .05
□ 374 Marvin Freeman .... .10 .05
□ 375 Deion Sanders .... .20 .09
□ 376 Roger Salkeld .... .10 .05
□ 377 Bernard Gilkey .... .10 .05
□ 378 Tony Fossas .... .10 .05
□ 379 Mark McLemore UER .10 .05
(Card number is 370)
□ 380 Darren Daulton .... .20 .09
□ 381 Chuck Finley .... .10 .05
□ 382 Mitch Webster .... .10 .05
□ 383 Gerald Williams .... .10 .05
□ 384 Frank Thomas AS .... .60 .25
Fred McGriff AS
□ 385 Roberto Alomar AS .... .20 .09
Robby Thompson AS
□ 386 Wade Boggs AS .... .20 .09
Matt Williams AS
□ 387 Cal Ripken AS .... .50 .23
Jeff Blauser AS
□ 388 Ken Griffey Jr. AS .... .50 .23
Len Dykstra AS

□ 389 Juan Gonzalez AS .40 .18
David Justice AS
□ 390 George Belle AS .20 .09
Bobby Bonds AS
□ 391 Mike Stanley AS .40 .18
Mike Piazza AS
□ 392 Jack McDowell AS .30 .14
Greg Maddux AS
□ 393 Jimmy Key AS .20 .09
Tom Glavine AS
□ 394 Jeff Montgomery AS .10 .05
Randy Myers AS
□ 395 Checklist 1-198 .... .10 .05
□ 396 Checklist 199-396 .... .10 .05
□ 397 Tim Salmon .... .40 .18
□ 398 Todd Benzinger .... .10 .05
□ 399 Frank Castillo .... .10 .05
□ 400 Ken Griffey Jr. .... 2.00 .90
□ 401 John Kruk .... .20 .09
□ 402 Dave Telgheder .... .10 .05
□ 403 Gary Gaetti .... .10 .05
□ 404 Jim Edmonds .... .40 .18
□ 405 Don Slaught .... .10 .05
□ 406 Jose Oquendo .... .10 .05
□ 407 Bruce Ruffin .... .10 .05
□ 408 Phil Clark .... .10 .05
□ 409 Joe Klink .... .10 .05
□ 410 Lou Whitaker .... .20 .09
□ 411 Kevin Seitzer .... .10 .05
□ 412 Darrin Fletcher .... .10 .05
□ 413 Kenny Rogers .... .10 .05
□ 414 Bill Pecota .... .10 .05
□ 415 Dave Fleming .... .10 .05
□ 416 Luis Alicea .... .10 .05
□ 417 Paul Quantrill .... .10 .05
□ 418 Damion Easley .... .10 .05
□ 419 Wes Chamberlain .... .10 .05
□ 420 Harold Baines .... .20 .09
□ 421 Scott Radinsky .... .10 .05
□ 422 Rey Sanchez .... .10 .05
□ 423 Junior Ortiz .... .10 .05
□ 424 Jeff Kent .... .10 .05
□ 425 Brian McRae .... .10 .05
□ 426 Ed Sprague .... .10 .05
□ 427 Tom Edens .... .10 .05
□ 428 Willie Greene .... .10 .05
□ 429 Bryan Hickerson .... .10 .05
□ 430 Dave Winfield .... .30 .14
□ 431 Pedro Astacio .... .10 .05
□ 432 Mike Gallego .... .10 .05
□ 433 Dave Burba .... .10 .05
□ 434 Bob Walk .... .10 .05
□ 435 Darryl Hamilton .... .10 .05
□ 436 Vince Horsman .... .10 .05
□ 437 Bob Natal .... .10 .05
□ 438 Mike Henneman .... .10 .05
□ 439 Willie Blair .... .10 .05
□ 440 Denny Martinez .... .20 .09
□ 441 Dan Peltier .... .10 .05
□ 442 Tony Tarasco .... .10 .05
□ 443 John Cummings .... .10 .05
□ 444 Geronimo Pena .... .10 .05
□ 445 Aaron Sele .... .10 .05
□ 446 Stan Javier .... .10 .05
□ 447 Mike Williams .... .10 .05
□ 448 First Base Prospects .. .30 .14
Greg Pirkl
Roberto Petagine
D.J.Boston
Shawn Wooten
□ 449 Jim Poole .... .10 .05
□ 450 Carlos Baerga .... .10 .05
□ 451 Bob Scanlan .... .10 .05
□ 452 Lance Johnson .... .10 .05
□ 453 Eric Hillman .... .10 .05
□ 454 Keith Miller .... .10 .05
□ 455 Dave Stewart .... .20 .09
□ 456 Pete Harnisch .... .10 .05
□ 457 Roberto Kelly .... .10 .05
□ 458 Tim Worrell .... .10 .05
□ 459 Pedro Munoz .... .10 .05
□ 460 Orel Hershiser .... .20 .09
□ 461 Randy Velarde .... .10 .05
□ 462 Trevor Wilson .... .10 .05
□ 463 Jerry Goff .... .10 .05
□ 464 Bill Wegman .... .10 .05

□ 465 Dennis Eckersley .... .20 .09
□ 466 Jeff Conine .... .20 .09
□ 467 Joe Boever .... .10 .05
□ 468 Dante Bichette .... .20 .09
□ 469 Jeff Shaw .... .10 .05
□ 470 Rafael Palmeiro .... .30 .14
□ 471 Phil Leftwich .... .10 .05
□ 472 Jay Buhner .... .30 .14
□ 473 Bob Tewksbury .... .10 .05
□ 474 Tim Naehring .... .10 .05
□ 475 Tom Glavine .... .20 .09
□ 476 Dave Hollins .... .10 .05
□ 477 Arthur Rhodes .... .10 .05
□ 478 Joey Cora .... .10 .05
□ 479 Mike Morgan .... .10 .05
□ 480 Albert Belle .... .50 .23
□ 481 John Franco .... .20 .09
□ 482 Hipolito Pichardo .... .10 .05
□ 483 Duane Ward .... .10 .05
□ 484 Luis Gonzalez .... .10 .05
□ 485 Joe Oliver .... .10 .05
□ 486 Wally Whitehurst .... .10 .05
□ 487 Mike Benjamin .... .10 .05
□ 488 Eric Davis .... .20 .09
□ 489 Scott Kamieniecki .... .10 .05
□ 490 Kent Hrbek .... .20 .09
□ 491 John Hope .... .10 .05
□ 492 Jesse Orosco .... .10 .05
□ 493 Troy Neel .... .10 .05
□ 494 Ryan Bowen .... .10 .05
□ 495 Mickey Tettleton .... .10 .05
□ 496 Chris Jones .... .10 .05
□ 497 John Wetteland .... .10 .05
□ 498 David Hulse .... .10 .05
□ 499 Greg Maddux .... 1.25 .55
□ 500 Bo Jackson .... .20 .09
□ 501 Donovan Osborne .... .10 .05
□ 502 Mike Greenwell .... .10 .05
□ 503 Steve Frey .... .10 .05
□ 504 Jim Eisenreich .... .10 .05
□ 505 Robby Thompson .... .10 .05
□ 506 Leo Gomez .... .10 .05
□ 507 Dave Staton .... .10 .05
□ 508 Wayne Kirby .... .10 .05
□ 509 Tim Bogar .... .10 .05
□ 510 David Cone .... .20 .09
□ 511 Devon White .... .10 .05
□ 512 Xavier Hernandez .... .10 .05
□ 513 Tim Costo .... .10 .05
□ 514 Gene Harris .... .10 .05
□ 515 Jack McDowell .... .10 .05
□ 516 Kevin Gross .... .10 .05
□ 517 Scott Leius .... .10 .05
□ 518 Lloyd McClendon .... .10 .05
□ 519 Alex Diaz .... .10 .05
□ 520 Wade Boggs .... .40 .18
□ 521 Bob Welch .... .10 .05
□ 522 Henry Cotto .... .10 .05
□ 523 Mike Moore .... .10 .05
□ 524 Tim Laker .... .10 .05
□ 525 Andres Galarraga .... .40 .18
□ 526 Jamie Moyer .... .10 .05
□ 527 Second Base Prospects .20 .09
Norberto Martin
Ruben Santana
Jason Hardtke
Chris Sexton
□ 528 Sid Bream .... .10 .05
□ 529 Erik Hanson .... .10 .05
□ 530 Ray Lankford .... .20 .09
□ 531 Rob Deer .... .10 .05
□ 532 Rod Correia .... .10 .05
□ 533 Roger Mason .... .10 .05
□ 534 Mike Devereaux .... .10 .05
□ 535 Jeff Montgomery .... .10 .05
□ 536 Dwight Smith .... .10 .05
□ 537 Jeremy Hernandez .... .10 .05
□ 538 Ellis Burks .... .20 .09
□ 539 Bobby Jones .... .20 .09
□ 540 Paul Molitor .... .40 .18
□ 541 Jeff Juden .... .10 .05
□ 542 Chris Sabo .... .10 .05
□ 543 Larry Casian .... .10 .05
□ 544 Jeff Gardner .... .10 .05
□ 545 Ramon Martinez .... .20 .09
□ 546 Paul O'Neill .... .20 .09

□ 547	Steve Hosey	.10	.05
□ 548	Dave Nilsson	.10	.05
□ 549	Ron Darling	.10	.05
□ 550	Matt Williams	.30	.14
□ 551	Jack Armstrong	.10	.05
□ 552	Bill Krueger	.10	.05
□ 553	Freddie Benavides	.10	.05
□ 554	Jeff Fassero	.10	.05
□ 555	Chuck Knoblauch	.40	.18
□ 556	Guillermo Velasquez	.10	.05
□ 557	Joel Johnston	.10	.05
□ 558	Tom Lampkin	.10	.05
□ 559	Todd Van Poppel	.10	.05
□ 560	Gary Sheffield	.40	.18
□ 561	Skeeter Barnes	.10	.05
□ 562	Darren Holmes	.10	.05
□ 563	John Vander Wal	.10	.05
□ 564	Mike Ignasiak	.10	.05
□ 565	Fred McGriff	.30	.14
□ 566	Luis Polonia	.10	.05
□ 567	Mike Perez	.10	.05
□ 568	John Valentin	.20	.09
□ 569	Mike Felder	.10	.05
□ 570	Tommy Greene	.10	.05
□ 571	David Segui	.10	.05
□ 572	Roberto Hernandez	.10	.05
□ 573	Steve Wilson	.10	.05
□ 574	Willie McGee	.10	.05
□ 575	Randy Myers	.10	.05
□ 576	Darrin Jackson	.10	.05
□ 577	Eric Plunk	.10	.05
□ 578	Mike Macfarlane	.10	.05
□ 579	Doug Brocail	.10	.05
□ 580	Steve Finley	.20	.09
□ 581	John Roper	.10	.05
□ 582	Danny Cox	.10	.05
□ 583	Chip Hale	.10	.05
□ 584	Scott Bullett	.10	.05
□ 585	Kevin Reimer	.10	.05
□ 586	Brent Gates	.10	.05
□ 587	Matt Turner	.10	.05
□ 588	Rich Rowland	.10	.05
□ 589	Kent Bottenfield	.10	.05
□ 590	Marquis Grissom	.20	.09
□ 591	Doug Strange	.10	.05
□ 592	Jay Howell	.10	.05
□ 593	Omar Vizquel	.20	.09
□ 594	Rheal Cormier	.10	.05
□ 595	Andre Dawson	.30	.14
□ 596	Hilly Hathaway	.10	.05
□ 597	Todd Pratt	.10	.05
□ 598	Mike Mussina	.40	.18
□ 599	Alex Fernandez	.10	.05
□ 600	Don Mattingly	.60	.25
□ 601	Frank Thomas ST	.75	.35
□ 602	Ryne Sandberg ST	.30	.14
□ 603	Wade Boggs ST	.40	.18
□ 604	Cal Ripken ST	.75	.35
□ 605	Barry Bonds ST	.30	.14
□ 606	Ken Griffey Jr. ST	1.00	.45
□ 607	Kirby Puckett ST	.40	.18
□ 608	Darren Daulton ST	.10	.05
□ 609	Paul Molitor ST	.20	.09
□ 610	Terry Steinbach	.10	.05
□ 611	Todd Worrell	.10	.05
□ 612	Jim Thome	.50	.23
□ 613	Chuck McElroy	.10	.05
□ 614	John Habyan	.10	.05
□ 615	Sid Fernandez	.10	.05
□ 616	Outfield Prospects	.20	.09
	Eddie Zambrano		
	Glenn Murray		
	Chad Mottola		
	Jermaine Allensworth		
□ 617	Steve Bedrosian	.10	.05
□ 618	Rob Ducey	.10	.05
□ 619	Tom Browning	.10	.05
□ 620	Tony Gwynn	1.00	.45
□ 621	Carl Willis	.10	.05
□ 622	Kevin Young	.10	.05
□ 623	Rafael Novoa	.10	.05
□ 624	Jerry Browne	.10	.05
□ 625	Charlie Hough	.10	.05
□ 626	Chris Gomez	.10	.05
□ 627	Steve Reed	.10	.05
□ 628	Kirk Rueter	.10	.05

□ 629	Matt Whiteside	.10	.05
□ 630	David Justice	.40	.18
□ 631	Brad Holman	.10	.05
□ 632	Brian Jordan	.20	.09
□ 633	Scott Bankhead	.10	.05
□ 634	Torey Lovullo	.10	.05
□ 635	Len Dykstra	.20	.09
□ 636	Ben McDonald	.10	.05
□ 637	Steve Howe	.10	.05
□ 638	Jose Vizcaino	.10	.05
□ 639	Bill Swift	.10	.05
□ 640	Darryl Strawberry	.20	.09
□ 641	Steve Farr	.10	.05
□ 642	Tom Kramer	.10	.05
□ 643	Joe Orsulak	.10	.05
□ 644	Tom Henke	.10	.05
□ 645	Joe Carter	.20	.09
□ 646	Ken Caminiti	.30	.14
□ 647	Reggie Sanders	.10	.05
□ 648	Andy Ashby	.10	.05
□ 649	Derek Parks	.10	.05
□ 650	Andy Van Slyke	.20	.09
□ 651	Juan Bell	.10	.05
□ 652	Roger Smithberg	.10	.05
□ 653	Chuck Carr	.10	.05
□ 654	Bill Gullickson	.10	.05
□ 655	Charlie Hayes	.10	.05
□ 656	Chris Nabholz	.10	.05
□ 657	Karl Rhodes	.10	.05
□ 658	Pete Smith	.10	.05
□ 659	Bret Boone	.10	.05
□ 660	Gregg Jefferies	.10	.05
□ 661	Bob Zupcic	.10	.05
□ 662	Steve Sax	.10	.05
□ 663	Mariano Duncan	.10	.05
□ 664	Jeff Tackett	.10	.05
□ 665	Mark Langston	.10	.05
□ 666	Steve Buechele	.10	.05
□ 667	Candy Maldonado	.10	.05
□ 668	Woody Williams	.10	.05
□ 669	Tim Wakefield	.10	.05
□ 670	Danny Tartabull	.10	.05
□ 671	Charlie O'Brien	.10	.05
□ 672	Felix Jose	.10	.05
□ 673	Bobby Ayala	.10	.05
□ 674	Scott Servais	.10	.05
□ 675	Roberto Alomar	.40	.18
□ 676	Pedro Martinez	.10	.05
□ 677	Eddie Guardado	.10	.05
□ 678	Mark Lewis	.10	.05
□ 679	Jaime Navarro	.10	.05
□ 680	Ruben Sierra	.20	.09
□ 681	Rick Renteria	.10	.05
□ 682	Storm Davis	.10	.05
□ 683	Cory Snyder	.10	.05
□ 684	Ron Karkovice	.10	.05
□ 685	Juan Gonzalez	1.00	.45
□ 686	Catchers Prospects	.40	.18
	Chris Howard		
	Carlos Delgado		
	Jason Kendall		
	Paul Bako		
□ 687	John Smoltz	.20	.09
□ 688	Brian Dorsett	.10	.05
□ 689	Omar Olivares	.10	.05
□ 690	Mo Vaughn	.50	.23
□ 691	Joe Grahe	.10	.05
□ 692	Mickey Morandini	.10	.05
□ 693	Tino Martinez	.40	.18
□ 694	Brian Barnes	.10	.05
□ 695	Mike Stanley	.10	.05
□ 696	Mark Clark	.10	.05
□ 697	Dave Hansen	.10	.05
□ 698	Willie Wilson	.10	.05
□ 699	Pete Schourek	.10	.05
□ 700	Barry Bonds	.50	.23
□ 701	Kevin Appier	.20	.09
□ 702	Tony Fernandez	.10	.05
□ 703	Darryl Kile	.20	.09
□ 704	Archi Cianfrocco	.10	.05
□ 705	Jose Rijo	.10	.05
□ 706	Brian Harper	.10	.05
□ 707	Zane Smith	.10	.05
□ 708	Dave Henderson	.10	.05
□ 709	Angel Miranda UER	.10	.05
	(no Topps logo on back)		

□ 710	Orestes Destrade	.10	.05
□ 711	Greg Gohr	.10	.05
□ 712	Eric Young	.10	.05
□ 713	Relief Pitchers	.20	.09
	Prospects		
	Todd Williams		
	Ron Watson		
	Kirk Bullinger		
	Mike Welch		
□ 714	Tim Spehr	.10	.05
□ 715	Hank Aaron	.50	.23
□ 716	Nate Minchey	.10	.05
□ 717	Mike Blowers	.10	.05
□ 718	Kent Mercker	.10	.05
□ 719	Tom Pagnozzi	.10	.05
□ 720	Roger Clemens	.75	.35
□ 721	Eduardo Perez	.10	.05
□ 722	Milt Thompson	.10	.05
□ 723	Gregg Olson	.10	.05
□ 724	Kirk McCaskill	.10	.05
□ 725	Sammy Sosa	.40	.18
□ 726	Alvaro Espinoza	.10	.05
□ 727	Henry Rodriguez	.10	.05
□ 728	Jim Leyritz	.10	.05
□ 729	Steve Scarsone	.10	.05
□ 730	Bobby Bonilla	.20	.09
□ 731	Chris Gwynn	.10	.05
□ 732	Al Leiter	.10	.05
□ 733	Bip Roberts	.10	.05
□ 734	Mark Portugal	.10	.05
□ 735	Terry Pendleton	.10	.05
□ 736	Dave Valle	.10	.05
□ 737	Paul Kilgus	.10	.05
□ 738	Greg A. Harris	.10	.05
□ 739	Jon Ratliff DP	.20	.09
□ 740	Kirk Presley DP	.20	.09
□ 741	Josue Estrada DP	.20	.09
□ 742	Wayne Gomes DP	.10	.05
□ 743	Pat Watkins DP	.20	.09
□ 744	Jamey Wright DP	.40	.18
□ 745	Jay Powell DP	.20	.09
□ 746	Ryan McGuire DP	.20	.09
□ 747	Marc Barcelo DP	.20	.09
□ 748	Sloan Smith DP	.20	.09
□ 749	John Wasdin DP	.20	.09
□ 750	Marc Vlades DP	.20	.09
□ 751	Dan Ehler DP	.20	.09
□ 752	Andre King DP	.20	.09
□ 753	Greg Keagle DP	.20	.09
□ 754	Jason Myers DP	.20	.09
□ 755	Dax Winslett DP	.20	.09
□ 756	Casey Whitten DP	.20	.09
□ 757	Tony Fuduric DP	.10	.05
□ 758	Greg Norton DP	.20	.09
□ 759	Jeff D'Amico DP	.40	.18
□ 760	Ryan Hancock DP	.20	.09
□ 761	David Cooper DP	.10	.05
□ 762	Kevin Orie DP	.75	.35
□ 763	John O'Donoghue DP	.10	.05
	Mike Oquist		
□ 764	Cory Bailey	.10	.05
	Scott Hatteberg		
□ 765	Mark Holzemer	.10	.05
	Paul Swingle		
□ 766	James Baldwin	.20	.09
	Rod Bolton		
□ 767	Jerry Di Poto	.20	.09
	Julian Tavarez		
□ 768	Danny Bautista	.10	.05
	Sean Bergman		
□ 769	Bob Hamelin	.10	.05
	Joe Vitiello		
□ 770	Mark Kiefer	.20	.09
	Troy O'Leary		
□ 771	Denny Hocking	.20	.09
	Oscar Munoz		
□ 772	Russ Davis	.20	.09
	Brien Taylor		
□ 773	Kyle Abbott	.10	.05
	Miguel Jimenez		
□ 774	Kevin King	.10	.05
	Eric Plantenberg		
□ 775	Jon Shave	.10	.05
	Desi Wilson		
□ 776	Domingo Cedeno	.10	.05
	Paul Spoljaric		

☐ 777	Chipper Jones	2.50	1.10	
	Ryan Klesko			
☐ 778	Steve Trachsel	.20	.09	
	Turk Wendell			
☐ 779	Johnny Ruffin	.10	.05	
	Jerry Spradlin			
☐ 780	Jason Bates	.10	.05	
	John Burke			
☐ 781	Carl Everett	.20	.09	
	Dave Weathers			
☐ 782	Gary Mota	.20	.09	
	James Mouton			
☐ 783	Raul Mondesi	.40	.18	
	Ben Van Ryn			
☐ 784	Gabe White	.30	.14	
	Rondell White			
☐ 785	Brook Fordyce	.20	.05	
	Bill Pulsipher			
☐ 786	Kevin Foster	.10	.05	
	Gene Schall			
☐ 787	Rich Aude	.10	.05	
	Midre Cummings			
☐ 788	Brian Barber	.20	.09	
	Rich Batchelor			
☐ 789	Brian Johnson	.10	.05	
	Scott Sanders			
☐ 790	Ricky Faneyte	.10	.05	
	J.R. Phillips			
☐ 791	Checklist 3	.10	.05	
☐ 792	Checklist 4	.10	.05	

1994 Topps Black Gold

Randomly inserted one in every 72 packs, this 44-card standard-size set was issued in two series of 22. Cards were also issued three per 1994 Topps factory set. Collectors had a chance, through redemption cards to receive all or part of the set. There are seven Winner redemption cards for a total 51 cards associated with this set. The set is considered complete with the 44 player cards. Card fronts feature color player action photos. The player's name at bottom and the team name at top are screened in gold foil. The backs contain a player photo and statistical rankings. The winner cards were redeemable until January 31, 1995

	MINT	NRMT
COMPLETE SET (44)	25.00	11.00
COMPLETE SERIES 1 (22)	15.00	6.75
COMPLETE SERIES 2 (22)	10.00	4.50
COMMON CARD (1-44)	.25	.11
STAT.ODDS 1:72H/R,1:18J,1:24RAC,1:36CEL		
THREE PER FACTORY SET.		

☐ 1	Roberto Alomar	.75	.35
☐ 2	Carlos Baerga	.25	.11

☐ 3	Albert Belle	1.00	.45
☐ 4	Joe Carter	.40	.18
☐ 5	Cecil Fielder	.40	.18
☐ 6	Travis Fryman	.40	.18
☐ 7	Juan Gonzalez	2.00	.90
☐ 8	Ken Griffey Jr.	4.00	1.80
☐ 9	Chris Hoiles	.25	.11
☐ 10	Randy Johnson	.75	.35
☐ 11	Kenny Lofton	1.00	.45
☐ 12	Jack McDowell	.25	.11
☐ 13	Paul Molitor	.75	.35
☐ 14	Jeff Montgomery	.25	.11
☐ 15	John Olerud	.40	.18
☐ 16	Rafael Palmeiro	.50	.23
☐ 17	Kirby Puckett	1.50	.70
☐ 18	Cal Ripken	3.00	1.35
☐ 19	Tim Salmon	.75	.35
☐ 20	Mike Stanley	.25	.11
☐ 21	Frank Thomas	3.00	1.35
☐ 22	Robin Ventura	.40	.18
☐ 23	Jeff Bagwell	1.50	.70
☐ 24	Jay Bell	.40	.18
☐ 25	Craig Biggio	.50	.23
☐ 26	Jeff Blauser	.40	.18
☐ 27	Barry Bonds	1.00	.45
☐ 28	Darren Daulton	.40	.18
☐ 29	Len Dykstra	.40	.18
☐ 30	Andres Galarraga	.75	.35
☐ 31	Ron Gant	.40	.18
☐ 32	Tom Glavine	.40	.18
☐ 33	Mark Grace	.50	.23
☐ 34	Marquis Grissom	.40	.18
☐ 35	Gregg Jefferies	.25	.11
☐ 36	David Justice	.75	.35
☐ 37	John Kruk	.40	.18
☐ 38	Greg Maddux	2.50	1.10
☐ 39	Fred McGriff	.50	.23
☐ 40	Randy Myers	.25	.11
☐ 41	Mike Piazza	2.50	1.10
☐ 42	Sammy Sosa	.75	.35
☐ 43	Robby Thompson	.25	.11
☐ 44	Matt Williams	.50	.23
☐ A	Winner A 1-11	.50	.23
☐ B	Winner B 12-22	.50	.23
☐ C	Winner C 23-33	.50	.23
☐ D	Winner D 34-44	.50	.23
☐ AB	Winner AB 1-22	1.00	.45
☐ CD	Winner CD 23-44	1.00	.45
☐ ABCD	Winner ABCD 1-44	2.00	.90

1994 Topps Traded

This set consists of 132 standard-size cards featuring traded players in their new uniforms, rookies and draft choices. Factory sets consisted of 140 cards including a set of eight Topps Finest cards. Card fronts feature a player photo with the player's name, team and position at the bottom. The horizontal backs have a player photo to the left with complete career statisics and highlights. The cards are numbered with a "T" suffix. Rookie Cards include

Brian Anderson, Rusty Greer, Ben Grieve, Paul Konerko, Chan Ho Park and Kevin Witt.

	MINT	NRMT
COMP.FACT.SET (140)	60.00	27.00
COMPLETE SET (132)	55.00	25.00
COMMON CARD (1T-132T)	.10	.05
MINOR STARS	.20	.09
UNLISTED STARS	.40	.18

☐ 1T	Paul Wilson	.50	.23
☐ 2T	Bill Taylor	.10	.05
☐ 3T	Dan Wilson	.20	.09
☐ 4T	Mark Smith	.10	.05
☐ 5T	Toby Borland	.10	.05
☐ 6T	Dave Clark	.10	.05
☐ 7T	Denny Martinez	.20	.09
☐ 8T	Dave Gallagher	.10	.05
☐ 9T	Josias Manzanillo	.10	.05
☐ 10T	Brian Anderson	.75	.35
☐ 11T	Damon Berryhill	.10	.05
☐ 12T	Alex Cole	.10	.05
☐ 13T	Jacob Shumate	.20	.09
☐ 14T	Oddibe McDowell	.10	.05
☐ 15T	Willie Banks	.10	.05
☐ 16T	Jerry Browne	.10	.05
☐ 17T	Donnie Elliott	.10	.05
☐ 18T	Ellis Burks	.20	.09
☐ 19T	Chuck McElroy	.10	.05
☐ 20T	Luis Polonia	.10	.05
☐ 21T	Brian Harper	.10	.05
☐ 22T	Mark Portugal	.10	.05
☐ 23T	Dave Henderson	.10	.05
☐ 24T	Mark Acre	.10	.05
☐ 25T	Julio Franco	.10	.05
☐ 26T	Darren Hall	.10	.05
☐ 27T	Eric Anthony	.10	.05
☐ 28T	Sid Fernandez	.10	.05
☐ 29T	Rusty Greer	4.00	1.80
☐ 30T	Riccardo Ingram	.10	.05
☐ 31T	Gabe White	.10	.05
☐ 32T	Tim Belcher	.10	.05
☐ 33T	Terrence Long	1.00	.45
☐ 34T	Mark Dalesandro	.10	.05
☐ 35T	Mike Kelly	.10	.05
☐ 36T	Jack Morris	.20	.09
☐ 37T	Jeff Brantley	.10	.05
☐ 38T	Larry Barnes	.20	.09
☐ 39T	Brian R. Hunter	.10	.05
☐ 40T	Otis Nixon	.10	.05
☐ 41T	Bret Wagner	.10	.05
☐ 42T	Pedro Martinez TR	.30	.14
	Delino Deshields		
☐ 43T	Heathcliff Slocumb	.10	.05
☐ 44T	Ben Grieve	30.00	13.50
☐ 45T	John Hudek	.10	.05
☐ 46T	Shawon Dunston	.10	.05
☐ 47T	Greg Colbrunn	.10	.05
☐ 48T	Joey Hamilton	.40	.18
☐ 49T	Marvin Freeman	.10	.05
☐ 50T	Terry Mulholland	.10	.05
☐ 51T	Keith Mitchell	.10	.05
☐ 52T	Dwight Smith	.10	.05
☐ 53T	Shawn Boskie	.10	.05
☐ 54T	Kevin Witt	5.00	2.20
☐ 55T	Ron Gant	.20	.09
☐ 56T	1994 Prospects	.75	.35
	Trenidad Hubbard		
	Jason Schmidt		
	Larry Sutton		
	Stephen Larkin		
☐ 57T	Jody Reed	.10	.05
☐ 58T	Rick Helling	.10	.05
☐ 59T	John Powell	.20	.09
☐ 60T	Eddie Murray	.40	.18
☐ 61T	Joe Hall	.10	.05
☐ 62T	Jorge Fabregas	.10	.05
☐ 63T	Mike Mordecai	.10	.05
☐ 64T	Ed Vosberg	.10	.05
☐ 65T	Rickey Henderson	.30	.14
☐ 66T	Tim Grieve	.10	.05
☐ 67T	Jon Lieber	.10	.05
☐ 68T	Chris Howard	.10	.05
☐ 69T	Matt Walbeck	.10	.05
☐ 70T	Chan Ho Park	4.00	1.80

☐ 71T	Bryan Eversgerd	.10	.05
☐ 72T	John Dettmer	.10	.05
☐ 73T	Erik Hanson	.10	.05
☐ 74T	Mike Thurman	.10	.05
☐ 75T	Bobby Ayala	.10	.05
☐ 76T	Rafael Palmeiro	.30	.14
☐ 77T	Bret Boone	.10	.05
☐ 78T	Paul Shuey	.10	.05
☐ 79T	Kevin Foster	.10	.05
☐ 80T	Dave Magadan	.10	.05
☐ 81T	Bip Roberts	.10	.05
☐ 82T	Howard Johnson	.10	.05
☐ 83T	Xavier Hernandez	.10	.05
☐ 84T	Ross Powell	.10	.05
☐ 85T	Doug Million	.10	.05
☐ 86T	Geronimo Berroa	.10	.05
☐ 87T	Mark Farris	.20	.09
☐ 88T	Butch Henry	.10	.05
☐ 89T	Junior Felix	.10	.05
☐ 90T	Bo Jackson	.20	.09
☐ 91T	Hector Carrasco	.10	.05
☐ 92T	Charlie O'Brien	.10	.05
☐ 93T	Omar Vizquel	.20	.09
☐ 94T	David Segui	.10	.05
☐ 95T	Dustin Hermanson	.10	.05
☐ 96T	Gar Finnvold	.10	.05
☐ 97T	Dave Stevens	.10	.05
☐ 98T	Corey Pointer	.20	.09
☐ 99T	Felix Fermin	.10	.05
☐ 100T	Lee Smith	.20	.09
☐ 101T	Reid Ryan	.20	.09
☐ 102T	Bobby Munoz	.10	.05
☐ 103T	Deion Sanders TR	.20	.09
	Roberto Kelly		
☐ 104T	Turner Ward	.10	.05
☐ 105T	W.VanLandingham	.20	.09
☐ 106T	Vince Coleman	.10	.05
☐ 107T	Stan Javier	.10	.05
☐ 108T	Darrin Jackson	.10	.05
☐ 109T	C.J. Nitkowski	.10	.05
☐ 110T	Anthony Young	.10	.05
☐ 111T	Kurt Miller	.10	.05
☐ 112T	Paul Konerko	25.00	11.00
☐ 113T	Walt Weiss	.10	.05
☐ 114T	Daryl Boston	.10	.05
☐ 115T	Will Clark	.30	.14
☐ 116T	Matt Smith	.20	.09
☐ 117T	Mark Leiter	.10	.05
☐ 118T	Gregg Olson	.10	.05
☐ 119T	Tony Pena	.10	.05
☐ 120T	Jose Vizcaino	.10	.05
☐ 121T	Rick White	.10	.05
☐ 122T	Rich Rowland	.10	.05
☐ 123T	Jeff Reboulet	.10	.05
☐ 124T	Greg Hibbard	.10	.05
☐ 125T	Chris Sabo	.10	.05
☐ 126T	Doug Jones	.10	.05
☐ 127T	Tony Fernandez	.10	.05
☐ 128T	Carlos Reyes	.10	.05
☐ 129T	Kevin Brown	.50	.23
☐ 130T	Ryne Sandberg	1.00	.45
	Farewell		
☐ 131T	Ryne Sandberg	1.00	.45
	Farewell		
☐ 132T	Checklist 1-132	.10	.05

1994 Topps Traded Finest Inserts

Each Topps Traded factory set contained a complete 8-card set of Finest Inserts. These cards are numbered separately and designed differently than the base cards. Each Finest Insert features a action shot of a player set against purple chrome background. The set highlights the top performers midway through the 1994 season, detailing their performances through July. The cards are numbered on back X of 8.

	MINT	NRMT
COMPLETE SET (8)	6.00	2.70
COMMON CARD (1-8)	.30	.14

ONE SET PER TRADED FACTORY SET

☐ 1	Greg Maddux	1.25	.55
☐ 2	Mike Piazza	1.25	.55
☐ 3	Matt Williams	.30	.14
☐ 4	Raul Mondesi	.40	.18
☐ 5	Ken Griffey Jr.	2.00	.90
☐ 6	Kenny Lofton	.40	.18
☐ 7	Frank Thomas	1.50	.70
☐ 8	Manny Ramirez	.50	.23

1995 Topps

These 660 standard-size cards feature color action photos with white borders on the fronts. This set was released in two series. The first series contained 396 cards. The second series had 264 cards. The player's name in gold-foil appears below the photo, with his position and team name underneath. The horizontal backs carry a color player close-up with a color player cut-out superimposed over it. Player biography, statistics and career highlights complete the backs. One "Own The Game" instant winner card has been inserted in every 120 packs. Rookie cards in this set include Karim Garcia and Rey Ordonez.

	MINT	NRMT
COMPLETE SET (660)	45.00	20.00
COMP.HOBBY SET (677)	60.00	27.00
COMP.RETAIL SET (677)	60.00	27.00
COMPLETE SERIES 1 (396)	25.00	11.00
COMPLETE SERIES 2 (264)	20.00	9.00
COMMON CARD (1-660)	.15	.07
MINOR STARS	.30	.14
UNLISTED STARS	.60	.25
COMP.CYBER.SET (396)	80.00	36.00
COMP.CYBER.SER.1 (198)	30.00	13.50
COMP.CYBER.SER.2 (198)	50.00	22.00

*CYBER.STARS: 1.25X to 2.5X HI COLUMN
*CYBER.YOUNG.STARS: 1X to 2X HI
ONE CYBERSTATS CARD PER PACK

☐ 1	Frank Thomas	2.50	1.10
☐ 2	Mickey Morandini	.15	.07
☐ 3	Babe Ruth 100th B-Day	2.00	.90
☐ 4	Scott Cooper	.15	.07
☐ 5	David Cone	.30	.14
☐ 6	Jacob Shumate	.30	.14
☐ 7	Trevor Hoffman	.15	.07
☐ 8	Shane Mack	.15	.07
☐ 9	Delino DeShields	.15	.07
☐ 10	Matt Williams	.40	.18
☐ 11	Sammy Sosa	.60	.25
☐ 12	Gary DiSarcina	.15	.07
☐ 13	Kenny Rogers	.15	.07
☐ 14	Jose Vizcaino	.15	.07
☐ 15	Lou Whitaker	.30	.14
☐ 16	Ron Darling	.15	.07
☐ 17	Dave Nilsson	.15	.07
☐ 18	Chris Hammond	.15	.07
☐ 19	Sid Bream	.15	.07
☐ 20	Denny Martinez	.30	.14
☐ 21	Orlando Merced	.15	.07
☐ 22	John Wetteland	.15	.07
☐ 23	Mike Devereaux	.15	.07
☐ 24	Rene Arocha	.15	.07
☐ 25	Jay Buhner	.40	.18
☐ 26	Darren Holmes	.15	.07
☐ 27	Hal Morris	.15	.07
☐ 28	Brian Buchanan	.30	.14
☐ 29	Keith Miller	.15	.07
☐ 30	Paul Molitor	.60	.25
☐ 31	Dave West	.15	.07
☐ 32	Tony Tarasco	.15	.07
☐ 33	Scott Sanders	.15	.07
☐ 34	Eddie Zambrano	.15	.07
☐ 35	Ricky Bones	.15	.07
☐ 36	John Valentin	.15	.07
☐ 37	Kevin Tapani	.15	.07
☐ 38	Tim Wallach	.15	.07
☐ 39	Darren Lewis	.15	.07
☐ 40	Travis Fryman	.30	.14
☐ 41	Mark Leiter	.15	.07
☐ 42	Jose Bautista	.15	.07
☐ 43	Pete Smith	.15	.07
☐ 44	Bret Barberie	.15	.07
☐ 45	Dennis Eckersley	.30	.14
☐ 46	Ken Hill	.15	.07
☐ 47	Chad Ogea	.15	.07
☐ 48	Pete Harnisch	.15	.07
☐ 49	James Baldwin	.15	.07
☐ 50	Mike Mussina	.60	.25
☐ 51	Al Martin	.15	.07
☐ 52	Mark Thompson	.30	.14
☐ 53	Matt Smith	.15	.07
☐ 54	Joey Hamilton	.30	.14
☐ 55	Edgar Martinez	.40	.18
☐ 56	John Smiley	.15	.07
☐ 57	Rey Sanchez	.15	.07
☐ 58	Mike Timlin	.15	.07
☐ 59	Ricky Bottalico	.30	.14
☐ 60	Jim Abbott	.15	.07
☐ 61	Mike Kelly	.15	.07
☐ 62	Brian Jordan	.15	.07
☐ 63	Ken Ryan	.15	.07
☐ 64	Matt Mieske	.15	.07
☐ 65	Rick Aguilera	.15	.07
☐ 66	Ismael Valdes	.40	.18
☐ 67	Royce Clayton	.15	.07
☐ 68	Junior Felix	.15	.07
☐ 69	Harold Reynolds	.15	.07
☐ 70	Juan Gonzalez	1.50	.70
☐ 71	Kelly Stinnett	.15	.07
☐ 72	Carlos Reyes	.15	.07
☐ 73	Dave Weathers	.15	.07
☐ 74	Mel Rojas	.15	.07
☐ 75	Doug Drabek	.15	.07
☐ 76	Charles Nagy	.30	.14
☐ 77	Tim Raines	.30	.14
☐ 78	Midre Cummings	.15	.07
☐ 79	First Base Prospects	.40	.18
	Gene Schall		
	Scott Talanoa		
	Harold Williams		

Ray Brown

□ 80	Rafael Palmeiro	.40	.18
□ 81	Charlie Hayes	.15	.07
□ 82	Ray Lankford	.30	.14
□ 83	Tim Davis	.15	.07
□ 84	C.J. Nitkowski	.15	.07
□ 85	Andy Ashby	.15	.07
□ 86	Gerald Williams	.15	.07
□ 87	Terry Shumpert	.15	.07
□ 88	Heathcliff Slocumb	.15	.07
□ 89	Domingo Cedeno	.15	.07
□ 90	Mark Grace	.40	.18
□ 91	Brad Woodall	.15	.07
□ 92	Gar Finnvold	.15	.07
□ 93	Jaime Navarro	.15	.07
□ 94	Carlos Hernandez	.15	.07
□ 95	Mark Langston	.15	.07
□ 96	Chuck Carr	.15	.07
□ 97	Mike Gardiner	.15	.07
□ 98	Dave McCarty	.15	.07
□ 99	Cris Carpenter	.15	.07
□ 100	Barry Bonds	.75	.35
□ 101	David Segui	.15	.07
□ 102	Scott Brosius	.15	.07
□ 103	Mariano Duncan	.15	.07
□ 104	Kenny Lofton	.75	.35
□ 105	Ken Caminiti	.40	.18
□ 106	Darrin Jackson	.15	.07
□ 107	Jim Poole	.15	.07
□ 108	Wil Cordero	.15	.07
□ 109	Danny Miceli	.15	.07
□ 110	Walt Weiss	.15	.07
□ 111	Tom Pagnozzi	.15	.07
□ 112	Terrence Long	.40	.18
□ 113	Bret Boone	.15	.07
□ 114	Daryl Boston	.15	.07
□ 115	Wally Joyner	.30	.14
□ 116	Rob Butler	.15	.07
□ 117	Rafael Belliard	.15	.07
□ 118	Luis Lopez	.15	.07
□ 119	Tony Fossas	.15	.07
□ 120	Len Dykstra	.30	.14
□ 121	Mike Morgan	.15	.07
□ 122	Denny Hocking	.15	.07
□ 123	Kevin Gross	.15	.07
□ 124	Todd Benzinger	.15	.07
□ 125	John Doherty	.15	.07
□ 126	Eduardo Perez	.15	.07
□ 127	Dan Smith	.15	.07
□ 128	Joe Orsulak	.15	.07
□ 129	Brent Gates	.15	.07
□ 130	Jeff Conine	.30	.14
□ 131	Doug Henry	.15	.07
□ 132	Paul Sorrento	.15	.07
□ 133	Mike Hampton	.15	.07
□ 134	Tim Spehr	.15	.07
□ 135	Julio Franco	.15	.07
□ 136	Mike Dyer	.15	.07
□ 137	Chris Sabo	.15	.07
□ 138	Rheal Cormier	.15	.07
□ 139	Paul Konerko	3.00	1.35
□ 140	Dante Bichette	.30	.14
□ 141	Chuck McElroy	.15	.07
□ 142	Mike Stanley	.15	.07
□ 143	Bob Hamelin	.15	.07
□ 144	Tommy Greene	.15	.07
□ 145	John Smoltz	.30	.14
□ 146	Ed Sprague	.15	.07
□ 147	Ray McDavid	.15	.07
□ 148	Otis Nixon	.15	.07
□ 149	Turk Wendell	.15	.07
□ 150	Chris James	.15	.07
□ 151	Derek Parks	.15	.07
□ 152	Jose Offerman	.15	.07
□ 153	Tony Clark	.75	.35
□ 154	Chad Curtis	.15	.07
□ 155	Mark Portugal	.15	.07
□ 156	Bill Pulsipher	.15	.07
□ 157	Troy Neel	.15	.07
□ 158	Dave Winfield	.40	.18
□ 159	Bill Wegman	.15	.07
□ 160	Benito Santiago	.15	.07
□ 161	Jose Mesa	.15	.07
□ 162	Luis Gonzalez	.15	.07
□ 163	Alex Fernandez	.15	.07
□ 164	Freddie Benavides	.15	.07
□ 165	Ben McDonald	.15	.07
□ 166	Blas Minor	.15	.07
□ 167	Bret Wagner	.15	.07
□ 168	Mac Suzuki	.15	.07
□ 169	Roberto Mejia	.15	.07
□ 170	Wade Boggs	.60	.25
□ 171	Calvin Reese	.15	.07
□ 172	Hipolito Pichardo	.15	.07
□ 173	Kim Batiste	.15	.07
□ 174	Darren Hall	.15	.07
□ 175	Tom Glavine	.30	.14
□ 176	Phil Plantier	.15	.07
□ 177	Chris Howard	.15	.07
□ 178	Karl Rhodes	.15	.07
□ 179	LaTroy Hawkins	.15	.07
□ 180	Raul Mondesi	.40	.18
□ 181	Jeff Reed	.15	.07
□ 182	Milt Cuyler	.15	.07
□ 183	Jim Edmonds	.40	.18
□ 184	Hector Fajardo	.15	.07
□ 185	Jeff Kent	.15	.07
□ 186	Wilson Alvarez	.15	.07
□ 187	Geronimo Berroa	.15	.07
□ 188	Billy Spiers	.15	.07
□ 189	Derek Lilliquist	.15	.07
□ 190	Craig Biggio	.40	.18
□ 191	Roberto Hernandez	.15	.07
□ 192	Bob Natal	.15	.07
□ 193	Bobby Ayala	.15	.07
□ 194	Travis Miller	.15	.07
□ 195	Bob Tewksbury	.15	.07
□ 196	Rondell White	.30	.14
□ 197	Steve Cooke	.15	.07
□ 198	Jeff Branson	.30	.14
□ 199	Derek Jeter	2.00	.90
□ 200	Tim Salmon	.60	.25
□ 201	Steve Frey	.15	.07
□ 202	Kent Mercker	.15	.07
□ 203	Randy Johnson	.60	.25
□ 204	Todd Worrell	.15	.07
□ 205	Mo Vaughn	.75	.35
□ 206	Howard Johnson	.15	.07
□ 207	John Wasdin	.15	.07
□ 208	Eddie Williams	.15	.07
□ 209	Tim Belcher	.15	.07
□ 210	Jeff Montgomery	.15	.07
□ 211	Kirt Manwaring	.15	.07
□ 212	Ben Grieve	4.00	1.80
□ 213	Pat Hentgen	.30	.14
□ 214	Shawon Dunston	.15	.07
□ 215	Mike Greenwell	.15	.07
□ 216	Alex Diaz	.15	.07
□ 217	Pat Mahomes	.15	.07
□ 218	Dave Hansen	.15	.07
□ 219	Kevin Rogers	.15	.07
□ 220	Cecil Fielder	.30	.14
□ 221	Andrew Lorraine	.15	.07
□ 222	Jack Armstrong	.15	.07
□ 223	Todd Hundley	.30	.14
□ 224	Mark Acre	.15	.07
□ 225	Darrell Whitmore	.15	.07
□ 226	Randy Milligan	.15	.07
□ 227	Wayne Kirby	.15	.07
□ 228	Darryl Kile	.30	.14
□ 229	Bob Zupcic	.15	.07
□ 230	Jay Bell	.30	.14
□ 231	Dustin Hermanson	.30	.14
□ 232	Harold Baines	.30	.14
□ 233	Alan Benes	.40	.18
□ 234	Felix Fermin	.15	.07
□ 235	Ellis Burks	.30	.14
□ 236	Jeff Brantley	.15	.07
□ 237	Outfield Prospects	1.50	.70
	Brian Hunter		
	Jose Malave		
	Karim Garcia		
	Shane Pullen		
□ 238	Matt Nokes	.15	.07
□ 239	Ben Rivera	.15	.07
□ 240	Joe Carter	.30	.14
□ 241	Jeff Granger	.15	.07
□ 242	Terry Pendleton	.15	.07
□ 243	Melvin Nieves	.30	.14
□ 244	Frankie Rodriguez	.30	.14
□ 245	Darryl Hamilton	.15	.07
□ 246	Brooks Kieschnick	.30	.14
□ 247	Todd Hollandsworth	.30	.14
□ 248	Joe Rosselli	.15	.07
□ 249	Bill Gullickson	.15	.07
□ 250	Chuck Knoblauch	.60	.25
□ 251	Kurt Miller	.15	.07
□ 252	Bobby Jones	.15	.07
□ 253	Lance Blankenship	.15	.07
□ 254	Matt Whiteside	.15	.07
□ 255	Darrin Fletcher	.15	.07
□ 256	Eric Plunk	.15	.07
□ 257	Shane Reynolds	.15	.07
□ 258	Norberto Martin	.15	.07
□ 259	Mike Thurman	.15	.07
□ 260	Andy Van Slyke	.30	.14
□ 261	Dwight Smith	.15	.07
□ 262	Allen Watson	.15	.07
□ 263	Dan Wilson	.15	.07
□ 264	Brent Mayne	.15	.07
□ 265	Bip Roberts	.15	.07
□ 266	Sterling Hitchcock	.15	.07
□ 267	Alex Gonzalez	.15	.07
□ 268	Greg Harris	.15	.07
□ 269	Ricky Jordan	.15	.07
□ 270	Johnny Ruffin	.15	.07
□ 271	Mike Stanton	.15	.07
□ 272	Rich Rowland	.15	.07
□ 273	Steve Trachsel	.15	.07
□ 274	Pedro Munoz	.15	.07
□ 275	Ramon Martinez	.30	.14
□ 276	Dave Henderson	.15	.07
□ 277	Chris Gomez	.15	.07
□ 278	Joe Grahe	.15	.07
□ 279	Rusty Greer	.60	.25
□ 280	John Franco	.30	.14
□ 281	Mike Bordick	.15	.07
□ 282	Jeff D'Amico	.30	.14
□ 283	Dave Magadan	.15	.07
□ 284	Tony Pena	.15	.07
□ 285	Greg Swindell	.15	.07
□ 286	Doug Million	.15	.07
□ 287	Gabe White	.15	.07
□ 288	Trey Beamon	.15	.07
□ 289	Arthur Rhodes	.15	.07
□ 290	Juan Guzman	.15	.07
□ 291	Jose Oquendo	.15	.07
□ 292	Willie Blair	.15	.07
□ 293	Eddie Taubensee	.15	.07
□ 294	Steve Howe	.15	.07
□ 295	Greg Maddux	2.00	.90
□ 296	Mike Macfarlane	.15	.07
□ 297	Curt Schilling	.30	.14
□ 298	Phil Clark	.15	.07
□ 299	Woody Williams	.15	.07
□ 300	Jose Canseco	.40	.18
□ 301	Aaron Sele	.15	.07
□ 302	Carl Willis	.15	.07
□ 303	Steve Buechele	.15	.07
□ 304	Dave Borba	.15	.07
□ 305	Orel Hershiser	.30	.14
□ 306	Damion Easley	.15	.07
□ 307	Mike Henneman	.15	.07
□ 308	Josias Manzanillo	.15	.07
□ 309	Kevin Seitzer	.15	.07
□ 310	Ruben Sierra	.15	.07
□ 311	Bryan Harvey	.15	.07
□ 312	Jim Thome	.60	.25
□ 313	Ramon Castro	.30	.14
□ 314	Lance Johnson	.15	.07
□ 315	Marquis Grissom	.30	.14
□ 316	Starting Pitcher Prospects	.40	.18
	Terrell Wade		
	Juan Acevedo		
	Matt Arrandale		
	Eddie Priest		
□ 317	Paul Wagner	.15	.07
□ 318	Jamie Moyer	.15	.07
□ 319	Todd Zeile	.15	.07
□ 320	Chris Bosio	.15	.07
□ 321	Steve Reed	.15	.07
□ 322	Erik Hanson	.15	.07
□ 323	Luis Polonia	.15	.07
□ 324	Ryan Klesko	.40	.18
□ 325	Kevin Appier	.30	.14
□ 326	Jim Eisenreich	.15	.07
□ 327	Randy Knorr	.15	.07

☐ 557 Danny Bautista	.15	.07
☐ 558 Will Clark	.40	.18
☐ 559 Rickey Henderson	.40	.18
☐ 560 Todd Jones	.15	.07
☐ 561 Jack McDowell	.15	.07
☐ 562 Carlos Rodriguez	.15	.07
☐ 563 Mark Eichhorn	.15	.07
☐ 564 Jeff Nelson	.15	.07
☐ 565 Eric Anthony	.15	.07
☐ 566 Randy Velarde	.15	.07
☐ 567 Javier Lopez	.30	.14
☐ 568 Kevin Mitchell	.15	.07
☐ 569 Steve Karsay	.15	.07
☐ 570 Brian Meadows	.30	.14
☐ 571 Rey Ordonez	.60	.25
Mike Metcalfe		
Kevin Orie		
Ray Holbert		
☐ 572 John Kruk	.30	.14
☐ 573 Scott Leius	.15	.07
☐ 574 John Patterson	.15	.07
☐ 575 Kevin Brown	.30	.14
☐ 576 Mike Moore	.15	.07
☐ 577 Manny Ramirez	.60	.25
☐ 578 Jose Lind	.15	.07
☐ 579 Derrick May	.15	.07
☐ 580 Cal Eldred	.15	.07
☐ 581 Third Base Prospects	.30	.14
David Bell		
Joel Chelmis		
Lino Diaz		
Aaron Boone		
☐ 582 J.T. Snow	.30	.14
☐ 583 Luis Sojo	.15	.07
☐ 584 Moises Alou	.30	.14
☐ 585 Dave Clark	.15	.07
☐ 586 Dave Hollins	.15	.07
☐ 587 Nomar Garciaparra	4.00	1.80
☐ 588 Cal Ripken	2.50	1.10
☐ 589 Pedro Astacio	.15	.07
☐ 590 J.R. Phillips	.15	.07
☐ 591 Jeff Frye	.15	.07
☐ 592 Bo Jackson	.30	.14
☐ 593 Steve Ontiveros	.15	.07
☐ 594 David Nied	.15	.07
☐ 595 Brad Ausmus	.15	.07
☐ 596 Carlos Baerga	.15	.07
☐ 597 James Mouton	.15	.07
☐ 598 Ozzie Guillen	.15	.07
☐ 599 Outfield Prospects	.60	.25
Ozzie Timmons		
Curtis Goodwin		
Johnny Damon		
Jeff Abbott		
☐ 600 Yorkis Perez	.15	.07
☐ 601 Rich Rodriguez	.15	.07
☐ 602 Mark McLemore	.15	.07
☐ 603 Jeff Fassero	.15	.07
☐ 604 John Roper	.15	.07
☐ 605 Mark Johnson	.15	.07
☐ 606 Wes Chamberlain	.15	.07
☐ 607 Felix Jose	.15	.07
☐ 608 Tony Longmire	.15	.07
☐ 609 Duane Ward	.15	.07
☐ 610 Brett Butler	.30	.14
☐ 611 William VanLandingham	.15	.07
☐ 612 Mickey Tettleton	.15	.07
☐ 613 Brady Anderson	.40	.18
☐ 614 Reggie Jefferson	.15	.07
☐ 615 Mike Kingery	.15	.07
☐ 616 Derek Bell	.15	.07
☐ 617 Scott Erickson	.15	.07
☐ 618 Bob Wickman	.15	.07
☐ 619 Phil Leftwich	.15	.07
☐ 620 David Justice	.60	.25
☐ 621 Paul Wilson	.30	.14
☐ 622 Pedro Martinez	.60	.25
☐ 623 Terry Mathews	.15	.07
☐ 624 Brian McRae	.30	.14
☐ 625 Bruce Ruffin	.15	.07
☐ 626 Steve Finley	.30	.14
☐ 627 Ron Gant	.30	.14
☐ 628 Rafael Bournigal	.15	.07
☐ 629 Darryl Strawberry	.30	.14
☐ 630 Luis Alicea	.15	.07
☐ 631 Orioles Prospects	.30	.14

Mark Smith		
Scott Klingenbeck		
☐ 632 Red Sox Prospects	.30	.14
Cory Bailey		
Scott Hatteberg		
☐ 633 Angels Prospects	.60	.25
Todd Greene		
Troy Percival		
☐ 634 White Sox Prospects	.15	.07
Rod Bolton		
Olmedo Saenz		
☐ 635 Indians Prospects	.30	.14
Steve Kline		
Herb Perry		
☐ 636 Tigers Prospects	.15	.07
Sean Bergman		
Shannon Penn		
☐ 637 Royals Prospects	.30	.14
Joe Randa		
Joe Vitiello		
☐ 638 Brewers Prospects	.15	.07
Jose Mercedes		
Duane Singleton		
☐ 639 Twins Prospects	.30	.14
Marc Barcelo		
Marty Cordova		
☐ 640 Yankees Prospects	1.25	.55
Andy Pettitte		
Ruben Rivera		
☐ 641 Athletics Prospects	.30	.14
Willie Adams		
Scott Spiezio		
☐ 642 Mariners Prospects	.30	.14
Eddy Diaz		
Desi Relaford		
☐ 643 Rangers Prospects	.15	.07
Terrell Lowery		
Jon Shave		
☐ 644 Blue Jays Prospects	.15	.07
Angel Martinez		
Paul Spoljaric		
☐ 645 Braves Prospects	.30	.14
Tony Graffanino		
Damon Hollins		
☐ 646 Cubs Prospects	.30	.14
Darron Cox		
Doug Glanville		
☐ 647 Reds Prospects	.30	.14
Tim Belk		
Pat Watkins		
☐ 648 Rockies Propsects	.15	.07
Rod Pedraza		
Phil Schneider		
☐ 649 Marlins Prospects	.30	.14
Vic Darensbourg		
Marc Valdes		
☐ 650 Astros Prospects	.15	.07
Rick Huisman		
Roberto Petagine		
☐ 651 Dodgers Prospects	.30	.14
Roger Cedeno		
Ron Coomer		
☐ 652 Expos Prospects	.30	.14
Shane Andrews		
Carlos Perez		
☐ 653 Mets Prospects	.30	.14
Jason Isringhausen		
Chris Roberts		
☐ 654 Phillies Prospects	.30	.14
Wayne Gomes		
Kevin Jordan		
☐ 655 Pirates Prospects	.30	.14
Esteban Loaiza		
Steve Pegues		
☐ 656 Cardinals Prospects	.15	.07
Terry Bradshaw		
John Frascatore		
☐ 657 Padres Prospects	.30	.14
Andres Berumen		
Bryce Florie		
☐ 658 Giants Prospects	.30	.14
Dan Carlson		
Keith Williams		
☐ 659 Checklist	.15	.07
☐ 660 Checklist	.15	.07

1995 Topps Finest

This 15-card standard-size set was inserted one every 36 Topps series two packs. This set featured the top 15 players in total bases from the 1994 season. The fronts feature a player photo, with his team identification and name on the bottom of the card. The horizontal backs feature another player photo along with a breakdown of how many of each type of hit each player got on the way to their season total. The set is sequenced in order of how they finished in the majors for the 1994 season.

	MINT	NRMT
COMPLETE SET (15)	70.00	32.00
COMMON CARD (1-15)	2.00	.90
SER.2 STAT.ODDS 1:36 HOB/RET, 1:20 JUM		

☐ 1 Jeff Bagwell	8.00	3.60
☐ 2 Albert Belle	5.00	2.20
☐ 3 Ken Griffey Jr.	20.00	9.00
☐ 4 Frank Thomas	15.00	6.75
☐ 5 Matt Williams	3.00	1.35
☐ 6 Dante Bichette	2.00	.90
☐ 7 Barry Bonds	5.00	2.20
☐ 8 Moises Alou	2.00	.90
☐ 9 Andres Galarraga	4.00	1.80
☐ 10 Kenny Lofton	5.00	2.20
☐ 11 Rafael Palmeiro	3.00	1.35
☐ 12 Tony Gwynn	10.00	4.50
☐ 13 Kirby Puckett	8.00	3.60
☐ 14 Jose Canseco	3.00	1.35
☐ 15 Jeff Conine	2.00	.90

1995 Topps League Leaders

Randomly inserted in jumbo packs at a rate of one in three and retail packs at a rate of one in six, this 50-card standard-size

set showcases those that were among league leaders in various categories. Card fronts feature a player photo with a black background. The player's name appears in gold foil at the bottom and the category with which he led the league or was among the leaders is in yellow letters up the right side. The backs contain various graphs and where the player placed among the leaders.

	MINT	NRMT
COMPLETE SET (50)	50.00	22.00
COMPLETE SERIES 1 (25)	20.00	9.00
COMPLETE SERIES 2 (25)	30.00	13.50
COMMON CARD (LL1-LL50)	.50	.23
STATED ODDS 1:6 RETAIL, 1:3 JUMBO		

		MINT	NRMT
☐ LL1	Albert Belle	1.50	.70
☐ LL2	Kevin Mitchell	.50	.23
☐ LL3	Wade Boggs	1.25	.55
☐ LL4	Tony Gwynn	3.00	1.35
☐ LL5	Moises Alou	.50	.23
☐ LL6	Andres Galarraga	.75	.35
☐ LL7	Matt Williams	1.00	.45
☐ LL8	Barry Bonds	1.50	.70
☐ LL9	Frank Thomas	5.00	2.20
☐ LL10	Jose Canseco	1.00	.45
☐ LL11	Jeff Bagwell	2.50	1.10
☐ LL12	Kirby Puckett	2.50	1.10
☐ LL13	Julio Franco	.50	.23
☐ LL14	Albert Belle	1.50	.70
☐ LL15	Fred McGriff	1.00	.45
☐ LL16	Kenny Lofton	1.50	.70
☐ LL17	Otis Nixon	.50	.23
☐ LL18	Brady Anderson	1.00	.45
☐ LL19	Deion Sanders	.75	.35
☐ LL20	Chuck Carr	.50	.23
☐ LL21	Pat Hentgen	.75	.35
☐ LL22	Andy Benes	.75	.35
☐ LL23	Roger Clemens	2.50	1.10
☐ LL24	Greg Maddux	4.00	1.80
☐ LL25	Pedro Martinez	1.25	.55
☐ LL26	Paul O'Neill	.75	.35
☐ LL27	Jeff Bagwell	2.50	1.10
☐ LL28	Frank Thomas	5.00	2.20
☐ LL29	Hal Morris	.50	.23
☐ LL30	Kenny Lofton	1.50	.70
☐ LL31	Ken Griffey Jr.	6.00	2.70
☐ LL32	Jeff Bagwell	2.50	1.10
☐ LL33	Albert Belle	1.25	.55
☐ LL34	Fred McGriff	1.00	.45
☐ LL35	Cecil Fielder	.75	.35
☐ LL36	Matt Williams	1.00	.45
☐ LL37	Joe Carter	.75	.35
☐ LL38	Dante Bichette	.75	.35
☐ LL39	Frank Thomas	5.00	2.20
☐ LL40	Mike Piazza	4.00	1.80
☐ LL41	Craig Biggio	1.00	.45
☐ LL42	Vince Coleman	.50	.23
☐ LL43	Marquis Grissom	.75	.35
☐ LL44	Chuck Knoblauch	1.25	.55
☐ LL45	Darren Lewis	.50	.23
☐ LL46	Randy Johnson	1.25	.55
☐ LL47	Jose Rijo	.50	.23
☐ LL48	Chuck Finley	.50	.23
☐ LL49	Bret Saberhagen	.50	.23
☐ LL50	Kevin Appier	.75	.35

1995 Topps Traded

This set contains 165 standard-size cards and was sold in 11-card packs for $1.29. The set features rookies, draft picks and players who had been traded. The fronts feature a photo with a white border. The backs have a player picture in a scoreboard and his statistics and information. All cards are numbered with a "T" prefix. Subsets fea-

tured are: At the Break (1T-10T) and All-Stars (156T-164T). Rookie Cards in this set include Ben Davis and Hideo Nomo.

		MINT	NRMT
	COMPLETE SET (165)	20.00	9.00
	COMMON CARD (1T-165T)	.15	.07
	MINOR STARS	.30	.14
	UNLISTED STARS	.60	.25

☐ 1T	Frank Thomas ATB	1.25	.55
☐ 2T	Ken Griffey Jr. ATB	1.50	.70
☐ 3T	Barry Bonds ATB	.40	.18
☐ 4T	Albert Belle ATB	.60	.25
☐ 5T	Cal Ripken ATB	1.25	.55
☐ 6T	Mike Piazza ATB	1.00	.45
☐ 7T	Tony Gwynn ATB	.75	.35
☐ 8T	Jeff Bagwell ATB	.60	.25
☐ 9T	Mo Vaughn ATB	.40	.18
☐ 10T	Matt Williams ATB	.40	.18
☐ 11T	Ray Durham	.30	.14
☐ 12T	Juan LeBron	1.00	.45
☐ 13T	Shawn Green	.30	.14
☐ 14T	Kevin Gross	.15	.07
☐ 15T	Jon Nunnally	.15	.07
☐ 16T	Brian Maxcy	.15	.07
☐ 17T	Mark Kiefer	.15	.07
☐ 18T	Carlos Beltran	.50	.23
☐ 19T	Mike Mimbs	.30	.14
☐ 20T	Larry Walker	.60	.25
☐ 21T	Chad Curtis	.15	.07
☐ 22T	Jeff Barry	.15	.07
☐ 23T	Joe Oliver	.15	.07
☐ 24T	Tomas Perez	.30	.14
☐ 25T	Michael Barrett	.50	.23
☐ 26T	Brian McRae	.15	.07
☐ 27T	Derek Bell	.15	.07
☐ 28T	Ray Durham	.30	.14
☐ 29T	Todd Williams	.15	.07
☐ 30T	Ryan Jaroncyk	.15	.07
☐ 31T	Todd Steverson	.15	.07
☐ 32T	Mike Devereaux	.15	.07
☐ 33T	Rheal Cormier	.15	.07
☐ 34T	Benny Santiago	.15	.07
☐ 35T	Bobby Higginson	1.00	.45
☐ 36T	Jack McDowell	.15	.07
☐ 37T	Mike Macfarlane	.15	.07
☐ 38T	Tony McKnight	.30	.14
☐ 39T	Brian Hunter	.40	.18
☐ 40T	Hideo Nomo	3.00	1.35
☐ 41T	Brett Butler	.30	.14
☐ 42T	Donovan Osborne	.15	.07
☐ 43T	Scott Karl	.15	.07
☐ 44T	Tony Phillips	.15	.07
☐ 45T	Marty Cordova	.30	.14
☐ 46T	Dave Mlicki	.15	.07
☐ 47T	Bronson Arroyo	.50	.23
☐ 48T	John Burkett	.15	.07
☐ 49T	J.D. Smart	.15	.07
☐ 50T	Mickey Tettleton	.15	.07
☐ 51T	Todd Stottlemyre	.15	.07
☐ 52T	Mike Perez	.15	.07
☐ 53T	Terry Mulholland	.15	.07
☐ 54T	Edgardo Alfonzo	.60	.25
☐ 55T	Zane Smith	.15	.07
☐ 56T	Jacob Brumfield	.15	.07
☐ 57T	Andujar Cedeno	.15	.07

☐ 58T	Jose Parra	.30	.14
☐ 59T	Manny Alexander	.15	.07
☐ 60T	Tony Tarasco	.15	.07
☐ 61T	Orel Hershiser	.30	.14
☐ 62T	Tim Scott	.15	.07
☐ 63T	Felix Rodriguez	.15	.07
☐ 64T	Ken Hill	.15	.07
☐ 65T	Marquis Grissom	.30	.14
☐ 66T	Lee Smith	.30	.14
☐ 67T	Jason Bates	.15	.07
☐ 68T	Felipe Lira	.15	.07
☐ 69T	Alex Hernandez	.50	.23
☐ 70T	Tony Fernandez	.15	.07
☐ 71T	Scott Radinsky	.15	.07
☐ 72T	Jose Canseco	.40	.18
☐ 73T	Mark Grudzielanek	.50	.23
☐ 74T	Ben Davis	1.50	.70
☐ 75T	Jim Abbott	.15	.07
☐ 76T	Roger Bailey	.15	.07
☐ 77T	Gregg Jefferies	.15	.07
☐ 78T	Erik Hanson	.15	.07
☐ 79T	Brad Radke	.75	.35
☐ 80T	Jaime Navarro	.15	.07
☐ 81T	John Wetteland	.15	.07
☐ 82T	Chad Fonville	.15	.07
☐ 83T	John Mabry	.30	.14
☐ 84T	Glenallen Hill	.15	.07
☐ 85T	Ken Caminiti	.40	.18
☐ 86T	Tom Goodwin	.15	.07
☐ 87T	Darren Bragg	.30	.14
☐ 88T	Pitching Prospects	.50	.23
	Pat Ahearne		
	Gary Rath		
	Larry Wimberly		
	Robbie Bell		
☐ 89T	Jeff Russell	.15	.07
☐ 90T	Dave Gallagher	.15	.07
☐ 91T	Steve Finley	.30	.14
☐ 92T	Vaughn Eshelman	.15	.07
☐ 93T	Kevin Jarvis	.15	.07
☐ 94T	Mark Gubicza	.15	.07
☐ 95T	Tim Wakefield	.15	.07
☐ 96T	Bob Tewksbury	.15	.07
☐ 97T	Sid Roberson	.15	.07
☐ 98T	Tom Henke	.15	.07
☐ 99T	Michael Tucker	.30	.14
☐ 100T	Jason Bates	.15	.07
☐ 101T	Otis Nixon	.15	.07
☐ 102T	Mark Whiten	.15	.07
☐ 103T	Dilson Torres	.15	.07
☐ 104T	Melvin Bunch	.15	.07
☐ 105T	Terry Pendleton	.15	.07
☐ 106T	Corey Jenkins	.60	.25
☐ 107T	Glenn Dishman	.30	.14
	Rob Grable		
☐ 108T	Reggie Taylor	.50	.23
☐ 109T	Curtis Goodwin	.15	.07
☐ 110T	David Cone	.30	.14
☐ 111T	Antonio Osuna	.15	.07
☐ 112T	Paul Shuey	.15	.07
☐ 113T	Doug Jones	.15	.07
☐ 114T	Mark McLemore	.15	.07
☐ 115T	Kevin Kitz	.15	.07
☐ 116T	John Kruk	.30	.14
☐ 117T	Trevor Wilson	.15	.07
☐ 118T	Jerald Clark	.15	.07
☐ 119T	Julian Tavarez	.15	.07
☐ 120T	Tim Pugh	.15	.07
☐ 121T	Todd Zeile	.15	.07
☐ 122T	Prospects	.75	.35
	Mark Sweeney UER		
	George Arias		
	Richie Sexson		
	Brian Schneider		
☐ 123T	Bobby Witt	.15	.07
☐ 124T	Hideo Nomo	1.50	.70
☐ 125T	Joey Cora	.30	.14
☐ 126T	Jim Scharrer	.30	.14
☐ 127T	Paul Quantrill	.15	.07
☐ 128T	Chipper Jones ROY	1.50	.70
☐ 129T	Kenny James	.15	.07
☐ 130T	Lyle Mouton	.60	.25
	Mariano Rivera		
☐ 131T	Tyler Green	.15	.07
☐ 132T	Brad Clontz	.15	.07
☐ 133T	Jon Nunnally	.15	.07

□ 134T Dave Magadan	.15	.07
□ 135T Al Leiter	.15	.07
□ 136T Bret Barberie	.15	.07
□ 137T Bill Swift	.15	.07
□ 138T Scott Cooper	.15	.07
□ 139T Roberto Kelly	.15	.07
□ 140T Charlie Hayes	.15	.07
□ 141T Pete Harnisch	.15	.07
□ 142T Rich Amaral	.15	.07
□ 143T Rudy Seanez	.15	.07
□ 144T Pat Listach	.15	.07
□ 145T Quilvio Veras	.15	.07
□ 146T Jose Olmeda	.15	.07
□ 147T Roberto Petagine	.15	.07
□ 148T Kevin Brown	.30	.14
□ 149T Phil Plantier	.15	.07
□ 150T Carlos Perez	.30	.14
□ 151T Pat Borders	.15	.07
□ 152T Tyler Green	.15	.07
□ 153T Stan Belinda	.15	.07
□ 154T Dave Stewart	.30	.14
□ 155T Andre Dawson	.40	.18
□ 156T Frank Thomas AS	.60	.25
Fred McGriff UER		
(McGriff's team shown as Blue Jays)		
□ 157T Carlos Baerga AS	.30	.14
Craig Biggio		
□ 158T Wade Boggs AS	.30	.14
Matt Williams		
□ 159T Cal Ripken AS	.60	.25
Ozzie Smith		
□ 160T Ken Griffey Jr. AS	.75	.35
Tony Gwynn		
□ 161T Albert Belle AS	.40	.18
Barry Bonds		
□ 162T Kirby Puckett	.60	.25
Len Dykstra		
□ 163T Ivan Rodriguez AS	.60	.25
Mike Piazza		
□ 164T Randy Johnson AS	.75	.35
Hideo Nomo		
□ 165T Checklist	.15	.07

1995 Topps Traded Power Boosters

This 10-card standard-size set was inserted in packs at a rate of one in 36. The set is comprised of parallel cards for the first 10 cards of the regular Topps Traded set which was the "At the Break" subset. The cards are done on extra-thick stock. The fronts have an action photo on a "Power Boosted" background, which is similar to diffraction technology, with the words "at the break" on the left side. The backs have a head shot and player information including his mid-season statistics for 1995 and previous years.

	MINT	NRMT
COMPLETE SET (10)	120.00	55.00
COMMON CARD (1-10)	5.00	2.20
STATED ODDS 1:36		
□ 1 Frank Thomas	25.00	11.00
□ 2 Ken Griffey Jr.	30.00	13.50
□ 3 Barry Bonds	8.00	3.60
□ 4 Albert Belle	8.00	3.60
□ 5 Cal Ripken	25.00	11.00
□ 6 Mike Piazza	20.00	9.00
□ 7 Tony Gwynn	15.00	6.75
□ 8 Jeff Bagwell	12.00	5.50
□ 9 Mo Vaughn	8.00	3.60
□ 10 Matt Williams	5.00	2.20

1996 Topps

This set consists of 440 standard-size cards. These cards were issued in 12-card foil packs with a suggested retail price of $1.29. The fronts feature full-color photos surrounded by a white background. Information on the backs includes a player photo, season and career stats and text. First series subsets include Star Power (1-6, 8-12), Draft Picks (13-26), AAA Stars (101-104), and Future Stars (210-219). A special Mickey Mantle card was issued as card #7 (his uniform number) and became the last card to be issued as card #7 in the Topps brand set. Rookie Cards in this set include Sean Casey, Matt Morris and Ron Wright.

	MINT	NRMT
COMPLETE SET (440)	30.00	13.50
COMP.HOBBY SET (449)	50.00	22.00
COMP.CEREAL SET (444)	50.00	22.00
COMPLETE SERIES 1 (220)	15.00	6.75
COMPLETE SERIES 2 (220)	15.00	6.75
COMMON CARD (1-440)	.10	.05
MINOR STARS	.20	.09
UNLISTED STARS	.40	.18
SUBSET CARDS HALF VALUE OF BASE CARDS		
ONE LAST DAY MANTLE PER FACT.SET		
□ 1 Tony Gwynn STP	.50	.23
□ 2 Mike Piazza STP	.50	.25
□ 3 Greg Maddux STP	.60	.25
□ 4 Jeff Bagwell STP	.40	.18
□ 5 Larry Walker STP	.20	.09
□ 6 Barry Larkin STP	.20	.09
□ 7 Mickey Mantle	4.00	1.80
□ 8 Tom Glavine STP UER	.10	.05
Won 21 games in June 95		
□ 9 Craig Biggio STP	.20	.09
□ 10 Barry Bonds STP	.30	.14
□ 11 Heathcliff Slocumb STP	.10	.05
□ 12 Matt Williams STP	.20	.09
□ 13 Todd Helton	1.50	.70
□ 14 Mark Redman	.20	.09
□ 15 Michael Barrett	.20	.09
□ 16 Ben Davis	.40	.18
□ 17 Juan LeBron	.30	.14
□ 18 Tony McKnight	.10	.05
□ 19 Ryan Jaroncyk	.20	.09
□ 20 Corey Jenkins	.20	.09
□ 21 Jim Scharrer	.10	.05
□ 22 Mark Bellhorn	.50	.23
□ 23 Jarrod Washburn	.30	.14
□ 24 Geoff Jenkins	.40	.18
□ 25 Sean Casey	1.00	.45
□ 26 Brett Tomko	.40	.18
□ 27 Tony Fernandez	.10	.05
□ 28 Rich Becker	.10	.05
□ 29 Andujar Cedeno	.10	.05
□ 30 Paul Molitor	.40	.18
□ 31 Brent Gates	.10	.05
□ 32 Glenallen Hill	.10	.05
□ 33 Mike Macfarlane	.10	.05
□ 34 Manny Alexander	.10	.05
□ 35 Todd Zeile	.10	.05
□ 36 Joe Girardi	.10	.05
□ 37 Tony Tarasco	.10	.05
□ 38 Tim Belcher	.10	.05
□ 39 Tom Goodwin	.10	.05
□ 40 Orel Hershiser	.20	.09
□ 41 Tripp Cromer	.10	.05
□ 42 Sean Bergman	.10	.05
□ 43 Troy Percival	.10	.05
□ 44 Kevin Stocker	.10	.05
□ 45 Albert Belle	.50	.23
□ 46 Tony Eusebio	.10	.05
□ 47 Sid Roberson	.10	.05
□ 48 Todd Hollandsworth	.10	.05
□ 49 Mark Wohlers	.10	.05
□ 50 Kirby Puckett	.75	.35
□ 51 Darren Holmes	.10	.05
□ 52 Ron Karkovice	.10	.05
□ 53 Al Martin	.10	.05
□ 54 Pat Rapp	.10	.05
□ 55 Mark Grace	.30	.14
□ 56 Greg Gagne	.10	.05
□ 57 Stan Javier	.10	.05
□ 58 Scott Sanders	.10	.05
□ 59 J.T. Snow	.20	.09
□ 60 David Justice	.40	.18
□ 61 Royce Clayton	.10	.05
□ 62 Kevin Foster	.10	.05
□ 63 Tim Naehring	.10	.05
□ 64 Orlando Miller	.10	.05
□ 65 Mike Mussina	.40	.18
□ 66 Jim Eisenreich	.10	.05
□ 67 Felix Fermin	.10	.05
□ 68 Bernie Williams	.40	.18
□ 69 Robb Nen	.10	.05
□ 70 Ron Gant	.20	.09
□ 71 Felipe Lira	.10	.05
□ 72 Jacob Brumfield	.10	.05
□ 73 John Mabry	.10	.05
□ 74 Mark Carreon	.10	.05
□ 75 Carlos Baerga	.10	.05
□ 76 Jim Dougherty	.10	.05
□ 77 Ryan Thompson	.10	.05
□ 78 Scott Leius	.10	.05
□ 79 Roger Pavlik	.10	.05
□ 80 Gary Sheffield	.40	.18
□ 81 Julian Tavarez	.10	.05
□ 82 Andy Ashby	.10	.05
□ 83 Mark Lemke	.10	.05
□ 84 Omar Vizquel	.20	.09
□ 85 Darren Daulton	.20	.09
□ 86 Mike Lansing	.10	.05
□ 87 Rusty Greer	.20	.09
□ 88 Dave Stevens	.10	.05
□ 89 Jose Offerman	.10	.05
□ 90 Tom Henke	.10	.05
□ 91 Troy O'Leary	.10	.05
□ 92 Michael Tucker	.20	.09
□ 93 Marvin Freeman	.10	.05
□ 94 Alex Diaz	.10	.05
□ 95 John Wetteland	.10	.05
□ 96 Cal Ripken 2131	2.00	.90
□ 97 Mike Mimbs	.10	.05
□ 98 Bobby Higginson	.20	.09
□ 99 Edgardo Alfonzo	.30	.14

100	Frank Thomas	1.50	.70
101	Steve Gibralter	.40	.18
	Bob Abreu		
102	Brian Givens	.10	.05
	T.J. Mathews		
103	Chris Pritchett	.10	.05
	Trenidad Hubbard		
104	Eric Owens	.20	.09
	Butch Huskey		
105	Doug Drabek	.10	.05
106	Tomas Perez	.10	.05
107	Mark Leiter	.10	.05
108	Joe Oliver	.10	.05
109	Tony Castillo	.10	.05
110	Checklist (1-110)	.10	.05
111	Kevin Seitzer	.10	.05
112	Pete Schourek	.10	.05
113	Sean Berry	.10	.05
114	Todd Stottlemyre	.10	.05
115	Joe Carter	.20	.09
116	Jeff King	.10	.05
117	Dan Wilson	.10	.05
118	Kurt Abbott	.10	.05
119	Lyle Mouton	.10	.05
120	Jose Rijo	.10	.05
121	Curtis Goodwin	.10	.05
122	Jose Valentin	.10	.05
123	Ellis Burks	.20	.09
124	David Cone	.20	.09
125	Eddie Murray	.40	.18
126	Brian Jordan	.20	.09
127	Darrin Fletcher	.10	.05
128	Curt Schilling	.20	.09
129	Ozzie Guillen	.10	.05
130	Kenny Rogers	.10	.05
131	Tom Pagnozzi	.10	.05
132	Garret Anderson	.20	.09
133	Bobby Jones	.10	.05
134	Chris Gomez	.10	.05
135	Mike Stanley	.10	.05
136	Hideo Nomo	1.00	.45
137	Jon Nunnally	.10	.05
138	Tim Wakefield	.10	.05
139	Steve Finley	.20	.09
140	Ivan Rodriguez	.50	.23
141	Quilvio Veras	.10	.05
142	Mike Fetters	.10	.05
143	Mike Greenwell	.10	.05
144	Bill Pulsipher	.10	.05
145	Mark McGwire	.75	.35
146	Frank Castillo	.10	.05
147	Greg Vaughn	.10	.05
148	Pat Hentgen	.20	.09
149	Walt Weiss	.10	.05
150	Randy Johnson	.40	.18
151	David Segui	.10	.05
152	Benji Gil	.10	.05
153	Tom Candiotti	.10	.05
154	Geronimo Berroa	.10	.05
155	John Franco	.20	.09
156	Jay Bell	.10	.05
157	Mark Gubicza	.10	.05
158	Hal Morris	.10	.05
159	Wilson Alvarez	.10	.05
160	Derek Bell	.10	.05
161	Ricky Bottalico	.10	.05
162	Bret Boone	.10	.05
163	Brad Radke	.20	.09
164	John Valentin	.10	.05
165	Steve Avery	.10	.05
166	Mark McLemore	.10	.05
167	Danny Jackson	.10	.05
168	Tino Martinez	.40	.18
169	Shane Reynolds	.10	.05
170	Terry Pendleton	.10	.05
171	Jim Edmonds	.30	.14
172	Esteban Loaiza	.10	.05
173	Ray Durham	.10	.05
174	Carlos Perez	.10	.05
175	Raul Mondesi	.30	.14
176	Steve Ontiveros	.10	.05
177	Chipper Jones	1.25	.55
178	Otis Nixon	.10	.05
179	John Burkett	.10	.05
180	Gregg Jefferies	.10	.05
181	Denny Martinez	.20	.09
182	Ken Caminiti	.30	.14
183	Doug Jones	.10	.05
184	Brian McRae	.10	.05
185	Don Mattingly	.60	.25
186	Mel Rojas	.10	.05
187	Marty Cordova	.20	.09
188	Vinny Castilla	.20	.09
189	John Smoltz	.20	.09
190	Travis Fryman	.20	.09
191	Chris Hoiles	.10	.05
192	Chuck Finley	.10	.05
193	Ryan Klesko	.30	.14
194	Alex Fernandez	.10	.05
195	Dante Bichette	.20	.09
196	Eric Karros	.20	.09
197	Roger Clemens	.75	.35
198	Randy Myers	.10	.05
199	Tony Phillips	.10	.05
200	Cal Ripken	1.50	.70
201	Rod Beck	.10	.05
202	Chad Curtis	.10	.05
203	Jack McDowell	.10	.05
204	Gary Gaetti	.10	.05
205	Ken Griffey Jr.	2.00	.90
206	Ramon Martinez	.20	.09
207	Jeff Kent	.10	.05
208	Brad Ausmus	.10	.05
209	Devon White	.10	.05
210	Jason Giambi	.20	.09
211	Nomar Garciaparra	1.50	.70
212	Billy Wagner	.20	.09
213	Todd Greene	.30	.14
214	Paul Wilson	.10	.05
215	Johnny Damon	.20	.09
216	Alan Benes	.20	.09
217	Karim Garcia	.30	.14
218	Dustin Hermanson	.10	.05
219	Derek Jeter	1.25	.55
220	Checklist (111-220)	.10	.05
221	Kirby Puckett STP	.40	.18
222	Cal Ripken STP	.75	.35
223	Albert Belle STP	.30	.14
224	Randy Johnson STP	.20	.09
225	Wade Boggs STP	.20	.09
226	Carlos Baerga STP	.10	.05
227	Ivan Rodriguez STP	.30	.14
228	Mike Mussina STP	.20	.09
229	Frank Thomas STP	.75	.35
230	Ken Griffey Jr. STP	1.00	.45
231	Jose Mesa STP	.10	.05
232	Matt Morris	.60	.25
233	Craig Wilson	.25	.11
234	Alvie Shepherd	.30	.14
235	Randy Winn	.30	.14
236	David Yocum	.30	.14
237	Jason Brester	.25	.11
238	Shane Monahan	.25	.11
239	Brian McNichol	.20	.09
240	Reggie Taylor	.30	.14
241	Garrett Long	.20	.09
242	Jonathan Johnson	.20	.09
243	Jeff Liefer	.25	.11
244	Brian Powell	.20	.09
245	Brian Buchanan	.20	.09
246	Mike Piazza	1.25	.55
247	Edgar Martinez	.30	.14
248	Chuck Knoblauch	.40	.18
249	Andres Galarraga	.40	.18
250	Tony Gwynn	1.00	.45
251	Lee Smith	.20	.09
252	Sammy Sosa	.40	.18
253	Jim Thome	.40	.18
254	Frank Rodriguez	.10	.05
255	Charlie Hayes	.10	.05
256	Bernard Gilkey	.10	.05
257	John Smiley	.10	.05
258	Brady Anderson	.30	.14
259	Rico Brogna	.10	.05
260	Kirt Manwaring	.10	.05
261	Len Dykstra	.20	.09
262	Tom Glavine	.20	.09
263	Vince Coleman	.10	.05
264	John Olerud	.20	.09
265	Orlando Merced	.10	.05
266	Kent Mercker	.10	.05
267	Terry Steinbach	.10	.05
268	Brian L. Hunter	.20	.09
269	Jeff Fassero	.10	.05
270	Jay Buhner	.30	.14
271	Jeff Brantley	.10	.05
272	Tim Raines	.20	.09
273	Jimmy Key	.10	.05
274	Mo Vaughn	.50	.23
275	Andre Dawson	.30	.14
276	Jose Mesa	.10	.05
277	Brett Butler	.20	.09
278	Luis Gonzalez	.20	.09
279	Steve Sparks	.10	.05
280	Chili Davis	.20	.09
281	Carl Everett	.10	.05
282	Jeff Cirillo	.20	.09
283	Thomas Howard	.10	.05
284	Paul O'Neill	.20	.09
285	Pat Meares	.10	.05
286	Mickey Tettleton	.10	.05
287	Rey Sanchez	.10	.05
288	Bip Roberts	.10	.05
289	Roberto Alomar	.40	.18
290	Ruben Sierra	.10	.05
291	John Flaherty	.10	.05
292	Bret Saberhagen	.10	.05
293	Barry Larkin	.30	.14
294	Sandy Alomar	.10	.05
295	Ed Sprague	.10	.05
296	Gary DiSarcina	.10	.05
297	Marquis Grissom	.20	.09
298	John Frascatore	.20	.09
299	Will Clark	.30	.14
300	Barry Bonds	.50	.23
301	Ozzie Smith	.50	.23
302	Dave Nilsson	.10	.05
303	Pedro Martinez	.40	.18
304	Joey Cora	.10	.05
305	Rick Aguilera	.10	.05
306	Craig Biggio	.30	.14
307	Jose Vizcaino	.10	.05
308	Jeff Montgomery	.10	.05
309	Moises Alou	.20	.09
310	Robin Ventura	.20	.09
311	David Wells	.10	.05
312	Delino DeShields	.10	.05
313	Trevor Hoffman	.10	.05
314	Andy Benes	.20	.09
315	Deion Sanders	.20	.09
316	Jim Bullinger	.10	.05
317	John Jaha	.10	.05
318	Greg Maddux	1.25	.55
319	Tim Salmon	.40	.18
320	Ben McDonald	.10	.05
321	Sandy Martinez	.10	.05
322	Dan Miceli	.10	.05
323	Wade Boggs	.40	.18
324	Ismael Valdes	.20	.09
325	Juan Gonzalez	1.00	.45
326	Charles Nagy	.20	.09
327	Ray Lankford	.20	.09
328	Mark Portugal	.10	.05
329	Bobby Bonilla	.20	.09
330	Reggie Sanders	.20	.09
331	Jamie Brewington	.10	.05
332	Aaron Sele	.10	.05
333	Pete Harnisch	.10	.05
334	Cliff Floyd	.20	.09
335	Cal Eldred	.10	.05
336	Jason Bates	.10	.05
337	Tony Clark	.40	.18
338	Jose Herrera	.10	.05
339	Alex Ochoa	.10	.05
340	Mark Loretta	.10	.05
341	Donne Wall	.10	.05
342	Jason Kendall	.30	.14
343	Shannon Stewart	.20	.09
344	Brooks Kieschnick	.20	.09
345	Chris Snopek	.10	.05
346	Ruben Rivera	.20	.09
347	Jeff Suppan	.20	.09
348	Phil Nevin	.10	.05
349	John Wasdin	.10	.05
350	Jay Payton	.20	.09
351	Tim Crabtree	.10	.05
352	Rick Krivda	.10	.05
353	Bob Wolcott	.10	.05

□			
□	354 Jimmy Haynes	.10	.05
□	355 Herb Perry	.10	.05
□	356 Ryne Sandberg	.50	.23
□	357 Harold Baines	.20	.09
□	358 Chad Ogea	.10	.05
□	359 Lee Tinsley	.10	.05
□	360 Matt Williams	.30	.14
□	361 Randy Velarde	.10	.05
□	362 Jose Canseco	.30	.14
□	363 Larry Walker	.40	.18
□	364 Kevin Appier	.20	.09
□	365 Darryl Hamilton	.10	.05
□	366 Jose Lima	.10	.05
□	367 Javy Lopez	.20	.09
□	368 Dennis Eckersley	.20	.09
□	369 Jason Isringhausen	.10	.05
□	370 Mickey Morandini	.10	.05
□	371 Scott Cooper	.10	.05
□	372 Jim Abbott	.10	.05
□	373 Paul Sorrento	.10	.05
□	374 Chris Hammond	.10	.05
□	375 Lance Johnson	.10	.05
□	376 Kevin Brown	.20	.09
□	377 Luis Alicea	.10	.05
□	378 Andy Pettitte	.50	.23
□	379 Dean Palmer	.10	.05
□	380 Jeff Bagwell	.75	.35
□	381 Jaime Navarro	.10	.05
□	382 Rondell White	.20	.09
□	383 Erik Hanson	.10	.05
□	384 Pedro Munoz	.10	.05
□	385 Heathcliff Slocumb	.10	.05
□	386 Wally Joyner	.20	.09
□	387 Bob Tewksbury	.10	.05
□	388 David Bell	.10	.05
□	389 Fred McGriff	.30	.14
□	390 Mike Henneman	.10	.05
□	391 Robby Thompson	.10	.05
□	392 Norm Charlton	.10	.05
□	393 Cecil Fielder	.20	.09
□	394 Benito Santiago	.10	.05
□	395 Rafael Palmeiro	.30	.14
□	396 Ricky Bones	.10	.05
□	397 Rickey Henderson	.30	.14
□	398 C.J. Nitkowski	.10	.05
□	399 Shawon Dunston	.10	.05
□	400 Manny Ramirez	.40	.18
□	401 Bill Swift	.10	.05
□	402 Chad Fonville	.10	.05
□	403 Joey Hamilton	.20	.09
□	404 Alex Gonzalez	.10	.05
□	405 Roberto Hernandez	.20	.09
□	406 Jeff Blauser	.20	.09
□	407 LaTroy Hawkins	.10	.05
□	408 Greg Colbrunn	.10	.05
□	409 Todd Hundley	.20	.09
□	410 Glenn Dishman	.10	.05
□	411 Joe Vitiello	.10	.05
□	412 Todd Worrell	.10	.05
□	413 Wil Cordero	.10	.05
□	414 Ken Hill	.10	.05
□	415 Carlos Garcia	.10	.05
□	416 Bryan Rekar	.10	.05
□	417 Shawn Green	.10	.05
□	418 Tyler Green	.10	.05
□	419 Mike Blowers	.10	.05
□	420 Kenny Lofton	.50	.23
□	421 Denny Neagle	.20	.09
□	422 Jeff Conine	.20	.09
□	423 Mark Langston	.10	.05
□	424 Steve Cox	1.00	.45
	Jesse Ibarra		
	Derrek Lee		
	Ron Wright		
□	425 Jim Bonnici	.50	.23
	Billy Owens		
	Richie Sexson		
	Daryle Ward		
□	426 Kevin Jordan	.20	.09
	Bobby Morris		
	Desi Relaford		
	Adam Riggs		
□	427 Tim Harkrider	.20	.09
	Rey Ordonez		
	Neifi Perez		
	Enrique Wilson		

□			
□	428 Bartolo Colon	.40	.18
	Doug Million		
	Rafael Orellano		
	Ray Ricken		
□	429 Jeff D'Amico	.20	.09
	Marty Janzen		
	Gary Rath		
	Clint Sodowsky		
□	430 Matt Drews	.20	.09
	Rich Hunter		
	Matt Ruebel		
	Bret Wagner		
□	431 Jaime Bluma	.30	.14
	David Coggin		
	Steve Montgomery		
	Brandon Reed		
□	432 Mike Figga	1.00	.45
	Raul Ibanez		
	Paul Konerko		
	Julio Mosquera		
□	433 Brian Barber	.20	.09
	Marc Kroon		
	Marc Valdes		
	Don Wengert		
□	434 George Arias	1.50	.70
	Chris Haas		
	Scott Rolen		
	Scott Spiezio		
□	435 Brian Banks	2.50	1.10
	Vladimir Guerrero		
	Andruw Jones		
	Billy McMillon		
□	436 Roger Cedeno	1.25	.55
	Derrick Gibson		
	Ben Grieve		
	Shane Spencer		
□	437 Anton French	.25	.11
	Demond Smith		
	DaRond Stovall		
	Keith Williams		
□	438 Michael Coleman	.50	.23
	Jacob Cruz		
	Richard Hidalgo		
	Charles Peterson		
□	439 Trey Beamon	.20	.09
	Yamil Benitez		
	Jermaine Dye		
	Angel Echevarria		
□	440 Checklist	.10	.05
□	F7 Mickey Mantle Last Day	12.00	5.50

1996 Topps Classic Confrontations

These cards were inserted at a rate of one in every 5-card Series 1 retail pack sold at Walmart. The first ten cards showcase hitters, while the last five cards feature pitchers. Inside white borders, the fronts show player cutouts on a brownish rock background featuring a shadow image of the player. The player's name is gold foil stamped across the bottom. The horizontal backs of the hitters' cards are aqua and present headshots and statistics. The backs of the pitchers cards are purple and present the same information.

	MINT	NRMT
COMPLETE SET (15)	6.00	2.70
COMMON CARD (CC1-CC15)	.25	.11
ONE PER SPECIAL SER.1 RETAIL PACK		

□			
□	CC1 Ken Griffey Jr.	1.50	.70
□	CC2 Cal Ripken	1.25	.55
□	CC3 Edgar Martinez	.40	.18
□	CC4 Kirby Puckett	.60	.25
□	CC5 Frank Thomas	1.25	.55
□	CC6 Barry Bonds	.60	.25
□	CC7 Reggie Sanders	.10	.05
□	CC8 Andres Galarraga	.60	.25
□	CC9 Tony Gwynn	.75	.35
□	CC10 Mike Piazza	1.00	.45
□	CC11 Randy Johnson	.60	.25
□	CC12 Mike Mussina	.60	.25
□	CC13 Roger Clemens	.75	.35
□	CC14 Tom Glavine	.25	.11
□	CC15 Greg Maddux	1.00	.45

1996 Topps Mantle

Randomly inserted in Series 1 packs, these cards are reprints of the original Mickey Mantle cards issued from 1951 through 1969. The fronts look the same except for a commemorative stamp, while the backs clearly state that they are "Mickey Mantle Commemorative" cards and have a 1996 copyright date. These cards honor Yankee great Mickey Mantle, who passed away in August 1995 after a gallant battle against cancer. Based on evidence from an uncut sheet auctioned off at the 1996 Kit Young Hawaii Trade Show, some collectors/dealers believe that cards 15 through 19 were slightly shorter printed in relation to the other 14 cards.

	MINT	NRMT
COMPLETE SET (19)	150.00	70.00
COMMON MANTLE (1-14)	8.00	3.60
COMMON MANTLE SP (15-19)	12.00	5.50
SER.1 STAT.ODDS 1:9 HOB, 1:6 RET, 1:2 JUM		
FOUR PER CEREAL FACT.SET		
COMP.CASE SET (19)	1000.00	450.00
COMMON CASE (1-14)	50.00	22.00
COMMON CASE SP (15-19)	60.00	27.00
*'51-'53 CARDS: 3X TO 6X LISTED CARDS		
ONE CASE PER SER.2 HOB/JUM/VEND CASE		
COMP.FINEST SET (19)	150.00	70.00

```
COMMON FINEST (1-14) ...... 8.00    3.60
COMMON FINEST SP (15-19) 12.00     5.50
*'51-'53 FINEST: .5X TO 1X LISTED CARDS
FINEST SER.2 ODDS 1:18 RET, 1:12 ANCO
COMP.REF.SET (19) .......... 800.00  350.00
COMMON REF. (1-14) .......... 40.00   18.00
COMMON REF.SP (15-19) .. 50.00      22.00
*'51-'53 REF: 2.5X TO 5X LISTED CARDS
REF.SER.2 ODDS 1:96 HOB, 1:144 RET
COMP.RDMP.SET (19) ...... 300.00   135.00
COMMON RDMP. (1-19) ...... 15.00     6.75
*'51-'53 RDMP: 1X TO 2X LISTED CARDS
RDMP.SER.2 ODDS 1:72 ANCO, 1:108 RET
```

		MINT	NRMT
□ 1	Mickey Mantle 1951 Bowman	15.00	6.75
□ 2	Mickey Mantle 1952 Topps	20.00	9.00
□ 3	Mickey Mantle 1953 Topps	10.00	4.50
□ 4	Mickey Mantle 1954 Bowman	8.00	3.60
□ 5	Mickey Mantle 1955 Bowman	8.00	3.60
□ 6	Mickey Mantle 1956 Topps	8.00	3.60
□ 7	Mickey Mantle 1957 Topps	8.00	3.60
□ 8	Mickey Mantle 1958 Topps	8.00	3.60
□ 9	Mickey Mantle 1959 Topps	8.00	3.60
□ 10	Mickey Mantle 1960 Topps	8.00	3.60
□ 11	Mickey Mantle 1961 Topps	8.00	3.60
□ 12	Mickey Mantle 1962 Topps	8.00	3.60
□ 13	Mickey Mantle 1963 Topps	8.00	3.60
□ 14	Mickey Mantle 1964 Topps	8.00	3.60
□ 15	Mickey Mantle 1965 Topps	12.00	5.50
□ 16	Mickey Mantle 1966 Topps	12.00	5.50
□ 17	Mickey Mantle 1967 Topps	12.00	5.50
□ 18	Mickey Mantle 1968 Topps	12.00	5.50
□ 19	Mickey Mantle 1969 Topps	12.00	5.50

1996 Topps Masters of the Game

Cards from this 20-card standard-size set were randomly inserted into first-series hobby packs. In addition, every factory set contained two Masters of the Game cards. The horizontal fronts comprise of silver foil set against white borders. The left side of the card has a player photo. The words "Master of the Game" and the player's name are printed on the right. The horizontal backs have a player photo, a brief write-up and some quick important dates in the player's career. The cards are numbered with a "MG" prefix in the lower left corner.

		MINT	NRMT
	COMPLETE SET (20)	30.00	13.50
	COMMON CARD (1-20)	.50	.23
	SER.1 STATED ODDS 1:18 HOBBY		
	TWO PER HOBBY FACTORY SET		

□ 1	Dennis Eckersley	1.00	.45
□ 2	Denny Martinez	1.00	.45
□ 3	Eddie Murray	2.00	.90
□ 4	Paul Molitor	2.00	.90
□ 5	Ozzie Smith	2.50	1.10
□ 6	Rickey Henderson	1.50	.70
□ 7	Tim Raines	1.00	.45
□ 8	Lee Smith	1.00	.45
□ 9	Cal Ripken	8.00	3.60
□ 10	Chili Davis	1.00	.45
□ 11	Wade Boggs	2.00	.90
□ 12	Tony Gwynn	5.00	2.20
□ 13	Don Mattingly	4.00	1.80
□ 14	Bret Saberhagen	.50	.23
□ 15	Kirby Puckett	4.00	1.80
□ 16	Joe Carter	1.00	.45
□ 17	Roger Clemens	3.00	1.35
□ 18	Barry Bonds	2.50	1.10
□ 19	Greg Maddux	6.00	2.70
□ 20	Frank Thomas	8.00	3.60

1996 Topps Mystery Finest

Randomly inserted in first-series packs, this 26-card standard-size set features a bit of a mystery. The fronts have opaque coating that must be removed before the player can be identified. After the opaque coating is removed, the fronts feature a player photo surrounded by silver borders. The backs feature a choice of players along with a corresponding mystery finest trivia fact. Some of these cards were also issued with refractor fronts.

		MINT	NRMT
	COMPLETE SET (26)	150.00	70.00
	COMMON CARD (M1-M26) ..	2.00	.90
	SER.1 STATED ODDS 1:36 HOB/RET, 1:8 JUM		
	COMP.REF.SET (22)	400.00	180.00
	*REFRACTORS: 1.25X TO 2.5X MYSTERY		
	REF.SER.1 ODDS 1:216 HOB/RET, 1:36 JUM		

□ M1	Hideo Nomo	8.00	3.60
□ M2	Greg Maddux	12.00	5.50
□ M3	Randy Johnson	4.00	1.80
□ M4	Chipper Jones	12.00	5.50
□ M5	Marty Cordova	2.00	.90
□ M6	Garret Anderson	2.00	.90
□ M7	Cal Ripken	15.00	6.75
□ M8	Kirby Puckett	8.00	3.60
□ M9	Tony Gwynn	10.00	4.50
□ M10	Manny Ramirez	4.00	1.80
□ M11	Jim Edmonds	2.50	1.10
□ M12	Mike Piazza	12.00	5.50
□ M13	Barry Bonds	5.00	2.20
□ M14	Raul Mondesi	2.50	1.10
□ M15	Sammy Sosa	4.00	1.80
□ M16	Ken Griffey Jr.	20.00	9.00
□ M17	Albert Belle	5.00	2.20
□ M18	Dante Bichette	2.00	.90
□ M19	Mo Vaughn	5.00	2.20
□ M20	Jeff Bagwell	8.00	3.60
□ M21	Frank Thomas	15.00	6.75
□ M22	Hideo Nomo	8.00	3.60
□ M23	Cal Ripken	15.00	6.75
□ M24	Mike Piazza	12.00	5.50
□ M25	Ken Griffey Jr.	20.00	9.00
□ M26	Frank Thomas	15.00	6.75

1996 Topps Power Boosters

Randomly inserted into packs, these cards are a metallic version of 25 of the first 26 cards from the basic Topps set. Card numbers 1-6 and 8-12 were issued in 1:36 retail packs, while numbers 13-26 were issued in 1:36 hobby packs. Inserted in place of two basic cards, they are printed on 28 point stock and the fronts have prismatic foil printing. Card number 7, which is Mickey Mantle in the regular set, was not issued in a Power Booster form.

		MINT	NRMT
	COMPLETE SET (25)	90.00	40.00
	COMP.STAR POW.SET (11)	50.00	22.00
	COMP.DRAFT PICKS SET (14)	40.00	18.00
	COMMON CARD (1-12)	1.50	.70
	COMMON DRAFT PICK (13-26)	2.00	.90
	SER.1 CARDS 13-26 STAT.ODDS 1:36 HOBBY		
	CARD #7 DOES NOT EXIST		

□ 1	Tony Gwynn	10.00	4.50
□ 2	Mike Piazza	12.00	5.50
□ 3	Greg Maddux	12.00	5.50
□ 4	Jeff Bagwell	8.00	3.60
□ 5	Larry Walker	4.00	1.80
□ 6	Barry Larkin	2.50	1.10
□ 7	Tom Glavine	2.00	.90
□ 8	Craig Biggio	2.50	1.10
□ 9	Barry Bonds	5.00	2.20
□ 10	Heathcliff Slocumb	1.50	.70
□ 11	Matt Williams	2.50	1.10

☐ 13 Todd Helton	15.00	6.75
☐ 14 Mark Redman	2.00	.90
☐ 15 Michael Barrett	2.00	.90
☐ 16 Ben Davis	6.00	2.70
☐ 17 Juan LeBron	4.00	1.80
☐ 18 Tony McKnight	2.00	.90
☐ 19 Ryan Jaroncyk	2.00	.90
☐ 20 Corey Jenkins	2.00	.90
☐ 21 Jim Scharrer	2.00	.90
☐ 22 Mark Bellhorn	5.00	2.20
☐ 23 Jarrod Washburn	3.00	1.35
☐ 24 Geoff Jenkins	4.00	1.80
☐ 25 Sean Casey	10.00	4.50
☐ 26 Brett Tomko	4.00	1.80

1996 Topps Profiles

Randomly inserted into Series 1 and 2 packs, this 20-card standard-size set features 10 players from each league. One card from each series was also included in all Topps factory sets. Topps spokesmen Kirby Puckett (AL) and Tony Gwynn (NL) give opinions on players within their league. The fronts feature a player photo set against a silver-foil background. The playeris name is on the bottom. A photo of either Gwynn or Puckett as well as the words "Profiles by ..." is on the right. The backs feature a player photo, some career data as well as Gwynn's or Puckett's opinion about the featured player. The cards are numbered with either an "AL or NL" prefix on the back depending on the playeris league. The cards is sequenced in alphabetical order within league.

	MINT	NRMT
COMPLETE SET (40)	40.00	18.00
COMPLETE SERIES 1 (20)	30.00	13.50
COMPLETE SERIES 2 (20)	10.00	4.50
COMMON CARD (AL1-NL20)	.50	.23
STAT.ODDS 1:12 HOB/RET,1:6 JUM,1:8 ANCO
1 SER.1 AND 2 SER.2 PER HOB.FACT.SET
☐ AL1 Roberto Alomar	1.00	.45
☐ AL2 Carlos Baerga	.25	.11
☐ AL3 Albert Belle	1.25	.55
☐ AL4 Cecil Fielder	.50	.23
☐ AL5 Ken Griffey Jr.	5.00	2.20
☐ AL6 Randy Johnson	1.00	.45
☐ AL7 Paul O'Neill	.50	.23
☐ AL8 Cal Ripken	4.00	1.80
☐ AL9 Frank Thomas	4.00	1.80
☐ AL10 Mo Vaughn	1.25	.55
☐ AL11 Jay Buhner	.75	.35
☐ AL12 Marty Cordova	.50	.23

☐ AL13 Jim Edmonds	.75	.35
☐ AL14 Juan Gonzalez	2.50	1.10
☐ AL15 Kenny Lofton	1.25	.55
☐ AL16 Edgar Martinez	.75	.35
☐ AL17 Don Mattingly	2.00	.90
☐ AL18 Mark McGwire	2.00	.90
☐ AL19 Rafael Palmeiro	.75	.35
☐ AL20 Tim Salmon	1.00	.45
☐ NL1 Jeff Bagwell	2.00	.90
☐ NL2 Derek Bell	.25	.11
☐ NL3 Barry Bonds	1.25	.55
☐ NL4 Greg Maddux	3.00	1.35
☐ NL5 Fred McGriff	.75	.35
☐ NL6 Raul Mondesi	.75	.35
☐ NL7 Mike Piazza	3.00	1.35
☐ NL8 Reggie Sanders	.25	.11
☐ NL9 Sammy Sosa	1.00	.45
☐ NL10 Larry Walker	1.00	.45
☐ NL11 Dante Bichette	1.00	.23
☐ NL12 Andres Galarraga	1.00	.45
☐ NL13 Ron Gant	.50	.23
☐ NL14 Tom Glavine	.50	.23
☐ NL15 Chipper Jones	3.00	1.35
☐ NL16 David Justice	1.00	.45
☐ NL17 Barry Larkin	.50	.23
☐ NL18 Hideo Nomo	2.00	.90
☐ NL19 Gary Sheffield	1.00	.45
☐ NL20 Matt Williams	.75	.35

1996 Topps Road Warriors

This 20-card set was inserted only into Series 2 WalMart packs and featured leading hitters of the majors. The set is sequenced in alphabetical order.

	MINT	NRMT
COMPLETE SET (20)	12.00	5.50
COMMON CARD (RW1-20)	.25	.11
ONE PER SPECIAL SER.2 RETAIL PACK
☐ RW1 Derek Bell	.25	.11
☐ RW2 Albert Belle	1.00	.45
☐ RW3 Craig Biggio	.50	.23
☐ RW4 Barry Bonds	1.00	.45
☐ RW5 Jay Buhner	.50	.23
☐ RW6 Jim Edmonds	.50	.23
☐ RW7 Gary Gaetti	.25	.11
☐ RW8 Ron Gant	.30	.14
☐ RW9 Edgar Martinez	.50	.23
☐ RW10 Tino Martinez	.75	.35
☐ RW11 Mark McGwire	1.50	.70
☐ RW12 Mike Piazza	3.00	1.35
☐ RW13 Manny Ramirez	.75	.35
☐ RW14 Tim Salmon	.75	.35
☐ RW15 Reggie Sanders	.25	.11
☐ RW16 Frank Thomas	3.00	1.35
☐ RW17 John Valentin	.25	.11
☐ RW18 Mo Vaughn	1.00	.45
☐ RW19 Robin Ventura	.30	.14
☐ RW20 Matt Williams	.50	.23

1996 Topps Wrecking Crew

Randomly inserted in Series 2 hobby packs, this 15-card set honors some of the hottest home run producers in the League. One card from this set was also inserted into Topps Hobby Factory sets. The cards feature color action player photos with foil stamping.

	MINT	NRMT
COMPLETE SET (15)	70.00	32.00
COMMON CARD (WC1-WC15)	2.00	.90
SER.2 STATED ODDS 1:18 HOBBY
ONE PER HOBBY FACTORY SET
☐ WC1 Jeff Bagwell	8.00	3.60
☐ WC2 Albert Belle	5.00	2.20
☐ WC3 Barry Bonds	5.00	2.20
☐ WC4 Jose Canseco	2.50	1.10
☐ WC5 Joe Carter	2.00	.90
☐ WC6 Cecil Fielder	2.00	.90
☐ WC7 Ron Gant	2.00	.90
☐ WC8 Juan Gonzalez	10.00	4.50
☐ WC9 Ken Griffey Jr.	20.00	9.00
☐ WC10 Fred McGriff	2.50	1.10
☐ WC11 Mark McGwire	8.00	3.60
☐ WC12 Mike Piazza	12.00	5.50
☐ WC13 Frank Thomas	15.00	6.75
☐ WC14 Mo Vaughn	5.00	2.20
☐ WC15 Matt Williams	2.50	1.10

1997 Topps

This 495-card set was primarily distributed in first and second series 11-card packs with a suggested retail price of $1.29. In addition, 8-card retail packs, 40-card jumbo packs and factory sets were made available. The card fronts feature a color action player photo with a gloss coating and a spot matte finish on the outside border with gold foil stamping. The backs carry another player photo, player information and statistics. The set includes the following sub-sets: Season Highlights (100-104, 462-466), Prospects (200-207, 487-494), the first ever expansion team cards of the Arizona Diamondbacks (249-251,468-469 and the Tampa Bay Devil Rays (252-253, 470-472) and Draft Picks (269-274, 477-483). Card 42 is a special Jackie Robinson tribute card commemorating the 50th anniversary of his contribution to baseball history and numbered for his Dodgers uniform number. Card #7 does not exist because it was retired in honor of Mickey Mantle. Card #84 does not exist because Mike Fetters' card was incorrectly numbered #61. Card #277 does not exist because Chipper Jones' card was incorrectly numbered #276. The 1996 number one draft pick Kris Benson's first card highlights the wide selection of Rookie Cards available in the set.

	MINT	NRMT
COMPLETE SET (496)	30.00	13.50
COMP.HOB.FACT.SET (497)	50.00	22.00
COMPLETE SERIES 1 (276)	15.00	6.75
COMPLETE SERIES 2 (220)	15.00	6.75
COMMON CARD (1-496)	.10	.05
MINOR STARS	.20	.09
UNLISTED STARS		.18

SUBSET CARDS HALF VALUE OF BASE CARDS
CARDS 7, 84 AND 277 DON'T EXIST
ELSTER AND FETTERS NUMBERED 61
CL 276 AND C.JONES NUMBERED 276

1	Barry Bonds	.50	.23
2	Tom Pagnozzi	.10	.05
3	Terrell Wade	.10	.05
4	Jose Valentin	.10	.05
5	Mark Clark	.10	.05
6	Brady Anderson	.30	.14
8	Wade Boggs	.40	.18
9	Scott Stahoviak	.10	.05
10	Andres Galarraga	.40	.18
11	Steve Avery	.10	.05
12	Rusty Greer	.20	.09
13	Derek Jeter	1.25	.55
14	Ricky Bottalico	.10	.05
15	Andy Ashby	.10	.05
16	Paul Shuey	.10	.05
17	F.P. Santangelo	.10	.05
18	Royce Clayton	.10	.05
19	Mike Mohler	.10	.05
20	Mike Piazza	1.25	.55
21	Jaime Navarro	.10	.05
22	Billy Wagner	.20	.09
23	Mike Timlin	.10	.05
24	Garret Anderson	.20	.09
25	Ben McDonald	.10	.05
26	Mel Rojas	.10	.05
27	John Burkett	.10	.05
28	Jeff King	.10	.05
29	Reggie Jefferson	.10	.05
30	Kevin Appier	.20	.09
31	Felipe Lira	.10	.05
32	Kevin Tapani	.10	.05
33	Mark Portugal	.10	.05
34	Carlos Garcia	.10	.05
35	Joey Cora	.20	.09
36	David Segui	.10	.05
37	Mark Grace	.30	.14
38	Erik Hanson	.10	.05
39	Jeff D'Amico	.10	.05
40	Jay Buhner	.30	.14
41	B.J. Surhoff	.10	.05
42	Jackie Robinson TRIB	2.00	.90

43	Roger Pavlik	.10	.05
44	Hal Morris	.10	.05
45	Mariano Duncan	.10	.05
46	Harold Baines	.20	.09
47	Jorge Fabregas	.10	.05
48	Jose Herrera	.10	.05
49	Jeff Cirillo	.20	.09
50	Tom Glavine	.20	.09
51	Pedro Astacio	.10	.05
52	Mark Gardner	.10	.05
53	Arthur Rhodes	.10	.05
54	Troy O'Leary	.10	.05
55	Bip Roberts	.10	.05
56	Mike Lieberthal	.10	.05
57	Shane Andrews	.10	.05
58	Scott Karl	.10	.05
59	Gary DiSarcina	.10	.05
60	Andy Pettitte	.40	.18
61	Kevin Elster	.10	.05
62	Mark McGwire	.75	.35
63	Dan Wilson	.10	.05
64	Mickey Morandini	.10	.05
65	Chuck Knoblauch	.40	.18
66	Tim Wakefield	.10	.05
67	Raul Mondesi	.30	.14
68	Todd Jones	.10	.05
69	Albert Belle	.50	.23
70	Trevor Hoffman	.10	.05
71	Eric Young	.10	.05
72	Robert Perez	.10	.05
73	Butch Huskey	.20	.09
74	Brian McRae	.10	.05
75	Jim Edmonds	.30	.14
76	Mike Henneman	.10	.05
77	Frank Rodriguez	.10	.05
78	Danny Tartabull	.10	.05
79	Robb Nen	.10	.05
80	Reggie Sanders	.10	.05
81	Ron Karkovice	.10	.05
82	Benito Santiago	.10	.05
83	Mike Lansing	.10	.05
84	Mike Fetters UER	.10	.05
	Card numbered 61		
85	Craig Biggio	.30	.14
86	Mike Bordick	.10	.05
87	Ray Lankford	.20	.09
88	Charles Nagy	.20	.09
89	Paul Wilson	.10	.05
90	John Wetteland	.10	.05
91	Tom Candiotti	.10	.05
92	Carlos Delgado	.20	.09
93	Derek Bell	.10	.05
94	Mark Lemke	.10	.05
95	Edgar Martinez	.30	.14
96	Rickey Henderson	.30	.14
97	Greg Myers	.10	.05
98	Jim Leyritz	.10	.05
99	Mark Johnson	.10	.05
100	Dwight Gooden HL	.10	.05
101	Al Leiter HL	.10	.05
102	John Mabry HL	.10	.05
103	Alex Ochoa HL	.10	.05
104	Mike Piazza HL	.60	.25
105	Jim Thome	.40	.18
106	Ricky Otero	.10	.05
107	Jamey Wright	.10	.05
108	Frank Thomas	1.50	.70
109	Jody Reed	.10	.05
110	Orel Hershiser	.20	.09
111	Terry Steinbach	.10	.05
112	Mark Loretta	.10	.05
113	Turk Wendell	.10	.05
114	Marvin Benard	.10	.05
115	Kevin Brown	.20	.09
116	Robert Person	.10	.05
117	Joey Hamilton	.20	.09
118	Francisco Cordova	.10	.05
119	John Smiley	.10	.05
120	Travis Fryman	.20	.09
121	Jimmy Key	.10	.05
122	Tom Goodwin	.10	.05
123	Mike Greenwell	.10	.05
124	Juan Guzman	1.00	.45
125	Pete Harnisch	.10	.05
126	Roger Cedeno	.10	.05
127	Ron Gant	.20	.09

128	Mark Langston	.10	.05
129	Tim Crabtree	.10	.05
130	Greg Maddux	1.25	.55
131	William VanLandingham	.10	.05
132	Wally Joyner	.20	.09
133	Randy Myers	.10	.05
134	John Valentin	.10	.05
135	Bret Boone	.10	.05
136	Bruce Ruffin	.10	.05
137	Chris Snopek	.10	.05
138	Paul Molitor	.40	.18
139	Mark McLemore	.10	.05
140	Rafael Palmeiro	.30	.14
141	Herb Perry	.10	.05
142	Luis Gonzalez	.10	.05
143	Doug Drabek	.10	.05
144	Ken Ryan	.10	.05
145	Todd Hundley	.20	.09
146	Ellis Burks	.20	.09
147	Ozzie Guillen	.10	.05
148	Rick Becker	.10	.05
149	Sterling Hitchcock	.10	.05
150	Bernie Williams	.40	.18
151	Mike Stanley	.10	.05
152	Roberto Alomar	.40	.18
153	Jose Mesa	.10	.05
154	Steve Trachsel	.10	.05
155	Alex Gonzalez	.10	.05
156	Troy Percival	.10	.05
157	John Smoltz	.20	.09
158	Pedro Martinez	.40	.18
159	Jeff Conine	.10	.05
160	Bernard Gilkey	.10	.05
161	Jim Eisenreich	.10	.05
162	Mickey Tettleton	.10	.05
163	Justin Thompson	.20	.09
164	Jose Offerman	.10	.05
165	Tony Phillips	.10	.05
166	Ismael Valdes	.20	.09
167	Ryne Sandberg	.50	.23
168	Matt Mieske	.10	.05
169	Geronimo Berroa	.10	.05
170	Otis Nixon	.10	.05
171	John Mabry	.10	.05
172	Shawon Dunston	.10	.05
173	Omar Vizquel	.20	.09
174	Chris Hoiles	.10	.05
175	Dwight Gooden	.20	.09
176	Wilson Alvarez	.10	.05
177	Todd Hollandsworth	.10	.05
178	Roger Salkeld	.10	.05
179	Rey Sanchez	.10	.05
180	Rey Ordonez	.20	.09
181	Denny Martinez	.20	.09
182	Ramon Martinez	.20	.09
183	Dave Nilsson	.10	.05
184	Marquis Grissom	.20	.09
185	Randy Velarde	.10	.05
186	Ron Coomer	.10	.05
187	Tino Martinez	.40	.18
188	Jeff Brantley	.10	.05
189	Steve Finley	.20	.09
190	Andy Benes	.20	.09
191	Terry Adams	.10	.05
192	Mike Blowers	.10	.05
193	Russ Davis	.10	.05
194	Darryl Hamilton	.10	.05
195	Jason Kendall	.20	.09
196	Johnny Damon	.10	.05
197	Dave Martinez	.10	.05
198	Mike Macfarlane	.10	.05
199	Norm Charlton	.10	.05
200	Doug Million	.25	.11
	Damian Moss		
	Bobby Rodgers		
201	Geoff Jenkins	.20	.09
	Raul Ibanez		
	Mike Cameron		
202	Sean Casey	.30	.14
	Jim Bonnici		
	Dmitri Young		
203	Jed Hansen	.10	.05
	Homer Bush		
	Felipe Crespo		
204	Kevin Orie	.20	.09
	Gabe Alvarez		

	Aaron Boone		
205	Ben Davis	.20	.09
	Kevin Brown		
	Bobby Estalella		
206	Billy McMillon	.40	.18
	Bubba Trammell		
	Dante Powell		
207	Jarrod Washburn	.20	.09
	Marc Wilkins		
	Glendon Rusch		
208	Brian Hunter	.20	.09
209	Jason Giambi	.20	.09
210	Henry Rodriguez	.10	.05
211	Edgar Renteria	.20	.09
212	Edgardo Alfonzo	.20	.09
213	Fernando Vina	.05	.02
214	Shawn Green	.10	.05
215	Ray Durham	.10	.05
216	Joe Randa	.10	.05
217	Armando Reynoso	.10	.05
218	Eric Davis	.20	.09
219	Bob Tewksbury	.10	.05
220	Jacob Cruz	.20	.09
221	Glenallen Hill	.10	.05
222	Gary Gaetti	.10	.05
223	Donne Wall	.10	.05
224	Brad Clontz	.10	.05
225	Marty Janzen	.10	.05
226	Todd Worrell	.10	.05
227	John Franco	.20	.09
228	David Wells	.10	.05
229	Gregg Jefferies	.10	.05
230	Tim Naehring	.10	.05
231	Thomas Howard	.10	.05
232	Roberto Hernandez	.10	.05
233	Kevin Ritz	.10	.05
234	Julian Tavarez	.10	.05
235	Ken Hill	.10	.05
236	Greg Gagne	.10	.05
237	Bobby Chouinard	.10	.05
238	Joe Carter	.20	.09
239	Jermaine Dye	.05	.02
240	Antonio Osuna	.10	.05
241	Julio Franco	.20	.09
242	Mike Grace	.10	.05
243	Aaron Sele	.10	.05
244	David Justice	.40	.18
245	Sandy Alomar Jr.	.20	.09
246	Jose Canseco	.30	.14
247	Paul O'Neill	.20	.09
248	Sean Berry	.10	.05
249	Nick Bierbrodt	.25	.11
	Kevin Sweeney		
250	Larry Rodriguez	.25	.11
	Vladimir Nunez		
251	Ron Hartman	.25	.11
	David Hayman		
252	Alex Sanchez	.30	.14
	Matthew Quatraro		
253	Ronni Seberino	.25	.11
	Pablo Ortega		
254	Rex Hudler	.10	.05
255	Orlando Miller	.10	.05
256	Mariano Rivera	.20	.09
257	Brad Radke	.20	.09
258	Bobby Higginson	.20	.09
259	Jay Bell	.20	.09
260	Mark Grudzielanek	.10	.05
261	Lance Johnson	.10	.05
262	Ken Caminiti	.30	.14
263	J.T. Snow	.20	.09
264	Gary Sheffield	.40	.18
265	Darrin Fletcher	.10	.05
266	Eric Owens	.10	.05
267	Luis Castillo	.20	.09
268	Scott Rolen	1.00	.45
269	Todd Noel	.25	.11
	John Oliver		
270	Robert Stratton	.25	.11
	Corey Lee		
271	Gil Meche	.25	.11
	Matt Halloran		
272	Eric Milton	1.00	.45
	Dermal Brown		
273	Josh Garrett	.25	.11
	Chris Reitsma		
274	A.J. Zapp	.75	.35
	Jason Marquis		
275	Checklist	.10	.05
276	Checklist	.10	.05
277	Chipper Jones UER	1.25	.55
	incorrectly numbered 276		
278	Orlando Merced	.10	.05
279	Ariel Prieto	.10	.05
280	Al Leiter	.10	.05
281	Pat Meares	.10	.05
282	Darryl Strawberry	.20	.09
283	Jamie Moyer	.10	.05
284	Scott Servais	.10	.05
285	Delino DeShields	.10	.05
286	Danny Graves	.10	.05
287	Gerald Williams	.10	.05
288	Todd Greene	.20	.09
289	Rico Brogna	.10	.05
290	Derrick Gibson	.30	.14
291	Joe Girardi	.10	.05
292	Darren Lewis	.10	.05
293	Nomar Garciaparra	1.25	.55
294	Greg Colbrunn	.10	.05
295	Jeff Bagwell	.75	.35
296	Brent Gates	.10	.05
297	Jose Vizcaino	.10	.05
298	Alex Ochoa	.10	.05
299	Sid Fernandez	.10	.05
300	Ken Griffey Jr.	2.00	.90
301	Chris Gomez	.10	.05
302	Wendell Magee	.10	.05
303	Darren Oliver	.10	.05
304	Mel Nieves	.10	.05
305	Sammy Sosa	.40	.18
306	George Arias	.10	.05
307	Jack McDowell	.10	.05
308	Stan Javier	.10	.05
309	Kimera Bartee	.10	.05
310	James Baldwin	.10	.05
311	Rocky Coppinger	.10	.05
312	Keith Lockhart	.10	.05
313	C.J. Nitkowski	.10	.05
314	Allen Watson	.10	.05
315	Darryl Kile	.20	.09
316	Amaury Telemaco	.10	.05
317	Jason Isringhausen	.10	.05
318	Manny Ramirez	.40	.18
319	Terry Pendleton	.10	.05
320	Tim Salmon	.40	.18
321	Eric Karros	.20	.09
322	Mark Whiten	.10	.05
323	Nick Krivda	.10	.05
324	Brett Butler	.20	.09
325	Randy Johnson	.40	.18
326	Eddie Taubensee	.10	.05
327	Mark Leiter	.10	.05
328	Kevin Gross	.10	.05
329	Ernie Young	.10	.05
330	Pat Hentgen	.20	.09
331	Rondell White	.20	.09
332	Bobby Witt	.10	.05
333	Eddie Murray	.40	.18
334	Tim Raines	.20	.09
335	Jeff Fassero	.10	.05
336	Chuck Finley	.10	.05
337	Willie Adams	.10	.05
338	Chan Ho Park	.40	.18
339	Jay Powell	.10	.05
340	Ivan Rodriguez	.50	.23
341	Jermaine Allensworth	.10	.05
342	Jay Payton	.10	.05
343	T.J. Mathews	.10	.05
344	Tony Batista	.10	.05
345	Ed Sprague	.10	.05
346	Jeff Kent	.10	.05
347	Scott Erickson	.10	.05
348	Jeff Suppan	.20	.09
349	Pete Schourek	.10	.05
350	Kenny Lofton	.50	.23
351	Alan Benes	.20	.09
352	Fred McGriff	.30	.14
353	Charlie O'Brien	.10	.05
354	Darren Bragg	.10	.05
355	Alex Fernandez	.20	.09
356	Al Martin	.10	.05
357	Bob Wells	.10	.05
358	Chad Mottola	.10	.05
359	Devon White	.10	.05
360	David Cone	.20	.09
361	Bobby Jones	.10	.05
362	Scott Sanders	.10	.05
363	Karim Garcia	.20	.09
364	Kirt Manwaring	.10	.05
365	Chili Davis	.20	.09
366	Mike Hampton	.10	.05
367	Chad Ogea	.10	.05
368	Curt Schilling	.20	.09
369	Phil Nevin	.10	.05
370	Roger Clemens	.75	.35
371	Willie Greene	.10	.05
372	Kenny Rogers	.10	.05
373	Jose Rijo	.10	.05
374	Bobby Bonilla	.20	.09
375	Mike Mussina	.40	.18
376	Curtis Pride	.10	.05
377	Todd Walker	.20	.09
378	Jason Bere	.10	.05
379	Heathcliff Slocumb	.10	.05
380	Dante Bichette	.20	.09
381	Carlos Baerga	.10	.05
382	Livan Hernandez	.30	.14
383	Jason Schmidt	.10	.05
384	Kevin Stocker	.10	.05
385	Matt Williams	.30	.14
386	Bartolo Colon	.20	.09
387	Will Clark	.30	.14
388	Dennis Eckersley	.20	.09
389	Brooks Kieschnick	.10	.05
390	Ryan Klesko	.30	.14
391	Mark Carreon	.10	.05
392	Tim Worrell	.10	.05
393	Dean Palmer	.10	.05
394	Wil Cordero	.10	.05
395	Javy Lopez	.20	.09
396	Rich Aurilia	.10	.05
397	Greg Vaughn	.20	.09
398	Vinny Castilla	.20	.09
399	Jeff Montgomery	.10	.05
400	Cal Ripken	1.50	.70
401	Walt Weiss	.10	.05
402	Brad Ausmus	.10	.05
403	Ruben Rivera	.20	.09
404	Mark Wohlers	.10	.05
405	Rick Aguilera	.10	.05
406	Tony Clark	.40	.18
407	Lyle Mouton	.10	.05
408	Bill Pulsipher	.10	.05
409	Jose Rosado	.20	.09
410	Tony Gwynn	1.00	.45
411	Cecil Fielder	.20	.09
412	John Flaherty	.10	.05
413	Lenny Dykstra	.20	.09
414	Ugueth Urbina	.20	.09
415	Brian Jordan	.20	.09
416	Bob Abreu	.20	.09
417	Craig Paquette	.10	.05
418	Sandy Martinez	.10	.05
419	Jeff Blauser	.20	.09
420	Barry Larkin	.30	.14
421	Kevin Seltzer	.10	.05
422	Tim Belcher	.10	.05
423	Paul Sorrento	.10	.05
424	Cal Eldred	.10	.05
425	Robin Ventura	.20	.09
426	John Olerud	.20	.09
427	Bob Wolcott	.10	.05
428	Matt Lawton	.10	.05
429	Rod Beck	.10	.05
430	Shane Reynolds	.10	.05
431	Mike James	.10	.05
432	Steve Wojciechowski	.10	.05
433	Vladimir Guerrero	.75	.35
434	Dustin Hermanson	.10	.05
435	Marty Cordova	.20	.09
436	Marc Newfield	.10	.05
437	Todd Stottlemyre	.10	.05
438	Jeffrey Hammonds	.10	.05
439	Dave Stevens	.10	.05
440	Hideo Nomo	1.00	.45
441	Mark Thompson	.10	.05
442	Mark Lewis	.10	.05
443	Quinton McCracken	.10	.05

		MINT	NRMT
☐ 444	Cliff Floyd	.10	.05
☐ 445	Denny Neagle	.20	.09
☐ 446	John Jaha	.10	.05
☐ 447	Mike Sweeney	.20	.09
☐ 448	John Wasdin	.10	.05
☐ 449	Chad Curtis	.10	.05
☐ 450	Mo Vaughn	.50	.23
☐ 451	Donovan Osborne	.10	.05
☐ 452	Ruben Sierra	.10	.05
☐ 453	Michael Tucker	.20	.05
☐ 454	Kurt Abbott	.10	.05
☐ 455	Andruw Jones UER	1.00	.45

Birthdate is incorrectly listed as 1-22-67, should be 1-22-77

		MINT	NRMT
☐ 456	Shannon Stewart	.20	.09
☐ 457	Scott Brosius	.10	.05
☐ 458	Juan Guzman	.10	.05
☐ 459	Ron Villone	.10	.05
☐ 460	Moises Alou	.20	.09
☐ 461	Larry Walker	.40	.18
☐ 462	Eddie Murray SH	.20	.09
☐ 463	Paul Molitor SH	.20	.09
☐ 464	Hideo Nomo SH	.50	.23
☐ 465	Barry Bonds SH	.30	.14
☐ 466	Todd Hundley SH	.10	.05
☐ 467	Rheal Cormier	.10	.05
☐ 468	Jason Conti	.40	.18
	Jhensy Sandoval		
☐ 469	Rod Barajas	.25	.11
	Jackie Rexrode		
☐ 470	Cedric Bowers	.40	.18
	Jared Sandberg		
☐ 471	Chei Gunner	.50	.23
	Paul Wilder		
☐ 472	Mike Decelle	.25	.11
	Marcus McCain		
☐ 473	Todd Zeile	.10	.05
☐ 474	Neifi Perez	.20	.09
☐ 475	Jeromy Burnitz	.10	.05
☐ 476	Trey Beamon	.10	.05
☐ 477	Braden Looper	.40	.18
	John Patterson		
☐ 478	Danny Peoples	.40	.18
	Jake Westbrook		
☐ 479	Eric Chavez	1.25	.55
	Adam Eaton		
☐ 480	Joe Lawrence	.25	.11
	Pete Tucci		
☐ 481	Kris Benson	.75	.35
	Billy Koch		
☐ 482	John Nicholson	.25	.11
	Andy Prater		
☐ 483	Mark Johnson	1.00	.45
	Mark Kotsay		
☐ 484	Armando Benitez	.10	.05
☐ 485	Mike Matheny	.10	.05
☐ 486	Jeff Reed	.10	.05
☐ 487	Mark Bellhorn	.20	.09
	Russ Johnson		
	Enrique Wilson		
☐ 488	Ben Grieve	.75	.35
	Richard Hidalgo		
	Scott Morgan		
☐ 489	Paul Konerko	.60	.25
	Derek Lee UER		
	spelled Derek on back		
	Ron Wright		
☐ 490	Wes Helms	.20	.09
	Bill Mueller		
	Brad Seitzer		
☐ 491	Jeff Abbott	.20	.09
	Shane Monahan		
	Edgard Velazquez		
☐ 492	Jimmy Anderson	.25	.11
	Ron Blazier		
	Gerald Witasick		
☐ 493	Darin Blood	.30	.14
	Heath Murray		
	Carl Pavano		
☐ 494	Nelson Figueroa	.25	.11
	Mark Redman		
	Mike Villano		
☐ 495	Checklist	.10	.05
☐ 496	Checklist	.10	.05
☐ NNO	Derek Jeter AU	100.00	45.00

1997 Topps All-Stars

Randomly inserted in Series 1 packs at a rate of one in 18, this 22-card set printed on rainbow foilboard features the top 11 players from each league and from each position as voted by the Topps Sports Department. The fronts carry a photo of a "first team" all-star player while the backs carry a different photo of that player alongside the "second team" and "third team" selections. Only the "first team" players are checklisted listed below.

		MINT	NRMT
	COMPLETE SET (22)	60.00	27.00
	COMMON CARD (AS1-AS22)	1.00	.45

SER.1 STATED ODDS 1:18 HOB/RET, 1:6 JUM

		MINT	NRMT
☐ AS1	Ivan Rodriguez	4.00	1.80
☐ AS2	Todd Hundley	1.50	.70
☐ AS3	Frank Thomas	12.00	5.50
☐ AS4	Andres Galarraga	3.00	1.35
☐ AS5	Chuck Knoblauch	3.00	1.35
☐ AS6	Eric Young	1.00	.45
☐ AS7	Jim Thome	3.00	1.35
☐ AS8	Chipper Jones	10.00	4.50
☐ AS9	Cal Ripken	12.00	5.50
☐ AS10	Barry Larkin	2.00	.90
☐ AS11	Albert Belle	4.00	1.80
☐ AS12	Barry Bonds	4.00	1.80
☐ AS13	Ken Griffey Jr.	15.00	6.75
☐ AS14	Ellis Burks	1.50	.70
☐ AS15	Juan Gonzalez	8.00	3.60
☐ AS16	Gary Sheffield	3.00	1.35
☐ AS17	Andy Pettitte	3.00	1.35
☐ AS18	Tom Glavine	1.50	.70
☐ AS19	Pat Hentgen	1.50	.70
☐ AS20	John Smoltz	1.50	.70
☐ AS21	Roberto Hernandez	1.00	.45
☐ AS22	Mark Wohlers	1.00	.45

1997 Topps Awesome Impact

Randomly inserted in second series 11-card retail packs at a rate of 1:18, cards from this 20-card set feature a selection of top young stars and prospects. Each card front features a color player action shot cut out against a silver prismatic background.

	MINT	NRMT
COMPLETE SET (20)	100.00	45.00
COMMON CARD (AI1-AI20)	1.50	.70
SEMISTARS	3.00	1.35

		MINT	NRMT
	UNLISTED STARS	5.00	2.20

SER.2 STATED ODDS 1:18 RETAIL

		MINT	NRMT
☐ AI1	Jaime Bluma	1.50	.70
☐ AI2	Tony Clark	5.00	2.20
☐ AI3	Jermaine Dye	1.50	.70
☐ AI4	Nomar Garciaparra	15.00	6.75
☐ AI5	Vladimir Guerrero	10.00	4.50
☐ AI6	Todd Hollandsworth	1.50	.70
☐ AI7	Derek Jeter	15.00	6.75
☐ AI8	Andruw Jones	12.00	5.50
☐ AI9	Chipper Jones	15.00	6.75
☐ AI10	Jason Kendall	2.50	1.10
☐ AI11	Brooks Kieschnick	1.50	.70
☐ AI12	Alex Ochoa	1.50	.70
☐ AI13	Rey Ordonez	1.50	.70
☐ AI14	Neifi Perez	2.50	1.10
☐ AI15	Edgar Renteria	2.50	1.10
☐ AI16	Mariano Rivera	2.50	1.10
☐ AI17	Ruben Rivera	2.50	1.10
☐ AI18	Scott Rolen	12.00	5.50
☐ AI19	Billy Wagner	2.50	1.10
☐ AI20	Todd Walker	2.50	1.10

1997 Topps Hobby Masters

Randomly inserted in first and second series hobby packs at a rate of one in 36, cards from this 10-card set honor twenty players picked by hobby dealers from across the country as their all-time favorites. Cards 1-10 were issued in first series packs and 11-20 in second series. Printed on 28-point diffraction foilboard, one card replaces two regular cards when inserted in packs. The fronts feature borderless color player photos on a background of the player's profile. The backs carry player information.

	MINT	NRMT
COMPLETE SET (20)	110.00	50.00
COMPLETE SERIES 1 (10)	60.00	27.00
COMPLETE SERIES 2 (10)	50.00	22.00

	MINT	NRMT
COMMON CARD (HM1-HM20)	2.00	.90
STATED ODDS 1:36 HOBBY		
☐ HM1 Ken Griffey Jr.	15.00	6.75
☐ HM2 Cal Ripken	12.00	5.50
☐ HM3 Greg Maddux	10.00	4.50
☐ HM4 Albert Belle	4.00	1.80
☐ HM5 Tony Gwynn	8.00	3.60
☐ HM6 Jeff Bagwell	6.00	2.70
☐ HM7 Randy Johnson	3.00	1.35
☐ HM8 Raul Mondesi	2.00	.90
☐ HM9 Juan Gonzalez	8.00	3.60
☐ HM10 Kenny Lofton	4.00	1.80
☐ HM11 Frank Thomas	12.00	5.50
☐ HM12 Mike Piazza	10.00	4.50
☐ HM13 Chipper Jones	10.00	4.50
☐ HM14 Brady Anderson	2.00	.90
☐ HM15 Ken Caminiti	2.00	.90
☐ HM16 Barry Bonds	4.00	1.80
☐ HM17 Mo Vaughn	4.00	1.80
☐ HM18 Derek Jeter	10.00	4.50
☐ HM19 Sammy Sosa	3.00	1.35
☐ HM20 Andres Galarraga	3.00	1.35

1997 Topps Inter-League Finest

Randomly inserted in Series 1 packs at a rate of one in 36, this 14-card set features top individual match-ups from inter-league rivalries. One player from each major league team is represented on each side of this double-sided card with a color photo and is covered with the patented Finest clear protector.

	MINT	NRMT
COMPLETE SET (14)	60.00	27.00
COMMON CARD (ILM1-ILM14)	1.50	.70
SER.1 STATED ODDS 1:36 HOB/RET,1:10 JUM		
COMP.REF.SET (14)	300.00	135.00
SER.1 STATED ODDS 1:36 HOB/RET,1:56 JUM		
*REFRACTORS: 2.5X TO 5X HI COLUMN		
COMMON REF. (ILM1-ILM14)	15.00	6.75
REF.SER.1 ODDS 1:216 HOB/RET,1:56 JUM		

☐ ILM1 Mark McGwire	6.00	2.70
Barry Bonds		
☐ ILM2 Tim Salmon	10.00	4.50
Mike Piazza		
☐ ILM3 Ken Griffey Jr.	15.00	6.75
Dante Bichette		
☐ ILM4 Juan Gonzalez	10.00	4.50
Tony Gwynn		
☐ ILM5 Frank Thomas	12.00	5.50
Sammy Sosa		
☐ ILM6 Albert Belle	4.00	1.80
Barry Larkin		
☐ ILM7 Johnny Damon	1.50	.70
Brian Jordan		
☐ ILM8 Paul Molitor	3.00	1.35
Jeff King		
☐ ILM9 John Jaha	5.00	2.20
Jeff Bagwell		
☐ ILM10 Bernie Williams	3.00	1.35

Todd Hundley		
☐ ILM11 Joe Carter	1.50	.70
Henry Rodriguez		
☐ ILM12 Cal Ripken	10.00	4.50
Gregg Jefferies		
☐ ILM13 Mo Vaughn	10.00	4.50
Chipper Jones		
☐ ILM14 Travis Fryman	3.00	1.35
Gary Sheffield		

1997 Topps Mantle

Randomly inserted at the rate of one in 12 Series 1 packs, this 16-card set features authentic reprints of Topps Mickey Mantle cards that were not reprinted last year. Each card is stamped with the commemorative gold foil logo.

	MINT	NRMT
COMPLETE SET (16)	125.00	55.00
COMMON MANTLE (21-36)	8.00	3.60
SER.1 STATED ODDS 1:12 HOB/RET,1:3 JUM		
COMP.FINEST SET (16)	125.00	55.00
COMMON FINEST (21-36)	8.00	3.60
FINEST SER.2 ODDS 1:24 HOB/RET,1:6 JUM		
COMP.REF.SET (16)	600.00	275.00
COMMON REF. (21-36)	40.00	18.00
REF.SER.2 ODDS 1:216 HOB/RET,1:60 JUM		

☐ 21 Mickey Mantle	8.00	3.60
Hank Bauer		
Yogi Berra		
1953 Bowman		
☐ 22 Mickey Mantle	8.00	3.60
1953 Bowman		
☐ 23 Mickey Mantle	8.00	3.60
Yogi Berra		
1957 Topps		
☐ 24 Mickey Mantle	8.00	3.60
Hank Aaron		
1958 Topps		
☐ 25 Mickey Mantle	8.00	3.60
1958 Topps AS		
☐ 26 Mickey Mantle	8.00	3.60
1959 Topps HL		
☐ 27 Mickey Mantle	8.00	3.60
1959 Topps AS		
☐ 28 Mickey Mantle	8.00	3.60
Ken Boyer		
1960 Topps		
☐ 29 Mickey Mantle	8.00	3.60
1960 Topps HL		
☐ 30 Mickey Mantle	8.00	3.60
1961 Topps HL		
☐ 31 Mickey Mantle	8.00	3.60
1961 Topps MVP		
☐ 32 Mickey Mantle	8.00	3.60
1961 Topps AS		
☐ 33 Mickey Mantle	8.00	3.60
Willie Mays		
1962 Topps		
Hank Aaron and Ernie Banks in background		
☐ 34 Mickey Mantle	8.00	3.60

1962 Topps IA		
☐ 35 Mickey Mantle	8.00	3.60
1962 AS		
☐ 36 Mickey Mantle	8.00	3.60
Roger Maris		
Al Kaline		
Norm Cash		
1964 Topps		

1997 Topps Mays

Randomly inserted at the rate of one in eight first series packs, cards from this 27-card set feature reprints of both the Topps and Bowman vintage Mays cards . Each card front is highlighted by a special commemorative gold foil stamp. Randomly inserted in first series hobby packs only (at the rate of one in 2,400) are personally signed cards. According to Topps, Mays signed about 65 each of the following cards: 51B, 52T, 53T, 55T, 57T, 58T, 60T, 60T AS, 61T, 61T AS, 63T, 64T, 65T, 66T, 69T, 70T, 72T, 73T. A special 4 1/4" by 5 3/4" jumbo reprint of the 1952 Topps Willie Mays card was made available exclusively in special series 1 Wal-Mart boxes. Each box (shaped much like a cereal box) contained ten 8-card retail packs and the aforementioned jumbo card and retailed for $10.

	MINT	NRMT
COMPLETE SET (27)	100.00	45.00
COMMON MAYS (1-27)	4.00	1.80
SER.1 STATED ODDS 1:8 HOB/RET, 1:2 JUM		
MAYS AUTOGRAPH	100.00	45.00
SER.1 AU ODDS 1:2400 HOB/RET, 1:625 JUM		
COMP.FINEST SET (27)	100.00	45.00
COMMON FINEST (1-27)	4.00	1.80
* '51-'52 FINEST: .5X TO 1X LISTED CARDS		
FINEST SER.2 ODDS 1:20 HOB/RET,1:4 JUM		
COMP.REF.SET (27)	400.00	180.00
COMMON REF. (1-27)	15.00	6.75
* '51-'52 REF: 2X TO 4X LISTED CARDS		
REF.SER.2 ODDS 1:180 HOB/RET,1:48 JUM		

☐ 1 Willie Mays	8.00	3.60
1951 Bowman		
☐ 2 Willie Mays	6.00	2.70
1952 Topps		
☐ 3 Willie Mays	4.00	1.80
1953 Topps		
☐ 4 Willie Mays	4.00	1.80
1954 Bowman		
☐ 5 Willie Mays	4.00	1.80
1954 Topps		
☐ 6 Willie Mays	4.00	1.80
1955 Bowman		
☐ 7 Willie Mays	4.00	1.80
1955 Topps		

	MINT	NRMT
☐ 8 Willie Mays	4.00	1.80
1956 Topps		
☐ 9 Willie Mays	4.00	1.80
1957 Topps		
☐ 10 Willie Mays	4.00	1.80
1958 Topps		
☐ 11 Willie Mays	4.00	1.80
1959 Topps		
☐ 12 Willie Mays	4.00	1.80
1960 Topps		
☐ 13 Willie Mays	4.00	1.80
1960 Topps AS		
☐ 14 Willie Mays	4.00	1.80
1961 Topps		
☐ 15 Willie Mays	4.00	1.80
1961 Topps AS		
☐ 16 Willie Mays	4.00	1.80
1962 Topps		
☐ 17 Willie Mays	4.00	1.80
1963 Topps		
☐ 18 Willie Mays	4.00	1.80
1964 Topps		
☐ 19 Willie Mays	4.00	1.80
1965 Topps		
☐ 20 Willie Mays	4.00	1.80
1966 Topps		
☐ 21 Willie Mays	4.00	1.80
1967 Topps		
☐ 22 Willie Mays	4.00	1.80
1968 Topps		
☐ 23 Willie Mays	25.00	11.00
1969 Topps		
☐ 24 Willie Mays	4.00	1.80
1970 Topps		
☐ 25 Willie Mays	4.00	1.80
1971 Topps		
☐ 26 Willie Mays	4.00	1.80
1972 Topps		
☐ 27 Willie Mays	4.00	1.80
1973 Topps		
☐ J261 Willie Mays 1952 Jumbo	10.00	4.50
☐ NNO Willie Mays AU	100.00	45.00

1997 Topps Season's Best

This 25-card set was randomly inserted into Topps Series 2 packs and features five top players from each of the following five statistical categories: Leading Looters (top base stealers), Bleacher Reachers (top home run hitters), Hill Toppers (most wins), Number Crunchers (most RBI's), Kings of Swings (top slugging percentages). The fronts display color player photos printed on prismatic illusion foilboard. The backs carry another player photo and statistics.

	MINT	NRMT
COMPLETE SET (25)	25.00	11.00
COMMON CARD (SB1-SB25)	.50	.23
SER.2 STATED ODDS 1:6 HOB/RET, 1:1 JUM		

		MINT	NRMT
☐ SB1	Tony Gwynn	4.00	1.80
☐ SB2	Frank Thomas	6.00	2.70
☐ SB3	Ellis Burks	.75	.35
☐ SB4	Paul Molitor	1.50	.70
☐ SB5	Chuck Knoblauch	1.50	.70
☐ SB6	Mark McGwire	3.00	1.35
☐ SB7	Brady Anderson	1.00	.45
☐ SB8	Ken Griffey Jr.	8.00	3.60
☐ SB9	Albert Belle	2.00	.90
☐ SB10	Andres Galarraga	1.50	.70
☐ SB11	Andres Galarraga	1.50	.70
☐ SB12	Albert Belle	2.00	.90
☐ SB13	Juan Gonzalez	4.00	1.80
☐ SB14	Mo Vaughn	2.00	.90
☐ SB15	Rafael Palmeiro	1.00	.45
☐ SB16	John Smoltz	.75	.35
☐ SB17	Andy Pettitte	1.50	.70
☐ SB18	Pat Hentgen	.75	.35
☐ SB19	Mike Mussina	1.50	.70
☐ SB20	Andy Benes	.75	.35
☐ SB21	Kenny Lofton	1.50	.70
☐ SB22	Tom Goodwin	.50	.23
☐ SB23	Otis Nixon	.50	.23
☐ SB24	Eric Young	.50	.23
☐ SB25	Lance Johnson	.50	.23

1997 Topps Sweet Strokes

This 15-card retail only set was randomly inserted in series one packs at a rate of one in 12. Printed on Rainbow foilboard, the set features color photos of some of Baseball's top hitters.

	MINT	NRMT
COMPLETE SET (15)	40.00	18.00
COMMON CARD (SS1-SS15)	1.25	.55
SER.1 STATED ODDS 1:12 RETAIL		

		MINT	NRMT
☐ SS1	Roberto Alomar	2.00	.90
☐ SS2	Jeff Bagwell	4.00	1.80
☐ SS3	Albert Belle	2.50	1.10
☐ SS4	Barry Bonds	2.50	1.10
☐ SS5	Mark Grace	1.25	.55
☐ SS6	Ken Griffey Jr.	10.00	4.50
☐ SS7	Tony Gwynn	5.00	2.20
☐ SS8	Chipper Jones	6.00	2.70
☐ SS9	Edgar Martinez	1.25	.55
☐ SS10	Mark McGwire	4.00	1.80
☐ SS11	Rafael Palmeiro	1.25	.55
☐ SS12	Mike Piazza	6.00	2.70
☐ SS13	Gary Sheffield	2.00	.90
☐ SS14	Frank Thomas	8.00	3.60
☐ SS15	Mo Vaughn	2.50	1.10

1997 Topps Team Timber

Randomly inserted into all second series packs at a rate of 1:36 and second series Hobby Collector packs at a rate of 1:8, cards from this 16-card set

highlight a selection of baseball's top sluggers. Each card features a simulated wood-grain stock, but the fronts are UV-coated, making the cards bow noticeably.

	MINT	NRMT
COMPLETE SET (16)	70.00	32.00
COMMON CARD (TT1-TT16)	2.00	.90
SER.2 STATED ODDS 1:36 HOB/RET, 1:8 JUM		

		MINT	NRMT
☐ TT1	Ken Griffey Jr.	15.00	6.75
☐ TT2	Ken Caminiti	2.00	.90
☐ TT3	Bernie Williams	3.00	1.35
☐ TT4	Jeff Bagwell	6.00	2.70
☐ TT5	Frank Thomas	12.00	5.50
☐ TT6	Andres Galarraga	3.00	1.35
☐ TT7	Barry Bonds	4.00	1.80
☐ TT8	Rafael Palmeiro	2.00	.90
☐ TT9	Brady Anderson	2.00	.90
☐ TT10	Juan Gonzalez	8.00	3.60
☐ TT11	Mo Vaughn	4.00	1.80
☐ TT12	Mark McGwire	6.00	2.70
☐ TT13	Gary Sheffield	3.00	1.35
☐ TT14	Albert Belle	4.00	1.80
☐ TT15	Chipper Jones	10.00	4.50
☐ TT16	Mike Piazza	10.00	4.50

1998 Topps

This 282-card set of Topps Series 1 was distributed in 11-card packs with a suggested retail price of $1.29. The fronts feature color action player photos printed on 16 pt. stock with player information and career statistics on the back. Card #7 was permanently retired in 1996 to honor Mickey Mantle. Series 1 contains the following subsets: Draft Picks (#245-249), Expansion Team Prospects (#250-253), and Prospects (#254-259). Hobby packs also included a redemption card program. Recipients of Memorabilia Madness and Wild Card inserts could win rare

Clemente Memorabilia including game-used bats, game-worn jersey, autographed photos, signed checks, autographed vintage Clemente Topps trading cards, original, unautographed Clemente cards, including three rookie cards, Pirates jerseys bearing Clemente's name and number, and uncut sheets of 1998 Topps Baseball Minted in Cooperstown cards. A Wild Card was seeded in hobby packs at the rate of one in 72.

	MINT	NRMT
COMPLETE SERIES 1 (282)	20.00	9.00
COMMON CARD (1-283)	.10	.05
MINOR STARS	.20	.09
UNLISTED STARS	.40	.18
COMP.MINTED SER.1 (282)	300.00	135.00
COMMON MINTED (1-283)	1.00	.45

*MINTED STARS: 6X TO 12X HI COLUMN
*MINTED YOUNG STARS: 5X TO 10X HI
*MINTED ROOKIES/PROSPECTS: 4X TO 8X HI
MINTED STATED ODDS: 1:8
CARD NUMBER 7 DOES NOT EXIST

Card	Player	MINT	NRMT
1	Tony Gwynn	1.00	.45
2	Larry Walker	.40	.18
3	Billy Wagner	.20	.09
4	Denny Neagle	.20	.09
5	Vladimir Guerrero	.60	.25
6	Kevin Brown	.20	.09
8	Mariano Rivera	.20	.09
9	Tony Clark	.40	.18
10	Deion Sanders	.20	.09
11	Francisco Cordova	.10	.05
12	Matt Williams	.30	.14
13	Carlos Baerga	.10	.05
14	Mo Vaughn	.50	.23
15	Bobby Witt	.10	.05
16	Matt Stairs	.10	.05
17	Chan Ho Park	.40	.18
18	Mike Bordick	.10	.05
19	Michael Tucker	.20	.09
20	Frank Thomas	1.50	.70
21	Roberto Clemente	1.00	.45
22	Dmitri Young	.10	.05
23	Steve Trachsel	.10	.05
24	Jeff Kent	.10	.05
25	Scott Rolen	1.00	.45
26	John Thomson	.10	.05
27	Joe Vitiello	.10	.05
28	Eddie Guardado	.10	.05
29	Charlie Hayes	.10	.05
30	Juan Gonzalez	1.00	.45
31	Garret Anderson	.20	.09
32	John Jaha	.10	.05
33	Omar Vizquel	.20	.09
34	Brian Hunter	.20	.09
35	Jeff Bagwell	.75	.35
36	Mark Lemke	.10	.05
37	Doug Glanville	.10	.05
38	Dan Wilson	.10	.05
39	Steve Cooke	.10	.05
40	Chili Davis	.10	.05
41	Mike Cameron	.20	.09
42	F.P. Santangelo	.10	.05
43	Brad Ausmus	.10	.05
44	Gary DiSarcina	.10	.05
45	Pat Hentgen	.20	.09
46	Wilton Guerrero	.10	.05
47	Devon White	.10	.05
48	Danny Patterson	.10	.05
49	Pat Meares	.10	.05
50	Rafael Palmeiro	.30	.14
51	Mark Gardner	.10	.05
52	Jeff Blauser	.20	.09
53	Dave Hollins	.10	.05
54	Carlos Garcia	.10	.05
55	Ben McDonald	.10	.05
56	John Mabry	.10	.05
57	Trevor Hoffman	.20	.09
58	Tony Fernandez	.10	.05
59	Rich Loiselle	.10	.05
60	Mark Leiter	.10	.05
61	Pat Kelly	.10	.05
62	John Flaherty	.10	.05
63	Roger Bailey	.10	.05
64	Tom Gordon	.10	.05
65	Ryan Klesko	.30	.14
66	Darryl Hamilton	.10	.05
67	Jim Eisenreich	.10	.05
68	Butch Huskey	.20	.09
69	Mark Grudzielanek	.10	.05
70	Marquis Grissom	.20	.09
71	Mark McLemore	.10	.05
72	Gary Gaetti	.10	.05
73	Greg Gagne	.10	.05
74	Lyle Mouton	.10	.05
75	Jim Edmonds	.30	.14
76	Shawn Green	.10	.05
77	Greg Vaughn	.10	.05
78	Terry Adams	.10	.05
79	Kevin Polcovich	.10	.05
80	Troy O'Leary	.10	.05
81	Jeff Shaw	.10	.05
82	Rich Becker	.10	.05
83	David Wells	.10	.05
84	Steve Karsay	.10	.05
85	Charles Nagy	.20	.09
86	B.J. Surhoff	.10	.05
87	Jamey Wright	.10	.05
88	James Baldwin	.10	.05
89	Edgardo Alfonzo	.10	.09
90	Jay Buhner	.30	.14
91	Brady Anderson	.30	.14
92	Scott Servais	.10	.05
93	Edgar Renteria	.20	.09
94	Mike Lieberthal	.10	.05
95	Rick Aguilera	.10	.05
96	Walt Weiss	.10	.05
97	Deivi Cruz	.10	.05
98	Kurt Abbott	.10	.05
99	Henry Rodriguez	.10	.05
100	Mike Piazza	1.25	.55
101	Bill Taylor	.10	.05
102	Todd Zeile	.10	.05
103	Rey Ordonez	.10	.05
104	Willie Greene	.10	.05
105	Tony Womack	.10	.05
106	Mike Sweeney	.10	.05
107	Jeffrey Hammonds	.10	.05
108	Kevin Orie	.20	.09
109	Alex Gonzalez	.10	.05
110	Jose Canseco	.30	.14
111	Paul Sorrento	.10	.05
112	Joey Hamilton	.20	.09
113	Brad Radke	.20	.09
114	Steve Avery	.10	.05
115	Esteban Loaiza	.10	.05
116	Stan Javier	.10	.05
117	Chris Gomez	.10	.05
118	Royce Clayton	.10	.05
119	Orlando Merced	.10	.05
120	Kevin Appier	.20	.09
121	Mel Nieves	.10	.05
122	Joe Girardi	.10	.05
123	Rico Brogna	.10	.05
124	Kent Mercker	.10	.05
125	Manny Ramirez	.40	.18
126	Jeromy Burnitz	.10	.05
127	Kevin Foster	.10	.05
128	Matt Morris	.20	.09
129	Jason Dickson	.10	.05
130	Tom Glavine	.20	.09
131	Wally Joyner	.10	.05
132	Rick Reed	.10	.05
133	Todd Jones	.10	.05
134	Dave Martinez	.10	.05
135	Sandy Alomar	.20	.09
136	Mike Lansing	.10	.05
137	Sean Berry	.10	.05
138	Doug Jones	.10	.05
139	Todd Stottlemyre	.10	.05
140	Jay Bell	.20	.09
141	Jaime Navarro	.10	.05
142	Chris Hoiles	.10	.05
143	Joey Cora	.10	.05
144	Scott Spiezio	.10	.05
145	Joe Carter	.20	.09
146	Jose Guillen	.40	.18
147	Damion Easley	.10	.05
148	Lee Stevens	.10	.05
149	Alex Fernandez	.10	.05
150	Randy Johnson	.40	.18
151	J.T. Snow	.20	.09
152	Chuck Finley	.10	.05
153	Bernard Gilkey	.10	.05
154	David Segui	.10	.05
155	Dante Bichette	.20	.09
156	Kevin Stocker	.10	.05
157	Carl Everett	.10	.05
158	Jose Valentin	.10	.05
159	Pokey Reese	.10	.05
160	Derek Jeter	1.00	.45
161	Roger Pavlik	.10	.05
162	Mark Wohlers	.10	.05
163	Ricky Bottalico	.10	.05
164	Ozzie Guillen	.10	.05
165	Mike Mussina	.40	.18
166	Gary Sheffield	.40	.18
167	Hideo Nomo	1.00	.45
168	Mark Grace	.30	.14
169	Aaron Sele	.10	.05
170	Darryl Kile	.20	.09
171	Shawn Estes	.20	.09
172	Vinny Castilla	.20	.09
173	Ron Coomer	.10	.05
174	Jose Rosado	.10	.05
175	Kenny Lofton	.50	.23
176	Jason Giambi	.20	.09
177	Hal Morris	.10	.05
178	Darren Bragg	.10	.05
179	Orel Hershiser	.20	.09
180	Ray Lankford	.20	.09
181	Hideki Irabu	.20	.09
182	Kevin Young	.10	.05
183	Javy Lopez	.20	.09
184	Jeff Montgomery	.10	.05
185	Mike Holtz	.10	.05
186	George Williams	.10	.05
187	Cal Eldred	.10	.05
188	Tom Candiotti	.10	.05
189	Glenallen Hill	.10	.05
190	Brian Giles	.10	.05
191	Dave Mlicki	.10	.05
192	Garrett Stephenson	.10	.05
193	Jeff Frye	.10	.05
194	Joe Oliver	.10	.05
195	Bob Hamelin	.10	.05
196	Luis Sojo	.10	.05
197	LaTroy Hawkins	.10	.05
198	Kevin Elster	.10	.05
199	Jeff Reed	.10	.05
200	Dennis Eckersley	.20	.09
201	Bill Mueller	.10	.05
202	Russ Davis	.10	.05
203	Armando Benitez	.10	.05
204	Quilvio Veras	.10	.05
205	Tim Naehring	.10	.05
206	Quinton McCracken	.10	.05
207	Raul Casanova	.10	.05
208	Matt Lawton	.10	.05
209	Luis Alicea	.10	.05
210	Luis Gonzalez	.10	.05
211	Allen Watson	.10	.05
212	Gerald Williams	.10	.05
213	David Bell	.10	.05
214	Todd Hollandsworth	.10	.05
215	Wade Boggs	.40	.18
216	Jose Mesa	.10	.05
217	Jamie Moyer	.10	.05
218	Darren Daulton	.20	.09
219	Mickey Morandini	.10	.05
220	Rusty Greer	.20	.09
221	Jim Bullinger	.10	.05
222	Jose Offerman	.10	.05
223	Matt Karchner	.10	.05
224	Woody Williams	.10	.05
225	Mark Loretta	.10	.05
226	Mike Hampton	.10	.05
227	Willie Adams	.10	.05
228	Scott Hatteberg	.10	.05
229	Rich Amaral	.10	.05
230	Terry Steinbach	.10	.05
231	Glendon Rusch	.10	.05

☐ 232 Bret Boone	.10	.05
☐ 233 Robert Person	.10	.05
☐ 234 Jose Hernandez	.10	.05
☐ 235 Doug Drabek	.10	.05
☐ 236 Jason McDonald	.10	.05
☐ 237 Chris Widger	.10	.05
☐ 238 Tom Martin	.10	.05
☐ 239 Dave Burba	.10	.05
☐ 240 Pete Rose Jr.	.20	.09
☐ 241 Bobby Ayala	.10	.05
☐ 242 Tim Wakefield	.10	.05
☐ 243 Dennis Springer	.10	.05
☐ 244 Tim Belcher	.10	.05
☐ 245 Jon Garland	.30	.14
Geoff Goetz		
☐ 246 Glenn Davis	.60	.25
Lance Berkman		
☐ 247 Vernon Wells	.40	.18
Aaron Akin		
☐ 248 Adam Kennedy	.20	.09
Jason Romano		
☐ 249 Jason Dellaero	.30	.14
Troy Cameron		
☐ 250 Alex Sanchez	.20	.09
Jared Sandberg		
☐ 251 Pablo Ortega	.20	.09
James Manias		
☐ 252 Jason Conti	.50	.23
Mike Stoner		
☐ 253 John Patterson	.30	.14
Larry Rodriguez		
☐ 254 Adrian Beltre	1.25	.55
Ryan Minor		
Aaron Boone		
☐ 255 Ben Grieve	.75	.35
Brian Buchanan		
Dermal Brown		
☐ 256 Carl Pavano	.50	.23
Kerrry Wood		
Gil Meche		
☐ 257 David Ortiz	.20	.09
Daryle Ward		
Richie Sexson		
☐ 258 Randy Winn	.20	.09
Juan Encarnacion		
Andrew Vessel		
☐ 259 Kris Benson	.30	.14
Travis Smith		
Courtney Duncan		
☐ 260 Chad Hermansen	.60	.25
Brent Butler		
Warren Morris		
☐ 261 Ben Davis	.20	.09
Eli Marrero		
Ramon Hernandez		
☐ 262 Eric Chavez	.50	.23
Russell Branyan		
Russ Johnson		
☐ 263 Todd Dunwoody	.25	.11
John Barnes		
Ryan Jackson		
☐ 264 Matt Clement	.25	.11
Roy Halladay		
Brian Fuentes		
☐ 265 Randy Johnson SH	.20	.09
☐ 266 Kevin Brown SH	.10	.05
☐ 267 Ricardo Rincon SH	.10	.05
Francisco Cordova		
☐ 268 Nomar Garciaparra SH	.60	.25
☐ 269 Tino Martinez SH	.20	.09
☐ 270 Chuck Knoblauch IL	.20	.09
☐ 271 Pedro Martinez IL	.20	.09
☐ 272 Denny Neagle IL	.10	.05
☐ 273 Juan Gonzalez IL	.50	.23
☐ 274 Andres Galarraga IL	.20	.09
☐ 275 Checklist	.10	.05
☐ 276 Checklist	.10	.05
☐ 277 Moises Alou WS	.20	.09
☐ 278 Sandy Alomar WS	.20	.09
☐ 279 Gary Sheffield WS	.20	.09
☐ 280 Matt Williams WS	.20	.09
☐ 281 Livan Hernandez WS	.20	.09
☐ 282 Chad Ogea WS	.10	.05
☐ 283 Marlins Champs	.10	.05
☐ NNO Wild Card	1.00	.45

1998 Topps Baby Boomers

MARK KOTSAY

Randomly inserted in retail packs only at the rate of one in 36, this 15-card set features color photos of young players who have already made their mark in the game dispite less than three years in the majors.

	MINT	NRMT
COMPLETE SET (15)	80.00	36.00
COMMON CARD (BB1-BB15)	2.00	.90
SER.1 STATED ODDS 1:36 RETAIL		

☐ BB1 Derek Jeter	10.00	4.50
☐ BB2 Scott Rolen	10.00	4.50
☐ BB3 Nomar Garciaparra	12.00	5.50
☐ BB4 Jose Cruz Jr.	15.00	6.75
☐ BB5 Darin Erstad	5.00	2.20
☐ BB6 Todd Helton	5.00	2.20
☐ BB7 Tony Clark	3.00	1.35
☐ BB8 Jose Guillen	4.00	1.80
☐ BB9 Andruw Jones	8.00	3.60
☐ BB10 Vladimir Guerrero	6.00	2.70
☐ BB11 Mark Kotsay	4.00	1.80
☐ BB12 Todd Greene	2.50	1.10
☐ BB13 Andy Pettitte	4.00	1.80
☐ BB14 Justin Thompson	2.50	1.10
☐ BB15 Alan Benes	2.00	.90

1998 Topps Clemente

BOB CLEMENTE • OUTFIELD

PIRATES

Randomly inserted in packs at the rate of one in 18, this 10-card set honors the memory of Roberto Clemente on the 25th anniversary of his untimely death with conventional reprints of his Topps cards that were originally printed in odd-numbered years (1955-1971). This set contains only odd-numbered cards.

	MINT	NRMT
COMPLETE SET (10)	60.00	27.00
COMMON CARD (1-19)	6.00	2.70
SER.1 STATED ODDS 1:18		
SKIP-NUMBERED SET		

☐ 1 Roberto Clemente 1955	12.00	5.50
☐ 3 Roberto Clemente 1957	6.00	2.70
☐ 5 Roberto Clemente 1959	6.00	2.70
☐ 7 Roberto Clemente 1961	6.00	2.70
☐ 9 Roberto Clemente 1963	6.00	2.70
☐ 11 Roberto Clemente 1965	6.00	2.70
☐ 13 Roberto Clemente 1967	6.00	2.70
☐ 15 Roberto Clemente 1969	6.00	2.70
☐ 17 Roberto Clemente 1971	6.00	2.70
☐ 19 Roberto Clemente 1973	6.00	2.70

1998 Topps Clemente Finest

PIRATES

Randomly inserted in packs at the rate of one in 72, this nine-card set honors the memory of Roberto Clemente on the 25th anniversary of his untimely death with Finest reprints of his Topps cards that were originally printed in even-numbered years (1956-1972). This set contains only even-numbered cards.

	MINT	NRMT
COMPLETE SET (9)	80.00	36.00
COMMON CARD (2-18)	12.00	5.50
SER.1 STATED ODDS 1:72		
COMP.REF.SET (9)	200.00	90.00
COMMON REF. (2-18)	30.00	13.50
REFRACTOR STATED SER.1 ODDS 1:288		
SKIP-NUMBERED SET		

☐ 2 Roberto Clemente 1956	12.00	5.50
☐ 4 Roberto Clemente 1958	12.00	5.50
☐ 6 Roberto Clemente 1960	12.00	5.50
☐ 8 Roberto Clemente 1962	12.00	5.50
☐ 10 Roberto Clemente 1964	12.00	5.50
☐ 12 Roberto Clemente 1966	12.00	5.50
☐ 14 Roberto Clemente 1968	12.00	5.50
☐ 16 Roberto Clemente 1970	12.00	5.50
☐ 18 Roberto Clemente 1972	12.00	5.50

1998 Topps Clemente Tribute

Randomly inserted in packs at the rate of one in 12, this five-card set honors the memory of Roberto Clemente on the 25th anniversary of his untimely death and features color photos printed on mirror foilboard on newly designed cards.

	MINT	NRMT
COMPLETE SET (5)	8.00	3.60
COMMON CARD (RC1-RC5)	2.00	.90
SER.1 STATED ODDS 1:12		

☐ RC1 Roberto Clemente	2.00	.90
Painting Bat from Rack		
☐ RC2 Roberto Clemente	2.00	.90
Posed batting shot		
☐ RC3 Roberto Clemente	2.00	.90
Follow through on swing		
☐ RC4 Roberto Clemente	2.00	.90
Portrait		
☐ RC5 Roberto Clemente	2.00	.90

1998 Topps Etch-A-Sketch

Randomly inserted in packs at the rate of one in 36, this nine-card set features drawings by artist George Vlosich III of some of baseball's hottest superstars using an Etch A Sketch as a canvas.

	MINT	NRMT
COMPLETE SET (9)	50.00	22.00
COMMON CARD (ES1-ES9)	3.00	1.35
SER.1 STATED ODDS 1:36		

☐ ES1 Albert Belle	3.00	1.35
☐ ES2 Barry Bonds	3.00	1.35
☐ ES3 Ken Griffey Jr.	12.00	5.50
☐ ES4 Greg Maddux	8.00	3.60
☐ ES5 Hideo Nomo	6.00	2.70
☐ ES6 Mike Piazza	8.00	3.60
☐ ES7 Cal Ripken	10.00	4.50
☐ ES8 Frank Thomas	10.00	4.50
☐ ES9 Mo Vaughn	3.00	1.35

1998 Topps Flashback

Randomly inserted in packs at the rate of one in 72, these two-

sided cards of top players feature photographs of how they looked "then" as rookies on one side and how they look "now" as stars on the other.

	MINT	NRMT
COMPLETE SET (10)	80.00	36.00
COMMON CARD (FB1-FB10)	3.00	1.35
SEMISTARS	4.00	1.80
UNLISTED STARS	6.00	2.70
SER.1 STATED ODDS 1:72		

☐ FB1 Barry Bonds	8.00	3.60
☐ FB2 Ken Griffey Jr.	30.00	13.50
☐ FB3 Paul Molitor	6.00	2.70
☐ FB4 Randy Johnson	6.00	2.70
☐ FB5 Cal Ripken	25.00	11.00
☐ FB6 Tony Gwynn	15.00	6.75
☐ FB7 Kenny Lofton	8.00	3.60
☐ FB8 Gary Sheffield	6.00	2.70
☐ FB9 Deion Sanders	3.00	1.35
☐ FB10 Brady Anderson	4.00	1.80

1998 Topps HallBound

Randomly inserted in hobby packs only at the rate of one in 36, this 15-card set features color photos of top stars who are bound for the Hall of Fame printed on foil mirrorboard cards.

	MINT	NRMT
COMPLETE SET (15)	100.00	45.00
COMMON CARD (HB1-HB15)	2.00	.90
UNLISTED STARS	4.00	1.80
SER.1 STATED ODDS 1:36 HOBBY		

☐ HB1 Paul Molitor	4.00	1.80
☐ HB2 Tony Gwynn	10.00	4.50
☐ HB3 Wade Boggs	4.00	1.80
☐ HB4 Roger Clemens	8.00	3.60
☐ HB5 Dennis Eckersley	2.00	.90
☐ HB6 Cal Ripken	15.00	6.75
☐ HB7 Greg Maddux	12.00	5.50
☐ HB8 Rickey Henderson	2.50	1.10
☐ HB9 Ken Griffey Jr.	20.00	9.00
☐ HB10 Frank Thomas	15.00	6.75
☐ HB11 Mark McGwire	10.00	4.50
☐ HB12 Barry Bonds	5.00	2.20
☐ HB13 Mike Piazza	12.00	5.50
☐ HB14 Juan Gonzalez	10.00	4.50
☐ HB15 Randy Johnson	4.00	1.80

1998 Topps Mystery Finest

Randomly inserted in packs at the rate of one in 36, this 20-card set features close action player photos which showcase five of the 1997 season's most intriguing inter-league matchups.

	MINT	NRMT
COMPLETE SET (20)	150.00	70.00
COMMON CARD (ILM1-ILM20)	2.00	.90
SEMISTARS	3.00	1.35
UNLISTED STARS	5.00	2.20
SER.1 STATED ODDS 1:36		
COMP.REF.SET (20)	400.00	180.00
*REFRACTORS: 1.25X TO 2.5X HI COLUMN		
REFRACTOR SER.1 STATED ODDS 1:144		

☐ ILM1 Chipper Jones	15.00	6.75
☐ ILM2 Cal Ripken	20.00	9.00
☐ ILM3 Greg Maddux	15.00	6.75
☐ ILM4 Rafael Palmeiro	3.00	1.35
☐ ILM5 Todd Hundley	2.00	.90
☐ ILM6 Derek Jeter	15.00	6.75
☐ ILM7 John Olerud	2.00	.90
☐ ILM8 Tino Martinez	5.00	2.20
☐ ILM9 Larry Walker	5.00	2.20
☐ ILM10 Ken Griffey Jr.	25.00	11.00
☐ ILM11 Andres Galarraga	5.00	2.20
☐ ILM12 Randy Johnson	5.00	2.20
☐ ILM13 Mike Piazza	15.00	6.75
☐ ILM14 Jim Edmonds	3.00	1.35
☐ ILM15 Eric Karros	2.00	.90
☐ ILM16 Tim Salmon	5.00	2.20
☐ ILM17 Sammy Sosa	5.00	2.20
☐ ILM18 Frank Thomas	20.00	9.00
☐ ILM19 Mark Grace	3.00	1.35
☐ ILM20 Albert Belle	6.00	2.70

1996 Topps Chrome

The 1996 Topps Chrome set was issued in one series totalling 165 cards and features the best old and new players from the 1996 Topps regular set. Each chromium card is a replica of its regular version with the exception of the Topps Chrome logo replacing the traditional logo. Included in the set is a Mickey Mantle #7

Commemorative card and a Cal Ripken Tribute card. The four-card packs retail for $3.00 each.

	MINT	NRMT
COMPLETE SET (165)	80.00	36.00
COMMON CARD (1-165)	.75	.18
MINOR STARS	.75	.35
UNLISTED STARS	1.50	.70
SUBSET CARDS HALF VALUE OF BASE CARDS		

		MINT	NRMT
☐ 1	Tony Gwynn STP	2.00	.90
☐ 2	Mike Piazza STP	2.50	1.10
☐ 3	Greg Maddux STP	2.50	1.10
☐ 4	Jeff Bagwell STP	1.50	.70
☐ 5	Larry Walker STP	.75	.35
☐ 6	Barry Larkin STP	.75	.35
☐ 7	Mickey Mantle COMM	10.00	4.50
☐ 8	Tom Glavine STP	.40	.18
☐ 9	Craig Biggio STP	.75	.35
☐ 10	Barry Bonds STP	1.00	.45
☐ 11	Heathcliff Slocumb STP	.40	.18
☐ 12	Matt Williams STP	.75	.35
☐ 13	Todd Helton	12.00	5.50
☐ 14	Paul Molitor	1.50	.70
☐ 15	Glenallen Hill	.40	.18
☐ 16	Troy Percival	.40	.18
☐ 17	Albert Belle	2.00	.90
☐ 18	Mark Wohlers	.40	.18
☐ 19	Kirby Puckett	3.00	1.35
☐ 20	Mark Grace	1.00	.45
☐ 21	J.T. Snow	.75	.35
☐ 22	David Justice	1.50	.70
☐ 23	Mike Mussina	1.50	.70
☐ 24	Bernie Williams	1.50	.70
☐ 25	Ron Gant	.75	.35
☐ 26	Carlos Baerga	.40	.18
☐ 27	Gary Sheffield	1.50	.70
☐ 28	Cal Ripken 2131	6.00	2.70
☐ 29	Frank Thomas	6.00	2.70
☐ 30	Kevin Seitzer	.40	.18
☐ 31	Joe Carter	.75	.35
☐ 32	Jeff King	.40	.18
☐ 33	David Cone	.75	.35
☐ 34	Eddie Murray	1.50	.70
☐ 35	Brian Jordan	.75	.35
☐ 36	Garret Anderson	.75	.35
☐ 37	Hideo Nomo	4.00	1.80
☐ 38	Steve Finley	.75	.35
☐ 39	Ivan Rodriguez	2.00	.90
☐ 40	Quilvio Veras	.40	.18
☐ 41	Mark McGwire	3.00	1.35
☐ 42	Greg Vaughn	.40	.18
☐ 43	Randy Johnson	1.50	.70
☐ 44	David Segui	.40	.18
☐ 45	Derek Bell	.40	.18
☐ 46	John Valentin	.40	.18
☐ 47	Steve Avery	.40	.18
☐ 48	Tino Martinez	1.50	.70
☐ 49	Shane Reynolds	.40	.18
☐ 50	Jim Edmonds	1.00	.45
☐ 51	Raul Mondesi	1.00	.45
☐ 52	Chipper Jones	5.00	2.20
☐ 53	Gregg Jefferies	.40	.18
☐ 54	Ken Caminiti	1.00	.45
☐ 55	Brian McRae	.40	.18
☐ 56	Don Mattingly	2.50	1.10
☐ 57	Marty Cordova	.75	.35
☐ 58	Vinny Castilla	.75	.35
☐ 59	John Smoltz	.75	.35
☐ 60	Travis Fryman	.75	.35
☐ 61	Ryan Klesko	1.00	.45
☐ 62	Alex Fernandez	.40	.18
☐ 63	Dante Bichette	.75	.35
☐ 64	Eric Karros	.75	.35
☐ 65	Roger Clemens	3.00	1.35
☐ 66	Randy Myers	.40	.18
☐ 67	Cal Ripken	6.00	2.70
☐ 68	Rod Beck	.40	.18
☐ 69	Jack McDowell	.40	.18
☐ 70	Ken Griffey Jr.	8.00	3.60
☐ 71	Ramon Martinez	.75	.35
☐ 72	Jason Giambi FS	.75	.35
☐ 73	Nomar Garciaparra FS	6.00	2.70
☐ 74	Billy Wagner FS	.75	.35
☐ 75	Todd Greene FS	1.00	.45
☐ 76	Paul Wilson FS	.40	.18
☐ 77	Johnny Damon FS	.75	.35
☐ 78	Alan Benes FS	.75	.35
☐ 79	Karim Garcia FS	1.00	.45
☐ 80	Derek Jeter FS	5.00	2.20
☐ 81	Kirby Puckett STP	1.50	.70
☐ 82	Cal Ripken STP	3.00	1.35
☐ 83	Albert Belle STP	1.00	.45
☐ 84	Randy Johnson STP	.75	.35
☐ 85	Wade Boggs STP	.75	.35
☐ 86	Carlos Baerga STP	.40	.18
☐ 87	Ivan Rodriguez STP	1.00	.45
☐ 88	Mike Mussina STP	.75	.35
☐ 89	Frank Thomas STP	3.00	1.35
☐ 90	Ken Griffey Jr. STP	4.00	1.80
☐ 91	Jose Mesa STP	.40	.18
☐ 92	Matt Morris	4.00	1.80
☐ 93	Mike Piazza	5.00	2.20
☐ 94	Edgar Martinez	1.00	.45
☐ 95	Chuck Knoblauch	1.50	.70
☐ 96	Andres Galarraga	1.50	.70
☐ 97	Tony Gwynn	4.00	1.80
☐ 98	Lee Smith	.75	.35
☐ 99	Sammy Sosa	1.50	.70
☐ 100	Jim Thome	1.50	.70
☐ 101	Bernard Gilkey	.40	.18
☐ 102	Brady Anderson	1.00	.45
☐ 103	Rico Brogna	.40	.18
☐ 104	Len Dykstra	.75	.35
☐ 105	Tom Glavine	.75	.35
☐ 106	John Olerud	.40	.18
☐ 107	Terry Steinbach	.40	.18
☐ 108	Brian Hunter	.75	.35
☐ 109	Jay Buhner	1.00	.45
☐ 110	Mo Vaughn	2.00	.90
☐ 111	Jose Mesa	.40	.18
☐ 112	Brett Butler	.75	.35
☐ 113	Chili Davis	.75	.35
☐ 114	Paul O'Neill	.75	.35
☐ 115	Roberto Alomar	1.50	.70
☐ 116	Barry Larkin	1.00	.45
☐ 117	Marquis Grissom	.75	.35
☐ 118	Will Clark	1.00	.45
☐ 119	Barry Bonds	2.00	.90
☐ 120	Ozzie Smith	2.00	.90
☐ 121	Pedro Martinez	1.50	.70
☐ 122	Craig Biggio	1.00	.45
☐ 123	Moises Alou	.75	.35
☐ 124	Robin Ventura	.75	.35
☐ 125	Greg Maddux	5.00	2.20
☐ 126	Tim Salmon	1.50	.70
☐ 127	Wade Boggs	1.50	.70
☐ 128	Ismael Valdes	.75	.35
☐ 129	Juan Gonzalez	4.00	1.80
☐ 130	Ray Lankford	.75	.35
☐ 131	Bobby Bonilla	.75	.35
☐ 132	Reggie Sanders	.40	.18
☐ 133	Alex Ochoa NOW	.40	.18
☐ 134	Mark Loretta NOW	.40	.18
☐ 135	Jason Kendall NOW	1.00	.45
☐ 136	Brooks Kieschnick NOW	.75	.35
☐ 137	Chris Snopek NOW	.40	.18
☐ 138	Ruben Rivera NOW	.75	.35
☐ 139	Jeff Suppan NOW	.75	.35
☐ 140	John Wasdin NOW	.40	.18
☐ 141	Jay Payton NOW	.75	.35
☐ 142	Rick Krivda NOW	.40	.18
☐ 143	Jimmy Haynes NOW	.40	.18
☐ 144	Ryne Sandberg	2.00	.90
☐ 145	Matt Williams	1.00	.45
☐ 146	Jose Canseco	1.00	.45
☐ 147	Larry Walker	1.50	.70
☐ 148	Kevin Appier	.75	.35
☐ 149	Javy Lopez	.75	.35
☐ 150	Dennis Eckersley	.75	.35
☐ 151	Jason Isringhausen	.40	.18
☐ 152	Dean Palmer	.40	.18
☐ 153	Jeff Bagwell	3.00	1.35
☐ 154	Rondell White	.75	.35
☐ 155	Wally Joyner	.75	.35
☐ 156	Fred McGriff	1.00	.45
☐ 157	Cecil Fielder	1.00	.45
☐ 158	Rafael Palmeiro	1.00	.45
☐ 159	Rickey Henderson	1.00	.45
☐ 160	Shawon Dunston	.40	.18
☐ 161	Manny Ramirez	1.50	.70
☐ 162	Alex Gonzalez	.40	.18
☐ 163	Shawn Green	.40	.18
☐ 164	Kenny Lofton	2.00	.90
☐ 165	Jeff Conine	.75	.35

1996 Topps Chrome Refractors

Randomly inserted at the rate of one in every 12 packs, this 165-card set is parallel to the regular Chrome set. The difference in design is the refractive quality of the cards.

	MINT	NRMT
COMPLETE SET (165)	3000.00	1350.00
COMMON CARD (1-165)	8.00	3.60
*STARS: 10X TO 20X HI COLUMN		
*YOUNG STARS: 6X TO 12X HI		
*ROOKIES: 3X TO 6X HI		
STATED ODDS 1:12 HOBBY		
CARDS 111-165 CONDITION SENSITIVE		

		MINT	NRMT
☐ 7	Mickey Mantle COMM	175.00	80.00
☐ 13	Todd Helton	70.00	32.00
☐ 19	Kirby Puckett	60.00	27.00
☐ 28	Cal Ripken TRIB	120.00	55.00
☐ 29	Frank Thomas	120.00	55.00
☐ 37	Hideo Nomo	80.00	36.00
☐ 41	Mark McGwire	80.00	36.00
☐ 52	Chipper Jones	80.00	36.00
☐ 65	Roger Clemens	60.00	27.00
☐ 67	Cal Ripken	120.00	55.00
☐ 70	Ken Griffey Jr.	150.00	70.00
☐ 73	Nomar Garciaparra	80.00	36.00
☐ 80	Derek Jeter FS	80.00	36.00
☐ 82	Cal Ripken STP	60.00	27.00
☐ 89	Frank Thomas STP	60.00	27.00
☐ 90	Ken Griffey Jr. STP	80.00	36.00
☐ 93	Mike Piazza	100.00	45.00
☐ 97	Tony Gwynn	80.00	36.00
☐ 125	Greg Maddux	100.00	45.00
☐ 129	Juan Gonzalez	80.00	36.00
☐ 153	Jeff Bagwell	60.00	27.00

1996 Topps Chrome Masters of the Game

Randomly inserted in packs at a rate of one in 12, this 20-card set honors players who are masters of their playing positions. The fronts feature color action photography with brilliant color metallization.

	MINT	NRMT
COMPLETE SET (20)	60.00	27.00
COMMON CARD (1-20)	1.00	.45
STATED ODDS 1:12 HOBBY		
COMP.REF.SET (20)	200.00	90.00

*REFRACTORS: 1.25X TO 3X BASIC MASTER
REF.STATED ODDS 1:36 HOBBY

☐	1 Dennis Eckersley	2.00	.90
☐	2 Denny Martinez	2.00	.90
☐	3 Eddie Murray	4.00	1.80
☐	4 Paul Molitor	4.00	1.80
☐	5 Ozzie Smith	5.00	2.20
☐	6 Rickey Henderson	2.50	1.10
☐	7 Tim Raines	2.00	.90
☐	8 Lee Smith	2.00	.90
☐	9 Cal Ripken	15.00	6.75
☐	10 Chili Davis	2.00	.90
☐	11 Wade Boggs	4.00	1.80
☐	12 Tony Gwynn	10.00	4.50
☐	13 Don Mattingly	8.00	3.60
☐	14 Bret Saberhagen	1.00	.45
☐	15 Kirby Puckett	8.00	3.60
☐	16 Joe Carter	2.00	.90
☐	17 Roger Clemens	6.00	2.70
☐	18 Barry Bonds	6.00	2.70
☐	19 Greg Maddux	12.00	5.50
☐	20 Frank Thomas	15.00	6.75

1996 Topps Chrome Wrecking Crew

Randomly inserted in packs at a rate of one in 24, this 15-card set features baseball's top hitters and is printed in color action photography with brilliant color metallization.

	MINT	NRMT
COMPLETE SET (15)	80.00	36.00
COMMON CARD (WC1-WC15) 2.50		1.10
STATED ODDS 1:24 HOBBY		
COMP.REF.SET (15)	250.00	110.00
*REFRACTORS: 1.25X TO 3X BASE CARD HI		
REF.STATED ODDS 1:72 HOBBY		

☐	WC1 Jeff Bagwell	10.00	4.50
☐	WC2 Albert Belle	6.00	2.70
☐	WC3 Barry Bonds	6.00	2.70
☐	WC4 Jose Canseco	4.00	1.80
☐	WC5 Joe Carter	2.50	1.10

☐	WC6 Cecil Fielder	2.50	1.10
☐	WC7 Ron Gant	2.50	1.10
☐	WC8 Juan Gonzalez	12.00	5.50
☐	WC9 Ken Griffey Jr.	25.00	11.00
☐	WC10 Fred McGriff	4.00	1.80
☐	WC11 Mark McGwire	10.00	4.50
☐	WC12 Mike Piazza	15.00	6.75
☐	WC13 Frank Thomas	20.00	9.00
☐	WC14 Mo Vaughn	6.00	2.70
☐	WC15 Matt Williams	4.00	1.80

1997 Topps Chrome

The 1997 Topps Chrome set was issued in one series totalling 165 cards and was distributed in four-card packs with a suggested retail price of $3. Using chromium technology to highlight the cards, this set features a metalized version of the cards of some of the best players from the 1997 regular Topps Series I and II. An attractive 8 1/2" by 11" chrome promo sheet was sent to dealers advertising this set.

	MINT	NRMT
COMPLETE SET (165)	80.00	36.00
COMMON CARD (1-165)	.40	.18
MINOR STARS	.75	.35
UNLISTED STARS	1.50	.70

☐	1 Barry Bonds	2.00	.90
☐	2 Jose Valentin	.40	.18
☐	3 Brady Anderson	1.00	.45
☐	4 Wade Boggs	1.50	.70
☐	5 Andres Galarraga	1.50	.70
☐	6 Rusty Greer	.75	.35
☐	7 Derek Jeter	5.00	2.20
☐	8 Ricky Bottalico	.40	.18
☐	9 Mike Piazza	5.00	2.20
☐	10 Garret Anderson	.75	.35
☐	11 Jeff King	.40	.18
☐	12 Kevin Appier	.75	.35
☐	13 Mark Grace	1.00	.45
☐	14 Jeff D'Amico	.40	.18
☐	15 Jay Buhner	1.00	.45
☐	16 Hal Morris	.40	.18
☐	17 Harold Baines	.75	.35
☐	18 Jeff Cirillo	.75	.35
☐	19 Tom Glavine	.75	.35
☐	20 Andy Pettitte	1.50	.70
☐	21 Mark McGwire	3.00	1.35
☐	22 Chuck Knoblauch	1.50	.70
☐	23 Raul Mondesi	1.00	.45
☐	24 Albert Belle	2.00	.90
☐	25 Trevor Hoffman	.40	.18
☐	26 Eric Young	.40	.18
☐	27 Brian McRae	.40	.18
☐	28 Jim Edmonds	1.00	.45
☐	29 Robb Nen	.40	.18
☐	30 Reggie Sanders	.40	.18
☐	31 Mike Lansing	.40	.18

☐	32 Craig Biggio	1.00	.45
☐	33 Ray Lankford	.75	.35
☐	34 Charles Nagy	.75	.35
☐	35 Paul Wilson	.40	.18
☐	36 John Wetteland	.40	.18
☐	37 Derek Bell	.40	.18
☐	38 Edgar Martinez	1.00	.45
☐	39 Rickey Henderson	1.00	.45
☐	40 Jim Thome	1.50	.70
☐	41 Frank Thomas	6.00	2.70
☐	42 Jackie Robinson	6.00	2.70
☐	43 Terry Steinbach	.40	.18
☐	44 Kevin Brown	.75	.35
☐	45 Joey Hamilton	.75	.35
☐	46 Travis Fryman	.75	.35
☐	47 Juan Gonzalez	4.00	1.80
☐	48 Ron Gant	.75	.35
☐	49 Greg Maddux	5.00	2.20
☐	50 Wally Joyner	.75	.35
☐	51 John Valentin	.40	.18
☐	52 Bret Boone	.40	.18
☐	53 Paul Molitor	1.50	.70
☐	54 Rafael Palmeiro	1.00	.45
☐	55 Todd Hundley	.75	.35
☐	56 Ellis Burks	.75	.35
☐	57 Bernie Williams	1.50	.70
☐	58 Roberto Alomar	1.50	.70
☐	59 Jose Mesa	.40	.18
☐	60 Troy Percival	.40	.18
☐	61 John Smoltz	.75	.35
☐	62 Jeff Conine	.75	.35
☐	63 Bernard Gilkey	.40	.18
☐	64 Mickey Tettleton	.40	.18
☐	65 Justin Thompson	.75	.35
☐	66 Tony Phillips	.40	.18
☐	67 Ryne Sandberg	2.00	.90
☐	68 Geronimo Berroa	.40	.18
☐	69 Todd Hollandsworth	.40	.18
☐	70 Rey Ordonez	.40	.18
☐	71 Marquis Grissom	.75	.35
☐	72 Tino Martinez	1.50	.70
☐	73 Steve Finley	.75	.35
☐	74 Andy Benes	.75	.35
☐	75 Jason Kendall	.75	.35
☐	76 Johnny Damon	.40	.18
☐	77 Jason Giambi	.75	.35
☐	78 Henry Rodriguez	.40	.18
☐	79 Edgar Renteria	.75	.35
☐	80 Ray Durham	.40	.18
☐	81 Gregg Jefferies	.40	.18
☐	82 Roberto Hernandez	.40	.18
☐	83 Joe Carter	.75	.35
☐	84 Jermaine Dye	.40	.18
☐	85 Julio Franco	.75	.35
☐	86 David Justice	1.50	.70
☐	87 Jose Canseco	1.00	.45
☐	88 Paul O'Neill	.75	.35
☐	89 Mariano Rivera	.75	.35
☐	90 Bobby Higginson	.75	.35
☐	91 Mark Grudzielanek	.40	.18
☐	92 Lance Johnson	.40	.18
☐	93 Ken Caminiti	1.00	.45
☐	94 Gary Sheffield	1.50	.70
☐	95 Luis Castillo	.75	.35
☐	96 Scott Rolen	4.00	1.80
☐	97 Chipper Jones	5.00	2.20
☐	98 Darryl Strawberry	.75	.35
☐	99 Nomar Garciaparra	5.00	2.20
☐	100 Jeff Bagwell	3.00	1.35
☐	101 Ken Griffey Jr.	8.00	3.60
☐	102 Sammy Sosa	1.50	.70
☐	103 Jack McDowell	.40	.18
☐	104 James Baldwin	.40	.18
☐	105 Rocky Coppinger	.40	.18
☐	106 Manny Ramirez	1.50	.70
☐	107 Tim Salmon	1.50	.70
☐	108 Eric Karros	.75	.35
☐	109 Brett Butler	.75	.35
☐	110 Randy Johnson	1.50	.70
☐	111 Pat Hentgen	.75	.35
☐	112 Rondell White	.75	.35
☐	113 Eddie Murray	1.50	.70
☐	114 Ivan Rodriguez	2.00	.90
☐	115 Jermaine Allensworth	.40	.18
☐	116 Ed Sprague	.40	.18
☐	117 Kenny Lofton	2.00	.90

		MINT	NRMT
☐ 118	Alan Benes .75		.35
☐ 119	Fred McGriff 1.00		.45
☐ 120	Alex Fernandez .75		.35
☐ 121	Al Martin .40		.18
☐ 122	Devon White .40		.18
☐ 123	David Cone .75		.35
☐ 124	Karim Garcia .75		.35
☐ 125	Chili Davis .75		.35
☐ 126	Roger Clemens 3.00		1.35
☐ 127	Bobby Bonilla .75		.35
☐ 128	Mike Mussina 1.50		.70
☐ 129	Todd Walker .75		.35
☐ 130	Dante Bichette .75		.35
☐ 131	Carlos Baerga .40		.18
☐ 132	Matt Williams 1.00		.45
☐ 133	Will Clark 1.00		.45
☐ 134	Dennis Eckersley .75		.35
☐ 135	Ryan Klesko 1.00		.45
☐ 136	Dean Palmer .40		.18
☐ 137	Javy Lopez .75		.35
☐ 138	Greg Vaughn .40		.18
☐ 139	Vinny Castilla .75		.35
☐ 140	Cal Ripken 6.00		2.70
☐ 141	Ruben Rivera .40		.18
☐ 142	Mark Wohlers .40		.18
☐ 143	Tony Clark 1.50		.70
☐ 144	Jose Rosado .75		.35
☐ 145	Tony Gwynn 4.00		1.80
☐ 146	Cecil Fielder .75		.35
☐ 147	Brian Jordan .75		.35
☐ 148	Bob Abreu .75		.35
☐ 149	Barry Larkin 1.00		.45
☐ 150	Robin Ventura .75		.35
☐ 151	John Olerud .75		.35
☐ 152	Rod Beck .40		.18
☐ 153	Vladimir Guerrero 3.00		1.35
☐ 154	Marty Cordova .75		.35
☐ 155	Todd Stottlemyre .40		.18
☐ 156	Hideo Nomo 4.00		1.80
☐ 157	Denny Neagle .75		.35
☐ 158	John Jaha .40		.18
☐ 159	Mo Vaughn 2.00		.90
☐ 160	Andruw Jones 4.00		1.80
☐ 161	Moises Alou .75		.35
☐ 162	Larry Walker 1.50		.70
☐ 163	Eddie Murray SH .75		.35
☐ 164	Paul Molitor SH .75		.35
☐ 165	Checklist .40		.18

1997 Topps Chrome Refractors

Randomly inserted in packs at a rate of one in 12, this 165-card set is a parallel version of the regular Topps Chrome set and is similar in design. The difference is found in the refractive quality of the cards.

	MINT	NRMT
COMPLETE SET (165)	2000.00	900.00
COMMON CARD (1-165)	6.00	2.70
*STARS: 7.5X TO 15X HI COLUMN		
*YOUNG STARS: 6X TO 12X HI		

STATED ODDS 1:12 ....
CONDITION SENSITIVE SET ....

		MINT	NRMT
☐ 7	Derek Jeter	60.00	27.00
☐ 9	Mike Piazza	80.00	36.00
☐ 21	Mark McGwire	50.00	22.00
☐ 41	Frank Thomas	100.00	45.00
☐ 42	Jackie Robinson	100.00	45.00
☐ 47	Juan Gonzalez	60.00	27.00
☐ 49	Greg Maddux	80.00	36.00
☐ 96	Scott Rolen	50.00	22.00
☐ 97	Chipper Jones	80.00	36.00
☐ 99	Nomar Garciaparra ..	60.00	27.00
☐ 100	Jeff Bagwell	50.00	22.00
☐ 101	Ken Griffey Jr.	120.00	55.00
☐ 126	Roger Clemens	50.00	22.00
☐ 140	Cal Ripken	100.00	45.00
☐ 145	Tony Gwynn	60.00	27.00
☐ 153	Vladimir Guerrero	40.00	18.00
☐ 156	Hideo Nomo	60.00	27.00
☐ 160	Andruw Jones	50.00	22.00

1997 Topps Chrome All-Stars

Randomly inserted in packs at a rate of one in 24, this 22-card set features color player photos printed on rainbow foilboard. The set showcases the top three players from each position from both the American and National leagues as voted by the Topps Sports Department.

	MINT	NRMT
COMPLETE SET (22)	120.00	55.00
COMMON CARD (AS1-AS22)	1.50	.70
UNLISTED STARS	5.00	2.20
STATED ODDS 1:24		
COMP.REF.SET (22)	500.00	220.00
*REFRACTORS: 2X TO 4X HI COLUMN		
REFRACTOR STATED ODDS 1:72		

		MINT	NRMT
☐ AS1	Ivan Rodriguez	6.00	2.70
☐ AS2	Todd Hundley	2.50	1.10
☐ AS3	Frank Thomas	20.00	9.00
☐ AS4	Andres Galarraga	5.00	2.20
☐ AS5	Chuck Knoblauch	5.00	2.20
☐ AS6	Eric Young	1.50	.70
☐ AS7	Jim Thome	5.00	2.20
☐ AS8	Chipper Jones	15.00	6.75
☐ AS9	Cal Ripken	20.00	9.00
☐ AS10	Barry Larkin	3.00	1.35
☐ AS11	Albert Belle	6.00	2.70
☐ AS12	Barry Bonds	6.00	2.70
☐ AS13	Ken Griffey Jr	25.00	11.00
☐ AS14	Ellis Burks	2.50	1.10
☐ AS15	Juan Gonzalez	12.00	5.50
☐ AS16	Gary Sheffield	5.00	2.20
☐ AS17	Andy Pettitte	5.00	2.20
☐ AS18	Tom Glavine	2.50	1.10
☐ AS19	Pat Hentgen	2.50	1.10
☐ AS20	John Smoltz	2.50	1.10
☐ AS21	Roberto Hernandez	1.50	.70
☐ AS22	Mark Wohlers	1.50	.70

1997 Topps Chrome Diamond Duos

Randomly inserted in packs at a rate of one in 36, this 10-card set features color player photos of two superstar teammates on double sided chromium cards.

	MINT	NRMT
COMPLETE SET (10)	100.00	45.00
COMMON CARD (DD1-DD10)	4.00	1.80
STATED ODDS 1:36		
COMP.REF.SET (10)........	400.00	180.00
*REFRACTORS: 2X TO 4X HI COLUMN		
REFRACTOR STATED ODDS 1:108		

		MINT	NRMT
☐ DD1	Chipper Jones	12.00	5.50
	Andruw Jones		
☐ DD2	Derek Jeter	10.00	4.50
	Bernie Williams		
☐ DD3	Ken Griffey Jr.	20.00	9.00
	Jay Buhner		
☐ DD4	Kenny Lofton	5.00	2.20
	Manny Ramirez		
☐ DD5	Jeff Bagwell	8.00	3.60
	Craig Biggio		
☐ DD6	Juan Gonzalez	10.00	4.50
	Ivan Rodriguez		
☐ DD7	Cal Ripken	15.00	6.75
	Brady Anderson		
☐ DD8	Mike Piazza	15.00	6.75
	Hideo Nomo		
☐ DD9	Andres Galarraga	4.00	1.80
	Dante Bichette		
☐ DD10	Frank Thomas	15.00	6.75
	Albert Belle		

1997 Topps Chrome Season's Best

Randomly inserted in packs at a rate of one in 18, this 25-card *set features color player photos of the five top players from five statistical categories: most steals (Leading Looters), most home runs (Bleacher Reachers), most wins (Hill Toppers), most RBIs (Number Crunchers), and best slugging percentage (Kings of Swing).*

	MINT	NRMT
COMPLETE SET (25)	100.00	45.00
COMMON CARD (1-25)	1.00	.45
UNLISTED STARS	4.00	1.80
STATED ODDS 1:18		
COMP.REF.SET (25)	400.00	180.00
*REFRACTORS: 2X TO 4X HI COLUMN		
REFRACTOR STATED ODDS 1:54		

☐ 1	Tony Gwynn	10.00	4.50
☐ 2	Frank Thomas	15.00	6.75
☐ 3	Ellis Burks	2.00	.90
☐ 4	Paul Molitor	4.00	1.80
☐ 5	Chuck Knoblauch	4.00	1.80
☐ 6	Mark McGwire	8.00	3.60
☐ 7	Brady Anderson	2.50	1.10
☐ 8	Ken Griffey Jr.	20.00	9.00
☐ 9	Albert Belle	5.00	2.20
☐ 10	Andres Galarraga	4.00	1.80
☐ 11	Andres Galarraga	4.00	1.80
☐ 12	Albert Belle	5.00	2.20
☐ 13	Juan Gonzalez	10.00	4.50
☐ 14	Mo Vaughn	5.00	2.20
☐ 15	Rafael Palmeiro	2.50	1.10
☐ 16	John Smoltz	2.00	.90
☐ 17	Andy Pettitte	4.00	1.80
☐ 18	Pat Hentgen	2.00	.90
☐ 19	Mike Mussina	4.00	1.80
☐ 20	Andy Benes	2.00	.90
☐ 21	Kenny Lofton	5.00	2.20
☐ 22	Tom Goodwin	1.00	.45
☐ 23	Otis Nixon	1.00	.45
☐ 24	Eric Young	1.00	.45
☐ 25	Lance Johnson	1.00	.45

1996 Topps Gallery

The 1996 Topps Gallery set was issued in one series totaling 180 cards. The eight-card packs retail for $3.00 each. The set is divided into 5 themes: Classics (1-90), New Editions (91-108), Modernists (109-126), Futurists (127-144) and Masters (145-180). Each theme features a different design on front, but the bulk of the set has full-bleed, color action shots.

	MINT	NRMT
COMPLETE SET (180)	40.00	18.00
COMMON CARD (1-180)	.25	.11
MINOR STARS	.50	.23
UNLISTED STARS	1.00	.45
COMP.PPI SET (180)	1000.00	450.00

COMMON PPI (1-180)		2.00	.90
*PPI STARS: 7.5X TO 15X HI COLUMN			
*PPI YOUNG STARS: 6X TO 12X HI			
PPI STATED ODDS 1:8			
PPI STAT.PRINT RUN 999 SERIAL #'d SETS			
FIRST 100 PPI CARDS SENT TO PLAYERS			
TOPPS ALSO DESTROYED 400 PPI SETS			
MANTLE STATED ODDS 1:48			

☐ 1	Tom Glavine	.50	.23
☐ 2	Carlos Baerga	.25	.11
☐ 3	Dante Bichette	.50	.23
☐ 4	Mark Langston	.25	.11
☐ 5	Ray Lankford	.25	.11
☐ 6	Moises Alou	.50	.23
☐ 7	Marquis Grissom	.50	.23
☐ 8	Ramon Martinez	.50	.23
☐ 9	Steve Finley	.50	.23
☐ 10	Todd Hundley	.50	.23
☐ 11	Brady Anderson	.75	.35
☐ 12	John Valentin	.25	.11
☐ 13	Heathcliff Slocumb	.25	.11
☐ 14	Ruben Sierra	.25	.11
☐ 15	Jeff Conine	.50	.23
☐ 16	Jay Buhner	.75	.35
☐ 17	Sammy Sosa	1.00	.45
☐ 18	Doug Drabek	.25	.11
☐ 19	Jose Mesa	.25	.11
☐ 20	Jeff King	.25	.11
☐ 21	Mickey Tettleton	.25	.11
☐ 22	Jeff Montgomery	.25	.11
☐ 23	Alex Fernandez	.25	.11
☐ 24	Greg Vaughn	.25	.11
☐ 25	Chuck Finley	.25	.11
☐ 26	Terry Steinbach	.25	.11
☐ 27	Rod Beck	.25	.11
☐ 28	Jack McDowell	.25	.11
☐ 29	Mark Wohlers	.25	.11
☐ 30	Leh Dykstra	.50	.23
☐ 31	Bernie Williams	1.00	.45
☐ 32	Travis Fryman	.25	.11
☐ 33	Jose Canseco	.75	.35
☐ 34	Ken Caminiti	.75	.35
☐ 35	Devon White	.25	.11
☐ 36	Bobby Bonilla	.50	.23
☐ 37	Paul Sorrento	.25	.11
☐ 38	Ryne Sandberg	1.25	.55
☐ 39	Derek Bell	.25	.11
☐ 40	Bobby Jones	.25	.11
☐ 41	J.T. Snow	.50	.23
☐ 42	Denny Neagle	.50	.23
☐ 43	Tim Wakefield	.25	.11
☐ 44	Andres Galarraga	1.00	.45
☐ 45	David Segui	.25	.11
☐ 46	Lee Smith	.50	.23
☐ 47	Mel Rojas	.25	.11
☐ 48	John Franco	.25	.11
☐ 49	Pete Schourek	.25	.11
☐ 50	John Wetteland	.25	.11
☐ 51	Paul Molitor	1.00	.45
☐ 52	Ivan Rodriguez	1.25	.55
☐ 53	Chris Hoiles	.25	.11
☐ 54	Mike Greenwell	.25	.11
☐ 55	Orel Hershiser	.50	.23
☐ 56	Brian McRae	.25	.11
☐ 57	Geronimo Berroa	.25	.11
☐ 58	Craig Biggio	.75	.35
☐ 59	David Justice	1.00	.45
☐ 60	Lance Johnson	.25	.11
☐ 61	Andy Ashby	.25	.11
☐ 62	Randy Myers	.25	.11
☐ 63	Gregg Jefferies	.25	.11
☐ 64	Kevin Appier	.50	.23
☐ 65	Rick Aguilera	.25	.11
☐ 66	Shane Reynolds	.25	.11
☐ 67	John Smoltz	.50	.23
☐ 68	Ron Gant	.50	.23
☐ 69	Eric Karros	.50	.23
☐ 70	Jim Thome	1.00	.45
☐ 71	Terry Pendleton	.25	.11
☐ 72	Kenny Rogers	.25	.11
☐ 73	Robin Ventura	.50	.23
☐ 74	Dave Nilsson	.25	.11
☐ 75	Brian Jordan	.50	.23
☐ 76	Glenallen Hill	.25	.11
☐ 77	Greg Colbrunn	.25	.11
☐ 78	Roberto Alomar	1.00	.45
☐ 79	Rickey Henderson	.75	.35
☐ 80	Carlos Garcia	.25	.11
☐ 81	Dean Palmer	.25	.11
☐ 82	Mike Stanley	.25	.11
☐ 83	Hal Morris	.25	.11
☐ 84	Wade Boggs	1.00	.45
☐ 85	Chad Curtis	.25	.11
☐ 86	Roberto Hernandez	.25	.11
☐ 87	John Olerud	.50	.23
☐ 88	Frank Castillo	.25	.11
☐ 89	Rafael Palmeiro	.75	.35
☐ 90	Trevor Hoffman	.25	.11
☐ 91	Marty Cordova	.50	.23
☐ 92	Hideo Nomo	2.50	1.10
☐ 93	Johnny Damon	.50	.23
☐ 94	Bill Pulsipher	.25	.11
☐ 95	Garret Anderson	.50	.23
☐ 96	Ray Durham	.25	.11
☐ 97	Ricky Bottalico	.25	.11
☐ 98	Carlos Perez	.25	.11
☐ 99	Troy Percival	.25	.11
☐ 100	Chipper Jones	3.00	1.35
☐ 101	Esteban Loaiza	.25	.11
☐ 102	John Mabry	.25	.11
☐ 103	Jon Nunnally	.25	.11
☐ 104	Andy Pettitte	1.25	.55
☐ 105	Lyle Mouton	.25	.11
☐ 106	Jason Isringhausen	.25	.11
☐ 107	Brian L.Hunter	.50	.23
☐ 108	Quilvio Veras	.25	.11
☐ 109	Jim Edmonds	.75	.35
☐ 110	Ryan Klesko	.75	.35
☐ 111	Pedro Martinez	1.00	.45
☐ 112	Joey Hamilton	.50	.23
☐ 113	Vinny Castilla	.50	.23
☐ 114	Alex Gonzalez	.25	.11
☐ 115	Raul Mondesi	.75	.35
☐ 116	Rondell White	.50	.23
☐ 117	Dan Miceli	.25	.11
☐ 118	Tom Goodwin	.25	.11
☐ 119	Bret Boone	.25	.11
☐ 120	Shawn Green	.25	.11
☐ 121	Jeff Cirillo	.50	.23
☐ 122	Rico Brogna	.25	.11
☐ 123	Chris Gomez	.25	.11
☐ 124	Ismael Valdes	.50	.23
☐ 125	Javy Lopez	.50	.23
☐ 126	Manny Ramirez	1.00	.45
☐ 127	Paul Wilson	.25	.11
☐ 128	Billy Wagner	.25	.11
☐ 129	Eric Owens	.25	.11
☐ 130	Todd Greene	.75	.35
☐ 131	Karim Garcia	.75	.35
☐ 132	Jimmy Haynes	.25	.11
☐ 133	Michael Tucker	.50	.23
☐ 134	John Wasdin	.25	.11
☐ 135	Brooks Kieschnick	.50	.23
☐ 136	Alex Ochoa	.25	.11
☐ 137	Ariel Prieto	.25	.11
☐ 138	Tony Clark	1.00	.45
☐ 139	Mark Loretta	.25	.11
☐ 140	Rey Ordonez	.50	.23
☐ 141	Chris Snopek	.25	.11
☐ 142	Roger Cedeno	.25	.11
☐ 143	Derek Jeter	3.00	1.35
☐ 144	Jeff Suppan	.50	.23
☐ 145	Greg Maddux	3.00	1.35
☐ 146	Ken Griffey Jr.	5.00	2.20
☐ 147	Tony Gwynn	2.50	1.10
☐ 148	Darren Daulton	.50	.23
☐ 149	Will Clark	.75	.35
☐ 150	Mo Vaughn	1.25	.55
☐ 151	Reggie Sanders	.25	.11
☐ 152	Kirby Puckett	2.00	.90
☐ 153	Paul O'Neill	.50	.23
☐ 154	Tim Salmon	1.00	.45
☐ 155	Mark McGwire	2.00	.90
☐ 156	Barry Bonds	1.25	.55
☐ 157	Albert Belle	1.25	.55
☐ 158	Edgar Martinez	.50	.23
☐ 159	Mike Mussina	1.00	.45
☐ 160	Cecil Fielder	.50	.23
☐ 161	Kenny Lofton	1.25	.55
☐ 162	Randy Johnson	1.00	.45
☐ 163	Juan Gonzalez	2.50	1.10

		MINT	NRMT
□ 164	Jeff Bagwell	2.00	.90
□ 165	Joe Carter	.50	.23
□ 166	Mike Piazza	3.00	1.35
□ 167	Eddie Murray	1.00	.45
□ 168	Cal Ripken	4.00	1.80
□ 169	Barry Larkin	.75	.35
□ 170	Chuck Knoblauch	1.00	.45
□ 171	Chili Davis	.50	.23
□ 172	Fred McGriff	.75	.35
□ 173	Matt Williams	.75	.35
□ 174	Roger Clemens	2.00	.90
□ 175	Frank Thomas	4.00	1.80
□ 176	Dennis Eckersley	.50	.23
□ 177	Gary Sheffield	1.00	.45
□ 178	David Cone	.50	.23
□ 179	Larry Walker	1.00	.45
□ 180	Mark Grace	.75	.35
□ NNO	Mantle Masterpiece	20.00	9.00

1996 Topps Gallery Expressionists

Randomly inserted in packs at a rate of one in 24, this 20-card set features 20 spiritual leaders printed on triple foil stamped and texture embossed cards. Card backs contain a second photo and narrative about the player.

	MINT	NRMT
COMPLETE SET (20)	120.00	55.00
COMMON CARD (1-20)	2.00	.90
SEMISTARS	4.00	1.80
UNLISTED STARS	6.00	2.70
STATED ODDS 1:24		

□ 1	Mike Piazza	20.00	9.00
□ 2	J.T. Snow	3.00	1.35
□ 3	Ken Griffey Jr.	30.00	13.50
□ 4	Kirby Puckett	12.00	5.50
□ 5	Carlos Baerga	2.00	.90
□ 6	Chipper Jones	20.00	9.00
□ 7	Hideo Nomo	15.00	6.75
□ 8	Mark McGwire	12.00	5.50
□ 9	Gary Sheffield	6.00	2.70
□ 10	Randy Johnson	6.00	2.70
□ 11	Ray Lankford	3.00	1.35
□ 12	Sammy Sosa	6.00	2.70
□ 13	Denny Martinez	3.00	1.35
□ 14	Jose Canseco	4.00	1.80
□ 15	Tony Gwynn	15.00	6.75
□ 16	Edgar Martinez	4.00	1.80
□ 17	Reggie Sanders	2.00	.90
□ 18	Andres Galarraga	6.00	2.70
□ 19	Albert Belle	8.00	3.60
□ 20	Barry Larkin	4.00	1.80

1996 Topps Gallery Photo Gallery

Randomly inserted in packs at a rate of one in 30, this 15-card set features top photography chronicling baseball's biggest stars and greatest moments from last year. Each double foil stamped card is printed on 24 pt. stock with customized designs to accentuate the photography.

	MINT	NRMT
COMPLETE SET (15)	100.00	45.00
COMMON CARD (PG1-15)	1.00	.45
STATED ODDS 1:30		

□ PG1	Eddie Murray	4.00	1.80
□ PG2	Randy Johnson	4.00	1.80
□ PG3	Cal Ripken	20.00	9.00
□ PG4	Bret Boone	1.00	.45
□ PG5	Frank Thomas	20.00	9.00
□ PG6	Jeff Conine	2.00	.90
□ PG7	Johnny Damon	2.00	.90
□ PG8	Roger Clemens	8.00	3.60
□ PG9	Albert Belle	5.00	2.20
□ PG10	Ken Griffey Jr.	25.00	11.00
□ PG11	Kirby Puckett	10.00	4.50
□ PG12	David Justice	4.00	1.80
□ PG13	Bobby Bonilla	2.00	.90
□ PG14	Colorado Rockies	4.00	1.80
□ PG15	Atlanta Braves	4.00	1.80

1997 Topps Gallery

The 1997 Topps Gallery set was issued in one series totalling 180 cards. The eight-card packs retail for $4.00 each. This hobby only set is divided into four themes: Veterans, Prospects, Rising Stars and Young Stars. Printed on 24-point card stock with a high-gloss film and etch stamped with one or more foils, each theme features a different design on front with a variety of informative statistics and revealing player text on the back.

	MINT	NRMT
COMPLETE SET (180)	55.00	25.00
COMMON CARD (1-180)	.25	.11
MINOR STARS	.50	.23
UNLISTED STARS	1.00	.45
COMP.PPI SET (180)	2000.00	900.00
COMMON PPI (1-180)	6.00	2.70
*PPI STARS: 12.5X TO 25X HI COLUMN		
*PPI YOUNG STARS: 10X TO 20X HI		
PPI STATED ODDS 1:12		
PPI STATED PRINT RUN 250 SETS		

□ 1	Paul Molitor	1.00	.45
□ 2	Devon White	.25	.11
□ 3	Andres Galarraga	1.00	.45
□ 4	Cal Ripken	4.00	1.80
□ 5	Tony Gwynn	2.50	1.10
□ 6	Mike Stanley	.25	.11
□ 7	Orel Hershiser	.50	.23
□ 8	Jose Canseco	.75	.35
□ 9	Chili Davis	.50	.23
□ 10	Harold Baines	.50	.23
□ 11	Rickey Henderson	.75	.35
□ 12	Darryl Strawberry	.50	.23
□ 13	Todd Worrell	.25	.11
□ 14	Cecil Fielder	.50	.23
□ 15	Gary Gaetti	.25	.11
□ 16	Bobby Bonilla	.50	.23
□ 17	Will Clark	.75	.35
□ 18	Kevin Brown	.50	.23
□ 19	Tom Glavine	.50	.23
□ 20	Wade Boggs	1.00	.45
□ 21	Edgar Martinez	.75	.35
□ 22	Lance Johnson	.25	.11
□ 23	Gregg Jefferies	.25	.11
□ 24	Bip Roberts	.25	.11
□ 25	Tony Phillips	.25	.11
□ 26	Greg Maddux	3.00	1.35
□ 27	Mickey Tettleton	.25	.11
□ 28	Terry Steinbach	.25	.11
□ 29	Ryne Sandberg	1.25	.55
□ 30	Wally Joyner	.50	.23
□ 31	Joe Carter	.50	.23
□ 32	Ellis Burks	.50	.23
□ 33	Fred McGriff	.75	.35
□ 34	Barry Larkin	.75	.35
□ 35	John Franco	.50	.23
□ 36	Rafael Palmeiro	.75	.35
□ 37	Mark McGwire	2.00	.90
□ 38	Ken Caminiti	.75	.35
□ 39	David Cone	.50	.23
□ 40	Julio Franco	.50	.23
□ 41	Roger Clemens	2.00	.90
□ 42	Barry Bonds	1.25	.55
□ 43	Dennis Eckersley	.50	.23
□ 44	Eddie Murray	1.00	.45
□ 45	Paul O'Neill	.50	.23
□ 46	Craig Biggio	.75	.35
□ 47	Roberto Alomar	1.00	.45
□ 48	Mark Grace	.75	.35
□ 49	Matt Williams	.75	.35
□ 50	Jay Buhner	.75	.35
□ 51	John Smoltz	.50	.23
□ 52	Randy Johnson	1.00	.45
□ 53	Ramon Martinez	.50	.23
□ 54	Curt Schilling	.50	.23
□ 55	Gary Sheffield	1.00	.45
□ 56	Jack McDowell	.25	.11
□ 57	Brady Anderson	.75	.35
□ 58	Dante Bichette	.50	.23
□ 59	Ron Gant	.50	.23
□ 60	Alex Fernandez	.50	.23
□ 61	Moises Alou	.50	.23
□ 62	Travis Fryman	.50	.23
□ 63	Dean Palmer	.25	.11
□ 64	Todd Hundley	.50	.23
□ 65	Jeff Brantley	.25	.11
□ 66	Bernard Gilkey	.25	.11
□ 67	Geronimo Berroa	.25	.11
□ 68	John Wetteland	.25	.11
□ 69	Robin Ventura	.50	.23
□ 70	Ray Lankford	.50	.23
□ 71	Kevin Appier	.50	.23
□ 72	Larry Walker	1.00	.45
□ 73	Juan Gonzalez	2.50	1.10
□ 74	Jeff King	.25	.11
□ 75	Greg Vaughn	.25	.11
□ 76	Steve Finley	.50	.23
□ 77	Brian McRae	.25	.11

78 Paul Sorrento	.25	.11
79 Ken Griffey Jr.	5.00	2.20
80 Omar Vizquel	.50	.23
81 Jose Mesa	.25	.11
82 Albert Belle	1.25	.55
83 Glenallen Hill	.25	.11
84 Sammy Sosa	1.00	.45
85 Andy Benes	.50	.23
86 David Justice	1.00	.45
87 Marquis Grissom	.50	.23
88 John Olerud	.50	.23
89 Tino Martinez	1.00	.45
90 Frank Thomas	4.00	1.80
91 Raul Mondesi	.75	.35
92 Steve Trachsel	.25	.11
93 Jim Edmonds	.75	.35
94 Rusty Greer	.50	.23
95 Joey Hamilton	.50	.23
96 Ismael Valdes	.50	.23
97 Dave Nilsson	.25	.11
98 John Jaha	.25	.11
99 Alex Gonzalez	.25	.11
100 Javy Lopez	.50	.23
101 Ryan Klesko	.75	.35
102 Tim Salmon	1.00	.45
103 Bernie Williams	1.00	.45
104 Roberto Hernandez	.25	.11
105 Chuck Knoblauch	1.00	.45
106 Mike Lansing	.25	.11
107 Vinny Castilla	.50	.23
108 Reggie Sanders	.25	.11
109 Mo Vaughn	1.00	.45
110 Rondell White	.50	.23
111 Ivan Rodriguez	1.25	.55
112 Mike Mussina	1.00	.45
113 Carlos Baerga	.25	.11
114 Jeff Conine	.50	.23
115 Jim Thome	1.00	.45
116 Manny Ramirez	1.00	.45
117 Kenny Lofton	1.25	.55
118 Wilson Alvarez	.25	.11
119 Eric Karros	.50	.23
120 Robb Nen	.25	.11
121 Mark Wohlers	.25	.11
122 Ed Sprague	.25	.11
123 Pat Hentgen	.50	.23
124 Juan Guzman	.25	.11
125 Derek Bell	.25	.11
126 Jeff Bagwell	2.00	.90
127 Eric Young	.25	.11
128 John Valentin	.25	.11
129 Al Martin UER	.25	.11
Picture of Javy Lopez		
130 Trevor Hoffman	.25	.11
131 Henry Rodriguez	.25	.11
132 Pedro Martinez	1.00	.45
133 Mike Piazza	3.00	1.35
134 Brian Jordan	.50	.23
135 Jose Valentin	.25	.11
136 Jeff Cirillo	.50	.23
137 Chipper Jones	3.00	1.35
138 Ricky Bottalico	.25	.11
139 Hideo Nomo	2.50	1.10
140 Troy Percival	.25	.11
141 Rey Ordonez	.25	.11
142 Edgar Renteria	.50	.23
143 Luis Castillo	.50	.23
144 Vladimir Guerrero	2.00	.90
145 Jeff D'Amico	.25	.11
146 Andruw Jones	2.50	1.10
147 Darin Erstad	1.50	.70
148 Bob Abreu	.50	.23
149 Carlos Delgado	.50	.23
150 Jamey Wright	.25	.11
151 Nomar Garciaparra	3.00	1.35
152 Jason Kendall	.50	.23
153 Jermaine Allensworth	.25	.11
154 Scott Rolen	2.50	1.10
155 Rocky Coppinger	.25	.11
156 Paul Wilson	.25	.11
157 Garret Anderson	.50	.23
158 Mariano Rivera	.50	.23
159 Ruben Rivera	.25	.11
160 Andy Pettitte	1.00	.45
161 Derek Jeter	3.00	1.35
162 Neifi Perez	.50	.23
163 Ray Durham	.25	.11
164 James Baldwin	.25	.11
165 Marty Cordova	.50	.23
166 Tony Clark	1.00	.45
167 Michael Tucker	.50	.23
168 Mike Sweeney	.50	.23
169 Johnny Damon	.25	.11
170 Jermaine Dye	.25	.11
171 Alex Ochoa	.25	.11
172 Jason Isringhausen	.25	.11
173 Mark Grudzielanek	.25	.11
174 Jose Rosado	.50	.23
175 Todd Hollandsworth	.25	.11
176 Alan Benes	.50	.23
177 Jason Giambi	.50	.23
178 Billy Wagner	.50	.23
179 Justin Thompson	.50	.23
180 Todd Walker	.50	.23

1997 Topps Gallery
Gallery of Heroes

Randomly inserted in packs at a rate of one in 36, this 10-card set features color player photos designed to command the attention paid to works hanging in art museums. The backs carry player information.

	MINT	NRMT
COMPLETE SET (10)	180.00	80.00
COMMON CARD (GH1-GH10)	10.00	4.50
STATED ODDS 1:36		
GH1 Derek Jeter	20.00	9.00
GH2 Chipper Jones	25.00	11.00
GH3 Frank Thomas	30.00	13.50
GH4 Ken Griffey Jr.	40.00	18.00
GH5 Cal Ripken	30.00	13.50
GH6 Mark McGwire	15.00	6.75
GH7 Mike Piazza	25.00	11.00
GH8 Jeff Bagwell	15.00	6.75
GH9 Tony Gwynn	20.00	9.00
GH10 Mo Vaughn	10.00	4.50

1997 Topps Gallery
Peter Max
Serigraphs

Randomly inserted in packs at a rate of one in 24, this 10-card set features painted renditions of ten superstars by the artist, Peter Max. The backs carry his commentary about the player.

	MINT	NRMT
COMPLETE SET (10)	100.00	45.00
COMMON CARD (1-10)	3.00	
STATED ODDS 1:24		
*AUTOGRAPHS: 15X TO 25X HI COLUMN		
AUTOGRAPHS: RANDOM INS.IN PACKS		

AUTO. PRINT RUN 40 SERIAL #'d SETS
AU'S SIGNED BY MAX BENEATH UV COATING

1 Derek Jeter	12.00	5.50
2 Albert Belle	6.00	2.70
3 Ken Caminiti	3.00	1.35
4 Chipper Jones	15.00	6.75
5 Ken Griffey Jr.	25.00	11.00
6 Frank Thomas	20.00	9.00
7 Cal Ripken	20.00	9.00
8 Mark McGwire	10.00	4.50
9 Barry Bonds	6.00	2.70
10 Mike Piazza	15.00	6.75

1997 Topps Gallery
Photo Gallery

Randomly inserted in packs at a rate of one in 24, this 16-card set features color photos of some of baseball's hottest stars and their most memorable moments. Each card is enhanced by customized designs and double foil-stamping.

	MINT	NRMT
COMPLETE SET (16)	180.00	80.00
COMMON CARD (PG1-PG16)	3.00	1.35
SEMISTARS	5.00	2.20
UNLISTED STARS	8.00	3.60
STATED ODDS 1:24		
PG1 John Wetteland	3.00	1.35
PG2 Paul Molitor	8.00	3.60
PG3 Eddie Murray	8.00	3.60
PG4 Ken Griffey Jr.	40.00	18.00
PG5 Chipper Jones	25.00	11.00
PG6 Derek Jeter	20.00	9.00
PG7 Frank Thomas	30.00	13.50
PG8 Mark McGwire	15.00	6.75
PG9 Kenny Lofton	10.00	4.50
PG10 Gary Sheffield	8.00	3.60
PG11 Mike Piazza	25.00	11.00
PG12 Vinny Castilla	4.00	1.80
PG13 Andres Galarraga	8.00	3.60
PG14 Andy Pettitte	8.00	3.60
PG15 Robin Ventura	4.00	1.80
PG16 Barry Larkin	5.00	2.20

1996 Topps Laser

The 1996 Topps Laser contains 128 regular cards that are found on one of four perfected designs. Every card is etch foil-stamped and laser-cut. The four-card packs retail for $5 each.

	MINT	NRMT
COMPLETE SET (128)	120.00	55.00
COMPLETE SERIES 1 (64)	60.00	27.00
COMPLETE SERIES 2 (64)	60.00	27.00
COMMON CARD (1-128)	.50	.23
MINOR STARS	1.00	.45
UNLISTED STARS	2.00	.90

☐ 1	Moises Alou	1.00	.45
☐ 2	Derek Bell	.50	.23
☐ 3	Joe Carter	1.00	.45
☐ 4	Jeff Conine	1.00	.45
☐ 5	Darren Daulton	1.00	.45
☐ 6	Jim Edmonds	1.50	.70
☐ 7	Ron Gant	1.00	.45
☐ 8	Juan Gonzalez	5.00	2.20
☐ 9	Brian Jordan	1.00	.45
☐ 10	Ryan Klesko	1.50	.70
☐ 11	Paul Molitor	2.00	.90
☐ 12	Tony Phillips	.50	.23
☐ 13	Manny Ramirez	2.00	.90
☐ 14	Sammy Sosa	2.00	.90
☐ 15	Devon White	.50	.23
☐ 16	Bernie Williams	2.00	.90
☐ 17	Garrett Anderson	1.00	.45
☐ 18	Jay Bell	1.00	.45
☐ 19	Craig Biggio	1.50	.70
☐ 20	Bobby Bonilla	1.00	.45
☐ 21	Ken Caminiti	1.50	.70
☐ 22	Shawon Dunston	.50	.23
☐ 23	Mark Grace	1.50	.70
☐ 24	Gregg Jefferies	1.00	.45
☐ 25	Jeff King	.50	.23
☐ 26	Javy Lopez	1.00	.45
☐ 27	Edgar Martinez	1.50	.70
☐ 28	Dean Palmer	.50	.23
☐ 29	J.T. Snow	1.00	.45
☐ 30	Mike Stanley	.50	.23
☐ 31	Terry Steinbach	.50	.23
☐ 32	Robin Ventura	1.00	.45
☐ 33	Roberto Alomar	2.00	.90
☐ 34	Jeff Bagwell	4.00	1.80
☐ 35	Dante Bichette	1.00	.45
☐ 36	Wade Boggs	2.00	.90
☐ 37	Barry Bonds	2.50	1.10
☐ 38	Jose Canseco	1.50	.70
☐ 39	Vinny Castilla	1.00	.45
☐ 40	Will Clark	1.50	.70
☐ 41	Marty Cordova	1.00	.45
☐ 42	Ken Griffey Jr.	10.00	4.50
☐ 43	Tony Gwynn	5.00	2.20
☐ 44	Rickey Henderson	1.50	.70
☐ 45	Chipper Jones	6.00	2.70
☐ 46	Mark McGwire	4.00	1.80
☐ 47	Brian McRae	.50	.23
☐ 48	Ryne Sandberg	2.50	1.10
☐ 49	Andy Ashby	.50	.23
☐ 50	Alan Benes	1.00	.45
☐ 51	Andy Benes	1.00	.45
☐ 52	Roger Clemens	4.00	1.80
☐ 53	Doug Drabek	.50	.23
☐ 54	Dennis Eckersley	1.00	.45
☐ 55	Tom Glavine	1.00	.45
☐ 56	Randy Johnson	2.00	.90
☐ 57	Mark Langston	.50	.23
☐ 58	Denny Martinez	1.00	.45
☐ 59	Jack McDowell	.50	.23
☐ 60	Hideo Nomo	5.00	2.20
☐ 61	Shane Reynolds	.50	.23
☐ 62	John Smoltz	1.00	.45
☐ 63	Paul Wilson	.50	.23
☐ 64	Mark Wohlers	.50	.23
☐ 65	Shawn Green	.50	.23
☐ 66	Marquis Grissom	1.00	.45
☐ 67	Dave Hollins	.50	.23
☐ 68	Todd Hundley	1.00	.45
☐ 69	David Justice	2.00	.90
☐ 70	Eric Karros	1.00	.45
☐ 71	Ray Lankford	1.00	.45
☐ 72	Fred McGriff	1.50	.70
☐ 73	Hal Morris	.50	.23
☐ 74	Eddie Murray	2.00	.90
☐ 75	Paul O'Neill	1.00	.45
☐ 76	Rey Ordonez	1.00	.45
☐ 77	Reggie Sanders	.50	.23
☐ 78	Gary Sheffield	2.00	.90
☐ 79	Jim Thome	2.00	.90
☐ 80	Rondell White	1.00	.45
☐ 81	Travis Fryman	1.00	.45
☐ 82	Derek Jeter	6.00	2.70
☐ 83	Chuck Knoblauch	2.00	.90
☐ 84	Barry Larkin	1.50	.70
☐ 85	Tino Martinez	1.50	.70
☐ 86	Raul Mondesi	1.50	.70
☐ 87	John Olerud	1.00	.45
☐ 88	Rafael Palmeiro	1.50	.70
☐ 89	Mike Piazza	6.00	2.70
☐ 90	Cal Ripken	8.00	3.60
☐ 91	Ivan Rodriguez	2.50	1.10
☐ 92	Frank Thomas	8.00	3.60
☐ 93	John Valentin	.50	.23
☐ 94	Mo Vaughn	2.50	1.10
☐ 95	Quivilo Veras	.50	.23
☐ 96	Matt Williams	1.50	.70
☐ 97	Brady Anderson	1.50	.70
☐ 98	Carlos Baerga	.50	.23
☐ 99	Albert Belle	2.50	1.10
☐ 100	Jay Buhner	1.50	.70
☐ 101	Johnny Damon	1.00	.45
☐ 102	Chili Davis	.50	.23
☐ 103	Ray Durham	.50	.23
☐ 104	Len Dykstra	1.00	.45
☐ 105	Cecil Fielder	1.00	.45
☐ 106	Andres Galarraga	2.00	.90
☐ 107	Brian L.Hunter	1.00	.45
☐ 108	Kenny Lofton	2.50	1.10
☐ 109	Kirby Puckett	4.00	1.80
☐ 110	Tim Salmon	2.00	.90
☐ 111	Greg Vaughn	.50	.23
☐ 112	Larry Walker	2.00	.90
☐ 113	Rick Aguilera	.50	.23
☐ 114	Kevin Appier	1.00	.45
☐ 115	Kevin Brown	1.00	.45
☐ 116	David Cone	1.00	.45
☐ 117	Alex Fernandez	.50	.23
☐ 118	Chuck Finley	.50	.23
☐ 119	Joey Hamilton	.50	.23
☐ 120	Jason Isringhausen	.50	.23
☐ 121	Greg Maddux	6.00	2.70
☐ 122	Pedro Martinez	2.00	.90
☐ 123	Jose Mesa	.50	.23
☐ 124	Jeff Montgomery	.50	.23
☐ 125	Mike Mussina	2.00	.90
☐ 126	Randy Myers	.50	.23
☐ 127	Kenny Rogers	.50	.23
☐ 128	Ismael Valdes	1.00	.45

1996 Topps Laser Bright Spots

Randomly inserted in packs at a rate of one in 20, this 16-card

set highlights top young star players. The cards are printed on etched silver and gold diffraction foil.

	MINT	NRMT
COMPLETE SET (16)	100.00	45.00
COMPLETE SERIES 1 (8)	40.00	18.00
COMPLETE SERIES 2 (8)	60.00	27.00
COMMON CARD (1-16)	3.00	1.35
MINOR STARS	5.00	2.20
STATED ODDS 1:20		

☐ 1	Brian L.Hunter	5.00	2.20
☐ 2	Derek Jeter	15.00	6.75
☐ 3	Jason Kendall	8.00	3.60
☐ 4	Brooks Kieschnick	5.00	2.20
☐ 5	Rey Ordonez	5.00	2.20
☐ 6	Jason Schmidt	5.00	2.20
☐ 7	Chris Snopek	3.00	1.35
☐ 8	Bob Wolcott	3.00	1.35
☐ 9	Alan Benes	5.00	2.20
☐ 10	Marty Cordova	5.00	2.20
☐ 11	Jimmy Haynes	3.00	1.35
☐ 12	Todd Hollandsworth	3.00	1.35
☐ 13	Derek Jeter	15.00	6.75
☐ 14	Chipper Jones	20.00	9.00
☐ 15	Hideo Nomo	15.00	6.75
☐ 16	Paul Wilson	3.00	1.35

1996 Topps Laser Power Cuts

Randomly inserted in packs at a rate of one in 40, this 16-card set features baseball's biggest bats on laser-cut stock polished off with etched silver and gold diffraction foil.

	MINT	NRMT
COMPLETE SET (16)	160.00	70.00
COMPLETE SERIES 1 (8)	80.00	36.00
COMPLETE SERIES 2 (8)	80.00	36.00
COMMON CARD (1-16)	4.00	1.80
UNLISTED STARS	8.00	3.60
STATED ODDS 1:40		

		MINT	NRMT
☐ 1	Albert Belle	10.00	4.50
☐ 2	Jay Buhner	6.00	2.70
☐ 3	Fred McGriff	6.00	2.70
☐ 4	Mike Piazza	25.00	11.00
☐ 5	Tim Salmon	8.00	3.60
☐ 6	Frank Thomas	30.00	13.50
☐ 7	Mo Vaughn	10.00	4.50
☐ 8	Matt Williams	6.00	2.70
☐ 9	Jeff Bagwell	15.00	6.75
☐ 10	Barry Bonds	10.00	4.50
☐ 11	Jose Canseco	6.00	2.70
☐ 12	Cecil Fielder	4.00	1.80
☐ 13	Juan Gonzalez	20.00	9.00
☐ 14	Ken Griffey Jr.	40.00	18.00
☐ 15	Sammy Sosa	8.00	3.60
☐ 16	Larry Walker	8.00	3.60

1996 Topps Laser Stadium Stars

Randomly inserted in packs at a rate of one in 60, this 16-card set features the best and the brightest stars of the baseball diamond. Each highly detailed, laser-sculpted cover folds back to reveal striated silver and gold etched diffraction foil on every card.

		MINT	NRMT
COMPLETE SET (16)		240.00	110.00
COMPLETE SERIES 1 (8)		120.00	55.00
COMPLETE SERIES 2 (8)		120.00	55.00
COMMON CARD (1-16)		5.00	2.20
UNLISTED STARS		10.00	4.50
STATED ODDS 1:60			

☐ 1	Carlos Baerga	5.00	2.20
☐ 2	Barry Bonds	12.00	5.50
☐ 3	Andres Galarraga	10.00	4.50
☐ 4	Ken Griffey Jr.	50.00	22.00
☐ 5	Barry Larkin	8.00	3.60
☐ 6	Raul Mondesi	8.00	3.60
☐ 7	Kirby Puckett	20.00	9.00
☐ 8	Cal Ripken	40.00	18.00
☐ 9	Will Clark	8.00	3.60
☐ 10	Roger Clemens	20.00	9.00
☐ 11	Tony Gwynn	25.00	11.00
☐ 12	Randy Johnson	10.00	4.50
☐ 13	Kenny Lofton	12.00	5.50
☐ 14	Edgar Martinez	8.00	3.60
☐ 15	Ryne Sandberg	12.00	5.50
☐ 16	Frank Thomas	40.00	18.00

1997 Topps Screenplays

The 1997 Topps Screenplays set was issued in one series totalling 20 cards and distributed in one-card packs with a suggested retail price of $9.99. Each card displays 24 frames of actual game footage with the

help of Kodak's revolutionary Kodamotion technology. The cards have a dura clear back. Each card is individually packaged in a fold metal finish collectible tin that resembles a movie reel canister and features a full-color image of the player inside. The tin contains a display stand for it and the card and includes player info, bio, and stats. The cards are unnumbered and checklisted below in alphabetical order. All values listed below are for a combination of the card and tin.

		MINT	NRMT
COMPLETE SET (20)		150.00	70.00
COMMON CARD (1-20)		4.00	1.80
UNLISTED STARS		5.00	2.20
PRICES BELOW ARE FOR TIN/CARD COMBO			

☐ 1	Jeff Bagwell	10.00	4.50
☐ 2	Albert Belle	6.00	2.70
☐ 3	Barry Bonds	6.00	2.70
☐ 4	Andres Galarraga	4.00	1.80
☐ 5	Nomar Garciaparra	15.00	6.75
☐ 6	Juan Gonzalez	12.00	5.50
☐ 7	Ken Griffey Jr.	25.00	11.00
☐ 8	Tony Gwynn	12.00	5.50
☐ 9	Derek Jeter	15.00	6.75
☐ 10	Randy Johnson	5.00	2.20
☐ 11	Andruw Jones	12.00	5.50
☐ 12	Chipper Jones	15.00	6.75
☐ 13	Kenny Lofton	6.00	2.70
☐ 14	Mark McGwire	10.00	4.50
☐ 15	Paul Molitor	5.00	2.20
☐ 16	Hideo Nomo	12.00	5.50
☐ 17	Cal Ripken	20.00	9.00
☐ 18	Sammy Sosa	4.00	1.80
☐ 19	Frank Thomas	20.00	9.00
☐ 20	Jim Thome	5.00	2.20

1997 Topps Screenplays Premium Series

This six-card limited production set features six top stars from the regular base set in additional action shots. The cards were seeded at a rate of 1:21 packs. The cards are unnumbered and checklisted below in alphabetical order. The values listed below are for a combination of the card and the tin it was issued in.

		MINT	NRMT
COMPLETE SET (6)		300.00	135.00
COMMON CARD (1-6)		15.00	6.75

STATED ODDS 1:21			
PRICES BELOW ARE FOR TIN/CARD COMBO			

☐ 1	Ken Griffey Jr.	80.00	36.00
☐ 2	Chipper Jones	50.00	22.00
☐ 3	Mike Piazza	50.00	22.00
☐ 4	Cal Ripken	60.00	27.00
☐ 5	Frank Thomas	60.00	27.00
☐ 6	Larry Walker	15.00	6.75

1997 Topps Stars

The 1997 Topps Stars set was issued in one series totalling 125 cards and was distributed in seven-card packs with a suggested retail price of $3. A checklisted card was added to every fifth pack as an extra card. The set was available exclusively to Home Team Advantage members and features color player photos printed on super-thick, 20-point stock with matte gold foil stamping and a textured matte laminate and spot UV coating. The backs carry another photo of the same player with biographical information and career statistics. Rookie cards include Lance Berkman, Mark Kotsay, Travis Lee and Kerry Wood.

		MINT	NRMT
COMPLETE SET (125)		40.00	18.00
COMMON CARD (1-125)		.30	.14
MINOR STARS		.30	.14
UNLISTED STARS		.60	.25
COMP.MINT SET (125)		800.00	350.00
COMMON MINT (1-125)		2.50	1.10
*ALWAYS MINT STARS: 7.5X TO 15X HI COL.			
*ALWAYS MINT YOUNG STARS: 6X TO 12X HI			
*ALWAYS MINT ROOKIES: 5X TO 10X HI			
ALWAYS MINT STATED ODDS 1:12			

☐ 1	Larry Walker	.60	.25
☐ 2	Tino Martinez	.60	.25
☐ 3	Cal Ripken	2.50	1.10
☐ 4	Ken Griffey Jr.	3.00	1.35

□			
□ 5	Chipper Jones	2.00	.90
□ 6	David Justice	.60	.25
□ 7	Mike Piazza	2.00	.90
□ 8	Jeff Bagwell	1.25	.55
□ 9	Ron Gant	.30	.14
□ 10	Sammy Sosa	.60	.25
□ 11	Tony Gwynn	1.50	.70
□ 12	Carlos Baerga	.15	.07
□ 13	Frank Thomas	2.50	1.10
□ 14	Moises Alou	.30	.14
□ 15	Barry Larkin	.40	.18
□ 16	Ivan Rodriguez	.75	.35
□ 17	Greg Maddux	2.00	.90
□ 18	Jim Edmonds	.40	.18
□ 19	Jose Canseco	.40	.18
□ 20	Rafael Palmeiro	.40	.18
□ 21	Paul Molitor	.60	.25
□ 22	Kevin Appier	.30	.14
□ 23	Raul Mondesi	.40	.18
□ 24	Lance Johnson	.15	.07
□ 25	Edgar Martinez	.40	.18
□ 26	Andres Galarraga	.60	.25
□ 27	Mo Vaughn	.75	.35
□ 28	Ken Caminiti	.40	.18
□ 29	Cecil Fielder	.30	.14
□ 30	Harold Baines	.30	.14
□ 31	Roberto Alomar	.60	.25
□ 32	Shawn Estes	.30	.14
□ 33	Tom Glavine	.30	.14
□ 34	Dennis Eckersley	.30	.14
□ 35	Manny Ramirez	.60	.25
□ 36	John Olerud	.30	.14
□ 37	Juan Gonzalez	1.50	.70
□ 38	Chuck Knoblauch	.60	.25
□ 39	Albert Belle	.75	.35
□ 40	Vinny Castilla	.30	.14
□ 41	John Smoltz	.30	.14
□ 42	Barry Bonds	.75	.35
□ 43	Randy Johnson	.60	.25
□ 44	Brady Anderson	.40	.18
□ 45	Jeff Blauser	.30	.14
□ 46	Craig Biggio	.40	.18
□ 47	Jeff Conine	.30	.14
□ 48	Marquis Grissom	.30	.14
□ 49	Mark Grace	.40	.18
□ 50	Roger Clemens	1.25	.55
□ 51	Mark McGwire	1.25	.55
□ 52	Fred McGriff	.40	.18
□ 53	Gary Sheffield	.60	.25
□ 54	Bobby Jones	.15	.07
□ 55	Eric Young	.15	.07
□ 56	Robin Ventura	.30	.14
□ 57	Wade Boggs	.60	.25
□ 58	Joe Carter	.30	.14
□ 59	Ryne Sandberg	.75	.35
□ 60	Matt Williams	.40	.18
□ 61	Todd Hundley	.30	.14
□ 62	Dante Bichette	.30	.14
□ 63	Chili Davis	.30	.14
□ 64	Kenny Lofton	.75	.35
□ 65	Jay Buhner	.40	.18
□ 66	Will Clark	.40	.18
□ 67	Travis Fryman	.30	.14
□ 68	Pat Hentgen	.30	.14
□ 69	Ellis Burks	.30	.14
□ 70	Mike Mussina	.60	.25
□ 71	Hideo Nomo	1.50	.70
□ 72	Sandy Alomar	.30	.14
□ 73	Bobby Bonilla	.30	.14
□ 74	Rickey Henderson	.40	.18
□ 75	David Cone	.30	.14
□ 76	Terry Steinbach	.15	.07
□ 77	Pedro Martinez	.60	.25
□ 78	Jim Thome	.60	.25
□ 79	Rod Beck	.15	.07
□ 80	Randy Myers	.15	.07
□ 81	Charles Nagy	.30	.14
□ 82	Mark Wohlers	.15	.07
□ 83	Paul O'Neill	.30	.14
□ 84	Curt Schilling	.30	.14
□ 85	Joey Cora	.30	.14
□ 86	John Franco	.30	.14
□ 87	Kevin Brown	.30	.14
□ 88	Benito Santiago	.15	.07
□ 89	Ray Lankford	.30	.14
□ 90	Bernie Williams	.60	.25

□ 91	Jason Dickson	.30	.14
□ 92	Jeff Cirillo	.30	.14
□ 93	Nomar Garciaparra	2.00	.90
□ 94	Mariano Rivera	.30	.14
□ 95	Javy Lopez	.30	.14
□ 96	Tony Womack	.75	.35
□ 97	Jose Rosado	.30	.14
□ 98	Denny Neagle	.30	.14
□ 99	Darryl Kile	.30	.14
□ 100	Justin Thompson	.30	.14
□ 101	Juan Encarnacion	.60	.25
□ 102	Brad Fullmer	.30	.14
□ 103	Kris Benson	1.50	.70
□ 104	Todd Helton	1.00	.45
□ 105	Paul Konerko	1.00	.45
□ 106	Travis Lee	8.00	3.60
□ 107	Todd Greene	.30	.14
□ 108	Mark Kotsay	2.00	.90
□ 109	Carl Pavano	.60	.25
□ 110	Kerry Wood	2.50	1.10
□ 111	Jason Romano	.50	.23
□ 112	Geoff Goetz	.40	.18
□ 113	Scott Hodges	.50	.23
□ 114	Aaron Akin	.40	.18
□ 115	Vernon Wells	2.00	.90
□ 116	Chris Stowe	.40	.18
□ 117	Brett Caradonna	1.00	.45
□ 118	Adam Kennedy	.50	.23
□ 119	Jayson Werth	1.50	.70
□ 120	Glenn Davis	.60	.25
□ 121	Troy Cameron	1.25	.55
□ 122	J.J. Davis	1.50	.70
□ 123	Jason Dellaero	.60	.25
□ 124	Jason Standridge	.50	.23
□ 125	Lance Berkman	3.00	1.35
□ NNO	Checklist	.15	.07

1997 Topps Stars All-Star Memories

Randomly inserted in packs at the rate of one in 24, this 10-card set features color photos printed on laser-cut foilboard of the best performing all-star players.

	MINT	NRMT
COMPLETE SET (10)	80.00	36.00
COMMON CARD (ASM1-ASM10)	2.00	.90
SEMISTARS	3.00	1.35
UNLISTED STARS	5.00	2.20
STATED ODDS 1:24		

□ ASM1	Cal Ripken	20.00	9.00
□ ASM2	Jeff Conine	2.00	.90
□ ASM3	Mike Piazza	15.00	6.75
□ ASM4	Randy Johnson	5.00	2.20
□ ASM5	Ken Griffey Jr.	25.00	11.00
□ ASM6	Fred McGriff	3.00	1.35
□ ASM7	Moises Alou	2.00	.90
□ ASM8	Hideo Nomo	12.00	5.50
□ ASM9	Larry Walker	5.00	2.20
□ ASM10	Sandy Alomar	2.00	.90

1997 Topps Stars Future All-Stars

Randomly inserted in packs at the rate of one in 12, this 15-card set features color photos printed on prismatic rainbow diffraction foilboard of players who are candidates to be next year's all-stars.

□ AS13	Larry Walker	12.00	5.50
□ AS14	Brady Anderson	8.00	3.60
□ AS15	Barry Bonds	15.00	6.75
□ AS16	Ken Griffey Jr.	60.00	27.00
□ AS17	Ray Lankford	5.00	2.20
□ AS18	Paul O'Neill	5.00	2.20
□ AS19	Jeff Blauser	5.00	2.20
□ AS20	Sandy Alomar	5.00	2.20

1997 Topps Stars '97 All-Stars

Randomly inserted in packs at the rate of one in 24, this 20-card set features color photos of players who represented their league in the 1997 All-Star Game in Cleveland and are printed on embossed uniluster.

	MINT	NRMT
COMPLETE SET (20)	300.00	135.00
COMMON CARD (AS1-AS20)	5.00	2.20
SEMISTARS	8.00	3.60
UNLISTED STARS	12.00	5.50
STATED ODDS 1:72		

□ AS1	Greg Maddux	40.00	18.00
□ AS2	Randy Johnson	12.00	5.50
□ AS3	Tino Martinez	12.00	5.50
□ AS4	Jeff Bagwell	25.00	11.00
□ AS5	Ivan Rodriguez	15.00	6.75
□ AS6	Mike Piazza	40.00	18.00
□ AS7	Cal Ripken	50.00	22.00
□ AS8	Ken Caminiti	8.00	3.60
□ AS9	Tony Gwynn	30.00	13.50
□ AS10	Edgar Martinez	8.00	3.60
□ AS11	Craig Biggio	8.00	3.60
□ AS12	Roberto Alomar	12.00	5.50

		MINT	NRMT
COMPLETE SET (15)		60.00	27.00
COMMON CARD (FAS1-FAS15)		1.00	.45
SEMISTARS		2.00	.90
UNLISTED STARS		3.00	1.35
STATED ODDS 1:12			

			MINT	NRMT
☐	FAS1	Derek Jeter	12.00	5.50
☐	FAS2	Andruw Jones	8.00	3.60
☐	FAS3	Vladimir Guerrero	6.00	2.70
☐	FAS4	Scott Rolen	8.00	3.60
☐	FAS5	Jose Guillen	4.00	1.80
☐	FAS6	Jose Cruz Jr.	25.00	11.00
☐	FAS7	Darin Erstad	5.00	2.20
☐	FAS8	Tony Clark	3.00	1.35
☐	FAS9	Scott Spiezio	1.50	.70
☐	FAS10	Kevin Orie	1.50	.70
☐	FAS11	Calvin Reese	1.00	.45
☐	FAS12	Billy Wagner	1.50	.70
☐	FAS13	Matt Morris	1.50	.70
☐	FAS14	Jeremi Gonzalez	1.50	.70
☐	FAS15	Hideki Irabu	2.50	1.10

1997 Topps Stars Rookie Reprints

Randomly inserted in packs at the rate of one in six, this 15-card set features reprints of the rookie cards of 15 top Hall of Famers.

		MINT	NRMT
COMPLETE SET (15)		40.00	18.00
COMMON CARD (1-15)		3.00	1.35
STATED ODDS 1:6			

			MINT	NRMT
☐	1	Luis Aparicio	3.00	1.35
☐	2	Richie Ashburn	3.00	1.35
☐	3	Jim Bunning	3.00	1.35
☐	4	Bob Feller	3.00	1.35
☐	5	Rollie Fingers	3.00	1.35
☐	6	Monte Irvin	3.00	1.35
☐	7	Al Kaline	6.00	2.70
☐	8	Ralph Kiner	3.00	1.35
☐	9	Eddie Mathews	5.00	2.20
☐	10	Hal Newhouser	3.00	1.35
☐	11	Gaylord Perry	3.00	1.35
☐	12	Robin Roberts	3.00	1.35
☐	13	Brooks Robinson	5.00	2.20
☐	14	Enos Slaughter	3.00	1.35
☐	15	Earl Weaver	3.00	1.35

1997 Topps Stars Rookie Reprint Autographs

Randomly inserted in packs at the rate of one in 30, this 14-card set is an autographed parallel version of the regular Topps Stars Rookie Reprint set. The Topps Certified Issue Autograph stamp is printed on

each card. Card No. 2 does not exist.

		MINT	NRMT
COMPLETE SET (14)		350.00	160.00
COMMON CARD (1/3-15)		20.00	9.00
STATED ODDS 1:30			
CARD NO.2 DOES NOT EXIST			

			MINT	NRMT
☐	1	Luis Aparicio	30.00	13.50
☐	3	Jim Bunning	30.00	13.50
☐	4	Bob Feller	25.00	11.00
☐	5	Rollie Fingers	20.00	9.00
☐	6	Monte Irvin	20.00	9.00
☐	7	Al Kaline	50.00	22.00
☐	8	Ralph Kiner	30.00	13.50
☐	9	Eddie Mathews	40.00	18.00
☐	10	Hal Newhouser	20.00	9.00
☐	11	Gaylord Perry	20.00	9.00
☐	12	Robin Roberts	25.00	11.00
☐	13	Brooks Robinson	40.00	18.00
☐	14	Enos Slaughter	25.00	11.00
☐	15	Earl Weaver	25.00	11.00

1998 Topps Stars 'N Steel

The 1998 Topps Stars 'N Steel set was issued in one series totaling 44 cards and was distributed in three-card tri-fold packs with a suggested retail price of $9.99. The fronts feature color action player photos printed using Serillustion technology on .25 gauge metal stock. The backs carry player information.

	MINT	NRMT
COMPLETE SET (44)	150.00	70.00
COMMON CARD (1-44)	1.50	.70
COMP.GOLD SET (44)	800.00	350.00
*GOLD STARS: 2X TO 4X HI COLUMN		
GOLD STATED ODDS 1:12		
COMP.HOLO.SET (44)	2000.00	900.00
*HOLO.STARS: 5X TO 10X HI COLUMN		
HOLOGRAPHIC STATED ODDS 1:40		

		MINT	NRMT
☐ 1	Roberto Alomar	4.00	1.80
☐ 2	Jeff Bagwell	8.00	3.60
☐ 3	Albert Belle	5.00	2.20
☐ 4	Dante Bichette	1.50	.70
☐ 5	Barry Bonds	5.00	2.20
☐ 6	Jay Buhner	2.50	1.10
☐ 7	Ken Caminiti	2.50	1.10
☐ 8	Vinny Castilla	2.00	.90
☐ 9	Roger Clemens	8.00	3.60
☐ 10	Jose Cruz Jr.	12.00	5.50
☐ 11	Andres Galarraga	3.00	1.35
☐ 12	Nomar Garciaparra	10.00	4.50
☐ 13	Juan Gonzalez	10.00	4.50
☐ 14	Mark Grace	2.00	.90
☐ 15	Ken Griffey Jr.	20.00	9.00
☐ 16	Tony Gwynn	10.00	4.50
☐ 17	Todd Hundley	1.50	.70
☐ 18	Derek Jeter	10.00	4.50
☐ 19	Randy Johnson	4.00	1.80
☐ 20	Andruw Jones	6.00	2.70
☐ 21	Chipper Jones	12.00	5.50
☐ 22	David Justice	3.00	1.35
☐ 23	Ray Lankford	2.50	1.10
☐ 24	Barry Larkin	2.50	1.10
☐ 25	Kenny Lofton	5.00	2.20
☐ 26	Greg Maddux	12.00	5.50
☐ 27	Edgar Martinez	2.50	1.10
☐ 28	Tino Martinez	3.00	1.35
☐ 29	Mark McGwire	10.00	4.50
☐ 30	Paul Molitor	4.00	1.80
☐ 31	Rafael Palmeiro	2.50	1.10
☐ 32	Mike Piazza	12.00	5.50
☐ 33	Manny Ramirez	4.00	1.80
☐ 34	Cal Ripken	15.00	6.75
☐ 35	Ivan Rodriguez	5.00	2.20
☐ 36	Scott Rolen	8.00	3.60
☐ 37	Tim Salmon	2.50	1.10
☐ 38	Gary Sheffield	3.00	1.35
☐ 39	Sammy Sosa	3.00	1.35
☐ 40	Frank Thomas	15.00	6.75
☐ 41	Jim Thome	4.00	1.80
☐ 42	Mo Vaughn	5.00	2.20
☐ 43	Larry Walker	4.00	1.80
☐ 44	Bernie Williams	3.00	1.35

1995 UC3

This 147-card standard-size set was issued by Pinnacle Brands. The cards were issued in 16-box cases with 36 packs per box and five cards per pack. The fronts feature a mix of horizontal and vertical designs. The player's photo is shown against a computer generated background. According to Pinnacle, this is the first set issued as an all-3D product. The key Rookie Card in this set is Hideo Nomo.

	MINT	NRMT
COMPLETE SET (147)	20.00	9.00
COMMON CARD (1-147)	.15	.07
MINOR STARS	.30	.14
UNLISTED STARS	.60	.25
SUBSET CARDS HALF VALUE OF BASE CARDS		

COMP.AP SET (147)	800.00	350.00
COMMON ART.PRF. (1-147)	2.50	1.10

*ART.PRF.STARS: 10X TO 25X HI COLUMN
*ART.PRF.YOUNG STARS: 8X TO 20X HI
AP STATED ODDS 1:36 ....

☐ 1 Frank Thomas	2.50	1.10
☐ 2 Wil Cordero	.15	.07
☐ 3 John Olerud	.30	.14
☐ 4 Deion Sanders	.30	.14
☐ 5 Mike Mussina	.60	.25
☐ 6 Mo Vaughn	.75	.35
☐ 7 Will Clark	.40	.18
☐ 8 Chili Davis	.30	.14
☐ 9 Jimmy Key	.30	.14
☐ 10 John Valentin	.15	.07
☐ 11 Tony Tarasco	.15	.07
☐ 12 Alan Trammell	.40	.18
☐ 13 David Cone	.30	.14
☐ 14 Tim Salmon	.60	.25
☐ 15 Danny Tartabull	.15	.07
☐ 16 Aaron Sele	.15	.07
☐ 17 Alex Fernandez	.15	.07
☐ 18 Barry Bonds	.75	.35
☐ 19 Andres Galarraga	.60	.25
☐ 20 Don Mattingly	1.00	.45
☐ 21 Kevin Appier	.30	.14
☐ 22 Paul Molitor	.60	.25
☐ 23 Omar Vizquel	.30	.14
☐ 24 Andy Benes	.30	.14
☐ 25 Rafael Palmeiro	.40	.18
☐ 26 Barry Larkin	.40	.18
☐ 27 Bernie Williams	.60	.25
☐ 28 Gary Sheffield	.60	.25
☐ 29 Wally Joyner	.30	.14
☐ 30 Wade Boggs	.60	.25
☐ 31 Rico Brogna	.15	.07
☐ 32 Ken Caminiti	.40	.18
☐ 33 Kirby Puckett	1.25	.55
☐ 34 Bobby Bonilla	.30	.14
☐ 35 Hal Morris	.15	.07
☐ 36 Moises Alou	.30	.14
☐ 37 Jim Thome	.60	.25
☐ 38 Chuck Knoblauch	.60	.25
☐ 39 Mike Piazza	2.00	.90
☐ 40 Travis Fryman	.30	.14
☐ 41 Rickey Henderson	.40	.18
☐ 42 Jack McDowell	.15	.07
☐ 43 Carlos Baerga	.30	.14
☐ 44 Gregg Jefferies	.15	.07
☐ 45 Kirk Gibson	.30	.14
☐ 46 Bret Saberhagen	.15	.07
☐ 47 Cecil Fielder	.30	.14
☐ 48 Manny Ramirez	.60	.25
☐ 49 Marquis Grissom	.30	.14
☐ 50 Dave Winfield	.40	.18
☐ 51 Mark McGwire	1.25	.55
☐ 52 Dennis Eckersley	.30	.14
☐ 53 Robin Ventura	.30	.14
☐ 54 Ryan Klesko	.40	.18
☐ 55 Jeff Bagwell	1.25	.55
☐ 56 Ozzie Smith	.75	.35
☐ 57 Brian McRae	.15	.07
☐ 58 Albert Belle	.75	.35
☐ 59 Darren Daulton	.30	.14
☐ 60 Jose Canseco	.40	.18
☐ 61 Greg Maddux	2.00	.90
☐ 62 Ben McDonald	.15	.07
☐ 63 Lenny Dykstra	.30	.14
☐ 64 Randy Johnson	.60	.25
☐ 65 Fred McGriff	.40	.18
☐ 66 Ray Lankford	.30	.14
☐ 67 Dave Justice	.60	.25
☐ 68 Paul O'Neill	.30	.14
☐ 69 Tony Gwynn	1.50	.70
☐ 70 Matt Williams	.40	.18
☐ 71 Dante Bichette	.30	.14
☐ 72 Craig Biggio	.40	.18
☐ 73 Ken Griffey Jr.	3.00	1.35
☐ 74 Juan Gonzalez	1.50	.70
☐ 75 Cal Ripken	2.50	1.10
☐ 76 Jay Bell	.15	.07
☐ 77 Joe Carter	.30	.14
☐ 78 Roberto Alomar	.60	.25
☐ 79 Mark Langston	.15	.07
☐ 80 Dave Hollins	.15	.07
☐ 81 Tom Glavine	.30	.14
☐ 82 Ivan Rodriguez	.75	.35
☐ 83 Mark Whiten	.15	.07
☐ 84 Raul Mondesi	.40	.18
☐ 85 Kenny Lofton	.75	.35
☐ 86 Ruben Sierra	.15	.07
☐ 87 Mark Grace	.40	.18
☐ 88 Royce Clayton	.15	.07
☐ 89 Billy Ashley	.15	.07
☐ 90 Larry Walker	.60	.25
☐ 91 Sammy Sosa	.60	.25
☐ 92 Jason Bere	.15	.07
☐ 93 Bob Hamelin	.15	.07
☐ 94 Greg Vaughn	.15	.07
☐ 95 Roger Clemens	1.25	.55
☐ 96 Scott Ruffcorn	.15	.07
☐ 97 Hideo Nomo	3.00	1.35
☐ 98 Michael Tucker	.30	.14
☐ 99 J.R. Phillips	.15	.07
☐ 100 Roberto Petagine	.15	.07
☐ 101 Chipper Jones	2.00	.90
☐ 102 Armando Benitez	.15	.07
☐ 103 Orlando Miller	.15	.07
☐ 104 Carlos Delgado	.30	.14
☐ 105 Jeff Cirillo	.30	.14
☐ 106 Shawn Green	.30	.14
☐ 107 Joe Randa	.15	.07
☐ 108 Vaughn Eshelman	.15	.07
☐ 109 Frank Rodriguez	.15	.07
☐ 110 Russ Davis	.15	.07
☐ 111 Todd Hollandsworth	.30	.14
☐ 112 Mark Grudzielanek	.50	.23
☐ 113 Jose Oliva	.15	.07
☐ 114 Ray Durham	.30	.14
☐ 115 Alex Rodriguez	2.50	1.10
☐ 116 Alex Gonzalez	.15	.07
☐ 117 Midre Cummings	.15	.07
☐ 118 Marty Cordova	.30	.14
☐ 119 John Mabry	.30	.14
☐ 120 Jason Jacome	.15	.07
☐ 121 Joe Vitiello	.15	.07
☐ 122 Charles Johnson	.30	.14
☐ 123 Cal Ripken ID	1.25	.55
☐ 124 Ken Griffey Jr. ID	1.50	.70
☐ 125 Frank Thomas ID	1.25	.55
☐ 126 Mike Piazza ID	1.00	.45
☐ 127 Matt Williams ID	.30	.14
☐ 128 Barry Bonds ID	.40	.18
☐ 129 Greg Maddux ID	1.00	.45
☐ 130 Randy Johnson ID	.30	.14
☐ 131 Albert Belle ID	.60	.25
☐ 132 Will Clark ID	.30	.14
☐ 133 Tony Gwynn ID	.75	.35
☐ 134 Manny Ramirez ID	.30	.14
☐ 135 Raul Mondesi ID	.30	.14
☐ 136 Mo Vaughn ID	.40	.18
☐ 137 Mark McGwire ID	.60	.25
☐ 138 Kirby Puckett ID	.60	.25
☐ 139 Don Mattingly ID	.40	.18
☐ 140 Carlos Baerga ID	.15	.07
☐ 141 Roger Clemens ID	.60	.25
☐ 142 Fred McGriff ID	.30	.14
☐ 143 Kenny Lofton ID	.40	.18
☐ 144 Jeff Bagwell ID	.60	.25
☐ 145 Larry Walker ID	.30	.14
☐ 146 Joe Carter ID	.15	.07
☐ 147 Rafael Palmeiro ID	.30	.14

1995 UC3 Clear Shots

This 12-card standard-size set was inserted approximately one in every 24 packs. The fronts have two photos that alternate when the card is tilted slightly. One photo is a portrait while the other is an action shot. Along with the two photos changing are the words "Clear Shots," and a "UC3 1995" logo which changes with the player's team logo. The backs are opaque, but do have the card number in

the upper left corner with a "CS" prefix.

	MINT	NRMT
COMPLETE SET (12)	60.00	27.00
COMMON PLAYER (CS1-CS12)	1.00	.45
SEMISTARS	2.50	1.10
STATED ODDS 1:24		

☐ CS1 Alex Rodriguez	20.00	9.00
☐ CS2 Shawn Green	1.50	.70
☐ CS3 Hideo Nomo	15.00	6.75
☐ CS4 Charles Johnson	1.50	.70
☐ CS5 Orlando Miller	1.00	.45
☐ CS6 Billy Ashley	1.00	.45
☐ CS7 Carlos Delgado	1.50	.70
☐ CS8 Cliff Floyd	1.00	.45
☐ CS9 Chipper Jones	15.00	6.75
☐ CS10 Alex Gonzalez	1.00	.45
☐ CS11 J.R. Phillips	1.00	.45
☐ CS12 Michael Tucker	1.50	.70
☐ PCS8 Cliff Floyd	2.00	.90
Promo		

1995 UC3 Cyclone Squad

This 20-card standard-size set was inserted approximately one in every four packs. The front features a player photo against a background of two circular objects. The "UC3" logo is in the upper left. The bottom has the words "Cyclone Squad" and the player's name and team. The horizontal backs contain a black and white player photo along with some information. The cards are numbered in the upper left with a "CS" prefix.

	MINT	NRMT
COMPLETE SET (20)	20.00	9.00
COMMON CARD(CS1-CS20)	.50	.23
STATED ODDS 1:4		

☐ CS1 Frank Thomas	3.00	1.35
☐ CS2 Ken Griffey Jr.	4.00	1.80

		MINT	NRMT
☐ CS3	Jeff Bagwell	1.50	.70
☐ CS4	Cal Ripken	3.00	1.35
☐ CS5	Barry Bonds	1.00	.45
☐ CS6	Mike Piazza	2.50	1.10
☐ CS7	Matt Williams	.60	.25
☐ CS8	Kirby Puckett	1.50	.70
☐ CS9	Jose Canseco	.60	.25
☐ CS10	Will Clark	.60	.25
☐ CS11	Don Mattingly	1.25	.55
☐ CS12	Albert Belle	1.00	.45
☐ CS13	Tony Gwynn	2.00	.90
☐ CS14	Raul Mondesi	.60	.25
☐ CS15	Bobby Bonilla	.50	.23
☐ CS16	Rafael Palmeiro	.60	.25
☐ CS17	Fred McGriff	.60	.25
☐ CS18	Tim Salmon	.75	.35
☐ CS19	Kenny Lofton	1.00	.45
☐ CS20	Joe Carter	.50	.23

1995 UC3 In Motion

This 10-card standard-size set was inserted approximately one in every 18 packs. The fronts feature a player photo that compresses into many pieces when the card is tilted slightly. The upper left features the words "In Motion 95" with the UC3 logo in the upper right and the player's name in the lower left. The horizontal back features two color photos along with a short informational blurb. The cards are numbered with an "IM" prefix in the upper right corner.

		MINT	NRMT
COMPLETE SET (10)		40.00	18.00
COMMON CARD(IM1-IM10)		.75	.35
STATED ODDS 1:18			
☐ IM1	Cal Ripken	6.00	2.70
☐ IM2	Ken Griffey Jr.	8.00	3.60
☐ IM3	Frank Thomas	6.00	2.70
☐ IM4	Mike Piazza	5.00	2.20
☐ IM5	Barry Bonds	2.00	.90
☐ IM6	Matt Williams	.75	.35
☐ IM7	Kirby Puckett	3.00	1.35
☐ IM8	Greg Maddux	5.00	2.20
☐ IM9	Don Mattingly	2.50	1.10
☐ IM10	Will Clark	.75	.35

1991 Ultra

This 400-card standard-size set marked Fleer's first entry into the premium card market. The cards were distributed exclusively in foil-wrapped packs. Fleer claimed in their original press release that there would only be 15 percent the amount of Ultra issued as there was of the regular issue. The cards feature full color action photography on the fronts and three full-color photos on the backs. Fleer also issued the sets in their now traditional alphabetical order as well as the teams in alphabetical order. Subsets include Major League Prospects (373-390), Elite Performance (391-396), and Checklists (397-400). The key Rookie Cards in this set are Jeff Conine, Eric Karros and Brian McRae, Denny Neagle and Henry Rodriguez.

		MINT	NRMT
COMPLETE SET (400)		20.00	9.00
COMMON CARD (1-400)		.10	.05
MINOR STARS		.20	.09
UNLISTED STARS		.40	.18
☐ 1	Steve Avery	.10	.05
☐ 2	Jeff Blauser	.10	.05
☐ 3	Francisco Cabrera	.10	.05
☐ 4	Ron Gant	.20	.09
☐ 5	Tom Glavine	.40	.18
☐ 6	Tommy Gregg	.10	.05
☐ 7	Dave Justice	.50	.23
☐ 8	Oddibe McDowell	.10	.05
☐ 9	Greg Olson	.10	.05
☐ 10	Terry Pendleton	.20	.09
☐ 11	Lonnie Smith	.10	.05
☐ 12	John Smoltz	.40	.18
☐ 13	Jeff Treadway	.10	.05
☐ 14	Glenn Davis	.10	.05
☐ 15	Mike Devereaux	.10	.05
☐ 16	Leo Gomez	.10	.05
☐ 17	Chris Hoiles	.10	.05
☐ 18	Dave Johnson	.10	.05
☐ 19	Ben McDonald	.10	.05
☐ 20	Randy Milligan	.10	.05
☐ 21	Gregg Olson	.10	.05
☐ 22	Joe Orsulak	.10	.05
☐ 23	Bill Ripken	.10	.05
☐ 24	Cal Ripken	1.50	.70
☐ 25	David Segui	.20	.09
☐ 26	Craig Worthington	.10	.05
☐ 27	Wade Boggs	.40	.18
☐ 28	Tom Bolton	.10	.05
☐ 29	Tom Brunansky	.10	.05
☐ 30	Ellis Burks	.20	.09
☐ 31	Roger Clemens	.75	.35
☐ 32	Mike Greenwell	.10	.05
☐ 33	Greg A. Harris	.10	.05
☐ 34	Daryl Irvine	.10	.05
☐ 35	Mike Marshall UER	.10	.05
	(1990 in stats is shown as 990)		
☐ 36	Tim Naehring	.10	.09
☐ 37	Tony Pena	.10	.05
☐ 38	Phil Plantier	.10	.05
☐ 39	Carlos Quintana	.10	.05
☐ 40	Jeff Reardon	.20	.09
☐ 41	Jody Reed	.10	.05
☐ 42	Luis Rivera	.10	.05
☐ 43	Jim Abbott	.10	.05
☐ 44	Chuck Finley	.20	.09
☐ 45	Bryan Harvey	.10	.05
☐ 46	Donnie Hill	.10	.05
☐ 47	Jack Howell	.10	.05
☐ 48	Wally Joyner	.20	.09
☐ 49	Mark Langston	.10	.05
☐ 50	Kirk McCaskill	.10	.05
☐ 51	Lance Parrish	.10	.05
☐ 52	Dick Schofield	.10	.05
☐ 53	Lee Stevens	.10	.05
☐ 54	Dave Winfield	.40	.18
☐ 55	George Bell	.10	.05
☐ 56	Damon Berryhill	.10	.05
☐ 57	Mike Bielecki	.10	.05
☐ 58	Andre Dawson	.40	.18
☐ 59	Shawon Dunston	.10	.05
☐ 60	Joe Girardi UER	.20	.09
	(Bats right, LH hitter shown is Doug Dascenzo)		
☐ 61	Mark Grace	.40	.18
☐ 62	Mike Harkey	.10	.05
☐ 63	Les Lancaster	.10	.05
☐ 64	Greg Maddux	1.25	.55
☐ 65	Derrick May	.10	.05
☐ 66	Ryne Sandberg	.50	.23
☐ 67	Luis Salazar	.10	.05
☐ 68	Dwight Smith	.10	.05
☐ 69	Hector Villanueva	.10	.05
☐ 70	Jerome Walton	.10	.05
☐ 71	Mitch Williams	.10	.05
☐ 72	Carlton Fisk	.40	.18
☐ 73	Scott Fletcher	.10	.05
☐ 74	Ozzie Guillen	.10	.05
☐ 75	Greg Hibbard	.10	.05
☐ 76	Lance Johnson	.10	.05
☐ 77	Steve Lyons	.10	.05
☐ 78	Jack McDowell	.10	.05
☐ 79	Dan Pasqua	.10	.05
☐ 80	Melido Perez	.10	.05
☐ 81	Tim Raines	.20	.09
☐ 82	Sammy Sosa	.50	.23
☐ 83	Cory Snyder	.10	.05
☐ 84	Bobby Thigpen	.10	.05
☐ 85	Frank Thomas	3.00	1.35
	(Card says he is an outfielder)		
☐ 86	Robin Ventura	.40	.18
☐ 87	Todd Benzinger	.10	.05
☐ 88	Glenn Braggs	.10	.05
☐ 89	Tom Browning UER	.10	.05
	(Front photo actually Norm Charlton)		
☐ 90	Norm Charlton	.10	.05
☐ 91	Eric Davis	.20	.09
☐ 92	Rob Dibble	.10	.05
☐ 93	Bill Doran	.10	.05
☐ 94	Mariano Duncan UER	.10	.05
	(Right back photo is Billy Hatcher)		
☐ 95	Billy Hatcher	.10	.05
☐ 96	Barry Larkin	.30	.14
☐ 97	Randy Myers	.10	.05
☐ 98	Hal Morris	.10	.05
☐ 99	Joe Oliver	.10	.05
☐ 100	Paul O'Neill	.20	.09
☐ 101	Jeff Reed	.10	.05
	(See also 104)		
☐ 102	Jose Rijo	.10	.05
☐ 103	Chris Sabo	.10	.05
	(See also 106)		
☐ 104	Beau Allred UER	.10	.05
	(Card number is 101)		
☐ 105	Sandy Alomar Jr.	.30	.14
☐ 106	Carlos Baerga UER	.20	.09
	(Card number is 103)		
☐ 107	Albert Belle	.60	.25
☐ 108	Jerry Browne	.10	.05
☐ 109	Tom Candiotti	.10	.05
☐ 110	Alex Cole	.10	.05
☐ 111	John Farrell	.10	.05
	(See also 114)		
☐ 112	Felix Fermin	.10	.05
☐ 113	Brook Jacoby	.10	.05
☐ 114	Chris James UER	.10	.05
	(Card number is 111)		
☐ 115	Doug Jones	.10	.05
☐ 116	Steve Olin	.10	.05

WILL CLARK GIANTS FIRST BASE

	(See also 119)		
☐ 117	Greg Swindell	.10	.05
☐ 118	Turner Ward	.10	.05
☐ 119	Mitch Webster UER	.10	.05
	(Card number is 116)		
☐ 120	Dave Bergman	.10	
☐ 121	Cecil Fielder	.20	.09
☐ 122	Travis Fryman	.40	.18
☐ 123	Mike Henneman	.10	.05
☐ 124	Lloyd Moseby	.10	.05
☐ 125	Dan Petry	.10	.05
☐ 126	Tony Phillips	.10	.05
☐ 127	Mark Salas	.10	.05
☐ 128	Frank Tanana	.10	.05
☐ 129	Alan Trammell	.30	.14
☐ 130	Lou Whitaker	.20	.09
☐ 131	Eric Anthony	.10	.05
☐ 132	Craig Biggio	.40	.18
☐ 133	Ken Caminiti	.40	.18
☐ 134	Casey Candaele	.10	.05
☐ 135	Andujar Cedeno	.10	.05
☐ 136	Mark Davidson	.10	.05
☐ 137	Jim Deshaies	.10	.05
☐ 138	Mark Portugal	.10	.05
☐ 139	Rafael Ramirez	.10	.05
☐ 140	Mike Scott	.10	.05
☐ 141	Eric Yelding	.10	.05
☐ 142	Gerald Young	.10	.05
☐ 143	Kevin Appier	.40	.18
☐ 144	George Brett	.75	.35
☐ 145	Jeff Conine	.50	.23
☐ 146	Jim Eisenreich	.10	.05
☐ 147	Tom Gordon	.10	.05
☐ 148	Mark Gubicza	.10	.05
☐ 149	Bo Jackson	.30	.14
☐ 150	Brent Mayne	.10	.05
☐ 151	Mike Macfarlane	.10	.05
☐ 152	Brian McRae	.40	.18
☐ 153	Jeff Montgomery	.20	.09
☐ 154	Bret Saberhagen	.10	.05
☐ 155	Kevin Seitzer	.10	.05
☐ 156	Terry Shumpert	.10	.05
☐ 157	Kurt Stillwell	.10	.05
☐ 158	Danny Tartabull	.10	.05
☐ 159	Tim Belcher	.10	.05
☐ 160	Kal Daniels	.10	.05
☐ 161	Alfredo Griffin	.10	.05
☐ 162	Lenny Harris	.10	.05
☐ 163	Jay Howell	.10	.05
☐ 164	Ramon Martinez	.20	.09
☐ 165	Mike Morgan	.10	.05
☐ 166	Eddie Murray	.40	.18
☐ 167	Jose Offerman	.10	.05
☐ 168	Juan Samuel	.10	.05
☐ 169	Mike Scioscia	.10	.05
☐ 170	Mike Sharperson	.10	.05
☐ 171	Darryl Strawberry	.20	.09
☐ 172	Greg Brock	.10	.05
☐ 173	Chuck Crim	.10	.05
☐ 174	Jim Gantner	.10	.05
☐ 175	Ted Higuera	.10	.05
☐ 176	Mark Knudson	.10	.05
☐ 177	Tim McIntosh	.10	.05
☐ 178	Paul Molitor	.40	.18
☐ 179	Dan Plesac	.10	.05
☐ 180	Gary Sheffield	.10	.05
☐ 181	Bill Spiers	.10	.05
☐ 182	B.J. Surhoff	.20	.09
☐ 183	Greg Vaughn	.10	.05
☐ 184	Robin Yount	.40	.18
☐ 185	Rick Aguilera	.20	.09
☐ 186	Greg Gagne	.10	.05
☐ 187	Dan Gladden	.10	.05
☐ 188	Brian Harper	.10	.05
☐ 189	Kent Hrbek	.20	.09
☐ 190	Gene Larkin	.10	.05
☐ 191	Shane Mack	.10	.05
☐ 192	Pedro Munoz	.10	.05
☐ 193	Al Newman	.10	.05
☐ 194	Junior Ortiz	.10	.05
☐ 195	Kirby Puckett	.75	.35
☐ 196	Kevin Tapani	.10	.05
☐ 197	Dennis Boyd	.10	.05
☐ 198	Tim Burke	.10	.05
☐ 199	Ivan Calderon	.10	.05
☐ 200	Delino DeShields	.10	.05
☐ 201	Mike Fitzgerald	.10	.05
☐ 202	Steve Frey	.10	.05
☐ 203	Andres Galarraga	.40	.18
☐ 204	Marquis Grissom	.40	.18
☐ 205	Dave Martinez	.10	.05
☐ 206	Dennis Martinez	.20	.09
☐ 207	Junior Noboa	.10	.05
☐ 208	Spike Owen	.10	.05
☐ 209	Scott Ruskin	.10	.05
☐ 210	Tim Wallach	.10	.05
☐ 211	Daryl Boston	.10	.05
☐ 212	Vince Coleman	.10	.05
☐ 213	David Cone	.20	.09
☐ 214	Ron Darling	.10	.05
☐ 215	Kevin Elster	.10	.05
☐ 216	Sid Fernandez	.10	.05
☐ 217	John Franco	.20	.09
☐ 218	Dwight Gooden	.20	.09
☐ 219	Tom Herr	.10	.05
☐ 220	Todd Hundley	.40	.18
☐ 221	Gregg Jefferies	.20	.09
☐ 222	Howard Johnson	.10	.05
☐ 223	Dave Magadan	.10	.05
☐ 224	Kevin McReynolds	.10	.05
☐ 225	Keith Miller	.10	.05
☐ 226	Mackey Sasser	.10	.05
☐ 227	Frank Viola	.10	.05
☐ 228	Jesse Barfield	.10	.05
☐ 229	Greg Cadaret	.10	.05
☐ 230	Alvaro Espinoza	.10	.05
☐ 231	Bob Geren	.10	.05
☐ 232	Lee Guetterman	.10	.05
☐ 233	Mel Hall	.10	.05
☐ 234	Andy Hawkins UER	.10	.05
	(Back center photo is not him)		
☐ 235	Roberto Kelly	.10	.05
☐ 236	Tim Leary	.10	.05
☐ 237	Jim Leyritz	.20	.09
☐ 238	Kevin Maas	.10	.05
☐ 239	Don Mattingly	.60	.25
☐ 240	Hensley Meulens	.10	.05
☐ 241	Eric Plunk	.10	.05
☐ 242	Steve Sax	.10	.05
☐ 243	Todd Burns	.10	.05
☐ 244	Jose Canseco	.30	.14
☐ 245	Dennis Eckersley	.20	.09
☐ 246	Mike Gallego	.10	.05
☐ 247	Dave Henderson	.10	.05
☐ 248	Rickey Henderson	.40	.18
☐ 249	Rick Honeycutt	.10	.05
☐ 250	Carney Lansford	.20	.09
☐ 251	Mark McGwire	.75	.35
☐ 252	Mike Moore	.10	.05
☐ 253	Terry Steinbach	.20	.09
☐ 254	Dave Stewart	.20	.09
☐ 255	Walt Weiss	.10	.05
☐ 256	Bob Welch	.10	.05
☐ 257	Curt Young	.10	.05
☐ 258	Wes Chamberlain	.10	.05
☐ 259	Pat Combs	.10	.05
☐ 260	Darren Daulton	.20	.09
☐ 261	Jose DeJesus	.10	.05
☐ 262	Len Dykstra	.10	.05
☐ 263	Charlie Hayes	.10	.05
☐ 264	Von Hayes	.10	.05
☐ 265	Ken Howell	.10	.05
☐ 266	John Kruk	.10	.05
☐ 267	Roger McDowell	.10	.05
☐ 268	Mickey Morandini	.10	.05
☐ 269	Terry Mulholland	.10	.05
☐ 270	Dale Murphy	.40	.18
☐ 271	Randy Ready	.10	.05
☐ 272	Dickie Thon	.10	.05
☐ 273	Stan Belinda	.10	.05
☐ 274	Jay Bell	.20	.09
☐ 275	Barry Bonds	.50	.23
☐ 276	Bobby Bonilla	.20	.09
☐ 277	Doug Drabek	.10	.05
☐ 278	Carlos Garcia	.10	.05
☐ 279	Neal Heaton	.10	.05
☐ 280	Jeff King	.20	.09
☐ 281	Bill Landrum	.10	.05
☐ 282	Mike LaValliere	.10	.05
☐ 283	Jose Lind	.10	.05
☐ 284	Orlando Merced	.20	.09
☐ 285	Gary Redus	.10	.05
☐ 286	Don Slaught	.10	.05
☐ 287	Andy Van Slyke	.20	.09
☐ 288	Jose DeLeon	.10	.05
☐ 289	Pedro Guerrero	.10	.05
☐ 290	Ray Lankford	.40	.18
☐ 291	Joe Magrane	.10	.05
☐ 292	Jose Oquendo	.10	.05
☐ 293	Tom Pagnozzi	.10	.05
☐ 294	Bryn Smith	.10	.05
☐ 295	Lee Smith	.20	.09
☐ 296	Ozzie Smith UER	.50	.23
	(Born 12-26, 54, should have hyphen)		
☐ 297	Milt Thompson	.10	.05
☐ 298	Craig Wilson	.10	.05
☐ 299	Todd Zeile	.20	.09
☐ 300	Shawn Abner	.10	.05
☐ 301	Andy Benes	.20	.09
☐ 302	Paul Faries	.10	.05
☐ 303	Tony Gwynn	1.00	.45
☐ 304	Greg W. Harris	.10	.05
☐ 305	Thomas Howard	.10	.05
☐ 306	Bruce Hurst	.10	.05
☐ 307	Craig Lefferts	.10	.05
☐ 308	Fred McGriff	.40	.18
☐ 309	Dennis Rasmussen	.10	.05
☐ 310	Bip Roberts	.10	.05
☐ 311	Benito Santiago	.10	.05
☐ 312	Garry Templeton	.10	.05
☐ 313	Ed Whitson	.10	.05
☐ 314	Dave Anderson	.10	.05
☐ 315	Kevin Bass	.10	.05
☐ 316	Jeff Brantley	.10	.05
☐ 317	John Burkett	.10	.05
☐ 318	Will Clark	.40	.18
☐ 319	Steve Decker	.10	.05
☐ 320	Scott Garrelts	.10	.05
☐ 321	Terry Kennedy	.10	.05
☐ 322	Mark Leonard	.10	.05
☐ 323	Darren Lewis	.10	.05
☐ 324	Greg Litton	.10	.05
☐ 325	Willie McGee	.10	.05
☐ 326	Kevin Mitchell	.20	.09
☐ 327	Don Robinson	.10	.05
☐ 328	Andres Santana	.10	.05
☐ 329	Robby Thompson	.10	.05
☐ 330	Jose Uribe	.10	.05
☐ 331	Matt Williams	.40	.18
☐ 332	Scott Bradley	.10	.05
☐ 333	Henry Cotto	.10	.05
☐ 334	Alvin Davis	.10	.05
☐ 335	Ken Griffey Sr.	.10	.05
☐ 336	Ken Griffey Jr.	3.00	1.35
☐ 337	Erik Hanson	.10	.05
☐ 338	Brian Holman	.10	.05
☐ 339	Randy Johnson	.50	.23
☐ 340	Edgar Martinez UER	.40	.18
	(Listed as playing SS)		
☐ 341	Tino Martinez	.40	.18
☐ 342	Pete O'Brien	.10	.05
☐ 343	Harold Reynolds	.10	.05
☐ 344	Dave Valle	.10	.05
☐ 345	Omar Vizquel	.40	.18
☐ 346	Brad Arnsberg	.10	.05
☐ 347	Kevin Brown	.20	.09
☐ 348	Julio Franco	.10	.05
☐ 349	Jeff Huson	.10	.05
☐ 350	Rafael Palmeiro	.40	.18
☐ 351	Geno Petralli	.10	.05
☐ 352	Gary Pettis	.10	.05
☐ 353	Kenny Rogers	.10	.05
☐ 354	Jeff Russell	.10	.05
☐ 355	Nolan Ryan	1.50	.70
☐ 356	Ruben Sierra	.40	.18
☐ 357	Bobby Witt	.10	.05
☐ 358	Roberto Alomar	.40	.18
☐ 359	Pat Borders	.10	.05
☐ 360	Joe Carter UER	.20	.09
	(Reverse negative on back photo)		
☐ 361	Kelly Gruber	.10	.05
☐ 362	Tom Henke	.10	.05
☐ 363	Glenallen Hill	.10	.05
☐ 364	Jimmy Key	.10	.05
☐ 365	Manny Lee	.10	.05

			MINT	NRMT
☐ 366	Rance Mulliniks	.10		.05
☐ 367	John Olerud UER	.20		.09
	(Throwing left on card; back has throws right; he does throw lefty)			
☐ 368	Dave Stieb	.10		.05
☐ 369	Duane Ward	.10		.05
☐ 370	David Wells	.10		.05
☐ 371	Mark Whiten	.10		.05
☐ 372	Mookie Wilson	.20		.09
☐ 373	Willie Banks MLP	.10		.05
☐ 374	Steve Carter MLP	.10		.05
☐ 375	Scott Chiamparino MLP	.10		.05
☐ 376	Steve Chitren MLP	.10		.05
☐ 377	Darrin Fletcher MLP	.10		.05
☐ 378	Rich Garces MLP	.10		.05
☐ 379	Reggie Jefferson MLP	.30		.14
☐ 380	Eric Karros MLP	.75		.35
☐ 381	Pat Kelly MLP	.10		.05
☐ 382	Chuck Knoblauch MLP	.75		.35
☐ 383	Denny Neagle MLP	1.25		.55
☐ 384	Dan Opperman MLP	.10		.05
☐ 385	John Ramos MLP	.10		.05
☐ 386	Henry Rodriguez MLP	.60		.25
☐ 387	Mo Vaughn MLP	.75		.35
☐ 388	Gerald Williams MLP	.10		.05
☐ 389	Mike York MLP	.10		.05
☐ 390	Eddie Zosky MLP	1.00		.45
☐ 391	Barry Bonds EP	.40		.18
☐ 392	Cecil Fielder EP	.20		.09
☐ 393	Rickey Henderson EP	.20		.09
☐ 394	Dave Justice EP	.20		.09
☐ 395	Nolan Ryan EP	.75		.35
☐ 396	Bobby Thigpen EP	.10		.05
☐ 397	Gregg Jefferies CL	.10		.05
☐ 398	Von Hayes CL	.10		.05
☐ 399	Terry Kennedy CL	.10		.05
☐ 400	Nolan Ryan CL	.40		.18

1991 Ultra Gold

This ten-card standard-size set presents Fleer's 1991 Ultra Team. These cards were randomly inserted into Ultra packs. On a gold background that fades as one moves toward the bottom of the card, the front design has a color head shot, with two cut-out action shots below. Player information is given in a dark blue strip at the bottom of the card face. In blue print on white background with gold borders, the back highlights the player's outstanding achievements. The set is sequenced in alphabetical order.

		MINT	NRMT
	COMPLETE SET (10)	10.00	4.50
	COMMON CARD (1-10)	.25	.11
	RANDOM INSERTS IN FOIL PACKS		
☐ 1	Barry Bonds	1.00	.45
☐ 2	Will Clark	.75	.35

			MINT	NRMT
☐ 3	Doug Drabek	.25		.11
☐ 4	Ken Griffey Jr.	6.00		2.70
☐ 5	Rickey Henderson	.75		.35
☐ 6	Bo Jackson	.60		.25
☐ 7	Ramon Martinez	.40		.18
☐ 8	Kirby Puckett UER	1.50		.70
	(Boggs won 1988 batting title, so Puckett didn't win consecutive titles)			
☐ 9	Chris Sabo	.25		.11
☐ 10	Ryne Sandberg UER	1.00		.45
	(Johnson and Hornsby didn't hit 40 homers in 1990, Fielder did hit 51 in '90)			

1991 Ultra Update

JUAN GUZMAN BLUE JAYS PITCHER

The 120-card set was distributed exclusively in factory set form along with 20 team logo stickers through hobby dealers. The set includes the year's hottest rookies and important veteran players traded after the original Ultra series was produced. Card design is identical to regular issue 1991 cards except for the U-prefixed numbering on back. Cards are ordered alphabetically within and according to teams for each league. Rookie Cards in this set include Jeff Bagwell, Juan Guzman, Mike Mussina, and Ivan Rodriguez.

		MINT	NRMT
	COMP.FACT.SET (120)	30.00	13.50
	COMMON CARD (1-120)	.25	.23
	MINOR STARS	.50	.23
	UNLISTED STARS	1.00	.45
☐ 1	Dwight Evans	.50	.11
☐ 2	Chito Martinez	.25	.11
☐ 3	Bob Melvin	.25	.11
☐ 4	Mike Mussina	6.00	2.70
☐ 5	Jack Clark	.50	.23
☐ 6	Dana Kiecker	.25	.11
☐ 7	Steve Lyons	.25	.11
☐ 8	Gary Gaetti	.25	.11
☐ 9	Dave Gallagher	.25	.11
☐ 10	Dave Parker	.50	.23
☐ 11	Luis Polonia	.25	.11
☐ 12	Luis Sojo	.25	.11
☐ 13	Wilson Alvarez	1.00	.45
☐ 14	Alex Fernandez	2.00	.90
☐ 15	Craig Grebeck	.25	.11
☐ 16	Ron Karkovice	.25	.11
☐ 17	Warren Newson	.25	.11
☐ 18	Scott Radinsky	.25	.11
☐ 19	Glenallen Hill	.25	.11
☐ 20	Charles Nagy	1.00	.45
☐ 21	Mark Whiten	.25	.11
☐ 22	Milt Cuyler	.25	.11
☐ 23	Paul Gibson	.25	.11

			MINT	NRMT
☐ 24	Mickey Tettleton	.50		.23
☐ 25	Todd Benzinger	.25		.11
☐ 26	Storm Davis	.25		.11
☐ 27	Kirk Gibson	.50		.23
☐ 28	Bill Pecota	.25		.11
☐ 29	Gary Thurman	.25		.11
☐ 30	Darryl Hamilton	.25		.11
☐ 31	Jaime Navarro	.25		.11
☐ 32	Willie Randolph	.50		.23
☐ 33	Bill Wegman	.25		.11
☐ 34	Randy Bush	.25		.11
☐ 35	Chili Davis	.50		.23
☐ 36	Scott Erickson	1.25		.55
☐ 37	Chuck Knoblauch	4.00		1.80
☐ 38	Scott Leius	.25		.11
☐ 39	Jack Morris	.50		.23
☐ 40	John Habyan	.25		.11
☐ 41	Pat Kelly	.25		.11
☐ 42	Matt Nokes	.25		.11
☐ 43	Scott Sanderson	.25		.11
☐ 44	Bernie Williams	4.00		1.80
☐ 45	Harold Baines	.50		.23
☐ 46	Brook Jacoby	.25		.11
☐ 47	Earnest Riles	.25		.11
☐ 48	Willie Wilson	.25		.11
☐ 49	Jay Buhner	1.00		.45
☐ 50	Rich DeLucia	.25		.11
☐ 51	Mike Jackson	.25		.11
☐ 52	Bill Krueger	.25		.11
☐ 53	Bill Swift	.25		.11
☐ 54	Brian Downing	.25		.11
☐ 55	Juan Gonzalez	15.00		6.75
☐ 56	Dean Palmer	1.25		.55
☐ 57	Kevin Reimer	.25		.11
☐ 58	Ivan Rodriguez	8.00		3.60
☐ 59	Tom Candiotti	.25		.11
☐ 60	Juan Guzman	.75		.35
☐ 61	Bob MacDonald	.25		.11
☐ 62	Greg Myers	.25		.11
☐ 63	Ed Sprague	.25		.11
☐ 64	Devon White	.25		.11
☐ 65	Rafael Belliard	.25		.11
☐ 66	Juan Berenguer	.25		.11
☐ 67	Brian R. Hunter	.25		.11
☐ 68	Kent Mercker	.25		.11
☐ 69	Otis Nixon	.50		.23
☐ 70	Danny Jackson	.25		.11
☐ 71	Chuck McElroy	.25		.11
☐ 72	Gary Scott	.25		.11
☐ 73	Heathcliff Slocumb	1.00		.45
☐ 74	Chico Walker	.25		.11
☐ 75	Rick Wilkins	.25		.11
☐ 76	Chris Hammond	.25		.11
☐ 77	Luis Quinones	.25		.11
☐ 78	Herm Winningham	.25		.11
☐ 79	Jeff Bagwell	15.00		6.75
☐ 80	Jim Corsi	.25		.11
☐ 81	Steve Finley	1.00		.45
☐ 82	Luis Gonzalez	1.00		.45
☐ 83	Pete Harnisch	.25		.11
☐ 84	Darryl Kile	2.00		.90
☐ 85	Brett Butler	.50		.23
☐ 86	Gary Carter	1.00		.45
☐ 87	Tim Crews	.25		.11
☐ 88	Orel Hershiser	.50		.23
☐ 89	Bob Ojeda	.25		.11
☐ 90	Bret Barbene	.25		.11
☐ 91	Barry Jones	.25		.11
☐ 92	Gilberto Reyes	.25		.11
☐ 93	Larry Walker	2.00		.90
☐ 94	Hubie Brooks	.25		.11
☐ 95	Tim Burke	.25		.11
☐ 96	Rick Cerone	.25		.11
☐ 97	Jeff Innis	.25		.11
☐ 98	Wally Backman	.25		.11
☐ 99	Tommy Greene	.25		.11
☐ 100	Ricky Jordan	.25		.11
☐ 101	Mitch Williams	.25		.11
☐ 102	John Smiley	.25		.11
☐ 103	Randy Tomlin	.25		.11
☐ 104	Gary Varsho	.25		.11
☐ 105	Cris Carpenter	.25		.11
☐ 106	Ken Hill	.50		.23
☐ 107	Felix Jose	.25		.11
☐ 108	Omar Olivares	.25		.11
☐ 109	Gerald Perry	.25		.11

□ 110 Jerald Clark	.25	.11
□ 111 Tony Fernandez	.25	.11
□ 112 Darrin Jackson	.25	.11
□ 113 Mike Maddux	.25	.11
□ 114 Tim Teufel	.25	.11
□ 115 Bud Black	.25	.11
□ 116 Kelly Downs	.25	.11
□ 117 Mike Felder	.25	.11
□ 118 Willie McGee	.25	.11
□ 119 Trevor Wilson	.25	.11
□ 120 Checklist 1-120	.25	.11

1992 Ultra

BRIAN McRAE
KANSAS CITY ROYALS • OUTFIELD

Consisting of 600 standard-size cards, the 1992 Fleer Ultra set was issued in two series of 300 cards each. Cards were distributed exclusively in foil packs. The glossy color action player photos on the fronts are full-bleed against a green marbleized border. The player's name and team appear on the marble-colored area in bars that are color-coded by team. The cards are numbered on the back and ordered below alphabetically within and according to teams for each league with AL preceding NL. There are no notable Rookie Cards in the set. Some cards have been found without the word Fleer on the front.

	MINT	NRMT
COMPLETE SET (600)	30.00	13.50
COMPLETE SERIES 1 (300)	20.00	9.00
COMPLETE SERIES 2 (300)	10.00	4.50
COMMON CARD (1-600)	.10	.05
MINOR STARS	.20	.09
UNLISTED STARS	.40	.18
COMP.GWYNN SET (10)	10.00	4.50
COMMON GWYNN (1-10)	1.00	.45
CERTIFIED GWYNN AUTO	175.00	80.00
GWYNN STATED AUTO ODDS 1:17,000		
COMMON GWYNN MAIL (S1-S2) 1.00		.45
GWYNN MAIL-IN AVAIL.VIA WRAPPER EXCH.		

□ 1 Glenn Davis	.10	.05
□ 2 Mike Devereaux	.10	.05
□ 3 Dwight Evans	.20	.09
□ 4 Leo Gomez	.10	.05
□ 5 Chris Hoiles	.10	.05
□ 6 Sam Horn	.10	.05
□ 7 Chito Martinez	.10	.05
□ 8 Randy Milligan	.10	.05
□ 9 Mike Mussina	.60	.25
□ 10 Billy Ripken	.10	.05
□ 11 Cal Ripken	1.50	.70
□ 12 Tom Brunansky	.10	.05
□ 13 Ellis Burks	.20	.09
□ 14 Jack Clark	.20	.09
□ 15 Roger Clemens	.75	.35
□ 16 Mike Greenwell	.10	.05

□ 17 Joe Hesketh	.10	.05
□ 18 Tony Pena	.10	.05
□ 19 Carlos Quintana	.10	.05
□ 20 Jeff Reardon	.20	.09
□ 21 Jody Reed	.10	.05
□ 22 Luis Rivera	.10	.05
□ 23 Mo Vaughn	.60	.25
□ 24 Gary DiSarcina	.10	.05
□ 25 Chuck Finley	.10	.05
□ 26 Gary Gaetti	.10	.05
□ 27 Bryan Harvey	.10	.05
□ 28 Lance Parrish	.10	.05
□ 29 Luis Polonia	.10	.05
□ 30 Dick Schofield	.10	.05
□ 31 Luis Sojo	.10	.05
□ 32 Wilson Alvarez	.20	.09
□ 33 Carlton Fisk	.40	.18
□ 34 Craig Grebeck	.10	.05
□ 35 Ozzie Guillen	.10	.05
□ 36 Greg Hibbard	.10	.05
□ 37 Charlie Hough	.10	.05
□ 38 Lance Johnson	.10	.05
□ 39 Ron Karkovice	.10	.05
□ 40 Jack McDowell	.10	.05
□ 41 Donn Pall	.10	.05
□ 42 Melido Perez	.10	.05
□ 43 Tim Raines	.20	.09
□ 44 Frank Thomas	2.00	.90
□ 45 Sandy Alomar Jr.	.20	.09
□ 46 Carlos Baerga	.10	.05
□ 47 Albert Belle	.50	.23
□ 48 Jerry Browne UER	.10	.05
(Reversed negative on card back)		
□ 49 Felix Fermin	.10	.05
□ 50 Reggie Jefferson UER	.20	.09
(Born 1968, not 1966)		
□ 51 Mark Lewis	.10	.05
□ 52 Carlos Martinez	.10	.05
□ 53 Steve Olin	.10	.05
□ 54 Jim Thome	1.25	.55
□ 55 Mark Whiten	.10	.05
□ 56 Dave Bergman	.10	.05
□ 57 Milt Cuyler	.10	.05
□ 58 Rob Deer	.10	.05
□ 59 Cecil Fielder	.20	.09
□ 60 Travis Fryman	.20	.09
□ 61 Scott Livingstone	.10	.05
□ 62 Tony Phillips	.10	.05
□ 63 Mickey Tettleton	.10	.05
□ 64 Alan Trammell	.30	.14
□ 65 Lou Whitaker	.20	.09
□ 66 Kevin Appier	.20	.09
□ 67 Mike Boddicker	.10	.05
□ 68 George Brett	.75	.35
□ 69 Jim Eisenreich	.10	.05
□ 70 Mark Gubicza	.10	.05
□ 71 David Howard	.10	.05
□ 72 Joel Johnson	.10	.05
□ 73 Mike Macfarlane	.10	.05
□ 74 Brent Mayne	.10	.05
□ 75 Brian McRae	.10	.05
□ 76 Jeff Montgomery	.10	.05
□ 77 Danny Tartabull	.20	.09
□ 78 Don August	.10	.05
□ 79 Dante Bichette	.30	.14
□ 80 Ted Higuera	.10	.05
□ 81 Paul Molitor	.40	.18
□ 82 Jaime Navarro	.10	.05
□ 83 Gary Sheffield	.40	.18
□ 84 Bill Spiers	.10	.05
□ 85 B.J. Surhoff	.10	.05
□ 86 Greg Vaughn	.10	.05
□ 87 Robin Yount	.30	.14
□ 88 Rick Aguilera	.10	.05
□ 89 Chili Davis	.20	.09
□ 90 Scott Erickson	.20	.09
□ 91 Brian Harper	.10	.05
□ 92 Kent Hrbek	.20	.09
□ 93 Chuck Knoblauch	.40	.18
□ 94 Scott Leius	.10	.05
□ 95 Shane Mack	.10	.05
□ 96 Mike Pagliarulo	.10	.05
□ 97 Kirby Puckett	.75	.35
□ 98 Kevin Tapani	.10	.05
□ 99 Jesse Barfield	.10	.05

□ 100 Alvaro Espinoza	.10	.05
□ 101 Mel Hall	.10	.05
□ 102 Pat Kelly	.10	.05
□ 103 Roberto Kelly	.10	.05
□ 104 Kevin Maas	.10	.05
□ 105 Don Mattingly	.60	.25
□ 106 Hensley Meulens	.10	.05
□ 107 Matt Nokes	.10	.05
□ 108 Steve Sax	.10	.05
□ 109 Harold Baines	.20	.09
□ 110 Jose Canseco	.30	.14
□ 111 Ron Darling	.10	.05
□ 112 Mike Gallego	.10	.05
□ 113 Dave Henderson	.10	.05
□ 114 Rickey Henderson	.30	.14
□ 115 Mark McGwire	.75	.35
□ 116 Terry Steinbach	.20	.09
□ 117 Dave Stewart	.20	.09
□ 118 Todd Van Poppel	.10	.05
□ 119 Bob Welch	.10	.05
□ 120 Greg Briley	.10	.05
□ 121 Jay Buhner	.30	.14
□ 122 Rick DeLucia	.10	.05
□ 123 Ken Griffey Jr.	2.50	1.10
□ 124 Erik Hanson	.10	.05
□ 125 Randy Johnson	.40	.18
□ 126 Edgar Martinez	.30	.14
□ 127 Tino Martinez	.40	.18
□ 128 Pete O'Brien	.10	.05
□ 129 Harold Reynolds	.10	.05
□ 130 Dave Valle	.10	.05
□ 131 Julio Franco	.10	.05
□ 132 Juan Gonzalez	1.25	.55
□ 133 Jeff Huson	.20	.09
(Shows Jose Canseco sliding into second)		
□ 134 Mike Jeffcoat	.10	.05
□ 135 Terry Mathews	.10	.05
□ 136 Rafael Palmeiro	.30	.14
□ 137 Dean Palmer	.20	.09
□ 138 Geno Petralli	.10	.05
□ 139 Ivan Rodriguez	.75	.35
□ 140 Jeff Russell	.10	.05
□ 141 Nolan Ryan	1.50	.70
□ 142 Ruben Sierra	.10	.05
□ 143 Roberto Alomar	.40	.18
□ 144 Pat Borders	.10	.05
□ 145 Joe Carter	.20	.09
□ 146 Kelly Gruber	.10	.05
□ 147 Jimmy Key	.10	.05
□ 148 Manny Lee	.10	.05
□ 149 Rance Mullinicks	.10	.05
□ 150 Greg Myers	.10	.05
□ 151 John Olerud	.20	.09
□ 152 Dave Stieb	.10	.05
□ 153 Todd Stottlemyre	.10	.05
□ 154 Duane Ward	.10	.05
□ 155 Devon White	.10	.05
□ 156 Eddie Zosky	.10	.05
□ 157 Steve Avery	.10	.05
□ 158 Rafael Belliard	.10	.05
□ 159 Jeff Blauser	.10	.05
□ 160 Sid Bream	.10	.05
□ 161 Ron Gant	.20	.09
□ 162 Tom Glavine	.30	.14
□ 163 Brian Hunter	.10	.05
□ 164 Dave Justice	.40	.18
□ 165 Mark Lemke	.10	.05
□ 166 Greg Olson	.10	.05
□ 167 Terry Pendleton	.20	.09
□ 168 Lonnie Smith	.10	.05
□ 169 John Smoltz	.30	.14
□ 170 Mike Stanton	.10	.05
□ 171 Jeff Treadway	.10	.05
□ 172 Paul Assenmacher	.10	.05
□ 173 George Bell	.10	.05
□ 174 Shawon Dunston	.10	.05
□ 175 Mark Grace	.30	.14
□ 176 Danny Jackson	.10	.05
□ 177 Les Lancaster	.10	.05
□ 178 Greg Maddux	1.25	.55
□ 179 Luis Salazar	.10	.05
□ 180 Rey Sanchez	.10	.05
□ 181 Ryne Sandberg	.50	.23
□ 182 Jose Vizcaino	.10	.05
□ 183 Chico Walker	.10	.05

☐ 184	Jerome Walton	.10	.05
☐ 185	Glenn Braggs	.10	.05
☐ 186	Tom Browning	.10	.05
☐ 187	Rob Dibble	.10	.05
☐ 188	Bill Doran	.10	.05
☐ 189	Chris Hammond	.10	.05
☐ 190	Billy Hatcher	.10	.05
☐ 191	Barry Larkin	.30	.14
☐ 192	Hal Morris	.10	.05
☐ 193	Joe Oliver	.10	.05
☐ 194	Paul O'Neill	.20	.09
☐ 195	Jeff Reed	.10	.05
☐ 196	Jose Rijo	.10	.05
☐ 197	Chris Sabo	.10	.05
☐ 198	Jeff Bagwell	1.25	.55
☐ 199	Craig Biggio	.30	.14
☐ 200	Ken Caminiti	.30	.14
☐ 201	Andujar Cedeno	.20	.09
☐ 202	Steve Finley	.20	.09
☐ 203	Luis Gonzalez	.10	.05
☐ 204	Pete Harnisch	.10	.05
☐ 205	Xavier Hernandez	.10	.05
☐ 206	Darryl Kile	.20	.09
☐ 207	Al Osuna	.10	.05
☐ 208	Curt Schilling	.30	.14
☐ 209	Brett Butler	.20	.09
☐ 210	Kal Daniels	.10	.05
☐ 211	Lenny Harris	.10	.05
☐ 212	Stan Javier	.10	.05
☐ 213	Ramon Martinez	.20	.09
☐ 214	Roger McDowell	.10	.05
☐ 215	Jose Offerman	.10	.05
☐ 216	Juan Samuel	.10	.05
☐ 217	Mike Scioscia	.10	.05
☐ 218	Mike Sharperson	.10	.05
☐ 219	Darryl Strawberry	.20	.09
☐ 220	Delino DeShields	.10	.05
☐ 221	Tom Foley	.10	.05
☐ 222	Steve Frey	.10	.05
☐ 223	Dennis Martinez	.20	.09
☐ 224	Spike Owen	.10	.05
☐ 225	Gilberto Reyes	.10	.05
☐ 226	Tim Wallach	.10	.05
☐ 227	Daryl Boston	.10	.05
☐ 228	Tim Burke	.10	.05
☐ 229	Vince Coleman	.10	.05
☐ 230	David Cone	.20	.09
☐ 231	Kevin Elster	.10	.05
☐ 232	Dwight Gooden	.20	.09
☐ 233	Todd Hundley	.30	.14
☐ 234	Jeff Innis	.10	.05
☐ 235	Howard Johnson	.10	.05
☐ 236	Dave Magadan	.10	.05
☐ 237	Mackey Sasser	.10	.05
☐ 238	Anthony Young	.10	.05
☐ 239	Wes Chamberlain	.10	.05
☐ 240	Darren Daulton	.20	.09
☐ 241	Len Dykstra	.20	.09
☐ 242	Tommy Greene	.10	.05
☐ 243	Charlie Hayes	.10	.05
☐ 244	Dave Hollins	.10	.05
☐ 245	Ricky Jordan	.10	.05
☐ 246	John Kruk	.20	.09
☐ 247	Mickey Morandini	.10	.05
☐ 248	Terry Mulholland	.10	.05
☐ 249	Dale Murphy	.40	.18
☐ 250	Jay Bell	.20	.09
☐ 251	Barry Bonds	.50	.23
☐ 252	Steve Buechele	.10	.05
☐ 253	Doug Drabek	.10	.05
☐ 254	Mike LaValliere	.10	.05
☐ 255	Jose Lind	.10	.05
☐ 256	Lloyd McClendon	.10	.05
☐ 257	Orlando Merced	.10	.05
☐ 258	Don Slaught	.10	.05
☐ 259	John Smiley	.10	.05
☐ 260	Zane Smith	.10	.05
☐ 261	Randy Tomlin	.10	.05
☐ 262	Andy Van Slyke	.20	.09
☐ 263	Pedro Guerrero	.10	.05
☐ 264	Felix Jose	.10	.05
☐ 265	Ray Lankford	.30	.14
☐ 266	Omar Olivares	.10	.05
☐ 267	Jose Oquendo	.10	.05
☐ 268	Tom Pagnozzi	.10	.05
☐ 269	Bryn Smith	.10	.05
☐ 270	Lee Smith UER (1991 record listed as 61-61)	.20	.09
☐ 271	Ozzie Smith UER (Comma before year of birth on card back)	.50	.23
☐ 272	Milt Thompson	.10	.05
☐ 273	Todd Zeile	.10	.05
☐ 274	Andy Benes	.20	.09
☐ 275	Jerald Clark	.10	.05
☐ 276	Tony Fernandez	.10	.05
☐ 277	Tony Gwynn	1.00	.45
☐ 278	Greg W. Harris	.10	.05
☐ 279	Thomas Howard	.10	.05
☐ 280	Bruce Hurst	.10	.05
☐ 281	Mike Maddux	.10	.05
☐ 282	Fred McGriff	.30	.14
☐ 283	Benito Santiago	.10	.05
☐ 284	Kevin Bass	.10	.05
☐ 285	Jeff Brantley	.10	.05
☐ 286	John Burkett	.10	.05
☐ 287	Will Clark	.30	.14
☐ 288	Royce Clayton	.10	.05
☐ 289	Steve Decker	.10	.05
☐ 290	Kelly Downs	.10	.05
☐ 291	Mike Felder	.10	.05
☐ 292	Darren Lewis	.10	.05
☐ 293	Kirt Manwaring	.10	.05
☐ 294	Willie McGee	.10	.05
☐ 295	Robby Thompson	.10	.05
☐ 296	Matt Williams	.30	.14
☐ 297	Trevor Wilson	.10	.05
☐ 298	Checklist 1-100	.10	.05
☐ 299	Checklist 101-200	.10	.05
☐ 300	Checklist 201-300	.10	.05
☐ 301	Brady Anderson	.30	.14
☐ 302	Todd Frohwirth	.10	.05
☐ 303	Ben McDonald	.10	.05
☐ 304	Mark McLemore	.10	.05
☐ 305	Jose Mesa	.10	.05
☐ 306	Bob Milacki	.10	.05
☐ 307	Gregg Olson	.10	.05
☐ 308	David Segui	.10	.05
☐ 309	Rick Sutcliffe	.10	.05
☐ 310	Jeff Tackett	.10	.05
☐ 311	Wade Boggs	.40	.18
☐ 312	Scott Cooper	.10	.05
☐ 313	John Flaherty	.10	.05
☐ 314	Wayne Housie	.10	.05
☐ 315	Peter Hoy	.10	.05
☐ 316	John Marzano	.10	.05
☐ 317	Tim Naehring	.20	.09
☐ 318	Phil Plantier	.10	.05
☐ 319	Frank Viola	.10	.05
☐ 320	Matt Young	.10	.05
☐ 321	Jim Abbott	.10	.05
☐ 322	Hubie Brooks	.10	.05
☐ 323	Chad Curtis	.40	.18
☐ 324	Alvin Davis	.10	.05
☐ 325	Junior Felix	.10	.05
☐ 326	Von Hayes	.10	.05
☐ 327	Mark Langston	.10	.05
☐ 328	Scott Lewis	.10	.05
☐ 329	Don Robinson	.10	.05
☐ 330	Bobby Rose	.10	.05
☐ 331	Lee Stevens	.10	.05
☐ 332	George Bell	.10	.05
☐ 333	Esteban Beltre	.10	.05
☐ 334	Joey Cora	.20	.09
☐ 335	Alex Fernandez	.20	.09
☐ 336	Roberto Hernandez	.40	.18
☐ 337	Mike Huff	.10	.05
☐ 338	Kirk McCaskill	.10	.05
☐ 339	Dan Pasqua	.10	.05
☐ 340	Scott Radinsky	.10	.05
☐ 341	Steve Sax	.10	.05
☐ 342	Bobby Thigpen	.10	.05
☐ 343	Robin Ventura	.20	.09
☐ 344	Jack Armstrong	.10	.05
☐ 345	Alex Cole	.10	.05
☐ 346	Dennis Cook	.10	.05
☐ 347	Glenallen Hill	.10	.05
☐ 348	Thomas Howard	.10	.05
☐ 349	Brook Jacoby	.10	.05
☐ 350	Kenny Lofton	1.50	.70
☐ 351	Charles Nagy	.20	.09
☐ 352	Rod Nichols	.10	.05
☐ 353	Junior Ortiz	.10	.05
☐ 354	Dave Otto	.10	.05
☐ 355	Tony Perezchica	.10	.05
☐ 356	Scott Scudder	.10	.05
☐ 357	Paul Sorrento	.10	.05
☐ 358	Skeeter Barnes	.10	.05
☐ 359	Mark Carreon	.10	.05
☐ 360	John Doherty	.10	.05
☐ 361	Dan Gladden	.10	.05
☐ 362	Bill Gullickson	.10	.05
☐ 363	Shawn Hare	.10	.05
☐ 364	Mike Henneman	.10	.05
☐ 365	Chad Kreuter	.10	.05
☐ 366	Mark Leiter	.10	.05
☐ 367	Mike Munoz	.10	.05
☐ 368	Kevin Ritz	.10	.05
☐ 369	Mark Davis	.10	.05
☐ 370	Tom Gordon	.10	.05
☐ 371	Chris Gwynn	.10	.05
☐ 372	Gregg Jefferies	.20	.09
☐ 373	Wally Joyner	.20	.09
☐ 374	Kevin McReynolds	.10	.05
☐ 375	Keith Miller	.10	.05
☐ 376	Rico Rossy	.10	.05
☐ 377	Curtis Wilkerson	.10	.05
☐ 378	Ricky Bones	.10	.05
☐ 379	Chris Bosio	.10	.05
☐ 380	Cal Eldred	.10	.05
☐ 381	Scott Fletcher	.10	.05
☐ 382	Jim Gantner	.10	.05
☐ 383	Darryl Hamilton	.10	.05
☐ 384	Doug Henry	.10	.05
☐ 385	Pat Listach	.10	.05
☐ 386	Tim McIntosh	.10	.05
☐ 387	Edwin Nunez	.10	.05
☐ 388	Dan Plesac	.10	.05
☐ 389	Kevin Seitzer	.10	.05
☐ 390	Franklin Stubbs	.10	.05
☐ 391	William Suero	.10	.05
☐ 392	Bill Wegman	.10	.05
☐ 393	Willie Banks	.10	.05
☐ 394	Jarvis Brown	.10	.05
☐ 395	Greg Gagne	.10	.05
☐ 396	Mark Guthrie	.10	.05
☐ 397	Bill Krueger	.10	.05
☐ 398	Pat Mahomes	.10	.05
☐ 399	Pedro Munoz	.10	.05
☐ 400	John Smiley	.10	.05
☐ 401	Gary Wayne	.10	.05
☐ 402	Lenny Webster	.10	.05
☐ 403	Carl Willis	.10	.05
☐ 404	Greg Cadaret	.10	.05
☐ 405	Steve Farr	.10	.05
☐ 406	Mike Gallego	.10	.05
☐ 407	Charlie Hayes	.10	.05
☐ 408	Steve Howe	.10	.05
☐ 409	Dion James	.10	.05
☐ 410	Jeff Johnson	.10	.05
☐ 411	Tim Leary	.10	.05
☐ 412	Jim Leyritz	.10	.05
☐ 413	Melido Perez	.10	.05
☐ 414	Scott Sanderson	.10	.05
☐ 415	Andy Stankiewicz	.10	.05
☐ 416	Mike Stanley	.10	.05
☐ 417	Danny Tartabull	.20	.09
☐ 418	Lance Blankenship	.10	.05
☐ 419	Mike Bordick	.10	.05
☐ 420	Scott Brosius	.20	.09
☐ 421	Dennis Eckersley	.20	.09
☐ 422	Scott Hemond	.10	.05
☐ 423	Carney Lansford	.10	.05
☐ 424	Henry Mercedes	.10	.05
☐ 425	Mike Moore	.10	.05
☐ 426	Gene Nelson	.10	.05
☐ 427	Randy Ready	.10	.05
☐ 428	Bruce Walton	.10	.05
☐ 429	Willie Wilson	.10	.05
☐ 430	Rich Amaral	.10	.05
☐ 431	Dave Cochrane	.10	.05
☐ 432	Henry Cotto	.10	.05
☐ 433	Calvin Jones	.10	.05
☐ 434	Kevin Mitchell	.20	.09
☐ 435	Clay Parker	.10	.05
☐ 436	Omar Vizquel	.20	.09
☐ 437	Floyd Bannister	.10	.05

□ 438 Kevin Brown	.20	.09
□ 439 John Cangelosi	.10	.05
□ 440 Brian Downing	.10	.05
□ 441 Monty Fariss	.10	.05
□ 442 Jose Guzman	.10	.05
□ 443 Donald Harris	.10	.05
□ 444 Kevin Reimer	.10	.05
□ 445 Kenny Rogers	.10	.05
□ 446 Wayne Rosenthal	.10	.05
□ 447 Dickie Thon	.10	.05
□ 448 Derek Bell	.20	.09
□ 449 Juan Guzman	.10	.05
□ 450 Tom Henke	.10	.05
□ 451 Candy Maldonado	.10	.05
□ 452 Jack Morris	.20	.09
□ 453 David Wells	.10	.05
□ 454 Dave Winfield	.40	.18
□ 455 Juan Berenguer	.10	.05
□ 456 Damon Berryhill	.10	.05
□ 457 Mike Bielecki	.10	.05
□ 458 Marvin Freeman	.10	.05
□ 459 Charlie Leibrandt	.10	.05
□ 460 Kent Mercker	.10	.05
□ 461 Otis Nixon	.20	.09
□ 462 Alejandro Pena	.10	.05
□ 463 Ben Rivera	.10	.05
□ 464 Deion Sanders	.20	.09
□ 465 Mark Wohlers	.30	.14
□ 466 Shawn Boskie	.10	.05
□ 467 Frank Castillo	.10	.05
□ 468 Andre Dawson	.30	.14
□ 469 Joe Girardi	.10	.05
□ 470 Chuck McElroy	.10	.05
□ 471 Mike Morgan	.10	.05
□ 472 Ken Patterson	.10	.05
□ 473 Bob Scanlan	.10	.05
□ 474 Gary Scott	.10	.05
□ 475 Dave Smith	.10	.05
□ 476 Sammy Sosa	.40	.18
□ 477 Hector Villanueva	.10	.05
□ 478 Scott Bankhead	.10	.05
□ 479 Tim Belcher	.10	.05
□ 480 Freddie Benavides	.10	.05
□ 481 Jacob Brumfield	.10	.05
□ 482 Norm Charlton	.10	.05
□ 483 Dwayne Henry	.10	.05
□ 484 Dave Martinez	.10	.05
□ 485 Bip Roberts	.10	.05
□ 486 Reggie Sanders	.20	.05
□ 487 Greg Swindell	.10	.05
□ 488 Ryan Bowen	.10	.05
□ 489 Casey Candaele	.10	.05
□ 490 Juan Guerrero UER	.10	.05
(photo on front is Andujar Cedeno)		
□ 491 Pete Incaviglia	.10	.05
□ 492 Jeff Juden	.10	.05
□ 493 Rob Murphy	.10	.05
□ 494 Mark Portugal	.10	.05
□ 495 Rafael Ramirez	.10	.05
□ 496 Scott Servais	.10	.05
□ 497 Ed Taubensee	.10	.05
□ 498 Brian Williams	.10	.05
□ 499 Todd Benzinger	.10	.05
□ 500 John Candelaria	.10	.05
□ 501 Tom Candiotti	.10	.05
□ 502 Tim Crews	.10	.05
□ 503 Eric Davis	.20	.09
□ 504 Jim Gott	.10	.05
□ 505 Dave Hansen	.10	.05
□ 506 Carlos Hernandez	.10	.05
□ 507 Orel Hershiser	.20	.09
□ 508 Eric Karros	.30	.14
□ 509 Bob Ojeda	.10	.05
□ 510 Steve Wilson	.10	.05
□ 511 Moises Alou	.30	.14
□ 512 Bret Barberie	.10	.05
□ 513 Ivan Calderon	.10	.05
□ 514 Gary Carter	.40	.18
□ 515 Archi Cianfrocco	.10	.05
□ 516 Jeff Fassero	.10	.05
□ 517 Darrin Fletcher	.10	.05
□ 518 Marquis Grissom	.20	.09
□ 519 Chris Haney	.10	.05
□ 520 Ken Hill	.10	.05
□ 521 Chris Nabholz	.10	.05
□ 522 Bill Sampen	.10	.05

□ 523 John Vander Wal	.10	.05
□ 524 Dave Wainhouse	.10	.05
□ 525 Larry Walker	.40	.18
□ 526 John Wetteland	.20	.09
□ 527 Bobby Bonilla	.20	.09
□ 528 Sid Fernandez	.10	.05
□ 529 John Franco	.20	.09
□ 530 Dave Gallagher	.10	.05
□ 531 Paul Gibson	.10	.05
□ 532 Eddie Murray	.40	.18
□ 533 Junior Noboa	.10	.05
□ 534 Charlie O'Brien	.10	.05
□ 535 Bill Pecota	.10	.05
□ 536 Willie Randolph	.20	.09
□ 537 Bret Saberhagen	.10	.05
□ 538 Dick Schofield	.10	.05
□ 539 Pete Schourek	.10	.05
□ 540 Ruben Amaro	.10	.05
□ 541 Andy Ashby	.10	.05
□ 542 Kim Batiste	.10	.05
□ 543 Cliff Brantley	.10	.05
□ 544 Mariano Duncan	.10	.05
□ 545 Jeff Grotewold	.10	.05
□ 546 Barry Jones	.10	.05
□ 547 Julio Peguero	.10	.05
□ 548 Curt Schilling	.30	.14
□ 549 Mitch Williams	.10	.05
□ 550 Stan Belinda	.10	.05
□ 551 Scott Bullett	.10	.05
□ 552 Cecil Espy	.10	.05
□ 553 Jeff King	.20	.09
□ 554 Roger Mason	.10	.05
□ 555 Paul Miller	.10	.05
□ 556 Denny Neagle	.30	.14
□ 557 Vicente Palacios	.10	.05
□ 558 Bob Patterson	.10	.05
□ 559 Tom Prince	.10	.05
□ 560 Gary Redus	.10	.05
□ 561 Gary Varsho	.10	.05
□ 562 Juan Agosto	.10	.05
□ 563 Cris Carpenter	.10	.05
□ 564 Mark Clark	.10	.05
□ 565 Jose DeLeon	.10	.05
□ 566 Rich Gedman	.10	.05
□ 567 Bernard Gilkey	.20	.09
□ 568 Rex Hudler	.10	.05
□ 569 Tim Jones	.10	.05
□ 570 Donovan Osborne	.10	.05
□ 571 Mike Perez	.10	.05
□ 572 Gerald Perry	.10	.05
□ 573 Bob Tewksbury	.10	.05
□ 574 Todd Worrell	.10	.05
□ 575 Dave Eiland	.10	.05
□ 576 Jeremy Hernandez	.10	.05
□ 577 Craig Lefferts	.10	.05
□ 578 Jose Melendez	.10	.05
□ 579 Randy Myers	.20	.09
□ 580 Gary Pettis	.10	.05
□ 581 Rich Rodriguez	.10	.05
□ 582 Gary Sheffield	.40	.18
□ 583 Craig Shipley	.10	.05
□ 584 Kurt Stillwell	.10	.05
□ 585 Tim Teufel	.10	.05
□ 586 Rod Beck	.40	.18
□ 587 Dave Burba	.10	.05
□ 588 Craig Colbert	.10	.05
□ 589 Bryan Hickerson	.10	.05
□ 590 Mike Jackson	.10	.05
□ 591 Mark Leonard	.10	.05
□ 592 Jim McNamara	.10	.05
□ 593 John Patterson	.10	.05
□ 594 Dave Righetti	.10	.05
□ 595 Cory Snyder	.10	.05
□ 596 Bill Swift	.10	.05
□ 597 Ted Wood	.10	.05
□ 598 Checklist 301-400	.10	.05
□ 599 Checklist 401-500	.10	.05
□ 600 Checklist 501-600	.10	.05

1992 Ultra All-Rookies

Cards from this ten-card standard-size set highlighting a

selection of top rookies were randomly inserted in 1992 Ultra II foil packs. The fronts feature borderless color action player photos except at the bottom where they are edged by a marbleized black wedge. The words "All-Rookie Team" in gold foil lettering appear in a black marbleized inverted triangle at the lower right corner, with the player's name on a color banner.

	MINT	NRMT
COMPLETE SET (10)	12.00	5.50
COMMON CARD (1-10)	.50	.23
SER.2 STATED ODDS 1:13		

□ 1 Eric Karros	1.50	.70
□ 2 Andy Stankiewicz	.50	.23
□ 3 Gary DiSarcina	.50	.23
□ 4 Archi Cianfrocco	.50	.23
□ 5 Jim McNamara	.50	.23
□ 6 Chad Curtis	2.00	.90
□ 7 Kenny Lofton	8.00	3.60
□ 8 Reggie Sanders	1.00	.45
□ 9 Pat Mahomes	.50	.23
□ 10 Donovan Osborne	.50	.23

1992 Ultra All-Stars

Featuring many of the 1992 season's stars, cards from this 20-card standard-size set were randomly inserted in 1992 Ultra II foil packs. The front design displays color action player photos enclosed by black marbleized borders. The word "All-Star" and the player's name are printed in gold foil lettering in the bottom border.

	MINT	NRMT
COMPLETE SET (20)	25.00	11.00
COMMON CARD (1-20)	.50	.23
SER.2 STATED ODDS 1:6.5		

	MINT	NRMT
□ 1 Mark McGwire	2.00	.90
□ 2 Roberto Alomar	1.50	.70
□ 3 Cal Ripken Jr.	5.00	2.20
□ 4 Wade Boggs	1.50	.70
□ 5 Mickey Tettleton	.50	.23
□ 6 Ken Griffey Jr.	8.00	3.60
□ 7 Roberto Kelly	.50	.23
□ 8 Kirby Puckett	2.50	1.10
□ 9 Frank Thomas	6.00	2.70
□ 10 Jack McDowell	.50	.23
□ 11 Will Clark	1.00	.45
□ 12 Ryne Sandberg	2.00	.90
□ 13 Barry Larkin	1.00	.45
□ 14 Gary Sheffield	1.50	.70
□ 15 Tom Pagnozzi	.50	.23
□ 16 Barry Bonds	2.00	.90
□ 17 Deion Sanders	.75	.35
□ 18 Darryl Strawberry	.75	.35
□ 19 David Cone	.75	.35
□ 20 Tom Glavine	1.00	.45

1992 Ultra Award Winners

TERRY PENDLETON

This 25-card standard-size set features 18 Gold Glove winners, both Cy Young Award winners, both Rookies of the Year, both league MVP's, and the World Series MVP. The cards were randomly inserted in 1992 Fleer Ultra I packs. The fronts carry full-bleed color player photos that have a diagonal blue marbleized border at the bottom. The player's name appears in this bottom border, and a diamond-shaped gold foil seal signifying the award the player won is superimposed in the lower right corner.

	MINT	NRMT
COMPLETE SET (25)	50.00	22.00
COMMON CARD(1-25)	.75	.35
RANDOM INSERTS IN SER.1 PACKS		
□ 1 Jack Morris	1.00	.45
□ 2 Chuck Knoblauch	2.00	.90
□ 3 Jeff Bagwell	6.00	2.70
□ 4 Terry Pendleton	1.00	.45
□ 5 Cal Ripken	8.00	3.60
□ 6 Roger Clemens	4.00	1.80
□ 7 Tom Glavine	1.50	.70
□ 8 Tom Pagnozzi	.75	.35
□ 9 Ozzie Smith	2.50	1.10
□ 10 Andy Van Slyke	.75	.35
□ 11 Barry Bonds	2.50	1.10
□ 12 Tony Gwynn	5.00	2.20
□ 13 Matt Williams	1.50	.70
□ 14 Will Clark	1.50	.70
□ 15 Robin Ventura	1.00	.45
□ 16 Mark Langston	.75	.35
□ 17 Tony Pena	.75	.35
□ 18 Devon White	.75	.35
□ 19 Don Mattingly	3.00	1.35

	MINT	NRMT
□ 20 Roberto Alomar	2.00	.90
□ 21A Cal Ripken ERR. (Reversed negative on card back)	15.00	6.75
□ 21B Cal Ripken COR.	6.00	2.70
□ 22 Ken Griffey Jr.	12.00	5.50
□ 23 Kirby Puckett	4.00	1.80
□ 24 Greg Maddux	6.00	2.70
□ 25 Ryne Sandberg	2.50	1.10

1993 Ultra

The 1993 Ultra baseball set was issued in two series and totaled 650 standard-size cards. The full-bleed color-enhanced action photos are edged at the bottom by a gold foil stripe and a fawn-colored border that is streaked with white on a marbleized effect. On a dimensionalized ball park background, the horizontal backs have an action shot, a portrait, last season statistics, and the player's entire professional career totals. The cards are numbered on the back, grouped alphabetically within teams, with NL preceding AL. The first series closes with checklist cards (298-300). The second series features 83 Ultra Rookies, 51 Rookies and Marlins, traded veteran players, and other major league veterans not included in the first series. The Rookie cards show a gold foil stamped Rookie "flag" as part of the card design. The key Rookie Card in this set is Jim Edmonds.

	MINT	NRMT
COMPLETE SET (650)	30.00	13.50
COMPLETE SERIES 1 (300)	15.00	6.75
COMPLETE SERIES 2 (350)	15.00	6.75
COMMON CARD (1-650)	.15	.07
MINOR STARS	.30	.14
UNLISTED STARS	.60	.25
COMP.ECKERSLEY SET (10)	4.00	1.80
COMMON ECKERSLEY (1-10)	.50	.23
CERTIFIED ECKERSLEY AUTO	40.00	18.00
ECKERSLEY:RANDOM INSERTS IN PACKS		
COMMON ECK.MAIL-IN (11-12)	1.00	.45
ECK.MAIL-IN AVAIL.VIA WRAPPER EXCH.		
□ 1 Steve Avery	.15	.07
□ 2 Rafael Belliard	.15	.07
□ 3 Damon Berryhill	.15	.07
□ 4 Sid Bream	.15	.07
□ 5 Ron Gant	.30	.14
□ 6 Tom Glavine	.40	.18
□ 7 Ryan Klesko	.75	.35
□ 8 Mark Lemke	.15	.07
□ 9 Javier Lopez	.60	.25
□ 10 Greg Olson	.15	.07
□ 11 Terry Pendleton	.30	.14

	MINT	NRMT
□ 12 Deion Sanders	.30	.14
□ 13 Mike Stanton	.15	.07
□ 14 Paul Assenmacher	.15	.07
□ 15 Steve Buechele	.15	.07
□ 16 Frank Castillo	.15	.07
□ 17 Shawon Dunston	.15	.07
□ 18 Mark Grace	.40	.18
□ 19 Derrick May	.15	.07
□ 20 Chuck McElroy	.15	.07
□ 21 Mike Morgan	.15	.07
□ 22 Bob Scanlan	.15	.07
□ 23 Dwight Smith	.15	.07
□ 24 Sammy Sosa	.60	.25
□ 25 Rick Wilkins	.15	.07
□ 26 Tim Belcher	.15	.07
□ 27 Jeff Branson	.15	.07
□ 28 Bill Doran	.15	.07
□ 29 Chris Hammond	.15	.07
□ 30 Barry Larkin	.40	.18
□ 31 Hal Morris	.15	.07
□ 32 Joe Oliver	.15	.07
□ 33 Jose Rijo	.15	.07
□ 34 Bip Roberts	.15	.07
□ 35 Chris Sabo	.15	.07
□ 36 Reggie Sanders	.30	.14
□ 37 Craig Biggio	.30	.14
□ 38 Ken Caminiti	.40	.18
□ 39 Steve Finley	.30	.14
□ 40 Luis Gonzalez	.15	.07
□ 41 Juan Guerrero	.15	.07
□ 42 Pete Harnisch	.15	.07
□ 43 Xavier Hernandez	.15	.07
□ 44 Doug Jones	.15	.07
□ 45 Al Osuna	.15	.07
□ 46 Eddie Taubensee	.15	.07
□ 47 Scooter Tucker	.15	.07
□ 48 Brian Williams	.15	.07
□ 49 Pedro Astacio	.15	.07
□ 50 Rafael Bournigal	.15	.07
□ 51 Brett Butler	.30	.14
□ 52 Tom Candiotti	.15	.07
□ 53 Eric Davis	.30	.14
□ 54 Lenny Harris	.15	.07
□ 55 Orel Hershiser	.30	.14
□ 56 Eric Karros	.30	.14
□ 57 Pedro Martinez	.60	.25
□ 58 Roger McDowell	.15	.07
□ 59 Jose Offerman	.15	.07
□ 60 Mike Piazza	3.00	1.35
□ 61 Moises Alou	.30	.14
□ 62 Kent Bottenfield	.15	.07
□ 63 Archi Cianfrocco	.15	.07
□ 64 Greg Colbrunn	.15	.07
□ 65 Wil Cordero	.15	.07
□ 66 Delino DeShields	.15	.07
□ 67 Darrin Fletcher	.15	.07
□ 68 Ken Hill	.15	.07
□ 69 Chris Nabholz	.15	.07
□ 70 Mel Rojas	.30	.14
□ 71 Larry Walker	.60	.25
□ 72 Sid Fernandez	.15	.07
□ 73 John Franco	.30	.14
□ 74 Dave Gallagher	.15	.07
□ 75 Todd Hundley	.40	.18
□ 76 Howard Johnson	.15	.07
□ 77 Jeff Kent	.30	.14
□ 78 Eddie Murray	.60	.25
□ 79 Bret Saberhagen	.15	.07
□ 80 Chico Walker	.15	.07
□ 81 Anthony Young	.15	.07
□ 82 Kyle Abbott	.15	.07
□ 83 Ruben Amaro	.15	.07
□ 84 Juan Bell	.15	.07
□ 85 Wes Chamberlain	.15	.07
□ 86 Darren Daulton	.30	.14
□ 87 Mariano Duncan	.15	.07
□ 88 Dave Hollins	.15	.07
□ 89 Ricky Jordan	.15	.07
□ 90 John Kruk	.30	.14
□ 91 Mickey Morandini	.15	.07
□ 92 Terry Mulholland	.15	.07
□ 93 Ben Rivera	.15	.07
□ 94 Mike Williams	.15	.07
□ 95 Stan Belinda	.15	.07
□ 96 Jay Bell	.30	.14
□ 97 Jeff King	.30	.14

☐ 98 Mike LaValliere	.15	.07	
☐ 99 Lloyd McClendon	.15	.07	
☐ 100 Orlando Merced	.15	.07	
☐ 101 Zane Smith	.15	.07	
☐ 102 Randy Tomlin	.15	.07	
☐ 103 Andy Van Slyke	.30	.14	
☐ 104 Tim Wakefield	.30	.14	
☐ 105 John Wehner	.15	.07	
☐ 106 Bernard Gilkey	.30	.14	
☐ 107 Brian Jordan	.30	.14	
☐ 108 Ray Lankford	.40	.18	
☐ 109 Donovan Osborne	.15	.07	
☐ 110 Tom Pagnozzi	.15	.07	
☐ 111 Mike Perez	.15	.07	
☐ 112 Lee Smith	.30	.14	
☐ 113 Ozzie Smith	.75	.35	
☐ 114 Bob Tewksbury	.15	.07	
☐ 115 Todd Zeile	.15	.07	
☐ 116 Andy Benes	.30	.14	
☐ 117 Greg W. Harris	.15	.07	
☐ 118 Darrin Jackson	.15	.07	
☐ 119 Fred McGriff	.40	.18	
☐ 120 Rich Rodriguez	.15	.07	
☐ 121 Frank Seminara	.15	.07	
☐ 122 Gary Sheffield	.60	.25	
☐ 123 Craig Shipley	.15	.07	
☐ 124 Kurt Stillwell	.15	.07	
☐ 125 Dan Walters	.15	.07	
☐ 126 Rod Beck	.30	.14	
☐ 127 Mike Benjamin	.15	.07	
☐ 128 Jeff Brantley	.15	.07	
☐ 129 John Burkett	.15	.07	
☐ 130 Will Clark	.40	.18	
☐ 131 Royce Clayton	.15	.07	
☐ 132 Steve Hosey	.15	.07	
☐ 133 Mike Jackson	.15	.07	
☐ 134 Darren Lewis	.15	.07	
☐ 135 Kirt Manwaring	.15	.07	
☐ 136 Bill Swift	.15	.07	
☐ 137 Robby Thompson	.15	.07	
☐ 138 Brady Anderson	.40	.18	
☐ 139 Glenn Davis	.15	.07	
☐ 140 Leo Gomez	.15	.07	
☐ 141 Chito Martinez	.15	.07	
☐ 142 Ben McDonald	.15	.07	
☐ 143 Alan Mills	.15	.07	
☐ 144 Mike Mussina	.65	.25	
☐ 145 Gregg Olson	.15	.07	
☐ 146 David Segui	.15	.07	
☐ 147 Jeff Tackett	.15	.07	
☐ 148 Jack Clark	.15	.07	
☐ 149 Scott Cooper	.15	.07	
☐ 150 Danny Darwin	.15	.07	
☐ 151 John Dopson	.15	.07	
☐ 152 Mike Greenwell	.15	.07	
☐ 153 Tim Naehring	.15	.07	
☐ 154 Tony Pena	.15	.07	
☐ 155 Paul Quantrill	.15	.07	
☐ 156 Mo Vaughn	.75	.35	
☐ 157 Frank Viola	.15	.07	
☐ 158 Bob Zupcic	.15	.07	
☐ 159 Chad Curtis	.30	.14	
☐ 160 Gary DiSarcina	.15	.07	
☐ 161 Damion Easley	.15	.07	
☐ 162 Chuck Finley	.15	.07	
☐ 163 Tim Fortugno	.15	.07	
☐ 164 Rene Gonzales	.15	.07	
☐ 165 Joe Grahe	.15	.07	
☐ 166 Mark Langston	.15	.07	
☐ 167 John Orton	.15	.07	
☐ 168 Luis Polonia	.15	.07	
☐ 169 Julio Valera	.15	.07	
☐ 170 Wilson Alvarez	.30	.14	
☐ 171 George Bell	.30	.14	
☐ 172 Joey Cora	.30	.14	
☐ 173 Alex Fernandez	.15	.07	
☐ 174 Lance Johnson	.15	.07	
☐ 175 Ron Karkovice	.15	.07	
☐ 176 Jack McDowell	.30	.14	
☐ 177 Scott Radinsky	.15	.07	
☐ 178 Tim Raines	.30	.14	
☐ 179 Steve Sax	.15	.07	
☐ 180 Bobby Thigpen	.15	.07	
☐ 181 Frank Thomas	2.50	1.10	
☐ 182 Sandy Alomar	.30	.14	
☐ 183 Carlos Baerga	.15	.07	

☐ 184 Felix Fermin	.15	.07	
☐ 185 Thomas Howard	.15	.07	
☐ 186 Mark Lewis	.15	.07	
☐ 187 Derek Lilliquist	.15	.07	
☐ 188 Carlos Martinez	.15	.07	
☐ 189 Charles Nagy	.30	.14	
☐ 190 Scott Scudder	.15	.07	
☐ 191 Paul Sorrento	.15	.07	
☐ 192 Jim Thome	1.25	.55	
☐ 193 Mark Whiten	.15	.07	
☐ 194 Milt Cuyler UER	.15	.07	
(Reversed negative			
on card front)			
☐ 195 Rob Deer	.15	.07	
☐ 196 John Doherty	.15	.07	
☐ 197 Travis Fryman	.30	.14	
☐ 198 Dan Gladden	.15	.07	
☐ 199 Mike Henneman	.15	.07	
☐ 200 John Kiely	.15	.07	
☐ 201 Chad Kreuter	.15	.07	
☐ 202 Scott Livingstone	.15	.07	
☐ 203 Tony Phillips	.15	.07	
☐ 204 Alan Trammell	.40	.18	
☐ 205 Mike Boddicker	.15	.07	
☐ 206 George Brett	1.25	.55	
☐ 207 Tom Gordon	.15	.07	
☐ 208 Mark Gubicza	.15	.07	
☐ 209 Gregg Jefferies	.15	.07	
☐ 210 Wally Joyner	.30	.14	
☐ 211 Kevin Koslofski	.15	.07	
☐ 212 Brent Mayne	.15	.07	
☐ 213 Brian McRae	.15	.07	
☐ 214 Kevin McReynolds	.15	.07	
☐ 215 Rusty Meacham	.15	.07	
☐ 216 Steve Shifflett	.15	.07	
☐ 217 James Austin	.15	.07	
☐ 218 Cal Eldred	.15	.07	
☐ 219 Darryl Hamilton	.15	.07	
☐ 220 Doug Henry	.15	.07	
☐ 221 John Jaha	.30	.14	
☐ 222 Dave Nilsson	.30	.14	
☐ 223 Jesse Orosco	.15	.07	
☐ 224 B.J. Surhoff	.30	.14	
☐ 225 Greg Vaughn	.15	.07	
☐ 226 Bill Wegman	.15	.07	
☐ 227 Robin Yount UER	.40	.18	
(Born in Illinois,			
not in Virginia)			
☐ 228 Rick Aguilera	.15	.07	
☐ 229 J.T. Bruett	.15	.07	
☐ 230 Scott Erickson	.15	.07	
☐ 231 Kent Hrbek	.30	.14	
☐ 232 Terry Jorgensen	.15	.07	
☐ 233 Scott Leius	.15	.07	
☐ 234 Pat Mahomes	.15	.07	
☐ 235 Pedro Munoz	.15	.07	
☐ 236 Kirby Puckett	1.25	.55	
☐ 237 Kevin Tapani	.15	.07	
☐ 238 Lenny Webster	.15	.07	
☐ 239 Carl Willis	.15	.07	
☐ 240 Mike Gallego	.15	.07	
☐ 241 John Habyan	.15	.07	
☐ 242 Pat Kelly	.15	.07	
☐ 243 Kevin Maas	.15	.07	
☐ 244 Don Mattingly	1.00	.45	
☐ 245 Hensley Meulens	.15	.07	
☐ 246 Sam Militello	.15	.07	
☐ 247 Matt Nokes	.15	.07	
☐ 248 Melido Perez	.15	.07	
☐ 249 Andy Stankiewicz	.15	.07	
☐ 250 Randy Velarde	.15	.07	
☐ 251 Bob Wickman	.15	.07	
☐ 252 Bernie Williams	.60	.25	
☐ 253 Lance Blankenship	.15	.07	
☐ 254 Mike Bordick	.15	.07	
☐ 255 Jerry Browne	.15	.07	
☐ 256 Ron Darling	.15	.07	
☐ 257 Dennis Eckersley	.30	.14	
☐ 258 Rickey Henderson	.40	.18	
☐ 259 Vince Horsman	.15	.07	
☐ 260 Troy Neel	.15	.07	
☐ 261 Jeff Parrett	.15	.07	
☐ 262 Terry Steinbach	.15	.07	
☐ 263 Bob Welch	.15	.07	
☐ 264 Bobby Witt	.15	.07	
☐ 265 Rich Amaral	.15	.07	

☐ 266 Bret Boone	.15	.07	
☐ 267 Jay Buhner	.40	.18	
☐ 268 Dave Fleming	.15	.07	
☐ 269 Randy Johnson	.60	.25	
☐ 270 Edgar Martinez	.40	.18	
☐ 271 Mike Schooler	.15	.07	
☐ 272 Russ Swan	.15	.07	
☐ 273 Dave Valle	.15	.07	
☐ 274 Omar Vizquel	.30	.14	
☐ 275 Kerry Woodson	.15	.07	
☐ 276 Kevin Brown	.30	.14	
☐ 277 Julio Franco	.15	.07	
☐ 278 Jeff Frye	.15	.07	
☐ 279 Juan Gonzalez	1.50	.70	
☐ 280 Jeff Huson	.15	.07	
☐ 281 Rafael Palmeiro	.40	.18	
☐ 282 Dean Palmer	.15	.07	
☐ 283 Roger Pavlik	.15	.07	
☐ 284 Ivan Rodriguez	.75	.35	
☐ 285 Kenny Rogers	.15	.07	
☐ 286 Derek Bell	.30	.14	
☐ 287 Pat Borders	.15	.07	
☐ 288 Joe Carter	.30	.14	
☐ 289 Bob MacDonald	.15	.07	
☐ 290 Jack Morris	.30	.14	
☐ 291 John Olerud	.15	.07	
☐ 292 Ed Sprague	.15	.07	
☐ 293 Todd Stottlemyre	.15	.07	
☐ 294 Mike Timlin	.15	.07	
☐ 295 Duane Ward	.15	.07	
☐ 296 David Wells	.15	.07	
☐ 297 Devon White	.15	.07	
☐ 298 Ray Lankford CL	.30	.14	
☐ 299 Bobby Witt CL	.15	.07	
☐ 300 Mike Piazza CL	.60	.25	
☐ 301 Steve Bedrosian	.15	.07	
☐ 302 Jeff Blauser	.15	.07	
☐ 303 Francisco Cabrera	.15	.07	
☐ 304 Marvin Freeman	.15	.07	
☐ 305 Brian Hunter	.15	.07	
☐ 306 David Justice	.60	.25	
☐ 307 Greg Maddux	2.00	.90	
☐ 308 Greg McMichael	.15	•.07	
☐ 309 Kent Mercker	.15	.07	
☐ 310 Otis Nixon	.15	.07	
☐ 311 Pete Smith	.15	.07	
☐ 312 John Smoltz	.30	.14	
☐ 313 Jose Guzman	.15	.07	
☐ 314 Mike Harkey	.15	.07	
☐ 315 Greg Hibbard	.15	.07	
☐ 316 Candy Maldonado	.15	.07	
☐ 317 Randy Myers	.30	.14	
☐ 318 Dan Plesac	.15	.07	
☐ 319 Rey Sanchez	.15	.07	
☐ 320 Ryne Sandberg	.75	.35	
☐ 321 Tommy Shields	.15	.07	
☐ 322 Jose Vizcaino	.15	.07	
☐ 323 Matt Walbeck	.15	.07	
☐ 324 Willie Wilson	.15	.07	
☐ 325 Tom Browning	.15	.07	
☐ 326 Tim Costo	.15	.07	
☐ 327 Rob Dibble	.15	.07	
☐ 328 Steve Foster	.15	.07	
☐ 329 Roberto Kelly	.15	.07	
☐ 330 Randy Milligan	.15	.07	
☐ 331 Kevin Mitchell	.30	.14	
☐ 332 Tim Pugh	.15	.07	
☐ 333 Jeff Reardon	.15	.07	
☐ 334 John Roper	.15	.07	
☐ 335 Juan Samuel	.15	.07	
☐ 336 John Smiley	.15	.07	
☐ 337 Dan Wilson	.30	.14	
☐ 338 Scott Aldred	.15	.07	
☐ 339 Andy Ashby	.15	.07	
☐ 340 Freddie Benavides	.15	.07	
☐ 341 Dante Bichette	.40	.18	
☐ 342 Willie Blair	.15	.07	
☐ 343 Daryl Boston	.15	.07	
☐ 344 Vinny Castilla	.60	.25	
☐ 345 Jerald Clark	.15	.07	
☐ 346 Alex Cole	.15	.07	
☐ 347 Andres Galarraga	.60	.25	
☐ 348 Joe Girardi	.15	.07	
☐ 349 Ryan Hawblitzel	.15	.07	
☐ 350 Charlie Hayes	.15	.07	
☐ 351 Butch Henry	.15	.07	

352	Darren Holmes	.15	.07
353	Dale Murphy	.40	.18
354	David Nied	.15	.07
355	Jeff Parrett	.15	.07
356	Steve Reed	.15	.07
357	Bruce Ruffin	.15	.07
358	Danny Sheaffer	.15	.07
359	Bryn Smith	.15	.07
360	Jim Tatum	.15	.07
361	Eric Young	.60	.25
362	Gerald Young	.15	.07
363	Luis Aquino	.15	.07
364	Alex Arias	.15	.07
365	Jack Armstrong	.15	.07
366	Bret Barberie	.15	.07
367	Ryan Bowen	.15	.07
368	Greg Briley	.15	.07
369	Cris Carpenter	.15	.07
370	Chuck Carr	.15	.07
371	Jeff Conine	.30	.14
372	Steve Decker	.15	.07
373	Orestes Destrade	.15	.07
374	Monty Fariss	.15	.07
375	Junior Felix	.15	.07
376	Chris Hammond	.15	.07
377	Bryan Harvey	.15	.07
378	Trevor Hoffman	.40	.18
379	Charlie Hough	.15	.07
380	Joe Klink	.15	.07
381	Richie Lewis	.15	.07
382	Dave Magadan	.15	.07
383	Bob McClure	.15	.07
384	Scott Pose	.15	.07
385	Rich Renteria	.15	.07
386	Benito Santiago	.15	.07
387	Walt Weiss	.15	.07
388	Nigel Wilson	.15	.07
389	Eric Anthony	.15	.07
390	Jeff Bagwell	1.25	.55
391	Andujar Cedeno	.15	.07
392	Doug Drabek	.15	.07
393	Darryl Kile	.30	.14
394	Mark Portugal	.15	.07
395	Karl Rhodes	.15	.07
396	Scott Servais	.15	.07
397	Greg Swindell	.15	.07
398	Tom Goodwin	.15	.07
399	Kevin Gross	.15	.07
400	Carlos Hernandez	.15	.07
401	Ramon Martinez	.30	.14
402	Raul Mondesi	.75	.35
403	Jody Reed	.15	.07
404	Mike Sharperson	.15	.07
405	Cory Snyder	.15	.07
406	Darryl Strawberry	.30	.14
407	Rick Trlicek	.15	.07
408	Tim Wallach	.15	.07
409	Todd Worrell	.15	.07
410	Tavo Alvarez	.15	.07
411	Sean Berry	.15	.07
412	Frank Bolick	.15	.07
413	Cliff Floyd	.30	.14
414	Mike Gardiner	.15	.07
415	Marquis Grissom	.30	.14
416	Tim Laker	.15	.07
417	Mike Lansing	.30	.14
418	Dennis Martinez	.30	.14
419	John Vander Wal	.15	.07
420	John Wetteland	.30	.14
421	Rondell White	.40	.18
422	Bobby Bonilla	.30	.14
423	Jeromy Burnitz	.15	.07
424	Vince Coleman	.15	.07
425	Mike Draper	.15	.07
426	Tony Fernandez	.15	.07
427	Dwight Gooden	.30	.14
428	Jeff Innis	.15	.07
429	Bobby Jones	.30	.14
430	Mike Maddux	.15	.07
431	Charlie O'Brien	.15	.07
432	Joe Orsulak	.15	.07
433	Pete Schourek	.15	.07
434	Frank Tanana	.15	.07
435	Ryan Thompson	.15	.07
436	Kim Batiste	.15	.07
437	Mark Davis	.15	.07
438	Jose DeLeon	.15	.07
439	Len Dykstra	.30	.14
440	Jim Eisenreich	.15	.07
441	Tommy Greene	.15	.07
442	Pete Incaviglia	.15	.07
443	Danny Jackson	.15	.07
444	Todd Pratt	.15	.07
445	Curt Schilling	.30	.14
446	Milt Thompson	.15	.07
447	David West	.15	.07
448	Mitch Williams	.15	.07
449	Steve Cooke	.15	.07
450	Carlos Garcia	.15	.07
451	Al Martin	.30	.14
452	Blas Minor	.15	.07
453	Dennis Moeller	.15	.07
454	Denny Neagle	.30	.14
455	Don Slaught	.15	.07
456	Lonnie Smith	.15	.07
457	Paul Wagner	.15	.07
458	Bob Walk	.15	.07
459	Kevin Young	.15	.07
460	Rene Arocha	.15	.07
461	Brian Barber	.15	.07
462	Rheal Cormier	.15	.07
463	Gregg Jefferies	.15	.07
464	Joe Magrane	.15	.07
465	Omar Olivares	.15	.07
466	Geronimo Pena	.15	.07
467	Allen Watson	.15	.07
468	Mark Whiten	.15	.07
469	Derek Bell	.30	.14
470	Phil Clark	.15	.07
471	Pat Gomez	.15	.07
472	Tony Gwynn	1.50	.70
473	Jeremy Hernandez	.15	.07
474	Bruce Hurst	.15	.07
475	Phil Plantier	.15	.07
476	Scott Sanders	.15	.07
477	Tim Scott	.15	.07
478	Darrell Sherman	.15	.07
479	Guillermo Velasquez	.15	.07
480	Tim Worrell	.15	.07
481	Todd Benzinger	.15	.07
482	Bud Black	.15	.07
483	Barry Bonds	.75	.35
484	Dave Burba	.15	.07
485	Bryan Hickerson	.15	.07
486	Dave Martinez	.15	.07
487	Willie McGee	.15	.07
488	Jeff Reed	.15	.07
489	Kevin Rogers	.15	.07
490	Matt Williams	.40	.18
491	Trevor Wilson	.15	.07
492	Harold Baines	.30	.14
493	Mike Devereaux	.15	.07
494	Todd Frohwirth	.15	.07
495	Chris Hoiles	.15	.07
496	Luis Mercedes	.15	.07
497	Sherman Obando	.15	.07
498	Brad Pennington	.15	.07
499	Harold Reynolds	.15	.07
500	Arthur Rhodes	.15	.07
501	Cal Ripken	2.50	1.10
502	Rick Sutcliffe	.15	.07
503	Fernando Valenzuela	.30	.14
504	Mark Williamson	.15	.07
505	Scott Bankhead	.15	.07
506	Greg Blosser	.15	.07
507	Ivan Calderon	.15	.07
508	Roger Clemens	1.25	.55
509	Andre Dawson	.40	.18
510	Scott Fletcher	.15	.07
511	Greg A. Harris	.15	.07
512	Billy Hatcher	.15	.07
513	Carlos Quintana	.15	.07
514	Luis Rivera	.15	.07
515	Jeff Russell	.15	.07
516	Ken Ryan	.15	.07
517	Ken Ryan	.15	.07
518	Chris Davis	.15	.07
519	Jim Edmonds	1.50	.70
520	Gary Gaetti	.15	.07
521	Torey Lovullo	.15	.07
522	Troy Percival	.30	.14
523	Tim Salmon	.75	.35
524	Scott Sanderson	.15	.07
525	J.T. Snow	.75	.35
526	Jerome Walton	.15	.07
527	Jason Bere	.30	.14
528	Rod Bolton	.15	.07
529	Ellis Burks	.30	.14
530	Carlton Fisk	.60	.25
531	Craig Grebeck	.15	.07
532	Ozzie Guillen	.15	.07
533	Roberto Hernandez	.30	.14
534	Bo Jackson	.30	.14
535	Kirk McCaskill	.15	.07
536	Dave Stieb	.15	.07
537	Robin Ventura	.30	.14
538	Albert Belle	.75	.35
539	Mike Bielecki	.15	.07
540	Glenallen Hill	.15	.07
541	Reggie Jefferson	.15	.07
542	Kenny Lofton	1.25	.55
543	Jeff Mutis	.15	.07
544	Junior Ortiz	.15	.07
545	Manny Ramirez	1.25	.55
546	Jeff Treadway	.15	.07
547	Kevin Wickander	.15	.07
548	Cecil Fielder	.30	.14
549	Kirk Gibson	.30	.14
550	Greg Gohr	.15	.07
551	David Haas	.15	.07
552	Bill Krueger	.15	.07
553	Mike Moore	.15	.07
554	Mickey Tettleton	.15	.07
555	Lou Whitaker	.30	.14
556	Kevin Appier	.30	.14
557	Billy Brewer	.15	.07
558	David Cone	.30	.14
559	Greg Gagne	.15	.07
560	Mark Gardner	.15	.07
561	Phil Hiatt	.15	.07
562	Felix Jose	.15	.07
563	Jose Lind	.15	.07
564	Mike Macfarlane	.15	.07
565	Keith Miller	.15	.07
566	Jeff Montgomery	.30	.14
567	Hipolito Pichardo	.15	.07
568	Ricky Bones	.15	.07
569	Tom Brunansky	.15	.07
570	Joe Kmak	.15	.07
571	Pat Listach	.15	.07
572	Graeme Lloyd	.15	.07
573	Carlos Maldonado	.15	.07
574	Josias Manzanillo	.15	.07
575	Matt Mieske	.30	.14
576	Kevin Reimer	.15	.07
577	Bill Spiers	.15	.07
578	Dickie Thon	.15	.07
579	Willie Banks	.15	.07
580	Jim Deshaies	.15	.07
581	Mark Guthrie	.15	.07
582	Brian Harper	.15	.07
583	Chuck Knoblauch	.60	.25
584	Gene Larkin	.15	.07
585	Shane Mack	.15	.07
586	David McCarty	.15	.07
587	Mike Pagliarulo	.15	.07
588	Mike Trombley	.15	.07
589	Dave Winfield	.40	.18
590	Jim Abbott	.30	.14
591	Wade Boggs	.60	.25
592	Russ Davis	.60	.25
593	Steve Farr	.15	.07
594	Steve Howe	.15	.07
595	Mike Humphreys	.15	.07
596	Jimmy Key	.30	.14
597	Jim Leyritz	.15	.07
598	Bobby Munoz	.15	.07
599	Paul O'Neill	.30	.14
600	Spike Owen	.15	.07
601	Mike Stanley	.15	.07
602	Danny Tartabull	.15	.07
603	Scott Brosius	.15	.07
604	Storm Davis	.15	.07
605	Eric Fox	.15	.07
606	Rich Gossage	.30	.14
607	Scott Hemond	.15	.07
608	Dave Henderson	.15	.07
609	Mark McGwire	1.25	.55

			MINT	NRMT
☐ 610	Mike Mohler	.15		.07
☐ 611	Edwin Nunez	.15		.07
☐ 612	Kevin Seitzer	.15		.07
☐ 613	Ruben Sierra	.15		.07
☐ 614	Chris Bosio	.15		.07
☐ 615	Norm Charlton	.15		.07
☐ 616	Jim Converse	.15		.07
☐ 617	John Cummings	.15		.07
☐ 618	Mike Felder	.15		.07
☐ 619	Ken Griffey Jr.	3.00		1.35
☐ 620	Mike Hampton	.40		.18
☐ 621	Erik Hanson	.15		.07
☐ 622	Bill Haselman	.15		.07
☐ 623	Tino Martinez	.60		.25
☐ 624	Lee Tinsley	.30		.14
☐ 625	Fernando Vina	.15		.07
☐ 626	David Wainhouse	.15		.07
☐ 627	Jose Canseco	.40		.18
☐ 628	Benji Gil	.15		.07
☐ 629	Tom Henke	.15		.07
☐ 630	David Hulse	.15		.07
☐ 631	Manuel Lee	.15		.07
☐ 632	Craig Lefferts	.15		.07
☐ 633	Robb Nen	.40		.18
☐ 634	Gary Redus	.15		.07
☐ 635	Bill Ripken	.15		.07
☐ 636	Nolan Ryan	2.50		1.10
☐ 637	Dan Smith	.15		.07
☐ 638	Matt Whiteside	.15		.07
☐ 639	Roberto Alomar	.60		.25
☐ 640	Juan Guzman	.15		.07
☐ 641	Pat Hentgen	.40		.18
☐ 642	Darrin Jackson	.15		.07
☐ 643	Randy Knorr	.15		.07
☐ 644	Domingo Martinez	.15		.07
☐ 645	Paul Molitor	.60		.25
☐ 646	Dick Schofield	.15		.07
☐ 647	Dave Stewart	.30		.14
☐ 648	Rey Sanchez CL	.15		.07
☐ 649	Jeremy Hernandez CL	.15		.07
☐ 650	Junior Ortiz CL	.15		.07

1993 Ultra All-Rookies

Inserted into series II packs at a rate of one in 18, this ten-card standard-size set features cutout color player action shots that are superposed upon a black background, which carries the player's uniform number, position, team name, and the set's title in multicolored lettering. The player's name appears in gold foil at the bottom. A posed color cutout player shot adorns the back, and is also projected upon a black background. The set's title appears at the top printed in gold foil and red lettering, and the player's name in gold foil precedes his career highlights, printed in white. The set is sequenced in alphabetical order. The key

cards in this set are Mike Piazza and Tim Salmon.

		MINT	NRMT
COMPLETE SET (10)		15.00	6.75
COMMON CARD(1-10)		.50	.23
SER.2 STATED ODDS 1:18			

		MINT	NRMT
☐ 1	Rene Arocha	.50	.23
☐ 2	Jeff Conine	.75	.35
☐ 3	Phil Hiatt	.50	.23
☐ 4	Mike Lansing	.75	.35
☐ 5	Al Martin	.75	.35
☐ 6	David Nied	.50	.23
☐ 7	Mike Piazza	12.00	5.50
☐ 8	Tim Salmon	4.00	1.80
☐ 9	J.T. Snow	2.00	.90
☐ 10	Kevin Young	.50	.23

1993 Ultra All-Stars

Inserted into series II packs at a rate of one in nine, this 20-card standard-size set features National League (1-10) and American League (11-20) All-Stars. The gray-bordered fronts carry color player action shots that are cutout and superposed upon their original, but faded and shifted, backgrounds. The player's name and the set's title are printed in gold foil upon simulated flames that issue from a baseball icon in the lower right. That same design of the player's name, the set's title, and flaming baseball icon appears again at the top of the gray-bordered back. The player's career highlights follow below.

		MINT	NRMT
COMPLETE SET (20)		40.00	18.00
COMMON CARD(1-20)		.75	.35
SER.2 STATED ODDS 1:9			

		MINT	NRMT
☐ 1	Darren Daulton	1.00	.45
☐ 2	Will Clark	1.50	.70
☐ 3	Ryne Sandberg	3.00	1.35
☐ 4	Barry Larkin	1.50	.70
☐ 5	Gary Sheffield	2.00	.90
☐ 6	Barry Bonds	3.00	1.35
☐ 7	Ray Lankford	1.50	.70
☐ 8	Larry Walker	2.00	.90
☐ 9	Greg Maddux	8.00	3.60
☐ 10	Lee Smith	1.00	.45
☐ 11	Ivan Rodriguez	3.00	1.35
☐ 12	Mark McGwire	5.00	2.20
☐ 13	Carlos Baerga	.75	.35
☐ 14	Cal Ripken	10.00	4.50
☐ 15	Edgar Martinez	1.50	.70
☐ 16	Juan Gonzalez	6.00	2.70
☐ 17	Ken Griffey Jr.	12.00	5.50
☐ 18	Kirby Puckett	5.00	2.20

			MINT	NRMT
☐ 19	Frank Thomas	10.00		4.50
☐ 20	Mike Mussina	2.00		.90

1993 Ultra Award Winners

Randomly inserted in first series packs, this first series of 1993 Ultra Award Winners presents the Top Glove for the National (1-9) and American (10-18) Leagues and other major award winners (19-25). The 25 standard-size cards comprising this set feature horizontal black-marbleized card designs and carry two color player photos: an action shot on the left and a posed photo on the right. The player's name appears in gold-foil cursive lettering near the bottom left. The category of award is shown in gold foil below. A gold-foil line highlights the card's lower edge. The horizontal and black-marbleized design continues on the back. A color player head shot appears on the left side. The player's name reappears in gold-foil cursive lettering near the top. Below is the player's award category in gold foil above a gold-foil underline. The player's career highlights are shown in white lettering below.

		MINT	NRMT
COMPLETE SET (25)		40.00	18.00
COMMON CARD(1-25)		.50	.23
RANDOM INSERTS IN SER.1 PACKS			

		MINT	NRMT
☐ 1	Greg Maddux	8.00	3.60
☐ 2	Tom Pagnozzi	.50	.23
☐ 3	Mark Grace	1.50	.70
☐ 4	Jose Lind	.50	.23
☐ 5	Terry Pendleton	.50	.23
☐ 6	Ozzie Smith	3.00	1.35
☐ 7	Barry Bonds	3.00	1.35
☐ 8	Andy Van Slyke	.50	.23
☐ 9	Larry Walker	2.00	.90
☐ 10	Mark Langston	.50	.23
☐ 11	Ivan Rodriguez	3.00	1.35
☐ 12	Don Mattingly	4.00	1.80
☐ 13	Roberto Alomar	2.00	.90
☐ 14	Robin Ventura	1.00	.45
☐ 15	Cal Ripken	10.00	4.50
☐ 16	Ken Griffey	12.00	5.50
☐ 17	Kirby Puckett	5.00	2.20
☐ 18	Devon White	.50	.23
☐ 19	Pat Listach	.50	.23
☐ 20	Eric Karros	1.00	.45
☐ 21	Pat Borders	.50	.23
☐ 22	Greg Maddux	8.00	3.60
☐ 23	Dennis Eckersley	1.00	.45

		MINT	NRMT
☐ 24	Barry Bonds	3.00	1.35
☐ 25	Gary Sheffield	2.00	.90

1993 Ultra Home Run Kings

Randomly inserted into all 1993 Ultra packs, this ten-card standard-size set features the best long ball hitters in baseball. The borderless cards carry cutout color action player photos that are superposed upon an outer space scene, which includes a baseball "planet" and background stars. The player's name and team, along with the set's logo, are printed in gold foil and rest at the bottom. The horizontal black-and-stellar back carries a color player close-up on the left side, and the player's name, nickname, and career highlights in white lettering on the right side. The set's logo, printed in gold foil at the upper right, rounds out the card.

		MINT	NRMT
COMPLETE SET (10)		15.00	6.75
COMMON CARD (1-10)		1.00	.45
RANDOM INSERTS IN PACKS ..			
☐ 1	Juan Gonzalez	8.00	3.60
☐ 2	Mark McGwire	5.00	2.20
☐ 3	Cecil Fielder	1.50	.70
☐ 4	Fred McGriff	2.00	.90
☐ 5	Albert Belle	6.00	2.70
☐ 6	Barry Bonds	4.00	1.80
☐ 7	Joe Carter	1.50	.70
☐ 8	Gary Sheffield	2.50	1.10
☐ 9	Darren Daulton	1.50	.70
☐ 10	Dave Hollins	1.00	.45

1993 Ultra Performers

This ten-card standard-size set could only be ordered directly from Fleer by sending in $9.95, five Fleer/Fleer Ultra baseball wrappers, and an order blank found in hobby and sports periodicals. Each borderless front features a color player action shot superposed upon four other player photos, which are ghosted and color-screened. The player's name and the set name, both stamped in gold foil, appear at the bottom. The Ultra Performers set logo, a gold-foil-rimmed baseball icon with a blue trail, lies just above. The gold-foil Fleer Ultra logo

appears in an upper corner. The back features a borderless color player action photo that is ghosted and color-screened on one side, where the player's name and career highlights appear. The set logo and gold-foil-stamped name appear below. The set's production number (out of 150,000 produced) rests within a ghosted rectangle at the bottom. The set is sequenced in alphabetical order.

		MINT	NRMT
COMPLETE SET (10)		25.00	11.00
COMMON CARD (1-10)		.50	.23
SETS DISTRIBUTED VIA MAIL-IN OFFER			
☐ 1	Barry Bonds	2.00	.90
☐ 2	Juan Gonzalez	4.00	1.80
☐ 3	Ken Griffey Jr.	10.00	4.50
☐ 4	Eric Karros	1.00	.45
☐ 5	Pat Listach	.50	.23
☐ 6	Greg Maddux	6.00	2.70
☐ 7	David Nied	.50	.23
☐ 8	Gary Sheffield	2.00	.90
☐ 9	J.T. Snow	2.00	.90
☐ 10	Frank Thomas	6.00	2.70

1993 Ultra Strikeout Kings

Inserted into series II packs at a rate of one in 37, this five-card standard-size set showcases outstanding pitchers from both leagues. The color cutout action player photo on the front of each card shows a pitcher on the mound superposed upon a background of stars and a metallic baseball. The player's name appears in gold foil at the bottom. The gold-foil-stamped set logo also appears on the front. Upon a metallic-baseball-and-stellar background, the hor-

izontal back carries a posed color player photo on the left side, and the player's career highlights in yellow lettering on the right side. The player's name and team, as well as the set's logo, appear in gold foil at the top. The set is sequenced in alphabetical order.

		MINT	NRMT
COMPLETE SET (5)		20.00	9.00
COMMON CARD(1-5)		1.00	.45
SER.2 STATED ODDS 1:37			
☐ 1	Roger Clemens	8.00	3.60
☐ 2	Juan Guzman	1.00	.45
☐ 3	Randy Johnson	2.50	1.10
☐ 4	Nolan Ryan	15.00	6.75
☐ 5	John Smoltz	1.50	.70

1994 Ultra

The 1994 Ultra baseball set consists of 600 standard-size cards that were issued in two series of 300. Each pack contains at least one insert card, while "Hot Packs" have nothing but insert cards in them. The front features a full-bleed color action player photo except at the bottom, where a gold foil strip edges the picture. The player's name, his position, team name, and company logo are gold foil stamped across the bottom of the front. The horizontal back has a montage of three different player cutouts on an action scene with a team color-coded border. Biography and statistics on a thin panel toward the bottom round out the back. The cards are numbered on the back, grouped alphabetically within teams, and checklisted below alphabetically according to teams for each league with AL preceding NL. Rookie Cards include Ray Durham and Chan Ho Park.

	MINT	NRMT
COMPLETE SET (600)	40.00	18.00
COMPLETE SERIES 1 (300)	20.00	9.00
COMPLETE SERIES 2 (300)	20.00	9.00
COMMON CARD (1-600)	.15	.07
MINOR STARS	.30	.14
UNLISTED STARS	.60	.25
COMP.FIREMAN SET (10)	5.00	2.20
COMMON FIREMAN (1-10)	.50	.23
FIREMAN: RANDOM INS.IN ALL SER.2 PACKS		
COMP.PHILLIES SET (20)	10.00	4.50
COMP.PHILLIES SER.1 (10)	5.00	2.20
COMP.PHILLIES SER.2 (10)	5.00	2.20
COMMON DAULTON (1-5/11/15)	.50	.23

COMMON KRUK (6-10/16-20)	.50		.23
CERTIFIED DAULTON AUTO	40.00		18.00
CERTIFIED KRUK AUTO	40.00		18.00
PHILLIES: RANDOM INS.IN BOTH SER.PACKS			
COMMON PHIL.MAIL (M1-M4)	1.00		.45
PHILLIES MAIL-IN DIST.VIA WRAPPER EXCH.			

#	Player	Value	Value
1	Jeffrey Hammonds	.30	.14
2	Chris Hoiles	.15	.07
3	Ben McDonald	.15	.07
4	Mark McLemore	.15	.07
5	Alan Mills	.15	.07
6	Jamie Moyer	.15	.07
7	Brad Pennington	.15	.07
8	Jim Poole	.15	.07
9	Cal Ripken Jr.	2.50	1.10
10	Jack Voigt	.15	.07
11	Roger Clemens	1.25	.55
12	Danny Darwin	.15	.07
13	Andre Dawson	.40	.18
14	Scott Fletcher	.15	.07
15	Greg A Harris	.15	.07
16	Billy Hatcher	.15	.07
17	Jeff Russell	.15	.07
18	Aaron Sele	.15	.07
19	Mo Vaughn	.75	.35
20	Mike Butcher	.15	.07
21	Rod Correia	.15	.07
22	Steve Frey	.15	.07
23	Phil Leftwich	.15	.07
24	Torey Lovullo	.15	.07
25	Ken Patterson	.15	.07
26	Eduardo Perez UER (listed as a Twin instead of Angel)	.15	.07
27	Tim Salmon	.60	.25
28	J.T. Snow	.60	.25
29	Chris Turner	.15	.07
30	Wilson Alvarez	.15	.07
31	Jason Bere	.15	.07
32	Joey Cora	.30	.14
33	Alex Fernandez	.15	.07
34	Roberto Hernandez	.15	.07
35	Lance Johnson	.15	.07
36	Ron Karkovice	.15	.07
37	Kirk McCaskill	.15	.07
38	Jeff Schwarz	.15	.07
39	Frank Thomas	2.50	1.10
40	Sandy Alomar Jr	.30	.14
41	Albert Belle	.75	.35
42	Felix Fermin	.15	.07
43	Wayne Kirby	.15	.07
44	Tom Kramer	.15	.07
45	Kenny Lofton	.75	.35
46	Jose Mesa	.15	.07
47	Eric Plunk	.15	.07
48	Paul Sorrento	.15	.07
49	Jim Thome	.75	.35
50	Bill Wertz	.15	.07
51	John Doherty	.15	.07
52	Cecil Fielder	.30	.14
53	Travis Fryman	.30	.14
54	Chris Gomez	.15	.07
55	Mike Henneman	.15	.07
56	Chad Kreuter	.15	.07
57	Bob MacDonald	.15	.07
58	Mike Moore	.15	.07
59	Tony Phillips	.15	.07
60	Lou Whitaker	.30	.14
61	Kevin Appier	.30	.14
62	Greg Gagne	.15	.07
63	Chris Gwynn	.15	.07
64	Bob Hamelin	.15	.07
65	Chris Haney	.15	.07
66	Phil Hiatt	.15	.07
67	Felix Jose	.15	.07
68	Jose Lind	.15	.07
69	Mike Macfarlane	.15	.07
70	Jeff Montgomery	.15	.07
71	Hipolito Pichardo	.15	.07
72	Juan Bell	.15	.07
73	Cal Eldred	.15	.07
74	Darryl Hamilton	.15	.07
75	Doug Henry	.15	.07
76	Mike Ignasiak	.15	.07
77	John Jaha	.15	.07
78	Graeme Lloyd	.15	.07
79	Angel Miranda	.15	.07
80	Dave Nilsson	.15	.07
81	Troy O'Leary	.15	.07
82	Kevin Reimer	.15	.07
83	Willie Banks	.15	.07
84	Larry Casian	.15	.07
85	Scott Erickson	.15	.07
86	Eddie Guardado	.15	.07
87	Kent Hrbek	.30	.14
88	Terry Jorgensen	.15	.07
89	Chuck Knoblauch	.60	.25
90	Pat Meares	.15	.07
91	Mike Trombley	.15	.07
92	Dave Winfield	.40	.18
93	Wade Boggs	.60	.25
94	Scott Kamieniecki	.15	.07
95	Pat Kelly	.15	.07
96	Jimmy Key	.30	.14
97	Jim Leyritz	.15	.07
98	Bobby Munoz	.15	.07
99	Paul O'Neill	.30	.14
100	Melido Perez	.15	.07
101	Mike Stanley	.15	.07
102	Danny Tartabull	.15	.07
103	Bernie Williams	.60	.25
104	Kurt Abbott	.15	.07
105	Mike Bordick	.15	.07
106	Ron Darling	.15	.07
107	Brent Gates	.15	.07
108	Miguel Jimenez	.15	.07
109	Steve Karsay	.15	.07
110	Scott Lydy	.15	.07
111	Mark McGwire	1.25	.55
112	Troy Neel	.15	.07
113	Craig Paquette	.15	.07
114	Bob Welch	.15	.07
115	Bobby Witt	.15	.07
116	Rich Amaral	.15	.07
117	Mike Blowers	.15	.07
118	Jay Buhner	.40	.18
119	Dave Fleming	.15	.07
120	Ken Griffey Jr.	3.00	1.35
121	Tino Martinez	.60	.25
122	Marc Newfield	.15	.07
123	Ted Power	.15	.07
124	Mackey Sasser	.15	.07
125	Omar Vizquel	.30	.14
126	Kevin Brown	.30	.14
127	Juan Gonzalez	1.50	.70
128	Tom Henke	.15	.07
129	David Hulse	.15	.07
130	Dean Palmer	.30	.14
131	Roger Pavlik	.15	.07
132	Ivan Rodriguez	.75	.35
133	Kenny Rogers	.15	.07
134	Doug Strange	.15	.07
135	Pat Borders	.15	.07
136	Joe Carter	.30	.14
137	Darnell Coles	.15	.07
138	Pat Hentgen	.30	.14
139	Al Leiter	.15	.07
140	Paul Molitor	.60	.25
141	John Olerud	.30	.14
142	Ed Sprague	.15	.07
143	Dave Stewart	.30	.14
144	Mike Timlin	.15	.07
145	Duane Ward	.15	.07
146	Devon White	.15	.07
147	Steve Avery	.30	.14
148	Steve Bedrosian	.15	.07
149	Damon Berryhill	.15	.07
150	Jeff Blauser	.15	.07
151	Tom Glavine	.30	.14
152	Chipper Jones	2.00	.90
153	Mark Lemke	.15	.07
154	Fred McGriff	.40	.18
155	Greg McMichael	.15	.07
156	Deion Sanders	.30	.14
157	John Smoltz	.30	.14
158	Mark Wohlers	.15	.07
159	Jose Bautista	.15	.07
160	Steve Buechele	.15	.07
161	Mike Harkey	.15	.07
162	Greg Hibbard	.15	.07
163	Chuck McElroy	.15	.07
164	Mike Morgan	.15	.07
165	Kevin Roberson	.15	.07
166	Ryne Sandberg	.75	.35
167	Jose Vizcaino	.15	.07
168	Rick Wilkins	.15	.07
169	Willie Wilson	.15	.07
170	Willie Greene	.15	.07
171	Roberto Kelly	.15	.07
172	Larry Luebbers	.15	.07
173	Kevin Mitchell	.15	.07
174	Joe Oliver	.15	.07
175	John Roper	.15	.07
176	Johnny Ruffin	.15	.07
177	Reggie Sanders	.15	.07
178	John Smiley	.15	.07
179	Jerry Spradlin	.15	.07
180	Freddie Benavides	.15	.07
181	Dante Bichette	.30	.14
182	Willie Blair	.15	.07
183	Kent Bottenfield	.15	.07
184	Jerald Clark	.15	.07
185	Joe Girardi	.15	.07
186	Roberto Mejia	.15	.07
187	Steve Reed	.15	.07
188	Armando Reynoso	.15	.07
189	Bruce Ruffin	.15	.07
190	Eric Young	.15	.07
191	Luis Aquino	.15	.07
192	Bret Barberie	.15	.07
193	Ryan Bowen	.15	.07
194	Chuck Carr	.15	.07
195	Orestes Destrade	.15	.07
196	Richie Lewis	.15	.07
197	Dave Magadan	.15	.07
198	Bob Natal	.15	.07
199	Gary Sheffield	.60	.25
200	Matt Turner	.15	.07
201	Darrell Whitmore	.15	.07
202	Eric Anthony	.15	.07
203	Jeff Bagwell	1.25	.55
204	Andujar Cedeno	.15	.07
205	Luis Gonzalez	.15	.07
206	Xavier Hernandez	.15	.07
207	Doug Jones	.15	.07
208	Darryl Kile	.30	.14
209	Scott Servais	.15	.07
210	Greg Swindell	.15	.07
211	Brian Williams	.15	.07
212	Pedro Astacio	.15	.07
213	Brett Butler	.30	.14
214	Omar Daal	.15	.07
215	Jim Gott	.15	.07
216	Raul Mondesi	.60	.25
217	Jose Offerman	.15	.07
218	Mike Piazza	2.00	.90
219	Cory Snyder	.15	.07
220	Tim Wallach	.15	.07
221	Todd Worrell	.15	.07
222	Moises Alou	.30	.14
223	Sean Berry	.15	.07
224	Wil Cordero	.15	.07
225	Jeff Fassero	.15	.07
226	Darrin Fletcher	.15	.07
227	Cliff Floyd	.30	.14
228	Marquis Grissom	.30	.14
229	Ken Hill	.15	.07
230	Mike Lansing	.30	.14
231	Kirk Rueter	.15	.07
232	John Wetteland	.15	.07
233	Rondell White	.40	.18
234	Tim Bogar	.15	.07
235	Jeromy Burnitz	.15	.07
236	Dwight Gooden	.30	.14
237	Todd Hundley	.30	.14
238	Jeff Kent	.15	.07
239	Josias Manzanillo	.15	.07
240	Joe Orsulak	.15	.07
241	Ryan Thompson	.15	.07
242	Kim Batiste	.15	.07
243	Darren Daulton	.30	.14
244	Tommy Greene	.15	.07
245	Dave Hollins	.15	.07
246	Pete Incaviglia	.15	.07
247	Danny Jackson	.15	.07
248	Ricky Jordan	.15	.07
249	John Kruk	.30	.14

☐ 250	Mickey Morandini	.15	.07
☐ 251	Terry Mulholland	.15	.07
☐ 252	Ben Rivera	.15	.07
☐ 253	Kevin Stocker	.15	.07
☐ 254	Jay Bell	.30	.14
☐ 255	Steve Cooke	.15	.07
☐ 256	Jeff King	.15	.07
☐ 257	Al Martin	.15	.07
☐ 258	Danny Miceli	.15	.07
☐ 259	Blas Minor	.15	.07
☐ 260	Don Slaught	.15	.07
☐ 261	Paul Wagner	.15	.07
☐ 262	Tim Wakefield	.15	.07
☐ 263	Kevin Young	.15	.07
☐ 264	Rene Arocha	.15	.07
☐ 265	Richard Batchelor	.15	.07
☐ 266	Gregg Jefferies	.15	.07
☐ 267	Brian Jordan	.30	.14
☐ 268	Jose Oquendo	.15	.07
☐ 269	Donovan Osborne	.15	.07
☐ 270	Erik Pappas	.15	.07
☐ 271	Mike Perez	.15	.07
☐ 272	Bob Tewksbury	.15	.07
☐ 273	Mark Whiten	.15	.07
☐ 274	Todd Zeile	.15	.07
☐ 275	Andy Ashby	.15	.07
☐ 276	Brad Ausmus	.15	.07
☐ 277	Phil Clark	.15	.07
☐ 278	Jeff Gardner	.15	.07
☐ 279	Ricky Gutierrez	.15	.07
☐ 280	Tony Gwynn	1.50	.70
☐ 281	Tim Mauser	.15	.07
☐ 282	Scott Sanders	.15	.07
☐ 283	Frank Seminara	.15	.07
☐ 284	Wally Whitehurst	.15	.07
☐ 285	Rod Beck	.15	.07
☐ 286	Barry Bonds	.75	.35
☐ 287	Dave Burba	.15	.07
☐ 288	Mark Carreon	.15	.07
☐ 289	Royce Clayton	.15	.07
☐ 290	Mike Jackson	.15	.07
☐ 291	Darren Lewis	.15	.07
☐ 292	Kirt Manwaring	.15	.07
☐ 293	Dave Martinez	.15	.07
☐ 294	Billy Swift	.15	.07
☐ 295	Salomon Torres	.15	.07
☐ 296	Matt Williams	.40	.18
☐ 297	Checklist 1-75	.15	.07
☐ 298	Checklist 76-150	.15	.07
☐ 299	Checklist 151-225	.15	.07
☐ 300	Checklist 226-300	.15	.07
☐ 301	Brady Anderson	.40	.18
☐ 302	Harold Baines	.30	.14
☐ 303	Damon Buford	.15	.07
☐ 304	Mike Devereaux	.15	.07
☐ 305	Sid Fernandez	.15	.07
☐ 306	Rick Krivda	.15	.07
☐ 307	Mike Mussina	.60	.25
☐ 308	Rafael Palmeiro	.40	.18
☐ 309	Arthur Rhodes	.15	.07
☐ 310	Chris Sabo	.15	.07
☐ 311	Lee Smith	.30	.14
☐ 312	Gregg Zaun	.15	.07
☐ 313	Scott Cooper	.15	.07
☐ 314	Mike Greenwell	.15	.07
☐ 315	Tim Naehring	.15	.07
☐ 316	Otis Nixon	.15	.07
☐ 317	Paul Quantrill	.15	.07
☐ 318	John Valentin	.30	.14
☐ 319	Dave Valle	.15	.07
☐ 320	Frank Viola	.15	.07
☐ 321	Brian Anderson	.60	.25
☐ 322	Garret Anderson	.60	.25
☐ 323	Chad Curtis	.15	.07
☐ 324	Chili Davis	.30	.14
☐ 325	Gary DiSarcina	.15	.07
☐ 326	Damion Easley	.15	.07
☐ 327	Jim Edmonds	.60	.25
☐ 328	Chuck Finley	.15	.07
☐ 329	Joe Grahe	.15	.07
☐ 330	Bo Jackson	.30	.14
☐ 331	Mark Langston	.15	.07
☐ 332	Harold Reynolds	.15	.07
☐ 333	James Baldwin	.30	.14
☐ 334	Ray Durham	.75	.35
☐ 335	Julio Franco	.15	.07
☐ 336	Craig Grebeck	.15	.07
☐ 337	Ozzie Guillen	.15	.07
☐ 338	Joe Hall	.15	.07
☐ 339	Darrin Jackson	.15	.07
☐ 340	Jack McDowell	.15	.07
☐ 341	Tim Raines	.30	.14
☐ 342	Robin Ventura	.30	.14
☐ 343	Carlos Baerga	.15	.07
☐ 344	Derek Lilliquist	.15	.07
☐ 345	Dennis Martinez	.30	.14
☐ 346	Jack Morris	.30	.14
☐ 347	Eddie Murray	.60	.25
☐ 348	Chris Nabholz	.15	.07
☐ 349	Charles Nagy	.30	.14
☐ 350	Chad Ogea	.30	.14
☐ 351	Manny Ramirez	.75	.35
☐ 352	Omar Vizquel	.30	.14
☐ 353	Tim Belcher	.15	.07
☐ 354	Eric Davis	.30	.14
☐ 355	Kirk Gibson	.30	.14
☐ 356	Rick Greene	.15	.07
☐ 357	Mickey Tettleton	.15	.07
☐ 358	Alan Trammell	.40	.18
☐ 359	David Wells	.15	.07
☐ 360	Stan Belinda	.15	.07
☐ 361	Vince Coleman	.15	.07
☐ 362	David Cone	.30	.14
☐ 363	Gary Gaetti	.15	.07
☐ 364	Tom Gordon	.15	.07
☐ 365	Dave Henderson	.15	.07
☐ 366	Wally Joyner	.30	.14
☐ 367	Brent Mayne	.15	.07
☐ 368	Brian McRae	.15	.07
☐ 369	Michael Tucker	.40	.18
☐ 370	Ricky Bones	.15	.07
☐ 371	Brian Harper	.15	.07
☐ 372	Tyrone Hill	.15	.07
☐ 373	Mark Kiefer	.15	.07
☐ 374	Pat Listach	.15	.07
☐ 375	Mike Matheny	.15	.07
☐ 376	Jose Mercedes	.15	.07
☐ 377	Jody Reed	.15	.07
☐ 378	Kevin Seitzer	.15	.07
☐ 379	B.J. Surhoff	.15	.07
☐ 380	Greg Vaughn	.15	.07
☐ 381	Turner Ward	.15	.07
☐ 382	Wes Weger	.15	.07
☐ 383	Bill Wegman	.15	.07
☐ 384	Rick Aguilera	.15	.07
☐ 385	Rich Becker	.15	.07
☐ 386	Alex Cole	.15	.07
☐ 387	Steve Dunn	.15	.07
☐ 388	Keith Garagozzo	.15	.07
☐ 389	LaTroy Hawkins	.30	.14
☐ 390	Shane Mack	.15	.07
☐ 391	David McCarty	.15	.07
☐ 392	Pedro Munoz	.15	.07
☐ 393	Derek Parks	.15	.07
☐ 394	Kirby Puckett	1.25	.55
☐ 395	Kevin Tapani	.15	.07
☐ 396	Matt Walbeck	.15	.07
☐ 397	Jim Abbott	.15	.07
☐ 398	Mike Gallego	.15	.07
☐ 399	Xavier Hernandez	.15	.07
☐ 400	Don Mattingly	1.00	.45
☐ 401	Terry Mulholland	.15	.07
☐ 402	Matt Nokes	.15	.07
☐ 403	Luis Polonia	.15	.07
☐ 404	Bob Wickman	.15	.07
☐ 405	Mark Acre	.15	.07
☐ 406	Fausto Cruz	.15	.07
☐ 407	Dennis Eckersley	.30	.14
☐ 408	Rickey Henderson	.40	.18
☐ 409	Stan Javier	.15	.07
☐ 410	Carlos Reyes	.15	.07
☐ 411	Ruben Sierra	.15	.07
☐ 412	Terry Steinbach	.15	.07
☐ 413	Bill Taylor	.15	.07
☐ 414	Todd Van Poppel	.15	.07
☐ 415	Eric Anthony	.15	.07
☐ 416	Bobby Ayala	.15	.07
☐ 417	Chris Bosio	.15	.07
☐ 418	Tim Davis	.15	.07
☐ 419	Randy Johnson	.60	.25
☐ 420	Kevin King	.15	.07
☐ 421	Anthony Manahan	.15	.07
☐ 422	Edgar Martinez	.40	.18
☐ 423	Keith Mitchell	.15	.07
☐ 424	Roger Salkeld	.15	.07
☐ 425	Mac Suzuki	.30	.14
☐ 426	Dan Wilson	.30	.14
☐ 427	Duff Brumley	.15	.07
☐ 428	Jose Canseco	.40	.18
☐ 429	Will Clark	.40	.18
☐ 430	Steve Dreyer	.15	.07
☐ 431	Rick Helling	.15	.07
☐ 432	Chris James	.15	.07
☐ 433	Matt Whiteside	.15	.07
☐ 434	Roberto Alomar	.60	.25
☐ 435	Scott Brow	.15	.07
☐ 436	Domingo Cedeno	.15	.07
☐ 437	Carlos Delgado	.40	.18
☐ 438	Juan Guzman	.15	.07
☐ 439	Paul Spoljaric	.15	.07
☐ 440	Todd Stottlemyre	.15	.07
☐ 441	Woody Williams	.15	.07
☐ 442	David Justice	.60	.25
☐ 443	Mike Kelly	.15	.07
☐ 444	Ryan Klesko	.60	.25
☐ 445	Javier Lopez	.40	.18
☐ 446	Greg Maddux	2.00	.90
☐ 447	Kent Mercker	.15	.07
☐ 448	Charlie O'Brien	.15	.07
☐ 449	Terry Pendleton	.15	.07
☐ 450	Mike Stanton	.15	.07
☐ 451	Tony Tarasco	.15	.07
☐ 452	Terrell Wade	.30	.14
☐ 453	Willie Banks	.15	.07
☐ 454	Shawon Dunston	.15	.07
☐ 455	Mark Grace	.40	.18
☐ 456	Jose Guzman	.15	.07
☐ 457	Jose Hernandez	.15	.07
☐ 458	Glenallen Hill	.15	.07
☐ 459	Blaise Ilsley	.15	.07
☐ 460	Brooks Kieschnick	.60	.25
☐ 461	Derrick May	.15	.07
☐ 462	Randy Myers	.15	.07
☐ 463	Karl Rhodes	.15	.07
☐ 464	Sammy Sosa	.60	.25
☐ 465	Steve Trachsel	.30	.14
☐ 466	Anthony Young	.15	.07
☐ 467	Eddie Zambrano	.15	.07
☐ 468	Bret Boone	.15	.07
☐ 469	Tom Browning	.15	.07
☐ 470	Hector Carrasco	.15	.07
☐ 471	Rob Dibble	.15	.07
☐ 472	Erik Hanson	.15	.07
☐ 473	Thomas Howard	.15	.07
☐ 474	Barry Larkin	.40	.18
☐ 475	Hal Morris	.15	.07
☐ 476	Jose Rijo	.15	.07
☐ 477	John Burke	.15	.07
☐ 478	Ellis Burks	.30	.14
☐ 479	Marvin Freeman	.15	.07
☐ 480	Andres Galarraga	.60	.25
☐ 481	Gary W. Harris	.15	.07
☐ 482	Charlie Hayes	.15	.07
☐ 483	Darren Holmes	.15	.07
☐ 484	Howard Johnson	.15	.07
☐ 485	Marcus Moore	.15	.07
☐ 486	David Nied	.15	.07
☐ 487	Mark Thompson	.15	.07
☐ 488	Walt Weiss	.15	.07
☐ 489	Kurt Abbott	.15	.07
☐ 490	Matias Carrillo	.15	.07
☐ 491	Jeff Conine	.30	.14
☐ 492	Chris Hammond	.15	.07
☐ 493	Bryan Harvey	.15	.07
☐ 494	Charlie Hough	.15	.07
☐ 495	Yorkis Perez	.15	.07
☐ 496	Pat Rapp	.15	.07
☐ 497	Benito Santiago	.15	.07
☐ 498	David Weathers	.15	.07
☐ 499	Craig Biggio	.40	.18
☐ 500	Ken Caminiti	.40	.18
☐ 501	Doug Drabek	.15	.07
☐ 502	Tony Eusebio	.15	.07
☐ 503	Steve Finley	.30	.14
☐ 504	Pete Harnisch	.15	.07
☐ 505	Brian L.Hunter	.60	.25
☐ 506	Domingo Jean	.15	.07
☐ 507	Todd Jones	.15	.07

☐ 508	Orlando Miller	.15	.07
☐ 509	James Mouton	.15	.07
☐ 510	Roberto Petagine	.15	.07
☐ 511	Shane Reynolds	.15	.07
☐ 512	Mitch Williams	.15	.07
☐ 513	Billy Ashley	.15	.07
☐ 514	Tom Candiotti	.15	.07
☐ 515	Delino DeShields	.15	.07
☐ 516	Kevin Gross	.15	.07
☐ 517	Orel Hershiser	.30	.14
☐ 518	Eric Karros	.30	.14
☐ 519	Ramon Martinez	.30	.14
☐ 520	Chan Ho Park	2.00	.90
☐ 521	Henry Rodriguez	.15	.07
☐ 522	Joey Eischen	.15	.07
☐ 523	Rod Henderson	.15	.07
☐ 524	Pedro J. Martinez	.60	.25
☐ 525	Mel Rojas	.15	.07
☐ 526	Larry Walker	.60	.25
☐ 527	Gabe White	.15	.07
☐ 528	Bobby Bonilla	.30	.14
☐ 529	Jonathan Hurst	.15	.07
☐ 530	Bobby Jones	.30	.14
☐ 531	Kevin McReynolds	.15	.07
☐ 532	Bill Pulsipher	.30	.14
☐ 533	Bret Saberhagen	.15	.07
☐ 534	David Segui	.15	.07
☐ 535	Pete Smith	.15	.07
☐ 536	Kelly Stinnett	.15	.07
☐ 537	Dave Telgheder	.15	.07
☐ 538	Quilvio Veras	.30	.14
☐ 539	Jose Vizcaino	.15	.07
☐ 540	Pete Walker	.15	.07
☐ 541	Ricky Bottalico	.60	.25
☐ 542	Wes Chamberlain	.15	.07
☐ 543	Mariano Duncan	.15	.07
☐ 544	Lenny Dykstra	.30	.14
☐ 545	Jim Eisenreich	.15	.07
☐ 546	Phil Geisler	.15	.07
☐ 547	Wayne Gomes	.15	.07
☐ 548	Doug Jones	.15	.07
☐ 549	Jeff Juden	.15	.07
☐ 550	Mike Lieberthal	.15	.07
☐ 551	Tony Longmire	.15	.07
☐ 552	Tom Marsh	.15	.07
☐ 553	Bobby Munoz	.15	.07
☐ 554	Curt Schilling	.30	.14
☐ 555	Carlos Garcia	.15	.07
☐ 556	Ravelo Manzanillo	.15	.07
☐ 557	Orlando Merced	.15	.07
☐ 558	Will Pennyfeather	.15	.07
☐ 559	Zane Smith	.15	.07
☐ 560	Andy Van Slyke	.30	.14
☐ 561	Rick White	.15	.07
☐ 562	Luis Alicea	.15	.07
☐ 563	Brian Barber	.15	.07
☐ 564	Clint Davis	.15	.07
☐ 565	Bernard Gilkey	.15	.07
☐ 566	Ray Lankford	.30	.14
☐ 567	Tom Pagnozzi	.15	.07
☐ 568	Ozzie Smith	.75	.35
☐ 569	Rick Sutcliffe	.15	.07
☐ 570	Allen Watson	.15	.07
☐ 571	Dmitri Young	.40	.18
☐ 572	Derek Bell	.15	.07
☐ 573	Andy Benes	.30	.14
☐ 574	Archi Cianfrocco	.15	.07
☐ 575	Joey Hamilton	.60	.25
☐ 576	Gene Harris	.15	.07
☐ 577	Trevor Hoffman	.15	.07
☐ 578	Tim Hyers	.15	.07
☐ 579	Brian Johnson	.15	.07
☐ 580	Keith Lockhart	.15	.07
☐ 581	Pedro A. Martinez	.15	.07
☐ 582	Ray McDavid	.15	.07
☐ 583	Phil Plantier	.15	.07
☐ 584	Bip Roberts	.15	.07
☐ 585	Dave Staton	.15	.07
☐ 586	Todd Benzinger	.15	.07
☐ 587	John Burkett	.15	.07
☐ 588	Bryan Hickerson	.15	.07
☐ 589	Willie McGee	.15	.07
☐ 590	John Patterson	.15	.07
☐ 591	Mark Portugal	.15	.07
☐ 592	Kevin Rogers	.15	.07
☐ 593	Joe Rosselli	.15	.07
☐ 594	Steve Soderstrom	.30	.14
☐ 595	Robby Thompson	.15	.07
☐ 596	125th Anniversary Card	.15	.07
☐ 597	Checklist	.15	.07
☐ 598	Checklist	.15	.07
☐ 599	Checklist	.15	.07
☐ 600	Checklist	.15	.07
☐ P243	Darren Daulton Promo	2.00	.90
☐ P249	John Kruk Promo ..	2.00	.90

1994 Ultra All-Rookies

This 10-card standard-size set features top rookies of 1994 and were randomly inserted in second series jumbo and foil packs at a rate of one in 10. Card fronts have a color player photo cut-out over a computer generated background that resembles volcanic activity. The player's name and All-Rookie Team logo appear in gold foil at the bottom. On the backs, the player cut-out appears toward the right with text over the left. The background is much the same as the front. The set is sequenced in alphabetical order. Every second series Ultra hobby case included this set in jumbo (3 1/2" by 5") form.

		MINT	NRMT
	COMPLETE SET (10)	10.00	4.50
	COMMON CARD (1-10)	.50	.23
	MINOR STARS	1.00	.45

RANDOM INSERTS IN ALL SER.2 PACKS
*JUMBOS: 1X TO 2X HI COLUMN
ONE JUMBO SET PER HOBBY CASE

☐ 1	Kurt Abbott	.50	.23
☐ 2	Carlos Delgado	1.50	.70
☐ 3	Cliff Floyd	1.00	.45
☐ 4	Jeffrey Hammonds	1.00	.45
☐ 5	Ryan Klesko	2.00	.90
☐ 6	Javier Lopez	1.50	.70
☐ 7	Raul Mondesi	2.00	.90
☐ 8	James Mouton	.50	.23
☐ 9	Chan Ho Park	2.00	.90
☐ 10	Dave Staton	.50	.23

1994 Ultra All-Stars

Randomly inserted in second series foil and jumbo packs at a rate of one in three, this 20-card standard-size set contains top major league stars. The fronts have a color player photo superimposed over a bright red (American League players) or dark blue (National League) background. The backs are much the same except they include highlights from 1993.

		MINT	NRMT
	COMPLETE SET (20)	18.00	8.00
	COMMON CARD (1-20)	.25	.11

RANDOM INSERTS IN ALL SER.2 PACKS

☐ 1	Chris Hoiles	.25	.11
☐ 2	Frank Thomas	4.00	1.80
☐ 3	Roberto Alomar	1.00	.45
☐ 4	Cal Ripken Jr.	4.00	1.80
☐ 5	Robin Ventura	.50	.23
☐ 6	Albert Belle	1.00	.45
☐ 7	Juan Gonzalez	2.50	1.10
☐ 8	Ken Griffey Jr.	5.00	2.20
☐ 9	John Olerud	.50	.23
☐ 10	Jack McDowell	.25	.11
☐ 11	Mike Piazza	3.00	1.35
☐ 12	Fred McGriff	.75	.35
☐ 13	Ryne Sandberg	1.25	.55
☐ 14	Jay Bell	.50	.23
☐ 15	Matt Williams	.75	.35
☐ 16	Barry Bonds	1.25	.55
☐ 17	Lenny Dykstra	.50	.23
☐ 18	David Justice	1.00	.45
☐ 19	Tom Glavine	.50	.23
☐ 20	Greg Maddux	3.00	1.35

1994 Ultra Award Winners

Randomly inserted in all first series packs at a rate of one in three, this 25-card standard-size set features three MVP's, two Rookies of the Year, and 18 Top Glove defensive standouts. The set is divided into American League Top Gloves (1-9), National League Top Gloves (10-18), and Award Winners (19-25). A horizontal design includes a color player cut-out over a gold background on front. Also on front, is a gold foil logo *that indicates the honor. The backs have a small photo and text.*

	MINT	NRMT
COMPLETE SET (25)	15.00	6.75
COMMON CARD(1-25)	.25	.11
RANDOM INSERTS IN ALL SER.1 PACKS		

		MINT	NRMT
☐ 1	Ivan Rodriguez	1.25	.55
☐ 2	Don Mattingly	1.50	.70
☐ 3	Roberto Alomar	1.00	.45
☐ 4	Robin Ventura	.50	.23
☐ 5	Omar Vizquel	.50	.23
☐ 6	Ken Griffey Jr.	5.00	2.20
☐ 7	Kenny Lofton	1.25	.55
☐ 8	Devon White	.25	.11
☐ 9	Mark Langston	.25	.11
☐ 10	Kirt Manwaring	.25	.11
☐ 11	Mark Grace	.75	.35
☐ 12	Robby Thompson	.25	.11
☐ 13	Matt Williams	.75	.35
☐ 14	Jay Bell	.50	.23
☐ 15	Barry Bonds	1.25	.55
☐ 16	Marquis Grissom	.50	.23
☐ 17	Larry Walker	1.00	.45
☐ 18	Greg Maddux	3.00	1.35
☐ 19	Frank Thomas	4.00	1.80
☐ 20	Barry Bonds	1.25	.55
☐ 21	Paul Molitor	1.00	.45
☐ 22	Jack McDowell	.25	.11
☐ 23	Greg Maddux	3.00	1.35
☐ 24	Tim Salmon	1.00	.45
☐ 25	Mike Piazza	3.00	1.35

1994 Ultra Career Achievement

Randomly inserted in all second series packs at a rate of one in 21, this five card standard-size set highlights veteran stars and milestones they have reached during their brilliant careers. Horizontally designed cards have fronts that feature a color player photo superimposed over solid color background that contains another player photo. A photo of the player earlier in his career is on back along with text. The cards are sequenced in alphabetical order.

		MINT	NRMT
COMPLETE SET (5)		12.00	5.50
COMMON CARD(1-5)		1.00	.45
RANDOM INSERTS IN ALL SER.2 PACKS			

		MINT	NRMT
☐ 1	Joe Carter	1.00	.45
☐ 2	Paul Molitor	2.00	.90
☐ 3	Cal Ripken Jr.	8.00	3.60
☐ 4	Ryne Sandberg	2.50	1.10
☐ 5	Dave Winfield	1.50	.70

1994 Ultra Hitting Machines

Randomly inserted in all second series packs at a rate of one in five, this 10-card horizontally designed standard-size set features top hitters from 1993. The fronts have a color player cut-out over a "Hitting Machines" background. The back has a smaller player cut-out and text. The set is sequenced in alphabetical order.

		MINT	NRMT
COMPLETE SET (10)		12.00	5.50
COMMON CARD(1-10)		.25	.11
RANDOM INSERTS IN ALL SER.2 PACKS			

		MINT	NRMT
☐ 1	Roberto Alomar	1.00	.45
☐ 2	Carlos Baerga	.25	.11
☐ 3	Barry Bonds	1.25	.55
☐ 4	Andres Galarraga	1.00	.45
☐ 5	Juan Gonzalez	2.50	1.10
☐ 6	Tony Gwynn	2.50	1.10
☐ 7	Paul Molitor	1.00	.45
☐ 8	John Olerud	.50	.23
☐ 9	Mike Piazza	3.00	1.35
☐ 10	Frank Thomas	4.00	1.80

1994 Ultra Home Run Kings

Randomly inserted exclusively in first series foil packs at a rate of one in 36, these 12 standard-size cards highlight home run hitters by an etched metalized look. Cards 1-6 feature American League Home Run Kings while cards 7-12 present National League Home Run Kings.

	MINT	NRMT
COMPLETE SET (12)	80.00	36.00
COMMON CARD(1-12)	2.50	1.10
RANDOM INS.IN SER.1 FOIL/JUMBO PACKS		

		MINT	NRMT
☐ 1	Juan Gonzalez	12.00	5.50
☐ 2	Ken Griffey Jr.	25.00	11.00
☐ 3	Frank Thomas	20.00	9.00
☐ 4	Albert Belle	4.00	1.80
☐ 5	Rafael Palmeiro	3.00	1.35
☐ 6	Joe Carter	2.50	1.10
☐ 7	Barry Bonds	6.00	2.70
☐ 8	David Justice	5.00	2.20
☐ 9	Matt Williams	3.00	1.35
☐ 10	Fred McGriff	3.00	1.35
☐ 11	Ron Gant	2.50	1.10
☐ 12	Mike Piazza	15.00	6.75

1994 Ultra League Leaders

Randomly inserted in all first series packs at a rate of one in 11, this ten-card standard-size set features ten of 1993's leading players. The fronts feature borderless color player action shots, with a color-screening that shades from being imperceptible at the top to washing out the photos' true colors at the bottom. The player's name in gold foil appears across the card face. The borderless back carries a color player head shot in a lower corner with his career highlights appearing above, all on a monochrome background that shades from dark to light, from top to bottom. The set is arranged according to American League (1-5) and National League (6-10) players.

	MINT	NRMT
COMPLETE SET (10)	5.00	2.20
COMMON CARD(1-10)	.25	.11
RANDOM INSERTS IN ALL SER.1 PACKS		

		MINT	NRMT
☐ 1	John Olerud	.50	.23
☐ 2	Rafael Palmeiro	1.00	.45
☐ 3	Kenny Lofton	2.00	.90
☐ 4	Jack McDowell	.25	.11
☐ 5	Randy Johnson	1.50	.70
☐ 6	Andres Galarraga	1.50	.70
☐ 7	Lenny Dykstra	.50	.23
☐ 8	Chuck Carr	.25	.11
☐ 9	Tom Glavine	.50	.23
☐ 10	Jose Rijo	.25	.11

1994 Ultra On-Base Leaders

Randomly inserted in second series jumbo packs at a rate of

one in 36, this 12-card standard-size set features those that were among the Major League leaders in on-base percentage. Card fronts have the player superimposed over a metallic background that simulates statistics from a sports page. The backs have a player cut-out and text over a statistical background that is not metallic. The set is sequenced in alphabetical order.

	MINT	NRMT
COMPLETE SET (12)	150.00	70.00
COMMON CARD (1-12)	4.00	1.80
SEMISTARS	8.00	3.60
UNLISTED STARS	12.00	5.50
RANDOM INSERTS IN SER.2 JUMBO PACKS		

		MINT	NRMT
☐ 1	Roberto Alomar	12.00	5.50
☐ 2	Barry Bonds	15.00	6.75
☐ 3	Lenny Dykstra	6.00	2.70
☐ 4	Andres Galarraga	12.00	5.50
☐ 5	Mark Grace	8.00	3.60
☐ 6	Ken Griffey Jr.	60.00	27.00
☐ 7	Gregg Jefferies	4.00	1.80
☐ 8	Orlando Merced	4.00	1.80
☐ 9	Paul Molitor	12.00	5.50
☐ 10	John Olerud	6.00	2.70
☐ 11	Tony Phillips	4.00	1.80
☐ 12	Frank Thomas	50.00	22.00

1994 Ultra RBI Kings

Randomly inserted in first series jumbo packs at a rate of one in 36, this 12-card standard-size set features RBI leaders. These horizontal, metallized cards have a color player photo on front that superimposes a player image. The backs have a write-up and a small color player photo. Cards 1-6 feature American League RBI Kings

while cards 7-12 present National League RBI Kings.

	MINT	NRMT
COMPLETE SET (12)	150.00	70.00
COMMON CARD (1-12)	4.00	1.80
SEMISTARS	8.00	3.60
UNLISTED STARS	12.00	5.50
RANDOM INS.IN SER.1 JUMBO PACKS		

		MINT	NRMT
☐ 1	Albert Belle	15.00	6.75
☐ 2	Frank Thomas	50.00	22.00
☐ 3	Joe Carter	6.00	2.70
☐ 4	Juan Gonzalez	30.00	13.50
☐ 5	Cecil Fielder	6.00	2.70
☐ 6	Carlos Baerga	4.00	1.80
☐ 7	Barry Bonds	15.00	6.75
☐ 8	David Justice	12.00	5.50
☐ 9	Ron Gant	6.00	2.70
☐ 10	Mike Piazza	40.00	18.00
☐ 11	Matt Williams	8.00	3.60
☐ 12	Darren Daulton	6.00	2.70

1994 Ultra Rising Stars

Randomly inserted in second series foil packs and jumbo packs at a rate of one in 36, this 12-card set spotlights top young major league stars. Metallic fronts have the player superimposed over icons resembling outer space. The backs feature the player in the same format along with text. The set is sequenced in alphabetical order.

	MINT	NRMT
COMPLETE SET (12)	120.00	55.00
COMMON CARD (1-12)	4.00	1.80
SEMISTARS	8.00	3.60
UNLISTED STARS	12.00	5.50
RANDOM INS.IN SER.2 FOIL/JUMBO PACKS		

		MINT	NRMT
☐ 1	Carlos Baerga	4.00	1.80
☐ 2	Jeff Bagwell	25.00	11.00
☐ 3	Albert Belle	15.00	6.75
☐ 4	Cliff Floyd	6.00	2.70
☐ 5	Travis Fryman	6.00	2.70
☐ 6	Marquis Grissom	6.00	2.70
☐ 7	Kenny Lofton	15.00	6.75
☐ 8	John Olerud	6.00	2.70
☐ 9	Mike Piazza	40.00	18.00
☐ 10	Mark Grace	4.00	1.80
☐ 11	Tim Salmon	12.00	5.50
☐ 12	Aaron Sele	4.00	1.80

1994 Ultra Second Year Standouts

Randomly inserted in all first series packs at a rate of one in 11, this 10-card standard-size

set included 10 1993 outstanding rookies who are destined to become future stars. The fronts feature two color player action cutouts superimposed upon borderless team-colored backgrounds. The player's name appears in gold foil at the bottom. The back carries a color player head shot in a lower corner with his career highlights appearing alongside, all on a borderless team color-coded background. The set is arranged in alphabetical order according to American League (1-5) and National League (6-10) players.

	MINT	NRMT
COMPLETE SET (10)	15.00	6.75
COMMON CARD (1-10)	.50	.23
SER.1 STATED ODDS 1:11		

		MINT	NRMT
☐ 1	Jason Bere	.50	.23
☐ 2	Brent Gates	.50	.23
☐ 3	Jeffrey Hammonds	1.00	.45
☐ 4	Tim Salmon	2.00	.90
☐ 5	Aaron Sele	.50	.23
☐ 6	Chuck Carr	.50	.23
☐ 7	Jeff Conine	1.00	.45
☐ 8	Greg McMichael	.50	.23
☐ 9	Mike Piazza	12.00	5.50
☐ 10	Kevin Stocker	.50	.23

1994 Ultra Strikeout Kings

Randomly inserted in all second series packs at a rate of one in seven, this five-card standard-size set features top strikeout artists. Full-bleed fronts offer triple exposure photos and a gold foil Strikeout King logo. The backs contain a photo and write-up with the Strikeout King logo as background. The set is sequenced in alphabetical order.

	MINT	NRMT
COMPLETE SET (5)	5.00	2.20
COMMON CARD(1-6)	.25	.11
SER.2 STATED ODDS 1:7		

□ 1 Randy Johnson	1.00	.45
□ 2 Mark Langston	.25	.11
□ 3 Greg Maddux	3.00	1.35
□ 4 Jose Rijo	.25	.11
□ 5 John Smoltz	.50	.23

1995 Ultra

This 450-card standard-size set was issued in two series. The first series contained 250 cards while the second series consisted of 200 cards. They were issued in 12-card packs (either hobby or retail) with a suggested retail price of $1.99. Also, 15-card pre-priced packs with a suggested retail of $2.69. Each pack contained two inserts: one is a Gold Medallion parallel while the other is from one of Ultra's many insert sets. "Hot Packs" contain nothing but insert cards. The full-bleed fronts feature the player's photo with the team name and player's name at the bottom. The "95 Fleer Ultra" logo is in the upper right corner. The backs have a two-photo design; one of which is a full-size duotone shot with the other being a full-color action shot. Personal bio, seasonal and career information are also included on the back. In each series the cards were grouped alphabetically within teams and checklisted alphabetically according to teams for each league with AL preceding NL. There are no key Rookie Cards in this set.

	MINT	NRMT
COMPLETE SET (450)	30.00	13.50
COMPLETE SERIES 1 (250)	18.00	8.00
COMPLETE SERIES 2 (200)	12.00	5.50
COMMON CARD (1-450)	.15	.07
MINOR STARS	.30	.14
UNLISTED STARS	.60	.25
COMP.G.MED.SET (450)	110.00	
COMP.G.MED.SER.1 (250)	60.00	27.00
COMP.G.MED.SER.2 (200)	50.00	22.00
COMMON G.MED. (1-450)	.30	.14
*G.MED.STARS: 1.5X TO 4X HI COLUMN		
*G.MED.YOUNG STARS: 1.25X TO 3X HI		
ONE GOLD MEDALLION PER PACK		

□ 1 Brady Anderson	.40	.18
□ 2 Sid Fernandez	.15	.07
□ 3 Jeffrey Hammonds	.30	.14
□ 4 Chris Hoiles	.15	.07
□ 5 Ben McDonald	.15	.07
□ 6 Mike Mussina	.60	.25
□ 7 Rafael Palmeiro	.40	.18
□ 8 Jack Voigt	.15	.07
□ 9 Wes Chamberlain	.15	.07
□ 10 Roger Clemens	1.25	.55
□ 11 Chris Howard	.15	.07
□ 12 Tim Naehring	.15	.07
□ 13 Otis Nixon	.15	.07
□ 14 Rich Rowland	.15	.07
□ 15 Ken Ryan	.15	.07
□ 16 John Valentin	.15	.07
□ 17 Mo Vaughn	.75	.35
□ 18 Brian Anderson	.30	.14
□ 19 Chili Davis	.30	.14
□ 20 Damion Easley	.15	.07
□ 21 Jim Edmonds	.40	.18
□ 22 Mark Langston	.15	.07
□ 23 Tim Salmon	.60	.25
□ 24 J.T. Snow	.30	.14
□ 25 Chris Turner	.15	.07
□ 26 Wilson Alvarez	.15	.07
□ 27 Joey Cora	.30	.14
□ 28 Alex Fernandez	.15	.07
□ 29 Roberto Hernandez	.15	.07
□ 30 Lance Johnson	.15	.07
□ 31 Ron Karkovice	.15	.07
□ 32 Kirk McCaskill	.15	.07
□ 33 Tim Raines	.30	.14
□ 34 Frank Thomas	2.50	1.10
□ 35 Sandy Alomar Jr.	.30	.14
□ 36 Albert Belle	.75	.35
□ 37 Mark Clark	.15	.07
□ 38 Kenny Lofton	.75	.35
□ 39 Eddie Murray	.60	.25
□ 40 Eric Plunk	.15	.07
□ 41 Manny Ramirez	.60	.25
□ 42 Jim Thome	.60	.25
□ 43 Omar Vizquel	.30	.14
□ 44 Danny Bautista	.15	.07
□ 45 Junior Felix	.15	.07
□ 46 Cecil Fielder	.30	.14
□ 47 Chris Gomez	.15	.07
□ 48 Chad Kreuter	.15	.07
□ 49 Mike Moore	.15	.07
□ 50 Tony Phillips	.15	.07
□ 51 Alan Trammell	.40	.18
□ 52 David Wells	.15	.07
□ 53 Kevin Appier	.30	.14
□ 54 Billy Brewer	.15	.07
□ 55 David Cone	.30	.14
□ 56 Greg Gagne	.15	.07
□ 57 Bob Hamelin	.15	.07
□ 58 Jose Lind	.15	.07
□ 59 Brent Mayne	.15	.07
□ 60 Brian McRae	.15	.07
□ 61 Terry Shumpert	.15	.07
□ 62 Ricky Bones	.15	.07
□ 63 Mike Fetters	.15	.07
□ 64 Darryl Hamilton	.15	.07
□ 65 John Jaha	.15	.07
□ 66 Graeme Lloyd	.15	.07
□ 67 Matt Mieske	.15	.07
□ 68 Kevin Seitzer	.15	.07
□ 69 Jose Valentin	.15	.07
□ 70 Turner Ward	.15	.07
□ 71 Rick Aguilera	.15	.07
□ 72 Rich Becker	.15	.07
□ 73 Alex Cole	.15	.07
□ 74 Scott Leius	.15	.07
□ 75 Pat Meares	.15	.07
□ 76 Kirby Puckett	1.25	.55
□ 77 Dave Stevens	.15	.07
□ 78 Kevin Tapani	.15	.07
□ 79 Matt Walbeck	.15	.07
□ 80 Wade Boggs	.60	.25
□ 81 Scott Kamieniecki	.15	.07
□ 82 Pat Kelly	.15	.07
□ 83 Jimmy Key	.30	.14
□ 84 Paul O'Neill	.30	.14
□ 85 Luis Polonia	.15	.07
□ 86 Mike Stanley	.15	.07
□ 87 Danny Tartabull	.15	.07
□ 88 Bob Wickman	.15	.07
□ 89 Mark Acre	.15	.07
□ 90 Geronimo Berroa	.15	.07
□ 91 Mike Bordick	.15	.07
□ 92 Ron Darling	.15	.07
□ 93 Stan Javier	.15	.07
□ 94 Mark McGwire	1.25	.55
□ 95 Troy Neel	.15	.07
□ 96 Ruben Sierra	.15	.07
□ 97 Terry Steinbach	.15	.07
□ 98 Eric Anthony	.15	.07
□ 99 Chris Bosio	.15	.07
□ 100 Dave Fleming	.15	.07
□ 101 Ken Griffey Jr.	3.00	1.35
□ 102 Reggie Jefferson	.15	.07
□ 103 Randy Johnson	.60	.25
□ 104 Edgar Martinez	.40	.18
□ 105 Bill Risley	.15	.07
□ 106 Dan Wilson	.15	.07
□ 107 Cris Carpenter	.15	.07
□ 108 Will Clark	.40	.18
□ 109 Juan Gonzalez	1.50	.70
□ 110 Rusty Greer	.60	.25
□ 111 David Hulse	.15	.07
□ 112 Roger Pavlik	.15	.07
□ 113 Ivan Rodriguez	.75	.35
□ 114 Doug Strange	.15	.07
□ 115 Matt Whiteside	.15	.07
□ 116 Roberto Alomar	.60	.25
□ 117 Brad Cornett	.15	.07
□ 118 Carlos Delgado	.30	.14
□ 119 Alex Gonzalez	.30	.14
□ 120 Darren Hall	.15	.07
□ 121 Pat Hentgen	.30	.14
□ 122 Paul Molitor	.60	.25
□ 123 Ed Sprague	.15	.07
□ 124 Devon White	.15	.07
□ 125 Tom Glavine	.30	.14
□ 126 David Justice	.60	.25
□ 127 Roberto Kelly	.15	.07
□ 128 Mark Lemke	.15	.07
□ 129 Greg Maddux	2.00	.90
□ 130 Greg McMichael	.15	.07
□ 131 Kent Mercker	.15	.07
□ 132 Charlie O'Brien	.15	.07
□ 133 John Smoltz	.30	.14
□ 134 Willie Banks	.15	.07
□ 135 Steve Buechele	.15	.07
□ 136 Kevin Foster	.15	.07
□ 137 Glenallen Hill	.15	.07
□ 138 Rey Sanchez	.15	.07
□ 139 Sammy Sosa	.60	.25
□ 140 Steve Trachsel	.15	.07
□ 141 Rick Wilkins	.15	.07
□ 142 Jeff Brantley	.15	.07
□ 143 Hector Carrasco	.15	.07
□ 144 Kevin Jarvis	.15	.07
□ 145 Barry Larkin	.40	.18
□ 146 Chuck McElroy	.15	.07
□ 147 Jose Rijo	.15	.07
□ 148 Johnny Ruffin	.15	.07
□ 149 Deion Sanders	.30	.14
□ 150 Eddie Taubensee	.15	.07
□ 151 Dante Bichette	.30	.14
□ 152 Ellis Burks	.30	.14
□ 153 Joe Girardi	.15	.07
□ 154 Charlie Hayes	.15	.07
□ 155 Mike Kingery	.15	.07
□ 156 Steve Reed	.15	.07
□ 157 Kevin Ritz	.15	.07
□ 158 Bruce Ruffin	.15	.07
□ 159 Eric Young	.15	.07
□ 160 Kurt Abbott	.15	.07
□ 161 Chuck Carr	.15	.07
□ 162 Chris Hammond	.15	.07
□ 163 Bryan Harvey	.15	.07
□ 164 Terry Mathews	.15	.07
□ 165 Yorkis Perez	.15	.07
□ 166 Pat Rapp	.15	.07
□ 167 Gary Sheffield	.50	.25
□ 168 Dave Weathers	.15	.07
□ 169 Jeff Bagwell	1.25	.55
□ 170 Ken Caminiti	.40	.18
□ 171 Doug Drabek	.15	.07
□ 172 Steve Finley	.30	.14
□ 173 John Hudek	.15	.07
□ 174 Todd Jones	.15	.07

175	James Mouton	.15	.07
176	Shane Reynolds	.15	.07
177	Scott Servais	.15	.07
178	Tom Candiotti	.15	.07
179	Omar Daal	.15	.07
180	Darren Dreifort	.15	.07
181	Eric Karros	.30	.14
182	Ramon J.Martinez	.30	.14
183	Raul Mondesi	.40	.18
184	Henry Rodriguez	.15	.07
185	Todd Worrell	.15	.07
186	Moises Alou	.30	.14
187	Sean Berry	.15	.07
188	Wil Cordero	.15	.07
189	Jeff Fassero	.15	.07
190	Darrin Fletcher	.15	.07
191	Butch Henry	.15	.07
192	Ken Hill	.15	.07
193	Mel Rojas	.15	.07
194	John Wetteland	.15	.07
195	Bobby Bonilla	.30	.14
196	Rico Brogna	.15	.07
197	Bobby Jones	.15	.07
198	Jeff Kent	.15	.07
199	Josias Manzanillo	.15	.07
200	Kelly Stinnett	.15	.07
201	Ryan Thompson	.15	.07
202	Jose Vizcaino	.15	.07
203	Lenny Dykstra	.30	.14
204	Jim Eisenreich	.15	.07
205	Dave Hollins	.15	.07
206	Mike Lieberthal	.15	.07
207	Mickey Morandini	.15	.07
208	Bobby Munoz	.15	.07
209	Curt Schilling	.30	.14
210	Heathcliff Slocumb	.15	.07
211	David West	.15	.07
212	Dave Clark	.15	.07
213	Steve Cooke	.15	.07
214	Midre Cummings	.15	.07
215	Carlos Garcia	.15	.07
216	Jeff King	.15	.07
217	Jon Lieber	.15	.07
218	Orlando Merced	.15	.07
219	Don Slaught	.15	.07
220	Rick White	.15	.07
221	Rene Arocha	.15	.07
222	Bernard Gilkey	.15	.07
223	Brian Jordan	.30	.14
224	Tom Pagnozzi	.15	.07
225	Vicente Palacios	.15	.07
226	Geronimo Pena	.15	.07
227	Ozzie Smith	.75	.35
228	Allen Watson	.15	.07
229	Mark Whiten	.15	.07
230	Brad Ausmus	.15	.07
231	Derek Bell	.15	.07
232	Andy Benes	.30	.14
233	Tony Gwynn	1.50	.70
234	Joey Hamilton	.30	.14
235	Luis Lopez	.15	.07
236	Pedro A.Martinez	.15	.07
237	Scott Sanders	.15	.07
238	Eddie Williams	.15	.07
239	Rod Beck	.15	.07
240	Dave Burba	.15	.07
241	Darren Lewis	.15	.07
242	Kirt Manwaring	.15	.07
243	Mark Portugal	.15	.07
244	Darryl Strawberry	.30	.14
245	Robby Thompson	.15	.07
246	Wm.VanLandingham	.15	.07
247	Matt Williams	.40	.18
248	Checklist	.15	.07
249	Checklist	.15	.07
250	Checklist	.15	.07
251	Harold Baines	.30	.14
252	Bret Barberie	.15	.07
253	Armando Benitez	.15	.07
254	Mike Devereaux	.15	.07
255	Leo Gomez	.15	.07
256	Jamie Moyer	.15	.07
257	Arthur Rhodes	.15	.07
258	Cal Ripken	2.50	1.10
259	Luis Alicea	.15	.07
260	Dave Canseco	.40	.18
261	Scott Cooper	.15	.07
262	Andre Dawson	.40	.18
263	Mike Greenwell	.15	.07
264	Aaron Sele	.15	.07
265	Garret Anderson	.40	.18
266	Chad Curtis	.15	.07
267	Gary DiSarcina	.15	.07
268	Chuck Finley	.15	.07
269	Rex Hudler	.15	.07
270	Andrew Lorraine	.15	.07
271	Spike Owen	.15	.07
272	Lee Smith	.30	.14
273	Jason Bere	.15	.07
274	Ozzie Guillen	.15	.07
275	Norberto Martin	.15	.07
276	Scott Ruffcorn	.15	.07
277	Robin Ventura	.30	.14
278	Carlos Baerga	.15	.07
279	Jason Grimsley	.15	.07
280	Dennis Martinez	.30	.14
281	Charles Nagy	.30	.14
282	Paul Sorrento	.15	.07
283	Dave Winfield	.40	.18
284	John Doherty	.15	.07
285	Travis Fryman	.30	.14
286	Kirk Gibson	.15	.07
287	Lou Whitaker	.30	.14
288	Gary Gaetti	.15	.07
289	Tom Gordon	.15	.07
290	Mark Gubicza	.15	.07
291	Wally Joyner	.30	.14
292	Mike Macfarlane	.15	.07
293	Jeff Montgomery	.15	.07
294	Jeff Cirillo	.30	.14
295	Cal Eldred	.15	.07
296	Pat Listach	.15	.07
297	Jose Mercedes	.15	.07
298	Dave Nilsson	.15	.07
299	Duane Singleton	.15	.07
300	Greg Vaughn	.15	.07
301	Scott Erickson	.15	.07
302	Denny Hocking	.15	.07
303	Chuck Knoblauch	.60	.25
304	Pat Mahomes	.15	.07
305	Pedro Munoz	.15	.07
306	Erik Schullstrom	.15	.07
307	Jim Abbott	.15	.07
308	Tony Fernandez	.15	.07
309	Sterling Hitchcock	.15	.07
310	Jim Leyritz	.15	.07
311	Don Mattingly	1.00	.45
312	Jack McDowell	.15	.07
313	Melido Perez	.15	.07
314	Bernie Williams	.60	.25
315	Scott Brosius	.15	.07
316	Dennis Eckersley	.30	.14
317	Brent Gates	.15	.07
318	Rickey Henderson	.40	.18
319	Steve Karsay	.15	.07
320	Steve Ontiveros	.15	.07
321	Bill Taylor	.15	.07
322	Todd Van Poppel	.15	.07
323	Bob Welch	.15	.07
324	Bobby Ayala	.15	.07
325	Mike Blowers	.15	.07
326	Jay Buhner	.40	.18
327	Felix Fermin	.15	.07
328	Tino Martinez	.60	.25
329	Marc Newfield	.15	.07
330	Greg Pirkl	.15	.07
331	Alex Rodriguez	2.50	1.10
332	Kevin Brown	.30	.14
333	John Burkett	.15	.07
334	Jeff Frye	.15	.07
335	Kevin Gross	.15	.07
336	Dean Palmer	.30	.14
337	Joe Carter	.30	.14
338	Shawn Green	.30	.14
339	Juan Guzman	.15	.07
340	Mike Huff	.15	.07
341	Al Leiter	.15	.07
342	John Olerud	.30	.14
343	Dave Stewart	.30	.14
344	Todd Stottlemyre	.15	.07
345	Steve Avery	.15	.07
346	Jeff Blauser	.30	.14
347	Chipper Jones	2.00	.90
348	Mike Kelly	.15	.07
349	Ryan Klesko	.40	.18
350	Javier Lopez	.30	.14
351	Fred McGriff	.40	.18
352	Jose Oliva	.15	.07
353	Terry Pendleton	.15	.07
354	Mike Stanton	.15	.07
355	Tony Tarasco	.15	.07
356	Mark Wohlers	.15	.07
357	Jim Bullinger	.15	.07
358	Shawon Dunston	.15	.07
359	Mark Grace	.40	.18
360	Derrick May	.15	.07
361	Randy Myers	.15	.07
362	Karl Rhodes	.15	.07
363	Bret Boone	.15	.07
364	Brian Dorsett	.15	.07
365	Ron Gant	.30	.14
366	Brian R.Hunter	.15	.07
367	Hal Morris	.15	.07
368	Jack Morris	.30	.14
369	John Roper	.15	.07
370	Reggie Sanders	.15	.07
371	Pete Schourek	.15	.07
372	John Smiley	.15	.07
373	Marvin Freeman	.15	.07
374	Andres Galarraga	.60	.25
375	Mike Hampton	.15	.07
376	David Nied	.15	.07
377	Walt Weiss	.15	.07
378	Greg Colbrunn	.15	.07
379	Jeff Conine	.30	.14
380	Charles Johnson	.30	.14
381	Kurt Miller	.15	.07
382	Robb Nen	.15	.07
383	Benito Santiago	.15	.07
384	Craig Biggio	.40	.18
385	Tony Eusebio	.15	.07
386	Luis Gonzalez	.15	.07
387	Brian L.Hunter	.40	.18
388	Darryl Kile	.30	.14
389	Orlando Miller	.15	.07
390	Phil Plantier	.15	.07
391	Greg Swindell	.15	.07
392	Billy Ashley	.15	.07
393	Pedro Astacio	.15	.07
394	Brett Butler	.30	.14
395	Delino DeShields	.15	.07
396	Orel Hershiser	.30	.14
397	Garey Ingram	.15	.07
398	Chan Ho Park	.60	.25
399	Mike Piazza	2.00	.90
400	Ismael Valdes	.40	.18
401	Tim Wallach	.15	.07
402	Cliff Floyd	.15	.07
403	Marquis Grissom	.30	.14
404	Mike Lansing	.15	.07
405	Pedro J.Martinez	.60	.25
406	Kirk Rueter	.15	.07
407	Tim Scott	.15	.07
408	Jeff Shaw	.15	.07
409	Larry Walker	.60	.25
410	Rondell White	.30	.14
411	John Franco	.15	.07
412	Todd Hundley	.30	.14
413	Jason Jacome	.15	.07
414	Joe Orsulak	.15	.07
415	Bret Saberhagen	.15	.07
416	David Segui	.15	.07
417	Darren Daulton	.30	.14
418	Mariano Duncan	.15	.07
419	Tommy Greene	.15	.07
420	Gregg Jefferies	.15	.07
421	John Kruk	.30	.14
422	Kevin Stocker	.15	.07
423	Jay Bell	.30	.14
424	Al Martin	.15	.07
425	Denny Neagle	.30	.14
426	Zane Smith	.15	.07
427	Andy Van Slyke	.30	.14
428	Paul Wagner	.15	.07
429	Tom Henke	.15	.07
430	Danny Jackson	.15	.07
431	Ray Lankford	.30	.14
432	John Mabry	.30	.14

		MINT	NRMT
☐ 433	Bob Tewksbury	.15	.07
☐ 434	Todd Zeile	.15	.07
☐ 435	Andy Ashby	.15	.07
☐ 436	Andujar Cedeno	.15	.07
☐ 437	Donnie Elliott	.15	.07
☐ 438	Bryce Florie	.15	.07
☐ 439	Trevor Hoffman	.15	.07
☐ 440	Melvin Nieves	.15	.07
☐ 441	Bip Roberts	.15	.07
☐ 442	Barry Bonds	.75	.35
☐ 443	Royce Clayton	.15	.07
☐ 444	Mike Jackson	.15	.07
☐ 445	John Patterson	.15	.07
☐ 446	J.R. Phillips	.15	.07
☐ 447	Bill Swift	.15	.07
☐ 448	Checklist	.15	.07
☐ 449	Checklist	.15	.07
☐ 450	Checklist	.15	.07

1995 Ultra All-Rookies

This 10-card standard-size set features rookies who emerged with an impact in 1994. These cards were inserted one in every five second series packs. The fronts feature a player's photo in the middle of the card with each corner devoted to a close-up of part of that action shot. The horizontal backs feature some player information as well as a photo. That same photo is also included in the background as well to a duotone photo. The cards are numbered in the lower left as "X" of 10 and are sequenced in alphabetical order.

	MINT	NRMT
COMPLETE SET (10)	5.00	2.20
COMMON CARD(1-10)	.25	.11
SER.2 STATED ODDS 1:5		
*GOLD MEDAL: 1X TO 2X HI COLUMN		
GM SER.2 STATED ODDS 1:50		

		MINT	NRMT
☐ 1	Cliff Floyd	.25	.11
☐ 2	Chris Gomez	.25	.11
☐ 3	Rusty Greer	1.25	.55
☐ 4	Bob Hamelin	.25	.11
☐ 5	Joey Hamilton	.50	.23
☐ 6	John Hudek	.25	.11
☐ 7	Ryan Klesko	.75	.35
☐ 8	Raul Mondesi	.75	.35
☐ 9	Manny Ramirez	1.50	.70
☐ 10	Steve Trachsel	.25	.11

1995 Ultra All-Stars

This 20-card standard-size set feature players who are considered to be the top players in the

game. Cards were inserted one in every four second series packs. The fronts feature two photos. One photo is in full-color while the other is a shaded black and white shot. The player's name, "All-Star" and his team name are at the bottom. The back is split between a player photo and career highlights. The cards are numbered in the bottom left as "X" of 20 and are sequenced in alphabetical order.

	MINT	NRMT
COMPLETE SET (20)	20.00	9.00
COMMON CARD(1-20)	.25	.11
SER.2 STATED ODDS 1:4		
*GOLD MEDAL: 1X TO 2X HI COLUMN		
GM SER.2 STATED ODDS 1:40		

		MINT	NRMT
☐ 1	Moises Alou	.50	.23
☐ 2	Albert Belle	1.25	.55
☐ 3	Craig Biggio	.75	.35
☐ 4	Wade Boggs	1.00	.45
☐ 5	Barry Bonds	1.25	.55
☐ 6	David Cone	.50	.23
☐ 7	Ken Griffey Jr.	5.00	2.20
☐ 8	Tony Gwynn	2.00	.90
☐ 9	Chuck Knoblauch	1.00	.45
☐ 10	Barry Larkin	.75	.35
☐ 11	Kenny Lofton	1.25	.55
☐ 12	Greg Maddux	3.00	1.35
☐ 13	Fred McGriff	.75	.35
☐ 14	Paul O'Neill	.50	.23
☐ 15	Mike Piazza	3.00	1.35
☐ 16	Kirby Puckett	2.00	.90
☐ 17	Cal Ripken	4.00	1.80
☐ 18	Ivan Rodriguez	1.25	.55
☐ 19	Frank Thomas	4.00	1.80
☐ 20	Matt Williams	.75	.35

1995 Ultra Award Winners

Featuring players who won major awards in 1994, this 25-card standard-size set was

inserted one in every four first series packs. The horizontal fronts feature a full-color photo as well as a "stretched" duotone photo. The award the player won is indicated at the top while the player's name is on the bottom. The backs feature two more photos as well as reasons for the player winning the given award. The cards are numbered as "X" of 25.

	MINT	NRMT
COMPLETE SET (25)	20.00	9.00
COMMON CARD(1-25)	.25	.11
SER.1 STATED ODDS 1:4		
*GOLD MEDAL: 1X TO 2X HI COLUMN		
GM SER.1 STATED ODDS 1:40		

		MINT	NRMT
☐ 1	Ivan Rodriguez	1.25	.55
☐ 2	Don Mattingly	2.00	.90
☐ 3	Roberto Alomar	1.00	.45
☐ 4	Wade Boggs	1.00	.45
☐ 5	Omar Vizquel	.50	.23
☐ 6	Ken Griffey Jr.	5.00	2.20
☐ 7	Kenny Lofton	1.25	.55
☐ 8	Devon White	.25	.11
☐ 9	Mark Langston	.25	.11
☐ 10	Tom Pagnozzi	.25	.11
☐ 11	Jeff Bagwell	2.00	.90
☐ 12	Craig Biggio	.75	.35
☐ 13	Matt Williams	.75	.35
☐ 14	Barry Larkin	.75	.35
☐ 15	Barry Bonds	1.25	.55
☐ 16	Marquis Grissom	.50	.23
☐ 17	Darren Lewis	.25	.11
☐ 18	Greg Maddux	3.00	1.35
☐ 19	Frank Thomas	4.00	1.80
☐ 20	Jeff Bagwell	2.00	.90
☐ 21	David Cone	.50	.23
☐ 22	Greg Maddux	3.00	1.35
☐ 23	Bob Hamelin	.25	.11
☐ 24	Raul Mondesi	.75	.35
☐ 25	Moises Alou	.50	.23

1995 Ultra Gold Medallion Rookies

This 20-card standard-size set was available through a mail-in wrapper offer that expired 9/30/95. These players featured were all rookies in 1995 and were not included in the regular Ultra set. The design is essentially the same as the corresponding basic cards save for the medallion in the upper left-hand corner. The cards are numbered with an "M" prefix. The set is sequenced in alphabetical order.

	MINT	NRMT
COMPLETE SET (20)	12.00	5.50
COMMON CARD (M1-M20)	.25	.11

	MINT	NRMT
SEMISTARS	.50	.23
UNLISTED STARS	1.00	.45
SET DIST.VIA MAIL-IN WRAPPER OFFER		

		MINT	NRMT
☐ M1	Manny Alexander	.25	.11
☐ M2	Edgardo Alfonzo	1.00	.45
☐ M3	Jason Bates	.25	.11
☐ M4	Andres Berumen	.25	.11
☐ M5	Darren Bragg	.25	.11
☐ M6	Jamie Brewington	.25	.11
☐ M7	Jason Christiansen	.25	.11
☐ M8	Brad Clontz	.25	.11
☐ M9	Marty Cordova	.30	.14
☐ M10	Johnny Damon	.30	.14
☐ M11	Vaughn Eshelman	.25	.11
☐ M12	Chad Fonville	.25	.11
☐ M13	Curtis Goodwin	.25	.11
☐ M14	Tyler Green	.25	.11
☐ M15	Bob Higginson	2.00	.90
☐ M16	Jason Isringhausen	.30	.14
☐ M17	Hideo Nomo	6.00	2.70
☐ M18	Jon Nunnally	.25	.11
☐ M19	Carlos Perez	.25	.11
☐ M20	Julian Tavarez	.25	.11

1995 Ultra Golden Prospects

Inserted one every eight first series hobby packs, this 10-card standard-size set features potential impact players. The horizontal fronts feature the same photo with multiple viewpoints giving the impression the photo has been "cut up" into various parts. The words "Golden Prospect" as well as the player's name and team are across the bottom. The horizontal backs have information about his career as well as a normal full-color photo. The cards are numbered as "X" of 10 and are sequenced alphabetically.

		MINT	NRMT
COMPLETE SET (10)		12.00	5.50
COMMON CARD (1-10)		.50	.23
SEMISTARS		1.00	.45
SER.1 STATED ODDS 1:8 HOBBY			
*GOLD MEDAL: 1X TO 2X HI COLUMN			
GM SER.1 STATED ODDS 1:80			

		MINT	NRMT
☐ 1	James Baldwin	.50	.23
☐ 2	Alan Benes	1.00	.45
☐ 3	Armando Benitez	.50	.23
☐ 4	Ray Durham	.75	.35
☐ 5	LaTroy Hawkins	.50	.23
☐ 6	Brian L.Hunter	1.00	.45
☐ 7	Derek Jeter	5.00	2.20
☐ 8	Charles Johnson	.75	.35
☐ 9	Alex Rodriguez	6.00	2.70
☐ 10	Michael Tucker	.75	.35

1995 Ultra Hitting Machines

This 10-card standard-size set features some of baseball's leading batters. Inserted one in every eight second-series retail packs, these horizontal cards have the player's photo against a background of the words "Hitting Machine." The player's name and team are identified on the bottom. The horizontal backs feature another player photo and reasons why they are great batters. The cards are numbered as "X" of 10 in the upper right and are sequenced in alphabetical order.

		MINT	NRMT
COMPLETE SET (10)		12.00	5.50
COMMON CARD (1-10)		.50	.23
SER.2 STATED ODDS 1:8 RETAIL			
*GOLD MEDAL: 1X TO 2X BASE CARD HI			
GM SER.2 STATED ODDS 1:80 RETAIL			

		MINT	NRMT
☐ 1	Jeff Bagwell	2.00	.90
☐ 2	Albert Belle	1.25	.55
☐ 3	Dante Bichette	.50	.23
☐ 4	Barry Bonds	1.25	.55
☐ 5	Jose Canseco	.75	.35
☐ 6	Ken Griffey Jr.	5.00	2.20
☐ 7	Tony Gwynn	2.00	.90
☐ 8	Fred McGriff	.75	.35
☐ 9	Mike Piazza	3.00	1.35
☐ 10	Frank Thomas	4.00	1.80

1995 Ultra Home Run Kings

This 10-card standard-size set featured the five leading home run hitters in each league. These cards were issued one every eight first series retail packs. These cards have a player photo on one side with the letters HRK on the other side. The player is identified vertically in the middle. The backs have information about the player's home run prowess as well as another action photo. The cards are numbered as "X" of 10 and are sequenced by league according to 1994's home rum standings.

		MINT	NRMT
COMPLETE SET (10)		30.00	13.50
COMMON CARD (1-10)		1.00	.45
SER.1 STATED ODDS 1:8 RETAIL			
*GOLD MEDAL: 1X TO 2X BASE CARD HI			
GM SER.1 STATED ODDS 1:80 RETAIL			

		MINT	NRMT
☐ 1	Ken Griffey Jr.	12.00	5.50
☐ 2	Frank Thomas	10.00	4.50
☐ 3	Albert Belle	3.00	1.35
☐ 4	Jose Canseco	1.50	.70
☐ 5	Cecil Fielder	1.00	.45
☐ 6	Matt Williams	1.50	.70
☐ 7	Jeff Bagwell	5.00	2.20
☐ 8	Barry Bonds	3.00	1.35
☐ 9	Fred McGriff	1.50	.70
☐ 10	Andres Galarraga	2.50	1.10

1995 Ultra League Leaders

This 10-card standard-size set was inserted one in three first series packs. The horizontal fronts feature a player photo against a background of his league's logo. The player is identified in one corner and the category he led the league in is featured in the other corner. The horizontal backs have a player photo as well as explaining more about the stat with which he paced the field.

		MINT	NRMT
COMPLETE SET (10)		6.00	2.70
COMMON CARD (1-10)		.25	.11
SER.1 STATED ODDS 1:3			
*GOLD MEDAL: 1X TO 2X HI COLUMN			
GM SER.1 STATED ODDS 1:30			

		MINT	NRMT
☐ 1	Paul O'Neil	.25	.11
☐ 2	Kenny Lofton	1.25	.55
☐ 3	Jimmy Key	.25	.11
☐ 4	Randy Johnson	.75	.35
☐ 5	Lee Smith	.25	.11
☐ 6	Tony Gwynn	2.00	.90
☐ 7	Craig Biggio	.50	.23
☐ 8	Greg Maddux	3.00	1.35
☐ 9	Andy Benes	.25	.11
☐ 10	John Franco	.25	.11

1995 Ultra On-Base Leaders

This 10-card standard-size set features ten players who are constantly reaching base safely. These cards were inserted one in every eight pre-priced second series jumbo packs. The fronts have an action photo against a background of several smaller action photos. The words "On-Base Leaders" are featured in the upper right corner along with the player's name. The horizontal backs contain the player's team, some information on how often they get on base and a player photo. The cards are numbered in the upper right corner as "X" of 10 and are sequenced in alphabetical order.

	MINT	NRMT
COMPLETE SET (10)	40.00	18.00
COMMON CARD (1-10)	2.50	1.10
SER.2 STATED ODDS 1:8 JUMBO		
*GOLD MEDAL: 1X TO 2X HI COLUMN		
GM SER.2 STATED ODDS 1:80 JUMBO		

☐ 1 Jeff Bagwell	8.00	3.60
☐ 2 Albert Belle	5.00	2.20
☐ 3 Craig Biggio	3.00	1.35
☐ 4 Wade Boggs	4.00	1.80
☐ 5 Barry Bonds	5.00	2.20
☐ 6 Will Clark	3.00	1.35
☐ 7 Tony Gwynn	10.00	4.50
☐ 8 David Justice	4.00	1.80
☐ 9 Paul O'Neill	2.50	1.10
☐ 10 Frank Thomas	15.00	6.75

1995 Ultra Power Plus

This six-card standard-size set was inserted one in every 37

first series packs. The six players portrayed are not only sluggers, but also excel at another part of the game. Unlike the 1995 Ultra cards and the other insert sets, these cards are 100 percent foil. The fronts have a player photo against a background that has the words "Power Plus" spelled in various size letters. The player and his team are identified on the bottom in gold foil. The backs have a player photo and some player information. The cards are numbered on the bottom right as "X" of 6 and are sequenced in alphabetical order by league.

	MINT	NRMT
COMPLETE SET (6)	50.00	22.00
COMMON CARD (1-6)	3.00	1.35
SER.1 STATED ODDS 1:37		
*GOLD MEDAL: 1X TO 2X HI COLUMN		
GM SER.1 STATED ODDS 1:370		

☐ 1 Albert Belle	5.00	2.20
☐ 2 Ken Griffey Jr.	20.00	9.00
☐ 3 Frank Thomas	15.00	6.75
☐ 4 Jeff Bagwell	8.00	3.60
☐ 5 Barry Bonds	5.00	2.20
☐ 6 Matt Williams	3.00	1.35

1995 Ultra RBI Kings

This 10-card standard-size set was inserted into series one jumbo packs at a rate of one every 11. The cards feature a player photo against a multi-colored background. The player's name, the words "RBI King" as well as his team identity are printed in gold foil in the middle. The backs have a player photo as well as some information about the players batting prowess. The cards are numbered in the upper left as "X" of 10 and are sequenced in order by league.

	MINT	NRMT
COMPLETE SET (10)	50.00	22.00
COMMON CARD (1-10)	1.00	.45
SER.1 STATED ODDS 1:11 JUMBO		
*GOLD MEDAL: 1X TO 2X BASE CARD HI		
GM SER.1 STATED ODDS 1:110 JUMBO		

☐ 1 Kirby Puckett	8.00	3.60
☐ 2 Joe Carter	2.00	.90
☐ 3 Albert Belle	4.00	1.80
☐ 4 Frank Thomas	15.00	6.75
☐ 5 Julio Franco	1.00	.45
☐ 6 Jeff Bagwell	8.00	3.60

☐ 7 Matt Williams	2.50	1.10
☐ 8 Dante Bichette	2.00	.90
☐ 9 Fred McGriff	2.50	1.10
☐ 10 Mike Piazza	12.00	5.50

1995 Ultra Rising Stars

This nine-card standard-size set was inserted one every 37 second series packs. Horizontal fronts feature two photos with the words "Rising Stars" as well as the player's name and team on the bottom left. This front design is set against a shiny background. The backs contain player information as well as a player photo. The cards are numbered "X" of 9 and are sequenced in alphabetical order.

	MINT	NRMT
COMPLETE SET (9)	80.00	36.00
COMMON CARD (1-10)	3.00	1.35
SER.2 STATED ODDS 1:37		
*GOLD MEDAL: 1X TO 2X HI COLUMN		
GM SER.2 STATED ODDS 1:370		

☐ 1 Moises Alou	3.00	1.35
☐ 2 Jeff Bagwell	12.00	5.50
☐ 3 Albert Belle	8.00	3.60
☐ 4 Juan Gonzalez	15.00	6.75
☐ 5 Chuck Knoblauch	6.00	2.70
☐ 6 Kenny Lofton	4.00	1.80
☐ 7 Raul Mondesi	4.00	1.80
☐ 8 Mike Piazza	20.00	9.00
☐ 9 Frank Thomas	25.00	11.00

1995 Ultra Second Year Standouts

This 15-card standard-size set was inserted into first series packs at a rate of not greater than one in six packs. The players in this set were all rookies in 1994 whom big things were expected from in 1995. The horizontal fronts feature the player's photo against a yellowish background. The player, his team's identification as well as the team logo are all printed in gold foil in the middle. The horizontal backs have another player photo as well as information about the player's 1994 season. The cards are numbered in the lower right as "X" of 15 and are sequenced in alphabetical order.

	MINT	NRMT
COMPLETE SET (15)	10.00	4.50
COMMON CARD (1-15)	.50	.23
SER.1 STATED ODDS 1:6		
*GOLD MEDAL: 1X TO 2X HI COLUMN		
GM SER.1 STATED ODDS 1:60		

		MINT	NRMT
☐ 1	Cliff Floyd	.50	.23
☐ 2	Chris Gomez	.50	.23
☐ 3	Rusty Greer	2.00	.90
☐ 4	Darren Hall	.50	.23
☐ 5	Bob Hamelin	.50	.23
☐ 6	Joey Hamilton	1.00	.45
☐ 7	Jeffrey Hammonds	1.00	.45
☐ 8	John Hudek	.50	.23
☐ 9	Ryan Klesko	1.50	.70
☐ 10	Raul Mondesi	1.50	.70
☐ 11	Manny Ramirez	2.50	1.10
☐ 12	Bill Risley	.50	.23
☐ 13	Steve Trachsel	.50	.23
☐ 14	W.VanLandingham	.50	.23
☐ 15	Rondell White	1.00	.45

1995 Ultra Strikeout Kings

This six-card standard-size set was inserted one every five second series packs. The fronts have a player photo as well as photos of grips for four major pitches. The player's name as well as the words "Strikeout King" is printed in a bottom corner. The horizontal backs feature a player photo, a brief blurb as well as a team logo. The cards are numbered as "X" of 6 and are sequenced in alphabetical order.

	MINT	NRMT
COMPLETE SET (6)	5.00	2.20
COMMON CARD (1-6)	.25	.11
SER.2 STATED ODDS 1:5		
*GOLD MEDAL: 1X TO 2X HI COLUMN		
GM SER.2 STATED ODDS 1:50		

		MINT	NRMT
☐ 1	Andy Benes	.75	.35
☐ 2	Roger Clemens	2.00	.90

		MINT	NRMT
☐ 3	Randy Johnson	1.00	.45
☐ 4	Greg Maddux	3.00	1.35
☐ 5	Pedro Martinez	1.00	.45
☐ 6	Jose Rijo	.25	.11

1996 Ultra

The 1996 Ultra set, produced by Fleer, contains 600 standard-size cards. The cards were distributed in packs that included two inserts. One insert is a Gold Medallion parallel while the other insert comes from one of the many Ultra insert sets. The cards are thicker than their 1995 counterparts and the fronts feature the player in an action shot in full-bleed color. Player's name and team are emblazoned across the bottom in silver foil. Backs show the players in two action shots and one pose. The backs are full-bleed color and include biography and player 1995 statistics in gold print across the bottom. The cards are sequenced in alphabetical order within league and team order.

	MINT	NRMT
COMPLETE SET (600)	60.00	27.00
COMPLETE SERIES 1 (300)	30.00	13.50
COMPLETE SERIES 2 (300)	30.00	13.50
COMMON CARD (1-600)	.15	.07
MINOR STARS	.30	.14
UNLISTED STARS	.60	.25
SUBSET CARDS HALF VALUE OF BASE CARDS		
COMP.G.MED.SET (600)	200.00	90.00
COMP.G.MED.SER.1 (300)	100.00	45.00
COMP.G.MED.SER.2 (300)	100.00	45.00
COMMON G.MED (1-600)	.25	.11
*G.MED.STARS: 1.5X TO 4X HI COLUMN		
*G.MED.YOUNG STARS: 1.25X TO 3X HI		
ONE GOLD MEDALLION PER PACK		

		MINT	NRMT
☐ 1	Manny Alexander	.15	.07
☐ 2	Brady Anderson	.40	.18
☐ 3	Bobby Bonilla	.30	.14
☐ 4	Scott Erickson	.15	.07
☐ 5	Curtis Goodwin	.15	.07
☐ 6	Chris Hoiles	.15	.07
☐ 7	Doug Jones	.15	.07
☐ 8	Jeff Manto	.15	.07
☐ 9	Mike Mussina	.60	.25
☐ 10	Rafael Palmeiro	.40	.18
☐ 11	Cal Ripken	2.50	1.10
☐ 12	Rick Aguilera	.15	.07
☐ 13	Luis Alicea	.15	.07
☐ 14	Stan Belinda	.15	.07
☐ 15	Jose Canseco	.40	.18
☐ 16	Roger Clemens	1.25	.55
☐ 17	Mike Greenwell	.15	.07
☐ 18	Mike Macfarlane	.15	.07
☐ 19	Tim Naehring	.15	.07
☐ 20	Troy O'Leary	.15	.07
☐ 21	John Valentin	.15	.07

		MINT	NRMT
☐ 22	Mo Vaughn	.75	.35
☐ 23	Tim Wakefield	.15	.07
☐ 24	Brian Anderson	.15	.07
☐ 25	Garret Anderson	.30	.14
☐ 26	Chili Davis	.15	.07
☐ 27	Gary DiSarcina	.15	.07
☐ 28	Jim Edmonds	.40	.18
☐ 29	Jorge Fabregas	.15	.07
☐ 30	Chuck Finley	.15	.07
☐ 31	Mark Langston	.15	.07
☐ 32	Troy Percival	.15	.07
☐ 33	Tim Salmon	.60	.25
☐ 34	Lee Smith	.30	.14
☐ 35	Wilson Alvarez	.15	.07
☐ 36	Ray Durham	.15	.07
☐ 37	Alex Fernandez	.15	.07
☐ 38	Ozzie Guillen	.15	.07
☐ 39	Roberto Hernandez	.15	.07
☐ 40	Lance Johnson	.15	.07
☐ 41	Ron Karkovice	.15	.07
☐ 42	Lyle Mouton	.15	.07
☐ 43	Tim Raines	.30	.14
☐ 44	Frank Thomas	2.50	1.10
☐ 45	Carlos Baerga	.15	.07
☐ 46	Albert Belle	.75	.35
☐ 47	Orel Hershiser	.30	.14
☐ 48	Kenny Lofton	.75	.35
☐ 49	Dennis Martinez	.30	.14
☐ 50	Jose Mesa	.15	.07
☐ 51	Eddie Murray	.60	.25
☐ 52	Chad Ogea	.15	.07
☐ 53	Manny Ramirez	.60	.25
☐ 54	Jim Thome	.60	.25
☐ 55	Omar Vizquel	.30	.14
☐ 56	Dave Winfield	.40	.18
☐ 57	Chad Curtis	.15	.07
☐ 58	Cecil Fielder	.30	.14
☐ 59	John Flaherty	.15	.07
☐ 60	Travis Fryman	.30	.14
☐ 61	Chris Gomez	.15	.07
☐ 62	Bob Higginson	.40	.18
☐ 63	Felipe Lira	.15	.07
☐ 64	Brian Maxcy	.15	.07
☐ 65	Alan Trammell	.40	.18
☐ 66	Lou Whitaker	.30	.14
☐ 67	Kevin Appier	.30	.14
☐ 68	Gary Gaetti	.15	.07
☐ 69	Tom Goodwin	.15	.07
☐ 70	Tom Gordon	.15	.07
☐ 71	Jason Jacome	.15	.07
☐ 72	Wally Joyner	.30	.14
☐ 73	Brent Mayne	.15	.07
☐ 74	Jeff Montgomery	.15	.07
☐ 75	Jon Nunnally	.15	.07
☐ 76	Joe Vitiello	.15	.07
☐ 77	Ricky Bones	.15	.07
☐ 78	Jeff Cirillo	.30	.14
☐ 79	Mike Fetters	.15	.07
☐ 80	Darryl Hamilton	.15	.07
☐ 81	David Hulse	.15	.07
☐ 82	Dave Nilsson	.15	.07
☐ 83	Kevin Seitzer	.15	.07
☐ 84	Steve Sparks	.15	.07
☐ 85	B.J. Surhoff	.15	.07
☐ 86	Jose Valentin	.15	.07
☐ 87	Greg Vaughn	.15	.07
☐ 88	Marty Cordova	.30	.14
☐ 89	Chuck Knoblauch	.60	.25
☐ 90	Pat Meares	.15	.07
☐ 91	Pedro Munoz	.15	.07
☐ 92	Kirby Puckett	1.25	.55
☐ 93	Brad Radke	.30	.14
☐ 94	Scott Stahoviak	.15	.07
☐ 95	Dave Stevens	.15	.07
☐ 96	Mike Trombley	.15	.07
☐ 97	Matt Walbeck	.15	.07
☐ 98	Wade Boggs	.60	.25
☐ 99	Russ Davis	.15	.07
☐ 100	Jim Leyritz	.15	.07
☐ 101	Don Mattingly	1.00	.45
☐ 102	Jack McDowell	.15	.07
☐ 103	Paul O'Neill	.30	.14
☐ 104	Andy Pettitte	.75	.35
☐ 105	Mariano Rivera	.40	.18
☐ 106	Ruben Sierra	.15	.07
☐ 107	Darryl Strawberry	.30	.14

☐ 108	John Wetteland	.15	.07	☐ 194	Larry Walker	.60	.25	☐ 280	Andy Ashby	.15	.07
☐ 109	Bernie Williams	.60	.25	☐ 195	Kurt Abbott	.15	.07	☐ 281	Brad Ausmus	.15	.07
☐ 110	Geronimo Berroa	.15	.07	☐ 196	John Burkett	.15	.07	☐ 282	Ken Caminiti	.40	.18
☐ 111	Scott Brosius	.15	.07	☐ 197	Greg Colbrunn	.15	.07	☐ 283	Glenn Dishman	.15	.07
☐ 112	Dennis Eckersley	.30	.14	☐ 198	Jeff Conine	.30	.14	☐ 284	Tony Gwynn	1.50	.70
☐ 113	Brent Gates	.15	.07	☐ 199	Andre Dawson	.40	.18	☐ 285	Joey Hamilton	.30	.14
☐ 114	Rickey Henderson	.40	.18	☐ 200	Chris Hammond	.15	.07	☐ 286	Trevor Hoffman	.15	.07
☐ 115	Mark McGwire	1.25	.55	☐ 201	Charles Johnson	.30	.14	☐ 287	Phil Plantier	.15	.07
☐ 116	Ariel Prieto	.15	.07	☐ 202	Robb Nen	.15	.07	☐ 288	Jody Reed	.15	.07
☐ 117	Terry Steinbach	.15	.07	☐ 203	Terry Pendleton	.15	.07	☐ 289	Eddie Williams	.15	.07
☐ 118	Todd Stottlemyre	.15	.07	☐ 204	Quilvio Veras	.15	.07	☐ 290	Barry Bonds	.75	.35
☐ 119	Todd Van Poppel	.15	.07	☐ 205	Jeff Bagwell	1.25	.55	☐ 291	Jamie Brewington	.15	.07
☐ 120	Steve Wojciechowski	.15	.07	☐ 206	Derek Bell	.15	.07	☐ 292	Mark Carreon	.15	.07
☐ 121	Rich Amaral	.15	.07	☐ 207	Doug Drabek	.15	.07	☐ 293	Royce Clayton	.15	.07
☐ 122	Bobby Ayala	.15	.07	☐ 208	Tony Eusebio	.15	.07	☐ 294	Glenallen Hill	.15	.07
☐ 123	Mike Blowers	.15	.07	☐ 209	Mike Hampton	.15	.07	☐ 295	Mark Leiter	.15	.07
☐ 124	Chris Bosio	.15	.07	☐ 210	Brian L. Hunter	.30	.14	☐ 296	Kirt Manwaring	.15	.07
☐ 125	Joey Cora	.30	.14	☐ 211	Todd Jones	.15	.07	☐ 297	J.R. Phillips	.15	.07
☐ 126	Ken Griffey Jr.	3.00	1.35	☐ 212	Orlando Miller	.15	.07	☐ 298	Deion Sanders	.30	.14
☐ 127	Randy Johnson	.60	.25	☐ 213	James Mouton	.15	.07	☐ 299	Wm. VanLandingham	.15	.07
☐ 128	Edgar Martinez	.40	.18	☐ 214	Shane Reynolds	.15	.07	☐ 300	Matt Williams	.40	.18
☐ 129	Tino Martinez	.60	.25	☐ 215	Dave Veres	.15	.07	☐ 301	Roberto Alomar	.60	.25
☐ 130	Alex Rodriguez	2.00	.90	☐ 216	Billy Ashley	.15	.07	☐ 302	Armando Benitez	.15	.07
☐ 131	Dan Wilson	.15	.07	☐ 217	Brett Butler	.30	.14	☐ 303	Mike Devereaux	.15	.07
☐ 132	Will Clark	.40	.18	☐ 218	Chad Fonville	.15	.07	☐ 304	Jeffrey Hammonds	.15	.07
☐ 133	Jeff Frye	.15	.07	☐ 219	Todd Hollandsworth	.15	.07	☐ 305	Jimmy Haynes	.15	.07
☐ 134	Benji Gil	.15	.07	☐ 220	Eric Karros	.30	.14	☐ 306	Scott McClain	.15	.07
☐ 135	Juan Gonzalez	1.50	.70	☐ 221	Ramon Martinez	.30	.14	☐ 307	Kent Mercker	.15	.07
☐ 136	Rusty Greer	.30	.14	☐ 222	Raul Mondesi	.40	.18	☐ 308	Randy Myers	.15	.07
☐ 137	Mark McLemore	.15	.07	☐ 223	Hideo Nomo	1.50	.70	☐ 309	B.J. Surhoff	.15	.07
☐ 138	Roger Pavlik	.15	.07	☐ 224	Mike Piazza	2.00	.90	☐ 310	Tony Tarasco	.15	.07
☐ 139	Ivan Rodriguez	.75	.35	☐ 225	Kevin Tapani	.15	.07	☐ 311	David Wells	.15	.07
☐ 140	Kenny Rogers	.15	.07	☐ 226	Ismael Valdes	.30	.14	☐ 312	Wil Cordero	.15	.07
☐ 141	Mickey Tettleton	.15	.07	☐ 227	Todd Worrell	.15	.07	☐ 313	Alex Delgado	.15	.07
☐ 142	Roberto Alomar	.60	.25	☐ 228	Moises Alou	.30	.14	☐ 314	Tom Gordon	.15	.07
☐ 143	Joe Carter	.30	.14	☐ 229	Wil Cordero	.15	.07	☐ 315	Dwayne Hosey	.15	.07
☐ 144	Tony Castillo	.15	.07	☐ 230	Jeff Fassero	.15	.07	☐ 316	Jose Malave	.15	.07
☐ 145	Alex Gonzalez	.15	.07	☐ 231	Darrin Fletcher	.15	.07	☐ 317	Kevin Mitchell	.15	.07
☐ 146	Shawn Green	.15	.07	☐ 232	Mike Lansing	.15	.07	☐ 318	Jamie Moyer	.15	.07
☐ 147	Pat Hentgen	.30	.14	☐ 233	Pedro J.Martinez	.60	.25	☐ 319	Aaron Sele	.15	.07
☐ 148	Sandy Martinez	.15	.07	☐ 234	Carlos Perez	.15	.07	☐ 320	Heathcliff Slocumb	.15	.07
☐ 149	Paul Molitor	.60	.25	☐ 235	Mel Rojas	.15	.07	☐ 321	Mike Stanley	.15	.07
☐ 150	John Olerud	.30	.14	☐ 236	David Segui	.15	.07	☐ 322	Jeff Suppan	.30	.14
☐ 151	Ed Sprague	.15	.07	☐ 237	Tony Tarasco	.15	.07	☐ 323	Jim Abbott	.15	.07
☐ 152	Jeff Blauser	.30	.14	☐ 238	Rondell White	.30	.14	☐ 324	George Arias	.15	.07
☐ 153	Brad Clontz	.15	.07	☐ 239	Edgardo Alfonzo	.40	.18	☐ 325	Todd Greene	.40	.18
☐ 154	Tom Glavine	.30	.14	☐ 240	Rico Brogna	.15	.07	☐ 326	Bryan Harvey	.15	.07
☐ 155	Marquis Grissom	.30	.14	☐ 241	Carl Everett	.15	.07	☐ 327	J.T. Snow	.30	.14
☐ 156	Chipper Jones	2.00	.90	☐ 242	Todd Hundley	.30	.14	☐ 328	Randy Velarde	.15	.07
☐ 157	David Justice	.60	.25	☐ 243	Butch Huskey	.30	.14	☐ 329	Tim Wallach	.15	.07
☐ 158	Ryan Klesko	.40	.18	☐ 244	Jason Isringhausen	.15	.07	☐ 330	Harold Baines	.30	.14
☐ 159	Javier Lopez	.30	.14	☐ 245	Bobby Jones	.15	.07	☐ 331	Jason Bere	.15	.07
☐ 160	Greg Maddux	2.00	.90	☐ 246	Jeff Kent	.15	.07	☐ 332	Darren Lewis	.15	.07
☐ 161	John Smoltz	.30	.14	☐ 247	Bill Pulsipher	.15	.07	☐ 333	Norberto Martin	.15	.07
☐ 162	Mark Wohlers	.15	.07	☐ 248	Jose Vizcaino	.15	.07	☐ 334	Tony Phillips	.15	.07
☐ 163	Jim Bullinger	.15	.07	☐ 249	Ricky Bottalico	.15	.07	☐ 335	Bill Simas	.15	.07
☐ 164	Frank Castillo	.15	.07	☐ 250	Darren Daulton	.30	.14	☐ 336	Chris Snopek	.15	.07
☐ 165	Shawon Dunston	.15	.07	☐ 251	Jim Eisenreich	.15	.07	☐ 337	Kevin Tapani	.15	.07
☐ 166	Kevin Foster	.15	.07	☐ 252	Tyler Green	.15	.07	☐ 338	Danny Tartabull	.15	.07
☐ 167	Luis Gonzalez	.15	.07	☐ 253	Charlie Hayes	.15	.07	☐ 339	Robin Ventura	.30	.14
☐ 168	Mark Grace	.40	.18	☐ 254	Gregg Jefferies	.30	.14	☐ 340	Sandy Alomar Jr.	.30	.14
☐ 169	Rey Sanchez	.15	.07	☐ 255	Tony Longmire	.15	.07	☐ 341	Julio Franco	.15	.07
☐ 170	Scott Servais	.15	.07	☐ 256	Michael Mimbs	.15	.07	☐ 342	Jack McDowell	.15	.07
☐ 171	Sammy Sosa	.60	.25	☐ 257	Mickey Morandini	.15	.07	☐ 343	Charles Nagy	.30	.14
☐ 172	Ozzie Timmons	.15	.07	☐ 258	Paul Quantrill	.15	.07	☐ 344	Julian Tavarez	.15	.07
☐ 173	Steve Trachsel	.15	.07	☐ 259	Heathcliff Slocumb	.15	.07	☐ 345	Kimera Bartee	.15	.07
☐ 174	Bret Boone	.15	.07	☐ 260	Jay Bell	.30	.14	☐ 346	Greg Keagle	.15	.07
☐ 175	Jeff Branson	.15	.07	☐ 261	Jacob Brumfield	.15	.07	☐ 347	Mark Lewis	.15	.07
☐ 176	Jeff Brantley	.15	.07	☐ 262	Angelo Encarnacion	.15	.07	☐ 348	Jose Lima	.15	.07
☐ 177	Dave Burba	.15	.07	☐ 263	John Ericks	.15	.07	☐ 349	Melvin Nieves	.15	.07
☐ 178	Ron Gant	.30	.14	☐ 264	Mark Johnson	.15	.07	☐ 350	Mark Parent	.15	.07
☐ 179	Barry Larkin	.40	.18	☐ 265	Esteban Loaiza	.15	.07	☐ 351	Eddie Williams	.15	.07
☐ 180	Darren Lewis	.15	.07	☐ 266	Al Martin	.15	.07	☐ 352	Johnny Damon	.30	.14
☐ 181	Mark Portugal	.15	.07	☐ 267	Orlando Merced	.15	.07	☐ 353	Sal Fasano	.15	.07
☐ 182	Reggie Sanders	.15	.07	☐ 268	Dan Miceli	.15	.07	☐ 354	Mark Gubicza	.15	.07
☐ 183	Pete Schourek	.15	.07	☐ 269	Denny Neagle	.30	.14	☐ 355	Bob Hamelin	.15	.07
☐ 184	John Smiley	.15	.07	☐ 270	Brian Barber	.15	.07	☐ 356	Chris Haney	.15	.07
☐ 185	Jason Bates	.15	.07	☐ 271	Scott Cooper	.15	.07	☐ 357	Keith Lockhart	.15	.07
☐ 186	Dante Bichette	.30	.14	☐ 272	Tripp Cromer	.15	.07	☐ 358	Mike Macfarlane	.15	.07
☐ 187	Ellis Burks	.30	.14	☐ 273	Bernard Gilkey	.15	.07	☐ 359	Jose Offerman	.15	.07
☐ 188	Vinny Castilla	.30	.14	☐ 274	Tom Henke	.15	.07	☐ 360	Bip Roberts	.15	.07
☐ 189	Andres Galarraga	.60	.25	☐ 275	Brian Jordan	.30	.14	☐ 361	Michael Tucker	.30	.14
☐ 190	Darren Holmes	.15	.07	☐ 276	John Mabry	.15	.07	☐ 362	Chuck Carr	.15	.07
☐ 191	Armando Reynoso	.15	.07	☐ 277	Tom Pagnozzi	.15	.07	☐ 363	Bobby Hughes	.15	.07
☐ 192	Kevin Ritz	.15	.07	☐ 278	Mark Petkovsek	.15	.07	☐ 364	John Jaha	.15	.07
☐ 193	Bill Swift	.15	.07	☐ 279	Ozzie Smith	.75	.35	☐ 365	Mark Loretta	.15	.07

☐ 366	Mike Matheny	.15	.07
☐ 367	Ben McDonald	.15	.07
☐ 368	Matt Mieske	.15	.07
☐ 369	Angel Miranda	.15	.07
☐ 370	Fernando Vina	.15	.07
☐ 371	Rick Aguilera	.15	.07
☐ 372	Rich Becker	.15	.07
☐ 373	LaTroy Hawkins	.15	.07
☐ 374	Dave Hollins	.15	.07
☐ 375	Roberto Kelly	.15	.07
☐ 376	Matt Lawton	.40	.18
☐ 377	Paul Molitor	.60	.25
☐ 378	Dan Naulty	.15	.07
☐ 379	Rich Robertson	.15	.07
☐ 380	Frank Rodriguez	.15	.07
☐ 381	David Cone	.30	.14
☐ 382	Mariano Duncan	.15	.07
☐ 383	Andy Fox	.15	.07
☐ 384	Joe Girardi	.15	.07
☐ 385	Dwight Gooden	.30	.14
☐ 386	Derek Jeter	2.00	.90
☐ 387	Pat Kelly	.15	.07
☐ 388	Jimmy Key	.30	.14
☐ 389	Matt Luke	.15	.07
☐ 390	Tino Martinez	.60	.25
☐ 391	Jeff Nelson	.15	.07
☐ 392	Melido Perez	.15	.07
☐ 393	Tim Raines	.30	.14
☐ 394	Ruben Rivera	.30	.14
☐ 395	Kenny Rogers	.15	.07
☐ 396	Tony Batista	.30	.14
☐ 397	Allen Battle	.15	.07
☐ 398	Mike Bordick	.15	.07
☐ 399	Steve Cox	.15	.07
☐ 400	Jason Giambi	.30	.14
☐ 401	Doug Johns	.15	.07
☐ 402	Pedro Munoz	.15	.07
☐ 403	Phil Plantier	.15	.07
☐ 404	Scott Spiezio	.40	.18
☐ 405	George Williams	.15	.07
☐ 406	Ernie Young	.15	.07
☐ 407	Darren Bragg	.15	.07
☐ 408	Jay Buhner	.40	.18
☐ 409	Norm Charlton	.15	.07
☐ 410	Russ Davis	.15	.07
☐ 411	Sterling Hitchcock	.15	.07
☐ 412	Edwin Hurtado	.15	.07
☐ 413	Raul Ibanez	.40	.18
☐ 414	Mike Jackson	.15	.07
☐ 415	Luis Sojo	.15	.07
☐ 416	Paul Sorrento	.15	.07
☐ 417	Bob Wolcott	.15	.07
☐ 418	Damon Buford	.15	.07
☐ 419	Kevin Gross	.15	.07
☐ 420	Darryl Hamilton UER	.15	.07
☐ 421	Mike Henneman	.15	.07
☐ 422	Ken Hill	.15	.07
☐ 423	Dean Palmer	.15	.07
☐ 424	Bobby Witt	.15	.07
☐ 425	Tilson Brito	.15	.07
☐ 426	Giovanni Carrara	.15	.07
☐ 427	Domingo Cedeno	.15	.07
☐ 428	Felipe Crespo	.15	.07
☐ 429	Carlos Delgado	.30	.14
☐ 430	Juan Guzman	.15	.07
☐ 431	Erik Hanson	.15	.07
☐ 432	Marty Janzen	.15	.07
☐ 433	Otis Nixon	.15	.07
☐ 434	Robert Perez	.15	.07
☐ 435	Paul Quantrill	.15	.07
☐ 436	Bill Risley	.15	.07
☐ 437	Steve Avery	.15	.07
☐ 438	Jermaine Dye	.30	.14
☐ 439	Mark Lemke	.15	.07
☐ 440	Marty Malloy	.30	.14
☐ 441	Fred McGriff	.15	.07
☐ 442	Greg McMichael	.15	.07
☐ 443	Wonderful Monds	.15	.07
☐ 444	Eddie Perez	.15	.07
☐ 445	Jason Schmidt	.30	.14
☐ 446	Terrell Wade	.15	.07
☐ 447	Terry Adams	.15	.07
☐ 448	Scott Bullett	.15	.07
☐ 449	Robin Jennings	.15	.07
☐ 450	Doug Jones	.15	.07
☐ 451	Brooks Kieschnick	.30	.14
☐ 452	Dave Magadan	.15	.07
☐ 453	Jason Maxwell	.15	.07
☐ 454	Brian McRae	.15	.07
☐ 455	Rodney Myers	.15	.07
☐ 456	Jaime Navarro	.15	.07
☐ 457	Ryne Sandberg	.40	.18
☐ 458	Vince Coleman	.15	.07
☐ 459	Eric Davis	.30	.14
☐ 460	Steve Gibralter	.15	.07
☐ 461	Thomas Howard	.15	.07
☐ 462	Mike Kelly	.15	.07
☐ 463	Hal Morris	.15	.07
☐ 464	Eric Owens	.15	.07
☐ 465	Jose Rijo	.15	.07
☐ 466	Chris Sabo	.15	.07
☐ 467	Eddie Taubensee	.15	.07
☐ 468	Trenidad Hubbard	.15	.07
☐ 469	Curt Leskanic	.15	.07
☐ 470	Quinton McCracken	.15	.07
☐ 471	Jayhawk Owens	.15	.07
☐ 472	Steve Reed	.15	.07
☐ 473	Bryan Rekar	.15	.07
☐ 474	Bruce Ruffin	.15	.07
☐ 475	Bret Saberhagen	.15	.07
☐ 476	Walt Weiss	.15	.07
☐ 477	Eric Young	.15	.07
☐ 478	Kevin Brown	.30	.14
☐ 479	Al Leiter	.15	.07
☐ 480	Pat Rapp	.15	.07
☐ 481	Gary Sheffield	.60	.25
☐ 482	Devon White	.15	.07
☐ 483	Bob Abreu	.40	.18
☐ 484	Sean Berry	.15	.07
☐ 485	Craig Biggio	.40	.18
☐ 486	Jim Dougherty	.15	.07
☐ 487	Richard Hidalgo	.60	.25
☐ 488	Darryl Kile	.30	.14
☐ 489	Derrick May	.15	.07
☐ 490	Greg Swindell	.15	.07
☐ 491	Rick Wilkins	.15	.07
☐ 492	Mike Blowers	.15	.07
☐ 493	Tom Candiotti	.15	.07
☐ 494	Roger Cedeno	.15	.07
☐ 495	Delino DeShields	.15	.07
☐ 496	Greg Gagne	.15	.07
☐ 497	Karim Garcia	.40	.18
☐ 498	Wilton Guerrero	.60	.25
☐ 499	Chan Ho Park	.60	.25
☐ 500	Isreal Alcantara	.15	.07
☐ 501	Shane Andrews	.15	.07
☐ 502	Yamil Benitez	.30	.14
☐ 503	Cliff Floyd	.15	.07
☐ 504	Mark Grudzielanek	.30	.14
☐ 505	Ryan McGuire	.15	.07
☐ 506	Sherman Obando	.15	.07
☐ 507	Jose Paniagua	.15	.07
☐ 508	Henry Rodriguez	.15	.07
☐ 509	Kirk Rueter	.15	.07
☐ 510	Juan Acevedo	.15	.07
☐ 511	John Franco	.30	.14
☐ 512	Bernard Gilkey	.15	.07
☐ 513	Lance Johnson	.15	.07
☐ 514	Rey Ordonez	.30	.14
☐ 515	Robert Person	.15	.07
☐ 516	Paul Wilson	.15	.07
☐ 517	Toby Borland	.15	.07
☐ 518	David Doster	.15	.07
☐ 519	Lenny Dykstra	.30	.14
☐ 520	Sid Fernandez	.15	.07
☐ 521	Mike Grace	.15	.07
☐ 522	Rich Hunter	.15	.07
☐ 523	Benito Santiago	.15	.07
☐ 524	Gene Schall	.15	.07
☐ 525	Curt Schilling	.30	.14
☐ 526	Kevin Sefcik	.15	.07
☐ 527	Lee Tinsley	.15	.07
☐ 528	David West	.15	.07
☐ 529	Mark Whiten	.15	.07
☐ 530	Todd Zeile	.15	.07
☐ 531	Carlos Garcia	.15	.07
☐ 532	Charlie Hayes	.15	.07
☐ 533	Jason Kendall	.40	.18
☐ 534	Jeff King	.15	.07
☐ 535	Mike Kingery	.15	.07
☐ 536	Nelson Liriano	.15	.07
☐ 537	Dan Plesac	.15	.07
☐ 538	Paul Wagner	.15	.07
☐ 539	Luis Alicea	.15	.07
☐ 540	David Bell	.15	.07
☐ 541	Alan Benes	.30	.14
☐ 542	Andy Benes	.30	.14
☐ 543	Mike Busby	.15	.07
☐ 544	Royce Clayton	.15	.07
☐ 545	Dennis Eckersley	.30	.14
☐ 546	Gary Gaetti	.15	.07
☐ 547	Ron Gant	.30	.14
☐ 548	Aaron Holbert	.15	.07
☐ 549	Ray Lankford	.30	.14
☐ 550	T.J. Mathews	.15	.07
☐ 551	Willie McGee	.15	.07
☐ 552	Miguel Mejia	.15	.07
☐ 553	Todd Stottlemyre	.15	.07
☐ 554	Sean Bergman	.15	.07
☐ 555	Willie Blair	.15	.07
☐ 556	Andujar Cedeno	.15	.07
☐ 557	Steve Finley	.30	.14
☐ 558	Rickey Henderson	.40	.18
☐ 559	Wally Joyner	.30	.14
☐ 560	Scott Livingstone	.15	.07
☐ 561	Marc Newfield	.15	.07
☐ 562	Bob Tewksbury	.15	.07
☐ 563	Fernando Valenzuela	.30	.14
☐ 564	Rod Beck	.15	.07
☐ 565	Doug Creek	.15	.07
☐ 566	Shawon Dunston	.15	.07
☐ 567	Osvaldo Fernandez	.30	.14
☐ 568	Stan Javier	.15	.07
☐ 569	Marcus Jensen	.15	.07
☐ 570	Steve Scarsone	.15	.07
☐ 571	Robby Thompson	.15	.07
☐ 572	Allen Watson	.15	.07
☐ 573	Roberto Alomar STA	.30	.14
☐ 574	Jeff Bagwell STA	.60	.25
☐ 575	Albert Belle STA	.40	.18
☐ 576	Wade Boggs STA	.30	.14
☐ 577	Barry Bonds STA	.40	.18
☐ 578	Juan Gonzalez STA	.75	.35
☐ 579	Ken Griffey Jr. STA	1.50	.70
☐ 580	Tony Gwynn STA	.75	.35
☐ 581	Randy Johnson STA	.30	.14
☐ 582	Chipper Jones STA	1.00	.45
☐ 583	Barry Larkin STA	.30	.14
☐ 584	Kenny Lofton STA	.40	.18
☐ 585	Greg Maddux STA	1.00	.45
☐ 586	Raul Mondesi STA	.30	.14
☐ 587	Mike Piazza STA	1.00	.45
☐ 588	Cal Ripken STA	1.25	.55
☐ 589	Tim Salmon STA	.30	.14
☐ 590	Frank Thomas STA	1.25	.55
☐ 591	Mo Vaughn STA	.40	.18
☐ 592	Matt Williams STA	.30	.14
☐ 593	Marty Cordova RAW	.15	.07
☐ 594	Jim Edmonds RAW	.30	.14
☐ 595	Cliff Floyd RAW	.15	.07
☐ 596	Chipper Jones RAW	1.00	.45
☐ 597	Ryan Klesko RAW	.30	.14
☐ 598	Raul Mondesi RAW	.30	.14
☐ 599	Manny Ramirez RAW	.30	.14
☐ 600	Ruben Rivera RAW	.15	.07

1996 Ultra Call to the Hall

Randomly inserted in packs at a rate of one in 24, this ten-card set features original illustrations of possible future Hall of Famers. The backs state why the player is a possible HOF.

	MINT	NRMT
COMPLETE SET (10)	80.00	36.00
COMMON CARD (1-10)	2.50	1.10
SER.2 STATED ODDS 1:24		
*GOLD MEDAL: 1X TO 2X BASE CARD HI		
GM SER.2 STATED ODDS 1:240		
☐ 1 Barry Bonds	5.00	2.20
☐ 2 Ken Griffey Jr.	20.00	9.00
☐ 3 Tony Gwynn	10.00	4.50

			MINT	NRMT
☐ B5	Derek Jeter		2.50	1.10
☐ B6	Jason Kendall		.60	.25
☐ B7	Ryan Klesko		.75	.35
☐ B8	Greg Maddux		2.50	1.10
☐ B9	Cal Ripken		3.00	1.35
☐ B10	Frank Thomas		3.00	1.35

1996 Ultra Diamond Producers

This 12-card standard-size set highlights the achievements of Major League stars. The cards were randomly inserted at a rate of one in 20. The horizontal fronts show the player close-up and an action photo on a metallic-silver paper. "Diamond Producers" and the player's name are printed in silver foil at the bottom of the card. The backs feature the player in an action shot on the left half and a white on black description of the player's career achievements. The cards are sequenced in alphabetical order and there are also gold medallion versions of these cards.

	MINT	NRMT
COMPLETE SET (12)	60.00	27.00
COMMON CARD(1-12)	3.00	1.35
SER.1 STATED ODDS 1:20		
*GOLD MEDAL: 1X TO 2X HI COLUMN		
GM SER.1 STATED ODDS 1:200		

		MINT	NRMT
☐ 1	Albert Belle	4.00	1.80
☐ 2	Barry Bonds	4.00	1.80
☐ 3	Ken Griffey Jr.	15.00	6.75
☐ 4	Tony Gwynn	8.00	3.60
☐ 5	Greg Maddux	10.00	4.50
☐ 6	Hideo Nomo	6.00	2.70
☐ 7	Mike Piazza	10.00	4.50
☐ 8	Kirby Puckett	6.00	2.70
☐ 9	Cal Ripken	12.00	5.50
☐ 10	Frank Thomas	12.00	5.50
☐ 11	Mo Vaughn	4.00	1.80
☐ 12	Matt Williams	3.00	1.35

1996 Ultra Fresh Foundations

Randomly inserted one every three packs, this 10-card standard-size set highlights the play of hot young players. The fronts feature the player in a full-color action cut-out with a red prismatic background. The Ultra seal, card title, player name and team are printed in silver-foil down the left side of the card.

Backs are full-bleed color action shots with player information. The cards are sequenced in alphabetical order and there are also gold medallion versions of these cards.

	MINT	NRMT
COMPLETE SET (10)	3.00	1.35
COMMON CARD(1-10)		.11
SER.1 STATED ODDS 1:3		
*GOLD MEDAL: .75X TO 2X HI COLUMN		
GM SER.1 STATED ODDS 1:30		

		MINT	NRMT
☐ 1	Garret Anderson	.25	.11
☐ 2	Marty Cordova	.25	.11
☐ 3	Jim Edmonds	.40	.18
☐ 4	Brian L.Hunter	.25	.11
☐ 5	Chipper Jones	2.00	.90
☐ 6	Ryan Klesko	.40	.18
☐ 7	Raul Mondesi	.40	.18
☐ 8	Hideo Nomo	1.00	.45
☐ 9	Manny Ramirez	.60	.25
☐ 10	Rondell White	.25	.11

1996 Ultra Golden Prospects

Randomly inserted at a rate of one in five hobby packs, this 10-card standard-size set features players who are likely to make it as major leaguers. The full-bleed fronts have team color-coded tinting over a stadium background. The player is featured in a horizontal action shot with the player's name and team name printed in gold foil. The horizontal backs also feature the minor leaguer in action and player information printed in white type. The cards are sequenced in alphabetical order and there are also gold medallion versions of these cards.

		MINT	NRMT
☐ 4	Rickey Henderson	2.50	1.10
☐ 5	Greg Maddux	12.00	5.50
☐ 6	Eddie Murray	4.00	1.80
☐ 7	Cal Ripken	15.00	6.75
☐ 8	Ryne Sandberg	5.00	2.20
☐ 9	Ozzie Smith	5.00	2.20
☐ 10	Frank Thomas	15.00	6.75

1996 Ultra Checklists

Randomly inserted in packs, this set of 10 standard-size cards features superstars of the game. Fronts are full-bleed color action photos of players with "Checklist" written in gold foil across the card. The horizontal backs are numbered and show the different card sets that are included in the Ultra line. The cards are sequenced in alphabetical order. A gold medallion parallel version of each card was issued.

	MINT	NRMT
COMPLETE SERIES 1 (10)	10.00	4.50
COMPLETE SERIES 2 (10)	8.00	3.60
COMMON CARD(A1-B10)	.60	.25
STATED ODDS 1:4	.75	.35
*GOLD MEDAL: 1X TO 2X HI COLUMN		
GM STATED ODDS 1:40		

		MINT	NRMT
☐ A1	Jeff Bagwell	1.50	.70
☐ A2	Barry Bonds	1.00	.45
☐ A3	Juan Gonzalez	2.00	.90
☐ A4	Ken Griffey Jr.	4.00	1.80
☐ A5	Chipper Jones	2.50	1.10
☐ A6	Mike Piazza	2.50	1.10
☐ A7	Manny Ramirez	.75	.35
☐ A8	Cal Ripken	3.00	1.35
☐ A9	Frank Thomas	3.00	1.35
☐ A10	Matt Williams	.75	.35
☐ B1	Albert Belle	1.00	.45
☐ B2	Cecil Fielder	.40	.18
☐ B3	Ken Griffey Jr.	4.00	1.80
☐ B4	Tony Gwynn	2.00	.90

	MINT	NRMT
COMPLETE SET (10)	5.00	2.20
COMMON CARD (1-10)	.25	.11

SER.1 STATED ODDS 1:5 HOBBY
*GOLD MEDAL: 1X TO 2X HI COLUMN
GM SER.1 STATED ODDS 1:50 HOBBY

□ 1 Yamil Benitez	.50	.23
□ 2 Alberto Castillo	.25	.11
□ 3 Roger Cedeno	.25	.11
□ 4 Johnny Damon	.50	.23
□ 5 Micah Franklin	.25	.11
□ 6 Jason Giambi	.50	.23
□ 7 Jose Herrera	.25	.11
□ 8 Derek Jeter	5.00	2.20
□ 9 Kevin Jordan	.25	.11
□ 10 Ruben Rivera	.50	.23

1996 Ultra Golden Prospects Hobby

Randomly inserted in hobby packs only at a rate of one in 72, this 15-card set is printed on crystal card stock and showcases players awaiting their Major League debut. The backs carry some of their accomplishments in the Minor League.

	MINT	NRMT
COMPLETE SET (15)	100.00	45.00
COMMON CARD (1-15)	6.00	2.70

SER.2 STATED ODDS 1:72 HOBBY
*GOLD MEDAL: 1X TO 2X HI COLUMN
GM SER.2 STATED ODDS 1:720 HOBBY

□ 1 Bob Abreu	8.00	3.60
□ 2 Israel Alcantara	6.00	2.70
□ 3 Tony Batista	6.00	2.70
□ 4 Mike Cameron	20.00	9.00
□ 5 Steve Cox	6.00	2.70
□ 6 Jermaine Dye	6.00	2.70
□ 7 Wilton Guerrero	10.00	4.50
□ 8 Richard Hidalgo	15.00	6.75
□ 9 Raul Ibanez	10.00	4.50
□ 10 Marty Janzen	6.00	2.70
□ 11 Robin Jennings	6.00	2.70
□ 12 Jason Maxwell	6.00	2.70
□ 13 Scott McClain	6.00	2.70
□ 14 Wonderful Monds	6.00	2.70
□ 15 Chris Singleton	6.00	2.70

1996 Ultra Hitting Machines

Randomly inserted in second series packs at a rate of one in 288, this 10-card set features players who hit the ball hard and often. The fronts display color action player photos on a die-cut machine gear background. The backs carry a color

player portrait and player information.

	MINT	NRMT
COMPLETE SET (10)	400.00	180.00
COMMON CARD (1-10)	15.00	6.75

SER.2 STATED ODDS 1:288.
*GOLD MEDAL: 1X TO 2X HI COLUMN
GM SER.2 STATED ODDS 1:2880

□ 1 Albert Belle	30.00	13.50
□ 2 Barry Bonds	30.00	13.50
□ 3 Juan Gonzalez	60.00	27.00
□ 4 Ken Griffey Jr.	120.00	55.00
□ 5 Edgar Martinez	15.00	6.75
□ 6 Rafael Palmeiro	15.00	6.75
□ 7 Mike Piazza	80.00	36.00
□ 8 Tim Salmon	25.00	11.00
□ 9 Frank Thomas	100.00	45.00
□ 10 Matt Williams	15.00	6.75

1996 Ultra Home Run Kings

This 12-card standard-size set features leading power hitters. These cards were randomly inserted at a rate of one in 75 packs. The card fronts are thin wood with a color cut out of the player and HR KING printed diagonally in copper foil down the left side. The Fleer company was not happy with the final look of the card because of the transfer of the copper foil. Therefore all cards were made redemption cards. Backs of the cards have information about how to redeem the cards for replacement. The exchange offer expired on December 1, 1996. The cards are sequenced in alphabetical order.

	MINT	NRMT
COMPLETE SET (12)	60.00	27.00
COMMON CARD (1-12)	2.00	.90

SER.1 STATED ODDS 1:75

*GOLD MEDAL: 5X TO 10X HI COLUMN
GM SER.1 STATED ODDS 1:750
*REDEMPTION: 1X TO 1.2X HI COLUMN
ONE RDMP.CARD VIA MAIL PER HR CARD

□ 1 Albert Belle	5.00	2.20
□ 2 Dante Bichette	2.00	.90
□ 3 Barry Bonds	5.00	2.20
□ 4 Jose Canseco	2.50	1.10
□ 5 Juan Gonzalez	10.00	4.50
□ 6 Ken Griffey Jr.	20.00	9.00
□ 7 Mark McGwire	8.00	3.60
□ 8 Manny Ramirez	4.00	1.80
□ 9 Tim Salmon	4.00	1.80
□ 10 Frank Thomas	15.00	6.75
□ 11 Mo Vaughn	5.00	2.20
□ 12 Matt Williams	2.50	1.10

1996 Ultra On-Base Leaders

Randomly inserted in second series packs at a rate of one in four, this 10-card set features players with consistently high on-base percentage. The fronts display a color action player image on a black-and-white player background photo with images of bases along the side. The backs carry a color player portrait and player information.

	MINT	NRMT
COMPLETE SET (10)	5.00	2.20
COMMON CARD (1-10)	.60	.25

SER.2 STATED ODDS 1:4.
*GOLD MEDAL: 1X TO 2X HI COLUMN
GM SER.2 STATED ODDS 1:40

□ 1 Wade Boggs	.75	.35
□ 2 Barry Bonds	1.00	.45
□ 3 Tony Gwynn	2.00	.90
□ 4 Rickey Henderson	.60	.25
□ 5 Chuck Knoblauch	.75	.35
□ 6 Edgar Martinez	.60	.25
□ 7 Mike Piazza	2.50	1.10
□ 8 Tim Salmon	.75	.35
□ 9 Frank Thomas	3.00	1.35
□ 10 Jim Thome	.75	.35

1996 Ultra Power Plus

Randomly inserted at a rate of one in ten packs, this 12-card standard-size set features top all-around players. The horizontal fronts feature the player in two cut-out action photos against a multi-colored prismatic wheel background. The player's name and "Power Plus" are stamped in foil across the bot-

tom. The backs are split between a full-color close-up shot of the player and player information printed in white type against a multi-colored circular background. The cards are sequenced in alphabetical order and gold medallion versions of these cards were also issued.

	MINT	NRMT
COMPLETE SET (12)	25.00	11.00
COMMON CARD (1-12)	.50	.23
SER.1 STATED ODDS 1:10		
*GOLD MEDAL: 1X TO 2X HI COLUMN		
GM SER.1 STATED ODDS 1:100		

		MINT	NRMT
☐ 1	Jeff Bagwell	4.00	1.80
☐ 2	Barry Bonds	2.50	1.10
☐ 3	Ken Griffey Jr.	10.00	4.50
☐ 4	Raul Mondesi	1.50	.70
☐ 5	Rafael Palmeiro	1.50	.70
☐ 6	Mike Piazza	6.00	2.70
☐ 7	Manny Ramirez	2.00	.90
☐ 8	Tim Salmon	2.00	.90
☐ 9	Reggie Sanders	.50	.23
☐ 10	Frank Thomas	8.00	3.60
☐ 11	Larry Walker	2.00	.90
☐ 12	Matt Williams	1.50	.70

1996 Ultra Prime Leather

Eighteen outstanding defensive players are featured in this standard-size set which is inserted approximately one in every eight packs. The horizontal fronts feature a color cut-out shot of the player against an embossed leather-like background. The player's name and team are embossed across the bottom with a black shadow effect. The backs have player's achievements noted in black type with a red outline against a glossy leather background. The

other half of the back is a full color shot of the player. The cards are sequenced in alphabetical order and gold medallion versions of these cards were also issued.

	MINT	NRMT
COMPLETE SET (18)	25.00	11.00
COMMON CARD (1-18)	.50	.23
SER.1 STATED ODDS 1:8		
*GOLD MEDAL: 1X TO 2X HI COLUMN		
GM SER.1 STATED ODDS 1:80		

		MINT	NRMT
☐ 1	Ivan Rodriguez	2.50	1.10
☐ 2	Will Clark	1.50	.70
☐ 3	Roberto Alomar	2.00	.90
☐ 4	Cal Ripken	8.00	3.60
☐ 5	Wade Boggs	2.00	.90
☐ 6	Ken Griffey Jr.	10.00	4.50
☐ 7	Kenny Lofton	2.50	1.10
☐ 8	Kirby Puckett	4.00	1.80
☐ 9	Tim Salmon	2.00	.90
☐ 10	Mike Piazza	6.00	2.70
☐ 11	Mark Grace	1.50	.70
☐ 12	Craig Biggio	1.50	.70
☐ 13	Barry Larkin	1.50	.70
☐ 14	Matt Williams	1.50	.70
☐ 15	Barry Bonds	2.50	1.10
☐ 16	Tony Gwynn	5.00	2.20
☐ 17	Brian McRae	.50	.23
☐ 18	Raul Mondesi	1.50	.70

1996 Ultra Rawhide

Randomly inserted in second series packs at a rate of one in 8, this 10-card set features leading defensive players. The embossed cards feature the Ultra logo, the word "Rawhide" and the players name against a background of a glove. The back gives a description of the player's defensive abilities.

	MINT	NRMT
COMPLETE SET (10)	15.00	6.75
COMMON CARD (1-10)	1.00	.45
SER.2 STATED ODDS 1:8		
*GOLD MEDAL: 1X TO 2X HI COLUMN		
GM SER.2 STATED ODDS 1:80		

		MINT	NRMT
☐ 1	Roberto Alomar	1.25	.55
☐ 2	Barry Bonds	1.50	.70
☐ 3	Mark Grace	1.00	.45
☐ 4	Ken Griffey Jr.	6.00	2.70
☐ 5	Kenny Lofton	1.50	.70
☐ 6	Greg Maddux	4.00	1.80
☐ 7	Raul Mondesi	1.00	.45
☐ 8	Mike Piazza	4.00	1.80
☐ 9	Cal Ripken	5.00	2.20
☐ 10	Matt Williams	1.00	.45

1996 Ultra RBI Kings

This 10-card standard-size set was randomly inserted at a rate of one in five retail packs. This set features top run producers. The full-color, full-bleed fronts feature player cutouts set against a background of baseballs. The player's name and team logo are printed in silver foil across the bottom. The backs show the players on a full-bleed surface with baseballs in the background and player name and accomplishments printed in white surrounding the type. The cards are sequenced in alphabetical order and gold medallion versions of these cards were also issued.

	MINT	NRMT
COMPLETE SET (10)	30.00	13.50
COMMON CARD (1-10)	1.50	.70
SER.1 STATED ODDS 1:5 RETAIL		
*GOLD MEDAL: 1X TO 2X HI COLUMN		
GM SER.1 STATED ODDS 1:50 RETAIL		

		MINT	NRMT
☐ 1	Derek Bell	1.50	.70
☐ 2	Albert Belle	6.00	2.70
☐ 3	Dante Bichette	2.00	.90
☐ 4	Barry Bonds	6.00	2.70
☐ 5	Jim Edmonds	3.00	1.35
☐ 6	Manny Ramirez	4.00	1.80
☐ 7	Reggie Sanders	1.50	.70
☐ 8	Sammy Sosa	4.00	1.80
☐ 9	Frank Thomas	20.00	9.00
☐ 10	Mo Vaughn	6.00	2.70

1996 Ultra Respect

Randomly inserted in second series packs at a rate of one in

18, this 10-card set features players who are well regarded by their peers for both on- and off-field activies. The fronts consist of a player photo with the word "Respect" as well as his name and the Ultra logo on the right. The back has another player photo as well as reasons why the player has earned his reputation.

	MINT	NRMT
COMPLETE SET (10)	60.00	27.00
COMMON CARD(1-10)	1.50	.70
SER.2 STATED ODDS 1:18		
*GOLD MEDAL: 1X TO 2X HI COLUMN		
GM SER.2 STATED ODDS 1:180		

		MINT	NRMT
☐ 1	Joe Carter	1.50	.70
☐ 2	Ken Griffey Jr.	15.00	6.75
☐ 3	Tony Gwynn	8.00	3.60
☐ 4	Greg Maddux	10.00	4.50
☐ 5	Eddie Murray	3.00	1.35
☐ 6	Kirby Puckett	6.00	2.70
☐ 7	Cal Ripken	12.00	5.50
☐ 8	Ryne Sandberg	4.00	1.80
☐ 9	Frank Thomas	12.00	5.50
☐ 10	Mo Vaughn	4.00	1.80

1996 Ultra Rising Stars

Randomly inserted in second series packs at a rate of one in four, this 10-card set features leading players of tomorrow. The fronts have a player photo superimposed on a stadium background. The words "Rising Star" as well as the player's name and the Ultra logo are in the middle of the front. The back has another player photo and informaton on the future of these young stars.

	MINT	NRMT
COMPLETE SET (10)	4.00	1.80
COMMON CARD(1-10)	.25	.11
SER.2 STATED ODDS 1:4		
*GOLD MEDAL: .75X TO X HI COLUMN		
GM SER.2 STATED ODDS 1:40		

		MINT	NRMT
☐ 1	Garret Anderson	.40	.18
☐ 2	Marty Cordova	.40	.18
☐ 3	Jim Edmonds	.60	.25
☐ 4	Cliff Floyd	.25	.11
☐ 5	Brian L.Hunter	.40	.18
☐ 6	Chipper Jones	2.50	1.10
☐ 7	Ryan Klesko	.60	.25
☐ 8	Hideo Nomo	1.50	.70
☐ 9	Manny Ramirez	.75	.35
☐ 10	Rondell White	.40	.18

1996 Ultra Season Crowns

This set features ten award winners and stat leaders. The cards were randomly inserted at a rate of one in ten. The clear acetate cards feature a full-color player cutout against a background of colored foliage and laurels. Backs include the player's 1995 statistics and other facts on a multi-colored background. The cards are sequenced in alphabetical order and gold medallion versions of these cards were also issued.

	MINT	NRMT
COMPLETE SET (10)	30.00	13.50
COMMON CARD(1-10)	.50	.23
SER.1 STATED ODDS 1:10		
*GOLD MEDAL: 1X TO 2X HI COLUMN		
GM SER.1 STATED ODDS 1:100		

		MINT	NRMT
☐ 1	Barry Bonds	2.50	1.10
☐ 2	Tony Gwynn	5.00	2.20
☐ 3	Randy Johnson	2.00	.90
☐ 4	Kenny Lofton	2.50	1.10
☐ 5	Greg Maddux	6.00	2.70
☐ 6	Edgar Martinez	1.50	.70
☐ 7	Hideo Nomo	4.00	1.80
☐ 8	Cal Ripken	8.00	3.60
☐ 9	Frank Thomas	8.00	3.60
☐ 10	Tim Wakefield	.50	.23

1996 Ultra Thunderclap

Randomly inserted one in 72 retail packs, these cards feature the leading power hitters. The player's photo is against a background of thunder and lightning and the words "Thunder Clap" and the player's name are on the bottom. The back consists of another player photo as well as a biography as to the player's power skills.

	MINT	NRMT
COMPLETE SET (20)	500.00	220.00
COMMON CARD (1-20)	12.00	5.50
SER.2 STATED ODDS 1:72 RETAIL		
*GOLD MEDAL: 3X BASIC CARDS		
GM SER.2 STATED ODDS 1:720 RETAIL		

		MINT	NRMT
☐ 1	Albert Belle	25.00	11.00
☐ 2	Barry Bonds	25.00	11.00
☐ 3	Bobby Bonilla	12.00	5.50
☐ 4	Jose Canseco	15.00	6.75
☐ 5	Joe Carter	12.00	5.50
☐ 6	Will Clark	15.00	6.75
☐ 7	Andre Dawson	15.00	6.75
☐ 8	Cecil Fielder	12.00	5.50
☐ 9	Andres Galarraga	20.00	9.00
☐ 10	Juan Gonzalez	50.00	22.00
☐ 11	Ken Griffey Jr.	100.00	45.00
☐ 12	Fred McGriff	15.00	6.75
☐ 13	Mark McGwire	40.00	18.00
☐ 14	Eddie Murray	25.00	11.00
☐ 15	Rafael Palmeiro	15.00	6.75
☐ 16	Kirby Puckett	50.00	22.00
☐ 17	Cal Ripken	80.00	36.00
☐ 18	Ryne Sandberg	30.00	13.50
☐ 19	Frank Thomas	80.00	36.00
☐ 20	Matt Williams	15.00	6.75

1997 Ultra

The 1997 Ultra was issued in two series totalling 553 cards. The first series consisted of 300 cards with the second containing 253. The 10-card packs had a suggested retail price of 2.49 each. Each pack had two insert cards, with one insert being a gold medallion parallel and the other insert being from one of serveral other insert sets. The fronts features borderless color action player photos with career statistics on the backs. As in most Fleer produced sets, the cards are arranged in alphabetical order by league, player and team. Second series retail packs contained only cards 301-450 while second series hobby packs contained all cards from 301-553. Rookie Cards include Jose Cruz Jr. and Fernando Tatis.

	MINT	NRMT
COMPLETE SET (553)	60.00	27.00
COMPLETE SERIES 1 (300)	30.00	13.50
COMPLETE SERIES 2 (253)	30.00	13.50
COMMON CARD (1-450)	.15	.07
MINOR STARS	.30	.14
UNLISTED STARS	.60	.25
COMMON CARD (451-553)	.20	.09

MINOR STARS 451-553 .... .40
UNLISTED STARS 451-553 ..... .75
COMP.G.MED.SET (553) .... 270.00 .... 120.00
COMP.G.MED.SER.1 (300) 150.00 .... 70.00
COMP.G.MED.SER.2 (253) 120.00 .... 55.00
COMMON G.MED (1-450) ...... .25 ...... .11
COMMON G.MED (451-553) .. .30 ...... .14
*G.MED.STARS: 2X TO 4X HI COLUMN
*G.MED YOUNG STARS: 1.5X TO 3X HI
*G.MED ROOKIES: 1X TO 2X HI
ONE GOLD MEDALLION PER PACK
COMP.PLAT.SET (553) .. 6500.00 2900.00
COMP.PLAT.SER.1 (300) 4000.00 1800.00
COMP.PLAT.SER.2 (253) 2500.00 1100.00
COMMON PLAT. (1-553) .... 10.00 .... 4.50
*PLAT.MED.STARS: 30X TO 60X HI COLUMN
*PLAT.MED.YOUNG STARS: 25X TO 50X HI
*PLAT.MED.ROOKIES: 10X TO 20X HI
PLATINUM MED.STATED ODDS 1:100
PLAT.MED.PRINT RUN LESS THAN 200 SETS
MEDALLIONS HAVE DIFFERENT PHOTOS
CARDS 451-553 ARE HOBBY ONLY

☐	1	Roberto Alomar	.60	.25				
☐	2	Brady Anderson	.40	.18				
☐	3	Rocky Coppinger	.15	.07				
☐	4	Jeffrey Hammonds	.15	.07				
☐	5	Chris Hoiles	.15	.07				
☐	6	Eddie Murray	.60	.25				
☐	7	Mike Mussina	.60	.25				
☐	8	Jimmy Myers	.15	.07				
☐	9	Randy Myers	.15	.07				
☐	10	Arthur Rhodes	.15	.07				
☐	11	Cal Ripken	2.50	1.10				
☐	12	Jose Canseco	.40	.18				
☐	13	Roger Clemens	1.25	.55				
☐	14	Tom Gordon	.15	.07				
☐	15	Jose Malave	.15	.07				
☐	16	Tim Naehring	.15	.07				
☐	17	Troy O'Leary	.15	.07				
☐	18	Bill Selby	.15	.07				
☐	19	Heathcliff Slocumb	.15	.07				
☐	20	Mike Stanley	.15	.07				
☐	21	Mo Vaughn	.75	.35				
☐	22	Garret Anderson	.30	.14				
☐	23	George Arias	.15	.07				
☐	24	Chili Davis	.30	.14				
☐	25	Jim Edmonds	.40	.18				
☐	26	Darin Erstad	1.00	.45				
☐	27	Chuck Finley	.15	.07				
☐	28	Todd Greene	.30	.14				
☐	29	Troy Percival	.15	.07				
☐	30	Tim Salmon	.60	.25				
☐	31	Jeff Schmidt	.15	.07				
☐	32	Randy Velarde	.15	.07				
☐	33	Shad Williams	.15	.07				
☐	34	Wilson Alvarez	.15	.07				
☐	35	Harold Baines	.30	.14				
☐	36	James Baldwin	.15	.07				
☐	37	Mike Cameron	.40	.18				
☐	38	Ray Durham	.15	.07				
☐	39	Ozzie Guillen	.15	.07				
☐	40	Roberto Hernandez	.15	.07				
☐	41	Darren Lewis	.15	.07				
☐	42	Jose Munoz	.15	.07				
☐	43	Tony Phillips	.15	.07				
☐	44	Frank Thomas	2.50	1.10				
☐	45	Sandy Alomar Jr.	.30	.14				
☐	46	Albert Belle	.75	.35				
☐	47	Mark Carreon	.15	.07				
☐	48	Julio Franco	.15	.07				
☐	49	Orel Hershiser	.30	.14				
☐	50	Kenny Lofton	.75	.35				
☐	51	Jack McDowell	.15	.07				
☐	52	Jose Mesa	.15	.07				
☐	53	Charles Nagy	.30	.14				
☐	54	Manny Ramirez	.60	.25				
☐	55	Julian Tavarez	.15	.07				
☐	56	Omar Vizquel	.30	.14				
☐	57	Raul Casanova	.15	.07				
☐	58	Tony Clark	.60	.25				
☐	59	Travis Fryman	.30	.14				
☐	60	Bob Higginson	.15	.07				
☐	61	Melvin Nieves	.15	.07				
☐	62	Curtis Pride	.15	.07				
☐	63	Justin Thompson	.30	.14				
☐	64	Alan Trammell	.30	.14				
☐	65	Kevin Appier	.30	.14				
☐	66	Johnny Damon	.15	.07				
☐	67	Keith Lockhart	.15	.07				
☐	68	Jeff Montgomery	.15	.07				
☐	69	Jose Offerman	.15	.07				
☐	70	Bip Roberts	.15	.07				
☐	71	Jose Rosado	.30	.14				
☐	72	Chris Stynes	.15	.07				
☐	73	Mike Sweeney	.30	.14				
☐	74	Jeff Cirillo	.30	.14				
☐	75	Jeff D'Amico	.15	.07				
☐	76	John Jaha	.15	.07				
☐	77	Scott Karl	.15	.07				
☐	78	Mike Matheny	.15	.07				
☐	79	Ben McDonald	.15	.07				
☐	80	Matt Mieske	.15	.07				
☐	81	Marc Newfield	.15	.07				
☐	82	Dave Nilsson	.15	.07				
☐	83	Jose Valentin	.15	.07				
☐	84	Fernando Vina	.15	.07				
☐	85	Rick Aguilera	.15	.07				
☐	86	Marty Cordova	.30	.14				
☐	87	Chuck Knoblauch	.60	.25				
☐	88	Matt Lawton	.15	.07				
☐	89	Pat Meares	.15	.07				
☐	90	Paul Molitor	.60	.25				
☐	91	Greg Myers	.15	.07				
☐	92	Dan Naulty	.15	.07				
☐	93	Kirby Puckett	1.25	.55				
☐	94	Frank Rodriguez	.15	.07				
☐	95	Wade Boggs	.60	.25				
☐	96	Cecil Fielder	.30	.14				
☐	97	Joe Girardi	.15	.07				
☐	98	Dwight Gooden	.30	.14				
☐	99	Derek Jeter	2.00	.90				
☐	100	Tino Martinez	.60	.25				
☐	101	Ramiro Mendoza	.40	.18				
☐	102	Andy Pettitte	.60	.25				
☐	103	Mariano Rivera	.30	.14				
☐	104	Ruben Rivera	.30	.14				
☐	105	Kenny Rogers	.15	.07				
☐	106	Darryl Strawberry	.30	.14				
☐	107	Bernie Williams	.60	.25				
☐	108	Tony Batista	.15	.07				
☐	109	Geronimo Berroa	.15	.07				
☐	110	Bobby Chouinard	.15	.07				
☐	111	Brent Gates	.15	.07				
☐	112	Jason Giambi	.30	.14				
☐	113	Damon Mashore	.15	.07				
☐	114	Mark McGwire	1.25	.55				
☐	115	Scott Spiezio	.30	.14				
☐	116	John Wasdin	.15	.07				
☐	117	Steve Wojciechowski	.15	.07				
☐	118	Ernie Young	.15	.07				
☐	119	Norm Charlton	.15	.07				
☐	120	Joey Cora	.30	.14				
☐	121	Ken Griffey Jr.	3.00	1.35				
☐	122	Sterling Hitchcock	.15	.07				
☐	123	Raul Ibanez	.15	.07				
☐	124	Randy Johnson	.60	.25				
☐	125	Edgar Martinez	.40	.18				
☐	126	Alex Rodriguez	2.00	.90				
☐	127	Matt Wagner	.15	.07				
☐	128	Bob Wells	.15	.07				
☐	129	Dan Wilson	.15	.07				
☐	130	Will Clark	.40	.18				
☐	131	Kevin Elster	.15	.07				
☐	132	Juan Gonzalez	1.50	.70				
☐	133	Rusty Greer	.30	.14				
☐	134	Darryl Hamilton	.15	.07				
☐	135	Mike Henneman	.15	.07				
☐	136	Ken Hill	.15	.07				
☐	137	Mark McLemore	.15	.07				
☐	138	Dean Palmer	.15	.07				
☐	139	Roger Pavlik	.15	.07				
☐	140	Ivan Rodriguez	.75	.35				
☐	141	Joe Carter	.30	.14				
☐	142	Carlos Delgado	.30	.14				
☐	143	Alex Gonzalez	.15	.07				
☐	144	Juan Guzman	.15	.07				
☐	145	Pat Hentgen	.30	.14				
☐	146	Marty Janzen	.15	.07				
☐	147	Otis Nixon	.15	.07				
☐	148	Charlie O'Brien	.15	.07				
☐	149	John Olerud	.30	.14				
☐	150	Robert Perez	.15	.07				
☐	151	Jermaine Dye	.15	.07				
☐	152	Tom Glavine	.30	.14				
☐	153	Andruw Jones	1.50	.70				
☐	154	Chipper Jones	2.00	.90				
☐	155	Ryan Klesko	.40	.18				
☐	156	Javier Lopez	.30	.14				
☐	157	Greg Maddux	2.00	.90				
☐	158	Fred McGriff	.40	.18				
☐	159	Wonderful Monds	.15	.07				
☐	160	John Smoltz	.30	.14				
☐	161	Terrell Wade	.15	.07				
☐	162	Mark Wohlers	.15	.07				
☐	163	Brant Brown	.15	.07				
☐	164	Mark Grace	.40	.18				
☐	165	Tyler Houston	.15	.07				
☐	166	Robin Jennings	.15	.07				
☐	167	Jason Maxwell	.15	.07				
☐	168	Ryne Sandberg	.75	.35				
☐	169	Sammy Sosa	.60	.25				
☐	170	Amaury Telemaco	.15	.07				
☐	171	Steve Trachsel	.15	.07				
☐	172	Pedro Valdes	.15	.07				
☐	173	Tim Belk	.15	.07				
☐	174	Bret Boone	.15	.07				
☐	175	Jeff Brantley	.15	.07				
☐	176	Eric Davis	.30	.14				
☐	177	Barry Larkin	.40	.18				
☐	178	Chad Mottola	.15	.07				
☐	179	Mark Portugal	.15	.07				
☐	180	Reggie Sanders	.15	.07				
☐	181	John Smiley	.15	.07				
☐	182	Eddie Taubensee	.15	.07				
☐	183	Dante Bichette	.30	.14				
☐	184	Ellis Burks	.30	.14				
☐	185	Andres Galarraga	.60	.25				
☐	186	Curt Leskanic	.15	.07				
☐	187	Quinton McCracken	.15	.07				
☐	188	Jeff Reed	.15	.07				
☐	189	Kevin Ritz	.15	.07				
☐	190	Walt Weiss	.15	.07				
☐	191	Jamey Wright	.15	.07				
☐	192	Eric Young	.15	.07				
☐	193	Kevin Brown	.30	.14				
☐	194	Luis Castillo	.30	.14				
☐	195	Jeff Conine	.30	.14				
☐	196	Andre Dawson	.40	.18				
☐	197	Charles Johnson	.30	.14				
☐	198	Al Leiter	.15	.07				
☐	199	Ralph Milliard	.15	.07				
☐	200	Robb Nen	.15	.07				
☐	201	Edgar Renteria	.30	.14				
☐	202	Gary Sheffield	.60	.25				
☐	203	Bob Abreu	.30	.14				
☐	204	Jeff Bagwell	1.25	.55				
☐	205	Derek Bell	.15	.07				
☐	206	Sean Berry	.15	.07				
☐	207	Richard Hidalgo	.30	.14				
☐	208	Todd Jones	.15	.07				
☐	209	Darryl Kile	.15	.07				
☐	210	Orlando Miller	.15	.07				
☐	211	Shane Reynolds	.15	.07				
☐	212	Billy Wagner	.30	.14				
☐	213	Donne Wall	.15	.07				
☐	214	Roger Cedeno	.15	.07				
☐	215	Greg Gagne	.15	.07				
☐	216	Karim Garcia	.30	.14				
☐	217	Wilton Guerrero	.15	.07				
☐	218	Todd Hollandsworth	.15	.07				
☐	219	Ramon Martinez	.30	.14				
☐	220	Raul Mondesi	.40	.18				
☐	221	Hideo Nomo	1.50	.70				
☐	222	Chan Ho Park	.60	.25				
☐	223	Mike Piazza	2.00	.90				
☐	224	Ismael Valdes	.30	.14				
☐	225	Moises Alou	.30	.14				
☐	226	Derek Aucoin	.15	.07				
☐	227	Yamil Benitez	.15	.07				
☐	228	Jeff Fassero	.15	.07				
☐	229	Darrin Fletcher	.15	.07				
☐	230	Mark Grudzielanek	.15	.07				
☐	231	Barry Manuel	.15	.07				
☐	232	Pedro Martinez	.60	.25				
☐	233	Henry Rodriguez	.15	.07				
☐	234	Ugueth Urbina	.15	.07				
☐	235	Rondell White	.30	.14				

236	Carlos Baerga	.15	.07
237	John Franco	.30	.14
238	Bernard Gilkey	.15	.07
239	Todd Hundley	.30	.14
240	Butch Huskey	.15	.07
241	Jason Isringhausen	.15	.07
242	Lance Johnson	.15	.07
243	Bobby Jones	.15	.07
244	Alex Ochoa	.15	.07
245	Rey Ordonez	.15	.07
246	Paul Wilson	.15	.07
247	Ron Blazier	.15	.07
248	David Doster	.15	.07
249	Jim Eisenreich	.15	.07
250	Mike Grace	.15	.07
251	Mike Lieberthal	.15	.07
252	Wendell Magee	.15	.07
253	Mickey Morandini	.15	.07
254	Ricky Otero	.15	.07
255	Scott Rolen	1.50	.70
256	Curt Schilling	.30	.14
257	Todd Zeile	.15	.07
258	Jermaine Allensworth	.15	.07
259	Trey Beamon	.15	.07
260	Carlos Garcia	.15	.07
261	Mark Johnson	.30	.14
262	Jason Kendall	.30	.14
263	Jeff King	.15	.07
264	Al Martin	.15	.07
265	Denny Neagle	.30	.14
266	Matt Ruebel	.15	.07
267	Marc Wilkins	.15	.07
268	Alan Benes	.30	.14
269	Dennis Eckersley	.30	.14
270	Ron Gant	.30	.14
271	Aaron Holbert	.15	.07
272	Brian Jordan	.30	.14
273	Ray Lankford	.30	.14
274	John Mabry	.15	.07
275	T.J. Mathews	.15	.07
276	Ozzie Smith	.75	.35
277	Todd Stottlemyre	.15	.07
278	Mark Sweeney	.15	.07
279	Andy Ashby	.15	.07
280	Steve Finley	.30	.14
281	John Flaherty	.15	.07
282	Chris Gomez	.15	.07
283	Tony Gwynn	1.50	.70
284	Joey Hamilton	.30	.14
285	Rickey Henderson	.40	.18
286	Trevor Hoffman	.15	.07
287	Jason Thompson	.15	.07
288	Fernando Valenzuela	.30	.14
289	Greg Vaughn	.15	.07
290	Barry Bonds	.75	.35
291	Jay Canizaro	.15	.07
292	Jacob Cruz	.30	.14
293	Shawon Dunston	.15	.07
294	Shawn Estes	.30	.14
295	Mark Gardner	.15	.07
296	Marcus Jensen	.15	.07
297	Bill Mueller	.15	.07
298	Chris Singleton	.15	.07
299	Allen Watson	.15	.07
300	Matt Williams	.40	.18
301	Rod Beck	.15	.07
302	Jay Bell	.30	.14
303	Shawon Dunston	.15	.07
304	Reggie Jefferson	.15	.07
305	Darren Oliver	.15	.07
306	Benito Santiago	.15	.07
307	Gerald Williams	.15	.07
308	Damon Buford	.15	.07
309	Jeromy Burnitz	.15	.07
310	Sterling Hitchcock	.15	.07
311	Dave Hollins	.15	.07
312	Mel Rojas	.15	.07
313	Robin Ventura	.30	.14
314	David Wells	.15	.07
315	Cal Eldred	.15	.07
316	Gary Gaetti	.15	.07
317	John Hudek	.15	.07
318	Brian Johnson	.15	.07
319	Denny Neagle	.30	.14
320	Larry Walker	.60	.25
321	Russ Davis	.15	.07
322	Delino DeShields	.15	.07
323	Charlie Hayes	.15	.07
324	Jermaine Dye	.15	.07
325	John Ericks	.15	.07
326	Jeff Fassero	.15	.07
327	Nomar Garciaparra	2.00	.90
328	Willie Greene	.15	.07
329	Greg McMichael	.15	.07
330	Damion Easley	.15	.07
331	Ricky Bones	.15	.07
332	John Burkett	.15	.07
333	Royce Clayton	.15	.07
334	Greg Colbrunn	.15	.07
335	Tony Eusebio	.15	.07
336	Gregg Jefferies	.15	.07
337	Wally Joyner	.30	.14
338	Jim Leyritz	.15	.07
339	Paul O'Neill	.30	.14
340	Bruce Ruffin	.15	.07
341	Michael Tucker	.30	.14
342	Andy Benes	.30	.14
343	Craig Biggio	.40	.18
344	Rex Hudler	.15	.07
345	Brad Radke	.30	.14
346	Deion Sanders	.30	.14
347	Moises Alou	.30	.14
348	Brad Ausmus	.15	.07
349	Armando Benitez	.15	.07
350	Mark Gubicza	.15	.07
351	Terry Steinbach	.15	.07
352	Mark Whiten	.15	.07
353	Ricky Bottalico	.15	.07
354	Brian Giles	.15	.07
355	Eric Karros	.30	.14
356	Jimmy Key	.30	.14
357	Carlos Perez	.15	.07
358	Alex Fernandez	.15	.07
359	J.T. Snow	.30	.14
360	Bobby Bonilla	.30	.14
361	Scott Brosius	.15	.07
362	Greg Swindell	.15	.07
363	Jose Vizcaino	.15	.07
364	Matt Williams	.40	.18
365	Darren Daulton	.30	.14
366	Shane Andrews	.15	.07
367	Jim Eisenreich	.15	.07
368	Ariel Prieto	.15	.07
369	Bob Tewksbury	.15	.07
370	Mike Bordick	.15	.07
371	Rheal Cormier	.15	.07
372	Cliff Floyd	.15	.07
373	David Justice	.60	.25
374	John Wetteland	.15	.07
375	Mike Blowers	.15	.07
376	Jose Canseco	.40	.18
377	Roger Clemens	1.25	.55
378	Kevin Mitchell	.15	.07
379	Todd Zeile	.15	.07
380	Jim Thome	.60	.25
381	Turk Wendell	.15	.07
382	Rico Brogna	.15	.07
383	Eric Davis	.30	.14
384	Mike Lansing	.15	.07
385	Devon White	.15	.07
386	Marquis Grissom	.30	.14
387	Todd Worrell	.15	.07
388	Jeff Kent	.15	.07
389	Mickey Tettleton	.15	.07
390	Steve Avery	.15	.07
391	David Cone	.30	.14
392	Scott Cooper	.15	.07
393	Lee Stevens	.15	.07
394	Kevin Elster	.15	.07
395	Tom Goodwin	.15	.07
396	Shawn Green	.15	.07
397	Pete Harnisch	.15	.07
398	Eddie Murray	.60	.25
399	Joe Randa	.15	.07
400	Scott Sanders	.15	.07
401	John Valentin	.15	.07
402	Todd Jones	.15	.07
403	Terry Adams	.15	.07
404	Brian Hunter	.30	.14
405	Pat Listach	.15	.07
406	Kenny Lofton	.75	.35
407	Hal Morris	.15	.07
408	Ed Sprague	.15	.07
409	Rich Becker	.15	.07
410	Edgardo Alfonzo	.30	.14
411	Albert Belle	.75	.35
412	Jeff King	.15	.07
413	Kirt Manwaring	.15	.07
414	Jason Schmidt	.15	.07
415	Allen Watson	.15	.07
416	Lee Tinsley	.15	.07
417	Brett Butler	.30	.14
418	Carlos Garcia	.15	.07
419	Mark Lemke	.15	.07
420	Jaime Navarro	.15	.07
421	David Segui	.15	.07
422	Ruben Sierra	.15	.07
423	B.J. Surhoff	.15	.07
424	Julian Tavarez	.15	.07
425	Billy Taylor	.15	.07
426	Ken Caminiti	.40	.18
427	Chuck Carr	.15	.07
428	Benji Gil	.15	.07
429	Terry Mulholland	.15	.07
430	Mike Stanton	.15	.07
431	Wil Cordero	.15	.07
432	Chili Davis	.30	.14
433	Mariano Duncan	.15	.07
434	Orlando Merced	.15	.07
435	Kent Mercker	.15	.07
436	John Olerud	.30	.14
437	Quilvio Veras	.15	.07
438	Mike Fetters	.15	.07
439	Glenallen Hill	.15	.07
440	Bill Swift	.15	.07
441	Tim Wakefield	.15	.07
442	Pedro Astacio	.15	.07
443	Vinny Castilla	.30	.14
444	Doug Drabek	.15	.07
445	Alan Embree	.15	.07
446	Lee Smith	.30	.14
447	Darryl Hamilton	.15	.07
448	Brian McRae	.15	.07
449	Mike Timlin	.15	.07
450	Bob Wickman	.15	.07
451	Jason Dickson	.40	.18
452	Chad Curtis	.20	.09
453	Mark Leiter	.20	.09
454	Damon Berryhill	.20	.09
455	Kevin Orie	.40	.18
456	Dave Burba	.20	.09
457	Chris Holt	.20	.09
458	Ricky Ledee	2.00	.90
459	Mike Devereaux	.20	.09
460	Pokey Reese	.20	.09
461	Tim Raines	.40	.18
462	Ryan Jones	.20	.09
463	Shane Mack	.20	.09
464	Darren Dreifort	.20	.09
465	Mark Parent	.20	.09
466	Mark Portugal	.20	.09
467	Dante Powell	.20	.09
468	Craig Grebeck	.20	.09
469	Ron Villone	.20	.09
470	Dmitri Young	.20	.09
471	Shannon Stewart	.40	.18
472	Rick Helling	.20	.09
473	Bill Haselman	.20	.09
474	Albie Lopez	.20	.09
475	Glendon Rusch	.20	.09
476	Derrick May	.20	.09
477	Chad Ogea	.20	.09
478	Kirk Rueter	.20	.09
479	Chris Hammond	.20	.09
480	Russ Johnson	.20	.09
481	James Mouton	.20	.09
482	Mike Macfarlane	.20	.09
483	Scott Ruffcorn	.20	.09
484	Jeff Frye	.20	.09
485	Richie Sexson	.40	.18
486	Emil Brown	.50	.23
487	Desi Wilson	.20	.09
488	Brent Gates	.20	.09
489	Tony Graffanino	.20	.09
490	Dan Miceli	.20	.09
491	Orlando Cabrera	.50	.23
492	Tony Womack	.75	.35
493	Jerome Walton	.20	.09

		MINT	NRMT
☐ 494	Mark Thompson	.20	.09
☐ 495	Jose Guillen	1.00	.45
☐ 496	Willie Blair	.20	.09
☐ 497	T.J. Staton	.50	.23
☐ 498	Scott Kamieniecki	.20	.09
☐ 499	Vince Coleman	.20	.09
☐ 500	Jeff Abbott	.20	.09
☐ 501	Chris Widger	.20	.09
☐ 502	Kevin Tapani	.20	.09
☐ 503	Carlos Castillo	.50	.23
☐ 504	Luis Gonzalez	.20	.09
☐ 505	Tim Belcher	.20	.09
☐ 506	Armando Reynoso	.20	.09
☐ 507	Jamie Moyer	.20	.09
☐ 508	Randall Simon	2.00	.90
☐ 509	Vladimir Guerrero	1.50	.70
☐ 510	Wady Almonte	.60	.25
☐ 511	Dustin Hermanson	.20	.09
☐ 512	Deivi Cruz	.60	.25
☐ 513	Luis Alicea	.20	.09
☐ 514	Felix Heredia	.50	.23
☐ 515	Don Slaught	.20	.09
☐ 516	Shigetoshi Hasegawa	.50	.23
☐ 517	Matt Walbeck	.20	.09
☐ 518	David Arias-Ortiz	1.50	.70
☐ 519	Brady Raggio	.20	.09
☐ 520	Rudy Pemberton	.20	.09
☐ 521	Wayne Kirby	.20	.09
☐ 522	Calvin Maduro	.20	.09
☐ 523	Mark Lewis	.20	.09
☐ 524	Mike Jackson	.20	.09
☐ 525	Sid Fernandez	.20	.09
☐ 526	Mike Bielecki	.20	.09
☐ 527	Bubba Trammell	1.00	.45
☐ 528	Brent Brede	.40	.18
☐ 529	Matt Morris	.40	.18
☐ 530	Joe Borowski	.20	.09
☐ 531	Orlando Miller	.20	.09
☐ 532	Jim Bullinger	.20	.09
☐ 533	Robert Person	.20	.09
☐ 534	Doug Glanville	.20	.09
☐ 535	Terry Pendleton	.20	.09
☐ 536	Jorge Posada	.20	.09
☐ 537	Marc Sagmoen	.20	.09
☐ 538	Fernando Tatis	2.50	1.10
☐ 539	Aaron Sele	.20	.09
☐ 540	Brian Banks	.20	.09
☐ 541	Derrek Lee	.50	.23
☐ 542	John Wasdin	.20	.09
☐ 543	Justin Towle	1.00	.45
☐ 544	Pat Cline	.20	.09
☐ 545	Dave Magadan	.20	.09
☐ 546	Jeff Blauser	.40	.18
☐ 547	Phil Nevin	.20	.09
☐ 548	Todd Walker	.40	.18
☐ 549	Eli Marrero	.40	.18
☐ 550	Bartolo Colon	.40	.18
☐ 551	Jose Cruz Jr.	8.00	3.60
☐ 552	Todd Dunwoody	.50	.23
☐ 553	Hideki Irabu	1.00	.45
☐ P11	Cal Ripken Promo	4.00	1.80
	Three Card Strip		

1997 Ultra Autographstix Emeralds

This six-card hobby exclusive Series 2 insert set consists of individually numbered Redemption cards for autographed bats from the players checklisted below. Only 25 of each card was produced. The deadline to exchange cards was July 1, 1998.

	MINT	NRMT
COMPLETE SET (6)	1500.00	700.00
COMMON CARD (1-6)	60.00	27.00
RANDOM INSERTS IN SER.2 HOBBY PACKS		
STATED PRINT RUN 25 SERIAL #'d SETS		
EXCHANGE DEADLINE: 7/1/98..		

		MINT	NRMT
☐ 1	Alex Ochoa	60.00	27.00
☐ 2	Todd Walker	100.00	45.00
☐ 3	Scott Rolen	400.00	180.00
☐ 4	Darin Erstad	250.00	110.00
☐ 5	Alex Rodriguez	800.00	350.00
☐ 6	Todd Hollandsworth	80.00	36.00

1997 Ultra Baseball Rules

Randomly inserted into first series retail packs of 1997 Ultra at a rate of 1:36, cards from this 10-card set feature a selection of baseball's top performers from the 1996 season. The die cut cards feature a player photo surrounded by a group of baseballs. The back explains some of the rules involved in making various awards.

	MINT	NRMT
COMPLETE SET (10)	120.00	55.00
COMMON CARD (1-10)	2.00	.90
SER.1 STATED ODDS 1:36 RETAIL		

		MINT	NRMT
☐ 1	Barry Bonds	6.00	2.70
☐ 2	Ken Griffey Jr.	25.00	11.00
☐ 3	Derek Jeter	12.00	5.50
☐ 4	Chipper Jones	15.00	6.75
☐ 5	Greg Maddux	15.00	6.75
☐ 6	Mark McGwire	10.00	4.50
☐ 7	Troy Percival	2.00	.90
☐ 8	Mike Piazza	15.00	6.75
☐ 9	Cal Ripken	20.00	9.00
☐ 10	Frank Thomas	20.00	9.00

1997 Ultra Checklists

Randomly inserted in all first and second series packs at a rate of one in four, this 20-card set features borderless player photos on the front along with the word "Checklist," the play-

er's name as well as the "ultra" logo at the bottom. The backs are checklists. The checklists for Series 1 are listed below with an "A" prefix and for Series 2 with a "B" prefix.

	MINT	NRMT
COMPLETE SERIES 1 (10)	8.00	3.60
COMPLETE SERIES 2 (10)	12.00	5.50
COMMON CARD (A1-B10)	.25	.11
STATED ODDS 1:4 HOBBY		

		MINT	NRMT
☐ A1	Dante Bichette	.25	.11
☐ A2	Barry Bonds	.75	.35
☐ A3	Ken Griffey Jr.	2.00	.90
☐ A4	Greg Maddux	2.00	.90
☐ A5	Mark McGwire	1.25	.55
☐ A6	Mike Piazza	2.00	.90
☐ A7	Cal Ripken	2.00	.90
☐ A8	John Smoltz	.25	.11
☐ A9	Sammy Sosa	.50	.23
☐ A10	Frank Thomas	2.00	.90
☐ B1	Andruw Jones	1.50	.70
☐ B2	Ken Griffey Jr.	3.00	1.35
☐ B3	Frank Thomas	2.00	.90
☐ B4	Alex Rodriguez	2.00	.90
☐ B5	Cal Ripken	2.00	.90
☐ B6	Mike Piazza	2.00	.90
☐ B7	Greg Maddux	2.00	.90
☐ B8	Chipper Jones	2.00	.90
☐ B9	Derek Jeter	2.00	.90
☐ B10	Juan Gonzalez	1.50	.70

1997 Ultra Diamond Producers

Randomly inserted in all first series packs at a rate of one in 288, this 12-card set features "flannel" material mounted on card stock and attempt to look and feel like actual uniforms.

	MINT	NRMT
COMPLETE SET (12)	600.00	275.00
COMMON CARD (1-12)	12.00	5.50
SER.1 STATED ODDS 1:288		

☐ 1 Jeff Bagwell	40.00	18.00
☐ 2 Barry Bonds	25.00	11.00
☐ 3 Ken Griffey Jr.	100.00	45.00
☐ 4 Chipper Jones	60.00	27.00
☐ 5 Kenny Lofton	25.00	11.00
☐ 6 Greg Maddux	60.00	27.00
☐ 7 Mark Piazza	40.00	18.00
☐ 8 Mike Piazza	60.00	27.00
☐ 9 Cal Ripken	80.00	36.00
☐ 10 Alex Rodriguez	60.00	27.00
☐ 11 Frank Thomas	80.00	36.00
☐ 12 Matt Williams	12.00	5.50

1997 Ultra Double Trouble

Randomly inserted in series 1 packs at a rate of one in four, this 20-card set features two players from each team. The horizontal cards feature players photos with their names in silver foil on the bottom and the words "double trouble" on the top. The backs feature information on what the players contributed to their team in 1996.

	MINT	NRMT
COMPLETE SET (20)	12.00	5.50
COMMON CARD (1-20)	.25	.11
SER.1 STATED ODDS 1:4		

☐ 1 Roberto Alomar	2.00	.90
Cal Ripken		
☐ 2 Mo Vaughn	.60	.25
Jose Canseco		
☐ 3 Jim Edmonds	.75	.35
Tim Salmon		
☐ 4 Harold Baines	2.00	.90
Frank Thomas		
☐ 5 Albert Belle	.75	.35
Kenny Lofton		
☐ 6 Marty Cordova	.75	.35
Chuck Knoblauch		
☐ 7 Derek Jeter	1.50	.70
Andy Pettitte		
☐ 8 Jason Giambi	1.00	.45
Mark McGwire		
☐ 9 Ken Griffey Jr.	4.00	1.80
Alex Rodriguez		
☐ 10 Juan Gonzalez	1.25	.55
Will Clark		
☐ 11 Greg Maddux	2.00	.90
Chipper Jones		
☐ 12 Mark Grace	.75	.35
Sammy Sosa		
☐ 13 Dante Bichette	.75	.35
Andres Galarraga		
☐ 14 Jeff Bagwell	1.00	.45
Derek Bell		
☐ 15 Hideo Nomo	2.00	.90
Mike Piazza		
☐ 16 Henry Rodriguez	.25	.11
Moises Alou		
☐ 17 Rey Ordonez	.25	.11

Alex Ochoa		
☐ 18 Ray Lankford	.25	.11
Ron Gant		
☐ 19 Tony Gwynn	1.25	.55
Rickey Henderson		
☐ 20 Barry Bonds	.60	.25
Matt Williams		

1997 Ultra Fame Game

Randomly inserted in Series 2 hobby packs only at a rate of one in eight, this 18-card set features color photos of players who have displayed Hall of Fame potential on an elegant card design.

	MINT	NRMT
COMPLETE SET (18)	70.00	32.00
COMMON CARD(1-18)	2.50	1.10
SER.2 STATED ODDS 1:8 HOBBY		

☐ 1 Ken Griffey Jr.	12.00	5.50
☐ 2 Frank Thomas	10.00	4.50
☐ 3 Alex Rodriguez	8.00	3.60
☐ 4 Cal Ripken	10.00	4.50
☐ 5 Mike Piazza	8.00	3.60
☐ 6 Greg Maddux	8.00	3.60
☐ 7 Derek Jeter	8.00	3.60
☐ 8 Jeff Bagwell	5.00	2.20
☐ 9 Juan Gonzalez	6.00	2.70
☐ 10 Albert Belle	3.00	1.35
☐ 11 Tony Gwynn	6.00	2.70
☐ 12 Mark McGwire	5.00	2.20
☐ 13 Andy Pettitte	2.50	1.10
☐ 14 Kenny Lofton	2.50	1.10
☐ 15 Roberto Alomar	2.50	1.10
☐ 16 Ryne Sandberg	3.00	1.35
☐ 17 Barry Bonds	3.00	1.35
☐ 18 Eddie Murray	2.50	1.10

1997 Ultra Fielder's Choice

Randomly inserted in Series 1 packs at a rate of one in 144, this 18-card set uses leather and gold foil to honor leading defensive players. The horizontal cards also include a player photo on the front as well as the big bold words "97 Fleer Ultra", "Fielder's Choice" and the player's name. The horizontal backs have another player photo as well as information about their defensive prowess.

	MINT	NRMT
COMPLETE SET (18)	300.00	135.00
COMMON CARD (1-18)	8.00	3.60
SEMISTARS	10.00	4.50

	MINT	NRMT
UNLISTED STARS	15.00	6.75
SER.1 STATED ODDS 1:144		

☐ 1 Roberto Alomar	15.00	6.75
☐ 2 Jeff Bagwell	30.00	13.50
☐ 3 Wade Boggs	15.00	6.75
☐ 4 Barry Bonds	20.00	9.00
☐ 5 Mark Grace	10.00	4.50
☐ 6 Ken Griffey Jr.	80.00	36.00
☐ 7 Marquis Grissom	8.00	3.60
☐ 8 Charles Johnson	8.00	3.60
☐ 9 Chuck Knoblauch	15.00	6.75
☐ 10 Barry Larkin	10.00	4.50
☐ 11 Kenny Lofton	20.00	9.00
☐ 12 Greg Maddux	50.00	22.00
☐ 13 Raul Mondesi	10.00	4.50
☐ 14 Rey Ordonez	8.00	3.60
☐ 15 Cal Ripken	60.00	27.00
☐ 16 Alex Rodriguez	50.00	22.00
☐ 17 Ivan Rodriguez	20.00	9.00
☐ 18 Matt Williams	10.00	4.50

1997 Ultra Golden Prospects

Randomly inserted in Series 2 hobby packs only at a rate of one in four, this 10-card set features color action player images on a gold baseball background with commentary on what makes these players so promising.

	MINT	NRMT
COMPLETE SET (10)	6.00	2.70
COMMON CARD(1-10)	.40	.18
SER.2 STATED ODDS 1:4 HOBBY		

☐ 1 Andruw Jones	2.00	.90
☐ 2 Vladimir Guerrero	1.50	.70
☐ 3 Todd Walker	.40	.18
☐ 4 Karim Garcia	.40	.18
☐ 5 Kevin Orie	.40	.18
☐ 6 Brian Giles	.40	.18
☐ 7 Jason Dickson	.40	.18
☐ 8 Jose Guillen	1.00	.45
☐ 9 Ruben Rivera	.40	.18
☐ 10 Derrek Lee	.50	.23

1997 Ultra Hitting Machines

Randomly inserted in Series 2 hobby packs only at a rate of one in 36, this 18-card set features color action player images of the MLB's most productive hitters in "machine-style" die-cut settings.

	MINT	NRMT
COMPLETE SET (18)	200.00	90.00
COMMON CARD (1-18)	4.00	1.80
SEMISTARS	4.00	1.80
UNLISTED STARS	6.00	2.70
SER.2 STATED ODDS 1:36 HOBBY		

		MINT	NRMT
☐ 1	Andruw Jones	12.00	5.50
☐ 2	Ken Griffey Jr.	30.00	13.50
☐ 3	Frank Thomas	25.00	11.00
☐ 4	Alex Rodriguez	20.00	9.00
☐ 5	Cal Ripken	25.00	11.00
☐ 6	Mike Piazza	20.00	9.00
☐ 7	Derek Jeter	15.00	6.75
☐ 8	Albert Belle	8.00	3.60
☐ 9	Tony Gwynn	15.00	6.75
☐ 10	Jeff Bagwell	12.00	5.50
☐ 11	Mark McGwire	12.00	5.50
☐ 12	Kenny Lofton	8.00	3.60
☐ 13	Manny Ramirez	6.00	2.70
☐ 14	Roberto Alomar	6.00	2.70
☐ 15	Ryne Sandberg	8.00	3.60
☐ 16	Eddie Murray	6.00	2.70
☐ 17	Sammy Sosa	6.00	2.70
☐ 18	Ken Caminiti	4.00	1.80

1997 Ultra Leather Shop

Randomly inserted in Series 2 hobby packs only at a rate of one in six, this 12-card set features color player images of some of the best fielders in the game highlighted by simulated leather backgrounds.

	MINT	NRMT
COMPLETE SET (12)	20.00	9.00
COMMON CARD(1-12)	.50	.23
SER.2 STATED ODDS 1:6 HOBBY		

		MINT	NRMT
☐ 1	Ken Griffey Jr.	5.00	2.20
☐ 2	Alex Rodriguez	3.00	1.35
☐ 3	Cal Ripken	4.00	1.80
☐ 4	Derek Jeter	3.00	1.35
☐ 5	Juan Gonzalez	2.50	1.10
☐ 6	Tony Gwynn	2.50	1.10
☐ 7	Jeff Bagwell	2.00	.90
☐ 8	Roberto Alomar	1.00	.45
☐ 9	Ryne Sandberg	1.25	.55
☐ 10	Ken Caminiti	.75	.35
☐ 11	Kenny Lofton	1.00	.45
☐ 12	John Smoltz	.50	.23

1997 Ultra Home Run Kings

Randomly inserted in Series 1 hobby packs only at a rate of one in 36, this 12-card set features ultra crystal cards with transparent refractive holo-foil technology. The players pictured are all leading power hitters.

	MINT	NRMT
COMPLETE SET (12)	100.00	45.00
COMMON CARD (1-12)	2.50	1.10
UNLISTED STARS	4.00	1.80
SER.1 STATED ODDS 1:36 HOBBY		

		MINT	NRMT
☐ 1	Albert Belle	6.00	2.70
☐ 2	Barry Bonds	6.00	2.70
☐ 3	Juan Gonzalez	12.00	5.50
☐ 4	Ken Griffey Jr.	25.00	11.00
☐ 5	Todd Hundley	2.50	1.10
☐ 6	Ryan Klesko	3.00	1.35
☐ 7	Mark McGwire	10.00	4.50
☐ 8	Mike Piazza	15.00	6.75
☐ 9	Sammy Sosa	4.00	1.80
☐ 10	Frank Thomas	20.00	9.00
☐ 11	Mo Vaughn	6.00	2.70
☐ 12	Matt Williams	3.00	1.35

1997 Ultra Power Plus

Randomly inserted in Series 1 packs at a rate of one in 24 and Series 2 hobby only packs at the rate of one in eight, this 12-card set utilizes silver rainbow holo-foil and features players who not only hit with power but also excel at other parts of the game. The cards in the Series 1 insert set have an "A" prefix while the cards in the Series 2 insert set carry a "B" prefix in the checklist below.

	MINT	NRMT
COMPLETE SERIES 1 (12)	100.00	45.00
COMMON CARD (A1-A12)	2.50	1.10
SER.1 STATED ODDS 1:24		
COMPLETE SERIES 2 (12)	30.00	13.50
COMMON CARD(B1-B12)	1.50	.70
SER.2 STATED ODDS 1:8 HOBBY		

		MINT	NRMT
☐ A1	Jeff Bagwell	8.00	3.60
☐ A2	Barry Bonds	5.00	2.20
☐ A3	Juan Gonzalez	10.00	4.50
☐ A4	Ken Griffey Jr.	20.00	9.00
☐ A5	Chipper Jones	12.00	5.50
☐ A6	Mark McGwire	8.00	3.60
☐ A7	Mike Piazza	12.00	5.50
☐ A8	Cal Ripken	15.00	6.75
☐ A9	Alex Rodriguez	12.00	5.50
☐ A10	Sammy Sosa	3.00	1.35
☐ A11	Frank Thomas	15.00	6.75
☐ A12	Matt Williams	2.50	1.10
☐ B1	Ken Griffey Jr.	6.00	2.70
☐ B2	Frank Thomas	5.00	2.20
☐ B3	Alex Rodriguez	4.00	1.80
☐ B4	Cal Ripken	5.00	2.20
☐ B5	Mike Piazza	4.00	1.80
☐ B6	Chipper Jones	4.00	1.80
☐ B7	Albert Belle	1.50	.70
☐ B8	Juan Gonzalez	3.00	1.35
☐ B9	Jeff Bagwell	2.50	1.10
☐ B10	Mark McGwire	2.50	1.10
☐ B11	Mo Vaughn	1.50	.70
☐ B12	Barry Bonds	1.50	.70

1997 Ultra RBI Kings

Randomly inserted in Series 1 packs at a rate of one in 18, this 10-card set features 100 percent etched-foil cards. The cards feature players who drive in many runs. The horizontal backs contain player information and another player photo.

	MINT	NRMT
COMPLETE SET (10)	50.00	22.00
COMMON CARD (1-10)	1.50	.70
SER.1 STATED ODDS 1:18		

☐ 1 Jeff Bagwell	6.00	2.70
☐ 2 Albert Belle	4.00	1.80
☐ 3 Dante Bichette	1.50	.70
☐ 4 Barry Bonds	4.00	1.80
☐ 5 Jay Buhner	2.00	.90
☐ 6 Juan Gonzalez	8.00	3.60
☐ 7 Ken Griffey Jr.	15.00	6.75
☐ 8 Sammy Sosa	2.50	1.10
☐ 9 Frank Thomas	12.00	5.50
☐ 10 Mo Vaughn	4.00	1.80

1997 Ultra Rookie Reflections

Randomly inserted in Series 1 packs at a rate of one in four, this 10-card set uses a silver foil design to feature young players. The horizontal backs contain player information as well as another player photo.

	MINT	NRMT
COMPLETE SET (10)	4.00	1.80
COMMON CARD(1-10)	.25	.11
SER.1 STATED ODDS 1:4		

☐ 1 James Baldwin	.25	.11
☐ 2 Jermaine Dye	.25	.11
☐ 3 Darin Erstad	1.25	.55
☐ 4 Todd Hollandsworth	.25	.11
☐ 5 Derek Jeter	2.50	1.10
☐ 6 Jason Kendall	.40	.18
☐ 7 Alex Ochoa	.25	.11
☐ 8 Rey Ordonez	.25	.11
☐ 9 Edgar Renteria	.40	.18
☐ 10 Scott Rolen	2.00	.90

1997 Ultra Season Crowns

Randomly inserted in Series 1 packs at a rate of one in eight, this 12-card set features color photos of baseball's top stars with etched foil backgrounds.

	MINT	NRMT
COMPLETE SET (12)	15.00	6.75
COMMON CARD(1-12)	.50	.23
SER.1 STATED ODDS 1:8		

☐ 1 Albert Belle	1.25	.55
☐ 2 Dante Bichette	.50	.23
☐ 3 Barry Bonds	1.25	.55
☐ 4 Kenny Lofton	1.25	.55
☐ 5 Edgar Martinez	.75	.35
☐ 6 Mark McGwire	2.00	.90
☐ 7 Andy Pettitte	1.00	.45
☐ 8 Mike Piazza	3.00	1.35
☐ 9 Alex Rodriguez	3.00	1.35
☐ 10 John Smoltz	.50	.23
☐ 11 Sammy Sosa	1.00	.45
☐ 12 Frank Thomas	4.00	1.80

1997 Ultra Starring Role

Randomly inserted in Series 2 hobby packs only at a rate of one in 288, this 12-card set featues color photos of tried-and-true clutch performers on die-cut plastic cards with foil stamping.

	MINT	NRMT
COMPLETE SET (12)	600.00	275.00
COMMON CARD (1-12)	25.00	11.00
SER.2 STATED ODDS 1:288 HOBBY		

☐ 1 Andruw Jones	40.00	18.00
☐ 2 Ken Griffey Jr.	100.00	45.00
☐ 3 Frank Thomas	80.00	36.00
☐ 4 Alex Rodriguez	60.00	27.00
☐ 5 Cal Ripken	80.00	36.00
☐ 6 Mike Piazza	60.00	27.00
☐ 7 Greg Maddux	60.00	27.00
☐ 8 Chipper Jones	60.00	27.00
☐ 9 Derek Jeter	50.00	22.00
☐ 10 Juan Gonzalez	50.00	22.00
☐ 11 Albert Belle	25.00	11.00
☐ 12 Tony Gwynn	50.00	22.00

1997 Ultra Thunderclap

Randomly inserted in Series 2 hobby packs only at a rate of one in 18, this 10-card set features color images of superstars who are feared by opponents for their ability to totally dominate a game on a background displaying lightning from a thunderstorm.

	MINT	NRMT
COMPLETE SET (10)	80.00	36.00
COMMON CARD(1-10)	4.00	1.80
SER.2 STATED ODDS 1:18 HOBBY		

☐ 1 Barry Bonds	4.00	1.80
☐ 2 Mo Vaughn	4.00	1.80
☐ 3 Mark McGwire	6.00	2.70
☐ 4 Jeff Bagwell	6.00	2.70
☐ 5 Juan Gonzalez	8.00	3.60
☐ 6 Alex Rodriguez	10.00	4.50
☐ 7 Chipper Jones	10.00	4.50
☐ 8 Ken Griffey Jr.	15.00	6.75
☐ 9 Mike Piazza	10.00	4.50
☐ 10 Frank Thomas	12.00	5.50

1997 Ultra Top 30

Randomly inserted one in every Ultra Series 2 retail packs only, this 30-card set features color action player images of top stars with a "Top 30" circle in the team-colored background. The backs carry another player image with his team logo the background circle.

	MINT	NRMT
COMPLETE SET (30)	30.00	13.50
COMMON CARD(1-30)	.40	.18
SER.2 STATED ODDS 1:1 RETAIL		
COMP.G.MED.SET (30)	300.00	135.00
*GOLD MED: 5X TO 10X BASE CARD HI		
G.MED SER.2 STATED ODDS 1:18 RETAIL		

☐ 1 Andruw Jones	2.00	.90
☐ 2 Ken Griffey	4.00	1.80
☐ 3 Frank Thomas	3.00	1.35
☐ 4 Alex Rodriguez	2.50	1.10
☐ 5 Cal Ripken	3.00	1.35
☐ 6 Mike Piazza	2.50	1.10
☐ 7 Greg Maddux	2.50	1.10
☐ 8 Chipper Jones	2.50	1.10
☐ 9 Derek Jeter	2.50	1.10
☐ 10 Juan Gonzalez	2.00	.90
☐ 11 Albert Belle	1.00	.45
☐ 12 Tony Gwynn	2.00	.90
☐ 13 Jeff Bagwell	1.50	.70
☐ 14 Mark McGwire	1.50	.70
☐ 15 Andy Pettitte	.75	.35
☐ 16 Mo Vaughn	1.00	.45
☐ 17 Kenny Lofton	1.00	.45
☐ 18 Manny Ramirez	.75	.35
☐ 19 Roberto Alomar	.75	.35

□ 20 Ryne Sandberg	1.00	.45
□ 21 Hideo Nomo	2.00	.90
□ 22 Barry Bonds	1.00	.45
□ 23 Eddie Murray	.75	.35
□ 24 Ken Caminiti	.50	.23
□ 25 John Smoltz	.40	.18
□ 26 Pat Hentgen	.40	.18
□ 27 Todd Hollandsworth	.40	.18
□ 28 Matt Williams	.50	.23
□ 29 Bernie Williams	.75	.35
□ 30 Brady Anderson	.50	.23

1998 Ultra

The 1998 Ultra Series 1 set features 250 cards and was distributed in 10-card packs with a suggested retail price of $2.59. The fronts carry UV coated color action player photos printed on 20 pt. card stock. The backs display another player photo with player information and career statistics. The set contains the following subsets: Season's Crown (211-220) seeded 1:12 packs, Prospects (221-245) seeded 1:4 packs, and Checklists (246-250) seeded 1:4 packs. Also seeded one in every pack, was one of 50 Million Dollar Moment cards which pictured some of the greatest moments in baseball history and gave the collector a chance to win a million dollars.

	MINT	NRMT
COMPLETE SERIES 1 (250)	120.00	55.00
COMP.SER.1 w/o SP's (210)	15.00	6.75
COMMON CARD (1-250)	.15	.07
MINOR STARS	.30	.14
UNLISTED STARS	.60	.25
CHECKLISTS ODDS 1:4		
SC MINOR STARS	1.00	.45
SC SEMISTARS	1.50	.70
SC UNLISTED STARS	2.50	1.10
SEASON CROWN ODDS 1:12		
COMMON PROSPECT (221-245)	.75	.35
PROS.MINOR STARS	1.50	.70
PROS.SEMISTARS	2.00	.90
PROS.UNLISTED STARS	3.00	1.35
PROSPECTS ODDS 1:4		
COMP.G.MED.SER.1 (250)	120.00	55.00
COMMON G.MED (1-250)	.50	.23

*G.MED.STARS: 2X TO 4X HI COLUMN
*G.MED.YOUNG STARS: 1.5X TO 3X HI
*G.MED.SEA.CROWNS: .6X TO 1.2X HI
*G.MED.PROSPECTS: .6X TO 1.2X HI
*G.MED.CHECKLISTS: 2X TO 4X HI
ONE GOLD MEDALLION PER HOBBY PACK
SUBSETS ARE NOT SP'S IN PARALLEL SETS

□ 1 Ken Griffey Jr.	3.00	1.35
□ 2 Matt Morris	.30	.14
□ 3 Roger Clemens	1.25	.55
□ 4 Matt Williams	.40	.18
□ 5 Roberto Hernandez	.15	.07
□ 6 Rondell White	.30	.14
□ 7 Tim Salmon	.60	.25
□ 8 Brad Radke	.30	.14
□ 9 Brett Butler	.30	.14
□ 10 Carl Everett	.15	.07
□ 11 Chili Davis	.30	.14
□ 12 Chuck Finley	.15	.07
□ 13 Darryl Kile	.30	.14
□ 14 Deivi Cruz	.15	.07
□ 15 Gary Gaetti	.15	.07
□ 16 Matt Stairs	.15	.07
□ 17 Pat Meares	.15	.07
□ 18 Will Cunnane	.15	.07
□ 19 Steve Woodard	.30	.14
□ 20 Andy Ashby	.15	.07
□ 21 Bobby Higginson	.30	.14
□ 22 Brian Jordan	.30	.14
□ 23 Craig Biggio	.40	.18
□ 24 Jim Edmonds	.40	.18
□ 25 Ryan McGuire	.15	.07
□ 26 Scott Hatteberg	.15	.07
□ 27 Willie Greene	.15	.07
□ 28 Albert Belle	.75	.35
□ 29 Ellis Burks	.30	.14
□ 30 Hideo Nomo	1.50	.70
□ 31 Jeff Bagwell	1.25	.55
□ 32 Kevin Brown	.30	.14
□ 33 Nomar Garciaparra	2.00	.90
□ 34 Pedro Martinez	.60	.25
□ 35 Raul Mondesi	.40	.18
□ 36 Ricky Bottalico	.15	.07
□ 37 Shawn Estes	.15	.07
□ 38 Otis Nixon	.15	.07
□ 39 Terry Steinbach	.15	.07
□ 40 Tom Glavine	.30	.14
□ 41 Todd Dunwoody	.30	.14
□ 42 Deion Sanders	.30	.14
□ 43 Gary Sheffield	.60	.25
□ 44 Mike Lansing	.15	.07
□ 45 Mike Lieberthal	.15	.07
□ 46 Paul Sorrento	.15	.07
□ 47 Paul O'Neill	.30	.14
□ 48 Tom Goodwin	.15	.07
□ 49 Andruw Jones	1.25	.55
□ 50 Barry Bonds	.75	.35
□ 51 Bernie Williams	.60	.25
□ 52 Jeremi Gonzalez	.30	.14
□ 53 Mike Piazza	2.00	.90
□ 54 Russ Davis	.15	.07
□ 55 Vinny Castilla	.30	.14
□ 56 Rod Beck	.15	.07
□ 57 Andres Galarraga	.60	.25
□ 58 Ben McDonald	.15	.07
□ 59 Billy Wagner	.30	.14
□ 60 Charles Johnson	.30	.14
□ 61 Fred McGriff	.40	.18
□ 62 Dean Palmer	.15	.07
□ 63 Frank Thomas	2.50	1.10
□ 64 Ismael Valdes	.30	.14
□ 65 Mark Bellhorn	.30	.14
□ 66 Jeff King	.15	.07
□ 67 John Wetteland	.15	.07
□ 68 Mark Grace	.40	.18
□ 69 Mark Kotsay	.25	.11
□ 70 Scott Rolen	1.50	.70
□ 71 Todd Hundley	.30	.14
□ 72 Todd Worrell	.15	.07
□ 73 Wilson Alvarez	.15	.07
□ 74 Bobby Jones	.15	.07
□ 75 Jose Canseco	.40	.18
□ 76 Kevin Appier	.30	.14
□ 77 Neifi Perez	.30	.14
□ 78 Paul Molitor	.60	.25
□ 79 Quilvio Veras	.15	.07
□ 80 Randy Johnson	.60	.25
□ 81 Glendon Rusch	.15	.07
□ 82 Curt Schilling	.30	.14
□ 83 Alex Rodriguez	2.00	.90
□ 84 Rey Ordonez	.30	.14
□ 85 Jeff Juden	.15	.07
□ 86 Mike Cameron	.30	.14
□ 87 Ryan Klesko	.40	.18
□ 88 Trevor Hoffman	.15	.07
□ 89 Chuck Knoblauch	.60	.25
□ 90 Larry Walker	.60	.25
□ 91 Mark McLemore	.15	.07
□ 92 B.J. Surhoff	.15	.07
□ 93 Darren Daulton	.30	.14
□ 94 Ray Durham	.15	.07
□ 95 Sammy Sosa	.60	.25
□ 96 Eric Young	.15	.07
□ 97 Gerald Williams	.15	.07
□ 98 Javy Lopez	.30	.14
□ 99 John Smiley	.15	.07
□ 100 Juan Gonzalez	1.50	.70
□ 101 Shawn Green	.15	.07
□ 102 Charles Nagy	.30	.14
□ 103 David Justice	.60	.25
□ 104 Joey Hamilton	.30	.14
□ 105 Pat Hentgen	.30	.14
□ 106 Raul Casanova	.15	.07
□ 107 Tony Phillips	.15	.07
□ 108 Tony Gwynn	1.50	.70
□ 109 Will Clark	.40	.18
□ 110 Jason Giambi	.30	.14
□ 111 Jay Bell	.30	.14
□ 112 Johnny Damon	.15	.07
□ 113 Alan Benes	.30	.14
□ 114 Jeff Suppan	.15	.07
□ 115 Kevin Polcovich	.15	.07
□ 116 Shigetoshi Hasegawa	.30	.14
□ 117 Steve Finley	.30	.14
□ 118 Tony Clark	.60	.25
□ 119 David Cone	.30	.14
□ 120 Jose Guillen	.60	.25
□ 121 Kevin Millwood	.60	.25
□ 122 Greg Maddux	2.00	.90
□ 123 Dave Nilsson	.15	.07
□ 124 Hideki Irabu	.30	.14
□ 125 Jason Kendall	.30	.14
□ 126 Jim Thome	.60	.25
□ 127 Delino DeShields	.15	.07
□ 128 Edgar Renteria	.30	.14
□ 129 Edgardo Alfonzo	.30	.14
□ 130 J.T. Snow	.30	.14
□ 131 Jeff Abbott	.15	.07
□ 132 Jeffrey Hammonds	.15	.07
□ 133 Todd Greene	.30	.14
□ 134 Vladimir Guerrero	1.00	.45
□ 135 Jay Buhner	.40	.18
□ 136 Jeff Cirillo	.30	.14
□ 137 Jeromy Burnitz	.30	.14
□ 138 Mickey Morandini	.15	.07
□ 139 Tino Martinez	.60	.25
□ 140 Jeff Shaw	.15	.07
□ 141 Rafael Palmeiro	.40	.18
□ 142 Bobby Bonilla	.30	.14
□ 143 Cal Ripken	2.50	1.10
□ 144 Chad Fox	.15	.07
□ 145 Dante Bichette	.30	.14
□ 146 Dennis Eckersley	.30	.14
□ 147 Mariano Rivera	.30	.14
□ 148 Mo Vaughn	.75	.35
□ 149 Reggie Sanders	.15	.07
□ 150 Derek Jeter	1.50	.70
□ 151 Rusty Greer	.15	.07
□ 152 Brady Anderson	.40	.18
□ 153 Brett Tomko	.15	.07
□ 154 Jaime Navarro	.15	.07
□ 155 Kevin Orie	.15	.07
□ 156 Roberto Alomar	.60	.25
□ 157 Edgar Martinez	.40	.18
□ 158 John Olerud	.30	.14
□ 159 John Smoltz	.30	.14
□ 160 Ryne Sandberg	.75	.35
□ 161 Billy Taylor	.15	.07
□ 162 Chris Holt	.15	.07
□ 163 Damion Easley	.15	.07
□ 164 Darin Erstad	.75	.35
□ 165 Joe Carter	.30	.14
□ 166 Kelvim Escobar	.15	.07
□ 167 Ken Caminiti	.40	.18
□ 168 Pokey Reese	.15	.07
□ 169 Ray Lankford	.30	.14
□ 170 Livan Hernandez	.40	.18
□ 171 Steve Kline	.15	.07
□ 172 Tom Gordon	.15	.07
□ 173 Travis Fryman	.30	.14
□ 174 Al Martin	.15	.07
□ 175 Andy Pettitte	.60	.25
□ 176 Jeff Kent	.15	.07

		MINT	NRMT
☐ 177	Jimmy Key	.30	.14
☐ 178	Mark Grudzielanek	.15	.07
☐ 179	Tony Saunders	.15	.07
☐ 180	Barry Larkin	.40	.18
☐ 181	Bubba Trammell	.30	.14
☐ 182	Carlos Delgado	.30	.14
☐ 183	Carlos Baerga	.15	.07
☐ 184	Derek Bell	.15	.07
☐ 185	Henry Rodriguez	.15	.07
☐ 186	Jason Dickson	.30	.14
☐ 187	Ron Gant	.30	.14
☐ 188	Tony Womack	.30	.14
☐ 189	Justin Thompson	.30	.14
☐ 190	Fernando Tatis	.60	.25
☐ 191	Mark Wohlers	.15	.07
☐ 192	Takashi Kashiwada	.30	.14
☐ 193	Garret Anderson	.30	.14
☐ 194	Jose Cruz Jr.	2.50	1.10
☐ 195	Ricardo Rincon	.15	.07
☐ 196	Tim Naehring	.15	.07
☐ 197	Moises Alou	.30	.14
☐ 198	Eric Karros	.30	.14
☐ 199	John Jaha	.15	.07
☐ 200	Marty Cordova	.30	.14
☐ 201	Ken Hill	.15	.07
☐ 202	Chipper Jones	2.00	.90
☐ 203	Kenny Lofton	.75	.35
☐ 204	Mike Mussina	.60	.25
☐ 205	Manny Ramirez	.60	.25
☐ 206	Todd Hollandsworth	.15	.07
☐ 207	Cecil Fielder	.30	.14
☐ 208	Mark McGwire	1.50	.70
☐ 209	Jim Leyritz	.15	.07
☐ 210	Ivan Rodriguez	.75	.35
☐ 211	Jeff Bagwell SC	2.20	1.00
☐ 212	Barry Bonds SC	3.00	1.35
☐ 213	Roger Clemens SC	.75	.35
☐ 214	Nomar Garciaparra SC	8.00	3.60
☐ 215	Ken Griffey Jr. SC	12.00	5.50
☐ 216	Tony Gwynn SC	6.00	2.70
☐ 217	Randy Johnson SC	2.50	1.10
☐ 218	Mark McGwire SC	6.00	2.70
☐ 219	Scott Rolen SC	6.00	2.70
☐ 220	Frank Thomas SC	10.00	4.50
☐ 221	Matt Perisho PROS	.75	.35
☐ 222	Wes Helms PROS	1.50	.70
☐ 223	Dave Dellucci PROS	.75	.35
☐ 224	Todd Helton PROS	4.00	1.80
☐ 225	Brian Rose PROS	2.00	.90
☐ 226	Aaron Boone PROS	.75	.35
☐ 227	Keith Foulke PROS	.75	.35
☐ 228	Homer Bush PROS	.75	.35
☐ 229	Shannon Stewart PROS	1.50	.70
☐ 230	Richard Hidalgo PROS	1.50	.70
☐ 231	Russ Johnson PROS	.75	.35
☐ 232	Henry Blanco PROS	.75	.35
☐ 233	Paul Konerko PROS	5.00	2.20
☐ 234	Antone Williamson PROS	.75	.35
☐ 235	Shane Bowers PROS	.75	.35
☐ 236	Jose Vidro PROS	1.50	.70
☐ 237	Derek Wallace PROS	.75	.35
☐ 238	Ricky Ledee PROS	2.50	1.10
☐ 239	Ben Grieve PROS	6.00	2.70
☐ 240	Lou Collier PROS	.75	.35
☐ 241	Derrek Lee PROS	2.00	.90
☐ 242	Ruben Rivera PROS	1.50	.70
☐ 243	Jorge Velandia PROS	.75	.35
☐ 244	Andrew Vessel PROS	.75	.35
☐ 245	Chris Carpenter PROS	.75	.35
☐ 246	Ken Griffey Jr. CL	1.50	.70
☐ 247	Alex Rodriguez CL	1.25	.55
☐ 248	Diamond Ink CL	.15	.07
☐ 249	Frank Thomas CL	1.25	.55
☐ 250	Cal Ripken CL	1.25	.55

1998 Ultra Platinum Medallion

Randomly inserted in hobby only packs at the rate of one in 100, this 250-card set is parallel to the base set. Only 100 of this set were produced and are serially numbered. Ten exchange cards good for a complete Platinum set were inserted into packs. Since there are so few of these cards issued and almost no market information -- no price is provided.

		MINT	NRMT
COMMON CARD (1-250)		20.00	9.00
MINOR STARS		30.00	13.50
SEMISTARS		50.00	22.00
UNLISTED STARS		80.00	36.00
STATED PRINT RUN 100 SERIAL #'d SETS			

		MINT	NRMT
☐ 1	Ken Griffey Jr.	400.00	180.00
☐ 3	Roger Clemens	150.00	70.00
☐ 28	Albert Belle	100.00	45.00
☐ 30	Hideo Nomo	250.00	110.00
☐ 31	Jeff Bagwell	150.00	70.00
☐ 33	Nomar Garciaparra	200.00	90.00
☐ 49	Andruw Jones	120.00	55.00
☐ 50	Barry Bonds	100.00	45.00
☐ 53	Mike Piazza	250.00	110.00
☐ 63	Frank Thomas	300.00	135.00
☐ 70	Scott Rolen	150.00	70.00
☐ 83	Alex Rodriguez	250.00	110.00
☐ 100	Juan Gonzalez	200.00	90.00
☐ 108	Tony Gwynn	200.00	90.00
☐ 122	Greg Maddux	250.00	110.00
☐ 134	Vladimir Guerrero	200.00	90.00
☐ 143	Cal Ripken	300.00	135.00
☐ 148	Mo Vaughn	200.00	90.00
☐ 150	Derek Jeter	200.00	90.00
☐ 160	Ryne Sandberg	100.00	45.00
☐ 194	Jose Cruz Jr.	200.00	90.00
☐ 202	Chipper Jones	200.00	90.00
☐ 203	Kenny Lofton	100.00	45.00
☐ 208	Mark McGwire	200.00	90.00
☐ 211	Jeff Bagwell SC	100.00	45.00
☐ 213	Roger Clemens SC	100.00	45.00
☐ 214	Nomar Garciaparra SC	120.00	55.00
☐ 215	Ken Griffey Jr. SC	250.00	110.00
☐ 216	Tony Gwynn SC	120.00	55.00
☐ 218	Mark McGwire SC	120.00	55.00
☐ 219	Scott Rolen SC	100.00	45.00
☐ 233	Paul Konerko PROS	100.00	45.00
☐ 239	Ben Grieve PROS	120.00	55.00
☐ 246	Ken Griffey Jr. CL	200.00	90.00
☐ 247	Alex Rodriguez CL	120.00	55.00
☐ 249	Frank Thomas CL	150.00	70.00
☐ 250	Cal Ripken CL	150.00	70.00

1998 Ultra Artistic Talents

Randomly inserted in Series 1 packs at the rate of one in eight, this 18-card set features color pictures of top players on art enhanced cards.

1998 Ultra Back to the Future

Randomly inserted in Series 1 packs at the rate of one in six, this 15-card set features color photos of top Rookies. The backs carry player information.

		MINT	NRMT
COMPLETE SET (18)		80.00	36.00
COMMON CARD (1-18)		2.50	1.10
SER.1 STATED ODDS 1:8.			

		MINT	NRMT
☐ 1	Ken Griffey Jr.	10.00	4.50
☐ 2	Andruw Jones	4.00	1.80
☐ 3	Alex Rodriguez	6.00	2.70
☐ 4	Frank Thomas	8.00	3.60
☐ 5	Cal Ripken	8.00	3.60
☐ 6	Derek Jeter	5.00	2.20
☐ 7	Chipper Jones	6.00	2.70
☐ 8	Greg Maddux	6.00	2.70
☐ 9	Mike Piazza	6.00	2.70
☐ 10	Albert Belle	2.50	1.10
☐ 11	Darin Erstad	2.50	1.10
☐ 12	Juan Gonzalez	5.00	2.20
☐ 13	Jeff Bagwell	4.00	1.80
☐ 14	Tony Gwynn	5.00	2.20
☐ 15	Mark McGwire	5.00	2.20
☐ 16	Scott Rolen	5.00	2.20
☐ 17	Barry Bonds	2.50	1.10
☐ 18	Kenny Lofton	2.50	1.10

		MINT	NRMT
COMPLETE SET (15)		20.00	9.00
COMMON CARD (1-15)		.50	.23
UNLISTED STARS		1.25	.55
SER.1 STATED ODDS 1:6.			

		MINT	NRMT
☐ 1	Andruw Jones	2.50	1.10
☐ 2	Alex Rodriguez	4.00	1.80
☐ 3	Derek Jeter	3.00	1.35
☐ 4	Darin Erstad	1.50	.70
☐ 5	Mike Cameron	.50	.23
☐ 6	Scott Rolen	3.00	1.35
☐ 7	Nomar Garciaparra	4.00	1.80
☐ 8	Hideki Irabu	.50	.23
☐ 9	Jose Cruz Jr.	5.00	2.20
☐ 10	Vladimir Guerrero	2.00	.90
☐ 11	Mark Kotsay	1.25	.55
☐ 12	Tony Womack	.50	.23
☐ 13	Jason Dickson	.50	.23
☐ 14	Jose Guillen	1.25	.55
☐ 15	Tony Clark	1.25	.55

1998 Ultra Big Shots

Randomly inserted in Series 1 packs at the rate of one in four, this 15-card set features color photos of players who hit the longest home runs in the 1997 season.

MARK McGWIRE

	MINT	NRMT
COMPLETE SET (15)	12.00	5.50
COMMON (1-15)	.50	.23
UNLISTED STARS	.75	.35
SER.1 STATED ODDS 1:4		

		MINT	NRMT
☐ 1	Ken Griffey Jr.	4.00	1.80
☐ 2	Frank Thomas	3.00	1.35
☐ 3	Chipper Jones	2.50	1.10
☐ 4	Albert Belle	1.00	.45
☐ 5	Juan Gonzalez	2.00	.90
☐ 6	Jeff Bagwell	1.50	.70
☐ 7	Mark McGwire	2.00	.90
☐ 8	Barry Bonds	1.00	.45
☐ 9	Manny Ramirez	.75	.35
☐ 10	Mo Vaughn	1.00	.45
☐ 11	Matt Williams	.50	.23
☐ 12	Jim Thome	.75	.35
☐ 13	Tino Martinez	.75	.35
☐ 14	Mike Piazza	2.50	1.10
☐ 15	Tony Clark	.75	.35

1998 Ultra Diamond Producers

Randomly inserted in Series 1 packs at the rate of one in 288, this 15-card set features color photos of Major League Baseball's top players.

	MINT	NRMT
COMPLETE SET (15)	1000.00	450.00
COMMON CARD (1-15)	30.00	13.50
SER.1 STATED ODDS 1:288		
CONDITION SENSITIVE SET		

		MINT	NRMT
☐ 1	Ken Griffey Jr.	120.00	55.00
☐ 2	Andruw Jones	40.00	18.00
☐ 3	Alex Rodriguez	80.00	36.00
☐ 4	Frank Thomas	100.00	45.00
☐ 5	Cal Ripken	100.00	45.00
☐ 6	Derek Jeter	60.00	27.00
☐ 7	Chipper Jones	80.00	36.00
☐ 8	Greg Maddux	80.00	36.00

		MINT	NRMT
☐ 9	Mike Piazza	80.00	36.00
☐ 10	Juan Gonzalez	60.00	27.00
☐ 11	Jeff Bagwell	50.00	22.00
☐ 12	Tony Gwynn	60.00	27.00
☐ 13	Mark McGwire	60.00	27.00
☐ 14	Barry Bonds	30.00	13.50
☐ 15	Jose Cruz Jr.	80.00	36.00

1998 Ultra Double Trouble

Randomly inserted in Series 1 packs at the rate of one in four, this 20-card set features color photos of two star players per card.

	MINT	NRMT
COMPLETE SET (20)	12.00	5.50
COMMON CARD (1-20)	.50	.23
SER.1 STATED ODDS 1:4		

		MINT	NRMT
☐ 1	Ken Griffey Jr. Alex Rodriguez	5.00	2.20
☐ 2	Vladimir Guerrero Pedro Martinez	.75	.35
☐ 3	Andruw Jones Kenny Lofton	1.50	.70
☐ 4	Chipper Jones Greg Maddux	3.00	1.35
☐ 5	Derek Jeter Tino Martinez	1.50	.70
☐ 6	Frank Thomas Albert Belle	3.00	1.35
☐ 7	Cal Ripken Roberto Alomar	3.00	1.35
☐ 8	Mike Piazza Hideo Nomo	3.00	1.35
☐ 9	Darin Erstad Jason Dickson	.75	.35
☐ 10	Juan Gonzalez Ivan Rodriguez	2.00	.90
☐ 11	Jeff Bagwell Darryl Kile UER front Kyle	1.25	.55
☐ 12	Tony Gwynn Steve Finley	1.50	.70
☐ 13	Mark McGwire Ray Lankford	1.25	.55
☐ 14	Barry Bonds Jeff Kent	.75	.35
☐ 15	Andy Pettitte Bernie Williams	.50	.23
☐ 16	Mo Vaughn Nomar Garciaparra	2.00	.90
☐ 17	Matt Williams Jim Thome	.50	.23
☐ 18	Hideki Irabu Mariano Rivera	.50	.23
☐ 19	Roger Clemens Jose Cruz Jr.	2.50	1.10
☐ 20	Manny Ramirez David Justice	.50	.23

1998 Ultra Fall Classics

Greg Maddux

Randomly inserted in Series 1 packs at the rate of one in 18, this 15-card set features color photos of the top potential post-season heroes. The backs carry player information.

	MINT	NRMT
COMPLETE SET (15)	120.00	55.00
COMMON CARD (1-15)	5.00	2.20
SER.1 STATED ODDS 1:18		

		MINT	NRMT
☐ 1	Ken Griffey Jr.	20.00	9.00
☐ 2	Andruw Jones	6.00	2.70
☐ 3	Alex Rodriguez	12.00	5.50
☐ 4	Frank Thomas	15.00	6.75
☐ 5	Cal Ripken	15.00	6.75
☐ 6	Derek Jeter	10.00	4.50
☐ 7	Chipper Jones	12.00	5.50
☐ 8	Greg Maddux	12.00	5.50
☐ 9	Mike Piazza	12.00	5.50
☐ 10	Albert Belle	5.00	2.20
☐ 11	Juan Gonzalez	10.00	4.50
☐ 12	Jeff Bagwell	8.00	3.60
☐ 13	Tony Gwynn	10.00	4.50
☐ 14	Mark McGwire	10.00	4.50
☐ 15	Barry Bonds	5.00	2.20

1998 Ultra Kid Gloves

Randomly inserted in Series 1 packs at the rate of one in eight, this 12-card set features color photos of top young defensive players. The backs carry player information.

	MINT	NRMT
COMPLETE SET (12)	20.00	9.00
COMMON CARD (1-12)	.50	.23
MINOR STARS	.50	
SER.1 STATED ODDS 1:8		

		MINT	NRMT
☐ 1	Andruw Jones	2.50	1.10
☐ 2	Alex Rodriguez	4.00	1.80
☐ 3	Derek Jeter	3.00	1.35
☐ 4	Chipper Jones	4.00	1.80
☐ 5	Darin Erstad	1.50	.70
☐ 6	Todd Walker	.50	.23
☐ 7	Scott Rolen	3.00	1.35
☐ 8	Nomar Garciaparra	4.00	1.80
☐ 9	Jose Cruz Jr.	5.00	2.20
☐ 10	Charles Johnson	.50	.23
☐ 11	Rey Ordonez	.50	.23
☐ 12	Vladimir Guerrero	2.00	.90

1998 Ultra Power Plus

Randomly inserted in Series 1 packs at the rate of one in 36, this 10-card set features color action photos of top young and veteran players. The backs carry player information.

		MINT	NRMT
COMPLETE SET (10)		120.00	55.00
COMMON CARD (1-10)		8.00	3.60
SER.1 STATED ODDS 1:36			

		MINT	NRMT
☐ 1	Ken Griffey Jr.	30.00	13.50
☐ 2	Andruw Jones	10.00	4.50
☐ 3	Alex Rodriguez	20.00	9.00
☐ 4	Frank Thomas	25.00	11.00
☐ 5	Mike Piazza	20.00	9.00
☐ 6	Albert Belle	8.00	3.60
☐ 7	Juan Gonzalez	15.00	6.75
☐ 8	Jeff Bagwell	12.00	5.50
☐ 9	Barry Bonds	8.00	3.60
☐ 10	Jose Cruz Jr.	20.00	9.00

1998 Ultra Prime Leather

Randomly inserted in Series 1 packs at the rate of one in 144, this 18-card set features color photos of young and veteran players considered to be good glove men. The backs carry player information.

		MINT	NRMT
COMPLETE SET (18)		600.00	275.00
COMMON CARD (1-18)		15.00	6.75
SER.1 STATED ODDS 1:144			

		MINT	NRMT
☐ 1	Ken Griffey Jr.	80.00	36.00
☐ 2	Andruw Jones	25.00	11.00
☐ 3	Alex Rodriguez	50.00	22.00
☐ 4	Frank Thomas	60.00	27.00
☐ 5	Cal Ripken	60.00	27.00
☐ 6	Derek Jeter	40.00	18.00
☐ 7	Chipper Jones	50.00	22.00
☐ 8	Greg Maddux	50.00	22.00
☐ 9	Mike Piazza	50.00	22.00
☐ 10	Albert Belle	20.00	9.00
☐ 11	Darin Erstad	15.00	6.75
☐ 12	Juan Gonzalez	40.00	18.00
☐ 13	Jeff Bagwell	30.00	13.50
☐ 14	Tony Gwynn	40.00	18.00
☐ 15	Roberto Alomar	15.00	6.75
☐ 16	Barry Bonds	20.00	9.00
☐ 17	Kenny Lofton	20.00	9.00
☐ 18	Jose Cruz Jr.	50.00	22.00

1989 Upper Deck

This attractive 800-card standard-size set was introduced in 1989 as the premier issue by the then-fledgling Upper Deck company. Unlike other 1989 releases, this set was issued in two separate series - a low series numbered 1-700 and a high series numbered 701-800. Cards were primarily issued in fin-wrapped low and high series foil packs, complete 800-card factory sets and 100-card high series factory sets. High series packs contained a mixture of both low and high series cards. Collectors should also note that many dealers consider that Upper Deck's "planned" production of 1,000,000 of each player was increased (perhaps even doubled) later in the year due to the explosion in popularity of the product. The cards feature slick paper stock, full color on both the front and the back and carry a hologram on the reverse to protect against counterfeiting. Subsets include Rookie Stars (1-26) and Collector's Choice art cards (668-693). The more significant variations involving changed photos or changed type are listed below. According to the company, the Murphy and Sheridan cards were corrected very early, after only two percent of the cards had been produced. Similarly, the Sheffield was corrected after 15 percent had been printed; Varsho, Gallego, and Schroeder were corrected after 20 percent; and Holton, Manrique, and Winningham were corrected 30 percent of the way through. Rookie Cards in the set include Jim Abbott, Sandy Alomar Jr., Dante Bichette, Craig Biggio, Steve Finley, Ken Griffey Jr., Erik Hanson, Charlie Hayes, Randy Johnson, Ramon Martinez, Gary Sheffield, John Smoltz and Todd Zeile. Cards with missing or duplicate holograms appear to be relatively common and are generally considered to be flawed cards that sell for substantial discounts.

	MINT	NRMT
COMPLETE SET (800)	120.00	55.00
COMP.FACT.SET (800)	120.00	55.00
COMPLETE LO SET (700)	110.00	50.00
COMPLETE HI SET (100)	10.00	4.50
COMMON CARD (1-800)	.20	.09
MINOR STARS	.40	.18
UNLISTED STARS	.75	.35

		MINT	NRMT
☐ 1	Ken Griffey Jr.	100.00	45.00
☐ 2	Luis Medina	.20	.09
☐ 3	Tony Chance	.20	.09
☐ 4	Dave Otto	.20	.09
☐ 5	Sandy Alomar Jr. UER	2.50	1.10
	(Born 6/16/66, should be 6/18/66)		
☐ 6	Rolando Roomes	.20	.09
☐ 7	Dave West	.20	.09
☐ 8	Cris Carpenter	.20	.09
☐ 9	Gregg Jefferies	.60	.25
☐ 10	Doug Dascenzo	.20	.09
☐ 11	Ron Jones	.20	.09
☐ 12	Luis DeLosSantos	.20	.09
☐ 13	Gary Sheffield COR	4.00	1.80
☐ 13A	Gary Sheffield ERR	.20	.09
	(SS upside down on card front)		
☐ 14	Mike Harkey	.20	.09
☐ 15	Lance Blankenship	.20	.09
☐ 16	William Brennan	.20	.09
☐ 17	John Smoltz	2.50	1.10
☐ 18	Ramon Martinez	1.00	.45
☐ 19	Mark Lemke	.60	.25
☐ 20	Juan Bell	.20	.09
☐ 21	Rey Palacios	.20	.09
☐ 22	Felix Jose	.20	.09
☐ 23	Van Snider	.20	.09
☐ 24	Dante Bichette	2.00	.90
☐ 25	Randy Johnson	6.00	2.70
☐ 26	Carlos Quintana	.20	.09
☐ 27	Star Rookie CL	.20	.09
☐ 28	Mike Schooler	.20	.09
☐ 29	Randy St.Claire	.20	.09
☐ 30	Jerald Clark	.20	.09
☐ 31	Kevin Gross	.20	.09
☐ 32	Dan Firova	.20	.09
☐ 33	Jeff Calhoun	.20	.09
☐ 34	Tommy Hinzo	.20	.09
☐ 35	Ricky Jordan	.40	.18
☐ 36	Larry Parrish	.20	.09
☐ 37	Bret Saberhagen UER	.20	.09
	(Hit total 931, should be 1031)		
☐ 38	Mike Smithson	.20	.09
☐ 39	Dave Dravecky	.40	.18
☐ 40	Ed Romero	.20	.09
☐ 41	Jeff Musselman	.20	.09
☐ 42	Ed Hearn	.20	.09
☐ 43	Rance Mulliniks	.20	.09
☐ 44	Jim Eisenreich	.20	.09
☐ 45	Sil Campusano	.20	.09
☐ 46	Mike Krukow	.20	.09
☐ 47	Paul Gibson	.20	.09
☐ 48	Mike LaCoss	.20	.09

□	#	Player		
□	49	Larry Herndon	.20	.09
□	50	Scott Garrelts	.20	.09
□	51	Dwayne Henry	.20	.09
□	52	Jim Acker	.20	.09
□	53	Steve Sax	.20	.09
□	54	Pete O'Brien	.20	.09
□	55	Paul Runge	.20	.09
□	56	Rick Rhoden	.20	.09
□	57	John Dopson	.20	.09
□	58	Casey Candaele UER	.20	
		(No stats for Astros for '88 season)		
□	59	Dave Righetti	.20	.09
□	60	Joe Hesketh	.20	.09
□	61	Frank DiPino	.20	.09
□	62	Tim Laudner	.20	.09
□	63	Jamie Moyer	.20	.09
□	64	Fred Toliver	.20	.09
□	65	Mitch Webster	.20	.09
□	66	John Tudor	.20	.09
□	67	John Cangelosi	.20	.09
□	68	Mike Devereaux	.20	.09
□	69	Brian Fisher	.20	.09
□	70	Mike Marshall	.20	.09
□	71	Zane Smith	.20	.09
□	72A	Brian Holton ERR	1.00	.45
		(Photo actually Shawn Hillegas)		
□	72B	Brian Holton COR	.40	.18
□	73	Jose Guzman	.20	.09
□	74	Rick Mahler	.20	.09
□	75	John Shelby	.20	.09
□	76	Jim Deshaies	.20	.09
□	77	Bobby Meacham	.20	.09
□	78	Bryn Smith	.20	.09
□	79	Joaquin Andujar	.20	.09
□	80	Richard Dotson	.20	.09
□	81	Charlie Lea	.20	.09
□	82	Calvin Schiraldi	.20	.09
□	83	Les Straker	.20	.09
□	84	Les Lancaster	.20	.09
□	85	Allan Anderson	.20	.09
□	86	Junior Ortiz	.20	.09
□	87	Jesse Orosco	.20	.09
□	88	Felix Fermin	.20	.09
□	89	Dave Anderson	.20	.09
□	90	Rafael Belliard UER	.20	.09
		(Born '61, not '51)		
□	91	Franklin Stubbs	.20	.09
□	92	Cecil Espy	.20	.09
□	93	Albert Hall	.20	.09
□	94	Tim Leary	.20	.09
□	95	Mitch Williams	.20	.09
□	96	Tracy Jones	.20	.09
□	97	Danny Darwin	.20	.09
□	98	Gary Ward	.20	.09
□	99	Neal Heaton	.20	.09
□	100	Jim Pankovits	.20	.09
□	101	Bill Doran	.20	.09
□	102	Tim Wallach	.20	.09
□	103	Joe Magrane	.20	.09
□	104	Ozzie Virgil	.20	.09
□	105	Alvin Davis	.20	.09
□	106	Tom Brookens	.20	.09
□	107	Shawon Dunston	.20	.09
□	108	Tracy Woodson	.20	.09
□	109	Nelson Liriano	.20	.09
□	110	Devon White UER	.20	.09
		(Doubles total 46, should be 56)		
□	111	Steve Balboni	.20	.09
□	112	Buddy Bell	.40	.18
□	113	German Jimenez	.20	.09
□	114	Ken Dayley	.20	.09
□	115	Andres Galarraga	.75	.35
□	116	Mike Scioscia	.20	.09
□	117	Gary Pettis	.20	.09
□	118	Ernie Whitt	.20	.09
□	119	Bob Boone	.40	.18
□	120	Ryne Sandberg	1.00	.45
□	121	Bruce Benedict	.20	.09
□	122	Hubie Brooks	.20	.09
□	123	Mike Moore	.20	.09
□	124	Wallace Johnson	.20	.09
□	125	Bob Horner	.20	.09
□	126	Chili Davis	.40	.18
□	127	Manny Trillo	.20	.09
□	128	Chet Lemon	.20	.09
□	129	John Cerutti	.20	.09
□	130	Orel Hershiser	.40	.18
□	131	Terry Pendleton	.20	.09
□	132	Jeff Blauser	.40	.18
□	133	Mike Fitzgerald	.20	.09
□	134	Henry Cotto	.20	.09
□	135	Gerald Young	.20	.09
□	136	Luis Salazar	.20	.09
□	137	Alejandro Pena	.20	.09
□	138	Jack Howell	.20	.09
□	139	Tony Fernandez	.20	.09
□	140	Mark Grace	.75	.35
□	141	Ken Caminiti	1.00	.45
□	142	Mike Jackson	.20	.09
□	143	Larry McWilliams	.20	.09
□	144	Andres Thomas	.20	.09
□	145	Nolan Ryan 3X	3.00	1.35
□	146	Mike Davis	.20	.09
□	147	DeWayne Buice	.20	.09
□	148	Jody Davis	.20	.09
□	149	Jesse Barfield	.20	.09
□	150	Matt Nokes	.20	.09
□	151	Jerry Reuss	.20	.09
□	152	Rick Cerone	.20	.09
□	153	Storm Davis	.20	.09
□	154	Marvell Wynne	.20	.09
□	155	Will Clark	.75	.35
□	156	Luis Aguayo	.20	.09
□	157	Willie Upshaw	.20	.09
□	158	Randy Bush	.20	.09
□	159	Ron Darling	.20	.09
□	160	Kal Daniels	.20	.09
□	161	Spike Owen	.20	.09
□	162	Luis Polonia	.20	.09
□	163	Kevin Mitchell UER	.40	.18
		('88/total HR's 18/52, should be 19/53)		
□	164	Dave Gallagher	.20	.09
□	165	Benito Santiago	.20	.09
□	166	Greg Gagne	.20	.09
□	167	Ken Phelps	.20	.09
□	168	Sid Fernandez	.20	.09
□	169	Bo Diaz	.20	.09
□	170	Cory Snyder	.20	.09
□	171	Eric Show	.20	.09
□	172	Robby Thompson	.20	.09
□	173	Marty Barrett	.20	.09
□	174	Dave Henderson	.20	.09
□	175	Ozzie Guillen	.20	.09
□	176	Barry Lyons	.20	.09
□	177	Kelvin Torve	.20	.09
□	178	Don Slaught	.20	.09
□	179	Steve Lombardozzi	.20	.09
□	180	Chris Sabo	.20	.09
□	181	Jose Uribe	.20	.09
□	182	Shane Mack	.20	.09
□	183	Ron Karkovice	.20	.09
□	184	Todd Benzinger	.20	.09
□	185	Dave Stewart	.40	.18
□	186	Julio Franco	.20	.09
□	187	Ron Robinson	.20	.09
□	188	Wally Backman	.20	.09
□	189	Randy Velarde	.20	.09
□	190	Joe Carter	.75	.35
□	191	Bob Welch	.20	.09
□	192	Kelly Paris	.20	.09
□	193	Chris Brown	.20	.09
□	194	Rick Reuschel	.20	.09
□	195	Roger Clemens	1.50	.70
□	196	Dave Concepcion	.40	.18
□	197	Al Newman	.20	.09
□	198	Brook Jacoby	.20	.09
□	199	Mookie Wilson	.40	.18
□	200	Don Mattingly	1.25	.55
□	201	Dick Schofield	.20	.09
□	202	Mark Gubicza	.20	.09
□	203	Gary Gaetti	.20	.09
□	204	Dan Pasqua	.20	.09
□	205	Andre Dawson	.75	.35
□	206	Chris Speier	.20	.09
□	207	Kent Tekulve	.20	.09
□	208	Rod Scurry	.20	.09
□	209	Scott Bailes	.20	.09
□	210	Rickey Henderson UER	.75	.35
		(Throws Right)		
□	211	Harold Baines	.40	.18
□	212	Tony Armas	.20	.09
□	213	Kent Hrbek	.40	.18
□	214	Darrin Jackson	.20	.09
□	215	George Brett	1.50	.70
□	216	Rafael Santana	.20	.09
□	217	Andy Allanson	.20	.09
□	218	Brett Butler	.40	.18
□	219	Steve Jeltz	.20	.09
□	220	Jay Buhner	.75	.35
□	221	Bo Jackson	.75	.35
□	222	Angel Salazar	.20	.09
□	223	Kirk McCaskill	.20	.09
□	224	Steve Lyons	.20	.09
□	225	Bert Blyleven	.40	.18
□	226	Scott Bradley	.20	.09
□	227	Bob Melvin	.20	.09
□	228	Ron Kittle	.20	.09
□	229	Phil Bradley	.20	.09
□	230	Tommy John	.40	.18
□	231	Greg Walker	.20	.09
□	232	Juan Berenguer	.20	.09
□	233	Pat Tabler	.20	.09
□	234	Terry Clark	.20	.09
□	235	Rafael Palmeiro	.75	.35
□	236	Paul Zuvella	.20	.09
□	237	Willie Randolph	.40	.18
□	238	Bruce Fields	.20	.09
□	239	Mike Aldrete	.20	.09
□	240	Lance Parrish	.20	.09
□	241	Greg Maddux	4.00	1.80
□	242	John Moses	.20	.09
□	243	Melido Perez	.20	.09
□	244	Willie Wilson	.20	.09
□	245	Mark McLemore	.20	.09
□	246	Von Hayes	.20	.09
□	247	Matt Williams	.75	.35
□	248	John Candelaria UER	.20	.09
		(Listed as Yankee for part of '87, should be Mets)		
□	249	Harold Reynolds	.20	.09
□	250	Greg Swindell	.20	.09
□	251	Juan Agosto	.20	.09
□	252	Mike Felder	.20	.09
□	253	Vince Coleman	.20	.09
□	254	Larry Sheets	.20	.09
□	255	George Bell	.20	.09
□	256	Terry Steinbach	.40	.18
□	257	Jack Armstrong	.20	.09
□	258	Dickie Thon	.20	.09
□	259	Ray Knight	.20	.09
□	260	Darryl Strawberry	.40	.18
□	261	Doug Sisk	.20	.09
□	262	Alex Trevino	.20	.09
□	263	Jeffrey Leonard	.20	.09
□	264	Tom Henke	.20	.09
□	265	Ozzie Smith	1.00	.45
□	266	Dave Bergman	.20	.09
□	267	Tony Phillips	.20	.09
□	268	Mark Davis	.20	.09
□	269	Kevin Elster	.20	.09
□	270	Barry Larkin	.75	.35
□	271	Manny Lee	.20	.09
□	272	Tom Brunansky	.20	.09
□	273	Craig Biggio	2.50	1.10
□	274	Jim Gantner	.20	.09
□	275	Eddie Murray	.75	.35
□	276	Jeff Reed	.20	.09
□	277	Tim Teufel	.20	.09
□	278	Rick Honeycutt	.20	.09
□	279	Guillermo Hernandez	.20	.09
□	280	John Kruk	.40	.18
□	281	Luis Alicea	.20	.09
□	282	Jim Clancy	.20	.09
□	283	Billy Ripken	.20	.09
□	284	Craig Reynolds	.20	.09
□	285	Robin Yount	.75	.35
□	286	Jimmy Jones	.20	.09
□	287	Ron Oester	.20	.09
□	288	Terry Leach	.20	.09
□	289	Dennis Eckersley	.40	.18
□	290	Alan Trammell	.60	.25
□	291	Jimmy Key	.40	.18
□	292	Chris Bosio	.20	.09

293	Jose DeLeon	.20	.09
294	Jim Traber	.20	.09
295	Mike Scott	.20	.09
296	Roger McDowell	.20	.09
297	Garry Templeton	.20	.09
298	Doyle Alexander	.20	.09
299	Nick Esasky	.20	.09
300	Mark McGwire UER	1.50	.70
	(Doubles total 52, should be 51)		
301	Darryl Hamilton	.20	.09
302	Dave Smith	.20	.09
303	Rick Sutcliffe	.20	.09
304	Dave Stapleton	.20	.09
305	Alan Ashby	.20	.09
306	Pedro Guerrero	.40	.18
307	Ron Guidry	.20	.09
308	Steve Farr	.20	.09
309	Curt Ford	.20	.09
310	Claudell Washington	.20	.09
311	Tom Prince	.20	.09
312	Chad Kreuter	.20	.09
313	Ken Oberkfell	.20	.09
314	Jerry Browne	.20	.09
315	R.J. Reynolds	.20	.09
316	Scott Bankhead	.20	.09
317	Milt Thompson	.20	.09
318	Mario Diaz	.20	.09
319	Bruce Ruffin	.20	.09
320	Dave Valle	.20	.09
321A	Gary Varsho ERR	2.00	.90
	(Back photo actually Mike Bielecki bunting)		
321B	Gary Varsho COR	.20	.09
	(In road uniform)		
322	Paul Mirabella	.20	.09
323	Chuck Jackson	.20	.09
324	Drew Hall	.20	.09
325	Don August	.20	.09
326	Israel Sanchez	.20	.09
327	Denny Walling	.20	.09
328	Joel Skinner	.20	.09
329	Danny Tartabull	.20	.09
330	Tony Pena	.20	.09
331	Jim Sundberg	.20	.09
332	Jeff D. Robinson	.20	.09
333	Oddibe McDowell	.20	.09
334	Jose Lind	.20	.09
335	Paul Kilgus	.20	.09
336	Juan Samuel	.20	.09
337	Mike Campbell	.20	.09
338	Mike Maddux	.20	.09
339	Darnell Coles	.20	.09
340	Bob Bernier	.20	.09
341	Rafael Ramirez	.20	.09
342	Scott Sanderson	.20	.09
343	B.J. Surhoff	.40	.18
344	Billy Hatcher	.20	.09
345	Pat Perry	.20	.09
346	Jack Clark	.40	.18
347	Gary Thurman	.20	.09
348	Tim Jones	.20	.09
349	Dave Winfield	.75	.35
350	Frank White	.40	.18
351	Dave Collins	.20	.09
352	Jack Morris	.40	.18
353	Eric Plunk	.20	.09
354	Leon Durham	.20	.09
355	Ivan DeJesus	.20	.09
356	Brian Holman	.20	.09
357A	Dale Murphy ERR	15.00	6.75
	(Front has reverse negative)		
357B	Dale Murphy COR	.75	.35
358	Mark Portugal	.20	.09
359	Andy McGaffigan	.20	.09
360	Tom Glavine	.75	.35
361	Keith Moreland	.20	.09
362	Todd Stottlemyre	.40	.18
363	Dave Leiper	.20	.09
364	Cecil Fielder	.60	.25
365	Carmelo Martinez	.20	.09
366	Dwight Evans	.40	.18
367	Kevin McReynolds	.20	.09
368	Rich Gedman	.20	.09
369	Len Dykstra	.40	.18
370	Jody Reed	.20	.09
371	Jose Canseco UER	.75	.35
	(Strikeout total 391, should be 491)		
372	Rob Murphy	.20	.09
373	Mike Henneman	.20	.09
374	Walt Weiss	.20	.09
375	Rob Dibble	.40	.18
376	Kirby Puckett	1.50	.70
	(Mark McGwire in background)		
377	Dennis Martinez	.40	.18
378	Ron Gant	.40	.18
379	Brian Harper	.20	.09
380	Nelson Santovenia	.20	.09
381	Lloyd Moseby	.20	.09
382	Lance McCullers	.20	.09
383	Dave Stieb	.20	.09
384	Tony Gwynn	2.00	.90
385	Mike Flanagan	.20	.09
386	Bob Ojeda	.20	.09
387	Bruce Hurst	.20	.09
388	Dave Magadan	.20	.09
389	Wade Boggs	.75	.35
390	Gary Carter	.75	.35
391	Frank Tanana	.20	.09
392	Curt Young	.20	.09
393	Jeff Treadway	.20	.09
394	Darrell Evans	.40	.18
395	Glenn Hubbard	.20	.09
396	Chuck Cary	.20	.09
397	Frank Viola	.20	.09
398	Jeff Parrett	.20	.09
399	Terry Blocker	.20	.09
400	Dan Gladden	.20	.09
401	Louie Meadows	.20	.09
402	Tim Raines	.40	.18
403	Joey Meyer	.20	.09
404	Larry Andersen	.20	.09
405	Rex Hudler	.20	.09
406	Mike Schmidt	1.00	.45
407	John Franco	.40	.18
408	Brady Anderson	2.50	1.10
409	Don Carman	.20	.09
410	Eric Davis	.40	.18
411	Bob Stanley	.20	.09
412	Pete Smith	.20	.09
413	Jim Rice	.40	.18
414	Bruce Sutter	.20	.09
415	Oil Can Boyd	.20	.09
416	Ruben Sierra	.20	.09
417	Mike LaValliere	.20	.09
418	Steve Buechele	.20	.09
419	Gary Redus	.20	.09
420	Scott Fletcher	.20	.09
421	Dale Sveum	.20	.09
422	Bob Knepper	.20	.09
423	Luis Rivera	.20	.09
424	Ted Higuera	.20	.09
425	Kevin Bass	.20	.09
426	Ken Gerhart	.20	.09
427	Shane Rawley	.20	.09
428	Paul O'Neil	.40	.18
429	Joe Orsulak	.20	.09
430	Jackie Gutierrez	.20	.09
431	Gerald Perry	.20	.09
432	Mike Greenwell	.20	.09
433	Jerry Royster	.20	.09
434	Ellis Burks	.40	.18
435	Ed Olwine	.20	.09
436	Dave Rucker	.20	.09
437	Charlie Hough	.40	.18
438	Bob Walk	.20	.09
439	Bob Brower	.20	.09
440	Barry Bonds	1.50	.70
441	Tom Foley	.20	.09
442	Rob Deer	.20	.09
443	Glenn Davis	.20	.09
444	Dave Martinez	.20	.09
445	Bill Wegman	.20	.09
446	Lloyd McClendon	.20	.09
447	Dave Schmidt	.20	.09
448	Darren Daulton	.40	.18
449	Frank Williams	.20	.09
450	Don Aase	.20	.09
451	Lou Whitaker	.40	.18
452	Goose Gossage	.40	.18
453	Ed Whitson	.20	.09
454	Jim Walewander	.20	.09
455	Damon Berryhill	.20	.09
456	Tim Burke	.20	.09
457	Barry Jones	.20	.09
458	Joel Youngblood	.20	.09
459	Floyd Youmans	.20	.09
460	Mark Salas	.20	.09
461	Jeff Russell	.20	.09
462	Darrell Miller	.20	.09
463	Jeff Kunkel	.20	.09
464	Sherman Corbett	.20	.09
465	Curtis Wilkerson	.20	.09
466	Bud Black	.20	.09
467	Cal Ripken	3.00	1.35
468	John Farrell	.20	.09
469	Terry Kennedy	.20	.09
470	Tom Candiotti	.20	.09
471	Roberto Alomar	1.25	.55
472	Jeff M. Robinson	.20	.09
473	Vance Law	.20	.09
474	Randy Ready UER	.20	.09
	(Strikeout total 136, should be 115)		
475	Walt Terrell	.20	.09
476	Kelly Downs	.20	.09
477	Johnny Paredes	.20	.09
478	Shawn Hillegas	.20	.09
479	Bob Brenly	.20	.09
480	Otis Nixon	.40	.18
481	Johnny Ray	.20	.09
482	Geno Petralli	.20	.09
483	Stu Cliburn	.20	.09
484	Pete Incaviglia	.20	.09
485	Brian Downing	.20	.09
486	Jeff Stone	.20	.09
487	Carmen Castillo	.20	.09
488	Tom Niedenfuer	.20	.09
489	Jay Bell	.40	.18
490	Rick Schu	.20	.09
491	Jeff Pico	.20	.09
492	Mark Parent	.20	.09
493	Eric King	.20	.09
494	Al Nipper	.20	.09
495	Andy Hawkins	.20	.09
496	Daryl Boston	.20	.09
497	Ernie Riles	.20	.09
498	Pascual Perez	.20	.09
499	Bill Long UER	.20	.09
	(Games started total 70, should be 44)		
500	Kirt Manwaring	.20	.09
501	Chuck Crim	.20	.09
502	Candy Maldonado	.20	.09
503	Dennis Lamp	.20	.09
504	Glenn Braggs	.20	.09
505	Joe Price	.20	.09
506	Ken Williams	.20	.09
507	Bill Pecota	.20	.09
508	Rey Quinones	.20	.09
509	Jeff Bittiger	.20	.09
510	Kevin Seitzer	.20	.09
511	Steve Bedrosian	.20	.09
512	Todd Worrell	.40	.18
513	Chris James	.20	.09
514	Jose Oquendo	.20	.09
515	David Palmer	.20	.09
516	John Smiley	.20	.09
517	Dave Clark	.20	.09
518	Mike Dunne	.20	.09
519	Ron Washington	.20	.09
520	Bob Kipper	.20	.09
521	Lee Smith	.40	.18
522	Juan Castillo	.20	.09
523	Don Robinson	.20	.09
524	Kevin Romine	.20	.09
525	Paul Molitor	.75	.35
526	Mark Langston	.20	.09
527	Donnie Hill	.20	.09
528	Larry Owen	.20	.09
529	Jerry Reed	.20	.09
530	Jack McDowell	.40	.18
531	Greg Mathews	.20	.09
532	John Russell	.20	.09
533	Dan Quisenberry	.20	.09

#	Player		
☐ 534	Greg Gross	.20	.09
☐ 535	Danny Cox	.20	.09
☐ 536	Terry Francona	.20	.09
☐ 537	Andy Van Slyke	.40	.18
☐ 538	Mel Hall	.20	.09
☐ 539	Jim Gott	.20	.09
☐ 540	Doug Jones	.20	.09
☐ 541	Craig Lefferts	.20	.09
☐ 542	Mike Boddicker	.20	.09
☐ 543	Greg Brock	.20	.09
☐ 544	Atlee Hammaker	.20	.09
☐ 545	Tom Bolton	.20	.09
☐ 546	Mike Macfarlane	.40	.18
☐ 547	Rich Renteria	.20	.09
☐ 548	John Davis	.20	.09
☐ 549	Floyd Bannister	.20	.09
☐ 550	Mickey Brantley	.20	.09
☐ 551	Duane Ward	.20	.09
☐ 552	Dan Petry	.20	.09
☐ 553	Mickey Tettleton UER	.40	.18
	(Walks total 175, should be 136)		
☐ 554	Rick Leach	.20	.09
☐ 555	Mike Witt	.20	.09
☐ 556	Sid Bream	.20	.09
☐ 557	Bobby Witt	.20	.09
☐ 558	Tommy Herr	.20	.09
☐ 559	Randy Milligan	.20	.09
☐ 560	Jose Cecena	.20	.09
☐ 561	Mackey Sasser	.20	.09
☐ 562	Carney Lansford	.40	.18
☐ 563	Rick Aguilera	.40	.18
☐ 564	Ron Hassey	.20	.09
☐ 565	Dwight Gooden	.40	.18
☐ 566	Paul Assenmacher	.20	.09
☐ 567	Neil Allen	.20	.09
☐ 568	Jim Morrison	.20	.09
☐ 569	Mike Pagliarulo	.20	.09
☐ 570	Ted Simmons	.40	.18
☐ 571	Mark Thurmond	.20	.09
☐ 572	Fred McGriff	.75	.35
☐ 573	Wally Joyner	.40	.18
☐ 574	Jose Bautista	.20	.09
☐ 575	Kelly Gruber	.20	.09
☐ 576	Cecilio Guante	.20	.09
☐ 577	Mark Davidson	.20	.09
☐ 578	Bobby Bonilla UER	.60	.25
	(Total steals 2 in '87, should be 3)		
☐ 579	Mike Stanley	.20	.09
☐ 580	Gene Larkin	.20	.09
☐ 581	Stan Javier	.20	.09
☐ 582	Howard Johnson	.20	.09
☐ 583A	Mike Gallego ERR	1.00	.45
	(Front wording negative)		
☐ 583B	Mike Gallego COR	.75	.35
☐ 584	David Cone	.75	.35
☐ 585	Doug Jennings	.20	.09
☐ 586	Charles Hudson	.20	.09
☐ 587	Dion James	.20	.09
☐ 588	Al Leiter	.75	.35
☐ 589	Charlie Puleo	.20	.09
☐ 590	Roberto Kelly	.40	.18
☐ 591	Thad Bosley	.20	.09
☐ 592	Pete Stanicek	.20	.09
☐ 593	Pat Borders	.40	.18
☐ 594	Bryan Harvey	.40	.18
☐ 595	Jeff Ballard	.20	.09
☐ 596	Jeff Reardon	.40	.18
☐ 597	Doug Drabek	.40	.18
☐ 598	Edwin Correa	.20	.09
☐ 599	Keith Atherton	.20	.09
☐ 600	Dave LaPoint	.20	.09
☐ 601	Don Baylor	.40	.18
☐ 602	Tom Pagnozzi	.20	.09
☐ 603	Tim Flannery	.20	.09
☐ 604	Gene Walter	.20	.09
☐ 605	Dave Parker	.40	.18
☐ 606	Mike Diaz	.20	.09
☐ 607	Chris Gwynn	.20	.09
☐ 608	Odell Jones	.20	.09
☐ 609	Carlton Fisk	.75	.35
☐ 610	Jay Howell	.20	.09
☐ 611	Tim Crews	.20	.09
☐ 612	Keith Hernandez	.40	.18
☐ 613	Willie Fraser	.20	.09
☐ 614	Jim Eppard	.20	.09
☐ 615	Jeff Hamilton	.20	.09
☐ 616	Kurt Stillwell	.20	.09
☐ 617	Tom Browning	.20	.09
☐ 618	Jeff Montgomery	.40	.18
☐ 619	Jose Rijo	.20	.09
☐ 620	Jamie Quirk	.20	.09
☐ 621	Willie McGee	.40	.18
☐ 622	Mark Grant UER	.20	.09
	(Glove on wrong hand)		
☐ 623	Bill Swift	.20	.09
☐ 624	Orlando Mercado	.20	.09
☐ 625	John Costello	.20	.09
☐ 626	Jose Gonzalez	.20	.09
☐ 627A	Bill Schroeder ERR	1.00	.45
	(Back photo actually Ronn Reynolds buckling shin guards)		
☐ 627B	Bill Schroeder COR	.75	.35
☐ 628A	Fred Manrique ERR	.75	.35
	(Back photo actually Ozzie Guillen throwing)		
☐ 628B	Fred Manrique COR	.20	.09
	(Swinging bat on back)		
☐ 629	Ricky Horton	.20	.09
☐ 630	Dan Plesac	.20	.09
☐ 631	Alfredo Griffin	.20	.09
☐ 632	Chuck Finley	.40	.18
☐ 633	Kirk Gibson	.40	.18
☐ 634	Randy Myers	.40	.18
☐ 635	Greg Minton	.20	.09
☐ 636A	Herm Winningham	.75	.35
	ERR (W1nningham on back)		
☐ 636B	Herm Winningham COR	.20	.09
☐ 637	Charlie Leibrandt	.20	.09
☐ 638	Tim Birtsas	.20	.09
☐ 639	Bill Buckner	.40	.18
☐ 640	Danny Jackson	.20	.09
☐ 641	Greg Booker	.20	.09
☐ 642	Jim Presley	.20	.09
☐ 643	Gene Nelson	.20	.09
☐ 644	Rod Booker	.20	.09
☐ 645	Dennis Rasmussen	.20	.09
☐ 646	Juan Nieves	.20	.09
☐ 647	Bobby Thigpen	.20	.09
☐ 648	Tim Belcher	.20	.09
☐ 649	Mike Young	.20	.09
☐ 650	Ivan Calderon	.20	.09
☐ 651	Oswaldo Peraza	.20	.09
☐ 652A	Pat Sheridan ERR	5.00	2.20
	(No position on front)		
☐ 652B	Pat Sheridan COR	.20	.09
☐ 653	Mike Morgan	.20	.09
☐ 654	Mike Heath	.20	.09
☐ 655	Jay Tibbs	.20	.09
☐ 656	Fernando Valenzuela	.40	.18
☐ 657	Lee Mazzilli	.20	.09
☐ 658	Frank Viola AL CY	.20	.09
☐ 659A	Jose Canseco AL MVP	.40	.18
	(Eagle logo in black)		
☐ 659B	Jose Canseco AL MVP	.40	.18
	(Eagle logo in blue)		
☐ 660	Walt Weiss AL ROY	.20	.09
☐ 661	Orel Hershiser NL CY	.40	.18
☐ 662	Kirk Gibson NL MVP	.20	.09
☐ 663	Chris Sabo NL ROY	.20	.09
☐ 664	Dennis Eckersley ALCS MVP	.20	.09
☐ 665	Orel Hershiser NLCS MVP	.40	.18
☐ 666	Kirk Gibson WS	.75	.35
☐ 667	Orel Hershiser WS MVP	.40	.18
☐ 668	Wally Joyner TC	.20	.09
☐ 669	Nolan Ryan TC	1.00	.45
☐ 670	Jose Canseco TC	.40	.18
☐ 671	Fred McGriff TC	.40	.18
☐ 672	Dale Murphy TC	.40	.18
☐ 673	Paul Molitor TC	.40	.18
☐ 674	Ozzie Smith TC	.60	.25
☐ 675	Ryne Sandberg TC	.60	.25
☐ 676	Kirk Gibson TC	.20	.09
☐ 677	Andres Galarraga TC	.40	.18
☐ 678	Will Clark TC	.40	.18
☐ 679	Cory Snyder TC	.20	.09
☐ 680	Alvin Davis TC	.20	.09
☐ 681	Darryl Strawberry TC	.20	.09
☐ 682	Cal Ripken TC	1.00	.45
☐ 683	Tony Gwynn TC	1.00	.45
☐ 684	Mike Schmidt TC	.60	.25
☐ 685	Andy Van Slyke TC UER	.20	.09
	(96 Junior Ortiz)		
☐ 686	Ruben Sierra TC	.20	.09
☐ 687	Wade Boggs TC	.40	.18
☐ 688	Eric Davis TC	.20	.09
☐ 689	George Brett TC	.75	.35
☐ 690	Alan Trammell TC	.40	.18
☐ 691	Frank Viola TC	.20	.09
☐ 692	Harold Baines TC	.20	.09
☐ 693	Don Mattingly TC	.60	.25
☐ 694	Checklist 1-100	.20	.09
☐ 695	Checklist 101-200	.20	.09
☐ 696	Checklist 201-300	.20	.09
☐ 697	Checklist 301-400	.20	.09
☐ 698	Checklist 401-500 UER	.20	.09
	(467 Cal Ripken Jr.)		
☐ 699	Checklist 501-600 UER	.20	.09
	(543 Greg Booker)		
☐ 700	Checklist 601-700	.20	.09
☐ 701	Checklist 701-800	.20	.09
☐ 702	Jesse Barfield	.20	.09
☐ 703	Walt Terrell	.20	.09
☐ 704	Dickie Thon	.20	.09
☐ 705	Al Leiter	.75	.35
☐ 706	Dave LaPoint	.20	.09
☐ 707	Charlie Hayes	.75	.35
☐ 708	Andy Hawkins	.20	.09
☐ 709	Mickey Hatcher	.20	.09
☐ 710	Lance McCullers	.20	.09
☐ 711	Ron Kittle	.20	.09
☐ 712	Bert Blyleven	.40	.18
☐ 713	Rick Dempsey	.20	.09
☐ 714	Ken Williams	.20	.09
☐ 715	Steve Rosenberg	.20	.09
☐ 716	Joe Skalski	.20	.09
☐ 717	Spike Owen	.20	.09
☐ 718	Todd Burns	.20	.09
☐ 719	Kevin Gross	.20	.09
☐ 720	Tommy Herr	.20	.09
☐ 721	Rob Ducey	.20	.09
☐ 722	Gary Green	.20	.09
☐ 723	Gregg Olson	.40	.18
☐ 724	Greg W. Harris	.20	.09
☐ 725	Craig Worthington	.20	.09
☐ 726	Tom Howard	.20	.09
☐ 727	Dale Mohorcic	.20	.09
☐ 728	Rich Yett	.20	.09
☐ 729	Mel Hall	.20	.09
☐ 730	Floyd Youmans	.20	.09
☐ 731	Lonnie Smith	.20	.09
☐ 732	Wally Backman	.20	.09
☐ 733	Trevor Wilson	.20	.09
☐ 734	Jose Alvarez	.20	.09
☐ 735	Bob Milacki	.20	.09
☐ 736	Tom Gordon	.75	.35
☐ 737	Wally Whitehurst	.20	.09
☐ 738	Mike Aldrete	.20	.09
☐ 739	Keith Miller	.20	.09
☐ 740	Randy Milligan	.20	.09
☐ 741	Jeff Parrett	.20	.09
☐ 742	Steve Finley	1.00	.45
☐ 743	Junior Felix	.40	.18
☐ 744	Pete Harnisch	.40	.18
☐ 745	Bill Spiers	.20	.09
☐ 746	Hensley Meulens	.20	.09
☐ 747	Juan Bell	.20	.09
☐ 748	Steve Sax	.20	.09
☐ 749	Phil Bradley	.20	.09
☐ 750	Rey Quinones	.20	.09
☐ 751	Tommy Gregg	.20	.09
☐ 752	Kevin Brown	.75	.35
☐ 753	Derek Lilliquist	.20	.09
☐ 754	Todd Zeile	.75	.35
☐ 755	Jim Abbott	.75	.35
	(Triple exposure)		
☐ 756	Ozzie Canseco	.20	.09
☐ 757	Nick Esasky	.20	.09
☐ 758	Mike Moore	.20	.09
☐ 759	Rob Murphy	.20	.09
☐ 760	Rick Mahler	.20	.09
☐ 761	Fred Lynn	.20	.09

		MINT	NRMT
☐ 762	Kevin Blankenship	.20	.09
☐ 763	Eddie Murray	.75	.35
☐ 764	Steve Searcy	.20	.09
☐ 765	Jerome Walton	.75	.35
☐ 766	Erik Hanson	.40	.18
☐ 767	Bob Boone	.40	.18
☐ 768	Edgar Martinez	.75	.35
☐ 769	Jose DeJesus	.20	.09
☐ 770	Greg Briley	.20	.09
☐ 771	Steve Peters	.20	.09
☐ 772	Rafael Palmeiro	.75	.35
☐ 773	Jack Clark	.40	.18
☐ 774	Nolan Ryan	3.00	1.35
	(Throwing football)		
☐ 775	Lance Parrish	.20	.09
☐ 776	Joe Girardi	.75	.35
☐ 777	Willie Wilson	.40	.18
☐ 778	Mitch Williams	.20	.09
☐ 779	Dennis Cook	.20	.09
☐ 780	Dwight Smith	.40	.18
☐ 781	Lenny Harris	.20	.09
☐ 782	Torey Lovullo	.20	.09
☐ 783	Norm Charlton	.40	.18
☐ 784	Chris Brown	.20	.09
☐ 785	Todd Benzinger	.20	.09
☐ 786	Shane Rawley	.20	.09
☐ 787	Omar Vizquel	2.00	.90
☐ 788	LaVel Freeman	.20	.09
☐ 789	Jeffrey Leonard	.20	.09
☐ 790	Eddie Williams	.20	.09
☐ 791	Jamie Moyer	.20	.09
☐ 792	Bruce Hurst UER	.20	.09
	(Workd Series)		
☐ 793	Julio Franco	.20	.09
☐ 794	Claudell Washington	.20	.09
☐ 795	Jody Davis	.20	.09
☐ 796	Oddibe McDowell	.20	.09
☐ 797	Paul Kilgus	.20	.09
☐ 798	Tracy Jones	.20	.09
☐ 799	Steve Wilson	.20	.09
☐ 800	Pete O'Brien	.20	.09

1990 Upper Deck

Kevin Maas

The 1990 Upper Deck set contains 800 standard-size cards issued in two series, low numbers (1-700) and high numbers (701-800). Cards were distributed in fin-wrapped low and high series foil packs, complete 800-card factory sets and 100-card high series factory sets. High series foil packs contained a mixture of low and high series cards. The front and back borders are white, and both sides feature full-color photos. The horizontally oriented backs have recent stats and anti-counterfeiting holograms. Team checklist cards are mixed in with the first 100 cards of the set. Rookie Cards in the set include Wilson Alvarez, Carlos Baerga, Juan Gonzalez, Marquis Grissom, Todd Hundley, David Justice, Ray Lankford, Ben McDonald, Dean Palmer, Sammy Sosa and Larry Walker. The high series contains a Nolan Ryan variation; all cards produced before August 12th only discuss Ryan's sixth no-hitter while the later-issue cards include a stripe honoring Ryan's 300th victory. Card 702 (Rookie Threats) was originally scheduled to be Mike Witt. A few Witt cards with 702 on back and checklist cards showing Witt as 702 escaped into early packs; they are characterized by a black rectangle covering much of the card's back.

	MINT	NRMT
COMPLETE SET (800)	20.00	9.00
COMPLETE LO SET (700)	16.00	7.25
COMPLETE HI SET (100)	4.00	1.80
COMMON CARD (1-800)	.10	.05
MINOR STARS	.20	.09
UNLISTED STARS	.40	.18
COMP.REGGIE SET (10)	15.00	6.75
COMMON REGGIE (1-9)	1.50	.70
REGGIE HEADER (NNO)	3.00	1.35
REGGIE AUTO/2500 (AU1)	250.00	110.00
REGGIE: RANDOM INSERTS IN HI SERIES		

		MINT	NRMT
☐ 1	Star Rookie Checklist	.10	.05
☐ 2	Randy Nosek	.10	.05
☐ 3	Tom Drees UER	.10	.05
	(11th line, hurled, should be hurled)		
☐ 4	Curt Young	.10	.05
☐ 5	Devon White TC	.10	.05
☐ 6	Luis Salazar	.10	.05
☐ 7	Von Hayes TC	.10	.05
☐ 8	Jose Bautista	.10	.05
☐ 9	Marquis Grissom	.75	.35
☐ 10	Orel Hershiser TC	.10	.05
☐ 11	Rick Aguilera	.20	.09
☐ 12	Benito Santiago TC	.10	.05
☐ 13	Deion Sanders	.40	.18
☐ 14	Marvell Wynne	.10	.05
☐ 15	Dave West	.10	.05
☐ 16	Bobby Bonilla TC	.10	.05
☐ 17	Sammy Sosa	1.50	.70
☐ 18	Steve Sax TC	.10	.05
☐ 19	Jack Howell	.10	.05
☐ 20	Mike Schmidt Special UER	.50	.23
	(Suprising, should be surprising)		
☐ 21	Robin Ventura UER	.40	.18
	(Samta Maria)		
☐ 22	Brian Meyer	.10	.05
☐ 23	Blaine Beatty	.10	.05
☐ 24	Ken Griffey Jr. TC	1.00	.45
☐ 25	Greg Vaughn UER	.20	.09
	(Association misspelled as assoication)		
☐ 26	Xavier Hernandez	.10	.05
☐ 27	Jason Grimsley	.10	.05
☐ 28	Eric Anthony UER	.20	.09
	(Ashville, should be Asheville)		
☐ 29	Tim Raines TC UER	.10	.05
	(Wallach listed before Walker)		
☐ 30	David Wells	.10	.05
☐ 31	Hal Morris	.10	.05
☐ 32	Bo Jackson TC	.20	.09
☐ 33	Kelly Mann	.10	.05
☐ 34	Nolan Ryan Special	.75	.35
☐ 35	Scott Service UER	.10	.05
	(Born Cincinatti on 7/27/67, should be Cincinnati 2/27)		
☐ 36	Mark McGwire UER	.40	.18
☐ 37	Tino Martinez	.75	.35
☐ 38	Chili Davis	.20	.09
☐ 39	Scott Sanderson	.10	.05
☐ 40	Kevin Mitchell TC	.10	.05

		MINT	NRMT
☐ 41	Lou Whitaker TC	.10	.05
☐ 42	Scott Coolbaugh UER	.10	.05
	(Definately)		
☐ 43	Jose Cano UER	.10	.05
	(Born 9/7/62, should be 3/7/62)		
☐ 44	Jose Vizcaino	.40	.18
☐ 45	Bob Hamelin	.40	.18
☐ 46	Jose Offerman UER	.40	.18
	(Possesses)		
☐ 47	Kevin Blankenship	.10	.05
☐ 48	Kirby Puckett TC	.40	.18
☐ 49	Tommy Greene UER	.10	.05
	(Livest, should be liveliest)		
☐ 50	Will Clark Special UER	.40	.18
	(Perenial, should be perennial)		
☐ 51	Rob Nelson	.10	.05
☐ 52	Chris Hammond UER	.10	.05
	(Chatanooga)		
☐ 53	Joe Carter TC	.10	.05
☐ 54A	Ben McDonald ERR..	5.00	2.20
	(No Rookie designation on card front)		
☐ 54B	Ben McDonald COR ..	.40	.18
☐ 55	Andy Benes UER	.40	.18
	(Whichita)		
☐ 56	John Olerud	.40	.18
☐ 57	Roger Clemens TC	.40	.18
☐ 58	Tony Armas	.10	.05
☐ 59	George Canale	.10	.05
☐ 60A	Mickey Tettleton TC ERR (683 Jamie Weston)	2.00	.90
☐ 60B	Mickey Tettleton TC COR (683 Mickey Weston)	.10	.05
☐ 61	Mike Stanton	.10	.05
☐ 62	Dwight Gooden TC	.10	.05
☐ 63	Kent Mercker UER	.20	.09
	(Albuquerque)		
☐ 64	Francisco Cabrera	.10	.05
☐ 65	Steve Avery UER	.10	.05
	(Born NJ, should be MI, Merker should be Mercker)		
☐ 66	Jose Canseco	.40	.18
☐ 67	Matt Merullo	.10	.05
☐ 68	Vince Coleman TC UER	.10	.05
	(Guererro)		
☐ 69	Ron Karkovice	.10	.05
☐ 70	Kevin Maas	.20	.09
☐ 71	Dennis Cook UER	.10	.05
	(Shown with rightly glove on card back)		
☐ 72	Juan Gonzalez UER ..	4.00	1.80
	(135 games for Tulsa in '89, should be 133)		
☐ 73	Andre Dawson TC	.20	.09
☐ 74	Dean Palmer UER	.50	.23
	(Permanent misspelled as perminant)		
☐ 75	Bo Jackson Special UER	.20	.09
	(Monsterous, should be monstrous)		
☐ 76	Rob Richie	.10	.05
☐ 77	Bobby Rose UER	.10	.05
	(Pickin, should be pick in)		
☐ 78	Brian DuBois UER	.10	.05
	(Commiting)		
☐ 79	Ozzie Guillen TC	.10	.05
☐ 80	Gene Nelson	.10	.05
☐ 81	Bob McClure	.10	.05
☐ 82	Julio Franco TC	.10	.05
☐ 83	Greg Minton	.10	.05
☐ 84	John Smoltz TC UER	.20	.09
	(Oddibe not Odibbe)		
☐ 85	Willie Fraser	.10	.05
☐ 86	Neal Heaton	.10	.05
☐ 87	Kevin Tapani UER	.10	.05
	(24th line has excpet, should be except)		
☐ 88	Mike Scott TC	.10	.05
☐ 89A	Jim Gott ERR ..	2.50	1.10
	(Photo actually Rick Reed)		
☐ 89B	Jim Gott COR	.10	.05

□	#	Name	Price 1	Price 2
□	90	Lance Johnson	.10	.05
□	91	Robin Yount TC UER .... (Checklist on back has 178 Rob Deer and 176 Mike Felder)	.20	.09
□	92	Jeff Parrett	.10	.05
□	93	Julio Machado UER (Valencelan, should be Venezuelan)	.10	.05
□	94	Ron Jones	.10	.05
□	95	George Bell TC	.10	.05
□	96	Jerry Reuss	.10	.05
□	97	Brian Fisher	.10	.05
□	98	Kevin Ritz UER (Amercian)	.10	.05
□	99	Barry Larkin TC	.30	.14
□	100	Checklist 1-100	.10	.05
□	101	Gerald Perry	.10	.05
□	102	Kevin Appier	.40	.18
□	103	Julio Franco	.10	.05
□	104	Craig Biggio	.40	.18
□	105	Bo Jackson UER ('89 BA wrong, should be .256)	.40	.18
□	106	Junior Felix	.10	.05
□	107	Mike Harkey	.10	.05
□	108	Fred McGriff	.40	.18
□	109	Rick Sutcliffe	.10	.05
□	110	Pete O'Brien	.10	.05
□	111	Kelly Gruber	.10	.05
□	112	Dwight Evans	.20	.09
□	113	Pat Borders	.10	.05
□	114	Dwight Gooden	.20	.09
□	115	Kevin Batiste	.10	.05
□	116	Eric Davis	.20	.09
□	117	Kevin Mitchell UER (Career HR total 99, should be 100)	.20	.09
□	118	Ron Oester	.10	.05
□	119	Brett Butler	.20	.09
□	120	Danny Jackson	.10	.05
□	121	Tommy Gregg	.10	.05
□	122	Ken Caminiti	.40	.18
□	123	Kevin Brown	.40	.18
□	124	George Brett UER (133 runs, should be 1300)	.75	.35
□	125	Mike Scott	.10	.05
□	126	Cory Snyder	.10	.05
□	127	George Bell	.10	.05
□	128	Mark Grace	.40	.18
□	129	Devon White	.10	.05
□	130	Tony Fernandez	.10	.05
□	131	Don Aase	.10	.05
□	132	Rance Mulliniks	.10	.05
□	133	Marty Barrett	.10	.05
□	134	Nelson Liriano	.10	.05
□	135	Mark Carreon	.10	.05
□	136	Candy Maldonado	.10	.05
□	137	Tim Birtsas	.10	.05
□	138	Tom Brookens	.10	.05
□	139	John Franco	.20	.09
□	140	Mike LaCoss	.10	.05
□	141	Jeff Treadway	.10	.05
□	142	Pat Tabler	.10	.05
□	143	Darrell Evans	.20	.09
□	144	Rafael Ramirez	.10	.05
□	145	Oddibe McDowell UER (Misspelled Odibbe)	.10	.05
□	146	Brian Downing	.10	.05
□	147	Curt Wilkerson	.10	.05
□	148	Ernie Whitt	.10	.05
□	149	Bill Schroeder	.10	.05
□	150	Domingo Ramos UER (Says throws right, but shows him throwing lefty)	.10	.05
□	151	Rick Honeycutt	.10	.05
□	152	Don Slaught	.10	.05
□	153	Mitch Webster	.10	.05
□	154	Tony Phillips	.10	.05
□	155	Paul Kilgus	.10	.05
□	156	Ken Griffey Jr. UER .. (Simultaniously)	4.00	1.80
□	157	Gary Sheffield	.50	.23
□	158	Wally Backman	.10	.05
□	159	B.J. Surhoff	.20	.09
□	160	Louie Meadows	.10	.05
□	161	Paul O'Neill	.20	.09
□	162	Jeff McKnight	.10	.05
□	163	Alvaro Espinoza	.10	.05
□	164	Scott Scudder	.10	.05
□	165	Jeff Reed	.10	.05
□	166	Gregg Jefferies	.20	.09
□	167	Barry Larkin	.40	.18
□	168	Gary Carter	.20	.09
□	169	Robby Thompson	.10	.05
□	170	Rolando Roomes	.10	.05
□	171	Mark McGwire UER (Total games 427 and hits 479, should be 467 and 427)	.75	.35
□	172	Steve Sax	.10	.05
□	173	Mark Williamson	.10	.05
□	174	Mitch Williams	.10	.05
□	175	Brian Holton	.10	.05
□	176	Rob Deer	.10	.05
□	177	Tim Raines	.20	.09
□	178	Mike Felder	.10	.05
□	179	Harold Reynolds	.10	.05
□	180	Terry Francona	.10	.05
□	181	Chris Sabo	.20	.09
□	182	Darryl Strawberry	.20	.09
□	183	Willie Randolph	.10	.05
□	184	Bill Ripken	.10	.05
□	185	Mackey Sasser	.10	.05
□	186	Todd Benzinger	.10	.05
□	187	Kevin Elster UER (16 homers in 1989, should be 10)	.10	.05
□	188	Jose Uribe	.10	.05
□	189	Tom Browning	.10	.05
□	190	Keith Miller	.10	.05
□	191	Don Mattingly	.60	.25
□	192	Dave Parker	.20	.09
□	193	Roberto Kelly UER (96 RBI, should be 62)	.20	.09
□	194	Phil Bradley	.10	.05
□	195	Ron Hassey	.10	.05
□	196	Gerald Young	.10	.05
□	197	Hubie Brooks	.10	.05
□	198	Bill Doran	.10	.05
□	199	Al Newman	.10	.05
□	200	Checklist 101-200	.10	.05
□	201	Terry Puhl	.10	.05
□	202	Frank DiPino	.10	.05
□	203	Jim Clancy	.10	.05
□	204	Bob Ojeda	.10	.05
□	205	Alex Trevino	.10	.05
□	206	Dave Henderson	.10	.05
□	207	Henry Cotto	.10	.05
□	208	Rafael Belliard UER (Born 1961, not 1951)	.10	.05
□	209	Stan Javier	.10	.05
□	210	Jerry Reed	.10	.05
□	211	Doug Dascenzo	.10	.05
□	212	Andres Thomas	.10	.05
□	213	Greg Maddux	1.25	.55
□	214	Mike Schooler	.10	.05
□	215	Lonnie Smith	.10	.05
□	216	Jose Rijo	.10	.05
□	217	Greg Gagne	.10	.05
□	218	Jim Gantner	.10	.05
□	219	Allan Anderson	.10	.05
□	220	Rick Mahler	.10	.05
□	221	Jim Deshaies	.10	.05
□	222	Keith Hernandez	.20	.09
□	223	Vince Coleman	.10	.05
□	224	David Cone	.40	.18
□	225	Ozzie Smith	.50	.23
□	226	Matt Nokes	.10	.05
□	227	Barry Bonds	.50	.23
□	228	Felix Jose	.10	.05
□	229	Dennis Powell	.10	.05
□	230	Mike Gallego	.10	.05
□	231	Shawon Dunston UER ('89 stats are Andre Dawson's)	.10	.05
□	232	Ron Gant	.20	.09
□	233	Omar Vizquel	.40	.18
□	234	Derek Lilliquist	.10	.05
□	235	Erik Hanson	.10	.05
□	236	Kirby Puckett UER (824 games, should be 924)	.75	.35
□	237	Bill Spiers	.10	.05
□	238	Dan Gladden	.10	.05
□	239	Bryan Clutterbuck	.10	.05
□	240	John Moses	.10	.05
□	241	Ron Darling	.10	.05
□	242	Joe Magrane	.10	.05
□	243	Dave Magadan	.10	.05
□	244	Pedro Guerrero UER .. (Misspelled Guererro)	.10	.05
□	245	Glenn Davis	.10	.05
□	246	Terry Steinbach	.20	.09
□	247	Fred Lynn	.10	.05
□	248	Gary Redus	.10	.05
□	249	Ken Williams	.10	.05
□	250	Sid Bream	.10	.05
□	251	Bob Welch UER (2587 career strike- outs, should be 1587)	.10	.05
□	252	Bill Buckner	.10	.05
□	253	Carney Lansford	.20	.09
□	254	Paul Molitor	.40	.18
□	255	Jose DeJesus	.10	.05
□	256	Orel Hershiser	.20	.09
□	257	Tom Brunansky	.20	.09
□	258	Mike Davis	.10	.05
□	259	Jeff Ballard	.10	.05
□	260	Scott Terry	.10	.05
□	261	Sid Fernandez	.10	.05
□	262	Mike Marshall	.10	.05
□	263	Howard Johnson UER (192 SO, should be 592)	.20	.09
□	264	Kirk Gibson UER (659 runs, should be 669)	.20	.09
□	265	Kevin McReynolds	.10	.05
□	266	Cal Ripken	1.50	.70
□	267	Ozzie Guillen UER (Career triples 27, should be 29)	.10	.05
□	268	Jim Traber	.10	.05
□	269	Bobby Thigpen UER .. (31 saves in 1989, should be 34)	.10	.05
□	270	Joe Orsulak	.10	.05
□	271	Bob Boone	.20	.09
□	272	Dave Stewart UER ... (Totals wrong due to omission of '86 stats)	.20	.09
□	273	Tim Wallach	.10	.05
□	274	Luis Aquino UER (Says throws lefty, but shows him throwing righty)	.10	.05
□	275	Mike Moore	.10	.05
□	276	Tony Pena	.10	.05
□	277	Eddie Murray UER (Several typos in career total stats)	.40	.18
□	278	Milt Thompson	.10	.05
□	279	Alejandro Pena	.10	.05
□	280	Ken Dayley	.10	.05
□	281	Carmen Castillo	.10	.05
□	282	Tom Henke	.10	.05
□	283	Mickey Hatcher	.10	.05
□	284	Roy Smith	.10	.05
□	285	Manny Lee	.10	.05
□	286	Dan Pasqua	.10	.05
□	287	Larry Sheets	.10	.05
□	288	Garry Templeton	.10	.05
□	289	Eddie Williams	.10	.05
□	290	Brady Anderson UER.. (Home: Silver Springs, not Siver Springs)	.40	.18
□	291	Spike Owen	.10	.05
□	292	Storm Davis	.10	.05
□	293	Chris Bosio	.10	.05
□	294	Jim Eisenreich	.10	.05
□	295	Don August	.10	.05
□	296	Jeff Hamilton	.10	.05
□	297	Mickey Tettleton	.20	.09
□	298	Mike Scioscia	.10	.05
□	299	Kevin Hickey	.10	.05
□	300	Checklist 201-300	.10	.05

□	#	Player	Price1	Price2
□	301	Shawn Abner	.10	.05
□	302	Kevin Bass	.10	.05
□	303	Bip Roberts	.10	.05
□	304	Joe Girardi	.20	.05
□	305	Danny Darwin	.10	.05
□	306	Mike Heath	.10	.05
□	307	Mike Macfarlane	.10	.05
□	308	Ed Whitson	.10	.05
□	309	Tracy Jones	.10	.05
□	310	Scott Fletcher	.10	.05
□	311	Darnell Coles	.10	.05
□	312	Mike Brumley	.10	.05
□	313	Bill Swift	.10	.05
□	314	Charlie Hough	.10	.05
□	315	Jim Presley	.10	.05
□	316	Luis Polonia	.10	.05
□	317	Mike Morgan	.10	.05
□	318	Lee Guetterman	.10	.05
□	319	Jose Oquendo	.10	.05
□	320	Wayne Tolleson	.10	.05
□	321	Jody Reed	.10	.05
□	322	Damon Berryhill	.10	.05
□	323	Roger Clemens	.75	.35
□	324	Ryne Sandberg	.50	.23
□	325	Benito Santiago UER (Misspelled Santago on card back)	.10	.05
□	326	Bret Saberhagen UER (1140 hits, should be 1240; 56 CG, should be 52)	.10	.05
□	327	Lou Whitaker	.20	.09
□	328	Dave Gallagher	.10	.05
□	329	Mike Pagliarulo	.10	.05
□	330	Doyle Alexander	.10	.05
□	331	Jeffrey Leonard	.10	.05
□	332	Torey Lovullo	.10	.05
□	333	Pete Incaviglia	.10	.05
□	334	Rickey Henderson	.40	.18
□	335	Rafael Palmeiro	.40	.18
□	336	Ken Hill	.30	.14
□	337	Dave Winfield UER (1418 RBI, should be 1438)	.40	.18
□	338	Alfredo Griffin	.10	.05
□	339	Andy Hawkins	.10	.05
□	340	Ted Power	.10	.05
□	341	Steve Wilson	.10	.05
□	342	Jack Clark UER (916 BB, should be 1006; 1142 SO, should be 1130)	.20	.09
□	343	Ellis Burks	.30	.14
□	344	Tony Gwynn UER (Doubles stats on card back are wrong)	1.00	.45
□	345	Jerome Walton UER (Total At Bats 476, should be 475)	.10	.05
□	346	Roberto Alomar UER (61 doubles, should be 51)	.40	.18
□	347	Carlos Martinez UER (Born 8/11/64, should be 8/11/65)	.10	.05
□	348	Chet Lemon	.10	.05
□	349	Willie Wilson	.10	.05
□	350	Greg Walker	.10	.05
□	351	Tom Bolton	.10	.05
□	352	German Gonzalez	.10	.05
□	353	Harold Baines	.20	.09
□	354	Mike Greenwell	.10	.05
□	355	Ruben Sierra	.40	.18
□	356	Andres Galarraga	.40	.18
□	357	Andre Dawson	.40	.18
□	358	Jeff Brantley	.10	.05
□	359	Mike Bielecki	.10	.05
□	360	Ken Oberkfell	.10	.05
□	361	Kurt Stillwell	.10	.05
□	362	Brian Holman	.10	.05
□	363	Kevin Seitzer UER (Career triples total does not add up)	.10	.05
□	364	Alvin Davis	.10	.05
□	365	Tom Gordon	.10	.05
□	366	Bobby Bonilla UER (Two steals in 1987, should be 3)	.20	.09
□	367	Carlton Fisk	.40	.18
□	368	Steve Carter UER (Charlotesville)	.10	.05
□	369	Joel Skinner	.10	.05
□	370	John Cangelosi	.10	.05
□	371	Cecil Espy	.10	.05
□	372	Gary Wayne	.10	.05
□	373	Jim Rice	.20	.09
□	374	Mike Dyer	.10	.05
□	375	Joe Carter	.20	.09
□	376	Dwight Smith	.10	.05
□	377	John Wetteland	.40	.18
□	378	Earnie Riles	.10	.05
□	379	Otis Nixon	.10	.05
□	380	Vance Law	.10	.05
□	381	Dave Bergman	.10	.05
□	382	Frank White	.20	.09
□	383	Scott Bradley	.10	.05
□	384	Israel Sanchez UER (Totals don't include '89 stats)	.10	.05
□	385	Gary Pettis	.10	.05
□	386	Donn Pall	.10	.05
□	387	John Smiley	.10	.05
□	388	Tom Candiotti	.10	.05
□	389	Junior Ortiz	.10	.05
□	390	Steve Lyons	.10	.05
□	391	Brian Harper	.10	.05
□	392	Fred Manrique	.10	.05
□	393	Lee Smith	.20	.09
□	394	Jeff Kunkel	.10	.05
□	395	Claudell Washington	.10	.05
□	396	John Tudor	.10	.05
□	397	Terry Kennedy UER (Career totals all wrong)	.10	.05
□	398	Lloyd McClendon	.10	.05
□	399	Craig Lefferts	.10	.05
□	400	Checklist 301-400	.10	.05
□	401	Keith Moreland	.10	.05
□	402	Rich Gedman	.10	.05
□	403	Jeff D. Robinson	.10	.05
□	404	Randy Ready	.10	.05
□	405	Rick Cerone	.10	.05
□	406	Jeff Blauser	.20	.09
□	407	Larry Andersen	.10	.05
□	408	Joe Boever	.10	.05
□	409	Felix Fermin	.10	.05
□	410	Glenn Wilson	.10	.05
□	411	Rex Hudler	.10	.05
□	412	Mark Grant	.10	.05
□	413	Dennis Martinez	.20	.09
□	414	Darrin Jackson	.10	.05
□	415	Mike Aldrete	.10	.05
□	416	Roger McDowell	.10	.05
□	417	Jeff Reardon	.20	.09
□	418	Darren Daulton	.20	.09
□	419	Tim Laudner	.10	.05
□	420	Don Carman	.10	.05
□	421	Lloyd Moseby	.10	.05
□	422	Doug Drabek	.10	.05
□	423	Lenny Harris UER (Walks 2 in '89, should be 20)	.10	.05
□	424	Jose Lind	.10	.05
□	425	Dave Johnson (P)	.10	.05
□	426	Jerry Browne	.10	.05
□	427	Eric Yelding	.10	.05
□	428	Brad Komminsk	.10	.05
□	429	Jody Davis	.10	.05
□	430	Mariano Duncan	.10	.05
□	431	Mark Davis	.10	.05
□	432	Nelson Santovenia	.10	.05
□	433	Bruce Hurst	.10	.05
□	434	Jeff Hamilton	.10	.05
□	435	Chris James	.10	.05
□	436	Mark Guthrie	.10	.05
□	437	Charlie Hayes	.10	.05
□	438	Shane Rawley	.10	.05
□	439	Dickie Thon	.10	.05
□	440	Juan Berenguer	.10	.05
□	441	Kevin Romine	.10	.05
□	442	Bill Landrum	.10	.05
□	443	Todd Frohwirth	.10	.05
□	444	Craig Worthington	.10	.05
□	445	Fernando Valenzuela	.20	.09
□	446	Joey Belle	1.00	.45
□	447	Ed Whited UER (Ashville, should be Asheville)	.10	.05
□	448	Dave Smith	.10	.05
□	449	Dave Clark	.10	.05
□	450	Juan Agosto	.10	.05
□	451	Dave Valle	.10	.05
□	452	Kent Hrbek	.20	.09
□	453	Von Hayes	.10	.05
□	454	Gary Gaetti	.10	.05
□	455	Greg Briley	.10	.05
□	456	Glenn Braggs	.10	.05
□	457	Kirt Manwaring	.10	.05
□	458	Mel Hall	.10	.05
□	459	Brook Jacoby	.10	.05
□	460	Pat Sheridan	.10	.05
□	461	Rob Murphy	.10	.05
□	462	Jimmy Key	.20	.09
□	463	Nick Esasky	.10	.05
□	464	Rob Ducey	.10	.05
□	465	Carlos Quintana UER (International)	.10	.05
□	466	Larry Walker	2.00	.90
□	467	Todd Worrell	.10	.05
□	468	Kevin Gross	.10	.05
□	469	Terry Pendleton	.20	.09
□	470	Dave Martinez	.10	.05
□	471	Gene Larkin	.10	.05
□	472	Len Dykstra UER ('89 and total runs understated by 10)	.20	.09
□	473	Barry Lyons	.10	.05
□	474	Terry Mulholland	.10	.05
□	475	Chip Hale	.10	.05
□	476	Jesse Barfield	.10	.05
□	477	Dan Plesac	.10	.05
□	478A	Scott Garrelts ERR (Photo actually Bill Bathe)	2.00	.90
□	478B	Scott Garrelts COR	.10	.05
□	479	Dave Righetti	.10	.05
□	480	Gus Polidor UER (Wearing 14 on front, but 10 on back)	.10	.05
□	481	Mookie Wilson	.10	.05
□	482	Luis Rivera	.10	.05
□	483	Mike Flanagan	.10	.05
□	484	Dennis Boyd	.10	.05
□	485	John Cerutti	.10	.05
□	486	John Costello	.10	.05
□	487	Pascual Perez	.10	.05
□	488	Tommy Herr	.10	.05
□	489	Tom Foley	.10	.05
□	490	Curt Ford	.10	.05
□	491	Steve Lake	.10	.05
□	492	Tim Teufel	.10	.05
□	493	Randy Bush	.10	.05
□	494	Mike Jackson	.10	.05
□	495	Steve Jeltz	.10	.05
□	496	Paul Gibson	.10	.05
□	497	Steve Balboni	.10	.05
□	498	Bud Black	.10	.05
□	499	Dale Sveum	.10	.05
□	500	Checklist 401-500	.10	.05
□	501	Tim Jones	.10	.05
□	502	Mark Portugal	.10	.05
□	503	Ivan Calderon	.10	.05
□	504	Rick Rhoden	.10	.05
□	505	Willie McGee	.20	.09
□	506	Kirk McCaskill	.10	.05
□	507	Dave LaPoint	.10	.05
□	508	Jay Howell	.10	.05
□	509	Johnny Ray	.10	.05
□	510	Dave Anderson	.10	.05
□	511	Chuck Crim	.10	.05
□	512	Joe Hesketh	.10	.05
□	513	Dennis Eckersley	.20	.09
□	514	Greg Brock	.10	.05
□	515	Tim Burke	.10	.05
□	516	Frank Tanana	.10	.05
□	517	Jay Bell	.20	.09
□	518	Guillermo Hernandez	.10	.05
□	519	Randy Kramer UER	.10	.05

	(Codiroli misspelled as Codoroli)		
520	Charles Hudson	.10	.05
521	Jim Corsi	.10	.05
	(Word "originally" is misspelled on back)		
522	Steve Rosenberg	.10	.05
523	Cris Carpenter	.10	.05
524	Matt Winters	.10	.05
525	Melido Perez	.10	.05
526	Chris Gwynn UER	.10	.05
	(Albequerque)		
527	Bert Blyleven UER	.20	.09
	(Games career total is wrong, should be 644)		
528	Chuck Cary	.10	.05
529	Daryl Boston	.10	.05
530	Dale Mohorcic	.10	.05
531	Geronimo Berroa	.20	.09
532	Edgar Martinez	.40	.18
533	Dale Murphy	.40	.18
534	Jay Buhner	.40	.18
535	John Smoltz UER	.40	.18
	(HEA Stadium)		
536	Andy Van Slyke	.20	.09
537	Mike Henneman	.10	.05
538	Miguel Garcia	.10	.05
539	Frank Williams	.10	.05
540	R.J. Reynolds	.10	.05
541	Shawn Hillegas	.10	.05
542	Walt Weiss	.10	.05
543	Greg Hibbard	.10	.05
544	Nolan Ryan	1.50	.70
545	Todd Zeile	.20	.09
546	Hensley Meulens	.10	.05
547	Tim Belcher	.10	.05
548	Mike Witt	.10	.05
549	Greg Cadaret UER	.10	.05
	(Aquiring, should be Acquiring)		
550	Franklin Stubbs	.10	.05
551	Tony Castillo	.10	.05
552	Jeff M. Robinson	.10	.05
553	Steve Olin	.20	.09
554	Alan Trammell	.30	.14
555	Wade Boggs 4X	.40	.18
	(Bo Jackson in background)		
556	Will Clark	.40	.18
557	Jeff King	.20	.09
558	Mike Fitzgerald	.10	.05
559	Ken Howell	.10	.05
560	Bob Kipper	.10	.05
561	Scott Bankhead	.10	.05
562A	Jeff Innis ERR	2.00	.90
	(Photo actually David West)		
562B	Jeff Innis COR	.10	.05
563	Randy Johnson	.60	.25
564	Wally Whitehurst	.10	.05
565	Gene Harris	.10	.05
566	Norm Charlton	.10	.05
567	Robin Yount UER	.20	.09
	(7602 career hits, should be 2606)		
568	Joe Oliver UER	.10	.05
	(Florida)		
569	Mark Parent	.10	.05
570	John Farrell UER	.10	.05
	(Loss total added wrong)		
571	Tom Glavine	.40	.18
572	Rod Nichols	.10	.05
573	Jack Morris	.20	.09
574	Greg Swindell	.10	.05
575	Steve Searcy	.10	.05
576	Ricky Jordan	.10	.05
577	Matt Williams	.40	.18
578	Mike LaValliere	.10	.05
579	Bryn Smith	.10	.05
580	Bruce Ruffin	.10	.05
581	Randy Myers	.20	.09
582	Rick Wrona	.10	.05
583	Juan Samuel	.10	.05
584	Les Lancaster	.10	.05
585	Jeff Musselman	.10	.05
586	Rob Dibble	.10	.05
587	Eric Show	.10	.05
588	Jesse Orosco	.10	.05
589	Herm Winningham	.10	.05
590	Andy Allanson	.10	.05
591	Dion James	.10	.05
592	Carmelo Martinez	.10	.05
593	Luis Quinones	.10	.05
594	Dennis Rasmussen	.10	.05
595	Rich Yett	.10	.05
596	Bob Walk	.10	.05
597A	Andy McGaffigan ERR	.20	.09
	(Photo actually Rich Thompson)		
597B	Andy McGaffigan COR	.10	.05
598	Billy Hatcher	.10	.05
599	Bob Knepper	.10	.05
	(599 Bob Kneppers)		
600	Checklist 501-600 UER	.10	.05
601	Joey Cora	.40	.18
602	Steve Finley	.40	.18
603	Kal Daniels UER	.10	.05
	(12 hits in '87, should be 123; 335 runs, should be 235)		
604	Gregg Olson	.10	.05
605	Dave Stieb	.10	.05
606	Kenny Rogers	.10	.05
	(Shown catching football)		
607	Zane Smith	.10	.05
608	Bob Geren UER	.10	.05
	(Originally)		
609	Chad Kreuter	.10	.05
610	Mike Smithson	.10	.05
611	Jeff Wetherby	.10	.05
612	Gary Mielke	.10	.05
613	Pete Smith	.10	.05
614	Jack Daugherty UER	.10	.05
	(Born 7/30/60, should be 7/3/60)		
615	Lance McCullers	.10	.05
616	Don Robinson	.10	.05
617	Jose Guzman	.10	.05
618	Steve Bedrosian	.10	.05
619	Jamie Moyer	.10	.05
620	Atlee Hammaker	.10	.05
621	Rick Luecken UER	.10	.05
	(Innings pitched wrong)		
622	Greg W. Harris	.10	.05
623	Pete Harnisch	.10	.05
624	Jerald Clark	.10	.05
625	Jack McDowell UER	.10	.05
	(Career totals for Games and GS don't include 1987 season)		
626	Frank Viola	.10	.05
627	Teddy Higuera	.10	.05
628	Marty Pevey	.10	.05
629	Bill Wegman	.10	.05
630	Eric Plunk	.10	.05
631	Drew Hall	.10	.05
632	Doug Jones	.10	.05
633	Geno Petralli UER	.10	.05
	(Sacramento)		
634	Jose Alvarez	.10	.05
635	Bob Milacki	.10	.05
636	Bobby Witt	.10	.05
637	Trevor Wilson	.10	.05
638	Jeff Russell UER	.10	.05
	(Shutout stats wrong)		
639	Mike Krukow	.10	.05
640	Rick Leach	.10	.05
641	Dave Schmidt	.10	.05
642	Terry Leach	.10	.05
643	Calvin Schiraldi	.10	.05
644	Bob Melvin	.10	.05
645	Jim Abbott	.20	.09
646	Jaime Navarro	.10	.05
647	Mark Langston UER	.10	.05
	(Several errors in stats totals)		
648	Juan Nieves	.10	.05
649	Damaso Garcia	.10	.05
650	Charlie O'Brien	.10	.05
651	Eric King	.10	.05
652	Mike Boddicker	.10	.05
653	Duane Ward	.10	.05
654	Bob Stanley	.10	.05
655	Sandy Alomar Jr.	.40	.18
656	Danny Tartabull UER	.10	.05
	(395 BB, should be 295)		
657	Randy McCament	.10	.05
658	Charlie Leibrandt	.10	.05
659	Dan Quisenberry	.10	.05
660	Paul Assenmacher	.10	.05
661	Walt Terrell	.10	.05
662	Tim Leary	.10	.05
663	Randy Milligan	.10	.05
664	Bo Diaz	.10	.05
665	Mark Lemke UER	.10	.05
	(Richmond misspelled as Richomond)		
666	Jose Gonzalez	.10	.05
667	Chuck Finley UER	.20	.09
	(Born 11/16/62, should be 11/26/62)		
668	Randy Kutcher	.20	.09
669	Dick Schofield	.10	.05
670	Tim Crews	.10	.05
671	John Orton	.10	.05
672	John Orton	.10	.05
673	Eric Hetzel	.10	.05
674	Lance Parrish	.10	.05
675	Ramon Martinez	.30	.14
676	Mark Gubicza	.10	.05
677	Greg Litton	.10	.05
678	Greg Mathews	.10	.05
679	Dave Dravecky	.20	.09
680	Steve Farr	.10	.05
681	Mike Devereaux	.10	.05
682	Ken Griffey Sr.	.10	.05
683A	Mickey Weston ERR	2.00	.90
	(Listed as Jamie on card)		
683B	Mickey Weston COR	.10	.05
	(Technically still an error as birthdate is listed as 3/26/81)		
684	Jack Armstrong	.10	.05
685	Steve Buechele	.10	.05
686	Bryan Harvey	.10	.05
687	Lance Blankenship	.10	.05
688	Dante Bichette	.40	.18
689	Todd Burns	.10	.05
690	Dan Petry	.10	.05
691	Kent Anderson	.10	.05
692	Todd Stottlemyre	.10	.05
693	Wally Joyner UER	.20	.09
	(Several stats errors)		
694	Mike Rochford	.10	.05
695	Floyd Bannister	.10	.05
696	Rick Reuschel	.10	.05
697	Jose DeLeon	.10	.05
698	Jeff Montgomery	.20	.09
699	Kelly Downs	.10	.05
700A	Checklist 601-700	2.00	.90
	(683 Jamie Weston)		
700B	Checklist 601-700	.10	.05
	(683 Mickey Weston)		
701	Jim Gott	.10	.05
702	Rookie Threats	.50	.23
	Delino DeShields Marquis Grissom Larry Walker		
703	Alejandro Pena	.10	.05
704	Willie Randolph	.20	.09
705	Tim Leary	.10	.05
706	Chuck McElroy	.10	.05
707	Gerald Perry	.10	.05
708	Tom Brunansky	.20	.09
709	John Franco	.20	.09
710	Mark Davis	.10	.05
711	David Justice	1.50	.70
712	Storm Davis	.10	.05
713	Scott Ruskin	.10	.05
714	Glenn Braggs	.10	.05
715	Kevin Bearse	.10	.05
716	Jose Nunez	.10	.05
717	Tim Layana	.10	.05
718	Greg Myers	.10	.05
719	Pete O'Brien	.10	.05

☐ 720	John Candelaria	.10	.05
☐ 721	Craig Grebeck	.10	.05
☐ 722	Shawn Boskie	.10	.05
☐ 723	Jim Leyritz	.40	.18
☐ 724	Bill Sampen	.10	.05
☐ 725	Scott Radinsky	.10	.05
☐ 726	Todd Hundley	.75	.35
☐ 727	Scott Hemond	.10	.05
☐ 728	Lenny Webster	.10	.05
☐ 729	Jeff Reardon	.20	.09
☐ 730	Mitch Webster	.10	.05
☐ 731	Brian Bohanon	.10	.05
☐ 732	Rick Parker	.10	.05
☐ 733	Terry Shumpert	.10	.05
☐ 734A	Ryan's 6th No-Hitter (No stripe on front)	2.50	1.10
☐ 734B	Ryan's 6th No-Hitter (stripe added on card front for 300th win)	.75	.35
☐ 735	John Burkett	.10	.05
☐ 736	Derrick May	.20	.09
☐ 737	Carlos Baerga	.50	.23
☐ 738	Greg Smith	.10	.05
☐ 739	Scott Sanderson	.10	.05
☐ 740	Joe Kraemer	.10	.05
☐ 741	Hector Villanueva	.10	.05
☐ 742	Mike Fetters	.10	.05
☐ 743	Mark Gardner	.10	.05
☐ 744	Matt Nokes	.10	.05
☐ 745	Dave Winfield	.40	.18
☐ 746	Delino DeShields	.40	.18
☐ 747	Dann Howitt	.10	.05
☐ 748	Tony Pena	.10	.05
☐ 749	Oil Can Boyd	.10	.05
☐ 750	Mike Benjamin	.10	.05
☐ 751	Alex Cole	.10	.05
☐ 752	Eric Gunderson	.10	.05
☐ 753	Howard Farmer	.10	.05
☐ 754	Joe Carter	.20	.09
☐ 755	Ray Lankford	1.00	.45
☐ 756	Sandy Alomar Jr.	.40	.18
☐ 757	Alex Sanchez	.10	.05
☐ 758	Nick Esasky	.10	.05
☐ 759	Stan Belinda	.10	.05
☐ 760	Jim Presley	.10	.05
☐ 761	Gary DiSarcina	.40	.18
☐ 762	Wayne Edwards	.10	.05
☐ 763	Pat Combs	.10	.05
☐ 764	Mickey Pina	.10	.05
☐ 765	Wilson Alvarez	.50	.23
☐ 766	Dave Parker	.20	.09
☐ 767	Mike Blowers	.40	.18
☐ 768	Tony Phillips	.10	.05
☐ 769	Pascual Perez	.10	.05
☐ 770	Gary Pettis	.10	.05
☐ 771	Fred Lynn	.10	.05
☐ 772	Mel Rojas	.40	.18
☐ 773	David Segui	.10	.05
☐ 774	Gary Carter	.40	.18
☐ 775	Rafael Valdez	.10	.05
☐ 776	Glenallen Hill	.10	.05
☐ 777	Keith Hernandez	.20	.09
☐ 778	Billy Hatcher	.10	.05
☐ 779	Marty Clary	.10	.05
☐ 780	Candy Maldonado	.10	.05
☐ 781	Mike Marshall	.10	.05
☐ 782	Billy Joe Robidoux	.10	.05
☐ 783	Mark Langston	.10	.05
☐ 784	Paul Sorrento	.40	.18
☐ 785	Dave Hollins	.40	.18
☐ 786	Cecil Fielder	.20	.09
☐ 787	Matt Young	.10	.05
☐ 788	Jeff Huson	.10	.05
☐ 789	Lloyd Moseby	.10	.05
☐ 790	Ron Kittle	.10	.05
☐ 791	Hubie Brooks	.10	.05
☐ 792	Craig Lefferts	.10	.05
☐ 793	Kevin Bass	.10	.05
☐ 794	Bryn Smith	.10	.05
☐ 795	Juan Samuel	.10	.05
☐ 796	Sam Horn	.10	.05
☐ 797	Randy Myers	.20	.09
☐ 798	Chris James	.10	.05
☐ 799	Bill Gullickson	.10	.05
☐ 800	Checklist 701-800	.10	.05

1991 Upper Deck

Frank Thomas

This set marked the third year Upper Deck issued a 800-card standard-size set in two separate series of 700 and 100 cards respectively. Cards were distributed in low and high series foil packs and factory sets. The 100-card extended or high-number series was issued by Upper Deck several months after the release of their first series. For the first time in Upper Deck's three-year history, they did not issue a factory Extended set. The basic cards are made on the typical Upper Deck slick, white card stock and features full-color photos on both the front and the back. Subsets include Star Rookies (1-26), Team Cards (28-34, 43-49, 77-82, 95-99) and Top Prospects (50-76). Several other special achievement cards are seeded throughout the set. The team checklist (TC) cards in the set feature an attractive Vernon Wells drawing of a featured player for that particular team. Rookie Cards in this set include Jeff Bagwell, Jeff Conine, Chipper Jones, Eric Karros, Brian McRae, Mike Mussina and Reggie Sanders. A special Michael Jordan card (numbered SP1) was randomly included in packs on a somewhat limited basis. The Hank Aaron hologram card was randomly inserted in the 1991 Upper Deck high number foil packs. Neither card is included in the price of the regular issue set.

	MINT	NRMT
COMPLETE SET (800)	20.00	9.00
COMPLETE LO SET (700)	16.00	7.25
COMPLETE HI SET (100)	4.00	1.80
COMMON CARD (1-800)	.05	.02
MINOR STARS	.10	.05
UNLISTED STARS	.20	.09
COMP.AARON SET (10)	5.00	2.20
COMMON AARON (19-27)	.50	.23
AARON HEADER SP (NNO)	1.00	.45
AARON AUTO/2500 (AU3)	300.00	135.00
AARON: RANDOM INSERTS IN HI SERIES		
COMP.RYAN SET (10)	5.00	2.20
COMMON RYAN (10-18)	.50	.23
RYAN HEADER SP (NNO)	1.00	.45
RYAN AUTO/2500 (AU2)	600.00	275.00
RYAN: RANDOM INSERTS IN LO SERIES		

☐ 1	Star Rookie Checklist	.05	.02
☐ 2	Phil Plantier	.10	.05
☐ 3	D.J. Dozier	.05	.02
☐ 4	Dave Hansen	.05	.02
☐ 5	Maurice Vaughn	.40	.18
☐ 6	Leo Gomez	.05	.02
☐ 7	Scott Aldred	.05	.02
☐ 8	Scott Chiamparino	.05	.02
☐ 9	Lance Dickson	.05	.02
☐ 10	Sean Berry	.10	.05
☐ 11	Bernie Williams	.25	.11
☐ 12	Brian Barnes UER (Photo either not him or in wrong jersey)	.05	.02
☐ 13	Narciso Elvira	.05	.02
☐ 14	Mike Gardiner	.05	.02
☐ 15	Greg Colbrunn	.05	.02
☐ 16	Bernard Gilkey	.10	.05
☐ 17	Mark Lewis	.05	.02
☐ 18	Mickey Morandini	.05	.02
☐ 19	Charles Nagy	.20	.09
☐ 20	Geronimo Pena	.05	.02
☐ 21	Henry Rodriguez	.40	.18
☐ 22	Scott Cooper	.05	.02
☐ 23	Andujar Cedeno UER (Shown batting left, back says right)	.05	.02
☐ 24	Eric Karros	.50	.23
☐ 25	Steve Decker UER (Lewis-Clark State College, not Lewis and Clark)	.05	.02
☐ 26	Kevin Belcher	.05	.02
☐ 27	Jeff Conine	.25	.11
☐ 28	Dave Stewart TC	.05	.02
☐ 29	Carlton Fisk TC	.10	.05
☐ 30	Rafael Palmeiro TC	.10	.05
☐ 31	Chuck Finley TC	.05	.02
☐ 32	Harold Reynolds TC	.05	.02
☐ 33	Bret Saberhagen TC	.05	.02
☐ 34	Gary Gaetti TC	.05	.02
☐ 35	Scott Leius	.05	.02
☐ 36	Neal Heaton	.05	.02
☐ 37	Terry Lee	.05	.02
☐ 38	Gary Redus	.05	.02
☐ 39	Barry Jones	.05	.02
☐ 40	Chuck Knoblauch	.25	.11
☐ 41	Larry Andersen	.05	.02
☐ 42	Darryl Hamilton	.05	.02
☐ 43	Mike Greenwell TC	.05	.02
☐ 44	Kelly Gruber TC	.05	.02
☐ 45	Jack Morris TC	.10	.05
☐ 46	Sandy Alomar Jr. TC	.05	.02
☐ 47	Gregg Olson TC	.05	.02
☐ 48	Dave Parker TC	.05	.02
☐ 49	Roberto Kelly TC	.05	.02
☐ 50	Top Prospect Checklist	.05	.02
☐ 51	Kyle Abbott	.05	.02
☐ 52	Jeff Juden	.05	.02
☐ 53	Todd Van Poppel UER (Born Arlington and attended John Martin HS, should say Hinsdale and James Martin HS)	.05	.02
☐ 54	Steve Karsay	.10	.05
☐ 55	Chipper Jones	4.00	1.80
☐ 56	Chris Johnson UER (Called Tim on back)	.05	.02
☐ 57	John Ericks	.05	.02
☐ 58	Gary Scott	.05	.02
☐ 59	Kiki Jones	.05	.02
☐ 60	Wil Cordero	.05	.02
☐ 61	Royce Clayton	.10	.05
☐ 62	Tim Costo	.05	.02
☐ 63	Roger Salkeld	.05	.02
☐ 64	Brook Fordyce	.05	.02
☐ 65	Mike Mussina	1.25	.55
☐ 66	Dave Staton	.05	.02
☐ 67	Mike Lieberthal	.25	.11
☐ 68	Kurt Miller	.05	.02
☐ 69	Dan Peltier	.05	.02
☐ 70	Greg Blosser	.05	.02
☐ 71	Reggie Sanders	.25	.11
☐ 72	Brent Mayne	.05	.02
☐ 73	Rico Brogna	.10	.05
☐ 74	Willie Banks	.05	.02
☐ 75	Len Brutcher	.05	.02
☐ 76	Pat Kelly	.05	.02
☐ 77	Chris Sabo TC	.05	.02
☐ 78	Ramon Martinez TC	.05	.02

□			
79	Matt Williams TC	.10	.05
80	Roberto Alomar TC	.10	.05
81	Glenn Davis TC	.05	.02
82	Ron Gant TC	.05	.02
83	Cecil Fielder FEAT	.05	.02
84	Orlando Merced	.10	.05
85	Domingo Ramos	.05	.02
86	Tom Bolton	.05	.02
87	Andres Santana	.05	.02
88	John Dopson	.05	.02
89	Kenny Williams	.05	.02
90	Marty Barrett	.05	.02
91	Tom Pagnozzi	.05	.02
92	Carmelo Martinez	.05	.02
93	Bobby Thigpen SAVE	.05	.02
94	Barry Bonds TC	.20	.09
95	Gregg Jefferies TC	.05	.02
96	Tim Wallach TC	.05	.02
97	Len Dykstra TC	.05	.02
98	Pedro Guerrero TC	.05	.02
99	Mark Grace TC	.10	.05
100	Checklist 1-100	.05	.02
101	Kevin Elster	.05	.02
102	Tom Brookens	.05	.02
103	Mackey Sasser	.05	.02
104	Felix Fermin	.05	.02
105	Kevin McReynolds	.05	.02
106	Dave Stieb	.05	.02
107	Jeffrey Leonard	.05	.02
108	Dave Henderson	.05	.02
109	Sid Bream	.05	.02
110	Henry Cotto	.05	.02
111	Shawon Dunston	.05	.02
112	Mariano Duncan	.05	.02
113	Joe Girardi	.05	.02
114	Billy Hatcher	.05	.02
115	Greg Maddux	.60	.25
116	Jerry Browne	.05	.02
117	Juan Samuel	.05	.02
118	Steve Olin	.05	.02
119	Alfredo Griffin	.05	.02
120	Mitch Webster	.05	.02
121	Joel Skinner	.05	.02
122	Frank Viola	.05	.02
123	Cory Snyder	.05	.02
124	Howard Johnson	.05	.02
125	Carlos Baerga	.10	.05
126	Tony Fernandez	.05	.02
127	Dave Stewart	.10	.05
128	Jay Buhner	.20	.09
129	Mike LaValliere	.05	.02
130	Scott Bradley	.05	.02
131	Tony Phillips	.05	.02
132	Ryne Sandberg	.25	.11
133	Paul O'Neill	.05	.02
134	Mark Grace	.20	.09
135	Chris Sabo	.05	.02
136	Ramon Martinez	.10	.05
137	Brook Jacoby	.05	.02
138	Candy Maldonado	.05	.02
139	Mike Scioscia	.05	.02
140	Chris James	.05	.02
141	Craig Worthington	.05	.02
142	Manny Lee	.05	.02
143	Tim Raines	.05	.02
144	Sandy Alomar Jr.	.15	.07
145	John Olerud	.10	.05
146	Ozzie Canseco	.10	.05
	(With Jose)		
147	Pat Borders	.05	.02
148	Harold Reynolds	.05	.02
149	Tom Henke	.05	.02
150	R.J. Reynolds	.05	.02
151	Mike Gallego	.05	.02
152	Bobby Bonilla	.10	.05
153	Terry Steinbach	.05	.02
154	Barry Bonds	.25	.11
155	Jose Canseco	.15	.07
156	Gregg Jefferies	.05	.02
157	Matt Williams	.20	.09
158	Craig Biggio	.20	.09
159	Daryl Boston	.05	.02
160	Ricky Jordan	.05	.02
161	Stan Belinda	.05	.02
162	Ozzie Smith	.25	.11
163	Tom Brunansky	.05	.02
164	Todd Zeile	.10	.05
165	Mike Greenwell	.05	.02
166	Kal Daniels	.05	.02
167	Kent Hrbek	.10	.05
168	Franklin Stubbs	.05	.02
169	Dick Schofield	.05	.02
170	Junior Ortiz	.05	.02
171	Hector Villanueva	.05	.02
172	Dennis Eckersley	.10	.05
173	Mitch Williams	.05	.02
174	Mark McGwire	.40	.18
175	Fernando Valenzuela 3X	.05	.02
176	Gary Carter	.20	.09
177	Dave Magadan	.05	.02
178	Robby Thompson	.05	.02
179	Bob Ojeda	.05	.02
180	Ken Caminiti	.20	.09
181	Don Slaught	.05	.02
182	Luis Rivera	.05	.02
183	Jay Bell	.10	.05
184	Jody Reed	.05	.02
185	Wally Backman	.05	.02
186	Dave Martinez	.05	.02
187	Luis Polonia	.05	.02
188	Shane Mack	.05	.02
189	Spike Owen	.05	.02
190	Scott Bailes	.05	.02
191	John Russell	.05	.02
192	Walt Weiss	.05	.02
193	Jose Oquendo	.05	.02
194	Carney Lansford	.10	.05
195	Jeff Huson	.05	.02
196	Keith Miller	.05	.02
197	Eric Yelding	.05	.02
198	Ron Darling	.05	.02
199	John Kruk	.10	.05
200	Checklist 101-200	.05	.02
201	John Shelby	.05	.02
202	Bob Geren	.05	.02
203	Lance McCullers	.05	.02
204	Alvaro Espinoza	.05	.02
205	Mark Salas	.05	.02
206	Mike Pagliarulo	.05	.02
207	Jose Uribe	.05	.02
208	Jim Deshaies	.05	.02
209	Ron Karkovice	.05	.02
210	Rafael Ramirez	.05	.02
211	Donnie Hill	.05	.02
212	Brian Harper	.05	.02
213	Jack Howell	.05	.02
214	Wes Gardner	.05	.02
215	Tim Burke	.05	.02
216	Doug Jones	.05	.02
217	Hubie Brooks	.05	.02
218	Tom Candiotti	.05	.02
219	Gerald Perry	.05	.02
220	Jose DeLeon	.05	.02
221	Wally Whitehurst	.05	.02
222	Alan Mills	.05	.02
223	Alan Trammell	.15	.07
224	Dwight Gooden	.15	.07
225	Travis Fryman	.20	.09
226	Joe Carter	.10	.05
227	Julio Franco	.05	.02
228	Craig Lefferts	.05	.02
229	Gary Pettis	.05	.02
230	Dennis Rasmussen	.05	.02
231A	Brian Downing ERR	.05	
	(No position on front)		
231B	Brian Downing COR	.15	.07
	(DH on front)		
232	Carlos Quintana	.05	.02
233	Gary Gaetti	.05	.02
234	Mark Langston	.05	.02
235	Tim Wallach	.05	.02
236	Greg Swindell	.05	.02
237	Eddie Murray	.20	.09
238	Jeff Manto	.05	.02
239	Lenny Harris	.05	.02
240	Jesse Orosco	.05	.02
241	Scott Lusader	.05	.02
242	Sid Fernandez	.05	.02
243	Jim Leyritz	.10	.05
244	Cecil Fielder	.20	.09
245	Darryl Strawberry	.05	.02
246	Frank Thomas UER	1.50	.70
	(Comiskey Park) misspelled Comisky)		
247	Kevin Mitchell	.10	.05
248	Lance Johnson	.05	.02
249	Rick Reuschel	.05	.02
250	Mark Portugal	.05	.02
251	Derek Lilliquist	.05	.02
252	Brian Holman	.05	.02
253	Rafael Valdez UER	.05	.02
	(Born 4/17/68, should be 12/17/67)		
254	B.J. Surhoff	.10	.05
255	Tony Gwynn	.50	.23
256	Andy Van Slyke	.10	.05
257	Todd Stottlemyre	.05	.02
258	Jose Lind	.05	.02
259	Greg Myers	.05	.02
260	Jeff Ballard	.05	.02
261	Bobby Thigpen	.05	.02
262	Jimmy Kremers	.05	.02
263	Robin Ventura	.20	.09
264	John Smoltz	.20	.09
265	Sammy Sosa	.25	.11
266	Gary Sheffield	.20	.09
267	Len Dykstra	.10	.05
268	Bill Spiers	.05	.02
269	Charlie Hayes	.05	.02
270	Brett Butler	.10	.05
271	Bip Roberts	.05	.02
272	Rob Deer	.05	.02
273	Fred Lynn	.05	.02
274	Dave Parker	.10	.05
275	Andy Benes	.10	.05
276	Glenallen Hill	.05	.02
277	Steve Howard	.05	.02
278	Doug Drabek	.05	.02
279	Joe Oliver	.05	.02
280	Todd Benzinger	.05	.02
281	Eric King	.05	.02
282	Jim Presley	.05	.02
283	Ken Patterson	.05	.02
284	Jack Daugherty	.05	.02
285	Ivan Calderon	.05	.02
286	Edgar Diaz	.05	.02
287	Kevin Bass	.05	.02
288	Don Carman	.05	.02
289	Greg Brock	.05	.02
290	John Franco	.10	.05
291	Joey Cora	.15	.07
292	Bill Wegman	.05	.02
293	Eric Show	.05	.02
294	Scott Bankhead	.05	.02
295	Garry Templeton	.05	.02
296	Mickey Tettleton	.10	.05
297	Luis Sojo	.05	.02
298	Jose Rijo	.05	.02
299	Dave Johnson	.05	.02
300	Checklist 201-300	.05	.02
301	Mark Grant	.05	.02
302	Pete Harnisch	.05	.02
303	Greg Olson	.05	.02
304	Anthony Telford	.05	.02
305	Lonnie Smith	.05	.02
306	Chris Hoiles	.05	.02
307	Bryn Smith	.05	.02
308	Mike Devereaux	.05	.02
309A	Milt Thompson ERR	.20	.09
	(Under air information has print dot)		
309B	Milt Thompson COR	.05	.02
	(Under air information says 86)		
310	Bob Melvin	.05	.02
311	Luis Salazar	.05	.02
312	Ed Whitson	.05	.02
313	Charlie Hough	.05	.02
314	Dave Clark	.05	.02
315	Eric Gunderson	.05	.02
316	Dan Petry	.05	.02
317	Dante Bichette UER	.20	.09
	(Assists misspelled as assists)		
318	Mike Heath	.05	.02
319	Damon Berryhill	.05	.02
320	Walt Terrell	.05	.02
321	Scott Fletcher	.05	.02

322	Dan Plesac	.05	.02
323	Jack McDowell	.05	.02
324	Paul Molitor	.20	.09
325	Ozzie Guillen	.05	.02
326	Gregg Olson	.05	.02
327	Pedro Guerrero	.05	.02
328	Bob Milacki	.05	.02
329	John Tudor UER	.05	.02
	('90 Cardinals, should be '90 Dodgers)		
330	Steve Finley UER	.20	.09
	(Born 3/12/65, should be 5/12)		
331	Jack Clark	.10	.02
332	Jerome Walton	.05	.02
333	Andy Hawkins	.05	.02
334	Derrick May	.05	.02
335	Roberto Alomar	.20	.09
336	Jack Morris	.10	.02
337	Dave Winfield	.20	.09
338	Steve Searcy	.05	.02
339	Chili Davis	.10	.02
340	Larry Sheets	.05	.02
341	Ted Higuera	.05	.02
342	David Segui	.10	.05
343	Greg Cadaret	.05	.02
344	Robin Yount	.20	.09
345	Nolan Ryan	.75	.35
346	Ray Lankford	.20	.09
347	Cal Ripken	.75	.35
348	Lee Smith	.10	.05
349	Brady Anderson	.20	.09
350	Frank DiPino	.05	.02
351	Hal Morris	.05	.02
352	Deion Sanders	.10	.05
353	Barry Larkin	.15	.07
354	Don Mattingly	.30	.14
355	Eric Davis	.10	.05
356	Jose Offerman	.05	.02
357	Mel Rojas	.20	.09
358	Rudy Seanez	.05	.02
359	Oil Can Boyd	.05	.02
360	Nelson Liriano	.05	.02
361	Ron Gant	.05	.02
362	Howard Farmer	.05	.02
363	David Justice	.25	.11
364	Delino DeShields	.20	.09
365	Steve Avery	.05	.02
366	David Cone	.10	.05
367	Lou Whitaker	.10	.05
368	Von Hayes	.05	.02
369	Frank Tanana	.05	.02
370	Tim Teufel	.05	.02
371	Randy Myers	.05	.02
372	Roberto Kelly	.05	.02
373	Jack Armstrong	.05	.02
374	Kelly Gruber	.05	.02
375	Kevin Maas	.25	.11
376	Randy Johnson	.25	.11
377	David West	.05	.02
378	Brent Knackert	.05	.02
379	Rick Honeycutt	.05	.02
380	Kevin Gross	.05	.02
381	Tom Foley	.05	.02
382	Jeff Blauser	.05	.02
383	Scott Ruskin	.05	.02
384	Andres Thomas	.05	.02
385	Dennis Martinez	.10	.05
386	Mike Henneman	.05	.02
387	Felix Jose	.05	.02
388	Alejandro Pena	.05	.02
389	Chet Lemon	.05	.02
390	Craig Wilson	.05	.02
391	Chuck Crim	.05	.02
392	Mel Hall	.05	.02
393	Mark Knudson	.05	.02
394	Norm Charlton	.05	.02
395	Mike Felder	.05	.02
396	Tim Layana	.05	.02
397	Steve Frey	.05	.02
398	Bill Doran	.05	.02
399	Dion James	.05	.02
400	Checklist 301-400	.05	.02
401	Ron Hassey	.05	.02
402	Don Robinson	.05	.02
403	Gene Nelson	.05	.02
404	Terry Kennedy	.05	.02
405	Todd Burns	.05	.02
406	Roger McDowell	.05	.02
407	Bob Kipper	.05	.02
408	Darren Daulton	.10	.05
409	Chuck Cary	.05	.02
410	Bruce Ruffin	.05	.02
411	Juan Berenguer	.05	.02
412	Gary Ward	.05	.02
413	Al Newman	.05	.02
414	Danny Jackson	.05	.02
415	Greg Gagne	.05	.02
416	Tom Herr	.05	.02
417	Jeff Parrett	.05	.02
418	Jeff Reardon	.10	.05
419	Mark Lemke	.05	.02
420	Charlie O'Brien	.05	.02
421	Willie Randolph	.10	.05
422	Steve Bedrosian	.05	.02
423	Mike Moore	.05	.02
424	Jeff Brantley	.05	.02
425	Bob Welch	.05	.02
426	Terry Mulholland	.05	.02
427	Willie Blair	.05	.02
428	Darrin Fletcher	.05	.02
429	Mike Witt	.05	.02
430	Joe Boever	.05	.02
431	Tom Gordon	.05	.02
432	Pedro Munoz	.20	.09
433	Kevin Seitzer	.05	.02
434	Kevin Tapani	.05	.02
435	Bret Saberhagen	.05	.02
436	Ellis Burks	.10	.05
437	Chuck Finley	.05	.02
438	Mike Boddicker	.05	.02
439	Francisco Cabrera	.05	.02
440	Todd Hundley	.20	.09
441	Kelly Downs	.05	.02
442	Dann Howitt	.05	.02
443	Scott Garrelts	.05	.02
444	Rickey Henderson 3X	.20	.09
445	Will Clark	.20	.09
446	Ben McDonald	.20	.09
447	Dale Murphy	.10	.05
448	Dave Righetti	.05	.02
449	Dickie Thon	.05	.02
450	Ted Power	.05	.02
451	Scott Coolbaugh	.05	.02
452	Dwight Smith	.05	.02
453	Pete Incaviglia	.05	.02
454	Andre Dawson	.20	.09
455	Ruben Sierra	.05	.02
456	Andres Galarraga	.05	.02
457	Alvin Davis	.05	.02
458	Tony Castillo	.05	.02
459	Pete O'Brien	.05	.02
460	Charlie Leibrandt	.05	.02
461	Vince Coleman	.05	.02
462	Steve Sax	.05	.02
463	Omar Olivares	.05	.02
464	Oscar Azocar	.05	.02
465	Joe Magrane	.05	.02
466	Karl Rhodes	.05	.02
467	Benito Santiago	.05	.02
468	Joe Klink	.05	.02
469	Sil Campusano	.05	.02
470	Mark Parent	.05	.02
471	Shawn Boskie UER	.05	.02
	(Depleted misspelled as depleated)		
472	Kevin Brown	.10	.05
473	Rick Sutcliffe	.05	.02
474	Rafael Palmeiro	.20	.09
475	Mike Harkey	.05	.02
476	Jaime Navarro	.05	.02
477	Marquis Grissom UER	.20	.09
	(DeShields misspelled as DeSheilds)		
478	Marty Clary	.05	.02
479	Greg Briley	.05	.02
480	Tom Glavine	.20	.09
481	Lee Guetterman	.05	.02
482	Rex Hudler	.05	.02
483	Dave LaPoint	.05	.02
484	Terry Pendleton	.10	.05
485	Jesse Barfield	.05	.02
486	Jose DeJesus	.05	.02
487	Paul Abbott	.05	.02
488	Ken Howell	.05	.02
489	Greg W. Harris	.05	.02
490	Roy Smith	.05	.02
491	Paul Assenmacher	.05	.02
492	Geno Petralli	.05	.02
493	Steve Wilson	.05	.02
494	Kevin Reimer	.05	.02
495	Bill Long	.05	.02
496	Mike Jackson	.05	.02
497	Oddibe McDowell	.05	.02
498	Bill Swift	.05	.02
499	Jeff Treadway	.05	.02
500	Checklist 401-500	.05	.02
501	Gene Larkin	.05	.02
502	Bob Boone	.10	.05
503	Allan Anderson	.05	.02
504	Luis Aquino	.05	.02
505	Mark Guthrie	.05	.02
506	Joe Orsulak	.05	.02
507	Dana Kiecker	.05	.02
508	Dave Gallagher	.05	.02
509	Greg A. Harris	.05	.02
510	Mark Williamson	.05	.02
511	Casey Candaele	.05	.02
512	Mookie Wilson	.10	.05
513	Dave Smith	.05	.02
514	Chuck Carr	.05	.02
515	Glenn Wilson	.05	.02
516	Mike Fitzgerald	.05	.02
517	Devon White	.05	.02
518	Dave Hollins	.05	.02
519	Mark Eichhorn	.05	.02
520	Otis Nixon	.10	.05
521	Terry Shumpert	.05	.02
522	Scott Erickson	.10	.05
523	Danny Tartabull	.05	.02
524	Orel Hershiser	.10	.05
525	George Brett	.40	.18
526	Greg Vaughn	.05	.02
527	Tim Naehring	.05	.02
528	Curt Schilling	.20	.09
529	Chris Bosio	.05	.02
530	Sam Horn	.05	.02
531	Mike Scott	.05	.02
532	George Bell	.05	.02
533	Eric Anthony	.05	.02
534	Julio Valera	.05	.02
535	Glenn Davis	.05	.02
536	Larry Walker UER	.30	.14
	(Should have comma after Expos in text)		
537	Pat Combs	.05	.02
538	Chris Nabholz	.05	.02
539	Kirk McCaskill	.05	.02
540	Randy Ready	.05	.02
541	Mark Gubicza	.05	.02
542	Rick Aguilera	.10	.05
543	Brian McRae	.20	.09
544	Kirby Puckett	.40	.18
545	Bo Jackson	.15	.07
546	Wade Boggs	.20	.09
547	Tim McIntosh	.05	.02
548	Randy Milligan	.05	.02
549	Dwight Evans	.10	.05
550	Billy Ripken	.05	.02
551	Erik Hanson	.05	.02
552	Lance Parrish	.05	.02
553	Tino Martinez	.20	.09
554	Jim Abbott	.05	.02
555	Ken Griffey Jr. UER	1.50	.70
	(Second most votes for 1991 All-Star Game)		
556	Milt Cuyler	.05	.02
557	Mark Leonard	.05	.02
558	Jay Howell	.05	.02
559	Lloyd Moseby	.05	.02
560	Chris Gwynn	.05	.02
561	Mark Whiten	.05	.02
562	Harold Baines	.10	.05
563	Junior Felix	.05	.02
564	Darren Lewis	.05	.02
565	Fred McGriff	.20	.09
566	Kevin Appier	.20	.09
567	Luis Gonzalez	.20	.09

568	Frank White	.10	.05
569	Juan Agosto	.05	.02
570	Mike Macfarlane	.05	.02
571	Bert Blyleven	.10	.05
572	Ken Griffey Sr.	.50	.23
	Ken Griffey Jr.		
573	Lee Stevens	.05	.02
574	Edgar Martinez	.20	.09
575	Wally Joyner	.10	.05
576	Tim Belcher	.05	.02
577	John Burkett	.05	.02
578	Mike Morgan	.05	.02
579	Paul Gibson	.05	.02
580	Jose Vizcaino	.05	.02
581	Duane Ward	.05	.02
582	Scott Sanderson	.05	.02
583	David Wells	.05	.02
584	Willie McGee	.05	.02
585	John Cerutti	.05	.02
586	Danny Darwin	.05	.02
587	Kurt Stillwell	.05	.02
588	Rich Gedman	.05	.02
589	Mark Davis	.05	.02
590	Bill Gullickson	.05	.02
591	Matt Young	.05	.02
592	Bryan Harvey	.05	.02
593	Omar Vizquel	.20	.09
594	Scott Lewis	.05	.02
595	Dave Valle	.05	.02
596	Tim Crews	.05	.02
597	Mike Bielecki	.05	.02
598	Mike Sharperson	.05	.02
599	Dave Bergman	.05	.02
600	Checklist 501-600	.05	.02
601	Steve Lyons	.05	.02
602	Bruce Hurst	.05	.02
603	Donn Pall	.05	.02
604	Jim Vatcher	.05	.02
605	Dan Pasqua	.05	.02
606	Kenny Rogers	.05	.02
607	Jeff Schulz	.05	.02
608	Brad Arnsberg	.05	.02
609	Willie Wilson	.05	.02
610	Jamie Moyer	.05	.02
611	Ron Oester	.05	.02
612	Dennis Cook	.05	.02
613	Rick Mahler	.05	.02
614	Bill Landrum	.05	.02
615	Scott Scudder	.05	.02
616	Tom Edens	.05	.02
617	1917 Revisited	.10	.05
	(White Sox in vintage uniforms)		
618	Jim Gantner	.05	.02
619	Darrel Akerfelds	.05	.02
620	Ron Robinson	.05	.02
621	Scott Radinsky	.05	.02
622	Pete Smith	.05	.02
623	Melido Perez	.05	.02
624	Jerald Clark	.05	.02
625	Carlos Martinez	.05	.02
626	Wes Chamberlain	.05	.02
627	Bobby Witt	.05	.02
628	Ken Dayley	.05	.02
629	John Barfield	.05	.02
630	Bob Tewksbury	.05	.02
631	Glenn Braggs	.05	.02
632	Jim Neidlinger	.05	.02
633	Tom Browning	.05	.02
634	Kirk Gibson	.10	.05
635	Rob Dibble	.05	.02
636	Rickey Henderson SB	.30	.14
	Lou Brock May 1, 1991 on front)		
636A	Rickey Henderson SB	.20	.09
	Lou Brock no date on card)		
637	Jeff Montgomery	.10	.05
638	Mike Schooler	.05	.02
639	Storm Davis	.05	.02
640	Rich Rodriguez	.05	.02
641	Phil Bradley	.05	.02
642	Kent Mercker	.05	.02
643	Carlton Fisk	.20	.09
644	Mike Bell	.05	.02
645	Alex Fernandez	.10	.05
646	Juan Gonzalez	.75	.35
647	Ken Hill	.10	.05
648	Jeff Russell	.05	.02
649	Chuck Malone	.05	.02
650	Steve Buechele	.05	.02
651	Mike Benjamin	.05	.02
652	Tony Pena	.05	.02
653	Trevor Wilson	.05	.02
654	Alex Cole	.05	.02
655	Roger Clemens	.40	.18
656	Mark McGwire BASH	.20	.09
657	Joe Grahe	.05	.02
658	Jim Eisenreich	.05	.02
659	Dan Gladden	.05	.02
660	Steve Farr	.05	.02
661	Bill Sampen	.05	.02
662	Dave Rohde	.05	.02
663	Mark Gardner	.05	.02
664	Mike Simms	.05	.02
665	Moises Alou	.20	.09
666	Mickey Hatcher	.05	.02
667	Jimmy Key	.10	.05
668	John Wetteland	.20	.09
669	John Smiley	.05	.02
670	Jim Acker	.05	.02
671	Pascual Perez	.05	.02
672	Reggie Harris UER	.05	.02
	(Opportunity misspelled as opportnity)		
673	Matt Nokes	.05	.02
674	Rafael Novoa	.05	.02
675	Hensley Meulens	.05	.02
676	Jeff M. Robinson	.05	.02
677	Ground Breaking	.10	.05
	(New Comiskey Park; Carlton Fisk and Robin Ventura)		
678	Johnny Ray	.05	.02
679	Greg Hibbard	.05	.02
680	Paul Sorrento	.10	.05
681	Mike Marshall	.05	.02
682	Jim Clancy	.05	.02
683	Rob Murphy	.05	.02
684	Dave Schmidt	.05	.02
685	Jeff Gray	.05	.02
686	Mike Hartley	.05	.02
687	Jeff King	.10	.05
688	Stan Javier	.05	.02
689	Bob Walk	.05	.02
690	Jim Gott	.05	.02
691	Mike LaCoss	.05	.02
692	John Farrell	.05	.02
693	Tim Leary	.05	.02
694	Mike Walker	.05	.02
695	Eric Plunk	.05	.02
696	Mike Fetters	.05	.02
697	Wayne Edwards	.05	.02
698	Tim Drummond	.05	.02
699	Willie Fraser	.05	.02
700	Checklist 601-700	.05	.02
701	Mike Heath	.05	.02
702	Rookie Threats	.75	.35
	Luis Gonzalez Karl Rhodes Jeff Bagwell		
703	Jose Mesa	.05	.02
704	Dave Smith	.05	.02
705	Danny Darwin	.05	.02
706	Rafael Belliard	.05	.02
707	Rob Murphy	.05	.02
708	Terry Pendleton	.10	.05
709	Mike Pagliarulo	.05	.02
710	Sid Bream	.05	.02
711	Junior Felix	.05	.02
712	Dante Bichette	.20	.09
713	Kevin Gross	.05	.02
714	Luis Sojo	.05	.02
715	Bob Ojeda	.05	.02
716	Julio Machado	.05	.02
717	Steve Farr	.05	.02
718	Franklin Stubbs	.05	.02
719	Mike Boddicker	.05	.02
720	Willie Randolph	.10	.05
721	Willie McGee	.05	.02
722	Chili Davis	.10	.05
723	Danny Jackson	.05	.02
724	Cory Snyder	.05	.02
725	MVP Lineup	.20	.09
	Andre Dawson George Bell Ryne Sandberg		
726	Rob Deer	.05	.02
727	Rich DeLucia	.05	.02
728	Mike Perez	.05	.02
729	Mickey Tettleton	.10	.05
730	Mike Stanley	.05	.02
731	Gary Gaetti	.05	.02
732	Brett Butler	.10	.05
733	Dave Parker	.10	.05
734	Eddie Zosky	.05	.02
735	Jack Clark	.05	.02
736	Jack Morris	.10	.05
737	Kirk Gibson	.10	.05
738	Steve Bedrosian	.05	.02
739	Candy Maldonado	.05	.02
740	Matt Young	.05	.02
741	Rich Garces	.05	.02
742	George Bell	.05	.02
743	Deion Sanders	.10	.05
744	Bo Jackson	.15	.07
745	Luis Mercedes	.15	.07
746	Reggie Jefferson UER	.15	.07
	(Throwing left on card; back has throws right)		
747	Pete Incaviglia	.05	.02
748	Chris Hammond	.05	.02
749	Mike Stanton	.05	.02
750	Scott Sanderson	.05	.02
751	Paul Faries	.05	.02
752	Al Osuna	.05	.02
753	Steve Chitren	.05	.02
754	Tony Fernandez	.05	.02
755	Jeff Bagwell UER	2.50	1.10
	(Strikeout and walk totals reversed)		
756	Kirk Dressendorfer	.05	.02
757	Glenn Davis	.05	.02
758	Gary Carter	.20	.09
759	Zane Smith	.05	.02
760	Vance Law	.05	.02
761	Denis Boucher	.05	.02
762	Turner Ward	.05	.02
763	Roberto Alomar	.20	.09
764	Albert Belle	.30	.14
765	Joe Carter	.05	.02
766	Pete Schourek	.10	.05
767	Heathcliff Slocumb	.20	.09
768	Vince Coleman	.05	.02
769	Mitch Williams	.05	.02
770	Brian Downing	.05	.02
771	Dana Allison	.05	.02
772	Pete Harnisch	.05	.02
773	Tim Raines	.10	.05
774	Darryl Kile	.20	.09
775	Fred McGriff	.20	.09
776	Dwight Evans	.10	.05
777	Joe Slusarski	.05	.02
778	Dave Righetti	.05	.02
779	Jeff Hamilton	.05	.02
780	Ernest Riles	.05	.02
781	Ken Dayley	.05	.02
782	Eric King	.05	.02
783	Devon White	.05	.02
784	Beau Allred	.05	.02
785	Mike Timlin	.05	.02
786	Ivan Calderon	.05	.02
787	Hubie Brooks	.05	.02
788	Juan Agosto	.05	.02
789	Barry Jones	.05	.02
790	Wally Backman	.05	.02
791	Jim Presley	.05	.02
792	Charlie Hough	.05	.02
793	Larry Andersen	.05	.02
794	Steve Finley	.20	.09
795	Shawn Abner	.05	.02
796	Jeff M. Robinson	.05	.02
797	Joe Bitker	.05	.02
798	Eric Show	.05	.02
799	Bud Black	.05	.02
800	Checklist 701-800	.05	.02
HH1	Hank Aaron Hologram	1.50	.70
SP1	Michael Jordan SP	15.00	6.75

(Shown batting in
White Sox uniform)
☐ SP2 Rickey Henderson.... 1.50   .70
Nolan Ryan
May 1, 1991 Records

1991 Upper Deck
Heroes of Baseball

These standard-size cards were randomly inserted in Upper Deck Baseball Heroes wax packs. On a white card face, the fronts of the first three cards have sepia-toned player photos, with red, gold, and blue border stripes. The player's name appears in a gold border stripe beneath the picture, with the Upper Deck "Heroes of Baseball" logo in the lower right corner. The backs have a similar design to the fronts, except with a career summary and an advertisement for Upper Deck "Heroes of Baseball" games that will be played prior to regularly scheduled Major League games. The fourth card features a color portrait of the three players by noted sports artist Vernon Wells.

	MINT	NRMT
COMPLETE SET (4)	20.00	9.00
COMMON CARD (H1-H4)....	6.00	2.70
RANDOM INSERTS IN HEROES FOIL		

		MINT	NRMT
☐ H1	Harmon Killebrew.....	6.00	2.70
☐ H2	Gaylord Perry	6.00	2.70
☐ H3	Ferguson Jenkins	6.00	2.70
☐ H4	Harmon Killebrew DRAW	6.00	2.70
	Ferguson Jenkins		
	Gaylord Perry		
☐ AU1	Harmon Killebrew AU/3000	60.00	27.00
☐ AU2	Gaylord Perry AU/3000	60.00	27.00
☐ AU3	Ferguson Jenkins AU/3000	60.00	27.00

1991 Upper Deck
Silver Sluggers

The Upper Deck Silver Slugger set features nine players from each league, representing the nine batting positions on the team. The cards were issued one per 1991 Upper Deck jumbo pack. The cards measure the standard size. The fronts have glossy color action player photos, with white borders on three sides and a "Silver Slugger" bat serving as the border on the left side. The player's name appears in a tan stripe

---

below the picture, with the team logo superimposed at the lower right corner. The card back is dominated by another color action photo with career highlights in a horizontally oriented rectangle to the left of the picture. The cards are numbered on the back with an SS prefix.

	MINT	NRMT
COMPLETE SET (18)	15.00	6.75
COMMON CARD (SS1-SS18) ..	.50	.23
ONE PER LO OR HI JUMBO PACK		

		MINT	NRMT
☐ SS1	Julio Franco	.50	.23
☐ SS2	Alan Trammell	1.00	.45
☐ SS3	Rickey Henderson	1.25	.55
☐ SS4	Jose Canseco	1.00	.45
☐ SS5	Barry Bonds	2.00	.90
☐ SS6	Eddie Murray	1.25	.55
☐ SS7	Kelly Gruber	.50	.23
☐ SS8	Ryne Sandberg	2.00	.90
☐ SS9	Darryl Strawberry	.75	.35
☐ SS10	Ellis Burks	.75	.35
☐ SS11	Lance Parrish	.50	.23
☐ SS12	Cecil Fielder	.75	.35
☐ SS13	Matt Williams	1.25	.55
☐ SS14	Dave Parker	.75	.35
☐ SS15	Bobby Bonilla	.75	.35
☐ SS16	Don Robinson...........	.50	.23
☐ SS17	Benito Santiago........	.50	.23
☐ SS18	Barry Larkin	1.00	.45

1991 Upper Deck
Final Edition

The 1991 Upper Deck Final Edition boxed set contains 100 standard-size cards and showcases players who made major contributions during their team's late-season pennant drive. In addition to the late season traded and impact rookie cards (22-78), the set includes two special subsets: Diamond Skills cards (1-21), depicting the best Minor League prospects, and All-Star

---

cards (80-99). Six assorted team logo hologram cards were issued with each set. The basic card fronts feature posed or action color player photos on a white card face, with the upper left corner of the picture cut out to provide space for the Upper Deck logo. The pictures are bordered in green on the left, with the player's name in a tan border below the picture. The cards are numbered on the back with an F suffix. Among the outstanding Rookie Cards in this set are Ryan Klesko, Kenny Lofton, Pedro Martinez, Ivan Rodriguez, Jim Thome, Rondell White, and Dmitri Young.

	MINT	NRMT
COMPLETE SET (100)	5.00	2.20
COMMON CARD (1F-100F) ..	.05	.02
MINOR STARS	.10	.05
UNLISTED STARS	.20	.09

		MINT	NRMT
☐ 1F	Ryan Klesko CL	.20	.09
	Reggie Sanders		
☐ 2F	Pedro Martinez	1.00	.45
☐ 3F	Lance Dickson	.05	.02
☐ 4F	Royce Clayton	.10	.05
☐ 5F	Scott Bryant.............	.05	.02
☐ 6F	Dan Wilson	.25	.11
☐ 7F	Dmitri Young	.25	.11
☐ 8F	Ryan Klesko..............	.75	.35
☐ 9F	Tom Goodwin	.10	.05
☐ 10F	Rondell White	.30	.14
☐ 11F	Reggie Sanders	.15	.07
☐ 12F	Todd Van Poppel.......	.05	.02
☐ 13F	Arthur Rhodes...........	.10	.05
☐ 14F	Eddie Zosky	.05	.02
☐ 15F	Gerald Williams	.05	.02
☐ 16F	Robert Eenhoorn........	.05	.02
☐ 17F	Jim Thome	1.25	.55
☐ 18F	Marc Newfield	.15	.07
☐ 19F	Kerwin Moore	.05	.02
☐ 20F	Jeff McNeely.............	.05	.02
☐ 21F	Frankie Rodriguez	.20	.09
☐ 22F	Andy Mota	.05	.02
☐ 23F	Chris Haney..............	.05	.02
☐ 24F	Kenny Lofton	1.50	.70
☐ 25F	Dave Nilsson	.20	.09
☐ 26F	Derek Bell	.20	.09
☐ 27F	Frank Castillo............	.10	.05
☐ 28F	Candy Maldonado	.05	.02
☐ 29F	Chuck McElroy	.05	.02
☐ 30F	Chito Martinez	.05	.02
☐ 31F	Steve Howe	.05	.02
☐ 32F	Freddie Benavides	.05	.02
☐ 33F	Scott Kamieniecki......	.05	.02
☐ 34F	Denny Neagle	.60	.25
☐ 35F	Mike Humphreys	.05	.02
☐ 36F	Mike Remlinger	.05	.02
☐ 37F	Scott Coolbaugh	.05	.02
☐ 38F	Darren Lewis	.05	.02
☐ 39F	Thomas Howard	.05	.02
☐ 40F	John Candelaria.........	.05	.02
☐ 41F	Todd Benzinger	.05	.02
☐ 42F	Wilson Alvarez	.20	.09
☐ 43F	Patrick Lennon	.05	.02
☐ 44F	Rusty Meacham..........	.05	.02
☐ 45F	Ryan Bowen	.05	.02
☐ 46F	Rick Wilkins..............	.05	.02
☐ 47F	Ed Sprague	.05	.02
☐ 48F	Bob Scanlan	.05	.02
☐ 49F	Tom Candiotti	.05	.02
☐ 50F	Dennis Martinez.........	.05	.02
	(Perfecto)		
☐ 51F	Oil Can Boyd	.05	.02
☐ 52F	Glenallen Hill	.05	.02
☐ 53F	Scott Livingstone.......	.05	.02
☐ 54F	Brian R. Hunter	.05	.02
☐ 55F	Ivan Rodriguez	1.50	.70
☐ 56F	Keith Mitchell............	.05	.02
☐ 57F	Roger McDowell	.05	.02
☐ 58F	Otis Nixon	.10	.05

☐ 59F Juan Bell	.05	.02
☐ 60F Bill Krueger	.05	.02
☐ 61F Chris Donnels	.05	.02
☐ 62F Tommy Greene	.05	.02
☐ 63F Doug Simons	.05	.02
☐ 64F Andy Ashby	.20	.09
☐ 65F Anthony Young	.05	.02
☐ 66F Kevin Morton	.05	.02
☐ 67F Bret Barberie	.05	.02
☐ 68F Scott Servais	.05	.02
☐ 69F Ron Darling	.05	.02
☐ 70F Tim Burke	.05	.02
☐ 71F Vicente Palacios	.05	.02
☐ 72F Gerald Alexander	.05	.02
☐ 73F Reggie Jefferson	.15	.07
☐ 74F Dean Palmer	.10	.05
☐ 75F Mark Whiten	.05	.02
☐ 76F Randy Tomlin	.05	.02
☐ 77F Mark Wohlers	.15	.07
☐ 78F Brook Jacoby	.05	.02
☐ 79F Ken Griffey Jr. CL	.40	.18
Ryne Sandberg		
☐ 80F Jack Morris AS	.05	.02
☐ 81F Sandy Alomar Jr. AS	.10	.05
☐ 82F Cecil Fielder AS	.05	.02
☐ 83F Roberto Alomar AS	.10	.05
☐ 84F Wade Boggs AS	.10	.05
☐ 85F Cal Ripken AS	.40	.18
☐ 86F Rickey Henderson AS	.10	.05
☐ 87F Ken Griffey Jr. AS	.75	.35
☐ 88F Dave Henderson AS	.05	.02
☐ 89F Danny Tartabull AS	.05	.02
☐ 90F Tom Glavine AS	.10	.05
☐ 91F Benito Santiago AS	.05	.02
☐ 92F Will Clark AS	.10	.05
☐ 93F Ryne Sandberg AS	.20	.09
☐ 94F Chris Sabo AS	.05	.02
☐ 95F Ozzie Smith AS	.20	.09
☐ 96F Ivan Calderon AS	.05	.02
☐ 97F Tony Gwynn AS	.25	.11
☐ 98F Andre Dawson AS	.10	.05
☐ 99F Bobby Bonilla AS	.05	.02
☐ 100F Checklist 1-100	.05	.02

1992 Upper Deck

The 1992 Upper Deck set contains two standard-size cards issued in two separate series of 700 and 100 cards respectively. The cards were distributed in low and high series foils packs in addition to factory sets. Factory sets feature a unique gold-foil hologram on the card backs in contrast to the silver hologram on foil pack cards). The basic issue card fronts features shadow-bordered action color player photos on a white card face. The player's name appears above the photo, with the team name superimposed at the lower right corner. Special subsets included in the set are Star Rookies (1-27), Team Checklists (29-40/86-99), with player portraits by Vernon Wells; Top Prospects (52-77); Bloodlines (79-85), Diamond Skills (640-650/711-721) and Diamond Debuts (771-780). Rookie Cards in the set include Shawn Green, Joey Hamilton, Brian Jordan and Manny Ramirez. A special card picturing Tom Selleck and Frank Thomas, commemorating the forgettable movie "Mr. Baseball," was randomly inserted into high series packs. A standard-size Ted Williams hologram card was randomly inserted into low series packs. By mailing in 15 low series foil wrappers, a completed order form, and a handling fee, the collector could receive an 8 1/2" by 11" numbered, black and white lithograph picturing Ted Williams in his batting swing.

	MINT	NRMT
COMPLETE SET (800)	15.00	6.75
COMP.FACT.SET (800)	20.00	9.00
COMPLETE LO SET (700)	12.00	5.50
COMPLETE HI SET (100)	3.00	1.35
COMMON CARD (1-800)	.05	.02
MINOR STARS	.10	.05
UNLISTED STARS	.20	.09
SUBSET CARDS HALF VALUE OF BASE CARDS		
COMP.BEN./MORG.SET (10) 10.00		4.50
COMMON BEN./MORG. (37-45) 1.00		.45
BENCH/MORG.HDR SP (NNO) 2.50		1.10
BENCH/MORGAN AU2500 150.00		70.00
BENCH/MORG: RANDOM INS.IN HI PACKS		
COMP.COLLEGE POY SET (3) 2.00		.90
COLL.POY: RANDOM INSERTS IN HI PACKS		
COMP.T.WILLIAMS SET (10) 6.00		2.70
COMMON T.WILLIAMS (28-36)		.23
T.WILLIAMS HDR SP (NNO) 2.00		.90
T.WILLIAMS AU2500 500.00		220.00
T.WILLIAMS: RANDOM INSERTS IN LO PACKS		

☐ 1 Ryan Klesko CL	.40	.18
Jim Thome		
☐ 2 Royce Clayton SR	.05	.02
☐ 3 Brian Jordan SR	.25	.11
☐ 4 Dave Fleming SR	.05	.02
☐ 5 Jim Thome SR	.60	.25
☐ 6 Jeff Juden SR	.05	.02
☐ 7 Roberto Hernandez SR	.20	.09
☐ 8 Kyle Abbott SR	.05	.02
☐ 9 Chris George SR	.05	.02
☐ 10 Rob Maurer SR	.05	.02
☐ 11 Donald Harris SR	.05	.02
☐ 12 Ted Wood SR	.05	.02
☐ 13 Patrick Lennon SR	.05	.02
☐ 14 Willie Banks SR	.05	.02
☐ 15 Roger Salkeld SR UER	.05	.02
(Bill was his grandfather, not his father)		
☐ 16 Wil Cordero SR	.05	.02
☐ 17 Arthur Rhodes SR	.05	.02
☐ 18 Pedro Martinez SR	.40	.18
☐ 19 Andy Ashby SR	.05	.02
☐ 20 Tom Goodwin SR	.05	.02
☐ 21 Braulio Castillo SR	.05	.02
☐ 22 Todd Van Poppel SR	.05	.02
☐ 23 Brian Williams SR	.05	.02
☐ 24 Ryan Klesko SR	.40	.18
☐ 25 Kenny Lofton SR	.75	.35
☐ 26 Derek Bell SR	.10	.05
☐ 27 Reggie Sanders SR	.10	.05
☐ 28 Dave Winfield's 400th	.10	.05
☐ 29 David Justice TC	.10	.05
☐ 30 Rob Dibble TC	.05	.02
☐ 31 Craig Biggio TC	.10	.05
☐ 32 Eddie Murray TC	.05	.02
☐ 33 Fred McGriff TC	.10	.05
☐ 34 Willie McGee TC	.05	.02
☐ 35 Shawon Dunston TC	.05	.02
☐ 36 Delino DeShields TC	.05	.02

☐ 37 Howard Johnson TC	.05	.02
☐ 38 John Kruk TC	.05	.02
☐ 39 Doug Drabek TC	.05	.02
☐ 40 Todd Zeile TC	.05	.02
☐ 41 Steve Avery	.05	.02
Playoff Perfection		
☐ 42 Jeremy Hernandez	.05	.02
☐ 43 Doug Henry	.05	.02
☐ 44 Chris Donnels	.05	.02
☐ 45 Mo Sanford	.05	.02
☐ 46 Scott Kamieniecki	.05	.02
☐ 47 Mark Lemke	.05	.02
☐ 48 Steve Farr	.05	.02
☐ 49 Francisco Oliveras	.05	.02
☐ 50 Ced Landrum	.05	.02
☐ 51 Rondell White CL	.20	.09
Mark Newfield		
☐ 52 Eduardo Perez TP	.05	.02
☐ 53 Tom Nevers TP	.05	.02
☐ 54 David Zancanaro TP	.05	.02
☐ 55 Shawn Green TP	.25	.11
☐ 56 Mark Wohlers TP	.10	.05
☐ 57 Dave Nilsson TP	.10	.05
☐ 58 Dmitri Young TP	.20	.09
☐ 59 Ryan Hawblitzel TP	.05	.02
☐ 60 Raul Mondesi TP	.40	.18
☐ 61 Rondell White TP	.20	.09
☐ 62 Steve Hosey TP	.05	.02
☐ 63 Manny Ramirez TP	1.25	.55
☐ 64 Marc Newfield TP	.15	.07
☐ 65 Jeromy Burnitz TP	.05	.02
☐ 66 Mark Smith TP	.05	.02
☐ 67 Joey Hamilton TP	.40	.18
☐ 68 Tyler Green TP	.05	.02
☐ 69 Jon Farrell TP	.05	.02
☐ 70 Kurt Miller TP	.05	.02
☐ 71 Jeff Plympton TP	.05	.02
☐ 72 Dan Wilson TP	.10	.05
☐ 73 Joe Vitiello TP	.05	.02
☐ 74 Rico Brogna TP	.10	.05
☐ 75 David McCarty TP	.05	.02
☐ 76 Bob Wickman TP	.05	.02
☐ 77 Carlos Rodriguez TP	.05	.02
☐ 78 Jim Abbott	.05	.02
Stay in School		
☐ 79 Ramon Martinez	.20	.09
Pedro Martinez		
☐ 80 Kevin Mitchell	.05	.02
Keith Mitchell		
☐ 81 Sandy Alomar Jr.	.20	.09
Roberto Alomar		
☐ 82 Cal Ripken	.50	.23
Billy Ripken		
☐ 83 Tony Gwynn	.20	.09
Chris Gwynn		
☐ 84 Dwight Gooden	.15	.07
Gary Sheffield		
☐ 85 Ken Griffey Sr.	.60	.25
Ken Griffey Jr.		
Craig Griffey		
☐ 86 Jim Abbott TC	.05	.02
☐ 87 Frank Thomas TC	.60	.25
☐ 88 Danny Tartabull TC	.05	.02
☐ 89 Scott Erickson TC	.05	.02
☐ 90 Rickey Henderson TC	.10	.05
☐ 91 Edgar Martinez TC	.05	.02
☐ 92 Nolan Ryan TC	.40	.18
☐ 93 Ben McDonald TC	.05	.02
☐ 94 Ellis Burks TC	.05	.02
☐ 95 Greg Swindell TC	.05	.02
☐ 96 Cecil Fielder TC	.05	.02
☐ 97 Greg Vaughn TC	.05	.02
☐ 98 Kevin Maas TC	.05	.02
☐ 99 Dave Stieb TC	.05	.02
☐ 100 Checklist 1-100	.05	.02
☐ 101 Joe Oliver	.05	.02
☐ 102 Hector Villanueva	.05	.02
☐ 103 Ed Whitson	.05	.02
☐ 104 Danny Jackson	.05	.02
☐ 105 Chris Hammond	.05	.02
☐ 106 Ricky Jordan	.05	.02
☐ 107 Kevin Bass	.05	.02
☐ 108 Darrin Fletcher	.05	.02
☐ 109 Junior Ortiz	.05	.02
☐ 110 Tom Bolton	.05	.02
☐ 111 Jeff King	.10	.05

112	Dave Magadan	.05	.02
113	Mike LaValliere	.05	.02
114	Hubie Brooks	.05	.02
115	Jay Bell	.10	.05
116	David Wells	.05	.02
117	Jim Leyritz	.05	.02
118	Manuel Lee	.05	.02
119	Alvaro Espinoza	.05	.02
120	B.J. Surhoff	.10	.05
121	Hal Morris	.05	.02
122	Shawon Dawson	.05	.02
123	Chris Sabo	.05	.02
124	Andre Dawson	.15	.07
125	Eric Davis	.10	.05
126	Chili Davis	.10	.05
127	Dale Murphy	.20	.09
128	Kirk McCaskill	.05	.02
129	Terry Mulholland	.05	.02
130	Rick Aguilera	.05	.02
131	Vince Coleman	.05	.02
132	Andy Van Slyke	.10	.05
133	Gregg Jefferies	.05	.02
134	Barry Bonds	.25	.11
135	Dwight Gooden	.10	.05
136	Dave Stieb	.05	.02
137	Albert Belle	.25	.11
138	Teddy Higuera	.05	.02
139	Jesse Barfield	.05	.02
140	Pat Borders	.05	.02
141	Bip Roberts	.05	.02
142	Rob Dibble	.05	.02
143	Mark Grace	.15	.07
144	Barry Larkin	.15	.07
145	Ryne Sandberg	.25	.11
146	Scott Erickson	.10	.05
147	Luis Polonia	.05	.02
148	John Burkett	.05	.02
149	Luis Sojo	.05	.02
150	Dickie Thon	.05	.02
151	Walt Weiss	.05	.02
152	Mike Scioscia	.05	.02
153	Mark McGwire	.40	.18
154	Matt Williams	.15	.07
155	Rickey Henderson	.15	.07
156	Sandy Alomar Jr.	.10	.05
157	Brian McRae	.10	.05
158	Harold Baines	.10	.05
159	Kevin Appier	.05	.02
160	Felix Fermin	.05	.02
161	Leo Gomez	.15	.07
162	Craig Biggio	.15	.07
163	Ben McDonald	.05	.02
164	Randy Johnson	.20	.09
165	Cal Ripken	.75	.35
166	Frank Thomas	1.00	.45
167	Delino DeShields	.05	.02
168	Greg Gagne	.05	.02
169	Ron Karkovice	.05	.02
170	Charlie Leibrandt	.05	.02
171	Dave Righetti	.05	.02
172	Dave Henderson	.05	.02
173	Steve Decker	.05	.02
174	Darryl Strawberry	.10	.05
175	Will Clark	.25	.07
176	Ruben Sierra	.25	.11
177	Ozzie Smith	.25	.11
178	Charles Nagy	.10	.05
179	Gary Pettis	.05	.02
180	Kirk Gibson	.10	.05
181	Randy Milligan	.05	.02
182	Dave Valle	.05	.02
183	Chris Hoiles	.10	.05
184	Tony Phillips	.05	.02
185	Brady Anderson	.15	.07
186	Scott Fletcher	.05	.02
187	Gene Larkin	.05	.02
188	Lance Johnson	.05	.02
189	Greg Olson	.05	.02
190	Melido Perez	.05	.02
191	Lenny Harris	.05	.02
192	Terry Kennedy	.05	.02
193	Mike Gallego	.05	.02
194	Willie McGee	.05	.02
195	Juan Samuel	.05	.02
196	Jeff Huson	.10	.05
197	Alex Cole	.05	.02
198	Ron Robinson	.05	.02
199	Joel Skinner	.05	.02
200	Checklist 101-200	.05	.02
201	Kevin Reimer	.05	.02
202	Stan Belinda	.05	.02
203	Pat Tabler	.05	.02
204	Jose Guzman	.05	.02
205	Jose Lind	.05	.02
206	Spike Owen	.05	.02
207	Joe Orsulak	.05	.02
208	Charlie Hayes	.05	.02
209	Mike Devereaux	.05	.02
210	Mike Fitzgerald	.05	.02
211	Willie Randolph	.10	.05
212	Rod Nichols	.05	.02
213	Mike Boddicker	.05	.02
214	Bill Spiers	.05	.02
215	Steve Olin	.05	.02
216	David Howard	.05	.02
217	Gary Varsho	.05	.02
218	Mike Harkey	.05	.02
219	Luis Aquino	.05	.02
220	Chuck McElroy	.05	.02
221	Doug Drabek	.05	.02
222	Dave Winfield	.20	.09
223	Rafael Palmeiro	.15	.07
224	Joe Carter	.10	.05
225	Bobby Bonilla	.10	.05
226	Ivan Calderon	.05	.02
227	Gregg Olson	.05	.02
228	Tim Wallach	.05	.02
229	Terry Pendleton	.10	.05
230	Gilberto Reyes	.05	.02
231	Carlos Baerga	.20	.09
232	Greg Vaughn	.05	.02
233	Bret Saberhagen	.05	.02
234	Gary Sheffield	.20	.09
235	Mark Lewis	.05	.02
236	George Bell	.05	.02
237	Danny Tartabull	.05	.02
238	Willie Wilson	.05	.02
239	Doug Dascenzo	.05	.02
240	Bill Pecota	.05	.02
241	Julio Franco	.05	.02
242	Ed Sprague	.05	.02
243	Juan Gonzalez	.60	.25
244	Chuck Finley	.05	.02
245	Ivan Rodriguez	.40	.18
246	Len Dykstra	.10	.05
247	Deion Sanders	.10	.05
248	Dwight Evans	.10	.05
249	Larry Walker	.20	.09
250	Billy Ripken	.05	.02
251	Mickey Tettleton	.05	.02
252	Tony Pena	.05	.02
253	Benito Santiago	.05	.02
254	Kirby Puckett	.40	.18
255	Cecil Fielder	.10	.05
256	Howard Johnson	.05	.02
257	Andujar Cedeno	.05	.02
258	Jose Rijo	.05	.02
259	Al Osuna	.05	.02
260	Todd Hundley	.05	.02
261	Orel Hershiser	.10	.05
262	Ray Lankford	.20	.09
263	Robin Ventura	.10	.05
264	Felix Jose	.05	.02
265	Eddie Murray	.20	.09
266	Kevin Mitchell	.05	.02
267	Gary Carter	.20	.09
268	Mike Benjamin	.05	.02
269	Dick Schofield	.05	.02
270	Jose Uribe	.05	.02
271	Pete Incaviglia	.05	.02
272	Tony Fernandez	.05	.02
273	Alan Trammell	.15	.07
274	Tony Gwynn	.50	.23
275	Mike Greenwell	.05	.02
276	Jeff Bagwell	.60	.25
277	Frank Viola	.05	.02
278	Randy Myers	.05	.02
279	Ken Caminiti	.15	.07
280	Bill Doran	.05	.02
281	Dan Pasqua	.05	.02
282	Alfredo Griffin	.05	.02
283	Jose Oquendo	.05	.02
284	Kal Daniels	.05	.02
285	Bobby Thigpen	.05	.02
286	Robby Thompson	.05	.02
287	Mark Eichhorn	.05	.02
288	Mike Felder	.05	.02
289	Dave Gallagher	.05	.02
290	Dave Anderson	.05	.02
291	Mel Hall	.05	.02
292	Jerald Clark	.05	.02
293	Al Newman	.05	.02
294	Rob Deer	.05	.02
295	Matt Nokes	.05	.02
296	Jack Armstrong	.05	.02
297	Jim Deshaies	.05	.02
298	Jeff Innis	.05	.02
299	Jeff Reed	.05	.02
300	Checklist 201-300	.05	.02
301	Lonnie Smith	.05	.02
302	Jimmy Key	.10	.05
303	Junior Felix	.05	.02
304	Mike Heath	.05	.02
305	Mark Langston	.05	.02
306	Greg W. Harris	.05	.02
307	Brett Butler	.10	.05
308	Luis Rivera	.05	.02
309	Bruce Ruffin	.05	.02
310	Paul Faries	.05	.02
311	Terry Leach	.05	.02
312	Scott Brosius	.05	.02
313	Scott Leius	.05	.02
314	Harold Reynolds	.05	.02
315	Jack Morris	.10	.05
316	David Segui	.05	.02
317	Bill Gullickson	.05	.02
318	Todd Frohwirth	.05	.02
319	Mark Leiter	.05	.02
320	Jeff M. Robinson	.05	.02
321	Gary Gaetti	.05	.02
322	John Smoltz	.15	.07
323	Andy Benes	.10	.05
324	Kelly Gruber	.05	.02
325	Jim Abbott	.15	.07
326	John Kruk	.10	.05
327	Kevin Seitzer	.05	.02
328	Darrin Jackson	.05	.02
329	Kurt Stillwell	.05	.02
330	Mike Maddux	.05	.02
331	Dennis Eckersley	.10	.05
332	Dan Gladden	.05	.02
333	Jose Canseco	.25	.07
334	Kent Hrbek	.10	.05
335	Ken Griffey Sr.	.05	.02
336	Greg Swindell	.05	.02
337	Trevor Wilson	.05	.02
338	Sam Horn	.05	.02
339	Mike Henneman	.05	.02
340	Jerry Browne	.05	.02
341	Glenn Braggs	.05	.02
342	Tom Glavine	.15	.07
343	Wally Joyner	.10	.05
344	Fred McGriff	.15	.07
345	Ron Gant	.10	.05
346	Ramon Martinez	.10	.05
347	Wes Chamberlain	.05	.02
348	Terry Shumpert	.05	.02
349	Tim Teufel	.05	.02
350	Wally Backman	.05	.02
351	Joe Girardi	.05	.02
352	Devon White	.05	.02
353	Greg Maddux	.60	.25
354	Ryan Bowen	.05	.02
355	Roberto Alomar	.20	.09
356	Don Mattingly	.30	.14
357	Pedro Guerrero	.05	.02
358	Steve Sax	.05	.02
359	Joey Cora	.05	.02
360	Jim Gantner	.05	.02
361	Brian Barnes	.05	.02
362	Kevin McReynolds	.05	.02
363	Bret Barberie	.05	.02
364	David Cone	.10	.05
365	Dennis Martinez	.10	.05
366	Brian Hunter	.05	.02
367	Edgar Martinez	.15	.07

(Shows Jose Canseco sliding into second)

Card	Player	Hi	Lo
368	Steve Finley	.10	.05
369	Greg Briley	.05	.02
370	Jeff Blauser	.05	.02
371	Todd Stottlemyre	.05	.02
372	Luis Gonzalez	.05	.02
373	Rick Wilkins	.05	.02
374	Darryl Kile	.10	.05
375	John Olerud	.10	.05
376	Lee Smith	.10	.05
377	Kevin Maas	.05	.02
378	Dante Bichette	.15	.07
379	Tom Pagnozzi	.05	.02
380	Mike Flanagan	.05	.02
381	Charlie O'Brien	.05	.02
382	Dave Martinez	.05	.02
383	Keith Miller	.05	.02
384	Scott Ruskin	.05	.02
385	Kevin Elster	.05	.02
386	Alvin Davis	.05	.02
387	Casey Candaele	.05	.02
388	Pete O'Brien	.05	.02
389	Jeff Treadway	.05	.02
390	Scott Bradley	.05	.02
391	Mookie Wilson	.05	.02
392	Jimmy Jones	.05	.02
393	Candy Maldonado	.05	.02
394	Eric Yelding	.05	.02
395	Tom Henke	.05	.02
396	Franklin Stubbs	.05	.02
397	Milt Thompson	.05	.02
398	Mark Carreon	.05	.02
399	Randy Velarde	.05	.02
400	Checklist 301-400	.05	.02
401	Omar Vizquel	.10	.05
402	Joe Boever	.05	.02
403	Bill Krueger	.05	.02
404	Jody Reed	.05	.02
405	Mike Schooler	.05	.02
406	Jason Grimsley	.05	.02
407	Greg Myers	.05	.02
408	Randy Ready	.05	.02
409	Mike Timlin	.05	.02
410	Mitch Williams	.05	.02
411	Garry Templeton	.05	.02
412	Greg Cadaret	.05	.02
413	Donnie Hill	.05	.02
414	Wally Whitehurst	.05	.02
415	Scott Sanderson	.05	.02
416	Thomas Howard	.05	.02
417	Neal Heaton	.05	.02
418	Charlie Hough	.05	.02
419	Jack Howell	.05	.02
420	Greg Hibbard	.05	.02
421	Carlos Quintana	.05	.02
422	Kim Batiste	.05	.02
423	Paul Molitor	.05	.02
424	Ken Griffey Jr.	1.25	.55
425	Phil Plantier	.15	.07
426	Denny Neagle	.15	.07
427	Von Hayes	.05	.02
428	Shane Mack	.05	.02
429	Darren Daulton	.10	.05
430	Dwayne Henry	.05	.02
431	Lance Parrish	.05	.02
432	Mike Humphreys	.05	.02
433	Tim Burke	.05	.02
434	Bryan Harvey	.05	.02
435	Pat Kelly	.05	.02
436	Ozzie Guillen	.05	.02
437	Bruce Hurst	.05	.02
438	Sammy Sosa	.20	.09
439	Dennis Rasmussen	.05	.02
440	Ken Patterson	.05	.02
441	Jay Buhner	.15	.07
442	Pat Combs	.05	.02
443	Wade Boggs	.20	.09
444	George Brett	.40	.18
445	Mo Vaughn	.30	.14
446	Chuck Knoblauch	.20	.09
447	Tom Candiotti	.05	.02
448	Mark Portugal	.05	.02
449	Mickey Morandini	.05	.02
450	Duane Ward	.05	.02
451	Otis Nixon	.10	.05
452	Bob Welch	.05	.02
453	Rusty Meacham	.05	.02
454	Keith Mitchell	.05	.02
455	Marquis Grissom	.10	.02
456	Robin Yount	.15	.07
457	Harvey Pulliam	.05	.02
458	Jose DeLeon	.05	.02
459	Mark Gubicza	.05	.02
460	Darryl Hamilton	.05	.02
461	Tom Browning	.05	.02
462	Monty Fariss	.05	.02
463	Jerome Walton	.05	.02
464	Paul O'Neill	.10	.05
465	Dean Palmer	.05	.02
466	Travis Fryman	.10	.05
467	John Smiley	.05	.02
468	Lloyd Moseby	.05	.02
469	John Wehner	.05	.02
470	Skeeter Barnes	.05	.02
471	Steve Chitren	.05	.02
472	Kent Mercker	.05	.02
473	Terry Steinbach	.10	.05
474	Andres Galarraga	.20	.09
475	Steve Avery	.05	.02
476	Tom Gordon	.05	.02
477	Cal Eldred	.05	.02
478	Omar Olivares	.05	.02
479	Julio Machado	.05	.02
480	Bob Milacki	.05	.02
481	Les Lancaster	.05	.02
482	John Candelaria	.05	.02
483	Brian Downing	.05	.02
484	Roger McDowell	.05	.02
485	Scott Scudder	.05	.02
486	Zane Smith	.05	.02
487	John Cerutti	.05	.02
488	Steve Buechele	.05	.02
489	Paul Gibson	.05	.02
490	Curtis Wilkerson	.05	.02
491	Marvin Freeman	.05	.02
492	Tom Foley	.05	.02
493	Juan Berenguer	.05	.02
494	Ernest Riles	.05	.02
495	Sid Bream	.05	.02
496	Chuck Crim	.05	.02
497	Mike Macfarlane	.05	.02
498	Dale Sveum	.05	.02
499	Storm Davis	.05	.02
500	Checklist 401-500	.05	.02
501	Jeff Reardon	.10	.05
502	Shawn Abner	.05	.02
503	Tony Fossas	.05	.02
504	Cory Snyder	.05	.02
505	Matt Young	.05	.02
506	Allan Anderson	.05	.02
507	Mark Lee	.05	.02
508	Gene Nelson	.05	.02
509	Mike Pagliarulo	.05	.02
510	Rafael Belliard	.05	.02
511	Jay Howell	.05	.02
512	Bob Tewksbury	.05	.02
513	Mike Morgan	.05	.02
514	John Franco	.10	.05
515	Kevin Gross	.05	.02
516	Lou Whitaker	.10	.05
517	Orlando Merced	.05	.02
518	Todd Benzinger	.05	.02
519	Gary Redus	.05	.02
520	Walt Terrell	.05	.02
521	Jack Clark	.10	.05
522	Dave Parker	.10	.05
523	Tim Naehring	.10	.05
524	Mark Whiten	.05	.02
525	Ellis Burks	.05	.02
526	Frank Castillo	.05	.02
527	Brian Harper	.05	.02
528	Brook Jacoby	.05	.02
529	Rick Sutcliffe	.05	.02
530	Joe Klink	.05	.02
531	Terry Bross	.05	.02
532	Jose Offerman	.05	.02
533	Todd Zeile	.05	.02
534	Eric Karros	.15	.07
535	Anthony Young	.05	.02
536	Milt Cuyler	.05	.02
537	Randy Tomlin	.05	.02
538	Scott Livingstone	.05	.02
539	Jim Eisenreich	.05	.02
540	Don Slaught	.05	.02
541	Scott Cooper	.05	.02
542	Joe Grahe	.05	.02
543	Tom Brunansky	.05	.02
544	Eddie Zosky	.05	.02
545	Roger Clemens	.40	.18
546	David Justice	.20	.09
547	Dave Stewart	.10	.05
548	David West	.05	.02
549	Dave Smith	.05	.02
550	Dan Plesac	.05	.02
551	Alex Fernandez	.10	.05
552	Bernard Gilkey	.10	.05
553	Jack McDowell	.05	.02
554	Tino Martinez	.20	.09
555	Bo Jackson	.10	.05
556	Bernie Williams	.20	.09
557	Mark Gardner	.05	.02
558	Glenallen Hill	.05	.02
559	Oil Can Boyd	.05	.02
560	Chris James	.05	.02
561	Scott Servais	.05	.02
562	Rey Sanchez	.05	.02
563	Paul McClellan	.05	.02
564	Andy Mota	.05	.02
565	Darren Lewis	.05	.02
566	Jose Melendez	.05	.02
567	Tommy Greene	.05	.02
568	Rich Rodriguez	.05	.02
569	Heathcliff Slocumb	.05	.02
570	Joe Hesketh	.05	.02
571	Carlton Fisk	.20	.09
572	Erik Hanson	.05	.02
573	Wilson Alvarez	.10	.05
574	Rheal Cormier	.05	.02
575	Tim Raines	.10	.05
576	Bobby Witt	.05	.02
577	Roberto Kelly	.05	.02
578	Kevin Brown	.10	.05
579	Chris Nabholz	.05	.02
580	Jesse Orosco	.05	.02
581	Jeff Brantley	.05	.02
582	Rafael Ramirez	.05	.02
583	Kelly Downs	.05	.02
584	Mike Simms	.05	.02
585	Mike Remlinger	.05	.02
586	Dave Hollins	.05	.02
587	Larry Andersen	.05	.02
588	Mike Gardiner	.05	.02
589	Craig Lefferts	.05	.02
590	Paul Assenmacher	.05	.02
591	Bryn Smith	.05	.02
592	Donn Pall	.05	.02
593	Mike Greenwell	.05	.02
594	Scott Radinsky	.05	.02
595	Brian Holman	.05	.02
596	Geronimo Pena	.05	.02
597	Mike Jeffcoat	.05	.02
598	Carlos Martinez	.05	.02
599	Geno Petralli	.05	.02
600	Checklist 501-600	.05	.02
601	Jerry Don Gleaton	.05	.02
602	Adam Peterson	.05	.02
603	Craig Grebeck	.05	.02
604	Mark Guthrie	.05	.02
605	Frank Tanana	.05	.02
606	Hensley Meulens	.05	.02
607	Mark Davis	.05	.02
608	Eric Plunk	.05	.02
609	Mark Williamson	.05	.02
610	Lee Guetterman	.05	.02
611	Bobby Rose	.05	.02
612	Bill Wegman	.05	.02
613	Mike Hartley	.05	.02
614	Chris Beasley	.05	.02
615	Chris Bosio	.05	.02
616	Henry Cotto	.05	.02
617	Chico Walker	.05	.02
618	Russ Swan	.05	.02
619	Bob Walk	.05	.02
620	Billy Swift	.05	.02
621	Warren Newson	.05	.02
622	Steve Bedrosian	.05	.02
623	Ricky Bones	.05	.02
624	Kevin Tapani	.05	.02
625	Juan Guzman	.05	.02

□ 626 Jeff Johnson	.05	.02
□ 627 Jeff Montgomery	.10	.05
□ 628 Ken Hill	.05	.02
□ 629 Gary Thurman	.05	.02
□ 630 Steve Howe	.05	.02
□ 631 Jose DeJesus	.05	.02
□ 632 Kirk Dressendorfer	.05	.02
□ 633 Jaime Navarro	.05	.02
□ 634 Lee Stevens	.05	.02
□ 635 Pete Harnisch	.05	.02
□ 636 Bill Landrum	.05	.02
□ 637 Rich DeLucia	.05	.02
□ 638 Luis Salazar	.05	.02
□ 639 Rob Murphy	.05	.02
□ 640 Jose Canseco CL	.20	.09
Rickey Henderson		
□ 641 Roger Clemens DS	.20	.09
□ 642 Jim Abbott DS	.05	.02
□ 643 Travis Fryman DS	.05	.02
□ 644 Jesse Barfield DS	.05	.02
□ 645 Cal Ripken DS	.20	.09
□ 646 Wade Boggs DS	.10	.05
□ 647 Cecil Fielder DS	.05	.02
□ 648 Rickey Henderson DS	.10	.05
□ 649 Jose Canseco DS	.10	.05
□ 650 Ken Griffey Jr. DS	1.00	.45
□ 651 Kenny Rogers	.05	.02
□ 652 Luis Mercedes	.05	.02
□ 653 Mike Stanton	.05	.02
□ 654 Glenn Davis	.05	.02
□ 655 Nolan Ryan	.75	.35
□ 656 Reggie Jefferson	.10	.05
□ 657 Javier Ortiz	.05	.02
□ 658 Greg A. Harris	.05	.02
□ 659 Mariano Duncan	.05	.02
□ 660 Jeff Shaw	.05	.02
□ 661 Mike Moore	.05	.02
□ 662 Chris Haney	.05	.02
□ 663 Joe Slusarski	.05	.02
□ 664 Wayne Housie	.05	.02
□ 665 Carlos Garcia	.05	.02
□ 666 Bob Ojeda	.05	.02
□ 667 Bryan Hickerson	.05	.02
□ 668 Tim Belcher	.05	.02
□ 669 Ron Darling	.05	.02
□ 670 Rex Hudler	.05	.02
□ 671 Sid Fernandez	.05	.02
□ 672 Chito Martinez	.05	.02
□ 673 Pete Schourek	.05	.02
□ 674 Armando Reynoso	.05	.02
□ 675 Mike Mussina	.30	.14
□ 676 Kevin Morton	.05	.02
□ 677 Norm Charlton	.05	.02
□ 678 Danny Darwin	.05	.02
□ 679 Eric King	.05	.02
□ 680 Ted Power	.05	.02
□ 681 Barry Jones	.05	.02
□ 682 Carney Lansford	.10	.05
□ 683 Mel Rojas	.10	.05
□ 684 Rick Honeycutt	.05	.02
□ 685 Jeff Fassero	.05	.02
□ 686 Cris Carpenter	.05	.02
□ 687 Tim Crews	.05	.02
□ 688 Scott Terry	.05	.02
□ 689 Chris Gwynn	.05	.02
□ 690 Gerald Perry	.05	.02
□ 691 John Barfield	.05	.02
□ 692 Bob Melvin	.05	.02
□ 693 Juan Agosto	.05	.02
□ 694 Alejandro Pena	.05	.02
□ 695 Jeff Russell	.05	.02
□ 696 Carmelo Martinez	.05	.02
□ 697 Bud Black	.05	.02
□ 698 Dave Otto	.05	.02
□ 699 Billy Hatcher	.05	.02
□ 700 Checklist 601-700	.05	.02
□ 701 Clemente Nunez	.05	.02
□ 702 Rookie Threats	.05	.02
Mark Clark		
Donovan Osborne		
Brian Jordan		
□ 703 Mike Morgan	.05	.02
□ 704 Keith Miller	.05	.02
□ 705 Kurt Stillwell	.05	.02
□ 706 Damon Berryhill	.05	.02
□ 707 Von Hayes	.05	.02

□ 708 Rick Sutcliffe	.05	.02
□ 709 Hubie Brooks	.05	.02
□ 710 Ryan Turner	.05	.02
□ 711 Barry Bonds CL	.10	.05
Andy Van Slyke		
□ 712 Jose Rijo DS	.05	.02
□ 713 Tom Glavine DS	.10	.05
□ 714 Shawon Dunston DS	.05	.02
□ 715 Andy Van Slyke DS	.05	.02
□ 716 Ozzie Smith DS	.20	.09
□ 717 Tony Gwynn DS	.25	.11
□ 718 Will Clark DS	.05	.02
□ 719 Marquis Grissom DS	.10	.05
□ 720 Howard Johnson DS	.05	.02
□ 721 Barry Bonds DS	.20	.09
□ 722 Kirk McCaskill	.05	.02
□ 723 Sammy Sosa	.20	.09
□ 724 George Bell	.05	.02
□ 725 Gregg Jefferies	.05	.02
□ 726 Gary DiSarcina	.05	.02
□ 727 Mike Bordick	.05	.02
□ 728 Eddie Murray	.20	.09
400 Home Run Club		
□ 729 Rene Gonzales	.05	.02
□ 730 Mike Bielecki	.05	.02
□ 731 Calvin Jones	.05	.02
□ 732 Jack Morris	.10	.05
□ 733 Frank Viola	.05	.02
□ 734 Dave Winfield	.20	.09
□ 735 Kevin Mitchell	.10	.05
□ 736 Bill Swift	.05	.02
□ 737 Dan Gladden	.05	.02
□ 738 Mike Jackson	.05	.02
□ 739 Mark Carreon	.05	.02
□ 740 Kirt Manwaring	.05	.02
□ 741 Randy Myers	.10	.05
□ 742 Kevin McReynolds	.05	.02
□ 743 Steve Sax	.05	.02
□ 744 Wally Joyner	.10	.05
□ 745 Gary Sheffield	.20	.09
□ 746 Danny Tartabull	.05	.02
□ 747 Julio Valera	.05	.02
□ 748 Denny Neagle	.05	.07
□ 749 Lance Blankenship	.05	.02
□ 750 Mike Gallego	.05	.02
□ 751 Bret Saberhagen	.05	.02
□ 752 Ruben Amaro	.05	.02
□ 753 Eddie Murray	.20	.09
□ 754 Kyle Abbott	.05	.02
□ 755 Bobby Bonilla	.10	.05
□ 756 Eric Davis	.10	.05
□ 757 Eddie Taubensee	.05	.02
□ 758 Andres Galarraga	.20	.09
□ 759 Pete Incaviglia	.05	.02
□ 760 Tom Candiotti	.05	.02
□ 761 Tim Belcher	.05	.02
□ 762 Ricky Bones	.05	.02
□ 763 Bip Roberts	.05	.02
□ 764 Pedro Munoz	.05	.02
□ 765 Greg Swindell	.05	.02
□ 766 Kenny Lofton	.75	.35
□ 767 Gary Carter	.20	.09
□ 768 Charlie Hayes	.05	.02
□ 769 Dickie Thon	.05	.02
□ 770 Donovan Osborne DD CL	.05	.02
□ 771 Bret Boone DD	.10	.05
□ 772 Archi Cianfrocco DD	.05	.02
□ 773 Mark Clark DD	.05	.02
□ 774 Chad Curtis DD	.20	.09
□ 775 Pat Listach DD	.05	.02
□ 776 Pat Mahomes DD	.05	.02
□ 777 Donovan Osborne DD	.05	.02
□ 778 John Patterson DD	.05	.02
□ 779 Andy Stankiewicz DD	.05	.02
□ 780 Turk Wendell DD	.10	.05
□ 781 Bill Krueger	.05	.02
□ 782 Rickey Henderson	.15	.07
Grand Theft		
□ 783 Kevin Seitzer	.05	.02
□ 784 Dave Martinez	.05	.02
□ 785 John Smiley	.05	.02
□ 786 Matt Stairs	.05	.02
□ 787 Scott Scudder	.05	.02
□ 788 John Wetteland	.10	.05
□ 789 Jack Armstrong	.05	.02
□ 790 Ken Hill	.05	.02

□ 791 Dick Schofield	.05	.02
□ 792 Mariano Duncan	.05	.02
□ 793 Bill Pecota	.05	.02
□ 794 Mike Kelly	.05	.02
□ 795 Willie Randolph	.10	.05
□ 796 Butch Henry	.05	.02
□ 797 Carlos Hernandez	.05	.02
□ 798 Doug Jones	.05	.02
□ 799 Melido Perez	.05	.02
□ 800 Checklist 701-800	.05	.02
HH2 Ted Williams Hologram	2.00	.90
(Top left corner says 91 Upper Deck 92)		
□ SP3 Deion Sanders FB/BB	1.00	.45
□ SP4 Tom Selleck	2.50	1.10
Frank Thomas SP		
(Mr. Baseball)		

1992 Upper Deck Heroes of Baseball

Continuing a popular insert set introduced the previous year, Upper Deck produced four new commemorative cards, including three player cards and one portrait card by sports artist Vernon Wells. These cards were randomly inserted in 1992 Upper Deck baseball low number foil packs. Three thousand of each card were personally numbered and autographed by each player. On a white card face, the fronts carry sepia-tone player photos with red, gold, and blue border stripes. The player's name appears in a gold border stripe beneath the picture, with the Upper Deck "Heroes of Baseball" logo in the lower right corner.

	MINT	NRMT
COMPLETE SET (4)	8.00	3.60
COMMON CARD (H5-H8)	1.00	.45
RANDOM INSERTS IN HEROES FOIL		
□ H5 Vida Blue	1.00	.45
□ H6 Lou Brock	4.00	1.80
□ H7 Rollie Fingers	2.00	.90
□ H8 Vida Blue ART	3.00	1.35
Lou Brock		
Rollie Fingers		
□ AU5 Vida Blue AU/3000	15.00	6.75
□ AU6 Lou Brock AU/3000	60.00	27.00
□ AU7 R.Fingers AU/3000	30.00	13.50

1992 Upper Deck Home Run Heroes

This 26-card standard-size set was inserted one per pack into 1992 Upper Deck low series jumbo packs. The set spotlights

the 1991 home run leaders from each of the 26 Major League teams. The fronts display color action player photos with a shadow strip around the picture for a three-dimensional effect. A gold bat icon runs vertically down the left side and contains the words "Homerun Heroes" printed in white.

	MINT	NRMT
COMPLETE SET (26)	12.00	5.50
COMMON CARD(HR1-HR26)	.25	.11
ONE PER LO SERIES JUMBO		

		MINT	NRMT
□ HR1	Jose Canseco	.60	.25
□ HR2	Cecil Fielder	.40	.18
□ HR3	Howard Johnson	.25	.11
□ HR4	Cal Ripken	2.00	.90
□ HR5	Matt Williams	.60	.25
□ HR6	Joe Carter	.40	.18
□ HR7	Ron Gant	.40	.18
□ HR8	Frank Thomas	3.00	1.35
□ HR9	Andre Dawson	.60	.25
□ HR10	Fred McGriff	.60	.25
□ HR11	Danny Tartabull	.25	.11
□ HR12	Chili Davis	.40	.18
□ HR13	Albert Belle	.75	.35
□ HR14	Jack Clark	.25	.11
□ HR15	Paul O'Neill	.40	.18
□ HR16	Darryl Strawberry	.40	.18
□ HR17	Dave Winfield	.75	.35
□ HR18	Jay Buhner	.60	.25
□ HR19	Juan Gonzalez	2.00	.90
□ HR20	Greg Vaughn	.25	.11
□ HR21	Barry Bonds	.75	.35
□ HR22	Matt Nokes	.25	.11
□ HR23	John Kruk	.40	.18
□ HR24	Ivan Calderon	.25	.11
□ HR25	Jeff Bagwell	2.00	.90
□ HR26	Todd Zeile	.25	.11

1992 Upper Deck Scouting Report

Inserted one per high series jumbo pack, cards from this 25-card standard-size set feature

outstanding prospects in baseball. The fronts carry color action player photos that are full-bleed on the top and right, bordered below by a black stripe with the player's name, and by a black jagged left border that resembles torn paper. The words "Scouting Report" are printed vertically in silver lettering in the left border.

	MINT	NRMT
COMPLETE SET (25)	15.00	6.75
COMMON CARD (SR1-SR25)	.50	.23
MINOR STARS	1.00	.45
UNLISTED STARS	1.50	.70
ONE PER HI SERIES JUMBO		

		MINT	NRMT
□ SR1	Andy Ashby	.50	.23
□ SR2	Willie Banks	.50	.23
□ SR3	Kim Batiste	.50	.23
□ SR4	Derek Bell	1.00	.45
□ SR5	Archi Cianfrocco	.50	.23
□ SR6	Royce Clayton	.50	.23
□ SR7	Gary DiSarcina	.50	.23
□ SR8	Dave Fleming	.50	.23
□ SR9	Butch Henry	.50	.23
□ SR10	Todd Hundley	1.25	.55
□ SR11	Brian Jordan	1.50	.70
□ SR12	Eric Karros	1.25	.55
□ SR13	Pat Listach	.50	.23
□ SR14	Scott Livingstone	.50	.23
□ SR15	Kenny Lofton	8.00	3.60
□ SR16	Pat Mahomes	.50	.23
□ SR17	Denny Neagle	1.25	.55
□ SR18	Dave Nilsson	1.00	.45
□ SR19	Donovan Osborne	.50	.23
□ SR20	Reggie Sanders	1.00	.45
□ SR21	Andy Stankiewicz	.50	.23
□ SR22	Jim Thome	6.00	2.70
□ SR23	Julio Valera	.50	.23
□ SR24	Mark Wohlers	1.25	.55
□ SR25	Anthony Young	.50	.23

1992 Upper Deck Williams Best

This 20-card standard-size set contains Ted Williams' choices of best current and future hitters in the game. The cards were randomly inserted in Upper Deck high series foil packs. The fronts feature full-bleed color action photos with the player's name in a black field separated from the picture by Ted Williams' gold-stamped signature.

	MINT	NRMT
COMPLETE SET (20)	25.00	11.00
COMMON CARD (T1-T20)	.50	.23
RANDOM INSERTS IN HI SERIES		

		MINT	NRMT
□ T1	Wade Boggs	1.50	.70
□ T2	Barry Bonds	1.50	.70
□ T3	Jose Canseco	1.00	.45
□ T4	Will Clark	1.00	.45
□ T5	Cecil Fielder	.75	.35
□ T6	Tony Gwynn	2.50	1.10
□ T7	Rickey Henderson	1.00	.45
□ T8	Fred McGriff	1.00	.45
□ T9	Kirby Puckett	2.00	.90
□ T10	Ruben Sierra	.50	.23
□ T11	Roberto Alomar	1.50	.70
□ T12	Jeff Bagwell	3.00	1.35
□ T13	Albert Belle	1.25	.55
□ T14	Juan Gonzalez	4.00	1.80
□ T15	Ken Griffey Jr.	8.00	3.60
□ T16	Chris Hoiles	.50	.23
□ T17	David Justice	1.50	.70
□ T18	Phil Plantier	.50	.23
□ T19	Frank Thomas	5.00	2.20
□ T20	Robin Ventura	.75	.35

1993 Upper Deck

The 1993 Upper Deck set consists of two series of 420 standard-size cards. A special card (SP5) was randomly inserted in first series packs to commemorate the 3,000th hit of George Brett and Robin Yount. A special card (SP6) commemorating Nolan Ryan's last season was randomly inserted into second series packs. Both SP cards were inserted at a rate of one every 72 packs. The front designs features color action player photos bordered in white. The company name is printed along the photo surface of the card top. The player's name appears in script in a color stripe cutting across the bottom of the picture while the team name and his position appear in another color stripe immediately below. The backs have a color close-up photo on the upper portion and biography, statistics, and career highlights on the lower portion. Special subsets featured include Star Rookies (1-29), Community Heroes (30-40), and American League Teammates (41-55), Top Prospects (421-449), Inside the Numbers (450-470), Team Stars (471-485), Award Winners (486-499), and Diamond Debuts (500-510). Derek Jeter is the only notable Rookie Card in this set.

	MINT	NRMT
COMPLETE SET (840)	30.00	13.50
COMP.FACT.SET (840)	40.00	18.00
COMPLETE SERIES 1 (420)	15.00	6.75

COMPLETE SERIES 2 (420) 15.00 6.75
COMMON CARD (1-840) .10 .05
MINOR STARS .20 .09
UNLISTED STARS .40 .18
SUBSET CARDS HALF VALUE OF BASE CARDS
COMP.GOLD FACT.SET (840) 80.00 36.00
*GOLD HOLOGRAM: 1X TO 2.5X HI COLUMN
GOLD DIST.ONLY IN FACTORY SET FORM
COMP.MAYS SET (10) 3.00 1.35
COMMON MAYS (46-54/HDR) .50 .23
MAYS SER.1 STATED ODDS 1:9
SP CARDS STATED ODDS 1:72

□ 1 Tim Salmon CL .40 .18
□ 2 Mike Piazza SR 2.00 .90
□ 3 Rene Arocha SR .10 .05
□ 4 Willie Greene SR .20 .09
□ 5 Manny Alexander SR .10 .05
□ 6 Dan Wilson SR .20 .05
□ 7 Dan Smith SR .10 .05
□ 8 Kevin Rogers SR .10 .05
□ 9 Kurt Miller SR .10 .05
□ 10 Joe Vitko SR .10 .05
□ 11 Tim Costo SR .10 .05
□ 12 Alan Embree SR .10 .05
□ 13 Jim Tatum SR .10 .05
□ 14 Cris Colon SR .10 .05
□ 15 Steve Hosey SR .10 .05
□ 16 Sterling Hitchcock SR .20 .09
□ 17 Dave Mlicki SR .10 .05
□ 18 Jessie Hollins SR .10 .05
□ 19 Bobby Jones SR .20 .09
□ 20 Kurt Miller SR .10 .05
□ 21 Melvin Nieves SR .20 .09
□ 22 Billy Ashley SR .10 .05
□ 23 J.T. Snow SR .50 .23
□ 24 Chipper Jones SR 2.00 .90
□ 25 Tim Salmon SR .50 .23
□ 26 Tim Pugh SR .10 .05
□ 27 David Nied SR .10 .05
□ 28 Mike Trombley SR .10 .05
□ 29 Javier Lopez SR .40 .18
□ 30 Jim Abbott CL .10 .05
□ 31 Jim Abbott CH .10 .05
□ 32 Dale Murphy CH .20 .09
□ 33 Tony Pena CH .10 .05
□ 34 Kirby Puckett CH .40 .18
□ 35 Harold Reynolds CH .10 .05
□ 36 Cal Ripken CH .75 .35
□ 37 Nolan Ryan CH .75 .35
□ 38 Ryne Sandberg CH .30 .14
□ 39 Dave Stewart CH .10 .05
□ 40 Dave Winfield CH .20 .09
□ 41 Joe Carter CL .40 .18
  Mark McGwire
□ 42 Blockbuster Trade .40 .18
  Joe Carter
  Roberto Alomar
□ 43 Brew Crew .40 .18
  Paul Molitor
  Pat Listach
  Robin Yount
□ 44 Iron and Steel .40 .18
  Cal Ripken
  Brady Anderson
□ 45 Youthful Tribe .20 .09
  Albert Belle
  Sandy Alomar Jr.
  Jim Thome
  Carlos Baerga
  Kenny Lofton
□ 46 Motown Mashers .20 .09
  Cecil Fielder
  Mickey Tettleton
□ 47 Yankee Pride .20 .09
  Roberto Kelly
  Don Mattingly
□ 48 Boston Cy Sox .20 .09
  Frank Viola
  Roger Clemens
□ 49 Bash Brothers .20 .09
  Ruben Sierra
  Mark McGwire
□ 50 Twin Titles .40 .18
  Kent Hrbek
  Kirby Puckett

□ 51 Southside Sluggers .40 .18
  Robin Ventura
  Frank Thomas
□ 52 Latin Stars .50 .23
  Juan Gonzalez
  Jose Canseco
  Ivan Rodriguez
  Rafael Palmeiro
□ 53 Lethal Lefties .10 .05
  Mark Langston
  Jim Abbott
  Chuck Finley
□ 54 Royal Family .10 .05
  Wally Joyner
  Gregg Jefferies
  George Brett
□ 55 Pacific Sock Exchange .50 .23
  Kevin Mitchell
  Ken Griffey Jr.
  Jay Buhner
□ 56 George Brett .75 .35
□ 57 Scott Cooper .10 .05
□ 58 Mike Maddux .10 .05
□ 59 Rusty Meacham .10 .05
□ 60 Wil Cordero .10 .05
□ 61 Tim Teufel .10 .05
□ 62 Jeff Montgomery .20 .09
□ 63 Scott Livingstone .10 .05
□ 64 Doug Dascenzo .10 .05
□ 65 Bret Boone .10 .05
□ 66 Tim Wakefield .20 .09
□ 67 Curt Schilling .20 .09
□ 68 Frank Tanana .10 .05
□ 69 Len Dykstra .20 .09
□ 70 Derek Lilliquist .10 .05
□ 71 Anthony Young .10 .05
□ 72 Hipolito Pichardo .10 .05
□ 73 Rod Beck .10 .05
□ 74 Kent Hrbek .20 .09
□ 75 Tom Glavine .30 .14
□ 76 Kevin Brown .20 .09
□ 77 Chuck Finley .10 .05
□ 78 Bob Walk .10 .05
□ 79 Rheal Cormier UER .10 .05
  (Born in New Brunswick,
  not British Columbia)
□ 80 Rick Sutcliffe .10 .05
□ 81 Harold Baines .20 .09
□ 82 Lee Smith .20 .09
□ 83 Geno Petralli .10 .05
□ 84 Jose Oquendo .10 .05
□ 85 Mark Gubicza .10 .05
□ 86 Mickey Tettleton .20 .09
□ 87 Bobby Witt .10 .05
□ 88 Mark Lewis .10 .05
□ 89 Kevin Appier .20 .09
□ 90 Mike Stanton .10 .05
□ 91 Rafael Belliard .10 .05
□ 92 Kenny Rogers .10 .05
□ 93 Randy Velarde .10 .05
□ 94 Luis Sojo .10 .05
□ 95 Mark Leiter .10 .05
□ 96 Jody Reed .10 .05
□ 97 Pete Harnisch .10 .05
□ 98 Tom Candiotti .10 .05
□ 99 Mark Portugal .10 .05
□ 100 Dave Valle .10 .05
□ 101 Shawon Dunston .10 .05
□ 102 B.J. Surhoff .20 .09
□ 103 Jay Bell .20 .09
□ 104 Sid Bream .10 .05
□ 105 Frank Thomas CL .40 .18
□ 106 Mike Morgan .10 .05
□ 107 Bill Doran .10 .05
□ 108 Lance Blankenship .10 .05
□ 109 Mark Lemke .10 .05
□ 110 Brian Harper .10 .05
□ 111 Brady Anderson .30 .14
□ 112 Bip Roberts .10 .05
□ 113 Mitch Williams .10 .05
□ 114 Craig Biggio .30 .14
□ 115 Eddie Murray .40 .18
□ 116 Matt Nokes .10 .05
□ 117 Lance Parrish .10 .05
□ 118 Bill Swift .10 .05
□ 119 Jeff Innis .10 .05

□ 120 Mike LaValliere .10 .05
□ 121 Hal Morris .10 .05
□ 122 Walt Weiss .10 .05
□ 123 Ivan Rodriguez .50 .23
□ 124 Andy Van Slyke .20 .09
□ 125 Roberto Alomar .40 .18
□ 126 Robby Thompson .10 .05
□ 127 Sammy Sosa .40 .18
□ 128 Mark Langston .10 .05
□ 129 Jerry Browne .10 .05
□ 130 Chuck McElroy .10 .05
□ 131 Frank Viola .10 .05
□ 132 Leo Gomez .10 .05
□ 133 Ramon Martinez .20 .09
□ 134 Don Mattingly .60 .25
□ 135 Roger Clemens .75 .35
□ 136 Rickey Henderson .40 .18
□ 137 Darren Daulton .20 .09
□ 138 Ken Hill .10 .05
□ 139 Ozzie Guillen .10 .05
□ 140 Jerald Clark .10 .05
□ 141 Dave Fleming .10 .05
□ 142 Delino DeShields .10 .05
□ 143 Matt Williams .30 .14
□ 144 Larry Walker .40 .18
□ 145 Ruben Sierra .10 .05
□ 146 Ozzie Smith .50 .23
□ 147 Chris Sabo .10 .05
□ 148 Carlos Hernandez .10 .05
□ 149 Pat Borders .10 .05
□ 150 Orlando Merced .10 .05
□ 151 Royce Clayton .10 .05
□ 152 Kurt Stillwell .10 .05
□ 153 Dave Hollins .10 .05
□ 154 Mike Greenwell .10 .05
□ 155 Nolan Ryan 1.50 .70
□ 156 Felix Jose .10 .05
□ 157 Junior Felix .10 .05
□ 158 Derek Bell .20 .09
□ 159 Steve Buechele .10 .05
□ 160 John Burkett .10 .05
□ 161 Pat Howell .10 .05
□ 162 Milt Cuyler .10 .05
□ 163 Terry Pendleton .20 .09
□ 164 Jack Morris .20 .09
□ 165 Tony Gwynn 1.00 .45
□ 166 Deion Sanders .20 .09
□ 167 Mike Devereaux .10 .05
□ 168 Ron Darling .10 .05
□ 169 Orel Hershiser .20 .09
□ 170 Mike Jackson .10 .05
□ 171 Doug Jones .10 .05
□ 172 Dan Walters .10 .05
□ 173 Darren Lewis .10 .05
□ 174 Carlos Baerga .20 .09
□ 175 Ryne Sandberg .50 .23
□ 176 Gregg Jefferies .10 .05
□ 177 John Jaha .20 .09
□ 178 Luis Polonia .10 .05
□ 179 Kirt Manwaring .10 .05
□ 180 Mike Magnante .10 .05
□ 181 Billy Ripken .10 .05
□ 182 Mike Moore .10 .05
□ 183 Eric Anthony .10 .05
□ 184 Lenny Harris .10 .05
□ 185 Tony Pena .10 .05
□ 186 Mike Felder .10 .05
□ 187 Greg Olson .10 .05
□ 188 Rene Gonzales .10 .05
□ 189 Mike Bordick .10 .05
□ 190 Mel Rojas .20 .09
□ 191 Todd Frohwirth .10 .05
□ 192 Darryl Hamilton .10 .05
□ 193 Mike Fetters .10 .05
□ 194 Omar Olivares .10 .05
□ 195 Tony Phillips .10 .05
□ 196 Paul Sorrento .10 .05
□ 197 Trevor Wilson .10 .05
□ 198 Kevin Gross .10 .05
□ 199 Ron Karkovice .10 .05
□ 200 Brook Jacoby .10 .05
□ 201 Mariano Duncan .10 .05
□ 202 Dennis Cook .10 .05
□ 203 Daryl Boston .10 .05
□ 204 Mike Perez .10 .05
□ 205 Manuel Lee .10 .05

206	Steve Olin	.10	.05
207	Charlie Hough	.10	.05
208	Scott Scudder	.10	.05
209	Charlie O'Brien	.10	.05
210	Barry Bonds CL	.40	.18
211	Jose Vizcaino	.10	.05
212	Scott Leius	.10	.05
213	Kevin Mitchell	.20	.09
214	Brian Barnes	.10	.05
215	Pat Kelly	.10	.05
216	Chris Hammond	.10	.05
217	Rob Deer	.10	.05
218	Cory Snyder	.10	.05
219	Gary Carter	.30	.14
220	Danny Darwin	.10	.05
221	Tom Gordon	.10	.05
222	Gary Sheffield	.40	.18
223	Joe Carter	.20	.09
224	Jay Buhner	.30	.14
225	Jose Offerman	.10	.05
226	Jose Rijo	.10	.05
227	Mark Whiten	.10	.05
228	Randy Milligan	.10	.05
229	Bud Black	.10	.05
230	Gary DiSarcina	.10	.05
231	Steve Finley	.10	.05
232	Dennis Martinez	.20	.09
233	Mike Mussina	.40	.18
234	Joe Oliver	.10	.05
235	Chad Curtis	.20	.09
236	Shane Mack	.10	.05
237	Jaime Navarro	.10	.05
238	Brian McRae	.10	.05
239	Chili Davis	.20	.09
240	Jeff King	.10	.05
241	Dean Palmer	.10	.05
242	Danny Tartabull	.20	.09
243	Charles Nagy	.20	.09
244	Ray Lankford	.30	.14
245	Barry Larkin	.30	.14
246	Steve Avery	.10	.05
247	John Kruk	.20	.09
248	Derrick May	.10	.05
249	Stan Javier	.10	.05
250	Roger McDowell	.10	.05
251	Dan Gladden	.10	.05
252	Wally Joyner	.20	.09
253	Pat Listach	.10	.05
254	Chuck Knoblauch	.40	.18
255	Sandy Alomar Jr.	.20	.09
256	Jeff Bagwell	.75	.35
257	Andy Stankiewicz	.10	.05
258	Darrin Jackson	.10	.05
259	Brett Butler	.20	.09
260	Joe Orsulak	.10	.05
261	Andy Benes	.20	.09
262	Kenny Lofton	.75	.35
263	Robin Ventura	.20	.09
264	Ron Gant	.20	.09
265	Ellis Burks	.20	.09
266	Juan Guzman	.10	.05
267	Wes Chamberlain	.10	.05
268	John Smiley	.10	.05
269	Franklin Stubbs	.10	.05
270	Tom Browning	.10	.05
271	Dennis Eckersley	.20	.09
272	Carlton Fisk	.40	.18
273	Lou Whitaker	.20	.09
274	Phil Plantier	.10	.05
275	Bobby Bonilla	.20	.09
276	Ben McDonald	.10	.05
277	Bob Zupcic	.10	.05
278	Terry Steinbach	.10	.05
279	Terry Mulholland	.10	.05
280	Lance Johnson	.10	.05
281	Willie McGee	.10	.05
282	Bret Saberhagen	.10	.05
283	Randy Myers	.20	.09
284	Randy Tomlin	.10	.05
285	Mickey Morandini	.10	.05
286	Brian Williams	.10	.05
287	Tino Martinez	.40	.18
288	Jose Melendez	.10	.05
289	Jeff Huson	.10	.05
290	Joe Grahe	.10	.05
291	Mel Hall	.10	.05
292	Otis Nixon	.10	.05
293	Todd Hundley	.30	.14
294	Casey Candaele	.10	.05
295	Kevin Seitzer	.10	.05
296	Eddie Taubensee	.10	.05
297	Moises Alou	.20	.09
298	Scott Radinsky	.10	.05
299	Thomas Howard	.10	.05
300	Kyle Abbott	.10	.05
301	Omar Vizquel	.20	.09
302	Keith Miller	.10	.05
303	Rick Aguilera	.10	.05
304	Bruce Hurst	.10	.05
305	Ken Caminiti	.30	.14
306	Mike Pagliarulo	.10	.05
307	Frank Seminara	.10	.05
308	Andre Dawson	.30	.14
309	Jose Lind	.10	.05
310	Joe Boever	.10	.05
311	Jeff Parrett	.10	.05
312	Alan Mills	.10	.05
313	Kevin Tapani	.10	.05
314	Darryl Kile	.20	.09
315	Will Clark CL	.20	.09
316	Mike Sharperson	.10	.05
317	John Orton	.10	.05
318	Bob Tewksbury	.10	.05
319	Xavier Hernandez	.10	.05
320	Paul Assenmacher	.10	.05
321	John Franco	.20	.09
322	Mike Timlin	.10	.05
323	Jose Guzman	.10	.05
324	Pedro Martinez	.40	.18
325	Bill Spiers	.10	.05
326	Melido Perez	.10	.05
327	Mike Macfarlane	.10	.05
328	Ricky Bones	.10	.05
329	Scott Bankhead	.10	.05
330	Rich Rodriguez	.10	.05
331	Geronimo Pena	.10	.05
332	Bernie Williams	.40	.18
333	Paul Molitor	.40	.18
334	Carlos Garcia	.10	.05
335	David Cone	.20	.09
336	Randy Johnson	.40	.18
337	Pat Mahomes	.10	.05
338	Erik Hanson	.10	.05
339	Duane Ward	.10	.05
340	Al Martin	.20	.09
341	Pedro Munoz	.10	.05
342	Greg Colbrunn	.10	.05
343	Julio Valera	.10	.05
344	John Olerud	.20	.09
345	George Bell	.20	.09
346	Devon White	.10	.05
347	Donovan Osborne	.10	.05
348	Mark Gardner	.10	.05
349	Zane Smith	.10	.05
350	Wilson Alvarez	.20	.09
351	Kevin Koslofski	.10	.05
352	Roberto Hernandez	.20	.09
353	Glenn Davis	.10	.05
354	Reggie Sanders	.20	.09
355	Ken Griffey Jr.	2.00	.90
356	Marquis Grissom	.20	.09
357	Jack McDowell	.10	.05
358	Stan Belinda	.10	.05
359	Stan Belinda	.10	.05
360	Gerald Williams	.10	.05
361	Sid Fernandez	.10	.05
362	Alex Fernandez	.20	.09
363	John Smoltz	.20	.09
364	Travis Fryman	.20	.09
365	Jose Canseco	.30	.14
366	David Justice	.40	.18
367	Pedro Astacio	.10	.05
368	Tim Belcher	.10	.05
369	Steve Sax	.10	.05
370	Gary Gaetti	.10	.05
371	Jeff Frye	.10	.05
372	Bob Wickman	.10	.05
373	Ryan Thompson	.20	.09
374	David Hulse	.10	.05
375	Cal Eldred	.20	.09
376	Ryan Klesko	.50	.23
377	Damion Easley	.10	.05
378	John Kiely	.10	.05
379	Jim Bullinger	.10	.05
380	Brian Bohanon	.10	.05
381	Rod Brewer	.10	.05
382	Fernando Ramsey	.10	.05
383	Sam Militello	.10	.05
384	Arthur Rhodes	.20	.09
385	Eric Karros	.20	.09
386	Rico Brogna	.20	.09
387	John Valentin	.20	.09
388	Kerry Woodson	.10	.05
389	Ben Rivera	.10	.05
390	Matt Whiteside	.10	.05
391	Henry Rodriguez	.20	.09
392	John Wetteland	.20	.09
393	Kent Mercker	.10	.05
394	Bernard Gilkey	.20	.09
395	Doug Henry	.10	.05
396	Mo Vaughn	.50	.23
397	Scott Erickson	.10	.05
398	Bill Gullickson	.10	.05
399	Mark Guthrie	.10	.05
400	Dave Martinez	.10	.05
401	Jeff Kent	.20	.09
402	Chris Hoiles	.10	.05
403	Mike Henneman	.10	.05
404	Chris Nabholz	.10	.05
405	Tom Pagnozzi	.10	.05
406	Kelly Gruber	.10	.05
407	Bob Welch	.10	.05
408	Frank Castillo	.10	.05
409	John Dopson	.10	.05
410	Steve Farr	.10	.05
411	Henry Cotto	.10	.05
412	Bob Patterson	.10	.05
413	Todd Stottlemyre	.10	.05
414	Greg A. Harris	.10	.05
415	Denny Neagle	.20	.09
416	Bill Wegman	.10	.05
417	Willie Wilson	.10	.05
418	Terry Leach	.10	.05
419	Willie Randolph	.20	.09
420	Mark McGwire CL	.40	.18
421	Calvin Murray CL	.10	.05
422	Pete Janicki TP	.10	.05
423	Todd Jones TP	.20	.09
424	Mike Neill TP	.10	.05
425	Carlos Delgado TP	.40	.18
426	Jose Oliva TP	.10	.05
427	Tyrone Hill TP	.10	.05
428	Dmitri Young TP	.40	.18
429	Derek Wallace TP	.10	.05
430	Michael Moore TP	.10	.05
431	Cliff Floyd TP	.20	.09
432	Calvin Murray TP	.10	.05
433	Manny Ramirez TP	.75	.35
434	Marc Newfield TP	.20	.09
435	Charles Johnson TP	.40	.18
436	Butch Huskey TP	.40	.18
437	Brad Pennington TP	.10	.05
438	Ray McDavid TP	.10	.05
439	Chad McConnell TP	.10	.05
440	Andre Cummings TP	.10	.05
441	Benji Gil TP	.20	.09
442	Frankie Rodriguez TP	.10	.05
443	Chad Mottola TP	.20	.09
444	John Burke TP	.10	.05
445	Michael Tucker TP	.40	.18
446	Rick Greene TP	.10	.05
447	Rich Becker TP	.20	.09
448	Mike Robertson TP	.10	.05
449	Derek Jeter TP	4.00	1.80
450	Ivan Rodriguez CL	.20	.09
	David McCarty		
451	Jim Abbott IN	.10	.05
452	Jeff Bagwell IN	.40	.18
453	Jason Bere IN	.10	.05
454	Delino DeShields IN	.10	.05
455	Travis Fryman IN	.10	.05
456	Alex Gonzalez IN	.30	.14
457	Phil Hiatt IN	.10	.05
458	Dave Hollins IN	.10	.05
459	Chipper Jones IN	1.25	.55
460	David Justice IN	.20	.09
461	Ray Lankford IN	.20	.09
462	David McCarty IN	.10	.05

☐ 463	Mike Mussina IN	.20	.09
☐ 464	Jose Offerman IN	.10	.05
☐ 465	Dean Palmer IN	.10	.05
☐ 466	Geronimo Pena IN	.10	.05
☐ 467	Eduardo Perez IN	.10	.05
☐ 468	Ivan Rodriguez IN	.40	.18
☐ 469	Reggie Sanders IN	.10	.05
☐ 470	Bernie Williams IN	.40	.18
☐ 471	Barry Bonds CL	.40	.18
	Matt Williams		
	Will Clark		
☐ 472	Strike Force	.40	.18
	Greg Maddux		
	Steve Avery		
	John Smoltz		
	Tom Glavine		
☐ 473	Red October	.10	.05
	Jose Rijo		
	Rob Dibble		
	Roberto Kelly		
	Reggie Sanders		
	Barry Larkin		
☐ 474	Four Corners	.30	.14
	Gary Sheffield		
	Phil Plantier		
	Tony Gwynn		
	Fred McGriff		
☐ 475	Shooting Stars	.10	.05
	Doug Drabek		
	Craig Biggio		
	Jeff Bagwell		
☐ 476	Giant Sticks	.30	.14
	Will Clark		
	Barry Bonds		
	Matt Williams		
☐ 477	Boyhood Friends	.20	.09
	Eric Davis		
	Darryl Strawberry		
☐ 478	Rock Solid Foundation	.30	.14
	Dante Bichette		
	David Nied		
	Andres Galarraga		
☐ 479	Inaugural Catch	.10	.05
	Dave Magadan		
	Orestes Destrade		
	Bret Barbere		
	Jeff Conine		
☐ 480	Steel City Champions	.10	.05
	Tim Wakefield		
	Andy Van Slyke		
	Jay Bell		
☐ 481	Les Grandes Etoiles	.20	.09
	Marquis Grissom		
	Delino DeShields		
	Dennis Martinez		
	Larry Walker		
☐ 482	Runnin' Redbirds	.20	.09
	Geronimo Pena		
	Ray Lankford		
	Ozzie Smith		
	Bernard Gilkey		
☐ 483	Ivy Leaguers	.20	.09
	Randy Myers		
	Ryne Sandberg		
	Mark Grace		
☐ 484	Big Apple Power Switch	.20	.09
	Eddie Murray		
	Howard Johnson		
	Bobby Bonilla		
☐ 485	Hammers and Nails	.10	.05
	John Kruk		
	Dave Hollins		
	Darren Daulton		
	Len Dykstra		
☐ 486	Barry Bonds AW	.40	.18
☐ 487	Dennis Eckersley AW	.10	.05
☐ 488	Greg Maddux AW	.60	.25
☐ 489	Dennis Eckersley AW	.10	.05
☐ 490	Eric Karros AW	.10	.05
☐ 491	Pat Listach AW	1.00	.05
☐ 492	Gary Sheffield AW	.20	.09
☐ 493	Mark McGwire AW	.50	.23
☐ 494	Gary Sheffield AW	.20	.09
☐ 495	Edgar Martinez AW	.20	.09
☐ 496	Fred McGriff AW	.20	.09
☐ 497	Juan Gonzalez AW	.50	.23
☐ 498	Darren Daulton AW	.10	.05
☐ 499	Cecil Fielder AW	.10	.05
☐ 500	Brent Gates CL	.10	.05
☐ 501	Tavo Alvarez DD	.10	.05
☐ 502	Rod Bolton DD	.10	.05
☐ 503	John Cummings DD	.10	.05
☐ 504	Brent Gates DD	.10	.05
☐ 505	Tyler Green DD	.10	.05
☐ 506	Jose Martinez DD	.10	.05
☐ 507	Troy Percival DD	.20	.09
☐ 508	Kevin Stocker DD	.10	.05
☐ 509	Matt Walbeck DD	.10	.05
☐ 510	Rondell White DD	.30	.14
☐ 511	Billy Ripken	.10	.05
☐ 512	Mike Moore	.10	.05
☐ 513	Jose Lind	.10	.05
☐ 514	Chito Martinez	.10	.05
☐ 515	Jose Guzman	.10	.05
☐ 516	Kim Batiste	.10	.05
☐ 517	Jeff Tackett	.10	.05
☐ 518	Charlie Hough	.10	.05
☐ 519	Marvin Freeman	.10	.05
☐ 520	Carlos Martinez	.10	.05
☐ 521	Eric Young	.40	.18
☐ 522	Pete Incaviglia	.10	.05
☐ 523	Scott Fletcher	.10	.05
☐ 524	Orestes Destrade	.10	.05
☐ 525	Ken Griffey Jr. CL	.40	.18
☐ 526	Ellis Burks	.20	.09
☐ 527	Juan Samuel	.10	.05
☐ 528	Dave Magadan	.10	.05
☐ 529	Jeff Parrett	.10	.05
☐ 530	Bill Krueger	.10	.05
☐ 531	Frank Bolick	.10	.05
☐ 532	Alan Trammell	.30	.14
☐ 533	Walt Weiss	.10	.05
☐ 534	David Cone	.20	.09
☐ 535	Greg Maddux	1.25	.55
☐ 536	Kevin Young	.10	.05
☐ 537	Dave Hansen	.10	.05
☐ 538	Alex Cole	.10	.05
☐ 539	Greg Maddux	.10	.05
☐ 540	Gene Larkin	.10	.05
☐ 541	Jeff Reardon	.20	.09
☐ 542	Felix Jose	.10	.05
☐ 543	Jimmy Key	.20	.09
☐ 544	Reggie Jefferson	.10	.05
☐ 545	Gregg Jefferies	.10	.05
☐ 546	Dave Stewart	.20	.09
☐ 547	Tim Wallach	.10	.05
☐ 548	Spike Owen	.10	.05
☐ 549	Tommy Greene	.10	.05
☐ 550	Fernando Valenzuela	.20	.09
☐ 551	Rich Amaral	.10	.05
☐ 552	Bret Barberie	.10	.05
☐ 553	Edgar Martinez	.30	.14
☐ 554	Jim Abbott	.10	.05
☐ 555	Frank Thomas	1.50	.70
☐ 556	Wade Boggs	.40	.18
☐ 557	Tom Henke	.10	.05
☐ 558	Milt Thompson	.10	.05
☐ 559	Lloyd McClendon	.10	.05
☐ 560	Vinny Castilla	.40	.18
☐ 561	Ricky Jordan	.10	.05
☐ 562	Andujar Cedeno	.10	.05
☐ 563	Greg Vaughn	.10	.05
☐ 564	Cecil Fielder	.20	.09
☐ 565	Kirby Puckett	.75	.35
☐ 566	Mark McGwire	1.00	.45
☐ 567	Barry Bonds	.50	.23
☐ 568	Jody Reed	.10	.05
☐ 569	Todd Zeile	.10	.05
☐ 570	Mark Carreon	.10	.05
☐ 571	Joe Girardi	.10	.05
☐ 572	Luis Gonzalez	.10	.05
☐ 573	Mark Grace	.30	.14
☐ 574	Rafael Palmeiro	.30	.14
☐ 575	Darryl Winfield	.20	.09
☐ 576	Will Clark	.30	.14
☐ 577	Fred McGriff	.30	.14
☐ 578	Kevin Reimer	.10	.05
☐ 579	Dave Righetti	.10	.05
☐ 580	Juan Bell	.10	.05
☐ 581	Jeff Parrett	.10	.05
☐ 582	Brian Hunter	.10	.05
☐ 583	Tim Naehring	.10	.05
☐ 584	Glenallen Hill	.10	.05
☐ 585	Cal Ripken	1.50	.70
☐ 586	Albert Belle	.50	.23
☐ 587	Robin Yount	.30	.14
☐ 588	Chris Bosio	.10	.05
☐ 589	Pete Smith	.10	.05
☐ 590	Chuck Carr	.10	.05
☐ 591	Jeff Blauser	.10	.05
☐ 592	Kevin McReynolds	.10	.05
☐ 593	Andres Galarraga	.40	.18
☐ 594	Kevin Maas	.10	.05
☐ 595	Eric Davis	.20	.09
☐ 596	Brian Jordan	.20	.09
☐ 597	Tim Raines	.20	.09
☐ 598	Rick Wilkins	.10	.05
☐ 599	Steve Cooke	.10	.05
☐ 600	Mike Gallego	.10	.05
☐ 601	Mike Munoz	.10	.05
☐ 602	Luis Rivera	.10	.05
☐ 603	Junior Ortiz	.10	.05
☐ 604	Brent Mayne	.10	.05
☐ 605	Luis Alicea	.10	.05
☐ 606	Damon Berryhill	.10	.05
☐ 607	Dave Henderson	.10	.05
☐ 608	Kirk McCaskill	.10	.05
☐ 609	Jeff Fassero	.10	.05
☐ 610	Mike Harkey	.10	.05
☐ 611	Francisco Cabrera	.10	.05
☐ 612	Rey Sanchez	.10	.05
☐ 613	Scott Servais	.10	.05
☐ 614	Darrin Fletcher	.10	.05
☐ 615	Felix Fermin	.10	.05
☐ 616	Kevin Seitzer	.10	.05
☐ 617	Bob Scanlan	.10	.05
☐ 618	Billy Hatcher	.10	.05
☐ 619	John Vander Wal	.10	.05
☐ 620	Joe Hesketh	.10	.05
☐ 621	Hector Villanueva	.10	.05
☐ 622	Randy Milligan	.10	.05
☐ 623	Tony Tarasco	.10	.05
☐ 624	Russ Swan	.10	.05
☐ 625	Willie Wilson	.10	.05
☐ 626	Frank Tanana	.10	.05
☐ 627	Pete O'Brien	.10	.05
☐ 628	Lenny Webster	.10	.05
☐ 629	Mark Clark	.10	.05
☐ 630	Roger Clemens CL	.40	.18
☐ 631	Alex Arias	.10	.05
☐ 632	Chris Gwynn	.10	.05
☐ 633	Tom Bolton	.10	.05
☐ 634	Greg Briley	.10	.05
☐ 635	Kent Bottenfield	.10	.05
☐ 636	Kelly Downs	.10	.05
☐ 637	Manuel Lee	.10	.05
☐ 638	Al Leiter	.20	.09
☐ 639	Jeff Gardner	.10	.05
☐ 640	Mike Gardiner	.10	.05
☐ 641	Mark Gardner	.10	.05
☐ 642	Jeff Branson	.10	.05
☐ 643	Paul Wagner	.10	.05
☐ 644	Sean Berry	.10	.05
☐ 645	Phil Hiatt	.10	.05
☐ 646	Kevin Mitchell	.20	.09
☐ 647	Charlie Hayes	.10	.05
☐ 648	Jim Deshaies	.10	.05
☐ 649	Dan Pasqua	.10	.05
☐ 650	Mike Maddux	.10	.05
☐ 651	Domingo Martinez	.10	.05
☐ 652	Greg McMichael	.10	.05
☐ 653	Eric Wedge	.10	.05
☐ 654	Mark Whiten	.10	.05
☐ 655	Roberto Kelly	.10	.05
☐ 656	Julio Franco	.10	.05
☐ 657	Gene Harris	.10	.05
☐ 658	Pete Schourek	.10	.05
☐ 659	Mike Bielecki	.10	.05
☐ 660	Ricky Gutierrez	.10	.05
☐ 661	Chris Hammond	.10	.05
☐ 662	Tim Scott	.10	.05
☐ 663	Norm Charlton	.10	.05
☐ 664	Doug Drabek	.10	.05
☐ 665	Dwight Gooden	.20	.09
☐ 666	Jim Gott	.10	.05
☐ 667	Randy Myers	.20	.09
☐ 668	Darren Holmes	.10	.05
☐ 669	Tim Spehr	.10	.05

□ 670 Bruce Ruffin	.10	.05	□ 756 Mike Kelly	.10	.05
□ 671 Bobby Thigpen	.10	.05	□ 757 John Doherty	.10	.05
□ 672 Tony Fernandez	.10	.05	□ 758 Jack Armstrong	.10	.05
□ 673 Darrin Jackson	.10	.05	□ 759 John Wehner	.10	.05
□ 674 Gregg Olson	.10	.05	□ 760 Scott Bankhead	.10	.05
□ 675 Rob Dibble	.10	.05	□ 761 Jim Tatum	.10	.05
□ 676 Howard Johnson	.10	.05	□ 762 Scott Pose	.10	.05
□ 677 Mike Lansing	.20	.09	□ 763 Andy Ashby	.10	.05
□ 678 Charlie Leibrandt	.10	.05	□ 764 Ed Sprague	.10	.05
□ 679 Kevin Bass	.10	.05	□ 765 Harold Baines	.20	.09
□ 680 Hubie Brooks	.10	.05	□ 766 Kirk Gibson	.20	.09
□ 681 Scott Brosius	.10	.05	□ 767 Troy Neel	.10	.05
□ 682 Randy Knorr	.10	.05	□ 768 Dick Schofield	.10	.05
□ 683 Dante Bichette	.30	.14	□ 769 Dickie Thon	.10	.05
□ 684 Bryan Harvey	.10	.05	□ 770 Butch Henry	.10	.05
□ 685 Greg Gohr	.10	.05	□ 771 Junior Felix	.10	.05
□ 686 Willie Banks	.10	.05	□ 772 Ken Ryan	.10	.05
□ 687 Robb Nen	.30	.14	□ 773 Trevor Hoffman	.30	.14
□ 688 Mike Sciosia	.10	.05	□ 774 Phil Plantier	.10	.05
□ 689 John Farrell	.10	.05	□ 775 Bo Jackson	.20	.09
□ 690 John Candelaria	.10	.05	□ 776 Benito Santiago	.10	.05
□ 691 Damon Buford	.10	.05	□ 777 Andre Dawson	.30	.14
□ 692 Todd Worrell	.10	.05	□ 778 Bryan Hickerson	.10	.05
□ 693 Pat Hentgen	.30	.14	□ 779 Dennis Moeller	.10	.05
□ 694 John Smiley	.10	.05	□ 780 Ryan Bowen	.10	.05
□ 695 Greg Swindell	.10	.05	□ 781 Eric Fox	.10	.05
□ 696 Derek Bell	.20	.09	□ 782 Joe Kmak	.10	.05
□ 697 Terry Jorgensen	.10	.05	□ 783 Mike Hampton	.30	.14
□ 698 Jimmy Jones	.10	.05	□ 784 Darrell Sherman	.10	.05
□ 699 David Wells	.10	.05	□ 785 J.T. Snow	.40	.18
□ 700 Dave Martinez	.10	.05	□ 786 Dave Winfield	.30	.14
□ 701 Steve Bedrosian	.10	.05	□ 787 Jim Austin	.10	.05
□ 702 Jeff Russell	.10	.05	□ 788 Craig Shipley	.10	.05
□ 703 Joe Magrane	.10	.05	□ 789 Greg Myers	.10	.05
□ 704 Matt Mieske	.20	.09	□ 790 Todd Benzinger	.10	.05
□ 705 Paul Molitor	.40	.18	□ 791 Cory Snyder	.10	.05
□ 706 Dale Murphy	.30	.14	□ 792 David Segui	.10	.05
□ 707 Steve Howe	.10	.05	□ 793 Armando Reynoso	.10	.05
□ 708 Greg Gagne	.10	.05	□ 794 Chili Davis	.20	.09
□ 709 Dave Eiland	.10	.05	□ 795 Dave Nilsson	.20	.09
□ 710 David West	.10	.05	□ 796 Paul O'Neill	.20	.09
□ 711 Luis Aquino	.10	.05	□ 797 Jerald Clark	.10	.05
□ 712 Joe Orsulak	.10	.05	□ 798 Jose Mesa	.10	.05
□ 713 Eric Plunk	.10	.05	□ 799 Brian Holman	.10	.05
□ 714 Mike Felder	.10	.05	□ 800 Jim Eisenreich	.10	.05
□ 715 Joe Klink	.10	.05	□ 801 Mark McLemore	.10	.05
□ 716 Lonnie Smith	.10	.05	□ 802 Luis Sojo	.10	.05
□ 717 Monty Fariss	.10	.05	□ 803 Harold Reynolds	.10	.05
□ 718 Craig Lefferts	.10	.05	□ 804 Dan Plesac	.10	.05
□ 719 John Habyan	.10	.05	□ 805 Dave Stieb	.10	.05
□ 720 Willie Blair	.10	.05	□ 806 Tom Brunansky	.10	.05
□ 721 Darnell Coles	.10	.05	□ 807 Kelly Gruber	.10	.05
□ 722 Mark Williamson	.10	.05	□ 808 Bob Ojeda	.10	.05
□ 723 Bryn Smith	.10	.05	□ 809 Dave Burba	.10	.05
□ 724 Greg W. Harris	.10	.05	□ 810 Joe Boever	.10	.05
□ 725 Graeme Lloyd	.10	.05	□ 811 Jeremy Hernandez	.10	.05
□ 726 Cris Carpenter	.10	.05	□ 812 Tim Salmon TC	.40	.18
□ 727 Chico Walker	.10	.05	□ 813 Jeff Bagwell TC	.40	.18
□ 728 Tracy Woodson	.10	.05	□ 814 Dennis Eckersley TC	.10	.05
□ 729 Jose Uribe	.10	.05	□ 815 Roberto Alomar TC	.20	.09
□ 730 Stan Javier	.10	.05	□ 816 Steve Avery TC	.10	.05
□ 731 Jay Howell	.10	.05	□ 817 Pat Listach TC	.10	.05
□ 732 Freddie Benavides	.10	.05	□ 818 Gregg Jefferies TC	.10	.05
□ 733 Jeff Reboulet	.10	.05	□ 819 Sammy Sosa TC	.20	.09
□ 734 Scott Sanderson	.10	.05	□ 820 Darryl Strawberry TC	.10	.05
□ 735 Ryne Sandberg CL	.40	.18	□ 821 Dennis Martinez TC	.10	.05
□ 736 Archi Cianfrocco	.10	.05	□ 822 Robby Thompson TC	.10	.05
□ 737 Daryl Boston	.10	.05	□ 823 Albert Belle TC	.40	.18
□ 738 Craig Grebeck	.10	.05	□ 824 Randy Johnson TC	.20	.09
□ 739 Doug Dascenzo	.10	.05	□ 825 Nigel Wilson TC	.10	.05
□ 740 Gerald Young	.10	.05	□ 826 Bobby Bonilla TC	.10	.05
□ 741 Candy Maldonado	.10	.05	□ 827 Glenn Davis TC	.10	.05
□ 742 Joey Cora	.20	.09	□ 828 Gary Sheffield TC	.20	.09
□ 743 Don Slaught	.10	.05	□ 829 Darren Daulton TC	.10	.05
□ 744 Steve Decker	.10	.05	□ 830 Jay Bell TC	.10	.05
□ 745 Blas Minor	.10	.05	□ 831 Juan Gonzalez TC	.50	.23
□ 746 Storm Davis	.10	.05	□ 832 Andre Dawson TC	.10	.05
□ 747 Carlos Quintana	.10	.05	□ 833 Hal Morris TC	.10	.05
□ 748 Vince Coleman	.10	.05	□ 834 David Nied TC	.10	.05
□ 749 Todd Burns	.10	.05	□ 835 Felix Jose TC	.10	.05
□ 750 Steve Frey	.10	.05	□ 836 Travis Fryman TC	.10	.05
□ 751 Ivan Calderon	.10	.05	□ 837 Shane Mack TC	.10	.05
□ 752 Steve Reed	.10	.05	□ 838 Robin Ventura TC	.20	.09
□ 753 Danny Jackson	.10	.05	□ 839 Danny Tartabull TC	.10	.05
□ 754 Jeff Conine	.20	.09	□ 840 Roberto Alomar CL	.40	.18
□ 755 Juan Gonzalez	1.00	.45	□ SP5 George Brett	1.50	.70

Robin Yount
3,000th Hit
□ SP6 Nolan Ryan 3.00 1.35

1993 Upper Deck Clutch Performers

These 20 standard-size cards were inserted one in series II retail foil packs, as well as inserted one per series II retail jumbo packs. The fronts feature color player action shots that are borderless, except at the bottom, where a black stripe is set off by a gold-foil line and carries the card's title and Reggie Jackson's gold-foil signature. The player's name is printed in white lettering rests at the bottom of the photo. The back carries a color player action shot below a black bar at the top that carries the player's name in gold-colored lettering. Below the picture appears a small black-and-white head shot of Reggie Jackson alongside his comments on the player. A player stat table appears below. The cards are numbered on the back with an "R" prefix and appear in alphabetical order. These 20 cards represent Reggie Jackson's selection of players who have come through under pressure.

	MINT	NRMT
COMPLETE SET (20)	20.00	9.00
COMMON CARD(R1-R20)	.25	.11
SER.2 STAT.ODDS: 1:9 RET, 1:1 RED JUMBO		
□ R1 Roberto Alomar	1.00	.45
□ R2 Wade Boggs	1.00	.45
□ R3 Barry Bonds	1.25	.55
□ R4 Jose Canseco	.75	.35
□ R5 Joe Carter	.50	.23
□ R6 Will Clark	.75	.35
□ R7 Roger Clemens	2.00	.90
□ R8 Dennis Eckersley	.50	.23
□ R9 Cecil Fielder	.50	.23
□ R10 Juan Gonzalez	2.50	1.10
□ R11 Ken Griffey Jr.	5.00	2.20
□ R12 Rickey Henderson	.75	.35
□ R13 Barry Larkin	.75	.35
□ R14 Don Mattingly	2.00	.90
□ R15 Fred McGriff	.75	.35
□ R16 Terry Pendleton	.25	.11
□ R17 Kirby Puckett	2.00	.90
□ R18 Ryne Sandberg	1.25	.55
□ R19 John Smoltz	.50	.23
□ R20 Frank Thomas	4.00	1.80

1993 Upper Deck Fifth Anniversary

This 15-card standard-size set celebrates Upper Deck's five years in the sports card business. The cards are essentially reprinted versions of some of Upper Deck's most popular cards in the last five years. These cards were inserted one every nine second series hobby packs. The black-bordered fronts feature player photos that previously appeared on an Upper Deck card. The Five-Year Anniversary logo is located in one of the corners and the player's name is printed in gold-foil along the lower black border. The black backs carry a picture of the original card on the left side with narrative historical information on Upper Deck and a brief career summary of the player. The gold-colored year of issue of the original card is prominently displayed in the middle of the text. The cards are numbered on the back with an "A" prefix. One over-sized (3 1/2" by 5") version of each of these cards was initially inserted into retail blister repacks, which contained one foil pack each of 1993 Upper Deck Series I and II. These cards are individually numbered out of 10,000 and were later inserted into various forms of repackaging.

	MINT	NRMT
COMPLETE SET (15)	20.00	9.00
COMMON CARD(A1-A15)	.25	.11
SER.2 STATED ODDS 1:9 HOBBY		
☐ A1 Ken Griffey Jr.	5.00	2.20
☐ A2 Gary Sheffield	1.00	.45
☐ A3 Roberto Alomar	1.00	.45
☐ A4 Jim Abbott	.25	.11
☐ A5 Nolan Ryan	4.00	1.80
☐ A6 Juan Gonzalez	2.50	1.10
☐ A7 David Justice	1.00	.45
☐ A8 Carlos Baerga	.25	.11
☐ A9 Reggie Jackson	1.00	.45
☐ A10 Eric Karros	.50	.23
☐ A11 Chipper Jones	5.00	2.20
☐ A12 Ivan Rodriguez	1.25	.55
☐ A13 Pat Listach	.25	.11
☐ A14 Frank Thomas	4.00	1.80
☐ A15 Tim Salmon	1.25	.55

1993 Upper Deck Future Heroes

Inserted in second series foil packs at a rate of one every nine pack; this set continues the Heroes insert set begun in the 1990 Upper Deck high-number set, this ten-card standard-size set features eight different "Future Heroes" along with a checklist and header card. The fronts feature borderless color player action shots that bear the player's simulated autograph in gold foil in an upper corner. The player's name appears within a black stripe formed by the simulated tearing away of a piece of the photo. The player's team appears below. The back carries the player's name vertically within a black "tear-away" stripe along the right edge. Career highlights are displayed within a white, gray, and tan panel on the left.

	MINT	NRMT
COMPLETE SET (10)	12.00	5.50
COMMON CARD(55-63,NNO)	.25	.11
SER.2 STATED ODDS 1:9		
☐ 55 Roberto Alomar	1.00	.45
☐ 56 Barry Bonds	1.25	.55
☐ 57 Roger Clemens	2.00	.90
☐ 58 Juan Gonzalez	2.00	1.10
☐ 59 Ken Griffey Jr.	5.00	2.20
☐ 60 Mark McGwire	2.00	1.10
☐ 61 Kirby Puckett	2.00	.90
☐ 62 Frank Thomas	4.00	1.80
☐ 63 Checklist	.25	.11
☐ NNO Header Card SP	.75	.35

1993 Upper Deck Home Run Heroes

This 28-card standard-size set features the home run leader from each Major League team. Each 1993 first series 27-card jumbo pack contained one of these cards. The cards feature action color player photos with a three-dimensional baseball bat design at the bottom. Featuring embossed printing, the bat looks and feels as if it stands off the card, and a shadow design below it adds to the effect. The words "Homerun Heroes" are printed vertically down the left. The backs show a team color-coded photo as the background

for player information. The player's name appears in a white border on the right. The baseball bat design is repeated at the bottom. The cards are numbered on the back with an "HR" prefix and the set is arranged in descending order according to the number of home runs.

	MINT	NRMT
COMPLETE SET (28)	15.00	6.75
COMMON CARD(HR1-HR28)	.25	.11
ONE PER SER.1 JUMBO PACK..		
☐ HR1 Juan Gonzalez	2.50	1.10
☐ HR2 Mark McGwire	2.50	1.10
☐ HR3 Cecil Fielder	.50	.23
☐ HR4 Fred McGriff	.75	.35
☐ HR5 Albert Belle	1.25	.55
☐ HR6 Barry Bonds	1.00	.45
☐ HR7 Joe Carter	.50	.23
☐ HR8 Darren Daulton	.50	.23
☐ HR9 Ken Griffey Jr.	5.00	2.20
☐ HR10 Dave Hollins	.25	.11
☐ HR11 Ryne Sandberg	1.25	.55
☐ HR12 George Bell	.25	.11
☐ HR13 Danny Tartabull	.25	.11
☐ HR14 Mike Devereaux	.25	.11
☐ HR15 Greg Vaughn	.25	.11
☐ HR16 Larry Walker	1.00	.45
☐ HR17 David Justice	.50	.23
☐ HR18 Terry Pendleton	.25	.11
☐ HR19 Eric Karros	.50	.23
☐ HR20 Ray Lankford	.75	.35
☐ HR21 Matt Williams	.75	.35
☐ HR22 Eric Anthony	.25	.11
☐ HR23 Bobby Bonilla	.50	.23
☐ HR24 Kirby Puckett	2.00	.90
☐ HR25 Mike Macfarlane	.25	.11
☐ HR26 Tom Brunansky	.25	.11
☐ HR27 Paul O'Neill	.50	.23
☐ HR28 Gary Gaetti	.25	.11

1993 Upper Deck Iooss Collection

This 27-card standard-size set spotlights the work of famous sports photographer Walter looss Jr. by presenting 26 of the game's current greats in a candid photo set. The cards were inserted in series I retail foil packs at a rate of one every nine packs. They were also in retail jumbo packs at a rate of one in five packs. The posed color player photos on the fronts are full-bleed and either horizontally or vertically oriented. The words "The Upper Deck looss Collection" are printed in gold foil. The back carries a quote from looss about the shoot and the player's career highlights. The text blocks on the card backs are separated by a gradated bars of varying colors. The cards are numbered on the back with a "WI" prefix. One over-sized version of each of these cards were initially inserted into retail blister repacks containing one foil pack each of 1993 Upper Deck Series I and II. These over-sized (3 1/2" by 5") cards are individually numbered out of 10,000 and were later inserted in various forms of repackaging.

	MINT	NRMT
COMPLETE SET (27)	25.00	11.00
COMMON CARD(W1-W126)	.25	.11
SER.1 STATED ODDS 1:9 RET, 1:5 JUM		

		MINT	NRMT
☐ WI1	Tim Salmon	1.50	.70
☐ WI2	Jeff Bagwell	2.50	1.10
☐ WI3	Mark McGwire	3.00	1.35
☐ WI4	Roberto Alomar	1.50	.70
☐ WI5	Steve Avery	.25	.11
☐ WI6	Paul Molitor	1.00	.45
☐ WI7	Ozzie Smith	1.50	.70
☐ WI8	Mark Grace	.75	.35
☐ WI9	Eric Karros	.50	.23
☐ WI10	Delino DeShields	.25	.11
☐ WI11	Will Clark	.75	.35
☐ WI12	Albert Belle	1.50	.70
☐ WI13	Ken Griffey Jr.	6.00	2.70
☐ WI14	Howard Johnson	.25	.11
☐ WI15	Cal Ripken Jr.	5.00	2.20
☐ WI16	Fred McGriff	.75	.35
☐ WI17	Darren Daulton	.50	.23
☐ WI18	Andy Van Slyke	.25	.11
☐ WI19	Nolan Ryan	5.00	2.20
☐ WI20	Wade Boggs	1.00	.45
☐ WI21	Barry Larkin	.75	.35
☐ WI22	George Brett	2.50	1.10
☐ WI23	Cecil Fielder	.50	.23
☐ WI24	Kirby Puckett	2.50	1.10
☐ WI25	Frank Thomas	5.00	2.20
☐ WI26	Don Mattingly	2.50	1.10
☐ NNO	Title Card	.50	.23
	looss Header		

1993 Upper Deck On Deck

Inserted one per series II jumbo packs, these 25 standard-size cards profile baseball's top players. The fronts feature borderless color player photos, some action, others posed, and carry the player's simulated gold-foil signature within a team color-coded stripe that appears as part of the set's logo. The gradated-tan-colored back carries the player's name, position, and team vertically within a team color-coded stripe near the left

edge. The player's answers to personal questions rounds out the back. The cards are numbered on the back with a "D" prefix in alphabetical order by name.

		MINT	NRMT
COMPLETE SET (25)		20.00	9.00
COMMON CARD(D1-D25)		.25	.11
SER.2 STAT.ODDS 1:1 RED/BLUE JUMBO			

		MINT	NRMT
☐ D1	Jim Abbott	.25	.11
☐ D2	Roberto Alomar	1.00	.45
☐ D3	Carlos Baerga	.25	.11
☐ D4	Albert Belle	1.25	.55
☐ D5	Wade Boggs	1.00	.45
☐ D6	George Brett	2.00	.90
☐ D7	Jose Canseco	.75	.35
☐ D8	Will Clark	.75	.35
☐ D9	Roger Clemens	2.00	.90
☐ D10	Dennis Eckersley	.50	.23
☐ D11	Cecil Fielder	.50	.23
☐ D12	Juan Gonzalez	2.50	1.10
☐ D13	Ken Griffey Jr.	5.00	2.20
☐ D14	Tony Gwynn	2.50	1.10
☐ D15	Bo Jackson	.50	.23
☐ D16	Chipper Jones	5.00	2.20
☐ D17	Eric Karros	.50	.23
☐ D18	Mark McGwire	2.50	1.10
☐ D19	Kirby Puckett	2.00	.90
☐ D20	Nolan Ryan	4.00	1.80
☐ D21	Tim Salmon	1.25	.55
☐ D22	Ryne Sandberg	1.25	.55
☐ D23	Darryl Strawberry	.50	.23
☐ D24	Frank Thomas	4.00	1.80
☐ D25	Andy Van Slyke	.25	.11

1993 Upper Deck Season Highlights

This 20-card standard-size insert set captures great moments of the 1992 Major League Baseball season. The cards were exclusively distributed in specially marked cases that were available only at Upper Deck Heroes of Baseball

Card Shows and through the purchase of a specified quantity of second series cases. In these packs, the cards were inserted at a rate of one every nine. The fronts display a full-bleed color action photo with a special "'92 Season Highlights" logo running across the bottom. The ribbon intersecting the logo is blue on the American League cards and red on the National League. The date of the player's outstanding achievement is gold-foil stamped at the lower right. On backs that fade from the league color to white, a description of the achievement is presented. The year 1992 is printed diagonally across the backs. The cards are numbered on the back with an "HI" prefix in alphabetical order by player's name.

		MINT	NRMT
COMPLETE SET (20)		150.00	70.00
COMMON CARD (HI1-HI20)		2.50	1.10
SEMISTARS		5.00	2.20
UNLISTED STARS		10.00	4.50
STATED ODDS 1:9 HOBBY SEASON HL			

		MINT	NRMT
☐ HI1	Roberto Alomar	10.00	4.50
☐ HI2	Steve Avery	2.50	1.10
☐ HI3	Harold Baines	4.00	1.80
☐ HI4	Damon Berryhill	2.50	1.10
☐ HI5	Barry Bonds	12.00	5.50
☐ HI6	Bret Boone	2.50	1.10
☐ HI7	George Brett	20.00	9.00
☐ HI8	Francisco Cabrera	2.50	1.10
☐ HI9	Ken Griffey Jr.	50.00	22.00
☐ HI10	Rickey Henderson	5.00	2.20
☐ HI11	Kenny Lofton	15.00	6.75
☐ HI12	Mickey Morandini	2.50	1.10
☐ HI13	Eddie Murray	10.00	4.50
☐ HI14	David Nied	2.50	1.10
☐ HI15	Jeff Reardon	4.00	1.80
☐ HI16	Bip Roberts	2.50	1.10
☐ HI17	Nolan Ryan	50.00	22.00
☐ HI18	Ed Sprague	2.50	1.10
☐ HI19	Dave Winfield	5.00	2.20
☐ HI20	Robin Yount	5.00	2.20

1993 Upper Deck Then And Now

This 18-card, standard-size hologram set highlights veteran stars in their rookie year and today, reflecting on how they and the game have changed. Cards 1-9 were randomly inserted in series I foil packs; cards 10-18 were randomly inserted in series II foil packs. In either series, the cards were inserted

one every 27 packs. The nine lithogram cards in the second series feature one card each of Hall of Famers Reggie Jackson, Mickey Mantle, and Willie Mays, as well as six active players. The horizontal fronts have a color close-up photo cutout and superimposed at the left corner of a full-bleed hologram portraying the player in an action scene. The skyline of the player's city serves as the background for the holograms. The player's name and the manufacturer's name form a right angle at the upper right corner. At the upper left corner, a "Then And Now" logo which includes the length of the player's career in years rounds out the front. On a sand-colored panel that resembles a postage stamp, the backs present career summary. The cards are numbered on the back with a "TN" prefix and arranged alphabetically within subgroup according to player's last name.

	MINT	NRMT
COMPLETE SET (18)	50.00	22.00
COMPLETE SERIES 1 (9)	20.00	9.00
COMPLETE SERIES 2 (9)	30.00	13.50
COMMON CARD(TN1-TN18)	.50	.23
STATED ODDS 1:27 HOBBY		

		MINT	NRMT
☐ TN1	Wade Boggs	1.50	.70
☐ TN2	George Brett	4.00	1.80
☐ TN3	Rickey Henderson	1.00	.45
☐ TN4	Cal Ripken	8.00	3.60
☐ TN5	Nolan Ryan	8.00	3.60
☐ TN6	Ryne Sandberg	2.50	1.10
☐ TN7	Ozzie Smith	2.50	1.10
☐ TN8	Darryl Strawberry	.75	.35
☐ TN9	Dave Winfield	1.00	.45
☐ TN10	Dennis Eckersley	.75	.35
☐ TN11	Tony Gwynn	5.00	2.20
☐ TN12	Howard Johnson	.50	.23
☐ TN13	Don Mattingly	4.00	1.80
☐ TN14	Eddie Murray	1.50	.70
☐ TN15	Robin Yount	1.00	.45
☐ TN16	Reggie Jackson	2.50	1.10
☐ TN17	Mickey Mantle	15.00	6.75
☐ TN18	Willie Mays	8.00	3.60

1993 Upper Deck Triple Crown

This ten-card, standard-size insert set highlights ten players who were selected by Upper Deck as having the best shot at winning Major League Baseball's Triple Crown. The cards were randomly inserted in

series I hobby foil packs at a rate of one in 15. The fronts display glossy full-bleed color player photos. At the bottom, a purple ribbon edged in gold foil carries the words "Triple Crown Contenders," while the player's name appears in gold foil lettering immediately below on a gradated black background. A crown overlays the ribbon at the lower left corner and rounds out the front. On a gradated black background, the backs summarize the player's performance in home runs, RBIs, and batting average. The cards are numbered on the back with a "TC" prefix and arranged alphabetically by player's last name.

	MINT	NRMT
COMPLETE SET (10)	30.00	13.50
COMMON CARD(TC1-TC10)	1.50	.70
STATED ODDS 1:15 HOBBY		

		MINT	NRMT
☐ TC1	Barry Bonds	2.50	1.10
☐ TC2	Jose Canseco	1.50	.70
☐ TC3	Will Clark	1.50	.70
☐ TC4	Ken Griffey Jr.	10.00	4.50
☐ TC5	Fred McGriff	1.25	.55
☐ TC6	Kirby Puckett	4.00	1.80
☐ TC7	Cal Ripken Jr.	8.00	3.60
☐ TC8	Gary Sheffield	2.00	.90
☐ TC9	Frank Thomas	8.00	3.60
☐ TC10	Larry Walker	2.00	.90

1994 Upper Deck

The 1994 Upper Deck set was issued in two series of 280 and 270 standard-size cards for a total of 550. Card fronts feature a color photo of the player with a smaller version of the same photo along the left-hand border. The player's name appears in a black box in the upper left-hand corner. There are number of topical subsets including Star Rookies (1-30), Fantasy Team (31-40), The Future Is Now (41-55), Home Field Advantage (267-294), Upper Deck Classic Alumni (295-299), Diamond Debuts (511-522) and Top Prospects (523-550). Three autograph cards were randomly inserted into first series retail packs. They are Ken Griffey Jr. (KG), Mickey Mantle (MM) and a combo card with Griffey and Mantle (GM). An Alex Rodriguez (298A) autograph card was randomly inserted into second series retail packs. Rookie Cards include Alan

Benes, Michael Jordan, Derrek Lee, Chan Ho Park, Alex Rodriguez and Billy Wagner. Many cards have been found with a significant variation on the back. The player's name, the horizontal bar containing the biographical information and the vertical bar containing the stats header are normally printed in copper-gold color. On the variation cards, these areas are printed in silver. It is not known exactly how many of the 550 cards have silver versions, nor has any premium been established for them. Also, all of the American League Home Field Advantage subset cards (#281-294) are minor uncorrected errors because the Upper Deck logos on the front are missing the year "1994."

	MINT	EXC
COMPLETE SET (550)	50.00	22.00
COMPLETE SERIES 1 (280)	30.00	13.50
COMPLETE SERIES 2 (270)	20.00	9.00
COMMON CARD (1-550)	.15	.07
MINOR STARS	.30	.14
UNLISTED STARS	.60	.25
SUBSET CARDS HALF VALUE OF BASE CARDS		
COMP.ED SET (550)	130.00	57.50
COMP.ED SER.1 (280)	80.00	36.00
COMP.ED SER.2 (270)	50.00	22.00
COMMON ELEC.DIAM. (1-550)	.20	.09
*ELEC.DIAM.STARS: 1.5X TO 4X HI COLUMN		
*ELEC.DIAM.YOUNG STARS: 1.25X TO 3X HI		
*ELEC.DIAM.ROOKIES: 1X TO 2X HI		
ONE ELECTRIC DIAMOND PER PACK		
COMP.MANTLE SET (10)	100.00	45.00
COMMON MANTLE (64-72/HDR)	12.00	5.50
MANTLE SER.2 STATED ODDS 1:35		
GRIFFEY/MANTLE AU INSERTS IN SER.1 RET.		
A.RODRIGUEZ AU INSERT IN SER.2 RET.		

		MINT	EXC
☐ 1	Brian Anderson	.60	.25
☐ 2	Shane Andrews	.15	.07
☐ 3	James Baldwin	.30	.14
☐ 4	Rich Becker	.15	.07
☐ 5	Greg Blosser	.15	.07
☐ 6	Ricky Bottalico	.60	.25
☐ 7	Midre Cummings	.15	.07
☐ 8	Carlos Delgado	.40	.18
☐ 9	Steve Dreyer	.15	.07
☐ 10	Joey Eischen	.15	.07
☐ 11	Carl Everett	.15	.07
☐ 12	Cliff Floyd UER	.30	.14
	(text indicates he throws left; should be right)		
☐ 13	Alex Gonzalez	.30	.14
☐ 14	Jeff Granger	.15	.07
☐ 15	Shawn Green	.30	.14
☐ 16	Brian L. Hunter	.60	.25
☐ 17	Butch Huskey	.30	.14
☐ 18	Mark Hutton	.15	.07
☐ 19	Michael Jordan	10.00	4.50
☐ 20	Steve Karsay	.15	.07
☐ 21	Jeff McNeely	.15	.07
☐ 22	Marc Newfield	.30	.14
☐ 23	Manny Ramirez	.75	.35
☐ 24	Alex Rodriguez	8.00	3.60
☐ 25	Scott Ruffcorn UER	.15	.07
	(photo on back is Robert Ellis)		
☐ 26	Paul Spoljaric UER	.15	.07
	(Expos logo on back)		
☐ 27	Salomon Torres	.15	.07
☐ 28	Steve Trachsel	.30	.14
☐ 29	Chris Turner	.15	.07
☐ 30	Gabe White	.15	.07
☐ 31	Randy Johnson FT	.30	.14
☐ 32	John Wetteland FT	.15	.07
☐ 33	Mike Piazza FT	1.00	.45
☐ 34	Rafael Palmeiro FT	.30	.14
☐ 35	Roberto Alomar FT	.30	.14
☐ 36	Matt Williams FT	.30	.14

☐ 37	Travis Fryman FT	.15	.07
☐ 38	Barry Bonds FT	.40	.18
☐ 39	Marquis Grissom FT	.15	.07
☐ 40	Albert Belle FT	.40	.18
☐ 41	Steve Avery FUT	.15	.07
☐ 42	Jason Bere FUT	.15	.07
☐ 43	Alex Fernandez FUT	.15	.07
☐ 44	Mike Mussina FUT	.30	.14
☐ 45	Aaron Sele FUT	.15	.07
☐ 46	Rod Beck FUT	.15	.07
☐ 47	Mike Piazza FUT	1.00	.45
☐ 48	John Olerud FUT	.15	.07
☐ 49	Carlos Baerga FUT	.15	.07
☐ 50	Gary Sheffield FUT	.30	.14
☐ 51	Travis Fryman FUT	.15	.07
☐ 52	Juan Gonzalez FUT	.75	.35
☐ 53	Ken Griffey Jr. FUT	1.50	.70
☐ 54	Tim Salmon FUT	.30	.14
☐ 55	Frank Thomas FUT	1.25	.55
☐ 56	Tony Phillips	.15	.07
☐ 57	Julio Franco	.15	.07
☐ 58	Kevin Mitchell	.15	.07
☐ 59	Raul Mondesi	.50	.25
☐ 60	Rickey Henderson	.40	.18
☐ 61	Jay Buhner	.15	.07
☐ 62	Bill Swift	.15	.07
☐ 63	Brady Anderson	.40	.18
☐ 64	Ryan Klesko	.60	.25
☐ 65	Darren Daulton	.30	.14
☐ 66	Damion Easley	.15	.07
☐ 67	Mark McGwire	1.25	.55
☐ 68	John Roper	.15	.07
☐ 69	Dave Telgheder	.15	.07
☐ 70	Dave Nied	.15	.07
☐ 71	Mo Vaughn	.75	.35
☐ 72	Tyler Green	.15	.07
☐ 73	Dave Magadan	.15	.07
☐ 74	Chili Davis	.30	.14
☐ 75	Archi Cianfrocco	.15	.07
☐ 76	Joe Girardi	.15	.07
☐ 77	Chris Hoiles	.15	.07
☐ 78	Ryan Bowen	.15	.07
☐ 79	Greg Gagne	.15	.07
☐ 80	Aaron Sele	.15	.07
☐ 81	Dave Winfield	.40	.18
☐ 82	Chad Curtis	.15	.07
☐ 83	Andy Van Slyke	.30	.14
☐ 84	Kevin Stocker	.15	.07
☐ 85	Deion Sanders	.30	.14
☐ 86	Bernie Williams	.60	.25
☐ 87	John Smoltz	.30	.14
☐ 88	Ruben Santana	.15	.07
☐ 89	Dave Stewart	.30	.14
☐ 90	Don Mattingly	1.00	.45
☐ 91	Joe Carter	.30	.14
☐ 92	Ryne Sandberg	.75	.35
☐ 93	Chris Gomez	.15	.07
☐ 94	Tino Martinez	.60	.25
☐ 95	Terry Pendleton	.15	.07
☐ 96	Andre Dawson	.40	.18
☐ 97	Wil Cordero	.15	.07
☐ 98	Kent Hrbek	.30	.14
☐ 99	John Olerud	.30	.14
☐ 100	Kirt Manwaring	.15	.07
☐ 101	Tim Bogar	.15	.07
☐ 102	Mike Mussina	.60	.25
☐ 103	Nigel Wilson	.15	.07
☐ 104	Ricky Gutierrez	.15	.07
☐ 105	Roberto Mejia	.15	.07
☐ 106	Tom Pagnozzi	.15	.07
☐ 107	Mike Macfarlane	.15	.07
☐ 108	Jose Bautista	.15	.07
☐ 109	Luis Ortiz	.15	.07
☐ 110	Brent Gates	.15	.07
☐ 111	Tim Salmon	.60	.25
☐ 112	Wade Boggs	.60	.25
☐ 113	Tripp Cromer	.15	.07
☐ 114	Denny Hocking	.15	.07
☐ 115	Carlos Baerga	.15	.07
☐ 116	J.R. Phillips	.15	.07
☐ 117	Bo Jackson	.30	.14
☐ 118	Lance Johnson	.15	.07
☐ 119	Bobby Jones	.30	.14
☐ 120	Bobby Witt	.15	.07
☐ 121	Ron Karkovice	.15	.07
☐ 122	Jose Vizcaino	.15	.07
☐ 123	Danny Darwin	.15	.07
☐ 124	Eduardo Perez	.15	.07
☐ 125	Brian Looney	.15	.07
☐ 126	Pat Hentgen	.30	.14
☐ 127	Frank Viola	.15	.07
☐ 128	Darren Holmes	.15	.07
☐ 129	Wally Whitehurst	.15	.07
☐ 130	Matt Walbeck	.15	.07
☐ 131	Albert Belle	.75	.35
☐ 132	Steve Cooke	.15	.07
☐ 133	Kevin Appier	.30	.14
☐ 134	Joe Oliver	.15	.07
☐ 135	Benji Gil	.15	.07
☐ 136	Steve Buechele	.15	.07
☐ 137	Devon White	.15	.07
☐ 138	Sterling Hitchcock UER (two losses for career; should be four)	.15	.07
☐ 139	Phil Leftwich	.15	.07
☐ 140	Jose Canseco	.40	.18
☐ 141	Rick Aguilera	.15	.07
☐ 142	Rod Beck	.15	.07
☐ 143	Jose Rijo	.15	.07
☐ 144	Tom Glavine	.30	.14
☐ 145	Phil Plantier	.15	.07
☐ 146	Jason Bere	.15	.07
☐ 147	Jamie Moyer	.15	.07
☐ 148	Wes Chamberlain	.15	.07
☐ 149	Glenallen Hill	.15	.07
☐ 150	Mark Whiten	.15	.07
☐ 151	Bret Barberie	.15	.07
☐ 152	Chuck Knoblauch	.60	.25
☐ 153	Trevor Hoffman	.15	.07
☐ 154	Rick Wilkins	.15	.07
☐ 155	Juan Gonzalez	1.50	.70
☐ 156	Ozzie Guillen	.15	.07
☐ 157	Jim Eisenreich	.15	.07
☐ 158	Pedro Astacio	.15	.07
☐ 159	Joe Magrane	.15	.07
☐ 160	Ryan Thompson	.15	.07
☐ 161	Jose Lind	.15	.07
☐ 162	Jeff Conine	.30	.14
☐ 163	Todd Benzinger	.15	.07
☐ 164	Roger Salkeld	.15	.07
☐ 165	Gary DiSarcina	.15	.07
☐ 166	Kevin Gross	.15	.07
☐ 167	Charlie Hayes	.15	.07
☐ 168	Tim Costo	.15	.07
☐ 169	Wally Joyner	.30	.14
☐ 170	Johnny Ruffin	.15	.07
☐ 171	Kirk Rueter	.15	.07
☐ 172	Lenny Dykstra	.30	.14
☐ 173	Ken Hill	.15	.07
☐ 174	Mike Bordick	.15	.07
☐ 175	Billy Hall	.15	.07
☐ 176	Rob Butler	.15	.07
☐ 177	Jay Bell	.30	.14
☐ 178	Jeff Kent	.25	.11
☐ 179	David Wells	.15	.07
☐ 180	Dean Palmer	.15	.07
☐ 181	Mariano Duncan	.15	.07
☐ 182	Orlando Merced	.15	.07
☐ 183	Brett Butler	.30	.14
☐ 184	Milt Thompson	.15	.07
☐ 185	Chipper Jones	2.00	.90
☐ 186	Paul O'Neill	.30	.14
☐ 187	Mike Greenwell	.15	.07
☐ 188	Harold Baines	.30	.14
☐ 189	Todd Stottlemyre	.15	.07
☐ 190	Jeromy Burnitz	.15	.07
☐ 191	Rene Arocha	.15	.07
☐ 192	Jeff Fassero	.15	.07
☐ 193	Robby Thompson	.15	.07
☐ 194	Greg W. Harris	.15	.07
☐ 195	Todd Van Poppel	.15	.07
☐ 196	Jose Guzman	.15	.07
☐ 197	Shane Mack	.15	.07
☐ 198	Carlos Garcia	.15	.07
☐ 199	Kevin Roberson	.15	.07
☐ 200	David McCarty	.15	.07
☐ 201	Alan Trammell	.40	.18
☐ 202	Chuck Carr	.15	.07
☐ 203	Tommy Greene	.15	.07
☐ 204	Wilson Alvarez	.15	.07
☐ 205	Dwight Gooden	.30	.14
☐ 206	Tony Tarasco	.15	.07
☐ 207	Darren Lewis	.15	.07
☐ 208	Eric Karros	.30	.14
☐ 209	Chris Hammond	.15	.07
☐ 210	Jeffrey Hammonds	.30	.14
☐ 211	Rich Amaral	.15	.07
☐ 212	Danny Tartabull	.15	.07
☐ 213	Jeff Russell	.15	.07
☐ 214	Dave Staton	.15	.07
☐ 215	Kenny Lofton	.75	.35
☐ 216	Manuel Lee	.15	.07
☐ 217	Brian Koelling	.15	.07
☐ 218	Scott Lydy	.15	.07
☐ 219	Tony Gwynn	1.50	.70
☐ 220	Cecil Fielder	.30	.14
☐ 221	Royce Clayton	.15	.07
☐ 222	Reggie Sanders	.15	.07
☐ 223	Brian Jordan	.30	.14
☐ 224	Ken Griffey Jr.	3.00	1.35
☐ 225	Fred McGriff	.40	.18
☐ 226	Felix Jose	.15	.07
☐ 227	Brad Pennington	.15	.07
☐ 228	Chris Bosio	.15	.07
☐ 229	Mike Stanley	.15	.07
☐ 230	Willie Greene	.15	.07
☐ 231	Alex Fernandez	.15	.07
☐ 232	Brad Ausmus	.15	.07
☐ 233	Darrell Whitmore	.15	.07
☐ 234	Marcus Moore	.15	.07
☐ 235	Allen Watson	.15	.07
☐ 236	Jose Offerman	.15	.07
☐ 237	Rondell White	.40	.18
☐ 238	Jeff King	.15	.07
☐ 239	Luis Alicea	.15	.07
☐ 240	Dan Wilson	.30	.14
☐ 241	Ed Sprague	.15	.07
☐ 242	Todd Hundley	.30	.14
☐ 243	Al Martin	.15	.07
☐ 244	Mike Lansing	.30	.14
☐ 245	Ivan Rodriguez	.75	.35
☐ 246	Dave Fleming	.15	.07
☐ 247	John Doherty	.15	.07
☐ 248	Mark McLemore	.15	.07
☐ 249	Bob Hamelin	.15	.07
☐ 250	Curtis Pride	.15	.07
☐ 251	Zane Smith	.15	.07
☐ 252	Eric Young	.15	.07
☐ 253	Brian McRae	.15	.07
☐ 254	Tim Raines	.30	.14
☐ 255	Javier Lopez	.40	.18
☐ 256	Melvin Nieves	.15	.07
☐ 257	Randy Myers	.15	.07
☐ 258	Willie McGee	.15	.07
☐ 259	Jimmy Key UER (birthdate missing on back)	.30	.14
☐ 260	Tom Candiotti	.15	.07
☐ 261	Eric Davis	.30	.14
☐ 262	Craig Paquette	.15	.07
☐ 263	Robin Ventura	.30	.14
☐ 264	Pat Kelly	.15	.07
☐ 265	Gregg Jefferies	.15	.07
☐ 266	Cory Snyder	.15	.07
☐ 267	David Justice HFA	.30	.14
☐ 268	Sammy Sosa HFA	.30	.14
☐ 269	Barry Larkin HFA	.30	.14
☐ 270	Andres Galarraga HFA	.30	.14
☐ 271	Gary Sheffield HFA	.30	.14
☐ 272	Jeff Bagwell HFA	.75	.35
☐ 273	Mike Piazza HFA	1.00	.45
☐ 274	Larry Walker HFA	.30	.14
☐ 275	Bobby Bonilla HFA	.15	.07
☐ 276	John Kruk HFA	.15	.07
☐ 277	Jay Bell HFA	.15	.07
☐ 278	Ozzie Smith HFA	.60	.25
☐ 279	Tony Gwynn HFA	.75	.35
☐ 280	Barry Bonds HFA	.40	.18
☐ 281	Cal Ripken Jr. HFA	1.25	.55
☐ 282	Mo Vaughn HFA	.40	.18
☐ 283	Tim Salmon HFA	.30	.14
☐ 284	Frank Thomas HFA	1.25	.55
☐ 285	Albert Belle HFA	.40	.18
☐ 286	Cecil Fielder HFA	.15	.07
☐ 287	Wally Joyner HFA	.15	.07
☐ 288	Greg Vaughn HFA	.15	.07
☐ 289	Kirby Puckett HFA	.60	.25
☐ 290	Don Mattingly HFA	.40	.18
☐ 291	Terry Steinbach HFA	.15	.07

	MINT	NRMT
☐ 550 Derek Jeter TP	2.50	1.10
☐ A298 Alex Rodriguez AU	150.00	70.00
☐ P224 Ken Griffey Jr. Promo	3.00	1.35
☐ GM1 Ken Griffey Jr. AU 1200.00	550.00	
Mickey Mantle AU/1000		
☐ KG1 Ken Griffey Jr. AU1000	250.00	110.00
☐ MM1 Mickey Mantle AU1000	600.00	275.00

1994 Upper Deck Diamond Collection

This 30-card standard-size set was inserted regionally in first series hobby packs at a rate of one in 18. The three regions are Central (C1-C10), East (E1-E10) and West (W1-W10). While each card has the same horizontal format, the color scheme differs by region. The Central cards have a blue background, the East green and the West a deep shade of red. Color player photos are superimposed over the backgrounds. Each card has, "The Upper Deck Diamond Collection" as part of the background. The backs have a small photo and career highlights.

	MINT	NRMT
COMPLETE SET (30)	300.00	135.00
COMPLETE CENTRAL (10)	140.00	65.00
COMPLETE EAST (10)	60.00	27.00
COMPLETE WEST (10)	100.00	45.00
COMMON CARD	2.50	1.10
SEMISTARS	5.00	2.20
UNLISTED STARS	8.00	3.60
SER.1 STATED ODDS 1:18 HOBBY REGIONAL		

		MINT	NRMT
☐ C1	Jeff Bagwell	15.00	6.75
☐ C2	Michael Jordan	50.00	22.00
☐ C3	Barry Larkin	5.00	2.20
☐ C4	Kirby Puckett	15.00	6.75
☐ C5	Manny Ramirez	10.00	4.50
☐ C6	Ryne Sandberg	10.00	4.50
☐ C7	Ozzie Smith	10.00	4.50
☐ C8	Frank Thomas	30.00	13.50
☐ C9	Andy Van Slyke	4.00	1.80
☐ C10	Robin Yount	5.00	2.20
☐ E1	Roberto Alomar	8.00	3.60
☐ E2	Roger Clemens	15.00	6.75
☐ E3	Lenny Dykstra	4.00	1.80
☐ E4	Cecil Fielder	4.00	1.80
☐ E5	Cliff Floyd	4.00	1.80
☐ E6	Dwight Gooden	4.00	1.80
☐ E7	David Justice	8.00	3.60
☐ E8	Don Mattingly	12.00	5.50
☐ E9	Cal Ripken Jr.	30.00	13.50
☐ E10	Gary Sheffield	8.00	3.60
☐ W1	Barry Bonds	10.00	4.50
☐ W2	Andres Galarraga	8.00	3.60

		MINT	NRMT
☐ W3	Juan Gonzalez	20.00	9.00
☐ W4	Ken Griffey Jr.	40.00	18.00
☐ W5	Tony Gwynn	20.00	9.00
☐ W6	Rickey Henderson	5.00	2.20
☐ W7	Bo Jackson	4.00	1.80
☐ W8	Mark McGwire	15.00	6.75
☐ W9	Mike Piazza	25.00	11.00
☐ W10	Tim Salmon	8.00	3.60

1994 Upper Deck Griffey Jumbos

Measuring 4 7/8" by 6 13/16", these four Griffey cards serve as checklists for first series Upper Deck issues. They were issued one per first series hobby foil box. Card fronts have a full color photo with a small Griffey hologram. The first three cards provide a numerical, alphabetical and team organized checklist for the basic set. The fourth card is a checklist of inserts. Each card was printed in different quantities with CL1 the most plentiful and CL4 the more scarce. The backs are numbered with a CL prefix.

	MINT	NRMT
COMPLETE SET (4)	20.00	9.00
COMMON GRIFFEY (CL1-CL4)	4.00	1.80
ONE PER SEALED SER.1 HOBBY FOIL BOX		

		MINT	NRMT
☐ CL1	Numerical CL TP	4.00	1.80
☐ CL2	Alphabetical CL DP	5.00	2.20
☐ CL3	Team CL	6.00	2.70
☐ CL4	Insert CL SP	8.00	3.60

1994 Upper Deck Mantle's Long Shots

Randomly inserted in first series retail packs at a rate of one in

18, this 21-card silver foil standard-size set features top longball hitters as selected by Mickey Mantle. Card fronts are horizontal with a color player photo standing out from a dulled holographic image. The backs have a vertical format with a player photo at the top, a small photo of Mickey Mantle, a quote from The Mick and their power numbers. The cards are numbered on the back with a "MM" prefix and sequenced in alphabetical order. Two trade cards, were also random inserts and were redeemable (expiration: December 31, 1994) for either the basic silver foil set version (Silver Trade card) or the Electric Diamond version (blue Trade card).

	MINT	NRMT
COMPLETE SET (21)	50.00	22.00
UNLISTED STARS	2.00	.90
COMMON CARD (MM1-MM21)	.50	.23
SER.1 STATED ODDS 1:18 RETAIL		
ONE SET VIA MAIL PER SILVER TRADE CARD		
COMP.ELEC.DIAM.SET (21)	60.00	27.00
*ELEC.DIAMOND: .5X TO 1.2X BASIC MANTLE		
ONE ED SET VIA MAIL PER BLUE TRD.CARD		
TRADES: RANDOM INS.IN SER.1 HOB.PACKS		

		MINT	NRMT
☐ MM1	Jeff Bagwell	4.00	1.80
☐ MM2	Albert Belle	2.00	.90
☐ MM3	Barry Bonds	2.50	1.10
☐ MM4	Jose Canseco	1.50	.70
☐ MM5	Joe Carter	1.00	.45
☐ MM6	Carlos Delgado	1.50	.70
☐ MM7	Cecil Fielder	1.00	.45
☐ MM8	Cliff Floyd	1.00	.45
☐ MM9	Juan Gonzalez	5.00	2.20
☐ MM10	Ken Griffey Jr.	10.00	4.50
☐ MM11	David Justice	2.00	.90
☐ MM12	Fred McGriff	1.50	.70
☐ MM13	Mark McGwire	4.00	1.80
☐ MM14	Dean Palmer	.50	.23
☐ MM15	Mike Piazza	6.00	2.70
☐ MM16	Manny Ramirez	2.00	.90
☐ MM17	Tim Salmon	2.00	.90
☐ MM18	Frank Thomas	8.00	3.60
☐ MM19	Mo Vaughn	2.50	1.10
☐ MM20	Matt Williams	1.50	.70
☐ MM21	Mickey Mantle	15.00	6.75
☐ NNO	M.Mantle Blue ED Trade	12.00	5.50
☐ NNO	M.Mantle Silver Trade	6.00	2.70

1994 Upper Deck Next Generation

Randomly inserted in second series retail packs at a rate of one in 20, this 18-card standard-size set spotlights young established stars and promising

prospects. The set is sequenced in alphabetical order. Metallic fronts feature a color player photo on solid background. A small player hologram is halfway up the card on the right and comes between the player's first and last name. The Next Generation logo is at bottom left. Horizontal backs contain statistical comparisons, where applicable, to Hall of Famers and brief write-up noting the comparisons. A Next Generation Electric Diamond Trade Card and a Next Generation Trade Card were seeded randomly in second series hobby packs. Each card could be redeemed for that set. Expiration date for redemption was October 31, 1994.

	MINT	NRMT
COMPLETE SET (18)	140.00	65.00
COMMON CARD (1-18)	3.00	1.35
SER.2 STATED ODDS 1:20 RETAIL		
ONE SET VIA MAIL PER TRADE CARD		
COMP.ELEC.DIAM.SET (18)	175.00	80.00
*ELEC.DIAMOND: .5X TO 1.2X BASIC MINT		
ONE ED SET VIA MAIL PER ED TRADE CARD		
TRADES: RANDOM INS.IN SER.2 HOB.PACKS		

☐ 1 Roberto Alomar	6.00	2.70
☐ 2 Carlos Delgado	4.00	1.80
☐ 3 Cliff Floyd	3.00	1.35
☐ 4 Alex Gonzalez	3.00	1.35
☐ 5 Juan Gonzalez	15.00	6.75
☐ 6 Ken Griffey Jr.	30.00	13.50
☐ 7 Jeffrey Hammonds	3.00	1.35
☐ 8 Michael Jordan	40.00	18.00
☐ 9 David Justice	6.00	2.70
☐ 10 Ryan Klesko	6.00	2.70
☐ 11 Javier Lopez	4.00	1.80
☐ 12 Raul Mondesi	6.00	2.70
☐ 13 Mike Piazza	20.00	9.00
☐ 14 Kirby Puckett	12.00	5.50
☐ 15 Manny Ramirez	6.00	2.70
☐ 16 Alex Rodriguez	30.00	13.50
☐ 17 Tim Salmon	6.00	2.70
☐ 18 Gary Sheffield	6.00	2.70
☐ NNO Expired NG Trade Card	4.00	1.80

1995 Upper Deck

The 1995 Upper Deck baseball set was issued in two series of 225 cards for a total of 450. The cards were distributed in 12-card packs (36 per box) with a suggested retail price of $1.99. The fronts display full-bleed color action photos, with the player's name in copper foil across the bottom. The backs carry another photo, biography, and season and career statistics. Subsets include Top Prospect (1-15, 251-265), 90's Midpoint (101-110), Star Rookie (211-240), and Diamond Debuts (241-250). Rookie Cards in this set include Karim Garcia and Hideo Nomo. Five randomly inserted Trade Cards were each redeemable for nine updated cards of new rookies or players who changed teams, comprising a 45-card Trade Redemption set. The Trade cards expired Feb 1, 1996. Autographed jumbo cards (Roger Clemens for series one, Alex Rodriguez for either series) were available through a wrapper redemption offer.

	MINT	NRMT
COMPLETE SET (450)	60.00	27.00
COMPLETE SERIES 1 (225)	30.00	13.50
COMPLETE SERIES 2 (225)	30.00	13.50
COMMON CARD (1-450)	.15	.07
MINOR STARS	.30	.14
UNLISTED STARS	.60	.25
SUBSET CARDS HALF VALUE OF BASE CARDS		
COMP.TRADE SET (45)	20.00	9.00
COMMON TRADE (451T-495T)	.25	.11
TRADE SEMISTARS	.50	.23
NINE TRADE CARDS PER TRADE EXCH.CARD		
COMP.TRADE EXCH.SET (5)	4.00	1.80
COMMON TRADE EXCH. (1-5)	1.00	.45
TRD.EXCH: RANDOM INS.IN SER.2 PACKS		
COMP.ED SET (450)	110.00	50.00
COMP.ED SER.1 (225)	50.00	22.00
COMP.ED SER.2 (225)	60.00	27.00
COMMON ELEC.DIAM. (1-450)	.25	.11
*ELEC.DIAM.STARS: 2X TO 4X HI COLUMN		
*ELEC.DIAM.YOUNG STARS: 1.5X TO 3X HI		
*ELEC.DIAM.ROOKIES: 1.5X TO 3X HI		
ONE ED PER RETAIL PACK		
COMP.ED GOLD SET (450)	2000.00	900.00
COMP.ED GOLD SER.1 (225)	1000.00	450.00
COMP.ED GOLD SER.2 (225)	1000.00	450.00
COMMON ED GOLD (1-450)	3.00	1.35
*ED GOLD STARS: 12.5X TO 30X HI COLUMN		
*ED GOLD YOUNG STARS: 8X TO 20X HI		
*ED GOLD ROOKIES: 8X TO 20X HI		
ED GOLD STATED ODDS 1:35 RETAIL		
COMP.B.RUTH SET (10)	120.00	55.00
COMMON RUTH (73-81/HDR)	15.00	6.75
RUTH SER.2 STATED ODDS 1:34 HOB/RET		
JUMBO AUS WERE REDEEMED W/WRAPPERS		

☐ 1 Ruben Rivera	.60	.25
☐ 2 Bill Pulsipher	.15	.07
☐ 3 Ben Grieve	4.00	1.80
☐ 4 Curtis Goodwin	.15	.07
☐ 5 Damon Hollins	.30	.14
☐ 6 Todd Greene	.60	.25
☐ 7 Glenn Williams	.30	.14
☐ 8 Bret Wagner	.15	.07
☐ 9 Karim Garcia	1.50	.70
☐ 10 Nomar Garciaparra	4.00	1.80
☐ 11 Raul Casanova	.50	.23
☐ 12 Matt Smith	.15	.07
☐ 13 Paul Wilson	.30	.14
☐ 14 Jason Isringhausen	.30	.14
☐ 15 Reid Ryan	.30	.14
☐ 16 Lee Smith	.30	.14
☐ 17 Chili Davis	.15	.07
☐ 18 Brian Anderson	.15	.07
☐ 19 Gary DiSarcina	.15	.07
☐ 20 Bo Jackson	.30	.14
☐ 21 Chuck Finley	.15	.07
☐ 22 Darryl Kile	.30	.14
☐ 23 Shane Reynolds	.30	.14
☐ 24 Tony Eusebio	.15	.07
☐ 25 Craig Biggio	.40	.18
☐ 26 Doug Drabek	.15	.07
☐ 27 Brian L. Hunter	.30	.14
☐ 28 James Mouton	.15	.07
☐ 29 Geronimo Berroa	.15	.07

☐ 30 Rickey Henderson	.40	.18
☐ 31 Steve Karsay	.15	.07
☐ 32 Steve Ontiveros	.15	.07
☐ 33 Ernie Young	.15	.07
☐ 34 Dennis Eckersley	.30	.14
☐ 35 Mark McGwire	1.25	.55
☐ 36 Dave Stewart	.30	.14
☐ 37 Pat Hentgen	.30	.14
☐ 38 Carlos Delgado	.30	.14
☐ 39 Joe Carter	.30	.14
☐ 40 Roberto Alomar	.60	.25
☐ 41 John Olerud	.30	.14
☐ 42 Devon White	.15	.07
☐ 43 Roberto Kelly	.15	.07
☐ 44 Jeff Blauser	.30	.14
☐ 45 Fred McGriff	.40	.18
☐ 46 Tom Glavine	.30	.14
☐ 47 Mike Kelly	.15	.07
☐ 48 Javier Lopez	.30	.14
☐ 49 Greg Maddux	2.00	.90
☐ 50 Matt Mieske	.15	.07
☐ 51 Troy O'Leary	.15	.07
☐ 52 Jeff Cirillo	.30	.14
☐ 53 Cal Eldred	.15	.07
☐ 54 Pat Listach	.15	.07
☐ 55 Jose Valentin	.15	.07
☐ 56 John Mabry	.30	.14
☐ 57 Bob Tewksbury	.15	.07
☐ 58 Brian Jordan	.30	.14
☐ 59 Gregg Jefferies	.15	.07
☐ 60 Ozzie Smith	.75	.35
☐ 61 Geronimo Pena	.15	.07
☐ 62 Mark Whiten	.15	.07
☐ 63 Rey Sanchez	.15	.07
☐ 64 Barry Banks	.15	.07
☐ 65 Mark Grace	.40	.18
☐ 66 Randy Myers	.15	.07
☐ 67 Steve Trachsel	.15	.07
☐ 68 Derrick May	.15	.07
☐ 69 Brett Butler	.30	.14
☐ 70 Eric Karros	.30	.14
☐ 71 Tim Wallach	.15	.07
☐ 72 Delino DeShields	.15	.07
☐ 73 Darren Dreifort	.15	.07
☐ 74 Orel Hershiser	.30	.14
☐ 75 Billy Ashley	.15	.07
☐ 76 Sean Berry	.15	.07
☐ 77 Ken Hill	.30	.14
☐ 78 John Wetteland	.15	.07
☐ 79 Moises Alou	.30	.14
☐ 80 Cliff Floyd	.15	.07
☐ 81 Marquis Grissom	.30	.14
☐ 82 Larry Walker	.60	.25
☐ 83 Rondell White	.30	.14
☐ 84 William VanLandingham	.15	.07
☐ 85 Matt Williams	.40	.18
☐ 86 Rod Beck	.15	.07
☐ 87 Darren Lewis	.15	.07
☐ 88 Robby Thompson	.15	.07
☐ 89 Darryl Strawberry	.30	.14
☐ 90 Kenny Lofton	.75	.35
☐ 91 Charles Nagy	.30	.14
☐ 92 Sandy Alomar Jr.	.30	.14
☐ 93 Mark Clark	.15	.07
☐ 94 Dennis Martinez	.30	.14
☐ 95 Dave Winfield	.40	.18
☐ 96 Jim Thome	.60	.25
☐ 97 Manny Ramirez	.50	.23
☐ 98 Goose Gossage	.30	.14
☐ 99 Tino Martinez	.60	.25
☐ 100 Ken Griffey Jr.	3.00	1.35
☐ 101 Greg Maddux ANA	1.00	.45
☐ 102 Randy Johnson ANA	.30	.14
☐ 103 Barry Bonds ANA	.40	.18
☐ 104 Juan Gonzalez ANA	.75	.35
☐ 105 Frank Thomas ANA	1.25	.55
☐ 106 Matt Williams ANA	.30	.14
☐ 107 Paul Molitor ANA	.30	.14
☐ 108 Fred McGriff ANA	.30	.14
☐ 109 Carlos Baerga ANA	.15	.07
☐ 110 Ken Griffey Jr. ANA	1.50	.70
☐ 111 Reggie Jefferson	.15	.07
☐ 112 Randy Johnson	.60	.25
☐ 113 Marc Newfield	.15	.07
☐ 114 Robb Nen	.15	.07
☐ 115 Jeff Conine	.30	.14

☐ 116	Kurt Abbott	.15	.07
☐ 117	Charlie Hough	.15	.07
☐ 118	Dave Weathers	.15	.07
☐ 119	Juan Castillo	.15	.07
☐ 120	Bret Saberhagen	.15	.07
☐ 121	Rico Brogna	.15	.07
☐ 122	John Franco	.30	.14
☐ 123	Todd Hundley	.30	.14
☐ 124	Jason Jacome	.15	.07
☐ 125	Bobby Jones	.15	.07
☐ 126	Bret Barberie	.15	.07
☐ 127	Ben McDonald	.15	.07
☐ 128	Harold Baines	.30	.14
☐ 129	Jeffrey Hammonds	.30	.14
☐ 130	Mike Mussina	.60	.25
☐ 131	Chris Hoiles	.15	.07
☐ 132	Brady Anderson	.40	.18
☐ 133	Eddie Williams	.15	.07
☐ 134	Andy Benes	.30	.14
☐ 135	Tony Gwynn	1.50	.70
☐ 136	Bip Roberts	.15	.07
☐ 137	Joey Hamilton	.30	.14
☐ 138	Luis Lopez	.15	.07
☐ 139	Ray McDavid	.15	.07
☐ 140	Lenny Dykstra	.30	.14
☐ 141	Mariano Duncan	.15	.07
☐ 142	Fernando Valenzuela	.30	.14
☐ 143	Bobby Munoz	.15	.07
☐ 144	Kevin Stocker	.15	.07
☐ 145	John Kruk	.30	.14
☐ 146	Jon Lieber	.15	.07
☐ 147	Zane Smith	.15	.07
☐ 148	Steve Cooke	.15	.07
☐ 149	Andy Van Slyke	.30	.14
☐ 150	Jay Bell	.30	.14
☐ 151	Carlos Garcia	.15	.07
☐ 152	John Dettmer	.15	.07
☐ 153	Darren Oliver	.15	.07
☐ 154	Dean Palmer	.15	.07
☐ 155	Otis Nixon	.15	.07
☐ 156	Rusty Greer	.60	.25
☐ 157	Rick Helling	.15	.07
☐ 158	Jose Canseco	.35	.16
☐ 159	Roger Clemens	1.25	.55
☐ 160	Andre Dawson	.40	.18
☐ 161	Mo Vaughn	.75	.35
☐ 162	Aaron Sele	.15	.07
☐ 163	John Valentin	.15	.07
☐ 164	Brian R. Hunter	.15	.07
☐ 165	Bret Boone	.15	.07
☐ 166	Hector Carrasco	.15	.07
☐ 167	Pete Schourek	.15	.07
☐ 168	Willie Greene	.15	.07
☐ 169	Kevin Mitchell	.15	.07
☐ 170	Deion Sanders	.30	.14
☐ 171	John Roper	.15	.07
☐ 172	Charlie Hayes	.15	.07
☐ 173	David Nied	.15	.07
☐ 174	Ellis Burks	.30	.14
☐ 175	Dante Bichette	.30	.14
☐ 176	Marvin Freeman	.15	.07
☐ 177	Eric Young	.15	.07
☐ 178	David Cone	.30	.14
☐ 179	Greg Gagne	.15	.07
☐ 180	Bob Hamelin	.15	.07
☐ 181	Wally Joyner	.30	.14
☐ 182	Jeff Montgomery	.15	.07
☐ 183	Jose Lind	.15	.07
☐ 184	Chris Gomez	.15	.07
☐ 185	Travis Fryman	.30	.14
☐ 186	Kirk Gibson	.30	.14
☐ 187	Mike Moore	.15	.07
☐ 188	Lou Whitaker	.30	.14
☐ 189	Sean Bergman	.15	.07
☐ 190	Shane Mack	.15	.07
☐ 191	Rick Aguilera	.15	.07
☐ 192	Denny Hocking	.15	.07
☐ 193	Chuck Knoblauch	.60	.25
☐ 194	Kevin Tapani	.15	.07
☐ 195	Kent Hrbek	.30	.14
☐ 196	Ozzie Guillen	.15	.07
☐ 197	Wilson Alvarez	.15	.07
☐ 198	Tim Raines	.30	.14
☐ 199	Scott Ruffcorn	.15	.07
☐ 200	Michael Jordan	3.00	1.35
☐ 201	Robin Ventura	.30	.14
☐ 202	Jason Bere	.15	.07
☐ 203	Darrin Jackson	.15	.07
☐ 204	Russ Davis	.15	.07
☐ 205	Jimmy Key	.30	.14
☐ 206	Jack McDowell	.15	.07
☐ 207	Jim Abbott	.15	.07
☐ 208	Paul O'Neill	.30	.14
☐ 209	Bernie Williams	.60	.25
☐ 210	Don Mattingly	1.00	.45
☐ 211	Orlando Miller	.15	.07
☐ 212	Alex Gonzalez	.15	.07
☐ 213	Terrell Wade	.15	.07
☐ 214	Jose Oliva	.15	.07
☐ 215	Alex Rodriguez	2.50	1.10
☐ 216	Garret Anderson	.40	.18
☐ 217	Alan Benes	.40	.18
☐ 218	Armando Benitez	.15	.07
☐ 219	Dustin Hermanson	.30	.14
☐ 220	Charles Johnson	.30	.14
☐ 221	Julian Tavarez	.15	.07
☐ 222	Jason Giambi	.60	.25
☐ 223	LaTroy Hawkins	.15	.07
☐ 224	Todd Hollandsworth	.30	.14
☐ 225	Derek Jeter	2.00	.90
☐ 226	Hideo Nomo	3.00	1.35
☐ 227	Tony Clark	.75	.35
☐ 228	Roger Cedeno	.30	.14
☐ 229	Scott Stahoviak	.15	.07
☐ 230	Michael Tucker	.30	.14
☐ 231	Joe Rosselli	.15	.07
☐ 232	Antonio Osuna	.15	.07
☐ 233	Bobby Higginson	1.00	.45
☐ 234	Mark Grudzielanek	.50	.23
☐ 235	Ray Durham	.30	.14
☐ 236	Frank Rodriguez	.15	.07
☐ 237	Quilvio Veras	.15	.07
☐ 238	Darren Bragg	.30	.14
☐ 239	Ugueth Urbina	.15	.07
☐ 240	Jason Bates	.15	.07
☐ 241	David Bell	.15	.07
☐ 242	Ron Villone	.15	.07
☐ 243	Joe Randa	.15	.07
☐ 244	Carlos Perez	.30	.14
☐ 245	Brad Clontz	.15	.07
☐ 246	Steve Rodriguez	.15	.07
☐ 247	Joe Vitiello	.15	.07
☐ 248	Ozzie Timmons	.15	.07
☐ 249	Rudy Pemberton	.15	.07
☐ 250	Marty Cordova	.30	.14
☐ 251	Tony Graffanino	.15	.07
☐ 252	Mark Johnson	.15	.07
☐ 253	Tomas Perez	.30	.14
☐ 254	Jimmy Hurst	.15	.07
☐ 255	Edgardo Alfonzo	.60	.25
☐ 256	Jose Malave	.15	.07
☐ 257	Brad Radke	.75	.35
☐ 258	Jon Nunnally	.15	.07
☐ 259	Dilson Torres	.15	.07
☐ 260	Esteban Loaiza	.30	.14
☐ 261	Freddy Garcia	.40	.18
☐ 262	Don Wengert	.15	.07
☐ 263	Robert Person	.15	.07
☐ 264	Tim Unroe	.15	.07
☐ 265	Juan Acevedo	.15	.07
☐ 266	Eduardo Perez	.15	.07
☐ 267	Tony Phillips	.15	.07
☐ 268	Jim Edmonds	.40	.18
☐ 269	Jorge Fabregas	.15	.07
☐ 270	Tim Salmon	.60	.25
☐ 271	Mark Langston	.15	.07
☐ 272	J.T. Snow	.30	.14
☐ 273	Phil Plantier	.15	.07
☐ 274	Derek Bell	.15	.07
☐ 275	Jeff Bagwell	1.25	.55
☐ 276	Luis Gonzalez	.15	.07
☐ 277	John Hudek	.15	.07
☐ 278	Todd Stottlemyre	.15	.07
☐ 279	Mark Acre	.15	.07
☐ 280	Ruben Sierra	.15	.07
☐ 281	Brent Gates	.15	.07
☐ 282	Ron Darling	.15	.07
☐ 283	Brent Gates	.15	.07
☐ 284	Todd Van Poppel	.15	.07
☐ 285	Paul Molitor	.60	.25
☐ 286	Ed Sprague	.15	.07
☐ 287	Juan Guzman	.15	.07
☐ 288	David Cone	.30	.14
☐ 289	Shawn Green	.30	.14
☐ 290	Marquis Grissom	.30	.14
☐ 291	Kent Mercker	.15	.07
☐ 292	Steve Avery	.15	.07
☐ 293	Chipper Jones	2.00	.90
☐ 294	John Smoltz	.30	.14
☐ 295	David Justice	.60	.25
☐ 296	Ryan Klesko	.40	.18
☐ 297	Joe Oliver	.15	.07
☐ 298	Ricky Bones	.15	.07
☐ 299	John Jaha	.15	.07
☐ 300	Greg Vaughn	.15	.07
☐ 301	Dave Nilsson	.15	.07
☐ 302	Kevin Seitzer	.15	.07
☐ 303	Bernard Gilkey	.15	.07
☐ 304	Allen Battle	.15	.07
☐ 305	Ray Lankford	.30	.14
☐ 306	Tom Pagnozzi	.15	.07
☐ 307	Allen Watson	.15	.07
☐ 308	Danny Jackson	.15	.07
☐ 309	Ken Hill	.15	.07
☐ 310	Todd Zeile	.15	.07
☐ 311	Kevin Roberson	.15	.07
☐ 312	Steve Buechele	.15	.07
☐ 313	Rick Wilkins	.15	.07
☐ 314	Kevin Foster	.15	.07
☐ 315	Sammy Sosa	.60	.25
☐ 316	Howard Johnson	.15	.07
☐ 317	Greg Hansell	.15	.07
☐ 318	Pedro Astacio	.15	.07
☐ 319	Rafael Bournigal	.15	.07
☐ 320	Mike Piazza	2.00	.90
☐ 321	Ramon Martinez	.30	.14
☐ 322	Raul Mondesi	.40	.18
☐ 323	Ismael Valdes	.40	.18
☐ 324	Wil Cordero	.15	.07
☐ 325	Tony Tarasco	.15	.07
☐ 326	Roberto Kelly	.15	.07
☐ 327	Jeff Fassero	.15	.07
☐ 328	Mike Lansing	.15	.07
☐ 329	Pedro J. Martinez	.60	.25
☐ 330	Kirk Rueter	.15	.07
☐ 331	Glenallen Hill	.15	.07
☐ 332	Kirt Manwaring	.15	.07
☐ 333	Royce Clayton	.15	.07
☐ 334	J.R. Phillips	.15	.07
☐ 335	Barry Bonds	.75	.35
☐ 336	Mark Portugal	.15	.07
☐ 337	Terry Mulholland	.15	.07
☐ 338	Omar Vizquel	.30	.14
☐ 339	Carlos Baerga	.15	.07
☐ 340	Albert Belle	.75	.35
☐ 341	Eddie Murray	.60	.25
☐ 342	Wayne Kirby	.15	.07
☐ 343	Chad Ogea	.15	.07
☐ 344	Tim Davis	.15	.07
☐ 345	Jay Buhner	.40	.18
☐ 346	Bobby Ayala	.15	.07
☐ 347	Mike Blowers	.15	.07
☐ 348	Dave Fleming	.15	.07
☐ 349	Edgar Martinez	.60	.25
☐ 350	Andre Dawson	.40	.18
☐ 351	Darrell Whitmore	.15	.07
☐ 352	Chuck Carr	.15	.07
☐ 353	John Burkett	.15	.07
☐ 354	Chris Hammond	.15	.07
☐ 355	Gary Sheffield	.60	.25
☐ 356	Pat Rapp	.15	.07
☐ 357	Greg Colbrunn	.15	.07
☐ 358	David Segui	.15	.07
☐ 359	Jeff Kent	.15	.07
☐ 360	Bobby Bonilla	.30	.14
☐ 361	Pete Harnisch	.15	.07
☐ 362	Ryan Thompson	.15	.07
☐ 363	Jose Vizcaino	.15	.07
☐ 364	Brett Butler	.30	.14
☐ 365	Cal Ripken Jr.	2.50	1.10
☐ 366	Rafael Palmeiro	.40	.18
☐ 367	Leo Gomez	.15	.07
☐ 368	Andy Van Slyke	.30	.14
☐ 369	Arthur Rhodes	.15	.07
☐ 370	Ken Caminiti	.40	.18
☐ 371	Steve Finley	.30	.14
☐ 372	Melvin Nieves	.15	.07
☐ 373	Andujar Cedeno	.15	.07

☐ 374	Trevor Hoffman	.15	.07	☐ 460	Todd Worrell TRADE	.25	.11
☐ 375	Fernando Valenzuela	.30	.14	☐ 461	Roberto Kelly TRADE	.25	.11
☐ 376	Ricky Bottalico	.30	.14	☐ 462	Chad Fonville TRADE	.25	.11
☐ 377	Dave Hollins	.15	.07	☐ 463	Shane Andrews TRADE	.25	.11
☐ 378	Charlie Hayes	.15	.07	☐ 464	David Segui TRADE	.25	.11
☐ 379	Tommy Greene	.15	.07	☐ 465	Deion Sanders TRADE	.35	.16
☐ 380	Darren Daulton	.30	.14	☐ 466	Orel Hershiser TRADE	.35	.16
☐ 381	Curt Schilling	.30	.14	☐ 467	Ken Hill TRADE	.25	.11
☐ 382	Midre Cummings	.15	.07	☐ 468	Andy Benes TRADE	.35	.16
☐ 383	Al Martin	.15	.07	☐ 469	Terry Pendleton TRADE	.25	.11
☐ 384	Jeff King	.15	.07	☐ 470	Bobby Bonilla TRADE	.35	.16
☐ 385	Orlando Merced	.15	.07	☐ 471	Scott Erickson TRADE	.25	.11
☐ 386	Denny Neagle	.30	.14	☐ 472	Kevin Brown TRADE	.35	.16
☐ 387	Don Slaught	.15	.07	☐ 473	Glenn Dishman TRADE	.25	.11
☐ 388	Dave Clark	.15	.07	☐ 474	Phil Plantier TRADE	.25	.11
☐ 389	Kevin Gross	.15	.07	☐ 475	Gregg Jefferies TRADE	.25	.11
☐ 390	Will Clark	.40	.18	☐ 476	Tyler Green TRADE	.25	.11
☐ 391	Ivan Rodriguez	.75	.35	☐ 477	Heathcliff Slocumb TRADE	.25	.11
☐ 392	Benji Gil	.15	.07	☐ 478	Mark Whiten TRADE	.25	.11
☐ 393	Jeff Frye	.15	.07	☐ 479	Mickey Tettleton TRADE	.25	.11
☐ 394	Kenny Rogers	.15	.07	☐ 480	Terry Wakefield TRADE	.25	.11
☐ 395	Juan Gonzalez	1.50	.70	☐ 481	Vaughn Eshelman TRADE	.25	.11
☐ 396	Mike Macfarlane	.15	.07	☐ 482	Rick Aguilera TRADE	.25	.11
☐ 397	Lee Tinsley	.15	.07	☐ 483	Erik Hanson TRADE	.25	.11
☐ 398	Tim Naehring	.15	.07	☐ 484	Willie McGee TRADE	.25	.11
☐ 399	Tim Vanegmond	.15	.07	☐ 485	Troy O'Leary TRADE	.25	.11
☐ 400	Mike Greenwell	.15	.07	☐ 486	Benito Santiago TRADE	.25	.11
☐ 401	Ken Ryan	.15	.07	☐ 487	Darren Lewis TRADE	.25	.11
☐ 402	John Smiley	.15	.07	☐ 488	Dave Burba TRADE	.25	.11
☐ 403	Tim Pugh	.15	.07	☐ 489	Ron Gant TRADE	.35	.16
☐ 404	Reggie Sanders	.15	.07	☐ 490	Bret Saberhagen TRADE	.35	.16
☐ 405	Barry Larkin	.40	.18	☐ 491	Vinny Castilla TRADE	.35	.16
☐ 406	Hal Morris	.15	.07	☐ 492	Frank Rodriguez TRADE	.35	.16
☐ 407	Jose Rijo	.15	.07	☐ 493	Andy Pettitte TRADE	6.00	2.70
☐ 408	Lance Painter	.15	.07	☐ 494	Ruben Sierra TRADE	.35	.16
☐ 409	Joe Girardi	.15	.07	☐ 495	David Cone TRADE	.25	.11
☐ 410	Andres Galarraga	.60	.25	☐ J159	R. Clemens Jumbo AU	40.00	18.00
☐ 411	Mike Kingery	.15	.07	☐ J215	A. Rodriguez Jumbo AU	80.00	36.00
☐ 412	Roberto Mejia	.15	.07	☐ P100	Ken Griffey Jr. Promo	3.00	1.35
☐ 413	Walt Weiss	.15	.07	☐ TC1	Orel Hershiser	1.00	.45
☐ 414	Bill Swift	.15	.07	☐ TC2	Terry Pendleton	1.00	.45
☐ 415	Larry Walker	.60	.25	☐ TC3	Benito Santiago	1.00	.45
☐ 416	Billy Brewer	.15	.07	☐ TC4	Kevin Brown	1.00	.45
☐ 417	Pat Borders	.15	.07	☐ TC5	Gregg Jefferies	1.00	.45
☐ 418	Tom Gordon	.15	.07				
☐ 419	Kevin Appier	.30	.14				
☐ 420	Gary Gaetti	.15	.07				
☐ 421	Greg Gohr	.15	.07				
☐ 422	Felipe Lira	.15	.07				
☐ 423	John Doherty	.15	.07				
☐ 424	Chad Curtis	.15	.07				
☐ 425	Cecil Fielder	.30	.14				
☐ 426	Alan Trammell	.40	.18				
☐ 427	David McCarty	.15	.07				
☐ 428	Scott Erickson	.15	.07				
☐ 429	Pat Mahomes	.15	.07				
☐ 430	Kirby Puckett	1.25	.55				
☐ 431	Dave Stevens	.15	.07				
☐ 432	Pedro Munoz	.15	.07				
☐ 433	Chris Sabo	.15	.07				
☐ 434	Alex Fernandez	.15	.07				
☐ 435	Frank Thomas	2.50	1.10				
☐ 436	Roberto Hernandez	.15	.07				
☐ 437	Lance Johnson	.15	.07				
☐ 438	Jim Abbott	.15	.07				
☐ 439	John Wetteland	.15	.07				
☐ 440	Melido Perez	.15	.07				
☐ 441	Tony Fernandez	.15	.07				
☐ 442	Pat Kelly	.15	.07				
☐ 443	Mike Stanley	.15	.07				
☐ 444	Danny Tartabull	.15	.07				
☐ 445	Wade Boggs	.60	.25				
☐ 446	Robin Yount	.40	.18				
☐ 447	Ryne Sandberg	.75	.35				
☐ 448	Nolan Ryan	2.50	1.10				
☐ 449	George Brett	1.25	.55				
☐ 450	Mike Schmidt	.75	.35				
☐ 451	Jim Abbott TRADE	.25	.11				
☐ 452	Danny Tartabull TRADE	.25	.11				
☐ 453	Ariel Prieto TRADE	.25	.16				
☐ 454	Scott Cooper TRADE	.25	.11				
☐ 455	Tom Henke TRADE	.25	.11				
☐ 456	Todd Zeile TRADE	.25	.11				
☐ 457	Brian McRae TRADE	.25	.11				
☐ 458	Luis Gonzalez TRADE	.25	.11				
☐ 459	Jaime Navarro TRADE	.25	.11				

numbered as "X" of 5 in the upper left.

	MINT	NRMT
COMPLETE SET (10)	15.00	6.75
COMPLETE SERIES 1 (5)	6.00	2.70
COMPLETE SERIES 2 (5)	10.00	4.50
COMMON CARD(A1-5B)	.75	.35
STATED ODDS 1:17 ALL PACKS		

☐ 1A	Montreal Expos	.75	.35
☐ 2A	Fred McGriff	1.25	.55
☐ 3A	John Valentin	.75	.35
☐ 4A	Kenny Rogers	.75	.35
☐ 5A	Greg Maddux	6.00	2.70
☐ 1B	Cecil Fielder	1.00	.45
☐ 2B	Tony Gwynn	3.00	1.35
☐ 3B	Greg Maddux	6.00	2.70
☐ 4B	Randy Johnson	1.25	.55
☐ 5B	Mike Schmidt	2.50	1.10

1995 Upper Deck Autographs

Trade cards to redeem these autographed issues were randomly seeded into second series packs. The actual signed cards share the same front design as the basic issue 1995 Upper Deck cards. The cards are unnumbered on back and therefore we have sequenced them in alphabetical order.

	MINT	NRMT
COMPLETE SET (5)	225.00	100.00
COMMON CARD (1-5)	40.00	18.00
SER.2 STATED ODDS 1:72 HOBBY		

☐ 1	Roger Clemens	50.00	22.00
☐ 2	Reggie Jackson	40.00	18.00
☐ 3	Willie Mays	80.00	18.00
☐ 4	Raul Mondesi	40.00	18.00
☐ 5	Frank Robinson	40.00	18.00

1995 Upper Deck Checklists

Each of these 10 cards features a star player(s) on the front and a checklist on the back. The cards were randomly inserted in hobby and retail packs at a rate of one in 17. The horizontal fronts feature a player image along with a sentence about the 1994 highlight. The cards are

1995 Upper Deck Predictor Award Winners

This set was inserted in hobby packs at a rate of approximately one in 30. This 40-card standard-size set features nine players and a Long Shot in each league for each of two categories -- MVP and Rookie of the Year. If the player pictured on the card won his category, the card was redeemable for a special foil version of all 20 Hobby Predictor cards. Fronts are full-color player action photos. Backs include the rules of the contest. These cards were redeemable until December 31, 1995. The cards are numbered in the upper left with an "H" prefix.

	MINT	NRMT
COMPLETE SET (40)	100.00	45.00
COMPLETE SERIES 1 (20)	60.00	27.00
COMPLETE SERIES 2 (20)	40.00	18.00
COMMON CARD(H1-H40)	.50	.23
STATED ODDS 1:30 HOBBY		
COMP.SER.1 EXCH.SET (20)	15.00	6.75
COMP.SER.2 EXCH.SET (20)	10.00	4.50

*AW EXCH.CARDS: 4X TO .8X BASE CARD HI
ONE EXCH.SET VIA MAIL PER PRED.WINNER

☐ H1 Albert Belle MVP	2.50	1.10
☐ H2 Juan Gonzalez MVP	5.00	2.20
☐ H3 Ken Griffey Jr. MVP	10.00	4.50
☐ H4 Kirby Puckett MVP	4.00	1.80
☐ H5 Frank Thomas MVP	8.00	3.60
☐ H6 Jeff Bagwell MVP	4.00	1.80
☐ H7 Barry Bonds MVP	2.50	1.10
☐ H8 Mike Piazza MVP	6.00	2.70
☐ H9 Matt Williams MVP	.50	.70
☐ H10 MVP Wild Card	.50	.23
☐ H11 Armando Benitez ROY	.50	.23
☐ H12 Alex Gonzalez ROY	.50	.23
☐ H13 Shawn Green ROY	1.00	.45
☐ H14 Derek Jeter ROY	6.00	2.70
☐ H15 Alex Rodriguez ROY	10.00	4.50
☐ H16 Alan Benes ROY	1.50	.70
☐ H17 Brian L.Hunter ROY	1.00	.45
☐ H18 Charles Johnson ROY	1.00	.45
☐ H19 Jose Oliva ROY	.50	.23
☐ H20 ROY Wild Card	.50	.23
☐ H21 Cal Ripken MVP	8.00	3.60
☐ H22 Don Mattingly MVP	4.00	1.80
☐ H23 Roberto Alomar MVP	2.00	.90
☐ H24 Kenny Lofton MVP	2.50	1.10
☐ H25 Will Clark MVP	1.50	.70
☐ H26 Mark McGwire MVP	4.00	1.80
☐ H27 Greg Maddux MVP	6.00	2.70
☐ H28 Fred McGriff MVP	1.50	.70
☐ H29 Andres Galarraga MVP	1.00	.45
☐ H30 Jose Canseco MVP	1.50	.70
☐ H31 Ray Durham ROY	1.00	.45
☐ H32 Mark Grudzielanek ROY	1.50	.70
☐ H33 Scott Ruffcorn ROY	.50	.23
☐ H34 Michael Tucker ROY	1.00	.45
☐ H35 Garret Anderson ROY	1.50	.70
☐ H36 Darren Bragg ROY	1.00	.45
☐ H37 Quilvio Veras ROY	.50	.23
☐ H38 Hideo Nomo ROY	6.00	2.70
☐ H39 Chipper Jones ROY W	6.00	2.70
☐ H40 Marty Cordova ROY W	1.00	.45

1995 Upper Deck Predictor League Leaders

This 60-card standard-size insert set was available only in retail packs. The set included nine players and a Long Shot in each league for each of three categories -- Batting Average Leader, Home Run Leader and

Runs Batted In Leader. If the player pictured on the card won his category, the card was redeemable for a special foil version of all 60 Retail Predictor cards. These cards were redeemable until December 31, 1995. Card fronts are full-color action photos of the player emerging from a marble diamond. Backs list the rules of the game. The cards are numbered in the upper left with an "R" prefix.

	MINT	NRMT
COMPLETE SET (60)	130.00	57.50
COMPLETE SERIES 1 (30)	80.00	36.00
COMPLETE SERIES 2 (30)	50.00	22.00
COMMON CARD(R1-R60)	.50	.23
STATED ODDS 1:30 RET, 1:17 ANCO		
COMP.SER.1 EXCH.SET (30)	20.00	9.00
COMP.SER.2 EXCH.SET (30)	12.00	5.50

*LL EXCH.CARDS: 4X TO .8X BASE CARD HI
ONE EXCH.SET VIA MAIL PER PRED.WINNER

☐ R1 Albert Belle HR W	2.50	1.10
☐ R2 Jose Canseco HR	1.50	.70
☐ R3 Juan Gonzalez HR	5.00	2.20
☐ R4 Ken Griffey Jr. HR	10.00	4.50
☐ R5 Frank Thomas HR	8.00	3.60
☐ R6 Jeff Bagwell HR	4.00	1.80
☐ R7 Barry Bonds HR	2.50	1.10
☐ R8 Fred McGriff HR	1.50	.70
☐ R9 Matt Williams HR	1.50	.70
☐ R10 HR Wild Card W (Bichette)	.50	.23
☐ R11 Albert Belle RBI W	2.50	1.10
☐ R12 Joe Carter RBI	1.00	.45
☐ R13 Cecil Fielder RBI	1.00	.45
☐ R14 Kirby Puckett RBI	4.00	1.80
☐ R15 Frank Thomas RBI	8.00	3.60
☐ R16 Jeff Bagwell RBI	4.00	1.80
☐ R17 Barry Bonds RBI	2.50	1.10
☐ R18 Mike Piazza RBI	6.00	2.70
☐ R19 Matt Williams RBI	1.50	.70
☐ R20 RBI W.Card W (M.Vaughn)	.50	.23
☐ R21 Wade Boggs BAT	2.00	.90
☐ R22 Kenny Lofton BAT	2.50	1.10
☐ R23 Paul Molitor BAT	2.00	.90
☐ R24 Paul O'Neill BAT	1.00	.45
☐ R25 Frank Thomas BAT	8.00	3.60
☐ R26 Jeff Bagwell BAT	4.00	1.80
☐ R27 Tony Gwynn BAT W	5.00	2.20
☐ R28 Gregg Jefferies BAT	.50	.23
☐ R29 Hal Morris BAT	.50	.23
☐ R30 Batting W.Card W (E.Martinez)	.50	.23
☐ R31 Joe Carter HR	1.50	.70
☐ R32 Cecil Fielder HR	1.00	.45
☐ R33 Rafael Palmeiro HR	1.50	.70
☐ R34 Larry Walker HR	2.00	.90
☐ R35 Manny Ramirez HR	2.00	.90
☐ R36 Tim Salmon HR	2.00	.90
☐ R37 Mike Piazza HR	6.00	2.70
☐ R38 Andres Galarraga HR	1.00	.45
☐ R39 David Justice HR	2.00	.90
☐ R40 Gary Sheffield HR	2.00	.90
☐ R41 Juan Gonzalez RBI	5.00	2.20
☐ R42 Jose Canseco RBI	1.50	.70
☐ R43 Will Clark RBI	1.50	.70
☐ R44 Rafael Palmeiro RBI	1.50	.70
☐ R45 Ken Griffey Jr. RBI	10.00	4.50
☐ R46 Ruben Sierra RBI	.50	.23
☐ R47 Larry Walker RBI	2.00	.90
☐ R48 Fred McGriff RBI	1.50	.70
☐ R49 Dante Bichette RBI W	1.00	.45
☐ R50 Darren Daulton BAT	1.00	.45
☐ R51 Will Clark BAT	1.50	.70
☐ R52 Ken Griffey Jr. BAT	10.00	4.50
☐ R53 Don Mattingly BAT	4.00	1.80
☐ R54 John Olerud BAT	1.00	.45
☐ R55 Kirby Puckett BAT	4.00	1.80
☐ R56 Raul Mondesi BAT	1.50	.70
☐ R57 Moises Alou BAT	.50	.23
☐ R58 Bret Boone BAT	.50	.23
☐ R59 Albert Belle BAT	2.50	1.10
☐ R60 Mike Piazza BAT	6.00	2.70

1995 Upper Deck Special Edition

Inserted at a rate of one per pack, this 270 standard-size card set features full color action shots of players on a silver foil background. The back highlights the player's previous performance, including 1994 and career statistics. Another player photo is also featured on the back.

	MINT	NRMT
COMPLETE SET (270)	200.00	90.00
COMPLETE SERIES 1 (135)	100.00	45.00
COMPLETE SERIES 2 (135)	100.00	45.00
COMMON CARD (1-270)	.25	.11
MINOR STARS	.50	.23
SEMISTARS	1.00	.45
UNLISTED STARS	2.00	.90
ONE PER HOBBY PACK		
COMP.SE GOLD SET (270)	2000.00	900.00
COMP.SE GOLD SER.1 (135)	1000.00	450.00
COMP.SE GOLD SER.2 (135)	1000.00	450.00

*SE GOLD STARS: 4X TO 10X HI COLUMN
*SE GOLD YOUNG STARS: 3X TO 8X HI
*SE GOLD ROOKIES: 3X TO 8X HI
SE GOLD STATED ODDS 1:35 HOBBY

☐ 1 Cliff Floyd	.25	.11
☐ 2 Wil Cordero	.25	.11
☐ 3 Pedro J. Martinez	2.00	.90
☐ 4 Larry Walker	2.00	.90
☐ 5 Derek Jeter	6.00	2.70
☐ 6 Mike Stanley	.25	.11
☐ 7 Melido Perez	.25	.11
☐ 8 Jim Leyritz	.25	.11
☐ 9 Danny Tartabull	.25	.11
☐ 10 Wade Boggs	2.00	.90
☐ 11 Ryan Klesko	1.00	.45
☐ 12 Steve Avery	.25	.11
☐ 13 Damon Hollins	.50	.23
☐ 14 Chipper Jones	6.00	2.70
☐ 15 David Justice	2.00	.90
☐ 16 Glenn Williams	.25	.23
☐ 17 Jose Oliva	.25	.11
☐ 18 Terrell Wade	.25	.11
☐ 19 Alex Fernandez	.25	.11
☐ 20 Frank Thomas	8.00	3.60
☐ 21 Ozzie Guillen	.25	.11
☐ 22 Roberto Hernandez	.25	.11
☐ 23 Albie Lopez	.25	.11
☐ 24 Eddie Murray	2.00	.90
☐ 25 Albert Belle	2.50	1.10
☐ 26 Omar Vizquel	.50	.23
☐ 27 Carlos Baerga	.25	.11
☐ 28 Jose Rijo	.25	.11
☐ 29 Hal Morris	.25	.11
☐ 30 Reggie Sanders	.25	.11
☐ 31 Jack Morris	.50	.23
☐ 32 Raul Mondesi	1.00	.45
☐ 33 Karim Garcia	5.00	2.20
☐ 34 Todd Hollandsworth	.50	.23
☐ 35 Mike Piazza	6.00	2.70
☐ 36 Chan Ho Park	2.00	.90

□ 37	Ramon Martinez	.50	.23
□ 38	Kenny Rogers	.25	.11
□ 39	Will Clark	1.00	.45
□ 40	Juan Gonzalez	5.00	2.20
□ 41	Ivan Rodriguez	2.50	1.10
□ 42	Orlando Miller	.25	.11
□ 43	John Hudek	.25	.11
□ 44	Luis Gonzalez	.25	.11
□ 45	Jeff Bagwell	4.00	1.80
□ 46	Cal Ripken	8.00	3.60
□ 47	Mike Oquist	.25	.11
□ 48	Armando Benitez	.25	.11
□ 49	Ben McDonald	.25	.11
□ 50	Rafael Palmeiro	1.00	.45
□ 51	Curtis Goodwin	.25	.11
□ 52	Vince Coleman	.25	.11
□ 53	Tom Gordon	.25	.11
□ 54	Mike Macfarlane	.25	.11
□ 55	Brian McRae	.25	.11
□ 56	Matt Smith	.25	.11
□ 57	David Segui	.25	.11
□ 58	Paul Wilson	.50	.23
□ 59	Bill Pulsipher	.25	.11
□ 60	Bobby Bonilla	.50	.23
□ 61	Jeff Kent	.25	.11
□ 62	Ryan Thompson	.25	.11
□ 63	Jason Isringhausen	.50	.23
□ 64	Ed Sprague	.25	.11
□ 65	Paul Molitor	2.00	.90
□ 66	Juan Guzman	.25	.11
□ 67	Alex Gonzalez	.25	.11
□ 68	Shawn Green	.50	.23
□ 69	Mark Portugal	.25	.11
□ 70	Barry Bonds	2.50	1.10
□ 71	Robby Thompson	.25	.11
□ 72	Royce Clayton	.25	.11
□ 73	Ricky Bottalico	.50	.23
□ 74	Doug Jones	.25	.11
□ 75	Darren Daulton	.50	.23
□ 76	Gregg Jefferies	.25	.11
□ 77	Scott Cooper	.25	.11
□ 78	Nomar Garciaparra	10.00	4.50
□ 79	Ken Ryan	.25	.11
□ 80	Mike Greenwell	.50	.23
□ 81	LaTroy Hawkins	.25	.11
□ 82	Rich Becker	.50	.23
□ 83	Scott Erickson	.25	.11
□ 84	Pedro Munoz	.25	.11
□ 85	Kirby Puckett	4.00	1.80
□ 86	Orlando Merced	.25	.11
□ 87	Jeff King	.25	.11
□ 88	Midre Cummings	.25	.11
□ 89	Bernard Gilkey	.25	.11
□ 90	Ray Lankford	.50	.23
□ 91	Todd Zeile	.25	.11
□ 92	Alan Benes	1.00	.45
□ 93	Bret Wagner	.25	.11
□ 94	Rene Arocha	.25	.11
□ 95	Cecil Fielder	.50	.23
□ 96	Alan Trammell	1.00	.45
□ 97	Tony Phillips	.25	.11
□ 98	Junior Felix	.25	.11
□ 99	Brian Harper	.25	.11
□ 100	Greg Vaughn	.25	.11
□ 101	Ricky Bones	.25	.11
□ 102	Walt Weiss	.25	.11
□ 103	Lance Painter	.25	.11
□ 104	Roberto Mejia	.25	.11
□ 105	Andres Galarraga	2.00	.90
□ 106	Todd Van Poppel	.25	.11
□ 107	Ben Grieve	10.00	4.50
□ 108	Brent Gates	.25	.11
□ 109	Jason Giambi	2.00	.90
□ 110	Ruben Sierra	.25	.11
□ 111	Terry Steinbach	.25	.11
□ 112	Chris Hammond	.25	.11
□ 113	Charles Johnson	.25	.23
□ 114	Jesus Tavarez	.25	.11
□ 115	Gary Sheffield	2.00	.90
□ 116	Chuck Carr	.25	.11
□ 117	Bobby Ayala	.25	.11
□ 118	Randy Johnson	2.00	.90
□ 119	Edgar Martinez	1.00	.45
□ 120	Alex Rodriguez	8.00	3.60
□ 121	Kevin Foster	.25	.11
□ 122	Kevin Roberson	.25	.11
□ 123	Sammy Sosa	2.00	.90
□ 124	Steve Trachsel	.25	.11
□ 125	Eduardo Perez	.25	.11
□ 126	Tim Salmon	2.00	.90
□ 127	Todd Greene	2.00	.90
□ 128	Jorge Fabregas	.25	.11
□ 129	Mark Langston	.25	.11
□ 130	Mitch Williams	.25	.11
□ 131	Raul Casanova	1.00	.45
□ 132	Mel Nieves	.25	.11
□ 133	Andy Benes	.50	.23
□ 134	Dustin Hermanson	.50	.23
□ 135	Trevor Hoffman	.25	.11
□ 136	Mark Grudzielanek	1.00	.45
□ 137	Ugueth Urbina	.25	.11
□ 138	Moises Alou	.50	.23
□ 139	Roberto Kelly	.25	.11
□ 140	Rondell White	.50	.23
□ 141	Paul O'Neill	.50	.23
□ 142	Jimmy Key	.25	.11
□ 143	Jack McDowell	.25	.11
□ 144	Ruben Rivera	2.00	.90
□ 145	Don Mattingly	3.00	1.35
□ 146	John Wetteland	.25	.11
□ 147	Tom Glavine	.50	.23
□ 148	Marquis Grissom	.50	.23
□ 149	Javier Lopez	.50	.23
□ 150	Fred McGriff	1.00	.45
□ 151	Greg Maddux	6.00	2.70
□ 152	Chris Sabo	.25	.11
□ 153	Ray Durham	.50	.23
□ 154	Robin Ventura	.50	.23
□ 155	Jim Abbott	.25	.11
□ 156	Jimmy Hurst	.25	.11
□ 157	Tim Raines	.50	.23
□ 158	Dennis Martinez	.50	.23
□ 159	Kenny Lofton	2.50	1.10
□ 160	Dave Winfield	1.00	.45
□ 161	Manny Ramirez	2.00	.90
□ 162	Jim Thome	2.00	.90
□ 163	Barry Larkin	1.00	.45
□ 164	Bret Boone	.25	.11
□ 165	Deion Sanders	.50	.23
□ 166	Ron Gant	.50	.23
□ 167	Benito Santiago	.50	.23
□ 168	Hideo Nomo	8.00	3.60
□ 169	Billy Ashley	.25	.11
□ 170	Roger Cedeno	.50	.23
□ 171	Ismael Valdes	1.00	.45
□ 172	Eric Karros	.50	.23
□ 173	Rusty Greer	2.00	.90
□ 174	Rick Helling	.25	.11
□ 175	Nolan Ryan	8.00	3.60
□ 176	Dean Palmer	.25	.11
□ 177	Phil Plantier	.25	.11
□ 178	Darryl Kile	.25	.11
□ 179	Derek Bell	.50	.23
□ 180	Doug Drabek	.25	.11
□ 181	Craig Biggio	1.00	.45
□ 182	Kevin Brown	.50	.23
□ 183	Harold Baines	.50	.23
□ 184	Jeffrey Hammonds	.50	.23
□ 185	Chris Hoiles	.25	.11
□ 186	Mike Mussina	2.00	.90
□ 187	Bob Hamelin	.25	.11
□ 188	Jeff Montgomery	.25	.11
□ 189	Michael Tucker	.50	.23
□ 190	George Brett	4.00	1.80
□ 191	Edgardo Alfonzo	2.00	.90
□ 192	Brett Butler	.25	.11
□ 193	Bobby Jones	.25	.11
□ 194	Todd Hundley	.25	.11
□ 195	Bret Saberhagen	.25	.11
□ 196	Pat Hentgen	.25	.11
□ 197	Roberto Alomar	2.00	.90
□ 198	David Cone	.50	.23
□ 199	Carlos Delgado	.50	.23
□ 200	Joe Carter	.50	.23
□ 201	Wm. VanLandingham	.25	.11
□ 202	Rod Beck	.25	.11
□ 203	J.R. Phillips	.25	.11
□ 204	Darren Lewis	.25	.11
□ 205	Matt Williams	1.00	.45
□ 206	Lenny Dykstra	.50	.23
□ 207	Dave Hollins	.25	.11
□ 208	Mike Schmidt	2.50	1.10
□ 209	Charlie Hayes	.25	.11
□ 210	Mo Vaughn	2.50	1.10
□ 211	Jose Malave	.25	.11
□ 212	Roger Clemens	4.00	1.80
□ 213	Jose Canseco	1.00	.45
□ 214	Mark Whiten	.25	.11
□ 215	Marty Cordova	.50	.23
□ 216	Rick Aguilera	.25	.11
□ 217	Kevin Tapani	.50	.23
□ 218	Chuck Knoblauch	2.00	.90
□ 219	Al Martin	.25	.11
□ 220	Jay Bell	.50	.23
□ 221	Carlos Garcia	.25	.11
□ 222	Freddy Garcia	1.00	.45
□ 223	Jon Lieber	.25	.11
□ 224	Danny Jackson	.25	.11
□ 225	Ozzie Smith	2.50	1.10
□ 226	Brian Jordan	.50	.23
□ 227	Ken Hill	.25	.11
□ 228	Scott Cooper	.25	.11
□ 229	[illegible]	.25	.11
□ 230	Lou Whitaker	.50	.23
□ 231	Kirk Gibson	.50	.23
□ 232	Travis Fryman	.50	.23
□ 233	Jose Valentin	.25	.11
□ 234	Dave Nilsson	.25	.11
□ 235	Cal Eldred	.25	.11
□ 236	Matt Mieske	.25	.11
□ 237	Bill Swift	.25	.11
□ 238	Marvin Freeman	.25	.11
□ 239	Jason Bates	.25	.11
□ 240	Larry Walker	2.00	.90
□ 241	Dave Nied	.25	.11
□ 242	Dante Bichette	.50	.23
□ 243	Dennis Eckersley	.50	.23
□ 244	Todd Stottlemyre	.25	.11
□ 245	Rickey Henderson	1.00	.45
□ 246	Geronimo Berroa	.25	.11
□ 247	Mark McGwire	4.00	1.80
□ 248	Quilvio Veras	.25	.11
□ 249	Terry Pendleton	.25	.11
□ 250	Andre Dawson	1.00	.45
□ 251	Jeff Conine	.50	.23
□ 252	Kurt Abbott	.25	.11
□ 253	Jay Buhner	1.00	.45
□ 254	Darren Bragg	.25	.11
□ 255	Ken Griffey Jr.	10.00	4.50
□ 256	Tino Martinez	2.00	.90
□ 257	Mark Grace	1.00	.45
□ 258	Ryne Sandberg	2.50	1.10
□ 259	Randy Myers	.25	.11
□ 260	Howard Johnson	.25	.11
□ 261	Lee Smith	.50	.23
□ 262	J.T. Snow	.50	.23
□ 263	Chili Davis	.50	.23
□ 264	Chuck Finley	.25	.11
□ 265	Eddie Williams	.25	.11
□ 266	Joey Hamilton	.50	.23
□ 267	Ken Caminiti	1.00	.45
□ 268	Andujar Cedeno	.50	.23
□ 269	Steve Finley	.50	.23
□ 270	Tony Gwynn	5.00	2.20

1995 Upper Deck Steal of a Deal

This set was inserted in hobby and retail packs at a rate of approximately one in 34. This 15-card standard-size set focuses on players who were acquired through, according to Upper Deck, "astute trades" or low round draft picks. The horizontal fronts feature a player cutout on a green background with a bronze seal. Backs feature information of how the player was acquired and past performance. The cards are numbered in the upper left with an "SD" prefix.

	MINT	NRMT
COMPLETE SET (15)	100.00	45.00
COMMON CARD(SD1-SD15)	2.00	.90
SER.1 STATED ODDS 1:34 ALL PACKS		

□ SD1 Mike Piazza	20.00	9.00
□ SD2 Fred McGriff	4.00	1.80
□ SD3 Kenny Lofton	8.00	3.60
□ SD4 Jose Oliva	2.00	.90
□ SD5 Jeff Bagwell	12.00	5.50
□ SD6 Roberto Alomar	6.00	2.70
Joe Carter		
□ SD7 Steve Karsay	2.00	.90
□ SD8 Ozzie Smith	8.00	3.60
□ SD9 Dennis Eckersley	3.00	1.35
□ SD10 Jose Canseco	4.00	1.80
□ SD11 Carlos Baerga	2.00	.90
□ SD12 Cecil Fielder	3.00	1.35
□ SD13 Don Mattingly	12.00	5.50
□ SD14 Bret Boone	2.00	.90
□ SD15 Michael Jordan	30.00	13.50

1996 Upper Deck

The 1996 Upper Deck set was issued in two series of 240 cards, and a 30 card update set, for a total of 510 cards. The cards were distributed in 10-card packs with a suggested retail price of $1.99, and 28 packs were contained in each box. The attractive fronts feature a full-bleed photo above a bronze foil bar that includes the player's name, team and position in a white oval. Subsets include Young at Heart (100-117), Beat the Odds (145-153), Postseason Checklist (218-222), Best of a Generation (370-387), Strange But True (415-423) and Managerial Salute Checklists (476-480). The only Rookie Card of note is Livan Hernandez.

	MINT	NRMT
COMPLETE SET (480)	70.00	32.00
COMP.FACT.SET (510)	80.00	36.00
COMPLETE SERIES 1 (240)	40.00	18.00
COMPLETE SERIES 2 (240)	30.00	13.50
COMMON CARD (1-480)	.15	.07
MINOR STARS	.30	.14
UNLISTED STARS	.60	.25
SUBSET CARDS HALF VALUE OF BASE CARDS		
COMP.UPDATE SET (30)	10.00	4.50
COMMON UPDATE (481U-510U)	.25	.11
ONE UPDATE SET PER FACTORY SET		
ONE UPDATE SET VIA SER.2 WRAP.OFFER		
COMP.NOMO SET (5)	20.00	9.00
COMMON NOMO (1-5)	5.00	2.20
NOMO SER.2 STATED ODDS 1:24		

□ 1 Cal Ripken 2131	4.00	1.80
□ 2 Eddie Murray 3000 Hits	.60	.25
□ 3 Mark Wohlers	.15	.07
□ 4 David Justice	.60	.25
□ 5 Chipper Jones	2.00	.90
□ 6 Javier Lopez	.30	.14
□ 7 Mark Lemke	.15	.07
□ 8 Marquis Grissom	.30	.14
□ 9 Tom Glavine	.30	.14
□ 10 Greg Maddux	2.00	.90
□ 11 Manny Alexander	.15	.07
□ 12 Curtis Goodwin	.15	.07
□ 13 Scott Erickson	.15	.07
□ 14 Chris Hoiles	.15	.07
□ 15 Rafael Palmeiro	.40	.18
□ 16 Rick Krivda	.15	.07
□ 17 Jeff Manto	.15	.07
□ 18 Mo Vaughn	.75	.35
□ 19 Tim Wakefield	.15	.07
□ 20 Roger Clemens	1.25	.55
□ 21 Tim Naehring	.15	.07
□ 22 Troy O'Leary	.15	.07
□ 23 Mike Greenwell	.15	.07
□ 24 Stan Belinda	.15	.07
□ 25 John Valentin	.15	.07
□ 26 J.T. Snow	.30	.14
□ 27 Gary DiSarcina	.15	.07
□ 28 Mark Langston	.15	.07
□ 29 Brian Anderson	.15	.07
□ 30 Jim Edmonds	.40	.18
□ 31 Garret Anderson	.30	.14
□ 32 Orlando Palmeiro	.15	.07
□ 33 Brian McRae	.15	.07
□ 34 Kevin Foster	.15	.07
□ 35 Sammy Sosa	.60	.25
□ 36 Todd Zeile	.15	.07
□ 37 Jim Bullinger	.15	.07
□ 38 Luis Gonzalez	.15	.07
□ 39 Lyle Mouton	.15	.07
□ 40 Ray Durham	.15	.07
□ 41 Ozzie Guillen	.15	.07
□ 42 Alex Fernandez	.15	.07
□ 43 Brian Keyser	.15	.07
□ 44 Robin Ventura	.30	.14
□ 45 Reggie Sanders	.15	.07
□ 46 Pete Schourek	.15	.07
□ 47 John Smiley	.15	.07
□ 48 Jeff Brantley	.15	.07
□ 49 Thomas Howard	.15	.07
□ 50 Bret Boone	.15	.07
□ 51 Kevin Jarvis	.15	.07
□ 52 Jeff Branson	.15	.07
□ 53 Carlos Baerga	.15	.07
□ 54 Jim Thome	.60	.25
□ 55 Manny Ramirez	.60	.25
□ 56 Omar Vizquel	.30	.14
□ 57 Jose Mesa	.15	.07
□ 58 Julian Tavarez UER	.15	.07
□ 59 Orel Hershiser	.30	.14
□ 60 Larry Walker	.60	.25
□ 61 Bret Saberhagen	.15	.07
□ 62 Vinny Castilla	.30	.14
□ 63 Eric Young	.15	.07
□ 64 Bryan Rekar	.15	.07
□ 65 Andres Galarraga	.60	.25
□ 66 Steve Reed	.15	.07
□ 67 Chad Curtis	.15	.07
□ 68 Bobby Higginson	.30	.14
□ 69 Phil Nevin	.15	.07
□ 70 Cecil Fielder	.30	.14
□ 71 Felipe Lira	.15	.07
□ 72 Chris Gomez	.15	.07
□ 73 Charles Johnson	.30	.14
□ 74 Quilvio Veras	.15	.07
□ 75 Jeff Conine	.30	.14
□ 76 John Burkett	.15	.07
□ 77 Greg Colbrunn	.15	.07
□ 78 Terry Pendleton	.15	.07
□ 79 Shane Reynolds	.15	.07
□ 80 Jeff Bagwell	1.25	.55
□ 81 Orlando Miller	.15	.07
□ 82 Mike Hampton	.15	.07
□ 83 James Mouton	.15	.07
□ 84 Brian L. Hunter	.30	.14
□ 85 Derek Bell	.15	.07
□ 86 Kevin Appier	.30	.14
□ 87 Joe Vitiello	.15	.07
□ 88 Wally Joyner	.30	.14
□ 89 Michael Tucker	.30	.14
□ 90 Johnny Damon	.30	.14
□ 91 Jon Nunnally	.15	.07
□ 92 Jason Jacome	.15	.07
□ 93 Chad Fonville	.15	.07
□ 94 Chan Ho Park	.60	.25
□ 95 Hideo Nomo	1.50	.70
□ 96 Ismael Valdes	.30	.14
□ 97 Greg Gagne	.15	.07
□ 98 Diamondbacks-Devil Rays	.60	.25
□ 99 Raul Mondesi	.40	.18
□ 100 Dave Winfield YH	.30	.14
□ 101 Dennis Eckersley YH	.15	.07
□ 102 Andre Dawson YH	.30	.14
□ 103 Dennis Martinez YH	.15	.07
□ 104 Lance Parrish YH	.15	.07
□ 105 Eddie Murray YH	.30	.14
□ 106 Alan Trammell YH	.15	.07
□ 107 Lou Whitaker YH	.15	.07
□ 108 Ozzie Smith YH	.40	.18
□ 109 Paul Molitor YH	.30	.14
□ 110 Rickey Henderson YH	.30	.14
□ 111 Tim Raines YH	.15	.07
□ 112 Harold Baines YH	.15	.07
□ 113 Lee Smith YH	.15	.07
□ 114 Fernando Valenzuela YH	.15	.07
□ 115 Cal Ripken YH	1.25	.55
□ 116 Tony Gwynn YH	.75	.35
□ 117 Wade Boggs	.60	.25
□ 118 Todd Hollandsworth	.15	.07
□ 119 Dave Nilsson	.15	.07
□ 120 Jose Valentin	.15	.07
□ 121 Steve Sparks	.15	.07
□ 122 Chuck Carr	.15	.07
□ 123 John Jaha	.15	.07
□ 124 Scott Karl	.15	.07
□ 125 Chuck Knoblauch	.60	.25
□ 126 Brad Radke	.30	.14
□ 127 Pat Meares	.15	.07
□ 128 Ron Coomer	.15	.07
□ 129 Pedro Munoz	.15	.07
□ 130 Kirby Puckett	1.25	.55
□ 131 David Segui	.15	.07
□ 132 Mark Grudzielanek	.30	.14
□ 133 Mike Lansing	.15	.07
□ 134 Sean Berry	.15	.07
□ 135 Rondell White	.30	.14
□ 136 Pedro J. Martinez	.60	.25
□ 137 Carl Everett	.15	.07
□ 138 Dave Mlicki	.15	.07
□ 139 Bill Pulsipher	.15	.07
□ 140 Jason Isringhausen	.15	.07
□ 141 Rico Brogna	.15	.07
□ 142 Edgardo Alfonzo	.40	.18
□ 143 Jeff Kent	.15	.07
□ 144 Andy Pettitte	.75	.35
□ 145 Mike Piazza BO	1.00	.45
□ 146 Cliff Floyd BO	.15	.07
□ 147 Jason Isringhausen BO	.15	.07
□ 148 Tim Wakefield BO	.15	.07
□ 149 Chipper Jones BO	1.00	.45
□ 150 Hideo Nomo BO	.75	.35
□ 151 Mark McGwire BO	.60	.25
□ 152 Ron Gant BO	.15	.07
□ 153 Gary Gaetti BO	.15	.07
□ 154 Don Mattingly	1.00	.45
□ 155 Paul O'Neill	.30	.14
□ 156 Derek Jeter	2.00	.90
□ 157 Joe Girardi	.15	.07
□ 158 Ruben Sierra	.15	.07

159	Jorge Posada	.15	.07
160	Geronimo Berroa	.15	.07
161	Steve Ontiveros	.15	.07
162	George Williams	.15	.07
163	Doug Johns	.15	.07
164	Ariel Prieto	.15	.07
165	Scott Brosius	.15	.07
166	Mike Bordick	.15	.07
167	Tyler Green	.15	.07
168	Mickey Morandini	.15	.07
169	Darren Daulton	.30	.14
170	Gregg Jefferies	.15	.07
171	Jim Eisenreich	.15	.07
172	Heathcliff Slocumb	.15	.07
173	Kevin Stocker	.15	.07
174	Esteban Loaiza	.15	.07
175	Jeff King	.15	.07
176	Mark Johnson	.15	.07
177	Denny Neagle	.30	.14
178	Orlando Merced	.15	.07
179	Carlos Garcia	.15	.07
180	Brian Jordan	.30	.14
181	Mike Morgan	.15	.07
182	Mark Petkovsek	.15	.07
183	Bernard Gilkey	.15	.07
184	John Mabry	.15	.07
185	Tom Henke	.15	.07
186	Glenn Dishman	.15	.07
187	Andy Ashby	.15	.07
188	Bip Roberts	.15	.07
189	Melvin Nieves	.15	.07
190	Ken Caminiti	.40	.18
191	Brad Ausmus	.15	.07
192	Deion Sanders	.30	.14
193	Jamie Brewington	.15	.07
194	Glenallen Hill	.15	.07
195	Barry Bonds	.75	.35
196	Wm. Van Landingham	.15	.07
197	Mark Carreon	.15	.07
198	Royce Clayton	.15	.07
199	Joey Cora	.30	.14
200	Ken Griffey Jr.	3.00	1.35
201	Jay Buhner	.40	.18
202	Alex Rodriguez	2.00	.90
203	Norm Charlton	.15	.07
204	Andy Benes	.30	.14
205	Edgar Martinez	.40	.18
206	Juan Gonzalez	1.50	.70
207	Will Clark	.40	.18
208	Kevin Gross	.15	.07
209	Roger Pavlik	.15	.07
210	Ivan Rodriguez	.75	.35
211	Rusty Greer	.30	.14
212	Angel Martinez	.15	.07
213	Tomas Perez	.15	.07
214	Alex Gonzalez	.15	.07
215	Joe Carter	.30	.14
216	Shawn Green	.15	.07
217	Edwin Hurtado	.15	.07
218	Edgar Martinez Tony Pena CL	.30	.14
219	Chipper Jones Barry Larkin CL	.75	.35
220	Orel Hershiser CL	.15	.07
221	Mike Devereaux CL	.15	.07
222	Tom Glavine CL	.15	.07
223	Karim Garcia	.40	.18
224	Arquimedez Pozo	.15	.07
225	Billy Wagner	.30	.14
226	John Wasdin	.15	.07
227	Jeff Suppan	.30	.14
228	Steve Gibralter	.15	.07
229	Jimmy Haynes	.15	.07
230	Ruben Rivera	.30	.14
231	Chris Snopek	.15	.07
232	Alex Ochoa	.15	.07
233	Shannon Stewart	.30	.14
234	Quinton McCracken	.15	.07
235	Trey Beamon	.15	.07
236	Billy McMillon	.15	.07
237	Steve Cox	.15	.07
238	George Arias	.15	.07
239	Jose Herrera	.15	.07
240	Todd Greene	.40	.18
241	Jason Kendall	.30	.14
242	Brooks Kieschnick	.30	.14
243	Osvaldo Fernandez	.30	.14
244	Livan Hernandez	2.00	.90
245	Rey Ordonez	.30	.14
246	Mike Grace	.15	.07
247	Jay Canizaro	.15	.07
248	Bob Wolcott	.15	.07
249	Jermaine Dye	.30	.14
250	Jason Schmidt	.30	.14
251	Mike Sweeney	.60	.25
252	Marcus Jensen	.15	.07
253	Mendy Lopez	.15	.07
254	Wilton Guerrero	.60	.25
255	Paul Wilson	.15	.07
256	Edgar Renteria	.40	.18
257	Richard Hidalgo	.60	.25
258	Bob Abreu	.40	.18
259	Robert Smith	.60	.25
260	Sal Fasano	.15	.07
261	Enrique Wilson	.30	.14
262	Rich Hunter	.15	.07
263	Sergio Nunez	.30	.14
264	Dan Serafini	.15	.07
265	David Doster	.15	.07
266	Ryan McGuire	.15	.07
267	Scott Spiezio	.40	.18
268	Rafael Orellano	.15	.07
269	Steve Avery	.15	.07
270	Fred McGriff	.40	.18
271	John Smoltz	.30	.14
272	Ryan Klesko	.40	.18
273	Jeff Blauser	.30	.14
274	Brad Clontz	.15	.07
275	Roberto Alomar	.60	.25
276	B.J. Surhoff	.15	.07
277	Jeffrey Hammonds	.15	.07
278	Brady Anderson	.40	.18
279	Bobby Bonilla	.30	.14
280	Cal Ripken	2.50	1.10
281	Mike Mussina	.60	.25
282	Wil Cordero	.15	.07
283	Mike Stanley	.15	.07
284	Aaron Sele	.15	.07
285	Jose Canseco	.40	.18
286	Tom Gordon	.15	.07
287	Heathcliff Slocumb	.15	.07
288	Lee Smith	.30	.14
289	Troy Percival	.15	.07
290	Tim Salmon	.60	.25
291	Chuck Finley	.15	.07
292	Jim Abbott	.15	.07
293	Chili Davis	.30	.14
294	Steve Trachsel	.15	.07
295	Mark Grace	.40	.18
296	Rey Sanchez	.15	.07
297	Scott Servais	.15	.07
298	Jaime Navarro	.15	.07
299	Frank Castillo	.15	.07
300	Frank Thomas	2.50	1.10
301	Jason Bere	.15	.07
302	Danny Tartabull	.15	.07
303	Darren Lewis	.15	.07
304	Roberto Hernandez	.15	.07
305	Tony Phillips	.15	.07
306	Wilson Alvarez	.15	.07
307	Jose Hijo	.15	.07
308	Hal Morris	.15	.07
309	Mark Portugal	.15	.07
310	Barry Larkin	.40	.18
311	Dave Burba	.15	.07
312	Ed Taubensee	.15	.07
313	Sandy Alomar Jr.	.30	.14
314	Dennis Martinez	.30	.14
315	Albert Belle	.75	.35
316	Eddie Murray	.40	.18
317	Charles Nagy	.30	.14
318	Chad Ogea	.15	.07
319	Kenny Lofton	.75	.35
320	Dante Bichette	.30	.14
321	Armando Reynoso	.15	.07
322	Walt Weiss	.15	.07
323	Ellis Burks	.30	.14
324	Kevin Ritz	.15	.07
325	Bill Swift	.15	.07
326	Jason Bates	.15	.07
327	Tony Clark	.60	.25
328	Travis Fryman	.30	.14
329	Mark Parent	.15	.07
330	Alan Trammell	.40	.18
331	C.J. Nitkowski	.15	.07
332	Jose Lima	.15	.07
333	Phil Plantier	.15	.07
334	Kurt Abbott	.15	.07
335	Andre Dawson	.40	.18
336	Chris Hammond	.15	.07
337	Robb Nen	.15	.07
338	Pat Rapp	.15	.07
339	Al Leiter	.15	.07
340	Gary Sheffield UER (HR total says 17	.60	.25
341	Todd Jones	.15	.07
342	Doug Drabek	.15	.07
343	Greg Swindell	.15	.07
344	Tony Eusebio	.15	.07
345	Craig Biggio	.40	.18
346	Darryl Kile	.30	.14
347	Mike Macfarlane	.15	.07
348	Jeff Montgomery	.15	.07
349	Chris Haney	.15	.07
350	Bip Roberts	.15	.07
351	Tom Goodwin	.15	.07
352	Mark Gubicza	.15	.07
353	Joe Randa	.15	.07
354	Ramon Martinez	.30	.14
355	Eric Karros	.30	.14
356	Delino DeShields	.15	.07
357	Brett Butler	.30	.14
358	Todd Worrell	.15	.07
359	Mike Blowers	.15	.07
360	Mike Piazza	2.00	.90
361	Ben McDonald	.15	.07
362	Ricky Bones	.15	.07
363	Greg Vaughn	.15	.07
364	Matt Mieske	.15	.07
365	Kevin Seitzer	.15	.07
366	Jeff Cirillo	.30	.14
367	LaTroy Hawkins	.15	.07
368	Frank Rodriguez	.15	.07
369	Rick Aguilera	.15	.07
370	Roberto Alomar BG	.30	.14
371	Albert Belle BG	.40	.18
372	Wade Boggs BG	.30	.14
373	Barry Bonds BG	.40	.18
374	Roger Clemens BG	.60	.25
375	Dennis Eckersley BG	.15	.07
376	Ken Griffey Jr. BG	1.50	.70
377	Tony Gwynn BG	.75	.35
378	Rickey Henderson BG	.30	.14
379	Greg Maddux BG	1.00	.45
380	Fred McGriff BG	.30	.14
381	Paul Molitor BG	.30	.14
382	Eddie Murray BG	.30	.14
383	Mike Piazza BG	1.00	.45
384	Kirby Puckett BG	.60	.25
385	Cal Ripken BG	1.25	.55
386	Ozzie Smith BG	.40	.18
387	Frank Thomas BG	1.25	.55
388	Matt Walbeck	.15	.07
389	Dave Stevens	.15	.07
390	Marty Cordova	.30	.14
391	Darrin Fletcher	.15	.07
392	Cliff Floyd	.15	.07
393	Mel Rojas	.15	.07
394	Shane Andrews	.15	.07
395	Moises Alou	.30	.14
396	Carlos Perez	.15	.07
397	Jeff Fassero	.15	.07
398	Bobby Jones	.30	.14
399	Todd Hundley	.30	.14
400	John Franco	.30	.14
401	Jose Vizcaino	.15	.07
402	Bernard Gilkey	.15	.07
403	Pete Harnisch	.15	.07
404	Pat Kelly	.15	.07
405	David Cone	.30	.14
406	Bernie Williams	.60	.25
407	Jim Wetteland	.15	.07
408	Scott Kamieniecki	.15	.07
409	Tim Raines	.30	.14
410	Wade Boggs	.60	.25
411	Terry Steinbach	.15	.07
412	Jason Giambi	.30	.14
413	Todd Van Poppel	.15	.07

☐ 414	Pedro Munoz	.15	.07
☐ 415	Eddie Murray SBT	.30	.14
☐ 416	Dennis Eckersley SBT	.15	.07
☐ 417	Bip Roberts SBT	.15	.07
☐ 418	Glenallen Hill SBT	.15	.07
☐ 419	John Hudek SBT	.15	.07
☐ 420	Derek Bell SBT	.15	.07
☐ 421	Larry Walker SBT	.30	.14
☐ 422	Greg Maddux SBT	1.00	.45
☐ 423	Ken Caminiti SBT	.30	.14
☐ 424	Brent Gates	.15	.07
☐ 425	Mark McGwire	1.25	.55
☐ 426	Mark Whiten	.15	.07
☐ 427	Sid Fernandez	.15	.07
☐ 428	Ricky Bottalico	.15	.07
☐ 429	Mike Mimbs	.15	.07
☐ 430	Lenny Dykstra	.30	.14
☐ 431	Todd Zeile	.15	.07
☐ 432	Benito Santiago	.15	.07
☐ 433	Danny Miceli	.15	.07
☐ 434	Al Martin	.15	.07
☐ 435	Jay Bell	.30	.14
☐ 436	Charlie Hayes	.15	.07
☐ 437	Mike Kingery	.15	.07
☐ 438	Paul Wagner	.15	.07
☐ 439	Tom Pagnozzi	.15	.07
☐ 440	Ozzie Smith	.75	.35
☐ 441	Ray Lankford	.30	.14
☐ 442	Dennis Eckersley	.30	.14
☐ 443	Ron Gant	.30	.14
☐ 444	Alan Benes	.30	.14
☐ 445	Rickey Henderson	.40	.18
☐ 446	Jody Reed	.15	.07
☐ 447	Trevor Hoffman	.15	.07
☐ 448	Andujar Cedeno	.15	.07
☐ 449	Steve Finley	.30	.14
☐ 450	Tony Gwynn	1.50	.70
☐ 451	Joey Hamilton	.30	.14
☐ 452	Mark Leiter	.15	.07
☐ 453	Rod Beck	.15	.07
☐ 454	Kirt Manwaring	.15	.07
☐ 455	Matt Williams	.40	.18
☐ 456	Robby Thompson	.15	.07
☐ 457	Shawon Dunston	.15	.07
☐ 458	Russ Davis	.15	.07
☐ 459	Paul Sorrento	.15	.07
☐ 460	Randy Johnson	.60	.25
☐ 461	Chris Bosio	.15	.07
☐ 462	Luis Sojo	.15	.07
☐ 463	Sterling Hitchcock	.15	.07
☐ 464	Benji Gil	.15	.07
☐ 465	Mickey Tettleton	.15	.07
☐ 466	Mark McLemore	.15	.07
☐ 467	Darryl Hamilton	.15	.07
☐ 468	Ken Hill	.15	.07
☐ 469	Dean Palmer	.15	.07
☐ 470	Carlos Delgado	.30	.14
☐ 471	Ed Sprague	.15	.07
☐ 472	Otis Nixon	.15	.07
☐ 473	Pat Hentgen	.30	.14
☐ 474	Juan Guzman	.15	.07
☐ 475	John Olerud	.30	.14
☐ 476	Buck Showalter CL	.15	.07
☐ 477	Bobby Cox CL	.15	.07
☐ 478	Tommy Lasorda CL	.30	.14
☐ 479	Buck Showalter CL	.15	.07
☐ 480	Sparky Anderson CL	.30	.14
☐ 481U	Randy Myers	.25	.11
☐ 482U	Kent Mercker	.25	.11
☐ 483U	David Wells	.25	.11
☐ 484U	Kevin Mitchell	.25	.11
☐ 485U	Randy Velarde	.25	.11
☐ 486U	Ryne Sandberg	1.50	.70
☐ 487U	Doug Jones	.25	.11
☐ 488U	Terry Adams	.25	.11
☐ 489U	Kevin Tapani	.25	.11
☐ 490U	Harold Baines	.50	.23
☐ 491U	Eric Davis	.50	.23
☐ 492U	Julio Franco	.25	.11
☐ 493U	Jack McDowell	.25	.11
☐ 494U	Devon White	.25	.11
☐ 495U	Kevin Brown	.50	.23
☐ 496U	Rick Wilkins	.25	.11
☐ 497U	Sean Berry	.25	.11
☐ 498U	Keith Lockhart	.25	.11
☐ 499U	Mark Loretta	.25	.11

☐ 500U	Paul Molitor	1.25	.55
☐ 501U	Roberto Kelly	.25	.11
☐ 502U	Lance Johnson	.25	.11
☐ 503U	Tino Martinez	1.00	.45
☐ 504U	Kenny Rogers	.25	.11
☐ 505U	Todd Stottlemyre	.25	.11
☐ 506U	Gary Gaetti	.25	.11
☐ 507U	Royce Clayton	.25	.11
☐ 508U	Andy Benes	.50	.23
☐ 509U	Wally Joyner	.50	.23
☐ 510U	Erik Hanson	.25	.11

1996 Upper Deck Blue Chip Prospects

Randomly inserted in retail packs at a rate of one in 72, this 20-card set, diecut on the top and bottom, features some of the best young stars in the majors against a bluish background.

	MINT	NRMT
COMPLETE SET (20)	200.00	90.00
COMMON CARD (BC1-BC20)	5.00	2.20
SEMISTARS	8.00	3.60
UNLISTED STARS	12.00	5.50
SER.1 STATED ODDS 1:72		

☐ BC1	Hideo Nomo	30.00	13.50
☐ BC2	Johnny Damon	6.00	2.70
☐ BC3	Jason Isringhausen	5.00	2.20
☐ BC4	Bill Pulsipher	5.00	2.20
☐ BC5	Marty Cordova	6.00	2.70
☐ BC6	Michael Tucker	5.00	2.20
☐ BC7	John Wasdin	5.00	2.20
☐ BC8	Karim Garcia	8.00	3.60
☐ BC9	Ruben Rivera	5.00	2.20
☐ BC10	Chipper Jones	40.00	18.00
☐ BC11	Billy Wagner	6.00	2.70
☐ BC12	Brooks Kieschnick	6.00	2.70
☐ BC13	Alan Benes	5.00	2.20
☐ BC14	Roger Cedeno	5.00	2.20
☐ BC15	Alex Rodriguez	40.00	18.00
☐ BC16	Jason Schmidt	6.00	2.70
☐ BC17	Derek Jeter	30.00	13.50
☐ BC18	Brian L.Hunter	6.00	2.70
☐ BC19	Garret Anderson	6.00	2.70
☐ BC20	Manny Ramirez	12.00	5.50

1996 Upper Deck Diamond Destiny

Issued one per Walmart pack, these 40 cards feature leading players of baseball. The cards have two photos on the front with the player's name listed on the bottom. The backs have another photo along with bio-

graphical information. The cards are numbered with a "DD" prefix.

	MINT	NRMT
COMPLETE SET (40)	120.00	55.00
COMMON CARD (DD1-DD40)	1.50	.70
ONE PER UD TECH RETAIL PACK		
COMP.GOLD DD SET (40)	1500.00	700.00
*GOLD DD: 6X TO 12X BASIC DD		
GOLD DD STATED ODDS 1:143 UD TECH		
COMP.SILVER DD SET (40)	500.00	220.00
*SILVER DD: 2X TO 4X BASIC DD		
SILVER DD STATED ODDS 1:35 UD TECH		

☐ DD1	Chipper Jones	10.00	4.50
☐ DD2	Fred McGriff	2.00	.90
☐ DD3	John Smoltz	1.50	.70
☐ DD4	Ryan Klesko	2.00	.90
☐ DD5	Greg Maddux	10.00	4.50
☐ DD6	Cal Ripken	12.00	5.50
☐ DD7	Roberto Alomar	3.00	1.35
☐ DD8	Eddie Murray	3.00	1.35
☐ DD9	Brady Anderson	2.00	.90
☐ DD10	Mo Vaughn	4.00	1.80
☐ DD11	Roger Clemens	4.00	1.80
☐ DD12	Darin Erstad	8.00	3.60
☐ DD13	Sammy Sosa	3.00	1.35
☐ DD14	Frank Thomas	12.00	5.50
☐ DD15	Barry Larkin	2.00	.90
☐ DD16	Albert Belle	4.00	1.80
☐ DD17	Manny Ramirez	3.00	1.35
☐ DD18	Kenny Lofton	4.00	1.80
☐ DD19	Dante Bichette	1.50	.70
☐ DD20	Gary Sheffield	2.00	.90
☐ DD21	Jeff Bagwell	6.00	2.70
☐ DD22	Hideo Nomo	6.00	2.70
☐ DD23	Mike Piazza	10.00	4.50
☐ DD24	Kirby Puckett	6.00	2.70
☐ DD25	Paul Molitor	3.00	1.35
☐ DD26	Chuck Knoblauch	3.00	1.35
☐ DD27	Wade Boggs	3.00	1.35
☐ DD28	Derek Jeter	10.00	4.50
☐ DD29	Ray Ordonez	1.50	.70
☐ DD30	Mark McGwire	6.00	2.70
☐ DD31	Ozzie Smith	4.00	1.80
☐ DD32	Tony Gwynn	8.00	3.60
☐ DD33	Barry Bonds	4.00	1.80
☐ DD34	Matt Williams	2.00	.90
☐ DD35	Ken Griffey Jr.	15.00	6.75
☐ DD36	Jay Buhner	2.00	.90
☐ DD37	Randy Johnson	3.00	1.35
☐ DD38	Alex Rodriguez	10.00	4.50
☐ DD39	Juan Gonzalez	8.00	3.60
☐ DD40	Joe Carter	1.50	.70

1996 Upper Deck Future Stock Prospects

Randomly inserted in packs at a rate of one in 6, this 20-card set highlights the top prospects who made their major league debuts in 1995. The cards are diecut at

	MINT	NRMT
COMPLETE SET (10)	12.00	5.50
COMMON CARD(GF1-GF10)	.40	.18
ONE PER SPECIAL SER.2 RETAIL PACK		

		MINT	NRMT
☐ GF1	Ken Griffey Jr.	3.00	1.35
☐ GF2	Frank Thomas	2.50	1.10
☐ GF3	Barry Bonds	.75	.35
☐ GF4	Albert Belle	.75	.35
☐ GF5	Cal Ripken	2.50	1.10
☐ GF6	Mike Piazza	2.00	.90
☐ GF7	Chipper Jones	2.00	.90
☐ GF8	Matt Williams	.40	.18
☐ GF9	Hideo Nomo	1.50	.70
☐ GF10	Greg Maddux	2.00	.90

the top and feature a purple border surrounding the player's picture.

	MINT	NRMT
COMPLETE SET (20)	10.00	4.50
COMMON CARD (FS1–FS20)	1.00	.45
SER.1 STATED ODDS 1:6 HOB/RET		

		MINT	NRMT
☐ FS1	George Arias	1.00	.45
☐ FS2	Brian Barber	1.00	.45
☐ FS3	Trey Beamon	1.00	.45
☐ FS4	Yamil Benitez	1.50	.70
☐ FS5	Jamie Brewington	1.00	.45
☐ FS6	Tony Clark	3.00	1.35
☐ FS7	Steve Cox	1.00	.45
☐ FS8	Carlos Delgado	1.50	.70
☐ FS9	Chad Fonville	1.00	.45
☐ FS10	Alex Ochoa	1.00	.45
☐ FS11	Curtis Goodwin	1.00	.45
☐ FS12	Todd Greene	2.00	.90
☐ FS13	Jimmy Haynes	1.00	.45
☐ FS14	Quinton McCracken	1.00	.45
☐ FS15	Billy McMillon	1.00	.45
☐ FS16	Chan Ho Park	2.00	.90
☐ FS17	Arquimedez Pozo	1.00	.45
☐ FS18	Chris Snopek	1.00	.45
☐ FS19	Shannon Stewart	1.50	.70
☐ FS20	Jeff Suppan	1.50	.70

1996 Upper Deck Gameface

These Gameface cards were seeded at a rate of one per Upper Deck and Collector's Choice Wal Mart retail pack. The Upper Deck packs contained eight cards and the Collector's Choice packs contained sixteen cards. Both packs carried a suggested retail price of $1.50. The card fronts feature the player's photo surrounded by a "cloudy" white border along with a Gameface logo at the bottom.

1996 Upper Deck Hot Commodities

Cards from this 20 card set double die-cut set were randomly inserted into series two Upper Deck packs at a rate of one in 37. The set features some of baseball's most popular players.

	MINT	NRMT
COMPLETE SET (20)	150.00	70.00
COMMON CARD (HC1–HC20)	4.00	1.80
UNLISTED STARS	6.00	2.70
SER.2 STATED ODDS 1:36 HOB/RET/ANCO		

		MINT	NRMT
☐ HC1	Ken Griffey Jr.	30.00	13.50
☐ HC2	Hideo Nomo	15.00	6.75
☐ HC3	Roberto Alomar	6.00	2.70
☐ HC4	Paul Wilson	4.00	1.80
☐ HC5	Albert Belle	8.00	3.60
☐ HC6	Manny Ramirez	6.00	2.70
☐ HC7	Kirby Puckett	12.00	5.50
☐ HC8	Johnny Damon	5.00	2.20
☐ HC9	Randy Johnson	6.00	2.70
☐ HC10	Greg Maddux	20.00	9.00
☐ HC11	Chipper Jones	20.00	9.00
☐ HC12	Barry Bonds	8.00	3.60
☐ HC13	Mo Vaughn	8.00	3.60
☐ HC14	Mike Piazza	20.00	9.00
☐ HC15	Cal Ripken	25.00	11.00
☐ HC16	Tim Salmon	6.00	2.70
☐ HC17	Sammy Sosa	6.00	2.70
☐ HC18	Kenny Lofton	8.00	3.60
☐ HC19	Tony Gwynn	15.00	6.75
☐ HC20	Frank Thomas	25.00	11.00

1996 Upper Deck V.J. Lovero Showcase

Upper Deck utilized photos from the files of V.J. Lovero to produce this set. The cards feature the photos along with a story of how Lovero took the photos. The cards are numbered with a "VJ" prefix.

	MINT	NRMT
COMPLETE SET (19)	25.00	11.00
COMMON CARD(VJ1-VJ19)	.50	.23
SER.2 STATED ODDS 1:6 HOB/RET,1:3 ANCO		

		MINT	NRMT
☐ VJ1	Jim Abbott	.50	.23
☐ VJ2	Hideo Nomo	3.00	1.35
☐ VJ3	Derek Jeter	5.00	2.20
☐ VJ4	Barry Bonds	2.00	.90
☐ VJ5	Greg Maddux	5.00	2.20
☐ VJ6	Mark McGwire	3.00	1.35
☐ VJ7	Jose Canseco	1.00	.45
☐ VJ8	Ken Caminiti	1.00	.45
☐ VJ9	Raul Mondesi	1.00	.45
☐ VJ10	Ken Griffey Jr.	8.00	3.60
☐ VJ11	Jay Buhner	1.00	.45
☐ VJ12	Randy Johnson	1.50	.70
☐ VJ13	Roger Clemens	2.00	.90
☐ VJ14	Brady Anderson	1.00	.45
☐ VJ15	Frank Thomas	5.00	2.20
☐ VJ16	Garret Anderson Jim Edmonds Tim Salmon	1.50	.70
☐ VJ17	Mike Piazza	5.00	2.20
☐ VJ18	Dante Bichette	.75	.35
☐ VJ19	Tony Gwynn	4.00	1.80

1996 Upper Deck Power Driven

Randomly inserted in first series packs at a rate of one in 36, this 20-card set consists of embossed rainbow foil inserts of baseball's top power hitters.

	MINT	NRMT
COMPLETE SET (20)	120.00	55.00
COMMON CARD (PD1-PD20)	2.50	1.10
SEMISTARS	4.00	1.80
UNLISTED STARS	6.00	2.70
SER.1 STATED ODDS 1:36 HOB/RET		

		MINT	NRMT
☐ PD1	Albert Belle	8.00	3.60
☐ PD2	Barry Bonds	8.00	3.60
☐ PD3	Jay Buhner	4.00	1.80
☐ PD4	Jose Canseco	4.00	1.80
☐ PD5	Cecil Fielder	3.00	1.35
☐ PD6	Juan Gonzalez	15.00	6.75

		MINT	NRMT
☐ PD7	Ken Griffey Jr........	30.00	13.50
☐ PD8	Eric Karros	3.00	1.35
☐ PD9	Fred McGriff	4.00	1.80
☐ PD10	Mark McGwire	12.00	5.50
☐ PD11	Rafael Palmeiro	4.00	1.80
☐ PD12	Mike Piazza..........	20.00	9.00
☐ PD13	Manny Ramirez	6.00	2.70
☐ PD14	Tim Salmon	6.00	2.70
☐ PD15	Reggie Sanders	2.50	1.10
☐ PD16	Sammy Sosa	6.00	2.70
☐ PD17	Frank Thomas........	25.00	11.00
☐ PD18	Mo Vaughn............	8.00	3.60
☐ PD19	Larry Walker	6.00	2.70
☐ PD20	Matt Williams	4.00	1.80

1996 Upper Deck Predictor Hobby

Randomly inserted in both series hobby packs at a rate of one in 12, this 60-card predictor set offers unique prizes as Major League Baseball players compete for monthly milestones and awards. The fronts feature a cutout player photo against a pinstriped background surrounded by a gray marble border.

	MINT	NRMT
COMPLETE SET (60)	110.00	50.00
COMPLETE SERIES 1 (30)..	60.00	27.00
COMPLETE SERIES 2 (30) ..	50.00	22.00
COMMON CARD(H1-H60) ..	1.00	.45
STATED ODDS 1:12 HOBBY...		
COMP.AL PLAY.EXCH.SET (10)	20.00	9.00
COMP.AL PITCH.EXCH.SET (10)	6.00	2.70
COMP.AL ROOK.EXCH.SET (10)	8.00	3.60
COMP.NL PLAY.EXCH.SET (10)	12.00	5.50
COMP.NL PITCH.EXCH.SET (10)	8.00	3.60
COMP.NL ROOK.EXCH.SET (10)	6.00	2.70
*EXCH.CARDS:.2X TO .5X BASIC PREDICTOR		
ONE EXCH.SET VIA MAIL PER PRED.WINNER		

☐ H1	Albert Belle	2.50	1.10
☐ H2	Kenny Lofton	2.50	1.10
☐ H3	Rafael Palmeiro......	1.50	.70
☐ H4	Ken Griffey Jr.........	10.00	4.50
☐ H5	Tim Salmon	2.00	.90
☐ H6	Cal Ripken.............	8.00	3.60
☐ H7	Mark McGwire	4.00	1.80
☐ H8	Frank Thomas........	8.00	3.60
☐ H9	Mo Vaughn W	2.50	1.10
☐ H10	Player of Month LShot	1.00	.45
☐ H11	Roger Clemens	3.00	1.35
☐ H12	David Cone	1.25	.55
☐ H13	Jose Mesa..............	1.00	.45
☐ H14	Randy Johnson.......	2.00	.90
☐ H15	Chuck Finley	1.00	.45
☐ H16	Mike Mussina	2.00	.90
☐ H17	Kevin Appier	1.25	.55
☐ H18	Kenny Rogers	1.00	.45
☐ H19	Lee Smith	1.25	.55
☐ H20	Pitcher of Month LShot W	1.00	.45
☐ H21	George Arias	1.00	.45

☐ H22	Jose Herrera	1.00	.45
☐ H23	Tony Clark..............	2.00	.90
☐ H24	Todd Greene	1.50	.70
☐ H25	Derek Jeter W	6.00	2.70
☐ H26	Arquimedez Pozo	1.00	.45
☐ H27	Matt Lawton...........	1.50	.70
☐ H28	Shannon Stewart	1.25	.55
☐ H29	Chris Snopek	1.00	.45
☐ H30	Most Rookie Hits LShot	1.00	.45
☐ H31	Jeff Bagwell W	4.00	1.80
☐ H32	Dante Bichette........	1.25	.55
☐ H33	Barry Bonds W	2.50	1.10
☐ H34	Tony Gwynn	5.00	2.20
☐ H35	Chipper Jones.........	6.00	2.70
☐ H36	Eric Karros	1.25	.55
☐ H37	Barry Larkin	1.50	.70
☐ H38	Mike Piazza...........	6.00	2.70
☐ H39	Matt Williams	1.50	.70
☐ H40	Long Shot Card	1.00	.45
☐ H41	Osvaldo Fernandez ..	1.25	.55
☐ H42	Tom Glavine	1.25	.55
☐ H43	Jason Isringhausen..	1.00	.45
☐ H44	Greg Maddux	6.00	2.70
☐ H45	Pedro Martinez	2.00	.90
☐ H46	Hideo Nomo	4.00	1.80
☐ H47	Pete Schourek	1.00	.45
☐ H48	Paul Wilson............	1.00	.45
☐ H49	Mark Wohlers	1.00	.45
☐ H50	Long Shot Card	1.00	.45
☐ H51	Bob Abreu	1.50	.70
☐ H52	Trey Beamon...........	1.00	.45
☐ H53	Yamil Benitez	1.25	.55
☐ H54	Roger Cedeno	1.00	.45
☐ H55	Todd Hollandsworth ..	1.00	.45
☐ H56	Marvin Benard	1.00	.45
☐ H57	Jason Kendall	1.50	.70
☐ H58	Brooks Kieschnick ..	1.25	.55
☐ H59	Rey Ordonez W	1.25	.55
☐ H60	Long Shot Card	1.00	.45

1996 Upper Deck Predictor Retail

Randomly inserted in both series retail packs at a rate of one in 12, this 60-card predictor set offers unique prizes as Major League Baseball players compete for "monthly milestones and awards." The fronts feature a "cutout" player photo against a pinstriped background surrounded by a gray marble border.

	MINT	NRMT
COMPLETE SET (60)	150.00	70.00
COMPLETE SERIES 1 (30)	100.00	45.00
COMPLETE SERIES 2 (30) ..	50.00	22.00
COMMON CARD(CR1-R60) ..	1.00	.45
STATED ODDS 1:12 RETAIL..		
COMP.AL HR EXCH.SET (10)	20.00	9.00
COMP.AL RBI EXCH.SET (10)	15.00	6.75
COMP.AL AVG.EXCH.SET (10)	15.00	6.75
COMP.NL HR EXCH.SET (10)	10.00	4.50
COMP.NL RBI EXCH.SET (10)	8.00	3.60

COMP.NL AVG.EXCH.SET (10) 10.00		4.50
*EXCH.CARDS:.2X TO .5X BASIC PREDICTORS		
ONE EXCH.SET VIA MAIL PER PRED.WINNER		

☐ R1	Albert Belle W	2.50	1.10
☐ R2	Jay Buhner W	1.50	.70
☐ R3	Juan Gonzalez	5.00	2.20
☐ R4	Ken Griffey Jr..........	10.00	4.50
☐ R5	Mark McGwire W	4.00	1.80
☐ R6	Rafael Palmeiro	1.50	.70
☐ R7	Tim Salmon	2.00	.90
☐ R8	Frank Thomas..........	8.00	3.60
☐ R9	Mo Vaughn W	2.50	1.10
☐ R10	Monthly HR Ldr LShot W	1.00	.45
☐ R11	Albert Belle W	2.50	1.10
☐ R12	Jay Buhner W	1.50	.70
☐ R13	Jim Edmonds	1.50	.70
☐ R14	Cecil Fielder	1.25	.55
☐ R15	Ken Griffey Jr..........	10.00	4.50
☐ R16	Edgar Martinez	1.50	.70
☐ R17	Manny Ramirez........	2.00	.90
☐ R18	Frank Thomas..........	8.00	3.60
☐ R19	Mo Vaughn W	2.50	1.10
☐ R20	Monthly RBI Ldr LShot	1.00	.45
☐ R21	Roberto Alomar W	2.00	.90
☐ R22	Carlos Baerga	1.00	.45
☐ R23	Wade Boggs	2.00	.90
☐ R24	Ken Griffey Jr..........	10.00	4.50
☐ R25	Chuck Knoblauch	2.00	.90
☐ R26	Kenny Lofton	2.50	1.10
☐ R27	Edgar Martinez	1.50	.70
☐ R28	Tim Salmon	2.00	.90
☐ R29	Frank Thomas..........	8.00	3.60
☐ R30	Monthly Avg Ldr LShot W	1.00	.45
☐ R31	Dante Bichette........	1.25	.55
☐ R32	Barry Bonds W	2.50	1.10
☐ R33	Ron Gant	1.25	.55
☐ R34	Chipper Jones.........	6.00	2.70
☐ R35	Fred McGriff	1.50	.70
☐ R36	Mike Piazza...........	6.00	2.70
☐ R37	Sammy Sosa	2.00	.90
☐ R38	Larry Walker	2.00	.90
☐ R39	Matt Williams	1.50	.70
☐ R40	Long Shot Card	1.00	.45
☐ R41	Jeff Bagwell W	4.00	1.80
☐ R42	Dante Bichette........	1.25	.55
☐ R43	Barry Bonds W	2.50	1.10
☐ R44	Jeff Conine	1.25	.55
☐ R45	Andres Galarraga	2.00	.90
☐ R46	Mike Piazza	6.00	2.70
☐ R47	Reggie Sanders.......	1.00	.45
☐ R48	Sammy Sosa	2.00	.90
☐ R49	Matt Williams	1.50	.70
☐ R50	Long Shot Card	1.00	.45
☐ R51	Jeff Bagwell	4.00	1.80
☐ R52	Derek Bell	1.00	.45
☐ R53	Dante Bichette.........	1.25	.55
☐ R54	Craig Biggio	1.50	.70
☐ R55	Barry Bonds	2.50	1.10
☐ R56	Bret Boone	1.00	.45
☐ R57	Tony Gwynn	5.00	2.20
☐ R58	Barry Larkin	1.50	.70
☐ R59	Mike Piazza W	6.00	2.70
☐ R60	Long Shot Card........	1.00	.45

1996 Upper Deck Ripken Collection

This 23 card set was issued across all the various Upper Deck brands. The cards were issued to commemorate Cal Ripken's career, which had been capped the previous season by the breaking of the consecutive game streak long held by Lou Gehrig. The cards were inserted at the following ratios: Cards 1-4 were in Collector Choice first series packs at a rate of one in 12. Cards 5-8 were inserted into Upper Deck series one packs at a rate of one in 24. Cards 9-12 were

placed into second series Collector Choice packs at a rate of one in 12. Cards 13-17 were in second series Upper Deck packs at a rate of one in 24. And Cards 18-22 were in SP Packs at a rate of one in 45. The header card (#23) was also inserted into only Collector Choice packs.

	MINT	NRMT
COMPLETE SET (23)	120.00	55.00
COMP.COLC SER.1 (5)	12.00	5.50
COMP.UD SER.1 (4)	25.00	11.00
COMP.COLC SER.2 (4)	10.00	4.50
COMP.UD SER.2 (5)	25.00	11.00
COMP.SP SET (5)	50.00	22.00
COMMON COLC (1-4/9-12)	3.00	1.35
COMMON UD (5-8/13-17)	6.00	2.70
COMMON SP (18-22)	12.00	5.50
HEADER CARD (CCH)	3.00	1.35
CARDS 1-4 STATED ODDS 1:12 CC SER.1		
CARDS 5-8 STATED ODDS 1:24 UD SER.1		
CARDS 9-12 STATED ODDS 1:12 CC SER.2		
CARDS13-17 STATED ODDS 1:24 UD SER.2		
CARDS18-22 STATED ODDS 1:45 SP		

☐ 1	Cal Ripken COLC	3.00	1.35
	After playing in 2,131 consecutive games		
☐ 2	Cal Ripken COLC	3.00	1.35
	Barry Bonds		
	1995 All-Star Game		
☐ 3	Cal Ripken COLC	3.00	1.35
	300th home run		
☐ 4	Cal Ripken COLC	3.00	1.35
	Chasing Pop-up		
	1994		
☐ 5	Cal Ripken UD	6.00	2.70
	Running to first		
	1995		
☐ 6	Cal Ripken UD	6.00	2.70
	Brian McRae sliding into second		
	1992		
☐ 7	Cal Ripken UD	6.00	2.70
	1992 Roberto Clemente Award		
☐ 8	Cal Ripken UD	6.00	2.70
	Batting pose		
	1991		
☐ 9	Cal Ripken COLC	3.00	1.35
	Batting follow-through		
	1991		
☐ 10	Cal Ripken COLC	3.00	1.35
	1991 1st Gold Glove		
☐ 11	Cal Ripken COLC	3.00	1.35
	Midway through swing		
	1991		
☐ 12	Cal Ripken COLC	3.00	1.35
	Fielding and throwing Ball		
	1990		
☐ 13	Cal Ripken UD	6.00	2.70
	Black uniform top in field		
	1990		
☐ 14	Cal Ripken UD	6.00	2.70
	Batting follow-through		
	1987		
☐ 15	Cal Ripken UD	6.00	2.70
	In Backswing		

	1986		
☐ 16	Cal Ripken UD	6.00	2.70
	Midway through swing		
	1984		
☐ 17	Cal Ripken UD	6.00	2.70
	Ball about to enter glove		
	1983		
☐ 18	Cal Ripken SP	12.00	5.50
	Throwing		
	1983		
☐ 19	Cal Ripken SP	12.00	5.50
	Batting, Orange Uniform		
	1983		
☐ 20	Cal Ripken SP	12.00	5.50
	Batting follow-through		
	1982		
☐ 21	Cal Ripken SP	12.00	5.50
	Fielding at third		
	Mark Belanger in background		
	1981		
☐ 22	Cal Ripken SP	12.00	5.50
	Eddie Murray		
	1981		
☐ NNO	Cal Ripken Header COLC	4.00	1.80

1996 Upper Deck Run Producers

This 20 card set was randomly inserted into series two packs at a rate of one every 71 packs. The cards are thermographically printed, which gives the card a rubber surface texture. The cards are double die-cut and are foil stamped. These cards are designed to show off the technology of the Upper Deck cards.

	NRMT	EX
COMPLETE SET (20)	200.00	90.00
COMMON CARD (RP1-RP20)	4.00	1.80
SEMISTARS	6.00	2.70
UNLISTED STARS	8.00	3.60
SER.2 ODDS 1:72 HOB/RET, 1:36 ANCO		
CONDITION SENSITIVE SET		
THIS SET PRICED IN NRMT CONDITION		

☐ RP1	Albert Belle	10.00	4.50
☐ RP2	Dante Bichette	4.00	1.80
☐ RP3	Barry Bonds	10.00	4.50
☐ RP4	Jay Buhner	6.00	2.70
☐ RP5	Jose Canseco	6.00	2.70
☐ RP6	Juan Gonzalez	20.00	9.00
☐ RP7	Ken Griffey Jr.	40.00	18.00
☐ RP8	Tony Gwynn	20.00	9.00
☐ RP9	Kenny Lofton	10.00	4.50
☐ RP10	Edgar Martinez	6.00	2.70
☐ RP11	Fred McGriff	6.00	2.70
☐ RP12	Mark McGwire	15.00	6.75
☐ RP13	Rafael Palmeiro	6.00	2.70
☐ RP14	Mike Piazza	25.00	11.00
☐ RP15	Manny Ramirez	8.00	3.60
☐ RP16	Tim Salmon	8.00	3.60
☐ RP17	Sammy Sosa	8.00	3.60
☐ RP18	Frank Thomas	30.00	13.50
☐ RP19	Mo Vaughn	10.00	4.50
☐ RP20	Matt Williams	6.00	2.70

1997 Upper Deck

The 1997 Upper Deck set was issued in two series (series one 1-240, series two 271-520). The 12-card packs retailed for $2.49 each. Many cards have dates on the front to identify when, and when possible, what significant event is pictured. The backs include a player photo, stats and a brief blurb to go with vital statistics. Subsets include Jackie Robinson Tribute (1-9), Strike Force (64-72), Defensive Gems (136-153), Global Impact (181-207), Season Highlight Checklists (214-222/316-324), Star Rookies (223-240/271-288), Capture the Flag (370-387), Griffey's Hot List (415-424) and Diamond Debuts (470-483). It's critical to note that the Griffey's Hot List subset cards (in an unannounced move by the manufacturer) were short-printed (about 1:7 packs) in relation to other cards in the Series 2 set. The comparatively low print run on these cards created a dramatic surge in demand amongst set collectors and the cards soared in value on the secondary market. A 30-card first series Update set (numbered 241-270) was available to collectors that mailed in 10 series one wrappers along with $3 for postage and handling. The Series 1 Update set is composed primarily of 1996 post-season highlights. An additional 30-card series two Trade set (numbered 521-550) was also released around the end of the season. It too was available to collectors that mailed in 10 Series 2 wrappers along with $3 for postage and handling. The Series 2 Trade set is composed primarily of traded players pictured in their new uniforms and a dynamic selection of rookies and prospects highlighted by the inclusion of Jose Cruz Jr. and Hideki Irabu.

	MINT	NRMT
COMP.MASTER SET (550)	200.00	90.00
COMPLETE SET (490)	130.00	57.50
COMPLETE SERIES 1 (240)	30.00	13.50
COMPLETE SERIES 2 (250)	100.00	45.00

COMP.SER.2 w/o GHL (240)	15.00	6.75
COMMON (1-240/271-520)	.15	.07
J.ROBINSON TRIB. (1-9)	.50	.23
MINOR STARS	.30	.14
UNLISTED STARS	.60	.25
SUBSET CARDS HALF VALUE OF BASE CARDS		
COMP.UPDATE SET (30)	50.00	22.00
COMMON UPDATE (241-270)	.50	.23
UPDATE MINOR STARS	1.00	.45
UPD.UNLISTED STARS	2.00	.90
ONE UPD.SET VIA MAIL PER 10 SER.1 WRAP.		
COMP.TRADE SET (30)	20.00	9.00
COMMON TRADE (521-550)	.25	.11
TRADE MINOR STARS	.30	.23
TRADE UNLISTED STARS	1.00	.45
ONE TRD.SET VIA MAIL PER 10 SER.2 WRAP.		
COMP.SET (490) EXCLUDES UPD/TRD SETS		

1	Jackie Robinson — The Beginnings	.50	.23
2	Jackie Robinson — Breaking the Barrier	.50	.23
3	Jackie Robinson — The MVP Season, 1949	.50	.23
4	Jackie Robinson — 1951 season	.50	.23
5	Jackie Robinson — 1952 and 1953 seasons	.50	.23
6	Jackie Robinson — 1954 season	.50	.23
7	Jackie Robinson — 1955 season	.50	.23
8	Jackie Robinson — 1956 season	.50	.23
9	Jackie Robinson — Hall of Fame	.50	.23
10	Chipper Jones	2.00	.90
11	Marquis Grissom	.30	.14
12	Jermaine Dye	.15	.07
13	Mark Lemke	.15	.07
14	Terrell Wade	.15	.07
15	Fred McGriff	.40	.18
16	Tom Glavine	.30	.14
17	Mark Wohlers	.15	.07
18	Randy Myers	.15	.07
19	Roberto Alomar	.60	.25
20	Cal Ripken	2.50	1.10
21	Rafael Palmeiro	.40	.18
22	Mike Mussina	.60	.25
23	Brady Anderson	.40	.18
24	Jose Canseco	.40	.18
25	Mo Vaughn	.75	.35
26	Roger Clemens	1.25	.55
27	Tim Naehring	.15	.07
28	Jeff Suppan	.30	.14
29	Troy Percival	.15	.07
30	Sammy Sosa	.60	.25
31	Amaury Telemaco	.15	.07
32	Rey Sanchez	.15	.07
33	Scott Servais	.15	.07
34	Steve Trachsel	.15	.07
35	Mark Grace	.40	.18
36	Wilson Alvarez	.15	.07
37	Harold Baines	.30	.14
38	Tony Phillips	.15	.07
39	James Baldwin	.15	.07
40	Frank Thomas UER — Bio information is Ken Griffey Jr.'s	2.50	1.10
41	Lyle Mouton	.15	.07
42	Chris Snopek	.15	.07
43	Hal Morris	.15	.07
44	Eric Davis	.30	.14
45	Barry Larkin	.40	.18
46	Reggie Sanders	.15	.07
47	Pete Schourek	.15	.07
48	Lee Smith	.30	.14
49	Charles Nagy	.30	.14
50	Albert Belle	.75	.35
51	Julio Franco	.30	.14
52	Kenny Lofton	.75	.35
53	Orel Hershiser	.30	.14
54	Omar Vizquel	.30	.14
55	Eric Young	.15	.07
56	Curtis Leskanic	.15	.07
57	Quinton McCracken	.15	.07
58	Kevin Ritz	.15	.07
59	Walt Weiss	.15	.07
60	Dante Bichette	.30	.14
61	Mark Lewis	.15	.07
62	Tony Clark	.60	.25
63	Travis Fryman	.30	.14
64	John Smoltz SF	.15	.07
65	Greg Maddux SF	1.00	.45
66	Tom Glavine SF	.15	.07
67	Mike Mussina SF	.30	.14
68	Andy Pettitte SF	.30	.14
69	Mariano Rivera SF	.15	.07
70	Hideo Nomo SF	.75	.35
71	Kevin Brown SF	.15	.07
72	Randy Johnson SF	.30	.14
73	Felipe Lira	.15	.07
74	Kimera Bartee	.15	.07
75	Alan Trammell	.30	.14
76	Kevin Brown	.15	.07
77	Edgar Renteria	.30	.14
78	Al Leiter	.15	.07
79	Charles Johnson	.15	.07
80	Andre Dawson	.40	.18
81	Billy Wagner	.30	.14
82	Donne Wall	.15	.07
83	Jeff Bagwell	1.25	.55
84	Keith Lockhart	.15	.07
85	Jeff Montgomery	.15	.07
86	Tom Goodwin	.15	.07
87	Tim Belcher	.15	.07
88	Mike Macfarlane	.15	.07
89	Joe Randa	.15	.07
90	Brett Butler	.30	.14
91	Todd Worrell	.15	.07
92	Todd Hollandsworth	.15	.07
93	Ismael Valdes	.30	.14
94	Hideo Nomo	1.50	.70
95	Mike Piazza	2.00	.90
96	Jeff Cirillo	.30	.14
97	Ricky Bones	.15	.07
98	Fernando Vina	.15	.07
99	Ben McDonald	.15	.07
100	John Jaha	.15	.07
101	Mark Loretta	.15	.07
102	Paul Molitor	.60	.25
103	Rick Aguilera	.15	.07
104	Marty Cordova	.30	.14
105	Kirby Puckett	1.25	.55
106	Dan Naulty	.15	.07
107	Frank Rodriguez	.15	.07
108	Shane Andrews	.15	.07
109	Henry Rodriguez	.15	.07
110	Mark Grudzielanek	.15	.07
111	Pedro Martinez	.60	.25
112	Ugueth Urbina	.15	.07
113	David Segui	.15	.07
114	Rey Ordonez	.15	.07
115	Bernard Gilkey	.15	.07
116	Butch Huskey	.30	.14
117	Paul Wilson	.15	.07
118	Alex Ochoa	.15	.07
119	John Franco	.30	.14
120	Dwight Gooden	.30	.14
121	Ruben Rivera	.15	.07
122	Andy Pettitte	.60	.25
123	Tino Martinez	.60	.25
124	Bernie Williams	.60	.25
125	Wade Boggs	.60	.25
126	Paul O'Neill	.30	.14
127	Scott Brosius	.15	.07
128	Ernie Young	.15	.07
129	Doug Johns	.15	.07
130	Geronimo Berroa	.15	.07
131	Jason Giambi	.30	.14
132	John Wasdin	.15	.07
133	Jim Eisenreich	.15	.07
134	Ricky Otero	.15	.07
135	Ricky Bottalico	.15	.07
136	Mark Langston DG	.15	.07
137	Greg Maddux DG	1.00	.45
138	Ivan Rodriguez DG	.40	.18
139	Charles Johnson DG	.15	.07
140	J.T. Snow DG	.15	.07
141	Mark Grace DG	.30	.14
142	Roberto Alomar DG	.30	.14
143	Craig Biggio DG	.30	.14
144	Ken Caminiti DG	.30	.14
145	Matt Williams DG	.30	.14
146	Omar Vizquel DG	.15	.07
147	Cal Ripken DG	1.25	.55
148	Ozzie Smith DG	.40	.18
149	Rey Ordonez DG	.15	.07
150	Ken Griffey Jr. DG	1.50	.70
151	Devon White DG	.15	.07
152	Barry Bonds DG	.40	.18
153	Kenny Lofton DG	.40	.18
154	Mickey Morandini	.15	.07
155	Gregg Jefferies	.15	.07
156	Curt Schilling	.30	.14
157	Jason Kendall	.30	.14
158	Francisco Cordova	.15	.07
159	Dennis Eckersley	.30	.14
160	Ron Gant	.30	.14
161	Ozzie Smith	.75	.35
162	Brian Jordan	.30	.14
163	John Mabry	.15	.07
164	Andy Ashby	.15	.07
165	Steve Finley	.15	.07
166	Fernando Valenzuela	.30	.14
167	Archi Cianfrocco	.15	.07
168	Wally Joyner	.15	.07
169	Greg Vaughn	.15	.07
170	Barry Bonds	.75	.35
171	William VanLandingham	.15	.07
172	Marvin Benard	.15	.07
173	Rich Aurilia	.15	.07
174	Jay Canizaro	.15	.07
175	Ken Griffey Jr.	3.00	1.35
176	Bob Wells	.15	.07
177	Jay Buhner	.40	.18
178	Sterling Hitchcock	.15	.07
179	Edgar Martinez	.40	.18
180	Rusty Greer	.30	.14
181	Dave Nilsson GI	.15	.07
182	Larry Walker GI	.30	.14
183	Edgar Renteria GI	.15	.07
184	Rey Ordonez GI	.15	.07
185	Rafael Palmeiro GI	.30	.14
186	Osvaldo Fernandez GI	.15	.07
187	Raul Mondesi GI	.30	.14
188	Manny Ramirez GI	.30	.14
189	Sammy Sosa GI	.30	.14
190	Robert Eenhoorn GI	.15	.07
191	Devon White GI	.15	.07
192	Hideo Nomo GI	.75	.35
193	Mac Suzuki GI	.15	.07
194	Chan Ho Park GI	.30	.14
195	Fernando Valenzuela GI	.15	.07
196	Andruw Jones GI	.75	.35
197	Vinny Castilla GI	.15	.07
198	Dennis Martinez GI	.15	.07
199	Ruben Rivera GI	.15	.07
200	Juan Gonzalez GI	.75	.35
201	Roberto Alomar GI	.30	.14
202	Edgar Martinez GI	.30	.14
203	Ivan Rodriguez GI	.40	.18
204	Carlos Delgado GI	.15	.07
205	Andres Galarraga GI	.30	.14
206	Ozzie Guillen GI	.15	.07
207	Midre Cummings GI	.15	.07
208	Roger Pavlik	.15	.07
209	Darren Oliver	.15	.07
210	Dean Palmer	.15	.07
211	Ivan Rodriguez	.75	.35
212	Otis Nixon	.15	.07
213	Pat Hentgen	.30	.14
214	Ozzie Smith / Andre Dawson / Kirby Puckett HL/CL (1-27)	.30	.14
215	Barry Bonds / Gary Sheffield / Brady Anderson HL/CL (28-54)	.30	.14
216	Ken Caminiti HL/CL	.30	.14
217	John Smoltz HL/CL	.15	.07
218	Eric Young HL/CL	.15	.07
219	Juan Gonzalez HL/CL	.75	.35
220	Eddie Murray HL/CL	.30	.14
221	Tommy Lasorda HL/CL	.15	.07
222	Paul Molitor HL/CL	.30	.14
223	Luis Castillo	.40	.18
224	Justin Thompson	.30	.14

225	Rocky Coppinger	.15	.07
226	Jermaine Allensworth	.15	.07
227	Jeff D'Amico	.15	.07
228	Jamey Wright	.15	.07
229	Scott Rolen	1.50	.70
230	Darin Erstad	1.00	.45
231	Marty Janzen	.15	.07
232	Jacob Cruz	.30	.14
233	Raul Ibanez	.15	.07
234	Nomar Garciaparra	2.00	.90
235	Todd Walker	.30	.14
236	Brian Giles	.15	.07
237	Matt Beech	.15	.07
238	Mike Cameron	.40	.18
239	Jose Paniagua	.15	.07
240	Andruw Jones	1.50	.70
241	Brant Brown UPD	.50	.23
242	Robin Jennings UPD	.50	.23
243	Willie Adams UPD	.50	.23
244	Ken Caminiti UPD	1.25	.55
245	Brian Jordan UPD	1.00	.45
246	Chipper Jones UPD	6.00	2.70
247	Juan Gonzalez UPD	5.00	2.20
248	Bernie Williams UPD	2.00	.90
249	Roberto Alomar UPD	2.00	.90
250	Bernie Williams UPD	2.00	.90
251	David Wells UPD	.50	.23
252	Cecil Fielder UPD	1.00	.45
253	Darryl Strawberry UPD	1.00	.45
254	Andy Pettitte UPD	2.00	.90
255	Javier Lopez UPD	1.00	.45
256	Gary Gaetti UPD	.50	.23
257	Ron Gant UPD	1.00	.45
258	Brian Jordan UPD	1.00	.45
259	John Smoltz UPD	1.00	.45
260	Greg Maddux UPD	6.00	2.70
261	Tom Glavine UPD	1.00	.45
262	Andruw Jones UPD	5.00	2.20
263	Greg Maddux UPD	6.00	2.70
264	David Cone UPD	1.00	.45
265	Jim Leyritz UPD	.50	.23
266	Andy Pettitte UPD	2.00	.90
267	John Wetteland UPD	.50	.23
268	Dario Veras UPD	1.00	.45
269	Neifi Perez UPD	1.00	.45
270	Bill Mueller UPD	.50	.23
271	Vladimir Guerrero	1.25	.55
272	Dmitri Young	.15	.07
273	Nerio Rodriguez	.30	.14
274	Kevin Orie	.30	.14
275	Felipe Crespo	.15	.07
276	Danny Graves	.15	.07
277	Rod Myers	.30	.14
278	Felix Heredia	.40	.18
279	Ralph Milliard	.15	.07
280	Greg Norton	.15	.07
281	Derek Wallace	.15	.07
282	Trot Nixon	.15	.07
283	Bobby Chouinard	.15	.07
284	Jay Witasick	.15	.07
285	Travis Miller	.15	.07
286	Brian Bevil	.15	.07
287	Bobby Estalella	.30	.14
288	Steve Soderstrom	.15	.07
289	Mark Langston	.15	.07
290	Tim Salmon	.60	.25
291	Jim Edmonds	.40	.18
292	Garret Anderson	.30	.14
293	George Arias	.15	.07
294	Gary DiSarcina	.15	.07
295	Chuck Finley	.15	.07
296	Todd Greene	.30	.14
297	Randy Velarde	.15	.07
298	David Justice	.60	.25
299	Ryan Klesko	.40	.18
300	John Smoltz	.30	.14
301	Javier Lopez	.30	.14
302	Greg Maddux	2.00	.90
303	Denny Neagle	.30	.14
304	B.J. Surhoff	.15	.07
305	Chris Hoiles	.15	.07
306	Eric Davis	.30	.14
307	Scott Erickson	.15	.07
308	Mike Bordick	.15	.07
309	John Valentin	.15	.07
310	Heathcliff Slocumb	.15	.07
311	Tom Gordon	.15	.07
312	Mike Stanley	.15	.07
313	Reggie Jefferson	.15	.07
314	Darren Bragg	.15	.07
315	Troy O'Leary	.15	.07
316	John Mabry SH CL	.15	.07
317	Mark Whiten SH CL	.15	.07
318	Edgar Martinez SH CL	.30	.14
319	Alex Rodriguez SH CL	1.00	.45
320	Mark McGwire SH CL	.60	.25
321	Hideo Nomo SH CL	.75	.35
322	Todd Hundley SH CL	.15	.07
323	Barry Bonds SH CL	.40	.18
324	Andruw Jones SH CL	.75	.35
325	Ryne Sandberg	.75	.35
326	Brian McRae	.15	.07
327	Frank Castillo	.15	.07
328	Shawon Dunston	.15	.07
329	Ray Durham	.15	.07
330	Robin Ventura	.30	.14
331	Ozzie Guillen	.15	.07
332	Roberto Hernandez	.15	.07
333	Albert Belle	.75	.35
334	Dave Martinez	.15	.07
335	Willie Greene	.15	.07
336	Jeff Brantley	.15	.07
337	Kevin Jarvis	.15	.07
338	John Smiley	.15	.07
339	Eddie Taubensee	.15	.07
340	Bret Boone	.15	.07
341	Kevin Seitzer	.15	.07
342	Jack McDowell	.15	.07
343	Sandy Alomar Jr.	.30	.14
344	Chad Curtis	.15	.07
345	Manny Ramirez	.60	.25
346	Chad Ogea	.15	.07
347	Jim Thome	.60	.25
348	Mark Thompson	.15	.07
349	Ellis Burks	.30	.14
350	Andres Galarraga	.60	.25
351	Vinny Castilla	.30	.14
352	Kirt Manwaring	.15	.07
353	Larry Walker	.50	.23
354	Omar Olivares	.15	.07
355	Bobby Higginson	.30	.14
356	Melvin Nieves	.15	.07
357	Brian Johnson	.15	.07
358	Devon White	.15	.07
359	Jeff Conine	.15	.07
360	Gary Sheffield	.60	.25
361	Robb Nen	.15	.07
362	Mike Hampton	.15	.07
363	Bob Abreu	.30	.14
364	Luis Castillo	.15	.07
365	Derek Bell	.15	.07
366	Sean Berry	.15	.07
367	Craig Biggio	.40	.18
368	Darryl Kile	.15	.07
369	Shane Reynolds	.15	.07
370	Jeff Bagwell CF	.60	.25
371	Ron Gant CF	.15	.07
372	Andy Benes CF	.15	.07
373	Gary Gaetti CF	.15	.07
374	Ramon Martinez CF	.15	.07
375	Raul Mondesi CF	.30	.14
376	Steve Finley CF	.15	.07
377	Ken Caminiti CF	.30	.14
378	Tony Gwynn CF	.75	.35
379	Dario Veras	.40	.18
380	Andy Pettitte CF	.30	.14
381	Ruben Rivera CF	.15	.07
382	David Cone CF	.15	.07
383	Roberto Alomar CF	.30	.14
384	Edgar Martinez CF	.15	.07
385	Ken Griffey Jr. CF	1.50	.70
386	Mark McGwire CF	.60	.25
387	Rusty Greer CF	.15	.07
388	Jose Rosado	.30	.14
389	Kevin Appier	.30	.14
390	Johnny Damon	.15	.07
391	Jose Offerman	.15	.07
392	Michael Tucker	.30	.14
393	Craig Paquette	.15	.07
394	Bip Roberts	.15	.07
395	Ramon Martinez	.15	.07
396	Greg Gagne	.15	.07
397	Chan Ho Park	.60	.25
398	Karim Garcia	.30	.14
399	Wilton Guerrero	.15	.07
400	Eric Karros	.30	.14
401	Raul Mondesi	.40	.18
402	Matt Mieske	.15	.07
403	Mike Fetters	.15	.07
404	Dave Nilsson	.15	.07
405	Jose Valentin	.15	.07
406	Scott Karl	.15	.07
407	Marc Newfield	.15	.07
408	Cal Eldred	.15	.07
409	Rich Becker	.15	.07
410	Terry Steinbach	.15	.07
411	Chuck Knoblauch	.60	.25
412	Pat Meares	.15	.07
413	Brad Radke	.30	.14
414	Kirby Puckett UER	1.25	.55
	Card numbered 415		
415	Andruw Jones GHL SP	6.00	2.70
416	Chipper Jones GHL SP	8.00	3.60
417	Mo Vaughn GHL SP	3.00	1.35
418	Frank Thomas GHL SP	12.00	5.50
419	Albert Belle GHL SP	3.00	1.35
420	Mark McGwire GHL SP	5.00	2.20
421	Derek Jeter GHL SP	8.00	3.60
422	Alex Rodriguez GHL SP	10.00	4.50
423	Juan Gonzalez GHL SP	6.00	2.70
424	Ken Griffey Jr. GHL SP	15.00	6.75
425	Rondell White	.30	.14
426	Darrin Fletcher	.15	.07
427	Cliff Floyd	.15	.07
428	Mike Lansing	.15	.07
429	F.P. Santangelo	.15	.07
430	Todd Hundley	.30	.14
431	Mark Clark	.15	.07
432	Pete Harnisch	.15	.07
433	Jason Isringhausen	.15	.07
434	Bobby Jones	.15	.07
435	Lance Johnson	.15	.07
436	Carlos Baerga	.15	.07
437	Mariano Duncan	.15	.07
438	David Cone	.30	.14
439	Mariano Rivera	.30	.14
440	Derek Jeter	2.00	.90
441	Joe Girardi	.15	.07
442	Charlie Hayes	.15	.07
443	Tim Raines	.15	.07
444	Darryl Strawberry	.30	.14
445	Cecil Fielder	.30	.14
446	Ariel Prieto	.15	.07
447	Tony Batista	.15	.07
448	Brent Gates	.15	.07
449	Scott Spiezio	.30	.14
450	Mark McGwire	1.25	.55
451	Don Wengert	.15	.07
452	Mike Lieberthal	.15	.07
453	Lenny Dykstra	.30	.14
454	Darren Daulton	.30	.14
455	Kevin Stocker	.15	.07
456	Trey Beamon	.15	.07
457	Midre Cummings	.15	.07
458	Mark Johnson	.15	.07
459	Al Martin	.15	.07
460	Kevin Elster	.15	.07
461	Jon Lieber	.15	.07
462	Jason Schmidt	.15	.07
463	Paul Wagner	.15	.07
464	Andy Benes	.30	.14
465	Alan Benes	.30	.14
466	Royce Clayton	.15	.07
467	Gary Gaetti	.15	.07
468	Curt Lyons	.15	.07
469	Eugene Kingsale DD	.15	.07
470	Damian Jackson DD	.15	.07
471	Wendel Magee DD	.15	.07
472	Kevin L. Brown DD	.15	.07
473	Raul Casanova DD	.15	.07
474	Ramiro Mendoza DD	.40	.18
475	Todd Dunn DD	.15	.07
476	Chad Mottola DD	.15	.07
477	Andy Larkin DD	.15	.07
478	Jaime Bluma DD	.15	.07
479	Mac Suzuki DD	.15	.07
480	Brian Banks DD	.15	.07
481	Desi Wilson DD	.15	.07

☐ 483 Einar Diaz DD	.15	.07
☐ 484 Tom Pagnozzi	.15	.07
☐ 485 Ray Lankford	.30	.14
☐ 486 Todd Stottlemyre	.15	.07
☐ 487 Donovan Osborne	.15	.07
☐ 488 Trevor Hoffman	.15	.07
☐ 489 Chris Gomez	.15	.07
☐ 490 Ken Caminiti	.40	.18
☐ 491 John Flaherty	.15	.07
☐ 492 Tony Gwynn	1.50	.70
☐ 493 Joey Hamilton	.30	.14
☐ 494 Rickey Henderson	.40	.18
☐ 495 Glenallen Hill	.15	.07
☐ 496 Rod Beck	.15	.07
☐ 497 Osvaldo Fernandez	.15	.07
☐ 498 Rick Wilkins	.15	.07
☐ 499 Joey Cora	.30	.14
☐ 500 Alex Rodriguez	2.00	.90
☐ 501 Randy Johnson	.60	.25
☐ 502 Paul Sorrento	.15	.07
☐ 503 Dan Wilson	.15	.07
☐ 504 Jamie Moyer	.15	.07
☐ 505 Will Clark	.40	.18
☐ 506 Mickey Tettleton	.15	.07
☐ 507 John Burkett	.15	.07
☐ 508 Ken Hill	.15	.07
☐ 509 Mark McLemore	.15	.07
☐ 510 Juan Gonzalez	1.50	.70
☐ 511 Bobby Witt	.15	.07
☐ 512 Carlos Delgado	.30	.14
☐ 513 Alex Gonzalez	.15	.07
☐ 514 Shawn Green	.15	.07
☐ 515 Joe Carter	.30	.14
☐ 516 Juan Guzman	.15	.07
☐ 517 Charlie O'Brien	.15	.07
☐ 518 Ed Sprague	.15	.07
☐ 519 Mike Timlin	.15	.07
☐ 520 Roger Clemens	1.25	.55
☐ 521 Eddie Murray TRADE	1.00	.45
☐ 522 Jason Dickson TRADE	.50	.23
☐ 523 Jim Leyritz TRADE	.25	.11
☐ 524 Michael Tucker TRADE	.50	.23
☐ 525 Kenny Lofton TRADE	1.25	.55
☐ 526 Jimmy Key TRADE	.25	.11
☐ 527 Mel Rojas TRADE	.25	.11
☐ 528 Deion Sanders TRADE	.50	.23
☐ 529 Bartolo Colon TRADE	.50	.23
☐ 530 Matt Williams TRADE	.75	.35
☐ 531 Marquis Grissom TRADE	.50	.23
☐ 532 David Justice TRADE	1.00	.45
☐ 533 Bubba Trammell TRADE	1.00	.45
☐ 534 Moises Alou TRADE	.50	.23
☐ 535 Bobby Bonilla TRADE	.50	.23
☐ 536 Alex Fernandez TRADE	.50	.23
☐ 537 Jay Bell TRADE	.50	.23
☐ 538 Chili Davis TRADE	.50	.23
☐ 539 Jeff King TRADE	.25	.11
☐ 540 Todd Zeile TRADE	.25	.11
☐ 541 John Olerud TRADE	.50	.23
☐ 542 Jose Guillen TRADE	1.25	.55
☐ 543 Derrek Lee TRADE	.75	.35
☐ 544 Dante Powell TRADE	.25	.11
☐ 545 J.T. Snow TRADE	.50	.23
☐ 546 Jeff Kent TRADE	.25	.11
☐ 547 Jose Cruz Jr. TRADE	10.00	4.50
☐ 548 John Wetteland TRADE	.25	.11
☐ 549 Orlando Merced TRADE	.25	.11
☐ 550 Hideki Irabu TRADE	1.00	.45

1997 Upper Deck Amazing Greats

Randomly inserted in all first series packs at a rate of one in 138, this 20-card set features a horizontal design along with two player photos on the front. The cards feature translucent player images against a real wood grain stock.

	MINT	NRMT
COMPLETE SET (20)	600.00	275.00
COMMON CARD (AG1-AG20)	10.00	4.50

UNLISTED STARS	15.00	6.75
SER.1 STATED ODDS 1:69		

☐ AG1 Ken Griffey Jr.	80.00	36.00
☐ AG2 Roberto Alomar	15.00	6.75
☐ AG3 Alex Rodriguez	50.00	22.00
☐ AG4 Paul Molitor	15.00	6.75
☐ AG5 Chipper Jones	50.00	22.00
☐ AG6 Tony Gwynn	40.00	18.00
☐ AG7 Kenny Lofton	20.00	9.00
☐ AG8 Albert Belle	20.00	9.00
☐ AG9 Matt Williams	10.00	4.50
☐ AG10 Frank Thomas	60.00	27.00
☐ AG11 Greg Maddux	50.00	22.00
☐ AG12 Sammy Sosa	15.00	6.75
☐ AG13 Kirby Puckett	30.00	13.50
☐ AG14 Jeff Bagwell	30.00	13.50
☐ AG15 Cal Ripken	60.00	27.00
☐ AG16 Manny Ramirez	15.00	6.75
☐ AG17 Barry Bonds	20.00	9.00
☐ AG18 Mo Vaughn	20.00	9.00
☐ AG19 Eddie Murray	15.00	6.75
☐ AG20 Mike Piazza	50.00	22.00

1997 Upper Deck Blue Chip Prospects

This rare 20-card set, randomly inserted into Series II packs, features color photos of high expectation prospects who are likely to have a big impact on Major League Baseball. Only 500 of this crash numbered, limited edition set was produced.

	MINT	NRMT
COMPLETE SET (20)	500.00	220.00
COMMON CARD (BC1-BC20)	8.00	3.60
SEMISTARS	15.00	6.75
UNLISTED STARS	25.00	11.00
RANDOM INSERTS IN SER.2 PACKS		
STATED PRINT RUN 500 SETS		

☐ BC1 Andruw Jones	60.00	27.00
☐ BC2 Derek Jeter	80.00	36.00
☐ BC3 Scott Rolen	60.00	27.00
☐ BC4 Manny Ramirez	25.00	11.00
☐ BC5 Todd Walker	12.00	5.50
☐ BC6 Rocky Coppinger	8.00	3.60
☐ BC7 Nomar Garciaparra	80.00	36.00
☐ BC8 Darin Erstad	40.00	18.00
☐ BC9 Jermaine Dye	8.00	3.60
☐ BC10 Vladimir Guerrero	50.00	22.00
☐ BC11 Edgar Renteria	12.00	5.50
☐ BC12 Bob Abreu	12.00	5.50
☐ BC13 Karim Garcia	12.00	5.50
☐ BC14 Jeff D'Amico	8.00	3.60
☐ BC15 Chipper Jones	80.00	36.00
☐ BC16 Todd Hollandsworth	8.00	3.60
☐ BC17 Andy Pettitte	25.00	11.00
☐ BC18 Ruben Rivera	12.00	5.50
☐ BC19 Jason Kendall	12.00	5.50
☐ BC20 Alex Rodriguez	80.00	36.00

1997 Upper Deck Game Jersey

Randomly inserted in all first series packs at a rate of one in 800, this 3-card set feauress swatches of real game-worn jerseys cut up and placed on the cards.

	MINT	NRMT
COMPLETE SET (3)	900.00	400.00
COMMON CARD (GJ1-GJ3)	80.00	36.00
SER.1 STATED ODDS 1:800		

☐ GJ1 Ken Griffey Jr.	650.00	300.00
☐ GJ2 Tony Gwynn	300.00	135.00
☐ GJ3 Rey Ordonez	80.00	36.00

1997 Upper Deck Hot Commodities

Randomly inserted in series two packs at a rate of one in 13, this 20-card set features color player images on a flame background in a black border. The backs carry a player head photo, statistics, and a com-

mentary by ESPN sportscaster Dan Patrick.

	MINT	NRMT
COMPLETE SET (20)	120.00	55.00
COMMON CARD (HC1-HC20)	1.25	.55
SER.2 STATED ODDS 1:13		

		MINT	NRMT
☐ HC1	Alex Rodriguez	8.00	3.60
☐ HC2	Andruw Jones	6.00	2.70
☐ HC3	Derek Jeter	8.00	3.60
☐ HC4	Frank Thomas	10.00	4.50
☐ HC5	Ken Griffey Jr.	12.00	5.50
☐ HC6	Chipper Jones	8.00	3.60
☐ HC7	Juan Gonzalez	6.00	2.70
☐ HC8	Cal Ripken	10.00	4.50
☐ HC9	John Smoltz	1.25	.55
☐ HC10	Mark McGwire	5.00	2.20
☐ HC11	Barry Bonds	3.00	1.35
☐ HC12	Albert Belle	3.00	1.35
☐ HC13	Mike Piazza	8.00	3.60
☐ HC14	Manny Ramirez	2.50	1.10
☐ HC15	Mo Vaughn	3.00	1.35
☐ HC16	Tony Gwynn	6.00	2.70
☐ HC17	Vladimir Guerrero	5.00	2.20
☐ HC18	Hideo Nomo	6.00	2.70
☐ HC19	Greg Maddux	10.00	4.50
☐ HC20	Kirby Puckett	5.00	2.20

1997 Upper Deck Long Distance Connection

Randomly inserted in series two packs at a rate of one in 35, this 20-card set features color player images of some of the League's top power hitters on backgrounds utilizing Light/FX technology. The backs carry the pictured player's statistics.

	MINT	NRMT
COMPLETE SET (20)	200.00	90.00
COMMON CARD (LD1-LD20)	4.00	1.80
SER.2 STATED ODDS 1:35		

		MINT	NRMT
☐ LD1	Mark McGwire	15.00	6.75
☐ LD2	Brady Anderson	5.00	2.20
☐ LD3	Ken Griffey Jr.	40.00	18.00
☐ LD4	Albert Belle	10.00	4.50
☐ LD5	Juan Gonzalez	20.00	9.00
☐ LD6	Andres Galarraga	8.00	3.60
☐ LD7	Jay Buhner	5.00	2.20
☐ LD8	Mo Vaughn	10.00	4.50
☐ LD9	Barry Bonds	10.00	4.50
☐ LD10	Gary Sheffield	8.00	3.60
☐ LD11	Todd Hundley	4.00	1.80
☐ LD12	Frank Thomas	30.00	13.50
☐ LD13	Sammy Sosa	8.00	3.60
☐ LD14	Rafael Palmeiro	5.00	2.20
☐ LD15	Alex Rodriguez	25.00	11.00
☐ LD16	Mike Piazza	25.00	11.00
☐ LD17	Ken Caminiti	5.00	2.20
☐ LD18	Chipper Jones	25.00	11.00

		MINT	NRMT
☐ LD19	Manny Ramirez	8.00	3.60
☐ LD20	Andruw Jones	15.00	6.75

1997 Upper Deck Memorable Moments

Cards from these sets were distributed exclusively in 6-card retail Collector's Choice series one and two packs. Each pack contained one of ten different Memorable Moments inserts. Each set features a selection of top stars captured in highlights of season's gone by. Each card features wave-like die cut top and bottom borders wth gold foil.

	MINT	NRMT
COMPLETE SERIES 1 (10)	15.00	6.60
COMPLETE SERIES 2 (10)	15.00	6.60
COMMON CARD (A1-B10)	.60	.25
ONE PER CC1 AND CC2 6-CARD RETAIL PACK		

		MINT	NRMT
☐ A1	Andruw Jones	1.50	.70
☐ A2	Chipper Jones	2.00	.90
☐ A3	Cal Ripken	2.50	1.10
☐ A4	Frank Thomas	2.50	1.10
☐ A5	Manny Ramirez	.60	.25
☐ A6	Mike Piazza	2.00	.90
☐ A7	Mark McGwire	1.25	.55
☐ A8	Barry Bonds	.75	.35
☐ A9	Ken Griffey Jr.	3.00	1.35
☐ A10	Alex Rodriguez	2.00	.90
☐ B1	Ken Griffey Jr.	3.00	1.35
☐ B2	Albert Belle	.75	.35
☐ B3	Derek Jeter	2.00	.90
☐ B4	Greg Maddux	2.00	.90
☐ B5	Tony Gwynn	1.50	.70
☐ B6	Ryne Sandberg	.75	.35
☐ B7	Juan Gonzalez	1.50	.70
☐ B8	Roger Clemens	1.25	.55
☐ B9	Jose Cruz Jr.	5.00	2.20
☐ B10	Mo Vaughn	.75	.35

1997 Upper Deck Power Package

Randomly inserted in all first series packs at a rate of one in 24, this 20-card set feaures some of the best longball hitters. The die cut cards feature some of baseball's leading power hitters. Non-die cut jumbo (5 x 7) versions were distributed one per 1997 Series 1 Upper Deck retail Sam's box on the bottom of the box under the packs.

	MINT	NRMT
COMPLETE SET (20)	120.00	55.00
COMMON CARD (PP1-PP20)	3.00	1.35
UNLISTED STARS	6.00	2.70
SER.1 STATED ODDS 1:24		

		MINT	NRMT
☐ PP1	Ken Griffey Jr.	30.00	13.50
☐ PP2	Joe Carter	3.00	1.35
☐ PP3	Rafael Palmeiro	4.00	1.80
☐ PP4	Jay Buhner	4.00	1.80
☐ PP5	Sammy Sosa	6.00	2.70
☐ PP6	Fred McGriff	4.00	1.80
☐ PP7	Jeff Bagwell	12.00	5.50
☐ PP8	Albert Belle	8.00	3.60
☐ PP9	Matt Williams	4.00	1.80
☐ PP10	Mark McGwire	12.00	5.50
☐ PP11	Gary Sheffield	6.00	2.70
☐ PP12	Tim Salmon	6.00	2.70
☐ PP13	Ryan Klesko	4.00	1.80
☐ PP14	Manny Ramirez	6.00	2.70
☐ PP15	Mike Piazza	20.00	9.00
☐ PP16	Barry Bonds	8.00	3.60
☐ PP17	Mo Vaughn	8.00	3.60
☐ PP18	Jose Canseco	4.00	1.80
☐ PP19	Juan Gonzalez	15.00	6.75
☐ PP20	Frank Thomas	25.00	11.00

1997 Upper Deck Predictor

Randomly inserted in series two packs at a rate of one in five, this 30-card set feaures a color player photo alongside a series of bats. The collector could activate the card by scratching off one of the bats to predict the performance of the pictured player during a single game. If the player matches or exceeds the predicted performance, the card could be mailed in with $2 to receive a Totally Virtual hightech cel-card of the player pictured on the front. The backs carry the rules of the game. The deadline to redeem these cards was November 22nd, 1997.

	MINT	NRMT
COMPLETE SET (30)	30.00	13.50
COMMON CARD (1-30)	.40	.18

*SCRATCHED SINGLES: .25X TO .5X BASE HI
*EXCHANGED WINNERS: 1.25X TO 2.5X BASE HI
SER.2 STATED ODDS 1:5

		MINT	NRMT
☐ 1	Andruw Jones L	2.00	.90
☐ 2	Chipper Jones L	2.50	1.10
☐ 3	Greg Maddux W	2.50	1.10
	Complete Game Shutout		
☐ 4	Fred McGriff W	.50	.23
	4 Hits/2HR/3B		
☐ 5	John Smoltz W	.40	.18
	Complete Game Shutout		
☐ 6	Brady Anderson W	.50	.23
	Leadoff HR		
☐ 7	Cal Ripken W	3.00	1.35
	Grand Slam		
☐ 8	Mo Vaughn W	1.00	.45
	3HR/6RBI		
☐ 9	Sammy Sosa L	.75	.35
☐ 10	Albert Belle W	1.00	.45
	Grand Slam/9th HR		
☐ 11	Frank Thomas L	3.00	1.35
☐ 12	Kenny Lofton W	1.00	.45
	5 Hits		
☐ 13	Jim Thome L	.75	.35
☐ 14	Dante Bichette W	.40	.18
	6RBI's		
☐ 15	Andres Galarraga L	.75	.35
☐ 16	Gary Sheffield L	.75	.35
☐ 17	Hideo Nomo W	2.00	.90
	Base Hit		
☐ 18	Mike Piazza W	2.50	1.10
	Steal/9th HR		
☐ 19	Derek Jeter W	2.50	1.10
	2HR		
☐ 20	Bernie Williams L	.75	.35
☐ 21	Mark McGwire W	1.50	.70
	Grand Slam/4HR		
☐ 22	Ken Caminiti W	.50	.23
	5RBI's		
☐ 23	Tony Gwynn W	2.00	.90
	2 2B/3RBI		
☐ 24	Barry Bonds W	1.00	.45
	5RBI's		
☐ 25	Jay Buhner W	.50	.23
	5RBI's		
☐ 26	Ken Griffey Jr. W	4.00	1.80
	3HR's		
☐ 27	Alex Rodriguez W	2.50	1.10
	Cycle		
☐ 28	Juan Gonzalez W	2.00	.90
	5RBI's/4 Hits		
☐ 29	Dean Palmer W	.40	.18
	2HR's/5RBI's		
☐ 30	Roger Clemens W	1.50	.70
	Complete Game Shutout		

1997 Upper Deck Rock Solid Foundation

Randomly inserted in all first series packs at a rate of one in seven, this 20-card set features players 25 and under who have made an impact in the majors. The fronts feature a player photo against a "silver" type background. The backs give player information as well as another player photo and are numbered with a "RS" prefix.

	MINT	NRMT
COMPLETE SET (20)	50.00	22.00
COMMON CARD(RS1-RS20)	1.00	.45

SER.1 STATED ODDS 1:7

☐ RS1	Alex Rodriguez	10.00	4.50
☐ RS2	Rey Ordonez	1.00	.45

☐ RS3	Derek Jeter	10.00	4.50
☐ RS4	Darin Erstad	5.00	2.20
☐ RS5	Chipper Jones	10.00	4.50
☐ RS6	Johnny Damon	1.00	.45
☐ RS7	Ryan Klesko	2.00	.90
☐ RS8	Charles Johnson	1.50	.70
☐ RS9	Andy Pettitte	3.00	1.35
☐ RS10	Manny Ramirez	3.00	1.35
☐ RS11	Ivan Rodriguez	4.00	1.80
☐ RS12	Jason Kendall	1.50	.70
☐ RS13	Rondell White	1.50	.70
☐ RS14	Alex Ochoa	1.00	.45
☐ RS15	Javier Lopez	1.50	.70
☐ RS16	Pedro Martinez	3.00	1.35
☐ RS17	Carlos Delgado	1.50	.70
☐ RS18	Paul Wilson	1.00	.45
☐ RS19	Alan Benes	1.50	.70
☐ RS20	Raul Mondesi	2.00	.90

1997 Upper Deck Run Producers

Randomly inserted in series two packs at a rate of one in 69, this 24-card set features color player images on die-cut cards that actually look and feel like home plate. The backs carry player information and career statistics.

	MINT	NRMT
COMPLETE SET (24)	350.00	160.00
COMMON CARD (RP1-RP24)	6.00	2.70
UNLISTED STARS	12.00	5.50

SER.2 STATED ODDS 1:69
CONDITION SENSITIVE SET

☐ RP1	Ken Griffey Jr	60.00	27.00
☐ RP2	Barry Bonds	15.00	6.75
☐ RP3	Albert Belle	15.00	6.75
☐ RP4	Mark McGwire	25.00	11.00
☐ RP5	Frank Thomas	50.00	22.00
☐ RP6	Juan Gonzalez	30.00	13.50
☐ RP7	Brady Anderson	8.00	3.60
☐ RP8	Andres Galarraga	8.00	3.60
☐ RP9	Rafael Palmeiro	8.00	3.60
☐ RP10	Alex Rodriguez	40.00	18.00
☐ RP11	Jay Buhner	8.00	3.60
☐ RP12	Gary Sheffield	12.00	5.50
☐ RP13	Sammy Sosa	12.00	5.50
☐ RP14	Dante Bichette	6.00	2.70
☐ RP15	Mike Piazza	40.00	18.00
☐ RP16	Manny Ramirez	12.00	5.50
☐ RP17	Kenny Lofton	15.00	6.75
☐ RP18	Mo Vaughn	15.00	6.75
☐ RP19	Tim Salmon	12.00	5.50
☐ RP20	Chipper Jones	40.00	18.00
☐ RP21	Jim Thome	12.00	5.50
☐ RP22	Ken Caminiti	8.00	3.60
☐ RP23	Jeff Bagwell	25.00	11.00
☐ RP24	Paul Molitor	12.00	5.50

1997 Upper Deck Ticket To Stardom

Randomly inserted in all first series packs at a rate of one in 34, this 20-card set is designed in the form of a ticket and are designed to be matched. The horizontal fronts feature two player photos as well as using "light f/x technology and embossed player images.

	MINT	NRMT
COMPLETE SET (20)	120.00	55.00
COMMON CARD (TS1-TS20)	2.00	.90
SEMISTARS	5.00	2.20
UNLISTED STARS	8.00	3.60

SER.1 STATED ODDS 1:34

☐ TS1	Chipper Jones	25.00	11.00
☐ TS2	Jermaine Dye	2.00	.90
☐ TS3	Rey Ordonez	2.00	.90
☐ TS4	Alex Ochoa	2.00	.90
☐ TS5	Derek Jeter	20.00	9.00
☐ TS6	Ruben Rivera	4.00	1.80
☐ TS7	Billy Wagner	4.00	1.80
☐ TS8	Jason Kendall	4.00	1.80
☐ TS9	Darin Erstad	12.00	5.50
☐ TS10	Alex Rodriguez	25.00	11.00
☐ TS11	Bob Abreu	4.00	1.80
☐ TS12	Richard Hidalgo	4.00	1.80
☐ TS13	Karim Garcia	4.00	1.80
☐ TS14	Andruw Jones	20.00	9.00
☐ TS15	Carlos Delgado	4.00	1.80
☐ TS16	Rocky Coppinger	2.00	.90
☐ TS17	Jeff D'Amico	2.00	.90
☐ TS18	Johnny Damon	2.00	.90
☐ TS19	Jim Wasdin	2.00	.90
☐ TS20	Manny Ramirez	8.00	3.60

1998 Upper Deck

The 1998 Upper Deck Series 1 set consisted of 270 cards and was distributed in 12-card packs with a suggested retail price of $2.49. The fronts feature game dated photographs of some of the Season's most unforgettable moments with the pictured player. The set contains the follow

ing subsets: History in the Making (1-8), Griffey's Hot List (9-18), Define the Game (136-153), Season Highlights (244-252), and Star Rookie (253-270).

	MINT	NRMT
COMPLETE SERIES 1 (270)	30.00	13.50
COMMON CARD (1-270)	.15	.07
MINOR STARS	.30	.14
UNLISTED STARS	.60	.25
COMP.GRIFFEY SER.1 (30)	120.00	55.00
COMMON GRIFFEY (1-30)	5.00	2.20
GRIFFEY HR SER.1 STATED ODDS 1:9		

☐ 1 Tino Martinez HIST	.30	.14
☐ 2 Jimmy Key HIST	.15	.07
☐ 3 Jay Buhner HIST	.30	.14
☐ 4 Mark Gardner HIST	.15	.07
☐ 5 Greg Maddux HIST	1.00	.45
☐ 6 Pedro Martinez HIST	.30	.14
☐ 7 Hideo Nomo HIST	.75	.35
☐ 8 Sammy Sosa HIST	.30	.14
☐ 9 Mark McGwire GHL	1.50	.70
☐ 10 Ken Griffey Jr. GHL	3.00	1.35
☐ 11 Larry Walker GHL	.60	.25
☐ 12 Tino Martinez GHL	.60	.25
☐ 13 Mike Piazza GHL	1.50	.70
☐ 14 Jose Cruz Jr. GHL	2.50	1.10
☐ 15 Tony Gwynn GHL	1.50	.70
☐ 16 Greg Maddux GHL	2.00	.90
☐ 17 Roger Clemens GHL	1.25	.55
☐ 18 Alex Rodriguez GHL	2.00	.90
☐ 19 Shigetoshi Hasegawa	.30	.14
☐ 20 Eddie Murray	.60	.25
☐ 21 Jason Dickson	.30	.14
☐ 22 Darin Erstad	.75	.35
☐ 23 Chuck Finley	.15	.07
☐ 24 Dave Hollins	.15	.07
☐ 25 Garret Anderson	.30	.14
☐ 26 Michael Tucker	.30	.14
☐ 27 Kenny Lofton	.75	.35
☐ 28 Javier Lopez	.30	.14
☐ 29 Fred McGriff	.40	.18
☐ 30 Greg Maddux	2.00	.90
☐ 31 Jeff Blauser	.30	.14
☐ 32 John Smoltz	.30	.14
☐ 33 Mark Wohlers	.15	.07
☐ 34 Scott Erickson	.15	.07
☐ 35 Jimmy Key	.15	.07
☐ 36 Harold Baines	.30	.14
☐ 37 Randy Myers	.15	.07
☐ 38 B.J. Surhoff	.15	.07
☐ 39 Eric Davis	.30	.14
☐ 40 Rafael Palmeiro	.40	.18
☐ 41 Jeffrey Hammonds	.15	.07
☐ 42 Mo Vaughn	.75	.35
☐ 43 Tom Gordon	.15	.07
☐ 44 Tim Naehring	.15	.07
☐ 45 Darren Bragg	.15	.07
☐ 46 Aaron Sele	.15	.07
☐ 47 Troy O'Leary	.15	.07
☐ 48 John Valentin	.15	.07
☐ 49 Doug Glanville	.15	.07
☐ 50 Ryne Sandberg	.75	.35
☐ 51 Steve Trachsel	.15	.07
☐ 52 Mark Grace	.40	.18
☐ 53 Kevin Foster	.15	.07
☐ 54 Kevin Tapani	.15	.07
☐ 55 Kevin Orie	.30	.14
☐ 56 Lyle Mouton	.15	.07
☐ 57 Ray Durham	.15	.07
☐ 58 Jaime Navarro	.15	.07
☐ 59 Mike Cameron	.30	.14
☐ 60 Albert Belle	.75	.35
☐ 61 Doug Drabek	.15	.07
☐ 62 Chris Snopek	.15	.07
☐ 63 Ed Taubensee	.15	.07
☐ 64 Terry Pendleton	.15	.07
☐ 65 Barry Larkin	.40	.18
☐ 66 Willie Greene	.15	.07
☐ 67 Deion Sanders	.30	.14
☐ 68 Pokey Reese	.15	.07
☐ 69 Jeff Shaw	.15	.07
☐ 70 Jim Thome	.60	.25
☐ 71 Orel Hershiser	.30	.14
☐ 72 Omar Vizquel	.30	.14
☐ 73 Brian Giles	.15	.07
☐ 74 David Justice	.60	.25
☐ 75 Bartolo Colon	.30	.14
☐ 76 Sandy Alomar Jr.	.30	.14
☐ 77 Neifi Perez	.30	.14
☐ 78 Dante Bichette	.30	.14
☐ 79 Vinny Castilla	.30	.14
☐ 80 Eric Young	.15	.07
☐ 81 Quinton McCracken	.15	.07
☐ 82 Jarney Wright	.15	.07
☐ 83 John Thomson	.15	.07
☐ 84 Damion Easley	.15	.07
☐ 85 Justin Thompson	.30	.14
☐ 86 Willie Blair	.15	.07
☐ 87 Raul Casanova	.15	.07
☐ 88 Bobby Higginson	.30	.14
☐ 89 Bubba Trammell	.30	.14
☐ 90 Tony Clark	.60	.25
☐ 91 Livan Hernandez	.40	.18
☐ 92 Charles Johnson	.30	.14
☐ 93 Edgar Renteria	.30	.14
☐ 94 Alex Fernandez	.15	.07
☐ 95 Gary Sheffield	.60	.25
☐ 96 Moises Alou	.30	.14
☐ 97 Tony Saunders	.30	.14
☐ 98 Robb Nen	.15	.07
☐ 99 Darryl Kile	.30	.14
☐ 100 Craig Biggio	.40	.18
☐ 101 Chris Holt	.15	.07
☐ 102 Bob Abreu	.30	.14
☐ 103 Luis Gonzalez	.15	.07
☐ 104 Billy Wagner	.30	.14
☐ 105 Brad Ausmus	.15	.07
☐ 106 Chili Davis	.30	.14
☐ 107 Tim Belcher	.15	.07
☐ 108 Dean Palmer	.15	.07
☐ 109 Jeff King	.15	.07
☐ 110 Jose Rosado	.15	.07
☐ 111 Mike Macfarlane	.15	.07
☐ 112 Jay Bell	.30	.14
☐ 113 Todd Worrell	.15	.07
☐ 114 Chan Ho Park	.60	.25
☐ 115 Raul Mondesi	.40	.18
☐ 116 Brett Butler	.30	.14
☐ 117 Greg Gagne	.15	.07
☐ 118 Hideo Nomo	1.50	.70
☐ 119 Todd Zeile	.15	.07
☐ 120 Eric Karros	.30	.14
☐ 121 Cal Eldred	.15	.07
☐ 122 Jeff D'Amico	.15	.07
☐ 123 Antone Williamson	.15	.07
☐ 124 Doug Jones	.15	.07
☐ 125 Dave Nilsson	.15	.07
☐ 126 Gerald Williams	.15	.07
☐ 127 Fernando Vina	.15	.07
☐ 128 Ron Coomer	.15	.07
☐ 129 Matt Lawton	.15	.07
☐ 130 Paul Molitor	.60	.25
☐ 131 Todd Walker	.30	.14
☐ 132 Rick Aguilera	.15	.07
☐ 133 Brad Radke	.30	.14
☐ 134 Bob Tewksbury	.15	.07
☐ 135 Vladimir Guerrero	1.00	.45
☐ 136 Tony Gwynn DG	.75	.35
☐ 137 Roger Clemens DG	.60	.25
☐ 138 Dennis Eckersley DG	.15	.07
☐ 139 Brady Anderson DG	.30	.14
☐ 140 Ken Griffey Jr. DG	1.50	.70
☐ 141 Derek Jeter DG	.75	.35
☐ 142 Ken Caminiti DG	.30	.14
☐ 143 Frank Thomas DG	1.25	.55
☐ 144 Barry Bonds DG	.40	.18
☐ 145 Cal Ripken DG	1.25	.55
☐ 146 Alex Rodriguez DG	1.00	.45
☐ 147 Greg Maddux DG	1.00	.45
☐ 148 Kenny Lofton DG	.40	.18
☐ 149 Mike Piazza DG	1.00	.45
☐ 150 Mark McGwire DG	.75	.35
☐ 151 Andruw Jones DG	.60	.25
☐ 152 Rusty Greer DG	.15	.07
☐ 153 F.P. Santangelo DG	.15	.07
☐ 154 Mike Lansing	.15	.07
☐ 155 Lee Smith	.30	.14
☐ 156 Carlos Perez	.15	.07
☐ 157 Pedro Martinez	.60	.25
☐ 158 Ryan McGuire	.15	.07
☐ 159 F.P. Santangelo	.15	.07
☐ 160 Rondell White	.30	.14
☐ 161 Takashi Kashiwada	.60	.25
☐ 162 Butch Huskey	.30	.14
☐ 163 Edgardo Alfonzo	.30	.14
☐ 164 John Franco	.30	.14
☐ 165 Todd Hundley	.30	.14
☐ 166 Rey Ordonez	.15	.07
☐ 167 Armando Reynoso	.15	.07
☐ 168 John Olerud	.30	.14
☐ 169 Bernie Williams	.60	.25
☐ 170 Andy Pettitte	.60	.25
☐ 171 Wade Boggs	.60	.25
☐ 172 Paul O'Neill	.30	.14
☐ 173 Cecil Fielder	.30	.14
☐ 174 Charlie Hayes	.15	.07
☐ 175 David Cone	.30	.14
☐ 176 Hideki Irabu	.30	.14
☐ 177 Mark Bellhorn	.30	.14
☐ 178 Steve Karsay	.15	.07
☐ 179 Damon Mashore	.15	.07
☐ 180 Jason McDonald	.15	.07
☐ 181 Scott Spiezio	.30	.14
☐ 182 Ariel Prieto	.15	.07
☐ 183 Jason Giambi	.30	.14
☐ 184 Wendell Magee	.15	.07
☐ 185 Rico Brogna	.15	.07
☐ 186 Garrett Stephenson	.15	.07
☐ 187 Wayne Gomes	.15	.07
☐ 188 Ricky Bottalico	.15	.07
☐ 189 Mickey Morandini	.15	.07
☐ 190 Mike Lieberthal	.15	.07
☐ 191 Kevin Polcovich	.15	.07
☐ 192 Francisco Cordova	.15	.07
☐ 193 Kevin Young	.15	.07
☐ 194 Jon Lieber	.15	.07
☐ 195 Kevin Elster	.15	.07
☐ 196 Tony Womack	.15	.07
☐ 197 Lou Collier	.15	.07
☐ 198 Mike Difelice	.15	.07
☐ 199 Gary Gaetti	.15	.07
☐ 200 Dennis Eckersley	.30	.14
☐ 201 Alan Benes	.15	.07
☐ 202 Willie McGee	.15	.07
☐ 203 Ron Gant	.30	.14
☐ 204 Fernando Valenzuela	.30	.14
☐ 205 Mark McGwire	1.50	.70
☐ 206 Archi Cianfrocco	.15	.07
☐ 207 Andy Ashby	.15	.07
☐ 208 Steve Finley	.30	.14
☐ 209 Quivio Veras	.15	.07
☐ 210 Ken Caminiti	.40	.18
☐ 211 Rickey Henderson	.40	.18
☐ 212 Joey Hamilton	.30	.14
☐ 213 Derrek Lee	.40	.18
☐ 214 Bill Mueller	.15	.07
☐ 215 Shawn Estes	.15	.07
☐ 216 J.T. Snow	.30	.14
☐ 217 Mark Gardner	.15	.07
☐ 218 Terry Mulholland	.15	.07
☐ 219 Dante Powell	.15	.07
☐ 220 Jeff Kent	.30	.14
☐ 221 Jamie Moyer	.15	.07
☐ 222 Joey Cora	.15	.07
☐ 223 Jeff Fassero	.15	.07
☐ 224 Dennis Martinez	.30	.14

☐ 225	Ken Griffey Jr.	3.00	1.35
☐ 226	Edgar Martinez	.40	.18
☐ 227	Russ Davis	.15	.07
☐ 228	Dan Wilson	.15	.07
☐ 229	Will Clark	.40	.18
☐ 230	Ivan Rodriguez	.75	.35
☐ 231	Benji Gil	.15	.07
☐ 232	Lee Stevens	.15	.07
☐ 233	Mickey Tettleton	.15	.07
☐ 234	Julio Santana	.15	.07
☐ 235	Rusty Greer	.30	.14
☐ 236	Bobby Witt	.15	.07
☐ 237	Ed Sprague	.15	.07
☐ 238	Pat Hentgen	.30	.14
☐ 239	Kelvim Escobar	.15	.07
☐ 240	Joe Carter	.30	.14
☐ 241	Carlos Delgado	.30	.14
☐ 242	Shannon Stewart	.30	.14
☐ 243	Benito Santiago	.15	.07
☐ 244	Tino Martinez SH	.30	.14
☐ 245	Ken Griffey Jr. SH	1.50	.70
☐ 246	Kevin Brown SH	.15	.07
☐ 247	Ryne Sandberg SH	.40	.18
☐ 248	Mo Vaughn SH	.40	.18
☐ 249	Darryl Hamilton SH	.15	.07
☐ 250	Randy Johnson SH	.30	.14
☐ 251	Steve Finley SH	.15	.07
☐ 252	Bobby Higginson SH	.15	.07
☐ 253	Brett Tomko	.30	.14
☐ 254	Mark Kotsay	.60	.25
☐ 255	Jose Guillen	.60	.25
☐ 256	Eli Marrero	.30	.14
☐ 257	Dennis Reyes	.30	.14
☐ 258	Richie Sexson	.30	.14
☐ 259	Pat Cline	.15	.07
☐ 260	Todd Helton	.75	.35
☐ 261	Juan Melo	.30	.14
☐ 262	Matt Morris	.30	.14
☐ 263	Jeremi Gonzalez	.30	.14
☐ 264	Jeff Abbott	.15	.07
☐ 265	Aaron Boone	.15	.07
☐ 266	Todd Dunwoody	.30	.14
☐ 267	Jaret Wright	1.50	.70
☐ 268	Derrick Gibson	.30	.14
☐ 269	Mario Valdez	.30	.14
☐ 270	Fernando Tatis	.60	.25

1998 Upper Deck 10th Anniversary Preview

Randomly inserted in Series 1 packs at the rate of one in five, this 60-card set features color player photos in a design similar to the inaugural 1989 Upper Deck series. The backs carry a photo of that player's previous Upper Deck card. A 10th Anniversary Ballot Card was inserted one in four packs which allowed the collector to vote for the players they wanted to see in the 1999 Upper Deck tenth anniversary series.

		MINT	NRMT
COMPLETE SET (60)		120.00	55.00
COMMON CARD (1-60)		.50	.33
MINOR STARS		1.00	.45
UNLISTED STARS		2.50	1.10
SER.1 STATED ODDS 1:5			
☐ 1	Greg Maddux	8.00	3.60
☐ 2	Mike Mussina	2.50	1.10
☐ 3	Roger Clemens	5.00	2.20
☐ 4	Hideo Nomo	6.00	2.70
☐ 5	David Cone	1.00	.45
☐ 6	Tom Glavine	1.00	.45
☐ 7	Andy Pettitte	2.50	1.10
☐ 8	Jimmy Key	1.00	.45
☐ 9	Randy Johnson	2.50	1.10
☐ 10	Dennis Eckersley	1.00	.45
☐ 11	Lee Smith	1.00	.45
☐ 12	John Franco	1.00	.45
☐ 13	Randy Myers	.50	.23
☐ 14	Mike Piazza	8.00	3.60
☐ 15	Ivan Rodriguez	3.00	1.35
☐ 16	Todd Hundley	1.00	.45
☐ 17	Sandy Alomar Jr.	1.00	.45
☐ 18	Frank Thomas	10.00	4.50
☐ 19	Rafael Palmeiro	1.50	.70
☐ 20	Mark McGwire	6.00	2.70
☐ 21	Mo Vaughn	3.00	1.35
☐ 22	Fred McGriff	1.50	.70
☐ 23	Andres Galarraga	2.50	1.10
☐ 24	Mark Grace	1.50	.70
☐ 25	Jeff Bagwell	5.00	2.20
☐ 26	Roberto Alomar	2.50	1.10
☐ 27	Chuck Knoblauch	2.50	1.10
☐ 28	Ryne Sandberg	3.00	1.35
☐ 29	Eric Young	.50	.23
☐ 30	Craig Biggio	1.50	.70
☐ 31	Carlos Baerga	1.00	.23
☐ 32	Robin Ventura	1.00	.45
☐ 33	Matt Williams	1.50	.70
☐ 34	Wade Boggs	2.50	1.10
☐ 35	Dean Palmer	.50	.23
☐ 36	Chipper Jones	8.00	3.60
☐ 37	Vinny Castilla	1.00	.45
☐ 38	Ken Caminiti	1.50	.70
☐ 39	Omar Vizquel	1.00	.45
☐ 40	Cal Ripken	10.00	4.50
☐ 41	Derek Jeter	6.00	2.70
☐ 42	Alex Rodriguez	8.00	3.60
☐ 43	Barry Larkin	1.50	.70
☐ 44	Mark Grudzielanek	.50	.23
☐ 45	Albert Belle	3.00	1.35
☐ 46	Manny Ramirez	2.50	1.10
☐ 47	Jose Canseco	1.50	.70
☐ 48	Ken Griffey Jr.	12.00	5.50
☐ 49	Juan Gonzalez	6.00	2.70
☐ 50	Kenny Lofton	3.00	1.35
☐ 51	Sammy Sosa	2.50	1.10
☐ 52	Larry Walker	2.50	1.10
☐ 53	Gary Sheffield	2.50	1.10
☐ 54	Rickey Henderson	1.50	.70
☐ 55	Tony Gwynn	6.00	2.70
☐ 56	Barry Bonds	3.00	1.35
☐ 57	Paul Molitor	2.50	1.10
☐ 58	Edgar Martinez	1.50	.70
☐ 59	Chili Davis	1.00	.45
☐ 60	Eddie Murray	2.50	1.10

1998 Upper Deck A Piece of the Action

Randomly inserted in Series 1 packs at the rate of one in 2,500, this 10-card set features color photos of top players with pieces of actual game worn jerseys and game used bats embedded in the cards. The cards are unnumbered and checklisted below in alphabetical order.

		MINT	NRMT
COMPLETE SET (6)		2000.00	900.00
COMMON CARD		80.00	36.00
SER.1 STATED ODDS 1:2500			
MULTI-COLOR PATCHES CARRY PREMIUMS			
ACTUAL CARDS ARE UNNUMBERED			
☐ 1	Jay Buhner Bat	100.00	45.00
☐ 2	Tony Gwynn Bat	250.00	110.00
☐ 3	Tony Gwynn Jersey	300.00	135.00
☐ 4	Todd Hollandsworth Bat	80.00	36.00
☐ 5	Todd Hollandsworth Jersey	100.00	45.00
☐ 6	Greg Maddux Jersey	400.00	180.00
☐ 7	Alex Rodriguez Bat	300.00	135.00
☐ 8	Alex Rodriguez Jersey	400.00	180.00
☐ 9	Gary Sheffield Bat	100.00	45.00
☐ 10	Gary Sheffield Jersey	120.00	55.00

1998 Upper Deck Amazing Greats

Randomly inserted in Series 1 packs, this 30-card set features color photos of amazing players printed on a hi-tech plastic card. Only 2000 of this set were produced and are crash numbered.

		MINT	NRMT
COMPLETE SET (30)		800.00	350.00
COMMON CARD (AG1-AG30)		12.00	5.50
UNLISTED STARS		15.00	6.75
STATED PRINT RUN 2000 SETS			
COMP.DIE CUT SET (30)		2000.00	900.00
*DIE CUT STARS: 1.25X TO 2.5X HI COLUMN			
DIE CUT PRINT RUN 250 SERIAL #'d SETS			
RANDOM INSERTS IN SER.1 PACKS			
☐ AG1	Ken Griffey Jr.	80.00	36.00
☐ AG2	Derek Jeter	40.00	18.00
☐ AG3	Alex Rodriguez	50.00	22.00
☐ AG4	Paul Molitor	15.00	6.75
☐ AG5	Jeff Bagwell	30.00	13.50
☐ AG6	Larry Walker	15.00	6.75
☐ AG7	Kenny Lofton	20.00	9.00
☐ AG8	Cal Ripken Jr.	60.00	27.00
☐ AG9	Juan Gonzalez	40.00	18.00
☐ AG10	Chipper Jones	50.00	22.00

	MINT	NRMT
☐ AG11 Greg Maddux	50.00	22.00
☐ AG12 Roberto Alomar	15.00	6.75
☐ AG13 Mike Piazza	50.00	22.00
☐ AG14 Andres Galarraga	12.00	5.50
☐ AG15 Barry Bonds	20.00	9.00
☐ AG16 Andy Pettitte	15.00	6.75
☐ AG17 Nomar Garciaparra	40.00	18.00
☐ AG18 Tino Martinez	12.00	5.50
☐ AG19 Tony Gwynn	40.00	18.00
☐ AG20 Frank Thomas	60.00	27.00
☐ AG21 Roger Clemens	30.00	13.50
☐ AG22 Sammy Sosa	12.00	5.50
☐ AG23 Jose Cruz Jr.	50.00	22.00
☐ AG24 Manny Ramirez	15.00	6.75
☐ AG25 Mark McGwire	40.00	18.00
☐ AG26 Randy Johnson	15.00	6.75
☐ AG27 Mo Vaughn	20.00	9.00
☐ AG28 Gary Sheffield	12.00	5.50
☐ AG29 Andruw Jones	25.00	11.00
☐ AG30 Albert Belle	20.00	9.00

1998 Upper Deck National Pride

Randomly inserted in Series 1 packs at the rate of one in 23, this 42-card set features color photos of some of the league's great players from countries other than the United States printed on die-cut ranbow foil cards. The backs carry player information.

	MINT	NRMT
COMPLETE SET (42)	350.00	160.00
COMMON CARD (NP1-NP42)	2.50	1.10
MINOR STARS	4.00	1.50
SEMISTARS	6.00	2.70
UNLISTED STARS	10.00	4.50
SER.1 STATED ODDS 1:23		

	MINT	NRMT
☐ NP1 Dave Nilsson	2.50	1.10
☐ NP2 Larry Walker	10.00	4.50
☐ NP3 Edgar Renteria	4.00	1.80
☐ NP4 Jose Canseco	6.00	2.70
☐ NP5 Rey Ordonez	2.50	1.10
☐ NP6 Rafael Palmeiro	6.00	2.70
☐ NP7 Livan Hernandez	6.00	2.70
☐ NP8 Andruw Jones	15.00	6.75
☐ NP9 Manny Ramirez	10.00	4.50
☐ NP10 Sammy Sosa	6.00	2.70
☐ NP11 Raul Mondesi	4.00	1.80
☐ NP12 Moises Alou	4.00	1.80
☐ NP13 Pedro Martinez	10.00	4.50
☐ NP14 Vladimir Guerrero	12.00	5.50
☐ NP15 Chili Davis	4.00	1.80
☐ NP16 Hideo Nomo	25.00	11.00
☐ NP17 Hideki Irabu	4.00	1.80
☐ NP18 Shigetoshi Hasegawa	4.00	1.80
☐ NP19 Takashi Kashiwada	4.00	1.80
☐ NP20 Chan Ho Park	10.00	4.50
☐ NP21 Fernando Valenzuela	4.00	1.80
☐ NP22 Vinny Castilla	4.00	1.80
☐ NP23 Armando Reynoso	2.50	1.10
☐ NP24 Karim Garcia	4.00	1.80

	MINT	NRMT
☐ NP25 Marvin Benard	2.50	1.10
☐ NP26 Mariano Rivera	4.00	1.80
☐ NP27 Juan Gonzalez	25.00	11.00
☐ NP28 Roberto Alomar	10.00	4.50
☐ NP29 Ivan Rodriguez	12.00	5.50
☐ NP30 Carlos Delgado	4.00	1.80
☐ NP31 Bernie Williams	10.00	4.50
☐ NP32 Edgar Martinez	6.00	2.70
☐ NP33 Frank Thomas	40.00	18.00
☐ NP34 Barry Bonds	12.00	5.50
☐ NP35 Mike Piazza	30.00	13.50
☐ NP36 Chipper Jones	30.00	13.50
☐ NP37 Cal Ripken Jr.	40.00	18.00
☐ NP38 Alex Rodriguez	30.00	13.50
☐ NP39 Ken Griffey Jr.	50.00	22.00
☐ NP40 Andres Galarraga	10.00	4.50
☐ NP41 Omar Vizquel	4.00	1.80
☐ NP42 Ozzie Guillen	2.50	1.10

1997 Upper Deck UD3

This 60-card standard-size super premium set was released by Upper Deck exclusively to retail outlets in mid-April 1997. The set is broken up into three distinct 20-card subsets: Homerun Heroes (1-20) featuring Electric Wood technology, Pro-Motion (21-40) featuring Light F/X technology and Future Impact (41-60) featuring Cel Chrome technology. Packs carried a suggested retail price of $3.99. Each pack contained three cards, one from each of the subsets. Boxes contained 24 packs.

	MINT	NRMT
COMPLETE SET (60)	60.00	27.00
COMMON CARD (1-60)	.50	.23
MINOR STARS	.50	.23
UNLISTED STARS	1.25	.55

	MINT	NRMT
☐ 1 Mark McGwire	2.50	1.10
☐ 2 Brady Anderson	.75	.35
☐ 3 Ken Griffey Jr.	6.00	2.70
☐ 4 Albert Belle	1.50	.70
☐ 5 Andres Galarraga	1.25	.55
☐ 6 Juan Gonzalez	3.00	1.35
☐ 7 Jay Buhner	.75	.35
☐ 8 Mo Vaughn	1.50	.70
☐ 9 Barry Bonds	1.50	.70
☐ 10 Gary Sheffield	1.25	.55
☐ 11 Todd Hundley	.50	.23
☐ 12 Ellis Burks	.50	.23
☐ 13 Ken Caminiti	.75	.35
☐ 14 Vinny Castilla	.50	.23
☐ 15 Sammy Sosa	1.25	.55
☐ 16 Frank Thomas	5.00	2.20
☐ 17 Rafael Palmeiro	.75	.35
☐ 18 Mike Piazza	4.00	1.80
☐ 19 Matt Williams	.75	.35
☐ 20 Eddie Murray	1.25	.55

	MINT	NRMT
☐ 21 Roger Clemens	2.50	1.10
☐ 22 Tim Salmon	1.25	.55
☐ 23 Robin Ventura	.50	.23
☐ 24 Ron Gant	.50	.23
☐ 25 Cal Ripken	5.00	2.20
☐ 26 Bernie Williams	1.25	.55
☐ 27 Hideo Nomo	3.00	1.35
☐ 28 Ivan Rodriguez	1.50	.70
☐ 29 John Smoltz	.50	.23
☐ 30 Paul Molitor	1.25	.55
☐ 31 Greg Maddux	4.00	1.80
☐ 32 Raul Mondesi	.75	.35
☐ 33 Roberto Alomar	1.25	.55
☐ 34 Barry Larkin	.75	.35
☐ 35 Tony Gwynn	3.00	1.35
☐ 36 Jim Thome	1.25	.55
☐ 37 Kenny Lofton	1.50	.70
☐ 38 Jeff Bagwell	2.50	1.10
☐ 39 Ozzie Smith	1.50	.70
☐ 40 Kirby Puckett	2.50	1.10
☐ 41 Andruw Jones	3.00	1.35
☐ 42 Vladimir Guerrero	2.50	1.10
☐ 43 Edgar Renteria	.50	.23
☐ 44 Luis Castillo	.50	.23
☐ 45 Darin Erstad	2.00	.90
☐ 46 Nomar Garciaparra	4.00	1.80
☐ 47 Todd Greene	.50	.23
☐ 48 Jason Kendall	.50	.23
☐ 49 Rey Ordonez	.50	.23
☐ 50 Alex Rodriguez	4.00	1.80
☐ 51 Manny Ramirez	1.25	.55
☐ 52 Todd Walker	.50	.23
☐ 53 Ruben Rivera	.50	.23
☐ 54 Andy Pettitte	1.25	.55
☐ 55 Derek Jeter	4.00	1.80
☐ 56 Todd Hollandsworth	.50	.23
☐ 57 Rocky Coppinger	.50	.23
☐ 58 Scott Rolen	3.00	1.35
☐ 59 Jermaine Dye	.50	.23
☐ 60 Chipper Jones	4.00	1.80

1997 Upper Deck UD3 Generation Next

Randomly seeded into one in every 11 packs, cards from this 20-card set feature a selection of the game's top prospects. The horizontal card fronts feature a full-color cut-out player photo set against a metallized background with another picture of the player in action. Card backs include 1996 season statistics, a rarity for insert issues.

	MINT	NRMT
COMPLETE SET (20)	120.00	55.00
COMMON CARD (1-20)	2.00	.90
UNLISTED STARS	5.00	2.20
STATED ODDS 1:11		

	MINT	NRMT
☐ GN1 Alex Rodriguez	15.00	6.75
☐ GN2 Vladimir Guerrero	10.00	4.50

☐ GN3 Luis Castillo	2.50	1.10
☐ GN4 Rey Ordonez	2.00	.90
☐ GN5 Andruw Jones	12.00	5.50
☐ GN6 Darin Erstad	8.00	3.60
☐ GN7 Edgar Renteria	2.50	1.10
☐ GN8 Jason Kendall	2.50	1.10
☐ GN9 Jermaine Dye	2.00	.90
☐ GN10 Chipper Jones	15.00	6.75
☐ GN11 Rocky Coppinger	2.00	.90
☐ GN12 Andy Pettitte	5.00	2.20
☐ GN13 Todd Greene	2.50	1.10
☐ GN14 Todd Hollandsworth	2.00	.90
☐ GN15 Derek Jeter	15.00	6.75
☐ GN16 Ruben Rivera	2.50	1.10
☐ GN17 Todd Walker	2.50	1.10
☐ GN18 Nomar Garciaparra	15.00	6.75
☐ GN19 Scott Rolen	12.00	5.50
☐ GN20 Manny Ramirez	5.00	2.20

1997 Upper Deck UD3 Marquee Attraction

photo, statistics on height, weight, date of birth and hometown, plus of course a real autograph at the base of the card. Card backs feature text congratulating the bearer of the card plus the signature of Upper Deck's president Brian Burr.

	MINT	NRMT
COMPLETE SET (4)	1000.00	450.00
COMMON CARD	80.00	36.00
STATED ODDS 1:1500		

☐ 1 Ken Caminiti	80.00	36.00
☐ 2 Ken Griffey Jr.	600.00	275.00
☐ 3 Vladimir Guerrero	150.00	70.00
☐ 4 Derek Jeter	250.00	110.00

1995 Zenith

The complete 1995 Zenith set consists of 150 standard-size cards. The cards are made of thick stock and are borderless. The fronts feature an action photo with a pyramid design serving as background. The player's name appears vertically up the left side with the Pinnacle logo in the upper right corner. The backs have a head shot and statistical information such as pitcher's strike frequency and what part of the field batters have the tendency to go to most. Included is a subset of 50 Rookies (111-150). The regular issued cards are in alphabetical order by first name. Rookie Cards in this set include Bobby Higginson and Hideo Nomo.

	MINT	NRMT
COMPLETE SET (150)	40.00	18.00
COMMON CARD (1-150)	.25	.11
MINOR STARS	.50	.23
UNLISTED STARS	1.00	.45

1997 Upper Deck UD3 Superb Signatures

Randomly seeded into one in every 1,500 packs, cards from this four-card set feature actual autographs from some of baseball's top stars. Horizontal wood-cel card fronts feature a rectangular clear plastic player

☐ 1 Albert Belle	1.25	.55
☐ 2 Alex Fernandez	.25	.11
☐ 3 Andy Benes	.50	.23
☐ 4 Barry Larkin	.50	.23
☐ 5 Barry Bonds	1.25	.55
☐ 6 Ben McDonald	.25	.11
☐ 7 Bernard Gilkey	.25	.11
☐ 8 Billy Ashley	.25	.11
☐ 9 Bobby Bonilla	.50	.23
☐ 10 Bret Saberhagen	.25	.11
☐ 11 Brian Jordan	.50	.23
☐ 12 Cal Ripken	4.00	1.80
☐ 13 Carlos Baerga	.25	.11
☐ 14 Carlos Delgado	.50	.23
☐ 15 Cecil Fielder	.50	.23
☐ 16 Chili Davis	.50	.23
☐ 17 Chuck Knoblauch	1.00	.45
☐ 18 Craig Biggio	.75	.35
☐ 19 Danny Tartabull	.25	.11
☐ 20 Dante Bichette	.50	.23
☐ 21 Darren Daulton	.50	.23
☐ 22 David Justice	1.00	.45
☐ 23 Dave Winfield	.75	.35
☐ 24 David Cone	.50	.23
☐ 25 Dean Palmer	.25	.11
☐ 26 Deion Sanders	.50	.23
☐ 27 Dennis Eckersley	.50	.23
☐ 28 Derek Bell	.25	.11
☐ 29 Don Mattingly	1.50	.70
☐ 30 Edgar Martinez	.75	.35
☐ 31 Eric Karros	.50	.23
☐ 32 James Mouton	.25	.11
☐ 33 Frank Thomas	4.00	1.80
☐ 34 Fred McGriff	.75	.35
☐ 35 Gary Sheffield	1.00	.45
☐ 36 Gary Gaetti	.25	.11
☐ 37 Greg Maddux	3.00	1.35
☐ 38 Gregg Jefferies	.25	.11
☐ 39 Ivan Rodriguez	1.25	.55
☐ 40 Kenny Rogers	.25	.11
☐ 41 J.T. Snow	.50	.23
☐ 42 Hal Morris	.25	.11
☐ 43 Eddie Murray 3000th Hit	.50	.23
☐ 44 Javier Lopez	.50	.23
☐ 45 Jay Bell	.50	.23
☐ 46 Jeff Conine	.50	.23
☐ 47 Jeff Bagwell	2.00	.90
☐ 48 Hideo Nomo Japanese	5.00	2.20
☐ 49 Jeff Kent	.25	.11
☐ 50 Jeff King	.25	.11
☐ 51 Jim Thome	1.00	.45
☐ 52 Jimmy Key	.50	.23
☐ 53 Joe Carter	.50	.23
☐ 54 John Valentin	.25	.11
☐ 55 John Olerud	.50	.23
☐ 56 Jose Canseco	.75	.35
☐ 57 Jose Rijo	.25	.11
☐ 58 Jose Offerman	.25	.11
☐ 59 Juan Gonzalez	2.50	1.10
☐ 60 Ken Caminiti	.75	.35
☐ 61 Ken Griffey Jr.	5.00	2.20
☐ 62 Kenny Lofton	1.25	.55
☐ 63 Kevin Appier	.50	.23
☐ 64 Kevin Seitzer	.25	.11
☐ 65 Kirby Puckett	2.00	.90
☐ 66 Kirk Gibson	.50	.23
☐ 67 Larry Walker	1.00	.45
☐ 68 Lenny Dykstra	.50	.23
☐ 69 Manny Ramirez	1.00	.45
☐ 70 Mark Grace	.75	.35
☐ 71 Mark McGwire	2.00	.90
☐ 72 Marquis Grissom	.50	.23
☐ 73 Jim Edmonds	.75	.35
☐ 74 Matt Williams	.75	.35
☐ 75 Mike Mussina	1.00	.45
☐ 76 Mike Piazza	3.00	1.35
☐ 77 Mo Vaughn	1.25	.55
☐ 78 Moises Alou	.50	.23
☐ 79 Ozzie Smith	1.25	.55
☐ 80 Paul O'Neill	.50	.23
☐ 81 Paul Molitor	1.00	.45
☐ 82 Rafael Palmeiro	.75	.35
☐ 83 Randy Johnson	1.00	.45
☐ 84 Raul Mondesi	.75	.35
☐ 85 Ray Lankford	.50	.23
☐ 86 Reggie Sanders	.25	.11

☐ 87 Rickey Henderson	.75	.35
☐ 88 Rico Brogna	.25	.11
☐ 89 Roberto Alomar	1.00	.45
☐ 90 Robin Ventura	.50	.23
☐ 91 Roger Clemens	2.00	.90
☐ 92 Ron Gant	.50	.23
☐ 93 Rondell White	.50	.23
☐ 94 Royce Clayton	.25	.11
☐ 95 Ruben Sierra	.25	.11
☐ 96 Rusty Greer	1.00	.45
☐ 97 Ryan Klesko	.75	.35
☐ 98 Sammy Sosa	1.00	.45
☐ 99 Shawon Dunston	.25	.11
☐ 100 Steve Ontiveros	.25	.11
☐ 101 Tim Naehring	.25	.11
☐ 102 Tim Salmon	1.00	.45
☐ 103 Tino Martinez	1.00	.45
☐ 104 Tony Gwynn	2.50	1.10
☐ 105 Travis Fryman	.50	.23
☐ 106 Vinny Castilla	.50	.23
☐ 107 Wade Boggs	1.00	.45
☐ 108 Wally Joyner	.50	.23
☐ 109 Wil Cordero	.25	.11
☐ 110 Will Clark	.75	.35
☐ 111 Chipper Jones	3.00	1.35
☐ 112 Armando Benitez	.25	.11
☐ 113 Curtis Goodwin	.25	.11
☐ 114 Gabe White	.25	.11
☐ 115 Vaughn Eshelman	.25	.11
☐ 116 Marty Cordova	.50	.23
☐ 117 Dustin Hermanson	.50	.23
☐ 118 Rich Becker	.25	.11
☐ 119 Ray Durham	.50	.23
☐ 120 Shane Andrews	.25	.11
☐ 121 Scott Ruffcorn	.25	.11
☐ 122 Mark Grudzielanek	.75	.35
☐ 123 James Baldwin	.25	.11
☐ 124 Carlos Perez	.50	.23
☐ 125 Julian Tavarez	.25	.11
☐ 126 Joe Vitiello	.25	.11
☐ 127 Jason Bates	.25	.11
☐ 128 Edgardo Alfonzo	1.00	.45
☐ 129 Juan Acevedo	.25	.11
☐ 130 Bill Pulsipher	.25	.11
☐ 131 Bob Higginson	1.50	.70
☐ 132 Russ Davis	.25	.11
☐ 133 Charles Johnson	.50	.23
☐ 134 Derek Jeter	3.00	1.35
☐ 135 Orlando Miller	.25	.11
☐ 136 LaTroy Hawkins	.25	.11
☐ 137 Brian L.Hunter	.50	.23
☐ 138 Roberto Petagine	.25	.11
☐ 139 Midre Cummings	.25	.11
☐ 140 Garret Anderson	.75	.35
☐ 141 Ugueth Urbina	.25	.11
☐ 142 Antonio Osuna	.25	.11
☐ 143 Michael Tucker	.50	.23
☐ 144 Benji Gil	.25	.11
☐ 145 Jon Nunnally	.25	.11
☐ 146 Alex Rodriguez	4.00	1.80
☐ 147 Todd Hollandsworth	.50	.23
☐ 148 Alex Gonzalez	.25	.11
☐ 149 Hideo Nomo	5.00	2.20
☐ 150 Shawn Green	.50	.23

1995 Zenith All-Star Salute

This 18-card set was randomly inserted in packs at a rate of one in six. The set commemorates many of the memorable plays of the 1995 All-Star Game played in Arlington, TX. The fronts have an action photo set out against the background of the game giving it a 3D look. The words "All-Star Salute" are in gold on the left with the player's name at the bottom. The backs have a color photo with personal All-Star Game tidbits. The cards are numbered "X of 18."

	MINT	NRMT
COMPLETE SET (18)	60.00	27.00
COMMON CARD (1-18)	.50	.23
STATED ODDS 1:6		

☐ 1 Cal Ripken	8.00	3.60
☐ 2 Frank Thomas	8.00	3.60
☐ 3 Mike Piazza	6.00	2.70
☐ 4 Kirby Puckett	4.00	1.80
☐ 5 Manny Ramirez	2.00	.90
☐ 6 Tony Gwynn	5.00	2.20
☐ 7 Hideo Nomo	10.00	4.50
☐ 8 Matt Williams	1.50	.70
☐ 9 Randy Johnson	2.00	.90
☐ 10 Raul Mondesi	1.50	.70
☐ 11 Albert Belle	2.50	1.10
☐ 12 Ivan Rodriguez	2.50	1.10
☐ 13 Barry Bonds	2.50	1.10
☐ 14 Carlos Baerga	.50	.23
☐ 15 Ken Griffey Jr.	10.00	4.50
☐ 16 Jeff Conine	.50	.23
☐ 17 Frank Thomas	8.00	3.60
☐ 18 Cal Ripken	6.00	2.70
Barry Bonds		

1995 Zenith Rookie Roll Call

This 18-card, Dufex-designed standard-size set was randomly inserted in packs at a rate of one in 24. The set is comprised of 18 top rookies from 1995. The fronts have two photos and a colorful star in the background with which rays of color emanate. The backs are laid out horizontally with a color photo on a multi-color foil background. Player information of previous accomplishments is also on the back and the cards are numbered "X of 18."

	MINT	NRMT
COMPLETE SET (18)	225.00	100.00
COMMON CARD (1-18)	8.00	3.60
UNLISTED STARS	12.00	5.50
STATED ODDS 1:24		

☐ 1 Alex Rodriguez	60.00	27.00
☐ 2 Derek Jeter	50.00	22.00
☐ 3 Chipper Jones	50.00	22.00
☐ 4 Shawn Green	10.00	4.50
☐ 5 Todd Hollandsworth	10.00	4.50
☐ 6 Bill Pulsipher	8.00	3.60
☐ 7 Hideo Nomo	50.00	22.00
☐ 8 Ray Durham	10.00	4.50
☐ 9 Curtis Goodwin	8.00	3.60
☐ 10 Brian L.Hunter	10.00	4.50
☐ 11 Julian Tavarez	8.00	3.60
☐ 12 Marty Cordova UER	10.00	4.50
Kevin Maas pictured		
☐ 13 Michael Tucker	10.00	4.50
☐ 14 Edgardo Alfonzo	12.00	5.50
☐ 15 LaTroy Hawkins	8.00	3.60
☐ 16 Carlos Perez	8.00	3.60
☐ 17 Charles Johnson	10.00	4.50
☐ 18 Benji Gil	8.00	3.60

1995 Zenith Z-Team

This 18-card standard-size set was randomly inserted in packs at a rate of one in 72. The set is comprised of the best players in baseball and is done in 3-D Dufex. The fronts have a player action photo positioned on home plate which has the words "Z Team." There are multi-colored rays coming out of the card background. The back is laid out horizontally with a color head shot and a stadium crowd background. The back also has player information and a "Z Team" emblem.

	MINT	NRMT
COMPLETE SET (18)	400.00	180.00
COMMON CARD (1-18)	8.00	3.60
UNLISTED STARS	12.00	5.50
STATED ODDS 1:72		

☐ 1 Cal Ripken	50.00	22.00
☐ 2 Ken Griffey Jr.	60.00	27.00
☐ 3 Frank Thomas	50.00	22.00
☐ 4 Matt Williams	10.00	4.50
☐ 5 Mike Piazza UER	40.00	18.00
(Card says started at first base Piazza was a catcher)		
☐ 6 Barry Bonds	15.00	6.75
☐ 7 Raul Mondesi	10.00	4.50
☐ 8 Greg Maddux	40.00	18.00
☐ 9 Jeff Bagwell	25.00	11.00
☐ 10 Manny Ramirez	12.00	5.50
☐ 11 Larry Walker	12.00	5.50
☐ 12 Tony Gwynn	30.00	13.50
☐ 13 Will Clark	10.00	4.50
☐ 14 Albert Belle	15.00	6.75
☐ 15 Kenny Lofton	15.00	6.75
☐ 16 Rafael Palmeiro	10.00	4.50
☐ 17 Don Mattingly	20.00	9.00
☐ 18 Carlos Baerga	8.00	3.60

1996 Zenith

This 1996 Zenith set was issued in one series totalling 150 cards. The six-card packs retail for $3.99 each. The set contains the subset: Honor Roll (131-150). The fronts feature a color player cutout over an arrangement of baseball bats on a black background. The backs carry a hit location chart and player statistics. The only notable Rookie Card is of Darin Erstad.

	MINT	NRMT
COMPLETE SET (150)	40.00	18.00
COMMON CARD (1-150)	.20	.09
MINOR STARS	.40	.18
UNLISTED STARS	.75	.35
SUBSET CARDS HALF VALUE OF BASE CARDS		
COMP. AP SET (150)	2000.00	900.00
COMMON ART.PRF. (1-150)	3.00	1.35
*AP STARS: 10X TO 25X HI COLUMN		
*AP YOUNG STARS: 8X TO 20X HI		
AP STATED ODDS 1:35		

		MINT	NRMT
☐ 1	Ken Griffey Jr.	4.00	1.80
☐ 2	Ozzie Smith	1.00	.45
☐ 3	Greg Maddux	2.50	1.10
☐ 4	Rondell White	.40	.18
☐ 5	Mark McGwire	1.00	.45
☐ 6	Jim Thome	.75	.35
☐ 7	Ivan Rodriguez	1.00	.45
☐ 8	Marc Newfield	.20	.09
☐ 9	Travis Fryman	.40	.18
☐ 10	Fred McGriff	.60	.25
☐ 11	Shawn Green	.20	.09
☐ 12	Mike Piazza	2.50	1.10
☐ 13	Dante Bichette	.40	.18
☐ 14	Tino Martinez	.75	.35
☐ 15	Sterling Hitchcock	.20	.09
☐ 16	Ryne Sandberg	1.00	.45
☐ 17	Rico Brogna	.20	.09
☐ 18	Roberto Alomar	.75	.35
☐ 19	Barry Larkin	.60	.25
☐ 20	Bernie Williams	.75	.35
☐ 21	Gary Sheffield	.75	.35
☐ 22	Frank Thomas	3.00	1.35
☐ 23	Gregg Jefferies	.20	.09
☐ 24	Jeff Bagwell	1.50	.70
☐ 25	Marty Cordova	.40	.18
☐ 26	Jim Edmonds	.60	.25
☐ 27	Jay Bell	.40	.18
☐ 28	Ben McDonald	.20	.09
☐ 29	Barry Bonds	1.00	.45
☐ 30	Mo Vaughn	1.00	.45
☐ 31	Johnny Damon	.40	.18
☐ 32	Dean Palmer	.20	.09
☐ 33	Ismael Valdes	.40	.18
☐ 34	Manny Ramirez	.75	.35
☐ 35	Edgar Martinez	.60	.25
☐ 36	Cecil Fielder	.40	.18
☐ 37	Ryan Klesko	.60	.25
☐ 38	Ray Lankford	.40	.18
☐ 39	Tim Salmon	.75	.35
☐ 40	Joe Carter	.40	.18
☐ 41	Jason Isringhausen	.20	.09
☐ 42	Rickey Henderson	.60	.25
☐ 43	Lenny Dykstra	.40	.18
☐ 44	Andre Dawson	.60	.25
☐ 45	Paul O'Neill	.40	.18
☐ 46	Ray Durham	.20	.09
☐ 47	Raul Mondesi	.60	.25
☐ 48	Jay Buhner	.60	.25
☐ 49	Eddie Murray	.75	.35
☐ 50	Henry Rodriguez	.20	.09
☐ 51	Hal Morris	.20	.09
☐ 52	Mike Mussina	.75	.35
☐ 53	Wally Joyner	.40	.18
☐ 54	Will Clark	.60	.25
☐ 55	Chipper Jones	2.50	1.10
☐ 56	Brian Jordan	.40	.18
☐ 57	Larry Walker	.75	.35
☐ 58	Wade Boggs	.75	.35
☐ 59	Melvin Nieves	.20	.09
☐ 60	Charles Johnson	.40	.18
☐ 61	Juan Gonzalez	2.00	.90
☐ 62	Carlos Delgado	.40	.18
☐ 63	Reggie Sanders	.20	.09
☐ 64	Brian L.Hunter	.40	.18
☐ 65	Edgardo Alfonzo	.60	.25
☐ 66	Kenny Lofton	1.00	.45
☐ 67	Paul Molitor	.75	.35
☐ 68	Mike Bordick	.20	.09
☐ 69	Garret Anderson	.40	.18
☐ 70	Orlando Merced	.20	.09
☐ 71	Craig Biggio	.60	.25
☐ 72	Chuck Knoblauch	.75	.35
☐ 73	Mark Grace	.60	.25
☐ 74	Jack McDowell	.20	.09
☐ 75	Randy Johnson	.75	.35
☐ 76	Cal Ripken	3.00	1.35
☐ 77	Matt Williams	.60	.25
☐ 78	Benji Gil	.20	.09
☐ 79	Moises Alou	.40	.18
☐ 80	Robin Ventura	.40	.18
☐ 81	Greg Vaughn	.20	.09
☐ 82	Carlos Baerga	.20	.09
☐ 83	Roger Clemens	1.50	.70
☐ 84	Hideo Nomo	2.00	.90
☐ 85	Pedro Martinez	.75	.35
☐ 86	John Valentin	.20	.09
☐ 87	Andres Galarraga	.75	.35
☐ 88	Andy Pettitte	1.00	.45
☐ 89	Derek Bell	.20	.09
☐ 90	Kirby Puckett	1.50	.70
☐ 91	Tony Gwynn	2.00	.90
☐ 92	Brady Anderson	.60	.25
☐ 93	Derek Jeter	2.50	1.10
☐ 94	Michael Tucker	.40	.18
☐ 95	Albert Belle	1.00	.45
☐ 96	David Cone	.40	.18
☐ 97	J.T. Snow	.40	.18
☐ 98	Tom Glavine	.40	.18
☐ 99	Alex Rodriguez	2.50	1.10
☐ 100	Sammy Sosa	.75	.35
☐ 101	Karim Garcia	.60	.25
☐ 102	Alan Benes	.40	.18
☐ 103	Chad Mottola	.20	.09
☐ 104	Robin Jennings	.20	.09
☐ 105	Bob Abreu	.60	.25
☐ 106	Tony Clark	.75	.35
☐ 107	George Arias	.20	.09
☐ 108	Jermaine Dye	.40	.18
☐ 109	Jeff Suppan	.40	.18
☐ 110	Ralph Milliard	.20	.09
☐ 111	Ruben Rivera	.40	.18
☐ 112	Billy Wagner	.40	.18
☐ 113	Jason Kendall	.60	.25
☐ 114	Mike Grace	.20	.09
☐ 115	Edgar Renteria	.60	.25
☐ 116	Jason Schmidt	.40	.18
☐ 117	Paul Wilson	.20	.09
☐ 118	Rey Ordonez	.40	.18
☐ 119	Rocky Coppinger	.75	.35
☐ 120	Wilton Guerrero	.75	.35
☐ 121	Brooks Kieschnick	.40	.18
☐ 122	Raul Casanova	.20	.09
☐ 123	Alex Ochoa	.20	.09
☐ 124	Chan Ho Park	.40	.18
☐ 125	John Wasdin	.20	.09
☐ 126	Eric Owens	.20	.09
☐ 127	Justin Thompson	.60	.25
☐ 128	Chris Snopek	.20	.09
☐ 129	Terrell Wade	.20	.09
☐ 130	Darin Erstad	4.00	1.80
☐ 131	Albert Belle HON	.60	.25
☐ 132	Cal Ripken HON	1.50	.70
☐ 133	Frank Thomas HON	1.50	.70
☐ 134	Greg Maddux HON	1.25	.55
☐ 135	Ken Griffey Jr. HON	2.00	.90
☐ 136	Mo Vaughn HON	.60	.25
☐ 137	Chipper Jones HON	1.25	.55
☐ 138	Mike Piazza HON	1.25	.55
☐ 139	Ryan Klesko HON	.40	.18
☐ 140	Hideo Nomo HON	1.00	.45
☐ 141	Roberto Alomar HON	.40	.18
☐ 142	Manny Ramirez HON	.40	.18
☐ 143	Gary Sheffield HON	.40	.18
☐ 144	Barry Bonds HON	.60	.25
☐ 145	Matt Williams HON	.40	.18
☐ 146	Jim Edmonds HON	.40	.18
☐ 147	Derek Jeter HON	1.25	.55
☐ 148	Sammy Sosa HON	.40	.18
☐ 149	Kirby Puckett HON	.40	.18
☐ 150	Tony Gwynn HON	1.00	.45

1996 Zenith Diamond Club

Randomly inserted in packs at a rate of one in 24, cards from this 20-card set honor top performers on a Spectroetch card design printed on thick foil stock with etched highlights. The fronts feature an above-the-waist color action player cutout over a diamond-shaped opening on a grass-green background. The backs carry player information.

	MINT	NRMT
COMPLETE SET (20)	250.00	110.00
COMMON CARD (1-20)	2.00	.90
SEMISTARS	4.00	1.80
UNLISTED STARS	6.00	2.70
STATED ODDS 1:24		
*REAL DIAMONDS: 3X TO 6X HI COLUMN		
REAL DIAMONDS STATED ODDS 1:350		

		MINT	NRMT
☐ 1	Albert Belle	8.00	3.60
☐ 2	Mo Vaughn	8.00	3.60
☐ 3	Ken Griffey Jr.	30.00	13.50
☐ 4	Mike Piazza	20.00	9.00
☐ 5	Cal Ripken	25.00	11.00
☐ 6	Jermaine Dye	3.00	1.35
☐ 7	Jeff Bagwell	12.00	5.50
☐ 8	Frank Thomas	25.00	11.00
☐ 9	Alex Rodriguez	20.00	9.00
☐ 10	Ryan Klesko	4.00	1.80
☐ 11	Roberto Alomar	6.00	2.70
☐ 12	Sammy Sosa	6.00	2.70
☐ 13	Matt Williams	4.00	1.80
☐ 14	Gary Sheffield	6.00	2.70
☐ 15	Ruben Rivera	3.00	1.35
☐ 16	Darin Erstad	20.00	9.00

		MINT	NRMT
☐ 17	Randy Johnson	6.00	2.70
☐ 18	Greg Maddux	20.00	9.00
☐ 19	Karim Garcia	4.00	1.80
☐ 20	Chipper Jones	20.00	9.00

1996 Zenith Mozaics

Randomly inserted in packs at a rate of one in 10, this 25-card set features three-player image cards of the hottest superstars. The fronts display multiple player images representing the core of each of the 28 teams and are printed on rainbow holographic foil.

		MINT	NRMT
COMPLETE SET (25)		200.00	90.00
COMMON CARD (1-25)		3.00	1.35
SEMISTARS		5.00	2.20
STATED ODDS 1:10			
☐ 1	Greg Maddux	20.00	9.00
	Chipper Jones		
	Ryan Klesko		
☐ 2	Juan Gonzalez	12.00	5.50
	Will Clark		
	Ivan Rodriguez		
☐ 3	Frank Thomas	20.00	9.00
	Robin Ventura		
	Ray Durham		
☐ 4	Matt Williams	6.00	2.70
	Barry Bonds		
	Osvaldo Fernandez		
☐ 5	Ken Griffey Jr.	30.00	13.50
	Randy Johnson		
	Alex Rodriguez		
☐ 6	Sammy Sosa	6.00	2.70
	Ryne Sandberg		
	Mark Grace		
☐ 7	Jim Edmonds	6.00	2.70
	Tim Salmon		
	Garret Anderson		
☐ 8	Cal Ripken	20.00	9.00
	Roberto Alomar		
	Mike Mussina		
☐ 9	Mo Vaughn	10.00	4.50
	Roger Clemens		
	John Valentin		
☐ 10	Barry Larkin	5.00	2.20
	Reggie Sanders		
	Hal Morris		
☐ 11	Ray Lankford	6.00	2.70
	Brian Jordan		
	Ozzie Smith		
☐ 12	Dante Bichette	6.00	2.70
	Larry Walker		
	Andres Galarraga		
☐ 13	Mike Piazza	20.00	9.00
	Hideo Nomo		
	Raul Mondesi		
☐ 14	Ben McDonald	3.00	1.35
	Greg Vaughn		
	Kevin Seitzer		

		MINT	NRMT
☐ 15	Joe Carter	3.00	1.35
	Carlos Delgado		
	Alex Gonzalez		
☐ 16	Gary Sheffield	6.00	2.70
	Charles Johnson		
	Jeff Conine		
☐ 17	Rondell White	3.00	1.35
	Moises Alou		
	Henry Rodriguez		
☐ 18	Albert Belle	6.00	2.70
	Manny Ramirez		
	Carlos Baerga		
☐ 19	Kirby Puckett	10.00	4.50
	Paul Molitor		
	Chuck Knoblauch		
☐ 20	Tony Gwynn	12.00	5.50
	Rickey Henderson		
	Wally Joyner		
☐ 21	Mark McGwire	10.00	4.50
	Mike Bordick		
	Scott Brosius		
☐ 22	Paul O'Neill	6.00	2.70
	Bernie Williams		
	Wade Boggs		
☐ 23	Jay Bell	3.00	1.35
	Orlando Merced		
	Jason Kendall		
☐ 24	Rico Brogna	3.00	1.35
	Paul Wilson		
	Jason Isringhausen		
☐ 25	Jeff Bagwell	10.00	4.50
	Craig Biggio		
	Derek Bell		

1996 Zenith Z-Team

Randomly inserted in packs at a rate of one in 72, this 18-card set features a color action player cutout on a clear micro-etched design with a gold foil Z-Team logo and a see-through green baseball field background. The backs carry player information printed on the back of the Z.

		MINT	NRMT
COMPLETE SET (18)		500.00	220.00
COMMON CARD (1-18)		10.00	4.50
UNLISTED STARS		15.00	6.75
STATED ODDS 1:72			
☐ 1	Ken Griffey Jr.	80.00	36.00
☐ 2	Albert Belle	20.00	9.00
☐ 3	Cal Ripken	60.00	27.00
☐ 4	Frank Thomas	60.00	27.00
☐ 5	Greg Maddux	50.00	22.00
☐ 6	Mo Vaughn	20.00	9.00
☐ 7	Chipper Jones	50.00	22.00
☐ 8	Mike Piazza	50.00	22.00
☐ 9	Ryan Klesko	10.00	4.50
☐ 10	Hideo Nomo	40.00	18.00
☐ 11	Roberto Alomar	15.00	6.75
☐ 12	Manny Ramirez	15.00	6.75

1997 Zenith

The 1997 Zenith set was issued in one series totalling 50 cards and was distributed in packs containing five standard-size cards and two 8" by 10" cards with a suggested retail price of $9.99. The fronts feature borderless color action player photos. The backs carry a black-and-white player photo with career statistics. The set contains 42 established player cards and eight rookie cards (43-50).

		MINT	NRMT
COMPLETE SET (50)		50.00	22.00
COMMON CARD (1-50)		.25	.11
MINOR STARS		.50	.23
UNLISTED STARS		1.00	.45
☐ 1	Frank Thomas	4.00	1.80
☐ 2	Tony Gwynn	2.50	1.10
☐ 3	Jeff Bagwell	2.00	.90
☐ 4	Paul Molitor	1.00	.45
☐ 5	Roberto Alomar	1.00	.45
☐ 6	Mike Piazza	3.00	1.35
☐ 7	Albert Belle	1.25	.55
☐ 8	Greg Maddux	3.00	1.35
☐ 9	Barry Larkin	.75	.35
☐ 10	Tony Clark	1.00	.45
☐ 11	Larry Walker	1.00	.45
☐ 12	Chipper Jones	3.00	1.35
☐ 13	Juan Gonzalez	2.50	1.10
☐ 14	Barry Bonds	1.25	.55
☐ 15	Ivan Rodriguez	1.25	.55
☐ 16	Sammy Sosa	1.00	.45
☐ 17	Derek Jeter	3.00	1.35
☐ 18	Hideo Nomo	2.50	1.10
☐ 19	Roger Clemens	2.00	.90
☐ 20	Ken Griffey Jr.	5.00	2.20
☐ 21	Andy Pettitte	1.00	.45
☐ 22	Alex Rodriguez	3.00	1.35
☐ 23	Tino Martinez	1.00	.45
☐ 24	Bernie Williams	1.00	.45
☐ 25	Ken Caminiti	.75	.35
☐ 26	John Smoltz	.50	.23
☐ 27	Javier Lopez	.50	.23
☐ 28	Mark McGwire	2.00	.90
☐ 29	Gary Sheffield	1.00	.45
☐ 30	David Justice	1.00	.45
☐ 31	Randy Johnson	1.00	.45
☐ 32	Chuck Knoblauch	1.00	.45
☐ 33	Mike Mussina	1.00	.45
☐ 34	Deion Sanders	.50	.23
☐ 35	Cal Ripken	4.00	1.80
☐ 36	Darin Erstad	1.50	.70
☐ 37	Kenny Lofton	1.25	.55

		MINT	NRMT
☐ 13	Gary Sheffield	10.00	4.50
☐ 14	Barry Bonds	20.00	9.00
☐ 15	Matt Williams	10.00	4.50
☐ 16	Jim Edmonds	10.00	4.50
☐ 17	Kirby Puckett	30.00	13.50
☐ 18	Sammy Sosa	15.00	6.75

		MINT	NRMT
☐ 38	Jay Buhner	.75	.35
☐ 39	Brady Anderson	.75	.35
☐ 40	Edgar Martinez	.75	.35
☐ 41	Mo Vaughn	1.25	.55
☐ 42	Ryne Sandberg	1.25	.55
☐ 43	Andruw Jones	2.50	1.10
☐ 44	Nomar Garciaparra	3.00	1.35
☐ 45	Hideki Irabu	1.00	.45
☐ 46	Wilton Guerrero	.25	.11
☐ 47	Jose Cruz Jr.	8.00	3.60
☐ 48	Vladimir Guerrero	2.00	.90
☐ 49	Scott Rolen	2.50	1.10
☐ 50	Jose Guillen	1.25	.55

1997 Zenith 8x10

Randomly inserted one in every pack, this 24-card set features 8" by 10" versions of the base set cards of the players listed below.

		MINT	NRMT
COMPLETE SET (24)		50.00	22.00
COMMON CARD(1-24)		.75	.35
ONE PER PACK			
COMP.DUFEX SET (24)		100.00	45.00
*DUFEX SINGLES : .8X TO .2X BASIC 8 BY 10			
ONE DUFEX PER PACK			
☐ 1	Frank Thomas	5.00	2.20
☐ 2	Tony Gwynn	3.00	1.35
☐ 3	Jeff Bagwell	2.50	1.10
☐ 4	Ken Griffey Jr.	6.00	2.70
☐ 5	Mike Piazza	4.00	1.80
☐ 6	Greg Maddux	4.00	1.80

		MINT	NRMT
☐ 7	Ken Caminiti	.75	.35
☐ 8	Albert Belle	1.50	.70
☐ 9	Ivan Rodriguez	1.50	.70
☐ 10	Sammy Sosa	1.00	.45
☐ 11	Mark McGwire	2.50	1.10
☐ 12	Roger Clemens	2.50	1.10
☐ 13	Alex Rodriguez	4.00	1.80
☐ 14	Chipper Jones	4.00	1.80
☐ 15	Juan Gonzalez	3.00	1.35
☐ 16	Barry Bonds	1.50	.70
☐ 17	Derek Jeter	4.00	1.80
☐ 18	Hideo Nomo	3.00	1.35
☐ 19	Cal Ripken	5.00	2.20
☐ 20	Hideki Irabu	1.50	.70
☐ 21	Andruw Jones	3.00	1.35
☐ 22	Nomar Garciaparra	4.00	1.80
☐ 23	Vladimir Guerrero	2.50	1.10
☐ 24	Scott Rolen	3.00	1.35

1997 Zenith V-2

Randomly inserted in packs at the rate of one in 47, this eight-card set features color action player photos produced with motion technology and state-of-the-art foil printing.

		MINT	NRMT
COMPLETE SET (8)		400.00	180.00
COMMON CARD (1-8)		25.00	
STATED ODDS 1:47			
☐ 1	Ken Griffey Jr.	80.00	36.00
☐ 2	Andruw Jones	30.00	13.50
☐ 3	Frank Thomas	60.00	27.00

		MINT	NRMT
☐ 4	Mike Piazza	50.00	22.00
☐ 5	Alex Rodriguez	50.00	22.00
☐ 6	Cal Ripken	60.00	27.00
☐ 7	Derek Jeter	40.00	18.00
☐ 8	Vladimir Guerrero	25.00	11.00

1997 Zenith Z-Team

Randomly inserted in packs, cards from this nine-card set feature color action photos of top players printed on full Mirror Gold Holographic Mylar foil card stock. Only 1,000 sets were produced and each card is sequentially numbered on back.

		MINT	NRMT
COMPLETE SET (9)		600.00	275.00
COMMON CARD (1-9)		25.00	11.00
RANDOM INSERTS IN PACKS ..			
STATED PRINT RUN 1000 SERIAL #'d SETS			
☐ 1	Ken Griffey Jr.	120.00	55.00
☐ 2	Larry Walker	25.00	11.00
☐ 3	Frank Thomas	100.00	45.00
☐ 4	Alex Rodriguez	80.00	36.00
☐ 5	Mike Piazza	80.00	36.00
☐ 6	Cal Ripken	100.00	45.00
☐ 7	Derek Jeter	60.00	27.00
☐ 8	Andruw Jones	50.00	22.00
☐ 9	Roger Clemens	50.00	22.00

Acknowledgments

Each year we refine the process of developing the most accurate and up-to-date information for this book. I believe this year's Price Guide is our best yet. Thanks again to all the contributors nationwide (listed below) as well as our staff here in Dallas.

Those who have worked closely with us on this and many other books have again proven themselves invaluable: Levi Bleam and Jim Fleck (707 Sportscards), Peter Brennan, Ray Bright, Card Collectors Co., Cartophilium (Andrew Pywowarczuk), Barry Colla, Bill and Diane Dodge, Donruss/Leaf (Shawn Heilbron, Eric Tijerina), David Festberg, Fleer/SkyBox (Rich Bradley, Doug Drotman and Ted Taylor), Steve Freedman, Gervise Ford, Larry and Jeff Fritsch, Tony Galovich, Georgia Music and Sports (Dick DeCourcey), Dick Gilkeson, Steve Gold (AU Sports), Bill Goodwin (St. Louis Baseball Cards), Mike and Howard Gordon, George Grauer, John Greenwald, Greg's Cards, Wayne Grove, Bill Henderson, Jerry and Etta Hersh, Mike Hersh, Neil Hoppenworth, Jay and Mary Kasper, David Kohler (SportsCards Plus), Paul Lewicki, Lew Lipset, Mike Livingston (University Trading Cards), Mark Macrae, Bill Madden, Bill Mastro, Michael McDonald (The Sports Page), Mid-Atlantic Sports Cards (Bill Bossert), Gary Mills, Brian Morris, Mike Mosier (Columbia City Collectibles Co.), B.A. Murry, Ralph Nozaki, Mike O'Brien, Oldies and Goodies (Nigel Spill), Pacific Trading Cards (Mike Cramer and Mike Monson), Pinnacle (Laurie Goldberg, Kurt Iverson), Jack Pollard, Jeff Prillaman, Pat Quinn, Jerald Reichstein (Fabulous Cardboard), Gavin Riley, Clifton Rouse, John Rumierz, San Diego Sport Collectibles (Bill Goepner and Nacho Arredondo), Kevin Savage (Sports Gallery), Gary Sawatski, Mike Schechter, Scoreboard (Brian Cahill), Barry Sloate, John E. Spalding, Phil Spector, Frank Steele, Don Steinbach, Murvin Sterling, Lee Temanson, Topps (Marty Appel, Sy Berger and Melissa Rosen), Treat (Harold Anderson), Ed Twombly (New England Bullpen), Upper Deck (Steve Ryan, Marilyn Van Dyke), Wayne Varner, Bill Vizas, Bill Wesslund (Portland Sports Card Co.), Kit Young and Bob Ivanjack (Kit Young Cards), Rick Young, Ted Zanidakis, Robert Zanze (Z-Cards and Sports), and Bill Zimpleman. Finally we give a special acknowledgment to the late Dennis W. Eckes, "Mr. Sport Americana." The success of the Beckett Price Guides has always been the result of a team effort.

It is very difficult to be "accurate" -- one can only do one's best. But this job is especially difficult since we're shooting at a moving target: Prices are fluctuating all the time. Having several full-time pricing experts has definitely proven to be better than just one, and I thank all of them for working together to provide you, our readers, with the most accurate prices possible.

Many people have provided price input, illustrative material, checklist verifications, errata, and/or background information. We should like to individually thank AbD Cards (Dale Wesolewski), Action Card Sales, Jerry Adamic, Johnny and Sandy Adams, Alex's MVP Cards & Comics, Doug Allen (Round Tripper Sportscards), Will Allison, Dennis Anderson, Ed Anderson, Shane Anderson, Bruce W. Andrews, Ellis Anmuth, Tom Antonowicz, Alan Applegate, Ric Apter, Jason Arasate, Clyde Archer, Randy Archer, Matt Argento, Burl Armstrong, Neil Armstrong (World Series Cards), Todd Armstrong, Ara Arzoumanian, B and J Sportscards, Shawn Bailey, Ball Four Cards (Frank and Steve Pemper), Frank and Vivian Barning, Bob Bartosz, Nathan Basford, Carl Berg, David Berman, Beulah Sports (Jeff Blatt), Brian Bigelow, George Birsic, B.J. Sportscollectables, David Boedicker (The Wild Pitch Inc.), Bob Boffa, Louis Bollman, Tim Bond (Tim's Cards & Comics), Andrew Bosarge, Brian W. Bottles, Kenneth Braatz, Bill Brandt, Jeff Breitenfield, John Brigandi, John Broggi, Chuck

Brooks, Dan Bruner, Lesha Bundrick, Michael Bunker, John E. Burick, Ed Burkey Jr.,
Bubba Burnett, Virgil Burns, California Card Co., Capital Cards, Danny Cariseo, Carl
Carlson (C.T.S.), Jim Carr, Patrick Carroll, Ira Cetron, Don Chaffee, Michael Chan,
Sandy Chan, Ric Chandgie, Dwight Chapin, Ray Cherry, Bigg Wayne Christian, Josh
Chidester, Dick Cianciotto, Michael and Abe Citron, Dr. Jeffrey Clair, Derrick F. Clark,
Bill Cochran, Don Coe, Michael Cohen, Tom Cohoon (Cardboard Dreams), Collection
de Sport AZ (Ronald Villaneuve), Gary Gollett, Andrew T. Collier, Charles A. Collins,
Curt Cooter, Steven Cooter, Pedro Cortes, Rick Cosmen (RC Card Co.), Lou Costanzo
(Champion Sports), Mike Coyne, Paul and Ryan Crabb, Tony Craig (T.C. Card Co.),
Kevin Crane, Taylor Crane, Chad Cripe, Brian Cunningham, Allen Custer, Donald L.
Cutler, Eugene C. Dalager, Dave Dame, Brett Daniel, Tony Daniele III, Scott Dantio,
Roy Datema, John Davidson, Travis Deaton, Dee's Baseball Cards (Dee Robinson), Joe
Delgrippo, Tim DelVecchio, Steve Dempski, John Derossett, Mark Diamond, Gilberto
Diaz Jr., Ken Dinerman (California Cruizers), Frank DiRoberto, Cliff Dolgins, Discount
Dorothy, Walter J. Dodds Sr., Bill Dodson, Richard Dolloff (Dolloff Coin Center), Ron
Dorsey, Double Play Baseball Cards, Richard Duglin (Baseball Cards-N-More), The
Dugout, Kyle Dunbar, B.M. Dungan, Ken Edick (Home Plate of Utah), Randall
Edwards, Rick Einhorn, Mark Ely, Todd Entenman, Doak Ewing, Bryan Failing, R.J.
Faletti, Terry Falkner, Mike and Chris Fanning, John Fedak, Stephen A. Ferradino,
Tom Ferrara, Dick Fields, Louis Fineberg, Jay Finglass, L.V. Fischer, Bob Flitter,
Fremont Fong, Perry Fong, Craig Frank, Mark Franke, Walter Franklin, Tom Freeman,
Bob Frye, Chris Gala, Richard Galasso, Ray Garner, David Garza, David Gaumer,
Georgetown Card Exchange, Richard Gibson Jr., Glenn A. Giesey, David Giove, Dick
Goddard, Alvin Goldblum, Brian Goldner, Jeff Goldstein, Ron Gomez, Rich Gove,
Joseph Griffin, Mike Grimm, Neil Gubitz (What-A-Card), Hall's Nostalgia, Hershell
Hanks, Gregg Hara, Zac Hargis, Floyd Haynes (H and H Baseball Cards), Ben Heckert,
Kevin Heffner, Kevin Heimbigner, Dennis Heitland, Joel Hellman, Arthur W. Henkel,
Kevin Hense, Hit and Run Cards (Jon, David, and Kirk Peterson), Gary Holcomb, Lyle
Holcomb, Rich Hovorka, John Howard, Mark Hromalik, H.P. Hubert, Dennis Hughes,
Harold Hull, Johnny Hustle Card Co., Tom Imboden, Chris Imbriaco, Vern Isenberg,
Dale Jackson, Marshall Jackson, Mike Jardina, Hal Jarvis, Paul Jastrzembski, Jeff's
Sports Cards, David Jenkins, Donn Jennings Cards, George Johnson, Robe Johnson,
Stephen Jones, Al Julian, Chuck Juliana, Dave Jurgensmeier, John Just, Robert Just,
Nick Kardoulias, Scott Kashner, Frank J. Katen, Jerry Katz (Bottom of the Ninth), Mark
Kauffman, Allan Kaye, Rick Keplinger, Sam Kessler, Kevin's Kards, Larry B. Killian,
Kingdom Collectibles, Inc., John Klassnik, Philip C. Klutts, Don Knutsen, Steven
Koenigsberg, Bob & Bryan Kornfeld, Blake Krier, Neil Krohn, Scott Ku, Thomas
Kunnecke, Gary Lambert, Matthew Lancaster (MC's Card and Hobby), Jason Lassic,
Allan Latawiec, Howard Lau, Gerald A. Lavelle, Dan Lavin, Richard S. Lawrence,
William Lawrence, Brent Lee, W.H. Lee, Morley Leeking, Ronald Lenhardt, Brian
Lentz, Tom Leon, Leo's Sports Collectibles, Irv Lerner, Larry and Sally Levine, Lisa
Licitra, James Litopoulos, Larry Loeschen (A and J Sportscards), Neil Lopez, Allan
Lowenberg, Kendall Loyd (Orlando Sportscards South), Robert Luce, David Macaray,
Jim Macie, Joe Maddigan, David Madison, Rob Maerten, Frank Magaha, Pierre
Marceau, Paul Marchant, Jim Marsh, Rich Markus, Bob Marquette, Brad L. Marten,
Ronald L. Martin, Scott Martinez, Frank J. Masi, Duane Matthes, James S. Maxwell Jr.,
Dr. William McAvoy, Michael McCormick, Paul McCormick, McDag Productions Inc.,
Tony McLaughlin, Mendal Mearkle, Carlos Medina, Ken Melanson, William Mendel,
Eric Meredith, Blake Meyer (Lone Star Sportscards), Tim Meyer, Joe Michalowicz, Lee
Milazzo, Jimmy Milburn, Cary S. Miller, David (Otis) Miller, Eldon Miller, George

Miller, Wayne Miller, Dick Millerd, Mitchell's Baseball Cards, Perry Miyashita, Douglas Mo, John Morales, William Munn, Mark Murphy, John Musacchio, Robert Nappe, National Sportscard Exchange, Roger Neufeldt, Bud Obermeyer, Francisco Ochoa, John O'Hara, Glenn Olson, Mike Orth, Ron Oser, Luther Owen, Earle Parrish, Clay Pasternack, Mickey Payne, Michael Perrotta, Doug and Zachary Perry, Tom Pfirrmann, Bob Pirro, George Pollitt, Don Prestia, Coy Priest, Loran Pulver, Bob Ragonese, Richard H. Ranck, Bryan Rappaport, Robert M. Ray, R.W. Ray, Phil Regli, Tom Reid, Glenn Renick, Rob Resnick, John Revell, Carson Ritchey, Bill Rodman, Craig Roehrig, David H. Rogers, Michael H. Rosen, Martin Rotunno, Michael Runyan, Mark Rush, George Rusnak, Mark Russell, Terry Sack, Joe Sak, Jennifer Salems, Barry Sanders, Everett Sands, Jon Sands, Tony Scarpa, John Schad, Dave Schau (Baseball Cards), Bruce M. Schwartz, Keith A. Schwartz, Charlie Seaver, Tom Shanyfelt, Steven C. Sharek, Eddie Silard, Art Smith, Ben Smith, Michael Smith, Jerry Sorice, Don Spagnolo, Carl Specht, Sports Card Fan-Attic, The Sport Hobbyist, Dauer Stackpole, Norm Stapleton, Bill Steinberg, Bob Stern, Lisa Stellato, Jason Stern, Andy Stoltz, Bill Stone, Tim Strandberg (East Texas Sports Cards), Edward Strauss, Strike Three, Richard Strobino, Superior Sport Card, Dr. Richard Swales, Paul Taglione, George Tahinos, Ian Taylor, Lyle Telfer, The Thirdhand Shoppe, Scott A. Thomas, Paul Thornton, Carl N. Thrower, Jim Thurtell, John Tomko, Bud Tompkins (Minnesota Connection), Philip J. Tremont, Ralph Triplette, Mike Trotta, Umpire's Choice Inc., Eric Unglaub, Hoyt Vanderpool, Rob Veres, Nathan Voss, Steven Wagman, Jonathan Waldman, Terry Walker, T. Wall, Gary A. Walter, Mark Weber, Joe and John Weisenburger (The Wise Guys), Brian Wentz, Richard West, Mike Wheat, Richard Wiercinski, Don Williams (Robin's Nest of Dolls), Jeff Williams, John Williams, Kent Williams, Craig Williamson, Opry Winston, Brandon Witz, Rich Wojtasick, John Wolf Jr., Jay Wolt (Cavalcade of Sports), Carl Womack, Pete Wooten, Peter Yee, Wes Young, Dean Zindler, Mark Zubrensky and Tim Zwick.

Every year we make active solicitations for expert input. We are particularly appreciative of help (however extensive or cursory) provided for this volume. We receive many inquiries, comments and questions regarding material within this book. In fact, each and every one is read and digested. Time constraints, however, prevent us from personally replying. But keep sharing your knowledge. Your letters and input are part of the "big picture" of hobby information we can pass along to readers in our books and magazines. Even though we cannot respond to each letter, you are making significant contributions to the hobby through your interest and comments.

The effort to continually refine and improve this book also involves a growing number of people and types of expertise on our home team. Our company boasts a substantial Sports Data Publishing team, which strengthens our ability to provide comprehensive analysis of the marketplace. SDP capably handled numerous technical details and provided able assistance in the preparation of this edition.

Our baseball analysts played a major part in compiling this year's book, traveling thousands of miles during the past year to attend sports card shows and visit card shops around the United States and Canada. The Beckett baseball specialists are, Mark Anderson, Mike Jaspersen, Steve Judd, Rich Klein and Grant Sandground (Senior Price Guide Editor). Their pricing analysis and careful proofreading were key contributions to the accuracy of this annual.

Grant Sandground's coordination and reconciling of prices as Beckett Baseball Card Monthly Price Guide Editor helped immeasurably. Rich Klein, as research analyst, contributed detailed pricing analysis and hours of proofing. They were ably assisted by Jeany Finch and Beverly Mills, who helped enter new sets and pricing information, and ably handled administration of our contributor Price Guide surveys. Card librarian Gabriel Rangel handled the ever-growing quantity of cards we need organized for efforts such as this.

The effort was led by the Manager of Technical Services Dan Hitt. They were ably assisted by the rest of the Price Guide analysts: Pat Blandford, Theo Chen, Steven Judd, Lon Levitan, Rob Springs and Bill Sutherland.

The price gathering and analytical talents of this fine group of hobbyists have helped make our Beckett team stronger, while making this guide and its companion monthly Price Guide more widely recognized as the hobby's most reliable and relied upon sources of pricing information.

The Beckett Interactive Department, ably headed by Mark Harwell, played a critical role in technology. Working with software designed by assistant manager Eric Best, they spent countless hours programming, testing, and implementing it to simplify the handling of thousands of prices that must be checked and updated for each edition.

In the Production Department, Paul Kerutis and Marlon DePaula were responsible for the typesetting and for the card photos you see throughout the book.

Don Pendergraft spent tireless hours on the phone attending to the wishes of our dealer advertisers. Once the ad specifications were delivered to our offices, Phaedra Strecher used her computer skills to turn raw copy into attractive display advertisements.

In the years since this guide debuted, Beckett Publications has grown beyond any rational expectation. A great many talented and hard working individuals have been instrumental in this growth and success. Our whole team is to be congratulated for what we together have accomplished. Our Beckett Publications team is led by President Jeff Amano, Vice Presidents Claire Backus and Joe Galindo, Directors Jeff Anthony, C.R.Conant, Beth Harwell and Margaret Steele. They are ably assisted by Pete Adauto, Dana Alecknavage, John Ayres, Joel Brown, Kaye Ball, Airey Baringer, Rob Barry, Therese Bellar, Julie Binion, Louise Bird, Amy Brougher, Bob Brown, Angie Calandro, Allen Christopherson, Randall Calvert, Cara Carmichael, Susan Catka, Albert Chavez, Marty Click, Amy Duret, Von Daniel, Deniel Derrick, Aaron Derr, Ryan Duckworth, Mitchell Dyson, Eric Evans, Kandace Elmore, Craig Ferris, Gean Paul Figari, Carol Fowler, Mary Gonzalez-Davis, Rosanna Gonzalez-Oleachea, Jeff Greer, Mary Gregory, Robert Gregory, Jenifer Grellhesl, Julie Grove, Barry HackerTracy Hackler, Patti Harris, Mark Hartley, Joanna Hayden, Chris Hellem, Pepper Hastings, Bob Johnson, Doug Kale, Kevin King, Justin Kanoya, Edie Kelly, Gayle Klancnik, Rudy J. Klancnik, Tom Layberger, Jane Ann Layton, Sara Leeman, Benedito Leme, Lori Lindsey, Stanley Lira, Louis Marroquin, John Marshall, Mike McAllister, Teri McGahey, Matt McGuire, Omar Mediano, Sherry Monday, Mila Morante, Daniel Moscoso Jr., Allan Muir, Hugh Murphy, Shawn Murphy, Mike Obert, Stacy Olivieri, Andrea Paul, Clark Palomino, Don Pendergraft, Missy Patton, Mike Pagel, Wendy Pallugna, Laura Patterson, Mike Payne, Tim Polzer, Bob Richardson, Lisa Runyon, Wade Rugenstein, Susan Sainz, Christine Seibert, Brett Setter, Len Shelton, Dave Sliepka, Judi Smalling, Sheri Smith, Jeff Stanton, Marcia Stoesz, Mark Stokes, Dawn Sturgeon, Margie Swoyer, Tina Tackett, Doree Tate, Jim Tereschuk, Jim Thompson, Doug Williams, Steve Wilson, Ed Wornson, David Yandry, Bryan Winstead, Jay Zwerner and Mark Zeske. The whole Beckett Publications team has my thanks for jobs well done. Thank you, everyone.

I also thank my family, especially my wife, Patti, and our daughters, Christina, Rebecca, and Melissa, for putting up with me again.